# Key British Enterprises 2015

## Britain's Top 50,000 Companies

Volume 3  P-Z

GAP
books

D&B

**Decide with Confidence**

Published by:

**GAP Books**
Dephna House
24-26 Arcadia Avenue
London N3 2JU
Tel: 020 8349 7199
Fax: 020 8349 7198
Web: www.gapbooks.com

In association with:

**D&B**
Marlow International
Parkway, Marlow
Bucks SL7 1AJ
Tel: 01628 492000
Fax: 01628 492332
Web: www.dnb.co.uk

# Key British Enterprises

ISBN 978-1-910556-00-9
ISSN 0142 5048

© Dun & Bradstreet Ltd
   United Kingdom 2015

First published 1961


Published by GAP Books in association with Dun & Bradstreet Ltd.

Legislation enables companies to register telephone and fax numbers against the Telephone Preference Service, Corporate Telephone Preference Service and Fax Preference Service (TPS, CTPS and FPS).

Data in these books is screened against this list and companies who have registered either their telephone or fax numbers with the TPS, CTPS and FPS preference services will not have this information listed within their entries.

For further information visit http://www.tpsonline.org.uk/ctps/what/

Printed and bound in Great Britain by CPI Antony Rowe

All paper for this publication comes from sustainable sources

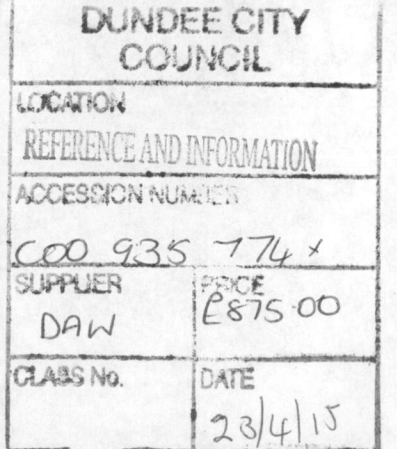

# Contents

# Within every customer there are 58 potential new customers

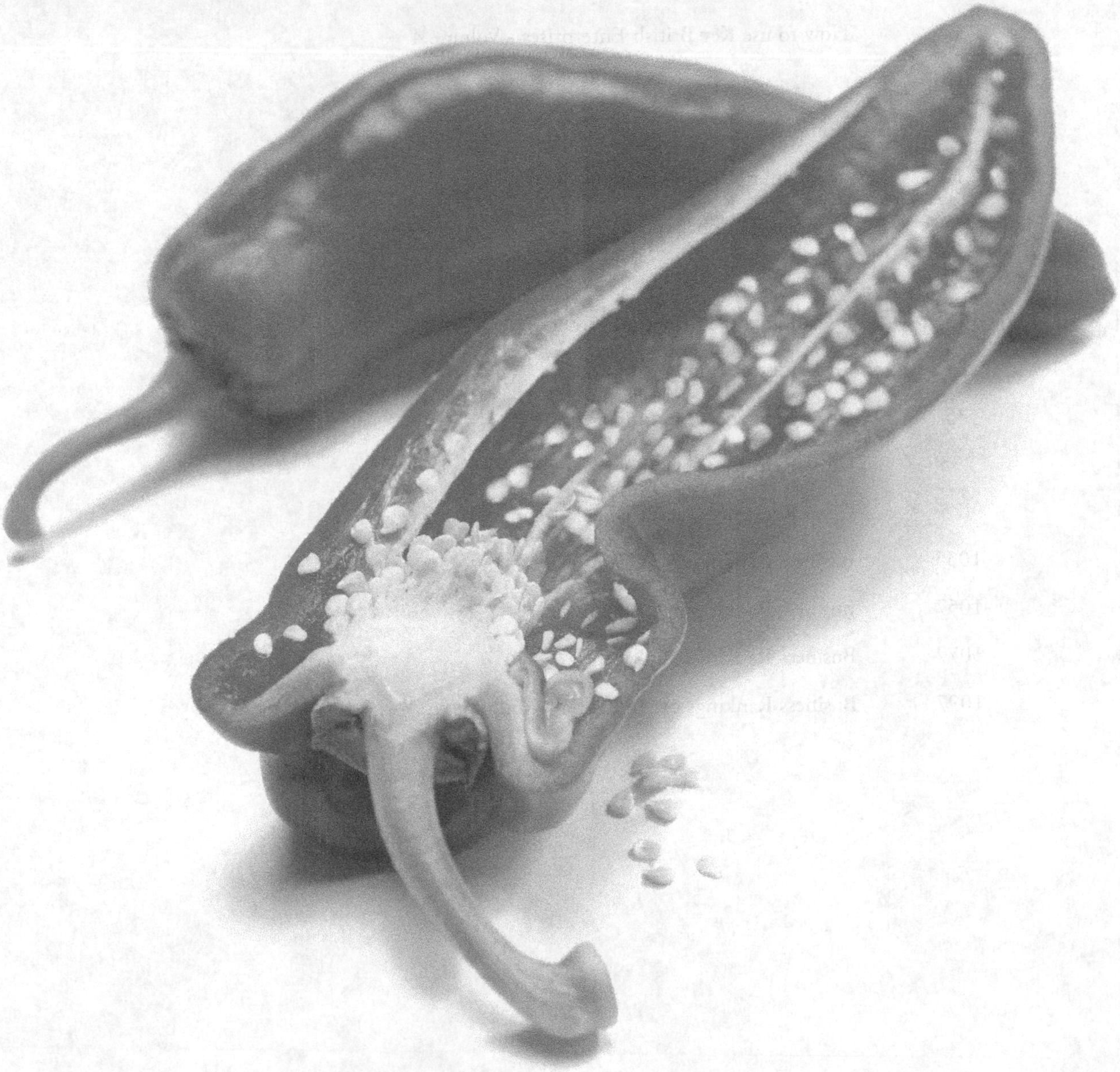

**Your customers give you more than just sales.**

In fact, on average,* each one has 58 sister companies which are statistically more likely to buy from you than other companies. If you can't identify them, Market Insight can.

Speak to us on 01628 492299 to get a free customised sample analysis and discover the fast way to improve your sales effectiveness.

*Based on a sample analysis of D&B customer and linkage data.

**D&B**

**Dun & Bradstreet**

# Preface

Welcome to the 2015 edition of **Key British Enterprises**. As one of the UK's most widely recognised and frequently used reference publications, **Key British Enterprises** has provided key business information on the top 50,000 UK businesses to librarians, sales and marketing managers, academics and all types of organisations for over forty five years.

**Key British Enterprises** is ideal for identifying sales prospects, locating suppliers, evaluating competition and takeover targets, simple credit checking and researching and planning marketing strategy. The 2015 edition includes some or all of the following for each company:

**Contact Details** - name and address, telephone and fax numbers, names and functions of principals; making approaching potential business partners easy.

**Financial Details** - issued capital, sales turnover, net worth, working capital, export sales turnover, profit figures and auditors.

**Operational Details** - line of business, markets, employees, branches, US & UK SIC codes. This data is essential for a full picture of potential customers or suppliers.

**Corporate Details** - parent company, date established, legal status, company registration number, VAT number and bankers.

**Key British Enterprises** provides unique benefits that only D&B is able to offer:

- **Impartial Quality Information** - no charge of any kind is made for a listing in this or any other D&B directory. By using appropriate listing criteria we ensure that only qualified businesses are included. Great care is taken in compiling each company entry.

- **Coverage** - the top 50,000 businesses in the UK are included, across all lines of business.

- **Cross Referencing** - cross reference indexes give contact information in each section making the directory very easy to use.

- **Validility** - all the businesses included have been checked and the information updated by telephone research. Dun & Bradstreet's dedicated call centre employs a permanent team to constantly update our database and ensure the accuracy of all records. Since company information changes, we recommend that you do not use this directory beyond April 2016.

The following pages provide a guide to getting the most from your the information provided.

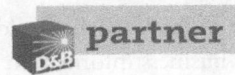

# Key British Enterprises – Overview

## CRITERIA FOR INCLUSION

All of the businesses featured in this edition have been specially selected to appear in **Key British Enterprises**. A panel of experts established the criteria that needed to be met in order to qualify as a Key British Enterprise. Every business within this book meets at least one of the criteria.

**Key British Enterprises 2015** features:

All UK businesses with 50 or more employees

Or All UK businesses with a sales turnover in excess of £7 million

Or All UK businesses with total assets in excess of £20 million

## FORMAT

Volumes 1-3 of **Key British Enterprises** list the 50,000 companies alphabetically, with full company information throughout.

Volume 4 provides cross-referencing to the 50,000 companies by industry and post town, county and post town and by principals' names. Volume 4 also includes British Business Rankings, listing the top 5,000 companies from volumes 1-3 and ranking them by employee size, by sales turnover, within each county and within industrial groupings.

# Key British Enterprises – Overview

## BUSINESS LISTINGS

A standard business entry in **Key British Enterprises** includes nearly thirty pieces of information. These are listed below. However it is not always possible to collect every piece of information. For instance sales turnover and profit figures may not be available or there may be no parent company or export markets. To show the incidence and quality of each data element a percentage figure is given in the table below, which indicates the number of business records that have the particular data element. This provides you with further insight into the data that you have at your fingertips.

| | % | | % |
|---|---|---|---|
| DUNS Number | 100 | Export Indicator | 19 |
| Full legal name | 100 | Export markets | 16 |
| Headquarters address | 100 | Date of formation | 96 |
| Telephone number | 92 | Legal status | 92 |
| Fax number | 42 | Company registration number | 87 |
| Website address | 32 | Issued capital | 81 |
| Location of branches | 44 | Principals' names | 97 |
| Line of business | 100 | Number of employees | 72 |
| Trading style | 25 | Sales turnover | 54 |
| UK SIC codes | 99 | Export sales turnover | 13 |
| US SIC codes | 100 | Profit figure | 67 |
| Parent company | 55 | Bankers | 62 |
| VAT number | 23 | Auditors | 75 |
| Net worth | 83 | Working Capital | 72 |

## TYPES OF BUSINESS

**Key British Enterprises** provides information for companies engaged in all types of business activity including:

Agriculture, Forestry & Fishing
Mining
Construction
Manufacturing
Transportation, Communication
& Public Utilities

Wholesale Trade
Retail Trade
Finance, Insurance & Real Estate
Business Services
Social Services
& Public Administration

Each business activity has been given equal emphasis, therefore **Key British Enterprises** gives an overview of the main businesses throughout the economy as a whole.

Please note that because of the fluctuating nature of the business world, organisations will constantly be moving into and out of the top 50,000.

# How to use Key British Enterprises: SIC Indexes

For indexing purposes **Key British Enterprises** uses the 1972 US Standard Industrial Classification (SIC) code system. However the UK SIC Codes appear as data elements in the main entry ensuring that no information is omitted.

SIC Codes are a vital tool in any business research. Market researchers and advertisers rely on them to pinpoint the kinds of business they want to reach. When economists study business segments they use the SIC Code to identify and compare industries - especially when they are analysing changes or trends in business and the economy. Job hunters use SIC's to identify appropriate or interesting prospective employers. Finally SIC Codes are used for hard copy and computer assisted searches in business research everywhere. The letters N.E.C. may appear in the business description, these occur when a full descriptive business operation has not been identified. N.E.C. refers to Not Elsewhere Classified.

US SIC Codes divide all economic activity into ten major groups. These business segments are represented by the first two digits of the SIC Codes:

| | | | |
|---|---|---|---|
| Agriculture, Forestry & Fishing | 01-09 | Wholesale Trade | 50-51 |
| Mining | 10-14 | Retail Trade | 52-59 |
| Construction | 15-17 | Finance, Insurance & Real Estate | 60-67 |
| Manufacturing | 20-39 | Business Services | 70-79 |
| Transportation, Communication & Public Utilities | 40-49 | Social Services & Public Administration | 80-97 |

Each line of business is categorised within one of these ten divisions and assigned a code. The first two digits of this code describe the general line of business. The third and fourth digits pinpoint a specific business activity, e.g.

| | |
|---|---|
| 22 | Manufacturing - Textile mill products |
| 227 | Manufacturing - Floor coverings |
| 2272 | Manufacturing - Tufted carpets, rugs |

**Key British Enterprises** and other D&B directories are cross referenced by US SIC Code.

To find the right US SIC Code, simply turn to the alphabetical index in volume 4

| | |
|---|---|
| Residential electric lighting fixtures | 3645 |
| Resistors, for electronic applications | 3676 |
| Retail bakeries, baking and selling | 5462 |
| Retail bakeries, selling only | 5463 |

Alternatively, if you need an explanation of a particular US SIC Code, it may be found in the numerical index in volume 4

| | |
|---|---|
| 3576 | Scales and balances, except laboratory |
| 3579 | Office machines n.e.c. |
| 3581 | Automatic merchandising machines |
| 3582 | Commercial laundry, dry cleaning pressing machines |

# How to use Key British Enterprises: Volumes 1-3

**Alphabetical Section**

A full business entry will appear as follows:

Unique Accession Number — DUNS 21-456-7885 — **Imp-Exp** — Import/Export Indicator

Full Legal Name — **Stubbs Distribution Ltd.**
(**Subsidiary of**: Stubbs Holdings — Ultimate Parent
International Ltd.)

Headquarters Address — Lambourne House, Western Road,
Romford, Essex, RM1 3ND

Telephone & Fax Numbers — **Tel:** 01708-567879 **Fax:** 01708-567880

**Reg No:** 434567 **VAT No:** 760730743 — VAT Registration Number

Company Registration Number — **Estd:** 1960 Private Limited Company — Date Started and Status of Company

Description of Business Activity — **Line of Business:** Manufacturers,
importers and exporters of staple
removers and other stationery accessories
including cardboard boxes

**Export Markets:** Germany; France; Spain — Export Market

**Export Sales:** £7,952,174 — Total for Overseas Sales

Business Trading Styles — **Trading Style:** Romford Staple Removers;
Wycombe Removers

Issued Capital — **Issued Capital:** £500,000

**Principals:** FR Palmer (*Chairman*), JH
Palmer (*Managing*), Mrs H Palmer — Directors' Names and Job Titles
(*Finance*), A Palmer (*Sales*)                    (up to eight)

Company Secretary's Name — **Co. Secretary:** Henry Ralston-Smith

**Responsibilities**

Managers Names, Responsibilities — **Finance:** H Palmer (*Finance Director*)
& Titles                          **Marketing:** B Reese (*Marketing Director*)
**Personnel:** J Collins (*Personnel Manager*)
**IT:** M Adams (*Head of IT*)
**Fleet:** B Stokes (*Fleet Purchase Manager*)
**Purchasing:** T Clark (*Head of Purchasing*)
**Sales:** A Palmer (*Sales Director*)
**Network:** I Smith (*IT Projects Manager*)
**Telecoms:** K Stevens (*Systems Manager*)

Location of Branches — **Branches:** High Wycombe, Dover

US and UK Standard Industrial — **US SIC:** 3579, 2451, 5112
Classification Codes — **UK SIC:** 33010, 47253, 61900

**Auditors:** Daffern & Co. — Auditors' Details

**Bankers:** Barclays Bank PLC (20-81-86) — Bankers' Details

| | 31-03-07 | 31-03-06 | 31-03-05 |
|---|---|---|---|
| TO | 4,073,219 | 3,099,720 | 2,964,762 |
| P/L | (1,018,988) | 1,703,554 | 489,373 |
| NW | 2,089,234 | 1,989,867 | 1,023,134 |
| WC | 2,010,966 | 1,678,987 | 1,256,096 |
| Emp. | 225 | 203 | 195 |

Total Sales Turnover (at date given)
Total Profit/Loss (in brackets)
Net Worth
Working Capital
Number of Employees

(All data are fictitious)

Volumes 1-3 of **Key British Enterprises** list Britain's top 50,000 companies alphabetically.

The following alphabetisation conventions have been used:

**ACRONYMS.** Businesses whose names comprise initials appear at the beginning of the relevant alphabetical system, e.g. N C R Ltd. appears before National Freight Co. Ltd., but where they appear as Ncr they are alphabetically listed.

**SURNAMES.** Where a company name consists of a person's name it will be listed under the christian name, e.g. Thomas H. Loveday Ltd. appears under 'T'.

**BUSINESS NAMES STARTING WITH 'St.'** are all listed as if the word 'Saint' was spelt out in full, e.g. St. Austell Brewery Co. Ltd. appears before Sandvik Ltd.

**BUSINESS NAMES STARTING 'THE'** are listed according to the next word in the business name, e.g. The Boots Co. PLC appears under 'B'.

**NUMERICAL ENTRIES.** Businesses whos names begin with a number or symbol are listed at the start of Volume 1.

# How to use Key British Enterprises: Volume 4 - Indexes

**Industrial Cross Reference**

All the businesses listed in **Key British Enterprises** grouped by industry. This Industrial Cross Reference section lists companys by type of business, as defined by US SIC Code and arranged alphabetically by county.

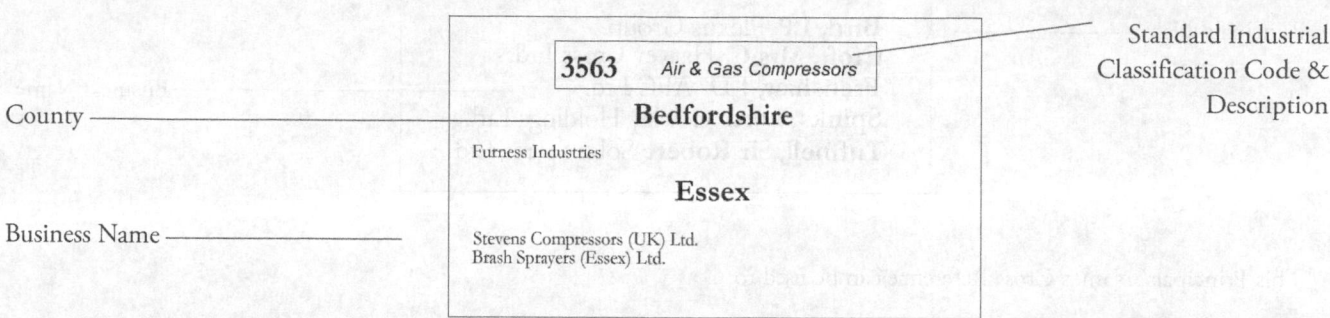

County

Business Name

| 3563 | Air & Gas Compressors |

Standard Industrial Classification Code & Description

**Bedfordshire**

Furness Industries

**Essex**

Stevens Compressors (UK) Ltd.
Brash Sprayers (Essex) Ltd.

This Industrial Cross Reference can be used to:

- identify sales prospects by line of business
- select suppliers
- conduct market research

- identify competitors
- discover where a particular industry is concentrated
- formulate direct marketing activity

**Geographical Cross Reference**

The 50,000 businesses listed are further cross referenced geographically. Business are arranged in alphabetical order within counties and then post towns.

County

Post town

*Aberdeenshire*

**Insch**
Abercrombie
P K T Tarmac Ltd.

**Inverurie**
A B C Importers
Danny Gillespie Contractors Ltd.
Electric Cars Co. Ltd.
Speciaity Shellfish Importers Ltd.

Business Name

This Geographical Cross Reference can be used to:

- identify businesses by county or post town
- compile targeted mailing lists by location and line of business
- approach prospective employers within a county

- assign sales territories based on the number of prospects within an area
- assess the potential of new markets
- contact local suppliers

# How to use Key British Enterprises: Volume 4 - Indexes

**Principals' Names Cross Reference**

Some two hundred thousand names of principals are given in alphabetical order by surname. Next to each listing appear details of the business on whose board they sit.

Principals' Name ───────────

> **Bird, LP** Plexus Group
> **Croft, Mrs C** Harvey Cross Ltd.
> **Frenshaw, J D** AFC Ltd. ──────────────────── Business Name
> **Spinks, Lord** Cowley Holdings Ltd.
> **Tuffnell, Sir Robert** Solar Stores Ltd.

This Principals' Names Cross Reference can be used to:

- identify business relationships
- contact known directors
- check out the range of an individual's directorships
- confirm board appointments

# How to use Key British Enterprises: Volume 4 - Rankings

The British Business Rankings section of **Key British Enterprises** takes the top 5,000 companies in each category and then ranks them accordingly:

**Rankings Within County**

Businesses within this section are ranked by employees within each county.

County ———————————

Business Name ———————————

| Aberdeenshire | | |
|---|---|---|
| Davidson Group PLC | 2818 | 1 |
| Oil & Gass Development Ltd. | 1699 | 2 |
| Sadler Holdings Ltd. | 1489 | 3 |

——— Employee Ranking

——— Employees

Use this ranking to:

• identify major businesses within a county

• compare the principal businesses across counties

**Rankings By Employee Size**

Businesses in this section are listed in descending order by employee size.

Business Name ———————————

| | | |
|---|---|---|
| BP Construction Ltd. | 7302 | 382 |
| GPG PLC | 7291 | 383 |
| Palmer Distribution Ltd. | 7248 | 384 |

——— Employee Ranking

——— Employees

Use this ranking to:

• compare major businesses by employees
• establish the largest employers

• contact businesses meeting your employee criteria

# How to use Key British Enterprises: Volume 4 - Rankings

**Rankings By Sales Turnover**

Companies in this section are listed in descending order by sales turnover. Businesses may appear in this section with the same sales figure. This occurs where companies are filing consolidated accounts.

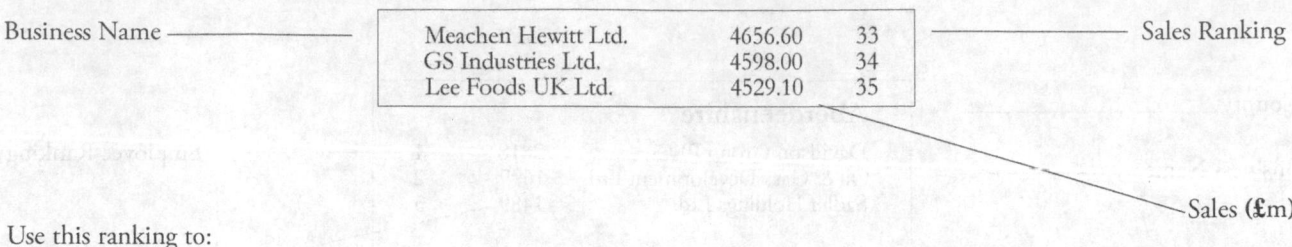

Business Name ——————————— | Meachen Hewitt Ltd. | 4656.60 | 33 | ——————————— Sales Ranking
GS Industries Ltd. | 4598.00 | 34
Lee Foods UK Ltd. | 4529.10 | 35

——— Sales (£m)

Use this ranking to:

- identify high volume sales businesses
- contact businesses meeting your sales criteria

- compare major businesses by sales or employees

**Rankings Within Industrial Groupings**

Companies in this section are ranked by employees within each major industrial grouping based upon the US SIC coding system.

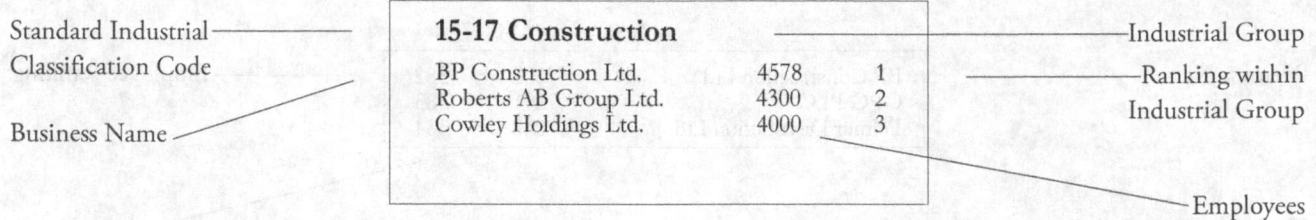

Standard Industrial ———————— Classification Code

Business Name ——

**15-17 Construction** ————————————— Industrial Group

BP Construction Ltd. | 4578 | 1 | ——————— Ranking within Industrial Group
Roberts AB Group Ltd. | 4300 | 2
Cowley Holdings Ltd. | 4000 | 3

——— Employees

Use this ranking to:

- identify industrial giants
- compare companies within a business sector

- contact key companies in a particular industry
- establish the industries with corporate leaders

# Key British Enterprises 2015

## Britain's Top 50,000 Companies

Volume 3  P-Z

# P

DUNS 22-522-4781

### P A Finlay and Co Ltd

Angel House, London E15 2HX
**Tel:** 02085558107 **Fax:** 02085368187
**Web:** www.pafinlay.co.uk
**Reg No:** 0988222 **VAT No:** 248846714
**Estd:** 1970 Private Limited Company
**Line of Business:** Building construction contractors
**Issued Capital:** £10,000
**Principals:** N R Athienitis *(Managing)*, P A Finlay, M Bradshaw
**Co. Secretary:** Mrs Catherine Athienitou
**Responsibilities**
**IT:** Paul Freedman *(Computer Manager)*
**Branches:** P A Finlay and Co Ltd, 6 Rowse Close, London E15 2HX
**US SIC:** 1522 **UK SIC:** 50100
**Auditors:** Alan Stanton & Co
**Bankers:** National Westminster Bank Plc (60-20-36)

| | 31-12-13 | 31-12-12 | 31-12-11 |
|---|---|---|---|
| TO | 5,088,315 | 6,757,064 | 3,376,708 |
| P/L | 407,865 | 691,101 | (309,285) |
| NW | 3,654,164 | 3,583,815 | 2,898,903 |
| WC | 1,150,389 | 1,170,250 | 516,872 |
| Emp. | N/A | N/A | 47 |

DUNS 39-910-2201 Exp

### P A Holdings Ltd

(**Subsidiary of:** Pacg2 Ltd)
123 Buckingham Palace Road, London SW1W 9SR
**Tel:** 020-7730-9000
**Web:** www.paconsulting.com
**Reg No:** 2235016 **Estd:** 1943 Private Limited Company
**Line of Business:** Management activities of holding companies
**Export Markets:** Europe, Scandinavia, N America Asia
**Trading Style:** P A Consulting
**Issued Capital:** £13,455,680
**Directors:** K Janjuah, A Middleton, C Barrett, M M Gordon
**Co. Secretary:** Robert King
**Responsibilities**
**Senior:** Jonathan Moynihan *(Chairperson)*
**US SIC:** 7392 **UK SIC:** 83951
**Auditors:** Ernst & Young LLP
**Bankers:** National Westminster Bank Plc (60-12-02)

| | 31-12-13 | 31-12-12 | 31-12-11 |
|---|---|---|---|
| TO | 178,752,985 | 161,958,423 | 148,040,388 |
| P/L | 25,440,299 | 17,633,690 | 5,319,900 |
| NW | 70,861,492 | 69,682,647 | 51,554,545 |
| WC | 8,817,679 | 52,747,971 | 34,516,684 |
| Emp. | 1,586 | 1,436 | 1,317 |

DUNS 22-651-0360 Imp-Exp

### P A S (Grantham) Ltd

(**Subsidiary of:** McCain Foods Group Inc)
Easton, Grantham, Lincolnshire NG33 5AY
**Tel:** 01476-581000
**Web:** www.mccain.com
**Reg No:** 1568027 **Estd:** 1981 Private Limited Company
**Line of Business:** Manufacturers of food products
**Export Markets:** Rest of Europe
**Export Sales:** £4,975,000
**Issued Capital:** £100
**Directors:** Ms A D Mccain, S S Chelley
**Co. Secretary:** John Legard
**Responsibilities**
**Operations:** Joseph Campion *(Supply Chain Manager)*
**Purchasing:** Joseph Campion *(Supply Chain Manager)*
**US SIC:** 2099 **UK SIC:** 42399
**Auditors:** PricewaterhouseCoopers LLP
**Bankers:** National Westminster Bank Plc (56-00-06)

| | 30-06-13 | 30-06-12 | 30-06-11 |
|---|---|---|---|
| TO | 73,797,000 | 72,253,000 | 74,466,000 |
| P/L | (4,895,000) | 4,269,000 | 178,000 |
| NW | 21,674,000 | 25,357,000 | 22,087,000 |
| WC | 3,132,000 | 7,600,000 | 12,534,000 |
| Emp. | 332 | 308 | 309 |

DUNS 29-069-6509

### P. A. V. H. International Ltd

East Street, Newquay, Cornwall TR7 1DB
**Tel:** 01637870350 **Fax:** 01637-859295
**Web:** www.senor-dicks.co.uk
**Reg No:** 1283143 **VAT No:** 133176194
**Estd:** 1976 Private Limited Company
**Line of Business:** Hotels and motels without restaurant
**Trading Style:** Hotel Victoria Newquay, Foster's Pub, Senor Dicks, Victoria Cabs
**Issued Capital:** £17,500
**Directors:** C T Law, D R Taylor
**Co. Secretary:** Ms Audrey Taylor
**Responsibilities**
**Senior:** Emma Huggins *(Manager)*, Zoe Layne *(Functions Manager)*
**Marketing:** Tony Townsend *(Marketing Manager)*
**Facilities:** Jim Turner *(Maintenance Manager)*
**Branches:** P. A. V. H. International Ltd, Chapel St, Penzance, Cornwall TR18 4AE
**US SIC:** 5812, 5813
**UK SIC:** 66110, 66200
**Auditors:** Francis Clark LLP
**Bankers:** The Royal Bank Of Scotland Plc (16-33-20)

| | 31-12-13 | 31-12-12 | 31-12-11 |
|---|---|---|---|
| TO | 2,657,325 | 2,803,322 | 3,133,998 |
| P/L | (32,335) | (347,756) | (303,036) |
| NW | 1,021,956 | 1,041,530 | 1,352,733 |
| WC | (261,102) | (2,041,841) | (1,901,055) |
| Emp. | 90 | 82 | 93 |

DUNS 76-921-8066

### P A Wright & Sons Ltd

Gopsall House Farm, 15 Bilstone Road, Atherstone, Warwickshire CV9 3PP
**Tel:** 01827-880472
**Web:** www.pawrightandsons.com
**Reg No:** 1886862 **Estd:** 1955 Private Limited Company
**Line of Business:** Growing of crops combined with farming of animals (mixed farming)
**Issued Capital:** £200
**Principals:** P A Wright *(Managing)*, D P Wright, T J Wright, R Wright, P H Wright
**US SIC:** 0291, 4953, 0214
**UK SIC:** 01001, 92110
**Bankers:** National Westminster Bank Plc (60-09-27)

| | 31-03-14 | 31-03-13 | 31-03-12 |
|---|---|---|---|
| TO | 18,726,980 | 14,598,210 | 15,679,933 |
| P/L | 2,680,723 | 3,024,474 | 4,223,181 |
| NW | 18,800,636 | 17,321,213 | 15,190,678 |
| WC | 4,602,689 | 3,900,419 | 3,058,312 |
| Emp. | 126 | 110 | 89 |

DUNS 39-693-7880

### P. & A. Packing (Northern) Ltd

Victoria House, 3 Huntsman Drive, Manchester M44 5EG
**Tel:** 01617778199 **Fax:** 01617778089
**Web:** www.papack.com
**Reg No:** 2150642 **Estd:** 1987 Private Limited Company
**Line of Business:** Other manufacturing not elsewhere classified
**Issued Capital:** £196
**Managing Director:** P Smith
**Co. Secretary:** Mrs Victoria Smith
**US SIC:** 3999 **UK SIC:** 49590
**Auditors:** Moors Andres Thomas & Co LLP

| | 30-11-13 | 30-11-12 | 30-11-11 |
|---|---|---|---|
| TA | 871,629 | 1,115,807 | 1,100,719 |
| NW | 602,535 | 725,640 | 635,919 |
| WC | 528,047 | 627,206 | 481,176 |

DUNS 73-728-4211

### P & A Receivables Services Plc

Kendall House, 41 Scotland Street, Sheffield, South Yorkshire S3 7BS
**Tel:** 01142-788868 **Fax:** 01142788824
**Web:** www.pandarecruitment.com
**Reg No:** 4986619 **Estd:** 2003 Public Limited Company
**Line of Business:** Business and management consultancy activities not elsewhere classified
**Issued Capital:** £50,000
**Directors:** S T Cooper, J J Priestley, Miss V S Hardwick, I S Wigfield
**Co. Secretary:** Ms Dawn Webster
**Responsibilities**
**Senior:** Laurie beagle *(Directors of investigations)*
**Finance:** Steve Dunwell *(Finance Manager)*
**US SIC:** 7392 **UK SIC:** 83951
**Auditors:** Garbutt & Elliott LLP
**Bankers:** Yorkshire Bank Plc (05-08-03)

| | 30-04-14 | 30-04-13 | 31-04-11 |
|---|---|---|---|
| TO | 3,097,134 | 4,706,756 | 4,100,574 |
| P/L | (175,557) | (438,448) | 43,356 |
| NW | (882,416) | (666,100) | (346,688) |
| WC | (894,133) | (879,715) | (598,994) |
| Emp. | 68 | 86 | 88 |

DUNS 23-669-0178

### P & A Wood

Great Easton, Dunmow, Essex CM6 2HD
**Web:** www.pa-wood.co.uk
**Estd:** 1980 Partnership
**Line of Business:** Sale of new motor vehicles
**Trading Style:** P and A Wood Llp
**Partners:** A Wood, P Wood
**Responsibilities**
**Finance:** Terry Malby *(Accounts Manager)*
**US SIC:** 5511 **UK SIC:** 65100
**Employees:** 50

DUNS 21-299-2333 Imp

### P. & B. (Foods) Ltd

(**Subsidiary of:** P. & B. Foods Holdings Ltd)
Bhagat Building, Bradfabs Ltd, 61a Planetrees Road, Bradford, West Yorkshire BD4 8AE
**Tel:** 01274-660118 **Fax:** 01274-668844
**Web:** www.pbfoods.co.uk
**Reg No:** 0988034 **VAT No:** 179913319
**Estd:** 1968 Private Limited Company
**Line of Business:** Agents involved in the sale of a variety of goods
**Export Sales:** £5,393,387
**Issued Capital:** £68,340
**Principals:** T V Patel *(Chairman)*, C Patel
**Co. Secretary:** Mohinder Bhatoa
**Responsibilities**
**Finance:** R Morker *(Accountant)*
**US SIC:** 5199 **UK SIC:** 61900
**Auditors:** Baker Tilly UK Audit LLP

| | 31-03-14 | 31-03-13 | 31-03-12 |
|---|---|---|---|
| TO | 44,680,648 | 41,046,954 | 38,325,894 |
| P/L | 3,695,178 | 3,152,922 | 3,700,148 |
| NW | 4,512,873 | 1,677,476 | 2,172,416 |
| WC | 7,904,841 | 6,872,864 | 7,698,889 |
| Emp. | 103 | 102 | 97 |

DUNS 49-000-0650

### P & B Kennedy Holdings Ltd

Herncliffe, Keighley, West Yorkshire BD20 6LH
**Tel:** 01535681484 **Fax:** 01535691693
**Web:** www.pbkennedy.co.uk
**Reg No:** 3068036 **Estd:** 1981 Private Limited Company
**Line of Business:** Clinics private
**Trading Style:** Herncliffe Nursing Home
**Issued Capital:** £10,002
**Directors:** P Kennedy, P Kennedy (Jnr), S Kennedy, Ms V Birch
**Co. Secretary:** John Kennedy
**Responsibilities**
**HR:** Sheila Lambert *(Home Manager)*
**Health & Safety:** Sheila Lambert *(Home Manager)*
**Purchasing:** Sheila Lambert *(Home Manager)*
**US SIC:** 8051 **UK SIC:** 95100
**Auditors:** Thompsons

| | 31-03-14 | 31-03-13 | 31-03-12 |
|---|---|---|---|
| TO | 3,800,365 | 3,779,221 | 3,879,748 |
| P/L | 164,850 | 239,780 | 218,081 |
| NW | 2,762,655 | 2,633,943 | 2,435,240 |
| WC | (408,913) | (353,379) | (532,350) |
| Emp. | 194 | 187 | 184 |

DUNS 21-706-3858 Imp-Exp

### P & B Metal Components Ltd

Tyler Way, Whitstable, Kent CT5 2RR
**Tel:** 01227-791-200 **Fax:** 01227794612
**Web:** www.p-and-b.com
**Reg No:** 0707502 **VAT No:** 201269895
**Estd:** 1961 Private Limited Company
**Line of Business:** Manufacture of tools
**Export Markets:** E C Countries, Far East, Africa, U.S.A.
**Export Sales:** £22,824,380
**Issued Capital:** £736,359
**Directors:** G D Bartlett, P A Bushell, S R Brown, J Howard, G P Miller
**Co. Secretary:** Mrs June Bushell
**Responsibilities**
**Senior:** Raymond Archer *(Financial Director)*
**Finance:** Raymond Archer *(Financial Director)*
**Branches:** P & B Metal Components Ltd, Westbrook Road, Margate, Kent CT9 5BB
**US SIC:** 3423 **UK SIC:** 31612
**Auditors:** Rayner Essex LLP
**Bankers:** National Westminster Bank Plc (60-04-27)

| | 31-05-13 | 31-05-12 | 31-05-11 |
|---|---|---|---|
| TO | 28,789,829 | 30,301,673 | 29,003,391 |
| P/L | 431,106 | 1,194,629 | 2,312,856 |
| NW | 14,047,827 | 14,026,172 | 13,166,104 |
| WC | 8,048,565 | 7,911,655 | 6,987,176 |
| Emp. | 214 | 220 | 214 |

DUNS 21-884-3134 Imp-Exp

### P. & F. Safepac Co. Ltd

Safepac House, Field Road, Mildenhall, Bury St Edmunds, Suffolk IP28 7AP
**Tel:** 01638-713323 **Fax:** 01638-713511
**Web:** www.safepac.co.uk
**Reg No:** 0872451 **VAT No:** 637893193
**Estd:** 1966 Private Limited Company
**Line of Business:** Ships agents
**Export Markets:** U S A, Africa
**Issued Capital:** £386,918
**Directors:** N Pearson, D Flynn
**Co. Secretary:** William Flynn
**Branches:** P. & F. Safepac Co. Ltd, H1 H2 East Way, Dales Manor Business Park, Swaston, Cambridge, Cambridgeshire CB22 3TJ
**US SIC:** 4712, 4213
**UK SIC:** 77002, 72300
**Auditors:** Stephenson Smart
**Bankers:** National Westminster Bank Plc (53-61-38)

| | 31-01-14 | 31-01-13 | 31-01-12 |
|---|---|---|---|
| TO | 7,354,629 | 6,794,587 | 7,675,863 |
| P/L | (634,156) | (487,604) | 58,773 |
| NW | 2,332,216 | 2,824,564 | 3,232,689 |
| WC | 515,411 | 779,531 | 1,198,600 |
| Emp. | 80 | 80 | 83 |

DUNS 23-804-2084

### P & H Contract Services Ltd

(**Subsidiary of:** Wallbank Holdings Ltd)
M4 Mulberry, Heywood, Lancashire OL10 2TR
**Tel:** 01617 052415 **Fax:** 01617972612
**Web:** www.phcs.co.uk
**Reg No:** 3796710 **Estd:** 1990 Private Limited Company
**Line of Business:** Freight transport by road not elsewhere classified
**Issued Capital:** £61
**Directors:** P J Houston, S D Gent
**Responsibilities**
**Finance:** Zoe Ball *(Accounts Manager)*
**HR:** Tracey Houston *(Human Resources Manager)*
**Health & Safety:** Richard Whittingham *(Health & Safety Officer)*
**Branches:** P & H Contract Services Ltd, Dukeminster Estate, Dunstable, Bedfordshire LU5 4HU
**US SIC:** 4213, 4226
**UK SIC:** 72300, 77003
**Auditors:** M.J. Forshaw

| | 31-07-14 | 31-07-13 | 31-07-12 |
|---|---|---|---|
| TO | 9,131,849 | 9,902,541 | 9,291,665 |
| P/L | 216,339 | 257,252 | 336,626 |
| NW | 701,351 | 831,467 | 629,920 |
| WC | 681,419 | 769,358 | 471,861 |
| Emp. | 176 | 187 | 165 |

DUNS 51-986-2689

### P & H Residential Cleaning Company Ltd

72-74 Gipsy Hill, London SE19 1PD
**Reg No:** 3993142 **Estd:** 2000 Private Limited Company
**Line of Business:** Traditional cleaning activities
**Issued Capital:** £1
**Director:** D J Parfitt
**Co. Secretary:** William Pellett
**US SIC:** 7349 **UK SIC:** 92300

| | 31-03-14 | 31-03-13 | 31-03-12 |
|---|---|---|---|
| TO | 45,908 | 50,178 | 47,496 |
| P/L | 22,985 | 2,050 | 3,726 |
| NW | 91,033 | 72,645 | 71,005 |
| WC | 91,033 | 72,645 | 71,005 |

DUNS 21-102-9205

### P & I Fruits Ltd

C69-C75, London SW8 5JJ
**Tel:** 02070628700 **Fax:** 020-749-82396
**Web:** www.freshproduce.org.uk
**Reg No:** 6460106 **Estd:** 2007 Private Limited Company
**Line of Business:** Wholesalers of fruit and vegetable
**Issued Capital:** £750,000
**Directors:** P Bishop, I C Taylor, P C Emmett
**Co. Secretary:** Ian Taylor
**US SIC:** 5148 **UK SIC:** 61700
**Auditors:** Crouch Chapman
**Bankers:** National Westminster Bank Plc (60-40-05)

| | 28-03-14 | 28-03-13 | 30-03-12 |
|---|---|---|---|
| TO | 29,255,812 | 29,996,192 | 27,592,646 |
| P/L | 1,214,921 | 1,053,797 | 998,277 |
| NW | 2,287,808 | 2,170,466 | 2,106,779 |
| WC | 2,078,141 | 1,950,776 | 1,956,793 |
| Emp. | 51 | 53 | 42 |

DUNS 39-694-6360

### P & L Joinery Sub-Contractors Ltd

Unit 8d, Mackenzie Industrial Estate, Bird Hall Lane, Stockport, Cheshire SK3 0SB
**Tel:** 0161-491-0066
**Web:** www.pandljoinery.com
**Reg No:** 2151528 **Estd:** 1987 Private Limited Company
**Line of Business:** Joinery and carpentry
**Issued Capital:** £100
**Principals:** F M Pratt *(Managing)*, S Wilkinson
**Co. Secretary:** Ms Teresa Pratt
**US SIC:** 2431 **UK SIC:** 46300
**Auditors:** Hallidays
**Bankers:** National Westminster Bank Plc (01-02-69)

| | 31-10-13 | 31-10-12 | 31-10-11 |
|---|---|---|---|
| TA | 982,453 | 982,164 | 864,031 |
| NW | 514,032 | 597,555 | 551,306 |
| WC | 502,043 | 591,008 | 543,309 |

DUNS 29-867-1454
### The P & M Group Ltd
27 Eastville Close, Eastern Avenue, Gloucester, Gloucestershire GL4 3SJ
**Tel:** 01452300073 **Fax:** 01452-416800
**Web:** www.pandm.co.uk
**Reg No:** 2070336 **VAT No:** 448444332
**Estd:** 1987 Private Limited Company
**Line of Business:** Manufacture of electric domestic appliances
**Export Sales:** £7,411,815
**Trading Style:** Cold Store Maintenance
**Issued Capital:** £325,000
**Principals:** A P Moon *(Managing)*, A Wall, G E Ross, P C Moon, A R Smith
**Branches:** The P & M Group Ltd, 28 Hempsted Lane, Gloucester, Gloucestershire GL2 5JA
**US SIC:** 3999, 1796
**UK SIC:** 49590, 50400
**Auditors:** Davies Mayers Barnett LLP
**Bankers:** Lloyds TSB Bank plc (30-93-48)

| | 31-01-14 | 31-01-13 | 31-01-12 |
|---|---|---|---|
| TO | 27,313,373 | 22,392,440 | 22,587,402 |
| P/L | 2,116,153 | 808,480 | 759,310 |
| NW | 4,355,513 | 3,220,969 | 2,827,733 |
| WC | 4,103,837 | 2,925,553 | 2,486,417 |
| Emp. | 93 | 91 | 90 |

DUNS 42-477-5679
### P & M Sinclair Ltd
**(Subsidiary of:** P & M Sinclair Holdings Ltd)
Thornton Road, Rosewell, Midlothian EH24 9DP
**Tel:** 0131-440-3438 **Fax:** 0131-440-4621
**Web:** www.pmsinclair.co.uk
**Reg No:** 0233066SC **Estd:** 1964 Private Limited Company
**Line of Business:** Builders
**Issued Capital:** £1,000
**Directors:** P Sinclair, Ms L C Sinclair
**Co. Secretary:** Douglas Sinclair
**US SIC:** 1522 **UK SIC:** 50100

| | 30-04-14 | 30-04-13 | 30-04-12 |
|---|---|---|---|
| TA | 924,117 | 828,364 | 1,053,660 |
| NW | 28,679 | 22,150 | 74,892 |
| WC | 350,602 | 413,772 | 334,965 |

DUNS 21-710-0091
### P & N Security Llp
16 Hanover Square, London W1S 1HT
**Web:** www.pnsecurity.co.uk
**Reg No:** 0361142OC **Estd:** 2011
**Line of Business:** Security activities
**US SIC:** 7393 **UK SIC:** 83954

| | 31-01-14 | 31-01-13 | 31-01-12 |
|---|---|---|---|
| TA | 30,730 | 15,278 | 1,225 |
| NW | 21,433 | 11,817 | 235 |
| WC | 26,698 | 10,360 | 725 |

DUNS 21-586-5865
### P & O Ferries
10 Redlands Road, Larne, Co Antrim BT40 1FD
**Tel:** 02828872200
**Web:** www.poferries.com
**Estd:** 1958 Partnership
**Line of Business:** Passenger sea and coastal water transport
**Partners:** M Ridley, R Peters, Mrs A Rogan, Ms H Deeble
**US SIC:** 4452 **UK SIC:** 74002
**Employees:** 70

DUNS 34-627-6400
### P & O Lloyd Ltd
Rhydwen Garage, Bagillt Road, Flint, Clwyd CH6 6JJ
**Tel:** 01352-710682 **Fax:** 01352-710093
**Reg No:** 5434004 **Estd:** 1925 Private Limited Company
**Line of Business:** Coach and bus hire
**Issued Capital:** £100
**Director:** D Lloyd
**Co. Secretary:** Ms Susan Allsopp
**US SIC:** 4119 **UK SIC:** 72200

| | 31-07-14 | 31-07-13 | 31-07-12 |
|---|---|---|---|
| TA | 1,438,705 | 1,209,571 | 1,235,049 |
| NW | 1,014,112 | 738,174 | 596,787 |
| WC | 270,703 | 166,071 | (123,809) |

DUNS 39-466-9246
### P & P Associates Ltd
**(Subsidiary of:** P&P Group Ltd)
Suite F13, Stevenage, Hertfordshire SG1 2DX
**Tel:** 01438-791-063 **Fax:** 01438311119
**Web:** www.ppassociates.co.uk
**Reg No:** 2124920 **VAT No:** 456052065
**Estd:** 1987 Private Limited Company
**Line of Business:** Activities of travel agencies
**Trading Style:** 2000 Travel Management, Chelsea Travel Management
**Issued Capital:** £100,000
**Principals:** P E Cook *(Managing)*, A Lewis, Ms J A Lacey, Ms A J Bagnell
**Co. Secretary:** Kristie Henderson
**Branches:** P & P Associates Ltd, Meadway Court, Unit 3, Stevenage, Hertfordshire SG1 2EF
**US SIC:** 4722 **UK SIC:** 77001
**Auditors:** MacIntyre Hudson LLP
**Bankers:** HSBC Bank plc (40-16-07)

| | 31-03-14 | 31-03-13 | 31-03-12 |
|---|---|---|---|
| TO | 44,857,678 | 44,740,541 | 46,335,209 |
| P/L | 91,784 | 176,419 | 135,468 |
| NW | 852,302 | 852,674 | 790,702 |
| WC | 38,122 | 152,642 | 226,544 |
| Emp. | 58 | 49 | 52 |

DUNS 23-493-2531
### P & P Duct Services Ltd
Zagale House, Kelpatrick Road, Slough, Berkshire SL1 6BW
**Tel:** 01628666616
**Web:** www.ppduct.uk
**Reg No:** 2828106 **VAT No:** 614910262
**Estd:** 1993 Private Limited Company
**Line of Business:** Blacksmiths
**Issued Capital:** £100
**Managing Director:** P Clements
**Co. Secretary:** Paul Taylor
**Responsibilities**
**Finance:** Taraq Ali *(Accountant)*
**US SIC:** 3469, 3499
**UK SIC:** 31200, 31694
**Auditors:** Mehta & Co
**Bankers:** HSBC Bank plc (40-47-02)

| | 31-01-14 | 31-01-13 | 31-01-12 |
|---|---|---|---|
| TA | 2,190,698 | 2,257,181 | 2,345,590 |
| NW | 891,880 | 1,119,325 | 1,089,393 |
| WC | 479,262 | 127,965 | 335,853 |

DUNS 22-594-4826
### P & P Glass Ltd
**(Subsidiary of:** P & P Holdings Ltd)
Unit 15 Old Portsmouth Road Quadrum Park, Guildford, Surrey GU3 1LU
**Tel:** 01483467250
**Web:** www.pandpglass.co.uk
**Reg No:** 2282602 **Estd:** 1988 Private Limited Company
**Line of Business:** Painting and glazing
**Issued Capital:** £1,262
**Principals:** U Stahlschmidt *(Managing)*, T P Scanlan, R Gilham
**Co. Secretary:** Kenneth Sauvarin
**Responsibilities**
**Senior:** Andy Musgrove *(Manager)*
**Sales:** Gary Merriott *(Sales Manager)*
**IT:** Andy Musgrove *(Manager)*
**Branches:** P & P Glass Ltd, Unit 15, Old Portsmouth Road, Guildford, Surrey GU3 1LU
**US SIC:** 3231, 1721
**UK SIC:** 24791, 50400
**Auditors:** Lever Bros & Co
**Bankers:** Barclays Bank Plc (20-35-35)

| | 31-10-13 | 31-10-12 | 31-10-11 |
|---|---|---|---|
| TO | 6,879,133 | 7,459,985 | 7,608,113 |
| P/L | 14,476 | (161,488) | 104,973 |
| NW | 81,841 | 67,059 | 206,783 |
| WC | (260,091) | (344,967) | (95,028) |
| Emp. | 60 | 68 | 64 |

DUNS 53-653-9331
### P & R Installation Company Ltd
6-8 Powerscroft Road, Sidcup, Kent DA14 5DT
**Tel:** 08003457000 **Fax:** 02088-516611
**Web:** www.pandr.com
**Reg No:** 3459190 **VAT No:** 714182064
**Estd:** 2011 Private Limited Company
**Line of Business:** Plumbers
**Issued Capital:** £1,000
**Directors:** D Richardson, P J Copolo, D T Ellingham, D P Dunnett, L Copolo
**Responsibilities**
**IT:** Fitz Hamilton *(IT Manager)*
**Branches:** P & R Installation Company Ltd, 178 Bexley Road, London SE9 2PH
**US SIC:** 1711 **UK SIC:** 50300
**Auditors:** Harrison Hill Castle & Co

| | 31-01-14 | 31-01-13 | 31-01-12 |
|---|---|---|---|
| TO | 9,455,806 | 8,459,633 | 7,607,647 |
| P/L | 733,660 | 496,819 | 700,415 |
| NW | 1,313,222 | 786,222 | 589,845 |
| WC | 630,393 | 57,050 | (27,371) |
| Emp. | 93 | 112 | 125 |

DUNS 56-939-1683
### P & R Morson & Company Ltd
Unit E3, Coombswood Way, Halesowen, West Midlands B62 8BH
**Tel:** 08712232051
**Web:** www.prmorson.co.uk
**Reg No:** 2838686 **Estd:** 1995 Private Limited Company
**Line of Business:** Building services
**Issued Capital:** £1,000
**Director:** P R Morris
**Co. Secretary:** Miss Ruth Hartell
**Responsibilities**
**Purchasing:** Gary Bayliss *(Buyer)*
**US SIC:** 1622 **UK SIC:** 50200
**Auditors:** Heathcote & Coleman

| | 31-07-13 | 31-07-12 | 31-07-11 |
|---|---|---|---|
| TO | 12,519,662 | 11,627,935 | 12,918,841 |
| P/L | 175,221 | 46,780 | 186,425 |
| NW | 962,429 | 865,317 | 908,770 |
| WC | 557,080 | 333,265 | 414,682 |
| Emp. | 56 | 56 | 51 |

DUNS 22-522-9194 Exp
### P B Design & Developments Ltd
**(Subsidiary of:** P B Design Holdings Ltd)
Unit 9-10, Hither Green Industrial Estate, Clevedon, Avon BS21 6XT
**Fax:** 01275-874428
**Web:** www.pbdesign.co.uk
**Reg No:** 1432936 **VAT No:** 336646833
**Estd:** 1979 Private Limited Company
**Line of Business:** Battery suppliers
**Export Markets:** countries worldwide
**Export Sales:** £215,981
**Trading Style:** P B Design & Developments Ltd
**Issued Capital:** £8,979
**Director:** A Hooper
**Co. Secretary:** Timothy Broomfield
**Responsibilities**
**Senior:** Richard Croad *(Warehouse Manager)*, Mark Crocker *(General Manager)*
**Sales:** Philip Tomkinson *(Business Development Manager)*
**US SIC:** 4911 **UK SIC:** 16101
**Auditors:** Robson Taylor LLP
**Bankers:** HSBC Bank plc (40-14-18)

| | 30-06-14 | 30-06-13 | 30-06-12 |
|---|---|---|---|
| TO | 6,900,343 | N/A | N/A |
| P/L | 923,810 | N/A | N/A |
| NW | 4,516,230 | 3,785,508 | 3,237,084 |
| WC | 3,816,820 | 3,058,531 | 2,610,290 |
| Emp. | 47 | N/A | N/A |

DUNS 76-910-0678
### P B Development Company Ltd
15 Summer Street, Aberdeen, Aberdeenshire AB10 1SB
**Tel:** 01224-626888
**Web:** www.pbdevco.com
**Reg No:** 0097813SC **Estd:** 1985 Private Limited Company
**Line of Business:** Activities of venture and development capital companies
**Issued Capital:** £10
**Managing Director:** S A Clarkson
**Co. Secretary:** Burness Paull Llp
**US SIC:** 7399 **UK SIC:** 83954
**Auditors:** Anderson Anderson & Brown

| | 31-03-14 | 31-03-13 | 31-03-12 |
|---|---|---|---|
| TO | 6,392,663 | 6,125,619 | 5,502,771 |
| P/L | 580,932 | 832,901 | 1,066,857 |
| NW | 12,066,143 | 11,631,222 | 10,993,825 |
| WC | 1,889,723 | 1,601,862 | 264,995 |
| Emp. | 179 | 158 | 164 |

DUNS 29-175-7045
### P. B. Donoghue (Construction) Ltd
**(Subsidiary of:** P.B. Donoghue (Haulage & Plant Hire) Ltd)
Donoghue Business Park, Claremont Road, London NW2 1RR
**Tel:** 02082082211 **Fax:** 02084522162
**Web:** www.pbdonoghue.com
**Reg No:** 1848478 **VAT No:** 544648816
**Estd:** 1991 Private Limited Company
**Line of Business:** Agents involved in the sale of timber and building materials
**Issued Capital:** £100
**Directors:** Mrs E B Mcgowan, P B Donoghue, P B Donoghue (Haulage & Plant Hi
**Co. Secretary:** Ms Elizabeth Donoghue
**US SIC:** 5072, 1541
**UK SIC:** 61500, 50100
**Auditors:** Hardy & Co
**Bankers:** Allied Irish Bank (gb) (23-84-84)

| | 31-12-13 | 31-12-12 | 31-12-11 |
|---|---|---|---|
| TO | 14,779,625 | 12,616,389 | 10,189,873 |
| P/L | 1,206,651 | 757,240 | 170,867 |
| NW | 2,534,924 | 1,625,689 | 1,076,541 |
| WC | 975,759 | (12,905) | (639,744) |
| Emp. | 63 | 54 | 62 |

DUNS 21-738-3321
### P B Donoghue (Waste Management) Ltd
Donoghue Buildings, 3 Shannon Close, London NW2 1RR
**Reg No:** 7720434 **Estd:** 2011 Private Limited Company
**Line of Business:** Sanitation, remediation and similar activities
**Issued Capital:** £1,000
**Director:** P B Donoghue
**US SIC:** 4959 **UK SIC:** 92110

| | 31-12-13 | 31-12-12 | 31-12-11 |
|---|---|---|---|
| TO | 14,779,625 | 12,616,389 | 10,189,873 |
| P/L | 1,280,516 | 927,284 | 263,160 |
| NW | 2,886,671 | 1,912,620 | 1,218,623 |
| WC | 1,146,033 | 158,694 | (544,024) |
| Emp. | 63 | 54 | 62 |

DUNS 21-929-0053 Imp-Exp
### P B Gelatins U.K. Ltd
**(Subsidiary of:** Tessenderlo Chemie Sa)
Unit A6, Pontypridd, Mid Glamorgan CF37 5SQ
**Tel:** 01443-849300 **Fax:** 01443-844209
**Web:** www.pbgelatins.com
**Reg No:** 1477674 **VAT No:** 484264428
**Estd:** 1980 Private Limited Company
**Line of Business:** Manufacturers general
**Export Markets:** Worldwide
**Issued Capital:** £9,825,000
**Directors:** R Dumont, W Y Poot, J Vandendriessche
**Co. Secretary:** Mark Evans
**Responsibilities**
**Senior:** Wendy Gerry *(Manager)*
**Finance:** Wendy Gerry *(Manager)*
**Health & Safety:** Alan Fitzpatrick *(Health & Safety Officer)*
**Operations:** Alan Fitzpatrick *(Health & Safety Officer)*
**US SIC:** 2099 **UK SIC:** 42399
**Auditors:** KPMG LLP
**Bankers:** HSBC Bank plc (40-16-18)

| | 31-12-13 | 31-12-12 | 31-12-11 |
|---|---|---|---|
| TO | 32,796,606 | 29,332,048 | 29,632,644 |
| P/L | 105,236 | (328,991) | 366,050 |
| NW | 4,294,179 | 4,137,663 | 5,015,519 |
| WC | 944,577 | 3,732,176 | 7,193,315 |
| Emp. | 71 | 71 | 68 |

DUNS 21-791-5376
### P B Heating Services
Unit 5 Shawfield Road, Barnsley, South Yorkshire S71 3HS
**Tel:** 01226730303
**Web:** www.pbhs.net
**Estd:** 2006 Proprietorship
**Line of Business:** Central heating systems (installation and servicing)
**Proprietor:** P Bates
**US SIC:** 4925 **UK SIC:** 25670
**Employees:** 50

DUNS 21-588-8641
### P Bryant
16 Park Lane, Fareham, Hampshire PO16 7JX
**Estd:** 2011 Proprietorship
**Line of Business:** Dentists
**Proprietor:** Dr P Bryant
**US SIC:** 8021 **UK SIC:** 95400
**Employees:** 74

DUNS 29-858-9987
### P.C. Contractors (Northern) Ltd
**(Subsidiary of:** P.C. Contractors Holdings Ltd)
The Hall, 10a Hazel Street, Nottingham, Nottinghamshire NG6 8EA
**Tel:** 01159-279191 **Fax:** 01159-274734
**Web:** www.pccontractors.co.uk
**Reg No:** 2062262 **VAT No:** 449984774
**Estd:** 1987 Private Limited Company
**Line of Business:** Ceilings (suspended)
**Trading Style:** P C Contractors
**Issued Capital:** £300,000
**Co. Secretary:** Ms June Charles
**Responsibilities**
**Senior:** Keith Charles *(Manager)*
**Marketing:** Keith Charles *(Manager)*
**US SIC:** 1799 **UK SIC:** 50000
**Auditors:** Richard J Hilton
**Bankers:** National Westminster Bank Plc (54-21-51)

| | 31-12-13 | 31-12-12 | 31-12-11 |
|---|---|---|---|
| TA | 537,392 | 588,811 | 719,697 |
| NW | 345,383 | 389,258 | 361,987 |
| WC | 231,218 | 251,887 | 403,288 |

DUNS 38-577-4922 Imp
### P C Cox Ltd
**(Subsidiary of:** Pc Cox Group Ltd.)
Turnpike Road Turnpike Industrial Estate, Newbury, Berkshire RG14 2NS
**Tel:** 01635-264-500
**Web:** www.pccox.co.uk
**Reg No:** 3338184 **VAT No:** 642285147
**Estd:** 1997 Private Limited Company
**Line of Business:** Sealing compounds and application
**Export Sales:** £11,973,000
**Issued Capital:** £1
**Directors:** F J Lumb, I Newberry, L M Smith, C E Beckett, R J Hart, Ms D Salisbury, G Hernandez Coria, D Inglut
**Co. Secretary:** Peter Crawford
**Responsibilities**
**HR:** Janet Hannah *(Personnel Manager)*
**Health & Safety:** Janet Hannah *(Personnel Manager)*
**Operations:** Janet Hannah *(Personnel Manager)*
**US SIC:** 1761, 3423, 3546
**UK SIC:** 50400, 31612, 32852
**Auditors:** H W

**Bankers:** Barclays Bank Plc (20-59-14)

| | 31-12-13 | 31-12-12 | 31-12-11 |
|---|---|---|---|
| TO | 13,788,000 | 12,701,000 | 13,881,000 |
| P/L | 2,054,000 | 18,086,000 | 1,501,000 |
| NW | 7,598,000 | 7,313,000 | (10,736,000) |
| WC | 4,680,000 | 3,850,000 | 2,886,000 |
| Emp. | 164 | 159 | 160 |

**DUNS 21-926-7101**

## P C E Ltd

(**Subsidiary of:** P.C.E. Group Holdings Ltd)
Unit 5, Mariner, Tamworth, Staffordshire B79 7UL

**Tel:** 01827-301020 **Fax:** 01827301021
**Web:** www.pceltd.co.uk
**Reg No:** 1146346 **VAT No:** 544903048
**Estd:** 1973 Private Limited Company
**Line of Business:** Specialised building trade contractors
**Issued Capital:** £50,000
**Directors:** S Harold, K Hubbard, G Langston, C M Mcreynolds, N Brown, G Firth
**Co. Secretary:** John Craig
**Responsibilities**
**Senior:** Vince Wetton (Chairman)
**HR:** Christina Hart (Human Resources Manager)
**US SIC:** 1799 **UK SIC:** 50000
**Auditors:** BDO Stoy Hayward LLP
**Bankers:** Lloyds TSB Bank plc (30-96-20)

| | 31-12-13 | 31-12-12 | 31-12-11 |
|---|---|---|---|
| TO | 12,988,399 | 6,762,154 | 10,176,706 |
| P/L | 109,520 | 93,350 | 1,118,521 |
| NW | 2,820,831 | 2,636,129 | 2,576,453 |
| WC | 687,125 | 1,296,206 | 1,448,650 |
| Emp. | 84 | 66 | 104 |

**DUNS 21-586-5856**

## P C L Transport

Charlton Mead Lane, Hoddesdon, Hertfordshire EN11 0DJ
**Tel:** 01992478072
**Web:** www.pcltransport.co.uk
**Estd:** 2000 Proprietorship
**Line of Business:** Road haulage and transport services
**Proprietor:** J Ricotta
**US SIC:** 4789 **UK SIC:** 77002
**Employees:** 200

**DUNS 23-275-5025**

## P C S Wholesale Motor Factors

4 Bay, Furnace Hill, Clay Cross, Chesterfield, Derbyshire S45 9NF
**Tel:** 01246250999
**Web:** www.pcsparts.co.uk
**VAT No:** 295602343 **Estd:** 2005 Partnership
**Line of Business:** Sale of motor vehicle parts and accessories
**Partners:** S Marsden, R Wilson, P Townsend
**US SIC:** 5531 **UK SIC:** 65100
**Bankers:** Lloyds TSB Bank plc (77-74-17)
**Employees:** 102

**DUNS 21-457-3826** Exp

## P. Clarke & Sons Ltd

Slushill Quarries, Enniskillen, Co Fermanagh BT92 0AF
**Tel:** 02867-721286
**Web:** www.clarkeltd.com
**Reg No:** 0003206NI **VAT No:** 251832569
**Estd:** 1935 Private Limited Company
**Line of Business:** Quarrying of stone
**Export Markets:** Republic of Ireland
**Trading Style:** Clarke Homes
**Issued Capital:** £16,334
**Directors:** P V Clarke, T J Clarke, D Clarke, Ms D A Somerville
**Co. Secretary:** David Clarke
**Responsibilities**
**Senior:** Paul McDermott (Transport Manager)
**Marketing:** Martin Lowry (Marketing Manager)
**Sales:** Liam Curran (Sales Director)
**HR:** Mairead Corr (Human Resources Manager)
**Health & Safety:** Wendy Beattie (Quality Officer)
**Facilities:** Paddy McManus (Quarry Manager)
**Operations:** Wendy Beattie (Quality Officer), Liam Curran (Sales Director)
**Purchasing:** Paddy McManus (Quarry Manager)
**Fleet:** Paul McDermott (Transport Manager)
**Engineering:** Paddy McManus (Quarry Manager)
**US SIC:** 1429, 3999
**UK SIC:** 23102, 49590
**Auditors:** Grant Thornton UK LLP
**Bankers:** Ulster Bank Ltd (98-09-70)

| | 31-03-14 | 31-03-13 | 31-03-12 |
|---|---|---|---|
| TO | 20,789,000 | 20,524,000 | 17,698,000 |
| P/L | 135,000 | (273,000) | 226,000 |
| NW | 4,347,000 | 4,272,000 | 4,634,000 |
| WC | (2,470,000) | 1,727,000 | (2,904,000) |
| Emp. | 111 | 96 | 89 |

**DUNS 53-548-2459**

## P D M Produce

Chadwell Park Farm, Great Chatwell, Newport, Shropshire TF10 9BN
**Tel:** 01952-691617
**Web:** www.pdmproduce.co.uk
**Estd:** 1991 Proprietorship
**Line of Business:** Wholesalers of fruit and vegetable
**Proprietor:** P D Maddocks
**Responsibilities**
**Senior:** Andrew Jeffery (Commercial Director), Dermot Tobin (Farms Manager)
**Sales:** Andrew Jeffery (Commercial Director)
**HR:** Dawn Jarmson (Human Resources Manager)
**Operations:** Stephen Kingdom (Technical, Production Manager)
**Engineering:** Stephen Kingdom (Technical, Production Manager)
**US SIC:** 5148 **UK SIC:** 61700
**Employees:** 128

**DUNS 38-586-5969**

## P D P Courier Services Ltd

(**Subsidiary of:** Spl Services Ltd)
Unit 2c Plane Tree Crescent, Feltham, Middlesex TW13 7HF
**Tel:** 01784420466 **Fax:** 01784 424300
**Web:** www.pdpcouriers.com
**Reg No:** 3341254 **Estd:** 1997 Private Limited Company
**Line of Business:** Freight transport by road not elsewhere classified
**Issued Capital:** £13,101
**Directors:** M E Joshi, Dr J W Totten, I A Mcleish
**Responsibilities**
**Senior:** Paul Balkwell (Operations Director), Robert Bier (Manager), Clive Bryant (Manager), Nick Butcher (Manager), Archibald Thomson (Manager)
**Finance:** Lorna Wright (Financial Controller)
**Facilities:** Paul Balkwell (Operations Director)
**Operations:** Kylie Thornhill (Operations Manager)
**Fleet:** Paul Balkwell (Operations Director)
**US SIC:** 4213, 4311
**UK SIC:** 72300, 79010
**Auditors:** Grant Thornton UK LLP
**Bankers:** HSBC Bank plc (40-05-23)

| | 31-07-14 | 31-07-13 | 31-07-12 |
|---|---|---|---|
| TO | 13,046,956 | 13,134,122 | 11,906,374 |
| P/L | 838,587 | (4,964,976) | 614,242 |
| NW | (4,687,422) | (5,486,136) | (521,160) |
| WC | (923,973) | (2,499,625) | 1,346,349 |
| Emp. | 59 | 59 | 53 |

**DUNS 29-122-0945**

## P D S A Trading Ltd

(**Subsidiary of:** Peoples Dispensary for Sick Animals)
White Chapel Way, Priorslee, Telford, Shropshire TF2 9PQ
**Tel:** 0800591248 **Fax:** 08455564906
**Web:** www.bdmlconnect.co.uk
**Reg No:** 1595637 **Estd:** 1981 Private Limited Company
**Line of Business:** Other retail sale in specialised stores not elsewhere classified
**Trading Style:** P D S A Trading Ltd
**Issued Capital:** £2
**Directors:** G J Pick, Ms J L Mc Loughlin, Ms M Heckel, S F Bailey
**Co. Secretary:** Russell Eaton
**Responsibilities**
**Senior:** Andrew Holl (Director of business services)
**Branches:** P D S A Trading Ltd, Unit 6 Bramley Centre, Leeds, West Yorkshire LS13 2ET
**US SIC:** 5999, 6111, 7399, 7999
**UK SIC:** 65600, 81501, 83954, 97913
**Auditors:** Deloitte LLP
**Bankers:** Lloyds TSB Bank plc (77-27-10)

| | 31-12-13 | 31-12-12 | 31-12-11 |
|---|---|---|---|
| TA | 1,333,686 | 1,927,684 | 1,710,403 |
| P/L | N/A | N/A | 2,438,678 |
| NW | 7,223 | 7,223 | 7,223 |
| WC | 7,223 | 7,223 | 7,223 |

**DUNS 23-283-6320** Imp

## P D Teesport Ltd

(**Subsidiary of:** Brookfield Asset Management Inc)
Craft Depot, Vulcan Street, Middlesbrough, Cleveland TS2 1LX
**Tel:** 01642877110
**Web:** www.pdports.co.uk
**Reg No:** 2636007 **VAT No:** 601853463
**Estd:** 1991 Private Limited Company
**Line of Business:** Operation of habours and ports
**Issued Capital:** £2
**Directors:** R W Mccallion, D J Robinson, J M Hopkinson
**Co. Secretary:** Dermot Russell

**Responsibilities**
**Marketing:** Kirstin Potter (Public Relations Manager)
**IT:** Michael Westmoreland (Business Systems Officer)
**Health & Safety:** John Simm (Health & Safety Officer)
**Branches:** P D Teesport Ltd, Tees Dock, Middlesbrough, Cleveland TS6 6UD
**US SIC:** 4469, 4411, 4226
**UK SIC:** 76300, 74001, 77003
**Auditors:** Deloitte LLP
**Bankers:** The Royal Bank Of Scotland Plc (16-26-32)

| | 31-12-13 | 31-12-12 | 31-12-11 |
|---|---|---|---|
| TO | 76,951,000 | 73,906,000 | 69,715,000 |
| P/L | (107,646,000) | (86,847,000) | (45,290,000) |
| NW | (234,579,000) | (129,395,000) | (42,034,000) |
| WC | 267,101,000 | 387,193,000 | 367,465,000 |
| Emp. | 271 | 277 | 369 |

**DUNS 51-740-2863**

## P E C Building Services

Pearl House, Commondale Way, Euroway Industrial Estate, Bradford, West Yorkshire BD4 6SF
**Tel:** 01274-686668
**Web:** www.p-e-c.co.uk
**Estd:** 2005 Partnership
**Line of Business:** Electrical contractors and electricians
**Partners:** M S Panesar, B Panesar, B Panesar, G S Panesar
**Responsibilities**
**Senior:** Sohan Panesar (Manager)
**US SIC:** 1731 **UK SIC:** 50300
**Employees:** 100

**DUNS 29-049-9250**

## P. Flannery Plant Hire (Oval) Ltd

Third Way, Wembley, Middlesex HA9 0RZ
**Tel:** 02089-009-290 **Fax:** 02089-027-357
**Web:** www.flanneryplant.co.uk
**Reg No:** 1058421 **Estd:** 2003 Private Limited Company
**Line of Business:** Plant hire and leasing
**Issued Capital:** £100
**Principals:** P Flannery (Managing), M C Flannery, P Flannery
**Co. Secretary:** Ms Mary Flannery
**Responsibilities**
**Senior:** Paul Flannery (Proprietor)
**Finance:** Fiona Ivory (Accountant)
**Branches:** P. Flannery Plant Hire (Oval) Limited, Third Way, Wembley, Middlesex HA9 0RZ
**US SIC:** 1799, 5082
**UK SIC:** 50000, 61490
**Auditors:** Buckingham & Co
**Bankers:** National Westminster Bank Plc (50-41-01)

| | 31-03-14 | 31-03-13 | 31-03-12 |
|---|---|---|---|
| TO | 35,812,863 | 21,245,075 | 21,029,827 |
| P/L | 7,768,598 | 3,935,203 | 3,529,101 |
| NW | 20,019,217 | 14,028,653 | 10,896,071 |
| WC | (3,384,339) | (4,754,056) | (6,829,181) |
| Emp. | 101 | 40 | 23 |

**DUNS 21-586-0147**

## P G L

Barton Hall, Kingskerswell Road, Torquay, Devon TQ2 8JY
**Tel:** 01803321400
**Estd:** 2011 Partnership
**Line of Business:** Other tourist or short-stay accommodation
**Partners:** D Moore, M Davis
**US SIC:** 7021 **UK SIC:** 66500
**Employees:** 176

**DUNS 22-622-7288**

## P G R Timber Ltd

(**Subsidiary of:** Pgr Enterprises Ltd)
Denbigh Road, Basildon, Essex SS15 6PY
**Tel:** 01268419424
**Web:** www.pgrtimber.co.uk
**Reg No:** 1832731 **VAT No:** 368747889
**Estd:** 1981 Private Limited Company
**Line of Business:** Agents involved in the sale of timber and building materials
**Issued Capital:** £800
**Directors:** S A Atkins, G J Toomey, P I Kruse
**Co. Secretary:** Mrs Rene Toomey
**Branches:** P G R Timber Ltd, 81 Tonbridge Road, Romford, Essex RM3 8TS
**US SIC:** 5072 **UK SIC:** 61500
**Auditors:** Sibley Chew
**Bankers:** Lloyds TSB Bank plc (30-10-52)

| | 31-03-14 | 31-03-13 | 31-03-12 |
|---|---|---|---|
| TO | 20,999,631 | 17,338,936 | 13,200,708 |
| P/L | 1,429,429 | 495,109 | 340,681 |
| NW | 2,905,978 | 2,803,856 | 2,921,858 |
| WC | 2,469,424 | 2,388,350 | 2,217,864 |
| Emp. | 91 | 84 | 67 |

**DUNS 21-773-4395**

## P H D

Avtech House, Hithercroft Road, Wallingford, Oxfordshire OX10 9DA
**Tel:** 01491825029
**Web:** www.plastichead.com
**Estd:** 1993 Partnership
**Line of Business:** Distribution service providers
**Partners:** S Beatty, Ms R Digweed
**US SIC:** 4712 **UK SIC:** 77002
**Employees:** 50

**DUNS 23-388-5628**

## P H Group Ltd

Royalty Studios, 105-109 Lancaster Road, London W11 1QF
**Tel:** 02079859700
**Web:** www.experian.co.uk
**Reg No:** 0053914NI **Estd:** 2003 Private Limited Company
**Line of Business:** Credit reporting and collection agency activities
**Issued Capital:** £2
**Director:** Ms G O'Hagan
**Co. Secretary:** Paul O'Hagan
**Responsibilities**
**Senior:** Max Firth (Manager), Paul Henry (Manager)
**Marketing:** Toby Alderson-Smith (Head of Business Development)
**Sales:** Toby Alderson-Smith (Head of Business Development)
**Admin:** Eve Thompson (Office Manager)
**IT:** Frederick Vander-Elst (IT Manager)
**Facilities:** Eve Thompson (Office Manager)
**US SIC:** 7321 **UK SIC:** 83954

| | 30-11-13 | 30-11-12 | 30-11-11 |
|---|---|---|---|
| TA | 5 | 5 | 5 |
| NW | 2 | 2 | 2 |
| WC | N/A | N/A | 2 |

**DUNS 21-592-9405**

## P H L

Oliver Road, Grays, Essex RM20 3EY
**Tel:** 01708863221
**Web:** www.dhl.com
**Estd:** 2000 Proprietorship
**Line of Business:** Distribution service providers
**Proprietor:** M Parry
**US SIC:** 4712 **UK SIC:** 77002
**Employees:** 68

**DUNS 89-616-8465**

## P H S All Clear Ltd

(**Subsidiary of:** Phs Group Holdings Ltd)
The Quadrant, Marlborough Road, Lancing, West Sussex BN15 8UW
**Tel:** 01903876006 **Fax:** 01903876182
**Web:** www.phs.co.uk
**Reg No:** 3314379 **Estd:** 1997 Private Limited Company
**Line of Business:** Representative office
**Issued Capital:** £50,008
**Director:** S A Woods
**Co. Secretary:** David Finlayson
**Responsibilities**
**Senior:** Anthony Pearlgood (Manager)
**Branches:** P H S All Clear Ltd, Hearthcote Rd, Swadlincote, Derbyshire DE11 9DU
**US SIC:** 7399, 4953
**UK SIC:** 83954, 92110
**Auditors:** PricewaterhouseCoopers LLP

| | 31-03-14 | 31-03-13 | 31-03-12 |
|---|---|---|---|
| TO | 41,917,000 | 54,744,000 | 62,357,000 |
| P/L | (13,996,000) | (42,359,000) | (1,169,000) |
| NW | (24,684,000) | (13,869,000) | (7,272,000) |
| WC | (24,684,000) | (19,768,000) | (13,268,000) |
| Emp. | 343 | 544 | 578 |

**DUNS 21-601-3857**

## P H S Waste Management

Unit 36 Moss Road Industrial Estate, Moss Road, Kearsley, Bolton, Lancashire BL4 8HS
**Tel:** 01204704633
**Web:** www.phs.co.uk
**Estd:** 2011 Proprietorship
**Line of Business:** Collection and treatment of other waste
**Proprietor:** G Highland
**US SIC:** 4953 **UK SIC:** 92110
**Employees:** 150

**DUNS 49-383-8759**

## P H Warr Plc

9th Floor, Christchurch, Dorset
**Web:** www.phwarr.com
**Reg No:** 3130893 **VAT No:** 673738302
**Estd:** 1992 Public Limited Company
**Line of Business:** Quantity surveyors
**Issued Capital:** £51,500
**Directors:** K J Butters, P H Warr, G F Page
**Co. Secretary:** Ms Paula Warburton
**Responsibilities**
**Fleet:** Sue Witcher (Transport Manager)

**Branches:** P H Warr Plc, 1 Kings Park Road, Southampton, Hampshire SO15 2AT
**US SIC:** 7397 **UK SIC:** 83702
**Auditors:** Grant Thornton UK LLP
**Bankers:** National Westminster Bank Plc (56-00-33)

| | 31-12-13 | 31-12-12 | 31-12-11 |
|---|---|---|---|
| TO | 2,901,413 | 2,464,025 | 2,546,363 |
| P/L | 265,159 | 168,254 | 95,163 |
| NW | (95,205) | (91,907) | (262,320) |
| WC | (134,447) | (111,905) | (103,270) |
| Emp. | 55 | 49 | 67 |

### DUNS 39-751-8317
## P. Hughes Construction Ltd
21 Main Road, Nottingham, Nottinghamshire NG16 5GP
**Web:** www.phughes.co.uk
**Reg No:** 2191240 **VAT No:** 455796889
**Estd:** 1987 Private Limited Company
**Line of Business:** Building of complete constructions or parts thereof; civil engineering
**Issued Capital:** £100
**Principals:** P Hughes *(Managing)*, D Hughes
**Co. Secretary:** Philip Hughes
**US SIC:** 1541, 1522
**UK SIC:** 50100
**Auditors:** Alliance Accountancy
**Bankers:** Barclays Bank Plc (20-23-55)

| | 31-03-14 | 31-03-13 | 31-03-12 |
|---|---|---|---|
| TO | 27,085,800 | 18,624,763 | 14,531,341 |
| P/L | 2,729,665 | 1,542,836 | 1,118,719 |
| NW | 4,981,166 | 3,876,826 | 3,146,709 |
| WC | 1,874,572 | 1,371,677 | 1,156,032 |
| Emp. | 99 | 79 | 85 |

### DUNS 21-584-4649
## P I C Uk
Llanhedric Farm, Clun, Bucknell, Shropshire SY7 8NG
**Tel:** 01588640951
**Web:** www.pic.com
**Estd:** 2011
**Line of Business:** Farming of sheep, goats, horses, asses, mules and hinnies
**Responsibilities**
**Senior:** Michelle Harvey *(Stud Manager)*
**US SIC:** 0214 **UK SIC:** 01001
**Employees:** 50

### DUNS 21-696-0427
## P I P Electrics Ltd
Fenton House, Fenton Way, Southfields Business Park, Basildon, Essex SS15 6TD
**Tel:** 01268-541651 **Fax:** 01268-541625
**Web:** www.pipelectrics.com
**Reg No:** 0968629 **VAT No:** 244210994
**Estd:** 1969 Private Limited Company
**Line of Business:** Electrical contractors and electricians
**Issued Capital:** £6,720
**Principals:** G Pascoe *(Managing)*, S Brewer
**Co. Secretary:** Gary Pascoe
**Responsibilities**
**Senior:** Richard Candler *(Financial Controller)*, Bob Moore *(Purchasing Officer)*
**Finance:** Richard Candler *(Financial Controller)*
**IT:** Tom Hawes *(IT Manager)*
**Facilities:** Bob Moore *(Purchasing Officer)*
**Purchasing:** Bob Moore *(Purchasing Officer)*
**Branches:** P I P Electrics Ltd, Fenton House, Fenton Way, Basildon, Essex SS15 6TD
**US SIC:** 1731 **UK SIC:** 50300
**Auditors:** Reddy Siddiqui & Kabani
**Bankers:** National Westminster Bank Plc (60-02-39)

| | 31-12-13 | 31-12-12 | 31-12-11 |
|---|---|---|---|
| TO | 24,365,524 | 23,124,228 | 18,399,155 |
| P/L | 146,325 | 151,240 | 120,315 |
| NW | 7,207,873 | 7,150,274 | 7,087,640 |
| WC | 6,280,596 | 6,258,110 | 6,126,527 |
| Emp. | 84 | 82 | 40 |

### DUNS 22-572-1109
## P J Brown Civil Engineering & Haulage Contractors
Charlwood Road, Ifield, Crawley, West Sussex RH11 0JZ
**Web:** www.pjbrown.co.uk
**VAT No:** 367447127 **Estd:** 1978 Proprietorship
**Line of Business:** Road haulage and transport services
**Proprietor:** P J Brown
**US SIC:** 4789, 8911
**UK SIC:** 77002, 83701
**Auditors:** TYas & Company
**Bankers:** National Westminster Bank Plc (60-06-20)
**Employees:** 15

### DUNS 21-597-6060
## P J C Exeter Tiling Services
15 Clarke Mead, Exeter, Devon EX2 5NA
**Estd:** 2011 Proprietorship
**Line of Business:** Ceiling contractors

**Proprietor:** P Hancock
**US SIC:** 1799 **UK SIC:** 50000
**Employees:** 50

### DUNS 49-381-5435
## P J I Security Ltd
Hunters Moon, Higher Harros, Roche, St Austell, Cornwall PL26 8LN
**Web:** www.pjisecurity.co.uk
**Reg No:** 3128587 **Estd:** 1989 Private Limited Company
**Line of Business:** Representative office
**Issued Capital:** £100
**Directors:** P J Inch, Ms L Inch, M J Inch
**Co. Secretary:** Ms Angela Inch
**US SIC:** 7399 **UK SIC:** 83954
**Bankers:** Lloyds TSB Bank plc (30-99-55)

| | 30-11-13 | 30-11-12 | 30-11-11 |
|---|---|---|---|
| TA | 427,638 | 488,896 | 444,411 |
| NW | 193,057 | 228,747 | 205,034 |
| WC | 175,819 | 214,128 | 191,702 |

### DUNS 73-458-9752
## P J Keary Holdings Ltd
Jubilee House, Townsend Lane, London NW9 8TZ
**Tel:** 02082052678 **Fax:** 020-8200-8591
**Web:** www.pjkeary.net
**Reg No:** 4723182 **Estd:** 2003 Private Limited Company
**Line of Business:** Management and business consultants
**Trading Style:** P J Keary Ltd
**Issued Capital:** £1
**Director:** P Joseph Keary (Jnr)
**Co. Secretary:**
Ms Sharon Majella O'Sullivan
**Responsibilities**
**Senior:** Patrick Joseph Keary *(Director)*, Micheal Keary *(Manager)*
**US SIC:** 7392 **UK SIC:** 83951

| | 30-04-14 | 30-04-13 | 30-04-11 |
|---|---|---|---|
| TA | 1 | 1 | 1 |
| NW | 1 | 1 | 1 |

### DUNS 23-013-6467
## P J Keary Ltd
Jubilee House, Townsend Lane, London NW9 8TZ
**Tel:** 02082023090 **Fax:** 02082008591
**Web:** www.pjkeary.co.uk
**Reg No:** 3041803 **Estd:** 1995 Private Limited Company
**Line of Business:** Business and management consultancy activities not elsewhere classified
**Issued Capital:** £1,000
**Directors:** P J Keary Jnr, P J Keary, Ms S O'Sullivan
**Co. Secretary:** Ms Ann Keary
**Responsibilities**
**Senior:** Deleres Connor *(CEO, Managing Director)*
**Fleet:** Michael Keary *(Fleet Manager)*
**US SIC:** 7392 **UK SIC:** 83951
**Auditors:** PSB Accountants Ltd

| | 31-12-13 | 31-12-12 | 31-12-11 |
|---|---|---|---|
| TA | 1,268,511 | 1,442,728 | 1,618,972 |
| NW | 474,382 | 587,671 | 475,767 |
| WC | 186,736 | 234,714 | 89,761 |

### DUNS 23-717-3427
## P J Lilley Ltd
(Subsidiary of: P J Lilley (Holdings) Ltd)
39-39a Beardall Street, Hucknall, Nottingham, Nottinghamshire NG15 7RJ
**Tel:** 01159634230 **Fax:** 01159-640176
**Web:** www.pjlilleyltd.co.uk
**Reg No:** 3712173 **VAT No:** 610637566
**Estd:** 1999 Private Limited Company
**Line of Business:** Other building installation
**Issued Capital:** £12,600
**Directors:** G Fisher, Mrs E N Evans, T G Travers, K J Lilley, Dr S A Lilley
**Co. Secretary:** Paul Lilley
**Responsibilities**
**Admin:** Paula Johnson *(Projects Administrator)*
**HR:** Debbie Hays *(Human Resources Manager)*
**Facilities:** Stuart Ashton *(Maintenance Manager)*
**Operations:** Paula Johnson *(Projects Administrator)*
**US SIC:** 1796, 1742, 1751
**UK SIC:** 50400
**Auditors:** Blythens
**Bankers:** Barclays Bank Plc (20-55-62)

| | 31-12-13 | 31-12-12 | 31-12-11 |
|---|---|---|---|
| TO | 4,670,921 | 5,580,457 | 7,783,702 |
| P/L | 9,504 | 23,107 | (117,467) |
| NW | 489,708 | 587,704 | 663,597 |
| WC | 488,606 | 594,769 | 671,659 |
| Emp. | 52 | 68 | 71 |

### DUNS 21-722-4476
## P J Scott & Sons
77 Staines Road East, Sunbury-On-Thames, Middlesex TW16 5AD
**Tel:** 01932782612
**Web:** www.pjscott.co.uk
**VAT No:** 208194665 **Estd:** 1926 Partnership
**Line of Business:** Builders merchants.
**Partners:** T Scott, G R Scott, D J Scott, Ms C E Scott, Ms M E Scott, M Scott
**Branches:** P J Scott & Sons, Kempton Rd, Middlesex Sunbury-On-Thames
**US SIC:** 5251 **UK SIC:** 64800
**Bankers:** Barclays Bank Plc (20-81-11)
**Employees:** 100

### DUNS 29-691-4591
## P J Spillings Ltd
41 Pinbush Road, Lowestoft, Suffolk NR33 7NL
**Tel:** 01502-585676
**Web:** www.pjspillings.co.uk
**Reg No:** 2014972 **VAT No:** 442944833
**Estd:** 1971 Private Limited Company
**Line of Business:** Management activities of holding companies
**Issued Capital:** £1,000
**Managing Director:** P J Spillings
**Co. Secretary:** Mrs Lesley Spillings
**Responsibilities**
**Finance:** Stephanie Smith *(Head of Finance)*
**Sales:** Darren Saunders *(manager)*, Mark flecther *(manager)*
**Branches:** P J Spillings Ltd, 2-4 Harvest Drive, Harvest Ct, Lowestoft, Suffolk NR33 7NB
**US SIC:** 6711 **UK SIC:** 83962
**Auditors:** Lovewell Blake
**Bankers:** HSBC Bank plc (40-30-28)

| | 31-05-13 | 31-05-12 | 31-05-11 |
|---|---|---|---|
| TO | N/A | 5,332,961 | 4,612,414 |
| P/L | N/A | (374,528) | (74,822) |
| NW | 1,633,644 | 5,234,280 | 5,530,439 |
| WC | 815,112 | 4,305,015 | 4,550,120 |
| Emp. | N/A | 49 | 54 |

### DUNS 49-058-9405
## P L V Enterprises Ltd
9-11 Frogmoor, High Wycombe, Buckinghamshire HP13 5DQ
**Web:** www.kfc.co.uk
**Reg No:** 3077267 **Estd:** 1986 Private Limited Company
**Line of Business:** Take away meal outlets
**Trading Style:** Kfc
**Issued Capital:** £100
**Director:** P Vujasevic
**Branches:** P L V Enterprises Ltd, 1 The Quadrant, St. Albans, Hertfordshire AL4 9RA
**US SIC:** 5812 **UK SIC:** 66110

| | 30-09-13 | 30-09-12 | 30-09-11 |
|---|---|---|---|
| TO | 6,955,622 | 7,067,363 | 6,801,705 |
| P/L | 361,616 | 406,878 | 458,763 |
| NW | 1,679,565 | 1,523,760 | 1,327,778 |
| WC | (145,823) | (391,748) | (687,245) |
| Emp. | 200 | 197 | 193 |

### DUNS 21-034-4752
## P L Workforce
7 King Edward Street, Normanton, West Yorkshire WF6 2AZ
**Tel:** 01924892075
**Web:** www.plworkforce.co.uk
**Line of Business:** Employment service
**US SIC:** 7361 **UK SIC:** 83954
**Employees:** 60

### DUNS 21-773-8125
## P M & M
Lodge House Lodge Square, Cow Lane, Burnley, Lancashire BB11 1NN
**Tel:** 01282438035
**Web:** www.pmm.co.uk
**Estd:** 1931 Proprietorship
**Line of Business:** Accounting activities
**Proprietor:** S Anderson
**US SIC:** 8931 **UK SIC:** 83600
**Employees:** 90

### DUNS 64-090-5774
## P M P Recruitment Ltd
(Subsidiary of: Cordant Group Plc)
35-37 Wellington Street, Luton, Bedfordshire LU1 2QH
**Tel:** 01302761260 **Fax:** 01582-484898
**Web:** www.pmprecruitment.co.uk
**Reg No:** 3485614 **Estd:** 2012 Private Limited Company
**Line of Business:** Labour recruitment and provision of personnel
**Issued Capital:** £79,200
**Directors:** P L Ullmann, S W Kirkpatrick, J R Ullmann
**Co. Secretary:** Alan Connor
**Responsibilities**
**Senior:** Alex Sochaczewski *(Branch Manager)*

**Branches:** P M P Recruitment Ltd, Millyard Way, Pike Road Industrial Estat, Eythorne, Dover, Kent CT15 4NL
**US SIC:** 7361 **UK SIC:** 83954
**Auditors:** HLB Vantis Audit PLC
**Bankers:** National Westminster Bank Plc (01-08-38)

| | 30-06-13 | 30-06-12 | 30-06-11 |
|---|---|---|---|
| TO | 106,299,289 | 97,849,900 | 89,490,886 |
| P/L | 1,567,561 | 1,494,153 | 1,524,405 |
| NW | 1,502,783 | 113,972 | (1,185,075) |
| WC | (8,178,144) | (8,052,436) | (2,373,467) |
| Emp. | 7,793 | 7,086 | 7,081 |

### DUNS 23-621-9895
## P M R Fixers
The Old Chapel, Mayfield Road, Ashbourne, Derbyshire DE6 2BJ
**Web:** www.pmrfixers.co.uk
**Estd:** 1989 Proprietorship
**Line of Business:** Construction of civil engineering constructions
**Proprietor:** S Robottom
**Responsibilities**
**Senior:** Darren Hooley *(Manager)*, Stephen Robotham *(Managing Director)*
**Finance:** Matthew O'Shaughnessy *(Finance Director)*
**US SIC:** 1622 **UK SIC:** 50200
**Employees:** 50

### DUNS 21-587-4517
## P McCann & Sons
9-11 Diviny Drive, Craigavon, Co Armagh BT63 5WE
**Tel:** 02838330401
**Web:** www.mccannapples.co.uk
**Estd:** 1972 Partnership
**Line of Business:** Manufacturers of food products
**Trading Style:** P McCann & Sons
**Partners:** O Mccann, P Mccann
**Responsibilities**
**Senior:** Oliver McCann *(Partner)*
**US SIC:** 2099 **UK SIC:** 42399
**Bankers:** Northern Bank Ltd (95-04-11)
**Employees:** 50

### DUNS 21-227-3805
## P O'Neill
Omagh Health Centre, Mountjoy Road, Omagh, Co Tyrone BT79 7BA
**Tel:** 08444773501
**Line of Business:** Doctors
**Responsibilities**
**Senior:** Carmel McGrath *(Practice Manager)*
**US SIC:** 8011 **UK SIC:** 95300
**Employees:** 132

### DUNS 77-542-1423
## P P Construction Ltd
Deepwater Yard, Reading, Berkshire RG7 1TB
**Tel:** 01189887211
**Web:** www.pp-construction.co.uk
**Reg No:** 2996377 **VAT No:** 641776913
**Estd:** 1994 Private Limited Company
**Line of Business:** Building of complete constructions or parts thereof; civil engineering
**Issued Capital:** £100
**Director:** P W Potter
**Co. Secretary:** Carl Trussler
**Responsibilities**
**Senior:** John Mckehon *(Health & Safety Manager)*
**Sales:** Richard Neville *(Sales Manager)*
**Health & Safety:** John Mckehon *(Health & Safety Manager)*
**US SIC:** 1541 **UK SIC:** 50100
**Auditors:** N Webster Smith & Sons
**Bankers:** Barclays Bank Plc (20-71-03)

| | 31-07-14 | 31-07-13 | 31-07-12 |
|---|---|---|---|
| TA | 1,111,220 | 1,179,167 | 1,071,550 |
| NW | (40,404) | 92,746 | 113,904 |
| WC | (13,910) | 93,927 | 122,614 |

### DUNS 22-657-6163      Imp-Exp
## P P D Global Ltd
(Subsidiary of: Ppd International Holdings Inc.)
Granta Park, Great Abington, Cambridge, Cambridgeshire CB21 6GQ
**Tel:** 01223374100 **Fax:** 01223-374101
**Web:** www.ppdi.com
**Reg No:** 1564604 **Estd:** 1981 Private Limited Company
**Line of Business:** Research institutions and organisations
**Export Markets:** Far East, Japan, Australasia, North America
**Trading Style:** P P D Developments
**Issued Capital:** £10,526,336
**Directors:** Mrs J M James, R S Newbery, P J Summerfield
**Co. Secretary:** Christopher Neild
**Responsibilities**
**Senior:** Brainard Hartman *(Manager)*
**IT:** Peter Simons *(Senior IT Executive)*

**Branches:** P P D Global Ltd, Southampton Internation Business Pk, George Curl Way, Southampton, Hampshire SO18 2RZ
**US SIC:** 7391 **UK SIC:** 94000
**Auditors:** Deloitte LLP
**Bankers:** National Westminster Bank Plc (60-04-23)

| | 31-12-13 | 31-12-12 | 31-12-11 |
|---|---|---|---|
| TO | 192,992,000 | 219,493,000 | 164,939,000 |
| P/L | 40,828,000 | 48,878,000 | 21,479,000 |
| NW | 97,940,000 | 185,876,000 | 135,154,000 |
| WC | 88,580,000 | 181,855,000 | 125,330,000 |
| Emp. | 1,290 | 1,265 | 1,123 |

DUNS 42-431-8897
## P P F Ltd
Unit 17-20, Home Farm, Luton Hoo Estate, Luton, Bedfordshire LU1 3TD
**Tel:** 01795432861
**Web:** www.ppfplc.com
**Reg No:** 3352071 **Estd:** 1997 Private Limited Company
**Line of Business:** Labour recruitment and provision of personnel
**Trading Style:** New Border Recruitments, Adr Network
**Issued Capital:** £135,043
**Directors:** G M Howitt, P J Howitt, A Waldron, K F Churchhouse, A Rodgers, S A Risbridger, N J Guyton
**Co. Secretary:** Steve Davis
**Branches:** P P F Ltd, Faraday Rd, Swindon, Wiltshire SN3 5HH
**US SIC:** 7361 **UK SIC:** 83954
**Auditors:** Rees Pollock
**Bankers:** Barclays Bank Plc (20-79-73)

| | 31-12-13 | 31-12-12 | 31-12-11 |
|---|---|---|---|
| TO | 98,430,031 | 89,323,600 | 64,746,249 |
| P/L | 3,025,626 | 2,309,336 | 2,088,602 |
| NW | 2,028,394 | 1,484,607 | 1,470,645 |
| WC | 1,804,102 | 1,367,999 | 1,376,775 |
| Emp. | 100 | 84 | 69 |

DUNS 21-782-2074
## P P M
45 Lakes Road, Derwent Howe Industrial Estate, Workington, Cumbria CA14 3YP
**Tel:** 0190061000
**Estd:** 2011
**Line of Business:** Building services
**Responsibilities**
**Senior:** Richard Moth *(Manager)*
**US SIC:** 1622 **UK SIC:** 50200
**Employees:** 51

DUNS 76-312-9905
## P P O'Connor Ltd
Woodrow Way, Irlam, Manchester M44 6NN
**Tel:** 0161-776-0333 **Fax:** 0161-776-0303
**Web:** www.ppoconnor.co.uk
**Reg No:** 2545561 **Estd:** 1990 Private Limited Company
**Line of Business:** Demolition and wrecking of buildings; earth moving
**Trading Style:** P P o"Connor Ltd
**Issued Capital:** £100
**Managing Director:** P P Oconnor
**Co. Secretary:** Ms Christine O'Connor
**Responsibilities**
**Senior:** Christine O' Connor *(Purchasing Manager)*
**Marketing:** Charmaine O'Connor *(Commercial Manager)*
**IT:** Charmaine O'Connor *(Commercial Manager)*
**HR:** Steve Doolan *(Human Resources Manager)*
**Purchasing:** Christine O' Connor *(Purchasing Manager)*
**Branches:** P P O'connor Ltd, Woodrow Way, Manchester M44 6NN
**US SIC:** 1795, 1799
**UK SIC:** 50000
**Auditors:** Crawfords

| | 31-10-13 | 31-10-12 | 31-10-11 |
|---|---|---|---|
| TO | 17,119,952 | 16,487,014 | 12,826,212 |
| P/L | 582,716 | 1,193,709 | 696,503 |
| NW | 4,275,748 | 3,985,159 | 3,171,676 |
| WC | (992,139) | (355,668) | (1,256,227) |
| Emp. | 143 | 118 | 106 |

DUNS 50-483-9572
## P P S Commercials Ltd
Pilsworth Industrial Estate, Bury, Lancashire BL9 8RR
**Tel:** 01617679554 **Fax:** 01617967645
**Web:** www.ppscommercials.co.uk
**Reg No:** 2457750 **Estd:** 1990 Private Limited Company
**Line of Business:** Manufacture of bodies (coachwork) for motor vehicles (except caravans)
**Issued Capital:** £99
**Director:** S S Whitworth
**Co. Secretary:** Gary Amos
**US SIC:** 3713, 7539
**UK SIC:** 35201, 67100

**Bankers:** Barclays Bank Plc (20-10-71)

| | 31-12-13 | 31-12-12 | 31-12-11 |
|---|---|---|---|
| TO | 13,120,850 | N/A | N/A |
| P/L | 1,269,719 | N/A | N/A |
| NW | 1,097,935 | 778,316 | 690,202 |
| WC | 762,374 | 540,268 | 564,382 |
| Emp. | 76 | N/A | N/A |

DUNS 21-309-6738 Exp
## P Plunkett (Tiling Contractors) Ltd
Dukes Way, Low Prudhoe Industrial Estate, Prudhoe, Northumberland NE42 6PQ
**Tel:** 01661-836960
**Web:** www.plunketttiling.co.uk
**Reg No:** 1354765 **VAT No:** 297591792
**Estd:** 1978 Private Limited Company
**Line of Business:** Tile laying and fitting contractors
**Export Markets:** Italy
**Issued Capital:** £105,500
**Principals:** P Plunkett *(Chairman and Managing)*, M Forster, Ms L Plunkett, G I Williams, S Allsopp, D Baker, P D Plunkett, J P Plunkett
**Co. Secretary:** Ms Susan Glaister
**US SIC:** 1752 **UK SIC:** 50400
**Auditors:** Bell Tindle Williamson LLP
**Bankers:** Barclays Bank Plc (20-59-97)

| | 31-05-14 | 31-05-13 | 31-05-12 |
|---|---|---|---|
| TA | 2,945,034 | 2,425,446 | 2,617,341 |
| NW | 1,998,974 | 1,800,718 | 1,815,657 |
| WC | 1,746,523 | 1,603,295 | 1,632,770 |

DUNS 23-377-7684
## P R M Enterprises Ltd
**(Subsidiary of:** Prm Group Ltd)
Rathdown Road, Lissue Industrial Estate, Lisburn, Co Antrim BT28 2RE
**Tel:** 028-9262-0200 **Fax:** 028-9262-1148
**Web:** www.prmgroup.co.uk
**Reg No:** 0044880NI **Estd:** 1992 Private Limited Company
**Line of Business:** Distribution service providers
**Trading Style:** Prm Group
**Issued Capital:** £10,002
**Director:** Ms L Morrow
**Co. Secretary:** Philip Morrow
**US SIC:** 4712, 5149
**UK SIC:** 77002, 61700
**Bankers:** The Bank Of Ireland (90-21-94)

| | 31-12-13 | 31-12-12 | 31-12-11 |
|---|---|---|---|
| TA | 7,195,552 | 7,720,203 | 5,120,915 |
| NW | 1,015,051 | 1,267,926 | 1,188,162 |
| WC | (4,838,709) | (4,744,896) | (2,171,042) |

DUNS 76-699-4594
## P R Marriott Drilling Ltd
Springwater House, Old Pit Lane, Danesmoor, Chesterfield, Derbyshire S45 9BQ
**Tel:** 01246861900
**Web:** www.marriottdrilling.com
**Reg No:** 2592487 **VAT No:** 593458107
**Estd:** 1991 Private Limited Company
**Line of Business:** Drilling contractors
**Issued Capital:** £73,002
**Directors:** A J Beswick, J W Hobday
**Co. Secretary:** Mrs Katrina Proctor
**Responsibilities**
**Senior:** Wendy Hobday *(Manager)*, Lee Thomson *(Manager)*
**US SIC:** 1381 **UK SIC:** 13000
**Auditors:** Voice & Co Accountancy Services Ltd
**Bankers:** National Westminster Bank Plc (60-40-09)

| | 31-12-13 | 30-04-13 | 30-12-12 |
|---|---|---|---|
| TO | 18,489,807 | 21,542,749 | 17,886,785 |
| P/L | (954,668) | 1,836,721 | 3,197,769 |
| NW | 9,519,881 | 10,583,009 | 9,656,300 |
| WC | (3,981,318) | (350,746) | 136,995 |
| Emp. | 110 | 119 | 118 |

DUNS 23-173-4851
## P R P Architect
10 Lindsey Street, London EC1A 9HP
**Web:** www.prparchitects.co.uk
**Estd:** 2000 Proprietorship
**Line of Business:** Architectural activities
**Proprietor:** A Vonbradzky
**Responsibilities**
**Senior:** Jenny Buterchi *(Manager)*, Frances Chaplin *(Partner)*, Sarah Harrison *(Manager)*, Mike Hawkins *(Manager)*, Stephen Hynds *(Manager)*, Manisha Patel *(Manager)*, Chris Wilford *(Associate Director)*
**Marketing:** David Pede *(Web Developer)*, Katie White *(Head of Communications)*
**IT:** Sarah Harrison *(Manager)*
**US SIC:** 8911 **UK SIC:** 83701
**Employees:** 180

DUNS 21-773-8735
## P R S for Music
Elwes House, Peterborough, Cambridgeshire PE1 2UZ
**Tel:** 08453093090
**Web:** www.prsformusic.com
**Estd:** 1990 Partnership
**Line of Business:** Other business activities not elsewhere classified
**Partners:** Mrs L Parker, Mrs C Heath
**Responsibilities**
**Senior:** Tracey Lowndes *(Centre Manager)*
**US SIC:** 7399 **UK SIC:** 83954
**Employees:** 65

DUNS 42-335-4146
## P S Financials Ltd
25 Harley Street, London W1G 9BR
**Tel:** 01733-367330
**Web:** www.psfinancials.com
**Reg No:** 4323067 **Estd:** 2001 Private Limited Company
**Line of Business:** Publishing of software
**Export Sales:** £71,278
**Issued Capital:** £100,000
**Directors:** R C Pierce, K N Binley, Ms S A Pierce, M Hay-Plumb, H G Jones
**Responsibilities**
**Finance:** David Bantin *(Operations Director)*
**Admin:** Carolyn Sutch *(Office Manager)*
**IT:** David Bantin *(Operations Director)*
**HR:** Carolyn Sutch *(Office Manager)*
**Health & Safety:** Carolyn Sutch *(Office Manager)*
**Facilities:** Carolyn Sutch *(Office Manager)*
**Branches:** P S Financials Ltd, Isis House, Minerva Business Park, Peterborough, Cambridgeshire PE2 6QR
**US SIC:** 7372 **UK SIC:** 83940
**Auditors:** Gerald Edelman
**Bankers:** The Royal Bank Of Scotland Plc (16-10-55)

| | 30-04-14 | 30-04-13 | 30-04-12 |
|---|---|---|---|
| TO | 6,762,024 | 5,101,367 | 4,425,294 |
| P/L | 1,573,272 | 593,301 | 550,736 |
| NW | 2,664,150 | 1,402,408 | 942,914 |
| WC | 2,535,908 | 1,146,072 | 681,838 |
| Emp. | 75 | 72 | 52 |

DUNS 21-318-9798 Imp-Exp
## P S I Global Ltd
South Industrial Estate, Bowburn, Durham, County Durham DH6 5AD
**Tel:** 01913777000
**Web:** www.psiglobal.co.uk
**Reg No:** 1252181 **VAT No:** 179011370
**Estd:** 1976 Private Limited Company
**Line of Business:** Manufacturers of filters
**Export Markets:** Worldwide
**Issued Capital:** £375,851
**Principals:** Ms S P Hunter *(Managing)*, H G Waltl, J S Hunter, R Theodoulou, D M Hunter
**Co. Secretary:** Daniel Hunter
**Responsibilities**
**Facilities:** Austin Comerford *(Maintenance Manager)*
**Engineering:** Austin Comerford *(Maintenance Manager)*
**US SIC:** 3559 **UK SIC:** 32863
**Auditors:** Deloitte LLP
**Bankers:** Barclays Bank Plc (20-25-29)

| | 02-05-14 | 30-04-13 | 30-04-12 |
|---|---|---|---|
| TA | 3,031,114 | 3,250,164 | 3,303,252 |
| NW | 1,814,164 | 1,672,274 | 1,431,517 |
| WC | 904,842 | 788,369 | 653,132 |

DUNS 22-062-2174
## P S Ridgway Group Ltd
**(Subsidiary of:** Strathmuir Holdings Ltd)
5 Smeaton Road, West Gourdie Industrial Estate, Dundee, Angus DD2 4UT
**Tel:** 01382-614500
**Web:** www.psridgway.co.uk
**Reg No:** 0210638SC **Estd:** 1970 Private Limited Company
**Line of Business:** Management activities of holding companies
**Trading Style:** P S Ridgway Ltd
**Issued Capital:** £76,527
**Managing Director:** D T Ridgway
**Co. Secretary:** John Lornie
**Responsibilities**
**Finance:** Karen Will *(Accounts Supervisor)*
**Sales:** Frank McGarry *(Sales Manager)*, Karen Will *(Accounts Supervisor)*
**Admin:** Craig Mudie *(Administration Manager)*
**US SIC:** 6711 **UK SIC:** 83962
**Bankers:** Bank Of Scotland (12-01-28)

| | 30-04-14 | 30-04-13 | 30-04-12 |
|---|---|---|---|
| TA | 921,507 | 945,038 | 967,209 |
| NW | 377,418 | 421,306 | 464,459 |
| WC | (503,996) | (481,695) | (460,930) |

DUNS 57-845-8168 Imp
## P S V Transport Systems Ltd
Impresa Park, Pindar Road, Hoddesdon, Hertfordshire EN11 0DL
**Tel:** 01992479950
**Web:** www.psv-transport-systems.co.uk
**Reg No:** 2898742 **VAT No:** 632361267
**Estd:** 1994 Private Limited Company
**Line of Business:** Manufacture of parts and accessories for motor vehicles and their engines
**Export Sales:** £138,090
**Issued Capital:** £250
**Principals:** Mrs B Barnwell *(Managing)*, L C Barnwell, T C Barnwell, J C King
**Co. Secretary:** Mrs Jean Barnwell
**Responsibilities**
**Senior:** Barry O'shea *(Manager)*
**IT:** Donna Barnwell *(Head of IT)*
**US SIC:** 3714, 5531
**UK SIC:** 35300, 65100
**Auditors:** Clarendons
**Bankers:** National Westminster Bank Plc (60-11-11)

| | 30-04-14 | 30-04-13 | 30-04-12 |
|---|---|---|---|
| TO | 11,022,261 | 10,358,698 | 9,785,986 |
| P/L | 742,313 | 1,142,023 | 632,688 |
| NW | 3,602,093 | 3,494,350 | 3,459,020 |
| WC | 3,273,721 | 3,230,507 | 3,144,382 |
| Emp. | 80 | 72 | 67 |

DUNS 21-783-6699
## P T S
Unit 2, Newcastle-Upon-Tyne, Tyne and Wear NE15 6LN
**Tel:** 01912266860
**Web:** www.ptsplumbing.co.uk
**Estd:** 2005 Proprietorship
**Line of Business:** Plumbers merchants
**Proprietor:** N Thornton
**Responsibilities**
**Senior:** Neil McClay *(manager)*
**US SIC:** 5074 **UK SIC:** 61300
**Employees:** 71

DUNS 28-972-4676 Exp
## P T S Consulting Group Ltd
60 New Broad Street, London EC2M 1JJ
**Tel:** 03303136200
**Web:** www.ptsconsulting.com
**Reg No:** 1738788 **VAT No:** 577565978
**Estd:** 1983 Private Limited Company
**Line of Business:** Hardware consultancy
**Export Markets:** Japan; Turkey; U S A; Singapore
**Issued Capital:** £1,063,829
**Principals:** K A Perrett *(Managing)*, S P Kidd, S Flaim, T P Whittard, D M Dewhurst, R J Stead, R H Pinchbeck
**Co. Secretary:** Mrs Holly Perrett
**Responsibilities**
**Senior:** Richard Seager *(Manager)*
**US SIC:** 7379, 6711
**UK SIC:** 83940, 83962
**Auditors:** KPMG LLP
**Bankers:** Barclays Bank Plc (20-77-67)

| | 31-03-14 | 31-03-13 | 31-03-12 |
|---|---|---|---|
| TO | 34,337,000 | 38,258,000 | 38,291,000 |
| P/L | (2,936,000) | 1,380,000 | 2,109,000 |
| NW | 3,748,000 | 3,050,000 | 3,234,000 |
| WC | 377,000 | 559,000 | 1,517,000 |
| Emp. | 278 | 258 | 267 |

DUNS 29-487-9135
## P T S Plumbing Trade Supplies Ltd
**(Subsidiary of:** Travis Perkins Plc)
117 Cobden Street, Leicester, Leicestershire LE1 2LB
**Tel:** 01162427700 **Fax:** 01162-427701
**Web:** www.ptsplumbing.com
**Reg No:** 1851210 **Estd:** 1984 Private Limited Company
**Line of Business:** Plumbers merchants
**Trading Style:** P T S Plumbing Trade Supplies Ltd
**Issued Capital:** £685,000
**Directors:** A D Buffin, J P Carter, Tp Directors Ltd
**Co. Secretary:**
Tpg Management Services Limited
**Branches:** P T S Plumbing Trade Supplies Ltd, Unit 10, Redkiln Close, Horsham, West Sussex RH13 5QL
**US SIC:** 5074 **UK SIC:** 61300
**Auditors:** PricewaterhouseCoopers LLP

| | 31-12-13 | 31-12-12 | 31-12-11 |
|---|---|---|---|
| TA | 1,000,000 | 10,000 | 1,000,000 |
| NW | 1,000,000 | 10,000 | 1,000,000 |

DUNS 22-622-4061
## P. Tuckwell Ltd
Ardleigh Hall, Dedham Road, Ardleigh, Colchester, Essex CO7 7LG
**Tel:** 01206230283
**Web:** www.tuckwell.co.uk
**Reg No:** 1189939 **Estd:** 1974 Private Limited Company

**Line of Business:** Agricultural machinery sales service and repair
**Export Sales:** £531,000
**Trading Style:** Tuckwells
**Issued Capital:** £800
**Principals:** P A Tuckwell *(Managing)*, J M Tuckwell, L E Tuckwell
**Co. Secretary:** Paul Tuckwell
**Responsibilities**
**Senior:** Tom Glover *(Sales & Marketing Director)*
**Marketing:** Tom Glover *(Sales & Marketing Director)*
**Sales:** Tom Glover *(Sales & Marketing Director)*, Tom Mason *(Sales Manager)*
**Admin:** Lynn Tanner *(Administration Manager)*
**HR:** Lynn Tanner *(Administration Manager)*
**Operations:** Kenny Cattee *(Parts Manager)*, David Flatt *(Service Manager)*
**Branches:** P. Tuckwell Ltd, 2 Windham Road, Sudbury, Suffolk CO10 2XD
**US SIC:** 3523, 0241
**UK SIC:** 32113, 01001
**Auditors:** Scrutton Bland
**Bankers:** Barclays Bank Plc (20-98-07)

| | 30-11-13 | 30-11-12 | 30-11-11 |
|---|---|---|---|
| TO | 56,335,630 | 45,221,072 | 42,998,149 |
| P/L | 1,905,644 | 1,149,404 | 1,516,407 |
| NW | 6,816,724 | 5,341,960 | 4,999,552 |
| WC | 6,221,863 | 5,161,842 | 4,462,016 |
| Emp. | 149 | 125 | 108 |

DUNS 21-216-1335     **Imp-Exp**

## P V Dobson & Sons

Ivy House Works, Levens, Kendal, Cumbria LA8 8PG
**Web:** www.pvdobson.com
**VAT No:** 153799917 **Estd:** 1959 Partnership
**Line of Business:** Agricultural engineers
**Export Markets:** European Union (E U)
**Partners:** Ms B Hammond, A Dobson, A Dobson
**Branches:** P V Dobson & Sons, Unit 4 Keighley Road Snaygill Industrial Estate, Skipton, North Yorkshire BD23 2QR
**US SIC:** 5083, 3523, 5511
**UK SIC:** 61490, 32113, 65100
**Bankers:** Barclays Bank Plc (20-45-28)
**Employees:** 46

DUNS 22-769-0294

## P V H Industries Ltd

Redhills Road, Milton, Stoke-On-Trent, Staffordshire ST2 7ER
**Tel:** 01782-534235 **Fax:** 01782-542207
**Reg No:** 0898396 **Estd:** 1967 Private Limited Company
**Line of Business:** Steel fabricators, materials handling equipment and dust control equipment manufacturers.
**Directors:** J Callaghan, T Barker, R M Bradbury, G L Perrott, B R Anderson, R B Newton
**Co. Secretary:** Iain Mckinlay
**US SIC:** 3444, 3536, 3564
**UK SIC:** 31694, 32554, 32843
**Bankers:** Lloyds TSB Bank plc (30-91-01)
**Employees:** 130

DUNS 73-278-4199     **Imp**

## P W Gates Distribution Ltd

2 Swallow End, Welwyn Garden City, Hertfordshire AL7 1JA
**Web:** www.pwgates.co.uk
**Reg No:** 4552128 **VAT No:** 806141658
**Estd:** 1978 Private Limited Company
**Line of Business:** Road haulage and transport services
**Issued Capital:** £2,000
**Directors:** A R Janes, Ms M J Gates, C Lynch, P W Gates
**US SIC:** 4789 **UK SIC:** 77002
**Auditors:** GKP
**Bankers:** Barclays Bank Plc (20-74-09)

| | 31-03-14 | 31-03-13 | 31-03-12 |
|---|---|---|---|
| TO | 7,583,284 | 6,713,365 | N/A |
| P/L | 215,497 | 300,603 | N/A |
| NW | 287,788 | 237,654 | 237,986 |
| WC | (252,433) | (308,042) | (338,165) |
| Emp. | 80 | 64 | N/A |

DUNS 77-519-0796     **Imp**

## P X Manufacturing & Distribution Company Ltd

*(Subsidiary of:* Chivgate Ltd*)*
40 Thorby Avenue, March, Cambridgeshire PE15 0AZ
**Tel:** 01354-653002 **Fax:** 01354-655782
**Web:** www.pxcables.com
**Reg No:** 2980841 **VAT No:** 424121207
**Estd:** 1984 Private Limited Company
**Line of Business:** Electrical wholesalers
**Export Sales:** £4,882,299
**Trading Style:** P X Cables
**Issued Capital:** £500,000
**Directors:** S F Tetnowski, Chivgate Limited, Dr P T Tetnowski, R Tetnowski
**Co. Secretary:** Ms Elzbieta Tetnowska

**Responsibilities**
**Senior:** Suresh Popat *(Financial Director)*
**Finance:** Suresh Popat *(Financial Director)*
**US SIC:** 5074, 3357, 5199
**UK SIC:** 61300, 22470, 61900
**Auditors:** Leon Haig & Co
**Bankers:** Barclays Bank Plc (20-37-16)

| | 31-12-13 | 31-12-12 | 31-12-11 |
|---|---|---|---|
| TO | 51,693,806 | 58,504,489 | 64,525,995 |
| P/L | 1,041,016 | 1,252,122 | 2,494,763 |
| NW | 12,135,987 | 11,347,077 | 10,411,160 |
| WC | 10,241,635 | 9,229,043 | 8,448,374 |
| Emp. | 51 | 54 | 59 |

DUNS 21-744-8745

## P1 Old Opco Ltd

Silverglade Business Park, Leatherhead Road, Chessington, Surrey KT9 2QL
**Tel:** 01372729560 **Fax:** 01372725050
**Web:** www.chessington.com
**Reg No:** 0406533 **Estd:** 1928 Private Limited Company
**Line of Business:** Operation of theme parks
**Trading Style:** Chessington World of Adventures, Alton Towers
**Issued Capital:** £2,600,000
**Directors:** N M Leslau, T J Evans
**Co. Secretary:** Miss Sandra Gumm
**Responsibilities**
**Senior:** Andy Green *(Stores Manager)*
**HR:** Linda Shackley *(Head of Human Resources)*
**Health & Safety:** Kevin Bainbridge *(Head of Engineering)*
**Facilities:** Ian Cunningham *(Maintenance Manager)*
**Engineering:** Kevin Bainbridge *(Head of Engineering)*
**US SIC:** 7996 **UK SIC:** 97913
**Auditors:** BDO Stoy Hayward LLP
**Bankers:** National Westminster Bank Plc (56-00-14)

| | 31-03-14 | 31-03-13 | 31-03-12 |
|---|---|---|---|
| TA | 353,634,574 | 353,634,574 | 353,634,574 |
| NW | 160,207,871 | 160,207,871 | 160,207,871 |

DUNS 23-625-9698

## P1 Tasmania Group Ltd

*(Subsidiary of:* Sir Theme Park Subholdco Ltd*)*
Leatherhead Road, Chessington, Surrey KT9 2NE
**Tel:** 08718943000 **Fax:** 0870-429-5500
**Web:** www.merlinentertainments.biz
**Reg No:** 3623056 **VAT No:** 905222754
**Estd:** 1998 Private Limited Company
**Line of Business:** Leisure & recreation centres.
**Trading Style:** Madame Tussauds, Thorpe Park, Chessington World of Adventures, Warwick Castle
**Issued Capital:** £401,393
**Directors:** T J Evans, N M Leslau
**Co. Secretary:** Miss Sandra Gumm
**US SIC:** 7999 **UK SIC:** 97913
**Auditors:** Deloitte & Touche LLP
**Bankers:** HSBC Bank plc (40-00-21)

| | 31-03-14 | 31-03-13 | 31-03-12 |
|---|---|---|---|
| TA | 189,278,424 | 189,278,424 | 189,278,424 |
| NW | 81,983,855 | 81,983,855 | 81,983,855 |

DUNS 73-552-3198     **Imp**

## P2I Ltd

127 North Milton Park, Abingdon, Oxfordshire OX14 4SA
**Tel:** 01235-833-100 **Fax:** 01235-861-214
**Web:** www.p2i.com
**Reg No:** 4814350 **VAT No:** 846560213
**Estd:** 2004 Private Limited Company
**Line of Business:** Other manufacturing not elsewhere classified
**Export Sales:** £8,628,764
**Issued Capital:** £4,128
**Directors:** P Dayal, J Chandra, C D Francis, A Hegarty, P D Mottershead, Dr L N Smith, Doctor S Coulson, W T Brown
**Co. Secretary:** Adrian Moores
**Responsibilities**
**Senior:** Mark Muth *(Non Executive Director)*, Nigel Young *(Director)*
**Sales:** Eric Cohill *(Chief Commercial Officer)*
**US SIC:** 3999, 7391
**UK SIC:** 49590, 94000
**Auditors:** Grant Thornton UK LLP
**Bankers:** HSBC Bank plc (40-40-14)

| | 31-12-13 | 31-12-12 | 31-12-12 |
|---|---|---|---|
| TO | 8,831,898 | 2,755,175 | 6,131,168 |
| P/L | (9,714,194) | (3,563,070) | (12,965,223) |
| NW | 6,449,369 | 15,948,394 | 13,499,668 |
| WC | 2,520,158 | 9,944,197 | 9,156,833 |
| Emp. | 90 | 115 | 129 |

DUNS 21-151-8337     **Exp**

## P3 Group Europe Ltd

Nimlock House, 45 Booth Drive, Park Farm Industrial Estate, Wellingborough, Northamptonshire NN8 6NL
**Tel:** 01933-409409
**Web:** www.nimlok.co.uk
**Reg No:** 0973784 **VAT No:** 239757517

**Estd:** 1970 Private Limited Company
**Line of Business:** Management activities of holding companies
**Export Markets:** Worldwide
**Trading Style:** Nimlok Display & Exhibition Systems
**Issued Capital:** £105,313
**Principals:** G E Perutz *(Chairman)*, T P Perutz *(Managing)*, S G Perutz
**Co. Secretary:** Jeremy Roberts
**Responsibilities**
**Senior:** Craig Dewart *(Production Manager)*
**Marketing:** Garry Clement-Boggis *(Marketing Manager)*
**Sales:** Jamie Zavoral-Brown *(Sales Director)*
**Operations:** Jo Tong *(Environmental Manager)*, Jamie Zavoral-Brown *(Sales Director)*
**Engineering:** Craig Dewart *(Production Manager)*
**US SIC:** 6711 **UK SIC:** 83962
**Auditors:** Grant Thornton UK LLP
**Bankers:** National Westminster Bank Plc (53-61-33)

| | 31-12-13 | 31-12-12 | 31-12-11 |
|---|---|---|---|
| TO | 30,548,244 | 25,506,649 | 20,683,964 |
| P/L | 1,727,100 | 888,220 | 1,339,162 |
| NW | 3,417,637 | 2,766,855 | 2,514,338 |
| WC | 5,098,377 | 4,553,206 | 4,122,203 |
| Emp. | 303 | 285 | 239 |

DUNS 21-721-4246     **Imp-Exp**

## P3 Medical Ltd

*(Subsidiary of:* Jardines (U.K.) Ltd*)*
Unit 1 Newbridge Close, Bristol, Avon BS4 4AX
**Web:** www.p3medical.com
**Reg No:** 1072913 **VAT No:** 138552556
**Estd:** 1971 Private Limited Company
**Line of Business:** Manufacturers of medical equipment
**Export Markets:** Middle East & Far East
**Export Sales:** £1,536,808
**Issued Capital:** £1,000,000
**Directors:** H Modi, I Mcevoy, W E Hughes, S C Talbot
**Responsibilities**
**IT:** Naren Mohan *(Engineering Manager)*
**Operations:** Naren Mohan *(Engineering Manager)*
**Engineering:** Naren Mohan *(Engineering Manager)*
**US SIC:** 3841 **UK SIC:** 37201
**Auditors:** Haysom Silverton & Partners Ltd

| | 31-10-13 | 31-10-12 | 31-10-11 |
|---|---|---|---|
| TO | 6,134,521 | 5,909,672 | 5,445,733 |
| P/L | 81,251 | 168,182 | 353,715 |
| NW | 1,220,962 | 1,130,259 | 982,083 |
| WC | 901,743 | 921,625 | 1,448,736 |
| Emp. | 82 | 82 | 74 |

DUNS 89-689-2056

## P55 Ltd

7 Folgate Road, North Walsham, Norfolk NR28 0AJ
**Tel:** 01692-406017 **Fax:** 01692406957
**Web:** www.pss.co.uk
**Reg No:** 3345358 **Estd:** 1997 Private Limited Company
**Line of Business:** Manufacture of machinery for the production and use of mechanical power, except aircraft, vehicle and cycle engines
**Export Sales:** £3,352,129
**Trading Style:** Pss - Steering & Hydraulics Division
**Issued Capital:** £2
**Directors:** A Brammer, M S Brooks, R M Pratt
**Co. Secretary:** Richard Pratt
**US SIC:** 3714, 3561
**UK SIC:** 35300, 32870
**Auditors:** Larking Gowen
**Bankers:** HSBC Bank plc (40-35-06)

| | 31-12-13 | 31-12-12 | 31-12-11 |
|---|---|---|---|
| TO | 6,290,839 | 8,092,221 | 8,597,231 |
| P/L | 341,598 | 284,558 | 962,242 |
| NW | 738,458 | 1,101,462 | 1,309,669 |
| WC | (289,598) | (523,985) | (469,960) |
| Emp. | 69 | 74 | 80 |

DUNS 21-863-3334

## Pa Consulting Group Ltd

123 Buckingham Palace Road, London SW1W 9SR
**Web:** www.paconsulting.co.uk
**Reg No:** 8249452 **Estd:** 2012 Private Limited Company
**Line of Business:** Holding companies management activities
**Export Sales:** £128,433,000
**Issued Capital:** £9
**Directors:** A Middleton, R C Wilson, A Hooke, T Mcewan, M J Queen, T Mullen, M A Agius, Ms E Dyson
**Co. Secretary:** Kully Janjuah
**US SIC:** 6711 **UK SIC:** 83962

| | 31-12-13 | 31-12-12 |
|---|---|---|
| TO | 427,861,000 | 365,943,000 |
| P/L | 47,532,000 | 41,701,000 |
| NW | 98,479,000 | 78,286,000 |
| WC | 142,337,000 | 139,131,000 |
| Emp. | 2,536 | 2,259 |

DUNS 21-100-0617

## Pa Consulting Services Ltd

*(Subsidiary of:* Pacg2 Ltd*)*
123 Buckingham Palace Road, London SW1W 9SR
**Web:** www.paconsulting.com
**Reg No:** 0414220 **Estd:** 1988 Private Limited Company
**Line of Business:** Management and business consultants
**Export Sales:** £27,766,000
**Trading Style:** Pa Consulting Group
**Issued Capital:** £200,000
**Directors:** D Vickerstaffe, A Middleton, K Janjuah, M M Gordon, C Barrett
**Co. Secretary:** Robert King
**Responsibilities**
**Senior:** Mike Gorham *(Chairman)*, Victor Halberstadt *(Non-Executive Director)*, Tim Lawrence *(Manager)*, Julie Metelko *(Member)*, Jonathan Moynihan *(Manager)*, Andrew Rea *(Partner)*, Martin Stapleton *(Non-Executive Director)*, Lisa Todd *(Manager)*
**Marketing:** Shivani Joshi *(?UK Communications Executive)*
**Admin:** Melissa Hooper *(Team Secretary)*, Cally McGlone *(Practice Secretary)*
**HR:** Aoife Webster *(People & Organisational Excell)*
**Branches:** Pa Consulting Services, Conference Ho, 152 Morrison St, Edinburgh, Midlothian EH3 8EB
**US SIC:** 7392 **UK SIC:** 83951
**Auditors:** Ernst & Young LLP
**Bankers:** National Westminster Bank Plc (50-30-09)

| | 31-12-13 | 31-12-12 | 31-12-11 |
|---|---|---|---|
| TO | 334,520,000 | 291,331,000 | 243,455,000 |
| P/L | 17,261,000 | 16,446,000 | 5,302,000 |
| NW | 49,655,000 | 32,480,000 | 16,377,000 |
| WC | 57,684,000 | 40,422,000 | 20,762,000 |

DUNS 77-471-8365

## P.A. Grant Electrical Contractors Ltd

*(Subsidiary of:* P.A. Grant Holding Co Ltd*)*
Danno House, Canterbury, Kent CT2 8JZ
**Tel:** 01227-472580
**Web:** www.pagrantelectrical.co.uk
**Reg No:** 2968438 **VAT No:** 661713050
**Estd:** 1994 Private Limited Company
**Line of Business:** Electrical contractors and electricians
**Issued Capital:** £1,200
**Director:** P Grant
**Co. Secretary:** Jon Love
**US SIC:** 1731 **UK SIC:** 50300
**Auditors:** Burgess Hodgson

| | 30-09-13 | 30-09-12 | 30-09-11 |
|---|---|---|---|
| TA | 2,109,996 | 2,287,644 | 2,440,804 |
| NW | 109,737 | 107,404 | 102,873 |
| WC | 509,114 | 446,253 | 346,408 |

DUNS 85-620-8736

## Pa Group (Uk) Ltd

Pinden End Farm, Dartford, Kent DA2 8EA
**Tel:** 0845-474-0172 **Fax:** 0845-474-0173
**Web:** www.pagroupuk.com
**Reg No:** 6257126 **VAT No:** 921945124
**Estd:** 2007 Private Limited Company
**Line of Business:** Other construction work involving special trades
**Issued Capital:** £1
**Director:** C Miller-Hanna
**Co. Secretary:** Matthew Clarke
**Responsibilities**
**Senior:** Christopher Miller-hanna *(Managing Director)*
**Admin:** Stephanie Gardiner *(Office Manager)*
**US SIC:** 1799 **UK SIC:** 50000
**Auditors:** Beverton & Co

| | 31-10-13 | 31-10-12 | 31-10-11 |
|---|---|---|---|
| TA | 579,202 | 985,454 | 553,283 |
| NW | 171,420 | 159,381 | 154,780 |
| WC | 67,509 | 53,363 | 88,016 |

DUNS 23-312-8771

## P.A. McKeever Ltd

16 Mount Charles, Belfast BT7 1NZ
**Tel:** 02837-518-383
**Web:** www.mckeevers-chemists.com
**Reg No:** 0046467NI **Estd:** 1965 Private Limited Company
**Line of Business:** Dispensing chemists
**Trading Style:** McKeevers Chemists
**Issued Capital:** £1
**Director:** P A Mckeever
**Co. Secretary:** Ms Mary Mckeever
**Responsibilities**
**Senior:** Ronan Mckeever *(Proprietor)*
**US SIC:** 5912 **UK SIC:** 64300
**Auditors:** Muldoon & Co

**Bankers:** First Trust Bank (aib Group (uk) Plc) (93-81-14)

| | 31-07-13 | 31-07-12 | 31-07-11 |
|---|---|---|---|
| TO | 15,569,210 | 16,665,564 | 19,542,035 |
| P/L | 125,013 | 679,162 | 817,001 |
| NW | (5,792,207) | (7,641,665) | (9,144,892) |
| WC | 560,360 | (333,530) | (877,623) |
| Emp. | 104 | 113 | 113 |

DUNS 21-041-5037    **Exp**
## Pa Photos
Pearl Assurance House, Friar Lane, Nottingham, Nottinghamshire NG1 6BT
**Tel:** 01158-447447
**Web:** www.pressassociation.com
**Partnership**
**Line of Business:** Photographers (general)
**Partners:** D Law, J Atkins, S Brown, Ms M Egan, P Spencer, P Lakin
**US SIC:** 7333   **UK SIC:** 83953
**Employees:** 70

DUNS 23-900-3507    **Exp**
## Pa Photos Ltd
**(Subsidiary of:** P A Group Ltd)
Pa News Centre, 292 Vauxhall Bridge Road, London SW1V 1SS
**Tel:** 02079637000
**Web:** www.pressassociation.com
**Reg No:** 3891060   **Estd:** 1868 Private Limited Company
**Line of Business:** News and photograph agencies
**Export Sales:** £777,000
**Trading Style:** Press Association
**Issued Capital:** £157,913
**Directors:** C P Marshall, A G Watson
**Co. Secretary:** Stephen Godsell
**US SIC:** 7351   **UK SIC:** 83954
**Auditors:** PricewaterhouseCoopers LLP
**Bankers:** HSBC Bank plc (40-25-07)

| | 31-12-13 | 31-12-12 | 31-12-11 |
|---|---|---|---|
| TO | 5,856,000 | 6,063,000 | 6,276,000 |
| P/L | 1,010,000 | (156,000) | 976,000 |
| NW | (2,615,000) | (3,701,000) | (3,824,000) |
| WC | (2,900,000) | (4,053,000) | (4,800,000) |
| Emp. | 54 | 61 | 68 |

DUNS 23-651-0876    **Imp**
## Pab Coventry Ltd
Cornwall House, Flakland Close, Charter Avenue Industrial Estate, Coventry, West Midlands CV4 8AU
**Tel:** 02476694419
**Web:** www.pabgroup.co.uk
**Reg No:** 3646267   **Estd:** 1998 Private Limited Company
**Line of Business:** Sheet metal fabricators
**Issued Capital:** £30,003
**Directors:** Mrs V Brazier, M W Brazier, D T Wheldon
**Co. Secretary:** Raymond Floyd
**Responsibilities**
**Senior:** Peter Brazier (CEO, Managing Director)
**Branches:** Pab Coventry Ltd, Cornwall Ho, Falkland Clo, Charter Avenue Indstl Est, Coventry, West Midlands CV4 8AU
**US SIC:** 3469, 3499, 3489
**UK SIC:** 31200, 31694, 32901
**Auditors:** Michael Dufty Partnership Ltd

| | 31-05-14 | 31-05-13 | 31-05-12 |
|---|---|---|---|
| TA | 2,699,652 | 2,389,548 | 1,524,932 |
| NW | 1,001,588 | 838,545 | 367,018 |
| WC | 389,757 | 132,728 | (88,804) |

DUNS 22-856-9133    **Exp**
## Pac International Ltd
**(Subsidiary of:** Black & Decker International Finance 3)
1 Bredbury Park Way Park Gate Close, Stockport, Cheshire SK6 2SZ
**Tel:** 0161-406-3400 **Fax:** 01614068984
**Web:** www.pac.co.uk
**Reg No:** 1363776   **Estd:** 1978 Private Limited Company
**Line of Business:** Manufacturers of security equipment suppliers and
**Export Markets:** Germany, France, Italy, U S A, Norway, Sweden, Far East, Middle East
**Issued Capital:** £10,000
**Directors:** Ms S Stubbs, A K Sood, M R Smiley
**Co. Secretary:** Steven Costello
**Responsibilities**
**Senior:** Bruce Ginnever (Manager), Fred Hayhurst (Manager), Simon Lidder (Manager), John Tripp (Manager), Jason Unsworth (Manager)
**US SIC:** 7393   **UK SIC:** 83954
**Bankers:** Barclays Bank Plc (20-82-14)

| | 31-12-13 | 31-12-12 | 31-12-11 |
|---|---|---|---|
| TA | 11,325,000 | 11,325,000 | 11,325,000 |
| NW | 11,325,000 | 11,325,000 | 11,325,000 |

DUNS 77-165-5511
## The Pace Centre Ltd
Philip Green House, Coventon Road, Aylesbury, Buckinghamshire HP19 9JL
**Tel:** 01296-392739
**Web:** www.thepacecentre.org
**Reg No:** 2707807   **Estd:** 1992 Private Company Limited By Guarantee
**Line of Business:** Charities and charitable organisations
**Directors:** Mrs L A Gomme, D F Craggs, M Doyle, J C Lovelock, A L Pikett, I C John, Mrs N T Rashid
**Co. Secretary:** Ms Susan Muir
**Responsibilities**
**Senior:** Patricia Bergqvist (Manager), Lorna Felce (Manager), Heather Last (Manager), Abigail Martin (Manager), Amanda Richardson (Chief Executive)
**IT:** Alyn Edwards (Head of IT), Duncan Walsh (Head of IT)
**US SIC:** 8211, 8299
**UK SIC:** 93200, 93300
**Auditors:** Taylor & Co
**Bankers:** National Westminster Bank Plc (60-01-31)

| | 31-12-13 | 31-12-12 | 31-12-11 |
|---|---|---|---|
| TO | 4,573,911 | 3,168,790 | 3,024,529 |
| P/L | 1,292,717 | 33,412 | 124,414 |
| NW | 2,899,258 | 1,606,541 | 1,573,129 |
| WC | 1,252,493 | 951,447 | 1,032,150 |
| Emp. | 110 | 101 | 97 |

DUNS 22-802-2075    **Imp-Exp**
## Pace Plc
Victoria Road, Shipley, West Yorkshire BD18 3LF
**Tel:** 01274-532000 **Fax:** 01274532010
**Web:** www.pace.co.uk
**Reg No:** 1672847   **VAT No:** 974841675
**Estd:** 1995 Public Limited Company
**Line of Business:** Telecommunications
**Export Markets:** Worldwide
**Directors:** Ms A Mesler, M Inglis, J A Grant, M Shuttleworth, Ms P Chapman-Pincher, M Pulli, A Leighton
**Co. Secretary:** Anthony Dixon
**Responsibilities**
**Senior:** Neil Gaydon (Manager), David McKinney (Manager), Mike McTighe (Chairman), Robert McTighe (Manager)
**Finance:** Belinda Ellis (Interim CFO)
**Marketing:** Chris Briggs (?SVP Products and Solutions)
**Engineering:** Jonathan Cantrell (Head of Component Engineering), Darren Fawcett (Chief Technician), Stephen Muir (Head of Lead Hardware Engineer)
**Branches:** Pace Plc, Berkshire Court, Building A, Bracknell, Berkshire RG12 1RE
**US SIC:** 4899, 3651, 7379
**UK SIC:** 79020, 34541, 83940
**Auditors:** KPMG Audit PLC
**Bankers:** HSBC Bank plc (40-13-15)
**Employees:** 2,051
**Turnover:** £2,469,200,000

DUNS 22-205-5852
## Pacemaker Cleaning Services Ltd
Unit 3b, Smithton Industrial Estate, Inverness, Inverness-Shire IV2 7WL
**Tel:** 01463-792288
**Web:** www.pacemakercleaning.com
**Reg No:** 0219630SC   **VAT No:** 297200749
**Estd:** 1970 Private Limited Company
**Line of Business:** Cleaning contracting commercial
**Issued Capital:** £100
**Managing Director:** R Panton
**Co. Secretary:** Mrs Lesley Panton
**US SIC:** 7349, 7341
**UK SIC:** 92300

| | 31-03-14 | 31-03-13 | 31-03-12 |
|---|---|---|---|
| TA | 366,158 | 319,828 | 310,117 |
| NW | 288,432 | 247,500 | 235,869 |
| WC | 231,409 | 217,591 | 196,637 |

DUNS 89-676-8363
## Pacific Care Ltd
Birdston Road, Glasgow, Lanarkshire G66 8BY
**Tel:** 0141-571-0056 **Fax:** 01417779157
**Web:** www.pacificcare.co.uk
**Reg No:** 0174016SC   **Estd:** 1997 Private Limited Company
**Line of Business:** Representative office
**Issued Capital:** £1,000
**Directors:** J Brawley, Ms J Allan, J Brawley Jnr
**Co. Secretary:** Brendan Brawley
**US SIC:** 7399   **UK SIC:** 83954
**Auditors:** Thomas A Moran

| | 30-04-14 | 30-04-13 | 30-04-12 |
|---|---|---|---|
| TO | 5,272,930 | 4,956,992 | 4,865,647 |
| P/L | 1,045,744 | 1,367,188 | 1,468,430 |
| NW | 5,700,263 | 4,831,479 | 3,814,495 |
| WC | 1,377,333 | 966,851 | 1,738,802 |
| Emp. | 215 | 197 | 196 |

DUNS 56-961-8945    **Imp-Exp**
## Pacific Direct Ltd
**(Subsidiary of:** Pacific Direct Holdings Ltd)
Dombey Court The Pilgrim Centre, Brickhill Drive, Bedford, Bedfordshire MK41 7PZ
**Tel:** 01234347140
**Web:** www.pacificdirect.co.uk
**Reg No:** 2850917   **Estd:** 1993 Private Limited Company
**Line of Business:** Toilet articles
**Export Sales:** £17,272,340
**Issued Capital:** £100
**Directors:** T A Leach, Ms H A Seeley, P J Hatherly, Dr L Wilding, G M Allan
**Responsibilities**
**Senior:** Carol Fake (Global Coordinator)
**Health & Safety:** Carolyn Norman (Health & Safety Officer)
**US SIC:** 5199   **UK SIC:** 61900
**Auditors:** BDO LLP
**Bankers:** HSBC Bank plc (40-10-02)

| | 31-12-13 | 31-12-12 | 31-12-11 |
|---|---|---|---|
| TO | 23,044,038 | 20,748,078 | 22,966,621 |
| P/L | 1,509,970 | 122,314 | 1,828,727 |
| NW | 7,544,499 | 6,711,798 | 7,008,325 |
| WC | 5,247,422 | 4,533,245 | 5,648,894 |
| Emp. | 194 | 196 | 212 |

DUNS 34-580-8307
## Pacific Health & Fitness Ltd
24-26 Baltic Street West, London EC1Y 0RP
**Tel:** 02084823000
**Web:** www.labspa.co.uk
**Reg No:** 2727984   **VAT No:** 564533140
**Estd:** 1995 Private Limited Company
**Line of Business:** Other entertainment activities not elsewhere classified
**Trading Style:** The Laboratory Spa & Health Club
**Issued Capital:** £1,000
**Principals:** J M Lyras (Managing), M J Lyras, V Hava
**Co. Secretary:** Cornhill Secretaries Limited
**Branches:** Pacific Health & Fitness Ltd, The Ave, London N10 2QJ
**US SIC:** 7999   **UK SIC:** 97913
**Auditors:** Moore Stephens LLP
**Bankers:** National Westminster Bank Plc (50-00-00)

| | 30-09-13 | 30-09-12 | 30-09-11 |
|---|---|---|---|
| TO | 3,375,742 | 3,377,215 | 3,296,111 |
| P/L | 1,154,147 | 1,102,459 | 1,068,675 |
| NW | 3,555,674 | 3,181,979 | 2,731,929 |
| WC | 606,353 | 332,168 | 3,677 |
| Emp. | 71 | 76 | 75 |

DUNS 22-814-4713    **Imp**
## Pacific Lifestyle Ltd
**(Subsidiary of:** Stafford Mills Holdings Ltd)
Stafford Mills, George Street, Huddersfield, West Yorkshire HD3 4JD
**Web:** www.pacific-lifestyle.co.uk
**Reg No:** 1625765   **VAT No:** 972584775
**Estd:** 1982 Private Limited Company
**Line of Business:** Cane and basketware
**Issued Capital:** £9,000
**Directors:** A S Hutchinson, D G Headey, N S Lawrence
**Co. Secretary:** Geoffrey Riley
**Responsibilities**
**Senior:** Elaine Budsfield (Manager)
**Sales:** Elaine Budsfield (Manager)
**US SIC:** 2392   **UK SIC:** 45550
**Auditors:** Clough & Co LLP
**Bankers:** HSBC Bank plc (40-25-10)

| | 31-12-13 | 31-12-12 | 31-12-11 |
|---|---|---|---|
| TO | 9,203,809 | 8,817,449 | 8,979,535 |
| P/L | 167,696 | 73,835 | 4,025 |
| NW | 213,059 | 25,770 | (39,342) |
| WC | 372,745 | 173,347 | (92,884) |
| Emp. | 66 | 65 | 70 |

DUNS 34-739-7593
## Pacifica Group Ltd
Picktree Court, Picktree Lane, Chester-Le-Street, County Durham DH3 3SY
**Tel:** 01913870774
**Web:** www.pacificagroup.co.uk
**Reg No:** 5541667   **Estd:** 2005 Private Limited Company
**Line of Business:** Secretarial and translation activities
**Issued Capital:** £15,000
**Directors:** P R Feek, K Brown
**Co. Secretary:** Scott Pallister
**US SIC:** 7339   **UK SIC:** 83954
**Bankers:** HSBC Bank plc (40-45-11)

| | 31-03-14 | 31-03-13 | 31-03-12 |
|---|---|---|---|
| TO | 26,370,896 | 20,214,274 | 14,021,803 |
| P/L | 161,234 | 185,649 | 372,733 |
| NW | 806,711 | 774,906 | 424,998 |
| WC | 302,279 | 276,365 | (253,232) |
| Emp. | 221 | 225 | 160 |

DUNS 29-558-3850    **Exp**
## The Pacifico Group Ltd
**(Subsidiary of:** Pacifico International Ltd)
5 Langley Street, London WC2H 9JA
**Tel:** 02072407075
**Web:** www.cafepacifico-laperla.com
**Reg No:** 1922730   **Estd:** 1985 Private Limited Company
**Line of Business:** Licensed restaurants
**Trading Style:** Cafe Pacifico, Perla Bar and Girl
**Issued Capital:** £100
**Principals:** T G Estes (Chairman), S M Tishler
**Co. Secretary:** Stephen Tishler
**Responsibilities**
**Senior:** Sheila Lakeman (General Manager), Carlos Londono (Manager)
**HR:** Sheila Lakeman (General Manager)
**Health & Safety:** Sheila Lakeman (General Manager)
**Facilities:** Sheila Lakeman (General Manager)
**US SIC:** 7399, 6711
**UK SIC:** 83954, 83962
**Auditors:** Sedley Richard Laurence Voulters
**Bankers:** National Westminster Bank Plc (60-50-00)

| | 31-12-13 | 31-12-12 | 31-12-11 |
|---|---|---|---|
| TA | 292,842 | 745,603 | 865,490 |
| NW | (2,124,083) | (2,155,404) | (2,042,468) |
| WC | (2,287,586) | (2,314,149) | (2,266,555) |

DUNS 21-834-2814    **Imp-Exp**
## Packaging Automation Ltd
Parkgate Industrial Park, Knutsford, Cheshire WA16 8XW
**Tel:** 01565755000 **Fax:** 01565-751015
**Web:** www.pal.co.uk
**Reg No:** 0761199   **VAT No:** 157580052
**Estd:** 1963 Private Limited Company
**Line of Business:** Manufacture of other special purpose machinery not elsewhere classified
**Export Markets:** worldwide
**Issued Capital:** £100,000
**Principals:** A A Penn (Chairman and Managing), Ms C A Royle (Managing), Doctor W G Holden, N Ashton, F J Cooke, Mrs S Ashton
**Co. Secretary:** Ms Carol Royle
**Responsibilities**
**HR:** Dorothy Wainscott (Human Resources Manager)
**Health & Safety:** Dorothy Wainscott (Human Resources Manager)
**Operations:** Dorothy Wainscott (Human Resources Manager)
**US SIC:** 3559   **UK SIC:** 32863
**Auditors:** PKF
**Bankers:** Barclays Bank Plc (20-53-77)

| | 30-09-13 | 30-09-12 | 30-09-11 |
|---|---|---|---|
| TO | 6,366,105 | 6,322,985 | 6,627,719 |
| P/L | 140,203 | (489,726) | 207,594 |
| NW | 2,580,161 | 2,455,303 | 2,895,716 |
| WC | 1,098,462 | 967,392 | 1,459,435 |
| Emp. | 94 | 93 | 89 |

DUNS 77-703-1592
## Packaging Innovation Ltd
1 Colville Mews, London W11 2AR
**Tel:** 02079080808
**Web:** www.piglobal.com
**Reg No:** 3006990   **Estd:** 1995 Private Limited Company
**Line of Business:** Design consultants
**Export Sales:** £2,414,677
**Trading Style:** P I Design International
**Issued Capital:** £14,955
**Principals:** C J Griffin (Managing), Ms K Krejberg, S F Kelsey, G M Obrien, D W Williams
**Co. Secretary:** Jeffrey Chew
**Responsibilities**
**Senior:** Amy Bridgman (Manager)
**US SIC:** 8911, 7311
**UK SIC:** 83701, 83800
**Auditors:** Lee Associates Ltd
**Bankers:** HSBC Bank plc (40-22-26)

| | 31-03-13 | 31-03-12 | 31-03-11 |
|---|---|---|---|
| TO | 3,400,953 | 3,603,531 | 4,810,867 |
| P/L | 63,303 | (140,354) | 70,119 |
| NW | 500,698 | 444,753 | 573,145 |
| WC | 710,033 | 696,216 | 830,917 |

DUNS 73-910-9770    **Imp**
## Packetexchange (Europe) Ltd
**(Subsidiary of:** Gtt Communications Inc.)
11a Curtain Road, London EC2A 3LT
**Tel:** 02074894200
**Web:** www.packetexchange.net
**Reg No:** 5164474   **Estd:** 2004 Private Limited Company
**Line of Business:** Other business activities not elsewhere classified
**Issued Capital:** £17,085
**Directors:** C T Mckee, R D Calder
**Co. Secretary:** Christopher Mckee
**US SIC:** 7399   **UK SIC:** 83954
**Auditors:** Grant Thornton

**Bankers:** The Royal Bank Of Scotland Plc (16-08-05)

| | 31-12-12 | 31-12-11 | 31-12-10 |
|---|---|---|---|
| TO | N/A | N/A | 8,540,617 |
| P/L | N/A | N/A | 1,107,769 |
| NW | (906,242) | (1,232,325) | (1,309,808) |
| WC | 211,447 | 634,667 | 666,776 |

DUNS 50-360-5081

## Packington Estate Enterprises Ltd

The Estate Office, Coventry, West Midlands CV7 7HF
**Tel:** 01676522020
**Web:** www.packingtonestate.net
**Reg No:** 2377594 **VAT No:** 544982313
**Estd:** 1989 Private Limited Company
**Line of Business:** Surveyors and valuers
**Trading Style:** Packington Fisheries
**Issued Capital:** £4,218,178
**Principals:** N P Barlow *(Managing)*, P A Finch-Knightley, H J Finch-Knightly, C H Finch-Knightley, R V Stone
**Co. Secretary:** Nicholas Barlow
**Responsibilities**
**Marketing:** Malcolm Wiggan *(Building Surveyor)*
**IT:** Malcolm Wiggan *(Building Surveyor)*
**Health & Safety:** Malcolm Wiggan *(Building Surveyor)*
**Facilities:** Malcolm Wiggan *(Building Surveyor)*
**US SIC:** 8911, 6531
**UK SIC:** 83701, 83400
**Auditors:** Burgis & Bullock

| | 31-03-14 | 31-03-13 | 31-03-12 |
|---|---|---|---|
| TA | 6,334,760 | 5,805,410 | 5,103,253 |
| NW | 3,131,209 | 3,345,815 | 3,159,172 |
| WC | 2,256,647 | 3,152,844 | 3,087,224 |

DUNS 45-824-6477 **Imp**

## Packpost International Ltd.

Griffin House, Griffin Lane, Aylesbury, Buckinghamshire HP19 8BE
**Tel:** 01296487493 **Fax:** 01296393469
**Web:** www.packpost.com
**Reg No:** 3177756 **Estd:** 1974 Private Limited Company
**Line of Business:** Direct mail service providers
**Trading Style:** Packpost Services Limited
**Issued Capital:** £300
**Directors:** Mrs M J Lucatello, J K Sandhu, N Sandhu
**Responsibilities**
**Senior:** Trudy Marshall *(Sales Director)*
**Marketing:** Trudy Marshall *(Sales Director)*
**Sales:** Trudy Marshall *(Sales Director)*
**Operations:** Trudy Marshall *(Sales Director)*
**US SIC:** 7319 **UK SIC:** 83800
**Auditors:** Whittenbury & Co

| | 31-12-13 | 31-12-12 | 31-12-11 |
|---|---|---|---|
| TA | 4,312,622 | 3,687,725 | 3,256,511 |
| NW | 3,010,541 | 2,033,250 | 1,742,104 |
| WC | 2,581,573 | 1,726,780 | 1,432,155 |

DUNS 76-942-7899

## Packwood Haugh School Ltd

Ruyton Xi Towns, Shrewsbury, Shropshire SY4 1HX
**Web:** www.packwood-haugh.co.uk
**Reg No:** 0563845 **Estd:** 1900 Private Limited Company
**Line of Business:** General secondary education
**Directors:** D R Stacey, R G Tovey, Ms E M Lewis, Ms F Humphreys, Dr C M Morton, M Turner, Mrs A G Mackeson-Sandbach, W A Johnston
**Co. Secretary:** Mrs Natalie Shaw
**Responsibilities**
**Senior:** Thomas Welti *(Bursar)*, Nigel Westlake *(Headmaster)*
**Finance:** Thomas Welti *(Bursar)*
**HR:** Nigel Westlake *(Headmaster)*
**US SIC:** 8211 **UK SIC:** 93200
**Auditors:** Whittingham Riddell
**Bankers:** Barclays Bank Plc (20-77-85)

| | 31-08-14 | 31-08-13 | 31-08-12 |
|---|---|---|---|
| TO | 3,644,323 | 3,728,297 | 4,008,211 |
| P/L | 6,193 | (48,510) | 149,978 |
| NW | 4,785,477 | 4,779,284 | 4,827,794 |
| WC | (163,535) | (344,974) | (485,673) |
| Emp. | 79 | 85 | 86 |

DUNS 54-814-7867

## Paco's Restaurant

21 Dumbarton Road, Stirling, Stirlingshire FK8 2LQ
**Tel:** 01786446414
**Web:** www.pacos.co.uk
**Estd:** 1996 Partnership
**Line of Business:** Continental Restaurant
**Partners:** Mrs I Galea, A Galea
**Branches:** Paco's Restaurant, Perth Concert Hall, Mill Street, Perth, Perthshire PH1 5HZ
**US SIC:** 5812 **UK SIC:** 66110
**Employees:** 100

DUNS 21-579-0867

## Paddington Academy

50 Marylands Road, London W9 2DR
**Tel:** 020-74793900
**Web:** www.paddington-academy.org
**Proprietorship**
**Line of Business:** Schools (foundation)
**Proprietor:** Mrs O Tomlinson
**US SIC:** 8211 **UK SIC:** 93200
**Employees:** 250

DUNS 21-454-4731

## Paddington Court Hotel & Suites

Devon Lodge, London W2 3DR
**Tel:** 02072622204
**Web:** www.paddingtonhotellondon.co.uk
**Estd:** 1996 Proprietorship
**Line of Business:** Hotels
**Proprietor:** R Arora
**Responsibilities**
**Senior:** Rahul Kanakgiri *(Hotel Manager)*, anne kita *(Reservation Manager)*
**Facilities:** Vinayak Girjune *(Facilities Manager)*
**US SIC:** 7011 **UK SIC:** 66500
**Employees:** 50

DUNS 21-546-3998

## Paddock Wood Town Council

The Podmore Building, St Andrews Road, Paddock Wood, Tonbridge, Kent TN12 6HT
**Tel:** 01892-837373
**Web:** www.paddockwoodtc.kentparishes.gov.uk
**Estd:** 2002 Proprietorship
**Line of Business:** Local government
**Proprietor:** Mrs N Reay
**Responsibilities**
**Senior:** Nichola Reay *(Manager)*
**US SIC:** 9121 **UK SIC:** 91110
**Employees:** 60

DUNS 55-074-0179

## Paddocks Residential Home

45 Cley Road, Swaffham, Norfolk PE37 7NP
**Tel:** 01760723416
**Web:** www.castlemeadowcare.co.uk
**Estd:** 1999 Partnership
**Line of Business:** Residential care establishments
**Partners:** Mrs M Green, J Green
**Responsibilities**
**Senior:** Ann Chilvers *(Care Manager)*
**US SIC:** 8321 **UK SIC:** 96111
**Employees:** 120

DUNS 76-576-8890

## Padi Emea Ltd

**(Subsidiary of:** Capital Investments & Ventures Corp.)
Bridgwater Road, Bristol, Avon BS13 8AE
**Tel:** 01173007234
**Web:** www.padi.co.uk
**Reg No:** 2575129 **Estd:** 1991 Private Limited Company
**Line of Business:** Education agencies and authorities
**Export Sales:** £18,262,000
**Issued Capital:** £10,000
**Directors:** M Caney, T A Richardson, C M Kuehn, M P Spiers, N R Fishburne
**Co. Secretary:** Neil Fishburne
**Responsibilities**
**Senior:** Mike Filer *(Operations Manager)*, Douglas Nash *(Manager)*, Gary Prenovost *(Manager)*
**Health & Safety:** Mike Filer *(Operations Manager)*
**Facilities:** Mike Filer *(Operations Manager)*
**US SIC:** 8299, 8631
**UK SIC:** 93300, 96313
**Auditors:** C V Mitchell & Co
**Bankers:** Barclays Bank Plc (20-33-83)

| | 31-12-13 | 31-12-12 | 31-12-11 |
|---|---|---|---|
| TO | 21,915,000 | 20,069,000 | 9,663,273 |
| P/L | 2,151,000 | 1,052,000 | 1,455,813 |
| NW | 791,000 | 1,832,000 | 4,642,420 |
| WC | (1,233,000) | (77,000) | 1,025,535 |
| Emp. | 85 | 82 | 70 |

DUNS 22-853-5613

## Padiham Glass Ltd

Glass Tech Centre Unit 10a, Burnley, Lancashire BB12 7NG
**Tel:** 01282-774124 **Fax:** 01282-774951
**Web:** www.padihamglass.co.uk
**Reg No:** 1520736 **VAT No:** 326052976
**Estd:** 1980 Private Limited Company
**Line of Business:** Builders merchants
**Issued Capital:** £5,000
**Principals:** S Clarkson *(Managing)*, W Clarkson, A J Clarkson, J K Kemp
**Co. Secretary:** Ms Tracy Clarkson
**US SIC:** 1721, 5199
**UK SIC:** 50400, 61900
**Auditors:** Ashworth Moulds

**Bankers:** National Westminster Bank Plc (01-00-04)

| | 30-09-13 | 30-09-12 | 30-09-11 |
|---|---|---|---|
| TA | 3,000,930 | 3,013,378 | 3,075,891 |
| NW | 1,574,226 | 1,524,893 | 1,558,460 |
| WC | 26,798 | (38,926) | (5,076) |

DUNS 34-691-9459 **Imp-Exp**

## Padley & Venables Ltd

**(Subsidiary of:** Brunner & Lay International Ltd)
Unit A-C, Callywhite Lane, Dronfield, South Yorkshire S18 2XT
**Tel:** 01246-299100 **Fax:** 01246-290354
**Web:** www.padley-venables.com
**Reg No:** 2778086 **VAT No:** 593467595
**Estd:** 1993 Private Limited Company
**Line of Business:** Other manufacturing not elsewhere classified
**Export Markets:** Worldwide
**Issued Capital:** £1,600,002
**Director:** F M Brunner
**Co. Secretary:** Darren Bradwell
**Responsibilities**
**Senior:** Philip Barlow *(General Manager)*
**Marketing:** Philip Barlow *(General Manager)*, Joan Whitehouse *(Sales & Marketing Manager)*
**Sales:** Joan Whitehouse *(Sales & Marketing Manager)*
**Branches:** Padley & Venables Ltd, Effingham Road, Sheffield, South Yorkshire S4 7YS
**US SIC:** 3531 **UK SIC:** 32541
**Auditors:** Barber Harrison & Platt
**Bankers:** National Westminster Bank Plc (56-00-09)

| | 31-12-13 | 31-12-12 | 31-12-11 |
|---|---|---|---|
| TO | 19,945,003 | 21,092,153 | 19,369,998 |
| P/L | 1,714,861 | 2,743,770 | 2,755,927 |
| NW | 26,019,818 | 24,298,608 | 23,450,820 |
| WC | 17,794,104 | 16,594,115 | 14,770,799 |
| Emp. | 186 | 188 | 179 |

DUNS 29-057-0746

## Padworth College Trust Ltd

Padworth College, Padworth, Reading, Berkshire RG7 4NR
**Tel:** 01189-832644
**Web:** www.padworth.com
**Reg No:** 1154199 **Estd:** 1974 Private Limited Company
**Line of Business:** Schools (independent)
**Directors:** Mrs D A Dyson, D G Crawford, Professor C N Mann, R G Ash, J F West, W M Hames, J P Rawes, J M Robertson
**Co. Secretary:** James Wilson
**Responsibilities**
**Senior:** John Augilar *(Principal)*, John Crawshaw *(Manager)*, Paul Tabberner *(Director)*
**US SIC:** 8211 **UK SIC:** 93200
**Auditors:** BDO Stoy Hayward
**Bankers:** Lloyds TSB Bank plc (30-96-96)

| | 31-08-13 | 31-08-12 | 31-08-11 |
|---|---|---|---|
| TO | 2,771,949 | 2,849,733 | 2,499,716 |
| P/L | 370,737 | 588,970 | 365,562 |
| NW | 2,176,614 | 1,805,877 | 1,216,907 |
| WC | 650,788 | 1,190,360 | 732,058 |
| Emp. | 48 | 45 | 45 |

DUNS 21-607-6299 **Exp**

## Pafra Adhesives Ltd

Bentalls, Basildon, Essex SS14 3BU
**Tel:** 01268290600 **Fax:** 012682906319
**Web:** www.pafra.com
**Reg No:** 0644949 **VAT No:** 250489554
**Estd:** 1959 Private Limited Company
**Line of Business:** Manufacturers and distribution of adhesive
**Export Markets:** Worldwide
**Issued Capital:** £713,710
**Directors:** J L Wosner, I E Gamse, Dr A G Steward, E A Kochmann
**Co. Secretary:** Stephen Martin
**US SIC:** 2891, 3559
**UK SIC:** 25620, 32863
**Auditors:** Jeffreys Henry
**Bankers:** Barclays Bank Plc (20-04-96)

| | 31-03-14 | 31-03-13 | 31-03-12 |
|---|---|---|---|
| TA | 4,589,666 | 4,399,546 | 4,475,741 |
| NW | 3,306,918 | 2,756,557 | 2,675,715 |
| WC | 1,519,191 | 1,313,869 | 1,492,666 |

DUNS 34-862-3666

## Pagan Osborne Discretionary Trustees Ltd

12 St Catherine Street, Cupar, Fife KY15 4HH
**Tel:** 01334653777
**Reg No:** 0294826SC **Estd:** 2005 Private Limited Company
**Line of Business:** Solicitors
**Issued Capital:** £4
**Directors:** C M Clark, A G Grant, Ms E L Calderwood, A L Morris
**Co. Secretary:** Pagan Osborne
**Branches:** Pagan Osborne Discretionary Trustees Ltd, 2-4 Comiston Road, Edinburgh, Midlothian EH10 5QE

**US SIC:** 8111 **UK SIC:** 83500

| | 31-12-13 | 31-12-12 | 31-12-11 |
|---|---|---|---|
| TA | 4 | 4 | 4 |
| NW | 4 | 4 | 4 |
| WC | 4 | N/A | N/A |
| Emp. | 100 | N/A | N/A |

DUNS 42-472-4396

## Pagazzi Lighting Ltd

Kirkhill House, Broom Road East, Newton Mearns, Glasgow, Lanarkshire G77 5LL
**Tel:** 01416395637
**Web:** www.pagazzi.com
**Reg No:** 0232732SC **Estd:** 2002 Private Limited Company
**Line of Business:** Lighting retailers
**Issued Capital:** £148,245
**Directors:** V A Gunn, A M Pagan, Mrs L Pagan, D W Needham, S Jones
**Co. Secretary:** Iain Doak
**Branches:** Pagazzi Lighting Ltd, Unit 4, Almondvale South Retail Park, Livingston, West Lothian EH54 6XG
**US SIC:** 5719 **UK SIC:** 64700
**Auditors:** KRP Chartered Certified Accountants & Registered Auditors
**Bankers:** The Royal Bank Of Scotland Plc (83-23-23)

| | 31-03-14 | 31-03-13 | 31-03-12 |
|---|---|---|---|
| TO | N/A | N/A | 5,939,315 |
| P/L | N/A | N/A | 88,327 |
| NW | 504,043 | 444,779 | 343,360 |
| WC | 211,131 | 200,627 | (125,717) |
| Emp. | N/A | N/A | 101 |

DUNS 21-630-7983 **Imp-Exp**

## Page Aerospace Ltd

**(Subsidiary of:** Page Engineering (Holdings) Ltd)
Page Works, Forge Lane, Sunbury-On-Thames, Middlesex TW16 6EQ
**Tel:** 01932-787661 **Fax:** 01932-780349
**Web:** www.pageaerospace.co.uk
**Reg No:** 0615793 **Estd:** 1944 Private Limited Company
**Line of Business:** Manufacture of electronic valves and tubes and other electronic components
**Export Markets:** E U & other countries
**Export Sales:** £21,902,000
**Trading Style:** Utc Aerospace
**Issued Capital:** £10,000
**Directors:** J S Erickson, N A Gregor Macgregor, M A Lipyeat, S R Anderson
**Co. Secretary:** Edwin Coe Secretaries Limited
**Responsibilities**
**Senior:** Nigel Marks *(Manager)*, Mark Spana *(Manager)*, Eve Wicks *(Manager)*
**IT:** Les Phelps *(IT Manager)*
**Facilities:** David Brench *(Facilities Manager)*
**Purchasing:** Mick Budd *(Senior Buyer)*
**Branches:** Page Aerospace Ltd, Pershore Trading Estate, Station Road, Wyre Piddle, Pershore, Pershore, Worcestershire WR10 2YA
**US SIC:** 3679 **UK SIC:** 34542
**Auditors:** PricewaterhouseCoopers LLP
**Bankers:** Bank Of Scotland (80-20-00)

| | 30-11-13 | 30-11-12 | 30-11-11 |
|---|---|---|---|
| TO | 23,934,000 | 22,916,000 | 18,082,000 |
| P/L | (2,898,000) | 5,430,000 | 2,817,000 |
| NW | 22,340,000 | 26,400,000 | 22,475,000 |
| WC | 27,880,000 | 24,813,000 | 21,087,000 |
| Emp. | 169 | 162 | 153 |

DUNS 22-650-9321 **Exp**

## Page & Moy Travel Group Air Holidays Ltd

**(Subsidiary of:** All Leisure Group Plc)
Compass House, Rockingham Road, Market Harborough, Market Harborough, Leicestershire LE16 7QD
**Tel:** 01858410456 **Fax:** 01858432202
**Web:** www.pageandmoytravelgroup.com
**Reg No:** 1329030 **VAT No:** 313060024
**Estd:** 1977 Private Limited Company
**Line of Business:** Activities of travel organisers
**Export Markets:** Canada, W Europe, Far East, China, U.S.A.
**Export Sales:** £1,062,000
**Issued Capital:** £100,000
**Directors:** I Smith, N J Arthur, Ms T Mckinnon, C Wilson, R J Allard
**Co. Secretary:** Nigel Arthur
**Responsibilities**
**Senior:** William Burton *(Chief Executive)*, Gillian Harvey *(Manager)*
**Marketing:** Caroline Welton *(Promotions Manager)*
**IT:** Kevin Keys *(IT Manager)*
**US SIC:** 4722 **UK SIC:** 77001
**Auditors:** KPMG LLP
**Bankers:** Barclays Bank Plc (20-49-11)

| | 31-10-13 | 31-10-12 | 30-10-11 |
|---|---|---|---|
| TO | 70,503,000 | 85,464,000 | 94,691,000 |
| P/L | 2,751,000 | 2,772,000 | (6,070,000) |
| NW | (2,455,000) | (5,166,000) | 304,000 |
| WC | (3,241,000) | (6,066,000) | 31,000 |
| Emp. | 283 | 267 | 295 |

DUNS 21-822-8567 **Exp**

## Page Bros. (Norwich) Ltd

(**Subsidiary of:** Milex Ltd)
Mile Cross Lane, Norwich, Norfolk NR6 6SA
**Tel:** 01603-778800
**Web:** www.pagebros.co.uk
**Reg No:** 0170008 **VAT No:** 595318508
**Estd:** 1920 Private Limited Company
**Line of Business:** Digital services
**Export Sales:** £1,602,000
**Issued Capital:** £33,412
**Principals:** C A Eastaugh *(Financial)*, D R Longfoot *(Technical)*, A M Spelman, D A Holt, S A Bryanton, G G Warner, S P Conway
**Responsibilities**
**Sales:** Stephen Commons *(Sales Director)*
**HR:** Jan Forkes *(Human Resources Coordinator)*
**Branches:** Page Bros. (Norwich) Ltd, St. James House, 10 Rosebery Avenue, London EC1R 4TF
**US SIC:** 2752, 2711
**UK SIC:** 47544, 47512
**Auditors:** PricewaterhouseCoopers LLP
**Bankers:** The Royal Bank Of Scotland Plc (83-07-06)

| | 30-09-13 | 30-09-12 | 30-09-11 |
|---|---|---|---|
| TO | 9,747,000 | 9,561,000 | 8,147,000 |
| P/L | 2,456,000 | 270,000 | (315,000) |
| NW | (557,000) | (2,269,000) | 145,000 |
| WC | 337,000 | 263,000 | (31,000) |
| Emp. | 103 | 97 | 88 |

DUNS 22-504-6465

## Page Holdings Ltd

20-24 East Street, Epsom, Surrey KT17 1HQ
**Tel:** 01202477468 **Fax:** 01372-745193
**Web:** www.pageholdings.co.uk
**Reg No:** 1400771 **VAT No:** 209884824
**Estd:** 1978 Private Limited Company
**Line of Business:** Management activities of holding companies
**Issued Capital:** £456,490
**Director:** R L Page
**Co. Secretary:** Mark Page
**US SIC:** 6711 **UK SIC:** 83962
**Auditors:** Finley & Partners
**Bankers:** HSBC Bank plc (40-20-24)

| | 31-12-13 | 31-12-12 | 31-12-11 |
|---|---|---|---|
| TA | 5,507,520 | 5,900,912 | 5,798,945 |
| NW | 2,888,644 | 3,029,218 | 3,239,783 |
| WC | (414,745) | (356,152) | (329,303) |

DUNS 76-964-9740

## The Page Media Group Ltd

3 Capricorn Centre, Basildon, Essex SS14 3JJ
**Tel:** 01268-271858
**Web:** wwwpagemediagroup.com
**Reg No:** 2629654 **Estd:** 1990 Public Limited Company
**Line of Business:** Interior designers
**Issued Capital:** £50,000
**Managing Director:** M Hughes
**Co. Secretary:** Mark Hughes
**Branches:** The Page Media Group Ltd, 4 Kingly Street, London W1B 5PE
**US SIC:** 6711, 8911
**UK SIC:** 83962, 83701
**Bankers:** Barclays Bank Plc (20-70-93)

| | 31-12-13 | 31-12-12 | 31-12-11 |
|---|---|---|---|
| TA | 375,248 | 346,983 | 577,113 |
| NW | (344,792) | (434,085) | (252,855) |
| WC | (407,342) | (568,970) | (361,057) |

DUNS 21-811-4685

## Page Personnel Finance

Victoria House, Southampton Row, London WC1B 4JB
**Tel:** 02072692160
**Web:** www.pagepersonnel.co.uk
**Estd:** 2012
**Line of Business:** Employment and recruitment companies and consultants
**US SIC:** 7361 **UK SIC:** 83954
**Employees:** 400

DUNS 53-624-6333 **Imp**

## Pageant Media Ltd

(**Subsidiary of:** Pageant Media Holdings Ltd)
Thavies Inn House, London EC1N 2HA
**Tel:** 02078326500 **Fax:** 020-7269-7570
**Web:** www.pageantmedia.com
**Reg No:** 3429596 **Estd:** 1997 Private Limited Company
**Line of Business:** Publishing of journals and periodicals
**Issued Capital:** £1,000
**Principals:** C R Kerr *(Managing)*, R M Flaye
**Co. Secretary:** Sebastian Timpson
**Responsibilities**
**Sales:** Thomas O' Riordan *(Sales Executive)*
**US SIC:** 2721 **UK SIC:** 47522
**Auditors:** Dua & Co
**Bankers:** HSBC Bank plc (40-07-06)

| | 28-02-14 | 28-02-13 | 29-02-12 |
|---|---|---|---|
| TO | 7,838,506 | 8,823,468 | 7,790,921 |
| P/L | 2,169,924 | 1,540,179 | 1,324,778 |
| NW | 734,698 | 517,772 | 91,834 |
| WC | 149,865 | (58,697) | (186,673) |
| Emp. | 83 | N/A | N/A |

DUNS 21-308-0360

## Pagoda Film & Television Corporation

31-32 Soho Square, London W1D 3AP
**Tel:** 02075343500
**Estd:** 1998 Partnership
**Line of Business:** Film production services and studios
**Partners:** C Barker, K Mansfield, D Elstein, J Auty, M Samuelson
**US SIC:** 7819 **UK SIC:** 97111
**Employees:** 50

DUNS 23-873-1215

## P.A.I. Group Ltd

(**Subsidiary of:** Pai Holdings Ltd)
Unit 3-4 Heol Rhosyn, Llanelli, Dyfed SA14 8QG
**Tel:** 01554-740500 **Fax:** 01554740501
**Web:** www.paigroup.com
**Reg No:** 3864452 **Estd:** 2000 Private Limited Company
**Line of Business:** Installation of electrical wiring and fittings
**Issued Capital:** £100
**Director:** R G Vaughan
**Co. Secretary:** Paul Adams
**Responsibilities**
**Senior:** Keith Badman *(General Manager)*, Keith Fish *(Business Development Manager)*
**Sales:** Keith Fish *(Business Development Manager)*
**IT:** Andy Bonehill *(Group Technical Director)*
**Operations:** Keith Elms *(Operations Director, Lighting)*, Tony Moruzzi *(Operations Manager)*
**Engineering:** Andy Bonehill *(Group Technical Director)*
**US SIC:** 1731 **UK SIC:** 50300
**Auditors:** Bevan & Buckland

| | 31-12-13 | 31-12-12 | 31-12-11 |
|---|---|---|---|
| TA | 100 | 100 | 100 |
| NW | 100 | 100 | 100 |

DUNS 21-613-6408

## Paice Group Ltd

Park Wood, Byers Lane, Godstone, Surrey RH9 8JH
**Tel:** 01342322240
**Reg No:** 0648332 **Estd:** 1960 Private Limited Company
**Line of Business:** Other letting of own property
**Issued Capital:** £120,575
**Principals:** P M Paice *(Managing)*, E C Paice, Ms B J Wickenden
**Co. Secretary:** Ms Amanda Medlam
**Branches:** Paice Group Ltd, Felbridge Forge, London Road, East Grinstead, West Sussex RH19 2RQ
**US SIC:** 6519, 5511
**UK SIC:** 85000, 65100
**Auditors:** Grant Thornton
**Bankers:** Lloyds TSB Bank plc (30-92-92)

| | 30-09-13 | 30-09-12 | 30-09-11 |
|---|---|---|---|
| TA | 3,615,056 | 3,579,007 | 3,726,498 |
| NW | 3,321,063 | 3,253,537 | 3,415,766 |
| WC | 290,833 | 257,950 | 396,213 |

DUNS 22-761-1738 **Imp-Exp**

## Pailton Engineering Ltd

Phoenix House, Holbrook Lane, Coventry, West Midlands CV6 4AD
**Tel:** 024-7668-0445
**Web:** www.pailton.com
**Reg No:** 1377101 **Estd:** 1978 Private Limited Company
**Line of Business:** Manufacture of parts and accessories for motor vehicles and their engines
**Export Markets:** Australasia; European Union (E U)
**Export Sales:** £7,056,001
**Issued Capital:** £48,775
**Directors:** J R Nollett, I M Palmer, S Williams, C T Wilkinson, K B Humphrey
**Responsibilities**
**Senior:** Trevor Townsend *(Training Manager)*
**Finance:** Greg Simpson *(Senior Finance Administrator)*
**Sales:** Markison Kynaston *(Senior Sales Executive)*
**Admin:** Greg Simpson *(Senior Finance Administrator)*
**IT:** Ryan Fawcett *(IT Technician)*, Trevor Rainsford *(IT Manager)*
**HR:** Trevor Townsend *(Training Manager)*
**US SIC:** 3714 **UK SIC:** 35300
**Auditors:** RSM Tenon Audit Ltd
**Bankers:** Barclays Bank Plc (20-23-55)

| | 31-12-13 | 31-12-12 | 31-12-11 |
|---|---|---|---|
| TO | 13,012,587 | 12,973,404 | 13,612,349 |
| P/L | (924,434) | (1,731,288) | 267,992 |
| NW | 5,507,828 | 6,305,620 | 7,919,527 |
| WC | 2,748,650 | 3,893,959 | 4,590,280 |
| Emp. | 179 | 181 | 178 |

DUNS 23-593-7567

## Paine Manwaring Heating Ltd

Unit D Easting Trading Estate, Worthing, West Sussex BN14 8HQ
**Tel:** 01903-237522
**Web:** www.painemanwaring.com
**Reg No:** 3591258 **Estd:** 1998 Private Limited Company
**Line of Business:** Installation of electrical wiring and fittings
**Issued Capital:** £97,500
**Directors:** M A Langdell, J M Preston
**Co. Secretary:** Feargal Woods
**Responsibilities**
**Senior:** Robert Grigson *(Manager)*
**IT:** Robert Grigson *(Manager)*
**US SIC:** 1731, 1711
**UK SIC:** 50300
**Auditors:** Carpenter Box
**Bankers:** National Westminster Bank Plc (60-24-31)

| | 31-03-14 | 31-03-13 | 31-03-12 |
|---|---|---|---|
| TO | 11,488,152 | 202,047 | 172,804 |
| P/L | 302,057 | 249,872 | 219,284 |
| NW | 815,656 | 486,295 | 382,207 |
| WC | 755,545 | 226,678 | 140,291 |
| Emp. | 99 | N/A | N/A |

DUNS 21-018-4745

## Paintbox Group Ltd

36-44 Melchett Road, Kings Norton Business Centre, Birmingham, West Midlands B30 3HS
**Tel:** 01212-506600
**Web:** www.paintboxuk.com
**Reg No:** 6402509 **VAT No:** 705343852
**Estd:** 2007 Private Limited Company
**Line of Business:** Manufacture of parts and accessories for motor vehicles and their engines
**Export Sales:** £2,080,370
**Issued Capital:** £42,500
**Directors:** D Alexander, R M Gilbert, K Durham, J G Sharp, P R London
**Co. Secretary:** Phillip London
**US SIC:** 3714, 6711
**UK SIC:** 35300, 83962
**Auditors:** Crowe Clark Whitehill LLP
**Bankers:** Barclays Bank Plc (20-03-84)

| | 31-12-13 | 31-12-12 | 31-12-11 |
|---|---|---|---|
| TO | 39,542,737 | 43,538,949 | 41,662,210 |
| P/L | 1,004,147 | 1,403,745 | 1,946,003 |
| NW | 6,442,341 | 5,769,924 | 4,435,911 |
| WC | 3,485,430 | 2,936,613 | 1,636,194 |
| Emp. | 311 | 338 | 288 |

DUNS 73-509-2710

## Pajef Ltd

Rhys House Minerva Business Park, Lynchwood, Peterborough, Cambridgeshire PE2 6FT
**Tel:** 01733371311
**Web:** www.comcertca.com
**Reg No:** 2913433 **Estd:** 1994 Private Limited Company
**Line of Business:** Business and management consultancy activities not elsewhere classified
**Export Sales:** £1,576,775
**Issued Capital:** £50,002
**Directors:** E R Friend, P A Friend, I R Friend
**Co. Secretary:** Ms Janice Friend
**US SIC:** 7392 **UK SIC:** 83951
**Bankers:** Barclays Bank Plc (20-67-37)

| | 31-12-13 | 31-12-12 | 31-12-11 |
|---|---|---|---|
| TO | 6,157,106 | 3,921,806 | 3,410,372 |
| P/L | 1,506,883 | 816,143 | 805,869 |
| NW | 2,068,261 | 2,360,973 | 1,839,522 |
| WC | 1,171,472 | 1,336,309 | 767,090 |
| Emp. | 50 | 39 | 30 |

DUNS 52-019-5728

## Pak Mecca Meats Ltd

162-194 Bishop Street, Birmingham, West Midlands B5 7EJ
**Tel:** 0121-622-1497 **Fax:** 0121-666-6071
**Web:** www.pakmeccameats.co.uk
**Reg No:** 3386185 **Estd:** 1997 Private Limited Company
**Line of Business:** Wholesale of meat and meat products
**Export Sales:** £1,682,314
**Trading Style:** Birmingham Halal Abattoir
**Issued Capital:** £37,500
**Director:** M Akram
**Co. Secretary:** Mrs Azra Sultana
**Responsibilities**
**Senior:** Mahammad Akram *(Managing Director)*
**Finance:** Imran Moghal *(Financial Director)*
**Marketing:** Mahammad Akram *(Managing Director)*
**Sales:** Amir Choudhery *(Sales Manager)*, Aman Gill *(Sales Manager)*
**Health & Safety:** Aman Gill *(Sales Manager)*
**US SIC:** 5147 **UK SIC:** 61700
**Auditors:** Sivapalan & Co
**Bankers:** National Westminster Bank Plc (60-02-35)

| | 31-08-13 | 31-08-12 | 02-08-11 |
|---|---|---|---|
| TO | 28,728,476 | 34,109,093 | 31,987,864 |
| P/L | 475,026 | 616,306 | 510,027 |
| NW | 2,662,140 | 2,338,796 | 2,028,831 |
| WC | (942,768) | (899,717) | (868,285) |
| Emp. | 54 | 57 | 63 |

DUNS 21-325-3438 **Imp-Exp**

## Pakawaste Ltd

(**Subsidiary of:** Pakawaste Holdings Ltd)
Rough Hey Road, Preston, Lancashire PR2 5AR
**Tel:** 01772796688
**Web:** www.pakawaste.co.uk
**Reg No:** 1256393 **VAT No:** 156551165
**Estd:** 1990 Private Limited Company
**Line of Business:** Handling equipment
**Export Markets:** Worldwide
**Issued Capital:** £8,000
**Director:** D Hamer
**Co. Secretary:** Ms Annette Smith
**Responsibilities**
**IT:** Andrew Ekins *(Buyer)*, Roy Potter *(IT Manager)*
**Purchasing:** Andrew Ekins *(Buyer)*
**Branches:** Pakawaste Ltd, 8 Winnersh Gate, Wokingham, Berkshire RG41 5PL
**US SIC:** 3534 **UK SIC:** 32553
**Auditors:** Moore & Smalley LLP
**Bankers:** The Royal Bank Of Scotland Plc (16-28-33)

| | 31-01-14 | 31-01-13 | 31-01-12 |
|---|---|---|---|
| TA | 2,142,447 | 2,856,246 | 2,777,223 |
| NW | 593,736 | 1,035,544 | 1,052,099 |
| WC | 120,158 | 391,370 | 588,444 |

DUNS 21-657-0020 **Imp**

## Pakeeza Dairies Ltd

Kingsway West Business Park, Moss Bridge Road, Rochdale, Lancashire OL16 5LX
**Tel:** 01706641551
**Web:** www.pakeeza.co.uk
**Reg No:** 7136404 **Estd:** 2010 Private Limited Company
**Line of Business:** Liquid milk and cream production
**Issued Capital:** £300
**Directors:** G Q Zouq, M A Zouq
**US SIC:** 2026 **UK SIC:** 41301

| | 31-01-14 | 31-01-13 | 31-01-12 |
|---|---|---|---|
| TO | 21,574,560 | 14,884,113 | 11,842,142 |
| P/L | 507,152 | 355,274 | 245,238 |
| NW | 622,197 | 245,393 | (37,019) |
| WC | (498,307) | (992,811) | (1,115,289) |
| Emp. | 128 | 89 | 74 |

DUNS 21-807-0759

## Pakefield High School

Kilbourn Road, Lowestoft, Suffolk NR33 7DS
**Web:** www.pakefield.org.uk
**Estd:** 2012
**Line of Business:** Schools (local authority)
**Responsibilities**
**Senior:** Perry Linsley *(Head Teacher)*
**US SIC:** 8211 **UK SIC:** 93200
**Employees:** 70

DUNS 22-770-0853 **Imp-Exp**

## Pal Group (Operations) Ltd

(**Subsidiary of:** Pal Group (2014) Ltd)
Darlaston Road Industrial Estate, Wednesbury, West Midlands WS10 7TN
**Tel:** 01215 264048 **Fax:** 01215 264658
**Web:** www.palgroup.co.uk
**Reg No:** 1511634 **VAT No:** 361823555
**Estd:** 1994 Private Limited Company
**Line of Business:** Plastic extruders
**Export Markets:** E U
**Export Sales:** £324,952
**Trading Style:** Pal Group Ltd
**Issued Capital:** £65,566
**Principals:** P A Lowe *(Chairman)*, Ms H C Tanner, Mrs G T Lowe, D K Lowe, M C Harrison, S A Lowe
**Co. Secretary:** Peter Walton
**Responsibilities**
**Health & Safety:** Mike Ward *(Engineering Manager)*
**Operations:** Mike Ward *(Engineering Manager)*
**Engineering:** Mike Ward *(Engineering Manager)*
**Branches:** Pal Group (Operations) Ltd, Bescot Trdg Est Woden Rd Wst, Wednesbury, West Midlands WS10 7SG
**US SIC:** 2821, 3079
**UK SIC:** 25140, 48360
**Auditors:** Clement Keys
**Bankers:** The Royal Bank Of Scotland Plc (16-33-31)

| | 31-03-14 | 31-03-13 | 31-03-12 |
|---|---|---|---|
| TO | 10,162,384 | 8,801,287 | 8,206,685 |
| P/L | 507,305 | 312,503 | 226,238 |
| NW | 1,224,836 | 883,954 | 918,390 |
| WC | 152,102 | (341,150) | 1,147,382 |
| Emp. | 118 | 110 | 102 |

DUNS 54-426-2413 **Imp-Exp**

## Pal International Ltd

Eagle House, Bilton Way, Lutterworth, Leicestershire LE17 4HJ
**Tel:** 01455558946 **Fax:** 01455-555777
**Web:** www.pclsurveyors.co.uk
**Reg No:** 3272370 **VAT No:** 399819471
**Estd:** 1975 Private Limited Company
**Line of Business:** Manufacture of workwear
**Export Markets:** Europe and Worldwide
**Trading Style:** Pal International Limited
**Issued Capital:** £2,850,218
**Directors:** P S Rupra, A Brucciani, Mrs S M Brucciani, R L Brucciani
**Co. Secretary:** Peter Bryan
**Responsibilities**
**Senior:** Steven Mycock *(Manager)*
**Operations:** Tim Dearing *(Supply Chain Manager)*
**Purchasing:** Tim Dearing *(Supply Chain Manager)*
**US SIC:** 3999 **UK SIC:** 49590
**Auditors:** RSM Tenon Audit Ltd
**Bankers:** National Westminster Bank Plc (56-00-55)

| | 31-12-13 | 31-12-12 | 31-12-11 |
|---|---|---|---|
| TO | 10,795,616 | 10,240,295 | 10,474,904 |
| P/L | 302,045 | 73,383 | 27,514 |
| NW | 6,276,632 | 6,221,028 | 6,243,914 |
| WC | 2,596,018 | 2,738,977 | 2,668,885 |
| Emp. | 70 | 70 | 67 |

DUNS 21-096-8544

## Pal Security & Cleaning Services Management Ltd

53 New Zealand Avenue Walton On Thames, Walton-On-Thames, Surrey KT12 1AD
**Tel:** 01932241973
**Web:** www.palservices.co.uk
**Reg No:** 6413192 **Estd:** 2007 Private Limited Company
**Line of Business:** Security and related activities
**Issued Capital:** £1
**Director:** P A Lumor
**Responsibilities**
**Senior:** Godwin Sabah *(Senior Accountant)*
**Finance:** Godwin Sabah *(Senior Accountant)*
**US SIC:** 7393, 7349
**UK SIC:** 83954, 92300

| | 31-10-13 | 31-10-12 | 31-10-11 |
|---|---|---|---|
| TA | 138,061 | 123,808 | 192,060 |
| NW | (21,837) | 43,665 | 66,220 |
| WC | (23,459) | 41,550 | 63,433 |

DUNS 22-129-1110 **Imp**

## Pal Technologies Ltd

Graham Hill Buildings, 50 Richmond Street, Glasgow, Lanarkshire G1 1XP
**Tel:** 01413038380 **Fax:** 0141-552-6085
**Web:** www.paltechnologies.com
**Reg No:** 0215123SC **Estd:** 2001 Private Limited Company
**Line of Business:** Manufacturers of scientific machinery and instrument
**Issued Capital:** £110
**Directors:** N Mourselas, D Maxwell
**Co. Secretary:** Dr Malcolm Granat
**US SIC:** 3829 **UK SIC:** 37100
**Bankers:** Bank Of Scotland (80-11-80)

| | 30-06-13 | 30-06-12 | 30-06-11 |
|---|---|---|---|
| TA | 190,374 | 107,615 | 115,353 |
| NW | 67,690 | (2,016) | 28,866 |
| WC | 60,686 | (11,191) | 29,036 |

DUNS 21-320-5172 **Imp-Exp**

## Palace Chemicals Ltd

**(Subsidiary of:** Micrown Ltd)
Unit 49, Liverpool, Merseyside L24 1YA
**Tel:** 0151-486-6101 **Fax:** 0151-448-1982
**Web:** www.palacechemicals.co.uk
**Reg No:** 1377241 **VAT No:** 618619520
**Estd:** 1978 Private Limited Company
**Line of Business:** Builders merchants
**Export Markets:** Saudia Arabia and the United Arab Emirates.
**Export Sales:** £2,848,562
**Issued Capital:** £20,000
**Principals:** C Clapham *(Chairman and Managing)*, S Clough, J Percival, W Clapham
**Co. Secretary:** Christopher Sweeney
**Responsibilities**
**Admin:** Mary Howard *(Office Manager)*
**HR:** Mary Howard *(Office Manager)*
**US SIC:** 2899 **UK SIC:** 25670
**Auditors:** Duncan Sheard Glass
**Bankers:** HSBC Bank plc (40-29-12)

| | 31-08-13 | 31-08-12 | 31-08-11 |
|---|---|---|---|
| TO | 15,724,774 | 14,773,551 | 15,232,206 |
| P/L | 1,199,801 | 1,058,416 | 491,492 |
| NW | 10,246,551 | 9,665,870 | 9,073,783 |
| WC | 5,875,031 | 5,365,479 | 6,006,410 |
| Emp. | 84 | 81 | 83 |

DUNS 21-121-2649

## The Palace Hotel

Oxford Road, Manchester M60 7HA
**Web:** www.principal-hayley.com
**Estd:** 2013 Proprietorship
**Line of Business:** Hotels
**Proprietor:** R Morrell
**US SIC:** 7011 **UK SIC:** 66500
**Employees:** 300

DUNS 23-963-1257

## Palace Hotel (Peterhead) Ltd

Prince Street, Peterhead, Aberdeenshire AB42 1PL
**Tel:** 01779-474821 **Fax:** 01779-476119
**Web:** www.palacehotel.co.uk
**Reg No:** 0205289SC **Estd:** 2000 Private Limited Company
**Line of Business:** Hotels
**Issued Capital:** £10,000
**Managing Director:** K Watt
**Co. Secretary:** Masson & Glennie
**US SIC:** 7011 **UK SIC:** 66500

| | 31-03-14 | 31-03-13 | 31-03-12 |
|---|---|---|---|
| TA | 3,317,728 | 3,198,092 | 3,125,117 |
| NW | 552,083 | 324,422 | 251,661 |
| WC | (260,112) | (1,575,789) | (1,462,618) |

DUNS 49-387-8870 **Imp**

## Palace International Ltd

Unit 51 Tong Park, Baildon, Shipley, West Yorkshire BD17 7QD
**Web:** www.metallography.co.uk
**Reg No:** 3134942 **Estd:** 1995 Private Limited Company
**Line of Business:** Other business activities not elsewhere classified
**Export Sales:** £6,191,104
**Trading Style:** Spectro, Spectro-Laboratories, Jet-Care, Aviation and Marine
**Issued Capital:** £10,500
**Principals:** D E Glass *(Managing)*, G J Glass *(Financial)*
**Co. Secretary:** Mrs Nicola Sjostrom
**Responsibilities**
**Senior:** Paul Chippendale *(Manager)*
**US SIC:** 7399, 7397
**UK SIC:** 83954, 83702
**Auditors:** Fitzgerald Mithia

| | 31-12-13 | 31-12-12 | 31-12-11 |
|---|---|---|---|
| TO | 8,198,687 | 7,589,930 | 7,759,534 |
| P/L | 501,052 | 470,666 | 493,867 |
| NW | 1,569,875 | 1,493,679 | 1,115,663 |
| WC | (2,917,935) | (3,093,291) | (2,268,754) |
| Emp. | 104 | 105 | 100 |

DUNS 64-741-4812

## Palace of Holyrood House

Abbey Strand, Edinburgh, Midlothian EH8 8DX
**Tel:** 01315241120
**Web:** www.the-royal-collection.org.uk
**Estd:** 2002 Proprietorship
**Line of Business:** Historic houses & gardens
**Proprietor:** G Mackrell
**US SIC:** 8411 **UK SIC:** 97700
**Employees:** 50

DUNS 45-881-0934

## The Palace Theatre Watford Ltd

20 Clarendon Road, North Watford, Watford, Hertfordshire WD17 1JZ
**Web:** www.watfordpalacetheatre.co.uk
**Reg No:** 3218719 **Estd:** 1908 Private Company Limited By Guarantee
**Line of Business:** Theatres & concert halls
**Directors:** A K Mitra, M J Baker, S Khilay, O A Blustin, Ms K O Dabiri, J B Hunt, Ms B G Jullien, Ms K Mcmahon
**Co. Secretary:** Jamie Arden
**Responsibilities**
**Senior:** Alex Bottom *(Director)*, George Derbyshire *(Director)*, Patricia Munn *(Director)*, Mathew Russell *(Executive Director)*, Patrick Stoddart *(Director)*, Amber Townsend *(Director)*
**US SIC:** 8999, 7911
**UK SIC:** 83954, 97913
**Auditors:** Fraser Russell
**Bankers:** National Westminster Bank Plc (60-00-08)

| | 31-03-14 | 31-03-13 | 31-03-12 |
|---|---|---|---|
| TO | 2,618,181 | 2,474,232 | 2,669,535 |
| P/L | (134,581) | (205,358) | (253,355) |
| NW | 6,609,011 | 6,743,592 | 6,948,950 |
| WC | 254,261 | 210,657 | 271,881 |
| Emp. | 68 | 73 | 68 |

DUNS 34-815-0491 **Imp**

## Palatial Leisure Ltd

Church Plain, Great Yarmouth, Norfolk NR30 1PL
**Tel:** 01493 844455
**Web:** www.thepalaces.com
**Reg No:** 2794499 **VAT No:** 665672989
**Estd:** 1996 Private Limited Company
**Line of Business:** Bingo halls
**Trading Style:** Palace Bingo Club
**Issued Capital:** £102
**Directors:** J Andersen, P M Duffy
**Co. Secretary:** Brian Pugh
**Branches:** Palatial Leisure Ltd, Palace Bingo Club, Crescent Road, Felixstowe, Suffolk IP11 7NL
**US SIC:** 7999 **UK SIC:** 97913
**Auditors:** PricewaterhouseCoopers LLP
**Bankers:** National Westminster Bank Plc (60-14-10)

| | 31-12-13 | 31-12-12 | 02-12-12 |
|---|---|---|---|
| TO | 9,318,199 | 10,306,334 | 10,249,758 |
| P/L | (607,198) | 239,960 | 1,134,110 |
| NW | 3,017,414 | 3,520,739 | 3,374,126 |
| WC | (2,489,939) | (1,703,019) | (1,753,985) |
| Emp. | 129 | 139 | 145 |

DUNS 21-391-3246

## Palatine Leisure Centre

207 St Annes Road, Blackpool, Lancashire FY4 2AP
**Tel:** 01253474874
**Estd:** 2005 Proprietorship
**Line of Business:** Leisure centres
**Proprietor:** E Noblett
**Responsibilities**
**Senior:** Martin Cardwell *(Sports Manager)*
**US SIC:** 7999 **UK SIC:** 97913
**Employees:** 50

DUNS 22-797-5638

## Palatine Products

Stamfordham Road Westerhope, Newcastle-Upon-Tyne, Tyne and Wear NE5 5HH
**Web:** www.palatinebeds.co.uk
**VAT No:** 176623740 **Estd:** 2000
**Line of Business:** Beds and bedding
**Trading Style:** Palatine Beds
**Principals:** J Cunningham *(Chairman)*, E W Gray *(General Manager)*
**Responsibilities**
**Marketing:** Antonia Debrason *(Sales Marketing Coordinator)*
**Sales:** Antonia Debrason *(Sales Marketing Coordinator)*
**Health & Safety:** Shirley Scobie *(Quality Manager)*
**Purchasing:** Petra Brown *(Purchasing Manager)*
**US SIC:** 2392, 2515
**UK SIC:** 45550, 46715
**Bankers:** Barclays Bank Plc (20-59-42)
**Employees:** 50

DUNS 21-773-3160

## Palatine School

Palatine Road, Goring-By-Sea, Worthing, West Sussex BN12 6JP
**Tel:** 01903242835
**Web:** www.palatineschool.org
**Estd:** 1965 Partnership
**Line of Business:** Schools (special)
**Partner:** N Dry
**Responsibilities**
**Senior:** Catriona Goldsmith *(Head Teacher)*
**US SIC:** 8299 **UK SIC:** 93300
**Employees:** 60

DUNS 21-580-4780

## Palatine Sports College

St Annes Road, Blackpool, Lancashire FY4 2AR
**Tel:** 01253336500
**Web:** www.palatinesportscollege.co.uk
**Estd:** 1993 Proprietorship
**Line of Business:** General secondary education
**Proprietor:** C Powell
**US SIC:** 8211 **UK SIC:** 93200
**Employees:** 150

DUNS 73-440-7674

## Palfrey Community Association

106 Milton Street, Walsall, West Midlands WS1 4LA
**Tel:** 01922-649716 **Fax:** 01922641729
**Web:** www.palfreycommunity.co.uk
**Reg No:** 4691879 **Estd:** 2003 Private Company Limited By Guarantee
**Line of Business:** Childcare services
**Directors:** M Hussain, A A Nawaz, M Mistry, T D Patel, K Sallu, T N Ajmal, Ms H Nadat, A Vadukul
**Co. Secretary:** Sean Coughlan
**Responsibilities**
**Senior:** Mohammed Bari *(Director)*, Allah Ditta *(Director)*, Shardaben Patel *(Director)*, Mark Pulford *(Director)*, Shehnaz Tarajia *(Director)*, Reshma Uddin *(Director)*
**US SIC:** 8221, 8299, 8091, 8321
**UK SIC:** 93100, 93300, 95200, 96111
**Bankers:** HSBC Bank plc (40-45-19)

| | 30-09-13 | 30-09-12 | 30-09-11 |
|---|---|---|---|
| TO | 1,394,482 | 1,503,311 | 1,514,392 |
| P/L | 44,971 | 87,289 | 35,679 |
| NW | 1,037,233 | 992,262 | 904,973 |
| WC | 1,037,233 | 992,262 | 904,973 |
| Emp. | 69 | 71 | 69 |

DUNS 39-948-0227

## Palfrey Service Station Ltd

Fairway, Cannock, Staffordshire WS11 0DJ
**Tel:** 01543466455 **Fax:** 01543435135
**Web:** www.edscouriers.co.uk
**Reg No:** 2254103 **VAT No:** 101070937
**Estd:** 2003 Private Limited Company
**Line of Business:** Distribution service providers
**Trading Style:** E D S Couriers
**Issued Capital:** £40,004
**Director:** A F Evans
**Responsibilities**
**Senior:** Sandra Evans *(Manager)*
**US SIC:** 4712, 4311
**UK SIC:** 77002, 79010
**Bankers:** HSBC Bank plc (40-45-19)

| | 30-11-13 | 30-11-12 | 30-11-11 |
|---|---|---|---|
| TA | 1,241,894 | 1,071,660 | 915,274 |
| NW | 48,874 | (19,682) | (71,082) |
| WC | (239,146) | (252,595) | (297,812) |

DUNS 21-667-6225

## Pall Europe Ltd

**(Subsidiary of:** Pall Manufacturing Uk Ltd)
Unit 5, Harbour Gate Business Park, Southampton Road, Portsmouth, Hampshire PO6 4BQ
**Tel:** 02392338000
**Web:** www.pall.com
**Reg No:** 7211681 **Estd:** 2010 Private Limited Company
**Line of Business:** Manufacture of other general purpose machinery not elsewhere classified
**Export Sales:** £77,705,000
**Trading Style:** Pall-Newquay
**Issued Capital:** £1,000,000
**Directors:** S Hart, Ms C E Munslow, M P Ayres
**Co. Secretary:** Ms Christina Munslow
**Responsibilities**
**Senior:** Huw Chapman *(Director)*, Jamie Collard *(Advanced Engineering Director)*
**Marketing:** Doug Harris *(?Tactical Marketing Manager)*
**Engineering:** Jamie Collard *(Advanced Engineering Director)*
**US SIC:** 3549 **UK SIC:** 32212
**Auditors:** KPMG LLP
**Bankers:** HSBC Bank plc (40-42-16)

| | 31-07-13 | 31-07-12 | 31-07-11 |
|---|---|---|---|
| TO | 122,658,000 | 151,770,000 | 204,912,000 |
| P/L | 5,834,000 | 14,509,000 | 13,029,000 |
| NW | 24,603,000 | 21,024,000 | 15,456,000 |
| WC | 21,599,000 | 29,595,000 | 327,000 |
| Emp. | 737 | 801 | 797 |

DUNS 52-310-3844

## Pall-Ex Group Ltd

Unit 1 Victoria Road, Ellistown, Coalville, Leicestershire LE67 1FH
**Tel:** 01530-239000 **Fax:** 01530239001
**Web:** www.pallex.co.uk
**Reg No:** 6051516 **Estd:** 2007 Private Limited Company
**Line of Business:** Management activities of holding companies
**Export Sales:** £266,000
**Issued Capital:** £40,476
**Directors:** G M Gillo, A Russell, Mrs H L Devey, K Buchanan
**Co. Secretary:** Martin Field
**US SIC:** 6711, 4213
**UK SIC:** 83962, 72300

| | 31-01-14 | 31-01-13 | 31-01-12 |
|---|---|---|---|
| TO | 64,906,000 | 58,212,000 | 59,742,000 |
| P/L | 2,213,000 | 2,331,000 | 2,009,000 |
| NW | 5,917,000 | 5,896,000 | 6,768,000 |
| WC | (1,152,000) | (7,440,000) | (824,000) |
| Emp. | 149 | 164 | 195 |

DUNS 21-708-4839 **Imp**

## Pall Manufacturing Uk Ltd

Unit 5 Harbour Gate Business Park, Southampton Road, Portsmouth, Hampshire PO6 4BQ
**Tel:** 02392303303
**Web:** www.pall.com
**Reg No:** 0769075 **VAT No:** 107772467
**Estd:** 1963 Private Limited Company
**Line of Business:** Manufacture of other general purpose machinery not elsewhere classified
**Trading Style:** Pall Aerospace & Industrial
**Issued Capital:** £21,000,000
**Directors:** M P Ayres, S Hart
**Co. Secretary:** Ms Christina Munslow
**Responsibilities**
**Senior:** Huw Chapman *(Director)*
**Branches:** Pall Manufacturing Uk Ltd, Anderson House, 389 Argyle Street, Glasgow, Lanarkshire G2 8LR
**US SIC:** 3999, 3559
**UK SIC:** 49590, 32863
**Auditors:** KPMG LLP

**Bankers:** National Westminster Bank Plc (56-00-64)

| | 31-07-13 | 31-07-12 | 31-07-11 |
|---|---|---|---|
| TO | 73,130,000 | 71,357,000 | 60,655,000 |
| P/L | 1,659,000 | 11,505,000 | 27,514,000 |
| NW | 47,927,000 | 49,295,000 | 60,887,000 |
| WC | 72,747,000 | 78,876,000 | 88,592,000 |
| Emp. | 1,037 | 1,071 | 955 |

DUNS 22-925-7878 **Exp**

## The Pallet Centre Ltd

(**Subsidiary of:** Eagle Holdings Ireland Ltd)
Houstons Corner, Doagh Road, Newtownabbey, Co Antrim BT36 4TP
**Tel:** 02890843434 **Fax:** 028-9084-3898
**Web:** www.thepalletcentre.com
**Reg No:** 0015056NI **VAT No:** 331778938
**Estd:** 1980 Private Limited Company
**Line of Business:** Manufacture of wooden containers
**Export Markets:** Republic of Ireland
**Issued Capital:** £100,000
**Director:** M J Morrow
**Co. Secretary:**
Moyne Moyne Secretarial Limited
**Responsibilities**
**Senior:** Jim Morrow *(Manager)*
**Finance:** Paul Kirkwood *(General Manager)*
**Marketing:** Paul Kirkwood *(General Manager)*
**Sales:** Paul Kirkwood *(General Manager)*
**IT:** Donna Montgomery *(Computer Manager)*
**HR:** Paul Kirkwood *(General Manager)*
**Health & Safety:** Paul Kirkwood *(General Manager)*
**Facilities:** Terry Elton *(Production Manager)*
**Operations:** Paul Kirkwood *(General Manager)*
**Engineering:** Terry Elton *(Production Manager)*
**US SIC:** 2449 **UK SIC:** 46402
**Auditors:** KPMG
**Bankers:** Ulster Bank Ltd (98-06-50)

| | 31-01-14 | 01-02-13 | 03-01-12 |
|---|---|---|---|
| TA | 2,492,000 | 2,581,000 | 2,420,000 |
| NW | 1,329,000 | 1,838,000 | 1,550,000 |
| WC | 1,505,000 | 1,511,000 | 1,442,000 |

DUNS 23-877-0783

## The Pallet Network Ltd

(**Subsidiary of:** Lloyds Banking Group Plc)
Prologis Park Midpoint, Midpoint Way, Minworth, Sutton Coldfield, West Midlands B76 9EH
**Tel:** 01213134000 **Fax:** 01788-552829
**Web:** www.thepalletnetworkltd.co.uk
**Reg No:** 3868401 **Estd:** 1999 Private Limited Company
**Line of Business:** Other supporting land transport activities
**Export Sales:** £595,346
**Issued Capital:** £133
**Directors:** R Schofield, R L Burdett, A Leonard, M Duggan, M Kendell, P Robinson
**Co. Secretary:** Paul Robinson
**Branches:** The Pallet Network Ltd, Boughton Rd Indstl Est, Boughton Rd, Rugby, Warwickshire CV21 1BF
**US SIC:** 4789 **UK SIC:** 77002
**Auditors:** Smith Craven

| | 31-03-14 | 31-03-13 | 31-03-12 |
|---|---|---|---|
| TO | 61,354,199 | 53,602,978 | 52,331,358 |
| P/L | 2,523,498 | 2,253,387 | 2,752,915 |
| NW | 2,696,984 | 12,647,476 | 10,828,667 |
| WC | 431,527 | 11,618,433 | 9,682,323 |
| Emp. | 105 | 97 | 88 |

DUNS 22-086-6706

## Palletforce P L C

Callister Way, Burton-On-Trent, Staffordshire DE14 2SY
**Tel:** 01283539392 **Fax:** 01543443969
**Web:** www.palletforce.com
**Reg No:** 4088035 **Estd:** 2000 Public Limited Company
**Line of Business:** Packing crate and pallet suppliers
**Export Sales:** £363,944
**Issued Capital:** £1,018,251
**Directors:** Pass J Holdings Limited, J Brotherton, D J Hughes, Redhead Freight Limited, J Hamill, D Holland, N A Carpenter, Bedfords Limited
**Co. Secretary:** Neil Carpenter
**Responsibilities**
**Senior:** Michael Conroy *(Director)*
**Marketing:** Trevor Mudd *(Business Development Manager)*
**Sales:** Trevor Mudd *(Business Development Manager)*
**IT:** Simon Gibbard *(Network Operations Manager)*
**US SIC:** 2449, 4712
**UK SIC:** 46402, 77002
**Auditors:** Lovewell Blake

**Bankers:** Bank Of Scotland (12-09-25)

| | 31-08-14 | 31-08-13 | 31-08-12 |
|---|---|---|---|
| TO | 18,358,156 | 14,691,676 | 12,807,135 |
| P/L | 3,071,334 | 2,578,785 | 2,579,889 |
| NW | 5,351,894 | 7,813,703 | 6,984,321 |
| WC | 4,594,431 | 7,133,431 | 6,510,401 |
| Emp. | 130 | 110 | 106 |

DUNS 39-981-4789

## Palletline Plc

The Palletline Centre, Birmingham, West Midlands B37 7HB
**Tel:** 0121-767-6870 **Fax:** 01217828682
**Web:** www.palletline.com
**Reg No:** 2277533 **Estd:** 1988 Public Limited Company
**Line of Business:** Distribution service providers
**Issued Capital:** £427,825
**Directors:** K J Hackling, J N Welch, J T Edge, N W Rushworth, P G Greenhalgh, I C Brown, P F Welsh, T C Ellis
**Co. Secretary:** Miss Ruth Moor
**Responsibilities**
**Senior:** Troy Bailey *(Operations Manager)*, Amy Liston *(General Manager, Business Deve)*
**Marketing:** Maria Holmes-Keeling *(Marketing Manager)*
**IT:** Steve Butter *(Head of Network Services)*
**Facilities:** Troy Bailey *(Operations Manager)*
**Operations:** Troy Bailey *(Operations Manager)*
**Branches:** Palletline Plc, William Street, Gateshead, Tyne and Wear NE10 0JP
**US SIC:** 4789, 4712
**UK SIC:** 77002
**Auditors:** Bentley Jennison

| | 30-06-14 | 30-06-13 | 30-06-12 |
|---|---|---|---|
| TO | 17,513,000 | 14,377,000 | 13,453,000 |
| P/L | 2,089,000 | 1,661,000 | 1,226,000 |
| NW | 11,982,000 | 10,662,000 | 9,599,000 |
| WC | 3,542,000 | 2,315,000 | 1,228,000 |
| Emp. | 167 | 154 | 149 |

DUNS 21-916-7756 **Imp-Exp**

## Palletower (G B) Ltd

(**Subsidiary of:** Palletower Group Holdings Ltd)
Unit 7 Dane Road Industrial Estate, Sale, Cheshire M33 7BH
**Tel:** 01619852233 **Fax:** 01619-720922
**Web:** www.palletower.com
**Reg No:** 0908180 **VAT No:** 611729749
**Estd:** 1967 Private Limited Company
**Line of Business:** Holding companies management activities
**Export Markets:** Far East, Middle East, E U
**Export Sales:** £1,688,974
**Issued Capital:** £5,000
**Directors:** L Spratt, R J Palmer, M R Palmer
**Responsibilities**
**Senior:** Pat Chubb *(Administration Manager)*, Paul Hutchins *(Manager)*, Paul Sheldon *(Head of Accounts)*, Ian Tate *(Logistics Manager)*
**Finance:** Paul Sheldon *(Head of Accounts)*
**Admin:** Pat Chubb *(Administration Manager)*
**IT:** Paul Hutchins *(Manager)*, Paul Sheldon *(Head of Accounts)*
**HR:** Pat Chubb *(Administration Manager)*
**Facilities:** Paul Hutchins *(Manager)*
**US SIC:** 4712 **UK SIC:** 77002
**Auditors:** Tenon Audit Ltd
**Bankers:** HSBC Bank plc (40-46-36)

| | 31-12-13 | 31-12-12 | 31-12-11 |
|---|---|---|---|
| TO | 15,708,187 | 17,510,520 | 16,272,472 |
| P/L | 1,377,857 | 1,460,143 | 1,499,335 |
| NW | 6,222,238 | 5,113,316 | 4,010,571 |
| WC | 7,546,543 | 7,196,908 | 3,882,051 |
| Emp. | 49 | 47 | 43 |

DUNS 73-922-3308

## Palletways Group Ltd

Fradley Distribution Park, Wood End Lane, Fradley, Lichfield, Staffordshire WS13 8NE
**Tel:** 01543-418000 **Fax:** 01543-418111
**Web:** www.palletways.com
**Reg No:** 5175499 **Estd:** 2004 Private Limited Company
**Line of Business:** Manufacture of wooden containers
**Issued Capital:** £10,334,349
**Directors:** J Wilson, R Daw, A D Reynolds, M P Sargeant, W A Cathcart
**Co. Secretary:** Andrew Reynolds
**US SIC:** 2449, 6711
**UK SIC:** 46402, 83962
**Auditors:** Ernst & Young LLP

| | 31-05-13 | 31-05-12 | 31-05-11 |
|---|---|---|---|
| TO | 188,073,000 | 177,491,000 | 157,892,000 |
| P/L | (4,658,000) | (2,183,000) | (820,000) |
| NW | (54,028,000) | (50,571,000) | (48,015,000) |
| WC | 2,157,000 | 1,563,000 | 813,000 |
| Emp. | 490 | 455 | 370 |

DUNS 42-343-1352

## Pallot Glass & Glazing Ltd

11 L And L And L'Avenue Le Bas, Lane Rue Des Pres Trading Estate, Jersey, Channel Islands JE2 7QN
**Tel:** 01534-760500
**Web:** www.pallotglass.com
**Reg No:** 0063805J **Estd:** 1952 Private Limited Company
**Line of Business:** Glass boarding up and replacement
**Issued Capital:** £100
**Principals:** W W Toporis *(Managing)*, G Gilbertson, R A Pallot
**Co. Secretary:** Widukind Toporis
**Responsibilities**
**Senior:** Sarah Pallot *(Proprietor)*
**US SIC:** 1721, 2371, 5199
**UK SIC:** 50400, 45600, 61900
**Bankers:** HSBC Bank plc (40-25-34)
**Employees:** 47

DUNS 21-582-6113

## The Palm

1 Pont Street, London SW1X 9EJ
**Tel:** 02072010710
**Web:** www.thepalm.com
**Estd:** 2009 Proprietorship
**Line of Business:** Restaurant - american
**Proprietor:** S Fish
**Responsibilities**
**Senior:** Sam Hallak *(General Manager)*
**US SIC:** 5812 **UK SIC:** 66110
**Employees:** 50

DUNS 77-108-8515

## Palm Beach Club Ltd

(**Subsidiary of:** Genting Bhd.)
30 Berkeley Street, London W1J 8EH
**Tel:** 020-7493-6585
**Web:** www.thepalmbeach.com
**Reg No:** 2685735 **Estd:** 1992 Private Limited Company
**Line of Business:** Casinos
**Trading Style:** Palm Beach Casino
**Issued Capital:** £2
**Directors:** P M Brooks, R R Salmond
**Co. Secretary:** Ms Elizabeth Tarn
**Responsibilities**
**Senior:** Colin Miller *(Manager)*, Richard Poyner *(General Manager)*
**Finance:** Richard Poyner *(General Manager)*
**Marketing:** Virginie Bigand *(Marketing Manager)*
**Sales:** Richard Poyner *(General Manager)*
**Admin:** Annie Hewson *(Administrator)*, Becky Miller *(Administrator)*
**IT:** Richard Poyner *(General Manager)*
**Health & Safety:** Annie Hewson *(Administrator)*, Liz Steyan *(Health & Safety Officer)*
**Facilities:** Richard Poyner *(General Manager)*
**Purchasing:** Annie Hewson *(Administrator)*
**US SIC:** 7999 **UK SIC:** 97913
**Auditors:** PricewaterhouseCoopers

| | 31-12-13 | 31-12-12 | 31-12-11 |
|---|---|---|---|
| TA | 16,233,203 | 16,233,203 | 16,233,203 |
| NW | 16,233,203 | 16,233,203 | 16,233,203 |

DUNS 21-033-2017

## Palm Court Hotel

81 Seafield Road, Aberdeen, Aberdeenshire AB15 7YX
**Web:** www.palmcourthotel.co.uk
**Estd:** 1992
**Line of Business:** Hotels and motels without restaurant
**Trading Style:** G 1 Group
**Proprietor:** G Urquhart
**Responsibilities**
**Health & Safety:** Scott Horner *(Hotel Manager)*
**US SIC:** 7011 **UK SIC:** 66500
**Employees:** 60

DUNS 22-575-1916 **Imp**

## Palm Equipment International Ltd

(**Subsidiary of:** Palm Equipment Holdings Ltd)
Kenn Road, Kenn, Clevedon, Avon BS21 6TH
**Tel:** 01275-798100
**Web:** www.palmequipmenteurope.com
**Reg No:** 2000120 **VAT No:** 997328067
**Estd:** 1980 Private Limited Company
**Line of Business:** Manufacturers of sports goods
**Trading Style:** Dagger Europe
**Issued Capital:** £100
**Principals:** A P Knight *(Managing)*, R K Slee, T J Chapple
**Co. Secretary:** Andrew Knight
**US SIC:** 3949, 3079
**UK SIC:** 49420, 48360
**Auditors:** PKF (UK) LLP

**Bankers:** HSBC Bank plc (40-37-33)

| | 31-12-13 | 31-12-12 | 31-12-11 |
|---|---|---|---|
| TA | 4,979,305 | 3,745,275 | 5,076,910 |
| NW | 3,042,717 | 2,725,588 | 2,493,494 |
| WC | 2,826,398 | 2,492,566 | 1,052,936 |

DUNS 21-198-0826 **Imp**

## Palm Paper Ltd

(**Subsidiary of:** Hera Gmbh)
Poplar Avenue, Saddlebow Industrial Estates, King's Lynn, Norfolk PE34 3AL
**Tel:** 01553782222 **Fax:** 01553-78-22-23
**Web:** www.palmpaper.co.uk
**Reg No:** 0813701 **VAT No:** 844270040
**Estd:** 2012 Private Limited Company
**Line of Business:** Manufacture of other containers
**Export Sales:** £22,576,873
**Trading Style:** Palm Paper Ltd
**Issued Capital:** £446,006,000
**Directors:** S Gruber, D R Harman, W Palm
**Co. Secretary:** Jose Villatoro
**US SIC:** 2654, 2631
**UK SIC:** 47280, 47017
**Auditors:** Ernst & Young LLP

| | 31-12-13 | 31-12-12 | 31-12-11 |
|---|---|---|---|
| TO | 167,435,718 | 173,645,253 | 171,773,297 |
| P/L | (7,609,397) | 1,892,280 | 1,911,294 |
| NW | 366,365,081 | 373,845,652 | 416,998,545 |
| WC | 16,506,242 | 5,424,784 | 27,844,455 |
| Emp. | 198 | 202 | 191 |

DUNS 21-668-2301

## Palman Ltd

Titan Distribution Centre, Millfields Road, Wolverhampton, West Midlands WV4 6JH
**Tel:** 01902355100
**Web:** www.pallet-track.co.uk
**Reg No:** 7216273 **Estd:** 2010 Private Limited Company
**Line of Business:** Management activities of holding companies
**Issued Capital:** £75,000
**Directors:** C Jones, N T Parkes
**Co. Secretary:** Ms Gail Malthy
**US SIC:** 6711 **UK SIC:** 83962

| | 31-01-14 | 31-01-13 | 31-01-12 |
|---|---|---|---|
| TO | 10,937,495 | 9,549,708 | 8,963,394 |
| P/L | 1,727,117 | 1,482,641 | 909,006 |
| NW | 2,562,933 | 1,807,157 | 1,086,201 |
| WC | 3,121,380 | 2,435,141 | 2,047,128 |
| Emp. | 106 | 96 | 94 |

DUNS 21-104-1896

## Palmer & Harvey (Holdings) Plc

106-112 Davigdor Road, Hove, East Sussex BN3 1RE
**Tel:** 01273222100
**Web:** www.palmerharvey.co.uk
**Reg No:** 6470058 **Estd:** 2008 Public Limited Company
**Line of Business:** Other retail sale in specialised stores not elsewhere classified
**Issued Capital:** £1,492,867
**Directors:** J D Moxon, C Etherington, S Oades, M R Ward, R S Grainger, J S Streeter
**Co. Secretary:** David Scudder
**Responsibilities**
**Finance:** Steve Watson *(Commercial Finance Director)*
**Marketing:** Clive Bacon *(Events Organizer)*
**Sales:** Russell Armstrong *(National Account Manager)*, Paul Hagon *(Group Strategy and Business De)*, Steve Watson *(Commercial Finance Director)*
**Admin:** Brian Bower *(Systems Administrator)*
**IT:** Brian Bower *(Systems Administrator)*
**HR:** Brian Hurley *(Group HR Director)*
**US SIC:** 5199, 6711
**UK SIC:** 61900, 83962
**Auditors:** KPMG LLP
**Bankers:** Barclays Bank Plc (20-00-34)
**Following financial data are in thousands**

| | 05-04-14 | 06-04-13 | 07-04-12 |
|---|---|---|---|
| TO | 4,197,000 | 4,232,700 | 4,227,500 |
| P/L | (1,300) | (8,600) | 4,900 |
| NW | (357,900) | (349,200) | (337,500) |
| WC | (232,400) | (234,700) | (221,600) |
| Emp. | 3,706 | 3,542 | 3,192 |

DUNS 29-146-0327 **Exp**

## Palmer Hargreaves Ltd

(**Subsidiary of:** Palmer Hargreaves Holdings Ltd)
16 A-20 Parade, Leamington Spa, Warwickshire CV32 4DW
**Fax:** 01926-335841
**Web:** www.palmerhargreaves.com
**Reg No:** 1716002 **Estd:** 1983 Private Limited Company
**Line of Business:** Advertising agency services
**Export Markets:** E C countries.
**Issued Capital:** £13,102
**Principals:** A C Clift *(Managing)*, M Stoves, R W Weeks, Mrs J D Clift, J Langensiepen
**Co. Secretary:** Andrew Clift

**Responsibilities**
**Senior:** Nicola Armstrong *(Account Director)*, Ria Kang *(Financial Controller)*, Simon Kitson *(Deputy Creative Director)*, Karen McKim *(Account Director)*, Priya Mistry *(Art Director)*, Rebecca Pell *(Account Director)*, Vineet Raheja *(Creative Director)*, Katie Sutton *(Account Executive)*, Sophie Taylor *(Client Services Director)*, Nikki Watts *(Manager)*
**Finance:** Adam Hall *(Group Finance Director)*, Ria Kang *(Financial Controller)*, Matt Lindsay *(Finance Assistant)*, Sue Perry *(Finance Assistant)*
**Marketing:** Ben Atkins *(Head of Digital)*, Leon Deeming *(Copywriter)*, Louise Wilce *(Sales and Marketing Manager)*
**Sales:** Nicola Armstrong *(Account Director)*, Paul Bennison *(Account Director)*, Rhian Cooling *(Account Executive)*, Toby Costar *(Senior Account Manager)*, James Crerar *(Account Manager)*, Adam Edgeller *(?Senior Account Manager)*, Alexandra Follett *(Account Manager)*, Kate Muller *(Account Director)*, Rebecca Pell *(Account Director)*, Simon Tierney *(Account Director)*, Will Weeks *(Account Executive)*, Louise Wilce *(Sales and Marketing Manager)*
**Admin:** Fiona Forrest *(Operations Administrator)*, Gemma Higham *(Administration and Operations)*
**Operations:** Fiona Forrest *(Operations Administrator)*
**US SIC:** 7319 **UK SIC:** 83800
**Auditors:** Grant Thornton UK LLP
**Bankers:** National Westminster Bank Plc (56-00-45)

| | 30-09-13 | 30-09-12 | 30-09-11 |
|---|---|---|---|
| TA | 286,468 | 270,409 | 247,488 |
| P/L | 97,175 | 84,660 | 56,059 |
| NW | 247,488 | 247,488 | 247,488 |
| WC | 231,685 | 231,685 | N/A |

DUNS 21-860-9550 **Imp**
## Palmer Timber Ltd
Granville Works, Cradley Heath, West Midlands B64 6PW
**Tel:** 01215-595511 **Fax:** 01215-614562
**Web:** www.palmertimber.com
**Reg No:** 0365289 **VAT No:** 277080937
**Estd:** 1916 Private Limited Company
**Line of Business:** Timber merchants
**Export Sales:** £134,660
**Issued Capital:** £101,552
**Principals:** S Russ *(Financial)*, P E Hill, S Russ, P W Kerr, I J Cox, R H Palmer, K F Edmonds
**Responsibilities**
**Fleet:** Bob Simpson *(Transport Manager)*
**Branches:** Palmer Timber Ltd, Coppice Gate, Tanners Hill, Bewdley, Worcestershire DY12 2LP
**US SIC:** 2421, 5039
**UK SIC:** 46101, 61300
**Auditors:** Crowe Clark Whitehill LLP
**Bankers:** Lloyds TSB Bank plc (30-90-88)

| | 30-09-13 | 30-09-12 | 30-09-11 |
|---|---|---|---|
| TO | 32,475,590 | 31,422,204 | 29,717,267 |
| P/L | 745,319 | 420,667 | 942,671 |
| NW | 6,140,664 | 5,945,072 | 5,964,049 |
| WC | 3,280,422 | 3,272,329 | 3,234,101 |
| Emp. | 215 | 221 | 210 |

DUNS 21-743-4551
## Palmers At Ullesthorpe Ltd
Lutterworth Road, Ullesthorpe, Lutterworth, Leicestershire LE17 5DR
**Tel:** 01455202144 **Fax:** 01455202585
**Web:** www.palmersgardencentre.co.uk
**Reg No:** 7759445 **Estd:** 2011 Private Limited Company
**Line of Business:** Garden centres
**Issued Capital:** £1,000
**Directors:** Mrs F J Palmer, Ms C F Jackson, I F Colledge, R B Palmer
**Responsibilities**
**Senior:** Natalie Spencer *(Manager)*
**US SIC:** 5999 **UK SIC:** 65600

| | 31-07-13 | 31-07-12 |
|---|---|---|
| TA | 897,794 | 770,578 |
| NW | (2,800) | 15,973 |
| WC | 158,697 | 78,266 |

DUNS 64-221-9380 **Imp**
## Palmers College
Chadwell Road, Grays, Essex RM17 5TD
**Tel:** 01375370121
**Web:** www.palmers.ac.uk
**Estd:** 2009
**Line of Business:** Further education schools and colleges
**Director:** P Fenwick
**Responsibilities**
**IT:** Ian Bayliss *(Desktop Support)*, Daniel Byne *(Computer Operations Manager)*, Alistair Dunkwu *(IT Manager)*
**US SIC:** 8221 **UK SIC:** 93100
**Employees:** 250

DUNS 29-017-8045
## Palmers Green High School Ltd
Palmers Green High School, London N21 3LJ
**Tel:** 020-8886-1135
**Web:** www.pghs.co.uk
**Reg No:** 0537727 **Estd:** 1905 Private Company Limited By Guarantee
**Line of Business:** Schools (independent)
**Directors:** Mrs G S Kettle, Dr A Goraya, Ms M B Curtis, J D Zinkin, Ms A Averkiou, R D Keys, D G Orfeur, D G Lewis
**Co. Secretary:** Kenneth Evans
**Responsibilities**
**Senior:** Loraine Cavanagh *(Director)*, Christine Edmundson *(Headmistress)*, Deborah Ivory-Webb *(Bursar)*, Margaret Lawrence *(Director)*, Joyce Mayhew *(Manager)*
**Finance:** Deborah Ivory-Webb *(Bursar)*
**Marketing:** Deborah Ivory-Webb *(Bursar)*
**Admin:** Deborah Ivory-Webb *(Bursar)*
**IT:** Karen Thompson *(IT Manager)*
**HR:** Deborah Ivory-Webb *(Bursar)*
**Health & Safety:** Deborah Ivory-Webb *(Bursar)*
**Facilities:** David Spurling *(Caretaker)*
**Operations:** Deborah Ivory-Webb *(Bursar)*
**US SIC:** 8211 **UK SIC:** 93200
**Auditors:** Hillier Hopkins
**Bankers:** HSBC Bank plc (40-05-21)

| | 31-07-14 | 31-07-13 | 31-07-12 |
|---|---|---|---|
| TO | 2,958,462 | 2,962,517 | 2,915,038 |
| P/L | 101,432 | 56,017 | 123,016 |
| NW | 4,427,958 | 4,260,998 | 4,475,108 |
| WC | 1,133,229 | 1,278,149 | 1,497,882 |
| Emp. | 65 | 64 | 67 |

DUNS 21-175-2196
## Palmers Solicitors
19 Town Square, Basildon, Essex SS14 1BD
**Tel:** 01268-240000
**Web:** www.palmerslaw.co.uk
**VAT No:** 394924214 **Estd:** 1978 Partnership
**Line of Business:** Solicitors
**Partners:** M Hunter, A Skinner, Ms C Jacobs, J Sirrell, C Mowat, T Steele, L Mcclellan, C Tant
**Responsibilities**
**Senior:** BJ Chong *(Partner)*, Enghet Chong *(Partner)*, Crhis Mowat *(Partner)*
**IT:** Neil Mansell *(IT Manager)*
**Branches:** Palmers Solicitors, Palmers, Prospect House, Chelmsford, Essex CM3 5XB
**US SIC:** 8111 **UK SIC:** 83500
**Employees:** 70

DUNS 53-632-3314
## Palmers (St Albans) Ltd
**(Subsidiary of:** Palmers & Sons Holdings Ltd)
Penine Way, Hemel Hempstead, Hertfordshire HP2 7AZ
**Tel:** 01442232300 **Fax:** 01727-841002
**Web:** www.palmerscars.co.uk
**Reg No:** 3437233 **VAT No:** 804803253
**Estd:** 1996 Private Limited Company
**Line of Business:** Sale of new motor vehicles
**Trading Style:** Palmers Group
**Issued Capital:** £50,000
**Directors:** D C Palmer, Ms C Palmer
**Responsibilities**
**Senior:** Christine Cullen *(Manager)*
**Finance:** Craig Milton *(Group Finance Director)*
**Branches:** Palmers (St Albans) Ltd, 16 St. Albans Road, Watford, Hertfordshire WD17 1UN
**US SIC:** 5511, 5521, 5571
**UK SIC:** 65100
**Auditors:** Trevor Jones

| | 31-12-13 | 31-12-12 | 31-12-11 |
|---|---|---|---|
| TO | 44,991,214 | 44,533,605 | 45,413,264 |
| P/L | 241,631 | 141,243 | 88,588 |
| NW | 2,450,318 | 2,414,705 | 2,435,528 |
| WC | 1,172,097 | 1,044,737 | 985,305 |
| Emp. | 134 | 134 | 137 |

DUNS 21-813-3494
## Palmers(Gt.Yarmouth)Ltd
37-39 Market Place, Great Yarmouth, Norfolk NR30 1LU
**Tel:** 01493844291 **Fax:** 01493-331208
**Web:** www.palmerstores.com
**Reg No:** 0349026 **VAT No:** 105561888
**Estd:** 1837 Private Limited Company
**Line of Business:** Other retail sale in non-specialised stores
**Issued Capital:** £534,200
**Principals:** B G Sturrock *(Chairman and Managing)*, T J Green, Ms W A Cole, D J Howard
**Co. Secretary:** Tony Green
**Responsibilities**
**Senior:** Stuart McGee *(Manager)*, Elizabeth Sturrock *(Director)*
**Branches:** Palmers(Gt.yarmouth)ltd, 61-64 St. Andrews Street South, Bury St. Edmunds, Suffolk IP33 1SD
**US SIC:** 5399, 5719
**UK SIC:** 65600, 64700
**Auditors:** Lovewell Blake
**Bankers:** Lloyds TSB Bank plc (30-99-97)

| | 01-02-14 | 26-01-13 | 28-02-12 |
|---|---|---|---|
| TO | 9,013,318 | 8,767,825 | 9,103,675 |
| P/L | (97,459) | 33,369 | (128,362) |
| NW | 3,712,811 | 3,890,823 | 3,939,350 |
| WC | 771,488 | 936,011 | 727,016 |
| Emp. | 286 | 297 | 307 |

DUNS 23-854-5144
## Palmerston Investment Holdings (Uk) Ltd
Brocket Hall, Brocket Park, Lemsford, Welwyn Garden City, Hertfordshire AL8 7XG
**Tel:** 01707368750
**Web:** www.palmerstonhotels.com
**Reg No:** 3846347 **Estd:** 1999 Private Limited Company
**Line of Business:** Restaurants
**Issued Capital:** £1
**Director:** D Klostermann
**Co. Secretary:** James Moore
**US SIC:** 7011, 7999
**UK SIC:** 66500, 97913

| | 31-12-13 | 31-12-12 | 31-12-11 |
|---|---|---|---|
| TO | 8,580,077 | 8,834,659 | 9,409,472 |
| P/L | (2,131,281) | (1,570,608) | (1,405,701) |
| NW | (10,608,089) | (8,476,808) | (6,906,200) |
| WC | 421,249 | 565,189 | 410,898 |
| Emp. | 207 | 211 | 228 |

DUNS 21-779-2858
## Palmerston School
Beaconsfield Road, Woolton, Liverpool, Merseyside L25 6EE
**Tel:** 01514282128
**Web:** www.schoolswire.org
**Estd:** 2011 Proprietorship
**Line of Business:** Schools (special)
**Proprietor:** Mrs S Bowden
**US SIC:** 8299 **UK SIC:** 93300
**Employees:** 54

DUNS 29-121-1357
## Palmglen Ltd
**(Subsidiary of:** The Ronnie Scott's Jazz Club Ltd)
47 Frith Street, Soho, London W1D 4HT
**Tel:** 020-7439-0747
**Web:** www.ronniescotts.co.uk
**Reg No:** 1590762 **Estd:** 1959 Private Limited Company
**Line of Business:** Jazz and soul clubs and pubs
**Trading Style:** Ronnie Scott's Club
**Issued Capital:** £548,024
**Directors:** Ms S A Greene, S F Cooke
**Co. Secretary:** Ms Angela Davies
**Responsibilities**
**Senior:** Ray Duhaney *(Manager)*
**US SIC:** 5813 **UK SIC:** 66200
**Auditors:** Gainsleys
**Bankers:** National Westminster Bank Plc (60-80-05)

| | 31-03-14 | 31-03-13 | 31-03-12 |
|---|---|---|---|
| TO | 9,054,460 | 8,532,228 | 7,324,355 |
| P/L | 817,439 | 674,872 | 464,253 |
| NW | 2,509,127 | 1,954,408 | 1,390,831 |
| WC | (1,814,977) | (2,749,994) | (3,463,169) |
| Emp. | 95 | 89 | 90 |

DUNS 39-821-2647 **Imp-Exp**
## Palmhive Technical Textiles Ltd
**(Subsidiary of:** A.C.Gill Ltd)
N T G House, Willow Road, Nottingham, Nottinghamshire NG7 2TA
**Tel:** 01159-707900
**Web:** www.palmhive.co.uk
**Reg No:** 2219323 **VAT No:** 496349788
**Estd:** 1988 Private Limited Company
**Line of Business:** Manufacturers of textiles
**Export Markets:** E U
**Issued Capital:** £100
**Principals:** J D Mcmeeking *(Managing)*, M D Connors, J M Mcmeeking, Ms C Richardson
**Co. Secretary:** Adrian Wright
**Responsibilities**
**Senior:** Michael Shearman *(Sales & Marketing Director)*
**Marketing:** Michael Shearman *(Sales & Marketing Director)*
**Sales:** Michael Shearman *(Sales & Marketing Director)*
**Facilities:** Michael Shearman *(Sales & Marketing Director)*
**US SIC:** 2392, 3079
**UK SIC:** 45550, 48360
**Auditors:** Cooper-Parry
**Bankers:** Barclays Bank Plc (20-63-25)

| | 31-03-14 | 31-03-13 | 31-03-12 |
|---|---|---|---|
| TA | 1,721,200 | 1,972,339 | 1,938,773 |
| NW | 1,344,409 | 1,296,961 | 1,277,576 |
| WC | 1,342,165 | 1,288,765 | 1,263,799 |

DUNS 21-231-1714
## Palms Hotel
Southend Arterial Road, Hornchurch, Essex RM11 3UJ
**Tel:** 01708-346789
**Web:** www.palmshotel.activehotels.com
**Estd:** 1999 Partnership
**Line of Business:** Hotels
**Partners:** A Sanger, G O'Malley
**Responsibilities**
**Senior:** Mohamed Nilam *(Manager)*
**US SIC:** 7011 **UK SIC:** 66500
**Employees:** 102

DUNS 77-262-2858
## Palms Row Health Care Ltd
60 Westbourne Road, Sheffield, South Yorkshire S10 2QT
**Tel:** 01142684400 **Fax:** 01142638176
**Web:** www.westbourneschool.co.uk
**Reg No:** 2713151 **Estd:** 2005 Private Limited Company
**Line of Business:** Medical nursing home activities
**Trading Style:** Newfield Nursing Home, Northfield Nursing Home, Westbourne Home, Kingsdales
**Issued Capital:** £46,562
**Director:** J M Hume Kendall
**Co. Secretary:** Mrs Nicola Richards
**Responsibilities**
**Senior:** Julian Kendall *(Manager)*, Karen Mullins *(Office Manager)*
**Branches:** Palms Row Health Care Ltd, 93 Knollys Road, London SW16 2JP
**US SIC:** 7399 **UK SIC:** 83954
**Auditors:** Haywood & Co
**Bankers:** National Westminster Bank Plc (54-41-47)

| | 31-05-13 | 31-05-12 | 31-05-11 |
|---|---|---|---|
| TO | 4,359,909 | 5,237,551 | 5,911,604 |
| P/L | (92,195) | (591,819) | (462,792) |
| NW | 6,650,429 | 7,467,019 | 9,013,264 |
| WC | 2,293,513 | 3,312,759 | 1,698,530 |
| Emp. | 214 | 246 | 281 |

DUNS 23-511-5206
## Palmstead Nurseries Ltd
Harville Road, Ashford, Kent TN25 5EU
**Tel:** 01233-813340
**Web:** www.palmstead.co.uk
**Reg No:** 3510694 **Estd:** 1968 Private Limited Company
**Line of Business:** Wholesale of flowers and plants
**Trading Style:** Palmstead Nurseries
**Issued Capital:** £500,000
**Principals:** J F Langman *(Managing)*, Mrs L F Langman, R I Chapman
**Co. Secretary:** Mark Hutchinson
**Responsibilities**
**HR:** Vanessa Chapman *(Human Resources Officer)*
**Health & Safety:** Vanessa Chapman *(Human Resources Officer)*
**US SIC:** 5199 **UK SIC:** 61900
**Auditors:** Larkings
**Bankers:** HSBC Bank plc (40-08-32)

| | 31-07-13 | 31-07-12 | 31-07-11 |
|---|---|---|---|
| TO | 3,291,522 | 3,487,448 | N/A |
| P/L | 68,403 | 95,529 | N/A |
| NW | 2,806,639 | 2,815,909 | 2,889,386 |
| WC | 1,530,335 | 1,361,979 | 1,254,035 |
| Emp. | 51 | 52 | N/A |

DUNS 34-581-6128 **Imp-Exp**
## Palram Dpl Ltd
**(Subsidiary of:** Ramat Yohanan Agriculture Development)
Coatham Avenue, Aycliffe Business Park, Newton Aycliffe, County Durham DL5 6DB
**Tel:** 01325300437 **Fax:** 01325318173
**Web:** www.palram.com
**Reg No:** 2728300 **Estd:** 1992 Private Limited Company
**Line of Business:** Manufacture of plastics in primary forms
**Issued Capital:** £549,138
**Directors:** I Rodoy, I Sunik
**Co. Secretary:** Michael Burton
**Responsibilities**
**Senior:** Mike Callaghan *(Distribution Manager)*, Gary Clement *(Plant Manager)*, Arnon Eshed *(Manager)*, Amir Zohar *(Manager)*
**Health & Safety:** Stuart Finnie *(Health & Safety Officer)*
**US SIC:** 2821 **UK SIC:** 25140
**Auditors:** Levy Cohen & Co

| | 31-12-13 | 31-12-12 | 31-12-11 |
|---|---|---|---|
| TO | 24,599,753 | 25,515,450 | 25,670,134 |
| P/L | (2,468,864) | (1,463,839) | (164,414) |
| NW | 2,570,503 | 4,731,880 | 5,884,317 |
| WC | 1,806,037 | 1,470,988 | 2,840,339 |
| Emp. | 121 | 125 | 112 |

DUNS 77-747-3547 **Imp-Exp**

## Palram Polycarb Ltd

**(Subsidiary of:** Ramat Yohanan Agriculture Development)
Unit 2 White Rose Way, Doncaster Carr Industrial Estate, Doncaster, South Yorkshire DN4 5JH
**Tel:** 01302360161 **Fax:** 01302-344121
**Web:** www.palram.com
**Reg No:** 3013725 **VAT No:** 656332924
**Estd:** 1996 Private Limited Company
**Line of Business:** Manufacture of other plastic products
**Export Markets:** Europe
**Issued Capital:** £1,000,000
**Directors:** I Sunik, I Rodoy
**Co. Secretary:** Michael Burton
**Responsibilities**
**Senior:** Arnon Eshed *(Manager)*, Carl Walker *(Warehouse Manager)*, Amir Zohar *(Manager)*
**Engineering:** Carl Burwell *(Plant Manager)*
**US SIC:** 3079 **UK SIC:** 48360
**Auditors:** Levy Cohen & Co
**Bankers:** Barclays Bank Plc (20-26-55)

| | 31-12-13 | 31-12-12 | 31-12-11 |
|---|---|---|---|
| TO | 21,215,833 | 25,176,515 | 26,216,175 |
| P/L | 281,668 | 985,507 | 244,777 |
| NW | 6,318,617 | 6,052,389 | 5,279,980 |
| WC | 4,005,814 | 1,977,008 | 1,337,641 |
| Emp. | 80 | 81 | 84 |

DUNS 53-636-9887 **Imp**

## Pama & Co. Ltd

Pama House, Pama House, Stockport Road East, Cheshire, Stockport, Cheshire SK6 2AA
**Tel:** 01614944230 **Fax:** 08707531561
**Web:** www.pama.com
**Reg No:** 3441841 **Estd:** 1997 Private Limited Company
**Line of Business:** Wholesale of other electronic parts and equipment
**Export Sales:** £1,820,460
**Trading Style:** Pama Export Distribution, Pama Cellular
**Issued Capital:** £250,000
**Principals:** E Farshi *(Managing)*, I Farshi *(Managing)*, K Mchugh
**Co. Secretary:** Igal Farshi
**Responsibilities**
**Senior:** Micheal Hopkinson *(Sales Director)*
**Marketing:** Ricky Harvey *(Sales & Marketing Manager)*
**Sales:** Ricky Harvey *(Sales & Marketing Manager)*, Micheal Hopkinson *(Sales Director)*
**IT:** Mark Smitham *(Computer Manager)*
**Purchasing:** Graham Barber *(Purchasing Manager)*
**US SIC:** 5065 **UK SIC:** 61500
**Auditors:** Wilds Ltd
**Bankers:** HSBC Bank plc (40-08-22)

| | 30-04-14 | 30-04-13 | 30-04-12 |
|---|---|---|---|
| TO | 16,822,656 | 17,335,592 | 15,203,009 |
| P/L | 195,502 | 163,277 | 145,438 |
| NW | 2,309,096 | 2,124,726 | 2,137,840 |
| WC | 2,565,271 | 2,483,066 | 2,733,239 |
| Emp. | 152 | 226 | 133 |

DUNS 22-782-5007 **Imp-Exp**

## Pamargan Products Ltd

**(Subsidiary of:** Total Sa)
Unit 47 Mochdre Industrial Estate, Newtown, Powys SY16 4LE
**Tel:** 01686-625181 **Fax:** 01686-627849
**Web:** www.pamargan.co.uk
**Reg No:** 1597523 **VAT No:** 351772746
**Estd:** 1981 Private Limited Company
**Line of Business:** Manufacture of other rubber products
**Export Markets:** E C Countries
**Export Sales:** £9,843,248
**Issued Capital:** £4,000
**Director:** P R Olivier
**Co. Secretary:** Mark Pace-Bonello
**Responsibilities**
**Senior:** Braut Patrick *(Manager)*
**Finance:** Dylan Woodhouse *(Accountant)*
**Sales:** Phil Kenyon *(Sales Manager)*
**IT:** Chris Halling *(IT Manager)*, Iwan Jones *(Technical Director)*
**Health & Safety:** Brendan Murray *(Operations Manager)*
**Facilities:** Barry Morris *(Maintenance Coordinator)*
**Operations:** Iwan Jones *(Technical Director)*, Phil Kenyon *(Sales Manager)*, Brendan Murray *(Operations Manager)*
**Purchasing:** Russell Pond *(Purchaser)*
**Engineering:** Iwan Jones *(Technical Director)*
**US SIC:** 3069, 3452
**UK SIC:** 48123, 31371
**Auditors:** Ernst & Young LLP
**Bankers:** HSBC Bank plc (40-34-33)

| | 31-12-13 | 31-12-12 | 31-12-11 |
|---|---|---|---|
| TO | 10,959,163 | 9,934,397 | 10,750,544 |
| P/L | 2,361,619 | 2,114,270 | 2,446,500 |
| NW | 4,730,754 | 4,626,174 | 4,238,718 |
| WC | 4,076,803 | 3,931,691 | 3,581,459 |
| Emp. | 68 | 69 | 70 |

DUNS 22-126-6377

## Pamper Cleaning Services Ltd

Innovation Centre, 2 Veridion Way, Erith, Kent DA18 4AL
**Tel:** 08009540245
**Web:** www.pampercleaning.com
**Reg No:** 4145647 **Estd:** 1989 Private Limited Company
**Line of Business:** Traditional cleaning activities
**Issued Capital:** £100
**Co. Secretary:** Terrence Allen
**US SIC:** 7349 **UK SIC:** 92300

| | 31-01-14 | 31-01-13 | 31-01-12 |
|---|---|---|---|
| TA | 373,408 | 567,371 | 572,206 |
| NW | 121,941 | 281,732 | 93,775 |
| WC | 49,844 | (41,656) | 10,107 |

DUNS 71-890-5859

## Pamplona Capital Management Llp

25 Park Lane, London W1K 1RA
**Tel:** 020-7079-8000
**Web:** www.pamplonafunds.com
**Reg No:** 0309813OC **Estd:** 2005
**Line of Business:** Investment consultants
**Responsibilities**
**Senior:** Amy Abob *(Non-designated Limited Liabili)*, Andrew Berardi *(Non-designated Limited Liabili)*, Nitin Bhandari *(Non-designated Limited Liabili)*, Eric Bidinger *(Non-designated Limited Liabili)*, Christian Boekhorst *(Non-designated Limited Liabili)*, Edward Chai *(Non-designated Limited Liabili)*, Olivier Dieudonne *(Non-designated Limited Liabili)*, Joao Felix Saraiva E Silva *(Non-designated Limited Liabili)*, Zoran Kozic *(Non-designated Limited Liabili)*, David Lang *(Non-designated Limited Liabili)*, Yves Leysen *(Non-designated Limited Liabili)*, Markku Lonnqvist *(Non-designated Limited Liabili)*, Anna Nikitina *(Office Manager)*, Michael Rosen *(Non-designated Limited Liabili)*, Martin Schwab *(Non-designated Limited Liabili)*
**US SIC:** 6111 **UK SIC:** 81501
**Auditors:** Ernst & Young LLP
**Bankers:** HSBC Bank plc (40-03-40)

| | 31-12-13 | 31-12-12 | 31-12-11 |
|---|---|---|---|
| TA | 33,247,170 | 11,929,444 | 17,530,591 |
| P/L | 29,800,873 | 20,187,188 | 15,454,946 |
| NW | 30,342,058 | 11,286,023 | 17,377,975 |
| WC | 30,342,058 | 11,286,023 | 17,377,975 |

DUNS 42-406-1823

## Pampurredpets (Holdings) Ltd

33 Black Moor Road, Ebblake Industrial Estate, Verwood, Dorset BH31 6BB
**Tel:** 01202-814414
**Web:** www.pampurredpets.com
**Reg No:** 4393875 **Estd:** 2002 Private Limited Company
**Line of Business:** Management activities of other non-financial holding companies not elsewhere classified
**Issued Capital:** £314,490
**Directors:** J A Kennedy, S W Fowler
**Co. Secretary:** Mrs Deborah Fowler
**Responsibilities**
**Senior:** Charlotte Sturmey *(Marketing & Property Manager)*
**Marketing:** Charlotte Sturmey *(Marketing & Property Manager)*
**Facilities:** Charlotte Sturmey *(Marketing & Property Manager)*
**Branches:** Pampurredpets (Holdings) Ltd, Bursledon House, Unit 1-2, New Milton, Hampshire BH25 6HS
**US SIC:** 6711, 5999
**UK SIC:** 83962, 65600
**Auditors:** Princecroft Willis LLP
**Bankers:** HSBC Bank plc (40-21-21)

| | 31-03-14 | 31-03-13 | 31-03-12 |
|---|---|---|---|
| TO | 13,214,467 | 12,846,368 | 12,364,721 |
| P/L | 278,205 | 269,146 | 265,407 |
| NW | 2,087,107 | 1,861,474 | 1,653,968 |
| WC | 1,331,302 | 1,143,908 | 861,084 |
| Emp. | 307 | 290 | 283 |

DUNS 22-824-3291

## Pampurredpets Ltd

**(Subsidiary of:** Pampurredpets (Holdings) Ltd)
61 Fairview Avenue, Wigmore, Gillingham, Kent ME8 0QP
**Tel:** 01634232558
**Web:** www.graemeandco.co.uk
**Reg No:** 2097566 **Estd:** 1987 Private Limited Company
**Line of Business:** Other retail sale in non-specialised stores
**Export Sales:** £46,954
**Issued Capital:** £82,798
**Director:** S W Fowler
**Co. Secretary:** Mrs Deborah Fowler
**Branches:** Pampurredpets Ltd, Unit 2 Retail Park, High Street, Gosport, Hampshire PO12 1BX
**US SIC:** 5399, 6711
**UK SIC:** 65600, 83962
**Auditors:** Princecroft Willis LLP

| | 31-03-14 | 31-03-13 | 31-03-12 |
|---|---|---|---|
| TO | 13,214,467 | 12,846,368 | 12,364,721 |
| P/L | 278,205 | 269,147 | 263,292 |
| NW | 1,598,186 | 1,372,553 | 1,165,046 |
| WC | 1,346,001 | 1,158,607 | 875,782 |
| Emp. | 307 | 290 | 283 |

DUNS 64-121-0737

## Pams of Gainsborough

Unit 30, Gainsborough, Lincolnshire DN21 1QB
**Tel:** 01427610011
**Web:** www.pams.co.uk
**Estd:** 1986 Partnership
**Line of Business:** Business information services
**Partners:** J Lyden, Mrs C Lyden
**US SIC:** 5199 **UK SIC:** 61900
**Employees:** 55

DUNS 29-862-9536 **Imp-Exp**

## Pam's of Gainsborough Ltd

**(Subsidiary of:** Lyden Holdings Ltd)
Unit 30, Corringham Road Industrial Estate, Corri, Gainsborough, Lincolnshire DN21 1QB
**Tel:** 01427-676300
**Web:** www.pams.co.uk
**Reg No:** 2066219 **Estd:** 1986 Private Limited Company
**Line of Business:** Cleaning materials and equipment
**Export Markets:** Worldwide
**Issued Capital:** £1,000
**Directors:** Miss L Gillum, C Taylor
**Co. Secretary:** Mrs Carolyn Lyden
**US SIC:** 5199, 3999
**UK SIC:** 61900, 49590
**Auditors:** Streets & Co
**Bankers:** Barclays Bank Plc (20-50-21)

| | 31-08-14 | 31-08-13 | 31-08-12 |
|---|---|---|---|
| TA | 1,718,186 | 1,796,209 | 1,959,366 |
| NW | 1,447,372 | 1,445,537 | 1,454,070 |
| WC | 1,438,000 | 1,421,614 | 1,414,341 |

DUNS 29-132-6122 **Exp**

## Pan Macmillan Ltd

**(Subsidiary of:** Georg Von Holtzbrinck Gmbh & Co.Kg)
20 New Wharf Road, London N1 9RR
**Fax:** 02070146001
**Web:** www.macmillan.co.uk
**Reg No:** 1650381 **Estd:** 1990 Private Limited Company
**Line of Business:** The Notes to the accounts for the period ending 31.12.2013 state that the subject acts as an agent for Macmillan Publishers Ltd.
**Issued Capital:** £100
**Directors:** Miss R E Jacobs, S P Cramond, A D Forbes Watson, G M Duffield
**Co. Secretary:**
Mrs Gabrielle Williams Hamer
**Responsibilities**
**Senior:** Katie James *(Publicity Director)*, Jeremy Trevathan *(Publishing Director)*
**Marketing:** Lee Dibble *(Marketing & Communications Dir)*, Katie James *(Publicity Director)*, Jeremy Trevathan *(Publishing Director)*
**IT:** Andrew Maymiller *(IT Director)*
**HR:** Suzy Shepherd *(Personnel Manager)*
**Health & Safety:** Trish McCulley *(Central Services Manager)*
**Operations:** Trish McCulley *(Central Services Manager)*
**Purchasing:** Anne Ash *(Head of Purchasing)*
**US SIC:** 2731 **UK SIC:** 47532
**Bankers:** National Westminster Bank Plc (60-02-49)

| | 31-12-13 | 31-12-05 | 31-12-04 |
|---|---|---|---|
| TA | 100 | 100 | 100 |
| NW | 100 | 100 | 100 |
| WC | 100 | N/A | N/A |
| Emp. | 250 | N/A | N/A |

DUNS 22-803-3734 **Imp**

## Panache Lingerie Ltd

7 Drake House Crescent, Waterthorpe, Sheffield, South Yorkshire S20 7HT
**Tel:** 01142-418888 **Fax:** 01142-418889
**Web:** www.panachelingerie.com
**Reg No:** 1524006 **Estd:** 1980 Private Limited Company
**Line of Business:** Clothing wholesale and suppliers
**Export Sales:** £11,809,000
**Issued Capital:** £4,800
**Directors:** D T Power, Ms S M Grantham, Ms L E Power, J A Power
**Co. Secretary:** Mrs Jennifer Gayle
**Responsibilities**
**Senior:** Stuart Knipe *(ITAnalyst)*, Tim Lestley *(Warehouse Manager)*
**IT:** Stuart Knipe *(IT Analyst)*
**HR:** Caroline Christopher *(Human Resources Manager)*
**Facilities:** Tim Lestley *(Warehouse Manager)*
**Purchasing:** Tim Lestley *(Warehouse Manager)*
**US SIC:** 2341, 7399
**UK SIC:** 45362, 83954
**Auditors:** Grant Thornton UK LLP
**Bankers:** Yorkshire Bank Plc (05-08-08)

| | 30-06-13 | 30-06-12 | 30-06-11 |
|---|---|---|---|
| TO | 25,775,000 | 23,084,000 | 23,139,000 |
| P/L | 247,000 | (175,000) | 710,000 |
| NW | 7,265,000 | 7,197,000 | 7,408,000 |
| WC | 4,619,000 | 4,459,000 | 4,601,000 |
| Emp. | 152 | 148 | 163 |

DUNS 21-634-4970

## Panad Site Services Ltd

12-14 Macon Court, Herald Drive, Crewe, Cheshire CW1 6UZ
**Web:** www.panadgroup.org
**Reg No:** 7121939 **Estd:** 2010 Private Limited Company
**Line of Business:** Management of real estate on a fee or contract basis
**Issued Capital:** £65
**Directors:** A Mckie, Mrs J E Goodier
**Responsibilities**
**Senior:** David Seale *(Manager)*
**US SIC:** 6531 **UK SIC:** 83400

| | 31-03-14 | 31-03-13 | 31-03-12 |
|---|---|---|---|
| TA | 490,920 | 745,819 | 621,752 |
| NW | (7,468) | (7,893) | 5,132 |
| WC | (29,384) | (33,264) | (14,292) |

DUNS 21-022-3632 **Imp-Exp**

## Panalpina World Transport Ltd

**(Subsidiary of:** Panalpina Welttransport (Holding) Ag)
Panalpina House, Great South West Road, Feltham, Middlesex TW14 8NU
**Tel:** 02085879000 **Fax:** 02085879200
**Web:** www.panalpina.com
**Reg No:** 0357697 **VAT No:** 785411025
**Estd:** 1939 Private Limited Company
**Line of Business:** Freight forwarders
**Issued Capital:** £12,350,000
**Directors:** F Simmen, C Cooper
**Co. Secretary:** Robert Chambers
**Responsibilities**
**Senior:** Peter Triebel *(Manager)*
**IT:** Daniel Mayor *(IT Manager)*
**Facilities:** Clive Holley *(Facilities Manager)*
**Branches:** Panalpina World Transport Ltd, 75 Carnegie Road, Glasgow, Lanarkshire G52 4JZ
**US SIC:** 4712 **UK SIC:** 77002
**Auditors:** KPMG LLP
**Bankers:** Citibank Na (18-50-08)

| | 31-12-13 | 31-12-12 | 31-12-11 |
|---|---|---|---|
| TO | 193,492,000 | 138,227,000 | 140,986,000 |
| P/L | 1,344,000 | (1,927,000) | (3,862,000) |
| NW | 4,682,000 | 2,605,000 | 3,790,000 |
| WC | 8,302,000 | 3,828,000 | 172,000 |
| Emp. | 428 | 401 | 375 |

DUNS 22-179-4600

## Panalux Ltd

**(Subsidiary of:** Panavision Inc)
Unit 21, The Metropolitan Centre, Derby Road, Greenford, Middlesex UB6 8UJ
**Tel:** 02088324800
**Web:** www.panalux.biz
**Reg No:** 4197837 **Estd:** 2001 Private Limited Company
**Line of Business:** Renting of radios, televisions, video recorders and dvd players
**Export Sales:** £2,108,000
**Issued Capital:** £100
**Directors:** D O Boston, S Savjani, K A Snyder, C J Millard, J T Allen
**Co. Secretary:** Pitsec Limited
**Responsibilities**
**Senior:** Sneahal Savjani *(Financial Director)*
**Finance:** Sneahal Savjani *(Financial Director)*
**Marketing:** Ian Sherborn *(Sales & Marketing Manager)*
**Sales:** Ian Sherborn *(Sales & Marketing Manager)*
**Facilities:** Stewart Hadley *(Facilities Manager)*
**Branches:** Panalux Ltd, Manchester Road, Bolton, Lancashire BL4 8RL
**US SIC:** 7394 **UK SIC:** 84000
**Auditors:** Ernst & Young LLP
**Bankers:** Bank Of Scotland (12-09-49)

| | 31-12-13 | 31-12-12 | 31-12-11 |
|---|---|---|---|
| TO | 29,040,000 | 30,413,000 | 31,706,000 |
| P/L | 2,831,000 | 3,251,000 | 3,098,000 |
| NW | 13,414,000 | 15,011,000 | 12,552,000 |
| WC | 2,778,000 | 9,662,000 | 7,093,000 |
| Emp. | 249 | 274 | 275 |

DUNS 54-891-0322 **Imp**

## Panasonic Avionics Corporation

(**Subsidiary of:** Panasonic Corporation)
Quadrant House, 50 Heron Drive, Slough, Berkshire SL3 8XP
**Tel:** 01753741400 **Fax:** 01753-741480
**Web:** www.mascorp.com
**Reg No:** 0018534FC **Estd:** 1995 Foreign Company
**Line of Business:** Airline related services
**Directors:** Y Miyabe, J M Taylor, Y Yamada, M Kume, T Takagi, M G Riccio, S I Safier, P A Margis
**Co. Secretary:** Robert Marin
**Responsibilities**
**Senior:** Bob Dick *(Chief Executive)*, Yasuji Enokido *(Director)*, Linda Isherwood *(Manager)*, Myung Lee *(Director)*, Hideo Nakano *(Manager)*, Naoto Noguchi *(Director)*, Robert Parson *(Director)*, Yoshihiro Yamashita *(Director)*
**US SIC:** 3721 **UK SIC:** 36400

DUNS 38-547-7427 **Imp**

## Panasonic Europe Ltd.

(**Subsidiary of:** Panasonic Corporation)
Panasonic Building A, Willoughby Road, Bracknell, Berkshire RG12 8FP
**Fax:** 020-8899-2211
**Web:** www.business.panasonic.co.uk
**Reg No:** 3329345 **Estd:** 1997 Private Limited Company
**Line of Business:** Management activities of holding companies
**Export Sales:** £66,431,000
**Issued Capital:** £199,922,641
**Directors:** M G Irving, K Katsuragi, L Abadie, Y Hirota, T Lammel
**Co. Secretary:** Ms Daniela Gardiner
**Responsibilities**
**Senior:** Junichi Suzuki *(Ceo Director Of Europe)*
**US SIC:** 6711, 5065
**UK SIC:** 83962, 61500
**Auditors:** KPMG LLP
**Following financial data are in thousands**

| | 31-03-14 | 31-03-13 | 31-03-12 |
|---|---|---|---|
| TO | 87,856 | 79,346 | 86,757 |
| P/L | (76,590) | 69,714 | 54,058 |
| NW | 1,057,220 | 1,098,279 | 820,480 |
| WC | 135,946 | 158,213 | 164,424 |
| Emp. | 427 | 473 | 390 |

DUNS 21-724-9937 **Imp-Exp**

## Panasonic Manufacturing U.K. Ltd.

(**Subsidiary of:** Panasonic Corporation)
Wharfdale Road, Cardiff, South Glamorgan CF23 7XB
**Tel:** 029-2054-0011
**Web:** www.panasonic.com
**Reg No:** 1174086 **VAT No:** 282433951
**Estd:** 1975 Private Limited Company
**Line of Business:** Manufacture of computers and other information processing equipment
**Export Sales:** £166,202,000
**Trading Style:** Panasonic
**Issued Capital:** £4,128,000
**Directors:** S Dohno, Y Inoue, N Akari, K Jones, L R Abadie, C J Bermingham-Mcdonogh
**Co. Secretary:** Ashley Kindred
**Responsibilities**
**Senior:** Daniel Humphrey *(Production Manager)*, John McNicholas *(Marketing Director)*, Toshiyuki Onoe *(Manager)*, Steven Randall Smith *(Manager)*, Masaru Sonoda *(Manager)*
**Marketing:** John McNicholas *(Marketing Director)*
**IT:** Ken Wareham *(Computer Manager)*
**HR:** Lisa Angus *(Human Resources Manager)*
**Health & Safety:** Pelham Morgan *(Health & Safety Officer)*
**Operations:** John McNicholas *(Marketing Director)*
**Fleet:** John McNicholas *(Marketing Director)*
**Engineering:** Daniel Humphrey *(Production Manager)*
**Branches:** Panasonic Manufacturing U.k. Ltd., Pentwyn Business Centre, Unit 2, Cardiff, South Glamorgan CF23 7HB
**US SIC:** 3573, 3651
**UK SIC:** 33020, 34541
**Auditors:** KPMG LLP
**Bankers:** Barclays Bank Plc (20-18-15)

| | 31-03-14 | 31-03-13 | 31-03-12 |
|---|---|---|---|
| TO | 209,698,000 | 183,917,000 | 184,158,000 |
| P/L | 9,793,000 | 13,551,000 | 3,539,000 |
| NW | 67,445,000 | 64,060,000 | 54,854,000 |
| WC | 74,553,000 | 70,903,000 | 65,184,000 |
| Emp. | 421 | 396 | 397 |

DUNS 21-360-8544

## Panasonic Store

The Harlequin Centre, Paul Street, Exeter, Devon EX4 3TT
**Web:** www.panastores.co.uk
**Estd:** 2001 Proprietorship
**Line of Business:** Cds dvds vinyl & tapes
**Proprietor:** J Holroyd
**Responsibilities**
**Senior:** Joe Holroyde *(Manager)*
**US SIC:** 5732 **UK SIC:** 64800
**Employees:** 46

DUNS 21-586-6025

## Panasonic Uk

Northampton, Northampton, Northamptonshire NN1 1BA
**Tel:** 08448443899
**Estd:** 2011 Partnership
**Line of Business:** Domestic Appliance Retailers
**Partners:** D Pratt, K Evans, D Miyake, M Matsushita
**US SIC:** 5722 **UK SIC:** 64800
**Employees:** 390

DUNS 21-113-4671 **Exp**

## Panasonic U.K. Ltd

(**Subsidiary of:** Panasonic Corporation)
Panasonic House, Willoughby Road, Bracknell, Berkshire RG12 8FP
**Tel:** 01344-862444 **Fax:** 01344-853564
**Web:** www.panasonic.co.uk
**Reg No:** 1069148 **Estd:** 1972 Private Limited Company
**Line of Business:** Wholesale of radio and television goods; wholesale of electrical household appliances not elsewhere classified
**Issued Capital:** £1
**Directors:** H Soejima, A G Denham
**Co. Secretary:** Darrell-John Pratt
**Responsibilities**
**Marketing:** Zeena Hill *(Head Of Marketing)*, Barnaby Sykes *(Head Of Product Marketing)*
**Sales:** Tony Jefcut *(Area Sales Manager)*, Robert Scholes *(Sales Director)*
**Engineering:** Adam Neale *(Technical Specialist)*, Valerie Townsend *(Chief Engineer)*, Ramona Zaharia *(Chief Engineer)*
**Branches:** Panasonic U.K. Ltd, Panasonic Store, 56 Cornwall Street, Plymouth, Devon PL1 1LR
**US SIC:** 5064, 5081
**UK SIC:** 61500, 61490
**Auditors:** KPMG LLP
**Bankers:** National Westminster Bank Plc (01-08-15)

| | 31-03-12 |
|---|---|
| P/L | 2,836,000 |

DUNS 50-593-3283 **Imp-Exp**

## Panavision Europe Ltd

(**Subsidiary of:** Panavision Inc)
The Metropolitan Centre, Bristol Road, Greenford, Middlesex UB6 8GD
**Tel:** 02088397333 **Fax:** 02085786769
**Web:** www.panavision.co.uk
**Reg No:** 2532311 **VAT No:** 581855115
**Estd:** 1990 Private Limited Company
**Line of Business:** Film production services and studios
**Export Markets:** Europe, U S A and Countries Worldwide
**Trading Style:** Panalux, Panavision U K, Lee Filters
**Issued Capital:** £78,825,364
**Directors:** J T Allen, W F Gosland
**Co. Secretary:** William Gosland
**Branches:** Panavision Europe Ltd, The Metropolitan Centre, Unit 27-29, Greenford, Middlesex UB6 8UQ
**US SIC:** 7819 **UK SIC:** 97111
**Auditors:** Ernst & Young LLP
**Bankers:** Barclays Bank Plc (20-91-79)

| | 31-12-13 | 31-12-12 | 31-12-11 |
|---|---|---|---|
| TO | 91,661,000 | 91,457,000 | 93,666,000 |
| P/L | (4,190,000) | (652,000) | (5,932,000) |
| NW | (12,237,000) | (10,878,000) | (11,523,000) |
| WC | (8,201,000) | (5,001,000) | (8,737,000) |
| Emp. | 740 | 764 | 786 |

DUNS 21-136-8933

## Panaz Holdings Ltd

Spring Mill, Wheatley Lane Road, Fence, Burnley, Lancashire BB12 9HP
**Tel:** 01282696969
**Web:** www.panaz.co.uk
**Reg No:** 6697759 **Estd:** 2008 Private Limited Company
**Line of Business:** Manufacture of soft furnishings
**Export Sales:** £2,787,815
**Issued Capital:** £20,000
**Directors:** S Chippendale, A J Attard, K Chippendale
**US SIC:** 2391 **UK SIC:** 45550
**Bankers:** HSBC Bank plc (40-15-17)

| | 31-03-14 | 31-03-13 | 31-03-12 |
|---|---|---|---|
| TO | 13,154,850 | 13,225,282 | 12,938,055 |
| P/L | 825,807 | 1,195,676 | 1,035,170 |
| NW | 6,319,029 | 5,995,023 | 5,344,194 |
| WC | 5,798,935 | 5,529,790 | 4,896,613 |
| Emp. | 72 | 75 | 73 |

DUNS 22-755-7451

## The Pancake Place Ltd

22 King Edward Street, Perth, Perthshire PH1 5SU
**Tel:** 01738444699 **Fax:** 01738-624403
**Web:** www.thepancakeplace.net
**Reg No:** 0065276SC **Estd:** 1978 Private Limited Company
**Line of Business:** Licensed restaurants
**Issued Capital:** £75,000
**Director:** E C Dunn
**Co. Secretary:** Ms Angela Dunn
**Branches:** The Pancake Place Ltd, 95-97 George Street, Oban, Argyll PA34 5NR
**US SIC:** 5812 **UK SIC:** 66110
**Auditors:** Johnston Carmichael
**Bankers:** The Royal Bank Of Scotland Plc (83-23-47)

| | 31-01-14 | 31-01-13 | 31-01-12 |
|---|---|---|---|
| TA | 1,105,544 | 1,102,011 | 1,068,020 |
| NW | 806,999 | 730,964 | 608,492 |
| WC | 701,207 | 589,881 | 394,960 |

DUNS 23-603-7557

## P&A Food Management Services Ltd

(**Subsidiary of:** Contract Catering Services (P&A) Group Ltd)
Kingsfield House, Carthorpe, Leyburn, North Yorkshire DL8 2LL
**Tel:** 01845567804 **Fax:** 01845565450
**Web:** www.pafoodmanagement.co.uk
**Reg No:** 3601088 **Estd:** 1998 Private Limited Company
**Line of Business:** Catering
**Issued Capital:** £100
**Directors:** E A Naylor, D J Hall
**Co. Secretary:** David Hall
**Branches:** P&a Food Management Services Ltd, Consett Road, Gateshead, Tyne and Wear NE11 0AN
**US SIC:** 5812 **UK SIC:** 66110
**Auditors:** RSM Tenon Audit Ltd
**Bankers:** HSBC Bank plc (40-19-03)

| | 31-03-14 | 31-03-13 | 31-03-12 |
|---|---|---|---|
| TO | N/A | 6,423,633 | 5,788,442 |
| P/L | N/A | 115,250 | 128,471 |
| NW | 1,107,822 | 1,291,138 | 1,258,193 |
| WC | 1,027,149 | 1,166,151 | 1,111,321 |

DUNS 21-699-8963 **Imp-Exp**

## Pandect Precision Components Ltd

Wellington Road, Cressex Business Park, High Wycombe, Buckinghamshire HP12 3PX
**Tel:** 01494-526303
**Web:** www.slipring.co.uk
**Reg No:** 0806716 **VAT No:** 385860412
**Estd:** 1964 Private Limited Company
**Line of Business:** Manufacture of electronic valves and tubes and other electronic components
**Export Markets:** Worldwide
**Trading Style:** Pandect Precision Components Limited
**Issued Capital:** £590
**Managing Director:** R Pope
**Co. Secretary:** Mrs Carole Harvey
**Responsibilities**
**Health & Safety:** Gary Alger *(Health & Safety Officer)*, Helen Blair *(Health & Safety Officer)*
**Operations:** Helen Blair *(Health & Safety Officer)*
**US SIC:** 3679 **UK SIC:** 34542
**Auditors:** Seymour Taylor Audit Ltd
**Bankers:** Barclays Bank Plc (20-40-71)

| | 31-03-14 | 31-03-13 | 31-03-12 |
|---|---|---|---|
| TO | N/A | N/A | 2,301,302 |
| P/L | N/A | N/A | 24,884 |
| NW | 1,261,836 | 1,367,170 | 1,199,298 |
| WC | 1,207,875 | 1,297,497 | 1,123,932 |

DUNS 29-052-3554

## P&Mm Ltd

(**Subsidiary of:** Sodexo)
Avalon House, Breckland, Linford Wood, Milton Keynes, Buckinghamshire MK14 6LD
**Tel:** 08450543333
**Web:** www.p-mm.co.uk
**Reg No:** 1090180 **VAT No:** 608407841
**Estd:** 1973 Private Limited Company
**Line of Business:** Labour recruitment and provision of personnel
**Trading Style:** Performance & Motivation, Event & Communication, Filmology
**Issued Capital:** £312,500
**Directors:** S R De Tramasure, D C Lebond, D P Machuel, S D Godet, J M Sylvester
**Co. Secretary:** Miss Susan Hocken
**Responsibilities**
**Senior:** James Malia *(Manager)*
**Marketing:** James Malia *(Manager)*
**HR:** Sue Giles *(Human Resources Manager)*
**US SIC:** 7399, 4899, 7999
**UK SIC:** 83954, 79020, 97913
**Auditors:** Grant Thornton UK LLP
**Bankers:** The Royal Bank Of Scotland Plc (16-25-27)

| | 31-12-13 | 31-12-12 | 31-12-11 |
|---|---|---|---|
| TO | 58,841,215 | 71,875,982 | 67,285,268 |
| P/L | 3,213,734 | 1,947,642 | 1,710,368 |
| NW | 9,099,662 | 8,669,259 | 7,191,643 |
| WC | 8,363,785 | 7,853,712 | 6,182,741 |
| Emp. | 188 | 181 | 173 |

DUNS 21-001-5962

## P&O European Ferries (Irish Sea) Ltd

(**Subsidiary of:** Dubai World Corporation)
Channel House, Channel View Road, Dover, Kent CT17 9TJ
**Tel:** 08716645645 **Fax:** 01304863223
**Web:** www.poferries.com
**Reg No:** 0318227 **VAT No:** 496850296
**Estd:** 1936 Private Limited Company
**Line of Business:** Passenger sea and coastal water transport
**Trading Style:** P&O European Ferries (Irish Sea) Ltd
**Issued Capital:** £40,600,000
**Directors:** Mrs H Deeble, L A Cotton, K Howarth, Ms J S Bell, J P Garner, Ms S M Mackenzie
**Co. Secretary:** Ms Susan Kitchin
**Responsibilities**
**Marketing:** Natalie Hardy *(Communications Executive)*, Christopher Laming *(Communications Director)*
**HR:** Peter Capon *(Human Resources Manager)*
**Branches:** P&o European Ferries (Irish Sea) Ltd, Torbitts, 10 Redlands Road, Larne, Co Antrim BT40 1FD
**US SIC:** 4452 **UK SIC:** 74002
**Auditors:** Ernst & Young LLP
**Bankers:** Barclays Bank Plc (20-00-00)

| | 31-12-13 | 31-12-12 | 31-12-11 |
|---|---|---|---|
| TO | 101,942,000 | 101,843,000 | 113,028,000 |
| P/L | (17,597,000) | (9,029,000) | 3,781,000 |
| NW | (42,120,000) | (25,923,000) | 29,167,000 |
| WC | (20,398,000) | (10,906,000) | (114,000) |
| Emp. | 213 | 223 | 241 |

DUNS 67-208-1721

## P&O Ferries Division Holdings Ltd

(**Subsidiary of:** Dubai World Corporation)
Channel House, Channel View Road, Dover, Kent CT17 9TJ
**Tel:** 01304-863000
**Web:** www.poferries.com
**Reg No:** 6038090 **Estd:** 2006 Private Limited Company
**Line of Business:** Passenger sea and coastal water transport
**Trading Style:** P & O Ferries
**Issued Capital:** £42,854,200
**Directors:** J M Bin Theniyeh, Mrs H Deeble, R S Ntuli, Y Narayan, R B Woods, S A Rais, K Howarth
**Co. Secretary:** Ms Susan Kitchin
**US SIC:** 4452 **UK SIC:** 74002

| | 31-12-13 | 31-12-12 | 31-12-11 |
|---|---|---|---|
| TO | 966,942,000 | 971,875,000 | 999,547,000 |
| P/L | (10,226,000) | 4,283,000 | 6,573,000 |
| NW | 29,067,000 | 46,378,000 | 185,391,000 |
| WC | 47,389,000 | 54,352,000 | 47,425,000 |
| Emp. | 3,996 | 4,121 | 4,238 |

DUNS 21-893-0089 **Imp-Exp**

## P&O Ferrymasters Ltd

(**Subsidiary of:** Dubai World Corporation)
Redlands Estate, Larne, Co Antrim BT40 1AX
**Tel:** 02828871500 **Fax:** 02828 871 516
**Web:** www.poferrymasters.com
**Reg No:** 0004115NI **VAT No:** 145066380
**Estd:** 1958 Private Limited Company
**Line of Business:** Road haulage and transport services
**Export Markets:** Worldwide
**Export Sales:** £288,032,000
**Issued Capital:** £46,830,000
**Directors:** Mrs H Deeble, M E Mulder, B Belder, C N Cassidy, H H Braam
**Co. Secretary:** Bastiaan Belder
**Responsibilities**
**Senior:** Wim Blomme *(Director)*
**Finance:** Wim Blomme *(Director)*
**Branches:** P&o Ferrymasters Limited, Leacroft Rd, Risley, Warrington, Cheshire WA3 6NW
**US SIC:** 4789, 4213
**UK SIC:** 77002, 72300
**Auditors:** KPMG LLP
**Bankers:** Barclays Bank Plc (20-00-00)

| | 31-12-13 | 31-12-12 | 31-12-11 |
|---|---|---|---|
| TO | 410,468,000 | 387,433,000 | 434,435,000 |
| P/L | 163,000 | (416,000) | 430,000 |
| NW | 3,397,000 | 2,193,000 | 6,002,000 |
| WC | 8,209,000 | 8,410,000 | 9,284,000 |
| Emp. | 383 | 377 | 387 |

DUNS 36-535-5403
## P&O Short Sea Ferries Ltd
(**Subsidiary of:** Dubai World Corporation)
Channel House, Channel View Road, Dover, Kent CT17 9TJ
**Tel:** 08716641641
**Web:** www.poferries.com
**Reg No:** 3291852 **Estd:** 1996 Private Limited Company
**Line of Business:** Passenger sea and coastal water transport
**Issued Capital:** £14,062,500
**Directors:** L A Cotton, Ms S M Mackenzie, Ms J S Bell, K Howarth, Mrs H Deeble, J P Garner
**Co. Secretary:** Ms Susan Kitchin
**Branches:** P&o Short Sea Ferries Ltd, 3 Gladstone Dock, North Quay, Liverpool, Merseyside L20 1BG
**US SIC:** 4452 **UK SIC:** 74002
**Auditors:** Ernst & Young LLP

| | 31-12-13 | 31-12-12 | 31-12-11 |
|---|---|---|---|
| TO | 283,616,000 | 322,494,000 | 271,900,000 |
| P/L | (169,990,000) | 23,545,000 | 6,263,000 |
| NW | 83,885,000 | 64,088,000 | 101,786,000 |
| WC | 18,002,000 | 172,076,000 | 135,803,000 |
| Emp. | 874 | 978 | 1,061 |

DUNS 21-131-5258
## Pandora Jewellery Uk Ltd
(**Subsidiary of:** Pandora A/S)
33 George Street, London W1U 3QB
**Tel:** 08448731442 **Fax:** 08448731444
**Web:** www.pandora.net
**Reg No:** 6654012 **Estd:** 2008 Private Limited Company
**Line of Business:** Wholesale of jewellery
**Export Sales:** £126,000
**Issued Capital:** £65,686,224
**Directors:** P A Andersen, Mrs A Hope-Richardson, L Jensen, P M Vekslund
**Co. Secretary:** Mrs Amanda Hope-Richardson
**Responsibilities**
**Senior:** David Stringer *(Store Manager)*
**Branches:** Pandora Jewellery Uk Ltd, 15 29 Cabot Square, London E14 4QS
**US SIC:** 5094, 5944
**UK SIC:** 61900, 65400
**Auditors:** Ernst & Young LLP
**Bankers:** Unibank A/s (40-48-78)

| | 31-12-13 | 31-12-12 | 31-12-11 |
|---|---|---|---|
| TO | 125,679,000 | 108,037,000 | 110,298,000 |
| P/L | 11,569,000 | 14,464,000 | 1,888,000 |
| NW | 75,198,000 | 77,617,000 | 65,173,000 |
| WC | 20,412,000 | 23,699,000 | 10,844,000 |
| Emp. | 123 | 154 | 130 |

DUNS 21-018-2556 **Imp-Exp**
## Pandrol Ltd
(**Subsidiary of:** Sodelho Sa)
63-65 Station Road, Addlestone, Surrey KT15 2AR
**Tel:** 01932-834500
**Web:** www.pandrol.com
**Reg No:** 0521438 **VAT No:** 232695162
**Estd:** 1937 Private Limited Company
**Line of Business:** Manufacture of other fabricated metal products not elsewhere classified
**Export Markets:** Europe
**Export Sales:** £60,361,000
**Trading Style:** Pandrol Uk, Pandrol International
**Issued Capital:** £1,000
**Directors:** D H Bourdon, G H Talbourdet, S J Cox, B Forster, D J Webster, W M Peacock, D J Cooke
**Co. Secretary:** David Cooke
**Responsibilities**
**Senior:** John Byles *(Manager)*
**Branches:** Pandrol Ltd, Gateford Rd, Worksop, Nottinghamshire S81 7AX
**US SIC:** 3499 **UK SIC:** 31694
**Auditors:** Mazars LLP
**Bankers:** Barclays Bank Plc (20-03-53)

| | 31-12-13 | 31-12-12 | 31-12-11 |
|---|---|---|---|
| TO | 80,498,000 | 74,977,000 | 71,728,000 |
| P/L | 8,924,000 | 6,774,000 | 8,079,000 |
| NW | 19,886,000 | 18,186,000 | 14,390,000 |
| WC | 21,592,000 | 20,468,000 | 16,851,000 |
| Emp. | 234 | 240 | 232 |

DUNS 36-523-3774 **Imp**
## Panduit Europe Ltd.
(**Subsidiary of:** Panduit Corp)
Westworld, West Gate, London W5 1UD
**Tel:** 02086017200
**Reg No:** 3287919 **Estd:** 1996 Private Limited Company
**Line of Business:** Cable and wire supply and distribution
**Export Sales:** £27,742,512
**Trading Style:** Panduit Europe
**Issued Capital:** £400,000
**Directors:** G W Lange, M G Kenny
**Co. Secretary:** Thomas Anthony
**Responsibilities**
**Senior:** Leighanne Bojarski *(Administration Assistant)*, Ralph Lolies *(Director)*, Jack R *(Manager)*, Carlos Ramirez *(Manager)*
**US SIC:** 3357 **UK SIC:** 22470
**Auditors:** Grant Thornton UK LLP
**Bankers:** Bank Of America, Na (30-16-35)

| | 31-12-13 | 31-12-12 | 31-12-11 |
|---|---|---|---|
| TO | 27,742,512 | 25,166,398 | 22,426,748 |
| P/L | 567,034 | 322,869 | 169,866 |
| NW | 1,099,339 | 712,741 | 902,070 |
| WC | 130,505 | (119,456) | 10,048 |
| Emp. | 214 | 220 | 197 |

DUNS 21-067-5486
## Pane E Vino
3 Hunter Street, Kirkcaldy, Fife KY1 1ED
**Tel:** 01592-200050
**Web:** www.paneevino.co.uk
**Estd:** 1997 Proprietorship
**Line of Business:** Restaurant - italian
**Proprietor:** A Citro
**Responsibilities**
**Senior:** Antonio Citro *(Proprietor)*
**US SIC:** 5812 **UK SIC:** 66110
**Employees:** 48

DUNS 21-321-4729 **Imp-Exp**
## Panel Systems Ltd
(**Subsidiary of:** Panel Systems (Holdings) Ltd)
Welland Close, Sheffield, South Yorkshire S3 9QY
**Tel:** 01142-752881 **Fax:** 01142-768807
**Web:** www.panelsystemsgroup.co.uk
**Reg No:** 1179701 **Estd:** 1974 Private Limited Company
**Line of Business:** Cladding and insulation materials
**Export Markets:** E U (0.1%)
**Issued Capital:** £1,000
**Managing Director:** C M Ibbotson
**Co. Secretary:** Ms Carol Fairburn
**Responsibilities**
**Sales:** Danny Phelan *(Sales Manager)*
**Operations:** Sue Stafford *(Parkwood Operations Manager)*
**US SIC:** 3079 **UK SIC:** 48360
**Auditors:** Barber Harrison & Platt
**Bankers:** The Royal Bank Of Scotland Plc (16-00-08)

| | 31-12-13 | 31-12-12 | 31-12-11 |
|---|---|---|---|
| TO | 8,053,966 | 8,143,801 | 8,656,308 |
| P/L | 230,394 | 359,760 | 455,219 |
| NW | 1,623,035 | 1,516,638 | 1,355,248 |
| WC | 1,395,610 | 1,306,677 | 1,147,967 |
| Emp. | 49 | 50 | 50 |

DUNS 64-083-0246
## Panelco Ltd
(**Subsidiary of:** The Meade Family Office Limited)
Grindley Lane, Blythe Bridge, Stoke-On-Trent, Staffordshire ST11 9LS
**Tel:** 01782-392100
**Web:** www.panelco.com
**Reg No:** 3478246 **Estd:** 1997 Private Limited Company
**Line of Business:** Distribution service providers
**Issued Capital:** £490
**Directors:** C J Rudd, D K Barnett, D I Siggins
**Co. Secretary:** Darren Barnett
**Responsibilities**
**Senior:** Jonathan Cameron *(Manager)*, Philip Ellis *(Manager)*
**US SIC:** 5072 **UK SIC:** 61500
**Auditors:** Walletts
**Bankers:** National Westminster Bank Plc (01-03-69)

| | 31-12-13 | 31-12-12 | 31-12-11 |
|---|---|---|---|
| TO | 35,763,000 | 31,787,000 | 28,174,000 |
| P/L | 2,441,000 | 1,125,000 | 827,000 |
| NW | 6,520,000 | 4,716,000 | 7,250,000 |
| WC | 3,836,000 | 2,516,000 | 5,937,000 |
| Emp. | 139 | 134 | 104 |

DUNS 21-586-6077
## Panels & Profiles
Shotton Works, Weighbridge Road, Deeside Industrial Park, Deeside, Clwyd CH5 2NH
**Tel:** 08453088330
**Web:** www.tatasteel.com
**Estd:** 2011 Partnership
**Line of Business:** Cladding suppliers and contractors
**Partners:** I Taylor, M Boyle, S Farrell
**Responsibilities**
**Senior:** Malcolm Boyles *(Managing Director)*
**US SIC:** 1799 **UK SIC:** 50000
**Employees:** 160

DUNS 76-852-0223
## Paneltex Ltd
Kingston International Business Park, Somerden Road, Hull, North Humberside HU9 5PE
**Tel:** 01427667600 **Fax:** 01482787238
**Web:** www.paneltex.co.uk
**Reg No:** 2607586 **VAT No:** 552010006
**Estd:** 2001 Private Limited Company
**Line of Business:** Manufacture of bodies (coachwork) for motor vehicles (except caravans)
**Export Sales:** £291,611
**Issued Capital:** £28,000
**Principals:** C T Berridge *(Managing)*, M Richardson, N E Wilde, K Drake
**Co. Secretary:** Mrs Jane Berridge
**Responsibilities**
**Senior:** Jason Hall *(Business Manager)*, Kevin Pinder *(Stores Manager)*
**US SIC:** 3713, 3079
**UK SIC:** 35201, 48360
**Auditors:** Baker Tilly UK Audit LLP
**Bankers:** HSBC Bank plc (40-32-06)

| | 30-06-13 | 30-06-12 | 30-06-11 |
|---|---|---|---|
| TO | 24,464,532 | 20,930,814 | 18,832,734 |
| P/L | 203,645 | (283,247) | 197,065 |
| NW | 2,843,495 | 2,635,113 | 2,835,667 |
| WC | 1,739,503 | 1,442,257 | 1,990,843 |
| Emp. | 257 | 236 | 235 |

DUNS 21-392-9232
## Panesar
Unit 2, Cliff Drive, Tipton, West Midlands DY4 0PZ
**Tel:** 0121-5067870
**Web:** www.panesarfoods.co.uk
**Proprietorship**
**Line of Business:** Manufacture of other food products not elsewhere classified
**Proprietor:** B Panesar
**US SIC:** 2099 **UK SIC:** 42399
**Employees:** 100

DUNS 34-590-2774 **Imp**
## Pang (2005) Ltd
Chiswick Avenue, Mildenhall, Bury St Edmunds, Suffolk IP28 7AX
**Tel:** 01638663575 **Fax:** 01638662274
**Web:** www.panguk.com
**Reg No:** 5397789 **Estd:** 2005 Private Limited Company
**Line of Business:** Sale of motor vehicle parts and accessories
**Export Sales:** £22,463
**Issued Capital:** £10,000
**Directors:** M P Parkinson, Mrs H Mcguirk, T R Cheek, J E Mcguirk
**Co. Secretary:** Martin Parkinson
**Responsibilities**
**Senior:** Barry Mcguirk *(Manager)*
**US SIC:** 5531 **UK SIC:** 65100

| | 31-12-13 | 31-12-12 | 31-12-11 |
|---|---|---|---|
| TO | 7,744,030 | 8,835,446 | N/A |
| P/L | 19,643 | (472,262) | N/A |
| NW | (438,943) | (525,089) | (499,999) |
| WC | (288,474) | (655,508) | N/A |
| Emp. | 56 | 77 | N/A |

DUNS 76-942-4540
## Pangbourne College Ltd
Shooters Hill, Pangbourne, Reading, Berkshire RG8 7DU
**Tel:** 01189844494
**Web:** www.pangbournecollege.com
**Reg No:** 0260104 **Estd:** 1931 Private Limited Company
**Line of Business:** Schools (foundation)
**Issued Capital:** £2,500
**Directors:** A T Bond, F J Slevin, C J Gould, Dr C J Boulter, Ms C L Butterworth, R C Barklett, G Macpherson, Mrs S Stevens
**Co. Secretary:** Ronald Obbard
**Responsibilities**
**Senior:** Michael Allsop *(Chair Of Governors)*, Pamela Bale *(Director)*, David Herbert *(Director)*, Roger Lane-Nott *(Director)*, Matilda Oppenheimer *(Director)*
**Facilities:** Ross Denny *(Works Manager)*
**Branches:** Pangbourne College Ltd, Bere Court Road, Reading, Berkshire RG8 8LA
**US SIC:** 8211 **UK SIC:** 93200
**Auditors:** Ernest & Young
**Bankers:** National Westminster Bank Plc (60-17-21)

| | 31-08-13 | 31-08-12 | 31-08-11 |
|---|---|---|---|
| TO | 8,660,547 | 12,277,270 | 8,477,744 |
| P/L | 93,110 | 3,867,631 | 537,261 |
| NW | 9,586,032 | 9,492,922 | 5,625,291 |
| WC | (939,098) | (768,754) | (1,023,520) |
| Emp. | 114 | 115 | 114 |

DUNS 52-013-5971
## Pangolin Editions Ltd
4 Chapel Row Queen Square, Bristol, Avon BS1 1HN
**Tel:** 01453731499 **Fax:** 01453-731499
**Web:** www.pangolin-editions.com
**Reg No:** 3380293 **Estd:** 1997 Private Limited Company
**Line of Business:** Bronze fine art castings foundry
**Issued Capital:** £2
**Director:** R D Kingdon
**Co. Secretary:** Total Solutions Uk Limited
**Responsibilities**
**Finance:** Jackie Evans *(Financial Manager)*
**HR:** Jackie Evans *(Financial Manager)*
**Health & Safety:** Helen Mitchell *(Health & Safety Officer)*
**Facilities:** Steve Maule *(Foundry Manager)*
**US SIC:** 3369 **UK SIC:** 31120

| | 30-11-13 | 30-11-12 | 30-11-11 |
|---|---|---|---|
| TA | 2 | 2 | 2 |
| NW | 2 | 2 | 2 |

DUNS 76-417-5261
## Panic Transport (Contracts) Ltd
Euro Park, Watling Street, Clifton Upon Dunsmore, Rugby, Warwickshire CV23 0AQ
**Tel:** 01788861200 **Fax:** 01788861206
**Web:** www.panictransport.co.uk
**Reg No:** 2559399 **Estd:** 1990 Private Limited Company
**Line of Business:** Activities of other transport agencies
**Issued Capital:** £100
**Managing Director:** K N Johnson
**Co. Secretary:** Mrs Nicola Henson
**Responsibilities**
**Marketing:** Phillip McBean *(Sales & Marketing Manager)*
**Sales:** Phillip McBean *(Sales & Marketing Manager)*
**IT:** Mark Wildgoose *(Computer Manager)*
**US SIC:** 4712, 4226
**UK SIC:** 77002, 77003
**Auditors:** Price Pearson
**Bankers:** Lloyds TSB Bank plc (30-97-17)

| | 31-12-13 | 31-12-12 | 31-12-11 |
|---|---|---|---|
| TA | 4,227,414 | 2,704,133 | 2,468,967 |
| NW | 1,810,287 | 1,465,605 | 1,319,380 |
| WC | 834,321 | 789,081 | 566,181 |

DUNS 64-102-9533
## Pankl Racing Systems Uk Ltd
(**Subsidiary of:** Wp Ag)
Telford Road, Bicester, Oxfordshire OX26 4LD
**Tel:** 01869-243344
**Web:** www.pankl.com
**Reg No:** 3497831 **VAT No:** 705180169
**Estd:** 1998 Private Limited Company
**Line of Business:** General mechanical engineering
**Export Sales:** £4,398,670
**Trading Style:** Northbridge Motorsport
**Issued Capital:** £510,000
**Directors:** G Sarkoezi, S Seidel
**Responsibilities**
**Senior:** Christian Brunner *(Manager)*, Bernd Ekhart *(Manager)*, Michael Neubauer *(Manager)*, Eric Newell *(Head Of Operations)*
**HR:** Carla Constantinou *(Human Resources Manager)*
**Operations:** Eric Newell *(Head Of Operations)*
**Branches:** Pankl Racing Systems Uk Ltd, Unit 16 Viking Road, Wigston, Leicestershire LE18 2BL
**US SIC:** 8911, 3452, 3499, 3714
**UK SIC:** 83701, 31371, 31694, 35300
**Auditors:** Richard Anthony & Co
**Bankers:** National Westminster Bank Plc (51-70-15)

| | 31-12-13 | 31-12-12 | 31-12-11 |
|---|---|---|---|
| TO | 6,519,213 | 7,139,358 | 5,571,650 |
| P/L | 733,567 | 662,802 | 257,821 |
| NW | 644,810 | 6,575 | (555,298) |
| WC | 1,777,143 | 1,530,807 | 1,064,793 |
| Emp. | 65 | 64 | 59 |

DUNS 21-034-0418
## Panks Engineers
7 Sabre Way, Peterborough, Cambridgeshire PE1 5EJ
**Tel:** 01733358989
**Web:** www.panks.co.uk
**Estd:** 2010 Proprietorship
**Line of Business:** Pumps sales and servicing
**Proprietor:** C Pank
**Responsibilities**
**Senior:** Gennaro Poli *(Branch Manager)*
**US SIC:** 5084 **UK SIC:** 61490
**Employees:** 50

DUNS 23-481-2543
## Panmedia Ltd
31 York Rise, Dartmouth Park London, London NW5 1SR
**Tel:** 02072841477 **Fax:** 0171-226-9701
**Web:** www.panmedia.co.uk
**Reg No:** 2815223 **Estd:** 1983 Private Limited Company
**Line of Business:** Activities of exhibition and fair organisers
**Trading Style:** Panmedia
**Issued Capital:** £100
**Director:** F V Wintle
**Co. Secretary:** Miss Juliet May
**US SIC:** 7399 **UK SIC:** 83954

**Auditors:** Brannas

| | 31-07-13 | 31-07-12 | 31-07-11 |
|---|---|---|---|
| TA | 24,390 | 45,124 | 45,721 |
| NW | (6,420) | 625 | 8,292 |
| WC | (8,044) | (692) | 7,368 |

DUNS 77-130-1918
## Panmure Gordon & Co. Plc
One New Change, London EC4M 9AF
**Tel:** 02078862500 **Fax:** 02074-593609
**Web:** www.panmure.com
**Reg No:** 2700769 **Estd:** 1876 Public Limited Company
**Line of Business:** Stockbrokers
**Issued Capital:** £6,183,247
**Directors:** J W Cann, M Katounas, C A Warre, L S Watkins, P Tansey, T H Al-Kawari, P A Wale, E W Warner
**Co. Secretary:** Capita Company Secretarial Servi
**Responsibilities**
**Senior:** Asar Mashkoor *(Manager)*, Shahzad Shahbaz *(Manager)*, Nader Shenouda *(Manager)*, Sarah Wigley *(Manager)*
**HR:** Anita Mason *(Head of Human Resources)*
**US SIC:** 6711 **UK SIC:** 83962
**Auditors:** KPMG Audit PLC
**Bankers:** Lloyds TSB Bank plc (30-98-71)

| | 31-12-13 | 31-12-12 | 31-12-11 |
|---|---|---|---|
| TO | 29,367,000 | 21,223,000 | 40,477,000 |
| P/L | 1,167,000 | 595,000 | (28,560,000) |
| NW | 18,276,000 | 18,091,000 | 23,818,000 |
| WC | 15,041,000 | 14,097,000 | 17,642,000 |
| Emp. | 128 | 112 | 232 |

DUNS 39-706-2399
## Pannells Financial Planning Ltd
**(Subsidiary of:** Pannells Llp)
20 Farringdon Road, London EC1M 3AP
**Tel:** 020-7065-0000 **Fax:** 02070650650
**Web:** www.pkf.co.uk
**Reg No:** 2158849 **Estd:** 1990 Private Limited Company
**Line of Business:** Other business activities not elsewhere classified
**Trading Style:** Pkf Financial Planning Limited
**Issued Capital:** £1,000,000
**Directors:** A B Davison, T J Entwistle, F Williamson, M J Gill, M R Goodchild
**Co. Secretary:** Graham Betts
**Responsibilities**
**Senior:** Richard Bint *(Director)*
**Branches:** Pannells Financial Planning Limited, Pannell Houseclifton Downlitfiel, Bristol, Avon BS8 3LX
**US SIC:** 7399 **UK SIC:** 83954
**Auditors:** McLay, McAlister & McGibbon LLP
**Bankers:** Bank Of Scotland (80-02-77)

| | 31-03-14 | 31-03-13 | 31-03-12 |
|---|---|---|---|
| TO | 4,393,771 | 4,623,740 | 4,483,683 |
| P/L | 229,812 | 283,663 | (212,338) |
| NW | 970,562 | 791,346 | 284,120 |
| WC | 804,899 | 658,559 | 367,142 |
| Emp. | 57 | 59 | 59 |

DUNS 22-860-4799
## Pannone & Partners
Ollerbarrow House, 209-211 Ashley Road, Altrincham, Cheshire WA15 9SQ
**Tel:** 01619261960
**Web:** www.pannone.com
**Estd:** 1844 Partnership
**Line of Business:** Solicitors
**Partners:** S R Grant, V O'Farrell, R Pannone, C R Fozard, Ms C E Jones, Ms B Wilkins, S W Lister, J Kitchinmen
**Responsibilities**
**Senior:** Robert Ashworth *(Partner)*, Christine Bradley *(Partner)*, Joy Kingsley *(Partner)*, Anthony Lyons *(Partner)*, Andrew Simkin *(Partner)*, C Tattam *(Partner)*
**US SIC:** 8111 **UK SIC:** 83500
**Bankers:** Bank Of Scotland (12-08-95)
**Employees:** 550

DUNS 23-694-1279
## Panoply Group Ltd
Bond House, Hardwick Road, Great Gransden, Sandy, Bedfordshire SG19 3BJ
**Tel:** 01767-676130
**Web:** www.thepanoply.com
**Reg No:** 3688988 **Estd:** 1998 Private Limited Company
**Line of Business:** Management activities of other non-financial holding companies not elsewhere classified
**Issued Capital:** £3,647,114
**Directors:** T A Pickford, K Mellor
**Co. Secretary:** Mrs Ann Mellor
**Responsibilities**
**Senior:** Bob Edwads *(Manager)*
**Finance:** Des Erwine *(Financial Director)*
**US SIC:** 6711 **UK SIC:** 83962
**Bankers:** National Westminster Bank Plc (60-80-09)

| | 31-12-13 | 31-12-12 | 31-12-11 |
|---|---|---|---|
| TA | 962,484 | 1,097,923 | 1,188,083 |
| NW | (1,647,794) | (1,696,973) | (1,745,942) |
| WC | (1,820,737) | (1,747,707) | (1,738,019) |

DUNS 21-155-1312 **Imp-Exp**
## Panorama Antennas Ltd
61 Frogmore, London SW18 1HF
**Web:** www.panorama-antennas.com
**Reg No:** 1203531 **VAT No:** 217216000
**Estd:** 1975 Private Limited Company
**Line of Business:** Manufacture of radio and electronic capital goods
**Export Markets:** Worldwide
**Export Sales:** £6,188,194
**Issued Capital:** £1,437
**Principals:** A P Jesman *(Managing)*, Ms S C Jesman, Mrs V L Wilson, J L Jesman, R A Jesman, M E Jesman
**Co. Secretary:** Christopher Jesman
**Responsibilities**
**Senior:** Irena Jesman *(Chairman of the Board and Dire)*
**Sales:** Ken Pattison *(Sales Manager)*
**HR:** Pravina Joshi *(Human Resources Manager)*
**Purchasing:** Arvin Parmar *(Purchasing Manager)*
**US SIC:** 3662, 3999
**UK SIC:** 34430, 49590
**Auditors:** Agn Shipleys
**Bankers:** Barclays Bank Plc (20-30-19)

| | 31-12-13 | 31-12-12 | 31-12-12 |
|---|---|---|---|
| TO | 7,703,569 | 6,544,887 | 7,442,936 |
| P/L | 16,125 | 15,377 | 110,104 |
| NW | 1,498,544 | 1,597,183 | 1,537,324 |
| WC | 1,674,822 | 1,738,590 | 1,839,855 |
| Emp. | 66 | 62 | 57 |

DUNS 22-855-4861
## Panorama Furnishing Mart Ltd
**(Subsidiary of:** Panorama Kitchens (Holdings) Ltd)
11 Belmont Road, Liverpool, Merseyside L6 5BG
**Tel:** 0151-260-7749
**Web:** www.panoramakitchens.co.uk
**Reg No:** 1628124 **VAT No:** 387217331
**Estd:** 1979 Private Limited Company
**Line of Business:** Manufacture of other kitchen furniture
**Trading Style:** Panorama Kitchens
**Issued Capital:** £1,100
**Managing Director:** R S Rotheram
**Responsibilities**
**Senior:** Sandra Driscoll *(Finance Director)*, Susan Rotheram *(Manager)*
**Finance:** Sandra Driscoll *(Finance Director)*, Susan Rotheram *(Manager)*
**Admin:** Diane Wells *(Office Manager)*
**HR:** Diane Wells *(Office Manager)*
**Health & Safety:** Diane Wells *(Office Manager)*
**Branches:** Panorama Furnishing Mart Ltd, 357 Woodchurch Rd, Birkenhead, Merseyside CH42 8PE
**US SIC:** 2599, 5719
**UK SIC:** 46720, 64700
**Bankers:** National Westminster Bank Plc (60-13-19)

| | 31-12-13 | 31-12-12 | 31-12-11 |
|---|---|---|---|
| TA | 2,455,621 | 2,204,900 | 1,872,716 |
| NW | 823,599 | 470,354 | 490,638 |
| WC | 4,653 | (284,809) | (254,212) |

DUNS 23-689-7612
## The Panoramic Management Co Ltd
152 Grosvenor Road, London SW1V 3JL
**Tel:** 02079329470
**Web:** www.panoramicmanagement.co.uk
**Reg No:** 3684701 **Estd:** 1998 Private Limited Company
**Line of Business:** Management of real estate on a fee or contract basis
**Directors:** L Feinstein, T D Gill
**Co. Secretary:** Douglas Lovatt
**Responsibilities**
**Senior:** Esme Wood *(Manager)*
**US SIC:** 6531 **UK SIC:** 83400
**Employees:** 70

DUNS 23-623-1577
## Panteg Nursing Home
Wern Road, Sebastopol, Pontypool, Gwent NP4 5DT
**Tel:** 08714232604
**Web:** www.summerhillgroup.co.uk
**Estd:** 2013 Partnership
**Line of Business:** Nursing homes
**Partners:** F Childs, Ms B A Childs
**Responsibilities**
**Senior:** Alex Kelleher *(Director Of Nursing)*
**US SIC:** 8051 **UK SIC:** 95100
**Bankers:** Barclays Bank Plc (20-60-58)
**Employees:** 50

DUNS 51-986-1850
## Pantek Ltd
Unit 1 Oakfield Road, Cheadle, Cheshire SK8 3GX
**Tel:** 01614954640 **Fax:** 0161-495-4690
**Web:** www.solutionspt.com
**Reg No:** 3353540 **Estd:** 1997 Private Limited Company
**Line of Business:** Management activities of holding companies
**Export Sales:** £3,284,012
**Issued Capital:** £5,000
**Directors:** Ms C Bailey, J E Bailey
**Co. Secretary:** Oakwood Corporate Secretary Limi
**US SIC:** 6711 **UK SIC:** 83962
**Auditors:** Chadwick

| | 31-08-14 | 31-08-13 | 31-08-12 |
|---|---|---|---|
| TO | 12,667,651 | 11,910,435 | 11,722,769 |
| P/L | 1,367,826 | 1,360,828 | 1,022,259 |
| NW | 3,436,972 | 2,800,065 | 1,788,896 |
| WC | 3,384,157 | 2,645,386 | 1,970,263 |
| Emp. | 98 | 96 | 76 |

DUNS 22-282-6211
## Pantheon Financial Ltd
Springfield House, 76 Wellington Street, Leeds, West Yorkshire LS1 2AY
**Web:** www.pantheonfinancialinvestments.co.uk
**Reg No:** 4300595 **Estd:** 2001 Private Limited Company
**Line of Business:** Management activities of holding companies
**Issued Capital:** £488,919
**Directors:** D P Sharp, J C Kaberry, R J Price, C R Rose
**Responsibilities**
**Finance:** Hugh Phillips-Baker *(Financial Director)*
**IT:** Lee Line *(IT Manager)*
**US SIC:** 6711 **UK SIC:** 83962
**Auditors:** Deloitte & Touche LLP

| | 31-12-13 | 31-12-12 | 31-12-11 |
|---|---|---|---|
| TO | 7,110,349 | 8,090,097 | 8,994,746 |
| P/L | 33,705 | (537,417) | (763,472) |
| NW | 1,262,610 | 794,391 | 651,724 |
| WC | (762,738) | (1,010,988) | 359,525 |
| Emp. | 64 | 68 | 76 |

DUNS 22-718-6350
## Pantheon Hotels & Leisure Ltd
**(Subsidiary of:** S N B Holdings Ltd)
West End Road, Ruislip, Middlesex HA4 6JB
**Tel:** 01895636057
**Web:** www.hotels.uk.com
**Reg No:** 1566794 **VAT No:** 340828756
**Estd:** 1981 Private Limited Company
**Line of Business:** Restaurants
**Trading Style:** Pantheon Hotels & Leisure Ltd
**Issued Capital:** £100
**Directors:** S Bhattessa, Ms S G Bhattessa
**Co. Secretary:** Kathirgamathamby Jegeswaran
**Branches:** Pantheon Hotels & Leisure Ltd, 60 Hyde Park Gate, London SW7 5BB
**US SIC:** 7011 **UK SIC:** 66500
**Auditors:** Helmores
**Bankers:** Barclays Bank Plc (20-20-37)

| | 31-03-14 | 31-03-13 | 31-03-12 |
|---|---|---|---|
| TO | 4,854,644 | 4,886,464 | 4,738,752 |
| P/L | 238,552 | 342,316 | 341,516 |
| NW | 10,184,270 | 10,105,718 | 9,787,402 |
| WC | (912,810) | (702,968) | (842,730) |
| Emp. | 133 | 134 | 128 |

DUNS 29-849-3867 **Imp**
## Pantheon Ventures Ltd
**(Subsidiary of:** Affiliated Managers Group Inc.)
Norfolk House, 31 St James's Square, London SW1Y 4JR
**Tel:** 020-7484-6200
**Web:** www.pantheonventures.com
**Reg No:** 2052746 **Estd:** 1986 Private Limited Company
**Line of Business:** Financial services
**Directors:** D M Billings, D A Maines
**Co. Secretary:** David Billings
**Responsibilities**
**Senior:** Robert Amis *(Partner)*, Alastair Bruce *(Financial Director)*, Helen Steers *(Manager)*, Frederick Swire *(Manager)*
**Finance:** Alastair Bruce *(Financial Director)*
**HR:** Rena Makadia *(Human Resources Officer)*
**Health & Safety:** Marie Ellenbroek *(Health & Safety Officer)*
**Facilities:** Steve Scarff *(Buildings Manager)*
**US SIC:** 6111, 6371
**UK SIC:** 81501, 82002
**Auditors:** PricewaterhouseCoopers LLP
**Bankers:** The Royal Bank Of Scotland Plc (15-10-00)
**Employees:** 81

DUNS 52-032-9756
## Panther 1919 Ltd
Unit 17, Hallgrove Farm, Grove End, Bagshot, Surrey GU19 5HY
**Tel:** 01276470300
**Web:** www.wooldridgegroup.co.uk
**Reg No:** 3399391 **Estd:** 1997 Private Limited Company
**Line of Business:** Management activities of holding companies
**Trading Style:** Wooldridge Group
**Issued Capital:** £25,000
**Directors:** G Wooldridge, P Merry, Ms J Thomas, Brigadier A Parker Bowles
**Co. Secretary:** Peter Merry
**Responsibilities**
**Finance:** Heather Gash *(Accountant Manager)*, Robin Mills *(Group Financial Controller)*
**Sales:** Natalie Ferreira *(Compliance Coordinator)*, Vince Padbury *(Senior Commercial Manager)*, Charlie Wooldridge *(Group Commercial Director)*
**IT:** Matt Hindmarch *(IT Assistant)*
**Operations:** Nick Anderson *(Demolition Director)*, Sophie Bowsher *(Projects Coordinator)*, Steve Bryne *(Senior Groundwork's Manager)*, Nobby Grimes *(Senior Groundwork's Manager)*
**Fleet:** Duncan Hartnell *(Transport Manager)*
**US SIC:** 6711, 6111
**UK SIC:** 83962, 81501
**Auditors:** Grant Thornton
**Bankers:** HSBC Bank plc (40-20-06)

| | 31-01-14 | 31-01-13 | 31-01-12 |
|---|---|---|---|
| TA | 10,398,199 | 10,099,704 | 8,910,688 |
| P/L | 82,372 | (65,357) | 1,095 |
| NW | 946,352 | 884,382 | 950,815 |
| WC | (952,639) | (693,916) | (574,571) |
| Emp. | 98 | 102 | 114 |

DUNS 21-750-8795
## Panther Platform Rentals Ltd
**(Subsidiary of:** Lavendon Group Plc)
Premier Business Park, Luton, Bedfordshire LU3 3HP
**Tel:** 08448560004 **Fax:** 01582-578080
**Web:** www.platform-rentals.co.uk
**Reg No:** 1360853 **VAT No:** 301890186
**Estd:** 1998 Private Limited Company
**Line of Business:** Renting of other machinery and equipment not elsewhere classified
**Issued Capital:** £175
**Director:** D T Kenny
**Co. Secretary:** Alan Merrell
**Branches:** Panther Platform Rentals Ltd, Unit 2D, Pearsall Drive, Oldbury, West Midlands B69 2RA
**US SIC:** 7394 **UK SIC:** 84000
**Auditors:** Bentley Jennison
**Bankers:** National Westminster Bank Plc (60-07-08)

| | 31-12-13 | 31-12-12 | 31-12-11 |
|---|---|---|---|
| TO | N/A | 1,851,000 | 24,166,000 |
| P/L | 286,000 | 676,000 | 4,103,000 |
| NW | 11,539,000 | 11,319,000 | 10,632,000 |
| WC | 11,539,000 | 11,319,000 | (5,691,000) |
| Emp. | N/A | 12 | 157 |

DUNS 21-627-4652
## Panther Warehousing Plc
Lodge Way Lodge Way, Lodge Farm Industrial Estate, Northampton, Northamptonshire NN5 7US
**Tel:** 01788823656
**Web:** www.panthergroup.co.uk
**Reg No:** 7068367 **Estd:** 2009 Public Limited Company
**Line of Business:** Freight transport by road not elsewhere classified
**Issued Capital:** £83,333
**Directors:** C Mccarthy, S W George, R E Bungey, W Barrett
**Co. Secretary:** Simon George
**US SIC:** 4213 **UK SIC:** 72300
**Bankers:** Lloyds TSB Bank plc (30-97-17)

| | 31-12-13 | 31-12-12 | 31-12-11 |
|---|---|---|---|
| TO | 12,910,594 | 7,582,836 | 820,755 |
| P/L | 917,026 | 39,611 | 15,579 |
| NW | 558,291 | (348,716) | 62,781 |
| WC | (755,005) | (409,823) | 57,393 |
| Emp. | 74 | N/A | N/A |

DUNS 22-117-1825
## Pantherella Ltd
**(Subsidiary of:** H J Hall Ltd)
Hallaton Street, Leicester, Leicestershire LE2 8QY
**Tel:** 01162-831111
**Web:** www.pantherella.co.uk
**Reg No:** 4136274 **VAT No:** 876320414
**Estd:** 2001 Private Limited Company
**Line of Business:** Lingerie retail
**Export Sales:** £2,234,429
**Issued Capital:** £100,000
**Director:** N P Hall
**Co. Secretary:** Mrs Kim Hall
**Responsibilities**
**Senior:** Justin Hall *(Chief Executive Officer)*, Lesley Turland *(Production Manager)*

**Finance:** Nina Daws *(Financial Manager)*
**IT:** Kelly Cosgrove *(IT Manager)*
**Purchasing:** Lesley Turland *(Production Manager)*
**Engineering:** Lesley Turland *(Production Manager)*
**US SIC:** 5621 **UK SIC:** 64500
**Bankers:** Bank Of Scotland (12-08-81)

| | 30-04-14 | 30-06-13 | 30-04-12 |
|---|---|---|---|
| TO | 3,610,428 | 4,059,078 | 4,482,323 |
| P/L | 128,302 | (2,321) | (43,900) |
| NW | 1,077,725 | 950,923 | 944,935 |
| WC | 2,090,090 | 1,859,055 | 1,994,701 |
| Emp. | 94 | 95 | 101 |

DUNS 50-655-6885
### Pantry Fayre
298 Bradford Road, Batley, West Yorkshire WF17 5PW
**Tel:** 01924-420950
**Web:** www.pantryfayre.co.uk
**Estd:** 2002 Proprietorship
**Line of Business:** Take away meal outlets
**Proprietor:** Mrs M Miller
**US SIC:** 5812 **UK SIC:** 66110
**Employees:** 50

DUNS 21-775-6623
### Papa G's
Unit 15 The Printworks, 27 Withy Grove, Manchester M4 2BS
**Tel:** 01618348668
**Web:** www.papags.co.uk
**Estd:** 2011 Proprietorship
**Line of Business:** Licensed restaurants
**Proprietor:** A Gabrilatsou
**Responsibilities**
**HR:** Danny Fong *(Purchasing Director)*
**US SIC:** 5812 **UK SIC:** 66110
**Employees:** 50

DUNS 76-537-1075
### Papa John's (Gb) Ltd
(**Subsidiary of:** Papa John's International Inc.)
The Forum, Chertsey, Surrey KT16 9JX
**Tel:** 01926888321
**Web:** www.papajohns.co.uk
**Reg No:** 2569801 **Estd:** 2012 Private Limited Company
**Line of Business:** Cafes and snack bars
**Export Sales:** £935,000
**Issued Capital:** £14
**Directors:** J H Swaysland, L F Tucker, G B Davies
**Responsibilities**
**Senior:** Gurneik Singh *(Proprietor)*
**Finance:** Barry Rodnight *(Financial Director)*
**Facilities:** Jeremy Peachey *(Estates Manager)*
**Branches:** Papa John's (Gb) Ltd, Papa Johns, 4 The Valley Shopping Village Villages, Gateshead, Tyne and Wear NE11 0EN
**US SIC:** 5812 **UK SIC:** 66110
**Auditors:** Ernst & Young LLP
**Bankers:** National Westminster Bahk Plc (60-05-17)

| | 29-12-13 | 30-12-12 | 25-12-11 |
|---|---|---|---|
| TO | 32,724,000 | 28,415,000 | 22,943,000 |
| P/L | 523,000 | 102,000 | (1,028,000) |
| NW | (64,000) | (704,000) | (857,000) |
| WC | (4,313,000) | (4,650,000) | (4,546,000) |
| Emp. | 84 | 69 | 65 |

DUNS 23-881-6172 **Imp**
### Papa John's Pizza Ltd
(**Subsidiary of:** Papa John's International Inc.)
5-6 Hanworth Lane, Chertsey, Surrey KT16 9JX
**Tel:** 02036936800
**Web:** www.papajohns.co.uk
**Reg No:** 3872801 **Estd:** 1999 Private Limited Company
**Line of Business:** Representative office
**Trading Style:** Perfect Pizza
**Issued Capital:** £10,240,445
**Directors:** L F Tucker, G B Davies, J H Swaysland
**Branches:** Papa John's Pizza Ltd, 62 Thornhill Park Road, Southampton, Hampshire SO18 5TQ
**US SIC:** 6711 **UK SIC:** 83962
**Auditors:** Ernst & Young LLP

| | 29-12-13 | 30-12-12 | 25-12-11 |
|---|---|---|---|
| TA | 11,324,000 | 11,324,000 | 11,324,000 |
| NW | 2,340,000 | 2,340,000 | 2,340,000 |

DUNS 21-920-2348
### Paper Chain (East Anglia) Ltd
(**Subsidiary of:** Tesco Plc)
125 London Road, Benfleet, Essex SS7 5UH
**Tel:** 01268758611 **Fax:** 01543-361073
**Reg No:** 0256555 **VAT No:** 287752901
**Estd:** 1931 Private Limited Company
**Line of Business:** Newsagents
**Trading Style:** Paper Shops, Village Store, Paper Chain
**Issued Capital:** £5,005,000
**Directors:** A W Reed, Tesco Services Limited
**Co. Secretary:** Mark Everitt
**Branches:** Paper Chain (East Anglia) Ltd, Exchange Ho, Exchange Sq, Beccles, Suffolk NR34 9HH
**US SIC:** 5942 **UK SIC:** 65300
**Bankers:** Barclays Bank Plc (20-62-53)

| | 22-02-14 | 23-02-13 | 25-02-12 |
|---|---|---|---|
| TA | 4,842,000 | 4,842,000 | 4,842,000 |
| NW | 4,842,000 | 4,842,000 | 4,842,000 |

DUNS 29-669-1538 **Imp**
### The Paper Company Ltd
(**Subsidiary of:** Paperlinx Limited)
Unit 1, London SE1 5SP
**Web:** www.paperco.co.uk
**Reg No:** 1995271 **VAT No:** 554500560
**Estd:** 1986 Private Limited Company
**Line of Business:** Wholesale of other intermediate products
**Export Sales:** £1,987,000
**Trading Style:** Donald Murray Paper, Masons Paper, Southern Paper, Paperlinx
**Issued Capital:** £86,567,022
**Directors:** Mrs G Mccolm, J W Smallenbroek, M Siwak
**Co. Secretary:** Mrs Michelle Brightman
**Responsibilities**
**Senior:** Marc Jacobs *(Director)*
**HR:** Sally Currie *(Human Resources Director)*
**Branches:** The Paper Company Limited, Island Housc, 1 Bluestem Road, Ransomes Industrial Estate, Ipswich, Suffolk IP3 9RR
**US SIC:** 5199 **UK SIC:** 61900
**Auditors:** KPMG LLP

| | 30-06-13 | 30-06-12 | 30-06-11 |
|---|---|---|---|
| TO | 234,908,000 | 273,329,000 | 296,720,000 |
| P/L | (6,018,000) | (3,890,000) | 1,310,000 |
| NW | 100,149,000 | 106,173,000 | 107,876,000 |
| WC | 99,121,000 | 105,626,000 | 106,658,000 |
| Emp. | 360 | 361 | 383 |

DUNS 67-215-6502 **Imp**
### Paper Island Ltd
5 Denby Way, Hellaby, Rotherham, South Yorkshire S66 8HR
**Tel:** 01709730700
**Web:** www.historyheraldry.com
**Reg No:** 6023474 **Estd:** 2000 Private Limited Company
**Line of Business:** Distribution service providers
**Export Sales:** £3,853,959
**Issued Capital:** £49,698
**Directors:** Ms D Clothier, M C Ogg
**Co. Secretary:** Miss Amanda Hill
**Responsibilities**
**Senior:** Christine Daniels *(Manager)*, Darryl Hudspeth *(Manager)*
**Admin:** Kay Waters *(Manager)*
**US SIC:** 4712 **UK SIC:** 77002
**Auditors:** Allotts

| | 31-12-13 | 31-12-12 | 31-12-11 |
|---|---|---|---|
| TO | 7,620,880 | 7,067,734 | 8,646,167 |
| P/L | (210,742) | 44,287 | 788,333 |
| NW | 496,741 | 712,337 | 667,516 |
| WC | 461,854 | 675,874 | 545,152 |
| Emp. | 50 | 47 | 52 |

DUNS 21-223-3950
### Paper Mill
Pilsworth Road, Bury, Lancashire BL9 8RP
**Tel:** 0161-7679504
**Web:** www.thespiritgroup.com
**Estd:** 2001 Proprietorship
**Line of Business:** Public house
**Proprietor:** G Campbell
**Responsibilities**
**Senior:** Dave Fowler *(General Manager)*
**Health & Safety:** Dave Fowler *(General Manager)*
**Facilities:** Dave Fowler *(General Manager)*
**US SIC:** 5813 **UK SIC:** 66200
**Employees:** 46

DUNS 21-680-8907
### Paper Planet Ltd
(**Subsidiary of:** Pearce Holdings St Albans Ltd)
Pearce House, St Albans, Hertfordshire AL4 0JY
**Tel:** 01727-861522 **Fax:** 01727737691
**Web:** www.pearce-recycling.co.uk
**Reg No:** 0707428 **Estd:** 1997 Private Limited Company
**Line of Business:** Wholesale of waste and scrap
**Trading Style:** Pearce Recycling
**Issued Capital:** £20,200
**Directors:** Ms S Jones, A C Berridge, S M Pearce
**Co. Secretary:** Niall Blackwell
**Responsibilities**
**Senior:** Edgar Pearce *(Manager)*
**US SIC:** 5093, 4953
**UK SIC:** 62200, 92110
**Auditors:** Hillier Hopkins LLP
**Bankers:** Barclays Bank Plc (20-74-09)

| | 31-03-14 | 31-03-13 | 31-03-12 |
|---|---|---|---|
| TA | 104,055 | 20,200 | 20,200 |
| NW | (288,985) | 20,200 | 20,200 |
| WC | (288,985) | N/A | N/A |

DUNS 21-879-2648
### Paper Round
Unit 38-39 Juliet Way, Purfleet Industrial Park, Aveley, South Ockendon, Essex RM15 4YA
**Tel:** 02074422202
**Web:** www.paper-round.co.uk
**Estd:** 2012
**Line of Business:** Recycling
**Responsibilities**
**Senior:** Nigel O'dell *(Operations Manager)*
**US SIC:** 3031 **UK SIC:** 48123
**Employees:** 120

DUNS 45-835-1947 **Imp**
### Paperchase Products Ltd
(**Subsidiary of:** Paperchase Worldwide Holdings Ltd)
12 Alfred Place, London WC1E 7EB
**Tel:** 02074676200 **Fax:** 020-7636-1322
**Web:** www.paperchaseproducts.co.uk
**Reg No:** 3185938 **Estd:** 2010 Private Limited Company
**Line of Business:** Stationery suppliers
**Export Sales:** £641,000
**Issued Capital:** £100,000
**Directors:** R J Warden, D P Bateman, Earl T Melgund
**Co. Secretary:** Kevin Heath
**Responsibilities**
**IT:** Gary Moodie *(IT Manager)*, Kirsty Willey *(IT Manager)*
**Health & Safety:** Kelly Warmbold *(Retail Operations Manager)*
**Facilities:** Kelly Warmbold *(Retail Operations Manager)*
**Branches:** Paperchase Products Ltd, Unit 3 Jubilee Place, 45 Bank Street, London E14 5NY
**US SIC:** 5942, 5999
**UK SIC:** 65300, 65600
**Auditors:** Ernst & Young LLP
**Bankers:** National Westminster Bank Plc (60-12-02)

| | 01-02-14 | 02-02-13 | 28-02-12 |
|---|---|---|---|
| TO | 95,849,000 | 84,891,000 | 77,590,000 |
| P/L | 741,000 | 629,000 | 846,000 |
| NW | 20,758,000 | 20,195,000 | 19,730,000 |
| WC | 2,878,000 | 4,277,000 | 4,680,000 |
| Emp. | 1,733 | 1,539 | 1,440 |

DUNS 73-434-2145
### Paperlinx Services (Europe) Ltd
(**Subsidiary of:** Paperlinx Limited)
Huntsman House, Mansion Close, Moulton Park Industrial Estate, Northampton, Northamptonshire NN3 6RU
**Tel:** 07541556133
**Web:** www.imperialexpresslimited.com
**Reg No:** 4707150 **Estd:** 2003 Private Limited Company
**Line of Business:** Management activities of holding companies
**Issued Capital:** £100
**Directors:** M Siwak, J W Smallenbroek, Mrs G Mccolm
**Co. Secretary:** Mrs Michelle Brightman
**US SIC:** 6711 **UK SIC:** 83962

| | 30-06-13 | 30-06-12 | 30-06-11 |
|---|---|---|---|
| TO | 51,087,000 | 41,990,685 | 43,470,917 |
| P/L | (2,766,000) | (1,871,897) | (4,917,758) |
| NW | 12,280,000 | 15,129,691 | 16,759,795 |
| WC | 12,615,000 | 15,169,000 | 15,767,914 |
| Emp. | 549 | 482 | 528 |

DUNS 23-617-7044
### Papplewick
Windsor Road, Ascot, Berkshire SL5 7LH
**Tel:** 01344621488
**Web:** www.papplewick.org.uk
**Estd:** 2012
**Line of Business:** Schools (independent)
**Responsibilities**
**Senior:** Tom Bunbury *(Headmaster)*
**US SIC:** 8211 **UK SIC:** 93200
**Employees:** 60

DUNS 21-042-9869
### Papworth Hospital Nhs Foundation Trust
Papworth Everard, Cambridge, Cambridgeshire CB2 3RE
**Tel:** 01480-830-541
**Web:** www.papworth-hospital.org.uk
**Estd:** 1917
**Line of Business:** Hospitals
**Trading Style:** Papworth Hospital
**Principals:** R Burgin *(Chairman)*, Ms J Payling *(Financial)*, Ms E Horne *(Personnel)*, Mrs C Tripp, S Bridge, J Lodge, Mrs A Bailey, A Bradley
**Responsibilities**
**Senior:** Nicola Mullan *(Non Executive Member)*, Howard Rolfe *(Non Executive Member)*
**IT:** Richard Bowes *(IT Manager)*
**Branches:** Papworth Hospital Nhs Foundation Trust, Ermine Street, Papworth Everard, Cambridge, Cambridgeshire CB23 8RE
**US SIC:** 9121, 8062, 6732
**UK SIC:** 91110, 95100, 83100
**Auditors:** PricewaterhouseCoopers LLP

| | 31-03-14 | 31-03-13 | 31-03-12 |
|---|---|---|---|
| TO | 128,519,000 | 123,587,000 | 118,429,000 |
| P/L | 5,334,000 | 8,022,000 | 6,450,000 |
| NW | 102,492,000 | 85,064,000 | 80,172,000 |
| WC | 34,675,000 | 29,739,000 | 21,271,000 |
| Emp. | 1,705 | 1,612 | 1,567 |

DUNS 21-601-4000
### Papworth Trust
Papworth Everard, Cambridge, Cambridgeshire CB23 3RG
**Tel:** 08009525000
**Web:** www.papworth.org.uk
**Estd:** 1917 Proprietorship
**Line of Business:** Charities and charitable organisations
**Proprietor:** A Bagg
**US SIC:** 8699 **UK SIC:** 96902
**Employees:** 100

DUNS 21-922-9994 **Exp**
### The Papworth Trust
Bernard Sunley Building, Cambridge, Cambridgeshire CB2 3RG
**Tel:** 01502531872
**Web:** www.papworth.org.uk
**Reg No:** 0148906 **Estd:** 1915 Private Company Limited By Guarantee
**Line of Business:** Construction of domestic buildings
**Export Markets:** Japan, U.S.A.
**Trading Style:** Papworth Trust
**Directors:** D J Ogilvy, A R Dixon, Ms S J Mitchell, Ms D M Sorkin, W P Cuell, P L Agar, Mrs J M Womack, G R Burnand
**Co. Secretary:** Antony Osborne
**Responsibilities**
**Senior:** Jill Millns *(Director)*
**Branches:** The Papworth Trust, Bridgets Trust, Tennis Court Rd, Cambridge, Cambridgeshire CB2 1QF
**US SIC:** 1522, 7399, 7361, 8321
**UK SIC:** 50100, 83954, 96111
**Auditors:** Grant Thornton UK LLP
**Bankers:** Barclays Bank Plc (20-17-19)

| | 31-03-14 | 31-03-13 | 31-03-12 |
|---|---|---|---|
| TO | 22,411,000 | 19,476,000 | 19,970,000 |
| P/L | (301,000) | (330,000) | 297,000 |
| NW | 24,614,000 | 25,187,000 | 24,822,000 |
| WC | (910,000) | (653,000) | (485,000) |
| Emp. | 730 | 416 | 525 |

DUNS 21-925-9975 **Imp-Exp**
### Par Jewellery Company Ltd
13-21 Vittoria Street, Birmingham, West Midlands B1 3ND
**Tel:** 0121-233-1705 **Fax:** 01212366704
**Web:** www.jewellery-innovation.co.uk
**Reg No:** 1484765 **VAT No:** 338157349
**Estd:** 1973 Private Limited Company
**Line of Business:** Manufacturers and repair of jewellery
**Export Markets:** U S A; Republic of Ireland
**Trading Style:** Par Jewellery Company Ltd
**Issued Capital:** £60,000
**Principals:** A J Mcleish *(Managing)*, S A Mcleish
**Co. Secretary:** Ms Janet Mcleish
**US SIC:** 3911 **UK SIC:** 49101
**Auditors:** Sadler Samson
**Bankers:** HSBC Bank plc (40-11-36)

| | 31-05-14 | 31-05-13 | 31-05-12 |
|---|---|---|---|
| TA | 1,168,839 | 1,286,861 | 1,531,444 |
| NW | 386,918 | 348,272 | 320,558 |
| WC | 367,977 | 334,238 | 302,531 |

DUNS 73-722-6951 **Imp**
### Par-Pak Europe Ltd
37-39 Burners Lane, Kiln Farm, Milton Keynes, Buckinghamshire MK11 3HA
**Tel:** 01908 260 900 **Fax:** 01908 261 900
**Web:** www.parpak.co.uk
**Reg No:** 2919936 **VAT No:** 608775902
**Estd:** 1993 Private Limited Company
**Line of Business:** Manufacture of other plastic products
**Export Sales:** £1,592,064
**Issued Capital:** £100
**Directors:** M Horan, M Evans, M Bettegowda, K A Ingram, M J Christopher
**Co. Secretary:** Philip Sisson
**Responsibilities**
**Senior:** Ali Ebrahim *(Manager)*, Sajjad Ebrahim *(CEO Managing Director)*, Mehboob Ladak *(Manager)*
**IT:** Nigel Gwillims *(Technical Manager)*
**Facilities:** Nigel Gwillims *(Technical Manager)*

**Operations:** Steve Banks (*Production Manager*)
**Purchasing:** Steve Banks (*Production Manager*)
**Engineering:** Steve Banks (*Production Manager*), Nigel Gwillims (*Technical Manager*)
**US SIC:** 3079  **UK SIC:** 48360
**Auditors:** Menzies LLP

|     | 29-03-14 | 06-06-13 | 30-03-12 |
| --- | --- | --- | --- |
| TO | 17,031,069 | 19,974,621 | 18,837,435 |
| P/L | 2,239,750 | (1,743,164) | 1,171,352 |
| NW | 12,028,219 | 10,312,800 | 12,448,348 |
| WC | 8,849,714 | 6,952,734 | 5,382,414 |
| Emp. | 104 | 104 | 100 |

DUNS 34-798-9571
## Parabis Law Llp
21 Riverside Studios, Amethyst Road, Newcastle Business Park, Newcastle-Upon-Tyne, Tyne and Wear NE4 7YL
**Tel:** 08443341287
**Web:** www.argentadjusters.co.uk
**Reg No:** 0315763OC  **VAT No:** 888236377
**Estd:** 2011
**Line of Business:** Accident administration & management services
**Trading Style:** Plexus Law
**Responsibilities**
**Senior:** Stephen Cornfield (*Non-designated Limited Liabili*), Peter Court (*Non-designated Limited Liabili*), Paul De La Porte (*Non-designated Limited Liabili*), Keith Donnelly (*Branch Manager*), Mark Dyson (*Non-designated Limited Liabili*), Daniel Hall (*Non-designated Limited Liabili*), Malcolm Henke (*Non-designated Limited Liabili*), Emma Hockley (*Non-designated Limited Liabili*), Bryn Hodges (*Non-designated Limited Liabili*), Jason Howarth (*Non-designated Limited Liabili*), Claire Mulligan (*Non-designated Limited Liabili*), Kathryn Oldfield (*Non-designated Limited Liabili*), Jarrod Parker (*Non-designated Limited Liabili*), Julie Sleath (*General Manager*)
**Health & Safety:** Joanne Alexander (*Health & Safety Officer*)
**Operations:** Julie Sleath (*General Manager*)
**Branches:** Parabis Law Llp, Plexus Law, 886 The Crescent, Colchester, Essex CO4 9YQ
**US SIC:** 7539  **UK SIC:** 67100
**Auditors:** PKF (UK) LLP
**Bankers:** The Royal Bank Of Scotland Plc (15-00-00)

|     | 31-03-14 | 31-03-13 | 31-03-12 |
| --- | --- | --- | --- |
| TO | 112,325,000 | 101,571,000 | 129,972,000 |
| P/L | 9,004,000 | 9,618,000 | 19,712,000 |
| NW | (17,489,000) | (18,537,000) | (11,655,000) |
| WC | (8,325,000) | (11,106,000) | 24,164,000 |
| Emp. | 1,263 | 1,008 | 1,536 |

DUNS 42-424-2373
## Parabis Ltd
(*Subsidiary of:* Trilliam Holdco Ltd)
Renaissance 12 Dingwall Road, Croydon, Surrey CR0 2NA
**Tel:** 08449844900 **Fax:** 01422322940
**Web:** www.parabisltd.co.uk
**Reg No:** 4411786  **Estd:** 1902 Private Limited Company
**Line of Business:** Financial services
**Issued Capital:** £5,000
**Directors:** J E Powell, Ms K Newton
**Co. Secretary:** Robert Gray
**Responsibilities**
**Senior:** Frances Firmin (*Manager*), Julie Sleath (*Manager*)
**US SIC:** 8111, 6411
**UK SIC:** 83500, 83200

|     | 31-03-14 | 31-03-13 | 31-03-12 |
| --- | --- | --- | --- |
| TO | 19,573,454 | 26,887,020 | 25,738,331 |
| P/L | (1,846,274) | 1,429,927 | 1,598,329 |
| NW | 2,597,478 | 4,397,598 | 3,346,274 |
| WC | 2,371,682 | 3,854,834 | 2,429,287 |
| Emp. | 545 | 637 | 560 |

DUNS 23-421-3309
## Parable Trust Ltd
Primavera, Village Street, Goodworth Clatford, Andover, Hampshire SP11 7QX
**Tel:** 01264338089
**Web:** www.parabletrust.com
**Reg No:** 5603939  **Estd:** 2005 Private Company Limited By Guarantee
**Line of Business:** Holding companies management activities
**Export Sales:** £11,402,000
**Directors:** P W Louis, R A Hume, Rev V E Lorenzo Moreno
**Co. Secretary:** Robert Conway
**US SIC:** 6711  **UK SIC:** 83962

|     | 31-12-13 | 31-12-12 | 31-12-11 |
| --- | --- | --- | --- |
| TO | 17,270,000 | 74,973 | 68,589 |
| P/L | 473,000 | 28,380 | 4,678 |
| NW | 581,000 | 160,676 | 132,296 |
| WC | 5,115,000 | 59,134 | 30,754 |
| Emp. | 136 | N/A | N/A |

DUNS 34-909-3476
## Paradigm Geophysical (U.K.) Ltd
(*Subsidiary of:* Paradigm (Uk) Holding Ltd)
Building C Dukes Court, Duke Street, Woking, Surrey GU21 5BH
**Tel:** 01483-758000 **Fax:** 01483-758001
**Web:** www.pdgm.com
**Reg No:** 2831267  **Estd:** 1993 Private Limited Company
**Line of Business:** Oil and gas exploration services
**Export Sales:** £6,535,897
**Issued Capital:** £2,336,021
**Directors:** A Laurent, S J Brownlee, C S Zunder
**Responsibilities**
**Senior:** Richard Jefferies (*Manager*), Jonathan Keller (*Manager*), Sherrie Palmer (*General Manager*)
**Finance:** Elijio Serrano (*Chief Financial Officer*)
**Marketing:** Sherrie Palmer (*General Manager*)
**Sales:** Robyn Russell-Hughes (*Head of Sales*)
**IT:** Andy Todd (*IT Manager*)
**Health & Safety:** Sherrie Palmer (*General Manager*)
**Facilities:** Sherrie Palmer (*General Manager*)
**US SIC:** 7379  **UK SIC:** 83940
**Auditors:** Ernst & Young
**Bankers:** Barclays Bank Plc (20-71-74)

|     | 31-12-13 | 31-12-12 | 31-12-11 |
| --- | --- | --- | --- |
| TO | 9,094,983 | 10,276,237 | 12,405,357 |
| P/L | 154,503 | (216,465) | 534,521 |
| NW | (236,845) | (257,195) | 691,990 |
| WC | 3,464,099 | 3,117,348 | 434,058 |
| Emp. | 66 | 59 | 59 |

DUNS 23-118-6466
## Paradigm Housing Group Ltd
1 Glory Park Avenue, Wooburn Green, High Wycombe, Buckinghamshire HP10 0DF
**Tel:** 01494830991
**Web:** www.paradigmhousing.co.uk
**Reg No:** 0028844IP  **Estd:** 2000 Private Limited Company
**Line of Business:** Housing associations societies trusts & co-operatives
**Responsibilities**
**Senior:** Alison Hadden (*CEO, Managing Director*)
**Finance:** Andy Nicol (*Senior Finance Administrator*)
**Admin:** Chrissie Barnes (*Executive Assistant*), Sherry Gifford (*Personal Assistant to CEO*)
**IT:** Mike Silk (*Head of IT*)
**HR:** Sarah Bowyer (*Human Resources*)
**US SIC:** 6531  **UK SIC:** 83400
**Auditors:** Grant Thornton UK LLP

|     | 31-03-13 | 31-03-12 | 31-03-11 |
| --- | --- | --- | --- |
| TO | 101,220,000 | 74,842,000 | 77,270,000 |
| P/L | 11,468,000 | 5,177,000 | 3,880,000 |
| NW | 329,202,000 | 296,615,000 | 225,927,000 |
| WC | 48,276,000 | 32,235,000 | 50,680,000 |
| Emp. | 381 | 391 | 396 |

DUNS 52-302-9668
## Paradigm Partners Llp
Brooke Court, Lower Meadow Road, Handforth, Wilmslow, Cheshire SK9 3ND
**Tel:** 08453036333
**Web:** www.paradigmsavings.co.uk
**Reg No:** 0323405OC  **Estd:** 2007 Private Limited Company
**Line of Business:** Financial services
**Responsibilities**
**Senior:** Lothar Mentel (*Non-designated Limited Liabili*), Anthony Murrell (*Non-designated Limited Liabili*), Graeme Nicholson (*Non-designated Limited Liabili*), David Ryder (*Non-designated Limited Liabili*)
**US SIC:** 6111  **UK SIC:** 81501
**Bankers:** Adam & Company Plc (83-75-55)

|     | 30-04-13 | 30-04-12 | 30-04-11 |
| --- | --- | --- | --- |
| TA | 4,960,127 | 4,359,856 | 1,995,646 |
| P/L | 210,166 | 1,170,683 | 939,873 |
| NW | (102,003) | (312,164) | (1,747,905) |
| WC | 332 | 158,211 | (1,819,321) |
| Emp. | 76 | 69 | 50 |

DUNS 73-883-6738                       Imp-Exp
## Paradigm Precision Burnley Ltd
(*Subsidiary of:* Paradigm Burnley Holdings Ltd)
Bentley Wood Way, Hapton, Burnley, Lancashire BB11 5GT
**Tel:** 01282 831199 **Fax:** 01282478843
**Web:** www.paradigmprecision.com
**Reg No:** 5137829  **Estd:** 2004 Private Limited Company
**Line of Business:** Aircraft Engine Parts
**Export Sales:** £15,788,000
**Trading Style:** Unison Engine Components - Burnley
**Issued Capital:** £25,653,816

**Directors:** G Bennett, R B Grochowski, C Q Hughes, I W Bushell
**Co. Secretary:** 7side Secretarial Limited
**Responsibilities**
**Senior:** David Cruise (*Manager*), Nathan Manning (*Manager*), Bruce Mcalister (*Manager*)
**IT:** Steve Oddy (*Senior IT Executive*)
**HR:** Hayley Morris (*Personnel Manager*)
**Health & Safety:** Jonathan Wensley (*Health & Safety Manager*)
**Purchasing:** Nadeem Ayyub (*Purchasing Manager*)
**US SIC:** 3724  **UK SIC:** 36400
**Auditors:** KPMG Audit PLC
**Bankers:** Barclays Bank Plc (20-03-53)

|     | 01-12-13 | 31-12-12 | 31-12-11 |
| --- | --- | --- | --- |
| TO | 36,300,000 | 38,856,000 | 52,955,000 |
| P/L | 1,349,000 | (3,565,000) | 29,923,000 |
| NW | 51,101,000 | 88,389,000 | 91,877,000 |
| WC | 49,485,000 | 86,018,000 | 88,791,000 |
| Emp. | 321 | 334 | 379 |

DUNS 73-288-9014
## Paradigm Secure Communications Ltd
(*Subsidiary of:* Airbus Group N.V.)
Gunnels Wood Road, Stevenage, Hertfordshire SG1 2AS
**Tel:** 01249853555 **Fax:** 01249853800
**Web:** www.paradigmsecure.com
**Reg No:** 4562657  **Estd:** 2002 Private Limited Company
**Line of Business:** Other service activities not elsewhere classified
**Export Sales:** £24,294,000
**Issued Capital:** £1,000
**Directors:** Ms C Masters, E W Dudok, J H Beazley
**Co. Secretary:** Didier Cahn
**Responsibilities**
**Sales:** Ken Hadfield (*Director of UK Business Develo*)
**US SIC:** 8999, 7399
**UK SIC:** 83954
**Auditors:** KPMG LLP

|     | 31-12-13 | 31-12-12 | 31-12-11 |
| --- | --- | --- | --- |
| TO | 381,148,000 | 360,146,000 | 351,878,000 |
| P/L | 10,995,000 | 36,047,000 | 30,353,000 |
| NW | 120,975,000 | 106,356,000 | 75,365,000 |
| WC | (78,820,000) | (80,848,000) | (94,432,000) |
| Emp. | 81 | 86 | 81 |

DUNS 73-298-6125                              Imp
## Paradigm Services Ltd
(*Subsidiary of:* Airbus Group N.V.)
Gunnels Wood Road, Stevenage, Hertfordshire SG1 2AS
**Tel:** 01438282828 **Fax:** 01438-282-828
**Web:** www.paradigmservices.net
**Reg No:** 4572481  **Estd:** 2002 Private Limited Company
**Line of Business:** Other service activities not elsewhere classified
**Export Sales:** £11,415,000
**Issued Capital:** £100
**Directors:** Ms C Masters, P C Bruton
**Co. Secretary:** Didier Cahn
**Responsibilities**
**Senior:** Peter Kershaw (*Manager*)
**US SIC:** 8999  **UK SIC:** 83954
**Auditors:** KPMG LLP

|     | 31-12-13 | 31-12-12 | 31-12-11 |
| --- | --- | --- | --- |
| TO | 176,561,000 | 179,628,000 | 169,196,000 |
| P/L | 16,405,000 | 20,593,000 | 14,529,000 |
| NW | 103,290,000 | 89,811,000 | 74,393,000 |
| WC | 56,930,000 | 48,341,000 | 34,780,000 |
| Emp. | 265 | 247 | 215 |

DUNS 22-533-1289
## Paradise Park Ltd
Lowin House, Tregolls Road, Truro, Cornwall TR1 2NA
**Tel:** 01736751020 **Fax:** 01736-756438
**Web:** www.paradisepark.org.uk
**Reg No:** 0986892  **Estd:** 1978 Private Limited Company
**Line of Business:** Tourist attraction
**Issued Capital:** £2
**Directors:** A J Hales, N S Reynolds
**Co. Secretary:** Ms Audrey Reynolds
**US SIC:** 7999  **UK SIC:** 97913
**Bankers:** HSBC Bank plc (40-20-32)

|     | 31-01-14 | 31-01-13 | 31-01-12 |
| --- | --- | --- | --- |
| NW | (11,429) | (11,429) | (11,429) |

DUNS 23-692-8313
## Paradise Park Wild Life Sanctuary
16 Trelissick Road, Hayle, Cornwall TR27 4HB
**Web:** http://localdirectory.thisiscornwall.co.uk
**VAT No:** 132594472  **Estd:** 1970 Proprietorship
**Line of Business:** Places of interest
**Partners:** Mrs A M Reynolds, N Reynolds, M W Reynolds, Mrs A Hales
**Responsibilities**
**Senior:** Allison Hales (*Director*)
**Finance:** Allison Hales (*Director*)

**US SIC:** 0279, 8421
**UK SIC:** 01001, 97700
**Bankers:** HSBC Bank plc (40-20-32)
**Employees:** 50

DUNS 21-684-3512
## Paradise Primary School Ltd
1 Bretton Street, Dewsbury, West Yorkshire WF12 9BB
**Tel:** 01924439803
**Web:** www.paradiseschool.org.uk
**Reg No:** 7341618  **Estd:** 2010 Private Company Limited By Guarantee
**Line of Business:** Schools (local authority)
**Directors:** A A Patel, I E Dalal
**Co. Secretary:** Abdul Patel
**Responsibilities**
**Senior:** Salna Kadia (*Head Teacher*), Moulana Kola (*Head Teacher*), Najam Sheikh (*Chairman*)
**US SIC:** 8211  **UK SIC:** 93200

|     | 31-08-13 | 31-08-12 |
| --- | --- | --- |
| TA | 115,459 | 35,391 |
| NW | 27,402 | 4,605 |
| WC | 27,402 | 4,605 |

DUNS 71-922-5836
## Parafix Holdings Ltd
Spencer Road, Lancing, West Sussex BN15 8UA
**Tel:** 01903750000
**Reg No:** 5303075  **Estd:** 2004 Private Limited Company
**Line of Business:** Management activities of holding companies
**Export Sales:** £4,486,165
**Issued Capital:** £100,000
**Director:** M A Punter
**Co. Secretary:** Colin Wills
**US SIC:** 6711  **UK SIC:** 83962
**Bankers:** Lloyds TSB Bank plc (30-00-00)

|     | 31-12-13 | 31-12-12 | 31-12-11 |
| --- | --- | --- | --- |
| TO | 9,103,248 | 8,546,718 | 8,534,834 |
| P/L | 311,695 | 37,065 | (188,498) |
| NW | 1,091,033 | 864,693 | 801,580 |
| WC | (100,060) | (70,478) | (42,374) |
| Emp. | 113 | 97 | 93 |

DUNS 23-684-6619
## Paragon Advance Ltd
Waterberry Drive, Waterlooville, Hampshire PO7 7YH
**Tel:** 08443759604 **Fax:** 08443 759605
**Web:** www.paragonadvance.com
**Reg No:** 3679691  **VAT No:** 880988364
**Estd:** 1998 Private Limited Company
**Line of Business:** Other business activities not elsewhere classified
**Issued Capital:** £101
**Directors:** B R Cole, Ms K Aston
**Co. Secretary:** Ms Sharon Cole
**US SIC:** 7399  **UK SIC:** 83954

|     | 31-12-13 | 31-12-12 | 31-12-11 |
| --- | --- | --- | --- |
| TA | 349,685 | 517,799 | 332,030 |
| NW | 100,461 | 72,489 | 42,781 |
| WC | 100,461 | 72,489 | 42,781 |

DUNS 73-699-8597
## Paragon Automotive Logistics Ltd
Baird Road, Kettering, Northamptonshire NN15 6RX
**Tel:** 01536443161
**Web:** www.paragonautomotive.co.uk
**Reg No:** 4958639  **Estd:** 2003 Private Limited Company
**Line of Business:** Freight forwarders
**Issued Capital:** £100
**Director:** B J Murphy
**Co. Secretary:** Paul Cox
**Responsibilities**
**Senior:** Mike Pilkington (*Manager*)
**Finance:** Ian Holroyd (*Group Finance Controller*)
**Operations:** Steve Maltby (*Operations Director*), Steve Stanger (*Group Operations Director*)
**Fleet:** Jake Mummery (*Group Logistics Director*)
**US SIC:** 4213  **UK SIC:** 72300
**Auditors:** C.R. Neville

|     | 30-11-13 | 30-11-12 | 30-11-11 |
| --- | --- | --- | --- |
| TO | 10,144,557 | 9,056,276 | 8,663,630 |
| P/L | 148,136 | 180,596 | 198,544 |
| NW | 256,645 | 226,294 | 143,790 |
| WC | (515,182) | (626,657) | (650,633) |
| Emp. | 92 | 76 | 67 |

DUNS 34-569-0791
## Paragon Automotive Ltd
Hangar 1, Thurleigh Business Park, Bedford, Bedfordshire MK44 2YP
**Tel:** 01234355075 **Fax:** 01234353158
**Web:** www.paragonautomotive.co.uk
**Reg No:** 5377252  **Estd:** 2005 Private Limited Company
**Line of Business:** Sale of used motor vehicles
**Issued Capital:** £95,000
**Directors:** K Riddle, S C Hucklesby

**Co. Secretary:** Jonathan Tate
**Responsibilities**
**Marketing:** Judy Ward *(Client Relations Director)*
**Operations:** Judy Ward *(Client Relations Director)*
**Branches:** Paragon Automotive Ltd, Kiln Lane, Grimsby, South Humberside DN41 8DQ
**US SIC:** 5521 **UK SIC:** 65100
**Auditors:** Grant Thornton UK LLP
**Bankers:** Lloyds TSB Bank plc (30-00-02)

| | 31-03-14 | 31-03-13 | 31-03-12 |
|---|---|---|---|
| TO | 138,691,000 | 99,286,000 | 84,578,000 |
| P/L | 3,498,000 | 3,128,000 | 4,753,000 |
| NW | 2,262,000 | 478,000 | 7,969,000 |
| WC | 3,051,000 | 3,229,000 | 5,508,000 |
| Emp. | 1,054 | 840 | 812 |

DUNS 21-120-7905
## Paragon Community Housing Group Ltd
Case House, 85-89 High Street, Walton-On-Thames, Surrey KT12 1DZ
**Tel:** 03001232221
**Web:** www.paragonchg.co.uk
**Reg No:** 0030090R **Estd:** 1999 Private Limited Company
**Line of Business:** Housing associations societies trusts & co-operatives
**Responsibilities**
**Senior:** Graham Bellinger *(Manager)*, Jacqueline Hird *(Manager)*, Philip Kabi *(Chief Executive)*, Dilip Kavi *(Chief Executive)*, Anna Sartori *(Manager)*, James Vickers *(Manager)*
**Branches:** Paragon Community Housing Group Ltd, 163 Fulmer Close, Hampton, Middlesex TW12 3YP
**US SIC:** 8699 **UK SIC:** 96902
**Bankers:** The Royal Bank Of Scotland Plc (15-00-00)
**Employees:** 300
**Turnover:** £46,755,000

DUNS 22-193-2630
## Paragon Construction Group Ltd
Unit 1 Paragon House, Ketterer Court, St Helens, Merseyside WA9 3AH
**Tel:** 01744458720
**Web:** www.paragonconstructiongroup.com
**Reg No:** 4211426 **Estd:** 2002 Private Limited Company
**Line of Business:** Residential building contractors
**Issued Capital:** £50
**Principals:** P G Barrow *(Managing)*, N Bamber
**Co. Secretary:** Ms Diane Thomas
**Responsibilities**
**Senior:** Frederick Kenyon *(Proprietor)*
**US SIC:** 1522, 1731
**UK SIC:** 50100, 50300

| | 31-03-14 | 31-03-13 | 31-03-12 |
|---|---|---|---|
| TA | 2,488,878 | 1,797,413 | 1,904,447 |
| NW | 371,595 | 512,696 | 470,209 |
| WC | 324,447 | 468,224 | 432,119 |

DUNS 21-112-6998
## Paragon Education & Skills Group Holdings Ltd
(**Subsidiary of:** Sovereign Capital Limited Partnership Ii)
Station Approach, Ashley Road, Bournemouth, Dorset BH1 4NB
**Tel:** 01202646470 **Fax:** 01202581116
**Web:** www.paragonskills.co.uk
**Reg No:** 6536512 **Estd:** 2008 Private Limited Company
**Line of Business:** Activities of private training providers
**Trading Style:** Paragon Skills for Industry
**Issued Capital:** £2,409
**Directors:** D P Bogg, Ms H J Frankham, M S Thurston, M R Evans, J J Rodriguez Cesenas
**Co. Secretary:** Mark Thurston
**Responsibilities**
**Finance:** Adam Carswell *(Financial Manager)*
**Operations:** stuart prior *(operations director)*
**US SIC:** 8299 **UK SIC:** 93300

| | 31-07-13 | 31-07-12 | 31-07-11 |
|---|---|---|---|
| TO | 13,819,016 | 12,634,778 | 13,767,947 |
| P/L | (2,000,364) | (1,277,236) | (792,068) |
| NW | (10,537,678) | (9,363,736) | (8,890,041) |
| WC | (3,808,783) | (1,928,866) | (1,975,498) |
| Emp. | 300 | 292 | 314 |

DUNS 76-987-4488
## Paragon Electronics Ltd
Wolseley Road, Kempston, Bedford, Bedfordshire MK42 7UP
**Tel:** 01234-840101 **Fax:** 01234840707
**Web:** www.paragon-electronics.com
**Reg No:** 2645657 **Estd:** 1991 Private Limited Company
**Line of Business:** Manufacture of electronic valves and tubes and other electronic components
**Export Sales:** £10,674,701
**Issued Capital:** £45,002
**Directors:** J G Mayes, C M Johnson
**Co. Secretary:** Simon Dabson
**US SIC:** 3679 **UK SIC:** 34542
**Auditors:** KPMG LLP
**Bankers:** Barclays Bank Plc (20-05-74)

| | 30-09-13 | 30-09-12 | 30-09-11 |
|---|---|---|---|
| TO | 28,188,700 | 30,247,570 | 29,231,493 |
| P/L | 500,558 | 963,631 | (173,412) |
| NW | 2,547,250 | 2,118,362 | 1,150,759 |
| WC | 1,609,513 | 1,200,334 | 103,570 |
| Emp. | 334 | 331 | 312 |

DUNS 29-550-7537
## Paragon Finance Plc
(**Subsidiary of:** The Paragon Group of Companies Plc)
Herbert Road, Solihull, West Midlands B91 3QE
**Tel:** 08458494070
**Web:** www.paragon-mortgages.co.uk
**Reg No:** 1917566 **Estd:** 1985 Public Limited Company
**Line of Business:** Credit granting by non-deposit taking finance houses and other specialist consumer credit grantors
**Trading Style:** National Home Loans
**Issued Capital:** £53,446,891
**Principals:** N Keen *(Financial)*, N S Terrington, J A Heron, R D Shelton, J A Harvey, R J Woodman
**Co. Secretary:** Miss Pandora Sharp
**Responsibilities**
**Senior:** John Gemmell *(Manager)*
**Branches:** Paragon Finance Plc, 6-8 Greencoat Place, London SW1P 1PL
**US SIC:** 6111, 7399
**UK SIC:** 81501, 83954
**Auditors:** Deloitte & Touche LLP
**Bankers:** The Hongkong And Shanghai Banking Corporation Ltd (40 48 60)

| | 30-09-13 | 30-09-12 | 30-09-11 |
|---|---|---|---|
| TA | 579,906,000 | 577,527,000 | 481,934,000 |
| P/L | 16,495,000 | 10,463,000 | 5,457,000 |
| NW | 130,684,000 | 117,279,000 | 111,169,000 |
| WC | (4,811,000) | (8,250,000) | (19,067,000) |
| Emp. | 793 | 703 | 628 |

DUNS 76-979-7408
## Paragon Fleet Solutions Ltd
(**Subsidiary of:** Paragon Automotive Ltd)
125 Camp Road Heyford Park, Bicester, Oxfordshire OX25 5HA
**Tel:** 01869-237000
**Web:** www.paragonfleetsolutions.co.uk
**Reg No:** 2638543 **Estd:** 2009 Private Limited Company
**Line of Business:** Fleet management
**Issued Capital:** £500,000
**Directors:** S C Hucklesby, K Riddle
**Co. Secretary:** Jonathan Tate
**Responsibilities**
**Finance:** Andrew Hetzel *(Financial Director)*
**Sales:** Mike Bingham *(Sales Director)*
**Purchasing:** Gary Nailor *(Purchasing Manager)*
**Branches:** Paragon Fleet Solutions Ltd, Estate Road 5, South Humberside Indust Estate, Grimsby, South Humberside DN31 2TG
**US SIC:** 7399 **UK SIC:** 83954
**Auditors:** Grant Thornton UK LLP
**Bankers:** Lloyds TSB Bank plc (30-99-72)

| | 31-03-14 | 31-03-13 | 31-03-12 |
|---|---|---|---|
| TO | 28,949,000 | 28,934,000 | 29,118,000 |
| P/L | 1,380,000 | 595,000 | 1,312,000 |
| NW | 11,594,000 | 10,571,000 | 10,140,000 |
| WC | 11,213,000 | 10,034,000 | 9,490,000 |
| Emp. | 337 | 357 | 373 |

DUNS 71-875-6070
## Paragon Group Ltd
Pallion Trading Estate, Sunderland, Tyne and Wear SR4 6ST
**Tel:** 01915140716 **Fax:** 01915146361
**Web:** www.paragonuk.com
**Reg No:** 5258175 **Estd:** 2004 Private Limited Company
**Line of Business:** Printing not elsewhere classified
**Issued Capital:** £35,000,000
**Directors:** P J Crean, L T Salmon
**Co. Secretary:** Richard Cahill
**US SIC:** 2752 **UK SIC:** 47544
**Auditors:** Ernst & Young LLP
**Bankers:** Barclays Bank Plc (20-59-61)

| | 30-06-13 | 30-06-12 | 30-06-11 |
|---|---|---|---|
| TO | 137,910,000 | 135,957,000 | 165,039,000 |
| P/L | 1,569,000 | (2,891,000) | 1,525,000 |
| NW | 6,995,000 | 6,648,000 | 11,596,000 |
| WC | 12,552,000 | 10,776,000 | 10,109,000 |
| Emp. | 1,294 | 1,369 | 1,328 |

DUNS 23-753-5570
## The Paragon Group of Companies Plc
51 Homer Road, Solihull, West Midlands B91 3QJ
**Tel:** 08458494000 **Fax:** 08458494002
**Web:** www.paragon-group.co.uk
**Reg No:** 2336032 **Estd:** 1989 Public Limited Company
**Line of Business:** Credit granting by non-deposit taking finance houses and other specialist consumer credit grantors
**Issued Capital:** £303,541,614
**Principals:** N S Terrington *(Financial)*, N Keen *(Financial)*, Ms F J Clutterbuck, R J Woodman, J A Heron, A K Fletcher, E A Tilly, R G Dench
**Co. Secretary:** Miss Pandora Sharp
**Responsibilities**
**Senior:** John Gemmell *(Manager)*, Hugh Tudor *(Director)*
**Finance:** John Gemmell *(Manager)*
**Branches:** The Paragon Group Of Companies Plc, 8 St. Catherines Court, Herbert Road, Solihull, West Midlands B91 3QE
**US SIC:** 6111 **UK SIC:** 81501
**Auditors:** Deloitte LLP
**Following financial data are in thousands**

| | 30-09-14 | 30-09-13 | 30-09-12 |
|---|---|---|---|
| TA | 10,895,100 | 10,328,300 | 10,037,100 |
| P/L | 122,800 | 105,400 | 95,500 |
| NW | 939,200 | 864,800 | 794,400 |
| WC | 788,300 | 549,800 | 460,100 |
| Emp. | 933 | 814 | 722 |

DUNS 21-017-2011 **Imp**
## Paragon Group Uk Ltd
(**Subsidiary of:** Paragon Group Limited)
Pallion Trading Estate, Sunderland, Tyne and Wear SR4 6ST
**Tel:** 0191-514-6200 **Fax:** 0191-514-6362
**Web:** www.paragonuk.com
**Reg No:** 0551336 **Estd:** 1955 Private Limited Company
**Line of Business:** Retail sale of books, newspapers and stationery
**Trading Style:** Paragon Group
**Issued Capital:** £6,144,000
**Directors:** P J Crean, L T Salmon
**Co. Secretary:** Richard Cahill
**Responsibilities**
**Senior:** Iain Black *(Manager)*, Phil Constantine *(General Manager)*, Cornelius Donnelly *(Manager)*, Connor Donnelly *(Non-Executive Chairman)*, Ann Harrington *(Commercial Director)*
**Sales:** Ann Harrington *(Commercial Director)*
**Branches:** Paragon Group Uk Limited, Nelson Ho, Park Rd, Altrincham, Cheshire WA14 5BZ
**US SIC:** 5942 **UK SIC:** 65300
**Auditors:** Ernst & Young LLP
**Bankers:** Barclays Bank Plc (20-59-42)

| | 30-06-13 | 30-06-12 | 30-06-11 |
|---|---|---|---|
| TO | 26,742,000 | 32,014,000 | 42,327,000 |
| P/L | (754,000) | 1,721,000 | 84,000 |
| NW | 3,905,000 | 14,269,000 | 14,100,000 |
| WC | (1,728,000) | 8,246,000 | 668,000 |
| Emp. | 297 | 336 | 334 |

DUNS 21-043-9523
## Paragon Hotel
145 Alcester Street, Birmingham, West Midlands B12 0PJ
**Tel:** 0121-627-0627
**Web:** www.theparagonhotel.co.uk
**Estd:** 2001
**Line of Business:** Hotels
**Proprietor:** Mrs B James
**Responsibilities**
**Senior:** Priyanka Hikkaduwa *(Financial Director)*, Peter Hirons *(Senior Marketing Executive)*, Terry McAvoy *(Operations Manager)*, Kelly Philips *(Sales & Marketing Manager)*
**Finance:** Priyanka Hikkaduwa *(Financial Director)*
**Marketing:** Peter Hirons *(Senior Marketing Executive)*, Kelly Philips *(Sales & Marketing Manager)*
**Sales:** Kelly Philips *(Sales & Marketing Manager)*
**Operations:** Terry McAvoy *(Operations Manager)*
**US SIC:** 7011 **UK SIC:** 66500
**Employees:** 80

DUNS 77-484-7768
## Paragon Hotels Ltd
(**Subsidiary of:** Calgarth Ltd)
Conway House, Ackhurst Park, Chorley, Lancashire PR7 1NY
**Tel:** 01257238754 **Fax:** 01257-454369
**Web:** www.paragonhotels.co.uk
**Reg No:** 2971215 **Estd:** 1994 Private Limited Company
**Line of Business:** Holding companies management activities
**Trading Style:** Savill Court Hotel
**Issued Capital:** £2,500,000
**Directors:** C J Hemmings, Miss K Revitt
**Co. Secretary:** John Kay
**Branches:** Paragon Hotels Ltd, Taplow Common Road, Slough, Berkshire SL1 8LR
**US SIC:** 6711, 7392
**UK SIC:** 83962, 83951
**Auditors:** Ernst & Young LLP
**Bankers:** Bank Of Scotland (80-20-00)

| | 31-03-14 | 28-03-13 | 29-03-12 |
|---|---|---|---|
| TO | 28,635,000 | 27,673,000 | 27,652,000 |
| P/L | (2,910,000) | (1,965,000) | (1,901,000) |
| NW | (4,729,000) | (2,482,000) | (893,000) |
| WC | (68,309,000) | (67,778,000) | (24,885,000) |
| Emp. | 558 | 428 | 431 |

DUNS 29-655-6244
## Paragon Interiors Group Plc
Paragon House, Orchard Place, Nottingham, Nottinghamshire NG8 6PX
**Tel:** 01159519514
**Web:** www.paragonplc.com
**Reg No:** 1981976 **VAT No:** 439653224
**Estd:** 1986 Public Limited Company
**Line of Business:** Other construction work involving special trades
**Issued Capital:** £50,000
**Principals:** A Hardy *(Managing)*, G M Dibley, A Sandell
**Co. Secretary:** Alan Hardy
**Responsibilities**
**Senior:** Michael Keown *(Manager)*, Michael Mckeown *(sales Director)*, Howard Thomas *(Manager)*
**Marketing:** Greg Simpson *(Marketing Manager)*
**Sales:** Michael Mckeown *(sales Director)*
**Admin:** Jackie Hardy *(Office Manager)*
**Facilities:** Emma Bailey *(Facilities Manager)*
**US SIC:** 1799 **UK SIC:** 50000
**Auditors:** Parkinson Matthews LLP
**Bankers:** The Royal Bank Of Scotland Plc (10-14-18)

| | 31-03-14 | 31-03-13 | 31-03-12 |
|---|---|---|---|
| TO | 29,316,232 | 23,290,788 | 21,232,379 |
| P/L | 2,142,011 | 527,266 | 155,820 |
| NW | 3,821,665 | 2,201,580 | 1,823,314 |
| WC | 3,696,243 | 2,168,021 | 1,932,026 |
| Emp. | 59 | 63 | 70 |

DUNS 45-872-8888
## Paragon International Insurance Brokers Ltd
(**Subsidiary of:** Paragon International Holdings Ltd)
140 Leadenhall Street, London EC3V 4QT
**Tel:** 02072808200 **Fax:** 02072808270
**Web:** www.paragonbrokers.com
**Reg No:** 3215272 **Estd:** 1996 Private Limited Company
**Line of Business:** Insurance brokers
**Export Sales:** £6,243,000
**Trading Style:** Paragon International Insurance Brokers Ltd
**Issued Capital:** £290,614
**Directors:** J Kalbassi, S Lee, G Obermaier, A Milsom, N O Lewin, S Witham, Ms T L Falk, A J Mcphie
**Co. Secretary:** Jonathan Burstin
**Responsibilities**
**Senior:** Helen Leary *(Company Executive Secretary)*, Christopher London *(Director)*
**Marketing:** Natasha Watson *(Marketing Director)*
**Health & Safety:** Helen Leary *(Company Executive Secretary)*
**Branches:** PARAGON INTERNATIONAL INSURANCE BROKERS LTD, 27 Reid St, Hamilton, Bermuda, HM11
**US SIC:** 6411 **UK SIC:** 83200
**Auditors:** KPMG Audit PLC
**Bankers:** The Royal Bank Of Scotland Plc (16-00-19)

| | 04-01-14 | 04-01-13 | 04-01-12 |
|---|---|---|---|
| TO | 8,472,000 | 7,220,000 | 6,143,000 |
| P/L | 341,000 | (164,000) | 167,000 |
| NW | 1,819,000 | 1,554,000 | 1,760,000 |
| WC | 1,747,000 | 1,479,000 | 1,700,000 |
| Emp. | 51 | 46 | 43 |

DUNS 21-582-9017
## Paragon Laundry
Canterbury Road, Nottingham, Nottinghamshire NG8 1PQ
**Tel:** 08458732466
**Estd:** 2011 Proprietorship
**Line of Business:** Laundries
**Proprietor:** C French
**Responsibilities**
**Senior:** Chris Gowers *(General Manager)*
**US SIC:** 7211 **UK SIC:** 98110
**Employees:** 120

**DUNS 34-631-1967**
## Paragon Management Uk Ltd
**(Subsidiary of:** Interserve Plc)
23 Austin Friars, London EC2N 2QP
**Tel:** 020 3008 7625
**Web:** www.intparagon.com
**Reg No:** 5437375 **Estd:** 2005 Private Limited Company
**Line of Business:** Secretarial and translation activities
**Issued Capital:** £282,000
**Directors:** G P Kew, B E Badcock, S J Sproat, M J Bray
**Co. Secretary:** Benjamin Badcock
**Responsibilities**
**Senior:** Stephen Eades (Manager), Gary Heard (Product Director), Paul Mari (Manager)
**Marketing:** Paul Mari (Manager)
**US SIC:** 7399 **UK SIC:** 83954
**Auditors:** PB Associates

| | 31-12-13 | 31-12-12 | 30-12-11 |
|---|---|---|---|
| TO | 43,921,211 | 46,399,049 | 22,263,872 |
| P/L | 1,038,841 | 547,543 | 637,850 |
| NW | 2,908,847 | 2,136,761 | 1,725,567 |
| WC | 2,832,290 | 2,093,206 | 1,684,955 |
| Emp. | 59 | 38 | 23 |

**DUNS 85-618-9782**
## Paragon Mortgages (No 15) Plc
**(Subsidiary of:** The Paragon Group of Companies Plc)
51 Holmer Road, Solihull, West Midlands B91 3QJ
**Tel:** 01217124242
**Reg No:** 6212267 **Estd:** 2007 Public Limited Company
**Line of Business:** Financial intermediation not elsewhere classified
**Issued Capital:** £50,000
**Directors:** D P Stolp, R J Woodman, J A Harvey, J P Fairrie, R D Shelton
**Co. Secretary:** Miss Pandora Sharp
**Responsibilities**
**Senior:** John Gemmell (Manager)
**US SIC:** 6111 **UK SIC:** 81501
Following financial data are in thousands

| | 30-09-13 | 30-09-12 | 30-09-11 |
|---|---|---|---|
| TA | 989,963 | 1,003,220 | 1,067,895 |
| NW | 417 | 232 | 234 |
| WC | 3,985 | 3,889 | 7,887 |

**DUNS 21-152-9182**
## Paragon Property Investments Ltd
Quadrant 3, Yorkshire Way, Doncaster, South Yorkshire DN3 3FB
**Tel:** 01302834141
**Reg No:** 6816668 **Estd:** 2009 Private Limited Company
**Line of Business:** Other letting of own property
**Export Sales:** £3,386,418
**Issued Capital:** £100
**Director:** M Pekin
**US SIC:** 6519 **UK SIC:** 85000

| | 28-02-14 | 28-02-13 | 28-02-12 |
|---|---|---|---|
| TO | 32,159,653 | 30,312,332 | 24,770,568 |
| P/L | 1,286,609 | 171,092 | 20,392 |
| NW | 5,920,722 | 4,572,888 | 4,608,996 |
| WC | 1,997,390 | 331,746 | (187,233) |
| Emp. | 118 | 118 | 111 |

**DUNS 45-819-0725**
## Paragon Scheme Management Services Ltd
45 & 6 Quay Point, Portsmouth, Hampshire PO6 3TD
**Tel:** 08443759606 **Fax:** 02392232126
**Web:** http://fccparagon.com
**Reg No:** 3176719 **Estd:** 1996 Private Limited Company
**Line of Business:** Non-life insurance
**Trading Style:** F C C Paragon, Paragon Advance
**Issued Capital:** £50,201
**Directors:** Ms J B Gaston, Ms K Aston, B R Cole
**Co. Secretary:** Ms Sharon Cole
**Responsibilities**
**IT:** Stuart Lindsey (Computer Manager)
**US SIC:** 6399, 7392
**UK SIC:** 82001, 83951
**Auditors:** Murray McIntosh O'Brien

| | 31-12-13 | 31-12-12 | 31-12-11 |
|---|---|---|---|
| TA | 706,015 | 928,337 | 816,127 |
| NW | 285,417 | 313,280 | 255,786 |
| WC | 90,115 | 84,782 | (63,191) |

**DUNS 21-319-2268**
## The Paragon School
Lyncombe Vale, Bath, Avon BA2 4LT
**Tel:** 01225310837
**Web:** www.paragonschool.co.uk
**Estd:** 1984
**Line of Business:** Primary education
**Sales Director:** P J Martin

**Responsibilities**
**Senior:** Titus Mills (Head Teacher)
**US SIC:** 8211 **UK SIC:** 93200
**Employees:** 80

**DUNS 73-852-8640**
## Parallel Consulting Ltd
Grayton House 498 - 504 Fulham Road, London SW6 5NH
**Tel:** 02033264100
**Web:** www.parallelconsulting.com
**Reg No:** 5107940 **Estd:** 2004 Private Limited Company
**Line of Business:** Labour recruitment and provision of personnel
**Export Sales:** £8,606,000
**Issued Capital:** £1,000
**Director:** I A Al-Tarafi
**Co. Secretary:** Steven Lamport-Went
**US SIC:** 7361 **UK SIC:** 83954

| | 31-12-13 | 31-12-12 | 31-12-11 |
|---|---|---|---|
| TO | 19,605,000 | 15,855,000 | N/A |
| P/L | 1,735,000 | 1,677,000 | N/A |
| NW | 3,519,000 | 3,090,000 | 1,524,515 |
| WC | 4,337,000 | 3,577,000 | 1,297,309 |
| Emp. | 61 | 49 | N/A |

**DUNS 73-877-4194**
## Parametric Investments Ltd
Unit 6 Lancaster Way Business Park, Ely, Cambridgeshire CB6 3NW
**Tel:** 01353666632
**Reg No:** 5131832 **Estd:** 2004 Private Limited Company
**Line of Business:** Plastic injection moulding
**Export Sales:** £26,507,972
**Issued Capital:** £8,975,000
**Directors:** T Casati, Mrs M A Salmon, M Bannister, J J Salmon
**Co. Secretary:** John Chaffe
**US SIC:** 3079 **UK SIC:** 48360
**Auditors:** Grant Thornton UK LLP
**Bankers:** Lloyds TSB Bank plc (30-93-54)

| | 31-12-13 | 31-12-12 | 31-12-11 |
|---|---|---|---|
| TO | 26,507,972 | 23,203,977 | 23,509,273 |
| P/L | 2,485,895 | 1,036,613 | 2,104,018 |
| NW | 10,244,731 | 8,164,022 | 7,300,057 |
| WC | 8,321,082 | 6,348,144 | 5,374,294 |
| Emp. | 231 | 219 | 194 |

**DUNS 50-565-2719** *Imp*
## Parametric Technology (U K) Ltd
**(Subsidiary of:** Ptc Inc.)
Chester House, Aeorspace Blvd, Farnborough Business, Farnborough, Hampshire GU14 6TQ
**Tel:** 01252453611
**Web:** www.ptc.com
**Reg No:** 2513030 **Estd:** 1990 Private Limited Company
**Line of Business:** Computer services
**Export Sales:** £975,000
**Trading Style:** Ptc
**Issued Capital:** £138,968
**Directors:** Ms P Heck, C C Dunn
**Co. Secretary:** Charles Dunn
**Branches:** Parametric Technology (U K) Ltd, Lochside Ho, 3 Lochside Way, Edinburgh, Midlothian EH12 9DT
**US SIC:** 7379 **UK SIC:** 83940
**Auditors:** PricewaterhouseCoopers LLP
**Bankers:** Barclays Bank Plc (20-05-06)

| | 30-09-13 | 30-09-12 | 30-09-11 |
|---|---|---|---|
| TO | 19,028,000 | 21,069,000 | 16,406,000 |
| P/L | (1,364,000) | 248,000 | (133,000) |
| NW | (1,996,000) | (95,000) | (747,000) |
| WC | (1,993,000) | (351,000) | (1,053,000) |
| Emp. | 182 | 178 | 169 |

**DUNS 50-005-9167** *Imp*
## Paramount 21 Ltd
Old Newton Road, Heathfield, Newton Abbot, Devon TQ12 6RA
**Web:** www.paramount21.co.uk
**Reg No:** 2295454 **VAT No:** 501441012
**Estd:** 1988 Private Limited Company
**Line of Business:** Frozen food processors and distributors
**Trading Style:** Paramount, Hannaford's
**Issued Capital:** £150,000
**Directors:** J G Hannaford, Mrs A B Hannaford, P J Wilkinson Obe, J E Phillips, S Lamont, Mrs S Cullum
**Co. Secretary:** Paul Hannaford
**Responsibilities**
**Senior:** Howard Heather (Warehouse Manager)
**IT:** Emma Willis (Technical Manager)
**Operations:** Emma Willis (Technical Manager)
**Branches:** Paramount 21 Ltd, Unit 4, Northfield Indstl Est, Brixham, Devon TQ5 8UA
**US SIC:** 5149, 2033
**UK SIC:** 61700, 41473
**Auditors:** Nigel Webster & Co

**Bankers:** HSBC Bank plc (40-20-30)

| | 31-10-13 | 31-10-12 | 31-10-11 |
|---|---|---|---|
| TA | 5,481,121 | 5,630,201 | 4,947,905 |
| P/L | 568,812 | 576,102 | 535,017 |
| NW | 2,104,852 | 1,765,251 | 1,428,476 |
| WC | (330,176) | (407,652) | (388,522) |
| Emp. | 95 | 79 | 69 |

**DUNS 29-844-3888** *Imp-Exp*
## Paramount Powders (U.K.) Ltd
4 Viveash Close, Hayes, Middlesex UB3 4RY
**Tel:** 020-8561-5588 **Fax:** 020-8561-5599
**Web:** www.paramountpowders.co.uk
**Reg No:** 2047691 **VAT No:** 452990524
**Estd:** 1986 Private Limited Company
**Line of Business:** Metal finishing and polishing services
**Export Markets:** Middle East; Far East
**Issued Capital:** £100
**Principals:** T S Badyal (Managing), V Bij (Financial), M S Badyal, S S Badyal
**Responsibilities**
**IT:** Ajay Munro (Technical Director)
**Health & Safety:** Adi Kansra (Health & Safety Officer)
**US SIC:** 2891 **UK SIC:** 25620
**Auditors:** Michael F G Cope
**Bankers:** National Westminster Bank Plc (01-08-15)

| | 31-03-14 | 31-03-13 | 31-03-12 |
|---|---|---|---|
| TA | 4,373,603 | 4,312,798 | 4,600,565 |
| NW | 1,677,232 | 1,794,130 | 1,967,835 |
| WC | 114,978 | 258,450 | 501,870 |

**DUNS 23-706-9955**
## Paramount Services (Uk) Ltd
Old Post Office, Telford, Shropshire TF6 6BJ
**Tel:** 01952-771111
**Web:** www.paramountservices.co.uk
**Reg No:** 3702068 **VAT No:** 549406524
**Estd:** 1994 Private Limited Company
**Line of Business:** Cleaning contracting commercial
**Issued Capital:** £2
**Director:** C Astle
**Co. Secretary:** Ms Karen Astle
**US SIC:** 7349 **UK SIC:** 92300
**Auditors:** The Integrity Partnership Ltd

| | 31-03-14 | 31-03-13 | 31-03-12 |
|---|---|---|---|
| TA | 171,166 | 137,756 | 112,092 |
| NW | 101,985 | 72,745 | 48,234 |
| WC | 85,864 | 63,673 | 38,104 |

**DUNS 50-316-4188** *Imp*
## Parasense Ltd
Unit 12 Olympus Park Bristol Road, Gloucester, Gloucestershire GL2 4NF
**Tel:** 01452724123
**Web:** www.parasense.co.uk
**Reg No:** 2341314 **Estd:** 1989 Private Limited Company
**Line of Business:** Energy management control systems
**Export Sales:** £1,555,589
**Issued Capital:** £2,536
**Principals:** L A Gallop (Managing), A G Ryan, Ms M Collier, Ms S J Land, P E Radford, J Ayres, D Radford
**Co. Secretary:** Leslie Gallop
**Responsibilities**
**Senior:** Glenn Roberts (Production Manager)
**HR:** Charlotte Gurney (Financial controller & Head of)
**Health & Safety:** Glenn Roberts (Production Manager)
**Facilities:** Glenn Roberts (Production Manager)
**Operations:** Glenn Roberts (Production Manager)
**Purchasing:** Glenn Roberts (Production Manager)
**Engineering:** Glenn Roberts (Production Manager)
**US SIC:** 3643 **UK SIC:** 34203
**Auditors:** Deloitte & Touche LLP
**Bankers:** Bank Of Scotland (12-05-77)

| | 31-12-13 | 31-12-12 | 31-12-11 |
|---|---|---|---|
| TO | 3,043,610 | 3,680,749 | 3,423,647 |
| P/L | (559,901) | (442,667) | 250,150 |
| NW | (2,369,064) | (1,626,917) | (1,244,184) |
| WC | (2,478,984) | (1,779,886) | (1,443,309) |
| Emp. | N/A | 40 | 45 |

**DUNS 23-951-3455** *Imp*
## Parasol Ltd
**(Subsidiary of:** Optionis Holdco Ltd)
Parasol House, Warrington, Cheshire WA1 1RL
**Tel:** 08448750079 **Fax:** 08707443909
**Web:** www.parasolgroup.co.uk
**Reg No:** 3940716 **Estd:** 2000 Private Limited Company
**Line of Business:** Holding companies management activities
**Trading Style:** Parasol It Public Limited Company
**Issued Capital:** £50,002
**Director:** R J Crossland
**Co. Secretary:** Derek Kelly

**Responsibilities**
**Finance:** Rob Easton (Group Financial Controller)
**Marketing:** Susie Lee-Kiltariff (General Manager)
**Facilities:** Susie Lee-Kiltariff (General Manager)
**US SIC:** 6711 **UK SIC:** 83962
**Auditors:** N.R. Barton & Co
**Bankers:** National Westminster Bank Plc (60-70-08)

| | 05-04-14 | 05-04-13 | 01-04-12 |
|---|---|---|---|
| TO | 310,092,000 | 327,042,000 | 377,926,000 |
| P/L | 3,391,000 | 3,430,000 | 4,658,000 |
| NW | 5,453,000 | 20,511,000 | 17,690,000 |
| WC | 4,844,000 | 20,141,000 | 17,212,000 |
| Emp. | 7,656 | 7,327 | 8,321 |

**DUNS 64-094-0086**
## Paratus Amc Ltd
**(Subsidiary of:** Sterling Holdings Lp)
Po Box 4189, Bracknell, Berkshire RG42 9LY
**Tel:** 08447-708030 **Fax:** 01344478050
**Web:** www.paratusamc.co.uk
**Reg No:** 3489004 **Estd:** 1998 Private Limited Company
**Line of Business:** Financial intermediation not elsewhere classified
**Issued Capital:** £45,117,941
**Directors:** C C Linkas, A J Keeble, N P Fegan, H Geberbauer
**Co. Secretary:** Hans Geberbauer
**US SIC:** 6111, 6012
**UK SIC:** 81501, 81402
**Auditors:** PricewaterhouseCoopers LLP

| | 31-12-13 | 31-12-12 | 31-12-11 |
|---|---|---|---|
| TA | 868,100,000 | 870,100,000 | 703,300,000 |
| P/L | 11,100,000 | 2,200,000 | 3,300,000 |
| NW | 72,300,000 | 61,200,000 | 60,900,000 |
| WC | 41,100,000 | 41,000,000 | 43,500,000 |
| Emp. | N/A | 122 | 118 |

**DUNS 21-584-7824**
## The Parc Hotel Cardiff
Park Place, Cardiff, South Glamorgan CF10 3UD
**Tel:** 08713769011
**Web:** www.thistle.com
**Estd:** 2011 Proprietorship
**Line of Business:** Other tourist assistance activities not elsewhere classified
**Proprietor:** R O'Bren
**Responsibilities**
**Senior:** Gareth Coles (Operations Manager)
**US SIC:** 7999 **UK SIC:** 97913
**Employees:** 100

**DUNS 76-691-8338** *Imp*
## PaRCEL2GO.Com Ltd
**(Subsidiary of:** P2g.Com Worldwide Ltd)
Coe House Coe Street, Off Bridgeman Street, Bolton, Lancashire BL3 6BU
**Tel:** 01204488900 **Fax:** 01204-384427
**Web:** www.parcel2go.com
**Reg No:** 2591405 **Estd:** 1991 Private Limited Company
**Line of Business:** Activities of other transport agencies
**Export Sales:** £488,000
**Issued Capital:** £1,157
**Directors:** H P Adams-Mercer, C Simpson, S Kramer, J B Greenbury, R H Adams-Mercer
**Co. Secretary:** Richard Adams-Mercer
**US SIC:** 4712 **UK SIC:** 77002
**Auditors:** Hill Ecketsley & Co
**Bankers:** National Westminster Bank Plc (01-30-99)

| | 31-03-14 | 31-03-13 | 31-03-12 |
|---|---|---|---|
| TO | 35,839,000 | 27,754,567 | 22,276,340 |
| P/L | 2,061,000 | 2,112,379 | 1,383,140 |
| NW | 3,154,000 | 1,508,323 | 1,008,650 |
| WC | 2,991,000 | 1,335,878 | 912,204 |
| Emp. | 110 | 101 | 96 |

**DUNS 22-111-2605**
## Parceline Ltd
Po Box 6979, Roebuck Lane, Smethwick, West Midlands B66 1BN
**Tel:** 08459505505
**Web:** www.geopostuk.com
**Reg No:** 4130503 **Estd:** 2000 Private Limited Company
**Line of Business:** Goods delivery services
**Issued Capital:** £1
**Director:** D M Mcdonald
**Co. Secretary:** David Adams
**Branches:** Parceline Ltd, Roebuck Lane, Smethwick, West Midlands B66 1BY
**US SIC:** 4213 **UK SIC:** 72300

| | 29-12-13 | 30-12-12 | 01-12-12 |
|---|---|---|---|
| TA | 1 | 1 | 1 |
| NW | 1 | 1 | 1 |

DUNS 21-132-1820

### Parcelpoke Ltd

22 Brighton Square, Brighton, East Sussex BN1 1HD
**Tel:** 01273775003
**Web:** www.parcelgenie.com
**Reg No:** 6659181 **Estd:** 2008 Private Limited Company
**Line of Business:** Other non-store retail sale
**Issued Capital:** £339
**Directors:** B C Garvey, R Tolcher, Dr J J Taylor, Sir C Powell
**Co. Secretary:** Dr John Taylor
**US SIC:** 5963, 7379
**UK SIC:** 65600, 83940

| | 31-01-14 | 31-01-13 | 31-01-12 |
|---|---|---|---|
| TA | 892,509 | 282,859 | 891,149 |
| NW | 827,624 | 164,609 | 819,950 |
| WC | 824,177 | 161,346 | 817,235 |

DUNS 34-843-3108

### Parcelroute Services Ltd

(**Subsidiary of:** B2c Europe (Netherlands) B.V.)
Gatehouse Close, Gatehouse Industrial Area, Aylesbury, Buckinghamshire HP19 8DE
**Tel:** 01296-338313
**Web:** www.parcelroute.co.uk
**Reg No:** 5642383 **Estd:** 2006 Private Limited Company
**Line of Business:** Storage and warehousing
**Export Sales:** £4,331,575
**Issued Capital:** £180,000
**Directors:** S W Rivett, J R Vega Vazquez, R H Van Meekeren
**Co. Secretary:** Mrs Carolyn Rivett
**Responsibilities**
**Senior:** Kerr Findeley *(Facilities Manager)*
**Facilities:** Tom Temple *(Facilities Manager)*
**US SIC:** 4226, 4311
**UK SIC:** 77003, 79010
**Auditors:** CH Auditing Solutions Ltd

| | 31-12-13 | 31-12-12 | 31-12-11 |
|---|---|---|---|
| TO | 11,899,932 | 9,202,431 | 5,877,750 |
| P/L | 437,494 | 304,644 | 29,103 |
| NW | 702,007 | 411,960 | 182,154 |
| WC | 409,472 | 231,013 | 221,926 |

DUNS 23-930-5282

### Parchment Trust

Ore Place Farm, The Ridge, Hastings, East Sussex TN34 2RA
**Tel:** 01424-755800 **Fax:** 01424-755777
**Web:** www.parchment-trust.org.uk
**Reg No:** 3920430 **Estd:** 2000 Private Company Limited By Guarantee
**Line of Business:** Day and care centres
**Directors:** J H Cosson, Ms K T Walker, J E Purle, D M Walker, J A Hassell
**Co. Secretary:** Ms Susan Geater
**Responsibilities**
**Senior:** Laurel Barnes *(Manager)*
**Finance:** Lesley Warmington *(Trust Administrator)*
**Branches:** Parchment Trust, 1A Nelson Road, Hastings, East Sussex TN34 3RX
**US SIC:** 8321 **UK SIC:** 96111
**Bankers:** National Westminster Bank Plc (60-10-15)

| | 31-07-14 | 31-07-13 | 31-07-12 |
|---|---|---|---|
| TO | 1,309,369 | 1,323,508 | 1,302,593 |
| P/L | 42,998 | 21,666 | 70,376 |
| NW | 1,204,112 | 1,161,114 | 1,139,448 |
| WC | 225,375 | 164,073 | 142,364 |
| Emp. | 51 | 53 | 52 |

DUNS 21-786-0779

### Parents' Association Merchant Taylors' Girls' School and Stanfield School

134 Liverpool Road, Crosby, Liverpool, Merseyside L23 5TH
**Tel:** 01519241506
**Web:** www.merchanttaylors.com
**Estd:** 1899
**Line of Business:** Schools (independent)
**Proprietor:** Miss J Yardley
**US SIC:** 8211 **UK SIC:** 93200
**Employees:** 50

DUNS 50-471-6648 **Exp**

### Parex Ltd

Abeles Way, Atherstone, Warwickshire CV9 2QZ
**Tel:** 01827-711755
**Web:** www.parex.co.uk
**Reg No:** 2450579 **VAT No:** 661541936
**Estd:** 1989 Private Limited Company
**Line of Business:** Manufacturers of cement
**Export Markets:** Republic of Ireland
**Export Sales:** £374,666
**Issued Capital:** £318,750
**Directors:** M A Shorrock, E C Berge, G De La Roche Aymon
**Co. Secretary:** Ms Anne Cogbill
**Responsibilities**
**Senior:** Frederic Herbaut *(Manager)*, Glyn Russell *(Health & Safety Manager)*
**Sales:** Glyn Russell *(Health & Safety Manager)*
**Health & Safety:** Glyn Russell *(Health & Safety Manager)*
**Branches:** Parex Ltd, Drumhead Road, Chorley North Business Park, Chorley, Lancashire PR6 7DE
**US SIC:** 3241, 3069
**UK SIC:** 24200, 48123
**Auditors:** Ernst & Young LLP

| | 31-12-13 | 31-12-12 | 31-12-11 |
|---|---|---|---|
| TO | 18,827,452 | 13,812,298 | 11,419,940 |
| P/L | 3,110,904 | 1,865,619 | 1,281,035 |
| NW | 1,640,122 | 132,450 | 345,711 |
| WC | 912,646 | 2,517,827 | 2,790,407 |
| Emp. | 68 | 63 | 64 |

DUNS 50-136-7544 **Imp-Exp**

### Parexel International Ltd

(**Subsidiary of:** Parexel International Corporation)
The Quays, 101-105 Oxford Road, Uxbridge, Middlesex UB8 1LZ
**Tel:** 01895-238000 **Fax:** 01895-238494
**Web:** www.parexcel.com
**Reg No:** 2322645 **VAT No:** 527841627
**Estd:** 1988 Private Limited Company
**Line of Business:** Manufacture of insulated wire and cable
**Issued Capital:** £18,859,360
**Principals:** J H Von Rickenbach *(President)*, D A Batt
**Co. Secretary:** Douglas Batt
**Responsibilities**
**Senior:** Joseph Rickenbach *(Manager)*, Michael Walshe *(Manager)*
**Branches:** Parexel International Ltd, 1 Chancellor Court, 50 Occam Rd, Guildford, Surrey GU2 7YT
**US SIC:** 3357 **UK SIC:** 22470
**Auditors:** Ernst & Young LLP
**Bankers:** Barclays Bank Plc (20-35-93)

| | 30-06-13 | 30-06-12 | 30-06-11 |
|---|---|---|---|
| TO | 106,151,000 | 101,594,000 | 61,638,000 |
| P/L | 13,280,000 | 3,333,000 | 834,000 |
| NW | 23,909,000 | 10,794,000 | 6,679,000 |
| WC | 18,416,000 | 5,056,000 | 7,629,000 |
| Emp. | 884 | 802 | 741 |

DUNS 21-196-4333 **Imp**

### Parfums Christian Dior(U.K.) Ltd

(**Subsidiary of:** Lvmh Moet Hennessy Louis Vuitton)
United Kingdom House, 180 Oxford Street, London W1D 1AB
**Tel:** 020-7563-6300
**Web:** www.dior.com
**Reg No:** 1012371 **VAT No:** 238953623
**Estd:** 1971 Private Limited Company
**Line of Business:** Beauty products
**Issued Capital:** £100,000
**Directors:** C P Vlieghe, H P Dusseaux, C M Martinez, Ms C Freund, Mrs M Attwooll, B Angibeau, B A Tefra
**Co. Secretary:** Christophe Vlieghe
**Responsibilities**
**Senior:** Elizabeth Cowper *(Human Resources Director)*, Vincent Jeanniard *(Manager)*
**Finance:** Christophe Wygas *(Finance Director)*
**Admin:** Marianne Russell *(Office Manager)*
**IT:** Kemal Suleyman *(IT Support)*
**HR:** Elizabeth Cowper *(Human Resources Director)*
**Health & Safety:** Marianne Russell *(Office Manager)*
**Facilities:** Marianne Russell *(Office Manager)*
**Branches:** Parfums Christian Dior(U.k.) Ltd, United Kingdom House, 180 Oxford Street, London W1D 1AB
**US SIC:** 2844 **UK SIC:** 25820
**Auditors:** Ernst & Young
**Bankers:** S G Hambros Bank & Trust Ltd (40-48-58)

| | 31-12-13 | 31-12-12 | 31-12-11 |
|---|---|---|---|
| TO | 54,522,507 | 50,927,598 | 52,264,185 |
| P/L | 2,457,485 | 3,190,679 | 2,462,219 |
| NW | 6,136,520 | 5,371,544 | 3,144,787 |
| WC | 1,996,281 | 2,483,255 | 1,325,005 |
| Emp. | 729 | 705 | 682 |

DUNS 39-761-9123 **Imp**

### Pargat & Co Ltd

40 Birmingham Road, West Bromwich, West Midlands B71 4JZ
**Tel:** 01215-251218 **Fax:** 01215-254843
**Web:** www.pargat.com
**Reg No:** 2198962 **VAT No:** 295809116
**Estd:** 1978 Private Limited Company
**Line of Business:** Hardware
**Export Sales:** £1,060,209
**Trading Style:** Pargat Houseware
**Issued Capital:** £220
**Director:** M Singh
**Responsibilities**
**Senior:** Manni Singh *(Managing Director)*
**US SIC:** 3499 **UK SIC:** 31694
**Auditors:** Mazars LLP

| | 30-09-13 | 30-09-12 | 30-09-11 |
|---|---|---|---|
| TO | 27,736,484 | 21,699,463 | 23,047,984 |
| P/L | 1,737,886 | 1,447,682 | 1,703,948 |
| NW | 5,612,016 | 4,245,544 | 2,983,814 |
| WC | 9,193,993 | 5,459,696 | 4,771,054 |
| Emp. | 134 | 123 | 131 |

DUNS 29-085-4264

### Parham Park Ltd

Parham Park, Parham, Pulborough, West Sussex RH20 4HS
**Tel:** 01903744888
**Web:** www.parhaminsussex.co.uk
**Reg No:** 1392448 **Estd:** 1978 Private Company Limited By Guarantee
**Line of Business:** Historic houses & gardens
**Trading Style:** Purham House & Gardens
**Directors:** R T Longstaffe-Gowan, Mrs L Petts, Lady E L Barnard, C J Schooling, J V Naunton Davies
**Co. Secretary:** Currey & Co Llp
**Responsibilities**
**Senior:** Richard Pailthorpe *(General Manager)*
**Finance:** Diana Edwards *(Financial Controller)*
**Marketing:** Alison Sweeney *(Marketing Manager)*
**HR:** Richard Pailthorpe *(General Manager)*
**Health & Safety:** Danny Lucas *(Health & Safety Officer)*
**Facilities:** Richard Pailthorpe *(General Manager)*
**US SIC:** 8411 **UK SIC:** 97700
**Auditors:** Macnair Mason
**Bankers:** Barclays Bank Plc (20-98-74)

| | 31-12-13 | 31-12-12 | 31-12-11 |
|---|---|---|---|
| TO | 1,011,856 | 1,043,392 | 992,679 |
| P/L | (4,002) | 172,388 | 143,415 |
| NW | 2,352,142 | 2,225,457 | 2,053,069 |
| WC | 210,198 | 233,882 | 311,000 |
| Emp. | 95 | 85 | 76 |

DUNS 73-951-2692

### Paris Smith Llp

1 London Road, Southampton, Hampshire SO15 2AE
**Tel:** 02380-482482
**Web:** www.parissmith.co.uk
**Reg No:** 0308962OC **Estd:** 2004
**Line of Business:** Notaries
**Responsibilities**
**Senior:** Richard Atcherley *(Non-designated Limited Liabili)*, Nicholas Borne *(Senior Partner)*, Sean Davies *(Partner - Head of Company/Comm)*, Clive Dobbin *(Partner - Employment)*, David Eminton *(Non-designated Limited Liabili)*, Peter Gammie *(Non-designated Limited Liabili)*, Thomas Georgiou *(Non-designated Limited Liabili)*, Andrew Heathcock *(Managing Partner)*, Crispin Jameson *(Partner - Tax)*, Neil Mcneil *(Non-designated Limited Liabili)*, Geraint Miles *(Non-designated Limited Liabili)*, Sarah Passemard *(Non-designated Limited Liabili)*, Mike Pavitt *(Partner - Insolvency)*, Frank Prior *(Non-designated Limited Liabili)*, David Roath *(Non-designated Limited Liabili)*, Sarah Wheadon *(Non-designated Limited Liabili)*, Mark Withers *(Partner)*
**Finance:** Crispin Jameson *(Partner - Tax)*
**US SIC:** 8111 **UK SIC:** 83500
**Auditors:** BDO LLP

| | 31-12-13 | 31-12-12 | 31-12-11 |
|---|---|---|---|
| TO | 10,760,006 | 10,380,874 | 10,274,203 |
| WC | 3,980,354 | 3,967,790 | 3,775,145 |
| Emp. | 112 | 114 | 123 |

DUNS 21-780-5309

### Parish C of E Primary School

London Lane, Bromley, Kent BR1 4HF
**Tel:** 02084607336
**Web:** www.parishceschool.com
**Estd:** 1988 Proprietorship
**Line of Business:** Schools (local authority)
**Proprietor:** H Richardson
**US SIC:** 8211 **UK SIC:** 93200
**Employees:** 60

DUNS 23-586-8648

### Parity for Disability

93-94 Whetstone Road, Farnborough, Hampshire GU14 9SX
**Web:** www.parityfordisability.org.uk
**Reg No:** 3584503 **Estd:** 1998 Private Limited Company
**Line of Business:** Representative office
**Trading Style:** Parity for Disability
**Directors:** P J Roper, Ms A S Brunton, Mrs A Cullen, D M Turnidge, K Smith, W I Mcneill, Mrs B J Hurst, J O Durrett
**Co. Secretary:** Ms Alison Cooper
**Responsibilities**
**Senior:** Helene Abbiss *(Commercial Manager)*, Brian Blewett *(Director)*, Gill Coley *(Manager)*, Susan Meldrum *(Director)*
**Finance:** Lisa Dowcett *(Head of Finance)*
**Marketing:** Helene Abbiss *(Commercial Manager)*
**Facilities:** Helene Abbiss *(Commercial Manager)*
**Branches:** Parity For Disability, 62 Park St, Camberley, Surrey GU15 3PT
**US SIC:** 7399 **UK SIC:** 83954
**Auditors:** Radford & Sergeant
**Bankers:** HSBC Bank plc (40-35-45)

| | 31-03-14 | 31-03-13 | 31-03-12 |
|---|---|---|---|
| TO | 1,096,765 | 965,918 | 842,619 |
| P/L | 130,200 | 37,489 | (27,252) |
| NW | 477,335 | 351,535 | 314,046 |
| WC | 254,330 | 132,935 | 121,031 |
| Emp. | 50 | 47 | 48 |

DUNS 23-540-8007 **Exp**

### Parity Group Plc

Wimbledon Bridge House, 1 Hartfield Road, London SW19 3RU
**Web:** www.parity.net
**Reg No:** 3539413 **Estd:** 1981 Public Limited Company
**Line of Business:** Other computer related activities
**Issued Capital:** £1,433,285,624
**Directors:** N J Ransome, D J Courtley, P Davies, A J Woolley, Lord R N Freeman, A J Law, P E Swinstead
**Co. Secretary:** Mrs Suzanne Chase
**US SIC:** 7379 **UK SIC:** 83940
**Auditors:** KPMG Audit PLC
**Bankers:** The Royal Bank Of Scotland Plc (15-00-00)

| | 31-12-13 | 31-12-12 | 31-12-11 |
|---|---|---|---|
| TO | 91,949,000 | 85,887,000 | 80,142,000 |
| P/L | (949,000) | (1,066,000) | (2,149,000) |
| NW | 1,202,000 | (3,878,000) | 172,000 |
| WC | 2,564,000 | (1,594,000) | 1,728,000 |
| Emp. | 156 | 162 | 169 |

DUNS 22-933-9882

### Parity Solutions Ire

(**Subsidiary of:** Parity Group Plc)
15 Dargan Road, Belfast BT3 9JU
**Tel:** 01925861046 **Fax:** 08707-625561
**Web:** www.parity.net
**Reg No:** 0019418NI **Estd:** 1975 Private Limited Company
**Line of Business:** Other computer related activities
**Trading Style:** Parity Ireland
**Issued Capital:** £1
**Director:** A J Woolley
**Co. Secretary:** Alastair Woolley
**US SIC:** 7379 **UK SIC:** 83940
**Bankers:** Northern Bank Ltd (95-02-02)

| | 31-12-13 | 31-12-12 | 31-12-11 |
|---|---|---|---|
| TA | 8,503,000 | 8,503,000 | 8,503,000 |
| NW | 2,122,000 | 2,122,000 | 2,122,000 |
| WC | 2,122,000 | 2,122,000 | N/A |

DUNS 21-930-3104

### Parity Solutions Ltd

(**Subsidiary of:** Parity Group Plc)
2 Bath Place, London EC2A 3DR
**Tel:** 08458730790
**Web:** www.parity.net
**Reg No:** 0969618 **Estd:** 1970 Private Limited Company
**Line of Business:** Employment and recruitment companies and consultants
**Issued Capital:** £10,000,000
**Directors:** A J Woolley, P Davies, P E Swinstead
**Co. Secretary:** Mrs Suzanne Chase
**Branches:** Parity Solutions Limited, Maybrook House, 40 Blackfriars Street, Manchester M3 2EG
**US SIC:** 7379, 8299
**UK SIC:** 83940, 93300
**Auditors:** KPMG Audit PLC
**Bankers:** Lloyds TSB Bank plc (30-94-08)

| | 31-12-13 | 31-12-12 | 31-12-11 |
|---|---|---|---|
| TO | 7,681,000 | 8,718,000 | 11,493,000 |
| P/L | 126,000 | (254,000) | (520,000) |
| NW | (2,130,000) | (1,806,000) | (66,000) |
| WC | 6,493,000 | 1,088,000 | (1,938,000) |
| Emp. | 55 | 69 | 87 |

DUNS 21-770-9081

### The Park

40 St Marks Road, Derby, Derbyshire DE21 6AH
**Tel:** 01332200422
**Web:** www.embracegroup.co.uk
**Estd:** 1997 Proprietorship
**Line of Business:** Nursing homes
**Proprietor:** Mrs S Johnston
**US SIC:** 8051 **UK SIC:** 95100
**Employees:** 53

DUNS 29-625-3578 **Imp-Exp**

### Park Air Systems Ltd

(**Subsidiary of:** Northrop Grumman Corporation)
Northfields Industrial Estate, Market Deeping, Peterborough, Cambridgeshire PE6 8UE
**Tel:** 01778-345434
**Web:** www.parkairsystems.com
**Reg No:** 1951792 **VAT No:** 551086749
**Estd:** 1985 Private Limited Company
**Line of Business:** Radio equipment

**Export Markets:** E U, Middle East, U.S.A., S America, Africa, S & S E Asia, Australasia, Canada
**Issued Capital:** £278,903
**Principals:** C J Houseago (Managing), R K Merker, D Milligan, J M Myers, D M Chandler, N T Bhatti, R C Wiltshire
**Co. Secretary:** Roger Wiltshire
**Responsibilities**
**Senior:** Larry Edelman (Manager), Michael Iszatt (Manager), Alan Leckenby (Board Director), Wolf Von Kumberg (Manager)
**IT:** Richard Allis (IT Director)
**HR:** Rachel Naylor (Training Coordinator)
**US SIC:** 3662  **UK SIC:** 34430
**Auditors:** Deloitte & Touche LLP
**Bankers:** Barclays Bank Plc (20-00-00)

|      | 31-12-13   | 31-12-12   | 31-12-11   |
|------|-----------|-----------|-----------|
| TO   | 37,799,000 | 29,512,000 | 33,459,000 |
| P/L  | 2,625,000  | 2,285,000  | 3,341,000  |
| NW   | 26,282,000 | 20,212,000 | 18,411,000 |
| WC   | 22,472,000 | 21,126,000 | 20,376,000 |
| Emp. | 150        | 151        | 149        |

DUNS 21-579-9273
## Park Avenue Healthcare
69 Park Avenue, Bromley, Kent BR1 4EW
**Tel:** 02084665267
**Web:** www.excelcareholdings.com
**Estd:** 2005 Proprietorship
**Line of Business:** Nursing homes
**Proprietor:** Mrs A Beebeejaun
**US SIC:** 8051  **UK SIC:** 95100
**Employees:** 72

DUNS 22-752-9484
## Park Avenue Hotel Ltd
158 Holywood Road, Belfast BT4 1PB
**Tel:** 028-9065-6520
**Web:** www.parkavenuehotel.co.uk
**Reg No:** 0006459NI  **VAT No:** 252648257
**Estd:** 1965 Private Limited Company
**Line of Business:** Hotels and motels without restaurant
**Issued Capital:** £14,998
**Director:** W Stephens
**Co. Secretary:** Paul Frame
**Responsibilities**
**Senior:** Mandy Patrick (Manager), Billy Stevens (CEO, Managing Director)
**IT:** Katrina Martin (IT Manager)
**HR:** Simon Harvey (Human Resources Director)
**US SIC:** 7011  **UK SIC:** 66500
**Auditors:** Lynn Drake & Co

|      | 31-03-14    | 31-03-13    | 31-03-12   |
|------|------------|------------|-----------|
| TO   | N/A        | 2,502,453  | 2,458,689 |
| P/L  | N/A        | (46,510)   | (38,796)  |
| NW   | (171,126)  | (207,017)  | (80,507)  |
| WC   | (1,083,417)| (1,013,945)| (975,877) |
| Emp. | N/A        | 73         | 78        |

DUNS 67-139-5759
## Park Cakes Ltd
**(Subsidiary of:** Park Cakes Acquisition Ltd)
Ashton Road, Oldham, Lancashire OL8 2ND
**Tel:** 01616 331 181 **Fax:** 01616 266 199
**Web:** http://parkcakes.com
**Reg No:** 5998327  **Estd:** 2006 Private Limited Company
**Line of Business:** Manufacture of bread; manufacture of fresh pastry goods and cakes
**Trading Style:** Park Cakes Bakeries, The Park Cake Bakeries
**Issued Capital:** £870
**Directors:** K A Mcgill, Ms A Allen, G J Voyle
**Co. Secretary:** Ms Anne Allen
**Responsibilities**
**IT:** Martin Stockdale (IT Manager)
**Branches:** Park Cakes Limited, Bella Street, Bolton, Lancashire BL3 4DU
**US SIC:** 2051  **UK SIC:** 41960
**Auditors:** KPMG LLP

|      | 29-03-14     | 30-03-13     | 31-03-12    |
|------|-------------|-------------|------------|
| TO   | 112,245,000 | 116,854,000 | 121,185,000|
| P/L  | (3,044,000) | (414,000)   | (3,367,000)|
| NW   | (26,312,000)| (23,268,000)| (21,842,000)|
| WC   | (5,902,000) | 2,654,000   | (1,823,000)|
| Emp. | 1,144       | 1,140       | 1,086      |

DUNS 34-959-2613
## Park Cameras Holdings Ltd
**(Subsidiary of:** Park Cameras Group Ltd)
York Road, Victoria Business Park, Burgess Hill, West Sussex RH15 9TT
**Web:** www.parkcameras.com
**Reg No:** 5754896  **Estd:** 2006 Private Limited Company
**Line of Business:** Management activities of other non-financial holding companies not elsewhere classified
**Export Sales:** £127,991
**Trading Style:** Park Cameras Holdings Ltd
**Issued Capital:** £1,000
**Director:** R W Atkins
**Co. Secretary:** Mrs Caroline Atkins
**Responsibilities**
**Senior:** Reginald Atkins (Manager)

---

**US SIC:** 7399  **UK SIC:** 83954

|      | 28-02-14   | 28-02-13   | 29-02-12   |
|------|-----------|-----------|-----------|
| TO   | 15,880,472 | 15,848,166 | 14,993,160 |
| P/L  | 577,336    | 532,893    | 15,243     |
| NW   | 2,929,277  | 2,601,052  | 2,418,368  |
| WC   | 749,559    | 339,080    | 233,779    |
| Emp. | 56         | 56         | 66         |

DUNS 22-503-2960
## Park Cameras Ltd
**(Subsidiary of:** Park Cameras Group Ltd)
York Road, Burgess Hill, West Sussex RH15 9TT
**Tel:** 08450550554 **Fax:** 0845-058-0488
**Web:** www.parkcameras.com
**Reg No:** 1449928  **Estd:** 1979 Private Limited Company
**Line of Business:** Other retail sale in specialised stores not elsewhere classified
**Export Sales:** £127,991
**Issued Capital:** £40,000
**Directors:** R W Atkins, D Admas
**Responsibilities**
**Senior:** Reginald Atkins (Manager)
**US SIC:** 5999  **UK SIC:** 65600
**Auditors:** UHY Hacker Young (S E) Ltd
**Bankers:** Lloyds TSB Bank plc (30-91-44)

|      | 28-02-14   | 28-02-13   | 29-02-12   |
|------|-----------|-----------|-----------|
| TO   | 15,880,472 | 15,848,166 | 14,993,160 |
| P/L  | 477,882    | 428,855    | (74,504)   |
| NW   | 2,617,706  | 2,355,038  | 2,249,376  |
| WC   | 2,354,258  | 2,327,886  | 2,206,111  |
| Emp. | 55         | 56         | 66         |

DUNS 21-786-4361
## Park Care Meals
Sycamore Centre, Sycamore Road Eastwood Trading E, Rotherham, South Yorkshire S65 1EN
**Web:** www.parkcaremealsltd.co.uk
**Estd:** 2011 Proprietorship
**Line of Business:** Home care service providers
**Proprietor:** Shipley
**Responsibilities**
**Senior:** Rick Shipley (Manager)
**US SIC:** 8091  **UK SIC:** 95200
**Employees:** 50

DUNS 21-150-7327
## Park College
Kings Drive, Eastbourne, East Sussex BN21 2UN
**Tel:** 01323-637111
**Web:** www.sussexdowns.ac.uk
**Estd:** 1960
**Line of Business:** Further education schools and colleges
**Trading Style:** Sussex Downs College
**Director:** P Frier
**Responsibilities**
**Senior:** Sally Bromley (Head Of Park), Melanie Hunt (CEO)
**IT:** James Poulter (College Manager - Creative Med)
**US SIC:** 8221  **UK SIC:** 93100
**Employees:** 120

DUNS 76-905-3794                                    Exp
## Park Communications Ltd
**(Subsidiary of:** Park Group Holdings Ltd)
Solar House, Alpine Way, London E6 6LA
**Tel:** 020-7055-6500 **Fax:** 02070556600
**Web:** www.parkcom.co.uk
**Reg No:** 2581687  **VAT No:** 577737974
**Estd:** 1991 Private Limited Company
**Line of Business:** Printing not elsewhere classified
**Export Sales:** £229,183
**Issued Capital:** £600,000
**Principals:** A G Branch (Managing), P Walker, H Mason
**Co. Secretary:** Alison Branch
**Responsibilities**
**Senior:** Kenneth Kerman (Manager)
**Finance:** Martin Rothera (Financial Director)
**IT:** Daniel Hopkins (Technical Director)
**HR:** Maria Shepard (Human Resources Manager)
**Operations:** Daniel Hopkins (Technical Director)
**US SIC:** 2752  **UK SIC:** 47544
**Auditors:** MacIntyre Hudson LLP
**Bankers:** Bank Of Scotland (12-01-03)

|      | 31-12-13   | 31-12-12   | 31-12-11   |
|------|-----------|-----------|-----------|
| TO   | 13,022,356 | 13,779,982 | 12,635,075 |
| P/L  | 395,787    | 335,658    | 344,822    |
| NW   | 5,550,307  | 5,594,213  | 5,452,662  |
| WC   | 2,970,780  | 2,489,499  | 1,797,227  |
| Emp. | 124        | 118        | 98         |

DUNS 21-770-9274
## Park Community School
Park Lane, Barnstaple, Devon EX32 9AX
**Tel:** 01271373131
**Web:** www.parkcommunity.devon.sch.uk
**Estd:** 2004
**Line of Business:** Schools (local authority)

---

**Responsibilities**
**IT:** J. Williams (Senior IT Executive)
**US SIC:** 8211  **UK SIC:** 93200
**Employees:** 100

DUNS 21-032-0692
## Park Court Chambers
16 Park Place, Leeds, West Yorkshire LS1 2SJ
**Web:** www.parkcourtchambers.co.uk
**Estd:** 1998
**Line of Business:** Barristers at law
**Trading Style:** New Park Court Chambers
**Proprietor:** Miss J Pickersgill
**Responsibilities**
**Senior:** Kirsten Frankland (Executive), Michael Meeson (Chief Executive)
**Finance:** Ellen Reid (Family Fees Clerk), Nicola Young (Senior Fees Clerk)
**Admin:** Carol Arundel (Receptionist), Elaine Herring (Administrator), Karen Wade (Administrator)
**US SIC:** 8111  **UK SIC:** 83500
**Employees:** 46

DUNS 29-929-3167
## Park Entertainment Ltd
54 Broadwick Street, London W1F 7AH
**Tel:** 020-7434-4176
**Web:** www.parkentertainment.com
**Reg No:** 2097916  **Estd:** 1987 Private Limited Company
**Line of Business:** Film production services and studios
**Trading Style:** Park Televisoin Production
**Issued Capital:** £800
**Managing Director:** J A Howell
**Co. Secretary:** Ms Gillian Howell
**US SIC:** 4833  **UK SIC:** 97411
**Auditors:** Wilkins Kennedy
**Bankers:** National Westminster Bank Plc (60-07-20)

|    | 31-05-13 | 31-05-12  | 31-05-11  |
|----|----------|-----------|-----------|
| TA | 458,058  | 528,985   | 257,424   |
| NW | 46,297   | (43,459)  | (40,192)  |
| WC | 44,894   | (43,767)  | (41,049)  |

DUNS 73-525-9694
## Park Families Ltd
Sandleford Road, Havant, Hampshire PO9 4LR
**Tel:** 02392478051 **Fax:** 02392-424985
**Web:** www.parkholidaysuk.com
**Reg No:** 4788663  **Estd:** 2002 Private Company Limited By Guarantee
**Line of Business:** Business and management consultancy activities not elsewhere classified
**Trading Style:** The Sure Start Ctr, Park Families
**Directors:** Ms E Aquilina, M I Khan, Reverend J G Jeffery, C D Thresher, Mrs L M Hoole, Ms F Ponsenby, Mrs C Godman
**Co. Secretary:** Ms Sarah Lamburne
**Responsibilities**
**Senior:** Alison Henry (Manager)
**US SIC:** 7392, 8091
**UK SIC:** 83951, 95200
**Auditors:** Rothman Pantall & Co
**Bankers:** National Westminster Bank Plc (60-04-23)

|      | 31-03-14  | 31-03-13  | 31-03-12  |
|------|-----------|-----------|-----------|
| TO   | 1,312,012 | 1,196,924 | 1,552,904 |
| P/L  | 47,283    | 16,770    | 233,455   |
| NW   | 942,161   | 894,798   | 878,028   |
| WC   | 300,821   | 236,794   | 200,742   |
| Emp. | 89        | 87        | 94        |

DUNS 21-156-5838
## Park Farm Primary School
Century House, Park Farm Road, Park Farm Industrial Estate, Folkestone, Kent CT19 5DW
**Tel:** 01303256031
**Web:** www.parkfarmjoinery.co.uk
**Estd:** 1972
**Line of Business:** Manufacturers of joinery
**Director:** I Geddes
**Responsibilities**
**Senior:** Arthur King (Manager)
**US SIC:** 8211  **UK SIC:** 93200
**Employees:** 60

DUNS 34-799-6845
## Park Finance Holdings Ltd
**(Subsidiary of:** Blue Finance Holdings Ltd)
Victoria House, Stanbridge Park, Staplefield Lane, Staplefield, Haywards Heath, West Sussex RH17 6AS
**Tel:** 01253735656 **Fax:** 02922664438
**Web:** www.parkfinance.com
**Reg No:** 2787748  **Estd:** 1993 Private Limited Company
**Line of Business:** Management activities of holding companies
**Issued Capital:** £23,737,668
**Director:** S R Jones

---

**Branches:** Park Finance Holdings Ltd, 54 Artillery Lane, London E1 7LS
**US SIC:** 6711, 6552
**UK SIC:** 83962, 85000
**Bankers:** Barclays Bank Plc (20-18-15)

|      | 31-12-13   | 31-12-12    | 31-12-11   |
|------|-----------|------------|-----------|
| TO   | N/A       | 1,500,000  | 1,650,283 |
| P/L  | N/A       | (5,736,132)| 5,992     |
| NW   | 10,036    | 13,075,237 | 18,811,370|
| WC   | N/A       | 13,075,237 | 18,811,370|
| Emp. | N/A       | 2          | N/A       |

DUNS 22-507-3501
## Park Furnishers (Bristol) Ltd
Willway Street, Bristol, Avon BS3 4AZ
**Tel:** 01179-669253
**Web:** www.parkfurnishers.co.uk
**Reg No:** 1537076  **Estd:** 1970 Private Limited Company
**Line of Business:** Retail sale of furniture, lighting equipment and household articles not elsewhere classified
**Issued Capital:** £50
**Principals:** T S Coller (Managing), D N Coller (Managing), S Foster, J D Coller
**Co. Secretary:** Michael Wilks
**US SIC:** 5719  **UK SIC:** 64700
**Auditors:** Burton Sweet
**Bankers:** National Westminster Bank Plc (52-10-00)

|      | 31-01-14  | 31-01-13  | 31-01-12  |
|------|-----------|-----------|-----------|
| TO   | 8,620,766 | 9,052,379 | N/A       |
| P/L  | 50,686    | 146,339   | 70,638    |
| NW   | 4,059,952 | 4,024,484 | 3,867,099 |
| WC   | 267,080   | 236,898   | 44,241    |
| Emp. | 65        | 66        | 67        |

DUNS 64-102-0599
## Park Garage Group Plc
106-108 Park Lane, Croydon, Surrey CR0 1JB
**Tel:** 02082530260 **Fax:** 02082530261
**Web:** www.parkandshop.co.uk
**Reg No:** 3497029  **Estd:** 2011 Public Limited Company
**Line of Business:** Representative office
**Issued Capital:** £50,000
**Director:** S Tandon
**Co. Secretary:** Balraj Tandon
**Responsibilities**
**Senior:** Sengul James (Financial Director)
**Finance:** Sengul James (Financial Director)
**Marketing:** Miles Harvey (Operations Manager)
**IT:** Miles Harvey (Operations Manager)
**Operations:** Miles Harvey (Operations Manager)
**Branches:** Park Garage Group Plc, 536-540 Falmer Road, Brighton, East Sussex BN2 6ND
**US SIC:** 5411  **UK SIC:** 64100
**Auditors:** BDO LLP

|      | 30-06-13    | 30-06-12    | 30-06-11    |
|------|------------|------------|------------|
| TO   | 150,069,056| 183,572,891| 172,268,995|
| P/L  | 534,441    | 383,511    | 474,048    |
| NW   | 12,252,250 | 11,954,934 | 11,669,977 |
| WC   | 312,809    | 300,549    | 264,709    |
| Emp. | 260        | 663        | 663        |

DUNS 50-531-9442
## Park Garden Centre Ltd
Over Lane, Almondsbury, Bristol, Avon BS32 4BP
**Tel:** 01454-457300 **Fax:** 01454-457332
**Web:** www.parkgardencentres.co.uk
**Reg No:** 2489833  **VAT No:** 302626984
**Estd:** 1990 Private Limited Company
**Line of Business:** Garden centres
**Trading Style:** Almondsbury Garden Centre, Lechlade Garden Centre, Cheddar Garden Centre
**Issued Capital:** £64
**Principals:** P J Hodges (Managing), G K Cairns, A K Hodges
**Co. Secretary:** Philip Hodges
**Branches:** Park Garden Centre Ltd, Fairford Road, Warrens Cross, Cirencester, Gloucestershire GL7 5BT
**US SIC:** 5999  **UK SIC:** 65600
**Auditors:** Solomon Hare
**Bankers:** National Westminster Bank Plc (56-00-05)

|      | 31-08-13   | 31-08-12   | 31-08-11   |
|------|-----------|-----------|-----------|
| TO   | 10,678,000 | 10,081,000 | 10,687,000 |
| P/L  | 3,542,000  | 294,000    | 702,000    |
| NW   | 7,798,000  | 4,407,000  | 5,215,000  |
| WC   | 8,180,000  | 602,000    | 1,513,000  |
| Emp. | 245        | 241        | 244        |

DUNS 21-313-6492                                    Imp
## Park Gate & Co Ltd
87 Kingstown Broadway, Kingstown Industrial Estate, Carlisle, Cumbria CA3 0HA
**Tel:** 01228552000 **Fax:** 01228-552001
**Web:** www.park-gate.co.uk
**Reg No:** 0422148  **VAT No:** 256600763
**Estd:** 1946 Private Limited Company
**Line of Business:** Other engineering activities
**Export Sales:** £44,000
**Issued Capital:** £1,000

**Principals:** G W Park (Chairman), I E Park (Managing), R A Park (Managing)
**Co. Secretary:** Ian Park
**Responsibilities**
**Marketing:** Sean Thornborrow (Sales Manager)
**Sales:** Michael Harding (Internal Sales Engineer), Sean Thornborrow (Sales Manager)
**HR:** Alison Killen (Personnel Manager)
**Health & Safety:** Jim MacDonald (Health & Safety Officer)
**Operations:** Shaun Bell (Control Panel Dept. Manager)
**Purchasing:** Paul Emmerson (Contracts Manager)
**Engineering:** Martin Shields (Commissioning Engineer)
**US SIC:** 8911 **UK SIC:** 83701
**Auditors:** RST Kyles
**Bankers:** HSBC Bank plc (40-16-22)

|       | 31-10-13   | 31-10-12   | 31-10-11  |
|-------|------------|------------|-----------|
| TO    | 10,979,286 | 10,376,264 | 9,665,157 |
| P/L   | 856,451    | 618,698    | 601,304   |
| NW    | 3,752,454  | 3,533,916  | 3,255,938 |
| WC    | 2,297,788  | 2,274,814  | 1,977,001 |
| Emp.  | 102        | 86         | 80        |

DUNS 34-626-0578
**Park Gate Financial Ltd**
10 Park Gate, Bradford, West Yorkshire BD1 5BS
**Tel:** 01274701888
**Web:** www.10parkgate.co.uk
**Reg No:** 5432470 **Estd:** 2000 Private Limited Company
**Line of Business:** Mortgage brokers
**Issued Capital:** £2
**Director:** G P Lawford
**Co. Secretary:** Mrs Gillian Lawford
**US SIC:** 6111 **UK SIC:** 81501

|    | 30-04-14 | 30-04-13 | 30-04-12 |
|----|----------|----------|----------|
| TA | 32,522   | 47,179   | 87,023   |
| NW | 11       | 4,980    | 1,406    |
| WC | (9,970)  | (3,663)  | (7,847)  |

DUNS 21-586-6048
**Park Gate Post Office**
26 Bridge Road, Park Gate, Southampton, Hampshire SO31 7GE
**Tel:** 01489572264
**Web:** www.postoffice.co.uk
**Estd:** 1990 Proprietorship
**Line of Business:** Post offices
**Proprietor:** Mrs K Henbest
**US SIC:** 4311 **UK SIC:** 79010
**Employees:** 48

DUNS 22-861-0952                                Imp
**Park Group Plc**
Valley Road, Birkenhead, Merseyside CH41 7ED
**Tel:** 01516-531700
**Web:** www.davidharrisons.com
**Reg No:** 1711939 **Estd:** 1969 Public Limited Company
**Line of Business:** Residential care establishments
**Trading Style:** Park Group Plc
**Issued Capital:** £3,387,050
**Directors:** J A Dembitz, M Dekare Silver, M R Stewart, Mrs L M Carstensen, C Houghton, G A Woods, P R Johnson
**Co. Secretary:** Russell Fairbrother
**Responsibilities**
**Senior:** Lawrence Alexander (Proprietor), Roger Flashman (Transport Manager)
**Sales:** Neil Johnstone (Brand Manager)
**HR:** Rachael Lees (Human Resources Manager)
**Health & Safety:** Rachael Lees (Human Resources Manager)
**Facilities:** Paul Parry (Production Manager)
**Fleet:** Roger Flashman (Transport Manager)
**Engineering:** Paul Parry (Production Manager)
**US SIC:** 6711, 5961, 7399
**UK SIC:** 83962, 65600, 83954
**Auditors:** KPMG Audit PLC
**Bankers:** Barclays Bank Plc (20-35-81)

|      | 31-03-14     | 31-03-13     | 31-03-12     |
|------|--------------|--------------|--------------|
| TO   | 269,563,000  | 278,984,000  | 279,025,000  |
| P/L  | 9,404,000    | 9,531,000    | 8,582,000    |
| NW   | (8,934,000)  | (16,600,000) | (21,311,000) |
| WC   | (16,364,000) | (25,352,000) | (29,368,000) |
| Emp. | 306          | 304          | 286          |

DUNS 21-781-1821
**Park Hall Care Home**
Ubberley Road, Stoke-On-Trent, Staffordshire ST2 0QS
**Tel:** 01782406920
**Web:** www.idealcarehomes.co.uk
**Estd:** 2011 Proprietorship
**Line of Business:** Residential care establishments
**Proprietor:** Mrs T Brough

**Responsibilities**
**Senior:** Melanie Fenton (Home Manager)
**US SIC:** 8321 **UK SIC:** 96111
**Employees:** 50

DUNS 23-478-0609
**Park Head Hotel**
New Coundon, Bishop Auckland, County Durham DL14 8QB
**Tel:** 01388-661727
**Web:** www.parkheadcountryhotel.co.uk
**Estd:** 1993 Proprietorship
**Line of Business:** Hotels
**Proprietor:** M Mckey
**Responsibilities**
**Senior:** Claire Gibbons (Proprietor), malcolm McKey (Proprietor)
**Finance:** Tony Gibbons (Manager)
**IT:** Tony Gibbons (Manager)
**Purchasing:** Tony Gibbons (Manager)
**US SIC:** 7011 **UK SIC:** 66500
**Employees:** 50

DUNS 29-162-5135
**Park Healthcare Ltd**
15 Queen Annes Gate, London SW1H 9BU
**Tel:** 01747830282
**Web:** www.park-healthcare.co.uk
**Reg No:** 1793096 **VAT No:** 563041271
**Estd:** 1984 Private Limited Company
**Line of Business:** Other human health activities
**Issued Capital:** £175,000
**Managing Director:** R M Clarkson
**Co. Secretary:** Currey & Co Llp
**Responsibilities**
**Finance:** Sharon Blake (Head of Finance)
**Branches:** Hays Ho, Nr Shaftesbury Dorset SP7 9JR
**US SIC:** 8091, 6531
**UK SIC:** 95200, 83400
**Auditors:** Baker Tilly
**Bankers:** The Royal Bank Of Scotland Plc (15-10-00)

|     | 31-08-13  | 31-08-12  | 31-08-11  |
|-----|-----------|-----------|-----------|
| TO  | N/A       | N/A       | 2,684,507 |
| P/L | N/A       | N/A       | (32,065)  |
| NW  | 2,481,209 | 2,637,426 | 1,668,844 |
| WC  | 1,266,407 | 1,429,470 | (796,057) |

DUNS 21-481-5578
**Park Hill Hospital**
Thorne Road, Doncaster, South Yorkshire DN2 5TH
**Tel:** 01302730300
**Web:** www.parkhillhospital.co.uk
**Estd:** 1996 Partnership
**Line of Business:** Physiotherapists
**Trading Style:** Ramsay Health Care Uk Operations Limited
**Partners:** Ms J Bedford, Ms D Abbott, Ms R Bradbury, Ms T Williamson
**Responsibilities**
**Finance:** Tracy Kaye (Accountant)
**US SIC:** 8062 **UK SIC:** 95100
**Employees:** 100

DUNS 50-451-4860
**Park Holidays Uk Ltd**
(Subsidiary of: Caledonia Investments P L C)
Coghurst Hall, Hastings, East Sussex TN35 4NP
**Tel:** 01424751185
**Web:** www.parkholidaysuk.com
**Reg No:** 2434151 **Estd:** 1989 Private Limited Company
**Line of Business:** Caravan parks
**Issued Capital:** £1,650
**Directors:** A N Clish, J A Sills
**Co. Secretary:** Alasdair Loch
**Responsibilities**
**Senior:** Geoff Barnes (Marketing Director)
**Finance:** K McPherson (Finance Director)
**Marketing:** Geoff Barnes (Marketing Director)
**IT:** Kevin Padgham (IT Director)
**HR:** P Devlia (Personnel Director), Marguerite Gillougley (Human Resources Director)
**Health & Safety:** Marguerite Gillougley (Human Resources Director)
**Facilities:** Gary Gough (Park Manager)
**Branches:** Park Holidays Uk Ltd, Cinque Ports Leisure, Felixstowe Beach Caravan Park, Felixstowe, Suffolk IP11 2HA
**US SIC:** 7033 **UK SIC:** 66701
**Auditors:** Baker Tilly
**Bankers:** National Westminster Bank Plc (51-70-12)

|      | 31-03-14     | 31-12-12     | 31-03-11     |
|------|--------------|--------------|--------------|
| TO   | 105,327,879  | 83,606,765   | 73,807,120   |
| P/L  | 14,508,495   | 15,817,311   | 14,305,210   |
| NW   | 190,719,735  | 202,362,168  | 207,203,351  |
| WC   | (14,763,195) | (26,155,239) | (34,513,607) |
| Emp. | 529          | 579          | 581          |

DUNS 51-981-9106
**Park Homes (U K) Ltd**
120 City Road, Bradford, West Yorkshire BD8 8JT
**Tel:** 01274-496321
**Web:** www.parkhomesuk.co.uk
**Reg No:** 3349379 **Estd:** 1997 Private Limited Company
**Line of Business:** Other business activities not elsewhere classified
**Issued Capital:** £100
**Directors:** Dr M Khan, M Hussain
**Co. Secretary:** Ms Fatima Shahid
**Branches:** Park Homes (U K) Ltd, Claremont Gardens, Pudsey, West Yorkshire LS28 5BF
**US SIC:** 7399 **UK SIC:** 83954
**Auditors:** Unknown Auditor
**Bankers:** National Westminster Bank Plc (60-60-05)

|      | 31-03-14  | 31-03-13  | 31-03-12  |
|------|-----------|-----------|-----------|
| TO   | 6,802,791 | 6,248,824 | 6,754,702 |
| P/L  | 1,163,290 | 303,736   | 716,834   |
| NW   | 5,091,963 | 3,819,554 | 3,545,056 |
| WC   | 4,944,188 | 4,230,482 | 4,314,795 |
| Emp. | 312       | 314       | 314       |

DUNS 77-820-3380
**Park House Court (Building No.5) Management Ltd**
(Subsidiary of: Homeselect Finance (No.3) Ltd)
Park House Hotel Narberth Road, Tenby, Dyfed SA70 8TJ
**Tel:** 01834843955
**Reg No:** 3028692 **Estd:** 1995 Private Limited Company
**Line of Business:** Management of real estate on a fee or contract basis
**Issued Capital:** £8
**Directors:** C S Parker, P J Parker
**Co. Secretary:** Phillip Parker
**US SIC:** 6531 **UK SIC:** 83400
**Auditors:** Ashmole & Co

|     | 24-03-14 | 24-03-13 | 24-03-12 |
|-----|----------|----------|----------|
| TA  | 1,661    | N/A      | N/A      |
| NW  | (6,120)  | (9,961)  | (8,061)  |
| WC  | (6,120)  | N/A      | N/A      |

DUNS 29-171-3881                          Imp-Exp
**Park House Healthcare Ltd**
Whitehall 26 Business Park, Bradford, West Yorkshire BD11 2HW
**Tel:** 0845-060-0333 **Fax:** 08450600334
**Web:** www.parkhouse-hc.com
**Reg No:** 1831906 **VAT No:** 406003216
**Estd:** 1984 Private Limited Company
**Line of Business:** Hospital equipment
**Export Markets:** U S A; Germany; France; Switzerland; Russia
**Export Sales:** £807,726
**Issued Capital:** £5,000
**Principals:** S G Owens (Managing), D J Perry, A Dawson, Ms P J Towey, R Slater
**Co. Secretary:** Mrs Collette Owens
**Branches:** Park House Healthcare Ltd, Chells Enterprise Village, Chells Way, Stevenage, Hertfordshire SG2 0LQ
**US SIC:** 5199, 3841
**UK SIC:** 61900, 37201
**Auditors:** Buckle Barton
**Bankers:** Yorkshire Bank Plc (05-06-56)

|      | 31-12-13   | 31-12-12   | 31-12-11   |
|------|------------|------------|------------|
| TO   | 16,154,519 | 15,494,634 | 13,326,094 |
| P/L  | 2,726,981  | 2,215,117  | 2,077,565  |
| NW   | 9,201,387  | 7,136,675  | 5,487,904  |
| WC   | 7,363,027  | 5,321,286  | 4,111,837  |
| Emp. | 162        | 152        | 120        |

DUNS 49-312-6759
**Park House Ltd**
(Subsidiary of: Blackshaw Investment Group Ltd)
93 Park Road South, Prenton, Merseyside CH43 4UU
**Tel:** 01516521021
**Reg No:** 3121024 **Estd:** 1995 Private Limited Company
**Line of Business:** Other letting of own property
**Issued Capital:** £100
**Director:** J S Brooksbank
**Co. Secretary:** Mrs Susan Brooksbank
**US SIC:** 6519 **UK SIC:** 85000

|    | 30-11-11 | 30-05-10 |
|----|----------|----------|
| TA | 170,124  | 170,124  |
| NW | 170,124  | 170,124  |

DUNS 21-526-4107
**Park House Nursing Home**
27 Park Crescent, Peterborough, Cambridgeshire PE1 4DX
**Tel:** 01733555700
**Web:** www.parkhousenursinghome.co.uk
**Estd:** 1989 Partnership
**Line of Business:** Medical nursing home activities
**Partners:** Mrs A Waller, A Waller

**Responsibilities**
**Senior:** Alan Waller (Proprietor)
**US SIC:** 8051 **UK SIC:** 95100
**Employees:** 50

DUNS 22-650-5055                                Imp
**Park Industrial & Agricultural Holdings Ltd**
4 Private Road, Nottingham, Nottinghamshire NG5 4DB
**Tel:** 01159403332 **Fax:** 01159-402728
**Web:** www.parklogistics.co.uk
**Reg No:** 1359576 **Estd:** 1978 Private Limited Company
**Line of Business:** Warehouses
**Trading Style:** Park Logistics
**Issued Capital:** £100
**Managing Director:** S R Gibson
**Responsibilities**
**Senior:** Ann Randell (Manager)
**US SIC:** 4226 **UK SIC:** 77003
**Auditors:** MGC Hayles Ltd
**Bankers:** HSBC Bank plc (40-35-18)

|      | 30-04-14    | 30-04-13  | 30-04-12  |
|------|-------------|-----------|-----------|
| TO   | 4,684,116   | 6,268,175 | 5,993,997 |
| P/L  | (883,717)   | 1,348,389 | (165,933) |
| NW   | 6,310,652   | 7,872,369 | 8,440,048 |
| WC   | (1,528,671) | (80,064)  | (946,297) |
| Emp. | 63          | 83        | 76        |

DUNS 21-320-2538
**Park Inn**
Birmingham Road, West Bromwich, West Midlands B70 6RS
**Tel:** 08713308201
**Web:** www.parkinn.co.uk
**Proprietorship**
**Line of Business:** Hotels
**Proprietor:** A Pickard
**Responsibilities**
**Finance:** Beckie Teale (Finance Controller)
**Sales:** Sarah Tennant (Sales Manager)
**US SIC:** 7999, 6531
**UK SIC:** 97913, 83400
**Employees:** 48

DUNS 21-555-6290
**Park Inn Belfast**
4 Clarence St West, Belfast BT2 7GP
**Tel:** 02890677700
**Web:** www.parkinn.co.uk
**Estd:** 2010 Proprietorship
**Line of Business:** Other tourist assistance activities not elsewhere classified
**Proprietor:** G Kelly
**Responsibilities**
**Senior:** Jan Hanak (Manager)
**US SIC:** 7999 **UK SIC:** 97913
**Employees:** 70

DUNS 21-620-9947
**Park Inn Palace**
Church Road, Southend-On-Sea, Essex SS1 2AL
**Tel:** 01702455100
**Web:** www.parkinn.co.uk
**Estd:** 2011 Proprietorship
**Line of Business:** Other tourist assistance activities not elsewhere classified
**Proprietor:** R Smith
**US SIC:** 7999, 7011
**UK SIC:** 97913, 66500
**Employees:** 60

DUNS 23-701-3925
**Park Lands Hospital**
Aldermaston Road, Basingstoke, Hampshire RG24 9RH
**Tel:** 01256-817718
**Web:** www.northhampshire.nhs.uk
**Proprietorship**
**Line of Business:** Hospitals
**Proprietor:** Mrs K Beaks
**US SIC:** 8062 **UK SIC:** 95100
**Employees:** 1,500

DUNS 21-230-6631
**Park Lane Care Home**
45 Park Lane, Barnstaple, Devon EX32 9AL
**Tel:** 01271-373600
**Web:** www.parklanenh.co.uk
**Estd:** 1971 Proprietorship
**Line of Business:** Nursing homes
**Proprietor:** Mrs L Orm
**Responsibilities**
**Senior:** Deborah Shears (Manager)
**US SIC:** 8051 **UK SIC:** 95100
**Employees:** 60

DUNS 29-435-1069
## Park Lane Ltd
**(Subsidiary of:** Bayerische Motoren Werke Ag)
77 Park Lane, London W1K 7TP
**Fax:** 02074938333
**Web:** www.bmwparklane.com
**Reg No:** 1569304 **Estd:** 1981 Private Limited Company
**Line of Business:** Car accessories and parts
**Trading Style:** B M W Authorities
**Issued Capital:** £10,000
**Directors:** K Davidson, M E Worthington
**Co. Secretary:** Ms Gillian Woolley
**Responsibilities**
**Senior:** Kavita Bengali *(Chef)*
**Finance:** Petra Synowzik *(Financial Director)*
**Sales:** Lukas Ryan *(?BMW and MINI Corporate Sales)*
**HR:** Matthew Ruck *(Human Resources Director)*
**Facilities:** Eddie Sycamore *(Maintenance Manager)*
**Branches:** Park Lane Ltd, 63-64 Park La, London W1K 7TP
**US SIC:** 5511, 7539, 5531, 5571
**UK SIC:** 65100, 67100
**Auditors:** KPMG LLP

| | 31-12-13 | 31-12-12 | 31-12-11 |
|---|---|---|---|
| TO | 246,855,000 | 242,203,000 | 239,848,000 |
| P/L | (5,740,000) | (6,093,000) | (1,063,000) |
| NW | 4,327,000 | 5,754,000 | 7,119,000 |
| WC | (4,958,000) | (4,191,000) | 5,593,000 |
| Emp. | 214 | 206 | 202 |

DUNS 49-136-6647
## Park Lane Properties (Leeds) Ltd
25 27 Otley Road, Leeds, West Yorkshire LS6 3AA
**Tel:** 01132-304949 **Fax:** 01132-260800
**Web:** www.parklaneproperties.com
**Reg No:** 3107217 **Estd:** 1995 Private Limited Company
**Line of Business:** Other letting of own property
**Issued Capital:** £1,030
**Directors:** N Ahmed, N Ahmed, R Ahmed, N Ahmed
**Co. Secretary:** Sameer Ahmed
**Branches:** Park Lane Properties (Leeds) Ltd, 12 Swinegate, Leeds, West Yorkshire LS1 4AG
**US SIC:** 6519, 6531
**UK SIC:** 85000, 83400
**Auditors:** Horwath Clark Whitehill
**Bankers:** Yorkshire Bank Plc (05-04-04)

| | 30-09-13 | 30-09-12 | 30-09-11 |
|---|---|---|---|
| TO | 10,814,663 | 10,107,113 | 9,722,275 |
| P/L | 1,776,305 | 1,774,872 | 2,120,794 |
| NW | 12,747,623 | 11,195,195 | 9,572,329 |
| WC | 3,463,639 | (3,836,948) | 3,468,977 |
| Emp. | 91 | 90 | 90 |

DUNS 39-686-0231 **Imp-Exp**
## Park Lane (U K) Ltd
9 Alton Business Centre, Omega Park, Alton, Hampshire GU34 2YU
**Tel:** 01420544300
**Web:** www.parklaneuk.com
**Reg No:** 2144597 **VAT No:** 466594501
**Estd:** 1987 Private Limited Company
**Line of Business:** Sale of new motor vehicles
**Export Markets:** Worldwide
**Export Sales:** £23,088,474
**Issued Capital:** £40,002
**Principals:** R W Dane *(Managing)*, S P Wright
**Co. Secretary:** Andrew Jackson
**US SIC:** 5511, 5521
**UK SIC:** 65100
**Auditors:** Hextall Meakin
**Bankers:** HSBC Bank plc (40-05-15)

| | 31-12-13 | 31-12-12 | 31-12-11 |
|---|---|---|---|
| TO | 24,182,804 | 29,417,627 | 21,659,388 |
| P/L | 1,222,809 | 177,322 | 2,694,324 |
| NW | 4,245,247 | 4,735,122 | 4,385,725 |
| WC | 5,188,018 | 2,513,878 | 4,214,328 |
| Emp. | 59 | 64 | 60 |

DUNS 51-984-5762
## Park Leisure 2000 Ltd
Frosterley, Bishop Auckland, County Durham DL13 2SJ
**Tel:** 08448263178
**Web:** www.parkleisure.co.uk
**Reg No:** 3352005 **Estd:** 1996 Private Limited Company
**Line of Business:** Holiday centres and holiday villages
**Issued Capital:** £100
**Directors:** Ms C Molloy, J Gourlay, P Burton, J Gourlay, G M Molloy, C Allerston, M Dewhurst, Ms J Cowl
**Co. Secretary:** Steven Davidson
**Branches:** Park Leisure 2000 Ltd, Heatherview Leisure Park, Bishop Auckland, County Durham DL13 2PS
**US SIC:** 7032 **UK SIC:** 66702

**Auditors:** Lloyd Dowson & Co
**Bankers:** Barclays Bank Plc (20-75-92)

| | 31-12-13 | 31-12-12 | 31-12-11 |
|---|---|---|---|
| TO | 32,888,161 | 27,324,849 | 22,843,620 |
| P/L | 3,054,393 | 2,357,946 | 2,305,321 |
| NW | 23,937,684 | 22,312,630 | 21,079,612 |
| WC | (5,687,518) | (2,777,699) | (3,360,652) |
| Emp. | 187 | 146 | 132 |

DUNS 21-028-3329
## Park Lodge Hotel
Parc Y Llyn Retail Park, Llanbadarn Fawr, Llanon, Dyfed SY23 3TL
**Tel:** 01970-636333
**Web:** www.aberpark.com
**Estd:** 2003 Partnership
**Line of Business:** Hotels and motels without restaurant
**Partners:** V Morgans, Mrs A Morgans
**US SIC:** 7011 **UK SIC:** 66500
**Employees:** 87

DUNS 21-783-0352
## Park Mains High School
Barrhill Road, Erskine, Renfrewshire PA8 6EY
**Tel:** 01418122801
**Web:** www.parkmainshigh.renfrewshire.sch.uk
**Estd:** 2002 Partnership
**Line of Business:** Schools (local authority)
**Partners:** M Dewar, M Dewar
**Responsibilities**
**IT:** Ann McGowan *(IT Manager)*, Ricky Taylor *(Network Manager)*
**US SIC:** 8211 **UK SIC:** 93200
**Employees:** 150

DUNS 21-589-0979
## Park Manor Nursing Home
6 Thornhill Road, Dunmurry, Belfast BT17 9EJ
**Tel:** 02890307700
**Web:** www.macklingroup.com
**Estd:** 2010 Proprietorship
**Line of Business:** Medical nursing home activities
**Proprietor:** G Macklin
**Responsibilities**
**Senior:** Liz Thompson *(Manager)*
**US SIC:** 8051 **UK SIC:** 95100
**Employees:** 120

DUNS 21-584-7817
## Park Motor Finance
Dallam Court, Dallam Lane, Warrington, Cheshire WA2 7LT
**Tel:** 08703200444
**Web:** www.bluemotorfinance.co.uk
**Estd:** 2011 Proprietorship
**Line of Business:** Financial services
**Proprietor:** J Summers
**Responsibilities**
**Senior:** Claire Boon *(Supervisor)*
**US SIC:** 6111 **UK SIC:** 81501
**Employees:** 200

DUNS 21-587-7015
## Park Plaza
Park Plaza, 41 Maid Marian Way, Nottingham, Nottinghamshire NG1 6GD
**Tel:** 01159477200
**Web:** www.parkplazanottingham.com
**Estd:** 2003 Proprietorship
**Line of Business:** Hotels
**Proprietor:** S Bench
**Responsibilities**
**Senior:** Tom Waldron-Lynch *(General Manager)*
**Health & Safety:** Tony Joynes *(Maintenance Manager)*
**Facilities:** Tony Joynes *(Maintenance Manager)*
**US SIC:** 7011 **UK SIC:** 66500
**Employees:** 90

DUNS 21-623-3348
## Park Plaza Hospitality Services (Uk) Ltd
**(Subsidiary of:** Park Plaza Coöperatief U.A.)
12 David Mews, London W1U 6EG
**Tel:** 02070344800
**Web:** www.parkplaza.com
**Reg No:** 7036248 **Estd:** 2009 Private Limited Company
**Line of Business:** Hotels
**Issued Capital:** £1
**Directors:** B E Ivesha, C C Moravsky
**Co. Secretary:** Mrs Inbar Zilberman
**US SIC:** 7011 **UK SIC:** 66500

| | 31-12-13 | 31-12-12 | 31-12-11 |
|---|---|---|---|
| TO | 19,776,000 | 18,414,000 | 17,488,000 |
| P/L | (552,000) | (48,000) | (1,093,000) |
| NW | (4,028,000) | (3,476,000) | (3,428,000) |
| WC | 2,498,000 | 3,679,000 | 1,676,000 |
| Emp. | 226 | 246 | 259 |

DUNS 21-038-7359
## Park Plaza Hotels & Resorts
239 Vauxhall Bridge Road, London SW1V 1EQ
**Tel:** 08444156750
**Web:** www.parkplaza.com
**Proprietorship**
**Line of Business:** Hotels
**Proprietor:** R Costa
**US SIC:** 7011 **UK SIC:** 66500
**Employees:** 46

DUNS 22-160-4296
## Park Resorts Holdings Ltd
**(Subsidiary of:** Dome Holdings Ltd)
Swan Court, Waterhouse Street, Hemel Hempstead, Hertfordshire HP1 1FN
**Web:** www.park-resorts.com
**Reg No:** 4178974 **Estd:** 2001 Private Limited Company
**Line of Business:** Holiday parks and camps
**Issued Capital:** £12,500
**Directors:** M Clark, N D Brewster, A Castledine, D Boden
**Co. Secretary:**
T & H Secretarial Services (Park
**Branches:** Park Resorts Holdings Ltd, Bideford Bay Holiday Village, Bideford, Devon EX39 5DU
**US SIC:** 6711 **UK SIC:** 83902
**Auditors:** KPMG LLP
**Bankers:** Bank Of Scotland (80-11-45)

| | 31-03-14 | 31-03-13 | 31-03-12 |
|---|---|---|---|
| TA | 56,716,000 | 56,716,000 | 56,716,000 |
| NW | 56,716,000 | 56,716,000 | 56,716,000 |

DUNS 22-114-8948
## Park Resorts Ltd
**(Subsidiary of:** Dome Holdings Ltd)
Swan Court, Swan Court, Hemel Hempstead, Hertfordshire HP1 1FN
**Tel:** 01442-414-100 **Fax:** 01442830200
**Web:** www.park-resorts.com
**Reg No:** 4133998 **Estd:** 2000 Private Limited Company
**Line of Business:** Representative office
**Issued Capital:** £20,503,693
**Directors:** D F Vaughan, N D Brewster, A Castledine, M Clark, D Boden
**Co. Secretary:**
T & H Secretarial Services (Park
**Responsibilities**
**Senior:** Richie Jones *(Marketing Director)*
**Marketing:** Andy Edge *(Sales & Marketing Director)*, Richie Jones *(Marketing Director)*, Francesca Read *(Marketing Exec)*
**Sales:** Andy Edge *(Sales & Marketing Director)*
**IT:** Mike Pitaman-Willcock *(IT Manager)*
**HR:** Beverley Murphy *(Human Resources Manager)*, Beverley Priest *(Human Resources Manager)*
**Health & Safety:** Beverley Murphy *(Human Resources Manager)*, Beverley Priest *(Human Resources Manager)*
**Branches:** Park Resorts Ltd, Mill Lane, Scarborough, North Yorkshire YO11 3NN
**US SIC:** 7399 **UK SIC:** 83954
**Auditors:** Deloitte & Touche LLP
**Bankers:** Bank Of Scotland (80-11-45)

| | 31-03-14 | 31-03-13 | 31-03-12 |
|---|---|---|---|
| TO | 162,591,000 | 167,484,000 | 173,339,000 |
| P/L | (4,689,000) | (4,025,000) | (2,186,000) |
| NW | 122,751,000 | 127,440,000 | 131,465,000 |
| WC | (34,277,000) | 143,610,000 | 138,290,000 |
| Emp. | 1,908 | 1,977 | 1,861 |

DUNS 34-593-0713
## Park School (Bournemouth) Ltd
43 South Road, Bournemouth, Dorset BH1 4PB
**Tel:** 01202396640
**Web:** www.parkschool.co.uk
**Reg No:** 2737223 **Estd:** 1999 Private Limited Company
**Line of Business:** Schools (independent)
**Trading Style:** Park School
**Issued Capital:** £112
**Directors:** A Main, M M Smyth
**Co. Secretary:** Mrs Sally Smyth
**US SIC:** 8211 **UK SIC:** 93200
**Auditors:** Thomas & Young
**Bankers:** National Westminster Bank Plc (56-00-35)

| | 31-08-14 | 31-08-13 | 31-08-12 |
|---|---|---|---|
| TA | 1,111,677 | 985,505 | 876,640 |
| NW | 485,286 | 415,881 | 320,943 |
| WC | 97,524 | 147,744 | 67,950 |

DUNS 29-020-6291
## The Park School (Yeovil) Ltd
The Park, Yeovil, Somerset BA20 1DH
**Web:** www.parkschool.com
**Reg No:** 0593878 **Estd:** 1957 Private Limited Company
**Line of Business:** Schools (independent)
**Directors:** K R Stevens, S G Hart, Ms S M Dare, C J Blackburn, R M Moody, Mrs F Wilson, N C Baker, Mrs L L Sanders
**Co. Secretary:** John Brookes
**Responsibilities**
**Senior:** Paul Bate *(Headmaster)*, Paul Cattermole *(Governor)*, Nicholas Forrest *(Manager)*, Ian Green *(Chairman)*, David Herring *(Manager)*, Jane Huntington *(Headmaster)*
**Finance:** Judy Gentis *(Bursar)*
**HR:** Paul Bate *(Headmaster)*, Jane Huntington *(Headmaster)*
**Health & Safety:** Judy Gentis *(Bursar)*
**Facilities:** Judy Gentis *(Bursar)*
**US SIC:** 8211 **UK SIC:** 93200
**Auditors:** Sully & Co

| | 31-08-13 | 31-08-12 | 31-08-11 |
|---|---|---|---|
| TO | 1,767,621 | 1,878,468 | 1,997,653 |
| P/L | (215,872) | (168,626) | 7,098 |
| NW | 1,707,977 | 1,923,849 | 2,092,475 |
| WC | 123,888 | 224,566 | 557,471 |
| Emp. | 70 | 79 | 79 |

DUNS 21-051-9604
## Park Surgery
Albion Way, Horsham, West Sussex RH12 1BG
**Tel:** 01403330266
**Web:** www.parksurgery.com
**Estd:** 2011 Partnership
**Line of Business:** Doctors
**Partners:** Dr J E Clarke, Dr D W Holwell, Dr D G Skipp, Dr J M Mulvey, Dr S R Fisher, Dr M Tariq, Dr S J Dean, Dr M K Noel-Paton
**Responsibilities**
**Senior:** Paula Salerno *(Practice Manager)*
**US SIC:** 8011 **UK SIC:** 95300
**Employees:** 50

DUNS 22-700-5089
## The Park Tower Hotel Ltd
**(Subsidiary of:** Park Tower Holdings Establishment)
101 Knightsbridge, London SW1X 7RN
**Tel:** 02072358050 **Fax:** 020-7235-8231
**Web:** www.theparktowerknightsbridge.com
**Reg No:** 1009626 **Estd:** 1971 Private Limited Company
**Line of Business:** Hotels
**Trading Style:** Sheraton Park Tower Hotel
**Issued Capital:** £1,400,000
**Directors:** His Excellency M M Al Tajir, A M Altajir, M S Al Tajir
**Responsibilities**
**Senior:** Sue Finlay *(Manager)*, Charles Parte *(Manager)*
**Purchasing:** Angella Tomlinson *(Purchasing Manager)*
**US SIC:** 7011, 5812
**UK SIC:** 66500, 66110
**Auditors:** Wheawill & Sudworth
**Bankers:** The Royal Bank Of Scotland Plc (16-01-29)

| | 31-12-13 | 31-12-12 | 31-12-11 |
|---|---|---|---|
| TO | 28,814,870 | 30,978,014 | 27,940,769 |
| P/L | 8,235,371 | 10,898,344 | 10,040,768 |
| NW | 952,447 | 1,045,537 | 2,666,407 |
| WC | (5,892,066) | (5,973,842) | (4,423,130) |
| Emp. | 235 | 248 | 232 |

DUNS 34-648-8901
## Park Tower Investments Ltd
**(Subsidiary of:** Park Tower Holdings Establishment)
101 Knightsbridge, London SW1X 7RQ
**Tel:** 02072356161
**Web:** www.grosvenorcasinos.com
**Reg No:** 2773984 **Estd:** 1992 Private Limited Company
**Line of Business:** Casinos
**Issued Capital:** £100
**Directors:** A M Al Tajir, M S Al Tajir, His Excellency M M Al Tajir
**Responsibilities**
**Senior:** James Ferrary *(General Manager)*
**US SIC:** 7999 **UK SIC:** 97913
**Auditors:** Wheawill & Sudworth

| | 31-12-13 | 31-12-12 | 31-12-11 |
|---|---|---|---|
| TO | 31,404,875 | 34,067,000 | 30,384,746 |
| P/L | 3,841,160 | 6,428,399 | 3,889,312 |
| NW | (20,246,627) | (17,904,297) | (16,399,076) |
| WC | (85,515,144) | 6,966,007 | 10,591,736 |
| Emp. | 259 | 280 | 264 |

DUNS 21-823-6937
## Park View Educational Trust
Park View School - The Academy Of, Mathematics & School, Birmingham, West Midlands B8 3HG
**Tel:** 01215666500
**Web:** www.pvet.co.uk
**Reg No:** 7949154 **Estd:** 2012 Private Company Limited By Guarantee
**Line of Business:** Schools (local authority)
**Directors:** Ms P M Smart, Ms B A Flint, W Saleem, K Hanif, A G Packer, Mrs Y L Wilkinson, A A Majid
**Co. Secretary:** Miss Sharon Griffiths

**Responsibilities**
**Senior:** Shahid Akmal *(Manager)*, Tahir Alam *(Chairman)*
**US SIC:** 8211 **UK SIC:** 93200
**Bankers:** Lloyds TSB Bank plc (30-93-66)

| | 31-08-13 | 31-08-12 |
|---|---|---|
| TO | 17,232,912 | 13,146,448 |
| P/L | 8,728,105 | 11,234,864 |
| NW | 19,640,969 | 11,130,864 |
| WC | 1,174,386 | 584,978 |
| Emp. | 238 | 102 |

DUNS 23-643-4775
## Park View Landscape Maintenance Ltd
(**Subsidiary of:** Nurture Landscapes Holdings Ltd)
Park Road, Blackburn, Lancashire BB1 4NG
**Tel:** 01254-886126
**Web:** www.parkviewlandscapes.co.uk
**Reg No:** 1378663 **VAT No:** 326099645
**Estd:** 1965 Private Limited Company
**Line of Business:** Agricultural services
**Issued Capital:** £100
**Directors:** P J Fane, P G Bean
**US SIC:** 0729 **UK SIC:** 01003

| | 31-03-14 | 31-03-13 | 31-03-11 |
|---|---|---|---|
| TO | N/A | 4,547,156 | N/A |
| P/L | N/A | 79,316 | N/A |
| NW | 4,785 | 635,674 | 802,553 |
| WC | 4,785 | 635,674 | 378,430 |

DUNS 22-806-9977 **Imp-Exp**
## Parkam Foods Ltd
(**Subsidiary of:** Tulip International (U K) Ltd)
Spen Valley Mills, Halifax Road, Liversedge, West Yorkshire WF15 6JL
**Tel:** 01924-522222 **Fax:** 01924516516
**Web:** www.parkam.com
**Reg No:** 1697175 **VAT No:** 361758337
**Estd:** 1983 Private Limited Company
**Line of Business:** Wholesale of meat and meat products
**Export Markets:** Switzerland; E U
**Issued Capital:** £287,725
**Directors:** H Jensen, C Thomas
**Co. Secretary:** Herluf Jensen
**Responsibilities**
**HR:** Rachel Rose *(Human Resources Manager)*
**Health & Safety:** Ralph Danby *(Manager)*
**Operations:** Ralph Danby *(Manager)*
**Branches:** Parkam Foods Ltd, Unit 4, Hanging Wood Way, Cleckheaton, West Yorkshire BD19 4TS
**US SIC:** 5147, 2013
**UK SIC:** 61700, 41223
**Auditors:** Murphy Salisbury
**Bankers:** Barclays Bank Plc (20-35-84)

| | 29-09-13 | 30-09-12 | 31-09-11 |
|---|---|---|---|
| TO | 25,806,270 | 29,482,896 | 47,340,529 |
| P/L | (3,554,616) | (4,432) | (5,528,785) |
| NW | 181,337 | 606,727 | 708,514 |
| WC | (834,352) | 3,930,466 | 6,926,218 |
| Emp. | 128 | 254 | 290 |

DUNS 77-951-6343
## Parkburn Precision Handling Systems Ltd
Unit 26, Hamilton, Lanarkshire ML3 0ED
**Web:** www.parkburn.com
**Reg No:** 0158127SC **VAT No:** 774836778
**Estd:** 1995 Private Limited Company
**Line of Business:** Manufacture of electricity distribution and control apparatus
**Export Sales:** £3,711,903
**Trading Style:** Parkburn Precision Handling Systems Ltd
**Issued Capital:** £2,000
**Directors:** D Ohara, A Lawson
**Co. Secretary:** Martin Mcfall
**Responsibilities**
**Senior:** Campbell Mcfell *(Manager)*, Dennis O'Hara *(Joint Managing Director)*
**Health & Safety:** Sandy Currie *(Health & Safety Officer)*
**Facilities:** Dennis O'Hara *(Joint Managing Director)*
**Branches:** Parkburn Precision Handling Systems Ltd, Glencairn Indust Est, Kilmarnock, Ayrshire KA1 4AY
**US SIC:** 3643, 5084
**UK SIC:** 34203, 61490
**Auditors:** Bannerman Johnstone Maclay
**Bankers:** Bank Of Scotland (80-11-66)

| | 30-06-13 | 30-06-12 | 30-06-11 |
|---|---|---|---|
| TO | 11,975,426 | 12,673,284 | 10,064,796 |
| P/L | 452,564 | 15,048 | 1,257,367 |
| NW | 1,870,870 | 1,302,978 | 1,282,091 |
| WC | 824,234 | 2,921,467 | 2,750,066 |
| Emp. | 65 | 61 | 65 |

DUNS 39-701-7013
## Parkcare Homes Ltd
(**Subsidiary of:** Advent International Corporation)
Weir End House, Weir End, Ross-On-Wye, Herefordshire HR9 6AL
**Tel:** 01214346140 **Fax:** 01989767077
**Web:** www.craegmoor.co.uk
**Reg No:** 2155276 **Estd:** 2002 Private Limited Company
**Line of Business:** Other human health activities
**Trading Style:** Craegmoor Health Care, Kilncroft Residential Home
**Issued Capital:** £4,772,000
**Directors:** A Pancott, Ms C Denny, J D Lock, T Riall, Ms N Bales
**Co. Secretary:** David Hall
**Responsibilities**
**Senior:** Donna Daniels *(Manager)*
**Branches:** Parkcare Homes Ltd, Derwent Street, Sheffield, South Yorkshire S2 5BN
**US SIC:** 8091 **UK SIC:** 95200
**Auditors:** PricewaterhouseCoopers LLP
**Bankers:** National Westminster Bank Plc (60-05-13)

| | 31-12-13 | 31-12-12 | 31-12-11 |
|---|---|---|---|
| TO | 25,079,000 | 26,506,000 | 45,704,000 |
| P/L | (9,428,000) | 3,216,000 | 2,721,000 |
| NW | 32,042,000 | 41,449,000 | 38,238,000 |
| WC | (4,290,000) | (6,940,000) | (5,946,000) |
| Emp. | 1,185 | 1,222 | 1,696 |

DUNS 22-085-2839
## Parkdean Holiday Parks Ltd
(**Subsidiary of:** Pd Parks Holdings Ltd)
2nd Floor, Newcastle-Upon-Tyne, Tyne and Wear NE12 8ET
**Tel:** 01912560795 **Fax:** 01912686018
**Web:** www.parkdeanholidays.co.uk
**Reg No:** 4086679 **Estd:** 2000 Private Limited Company
**Line of Business:** Caravan parks
**Trading Style:** Grannie's Heilan'Hame, Nairn Lochloy Holiday Park, Tummel Valley Holiday Park, Sundrum Castle Holiday Park
**Issued Capital:** £8,027,167
**Directors:** J A Waterworth, M J Wilmot, D Bamsey
**Co. Secretary:** Ms Judith Archibold
**Responsibilities**
**Senior:** David Hopper *(Operations Manager)*
**Branches:** Parkdean Holiday Parks Ltd, Embo, Dornoch, Sutherland IV25 3QD
**US SIC:** 7033 **UK SIC:** 66701
**Auditors:** KPMG LLP

| | 31-01-14 | 31-01-13 | 31-01-12 |
|---|---|---|---|
| TO | 53,450,000 | 49,693,000 | 50,093,000 |
| P/L | (520,000) | 536,000 | 1,926,000 |
| NW | 46,171,000 | 46,775,000 | 46,702,000 |
| WC | (47,843,000) | (50,064,000) | (53,754,000) |
| Emp. | 831 | 789 | 755 |

DUNS 23-872-8021 **Imp**
## Parkdean Holidays Ltd
(**Subsidiary of:** Pd Parks Holdings Ltd)
2nd Floor, Newcastle-Upon-Tyne, Tyne and Wear NE12 8ET
**Tel:** 08443353450 **Fax:** 01912 686018
**Web:** www.parkdeanholidays.co.uk
**Reg No:** 3864124 **Estd:** 2000 Private Limited Company
**Line of Business:** Management activities of holding companies
**Issued Capital:** £10,756,444
**Directors:** D Bamsey, J A Waterworth, M J Wilmot
**Co. Secretary:** Ms Judith Archibold
**Responsibilities**
**Senior:** David Hopper *(Operations Manager)*
**Finance:** Michael Norden *(Finance Director)*
**US SIC:** 6711, 7032
**UK SIC:** 83962, 66702
**Auditors:** KPMG LLP
**Bankers:** Bank Of Scotland (12-08-95)

| | 31-01-14 | 31-01-13 | 31-01-12 |
|---|---|---|---|
| TA | 228,107,000 | 204,038,000 | 191,767,000 |
| P/L | 12,642,000 | 294,000 | 609,000 |
| NW | 67,540,000 | 54,894,000 | 54,564,000 |
| WC | (20,363,000) | (20,795,000) | (21,125,000) |

DUNS 42-471-9037 **Imp-Exp**
## Parkelect Ltd
(**Subsidiary of:** Westbank Business Park Ltd)
84 Dargan Road, Belfast BT3 9JU
**Tel:** 02890772773
**Web:** www.parkelect.co.uk
**Reg No:** 0026999NI **Estd:** 1973 Private Limited Company
**Line of Business:** Wholesale of hardware, plumbing and heating equipment and supplies
**Export Markets:** Republic of Ireland
**Trading Style:** Park Automation, Park Electrical Services, Satellite Lighting, Sinelco Controlgear
**Issued Capital:** £1,032
**Directors:** T Mcconnell, R Mcconachie, J W Mcconachie
**Co. Secretary:** Trevor Crawford
**Branches:** Parkelect Ltd, Lakeside, Unit 2, Sheffield, South Yorkshire S20 3RW
**US SIC:** 5074 **UK SIC:** 61300
**Auditors:** DNT
**Bankers:** Northern Bank Ltd (95-01-18)

| | 31-08-13 | 31-08-12 | 31-08-11 |
|---|---|---|---|
| TO | 15,189,213 | 14,461,144 | 13,681,354 |
| P/L | 1,122,498 | 878,069 | 1,111,939 |
| NW | 3,025,083 | 2,388,062 | 2,179,125 |
| WC | 1,792,231 | 1,150,323 | 1,012,503 |
| Emp. | 49 | 50 | 49 |

DUNS 73-608-0495
## Parkeon Ltd
10 Willis Way, Poole, Dorset BH15 3SS
**Tel:** 01202670671 **Fax:** 01202-339-369
**Web:** www.parkeon.com
**Reg No:** 4869035 **Estd:** 2003 Private Limited Company
**Line of Business:** Other business activities not elsewhere classified
**Issued Capital:** £2,320,001
**Directors:** D Hassett, B Barthelemy
**Co. Secretary:** Stephen Horton
**US SIC:** 7399, 1611
**UK SIC:** 83954, 50200
**Auditors:** Deloitte LLP
**Bankers:** National Westminster Bank Plc (52-41-37)

| | 31-12-13 | 31-12-12 | 31-12-11 |
|---|---|---|---|
| TO | 14,857,000 | 13,672,000 | 14,688,000 |
| P/L | 46,000 | 688,000 | 1,308,000 |
| NW | 3,941,000 | 3,570,000 | 2,645,000 |
| WC | 3,941,000 | 3,570,000 | 2,645,000 |
| Emp. | 64 | 64 | 64 |

DUNS 21-741-6262 **Imp-Exp**
## Parkeon Transit Ltd
(**Subsidiary of:** Intermediate Capital Group Plc)
Fleets Industrial Estate, Willis Way, Poole, Dorset BH15 3SS
**Tel:** 01202339339 **Fax:** 01202339369
**Web:** www.parkeon.co.uk
**Reg No:** 1232487 **VAT No:** 187700249
**Estd:** 1975 Private Limited Company
**Line of Business:** Manufacturers of electronic equipment and components
**Export Sales:** £5,801,000
**Issued Capital:** £900,312
**Directors:** O T Griffith, B Barthelemy
**Co. Secretary:** Stephen Horton
**Responsibilities**
**Senior:** Yves Chambeau *(Manager)*, Johannes Lindeman *(Manager)*, Philippe Millet *(Manager)*
**Sales:** Chris Octon *(Head of Export Sales)*
**IT:** Tony Cutler *(Facilities Manager)*
**Facilities:** T Culter *(Facilities Manager)*, Tony Cutler *(Facilities Manager)*, Ron Stevens *(Facilities Manager)*
**US SIC:** 7011, 3799
**UK SIC:** 66500, 36502
**Auditors:** Deloitte LLP
**Bankers:** Barclays Bank Plc (20-30-47)

| | 31-12-13 | 31-12-12 | 31-12-11 |
|---|---|---|---|
| TO | 17,047,000 | 23,186,000 | 21,934,000 |
| P/L | 1,020,000 | 1,193,000 | 1,570,000 |
| NW | 5,054,000 | 3,761,000 | 2,296,000 |
| WC | 4,970,000 | 3,661,000 | 2,041,000 |
| Emp. | 190 | 198 | 206 |

DUNS 21-640-8799
## Parker Brothers (Holdings) Ltd
Glyncoed Terrace, Llanelli, Dyfed SA15 1HQ
**Tel:** 01554-778666
**Web:** www.parker-hire.co.uk
**Reg No:** 0000910 **Estd:** 1958 Private Limited Company
**Line of Business:** Management activities of construction holding companies
**Issued Capital:** £900
**Managing Director:** S L Parker
**Co. Secretary:** George Parker
**US SIC:** 6711 **UK SIC:** 83962
**Auditors:** PricewaterhouseCooers
**Bankers:** HSBC Bank plc (40-30-10)

| | 31-03-14 | 31-03-13 | 31-03-12 |
|---|---|---|---|
| TO | 4,770,106 | 4,950,130 | 4,934,843 |
| P/L | 408,574 | (25,922) | 172,070 |
| NW | 3,758,946 | 3,501,660 | 3,499,139 |
| WC | 152,092 | (353,756) | (520,115) |
| Emp. | 54 | 52 | 52 |

DUNS 22-846-8153
## Parker Building Supplies Ltd
Westminster House, Bolton Close, Bellbrook Industrial Estate, Uckfield, East Sussex TN22 1QZ
**Web:** www.helpmebuildit.co.uk
**Reg No:** 2045211 **VAT No:** 403210719
**Estd:** 1986 Private Limited Company
**Line of Business:** Builders merchants
**Issued Capital:** £100,000
**Managing Director:** T C Parker
**Co. Secretary:** Stewart Pierce
**Responsibilities**
**Sales:** Byron Danahay *(Sales Manager)*
**Purchasing:** Grahame Coombs *(Procurement)*
**Branches:** Parker Building Supplies Ltd, Priory Road, Tonbridge, Kent TN9 2BB
**US SIC:** 5072 **UK SIC:** 61500
**Auditors:** Spain Brothers & Co
**Bankers:** Barclays Bank Plc (20-88-13)

| | 31-12-13 | 31-12-12 | 31-12-11 |
|---|---|---|---|
| TO | 44,200,785 | 32,715,711 | 31,879,552 |
| P/L | 310,390 | (167,039) | 594,637 |
| NW | 2,433,572 | 2,226,128 | 3,446,928 |
| WC | (86,413) | 448,723 | 1,453,234 |
| Emp. | 231 | 164 | 157 |

DUNS 73-996-5957
## Parker Cars Ltd
279 The Broadway, London SW19 1SD
**Tel:** 02085435555 **Fax:** 02089418005
**Web:** www.parkercarservice.co.uk
**Reg No:** 5247014 **Estd:** 2008 Private Limited Company
**Line of Business:** Taxis and private hire vehicles
**Issued Capital:** £100
**Director:** J Polley
**Co. Secretary:** Ms Andrea Polley
**Responsibilities**
**Senior:** Dave Weston *(Manager)*
**Branches:** Parker Cars Ltd, 279 The Broadway, London SW19 1SD
**US SIC:** 4121 **UK SIC:** 72200
**Auditors:** Bright Grahame Murray

| | 31-10-13 | 31-10-12 | 31-10-11 |
|---|---|---|---|
| TA | 567,386 | 490,067 | 686,093 |
| NW | 298,367 | 87,509 | 195,453 |
| WC | 298,367 | 70,051 | 145,474 |

DUNS 34-759-9177
## Parker Diving Ltd
(**Subsidiary of:** Clipper Data Ltd)
Water Ma Trout Industrial Estate, Helston, Cornwall TR13 0LW
**Tel:** 01326-561040
**Web:** www.apvalves.com
**Reg No:** 2785572 **Estd:** 1993 Private Limited Company
**Line of Business:** Manufacture of sports goods
**Trading Style:** A P Valves
**Issued Capital:** £3
**Director:** M J Parker
**Co. Secretary:** Ms Angela Parker
**Responsibilities**
**Purchasing:** Allison Clark *(Purchasing Manager)*
**US SIC:** 3949 **UK SIC:** 49420
**Auditors:** Kitchen & Brown

| | 31-01-14 | 31-01-13 | 31-01-12 |
|---|---|---|---|
| TA | 1,400,385 | 1,448,780 | 1,218,342 |
| NW | 41,373 | 109,270 | 43,997 |
| WC | 611,815 | 685,877 | 606,738 |

DUNS 21-721-9850 **Imp**
## Parker Hannifin Ltd
(**Subsidiary of:** Parker-Hannifin Corporation)
Parker House, Maylands Avenue, Hemel Hempstead Industrial Estate, Hemel Hempstead, Hertfordshire HP2 4SJ
**Web:** www.parker.com
**Reg No:** 7595632 **VAT No:** 366991400
**Estd:** 2011 Private Limited Company
**Line of Business:** Manufacture of machinery for the production and use of mechanical power, except aircraft, vehicle and cycle engines
**Export Sales:** £67,267,000
**Issued Capital:** £1
**Directors:** N W Judd, G M Ellinor, J A Elsey
**Branches:** PARKER HANNIFIN LIMITED: Chomerics Division Europe, Unit 6 Century Point, Halifax Road, High Wycombe, HP12 3SL, BUCKINGHAMSHIRE.
**US SIC:** 3519 **UK SIC:** 32811
**Auditors:** Deloitte LLP

| | 30-06-13 | 30-06-12 |
|---|---|---|
| TO | 258,707,000 | 252,708,000 |
| P/L | 11,905,000 | 6,913,000 |
| NW | (22,133,000) | (30,858,000) |
| WC | (32,768,000) | (41,792,000) |
| Emp. | 502 | 466 |

DUNS 21-022-4556
## Parker Merchanting Ltd
(**Subsidiary of:** Rexel)
John O Grant Industrial Estate, Leeds Road, Leeds, West Yorkshire LS26 0DU
**Tel:** 01514207787 **Fax:** 01132-822620
**Web:** www.parker-direct.com
**Reg No:** 0224779 **VAT No:** 243428962
**Estd:** 1896 Private Limited Company
**Line of Business:** Manufacture of other wearing apparel and accessories not elsewhere classified
**Issued Capital:** £50,500
**Directors:** H Laschkar, N M Croxson
**Responsibilities**
**Senior:** Dominic Procter *(Ceo)*
**Branches:** Parker Merchanting Ltd, Cofton Road, Exeter, Devon EX2 8QW
**US SIC:** 2389 **UK SIC:** 45393

**Bankers:** The Royal Bank Of Scotland Plc (16-04-00)

| | 31-12-13 | 31-12-12 | 31-12-11 |
|---|---|---|---|
| TA | 51,000 | 51,000 | 51,000 |
| NW | 51,000 | 51,000 | 51,000 |

DUNS 73-648-8276                                                 Imp
## Parker Plant Ltd
(Subsidiary of: Phoenix Parker Holdings Ltd)
Viaduct Works, Canon Street, Leicester, Leicestershire LE4 6GH
**Tel:** 01162-665999 **Fax:** 01162-681254
**Web:** www.parkerplant.com
**Reg No:** 4908756 **Estd:** 1912 Private Limited Company
**Line of Business:** Manufacturers of crushing plants
**Export Sales:** £12,997,000
**Trading Style:** Parker Plant, Universal Conveyors
**Issued Capital:** £200,000
**Directors:** R D Sciville, G B Dalby, G J Wheeler, A K Butler
**Co. Secretary:** Simon Wilkinson
**Responsibilities**
**IT:** Dave Reynolds (IT Manager)
**US SIC:** 3549 **UK SIC:** 32212
**Auditors:** KPMG LLP

| | 31-12-13 | 31-12-12 | 31-12-11 |
|---|---|---|---|
| TO | 18,501,000 | 15,229,000 | 15,607,401 |
| P/L | 1,510,000 | 552,000 | 725,893 |
| NW | 6,486,000 | 4,976,000 | 4,195,447 |
| WC | 5,496,000 | 4,312,000 | 3,550,549 |
| Emp. | 105 | 124 | 147 |

DUNS 64-251-5548
## Parker Rhodes Field With Pashley & Hodgkinson
16 Moorgate Street, Rotherham, South Yorkshire S60 2DG
**Tel:** 01709830757
**Web:** www.lsllandandnewhomes.co.uk
**Estd:** 1895 Partnership
**Line of Business:** Solicitors
**Trading Style:** Parker Rhodes
**Partners:** Miss D Tickle, D W Coopland, J P Wooffenden, Mrs F Greene
**Responsibilities**
**Senior:** Tom Stainthorpe (Area Manager)
**US SIC:** 7399 **UK SIC:** 83954
**Employees:** 50

DUNS 42-469-8611
## Parker Transport
Unit 32a, Second Avenue Westfield Industrial, Estate, Bath, Avon BA3 4BH
**Tel:** 01761-416611
**Web:** www.parkertransport.com
**Estd:** 2000 Partnership
**Line of Business:** Other supporting land transport activities
**Trading Style:** Parker Transport Sw Ltd
**Partners:** Mrs C Parker, K Parker
**US SIC:** 4789 **UK SIC:** 77002
**Employees:** 50

DUNS 64-101-0293                                                 Imp
## Parkeray Ltd
(Subsidiary of: Parkeray Holdings Ltd)
Bridge House, 4 Borough High Street, London SE1 9QQ
**Web:** www.parkeray.co.uk
**Reg No:** 3493453 **Estd:** 1998 Private Limited Company
**Line of Business:** Office refurbishment services
**Issued Capital:** £60,008
**Directors:** I Collins, Miss C Ashmore, P R Kerr, P J Pearce, D Elphick, M J Murray, I G Collins, G M Watson
**Co. Secretary:** Adrian Grint
**Responsibilities**
**Senior:** Ian Garrett (Manager), Clare Murdoch (Manager)
**Finance:** Jamie Cooper (Finance Manager), Jessica Kelly (Finance Assistant)
**Marketing:** Carrieanne Beer (Sales and Marketing Trainee), Jodie Green (Sales and Marketing Manager)
**Sales:** Carrieanne Beer (Sales and Marketing Trainee), Iain Dodson (Commercial Manager), Jodie Green (Sales and Marketing Manager), Ryan Hignell (Commercial Manager), Greg Lloyd (Commercial Manager), Tony Murrell (Commercial Manager), Alex Soltynski (Business Development Manager), James Sturrock (Commercial Manager)
**HR:** Aileen Partner (Human Resources Manager)
**Purchasing:** Jason Pitts (Contracts Director), Bob Wills (Contracts Director)
**Engineering:** Martin Barnett (Construction Director)
**Branches:** Parkeray Ltd, 107 Cannon St, London EC4N 5AF
**US SIC:** 2599, 1799
**UK SIC:** 46720, 50000

**Auditors:** BDO Stoy Hayward LLP

| | 31-12-13 | 31-12-12 | 31-12-11 |
|---|---|---|---|
| TO | 47,796,419 | 52,993,011 | 53,129,423 |
| P/L | 34,740 | (69,371) | 48,903 |
| NW | 4,068,450 | 4,140,406 | 4,212,114 |
| WC | 3,935,587 | 4,004,785 | 4,101,648 |
| Emp. | 90 | 96 | 92 |

DUNS 21-640-8823
## Parkers Leisure (Holdings) Ltd
Queens Chambers, Sussex Street, Rhyl, Clwyd LL18 1SE
**Tel:** 01745-343525
**Reg No:** 0609150 **Estd:** 1932 Private Limited Company
**Line of Business:** Gambling and betting activities
**Issued Capital:** £34,500
**Directors:** J G Parker, B W Parker
**Co. Secretary:** Brian Stables
**Responsibilities**
**Senior:** Vanessa Williams (IT Director)
**IT:** Vanessa Williams (IT Director)
**Branches:** Parkers Leisure (Holdings) Ltd, 96 Church Street, Flint, Clwyd CH6 5AF
**US SIC:** 7999, 6531
**UK SIC:** 97913, 83400
**Auditors:** Sage & Co
**Bankers:** Barclays Bank Plc (20-25-76)

| | 31-12-13 | 31-12-12 | 31-12-11 |
|---|---|---|---|
| TA | 3,987,157 | 4,187,130 | 4,204,422 |
| NW | 3,170,070 | 3,540,070 | 3,843,429 |
| WC | (210,548) | 28,664 | 302,411 |

DUNS 29-235-3471
## Parkers Motor Services (Syston) Ltd
48-52 Wanlip Road, Leicester, Leicestershire LE7 1PA
**Tel:** 01162-600625 **Fax:** 01162-645931
**Web:** www.thepartspeople.co.uk
**Reg No:** 1215528 **VAT No:** 115788450
**Estd:** 1975 Private Limited Company
**Line of Business:** Management activities of holding companies
**Issued Capital:** £64,044
**Principals:** J M Parker (Managing), Mrs H Parker, W G Parker, Mrs P A Parker, Mrs S Parker, J W Parker, R D Parker
**Co. Secretary:** James Parker
**Responsibilities**
**Senior:** Gary Riley (Branch Manager)
**Branches:** Parkers Motor Services (Syston) Ltd, 54-56 Green Lane Road, Leicester, Leicestershire LE5 3TH
**US SIC:** 6711 **UK SIC:** 83962
**Auditors:** Pole Arnold
**Bankers:** National Westminster Bank Plc (60-02-17)

| | 31-12-13 | 31-12-12 | 31-12-11 |
|---|---|---|---|
| TO | 26,232,580 | 25,156,253 | 22,808,102 |
| P/L | 831,104 | 710,783 | 279,276 |
| NW | 3,935,493 | 3,320,745 | 2,673,228 |
| WC | 2,774,851 | 1,997,410 | 1,166,003 |
| Emp. | 239 | 234 | 220 |

DUNS 21-779-0759
## Parkfields Middle School
Park Road, Toddington, Dunstable, Bedfordshire LU5 6AB
**Tel:** 01525872555
**Web:** www.parkfieldsschool.co.uk
**Estd:** 1975 Proprietorship
**Line of Business:** Schools (local authority)
**Proprietor:** D Brandon
**Responsibilities**
**Senior:** David Brandon-Bravo (Head Teacher)
**US SIC:** 8211 **UK SIC:** 93200
**Employees:** 80

DUNS 49-459-1126
## Parkfields Nursing Home Ltd
556 Wolverhampton Road East, Wolverhampton, West Midlands WV4 6AA
**Tel:** 01902-621721 **Fax:** 01902-339915
**Reg No:** 3147365 **Estd:** 1996 Private Limited Company
**Line of Business:** Other human health activities
**Issued Capital:** £20,000
**Director:** U Passi
**Co. Secretary:** Dr Uma Passi
**Responsibilities**
**Senior:** Cheryl Fenton (Home Manager)
**Finance:** Man Passi (Finance Director)
**US SIC:** 8091, 6732
**UK SIC:** 95200, 83100
**Auditors:** J S Slater
**Bankers:** National Westminster Bank Plc (56-00-69)

| | 31-03-14 | 31-03-13 | 31-03-12 |
|---|---|---|---|
| TA | 1,012,714 | 971,142 | 900,794 |
| NW | 539,507 | 449,082 | 430,860 |
| WC | (94,937) | (133,170) | (93,612) |

DUNS 21-069-6272
## Parkgate Property (U K) Ltd
4 Turners View, Parkgate, Neston, Cheshire CH64 3SH
**Tel:** 01513538168
**Reg No:** 6442878 **Estd:** 2007 Private Limited Company
**Line of Business:** Estate agents
**Issued Capital:** £3
**Director:** D J Jenkins
**US SIC:** 6531 **UK SIC:** 83400

| | 30-04-13 | 30-04-12 | 30-04-11 |
|---|---|---|---|
| TO | 279,302 | N/A | N/A |
| P/L | 8,365 | N/A | N/A |
| NW | (1,051,943) | (3,828) | (3,017) |
| WC | (938,468) | (3,828) | (3,017) |
| Emp. | 82 | N/A | N/A |

DUNS 23-088-6665
## Parkhall Leisure
Park Hall Complex, Park Hall Road, Charnock Richard, Chorley, Lancashire PR7 5LP
**Tel:** 08716636500
**Web:** www.bestwestern.co.uk
**Estd:** 2002 Proprietorship
**Line of Business:** Sports clubs
**Proprietor:** Ms J Marshall
**Responsibilities**
**Senior:** Simon Doherty (Operations Director)
**US SIC:** 7999, 6531
**UK SIC:** 97913, 83400
**Employees:** 100

DUNS 22-853-5696
## Parkhaven Trust
Administration Office, Liverpool, Merseyside L31 8BR
**Tel:** 0151-526-4133
**Web:** www.parkhaven.org.uk
**Reg No:** 0361505 **Estd:** 1888 Private Company Limited By Guarantee
**Line of Business:** Non-charitable social work activities with accommodation
**Trading Style:** The Kyffin-Taylor, Bartlett Home
**Directors:** Mrs H Torpey, J M Brennand, R S Croft, Ms K M Matthews, Ms E Kitt, Mrs P J Ryder, Ms R Eley
**Co. Secretary:** Mrs Katherine Randall
**Responsibilities**
**Senior:** Susan Roland (Chief Executive), Hilary Rowland (CEO)
**Finance:** Claire Winstanley (Accountant)
**Health & Safety:** Jon McGee (Estates Manager)
**Facilities:** Jon McGee (Estates Manager)
**US SIC:** 8321, 6732
**UK SIC:** 96111, 83100
**Auditors:** Macfarlane & Co
**Bankers:** Lloyds TSB Bank plc (30-95-11)

| | 31-03-14 | 31-03-13 | 31-03-12 |
|---|---|---|---|
| TO | 4,120,994 | 3,977,191 | 4,109,093 |
| P/L | 318,981 | 207,767 | 568,213 |
| NW | 7,930,495 | 7,465,927 | 7,364,333 |
| WC | 869,319 | 627,009 | 614,570 |
| Emp. | 200 | 198 | 187 |

DUNS 39-158-8258                                                 Exp
## Parkin International Engineering Services Ltd
Sovereign House, Turner Way, Wakefield, West Yorkshire WF2 8EF
**Tel:** 01924-331700
**Web:** www.parkingroup.co.uk
**Reg No:** 1252141 **Estd:** 1976 Private Limited Company
**Line of Business:** Property leasing
**Export Markets:** E E C
**Issued Capital:** £99
**Principals:** F N Parkin (Managing), Ms K R Parkin, R N Parkin
**Co. Secretary:** Mrs Norma Parkin
**US SIC:** 6519, 6531
**UK SIC:** 85000, 83400
**Auditors:** Andrew Pollock
**Bankers:** HSBC Bank plc (40-45-11)

| | 31-07-13 | 31-07-12 | 31-07-11 |
|---|---|---|---|
| TA | 7,600,805 | 7,696,725 | 7,611,864 |
| NW | 821,127 | 823,423 | 653,739 |
| WC | 2,567,529 | 2,669,959 | 2,174,099 |

DUNS 21-215-6749
## Parkinson Ltd
B C S House, Peel Road Industrial Estate, Douglas, Douglas, Isle of Man IM4 4LE
**Tel:** 01624-681400
**Web:** www.parkinson.co.uk
**Reg No:** 0001073M **Estd:** 1947 Private Limited Company
**Line of Business:** Builders
**Principals:** C H Turner (Managing), Ms E Parkinson
**Co. Secretary:** John Shimmin
**Responsibilities**
**Senior:** Malcolm Blackburn (Manager)

**US SIC:** 1522 **UK SIC:** 50100
**Bankers:** Isle Of Man Bank (55-91-10)
**Employees:** 88

DUNS 21-031-8861
## Parkinson Properties (Number 2) Ltd
(Subsidiary of: Rotrex Group Ltd)
120 Bolton Road, Manchester M46 9JZ
**Tel:** 01942-896565
**Reg No:** 0242668 **Estd:** 1929 Private Limited Company
**Line of Business:** Business services
**Issued Capital:** £3,153
**Directors:** I W Parkinson, S H Butterworth
**Co. Secretary:** Simon Butterworth
**Branches:** Parkinson Properties (Number 2) Ltd, Unit 1C, Walney Rd Indust Est, Barrow-In-Furness, Cumbria LA14 5UG
**US SIC:** 7399 **UK SIC:** 83954

| | 30-06-13 | 30-06-12 | 30-06-11 |
|---|---|---|---|
| TA | 6,624 | 6,624 | 6,624 |
| NW | 6,624 | 6,624 | 6,624 |

DUNS 29-041-9761
## Parkinson's Disease Society of the United Kingdom
215 Vauxhall Bridge Road, London SW1V 1EJ
**Tel:** 020-7931-8080 **Fax:** 020-7233-9908
**Web:** www.parkinsons.org.uk
**Reg No:** 0948776 **Estd:** 1969 Private Company Limited By Guarantee
**Line of Business:** Charities and charitable organisations
**Directors:** C Cheesman, Dr D Macmahon, R D Raine, J A Glenn, P L Boothman, M Goodridge, Miss M Chamberlain, T G Tamblyn
**Co. Secretary:** Miss Sarah Day
**Responsibilities**
**Senior:** Hilary Ackland (Director), Caroline Bartlett (Regional Manager), Kieran Breen (Director of Research and Innov), Paula Carey (Area Manager), Terence Kavanagh (Manager), Teresa Watson (Director), Elizabeth Wolstenholme (Manager)
**Finance:** Paul Jackson-Clark (Director, Fundraising), Richard Penney (Director of Finance)
**Marketing:** Clare Allen (Senior Marketing Officer), Lee Armitt (Media and Communications Offic), Freya Barnes (Media and Communications Offic), Val Buxton (Director of External Relations), Jill Davis (Media and Communications Offic), Sandra Mattocks (Celebrity and VIP Manager), Alison Tebbutt (Media and Communications Offic)
**Sales:** Caroline Nutkins (Director of Organisational Dev), Carol Stork (Regional Fundraiser)
**IT:** Emily Hughes (Research Support Network Manag)
**HR:** Claire Hewitt (Education and Training Officer)
**Branches:** Parkinson's Disease Society Of The United Kingdom, 4 Walesby Close, Grimsby, South Humberside DN33 3HQ
**US SIC:** 8699 **UK SIC:** 96902
**Auditors:** Deloitte & Touche LLP
**Bankers:** The Royal Bank Of Scotland Plc (16-00-28)

| | 31-12-13 | 31-12-12 | 31-12-11 |
|---|---|---|---|
| TO | 24,518,000 | 23,937,000 | 21,923,000 |
| P/L | (3,621,000) | (2,654,000) | (1,758,000) |
| NW | 15,651,000 | 19,370,000 | 17,108,000 |
| WC | (1,807,000) | 1,236,000 | 3,057,000 |
| Emp. | 321 | 305 | 285 |

DUNS 21-322-7762                                              Imp-Exp
## Parkland Engineering Ltd
(Subsidiary of: Kiowa Holdings Ltd)
Unit 3 Whitley Road North Tyne, Industrial Estate, Newcastle-Upon-Tyne, Tyne and Wear NE12 9SZ
**Tel:** 01912709730 **Fax:** 01912709740
**Web:** www.parkland-eng.co.uk
**Reg No:** 1363157 **VAT No:** 297582891
**Estd:** 2012 Private Limited Company
**Line of Business:** Tube fittings
**Export Markets:** Western Europe
**Issued Capital:** £4,395
**Principals:** R D Sutherland (Managing), Mrs S Sutherland (Financial), A J Black, N Colman, A Towers, J D Needham, Ms F A Elstob, M E Needham
**Co. Secretary:** Martin Needham
**Responsibilities**
**Senior:** Jim Black (Sales Director), Graham Wall (Production Director)
**Marketing:** Jim Black (Sales Director)
**Sales:** Jim Black (Sales Director)
**IT:** Fiona Black (Administration Director)
**Health & Safety:** Graham Wall (Production Director)
**Facilities:** Graham Wall (Production Director)
**Purchasing:** Paul Carnegie (Purchasing Manager)

**Engineering:** Graham Wall *(Production Director)*
**Branches:** Parkland Engineering Ltd, 72 Dykehead Street, Glasgow, Lanarkshire G33 4AQ
**US SIC:** 3069, 5963
**UK SIC:** 48123, 65600
**Auditors:** Robson Laidler LLP
**Bankers:** National Westminster Bank Plc (01-05-31)

| | 31-03-14 | 31-03-13 | 31-03-12 |
|---|---|---|---|
| TA | 2,590,894 | 2,551,149 | 2,228,227 |
| NW | 1,039,625 | 717,926 | 629,092 |
| WC | 357,216 | 107,325 | 115,243 |

DUNS 21-242-0140
## Parkland House Residential Home
Barley Lane, Exeter, Devon EX4 1TA
**Tel:** 01392-251144
**Web:** www.peninsulacarehomes.co.uk
**Estd:** 2010 Partnership
**Line of Business:** Rest and retirement homes
**Partners:** Mrs L March, J March
**US SIC:** 8321 **UK SIC:** 96111
**Bankers:** Lloyds TSB Bank plc (30-93-14)
**Employees:** 48

DUNS 23-269-2707
## Parkland Nursing Home
33 Newport Road, Woolstone, Milton Keynes, Buckinghamshire MK15 0AA
**Tel:** 01908692690
**Estd:** 1990 Partnership
**Line of Business:** Nursing homes
**Partners:** Ms M J Baz, C Baz
**US SIC:** 8051 **UK SIC:** 95100
**Bankers:** Barclays Bank Plc (20-38-83)
**Employees:** 46

DUNS 21-783-7864
## Parkland Primary School
St Thomas Road, Wigston, Leicestershire LE18 4TA
**Tel:** 01162782142
**Web:** www.parklandprimary.co.uk
**Estd:** 2004 Proprietorship
**Line of Business:** General secondary education
**Proprietor:** Ms A Kirk
**Responsibilities**
**Senior:** Jane Windsor *(Head Teacher)*
**US SIC:** 8211 **UK SIC:** 93200
**Employees:** 75

DUNS 21-780-3234
## Parklands Care Centre
Newport Road, Bedwas, Caerphilly, Mid Glamorgan CF83 8AA
**Web:** http://hc-one.co.uk
**Estd:** 1995 Partnership
**Line of Business:** Nursing homes
**Partners:** Mrs P Hart, S George, Mrs T Shehan
**US SIC:** 8051 **UK SIC:** 95100
**Employees:** 60

DUNS 57-060-5931
## Parklands Ltd
Banff Road, Keith, Banffshire AB55 5GT
**Tel:** 01542-882925
**Web:** www.parklandsgroup.com
**Reg No:** 0148097SC **Estd:** 2002 Private Limited Company
**Line of Business:** Residential care establishments
**Trading Style:** Parklands Ltd
**Issued Capital:** £118,500
**Directors:** Mrs E Mcintosh, R S Taylor
**Co. Secretary:** Mrs Elaine Mcintosh
**Responsibilities**
**Senior:** Jane Stuart *(Manager)*
**Branches:** Parklands Ltd, High Street, Buckie, Banffshire AB56 4AD
**US SIC:** 8091 **UK SIC:** 95200
**Auditors:** McDonald & Co
**Bankers:** Clydesdale Bank Plc (82-61-14)

| | 31-12-13 | 31-12-12 | 31-12-11 |
|---|---|---|---|
| TO | 5,650,848 | 5,077,084 | 4,971,148 |
| P/L | (18,232) | 453,764 | 405,880 |
| NW | 6,926,925 | 7,697,153 | 7,383,364 |
| WC | (2,731,465) | 248,533 | (171,359) |
| Emp. | 330 | 295 | 302 |

DUNS 21-812-1966
## Parklands Middlesbrough Intermediate Care
Homerton Road, Middlesbrough, Cleveland TS3 8PN
**Tel:** 01642513120
**Estd:** 2012
**Line of Business:** Rehabilitation centres
**Responsibilities**
**Senior:** June Hunt *(Manager)*
**US SIC:** 8062 **UK SIC:** 95100
**Employees:** 60

DUNS 29-863-8818
## Parkman South East Ltd
**(Subsidiary of:** Mrbl Ltd)
307-317 Euston Road, London NW1 3AD
**Tel:** 02073835393
**Reg No:** 2067191 **Estd:** 1987 Private Limited Company
**Line of Business:** Other engineering activities
**Trading Style:** Muchel Parkman
**Issued Capital:** £195,001
**Directors:** P A Rayner, G S Pearson
**Branches:** Parkman South East Ltd, Blackwall Tunnel Depot, Naval Row, London E14 9PS
**US SIC:** 8911 **UK SIC:** 83701
**Bankers:** National Westminster Bank Plc (60-13-19)

| | 31-03-14 | 31-03-13 | 31-03-12 |
|---|---|---|---|
| TA | 17,724 | 17,724 | 17,724 |
| NW | 17,724 | 17,724 | 17,724 |

DUNS 34-516-3021
## Parkmore Hotel Ltd
**(Subsidiary of:** Ja Hotels Ltd)
636 Yarm Road, Eaglescliffe, Stockton-On-Tees, Cleveland TS16 0DH
**Tel:** 01642786815
**Web:** www.bestwestern.co.uk
**Reg No:** 5327103 **Estd:** 2005 Private Limited Company
**Line of Business:** Hotels
**Issued Capital:** £1,000
**Director:** J P Leeds
**Co. Secretary:** Ms Louise Leeds
**Responsibilities**
**Finance:** Carol Pickles *(Accounts Manager)*
**IT:** Carol Pickles *(Accounts Manager)*
**US SIC:** 7011, 7999
**UK SIC:** 66500, 97913

| | 31-03-14 | 31-03-13 | 31-03-12 |
|---|---|---|---|
| TA | 2,128,159 | 2,124,050 | 2,351,208 |
| NW | 1,891,402 | 1,889,124 | 1,892,309 |
| WC | 573,338 | 557,526 | 547,006 |

DUNS 21-414-4720
## Park's
143-159 Almada Street, Hamilton, Lanarkshire ML3 0ET
**Tel:** 01698303999
**Web:** www.parks.uk.com
**Estd:** 1969 Proprietorship
**Line of Business:** Car dealers (new & used)
**Proprietor:** C Little
**Responsibilities**
**Senior:** Maragaret Mcnish *(Dealer Principal)*
**US SIC:** 5511 **UK SIC:** 65100
**Employees:** 46

DUNS 21-780-3141
## Parks & Open Spaces
Holywells Park Stable, Cliff Lane, Ipswich, Suffolk IP3 0PG
**Tel:** 01473433996
**Estd:** 2011 Proprietorship
**Line of Business:** Parks & gardens
**Proprietor:** N Wilcox
**US SIC:** 8411 **UK SIC:** 97700
**Employees:** 90

DUNS 21-779-1724
## Park's Motor Group
1 Braeview Place, East Kilbride, Glasgow, Lanarkshire G74 3XH
**Tel:** 01355818000
**Web:** www.parks.uk.com
**Estd:** 2011
**Line of Business:** Car dealers (new & used)
**US SIC:** 5511 **UK SIC:** 65100
**Employees:** 150

DUNS 21-591-0340
## Park's of Hamilton (Holdings) Ltd
Park House, Hamilton, Lanarkshire ML3 0AY
**Tel:** 01698303900 **Fax:** 01698-303901
**Web:** www.parks.uk.com
**Reg No:** 0066568SC **Estd:** 1978 Private Limited Company
**Line of Business:** Holding companies management activities
**Trading Style:** Parks Motor Group
**Issued Capital:** £16,250,001
**Principals:** D I Park *(Chairman and Managing)*, I B Mackay, W Cumming, G T Park, A S Bryce, R W Park
**Co. Secretary:** Gerard Donnachie
**Branches:** Park's Of Hamilton (Holdings) Ltd, Royle Works, Royle Road, Rochdale, Lancashire OL11 3EH
**US SIC:** 6711 **UK SIC:** 83962
**Auditors:** Thomas Barrie & Co
**Bankers:** Bank Of Scotland (80-08-24)

| | 31-03-14 | 31-03-13 | 31-03-12 |
|---|---|---|---|
| TO | 399,422,165 | 347,091,459 | 339,772,310 |
| P/L | 14,292,814 | 12,174,471 | 10,535,221 |
| NW | 45,112,424 | 39,784,568 | 35,040,610 |
| WC | (21,385,795) | (18,290,418) | (22,984,668) |
| Emp. | 1,201 | 1,104 | 1,111 |

DUNS 23-836-3456
## Parks Options Ltd
23 Corn Street, Liverpool, Merseyside L7 2QR
**Tel:** 01513008420
**Web:** www.parksoptions.co.uk
**Reg No:** 3828083 **Estd:** 1999 Private Limited Company
**Line of Business:** Management activities of holding companies
**Directors:** S W Mcelroy, P Moore, K Newbolds, F J Doran, R Keenan
**Co. Secretary:** Mrs Lori Murdock
**US SIC:** 6711 **UK SIC:** 83962
**Bankers:** HSBC Bank plc (40-29-08)

| | 31-03-14 | 31-03-13 | 31-03-12 |
|---|---|---|---|
| TO | 2,154,156 | 2,199,842 | 2,080,104 |
| P/L | (57,946) | (1,243) | (68,953) |
| NW | 3,986,492 | 4,044,439 | 2,471,175 |
| WC | 246,673 | 257,519 | 294,295 |
| Emp. | 26 | 106 | 96 |

DUNS 21-820-9421
## Parkside Academy
Hall Lane Estate, Willington, Crook, County Durham DL15 0QF
**Tel:** 01388746396 **Fax:** 01388746782
**Web:** www.parksideacademy.org.uk
**Reg No:** 7928558 **Estd:** 2002 Private Company Limited By Guarantee
**Line of Business:** General secondary education
**Directors:** R G Wolff, A Rowell, Ms O E Gunn, Ms L A Davies, Mrs E C Blackett, K Reynolds, D G Liddle, G Hardy
**Co. Secretary:** Mrs Claire Oates
**Responsibilities**
**Senior:** Edward Buckham *(Director)*, John Deller *(Director)*, Julie Gallon *(Director)*, Pauline Gordon *(Director)*, Eileen Graham *(Director)*, Kenneth Henfrey *(Director)*, Anna Horner *(Director)*, Simon Lipscombe *(Director)*, Kelly Martin *(Director)*
**US SIC:** 8211 **UK SIC:** 93200
**Bankers:** Lloyds TSB Bank plc (77-20-16)

| | 31-08-13 | 31-08-12 |
|---|---|---|
| TO | 4,808,773 | 7,184,346 |
| P/L | 97,814 | 4,928,592 |
| NW | 4,929,406 | 4,823,592 |
| WC | 428,975 | 248,558 |
| Emp. | 87 | 91 |

DUNS 21-107-3427
## Parkside Care Ltd
6 Parkside, North Shields, Tyne and Wear NE30 4JN
**Tel:** 01912-573859
**Web:** www.parksidecare.co.uk
**Reg No:** 6494922 **Estd:** 2008 Private Limited Company
**Line of Business:** Social work activities with accommodation
**Issued Capital:** £120
**Directors:** G R Kerr, A S Kerr, R Kerr
**Co. Secretary:** Graham Kerr
**US SIC:** 8321 **UK SIC:** 96111

| | 31-03-14 | 31-03-13 | 31-03-12 |
|---|---|---|---|
| TA | 1,039,660 | 1,183,031 | 1,170,247 |
| NW | (400,329) | (562,754) | (675,210) |
| WC | 45,005 | (36,886) | (118,864) |

DUNS 34-514-5101 **Imp**
## Parkside Flexibles (Europe) Ltd
**(Subsidiary of:** Bushman Limited)
Tyler Close, Normanton Industrial Estate, Normanton, West Yorkshire WF6 1RL
**Tel:** 01924-898074 **Fax:** 01924893263
**Web:** www.parksideflex.com
**Reg No:** 5325366 **VAT No:** 853073432
**Estd:** 2000 Private Limited Company
**Line of Business:** Printing not elsewhere classified
**Export Sales:** £16,954,501
**Issued Capital:** £500,000
**Directors:** R S Adamson, M N Aldridge, N J Smith, Ms R Grace, S Mccormick, C Kozlik, N J Worton
**Co. Secretary:** Nicholas Worton
**Responsibilities**
**Senior:** Tracy Cardell *(Manager)*, Donna Needham *(Manager)*, Stephen Parry *(Manager)*
**IT:** Andy Fox *(?IT Leader)*
**US SIC:** 2752 **UK SIC:** 47544
**Auditors:** KPMG LLP
**Bankers:** Barclays Bank Plc (20-25-42)

| | 31-12-13 | 31-12-12 | 31-12-11 |
|---|---|---|---|
| TO | 30,707,983 | 24,834,089 | 24,726,946 |
| P/L | 2,874,960 | 1,816,912 | 3,124,520 |
| NW | 5,127,851 | 5,774,152 | 4,772,585 |
| WC | 3,132,831 | 3,403,079 | 2,114,267 |
| Emp. | 151 | 155 | 146 |

DUNS 21-819-6876
## Parkside Foundation Fund
Parkside Community College, Cambridge, Cambridgeshire CB1 1EH
**Tel:** 01223-712600
**Web:** www.parkside.cambs.sch.uk
**Estd:** 1994
**Line of Business:** General secondary education
**US SIC:** 8211 **UK SIC:** 93200
**Employees:** 104

DUNS 21-708-3674 **Imp**
## The Parkside Group Ltd
Unit 5 The Willow Centre, Mitcham, Surrey CR4 4NX
**Tel:** 020-8685-9685 **Fax:** 020-8646-5096
**Web:** www.comar-alu.co.uk
**Reg No:** 0921619 **Estd:** 1967 Private Limited Company
**Line of Business:** Aluminium stockholders
**Trading Style:** Comar Architectural Aluminium Systems, Comar Architecture Aluminium Systems
**Issued Capital:** £48,000
**Principals:** D W Cook *(Managing)*, M D Hayward, S J Jones, P T Dziurzynski, D M Trussell
**Co. Secretary:** Peter Dziurzynski
**Responsibilities**
**Senior:** Warren Silk *(Manager)*, Alan Stocks *(Managor)*
**Marketing:** Alison Davey *(Sales & Marketing Manager)*
**Sales:** Alison Davey *(Sales & Marketing Manager)*
**HR:** Lisa Alexander *(Human Resources Manager)*
**Purchasing:** Esther Marchese *(Purchasing Manager)*
**US SIC:** 5051 **UK SIC:** 61200
**Auditors:** Sinclairs Leigh Sorene
**Bankers:** Barclays Bank Plc (20-24-61)

| | 31-12-13 | 31-12-12 | 31-12-11 |
|---|---|---|---|
| TO | 17,164,083 | 16,373,640 | 15,870,562 |
| P/L | 93,145 | 52,379 | (38,798) |
| NW | 8,686,664 | 8,817,944 | 8,811,632 |
| WC | 8,285,590 | 8,275,445 | 8,145,845 |
| Emp. | 92 | 95 | 92 |

DUNS 22-713-0747
## Parkside Hospital Ltd
**(Subsidiary of:** European Surgical Partners Ltd)
The Lodge, 53 Parkside, London SW19 5NX
**Tel:** 02089440665 **Fax:** 02089718001
**Web:** www.wimbledonclinics.co.uk
**Reg No:** 1328198 **Estd:** 1977 Private Limited Company
**Line of Business:** Sporting injury therapists and clinics
**Issued Capital:** £468,400
**Co. Secretary:** Desmond Shiels
**Responsibilities**
**Senior:** Phillip Albert *(Manager)*, Hilda Bradbury *(Hospital Director)*, Malcolm Bream *(Stores Manager)*
**HR:** Louise Lott *(Human Resources Manager)*
**Health & Safety:** Elizabeth Lindsey *(Director of Nursing)*
**Facilities:** Dean Burton *(Maintenance Manager)*
**Operations:** Hilda Bradbury *(Hospital Director)*
**US SIC:** 8062 **UK SIC:** 95100
**Bankers:** National Westminster Bank Plc (60-24-07)
**Employees:** 300

DUNS 21-722-1837 **Imp**
## Parkside Leisure Ltd
Paradise Park, White Stubbs Lane, Broxbourne, Hertfordshire EN10 7QA
**Tel:** 01992-470490
**Web:** www.pwpark.com
**Reg No:** 0842819 **Estd:** 1965 Private Limited Company
**Line of Business:** Management activities of other non-financial holding companies not elsewhere classified
**Issued Capital:** £3,500
**Principals:** P C Sampson *(Managing)*, Ms L K Whitnall
**Co. Secretary:** Ms Grace Sampson
**Branches:** Parkside Leisure Ltd, 37 Barnet Rd, Potters Bar, Hertfordshire EN6 2QX
**US SIC:** 6711, 6519
**UK SIC:** 83962, 85000
**Auditors:** Solazzo & Co
**Bankers:** Barclays Bank Plc (20-20-37)

| | 31-12-13 | 31-12-12 | 31-12-11 |
|---|---|---|---|
| TO | 4,344,260 | 3,751,545 | 3,361,496 |
| P/L | 476,477 | 211,441 | 189,143 |
| NW | 6,711,985 | 6,416,575 | 6,332,783 |
| WC | 940,229 | 742,751 | 559,949 |
| Emp. | 169 | 161 | 164 |

DUNS 21-781-0793
## Parkside Nursing Home
Olive Grove, Mansfield, Nottinghamshire NG19 0AR
**Tel:** 01623655341
**Estd:** 2011
**Line of Business:** Clinics private
**US SIC:** 8051 **UK SIC:** 95100
**Employees:** 85

DUNS 22-523-3444
## Parkside Recruitment Ltd
(**Subsidiary of:** Antal International Ltd)
268-270 High Street, Uxbridge, Middlesex UB8 1LQ
**Tel:** 01895-255007 **Fax:** 01895-812111
**Web:** www.parksiderec.com
**Reg No:** 1655502 **VAT No:** 493725611
**Estd:** 1982 Private Limited Company
**Line of Business:** Employment and recruitment companies and consultants
**Trading Style:** Parkside Recruitment Limited
**Issued Capital:** £15,200
**Director:** A M Goodwin
**Co. Secretary:** Sagar Ruparelia
**Responsibilities**
**Senior:** Tremayne Elson *(Manager)*, Vanessa Lungley *(Site Manager)*
**Branches:** Parkside Recruitmont Limited, 59 Church Street, Staines, Middlesex TW18 4XS
**US SIC:** 7361 **UK SIC:** 83954
**Auditors:** BDO LLP
**Bankers:** HSBC Bank plc (40-34-25)

| | 31-12-13 | 31-12-12 | 31-12-11 |
|---|---|---|---|
| TO | 8,523,207 | N/A | N/A |
| P/L | 111,307 | N/A | N/A |
| NW | 651,473 | 540,802 | 564,402 |
| WC | 647,284 | 531,712 | 549,371 |
| Emp. | 50 | N/A | N/A |

DUNS 29-024-8970
## Parkside School Trust
78-80 Stoke Road, Cobham, Surrey KT11 3PX
**Tel:** 01932862749
**Web:** www.parkside-school.co.uk
**Reg No:** 0667817 **Estd:** 1900 Private Company Limited By Guarantee
**Line of Business:** General secondary education
**Directors:** P J Ostley, P R Brooks, R M Morris, R A Lo, M W Hoskins, Mrs P J Stoffberg, B M Kesterton, R S Southwell
**Co. Secretary:** Eve-Lucille Mccann
**Responsibilities**
**Senior:** David Aylward *(Headmaster)*, Miles Beeson *(Director)*, Celia Gregory *(Director)*, David Jarrett *(Director)*
**HR:** David Aylward *(Headmaster)*
**US SIC:** 8211 **UK SIC:** 93200
**Auditors:** Horwath Clark Whitehill
**Bankers:** Lloyds TSB Bank plc (30-93-74)

| | 31-08-14 | 31-08-13 | 31-08-12 |
|---|---|---|---|
| TO | 3,814,222 | 3,979,432 | 4,084,934 |
| P/L | (72,018) | 185,685 | 349,535 |
| NW | 4,964,731 | 5,036,749 | 4,851,064 |
| WC | 594,080 | 545,844 | 294,574 |
| Emp. | 73 | 73 | 79 |

DUNS 73-373-0514
## Parkside Taxis Ltd
Unit 2/N, Admiral Business Park, Nelson Way, Nelson Park West, Cramlington, Northumberland NE23 1WG
**Tel:** 01670-735555 **Fax:** 01670-735544
**Web:** www.parkside-taxis.co.uk
**Reg No:** 4646682 **Estd:** 2003 Private Limited Company
**Line of Business:** Taxis
**Issued Capital:** £2
**Director:** R E Wrightson
**Responsibilities**
**Senior:** Barry Wrightson *(Transport Manager)*
**Fleet:** Barry Wrightson *(Transport Manager)*
**US SIC:** 4119, 4142
**UK SIC:** 72200, 72102
**Auditors:** BW Atherton Ltd

| | 31-03-14 | 31-03-13 | 31-03-12 |
|---|---|---|---|
| TA | 137,613 | 158,571 | 167,496 |
| NW | (9,774) | (26,826) | (10,060) |
| WC | (86,989) | (132,984) | (99,607) |

DUNS 23-989-7770
## Parkstone Grammar School
Upton House, Poole Road, Poole, Dorset BH17 7BJ
**Tel:** 01202-605605
**Web:** www.parkstone.poole.sch.uk
**Estd:** 1966 Proprietorship
**Line of Business:** Schools (local authority)
**Director:** Mrs A Shinwell
**US SIC:** 8211 **UK SIC:** 93200
**Employees:** 250

DUNS 22-553-1763
## Parkstone Ltd
(**Subsidiary of:** Hoopers Ltd)
Strand Road, Torquay, Devon TQ1 1BJ
**Tel:** 01803-299226
**Web:** www.hoopers.ltd.uk
**Reg No:** 1603910 **VAT No:** 456285230
**Estd:** 1982 Private Limited Company
**Line of Business:** Other retail sale in non-specialised stores
**Trading Style:** Hoopers
**Issued Capital:** £180,000
**Directors:** Ms D Angus, Ms K P Woodward, Ms P Thompson, D B Thompson, R B Copus
**Co. Secretary:** Christopher Dant
**Responsibilities**
**Senior:** Anne Horton *(Manager)*
**Finance:** Mo Mahdadi *(Financial Controller)*
**IT:** Sarah McKerrell *(Customer Accounts Controller)*
**Branches:** Parkstone Ltd, 142-144 Kenton La, Harrow, Middlesex HA3 8UG
**US SIC:** 5399 **UK SIC:** 65600
**Auditors:** Baker Tilly Audit Ltd
**Bankers:** Barclays Bank Plc (20-13-42)

| | 01-02-14 | 02-02-13 | 28-02-12 |
|---|---|---|---|
| TO | 25,460,130 | 28,762,898 | 29,727,650 |
| P/L | (189,194) | (1,685,475) | 407,531 |
| NW | 4,729,721 | 4,990,924 | 6,486,324 |
| WC | 2,476,761 | 2,835,013 | 5,415,274 |
| Emp. | 481 | 507 | 523 |

DUNS 21-450-0360
## Parkstone Sea Cadets
Ringwood Road, Poole, Dorset BH12 4NB
**Tel:** 01202-732012
**Estd:** 2009
**Line of Business:** Associations
**Principals:** Captain N P Brown *(Chairman)*, Mrs P Goodson
**Responsibilities**
**Senior:** Fiona Dodds *(Chair Person)*
**US SIC:** 8699 **UK SIC:** 96902
**Employees:** 81

DUNS 21-772-4172
## Parkview Clinic
Park View, Birmingham, West Midlands B13 8QE
**Tel:** 01213339955
**Web:** www.bch.nhs.uk
**Estd:** 2002 Proprietorship
**Line of Business:** Nhs clinics
**Proprietor:** C Gibbs
**Responsibilities**
**Senior:** Sarah-Jane Marsh *(Chief Executive Officer)*, Sandra Wallace *(Camhs Service Manager)*, Sandra Wallis *(CEO, Managing Director)*
**Sales:** Theresa Nelson *(Chief Officer for Workforce De)*
**US SIC:** 8062 **UK SIC:** 95100
**Employees:** 143

DUNS 64-254-5248
## Parkview Residential Home
Parkview House, 12 Houndsfield Road, London N9 7RQ
**Web:** www.sanctuary-housing.co.uk
**Estd:** 1992
**Line of Business:** Residential care establishments
**Proprietor:** Mrs M Rockcliffe
**Responsibilities**
**Senior:** Jenny Goddard *(Home Manager)*
**US SIC:** 8321 **UK SIC:** 96111
**Employees:** 50

DUNS 21-042-9712
## Parkville Care Home
Walpole Street, Middlesbrough, Cleveland TS1 4HA
**Tel:** 01642-223334
**Web:** www.parkvillecarecentre.com
**Estd:** 2005
**Line of Business:** Residential care establishments
**Proprietor:** Mrs M Moss
**Responsibilities**
**Senior:** Natalie Mccartin *(Manager)*
**US SIC:** 8321 **UK SIC:** 96111
**Employees:** 70

DUNS 23-791-4762
## Parkway Derby Ltd
252 Upper Third Street, Grafton Gate East, Milton Keynes, Buckinghamshire MK9 1DZ
**Tel:** 08436590592
**Web:** www.myvolkswagen.co.uk
**Reg No:** 3784257 **Estd:** 1999 Private Limited Company
**Line of Business:** Sale of motor vehicles
**Issued Capital:** £100,000
**Directors:** Mrs A Booth, S R Booth
**Co. Secretary:** Alison Booth
**Branches:** Parkway Derby Ltd, Locomotive Way, Derby, Derbyshire DE24 8PU
**US SIC:** 5511 **UK SIC:** 65100
**Auditors:** Trevor Jones & Co
**Bankers:** National Westminster Bank Plc (60-14-55)

| | 30-11-13 | 30-11-12 | 30-11-11 |
|---|---|---|---|
| TO | 109,663,447 | 97,515,487 | 87,026,793 |
| P/L | 1,090,114 | 533,684 | 709,087 |
| NW | 4,092,354 | 3,562,311 | 3,106,963 |
| WC | (243,889) | (956,120) | (80,965) |
| Emp. | 232 | 229 | 230 |

DUNS 29-157-1586
## Parkway Entertainment Co Ltd
Kings Road, Cleethorpes, South Humberside DN35 0AQ
**Tel:** 01472204085
**Web:** www.parkwaycinemas.co.uk
**Reg No:** 1768567 **Estd:** 1983 Private Limited Company
**Line of Business:** Cinemas
**Issued Capital:** £103
**Directors:** K J Edwards, G D Parkes, R J Parkes, S G Marshall
**Co. Secretary:** Mrs Denise Parkes
**Branches:** Parkway Entertainment Co Ltd, 28 Queen St, Peterhead, Aberdeenshire AB42 1TS
**US SIC:** 7829, 7832
**UK SIC:** 97112, 97113

| | 31-03-14 | 31-03-13 | 31-03-12 |
|---|---|---|---|
| TA | 2,892,943 | 3,170,604 | 3,016,753 |
| NW | 1,468,503 | 1,489,092 | 1,506,552 |
| WC | 652,367 | 640,695 | 663,155 |

DUNS 73-969-3054
## Parkway Green Housing Trust
Parkway Green House, Palatine Road, Manchester M22 4DJ
**Tel:** 03001110000
**Web:** www.parkwaygreen.co.uk
**Reg No:** 5220157 **Estd:** 2004 Private Company Limited By Guarantee
**Line of Business:** Housing associations societies trusts & co-operatives
**Directors:** Ms W Casey, S A Russell, G Evans, D A Teale, S S Coutsavlis, S A Thompson, M Wiggins, P G Andrews
**Co. Secretary:** Richard Coughlan
**Responsibilities**
**Senior:** Jon Farr *(Director)*
**US SIC:** 6519 **UK SIC:** 85000
**Bankers:** National Westminster Bank Plc (60-15-25)

| | 31-03-14 | 31-03-13 | 31-03-12 |
|---|---|---|---|
| TO | 23,014,000 | 26,326,000 | 27,622,000 |
| P/L | 451,000 | 2,813,000 | (173,000) |
| NW | 73,122,000 | 7,938,000 | 6,813,000 |
| WC | (24,219,000) | (23,343,000) | (24,316,000) |
| Emp. | 175 | 173 | 179 |

DUNS 22-782-7516
## The Parkway Hotel & Spa Ltd
(**Subsidiary of:** Havana West Ltd)
Cwmbran Drive, Cwmbran, Gwent NP44 3UW
**Tel:** 01633-871199
**Web:** www.bestwestern.co.uk
**Reg No:** 1740869 **Estd:** 1983 Private Limited Company
**Line of Business:** Hotels
**Trading Style:** The Parkway Hotel
**Issued Capital:** £250,000
**Directors:** I D Solkin, Mrs L L De Savary
**Co. Secretary:** Joseph Keefe
**Responsibilities**
**Senior:** Kerry Jennings *(Conference Manager)*, Laura Szmaglik *(Food & Beverage Manager)*, Julian Vance-Daniel *(Finance Director)*, Alison Woodcock *(Manager)*
**Finance:** Sue Hamilton *(Financial Director)*, Julian Vance-Daniel *(Finance Director)*
**Marketing:** Kerry Jennings *(Conference Manager)*
**Sales:** Kerry Jennings *(Conference Manager)*
**IT:** Sue Hamilton *(Financial Director)*
**HR:** Alison Woodcock *(Manager)*
**Health & Safety:** Charles Baldwin *(Head Porter)*
**Facilities:** Alison Woodcock *(Manager)*
**Purchasing:** Alison Woodcock *(Manager)*
**US SIC:** 7011 **UK SIC:** 66500
**Auditors:** Kilsby & Williams
**Bankers:** Bank Of Scotland (80-02-52)

| | 31-12-13 | 31-12-12 | 31-12-11 |
|---|---|---|---|
| TO | 3,208,413 | 3,062,095 | 2,832,993 |
| P/L | 367,145 | 478,932 | 231,144 |
| NW | 3,916,309 | 3,655,345 | 3,397,637 |
| WC | (100,627) | 222,813 | (119,958) |
| Emp. | 102 | 108 | 114 |

DUNS 67-224-5003
## Parkwood Community Leisure Ltd
Perdiswell Park, Worcester, Worcestershire WR3 7NW
**Tel:** 01299-253400 **Fax:** 01299253444
**Web:** www.leisurecentre.com
**Reg No:** 6054092 **Estd:** 1994 Private Company Limited By Guarantee
**Line of Business:** Other sporting activities not elsewhere classified
**Directors:** A G Holt, A J Tucker, W G Rawlinson
**Responsibilities**
**Senior:** Paul Cluett *(Manager)*, Douglas Eadie *(Manager)*
**US SIC:** 7399, 5812
**UK SIC:** 83954, 66110
**Auditors:** PricewaterhouseCoopers LLP
**Bankers:** Abbey National Plc (09-00-29)

| | 31-12-13 | 31-12-12 | 31-12-11 |
|---|---|---|---|
| TO | 47,087,000 | 43,610,000 | 26,670,000 |
| P/L | 28,000 | (10,000) | 25,000 |
| NW | 8,000 | (12,000) | (3,000) |
| WC | (1,351,000) | (1,506,000) | (1,087,000) |
| Emp. | 1,433 | 1,508 | 987 |

DUNS 34-589-4661
## Parkwood Holdings Ltd
(**Subsidiary of:** Alston Acquisitions Ltd)
Parkwood House-Cuerden Park, Preston, Lancashire PR5 6BY
**Tel:** 01772-627111
**Web:** www.parkwood-holdings.co.uk
**Reg No:** 2733592 **Estd:** 1992 Private Limited Company
**Line of Business:** Management activities of holding companies
**Issued Capital:** £132,184
**Principals:** A W Hewitt *(Chairman)*, Ms M P Hewitt, A G Holt, M J Quayle
**Co. Secretary:** Mike Quayle
**Responsibilities**
**Senior:** Julie Anthony *(Office Manager)*, Carolyn Stockdale *(Manager)*
**Finance:** Nadine NG *(Financial Controller)*, Jill Rawlinson *(Finance Director)*
**Admin:** Julie Anthony *(Office Manager)*
**HR:** Alexandria Gibson *(Human Resources Manager)*
**Facilities:** Julie Anthony *(Office Manager)*
**Branches:** Parkwood Holdings Ltd, Netherfield Hill, Battle, East Sussex TN33 0LL
**US SIC:** 6711, 0729
**UK SIC:** 83962, 01003
**Auditors:** PricewaterhouseCoopers LLP
**Bankers:** National Westminster Bank Plc (60-14-20)

| | 31-12-13 | 31-12-12 | 31-12-11 |
|---|---|---|---|
| TO | 122,163,000 | 116,749,000 | 114,403,000 |
| P/L | 1,899,000 | 1,502,000 | 1,486,000 |
| NW | 1,621,000 | 2,528,000 | 3,680,000 |
| WC | (8,472,000) | (5,836,000) | (4,412,000) |
| Emp. | 2,910 | 2,956 | 3,110 |

DUNS 21-530-4291
## Parkwood House Residential & Nursing Home
72 Exmouth Road, Plymouth, Devon PL1 4QJ
**Tel:** 01752-560000
**Web:** www.southernhealthcare.co.uk
**Estd:** 1986 Proprietorship
**Line of Business:** Nursing homes
**Proprietor:** G Cox
**Responsibilities**
**Senior:** Lorna Smith *(CEO, Managing Director)*
**Admin:** Melanie Scott *(Administrator)*
**US SIC:** 8051 **UK SIC:** 95100
**Employees:** 50

DUNS 52-527-1292
## Parkwood Leisure Ltd
(**Subsidiary of:** Alston Acquisitions Ltd)
Crook Log, Brampton Road, Bexleyheath, Kent DA7 4HH
**Tel:** 02083049090 **Fax:** 02083044604
**Web:** www.leisurecentre.com
**Reg No:** 3232979 **Estd:** 1995 Private Limited Company
**Line of Business:** Other business activities not elsewhere classified
**Trading Style:** Erith Sports Centre
**Issued Capital:** £2
**Directors:** A G Holt, W G Rawlinson, G Hall, A W Hewitt, A J Tucker, Ms S J Martin, Ms M P Hewitt
**Responsibilities**
**Senior:** Carolyn Stockdale *(Manager)*
**HR:** Lindsay Holbraith *(Human Resources Manager)*
**Branches:** Parkwood Leisure Ltd, The Bridge Sports & Leisure Centre, Kangley Bridge Road, London SE26 5AQ
**US SIC:** 7399, 7999
**UK SIC:** 83954, 97913
**Auditors:** PricewaterhouseCoopers LLP
**Bankers:** Abbey National Plc (09-00-29)

| | 31-12-13 | 31-12-12 | 31-12-11 |
|---|---|---|---|
| TO | 70,992,000 | 70,567,000 | 67,400,000 |
| P/L | 3,467,000 | 2,404,000 | 2,144,000 |
| NW | 3,677,000 | 3,586,000 | 4,951,000 |
| WC | (3,295,000) | (3,588,000) | (2,309,000) |
| Emp. | 1,799 | 1,879 | 2,026 |

## DUNS 22-550-2160     Imp-Exp
### Parlex (Europe) Ltd
(Subsidiary of: Johnson Electric Holdings Limited)
Unit 3 Taylor Road, Newport, Isle of Wight PO30 5LG
Tel: 01983-526535
Web: www.johnsonelectric.com
Reg No: 1345578   Estd: 1966 Private Limited Company
Line of Business: Printed and integrated circuit services
Export Markets: U S A; Europe
Export Sales: £3,297,806
Issued Capital: £2,000,000
Directors: D J Ward, C J Hasson, J L Obermayer
Co. Secretary: Ms Lai Cheng
Responsibilities
Senior: Clive Kydd (Manager), Angela Norton (Customer Service Assistant), Chee Yip (Manager)
US SIC: 3679, 3629
UK SIC: 34542, 34350
Auditors: Deloitte & Touche
Bankers: Lloyds TSB Bank plc (30-95-99)

|      | 31-03-14  | 31-03-13  | 31-03-12  |
|------|-----------|-----------|-----------|
| TO   | 3,901,782 | 4,435,179 | 4,758,700 |
| P/L  | 203,431   | 781,961   | 1,200,381 |
| NW   | 4,404,167 | 4,192,746 | 3,144,354 |
| WC   | 4,347,966 | 4,269,597 | 3,188,012 |
| Emp. | 56        | 58        | 51        |

## DUNS 23-220-2226
### Parliamentary Estate Directorate
1 Canon Row, London SW1A 2JN
Web: www.parliament.uk
Estd: 1992
Line of Business: Administration of the state and the economic and social policy of the community
Director: P F Linge
Responsibilities
Senior: Mel Barlex (Director of Parliamentary), Lester Benjamin (Facilities Manager)
HR: Judith Welham (Human Resources Manager)
Facilities: Lester Benjamin (Facilities Manager)
US SIC: 9121   UK SIC: 91110
Employees: 100

## DUNS 77-958-3405
### Parmenion Capital Partners Llp
2 College Square, Anchor Road, Bristol, Avon BS1 5UE
Tel: 01179349792
Web: www.parmenion.co.uk
Reg No: 0322243OC   Estd: 2006 Private Limited Company
Line of Business: Miscellaneous Investors
Responsibilities
Senior: Bimal Balasingham (Non-designated Limited Liabili), Mark Bonehill (Non-designated Limited Liabili), Edward Brett (Non-designated Limited Liabili), Madhu Garala (Non-designated Limited Liabili), Jaymini Garala (Non-designated Limited Liabili)
US SIC: 6799   UK SIC: 81502
Auditors: Nexia Smith & Williamson

|      | 31-03-14  | 31-03-13  | 31-03-12  |
|------|-----------|-----------|-----------|
| TO   | 5,276,725 | 3,353,211 | 2,249,470 |
| P/L  | 1,221,950 | 568,903   | 251,128   |
| NW   | 1,738,955 | 1,075,981 | 777,321   |
| WC   | 782,261   | 610,039   | 616,042   |
| Emp. | 48        | 35        | 22        |

## DUNS 21-730-8135
### Parmiter's School
High Elms Lane, Watford, Hertfordshire WD25 0UU
Tel: 01923671424
Web: www.parmiters.herts.sch.uk
Reg No: 7662765   Estd: 2011 Private Company Limited By Guarantee
Line of Business: Schools (foundation)
Directors: Mrs J E Glossop, D K Robertson, A Mehmet, J F Hubbard, A Heathcote, C Partridge, N J Daymond, C Farrelly
Responsibilities
Senior: Laurence Pilgrim (Director), Lindsey Rigby (Director), Stephen Westwood (Director)
US SIC: 8211   UK SIC: 93200
Bankers: Barclays Bank Plc (20-91-79)

|      | 31-08-14  | 31-08-13  | 31-08-12  |
|------|-----------|-----------|-----------|
| TO   | 8,594,706 | 7,542,000 | 9,865,000 |
| P/L  | 229,045   | 187,000   | 499,000   |
| NW   | 789,447   | 517,000   | 281,000   |
| WC   | 100,607   | 141,000   | 208,000   |
| Emp. | 150       | 190       | 191       |

## DUNS 21-232-2903     Imp-Exp
### Parmley Graham Ltd
South Shore Road, Gateshead, Tyne and Wear NE8 3AE
Tel: 01914780400
Web: www.parmley-graham.co.uk
Reg No: 0172842   VAT No: 176700654
Estd: 1903 Private Limited Company
Line of Business: Electrical wholesalers
Export Markets: Rest of the World
Export Sales: £798,000
Issued Capital: £399,570
Principals: M Wilson (Chairman), N J Wilson (Managing), Mrs K Wilson, G Mackey
Co. Secretary: Ian Gillies
Branches: Parmley Graham Ltd, Unit 6, Ashurst Drive, Stockport, Cheshire SK3 0SD
US SIC: 5074   UK SIC: 61300
Auditors: Stephenson Coates
Bankers: Lloyds TSB Bank plc (30-93-71)

|      | 31-12-13   | 31-12-12   | 31-12-11   |
|------|------------|------------|------------|
| TO   | 37,978,000 | 36,030,000 | 34,161,000 |
| P/L  | 955,000    | 999,000    | 1,017,000  |
| NW   | 3,973,000  | 4,328,000  | 3,795,000  |
| WC   | 3,967,000  | 4,770,000  | 4,082,000  |
| Emp. | 98         | 97         | 92         |

## DUNS 39-946-7745     Imp-Exp
### Parragon Books Ltd
(Subsidiary of: D C Thomson & Company Ltd)
Queen St House, Bath, Avon BA1 1HE
Web: www.parragon.com
Reg No: 2252808   VAT No: 873291406
Estd: 1989 Private Limited Company
Line of Business: Publishing of books
Export Markets: U S A; France; Australia; Asia
Export Sales: £31,376,000
Trading Style: Parragon Publishers, Parragon Book Services
Issued Capital: £25,027,972
Directors: A F Thomson, S A Bailey, C H Thomson, P Taylor, A R Hall
Co. Secretary: Ms Susan Staunton
US SIC: 2731   UK SIC: 47532
Auditors: Henderson Loggie
Bankers: Barclays Bank Plc (20-13-42)

|      | 31-03-14   | 31-03-13   | 31-03-12   |
|------|------------|------------|------------|
| TO   | 48,171,000 | 56,242,000 | 59,321,000 |
| P/L  | 19,490,000 | (6,080,000) | (386,000) |
| NW   | 50,964,000 | 23,452,000 | 28,128,000 |
| WC   | 49,412,000 | 26,834,000 | 31,770,000 |
| Emp. | 186        | 188        | 168        |

## DUNS 21-319-9214
### Parrott & Coales
14-16 Bourbon Street, Aylesbury, Buckinghamshire HP20 2RS
Web: www.parrottandcoalesllp.co.uk
Estd: 1997 Partnership
Line of Business: Solicitors
Partners: T Freelander, J Couzens, J Leggett, Miss S Plumridge, S Ellis, T Dawe, Mrs H Reid
Responsibilities
Senior: Tim Friedlander (Partner), Richard Friedlander (Designated Limited Liability P), Richard Sauvain (Partner), Sharon Stone (Commercial Director)
Sales: Sharon Stone (Commercial Director)
US SIC: 8111   UK SIC: 83500
Employees: 55

## DUNS 21-108-1980
### Parry & Evans Ltd
Severn Farm Industrial Estate, Welshpool, Powys SY21 7DF
Tel: 01938552185
Web: www.parryandevans.co.uk
Reg No: 6501567   Estd: 1961 Private Limited Company
Line of Business: Waste paper merchants
Export Sales: £59,261
Trading Style: Parry & Evans Limited
Issued Capital: £1,000
Directors: J R Evans, J E Evans
Co. Secretary: Stephen Evans
US SIC: 3031, 3341, 4959
UK SIC: 48123, 22470, 92110
Bankers: HSBC Bank plc (40-46-07)

|      | 31-05-13  | 31-05-12  | 31-05-11  |
|------|-----------|-----------|-----------|
| TO   | 7,895,955 | 7,958,839 | 7,984,736 |
| P/L  | 233,985   | 1,281,058 | 1,332,805 |
| NW   | 2,925,060 | 2,556,668 | 1,578,207 |
| WC   | 1,670,990 | 1,809,201 | 927,319   |
| Emp. | 85        | 62        | 61        |

## DUNS 21-811-6887     Imp-Exp
### Parry Group Ltd
The New Factory, Town End Road, Draycott, Derby, Derbyshire DE72 3PT
Tel: 01332-875544
Web: www.parry.co.uk
Reg No: 0395292   VAT No: 125207895
Estd: 1946 Private Limited Company
Line of Business: Manufacture of other electrical equipment not elsewhere classified
Export Markets: Worldwide
Issued Capital: £500,000

Director: M W Banton
Co. Secretary: Gary Rose
Branches: Parry Group Ltd, Wilson's Yd, Clifton Ave, Long Eaton, Nottingham, Nottinghamshire NG10 2GA
US SIC: 3629   UK SIC: 34350
Auditors: Cooper Parry Group Ltd
Bankers: HSBC Bank plc (40-10-06)

|      | 02-05-14  | 26-04-13  | 27-05-12  |
|------|-----------|-----------|-----------|
| TO   | 6,322,767 | 7,408,750 | 8,006,109 |
| P/L  | (395,777) | (346,828) | 99,379    |
| NW   | 751,908   | 1,443,747 | 2,528,507 |
| WC   | 1,719,918 | 2,180,182 | 2,601,226 |
| Emp. | 67        | 81        | 80        |

## DUNS 21-244-2917     Imp
### Parry's Motor Parts Ltd
(Subsidiary of: Parry's Holdings Ltd)
104 Frog Lane, Wigan, Lancashire WN6 7DA
Tel: 01942244669
Web: www.upd.co.uk
Reg No: 0845508   Estd: 1955 Private Limited Company
Line of Business: Motor factors
Trading Style: Ap Paints
Issued Capital: £2,000
Principals: N Parry (Managing), Ms B Parry, M Parry
Co. Secretary: Norman Parry
Branches: Parry's Motor Parts Ltd, Unit 1, Booth Road, Sale, Cheshire M33 7JS
US SIC: 5531   UK SIC: 65100
Auditors: Tenon Ltd
Bankers: The Co-Operative Bank Plc (08-90-96)

|      | 30-04-14  | 30-04-13  | 30-04-12  |
|------|-----------|-----------|-----------|
| TO   | N/A       | 3,243,748 | 4,638,614 |
| P/L  | N/A       | 9,665     | (243,778) |
| NW   | 7,522,980 | 7,645,247 | 7,629,582 |
| WC   | 7,072,271 | 7,209,602 | 7,112,575 |
| Emp. | N/A       | 48        | 56        |

## DUNS 23-783-3541
### Pars Group Ltd.
Unit 21, Dunfermline Business Park, Inverkeithing, Fife KY11 2RN
Web: www.parsproperties.co.uk
Reg No: 0196593SC   Estd: 1999 Private Limited Company
Line of Business: Management activities of holding companies
Issued Capital: £1,000
Director: A Sarafilovic
Co. Secretary: Alexander Sarafilovic
Branches: Pars Group Ltd., 2 Station Road, Dollar, Clackmannanshire FK14 7EJ
US SIC: 6711   UK SIC: 83962
Bankers: The Royal Bank Of Scotland Plc (83-07-06)

|      | 30-06-13  | 30-06-12  | 30-06-11  |
|------|-----------|-----------|-----------|
| TO   | 7,778,508 | 6,967,753 | 6,433,636 |
| P/L  | 1,417,180 | 893,449   | 942,162   |
| NW   | 6,189,898 | 5,214,524 | 4,706,946 |
| WC   | 2,478,789 | 1,645,360 | 1,123,628 |
| Emp. | 152       | 140       | 138       |

## DUNS 77-912-5652
### Parseq Ltd
Lowton Way, Hellaby, Rotherham, South Yorkshire S66 8RY
Tel: 01709448000
Web: www.parseq.com
Reg No: 5815806   VAT No: 927352809
Estd: 1990 Private Limited Company
Line of Business: Data storage solutions
Issued Capital: £192
Directors: Mrs T E Spencer, R Cassis, J D Seal, D H Jones
Co. Secretary: Mrs Theresa Spencer
US SIC: 7374, 6711
UK SIC: 83940, 83962
Auditors: PricewaterhouseCoopers LLP
Bankers: The Co-Operative Bank Plc (08-90-86)

|      | 31-12-13   | 31-12-12   | 31-12-11    |
|------|------------|------------|-------------|
| TO   | 30,185,000 | 12,120,000 | 10,174,000  |
| P/L  | 118,000    | 8,394,000  | (161,000)   |
| NW   | 379,000    | 4,154,000  | 408,000     |
| WC   | (1,972,000) | (262,000) | (12,951,000) |
| Emp. | 1,196      | 379        | 320         |

## DUNS 50-493-7350
### Parseq Services Ltd
(Subsidiary of: Parseq Ltd)
90-92 Pentonville Road, London N1 9HS
Tel: 02071877187   Fax: 01709-778801
Web: www.parseq.com
Reg No: 2461931   Estd: 1990 Private Limited Company
Line of Business: Computer games
Trading Style: Active Business Services
Issued Capital: £2,459,000
Directors: R Cassis, D H Jones, Mrs T E Spencer
Co. Secretary: Mrs Theresa Spencer
US SIC: 7372, 8931
UK SIC: 83940, 83600
Auditors: PricewaterhouseCoopers

Bankers: National Westminster Bank Plc (60-24-30)

|    | 31-12-13   | 31-12-12   | 31-12-11   |
|----|------------|------------|------------|
| TA | 11,793,000 | 11,793,000 | 11,793,000 |

## DUNS 23-601-9654
### Parsons Brinckerhoff Investments Ltd
(Subsidiary of: Balfour Beatty Plc)
6 Devonshire Square, London EC2M 4YE
Tel: 02073371700   Fax: 02073371701
Web: www.pbworld.com
Reg No: 3599313   Estd: 1997 Private Limited Company
Line of Business: Management activities of holding companies
Issued Capital: £9,578,412
Directors: S J Reffitt, S D Bingham
Co. Secretary: Nikolas Weston
Responsibilities
Senior: Gary Craigie (Deputy Projects Director)
Marketing: Tracey Chong (Marketing Manager), Maria Laffey (Public Relations & Media Direc), Rachel Skinner (Director Marketing & Communica)
IT: Bob Brannan (Projects Director), Gary Craigie (Deputy Projects Director)
Engineering: Gary Craigie (Deputy Projects Director), Raymond Leach (Principal Engineer), Tomas Luquez (Project Director), Darren Reed (Head of Rail (UK)), Russell Thomas (Technical Director), Jon Yarker (Head of Rail Engineering Desig)
US SIC: 6711, 8911
UK SIC: 83962, 83701
Auditors: Ernst & Young
Bankers: HSBC Bank plc (40-22-12)

|      | 31-12-13   | 31-12-12    | 31-12-11   |
|------|------------|-------------|------------|
| TA   | 19,421,000 | 19,733,000  | 19,488,000 |
| P/L  | N/A        | (1,273,000) | N/A        |
| NW   | 17,550,000 | 17,862,000  | 18,823,000 |
| WC   | (1,545,000) | (1,233,000) | (272,000) |

## DUNS 76-383-4587     Exp
### Parsons Brinckerhoff Ltd
(Subsidiary of: Balfour Beatty Plc)
William Armstrong Drive, Newcastle-Upon-Tyne, Tyne and Wear NE4 7YQ
Tel: 01912262000
Web: www.pbworld.com
Reg No: 2554514   VAT No: 217967235
Estd: 1899 Private Limited Company
Line of Business: Engineers (consulting)
Export Markets: Worldwide
Issued Capital: £33,075,501
Directors: S D Bingham, S J Reffitt
Co. Secretary: Nikolas Weston
Responsibilities
Senior: Nicholas Flew (Manager)
Sales: Tony Appleton (Business Development Director)
IT: Steven Terry (IT Infastructure Manager)
Purchasing: Paul Tumilty (Purchasing Manager)
Engineering: Chris Lomax (Technical Director)
Branches: Parsons Brinckerhoff Ltd, Quadrant Court, 44-45 Calthorpe Road, Birmingham, West Midlands B15 1TH
US SIC: 8911, 7392
UK SIC: 83701, 83951
Auditors: Deloitte LLP
Bankers: HSBC Bank plc (40-22-12)

|      | 31-12-13    | 31-12-12    | 31-12-11    |
|------|-------------|-------------|-------------|
| TO   | 170,391,000 | 167,500,000 | 166,773,000 |
| P/L  | (1,973,000) | (2,405,000) | (6,822,000) |
| NW   | 38,108,000  | 46,338,000  | 51,308,000  |
| WC   | 42,703,000  | 45,892,000  | 50,119,000  |
| Emp. | 1,986       | 1,133       | 1,267       |

## DUNS 52-026-8293     Imp
### Parsons Group International Ltd
(Subsidiary of: The Parsons Corporation)
65-67 Mansfield Road, Sheffield, South Yorkshire S21 2BW
Tel: 01142479100
Web: www.parsonsgroup.co.uk
Reg No: 3393325   Estd: 1997 Private Limited Company
Line of Business: Business and management consultancy activities not elsewhere classified
Issued Capital: £40,000
Directors: Ms V L Grebbien, T K Wager
Co. Secretary: Terence Hazell
Responsibilities
Marketing: tony Gowland (Sales and Marketing)
Sales: tony Gowland (Sales and Marketing)
US SIC: 7392   UK SIC: 83951
Auditors: Chantrey Vellacott DFK LLP

|      | 27-12-13  | 28-12-12  | 30-12-11  |
|------|-----------|-----------|-----------|
| TO   | 5,533,552 | 5,530,816 | 4,831,597 |
| P/L  | 221,378   | 1,110,982 | 406,018   |
| NW   | 1,893,275 | 1,768,465 | 933,249   |
| WC   | 9,533,544 | 11,350,183 | 11,935,100 |
| Emp. | 48        | 43        | 45        |

DUNS 23-752-9768
## Parsons Nationwide Distribution Ltd.
Aylesbeare Common Business Park, Exeter, Devon EX5 2DG
**Tel:** 01395-232252
**Web:** www.parsonsnationwide.com
**Reg No:** 3746821 **Estd:** 1999 Private Limited Company
**Line of Business:** Road haulage and transport services
**Trading Style:** Parsons Nationwide Distribution Ltd
**Issued Capital:** £100
**Director:** Ms N A Hoskin
**Co. Secretary:** Keith Hoskin
**Responsibilities**
**Finance:** Noyen Hoskins *(Senior Finance Administrator)*
IT: Winston Hoskins *(Senior IT Executive)*
**US SIC:** 4789 **UK SIC:** 77002
**Auditors:** Redwoods

| | 31-03-14 | 31-03-13 | 31-03-12 |
|---|---|---|---|
| TA | 3,551,378 | 3,041,174 | 2,649,620 |
| NW | 457,861 | 325,590 | 280,269 |
| WC | (757,222) | (775,084) | (649,958) |

DUNS 34-584-7086
## Parsons Peebles Generation Ltd
(**Subsidiary of:** Cbc Electric Machines Group Ltd)
Wood Road, Dunfermline, Fife KY11 2EA
**Tel:** 01383-421150 **Fax:** 01383-421198
**Web:** www.parsons-peebles.com
**Reg No:** 0281567SC **VAT No:** 556638017
**Estd:** 2005 Private Limited Company
**Line of Business:** Manufacturers of electric motors
**Issued Capital:** £500,000
**Directors:** G J Mccallum, K Gibson, F G Barrett, W K Picken, N G Black
**Co. Secretary:** Martin Ward
**Responsibilities**
**Senior:** Arnold Kosky *(Proprietor)*, Sandy Macvoy *(Manager)*, Troy Saunders *(Manager)*
**Marketing:** Allan Robinson *(Market Anaylist)*
**Operations:** Troy Saunders *(Manager)*
**US SIC:** 3621 **UK SIC:** 34201
**Auditors:** KPMG LLP
**Bankers:** Clydesdale Bank Plc (82-60-18)

| | 30-11-13 | 30-11-12 | 30-11-11 |
|---|---|---|---|
| TO | 4,810,782 | 5,341,831 | 5,927,686 |
| P/L | 214,559 | 1,166,786 | 1,296,688 |
| NW | 734,785 | 4,878,071 | 4,009,616 |
| WC | 538,386 | 4,776,709 | 3,873,073 |
| Emp. | 47 | 41 | 42 |

DUNS 21-065-7131
## Part 2
7a King Street, Frome, Somerset BA11 1BH
**Tel:** 01373-453212
**Estd:** 1983 Proprietorship
**Line of Business:** Hairdressers (unisex)
**Proprietor:** Mrs B Gregorczyk
**US SIC:** 7231 **UK SIC:** 98200
**Bankers:** Lloyds TSB Bank plc (30-93-40)
**Employees:** 49

DUNS 42-389-5239
## Parthenon Entertainment Ltd
(**Subsidiary of:** Sky Plc)
Parthenon House, 4-5 Station Approach, Rickmansworth, Hertfordshire WD3 5PF
**Tel:** 01923-286886 **Fax:** 01923286686
**Web:** www.bskyb.com
**Reg No:** 4377175 **Estd:** 2004 Private Limited Company
**Line of Business:** Other motion picture and video production activities
**Export Sales:** £7,894,000
**Trading Style:** Sky Vision
**Issued Capital:** £100
**Directors:** C R Jones, C J Taylor
**Co. Secretary:** Christopher Taylor
**Responsibilities**
**Senior:** Beverley Chappell *(Office Manager)*, Karl Hall *(Manager)*, Jane Millichip *(Manager)*
**Finance:** Mike Shanks *(Director of Finance and Operat)*
**Marketing:** Sean Harris *(Head of PR & Marketing)*
**Sales:** Leona Connell *(Head of Global Sales & Acquisi)*, Mirjam Strasser *(Senior Sales Manager)*
**Admin:** Beverly Chapel *(Office Manager)*
**Branches:** Parthenon Entertainment Ltd, 34 Whiteladies Road, Bristol, Avon BS8 2LG
**US SIC:** 7819, 7829
**UK SIC:** 97111, 97112
**Bankers:** Coutts & Co (18-00-02)

| | 30-06-14 | 30-06-13 | 30-06-12 |
|---|---|---|---|
| TO | 10,355,000 | 9,824,700 | 10,346,585 |
| P/L | (2,913,000) | (1,291,008) | 1,888,220 |
| NW | (20,850,000) | (14,561,101) | (11,846,106) |
| WC | (20,330,000) | (14,055,971) | (11,138,567) |
| Emp. | 45 | 53 | 53 |

DUNS 29-087-8271
## Partic Motor Spares Ltd
Brunel Drive, Northern Road Industrial Estate, Newark, Nottinghamshire NG24 2EG
**Tel:** 01636702479 **Fax:** 01636-705362
**Web:** www.tescos.net
**Reg No:** 1410324 **Estd:** 1979 Private Limited Company
**Line of Business:** Sale of motor vehicle parts and accessories
**Issued Capital:** £66
**Managing Director:** I R Beard
**Co. Secretary:** Mrs Olive Beard
**Responsibilities**
**Finance:** Danielle Page *(Credit Manager)*
**Sales:** Danielle Page *(Credit Manager)*
**Branches:** Partic Motor Spares Ltd, 8 Pioneer Way, Lincoln, Lincolnshire LN6 3DH
**US SIC:** 5531 **UK SIC:** 65100
**Auditors:** BDO Stoy Hayward
**Bankers:** National Westminster Bank Plc (54-10-23)

| | 30-04-14 | 30-04-13 | 30-04-12 |
|---|---|---|---|
| TO | 7,217,144 | 6,534,766 | N/A |
| P/L | 750,380 | 590,027 | N/A |
| NW | 3,639,291 | 3,481,020 | 3,022,284 |
| WC | 2,564,191 | 2,724,492 | 2,318,830 |
| Emp. | 57 | 55 | N/A |

DUNS 28-997-7415
## The Partick Thistle Football Club Ltd
Firhill Stadium, 90 Firhill Road, Glasgow, Lanarkshire G20 7AL
**Tel:** 08714021971 **Fax:** 08714101876
**Web:** www.ptfc.co.uk
**Reg No:** 0005417SC **VAT No:** 260826560
**Estd:** 1903 Private Limited Company
**Line of Business:** Sports clubs
**Issued Capital:** £1,574,767
**Directors:** G R Brown, B Donald, I G Maxwell, W M Allan, A Chopra, D Beattie, I R Dodd
**Co. Secretary:** David Kelly
**Responsibilities**
**Senior:** Grant Bannerman *(Manager)*, Gerry Britton *(Assistant Manager)*, Allan Cowan *(Manager)*, Ronald Gilfillan *(Manager)*, Thomas McMaster *(Manager)*, Eddie Pice *(Manager)*
**Marketing:** George Francis *(?Media and Communications Mana)*
**Sales:** Kirsten Fordham *(Sales & Events Executive)*, Stacey Greig *(Sales & Events Executive)*
**US SIC:** 7999 **UK SIC:** 97913
**Auditors:** BKR Haines Watts
**Bankers:** Bank Of Scotland (80-83-88)

| | 31-05-14 | 31-05-13 | 31-05-12 |
|---|---|---|---|
| TO | 2,852,295 | N/A | N/A |
| P/L | (5,267) | N/A | N/A |
| NW | 4,547,144 | 4,552,411 | 4,546,875 |
| WC | (560,175) | (816,979) | (795,053) |
| Emp. | 76 | N/A | N/A |

DUNS 29-012-5582
## Partingtons Holiday Centres Ltd
(**Subsidiary of:** The Partington Group Ltd)
Chapel Court, 204 Fleetwood Road North, Thornton-Cleveleys, Lancashire FY5 4BJ
**Tel:** 01253338260 **Fax:** 01253-893101
**Web:** www.partingtons.com
**Reg No:** 0391104 **Estd:** 1944 Private Limited Company
**Line of Business:** Caravan parks
**Trading Style:** Partingtons Caravan Holiday Centre
**Issued Capital:** £2,000
**Directors:** Mrs C M Kearsley, R P Kearsley, T A Kearsley, Mrs A M Challis
**Responsibilities**
**Senior:** Donna Armstead *(Personal Assistant)*
**Branches:** Partingtons Holiday Centres Ltd, Fleetwood Road, Fleetwood, Lancashire FY7 8JX
**US SIC:** 7033 **UK SIC:** 66701
**Auditors:** Haworth Moore
**Bankers:** Barclays Bank Plc (20-10-03)

| | 31-03-14 | 31-03-13 | 31-03-12 |
|---|---|---|---|
| TO | 9,807,124 | 8,961,513 | 8,911,039 |
| P/L | 268,430 | 499,008 | 163,233 |
| NW | 944,802 | 765,361 | 640,595 |
| WC | (95,861) | (422,274) | (385,026) |
| Emp. | 159 | 158 | 156 |

DUNS 21-634-9762
## Partner Logistics Wisbech Bv
(**Subsidiary of:** Partner Logistics Investment B.V.)
101 Boleness Road, Wisbech, Cambridgeshire PE13 2XQ
**Tel:** 01945428860
**Web:** www.partnerlogistics.eu
**Reg No:** 0029124FC **Estd:** 2009 Foreign Company
**Line of Business:** Frozen food processors and distributors

**Proprietor:** S Garratt
**Responsibilities**
**Senior:** Mark Swash *(Site Manager)*
**US SIC:** 5149 **UK SIC:** 61700

DUNS 29-863-5616
## Partners B D D H Ltd
(**Subsidiary of:** Havas)
Cupola House, 15 Alfred Place, London WC1E 7EB
**Tel:** 02074679200 **Fax:** 02074679201
**Web:** www.havaspr.co.uk
**Reg No:** 2066862 **Estd:** 1987 Private Limited Company
**Line of Business:** Advertising
**Issued Capital:** £52,358
**Directors:** A Chapman, P F Woodhouse
**Co. Secretary:** Allan Ross
**Responsibilities**
**Senior:** Steve Marinker *(Manager)*
**Marketing:** Piyush Pankaj *(Head of Search)*, Claire Twohill *(Head of Social)*
**Sales:** Jess Tarpey *(New Business Manager)*
**US SIC:** 7311 **UK SIC:** 83800
**Auditors:** Arthur Andersen
**Bankers:** Lloyds TSB Bank plc (77-91-65)

| | 31-12-13 | 31-12-12 | 31-12-11 |
|---|---|---|---|
| TA | 52,358 | 52,358 | 52,358 |
| NW | 52,358 | 52,358 | 52,358 |

DUNS 21-098-8615
## Partners Capital Llp
5th Floor 5 Young Street, London W8 5EH
**Tel:** 02073617610
**Web:** www.weightpartners.com
**Reg No:** 0332859OC **Estd:** 2007 Private Limited Company
**Line of Business:** Activities auxiliary to financial intermediation not elsewhere classified
**Export Sales:** £6,462,196
**US SIC:** 6111 **UK SIC:** 81501

| | 31-12-13 | 31-12-12 | 31-12-11 |
|---|---|---|---|
| TA | 13,381,860 | 8,574,761 | 5,676,464 |
| NW | 3,962,783 | 3,962,783 | 3,148,522 |
| WC | 8,617,036 | 5,845,437 | 4,224,736 |
| Emp. | 52 | 40 | 36 |

DUNS 22-878-2249
## Partners Credit Union Ltd
New Oxford House, Liverpool, Merseyside L2 2HT
**Tel:** 01512581014
**Web:** www.partnerscreditunion.co.uk
**Reg No:** 0000354IP **Estd:** 1842 Friendly Society
**Line of Business:** Credit unions
**Principals:** R Woods *(President)*, H Piggott *(Chairman)*, P Caldwell, D Maidment, Ms S Hartstone, D Challenger, J Hare, A Long
**Responsibilities**
**Senior:** Allan Chalkley *(Chief Executive Officer)*, Tracy Fletcher *(Chief Executive Officer)*, Arnold Jones *(Vice President)*, Norman Lee *(Vice Chairman)*, Tracy Schuler *(Proprietor)*
**US SIC:** 6111 **UK SIC:** 81501
**Auditors:** J M P Bishop
**Bankers:** HSBC Bank plc (40-27-15)
**Employees:** 137

DUNS 73-769-4039
## Partners for Inclusion
84 Portland Street, Kilmarnock, Ayrshire KA3 1AA
**Tel:** 01563825555 **Fax:** 01563-825556
**Web:** www.partnersforinclusion.org
**Reg No:** 0262549SC **Estd:** 2004 Private Limited Company
**Line of Business:** Activities of households as employers of domestic staff
**Directors:** J A Maxton, Ms L Webster, Ms C Currie, D Watson, C Edgar, Mrs J A Barbour, Ms M H Imrie
**Co. Secretary:** Ms Doreen Kelly
**Responsibilities**
**Health & Safety:** Ken Fentie *(Health & Safety Manager)*
**US SIC:** 8811, 7392
**UK SIC:** 99000, 83951
**Bankers:** The Royal Bank Of Scotland Plc (83-06-08)

| | 31-03-14 | 31-03-13 | 31-03-12 |
|---|---|---|---|
| TO | 5,651,286 | 5,499,299 | 5,056,803 |
| P/L | 107,662 | (1,062) | 48,490 |
| NW | 2,092,466 | 1,984,804 | 1,985,866 |
| WC | 1,301,967 | 1,212,293 | 1,323,529 |
| Emp. | 309 | 289 | 272 |

DUNS 73-858-5061
## Partners Group (Uk) Ltd
(**Subsidiary of:** Partners Group Holding Ag)
Heron Tower, 14th Floor, London EC2N 4AY
**Tel:** 02075752500 **Fax:** 02075752501
**Web:** www.partnersgroup.com
**Reg No:** 5113447 **Estd:** 2004 Private Limited Company

**Line of Business:** Financial services
**Export Sales:** £2,916,120
**Issued Capital:** £450,000
**Directors:** M Studer, A M Campbell, P J Ward, S Jovele
**Co. Secretary:** Christopher Toone
**US SIC:** 6371 **UK SIC:** 82002
**Bankers:** HSBC Bank plc (40-05-20)

| | 31-12-13 | 31-12-12 | 31-12-11 |
|---|---|---|---|
| TO | 21,161,881 | 18,822,721 | 11,179,823 |
| P/L | 6,243,671 | 4,208,878 | 1,718,735 |
| NW | 5,579,403 | 6,873,881 | 4,191,219 |
| WC | 5,412,576 | 6,675,249 | 3,485,607 |
| Emp. | 64 | 58 | 43 |

DUNS 77-973-6862
## Partners in Hygiene Ltd
12 Charnwood Drive, Faverdale, Darlington, County Durham DL3 0EG
**Web:** www.partnersinhygiene.co.uk
**Reg No:** 5942234 **Estd:** 2006 Private Limited Company
**Line of Business:** Specialised cleaning services
**Issued Capital:** £1,000
**Directors:** P Barker, D S Twemlow, M J Twemlow
**Co. Secretary:** Mrs Christina Barker
**Responsibilities**
**Senior:** Michael Mikkelsen *(Manager)*
**US SIC:** 7349 **UK SIC:** 92300

| | 31-03-14 | 31-03-13 | 31-03-12 |
|---|---|---|---|
| TO | 7,176,194 | N/A | N/A |
| P/L | 488,944 | N/A | N/A |
| NW | 413,756 | 227,043 | 212,791 |
| WC | 175,961 | (78,100) | (130,331) |
| Emp. | 281 | N/A | N/A |

DUNS 23-986-3389
## Partners in Property Ltd
(**Subsidiary of:** Washbrook Capital Ltd)
T/A Movewithus, St Ives, Cambridgeshire PE27 4AA
**Fax:** 01480358501
**Web:** www.movewithus.co.uk
**Reg No:** 3974653 **Estd:** 1999 Private Limited Company
**Line of Business:** Relocation services
**Trading Style:** Move With Us
**Issued Capital:** £100
**Directors:** R G Jeffrey, S King
**Co. Secretary:** Nigel Berry
**US SIC:** 6531 **UK SIC:** 83400
**Auditors:** King & Partners

| | 30-09-13 | 30-09-12 | 30-09-11 |
|---|---|---|---|
| TA | 10 | 10 | 10 |
| NW | 10 | 10 | 10 |

DUNS 21-001-7389
## Partners in Support Ltd
Unit 11 Meadway Court, Rutherford Close, Stevenage, Hertfordshire SG1 2EF
**Tel:** 01438-746-243
**Web:** www.partnersinsupport.org.uk
**Reg No:** 6272741 **Estd:** 2007 Private Company Limited By Guarantee
**Line of Business:** Home care service providers
**Director:** M J Nicholas
**US SIC:** 8091 **UK SIC:** 95200
**Auditors:** Cook & Partners Ltd

| | 31-03-14 | 31-03-13 | 31-03-12 |
|---|---|---|---|
| TA | 222,960 | 161,442 | 117,687 |
| NW | 179,807 | 140,697 | 111,279 |
| WC | 170,390 | 132,441 | 111,127 |

DUNS 77-964-1182
## Partners of Prisoners & Families Support Group
1079 Rochdale Road, Manchester M9 8AJ
**Tel:** 0161-702-1000
**Web:** www.partnersofprisoners.co.uk
**Reg No:** 3067385 **Estd:** 2000 Private Limited Company
**Line of Business:** Counselling & advice services
**Directors:** S Cook, Ms A Davie, Miss S J Leach, Mrs E J Asante-Mensah, S Wallace, G B Black, W R Ashberry, Ms V Charles
**Responsibilities**
**Senior:** Diane Curry *(Chief Executive)*
**US SIC:** 8321 **UK SIC:** 96111
**Auditors:** Slade & Cooper Ltd
**Bankers:** Unity Trust Bank Plc (08-60-01)

| | 31-03-14 | 31-03-13 | 31-03-12 |
|---|---|---|---|
| TO | 1,532,284 | 1,669,080 | 1,466,295 |
| P/L | 21,102 | (4,404) | (4,833) |
| NW | 660,613 | 639,511 | 643,915 |
| WC | 480,827 | 442,026 | 451,714 |
| Emp. | 47 | 47 | 39 |

DUNS 21-927-7148
### Partnership Assurance Group Plc
5th Floor 110 Bishopsgate, London EC2N 4AY
**Tel:** 08451087240 **Fax:** 08451087238
**Web:** www.partnership.co.uk
**Reg No:** 8419490 **Estd:** 2013 Public Limited Company
**Line of Business:** Activities auxiliary to insurance and pension funding
**Issued Capital:** £50,000
**Directors:** Dr C S Gibson Smith, Dr R C Ward, P Bishop, D Ferrans, D L Richardson, S J Groves, S J Waugh, Ms C Spottiswoode
**Co. Secretary:** Prism Cosec Limited
**US SIC:** 6411 **UK SIC:** 83200
**Auditors:** Deloitte LLP

| | 31-12-13 |
|---|---|
| TO | 425,713,000 |
| P/L | 82,661,000 |
| NW | 456,007,000 |
| WC | 837,421,000 |
| Emp. | 539 |

DUNS 21-584-7488
### Partnership Card Customer Services
Po Box 11403, Birmingham, West Midlands B3 2YW
**Tel:** 08453003833
**Web:** www.partnershipcard.co.uk
**Estd:** 2011
**Line of Business:** Call centres
**US SIC:** 7399 **UK SIC:** 83954
**Employees:** 100

DUNS 29-845-3986
### The Partnership in Care Ltd
Lethrede, Hall Lane, Bury St Edmunds, Suffolk IP28 6RS
**Tel:** 01284811297
**Web:** www.thepartnershipincare.co.uk
**Reg No:** 2048736 **Estd:** 2011 Private Limited Company
**Line of Business:** Other adult and other education not elsewhere classified
**Trading Style:** Risby Hall Nursing Home
**Issued Capital:** £150
**Directors:** Mrs R E Fitton, I D Turner, Mrs E C John
**Co. Secretary:** Ms Elaine Turner
**Responsibilities**
**Senior:** Harry Kambadza *(Manager)*
**Branches:** The Partnership In Care Ltd, Boxclever, Atherton Street, Manchester M60 9EB
**US SIC:** 8299 **UK SIC:** 93300
**Auditors:** Jacobs Allen
**Bankers:** National Westminster Bank Plc (60-04-16)

| | 31-03-14 | 31-03-13 | 31-03-12 |
|---|---|---|---|
| TO | 8,471,550 | 8,548,609 | 7,344,556 |
| P/L | 615,642 | 1,277,432 | 481,941 |
| NW | 4,262,353 | 4,124,701 | 3,521,430 |
| WC | (245,988) | (512,339) | (1,047,026) |
| Emp. | 425 | 400 | 390 |

DUNS 37-874-5087
### Partnership Media Group Ltd
St James Buildings, Oxford Street, Manchester M1 6PP
**Tel:** 01612113000
**Web:** www.govnet.co.uk
**Reg No:** 3307092 **VAT No:** 686277974
**Estd:** 1997 Private Limited Company
**Line of Business:** Advertising
**Trading Style:** Govnet Communications
**Issued Capital:** £66
**Director:** Ms J Walsh
**Co. Secretary:** T P D S Limited
**Responsibilities**
**Senior:** Mohammed Umerji *(Sales Director)*
**Marketing:** Rebekkah Tabern *(Marketing and Communications D)*
**Sales:** Mohammed Umerji *(Sales Director)*
**Health & Safety:** Ian Nally *(Health & Safety Officer)*
**US SIC:** 7311, 7399
**UK SIC:** 83800, 83954

| | 31-12-13 | 31-12-12 | 31-12-11 |
|---|---|---|---|
| TO | 11,823,070 | 9,324,377 | 8,331,094 |
| P/L | 1,879,962 | 1,185,321 | 531,285 |
| NW | 2,651,510 | 1,929,538 | 1,038,667 |
| WC | 2,556,093 | 1,882,149 | 945,760 |
| Emp. | 114 | 107 | 108 |

DUNS 21-601-3816
### Partnerships in Care
Burston House, Rectory Road, Burston, Diss, Norfolk IP22 5TU
**Tel:** 01379741562
**Web:** www.partnershipsincare.co.uk
**Estd:** 2011 Proprietorship
**Line of Business:** Public sector hospital activities, including nhs trusts
**Proprietor:** Ms R O'Connell
**Responsibilities**
**Senior:** Rosario O'Connell *(Regional Executive Director)*
**US SIC:** 8062 **UK SIC:** 95100
**Employees:** 100

DUNS 76-958-4145 **Exp**
### Partnerships in Care Ltd
(**Subsidiary of:** Acadia Healthcare Company Inc.)
Unit 2 Imperial Place, Maxwell Road, Borehamwood, Hertfordshire WD6 1JN
**Tel:** 020-8327-1800
**Web:** www.partnershipsincare.co.uk
**Reg No:** 2622784 **Estd:** 2011 Private Limited Company
**Line of Business:** Representative office
**Export Markets:** Sweden
**Trading Style:** Partnerships in Care, The Dene Hospital, Redford Lodge
**Issued Capital:** £500,000
**Directors:** Ms L J Chamberlain, Dr Q Haque, S J Woolgar
**Co. Secretary:** Ms Sarah Livingston
**Responsibilities**
**Senior:** Tony Rook *(Manager)*, Fred Sinclair-Brown *(Chief Executive)*
**Branches:** Partnerships In Care Ltd, Longsight Road, Blackburn, Lancashire BB6 8AD
**US SIC:** 8062 **UK SIC:** 95100
**Auditors:** PricewaterhouseCoopers LLP
**Bankers:** Barclays Bank Plc (20-65-82)

| | 31-12-13 | 31-12-12 | 31-12-11 |
|---|---|---|---|
| TO | 157,808,785 | 157,936,715 | 160,301,731 |
| P/L | 3,081,184 | 5,220,538 | 56,291,769 |
| NW | 52,070,290 | 51,246,600 | 46,174,750 |
| WC | 50,245,950 | 50,273,238 | 47,581,079 |
| Emp. | 2,943 | 2,945 | 2,865 |

DUNS 21-913-2420 **Imp-Exp**
### Partnertech Ltd
(**Subsidiary of:** Partnertech Ab)
Unit 6-8, Coldhams Lane College Park, Cambridge, Cambridgeshire CB1 3HD
**Tel:** 01223278850
**Web:** www.partnertech.co.uk
**Reg No:** 1041448 **VAT No:** 105565092
**Estd:** 1972 Private Limited Company
**Line of Business:** Manufacture of electronic valves and tubes and other electronic components
**Export Markets:** Worldwide
**Export Sales:** £802,028
**Issued Capital:** £1,000,226
**Directors:** L T Thorwaldsson, K A Bengtsson
**Responsibilities**
**Senior:** Angela Wootton *(Manager)*
**Health & Safety:** Wayne Barrett *(Health & Safety Coordinator)*
**Engineering:** Stewart Green *(Production Manager)*
**Branches:** Partnertech Limited, Unit 6-7, Coldhams Lane, Cambridge, Cambridgeshire CB1 3HD
**US SIC:** 3679, 3651
**UK SIC:** 34542, 34541
**Auditors:** Deloitte LLP
**Bankers:** National Westminster Bank Plc (53-61-38)

| | 31-12-13 | 31-12-12 | 31-12-11 |
|---|---|---|---|
| TO | 4,441,299 | 5,812,648 | 9,926,261 |
| P/L | (736,792) | (881,404) | (1,677,253) |
| NW | (76,991) | (540,199) | (658,795) |
| WC | (225,677) | (783,921) | (1,808,200) |
| Emp. | 50 | 54 | 87 |

DUNS 21-811-0209
### Partridge Care Centre
Partridge Road, Harlow, Essex CM18 6TD
**Tel:** 01279452990
**Web:** www.rushcliffecare.co.uk
**Estd:** 2012
**Line of Business:** Children's homes
**Responsibilities**
**Senior:** Andrea Gamble *(Senior Manager)*, Jayne Wood *(Manager)*
**US SIC:** 8321 **UK SIC:** 96111
**Employees:** 120

DUNS 52-537-4633 **Imp**
### Partspanel Ltd
(**Subsidiary of:** B N D Holdings Ltd)
Unit 4 29-35, North Acton Road, London NW10 6PE
**Fax:** 020-8965-1966
**Web:** www.partspanelonline.com
**Reg No:** 3241006 **VAT No:** 672721823
**Estd:** 1996 Private Limited Company
**Line of Business:** Car accessories and parts
**Issued Capital:** £890,100
**Director:** H C Patel
**Co. Secretary:** Jayesh Patel
**Responsibilities**
**Health & Safety:** Mahesh Jethwa *(General Manager)*
**US SIC:** 5531 **UK SIC:** 65100
**Auditors:** Patens & Co Ltd

| | 30-09-13 | 30-09-12 | 30-09-11 |
|---|---|---|---|
| TA | 3,034,429 | 3,044,906 | 3,238,674 |
| NW | 267,279 | 259,629 | 252,341 |
| WC | 215,589 | 249,799 | 500,898 |

DUNS 21-029-6911
### Partswarehouse
22-24 Hornsby Square, Southfields Business Park, Basildon, Essex SS15 6SD
**Tel:** 0870-870-1220
**Web:** www.partswarehouse.co.uk
**Estd:** 2010 Proprietorship
**Line of Business:** Printers services and supplies
**Proprietor:** S Kotadia
**Responsibilities**
**Senior:** Dave Holyfield *(Proprietor)*, Eamonn O'connor *(Manager)*, Phil Wheeler *(Manager)*
**US SIC:** 5081 **UK SIC:** 61490
**Employees:** 50

DUNS 54-851-6038
### Party Express-the Party Bus
Argo House, London NW6 5LF
**Tel:** 08458385400
**Web:** www.partyexpressbus.com
**VAT No:** 629430830 **Estd:** 1989 Partnership
**Line of Business:** Activities of exhibition and fair organisers
**Partners:** D Chapman, D Mccourt
**US SIC:** 7299 **UK SIC:** 98902
**Bankers:** National Westminster Bank Plc (56-00-33)
**Employees:** 100

DUNS 67-230-5497
### The Partyman Co Ltd
Unit 13 Repton Close, Basildon, Essex SS13 1LJ
**Tel:** 08450345123 **Fax:** 01702-522048
**Web:** www.thepartymancompany.co.uk
**Reg No:** 6057445 **Estd:** 2007 Private Limited Company
**Line of Business:** Social work activities without accommodation
**Issued Capital:** £200
**Directors:** J Sinclair, Ms V J Barton-Wright
**US SIC:** 8321, 7922
**UK SIC:** 96111, 97412

| | 31-03-14 | 31-03-13 | 31-03-12 |
|---|---|---|---|
| TA | 1,172,718 | 876,930 | 630,760 |
| NW | (174,119) | (34,771) | (98,534) |
| WC | (714,467) | (282,625) | (182,201) |

DUNS 21-603-7747 **Imp-Exp**
### Parvalux Electric Motors Ltd
(**Subsidiary of:** Parvalux Ltd)
490-492 Wallisdown Road, Bournemouth, Dorset BH11 8PU
**Tel:** 01202-512575 **Fax:** 01202-530885
**Web:** www.parvalux.com
**Reg No:** 0446422 **VAT No:** 185952225
**Estd:** 1947 Private Limited Company
**Line of Business:** Manufacturers of electric motors
**Export Markets:** Middle East, U S A, E U, Canada
**Export Sales:** £8,726,035
**Issued Capital:** £135,000
**Directors:** S J Clark, M P Pennock, M A Shearer, C L Reynolds, J P Severn, N S Spetch
**Co. Secretary:** Stephen Siggs
**Responsibilities**
**Marketing:** Rudi Dias *(E-Business Strategist)*
**Purchasing:** Joanne Kerley *(Purchasing Manager)*
**Branches:** Parvalux Electric Motors Ltd, Unit 4, 26 Avenue Road, Birmingham, West Midlands B6 4DY
**US SIC:** 3621, 3999
**UK SIC:** 34201, 49590
**Auditors:** Mazars LLP
**Bankers:** National Westminster Bank Plc (54-30-03)

| | 30-06-13 | 30-06-12 | 30-06-11 |
|---|---|---|---|
| TO | 17,265,790 | 18,009,948 | 14,186,635 |
| P/L | 634,684 | 1,222,560 | (111,638) |
| NW | 1,335,478 | 682,931 | (590,806) |
| WC | 3,390,606 | 4,618,859 | 5,133,695 |
| Emp. | 198 | 188 | 178 |

DUNS 73-528-6242
### Pasab Ltd
70 Station Road, Erdington, Birmingham, West Midlands B23 6UE
**Tel:** 01213732796
**Web:** www.jhoots.co.uk
**Reg No:** 4791222 **Estd:** 1961 Private Limited Company
**Line of Business:** Chemists consulting
**Trading Style:** Badham Pharmacy
**Issued Capital:** £7
**Directors:** M S Jhooty, Dr J P Kingsland, S S Jhooty, R T Sugden, B S Guest, R P Herbert, S K Jhooty, S A Haywood
**Co. Secretary:** Sandip Jhooty
**Responsibilities**
**Senior:** Michael Galyas *(Manager)*
**US SIC:** 5912 **UK SIC:** 64300

| | 31-08-13 | 31-08-12 | 31-08-11 |
|---|---|---|---|
| TO | 14,414,268 | 13,226,561 | 13,559,760 |
| P/L | 299,673 | 952,436 | 531,036 |
| NW | (1,457,078) | (1,501,293) | (2,555,280) |
| WC | (536,012) | (98,596) | (212,488) |
| Emp. | 121 | 122 | 126 |

DUNS 29-144-9841
### Pascall + Watson Ltd
The Warehouses, 10 Black Friars Lane, London EC4V 6EJ
**Tel:** 02038372500 **Fax:** 02038372600
**Web:** www.pascalls.co.uk
**Reg No:** 1711056 **Estd:** 1983 Private Limited Company
**Line of Business:** Architectural activities
**Export Sales:** £4,495,809
**Issued Capital:** £9,950
**Directors:** J Carlson, P J Ruggles, P K Holden, M W Butters, M C Haste, P J Allen, S G West, J R Speed
**Co. Secretary:** Alan Lamond
**Responsibilities**
**HR:** Leena Meisuria *(Human Resources Manager)*
**US SIC:** 7399 **UK SIC:** 83954
**Auditors:** Saffery Champness
**Bankers:** Lloyds TSB Bank plc (30-97-71)

| | 30-04-14 | 30-04-13 | 30-04-12 |
|---|---|---|---|
| TO | 10,491,036 | 16,833,157 | 16,762,903 |
| P/L | 143,312 | 958,753 | 548,247 |
| NW | 3,633,008 | 3,501,557 | 2,994,618 |
| WC | 3,085,892 | 2,944,106 | 2,529,873 |
| Emp. | 156 | 175 | 183 |

DUNS 21-745-3141 **Imp-Exp**
### Pascall Electronics Ltd
(**Subsidiary of:** Emrise Electronics Ltd)
Westridge Business Park, Cothey Way, Ryde, Isle of Wight PO33 1QT
**Tel:** 01983-817300 **Fax:** 01983-564708
**Web:** www.pascall.co.uk
**Reg No:** 1316674 **Estd:** 1977 Private Limited Company
**Line of Business:** Manufacturers of electronic equipment and components
**Export Markets:** Worldwide
**Export Sales:** £6,779,886
**Trading Style:** Pascall Electronics Ltd
**Issued Capital:** £53,822
**Directors:** R L Weller, M K Blake, C T Oliva, G M Jefferies
**Co. Secretary:** Graham Jefferies
**Responsibilities**
**Senior:** Dennis Donovan *(Manager)*
**Marketing:** Adele Maclachlan *(Sales & Marketing Director)*
**Sales:** Adele Maclachlan *(Sales & Marketing Director)*
**IT:** Olli Poole *(IT Manager)*
**HR:** Emma Crabbe *(Personnel Manager)*
**Health & Safety:** Emma Crabbe *(Personnel Manager)*
**Operations:** Andy Baskill *(Operations Manager)*, Emma Crabbe *(Personnel Manager)*
**Purchasing:** Andy Baskill *(Operations Manager)*
**Branches:** Pascall Electronics Ltd, Suite 16E, Manchester International Office Centre, Styal Rd, Manchester M22 5WB
**US SIC:** 3679 **UK SIC:** 34542
**Auditors:** Grant Thornton UK LLP
**Bankers:** Barclays Bank Plc (20-84-58)

| | 31-12-13 | 31-12-12 | 31-12-11 |
|---|---|---|---|
| TO | 9,449,973 | 10,636,725 | 10,245,796 |
| P/L | 877,923 | 1,130,936 | 980,727 |
| NW | 3,807,359 | 3,418,648 | 2,619,456 |
| WC | 3,268,615 | 3,334,610 | 2,465,073 |
| Emp. | 117 | 120 | 114 |

DUNS 77-490-4429 **Exp**
### Pashley Holdings Ltd
Masons Road, Stratford-Upon-Avon, Warwickshire CV37 9NL
**Tel:** 01789-292263 **Fax:** 01789-414201
**Web:** www.pashleycollection.co.uk
**Reg No:** 2974132 **Estd:** 1994 Private Limited Company
**Line of Business:** Manufacturers and wholesalers of cycles
**Issued Capital:** £153,000
**Director:** A M Williams
**Co. Secretary:** Ms Kathleen Warren
**Responsibilities**
**Marketing:** Lee Pillinger *(Marketing Manager)*
**Branches:** Pashley Holdings Ltd, 37 St Georges Terr, Newcastle Upon Tyne, Tyne and Wear NE2 2SX
**US SIC:** 3751 **UK SIC:** 36330
**Auditors:** Bentley Jennison

| | 31-12-13 | 31-12-12 | 31-12-11 |
|---|---|---|---|
| TA | 3,253,098 | 2,858,141 | 2,718,609 |
| NW | 2,102,147 | 1,991,780 | 1,856,905 |
| WC | 1,838,665 | 1,734,741 | 1,583,265 |

DUNS 64-740-1132
## Pashley Manor Gardens
Pashley Manor, Pashley Road, Wadhurst, East Sussex TN5 7HE
**Tel:** 01580-200888
**Web:** www.pashleymanorgardens.com
**Estd:** 1992 Proprietorship
**Line of Business:** Parks & gardens
**Proprietor:** J A Selleck
**Responsibilities**
**Senior:** James Selleck *(Managing Director)*
**US SIC:** 8411 **UK SIC:** 97700
**Employees:** 50

DUNS 29-622-5691
## Pass J. Holdings Ltd
**(Subsidiary of:** o'Leary Group Ltd)
Online Roadways, Online House, Dagenham, Essex RM8 1RX
**Tel:** 02085977404 **Fax:** 02089838948
**Web:** www.pjholdings.com
**Reg No:** 1949116 **Estd:** 1985 Private Limited Company
**Line of Business:** Freight transport by road not elsewhere classified
**Export Sales:** £3,399,154
**Trading Style:** Online Roadways
**Issued Capital:** £500,000
**Principals:** S J Oleary *(Managing)*, Ms P R Oleary, Ms J D Oleary
**Co. Secretary:** Geoffrey Lane
**US SIC:** 4213, 4226
**UK SIC:** 72300, 77003
**Auditors:** The Hart Partnership
**Bankers:** HSBC Bank plc (40-02-34)

| | 31-01-14 | 31-01-13 | 31-01-12 |
|---|---|---|---|
| TO | 21,930,439 | 22,596,998 | 25,352,175 |
| P/L | 627,890 | 20,472 | (450,820) |
| NW | 412,426 | (127,038) | (332,223) |
| WC | (1,785,656) | (1,670,920) | (1,998,852) |
| Emp. | 210 | 218 | 212 |

DUNS 23-894-7217
## Passage 2000
Great Peter Street, London SW1P 3NQ
**Tel:** 02075921850
**Web:** www.passage.org.uk
**Reg No:** 3885593 **Estd:** 1980 Private Company Limited By Guarantee
**Line of Business:** Day and care centres
**Directors:** V J Felzmann, M J Kelly, M Raw, J J Studzinski, C Williams, E Glancy, P R Macklin, Dr I Sattar
**Co. Secretary:** Brian Hollingsworth
**Responsibilities**
**Senior:** Mick Clarke *(Chief Executive Officer)*, Ellen Flynn *(CEO, Managing Director)*
**HR:** Samantha Rowe *(HR Manager)*
**Health & Safety:** Les Wood *(Maintenance Officer)*
**Facilities:** Les Wood *(Maintenance Officer)*
**Operations:** Tamsin Mallion *(Services Director)*
**US SIC:** 8321, 8249
**UK SIC:** 96111, 93300
**Auditors:** Buzzacott LLP
**Bankers:** HSBC Bank plc (40-01-13)

| | 31-03-14 | 31-03-13 | 31-03-12 |
|---|---|---|---|
| TO | 11,416,574 | 4,692,803 | 5,041,389 |
| P/L | 7,394,499 | 579,706 | 1,053,168 |
| NW | 19,145,473 | 11,750,974 | 11,171,268 |
| WC | 12,471,895 | 5,230,431 | 4,268,995 |
| Emp. | 85 | 89 | 91 |

DUNS 21-152-3600
## Passage Properties Ltd
106 Islington High Street, Islington, London N1 8EG
**Tel:** 02073592888
**Web:** www.fredericks.co.uk
**Reg No:** 0942104 **Estd:** 1969 Private Limited Company
**Line of Business:** Restaurants
**Trading Style:** Fredericks Restaurant
**Issued Capital:** £8,240
**Directors:** Ms V L Segal, Ms E C Nyavie
**Co. Secretary:** Nicholas Segal
**US SIC:** 6519 **UK SIC:** 85000
**Auditors:** Craig Goodman
**Bankers:** National Westminster Bank Plc (60-02-13)

| | 31-12-13 | 31-12-12 | 31-12-11 |
|---|---|---|---|
| TA | 2,646,375 | 2,715,737 | 2,698,496 |
| NW | 801,946 | 638,194 | 463,028 |
| WC | (257,743) | (117,443) | (129,276) |

DUNS 39-974-7633
## Passcrystal Ltd
105 Station Road, Llanishen, Cardiff, South Glamorgan CF14 5UW
**Tel:** 029-2074-7575
**Web:** www.tycoch.com
**Reg No:** 2271407 **Estd:** 1994 Private Limited Company
**Line of Business:** Nursing homes
**Issued Capital:** £2,380
**Directors:** Mrs G Williams, S G Williams, P Clarke
**Co. Secretary:** Mrs Dianne Parsons
**Responsibilities**
**Marketing:** Jan Cruwys *(Administrator)*
**Admin:** Jan Cruwys *(Administrator)*
**HR:** Jan Cruwys *(Administrator)*
**Health & Safety:** Gaynor Hayes *(Matron)*
**US SIC:** 8051 **UK SIC:** 95100
**Auditors:** Johns Jones & Co Ltd
**Bankers:** Barclays Bank Plc (20-18-27)

| | 31-03-14 | 31-03-13 | 31-03-12 |
|---|---|---|---|
| TO | 2,563,844 | 2,522,947 | 2,514,742 |
| P/L | 668,468 | 170,781 | 225,061 |
| NW | 2,261,668 | 1,842,010 | 1,808,126 |
| WC | 1,122,089 | 650,766 | 638,908 |
| Emp. | 115 | 123 | 119 |

DUNS 23-225-8017
## Passenger Focus
9th Floor Rail House, Store Street, Manchester M1 2RP
**Tel:** 03001232350
**Web:** www.passengerfocus.org.uk
**Estd:** 2002
**Line of Business:** Trade assoc & regulatory bodies
**Principals:** A Smith, P Davis, D Burton, Ms J Barrow, C Foxall, B Cook, Ms C Knights, Ms K Gordon
**Branches:** Passenger Focus, Tower House, Fairfax Street, Bristol, Avon BS1 3BN
**US SIC:** 9121 **UK SIC:** 91110
**Employees:** 500

DUNS 76-321-9136
## Passenger Lift Services Ltd
**(Subsidiary of:** Roxana Investments Ltd)
Unit 1c Pearsall Drive, Oldbury, West Midlands B69 2RA
**Tel:** 0121-552-0660
**Web:** www.passengerliftservices.co.uk
**Reg No:** 2544902 **VAT No:** 547565804
**Estd:** 1990 Private Limited Company
**Line of Business:** Manufacture of invalid carriages
**Issued Capital:** £20,000
**Directors:** M W Pitt, M R Simmonds, P B O'Connor, A Beck
**Co. Secretary:** Michael Simmonds
**Responsibilities**
**Senior:** Anthony Bull *(Manager)*, Carl O'Connor *(Manager)*
**Finance:** Alan Godfrey *(Finance Controller)*
**US SIC:** 3799 **UK SIC:** 36502
**Auditors:** Clement Keys
**Bankers:** HSBC Bank plc (40-23-03)

| | 31-03-14 | 31-03-13 | 31-03-12 |
|---|---|---|---|
| TA | 3,647,065 | 3,877,857 | 4,113,933 |
| NW | 1,993,055 | 1,949,473 | 2,067,470 |
| WC | 1,800,058 | 1,782,395 | 1,899,688 |

DUNS 39-735-9787 **Imp-Exp**
## Passion Pictures Ltd
Kirkman House, London W1T 2RF
**Tel:** 020-7323-9933 **Fax:** 020-7323-9030
**Web:** www.passion-pictures.com
**Reg No:** 2177709 **Estd:** 1987 Private Limited Company
**Line of Business:** Theatrical presentation companies
**Export Markets:** Worldwide
**Export Sales:** £4,915,180
**Issued Capital:** £50
**Director:** A R Ruhemann
**Co. Secretary:** Raymond Hobbs
**Responsibilities**
**Senior:** John Battsek *(Producer executive ? MD)*
**Sales:** Nicole Stott *(Producer/Head of Development)*
**Facilities:** Kate Parker *(?Production Coordinator)*
**Operations:** Hugo Sands *(Executive Producer)*
**Engineering:** Julian Hodgson *(Senior Technical)*, Nicole Stott *(Producer/Head of Development)*
**US SIC:** 7819 **UK SIC:** 97111
**Auditors:** Casson Beckman

| | 31-03-14 | 31-03-13 | 31-03-12 |
|---|---|---|---|
| TO | 18,182,315 | 13,373,673 | 13,876,050 |
| P/L | 809,860 | 691,674 | (398,632) |
| NW | 782,739 | 473,884 | 30,744 |
| WC | 261,847 | 364,418 | (119,569) |
| Emp. | 94 | N/A | N/A |

DUNS 22-016-5107
## PaSSIONATE24/7 Healthcare Service Ltd
907-909 907-909, Aston New Road, Manchester M11 4PB
**Tel:** 01618794069
**Reg No:** 9062847 **Estd:** 2014 Private Limited Company
**Line of Business:** Accommodation advice
**Director:** Mrs F Iguodala
**US SIC:** 8091 **UK SIC:** 95200
**Employees:** 100

DUNS 23-012-6554
## Password Services Air Conditioning Ltd
**(Subsidiary of:** Password Services (Holdings) Ltd)
Unit H Ryelands Business Centre, Ryelands Lane, Elmley Lovett, Droitwich, Worcestershire WR9 0PT
**Tel:** 01299 253344
**Web:** www.passwordservices.co.uk
**Reg No:** 3891122 **Estd:** 1999 Private Limited Company
**Line of Business:** Business services
**Issued Capital:** £100
**Directors:** R Schlanker, Ms E Tovey
**Co. Secretary:** Alison Purnell
**Responsibilities**
**Senior:** Mark Purnell *(Manager)*
**US SIC:** 7399 **UK SIC:** 83954
**Auditors:** RSM Tenon Ltd

| | 31-01-14 | 31-01-13 | 31-01-12 |
|---|---|---|---|
| TA | 1,422,763 | 1,025,172 | 993,651 |
| NW | 576,000 | 435,557 | 471,817 |
| WC | 546,996 | 282,155 | 281,905 |

DUNS 21-236-5936 **Imp-Exp**
## Pasta Foods Ltd
**(Subsidiary of:** Pretty 210 Ltd)
Pasteur Road, Great Yarmouth, Norfolk NR31 0DW
**Tel:** 01493416200
**Web:** www.pastafoods.com
**Reg No:** 0566338 **VAT No:** 197021462
**Estd:** 1956 Private Limited Company
**Line of Business:** Manufacture of macaroni, noodles, couscous and similar farinaceous products
**Export Markets:** Europe, Worldwide
**Export Sales:** £8,738,619
**Issued Capital:** £10,000,000
**Directors:** P N Barry, Ms T Woolner, S M Webber, D Lewis
**Co. Secretary:** Karl Jermyn
**Responsibilities**
**Sales:** Mike Cooper *(Export Manager)*, Sophie Fauvel *(Sales Director)*, Barrie Turner *(European Sales Manager)*
**HR:** Kerri Johnson *(Human Resources Officer)*
**Branches:** Pasta Foods Ltd, Unit 1, Verulam Industrial Estate, London Road, St. Albans, Hertfordshire AL1 1JB
**US SIC:** 2099 **UK SIC:** 42399
**Auditors:** PKF (UK) LLP
**Bankers:** HSBC Bank plc (40-22-22)

| | 03-05-14 | 04-05-13 | 05-05-12 |
|---|---|---|---|
| TO | 25,230,007 | 25,328,040 | 24,957,935 |
| P/L | (10,934) | 876,806 | (611,645) |
| NW | 12,133,092 | 12,017,291 | 11,397,074 |
| WC | 9,612,473 | 10,602,813 | 9,994,308 |
| Emp. | 139 | 137 | 137 |

DUNS 21-580-1030
## Pasta Reale
Station Road, Gillingham, Dorset SP8 4QA
**Web:** www.joubere.com
**Estd:** 2011 Partnership
**Line of Business:** Manufacturers of food products
**Partners:** Mrs M Jeffrey, R Herbert
**Responsibilities**
**Senior:** Bryan Linn *(Manager)*
**US SIC:** 2099 **UK SIC:** 42399
**Employees:** 50

DUNS 54-899-9481
## Paston College
Grammar School Road, North Walsham, Norfolk NR28 9JL
**Tel:** 01692402334
**Web:** www.paston.ac.uk
**Estd:** 2009
**Line of Business:** Sixth form colleges
**Proprietor:** P Mayne
**Responsibilities**
**Senior:** Kevin Grieve *(Principal)*
**Marketing:** George Norton *(Head of English)*
**IT:** Micky Martin *(Head of IT)*
**US SIC:** 8221 **UK SIC:** 93100
**Employees:** 120

DUNS 34-926-1375
## Pastoral Cymru (Cardiff) Ltd
**(Subsidiary of:** Pastoral Cymru Care Group Ltd)
Ty Catrin Dyffrig Road, Ely, Cardiff, South Glamorgan CF5 5AD
**Tel:** 02920552966
**Reg No:** 5722804 **Estd:** 2006 Private Limited Company
**Line of Business:** Hospitals
**Issued Capital:** £100
**Directors:** M B Catris, R J Fennell
**Co. Secretary:** Simon Parry
**US SIC:** 8062 **UK SIC:** 95100

| | 31-03-14 | 31-03-13 | 31-03-12 |
|---|---|---|---|
| TO | 5,545,688 | 4,463,100 | 5,733,683 |
| P/L | 799,458 | 395,486 | 292,163 |
| NW | 537,631 | (86,586) | (416,572) |
| WC | (222,546) | (680,866) | (785,632) |
| Emp. | 156 | 137 | 155 |

DUNS 34-918-6549
## Pastoral Cymru Ltd
**(Subsidiary of:** Pastoral Cymru Care Group Ltd)
Tyntyla Avenue, Ystrad, Pentre, Mid Glamorgan CF41 7SU
**Tel:** 01443424940
**Web:** www.pastoralhealthcare.co.uk
**Reg No:** 5715589 **Estd:** 2006 Private Limited Company
**Line of Business:** Hospital activities
**Issued Capital:** £900
**Directors:** R J Fennell, M B Catris
**Co. Secretary:** Simon Parry
**Responsibilities**
**Senior:** Theresa Galazka *(Manager)*
**US SIC:** 8062 **UK SIC:** 95100

| | 31-03-14 | 31-03-13 | 31-03-12 |
|---|---|---|---|
| TO | 2,477,356 | 2,322,461 | 2,709,362 |
| P/L | 101,801 | 23,693 | 89,436 |
| NW | 59,648 | (22,635) | (49,819) |
| WC | (122,474) | (56,318) | 135,982 |
| Emp. | N/A | 64 | 65 |

DUNS 53-040-0429
## Pastures Leisure Ltd
Pastures Road, Mexborough, South Yorkshire S64 0JJ
**Tel:** 01709579599 **Fax:** 01709578756
**Web:** www.pastureslodge.co.uk
**Reg No:** 3453588 **Estd:** 1998 Private Limited Company
**Line of Business:** Public house
**Trading Style:** Pastures Hotel
**Issued Capital:** £372,500
**Director:** M S Chappell
**Co. Secretary:** Ms Maxine Chappell
**Responsibilities**
**Senior:** Kevin Gaze *(Licensee)*
**Branches:** Pastures Leisure Ltd, Pastures Road, Mexborough, South Yorkshire S64 0JJ
**US SIC:** 5813 **UK SIC:** 66200
**Auditors:** Andertons Liversidge & Co
**Bankers:** Yorkshire Bank Plc (05-04-14)

| | 31-10-13 | 31-10-12 | 31-10-11 |
|---|---|---|---|
| TO | 3,374,923 | 3,446,812 | 3,525,784 |
| P/L | 474,595 | 337,026 | 160,013 |
| NW | 2,912,326 | 2,606,862 | 2,397,737 |
| WC | (350,923) | (714,122) | (734,595) |
| Emp. | 95 | 98 | 101 |

DUNS 34-627-5472
## Pasuda (Hire) Ltd
**(Subsidiary of:** Pasuda Group Holdings Ltd)
Highfield Lane, Sheffield, South Yorkshire S13 9NA
**Tel:** 0845-094-4487 **Fax:** 0845-094-4497
**Web:** www.pasuda.co.uk
**Reg No:** 2761701 **VAT No:** 646429125
**Estd:** 1994 Private Limited Company
**Line of Business:** Engineering machine services
**Issued Capital:** £2
**Directors:** G Jones, B G Jones
**Co. Secretary:** Mrs Susan Jones
**US SIC:** 7394 **UK SIC:** 84000
**Auditors:** Landin, Wilcock & Co
**Bankers:** National Westminster Bank Plc (56-00-09)

| | 30-06-13 | 30-06-12 | 30-06-11 |
|---|---|---|---|
| TA | 3,158,731 | 2,804,152 | 2,649,495 |
| NW | 1,238,629 | 1,144,643 | 1,104,212 |
| WC | 493,012 | 551,079 | 629,028 |

DUNS 21-401-0563
## Pat Munro (Alness) Ltd
Caplich Quarry, Alness, Ross-Shire IV17 0XU
**Tel:** 01349-882377
**Web:** www.patmunro.co.uk
**Reg No:** 0033294SC **VAT No:** 266232954
**Estd:** 1945 Private Limited Company
**Line of Business:** Builders merchants
**Issued Capital:** £513,335
**Principals:** A C Munro *(Managing)*, S J Munro, B K Munro, P Munro, M S Bramley
**Co. Secretary:** Alastair Munro
**Branches:** Pat Munro (Alness) Ltd, Clashmore Quarry, Dornoch, Sutherland IV25 1XX
**US SIC:** 5039, 3273, 1522, 1541
**UK SIC:** 61300, 24360, 50100
**Auditors:** Johnston Carmichael
**Bankers:** The Royal Bank Of Scotland Plc (83-15-17)

| | 31-03-14 | 31-03-13 | 31-03-12 |
|---|---|---|---|
| TO | 15,416,267 | 13,382,556 | 11,519,223 |
| P/L | (436,488) | 407,021 | 301,511 |
| NW | 8,149,230 | 8,575,963 | 7,760,935 |
| WC | 6,464,993 | 6,846,018 | 6,259,300 |
| Emp. | 141 | 133 | 122 |

DUNS 51-739-6222

## Pat Security Systems Ltd

162 Middleton Road, Royton, Oldham, Lancashire OL2 5LS
**Web:** www.secureoptionsgroup.co.uk
**Proprietorship**
**Line of Business:** Install & maintain alarm systems part of secure options group
**Proprietor:** M Wood
**US SIC:** 1731 **UK SIC:** 50300
**Employees:** 50

DUNS 51-987-9055

## Patagonia Gold P L C

15 Upper Grosvenor Street, London W1K 7PJ
**Web:** www.patagoniagold.com
**Reg No:** 3994744 **Estd:** 2000 Public Limited Company
**Line of Business:** Mining of metals
**Directors:** G R Featherby, G Tanoira, M De Prado Eulate, C J Miguens, E J Badida, W H Humphries
**Co. Secretary:** Nigel Everest
**Responsibilities**
**Finance:** Philip Yee *(Chief Financial Officer)*
**Operations:** Matthew Boyes *(Chief Operating Officer)*
**US SIC:** 1099 **UK SIC:** 21000
**Auditors:** Grant Thornton UK LLP
**Employees:** 2
**Turnover:** £10,182,000

DUNS 53-634-0334

## Patech Solutions Ltd

Tame House, Wellington Crescent, Fradley Park, Fradley Park, Lichfield, Staffordshire WS13 8RZ
**Tel:** 01543-444707
**Web:** www.patech-solutions.com
**Reg No:** 3438874 **Estd:** 1997 Private Limited Company
**Line of Business:** Computer consumables suppliers
**Issued Capital:** £20,000
**Directors:** J Dooley, J Keating
**Co. Secretary:** Ms Rita Crowley
**Responsibilities**
**Admin:** Amie Whincup *(Administration Manager)*
**Health & Safety:** Amie Whincup *(Administration Manager)*
**Facilities:** Amie Whincup *(Administration Manager)*
**US SIC:** 7379, 7374
**UK SIC:** 83940
**Auditors:** Hawsons Chartered Accountants
**Bankers:** The Royal Bank Of Scotland Plc (16-16-18)

| | 31-10-13 | 31-10-12 | 31-10-11 |
|---|---|---|---|
| TO | 8,286,217 | N/A | N/A |
| P/L | 897,490 | N/A | N/A |
| NW | 1,615,028 | 1,477,674 | 1,243,143 |
| WC | 1,541,496 | 1,419,827 | 1,183,173 |
| Emp. | 54 | N/A | N/A |

DUNS 21-825-3433

## Paten & Co Ltd

(**Subsidiary of:** Bdl Select Hotels Ltd)
C/O Redefine Bdl Hotels Commerce Road, Brentford, Middlesex TW8 8GA
**Fax:** 01733-552335
**Web:** www.patenhk.com
**Reg No:** 0227473 **VAT No:** 119235676
**Estd:** 1928 Private Limited Company
**Line of Business:** Management activities of holding companies
**Trading Style:** Paten Hotels
**Issued Capital:** £1,135,000
**Directors:** S Scott, A C Lapping
**Co. Secretary:** Stuart Mccaffer
**Branches:** Paten & Co Ltd, Rutland Arms Hotel, High Street, Newmarket, Suffolk CB8 8NB
**US SIC:** 6711 **UK SIC:** 83962
**Auditors:** Hawsons
**Bankers:** HSBC Bank plc (40-36-15)

| | 03-11-13 | 28-10-12 | 30-11-11 |
|---|---|---|---|
| TO | 6,958,000 | 6,746,000 | 6,522,000 |
| P/L | 11,000 | (67,000) | 255,000 |
| NW | 26,655,000 | 26,564,000 | 26,573,000 |
| WC | (5,533,000) | 13,318,000 | 12,994,000 |
| Emp. | 141 | 122 | 184 |

DUNS 21-686-8026

## Paten Hotels Ltd

(**Subsidiary of:** Bdl Select Hotels Ltd)
The Embankment, Bedford, Bedfordshire MK40 3PD
**Tel:** 01234346565 **Fax:** 01234-212009
**Web:** www.bedfordswanhotel.co.uk
**Reg No:** 0950976 **VAT No:** 119235676
**Estd:** 1969 Private Limited Company
**Line of Business:** Hotels
**Trading Style:** The Bedford Swan Hotel, Bdl Hotels
**Issued Capital:** £8,080
**Directors:** S Scott, A C Lapping
**Co. Secretary:** Stuart Mccaffer
**Responsibilities**
**Senior:** Louis Woodcock *(Manager)*
**Branches:** Paten Hotels Ltd, 12-14 Warwick Road, Stratford-Upon-Avon, Warwickshire CV37 6YT
**US SIC:** 7011 **UK SIC:** 66500
**Auditors:** Ernst & Young LLP
**Bankers:** The Royal Bank Of Scotland Plc (83-07-06)

| | 03-11-13 | 28-10-12 | 30-11-11 |
|---|---|---|---|
| TO | 6,654,000 | 6,302,000 | 6,603,000 |
| P/L | 1,207,000 | 989,000 | 1,110,000 |
| NW | 14,873,000 | 13,655,000 | 12,609,000 |
| WC | 11,004,000 | 9,702,000 | 8,625,000 |
| Emp. | 128 | 97 | 170 |

DUNS 21-231-0228

## Paternoster House

Watermoor Road, Cirencester, Gloucestershire GL7 1JR
**Tel:** 01285-653699
**Web:** www.osjct.co.uk
**Estd:** 1967 Proprietorship
**Line of Business:** Medical nursing home activities
**Proprietor:** Mrs J Warren
**Responsibilities**
**Senior:** Jey Warren *(CEO, Managing Director)*
**US SIC:** 8051 **UK SIC:** 95100
**Employees:** 56

DUNS 73-671-5082 **Imp**

## Paterson Enterprises Ltd

38-41 Castle Foregate, Shrewsbury, Shropshire SY1 2EL
**Tel:** 01743-232200
**Web:** www.morris-leisure.co.uk
**Reg No:** 4930959 **VAT No:** 838420327
**Estd:** 1943 Private Limited Company
**Line of Business:** Other treatment of petroleum products (excluding petrochemicals manufacture)
**Export Sales:** £10,117,000
**Trading Style:** Morris Lubricants, Morris Leisure
**Issued Capital:** £36,935,929
**Directors:** E W Goddard, D W Goddard, D G Jones, A J Goddard, J D Alton
**Co. Secretary:** Mrs Jane Shelton
**Responsibilities**
**Senior:** Graham Fewtrell *(Transport Manager)*
**HR:** Debbie Blayney *(Personnel Officer)*
**Facilities:** Jim Evans *(Production Manager)*
**Fleet:** Graham Fewtrell *(Transport Manager)*
**Engineering:** Jim Evans *(Production Manager)*
**US SIC:** 2999, 7033
**UK SIC:** 11150, 66701
**Auditors:** PricewaterhouseCoopers LLP

| | 02-08-14 | 03-08-13 | 04-08-12 |
|---|---|---|---|
| TO | 49,037,000 | 49,582,000 | 50,029,000 |
| P/L | 7,795,000 | 8,491,000 | 6,415,000 |
| NW | 32,250,000 | 28,903,000 | 23,538,000 |
| WC | 12,534,000 | 9,795,000 | 8,677,000 |
| Emp. | 140 | 139 | 141 |

DUNS 21-022-5983 **Exp**

## Paterson Simons & Co.(Africa)Ltd

4 The Offices, 10 Fleet Street, Brighton, East Sussex BN1 4ZE
**Tel:** 01273623843
**Web:** www.patersonsimons.com
**Reg No:** 0453843 **VAT No:** 497597366
**Estd:** 1948 Private Limited Company
**Line of Business:** Agents involved in the sale of machinery, industrial equipment, ships and aircraft
**Export Markets:** West Africa, Australasia
**Export Sales:** £20,931,431
**Issued Capital:** £400,000
**Directors:** K Okoh, E Lyne, S A Baker, J P Traynor, H M Lyne
**US SIC:** 5084, 5399
**UK SIC:** 61490, 65600
**Auditors:** John & Co
**Bankers:** Barclays Bank Plc (20-00-00)

| | 31-12-13 | 31-12-12 | 31-12-11 |
|---|---|---|---|
| TO | 21,142,860 | 26,587,689 | 21,635,211 |
| P/L | 245,286 | 344,495 | 912,366 |
| NW | 3,636,743 | 3,820,393 | 3,736,210 |
| WC | 1,313,993 | 455,294 | 1,198,625 |
| Emp. | 143 | 138 | 27 |

DUNS 50-357-7454

## Patersons Quarries Ltd

Gartsherrie Road, Coatbridge, Lanarkshire ML5 2EU
**Tel:** 01236-433351
**Web:** www.patersonsquarries.co.uk
**Reg No:** 0117448SC **Estd:** 1989 Private Limited Company
**Line of Business:** Waste reclamation
**Issued Capital:** £7,002,002
**Principals:** W Paterson *(Managing)*, J Richardson *(Financial)*, T D Anderson, Dr L M Gall, T M Paterson, J A Stickler
**Co. Secretary:** James Stickler
**Responsibilities**
**Senior:** Alexander Mcevoy *(Engineering Director)*, Margaret Paterson *(Manager)*, Harry Young *(Quarry Manager)*
**Finance:** Leslie Dunee *(Accounts)*
**Sales:** Alan Perry *(Sales Manager)*
**HR:** Laura Armstrong *(Human Resources Manager)*, Leslie Dunee *(Accounts)*, Harry Young *(Quarry Manager)*
**Health & Safety:** Harry Young *(Quarry Manager)*
**Facilities:** Ross Campbell *(Maintenance Manager)*
**Operations:** Harry Young *(Quarry Manager)*
**Purchasing:** Harry Young *(Quarry Manager)*
**Engineering:** Ross Campbell *(Maintenance Manager)*, Alexander Mcevoy *(Engineering Director)*
**Branches:** Patersons Quarries Ltd, Dunduff Quarry, Lesmahagow, Lanark, Lanarkshire ML11 0JQ
**US SIC:** 6711, 1429
**UK SIC:** 83962, 23102
**Auditors:** KPMG LLP
**Bankers:** Clydesdale Bank Plc (82-60-18)

| | 30-11-13 | 30-11-12 | 30-11-11 |
|---|---|---|---|
| TO | 50,391,952 | 55,744,082 | 51,539,453 |
| P/L | 13,927,796 | (1,450,126) | 203,858 |
| NW | 39,285,682 | 23,541,569 | 30,820,371 |
| WC | 7,462,493 | 2,920,720 | 2,468,835 |
| Emp. | 798 | 825 | 692 |

DUNS 21-689-3999

## Pate's Grammar School

Admissions Office, Oldbury Road, Cheltenham, Gloucestershire GL51 0HG
**Tel:** 01242523169
**Web:** www.patesgs.org
**Reg No:** 7369704 **Estd:** 2010 Private Company Limited By Guarantee
**Line of Business:** Schools (local authority)
**Directors:** Mrs S Park, J H Parker, Mrs A Barradell-Black, R Ellicott, Dr J Watts, W Ainsworth-Parker, J P Henry, R W Gue
**Co. Secretary:** Stephen Locke
**Responsibilities**
**Senior:** Trevor Allinson *(Director)*, Wallace Ascham *(Director)*, Guy Bradshaw *(Director)*, Nikki Clark *(Director)*, Alison Donnell *(Director)*, Russell Ellicott *(Headmaster)*, Shaun Fenton *(Headmaster)*, Nancy Western *(Director)*
**US SIC:** 8211 **UK SIC:** 93200
**Bankers:** Barclays Bank Plc (20-20-15)

| | 31-08-14 | 31-08-13 | 31-08-12 |
|---|---|---|---|
| TO | 6,406,734 | 6,038,592 | 6,611,990 |
| P/L | (523,313) | (778,150) | 130,045 |
| NW | 30,021,569 | 30,822,882 | 31,566,032 |
| WC | 366,289 | 478,466 | 1,397,428 |
| Emp. | 102 | 98 | 95 |

DUNS 23-771-0418 **Imp-Exp**

## Patheon Uk Ltd

(**Subsidiary of:** Jll Partners Inc.)
Patheon Building, Kingfisher Drive, Swindon, Wiltshire SN3 5BZ
**Tel:** 01793524411
**Web:** www.patheon.com
**Reg No:** 3764421 **VAT No:** 718239916
**Estd:** 1999 Private Limited Company
**Line of Business:** Pharmaceutical preparation manufacturers
**Export Sales:** £78,930,000
**Issued Capital:** £2,100,001
**Directors:** M E Lytton, J C Mullen
**Co. Secretary:** Nicholas Plummer
**Branches:** Patheon Uk Ltd, 151 Milton Park, Abingdon, Oxfordshire OX14 4SD
**US SIC:** 2834, 7397, 7399
**UK SIC:** 25700, 83702, 83954
**Auditors:** Ernst & Young LLP
**Bankers:** Barclays Bank Plc (20-71-03)

| | 31-10-13 | 31-10-12 | 31-10-11 |
|---|---|---|---|
| TO | 82,365,000 | 69,479,000 | 76,508,000 |
| P/L | (3,092,000) | (39,337,000) | 24,384,000 |
| NW | (11,224,000) | (4,794,000) | 31,014,000 |
| WC | 9,246,000 | 5,546,000 | 4,632,000 |
| Emp. | 486 | 537 | 603 |

DUNS 21-777-7708

## Pathfield Special School

Abbey Road, Barnstaple, Devon EX31 1JU
**Tel:** 01271342423
**Web:** www.pathfield.devon.sch.uk
**Estd:** 1998 Proprietorship
**Line of Business:** Schools (special)
**Proprietor:** R Conway
**Responsibilities**
**Senior:** Claire May *(Head Teacher)*
**US SIC:** 8299 **UK SIC:** 93300
**Employees:** 76

DUNS 23-714-3362

## Pathfinder Energy Services Ltd

(**Subsidiary of:** Schlumberger N.V.)
1-3 Howe Moss Drive, Aberdeen, Aberdeenshire AB21 0GL
**Tel:** 01224762000 **Fax:** 01224-762010
**Web:** www.pathfinderlwd.com
**Reg No:** 3709500 **VAT No:** 671363925
**Estd:** 1999 Private Limited Company
**Line of Business:** Extraction of crude petroleum and natural gas
**Issued Capital:** £15,000
**Directors:** Mrs K A Hoeing-Cosentino, R A Kidd, G G Ballard
**Co. Secretary:** Ms Pauline Droy Moore
**Responsibilities**
**Senior:** Eric Hendry *(Manager)*, Trever Mcalister *(Manager)*
**US SIC:** 1311 **UK SIC:** 13000
**Auditors:** Arthur Andersen
**Bankers:** HSBC Bank plc (40-01-25)

| | 31-12-13 | 31-12-12 | 31-12-11 |
|---|---|---|---|
| TO | 13,564,000 | 22,712,000 | 23,786,000 |
| P/L | (917,000) | (1,182,000) | 1,575,000 |
| NW | 11,665,000 | 12,727,000 | 14,166,000 |
| WC | 8,916,000 | 11,606,000 | 18,941,000 |
| Emp. | 60 | 117 | 123 |

DUNS 29-519-1621

## Pathfinder (Newark) Ltd

(**Subsidiary of:** Nottingham City Council)
Lower Parliament Street, Nottingham, Nottinghamshire NG1 1GN
**Tel:** 01159505745 **Fax:** 01636-611971
**Reg No:** 1882298 **Estd:** 1985 Private Limited Company
**Line of Business:** Other passenger land transport
**Issued Capital:** £67,500
**Director:** M J Fowles
**Co. Secretary:** Robert Hicklin
**US SIC:** 4141 **UK SIC:** 72102
**Auditors:** PricewaterhouseCoopers
**Bankers:** National Westminster Bank Plc (54-10-23)

| | 31-03-14 | 31-03-13 | 31-03-12 |
|---|---|---|---|
| NW | (7,000) | (7,000) | (7,000) |

DUNS 34-815-2281

## Pathfinder Park Homes Ltd

Armada House, Cavalier Road, Heathfield Industrial Estate, Newton Abbot, Devon TQ12 6FJ
**Tel:** 01626833799 **Fax:** 01626-834354
**Web:** www.pathfinderhomes.co.uk
**Reg No:** 2794691 **VAT No:** 384996578
**Estd:** 2002 Private Limited Company
**Line of Business:** Mobile homes
**Trading Style:** Pathfinder Park Homes Services
**Issued Capital:** £25,000
**Principals:** M A Wills *(Managing)*, Ms J D Wills, S A Jeff, Ms M J Durrant
**Co. Secretary:** Martin Hember
**US SIC:** 7033 **UK SIC:** 66701
**Auditors:** PEPLOWS
**Bankers:** National Westminster Bank Plc (54-21-21)

| | 31-03-14 | 31-03-13 | 31-03-12 |
|---|---|---|---|
| TO | 10,023,934 | 6,959,707 | 7,213,494 |
| P/L | 909,094 | 221,036 | 454,748 |
| NW | 1,768,018 | 1,313,893 | 1,279,101 |
| WC | 1,452,558 | 1,024,749 | 997,769 |
| Emp. | 88 | 79 | 71 |

DUNS 51-614-3141

## Pathfinders-Care (Ollerton) Ltd

Darwin Drive, New Ollerton, Newark, Nottinghamshire NG22 9GW
**Tel:** 01623 836639 **Fax:** 01623 836639
**Web:** www.pathfinders-care.co.uk
**Reg No:** 5894573 **Estd:** 2006 Private Limited Company
**Line of Business:** Residential care establishments
**Issued Capital:** £50,000
**Directors:** S Paterson, Dr A J Nall
**US SIC:** 8321, 8051
**UK SIC:** 96111, 95100
**Auditors:** Stopford Associates Ltd

| | 31-01-14 | 31-01-13 | 31-01-12 |
|---|---|---|---|
| TO | 2,933,071 | 2,661,625 | 2,448,130 |
| P/L | 332,207 | 139,582 | 348,804 |
| NW | 1,279,943 | 925,611 | 778,426 |
| WC | (384,398) | (414,837) | (484,969) |
| Emp. | N/A | 119 | 110 |

DUNS 73-529-4204

## Pathway Care Ltd

(**Subsidiary of:** Ontario Teachers' Pension Plan Board)
Unit 10, Cardiff, South Glamorgan CF15 7NE
**Tel:** 01626333787 **Fax:** 02920815300
**Web:** www.pathwayscaregroup.co.uk
**Reg No:** 4792049 **Estd:** 2005 Private Limited Company

**Line of Business:** Social work activities without accommodation
**Issued Capital:** £100
**Directors:** Dr N A Macdonald, J E Janet
**Co. Secretary:** Mrs Helen Lecky
**Responsibilities**
**Senior:** William Napier-Fenning *(Manager)*
**Branches:** Pathway Care Ltd, Bartleet House, 165A Birmingham Road, Bromsgrove, Worcestershire B61 0DJ
**US SIC:** 8321 **UK SIC:** 96111
**Auditors:** Deloitte LLP
**Bankers:** Barclays Bank Plc (20-00-00)

| | 31-08-13 | 31-08-12 | 31-08-11 |
|---|---|---|---|
| TO | 10,447,444 | 10,748,979 | 7,504,431 |
| P/L | 723,819 | 749,023 | 800,790 |
| NW | 5,187,835 | 4,604,287 | 4,065,163 |
| WC | 5,118,768 | 4,581,332 | 3,710,489 |
| Emp. | 58 | 45 | 48 |

DUNS 34-549-3485
### Pathways 4 Care Ltd
(**Subsidiary of:** Pathways Care Group Ltd)
New Road, Kidderminster, Worcestershire DY10 1AQ
**Tel:** 01562748660
**Web:** www.pathways4care.co.uk
**Reg No:** 5359403 **Estd:** 2005 Private Limited Company
**Line of Business:** Other human health activities
**Issued Capital:** £1
**Directors:** M S Patel, S S Patel
**Co. Secretary:** John Alflatt
**Responsibilities**
**Facilities:** Allison Tolley *(Branch Manager)*
**Operations:** Allison Tolley *(Branch Manager)*
**US SIC:** 8091 **UK SIC:** 95200

| | 31-03-14 | 31-03-13 | 31-03-12 |
|---|---|---|---|
| TO | 820,294 | 968,114 | 926,848 |
| P/L | 50,124 | 26,428 | 123,147 |
| NW | 260,832 | 213,723 | 186,637 |
| WC | 259,102 | 210,395 | 186,637 |
| Emp. | 51 | 63 | 58 |

DUNS 23-745-5642
### Patienceform Ltd
Keepmoat Stadium Stadium Way, Doncaster, South Yorkshire DN4 5JW
**Tel:** 01302762576
**Web:** www.doncasterroversfc.co.uk
**Reg No:** 3739676 **Estd:** 1999 Private Limited Company
**Line of Business:** Other sporting activities not elsewhere classified
**Issued Capital:** £12,265,606
**Directors:** A J Watson, D Blunt, R Watson, G P Baldwin, T G Bramall
**US SIC:** 7999 **UK SIC:** 97913
**Auditors:** PKF
**Bankers:** The Royal Bank Of Scotland Plc (16-71-38)

| | 30-06-13 | 31-05-12 | 31-06-11 |
|---|---|---|---|
| TO | 5,250,268 | 8,278,895 | 8,960,237 |
| P/L | (4,387,733) | (3,319,652) | (2,600,026) |
| NW | (13,344,383) | (9,198,421) | (6,543,776) |
| WC | (1,842,097) | (9,046,048) | (6,763,111) |
| Emp. | 191 | 109 | 89 |

DUNS 21-233-4504
### Patients Transport Service Non Emergency Nhs
Whalley Drive, Bletchley, Milton Keynes, Buckinghamshire MK3 6EN
**Tel:** 01908-365299
**Estd:** 2004 Proprietorship
**Line of Business:** Nhs clinics
**Proprietor:** M Clayton
**US SIC:** 8062 **UK SIC:** 95100
**Employees:** 100

DUNS 50-458-7353
### Patio Hotel (Aberdeen) Ltd
(**Subsidiary of:** Dlt Capital Ltd)
Beach Boulevard, Aberdeen, Aberdeenshire AB24 5EF
**Tel:** 01224590426
**Web:** www.patiohotels.com
**Reg No:** 2441321 **Estd:** 1989 Private Limited Company
**Line of Business:** Hotels
**Trading Style:** Double Tree Hotel
**Issued Capital:** £100
**Managing Director:** A N Story
**Co. Secretary:** Mrs Alison Dufresne
**Responsibilities**
**Senior:** Barry Attridge *(Manager)*
**US SIC:** 7011 **UK SIC:** 66500
**Auditors:** Anderson Anderson & Brown LLP
**Bankers:** Bank Of Scotland (80-29-01)

| | 31-12-13 | 31-12-12 | 31-12-11 |
|---|---|---|---|
| TO | 6,952,848 | 5,977,733 | 5,482,678 |
| P/L | (221,495) | (204,895) | (1,509,013) |
| NW | (2,614,109) | (2,392,614) | (2,187,719) |
| WC | (2,755,720) | (2,559,543) | (2,395,122) |

DUNS 21-885-9937
### Patisserie Acquisition Ltd
146-156 Sarehole Road, Birmingham, West Midlands B28 8DT
**Tel:** 01217-777000
**Web:** www.patisserie-valerie.co.uk
**Reg No:** 6070007 **Estd:** 2007 Private Limited Company
**Line of Business:** Management activities of holding companies
**Issued Capital:** £1,454
**Directors:** L O Johnson, J M Horler, P E May
**Co. Secretary:** Christopher Marsh
**Responsibilities**
**Senior:** Rob Hunch *(Manager)*, Benedict Redmond *(Director)*
**Finance:** Rob Hunch *(Manager)*
**US SIC:** 6711 **UK SIC:** 83962
**Auditors:** Grant Thornton UK LLP
**Bankers:** HSBC Bank plc (40-05-20)

| | 30-09-13 | 30-09-12 | 30-09-11 |
|---|---|---|---|
| TO | 60,112,215 | 49,511,423 | 40,482,648 |
| P/L | 4,707,657 | 5,895,285 | 4,595,649 |
| NW | (1,752,955) | (5,198,430) | (10,300,677) |
| WC | 1,692,688 | (1,458,364) | (2,656,633) |
| Emp. | 1,909 | 1,558 | 1,292 |

DUNS 21-578-3887
### Paton Plant Ltd
(**Subsidiary of:** Shepherd Building Group Ltd)
Whistleberry Road, Hamilton, Lanarkshire ML3 0EJ
**Tel:** 01698429414
**Web:** www.portakabin.co.uk
**Reg No:** 0045554SC **Estd:** 1968 Private Limited Company
**Line of Business:** Portable buildings
**Trading Style:** Portakabin
**Issued Capital:** £1,500,000
**Directors:** G Finlayson, D P Carter, J M Collins, C L Brown
**Co. Secretary:** Philip Clarke
**Responsibilities**
**HR:** Phil Marsland *(HR Manager)*
**Health & Safety:** Harry Erwin *(Operations Manager)*
**Facilities:** Harry Erwin *(Operations Manager)*
**Branches:** Paton Plant Ltd, 17-18 Lochend, Ratho Station, Ratho Station, Newbridge, Midlothian EH28 8SY
**US SIC:** 5039, 1541
**UK SIC:** 61300, 50100
**Auditors:** KPMG LLP
**Bankers:** HSBC Bank plc (40-47-31)

| | 30-06-14 | 30-06-13 | 30-06-12 |
|---|---|---|---|
| TO | 20,940,000 | 15,321,000 | 16,418,000 |
| P/L | 3,064,000 | 1,892,000 | 2,192,000 |
| NW | 14,254,000 | 11,821,000 | 12,360,000 |
| WC | 3,114,000 | 3,100,000 | 5,116,000 |
| Emp. | 115 | 110 | 106 |

DUNS 21-585-7970
### Patrick Bradley Ltd
Craigall Quarry, Kilrea, Coleraine, Co Londonderry BT51 5XR
**Tel:** 02829540285
**Web:** www.patrickbradley.co.uk
**Reg No:** 0001586NI **VAT No:** 252802281
**Estd:** 1942 Private Limited Company
**Line of Business:** Manufacturers of plant machinery
**Issued Capital:** £21,000
**Directors:** J Bradley, J Shannon
**Co. Secretary:** John Shannon
**Responsibilities**
**Senior:** Antoinette Bradley *(Manager)*
**Admin:** Barbara Darragh *(Private Development Administra)*
**US SIC:** 3531, 1499, 1799
**UK SIC:** 32541, 23960, 50000
**Auditors:** Moore Stephens
**Bankers:** Northern Bank Ltd (95-03-46)

| | 31-12-13 | 31-12-12 | 31-12-11 |
|---|---|---|---|
| TA | 9,718,300 | 10,622,408 | 10,399,462 |
| P/L | 287,018 | 79,740 | 166,075 |
| NW | 2,980,562 | 3,096,149 | 3,085,684 |
| WC | 2,624,373 | (705,244) | (663,211) |
| Emp. | 86 | 73 | 58 |

DUNS 21-709-7490 **Imp**
### Patron Capital Advisers Llp
7 Hanover Square, London W1S 1HQ
**Tel:** 02076299417
**Web:** www.patroncapital.com
**Reg No:** 0361119OC **Estd:** 2011
**Line of Business:** Activities of open-ended investment companies
**US SIC:** 8999 **UK SIC:** 83954

| | 31-12-13 | 31-12-12 | 31-12-11 |
|---|---|---|---|
| TO | 10,708,912 | 11,212,707 | 6,331,344 |
| P/L | 1,948,618 | 2,162,783 | 1,021,918 |
| NW | 1,221,265 | 1,692,642 | 1,093,271 |
| WC | 981,848 | 1,407,694 | 716,946 |
| Emp. | 60 | 58 | 55 |

DUNS 23-941-2468
### Patsystems Holdings Ltd
(**Subsidiary of:** Itt Sa)
30 St Mary Axe, Hays Lane, London EC3A 8EP
**Fax:** 02079400499
**Web:** www.patsystems.com
**Reg No:** 3930861 **Estd:** 2000 Private Limited Company
**Line of Business:** Computer games
**Issued Capital:** £1,315,381
**Directors:** C G Clinch, S Oliviero
**Co. Secretary:** Ashley Woods
**US SIC:** 7372, 7379, 6711
**UK SIC:** 83940, 83962
**Auditors:** PricewaterhouseCoopers
**Bankers:** The Royal Bank Of Scotland Plc (15-10-00)

| | 31-12-13 | 31-12-12 | 31-12-11 |
|---|---|---|---|
| TA | 12,378,046 | 12,408,979 | 12,426,789 |
| P/L | (30) | (16,576) | (44,935) |
| NW | 9,782,654 | 9,813,587 | 9,838,444 |
| WC | 3,973,210 | 4,004,143 | 4,029,000 |

DUNS 21-610-1311 **Exp**
### Pattemore's Transport (Crewkerne) Ltd
Mosterton Road, Misterton, Crewkerne, Somerset TA18 8NT
**Tel:** 01400-72046
**Web:** www.pattemores.com
**Reg No:** 0626343 **Estd:** 1920 Private Limited Company
**Line of Business:** Road haulage and transport services
**Export Markets:** Europe
**Trading Style:** Pattemores Dairy Ingredients, Pattemores Transport Crewkerne
**Issued Capital:** £152,000
**Principals:** G W Pattemore *(Managing)*, S G Pattemore, S S Pattemore, Mrs N S Hill, A W Pattemore
**Co. Secretary:** Ms Nicola Hill
**US SIC:** 4789, 4213
**UK SIC:** 77002, 72300
**Auditors:** Albert Goodman
**Bankers:** Lloyds TSB Bank plc (30-92-40)

| | 30-04-14 | 30-04-13 | 30-04-12 |
|---|---|---|---|
| TO | 32,327,702 | 31,115,920 | 34,285,174 |
| P/L | 247,321 | 277,171 | 225,314 |
| NW | 1,778,714 | 1,597,182 | 1,393,907 |
| WC | 648,044 | 637,488 | 338,164 |
| Emp. | 98 | 96 | 98 |

DUNS 21-111-2315
### Patterson & Rothwell Holdings Ltd
119 Lees Road, Oldham, Lancashire OL4 1JW
**Tel:** 01616529984 **Fax:** 01616215001
**Reg No:** 6526130 **Estd:** 2008 Private Limited Company
**Line of Business:** Management activities of holding companies
**Issued Capital:** £1
**Directors:** L F Tilley, A Rothwell
**Co. Secretary:** Robert Anderson
**US SIC:** 6711 **UK SIC:** 83962

| | 31-03-14 | 31-03-13 | 31-03-12 |
|---|---|---|---|
| TA | 1 | 1 | 1 |
| NW | 1 | 1 | 1 |

DUNS 29-175-6450 **Imp-Exp**
### Patterson & Rothwell Ltd
(**Subsidiary of:** Makemore Ltd)
Mount Pleasant Street, Mount Pleasant Industrial Estate, Oldham, Lancashire OL4 1HH
**Tel:** 0161-621-5000 **Fax:** 0161-621-5001
**Web:** www.patterson-rothwell.co.uk
**Reg No:** 1848302 **VAT No:** 408852538
**Estd:** 1981 Private Limited Company
**Line of Business:** Plastic injection moulding
**Export Markets:** Europe
**Issued Capital:** £100,000
**Principals:** A Rothwell *(Managing)*, L F Tilley
**Co. Secretary:** Robert Anderson
**Responsibilities**
**HR:** Amanda Flynn *(Personnel Manager)*
**Purchasing:** Rachel Dyer *(Head of Purchasing)*
**Engineering:** Trevor Mills *(Engineering Manager)*
**Branches:** Patterson & Rothwell Ltd, 119 Lees Rd, Oldham, Lancashire OL4 1JW
**US SIC:** 3079, 3545
**UK SIC:** 48360, 32223
**Auditors:** Baker Tilly
**Bankers:** Yorkshire Bank Plc (05-07-37)

| | 31-12-13 | 31-12-12 | 31-12-11 |
|---|---|---|---|
| TO | 13,921,037 | 13,552,379 | 13,249,570 |
| P/L | 712,195 | 627,042 | 760,146 |
| NW | 5,189,537 | 4,640,449 | 4,116,649 |
| WC | 757,264 | 996,962 | 1,688,066 |
| Emp. | 156 | 158 | 145 |

DUNS 42-387-1594 **Imp**
### Patterson Medical Ltd
(**Subsidiary of:** Patterson Companies Inc.)
Nunn Brook Road Huthwaite, Sutton-In-Ashfield, Nottinghamshire NG17 2HU
**Tel:** 08444124330 **Fax:** 08448730100
**Web:** https://www.pattersonmedical.co.uk
**Reg No:** 4374752 **Estd:** 2002 Private Limited Company
**Line of Business:** Clinic and hospital supplies
**Export Sales:** £14,408,000
**Issued Capital:** £200
**Directors:** Mrs A B Gugino, M J Orscheln, T S Daniels, C D Manning, I T Thomas, S P Anderson, A M Booker
**Co. Secretary:** Andrew Booker
**Responsibilities**
**Senior:** Colin Webb *(Manager)*
**Branches:** Patterson Medical Ltd, Nunn Brook Road, Sutton-In-Ashfield, Nottinghamshire NG17 2HU
**US SIC:** 5122, 5999
**UK SIC:** 61800, 65600
**Auditors:** PricewaterhouseCoopers LLP

| | 26-04-14 | 27-04-13 | 28-04-12 |
|---|---|---|---|
| TO | 58,070,000 | 63,832,000 | 68,434,000 |
| P/L | (94,000) | (877,000) | 5,086,000 |
| NW | (2,268,000) | (2,839,000) | (2,575,000) |
| WC | (10,603,000) | (14,173,000) | (14,463,000) |
| Emp. | 270 | 328 | 359 |

DUNS 22-042-6170
### Pattersons (Holdings) Ltd
Winterstoke Road, Bristol, Avon BS3 2NS
**Tel:** 0117-934-1270 **Fax:** 0117-929-3032
**Reg No:** 4044979 **Estd:** 2000 Private Limited Company
**Line of Business:** Management activities of holding companies
**Issued Capital:** £26,001
**Directors:** R C Ireland, C J Patterson, J B Patterson
**Co. Secretary:** Ms Sheila Patterson
**US SIC:** 6711 **UK SIC:** 83962
**Auditors:** BDO LLP
**Bankers:** National Westminster Bank Plc (01-00-53)

| | 30-04-14 | 30-04-13 | 30-04-12 |
|---|---|---|---|
| TO | 16,276,975 | 14,506,393 | 12,900,811 |
| P/L | 538,953 | 530,803 | 439,401 |
| NW | 3,455,799 | 3,422,133 | 3,095,080 |
| WC | 1,539,544 | 853,602 | 478,187 |
| Emp. | 89 | 74 | 73 |

DUNS 22-723-6098
### Pattinson & Brewer
30 Great James Street, London WC1N 3EY
**Tel:** 02076533200
**Web:** www.pattinsonbrewer.co.uk
**Estd:** 1850 Partnership
**Line of Business:** Solicitors
**Partners:** K Hughes, N J Mills, Ms P Y Stewart, S E Butcher, D Coburn, Ms J Chidgey, J A Couch, N O'Brady
**Responsibilities**
**Senior:** Graham Church *(Partner)*, Linda Levison *(Partner)*, Niamah O'brady *(Partner)*, Kathy Tailby *(Partner)*
**Finance:** Mike Dempsey *(Financial Director)*
**Sales:** Denise Kitchener *(Business Development Manager)*
**Admin:** Katrina Uting *(Office Manager)*
**IT:** Mike Dempsey *(Financial Director)*
**HR:** Dana Smith *(Human Resources Manager)*, Katrina Uting *(Office Manager)*
**Health & Safety:** Katrina Uting *(Office Manager)*
**Facilities:** Katrina Uting *(Office Manager)*
**Branches:** Pattinson & Brewer, 8-12 New Rd, Chatham, Kent ME4 4QR
**US SIC:** 8111 **UK SIC:** 83500
**Bankers:** The Royal Bank Of Scotland Plc (16-00-53)
**Employees:** 70

DUNS 21-722-6240 **Exp**
### Pattonair Ltd
(**Subsidiary of:** Exponent Private Equity Partners Lp)
Unit A3, Woking, Surrey GU21 5SA
**Tel:** 01483774600 **Fax:** 01483774619
**Web:** www.pattonair.com
**Reg No:** 0974964 **Estd:** 1970 Private Limited Company
**Line of Business:** Aviation supplies
**Export Sales:** £41,908,000
**Issued Capital:** £78,000
**Directors:** P Ahye, D G Puddifoot, W R Hollinshead
**Responsibilities**
**Senior:** Andy Nolan *(Head of Sales & Marketing)*, Polly Wu *(General Manager (china))*
**Marketing:** Andy Nolan *(Head of Sales & Marketing)*
**Sales:** Andy Nolan *(Head of Sales & Marketing)*
**Operations:** Steve Gifford *(Operations Manager)*, Steve Halford *(Chairman)*

**Purchasing:** David Bowdery *(Head of Supply Chain Solutions)*
**Branches:** Pattonair Ltd, Octimum, Unit 5, Woking, Surrey GU21 5SF
**US SIC:** 3721, 7392
**UK SIC:** 36400, 83951
**Auditors:** PricewaterhouseCoopers LLP
**Bankers:** Lloyds TSB Bank plc (30-95-89)

| | 31-03-14 | 31-03-13 | 31-03-12 |
|---|---|---|---|
| TO | 111,137,000 | 79,801,000 | 45,662,000 |
| P/L | 9,015,000 | 5,984,000 | 4,930,000 |
| NW | 25,212,000 | 18,217,000 | 13,671,000 |
| WC | 57,122,000 | 50,914,000 | 22,658,000 |
| Emp. | 155 | 139 | 103 |

DUNS 21-602-8225
## P.A.Turney Ltd
Middleton Stoney, Middleton Stoney, Bicester, Oxfordshire OX25 4AB
**Tel:** 01869343333
**Web:** www.turneygroup.com
**Reg No:** 0607154 **VAT No:** 119911073
**Estd:** 1958 Private Limited Company
**Line of Business:** Agricultural engineers
**Trading Style:** Turney Aquiforce, Turney Field Force
**Issued Capital:** £179,763
**Principals:** P Turney *(Chairman and Managing)*, J A Turney, J Turney
**Co. Secretary:** David Shorey
**Responsibilities**
**Senior:** Enid Turney *(Manager)*
**Finance:** Neil Houghton *(Accountant)*
**IT:** Neil Houghton *(Accountant)*
**HR:** Mike Grice *(Parts Manager)*
**Health & Safety:** Mike Grice *(Parts Manager)*
**Branches:** P.a.turney Ltd, Unit 3A, Worcester Road Industrial Estate, Chipping Norton, Oxfordshire OX7 5XW
**US SIC:** 0729 **UK SIC:** 01003
**Auditors:** Grant Thornton UK LLP
**Bankers:** National Westminster Bank Plc (60-17-21)

| | 31-12-13 | 31-12-12 | 31-12-11 |
|---|---|---|---|
| TO | 25,432,626 | 26,530,626 | 27,398,115 |
| P/L | 110,914 | 114,602 | 241,688 |
| NW | 4,768,626 | 4,716,361 | 4,673,314 |
| WC | 2,747,648 | 2,605,340 | 2,567,417 |
| Emp. | 105 | 103 | 102 |

DUNS 33-934-6074
## Paul Brighouse
Navigation Park, 810 London Road, Alvaston, Derby, Derbyshire DE24 8WA
**Tel:** 01332223850
**Web:** www.tradewindows.com
**Proprietorship**
**Line of Business:** Double glazing installers
**Proprietor:** P Brighouse
**US SIC:** 1793 **UK SIC:** 50400
**Employees:** 100

DUNS 29-624-7265 **Imp-Exp**
## Paul Dennicci Ltd
Unit 3c Galliford Road Industrial Estate, Heybridge, Maldon, Essex CM9 4XD
**Tel:** 01621859119
**Web:** www.dennicci.co.uk
**Reg No:** 1951127 **VAT No:** 434795619
**Estd:** 2004 Private Limited Company
**Line of Business:** Import and export agents
**Export Markets:** E U
**Issued Capital:** £49,999
**Director:** A J Farrow
**US SIC:** 5136 **UK SIC:** 61600
**Auditors:** Fricker & Co
**Bankers:** HSBC Bank plc (40-31-35)

| | 31-05-14 | 31-05-13 | 31-05-12 |
|---|---|---|---|
| TO | 27,978,711 | 28,854,108 | 22,307,388 |
| P/L | 2,339,556 | 2,335,383 | 1,697,120 |
| NW | 5,170,081 | 4,808,622 | 3,074,084 |
| WC | 4,970,649 | 4,601,503 | 2,859,866 |
| Emp. | 51 | 41 | 37 |

DUNS 50-492-4085
## Paul Earl Ltd
Albourne Court, Hassocks, West Sussex BN6 9FF
**Tel:** 08452106000 **Fax:** 01273-611036
**Web:** www.paulearl.co.uk
**Reg No:** 2460613 **VAT No:** 550407666
**Estd:** 1964 Private Limited Company
**Line of Business:** Building services
**Issued Capital:** £121,514
**Principals:** R K Moore *(Managing)*, D F Plant, Ms K B Coade, D R Moore, W P Moore, S T Everitt
**Co. Secretary:** Ms Louise Moore
**Responsibilities**
**Marketing:** Paul Gunn *(General Manager)*
**Sales:** Paul Gunn *(General Manager)*
**Health & Safety:** John Lawley *(Health & Safety Manager)*
**Facilities:** Paul Gunn *(General Manager)*
**US SIC:** 1622 **UK SIC:** 50200
**Auditors:** Plummer Parsons

**Bankers:** Allied Irish Bank (gb) (23-85-89)

| | 31-05-14 | 31-05-13 | 31-05-12 |
|---|---|---|---|
| TO | N/A | N/A | 9,319,673 |
| P/L | N/A | N/A | 57,965 |
| NW | 1,496,729 | 1,371,630 | 1,360,280 |
| WC | 953,657 | 765,796 | 873,787 |

DUNS 23-715-0417 **Imp-Exp**
## Paul Fabrications Ltd
**(Subsidiary of:** Agc Aerospace and Defense)
Unit 10a, Derby, Derbyshire DE74 2US
**Tel:** 01332-818000 **Fax:** 01332-818089
**Web:** www.paulfabrications.co.uk
**Reg No:** 3709882 **VAT No:** 852866490
**Estd:** 2000 Private Limited Company
**Line of Business:** Sheet metal fabrication equipment
**Export Sales:** £4,826,831
**Issued Capital:** £1,549,363
**Directors:** R R Nagel, A Burns
**Co. Secretary:** Vp Secretarial Limited
**Responsibilities**
**Senior:** Ingard Sagstad *(Manager)*
**Finance:** Ian Doe *(Senior Finance Administrator)*
**Marketing:** Christopher Cropley *(IT Manager)*, Kevin Dexter *(Business Development Manager)*
**Sales:** Kevin Dexter *(Business Development Manager)*
**IT:** Christopher Cropley *(IT Manager)*, Ingard Sagstad *(Manager)*
**Operations:** Christopher Cropley *(IT Manager)*, Ingard Sagstad *(Manager)*
**Purchasing:** Jackie Stonehouse *(Purchasing Manager)*
**Engineering:** Richard Higginbottom *(Production Manager)*
**US SIC:** 3441, 3499, 3721
**UK SIC:** 32042, 31694, 36400
**Auditors:** Smith Cooper
**Bankers:** HSBC Bank plc (40-11-18)

| | 31-12-13 | 31-12-12 | 31-12-11 |
|---|---|---|---|
| TO | 13,757,814 | 12,910,764 | 13,014,629 |
| P/L | 3,578,305 | 4,012,339 | 4,117,488 |
| NW | 16,838,554 | 13,804,010 | 10,228,985 |
| WC | 15,642,155 | 12,444,577 | 8,678,125 |
| Emp. | 124 | 122 | 121 |

DUNS 34-564-2982
## Paul Gearey Construction Ltd
21 Second Avenue, Horbury, Wakefield, West Yorkshire WF4 6HB
**Tel:** 07833101669
**Reg No:** 5373727 **Estd:** 2005 Private Limited Company
**Line of Business:** Property developers
**Issued Capital:** £1
**Managing Director:** P A Gearey
**Co. Secretary:** Ms Janice Gearey
**US SIC:** 1522 **UK SIC:** 50100

| | 31-03-14 | 31-03-13 | 31-03-12 |
|---|---|---|---|
| TA | 14,926 | 11,195 | 21,969 |
| NW | 95 | 31 | 380 |
| WC | (1,840) | (2,547) | (3,056) |

DUNS 22-728-8982 **Imp**
## Paul Hartmann Ltd
**(Subsidiary of:** Schwenk Limes Gmbh & Co. Kg)
Heywood Distribution Park, Heywood, Lancashire OL10 2TT
**Tel:** 01706-363200 **Fax:** 01706-363201
**Web:** www.hartmann.co.uk
**Reg No:** 1523121 **VAT No:** 362341768
**Estd:** 1981 Private Limited Company
**Line of Business:** Wholesale of pharmaceutical goods
**Trading Style:** Paul Hartmann Ltd
**Issued Capital:** £2,510,000
**Directors:** W Roehrl, O Heinzel, Dr W Casper
**Co. Secretary:** Trevor Coupe
**Responsibilities**
**Finance:** Diane Coupe *(Purchasing Manager)*
**Marketing:** Kim Rawlinson *(Business Development Manager)*
**Sales:** Peter Hulme *(Sales Manager)*
**HR:** Abid Al-Qasmi *(Human Resources Manager)*, Marilyn Ripley *(Personnel Officer)*
**Purchasing:** Diane Coupe *(Purchasing Manager)*
**US SIC:** 5122 **UK SIC:** 61800
**Auditors:** PricewaterhouseCoopers LLP
**Bankers:** Barclays Bank Plc (20-72-67)

| | 31-12-13 | 31-12-12 | 31-12-11 |
|---|---|---|---|
| TO | 33,295,853 | 28,412,434 | 25,295,970 |
| P/L | 781,636 | (665,153) | (1,121,626) |
| NW | 1,601,124 | 544,488 | 1,209,641 |
| WC | 1,040,387 | 14,094 | 752,170 |
| Emp. | 85 | 81 | 78 |

DUNS 73-759-5368
## Paul Hastings (Europe) Llp
Eighth Floor, Ten Bishops Square, London E1 6EG
**Tel:** 020-3023-5100
**Web:** www.paulhastings.com
**Reg No:** 0306535OC **Estd:** 2004
**Line of Business:** Solicitors
**Export Sales:** £42,345,806
**Trading Style:** Paul Hastings (Europe) Llp
**Responsibilities**
**Senior:** Erwan Barre *(Non-designated Limited Liabili)*, Arun Birla *(Non-designated Limited Liabili)*, Dominique Borde *(Non-designated Limited Liabili)*, Emma Bucknall *(Non-designated Limited Liabili)*, Karl Clowry *(Non-designated Limited Liabili)*, Bruno Cova *(Non-designated Limited Liabili)*, Pascal De Moidrey *(Non-designated Limited Liabili)*, Allard De Waal *(Non-designated Limited Liabili)*, Conor Downey *(Non-designated Limited Liabili)*, Regina Engelstadter *(Non-designated Limited Liabili)*, Ugo Giordano *(Non-designated Limited Liabili)*, Garrett Hayes *(Non-designated Limited Liabili)*, Lorenzo Parola *(Non-designated Limited Liabili)*, Aline Poncelet *(Non-designated Limited Liabili)*, David Revcolevschi *(Non-designated Limited Liabili)*, Seth Zachary *(Non-designated Limited Liabili)*
**US SIC:** 8111 **UK SIC:** 83500
**Auditors:** Chantrey Vellacott DFK LLP

| | 31-01-14 | 31-01-13 | 31-01-12 |
|---|---|---|---|
| TO | 77,984,910 | 64,409,976 | 60,769,721 |
| WC | 34,186,166 | 27,994,153 | 25,294,640 |
| Emp. | 217 | 213 | 209 |

DUNS 22-655-6173
## Paul John Construction (Leicester) Ltd
Telford Way, Stephenson Industrial Estate, Coalville, Leicestershire LE67 3HE
**Tel:** 01530-513400 **Fax:** 015330513452
**Web:** www.pauljohngroup.com
**Reg No:** 1263399 **VAT No:** 116029011
**Estd:** 1976 Private Limited Company
**Line of Business:** Construction of domestic buildings
**Issued Capital:** £155,000
**Principals:** J T Henry *(Managing)*, J P Henry
**Co. Secretary:** John Brouder
**Responsibilities**
**Senior:** Mark Poulson *(Group Accountant)*
**Finance:** Mark Poulson *(Group Accountant)*
**IT:** Mark Poulson *(Group Accountant)*
**Health & Safety:** Andy Cartridge *(Health & Safety Director)*
**US SIC:** 1522, 1541
**UK SIC:** 50100
**Auditors:** Law & Co
**Bankers:** The Bank Of Ireland (30-15-10)

| | 31-12-13 | 31-12-12 | 31-12-11 |
|---|---|---|---|
| TO | 29,268,081 | 23,677,262 | 23,584,888 |
| P/L | 336,912 | (1,160,751) | 145,761 |
| NW | 1,238,235 | 1,034,580 | 2,008,331 |
| WC | 176,544 | (5,845) | 684,937 |
| Emp. | 68 | 112 | 129 |

DUNS 34-738-1035 **Imp**
## Paul Macarthur Ltd
Phoenix Park, 1hq Building, Eaton Socon, St Neots, Cambridgeshire PE19 8EP
**Tel:** 01480-404888 **Fax:** 01480-404333
**Web:** www.sccssurvey.co.uk
**Reg No:** 5540080 **Estd:** 2005 Private Limited Company
**Line of Business:** Other construction work involving special trades
**Trading Style:** Sccs
**Issued Capital:** £75,100
**Director:** P W Macarthur
**Co. Secretary:** Mrs Catherine Macarthur
**US SIC:** 1799, 7394
**UK SIC:** 50000, 84000
**Auditors:** Brown Butler
**Bankers:** HSBC Bank plc (40-40-10)

| | 30-06-13 | 30-06-12 | 30-06-11 |
|---|---|---|---|
| TO | 9,949,663 | 9,623,310 | 8,467,314 |
| P/L | 1,134,594 | 1,428,225 | 668,557 |
| NW | 3,460,593 | 2,518,291 | 1,459,102 |
| WC | 246,796 | (150,535) | (649,453) |
| Emp. | 60 | 54 | 47 |

DUNS 22-125-3102
## Paul Mason Consulting Ltd
30-32 Blacklands Way, Abingdon, Oxfordshire OX14 1DY
**Tel:** 01235-521900
**Web:** www.pmcretail.com
**Reg No:** 4144304 **Estd:** 2007 Private Limited Company
**Line of Business:** It consultants
**Issued Capital:** £3,290
**Directors:** H Thomas, P Mason, I R Edwards, G C Ambidge, N Gilna
**Co. Secretary:** Mrs Iris Mason

**US SIC:** 7379 **UK SIC:** 83940

| | 31-03-14 | 31-03-13 | 31-03-12 |
|---|---|---|---|
| TO | 7,782,873 | 5,866,012 | 6,580,346 |
| P/L | 521,160 | (72,472) | 306,960 |
| NW | 1,073,452 | 844,819 | 908,548 |
| WC | 809,529 | 613,235 | 695,395 |
| Emp. | 165 | 136 | 122 |

DUNS 21-015-6696
## Paul Merrifield
27 Castle Foregate, Shrewsbury, Shropshire SY1 2EE
**Estd:** 1993 Proprietorship
**Line of Business:** Taxis and private hire vehicles
**Proprietor:** P Merrifield
**US SIC:** 4121 **UK SIC:** 72200
**Employees:** 50

DUNS 23-665-9439
## Paul Monyard
Tormarton, Badminton, Avon GL9 1JB
**Web:** www.compass-inn.co.uk
**Estd:** 1969 Proprietorship
**Line of Business:** Hotel
**Proprietor:** P Monyard
**US SIC:** 7011 **UK SIC:** 66500
**Employees:** 50

DUNS 21-104-8462
## Paul Moorman
Clarendon Road, Shanklin, Isle of Wight PO37 6DP
**Tel:** 01983-862286
**Web:** www.shanklinhotel.co.uk
**Proprietorship**
**Line of Business:** Hotels
**Responsibilities**
**Senior:** Paul Moorman *(Manager)*
**US SIC:** 7011 **UK SIC:** 66500
**Employees:** 60

DUNS 21-726-4167 **Imp-Exp**
## Paul Murray Plc
School Lane, Chandler's Ford, Eastleigh, Hampshire SO53 4YN
**Web:** www.murrayshealthandbeauty.com
**Reg No:** 1172728 **VAT No:** 189602922
**Estd:** 1974 Public Limited Company
**Line of Business:** Pharmaceutical suppliers and wholesalers
**Export Markets:** Worldwide
**Export Sales:** £786,918
**Trading Style:** Murrays/Clio/Sun Setters/ Miners Cosmetics, Head Girl/West Point/ Handy Guard, Safe & Sound/Meridiana/ Spring Island, Junior Macare/Cassandra
**Issued Capital:** £100,000
**Principals:** P T Murray *(Chairman)*, Ms C Murray, M Cox, T Eastwood, M J Murray, Mrs K J Murray, Mrs G L Robertson, N B Hayton
**Co. Secretary:** Susan Coatham
**Responsibilities**
**Senior:** Tony Pickford *(Manager)*
**Marketing:** Ally Mead *(Digital Marketing Executive)*
**Admin:** Sue Webb *(Office Manager)*
**Operations:** Sue Webb *(Office Manager)*
**Purchasing:** Leigh Hadaway *(Buyer)*
**US SIC:** 5122 **UK SIC:** 61800
**Auditors:** Rothman Pantall & Co
**Bankers:** Barclays Bank Plc (20-79-25)

| | 31-12-13 | 31-12-12 | 31-12-11 |
|---|---|---|---|
| TO | 18,109,647 | 16,369,066 | 11,769,421 |
| P/L | 1,210,043 | 1,006,689 | 559,736 |
| NW | 3,886,714 | 2,952,727 | 2,390,544 |
| WC | 2,734,552 | 2,119,797 | 1,745,704 |
| Emp. | 76 | 72 | 66 |

DUNS 53-642-5267
## Paul Nicholls Racing Ltd
Manor Farm, Shepton Mallet, Somerset BA4 6RD
**Tel:** 01749-860656
**Web:** www.paulnichollsracing.com
**Reg No:** 3448030 **Estd:** 1991 Private Limited Company
**Line of Business:** Horse trainers
**Issued Capital:** £100
**Managing Director:** P F Nicholls
**Co. Secretary:** Ms Carolina Chadburn
**US SIC:** 7999 **UK SIC:** 97913
**Auditors:** Blueprint Audit Ltd

| | 31-10-13 | 31-10-12 | 31-10-11 |
|---|---|---|---|
| TA | 1,950,043 | 1,881,238 | 1,179,570 |
| NW | 1,023,740 | 789,968 | 548,147 |
| WC | 511,064 | 322,172 | 191,360 |

DUNS 22-274-3259
## Paul Rhodes Precision Engineering Ltd
Quarry Mills, Oxford Road, Gomersal, Cleckheaton, West Yorkshire BD19 4HQ
**Tel:** 01274-851225
**Reg No:** 4292152 **Estd:** 1967 Private Limited Company
**Line of Business:** Precision engineers
**Issued Capital:** £2

**Director:** P Rhodes
**Co. Secretary:** Ms Elizabeth Rhodes
**US SIC:** 8911 **UK SIC:** 83701

| | 30-09-13 | 30-09-12 | 30-09-11 |
|---|---|---|---|
| TA | 832,189 | 787,436 | 705,387 |
| NW | 752,598 | 682,226 | 582,560 |
| WC | 449,890 | 439,993 | 345,399 |

DUNS 22-194-5145
## Paul Robinson Solicitors Llp
The Old Bank, Westcliff-On-Sea, Essex SS0 9LD
**Tel:** 01702-338338
**Web:** www.paulrobinson.co.uk
**Reg No:** 0300127OC **Estd:** 1984 Limited Partnership
**Line of Business:** Solicitors
**US SIC:** 8111 **UK SIC:** 83500

| | 31-03-14 | 31-03-13 | 31-03-12 |
|---|---|---|---|
| TA | 2,038,194 | 1,977,685 | 2,047,911 |
| NW | 742,500 | 742,500 | 742,500 |
| WC | 828,274 | 830,337 | 851,037 |

DUNS 21-327-2235
## Paul Rooney Partnership
Stanley Court, 19-23 Stanley Street, Liverpool, Merseyside L1 6AA
**Tel:** 0151-227-2851
**Web:** www.paulrooney.co.uk
**Estd:** 2005 Partnership
**Line of Business:** Solicitors
**Trading Style:** Paul Rooney Partnership Solicitors
**Principals:** S A Brassington *(Partner)*, D Lloyd *(Partner)*, P J Davis *(Partner)*, P Rooney
**Responsibilities**
**Finance:** Graham Beesley *(Practice Manager)*
**Marketing:** james rooney *(marketing manager)*
**Health & Safety:** Louise Boose *(Health & Safety Officer)*
**Purchasing:** Louise Boose *(Health & Safety Officer)*
**US SIC:** 7399 **UK SIC:** 83954
**Employees:** 60

DUNS 23-305-5479
## Paul Shaw
Priory Shopping Centre, Dartford, Kent DA1 2HR
**Tel:** 01322271425
**Web:** www.mcdonalds.co.uk
**Estd:** 2002 Proprietorship
**Line of Business:** Restaurants
**Proprietor:** P Shaw
**Branches:** Paul Shaw, Bean Road, Cobham Terrace, Greenhithe, Kent DA9 9HY
**US SIC:** 5812 **UK SIC:** 66110
**Employees:** 76

DUNS 34-732-7228
## Paul Smith Group Holdings Ltd
The Poplars, Lenton Lane, Nottingham, Nottinghamshire NG7 2PW
**Tel:** 01159685821
**Web:** www.paulsmith.co.uk
**Reg No:** 5534862 **Estd:** 2005 Private Limited Company
**Line of Business:** Management activities of holding companies
**Export Sales:** £129,337,000
**Issued Capital:** £44,405
**Directors:** M Morofuji, Sir P B Smith
**Co. Secretary:** Ashley Long
**US SIC:** 6711 **UK SIC:** 83962

| | 30-06-14 | 30-06-13 | 30-06-12 |
|---|---|---|---|
| TO | 202,708,000 | 202,484,000 | 202,096,000 |
| P/L | 20,779,000 | 23,808,000 | 31,703,000 |
| NW | 147,999,000 | 138,193,000 | 129,862,000 |
| WC | 86,273,000 | 68,748,000 | 70,531,000 |
| Emp. | 1,085 | 1,017 | 1,024 |

DUNS 21-916-3102 **Imp-Exp**
## Paul Smith Ltd
**(Subsidiary of:** Paul Smith Group Holdings Ltd)
Riverside Building, Riverside Way, Nottingham, Nottinghamshire NG2 1DP
**Tel:** 01159868877
**Web:** www.paulsmith.co.uk
**Reg No:** 1170719 **VAT No:** 648096114
**Estd:** 1970 Private Limited Company
**Line of Business:** Fashion shops
**Export Sales:** £107,914,000
**Issued Capital:** £47,940
**Principals:** Sir P B Smith *(Chairman and Managing)*, J D Francis, A J Long, G A Chilton, M Morofuji
**Co. Secretary:** Ashley Snowden Long
**Responsibilities**
**Senior:** Mark Wiggington *(Maintenance Manager)*
**IT:** Lee Bingham *(IT Manager)*
**Health & Safety:** Adam Stevens *(Health & Safety Officer)*
**Facilities:** Derek Severn *(Maintenance Manager)*, Mark Wiggington *(Maintenance Manager)*
**Branches:** Paul Smith Ltd, Sloane Avenue, London SW3 3DZ
**US SIC:** 7399, 5699
**UK SIC:** 83954, 64500
**Auditors:** PricewaterhouseCoopers LLP
**Bankers:** Yorkshire Bank Plc (05-06-41)

| | 30-06-14 | 30-06-13 | 30-06-12 |
|---|---|---|---|
| TO | 181,284,000 | 176,683,000 | 178,799,000 |
| P/L | 18,366,000 | 18,395,000 | 24,853,000 |
| NW | 156,175,000 | 147,704,000 | 148,268,000 |
| WC | 102,312,000 | 87,245,000 | 97,503,000 |
| Emp. | 903 | 856 | 836 |

DUNS 21-354-6158
## Paul Stothard
The Lakes, Northampton, Northamptonshire NN4 7YD
**Tel:** 01604543000
**Web:** www.shoosmiths.co.uk
**Estd:** 1800
**Line of Business:** Solicitors
**Proprietor:** J H Peet
**Responsibilities**
**Senior:** Claire Row *(Chief Executive)*
**US SIC:** 8111 **UK SIC:** 83500
**Employees:** 500

DUNS 23-683-3050
## Paul T Garthwaite
41-45 Skinnergate, Darlington, County Durham DL3 7NR
**Tel:** 01325-464716
**Web:** www.taylorsbutchers.com
**Estd:** 1924 Partnership
**Line of Business:** Butchers
**Trading Style:** H Taylor & Sons
**Partners:** Mrs P Garthwaite, P T Garthwaite, A Taylor, N Garthwaite
**US SIC:** 5423 **UK SIC:** 64100
**Bankers:** National Westminster Bank Plc (52-30-18)
**Employees:** 50

DUNS 23-847-4147
## Paul U.K. Ltd
302 Upper Street, London N1 2TU
**Tel:** 02072882721
**Web:** www.paul-uk.com
**Reg No:** 3839415 **Estd:** 1999 Private Limited Company
**Line of Business:** Bakers & baked goods retailers
**Issued Capital:** £5,136,492
**Directors:** M Holder, J M Orieux
**Co. Secretary:**
Reed Smith Corporate Services Ll
**Responsibilities**
**Senior:** Claudio Nogueira *(Manager)*
**Branches:** Paul U.k. Ltd, Unit RP390, 15 Cabot Square, London E14 4QS
**US SIC:** 5462 **UK SIC:** 64100
**Auditors:** Mazars LLP

| | 31-12-13 | 31-12-12 | 31-12-11 |
|---|---|---|---|
| TO | 23,773,540 | 23,366,832 | 22,675,402 |
| P/L | (115,496) | (1,432,484) | (596,969) |
| NW | 392,406 | 512,583 | 1,645,963 |
| WC | (2,675,632) | (2,362,080) | (1,221,989) |
| Emp. | 476 | 470 | 487 |

DUNS 23-523-7992 **Imp-Exp**
## Paula Rosa Ltd
**(Subsidiary of:** Stena Ab)
Robell Way, Storrington, Pulborough, West Sussex RH20 3DS
**Tel:** 01903743322
**Web:** www.paularosa.com
**Reg No:** 3522795 **Estd:** 1965 Private Limited Company
**Line of Business:** Manufacture of other kitchen furniture
**Export Markets:** Far East
**Trading Style:** Paula Rosa Kitchens
**Issued Capital:** £1
**Director:** I Flitcroft
**Co. Secretary:** Kevin Cook
**Responsibilities**
**Health & Safety:** Lee Golby *(health & Safety manager)*
**US SIC:** 2599 **UK SIC:** 46720
**Bankers:** Merita Bank Ltd (40-50-43)

| | 31-03-14 | 31-03-13 | 31-03-12 |
|---|---|---|---|
| TA | 1 | 1 | 1 |
| NW | 1 | 1 | 1 |

DUNS 21-154-4710
## Paull & Williamsons Llp
1 Union Wynd, Aberdeen, Aberdeenshire AB10 1DQ
**Tel:** 01224621621
**Web:** www.burnesspaull.com
**Reg No:** 0302228SO **Estd:** 2009 Private Limited Company
**Line of Business:** Solicitors
**Responsibilities**
**Senior:** Robin Clarkson *(Non-designated Limited Liabili)*, Helen Dickson *(Non-designated Limited Liabili)*, Margaret Gibson *(Non-designated Limited Liabili)*, Richard Goodfellow *(Non-designated Limited Liabili)*, Alan McNiven *(Senior Partner)*, James Stark *(Non-designated Limited Liabili)*, John Strachan *(Non-designated Limited Liabili)*
**Admin:** Norman Haggart *(Practice Manager)*
**IT:** Sandra Middleton *(IT Manager)*
**Health & Safety:** Norman Haggart *(Practice Manager)*
**Facilities:** Alan McNiven *(Senior Partner)*
**Purchasing:** Norman Haggart *(Practice Manager)*
**US SIC:** 8111 **UK SIC:** 83500
**Auditors:** KPMG LLP
**Bankers:** Bank Of Scotland (80-05-16)

| | 05-04-13 | 05-04-12 |
|---|---|---|
| TO | 9,756,000 | 13,249,000 |
| P/L | 4,388,000 | 5,367,000 |
| WC | N/A | 5,021,000 |
| Emp. | 104 | 103 |

DUNS 21-810-1529
## Paulo Giannis
New Street, Lancaster, Lancashire LA1 1EG
**Tel:** 01524383403
**Estd:** 2012
**Line of Business:** Restaurant - italian
**Responsibilities**
**Senior:** Helder Mendes *(Manager)*
**US SIC:** 5812 **UK SIC:** 66110
**Employees:** 50

DUNS 21-815-5109 **Exp**
## Pauls Malt Ltd
**(Subsidiary of:** Societe Cooperative Agricole Axe)
24-25 Eastern Way, Bury St Edmunds, Suffolk IP32 7AD
**Tel:** 01284772000
**Web:** www.boortmalt.com
**Reg No:** 0088929 **Estd:** 1906 Private Limited Company
**Line of Business:** Manufacture of malt
**Export Markets:** Japan, South America, Germany, Africa, Asia
**Export Sales:** £38,365,000
**Issued Capital:** £1,081,000
**Directors:** D R Wilkes, J Loiseau, Y Shaepman, P Chaudru De Raynal
**Co. Secretary:**
Goodbody Northern Ireland Secret
**Responsibilities**
**Senior:** Jean-francios Loiseau *(Director)*
**IT:** Andrew Akin *(IT Manager)*
**Branches:** Pauls Malt Ltd, Campmuir, Blairgowrie, Perthshire PH13 9JF
**US SIC:** 2083, 2082
**UK SIC:** 42702
**Auditors:** PricewaterhouseCoopers LLP
**Bankers:** Lloyds TSB Bank plc (30-94-55)

| | 30-06-13 | 30-06-12 | 30-06-11 |
|---|---|---|---|
| TO | 129,692,000 | 112,893,000 | 77,572,000 |
| P/L | 1,761,000 | 1,987,000 | 5,517,000 |
| NW | 31,102,000 | 30,201,000 | 29,173,000 |
| WC | 8,721,000 | 7,548,000 | 7,846,000 |
| Emp. | 115 | 116 | 122 |

DUNS 29-766-3130
## Paultons Park Ltd
Ower, Romsey, Hampshire SO51 6AL
**Tel:** 02380814442
**Web:** www.paultonsbreaks.com
**Reg No:** 2029374 **Estd:** 1983 Private Limited Company
**Line of Business:** Operation of theme parks
**Issued Capital:** £225,000
**Principals:** R W Mancey *(Managing)*, S J Lorton
**Co. Secretary:** Ms Sara Mancey
**US SIC:** 7996 **UK SIC:** 97913
**Auditors:** BKL Weeks Green
**Bankers:** Lloyds TSB Bank plc (30-99-71)

| | 01-12-13 | 02-12-12 | 27-12-11 |
|---|---|---|---|
| TO | 20,300,943 | 18,278,264 | 18,631,941 |
| P/L | 6,316,413 | 5,568,903 | 6,764,210 |
| NW | 25,133,730 | 19,150,161 | 14,995,619 |
| WC | 10,679,589 | 7,408,235 | 4,656,663 |
| Emp. | 338 | 331 | 305 |

DUNS 21-924-7681
## Pave-Aways Ltd
**(Subsidiary of:** Pave-Aways Holdings (2011) Ltd)
Avenue Mill, Knockin, Oswestry, Shropshire SY10 8HQ
**Tel:** 01691682111
**Web:** www.paveaways.co.uk
**Reg No:** 1136997 **Estd:** 1973 Private Limited Company
**Line of Business:** Building construction contractors
**Issued Capital:** £70
**Principals:** W R Evans *(Financial)*, Ms B H Jones, S P Owen, M G Donoghue, Mrs A J Evans
**Co. Secretary:** Ms Bernadette Jones
**Responsibilities**
**Senior:** Phillip Hodges *(Manager)*
**Branches:** Pave-Aways Ltd, Avenue Mill, Oswestry, Shropshire SY10 8HQ
**US SIC:** 1522 **UK SIC:** 50100
**Auditors:** D.R.E. & Co

| | 31-03-14 | 31-03-13 | 31-03-12 |
|---|---|---|---|
| TO | 19,281,107 | 13,483,938 | 13,554,604 |
| P/L | 735,636 | 362,403 | 305,147 |
| NW | 3,769,876 | 3,201,209 | 2,921,166 |
| WC | 3,083,970 | 2,617,254 | 2,316,444 |
| Emp. | 80 | 70 | 75 |

DUNS 34-629-3756
## Pavelodge Packaging Ltd
Enfield Industrial Estate, Redditch, Worcestershire B97 6BX
**Tel:** 07887627888 **Fax:** 01527-584495
**Reg No:** 2763141 **Estd:** 1967 Private Limited Company
**Line of Business:** Manufacture of other plastic products
**Issued Capital:** £2
**Directors:** D G Duthie, British Polythene Limited
**Co. Secretary:** Ms Hilary Kane
**Responsibilities**
**Senior:** Raymond Brooksbank *(Manager)*
**US SIC:** 3079 **UK SIC:** 48360
**Bankers:** Clydesdale Bank Plc (82-65-06)

| | 31-12-13 | 31-12-12 | 31-12-11 |
|---|---|---|---|
| TA | 341,000 | 341,000 | 341,000 |
| NW | 78,576 | 78,576 | 78,576 |
| WC | 78,576 | 78,576 | 78,576 |

DUNS 29-538-2816
## Paver Repair Services Ltd
Chorley Road, Preston, Lancashire PR5 4JA
**Tel:** 01772-697007
**Web:** www.bgp-group.co.uk
**Reg No:** 1905132 **Estd:** 1985 Private Limited Company
**Line of Business:** Management activities of other non-financial holding companies not elsewhere classified
**Issued Capital:** £16,400
**Managing Director:** T Fagan
**Co. Secretary:** Ms Gaynor Fagan
**Responsibilities**
**Senior:** Emma Feddon *(Manager)*
**US SIC:** 6711 **UK SIC:** 83962
**Auditors:** Jacksons
**Bankers:** National Westminster Bank Plc (01-00-53)

| | 31-12-13 | 31-12-12 | 31-12-11 |
|---|---|---|---|
| TA | 2,189,312 | 2,125,791 | 2,136,612 |
| NW | 1,712,126 | 1,673,382 | 1,781,996 |
| WC | 324,259 | 77,737 | 217,299 |

DUNS 39-466-5533
## Paver Systems Ltd
**(Subsidiary of:** Marshalls Plc)
Yieldshields Road, Carluke, Lanarkshire ML8 4QG
**Tel:** 08453040703 **Fax:** 01555772868
**Web:** www.stonemarket.co.uk
**Reg No:** 0104334SC **VAT No:** 464064942
**Estd:** 1987 Private Limited Company
**Line of Business:** Manufacture of cement
**Issued Capital:** £30,000
**Directors:** M Coffey, J J Clarke
**Co. Secretary:** Ms Catherine Baxandall
**US SIC:** 3241, 3291
**UK SIC:** 24200, 24600
**Auditors:** KPMG Audit PLC
**Bankers:** Clydesdale Bank Plc (82-60-19)

| | 31-12-13 | 31-12-12 | 31-12-11 |
|---|---|---|---|
| TA | 30,000 | 30,000 | 30,000 |
| NW | 30,000 | 30,000 | 30,000 |

DUNS 22-810-4097 **Imp**
## Pavers Ltd
**(Subsidiary of:** Pavers Holdings Ltd)
Catherine House, Northminster Business Park Harwood Road, York, North Yorkshire YO26 6QU
**Tel:** 01904528780
**Web:** www.pavers.co.uk
**Reg No:** 1014213 **VAT No:** 170030126
**Estd:** 1971 Private Limited Company
**Line of Business:** Footwear retailers
**Trading Style:** Pavers Shoes
**Issued Capital:** £24,471
**Managing Director:** S D Paver
**Co. Secretary:** Mrs Catherine Paver
**Responsibilities**
**Senior:** Ian Paver *(Manager)*
**Marketing:** Beth Morgan - Henderson *(Marketing Manager)*
**IT:** Chris Flynn *(IT Manager)*
**HR:** Helen Blake *(HR Manager)*
**Branches:** Pavers Ltd, 20 Piccadilly, York, North Yorkshire YO1 9NU
**US SIC:** 5948, 5961
**UK SIC:** 64600, 65600
**Auditors:** Clough & Co LLP

**Bankers:** HSBC Bank plc (40-47-31)

| | 01-02-14 | 02-02-13 | 28-02-12 |
|---|---|---|---|
| TO | 70,713,000 | 65,634,238 | 63,373,182 |
| P/L | 8,150,000 | 7,071,860 | 5,261,709 |
| NW | 32,257,000 | 27,073,898 | 22,529,058 |
| WC | 21,344,000 | 17,629,296 | 15,904,945 |
| Emp. | 1,070 | 916 | 865 |

DUNS 53-613-8878

## Pavey Group Ltd

(**Subsidiary of:** Pavey Group Holdings Ltd)
Minerva House, Orchard Way, Torquay, Devon TQ2 7FA
**Fax:** 01803217001
**Web:** www.michaelpavey.co.uk
**Reg No:** 3419086 **Estd:** 1971 Private Limited Company
**Line of Business:** Insurance brokers
**Trading Style:** Pavey Group
**Issued Capital:** £401,000
**Principals:** G M Brown *(Managing)*, Ms M Birchell, C Dean, G L Howe, G Gale, J A Cox, N D Sanders
**Co. Secretary:** Graham Howe
**Responsibilities**
**Senior:** Ray Illingworth *(Manager)*
**Sales:** Andy Gait *(Senior Account Manager)*
**Admin:** Alison Hopkins *(Administrative Support)*
**US SIC:** 6411, 6211, 6111
**UK SIC:** 83200, 83100, 81501
**Bankers:** The Royal Bank Of Scotland Plc (16-33-61)

| | 31-12-13 | 31-12-12 | 31-12-11 |
|---|---|---|---|
| TA | 2,779,483 | 2,565,241 | 2,515,598 |
| NW | 1,520,461 | 1,259,159 | 958,392 |
| WC | 1,917,054 | 1,589,132 | 1,161,842 |

DUNS 21-033-7459

## The Pavilion

33 Harbour Street, Broadstairs, Kent CT10 1EU
**Tel:** 01843-600999
**Web:** www.pavilion-broadstairs.co.uk
**Estd:** 2002 Proprietorship
**Line of Business:** Hotels and motels without restaurant
**Proprietor:** M Towe
**Responsibilities**
**Senior:** Mac Towe *(Manager)*
**US SIC:** 7011 **UK SIC:** 66500
**Employees:** 50

DUNS 34-765-6212 **Exp**

## Pavilion Books Group Ltd

(**Subsidiary of:** Pavilion Books Holdings Ltd)
The Old Magistrates Court, 10 Southcombe Street, London W14 0RA
**Web:** www.anovabooks.com
**Reg No:** 5566710 **Estd:** 2005 Private Limited Company
**Line of Business:** Publishing of books
**Issued Capital:** £100
**Directors:** N R Butterfield, Ms P A Powell
**Co. Secretary:** Allan Sams
**Responsibilities**
**Senior:** David Proffit *(Manager)*
**Finance:** Z Hanks *(Financial Director)*
**US SIC:** 2731 **UK SIC:** 47532
**Auditors:** Baker Tilly

| | 28-02-14 | 28-02-13 | 29-02-12 |
|---|---|---|---|
| TO | 8,503,291 | 8,844,886 | 11,014,326 |
| P/L | (295,342) | (21,956) | 330,861 |
| NW | 3,336,133 | 3,896,040 | 4,033,798 |
| WC | 3,308,421 | 3,828,323 | 3,883,484 |
| Emp. | 54 | 58 | 63 |

DUNS 21-812-0283

## Pavilion Court Care Home

Pavilion Court Care Home, Newcastle-Upon-Tyne, Tyne and Wear NE5 3AB
**Tel:** 01912867653
**Estd:** 2008
**Line of Business:** Medical nursing home activities
**Responsibilities**
**Senior:** Sharon Dixon *(Manager)*, Jude Goode *(Manager)*
**US SIC:** 8051 **UK SIC:** 95100
**Employees:** 60

DUNS 23-207-7586

## Pavilion Housing Association Ltd

Parsons House, Aldershot, Hampshire GU11 2AE
**Tel:** 08000191470
**Web:** https://www.firstwessex.org
**Reg No:** 0028040IP **VAT No:** 641595722
**Estd:** 1995 Friendly Society
**Line of Business:** Non-charitable social work activities with accommodation
**Trading Style:** First Wessex
**Principals:** R Lane *(Chairman)*, M Lindo *(Financial)*, M Jones, Ms L Conlon, Ms K Badger, S Rice, J Selby, A Straker
**Responsibilities**
**Senior:** Lynn Cobb *(Designated Limited Liability P)*, Richard Garside *(Designated Limited Liability P)*, Peter Grainger *(Designated Limited Liability P)*, Adrienne Harper *(Head of Housing Services)*, Alex Hughes *(Designated Limited Liability P)*, David January *(Designated Limited Liability P)*, Carol Knight *(Manager)*, Abi Little *(Manager)*, Marlina Mclaughlin *(Facilities Manager)*, Graham Plumbe *(Manager)*, Maurice Sheehan *(Partner)*, Veronica Stancer *(Designated Limited Liability P)*, Peter Walters *(Chief Executive)*
**Finance:** Hazel Warwick *(Asset Management Director & De)*
**Sales:** Mark Fitch *(?Head of Commercial Services)*
**Admin:** Jan Cass *(Sales Manager)*
**IT:** Neil Charlton *(Head of IT)*, Terry Cowdery *(Computer Operations Manager)*
**Health & Safety:** Julie Maddocks *(Facilities Manager)*
**Facilities:** Julie Maddocks *(Facilities Manager)*, Chris Teal *(Neighbourhood Manager)*
**Operations:** Adrienne Harper *(Head of Housing Services)*
**Fleet:** Marlina Mclaughlin *(Facilities Manager)*
**Branches:** Pavilion Housing Association Ltd, Pool Rd, Aldershot, Hampshire GU11 3SW
**US SIC:** 8321 **UK SIC:** 96111
**Auditors:** B D O Stoy Hayward
**Bankers:** Lloyds TSB Bank plc (30-90-09)
**Employees:** 60
**Turnover:** £25,807,000

DUNS 64-729-4933

## The Pavilion Leisure Centre

Pavilion Leisure Centre, Kentish Way, Bromley, Kent BR1 3EF
**Tel:** 020-8313-9911
**Web:** www.bromleymytime.org.uk
**Estd:** 2003 Partnership
**Line of Business:** Leisure centres
**Trading Style:** D C Leisure
**Partners:** P Conoway, C Gaywoods, Mrs K Gaywood, D Cross
**Responsibilities**
**Senior:** Adam Royall *(General Manager)*
**US SIC:** 7999 **UK SIC:** 97913
**Employees:** 90

DUNS 21-586-6222

## Pavilion Theatre

Pavilion Theatre, Westover Road, Bournemouth, Dorset BH1 2BU
**Tel:** 08445763000
**Web:** www.bic.co.uk
**Estd:** 1924 Proprietorship
**Line of Business:** Theatres & concert halls
**Proprietor:** P Gunn
**Responsibilities**
**Senior:** Bob Bentley *(Theatre Manager)*
**US SIC:** 7911 **UK SIC:** 97913
**Employees:** 150

DUNS 21-306-6959

## Pavillions of Harrogate

Great Yorkshire Showground, Railway Road, Harrogate, North Yorkshire HG2 8NZ
**Web:** www.pavilionsofharrogate.co.uk
**Estd:** 1994 Proprietorship
**Line of Business:** Conference centres and facilities
**Proprietor:** R Whiteley
**US SIC:** 6531 **UK SIC:** 83400
**Employees:** 50

DUNS 21-777-3060

## Pax Hill Care Home

Bentley, Farnham, Surrey GU10 5NG
**Tel:** 01420525882
**Web:** www.paxhill.co.uk
**Estd:** 2011 Proprietorship
**Line of Business:** Nursing homes
**Proprietor:** D Zaki
**Responsibilities**
**Senior:** N Zaki *(Manager)*
**US SIC:** 8321 **UK SIC:** 96111
**Employees:** 50

DUNS 73-470-1266

## Paxcorn Ltd

Kilbane Street, Fleetwood, Lancashire FY7 7PF
**Reg No:** 4734189 **Estd:** 2003 Private Limited Company
**Line of Business:** Holding companies management activities
**Issued Capital:** £100
**Director:** P D Worthington
**Co. Secretary:** James Barlow
**Branches:** Paxcorn Ltd, Dorset Avenue, Thornton-Cleveleys, Lancashire FY5 2DB
**US SIC:** 6711 **UK SIC:** 83962

**Bankers:** National Westminster Bank Plc (01-67-14)

| | 30-09-13 | 30-09-12 | 30-09-11 |
|---|---|---|---|
| TO | 11,599,975 | 11,209,177 | 10,790,206 |
| P/L | 242,165 | 199,375 | 337,840 |
| NW | 3,373,251 | 3,256,407 | 3,128,932 |
| WC | 1,934,773 | 1,809,801 | 1,770,006 |
| Emp. | 62 | 65 | 63 |

DUNS 57-837-8754

## Paxford Composites Ltd

(**Subsidiary of:** Paxford Holdings Ltd)
Redwongs Way, Huntingdon, Cambridgeshire PE29 7HB
**Tel:** 01480-453-537 **Fax:** 01480-413-125
**Web:** www.paxfordcomposites.co.uk
**Reg No:** 2891008 **Estd:** 2005 Private Limited Company
**Line of Business:** Coated Fabric Manufacturers, Ex Rubber
**Trading Style:** Paxford Composites
**Issued Capital:** £10,300
**Directors:** N F Appleby, G Ford
**Co. Secretary:** Glenn Ford
**Responsibilities**
**Finance:** James Pugh *(Financial Controller)*
**US SIC:** 2295 **UK SIC:** 43702
**Auditors:** George Hay Partnership LLP
**Bankers:** Barclays Bank Plc (20-09-72)

| | 30-09-13 | 30-09-12 | 30-09-11 |
|---|---|---|---|
| TA | 1,242,648 | 1,456,556 | 1,015,243 |
| NW | 556,580 | 421,188 | 160,031 |
| WC | 415,437 | 247,741 | (17,080) |

DUNS 77-494-3252

## Paxman Darts Ltd

(**Subsidiary of:** Cobra Industries Ltd)
Unit 3-4 Cobra Works, Pindar Road, Hoddesdon, Hertfordshire EN11 0JX
**Tel:** 01992300000
**Web:** www.harrowsdarts.com
**Reg No:** 2977014 **Estd:** 1996 Private Limited Company
**Line of Business:** Manufacturers of sports goods
**Issued Capital:** £2
**Directors:** G C Paxman, R J Pringle
**Co. Secretary:** Colin Harris
**Responsibilities**
**Senior:** Adam Lanes *(Manager)*
**US SIC:** 3949 **UK SIC:** 49420

| | 31-12-13 | 31-12-12 | 31-12-11 |
|---|---|---|---|
| TA | 2 | 2 | 2 |
| NW | 2 | 2 | 2 |

DUNS 29-516-2713 **Imp-Exp**

## Paxton Access Ltd

(**Subsidiary of:** Paxton Access Group Ltd)
Paxton House, Home Farm Road, Brighton, East Sussex BN1 9HU
**Tel:** 01273811011 **Fax:** 01273-811089
**Web:** www.paxton.co.uk
**Reg No:** 1879474 **VAT No:** 423167374
**Estd:** 1985 Private Limited Company
**Line of Business:** Manufacture of lifting and handling equipment
**Export Markets:** Worldwide
**Export Sales:** £7,438,237
**Issued Capital:** £200,001
**Directors:** V Parekh, P S Rawlinson, G O'Hara, A Brotherton-Ratcliffe, P R Bannister, A J Stroud, S G Young
**Responsibilities**
**Senior:** Anthony Brotherton-ratcliffe *(Director)*, Janis Dartnell *(Manager)*, Drew Hoggatt *(Manager)*, Vinny Parekh *(Chief Financial Officer)*
**Finance:** J Dartnell *(Financial Director)*, Vinny Parekh *(Chief Financial Officer)*
**Marketing:** Trish Bambury *(Marketing Manager)*
**Sales:** Ramon Surrey *(Sales Manager)*
**US SIC:** 3999 **UK SIC:** 49590
**Auditors:** Humphrey & Co
**Bankers:** National Westminster Bank Plc (60-04-35)

| | 31-12-13 | 31-12-12 | 31-12-11 |
|---|---|---|---|
| TO | 23,245,136 | 20,659,483 | 17,188,406 |
| P/L | 1,444,160 | 1,000,204 | 340,866 |
| NW | 7,830,903 | 6,386,743 | 5,386,539 |
| WC | 8,560,396 | 3,780,650 | 3,185,626 |
| Emp. | 174 | 143 | 152 |

DUNS 21-675-4381

## Paxton Veterinary Clinics Ltd

30 Clifton Road, London SE25 6NJ
**Tel:** 02086533355
**Web:** www.paxtonvets.co.uk
**Reg No:** 7271614 **Estd:** 2010 Private Limited Company
**Line of Business:** Veterinary activities
**Issued Capital:** £100
**Director:** Miss H E Spencer
**Responsibilities**
**Senior:** Louisa Ellis *(Manager)*
**Branches:** Paxton Veterinary Clinics Ltd, 231 Gipsy Road, SE27 9QY Norwood

**US SIC:** 0741 **UK SIC:** 95601

| | 30-06-14 | 30-06-13 | 30-06-12 |
|---|---|---|---|
| TA | 747,351 | 746,781 | 695,087 |
| NW | (27,290) | (138,397) | (260,032) |
| WC | (65,555) | (174,419) | (302,291) |

DUNS 21-740-5422 **Exp**

## Paydens Ltd

(**Subsidiary of:** Paydens Group Holdings Ltd)
Parkwood, Sutton Road, Maidstone, Kent ME15 9NE
**Tel:** 01622-754977
**Web:** www.sangersmaidstone.co.uk
**Reg No:** 0574716 **VAT No:** 210713222
**Estd:** 1956 Private Limited Company
**Line of Business:** Chemists dispensing
**Export Markets:** Europe
**Issued Capital:** £1,623
**Principals:** D C Pay *(Chairman and Managing)*, Mrs R E Pay *(Financial)*, J P Mcconville
**Co. Secretary:** John Seal
**Branches:** Paydens Ltd, 98 High Street, Maidstone, Kent ME14 1SA
**US SIC:** 5912, 5999
**UK SIC:** 64300, 65600
**Auditors:** Crowe Clark Whitehill LLP
**Bankers:** National Westminster Bank Plc (53-81-51)

| | 31-03-14 | 31-03-13 | 31-03-12 |
|---|---|---|---|
| TO | 113,245,595 | 112,287,298 | 114,361,441 |
| P/L | 7,349,880 | 6,690,557 | 5,868,930 |
| NW | 66,444,393 | 60,822,827 | 54,720,312 |
| WC | 57,446,477 | 58,369,462 | 38,840,583 |
| Emp. | 1,428 | 1,290 | 1,421 |

DUNS 34-602-4607 **Imp**

## Paye Stonework & Restoration Ltd

(**Subsidiary of:** Paye Stonework Holdings Ltd)
Stationmasters House, Mottingham Station Approach, London SE9 4EL
**Tel:** 02088579111
**Web:** www.paye.net
**Reg No:** 2743908 **Estd:** 1992 Private Limited Company
**Line of Business:** Other construction work involving special trades
**Issued Capital:** £50,000
**Principals:** A P Paye *(Managing)*, G Staple, M J Kember, P P Newsam, R W Greer, D J Devon, P D Lloyd, A Mcneill
**Co. Secretary:** Martin Harvey
**Responsibilities**
**Sales:** David Manktelow *(Business Development Manager)*
**Admin:** Joanna Curtis *(Administrative Assistant)*, Karrie White *(Administrative Assistant)*
**US SIC:** 1799 **UK SIC:** 50000
**Auditors:** Horwath Clark Whitehill
**Bankers:** National Westminster Bank Plc (55-70-13)

| | 31-08-13 | 31-08-12 | 31-08-11 |
|---|---|---|---|
| TO | 22,112,871 | 24,071,517 | 18,024,188 |
| P/L | 438,518 | 31,421 | 69,992 |
| NW | 1,239,357 | 912,192 | 913,182 |
| WC | 2,183,722 | 1,677,020 | 1,666,230 |
| Emp. | 72 | 72 | 64 |

DUNS 21-141-2526

## Paymentsense Ltd

401 Westbourne Studios, 242 Acklam Road, London W10 5JJ
**Tel:** 08717161118
**Web:** www.paymentsense.co.uk
**Reg No:** 6730690 **Estd:** 2008 Private Limited Company
**Line of Business:** Financial intermediation not elsewhere classified
**Issued Capital:** £104
**Directors:** G V Karibian, J Rose, J S Farrarons
**US SIC:** 6111 **UK SIC:** 81501
**Bankers:** HSBC Bank plc (40-01-06)

| | 31-03-14 | 31-03-13 | 31-03-12 |
|---|---|---|---|
| TA | 2,701,755 | 2,380,270 | 1,505,962 |
| P/L | (1,473,365) | 38,924 | N/A |
| NW | (3,860,351) | (2,395,081) | (2,752,704) |
| WC | 804,498 | 1,114,217 | 418,442 |
| Emp. | 140 | 134 | N/A |

DUNS 34-581-8017

## Paymentshield Ltd

(**Subsidiary of:** Towergate Partnershipco Ltd)
Unit 3, Southport, Merseyside PR8 4HQ
**Tel:** 08456011050 **Fax:** 01704518848
**Web:** www.paymentshield.co.uk
**Reg No:** 2728936 **VAT No:** 618811436
**Estd:** 1992 Private Limited Company
**Line of Business:** Insurance brokers
**Issued Capital:** £1,000
**Directors:** S Egan, A D Lyons
**Co. Secretary:** Ms Jennifer Owens

**Responsibilities**
**Senior:** Samuel Clark (*Manager*), Nicola Gifford (*Manager*), Paul Jarman (*Customer Operations Director*), Dean Newton (*Customer Operations Director*)
**Finance:** Jane Waters (*Head of Finance*)
**Sales:** Ellie Bond (*Account Manager*), Jeni Hamilton (*Business Development Manager*), Jeni Law (*Account Manager*), Marc Orme (*Account Manager*)
**Health & Safety:** Tracey Brough (*Facilities Manager*)
**Facilities:** Tracey Brough (*Facilities Manager*)
**US SIC:** 6111 **UK SIC:** 81501
**Auditors:** KPMG Audit PLC
**Bankers:** National Westminster Bank Plc (52-10-23)

|     | 31-12-13 | 31-12-12 | 31-12-11 |
| --- | --- | --- | --- |
| TA | 257,867,772 | 191,706,593 | 162,268,801 |
| P/L | 41,785,049 | 43,508,114 | 36,250,862 |
| NW | 72,504,220 | 71,192,260 | 39,944,692 |
| WC | 55,368,126 | 63,745,905 | 39,932,715 |
| Emp. | 301 | 292 | 319 |

DUNS 77-920-6056
**Paymex Ltd**
8 St John Street, Manchester M3 4DU
**Tel:** 08456345802
**Web:** www.paymex.co.uk
**Reg No:** 5823633 **Estd:** 2006 Private Limited Company
**Line of Business:** Financial intermediation not elsewhere classified
**Issued Capital:** £12,170
**Directors:** S Brilus, T J O'Neill
**Co. Secretary:** Paul Nicholson
**US SIC:** 6111, 6711
**UK SIC:** 81501, 83962

|     | 31-12-13 | 31-12-12 | 31-12-11 |
| --- | --- | --- | --- |
| TA | 27,283,000 | 28,897,972 | 32,255,948 |
| P/L | (4,017,000) | (87,348) | 6,356,109 |
| NW | (20,147,000) | (18,520,469) | (19,892,871) |
| WC | (6,330,000) | (7,598,538) | (7,801,614) |
| Emp. | 300 | 295 | 369 |

DUNS 34-514-3643
**Paymill Motor Holdings Ltd**
20 Raby Street, Wolverhampton, West Midlands WV2 1AS
**Tel:** 01902457000
**Web:** www.benhamwolvesbmw.co.uk
**Reg No:** 5325212 **Estd:** 2005 Private Limited Company
**Line of Business:** Holding companies management activities
**Issued Capital:** £300,000
**Directors:** Mrs R E Mills, S J Mills, Mrs S J Payne
**Co. Secretary:** Nigel Payne
**US SIC:** 6711 **UK SIC:** 83962
**Bankers:** Barclays Bank Plc (20-07-71)

|     | 31-12-13 | 31-12-12 | 31-12-11 |
| --- | --- | --- | --- |
| TO | 48,381,180 | 49,835,863 | 41,230,209 |
| P/L | (61,001) | 254,310 | 91,740 |
| NW | 302,419 | 400,042 | 112,885 |
| WC | (2,161,516) | (1,145,489) | (612,160) |
| Emp. | 99 | 89 | 87 |

DUNS 23-557-8684
**Paynes Dairies Ltd**
Bar Lane Boroughbridge, Boroughbridge, York, North Yorkshire YO51 9NN
**Tel:** 01423-326058 **Fax:** 01423-325702
**Web:** www.paynesdairies.co.uk
**Reg No:** 3556170 **VAT No:** 698391176
**Estd:** 1993 Private Limited Company
**Line of Business:** Liquid milk and cream production
**Issued Capital:** £1,000
**Principals:** C A Payne (*Managing*), Ms E Payne, B Payne
**Co. Secretary:** Charles Payne
**US SIC:** 2026 **UK SIC:** 41301
**Auditors:** Lishman Sidwell Campbell & Price LLP

|     | 30-04-14 | 30-04-13 | 30-04-12 |
| --- | --- | --- | --- |
| TO | 103,235,440 | 87,118,680 | 74,964,771 |
| P/L | (464,249) | (429,379) | 478,608 |
| NW | 6,463,080 | 6,934,512 | 7,244,640 |
| WC | 2,527,667 | 3,354,298 | 3,820,722 |
| Emp. | 128 | N/A | 85 |

DUNS 21-814-6488
**Paynes Garages Ltd**
(**Subsidiary of:** Paynes Garage (Holdings) Ltd)
Watling Street, Hinckley, Hinckley, Leicestershire LE10 3ED
**Tel:** 01455237777
**Web:** www.paynes-garages.co.uk
**Reg No:** 0442329 **Estd:** 1911 Private Limited Company
**Line of Business:** Sale of new motor vehicles
**Issued Capital:** £75,000
**Directors:** M Grainger, N R Payne, J L Davey
**Co. Secretary:** Stuart Spalding
**Responsibilities**
**Senior:** Russell Astley (*Parts Manager*)

**Marketing:** Charles Harlock (*Marketing Manager*)
**Branches:** Paynes Garages Ltd, Bayton Rd Indstl Est, Coventry, West Midlands CV7 9FY
**US SIC:** 5511, 7539, 5531
**UK SIC:** 65100, 67100
**Auditors:** Farrar & Partners
**Bankers:** National Westminster Bank Plc (60-11-06)

|     | 31-12-13 | 31-12-12 | 31-12-11 |
| --- | --- | --- | --- |
| TO | 28,224,375 | 26,161,649 | 27,930,975 |
| P/L | 145,178 | 89,165 | (64,895) |
| NW | 2,652,297 | 2,541,796 | 2,457,055 |
| WC | 885,108 | 723,730 | 452,228 |
| Emp. | 106 | 114 | 120 |

DUNS 34-805-2457
**Paynes Heating Appliance Services Ltd.**
(**Subsidiary of:** Php Group Ltd)
Oak Tree Barn, Scaines Hill, Blackboys, Uckfield, East Sussex TN22 5JL
**Tel:** 01825891720
**Web:** www.paynesheatcentre.co.uk
**Reg No:** 2789960 **Estd:** 1993 Private Limited Company
**Line of Business:** Plumbers
**Issued Capital:** £110
**Directors:** S R Payne, F W Payne, A F Payne
**Co. Secretary:** Stephen Payne
**US SIC:** 1711 **UK SIC:** 50300
**Bankers:** National Westminster Bank Plc (60-22-05)

|     | 31-12-14 | 31-12-13 | 31-12-12 |
| --- | --- | --- | --- |
| TA | 110 | 110 | 139 |
| NW | 110 | 110 | 110 |
| WC | N/A | N/A | 110 |

DUNS 23-407-7811
**Paypal (Uk) Ltd**
(**Subsidiary of:** Ebay Inc.)
Hotham House, 1 Heron Square, Richmond, Surrey TW9 1EJ
**Tel:** 02084392000
**Web:** www.paypal.com
**Reg No:** 5468033 **Estd:** 2005 Private Limited Company
**Line of Business:** Management and business consultants
**Issued Capital:** £1
**Directors:** N P Staheyeff, C A Mclean
**Co. Secretary:** Taylor Wessing Secretaries Limit
**US SIC:** 7392 **UK SIC:** 83951
**Auditors:** PricewaterhouseCoopers LLP

|     | 31-12-13 | 31-12-12 | 31-12-11 |
| --- | --- | --- | --- |
| TO | 25,504,697 | 27,253,260 | 19,214,606 |
| P/L | 3,235,016 | 4,339,805 | 1,229,420 |
| NW | 5,811,655 | 4,289,937 | 3,090,648 |
| WC | 5,641,993 | 4,140,473 | 2,937,152 |
| Emp. | 128 | 139 | 106 |

DUNS 77-488-8770
**Paypoint Network Ltd**
(**Subsidiary of:** Paypoint Plc)
Unit 1, Welwyn Garden City, Hertfordshire AL7 1EL
**Tel:** 07814504855 **Fax:** 01707-660333
**Web:** www.paypoint.co.uk
**Reg No:** 2973115 **Estd:** 1996 Private Limited Company
**Line of Business:** Other business activities not elsewhere classified
**Issued Capital:** £100,000
**Directors:** G W Earle, T D Watkin Rees, D C Von Trotha Taylor
**Co. Secretary:** Ms Susan Court
**Responsibilities**
**Senior:** Dominic Taylor (*Manager*)
**Marketing:** Hugh Arnott (*Marketing Manager*)
**Health & Safety:** Stewart Hendry (*Facilities Manager*)
**Facilities:** Stewart Hendry (*Facilities Manager*)
**US SIC:** 7399 **UK SIC:** 83954
**Auditors:** Deloitte & Touche
**Bankers:** Barclays Bank Plc (20-00-00)

|     | 31-03-14 | 31-03-13 | 25-03-12 |
| --- | --- | --- | --- |
| TO | 71,468,347 | 69,205,153 | 56,791,556 |
| P/L | 12,990,585 | 16,657,707 | 18,244,460 |
| NW | 36,805,335 | 25,144,842 | 15,138,330 |
| WC | 19,877,326 | 12,565,805 | 3,214,044 |
| Emp. | 379 | 342 | 296 |

DUNS 23-583-8542
**Paypoint Plc**
1 The Boulevard, Welwyn Garden City, Hertfordshire AL7 1EL
**Fax:** 01707-600-333
**Web:** www.paypoint.co.uk
**Reg No:** 3581541 **Estd:** 1998 Public Limited Company
**Line of Business:** Representative office
**Export Sales:** £43,977,000
**Issued Capital:** £226,293
**Principals:** D C Von Trotha Taylor (*Managing*), G W Earle, W G Tucker, E E Anstee, S P Rowley, N W Wiles, N A Carson, D J Morrison

**Co. Secretary:** Ms Susan Court
**Responsibilities**
**Senior:** Robin Bevan (*CEO PayByPhone*), Michael Norton (*Manager*), Seamus Smith (*Manager*), Dominic Taylor (*Chief Executive*)
**Marketing:** Tarli Cameron (*Marketing Communication Execut*), Suzanne Dewar-Smith (*Marketing Executive - Retail B*), Rob Fernandes (*Director of Products & Strateg*), Caroline Knight (*?Retail Marketing Manager*), Steve O'Neill (*Marketing Manager*), Dan Salmons (*Managing Director, E&M Commerc*), Jan Tebb (*Communications Executive*), Lesley Thomas (*In-House Marketing Design Exec*)
**Sales:** Simon Lambert (*Account Manager*)
**IT:** James Gupwell (*Group Head of IT Operations*), Jon Marchant (*Chief Information Officer*), Jay Payne (*IT / MIS Director*)
**HR:** Margaret Tamcken (*Human Resources Manager*)
**Health & Safety:** Margaret Tamcken (*Human Resources Manager*)
**Operations:** James Neesom (*UK Product and Operations Mana*)
**US SIC:** 7399 **UK SIC:** 83954
**Auditors:** Deloitte LLP

|     | 31-03-14 | 31-03-13 | 25-03-12 |
| --- | --- | --- | --- |
| TO | 212,158,000 | 208,526,000 | 200,029,000 |
| P/L | 46,008,000 | 41,267,000 | 37,201,000 |
| NW | 39,729,000 | 44,773,000 | 33,062,000 |
| WC | 14,848,000 | 24,422,000 | 16,626,000 |
| Emp. | 687 | 620 | 580 |

DUNS 21-722-4200
**Paystream My Max Holdings Ltd**
Mansion House, Manchester Road, Altrincham, Cheshire WA14 4RW
**Tel:** 08001976516
**Reg No:** 7598949 **Estd:** 2011 Private Limited Company
**Line of Business:** Management activities of other non-financial holding companies not elsewhere classified
**Issued Capital:** £2,714,823
**Directors:** J A Ball, P Malley, A Reeves
**Co. Secretary:** Miss Davina Heap
**US SIC:** 6711 **UK SIC:** 83962

|     | 31-03-14 | 31-03-13 | 31-03-12 |
| --- | --- | --- | --- |
| TO | 161,842,314 | 111,415,950 | 77,980,309 |
| P/L | 2,754,199 | 1,918,709 | 1,333,796 |
| NW | 1,596,963 | 549,457 | (912,190) |
| WC | 1,423,212 | 364,887 | (1,088,614) |
| Emp. | 4,151 | 3,100 | 2,411 |

DUNS 52-007-8742
**Paywizard Group Plc**
Chapelton Drive Cluny Court, Kirkcaldy, Fife KY2 6QJ
**Tel:** 08448557000 **Fax:** 0870-840-7001
**Web:** www.paywizard.com
**Reg No:** 0175703SC **Estd:** 1997 Public Limited Company
**Line of Business:** Call centres
**Trading Style:** Paywizard Plc
**Issued Capital:** £305,672
**Principals:** R Millar (*Managing*), J Guthrie (*Managing*), G A Jones, J G Mackinlay, P G Freeman, D J Morrison
**Co. Secretary:** Gordon Tainton
**Responsibilities**
**Senior:** Debbie Leishman (*Chief Operating Officer - Serv*)
**Finance:** Graeme Downie (*Finance Controller*), Chris Trueman (*Director of Financial Operatio*)
**Marketing:** Ann-Louise Buick (*Marketing Manager*)
**HR:** Moira Brown (*Human Resources Director*), Paul Hastie (*Training Manager*)
**Health & Safety:** Ken McFarlene (*Facilities Manager*)
**Facilities:** Ken McFarlene (*Facilities Manager*)
**Operations:** Debbie Leishman (*Chief Operating Officer - Serv*)
**US SIC:** 7399 **UK SIC:** 83954
**Auditors:** Ernst & Young LLP
**Bankers:** The Royal Bank Of Scotland Plc (83-00-01)

|     | 31-12-13 | 31-12-12 | 31-12-11 |
| --- | --- | --- | --- |
| TO | 9,047,056 | 13,745,106 | 15,357,823 |
| P/L | (1,727,633) | (2,089,101) | (3,267,573) |
| NW | 280,441 | 2,351,363 | 4,400,145 |
| WC | 1,641,367 | 1,131,126 | 1,652,479 |
| Emp. | 400 | 661 | 752 |

DUNS 49-123-3326
**Payzone Uk Ltd**
(**Subsidiary of:** Hm Treasury)
Davidson House, Northwich, Cheshire CW9 7TW
**Tel:** 01606333338 **Fax:** 01383648199
**Web:** www.payzone.co.uk
**Reg No:** 3102137 **Estd:** 2003 Private Limited Company
**Line of Business:** Business and management consultancy activities not elsewhere classified
**Issued Capital:** £2,478,212

**Directors:** Ms M M Turrell, M J Maloney, J G Rothwell
**Co. Secretary:** Ms Brenda Hogan
**Responsibilities**
**Senior:** John Hutchison (*Partner*)
**Branches:** Payzone Uk Ltd, Davidson House, Gadbrook Park, Northwich, Cheshire CW9 7TW
**US SIC:** 7392 **UK SIC:** 83951
**Auditors:** PricewaterhouseCoopers
**Bankers:** Lloyds TSB Bank plc (30-99-93)

|     | 30-09-13 | 30-09-12 | 30-09-11 |
| --- | --- | --- | --- |
| TO | 23,031,579 | 24,843,105 | 28,850,624 |
| P/L | (1,071,216) | (2,667,989) | (171,404) |
| NW | (12,429,618) | (11,366,929) | (7,920,479) |
| WC | (14,992,378) | (13,425,218) | (9,433,357) |
| Emp. | 186 | 182 | 144 |

DUNS 29-201-1814    Exp
**Pb Ltd**
(**Subsidiary of:** Balfour Beatty Plc)
Westbrook Mills, Borough Road, Godalming, Surrey GU7 2AZ
**Tel:** 01483528400 **Fax:** 01483-425136
**Web:** www.pbworld.com
**Reg No:** 0656314 **Estd:** 1889 Private Limited Company
**Line of Business:** Architectural services
**Export Markets:** Middle East; Far East; Australia; Africa; Europe; West Indies; America
**Issued Capital:** £8,138,878
**Directors:** S D Bingham, S J Reffitt
**Co. Secretary:** Nikolas Weston
**Responsibilities**
**Operations:** John Craigen (*Environmental Manager*)
**Branches:** Pb Ltd, Queen Victoria House, Redland Hill, Bristol, Avon BS6 6US
**US SIC:** 8911 **UK SIC:** 83701
**Auditors:** Deloitte LLP
**Bankers:** HSBC Bank plc (40-22-12)

|     | 31-12-13 | 31-12-12 | 31-12-11 |
| --- | --- | --- | --- |
| TO | 6,453,000 | 60,187,000 | 68,304,000 |
| P/L | (23,000) | (10,049,000) | (1,243,000) |
| NW | (35,491,000) | (24,940,000) | (12,140,000) |
| WC | 4,848,000 | 4,436,000 | 17,071,000 |
| Emp. | 446 | 1,113 | 1,499 |

DUNS 23-013-5910
**Pbdfm Ltd**
51a Forkhill Road, Newry, Co Down BT35 8QY
**Tel:** 02841753629
**Web:** www.spar.co.uk
**Reg No:** 0036976NI **Estd:** 1999 Private Limited Company
**Line of Business:** Convenience stores
**Trading Style:** Eurospar
**Issued Capital:** £100
**Directors:** D Mcveigh, Ms P Mclarnon, B Mcveigh
**Co. Secretary:** Mrs Frances Mcveigh
**US SIC:** 5411 **UK SIC:** 64100
**Auditors:** Daly Park & Co

|     | 31-12-13 | 31-12-12 | 31-12-11 |
| --- | --- | --- | --- |
| TA | 633,955 | 743,849 | 786,310 |
| NW | 395,600 | 322,690 | 303,487 |
| WC | 87,519 | 157,649 | 141,423 |

DUNS 57-032-0556
**P.B.P. Services Ltd**
85-87 Bayham Street, London NW1 0AG
**Tel:** 020-7099-9113
**Web:** www.pbp-services.com
**Reg No:** 2872813 **VAT No:** 629611629
**Estd:** 1993 Private Limited Company
**Line of Business:** Commercial premises cleaning
**Issued Capital:** £2
**Director:** G J Pollock
**Responsibilities**
**Senior:** Paola Pollock (*Founder and Managing Director*)
**US SIC:** 7349 **UK SIC:** 92300

|     | 30-04-14 | 30-04-13 | 30-04-12 |
| --- | --- | --- | --- |
| TA | 260,589 | 316,373 | 304,921 |
| NW | 122,890 | 139,716 | 102,049 |
| WC | 119,457 | 135,834 | 109,637 |

DUNS 29-767-1190    Imp-Exp
**Pbsi Group Ltd**
Belle Vue Works, Boundary Street, Manchester M12 5NG
**Tel:** 01612306363
**Web:** www.pbeng.co.uk
**Reg No:** 2030212 **VAT No:** 519549907
**Estd:** 1986 Private Limited Company
**Line of Business:** Manufacturers and wholesalers of electrical products
**Export Markets:** worldwide
**Export Sales:** £1,863,785
**Trading Style:** P & B Weir Electrical, P & B Engineering, P & B Power Engineering, P & B Technical Services
**Issued Capital:** £446,058
**Principals:** H A Corbin (*Chairman*), N A Whitbread (*Managing*), Mr Tony Harris, D Hampson
**Co. Secretary:** Ms Anne Denton

**Responsibilities**
**Senior:** L Whitbread (Proprietor)
**Marketing:** Phil York (Business & Development Manager)
**Sales:** Phil York (Business & Development Manager)
**Admin:** Julie Beaumont (Office Manager)
**IT:** Terence Andrews (IT Manager)
**HR:** Julie Beaumont (Office Manager)
**Facilities:** Phil York (Business & Development Manager)
**Purchasing:** Dawn Jones (Buyer)
**Branches:** Pbsi Group Ltd, Unit 1, Leafield Way, Corsham, Wiltshire SN13 9SW
**US SIC:** 3643, 3629
**UK SIC:** 34203, 34350
**Auditors:** UHY Hacker Young
**Bankers:** National Westminster Bank Plc (01-10-01)

|     | 30-06-13 | 30-06-12 | 30-06-11 |
|-----|----------|----------|----------|
| TO  | 8,264,143 | 6,549,796 | 6,373,038 |
| P/L | 1,043,133 | 90,069 | (148,361) |
| NW  | 4,785,637 | 4,030,276 | 3,995,302 |
| WC  | 2,456,028 | 2,009,412 | 2,437,022 |
| Emp.| 105 | 113 | 113 |

DUNS 29-165-1677     Imp-Exp
## P.B.T. International Ltd
Haydon Drove, Wells, Somerset BA5 3EH
**Tel:** 01749685686 **Fax:** 01749-834834
**Web:** www.pbtigroup.com
**Reg No:** 1805267 **VAT No:** 416701473
**Estd:** 1984 Private Limited Company
**Line of Business:** Printing not elsewhere classified
**Export Markets:** Europe
**Export Sales:** £435,783
**Trading Style:** Pbti Electronic Imaging Products, Xinia Imaging Supplies
**Issued Capital:** £100
**Principals:** P B Thompson (Managing), J S Thompson, J P Thompson, Mrs P A Price, G V Thompson, B Agar
**Co. Secretary:** Mrs Edith Thompson
**Responsibilities**
**Senior:** Rory Thompson (Senior Marketing Executive)
**Marketing:** Rory Thompson (Senior Marketing Executive)
**IT:** Jordan Fey (IT Manager)
**Purchasing:** Robert Braodwater (Purchasing Manager)
**US SIC:** 7399 **UK SIC:** 83954
**Auditors:** Chalmers & Co
**Bankers:** National Westminster Bank Plc (60-14-24)

|     | 30-06-14 | 30-06-13 | 30-06-12 |
|-----|----------|----------|----------|
| TO  | 4,376,495 | 4,621,296 | 5,019,678 |
| P/L | (232,225) | (80,670) | 120,202 |
| NW  | 1,309,375 | 1,632,443 | 1,691,389 |
| WC  | (260,729) | 182,965 | 394,366 |
| Emp.| 66 | 65 | 59 |

DUNS 21-716-0027     Imp-Exp
## P.C. Henderson Ltd
(**Subsidiary of:** Assa Abloy Ab)
Unit 1 Durham Road, Durham, County Durham DH6 5NG
**Tel:** 01913770701
**Web:** www.pchenderson.com
**Reg No:** 1188468 **VAT No:** 246297537
**Estd:** 1921 Private Limited Company
**Line of Business:** Manufacture of locks and hinges
**Export Markets:** E U, Australasia, Caribbean.
**Export Sales:** £7,019,792
**Trading Style:** Henderson
**Issued Capital:** £6,525,000
**Directors:** R Gurney, M Wilson, J R Vargues Huerta, P O Hansson, F W Pickard
**Co. Secretary:** Duncan Moncrieff
**Responsibilities**
**Senior:** Ake Bengtsson (Manager), Ove Bergkvist (Manager)
**Finance:** Stephaine Clark (Financial Controller)
**Marketing:** Kerry Baker (Marketing Manager)
**Sales:** Andrew Royle (Commercial Director)
**IT:** Dave Quickmire (Quality Manager)
**HR:** Victoria Hayes (Personnel Manager)
**Health & Safety:** Victoria Hayes (Personnel Manager)
**Operations:** Dave Quickmire (Quality Manager)
**Branches:** P.c. Henderson Ltd, Lyndale Estate, Grays, Essex RM20 3DR
**US SIC:** 3429 **UK SIC:** 31694
**Auditors:** Ernst & Young LLP
**Bankers:** National Westminster Bank Plc (56-00-09)

|     | 31-12-13 | 31-12-12 | 31-12-11 |
|-----|----------|----------|----------|
| TO  | 8,496,581 | 7,849,126 | 8,234,685 |
| P/L | 811,507 | 600,551 | 950,330 |
| NW  | 546,437 | 129,930 | 1,095,379 |
| WC  | 2,677,303 | 2,201,932 | 1,758,215 |
| Emp.| 75 | 75 | 75 |

DUNS 21-888-2504
## P.C. Howard Ltd
Kings Cliffe, Peterborough, Cambridgeshire PE8 6XX
**Tel:** 01780-444444
**Web:** www.pchoward.com
**Reg No:** 0496076 **Estd:** 1951 Private Limited Company
**Line of Business:** Other supporting land transport activities
**Issued Capital:** £2,377,434
**Principals:** A P Howard (Financial), A F Howard, P C Howard
**Co. Secretary:** Percival Howard
**Responsibilities**
**Senior:** Roy Howard (Manager), Bernard Howard (Manager)
**Branches:** P.c. Howard Ltd, Crucible Road, Corby, Northamptonshire NN17 5TS
**US SIC:** 4213, 4226
**UK SIC:** 72300, 77003
**Auditors:** Stephenson Smart & Co
**Bankers:** Lloyds TSB Bank plc (30-98-02)

|     | 31-03-14 | 31-03-13 | 31-03-12 |
|-----|----------|----------|----------|
| TO  | 17,518,387 | 15,951,247 | 14,477,554 |
| P/L | 332,104 | 121,204 | 379,108 |
| NW  | 5,677,149 | 5,490,813 | 5,478,627 |
| WC  | 482,444 | 241,322 | 554,797 |
| Emp.| 182 | 177 | 169 |

DUNS 22-350-9543
## P.C McQueenie Builders
Catchpell House, 5 Carpet Lane, Edinburgh, Midlothian EH6 6SS
**Tel:** 01314687061
**Estd:** 1998 Proprietorship
**Line of Business:** Building services
**Proprietor:** P Mcqueenie
**Responsibilities**
**Senior:** P McQueenie (Proprietor)
**US SIC:** 1622 **UK SIC:** 50200
**Employees:** 50

DUNS 42-349-4850
## Pc-Pos (U K) Ltd
(**Subsidiary of:** Digipos Store Solutions (Holdings) Ltd)
Unit 1 Beachwood, Basingstoke, Hampshire RG24 8WA
**Web:** www.pc-pos.co.uk
**Reg No:** 4337189 **Estd:** 1995 Private Limited Company
**Line of Business:** Other computer related activities
**Issued Capital:** £100,000
**Directors:** T G Bouzac, O C Archer
**Co. Secretary:** Richard Warwick-Saunders
**Responsibilities**
**Senior:** David Gibbon (Manager)
**Finance:** David Gibbon (Manager)
**Sales:** Barry Daniel (Sales Manager)
**US SIC:** 7379 **UK SIC:** 83940

|     | 30-09-13 | 30-09-12 | 29-09-12 |
|-----|----------|----------|----------|
| TA  | 100,000 | 100,000 | 100,000 |
| NW  | 100,000 | 100,000 | 100,000 |

DUNS 51-647-8927
## Pcj Solicitors Ltd
4th Floor, 2 Moorfields, Liverpool, Merseyside L2 2BS
**Tel:** 0151-236-6400 **Fax:** 01512364545
**Web:** www.pcjs.co.uk
**Reg No:** 5964692 **Estd:** 1999 Private Limited Company
**Line of Business:** Solicitors
**Issued Capital:** £101
**Director:** D Lloyd
**Co. Secretary:** Jason Lee
**US SIC:** 8111 **UK SIC:** 83500
**Bankers:** HSBC Bank plc (40-29-05)

|     | 30-04-13 | 30-04-12 | 30-04-11 |
|-----|----------|----------|----------|
| TO  | 5,376,431 | N/A | N/A |
| P/L | 261,341 | N/A | N/A |
| NW  | (967,548) | (3,066,513) | (4,114,654) |
| WC  | 97,735 | (1,451,366) | 225,820 |
| Emp.| 77 | N/A | N/A |

DUNS 29-887-8208
## P.C.L. Security Ltd
P C L House, 20-22 Belmont Road, Wallington, Surrey SM6 8TB
**Tel:** 020-8773-3133 **Fax:** 020-8773-3184
**Web:** www.kingdomsecurity.co.uk
**Reg No:** 2090782 **VAT No:** 452165659
**Estd:** 2011 Private Limited Company
**Line of Business:** Security activities
**Trading Style:** Kingdom Security
**Issued Capital:** £54,000
**Director:** P J Cullen
**Co. Secretary:** Robert Cullen
**Responsibilities**
**Senior:** Tracey Boult (Operations), Ian Holden (Manager)
**HR:** Ian Holden (Manager)
**Operations:** Tracey Boult (Operations)
**Branches:** P.c.l. Security Ltd, 55 High Holborn, London WC1V 6DX
**US SIC:** 7393 **UK SIC:** 83954
**Auditors:** Hilton Sharp & Clarke

**Bankers:** Barclays Bank Plc (20-24-61)

|     | 31-03-13 | 31-03-12 | 31-03-11 |
|-----|----------|----------|----------|
| TO  | 13,531,106 | 13,349,221 | 13,096,805 |
| P/L | 284,558 | 392,387 | 22,950 |
| NW  | 953,438 | 974,641 | 891,959 |
| WC  | 936,198 | 932,617 | 834,541 |
| Emp.| 515 | 773 | 751 |

DUNS 50-566-7436     Exp
## Pcme Ltd
Clearview Building, Edison Road, St Ives, Cambridgeshire PE27 3GH
**Tel:** 01480468200 **Fax:** 01480463400
**Web:** www.pcme.co.uk
**Reg No:** 2514486 **Estd:** 1990 Private Limited Company
**Line of Business:** Other manufacturing not elsewhere classified
**Export Markets:** Worldwide
**Issued Capital:** £44,207
**Directors:** C Chevillion, J Gallucci
**Co. Secretary:** William Averdieck
**Responsibilities**
**Senior:** Fran?s Gourdon (Director), St?ane Kempenar (Director), Roger Millington (Health & Safety Officer)
**Marketing:** Linda Furnell (Office Manager)
**Admin:** Linda Furnell (Office Manager)
**HR:** Linda Furnell (Office Manager)
**Health & Safety:** Roger Millington (Health & Safety Officer)
**Facilities:** Mike Hill (Service Manager)
**Branches:** Pcme Ltd, 17 Percy Gdns, Whitley Bay, Tyne and Wear NE25 8RF
**US SIC:** 3999 **UK SIC:** 49590
**Auditors:** Rawlinsons
**Bankers:** Barclays Bank Plc (20-45-77)

|     | 31-03-14 | 31-03-13 | 31-03-12 |
|-----|----------|----------|----------|
| TO  | 5,679,599 | N/A | N/A |
| P/L | 560,918 | N/A | N/A |
| NW  | 3,137,945 | 2,761,302 | 2,546,995 |
| WC  | 2,917,134 | 2,594,003 | 2,369,575 |
| Emp.| 52 | N/A | N/A |

DUNS 29-096-3917     Imp
## The Pcms Group Plc
(**Subsidiary of:** Pcms Holdings (International) Ltd)
P C M S House, Torwood Close, Westwood Business Park, Coventry, West Midlands CV4 8HX
**Tel:** 024-7669-4455 **Fax:** 024-7642-1390
**Web:** www.pcmsgroup.com
**Reg No:** 1459419 **VAT No:** 705338743
**Estd:** 1982 Public Limited Company
**Line of Business:** Hardware consultancy
**Export Sales:** £7,329,909
**Issued Capital:** £50,000
**Principals:** R A Smith (Managing), J Court, P R Smith, G Mclauchlan, R Goodall
**Co. Secretary:** Mrs Brenda Smith
**Responsibilities**
**HR:** Elaine Rowlands (Human Resources Manager)
**US SIC:** 7379 **UK SIC:** 83940
**Auditors:** Ernst & Young LLP
**Bankers:** Barclays Bank Plc (20-23-55)

|     | 30-09-13 | 30-09-12 | 30-09-11 |
|-----|----------|----------|----------|
| TO  | 26,700,763 | 28,443,618 | 30,664,502 |
| P/L | 4,545,629 | 8,046,904 | 7,105,883 |
| NW  | 21,719,980 | 23,257,197 | 21,260,014 |
| WC  | 20,809,363 | 22,456,337 | 20,507,890 |
| Emp.| 291 | 283 | 252 |

DUNS 36-484-9864
## Pco
36 Whitehall, London SW1A 2AY
**Tel:** 02072106611
**Web:** www.cabinetoffice.gov.uk
**Proprietorship**
**Line of Business:** Central government
**Proprietor:** Ms J Gilhooly
**Responsibilities**
**Senior:** Jim Barron (Chief Executive)
**US SIC:** 9121 **UK SIC:** 91110
**Employees:** 80

DUNS 21-230-9090     Exp
## P.C.Richardson & Co.(Middlesbrough) Ltd
(**Subsidiary of:** Pcr Holdings Ltd)
Courville House, 34 Ellerbeck Court, Stokesley Business Park, Stokesley, Middlesbrough, Cleveland TS9 5PT
**Web:** www.pcrichardson.co.uk
**Reg No:** 0196308 **VAT No:** 258515737
**Estd:** 1918 Private Limited Company
**Line of Business:** Other construction work involving special trades
**Export Markets:** Gibralta, Belgium, W Europe
**Export Sales:** £782,030
**Issued Capital:** £44,032
**Principals:** J F Richardson (Chairman), P C Richardson (Managing), Mrs T B Richardson, D J Richardson, G Ablett
**Co. Secretary:** Paul Flintoft

**Branches:** P.c.richardson & Co.(Middlesbrough) Ltd, Construction Site Office, B546.1 Selafield Wks, Seascale, Cumbria CA20 1PG
**US SIC:** 1799 **UK SIC:** 50000
**Auditors:** Gilchrist Tash
**Bankers:** HSBC Bank plc (40-33-01)

|     | 31-03-14 | 31-03-13 | 31-03-12 |
|-----|----------|----------|----------|
| TO  | 5,493,456 | 5,569,754 | 5,904,356 |
| P/L | 380,458 | 415,296 | 155,956 |
| NW  | 3,093,657 | 2,899,191 | 2,652,069 |
| WC  | 2,920,033 | 2,725,341 | 2,446,066 |
| Emp.| 59 | 61 | 71 |

DUNS 23-724-2144
## Pcs Business Systems Ltd
(**Subsidiary of:** Pcs Business Systems Holdings Ltd)
Unit 2 Northfield Point, Cunliffe Drive, Kettering, Northamptonshire NN16 9QJ
**Tel:** 0845-241-4155 **Fax:** 0845-241-4154
**Web:** www.pcs-systems.com
**Reg No:** 3082062 **VAT No:** 650773431
**Estd:** 1995 Private Limited Company
**Line of Business:** Maintenance and repair of office, accounting and computing machinery
**Export Sales:** £1,285,024
**Issued Capital:** £100
**Director:** Mrs L M Morrissey
**Co. Secretary:** Mrs Lynda Morrissey
**Responsibilities**
**Senior:** Steven Cream (Managing Director)
**Marketing:** Stuart Knott (Sales & Marketing Manager)
**Sales:** Stuart Knott (Sales & Marketing Manager)
**IT:** Stuart Knott (Sales & Marketing Manager)
**US SIC:** 7379 **UK SIC:** 83940
**Auditors:** Meadows & Co
**Bankers:** Lloyds TSB Bank plc (30-99-26)

|     | 31-05-14 | 31-05-13 | 31-05-12 |
|-----|----------|----------|----------|
| TO  | 25,711,954 | 20,337,871 | 20,350,701 |
| P/L | 975,730 | 1,093,032 | 1,121,101 |
| NW  | 2,643,130 | 2,473,692 | 1,935,631 |
| WC  | 2,294,419 | 2,132,552 | 1,616,972 |
| Emp.| 69 | 60 | 54 |

DUNS 21-386-6187
## Pcs Technical Services
70 Church Road, Aston, Birmingham, West Midlands B6 5TY
**Tel:** 01212121234
**Web:** www.taalus.co.uk
**Estd:** 2002 Partnership
**Line of Business:** Printing not elsewhere classified
**Trading Style:** Taalus Technical Solutions
**Partners:** J Gray, S Potter, L James, Ms C Gregory, S Corlis, I Hixon, I Horne
**Responsibilities**
**Senior:** Richard Makowski (Manager)
**HR:** Elaine Murphy (HR Manager)
**US SIC:** 2752 **UK SIC:** 47544
**Employees:** 70

DUNS 34-774-9256
## Pct Automotive Ltd
(**Subsidiary of:** Pct Holdings Ltd)
Holbrook Industrial Estate, Holbrook, Holbrook, Sheffield, South Yorkshire S20 3GH
**Tel:** 08451231111
**Web:** www.pctautomotive.com
**Reg No:** 5575830 **Estd:** 1926 Private Limited Company
**Line of Business:** Towing bars fitting and supply
**Issued Capital:** £2
**Directors:** J I Harding-Terry, P I Terry
**Co. Secretary:** Ms Judith Mccoy
**US SIC:** 7539 **UK SIC:** 67100

|     | 31-10-13 | 31-10-12 | 31-10-11 |
|-----|----------|----------|----------|
| TA  | 2 | 2 | 2 |
| NW  | 2 | 2 | 2 |

DUNS 22-900-1888     Imp-Exp
## Pct Group Sales Ltd
(**Subsidiary of:** Oakenash Group Ltd)
Etc Welding Ltd, Glasgow, Lanarkshire G15 8TE
**Tel:** 01419444000
**Web:** www.pctgroup.co.uk
**Reg No:** 0075642SC **Estd:** 1970 Private Limited Company
**Line of Business:** Lifting equipment
**Export Markets:** Middle East, E U, Canada, Korea
**Export Sales:** £9,389,372
**Trading Style:** Kings Hoists, Matterson Cranes, Procuts
**Issued Capital:** £1,041,666
**Principals:** W S Wilson (Chairman), P R Agnew (Managing), W N Agnew, B H Lemond
**Co. Secretary:** Laurence Grainger
**Responsibilities**
**IT:** Steve Messenger (IT Manager)
**Health & Safety:** Allan Mcdougall (Quality Manager)
**Facilities:** John Deatcher (Works Manager)

**Operations:** Allan Mcdougall *(Quality Manager)*
**Engineering:** John Deatcher *(Works Manager)*
**Branches:** Pct Group Sales Ltd, 45 Regent Street, Rochdale, Lancashire OL12 0HQ
**US SIC:** 3534 **UK SIC:** 32553
**Auditors:** Campbell Dallas LLP
**Bankers:** Bank Of Scotland (80-54-01)

| | 31-12-13 | 31-12-12 | 31-12-11 |
|---|---|---|---|
| TO | 12,168,077 | 11,734,566 | 11,289,138 |
| P/L | 602,098 | 426,989 | 520,653 |
| NW | 4,854,529 | 4,450,787 | 4,276,139 |
| WC | 3,668,183 | 3,472,273 | 3,316,800 |
| Emp. | 90 | 87 | 82 |

DUNS 29-157-2246
## Pct Healthcare Ltd
(**Subsidiary of:** Pct Healthcare (Holdings) Ltd)
Sycamore House, Smeckley Wood Close, Chesterfield, Derbyshire S41 9PZ
**Tel:** 01246-450470
**Web:** www.peakpharmacy.co.uk
**Reg No:** 1768840 **VAT No:** 405747256
**Estd:** 1983 Private Limited Company
**Line of Business:** Dispensing chemists
**Trading Style:** Peak Pharmacy, Market Street Pharmacy, Parks Pharmacy
**Issued Capital:** £263,006
**Principals:** P Cattee *(Managing)*, G A Tims
**Co. Secretary:** Mrs Angela Cattee
**Branches:** Pct Healthcare Ltd, 5 Edinburgh Court, Chesterfield, Derbyshire S42 6SH
**US SIC:** 5912, 4226
**UK SIC:** 64300, 77003
**Auditors:** Abrams Ashton
**Bankers:** National Westminster Bank Plc (60-40-09)

| | 30-11-13 | 30-11-12 | 30-11-11 |
|---|---|---|---|
| TO | 51,346,265 | 50,530,154 | 52,865,925 |
| P/L | 1,292,523 | 3,610,420 | 1,684,045 |
| NW | (3,013,592) | (1,564,153) | (6,377,593) |
| WC | (4,003,259) | (266,471) | (3,268,121) |
| Emp. | 495 | 431 | 425 |

DUNS 42-477-5711
## Pd & Ms Energy (Aberdeen) Ltd
(**Subsidiary of:** Pd & Ms Holdings Ltd)
Atholl House, Aberdeen, Aberdeenshire AB11 6LT
**Tel:** 01224282900 **Fax:** 01224581386
**Web:** www.pdmsenergy.com
**Reg No:** 0233070SC **Estd:** 2002 Private Limited Company
**Line of Business:** Oil and gas exploration services
**Export Sales:** £12,163,703
**Issued Capital:** £100
**Directors:** S Rio, J K Pearce, M Lunney, N Murray, R P Smeaton, D J Mackay, F Herlihy
**Co. Secretary:** Francis Herlihy
**US SIC:** 8911, 7399
**UK SIC:** 83701, 83954

| | 30-06-13 | 30-06-12 | 30-06-11 |
|---|---|---|---|
| TO | 47,032,515 | 32,084,644 | 29,404,725 |
| P/L | 4,506,795 | 2,202,939 | 3,528,222 |
| NW | 6,584,017 | 11,567,868 | 9,924,043 |
| WC | 5,840,637 | 10,926,946 | 9,470,081 |
| Emp. | 60 | 50 | 47 |

DUNS 23-638-6277
## Pd Edenhall Ltd
(**Subsidiary of:** Pd Edenhall Holdings Ltd)
Dan-Y-Graig, Newport, Gwent NP11 6DP
**Tel:** 01633-612671
**Web:** http://pd-edenhall.co.uk
**Reg No:** 3635485 **Estd:** 1998 Private Limited Company
**Line of Business:** Manufacturers of bricks
**Issued Capital:** £153,846
**Principals:** A P Cotton *(Managing)*, G Mounfield *(Financial)*
**Responsibilities**
**IT:** Anne-Marie Jenkins *(IT Coordinator)*
**Health & Safety:** Peter Stokes *(Operations Manager)*
**Operations:** Peter Stokes *(Operations Manager)*
**Branches:** Pd Edenhall Ltd, Blencowe Quarry, Penrith, Cumbria CA11 0DE
**US SIC:** 3251, 3271
**UK SIC:** 24100, 24370
**Bankers:** Lloyds TSB Bank plc (30-00-01)

| | 31-12-13 | 31-12-12 | 31-12-11 |
|---|---|---|---|
| TO | 17,872,000 | 15,337,000 | 15,542,000 |
| P/L | 395,000 | 368,000 | 101,000 |
| NW | 1,975,000 | 1,588,000 | 1,032,000 |
| WC | (1,422,000) | (1,115,000) | (1,707,000) |
| Emp. | 161 | 143 | 132 |

DUNS 22-161-2265
## Pd Portco Ltd
(**Subsidiary of:** Brookfield Asset Management Inc)
17-27 Queens Square, Middlesbrough, Cleveland TS2 1AH
**Tel:** 01642-877000 **Fax:** 01642-877056
**Web:** www.pdports.co.uk
**Reg No:** 4179797 **Estd:** 2001 Private Limited Company
**Line of Business:** Management activities of holding companies
**Issued Capital:** £313,626,602
**Director:** D J Robinson
**Co. Secretary:** Dermot Russell
**Branches:** Pd Portco Ltd, Station Road, Scunthorpe, South Humberside DN17 3BN
**US SIC:** 6711, 4469
**UK SIC:** 83962, 76300

| | 31-12-13 | 31-12-12 | 31-12-11 |
|---|---|---|---|
| TO | 117,082,000 | 116,708,000 | 113,466,000 |
| P/L | (127,979,000) | (99,500,000) | (56,579,000) |
| NW | (300,162,000) | (176,402,000) | (77,123,000) |
| WC | 311,444,000 | 320,587,000 | 322,262,000 |
| Emp. | 1,153 | 1,181 | 1,157 |

DUNS 21-232-5343
## Pd&Se Johnson
105 Front Street, Lockington, Driffield, North Humberside YO25 9SH
**Tel:** 01430-810655
**Estd:** 2002 Proprietorship
**Line of Business:** Farming (mixed)
**US SIC:** 0291 **UK SIC:** 01001
**Employees:** 55

DUNS 23-588-2821
## P.D.C. Utility Services Ltd
Unit 3, Chepstow, Gwent NP16 6UN
**Tel:** 01291-638980
**Web:** www.pdc-painters.co.uk
**Reg No:** 3585908 **VAT No:** 713708838
**Estd:** 1998 Private Limited Company
**Line of Business:** Construction of civil engineering constructions
**Trading Style:** P.D.C. Utility Services Ltd
**Issued Capital:** £1,500
**Directors:** M Bone, I E Forster
**Co. Secretary:** Ms Janet Bone
**Responsibilities**
**Senior:** Mark Freer *(Manager)*
**US SIC:** 1622 **UK SIC:** 50200
**Auditors:** Susan J. Arthur & Co

| | 31-12-13 | 31-12-12 | 31-12-11 |
|---|---|---|---|
| TO | 7,734,599 | 8,187,055 | 7,571,347 |
| P/L | 728,687 | 1,215,804 | 1,474,547 |
| NW | 2,209,586 | 2,243,861 | 1,297,792 |
| WC | 2,201,722 | 2,235,129 | 1,287,222 |
| Emp. | 95 | 106 | 93 |

DUNS 67-151-5724
## Pdhl Ltd
Pdhl House Carrs Road, Cheadle, Cheshire SK8 2LA
**Tel:** 08452417676 **Fax:** 01614348721
**Web:** www.pdhl.co.uk
**Reg No:** 5990423 **Estd:** 2004 Private Limited Company
**Line of Business:** Business and commerce centres
**Issued Capital:** £5,000
**Directors:** G P Finneran, M O Mcgrath, I N Millington, M J Dolan
**US SIC:** 7392 **UK SIC:** 83951

| | 28-02-14 | 28-02-13 | 29-02-12 |
|---|---|---|---|
| TA | 1,917,532 | 1,830,537 | 1,326,796 |
| NW | 412,096 | (91,131) | (413,540) |
| WC | 363,936 | (122,778) | 144,327 |

DUNS 21-142-1025
## Pdl Finance Ltd
(**Subsidiary of:** Sdj Enterprises Ltd)
6th Floor 25 Farringdon Street, London EC4A 4AB
**Tel:** 02085321969
**Web:** www.mrlender.com
**Reg No:** 6738633 **Estd:** 2008 Private Limited Company
**Line of Business:** Credit granting by non-deposit taking finance houses and other specialist consumer credit grantors
**Issued Capital:** £2,000
**Directors:** J D Shaffer, A L Shinebroom, Miss E L Nisbet, A R Freeman
**Responsibilities**
**Senior:** Joshus Landy *(Director)*
**US SIC:** 6111 **UK SIC:** 81501

| | 31-12-13 | 31-12-12 | 31-12-11 |
|---|---|---|---|
| TA | 17,856,124 | 10,000,883 | 3,252,698 |
| P/L | 7,813,439 | 3,243,555 | N/A |
| NW | 8,343,830 | 2,359,103 | (85,894) |
| WC | 8,048,455 | 2,012,332 | (293,543) |
| Emp. | 154 | 86 | N/A |

DUNS 23-838-2670
## Pdm Training & Consultancy Ltd
2 Eastgate House, 5-7 East Street, Andover, Hampshire SP10 1EP
**Tel:** 01264-321340 **Fax:** 01264-358506
**Web:** www.pdmtc.co.uk
**Reg No:** 3829972 **Estd:** 1999 Private Limited Company
**Line of Business:** Representative office
**Issued Capital:** £801,000
**Directors:** P D Moody, Mrs M B Moody, A W Collins
**US SIC:** 8299, 8249, 7392
**UK SIC:** 93300, 83951
**Auditors:** Seymour Taylor Audit Ltd
**Bankers:** National Westminster Bank Plc (51-81-41)

| | 23-07-13 | 23-07-12 | 23-07-11 |
|---|---|---|---|
| TA | 1,386,448 | 1,285,708 | 1,670,401 |
| NW | 150,242 | (212,539) | 251,270 |
| WC | 547,609 | 58,963 | 896,229 |

DUNS 38-585-5051
## Pdq Couriers Uk Ltd
Unit 26a Rufford Court, Hardwick Grange, Woolston, Warrington, Cheshire WA1 4RF
**Tel:** 01925817876
**Web:** www.pdqcouriers.co.uk
**Reg No:** 3340187 **VAT No:** 437825134
**Estd:** 1987 Private Limited Company
**Line of Business:** Freight transport by road not elsewhere classified
**Issued Capital:** £100
**Directors:** R D Dabbs, J O Robertson
**Co. Secretary:** Ms Julie Dabbs
**Branches:** Pdq Couriers Uk Ltd, Llys Gwynt, Old Mill Road, Penmaenmawr, Gwynedd LL34 6TB
**US SIC:** 4213 **UK SIC:** 72300
**Auditors:** Gareth Hughes & Co
**Bankers:** HSBC Bank plc (40-30-07)

| | 31-03-14 | 31-03-13 | 31-03-12 |
|---|---|---|---|
| TA | 133,917 | 134,598 | 109,827 |
| NW | 86,201 | 80,659 | 70,877 |
| WC | 58,992 | 50,307 | 46,066 |

DUNS 29-972-2843 **Exp**
## P.D.Q. Distribution Ltd
(**Subsidiary of:** Coöperatie Activision Blizzard International U.A.)
6 Pavilion Drive, Birmingham, West Midlands B6 7BB
**Tel:** 01216253377 **Fax:** 01213561652
**Web:** www.pdqdist.co.uk
**Reg No:** 2105582 **VAT No:** 580715534
**Estd:** 1987 Private Limited Company
**Line of Business:** Distribution service providers
**Export Markets:** Worldwide
**Issued Capital:** £100
**Directors:** R Kotick, D O'Sullivan, I D Mattingly, Mrs M Pearson, D Neal
**Co. Secretary:** Damian O'Sullivan
**Responsibilities**
**Senior:** Robert Kottick *(Chief Executive)*, Paul Sherry *(Group Operations Director)*, Steven Varnish *(Manager)*, Christopher Walther *(Board Member)*
**Finance:** Gemma Mcintyre *(Credit Controller)*, Jamie Morgan *(Credit Controller)*
**Marketing:** Ben Hooper *(Customer Services Representati)*, Baljinder Sahota *(Customer Services Representati)*, Ann Trentham *(Customer Services Representati)*
**Sales:** Tracie Worrall *(Account Manager)*
**Fleet:** Matt Cusack *(Goods In Supervisor)*, Keith Harley *(Stock Control Manager)*, Jason Sturch *(Stock Controller)*
**US SIC:** 4712 **UK SIC:** 77002
**Auditors:** PricewaterhouseCoopers
**Bankers:** Bank Of Scotland (12-05-65)

| | 31-12-13 | 31-12-12 | 31-12-11 |
|---|---|---|---|
| TO | 5,765,000 | 6,681,000 | 6,560,000 |
| P/L | 174,000 | 220,000 | 244,000 |
| NW | 6,596,000 | 6,552,000 | 6,393,000 |
| WC | 6,500,000 | 6,416,000 | 6,230,000 |
| Emp. | 56 | 58 | 63 |

DUNS 29-876-1875
## P.D.Q. Engineering Ltd
Industrial Road, Hertburn, Washington, Tyne and Wear NE37 2SA
**Tel:** 0191-417-2343 **Fax:** 0191-416-5518
**Web:** www.pdqengineering.com
**Reg No:** 2079310 **VAT No:** 408049561
**Estd:** 1986 Private Limited Company
**Line of Business:** Engineers (general)
**Issued Capital:** £27,149
**Director:** R J Mellett
**Co. Secretary:** Paul Jackson
**Responsibilities**
**Senior:** Gayle Jackson *(Accounts Manager)*
**Finance:** Gayle Jackson *(Accounts Manager)*
**Purchasing:** Nikki Handley *(Purchasing Manager)*
**US SIC:** 8911 **UK SIC:** 83701
**Auditors:** R Tait Walker & Co
**Bankers:** National Westminster Bank Plc (60-22-52)

| | 31-07-13 | 31-07-12 | 31-07-11 |
|---|---|---|---|
| TA | 2,545,046 | 2,812,008 | 2,625,594 |
| NW | 1,218,038 | 1,070,030 | 838,830 |
| WC | 64,491 | (51,329) | (237,007) |

DUNS 34-647-0180
## P.D.R. Construction Ltd
Salisbury House, Saxon Way, Priory Park, Hessle, North Humberside HU13 9PB
**Fax:** 01482-579888
**Web:** www.pdrconstruction.co.uk
**Reg No:** 2772148 **VAT No:** 599023020
**Estd:** 1992 Private Limited Company
**Line of Business:** Builders
**Trading Style:** Pdr Construction
**Issued Capital:** £111
**Directors:** D J Kilvington, P Dransfield, L R Newsham, N Weatherall, D H Maughan
**Co. Secretary:** Mrs Joanne Dransfield
**US SIC:** 1522 **UK SIC:** 50100
**Auditors:** Smailes Goldie
**Bankers:** The Royal Bank Of Scotland Plc (16-22-04)

| | 31-03-14 | 31-03-13 | 31-03-12 |
|---|---|---|---|
| TO | 26,652,564 | 30,582,804 | 38,056,570 |
| P/L | 577,915 | (500,822) | 64,627 |
| NW | 2,200,492 | 1,742,128 | 2,603,494 |
| WC | 1,279,676 | 829,965 | 711,306 |
| Emp. | N/A | 78 | 76 |

DUNS 39-232-7102 **Imp**
## P.E. Systems Ltd
Victoria Street, Leigh, Lancashire WN7 5SE
**Tel:** 01942260330
**Web:** www.pe-systems.co.uk
**Reg No:** 2117413 **VAT No:** 457967876
**Estd:** 1987 Private Limited Company
**Line of Business:** Manufacturers of electronic equipment and components
**Issued Capital:** £1,000
**Managing Director:** M Smith
**Co. Secretary:** Ms June Smith
**Responsibilities**
**IT:** Stephen Kendall *(IT Manager)*
**Purchasing:** Julie Nuttall *(Purchasing Manager)*
**US SIC:** 3679, 3621
**UK SIC:** 34542, 34201
**Auditors:** Lathams
**Bankers:** The Royal Bank Of Scotland Plc (16-00-09)

| | 31-12-13 | 31-12-12 | 30-12-11 |
|---|---|---|---|
| TA | 3,184,301 | 3,370,506 | 2,733,823 |
| NW | 1,182,573 | 1,107,352 | 1,137,620 |
| WC | 605,568 | 437,364 | 469,296 |

DUNS 29-057-9382
## Peabody Pension Trust Ltd
Minster Court 45-47, Westminster Bridge Road, London SE1 7JB
**Tel:** 08000224040
**Web:** www.peabody.org.uk
**Reg No:** 1164841 **Estd:** 1974 Private Limited Company
**Line of Business:** Pension companies
**Issued Capital:** £6
**Directors:** S Howlett, Mrs S L Hickey
**Co. Secretary:** Ms Susan Hickey
**Branches:** Peabody Pension Trust Ltd, Block K Peabody Bldgs, Rodney Rd, London SE17 1BX
**US SIC:** 6371 **UK SIC:** 82002
**Auditors:** Deloitte & Touche LLP

| | 31-03-14 | 31-03-13 | 31-03-12 |
|---|---|---|---|
| TO | 24,729 | 23,684 | 22,106 |
| P/L | 2,998 | 2,674 | 2,038 |
| NW | 33,186 | 30,188 | 27,514 |
| WC | 33,186 | 30,188 | 27,514 |

DUNS 22-733-9264
## Peabody Trust
Minster Court, 45-47 Westminster Bridge Road, London SE1 7JB
**Tel:** 02079287811
**Web:** www.peabody.org.uk
**Estd:** 1862
**Line of Business:** Housing associations societies trusts & co-operatives
**Principals:** P Harbard *(Financial)*, Ms C A Forbes, Ms S L Hickey, S Howlett, Ms E A Peace, Ms J Glass, G Barlow, D Robinson
**Responsibilities**
**Senior:** Claire Bennie *(Development Manager)*, Giles Colchester *(Manager)*, Vevet Deer *(Manager)*, Sue Forsyth *(Project Manager)*, Coralie Francis *(Manager)*, Glenda Huxley *(Manager)*, David Lavarack *(Executive Director Corporate S)*, Abdur Perwez *(Manager)*, Dorit Raymond *(Manager)*, Sandra Skeete *(Executive Director, Housing)*, June Welcome *(Manager)*, Terence Wheeler *(Manager)*
**Marketing:** Ebun Atinmo *(Communications Officer)*, Benjamin Blades *(Media and Public Affairs Manag)*
**Sales:** Claire Bennie *(Development Manager)*
**Admin:** H Doe *(Secretary)*

**Operations:** Sue Forsyth (Project Manager)
**Purchasing:** Stephen Lamprell (Senior Infrastructure Engineer)
**Engineering:** Stephen Lamprell (Senior Infrastructure Engineer)
**Branches:** Peabody Trust, Wellington Buildings, Flat 261, London SW1W 8RZ
**US SIC:** 8321 **UK SIC:** 96111
**Auditors:** Grant Thornton UK LLP
**Bankers:** Coutts & Co (18-00-02)

|  | 31-03-12 | 31-03-11 | 31-03-10 |
|---|---|---|---|
| TO | 122,399,000 | 112,648,000 | 105,966,000 |
| P/L | 19,592,000 | 9,144,000 | 23,422,000 |
| NW | 265,540,000 | 261,696,000 | 228,804,000 |
| WC | 43,000,000 | (7,697,000) | 27,220,000 |
| Emp. | 690 | 739 | 910 |

DUNS 76-838-6260
## Peace Hospice Care
Peace Drive, Watford, Hertfordshire WD17 1LA
**Tel:** 01923330330
**Web:** www.peacehospice.co.uk
**Reg No:** 2604892 **Estd:** 1991 Private Company Limited By Guarantee
**Line of Business:** Other human health activities
**Directors:** Ms J E Robinson, Ms I R Walker, P W Mitchell, R R Amin, Mrs V R Edwards, Mrs C A Stephens, J P Kesanto, C Piers
**Co. Secretary:** Mrs Susan Plummer
**Responsibilities**
**Senior:** Belinda Chadwick (Director), Ian Chait (Manager), Robert Elkeles (Director), Joe Feeley (Director of Trading), Raj Jobanputra (Manager), Sharon Kilbane (Manager), Jackie Tritton (Director of Patient Services)
**HR:** Kim Tolley (Human Resources)
**Operations:** Ropinder Gill (Director of Fundraising)
**US SIC:** 8091 **UK SIC:** 95200
**Auditors:** Hillier Hopkins
**Bankers:** National Westminster Bank Plc (60-00-08)

|  | 31-03-14 | 31-03-13 | 31-03-12 |
|---|---|---|---|
| TO | 5,287,625 | 5,088,622 | 4,840,121 |
| P/L | (19,054) | (18,250) | (89,098) |
| NW | 5,125,739 | 5,182,705 | 5,244,765 |
| WC | 1,507,501 | 1,915,540 | 1,882,196 |
| Emp. | 108 | 100 | 94 |

DUNS 21-920-8018
## Peace of Mind Care Ltd
Rownhams Lane, Southampton, Hampshire SO16 8AR
**Tel:** 02380735413 **Fax:** 08445047587
**Web:** www.peaceofmindcare.ork.uk
**Reg No:** 8366869 **Estd:** 2013 Private Limited Company
**Line of Business:** Other human health activities
**Issued Capital:** £100
**Directors:** Ms E Kitchen, Ms C Ely, R E Kitchen
**US SIC:** 8091 **UK SIC:** 95200

|  | 31-01-14 |
|---|---|
| TA | 100 |
| NW | 100 |

DUNS 21-579-5740
## Peacehavens Childrens Centre
Meridian Way, Peacehaven, East Sussex BN10 8NF
**Tel:** 01273335100
**Web:** www.eastsussex.gov.uk
**Estd:** 1990 Partnership
**Line of Business:** Primary education
**Partners:** Mrs J Maclean, Mrs S Edmonds
**Responsibilities**
**Senior:** Donna Mcadam (Havens Cluster Coordinator)
**US SIC:** 8211 **UK SIC:** 93200
**Employees:** 100

DUNS 42-477-1538
## Peach Personnel Services Ltd
129-133 High Street, Slough, Berkshire SL1 1DH
**Tel:** 01753532500
**Web:** www.peach.co.uk
**Reg No:** 4464771 **Estd:** 2002 Private Limited Company
**Line of Business:** Employment and recruitment companies and consultants
**Trading Style:** Peach Personnel Services Ltd
**Issued Capital:** £9,284
**Directors:** Ms A L Russell, R P Russell
**Co. Secretary:** Richard Russell
**US SIC:** 7361 **UK SIC:** 83954

|  | 30-04-14 | 30-04-13 | 30-04-12 |
|---|---|---|---|
| TA | 713,501 | 733,593 | 573,001 |
| NW | (264,109) | (462,492) | (674,534) |
| WC | 300,650 | 296,566 | 240,302 |

DUNS 23-281-1864
## The Peach Pub Company Ltd
The Peach Barns, Somerton Road, North Aston, Bicester, Oxfordshire OX25 6HX
**Tel:** 01869220110 **Fax:** 0870-712-9402
**Web:** www.peachpubs.com
**Reg No:** 4336195 **VAT No:** 806659996
**Estd:** 2009 Private Limited Company
**Line of Business:** Independent public houses and bars
**Issued Capital:** £5,000
**Directors:** L R Cash, W H Stoddart
**Co. Secretary:** Wilfrid Stoddart
**Responsibilities**
**Senior:** Janet Watts (Manager)
**Branches:** The Peach Pub Company Ltd, Fleece Hotel, 11 Church Green, Witney, Oxfordshire OX28 4AZ
**US SIC:** 5813 **UK SIC:** 66200
**Auditors:** Wellers
**Bankers:** HSBC Bank plc (40-45-25)

|  | 29-12-13 | 31-12-12 | 01-12-12 |
|---|---|---|---|
| TO | 4,174,625 | 3,882,499 | 4,123,853 |
| P/L | 218,111 | 177,913 | 179,760 |
| NW | 991,373 | 727,020 | 566,904 |
| WC | 2,717,431 | 2,367,337 | 1,748,847 |
| Emp. | 74 | 97 | 97 |

DUNS 77-929-5133
## Peach Technologies Ltd
St Andrews House, 4400 Parkway, Whiteley, Fareham, Hampshire PO15 7FJ
**Tel:** 0800 988 2002 **Fax:** 0800 988 2003
**Web:** www.peachtelecom.co.uk
**Reg No:** 5832338 **Estd:** 2006 Private Limited Company
**Line of Business:** Telecommunications
**Issued Capital:** £100
**Directors:** A D Miles, G M Mcquaid, J M Handley Potts, D J Scott-Healey
**US SIC:** 4899 **UK SIC:** 79020
**Auditors:** Winterstoke Financial Management Ltd

|  | 31-08-13 | 31-08-12 | 31-08-11 |
|---|---|---|---|
| TO | 7,731,119 | 8,118,132 | 7,711,346 |
| P/L | 349,816 | 273,744 | 568,573 |
| NW | 12,352 | 329,244 | 282,342 |
| WC | 360,581 | (237,131) | (239,207) |
| Emp. | 72 | 72 | 54 |

DUNS 21-721-2935    Imp
## Peachey (Basildon) Group Ltd
No 2 Pipps Hill Industrial Estate, Basildon, Essex SS14 3BS
**Web:** www.peacheys.com
**Reg No:** 0963603 **Estd:** 1969 Private Limited Company
**Line of Business:** Management activities of holding companies
**Issued Capital:** £1,100
**Managing Director:** T B Peachey
**Co. Secretary:** Gary Peachey
**Branches:** Peachey (Basildon) Group Ltd, 65 Hamilton Rd, Felixstowe, Suffolk IP11 7BE
**US SIC:** 6711, 5148
**UK SIC:** 83962, 61700
**Auditors:** Littlestone Martin Glenton
**Bankers:** Lloyds TSB Bank plc (30-14-56)

|  | 29-09-13 | 30-09-12 | 25-09-11 |
|---|---|---|---|
| TO | 14,681,920 | 17,273,861 | 18,036,696 |
| P/L | 346,974 | 979,739 | 665,616 |
| NW | 7,221,167 | 7,247,067 | 6,936,766 |
| WC | (1,343,720) | (1,083,675) | (636,037) |
| Emp. | 423 | 435 | 436 |

DUNS 21-807-3385
## Peacock & Binnington
(Subsidiary of: Peacock & Binnington Holdings Ltd)
Old Foundry, Brigg, South Humberside DN20 8NR
**Tel:** 01652-600200 **Fax:** 01652-657532
**Web:** www.peacock.co.uk
**Reg No:** 0328944 **VAT No:** 128128577
**Estd:** 1990 Private Unlimited Company
**Line of Business:** Agricultural engineers
**Export Sales:** £335,500
**Trading Style:** Peacock & Binnington
**Issued Capital:** £188,000
**Principals:** M A Peacock (Managing), L Bacon, G W Main, N A Peacock, A J Whiteley
**Co. Secretary:** Graham Wright
**Responsibilities**
**Senior:** Derek Blow (Manager)
**Branches:** Peacock & Binnington, High Street, Gainsborough, Lincolnshire DN21 5QP
**US SIC:** 5084 **UK SIC:** 61490
**Auditors:** Stephenson Smart & Co
**Bankers:** Barclays Bank Plc (20-76-14)

|  | 31-12-13 | 31-12-12 | 31-12-11 |
|---|---|---|---|
| TO | 38,894,011 | 38,135,255 | 35,981,956 |
| P/L | 308,174 | 505,620 | 361,341 |
| NW | 3,836,395 | 3,606,858 | 3,353,336 |
| WC | 2,379,013 | 2,303,754 | 2,126,691 |
| Emp. | 94 | 85 | 88 |

DUNS 21-223-4971
## Peacock Farm Public House
Peacock Lane, Bracknell, Berkshire RG12 8SS
**Tel:** 01344-423481
**Web:** www.peacockfarm.co.uk
**Proprietorship**
**Line of Business:** Public house
**Proprietors:** Rutter, Rutter
**Responsibilities**
**Senior:** Paul Rutter (General Manager)
**US SIC:** 5813 **UK SIC:** 66200
**Employees:** 48

DUNS 39-993-7861
## Peacock Medicare Ltd
Quentin Rise, Livingston, West Lothian EH54 6QR
**Tel:** 01506462545
**Reg No:** 0112618SC **Estd:** 1989 Private Limited Company
**Line of Business:** Medical nursing home activities
**Trading Style:** Peacock Nursing Home, Nightswood, Woodlands Nursing Home, Elsie Ingle Nursing Home
**Issued Capital:** £100,000
**Directors:** Dr J Bagaria, Miss A Bagaria
**Co. Secretary:** Dr Nawal Bagaria
**Branches:** Peacock Medicare Ltd, Quentin Rise, Livingston, West Lothian EH54 6QR
**US SIC:** 8051 **UK SIC:** 95100
**Auditors:** PKF
**Bankers:** Bank Of Scotland (80-08-80)

|  | 31-07-13 | 31-07-12 | 31-07-11 |
|---|---|---|---|
| TO | 4,591,871 | 4,479,404 | 5,790,672 |
| P/L | 682,907 | 718,958 | 448,763 |
| NW | 1,761,961 | 1,256,291 | 871,100 |
| WC | 837,577 | 472,592 | 360,569 |
| Emp. | 200 | 200 | 268 |

DUNS 21-232-7175    Imp
## Peacocks Medical Group Ltd
Unit C Benfield Business Park, Newcastle-Upon-Tyne, Tyne and Wear NE6 4NQ
**Tel:** 01912 769600
**Web:** www.peacocks.net
**Reg No:** 0560972 **VAT No:** 755998065
**Estd:** 1956 Private Limited Company
**Line of Business:** Manufacture of medical and surgical equipment and orthopaedic appliances
**Issued Capital:** £53,218
**Principals:** J C Peacock (Managing), D W Stevens, D W Ferguson, S J Cook, C D Peacock, T E Gumbley
**Co. Secretary:** David Hood
**Responsibilities**
**Senior:** C Denman (Manager), Robert Strong (Supply Chain Manager)
**Finance:** A Hansell (Financial Director)
**Marketing:** Clive Mitchell (Marketing & Sales Manager)
**Sales:** Clive Mitchell (Marketing & Sales Manager)
**Operations:** Robert Strong (Supply Chain Manager)
**Purchasing:** Robert Strong (Supply Chain Manager)
**Branches:** Peacocks Medical Group Ltd, Nathan House, 27 Hursley Rd, Eastleigh, Hampshire SO53 2FS
**US SIC:** 3841, 5999
**UK SIC:** 37201, 65600
**Auditors:** Joseph Miller & Co
**Bankers:** Lloyds TSB Bank plc (30-93-71)

|  | 31-05-13 | 31-05-12 | 31-05-11 |
|---|---|---|---|
| TO | 10,794,374 | 10,534,788 | 10,044,979 |
| P/L | 389,335 | 151,329 | 149,482 |
| NW | 2,290,996 | 2,038,516 | 1,976,732 |
| WC | 1,089,831 | 1,247,711 | 1,332,452 |
| Emp. | 150 | 157 | 166 |

DUNS 34-650-7499    Imp
## Peacocks Stores Ltd
(Subsidiary of: The Edinburgh Woollen Mill (Group) Ltd)
Capital Link, Windsor Road, Cardiff, South Glamorgan CF24 5NG
**Tel:** 02920-270-000 **Fax:** 02920-440-400
**Web:** www.peacocks.co.uk
**Reg No:** 0285031SC **Estd:** 1884 Private Limited Company
**Line of Business:** Retail sale of clothing
**Issued Capital:** £5,000,000
**Directors:** K B Lee, S R Simpson, Mrs C Leigh, P E Day
**Co. Secretary:** Ms June Carruthers
**Branches:** Peacocks Stores Ltd, Newport Retail Park, Spytty Road, Newport, Gwent NP19 4QQ
**US SIC:** 5699, 5621
**UK SIC:** 64500
**Auditors:** KPMG LLP
**Bankers:** Barclays Bank Plc (20-48-46)

|  | 01-03-14 | 02-03-13 | 25-03-12 |
|---|---|---|---|
| TO | 324,874,000 | 315,874,000 | 2,578,000 |
| P/L | 58,471,000 | 51,657,000 | 710,000 |
| NW | 90,545,000 | 45,325,000 | 100,000 |
| WC | 87,962,000 | 43,773,000 | (1,899,000) |
| Emp. | 5,455 | 5,575 | 65 |

DUNS 21-735-8398
## Peak Answers Ltd
Suite B 2nd Floor Grosvenor House, St Thomas' Plance, Stockport, Cheshire SK1 3TZ
**Tel:** 01614766655
**Web:** www.peakanswers.co.uk
**Reg No:** 7701080 **Estd:** 2011 Private Limited Company
**Line of Business:** Market research organisations
**Trading Style:** Peak Answers Limited
**Issued Capital:** £100
**Directors:** Mrs C Laybourne, D M Laybourne
**US SIC:** 7392 **UK SIC:** 83951

|  | 31-03-13 | 31-03-12 |
|---|---|---|
| TA | 419,035 | 172,154 |
| NW | 222,048 | 68,569 |
| WC | 215,417 | 62,033 |

DUNS 21-777-0096
## Peak Leisure Centre
Vue Stirling, Stirling, Stirlingshire FK8 1QZ
**Tel:** 01786273555
**Web:** www.activestirling.org.uk
**Estd:** 2011 Proprietorship
**Line of Business:** Other sporting activities not elsewhere classified
**Proprietor:** Miss L Mann
**US SIC:** 8999 **UK SIC:** 83954
**Employees:** 90

DUNS 23-288-3843
## Peak Park National Park Authority
Aldern House, Baslow Road, Bakewell, Derbyshire DE45 1AE
**Tel:** 01629816200
**Web:** www.peakdistrict.gov.uk
**Estd:** 1951 Incorporate By Act Of Parliament
**Line of Business:** Parks & gardens
**Trading Style:** Peak District National Park Authority
**Directors:** K Francis, C Harrison, K Parker, J Anfield, Ms P Goodall-Mcintosh
**Responsibilities**
**Finance:** Philip Naylor (Financial Manager)
**Marketing:** Barbara Crossley (Communications Officer), Maureen Eastgate (Head of Marketing and Communic), Rachel Gillis (Assistant Director Policy and), Alison Riley (Communications Officer)
**IT:** David Mc Mahon (IT Officer (Support)), Jeff Winston (Head of Information Management)
**HR:** Theresa Reid (Head of Human Resources)
**Operations:** Mary Bagley (Assistant Director Enterprise), Jane Chapman (Assistant Director Land Manage)
**Purchasing:** Josephine Allen (Purchasing Manager)
**Branches:** Peak Park National Park Authority, Langsett House, Langsett, Sheffield, South Yorkshire S36 4GY
**US SIC:** 9121 **UK SIC:** 91110
**Bankers:** The Co-Operative Bank Plc (08-90-05)
**Employees:** 200

DUNS 77-442-2117
## Peak-Ryzex Plc
Ryzex House, Chippenham, Wiltshire SN14 6LH
**Tel:** 08448750115 **Fax:** 08448750116
**Web:** www.ryzex.com
**Reg No:** 2951840 **Estd:** 1997 Private Limited Company
**Line of Business:** Computer software (development)
**Export Sales:** £582,647
**Issued Capital:** £54,000
**Directors:** A Doyle, D Greer, S Gwilliam, R M Young, B Chung
**Co. Secretary:** Aldex Limited
**US SIC:** 7379, 5065
**UK SIC:** 83940, 61500
**Auditors:** Mazars LLP
**Bankers:** Lloyds TSB Bank plc (30-00-02)

|  | 31-12-13 | 31-12-12 | 31-12-11 |
|---|---|---|---|
| TO | 15,838,975 | 18,528,989 | 19,277,816 |
| P/L | 186,115 | 501,981 | (3,378) |
| NW | 676,722 | 546,849 | 189,663 |
| WC | 560,085 | 425,991 | 858,572 |
| Emp. | 73 | 78 | 79 |

DUNS 52-002-4944    Exp
## Peak Scientific Instruments Ltd
(Subsidiary of: Peak Scientific Holdings Ltd)
Fountain Crescent, Renfrew, Renfrewshire PA4 9RE
**Tel:** 0141-812-8100
**Web:** www.peakscientific.com
**Reg No:** 0175368SC **Estd:** 1997 Private Limited Company

**Line of Business:** Electricity generating equipment
**Export Markets:** U S A
**Export Sales:** £21,957,863
**Issued Capital:** £1,602,310
**Directors:** M D Hamilton, R W Macgeachy
**Co. Secretary:** Ms June Macgeachy
**Responsibilities**
**Senior:** Brian Ritchie *(Manager)*
**Health & Safety:** Charlie Street *(Facilities Manager)*
**Facilities:** Charlie Street *(Facilities Manager)*
**US SIC:** 3643 **UK SIC:** 34203
**Auditors:** French Duncan LLP
**Bankers:** National Westminster Bank Plc (01-10-01)

| | 30-09-13 | 30-09-12 | 30-09-11 |
|---|---|---|---|
| TO | 25,399,219 | 18,738,559 | 14,841,736 |
| P/L | 4,926,501 | 4,235,183 | 2,519,824 |
| NW | 10,858,169 | 8,461,281 | 5,481,725 |
| WC | 5,638,558 | 4,925,287 | 3,540,125 |
| Emp. | 154 | 123 | 97 |

DUNS 22-667-5262
## Peak Waste Recycling Ltd
Wood Lane, Longrose Lane, Ashbourne, Derbyshire DE6 1JL
**Tel:** 01335342276
**Web:** www.peakwaste.co.uk
**Reg No:** 1587329 **Estd:** 1980 Private Limited Company
**Line of Business:** Waste disposal
**Export Sales:** £36
**Issued Capital:** £412,200
**Principals:** Ms E N Martin *(Managing)*, J D Partridge, R S Martin, K Martin
**Co. Secretary:** Ms Edna Martin
**Responsibilities**
**Admin:** Justin Foster *(Office Administrator)*
**IT:** Justin Foster *(Office Administrator)*
**Operations:** Justin Foster *(Office Administrator)*
**Purchasing:** Justin Foster *(Office Administrator)*
**US SIC:** 4953 **UK SIC:** 92110
**Auditors:** Robt A Page Kirk Cree Jepson
**Bankers:** National Westminster Bank Plc (60-01-19)

| | 30-09-13 | 30-09-12 | 30-09-11 |
|---|---|---|---|
| TO | 5,763,453 | 5,419,586 | 5,359,019 |
| P/L | 448,921 | 11,761 | 176,265 |
| NW | 1,993,241 | 1,726,006 | 1,741,391 |
| WC | 285,258 | 153,057 | (13,824) |
| Emp. | 71 | 70 | 62 |

DUNS 50-320-7896 **Imp**
## Peakdale Molecular Ltd
Peakdale Science Park, High Peak, Derbyshire SK23 0PG
**Tel:** 01298816700
**Web:** www.peakdale.com
**Reg No:** 2345676 **VAT No:** 606448834
**Estd:** 1989 Private Limited Company
**Line of Business:** Research institutions and organisations
**Export Sales:** £4,473,933
**Trading Style:** Peakdale Molecular
**Issued Capital:** £1,203,001
**Directors:** Dr P M Doyle, A S Morgan, R Fisher, P Mccluskey
**Co. Secretary:** Paul Mccluskey
**Responsibilities**
**Senior:** Rosie Barratt *(Purchasing Manager)*, Christine Fisher *(Operations Director)*, William Fraser Allen *(Share Holder)*, Michael McGoun *(Manager)*
**Sales:** Mick Durrant *(Business Development Director)*
**Health & Safety:** Christine Fisher *(Operations Director)*
**US SIC:** 7391 **UK SIC:** 94000
**Auditors:** CLB Coopers
**Bankers:** National Westminster Bank Plc (01-03-38)

| | 31-03-14 | 31-03-13 | 31-03-12 |
|---|---|---|---|
| TO | 9,185,022 | 9,107,763 | 9,083,106 |
| P/L | 637,915 | 634 | 207,091 |
| NW | 6,486,016 | 5,652,530 | 5,500,486 |
| WC | 2,055,932 | 964,402 | 793,606 |
| Emp. | 146 | 148 | 158 |

DUNS 23-691-7613
## Peake (G B) Ltd
Stoneybridge Park, Liskeard, Cornwall PL14 3NQ
**Web:** www.home.btconnect.com
**Reg No:** 2668564 **VAT No:** 557739394
**Estd:** 1991 Private Limited Company
**Line of Business:** Animal by-product processing
**Trading Style:** Sun Flower Hygine, Incineration South West
**Issued Capital:** £80,000
**Principals:** R J Peake *(Managing)*, M J Peake, Ms J A Peake, R W Brenton
**Co. Secretary:** Ms Nicola Brenton
**Responsibilities**
**Senior:** Trevor Heayns *(Manager)*
**Branches:** Peake (G B) Ltd, Stoneybridge Park, Liskeard, Cornwall PL14 3NQ
**US SIC:** 2013, 7539
**UK SIC:** 41223, 67100
**Auditors:** Geoffrey L Johnson & Co
**Bankers:** Barclays Bank Plc (20-50-40)

| | 31-12-13 | 31-12-12 | 31-12-11 |
|---|---|---|---|
| TA | 2,780,397 | 2,931,568 | 2,898,827 |
| NW | 2,017,343 | 2,019,610 | 1,893,058 |
| WC | (52,600) | (158,356) | (269,219) |

DUNS 37-865-0816
## Peakview Ltd
7-9 27 King Street, Aberdeen, Aberdeenshire AB24 5AA
**Tel:** 01224-636333
**Web:** www.carewatch.co.uk
**Reg No:** 0171462SC **Estd:** 1997 Private Limited Company
**Line of Business:** Home care service providers
**Trading Style:** Carewatch Grampian
**Issued Capital:** £20,402
**Directors:** A J Price, Mrs K L Duncan, N J Price
**Co. Secretary:** Mrs Hilary Price
**Responsibilities**
**Senior:** June Gunn *(Manager)*
**Purchasing:** Marie McBeath *(Receptionist)*
**US SIC:** 8091 **UK SIC:** 95200
**Auditors:** Meston Reid & Co
**Bankers:** Lloyds TSB Bank plc (30-10-01)

| | 31-03-14 | 31-03-13 | 31-03-12 |
|---|---|---|---|
| TA | 3,012,379 | 2,630,263 | 1,703,408 |
| NW | 1,318,728 | 978,878 | 876,774 |
| WC | (24,768) | (120,599) | 723,333 |

DUNS 21-139-5797 **Imp**
## Pear Track Systems Ltd
3000 Aviator Way, Manchester Business Park, Manchester M22 5TG
**Tel:** 01625820483
**Web:** www.peartrack.com
**Reg No:** 6717970 **Estd:** 2008 Private Limited Company
**Line of Business:** Activities of other transport agencies
**Issued Capital:** £1,800
**Directors:** Peartrack Systems Group Ltd, J Macey
**US SIC:** 4712 **UK SIC:** 77002

| | 31-08-13 | 31-10-12 | 31-08-11 |
|---|---|---|---|
| TA | 260,707 | 391,769 | 193,592 |
| NW | (240,334) | 51,606 | 60,250 |
| WC | (240,951) | 50,880 | 59,396 |

DUNS 34-626-7503
## Pear Tree Projects Ltd
Pear Tree House, Bolam, Darlington, County Durham DL2 2UP
**Tel:** 01388776799 **Fax:** 01325-369850
**Web:** www.peartreeprojects.co.uk
**Reg No:** 2760566 **Estd:** 1992 Private Limited Company
**Line of Business:** Agricultural service activities; landscape gardening
**Issued Capital:** £1,000
**Director:** D A Bartlett
**Co. Secretary:** Ms Andrea Bartlett
**Branches:** Pear Tree Projects Ltd, Peartree House, Darlington, County Durham DL2 2UP
**US SIC:** 8999 **UK SIC:** 83954
**Auditors:** Gregory Mitford Snowball
**Bankers:** Yorkshire Bank Plc (05-06-01)

| | 30-04-14 | 30-04-13 | 30-04-12 |
|---|---|---|---|
| TO | 3,801,672 | 3,929,674 | N/A |
| P/L | 725,623 | 644,972 | N/A |
| NW | 2,512,929 | 2,105,034 | 1,814,420 |
| WC | (42,187) | (251,278) | (448,004) |
| Emp. | 79 | 80 | N/A |

DUNS 21-721-2851
## Pearce Construction (Barnstaple) Ltd
**(Subsidiary of:** Pcbl Ltd)
Pearce House, Brannam Crescent, Barnstaple, Devon EX31 3TD
**Tel:** 01271345261 **Fax:** 01271852134
**Web:** www.pearcebarnstaple.co.uk
**Reg No:** 0408163 **VAT No:** 810757831
**Estd:** 1946 Private Limited Company
**Line of Business:** Development and selling of real estate
**Trading Style:** Pearce Homes
**Issued Capital:** £152,253
**Principals:** D M Parsons *(Managing)*, R C Jeffs *(Financial)*, R A Bevan, D T Lake, P S Knox
**Responsibilities**
**Senior:** Stephanie Coley *(Human Resources Manager)*
**HR:** Stephanie Coley *(Human Resources Manager)*
**US SIC:** 1522, 1541
**UK SIC:** 50100
**Auditors:** Ernst & Young LLP
**Bankers:** Lloyds TSB Bank plc (30-90-49)

| | 30-04-14 | 30-04-13 | 30-04-12 |
|---|---|---|---|
| TO | 20,676,995 | 12,395,495 | 12,991,757 |
| P/L | 128,490 | (80,377) | 5,207 |
| NW | 3,045,820 | 3,476,906 | 4,059,087 |
| WC | 1,599,516 | 2,015,387 | 2,561,593 |
| Emp. | 119 | 110 | 104 |

DUNS 45-835-2820
## Pearce Maintenance Ltd
**(Subsidiary of:** Pearce Group Ltd)
Chelsea House, Chelsea Street, Nottingham, Nottinghamshire NG7 7HP
**Tel:** 01159700371 **Fax:** 01159887047
**Web:** www.pannellsigns.co.uk
**Reg No:** 3186029 **Estd:** 1996 Private Limited Company
**Line of Business:** Signs and nameplate designers.
**Issued Capital:** £1,000
**Director:** P W Snaith
**Co. Secretary:** Mrs Elisabeth Snaith
**US SIC:** 7399 **UK SIC:** 83954

| | 31-03-14 | 31-03-13 | 31-03-12 |
|---|---|---|---|
| TA | 1,000 | 1,000 | 1,000 |
| NW | 1,000 | 1,000 | 1,000 |

DUNS 22-621-5739
## Pearce Recycling Co Ltd
**(Subsidiary of:** Pearce Holdings St Albans Ltd)
Pearce Recycling Group, St Albans, Hertfordshire AL4 0JZ
**Tel:** 01727737699
**Web:** www.pearce-recycling.co.uk
**Reg No:** 1105882 **Estd:** 1969 Private Limited Company
**Line of Business:** Collection and treatment of other waste
**Trading Style:** Pearce Recyclin Group
**Issued Capital:** £151
**Principals:** S M Pearce *(Managing)*, Ms S Jones, A C Berridge
**Co. Secretary:** Niall Blackwell
**Responsibilities**
**Facilities:** Brian Jepson *(Facilities Manager)*
**Branches:** Pearce Recycling Co Ltd, 673 Dunstable Road, Luton, Bedfordshire LU4 0DS
**US SIC:** 4953, 3341
**UK SIC:** 92110, 22470
**Auditors:** Smith & Williamson

| | 31-03-14 | 31-03-13 | 31-03-12 |
|---|---|---|---|
| TO | 11,952,805 | 13,263,877 | 19,022,171 |
| P/L | 190,022 | (647,758) | 2,373 |
| NW | 383,797 | 188,463 | 594,707 |
| WC | (429,362) | (887,801) | 12,481 |
| Emp. | 107 | 104 | 103 |

DUNS 77-680-8842
## Pearce Signs Ltd
**(Subsidiary of:** Pearce Group Ltd)
Castle Court, Duke Street, Nottingham, Nottinghamshire NG7 7JN
**Tel:** 01159409620 **Fax:** 01794 524490
**Web:** www.pearcegroup.com
**Reg No:** 3005322 **VAT No:** 865251319
**Estd:** 1995 Private Limited Company
**Line of Business:** Sign and nameplate suppliers
**Issued Capital:** £1,177
**Directors:** J Blackaby, D P Crosby, M D Hudson, P W Snaith, H Everington
**Co. Secretary:** Mrs Elisabeth Snaith
**Branches:** Pearce Signs Ltd, Romsey Indust Estate, Greatbridge Road, Romsey, Hampshire SO51 0HR
**US SIC:** 2599 **UK SIC:** 46720
**Auditors:** Page Kirk LLP
**Bankers:** HSBC Bank plc (40-35-18)

| | 31-03-14 | 31-12-12 | 31-03-11 |
|---|---|---|---|
| TA | 2,720,903 | 2,910,355 | 2,492,903 |
| NW | 651,508 | 598,134 | 1,025,253 |
| WC | 484,310 | 410,474 | 904,462 |

DUNS 50-029-6249
## Pearl 2004 Ltd
**(Subsidiary of:** Pearl Centre Holdings Ltd)
Military Road, Newport, Isle of Wight PO30 4DD
**Tel:** 01983740352
**Web:** www.iowpearl.co.uk
**Reg No:** 2307205 **Estd:** 1988 Private Limited Company
**Line of Business:** Retail sale of jewellery, clocks and watches
**Trading Style:** Cornwall Pearl
**Issued Capital:** £3
**Directors:** M L Scragg, J S Taylor
**US SIC:** 5944 **UK SIC:** 65400
**Auditors:** Deloitte & Touche

| | 31-10-13 | 31-10-12 | 31-10-11 |
|---|---|---|---|
| TA | 3 | 3 | 3 |
| NW | 3 | 3 | 3 |

DUNS 21-752-0782 **Imp-Exp**
## Pearl Automotive Ltd
**(Subsidiary of:** Pearl Automotive Holdings Ltd)
2 Manor Trading Estate Armstrong Road, Benfleet, Essex SS7 4PW
**Tel:** 01268756216 **Fax:** 01268-565589
**Web:** www.pearlautomotivegroup.com
**Reg No:** 1075111 **VAT No:** 250754174
**Estd:** 1972 Private Limited Company
**Line of Business:** Sale of motor vehicle parts and accessories
**Export Markets:** European Union (E U)
**Trading Style:** Pearl Products
**Issued Capital:** £894
**Directors:** R J Etherington, P G Ground
**Co. Secretary:** Stephen Catling
**Responsibilities**
**Senior:** Richard Withers *(Marketing Manager)*
**Marketing:** Richard Withers *(Marketing Manager)*
**Purchasing:** Jack Chambers *(Purchasing Manager)*
**Engineering:** Tony Catling *(Engineering Manager)*
**US SIC:** 5531 **UK SIC:** 65100
**Auditors:** Rickard Keen
**Bankers:** Lloyds TSB Bank plc (30-10-75)

| | 31-12-13 | 31-12-12 | 31-12-11 |
|---|---|---|---|
| TA | 3,209,807 | 2,974,342 | 3,102,094 |
| NW | 390,051 | 410,899 | 361,607 |
| WC | 577,910 | 601,981 | 545,435 |

DUNS 29-443-8023
## Pearl Bula Ltd
**(Subsidiary of:** Phoenix Life Holdings Ltd)
1 Wythall Green Way, Wythall, Birmingham, West Midlands B47 6WG
**Web:** www.thephoenixgroup.com
**Reg No:** 1621367 **Estd:** 1982 Private Limited Company
**Line of Business:** Insurance
**Issued Capital:** £1
**Directors:** A Moss, S Mohammed
**Co. Secretary:**
Pearl Group Secretariat Services
**US SIC:** 6311 **UK SIC:** 82002
**Auditors:** KPMG Audit Plc
**Employees:** 1,500

DUNS 21-771-8983
## Pearl Care Group
9 Fynney Street, Leek, Staffordshire ST13 5LF
**Estd:** 2011 Proprietorship
**Line of Business:** Rest and retirement homes
**Proprietor:** Mrs D Johnson
**Responsibilities**
**Senior:** Tracey Wright *(Manager)*
**US SIC:** 8321 **UK SIC:** 96111
**Employees:** 50

DUNS 21-827-3086
## Pearl Chemist Ltd
New Bridge Street House, 30-34 New Bridge Street, London EC4V 6BJ
**Tel:** 02086722157
**Web:** www.pearlchemist.co.uk
**Reg No:** 7976515 **Estd:** 2012 Private Limited Company
**Line of Business:** Dispensing chemists
**Issued Capital:** £2
**Directors:** M H Patel, V K Patel
**US SIC:** 5912 **UK SIC:** 64300
**Bankers:** Abbey National Plc (09-00-21)

| | 30-04-14 | 30-04-13 |
|---|---|---|
| TO | 19,155,756 | 18,334,496 |
| P/L | (321,668) | (690,815) |
| NW | (6,986,478) | (7,260,813) |
| WC | (1,777,290) | (4,902,579) |
| Emp. | 55 | 46 |

DUNS 34-745-7459
## Pearl Dusk Ltd
North Country Court, Hull, North Humberside HU9 3TQ
**Tel:** 01482-702750
**Reg No:** 2782831 **Estd:** 1993 Private Limited Company
**Line of Business:** Residential care establishments
**Trading Style:** Country Court Care Home
**Issued Capital:** £97
**Directors:** A Kitching, Ms P A Bucknell, M C Hall
**Co. Secretary:** Jean Kitching
**Responsibilities**
**Senior:** Gary Kitchen *(Manager)*, Garry Kitching *(Manager)*, Susan Welders *(Manager)*
**US SIC:** 8321 **UK SIC:** 96111

| | 31-03-14 | 31-03-13 | 31-03-12 |
|---|---|---|---|
| TO | N/A | N/A | 631,976 |
| P/L | N/A | N/A | 78,453 |
| NW | 536,509 | 491,631 | 456,085 |
| WC | 127,762 | 82,374 | 44,690 |
| Emp. | N/A | N/A | 48 |

DUNS 23-633-4335
## Pearl Group Holdings Ltd
New Farm, Newhouse Lane, Ongar, Essex CM5 0DJ
**Tel:** 01277-890274
**Web:** www.hughpearl.co.uk
**Reg No:** 3630337 **Estd:** 1951 Private Limited Company
**Line of Business:** Other construction work involving special trades
**Issued Capital:** £1,380
**Directors:** Mrs K J Pearl, R Ward, C Hart

**Co. Secretary:** Ms Lucinda Pearl
**Responsibilities**
**Finance:** Kim Fish *(Finance Manager)*
**US SIC:** 1799 **UK SIC:** 50000
**Auditors:** Baverstocks

| | 31-03-14 | 31-03-13 | 31-03-12 |
|---|---|---|---|
| TA | 598,102 | 598,750 | 599,393 |
| NW | 597,472 | 598,121 | 598,764 |
| WC | 10,603 | 11,252 | 11,895 |

DUNS 23-590-4609
## Pearl Group Management Services Ltd
(**Subsidiary of:** Phoenix Life Holdings Ltd)
1 Wythall Green Way, Birmingham, West Midlands B47 6WG
**Tel:** 08450020344
**Web:** www.phoenixlife.co.uk
**Reg No:** 3588063 **VAT No:** 369446510
**Estd:** 1997 Private Limited Company
**Line of Business:** Activities auxiliary to insurance and pension funding
**Trading Style:** Phoenix Group
**Issued Capital:** £38,613,037
**Directors:** S Fawcett, S Mohammed, A Kassimiotis, R K Thakrar
**Co. Secretary:** Pearl Group Secretariat Services
**Responsibilities**
**Senior:** Alan Roffey-Jones *(Manager)*
**US SIC:** 6411, 6311
**UK SIC:** 83200, 82002
**Auditors:** Ernst & Young LLP

| | 31-12-13 | 31-12-12 | 31-12-11 |
|---|---|---|---|
| TO | 186,832,000 | 223,873,000 | 247,142,000 |
| P/L | 14,601,000 | 14,879,000 | (11,513,000) |
| NW | 70,976,000 | 53,929,000 | 25,797,000 |
| WC | 31,565,000 | 20,765,000 | 16,140,000 |
| Emp. | 749 | 746 | 729 |

DUNS 77-960-7407
## Pearl Investments Ltd
Bentima House 168-172 Old Street, London EC1V 9BP
**Tel:** 02088382369
**Reg No:** 3064114 **Estd:** 1995 Private Limited Company
**Line of Business:** Licensed restaurants
**Issued Capital:** £580,000
**Director:** K K Cheng
**Co. Secretary:** To Lam
**US SIC:** 5812 **UK SIC:** 66110

| | 31-03-14 | 31-03-13 | 31-03-12 |
|---|---|---|---|
| TO | 5,622,723 | 4,947,430 | 4,068,963 |
| P/L | (48,751) | 696,920 | (492,186) |
| NW | 2,122,752 | 2,605,773 | 1,955,602 |
| WC | 625,625 | 613,461 | (429,920) |
| Emp. | 79 | 68 | 65 |

DUNS 76-982-6876
## Pearl Rlh Ltd
(**Subsidiary of:** Phoenix Life Holdings Ltd)
Juxon House, London EC4M 8BU
**Tel:** 02035679100 **Fax:** 0141-275-8755
**Web:** www.thephoenixgroup.com
**Reg No:** 0133636SC **Estd:** 2005 Private Limited Company
**Line of Business:** Financial services
**Trading Style:** Pearl Group Ltd
**Issued Capital:** £3,101,099,600
**Directors:** S Mohammed, A Moss
**Co. Secretary:** Pearl Group Secretariat Services
**Responsibilities**
**Senior:** Tony Kassimiotis *(Managing Director - Operations)*
**Finance:** Jim McConville *(Group Finance Director)*
**Marketing:** Shellie Wells *(Head of Media Relations)*
**Sales:** Bob Seaman *(Commercial and Procurement Dir)*
**IT:** Steve Nesbitt *(Head of IT)*
**US SIC:** 6111, 6711
**UK SIC:** 81501, 83962
**Auditors:** Ernst & Young LLP

| | 31-12-13 | 31-12-12 | 31-12-11 |
|---|---|---|---|
| TA | 637,692 | 637,692 | 637,692 |
| P/L | N/A | N/A | 338,611 |
| NW | 623,436 | 623,436 | 623,436 |
| WC | 275,635 | 275,635 | 275,635 |

DUNS 23-675-5786
## Pearl Window Systems Ltd
Unit 14, Bolton, Lancashire BL5 3XU
**Tel:** 01942-843586 **Fax:** 01942840619
**Web:** www.pearlwindows.co.uk
**Reg No:** 3670150 **Estd:** 1999 Private Limited Company
**Line of Business:** Painting & decorating contractors
**Issued Capital:** £2
**Directors:** J H Walsh, Mrs J M Walsh
**Co. Secretary:** Ms Judith Walsh
**Responsibilities**
**Marketing:** Mark Gore *(Marketing and IT Manager)*, Bryn Williams *(New Business Manager)*
**Sales:** Kelly Brown *(Account Manager)*
**Admin:** Ryan Fulop *(Office Manager)*
**IT:** Mike Morgan *(Senior IT Executive)*
**Operations:** Anthony Holliday *(Operations Manager)*
**US SIC:** 1721, 7399
**UK SIC:** 50400, 83954
**Auditors:** Edwards Veeder LLP
**Bankers:** Barclays Bank Plc (20-10-71)

| | 31-12-13 | 31-12-12 | 31-12-11 |
|---|---|---|---|
| TO | 7,860,421 | N/A | N/A |
| P/L | 445,760 | N/A | N/A |
| NW | 470,581 | 268,907 | 245,803 |
| WC | 416,590 | 201,968 | 164,460 |
| Emp. | 112 | N/A | N/A |

DUNS 21-158-5682
## Pearlcastle Ltd
(**Subsidiary of:** Castlepearl Ltd)
Unit 14a, London N11 1JL
**Web:** www.carsparesfactors.co.uk
**Reg No:** 1292813 **Estd:** 1976 Private Limited Company
**Line of Business:** Car accessories and parts
**Trading Style:** Car Spares Factors
**Issued Capital:** £140
**Principals:** K K Shah *(Managing)*, S Shah, M Shah
**Co. Secretary:** Avnish Shah
**Responsibilities**
**IT:** Syed Raza *(IT Manager)*
**Branches:** Pearlcastle Ltd, Unit 14 Brunswick Industrial Estate, Brunswick Way, London N11 1JL
**US SIC:** 5531 **UK SIC:** 65100
**Auditors:** Glazers

| | 31-12-13 | 31-12-12 | 31-12-11 |
|---|---|---|---|
| TO | N/A | 4,868,701 | 5,178,234 |
| P/L | N/A | (210,402) | 264,102 |
| NW | 2,547,582 | 2,702,677 | 3,114,420 |
| WC | 826,168 | 1,047,083 | 965,085 |
| Emp. | N/A | 47 | 51 |

DUNS 23-509-8662
## Pearlmans Finance Ltd
10-12 Murton Street, Sunderland, Tyne and Wear SR1 2RB
**Tel:** 0191-514-3399
**Web:** www.mmfltd.co.uk
**Reg No:** 0853991 **Estd:** 1965 Private Limited Company
**Line of Business:** Credit granting by non-deposit taking finance houses and other specialist consumer credit grantors
**Trading Style:** J Pearlmans, R D & P Warehouses
**Issued Capital:** £811
**Directors:** S D Pearlman, L D Pearlman, I S Mackenzie, D D'Arcy, D Liddle
**Branches:** Pearlmans Finance Ltd, 2 Ridge Road, Burnley, Lancashire BB11 3DD
**US SIC:** 6111 **UK SIC:** 81501
**Auditors:** RMT Accountants & Business Advisors Ltd
**Bankers:** Bank Of Scotland (12-09-19)

| | 30-06-13 | 30-06-12 | 30-06-11 |
|---|---|---|---|
| TA | 2,395,237 | 2,344,274 | 2,769,009 |
| NW | 1,542,351 | 1,297,849 | 1,500,032 |
| WC | 2,136,967 | 2,067,234 | 1,635,232 |

DUNS 50-479-3050
## Pearn's Pharmacies Ltd
36 Windsor Road, Penarth, South Glamorgan CF64 1YD
**Tel:** 02920707568
**Web:** www.pearns.co.uk
**Reg No:** 2453256 **Estd:** 2012 Private Limited Company
**Line of Business:** Chemists dispensing
**Issued Capital:** £100
**Principals:** D H Pearn *(Managing)*, M G Pearn, Mrs J Pearn
**Co. Secretary:** David Pearn
**Responsibilities**
**Senior:** Jenny Buckland *(Manager)*
**Branches:** Pearn's Pharmacies Ltd, 30 Victoria Street, Merthyr Tydfil, Mid Glamorgan CF48 3RN
**US SIC:** 5912 **UK SIC:** 64300
**Auditors:** Grant Thornton
**Bankers:** Lloyds TSB Bank plc (30-95-86)

| | 31-05-14 | 31-05-13 | 31-05-12 |
|---|---|---|---|
| TO | 18,326,535 | 18,309,385 | 19,602,752 |
| P/L | 1,782,899 | 1,639,234 | 1,716,814 |
| NW | 4,223,136 | 3,003,829 | 1,555,701 |
| WC | 3,195,673 | 2,708,183 | 1,748,046 |
| Emp. | 166 | 170 | 166 |

DUNS 73-644-2679 **Imp-Exp**
## Pearson Driving Assessments Ltd
(**Subsidiary of:** Pearson Plc)
Corporate Officethe Lighthouse 14 The, Quays, Salford, Lancashire M50 3BF
**Tel:** 01618557000 **Fax:** 0161 855 7331
**Web:** www.pearsonvue.co.uk
**Reg No:** 4904325 **Estd:** 2003 Private Limited Company
**Line of Business:** Medical practice activities
**Export Sales:** £2,823,000
**Trading Style:** Pearson Vue
**Issued Capital:** £1
**Directors:** Dr G Gates, R D Whelan, M Poiadgi, D C Kennedy, J Nijjar
**Co. Secretary:** Ms Natalie Dale
**Responsibilities**
**Senior:** Suzana Lopez *(Manager)*
**HR:** Louise Hudson *(Human Resources Manager)*, Alex Miell *(Human Resources Manager)*
**Facilities:** Rebecca Beirne *(Facilities Manager)*
**Branches:** Pearson Driving Assessments Ltd, The Lighthouse, 14 The Quays, Salford, Lancashire M50 3BF
**US SIC:** 8011 **UK SIC:** 95300
**Auditors:** PricewaterhouseCoopers LLP
**Bankers:** HSBC Bank plc (40-00-02)

| | 31-12-13 | 31-12-12 | 31-12-11 |
|---|---|---|---|
| TO | 61,042,000 | 53,771,000 | 47,874,000 |
| P/L | 10,086,000 | 9,970,000 | 10,078,000 |
| NW | 21,351,000 | 23,220,000 | 16,683,000 |
| WC | 21,080,000 | 21,521,000 | 13,186,000 |
| Emp. | 708 | 694 | 584 |

DUNS 21-018-4776 **Imp-Exp**
## Pearson Education Ltd
(**Subsidiary of:** Pearson Plc)
Edinburgh Gate, Harlow, Essex CM20 2JE
**Tel:** 01279623623 **Fax:** 08708505255
**Web:** www.pearsoned.co.uk
**Reg No:** 0872828 **VAT No:** 278537121
**Estd:** 1966 Private Limited Company
**Line of Business:** Book publishers
**Export Sales:** £172,699,000
**Issued Capital:** £90,000,000
**Directors:** R R Price, I A Mackinnon, A Singh Basi, Ms M M Wilson, S J Grix, Ms S K Johnson, Ms C A Sheret, K R Bristow
**Co. Secretary:** Ms Natalie Dale
**Responsibilities**
**Senior:** Gay Anderson *(IT Coordinator)*, Bill Anderson *(President, Global ELT)*, Rod Bristow *(Manager)*, Lesley Davies *(Director)*, Sharon Hague *(Director)*, Zeghum Liaquat *(Manager)*, David Melville *(Director)*
**Marketing:** Mike Howard *(PTE Academic Product Manager)*
**IT:** Gay Anderson *(IT Coordinator)*, Dave MacPherson *(IT Director)*
**HR:** Derek Frier *(Human Resources Manager)*
**Branches:** Pearson Education Ltd, 1 Shire Park, Falcon Way, Welwyn Garden City, Hertfordshire AL7 1TW
**US SIC:** 2731, 7392
**UK SIC:** 47532, 83951
**Auditors:** PricewaterhouseCoopers LLP
**Bankers:** National Westminster Bank Plc (60-00-01)

| | 31-12-13 | 31-12-12 | 31-12-11 |
|---|---|---|---|
| TO | 565,715,000 | 563,967,000 | 510,604,000 |
| P/L | 36,050,000 | 68,743,000 | 70,083,000 |
| NW | 180,947,000 | 139,239,000 | 114,397,000 |
| WC | 175,287,000 | 131,662,000 | 111,986,000 |
| Emp. | 2,633 | 2,685 | 2,562 |

DUNS 29-512-8748 **Exp**
## Pearson Engineering Ltd
(**Subsidiary of:** Reece Group Ltd)
Wincomblee Road, Newcastle-Upon-Tyne, Tyne and Wear NE6 3QS
**Tel:** 01912-340001
**Web:** www.pearson-eng.com
**Reg No:** 1876136 **VAT No:** 556269610
**Estd:** 1985 Private Limited Company
**Line of Business:** Engineers (general)
**Export Sales:** £43,924,000
**Issued Capital:** £100
**Directors:** M R Welstead, Ms H Livingstone, J P Reece, P J Kite, R D Anderton, C Priday, H R Flack, S P Gilroy
**Co. Secretary:** Philip Kite
**Responsibilities**
**Senior:** Randal Flack *(Sales & Marketing Manager)*, Alan Reece *(Owner)*
**Finance:** Terry Courtney *(Financial Manager)*
**Marketing:** Dennis Doble *(Sales & Marketing Manager)*, Randal Flack *(Sales & Marketing Manager)*
**Sales:** Dennis Doble *(Sales & Marketing Manager)*, Randal Flack *(Sales & Marketing Manager)*
**IT:** Richard Nesbitt *(IT Manager)*
**Health & Safety:** Tony Harte *(Health & Safety Manager)*
**Facilities:** Tony Harte *(Health & Safety Manager)*
**Operations:** Tony Harte *(Health & Safety Manager)*
**Purchasing:** Tom Clarke *(Purchasing Manager)*
**Engineering:** Randal Flack *(Sales & Marketing Manager)*
**US SIC:** 8911, 3489
**UK SIC:** 83701, 32901
**Auditors:** UNW LLP
**Bankers:** Barclays Bank Plc (20-59-42)

| | 31-12-13 | 31-12-12 | 31-12-11 |
|---|---|---|---|
| TO | 53,105,000 | 81,440,000 | 207,676,000 |
| P/L | 14,549,000 | 29,776,000 | 62,841,000 |
| NW | 96,711,000 | 100,218,000 | 110,518,000 |
| WC | 93,842,000 | 97,103,000 | 107,091,000 |
| Emp. | 56 | 59 | 60 |

DUNS 21-213-9062
## Pearson Hinchlisse
Albion House, 31 Queen Street, Oldham, Lancashire OL1 1RD
**Tel:** 08007311874
**Web:** www.pearson-hinchliffe.co.uk
**Partnership**
**Line of Business:** Solicitors
**Trading Style:** Pearson Hinchliffe
**Partners:** D Prince, D Hinchlisse, R Hinchlisse, A J Pearson
**Responsibilities**
**Senior:** Michael Talbot *(Partner)*
**US SIC:** 8111 **UK SIC:** 83500
**Employees:** 60

DUNS 50-391-0333
## Pearson Jones & Co (Trustees) Ltd
(**Subsidiary of:** Skipton Building Society)
Clayton Wood Close, Leeds, West Yorkshire LS16 6QE
**Tel:** 01132-280-900 **Fax:** 01332-280-901
**Web:** www.pearson-jones.co.uk
**Reg No:** 2397618 **VAT No:** 686783565
**Estd:** 1989 Private Limited Company
**Line of Business:** Other financial intermediation
**Trading Style:** The Bradbury Executive Trust
**Issued Capital:** £250,000
**Directors:** R Lee, Ms J C Williamson, T W Johnson, A C Robinson
**Co. Secretary:** Jeremy Dunne
**US SIC:** 6111 **UK SIC:** 81501
**Bankers:** Bank Of Scotland (12-08-83)

| | 31-12-13 | 31-12-12 | 31-12-11 |
|---|---|---|---|
| TA | 250,000 | 250,000 | 250,000 |
| NW | 250,000 | 250,000 | 250,000 |

DUNS 21-022-7468 **Exp**
## Pearson Plc
80 Strand, London WC2R 0RL
**Tel:** 020-7010-2000 **Fax:** 020-7010-6060
**Web:** www.pearson.com
**Reg No:** 0053723 **Estd:** 1995 Public Limited Company
**Line of Business:** Other publishing
**Export Sales:** £4,420,000,000
**Trading Style:** Pearson in Practice Ata
**Issued Capital:** £204,372,464
**Directors:** H Manwani, Dr V Cox, G R Moreno, Mrs E P Corley, T Score, J J Fallon, K J Hydon, Sir T D Arculus
**Co. Secretary:** Stephen Jones
**Responsibilities**
**Senior:** David Arculus *(Non-Executive Director)*, Brett Bartow *(Executive Editor)*, Abu Bundu-Kamara *(General Manager)*, Dean Condodina *(District Manager)*, Richard Ferrie *(Manager)*, Joanne Foster *(Manager)*, Tracey Jerauld *(General Manager)*, Debra Kerr *(Manager)*, Salim Lewis *(Director)*, Linda Lorimer *(Director)*, Gloria Maccow *(Representative)*, Grace Massey *(Manager)*, Anne Mckim *(Centre Manager)*, Christopher Penn *(Senior Manager)*, Aurelio Prifitera *(Chief Executive Officer)*, Kelly Rippolone *(Vice President)*, Senta Rivera *(Manager)*, David Rodgers *(Manager)*, Carole Sandefer *(Chairman)*, Colleen Tyson *(Manager)*, Brian Vickery *(Manager)*
**Finance:** Debbie Campbell *(Analyst)*, Richard Gyurko *(Director, the Treasury)*, Anthony Mitru *(Executive)*, Tom Simon *(Vice President Corporate Finan)*
**Marketing:** Brett Bartow *(Executive Editor)*, Lori Deshazo *(Executive Marketing Manager)*, Bob Hemmer *(Executive Editor, MyLanguageLa)*, Elizabeth Lehnertz *(Director, Product Management)*, Maxine Lyseight *(Communications Manager)*, Trina MacDonald *(Editor)*, Dave Ostrow *(Editor)*, Katherine Samson *(Website Associate)*, Pippa Vaux *(Director of Media Relations)*
**Sales:** Karen Barclay *(Account Executive)*, Mitchell Grossman *(Senior Vice President)*, Christine Harthan *(Account Executive)*, Teresa Low *(Account Executive)*, Janet Marsico *(Sales Executive)*, Sheryl Morris *(Account Executive)*, Jan Pereira *(Business Development Manager)*, Luke Rabbidge *(Senior Sales Representative)*, Arnoldo Rodriguez *(Account Executive)*, Jennifer Rojas *(Account Executive)*, engene Smith *(Sales Manager)*, Linda Winer *(Technology Manager)*
**Admin:** Helene Horn *(Executive Assistant)*, Kim Kristiansen *(Executive Assistant)*, Ina Mendelsohn *(Administrator)*, Brendan O' Grady *(Head of Corporate Affairs)*

**IT:** Mark Denyer (?Programme Manager), Frank Dipentima (Vice President), Tom Flieger (Applications Manager), David Fogden (Head of Online Delivery and Su), Chris Harland (IT Security Architect), Scott Kaplan (Information Systems Manager), Jackie Mascitelli (Project Manager), Terri Mitchell (Website Developer), Richard Wyler (Project Manager), Brad Yanta (Engineer)
**HR:** Liz Almeida (Workforce Planning & Analytics), Jennifer Diblasi (HR Manager), Cheryl Gayner (Human Resources Manager), Jill Hugunin (Director Human Resources Direc), Tracy Hulsebus (HR Manager), Peggy Lester (Training Director), Vicki Malecha (Analyst), Sarah Rades (Training Director), Natalie Robinson (Human Resources Manager), Denise Schaumberg (Human Resource Manager), Dee Zutshi (Manager)
**Operations:** Jim Campbell (Project Manager), Jenny Colley (Publisher), Justin Cracolice (Field Service Supervisor), Dan Doyle (Operations Manager), Jason Fournier (Editor), Robert Friedman (Production Manager), Marc Jolicoeur (Director, the Project Office), Rick Lent (Quality Initiatives Manager), Jim Lewis (Operations Director), Maureen Martin (Manager), Julie Nahil (Manager), Lynn Nelson (Operations Planning), Jill Pina (Production Services Manager), Greg Rosenow (Software Development Manager), Tracy Sankot (Director, Operations), Jay Selmos (Product Assistant), Katherine Sette (Field Service Supervisor), David Shafer (Senior Product Manager), Salil Sharma (Production and Operations Mana), Mario Thomas (Project Coordinator), Ariel Tribble (Product Manager), Arnold Vila (Project Executive), Cindy White (Director of Production and Ope), Linda Winer (Technology Manager), John de Jong (Senior Vice President Standard)
**Purchasing:** Simon Muir (Purchasing Manager Global Sour)
**Engineering:** Bryan Macdonald (Chief Technician), Grant Strom (Desktop Support Technician)
**US SIC:** 2741, 7311
**UK SIC:** 47541, 83800
**Auditors:** PricewaterhouseCoopers LLP
Following financial data are in thousands

|      | 31-12-13 | 31-12-12 | 31-12-11 |
|------|----------|----------|----------|
| TO   | 5,069,000 | 5,059,000 | 5,862,000 |
| P/L  | 382,000 | 434,000 | 1,155,000 |
| NW   | (101,000) | (532,000) | (399,000) |
| WC   | 689,000 | 1,812,000 | 1,731,000 |
| Emp. | 42,115 | 42,980 | 41,521 |

DUNS 21-612-6185
## Pearsons (Enfield) Ltd
11-14 The Town, Enfield, Middlesex EN2 6LJ
**Tel:** 020-8373-4200 **Fax:** 0203667749
**Web:** www.pearsons-enfield.co.uk
**Reg No:** 0368937 **VAT No:** 220320730
**Estd:** 1941 Private Limited Company
**Line of Business:** Departmental stores
**Trading Style:** Pearsons (Wood Green), Pearsons (Bishops Stortford), Pearsons Department Stores
**Issued Capital:** £268,000
**Directors:** D I Hordle, Mrs M Syed, B H Dreesmann
**Co. Secretary:** Mrs Maura Syed
**Branches:** Pearsons (Enfield) Ltd, New Warehouse, Bilton Way, Enfield, Middlesex EN3 6EU
**US SIC:** 5399, 7629, 3552
**UK SIC:** 65600, 67301, 32300
**Auditors:** Moore Stephens LLP
**Bankers:** Barclays Bank Plc (20-29-77)

|      | 01-02-14 | 26-01-13 | 28-02-12 |
|------|----------|----------|----------|
| TO   | 8,738,982 | 11,192,873 | 10,671,669 |
| P/L  | 972,627 | 847,425 | 725,130 |
| NW   | 7,953,665 | 6,965,893 | 6,385,622 |
| WC   | 1,501,776 | 2,636,866 | 806,425 |
| Emp. | 114 | 147 | 158 |

DUNS 29-073-4078                         **Imp-Exp**
## Pearsons Glass Ltd
32 Wellington Park, Dunes Way, Liverpool, Merseyside L5 9RJ
**Tel:** 0151 2071474 **Fax:** 0151 2072110
**Web:** www.pearsonsglass.com
**Reg No:** 1312627 **VAT No:** 303569272
**Estd:** 1977 Private Limited Company
**Line of Business:** Manufacture of glass fibres
**Export Markets:** Malta; Africa; Republic of Ireland
**Issued Capital:** £1,000
**Principals:** P G Vellins (Managing), A M Vellins, R Mawson
**Co. Secretary:** Mrs Diane Vellins
**Responsibilities**
**Marketing:** Robert Beaver (Senior Marketing Executive)
**Branches:** Pearsons Glass Ltd, 32 Dunes Way, Liverpool, Merseyside L5 9RJ
**US SIC:** 3999, 5039
**UK SIC:** 49590, 61300
**Auditors:** Haines Watts

**Bankers:** National Westminster Bank Plc (60-13-20)

|      | 28-02-14 | 28-02-13 | 29-02-12 |
|------|----------|----------|----------|
| TA   | 2,435,279 | 2,274,986 | 2,482,464 |
| NW   | 939,478 | 916,868 | 883,418 |
| WC   | 165,521 | 110,107 | 238,063 |

DUNS 23-515-9402
## Pearsons of Duns Ltd
Cheeklaw Centre, Station Road, Duns, Berwickshire TD11 3EL
**Tel:** 01361882277
**Web:** www.pearsonsofduns.co.uk
**Reg No:** 0183235SC **VAT No:** 269543228
**Estd:** 1998 Private Limited Company
**Line of Business:** Builders merchants
**Issued Capital:** £51,000
**Managing Director:** M P Pearson
**Branches:** Pearsons Of Duns Ltd, Stoup Hill Cott, Alnwick, Northumberland NE66 2AS
**US SIC:** 5072, 5039
**UK SIC:** 61500, 61300
**Auditors:** Hogg & Thorburn
**Bankers:** The Royal Bank Of Scotland Plc (83-18-40)

|      | 28-02-14 | 28-02-13 | 29-02-12 |
|------|----------|----------|----------|
| TA   | 1,996,735 | 1,893,326 | 1,890,744 |
| NW   | 785,879 | 695,797 | 552,842 |
| WC   | 184,314 | 147,139 | 2,401 |

DUNS 28-929-1361
## Pearsons Southern Ltd
(Subsidiary of: Hull Hampshire Estates Plc)
58-60 London Road, Southampton, Hampshire SO15 2AH
**Tel:** 023-8023-3288
**Web:** www.pearsons.com
**Reg No:** 1517996 **Estd:** 1980 Private Limited Company
**Line of Business:** Estate agents
**Trading Style:** Pearsons Estate Agents
**Issued Capital:** £1,000
**Principals:** P A Grover (Managing), Ms D J Passells, S C Pinkney, P D Powell, R N Parsons, J D Beckingsale, L J Turner, S Sprake
**Co. Secretary:** Ms Nicola Kennard
**Branches:** Pearsons Southern Ltd, 7 North Street, Havant, Hampshire PO9 1PW
**US SIC:** 6531 **UK SIC:** 83400
**Auditors:** Alliott Wingham Ltd
**Bankers:** Barclays Bank Plc (20-10-53)

|      | 31-12-13 | 31-12-12 | 31-12-11 |
|------|----------|----------|----------|
| TO   | 3,943,425 | 4,041,282 | 3,636,995 |
| P/L  | 472,619 | 449,296 | 422,703 |
| NW   | 1,297,011 | 1,165,305 | 991,199 |
| WC   | 692,554 | 550,213 | 409,694 |
| Emp. | 92 | 92 | 91 |

DUNS 73-790-0006
## Peart Access Ramps Ltd
Baltic Works, Baltic Street, Hartlepool, Cleveland TS25 1PW
**Tel:** 01429852152 **Fax:** 01429-262179
**Web:** www.peartaccessramps.co.uk
**Reg No:** 5046633 **Estd:** 2004 Private Limited Company
**Line of Business:** Oil companies
**Issued Capital:** £100,000
**Managing Directors:** D R Peart, C F Peart
**Co. Secretary:** Colin Stead
**US SIC:** 2999, 3325
**UK SIC:** 11150, 31110

|      | 30-06-13 | 30-06-12 | 30-06-11 |
|------|----------|----------|----------|
| TA   | 364,891 | 346,820 | 405,984 |
| NW   | 277,616 | 300,365 | 313,903 |
| WC   | 229,163 | 259,066 | 287,436 |

DUNS 21-660-9739
## Peart Fencing Ltd
Baltic Works, Baltic Street, Hartlepool, Cleveland TS25 1PW
**Tel:** 01429852352
**Web:** www.peartfencing.co.uk
**Reg No:** 7166841 **Estd:** 2010 Private Limited Company
**Line of Business:** Fence and gate suppliers
**Issued Capital:** £700,000
**Directors:** M G Mitchinson, C Stead, R D Peart, C F Peart, P J Blenkiron
**US SIC:** 3496 **UK SIC:** 31694

|      | 30-06-13 | 30-06-12 | 30-06-11 |
|------|----------|----------|----------|
| TA   | 2,320,381 | 2,668,611 | 2,335,423 |
| NW   | 810,600 | 758,719 | 708,295 |
| WC   | 456,799 | 321,685 | 275,583 |

DUNS 21-660-9740
## Peart Property Ltd
Baltic Works, Baltic Street, Hartlepool, Cleveland TS25 1PW
**Tel:** 01429860308 **Fax:** 01429233833
**Reg No:** 7166842 **Estd:** 2002 Private Limited Company
**Line of Business:** Manufacturers of lubricating oils
**Issued Capital:** £1,247,500
**Directors:** R D Peart, C F Peart
**Responsibilities**
**Senior:** Laura Jackson (Branch Manager)

**US SIC:** 2999 **UK SIC:** 11150

|      | 30-06-13 | 30-06-12 | 30-06-11 |
|------|----------|----------|----------|
| TA   | 1,839,982 | 1,859,584 | 1,885,636 |
| NW   | 1,431,895 | 1,328,463 | 1,306,849 |
| WC   | (68,410) | (391,462) | (440,175) |

DUNS 21-230-3068
## Peartree Care Centre
195-199 Sydenham Road, Lower Sydenham, London SE26 5HF
**Tel:** 020-84889000
**Web:** www.excelcareholdings.com
**Estd:** 1997
**Line of Business:** Residential care establishments
**Proprietor:** Ms L Pawley
**US SIC:** 8321 **UK SIC:** 96111
**Employees:** 73

DUNS 29-842-5166
## Peartree Cleaning Services Ltd
(Subsidiary of: Peartree Asset Management Ltd)
Peartree House, Brentwood, Essex CM14 5LD
**Tel:** 01277-201420 **Fax:** 01277-200114
**Web:** www.peartreecleaning.co.uk
**Reg No:** 2045868 **Estd:** 1986 Private Limited Company
**Line of Business:** Cleaning activities not elsewhere classified
**Issued Capital:** £828,800
**Principals:** B S Reames (Managing), D S Reames (Managing), Ms C T Fowler, S M Conroy, S J Cooney, Mrs B Ayling, M Rowley
**Co. Secretary:** Mrs Jacqueline Reames
**US SIC:** 8999 **UK SIC:** 83954
**Bankers:** National Westminster Bank Plc (60-11-15)

|      | 31-08-13 | 31-08-12 | 31-08-11 |
|------|----------|----------|----------|
| TO   | 10,483,446 | 9,211,373 | 8,755,889 |
| P/L  | 292,861 | 135,871 | 483,126 |
| NW   | 838,314 | 919,712 | 920,885 |
| WC   | 482,499 | 597,164 | 645,734 |
| Emp. | 953 | 927 | 866 |

DUNS 21-778-0468
## Peasedown St John Primary School
Bath Road, Peasedown St John, Bath, Avon BA2 8DH
**Tel:** 01761432311
**Web:** www.peasedownstjohnprimary.org.uk
**Estd:** 1901 Proprietorship
**Line of Business:** Schools (local authority)
**Proprietor:** D Killing
**US SIC:** 8211 **UK SIC:** 93200
**Employees:** 50

DUNS 23-931-4839
## Peaspring Ltd
Haincliffe Road, Keighley, West Yorkshire BD21 5BU
**Tel:** 01535-251902
**Reg No:** 3921344 **Estd:** 2000 Private Limited Company
**Line of Business:** Management activities of holding companies
**Export Sales:** £3,037,581
**Directors:** J E Scott, J B Jones
**Co. Secretary:** Andrew Booth
**US SIC:** 6711 **UK SIC:** 83962
**Bankers:** HSBC Bank plc (40-25-10)

|      | 31-12-13 | 31-12-12 | 31-12-11 |
|------|----------|----------|----------|
| TO   | 20,718,003 | 19,716,348 | 18,320,349 |
| P/L  | 1,803,133 | 991,531 | 1,584,406 |
| NW   | 4,321,845 | 3,397,313 | 3,108,106 |
| WC   | 3,052,642 | 2,052,488 | 1,680,288 |
| Emp. | 90 | 88 | 81 |

DUNS 77-952-3914
## Pebble Hotels Ltd
Hartley Place, Croft Road, Hook, Hampshire RG27 8HT
**Tel:** 02380277808
**Web:** www.pebblehotels.com
**Reg No:** 5921582 **Estd:** 2006 Private Limited Company
**Line of Business:** Hotels
**Issued Capital:** £99
**Directors:** Z Akguneyli, S E Kennedy, K Thomson, P D Walters
**Co. Secretary:** Keith Thomson
**US SIC:** 7011 **UK SIC:** 66500
**Bankers:** Anglo Irish Bank Corporation Plc (23-02-40)

|      | 31-03-14 | 31-03-13 | 31-03-12 |
|------|----------|----------|----------|
| TO   | 3,844,741 | 3,242,534 | 3,165,906 |
| P/L  | 410,567 | 239,686 | 367,370 |
| NW   | (1,892,033) | (2,207,831) | (2,447,517) |
| WC   | (6,792,266) | (7,155,916) | (7,270,517) |
| Emp. | 85 | 79 | 73 |

DUNS 33-939-4421
## Pebbles Restaurant
Burton Bradstock, Bridport, Dorset DT6 4PT
**Tel:** 01308897317
**Web:** www.freshwaterbeach.co.uk
**Partnership**
**Line of Business:** Restaurant - indian
**Partners:** R Condliffe, Mrs S Ireland
**US SIC:** 5812 **UK SIC:** 66110
**Employees:** 60

DUNS 77-146-7289
## Pecan Deluxe Candy (Europe) Ltd
(Subsidiary of: Pecan Deluxe Candy Company)
17 Moor Lane Trading Estate, Sherburn In Elmet, Leeds, West Yorkshire LS25 6ES
**Tel:** 01977681141
**Web:** www.pecandeluxe.com
**Reg No:** 2704966 **Estd:** 1992 Private Limited Company
**Line of Business:** Manufacturers of food products
**Export Sales:** £7,212,862
**Issued Capital:** £2,235,000
**Directors:** J Brigham, B Brigham, G N Kingston
**Co. Secretary:** Robert Cranston
**Responsibilities**
**Senior:** Allan Dew (Manager), Geoffrey Spinks (Manager), Roona Spinks (Manager)
**Sales:** Stephanie Cryer (Sales Manager)
**IT:** Stephanie Cryer (Sales Manager), Matthew Dobson (Technical Manager), Rachael Fewster (Technical Manager)
**HR:** Jackie Bester (Purchasing Manager)
**Health & Safety:** Matthew Dobson (Technical Manager), Rachael Fewster (Technical Manager)
**Purchasing:** Jackie Bester (Purchasing Manager)
**US SIC:** 2099 **UK SIC:** 42399
**Auditors:** Harrison Shipley

|      | 30-09-13 | 30-09-12 | 30-09-11 |
|------|----------|----------|----------|
| TO   | 11,032,836 | 12,411,826 | 10,164,903 |
| P/L  | 244,370 | 576,537 | 358,014 |
| NW   | 2,856,450 | 2,612,083 | 2,035,554 |
| WC   | 2,071,470 | 1,830,911 | 1,413,930 |
| Emp. | 85 | 83 | 69 |

DUNS 21-601-5882
## Pectel A Keltbray Division
Keltbray House, Burnt Mills Road, Basildon, Essex SS13 1DT
**Tel:** 01268591222
**Web:** www.keltbray.com
**Estd:** 2011
**Line of Business:** Asbestos products & removal
**Responsibilities**
**Senior:** Darren Wickins (Manager)
**US SIC:** 1799 **UK SIC:** 50000
**Employees:** 135

DUNS 23-696-3310
## Peddars Way Housing Association
(Subsidiary of: Flagship Housing Group Ltd)
Michael Chaplin House, Station Road, Dereham, Norfolk NR19 1DA
**Tel:** 01362694858 **Fax:** 01362656510
**Web:** www.flagship-housing.co.uk
**Reg No:** 0027582IP **Estd:** 1997 Friendly Society
**Line of Business:** Provider of affordable homes.
**Trading Style:** Flagship Peddars Way
**Issued Capital:** £1
**Principals:** F J Chaplin (Chairman), P Hargrave, I W Johnson, M J Wilson, J B Rawlings, E F Jolly, Ms M L Williams, N E Boldero
**Responsibilities**
**Senior:** Brenda Canham (Designated Limited Liability P), Stephen Chalmers (Designated Limited Liability P), Joan Fenning (Designated Limited Liability P), Eric Hubbard (Designated Limited Liability P), Joan Jenkins (Designated Limited Liability P), Cliff Jordan (Designated Limited Liability P), Lynne Riddoch (Team Leader), Alex Taylor (Designated Limited Liability P), Sylvia Welsh (Designated Limited Liability P)
**Operations:** Diane Allibone (Community Manager), Jackie Bryant (Community Manager), Debbie Hewson (Community Manager), Mandy Player (Community Manager), Amy-Louise Sangster (Community Manager), Natasha Spillet (Community Manager)
**Branches:** Peddars Way Housing Association, London St, Swaffham, Norfolk PE37 7EG
**US SIC:** 6733 **UK SIC:** 83100
**Auditors:** KPMG LLP

**Bankers:** National Westminster Bank Plc (60-07-47)
**Employees:** 54
**Turnover:** £38,968,000

DUNS 29-065-0936
## Pedersen Contracting Services Ltd
The Old Mill, Woodhall Spa, Lincolnshire LN10 6YQ
**Web:** www.pedersencontracting.co.uk
**Reg No:** 1242286 **VAT No:** 129852542
**Estd:** 1976 Private Limited Company
**Line of Business:** Manufacture of other transport equipment not elsewhere classified
**Issued Capital:** £258
**Principals:** M Pedersen (Managing), C S Blades, N M Pedersen, D Pedersen
**Co. Secretary:** Nicholas Pedersen
**Responsibilities**
**Senior:** Peter Giddens (Depot Manager)
**Operations:** Christopher Akid (Operations Manager)
**Branches:** Pedersen Contracting Services Ltd, Station Rd, King's Lynn, Norfolk PE32 1EJ
**US SIC:** 3799, 4213, 7349
**UK SIC:** 36502, 72300, 92300
**Auditors:** Streets
**Bankers:** Bank Of Scotland (12-17-35)

| | 30-06-14 | 30-06-13 | 30-06-12 |
|---|---|---|---|
| TO | 8,277,394 | 7,461,500 | 7,174,347 |
| P/L | 370,806 | 230,954 | 255,711 |
| NW | 1,489,521 | 1,259,207 | 1,060,525 |
| WC | 137,756 | (22,346) | (19,185) |
| Emp. | 90 | 78 | 85 |

DUNS 58-112-7222
## Pedersen Leisure Ltd
St Mellons, Castleton, St Mellons, Cardiff, South Glamorgan CF3 2XR
**Tel:** 01633-680355
**Web:** www.pedersenhotels.com
**Reg No:** 2906145 **Estd:** 1994 Private Limited Company
**Line of Business:** Hotels
**Trading Style:** St Mellons Hotel & Country Club
**Issued Capital:** £2
**Director:** M S Gourgey
**Co. Secretary:** Pedersen Holdings Limited
**US SIC:** 7011, 7999
**UK SIC:** 66500, 97913
**Auditors:** Enoch & Partners

| | 31-08-13 | 31-08-12 | 31-08-11 |
|---|---|---|---|
| TA | 4,382 | 143,567 | 144,316 |
| NW | (1,420,246) | (1,572,310) | (1,570,060) |
| WC | (1,422,615) | (1,574,942) | (1,572,984) |

DUNS 21-447-5774
## Peebles Hydro Ltd
Innerleithen Road, Peebles, Peeblesshire EH45 8LX
**Tel:** 01721720451
**Web:** www.peebleshydro.com
**Reg No:** 0005906SC **VAT No:** 269255135
**Estd:** 1905 Private Limited Company
**Line of Business:** Hotels and motels without restaurant
**Trading Style:** The Park Hotel
**Issued Capital:** £220,000
**Directors:** G K Leckie, J D Jennett
**Responsibilities**
**Senior:** Val Carrick (Manager), Mandy Colquhon (Personnel Manager), Fay Cowan (Manager)
**HR:** Ali Donnechie (Personnel Manager), Caroline Wood (Personnel Manager)
**Branches:** Peebles Hydro Ltd, Innerleithen Road, Peebles, Peeblesshire EH45 8BA
**US SIC:** 7011 **UK SIC:** 66500
**Auditors:** William Duncan & Co
**Bankers:** Bank Of Scotland (80-09-33)

| | 28-02-14 | 31-05-13 | 31-02-12 |
|---|---|---|---|
| TO | 3,177,137 | 4,369,111 | 4,265,118 |
| P/L | 198,184 | (60,415) | (151,574) |
| NW | 4,237,587 | 4,266,146 | 9,857,695 |
| WC | (419,859) | (413,341) | 190,344 |
| Emp. | 113 | 127 | 142 |

DUNS 21-107-6194
## Peel Holdings Land & Property (Uk) Ltd
(**Subsidiary of:** Tokenhouse Ltd)
The Dome, The Trafford Centre, Manchester M17 8PL
**Tel:** 01616298200
**Reg No:** 6497115 **Estd:** 2008 Private Limited Company
**Line of Business:** Development and selling of real estate
**Export Sales:** £3,272,000
**Issued Capital:** £406,259,707
**Directors:** P P Wainscott, S Underwood, P J Hosker, J Whittaker
**Co. Secretary:** Neil Lees
**US SIC:** 6552, 6531
**UK SIC:** 85000, 83400

**Auditors:** Deloitte LLP

| | 31-03-14 | 31-03-13 | 31-03-12 |
|---|---|---|---|
| TO | 84,616,000 | 85,540,000 | 91,700,000 |
| P/L | (36,101,000) | (6,721,000) | (22,078,000) |
| NW | 551,215,000 | 580,653,000 | 561,263,000 |
| WC | (80,808,000) | (269,559,000) | (48,942,000) |
| Emp. | 118 | 132 | 125 |

DUNS 64-078-4229
## Peel Hotels P L C
Westgate, Peterborough, Cambridgeshire PE1 1RB
**Tel:** 01733561364 **Fax:** 01733-557304
**Web:** www.peelhotels.co.uk
**Reg No:** 3473990 **VAT No:** 706050474
**Estd:** 1997 Public Limited Company
**Line of Business:** Hotels and motels without restaurant
**Trading Style:** Bull Hotel, Avon Gorge Hotel, The Golden Lion Hotel
**Issued Capital:** £1,412,612
**Principals:** R E Peel (Managing), C J Govett, N P Petersen, K P Benham, N D Parrish
**Co. Secretary:** Thrings Llp
**Responsibilities**
**Senior:** Jo Kasey (Food & Beverage Manager)
**Finance:** Gail Boreham (Financial Controller)
**Marketing:** Maria Oska (Sales & Marketing Manager)
**Sales:** Maria Oska (Sales & Marketing Manager)
**HR:** Sandra Parnham (Personnel Manager)
**Health & Safety:** Sandra Parnham (Personnel Manager)
**Facilities:** Howard Vacca (Maintenance Manager)
**Operations:** Sandra Parnham (Personnel Manager)
**Purchasing:** Gail Boreham (Financial Controller)
**Branches:** Peel Hotels P L C, 2 Briggate, Leeds, West Yorkshire LS1 4AE
**US SIC:** 7011, 5812
**UK SIC:** 66500, 66110
**Auditors:** Grant Thornton UK LLP
**Bankers:** The Royal Bank Of Scotland Plc (15-10-00)

| | 02-02-14 | 03-02-13 | 05-02-12 |
|---|---|---|---|
| TO | 15,509,911 | 15,233,026 | 14,647,126 |
| P/L | 341,863 | (97,411) | (227,802) |
| NW | 22,443,067 | 22,053,594 | 22,049,442 |
| WC | (2,268,362) | (4,520,216) | (4,223,494) |
| Emp. | 453 | 450 | 445 |

DUNS 21-206-6695
## Peel House Nursing & Residential Care Home
Peel House, Woodcote Lane, Fareham, Hampshire PO14 1AY
**Tel:** 01329-667724
**Web:** www.peelhouse.org.uk
**Estd:** 1992 Proprietorship
**Line of Business:** Nursing homes
**Proprietor:** Mrs P West
**Responsibilities**
**Senior:** Pari Asghan (Proprietor), Valenzina Purefoy (Home Manager)
**Finance:** Suzanne Pearce (Financial Administrator)
**HR:** Pari Asghan (Proprietor), Valenzina Purefoy (Home Manager)
**Health & Safety:** Valenzina Purefoy (Home Manager)
**Facilities:** Pari Asghan (Proprietor)
**Operations:** Valenzina Purefoy (Home Manager)
**US SIC:** 8051 **UK SIC:** 95100
**Employees:** 50

DUNS 21-684-4114
## Peel Hunt Llp
120 London Wall Fore Street, London EC2Y 5EJ
**Tel:** 02074188900
**Web:** www.peelhunt.com
**Reg No:** 0357088OC **Estd:** 2010
**Line of Business:** Insurance brokers
**Responsibilities**
**Senior:** Peter Hannes (Manager), Alexandra Hendy (Non-designated Limited Liabili), Richard Kauffer (Non-designated Limited Liabili), Aaqib Mirza (Non-designated Limited Liabili), Andrew Nussey (Non-designated Limited Liabili), Nick Pettman (Non-designated Limited Liabili), Guido Segers (Manager), Andrew Shepherd-Barron (Non-designated Limited Liabili), James Steel (Non-designated Limited Liabili), Karen Stevenson (Non-designated Limited Liabili), Guy Wiehahn (Non-designated Limited Liabili)
**US SIC:** 6211 **UK SIC:** 83100

| | 31-03-14 | 31-03-13 | 31-03-12 |
|---|---|---|---|
| TA | 512,010,000 | 370,686,000 | 348,867,000 |
| P/L | 24,879,000 | 2,838,000 | 4,230,000 |
| NW | 32,375,000 | 35,557,000 | 35,629,000 |
| WC | 37,546,000 | 40,370,000 | 39,490,000 |
| Emp. | 156 | 152 | 152 |

DUNS 67-145-1925
## Peel Media Hotels Ltd
(**Subsidiary of:** Tokenhouse Ltd)
Peel Dome, The Trafford Centre, Manchester M17 8PL
**Tel:** 01616603711
**Web:** www.peel.co.uk
**Reg No:** 6003799 **Estd:** 2006 Private Limited Company
**Line of Business:** Hotels
**Trading Style:** Peel Holdings
**Issued Capital:** £2
**Directors:** P J Hosker, J Whittaker, P P Wainscott, D J Glover, S Underwood
**Co. Secretary:** Neil Lees
**US SIC:** 7011 **UK SIC:** 66500

| | 31-03-14 | 31-03-13 | 31-03-12 |
|---|---|---|---|
| TO | 5,262,824 | 4,951,572 | 4,441,333 |
| P/L | 417,891 | 370,423 | 245,472 |
| NW | (2,140,926) | (2,495,117) | (2,854,960) |
| WC | (2,182,744) | (2,544,934) | (2,908,889) |
| Emp. | 54 | 55 | 61 |

DUNS 51-648-2937
## Peel Ports Group Ltd
(**Subsidiary of:** Tokenhouse Ltd)
Maritime Centre, Port Of Liverpool, Liverpool, Merseyside L21 1LA
**Web:** www.peelports.com
**Reg No:** 5965116 **Estd:** 2006 Private Limited Company
**Line of Business:** Management activities of holding companies
**Export Sales:** £98,200,000
**Issued Capital:** £337,492,988
**Directors:** T E Allison, I G Charnock, Dr M Whitworth, J Whittaker, H M Mackenzie, S Underwood, S Vyas
**Co. Secretary:** Ms Caroline Marrison G
**US SIC:** 6711 **UK SIC:** 83962
**Bankers:** The Royal Bank Of Scotland Plc (16-24-06)

| | 31-03-14 | 31-03-13 | 31-03-12 |
|---|---|---|---|
| TO | 623,700,000 | 501,900,000 | 380,500,000 |
| P/L | 3,900,000 | 28,400,000 | 26,900,000 |
| NW | (719,200,000) | (676,500,000) | (804,500,000) |
| WC | (92,000,000) | (126,800,000) | (78,600,000) |
| Emp. | 2,745 | 1,963 | 1,216 |

DUNS 21-307-9977
## The Peele
15 Walney Road, Manchester M22 9TP
**Tel:** 0161-490-8057
**Estd:** 2012 Proprietorship
**Line of Business:** Children's homes
**Responsibilities**
**Senior:** Lin Block (Manager)
**US SIC:** 8321 **UK SIC:** 96111
**Employees:** 134

DUNS 21-157-9603 **Imp**
## Peer 1 (Uk) Ltd.
The Quay, Southampton, Hampshire SO14 3TG
**Tel:** 08008407490 **Fax:** 023 802 30340
**Web:** www.peer1hosting.co.uk
**Reg No:** 6854675 **VAT No:** 971189590
**Estd:** 2009 Private Limited Company
**Line of Business:** Computer services
**Issued Capital:** £1
**Directors:** Mrs H Ives, R Woodham
**Responsibilities**
**Senior:** Christian Jolivet (Director)
**US SIC:** 7379, 7374
**UK SIC:** 83940
**Auditors:** Mazars LLP

| | 31-08-13 | 30-06-13 | 30-08-12 |
|---|---|---|---|
| TO | 1,895,548 | 8,143,205 | N/A |
| P/L | (1,279,031) | (10,263,775) | N/A |
| NW | 6,020,095 | 7,299,127 | (11,487,189) |
| WC | (11,496,666) | (8,431,890) | (1,224,038) |
| Emp. | 94 | 87 | N/A |

DUNS 22-772-2089 **Imp**
## Peers Hardy (U K) Ltd
Precision House, Birmingham, West Midlands B37 7GN
**Tel:** 01215258577
**Web:** www.peershardy.com
**Reg No:** 1391526 **Estd:** 1976 Private Limited Company
**Line of Business:** Watch and clock sales & repairs
**Export Sales:** £3,850,559
**Trading Style:** Icewatch
**Issued Capital:** £85,000
**Principals:** J E Story (Chairman), N C Baker, D N Crowe, P V Harry
**Co. Secretary:** David Crowe
**Responsibilities**
**IT:** John Kitts (Purchasing Manager)
**Purchasing:** John Kitts (Purchasing Manager)
**Branches:** Peers Hardy (U K) Ltd, Stokenchurch Business Park, Unit 6, High Wycombe, Buckinghamshire HP14 3FE
**US SIC:** 5199, 5064
**UK SIC:** 61900, 61500
**Auditors:** CK Audit

**Bankers:** The Hongkong And Shanghai Banking Corporation Ltd (40-48-69)

| | 31-12-13 | 31-12-12 | 31-12-11 |
|---|---|---|---|
| TO | 32,536,275 | 34,359,099 | 25,771,990 |
| P/L | 1,275,958 | 1,575,697 | 1,588,939 |
| NW | 7,142,035 | 6,821,416 | 5,652,427 |
| WC | 6,608,233 | 6,322,716 | 5,329,230 |
| Emp. | 105 | 104 | 95 |

DUNS 49-249-9215
## Peers Hunt Ltd
(**Subsidiary of:** Texas Holdings Ltd)
Barton Hall Works, Manchester M30 7SD
**Tel:** 01617879298 **Fax:** 0161-787-7280
**Web:** www.txholdings.com
**Reg No:** 3118369 **Estd:** 1995 Private Limited Company
**Line of Business:** Other letting of own property
**Trading Style:** Texas Holdings Limited.
**Issued Capital:** £50,000
**Directors:** R K Mcdonald, J M Mcdonald
**Co. Secretary:** Stuart Mollekin
**Branches:** Peers Hunt Ltd, Hobhill Farm, Hague St, Glossop, Derbyshire SK13 8NS
**US SIC:** 6519, 6531
**UK SIC:** 85000, 83400
**Auditors:** Morris Gregory
**Bankers:** Yorkshire Bank Plc (05-00-20)

| | 30-11-13 | 30-11-12 | 30-11-11 |
|---|---|---|---|
| TO | 111,000 | 240,000 | N/A |
| P/L | (14,000) | (55,000) | (15,000) |
| NW | (43,000) | (29,000) | 26,000 |
| WC | (1,247,000) | (780,000) | (471,000) |

DUNS 57-055-1952
## Pegasus Express Ltd
(**Subsidiary of:** Ecosse Transport Logistics Ltd)
Souter Head Road, Aberdeen, Aberdeenshire AB12 3LF
**Tel:** 01224890999
**Web:** www.pegasusexp.co.uk
**Reg No:** 0148046SC **Estd:** 1980 Private Limited Company
**Line of Business:** Representative office
**Issued Capital:** £864,519
**Directors:** J A Mcnab, J A Cowie, Ms J E Murphy, W Goodall
**Responsibilities**
**Senior:** Charles Ryrie (Warehouse Manager)
**Branches:** Pegasus Express Ltd, 10 Biggar Road, Motherwell, Lanarkshire ML1 5PB
**US SIC:** 7399, 4226
**UK SIC:** 83954, 77003
**Auditors:** Johnston Carmichael
**Bankers:** Bank Of Scotland (80-11-00)

| | 31-10-13 | 31-10-12 | 31-10-11 |
|---|---|---|---|
| TO | 7,570,925 | 7,195,658 | 6,680,517 |
| P/L | (44,039) | (202,209) | (93,440) |
| NW | 336,144 | 380,183 | 582,392 |
| WC | (37,602) | 263,852 | 400,062 |
| Emp. | 84 | 88 | 89 |

DUNS 53-616-1763
## Pegasus Fire Protection Co Ltd
25a Bankhead Drive, Edinburgh, Midlothian EH11 4DN
**Web:** www.pfpuk.com
**Reg No:** 0178102SC **VAT No:** 694117127
**Estd:** 2003 Private Limited Company
**Line of Business:** Partition installation of
**Trading Style:** P F P
**Issued Capital:** £12,000
**Managing Director:** W B Sinclair
**Co. Secretary:** Christopher Shaw
**Responsibilities**
**Senior:** Amanda Riley (Manager), Laura Sinclair (Office Manager)
**Admin:** Laura Sinclair (Office Manager)
**US SIC:** 1799, 1742
**UK SIC:** 50000, 50400
**Auditors:** Danzig & Co
**Bankers:** Bank Of Scotland (80-11-00)

| | 31-08-13 | 31-08-12 | 31-08-11 |
|---|---|---|---|
| TO | 9,686,170 | 10,366,094 | 9,449,658 |
| P/L | 629,980 | 766,213 | 1,855,212 |
| NW | 3,955,639 | 3,529,925 | 3,453,336 |
| WC | 3,785,188 | 3,302,685 | 3,258,321 |
| Emp. | 193 | 187 | 154 |

DUNS 21-676-1503
## Pegasus Planning Group Ltd
Querns Business Centre, Whitworth Road, Cirencester, Gloucestershire GL7 1RT
**Tel:** 01285641717
**Web:** www.pegasuspg.co.uk
**Reg No:** 7277000 **Estd:** 2003 Private Limited Company
**Line of Business:** Planning consultants
**Issued Capital:** £10,400
**Directors:** D J Stentiford, J Holden, M J Smith, S H Bawtree, A C Bateman, M E Dobson, P Burrell, G R Godwin
**Responsibilities**
**Senior:** Gary Lees (Director), Jeremy Peachey (Director), James Tarzey (Director)

**Branches:** Pegasus Planning Group Ltd, Pegasus Planning Group Ltd, Pioneer Court, Cambridge, Cambridgeshire CB24 9PT
**US SIC:** 8911 **UK SIC:** 83701
**Auditors:** Hazlewoods LLP
**Bankers:** Barclays Bank Plc (20-49-08)

| | 30-06-13 | 30-06-12 | 30-06-11 |
|---|---|---|---|
| TO | 16,875,056 | 14,328,155 | 11,654,401 |
| P/L | 3,289,916 | 3,048,980 | 1,456,878 |
| NW | (3,173,258) | (6,705,137) | (10,158,936) |
| WC | (3,303,208) | (6,821,892) | (10,214,475) |
| Emp. | 182 | 151 | 131 |

DUNS 77-670-5667

## Pegasus Public Relations Ltd

Sovereign House, Church Street, Brighton, East Sussex BN1 1UJ
**Web:** www.thisispegasus.co.uk
**Reg No:** 3005235 **Estd:** 1994 Private Limited Company
**Line of Business:** Public relations consultants
**Issued Capital:** £103
**Principals:** Ms L H Bradley *(Managing)*, S Hehir, Ms J Spadaccino, D I Mackenzie-Reid, S R Hackett, T P Adams, Ms H Goggin, R Calvert
**Responsibilities**
**Senior:** Helan Yeardsley *(Manager)*
**US SIC:** 7392 **UK SIC:** 83951
**Auditors:** L E V Masters & Co

| | 31-12-13 | 31-12-12 | 31-12-11 |
|---|---|---|---|
| TA | 3,935,198 | 2,735,694 | 2,180,190 |
| NW | 2,413,383 | 1,640,382 | 1,291,041 |
| WC | 2,259,309 | 1,393,327 | 1,103,323 |

DUNS 22-659-2533 **Exp**

## Pegasus Software Ltd

(**Subsidiary of:** Infor Lux Bond Company)
Orion House, Orion Way, Kettering, Northamptonshire NN15 6PE
**Fax:** 01536-495001
**Web:** www.pegasus.co.uk
**Reg No:** 1601542 **Estd:** 1981 Private Limited Company
**Line of Business:** Computer software (development)
**Export Markets:** U.S.A.; Hong Kong; Ireland; S Africa
**Export Sales:** £312,000
**Issued Capital:** £2,000,000
**Directors:** Ms J Allsop, G Czasznicki, J B Kasper
**Responsibilities**
**Senior:** George Bisnought *(Manager)*, Andrew Oldroyd *(Director)*
**Marketing:** Jennifer Harley *(Marketing Manager)*, Steve Power *(Product Specialist)*
**IT:** Shaun Hanna *(Development Director)*
**US SIC:** 7379 **UK SIC:** 83940
**Auditors:** KPMG Audit PLC
**Bankers:** Barclays Bank Plc (20-45-77)

| | 31-05-14 | 31-05-13 | 31-05-12 |
|---|---|---|---|
| TO | 6,600,000 | 6,603,000 | 6,621,000 |
| P/L | 2,927,000 | 3,985,000 | 19,243,000 |
| NW | 11,389,000 | 8,431,000 | 4,415,000 |
| WC | 10,364,000 | 5,914,000 | 1,887,000 |
| Emp. | 50 | 53 | 53 |

DUNS 22-513-8650 **Exp**

## Pegasus Solutions Ltd

(**Subsidiary of:** Perseus Holding Corp)
Unit 2670, Kings Court, The Crescent, Birmingham, West Midlands B37 7YE
**Tel:** 02086042400
**Web:** www.pegs.com
**Reg No:** 0181427 **VAT No:** 787449368
**Estd:** 1922 Private Limited Company
**Line of Business:** Other computer related activities
**Export Markets:** Worldwide
**Trading Style:** Summit International Hotels, A B C International, Official Airline Guides, Golden Tulip Worldwide
**Directors:** D Millili, T Weiss
**Responsibilities**
**Sales:** Chris Wichers *(Chief Sales Officer)*
**IT:** Bill Rose *(Chief Information Officer)*
**HR:** Rick Huntley *(Vice President Human Resources)*
**Branches:** Pegasus Solutions Ltd, 13-16 Addiscombe Rd, Croydon, Surrey CR9 6DS
**US SIC:** 7379 **UK SIC:** 83940
**Auditors:** KPMG LLP
**Bankers:** National Westminster Bank Plc (60-07-08)
**Employees:** 257
**Turnover:** £34,170,000

DUNS 57-615-3621 **Imp-Exp**

## Pegasystems Ltd

(**Subsidiary of:** Pegasystems Inc.)
Atrium Court, Forbury Road Apex Plaza, Reading, Berkshire RG1 1AX
**Tel:** 01189-591150 **Fax:** 01189-591174
**Web:** www.pega.com
**Reg No:** 2883981 **Estd:** 1994 Private Limited Company
**Line of Business:** Hardware consultancy
**Issued Capital:** £1,002
**Directors:** Ms J Mesrobian, E Kouninis, D Wells, Ms A E Warner
**Responsibilities**
**Senior:** Shawn Hoyt *(Vice President, Global Custome)*, Alan Trefler *(CEO / Managing Director and Fo)*
**Sales:** Shawn Hoyt *(Vice President, Global Custome)*
**HR:** Lesley Law *(Human Resources Manager)*
**Health & Safety:** Lesley Law *(Human Resources Manager)*
**Facilities:** Lesley Law *(Human Resources Manager)*
**Operations:** Lesley Law *(Human Resources Manager)*
**US SIC:** 7379 **UK SIC:** 83940
**Auditors:** Arthur Andersen
**Bankers:** Barclays Bank Plc (20-71-03)

| | 31-12-13 | 31-12-12 | 31-12-11 |
|---|---|---|---|
| TO | 36,522,526 | 38,399,076 | 34,460,328 |
| P/L | 2,783,235 | 3,206,226 | 2,299,111 |
| NW | 16,909,949 | 14,827,443 | 12,442,520 |
| WC | 14,383,265 | 11,652,501 | 8,518,776 |
| Emp. | 210 | 203 | 168 |

DUNS 29-012-8727

## Pegler Yorkshire Group Ltd

(**Subsidiary of:** Aalberts Industries N.V.)
Belmont Works, St Catherines Avenue, Doncaster, South Yorkshire DN4 8DF
**Tel:** 08442-434-400 **Fax:** 08442-439-870
**Web:** www.pegleryorkshire.co.uk
**Reg No:** 0401507 **VAT No:** 418013192
**Estd:** 1945 Private Limited Company
**Line of Business:** Manufacturers of commercial and residential plumbing and heating products
**Export Sales:** £43,159,000
**Trading Style:** Pegler Yorkshire
**Issued Capital:** £55,558,827
**Directors:** I M Howarth, N Mccarroll, W A Pelsma, G Fawcett, S K Craig
**Co. Secretary:** Kevin Parker
**Responsibilities**
**Finance:** Dale Bacon *(Key Accounts Manager)*
**Marketing:** Phill Jackson *(Senior Marketing Executive)*
**Sales:** Paul Arbon *(Sales Manager)*, Julie Ball *(Retail Sales Manager)*, Chris Barnham *(Sales Manager)*, David Feehan *(Sales Manager)*, Michael Link *(Sales Manager)*, Steve Molson *(Area Sales Manager)*, Chris Sowerby *(Senior Domestic Sales Executiv)*
**Admin:** Karen Sanderson *(Receptionist)*
**Operations:** Barrie Plant *(Product Market Manager)*, Paul Reasbeck *(Export Director)*
**Purchasing:** Roger Ablett *(Supply Chain Director)*, Tony Hirst *(Purchasing Manager)*
**Branches:** Pegler Yorkshire Group Ltd, Fyffe Works, Carolina Port, Dundee, Angus DD1 3LR
**US SIC:** 3494, 3433, 3585
**UK SIC:** 32880, 32041, 32841
**Auditors:** PricewaterhouseCoopers LLP
**Bankers:** Lloyds TSB Bank plc (30-00-05)

| | 31-12-13 | 31-12-12 | 31-12-11 |
|---|---|---|---|
| TO | 146,317,000 | 150,784,000 | 154,085,000 |
| P/L | 7,593,000 | 6,956,000 | 6,477,000 |
| NW | 44,451,000 | 43,099,000 | 43,029,000 |
| WC | 48,618,000 | 48,542,000 | 50,283,000 |
| Emp. | 271 | 275 | 289 |

DUNS 21-622-5716

## Pei Delta Group Ltd

Furness Drive, Poulton Industrial Estate, Poulton-Le-Fylde, Lancashire FY6 8JS
**Web:** www.pei-delta.co.uk
**Reg No:** 7031809 **Estd:** 2009 Private Limited Company
**Line of Business:** Electrical contractors and electricians
**Issued Capital:** £10,000
**Directors:** Ms C Gallagher, R Gallagher, D J Rothwell
**Co. Secretary:** Ms Caroline Gallagher
**US SIC:** 1731 **UK SIC:** 50300

| | 30-04-14 | 30-04-13 | 30-04-12 |
|---|---|---|---|
| TO | 7,191,002 | 9,010,235 | 10,467,288 |
| P/L | 367,436 | 806,563 | 959,322 |
| NW | 2,281,918 | 2,072,554 | 1,619,021 |
| WC | 2,236,152 | 1,994,817 | 1,542,231 |
| Emp. | 78 | 85 | 93 |

DUNS 36-530-1175 **Imp**

## Pei-Genesis (U.K.) Ltd

(**Subsidiary of:** Pei/Genesis Inc.)
George Curl Way, Southampton, Hampshire SO18 2RZ
**Tel:** 0844-871-6060 **Fax:** 08448716070
**Web:** www.peigenesis.com
**Reg No:** 3290190 **Estd:** 1997 Private Limited Company
**Line of Business:** Manufacture of electronic valves and tubes and other electronic components
**Export Sales:** £26,230,251
**Issued Capital:** £207,000
**Managing Director:** S L Fisher
**Co. Secretary:** Gregory Warshaw
**Responsibilities**
**Senior:** Tony Houghton *(Operations Manager)*
**Marketing:** Peter Christie *(Business Development Director)*
**Sales:** Linda Harrison *(Regional Sales Manager)*
**HR:** Kelly Sunderland *(Human Resources Manager)*
**Health & Safety:** Jerry Griffin *(Facilities Manager)*
**Facilities:** Jerry Griffin *(Facilities Manager)*
**Operations:** Tony Houghton *(Operations Manager)*
**Engineering:** Tony Houghton *(Operations Manager)*
**US SIC:** 3679, 5084
**UK SIC:** 34542, 61490
**Auditors:** Magee Gammon Corporate Ltd

| | 31-08-14 | 31-08-13 | 31-08-12 |
|---|---|---|---|
| TO | 34,153,973 | 33,472,664 | 30,049,065 |
| P/L | (35,639) | 374,710 | (540,391) |
| NW | 3,663,908 | 3,435,906 | 2,891,761 |
| WC | 2,821,897 | 2,527,933 | 1,937,557 |
| Emp. | 168 | 154 | 153 |

DUNS 21-954-3134

## Pei Media Group Ltd

Bastion House, 140 London Wall, London EC2Y 5DN
**Tel:** 020-7566-5444 **Fax:** 021-2633-2904
**Web:** www.peimedia.com
**Reg No:** 6135779 **Estd:** 2007 Private Limited Company
**Line of Business:** Management activities of holding companies
**Export Sales:** £8,274,850
**Issued Capital:** £9,450
**Directors:** R F O'Donohoe, T Mcloughlin, P K Borel, D C Hawkins
**Co. Secretary:** Mrs Cordulla Weisser-Borel
**US SIC:** 6711 **UK SIC:** 83962

| | 31-12-13 | 31-12-12 | 31-12-11 |
|---|---|---|---|
| TO | 12,008,460 | 10,405,193 | 9,404,885 |
| P/L | 1,296,578 | 400,248 | 119,261 |
| NW | (562,538) | (1,356,748) | (1,573,398) |
| WC | (796,643) | (1,693,130) | (1,967,172) |
| Emp. | 115 | 98 | 96 |

DUNS 21-861-0426 **Imp-Exp**

## Pektron Group Ltd

Alfreton Road, Derby, Derbyshire DE21 4AP
**Tel:** 01332-832424
**Web:** www.pektron.co.uk
**Reg No:** 0823259 **Estd:** 1964 Private Limited Company
**Line of Business:** Manufacture of electronic valves and tubes and other electronic components
**Export Markets:** E U, Middle East, U S A, Australasia, Canada
**Issued Capital:** £9,500
**Principals:** G Morgan *(Chairman and Managing)*, I S Harpham, J R Potts
**Co. Secretary:** Ms Barbara Morgan
**Responsibilities**
**IT:** Kevin Bark *(It Manager)*
**HR:** Tina Roberts *(Training Manager)*, Nesta Robinson *(Human Resources Coordinator)*
**Facilities:** Gary Brock *(Maintenance Coordinator)*
**Purchasing:** Jason Hatton *(Purchasing Manager)*
**US SIC:** 3679, 3621
**UK SIC:** 34542, 34201
**Auditors:** Smith Cooper
**Bankers:** The Royal Bank Of Scotland Plc (16-11-31)

| | 31-12-13 | 31-12-12 | 31-12-11 |
|---|---|---|---|
| TO | 39,105,320 | 32,620,710 | 27,400,218 |
| P/L | 6,539,356 | 5,623,082 | 5,225,400 |
| NW | 30,266,891 | 26,905,794 | 24,317,733 |
| WC | 24,274,789 | 19,930,436 | 17,089,761 |
| Emp. | 314 | 289 | 252 |

DUNS 29-823-0707 **Imp**

## Pel Services Ltd

Unit 1-2, Belvue Road Belvue Business Centre, Northolt, Middlesex UB5 5QQ
**Tel:** 020-8839-2100 **Fax:** 020-8841-1948
**Web:** www.pel.co.uk
**Reg No:** 2016666 **VAT No:** 449317922
**Estd:** 1986 Private Limited Company
**Line of Business:** Security and related activities
**Issued Capital:** £10,000
**Principals:** K I Faulks *(Managing)*, K L Hobbs, D A Jarman, V W Swain
**Co. Secretary:** Ms Karen Hobbs
**Responsibilities**
**HR:** David Barnhurst *(Health & Safety Officer)*
**Health & Safety:** David Barnhurst *(Health & Safety Officer)*
**US SIC:** 7393, 9224, 1731
**UK SIC:** 83954, 91400, 50300
**Auditors:** Haysmacintyre
**Bankers:** National Westminster Bank Plc (56-00-03)

| | 31-12-13 | 31-12-12 | 31-12-11 |
|---|---|---|---|
| TA | 2,323,088 | 2,035,685 | 1,815,696 |
| NW | 1,581,787 | 1,357,312 | 1,157,923 |
| WC | 1,345,239 | 1,226,753 | 1,095,862 |

DUNS 73-389-4542

## Peldon Rose Group Ltd

42 Worple Road, London SW19 4EQ
**Tel:** 020-8971-7777 **Fax:** 020-8971-7789
**Web:** www.peldonrose.co.uk
**Reg No:** 4662933 **Estd:** 2003 Private Limited Company
**Line of Business:** Other construction work involving special trades
**Export Sales:** £77,130
**Issued Capital:** £80
**Directors:** A R Jamieson, J N Patel, Ms C A Unsworth
**Co. Secretary:** Ms Christina Unsworth
**Responsibilities**
**Senior:** Marie Heaphy *(Financial Controller)*
**Finance:** Marie Heaphy *(Financial Controller)*
**HR:** Corinne Watkyns *(Human Resources Manager)*
**US SIC:** 1522, 1799
**UK SIC:** 50100, 50000

| | 31-03-14 | 31-03-13 | 31-03-12 |
|---|---|---|---|
| TO | 37,806,926 | 19,808,077 | 12,493,625 |
| P/L | 4,168,262 | 1,035,947 | 156,504 |
| NW | 5,412,137 | 2,672,413 | 2,402,830 |
| WC | 3,389,145 | 703,831 | 631,733 |
| Emp. | 62 | 56 | 59 |

DUNS 73-579-4492

## Pelham House Associates Ltd

St Andrews Lane, Lewes, East Sussex BN7 1UW
**Tel:** 01273-488600
**Web:** www.pelhamhouse.com
**Reg No:** 4840996 **Estd:** 2003 Private Limited Company
**Line of Business:** Hotels
**Issued Capital:** £196,126
**Directors:** D M Anderson, S I Horthy
**Co. Secretary:** Sharifin Gardiner
**Responsibilities**
**Senior:** Matt Linkin *(General Manager)*
**US SIC:** 7011, 5999
**UK SIC:** 66500, 65600
**Bankers:** HSBC Bank plc (40-28-15)

| | 31-01-14 | 31-01-13 | 31-01-12 |
|---|---|---|---|
| TO | 2,105,572 | 1,989,283 | 1,921,085 |
| P/L | 115,603 | 76,140 | 170,650 |
| NW | (58,577) | (409,023) | (485,163) |
| WC | (730,808) | (995,885) | (1,024,150) |
| Emp. | 54 | 55 | 50 |

DUNS 50-510-7920 **Imp**

## Pelham Leather Goods Ltd

The Pelham Centre, Borehamwood, Hertfordshire WD6 3SB
**Tel:** 020-8731-3500
**Web:** www.pelhamgroup.co.uk
**Reg No:** 2478674 **Estd:** 1990 Private Limited Company
**Line of Business:** Wholesale of hides, skins and leather
**Trading Style:** Tumi
**Issued Capital:** £191,301
**Principals:** J P Kraines *(Managing)*, P Mcguinness *(Sales)*, N Crossick, M J Crowe, R A Ettlinger, S B Spitz
**Co. Secretary:** Jonathan Kraines
**Responsibilities**
**Senior:** John Kraines *(Operations Director)*
**Marketing:** Shelley Williams *(Marketing Manager)*
**Operations:** John Kraines *(Operations Director)*
**US SIC:** 5159, 5661
**UK SIC:** 61100, 64600
**Auditors:** Rawlinson & Hunter

| | 31-01-14 | 31-01-13 | 31-01-12 |
|---|---|---|---|
| TO | 23,093,278 | 20,687,962 | 20,792,752 |
| P/L | 335,109 | 258,477 | 235,046 |
| NW | (2,454,653) | (2,923,785) | (3,320,285) |
| WC | (2,105,412) | (2,963,096) | (2,966,018) |
| Emp. | 144 | 131 | 125 |

DUNS 21-930-3106

## Pelham Primary School

Pelham Road, Bexleyheath, Kent DA7 4HL
**Web:** www.pelhamprimary.co.uk
**Reg No:** 8439184 **Estd:** 2013 Private Company Limited By Guarantee
**Line of Business:** Primary education
**Directors:** Miss E M Anderson, R O Mcdonnell, K R Barrett, Dr A M Rashid, G D Streatfield, Ms I M Holliss, D A Micklefield, A I Hogarth
**Responsibilities**
**Senior:** Derek Clements *(Director)*, Jill Hayman *(Director)*
**US SIC:** 8211 **UK SIC:** 93200

**Bankers:** Lloyds TSB Bank plc (30-25-80)

| | 31-08-14 | 31-08-13 |
|---|---|---|
| TO | 2,253,887 | 5,162,724 |
| P/L | 42,607 | 4,055,161 |
| NW | 4,039,768 | 4,079,161 |
| WC | 332,183 | 278,917 |
| Emp. | 41 | 53 |

DUNS 21-786-0937

## Pelhams Park Leisure Centre

Manor Farm Road, Kinson, Bournemouth, Dorset BH10 7LF
**Tel:** 01202437801
**Web:** www.pelhamsparkleisurecentre.co.uk
**Estd:** 2011 Proprietorship
**Line of Business:** Operation of swimming pools
**Proprietor:** Miss G Hawkett
**US SIC:** 7999 **UK SIC:** 97913
**Employees:** 60

DUNS 34-578-5372     Imp

## Peli Products (Uk) Ltd

Peli House, Peakdale Road Brookfield Industrial, Estate, Glossop, Derbyshire SK13 6LQ
**Fax:** 01457-869966
**Web:** www.peliproducts.co.uk
**Reg No:** 2725685 **VAT No:** 603414680
**Estd:** 1992 Private Limited Company
**Line of Business:** Distribution service providers
**Export Sales:** £160,995
**Issued Capital:** £3,338
**Principals:** E W Breeze (Managing), Ms G Howard, J C Hastings, A P Clark, P S Frost
**Co. Secretary:** Ms Sarah Breeze
**Responsibilities**
**Senior:** Neil McMillan (Manager)
**Marketing:** Gill Lack (Marketing director)
**US SIC:** 5065, 5199
**UK SIC:** 61500, 61900
**Auditors:** Chadwick & Co (Manchester) Ltd
**Bankers:** HSBC Bank plc (40-08-33)

| | 30-11-13 | 30-11-12 | 30-11-11 |
|---|---|---|---|
| TO | 10,516,240 | N/A | N/A |
| P/L | 936,767 | N/A | N/A |
| NW | 2,366,203 | 2,076,998 | 1,466,246 |
| WC | 1,288,120 | 1,806,622 | 1,189,441 |
| Emp. | 54 | N/A | N/A |

DUNS 21-218-1598

## Pelican Engineering Co. Ltd

Altofts Lane, Wakefield Europort, Castleford, West Yorkshire WF10 5UB
**Tel:** 01924227722
**Web:** www.pelicangenerators.co.uk
**Reg No:** 0212209 **Estd:** 1919 Private Limited Company
**Line of Business:** Van and truck dealers
**Issued Capital:** £2,856
**Principals:** R B Crump (Managing), R E Crump (Managing), Miss S J Newton
**Co. Secretary:** Richard Crump
**Responsibilities**
**Sales:** Ken Grindrod (Senior Sales Executive)
**US SIC:** 6711, 5511
**UK SIC:** 83962, 65100
**Auditors:** David Newton & Co Ltd
**Bankers:** HSBC Bank plc (40-19-17)

| | 31-03-14 | 31-03-13 | 31-03-12 |
|---|---|---|---|
| TO | 20,068,708 | 20,294,889 | 17,776,324 |
| P/L | 769,820 | 539,816 | 207,285 |
| NW | 6,079,624 | 5,759,501 | 5,543,701 |
| WC | 2,872,187 | 2,673,843 | 2,293,882 |
| Emp. | 121 | 123 | 114 |

DUNS 50-347-2557

## Pelican Procurement Services Ltd

Southern House, Flambard Way, Godalming, Surrey GU7 1HH
**Tel:** 01252705222 **Fax:** 01483-239-109
**Web:** www.pelicanbuying.co.uk
**Reg No:** 2367432 **VAT No:** 528073349
**Estd:** 1989 Private Limited Company
**Line of Business:** Procurement services
**Issued Capital:** £8,714
**Principals:** M O Hancock (Managing), S Mohammed, Ms C A Stimpson, S O Hancock, Ms V P Heffer
**Co. Secretary:** Mrs Christine Stimpson
**Responsibilities**
**Senior:** Nick Bish (Non-Executive Director), Bob Cotton OBE (Non Executive Director)
**Finance:** Gary Cockrel (Accountant), Gary Cottrell (Financial Controller), Franco Scannella (Head of Finance)
**Sales:** Ian Holliday (Head of Sales), Margaret Poulton (Senior Contract Manager)
**US SIC:** 7399 **UK SIC:** 83954
**Auditors:** Wise & Co
**Bankers:** Lloyds TSB Bank plc (30-94-77)

| | 31-12-13 | 31-12-12 | 31-12-11 |
|---|---|---|---|
| TO | 6,728,083 | 6,260,765 | 5,920,476 |
| P/L | 364,264 | 533,825 | 376,768 |
| NW | 2,103,027 | 1,894,599 | 2,137,290 |
| WC | 1,988,389 | 1,768,341 | 1,965,746 |

DUNS 76-840-4410     Imp-Exp

## Pelican Rouge Coffee Solutions Ltd

(**Subsidiary of:** Staunton Luxco Sca)
19 Aintree Road, Greenford, Middlesex UB6 7LG
**Tel:** 02089982828 **Fax:** 0208-498-8499
**Web:** www.bunzlvend.com
**Reg No:** 2605313 **VAT No:** 581705924
**Estd:** 1999 Private Limited Company
**Line of Business:** Canteens and catering
**Export Markets:** Italy
**Export Sales:** £179,000
**Issued Capital:** £3,561
**Directors:** D H Abrahams, K P Geysels
**Responsibilities**
**Finance:** Andrew Mooney (Financial Director)
**IT:** John Sheehan (IT Manager)
**Purchasing:** Becky Osmond (Purchasing Manager)
**Branches:** Pelican Rouge Coffee Solutions Ltd, Unit 28, Purfleet Industrial Park, South Ockendon, Essex RM15 4YA
**US SIC:** 5812, 1731
**UK SIC:** 66110, 50300
**Auditors:** PricewaterhouseCoopers LLP
**Bankers:** National Westminster Bank Plc (60-00-01)

| | 30-03-14 | 31-03-13 | 01-03-12 |
|---|---|---|---|
| TO | 128,669,000 | 94,516,000 | 77,751,000 |
| P/L | (5,047,000) | (262,000) | (8,275,000) |
| NW | 27,197,000 | 2,651,000 | (13,350,000) |
| WC | 29,333,000 | 26,586,000 | 6,148,000 |
| Emp. | 1,225 | 1,203 | 990 |

DUNS 22-730-3609

## Pelicans Manufacturing Co. Ltd

(**Subsidiary of:** Al-Noor Investments Ltd)
717 A, North Circular Road, London NW2 7AH
**Tel:** 020 8452 9111 **Fax:** 020 8452 9911
**Web:** www.pelicans.co.uk
**Reg No:** 1604582 **VAT No:** 396314628
**Estd:** 1981 Private Limited Company
**Line of Business:** Miscellaneous manufacturing industries
**Export Sales:** £7,265,729
**Issued Capital:** £117,000
**Principals:** A N Merchant (Chairman), S F Maxton (Managing), P Kabra, Ms S Merchant, C Acharya
**Co. Secretary:** Mrs Shireen Merchant
**Responsibilities**
**Senior:** Chetan Achariya (Production Manager)
**Finance:** Hamida Ali (Financial Controller)
**HR:** Kamlesh Shah (Quality Manager)
**Health & Safety:** Chetan Achariya (Production Manager)
**Facilities:** Chetan Achariya (Production Manager)
**Engineering:** Chetan Achariya (Production Manager)
**US SIC:** 3999, 5199
**UK SIC:** 49590, 61900
**Auditors:** Atkins & Partners
**Bankers:** National Westminster Bank Plc (50-30-05)

| | 31-05-14 | 31-05-13 | 31-05-12 |
|---|---|---|---|
| TO | 10,407,623 | 11,377,538 | 12,459,637 |
| P/L | 603,081 | 886,822 | 1,102,221 |
| NW | 4,427,011 | 1,917,107 | 1,521,920 |
| WC | 1,978,631 | 1,694,257 | 984,644 |
| Emp. | 62 | 60 | 62 |

DUNS 77-110-1292     Imp-Exp

## Pelikan Hardcopy Scotland Ltd

Markethill Road, Turriff, Aberdeenshire AB53 4AW
**Tel:** 01888564200
**Web:** www.pelikan-ttr.com
**Reg No:** 2686787 **VAT No:** 743002282
**Estd:** 1992 Private Limited Company
**Line of Business:** Manufacturers general
**Export Markets:** Europe
**Export Sales:** £6,411,757
**Trading Style:** Pelikan U K
**Issued Capital:** £7,882,201
**Director:** E Wilson
**Co. Secretary:** Maclay Murray & Spens
**Responsibilities**
**Senior:** Hicham Fadel (Manager), Jock Wilson (Manager)
**US SIC:** 3999, 3953
**UK SIC:** 49590, 49541
**Auditors:** BDO LLP
**Bankers:** Barclays Bank Plc (20-00-00)

| | 31-12-13 | 31-12-12 | 31-12-11 |
|---|---|---|---|
| TO | 7,604,800 | 8,429,063 | 9,225,764 |
| P/L | (2,702,564) | (2,110,548) | (2,586,712) |
| NW | (24,164,546) | (21,290,982) | (18,404,434) |
| WC | (15,752,571) | (13,691,824) | (10,730,816) |
| Emp. | 97 | 98 | 102 |

DUNS 29-159-1048     Exp

## Pell Frischmann Consultants Ltd

(**Subsidiary of:** Pell Frischmann Holdings Ltd)
George House, George Street, Wakefield, West Yorkshire WF1 1LY
**Tel:** 01924368145
**Web:** www.pellfrischmann.com
**Reg No:** 1777946 **Estd:** 1983 Private Limited Company
**Line of Business:** Civil engineers
**Export Markets:** worldwide
**Export Sales:** £3,087,728
**Trading Style:** Pell Frischmann Group
**Issued Capital:** £8,000
**Directors:** C P Mcbeath, Dr W W Frischmann, R J Barrett, T S Prabhu, L Goddard, C V Powell
**Co. Secretary:** Ms Linda Roberts
**Responsibilities**
**Senior:** Tracey Fozzard (Office Manager), Kevin Paylor (Structures Director), Chris Steele (Manager)
**Admin:** Tracey Fozzard (Office Manager)
**Facilities:** Andy Hoyland (Structures Director)
**Purchasing:** Louise Bostock (Administrator)
**Branches:** Pell Frischmann Consultants Ltd, Unit 12, Maryland Road, Tongwell, Milton Keynes, Buckinghamshire MK15 8HF
**US SIC:** 8911 **UK SIC:** 83701
**Auditors:** Berg Kaprow Lewis LLP
**Bankers:** Barclays Bank Plc (20-41-41)

| | 31-03-13 | 31-03-12 | 31-03-11 |
|---|---|---|---|
| TO | 21,413,676 | 21,443,770 | 24,787,375 |
| P/L | 547,085 | 575,379 | 962,569 |
| NW | 3,409,580 | 3,374,826 | 3,546,455 |
| WC | 3,884,468 | 3,520,729 | 3,571,664 |
| Emp. | 365 | 379 | 423 |

DUNS 42-415-3240

## Pell Frischmann Consulting Engineers Ltd.

(**Subsidiary of:** Pell Frischmann Holdings Ltd)
4-5 Manchester Square, London W1U 3PD
**Web:** www.pellfrischmann.com
**Reg No:** 4403030 **Estd:** 2002 Private Limited Company
**Line of Business:** Engineering related scientific and technical consulting activities
**Export Sales:** £3,918,000
**Trading Style:** Pell Frischmann
**Issued Capital:** £7
**Directors:** Dr W W Frischmann, L Goddard, R J Barrett, S S Prabhu, T S Prabhu, C P Mcbeath, C V Powell
**Co. Secretary:** Ms Linda Roberts
**Responsibilities**
**Senior:** Crawford Munro (Manager)
**Branches:** Pell Frischmann Consulting Engineers Ltd., 26 Horseshoe Park, Reading, Berkshire RG8 7JW
**US SIC:** 8911, 6711
**UK SIC:** 83701, 83962
**Auditors:** Berg Kaprow Lewis LLP

| | 31-03-13 | 31-03-12 | 31-03-11 |
|---|---|---|---|
| TO | 25,499,000 | 23,692,000 | 27,533,000 |
| P/L | 2,277,000 | 2,553,000 | 3,038,000 |
| NW | 10,470,000 | 7,700,000 | 8,856,000 |
| WC | 20,462,000 | 18,485,000 | 17,952,000 |
| Emp. | 366 | 376 | 418 |

DUNS 42-413-7177

## Pell Frischmann Holdings Ltd

5 Manchester Square, London W1U 3PD
**Reg No:** 4401327 **Estd:** 2002 Private Limited Company
**Line of Business:** Engineering design activities for industrial process and production
**Export Sales:** £8,893,000
**Issued Capital:** £8,600
**Directors:** R S Frischmann, Dr W W Frischmann, T S Prabhu
**Co. Secretary:** Ms Linda Roberts
**US SIC:** 7399 **UK SIC:** 83954

| | 31-03-13 | 31-03-12 | 31-03-11 |
|---|---|---|---|
| TO | 30,423,000 | 28,495,000 | 31,527,000 |
| P/L | 1,974,000 | 7,453,000 | 4,725,000 |
| NW | 52,994,000 | 49,982,000 | 45,867,000 |
| WC | 31,292,000 | 33,436,000 | 43,929,000 |
| Emp. | 608 | 659 | 649 |

DUNS 23-069-1354

## Pelsall Hall

Paradise Lane, Walsall, West Midlands WS3 4NH
**Tel:** 01922-693399
**Web:** www.greensleeves.org.uk
**Estd:** 1988
**Line of Business:** Rest and retirement homes
**Trading Style:** Greensleebes Homes Trust
**Proprietor:** Ms R O'Mara
**Responsibilities**
**Senior:** Steve Brookes (Manager)
**US SIC:** 8321 **UK SIC:** 96111
**Employees:** 50

DUNS 22-809-4033     Imp-Exp

## Pelsis Ltd

(**Subsidiary of:** Pelsis Holding (Uk) Ltd)
Unit 10, Knaresborough, North Yorkshire HG5 8QB
**Tel:** 08009885359 **Fax:** 01423-863497
**Web:** www.pandl.co.uk
**Reg No:** 1576542 **VAT No:** 392192440
**Estd:** 1984 Private Limited Company
**Line of Business:** Other business activities not elsewhere classified
**Export Markets:** Germany, Belgium, France, Saudia Arabia, Hong Kong and other worldwide countries.
**Export Sales:** £12,668,933
**Trading Style:** Direct Supply
**Issued Capital:** £550,000
**Directors:** D Stott, J C Spence, P A Mangion, M Rohl
**Co. Secretary:**
Squire Patton Boggs Secretarial
**US SIC:** 7399 **UK SIC:** 83954
**Auditors:** Auker Rhodes
**Bankers:** National Westminster Bank Plc (53-50-21)

| | 31-12-13 | 31-12-12 | 31-12-11 |
|---|---|---|---|
| TO | 18,140,436 | 16,888,224 | 16,783,514 |
| P/L | 1,017,852 | 687,047 | 1,653,336 |
| NW | 1,280,389 | (197,890) | (1,381,130) |
| WC | 1,939,167 | (111,725) | (1,001,647) |
| Emp. | 77 | 69 | 69 |

DUNS 73-256-5184

## Pem Vat Services Llp

Salisbury House, Station Road, Cambridge, Cambridgeshire CB1 2LA
**Tel:** 01223728205
**Web:** www.pemit.co.uk
**Reg No:** 0302961OC **Estd:** 2002
**Line of Business:** It consultants
**Responsibilities**
**Senior:** Warren Tilbury (Designated Limited Liability P)
**US SIC:** 7379 **UK SIC:** 83940

| | 31-03-14 | 31-03-13 | 31-03-12 |
|---|---|---|---|
| TA | 54,212 | 52,590 | 97,571 |
| NW | 30,000 | 30,000 | N/A |
| WC | 32,013 | 38,631 | 72,881 |

DUNS 22-088-5631     Exp

## Pembar Ltd

(**Subsidiary of:** Hatt Kitchens Ltd)
Unit 23, Kidderminster, Worcestershire DY10 4JB
**Tel:** 01299-251320
**Web:** www.hatt.co.uk
**Reg No:** 4089902 **Estd:** 2008 Private Limited Company
**Line of Business:** Manufacture of other kitchen furniture
**Trading Style:** Hatt Kitchens
**Issued Capital:** £390,939
**Directors:** D E Powell, C T Hatt, K Kane
**Co. Secretary:** Ms Sara Mcconville
**US SIC:** 2599 **UK SIC:** 46720
**Auditors:** CK Audit

| | 30-04-14 | 30-04-13 | 30-04-12 |
|---|---|---|---|
| TA | 2,814,236 | 2,252,451 | 2,704,885 |
| NW | 375,085 | 345,992 | 542,660 |
| WC | 518,640 | 242,155 | (343,352) |

DUNS 21-586-6305

## Pemberton & Robinpark

Hope Enterprise Centre, Scot Lane, Wigan, Lancashire WN5 0PN
**Tel:** 01942222111
**Estd:** 1998 Proprietorship
**Line of Business:** Taxis and private hire vehicles
**Proprietor:** C Ashcroft
**US SIC:** 4121 **UK SIC:** 72200
**Employees:** 80

DUNS 21-042-5235

## Pemberton Greenish

45 Pont Street, London SW1X 0BX
**Web:** www.pglaw.co.uk
**Partnership**
**Line of Business:** Solicitors
**Proprietor:** D Greenish
**US SIC:** 8111 **UK SIC:** 83500
**Employees:** 70

DUNS 21-773-0697

## Pemberton Health & Beauty

2 Marshalls Road, Belfast BT5 6SR
**Tel:** 02890702220
**Web:** www.united-drug.com
**Estd:** 2003
**Line of Business:** Pharmaceutical suppliers and wholesalers
**US SIC:** 5122 **UK SIC:** 61800
**Employees:** 240

**DUNS 36-487-0548**

## Pembroke College in the University of Cambridge

Trumpington Street, Cambridge, Cambridgeshire CB2 1RF
**Web:** www.cao.cam.ac.uk
**VAT No:** 214244208 **Estd:** 1347
**Line of Business:** Colleges (higher education)
**Trading Style:** The College Or Hall of Valence Mary Commonly Pembroke College, The University of Cambridge
**Principals:** Dr A Cates (Chairman), M Mellor, C Blencowe, Dr H Diemberger, Dr J Maciejowski, Sir R B Dearlove, Dr M R Wormald
**US SIC:** 8221 **UK SIC:** 93100
**Auditors:** Peters Elworthy & Moore

|  | 30-06-13 | 30-06-12 | 30-06-11 |
|---|---|---|---|
| TO | 12,331,492 | 11,930,336 | 11,258,881 |
| P/L | (258,803) | (38,159) | (190,326) |
| NW | 63,737,193 | 117,973,225 | 118,483,095 |
| WC | (851,883) | (572,416) | (734,107) |
| Emp. | 223 | 225 | 215 |

**DUNS 21-761-8154**

## Pembroke Lothbury Holdings Ltd

41 Lothbury, London EC2R 7HF
**Tel:** 02073971060
**Reg No:** 0047204G **Estd:** 2007 Private Limited Company
**Line of Business:** Holding companies management activities
**US SIC:** 6531 **UK SIC:** 83400
**Employees:** 200

**DUNS 77-929-2460**

## Pembroke Managing Agency Ltd

(**Subsidiary of:** Ironshore Inc.)
Plantation Place, 30 Fenchurch Street, London EC3M 3BD
**Tel:** 02073374400
**Web:** www.chaucerplc.com
**Reg No:** 5832065 **Estd:** 2006 Private Limited Company
**Line of Business:** Non-life insurance
**Issued Capital:** £400,000
**Directors:** J A Wash, I Garven, Ms G E Barnes, T A Glover, C D Brown, A Kaufman, T M Seymour, M H Wheeler
**Co. Secretary:** Philip Hicks
**Responsibilities**
**Senior:** Bob Stuchbery (Chief Executive)
**US SIC:** 6399 **UK SIC:** 82001
**Auditors:** Ernst & Young LLP

|  | 31-12-13 | 31-12-12 | 31-12-11 |
|---|---|---|---|
| TO | 28,862,000 | 25,324,000 | 17,380,000 |
| P/L | 5,622,000 | 4,871,000 | 766,000 |
| NW | 13,131,000 | 6,715,000 | 4,047,000 |
| WC | 13,835,000 | 8,268,000 | 4,843,000 |
| Emp. | 87 | 80 | 72 |

**DUNS 22-043-7086**

## Pembroke Nursing Homes Ltd

18 Coed Pella Road, Colwyn Bay, Clwyd LL29 7BB
**Fax:** 01492533484
**Web:** www.pembrokecarehomes.co.uk
**Reg No:** 4046041 **Estd:** 2000 Private Limited Company
**Line of Business:** Nursing homes
**Issued Capital:** £400,002
**Director:** S G Ford
**Co. Secretary:** Mrs Shirley Ford
**Responsibilities**
**Marketing:** Noreen Burns (Senior Nurse)
**Operations:** Noreen Burns (Senior Nurse)
**US SIC:** 8051, 6732
**UK SIC:** 95100, 83100

|  | 31-08-13 | 31-08-12 | 31-08-11 |
|---|---|---|---|
| TA | 368,821 | 275,246 | 313,021 |
| NW | 21,618 | 38,378 | 30,514 |
| WC | (76,230) | (31,284) | (40,717) |

**DUNS 21-783-2420**

## Pembroke Port

The Dockyard, Pembroke Dock, Dyfed SA72 6TD
**Tel:** 01646696110
**Web:** www.mhpa.co.uk
**Estd:** 2011 Proprietorship
**Line of Business:** Operation of habours and ports
**Proprietor:** M Ashworth
**US SIC:** 4469 **UK SIC:** 76300
**Employees:** 110

**DUNS 21-223-7047**

## Pembrokeshire & Carmarthenshire House Promotions Service

5 Merlins Court, Winch Lane, Haverfordwest, Dyfed SA61 1SB
**Tel:** 01437771221
**Proprietorship**

**Line of Business:** Health authorities
**US SIC:** 8062 **UK SIC:** 95100
**Employees:** 85

**DUNS 21-453-7701**

## Pembrokeshire & Derwyn N H S Trust

(**Subsidiary of:** Welsh Government)
Fishguard Road, Haverfordwest, Dyfed SA61 2PZ
**Tel:** 01437-764545
**Incorporate By Act Of Parliament**
**Line of Business:** Administration of the state and the economic and social policy of the community
**Trading Style:** Swn Y Gwynt Day Hospital, St Davids Hospital
**Issued Capital:** £1
**Principals:** Mrs L George (Chairman), Dr M Sargeant, K Jones, Dr C Merrill, Ms J Wilkinson, Mrs M Barnaby, Mrs C Oakley, Mrs G Davies
**Responsibilities**
**Senior:** J Thomas-Ferrand (Non Executive Member)
**Branches:** Pembrokeshire & Derwyn N H S Trust, Tirydail La, Ammanford, Dyfed SA18 3AS
**US SIC:** 9121, 8062
**UK SIC:** 91110, 95100
**Employees:** 50

**DUNS 21-369-8359**

## Pembrokeshire Coast National Park Author

Long St Bank Cottages, Newport, Dyfed SA42 0TN
**Tel:** 01239820912
**Web:** www.pembrokeshirecoast.org.uk
**Proprietorship**
**Line of Business:** Parks & gardens
**Proprietor:** Mrs J Davies
**Responsibilities**
**Senior:** Tegrym Jones (Chief Executive)
**US SIC:** 8411 **UK SIC:** 97700
**Employees:** 120

**DUNS 54-854-7785**

## Pembrokeshire Coast National Pk

Llanion Park, Pembroke Dock, Dyfed SA72 6DY
**Tel:** 08453457275
**Web:** www.pembrokeshirecoast.org.uk
**VAT No:** 618385813 **Estd:** 1996
**Line of Business:** National park authority
**Director:** N Wheeler
**Responsibilities**
**Senior:** Nick Wheeler (CEO, Managing Director)
**Sales:** John Worral (Sales Manager)
**IT:** Jan Waite (IT Manager)
**HR:** June Skilton (Personnel Manager)
**Operations:** John Worral (Sales Manager)
**Branches:** Pembrokeshire Coast National Pk, 40 High St, Haverfordwest, Dyfed SA61 2DA
**US SIC:** 9121 **UK SIC:** 91110
**Bankers:** HSBC Bank plc (40-23-21)
**Employees:** 120

**DUNS 23-684-5806**

## Pembrokeshire College

Merlins Bridge, Haverfordwest, Hakin, Merlins Bridge, Haverfordwest, Dyfed SA61 1SZ
**Tel:** 01437753000
**Web:** www.pembrokeshire.ac.uk
**Estd:** 1992
**Line of Business:** Further education schools and colleges
**Principals:** G Jones (Chairman), I Morgan, Ms S Lusher
**Responsibilities**
**Senior:** Barry Walters (Principal), Malcolm York (Centre Manager)
**Admin:** Nick Paul-James (Administrator)
**IT:** Simon Hitches (IT Director)
**HR:** Chris Curtis (Head of Workforce), Kathryn Robson (Human Resources Director)
**Purchasing:** Elesabeth Callard (Procurement Officer)
**Branches:** Pembrokeshire College, Merlins Bridge, Haverfordwest, Dyfed SA61 1SZ
**US SIC:** 8211 **UK SIC:** 93200
**Employees:** 500

**DUNS 36-800-7977**     Imp

## Pembrokeshire County Council

County Hall, Haverfordwest, Dyfed SA61 1TP
**Tel:** 01437764551 **Fax:** 01437775303
**Web:** www.pembrokeshire.gov.uk
**VAT No:** 655823710 **Estd:** 1996 Incorporate By Act Of Parliament
**Line of Business:** Local government
**Principals:** B Parry-Jones, A M Boobyer
**Responsibilities**
**Senior:** Darren Bowen (Centre Manager), Kay Codd (Partner), Ann Edmunds (Senior Manager), Sian Fair (Centre Manager), Laurence Harding (Manager), Dave Howells (Executive), Jeanette John (Manager), Matthew Johns (Manager), Marc Owen (Street Works Manager), Kim Puhl (Manager), Coleen Raymond (Senior Manager), Richard Staden (Executive), Trevor Theobald (Executive), Dekker Thomas (Executive), Lynne Thomas (Manager), Sean Tilling (Executive), Nigel Watts (Manager), Tryphena Williams (Manager)
**Finance:** Matt Cloud (Finance Manager), Kerry Mcdermott (Head of Revenue Services), Lynne Richards (Business Manager)
**Marketing:** Loretta Corp (Public Relations and Training), Len Mullins (Press and Public Relations Off), Gary Nicholas (Leisure Marketing & Developmen), Claire Rees (Tourism Marketing Officer), Emily Sheen (Relations Manager), Joanne Welch (Food Development Officer)
**Sales:** Claire George (Business Development Manager), Alison Mattson (Business Development Manager), Peter Sedgwick (Planning Officer)
**Admin:** Charlie Blythe (Administrative Assistant - Gov), Emily James (Review & Monitoring Officer), Wendy Lavender (Departmental Secretary, Develo), Ian Randell (Review and Monitoring Officer)
**HR:** Loretta Corp (Public Relations and Training), Sue Swan (Training Manager), Rosemary Tippett-Maudsley (Training Director)
**Health & Safety:** Jeff Beynon (Food Safety and Port Health Ma), Shaun Griffiths (Corporate System and Safety Ma)
**Operations:** Jill Jack (Regeneration Executive), Steve Keating (Energy Manager), Kate Morgan (Food Development Manager), Owen Roberts (Project Manager), Bob Smith (Senior Forward Planning Office)
**Purchasing:** Julie Randell (Procurement Officer)
**Fleet:** Shaun Griffiths (Corporate System and Safety Ma), Hubert Mathias (Transport Manager), Ceri Rees (?Transport Strategy & Project), Ian Westley (Director, Transportation and E)
**Engineering:** Karen John (Officer)
**Branches:** Pembrokeshire County Council, Fishguard Harbour, Goodwick, Dyfed SA64 0DE
**US SIC:** 9121, 6732
**UK SIC:** 91110, 83100
**Employees:** 6,500

**DUNS 23-352-7993**

## Pembrokeshire Housing Association Ltd

Meyler House, St Thomas Green, Haverfordwest, Dyfed SA61 1QP
**Tel:** 01437-763688 **Fax:** 01437-763997
**Web:** www.pembs-ha.co.uk
**Reg No:** 0023308IP **Estd:** 1981 Friendly Society
**Line of Business:** Housing associations societies trusts & co-operatives
**Principals:** G Doughty (Chairman), A Williams (Financial), N Sinnett, G Holmes, Mrs Y Evans, Mrs D Campbell, Mrs H Wright, N Sinnett
**Responsibilities**
**Senior:** B Charles (Designated Limited Liability P), Donna Dennison (Manager), Peter Maggs (Chief Executive), Nigel Sinnett (Director)
**IT:** Lindsey Dofoe (PC Manager), Lindsey Griffiths (PC Manager), Kingsley Oliver (Computer Operations Manager), Steve Townley (Head of IT)
**Health & Safety:** Aled Roberts (Health & Safety Officer)
**US SIC:** 6531, 9121
**UK SIC:** 83400, 91110
**Auditors:** Bevan & Buckland
**Employees:** 51
**Turnover:** £5,974,270

**DUNS 29-125-2906**

## Pemican Ltd

Kings Park, Canvey Island, Essex SS8 8HE
**Tel:** 01268-511555
**Web:** www.pemican.com
**Reg No:** 1612988 **Estd:** 1975 Private Limited Company
**Line of Business:** Construction of commercial buildings
**Issued Capital:** £100
**Directors:** Ms S J Palmer King, G I King
**US SIC:** 1541 **UK SIC:** 50100
**Auditors:** Harris Lipman LLP
**Bankers:** Barclays Bank Plc (20-79-73)

|  | 30-09-12 | 31-03-11 | 31-09-10 |
|---|---|---|---|
| TO | 7,295,595 | 5,028,154 | N/A |
| P/L | (2,154,464) | 5,081,760 | N/A |
| NW | 1,674,517 | 3,969,625 | 1,046,811 |
| WC | (3,327,249) | (3,257,784) | (3,898,189) |
| Emp. | 60 | 60 | N/A |

**DUNS 21-606-7994**

## Pen Y Bont Court Nursing Home

Ewenny Road, Ewenny, Bridgend, Mid Glamorgan CF35 5AW
**Tel:** 01656653897
**Estd:** 2008
**Line of Business:** Nursing homes
**Proprietor:** Mrs J Collins
**Responsibilities**
**Senior:** Avril Pickett (Manageress)
**US SIC:** 8051 **UK SIC:** 95100
**Employees:** 100

**DUNS 57-061-2333**

## Pen-y-Garth Care Homes Ltd

Sovereign House, Queen Street, Manchester M2 5HR
**Tel:** 01565830780
**Reg No:** 2882141 **Estd:** 1993 Private Limited Company
**Line of Business:** Social work activities with accommodation
**Issued Capital:** £12,600
**Directors:** K Symms, Mrs S E Symms
**Co. Secretary:** Jonathan Symms
**US SIC:** 8321 **UK SIC:** 96111
**Auditors:** Pannell Kerr Forster

|  | 31-12-13 | 31-12-12 | 31-12-11 |
|---|---|---|---|
| TA | 985,904 | 1,060,059 | 1,043,755 |
| NW | 200,477 | 182,588 | 188,366 |
| WC | 69,018 | 93,818 | 127,644 |

**DUNS 21-857-6526**

## Penalyn Ltd

(**Subsidiary of:** Pennaf Ltd)
72 Ffordd William Morgan, St Asaph Business Park, St Asaph, Clwyd LL17 0JD
**Tel:** 08001835757
**Web:** www.pennaf.co.uk
**Reg No:** 8206467 **Estd:** 2012 Private Limited Company
**Line of Business:** Construction of domestic buildings
**Issued Capital:** £1
**Directors:** G M Jones, R Waters, M Soffe, J F Poole, D J Lewis, T J Henderson
**Co. Secretary:** Trevor Henderson
**US SIC:** 1522, 1796, 1799
**UK SIC:** 50100, 50400, 50000
**Bankers:** Barclays Bank Plc (20-88-70)

|  | 31-03-14 | 31-03-13 |
|---|---|---|
| TO | 5,550,413 | 2,370,450 |
| NW | (720) | 1 |
| WC | (100,628) | (160,372) |
| Emp. | 73 | 68 |

**DUNS 21-923-5504**

## Penarth Commercial Properties Ltd

(**Subsidiary of:** Penarth Commercial Properties (Holdings) Ltd)
281 Penarth Road, Cardiff, South Glamorgan CF11 8YZ
**Tel:** 02920223100 **Fax:** 029-2038-1714
**Web:** www.fordthorne.co.uk
**Reg No:** 0668982 **VAT No:** 402662482
**Estd:** 1960 Private Limited Company
**Line of Business:** Management activities of holding companies
**Issued Capital:** £133,334
**Principals:** W M Barritt (Managing), R C Pugsley
**Co. Secretary:** Robert Evans
**Branches:** Penarth Commercial Properties Ltd, Gledrid Industrial Park, Gledrid, Wrexham, Clwyd LL14 5DG
**US SIC:** 6711, 2421
**UK SIC:** 83962, 46101
**Auditors:** KPMG
**Bankers:** HSBC Bank plc (40-16-15)

|  | 28-02-14 | 28-02-13 | 29-02-12 |
|---|---|---|---|
| TO | 54,740,954 | 47,214,340 | 45,987,519 |
| P/L | 539,523 | 806,490 | 746,545 |
| NW | 6,698,292 | 6,777,149 | 6,822,772 |
| WC | 998,387 | 642,208 | 467,166 |
| Emp. | 217 | 213 | 229 |

DUNS 21-926-2946

## Penarth Industrial Services Ltd

Coleridge Road, Cardiff, South Glamorgan CF11 8BT
**Tel:** 02920641555 **Fax:** 029-2064-1899
**Web:** www.tema-engineering.co.uk
**Reg No:** 1158345 **VAT No:** 137125487
**Estd:** 1974 Private Limited Company
**Line of Business:** Manufacture of other fabricated metal products not elsewhere classified
**Issued Capital:** £50,000
**Principals:** M Donovan *(Managing)*, A Marinos, A J Mulhern
**Co. Secretary:** Alan Rowles
**US SIC:** 3499 **UK SIC:** 31694
**Auditors:** Deloitte & Touche
**Bankers:** Lloyds TSB Bank plc (30-96-52)

| | 31-03-14 | 31-03-13 | 31-03-12 |
|---|---|---|---|
| TO | 10,114,927 | 5,925,317 | 9,688,000 |
| P/L | 516,205 | (125,189) | 127,495 |
| NW | 949,628 | 558,482 | 662,845 |
| WC | 565,878 | 173,730 | 198,620 |
| Emp. | 103 | 89 | 125 |

DUNS 21-738-8216

## Pencalenick

St Clement, Truro, Cornwall TR1 1TE
**Tel:** 01872520385
**Web:** www.pencalenick.net
**Reg No:** 7724160 **Estd:** 2011 Private Company Limited By Guarantee
**Line of Business:** General secondary education
**Directors:** J C Dorman, Mrs V K Coxhead, Mrs C A Smith, Ms A Phillips, A Taylor, G J Chappell, R M Ferrie, A C Barnett
**Responsibilities**
**Senior:** John Rail *(Director)*, Huw Rowswell *(Director)*, Suzanne Sutton *(Director)*
**US SIC:** 8211 **UK SIC:** 93200
**Bankers:** Lloyds TSB Bank plc (30-98-76)

| | 31-08-14 | 31-08-13 | 31-08-12 |
|---|---|---|---|
| TO | 2,481,708 | 2,850,544 | 6,368,785 |
| P/L | (64,340) | 380,753 | 3,643,493 |
| NW | 3,481,906 | 3,890,246 | 3,481,493 |
| WC | 603,241 | 609,793 | 421,965 |
| Emp. | 59 | 65 | 72 |

DUNS 21-036-1543

## Pencalenick School

St Clement, Truro, Cornwall TR1 1TE
**Tel:** 01872-520385
**Web:** www.pencalenick.org
**Estd:** 1988
**Line of Business:** Schools (local authority)
**Proprietor:** A Barnett
**US SIC:** 8299 **UK SIC:** 93300
**Employees:** 65

DUNS 52-004-7671 **Imp**

## Pencarrie Ltd

Pencarrie Ltd, Eagle Way, Sowton Industrial Estate, Exeter, Devon EX2 7HY
**Tel:** 01392209910
**Web:** www.pencarrieukl.com
**Reg No:** 3371637 **VAT No:** 730379047
**Estd:** 1997 Private Limited Company
**Line of Business:** Wholesale of clothing not elsewhere classified
**Issued Capital:** £5,000
**Directors:** Mrs S L Irving, Miss C V Persey, A J Lock, F L Bevan, Mrs N C Gratwicke
**Co. Secretary:** Francis Bevan
**Responsibilities**
**Senior:** Paul Persey *(Owner)*, Caroline Persey *(Finance Director)*
**Operations:** Andrea Charceris *(Customer Services Manager)*
**US SIC:** 5136 **UK SIC:** 61600
**Auditors:** Simpkins Edwards
**Bankers:** Lloyds TSB Bank plc (30-93-14)

| | 27-12-13 | 28-12-12 | 30-12-11 |
|---|---|---|---|
| TO | 42,778,624 | 38,936,952 | 66,934,948 |
| P/L | 1,940,236 | 2,798,765 | 5,407,678 |
| NW | 14,923,171 | 17,964,991 | 15,731,583 |
| WC | 12,966,081 | 17,497,961 | 15,111,095 |
| Emp. | 139 | 131 | 193 |

DUNS 29-018-5214

## Pendennis Foods Ltd

Kirton House, London Road, Kirton, Boston, Lincolnshire PE20 1JD
**Tel:** 01205724778
**Web:** www.woodlandsfarm.co.uk
**Reg No:** 0551786 **Estd:** 1955 Private Limited Company
**Line of Business:** Growing of cereals and other crops not elsewhere classified
**Issued Capital:** £2,500
**Director:** D M Dennis
**Branches:** Pendennis Foods Ltd, Station Rd, Doddington-On-Bain, Louth, Lincolnshire LN11 9TR
**US SIC:** 0119, 0161
**UK SIC:** 01001
**Auditors:** KPMG Audit Plc

**Bankers:** Lloyds TSB Bank plc (30-91-04)

| | 05-04-14 | 05-04-13 | 05-04-12 |
|---|---|---|---|
| TA | 2,433,562 | 2,547,511 | 2,831,564 |
| NW | 2,429,957 | 2,519,776 | 2,414,212 |
| WC | 22,406 | (14,293) | (380,129) |

DUNS 39-992-9561 **Imp-Exp**

## Pendennis Shipyard (Holdings) Ltd

The Docks, Falmouth, Cornwall TR11 4NR
**Tel:** 01326-211344 **Fax:** 01326-319253
**Web:** www.pendennis.com
**Reg No:** 2281468 **VAT No:** 557373221
**Estd:** 1988 Private Limited Company
**Line of Business:** Marine services
**Export Markets:** Europe
**Export Sales:** £35,507,580
**Issued Capital:** £3,881,348
**Principals:** M J Carr *(Managing)*, H Wiekens *(Managing)*, A A Hill *(Financial)*, C B Robertson, T J Allies, J P Arnold, T C Mordaunt
**Co. Secretary:** Ian Granville
**US SIC:** 3732, 7399
**UK SIC:** 36102, 83954
**Auditors:** Robinson Reed Layton
**Bankers:** National Westminster Bank Plc (52-41-31)

| | 31-12-13 | 31-12-12 | 31-12-11 |
|---|---|---|---|
| TO | 37,157,747 | 33,158,261 | 30,991,858 |
| P/L | 2,452,982 | 2,358,717 | 2,255,332 |
| NW | 22,735,949 | 16,719,354 | 14,831,961 |
| WC | 258,039 | 3,228 | (111,529) |
| Emp. | 339 | 334 | 354 |

DUNS 23-562-0957

## The Penderels Trust Ltd

St Andrews Park, Queens Lane, Bromfield Industrial Estate, Mold, Clwyd CH7 1XB
**Tel:** 01352706235
**Web:** www.penderelstrust.org.uk
**Reg No:** 3560335 **Estd:** 2011 Private Limited Company
**Line of Business:** Disability services
**Directors:** Ms P F Sadio, J Finnie, R J Harris, A J Wright, K J Barrett Mbe, I R Besant, Ms J Wakelin, Ms S Henson
**Co. Secretary:**
Hargreaves Mounteney Limited
**Responsibilities**
**Senior:** Peter Collard *(Manager)*, Penelope Collard *(Manager)*
**Branches:** The Penderels Trust Ltd, The Steadings Business Centre, Unit 7, Gloucester, Gloucestershire GL2 8EY
**US SIC:** 8321 **UK SIC:** 96111
**Bankers:** National Westminster Bank Plc (56-00-45)

| | 31-03-14 | 31-03-13 | 31-03-12 |
|---|---|---|---|
| TO | 4,149,554 | 4,323,858 | 3,996,768 |
| P/L | 54,541 | (134,884) | (133,318) |
| NW | 1,100,660 | 1,046,119 | 1,181,003 |
| WC | 990,045 | 976,267 | 1,134,355 |
| Emp. | 141 | 150 | 140 |

DUNS 22-865-0149

## Pendle Borough Council

Market Street, Nelson, Lancashire BB9 7LG
**Web:** www.pendle.gov.uk
**Estd:** 1978
**Line of Business:** Local government
**Trading Style:** Brierfield Community Centre, Marsden Park Golf Course, Brierfield Town Council
**Principals:** S Barnes, J Kirk, P Mousdale
**Responsibilities**
**Finance:** Dean Langton *(Financial Director)*
**Branches:** Pendle Borough Council, Post Office Buildings, Barnoldswick, Lancashire BB18 5DL
**US SIC:** 9121, 7999
**UK SIC:** 91110, 97913
**Bankers:** Barclays Bank Plc (20-15-70)
**Employees:** 700

DUNS 29-135-3316

## Pendle Hippodrome Theatre Ltd

New Market Street, Colne, Lancashire BB8 9BJ
**Tel:** 01282-863210
**Web:** www.phtheatre.co.uk
**Reg No:** 1664358 **Estd:** 1982 Private Limited Company
**Line of Business:** Artistic and literary creation and interpretation
**Directors:** D Farrer, S C Manley, Ms T Greenwood, M Greenwood, K Mason, K Walton, P S Thompson, A Walton
**Co. Secretary:** Mrs Sheila Keogh
**Responsibilities**
**Senior:** Mildred Greenwood *(Director)*, Frank Lomax *(Director)*, Joseph Whittam *(Director)*
**US SIC:** 7911 **UK SIC:** 97913
**Auditors:** Kneeshaw Moffatt

**Bankers:** Barclays Bank Plc (20-00-00)

| | 31-12-13 | 31-12-12 | 31-12-11 |
|---|---|---|---|
| TO | 91,599 | 85,715 | 79,054 |
| P/L | 11,244 | (6,539) | 6,590 |
| NW | 208,776 | 197,532 | 204,071 |
| WC | 40,011 | 25,483 | 38,378 |

DUNS 54-428-2650

## Pendle Personnel Ltd

**(Subsidiary of:** Cavendish Waterhouse Group Ltd)
The Maltkiln, Gisburn Road, Barrowford, Nelson, Lancashire BB9 6AJ
**Tel:** 01282612000
**Web:** www.pendlepersonnel.co.uk
**Reg No:** 3274361 **Estd:** 1995 Private Limited Company
**Line of Business:** Employment and recruitment companies and consultants
**Trading Style:** Pendle Personnel
**Issued Capital:** £200
**Directors:** G M Ellis, N P Stephenson, N Whittaker
**Responsibilities**
**Senior:** Mandy Hartley *(Accounts Manager)*
**Finance:** Mandy Hartley *(Accounts Manager)*
**Branches:** Pendle Personnel Ltd, 18 Wesley St, Castleford, West Yorkshire WF10 1AE
**US SIC:** 7361 **UK SIC:** 83954
**Auditors:** Walker & Co

| | 31-12-13 | 31-12-12 | 31-12-11 |
|---|---|---|---|
| TA | 429,298 | 262,438 | 320,607 |
| NW | 56,845 | 42,588 | 116,559 |
| WC | 39,497 | 27,212 | 104,083 |

DUNS 39-965-2031

## Pendle Polymer Engineering Ltd

**(Subsidiary of:** Pendle Fluid Sealing Ltd)
Warehouse Lane, Colne, Lancashire BB8 7PP
**Tel:** 01282-868916 **Fax:** 01282870529
**Web:** www.pendlepolymer.co.uk
**Reg No:** 2265026 **VAT No:** 498006915
**Estd:** 1988 Private Limited Company
**Line of Business:** Engineers (general)
**Trading Style:** Pendle Polymer Engineering Ltd
**Issued Capital:** £100
**Principals:** J Lorrison *(Managing)*, A D Wood, N H Burton, R J Lorrison
**Co. Secretary:**
Rowan Croft Business Services Li
**Responsibilities**
**Senior:** Anthony Bielby *(Manager)*
**US SIC:** 8911 **UK SIC:** 83701
**Auditors:** Montpelier Professional (Lancs) Ltd
**Bankers:** HSBC Bank plc (40-15-17)

| | 31-05-13 | 31-05-12 | 31-05-11 |
|---|---|---|---|
| TA | 2,270,827 | 2,338,255 | 2,129,285 |
| NW | 1,422,345 | 1,349,178 | 1,260,403 |
| WC | 921,642 | 972,629 | 922,339 |

DUNS 23-329-5422

## Pendle Village Mill

Hollin Bank, Brierfield, Nelson, Lancashire BB9 5NG
**Tel:** 01282 442424
**Web:** www.pendlevillagemill.co.uk
**Estd:** 1981 Partnership
**Line of Business:** Retail sale of furniture, lighting equipment and household articles not elsewhere classified
**Partners:** B Lockwood, Ms S Lockwood
**US SIC:** 5719 **UK SIC:** 64700
**Bankers:** Yorkshire Bank Plc (05-03-53)
**Employees:** 60

DUNS 21-583-3228

## Pendle Wavelengths

Leeds Road, Nelson, Lancashire BB9 9TD
**Tel:** 01282661717
**Web:** www.pendleleisuretrust.co.uk
**Estd:** 2011 Proprietorship
**Line of Business:** Other sporting activities not elsewhere classified
**Proprietor:** Mrs S Slater
**Responsibilities**
**Senior:** Quammer Iqbal *(Centre Manager)*
**US SIC:** 7999 **UK SIC:** 97913
**Employees:** 100

DUNS 23-294-0150

## Pendleton Property Services Ltd

54 Cobden Street, Salford, Lancashire M6 6WF
**Tel:** 01617-361637
**Web:** www.dlpservices.com
**Reg No:** 4354448 **Estd:** 2002 Private Limited Company
**Line of Business:** Other construction work involving special trades
**Issued Capital:** £1,000
**Director:** K J Greenhalgh
**Co. Secretary:** Lee Morris

**US SIC:** 1799, 6519
**UK SIC:** 50000, 85000
**Auditors:** Abrams Ashton

| | 28-02-14 | 28-02-13 | 29-02-12 |
|---|---|---|---|
| TO | 15,647,725 | 13,723,351 | 15,426,109 |
| P/L | 740,310 | 172,255 | 884,598 |
| NW | 1,454,723 | 1,112,831 | 1,501,355 |
| WC | 983,428 | 608,389 | 999,864 |
| Emp. | 153 | 154 | 157 |

DUNS 21-025-3638

## Pendlevale College

Oxford Road, Nelson, Lancashire BB9 8LF
**Tel:** 01282682240
**Web:** www.pendlevale.lancs.sch.uk
**Estd:** 2012
**Line of Business:** Schools (local authority)
**US SIC:** 8211 **UK SIC:** 93200
**Employees:** 75

DUNS 23-843-9264

## Pendragon Automotive Services Ltd

**(Subsidiary of:** Pendragon Plc)
2 Oakwood Court, Little Oak Drive, Annesley, Nottingham, Nottinghamshire NG15 0DR
**Tel:** 01623725000 **Fax:** 01623-725010
**Web:** www.pendragonplc.com
**Reg No:** 3836134 **Estd:** 1999 Private Limited Company
**Line of Business:** Sale of new motor vehicles
**Issued Capital:** £21,885,286
**Directors:** T G Finn, M S Casha, Pendragon Management Services Li, T P Holden
**Co. Secretary:** Miss Hilary Sykes
**Responsibilities**
**Marketing:** Victoria Finn *(Marketing Manager)*
**Branches:** Pendragon Automotive Services Ltd, 105 Queens Rd, Weybridge, Surrey KT13 9UJ
**US SIC:** 7399, 7512
**UK SIC:** 83954, 84801
**Auditors:** KPMG Audit Plc

| | 31-12-13 | 31-12-12 | 31-12-11 |
|---|---|---|---|
| TA | 21,885,000 | 21,885,000 | 21,885,000 |
| P/L | N/A | 2,000,000 | N/A |
| NW | 21,885,000 | 21,885,000 | 21,885,000 |
| Emp. | N/A | 5 | N/A |

DUNS 22-770-6330

## Pendragon Contracts Ltd

**(Subsidiary of:** Pendragon Plc)
Pendragon House, Sir Frank Whittle Road, Derby, Derbyshire DE21 4AZ
**Tel:** 01332-292777 **Fax:** 01332364270
**Web:** www.pendragon-contracts.uk.com
**Reg No:** 0141388 **VAT No:** 508029855
**Estd:** 1915 Private Limited Company
**Line of Business:** Renting of automobiles
**Issued Capital:** £1,250,000
**Directors:** T G Finn, Pendragon Management Services Li, T P Holden, M S Casha
**Co. Secretary:** Miss Hilary Sykes
**Responsibilities**
**Marketing:** Alan Hillier *(Marketing & Data Leader)*
**Branches:** Pendragon Contracts Ltd, Athena Avenue, Elgin, Swindon, Wiltshire SN2 8XT
**US SIC:** 7512 **UK SIC:** 84801
**Auditors:** KPMG Audit PLC
**Bankers:** Lloyds TSB Bank plc (30-92-59)

| | 31-12-13 | 31-12-12 | 31-12-11 |
|---|---|---|---|
| TO | 12,136,000 | 14,342,000 | 16,037,000 |
| P/L | 1,110,000 | 2,909,000 | 3,263,000 |
| NW | 8,994,000 | 8,215,000 | 8,089,000 |
| WC | 36,782,000 | 30,663,000 | 25,180,000 |
| Emp. | 57 | 58 | 65 |

DUNS 50-025-9437 **Imp**

## Pendragon Plc

1 Oakwood Court, Little Oak Drive, Annesley, Nottingham, Nottinghamshire NG15 0DR
**Tel:** 01623725200
**Web:** www.evanshalshaw.com
**Reg No:** 2304195 **VAT No:** 508029855
**Estd:** 1988 Public Limited Company
**Line of Business:** Representative office
**Trading Style:** Quickco Chatfields, Templars Volvo, Stratstones, Nottingham Power Sports
**Issued Capital:** £71,887,894
**Principals:** T G Finn *(Managing)*, Ms G D Kent, J S King, T P Holden, M S Casha, P Hampden Smith, C M Chambers, M J Egglenton
**Co. Secretary:** Ms Hilary Sykes
**Branches:** Pendragon Plc, Mill St, Slough, Berkshire SL2 5DR
**US SIC:** 5511, 5521, 6711
**UK SIC:** 65100, 83962
**Auditors:** KPMG Audit PLC

**Bankers:** Barclays Bank Plc (20-31-52)
**Following financial data are in thousands**

| | 31-12-13 | 31-12-12 | 31-12-11 |
|---|---|---|---|
| TO | 3,848,900 | 3,635,100 | 3,465,800 |
| P/L | 38,900 | 37,800 | 24,000 |
| NW | (65,200) | (131,000) | (138,600) |
| WC | (90,200) | (82,100) | (96,900) |
| Emp. | 9,171 | 9,261 | 9,521 |

DUNS 23-843-6484
## Pendragon Premier Ltd
**(Subsidiary of:** Pendragon Plc)
50-56 High Road, London E18 2QL
**Tel:** 020-8989-6644
**Web:** www.stratstone.com
**Reg No:** 3835850 **Estd:** 1999 Private Limited Company
**Line of Business:** Sale of new motor vehicles
**Trading Style:** Stratstone Jaguar Woodford
**Issued Capital:** £6,000,000
**Directors:** M S Casha, T G Finn, T P Holden, Pendragon Management Services Li
**Co. Secretary:** Ms Hilary Sykes
**Responsibilities**
**Senior:** Daniel Cross *(Dealer Principal)*
**Branches:** Pendragon Premier Ltd, Northfield Dri, Milton Keynes, Buckinghamshire MK15 0EB
**US SIC:** 5511 **UK SIC:** 65100
**Auditors:** KPMG Audit PLC

| | 31-12-13 | 31-12-12 | 31-12-11 |
|---|---|---|---|
| TO | 666,319,000 | 630,951,000 | 605,854,000 |
| P/L | 8,038,000 | (1,211,000) | (680,000) |
| NW | 710,000 | (6,967,000) | (8,114,000) |
| WC | (5,515,000) | (13,525,000) | (16,941,000) |
| Emp. | 1,139 | 1,265 | 1,236 |

DUNS 21-507-5982
## Pendruccombe House
23 Tavistock Road, Launceston, Cornwall PL15 9HF
**Tel:** 01566776800
**Web:** http://pendruccombe.co.uk
**Estd:** 1986 Partnership
**Line of Business:** Other human health activities
**Partners:** R Smallridge, D Smallridge
**Responsibilities**
**Senior:** Sally Glendinning *(Administration Manager)*, Lynda Winston *(Home Manager)*
**US SIC:** 8091 **UK SIC:** 95200
**Employees:** 75

DUNS 21-634-7864 **Imp-Exp**
## Penguin Books Ltd
**(Subsidiary of:** Bertelsmann Uk Ltd)
Shell Mex House, 80 Strand, London WC2R 0RL
**Tel:** 08453134444 **Fax:** 020 7010 6060
**Web:** www.penguin.com.au
**Reg No:** 0861590 **Estd:** 1936 Private Limited Company
**Line of Business:** Book publishers
**Export Markets:** Worldwide
**Export Sales:** £48,602,000
**Trading Style:** The Penguin Group (Uk)
**Issued Capital:** £10,300,000
**Directors:** J C Makinson, T D Weldon, M J Symons, M W Gardiner
**Co. Secretary:** Mrs Helena Peacock
**Responsibilities**
**Finance:** Brian Lownders *(Financial Director)*
**Health & Safety:** Steve Weston *(Health & Safety Officer)*
**Branches:** Penguin Books Ltd, 27 Wrights La, London W8 5SW
**US SIC:** 2731 **UK SIC:** 47532
**Auditors:** PricewaterhouseCoopers LLP
**Bankers:** National Westminster Bank Plc (60-00-01)

| | 31-12-13 | 31-12-12 | 31-12-11 |
|---|---|---|---|
| TO | 163,376,000 | 166,714,000 | 158,977,000 |
| P/L | 2,310,000 | 7,288,000 | 7,800,000 |
| NW | 121,238,000 | 125,485,000 | 123,573,000 |
| WC | 85,009,000 | 91,831,000 | 88,294,000 |
| Emp. | 808 | 818 | 822 |

DUNS 39-030-7627 **Imp-Exp**
## Penhaligon's Ltd
37-39 Artillery Lane, Whitechapel, London E1 7LP
**Tel:** 02075906110 **Fax:** 02075906137
**Web:** www.penhaligons.com
**Reg No:** 2110619 **VAT No:** 554127845
**Estd:** 1870 Private Limited Company
**Line of Business:** Retail sale of cosmetic and toilet articles
**Export Markets:** U S A; E U; Far East
**Export Sales:** £4,253,761
**Trading Style:** Penhaligons
**Issued Capital:** £38,437,585
**Director:** J Subramanian
**Responsibilities**
**Senior:** Sarah Rotheram *(Branch Manager)*
**Finance:** Duncan Miller *(Financial Director)*
**Branches:** Penhaligon's Ltd, 41 Wellington Street, London WC2E 7BN
**US SIC:** 5999 **UK SIC:** 65600
**Auditors:** BDO LLP

**Bankers:** National Westminster Bank Plc (56-00-27)

| | 31-12-13 | 31-12-12 | 31-12-11 |
|---|---|---|---|
| TO | 12,624,384 | 10,514,464 | 10,724,623 |
| P/L | 1,061,790 | 812,004 | 609,193 |
| NW | 9,588,198 | 6,420,279 | 4,232,824 |
| WC | 7,566,400 | 4,938,057 | 3,603,204 |
| Emp. | 126 | 117 | 116 |

DUNS 76-497-9803
## Peninsula Business Services Group Ltd
**(Subsidiary of:** Rainy City Investments Ltd)
2 Cheetham Hill Road, Manchester M4 4EW
**Tel:** 01618369000
**Reg No:** 2567996 **Estd:** 2012 Private Limited Company
**Line of Business:** Management and business consultants
**Export Sales:** £13,156,226
**Issued Capital:** £939
**Directors:** F Done, P E Done
**Co. Secretary:** Peter Swift
**US SIC:** 6711, 7999
**UK SIC:** 83962, 97913
**Auditors:** Hoban Nelson Lang
**Bankers:** National Westminster Bank Plc (01-10-01)

| | 31-03-14 | 31-03-13 | 31-03-12 |
|---|---|---|---|
| TO | 102,777,034 | 92,027,916 | 84,331,772 |
| P/L | 17,360,475 | 18,201,969 | 14,735,641 |
| NW | 66,947,932 | 62,380,401 | 58,170,033 |
| WC | 140,571,470 | 133,628,666 | 130,696,180 |
| Emp. | 968 | 936 | 873 |

DUNS 22-807-8655
## Peninsula Business Services Ltd
**(Subsidiary of:** Rainy City Investments Ltd)
2 Cheetham Hill Road, Manchester M4 4FB
**Fax:** 0161-833-9517
**Web:** www.peninsula-uk.com
**Reg No:** 1702759 **VAT No:** 383284728
**Estd:** 1983 Private Limited Company
**Line of Business:** Legal activities
**Issued Capital:** £94
**Principals:** P E Done *(Chairman and Managing)*, A Price, R Corlett, P N Swift, A Sutcliffe, N A Babington, Mrs J English, D S Chadwick
**Co. Secretary:** Peter Swift
**Responsibilities**
**Senior:** Dennis Upfold *(Director)*
**Health & Safety:** Noel Pilling *(Health & Safety Manager)*
**US SIC:** 8111 **UK SIC:** 83500
**Auditors:** Beever & Struthers
**Bankers:** National Westminster Bank Plc (01-05-31)

| | 31-03-14 | 31-03-13 | 31-03-12 |
|---|---|---|---|
| TO | 72,351,085 | 69,678,940 | 67,004,625 |
| P/L | 14,549,684 | 17,078,637 | 13,887,022 |
| NW | 58,018,455 | 55,588,927 | 62,017,538 |
| WC | 119,780,309 | 120,257,750 | 120,790,522 |
| Emp. | 762 | 735 | 746 |

DUNS 73-339-9922
## Peninsula Care Homes Ltd
Parkland House Residential Home, Barley Lane, Exeter, Devon EX4 1TA
**Tel:** 01803551207
**Web:** www.peninsulacarehomes.co.uk
**Reg No:** 4613800 **Estd:** 2002 Private Limited Company
**Line of Business:** Medical nursing home activities
**Issued Capital:** £1,002
**Directors:** Ms C J Arnold, Ms L C Arnold, Ms I Arnold, S J Arnold
**Co. Secretary:** David Arnold
**Branches:** Peninsula Care Homes Ltd, Parkland House, Barley Lane, Exeter, Devon EX4 1TA
**US SIC:** 8999 **UK SIC:** 83954
**Bankers:** National Westminster Bank Plc (01-09-51)

| | 31-03-14 | 31-03-13 | 31-03-12 |
|---|---|---|---|
| TO | 5,488,423 | 5,162,678 | 5,165,924 |
| P/L | 470,919 | 278,037 | 133,768 |
| NW | 939,933 | 431,956 | 146,280 |
| WC | (581,587) | (711,714) | (752,404) |
| Emp. | 218 | 212 | 212 |

DUNS 21-717-9299
## Peninsula Community Health C.I.C.
Sedgemoor Centre, Priory Road, St Austell, Cornwall PL25 5AS
**Tel:** 01726-627800
**Web:** www.peninsulacommunityhealth.co.uk
**Reg No:** 7564579 **Estd:** 2011 Private Company Limited By Guarantee
**Line of Business:** Hospital activities
**Directors:** S Jenkin, N B Buckland, Mrs E Marshall, Dr J Glazier, J M Day, Ms J D Kessell, M S Williams
**Co. Secretary:** Justin Day
**Responsibilities**
**Senior:** John Lander *(Manager)*
**US SIC:** 8062, 8091
**UK SIC:** 95100, 95200

**Auditors:** KPMG LLP

| | 31-03-14 | 31-03-13 |
|---|---|---|
| TO | 87,778,000 | 130,379,000 |
| P/L | (328,000) | 317,000 |
| NW | (382,000) | 169,000 |
| WC | (1,094,000) | (834,000) |
| Emp. | 1,710 | 1,691 |

DUNS 21-718-0051
## Peninsula Learning Trust
Charlestown Road, St Austell, Cornwall PL25 3NR
**Tel:** 0172672163
**Web:** www.penrice.cornwall.sch.uk
**Reg No:** 7565242 **Estd:** 1959 Private Company Limited By Guarantee
**Line of Business:** Schools (local authority)
**Trading Style:** Penrice Community College
**Directors:** S Disney-Pollard, Mrs J L Seyler, J K Barnard, P G Marshall, P F Towe, Ms E M Knowles, K M Pearce, K A Johns
**Co. Secretary:** Jeremy Alder
**Responsibilities**
**Senior:** Elise Alma *(Director)*, Marlene Behennah *(Director)*, Pani Bundy *(Director)*, Matthew De Villiers *(Director)*, Jacqueline Sage *(Director)*, Andrew Stittle *(Director)*
**US SIC:** 8211 **UK SIC:** 93200
**Bankers:** Lloyds TSB Bank plc (30-12-21)

| | 31-08-14 | 31-08-13 | 31-08-12 |
|---|---|---|---|
| TO | 8,012,082 | 8,633,412 | 22,688,121 |
| P/L | 387,844 | 1,408,843 | 12,750,538 |
| NW | 13,571,224 | 13,855,381 | 12,399,538 |
| WC | 733,677 | 1,145,725 | 687,978 |
| Emp. | 141 | 149 | 142 |

DUNS 37-849-5840
## Peninsula Medical Foundation
The John Bull Building, 16 Research Way, Plymouth, Devon PL6 8BU
**Tel:** 01752437444
**Web:** www.plymouth.ac.uk
**Reg No:** 3300591 **Estd:** 1997 Private Limited Company
**Line of Business:** Activities of other membership organisations not elsewhere classified
**Directors:** Ms S K Brimacombe, Professor M J Watkins, N H Proctor, D C Wilkins, R D Bayly, Dr B J Vann, A M Powell, I H Powell
**Co. Secretary:** James Groves
**Responsibilities**
**IT:** Nick Evens *(IT Manager)*
**Health & Safety:** Maurice Longley *(Facilities Manager)*
**Facilities:** Maurice Longley *(Facilities Manager)*
**US SIC:** 8999, 8211
**UK SIC:** 83954, 93200
**Auditors:** Northcott Trumfield
**Bankers:** National Westminster Bank Plc (60-20-26)

| | 31-01-14 | 31-01-13 | 31-01-12 |
|---|---|---|---|
| TO | 101,952 | 372,969 | 378,699 |
| P/L | (162,632) | (119,776) | (224,986) |
| NW | 585,537 | 726,072 | 789,773 |
| WC | 136,037 | 121,092 | 35,219 |

DUNS 21-586-6334
## Peninsula Medical School
Heavitree Road, Exeter, Devon EX1 2LU
**Tel:** 01392262929
**Web:** www.pcmd.ac.uk
**Estd:** 2011 Partnership
**Line of Business:** First-degree level higher education
**Partners:** Mrs W Wilson, J Tooke, Professor A Pinching
**US SIC:** 8221 **UK SIC:** 93100
**Employees:** 106

DUNS 21-810-7655
## Peninsula Radiology Academy
Peninsula Radiology Academy, William Prance Road, Plymouth, Devon PL6 5WR
**Tel:** 01752437437
**Web:** www.penra.org.uk
**Estd:** 2012
**Line of Business:** Adult and other education not elsewhere classified
**Responsibilities**
**Senior:** Deborah Sutton *(Business Manager)*
**US SIC:** 8249 **UK SIC:** 93300
**Employees:** 60

DUNS 21-022-8177 **Imp**
## The Peninsular & Oriental Steam Navigation Co
**(Subsidiary of:** Dubai World Corporation)
16 Palace Street, London SW1E 5JQ
**Tel:** 02079014000
**Web:** www.dpworld.com
**Reg No:** 0000073ZC **Estd:** 1954 Incorporate By Act Of Parliament
**Line of Business:** Management activities of holding companies
**Trading Style:** P & O P & O Ports, P & O European Ferries P-And-O.Com, P & O Cruises, D P World

**Issued Capital:** £843,223,348
**Directors:** S M Qureshi, J M Bin Thaniah, Y Narayan, A Wats, M Sharaf, G R Jayaraman
**Co. Secretary:** Mrs Bernadette Allinson
**Branches:** The Peninsular & Oriental Steam Navigation Co, 247 Tottenham Court Road, London W1T 7QX
**US SIC:** 6711, 4411, 4469
**UK SIC:** 83962, 74001, 76300
**Auditors:** KPMG LLP
**Bankers:** Barclays Bank Plc (20-00-00)
**Following financial data are in thousands**

| | 31-12-13 | 31-12-12 | 31-12-11 |
|---|---|---|---|
| TO | 733,500 | 752,500 | 822,400 |
| P/L | 151,700 | 335,100 | 1,015,400 |
| NW | 3,255,800 | 3,265,100 | 3,041,900 |
| WC | 2,353,900 | 2,113,800 | 2,289,900 |
| Emp. | 6,152 | 6,180 | 6,546 |

DUNS 22-853-3907
## Penketh's Ltd
Bassendale Road, Wirral, Merseyside CH62 3QL
**Tel:** 01513344417 **Fax:** 01517375001
**Web:** www.penkeths.com
**Reg No:** 1287607 **VAT No:** 166543646
**Estd:** 1976 Private Limited Company
**Line of Business:** Commercial stationery supplies
**Trading Style:** Penketh's, Penkeths Office Interiors
**Issued Capital:** £12,004
**Principals:** S W Penketh *(Managing)*, M S Penketh *(Financial)*, A J Penketh, P A Mann, D J Finn
**Co. Secretary:** Simon Penketh
**US SIC:** 5942 **UK SIC:** 65300
**Auditors:** Mitchell Charlesworth
**Bankers:** Barclays Bank Plc (20-50-36)

| | 31-12-13 | 31-12-12 | 31-12-11 |
|---|---|---|---|
| TO | 10,589,883 | 10,531,154 | 10,333,839 |
| P/L | 691,954 | 605,759 | 439,919 |
| NW | 1,384,613 | 1,216,408 | 1,028,290 |
| WC | 346,621 | 250,929 | 155,676 |
| Emp. | 66 | 68 | 67 |

DUNS 22-623-0902
## Penlaw & Co Ltd
Penlaw House, Robert Way, Wickford, Essex SS11 8DD
**Tel:** 01268764029 **Fax:** 01268-764043
**Web:** www.penlaw.co.uk
**Reg No:** 1332889 **VAT No:** 291685228
**Estd:** 1977 Private Limited Company
**Line of Business:** Plasterers' equipment and supplies
**Issued Capital:** £95
**Managing Director:** R J Gray
**Co. Secretary:** Eric Gray
**US SIC:** 5039 **UK SIC:** 61300
**Auditors:** K P Doherty& Co
**Bankers:** HSBC Bank plc (40-13-22)

| | 31-10-13 | 31-10-12 | 31-10-11 |
|---|---|---|---|
| TO | 20,604,712 | 21,556,385 | 19,920,966 |
| P/L | 307,337 | 351,165 | 412,547 |
| NW | 2,075,601 | 1,914,920 | 1,725,034 |
| WC | (135,638) | (220,464) | (296,922) |
| Emp. | 50 | 49 | 46 |

DUNS 45-894-2687 **Imp-Exp**
## Penlon Ltd
**(Subsidiary of:** Intermed Ltd)
Barton Lane, Abingdon Science Park, Abingdon, Oxfordshire OX14 3PH
**Tel:** 01235547000
**Web:** www.penlon.com
**Reg No:** 3228364 **Estd:** 1996 Private Limited Company
**Line of Business:** Manufacturers of instruments for medical purposes
**Export Markets:** Worldwide
**Export Sales:** £12,686,567
**Trading Style:** East Healthcare
**Issued Capital:** £565,340
**Directors:** P A Worrallo, S K Franklin, S E Moon
**Co. Secretary:** Stuart Franklin
**Responsibilities**
**Senior:** Ian Gil-Rodriguez *(General Manager)*, Max Kelly *(Operations Director)*, Dennis Knell *(Manager)*, Tony Serratore *(IT Manager)*
**Finance:** Sarah O'Dell *(Finance Controller)*
**Marketing:** Roger Crossley *(Head of Business Development)*
**Sales:** Roger Crossley *(Head of Business Development)*
**IT:** Tony Serratore *(IT Manager)*
**Operations:** Mike Barlow *(Materials Manager)*
**Branches:** Penlon Ltd, Unit 8, Guide Street, Salford, Lancashire M50 1EW
**US SIC:** 3841 **UK SIC:** 37201
**Auditors:** KPMG LLP
**Bankers:** Barclays Bank Plc (20-00-00)

| | 31-12-13 | 31-12-12 | 31-12-11 |
|---|---|---|---|
| TO | 15,142,428 | 20,541,158 | 21,483,644 |
| P/L | (1,382,402) | (940,514) | 9,965,821 |
| NW | 21,334,947 | 22,414,652 | 22,693,559 |
| WC | 26,681,483 | 27,743,471 | 28,550,708 |
| Emp. | 189 | 201 | 247 |

DUNS 34-641-6154

## Penman Engineering Holdings Ltd

**(Subsidiary of:** Penman Specialist Services Ltd)
Heathhall Industrial Estate, Heathhall, Dumfries, Dumfriesshire DG1 3NY
**Fax:** 01387267332
**Web:** www.penman.co.uk
**Reg No:** 0284498SC **Estd:** 2005 Private Limited Company
**Line of Business:** Management activities of holding companies
**Issued Capital:** £80,000
**Directors:** Brigadier P C Cort, S B St.John-Claire, Miss L J Breckell, C P Welsh, J L Craig, J Knox
**Co. Secretary:** Miss Lisa Breckell
**Responsibilities**
**Senior:** Stuart St John-Claire *(Director)*
**Sales:** Tony Rodgers *(Commercial Director)*
**US SIC:** 6711 **UK SIC:** 83962
**Auditors:** BDO LLP

| | 31-03-14 | 31-03-13 | 31-03-12 |
|---|---|---|---|
| TO | 10,209,365 | 13,075,653 | 18,559,518 |
| P/L | 2,068,034 | 475,411 | 1,727,578 |
| NW | 4,000,882 | 2,842,839 | 2,927,873 |
| WC | 3,900,003 | 2,774,169 | 2,124,235 |
| Emp. | 100 | 123 | 139 |

DUNS 54-919-4363

## Penmellyn Veterinary Group

Station Road, St Columb, Cornwall TR9 6BX
**Tel:** 01637880307
**Web:** www.penmellynvets.co.uk
**Estd:** 2012 Partnership
**Line of Business:** Veterinary activities
**Trading Style:** Penmellyn Veterinary Group Ltd
**Partners:** H Tanzer, P Rogers, P Lockett, Mrs R Barcoe
**Branches:** Penmellyn Veterinary Group, Riviera Surgery, Padstow, Cornwall PL28 8NP
**US SIC:** 0741 **UK SIC:** 95601
**Employees:** 51

DUNS 29-060-4537 **Imp-Exp**

## Penmoor U K Ltd

Eastfield Mills The Knowle, Huddersfield, West Yorkshire HD8 8EA
**Reg No:** 1194757 **VAT No:** 184545736
**Estd:** 1974 Private Limited Company
**Line of Business:** Renting of other machinery and equipment not elsewhere classified
**Export Markets:** Europe and Rest of World
**Issued Capital:** £14,004
**Principals:** J S Smith *(Managing)*, J M Smith, C A Smith
**Co. Secretary:** Alison Horn
**US SIC:** 7394 **UK SIC:** 84000
**Auditors:** Walker & Sutcliffe
**Bankers:** Barclays Bank Plc (20-43-04)

| | 31-01-14 | 31-01-13 | 31-01-12 |
|---|---|---|---|
| TO | 14,986,505 | 6,991,595 | N/A |
| P/L | 705,486 | 261,363 | N/A |
| NW | 3,344,671 | 2,918,938 | 2,206,366 |
| WC | (270,520) | (378,076) | (1,114,912) |
| Emp. | 60 | 32 | N/A |

DUNS 21-774-5200

## Penn Cottage

Stourbridge Road, Wolverhampton, West Midlands WV4 5NG
**Tel:** 01902896264
**Web:** www.millerandcarter.co.uk
**Estd:** 1987 Proprietorship
**Line of Business:** Restaurants
**Proprietor:** S Timmins
**US SIC:** 5812 **UK SIC:** 66110
**Employees:** 100

DUNS 73-505-6769

## Penn Elcom Ltd

**(Subsidiary of:** Penn Elcom Corporation)
Drury Lane, St Leonards-On-Sea, East Sussex
**Tel:** 01424718576
**Web:** www.penn-elcom.com
**Reg No:** 4768848 **Estd:** 2003 Private Limited Company
**Line of Business:** Management activities of holding companies
**Issued Capital:** £3,000,000
**Directors:** P J Stratford, R P Willems
**Responsibilities**
**Health & Safety:** Bob Hayley *(Health & Safety Officer)*
**US SIC:** 6711 **UK SIC:** 83962
**Auditors:** Wilder Coe

| | 30-11-13 | 30-11-12 | 30-11-11 |
|---|---|---|---|
| TO | 13,039,251 | 12,867,223 | 12,604,523 |
| P/L | 365,365 | 304,722 | 71,659 |
| NW | 2,260,553 | 1,805,371 | 1,410,608 |
| WC | 4,095,147 | 5,256,342 | 4,470,630 |
| Emp. | 150 | 149 | 155 |

DUNS 21-715-6967 **Exp**

## Penn Fabrication Ltd

**(Subsidiary of:** Offerfair Ltd)
9-10 Parsons Road, Parsons Industrial Estate, Washington, Tyne and Wear NE37 1HB
**Tel:** 01914161717
**Web:** www.penn-elcom.com
**Reg No:** 1161624 **VAT No:** 209100512
**Estd:** 1974 Private Limited Company
**Line of Business:** Other letting of own property
**Export Markets:** countries worldwide
**Trading Style:** Penn Visual Aids, M B Engineering
**Issued Capital:** £10,000
**Principals:** R P Willems *(Chairman and Managing)*, D C Brown *(Managing)*, P J Stratford, R Mehio
**Responsibilities**
**Senior:** Vince Bullman *(Warehouse Manager)*
**Health & Safety:** Bob Haley *(Facilities Manager)*
**Facilities:** Bob Haley *(Facilities Manager)*
**Branches:** Penn Fabrication Ltd, Drury Lane, St Leonards-On-Sea, St. Leonards-On-Sea, East Sussex TN38 9BA
**US SIC:** 6519 **UK SIC:** 85000
**Bankers:** HSBC Bank plc (40-24-17)

| | 30-11-13 | 30-11-12 | 30-11-11 |
|---|---|---|---|
| TA | 1,581,153 | 1,599,897 | 3,480,163 |
| NW | 225,794 | 19,603 | 3,480,163 |
| WC | (560,147) | (569,083) | N/A |

DUNS 22-627-7259 **Imp-Exp**

## Penn Pharmaceutical Services Ltd

**(Subsidiary of:** Lloyds Banking Group Plc)
Unit 23-24, Tafarnaubach Industrial Estate, Tafarnau, Tredegar, Gwent NP22 3AA
**Tel:** 01495-711222 **Fax:** 01495711225
**Web:** www.pennpharm.co.uk
**Reg No:** 1331447 **VAT No:** 321293487
**Estd:** 1977 Private Limited Company
**Line of Business:** Manufacturers of pharmaceutical products
**Export Markets:** Europe & Rest of the World
**Export Sales:** £24,242,000
**Issued Capital:** £430,694
**Directors:** R J Yarwood, M Dean-Netscher
**Responsibilities**
**Senior:** Darren Hassey *(Manager)*, Lee Mainwaring *(Manager)*
**Branches:** High Wycombe
**US SIC:** 2834 **UK SIC:** 25700
**Auditors:** PricewaterhouseCoopers LLP
**Bankers:** Lloyds TSB Bank plc (30-90-38)

| | 31-03-14 | 31-03-13 | 31-03-12 |
|---|---|---|---|
| TO | 35,117,000 | 46,784,000 | 26,892,000 |
| P/L | 6,960,000 | 5,845,000 | 5,666,000 |
| NW | 7,507,000 | 10,539,000 | 9,752,000 |
| WC | (9,249,000) | (6,664,000) | 1,353,000 |
| Emp. | 299 | 282 | 290 |

DUNS 49-431-7183

## Penna Consulting Plc

5 Fleet Place, London EC4M 7RD
**Tel:** 01412714414 **Fax:** 02076482450
**Web:** www.penna.com
**Reg No:** 3142685 **VAT No:** 605849719
**Estd:** 1996 Public Limited Company
**Line of Business:** Labour recruitment and provision of personnel
**Export Sales:** £1,290,000
**Trading Style:** Penna
**Issued Capital:** £1,303,755
**Directors:** G Browning, L J Ferrar, G L Paton, Ms J A Towers, S R Rowlinson, Ms B M White
**Co. Secretary:** David Firth
**Branches:** Penna Consulting Plc, 55 Gracechurch Street, London EC3V 0EE
**US SIC:** 7361 **UK SIC:** 83954
**Auditors:** Grant Thornton UK LLP
**Bankers:** Barclays Bank Plc (20-00-00)

| | 31-03-14 | 31-03-13 | 31-03-12 |
|---|---|---|---|
| TO | 69,022,000 | 66,640,000 | 68,480,000 |
| P/L | 83,000 | 2,173,000 | 1,759,000 |
| NW | (1,782,000) | 2,169,000 | 1,479,000 |
| WC | (3,171,000) | (498,000) | (1,412,000) |
| Emp. | 302 | 321 | 342 |

DUNS 29-551-3162

## Penna Plc

**(Subsidiary of:** Penna Consulting Plc)
5 Fleet Place, London EC4M 7RD
**Tel:** 02073327777 **Fax:** 02071609332
**Web:** www.penna.com
**Reg No:** 1918150 **VAT No:** 605849719
**Estd:** 2004 Public Limited Company
**Line of Business:** Representative office
**Export Sales:** £657,873
**Issued Capital:** £50,000
**Principals:** D S Firth *(Financial)*, G Browning, O J Morgan, F Cook, K R Pilling, Ms B M White, Ms J A Towers, G R Weemes
**Co. Secretary:** David Firth
**Responsibilities**
**Senior:** Penelope Devalk *(Director)*, Ruth Kaye *(Partner)*, Timothy Morton *(Director)*, Tracy Shuff *(Manager)*, Lesley Styles *(Manager)*, Declan Woods *(Director, Board and Executive)*
**Marketing:** Louise Lerego *(Marketing Executive)*, Kerry Simmons *(Head of Marketing)*
**Sales:** Loretta Maynard *(Business Operations Support)*
**HR:** David Mackey *(Head of Executive HR Recruitme)*
**Operations:** Alison Dexter *(Operations Manager)*
**Branches:** Penna Plc, Temple Court, Cardiff, South Glamorgan CF11 9HA
**US SIC:** 7361, 7392
**UK SIC:** 83954, 83951
**Auditors:** Grant Thornton UK LLP
**Bankers:** The Royal Bank Of Scotland Plc (15-10-00)

| | 31-03-14 | 31-03-13 | 31-03-12 |
|---|---|---|---|
| TO | 67,858,200 | 65,602,858 | 66,618,889 |
| P/L | 206,232 | 1,476,513 | 873,796 |
| NW | 2,126,652 | 2,739,076 | 555,592 |
| WC | 73,730 | 165,240 | (2,607,070) |

DUNS 73-370-8569

## Pennaf Ltd

72 Ffordd William Morgan, St Asaph, Clwyd LL17 0JD
**Tel:** 01745 536800 **Fax:** 01745 538392
**Web:** www.pennaf.co.uk
**Reg No:** 4644360 **Estd:** 2003 Private Company Limited By Guarantee
**Line of Business:** Holding companies nec
**Directors:** G Worthington, Dr S N Horrocks, Mrs J A Owen, D N Ifans, Dr A K Holdsworth, M Steel, G M Jones, M Hornsby
**Co. Secretary:** Trevor Henderson
**Responsibilities**
**Senior:** Eurwen Edwards *(Honorary President)*
**Marketing:** Kristen Jones *(Marketing Director)*
**Sales:** Brian Wooster *(Business Development Manager)*
**HR:** Gill Murgatroyd *(Human Resources Director)*
**Engineering:** Deiniol Evans *(Director, Development and Tech)*
**US SIC:** 6711, 7399, 7339
**UK SIC:** 83962, 83954
**Auditors:** Mazars LLP

| | 31-03-14 | 31-03-13 | 31-03-12 |
|---|---|---|---|
| TO | 31,324,000 | 29,181,000 | 26,964,000 |
| P/L | 1,421,000 | 220,000 | 157,000 |
| NW | 11,402,000 | 9,992,000 | 9,872,000 |
| WC | 1,251,000 | (2,183,000) | (3,393,000) |
| Emp. | 577 | 545 | 429 |

DUNS 45-837-3099

## Pennant International Group Plc

Pennant Court, Cheltenham, Gloucestershire GL51 6TL
**Tel:** 01452714881
**Web:** www.pennantplc.co.uk
**Reg No:** 3187528 **Estd:** 1996 Public Limited Company
**Line of Business:** Management activities of production holding companies
**Export Sales:** £3,495,755
**Trading Style:** Pennet Training System
**Issued Capital:** £1,400,000
**Directors:** P H Walker, C Snook, Ms J K Powell, C C Powell, J M Waller
**Co. Secretary:** Philip Walker
**Responsibilities**
**Sales:** Chris Mair *(International Sales Manager)*
**US SIC:** 7399 **UK SIC:** 83954
**Auditors:** Mazars LLP
**Bankers:** Barclays Bank Plc (20-20-15)

| | 31-12-13 | 31-12-12 | 31-12-11 |
|---|---|---|---|
| TO | 18,676,969 | 14,469,715 | 10,353,534 |
| P/L | 2,246,628 | 1,602,965 | 697,104 |
| NW | 5,111,817 | 4,215,880 | 3,758,383 |
| WC | 3,322,535 | 2,508,955 | 2,027,197 |
| Emp. | 125 | 119 | 110 |

DUNS 67-149-6995

## Pennell's Holdings Ltd

Newark Road, South Hykeham, Lincoln, Lincolnshire LN6 9NT
**Reg No:** 6008237 **Estd:** 2006 Private Limited Company
**Line of Business:** Other retail sale in specialised stores not elsewhere classified
**Issued Capital:** £38,670
**Directors:** W E Pennell, R N Pennell
**Co. Secretary:** Mrs Julie Pennell
**US SIC:** 5999 **UK SIC:** 65600

| | 31-01-14 | 31-01-13 | 31-01-12 |
|---|---|---|---|
| TO | 5,832,156 | 5,655,920 | 5,855,270 |
| P/L | 375,974 | 431,729 | 590,740 |
| NW | 7,568,938 | 7,744,915 | 7,634,556 |
| WC | 1,082,204 | 1,023,592 | 934,890 |
| Emp. | 123 | 122 | 124 |

DUNS 77-927-1266

## Penney's Ltd

123 Rutten Lane, Kidlington, Oxfordshire OX5 1LT
**Tel:** 01865-371866
**Web:** www.penneyscleaning.co.uk
**Reg No:** 5829970 **Estd:** 2006 Private Limited Company
**Line of Business:** Estate agents
**Issued Capital:** £100
**Directors:** E L Penney, Mrs S P Penney, P J Penney
**Co. Secretary:** Mrs Lucy Penney
**US SIC:** 6531 **UK SIC:** 83400

| | 31-05-13 | 31-05-12 | 31-05-11 |
|---|---|---|---|
| TA | 38,875 | 59,955 | 69,193 |
| NW | 9,688 | 15,745 | 12,294 |
| WC | 7,251 | 3,431 | (3,447) |

DUNS 64-101-9518

## Pennies Day Nursery Ltd

Newnham Court, Bearsted Road, Weavering, Maidstone, Kent ME14 5LH
**Tel:** 01622-737733 **Fax:** 01622737733
**Web:** www.pennies.co.uk
**Reg No:** 3496768 **Estd:** 1998 Private Limited Company
**Line of Business:** Nursery schools
**Trading Style:** Pennies Day Nursery Ltd
**Issued Capital:** £225,835
**Directors:** Ms Z M Scotton, L B Kaye
**Co. Secretary:** Dominic Scotton
**Branches:** Pennies Day Nursery Ltd, 149 Hockers Lane, Maidstone, Kent ME14 5JY
**US SIC:** 8211 **UK SIC:** 93200

| | 31-03-14 | 31-03-13 | 31-03-12 |
|---|---|---|---|
| TA | 2,155,109 | 2,108,185 | 2,131,448 |
| NW | 196,994 | 152,171 | 298,540 |
| WC | (75,206) | (155,125) | (13,182) |

DUNS 23-288-8714

## The Pennine Acute Hospital N H S Trust

Trust Headquarters, North Manchester General Hospital, Delaunays Road, Crumpsall, Manchester M8 5RB
**Tel:** 01616045460
**Web:** www.pat.nhs.uk
**VAT No:** 654418333 **Estd:** 2002
**Line of Business:** Hospitals & clinics
**Issued Capital:** £1
**Principals:** J Jesky *(Chairman)*, R Pickering *(Personnel)*, H Mullen, J Wilkes, J Saxby, E Ahmad, M Holly, Mrs C Guereca
**Responsibilities**
**Senior:** Nadine Broecker *(Manager)*, Fiona Burke *(Non-Executive Director)*, Marian Carroll *(Manager)*, Haydn Griffith *(Non-Executive Director)*, Nicola Nicholls *(Associate Director Nursing - C)*, Egware Odeka *(Manager)*, Tim Pickstone *(Non-Executive Director)*, Christine Walters *(Associate Director, IM&T)*
**Finance:** Barbara Herring *(Associate Director of Finance)*, Barry Waterhouse *(Accounts Manager)*
**HR:** Nadia Khan *(Human Resources Manager)*
**Facilities:** Pam Miller *(Associate Director, Facilities)*
**Operations:** John Allwork *(Head of Estate Operations)*, Gail Buggy *(Operations Manager)*, Lisa Parr *(Production and Operations Mana)*
**Branches:** The Pennine Acute Hospital N H S Trust, Fairfax Road, Manchester M25 1BT
**US SIC:** 9121, 8062
**UK SIC:** 91110, 95100
**Employees:** 9,500

DUNS 21-036-9903

## Pennine Care Nhs Foundation Trust

225 Old Street, Ashton-Under-Lyne, Lancashire OL6 7SR
**Tel:** 01617163000
**Web:** www.penninecare.nhs.uk
**Estd:** 1948
**Line of Business:** Hospitals
**Principals:** J Schofield *(Chairman)*, D Curtis, Dr S Kaligotla, M Roe, M Mccourt, J Archer, J Lane, Ms K Calvin-Thomas
**Responsibilities**
**Senior:** Carol Ainsworth *(Manager)*, Robert Ainsworth *(Designated Limited Liability P)*, Tim Chamberlain *(Designated Limited Liability P)*, Rex Charlton *(Designated Limited Liability P)*, Colin Mckinless *(Non Executive Director)*, Wendy Meikle *(Designated Limited Liability P)*, Alan Moran *(Non-Executive Director)*, Dale Mulgrew *(Partner)*, Mansoor Shah *(Designated Limited Liability P)*, Henry Ticehurst *(Medical Director)*
**Finance:** Judith Crosby *(Financial Director)*
**Marketing:** Richard Spearing *(Acting Director of Service Dev)*
**IT:** Barbara Hoyle *(ICT Director)*
**US SIC:** 8062 **UK SIC:** 95100

**Auditors:** PricewaterhouseCoopers LLP

| | 31-03-14 | 31-03-13 | 31-03-12 |
|---|---|---|---|
| TO | 271,377,000 | 231,986,000 | 228,434,000 |
| P/L | 758,000 | (3,223,000) | 2,857,000 |
| NW | 85,600,000 | 71,877,000 | 78,483,000 |
| WC | 9,975,000 | 8,677,000 | 13,077,000 |
| Emp. | 5,476 | 4,769 | 4,924 |

DUNS 29-517-5632 **Exp**

## Pennine Healthcare Ltd

City Gate, Derby, Derbyshire DE24 8WY
**Tel:** 01332794880
**Web:** www.penninehealthcare.com
**Reg No:** 1880762 **Estd:** 1953 Private Limited Company
**Line of Business:** Hospital equipment
**Export Markets:** Germany, U S A and France etc
**Issued Capital:** £4
**Managing Director:** Ms E J Fothergill
**Responsibilities**
**Senior:** Luke Fryer *(Chief Executive)*, Mick Marvel *(Warehouse Manager)*
**Finance:** Nicky Steinbac *(Financial Controller)*
**Marketing:** Andrea Robinson *(UK Business Manager)*
**Sales:** Delphine Demilly *(Plackett, Export Sales Manager)*
**IT:** Mark Gillanders *(Head of IT)*
**HR:** Helen Chambers *(Human Resources Manager)*
**Facilities:** Darryl Orridge *(Facilities Manager)*
**Operations:** Nick Lewins *(Engineering Design Manager)*
**Engineering:** Nick Lewins *(Engineering Design Manager)*
**US SIC:** 5199 **UK SIC:** 61900
**Auditors:** Bates Weston
**Bankers:** Lloyds TSB Bank plc (30-92-59)

| | 31-03-14 | 31-03-13 | 31-03-12 |
|---|---|---|---|
| TA | 4 | 4 | 4 |
| NW | 4 | 4 | 4 |

DUNS 21-878-3825

## Pennine Housing 2000 Ltd

Bull Green House, Bull Green, Halifax, West Yorkshire HX1 2EB
**Tel:** 03005555557 **Fax:** 01422284598
**Web:** http://togetherhousing.co.uk
**Reg No:** 0031839IP **Estd:** 2000 Friendly Society
**Line of Business:** Non-charitable social work activities with accommodation
**Trading Style:** Together Housing Group
**Responsibilities**
**Senior:** Geoffrey Butler *(Board Member)*, Jim Calland *(Tenant Board Member)*, Steve Close *(Group Chief Executive)*, Tom Miskell *(Chief Executive)*
**IT:** Frank Anderson *(ICT Officer)*
**Facilities:** Amanda Garrard *(Group Director of Neighbourhoo)*
**US SIC:** 8321 **UK SIC:** 96111
**Employees:** 405

DUNS 21-313-3291 **Imp-Exp**

## Pennine Industrial Equipment Ltd

Manorcroft House, Commercial Road, Skelmanthorpe, Huddersfield, West Yorkshire HD8 9DT
**Tel:** 01484864733
**Web:** www.pennine.org
**Reg No:** 1032904 **Estd:** 1971 Private Limited Company
**Line of Business:** Manufacturers of plastic products
**Export Markets:** E U; Middle East; Far East; Africa;
**Issued Capital:** £9,326
**Principals:** G K Hobbs *(Managing)*, C J Hobbs, Miss K J Hobbs, G Womersley
**Co. Secretary:** Christopher Hobbs
**US SIC:** 2821 **UK SIC:** 25140
**Auditors:** Charles Frieze & Co
**Bankers:** The Royal Bank Of Scotland Plc (16-22-04)

| | 30-09-13 | 30-09-12 | 30-09-11 |
|---|---|---|---|
| TA | 1,924,133 | 1,850,704 | 1,829,899 |
| NW | 955,582 | 818,709 | 859,125 |
| WC | 388,900 | 227,717 | 273,623 |

DUNS 73-463-7452

## Pennine Telecom (Holdings) Ltd

(**Subsidiary of:** Ptl (Holdings) Ltd)
Pennine House, Salford Street, Bury, Lancashire BL9 6YA
**Tel:** 01617633333
**Web:** www.penninetelecom.com
**Reg No:** 4727822 **Estd:** 2003 Private Limited Company
**Line of Business:** Telecom equipment and systems
**Issued Capital:** £202,500
**Directors:** G D King, A J Roberts, N H Beaumont, S K Watts
**Co. Secretary:** Nigel Beaumont
**US SIC:** 4899 **UK SIC:** 79020
**Bankers:** The Royal Bank Of Scotland Plc (16-15-17)

| | 31-12-13 | 31-12-12 | 31-12-11 |
|---|---|---|---|
| TO | 10,370,796 | 8,702,018 | 8,017,057 |
| P/L | 526,932 | 149,944 | 185,171 |
| NW | 553,063 | 21,420 | (73,355) |
| WC | 442,796 | 47,497 | 129,410 |
| Emp. | 68 | 62 | 56 |

DUNS 21-811-4698

## Pennine View School

Old Road, Conisbrough, Doncaster, South Yorkshire DN12 3LR
**Tel:** 01709864978
**Web:** www.pennineviewschool.org.uk
**Estd:** 2002
**Line of Business:** Schools (local authority)
**Responsibilities**
**Senior:** Glyn Davies *(Head Teacher)*
**US SIC:** 8299 **UK SIC:** 93300
**Employees:** 50

DUNS 85-603-1724

## Pennine Weavers Ltd

North Beck Mills, Becks Road, Keighley, West Yorkshire BD21 1SD
**Tel:** 01535-664341
**Reg No:** 6221106 **Estd:** 2007 Private Limited Company
**Line of Business:** Loom operators and weavers
**Issued Capital:** £60,001
**Director:** G Eastwood
**Co. Secretary:** John Hodges
**US SIC:** 2231 **UK SIC:** 43103

| | 30-04-14 | 30-04-13 | 30-04-12 |
|---|---|---|---|
| TA | 3,249,857 | 3,256,308 | 3,253,372 |
| NW | 2,813,484 | 2,859,186 | 2,588,867 |
| WC | 1,443,140 | 1,550,214 | 1,056,976 |

DUNS 21-360-8745

## Pennington Court

Hunslet Hall Road, Leeds, West Yorkshire LS11 6TT
**Tel:** 01132284040
**Web:** www.westwardcare.co.uk
**Estd:** 1994 Proprietorship
**Line of Business:** Residential care establishments
**Proprietor:** P Hodkingson
**Responsibilities**
**Senior:** Jennie Gillham *(Manager)*, Eugene Hopton *(Manager)*, Lynn Priest *(General Manager)*, Simon Shires *(Manager)*
**US SIC:** 8321 **UK SIC:** 96111
**Employees:** 70

DUNS 42-417-5375

## Penningtons Solicitors Ltd

(**Subsidiary of:** Penningtons Manches Llp)
33 Gutter Lane, London EC2V 8AR
**Tel:** 02074573000 **Fax:** 02074573240
**Web:** www.penningtons.co.uk
**Reg No:** 4405247 **Estd:** 2002 Private Limited Company
**Line of Business:** Solicitors
**Issued Capital:** £1
**Directors:** G Bosi, Penningtons Directors (No 1) Lim
**Co. Secretary:** Pennsec Limited
**Responsibilities**
**Senior:** David Raine *(Chief Executive)*
**HR:** Lorna Hector *(Recruitment & Training Manager)*, Rachel McCloud *(Human Resources Manager)*
**US SIC:** 8111, 7399
**UK SIC:** 83500, 83954

| | 31-03-14 | 31-03-13 | 31-03-12 |
|---|---|---|---|
| TA | 1 | 1 | 1 |
| NW | 1 | 1 | 1 |

DUNS 23-776-0392

## Pennon Group Plc

Peninsula House, Rydon Lane, Exeter, Devon EX2 7HR
**Tel:** 01392-446677 **Fax:** 01392-444175
**Web:** www.pennon-group.co.uk
**Reg No:** 2366640 **VAT No:** 540465165
**Estd:** 1989 Public Limited Company
**Line of Business:** Management activities of holding companies
**Export Sales:** £56,000,000
**Trading Style:** Pennon Group
**Issued Capital:** £148,897,854
**Principals:** C Loughlin, Ms S J Davy, N Cooper, I J Mcaulay, Ms G A Rider, G D Connell, M D Angle, K G Harvey
**Co. Secretary:** Kenneth Woodier
**Responsibilities**
**Senior:** Mike Davey *(Manager)*, Colin Drummond *(Chairman of Viridor)*, David Dupont *(Director)*, Andy Willicott *(Head of IS)*
**IT:** Andy Willicott *(Head of IS)*
**Health & Safety:** Huw Parry *(Health & Safety Officer)*, barry flicker *(health and safety manager)*
**Branches:** Pennon Group Plc, Peninsula House, Rydon Lane, Exeter, Devon EX2 7HR
**US SIC:** 6711, 4941
**UK SIC:** 83962, 17000
**Auditors:** PricewaterhouseCoopers LLP
**Bankers:** Lloyds TSB Bank plc (30-00-02)
**Following financial data are in thousands**

| | 31-03-14 | 31-03-13 | 31-03-12 |
|---|---|---|---|
| TO | 1,321,200 | 1,201,100 | 1,233,100 |
| P/L | 158,700 | 21,800 | 200,500 |
| NW | 827,700 | 712,800 | 477,500 |
| WC | 241,900 | 379,300 | 13,000 |
| Emp. | 4,451 | 4,584 | 4,529 |

DUNS 21-772-4944

## Pennoweth Primary School

Drump Road, Redruth, Cornwall TR15 1NA
**Tel:** 01209215671
**Web:** www.pennweth.cornwall.sch.uk
**Estd:** 1975 Proprietorship
**Line of Business:** Schools (local authority)
**Proprietor:** Ms P Crawford
**US SIC:** 8211 **UK SIC:** 93200
**Employees:** 83

DUNS 39-981-9630

## Pennthorpe School Trust Ltd

Church Street, Rudgwick, Horsham, West Sussex RH12 3HJ
**Tel:** 01403-822391
**Web:** www.pennthorpe.com
**Reg No:** 0799603 **Estd:** 1964 Private Company Limited By Guarantee
**Line of Business:** Schools (independent)
**Trading Style:** Pennthorpe School
**Directors:** M P King, N J Charman, K F Mcdonagh, Ms P Laurence, R W Nugent, M A Bell, Mrs A D Gilchrist, M R Lucas
**Co. Secretary:** Mrs Tracy Caveney
**Responsibilities**
**Senior:** Daniel Connolly *(Director)*, Hilary Dugdale *(Manager)*, Dominic Edginton *(Director)*, Mark Fielden *(Director)*, Toby Mullins *(Manager)*
**US SIC:** 8211 **UK SIC:** 93200
**Auditors:** RSM Robson Rhodes
**Bankers:** Barclays Bank Plc (20-23-97)

| | 31-08-13 | 31-08-12 | 31-08-11 |
|---|---|---|---|
| TO | 3,132,184 | 3,106,624 | 3,070,146 |
| P/L | 7,529 | (129,795) | 82,656 |
| NW | 3,461,911 | 3,454,382 | 3,584,177 |
| WC | (147,415) | (71,099) | 770,449 |
| Emp. | 77 | 64 | 65 |

DUNS 34-696-6286

## Pennwell International Ltd

(**Subsidiary of:** Pennwell Corporation)
The Water Tower, Gunpowder Mill, Powdermill Lane, Waltham Abbey, Essex EN9 1BN
**Tel:** 01992656600
**Web:** www.pennwell.com
**Reg No:** 2779246 **Estd:** 1993 Private Limited Company
**Line of Business:** Other business activities not elsewhere classified
**Issued Capital:** £999
**Directors:** Ms J A Gilsinger, R F Biolchini, M Wilmoth
**US SIC:** 7399 **UK SIC:** 83954
**Auditors:** Silver Levene
**Bankers:** The Royal Bank Of Scotland Plc (16-01-02)

| | 31-03-14 | 31-03-13 | 31-03-12 |
|---|---|---|---|
| TO | 7,460,776 | 8,393,734 | 7,523,688 |
| P/L | (959,600) | (757,288) | (30,181) |
| NW | (4,104,228) | (4,080,789) | (3,535,096) |
| WC | (4,087,747) | (4,064,425) | (3,533,040) |
| Emp. | 62 | 60 | 3 |

DUNS 21-609-1124 **Imp-Exp**

## Penny & Giles Controls Ltd

(**Subsidiary of:** Curtiss-Wright Corporation)
36 Nine Mile Point Industrial Estate, Newport, Gwent NP11 7HZ
**Tel:** 01495-202000
**Web:** www.pennyandgiles.com
**Reg No:** 0843903 **Estd:** 1965 Private Limited Company
**Line of Business:** Manufacturers and distributors of electronic components
**Export Markets:** U S A; Germany; European Union (E U)
**Export Sales:** £58,063,000
**Issued Capital:** £3,240,000
**Directors:** J K Watkins, N P Jones, K Rayment, A R Thornton, G E Tynan, G P Macdonald
**Co. Secretary:** Robert Shaw
**Responsibilities**
**Senior:** Neil Parke *(Manager)*
**HR:** Pat Bush *(Human Resources Representative)*
**Engineering:** Sean Tedstone *(Engineering Manager)*
**Branches:** Penny & Giles Controls Ltd, 1 Embankment Way, Ringwood, Hampshire BH24 1EU
**US SIC:** 3679 **UK SIC:** 34542
**Auditors:** Deloitte LLP
**Bankers:** HSBC Bank plc (40-32-04)

| | 31-12-13 | 31-12-12 | 31-12-11 |
|---|---|---|---|
| TO | 76,498,000 | 43,835,000 | 37,085,000 |
| P/L | 8,294,000 | 2,666,000 | 2,398,000 |
| NW | 6,911,000 | 265,000 | 25,728,000 |
| WC | 32,658,000 | 22,333,000 | 26,821,000 |
| Emp. | 515 | 396 | 369 |

DUNS 21-925-0040 **Imp-Exp**

## Penny Hydraulics Ltd

Station Road Industrial Estate, Station Road, Chesterfield, Derbyshire S43 4AB
**Tel:** 01246811475
**Web:** www.pennyhydraulics.com
**Reg No:** 1380206 **VAT No:** 295593603
**Estd:** 1978 Private Limited Company
**Line of Business:** Representative office
**Export Markets:** E U
**Issued Capital:** £1,500
**Directors:** T J Penny, R P Short, R G Penny, A J Holmes
**Co. Secretary:** Ms Helen Penny
**Responsibilities**
**Marketing:** Jess Penny *(PR Manager)*
**Operations:** Simon Pykett *(Project Manager)*
**US SIC:** 3534, 3532
**UK SIC:** 32553, 32510
**Auditors:** Shorts
**Bankers:** Barclays Bank Plc (20-20-50)

| | 30-06-14 | 30-06-13 | 30-06-12 |
|---|---|---|---|
| TO | 5,648,303 | 5,402,302 | 4,807,491 |
| P/L | 502,685 | 347,910 | 266,067 |
| NW | 3,038,265 | 2,666,689 | 2,577,322 |
| WC | 2,437,259 | 1,961,421 | 1,864,182 |
| Emp. | 77 | 78 | 72 |

DUNS 29-514-3564 **Imp**

## Penny Lane Foods Ltd

(**Subsidiary of:** Penny Lane Holdings Ltd)
Unit 1a-1e, Yeo Mill Business Park, Yeo Road, Bridgwater, Somerset TA6 5NA
**Tel:** 01278424244
**Web:** www.pennylanefoods.com
**Reg No:** 1877588 **VAT No:** 429077535
**Estd:** 1985 Private Limited Company
**Line of Business:** Production of sausages
**Export Sales:** £142,245
**Issued Capital:** £110
**Director:** A C Jones
**Co. Secretary:** Mrs Catherine Jones
**Responsibilities**
**Sales:** Barry Reeves *(Sales Manager)*
**US SIC:** 2013 **UK SIC:** 41223
**Auditors:** Churchill & Co
**Bankers:** Lloyds TSB Bank plc (30-98-45)

| | 31-12-13 | 31-12-12 | 31-12-11 |
|---|---|---|---|
| TO | 11,928,345 | 11,586,918 | 11,084,998 |
| P/L | 1,100,237 | 553,954 | 726,731 |
| NW | 3,165,581 | 2,680,388 | 2,663,216 |
| WC | 1,784,048 | 1,229,892 | 1,000,728 |
| Emp. | 95 | 97 | 97 |

DUNS 50-442-0712

## Pennyfarthing Construction Ltd

(**Subsidiary of:** Pennyfarthing Developments Ltd)
Pennyfarthings House, South Drive, Ossemsley, Ossemsley, New Milton, Hampshire BH25 5TL
**Tel:** 01425-613958
**Web:** www.pennyfarthinghomes.co.uk
**Reg No:** 2430019 **VAT No:** 579949746
**Estd:** 1991 Private Limited Company
**Line of Business:** Residential property developers
**Issued Capital:** £4,100
**Principals:** M Adams *(Managing)*, D Adams *(Sales)*, M S Dukes, T R Adams
**Co. Secretary:** Mark Adams
**US SIC:** 1522 **UK SIC:** 50100
**Auditors:** DNB Accounting Ltd
**Bankers:** Lloyds TSB Bank plc (30-92-02)

| | 31-01-14 | 31-01-13 | 31-01-12 |
|---|---|---|---|
| TO | 9,065,797 | 8,399,757 | 8,111,618 |
| P/L | 181,840 | 30,032 | 90,993 |
| NW | 2,181,492 | 2,041,163 | 2,015,240 |
| WC | 2,118,415 | 1,949,726 | 1,894,526 |
| Emp. | 53 | 29 | 54 |

DUNS 22-604-3883

## Pennyfarthing Estates Ltd

Pennyfarthing House, Ossemsley, New Milton, Hampshire BH25 5TL
**Tel:** 01425639393
**Web:** www.pennyfarthinghomes.co.uk
**Reg No:** 1280945 **Estd:** 1976 Private Limited Company
**Line of Business:** Development and selling of real estate
**Issued Capital:** £4,000
**Managing Director:** T R Adams
**Co. Secretary:** Ms Susanne Adams
**US SIC:** 6552 **UK SIC:** 85000
**Auditors:** HLB AV Audit Plc

**Bankers:** Lloyds TSB Bank plc (30-92-02)

| | 31-01-14 | 31-01-13 | 31-01-12 |
|---|---|---|---|
| TO | N/A | 600,000 | N/A |
| P/L | (1,767) | 250,438 | 17,135 |
| NW | 912,913 | 934,250 | 920,790 |
| WC | 912,913 | 934,250 | 751,066 |

DUNS 21-295-2787

## Penoyre & Prasad Architects

Discovery House, 28-42 Banner Street, London EC1Y 8QE
**Tel:** 020-7250-3477
**Web:** www.penoyre-prasad.net
**VAT No:** 480864128 **Estd:** 1988 Partnership
**Line of Business:** Architects
**Trading Style:** Penoyre & Prasad Architects
**Partners:** G Penoyre, S Prasad
**US SIC:** 8911 **UK SIC:** 83701
**Employees:** 60

DUNS 64-097-6838

## Penpergwm House Ltd

Penpergwm House Penpergwm, Abergavenny, Gwent NP7 9AE
**Tel:** 01873-840267
**Web:** www.penpergwmhouse.org.uk
**Reg No:** 4501174 **Estd:** 2002 Private Limited Company
**Line of Business:** Social work activities with accommodation
**Issued Capital:** £1,000
**Principals:** Ms P C Llewelyn *(Managing)*, H W Llewelyn
**Co. Secretary:** Hugo Llewelyn
**US SIC:** 8321 **UK SIC:** 96111

| | 31-03-14 | 31-03-13 | 31-03-12 |
|---|---|---|---|
| TA | 589,622 | 477,256 | 304,446 |
| NW | 237,180 | 231,064 | 148,178 |
| WC | 66,951 | 50,222 | 57,755 |

DUNS 21-585-0585

## Penrhos Polish Care Home

Penrhos Home, Penrhos, Pwllheli, Gwynedd LL53 7HN
**Tel:** 01758613825
**Web:** www.phsltd.org
**Estd:** 2011 Proprietorship
**Line of Business:** Residential care establishments
**Proprietor:** Mrs C Hughes Love
**Responsibilities**
**Senior:** Cathy Adams *(Care Home Manager)*
**US SIC:** 8321 **UK SIC:** 96111
**Employees:** 100

DUNS 23-005-9420

## The Penrith Farmers & Kidds Plc

Agricultural Hall, Skirsgill, Penrith, Cumbria CA11 0DN
**Web:** www.pfandk.co.uk
**Reg No:** 0010553 **VAT No:** 256498419
**Estd:** 2005 Public Limited Company
**Line of Business:** Other engineering activities
**Issued Capital:** £318,233
**Principals:** R C Morris *(Managing)*, J Stalker, K K Blue, R L Good, Mrs J Brown, W F Mossop
**Co. Secretary:** Richard Morris
**Branches:** The Penrith Farmers & Kidds Plc, Auction House, Station Road, Stokesley, Middlesbrough, Cleveland TS9 7AB
**US SIC:** 8911 **UK SIC:** 83701
**Auditors:** Grant Thornton
**Bankers:** Barclays Bank Plc (20-66-97)

| | 31-08-14 | 31-08-13 | 31-08-12 |
|---|---|---|---|
| TO | 2,367,313 | 2,127,251 | 1,976,292 |
| P/L | 362,635 | 154,164 | 126,003 |
| NW | 5,561,354 | 5,613,613 | 5,507,408 |
| WC | 1,177,596 | 1,214,901 | 1,183,720 |
| Emp. | 62 | 65 | 63 |

DUNS 76-908-1928

## Penrose Housing Association Ltd

Unit 1, Waterloo Gardens, Milner Square, London N1 1TY
**Tel:** 02036689270
**Web:** www.penrose.org.uk
**Reg No:** 0026973IP **Estd:** 1969
**Line of Business:** Activities of other membership organisations not elsewhere classified
**Principals:** J Ogbonna *(Chairman)*, J Horsman, J Cawley, E King, D Elliott, M Doherty, S Jacobs, M Jones
**Responsibilities**
**Senior:** S Haleema *(Principal)*, Helen Ralston *(Vice Chairman)*
**Finance:** E Acquaah *(Treasurer)*
**Branches:** Penrose Housing Association Ltd, 6 Kingswood Rd, Gillingham, Kent ME7 1EA
**US SIC:** 8699 **UK SIC:** 96902
**Auditors:** Horwath Clark Whitehill LLP
**Employees:** 121
**Turnover:** £5,928,536

DUNS 34-909-6631

## Pension Insurance Corporation Plc

**(Subsidiary of:** Pension Holding Co (Uk) 3 Ltd)
14 Cornhill, London EC3V 3ND
**Tel:** 02071052000
**Web:** www.pensioncorporation.com
**Reg No:** 5706720 **Estd:** 2006 Public Limited Company
**Line of Business:** Activities auxiliary to insurance and pension funding
**Issued Capital:** £401,304,196
**Directors:** Sir M A Weinberg, E U Michotte, T J Hanford, Ms C H Maunsell, S J Sarjant, Ms T Blackwell, T M Stephen, R P Sewell
**Co. Secretary:** David Thomson
**Responsibilities**
**Senior:** John Coomber *(Director)*, Christopher Mckechnie *(Director)*, William Winters *(Director)*
**Marketing:** Sandra Hatugari *(Business Development/ Marketin)*
**Sales:** Sandra Hatugari *(Business Development/ Marketin)*
**US SIC:** 6411 **UK SIC:** 83200
**Auditors:** KPMG Audit PLC
**Following financial data are in thousands**

| | 31-12-13 | 31-12-12 | 31-12-11 |
|---|---|---|---|
| TO | 3,340,000 | 1,358,800 | 588,333 |
| P/L | 114,000 | 184,200 | 11,974 |
| NW | 946,000 | 635,400 | 419,973 |
| WC | (496,000) | (4,808,700) | (5,127,072) |

DUNS 21-557-9554

## Pension Protection Fund

12 Dingwall Road, Croydon, Surrey CR0 2NA
**Tel:** 0845-600-2541 **Fax:** 020-8633-4910
**Web:** www.pensionprotectionfund.org.uk
**Estd:** 2006 Incorporate By Act Of Parliament
**Line of Business:** Pension companies
**Trading Style:** Fraud Compensation Fund
**Principals:** L Churchill *(Chairman)*, A Rubenstein, I Abrams, C Hughes, M Clarke, Ms A Berresford, M Baker, Ms J Drake
**Responsibilities**
**Senior:** Caroline Dear *(Facilities Manager)*
**Finance:** Andy McKinnon *(Chief Financial Officer)*
**Marketing:** Sharon Carson *(Media Manager)*, Ana Moreno *(Communications Manager)*
**IT:** Alan Losty *(Head of IT)*
**HR:** Katherine Easter *(Human Resources Director)*
**Facilities:** Caroline Dear *(Facilities Manager)*
**Branches:** Pension Protection Fund, Pension Protection Fund, Renaissance House, Croydon, Surrey CR0 2NA
**US SIC:** 6371, 6411
**UK SIC:** 82002, 83200
**Auditors:** Amyas C E Morse
**Following financial data are in thousands**

| | 31-03-13 | 31-03-12 | 31-03-11 |
|---|---|---|---|
| TO | 647,700 | 604,800 | 690,609 |
| P/L | 668,800 | 2,251,900 | 1,010,258 |
| NW | 1,760,700 | 1,064,500 | 671,214 |
| WC | 3,264,100 | 2,773,000 | 847,908 |
| Emp. | 262 | 256 | 291 |

DUNS 77-441-6739

## Pensionology.Uk Ltd

1 The Pavilions, Knutsford, Cheshire WA16 8DX
**Tel:** 08456341144 **Fax:** 08456-341145
**Web:** www.broker-support.com
**Reg No:** 2951351 **Estd:** 2002 Private Limited Company
**Line of Business:** Financial intermediation not elsewhere classified
**Issued Capital:** £1,000
**Directors:** M J Ruffles, C J Burgess, J R Mamelok
**Co. Secretary:** Ms Rachel Mamelok
**Responsibilities**
**Finance:** Amy Clarke *(Head of Annuities)*
**Admin:** Ursula Reeves *(Investment Administrator)*
**US SIC:** 6111 **UK SIC:** 81501
**Auditors:** Campbell Woolley LLP

| | 31-07-13 | 31-07-12 | 31-07-11 |
|---|---|---|---|
| TA | 110,967 | 231,236 | 252,530 |
| NW | 24,741 | 5,777 | (85,834) |
| WC | (25,489) | (43,503) | (266,280) |

DUNS 34-972-0438

## Pensions First Group Llp

6th Floor, 90 Long Acre, London WC2E 9RA
**Tel:** 020-7632-9100
**Web:** www.pensionsfirst.com
**Reg No:** 0318884OC **Estd:** 2006
**Line of Business:** Pension, Health and Welfare Funds
**Responsibilities**
**Senior:** Anabel Hoult *(Non-designated Limited Liabili)*
**US SIC:** 6371 **UK SIC:** 82002
**Auditors:** Deloitte LLP

| | 31-12-13 | 31-12-12 | 31-12-11 |
|---|---|---|---|
| TO | 10,030,460 | 3,772,047 | 1,567,411 |
| P/L | (6,819,443) | (9,669,745) | (12,220,882) |
| NW | 6,653,110 | (882,515) | 8,048,230 |
| WC | 5,545,477 | (1,509,981) | 7,795,500 |
| Emp. | 63 | 54 | 63 |

DUNS 55-073-0725

## The Pensions Regulator

Po Box 16314, Birmingham, West Midlands B23 3JP
**Tel:** 08456001011
**Web:** www.thepensionsregulator.gov.uk
**Estd:** 1996 Incorporate By Act Of Parliament
**Line of Business:** Pension advisers and consultants
**Principals:** J Hayes *(Chairman)*, Ms C Instance
**Responsibilities**
**Senior:** Tony Brierley *(Non-Executive Director)*, Tony Hobman *(Chief Executive)*, Robert Laslett *(Board Member)*, David Norgrove *(Chairman)*, Stephen Soper *(Interim CEO)*
**Finance:** Mark Ardron *(Finance Manager)*
**Marketing:** Matt Adams *(Media Relations Manager)*, Ciara Bridge-Butler *(Press Officer)*, Cat Dean *(Press Officer)*, Katherine Long *(Press Officer)*, Rebecca Sandles *(Senior Media Officer)*, Simon Steers *(Relations Manager)*
**HR:** Kathryn Mountford *(Training Officer)*
**Branches:** The Pensions Regulator, Po Box 878, Lincoln, Lincolnshire LN1 1ZF
**US SIC:** 9121 **UK SIC:** 91110
**Employees:** 300

DUNS 42-346-4999

## The Pensions Trust

Verity House, 6 Canal Wharf, Leeds, West Yorkshire LS11 5BQ
**Tel:** 01132345500
**Web:** www.thepensionstrust.org.uk
**VAT No:** 577834194 **Estd:** 2002
**Line of Business:** Pension companies
**Director:** R Stroud
**Responsibilities**
**Senior:** Stephen Nichols *(Chief Executive)*, Sarah Smart *(Chair)*
**Finance:** Mike Scrowston *(Head of Finance)*
**Marketing:** Logan Anderson *(Head of Customer Relations)*, Suzy Brear *(PR & Communications Manager)*, Katy Pollard *(PR & Communications Manager)*
**Sales:** Glenn Austen *(Account Manager)*, Jacki Johnston *(Account Manager)*
**Admin:** Simon Stead *(Administration Manager)*
**HR:** Lisa Brailsford *(HR Manager)*, Corinne Quin *(Human Resources Manager)*
**Branches:** The Pensions Trust, 45 Moorfields, London EC2Y 9AE
**US SIC:** 6411 **UK SIC:** 83200
**Auditors:** KPMG LLP
**Employees:** 160
**Turnover:** £235,500,000

DUNS 23-795-1541 **Imp**

## Penso Consulting Ltd

**(Subsidiary of:** Penso Holdings Ltd)
Woodhams Road, Coventry, West Midlands CV3 4FX
**Tel:** 02476-217760 **Fax:** 02476-217769
**Web:** www.penso.co.uk
**Reg No:** 3787877 **Estd:** 2010 Private Limited Company
**Line of Business:** Speciality design activities
**Issued Capital:** £300,100
**Directors:** J Thurston-Thorpe, D Hurcombe
**Co. Secretary:** David Roche
**US SIC:** 7399, 7392
**UK SIC:** 83954, 83951

| | 31-03-14 | 31-03-13 | 31-03-12 |
|---|---|---|---|
| TO | 11,238,923 | 9,890,653 | N/A |
| P/L | 1,086,502 | 1,147,023 | N/A |
| NW | 3,544,357 | 1,504,131 | 900,885 |
| WC | (40,764) | (353,535) | 620,549 |
| Emp. | 117 | 93 | N/A |

DUNS 21-701-0164 **Imp**

## Pensord Press Ltd

Tram Road, Pontllanfraith, Blackwood, Gwent NP12 2YA
**Tel:** 01495-223721
**Web:** www.pensord.co.uk
**Reg No:** 0939885 **VAT No:** 288944882
**Estd:** 1969 Private Limited Company
**Line of Business:** Newspapers publishing
**Issued Capital:** £1,630,000
**Directors:** K Gater, D Coxon
**Responsibilities**
**Finance:** Redford Best *(Finance Director)*, Graham Lambert *(Financial Director)*, Caryll Maggs *(Accounts Manager)*, Leigh Williams *(Credit Controller)*
**Admin:** Cathy Hewitt *(Administration Manager)*
**HR:** Cathy Hewitt *(Administration Manager)*
**Health & Safety:** Victor Spear *(Pre Press Coordinator)*
**Branches:** Pensord Press Ltd, 1 Gayford Rd, London W12 9BY
**US SIC:** 2711 **UK SIC:** 47512
**Auditors:** KPMG LLP
**Bankers:** National Westminster Bank Plc (60-00-04)

| | 31-12-13 | 31-12-12 | 31-12-11 |
|---|---|---|---|
| TO | 12,940,089 | 13,171,188 | 13,261,868 |
| P/L | 829,457 | 961,460 | 603,294 |
| NW | 4,133,725 | 3,630,151 | 2,989,414 |
| WC | 2,286,327 | 1,393,657 | 837,325 |
| Emp. | 148 | 148 | 146 |

DUNS 22-727-4537 **Exp**

## The Penspen Group Ltd

**(Subsidiary of:** Dar Al-Handasah Consultants Shair & Partners Holdi)
Darpen House, 3 Water Lane, Richmond, Surrey TW9 1TJ
**Tel:** 02083342700
**Web:** www.penspen.com
**Reg No:** 0980600 **Estd:** 1970 Private Limited Company
**Line of Business:** Management activities of holding companies
**Export Markets:** Africa, Middle East, Far East, E U
**Export Sales:** £98,031,000
**Trading Style:** The Penspen Group Ltd
**Issued Capital:** £29,528,557
**Directors:** P B O'Sullivan, D Aoun, T Shair, Ms C Brown
**Co. Secretary:** Miss Susan Mcdonald
**US SIC:** 6711, 8911
**UK SIC:** 83962, 83701
**Auditors:** Arthur Andersen
**Bankers:** Arab Bank Plc (40-50-44)

| | 31-12-13 | 31-12-12 | 31-12-11 |
|---|---|---|---|
| TO | 113,894,000 | 105,200,000 | 106,879,000 |
| P/L | 3,380,000 | 213,000 | 2,368,000 |
| NW | 19,211,000 | 15,046,000 | 16,878,000 |
| WC | 12,831,000 | 8,291,000 | 11,833,000 |
| Emp. | 859 | 966 | 1,404 |

DUNS 73-476-2771

## The Pensthorpe Conservation Trust Ltd

Pensthorpe Wildfowl Park Fakenham, Fakenham, Norfolk NR21 0LN
**Tel:** 01328863628
**Web:** www.pensthorpetrust.org.uk
**Reg No:** 4740162 **Estd:** 2003 Private Company Limited By Guarantee
**Line of Business:** Botanical and zoological gardens and nature reserve activities
**Directors:** Ms D A Jordan, J Jordan, W J Jordan, C R Papworth, G Archibald, Dr D J Bellamy, T D Nevard
**Co. Secretary:** Martin Bonynge
**Responsibilities**
**Facilities:** Rodney Haclin *(Plant & Facilities Manager)*
**US SIC:** 8421, 8699
**UK SIC:** 97700, 96902
**Bankers:** Barclays Bank Plc (20-27-41)

| | 31-12-13 | 31-12-12 | 31-12-12 |
|---|---|---|---|
| TO | 380,905 | 175,874 | 143,076 |
| P/L | (179,029) | 12,689 | 566 |
| NW | 349,886 | 528,915 | 520,346 |
| WC | 173,347 | 343,743 | 325,738 |

DUNS 21-161-5039

## Pent Valley Further Studies Centre

Surrenden Road, Folkestone, Kent CT19 4ED
**Tel:** 01303-277161
**Web:** www.pentvalley.com
**Estd:** 1971 Proprietorship
**Line of Business:** General secondary education
**Proprietor:** Miss G Spear
**Responsibilities**
**Senior:** Marion Citro *(Head Master)*, Mick Kelly *(Deputy Head Teacher)*, Giles Osborne *(Deputy Head Teacher)*, T Reene *(Site Manager)*
**Finance:** Laura Ilsley *(Financial Manager)*
**Marketing:** Samantha Spratley *(Human Resources Manager)*
**IT:** Christopher Farnfield *(Network & IT Manager)*
**HR:** Samantha Spratley *(Human Resources Manager)*
**Health & Safety:** Jane Rose *(Business Manager)*
**Facilities:** Jane Rose *(Business Manager)*
**US SIC:** 8211 **UK SIC:** 93200
**Employees:** 150

DUNS 23-526-6926 **Exp**

## Penta Consulting Ltd

Crosspoint House, 28 Stafford Road, Wallington, Surrey SM6 9AA
**Tel:** 02086473999 **Fax:** 020-8647-2777
**Web:** www.pentaconsulting.com
**Reg No:** 3525651 **Estd:** 1998 Private Limited Company

**Line of Business:** Labour recruitment and provision of personnel
**Export Sales:** £38,679
**Issued Capital:** £17,381
**Principals:** R Harverson *(Chairman)*, P R Clark *(Managing)*, R Wilson *(Sales)*, N A Iandoli, J A Sobrany, P A Collins, J R Foley
**Co. Secretary:** Ian Storrier
**Responsibilities**
**Senior:** Garry Renton *(Health & Safety Coordinator)*
**Marketing:** Chris Street *(Senior Consultant - Digital an)*
**Sales:** Gary Traisneau *(Account Manager and Contract C)*
**Admin:** John Cakebread *(Administration)*, Karen Eels *(Administrator)*
**IT:** Garry Renton *(Health & Safety Coordinator)*
**HR:** Kris England-Smith *(Training Manager)*
**Health & Safety:** Garry Renton *(Health & Safety Coordinator)*
**Operations:** Keith Gard *(Operations Manager)*, Luke Jolliffe *(Operations Manager)*, James Pickard *(Consultant)*
**US SIC:** 7361 **UK SIC:** 83954
**Auditors:** Cruse & Burke
**Bankers:** National Westminster Bank Plc (60-22-20)

| | 31-03-14 | 31-03-13 | 31-03-12 |
|---|---|---|---|
| TO | 45,226,313 | 46,749,612 | 45,069,671 |
| P/L | 3,055,591 | 3,285,186 | 3,305,153 |
| NW | 9,815,334 | 8,887,344 | 7,583,405 |
| WC | 9,649,594 | 8,676,026 | 7,285,050 |
| Emp. | 88 | 88 | 88 |

DUNS 76-964-0244 **Imp**

## Penta Foods Ltd

Penta House, Lynchford Lane, Farnborough, Hampshire GU14 6JF
**Tel:** 01252894800 **Fax:** 0845-051-0224
**Web:** www.pentafoods.com
**Reg No:** 2628701 **VAT No:** 572770520
**Estd:** 1991 Private Limited Company
**Line of Business:** Agents involved in the sale of food, beverages and tobacco
**Issued Capital:** £1,000
**Directors:** S R Rubbani, S M Rubbani, S A Rubbani
**Co. Secretary:** Nazir Rubbani
**Responsibilities**
**Senior:** Areej Abbi *(Manager)*, Manzer Rubbani *(Manager)*
**IT:** Ahtesham Hussain *(Head of IT)*
**US SIC:** 5149 **UK SIC:** 61700
**Auditors:** Deitch Cooper
**Bankers:** Lloyds TSB Bank plc (30-91-11)

| | 31-12-13 | 31-12-12 | 31-12-11 |
|---|---|---|---|
| TO | 31,996,061 | 28,125,089 | 27,512,494 |
| P/L | 484,212 | 287,283 | 226,231 |
| NW | (200,440) | (144,432) | (129,318) |
| WC | (659,281) | (551,981) | (570,871) |
| Emp. | 153 | 146 | 149 |

DUNS 21-618-6373

## Penta Hotel

Oxford Road, Reading, Berkshire RG1 7RH
**Tel:** 01189586222
**Web:** www.pentahotels.com
**Estd:** 2011 Partnership
**Line of Business:** Hotels
**Partners:** P Cox, R Hider, Mrs H Hassan, S Ho, Mrs A Day
**Responsibilities**
**Senior:** Andrew Munt *(CEO, Managing Director)*
**US SIC:** 7011 **UK SIC:** 66500
**Employees:** 110

DUNS 21-103-0253

## Pentagon 24HR Recruitment Ltd

31 Hakewill Way, Colchester, Essex CO4 5GX
**Tel:** 01206838968
**Web:** www.pentagon24hrnurses.co.uk
**Reg No:** 6460939 **Estd:** 2007 Private Limited Company
**Line of Business:** Employment and recruitment companies and consultants
**Issued Capital:** £10
**Director:** Ms B B Gwara
**Co. Secretary:** Yorlandah Gwara
**Responsibilities**
**Senior:** Becky Goldsmith *(Manager)*, Beauty Goldsmith *(Manager)*
**US SIC:** 7361 **UK SIC:** 83954

| | 31-03-14 | 31-03-13 | 31-03-12 |
|---|---|---|---|
| TA | 90,486 | 66,784 | 39,748 |
| NW | 2,632 | 2,330 | (1,765) |
| WC | 4,931 | 6,540 | (4,881) |

DUNS 42-337-2684 **Imp**

## Pentagon Chemicals (Holdings) Ltd

(**Subsidiary of:** Wind Point Partners L.P.)
Northside Road, Workington, Cumbria CA14 1BD
**Tel:** 01900-604371
**Web:** www.pentagonchemicals.co.uk
**Reg No:** 4324948 **Estd:** 2001 Private Limited Company
**Line of Business:** Manufacture of other organic basic chemicals
**Export Sales:** £40,831,000
**Trading Style:** Pentagon Chemicals (Holdings)
**Issued Capital:** £1,165
**Directors:** P R Gillespie, R V Preziotti, Ms A M Frye
**Co. Secretary:** Prima Secretary Limited
**Responsibilities**
**Senior:** Ronald Fisher *(Manager)*, Alastair Lloyd *(Director of Sales)*, Christopher Ravenscroft *(Non-Executive Director)*
**Marketing:** Susan Bench *(Business manager)*
**Operations:** David Work *(Production Development Directo)*
**US SIC:** 2869 **UK SIC:** 25120
**Auditors:** BDO LLP

| | 30-06-13 | 30-06-12 | 30-06-11 |
|---|---|---|---|
| TO | 50,859,000 | 43,387,000 | 39,582,000 |
| P/L | 2,624,000 | 1,445,000 | 1,000,000 |
| NW | 5,905,000 | 3,307,000 | 2,172,000 |
| WC | 1,277,000 | (74,000) | (839,000) |
| Emp. | 183 | 171 | 162 |

DUNS 73-604-4863 **Exp**

## Pentagon Fine Chemicals Ltd

Lower Road, Halebank, Widnes, Cheshire WA8 8NS
**Tel:** 01514-243671 **Fax:** 01514-201301
**Web:** www.pentagonchemicals.co.uk
**Reg No:** 4865584 **VAT No:** 790220253
**Estd:** 1992 Private Limited Company
**Line of Business:** Manufacture of other chemical products not elsewhere classified
**Export Sales:** £25,356,000
**Issued Capital:** £100
**Directors:** P R Gillespie, R V Preziotti, Ms A M Frye
**Co. Secretary:** Prima Secretary Limited
**Responsibilities**
**Senior:** Gillian Jacks *(Manager)*, Allan Laing *(Chief Executive Officer)*, Alastair Lloyd *(Manager)*, Allan Macbean-Laing *(Manager)*, Hafeez Mohammed *(Manager)*, Nigel Spruce *(Engineering Manager)*, David Work *(Manager)*
**Engineering:** Nigel Spruce *(Engineering Manager)*
**US SIC:** 2899 **UK SIC:** 25670
**Auditors:** BDO LLP
**Bankers:** Lloyds TSB Bank plc (30-00-02)

| | 30-06-13 | 30-06-12 | 30-06-11 |
|---|---|---|---|
| TO | 26,118,000 | 20,796,000 | 19,072,000 |
| P/L | 1,367,000 | 309,000 | 353,000 |
| NW | 1,953,000 | 696,000 | 52,000 |
| WC | 2,969,000 | 1,795,000 | (2,447,000) |
| Emp. | 111 | 104 | 97 |

DUNS 22-099-9978

## Pentagon Holdings Ltd

Unit 1 Main Road Crayfield Industrial, Park, Orpington, Kent BR5 3HP
**Tel:** 01689-877777
**Web:** www.pentagon-group.co.uk
**Reg No:** 4101313 **Estd:** 2000 Private Limited Company
**Line of Business:** Management activities of other non-financial holding companies not elsewhere classified
**Issued Capital:** £88,088
**Director:** G R Smith
**Co. Secretary:** Timothy Spittle
**Branches:** Pentagon Holdings Ltd, 159 Wright Street, Renfrew, Renfrewshire PA4 8AN
**US SIC:** 6711 **UK SIC:** 83962
**Auditors:** Chantrey Vellacott DFK LLP

| | 30-04-14 | 30-04-13 | 30-04-12 |
|---|---|---|---|
| TO | 200,818,521 | 186,038,188 | 157,649,010 |
| P/L | 10,363,760 | 7,740,266 | 6,479,379 |
| NW | 37,041,473 | 29,816,093 | 20,353,323 |
| WC | 25,824,596 | 23,600,863 | 15,102,572 |
| Emp. | 569 | 496 | 408 |

DUNS 21-807-6529

## Pentagon Investments Ltd

12 Chequers Road, West Meadows Industrial Estate, Derby, Derbyshire DE21 6EN
**Web:** www.mertrux.com
**Reg No:** 0721312 **Estd:** 1962 Private Limited Company
**Line of Business:** Management activities of other non-financial holding companies not elsewhere classified
**Trading Style:** Mertrux
**Issued Capital:** £51,020
**Directors:** Mrs H Marshall, I E Marshall, M E Marshall, G R Robson
**Co. Secretary:** Ms Sarah Robson
**Branches:** Pentagon Investments Ltd, Export Drive, Sutton-In-Ashfield, Nottinghamshire NG17 6AF
**US SIC:** 6711, 6519
**UK SIC:** 83962, 85000
**Auditors:** Bates Weston
**Bankers:** Bank Of Scotland (12-09-26)

| | 31-12-13 | 31-12-12 | 31-12-11 |
|---|---|---|---|
| TO | 172,915,000 | 137,722,000 | 144,866,000 |
| P/L | 3,848,000 | 3,111,000 | 3,183,000 |
| NW | 25,003,000 | 23,920,000 | 22,322,000 |
| WC | 10,226,000 | 9,546,000 | 9,932,000 |
| Emp. | 304 | 305 | 303 |

DUNS 21-584-8385

## Pentagon Oldham

Chadderton Way, Oldham, Lancashire OL1 2QL
**Tel:** 01616212720
**Web:** www.pentagon-group.co.uk
**Estd:** 2011 Proprietorship
**Line of Business:** Car dealers (new & used)
**Proprietor:** R Scofield
**US SIC:** 5511 **UK SIC:** 65100
**Employees:** 100

DUNS 21-604-8246

## Pentagon Sheffield

100 Savile Street, Sheffield, South Yorkshire S4 7UD
**Tel:** 01142537600
**Web:** www.pentagon-group.co.uk
**Estd:** 2011 Proprietorship
**Line of Business:** Car dealers (new & used)
**Proprietor:** J Bilums
**Responsibilities**
**Senior:** Danny Whitehead *(Manager)*
**US SIC:** 5511 **UK SIC:** 65100
**Employees:** 80

DUNS 21-233-4381

## Pentagon Toyota

Quest Park, Wheatley Hall Road, Doncaster, South Yorkshire DN2 4LT
**Tel:** 01302-762300
**Web:** www.pentagondoncaster.toyota.co.uk
**Estd:** 1974 Proprietorship
**Line of Business:** Sale of new motor vehicles
**Proprietor:** S Burrows
**Responsibilities**
**Finance:** Louise Holmes *(Group Accountant)*
**Sales:** Steve Daykin *(Sales Manager)*
**Admin:** Oonagh Hall *(Administration Manager)*
**IT:** Neil Henderson *(IT Manager)*
**HR:** Oonagh Hall *(Administration Manager)*
**Health & Safety:** Laurence Forbes *(Health & Safety Training & Com)*
**US SIC:** 5511 **UK SIC:** 65100
**Employees:** 102

DUNS 54-383-0004

## Pentagon (U K) Ltd

Franklin Court, Stannard Way, Bedford, Bedfordshire MK44 3JZ
**Tel:** 01234836352
**Reg No:** 3267970 **Estd:** 1996 Private Limited Company
**Line of Business:** Other service activities not elsewhere classified
**Issued Capital:** £100
**Directors:** K A Still, J P Davies, T D Williams, Ms L M Bramham, G R Dennis, Ms S J Duffin
**Co. Secretary:** Richard Bramham
**Branches:** Pentagon (U K) Ltd, Cayley Ct, George Cayley Dr, York, North Yorkshire YO30 4WH
**US SIC:** 8999 **UK SIC:** 83954
**Auditors:** Morrell Middleton Auditors Ltd
**Bankers:** Barclays Bank Plc (20-17-35)

| | 31-10-13 | 31-10-12 | 31-10-11 |
|---|---|---|---|
| TO | 9,434,314 | 9,058,711 | 9,556,674 |
| P/L | 790,444 | 283,935 | (13,489) |
| NW | 179,695 | 385,467 | 452,566 |
| WC | 37,677 | 213,436 | 320,050 |
| Emp. | 148 | 159 | 152 |

DUNS 22-719-7936 **Exp**

## Pentagram Design Ltd

(**Subsidiary of:** Pentagram Design Ag)
11 Needham Road, London W11 2RP
**Tel:** 02072293477
**Web:** www.pentagram.co.uk
**Reg No:** 1599748 **VAT No:** 241387762
**Estd:** 1972 Private Limited Company
**Line of Business:** Engineering design activities for industrial process and production
**Issued Capital:** £105,007
**Directors:** H Pearce, D Weil, A G Hyland, D Lippa, J W Oehler, N Ramchandani, J Rushworth
**Co. Secretary:** Jon O'Hern
**Responsibilities**
**Senior:** Lorenzo Apicella *(Manager)*, James Biber *(Manager)*, Julia Wyatt *(Studio Manager)*
**Finance:** Ceyrilia Francis-Kirton *(Manager)*
**HR:** Julia Wyatt *(Studio Manager)*
**Health & Safety:** Julia Wyatt *(Studio Manager)*
**Facilities:** Julia Wyatt *(Studio Manager)*
**Operations:** Julia Wyatt *(Studio Manager)*
**Purchasing:** Julia Wyatt *(Studio Manager)*
**US SIC:** 7399, 8999
**UK SIC:** 83954
**Auditors:** Grant Thornton
**Bankers:** Barclays Bank Plc (20-05-75)

| | 30-09-13 | 30-09-12 | 30-09-11 |
|---|---|---|---|
| TO | 7,620,503 | 8,031,205 | 6,142,783 |
| P/L | 49,990 | 144,992 | 51,522 |
| NW | 1,512,366 | 1,486,846 | 1,378,780 |
| WC | 1,389,685 | 1,379,270 | 1,250,607 |
| Emp. | 61 | 59 | 56 |

DUNS 23-895-7133 **Imp-Exp**

## Pentair Valves & Controls (Uk) Ltd

(**Subsidiary of:** Pentair Flow Control Holdings Limited)
Crosby Road, Market Harborough, Leicestershire LE16 9EE
**Tel:** 01858467281
**Web:** www.pentair.com
**Reg No:** 0202028SC **VAT No:** 787430889
**Estd:** 1999 Private Limited Company
**Line of Business:** Manufacturers of valves
**Export Sales:** £10,623,000
**Trading Style:** Pentair
**Issued Capital:** £2
**Directors:** T Toffolo, F H Langedijk, M S Boardman
**Co. Secretary:** Ms Sophie Grundy
**Responsibilities**
**Senior:** George Amabile *(Manager)*, Alison Boldison *(Manager)*, Jon Burgess *(Sales Director)*, Graham Latham *(Manager)*, Stuart Medford *(Manager)*
**Sales:** Jon Burgess *(Sales Director)*
**IT:** David Sterang *(Senior IT Executive)*
**Purchasing:** Ross Forbes *(Purchasing Manager)*
**Branches:** Pentair Valves & Controls (Uk) Ltd, Moss Lane View, Skelmersdale, Lancashire WN8 9TN
**US SIC:** 3494 **UK SIC:** 32880
**Auditors:** Deloitte LLP
**Bankers:** Barclays Bank Plc (20-53-30)

| | 31-12-13 | 31-12-12 | 30-12-11 |
|---|---|---|---|
| TO | 44,895,000 | 48,202,000 | 39,101,000 |
| P/L | (471,000) | (779,000) | (2,144,000) |
| NW | 13,003,000 | 13,336,000 | 14,188,000 |
| WC | 9,378,000 | 9,905,000 | 11,454,000 |
| Emp. | 164 | 181 | 178 |

DUNS 22-768-0725

## Pentalver Cannock Ltd

(**Subsidiary of:** Maersk Line Uk Ltd)
Pentalver Way, Cannock, Staffordshire WS11 8XY
**Tel:** 01543464000 **Fax:** 01543464044
**Reg No:** 1189068 **VAT No:** 101587494
**Estd:** 1974 Private Limited Company
**Line of Business:** Other supporting land transport activities
**Trading Style:** Pentalver Cannock Ltd
**Issued Capital:** £7,500
**Directors:** E M Spriggs, M A Van Dongen, C R Lawrenson
**Co. Secretary:** John Kilby
**Responsibilities**
**Senior:** Andrew Jellis *(Depot Manager)*, Martin Poulsen *(Manager)*
**Facilities:** Andrew Jellis *(Depot Manager)*
**Branches:** Pentalver Cannock Ltd, Pentalver Cannock Ltd, Pentalver Way, Cannock, Staffordshire WS11 8XY
**US SIC:** 4789 **UK SIC:** 77002
**Auditors:** KPMG LLP
**Bankers:** National Westminster Bank Plc (60-01-40)

| | 31-12-13 | 31-12-12 | 31-12-11 |
|---|---|---|---|
| TO | 26,271,000 | 23,938,000 | 24,882,000 |
| P/L | 1,448,000 | (195,000) | 246,000 |
| NW | 14,193,000 | 13,046,000 | 13,480,000 |
| WC | 5,665,000 | 3,273,000 | 2,391,000 |
| Emp. | 262 | 278 | 337 |

DUNS 21-743-5916

## Pentewan Sands Ltd

Pentewan, St Austell, Cornwall PL26 6BT
**Tel:** 01726843485
**Web:** www.pentewan.co.uk
**Reg No:** 0394475 **Estd:** 1945 Private Limited Company
**Line of Business:** Holiday parks and camps
**Trading Style:** Pentewan Sands Holiday Park
**Issued Capital:** £17,422
**Directors:** J R Willis, Ms P E Willis, P E Hawley
**Co. Secretary:** Ms Antonia Delia
**US SIC:** 7033 **UK SIC:** 66701
**Auditors:** Stephen Pearn & Co

**Bankers:** Lloyds TSB Bank plc (30-97-28)

| | 31-03-14 | 31-03-13 | 31-03-12 |
|---|---|---|---|
| TO | 3,707,781 | 3,849,069 | 3,785,573 |
| P/L | 87,827 | 509,599 | 384,575 |
| NW | 5,142,216 | 4,990,313 | 4,649,279 |
| WC | (1,895,560) | (1,571,838) | (1,663,774) |
| Emp. | 92 | 91 | 85 |

DUNS 29-566-8339 Imp-Exp

## Pentex Ltd

177-179 Commercial Road, London E1 2DA
**Tel:** 02077902722 **Fax:** 020-726-40778
**Web:** www.pentexwholesale.com
**Reg No:** 1928818 **VAT No:** 397169988
**Estd:** 1985 Private Limited Company
**Line of Business:** Manufacture of other women's outerwear
**Export Markets:** Denmark, Spain, Finland, Portugal, Dubai, Germany
**Issued Capital:** £1,000
**Director:** S Zeki
**Co. Secretary:** Serif Iyikan
**Branches:** Pentex Ltd, 94-100 Christian Street, London E1 1RS
**US SIC:** 2339 **UK SIC:** 45330
**Auditors:** Arram Berlyn Gardner
**Bankers:** HSBC Bank plc (40-02-20)

| | 31-12-12 | 31-12-11 | 31-12-10 |
|---|---|---|---|
| TO | 49,876,110 | 36,732,190 | 31,110,421 |
| P/L | 3,448,570 | 2,017,284 | 1,263,654 |
| NW | 6,414,929 | 4,432,382 | 3,549,584 |
| WC | 6,154,529 | 4,294,020 | 3,413,938 |
| Emp. | 51 | 37 | 33 |

DUNS 21-772-1407

## The Penthouse

1 Leicester Square, London WC2H 7NA
**Tel:** 02035881100
**Web:** www.thepenthouselondon.com
**Estd:** 2008 Proprietorship
**Line of Business:** Managed public houses and bars
**Proprietor:** T Flynn
**Responsibilities**
**Senior:** Wayne Roberts *(Operations Manager)*
**IT:** Freddie Rochford *(IT Manager)*
**US SIC:** 5813 **UK SIC:** 66200
**Employees:** 100

DUNS 77-507-6904 Exp

## Penthouse Carpets Holdings Ltd

Buckley Carpet Mill, Buckley Road, Rochdale, Lancashire OL12 9DU
**Tel:** 01706-341231 **Fax:** 01706-860577
**Web:** www.penthousecarpets.co.uk
**Reg No:** 2982102 **VAT No:** 652606345
**Estd:** 1994 Private Limited Company
**Line of Business:** Management activities of holding companies
**Export Sales:** £54,012
**Issued Capital:** £176,067
**Principals:** A J Dyson *(Managing)*, M Muschamp, J R Gamble, Ms S A Jackson
**Co. Secretary:** Alexander Dyson
**Responsibilities**
**Finance:** Steven Yu *(Financial Director)*
**IT:** Steven Yu *(Financial Director)*
**HR:** Steven Yu *(Financial Director)*
**US SIC:** 6711 **UK SIC:** 83962
**Auditors:** Ap Smith Atkins & Co

| | 30-06-13 | 30-06-12 | 30-06-11 |
|---|---|---|---|
| TO | 12,130,270 | 12,121,909 | 14,233,143 |
| P/L | (550,235) | (522,578) | 274,068 |
| NW | 5,829,885 | 5,146,396 | 5,525,808 |
| WC | 2,705,680 | 3,218,869 | 3,652,695 |
| Emp. | 79 | 81 | 85 |

DUNS 21-226-8047

## Pentland Distribution

Glover Industrial Estate, Spire Road, Washington, Tyne and Wear NE37 3ES
**Tel:** 0191-4154037
**Web:** www.pentland.com
**Estd:** 2003 Proprietorship
**Line of Business:** Activities of other transport agencies
**Proprietor:** T Marriner
**Responsibilities**
**Senior:** Tim Marriner *(Manager)*
**US SIC:** 4712 **UK SIC:** 77002
**Employees:** 51

DUNS 21-028-0806 Exp

## Pentland Group P L C

8 Manchester Square, London W1U 3PH
**Tel:** 020-7535-3800
**Web:** www.pentland.com
**Reg No:** 0793577 **Estd:** 1964 Public Limited Company
**Line of Business:** Management activities of holding companies
**Export Markets:** U S A, Canada, Europe, Asia, Australia, Africa, and South America.
**Export Sales:** £619,700,000
**Issued Capital:** £973,640
**Principals:** R S Rubin Obe *(Chairman and Managing)*, Mrs A S Rubin, T J Hockings, Ms C L Rubin, Mrs A J Mosheim, J D Morgan, A K Rubin, B A Mosheim
**Co. Secretary:** Patrick Campbell
**US SIC:** 6711, 5199
**UK SIC:** 83962, 61900
**Auditors:** PricewaterhouseCoopers LLP
**Bankers:** National Westminster Bank Plc (50-00-00)
**Following financial data are in thousands**

| | 31-12-13 | 31-12-12 | 31-12-11 |
|---|---|---|---|
| TO | 1,910,800 | 1,740,000 | 1,523,100 |
| P/L | 85,300 | 62,900 | 113,600 |
| NW | 337,100 | 294,400 | 286,800 |
| WC | 206,900 | 180,100 | 189,400 |
| Emp. | 17,746 | 18,301 | 15,468 |

DUNS 21-809-7278

## Pentland Landrover

Hallbarns Crescent, Newbridge, Midlothian EH28 8TH
**Tel:** 01313354150
**Web:** www.john-clark.co.uk
**Estd:** 2012
**Line of Business:** Car dealers (used)
**US SIC:** 5511 **UK SIC:** 65100
**Employees:** 90

DUNS 22-927-4360

## Pentland Plants

Pentland Nurseries, Loanhead, Midlothian EH20 9QG
**Tel:** 0131-440-0895
**Web:** www.pentlandplants.co.uk
**VAT No:** 270632277 **Estd:** 1964 Partnership
**Line of Business:** Horticultural supplies retailers and wholesalers.
**Partners:** R J Spray, Mrs H N Spray, Ms C E Spray, D W Spray
**US SIC:** 5261, 5199
**UK SIC:** 65400, 61900
**Bankers:** The Royal Bank Of Scotland Plc (83-17-26)
**Employees:** 50

DUNS 57-840-6803

## Pentlands Science Park Ltd

Pentlands Science Park, Bush Loan, Penicuik, Midlothian EH26 0PZ
**Tel:** 0131-445-5111
**Web:** www.moredun.ac.uk
**Reg No:** 0148767SC **Estd:** 1993 Private Limited Company
**Line of Business:** Science centres
**Issued Capital:** £2
**Directors:** G T Baird, P Scott Aiton, Dr D P Knox, E P Bacchus, Dr K D Winton
**Co. Secretary:** George Walker
**Responsibilities**
**Senior:** Robert Coop *(Manager)*, Loudon Hamilton *(Manager)*, John Matts *(Manager)*
**Facilities:** Lenny Marshall *(Facilities Manager)*
**US SIC:** 8299, 6519
**UK SIC:** 93300, 85000
**Auditors:** PKF
**Bankers:** Bank Of Scotland (80-20-19)

| | 31-03-14 | 31-03-13 | 31-03-12 |
|---|---|---|---|
| TO | 3,403,573 | 3,530,176 | 3,247,227 |
| P/L | 109,027 | 107,394 | 112,643 |
| NW | 906,867 | 822,780 | 728,905 |
| WC | 791,410 | 672,686 | 558,623 |

DUNS 21-580-1012

## Pentlow & Summerdown

59-63 Summerdown Road, Eastbourne, East Sussex BN20 8DQ
**Tel:** 01323722245
**Web:** www.canfordhealthcare.co.uk
**Estd:** 1974 Proprietorship
**Line of Business:** Nursing homes
**Proprietor:** Miss L Wicks
**US SIC:** 8051 **UK SIC:** 95100
**Employees:** 90

DUNS 21-205-4188

## Pentlow Nursing Home

59-63 Summerdown Road, Eastbourne, East Sussex BN20 8DQ
**Tel:** 01323723176
**Web:** www.pentlow.co.uk
**Estd:** 1974 Partnership
**Line of Business:** Other human health activities
**Trading Style:** Pentlow & Summerdown Nursing Home
**Partners:** Mrs C A Alford, B G Alford
**Responsibilities**
**Senior:** Sharon Hobden *(Hr Manager)*
**HR:** Sue Jaques *(Human Resources Manager)*
**Purchasing:** Sue Jaques *(Human Resources Manager)*
**Branches:** Pentlow Nursing Home, 26-28 Church Street, Eastbourne, East Sussex BN21 1HS
**US SIC:** 8091, 6732
**UK SIC:** 95200, 83100
**Employees:** 178

DUNS 49-732-1059

## Penton Hook Yacht Club

Staines Road, Chertsey, Surrey KT16 9DA
**Estd:** 2013
**Line of Business:** Sports clubs
**Responsibilities**
**Senior:** Christine Barnes *(Vice Commodore)*
**US SIC:** 8699 **UK SIC:** 96902
**Employees:** 200

DUNS 56-959-6356 Exp

## Pentons Haulage & Cold Storage

**(Subsidiary of:** Pentons Property Services)
Maes Y Clawdd, Maesbury Road Industrial Estate, Oswestry, Shropshire SY10 8NN
**Tel:** 01691-656922 **Fax:** 01691663533
**Web:** www.pentons.co.uk
**Reg No:** 2849859 **VAT No:** 594447108
**Estd:** 1994 Private Unlimited Company
**Line of Business:** Freight transport by road not elsewhere classified
**Issued Capital:** £500,000
**Directors:** S B Canlett, S R Penton, G P Penton
**Co. Secretary:** Barry Williams
**Responsibilities**
**IT:** Julian Lycett *(Computer Manager)*
**Facilities:** Malcolm Grindley *(Maintenance Manager)*
**US SIC:** 4213, 4226
**UK SIC:** 72300, 77003
**Bankers:** Lloyds TSB Bank plc (30-96-33)
**Employees:** 150

DUNS 57-843-3864

## Pentraeth Automotive Ltd

**(Subsidiary of:** Pentraeth Holdings Ltd)
Henffordd Garage, Pentraeth Road, Menai Bridge, Gwynedd LL59 5RW
**Tel:** 01492875991
**Web:** www.pentraeth.co.uk
**Reg No:** 2896353 **Estd:** 1980 Private Limited Company
**Line of Business:** Car dealers (new & used)
**Trading Style:** Pentraeth Group
**Issued Capital:** £100
**Director:** K W Jones
**Co. Secretary:** Ms Patricia Kirkham
**Branches:** Pentraeth Automotive Ltd, Manchester Audi, Brindley Road, Manchester M16 9UA
**US SIC:** 5511, 5521
**UK SIC:** 65100
**Auditors:** Fraser Wood
**Bankers:** National Westminster Bank Plc (54-10-01)

| | 28-02-14 | 28-02-13 | 31-02-11 |
|---|---|---|---|
| TA | 1,792,944 | 1,257,489 | 1,224,043 |
| NW | (204,632) | (290,183) | 82,570 |
| WC | (278,635) | (378,238) | (44,425) |

DUNS 73-658-5097 Exp

## Pentre Holdings Ltd

Unit 2, Leigh, Lancashire WN7 3PG
**Tel:** 01942676331
**Web:** www.pentregroup.com
**Reg No:** 4918239 **Estd:** 1991 Private Limited Company
**Line of Business:** Management activities of holding companies
**Export Sales:** £9,515,434
**Issued Capital:** £67
**Directors:** J P Orrell, S A Kilgallon, R P Johnstone, M F Seymour, Mrs J Meal, J V Carr, H W Platt
**Co. Secretary:** Mrs Julie Meal
**US SIC:** 6711, 2654
**UK SIC:** 83962, 47280
**Auditors:** Voisey & Co

| | 31-03-14 | 31-03-13 | 31-03-12 |
|---|---|---|---|
| TO | 21,102,218 | 20,216,990 | 20,451,019 |
| P/L | 1,921,467 | 1,627,279 | 2,177,045 |
| NW | 12,798,374 | 11,406,869 | 10,148,282 |
| WC | 8,254,096 | 6,747,558 | 5,596,378 |
| Emp. | 241 | 221 | 225 |

DUNS 50-005-8789 Exp

## Pentre Overseas Holdings Ltd

**(Subsidiary of:** Pentre Holdings Ltd)
Pentre Group, Neills Road, St Helens, Merseyside WA9 4TJ
**Tel:** 01744813225 **Fax:** 01744-819994
**Web:** www.pentregroup.com
**Reg No:** 2295416 **Estd:** 1988 Private Limited Company
**Line of Business:** Holding companies management activities
**Issued Capital:** £1,500,000
**Principals:** M F Seymour *(Managing)*, Mrs J Meal
**Co. Secretary:** Mrs Julie Meal
**Responsibilities**
**Engineering:** Andrew Orford *(Fabrication Manager)*
**US SIC:** 6711 **UK SIC:** 83962
**Auditors:** Deloitte & Touche

| | 31-03-14 | 31-03-13 | 31-03-12 |
|---|---|---|---|
| TA | 2,248,433 | 2,248,433 | 2,248,433 |
| NW | 2,248,433 | 2,248,433 | 2,248,433 |

DUNS 29-518-9187

## Penumbra

57 Albion Road, Edinburgh, Midlothian EH7 5QY
**Web:** www.penumbra.org.uk
**Reg No:** 0091542SC **Estd:** 1985 Private Company Limited By Guarantee
**Line of Business:** Social work activities
**Directors:** A Mcloughlin, Ms S Wedgwood, Ms L Reid, Mrs F A Henderson, S Keaveney, J F Lawrie, Ms S K Sinclair, Ms P Hall
**Co. Secretary:** Nigel Henderson
**Responsibilities**
**Senior:** Susan Reekie *(Manager)*, Graeme Reekie *(Manager)*, Jennifer Rees *(Manager)*
**Purchasing:** Stephen Powers *(Purchasing Manager)*
**Branches:** Penumbra, 8A Hawthorn Place, Broxburn, West Lothian EH52 5BX
**US SIC:** 7399, 8091, 8699
**UK SIC:** 83954, 95200, 96902
**Auditors:** McCabe Partnership
**Bankers:** Bank Of Scotland (80-02-34)

| | 31-03-14 | 31-03-13 | 31-03-12 |
|---|---|---|---|
| TO | 9,059,090 | 9,559,121 | 9,553,409 |
| P/L | (1,056,018) | (1,828) | 303,766 |
| NW | 2,749,617 | 3,846,635 | 3,900,463 |
| WC | 2,486,794 | 2,715,876 | 2,772,363 |
| Emp. | 348 | 311 | 352 |

DUNS 22-607-3526

## Penventon Hotel (1970) Ltd

West End, Redruth, Cornwall TR15 1TE
**Tel:** 01209203000
**Web:** www.penventon.com
**Reg No:** 0979483 **Estd:** 1970 Private Limited Company
**Line of Business:** Hotels
**Issued Capital:** £50
**Principals:** A D Pascoe *(Managing)*, M I Pascoe, A D Pascoe
**Co. Secretary:** Mrs Paola Pascoe
**Responsibilities**
**Finance:** Sarah Blenes *(Financial Director)*
**HR:** Laura Pascoe *(Human Resources Manager)*, Paul Rickett *(Human Resources Manager)*
**US SIC:** 7011 **UK SIC:** 66500
**Auditors:** Robinson Reed Layton
**Bankers:** HSBC Bank plc (40-44-34)

| | 31-03-14 | 31-03-13 | 31-03-12 |
|---|---|---|---|
| TO | 2,390,265 | 2,327,335 | 2,142,019 |
| P/L | 19,385 | 99,604 | 141,657 |
| NW | 1,012,836 | 989,349 | 954,807 |
| WC | (125,641) | (58,006) | (1,831) |

DUNS 22-666-4845

## Penwise Properties Ltd

Stamford Road, Oakham, Leicestershire LE15 8AB
**Tel:** 01572757901
**Web:** www.barnsdalehotel.co.uk
**Reg No:** 0708033 **VAT No:** 114536786
**Estd:** 1961 Private Limited Company
**Line of Business:** Beauty salons
**Trading Style:** Barnesdale Hall Hotel
**Issued Capital:** £958
**Directors:** Ms B E Hodges, A D Hine
**Co. Secretary:** Ms Barbara Hodges
**Responsibilities**
**Senior:** Derek Penman *(Manager)*, Russel Waters *(Ceo, Managing Director)*
**US SIC:** 7231, 8922
**UK SIC:** 98200, 94000
**Auditors:** Blueprint Audit Ltd
**Bankers:** The Royal Bank Of Scotland Plc (16-01-29)

| | 31-12-13 | 31-12-12 | 31-12-11 |
|---|---|---|---|
| TO | 2,770,351 | 2,635,711 | 2,691,515 |
| P/L | 12,248 | 10,935 | 163,084 |
| NW | 4,100,518 | 4,098,598 | 4,310,362 |
| WC | 912,316 | 817,778 | 963,322 |
| Emp. | 73 | 73 | 72 |

DUNS 64-247-7533

## Penwith College

St Clare Street, Penzance, Cornwall TR18 2SA
**Tel:** 01736335001
**Web:** www.truro-penwith.ac.uk
**Estd:** 2002
**Line of Business:** Post-graduate level higher education
**Director:** R M Andruszko
**Responsibilities**
**Marketing:** Marie Walton *(Marketing Manager)*
**HR:** Kevin Buzza *(Human Resources Manager)*
**Health & Safety:** Kevin Buzza *(Human Resources Manager)*

**Facilities:** Kevin Buzza *(Human Resources Manager)*
**US SIC:** 8221 **UK SIC:** 93100
**Employees:** 300

DUNS 21-354-7271
## Penyrheol Comprehensive School
Pontardulais Road, Gorseinon, Swansea, West Glamorgan SA4 4FG
**Tel:** 01792-533066
**Web:** www.penyrheol-comp.net
**Estd:** 2002 Proprietorship
**Line of Business:** Schools (local authority)
**Proprietor:** A Tootill
**Responsibilities**
**Admin:** Verna Jeffreys *(Administrator)*
**IT:** Joanna Evans *(Senior IT Executive)*
**US SIC:** 8211 **UK SIC:** 93200
**Employees:** 90

DUNS 76-404-4186
## People 1ST
2nd Floor, Armstrong House, Uxbridge, Middlesex UB8 1LH
**Tel:** 08700602550 **Fax:** 01895-17035
**Web:** www.people1st.co.uk
**Reg No:** 2557730 **VAT No:** 532329953
**Estd:** 1990 Private Company Limited By Guarantee
**Line of Business:** Business and management consultancy activities not elsewhere classified
**Directors:** Ms L Chandler, Ms F M Ryland, Mrs N Bickford, C H Prew, Ms S L Edwards, J A Mcewan, D O Fairhurst, P J Harvey
**Co. Secretary:** Simon Tarr
**Responsibilities**
**Senior:** Amanda Brady *(Director)*, Richard Carrick *(Director)*, Nicholas Howe *(Manager)*, Roisin Mckee *(Manager)*, Robin Mills *(Director)*, Therese Procter *(Director)*
**Sales:** Simon Kitto *(Head of Sales)*
**HR:** Gerry Brown *(Strategic Operations & Trainin)*, Linda Greenwood *(Training Manager)*, Phil Raynsford *(Director of Nations & Internat)*
**Operations:** Gerry Brown *(Strategic Operations & Trainin)*, Annabel Thomson *(Operations Manager)*, Nicola Ward *(Senior Operations Executive)*
**Branches:** People 1ST, Suite 2 Ground Floor, Henwood Pavilion, Henwood, Ashford, Kent TN24 8DH
**US SIC:** 7392 **UK SIC:** 83951
**Auditors:** haysmacintyre
**Bankers:** Barclays Bank Plc (20-92-60)

| | 31-03-14 | 31-03-13 | 31-03-12 |
|---|---|---|---|
| TO | 9,510,000 | 9,538,000 | 6,409,000 |
| P/L | (272,000) | 163,000 | 309,000 |
| NW | 3,968,000 | 4,240,000 | 4,077,000 |
| WC | 2,744,000 | 3,875,000 | 3,774,000 |
| Emp. | 101 | 101 | 72 |

DUNS 29-050-2145
## People 2000 Ltd
1 Wheal Northey, St Austell, Cornwall PL25 3EF
**Tel:** 01726626840
**Web:** www.whealnortheysurgery.co.uk
**Reg No:** 1062035 **VAT No:** 434395149
**Estd:** 1986 Private Limited Company
**Line of Business:** Credit granting by non-deposit taking finance houses and other specialist consumer credit grantors
**Trading Style:** Cornish Ford, Liskeard Ford, Western Truck & Van Exeter, Western Truck & Van Yeovil Western Truck & Van Redruth
**Issued Capital:** £11,000
**Chairman and Managing Director:** P A Browning
**Co. Secretary:** Mrs Ann Browning
**Branches:** People 2000 Ltd, Cardrew Industrial Estate, Redruth, Cornwall TR15 1SS
**US SIC:** 6111, 7399
**UK SIC:** 81501, 83954
**Auditors:** Grant Thornton

| | 31-12-13 | 31-12-12 | 31-12-11 |
|---|---|---|---|
| TA | 5,103,939 | 5,021,017 | 4,999,984 |
| NW | 5,079,908 | 5,005,594 | 4,962,140 |
| WC | 5,079,858 | 5,005,544 | 4,937,333 |

DUNS 21-691-8538
## People & Gardens Cic
Watering Lane Nursery Pentewan, St Austell, Cornwall PL26 6BE
**Tel:** 0172670721
**Web:** www.peopleandgardens.co.uk
**Reg No:** 7388684 **Estd:** 2010 Private Company Limited By Guarantee
**Line of Business:** Growing of vegetables, horticultural specialities and nursery products
**Directors:** K G Radford, Ms L Radford, Ms C E Russell, J E Collings, W R Simpson, Dr A J Griffiths

**US SIC:** 8999 **UK SIC:** 83954

| | 31-03-14 | 31-03-13 | 31-03-12 |
|---|---|---|---|
| TO | 70,757 | 59,256 | 57,745 |
| P/L | (830) | 3,203 | 27,469 |
| NW | 31,899 | 30,805 | 27,469 |
| WC | 20,032 | 19,225 | 16,651 |

DUNS 50-528-5726
## People in Action
44 High Street, Bedworth, Warwickshire CV12 8NF
**Tel:** 02476643776 **Fax:** 024-7664-0146
**Web:** www.people-in-action.com
**Reg No:** 2486564 **Estd:** 1990 Private Company Limited By Guarantee
**Line of Business:** Home care service providers
**Directors:** Ms R A Frankel, Ms M Mckee, J W Hunt, Ms S J Morris, J Seton
**Co. Secretary:** John Rigby
**Responsibilities**
**Senior:** Sara Doughty *(Marketing Manager)*
**Branches:** People In Action, 154 Coventry Rd, Coventry, West Midlands CV7 9EW
**US SIC:** 8091 **UK SIC:** 95200
**Auditors:** Muras Baker Jones & Co

| | 31-03-14 | 31-03-13 | 31-03-12 |
|---|---|---|---|
| TO | 10,926,126 | 10,419,606 | 8,955,908 |
| P/L | 594,202 | 833,438 | 461,719 |
| NW | 4,148,409 | 3,535,426 | 2,889,800 |
| WC | 1,135,608 | 1,514,285 | 461,035 |
| Emp. | 528 | 503 | 426 |

DUNS 50-337-5875
## People in Action (Leeds) Uk
Oxford Chambers, Oxford Place, Leeds, West Yorkshire LS1 3AU
**Tel:** 01132-470411
**Web:** www.peopleinaction.org.uk
**Reg No:** 2361654 **Estd:** 1989 Private Limited Company
**Line of Business:** Social work activities
**Directors:** C J Parlington, Ms L Musonza, Miss C P Cavadino, Ms J C Preston, Miss L Smickersgill
**Co. Secretary:** Ms Aqila Choudhry
**Responsibilities**
**Senior:** Tsheppiso Maganu *(Manager)*, Michelle Major *(Finance Manager)*
**Finance:** Michelle Major *(Finance Manager)*
**US SIC:** 6732 **UK SIC:** 83100
**Auditors:** Thomas Coombs & Son
**Bankers:** Cafcash Ltd (40-52-40)

| | 31-03-14 | 31-03-13 | 31-03-12 |
|---|---|---|---|
| TO | 793,431 | 676,018 | 541,301 |
| P/L | 71,759 | 2,145 | (38,747) |
| NW | 279,806 | 208,047 | 205,902 |
| WC | 279,806 | 208,047 | 205,902 |
| Emp. | 99 | 89 | 28 |

DUNS 45-826-5345
## People in Business Ltd
**(Subsidiary of:** Tmp Worldwide Advertising & Communications Llc)
200 Aldersgate Street, London EC1A 4HD
**Tel:** 02033754180 **Fax:** 020-7240-1977
**Web:** www.people-in-business.com
**Reg No:** 3179657 **Estd:** 1996 Private Limited Company
**Line of Business:** Management and business consultants
**Export Sales:** £15,414,000
**Issued Capital:** £2,400,022
**Directors:** Ms J Sippy, D P Richardson, D Prin
**Responsibilities**
**Senior:** Simon Barrow *(Chairman)*, Frances Davenport *(Manager)*, Richard Mosley *(Manager)*
**US SIC:** 7392 **UK SIC:** 83951
**Auditors:** Deloitte LLP
**Bankers:** National Westminster Bank Plc (50-00-00)

| | 31-12-13 | 31-12-12 | 31-12-11 |
|---|---|---|---|
| TO | 27,897,000 | 21,584,000 | 22,617,000 |
| P/L | (382,000) | (492,000) | 759,000 |
| NW | (574,000) | (424,000) | (253,000) |
| WC | (1,148,000) | (1,012,000) | (931,000) |
| Emp. | 129 | 123 | 110 |

DUNS 50-537-6236
## People Potential Possibilities
27 Thornley Street, Wolverhampton, West Midlands WV1 1JS
**Tel:** 01158008190 **Fax:** 01159302939
**Web:** www.p3charity.com
**Reg No:** 2495423 **Estd:** 1990 Private Limited Company
**Line of Business:** Other service activities not elsewhere classified
**Trading Style:** P3
**Directors:** M Green, D Riches, Ms E Brooks, Ms A Cairns, M J Cooper, A J Hackett, J F Spriggs Taylor
**Co. Secretary:** Dale Wilkins
**Branches:** People Potential Possibilities, 12 Hill Street, Swadlincote, Derbyshire DE11 8HL
**US SIC:** 8999 **UK SIC:** 83954
**Auditors:** Haysmacintyre

**Bankers:** Lloyds TSB Bank plc (30-19-40)

| | 31-03-14 | 31-03-13 | 31-03-12 |
|---|---|---|---|
| TO | 13,018,841 | 9,776,460 | 8,023,412 |
| P/L | 201,247 | 34,107 | 122,336 |
| NW | 2,737,859 | 2,536,612 | 2,502,505 |
| WC | 781,766 | 553,401 | 733,368 |
| Emp. | 406 | 317 | 243 |

DUNS 34-946-1793
## People Potential Uk Ltd
**(Subsidiary of:** Dns Holdings Ltd)
People Potential (Uk) Ltd, Alton, Hampshire GU34 1EF
**Tel:** 01420542447
**Web:** www.people-potential.org
**Reg No:** 5742232 **Estd:** 2006 Private Limited Company
**Line of Business:** Other human health activities
**Issued Capital:** £1,111
**Directors:** D N Stoodley, Ms R A Hurst
**Co. Secretary:** Ms Sally Stoodley
**US SIC:** 8091 **UK SIC:** 95200

| | 30-09-14 | 31-03-13 | 31-09-12 |
|---|---|---|---|
| TA | 260,619 | 1,409,805 | 2,031,658 |
| NW | (296,859) | 191,426 | 345,898 |
| WC | (296,859) | (93,239) | (153,390) |

DUNS 21-576-5564
## People to People
Clarendon Room, Ackholt Road, Aylesham, Canterbury, Kent CT3 3AJ
**Tel:** 01304-849020
**Estd:** 2005 Proprietorship
**Line of Business:** Home care service providers
**Proprietor:** R Horsler
**Responsibilities**
**Senior:** Lisa Morris *(Manager)*
**US SIC:** 8091 **UK SIC:** 95200
**Employees:** 79

DUNS 21-580-1004
## Peoples
Trinity Park, Orrell Lane, Bootle, Merseyside L20 6PD
**Tel:** 01519220070
**Web:** www.peoplescars.co.uk
**Estd:** 2011 Proprietorship
**Line of Business:** Car dealers (new & used)
**Proprietor:** J Brown
**Responsibilities**
**Senior:** Jackie Waterhouse *(Dealer Principal)*
**US SIC:** 5511 **UK SIC:** 65100
**Employees:** 200

DUNS 22-512-0963
## Peoples Dispensary for Sick Animals
Whitechapel Way, Priorslee, Telford, Shropshire TF2 9PQ
**Tel:** 0800591248 **Fax:** 08455564906
**Web:** www.pdsa.org.uk
**Reg No:** 0208217ZC **Estd:** 1917 Incorporate By Act Of Parliament
**Line of Business:** Charity shops
**Trading Style:** Pdsa Ltd
**Issued Capital:** £2
**Principals:** J Bodenham, Mrs J Mcloughlin, K L Clemmey, Sir R Guy, F Bircher, Mrs M Rydstrom, D J Inchbald, M Bolton
**Responsibilities**
**Senior:** Andrew Holl *(Manager)*, Sue Mayne *(Manager)*, Janice McLoughlin *(Director General)*, Gina Spicer *(Manager)*
**Marketing:** Mary Bawn *(Acting Head of PR)*, Jenny Davies *(Press Officer)*
**IT:** Matthew Connolly *(Web Technologies and System Ma)*, Philip Sleigh *(Network Manager)*
**HR:** Karen Hailes *(Human Resources Manager)*
**Health & Safety:** Karen Hailes *(Human Resources Manager)*
**Facilities:** Martin Cowell *(Head of Property Services)*
**Purchasing:** Martin Cowell *(Head of Property Services)*
**Branches:** Peoples Dispensary For Sick Animals, P D S A, 441 Wimborne Road, Bournemouth, Dorset BH9 2AN
**US SIC:** 0741, 6732
**UK SIC:** 95601, 83100
**Auditors:** Deloitte LLP
**Bankers:** Lloyds TSB Bank plc (30-18-55)
**Employees:** 1,615
**Turnover:** £93,463,000

DUNS 52-022-2258
## Peoples Ecosse Ltd
1 Cultins Road, Edinburgh, Midlothian EH11 4DF
**Tel:** 08456004433 **Fax:** 0131-453-0222
**Web:** www.peoplescars.co.uk
**Reg No:** 0176576SC **Estd:** 1997 Private Limited Company
**Line of Business:** Car dealers (new & used)
**Trading Style:** Peoples Ford
**Issued Capital:** £2
**Directors:** Ms J S Waterhouse, B P Gilda, K Clezy, Ms N S Gilda
**Co. Secretary:** Stewart Ramsay
**Responsibilities**
**Finance:** Lesley Moody *(Accounts Manager)*
**Marketing:** Iain McFarlane *(Marketing Manager)*
**IT:** Mike Kee *(IT assistant)*, Brian Peat *(Computer Manager)*
**Branches:** Peoples Ecosse Ltd, The Autocentre, Callendar Road, Falkirk, Stirlingshire FK1 1SQ
**US SIC:** 5511, 5521, 5531
**UK SIC:** 65100
**Auditors:** Arthur Andersen
**Bankers:** Bank Of Scotland (80-20-00)

| | 31-07-14 | 31-07-13 | 31-07-12 |
|---|---|---|---|
| TO | 64,507,455 | 60,402,286 | 49,442,501 |
| P/L | 1,274,127 | 1,296,926 | 731,645 |
| NW | (636,703) | (1,621,831) | (2,605,918) |
| WC | (1,116,167) | (2,242,288) | (3,196,650) |
| Emp. | 137 | 134 | 137 |

DUNS 29-003-9536
## Peoples Ltd
The Autocentre, Callendar Road, Falkirk, Stirlingshire FK1 1SQ
**Tel:** 01324621511
**Web:** www.peoplescars.co.uk
**Reg No:** 0080359SC **Estd:** 1982 Private Limited Company
**Line of Business:** Sale, maintenance and repair of motorcycles and related parts and accessories
**Issued Capital:** £100,000
**Chairman:** B P Gilda
**Co. Secretary:** Stewart Ramsay
**Responsibilities**
**Senior:** Thomas McAuley *(Parts Manager)*
**Finance:** Roy Morrison *(Financial Controller)*
**IT:** Brian Peat *(Group IT Director)*
**Branches:** Peoples Ltd, The Autocentre, Callendar Road, Falkirk, Stirlingshire FK1 1SQ
**US SIC:** 5571, 7539
**UK SIC:** 65100, 67100
**Auditors:** Deloitte & Touche LLP
**Bankers:** Bank Of Scotland (80-20-00)

| | 31-07-14 | 31-07-13 | 31-07-12 |
|---|---|---|---|
| TO | 204,997,949 | 185,901,476 | 146,735,134 |
| P/L | 4,151,590 | 3,836,536 | 1,817,075 |
| NW | 15,510,473 | 13,172,576 | 10,690,474 |
| WC | 6,269,488 | 3,438,235 | 1,618,389 |
| Emp. | 395 | 379 | 382 |

DUNS 73-433-4209
## Peopletek Group Ltd
Sceptre House, 8 Hornbeam Square North, Harrogate, North Yorkshire HG2 8PB
**Tel:** 01423859350
**Web:** www.putpeoplefirst.com
**Reg No:** 4706320 **VAT No:** 708257235
**Estd:** 2010 Private Limited Company
**Line of Business:** Employment and recruitment companies and consultants
**Issued Capital:** £1,000
**Directors:** A M Velvin, M Styles
**Responsibilities**
**Senior:** Mark Granger *(Joint Managing Director)*
**US SIC:** 7379 **UK SIC:** 83940
**Auditors:** Cardale Accountancy & Taxation Services

| | 31-03-14 | 31-03-13 | 31-03-12 |
|---|---|---|---|
| TA | 175,814 | 212,577 | 301,396 |
| NW | (86,478) | (106,180) | (120,328) |
| WC | (92,723) | (114,630) | (130,562) |

DUNS 21-402-3744
## Pepper School of Motoring
Unit 2 Vander House, Brunel Road, Newton Abbot, Devon TQ12 4YQ
**Tel:** 08000269165
**Web:** www.passwithpeppers.com
**Line of Business:** Driving schools
**Proprietor:** Mrs J Connor
**US SIC:** 8299 **UK SIC:** 93300
**Employees:** 52

DUNS 21-316-7950 **Imp-Exp**
## Pepperl+Fuchs Gb Ltd
**(Subsidiary of:** Pepperl + Fuchs Gmbh)
77 Ripponden Road, Oldham, Lancashire OL1 4EL
**Tel:** 0161-633-6431
**Web:** www.pepperl-fuchs.co.uk
**Reg No:** 1121083 **VAT No:** 562654430
**Estd:** 1973 Private Limited Company
**Line of Business:** Industrial instrument mfrs
**Export Markets:** Worldwide
**Export Sales:** £351,589
**Issued Capital:** £2,500,000
**Directors:** O Nordmark, S Albrecht
**Co. Secretary:** Ms Amanda Boyle
**Responsibilities**
**Health & Safety:** Winston Edwards *(Health & Safety Officer)*
**Facilities:** Steve Fairbrother *(Facilities Manager)*

**Branches:** Pepperl+fuchs Gb Ltd, Brighstone House, Flat 10, Farnborough, Hampshire GU14 6NZ
**US SIC:** 3823, 7399
**UK SIC:** 37100, 83954
**Auditors:** KPMG LLP
**Bankers:** HSBC Bank plc (40-35-26)

| | 31-12-13 | 31-12-12 | 31-12-11 |
|---|---|---|---|
| TO | 14,349,127 | 13,789,932 | 12,588,511 |
| P/L | 751,060 | 726,931 | 349,184 |
| NW | 4,204,305 | 3,631,514 | 3,110,059 |
| WC | 3,157,922 | 2,483,412 | 1,986,729 |
| Emp. | 73 | 72 | 67 |

DUNS 39-475-6316 **Imp**

## Peppers Marquees Ltd

Cross Hill Pontefract Road, Goole, North Humberside DN14 9JT
**Tel:** 01405-860249 **Fax:** 01405-862098
**Web:** www.peppersmarquees.co.uk
**Reg No:** 2128247 **Estd:** 1987 Private Limited Company
**Line of Business:** Other service activities not elsewhere classified
**Issued Capital:** £100
**Directors:** Ms M Pepper, T S Pepper
**Co. Secretary:** Ms Margaret Pepper
**Responsibilities**
**HR:** Sue Sherban *(Human Resources Manager)*
**US SIC:** 7394, 1799
**UK SIC:** 84000, 50000
**Auditors:** Townends

| | 31-03-14 | 31-03-13 | 31-03-12 |
|---|---|---|---|
| TA | 3,005,523 | 2,000,400 | 2,883,220 |
| NW | 2,469,840 | 2,296,119 | 2,149,248 |
| WC | 345,393 | 261,653 | 229,916 |

DUNS 76-959-3013 **Imp**

## Per Aarsleff (U K) Ltd

(**Subsidiary of:** Per Aarsleff A/S)
Hawton Lane, Newark, Nottinghamshire NG24 3BU
**Tel:** 01636611140
**Web:** www.aarsleff.co.uk
**Reg No:** 2623694 **VAT No:** 599367956
**Estd:** 1991 Private Limited Company
**Line of Business:** Construction of foundations
**Trading Style:** Aarsleff Piling
**Issued Capital:** £1,915,000
**Directors:** E M Iversen, L Rande
**Co. Secretary:** Christopher Primett
**Responsibilities**
**Senior:** Terence Bolsher *(Manager)*
**Sales:** Phil Woodcock *(Business Development Manager)*
**Admin:** Heather Jones *(Office Manager)*
**HR:** Chris Cookson *(Quality Manager)*, Heather Jones *(Office Manager)*
**Health & Safety:** Chris Cookson *(Quality Manager)*
**Operations:** Heather Jones *(Office Manager)*
**US SIC:** 1799, 1795
**UK SIC:** 50000
**Auditors:** Newton & Garner

| | 30-09-13 | 30-09-12 | 30-09-11 |
|---|---|---|---|
| TO | 11,039,489 | 8,626,957 | 6,097,289 |
| P/L | (586,869) | (3,585,207) | (1,635,466) |
| NW | 2,589,295 | 1,126,450 | 4,421,661 |
| WC | (2,912,106) | (5,064,884) | (4,938,633) |
| Emp. | 66 | 59 | 63 |

DUNS 73-994-7591 **Imp**

## Per-Scent Ltd

(**Subsidiary of:** Fragrance Acquisitions Ltd)
Churchill Point, Lake Edge Gre, Trafford Park Road, Trafford Park, Manchester M17 1BL
**Tel:** 01618732100
**Web:** www.per-scent.co.uk
**Reg No:** 5245148 **VAT No:** 844298889
**Estd:** 2005 Private Limited Company
**Line of Business:** Wholesale of perfume and cosmetics
**Export Sales:** £16,182,616
**Issued Capital:** £5,500,002
**Director:** V J Vadera
**Co. Secretary:** Sanjay Vadera
**US SIC:** 5122 **UK SIC:** 61800
**Auditors:** Grant Thornton UK LLP

| | 30-04-14 | 30-04-13 | 30-04-12 |
|---|---|---|---|
| TO | 62,983,115 | 56,629,160 | 56,837,343 |
| P/L | 6,811,167 | 6,735,493 | 6,078,123 |
| NW | 38,421,814 | 33,240,184 | 28,122,246 |
| WC | 38,358,180 | 33,172,911 | 28,042,871 |
| Emp. | 92 | 85 | 101 |

DUNS 21-841-2713

## Pera Training Ltd

Pera Business Park, Nottingham Road, Melton Mowbray, Leicestershire LE13 0PB
**Tel:** 01664501501
**Web:** www.peratraining.com
**Reg No:** 8082277 **Estd:** 2012 Private Limited Company
**Line of Business:** Business and management consultancy activities not elsewhere classified
**Issued Capital:** £500
**Directors:** J T Hill, R J Grice, G P Goddard, A J Baxter, P Tranter
**Co. Secretary:** Mrs Lorraine Gibson
**US SIC:** 7392 **UK SIC:** 83951

| | 31-03-14 | 31-03-13 |
|---|---|---|
| TO | 16,689,764 | 11,044,096 |
| P/L | 1,231,816 | 1,944,929 |
| NW | 2,618,881 | 1,696,972 |
| WC | 3,927,615 | 3,059,542 |
| Emp. | 171 | 131 |

DUNS 21-419-8252

## Peradon

128 Richmond Row, Liverpool, Merseyside L3 3BL
**Web:** www.peradon.co.uk
**Proprietorship**
**Line of Business:** Snooker tables and accessory suppliers
**Proprietor:** P Clare
**US SIC:** 3949 **UK SIC:** 49420
**Employees:** 100

DUNS 51-988-5797

## Percepta Uk Ltd

(**Subsidiary of:** Teletech Holdings Inc.)
Morrison Court, Glasgow, Lanarkshire G1 3LH
**Tel:** 01415713400
**Web:** www.perceptaeurope.com
**Reg No:** 3995396 **Estd:** 2000 Private Limited Company
**Line of Business:** Call centres
**Issued Capital:** £2
**Director:** A M Meldrum
**Co. Secretary:** Ms Rose Sexton
**Responsibilities**
**Senior:** Ron Chmara *(Chief Executive Officer)*
**Branches:** Percepta Uk Ltd, Room 555, Eagle Way, Brentwood, Essex CM13 3BW
**US SIC:** 7399 **UK SIC:** 83954
**Auditors:** Ernst & Young LLP
**Bankers:** HSBC Bank plc (40-13-22)

| | 31-12-13 | 31-12-12 | 31-12-11 |
|---|---|---|---|
| TO | 9,943,439 | 10,422,062 | 10,877,368 |
| P/L | 432,594 | 400,447 | 719,385 |
| NW | 1,343,735 | 1,315,276 | 1,522,333 |
| WC | 1,318,719 | 1,278,570 | 1,504,771 |
| Emp. | 340 | 350 | 345 |

DUNS 54-376-9251

## Perceptive Eclinical Ltd

(**Subsidiary of:** Clinphone Ltd)
Lady Bay House, Meadow Grove, Nottingham, Nottinghamshire NG2 3HF
**Tel:** 01159-557333
**Reg No:** 3264836 **Estd:** 1996 Private Limited Company
**Line of Business:** Data storage solutions
**Trading Style:** Clinphone
**Issued Capital:** £1,001
**Directors:** D A Batt, J H Von Rickenbach
**Co. Secretary:** Douglas Batt
**US SIC:** 7374 **UK SIC:** 83940
**Auditors:** PKF
**Bankers:** The Chase Manhattan Bank (60-91-41)

| | 30-06-13 | 30-06-12 | 30-06-11 |
|---|---|---|---|
| TO | 56,704,000 | 49,370,000 | 26,559,000 |
| P/L | (15,568,000) | 2,343,000 | 854,000 |
| NW | 47,489,000 | 63,587,000 | 61,488,000 |
| WC | 50,880,000 | 47,175,000 | 37,451,000 |
| Emp. | 583 | 538 | 507 |

DUNS 23-680-8676 **Exp**

## Perceptive Informatics Uk Ltd

(**Subsidiary of:** Clinphone Ltd)
8th Floor, Birmingham, West Midlands B5 4UA
**Tel:** 0121-616-5600
**Web:** www.perceptive.com
**Reg No:** 3675405 **Estd:** 1998 Private Limited Company
**Line of Business:** Computer systems and software (sales)
**Export Markets:** E U
**Issued Capital:** £2
**Director:** J H Von Rickenbach
**Co. Secretary:** Douglas Batt
**Responsibilities**
**Senior:** Christine Walker *(Office Manager)*
**Facilities:** Christine Walker *(Office Manager)*
**US SIC:** 7379 **UK SIC:** 83940
**Auditors:** Ernst & Young LLP
**Bankers:** The Chase Manhattan Bank (60-92-42)

| | 30-06-13 | 30-06-12 | 30-06-11 |
|---|---|---|---|
| TO | 9,549,000 | 9,233,000 | 9,921,000 |
| P/L | 2,397,000 | 2,519,000 | 4,507,000 |
| NW | 6,963,000 | 5,139,000 | 3,227,000 |
| WC | 6,150,000 | 4,332,000 | 2,555,000 |
| Emp. | 74 | 76 | 77 |

DUNS 36-535-8279

## Perceptive Insight Market Research Ltd

109b Bloomfield Avenue, Belfast BT5 5AB
**Tel:** 028-9073-7090 **Fax:** 02890737091
**Web:** www.perceptiveinsight.co.uk
**Reg No:** 0060629NI **Estd:** 2006 Private Limited Company
**Line of Business:** Market research organisations
**Issued Capital:** £2
**Directors:** D Treacy, Ms M Treacy
**Co. Secretary:** Daniel Treacy
**US SIC:** 7392 **UK SIC:** 83951

| | 31-08-13 | 31-08-12 | 31-08-11 |
|---|---|---|---|
| TA | 133,575 | 112,788 | 82,093 |
| NW | 89,497 | 71,866 | 49,535 |
| WC | 74,226 | 51,328 | 41,170 |

DUNS 29-096-2075 **Imp-Exp**

## Percival Aviation Ltd

15 Barnes Wallis Road, Fareham, Hampshire PO15 5TT
**Tel:** 01489569000 **Fax:** 01489-569050
**Web:** www.percival-aviation.co.uk
**Reg No:** 1458467 **VAT No:** 329790325
**Estd:** 1979 Private Limited Company
**Line of Business:** Aircraft - services for
**Export Markets:** Europe
**Trading Style:** Percival Aviation Ltd
**Issued Capital:** £490
**Managing Director:** N J Percival
**Co. Secretary:** Ms Karen Percival
**Responsibilities**
**Finance:** Debbie Plant *(Office Manager)*
**Admin:** Debbie Plant *(Office Manager)*
**HR:** Debbie Plant *(Office Manager)*
**Health & Safety:** Craig Challenor *(Production Manager)*
**Purchasing:** Debbie Plant *(Office Manager)*
**Engineering:** Craig Challenor *(Production Manager)*
**Branches:** Percival Aviation Ltd, The Sidings, Fareham, Hampshire PO17 5LZ
**US SIC:** 4582, 8999
**UK SIC:** 76400, 83954
**Bankers:** The Royal Bank Of Scotland Plc (16-19-28)

| | 30-11-13 | 30-11-12 | 30-11-11 |
|---|---|---|---|
| TA | 2,237,071 | 2,079,062 | 2,017,741 |
| NW | 1,441,063 | 1,282,581 | 1,107,794 |
| WC | 1,127,953 | 936,292 | 838,658 |

DUNS 21-007-1563

## Percurra Ltd

117 Trent Boulevard, West Bridgford, Nottingham, Nottinghamshire NG2 5BN
**Tel:** 01159696108
**Web:** www.percurra.com
**Reg No:** 6314569 **Estd:** 2010 Private Limited Company
**Line of Business:** Home care service providers
**Issued Capital:** £1
**Director:** Ms G A Heppell
**Co. Secretary:** Paul Gayton
**US SIC:** 8091 **UK SIC:** 95200

| | 31-12-12 | 31-12-11 | 31-12-10 |
|---|---|---|---|
| TA | 156,119 | 236,803 | 214,330 |
| NW | 58,686 | 81,624 | 67,241 |
| WC | 34,212 | 56,855 | 34,008 |

DUNS 29-491-5954

## The Percy Hedley Foundation

Lower School Station Road, Newcastle-Upon-Tyne, Tyne and Wear NE12 8YY
**Tel:** 01912665491 **Fax:** 01912665537
**Web:** www.percyhedley.org.uk
**Reg No:** 1855026 **Estd:** 1953 Private Company Limited By Guarantee
**Line of Business:** Day and care centres
**Trading Style:** Percy Hedley Foundation
**Directors:** N R Swales, G Walker, Professor M J Potts, Ms A Curran, J Jowett, P Wignall, D R Arthur, D J Burdus
**Co. Secretary:** Mrs Sarah Turner
**Responsibilities**
**Senior:** Tony Best *(Chief Executive)*, Jayne Curry *(Manager)*, Barbara Dennis *(Trustee)*, Jeanne Jackson *(Director)*, Susan Jopling *(Director)*, S McCormick *(Manager)*, Hari Shukla *(Manager)*
**Finance:** Sheila Coltman *(Fundraiser)*
**Marketing:** Des Bustard *(Fundraising Director)*, Sheila Coltman *(Fundraiser)*, Maria Hallett *(Fundraiser)*
**IT:** Paul Hansson *(Senior IT Executive)*
**US SIC:** 8321, 8211
**UK SIC:** 96111, 93200
**Auditors:** John Marshall & Co
**Bankers:** Barclays Bank Plc (20-59-61)

| | 31-08-14 | 31-08-13 | 31-08-12 |
|---|---|---|---|
| TO | 21,732,146 | 18,717,502 | 23,330,384 |
| P/L | 2,168,314 | 946,894 | (987,500) |
| NW | 12,958,920 | 11,107,606 | 8,099,713 |
| WC | 7,270,468 | 4,803,180 | 3,278,482 |
| Emp. | 748 | 713 | 587 |

DUNS 21-591-8455

## Percy Hedley Upper School

West Lane, Newcastle-Upon-Tyne, Tyne and Wear NE12 7BH
**Tel:** 01912161811
**Web:** www.percyhedley.org.uk
**Estd:** 2011 Proprietorship
**Line of Business:** Education services
**Proprietor:** Ms S Fisher
**Responsibilities**
**Senior:** Lynn Watson *(Head Teacher)*
**US SIC:** 8699 **UK SIC:** 96902
**Employees:** 60

DUNS 77-952-3661

## Percy Ingle Holdings Ltd

210 Church Road, London E10 7JQ
**Tel:** 02085569431
**Web:** www.percy-ingle.co.uk
**Reg No:** 3058130 **Estd:** 1995 Private Limited Company
**Line of Business:** Bakers and confectioners supplies
**Trading Style:** Ingle Percy Bakeries
**Issued Capital:** £9,697
**Director:** D P Ingle
**Co. Secretary:** Michael Ingle
**Responsibilities**
**Senior:** James Darby *(General Manager)*
**US SIC:** 2051, 6711
**UK SIC:** 41960, 83962
**Auditors:** Barnes Roffe
**Bankers:** Barclays Bank Plc (20-44-22)

| | 30-06-13 | 30-06-12 | 30-06-11 |
|---|---|---|---|
| TO | 11,898,432 | 11,932,733 | 11,271,417 |
| P/L | 139,393 | 244,938 | (89,791) |
| NW | 8,319,854 | 8,338,817 | 8,369,786 |
| WC | (740,543) | (626,495) | (388,054) |
| Emp. | 314 | 313 | 306 |

DUNS 29-043-0628

## Percy Ingle Services Ltd

(**Subsidiary of:** Percy Ingle Holdings Ltd)
210 Church Road, London E10 7JQ
**Tel:** 02085565338
**Web:** www.gbnselfdrive.co.uk
**Reg No:** 0964572 **Estd:** 1969 Private Limited Company
**Line of Business:** Management activities of other non-financial holding companies not elsewhere classified
**Issued Capital:** £9,697
**Directors:** P D Ingle, D P Ingle
**Co. Secretary:** Michael Ingle
**US SIC:** 6711, 5462
**UK SIC:** 83962, 64100
**Auditors:** Barnes Roffe
**Bankers:** National Westminster Bank Plc (60-09-23)

| | 30-06-13 | 30-06-12 | 30-06-11 |
|---|---|---|---|
| TA | 10,906,102 | 10,756,344 | 10,735,090 |
| NW | 8,685,332 | 8,445,336 | 8,358,237 |
| WC | 4,553,195 | 4,530,817 | 4,543,357 |

DUNS 22-234-7416

## Percy Lane Products Ltd

(**Subsidiary of:** L&P 176 Ltd)
Lichfield Road Staffs Moor Industrial, Estate, Tamworth, Staffordshire B79 7TL
**Tel:** 0182763821 **Fax:** 01827-310159
**Web:** www.percy-lane.co.uk
**Reg No:** 4252701 **Estd:** 2001 Private Limited Company
**Line of Business:** Portable buildings
**Export Sales:** £513,112
**Issued Capital:** £111,000
**Directors:** G H Fowler, P S Wright, N Greenhalgh, J W Whetton, Ms J G Hunt
**Co. Secretary:** Alison Fowler
**Responsibilities**
**HR:** Leah Coll *(human Resources Officer)*
**Purchasing:** Beth Hughes *(Buyer)*
**US SIC:** 3231 **UK SIC:** 24791
**Auditors:** PricewaterhouseCoopers LLP
**Bankers:** Alliance & Leicester Plc (72-50-00)

| | 31-12-13 | 31-12-12 | 31-12-11 |
|---|---|---|---|
| TO | 10,147,651 | 9,293,253 | 9,659,236 |
| P/L | 1,121,755 | 1,113,097 | 1,084,282 |
| NW | 6,257,129 | 5,612,702 | 5,004,892 |
| WC | 5,714,546 | 5,143,998 | 4,629,239 |
| Emp. | 140 | 134 | 131 |

DUNS 53-645-5009

## Percy R Brend & Sons (Holdings) Ltd

1 Park Villas, Tawvale, Barnstaple, Devon EX32 0EL
**Tel:** 01271-344496 **Fax:** 01271-378558
**Web:** www.hotelsindevonandcornwall.com
**Reg No:** 3450932 **Estd:** 1969 Private Limited Company
**Line of Business:** Management activities of other non-financial holding companies not elsewhere classified
**Issued Capital:** £922,250
**Directors:** J E Brend, P A Brend, J J Brend, R P Brend, M J Brend
**Co. Secretary:** Peter Brend

**Responsibilities**
Finance: Jenny Smith (Manager)
Admin: Sandra Handford (Office Manager)
IT: Tony Clarke (Computer Manager)
HR: Andrew Mosedale (Personnel Manager)
Health & Safety: Andrew Mosedale (Personnel Manager)
US SIC: 7399, 5812
UK SIC: 83954, 66110
Auditors: Bishop Fleming
Bankers: Lloyds TSB Bank plc (30-90-49)

|     | 31-03-14 | 31-03-13 | 31-03-12 |
|-----|----------|----------|----------|
| TO  | 50,508,092 | 47,458,240 | 48,574,415 |
| P/L | 968,805 | 701,828 | 646,665 |
| NW  | 6,671,765 | 6,568,396 | 6,512,435 |
| WC  | (10,812,286) | (10,673,704) | (10,289,251) |
| Emp. | 1,099 | 1,096 | 1,145 |

DUNS 21-705-0608
## Percy R.Brend & Sons(Hoteliers) Ltd
(Subsidiary of: Percy R Brend & Sons (Holdings) Ltd)
Saunton, Braunton, Devon EX33 1LQ
Tel: 01271890212 Fax: 01271323157
Web: www.brand-hotels.co.uk
Reg No: 0955450 VAT No: 684899648
Estd: 1969 Private Limited Company
Line of Business: Hotels
Trading Style: The Park Hotel, The Saunton Sands Hotel, Carlyon Bay Golf Hotel, Royal Duchy Hotel
Issued Capital: £100
Principals: J E Brend (Managing), J J Brend, M J Brend, P A Brend, R P Brend
Co. Secretary: Peter Brend
Responsibilities
Senior: Anthony Kingdon (Hotel Manager)
Facilities: Stuart Fewings (Maintenance Manager)
Branches: Percy R.brend & Sons(Hoteliers) Ltd, Exeter By-Pass, Exeter, Devon EX2 8XU
US SIC: 7011 UK SIC: 66500
Auditors: Bishop Fleming
Bankers: Lloyds TSB Bank plc (30-90-49)

|     | 31-03-14 | 31-03-13 | 31-03-12 |
|-----|----------|----------|----------|
| TO  | 30,476,160 | 30,205,817 | 30,658,525 |
| P/L | 397,646 | 330,377 | 320,059 |
| NW  | 6,760,144 | 6,364,995 | 6,088,900 |
| WC  | 778,680 | 760,278 | 903,863 |
| Emp. | 1,044 | 1,041 | 1,085 |

DUNS 21-772-1957
## Percy Shurmer
Longmore Street, Birmingham, West Midlands B12 9ED
Tel: 01214643431
Web: www.percyshurmer.bham.sch.uk
Estd: 2011 Proprietorship
Line of Business: Schools (local authority)
Proprietor: Ms E Simpson
Responsibilities
Senior: Joe Purnell (Head Teacher)
US SIC: 8211 UK SIC: 93200
Employees: 445

DUNS 23-700-5871
## Perdiswell Leisure Centre
Bilford Road, Worcester, Worcestershire WR3 8DX
Tel: 01905-457189
Web: www.1life.co.uk
Estd: 2011 Proprietorship
Line of Business: Leisure centres
Proprietor: D Pugh
US SIC: 7999 UK SIC: 97913
Employees: 50

DUNS 55-056-6277
## Peregrine House
1 Queen Elizabeth Drive, Scalby, Scarborough, North Yorkshire YO13 0SR
Tel: 01947603886
Web: www.peregrinehouse.co.uk
Estd: 1995 Partnership
Line of Business: Non-charitable social work activities with accommodation
Partners: Mrs T O'Sullivan, Dr K O'Sullivan
Responsibilities
Senior: Alison Bedford (Manager)
US SIC: 8321 UK SIC: 96111
Employees: 47

DUNS 42-428-3161                                    Imp
## Peregrine Livefoods Ltd
Rolls Farm Barns, Magdalen Laver, Ongar, Essex CM5 0EN
Tel: 01279438459 Fax: 08451307723
Web: http://peregrine-livefoods.co.uk
Reg No: 4415888 Estd: 2002 Private Limited Company
Line of Business: Wholesale of other intermediate products
Issued Capital: £102
Director: D C Perry
Co. Secretary: Timothy Green
Responsibilities
Sales: Darryl Chapman (Head of Sales)

HR: Dawn Green (HR and HS Manager)
Health & Safety: Joanne Daniel (Health and Safety Officer)
US SIC: 5199, 0279
UK SIC: 61900, 01001
Bankers: Barclays Bank Plc (20-29-86)

|     | 31-05-14 | 31-05-13 | 31-05-12 |
|-----|----------|----------|----------|
| TO  | 12,804,698 | 12,732,007 | 12,047,092 |
| P/L | 832,783 | 678,118 | 824,984 |
| NW  | 2,410,023 | 2,052,986 | 1,772,007 |
| WC  | 2,121,357 | 1,719,225 | 1,373,157 |
| Emp. | 113 | 101 | 94 |

DUNS 38-543-9575
## Peregrine Retail Ltd
(Subsidiary of: Forelle Estates Holdings Ltd.)
Strand House, Strand Street, Poole, Dorset BH15 1SB
Reg No: 3327423 Estd: 1997 Private Limited Company
Line of Business: Petrol service stations
Issued Capital: £2
Directors: T R Orford, M J Price, R C King, R B O'Connell, J Mason, D R Haikney
Co. Secretary: David Haikney
US SIC: 5541 UK SIC: 65200
Auditors: Princecroft Redman
Bankers: Lloyds TSB Bank plc (30-96-73)

|     | 31-01-14 | 31-01-13 | 31-01-12 |
|-----|----------|----------|----------|
| TO  | 24,603,934 | 19,557,144 | 0,070,177 |
| P/L | 81,750 | (7,226) | 61,377 |
| NW  | (1,050,512) | (1,243,408) | (621,234) |
| WC  | 400,527 | 584,603 | 434,871 |
| Emp. | 60 | N/A | N/A |

DUNS 22-513-9633                                    Imp-Exp
## Perei Group Ltd
(Subsidiary of: Deltronic Ltd)
Sunbury House, 4 Christy Estate, Aldershot, Hampshire GU12 4TX
Tel: 01252350833 Fax: 01252-350875
Web: www.perei.co.uk
Reg No: 0761224 Estd: 1963 Private Limited Company
Line of Business: Car accessories and parts
Export Markets: Western Europe, Middle East, Africa, South and South East Asia and Australasia
Export Sales: £1,530,555
Issued Capital: £101,000
Directors: R Corke, C O'Connell, R A Perei
Co. Secretary: William Perei
Responsibilities
Senior: Steve Bamber (Operations Manager)
Operations: Steve Bamber (Operations Manager)
US SIC: 3714 UK SIC: 35300
Auditors: Grant Thornton UK LLP
Bankers: Barclays Bank Plc (20-71-02)

|     | 30-06-13 | 30-06-12 | 30-06-11 |
|-----|----------|----------|----------|
| TO  | 16,865,292 | 14,223,651 | 11,562,322 |
| P/L | 1,466,878 | 1,308,962 | 666,069 |
| NW  | 3,573,485 | 3,994,273 | 3,497,002 |
| WC  | 2,394,790 | 2,786,953 | 2,192,341 |
| Emp. | 134 | 139 | 124 |

DUNS 34-989-1320                                    Imp
## Perella Weinberg Partners Uk Llp
Fitzroy House, 18-20 Grafton Street, London W1S 4DZ
Tel: 02072682800
Web: www.pwpartners.com
Reg No: 0319198OC Estd: 2006
Line of Business: Financial intermediation not elsewhere classified
Responsibilities
Senior: Graham Davidson (Non-designated Limited Liabili), Michael Dickman (Partner), Bernard Gault (Non-designated Limited Liabili), Joseph Perella (Non-designated Limited Liabili), Klaus Wuelfing (Partner)
IT: Tom Holloway (Head of IT)
US SIC: 6111 UK SIC: 81501

|     | 31-12-13 | 31-12-12 | 31-12-11 |
|-----|----------|----------|----------|
| TA  | 33,262,715 | 34,568,179 | 33,013,498 |
| P/L | 1,037,377 | 9,214,339 | 1,790,495 |
| NW  | 16,796,192 | 19,035,238 | 19,040,238 |
| WC  | 16,295,719 | 18,748,978 | 18,731,037 |
| Emp. | 77 | 71 | 64 |

DUNS 21-580-3591
## Perenco
Paston Road, Norwich, Norfolk NR12 0JF
Tel: 01263720791
Web: www.perenco.com
Estd: 2011 Proprietorship
Line of Business: Oil and gas exploration services
Proprietor: P Ratcliffe
Responsibilities
Senior: Adrian Fletcher (Terminal Manager)
US SIC: 1389 UK SIC: 13000
Employees: 50

DUNS 29-336-6332
## Perenco (Oil & Gas) International Ltd
(Subsidiary of: Perenco International Limited)
29 Duke Of York Square, London SW3 4LY
Fax: 02073764290
Reg No: 0061143SC Estd: 1976 Private Limited Company
Line of Business: Management activities of holding companies
Issued Capital: £1,000
Directors: J B Parr, N J Fallows
Co. Secretary: Mrs Averil Eager
US SIC: 6711 UK SIC: 83962
Auditors: Deloitte LLP
Bankers: The Royal Bank Of Scotland Plc (16-08-05)

|     | 31-12-13 | 31-12-12 | 31-12-11 |
|-----|----------|----------|----------|
| TO  | 179,029,000 | 207,715,000 | 182,430,000 |
| P/L | 98,145,000 | 152,101,000 | 125,463,000 |
| NW  | 387,231,000 | 534,163,000 | 426,478,000 |
| WC  | 313,849,000 | 479,286,000 | 381,522,000 |
| Emp. | 261 | 249 | 259 |

DUNS 73-379-5137
## Perenco Uk Ltd
(Subsidiary of: Perenco International Limited)
Anchor House, 15-19 Britten Street, London SW3 3TY
Fax: 02073689009
Web: www.perenco-uk.com
Reg No: 4653066 Estd: 2013 Private Limited Company
Line of Business: Oil and gas exploration services
Issued Capital: £47,080,980
Directors: J Rusin, N J Fallows, J B Parr, K Kallmeyer, B James
Co. Secretary: Mrs Elisabeth Sullivan
Responsibilities
Senior: Eric Faillenet (Manager), Francois Raux (Director)
Branches: Perenco Uk Limited, Yarmouth Business Park, Thamesfield Way, Great Yarmouth, Norfolk NR31 0DN
US SIC: 1389 UK SIC: 13000
Auditors: Deloitte LLP
Following financial data are in thousands

|     | 31-12-13 | 31-12-12 | 31-12-11 |
|-----|----------|----------|----------|
| TO  | 1,051,227 | 585,499 | 348,791 |
| P/L | 387,722 | 164,426 | 146,538 |
| NW  | 184,470 | 139,241 | 204,414 |
| WC  | 425,025 | 356,099 | 215,113 |
| Emp. | 829 | 548 | 329 |

DUNS 21-909-3481                                    Imp-Exp
## Perfectos Printing Inks Co Ltd.
(Subsidiary of: Perfectos Printing Inks Group Ltd)
Perfectos Mills, Normanton Lane, Bottesford, Nottingham, Nottinghamshire NG13 0EL
Web: www.perfectos.co.uk
Reg No: 1183880 VAT No: 119026589
Estd: 1974 Private Limited Company
Line of Business: Manufacturers of printing inks
Export Sales: £9,055,716
Issued Capital: £2,000
Principals: Dr J H Price (Chairman and Managing), E J Price, S J Price
Co. Secretary: Ms Jacqueline Dixon
US SIC: 2891 UK SIC: 25620
Auditors: Greenhalgh & Co

|     | 01-04-14 | 01-04-13 | 01-04-12 |
|-----|----------|----------|----------|
| TO  | 9,421,816 | 7,845,931 | N/A |
| P/L | 3,670,951 | 3,457,034 | N/A |
| NW  | 12,363,927 | 9,604,631 | 5,233,414 |
| WC  | 10,903,313 | 8,176,106 | 3,859,181 |
| Emp. | 56 | 46 | N/A |

DUNS 21-008-4058                                    Imp
## Perform Group Plc
Sussex House, 2 Plane Tree Crescent, Feltham, Middlesex TW13 7HE
Tel: 02033720600 Fax: 02089170803
Web: www.performgroup.co.uk
Reg No: 6324278 Estd: 2007 Public Limited Company
Line of Business: Advertising, radio, tv and other media
Export Sales: £154,619,000
Trading Style: Perform
Issued Capital: £7,358
Directors: A G Milton, S C Denyer, T C Harding, P A Walker, O M Slipper, J P Williams, H S Mohaupt
Co. Secretary: Richard Mcmorris
Responsibilities
Senior: Stefano D Anna (Manager)
Marketing: Stacey Cann (Head of Marketing)
HR: Paul Chesworth (Chief People Officer)
Purchasing: Jonathan Hyatt (Purchasing Manager)
US SIC: 7319 UK SIC: 83800

Auditors: Deloitte LLP

|     | 31-12-13 | 31-12-12 | 31-12-11 |
|-----|----------|----------|----------|
| TO  | 208,135,000 | 151,607,000 | 103,194,000 |
| P/L | 4,058,000 | 16,920,000 | 3,486,000 |
| NW  | 16,456,000 | (39,682,000) | 58,197,000 |
| WC  | 45,973,000 | (14,752,000) | 57,171,000 |
| Emp. | 1,345 | 906 | 590 |

DUNS 53-621-3952
## Perform Media Services Ltd
(Subsidiary of: Perform Group Plc)
Sussex House, 2 Plane Tree Crescent, Feltham, Middlesex TW13 7HE
Tel: 02033720600 Fax: 0284848080
Web: www.performgroup.com
Reg No: 3426471 Estd: 1997 Private Limited Company
Line of Business: Broadcasting services
Export Sales: £18,085,000
Issued Capital: £2,239,058
Directors: R E Mcmorris, S C Denyer, O M Slipper
Responsibilities
Senior: Andrew Croker (Manager), David Surtees (Manager)
US SIC: 4833 UK SIC: 97411
Auditors: Grant Thornton UK LLP
Bankers: Bristol And West Plc (57-14-62)

|     | 31-12-13 | 31-12-12 | 31-12-11 |
|-----|----------|----------|----------|
| TO  | 78,389,000 | 70,605,000 | 49,229,000 |
| P/L | 1,187,000 | 15,376,000 | 7,310,000 |
| NW  | 30,565,000 | 34,727,000 | 24,015,000 |
| WC  | (157,882,000) | (111,269,000) | 1,455,000 |
| Emp. | 538 | 493 | 257 |

DUNS 49-081-1353
## Performance Direct Ltd
Toll Gate House 96 Market Place, Romford, Essex RM1 3ER
Tel: 01708436801 Fax: 01708-436897
Web: www.performancedirect.co.uk
Reg No: 3087037 Estd: 1995 Private Limited Company
Line of Business: Non-life insurance
Issued Capital: £2
Director: P J Collett
Co. Secretary: Damian Collett
Branches: Performance Direct Ltd, 182-184 High Street, Hornchurch, Essex RM12 6QP
US SIC: 6399, 8999
UK SIC: 82001, 83954
Auditors: Balfour Sanson

|     | 31-05-13 | 31-05-12 | 31-05-11 |
|-----|----------|----------|----------|
| TA  | 6,233 | 6,233 | 6,233 |
| NW  | 6,162 | 6,162 | 6,162 |
| WC  | 6,162 | 6,162 | 6,162 |

DUNS 73-369-0312
## Performance Doorset Solutions Ltd
Greenvale Business Park, Todmorden Road, Littleborough, Lancashire OL15 9AZ
Tel: 01706370001 Fax: 01706370002
Web: www.pdsdoorsets.co.uk
Reg No: 4642499 Estd: 2003 Private Limited Company
Line of Business: Manufacturers of domestic doors
Trading Style: P D S
Issued Capital: £36,620
Directors: C Murphy, P Goggins, T J Fairley, J J Thompson
Co. Secretary: Timothy Fairley
US SIC: 2431, 2499
UK SIC: 46300, 46500
Auditors: Richard Smedley Ltd
Bankers: Barclays Bank Plc (20-72-67)

|     | 30-04-14 | 30-04-13 | 30-04-12 |
|-----|----------|----------|----------|
| TO  | 11,152,694 | 9,198,339 | 9,333,878 |
| P/L | 749,957 | 151,936 | 547,878 |
| NW  | 1,904,239 | 1,241,237 | 1,226,302 |
| WC  | 611,634 | 155,803 | 183,933 |
| Emp. | 123 | 113 | 107 |

DUNS 21-327-9524
## Performance Electrical Ltd
(Subsidiary of: Peg Ltd)
123 Radcliffe Road, Bury, Lancashire BL9 9LD
Tel: 0161-797-3476
Web: www.performanceelectrical.co.uk
Reg No: 1404578 VAT No: 323900093
Estd: 1978 Private Limited Company
Line of Business: Electrical contractors and electricians
Issued Capital: £50
Directors: M A Corris, D P Jones
US SIC: 1731 UK SIC: 50300
Auditors: RSM Tenon Ltd
Bankers: Barclays Bank Plc (20-16-08)

|     | 31-03-14 | 31-03-13 | 31-03-12 |
|-----|----------|----------|----------|
| TA  | 2,855,602 | 2,930,813 | 2,589,649 |
| NW  | 1,293,947 | 1,230,308 | 1,244,832 |
| WC  | 1,277,269 | 1,194,144 | 1,196,297 |

DUNS 42-356-8992
### Performance First Ltd
The Tower, Wareham, Dorset BH20 6AN
**Tel:** 07968-029638
**Web:** www.performancefirst.com
**Reg No:** 4344494 **Estd:** 1999 Private Limited Company
**Line of Business:** Business and management consultancy activities not elsewhere classified
**Trading Style:** Performance First Ltd
**Issued Capital:** £200
**Director:** G S Mackenzie Philps
**Co. Secretary:** Gordon Mackenzie-Philps
**US SIC:** 7392 **UK SIC:** 83951
**Auditors:** Gilbert Allen & Co

| | 31-03-14 | 31-03-13 | 31-03-12 |
|---|---|---|---|
| TA | 52,781 | 29,672 | 40,039 |
| NW | 27,523 | 21,578 | 32,029 |
| WC | 25,252 | 21,578 | 32,029 |

DUNS 38-567-4478
### Performance Improvements (P I) Ltd
(**Subsidiary of:** Amec Foster Wheeler Plc)
6 Albyn Terrace, Aberdeen, Aberdeenshire AB10 1YP
**Tel:** 01224-647770
**Web:** www.pi-ltd.com
**Reg No:** 0173714SC **Estd:** 1997 Private Limited Company
**Line of Business:** Engineers (consulting)
**Issued Capital:** £14,000
**Directors:** C R Fleming, G B Sleigh, A J Johnstone, R J Etherington
**Co. Secretary:** Christopher Fidler
**Responsibilities**
**Senior:** Michael Horgan *(Manager)*
**Finance:** Karen Laing *(Administration Manager)*
**Health & Safety:** Danial Grant *(Health & Safety Officer)*
**US SIC:** 1389 **UK SIC:** 13000
**Auditors:** Ernst & Young
**Bankers:** Clydesdale Bank Plc (82-60-11)

| | 31-12-13 | 31-12-12 | 31-12-11 |
|---|---|---|---|
| TO | 5,347,000 | 5,048,000 | 5,504,000 |
| P/L | 173,000 | (111,000) | 899,000 |
| NW | 3,811,000 | 3,641,000 | 3,752,000 |
| WC | 3,874,000 | 3,705,000 | 3,810,000 |
| Emp. | 54 | 56 | 23 |

DUNS 23-879-8750
### Performance in People Ltd
Murrays, 50 London Road, Stroud, Gloucestershire GL5 2AD
**Tel:** 01983-568080
**Web:** www.performanceinpeople.co.uk
**Reg No:** 3871085 **Estd:** 1999 Private Limited Company
**Line of Business:** Training services
**Issued Capital:** £2,031
**Directors:** M C Dalloz, A J Breingan
**Co. Secretary:** Simon Gibbs
**Responsibilities**
**Senior:** Nick Drake Knight *(Joint Managing Director)*
**Finance:** Nick Drake Knight *(Joint Managing Director)*
**US SIC:** 8299 **UK SIC:** 93300
**Auditors:** Bright Brown Ltd

| | 31-12-13 | 31-12-12 | 31-12-11 |
|---|---|---|---|
| TA | 1,004,941 | 1,243,874 | 1,394,079 |
| NW | (11,736) | 14,923 | 57,332 |
| WC | (114,637) | (179,676) | (193,227) |

DUNS 45-811-8924
### Performances Birmingham Ltd
Birmingham Forward, Baskerville House, Broad Street, Birmingham, West Midlands B1 2ND
**Tel:** 01212002000
**Web:** www.thsh.co.uk
**Reg No:** 3169600 **Estd:** 1996 Private Limited Company
**Line of Business:** Theatres & concert halls
**Directors:** J W Moir, A Bore, I P Myatt, Lord W M Morris, Ms M J Martin, Ms A K Bhalla, Professor C R Timms, D L Scard
**Co. Secretary:** Richard Paterson
**Responsibilities**
**Senior:** Andy Street *(Director)*, Mike Whitby *(Director)*
**US SIC:** 8999 **UK SIC:** 83954

| | 31-03-13 | 31-03-12 | 31-03-11 |
|---|---|---|---|
| TO | 11,674,000 | 11,746,000 | 11,795,000 |
| P/L | (174,000) | (180,000) | 65,000 |
| NW | 2,038,000 | 2,212,000 | 2,392,000 |
| WC | 1,315,000 | 1,414,000 | 1,582,000 |
| Emp. | 72 | 73 | 70 |

DUNS 22-703-6522 **Imp**
### Performing Right Society Ltd
29-33 Berners Street, London W1T 3AB
**Web:** www.mcps-prs-alliance.co.uk
**Reg No:** 0134396 **Estd:** 1922 Private Company Limited By Guarantee
**Line of Business:** Other artistic and literary creation and interpretation
**Directors:** R J Ashcroft, M D Leeson, J R Manners, M G Fletcher, E Gregson, J F Nott, J B Minch, C M Butler
**Co. Secretary:** Ms Victoria Burnett
**Responsibilities**
**Senior:** Barry Blue *(Director)*, Edwin Cox *(Director)*, Nicholas Graham *(Director)*, Stuart Hornall *(Director)*, Stephen Levine *(Director)*, Paulette Long *(Director)*, Estelle Morris *(Director)*, Mitch Murray *(Director)*, Molly Nyman *(Director)*, Simon Platz *(Director)*
**Branches:** Performing Right Society,Ltd, Elwes House, 19 Church Walk, Peterborough, Cambridgeshire PE1 2UZ
**US SIC:** 8999, 5064
**UK SIC:** 83954, 61500
**Auditors:** Ernst & Young LLP
**Bankers:** National Westminster Bank Plc (60-40-02)

| | 31-12-13 | 31-12-12 | 31-12-11 |
|---|---|---|---|
| TO | 522,873,000 | 474,992,000 | 473,840,000 |
| P/L | 444,005,000 | 405,758,000 | 421,127,000 |
| NW | (33,226,000) | N/A | 3,779,000 |
| WC | (51,178,000) | (558,000) | (11,054,000) |
| Emp. | 600 | 24 | 26 |

DUNS 77-127-3653
### The Perfume Shop Ltd
(**Subsidiary of:** A.S. Watson (Europe) Holdings B.V.)
1 The Gateway Centre, Coronation Road, High Wycombe, Buckinghamshire HP12 3SU
**Tel:** 01494-539900
**Web:** www.theperfumeshop.co.uk
**Reg No:** 2699577 **VAT No:** 582839203
**Estd:** 1992 Private Limited Company
**Line of Business:** Representative office
**Export Sales:** £11,652,248
**Issued Capital:** £100,000
**Directors:** Dr A J Heaton, C N Salbaing, Ms M K Fellows, D K Lai, Ms G G Smith
**Co. Secretary:** Ms Edith Shih
**Responsibilities**
**Finance:** Jill Smith *(Financial Director)*
**IT:** Alistair Cossins *(Computer Manager)*
**HR:** Vicky Richardson *(Human Resources Manager)*
**Health & Safety:** Matt Hanwell *(Health & Safety Manager)*
**Facilities:** Tom Marsh *(Project Manager)*
**Branches:** The Perfume Shop Ltd, Phelans, 12-14 Crown Walk, Milton Keynes, Buckinghamshire MK9 3AH
**US SIC:** 2844, 5999
**UK SIC:** 25820, 65600
**Auditors:** PricewaterhouseCoopers LLP
**Bankers:** Barclays Bank Plc (20-65-82)

| | 28-12-13 | 29-12-12 | 31-12-11 |
|---|---|---|---|
| TO | 218,080,497 | 211,572,523 | 202,134,683 |
| P/L | 23,722,812 | 25,375,030 | 26,592,098 |
| NW | 17,988,984 | 93,218,549 | 75,244,332 |
| WC | 7,532,942 | 82,628,261 | 65,506,966 |
| Emp. | 2,148 | 2,055 | 1,750 |

DUNS 50-397-0154 **Imp-Exp**
### Peri Ltd
(**Subsidiary of:** Peri-Werk Artur Schwörer Gmbh & Co. Kg)
Market Harborough Road, Clifton Upon Dunsmore, Rugby, Warwickshire CV23 0AN
**Tel:** 01788-861600
**Web:** www.peri.ltd.uk
**Reg No:** 2403512 **VAT No:** 523151388
**Estd:** 1989 Private Limited Company
**Line of Business:** Renting of construction and civil engineering machinery and equipment
**Export Markets:** Rest of the World
**Export Sales:** £1,606,502
**Trading Style:** Peri U K
**Issued Capital:** £1,000,000
**Principals:** C F Heathcote *(Managing)*, A L Stables
**Co. Secretary:** Ms Trudie Swift
**Responsibilities**
**Senior:** Christian Schwoerer *(Manager)*
**Branches:** Peri, 331 Charles Street, Glasgow, Lanarkshire G21 2QA
**US SIC:** 7394 **UK SIC:** 84000
**Auditors:** PricewaterhouseCoopers LLP
**Bankers:** Lloyds TSB Bank plc (30-92-86)

| | 31-12-13 | 31-12-12 | 31-12-11 |
|---|---|---|---|
| TO | 24,066,528 | 22,625,850 | 21,945,076 |
| P/L | 2,044,592 | 629,386 | 2,049,305 |
| NW | 17,220,069 | 15,370,175 | 16,606,284 |
| WC | 2,477,464 | 490,429 | 4,315,065 |
| Emp. | 136 | 134 | 134 |

DUNS 21-880-4709
### Perinatal Mental Health Team
Florence House, 49 Alumhurst Road, Bournemouth, Dorset BH4 8EP
**Tel:** 01202584329
**Web:** www.dorsethealthcare.nhs.uk
**Estd:** 2012
**Line of Business:** Mental health centres
**Responsibilities**
**Senior:** Jagoda Banovic *(Team Manager)*, Liz James *(Manager)*
**US SIC:** 8091 **UK SIC:** 95200
**Employees:** 50

DUNS 21-735-6592
### Perins School
Pound Hill, Alresford, Hampshire SO24 9BS
**Tel:** 01962735930
**Web:** www.perins.net
**Reg No:** 7699705 **Estd:** 2011 Private Company Limited By Guarantee
**Line of Business:** General secondary education
**Directors:** Miss L E Billington, Mrs J S Bernard, Mrs K J Toms, K R Mcpherson, R Lawes, B Tucker, Ms C Malam, Mrs B A Cazalet
**Co. Secretary:** Philip Burridge
**Responsibilities**
**Senior:** Ase Cave *(Director)*, Janet Conway *(Director)*, Penelope Garnett *(Director)*, Edward Johnstone *(Director)*, Alison Mayne *(Director)*, Susan Pakenham-Walsh *(Director)*, Andrew Wild *(Director)*, Ellis Williams *(Director)*
**US SIC:** 8211 **UK SIC:** 93200
**Bankers:** Lloyds TSB Bank plc (30-00-00)

| | 31-08-14 | 31-08-13 | 31-08-12 |
|---|---|---|---|
| TO | 7,097,024 | 6,863,478 | 19,678,359 |
| P/L | 696,373 | 271,830 | 13,206,523 |
| NW | 13,855,726 | 13,254,353 | 12,968,523 |
| WC | 1,775,209 | 1,978,545 | 1,505,623 |
| Emp. | 125 | 133 | 115 |

DUNS 73-442-7367
### Perivan Ltd
21 Worship Street, London EC2A 2DW
**Tel:** 020-7562-2200 **Fax:** 020-7562-2203
**Web:** www.perivan.co.uk
**Reg No:** 4694449 **Estd:** 2003 Private Limited Company
**Line of Business:** Printers general
**Export Sales:** £506,436
**Trading Style:** Perivan Ltd
**Issued Capital:** £260,450
**Directors:** P G Williams, G L Hudson, R D Bishop
**Co. Secretary:** London Registrars Plc
**Responsibilities**
**Operations:** Danny Cruse *(Production Manager)*
**US SIC:** 2752, 7379, 6711, 7399
**UK SIC:** 47544, 83940, 83962, 83954
**Bankers:** Lloyds TSB Bank plc (30-15-97)

| | 31-07-13 | 31-07-12 | 31-07-11 |
|---|---|---|---|
| TO | 9,637,616 | 8,882,206 | 8,871,547 |
| P/L | 668,064 | 430,507 | 428,949 |
| NW | 1,411,091 | 1,299,108 | 1,141,725 |
| WC | 934,478 | 856,707 | 708,957 |
| Emp. | 69 | 67 | 63 |

DUNS 23-764-7883 **Imp-Exp**
### Perkinelmer Ltd
(**Subsidiary of:** Perkinelmer International C.V.)
Chalfont Road, Beaconsfield, Buckinghamshire HP9 2FX
**Tel:** 01494874515 **Fax:** 01443234340
**Web:** www.perkinelmer.com
**Reg No:** 3758366 **Estd:** 1999 Private Limited Company
**Line of Business:** Pharmaceutical suppliers and wholesalers
**Issued Capital:** £11,466,049
**Directors:** J L Healy, A J Crook
**Co. Secretary:** Ms Sandra Ward
**Responsibilities**
**Finance:** Gareth Michin *(Senior Finance Administrator)*
**IT:** Grant Jones *(Computer Operations Manager)*
**HR:** Jackie Thomas *(Human Resources Manager)*
**Purchasing:** Lisa Wines *(Purchasing Manager)*
**Branches:** Perkinelmer Ltd, Llantrisant Business Park, Pontyclun, Mid Glamorgan CF72 8YW
**US SIC:** 5122 **UK SIC:** 61800
**Auditors:** Deloitte LLP

| | 29-12-13 | 30-12-12 | 01-12-12 |
|---|---|---|---|
| TO | 16,999,000 | 16,278,000 | 15,129,000 |
| P/L | 1,388,000 | 1,320,000 | 1,135,000 |
| NW | 36,681,000 | 35,235,000 | 34,493,000 |
| WC | 35,350,000 | 33,717,000 | 33,097,000 |
| Emp. | 184 | 179 | 173 |

DUNS 23-764-7917
### Perkinelmer (U K) Holdings Ltd
(**Subsidiary of:** Perkinelmer International C.V.)
Ilex, Fishponds Road Mulberry Business Park, Wokingham, Berkshire RG41 2GY
**Tel:** 01189773003
**Web:** www.perkinelmer.co.uk
**Reg No:** 3758369 **Estd:** 1990 Private Limited Company
**Line of Business:** Management activities of holding companies
**Issued Capital:** £10,493,827
**Director:** J L Healy
**Co. Secretary:** Andrew Crook
**US SIC:** 6711 **UK SIC:** 83962
**Auditors:** Deloitte LLP

| | 29-12-13 | 30-12-12 | 01-12-12 |
|---|---|---|---|
| TA | 68,106,000 | 68,092,000 | 35,396,000 |
| P/L | (120,000) | 31,152,000 | (478,000) |
| NW | 17,214,000 | 17,334,000 | (13,818,000) |
| WC | (26,662,000) | (26,373,000) | (27,317,000) |

DUNS 51-644-5942
### Perkins + Will Uk Ltd
(**Subsidiary of:** The Perkins & Will Group Ltd)
10 Bonhill Street, Finsbury, London EC2A 4QJ
**Tel:** 02074661000
**Web:** www.perkinswill.com
**Reg No:** 5961514 **Estd:** 2006 Private Limited Company
**Line of Business:** Architectural woodwork
**Export Sales:** £2,944,715
**Issued Capital:** £1
**Directors:** P Harrison, J Pringle, C J Brandon
**Co. Secretary:** Brodie Stephens
**US SIC:** 8911 **UK SIC:** 83701

| | 29-12-13 | 31-12-12 | 31-12-11 |
|---|---|---|---|
| TO | 13,324,642 | N/A | N/A |
| P/L | 670,816 | N/A | N/A |
| NW | (5,650,415) | (4,903,614) | (160,593) |
| WC | 3,108,061 | 1,096,452 | (161,685) |
| Emp. | 108 | N/A | N/A |

DUNS 29-886-3192 **Exp**
### Perkins Engines Company Ltd
(**Subsidiary of:** Caterpillar Inc.)
Frank Perkins Way, Peterborough, Cambridgeshire PE1 5NA
**Tel:** 01733583000 **Fax:** 01733 58 2240
**Web:** www.perkins.com
**Reg No:** 2089227 **VAT No:** 661546137
**Estd:** 1987 Private Limited Company
**Line of Business:** Manufacture of engines and turbines, except aircraft, vehicle and cycle engines
**Export Sales:** £1,151,097,000
**Trading Style:** Perkins
**Issued Capital:** £768,945,000
**Directors:** M R Stratton, R Younessi, K J Epley, N J Burroughs, P A Clegg, M Dorsett
**Co. Secretary:** Mrs Janette Nicholls
**Responsibilities**
**Senior:** Andy Wheatcroft *(Factory Manager)*
**Sales:** Howard Beeken *(Sales Manager)*
**IT:** Andy Wheatcroft *(Factory Manager)*
**HR:** Nicole Aldred *(Human Resources Manager)*, Susan Humpreys *(Training Manager)*
**Facilities:** Andy Wheatcroft *(Factory Manager)*
**Purchasing:** Jonathan Beardmore *(Purchasing Manager)*
**Engineering:** Becky Adams *(Manufacturing Supervisor & Eng)*
**Branches:** Perkins Engines Company Limited, Perkins Powerpart Distribution Centre, Frank Perkins Way, Manchester M44 5PP
**US SIC:** 3519, 7399
**UK SIC:** 32811, 83954
**Auditors:** PricewaterhouseCoopers LLP
**Following financial data are in thousands**

| | 31-12-13 | 31-12-12 | 31-12-11 |
|---|---|---|---|
| TO | 1,400,200 | 1,316,510 | 1,560,240 |
| P/L | (2,824) | (69,822) | 22,616 |
| NW | 220,979 | 221,432 | 223,735 |
| WC | 58,636 | 134,269 | 118,308 |
| Emp. | 2,623 | 2,961 | 2,990 |

DUNS 22-558-0240 **Imp**
### Perkins Group Services Ltd
(**Subsidiary of:** Cathay Investments 2 Ltd)
45 Cobham Road, Ferndown Industrial Estate, Wimborne, Dorset BH21 7QZ
**Tel:** 01202-891-890 **Fax:** 01202-897-898
**Web:** www.perkinsgroup.co.uk
**Reg No:** 0568115 **VAT No:** 355847910
**Estd:** 1956 Private Limited Company
**Line of Business:** Wholesale of toys and games
**Trading Style:** Humatt
**Issued Capital:** £50,000
**Directors:** K A Johnson, B K Chaing
**Responsibilities**
**Senior:** Edward Gardener *(Manager)*, Kevin Pickering *(Manager)*, Terence Pugh *(Sales Director)*, Bramley Sparkes *(Manager)*
**Sales:** Terence Pugh *(Sales Director)*, Laurence Watford *(Sales Manager)*
**Health & Safety:** Martin Mullins *(Product Safety Officer)*
**Purchasing:** Adam Watson *(Buyer Manager)*
**US SIC:** 5199 **UK SIC:** 61900
**Auditors:** Menzies LLP

**Bankers:** HSBC Bank plc (40-03-05)

| | 31-12-13 | 31-12-12 | 31-12-11 |
|---|---|---|---|
| TO | 9,667,818 | 12,619,082 | 12,268,717 |
| P/L | (300,950) | (211,987) | 273,192 |
| NW | 1,796,310 | 2,090,937 | 2,257,888 |
| WC | 2,050,998 | 2,111,719 | 2,222,083 |
| Emp. | N/A | 61 | 67 |

DUNS 22-758-3978
## Perkins Slade Ltd
**(Subsidiary of:** Perkins Slade Forrest Holdings Ltd)
3 Broadway, Broad Street, Birmingham, West Midlands B15 1BQ
**Web:** www.perkins-slade.com
**Reg No:** 0969374 **Estd:** 1970 Private Limited Company
**Line of Business:** Activities auxiliary to insurance and pension funding
**Issued Capital:** £100,000
**Principals:** D M Slade *(Chairman)*, N J Tamblyn, Mrs J M Hulton-Harrop, R J Doubleday, A Ismail, R W Forrest
**Co. Secretary:** Aslam Ismail
**Branches:** Perkins Slade Ltd, Town Hall Chambers, Heath Road, Petersfield, Hampshire GU31 4TF
**US SIC:** 6411, 6399
**UK SIC:** 83200, 82001
**Auditors:** BDO Stoy Hayward
**Bankers:** Barclays Bank Plc (20-97-78)

| | 31-08-13 | 31-08-12 | 31-08-11 |
|---|---|---|---|
| TO | 5,295,096 | 5,230,840 | 5,611,379 |
| P/L | 103,204 | 88,126 | 78,153 |
| NW | 3,202,653 | 3,110,720 | 3,010,159 |
| WC | 2,979,451 | 2,815,992 | 3,066,269 |
| Emp. | 84 | 80 | 81 |

DUNS 23-536-5108
## Permal Investment Management Services Ltd
**(Subsidiary of:** Legg Mason Global Holdings Ltd)
12 St James's Square, London SW1Y 4LB
**Tel:** 020-7389-1300
**Web:** www.permal.com
**Reg No:** 3535219 **Estd:** 1998 Private Limited Company
**Line of Business:** Investment consultants
**Directors:** O Kodmani, F P Becquaert
**Co. Secretary:** Michael Mcdonough
**Responsibilities**
**Senior:** Thomas Delitto *(Manager)*
**Sales:** Shane Clifford *(Head of Global Business Develo)*, Roberto Giuffrida *(Executive VP International Bus)*
**US SIC:** 6371, 6111
**UK SIC:** 82002, 81501
**Auditors:** PricewaterhouseCoopers LLP
**Employees:** 545
**Turnover:** £284,563,000

DUNS 23-547-7515 **Imp-Exp**
## Permali Gloucester Ltd
170 Bristol Road, Gloucester, Gloucestershire GL1 5TT
**Web:** www.permali.co.uk
**Reg No:** 3546214 **VAT No:** 682442232
**Estd:** 1937 Private Limited Company
**Line of Business:** Plastics - engineering materials
**Export Sales:** £4,718,637
**Issued Capital:** £222,222
**Principals:** G King *(Managing)*, P D Carter
**Co. Secretary:** Nicholas Baird
**Responsibilities**
**Finance:** Sarah Minchew *(Financial Controller)*
**HR:** Sue Farmer *(Human Resources Coordinator)*
**US SIC:** 2821 **UK SIC:** 25140
**Auditors:** Hazlewoods LLP

| | 31-05-13 | 31-05-12 | 31-05-11 |
|---|---|---|---|
| TO | 9,807,810 | 9,288,851 | 9,579,859 |
| P/L | 105,181 | 290,068 | 197,068 |
| NW | 6,371,590 | 6,420,668 | 6,266,436 |
| WC | 5,009,590 | 4,976,138 | 4,855,337 |
| Emp. | 76 | 77 | 87 |

DUNS 21-228-8096 **Imp-Exp**
## Permanoid Ltd
**(Subsidiary of:** Davro Investments Ltd)
107 Hulme Hall Lane, Manchester M40 8HH
**Tel:** 01612056161
**Web:** www.permanoid.co.uk
**Reg No:** 0352908 **VAT No:** 677312716
**Estd:** 1939 Private Limited Company
**Line of Business:** Manufacturers cable and wire equipment
**Export Markets:** Europe, Middle East, Far East
**Export Sales:** £561,056
**Issued Capital:** £759,997
**Directors:** B K Hay, P J Stott, Mrs S Hingston, J D Monello Jr, D L Hingston
**Co. Secretary:** David Cresswell
**Responsibilities**
**Senior:** Joseph Monello *(Director)*
**HR:** Carl Cheffins *(Training Officer)*
**Health & Safety:** Carl Cheffins *(Training Officer)*
**Purchasing:** S Sandham *(Purchasing Manager)*
**Branches:** Permanoid Ltd, Suite 28, Smyth Rd, Bristol, Avon BS3 2BX
**US SIC:** 3357 **UK SIC:** 22470
**Auditors:** Cowgill Holloway
**Bankers:** National Westminster Bank Plc (60-08-46)

| | 30-09-13 | 30-09-12 | 30-09-11 |
|---|---|---|---|
| TO | 8,242,135 | 9,713,794 | 12,112,918 |
| P/L | (179,054) | (245,556) | 370,610 |
| NW | (1,214,270) | (1,049,248) | (733,692) |
| WC | 105,792 | 98,048 | (520,011) |
| Emp. | 54 | 57 | 57 |

DUNS 22-288-3477 **Imp**
## Permastore Group Ltd
Eye Airfield Industrial Estate Airfield, Industrial Park, Eye, Suffolk IP23 7HS
**Tel:** 01379-870723
**Web:** www.permastore.com
**Reg No:** 4306332 **Estd:** 2001 Private Limited Company
**Line of Business:** Management activities of holding companies
**Trading Style:** Permastore Group Ltd
**Issued Capital:** £328,122
**Directors:** I T Henry, D J Mann, E M Mannis, A R Gare, B L Quarendon
**US SIC:** 6711 **UK SIC:** 83962
**Bankers:** Barclays Bank Plc (20-17-19)

| | 30-03-14 | 31-03-13 | 01-03-12 |
|---|---|---|---|
| TO | 25,905,494 | 21,724,834 | 27,260,885 |
| P/L | 3,086,648 | 2,081,331 | 4,304,935 |
| NW | 5,531,170 | 3,896,314 | 5,075,414 |
| WC | 4,737,364 | 4,320,822 | 6,710,216 |
| Emp. | 210 | 190 | 201 |

DUNS 67-143-9560
## Permira Advisers Holdings Ltd
**(Subsidiary of:** Permira Holdings Ltd)
80 Pall Mall, London SW1Y 5ES
**Tel:** 02076321000
**Web:** www.permira.com
**Reg No:** 5983113 **Estd:** 2006 Private Limited Company
**Line of Business:** Investment companies and vehicles
**Issued Capital:** £50,001
**Directors:** D J Smith, P Gibbs
**Co. Secretary:** David O'Brien
**US SIC:** 6111 **UK SIC:** 81501
**Auditors:** PricewaterhouseCoopers LLP
**Bankers:** The Royal Bank Of Scotland Plc (16-71-67)

| | 31-12-13 | 31-12-12 | 31-12-11 |
|---|---|---|---|
| TA | 28,852,000 | 19,065,000 | 28,488,000 |
| P/L | 29,140,000 | 22,456,000 | 32,112,000 |
| NW | 1,503,000 | 1,291,000 | 1,062,000 |
| WC | 17,444,000 | 3,111,000 | 8,028,000 |
| Emp. | 65 | 84 | 76 |

DUNS 29-507-2177 **Imp**
## Pernod Ricard Uk Ltd
**(Subsidiary of:** Pernod Ricard Uk Holdings Ltd)
Building 12, London W4 5AN
**Tel:** 02085384484
**Web:** www.pernod-ricard.com
**Reg No:** 1870414 **VAT No:** 394708220
**Estd:** 1994 Private Limited Company
**Line of Business:** Agents involved in the sale of food, beverages and tobacco
**Trading Style:** Pernodricard Uk
**Issued Capital:** £5,547
**Directors:** Ms O Lagache, S Macnab, C Porta, E Mayle, L Lacassagne, H D Fetter, D R O'Flynn
**Responsibilities**
**Senior:** Thierry Billot *(Manager)*, Romain Darcos *(Manager)*, Nicolas Krantz *(Manager)*, Jean-Manuel Spriet *(Chief Executive Officer)*
**Finance:** Julia Massies *(Finance Director)*
**Marketing:** Adam Boita *(Head of Marketing - Absolut)*, Joanna Steel *(Senior Brand Manager - Absolut)*, Patrick Venning *(Marketing Director)*
**Sales:** Simon van Moppes *(Commercial Director)*
**HR:** Pam Rowan *(Human Resources Director)*
**Branches:** Pernod Ricard, Miltonduff Distillery, Elgin, Morayshire IV30 8TQ
**US SIC:** 5149 **UK SIC:** 61700
**Auditors:** Mazars LLP
**Bankers:** Barclays Bank Plc (20-72-17)

| | 30-06-13 | 30-06-12 | 30-06-11 |
|---|---|---|---|
| TO | 166,840,000 | 166,858,000 | 178,408,000 |
| P/L | 17,028,000 | 31,841,000 | 28,028,000 |
| NW | 477,428,000 | 459,917,000 | 426,914,000 |
| WC | 475,643,000 | 457,981,000 | 425,825,000 |
| Emp. | 239 | 242 | 250 |

DUNS 22-019-8217
## Peros Ltd
8 Century Point, Halifax Road, Cressex Business Park, High Wycombe, Buckinghamshire HP12 3SL
**Tel:** 01494-436426 **Fax:** 01494-769545
**Web:** www.peros.co.uk
**Reg No:** 4022650 **VAT No:** 757244415
**Estd:** 2002 Private Limited Company
**Line of Business:** Unlicensed restaurants and cafes
**Trading Style:** Peros Ltd
**Issued Capital:** £100
**Directors:** J L Roberts, A B O'Hare, P H Goodey
**Co. Secretary:** Ms Tracy Roberts
**Responsibilities**
**Senior:** Jim Imrie *(General Manager)*
**US SIC:** 7399, 2086
**UK SIC:** 83954, 42831
**Auditors:** Cannon Moorcroft Ltd
**Bankers:** Barclays Bank Plc (20-40-71)

| | 31-08-13 | 31-08-12 | 31-08-11 |
|---|---|---|---|
| TO | 22,503,996 | 22,001,901 | 20,483,722 |
| P/L | 2,015,353 | 2,072,777 | 2,219,367 |
| NW | 3,977,915 | 3,227,052 | 2,624,469 |
| WC | 3,068,641 | 2,388,580 | 1,922,448 |
| Emp. | 104 | 97 | 88 |

DUNS 29-057-6438
## Perpetual Portfolio Management Ltd
**(Subsidiary of:** Invesco Ltd.)
Perpetual Park, Perpetual Park Drive, Henley-On-Thames, Oxfordshire RG9 1HH
**Tel:** 01491417000 **Fax:** 01491-416000
**Web:** www.invescoperpetual.co.uk
**Reg No:** 1161477 **Estd:** 1974 Private Limited Company
**Line of Business:** Investment companies and vehicles
**Issued Capital:** £1,000,000
**Directors:** M S Mcloughlin, J Rowland
**Co. Secretary:** Ms Emma Pearce
**US SIC:** 7399 **UK SIC:** 83954
**Auditors:** Ernst & Young LLP

| | 31-12-13 | 31-12-12 | 31-12-11 |
|---|---|---|---|
| TA | 5,013,831 | 4,965,136 | 4,929,394 |
| P/L | 48,695 | 53,454 | 55,039 |
| NW | 5,013,831 | 4,965,136 | 4,911,682 |
| WC | N/A | N/A | 4,911,682 |

DUNS 42-350-1209 **Imp**
## Perrett Laver Ltd
8-10 Great George Street, London SW1P 3AE
**Fax:** 02073406201
**Web:** www.perrettlaver.com
**Reg No:** 4337808 **Estd:** 2001 Private Limited Company
**Line of Business:** Labour recruitment and provision of personnel
**Export Sales:** £2,346,793
**Issued Capital:** £100
**Director:** D R Perrett
**Co. Secretary:** Simon Laver
**Responsibilities**
**Senior:** Clementine Mckinley *(Chief Operations Manager)*
**US SIC:** 7361 **UK SIC:** 83954

| | 31-12-13 | 31-12-12 | 31-12-11 |
|---|---|---|---|
| TO | 7,951,772 | N/A | N/A |
| P/L | 1,968,861 | N/A | N/A |
| NW | 313,270 | 333,871 | 209,025 |
| WC | 259,991 | 298,437 | 186,362 |
| Emp. | 62 | N/A | N/A |

DUNS 29-038-5806
## Perrott Hill School Trust Ltd
North Perrott, Crewkerne, Somerset TA18 7SL
**Tel:** 0146-072051 **Fax:** 01460-78246
**Web:** www.perrott-hill.sch.co.uk
**Reg No:** 0894719 **Estd:** 1945 Private Limited Company
**Line of Business:** General secondary education
**Directors:** A B Leach, Mrs S J Thomas, R J King, M Longbottom, K R Moore, Mrs K Latham, Ms H I Carless, C A Knott
**Co. Secretary:** Neil Mapletoft
**Responsibilities**
**Senior:** John Bradbury *(Director)*, Lewis Findlay *(Manager)*, Geraldine Kerton-Johnson *(Director)*, Annette Smallwood *(Director)*
**Finance:** Angus Dunlop *(Bursar)*
**HR:** Angus Dunlop *(Bursar)*
**Health & Safety:** Angus Dunlop *(Bursar)*
**US SIC:** 8211 **UK SIC:** 93200
**Auditors:** Chalmers & Co
**Bankers:** National Westminster Bank Plc (60-06-24)

| | 31-08-14 | 31-08-13 | 31-08-12 |
|---|---|---|---|
| TO | 2,846,742 | 2,762,390 | 2,500,458 |
| P/L | 208,032 | 211,538 | 103,971 |
| NW | 1,581,942 | 1,373,671 | 1,161,770 |
| WC | (68,986) | 24,501 | 13,392 |
| Emp. | 55 | 52 | 51 |

DUNS 21-194-5365 **Imp-Exp**
## Perry Ellis Europe Ltd
**(Subsidiary of:** Perry Ellis International Inc)
Crittall Road, Witham, Essex CM8 3DJ
**Tel:** 01376502345
**Web:** www.farah.co.uk
**Reg No:** 0981294 **VAT No:** 232867158
**Estd:** 1970 Private Limited Company
**Line of Business:** Clothing wholesale and suppliers
**Export Markets:** Western Europe
**Export Sales:** £2,794,093
**Trading Style:** Farah, Penguin
**Issued Capital:** £11,000
**Directors:** Mrs F Feldenkreis Hanono, G Feldenkreis, Mrs J A Reeve
**Co. Secretary:** Darren Brown
**Responsibilities**
**Senior:** Alfie D'Costa *(Warehouse Manager)*, Oscar Feldenkreis *(President)*, Francisco Hoffmann *(Manager)*, George Pita *(Chief Executive)*, Rosemary Trudeau *(Manager)*
**Finance:** Bernadette Keasley *(Financial Controller)*
**Marketing:** J O'Boyle *(Sales & Marketing Director)*
**Sales:** J O'Boyle *(Sales & Marketing Director)*
**IT:** Ian Fulcher *(Computer Manager)*
**HR:** Julie Dow *(Human Resources Manager)*
**Operations:** Alfie D'Costa *(Warehouse Manager)*
**Engineering:** Alfie D'Costa *(Warehouse Manager)*, Patricia Tosh *(Production Manager)*
**Branches:** Perry Ellis Europe Ltd, Clarks Village, Farm Road, Street, Somerset BA16 0BB
**US SIC:** 5136, 5699, 2329
**UK SIC:** 61600, 64500, 45350
**Auditors:** Deloitte LLP
**Bankers:** Barclays Bank Plc (20-97-40)

| | 01-02-14 | 02-02-13 | 28-02-12 |
|---|---|---|---|
| TO | 32,879,322 | 29,773,874 | 28,647,131 |
| P/L | (1,369,795) | (1,668,958) | (851,617) |
| NW | (3,132,736) | (1,763,942) | (96,344) |
| WC | 9,588,671 | 9,113,577 | 9,017,016 |
| Emp. | 158 | 143 | 115 |

DUNS 21-224-4670
## Perry Locks
Perry Locks Nursing Home, Birmingham, West Midlands B44 8BG
**Tel:** 0121-3560598
**Web:** www.bupacarehomes.co.uk
**Estd:** 2002 Partnership
**Line of Business:** Nursing homes
**Partners:** Mrs S Slym, Mrs H Hunter
**Responsibilities**
**Senior:** Sandra Grierson *(Deputy Manager)*
**Finance:** Elaine Watts *(Administrator)*
**US SIC:** 8051 **UK SIC:** 95100
**Employees:** 113

DUNS 23-813-4444
## Perry Scott Nash Training Ltd
**(Subsidiary of:** Acoura Holdings Ltd)
Whittle Way, Arlington Business Park, Stevenage, Hertfordshire SG1 2FS
**Tel:** 01438745771 **Fax:** 01438745772
**Web:** www.perryscottnash.co.uk
**Reg No:** 3805752 **Estd:** 1999 Private Limited Company
**Line of Business:** Adult and other education not elsewhere classified
**Issued Capital:** £1
**Directors:** F Dick, P R Egan, S Kelly
**US SIC:** 8249, 7392
**UK SIC:** 93300, 83951

| | 31-03-14 | 30-09-12 | 30-03-11 |
|---|---|---|---|
| TA | 100 | 100 | 100 |
| NW | 100 | 100 | 100 |

DUNS 21-101-0110
## Perrymans Buses Ltd
Ramparts Business Park, Berwick-Upon-Tweed, Northumberland TD15 1TX
**Tel:** 01289-308719
**Web:** www.perrymansbuses.com
**Reg No:** 6445349 **Estd:** 2000 Private Limited Company
**Line of Business:** Bus operators and stations
**Issued Capital:** £10,000
**Director:** R J Perryman
**Co. Secretary:** Ms Linda Perryman
**Responsibilities**
**Sales:** Derek Macgregor *(Sales Director)*
**Admin:** Perrymen Linda *(Office Manager)*
**Health & Safety:** Roddy Perryman *(General Manager)*
**US SIC:** 4119 **UK SIC:** 72200

| | 31-01-14 | 31-01-13 | 31-01-12 |
|---|---|---|---|
| TA | 3,384,107 | 1,934,909 | 1,939,851 |
| NW | 863,435 | 596,717 | 412,268 |
| WC | (466,276) | (354,966) | (483,016) |

DUNS 21-206-7110

## Perrys Bury Ltd

(**Subsidiary of:** Perrys Group Ltd)
Crostons Road, Bury, Lancashire BL8 1AJ
**Tel:** 0161-764-2434 **Fax:** 0161-762-5584
**Web:** www.perrys.co.uk
**Reg No:** 0246224 **VAT No:** 673557013
**Estd:** 1930 Private Limited Company
**Line of Business:** Car dealers (new & used)
**Issued Capital:** £12,000
**Director:** K Savage
**Co. Secretary:** Neil Taylor
**Responsibilities**
**Senior:** Garry Allum *(Manager)*, Gill Ashton *(Manager)*, Darren Knight *(General Manager)*, Andy Lockey *(Parts Manager)*
**Finance:** Darren Knight *(General Manager)*
**Admin:** Rika Kirkpatrick *(Office Manager)*
**HR:** Rika Kirkpatrick *(Office Manager)*
**Facilities:** Darren Knight *(General Manager)*
**Purchasing:** Darren Knight *(General Manager)*
**US SIC:** 5511, 7539
**UK SIC:** 65100, 67100
**Auditors:** BDO Stoy Hayward

| | 31-12-13 | 31-12-12 | 31-12-11 |
|---|---|---|---|
| TA | 878,349 | 878,349 | 878,349 |
| NW | 878,349 | 878,349 | 878,349 |

DUNS 21-693-1977

## Perrys Chartered Accountants

34 Threadneedle Street, London EC2R 8AY
**Tel:** 02030516106
**Web:** www.perry-company.co.uk
**Estd:** 1977 Partnership
**Line of Business:** Accounting activities primarily bookkeeping
**Partners:** S Pope, S Hale
**Responsibilities**
**Senior:** Alex Skinner *(Managing Partner)*, Allan Taylor *(Partner)*
**US SIC:** 8931 **UK SIC:** 83600
**Employees:** 6

DUNS 21-860-0518

## Perrys Lancashire Ltd

(**Subsidiary of:** Perrys Group Ltd)
Accrington Road, Burnley, Lancashire BB11 5EX
**Tel:** 01282427321
**Web:** www.perrys.co.uk
**Reg No:** 0916658 **VAT No:** 145882638
**Estd:** 1977 Private Limited Company
**Line of Business:** Sale of new motor vehicles
**Trading Style:** Perrys Motors
**Issued Capital:** £104,000
**Director:** K Savage
**Co. Secretary:** Neil Taylor
**Responsibilities**
**Senior:** Nigel Denaline *(General Manager)*
**Marketing:** Terry Davies *(General Manager)*, Nigel Denaline *(General Manager)*
**Sales:** Terry Davies *(General Manager)*, Nigel Denaline *(General Manager)*
**US SIC:** 5511 **UK SIC:** 65100
**Auditors:** Tenon Audit Ltd

| | 31-12-13 | 31-12-12 | 31-12-11 |
|---|---|---|---|
| TA | 8,718 | 8,718 | 8,718 |
| NW | (281,223) | (281,223) | (281,223) |

DUNS 21-585-1070

## Perry's Motor Sales

Retail World, Stadium Way, Parkgate, Rotherham, South Yorkshire S60 1TG
**Tel:** 01709828484
**Web:** www.perrys.co.uk
**Estd:** 2002 Proprietorship
**Line of Business:** Car dealers (new & used)
**Proprietor:** Miss J Taylor
**Responsibilities**
**Senior:** Stephen Eyre *(General Manager)*
**US SIC:** 5511 **UK SIC:** 65100
**Employees:** 70

DUNS 21-304-3029

## Perrys Motor Sales Ltd

(**Subsidiary of:** Perrys Group Ltd)
Suite One 500 Pavilion Drive, Northampton Business Park, Northampton, Northamptonshire NN4 7YJ
**Tel:** 01604667300 **Fax:** 01254262117
**Web:** www.perrys.co.uk
**Reg No:** 0972286 **Estd:** 1970 Private Limited Company
**Line of Business:** Sale of new motor vehicles
**Trading Style:** Perrys of Bolton (Peugeot), Rocar Moores, Perrys Citroen, Perrys Group Ltd
**Issued Capital:** £16,979,443
**Directors:** R G Ingram, K Savage, Ms D Millard, D Ardron, R Sommerville
**Co. Secretary:** Neil Taylor
**Responsibilities**
**Senior:** Dave Walker-Smith *(Dealer Principal)*
**Finance:** Tony Cowpe *(Financial Manager)*
**Sales:** Paul Fagar *(Sales Manager)*, Dave Walker-Smith *(Dealer Principal)*
**Health & Safety:** Gill Hargreaves *(Health & Safety Officer)*
**Branches:** Perrys Motor Sales Ltd, Leeds Road, Huddersfield, West Yorkshire HD5 0RP
**US SIC:** 5511, 5521, 7539, 5531, 8299
**UK SIC:** 65100, 67100, 93300
**Auditors:** RSM Tenon Audit Ltd

| | 31-12-13 | 31-12-12 | 31-12-11 |
|---|---|---|---|
| TO | 491,477,000 | 439,638,000 | 429,062,000 |
| P/L | 6,779,000 | 4,013,000 | 1,752,000 |
| NW | 49,573,000 | 45,220,000 | 42,310,000 |
| WC | 4,121,000 | 3,201,000 | 4,113,000 |
| Emp. | 1,389 | 1,282 | 1,337 |

DUNS 21-810-7701

## Perrys of Barnsley

Perrys Motor Village, Claycliffe Road, Barugh Green, Barnsley, South Yorkshire S75 1LR
**Tel:** 01226417221
**Estd:** 2002
**Line of Business:** Car dealers (used)
**US SIC:** 5521 **UK SIC:** 65100
**Employees:** 88

DUNS 22-363-7518

## Perrys of Bolton (Peugeot)

Bridgeman Street, Bolton, Lancashire BL3 6BS
**Tel:** 01204-362747
**Web:** www.perrys.co.uk
**Estd:** 2000 Proprietorship
**Line of Business:** Sale of new motor vehicles
**Proprietor:** Miss G Ashton
**Responsibilities**
**Senior:** Gill Ashton *(Dealer Principal)*, Roy Hughes *(Service Manager)*, Jason Kenneth *(Branch Manager)*
**Finance:** Lynne Singer *(Accounts Manager)*
**Marketing:** Linda Leyland *(Marketing Manager)*
**Sales:** Gill Ashton *(Dealer Principal)*, Jason Kenny *(Sales Manager)*
**HR:** Gill Ashton *(Dealer Principal)*
**Health & Safety:** Roy Hughes *(Service Manager)*
**Purchasing:** Jason Kenny *(Sales Manager)*
**US SIC:** 5511, 7539
**UK SIC:** 65100, 67100
**Employees:** 48

DUNS 21-586-6353

## Perrys of Rotherham

Rotherham Road, Parkgate, Rotherham, South Yorkshire S60 1TG
**Tel:** 01709711552
**Web:** www.perrys.co.uk
**Estd:** 2002 Proprietorship
**Line of Business:** Sale of motor vehicles
**Proprietor:** R Lockwood
**Responsibilities**
**Senior:** Stephen Eyre *(Manager)*
**US SIC:** 5511 **UK SIC:** 65100
**Employees:** 73

DUNS 21-228-2989

## Perrys Peugeot

Whalley New Road, Blackburn, Lancashire BB1 6JT
**Tel:** 01254477212
**Web:** www.perrys.co.uk
**Proprietorship**
**Line of Business:** Car dealers (used)
**Proprietor:** D Walker-Smith
**Responsibilities**
**Finance:** Carl Midgley *(Finance Director)*
**Marketing:** Cathy Keightley *(Marketing Manager)*
**Sales:** Paul Sagar *(Sales Manager)*
**US SIC:** 5511 **UK SIC:** 65100
**Employees:** 60

DUNS 21-708-8590 **Exp**

## Perrys Recycling Ltd

(**Subsidiary of:** Perrys Holdings Ltd)
Rimpton Road, Marston Magna, Yeovil, Somerset BA22 8DL
**Tel:** 01935850111
**Web:** www.perrys-recycling.co.uk
**Reg No:** 1195655 **VAT No:** 131357495
**Estd:** 1962 Private Limited Company
**Line of Business:** Manufacture of other special purpose machinery not elsewhere classified
**Export Markets:** France, Spain, Germany
**Trading Style:** Perry Recycling
**Issued Capital:** £3,200
**Principals:** B F Perry *(Chairman and Managing)*, N S Perry, M A Perry, C J Perry
**Co. Secretary:** Ms Samantha Perry
**Branches:** Perrys Recycling Ltd, Bidna Yard, Unit 3, Bideford, Devon EX39 1LZ
**US SIC:** 3559, 8231
**UK SIC:** 32863, 97700
**Auditors:** Ivan Rendall & Co
**Bankers:** National Westminster Bank Plc (60-01-21)

| | 31-12-13 | 31-12-12 | 31-12-11 |
|---|---|---|---|
| TO | 6,121,256 | 5,979,741 | 8,441,778 |
| P/L | 19,656 | (41,683) | 601,547 |
| NW | 3,008,135 | 3,153,780 | 3,358,185 |
| WC | 1,175,683 | 1,154,368 | 1,356,751 |
| Emp. | 58 | 56 | 52 |

DUNS 51-602-8453

## Perrywood Nurseries

Kelvedon Road, Inworth, Colchester, Essex CO5 9SX
**Web:** www.perrywood.co.uk
**Estd:** 1984 Partnership
**Line of Business:** Garden centres
**Partners:** Mrs K Bourne, A Bourne
**US SIC:** 5999 **UK SIC:** 65600
**Employees:** 50

DUNS 21-158-4672

## The Perse School

Hills Road, Cambridge, Cambridgeshire CB2 8QF
**Web:** www.perse.co.uk
**Estd:** 2006
**Line of Business:** General secondary education
**Trading Style:** The Perse School
**Principals:** A Cook *(Chairman)*, N Richardson
**Responsibilities**
**Senior:** John Aston *(Manager)*, Anita Bunyan *(Manager)*, Linda Capper *(Manager)*, Christopher Dell *(Manager)*, Gerald Ellison *(Manager)*, Ian Galbraith *(Manager)*, Michael Pooles *(Manager)*, Rosamund Rainey *(Manager)*, Diana Shave *(Manager)*, Mary Webber *(Manager)*
**Finance:** Helen Parkhouse *(Bursar)*
**US SIC:** 8211 **UK SIC:** 93200
**Employees:** 175

DUNS 29-869-1411

## Pershing Ltd

(**Subsidiary of:** Pershing Llc)
Capstan House, London E14 2BH
**Tel:** 020-7864-8000
**Web:** www.pershing.co.uk
**Reg No:** 2072264 **Estd:** 1987 Private Limited Company
**Line of Business:** Security broking and related activities
**Export Sales:** £5,778,000
**Issued Capital:** £18,092,415
**Directors:** G D Hutt, Ms L A Dolly, M C Cole-Fontayn, P J Mahon, K Bonar, Ms J M Johnstone
**Co. Secretary:** Bny Mellon Secretaries (Uk) Limi
**Responsibilities**
**Marketing:** Scott Coey *(Head of Institutional Relation)*
**US SIC:** 6211 **UK SIC:** 83100
**Auditors:** Ernst & Young LLP
**Bankers:** National Westminster Bank Plc (60-00-01)

| | 31-12-13 | 31-12-12 | 31-12-11 |
|---|---|---|---|
| TA | 444,535,000 | 822,531,000 | 775,660,000 |
| P/L | (463,000) | 402,000 | 3,824,000 |
| NW | 186,350,000 | 79,444,000 | 81,771,000 |
| WC | 181,623,000 | 75,501,000 | 76,406,000 |
| Emp. | 466 | 539 | 581 |

DUNS 21-591-5833

## Pershore Community Hospital

Queen Elizabeth House, Queen Elizabeth Drive, Pershore, Worcestershire WR10 1PS
**Tel:** 01386502071
**Estd:** 2010 Proprietorship
**Line of Business:** Hospitals
**Proprietor:** Mrs K Young
**US SIC:** 8062 **UK SIC:** 95100
**Employees:** 100

DUNS 21-731-1686

## Pershore High School

Station Road, Pershore, Worcestershire WR10 2BX
**Tel:** 01386552471 **Fax:** 01386555104
**Web:** www.pershore.worcs.sch.uk
**Reg No:** 7665364 **Estd:** 2011 Private Company Limited By Guarantee
**Line of Business:** General secondary education
**Directors:** R T Charles, Mrs M Chippendale, Mrs E B Tucker, R Evans, T R West, N A Young, R G Dalton, Mrs N F Gow
**Co. Secretary:** Mrs Annette Davenport
**Responsibilities**
**Senior:** Steven Bessant *(Director)*, Graham Booth *(Director)*, Philippa Cavilla *(Director)*, Clive Corbett *(Director)*, Paul Featonby *(Director)*, Anita Iddon *(Director)*, Kenneth Rowe *(Director)*
**US SIC:** 8211 **UK SIC:** 93200

| | 31-08-14 | 31-08-13 | 31-08-12 |
|---|---|---|---|
| TO | 9,955,000 | 6,804,000 | 19,457,000 |
| P/L | 3,111,000 | 390,000 | 10,318,000 |
| NW | 13,311,000 | 10,578,000 | 10,145,000 |
| WC | 3,460,000 | 506,000 | 279,000 |
| Emp. | 149 | 128 | 213 |

DUNS 21-626-3426

## Persimmon Homes (Essex) Ltd

(**Subsidiary of:** Persimmon Plc)
10 Collingwood Road, Witham, Essex CM8 2EA
**Tel:** 01376518811
**Web:** www.persimmonhomes.com
**Reg No:** 0293769 **VAT No:** 512380088
**Estd:** 1934 Private Limited Company
**Line of Business:** Residential property developers
**Issued Capital:** £490,417
**Directors:** N P Greenaway, G N Francis, J Fairburn, M H Killoran
**Co. Secretary:** Miss Tracy Davison
**Responsibilities**
**Senior:** Edward Hollis *(Manager)*, Gerald Pople *(Manager)*
**Marketing:** Gerald Pople *(Manager)*
**Sales:** Gerald Pople *(Manager)*
**HR:** M Thirstion *(Chief Buyer)*
**Branches:** Persimmon Homes (Essex) Ltd, The Caines Thorpe Marriott, Norwich, Norfolk NR8 6FU
**US SIC:** 1522 **UK SIC:** 50100
**Auditors:** Unknown Auditor
**Bankers:** National Westminster Bank Plc (56-00-34)

| | 31-12-13 | 31-12-12 | 31-12-11 |
|---|---|---|---|
| TA | 6,148,336 | 6,148,336 | 6,148,336 |
| NW | 6,148,336 | 6,148,336 | 6,148,336 |

DUNS 22-804-1752

## Persimmon Homes (Wessex) Ltd

(**Subsidiary of:** Persimmon Plc)
Verona House, Tetbury Hill, Malmesbury, Wiltshire SN16 9JR
**Tel:** 01666-824721 **Fax:** 01666-826152
**Web:** www.persimmonhomes.com
**Reg No:** 1311348 **Estd:** 1972 Private Limited Company
**Line of Business:** Builders
**Issued Capital:** £3,000
**Directors:** M H Killoran, G N Francis, N P Greenaway, J Fairburn
**Co. Secretary:** Miss Tracy Davison
**Responsibilities**
**Senior:** Michael Farley *(group CEO)*
**Admin:** Tracy Trimble *(Office Manager)*
**Health & Safety:** Tracy Trimble *(Office Manager)*
**Fleet:** Tracy Trimble *(Office Manager)*
**Branches:** Persimmon Homes (Wessex) Ltd, Helme Bank, Kendal, Cumbria LA9 7PS
**US SIC:** 1799 **UK SIC:** 50000
**Bankers:** Lloyds TSB Bank plc (30-98-45)

| | 31-12-13 | 31-12-12 | 31-12-11 |
|---|---|---|---|
| TA | 33,359,000 | 33,359,000 | 33,359,000 |
| NW | 3,000 | 3,000 | 3,000 |
| WC | 3,000 | 3,000 | 3,000 |

DUNS 23-185-9906

## Persimmon Homes (West Scotland) Ltd

(**Subsidiary of:** Persimmon Plc)
180 Findochty Street, Garthamlock, Glasgow, Lanarkshire G33 5EP
**Tel:** 0141 766 2600
**Reg No:** 2717246 **Estd:** 1992 Private Limited Company
**Line of Business:** Construction of domestic buildings
**Issued Capital:** £100
**Directors:** J Fairburn, M H Killoran, G N Francis, N P Greenaway
**Co. Secretary:** Miss Tracy Davison
**Responsibilities**
**Senior:** Doug Law *(Manager)*
**US SIC:** 1522 **UK SIC:** 50100

| | 31-12-13 | 31-12-12 | 31-12-11 |
|---|---|---|---|
| TA | 26,177,000 | 26,177,000 | 26,177,000 |
| NW | (1,000) | (1,000) | (1,000) |
| WC | (1,000) | (1,000) | (1,000) |

DUNS 22-813-7451

## Persimmon Plc

Persimmon House, Fulford, York, North Yorkshire YO19 4FE
**Tel:** 01904642199
**Web:** www.persimmonhomes.com
**Reg No:** 1818486 **Estd:** 1984 Public Limited Company
**Line of Business:** Development and selling of real estate
**Issued Capital:** £30,383,576
**Directors:** N P Greenway, M R Preston, J R Davie, R Pennycook, Ms M J Sears, J Fairburn, D Jenkinson, M H Killoran
**Co. Secretary:** Gerald Francis

**Responsibilities**
**Senior:** Michael Farley *(Chief Executive Officer)*
**Finance:** Richard Stenhouse *(Group Tax & Treasury Director)*
**Branches:** Persimmon Plc, Churchward House, Churchward Road, Yate, Bristol, Avon BS37 5NN
**US SIC:** 6552, 6711
**UK SIC:** 85000, 83962
**Auditors:** KPMG Audit PLC
**Bankers:** The Royal Bank Of Scotland Plc (16-34-80)
**Following financial data are in thousands**

| | 31-12-13 | 31-12-12 | 31-12-11 |
|---|---|---|---|
| TO | 2,085,900 | 1,721,400 | 1,535,000 |
| P/L | 337,100 | 221,800 | 147,200 |
| NW | 1,807,600 | 1,749,200 | 1,588,500 |
| WC | 1,742,800 | 1,701,400 | 1,538,000 |
| Emp. | 2,791 | 2,515 | 2,432 |

DUNS 73-828-4046
## The Personal Finance Society
20 Aldermanbury, London EC2V 7HY
**Tel:** 020-8530-0852
**Web:** www.thepfs.org
**Reg No:** 5084125 **Estd:** 2004 Private Company Limited By Guarantee
**Line of Business:** Insurance services
**Directors:** N J Turner, D J Thomson, Mrs S A Sutton, K Richards, D Ingram, Ms T M Perchard, Doctor A W Scott, D G Thomas
**Co. Secretary:** Rowan Paterson
**Responsibilities**
**Senior:** Jonathon Everill *(Manager)*, Fay Goddard *(Manager)*, Garry Hale *(Director)*, Cathleen Harrison *(Director)*, Brendan O'Ciobhain *(Director)*
**US SIC:** 6411 **UK SIC:** 83200

| | 31-12-13 | 31-12-12 | 31-12-11 |
|---|---|---|---|
| TO | 7,105,000 | 6,157,000 | 5,354,000 |
| P/L | 792,000 | 199,000 | 83,000 |
| NW | 3,637,000 | 2,884,000 | 2,693,000 |
| WC | 3,637,000 | 2,884,000 | 2,693,000 |

DUNS 45-848-3096
## Personal Group Holdings Plc
John Ormond House, 899 Silbury Boulevard, Milton Keynes, Buckinghamshire MK9 3XL
**Tel:** 01908-605000
**Web:** www.personal-group.com
**Reg No:** 3194991 **Estd:** 1996 Public Limited Company
**Line of Business:** Management activities of holding companies
**Issued Capital:** £1,503,233
**Directors:** M W Scanlon, C J Curling, K W Rooney, M Winlow, M I Dugdale
**Co. Secretary:** Mrs Sarah Mace
**Responsibilities**
**Senior:** Lynne Foster *(Manager)*
**Finance:** Simon Ingman *(Finance Director)*
**Marketing:** Alison Kidgell *(Group Marketing Director)*
**Sales:** Mike Govier *(Key Account Director)*
**IT:** Richard Tilbury *(IT Director)*
**Health & Safety:** Ben Begeant *(Health & Safety Officer)*
**US SIC:** 6711 **UK SIC:** 83962
**Auditors:** KPMG LLP
**Bankers:** The Co-Operative Bank Plc (08-90-01)

| | 31-12-13 | 31-12-12 | 31-12-11 |
|---|---|---|---|
| TO | 22,572,000 | 20,924,000 | 27,478,000 |
| P/L | 3,730,000 | 8,320,000 | 10,015,000 |
| NW | 25,163,000 | 24,592,000 | 22,757,000 |
| WC | 4,107,000 | 1,293,000 | (235,000) |
| Emp. | 171 | 163 | 164 |

DUNS 21-145-5690
## Personal Reclaims Ltd
20 Garrick Lane, New Waltham, Grimsby, South Humberside DN36 4WD
**Tel:** 08004581224
**Web:** www.ppiukclaims.co.uk
**Reg No:** 6760146 **Estd:** 2008 Private Limited Company
**Line of Business:** Activities auxiliary to financial intermediation not elsewhere classified
**Issued Capital:** £1,000
**Directors:** Mrs P J Marshall, E E Marshall
**Responsibilities**
**Senior:** Tricia Marshall *(Manager)*
**US SIC:** 6111 **UK SIC:** 81501

| | 31-03-14 | 31-03-13 | 31-03-12 |
|---|---|---|---|
| TA | 15,823 | 24,852 | 18,319 |
| NW | (6,940) | 3,896 | 9,219 |
| WC | (7,475) | 2,801 | 7,405 |

DUNS 42-404-0546
## Personal Telephone Fundraising Ltd
Tower Point, 44 North Road, Brighton, East Sussex BN1 1YR
**Fax:** 01273-819156
**Web:** www.ptf.org
**Reg No:** 4391744 **Estd:** 1992 Private Limited Company
**Line of Business:** Fund raising services charitable and non charitable
**Issued Capital:** £1
**Director:** Ms J A Cunningham
**Co. Secretary:** Ms Denise Bishop
**Responsibilities**
**Admin:** Debbie Knight *(Office Manager)*
**US SIC:** 8321 **UK SIC:** 96111

| | 31-03-14 | 31-03-13 | 31-03-12 |
|---|---|---|---|
| TA | 1,077,730 | 968,138 | 1,113,805 |
| NW | 612,176 | 491,242 | 448,725 |
| WC | 543,844 | 403,602 | 408,735 |

DUNS 51-592-1398
## Personal Touch Holdings Ltd
3 Bickenhill Lane Trinity Park, Birmingham, West Midlands B37 7ES
**Tel:** 01217671000
**Web:** www.personaltouchfs.com
**Reg No:** 5872883 **Estd:** 2006 Private Limited Company
**Line of Business:** Activities auxiliary to financial intermediation not elsewhere classified
**Trading Style:** Personal Touch Financial Services Ltd
**Issued Capital:** £2,084,747
**Directors:** M T Wadelin, A S Hurl-Hodges, D A Edwards, M J Wright, N A Bacon, Mrs M J Cross, D Carrington, Miss K Pearson
**Responsibilities**
**IT:** Donald Chin *(IT manager)*
**US SIC:** 6111, 6311
**UK SIC:** 81501, 82002
**Auditors:** Deloitte & Touche LLP

| | 31-12-13 | 31-12-12 | 31-12-11 |
|---|---|---|---|
| TA | 30,047,365 | 34,774,637 | 20,990,704 |
| P/L | (909,269) | (3,345,777) | (3,850,689) |
| NW | (6,096,189) | (17,653,963) | (14,996,592) |
| WC | 15,993,599 | 18,431,565 | 5,963,842 |
| Emp. | 156 | 195 | 220 |

DUNS 21-714-3072 **Imp-Exp**
## Personnel Hygiene Services Ltd
**(Subsidiary of:** Phs Group Holdings Ltd)
Block B, Western Industrial Estae, Lon-Y, Caerphilly, Mid Glamorgan CF83 1XH
**Tel:** 02920-851-000
**Web:** www.phs.co.uk
**Reg No:** 0770813 **VAT No:** 542951438
**Estd:** 1963 Private Limited Company
**Line of Business:** Other business activities not elsewhere classified
**Export Markets:** W Europe
**Trading Style:** P H S, Jpen Medical
**Issued Capital:** £14,634,800
**Directors:** J A Tydeman, S A Woods, C R Kemball
**Co. Secretary:** David Finlayson
**Responsibilities**
**Senior:** Gareth Rhys Williams *(Director)*, John Skidmore *(Manager)*, gareth williams *(Manager)*
**Branches:** Personnel Hygiene Services Ltd, Unit 1, Wessex Way, Winchester, Hampshire SO21 1WP
**US SIC:** 7399, 7349
**UK SIC:** 83954, 92300
**Auditors:** PricewaterhouseCoopers LLP
**Bankers:** Bank Of Scotland (80-20-00)

| | 31-03-14 | 31-03-13 | 31-03-12 |
|---|---|---|---|
| TO | 288,782,000 | 287,165,000 | 282,730,000 |
| P/L | (186,520,000) | 39,581,000 | 51,293,000 |
| NW | (334,856,000) | (311,153,000) | (323,015,000) |
| WC | (427,599,000) | (442,758,000) | (457,758,000) |
| Emp. | 3,646 | 3,437 | 3,356 |

DUNS 22-522-5986
## Personnel Selection Associates Ltd
3 High Street, Woking, Surrey GU21 6BG
**Tel:** 01483765544 **Fax:** 01483756258
**Web:** www.personnelselection.co.uk
**Reg No:** 1002037 **VAT No:** 492809902
**Estd:** 1997 Private Limited Company
**Line of Business:** Employment and recruitment companies and consultants
**Trading Style:** Personnel Selection
**Issued Capital:** £375,000
**Director:** J J Agace
**Co. Secretary:** Mark Carter
**Responsibilities**
**Senior:** Lorraine Lovelock *(General Manager)*
**Branches:** Personnel Selection Associates Ltd, 108A London Road, Bognor Regis, West Sussex PO21 1BD
**US SIC:** 7361 **UK SIC:** 83954
**Auditors:** Menzies
**Bankers:** Barclays Bank Plc (20-97-58)

| | 31-12-13 | 31-12-12 | 31-12-11 |
|---|---|---|---|
| TO | N/A | 6,293,857 | 7,139,285 |
| P/L | N/A | 92,402 | 208,229 |
| NW | 527,559 | 575,406 | 608,624 |
| WC | 457,279 | 507,029 | 579,054 |
| Emp. | N/A | 419 | 469 |

DUNS 21-102-3591
## Perspective Financial Group Ltd
Paradigm House, Wilmslow, Cheshire SK9 3ND
**Tel:** 08456881454
**Web:** www.pfgl.co.uk
**Reg No:** 6455775 **Estd:** 2007 Private Limited Company
**Line of Business:** Financial advisers (independent)
**Issued Capital:** £1,249
**Directors:** Mosaic Private Equity Limited, D J Hesketh, Mrs J S Hepworth, P M Newton, M P Rogan, I M Wilkinson, P H Hogarth
**Co. Secretary:** David Hesketh
**Responsibilities**
**Marketing:** Sharon Seed *(Marketing Manager)*
**US SIC:** 6111 **UK SIC:** 81501
**Auditors:** Langtons

| | 31-12-13 | 31-12-12 | 31-12-11 |
|---|---|---|---|
| TA | 26,816,028 | 32,814,228 | 32,011,292 |
| P/L | (5,422,990) | (1,454,253) | (1,971,772) |
| NW | (34,136,627) | (32,439,501) | (30,911,867) |
| WC | (16,312,319) | (5,851,500) | (5,246,404) |
| Emp. | 225 | 250 | 238 |

DUNS 23-678-6760 **Imp**
## Perstorp Uk Ltd.
**(Subsidiary of:** Pai Partners)
Baronet Road, Warrington, Cheshire WA4 6HA
**Tel:** 01925 591111
**Web:** www.perstorp.com
**Reg No:** 2715398 **VAT No:** 616034079
**Estd:** 1992 Private Limited Company
**Line of Business:** Manufacture of other chemical products not elsewhere classified
**Issued Capital:** £40,010,000
**Directors:** Mrs J M Driessen, Ms E Sohlberg
**Co. Secretary:** David Turner
**Branches:** Perstorp Uk Ltd., 40 Seaton, Tamworth, Staffordshire B77 2NP
**US SIC:** 2899 **UK SIC:** 25670
**Auditors:** PricewaterhouseCoopers LLP
**Bankers:** National Westminster Bank Plc (01-07-08)

| | 31-12-13 | 31-12-12 | 31-12-11 |
|---|---|---|---|
| TO | 77,704,000 | 76,594,000 | 82,831,000 |
| P/L | (9,201,000) | (2,737,000) | 4,777,000 |
| NW | (2,558,000) | (11,424,000) | (15,845,000) |
| WC | (11,337,000) | (9,282,000) | (18,075,000) |
| Emp. | 88 | 86 | 85 |

DUNS 34-639-1092
## Pert Bruce Construction Ltd
Broomfield Industrial Estate, Broomfield Road, Montrose, Angus DD10 8SY
**Tel:** 01674-673883 **Fax:** 01674-678533
**Web:** www.pertbruce.co.uk
**Reg No:** 0284392SC **Estd:** 2005 Private Limited Company
**Line of Business:** Construction of commercial buildings
**Issued Capital:** £50,000
**Directors:** J M Pert, G Davies, J K Bruce, B Bryant, C Bruce, G Forrest
**Co. Secretary:** Mrs Sharon Bruce
**Responsibilities**
**Health & Safety:** Lawrence Francis *(Health & Safety Officer)*
**US SIC:** 1541, 1522
**UK SIC:** 50100

| | 31-10-13 | 31-10-12 | 31-10-11 |
|---|---|---|---|
| TA | 3,425,796 | 3,064,616 | 2,858,751 |
| NW | 661,807 | 603,294 | 581,258 |
| WC | (17,038) | (48,038) | (21,303) |

DUNS 73-620-9334
## Pertemps Ltd
**(Subsidiary of:** Pertemps Network Group Ltd)
32-33 Foregate Street, Worcester, Worcestershire WR1 1EE
**Tel:** 0190524420
**Web:** www.pertemps.co.uk
**Reg No:** 4881571 **Estd:** 1999 Private Limited Company
**Line of Business:** Employment and recruitment companies and consultants
**Issued Capital:** £26,188
**Directors:** Miss T M Evans, S West, K Thompson, Ms C Perry, J E Smith, S C Mogano, Ms C Watson, Ms M White
**Co. Secretary:** Nigel Dudley
**Responsibilities**
**Senior:** Carl Dohery *(Branch Manager)*, Alan Ratcliffe *(Director)*
**Branches:** Pertemps Ltd, 8A Albert Road, Middlesbrough, Cleveland TS1 1QA
**US SIC:** 7361 **UK SIC:** 83954
**Auditors:** Deloitte & Touche LLP
**Bankers:** HSBC Bank plc (40-01-01)

| | 31-12-13 | 31-12-12 | 31-12-11 |
|---|---|---|---|
| TO | 352,204,000 | 357,589,000 | 310,174,000 |
| P/L | 10,359,000 | 5,315,000 | 4,563,000 |
| NW | 11,084,000 | 2,564,000 | (1,255,000) |
| WC | 20,090,000 | 13,181,000 | 8,604,000 |
| Emp. | 752 | 682 | 535 |

DUNS 21-745-7283
## Pertemps Network Group Ltd
Meriden Hall Main Road, Meriden, Coventry, West Midlands CV7 7PT
**Tel:** 01676525000
**Reg No:** 7776671 **Estd:** 2011 Private Limited Company
**Line of Business:** Labour recruitment and provision of personnel
**Issued Capital:** £73,596,216
**Directors:** C R Hurley, Ms J A Jackson, D J Waller, K Thompson, R Englefield, M R Owen, Mrs C Watson, S R Jones
**Co. Secretary:** Nigel Dudley
**US SIC:** 7361 **UK SIC:** 83954
**Bankers:** Lloyds TSB Bank plc (30-00-03)

| | 31-12-13 | 31-12-12 |
|---|---|---|
| TO | 468,419,000 | 411,041,000 |
| P/L | 6,127,000 | 4,649,000 |
| NW | (25,659,000) | (27,925,000) |
| WC | 12,608,000 | 10,951,000 |
| Emp. | 1,207 | 1,024 |

DUNS 29-005-1713
## Perth & Kinross Association of Voluntary Service Ltd
The Gateway, Perth, Perthshire PH1 5PP
**Tel:** 01738-567076
**Web:** www.pkavs.org.uk
**Reg No:** 0086065SC **Estd:** 1984 Private Company Limited By Guarantee
**Line of Business:** Charities and charitable organisations
**Trading Style:** Volunteering in Action
**Directors:** S Bolland, Mrs G E Mackay, J A Mcguinness, A Chan, A J Fyfe, Mrs D J Knight, Mrs L Paul, Ms K M Frew
**Co. Secretary:** Elliot & Company Ws
**Responsibilities**
**Senior:** Michael Duke *(Manager)*, Graham Fleming *(Manager)*, Raymond Jamieson *(Senior Manager)*, John Leggate *(Manager)*, Helen Mackinnon *(Chief Executive)*, George Millar *(General Manager)*
**Branches:** Perth & Kinross Association Of Voluntary Service Ltd, The Gateway Centre, North Methven Street, Perth, Perthshire PH1 5PP
**US SIC:** 8321 **UK SIC:** 96111
**Auditors:** Moir Wood & Co
**Bankers:** The Royal Bank Of Scotland Plc (83-47-00)

| | 31-03-14 | 31-03-13 | 31-03-12 |
|---|---|---|---|
| TO | 1,696,215 | 1,723,201 | 1,666,644 |
| P/L | 98,897 | 45,650 | (65,083) |
| NW | 920,253 | 821,356 | 775,706 |
| WC | 342,644 | 244,506 | 187,626 |
| Emp. | 61 | 62 | 68 |

DUNS 21-192-8114
## Perth & Kinross Council
2 High Street, Perth, Perthshire PH1 5PH
**Tel:** 01738-475000 **Fax:** 01738-475510
**Web:** www.pkc.gov.uk
**Estd:** 2011 Incorporate By Act Of Parliament
**Line of Business:** Central government
**Trading Style:** Blairgowrie High School, Collace Primary School, Goodburn School
**Principals:** A R Mcarthur *(Financial)*, R Jackson, H Robertson, G A Beaton
**Responsibilities**
**Finance:** A McArthur *(Financial Director)*
**Branches:** Perth & Kinross Council, 56 King Street, Crieff, Perthshire PH7 3AX
**US SIC:** 9121, 7399
**UK SIC:** 91110, 83954
**Bankers:** Bank Of Scotland (80-91-28)
**Employees:** 200

DUNS 23-226-0836
## Perth & Kinross N H S Trust
Trust Offices, Perth Royal Infirmary, Perth, Perthshire PH1 1NX
**Tel:** 01382423000
**Web:** www.cylex-uk.co.uk
**Estd:** 1994
**Line of Business:** Gen medical & surgical hospitals
**Principals:** Ms P Ballie *(Financial)*, F Brown
**Branches:** Perth & Kinross N H S Trust, Alyth Health Centre, New Alyth Road, Blairgowrie, Perthshire PH11 8EQ
**US SIC:** 8062 **UK SIC:** 95100
**Bankers:** The Royal Bank Of Scotland Plc (83-47-00)
**Employees:** 2,600

DUNS 29-860-3382
## Perthshire Visitor Centre Ltd
Bankfoot, Perth, Perthshire PH1 4EB
**Tel:** 01738-787696 **Fax:** 01738-787120
**Web:** www.perthshirevisitorcentre.co.uk
**Reg No:** 0101359SC **Estd:** 1987 Private Limited Company
**Line of Business:** Restaurants
**Issued Capital:** £30,000
**Principals:** G W Girvan *(Managing)*, C J Maclellan
**Co. Secretary:** Ms Catriona Girvan

**US SIC:** 5399, 5812
**UK SIC:** 65600, 66110
**Auditors:** Michael Revels & Co
**Bankers:** Bank Of Scotland (80-91-26)

| | 31-03-14 | 31-03-13 | 31-03-12 |
|---|---|---|---|
| TA | 1,416,955 | 1,414,010 | 1,444,281 |
| NW | 1,219,842 | 1,129,190 | 1,017,177 |
| WC | 266,194 | 125,172 | (27,853) |

DUNS 77-754-1608
## Perthyn
Vivian Court, Llys Felin Newydd, Swansea, West Glamorgan SA7 9FG
**Tel:** 01792-311980 **Fax:** 01792-311999
**Web:** www.perthyn.org.uk
**Reg No:** 3017158 **Estd:** 1995 Private Limited Company
**Line of Business:** Activities of households as employers of domestic staff
**Directors:** Mrs A Phillips, A L Thomas, N J Wood, Mrs A M Gasgoine, J Lord, D W Lloyd, Mrs D R Williams, Mrs F L Blakeley
**Co. Secretary:** Stephen Cox
**Branches:** Perthyn, Orion House, Nelson Quay, Milford Haven, Dyfed SA73 3AZ
**US SIC:** 8811, 8321
**UK SIC:** 99000, 96111
**Auditors:** Haines Watts Wales LLP
**Bankers:** HSBC Bank plc (40-43-31)

| | 31-03-14 | 31-03-13 | 31-03-12 |
|---|---|---|---|
| TO | 16,689,013 | 17,894,308 | 16,914,711 |
| P/L | 11,124 | 565,776 | 35,342 |
| NW | 1,870,189 | 1,768,341 | 1,191,372 |
| WC | 954,197 | 824,432 | 339,976 |
| Emp. | 667 | 765 | 733 |

DUNS 21-813-3510
## Pertwee & Back Ltd
Gapton Hall Road, Great Yarmouth, Norfolk NR31 0NJ
**Web:** www.pertweeandback.co.uk
**Reg No:** 0237370 **VAT No:** 105101835
**Estd:** 1929 Private Limited Company
**Line of Business:** Sale of new motor vehicles
**Issued Capital:** £2,012
**Principals:** M T Coller *(Chairman)*, R S Coller *(Managing)*, T M Coller, N L Coller
**Co. Secretary:** Stephen Hatton
**Branches:** Pertwee & Back,Ltd, Southgates Road, Great Yarmouth, Norfolk NR30 3LF
**US SIC:** 5511, 5521, 7539, 5531
**UK SIC:** 65100, 67100
**Auditors:** Larking Gowen
**Bankers:** Barclays Bank Plc (20-99-21)

| | 31-10-13 | 31-10-12 | 31-10-11 |
|---|---|---|---|
| TO | 47,749,135 | 27,335,111 | 26,830,462 |
| P/L | 101,526 | (141,542) | (75,984) |
| NW | 2,143,779 | 2,028,744 | 2,404,903 |
| WC | 1,201,673 | 1,091,306 | 1,331,383 |
| Emp. | 67 | 69 | 77 |

DUNS 34-881-2566
## Pervasive Ltd
Rivergate House, Newbury Business Park, London Road, Newbury, Berkshire RG14 2PZ
**Tel:** 0870-004-0002
**Web:** www.pervasive.co.uk
**Reg No:** 5679204 **Estd:** 2006 Private Limited Company
**Line of Business:** Miscellaneous computer services
**Issued Capital:** £214
**Directors:** K M Cahoon, A J Langley, R R Bennett
**Co. Secretary:** Bradley Shore
**US SIC:** 7379 **UK SIC:** 83940

| | 31-03-14 | 31-03-13 | 31-03-12 |
|---|---|---|---|
| TO | 21,465,478 | 12,667,536 | 11,028,784 |
| P/L | 1,889,652 | 1,299,857 | 1,211,018 |
| NW | 3,212,273 | 4,594,703 | 3,812,134 |
| WC | 2,683,796 | 4,262,038 | 3,487,230 |
| Emp. | 72 | 35 | 30 |

DUNS 76-369-0435
## P.E.S. Holdings Ltd
124 Emily Street, Birmingham, West Midlands B12 0XJ
**Tel:** 01214-405995
**Reg No:** 2551489 **Estd:** 1990 Private Limited Company
**Line of Business:** Management activities of holding companies
**Issued Capital:** £1,200
**Director:** J Evans
**Co. Secretary:** Mrs Linda Evans
**US SIC:** 6711, 6111
**UK SIC:** 83962, 81501

| | 31-03-14 | 31-03-13 | 31-03-12 |
|---|---|---|---|
| TA | 1,439,055 | 1,400,826 | 1,293,757 |
| NW | 1,411,081 | 1,343,351 | 1,244,652 |
| WC | 1,161,837 | 1,089,417 | 986,028 |

DUNS 71-937-2521
## Peshawear (U.K.) Ltd
Millers Three, Southmill Road, Bishops Stortford, Hertfordshire CM23 3DH
**Tel:** 01279306257 **Fax:** 01279306259
**Web:** www.peshawear.co.uk
**Reg No:** 5318077 **Estd:** 2004 Private Limited Company
**Line of Business:** Wholesale of clothing and footwear
**Export Sales:** £1,578,995
**Trading Style:** Boardman Brothers
**Issued Capital:** £225,000
**Directors:** P J Wright, G Miklaucich, J B Phillips, Mrs J E Wright
**Co. Secretary:** Mrs Jane Wright
**Responsibilities**
**Senior:** Joanne Worrall *(Manager)*
**US SIC:** 5136 **UK SIC:** 61600

| | 31-01-14 | 31-01-13 | 31-01-12 |
|---|---|---|---|
| TO | 16,666,507 | 17,035,280 | 18,692,768 |
| P/L | 10,005 | 784,408 | 794,796 |
| NW | 701,924 | 485,874 | (319,526) |
| WC | 521,713 | 879,826 | 411,691 |
| Emp. | 50 | 60 | 65 |

DUNS 21-412-5819
## Pestana Chelsea Bridge Hotel
354 Queenstown Road, London SW8 4AE
**Tel:** 02070628000
**Web:** www.pestana.com
**Estd:** 2010 Proprietorship
**Line of Business:** Hotels and motels without restaurant
**Proprietor:** Miss P Nascimento
**US SIC:** 7999 **UK SIC:** 97913
**Employees:** 100

DUNS 50-498-6472
## Pet City Ltd
**(Subsidiary of:** Pets At Home Holdings Limited)
Epsom Avenue, Stanley Green Tradin, Handforth, Wilmslow, Cheshire SK9 3RN
**Tel:** 01279422790
**Reg No:** 2466773 **Estd:** 1971 Private Limited Company
**Line of Business:** OTHER SPEC.RET.DIST(NON-FOOD)
**Issued Capital:** £43,390,000
**Directors:** I Kellett, N Wood
**Co. Secretary:** Ms Louise Stonier
**Branches:** Pet City Ltd, Worthington Way, Wigan, Lancashire WN3 6XA
**US SIC:** 5999 **UK SIC:** 65600
**Auditors:** KPMG LLP
**Bankers:** National Westminster Bank Plc (01-06-88)

| | 27-03-14 | 28-03-13 | 29-03-12 |
|---|---|---|---|
| TA | 4,947,000 | 4,947,000 | 4,947,000 |
| NW | 4,947,000 | 4,947,000 | 4,947,000 |

DUNS 23-776-5156
## Pet Doctors Ltd
**(Subsidiary of:** C V S Group Plc)
1 Vinces Road, Diss, Norfolk IP22 4AY
**Tel:** 02380255565 **Fax:** 08448584018
**Web:** www.petdoctors.co.uk
**Reg No:** 3769799 **Estd:** 2002 Private Limited Company
**Line of Business:** Veterinary activities
**Issued Capital:** £100
**Directors:** S Innes, N J Perrin, B H Pound
**Co. Secretary:** Mrs Rebecca Cleal
**Responsibilities**
**Senior:** Michael Hode *(Senior Vet)*
**Branches:** Pet Doctors Ltd, 145 Cobham Road, Leatherhead, Surrey KT22 9HX
**US SIC:** 0741 **UK SIC:** 95601
**Auditors:** Lewis Brownlee
**Bankers:** National Westminster Bank Plc (51-50-00)

| | 30-06-14 | 30-06-13 | 30-06-12 |
|---|---|---|---|
| TO | 11,626,000 | 12,148,000 | 11,865,000 |
| P/L | 1,015,000 | 1,601,000 | 1,181,000 |
| NW | 1,786,000 | 1,021,000 | (243,000) |
| WC | 892,000 | 128,000 | (1,082,000) |
| Emp. | 186 | 185 | 189 |

DUNS 52-566-6723
## Pet Vaccination Clinic Ltd
**(Subsidiary of:** Your Vets (Holdings) Ltd)
Unit 2 Rumbush Farm, Birmingham, West Midlands B9 5LW
**Tel:** 01564 701830
**Web:** www.petvaccinationclinic.com
**Reg No:** 3252801 **VAT No:** 859951952
**Estd:** 1996 Private Limited Company
**Line of Business:** Veterinary activities
**Trading Style:** Yourvets
**Issued Capital:** £2
**Directors:** Mrs L Bruce, Ms S Wright, Mrs J C Martin
**Co. Secretary:** Michael Bishop
**Responsibilities**
**Senior:** Jonathan Stirling *(Director)*
**Purchasing:** Anne O'Donnell *(Logistics Support)*
**Branches:** Pet Vaccination Clinic Ltd - 1-7 Whalebone Lane South, Dagenham, RM8 1AH Essex
**US SIC:** 0741 **UK SIC:** 95601
**Auditors:** Stewart Fletcher & Barrett
**Bankers:** The Royal Bank Of Scotland Plc (16-08-85)

| | 31-03-14 | 31-03-13 | 31-03-12 |
|---|---|---|---|
| TO | 9,171,217 | 8,212,223 | N/A |
| P/L | (36,081) | (321,639) | N/A |
| NW | 1,227,029 | 1,293,055 | 1,589,897 |
| WC | (7,817) | (13,536) | 204,878 |
| Emp. | 207 | 205 | N/A |

DUNS 49-095-0102
## Pet-Xi Training Ltd
Unit 10 Westwood House, Westwood Business Park, Coventry, West Midlands CV4 8HS
**Tel:** 02476-420-310 **Fax:** 02476-462-621
**Web:** www.pet-xi.co.uk
**Reg No:** 3092428 **Estd:** 1994 Private Limited Company
**Line of Business:** Educational training
**Trading Style:** Pet Learning
**Issued Capital:** £101
**Directors:** C G Sexton, Mrs F J Sexton
**Co. Secretary:** Mrs Gaye Darkins
**US SIC:** 8299, 8211
**UK SIC:** 93300, 93200
**Auditors:** Crowthers Chartered Accountants
**Bankers:** Lloyds TSB Bank plc (30-94-93)

| | 31-12-13 | 31-12-12 | 31-12-11 |
|---|---|---|---|
| TA | 825,506 | 486,537 | 315,833 |
| NW | 315,848 | 136,422 | 55,030 |
| WC | 262,871 | 126,201 | 43,580 |

DUNS 29-133-1593
## Peta Ltd
Access Point, Northarbour Road, Portsmouth, Hampshire PO6 3TE
**Tel:** 02392454445
**Web:** www.peta.co.uk
**Reg No:** 1653178 **VAT No:** 339092739
**Estd:** 1982 Private Company Limited By Guarantee
**Line of Business:** Training centres
**Principals:** R S Hiskey *(Managing)*, N V Iacobucci, A D Zemenides, Mrs A E New, A M Waring, S P Escott, N P Loader, K J Rough
**Co. Secretary:** Ms Janice Wynton
**Responsibilities**
**Senior:** Philip Deer *(Director)*, Dawn Halfacre *(Facilities Manager)*
**HR:** Sarah Duffett *(Personnel Officer)*
**Health & Safety:** Dawn Halfacre *(Facilities Manager)*
**Facilities:** Dawn Halfacre *(Facilities Manager)*
**Branches:** Peta Ltd, 5 New Lane, Kenwood Business Park, Havant, Hampshire PO9 2NT
**US SIC:** 8299 **UK SIC:** 93300
**Auditors:** Evans Pearce
**Bankers:** National Westminster Bank Plc (56-00-64)

| | 31-07-14 | 31-03-13 | 31-07-12 |
|---|---|---|---|
| TO | 4,903,800 | 3,457,907 | 3,530,302 |
| P/L | 251,193 | (82,089) | (82,943) |
| NW | 3,783,377 | 3,532,184 | 3,614,273 |
| WC | 803,948 | 578,813 | 573,354 |
| Emp. | 65 | 64 | 68 |

DUNS 21-041-1441
## Petagon Vauxhall
Pinnacle Storage Park, Cat & Fiddle Lane, Ilkeston, Derbyshire DE7 6HE
**Tel:** 01159-445505
**Estd:** 2002
**Line of Business:** Fleet management
**Partner:** R Sisson
**Responsibilities**
**Senior:** Keith West *(General Manager)*
**US SIC:** 7399 **UK SIC:** 83954
**Employees:** 50

DUNS 22-925-0949 **Imp-Exp**
## Petal Postforming Ltd
Dromore Road, Enniskillen, Co Fermanagh BT94 1ET
**Tel:** 028-6862-1766 **Fax:** 028-6862-1004
**Web:** www.petal.co.uk
**Reg No:** 0014306NI **Estd:** 1981 Private Limited Company
**Line of Business:** Manufacture of builders carpentry and joinery
**Export Markets:** Republic of Ireland
**Trading Style:** Petal Postforming Ltd
**Issued Capital:** £85,000
**Directors:** M D Monaghan, D J Monaghan
**Co. Secretary:** Patrick Monaghan
**Branches:** Petal Postforming Ltd, Gibbs House, Kennel Ride, Ascot, Berkshire SL5 7NT
**US SIC:** 2431, 8911, 3079
**UK SIC:** 46300, 83701, 48360
**Bankers:** The Bank Of Ireland (90-48-86)

| | 31-03-14 | 31-03-13 | 31-03-12 |
|---|---|---|---|
| TA | 1,866,915 | 2,336,385 | 2,280,926 |
| NW | 736,039 | 1,185,335 | 1,105,421 |
| WC | 867,134 | 1,316,641 | 1,148,928 |

DUNS 77-525-7157 **Exp**
## Petards Group Plc
390 Princesway North, Gateshead, Tyne and Wear NE11 0TU
**Fax:** 01914-203030
**Web:** www.petards.com
**Reg No:** 2990100 **VAT No:** 727287803
**Estd:** 1994 Public Limited Company
**Line of Business:** Management activities of holding companies
**Export Markets:** Rest of world
**Export Sales:** £777,000
**Issued Capital:** £6,367,100
**Directors:** T R Connolly, R M Abdullah, P J Negus, O Abdullah
**Co. Secretary:** Andrew Wonnacott
**Responsibilities**
**Senior:** Timothy Wightman *(Manager)*
**Marketing:** Steven Proudfoot *(Marketing Manager)*
**Health & Safety:** Brian Taite *(quality manufacturing engineer)*
**Engineering:** Brian Taite *(quality manufacturing engineer)*
**Branches:** Petards Group Plc, The Old Barn, Abingdon, Oxfordshire OX14 4PS
**US SIC:** 6711, 3662
**UK SIC:** 83962, 34430
**Auditors:** KPMG Audit PLC
**Bankers:** Bank Of Scotland (12-18-05)

| | 31-12-13 | 31-12-12 | 31-12-11 |
|---|---|---|---|
| TO | 6,259,000 | 9,013,000 | 12,127,000 |
| P/L | (2,388,000) | 206,000 | 215,000 |
| NW | 695,000 | 586,000 | (618,000) |
| WC | 1,523,000 | (51,000) | (1,429,000) |
| Emp. | 83 | 89 | 93 |

DUNS 23-208-0895
## Peter Bedford Housing Association Ltd
Gillett Street, London N16 8JH
**Tel:** 02079239255
**Web:** www.peterbedford.org.uk
**Reg No:** 0020037IP **Estd:** 1981
**Line of Business:** Non-charitable social work activities with accommodation
**Trading Style:** Peter Bedford Trust
**Responsibilities**
**Senior:** Clare Norton *(Chief Executive)*
**Branches:** Peter Bedford Housing Association Ltd, 27 Stacey St, London N7 7JQ
**US SIC:** 8321 **UK SIC:** 96111
**Auditors:** Beever & Struthers

| | 31-03-12 | 31-03-11 | 31-03-10 |
|---|---|---|---|
| TO | 3,919,022 | 3,923,048 | 3,716,280 |
| P/L | 727,098 | 190,953 | 46,742 |
| NW | 2,017,403 | 987,728 | 796,773 |
| WC | 1,209,012 | 540,165 | 677,104 |
| Emp. | 60 | 63 | 62 |

DUNS 21-788-7121
## Peter Black Footwear and Accessories
Woolworth House 242 246, Marylebone Road, London NW1 6JQ
**Estd:** 2011 Proprietorship
**Line of Business:** Footwear mnfrs - component suppliers
**Proprietor:** Miss D Young
**US SIC:** 3149 **UK SIC:** 45100
**Employees:** 80

DUNS 50-397-1871
## Peter Blake (Clumber) Ltd
**(Subsidiary of:** Vertu Motors Plc)
464 Chatsworth Road, Chesterfield, Derbyshire S40 3BD
**Tel:** 01246-245200
**Web:** www.bristolstreet.co.uk
**Reg No:** 2403690 **Estd:** 1989 Private Limited Company
**Line of Business:** Car dealers (new & used)
**Issued Capital:** £100,000
**Directors:** M Sherwin, Ms K Anderson, R T Forrester
**Co. Secretary:** Ms Karen Anderson
**Branches:** Peter Blake (Clumber) Ltd, Retford Road, Worksop, Nottinghamshire S80 2QD
**US SIC:** 5511, 7539
**UK SIC:** 65100, 67100
**Auditors:** Grant Thornton
**Bankers:** HSBC Bank plc (40-17-15)

| | 29-02-12 |
|---|---|
| NW | (275,154) |

DUNS 21-106-0703
## Peter Brett Associates Llp
Caversham Bridge House, Waterman Place, Reading, Berkshire RG1 8DN
**Tel:** 0118-950-0761
**Web:** www.peterbrett.com
**Reg No:** 0334398OC **Estd:** 2000
**Line of Business:** Engineers (consulting)

**Responsibilities**
**Senior:** Robert Brickwood *(Partner)*, Gregory Callaghan *(Non-designated Limited Liabili)*, Malcolm Cleaver *(Partner)*, Francis Connolley *(Partner)*, Stephen Dellow *(Partner)*, Martin Dix *(Non-designated Limited Liabili)*, Martin Duris *(Partner)*, Clive Edmonds *(Non-designated Limited Liabili)*, Nora Galley *(Partner)*, Iain Gibb *(Partner)*, Bernard Greep *(Non-designated Limited Liabili)*, Paul Jenkin *(Partner)*, Fergal Kelly *(Non-designated Limited Liabili)*, Sarah Matthews *(Non-designated Limited Liabili)*, Kieth Mitchel *(Partner)*, Rahul Patalia *(Non-designated Limited Liabili)*, Nicholas Patterson *(Non-designated Limited Liabili)*, Robert Pinkett *(Partner)*, Richard Puttock *(Partner)*, Kieran Rushe *(Non-designated Limited Liabili)*, Anthony Russel *(Partner)*, Richard Swinden *(Partner)*, Antony Wake *(Partner)*, Matthew Whiston *(Partner)*, Scott Witchalls *(Partner)*
**Finance:** Alec Stevens *(Head of Finance)*
**HR:** Claudia Desai *(Head of Human Resources)*, Nicola Shaw *(Training Manager)*
**Facilities:** Jeff Mead *(Facilities Manager)*
**Branches:** Peter Brett Associates Llp, Calgarth House, 39-41 Bank Street, Ashford, Kent TN23 1DQ
**US SIC:** 8911 **UK SIC:** 83701
**Auditors:** BDO LLP

| | 30-06-13 | 31-03-12 | 31-06-11 |
|---|---|---|---|
| TO | 44,937,518 | 32,209,224 | 25,896,754 |
| P/L | 3,129,581 | 1,336,919 | 764,651 |
| NW | (6,483,000) | (7,942,000) | (4,664,000) |
| WC | 8,520,825 | 8,199,592 | 7,446,821 |
| Emp. | 370 | 366 | 366 |

DUNS 22-608-7112
## Peter Cooper Motor Group Ltd
2-4 Botley Road, Southampton, Hampshire SO30 2WA
**Tel:** 01489-783434 **Fax:** 01489787600
**Web:** www.petercoopergroup.co.uk
**Reg No:** 1588003 **Estd:** 1981 Private Limited Company
**Line of Business:** Car dealers (new & used)
**Trading Style:** Cooper Roundabout
**Issued Capital:** £65,000
**Principals:** P J Cooper *(Managing)*, D J Cooper, G S Austin, P S Lee
**Co. Secretary:** Ms Marilyn Cooper
**Responsibilities**
**Senior:** Doug Viney *(Parts)*
**Sales:** Darren Batchelor *(Sales Manager)*, Harvey Hodgson *(Sales Manager)*, Lee Kelly *(Sales Manager)*, Kevin Mathewson *(Sales Manager)*, Graham New *(Senior Sales Executive)*
**US SIC:** 5511, 7539, 5531
**UK SIC:** 65100, 67100
**Auditors:** Fiander Tovell LLP
**Bankers:** Barclays Bank Plc (20-79-25)

| | 31-12-13 | 31-12-12 | 31-12-11 |
|---|---|---|---|
| TO | 65,102,363 | 56,961,308 | 35,824,704 |
| P/L | 818,883 | 702,492 | 165,082 |
| NW | 1,966,683 | 1,486,015 | 1,048,158 |
| WC | 1,404,156 | 846,432 | 745,008 |
| Emp. | 195 | 192 | 172 |

DUNS 23-618-3518
## Peter Cooper (Portsmouth) Ltd
(**Subsidiary of:** Peter Cooper Motor Group Ltd)
Bilton Way, Portsmouth, Hampshire PO3 5FH
**Tel:** 023-9266-1000 **Fax:** 023-9265-4166
**Web:** www.petercoopergroup.co.uk
**Reg No:** 3615486 **Estd:** 1999 Private Limited Company
**Line of Business:** Sale of new motor vehicles
**Issued Capital:** £100
**Principals:** P J Cooper *(Managing)*, D J Cooper, P S Lee
**Responsibilities**
**Marketing:** Phil Brine *(Sales & Marketing Manager)*
**Sales:** Phil Brine *(Sales & Marketing Manager)*
**Admin:** Gin Vincent *(Administrator)*
**HR:** Gin Vincent *(Administrator)*
**US SIC:** 5511, 7539, 5531
**UK SIC:** 65100, 67100
**Auditors:** Fiander Tovell & Co

| | 31-12-13 | 31-12-12 | 31-12-11 |
|---|---|---|---|
| TA | 214,284 | 214,284 | 2,448,835 |
| NW | 214,284 | 214,284 | (32,670) |
| WC | N/A | N/A | (95,313) |

DUNS 21-314-7259
## Peter Duffy Ltd
Park View, Wakefield, West Yorkshire WF3 3HA
**Tel:** 01924-871100
**Web:** www.peterduffyltd.com
**Reg No:** 1051852 **Estd:** 1972 Private Limited Company
**Line of Business:** Civil engineers
**Issued Capital:** £1,000
**Principals:** P G Duffy *(Managing)*, R J Hudson, K Duffy, N M Duffy, M F Duffy
**Co. Secretary:** John Davidson
**Responsibilities**
**Senior:** Robert Scroggins *(Manager)*
**US SIC:** 8911, 1541
**UK SIC:** 83701, 50100
**Auditors:** PKF (UK) LLP
**Bankers:** HSBC Bank plc (40-27-15)

| | 31-05-14 | 31-05-13 | 31-05-12 |
|---|---|---|---|
| TO | 38,275,178 | 32,474,179 | 25,153,446 |
| P/L | 4,597,297 | 1,790,066 | 1,813,377 |
| NW | 12,595,197 | 9,348,113 | 8,005,078 |
| WC | 5,418,517 | 2,735,503 | 1,825,308 |
| Emp. | 484 | 408 | 310 |

DUNS 21-225-4218
## Peter G Whiteman
Temple Queen Elizabeth Buildings, London EC4Y 9BS
**Tel:** 02079363131
**Web:** www.qebholliswhiteman.co.uk
**Estd:** 1975 Proprietorship
**Line of Business:** Solicitors
**Proprietor:** P G Whiteman
**US SIC:** 8111 **UK SIC:** 83500
**Employees:** 60

DUNS 29-053-2266
## Peter Gabriel Ltd
Real World Studios, Mill Lane, Box, Corsham, Wiltshire SN13 8PL
**Tel:** 0845-146-1730
**Web:** www.petergabriel.com
**Reg No:** 1102482 **Estd:** 1990 Private Limited Company
**Line of Business:** Publishing of sound recordings
**Export Sales:** £2,905,585
**Issued Capital:** £1,100
**Principals:** P B Gabriel *(Managing)*, M D Large, Mrs A F Goldsworthy
**Co. Secretary:** David Hatchman
**US SIC:** 3652 **UK SIC:** 34520
**Auditors:** Grant Thornton
**Bankers:** Coutts & Co (18-00-13)

| | 31-12-13 | 31-12-12 | 31-12-11 |
|---|---|---|---|
| TO | 12,394,572 | 13,136,322 | 13,301,345 |
| P/L | 770,786 | 701,046 | 185,377 |
| NW | (2,219,435) | (2,867,969) | (3,224,483) |
| WC | (2,062,772) | (2,623,363) | (3,113,470) |
| Emp. | 91 | 90 | 72 |

DUNS 23-963-3089
## Peter Gradon Meat & Poultry Marketing Ltd
Marsh Dene Farm, Marsh Lane, Halifax, West Yorkshire HX3 9NR
**Tel:** 01422-353033
**Web:** www.gradons.uk.com
**Reg No:** 3952266 **VAT No:** 333478157
**Estd:** 1979 Private Limited Company
**Line of Business:** Wholesale of meat and meat products
**Issued Capital:** £2,000
**Principals:** P W Gradon *(Managing)*, Ms B Gradon
**Co. Secretary:** Peter Gradon
**Responsibilities**
**Senior:** Mark Halliday *(Transport Manager)*
**Fleet:** Mark Halliday *(Transport Manager)*
**US SIC:** 5147, 2013
**UK SIC:** 61700, 41223
**Auditors:** Crowthers
**Bankers:** Yorkshire Bank Plc (05-04-49)

| | 01-11-13 | 02-11-12 | 04-11-11 |
|---|---|---|---|
| TO | 10,186,037 | 9,079,757 | 11,203,117 |
| P/L | 241,467 | 279,126 | 306,472 |
| NW | 5,633,987 | 5,440,627 | 5,203,537 |
| WC | 3,840,610 | 4,193,200 | 4,235,706 |
| Emp. | 61 | 60 | 59 |

DUNS 21-742-2815 **Imp-Exp**
## Peter Grant Papers Ltd
(**Subsidiary of:** Repap Holdings Ltd)
Stafford Park 12, Telford, Shropshire TF3 3BJ
**Tel:** 01952-292200 **Fax:** 08007835324
**Web:** www.petergrantpapers.com
**Reg No:** 1329787 **VAT No:** 314005811
**Estd:** 1978 Private Limited Company
**Line of Business:** Paper products
**Export Markets:** worldwide
**Issued Capital:** £2,060,000
**Directors:** P E King, A S Fecher, P Fecher
**Co. Secretary:** Paul King
**Responsibilities**
**Operations:** Mark Monk *(Production Manager)*
**Engineering:** Mark Monk *(Production Manager)*
**Branches:** Peter Grant Papers Ltd, Caton Road, Lansil Industrial Estate, Lancaster, Lancashire LA1 3NX
**US SIC:** 2654 **UK SIC:** 47280
**Auditors:** AdamsLeeClark
**Bankers:** Barclays Bank Plc (20-38-83)

| | 31-12-13 | 31-12-12 | 31-12-11 |
|---|---|---|---|
| TO | 19,076,445 | 22,471,490 | 23,667,492 |
| P/L | (2,208,053) | (1,122,544) | (1,688,592) |
| NW | (998,472) | 1,130,735 | 2,161,050 |
| WC | (779,503) | (2,586,757) | (1,794,123) |
| Emp. | 173 | 176 | 189 |

DUNS 21-712-5533 **Imp**
## Peter Green Haulage Ltd
(**Subsidiary of:** Fricor Ltd)
Leighton Lane, Shepton Mallet, Somerset BA4 6LQ
**Tel:** 01749830824 **Fax:** 01749-830825
**Web:** www.petergreenchilled.co.uk
**Reg No:** 1296004 **VAT No:** 290981623
**Estd:** 1960 Private Limited Company
**Line of Business:** Road haulage and transport services
**Export Sales:** £3,016,517
**Trading Style:** Peter Green Chilled
**Issued Capital:** £50,000
**Directors:** T A Binks, A W Binks, N J Haggett, W A Binks
**Co. Secretary:** Allan Binks
**Responsibilities**
**Senior:** Marjorie Egan *(Manager)*
**HR:** Isobel Binks *(Human Resources Manager)*
**Purchasing:** Jeanette Chance *(Purchasing Coordinator)*
**Branches:** Peter Green Haulage Ltd, Unit 12, Childerditch Hall Drive, Little Warley, Brentwood, Essex CM13 3HD
**US SIC:** 4789, 4226
**UK SIC:** 77002, 77003
**Auditors:** Grant Thornton

| | 31-12-13 | 31-12-12 | 31-12-12 |
|---|---|---|---|
| TO | 16,788,793 | 14,516,071 | 15,746,297 |
| P/L | (504,882) | (655,742) | (64,826) |
| NW | 2,823,190 | 3,307,072 | 3,847,234 |
| WC | (945,091) | (2,267,813) | (429,488) |
| Emp. | 170 | 179 | 152 |

DUNS 21-581-2349
## Peter Guild
Bonsall Street, Nottingham, Nottinghamshire NG10 2AL
**Tel:** 01159729863
**Web:** www.peterguild.co.uk
**Estd:** 2007 Proprietorship
**Line of Business:** Manufacture of chairs and seats
**Proprietor:** Mrs C Steed
**Responsibilities**
**Senior:** Michael Steed *(Manager)*
**US SIC:** 2599 **UK SIC:** 46720
**Employees:** 100

DUNS 21-103-7222
## Peter H Smith (Holdings) Ltd
Chain Caul Way, Ashton-On-Ribble, Preston, Lancashire PR2 2YL
**Tel:** 01772333000
**Web:** www.peterhsmith.com
**Reg No:** 6466371 **Estd:** 2008 Private Limited Company
**Line of Business:** Management activities of holding companies
**Issued Capital:** £10,000
**Director:** N P Smith
**Co. Secretary:** Ms Ann Rainford
**Responsibilities**
**Sales:** Martin Pritchard *(Sales Manager)*
**US SIC:** 6711 **UK SIC:** 83962

| | 30-09-13 | 30-09-12 | 30-09-11 |
|---|---|---|---|
| TO | 9,492,364 | 10,414,524 | 10,256,385 |
| P/L | 312,485 | 355,329 | 363,590 |
| NW | 1,556,238 | 1,388,134 | 1,207,513 |
| WC | 389,373 | 319,475 | 141,858 |
| Emp. | 71 | 68 | 67 |

DUNS 21-811-0480
## Peter Hodgkinson Centre
Greetwell Road, Lincoln, Lincolnshire LN2 5UA
**Estd:** 2012
**Line of Business:** Nhs clinics
**Responsibilities**
**Senior:** Gill Hunt *(Team Leader)*
**US SIC:** 8062 **UK SIC:** 95100
**Employees:** 700

DUNS 29-012-4320
## Peter Howard Ltd
25a High Street, Ramsbury, Marlborough, Wiltshire SN8 2QN
**Tel:** 01672-520466 **Fax:** 01672-520813
**Reg No:** 0387497 **Estd:** 1944 Private Limited Company
**Line of Business:** Gunsmiths
**Issued Capital:** £250
**Directors:** D P Mills, R W Mills
**Co. Secretary:** Mrs Frances Mills
**US SIC:** 3489, 5251
**UK SIC:** 32901, 64800
**Bankers:** Barclays Bank Plc (20-49-08)

| | 31-12-13 | 31-12-12 | 31-12-11 |
|---|---|---|---|
| TO | N/A | 136,702 | 127,393 |
| P/L | N/A | (2,002) | 429 |
| NW | 28,456 | 24,209 | 26,211 |
| WC | 33,537 | 26,137 | 23,497 |

DUNS 21-138-4521
## Peter Hunt's Bakery Ltd
(**Subsidiary of:** David Wood Baking Uk Ltd)
Unit 14 Lyon Road Industrial Estate, Kearsley, Bolton, Lancashire BL4 8NB
**Tel:** 08453011900
**Web:** www.dwbaking.com
**Reg No:** 6709170 **VAT No:** 940829901
**Estd:** 2009 Private Limited Company
**Line of Business:** Bakers shops
**Director:** D A Wood
**Co. Secretary:** Ms Karen Wood
**US SIC:** 2099 **UK SIC:** 42399
**Auditors:** WHS Accountants Ltd

| | 29-03-14 | 30-03-13 | 31-03-12 |
|---|---|---|---|
| TO | N/A | 21,163,471 | 15,168,825 |
| P/L | N/A | 67,028 | 162,454 |
| NW | 1 | 1,653,901 | 1,801,034 |
| WC | N/A | N/A | (472,525) |
| Emp. | N/A | 164 | 144 |

DUNS 22-140-0281
## Peter Lea Waste Management Ltd
2 Abbey Road, Birkenhead, Merseyside CI41 5FQ
**Tel:** 01516472647
**Web:** www.skiphiremerseyside.com
**Reg No:** 4158902 **Estd:** 2001 Private Limited Company
**Line of Business:** Recycling
**Issued Capital:** £2,000
**Director:** P R Lea
**Co. Secretary:** Ms Deborah Lea
**US SIC:** 3341, 4953
**UK SIC:** 22470, 92110
**Auditors:** Hamilton Burke Dufau
**Bankers:** National Westminster Bank Plc (60-05-07)

| | 30-06-14 | 30-06-13 | 30-06-12 |
|---|---|---|---|
| TA | 104,169 | 117,342 | 106,827 |
| NW | (9,229) | (3,755) | (29,138) |
| WC | (68,491) | (77,846) | (105,532) |

DUNS 21-221-1437 **Imp-Exp**
## Peter Marsh & Sons Ltd
47 Canal Street, Bootle, Merseyside L20 8AE
**Fax:** 0151-922-3804
**Web:** www.petermarsh.co.uk
**Reg No:** 0186560 **Estd:** 1837 Private Limited Company
**Line of Business:** Manufacture of corrugated paper and paperboard, sacks and bags
**Issued Capital:** £160,000
**Principals:** S P Marsh *(Chairman and Managing)*, P W Durrance, P H Marsh, N J Hinton, B A Marsh, C R Marlow
**Co. Secretary:** Alan Hughes
**Responsibilities**
**Senior:** John Dobbs *(Production Manager)*, David Ewen *(Manager)*
**Sales:** David Ewen *(Manager)*
**IT:** Paul Guilmin *(IT Manager)*
**Operations:** John Dobbs *(Production Manager)*
**Engineering:** John Dobbs *(Production Manager)*
**US SIC:** 2645, 2654
**UK SIC:** 47280
**Auditors:** Lonsdale & Marsh

| | 31-12-13 | 31-12-12 | 31-12-11 |
|---|---|---|---|
| TO | 6,220,524 | N/A | N/A |
| P/L | 317,964 | N/A | N/A |
| NW | 3,266,581 | 1,871,758 | 1,719,211 |
| WC | 2,550,491 | 1,296,113 | 1,235,869 |
| Emp. | 62 | N/A | N/A |

DUNS 64-268-8873
## Peter Marshall & Co
Muirton Farm, Alyth, Blairgowrie, Perthshire PH11 8JF
**Tel:** 01828-632227
**Web:** www.petermarshallfarms.com
**Estd:** 1948 Partnership
**Line of Business:** Fruit and vegetable (producers)
**Partners:** H Marshall, Ms M Marshall, Ms E Marshall, P Marshall
**Branches:** Peter Marshall & Co, Cairns Bungalow, Alyth, Blairgowrie, Perthshire PH11 8NN
**US SIC:** 0179, 0119
**UK SIC:** 01002, 01001
**Employees:** 200

DUNS 55-063-3978
## Peter Phillip
4 Victoria Street, Monifieth, Dundee, Angus DD5 4HL
**Tel:** 01382-532357
**Web:** www.tighnamuirn.co.uk
**Estd:** 1991 Proprietorship

**Line of Business:** Residential care establishments
**Proprietor:** P Phillip
**US SIC:** 8321 **UK SIC:** 96111
**Employees:** 70

DUNS 73-313-0400
### Peter Ramsey & Sons Ltd
Sawmills, Wellington Street, Bradford, West Yorkshire BD4 8BW
**Tel:** 01274-656563 **Fax:** 01274656505
**Web:** www.ramsey-uk.com
**Reg No:** 4586797 **Estd:** 2002 Private Limited Company
**Line of Business:** Other letting of own property
**Issued Capital:** £924,914
**Directors:** P R Ramsey, N P Ramsey, Ms P E Ramsey
**Co. Secretary:** Michael Ramsey
**Responsibilities**
**Admin:** Louise Merrifield *(Office Manager)*
**US SIC:** 6519 **UK SIC:** 85000

| | 30-09-14 | 30-09-13 | 30-09-12 |
|---|---|---|---|
| TO | 12,251,244 | 9,372,849 | 9,793,979 |
| P/L | 590,013 | 553,308 | 579,860 |
| NW | 3,855,111 | 3,595,892 | 3,652,153 |
| WC | 1,981,291 | 1,863,141 | 1,722,311 |
| Emp. | 91 | 98 | 84 |

DUNS 76-900-8962
### Peter Smith (Bridgend) Holdings Ltd
Tremains Road, Bridgend, Mid Glamorgan CF31 1UA
**Web:** www.bmf.uk.com
**Reg No:** 1456433 **Estd:** 1964 Private Limited Company
**Line of Business:** Management activities of holding companies
**Issued Capital:** £100
**Directors:** Ms M Smith, P Smith
**Co. Secretary:** David Smith
**US SIC:** 6711 **UK SIC:** 83962

| | 31-03-14 | 31-03-13 | 31-03-12 |
|---|---|---|---|
| TA | 209,293 | 167,420 | 135,163 |
| NW | 169,398 | 133,730 | 111,803 |
| WC | 75,619 | 42,149 | 19,496 |

DUNS 54-867-8465
### Peter Symonds College
Owens Road, Winchester, Hampshire SO22 6RX
**Tel:** 01962857500
**Web:** www.psc.ac.uk
**Estd:** 2003
**Line of Business:** Secretarial and business colleges
**Director:** N Hopkins
**Responsibilities**
**Senior:** Stephen Carville *(Principal)*
**Marketing:** Sandra Showell *(Marketing Manager)*
**Admin:** Hillary Lette *(Administrator)*
**IT:** Charles Parish *(Senior IT Executive)*
**HR:** Victoria Harland *(Instructor)*
**Facilities:** Sarah Vance *(Site Manager)*
**Operations:** Gill Gardiner *(Manager)*
**Purchasing:** Christina Russell *(Resources Manager)*
**Branches:** Peter Symonds College, Stoney Lane, Winchester, Hampshire SO22 6DR
**US SIC:** 8249 **UK SIC:** 93300
**Employees:** 400

DUNS 21-601-6053
### Peter Vardy
Whitemyres Avenue, Aberdeen, Aberdeenshire AB16 6HQ
**Tel:** 01224684848
**Web:** www.petervardy.com
**Estd:** 2000
**Line of Business:** Car dealers (new & used)
**Proprietor:** P Vardy
**Responsibilities**
**Senior:** Richie Cooper *(Managing Partner)*
**US SIC:** 5511 **UK SIC:** 65100
**Employees:** 70

DUNS 21-998-6937
### Peter Vardy Holdings Ltd
The Wright Business Centre, 1 Lonmay Road, Glasgow, Lanarkshire G33 4EL
**Tel:** 08444828999
**Reg No:** 0319442SC **Estd:** 2007 Private Limited Company
**Line of Business:** Sale of new motor vehicles
**Issued Capital:** £17,604,100
**Directors:** P D Vardy, Lady M B Vardy, Mrs C Maith
**Co. Secretary:** Mrs Claire Maith
**US SIC:** 5511, 7539
**UK SIC:** 65100, 67100
**Bankers:** Barclays Bank Plc (20-59-42)

| | 31-12-13 | 31-12-12 | 31-12-11 |
|---|---|---|---|
| TO | 340,740,000 | 239,035,000 | 206,982,000 |
| P/L | 6,524,000 | 5,583,000 | 1,407,000 |
| NW | 30,574,000 | 19,858,000 | 18,250,000 |
| WC | 6,995,000 | 9,917,000 | 11,995,000 |
| Emp. | 674 | 478 | 460 |

DUNS 29-178-8636
### Peter Vardy Land Rover Ltd
(**Subsidiary of:** Peter Vardy Holdings Ltd)
Greenwell Road, East Tullos Industrial Estate, Aberdeen, Aberdeenshire AB12 3AX
**Tel:** 01224871219
**Web:** www.petervardy.com
**Reg No:** 0055055SC **Estd:** 1985 Private Limited Company
**Line of Business:** Sale of new motor vehicles
**Trading Style:** Peter Vardy Landrover, Town & Country Porshe, Lexus Aberdeen
**Issued Capital:** £2
**Directors:** Sir P Vardy, Mrs C Maith, P D Vardy
**Co. Secretary:** Ms Claire Maith
**Responsibilities**
**Senior:** Tom Hail *(Area manager)*, Arthur Mcjenzie
**US SIC:** 5511 **UK SIC:** 65100
**Auditors:** PricewaterhouseCoopers
**Bankers:** Clydesdale Bank Plc (82-60-01)

| | 31-12-13 | 31-12-12 | 31-12-11 |
|---|---|---|---|
| TO | 62,169,000 | 67,126,000 | 53,703,974 |
| P/L | 1,111,000 | (62,000) | 77,847 |
| NW | 2,425,000 | 1,586,000 | 1,638,654 |
| WC | N/A | 1,448,000 | 1,443,963 |
| Emp. | 75 | 145 | 139 |

DUNS 54-864-4939
### Peterborough & Stamford Hospitals Nhs Foundation Trust
Edith Cavell Campus, Bretton Gate, Peterborough, Cambridgeshire PE3 9GZ
**Web:** www.peterboroughhospitals.co.uk
**Estd:** 1993
**Line of Business:** Public sector hospital activities, including nhs trusts
**Trading Style:** Peterborough Hospital Transformation
**Issued Capital:** £1
**Principals:** N Hards *(Chairman)*, C Hall *(Financial)*, Ms C Tolond *(Personnel)*, Ms R Barnes, Ms J Pigg, N Patten, J Radway, R Rahim
**Responsibilities**
**Senior:** Martin Chillcott *(Non-Executive Director)*, Susan Grey *(Non-Executive Director)*, Lorraine Moulton *(Manager)*
**Branches:** Peterborough & Stamford Hospitals Nhs Foundation Trust, Pelham House, Thorpe Road, Peterborough, Cambridgeshire PE3 6NH
**US SIC:** 8062 **UK SIC:** 95100
**Auditors:** KPMG LLP

| | 31-03-14 | 31-03-13 | 31-03-12 |
|---|---|---|---|
| TO | 217,435,000 | 202,404,000 | 189,502,000 |
| P/L | (37,757,000) | (39,373,000) | (45,839,000) |
| NW | (8,380,000) | (26,754,000) | (31,474,000) |
| WC | (8,955,000) | (8,187,000) | (9,939,000) |
| Emp. | 3,640 | 3,478 | 3,408 |

DUNS 22-747-3071
### Peterborough City Council
49 Lincoln Road, Peterborough, Cambridgeshire PE1 2RR
**Tel:** 01733207299
**Web:** www.peterborough.gov.uk
**VAT No:** 121533513 **Estd:** 1974 Incorporate By Act Of Parliament
**Line of Business:** Day and care centres
**Trading Style:** The Beeches Primary School, Standground College
**Directors:** B Samuel, R Palmer, P Lee, R Davis, M Leonard, G Blagden
**Responsibilities**
**Senior:** Gillian Beasley *(Chief Executive)*
**IT:** Elaine Alexander *(Head of Programme Projects Man)*
**Health & Safety:** Andy Baker *(Health & Safety Manager)*
**Facilities:** Sue Scott *(Facilities Management Officer)*
**Purchasing:** Yvonne Phair *(Purchasing Officer)*
**Branches:** Peterborough City Council, Bretton Library, Bretton Centre, Peterborough, Cambridgeshire PE3 8DS
**US SIC:** 9121 **UK SIC:** 91110
**Bankers:** The Co-Operative Bank Plc (08-90-40)
**Employees:** 3

DUNS 29-008-0217
### The Peterborough Diocesan Board of Finance
The Palace, Minster Precincts, Peterborough, Cambridgeshire PE1 1YB
**Tel:** 01733-887000
**Web:** www.peterborough-diocese.org.uk
**Reg No:** 0186179 **Estd:** 1922 Private Company Limited By Guarantee
**Line of Business:** Activities of religious organisations
**Directors:** D P Randell, N J Critchlow, Reverend S J Trott, Ms H J Daniels, J Orme, A W Heald, C W Taylor, C J Haynes
**Co. Secretary:** Andrew Roberts
**Responsibilities**
**Senior:** Christine Allsopp *(Trustee)*, Jane Baxter *(Director)*, Peter Burchell *(Director)*, Hilary Creek *(Director)*, Michael Hobart *(Director)*, John Holbrook *(Director)*, Kenneth Hope Jones *(Director)*, Alistair Macmahon *(Director)*, Alan March *(Director)*, Richard Ormston *(Director)*, Robert Purser *(Director)*, Anne Toms *(Director)*, Frank White *(Manager)*
**Finance:** Graham Cuthbert *(Senior Finance Administrator)*
**Branches:** The Peterborough Diocesan Board Of Finance, Twelvetree Avenue, Peterborough, Cambridgeshire PE4 5DT
**US SIC:** 7399 **UK SIC:** 83954
**Auditors:** Mazars LLP
**Bankers:** Barclays Bank Plc (20-67-37)

| | 31-12-13 | 31-12-12 | 31-12-11 |
|---|---|---|---|
| TO | 13,228,168 | 12,079,328 | 10,119,928 |
| P/L | 138,414 | 367,739 | (779,157) |
| NW | 108,395,838 | 104,335,394 | 101,381,683 |
| WC | 7,457,603 | 5,508,383 | 5,572,647 |
| Emp. | 173 | 169 | 153 |

DUNS 23-599-9737
### Peterborough Health Authority
41 Priestgate, Peterborough, Cambridgeshire PE1 1JL
**Tel:** 01733562101
**Web:** www.cityclubuk.co.uk
**Proprietorship**
**Line of Business:** Local government
**Branches:** Peterborough Health Authority, The Deepings Practice, 3-4 The Green, Peterborough, Cambridgeshire PE6 7JN
**US SIC:** 9121 **UK SIC:** 91110
**Employees:** 70

DUNS 21-825-3490
### Peterborough Sports Stadium Ltd
Peterborough Greyhound Stadium, First Drove, Fengate, Peterborough, Cambridgeshire PE1 5BJ
**Tel:** 01733-296939 **Fax:** 01733-296932
**Web:** www.thegreatfoundation.org.uk
**Reg No:** 0365131 **Estd:** 1930 Private Limited Company
**Line of Business:** Operation of other sports arenas and stadiums not elsewhere classified
**Issued Capital:** £11,800
**Directors:** D N Perkins, Mrs K M Perkins
**Co. Secretary:** Mrs Catherine Perkins
**US SIC:** 7999 **UK SIC:** 97913
**Bankers:** Barclays Bank Plc (20-67-37)

| | 31-03-14 | 31-03-13 | 31-03-12 |
|---|---|---|---|
| TO | 3,423,188 | 3,616,123 | 3,785,290 |
| P/L | 122,538 | 105,491 | 244,954 |
| NW | 3,684,324 | 3,741,786 | 3,744,846 |
| WC | (239,766) | (357,301) | (435,715) |
| Emp. | 192 | 191 | 196 |

DUNS 21-103-8687
### Peterhead Health Centre
Links Terrace, Peterhead, Aberdeenshire AB42 2XA
**Tel:** 01779474841
**Estd:** 2009 Partnership
**Line of Business:** Doctors
**Partner:** Dr I R Young
**Responsibilities**
**Senior:** Diane Buchan *(Practice Manager)*
**US SIC:** 8011 **UK SIC:** 95300
**Employees:** 60

DUNS 21-121-5866 **Imp**
### Peterhead Port Authority
West Pier, Peterhead, Aberdeenshire AB42 1DW
**Tel:** 01779483600
**Web:** www.peterheadport.co.uk
**Estd:** 1873
**Line of Business:** Operation of habours and ports
**Proprietor:** J Wallis
**US SIC:** 4469 **UK SIC:** 76300
**Employees:** 65

DUNS 36-487-7766
### Peterhouse
Trumpington Street, Cambridge, Cambridgeshire CB2 1RD
**Web:** www.peterhouse-conferences.co.uk
**Estd:** 2002
**Line of Business:** University
**Directors:** M S Golding, Prof P C Woodland, Prof A K Dixon, Dr P Pattenden, Prof M A Parker, Dr R A Crowther, Dr S N Solomou, Prof D J Watkin
**Responsibilities**
**Senior:** Pat Grassick *(Manager)*, Gerald Meade *(Head Porter)*, R Munday Steward *(Principal)*, ASHWIN PATEL *(Principal)*
**Finance:** Richard Grigson *(Bursar)*
**IT:** Andrew Clelland *(IT Manager)*
**HR:** Richard Grigson *(Bursar)*
**Health & Safety:** Richard Grigson *(Bursar)*
**Facilities:** Richard Grigson *(Bursar)*
**US SIC:** 8221 **UK SIC:** 93100
**Auditors:** Price Bailey LLP

| | 30-06-13 | 30-06-12 | 30-06-11 |
|---|---|---|---|
| TO | 10,723,000 | 10,509,000 | 9,530,000 |
| P/L | 45,000 | 808,000 | 131,000 |
| NW | 256,390,000 | 240,126,000 | 234,028,000 |
| WC | 10,683,000 | 11,303,000 | 5,515,000 |
| Emp. | 144 | 141 | 143 |

DUNS 22-802-3735 **Exp**
### Peterhouse Group Ltd
(**Subsidiary of:** Babcock International Group Plc)
2 Cavendish Square, London W1G 0PU
**Tel:** 01422374757 **Fax:** 01422-374710
**Reg No:** 1517100 **Estd:** 1980 Public Limited Company
**Line of Business:** Management activities of holding companies
**Export Markets:** Europe
**Issued Capital:** £10
**Directors:** P L Rogers, I S Urquhart, F Martinelli
**Co. Secretary:** Babcock Corporate Secretaries Li
**US SIC:** 6711, 8911
**UK SIC:** 83962, 83701
**Auditors:** PricewaterhouseCoopers LLP
**Bankers:** Bank Of Scotland (12-08-83)

| | 31-03-14 | 31-03-13 | 31-03-12 |
|---|---|---|---|
| TA | 46,076,000 | 45,790,000 | 46,814,000 |
| P/L | (1,396,000) | (1,573,000) | (1,580,000) |
| NW | (6,975,000) | (5,578,000) | (2,691,000) |
| WC | 29,950,000 | 31,308,000 | 34,195,000 |

DUNS 49-144-4980
### PeTERHOUSE6 (letg) Ltd
(**Subsidiary of:** Babcock International Group Plc)
Cross Greenway, Cross Green Industrial Estate, Leeds, West Yorkshire LS9 0SE
**Tel:** 01132-019700 **Fax:** 01422-374710
**Web:** www.idexcorp.com
**Reg No:** 3111794 **Estd:** 1995 Public Limited Company
**Line of Business:** Other business activities not elsewhere classified
**Trading Style:** I E T G 40 Seven
**Issued Capital:** £571,474
**Directors:** P L Rogers, F Martinelli, I S Urquhart
**Co. Secretary:** Babcock Corporate Secretaries Li
**Responsibilities**
**Senior:** Eunice Payne *(Manager)*, Valerie Teller *(Manager)*
**Branches:** PeterhouSE6 (letg) Ltd, Hayfield La, Doncaster, South Yorkshire DN9 3XA
**US SIC:** 7399, 7374
**UK SIC:** 83954, 83940
**Auditors:** Ernst & Young LPP
**Bankers:** HSBC Bank plc (40-13-15)

| | 31-03-14 | 31-03-13 | 31-03-12 |
|---|---|---|---|
| TA | 371,000 | 371,000 | 371,000 |
| NW | (4,095,000) | (4,095,000) | (4,095,000) |
| WC | (4,264,000) | (4,264,000) | (4,264,000) |

DUNS 23-986-5413
### Peterkins Solicitors
100 Union Street, Aberdeen, Aberdeenshire AB10 1QR
**Tel:** 01224428000
**Web:** www.peterkins.com
**Estd:** 2011 Partnership
**Line of Business:** Solicitors
**Trading Style:** Peterkins Solicitors
**Director:** P Kins
**Responsibilities**
**Finance:** Moira Carroll *(Finance Coordinator)*
**Sales:** Ray Baxter *(Sales Manager)*
**Branches:** Peterkins Solicitors, 75 High St, Banchory, Kincardineshire AB31 5TJ
**US SIC:** 6531 **UK SIC:** 83400
**Employees:** 70

DUNS 21-232-1346

## Peterlee Leisure Centre

St Cuthberts Way, Peterlee, County Durham SR8 1AF
**Tel:** 0191-5862400
**Web:** www.1-life.co.uk
**Estd:** 1970 Proprietorship
**Line of Business:** Leisure centres
**Proprietor:** M Grinstead
**Responsibilities**
**Health & Safety:** Wayne Adamson *(Health & Safety Officer)*
**Facilities:** Ian Gustard *(Maintenance Manager)*
**Operations:** Wayne Adamson *(Health & Safety Officer)*
**US SIC:** 7999 **UK SIC:** 97913
**Employees:** 50

DUNS 23-981-6465

## Peters & Peters Solicitors

15 Fetter Lane, London EC4A 1BW
**Tel:** 02078227777
**Web:** www.petersandpeters.com
**Estd:** 1938 Partnership
**Line of Business:** Solicitors
**Partners:** Miss J Rickards, K Oliver
**US SIC:** 8111 **UK SIC:** 83500
**Employees:** 60

DUNS 29-683-8683

## Peters Elworthy & Moore Ltd

Salisbury House, 2-3 Salisbury Villas, Cambridge, Cambridgeshire CB1 2LA
**Tel:** 01223-728222
**Web:** www.pem.co.uk
**Reg No:** 2007313 **Estd:** 1874 Private Limited Company
**Line of Business:** Accounting and auditing activities
**Issued Capital:** £2
**Director:** P R Chapman
**Co. Secretary:** Roger Guthrie
**Responsibilities**
**Senior:** Judith Coplowe *(Director, Charities)*, Roy Guy *(Partner)*
**Finance:** Helen Broadbent *(Head of Finance)*
**Marketing:** Vicky Hurst *(Marketing Manager)*
**Admin:** Lyn Tilley *(Office Manager)*
**IT:** Edward Wilkins *(IT Executive)*
**HR:** Toni Munro *(Human Resources Manager)*
**Purchasing:** Andy Munro *(Purchasing Manager)*
**US SIC:** 8931 **UK SIC:** 83600
**Employees:** 240

DUNS 22-741-6807

## Peters Elworthy Moore

Station Road, Cambridge, Cambridgeshire CB1 2LA
**Tel:** 01223362333
**Web:** www.pem.co.uk
**Estd:** 1874 Partnership
**Line of Business:** Accounting and auditing activities
**Trading Style:** Peters Elworthy Moore
**Principals:** D Shepherd, J Parry *(Partner)*, D Collison *(Partner)*, Mrs A Counsell *(Partner)*, A Dewey *(Partner)*, W Wilsden *(Partner)*, P Chapman *(Partner)*, R Webster *(Partner)*
**Responsibilities**
**Senior:** Roy Guy *(Partner)*
**US SIC:** 8931 **UK SIC:** 83600
**Employees:** 150

DUNS 21-810-2378

## Peter's Fish Bar

27 Sedlescombe Road North, St Leonards-On-Sea, East Sussex TN37 7DA
**Tel:** 01424433806
**Estd:** 2012
**Line of Business:** Fish and chip shops
**Responsibilities**
**Senior:** A Lai *(Proprietor)*
**US SIC:** 5812 **UK SIC:** 66110
**Employees:** 74

DUNS 38-587-1033

## Peters Food Service Ltd

(**Subsidiary of:** Peter's Holdings Ltd)
Bedwas House Industrial Estate, Caerphilly, Mid Glamorgan CF83 8XP
**Tel:** 02920853200 **Fax:** 01179586910
**Web:** www.petersfood.com
**Reg No:** 3341786 **Estd:** 1996 Private Limited Company
**Line of Business:** Manufacturers and suppliers of pies
**Export Sales:** £6,546,000
**Issued Capital:** £72,750
**Directors:** D Jackson, S A Jones, M J Grimwood
**Co. Secretary:** David Peek
**Responsibilities**
**Finance:** Mandy Evans *(Accounts Manager)*
**Marketing:** Claire Conway *(Marketing Events Manager)*, Clare Morgan *(Marketing Director)*
**Sales:** Huw Butler *(National Account Manager, Reta)*, John McAughtrie *(Sales Director)*, Ginny Priestley *(Retail Sales Manager)*
**HR:** Judith Caddy *(Human Resources Manager)*
**Branches:** Peters Food Service Ltd, Unit 29, Forge La, Sutton Coldfield, West Midlands B76 1AH
**US SIC:** 2099, 5147
**UK SIC:** 42399, 61700
**Auditors:** PricewaterhouseCoopers LLP
**Bankers:** National Westminster Bank Plc (52-10-40)

| | 31-05-14 | 31-05-13 | 31-05-12 |
|---|---|---|---|
| TO | 80,250,000 | 72,057,000 | 70,028,000 |
| P/L | 2,666,000 | (192,000) | 569,000 |
| NW | 6,943,000 | 4,916,000 | 5,169,000 |
| WC | 1,276,000 | (570,000) | (227,000) |
| Emp. | 813 | 775 | 752 |

DUNS 50-473-4492

## Peters Ltd

(**Subsidiary of:** J.S.Peters & Son Ltd)
120-130 Bromsgrove Street, Birmingham, West Midlands B5 6RJ
**Tel:** 0121-666-6646
**Web:** www.peters-educational-furniture.co.uk
**Reg No:** 2452340 **Estd:** 1989 Private Limited Company
**Line of Business:** Retail sale of books, newspapers and stationery
**Trading Style:** Peters Book Selling Services
**Issued Capital:** £10,000
**Principals:** M J Peters Macdougall *(Managing)*, R J Peters, R F Dyer, G J Newsome
**Responsibilities**
**Senior:** Jeanette Meikle *(Manager)*
**US SIC:** 5942 **UK SIC:** 65300
**Auditors:** Daw White Murrall

| | 30-04-14 | 30-04-13 | 30-04-12 |
|---|---|---|---|
| TO | 10,977,195 | 8,046,630 | 13,067,596 |
| P/L | (176,840) | (575,380) | (37,911) |
| NW | 2,860,485 | 3,037,325 | 3,612,705 |
| WC | 2,791,171 | 2,942,125 | 3,458,458 |
| Emp. | 99 | 83 | 121 |

DUNS 21-738-4957

## Petersfield & Reliance Launderers Ltd

(**Subsidiary of:** Belsat Investments Ltd)
Rushes Road, Petersfield, Hampshire GU32 3AR
**Tel:** 01730-262411
**Web:** www.petersfieldlaundry.co.uk
**Reg No:** 0061140 **VAT No:** 192946032
**Estd:** 1899 Private Limited Company
**Line of Business:** Washing and dry cleaning of textile and fur products
**Trading Style:** Workleen
**Issued Capital:** £16,000
**Principals:** R J James *(Managing)*, S G Pritchard, Mrs E A James
**Co. Secretary:** Mrs Sally Thoday
**US SIC:** 7219 **UK SIC:** 98110
**Auditors:** Cunningham Wishart

| | 30-11-13 | 30-11-12 | 30-11-11 |
|---|---|---|---|
| TA | 654,448 | 824,105 | 971,014 |
| NW | 216,302 | 310,496 | 367,412 |
| WC | 164,371 | 238,313 | 288,889 |

DUNS 21-772-6127

## Petersfield Infants School

St Peters Road, Petersfield, Hampshire GU32 3HX
**Tel:** 01730263048
**Web:** www.petersfield-inf.hants.sch.uk
**Estd:** 1981 Proprietorship
**Line of Business:** General secondary education
**Proprietor:** Mrs L Lee
**US SIC:** 8211 **UK SIC:** 93200
**Employees:** 50

DUNS 39-757-2637

## The Petersham Hotel Ltd

Petersham Hotel, Richmond, Surrey TW10 6UZ
**Tel:** 02089407471 **Fax:** 020-8939-1098
**Web:** www.petershamhotel.co.uk
**Reg No:** 2196266 **VAT No:** 468802222
**Estd:** 2001 Private Limited Company
**Line of Business:** Hotels and motels without restaurant
**Issued Capital:** £35,300
**Directors:** Mrs L C Luchterhand, Mrs M E Dare
**Co. Secretary:** Greville Dare
**Responsibilities**
**Senior:** Anne Atkinson *(Deputy General Manager)*, Feleck Wooden *(CEO, Managing Director)*
**Finance:** Edward Carr *(Accounts)*, Barbara Lee *(Accounts)*
**Marketing:** Karina Eremina *(Marketing Executive)*, Terence Filipe-O'Neill *(Events & Marketing)*, Kalpa Hirani *(Events & Marketing)*, Huyla Kose Ozer *(Events & Marketing)*, Laura Rochette *(Marketing Assistant)*
**Admin:** Elena Benitez *(Office Manager)*
**Facilities:** Keith Temple *(Maintenance Manager)*
**US SIC:** 7011 **UK SIC:** 66500
**Auditors:** Blueprint Audit Ltd
**Bankers:** HSBC Bank plc (40-02-17)

| | 31-01-14 | 31-01-13 | 31-01-12 |
|---|---|---|---|
| TO | 9,187,684 | 8,975,874 | 8,421,802 |
| P/L | 766,865 | 622,744 | 299,832 |
| NW | 12,208,790 | 11,865,565 | 11,651,040 |
| WC | (2,151,998) | (1,353,732) | (2,235,771) |
| Emp. | 258 | 244 | 240 |

DUNS 22-524-3104 **Imp**

## Petersham Nurseries Ltd

Church Terrace, Richmond, Surrey TW10 6SE
**Tel:** 02089405230
**Web:** www.petershamnurseries.com
**Reg No:** 0738272 **VAT No:** 216391179
**Estd:** 1962 Private Limited Company
**Line of Business:** Garden centres
**Issued Capital:** £100
**Directors:** Ms L A Boglione, Mrs G L Boglione
**Co. Secretary:** Francesco Boglione
**Responsibilities**
**Senior:** Charlotte Senn *(General Manager)*
**US SIC:** 5999 **UK SIC:** 65600
**Bankers:** Lloyds TSB Bank plc (30-94-77)

| | 31-12-13 | 31-12-12 | 31-12-11 |
|---|---|---|---|
| TA | 871,681 | 915,307 | 1,011,416 |
| NW | (1,229,620) | (1,336,663) | (1,174,412) |
| WC | 100,341 | (71,300) | 48,144 |

DUNS 21-772-5034

## Peterson S B S

Inglesmaldie, Luthermuir, Laurencekirk, Kincardineshire AB30 1QD
**Tel:** 01674840007
**Web:** www.onepeterson.com
**Estd:** 2011 Proprietorship
**Line of Business:** Operation of storage facilities
**Proprietor:** K Stephens
**Responsibilities**
**Senior:** Bill Blair *(Operations Manager)*, Jason Hendrie *(Area Manager)*
**US SIC:** 4226 **UK SIC:** 77003
**Employees:** 53

DUNS 22-657-2279 **Imp-Exp**

## Peterson Spring Europe Ltd

(**Subsidiary of:** Peterson American Corp.)
Heath House, Hewell Road, Redditch, Worcestershire B97 6AY
**Tel:** 0152761952
**Web:** www.btinternet.com
**Reg No:** 1363153 **VAT No:** 454826429
**Estd:** 1929 Private Limited Company
**Line of Business:** Manufacturers of springs
**Export Sales:** £3,792,832
**Trading Style:** Peterson Spring Uk Limited
**Issued Capital:** £4,022,250
**Directors:** R G Bray, D E Sceli, E C Peterson
**Co. Secretary:** Reginald Groseley
**Responsibilities**
**Senior:** Nick Scroggs *(Sales Manager)*
**Sales:** John Iliffe *(Technical Manager)*, Nick Scroggs *(Sales Manager)*
**IT:** Jonathan Heath *(IT Manager)*, John Iliffe *(Technical Manager)*
**HR:** Christen Taylor *(HR Manager)*
**Facilities:** Roger Nightingale *(Maintenance Manager)*
**Engineering:** John Iliffe *(Technical Manager)*, Roger Nightingale *(Maintenance Manager)*
**Branches:** Peterson Spring Europe Ltd, The Trafford Park Industrial Estate, Redditch, Worcestershire B98 7AH
**US SIC:** 3452, 3496
**UK SIC:** 31371, 31694
**Auditors:** KPMG LLP
**Bankers:** National Westminster Bank Plc (60-11-01)

| | 31-12-13 | 31-12-12 | 31-12-11 |
|---|---|---|---|
| TO | 5,967,463 | 5,579,763 | 5,424,455 |
| P/L | 439,462 | 226,896 | 127,924 |
| NW | 2,699,386 | 2,156,340 | 1,100,811 |
| WC | 1,694,153 | 1,442,550 | 1,363,531 |
| Emp. | 58 | 55 | 48 |

DUNS 21-801-4918 **Exp**

## Peterson Spring Uk Ltd

(**Subsidiary of:** Peterson American Corp.)
Hewell Road, Redditch, Worcestershire B97 6AY
**Tel:** 0152761952
**Web:** www.btinternet.com
**Reg No:** 0243917 **Estd:** 1929 Private Limited Company
**Line of Business:** Manufacturers of springs
**Export Markets:** France; Kenya
**Issued Capital:** £39,374
**Directors:** E C Peterson, D E Sceli, R G Bray
**Co. Secretary:** Reginald Groseley
**Branches:** Peterson Spring Uk Ltd, The Trafford Park Industrial Estate, Unit 21, Redditch, Worcestershire B98 7AH
**US SIC:** 3452 **UK SIC:** 31371
**Bankers:** Lloyds TSB Bank plc (30-93-66)

| | 31-12-13 | 31-12-12 | 31-12-11 |
|---|---|---|---|
| TA | 2,232,066 | 2,232,066 | 2,232,066 |
| NW | 2,232,066 | 2,232,066 | 2,232,066 |

DUNS 37-891-7405 **Imp**

## Peterson (United Kingdom) Ltd

(**Subsidiary of:** Peterson Offshore Group B.V.)
Nautilus House, 35 Waterloo Quay, Aberdeen, Aberdeenshire AB11 5BS
**Tel:** 01224288100 **Fax:** 01224-288101
**Web:** www.onepeterson.com
**Reg No:** 3311077 **VAT No:** 743049735
**Estd:** 1973 Private Limited Company
**Line of Business:** Miscellaneous transportation services
**Trading Style:** Sbsl
**Issued Capital:** £3,059,000
**Directors:** J W Bain, J Mcsporran
**Co. Secretary:** Stronachs Secretaries Limited
**Responsibilities**
**Senior:** Steven Mcdonald *(Manager)*, Laura Reynolds *(Personal Assistant)*
**HR:** Joyce Russell *(Human Resources Manager)*
**Purchasing:** Liz Gardiner *(Buyer)*
**Branches:** Peterson (United Kingdom) Ltd, Greenhead, Lerwick, Shetland, Shetland ZE1 0PY
**US SIC:** 4789, 4712
**UK SIC:** 77002
**Auditors:** Anderson Anderson & Brown LLP

| | 31-12-13 | 31-12-12 | 31-12-11 |
|---|---|---|---|
| TO | 165,678,000 | 153,013,000 | 151,787,000 |
| P/L | 3,218,000 | 2,619,000 | 1,113,000 |
| NW | 13,234,000 | 10,763,000 | 8,841,000 |
| WC | 4,893,000 | 3,663,000 | 3,019,000 |
| Emp. | 495 | 440 | 391 |

DUNS 22-763-0787 **Imp**

## Petford Tools Ltd

Unit 8 Lygon Buildings, Peartree Lane, Dudley, West Midlands DY2 0QU
**Tel:** 01384-246930 **Fax:** 01384-246939
**Web:** www.petfordtools.co.uk
**Reg No:** 1021332 **VAT No:** 277027450
**Estd:** 1971 Private Limited Company
**Line of Business:** Manufacturers of tools
**Export Sales:** £4,424,470
**Issued Capital:** £57
**Principals:** M J Parr *(Managing)*, I S Foy, D S Parr, N T Howard, M A Sinar
**Co. Secretary:** Michael Parr
**Responsibilities**
**Sales:** Owen McNally *(Mold Shop Manager)*
**US SIC:** 3423, 3499
**UK SIC:** 31612, 31694
**Auditors:** AGS Accountants & Business Advisors Ltd
**Bankers:** National Westminster Bank Plc (60-20-48)

| | 30-11-13 | 30-11-12 | 30-11-11 |
|---|---|---|---|
| TO | 15,075,029 | 14,805,358 | 9,496,368 |
| P/L | 259,699 | 910,111 | 601,228 |
| NW | 3,230,051 | 3,026,795 | 2,445,583 |
| WC | 1,077,310 | 1,472,916 | 1,246,280 |
| Emp. | 90 | 85 | 65 |

DUNS 54-428-6412

## Petit Bateau Uk Ltd

(**Subsidiary of:** Soc Financiere Yves Rocher)
2nd Floor Radiant House, London W1W 7RG
**Tel:** 02074625770
**Web:** www.petit-bateau.co.uk
**Reg No:** 3274758 **Estd:** 1996 Private Limited Company
**Line of Business:** Retail sale of clothing
**Issued Capital:** £40,000
**Directors:** Petit Bateau Sas, R Larose
**Co. Secretary:** Regis Larose
**Responsibilities**
**Senior:** Philipp Blanquet *(Manager)*
**Branches:** Petit Bateau Uk Ltd, 124-125 Upper Street, London N1 1QP
**US SIC:** 5699 **UK SIC:** 64500
**Auditors:** Deloitte & Touche LLP

| | 31-12-13 | 31-12-12 | 31-12-11 |
|---|---|---|---|
| TO | 8,055,000 | 8,316,000 | 7,568,000 |
| P/L | 407,000 | 401,000 | (50,000) |
| NW | 446,000 | 417,000 | 127,000 |
| WC | (34,000) | (213,000) | (626,000) |
| Emp. | 60 | 60 | 68 |

## DUNS 28-980-3074
## Petit Forestier Uk Ltd
(**Subsidiary of:** Petit Forestier)
Birch Coppice Industrial Estate, Tamworth, Staffordshire B78 1SZ
**Tel:** 01827-263100
**Web:** www.petitforestier.co.uk
**Reg No:** 1775955 **Estd:** 1986 Private Limited Company
**Line of Business:** Van hire
**Export Sales:** £1,077,323
**Issued Capital:** £18,800,000
**Directors:** E Forestier, J C Forestier, Y Forestier
**Co. Secretary:** Vincent Lachambre
**Responsibilities**
**Senior:** Guillaume Balon *(Finance Manager)*
**Finance:** Guillaume Balon *(Finance Manager)*
**Health & Safety:** Martin Farrand *(Engineering Director)*
**Branches:** Petit Forestier Uk Ltd, 37 Hardwick Grange, Warrington, Cheshire WA1 4RF
**US SIC:** 7513, 7539
**UK SIC:** 84802, 67100
**Auditors:** Baker Tilly UK Audit LLP
**Bankers:** Barclays Bank Plc (20-41-12)

|      | 31-12-13     | 31-12-12     | 31-12-11     |
|------|--------------|--------------|--------------|
| TO   | 40,770,699   | 39,141,454   | 38,825,931   |
| P/L  | 389,441      | (1,432,739)  | 89,747       |
| NW   | 11,673,894   | 11,533,453   | 13,141,948   |
| WC   | (23,202,160) | (19,808,632) | (19,559,898) |
| Emp. | 233          | 231          | 213          |

## DUNS 23-809-4275
## Petplanet.Co.Uk Ltd.
(**Subsidiary of:** M8 Group Ltd)
10 Lindsay Square, Livingston, West Lothian EH54 8RL
**Tel:** 08453450723 **Fax:** 08453450729
**Web:** www.petplanet.co.uk
**Reg No:** 0197870SC **Estd:** 1999 Private Limited Company
**Line of Business:** Retail sale via mail order house
**Trading Style:** Petplanet
**Issued Capital:** £100
**Directors:** J B Mcfarlane, Miss M L Peterson, R S Torrens
**Co. Secretary:** Kevin Hague
**US SIC:** 5961 **UK SIC:** 65600

|      | 30-09-14   | 30-09-13  | 30-09-12 |
|------|------------|-----------|----------|
| TO   | 11,485,651 | N/A       | N/A      |
| P/L  | 795,615    | N/A       | N/A      |
| NW   | 2,272,170  | 1,426,438 | 918,288  |
| WC   | 2,239,131  | 1,398,431 | 880,694  |

## DUNS 64-110-6505                                   Imp
## Petproject Ltd
(**Subsidiary of:** Gemini Fine Foods Ltd)
1king Mews, London N2 8DY
**Tel:** 020-8442-2552
**Web:** www.petproject.co.uk
**Reg No:** 4110818 **Estd:** 2000 Private Limited Company
**Line of Business:** Animal feed and pet foods
**Trading Style:** Pet Project
**Issued Capital:** £2
**Directors:** Ms M Reuben, A S Bard, P J Finger
**US SIC:** 2047 **UK SIC:** 42221

|      | 31-12-13  | 30-09-12 | 30-12-11 |
|------|-----------|----------|----------|
| TA   | 1,440,191 | 847,947  | 796,397  |
| NW   | 357,767   | 187,573  | 108,159  |
| WC   | 444,448   | 324,109  | 172,701  |

## DUNS 22-950-2646                                   Exp
## Petrocell Holdings Ltd
274-278 Wickham Road, Croydon, Surrey CR0 8BJ
**Tel:** 02086554444 **Fax:** 02086566111
**Web:** www.ptamotoringcentres.co.uk
**Reg No:** 1190922 **VAT No:** 284808034
**Estd:** 1974 Private Limited Company
**Line of Business:** Car breakers
**Export Markets:** U K
**Issued Capital:** £491,834
**Principals:** J B Dowling *(Chairman and Managing)*, A Spackman *(Managing)*, J T Dowling, P R Dowling
**Co. Secretary:** Ms Elaine Read
**Branches:** Petrocell Holdings Ltd, Burnham Rd Filling Station, Burnham Rd, Dartford, Kent DA1 5BL
**US SIC:** 7539, 5541
**UK SIC:** 67100, 65200
**Auditors:** Barnes Roffe
**Bankers:** National Westminster Bank Plc (60-06-33)

|      | 30-04-14   | 30-04-13   | 30-04-12   |
|------|------------|------------|------------|
| TO   | 37,646,005 | 34,035,037 | 33,070,388 |
| P/L  | 1,496,063  | 868,034    | 825,149    |
| NW   | 7,742,146  | 6,521,267  | 6,150,494  |
| WC   | 2,032,189  | 356,813    | 351,442    |
| Emp. | 120        | 113        | 116        |

## DUNS 21-196-7955                               Imp-Exp
## Petrochem Carless Ltd
(**Subsidiary of:** Hcs Gmbh)
Cedar Court, Guildford Road, Leatherhead, Surrey KT22 9RX
**Tel:** 01372-360000 **Fax:** 01372-380400
**Web:** www.petrochemcarless.com
**Reg No:** 0429315 **Estd:** 1947 Private Limited Company
**Line of Business:** Mineral oil refining
**Export Sales:** £235,315,000
**Issued Capital:** £2,000,000
**Directors:** D P Stonehouse, N J Wright
**Co. Secretary:** Nigel Wright
**Branches:** Petrochem Carless Ltd, Harwich Refinery, Foster Road, Harwich, Essex CO12 4SS
**US SIC:** 2911, 2869
**UK SIC:** 14010, 25120
**Auditors:** PricewaterhouseCoopers LLP
**Bankers:** Lloyds TSB Bank plc (30-00-02)

|      | 31-12-13    | 31-12-12    | 31-12-11    |
|------|-------------|-------------|-------------|
| TO   | 372,371,000 | 355,904,000 | 385,276,000 |
| P/L  | 15,653,000  | 18,923,000  | 24,626,000  |
| NW   | 98,812,000  | 86,062,000  | 69,448,000  |
| WC   | 71,126,000  | 57,888,000  | 42,877,000  |
| Emp. | 172         | 171         | 161         |

## DUNS 76-895-0073
## Petrofac Engineering Ltd
(**Subsidiary of:** Petrofac Ltd)
Chester House, Woking, Surrey GU21 5BJ
**Tel:** 01483-738500
**Web:** www.petrofac.com
**Reg No:** 2615887 **Estd:** 1991 Private Limited Company
**Line of Business:** Gas service engineers
**Issued Capital:** £3,225,000
**Directors:** M D Barnes, J M Scott, M U Darr
**Co. Secretary:** Robert Smith
**Responsibilities**
**Marketing:** Stewart Highett *(Sales & Marketing Manager)*
**Sales:** Stewart Highett *(Sales & Marketing Manager)*, Peter Ireton *(VP of Business Development)*
**IT:** Guillaume Roux *(Infrastructure Manager)*, Steve Salmon *(IT Director)*
**HR:** Sally Porter *(Human Resources Manager)*, Sarah Townsend *(Training Manager)*, Michelle walsch *(Human Resources Manager)*
**Engineering:** Sean Wilks *(Technology Manager)*
**US SIC:** 1799, 1311
**UK SIC:** 50000, 13000
**Auditors:** Ernst & Young LLP
**Bankers:** National Westminster Bank Plc (60-11-13)

|      | 31-12-13    | 31-12-12    | 31-12-11    |
|------|-------------|-------------|-------------|
| TO   | 118,501,543 | 126,616,814 | 184,482,157 |
| P/L  | 2,438,943   | 3,305,717   | 11,968,060  |
| NW   | 18,545,868  | 16,671,528  | 14,516,563  |
| WC   | 16,555,476  | 16,102,923  | 14,580,627  |
| Emp. | 205         | 169         | 139         |

## DUNS 29-338-3253                                   Imp
## Petrofac Facilities Management Ltd
(**Subsidiary of:** Petrofac Ltd)
1 North Esplanade West, Aberdeen, Aberdeenshire AB11 5QF
**Tel:** 01224247000 **Fax:** 01224247001
**Web:** www.petrofac.com
**Reg No:** 0075047SC **Estd:** 1988 Private Limited Company
**Line of Business:** Oil and gas exploration services
**Issued Capital:** £220
**Directors:** Mrs E Bentley, G Smith, W Thain, R S Mcknight, C H Muir, C W Thompson
**Responsibilities**
**Senior:** Gordon East *(Manager)*, John Methven *(Manager)*
**Marketing:** Louise Ferguson *(E-Business Strategist)*, Hazel Meldrum *(Marketing Manager)*
**Sales:** Tony Brady *(Business Development Manager)*
**HR:** Amy Brown *(HR Officer)*, Maureen Cowie *(Human Resources Manager)*
**Purchasing:** Tom Heron *(Director of Supply Chain)*, Sheila Pedder *(Purchasing Manager)*
**Branches:** Petrofac Facilities Management Ltd, Bridge View, 1 North Esplanade West, Aberdeen, Aberdeenshire AB11 5QF
**US SIC:** 1389, 7399
**UK SIC:** 13000, 83954
**Auditors:** Ernst & Young LLP
**Bankers:** Clydesdale Bank Plc (82-60-10)
**Following financial data are in thousands**

|      | 31-12-13  | 31-12-12 | 31-12-11 |
|------|-----------|----------|----------|
| TO   | 1,005,263 | 744,978  | 558,850  |
| P/L  | 15,401    | 2,233    | 3,698    |
| NW   | 52,692    | 29,309   | 27,135   |
| WC   | 14,920    | 1,837    | (301)    |
| Emp. | 1,659     | 1,617    | 1,424    |

## DUNS 23-349-0643
## Petrofac Ltd
44 Esplanade, St Helier, Jersey, Channel Islands JE4 9WG
**Web:** www.petrofac.com
**Reg No:** 0081792J **Estd:** 2002 Private Limited Company
**Line of Business:** Design, build, commission and operate surface facilities for oil and gas production.
**Principals:** T Weller *(Financial)*, M Chedid, Ms R Decyk, T T Anderson, Ms K Hogenson, R Medori, S Cao, N Murray
**Co. Secretary:** Ogier Secretaries Ltd
**Responsibilities**
**Senior:** Ayman Asfari *(Group Managing Director)*
**Branches:** Petrofac Ltd, 2 Jermyn Street, London SW1Y 4XA
**US SIC:** 6711, 1389, 1799
**UK SIC:** 83962, 13000, 50000
**Auditors:** Ernst & Young LLP
**Employees:** 13,212
**Turnover:** £5,800,719,000

## DUNS 23-955-1877                                   Imp
## Petrofac Training Group Ltd
(**Subsidiary of:** Petrofac Ltd)
Scota House, Blackness Avenue, Aberdeen, Aberdeenshire AB12 3PG
**Tel:** 01224-899707
**Web:** www.petrofactraining.com
**Reg No:** 0204847SC **Estd:** 1977 Private Limited Company
**Line of Business:** Service activities incidental to oil and gas extraction excluding surveying
**Issued Capital:** £3,435,002
**Directors:** C W Thompson, S P Bullock, D Thow
**Co. Secretary:** Mrs Alison Broughton
**Responsibilities**
**Senior:** Darren South *(Financial Director)*
**Finance:** Darren South *(Financial Director)*
**HR:** Meureen Cowre *(HR Manager)*
**Branches:** Petrofac Training Group Ltd, North Esplanade East, Aberdeen, Aberdeenshire AB11 5QD
**US SIC:** 1389, 6711
**UK SIC:** 13000, 83962
**Auditors:** PricewaterhouseCoopers
**Bankers:** The Royal Bank Of Scotland Plc (83-25-16)

|      | 31-12-13  | 31-12-12  | 31-12-11  |
|------|-----------|-----------|-----------|
| TA   | 5,571,000 | 5,571,000 | 5,571,000 |
| P/L  | N/A       | N/A       | 3,016,000 |
| NW   | 3,949,000 | 3,949,000 | 3,949,000 |
| WC   | 558,000   | 558,000   | 558,000   |

## DUNS 53-645-1693
## Petrofac Training Ltd
(**Subsidiary of:** Petrofac Ltd)
Montrose Training Centre, Forties Road, Montrose, Angus DD10 9ET
**Tel:** 01674672230
**Web:** www.petrofactraining.com
**Reg No:** 0179707SC **VAT No:** 699815753
**Estd:** 1972 Private Limited Company
**Line of Business:** Training centres
**Trading Style:** R G I T Montrose
**Issued Capital:** £1,850,000
**Directors:** D Thow, G A Caird, S P Bullock, C W Thompson
**Co. Secretary:** Mrs Alison Broughton
**Responsibilities**
**Senior:** Peter Dennett *(Business Unit Manager)*, Louise Ferguson *(Manager)*
**Finance:** Kay Sherrifs *(Financial Manager)*
**Facilities:** Peter Dennett *(Business Unit Manager)*
**Branches:** Petrofac Training Ltd, Blackness Avenue, Altens Industrial Estate, Aberdeen, Aberdeenshire AB12 3PG
**US SIC:** 8299, 8249
**UK SIC:** 93300
**Auditors:** PricewaterhouseCoopers
**Bankers:** Bank Of Scotland (80-17-59)

|      | 31-12-13   | 31-12-12   | 31-12-11   |
|------|------------|------------|------------|
| TO   | 35,133,000 | 37,807,000 | 40,778,000 |
| P/L  | 2,765,000  | 2,119,000  | 4,005,000  |
| NW   | 7,591,000  | 5,757,000  | 4,245,000  |
| WC   | 1,947,000  | 2,092,000  | 1,123,000  |
| Emp. | 309        | 289        | 270        |

## DUNS 21-177-3666
## Petroineos Fuels Ltd
(**Subsidiary of:** China National Petroleum Corporation)
5 Wilton Road, London SW1V 1AN
**Tel:** 02380287200
**Reg No:** 7003774 **Estd:** 2009 Private Limited Company
**Line of Business:** Fuel dealers
**Directors:** A R Gardner, F Demay
**Co. Secretary:** Ms Diane Devotta-Hill
**Responsibilities**
**Finance:** Martin Stokes *(Financial Director)*
**US SIC:** 5052 **UK SIC:** 61200

**Auditors:** PricewaterhouseCoopers LLP
**Employees:** 65
**Turnover:** £3,068,400,000

## DUNS 21-443-6024
## Petroineos Manufacturing Scotland Ltd
(**Subsidiary of:** Ineos Ag)
Po Box 21, Bo'Ness Road, Grangemouth, Stirlingshire FK3 9XH
**Tel:** 01324483422 **Fax:** 01324-476159
**Web:** www.ineos.com
**Reg No:** 0010612SC **Estd:** 1919 Private Limited Company
**Line of Business:** Mineral oil refining
**Trading Style:** Ineos Technologies
**Issued Capital:** £35,000
**Directors:** Y Luo, L Yang, R E Mann, A Traynor, A R Gardner, B Si
**Co. Secretary:** Ms Diane Devotta-Hill
**Responsibilities**
**Finance:** James Laird *(Financial Director)*
**Marketing:** Dave Clarke *(IT Manager)*
**IT:** Dave Clarke *(IT Manager)*
**HR:** Nicola Porco *(Training Coordinator)*
**Health & Safety:** Sandy Todd *(Health & Safety Officer)*
**Operations:** Dave Clarke *(IT Manager)*
**Branches:** Petroineos Manufacturing Scotland Ltd, Finnart Ocean Terminal, Helensburgh, Dunbartonshire G84 0EY
**US SIC:** 2911 **UK SIC:** 14010
**Auditors:** PricewaterhouseCoopers LLP
**Bankers:** National Westminster Bank Plc (50-00-00)

|      | 31-12-13     | 31-12-12     | 31-12-11     |
|------|--------------|--------------|--------------|
| TO   | 214,959,000  | 208,231,000  | 291,120,000  |
| P/L  | (20,851,000) | (17,615,000) | 93,932,000   |
| NW   | 312,278,000  | 346,322,000  | 373,049,000  |
| WC   | (158,551,000)| (92,879,000) | (20,909,000) |
| Emp. | 403          | 390          | 595          |

## DUNS 73-920-3094
## Petrolatina Energy Ltd
Stanmore House, 2nd Floor, Suite 23, 29-30 St James's Street, London SW1A 1HB
**Tel:** 02079176825
**Web:** www.petrolatinaenergy.com
**Reg No:** 5173588 **Estd:** 2004 Private Limited Company
**Line of Business:** Oil and gas extraction
**Directors:** L Gerard, C A Mendez Sampayo, M Wiebe, J C Rodriguez
**Co. Secretary:** Capita Company Secretarial Servi
**US SIC:** 1311 **UK SIC:** 13000
**Auditors:** BDO LLP
**Employees:** 138
**Turnover:** £54,908,000

## DUNS 50-584-6055
## Petroleum Experts Ltd
(**Subsidiary of:** Petex Management Company Limited)
10 Logie Mill, Edinburgh, Midlothian EH7 4HG
**Tel:** 0131 474 7030
**Web:** www.petex.com
**Reg No:** 0126553SC **Estd:** 1990 Private Limited Company
**Line of Business:** Research and experimental development on natural sciences and engineering
**Export Sales:** £33,825,857
**Trading Style:** Petex
**Issued Capital:** £120,000
**Directors:** A Guedroudj, M Deere, P G Hadjipieris, J A Woodrow, M Seijo
**Responsibilities**
**Senior:** Michel Chartron *(Manager)*
**Finance:** Michel Chartron *(Manager)*
**US SIC:** 7391 **UK SIC:** 94000
**Auditors:** PricewaterhouseCoopers LLP
**Bankers:** Bank Of Scotland (80-11-30)

|      | 30-09-14   | 30-09-13   | 30-09-12   |
|------|------------|------------|------------|
| TO   | 39,152,665 | 37,893,559 | 27,572,588 |
| P/L  | 30,515,762 | 29,063,203 | 19,359,991 |
| NW   | 45,354,028 | 49,722,945 | 27,058,091 |
| WC   | 39,048,682 | 43,825,140 | 21,375,209 |
| Emp. | 61         | 59         | 53         |

## DUNS 39-969-5543                                   Imp
## Petroleum Manufacturing Services Ltd
Todd Square, Houstoun Industrial Estate, Livingston, West Lothian EH54 5EF
**Tel:** 01506432233 **Fax:** 01506-431122
**Web:** www.petroleumservices.co.nz
**Reg No:** 0111835SC **Estd:** 1988 Private Limited Company
**Line of Business:** Oil and gas exploration services
**Export Sales:** £13,404,876
**Issued Capital:** £50,000
**Directors:** W D Taylor, M Betts, D A Johnston
**Co. Secretary:** Scot Clifton

**Responsibilities**
**Senior:** Gary Eshenroder *(Manager)*, Brian Horne *(Plant Manager)*, Denis Jolly *(Plant Manager)*, Ricky Luke *(Manager)*, Derek Mathieson *(Manager)*, Kenneth McAllister *(Manager)*
**Engineering:** Denis Jolly *(Plant Manager)*
**US SIC:** 1389 **UK SIC:** 13000
**Auditors:** PricewaterhouseCoopers
**Bankers:** Bank Of Scotland (80-05-14)

| | 31-12-13 | 31-12-12 | 31-12-11 |
|---|---|---|---|
| TO | 14,268,367 | 19,423,215 | 17,956,661 |
| P/L | 301,782 | 2,008,018 | 1,082,022 |
| NW | 10,936,728 | 10,711,914 | 9,198,515 |
| WC | 9,834,152 | 9,354,991 | 8,138,211 |
| Emp. | 68 | 68 | 69 |

DUNS 22-288-6033

## Petromedia Ltd.

First Floor Regency House, 4 Clarence Road, Windsor, Berkshire SL4 5AD
**Tel:** 01753-410940 **Fax:** 01753-272251
**Web:** www.petromediacorp.com
**Reg No:** 4306574 **Estd:** 2012 Private Limited Company
**Line of Business:** Publishers
**Trading Style:** Bunkerworld
**Issued Capital:** £113,108
**Directors:** D J Post, M B Cape, N J Murphy, B J Peters, P Ajmera, M P Perryman
**Co. Secretary:**
Kenwood Secretaries Limited
**Responsibilities**
**Senior:** Paula Cape *(Manager)*
**US SIC:** 2731 **UK SIC:** 47532
**Auditors:** Grosvenor Partners LLP

| | 31-10-13 | 31-10-12 | 31-10-11 |
|---|---|---|---|
| TA | 1,082,537 | 846,455 | 807,683 |
| NW | 9,186 | (74,451) | 139,035 |
| WC | (182,287) | (222,329) | (866) |

DUNS 51-991-7744 **Imp**

## Petronas Energy Trading Ltd

1st Floor, Grand Building, One Strand, Trafalgar Square, London WC2N 5EJ
**Tel:** 02079-258-686 **Fax:** 02085-820-161
**Web:** www.petronasenergy.com
**Reg No:** 3359379 **Estd:** 1997 Private Limited Company
**Line of Business:** Gas companies
**Issued Capital:** £129,363,666
**Directors:** H R Kadir Shah, M F Bin Mohd Adnan, A Bin Zainol Abidin, M A Taib, K Reinisch, A A Alias
**Responsibilities**
**Senior:** Anuar Bin Ahmad *(Manager)*, Dario Ghazi *(Head of Analytics)*, Terry Labunda *(Head of PETRONAS LNG)*, Kevin Selleslags *(Head of Business Development)*, Swee Yap *(Manager)*
**Marketing:** Stuart Helm *(Senior Originator)*
**Sales:** Kevin Selleslags *(Head of Business Development)*
**IT:** Daniel Suttle *(Head of IT)*
**HR:** Lance Tilley *(Head of Human Resources)*
**Operations:** Daniel Dunn *(Head of Operations)*
**US SIC:** 4925 **UK SIC:** 25670
**Auditors:** Ernst & Young LLP
**Bankers:** Bumiputra-Commerce Bank Berhad (30-16-31)
**Following financial data are in thousands**

| | 31-12-13 | 31-12-12 | 31-12-11 |
|---|---|---|---|
| TO | 2,147,940 | 973,605 | 434,121 |
| P/L | (15,353) | (39,852) | 3,495 |
| NW | 106,956 | 27,503 | 67,874 |
| WC | (13,059) | (179,155) | 33,473 |
| Emp. | 76 | 66 | 29 |

DUNS 42-356-1906

## Petropavlovsk Plc

11 Grosvenor Place, London SW1X 7HH
**Tel:** 020-7201-8900 **Fax:** 020-7201-8901
**Web:** www.petropavlovsk.net
**Reg No:** 4343841 **Estd:** 2001 Private Limited Company
**Line of Business:** Other mining and quarrying not elsewhere classified
**Directors:** A Samokhvalova, C R Guthrie, Sir R Lyne, Dr D S Humphreys, C S Mcveigh Iii, A Maruta, Sir M D Field, D Chekashkin
**Co. Secretary:** Ms Amanda Whalley
**Responsibilities**
**Senior:** Sergey Ermolenko *(Manager)*, Peter Hill-Wood *(Non-Executive Director)*, Roderick Lyne *(Non-Executive Director)*, Pavel Maslovsky *(Director)*, Anna Subczynska-Samberger *(Legal Director)*
**US SIC:** 1499, 6711
**UK SIC:** 23960, 83962
**Auditors:** Deloitte LLP
**Employees:** 11,789
**Turnover:** £1,199,784,000

DUNS 22-715-8102 **Exp**

## Petroplan Ltd

**(Subsidiary of:** Petroplan Holdings Ltd)
99 Walnut Tree Close, Guildford, Surrey GU1 4UQ
**Tel:** 01483-881500 **Fax:** 01483-881501
**Web:** www.petroplan.com
**Reg No:** 1266770 **VAT No:** 215108505
**Estd:** 1976 Private Limited Company
**Line of Business:** Employment and recruitment companies and consultants
**Export Markets:** U S A; Venezuela; Netherlands
**Export Sales:** £72,850,750
**Issued Capital:** £10,600
**Principals:** J C Reeder *(Managing)*, Mrs P A Horton, J Coles, A G Speers, G R Pyle, Mrs J S Thomerson
**Co. Secretary:** Jess Coles
**US SIC:** 7361 **UK SIC:** 83954
**Auditors:** Roffe Swayne
**Bankers:** The Royal Bank Of Scotland Plc (16-20-30)

| | 31-12-13 | 31-12-12 | 31-12-11 |
|---|---|---|---|
| TO | 123,475,848 | 129,969,993 | 87,902,721 |
| P/L | 3,971,265 | (133,347) | 651,937 |
| NW | 2,350,488 | 787,796 | 1,115,312 |
| WC | 2,058,566 | 1,297,846 | 1,239,786 |
| Emp. | 71 | 83 | 66 |

DUNS 21-807-3704

## Petrostrat

48 Verulam Road, St Albans, Hertfordshire AL3 4DH
**Estd:** 2012
**Line of Business:** Building services
**US SIC:** 1622 **UK SIC:** 50200
**Employees:** 50

DUNS 22-166-9026

## Petrostrat Ltd

Tan-Y-Graig, Parc Caer Seion, Conwy, Gwynedd LL32 8FA
**Tel:** 01492562252 **Fax:** 01492 581 240
**Web:** www.petrostrat.com
**Reg No:** 4185518 **VAT No:** 771659691
**Estd:** 2001 Private Limited Company
**Line of Business:** Engineering services
**Issued Capital:** £1,000
**Directors:** Dr D C Rutledge, Dr F J Gregory, M F Weldon, P A Cornick
**Co. Secretary:** Jonathan Castle
**Branches:** Petrostrat Ltd - Tyttenhanger House, Tyttenhanger Park, St Albans, AL4 0PG Hertfordshire
**US SIC:** 8911 **UK SIC:** 83701

| | 31-03-14 | 31-03-13 | 31-03-12 |
|---|---|---|---|
| TA | 3,289,572 | 2,909,107 | 1,619,502 |
| NW | 1,513,581 | 1,338,129 | 945,780 |
| WC | 699,126 | 333,508 | 263,074 |

DUNS 50-390-0029

## Petrotechnics Ltd

Pavilion 5, Aberdeen, Aberdeenshire AB12 3QH
**Tel:** 01224337200
**Web:** www.petrotechnics.com
**Reg No:** 0118652SC **VAT No:** 552986991
**Estd:** 1990 Private Limited Company
**Line of Business:** Computer software (development)
**Issued Capital:** £14,863
**Directors:** A M Jones, P Murray, I W Mackay, D A Harcus, H C Rothermund, M A Sibson
**Co. Secretary:** David Harcus
**Responsibilities**
**Senior:** Michael Neill *(Manager)*
**Finance:** Alec Harcus *(Financial Director)*
**Marketing:** Scott Lehmann *(VP Product Management & Market)*
**Sales:** David Bleackley *(Vice President Sales)*
**Admin:** Alec Harcus *(Financial Director)*
**IT:** Steve Cannon *(PC Manager)*
**Health & Safety:** Jim Cameron *(Facilities Manager)*
**Facilities:** Jim Cameron *(Facilities Manager)*
**US SIC:** 7379, 7372
**UK SIC:** 83940
**Auditors:** Anderson Anderson & Brown LLP
**Bankers:** Lloyds TSB Bank plc (30-10-01)

| | 31-03-14 | 31-03-13 | 31-03-12 |
|---|---|---|---|
| TO | 10,228,952 | 9,257,488 | 6,894,253 |
| P/L | (546,013) | 29,373 | (3,364,023) |
| NW | 5,421,226 | 2,973,153 | 2,809,434 |
| WC | 8,435,776 | 2,880,264 | 2,645,994 |
| Emp. | 117 | 113 | 128 |

DUNS 22-867-7209 **Imp**

## Pets At Home Ltd

**(Subsidiary of:** Pets At Home Holdings Limited)
Epsom Avenue, Stanley Green Trading Estate, Handforth, Wilmslow, Cheshire SK9 3RN
**Tel:** 01614866688 **Fax:** 01614-854846
**Web:** www.petsathome.co.uk
**Reg No:** 1822577 **VAT No:** 616431754
**Estd:** 1984 Private Limited Company
**Line of Business:** Other retail sale in specialised stores not elsewhere classified
**Issued Capital:** £1,020,000
**Directors:** P Pritchard, Ms S E Hopson, N Wood, I Kellett, P Hackney
**Co. Secretary:** Ms Louise Stonier
**Responsibilities**
**HR:** Alison McCarthy *(Training Manager)*
**Purchasing:** Trudi Hills *(Head of Trading)*
**Branches:** Pets At Home Ltd, Myton Road, Leamington Spa, Warwickshire CV31 3NY
**US SIC:** 5999 **UK SIC:** 65600
**Auditors:** KPMG LLP
**Bankers:** National Westminster Bank Plc (01-10-01)

| | 27-03-14 | 28-03-13 | 29-03-12 |
|---|---|---|---|
| TO | 633,429,000 | 586,350,000 | 536,410,000 |
| P/L | 83,858,000 | 77,707,000 | 72,864,000 |
| NW | 462,445,000 | 382,537,000 | 308,386,000 |
| WC | 426,655,000 | 336,227,000 | 258,135,000 |
| Emp. | 4,537 | 4,038 | 3,735 |

DUNS 39-740-0193 **Imp-Exp**

## Pets Choice Ltd

**(Subsidiary of:** Pet Food Brands (Holdings) Ltd)
Brentwood House, Lower Philips Road, Whitebirk Industrial Estate, Blackburn, Lancashire BB1 5UD
**Tel:** 01254-54545 **Fax:** 01254-681446
**Web:** www.petschoice.co.uk
**Reg No:** 2181268 **VAT No:** 507909334
**Estd:** 1990 Private Limited Company
**Line of Business:** Animal feed and pet foods
**Export Sales:** £1,224,465
**Issued Capital:** £567,099
**Directors:** H J Deuerer, A P Raeburn
**Co. Secretary:** Scott Campbell
**Responsibilities**
**Senior:** Philippe Bieler *(Manager)*, Joseph Davies *(Manager)*
**Admin:** Margaret Hudson *(Administration Manager)*
**HR:** Margaret Hudson *(Administration Manager)*
**Health & Safety:** Ian Greenlees *(Health & Safety Officer)*
**Facilities:** Ian Greenlees *(Health & Safety Officer)*
**Operations:** Margaret Hudson *(Administration Manager)*
**Purchasing:** Margaret Hudson *(Administration Manager)*
**Branches:** Pets Choice Ltd, Gorse Street, Blackburn, Lancashire BB1 3EU
**US SIC:** 2047 **UK SIC:** 42221
**Auditors:** Mazars LLP
**Bankers:** Lloyds TSB Bank plc (30-91-47)

| | 31-12-13 | 29-06-12 | 24-12-11 |
|---|---|---|---|
| TO | 40,651,461 | 24,407,023 | 22,019,388 |
| P/L | 1,150,025 | 1,060,015 | 1,131,972 |
| NW | 5,167,538 | 4,254,823 | 3,738,517 |
| WC | 271,171 | 338,256 | 208,461 |
| Emp. | 137 | 142 | 138 |

DUNS 23-552-7772

## Pets Corner (U K) Ltd

**(Subsidiary of:** Dechado Group Ltd)
33 Queensway, Crawley, West Sussex RH10 1EG
**Tel:** 01293560665 **Fax:** 01293-550554
**Web:** www.petscorner.co.uk
**Reg No:** 3551085 **Estd:** 1998 Private Limited Company
**Line of Business:** Other retail sale in specialised stores not elsewhere classified
**Issued Capital:** £1,510,000
**Principals:** D A Richmond *(Managing)*, I Dougal
**Co. Secretary:** Steven Charman
**Responsibilities**
**Senior:** Charlotte Williams *(Manager)*
**Branches:** Pets Corner (U K) Ltd, Wyevale Garden Centre, Bath Road, Hungerford, Berkshire RG17 0HE
**US SIC:** 7399 **UK SIC:** 83954
**Auditors:** Liberty Bishop
**Bankers:** Girobank Plc (72-00-00)

| | 30-09-13 | 30-09-12 | 30-09-11 |
|---|---|---|---|
| TO | 25,169,010 | 22,866,718 | 20,567,723 |
| P/L | 1,489,637 | 674,536 | 415,926 |
| NW | 2,054,326 | 1,592,489 | 1,549,053 |
| WC | 945,719 | (1,164,201) | 173,651 |
| Emp. | 419 | 375 | 350 |

DUNS 21-030-0923

## Pets Perfection

37 Ebury Bridge Road, London SW1W 8QX
**Tel:** 02077305080
**Web:** www.petsperfection.co.uk
**Proprietorship**
**Line of Business:** Pet services
**Proprietor:** P Cambridge
**US SIC:** 5154 **UK SIC:** 61100
**Employees:** 60

DUNS 21-633-3401

## Pettits of Wallingford Ltd

**(Subsidiary of:** Rowse Trading Ltd)
46-50 St Marys Street, Wallingford, Oxfordshire OX10 0EY
**Tel:** 01491-835253
**Web:** www.pettitsofwallingford.co.uk
**Reg No:** 0716637 **VAT No:** 614567731
**Estd:** 1996 Private Limited Company
**Line of Business:** Departmental stores
**Issued Capital:** £10,000
**Managing Director:** R M Rowse
**Responsibilities**
**Senior:** Kevin Willis *(Store Manager)*
**Marketing:** Kevin Willis *(Store Manager)*
**Sales:** Kevin Willis *(Store Manager)*
**HR:** Kevin Willis *(Store Manager)*
**Facilities:** Kevin Willis *(Store Manager)*
**Branches:** in the Oxford area.
**US SIC:** 5812 **UK SIC:** 66110
**Auditors:** Target Consulting Ltd
**Bankers:** Barclays Bank Plc (20-27-48)

| | 01-02-14 | 26-01-13 | 28-02-12 |
|---|---|---|---|
| TA | 953,310 | 993,181 | 892,270 |
| NW | 284,696 | 424,806 | 510,241 |
| WC | 146,224 | 283,169 | 361,009 |

DUNS 54-368-7529

## Petwood Hotel Ltd

Stixwould Road, Woodhall Spa, Lincolnshire LN10 6QG
**Tel:** 01526-352411 **Fax:** 01526-353473
**Web:** www.petwood.co.uk
**Reg No:** 3258579 **Estd:** 1996 Private Limited Company
**Line of Business:** Hotels
**Issued Capital:** £1,000
**Directors:** F J Brealey, Miss E T Brealey
**Co. Secretary:** Jeremiah Kelly
**Responsibilities**
**Senior:** John Mcculloch *(General Manager)*
**Finance:** Jenny Compton *(Accounts Manager)*, Sally Dickinson *(Accounts Manager)*
**Marketing:** Emma Brilly *(Sales and Marketing Director)*, Sue Newell *(Sales & Marketing Manager)*
**Sales:** Emma Brilly *(Sales and Marketing Director)*, Sue Newell *(Sales & Marketing Manager)*
**HR:** John Mcculloch *(General Manager)*
**Purchasing:** John Mcculloch *(General Manager)*
**US SIC:** 7011 **UK SIC:** 66500
**Auditors:** Bdo Stoy Hayward
**Bankers:** National Westminster Bank Plc (51-81-08)

| | 29-09-13 | 30-09-12 | 02-09-11 |
|---|---|---|---|
| TO | 2,458,515 | 2,290,157 | 2,354,190 |
| P/L | 83,298 | (11,223) | 89,113 |
| NW | 1,558,900 | 1,486,556 | 1,400,138 |
| WC | (63,145) | (65,532) | (258,641) |
| Emp. | 97 | 94 | 99 |

DUNS 21-615-3379

## Peugeot Citroen Retail Uk Ltd

**(Subsidiary of:** Peugeot Sa)
Pinley House, 2 Sunbeam Way, Coventry, West Midlands CV3 1ND
**Tel:** 02476449581
**Web:** www.robinsandday.co.uk
**Reg No:** 0129806 **VAT No:** 272369149
**Estd:** 1913 Private Limited Company
**Line of Business:** Sale of new motor vehicles
**Issued Capital:** £82,742,000
**Directors:** D Connell, J G Imparato, D I Peel, S D Lawrence, N J Willetts, Mrs L Jackson
**Co. Secretary:**
Shoosmiths Secretaries Limited
**Responsibilities**
**Senior:** St?ane Le Guevel *(Director)*
**Branches:** Peugeot Citroen Retail Uk Ltd, Edgware Infant School, High Street, Edgware, Middlesex HA8 7EQ
**US SIC:** 5511, 5521, 5531
**UK SIC:** 65100
**Auditors:** Ernst & Young LLP
**Bankers:** HSBC Bank plc (40-18-17)

| | 31-12-13 | 31-12-12 | 31-12-11 |
|---|---|---|---|
| TO | 447,339,000 | 457,976,000 | 438,453,000 |
| P/L | (10,129,000) | (18,212,000) | (13,388,000) |
| NW | (4,139,000) | (3,197,000) | 2,138,000 |
| WC | 37,980,000 | 34,573,000 | (2,754,000) |
| Emp. | 1,150 | 1,299 | 1,399 |

DUNS 21-025-2128

## Peugeot Motor Company Plc

**(Subsidiary of:** Peugeot Sa)
Pinley House, 2 Sunbeam Way, Coventry, West Midlands CV3 1ND
**Tel:** 02476884000
**Web:** www.peugeot.co.uk
**Reg No:** 0148545 **VAT No:** 272369149
**Estd:** 1917 Public Limited Company
**Line of Business:** Representative office
**Issued Capital:** £20,717,200
**Directors:** N Moscrop, M Picat, P De Rovira, K M O'Kelly, D J Connell, N J Willetts

**Co. Secretary:**
Shoosmiths Secretaries Limited
**Responsibilities**
**Senior:** Francois Bardon *(Manager)*, Christian Carsalade *(Manager)*, Kerry Farr *(Office Manager)*, St?ane Le Guevel *(Director)*, Marc Lechantre *(Global Marketing And Events Di)*
**Facilities:** Dave Metcalfe *(Facilities Manager)*
**Purchasing:** David Kettley *(Purchasing Director)*
**Branches:** Peugeot Motor Company Plc, Robins & Day, Kenpas Highway, Coventry, West Midlands CV3 6PE
**US SIC:** 5511, 5521
**UK SIC:** 65100
**Auditors:** Ernst & Young LLP
**Bankers:** National Westminster Bank Plc (60-00-01)

**Following financial data are in thousands**

| | 31-12-13 | 31-12-12 | 31-12-11 |
|---|---|---|---|
| TO | 1,331,515 | 1,322,675 | 1,291,200 |
| P/L | 1,559 | (2,108) | (786) |
| NW | 27,397 | 27,094 | 21,654 |
| WC | 87,429 | 80,342 | 52,701 |
| Emp. | 395 | 505 | 569 |

DUNS 21-780-5904

## Pevensey & Westham C of E Primary School

86 High Street, Westham, Pevensey, East Sussex BN24 5LP
**Tel:** 01323762269
**Web:** http://pev-west.esussex.dbprimary.com
**Estd:** 1990 Proprietorship
**Line of Business:** Primary education
**Proprietor:** Mrs J Gott
**Responsibilities**
**Finance:** K Brett *(Business Manager)*
**Marketing:** K Brett *(Business Manager)*
**US SIC:** 8211 **UK SIC:** 93200
**Employees:** 60

DUNS 21-198-1394 **Imp**

## Peverall Bros. Ltd

(**Subsidiary of:** Relden Ltd)
Unit 3c Tonbridge Road, Romford, Essex RM3 8TS
**Tel:** 01708-381525
**Web:** www.surveyexpress.co.uk
**Reg No:** 1417291 **VAT No:** 324189754
**Estd:** 1972 Private Limited Company
**Line of Business:** Other construction work involving special trades
**Trading Style:** Survey Express Services
**Issued Capital:** £3,000
**Directors:** C Ginnaw, S Jennings
**Co. Secretary:** Paul Harden
**Responsibilities**
**Senior:** Carl Proctor *(Manager)*
**Branches:** Peverall Bros. Ltd, Brownhill Rd, London SE6 1AT
**US SIC:** 1799 **UK SIC:** 50000
**Auditors:** Barnes Roffe LLP
**Bankers:** Barclays Bank Plc (20-48-46)

| | 30-04-14 | 30-04-13 | 30-04-12 |
|---|---|---|---|
| TA | 3,052,381 | 3,037,512 | 2,715,360 |
| NW | 756,803 | 740,591 | 746,217 |
| WC | 1,348,996 | 1,270,591 | 1,290,934 |

DUNS 42-394-6862

## Peveril Shipping Ltd

(**Subsidiary of:** Bernhard Schulte Gmbh & Co. Kg)
Belmont Hill, Douglas, Douglas, Isle of Man IM1 4RE
**Tel:** 01624631800
**Reg No:** 0056956M **Estd:** 1992 Private Limited Company
**Line of Business:** Ship management and technical management
**Issued Capital:** £2,000
**Directors:** F E Preece, G J Kelly, W R Mann
**Co. Secretary:** Michael Gisbourne
**US SIC:** 7392 **UK SIC:** 83951
**Employees:** 70

DUNS 23-086-0822

## Pewsey Vale School

Wilcot Road, Pewsey, Wiltshire SN9 5EW
**Tel:** 01672-565000
**Web:** www.pewsey-vale.wilts.sch.uk
**Estd:** 1969
**Line of Business:** Schools (local authority)
**Directors:** Mrs D Palnte-Cleall, M Anderson
**US SIC:** 8211 **UK SIC:** 93200
**Employees:** 50

DUNS 34-514-3924

## Peyton & Byrne Ltd

Trafalgar Square, London WC2N 5DN
**Web:** www.peytonandbyrne.com
**Reg No:** 5325242 **VAT No:** 917443420
**Estd:** 2005 Private Limited Company
**Line of Business:** Representative office
**Issued Capital:** £1
**Directors:** M A Johnson, O P Peyton, A J Brew, P Deeming, C M Peyton
**Co. Secretary:** Ms Siobhan Peyton
**Responsibilities**
**Senior:** Matthew Britton *(Manager)*
**US SIC:** 5199 **UK SIC:** 61900
**Auditors:** Brebners
**Bankers:** Bank Of Scotland (12-01-03)

| | 31-03-13 | 01-04-12 | 27-03-11 |
|---|---|---|---|
| TO | 18,717,055 | 19,971,346 | 16,207,785 |
| P/L | 221,909 | 359,943 | (662,845) |
| NW | (1,365,330) | (2,003,695) | (2,373,231) |
| WC | (2,127,871) | (4,061,538) | (4,616,382) |
| Emp. | 511 | 476 | 408 |

DUNS 21-120-7758

## P.F. Ahern & Sons Ltd

Oliver Close, Grays, Essex RM20 3EE
**Tel:** 01268293931
**Web:** www.ahern.co.uk
**Reg No:** 1228889 **Estd:** 1965 Private Limited Company
**Line of Business:** Waste disposal
**Issued Capital:** £288,400
**Principals:** Mrs L B Scott *(Managing)*, P R Scott, P B Ahern
**Co. Secretary:** Mrs Lilian Scott
**Responsibilities**
**Senior:** Mike Harvey *(Operations Director)*
**Branches:** P.f. Ahern & Sons Ltd, Tollgate Rd Becton, London E6 5YA
**US SIC:** 6711, 7399
**UK SIC:** 83962, 83954
**Auditors:** Fredericks
**Bankers:** The Royal Bank Of Scotland Plc (16-30-10)

| | 31-10-13 | 31-10-12 | 31-10-11 |
|---|---|---|---|
| TO | 9,009,529 | 8,981,047 | 8,891,856 |
| P/L | 919,176 | 200,072 | 83,488 |
| NW | 8,477,280 | 7,659,643 | 7,451,304 |
| WC | 650,105 | (45,808) | (190,345) |
| Emp. | 65 | 65 | 66 |

DUNS 50-398-0070 **Imp**

## P.F. Cusack (Tools Supplies) Ltd

Unit 1, Dencoram Business Centre, Dundee Way, Enfield, Middlesex EN3 7SX
**Tel:** 02083444100 **Fax:** 020-8808-6662
**Web:** www.cusack.co.uk
**Reg No:** 2404505 **VAT No:** 553887693
**Estd:** 2010 Private Limited Company
**Line of Business:** Builders equipment
**Export Sales:** £88,005
**Issued Capital:** £10,000
**Managing Director:** P F Cusack
**Co. Secretary:** Mrs Mary Cusack
**Branches:** P.f. Cusack (Tools Supplies) Ltd, Prince Of Wales Indstl Units, Vulcan St, Oldham, Lancashire OL1 4ER
**US SIC:** 3423 **UK SIC:** 31612
**Auditors:** Barron & Co
**Bankers:** Allied Irish Bank (gb) (23-83-95)

| | 30-09-13 | 30-09-12 | 30-09-11 |
|---|---|---|---|
| TO | 23,121,358 | 22,650,845 | 20,486,004 |
| P/L | 2,361,106 | 2,002,402 | 2,037,921 |
| NW | 13,957,300 | 12,349,027 | 10,989,814 |
| WC | 7,386,423 | 7,048,696 | 6,288,382 |
| Emp. | 120 | 110 | 110 |

DUNS 29-044-6988

## Pf Whitehead Transport Services Ltd

Unit 4, Coomber Way, Croydon, Surrey CR0 4TQ
**Tel:** 02086650110 **Fax:** 02086650110
**Web:** www.pfwhitehead.com
**Reg No:** 0987986 **Estd:** 1970 Private Limited Company
**Line of Business:** Misc special warehousing & storage
**Issued Capital:** £100
**Principals:** P F Whitehead *(Managing)*, Ms N M Whitehead, P N Whitehead
**Co. Secretary:** Peter Whitehead
**Branches:** Pf Whitehead Transport Services Ltd, Unit 4, Coomber Way, Croydon, Surrey CR0 4TQ
**US SIC:** 4226, 4213
**UK SIC:** 77003, 72300
**Auditors:** Kingston Smith LLP
**Bankers:** National Westminster Bank Plc (60-07-02)

| | 31-07-14 | 31-07-13 | 31-07-12 |
|---|---|---|---|
| TO | 6,779,440 | 5,759,363 | 6,348,283 |
| P/L | 410,675 | 308,438 | 79,456 |
| NW | 1,339,127 | 1,209,749 | 974,502 |
| WC | 1,210,822 | 1,034,787 | 766,144 |
| Emp. | N/A | N/A | 91 |

DUNS 39-758-1604 **Imp-Exp**

## Pfaudler Process Solutions Group Uk Ltd

(**Subsidiary of:** National Oilwell Varco Inc.)
Riverside, Leven, Fife KY8 4RT
**Tel:** 01333423020 **Fax:** 01333-427432
**Web:** www.pfaudlerbalfour.co.uk
**Reg No:** 2197267 **VAT No:** 379942489
**Estd:** 1810 Private Limited Company
**Line of Business:** Manufacture of other special purpose machinery not elsewhere classified
**Export Markets:** European Union (E U); U S A; S Africa; Far East
**Export Sales:** £23,485,471
**Trading Style:** Pfauduer-Balfour, Chemical Reactor Services, Chemineer
**Issued Capital:** £7,831
**Directors:** M Goldsmith, A C Wills, J A Drury
**Co. Secretary:** Ms Kathryn Mccann
**Responsibilities**
**Operations:** Ronald Black *(Quality Assurance Manager)*
**Purchasing:** Dougie Edwards *(Purchasing Manager)*
**Branches:** Pfaudler Process Solutions Group Uk Ltd, Mosterton, Beaminster, Dorset DT8 3HG
**US SIC:** 3559, 3999
**UK SIC:** 32863, 49590
**Auditors:** Ernst & Young LLP
**Bankers:** The Royal Bank Of Scotland Plc (83-24-24)

| | 31-12-13 | 31-08-12 | 31-12-11 |
|---|---|---|---|
| TO | 38,133,133 | 27,569,791 | 23,415,365 |
| P/L | 3,050,351 | 680,435 | 224,579 |
| NW | 6,847,410 | 6,810,421 | 11,645,427 |
| WC | 9,258,792 | 7,284,058 | 10,478,532 |
| Emp. | 250 | 259 | 259 |

DUNS 22-227-8934

## P.F.B.G. Ltd

Bryngelynen, Oswestry, Shropshire SY10 0BP
**Tel:** 01691780506
**Web:** www.progressivefarmers.co.uk
**Reg No:** 4245840 **Estd:** 2001 Private Limited Company
**Line of Business:** Animal feed and pet foods
**Trading Style:** Progressive Farmers Buying Group
**Issued Capital:** £10
**Director:** A Evans
**US SIC:** 2047, 5999
**UK SIC:** 42221, 65600
**Bankers:** National Westminster Bank Plc (55-70-40)

| | 31-03-14 | 31-03-13 | 31-03-12 |
|---|---|---|---|
| TA | 251,151 | 203,152 | 110,059 |
| NW | 223,909 | 164,354 | 87,673 |
| WC | 223,726 | 163,948 | 87,037 |

DUNS 21-000-1591

## Pfc Education Llp

1 Mcbride House, Penn Road, Beaconsfield, Buckinghamshire HP9 2FY
**Tel:** 01494670024
**Reg No:** 0328674OC **Estd:** 2007 Private Limited Company
**Line of Business:** Menswear retail
**US SIC:** 5611 **UK SIC:** 64500

| | 31-08-14 | 31-08-13 | 31-08-12 |
|---|---|---|---|
| TO | 4,242,529 | 4,046,807 | 4,282,499 |
| P/L | (276,230) | (480,137) | (260,093) |
| NW | 6,396,987 | 5,080,631 | 4,814,275 |
| WC | (1,013,288) | (612,893) | (283,435) |
| Emp. | 102 | 104 | 106 |

DUNS 21-207-2490

## P.F.D.(Carlisle)Ltd

Pioneer House, Montgomery Way, Carlisle, Cumbria CA1 2RR
**Tel:** 01228-523474
**Web:** www.pioneerfoods.co.uk
**Reg No:** 0557210 **VAT No:** 533445750
**Estd:** 2002 Private Limited Company
**Line of Business:** Catering supplies
**Trading Style:** Pioneer Food Distributors
**Issued Capital:** £17,301
**Principals:** H A Jenkins *(Chairman and Managing)*, Miss K E Abbott *(Financial)*, N G Jenkins, D A Jenkins, B G Garrett, Ms P D Jenkins
**Branches:** P.f.d.(Carlisle)ltd, Montgomery Way, Carlisle, Cumbria CA1 2RW
**US SIC:** 5149, 5146
**UK SIC:** 61700
**Auditors:** Moore & Smalley LLP
**Bankers:** National Westminster Bank Plc (60-04-30)

| | 30-04-14 | 30-04-13 | 30-04-12 |
|---|---|---|---|
| TO | 34,560,936 | 32,885,068 | 33,061,872 |
| P/L | 1,769,364 | 1,641,562 | 1,409,284 |
| NW | 12,798,194 | 11,785,809 | 10,501,608 |
| WC | 7,309,396 | 6,997,823 | 5,798,469 |
| Emp. | 296 | 296 | 294 |

DUNS 29-145-1938 **Imp-Exp**

## Pfe Express Ltd

Foremost House, Eastways, Witham, Essex CM8 3PL
**Tel:** 08707771400 **Fax:** 0870-777-1401
**Web:** www.pfeweb.com
**Reg No:** 1712129 **VAT No:** 407023887
**Estd:** 1984 Private Limited Company
**Line of Business:** Road haulage and transport services
**Issued Capital:** £10,000
**Principals:** P A Collins *(Managing)*, D Girling, A J Collins
**Co. Secretary:** Ms Doreen Toms
**Responsibilities**
**Senior:** Ray Cable *(Warehouse Manager)*
**Finance:** Simon Boulton *(Financial Coordinator)*
**HR:** Veronica Girling *(Human Resources Manager)*
**Health & Safety:** Ray Cable *(Warehouse Manager)*
**Facilities:** Ray Cable *(Warehouse Manager)*
**Purchasing:** Simon Boulton *(Financial Coordinator)*
**US SIC:** 4789 **UK SIC:** 77002
**Auditors:** Errington Langer Pinner
**Bankers:** Barclays Bank Plc (20-77-67)

| | 30-06-13 | 30-06-12 | 30-06-11 |
|---|---|---|---|
| TO | 40,776,901 | 35,355,819 | 42,138,875 |
| P/L | 1,010,333 | 993,934 | 690,859 |
| NW | 6,880,612 | 6,150,279 | 5,422,345 |
| WC | 4,086,924 | 3,288,158 | 2,608,675 |
| Emp. | 94 | 88 | 85 |

DUNS 22-855-7344 **Imp**

## Pfeifer Drako Ltd

(**Subsidiary of:** Pfeifer Holding Gmbh & Co. Kg)
Marshfield Bank, Crewe, Cheshire CW2 8UY
**Tel:** 01270-587-728
**Web:** www.pfeifer.co.uk
**Reg No:** 1515817 **VAT No:** 338403268
**Estd:** 1980 Private Limited Company
**Line of Business:** Lifting equipment
**Export Sales:** £152,732
**Issued Capital:** £250,000
**Principals:** A Morrison *(Financial)*, E H Pfeifer
**Co. Secretary:** Mrs Sandra Dutton Jones
**Responsibilities**
**Senior:** Wayne Shaw *(Warehouse Manager)*
**Admin:** Angie Dutton *(Administrator)*, Claire Standage *(Administrator)*
**Facilities:** Wayne Shaw *(Warehouse Manager)*
**Branches:** Pfeifer Drako Ltd, Crewe,Gates Farm Est,Lancaster Fields, Cheshire Crewe
**US SIC:** 3534 **UK SIC:** 32553
**Auditors:** Afford Bond LLP
**Bankers:** HSBC Bank plc (40-18-24)

| | 31-12-13 | 31-12-12 | 31-12-11 |
|---|---|---|---|
| TO | 11,683,351 | 11,444,407 | 10,974,926 |
| P/L | 566,525 | 660,922 | 483,581 |
| NW | 1,995,366 | 1,639,800 | 1,224,262 |
| WC | 1,158,065 | 800,543 | 387,062 |
| Emp. | 70 | 72 | 76 |

DUNS 76-994-2608

## Pff Packaging Ltd

(**Subsidiary of:** Pff Packaging Group Ltd)
Unit 3 Airedale Park, Royd Ings Avenue, Keighley, West Yorkshire BD21 4DG
**Tel:** 01535-662-800 **Fax:** 01535-606-533
**Web:** www.pff.uk.com
**Reg No:** 2648722 **VAT No:** 557297793
**Estd:** 2007 Private Limited Company
**Line of Business:** Manufacturer of sustainable, thermoformed packaging
**Export Sales:** £64,033
**Trading Style:** Pff Thermoformed Packaging
**Issued Capital:** £100
**Directors:** N H Bairstow, S W Dowe, Ms C Cox, Ms M A Bairstow, A R Bairstow, S J Carr
**Co. Secretary:** Mrs Michelle Bairstow
**US SIC:** 2821, 3079, 4783
**UK SIC:** 25140, 48360, 77002
**Auditors:** Walter Dawson & Son

| | 31-07-13 | 31-07-12 | 31-07-11 |
|---|---|---|---|
| TO | 17,693,242 | 11,188,883 | 12,229,436 |
| P/L | (62,288) | 108,614 | 41,939 |
| NW | 464,280 | 527,662 | 444,746 |
| WC | (992,679) | (777,141) | (655,719) |
| Emp. | 71 | 61 | 55 |

DUNS 29-017-2675 **Imp**

## Pfizer Ltd

(**Subsidiary of:** Pfizer Pharmaceuticals Global Coöperatief U.A.)
Ramsgate Road, Sandwich, Kent CT13 9NJ
**Tel:** 01304-616-161 **Fax:** 01304-656-221
**Web:** www.pfizer.co.uk
**Reg No:** 0526209 **VAT No:** 201048427
**Estd:** 1953 Private Limited Company
**Line of Business:** Wholesale of pharmaceutical goods
**Export Sales:** £249,527,000
**Issued Capital:** £86,300,000
**Directors:** Ms E M Greenfield, C M Seller, Ms R A Coles, Ms P Tully, I E Franklin, T F Dolan, J R Smith, D B Hughes
**Co. Secretary:** Ms Jacqueline Mount
**Responsibilities**
**Senior:** Jonathan Emms *(Director)*, Imogen Gill *(Manager)*, Ruth Mckernan *(Director)*, Berkeley Phillips *(Director)*
**Marketing:** Raquel Alcobia *(Brand Manager - Robitussin & T)*, Cormac Devery *(R&D & Marketing Director - Adv)*, Laura Duckworth *(Brand Manager - Emergen-c)*, Rajen Gohil *(Digital Marketing Manager)*, Helene Manga *(Senior Brand Manager - Centrum)*, Kelly Reed *(Digital Marketing Manager)*, Nolla Sleiman *(Senior European Brand Manager)*, Keitel Suri *(European Brand Director - Lipi)*

**IT:** Rajen Gohil (*Digital Marketing Manager*), Jon Gunne (*Regional Digital Service and O*), Kelly Reed (*Digital Marketing Manager*)
**HR:** Sue Adam-Reynolds (*Compensation Lead Pfizer Globa*)
**Branches:** Pfizer Ltd, 34 South Gyle Crescent, Edinburgh, Midlothian EH12 9EB
**US SIC:** 5122, 7391
**UK SIC:** 61800, 94000
**Auditors:** KPMG LLP
**Bankers:** Lloyds TSB Bank plc (30-00-00)
Following financial data are in thousands

|       | 30-11-13  | 30-11-12  | 30-11-11  |
|-------|-----------|-----------|-----------|
| TO    | 1,359,501 | 1,576,731 | 1,831,528 |
| P/L   | 84,736    | 97,935    | (759,700) |
| NW    | 286,347   | 78,412    | 35,524    |
| WC    | 25,123    | (381,317) | (511,065) |
| Emp.  | 2,357     | 3,280     | 4,134     |

**DUNS 21-925-6666**
### P.F.K. Ling Ltd
55 Mendham Lane, Harleston, Norfolk IP20 9DW
**Tel:** 01379851080 **Fax:** 01379-854373
**Web:** www.lings.co.uk
**Reg No:** 0710435 **Estd:** 1966 Private Limited Company
**Line of Business:** Motor cycles & scooters
**Issued Capital:** £521,200
**Principals:** D J Jary (*Managing*), C J Jary (*Managing*), Mrs A M Jary, P M Barkshire
**Branches:** P.f.k. Ling Ltd, Riverside Rd, Lowestoft, Suffolk NR33 0TU
**US SIC:** 5571, 5521
**UK SIC:** 65100
**Auditors:** Sexty & Co
**Bankers:** National Westminster Bank Plc (60-15-31)

|       | 31-12-13   | 31-12-12   | 31-12-11   |
|-------|------------|------------|------------|
| TO    | 18,176,427 | 17,279,662 | 15,852,904 |
| P/L   | 213,744    | 40,230     | (434,929)  |
| NW    | 4,954,625  | 4,809,163  | 4,831,713  |
| WC    | 2,035,123  | 1,843,679  | 1,705,511  |
| Emp.  | 86         | 85         | 86         |

**DUNS 64-098-8085**
### P.F.L. (Holdings) Ltd
Genesis Marketing Ltd, Worcester, Worcestershire WR3 8TJ
**Tel:** 01905342000
**Reg No:** 3494460 **Estd:** 1998 Private Limited Company
**Line of Business:** Management activities of other non-financial holding companies not elsewhere classified
**Issued Capital:** £29
**Director:** C M Westwood
**Co. Secretary:** Ms Maria Westwood
**US SIC:** 7399 **UK SIC:** 83954

|     | 31-12-13  | 31-12-12 | 31-12-11 |
|-----|-----------|----------|----------|
| TA  | 1,096,977 | 905,403  | 906,253  |
| NW  | 936,541   | 894,002  | 899,772  |
| WC  | 3,862     | 148,944  | 317,438  |

**DUNS 45-890-0305**
### Pfp Contracting Ltd
26 Abbotsinch Road, Grangemouth, Stirlingshire FK3 9UX
**Tel:** 01324-878180 **Fax:** 01324-878181
**Web:** www.pfpcontracting.com
**Reg No:** 0167125SC **Estd:** 1995 Private Limited Company
**Line of Business:** Fire protection consultants and engineers
**Issued Capital:** £2
**Directors:** C Frew, S P Ullyart
**Co. Secretary:** Malcolm Morgan
**Responsibilities**
**Senior:** Angela Frew (*Manager*)
**US SIC:** 8911, 1731, 1742
**UK SIC:** 83701, 50300, 50400
**Auditors:** RSM Tenon Audit Ltd
**Bankers:** Lloyds Tsb Scotland Plc (87-64-05)

|      | 31-07-13  | 31-07-12  | 31-07-11  |
|------|-----------|-----------|-----------|
| TO   | N/A       | N/A       | 2,702,194 |
| P/L  | N/A       | N/A       | 29,597    |
| NW   | 2,753,584 | 143,294   | 82,965    |
| WC   | 2,282,877 | 1,984,269 | 1,960,195 |
| Emp. | N/A       | N/A       | 31        |

**DUNS 73-570-3329**
### Pfpl (Holdings) Ltd.
(**Subsidiary of:** Places for People Group Ltd)
Otium House, 2 Freemantle Road, Bagshot, Surrey GU19 5LL
**Web:** www.dcleisure.co.uk
**Reg No:** 4832063 **Estd:** 2003 Private Limited Company
**Line of Business:** Holding companies management activities
**Trading Style:** D C L Management
**Issued Capital:** £250,000
**Directors:** D Cowans, Ms S Dodd, P Kirkham, S J Philpott, C R Phillips, T C Hewett
**Co. Secretary:** Christopher Martin
**Responsibilities**
**Senior:** Keith Pacey (*Manager*), Ryan Robson (*Manager*)
**Branches:** Pfpl (Holdings) Ltd., St. Margarets Street, Bradford-On-Avon, Wiltshire BA15 1DF

**US SIC:** 6711 **UK SIC:** 83962
**Auditors:** Grant Thornton UK LLP
**Bankers:** Lloyds TSB Bank plc (30-12-99)

|      | 31-03-14    | 31-03-13   | 31-03-12   |
|------|-------------|------------|------------|
| TO   | 102,780,000 | 89,732,000 | 88,007,000 |
| P/L  | 7,662,000   | 1,805,000  | 2,689,000  |
| NW   | 2,994,000   | (825,000)  | (2,350,000)|
| WC   | 5,605,000   | 4,811,000  | 2,483,000  |
| Emp. | 2,067       | 1,762      | 1,816      |

**DUNS 29-351-4816**
### Pft Ltd
(**Subsidiary of:** Marsh & McLennan Companies Inc.)
1 Tower Place West, Tower Place, London EC3R 5BU
**Tel:** 02083746907
**Reg No:** 0543180 **Estd:** 1955 Private Limited Company
**Line of Business:** Pension and Employee Benifit Consultants.
**Issued Capital:** £1,000
**Directors:** Ms C E Ross, Ms F Dunsire, D N Williams
**Co. Secretary:** Ms Romana Lewis
**US SIC:** 6371 **UK SIC:** 82002
**Bankers:** Citibank Na (18-50-08)

|     | 31-12-13 | 31-12-12 | 31-12-11 |
|-----|----------|----------|----------|
| TA  | 1,000    | 1,000    | 1,000    |
| NW  | 1,000    | 1,000    | 1,000    |

**DUNS 22-706-9523**   Imp-Exp
### Pfu Imaging Solutions Europe Ltd
(**Subsidiary of:** Fujitsu Limited)
Hayes Park, Hayes End Road, Hayes, Middlesex UB4 8EE
**Tel:** 02085-734444
**Web:** www.fujitsu-europe.com
**Reg No:** 1578652 **VAT No:** 340690076
**Estd:** 1981 Private Limited Company
**Line of Business:** Wholesale of computers, computer peripheral equipment and software
**Export Markets:** E U Countries & Rest of World
**Issued Capital:** £12,183,000
**Directors:** K Hasegawa, K Miyamoto, E Sato, T Yamada, T Higashida, M P Nelson, Y Shimizu, F Nishida
**Responsibilities**
**Senior:** Graham Makepeace (*General Manager*), Masamichi Yamamoto (*Manager*)
**Marketing:** Catrina Clulow (*Marketing Director*)
**IT:** Nick Taube (*IT Director*)
**Facilities:** Graham Makepeace (*General Manager*)
**Fleet:** Graham Makepeace (*General Manager*)
**US SIC:** 5081 **UK SIC:** 61490
**Auditors:** KPMG LLP
**Bankers:** Barclays Bank Plc (20-67-59)

|      | 31-03-14   | 31-03-13   | 31-03-12   |
|------|------------|------------|------------|
| TO   | 91,909,000 | 92,058,000 | 88,488,000 |
| P/L  | 1,588,000  | 4,758,000  | 5,500,000  |
| NW   | 41,942,000 | 42,300,000 | 39,965,000 |
| WC   | 45,313,000 | 46,294,000 | 44,308,000 |
| Emp. | 97         | 97         | 95         |

**DUNS 21-155-6253**   Exp
### Pg Media Services Ltd
(**Subsidiary of:** Publicis Groupe S.A.)
Warwick Building, Avonmore Road, London W14 8HQ
**Tel:** 020-7751-1662
**Web:** www.tescodemos.com
**Reg No:** 0926566 **Estd:** 1943 Private Limited Company
**Line of Business:** Advertising
**Export Markets:** Europe and USA
**Export Sales:** £16,453,000
**Trading Style:** Arc
**Issued Capital:** £5,382,509
**Directors:** M Karam, I B Jacob, R Johansson
**Co. Secretary:** Raj Basran
**Branches:** Pg Media Services Ltd, Dovecot Workshops, Barnsley Park, Barnsley, Cirencester, Gloucestershire GL7 5EG
**US SIC:** 7311 **UK SIC:** 83800
**Auditors:** Ernst & Young LLP
**Bankers:** National Westminster Bank Plc (56-00-03)

|      | 31-12-13   | 31-12-12   | 31-12-11    |
|------|------------|------------|-------------|
| TO   | 51,217,000 | 517,431,000| 518,292,000 |
| P/L  | 8,558,000  | 6,179,000  | 13,942,000  |
| NW   | 56,469,000 | 51,375,000 | 45,692,000  |
| WC   | 59,389,000 | 57,036,000 | 51,804,000  |
| Emp. | 533        | 493        | 436         |

**DUNS 22-257-3789**
### Pg Motors Ltd
Eastman House, Fleming Way, Crawley, West Sussex RH10 9JY
**Tel:** 01293618155
**Web:** www.unbeatablecar.com
**Reg No:** 4275433 **Estd:** 2001 Private Limited Company
**Line of Business:** Car dealers (used)
**Issued Capital:** £2,750,100
**Directors:** Ms L A Moore, F J Sopp, M F Sopp

**Co. Secretary:** Fred Sopp
**Responsibilities**
**Senior:** Charlotte Desousa (*Manager*)
**US SIC:** 5511 **UK SIC:** 65100
**Bankers:** HSBC Bank plc (40-14-03)

|      | 30-04-14   | 30-04-13   | 30-04-12   |
|------|------------|------------|------------|
| TO   | 37,466,657 | 35,458,104 | 35,738,371 |
| P/L  | 700,707    | 1,117,731  | 1,301,165  |
| NW   | 4,931,588  | 4,460,405  | 3,699,747  |
| WC   | 4,200,299  | 4,338,431  | 3,603,878  |
| Emp. | 91         | 72         | 67         |

**DUNS 29-504-7781**   Imp-Exp
### Pga European Tour
European Tour Building, Wentworth Drive, Virginia Water, Surrey GU25 4LX
**Tel:** 01344-840-400
**Web:** www.europeantour.com
**Reg No:** 1867610 **Estd:** 1984 Private Company Limited By Guarantee
**Line of Business:** Operation of other sports arenas and stadiums not elsewhere classified
**Trading Style:** European Tour
**Directors:** J S Spence, D G Williams, C L Hanell, O Sellberg, P Eales, D J Russell, D Jones, J E O'Leary
**Co. Secretary:** Jonathan Orr
**Responsibilities**
**Senior:** Angel Gallardo (*Vice-Chairman*), George O'Grady (*Chief Executive Officer*), Mark Roe (*Director*), Ove Selleberg (*Director*)
**Marketing:** Scott Kelly (*Group Marketing Director*)
**Admin:** Linda Soltysiak (*Facilities Manager*)
**Facilities:** Linda Soltysiak (*Facilities Manager*)
**Branches:** Mccormack House, London W4 2th Burlington Lane
**US SIC:** 7999, 7399
**UK SIC:** 97913, 83954
**Auditors:** Grant Thornton UK LLP
**Bankers:** The Royal Bank Of Scotland Plc (15-10-00)

|      | 31-12-13    | 31-12-12    | 31-12-11    |
|------|-------------|-------------|-------------|
| TO   | 119,102,233 | 123,280,250 | 124,106,143 |
| P/L  | (2,429,957) | 3,297,521   | (2,248,419) |
| NW   | 14,704,506  | 15,174,948  | 13,438,194  |
| WC   | 9,408,250   | 11,872,239  | 9,141,535   |
| Emp. | 167         | 157         | 152         |

**DUNS 21-826-1718**
### Pgi - Protection Group International Ltd.
Unit 8, Cotswold Business Park, Millfiel, Luton, Bedfordshire LU1 4AJ
**Web:** www.slsitl.com
**Reg No:** 7967865 **Estd:** 2012 Private Limited Company
**Line of Business:** Security and related activities
**Export Sales:** £41,001,375
**Issued Capital:** £86
**Directors:** N R Storey, B M Roche, C T Moore, Sir T P Mcclement, Dr M A Al Barwani, Mrs C I Green
**US SIC:** 7393 **UK SIC:** 83954
**Bankers:** Abbey National Plc (09-00-00)

|      | 31-12-13    | 31-12-12   |
|------|-------------|------------|
| TO   | 52,193,967  | 60,858,297 |
| P/L  | 350,806     | 2,002,245  |
| NW   | (3,390,101) | 3,511,846  |
| WC   | (6,879,684) | 464,551    |
| Emp. | 155         | 88         |

**DUNS 22-714-8780**   Exp
### Pgi Group Ltd
3rd Floor, 45 Ludgate Hill, London EC4M 7JU
**Tel:** 02072460210 **Fax:** 02072360997
**Web:** www.pgi-uk.com
**Reg No:** 1338135 **Estd:** 1977 Private Limited Company
**Line of Business:** Investment consultants
**Export Markets:** UK, Rest of Europe, Middle East, India, Africa, South East Asia, USA, Canada, South America, Caribbean, Australasia
**Issued Capital:** £31,627,750
**Directors:** Ms M A Gage, S N Roditi, D M Ryan, Dr L Hene, C E Ryan, R L Pennant-Rea, S S Hobhouse
**Co. Secretary:** Ms Margaret Gage
**Responsibilities**
**Senior:** Barry Hill (*Finance Director*), Roy Troup (*Manager*)
**Finance:** Barry Hill (*Finance Director*)
**US SIC:** 0161 **UK SIC:** 01001
**Auditors:** Baker Tilly UK Audit LLP
**Bankers:** Barclays Bank Plc (20-00-00)

|      | 31-12-13   | 31-12-12   | 31-12-11   |
|------|------------|------------|------------|
| TO   | 36,897,000 | 33,181,000 | 31,960,000 |
| P/L  | 9,252,000  | 12,631,000 | 5,937,000  |
| NW   | 27,326,000 | 23,628,000 | 23,096,000 |
| WC   | 7,609,000  | 8,740,000  | 5,122,000  |
| Emp. | 13,835     | 13,019     | 12,607     |

**DUNS 34-536-6798**
### Pgl Group Ltd
(**Subsidiary of:** Cox and Kings Limited)
Alton Court, Penyard Lane, Ross-On-Wye, Herefordshire HR9 5GL
**Tel:** 01989-764211
**Reg No:** 5346933 **Estd:** 2005 Private Limited Company
**Line of Business:** Management activities of holding companies
**Export Sales:** £2,079,000
**Issued Capital:** £7,000
**Directors:** J G Firth, N Bali, P J Churchus, A Goenka, T W May, Ms P M Walker
**Co. Secretary:** Timothy May
**US SIC:** 6711 **UK SIC:** 83962
**Auditors:** KPMG LLP
**Bankers:** The Royal Bank Of Scotland Plc (16-08-05)

|      | 31-03-14    | 31-03-13     | 31-03-12      |
|------|-------------|--------------|---------------|
| TO   | 62,679,000  | 65,155,000   | 81,487,000    |
| P/L  | 49,786,000  | 19,169,000   | 10,310,000    |
| NW   | 38,486,000  | 32,420,000   | 33,142,000    |
| WC   | (113,367,000)| (163,958,000)| (142,778,000)|
| Emp. | 1,698       | 1,734        | 1,568         |

**DUNS 21-932-1437**   Exp
### Pgl Travel Ltd
(**Subsidiary of:** Cox and Kings Limited)
Alton Court, Penyard Lane
**Tel:** 08443710101 **Fax:** 08700551561
**Web:** www.pgl.co.uk
**Reg No:** 1191534 **Estd:** 1958 Private Limited Company
**Line of Business:** Tour operators
**Export Sales:** £1,919,000
**Trading Style:** P G L Adventure Holidays, P G L School Tours, P G L International
**Issued Capital:** £13,550,000
**Principals:** P J Churchus (*Managing*), J G Firth, N Bali, A Goenka, A G Sadler, T W May, Mrs P M Walker, R Sanders
**Co. Secretary:** Timothy May
**Responsibilities**
**HR:** Kath Clayden (*Human Resources Manager*), Karen Hockenhull (*Training Projects Executive*)
**Health & Safety:** Paul Kenwright (*Head of Safety*)
**Branches:** Pgl Travel Ltd, 15 Parkland Dr, Exeter, Devon EX2 5RX
**US SIC:** 7021 **UK SIC:** 66500
**Auditors:** KPMG LLP
**Bankers:** The Royal Bank Of Scotland Plc (16-20-20)

|      | 31-03-13     | 31-03-12     | 30-03-10     |
|------|--------------|--------------|--------------|
| TO   | 66,154,000   | 82,847,000   | 67,899,000   |
| P/L  | 17,482,000   | 10,043,000   | 11,671,000   |
| NW   | 66,554,000   | 67,283,000   | 56,148,000   |
| WC   | (115,748,000)| (93,357,000) | (54,575,000) |
| Emp. | 1,700        | 1,530        | 1,730        |

**DUNS 57-899-9641**   Exp
### Pgs Exploration (Uk) Ltd
(**Subsidiary of:** Petroleum Geo-Services Asa)
4 The Heights, Brooklands, Weybridge, Surrey KT13 0NY
**Tel:** 01932376000 **Fax:** 01932376100
**Web:** www.pgs.com
**Reg No:** 2904391 **Estd:** 1994 Private Limited Company
**Line of Business:** Service activities incidental to oil and gas extraction excluding surveying
**Export Markets:** Worldwide
**Directors:** G Langseth, Ms C Steen Nilsen, J E Reinhardsen
**Co. Secretary:** Carl Richards
**Responsibilities**
**IT:** Mike Rowland (*Computer Manager*)
**HR:** Pat Cardwell (*Human Resources Administrator*)
**US SIC:** 1389 **UK SIC:** 13000
**Auditors:** KPMG LLP
**Bankers:** HSBC Bank plc (40-05-30)
**Employees:** 179
**Turnover:** £270,295,000

**DUNS 21-915-6320**   Imp-Exp
### P.H. Betts (Holdings) Ltd
Broadwater Road, Woodbridge, Suffolk IP13 9LL
**Tel:** 01728-723675 **Fax:** 01728-724475
**Web:** www.hatchercomp.co.uk
**Reg No:** 1157707 **Estd:** 1974 Private Limited Company
**Line of Business:** Management activities of production holding companies
**Export Markets:** E U
**Export Sales:** £5,342,277
**Trading Style:** Hatcher Components
**Issued Capital:** £100
**Principals:** P H Betts (*Chairman and Managing*), Mrs J A Nash, J G Simpkin Betts, Mrs I J Mcgovern, Mrs S A Sledmere
**Co. Secretary:** Mrs Judith Betts
**Responsibilities**
**Senior:** Brian Ghelly (*Manager*)
**Admin:** Lisa Lindey (*Manager*)

**US SIC:** 6711, 3714
**UK SIC:** 83962, 35300
**Auditors:** Scrutton Bland
**Bankers:** Barclays Bank Plc (20-98-07)

| | 31-01-14 | 31-01-13 | 31-01-12 |
|---|---|---|---|
| TO | 17,839,484 | 16,382,694 | 16,072,347 |
| P/L | 1,155,562 | 848,472 | 1,243,381 |
| NW | 4,297,191 | 3,687,832 | 3,335,764 |
| WC | 3,396,777 | 3,109,095 | 2,947,536 |
| Emp. | 171 | 163 | 151 |

**DUNS 21-104-7067**
## P.H Jones Group Ltd
**(Subsidiary of:** Centrica Plc)
Priory House, Runcorn, Cheshire WA7 1TN
**Tel:** 01614237800 **Fax:** 01948 820484
**Web:** www.phjones.co.uk
**Reg No:** 6474145 **Estd:** 1971 Private
Limited Company
**Line of Business:** Plumbers
**Issued Capital:** £104
**Directors:** K M Main, G Barbaro, P V Black
**Co. Secretary:** Centrica Secretaries Limited
**Responsibilities**
**Admin:** Yvonne Keay (Administrator)
**IT:** Simon Shillabeer (IT infostructure
Manager)
**US SIC:** 1799 **UK SIC:** 50000
**Auditors:** PricewaterhouseCoopers LLP

| | 31-12-13 | 31-12-12 | 31-12-11 |
|---|---|---|---|
| TA | 36,080,000 | 36,080,000 | 6,080,000 |
| P/L | N/A | N/A | (26,000) |
| NW | 29,151,000 | 29,240,000 | (760,000) |
| WC | 23,071,000 | 23,160,000 | N/A |

**DUNS 73-880-3373**
## Phaidon International (Uk) Ltd
**(Subsidiary of:** Phaidon Holdings Ltd)
21 Lombard Street, London EC3V 9AH
**Tel:** 02037588805 **Fax:** 020-7019-4101
**Web:** www.phaidoninternational.com
**Reg No:** 5134675 **Estd:** 2011 Private
Limited Company
**Line of Business:** Employment and
recruitment companies and consultants
**Export Sales:** £5,284,413
**Trading Style:** Viridium Associates
**Issued Capital:** £51,000
**Directors:** A J Buck, K Behan, S Yendell
**Co. Secretary:** Justyna Buck
**Responsibilities**
**Senior:** Natalie Basiratpour (Associate
Director), Dawn Campion (Associate
Director)
**Finance:** Clare Cooper (Head of Financial
Technology)
**HR:** Katherine Ibbotson (Head of Structuring
and Origin), Adriana Swift (Head of
Recruitment FIFX Team)
**Facilities:** Jake White (Head of
Commodities)
**US SIC:** 7361 **UK SIC:** 83954
**Auditors:** Saffery Champness

| | 31-10-13 | 31-10-12 | 31-10-11 |
|---|---|---|---|
| TO | 13,509,232 | 11,008,179 | 11,493,630 |
| P/L | 159,432 | 1,020,325 | 2,433,819 |
| NW | (313,793) | 2,656,238 | 2,004,749 |
| WC | 3,433,740 | 2,455,800 | 1,905,221 |
| Emp. | 105 | 94 | 90 |

**DUNS 50-583-1081**                                                  **Imp-Exp**
## Phaidon Press Ltd
**(Subsidiary of:** Jmwt Topco Ltd)
18 Regents Wharf, All Saints Street,
Islington, London N1 9PA
**Web:** www.phaidon.co.uk
**Reg No:** 2525791 **VAT No:** 537349229
**Estd:** 1923 Private Limited Company
**Line of Business:** Publishing of books
**Export Markets:** Europe; U.S.A & Worldwide
**Issued Capital:** £60,005
**Principals:** A J Price (Managing),
Ms E D Alexanderson, J J Murphy,
Ms D H Aaronson, K L Fox, Ms E Terragni,
J H Booth-Clibborn
**Co. Secretary:** Jonathan Whale
**Responsibilities**
**Senior:** Jonathan Feinmesser (Financial
Director)
**Finance:** Jonathan Feinmesser (Financial
Director)
**Marketing:** Samuel Bennett (Head of
International Editions), Nat Foreman
(Publicity Assistant), Michele Robecchi
(Project Editor, Contemporary A)
**Sales:** Dan Groenewald (Sales & Business
Development M)
**Branches:** Phaidon Press Ltd, Grove Lane,
Frome, Somerset BA11 4AT
**US SIC:** 2731 **UK SIC:** 47532
**Auditors:** Bdo Stoy Hayward
**Bankers:** Bank Of Scotland (80-20-00)

| | 30-06-13 | 30-06-12 | 30-06-11 |
|---|---|---|---|
| TO | 20,386,000 | 23,771,000 | 22,744,000 |
| P/L | (1,950,000) | 939,000 | 411,000 |
| NW | 8,685,000 | 8,205,000 | 3,128,000 |
| WC | 10,018,000 | 9,346,000 | 4,193,000 |
| Emp. | 114 | 131 | 126 |

**DUNS 49-343-9830**                                                         **Imp**
## Pharm-Olam International (U K) Ltd
**(Subsidiary of:** Pharm-Olam Group Ltd)
The Brackens, London Road, Ascot,
Berkshire SL5 8BJ
**Tel:** 01344-891121
**Web:** www.pharm-olam.com
**Reg No:** 3125708 **Estd:** 1996 Private
Limited Company
**Line of Business:** Research institutions and
organisations
**Export Sales:** £16,104,242
**Issued Capital:** £50,000
**Managing Director:** Z M Munk
**Co. Secretary:** Ms Susan Munk
**Responsibilities**
**Senior:** Yamim Khan (Manager)
**US SIC:** 7391 **UK SIC:** 94000
**Auditors:** UHY Hacker Young
**Bankers:** National Westminster Bank Plc
(60-09-21)

| | 31-12-13 | 31-12-12 | 31-12-11 |
|---|---|---|---|
| TO | 18,420,379 | 14,983,303 | 13,538,726 |
| P/L | 77,285 | 124,911 | 165,600 |
| NW | 2,231,455 | 2,153,277 | 2,060,326 |
| WC | 2,040,392 | 1,978,380 | 1,945,437 |
| Emp. | 133 | 108 | 99 |

**DUNS 52-561-6215**                                                         **Imp-Exp**
## Pharm Research Associates (U K) Ltd
**(Subsidiary of:** Pra International Operations
Inc.)
Pacific House, Imperial Way Worton Grange,
Reading, Berkshire RG2 0TD
**Tel:** 01189181000 **Fax:** 01189-181001
**Web:** www.prainternational.com
**Reg No:** 3247443 **VAT No:** 681970990
**Estd:** 1996 Private Limited Company
**Line of Business:** Data processing
**Export Markets:** E U and U S A
**Trading Style:** P R A International
**Issued Capital:** £1,340,848
**Directors:** C J Gray, C Shannon
**Co. Secretary:** Mitre Secretaries Limited
**Branches:** Pharm Research Associates (U
K) Ltd, Llys Tawe, Kings Road, Swansea,
West Glamorgan SA1 8PG
**US SIC:** 7374 **UK SIC:** 83940
**Auditors:** BDO Stoy Hayward LLP
**Bankers:** HSBC Bank plc (40-34-03)

| | 31-12-13 | 31-12-12 | 31-12-11 |
|---|---|---|---|
| TO | 168,900,615 | 137,497,913 | 126,616,986 |
| P/L | 10,027,591 | 4,164,465 | 15,588,214 |
| NW | 40,840,182 | 32,938,944 | 27,097,981 |
| WC | 35,164,055 | 29,580,621 | 25,087,752 |
| Emp. | 561 | 433 | 369 |

**DUNS 39-720-6418**
## Pharmaceutical Packaging (Leeds) Ltd
**(Subsidiary of:** Templeton M Ltd)
129 Water Lane, Leeds, West Yorkshire
LS11 9UD
**Tel:** 01132134343
**Web:** www.ppl-leeds.co.uk
**Reg No:** 2169560 **VAT No:** 477041640
**Estd:** 1987 Private Limited Company
**Line of Business:** Labels finishing and
supply
**Trading Style:** P P L
**Issued Capital:** £60,000
**Principals:** P T Mcvicker (Managing),
Ms S A Templeman
**Responsibilities**
**Senior:** Ian Pickles (Warehouse Manager)
**US SIC:** 2752 **UK SIC:** 47544
**Auditors:** Templeman Ross
**Bankers:** National Westminster Bank Plc
(60-60-05)

| | 31-10-13 | 31-10-12 | 31-10-11 |
|---|---|---|---|
| TA | 1,261,354 | 1,151,765 | 1,222,696 |
| NW | 157,734 | 88,990 | (39,164) |
| WC | 134,800 | 46,433 | (103,632) |

**DUNS 21-110-7176**
## Pharmacy Care Plus Ltd
69 Valley Road, Liversedge, West Yorkshire
WF15 6DL
**Tel:** 01924408488
**Web:** www.pharmacycareplus.co.uk
**Reg No:** 6521783 **Estd:** 2008 Private
Limited Company
**Line of Business:** Chemists dispensing
**Trading Style:** Pharmacy Care Plus Ltd
**Issued Capital:** £4,469,317
**Directors:** Dr R G Andrew, Dr D Shah
**Co. Secretary:** Michael Niblock
**Responsibilities**
**Senior:** Anna Dziob (Manager), Kev Patel
(Manager)
**US SIC:** 8091 **UK SIC:** 95200

| | 30-06-14 | 30-06-13 | 30-06-12 |
|---|---|---|---|
| TO | 8,835,470 | 9,085,801 | N/A |
| P/L | 5,919 | (87,759) | N/A |
| NW | (1,155,501) | (1,470,859) | (1,692,539) |
| WC | 220,006 | 337,279 | 510,382 |
| Emp. | 100 | 91 | N/A |

**DUNS 21-730-2772**                                                         **Imp**
## Pharmacy Supplies Ltd
Unit 3, Magherafelt, Co Londonderry BT45
7AG
**Tel:** 02879-627889 **Fax:** 02879-627111
**Web:** www.pharmacy-supplies.net
**Reg No:** 0057269NI **Estd:** 2005 Private
Limited Company
**Line of Business:** Pharmaceutical suppliers
and wholesalers
**Issued Capital:** £2
**Directors:** L O'Kane, P R Canning,
J P Mcguigan, S Kerlin
**Co. Secretary:** Mrs Maura O'Kane
**US SIC:** 5122 **UK SIC:** 61800
**Auditors:** ASM Horwath (S) Ltd

| | 31-03-14 | 31-03-13 | 31-03-12 |
|---|---|---|---|
| TO | 9,500,026 | 9,197,783 | 9,637,986 |
| P/L | 437,480 | 372,991 | 604,238 |
| NW | 1,094,680 | 950,917 | 1,257,830 |
| WC | 649,453 | 604,197 | 894,043 |
| Emp. | 38 | 55 | 53 |

**DUNS 23-810-2581**
## PhARMACY2U Ltd
1 Coal Road Hawthorn Park, Leeds, West
Yorkshire LS14 1PQ
**Tel:** 01132018120
**Web:** www.pharmacy2u.co.uk
**Reg No:** 3802593 **Estd:** 1999 Private
Limited Company
**Line of Business:** Dispensing chemists
**Trading Style:** Pharmacy2u Ltd
**Issued Capital:** £638,160
**Directors:** S L Fawcett, B S Haigh,
M L Glatman, A Hornby, G R Brand,
D M Lee, Dr J E Harrison, Dr K G Mccullagh
**Co. Secretary:** Scott Fawcett
**Responsibilities**
**Senior:** Karen Wollard (Manager)
**Marketing:** Steven Dobson (Head of IT)
**IT:** Steven Dobson (Head of IT)
**US SIC:** 5912, 5999
**UK SIC:** 64300, 65600
**Auditors:** PricewaterhouseCoopers LLP
**Bankers:** Barclays Bank Plc (20-04-48)

| | 31-03-14 | 31-03-13 | 31-03-12 |
|---|---|---|---|
| TO | 17,078,000 | 15,815,000 | 18,634,000 |
| P/L | (47,000) | (45,000) | 356,000 |
| NW | 1,138,000 | 981,000 | 3,070,000 |
| WC | 598,000 | 462,000 | 2,568,000 |
| Emp. | 53 | 51 | 52 |

**DUNS 23-505-8240**
## Pharmalink Consulting Ltd
**(Subsidiary of:** Genpact Limited)
Vandervell House, Vanwall Road,
Maidenhead, Berkshire SL6 4UB
**Tel:** 01628860300 **Fax:** 01628-509125
**Web:** www.pharmalinkconsulting.com
**Reg No:** 3505088 **Estd:** 1998 Private
Limited Company
**Line of Business:** Other business activities
not elsewhere classified
**Export Sales:** £7,144,910
**Trading Style:** Genpact Pharmalink
**Issued Capital:** £100
**Directors:** A J Mazhari, O Das, K L Webb
**Responsibilities**
**Senior:** Lucinda Full (Director), Stephen
Loughrey (Manager), Una Loughrey
(Manager), Desmond Mcmahon (Manager),
Heather White (Director)
**Sales:** Stephen Loughrey (Manager)
**US SIC:** 7399 **UK SIC:** 83954
**Auditors:** MHA MacIntyre Hudson
**Bankers:** The Royal Bank Of Scotland Plc
(16-24-48)

| | 30-04-14 | 30-04-13 | 30-04-12 |
|---|---|---|---|
| TO | 13,485,161 | 13,931,420 | 17,012,839 |
| P/L | 1,417,945 | 1,798,013 | 3,531,135 |
| NW | 1,729,625 | 1,679,674 | 1,485,926 |
| WC | 1,477,790 | 1,439,807 | 1,246,595 |
| Emp. | 135 | 129 | 59 |

**DUNS 51-998-6335**                                                         **Exp**
## Pharmanet Ltd
**(Subsidiary of:** Inventiv Group Holdings
Inc.)
Building 2, Glory Park Avenue, Wooburn
Green, Wooburn Green, High Wycombe,
Buckinghamshire HP10 0DF
**Tel:** 08702420780
**Web:** www.pharmanet.com
**Reg No:** 3365723 **Estd:** 1997 Private
Limited Company
**Line of Business:** Research institutions and
organisations
**Export Sales:** £3,153,217
**Issued Capital:** £1
**Directors:** T P Hanbury, J R Moore
**Responsibilities**
**Senior:** Caroline Carter (Human Resource
Executive), Robert Reekie (Manager)
**HR:** Julie Hudson (Recruitment Officer)
**US SIC:** 7392 **UK SIC:** 83951
**Auditors:** Ernst & Young LLP

**Bankers:** Barclays Bank Plc (20-78-58)

| | 31-12-13 | 31-12-12 | 31-12-11 |
|---|---|---|---|
| TO | 3,153,217 | 9,649,018 | 10,248,139 |
| P/L | 335,270 | 647,808 | 699,989 |
| NW | 4,441,709 | 4,112,595 | 3,596,899 |
| WC | 4,441,709 | 4,433,693 | 4,000,523 |
| Emp. | 71 | 82 | 98 |

**DUNS 45-855-4847**
## Pharmapac (U.K.) Ltd
**(Subsidiary of:** Pharmapac Holdings Ltd)
Unit 22 Valley Road, Birkenhead, Merseyside
CH41 7EL
**Tel:** 0151-670-9090 **Fax:** 0151-670-0990
**Web:** www.pharmapacuk.com
**Reg No:** 3201556 **VAT No:** 677312128
**Estd:** 1996 Private Limited Company
**Line of Business:** Manufacture of basic
pharmaceutical products
**Issued Capital:** £114,865
**Directors:** G Elliott, M Elliott, A M Sampson,
K Elliott, I P Robinson
**Co. Secretary:** Steven Scott
**Responsibilities**
**IT:** John Gauntlett (Head of IT)
**HR:** Sarah Sibeon (HR Manager)
**Health & Safety:** Graeme Hasson (Health &
Safety Manager)
**Operations:** Graeme Hasson (Health &
Safety Manager)
**US SIC:** 2834, 7399
**UK SIC:** 25700, 83954
**Auditors:** Cobham Murphy

| | 30-06-13 | 30-06-12 | 30-06-11 |
|---|---|---|---|
| TO | 12,818,641 | 10,396,549 | 8,903,071 |
| P/L | 399,536 | 178,193 | 5,128 |
| NW | 2,822,018 | 2,423,444 | 2,419,148 |
| WC | 1,572,797 | 1,147,535 | 1,193,861 |
| Emp. | 205 | 210 | 202 |

**DUNS 21-014-1282**                                                         **Imp**
## Pharmaserve (North West) Ltd
**(Subsidiary of:** Obg Pharmaceuticals Ltd)
9 Arkwright Road, Astmoor Industrial Estate,
Runcorn, Cheshire WA7 1NU
**Tel:** 01928502200
**Web:** www.pharmasol.co.uk
**Reg No:** 6368662 **Estd:** 2010 Private
Limited Company
**Line of Business:** Manufacturers of
pharmaceutical products
**Issued Capital:** £1
**Directors:** P M O'Brien, P Didlick,
G F Obrien
**Co. Secretary:** Philip Didlick
**Responsibilities**
**Senior:** Anastacia Loftus (Head of
Development)
**US SIC:** 2834 **UK SIC:** 25700
**Auditors:** Mitchell Charlesworth
**Bankers:** National Westminster Bank Plc
(60-12-25)

| | 31-12-13 | 31-12-12 | 31-12-11 |
|---|---|---|---|
| TO | 6,645,769 | 5,303,360 | 5,252,807 |
| P/L | 315,071 | (755,191) | (304,806) |
| NW | 1,036,085 | 629,867 | 519,617 |
| WC | (1,717,882) | 359,628 | 1,392,461 |
| Emp. | 71 | 47 | 56 |

**DUNS 29-631-5989**                                                         **Imp**
## Pharmatube Ltd
Wardley Industrual Estate, Manchester M28
2QB
**Tel:** 01617-947-391
**Web:** www.pharmatube.com
**Reg No:** 1957639 **VAT No:** 437573429
**Estd:** 1986 Private Limited Company
**Line of Business:** Manufacturers of
aluminium
**Trading Style:** Fact
**Issued Capital:** £20,000
**Managing Director:** S J Hay
**Co. Secretary:** Gordon Midgley
**Responsibilities**
**Senior:** Lee Pollitt (Works Manager)
**Health & Safety:** Lee Pollitt (Works
Manager)
**US SIC:** 3334, 3398
**UK SIC:** 22451, 31380
**Auditors:** Grant Thornton UK LLP
**Bankers:** The Royal Bank Of Scotland Plc
(16-24-06)

| | 31-07-13 | 31-07-12 | 31-07-11 |
|---|---|---|---|
| TO | N/A | 3,872,778 | 4,626,066 |
| P/L | N/A | (408,920) | 95,945 |
| NW | 1,326,740 | 1,611,482 | 2,021,801 |
| WC | 1,241,263 | 1,474,673 | 1,840,966 |
| Emp. | N/A | 61 | 68 |

**DUNS 50-482-6470**
## Pharmexx Uk Ltd
**(Subsidiary of:** Udg Healthcare Public
Limited Company)
Home Farm, Newbury, Berkshire RG20 8HR
**Tel:** 01488607350
**Web:** www.alchemy-uk.com
**Reg No:** 2456441 **Estd:** 1989 Private
Limited Company
**Line of Business:** Labour recruitment and
provision of personnel
**Issued Capital:** £1,040

**Directors:** Mrs C J Bates, N Mansford
**Co. Secretary:** Nigel Mansford
**US SIC:** 7361, 7399
**UK SIC:** 83954
**Auditors:** Grant Thornton
**Bankers:** National Westminster Bank Plc (60-01-17)

| | 30-09-13 | 31-12-12 | 30-09-11 |
|---|---|---|---|
| TO | 9,735,280 | 11,528,242 | 8,642,677 |
| P/L | 451,428 | 416,964 | (713,780) |
| NW | 1,241,297 | 2,166,696 | 2,502,479 |
| WC | 1,136,356 | 2,075,872 | 2,414,297 |
| Emp. | 167 | 171 | 132 |

DUNS 23-803-3125 Imp

## Pharos Group Ltd

228 Lythalls Lane, Coventry, West Midlands CV6 6HY
**Tel:** 024-7668-7235 **Fax:** 02476664397
**Web:** www.pharosgroupuk.com
**Reg No:** 3795831 **Estd:** 1956 Private Limited Company
**Line of Business:** Aviation engineering and engineers
**Trading Style:** Pharos Gear Technology Limited
**Issued Capital:** £337,100
**Director:** R W Apted
**Co. Secretary:** Stephen Jackson
**Responsibilities**
**Senior:** Matt Winstone *(Sales & Marketing Manager)*
**Marketing:** Matt Winstone *(Sales & Marketing Manager)*
**Sales:** Matt Winstone *(Sales & Marketing Manager)*
**Branches:** Pharos Group Ltd, Rother Way, Hellaby Indstl Est, Rotherham, South Yorkshire S66 8QN
**US SIC:** 6711 **UK SIC:** 83962
**Auditors:** The Richards Sandy Partnership Ltd
**Bankers:** Bank Of Scotland (80-11-00)

| | 30-09-13 | 30-09-12 | 31-12-11 |
|---|---|---|---|
| TO | 15,219,408 | 16,767,534 | 15,240,540 |
| P/L | 2,753,572 | 2,364,636 | 1,526,923 |
| NW | 4,918,173 | 3,384,294 | 2,532,756 |
| WC | 2,384,254 | 2,027,033 | 1,594,908 |
| Emp. | 70 | 55 | 50 |

DUNS 29-150-1484 Imp

## Phase Eight (Fashion & Designs) Ltd

**(Subsidiary of:** Poppy Holdco Limited)
90 Peterborough Road, London SW6 3HH
**Tel:** 02073-715-656
**Web:** www.phase-eight.co.uk
**Reg No:** 1735454 **VAT No:** 863864287
**Estd:** 1979 Private Limited Company
**Line of Business:** Fashion shops
**Export Sales:** £7,631,000
**Issued Capital:** £5,139
**Directors:** B L Barnett, G P Tambling, L E Harlow, C J Jack, M M Rahamim, Mrs J A Bremner, I E Wallis
**Responsibilities**
**HR:** Alex Didymiotis *(Head of HR)*
**Purchasing:** Amy Adams *(Buyers Assistant)*
**Branches:** Phase Eight (Fashion & Designs) Ltd, 21 Carnwath Road, SW6 3HR London
**US SIC:** 5621, 5661
**UK SIC:** 64500, 64600
**Auditors:** Deloitte LLP
**Bankers:** Bank Of Scotland (12-11-03)

| | 01-02-14 | 02-02-13 | 28-02-12 |
|---|---|---|---|
| TO | 132,141,000 | 121,080,000 | 108,378,000 |
| P/L | 22,821,000 | 19,865,000 | 17,767,000 |
| NW | 85,695,000 | 65,872,000 | 48,616,000 |
| WC | 73,678,000 | 56,856,000 | 41,179,000 |
| Emp. | 1,621 | 1,572 | 1,465 |

DUNS 42-436-9093 Imp

## Phase Electrical Distributors Ltd

Unit 10-11, Cubitt Way, St Leonards-On-Sea, East Sussex TN38 9SU
**Tel:** 01424-852552 **Fax:** 01424-852452
**Web:** www.phase-electrical.co.uk
**Reg No:** 4424536 **Estd:** 1902 Private Limited Company
**Line of Business:** Electrical wholesalers
**Trading Style:** Phase Electrical Distributors Ltd
**Issued Capital:** £4,128
**Directors:** M B Nealer, S R Millard, D P Hogg, D Poole, S D Godden
**Co. Secretary:** Mark Walker
**Branches:** Phase Electrical Distributors Ltd, Bell Lane, Uckfield, East Sussex TN22 1QL
**US SIC:** 5074, 3648
**UK SIC:** 61300, 34702
**Auditors:** Ashdown Hurrey

| | 31-03-14 | 31-03-13 | 31-03-12 |
|---|---|---|---|
| TO | 11,349,394 | 9,706,084 | 9,526,631 |
| P/L | 651,563 | 629,909 | 633,432 |
| NW | 819,879 | 663,254 | 531,490 |
| WC | 595,796 | 550,245 | 426,795 |
| Emp. | 56 | 48 | N/A |

DUNS 23-828-9201

## P.H.C. (Pharmacy) Ltd

**(Subsidiary of:** National Co-Operative Chemists Ltd)
21 Cowglen Road, Glasgow, Lanarkshire G53 6EQ
**Tel:** 01415316800 **Fax:** 01415316808
**Reg No:** 0115847SC **Estd:** 2002 Private Limited Company
**Line of Business:** Drug stores outlets
**Issued Capital:** £1,000
**Directors:** D L Robertson, A J Smith
**Co. Secretary:** Mrs Caroline Sellers
**Responsibilities**
**Senior:** Christine Mcneil *(Practice Manager)*
**US SIC:** 5912 **UK SIC:** 64300
**Auditors:** Hardie Caldwell
**Bankers:** Bank Of Scotland (80-14-26)

| | 31-03-14 | 31-03-13 | 31-03-12 |
|---|---|---|---|
| TA | 1,174,429 | 1,999,101 | 1,283,829 |
| NW | 3,377 | 2,704 | 2,890 |
| WC | (3,338) | (5,783) | (7,342) |

DUNS 50-435-9175

## Phd Media Ltd

**(Subsidiary of:** Omnicom Group Inc.)
The Telephone Exchange, 5 North Crescent, Chenies Street, London WC1E 7PH
**Tel:** 02074460555 **Fax:** 020-7446-7100
**Web:** www.phdmedia.com
**Reg No:** 2423952 **VAT No:** 495133729
**Estd:** 1990 Private Limited Company
**Line of Business:** Advertising agency services
**Issued Capital:** £3,034,196
**Directors:** Ms F Ralston-Good, D Rubins
**Co. Secretary:** Mrs Sally Bray
**Responsibilities**
**Senior:** Tim Caira *(Manager)*, Hugh Cameron *(Manager)*, Verica Djurdjevic *(Managing Partner)*, Paul Hawkey *(Manager)*, Sean Meikle *(Managing Partner)*, Darren Rubens *(CEO)*
**Marketing:** Tim Caira *(Manager)*, Dipesh Pattni *(Seo Manager)*
**HR:** Kate Corbett *(Human Resources Manager)*, Kate King *(Human Resources Director)*
**Operations:** Kate Corbett *(Human Resources Manager)*
**US SIC:** 7319 **UK SIC:** 83800
**Auditors:** KPMG Audit PLC
**Bankers:** HSBC Bank plc (40-02-50)

| | 31-12-13 | 31-12-12 | 31-12-11 |
|---|---|---|---|
| TO | N/A | 28,382,000 | 25,544,000 |
| P/L | 7,616,693 | 7,201,000 | 6,030,000 |
| NW | 8,907,654 | 8,387,000 | 7,079,000 |
| WC | 7,473,027 | 7,005,000 | 5,873,000 |
| Emp. | 264 | 236 | 229 |

DUNS 77-117-4992

## Phd Modular Access Services Ltd

14 Linden Square, Coppermill Lock, Harefield, Uxbridge, Middlesex UB9 6TQ
**Tel:** 01895-822292
**Web:** www.phdaccess.com
**Reg No:** 2690003 **Estd:** 1992 Private Limited Company
**Line of Business:** Other construction work involving special trades
**Issued Capital:** £100,000
**Directors:** L Hannon, M N Mayadeen, Mrs J T Dwyer
**Responsibilities**
**Senior:** Floyd Gammon *(Manager)*, William O'Donoghue *(Manager)*
**US SIC:** 3441 **UK SIC:** 32042
**Auditors:** Hillier Hopkins LLP

| | 28-02-14 | 28-02-13 | 29-02-12 |
|---|---|---|---|
| TO | 10,549,499 | 14,129,312 | N/A |
| P/L | 393,326 | 628,140 | N/A |
| NW | 1,274,137 | 875,009 | 356,241 |
| WC | (487,413) | (1,334,337) | (837,474) |
| Emp. | 13 | N/A | N/A |

DUNS 22-230-1082

## Phdmail Ltd

Unit 1 Falcon Close, Burton-On-Trent, Staffordshire DE14 1SG
**Tel:** 01283512733 **Fax:** 01283-510516
**Web:** www.phdmail.co.uk
**Reg No:** 4248052 **Estd:** 1995 Private Limited Company
**Line of Business:** Direct mail service providers
**Issued Capital:** £1,000
**Directors:** J L Mason, S J Murfin, C Brooks
**Co. Secretary:** Kevin Dunn
**US SIC:** 7319, 7399
**UK SIC:** 83800, 83954
**Auditors:** Thacker & Co

| | 31-03-14 | 30-09-12 | 30-03-11 |
|---|---|---|---|
| TA | 2,629,356 | 2,799,541 | 2,720,651 |
| NW | 1,554,357 | 1,607,374 | 1,509,734 |
| WC | 898,812 | 871,830 | 779,138 |

DUNS 39-689-5070

## Phelan Construction Ltd

1 Brunel Road, Gorse Lane Industrial Estate, Clacton-On-Sea, Essex CO15 4LU
**Tel:** 08712307666 **Fax:** 01255224649
**Web:** www.phelans.co.uk
**Reg No:** 2147266 **VAT No:** 466014852
**Estd:** 1987 Private Limited Company
**Line of Business:** Manufacture of non-domestic cooling and ventilation equipment
**Issued Capital:** £60
**Principals:** K W O'Phelan *(Managing)*, D W Mcgowan, N I Coy
**Branches:** Phelan Construction Ltd, 16 North St, Sudbury, Suffolk CO10 1RB
**US SIC:** 3585, 1541, 1522
**UK SIC:** 32841, 50100
**Auditors:** Passmore Weeks & Richardson

| | 31-12-13 | 31-12-12 | 31-12-11 |
|---|---|---|---|
| TO | 18,937,447 | 20,170,026 | 14,311,020 |
| P/L | 477,769 | 764,019 | 463,486 |
| NW | 1,988,487 | 2,733,198 | 2,145,133 |
| WC | 1,381,192 | 1,923,630 | 1,572,731 |
| Emp. | 57 | 46 | 40 |

DUNS 39-478-1504 Imp-Exp

## Phenomenex Ltd

Melville House, Queens Avenue, Macclesfield, Cheshire SK10 2BN
**Tel:** 01625501367
**Web:** www.phenomenex.com
**Reg No:** 2130831 **VAT No:** 466529024
**Estd:** 1987 Private Limited Company
**Line of Business:** Manufacturers of scientific machinery and instrument
**Export Markets:** European Union (E U)
**Export Sales:** £9,728,282
**Issued Capital:** £2
**Managing Director:** F Mahjoor
**Co. Secretary:** Ms Flora Sadeghi
**US SIC:** 3829 **UK SIC:** 37100
**Auditors:** Twist Hughes & Co
**Bankers:** Barclays Bank Plc (20-53-77)

| | 31-12-13 | 31-12-12 | 31-12-11 |
|---|---|---|---|
| TO | 15,465,703 | 13,828,814 | 14,273,674 |
| P/L | 913,802 | 582,030 | 1,432,933 |
| NW | 13,379,586 | 12,657,483 | 12,492,092 |
| WC | 12,963,786 | 12,089,584 | 11,801,037 |
| Emp. | 81 | 60 | 73 |

DUNS 21-584-1358

## Pheonix Health

Phoenix House, Little Henfaes Drive, Welshpool, Powys SY21 7BG
**Tel:** 01938552756
**Estd:** 2011
**Line of Business:** Clinics private
**Proprietor:** D Newson
**US SIC:** 8051 **UK SIC:** 95100
**Employees:** 60

DUNS 45-839-6371

## Phew (Scotland)

49 Hope Street, Motherwell, Lanarkshire ML1 1BS
**Tel:** 01698-404051 **Fax:** 01698-404061
**Web:** www.phewscotlandrespite.org
**Reg No:** 0165172SC **Estd:** 1989 Private Limited Company
**Line of Business:** Social work activities with accommodation
**Directors:** H ( Mcguigan, A S Bauld, W M Shanks, T J Mcmanus, D Mckendrick, Mrs J Mcguire, M G Lunny, Mrs L Gray
**Co. Secretary:** Alexanderina Craig
**Responsibilities**
**Senior:** Mary Callaghan *(Director)*, Margaret Johnston *(Director)*, William Lunny *(Manager)*
**US SIC:** 8321 **UK SIC:** 96111
**Auditors:** Grant Thornton
**Bankers:** Bank Of Scotland (80-09-93)

| | 31-03-14 | 31-03-13 | 31-03-12 |
|---|---|---|---|
| TO | 1,007,283 | 1,044,661 | 978,158 |
| P/L | 60,376 | 74,499 | (35,346) |
| NW | 2,236,116 | 2,175,740 | 2,101,241 |
| WC | 715,930 | 622,965 | 518,545 |
| Emp. | 52 | 51 | 51 |

DUNS 21-125-7797

## Phi Partners Global Ltd

Heron Tower, 110 Bishopsgate, London EC2N 4AY
**Tel:** 02031-706-355 **Fax:** 02031-706-356
**Web:** www.phipartners.com
**Reg No:** 6609685 **Estd:** 2004 Private Limited Company
**Line of Business:** Labour recruitment and provision of personnel
**Export Sales:** £3,602,555
**Trading Style:** Phi Partners, It Consultancy
**Issued Capital:** £1,000
**Directors:** J Detard, A W Kehoe, W R Bodilly, S Wadhar, Ms H Saunders, J P Radley, A Kapasi, D Stockdale
**Co. Secretary:** Snehal Wadhar
**Responsibilities**
**Senior:** Michael Mcfarlane *(Director)*
**US SIC:** 7361, 7372
**UK SIC:** 83954, 83940

**Auditors:** Sayers Butterworth LLP
**Bankers:** HSBC Bank plc (40-05-30)

| | 31-12-13 | 31-12-12 | 31-12-11 |
|---|---|---|---|
| TO | 6,433,134 | 3,881,152 | 3,992,208 |
| P/L | 78,931 | 311,967 | 16,104 |
| NW | 783,232 | 697,794 | 460,106 |
| WC | 532,259 | 649,981 | 375,507 |

DUNS 73-476-2128

## Phil McIntyre Holdings Ltd

Richard House, 9 Winckley Square, Preston, Lancashire PR1 3HP
**Tel:** 02074392270
**Reg No:** 4740096 **Estd:** 2003 Private Limited Company
**Line of Business:** Entertainment agencies
**Issued Capital:** £202
**Director:** P C Mcintyre
**Co. Secretary:** John Mcintyre
**US SIC:** 7999 **UK SIC:** 97913
**Bankers:** The Royal Bank Of Scotland Plc (16-28-33)

| | 30-06-13 | 30-09-12 | 30-06-11 |
|---|---|---|---|
| TO | 28,271,630 | 34,107,669 | 44,877,800 |
| P/L | 491,164 | 1,732,132 | (1,154,965) |
| NW | 2,246,759 | 1,744,469 | 323,803 |
| WC | 2,238,597 | 1,723,894 | 133,767 |
| Emp. | 64 | 19 | 60 |

DUNS 56-977-4235

## Philcap Two Ltd

10 Lower Grosvenor Place, London SW1W 0EN
**Tel:** 02077305565
**Reg No:** 2853794 **Estd:** 1993 Private Limited Company
**Line of Business:** Buying and selling of own real estate
**Issued Capital:** £100
**Directors:** T J Knowles, Ms C C Sharp, T D Hopkinson
**Co. Secretary:** Miss Claire Sharp
**US SIC:** 6531 **UK SIC:** 83400
**Auditors:** Moore & Smalley LLP

| | 31-01-14 | 31-01-13 | 31-01-12 |
|---|---|---|---|
| TA | 100 | 100 | 100 |
| NW | 100 | 100 | 100 |

DUNS 22-716-0314 Imp-Exp

## Philex Ltd

Philex House, Bedford, Bedfordshire MK42 0NX
**Tel:** 01234263700 **Fax:** 01234267400
**Web:** www.philex.com
**Reg No:** 1629476 **VAT No:** 371293452
**Estd:** 1982 Private Limited Company
**Line of Business:** Manufacturers and wholesalers of electrical products
**Export Markets:** Western Europe
**Export Sales:** £366,012
**Issued Capital:** £108,842
**Principals:** M Sabourian *(Managing)*, D Beattie, W M Kok, A N Hewson, K M Thomas, B E Chernett
**Co. Secretary:** Ms Hilary Price
**Responsibilities**
**Senior:** Andrew Newland *(Financial Director)*
**Finance:** Andrew Newland *(Financial Director)*
**Marketing:** Tony Barton *(Group Marketing Manager)*
**IT:** Mike Boorman *(Head Of IT)*, Nikolaos Gazis *(IT Infrastructure Manager)*
**Branches:** Philex Ltd, Philex House Kingfisher Wharf, London Road, Bedford, Bedfordshire MK42 0NX
**US SIC:** 3629, 5065
**UK SIC:** 34350, 61500
**Auditors:** BDO LLP

| | 31-03-14 | 31-03-13 | 31-03-12 |
|---|---|---|---|
| TO | 19,760,120 | 18,293,655 | 22,961,608 |
| P/L | 889,947 | 203,559 | (1,311,104) |
| NW | 4,391,711 | 4,149,034 | 4,019,291 |
| WC | 1,653,909 | 1,418,556 | 1,271,137 |
| Emp. | 77 | 84 | 79 |

DUNS 54-861-9642

## Philip Baker & Co

Somerset House, Temple Street, Birmingham, West Midlands B2 5DP
**Tel:** 0121-632-4199
**Web:** www.shakespeares.co.uk
**Estd:** 1963 Partnership
**Line of Business:** Solicitors
**Trading Style:** Philip Baker & Co
**US SIC:** 8111 **UK SIC:** 83500
**Employees:** 160

DUNS 21-618-8631

## Philip Dennis Foodservice Ltd

Brannam Crescent, Roundswell Business Park, Barnstaple, Devon EX31 3TD
**Tel:** 01271311122 **Fax:** 01271311138
**Web:** www.philipdennisfoodservice.co.uk
**Reg No:** 0571334 **Estd:** 1956 Private Limited Company
**Line of Business:** Frozen foods (wholesale)
**Trading Style:** The Devonia Supply Co
**Issued Capital:** £115,267

**Principals:** J P Dennis *(Chairman and Managing)*, S J Carr
**Co. Secretary:** Mrs Elizabeth Dennis
**Responsibilities**
**Finance:** Maurice Malloy *(Accountant)*
**Sales:** Nikki Fox *(Sales Manager)*
**HR:** Alison Corsten *(Human Resources Manager)*
**Branches:** Philip Dennis Foodservice Ltd, 1 Chancel Way, Halesowen Industrial Park, Halesowen, West Midlands B62 8SE
**US SIC:** 5149   **UK SIC:** 61700
**Auditors:** Francis Clark LLP
**Bankers:** Lloyds TSB Bank plc (30-94-52)

| | 01-02-14 | 26-01-13 | 28-02-12 |
|---|---|---|---|
| TO | 34,896,296 | 30,771,487 | 28,893,619 |
| P/L | 500,368 | 388,585 | (582,987) |
| NW | 3,560,246 | 3,179,878 | 2,898,293 |
| WC | 481,766 | (619,322) | (327,721) |
| Emp. | 212 | 200 | 189 |

---

**DUNS 22-752-7330**   Imp-Exp
### Philip M Bassett Ltd
*(Subsidiary of:* Compagnie De Saint Gobain Les Miroirs La Defense 3)
Mahon Industrial Estate Mahon Road, Craigavon, Co Armagh BT62 3EH
**Tel:** 02838339438 **Fax:** 028-3833-8813
**Web:** www.bassettsonline.com
**Reg No:** 0017675NI **Estd:** 1978 Private Limited Company
**Line of Business:** Plumbers merchants
**Export Markets:** Republic of Ireland
**Trading Style:** Bassetts
**Issued Capital:** £6,250
**Director:** P E Moore
**Co. Secretary:** Alun Oxenham
**Responsibilities**
**Senior:** Stephen Bassett *(Manager)*
**Marketing:** Stephen Bassett *(Manager)*
**Sales:** Stephen Bassett *(Manager)*
**Facilities:** Stephen Bassett *(Manager)*
**Purchasing:** Margaret Black *(Purchasing Manager)*
**Branches:** Philip M Bassett Ltd, Riverside Industrial Estate, Hillsborough Old Road, Lisburn, Co Antrim BT27 5EW
**US SIC:** 5074   **UK SIC:** 61300
**Bankers:** Ulster Bank Ltd (98-01-90)

| | 31-12-13 | 31-12-12 | 31-12-11 |
|---|---|---|---|
| TA | 6,000 | 6,000 | 6,000 |
| NW | 6,000 | 6,000 | 6,000 |

---

**DUNS 21-749-5179**
### The Philip Morant School & College Academy Trust
Rembrandt Way, Colchester, Essex CO3 4QS
**Tel:** 01206545222
**Web:** www.philipmorant.essex.sch.uk
**Reg No:** 7803969 **Estd:** 2011 Private Company Limited By Guarantee
**Line of Business:** Schools (local authority)
**Directors:** J F Pyman, R G Smith, R May, Ms A Lawrence, Miss C Hutley, Ms C D'Arcy Jones, J Daniels, P Bamford
**Co. Secretary:** Paul Harrison
**Responsibilities**
**Senior:** Lyndsay Fildes *(Director)*, Stewart Francis *(Director)*, Lorna Kean *(Director)*, Aleca Ramsey *(Director)*, Stephen Razzell *(Director)*, Glynis Rodgers *(Director)*, Charmaine Scott *(Director)*, Nardeep Sharma *(Director)*, Gareth Staines *(Director)*
**US SIC:** 8211   **UK SIC:** 93200
**Bankers:** Barclays Bank Plc (20-22-67)

| | 31-08-14 | 31-08-13 | 31-08-12 |
|---|---|---|---|
| TO | 10,193,567 | 9,715,791 | 32,418,019 |
| P/L | 51,804 | 27,373 | 24,748,090 |
| NW | 24,267,267 | 23,967,463 | 24,116,090 |
| WC | 1,288,342 | 1,505,906 | 1,811,002 |
| Emp. | 281 | 304 | 181 |

---

**DUNS 23-621-9841**   Imp-Exp
### Philip Morris Ltd
*(Subsidiary of:* Philip Morris International Inc.)
1 Parkshot, Richmond, Surrey TW9 2RD
**Fax:** 02082326050
**Web:** www.philpmorris.com
**Reg No:** 3619145 **Estd:** 1971 Private Limited Company
**Line of Business:** Manufacturers of tobacco products
**Export Markets:** Rest of world
**Export Sales:** £14,212,000
**Issued Capital:** £100,000
**Directors:** K Sousa, F Vroemen, M Inkster
**US SIC:** 2111   **UK SIC:** 42900
**Auditors:** PricewaterhouseCoopers LLP

| | 31-12-13 | 31-12-12 | 31-12-11 |
|---|---|---|---|
| TO | 160,453,000 | 173,668,000 | 171,356,000 |
| P/L | 4,833,000 | 4,591,000 | 3,862,000 |
| NW | 6,045,000 | 5,877,000 | 5,818,000 |
| WC | (3,073,000) | (3,241,000) | (2,674,000) |
| Emp. | 74 | 64 | 58 |

---

**DUNS 42-414-5993**
### Philip White Ltd
Station Road Industrial Estate, Station Road, Armagh, Co Armagh BT61 7NP
**Tel:** 02837525946
**Web:** www.philipwhitetyres.com
**Reg No:** 0021612NI **Estd:** 1988 Private Limited Company
**Line of Business:** Sale of motor vehicle parts and accessories
**Issued Capital:** £2
**Directors:** P M White, P H White
**Co. Secretary:** Philip White
**Branches:** Dublin, Dublin
**US SIC:** 5531   **UK SIC:** 65100
**Bankers:** The Bank Of Ireland (90-22-90)

| | 31-03-14 | 31-03-13 | 31-03-12 |
|---|---|---|---|
| TA | 28,036 | 28,036 | 28,036 |
| NW | 26,520 | 26,520 | 26,520 |
| WC | 26,520 | 26,520 | 26,520 |

---

**DUNS 22-931-7326**   Imp-Exp
### Philip White Tyres Ltd
2 Loughgall Road, Armagh, Co Armagh BT61 7NH
**Tel:** 02837511032
**Web:** www.philipwhitetyres.com
**Reg No:** 0019153NI **Estd:** 1982 Private Limited Company
**Line of Business:** Tyre dealers
**Export Markets:** Republic of Ireland
**Export Sales:** £6,886,340
**Issued Capital:** £10,000
**Directors:** L P White, P H White
**Co. Secretary:** Mrs Elizabeth Maxwell
**Responsibilities**
**Senior:** Sean Dougan *(Manager)*
**Health & Safety:** Sean Dougan *(Manager)*
**Branches:** Philip White Tyres Ltd, Rosevale Industrial Estate, Unit 15A-15D, Lisburn, Co Antrim BT28 1RW
**US SIC:** 5531   **UK SIC:** 65100
**Auditors:** B.P. Tanney & Co
**Bankers:** The Bank Of Ireland (90-20-47)

| | 31-03-14 | 31-03-13 | 31-03-12 |
|---|---|---|---|
| TO | 14,361,313 | 14,371,643 | 16,930,450 |
| P/L | 299,621 | 93,403 | 108,863 |
| NW | 2,528,570 | 2,285,611 | 2,221,450 |
| WC | 866,193 | 637,490 | 646,624 |
| Emp. | 56 | 60 | 58 |

---

**DUNS 21-104-5401**
### Philip Williams & Co
35 Walton Road, Stockton Heath, Warrington, Cheshire WA4 6NW
**Tel:** 08452301650
**Web:** www.philipwilliams.co.uk
**Estd:** 1997 Proprietorship
**Line of Business:** Insurance - household
**Proprietor:** P Williams
**Responsibilities**
**IT:** David Kilpatrick *(IT Manager)*
**Health & Safety:** David Kilpatrick *(IT Manager)*
**Facilities:** Melanie Carbet *(PA to Managing Director)*
**US SIC:** 6411   **UK SIC:** 83200
**Employees:** 50

---

**DUNS 21-023-0256**   Imp
### Philips Electronics Uk Ltd
*(Subsidiary of:* Koninklijke Philips N.V.)
Philips Centre, Guildford Business Park, Guildford, Surrey GU2 8XH
**Tel:** 08706 010101 **Fax:** 01483298860
**Web:** www.philips.co.uk
**Reg No:** 0446897 **VAT No:** 407850060
**Estd:** 1947 Private Limited Company
**Line of Business:** Manufacture of insulated wire and cable
**Export Sales:** £226,000,000
**Trading Style:** Philips Consumer Electronics, Philip Lighting, Philips Healthcare
**Issued Capital:** £620,000,000
**Directors:** P J Maskell, C Petrie, Mrs J Rogers, N A Mesher, H Vivash
**Co. Secretary:** Martin Armstrong
**Responsibilities**
**Senior:** Jodie Bridge *(Marketing Director)*, Brent Kokoskin *(Marketing And Sales Director)*, Mark Leftwich *(Marketing Director)*, Jo Schiller *(Marketing Director)*
**Finance:** Marta Kulpiecinska *(Chief Financial Officer)*
**Marketing:** Jodie Bridge *(Marketing Director)*, Brent Kokoskin *(Marketing And Sales Director)*, Alex Kypriotis *(Marketing And Sales Director)*, Mark Leftwich *(Marketing Director)*, Jo Schiller *(Marketing Director)*, Teresa Vallis *(Segment Marketing and Event Ma)*
**Sales:** Brent Kokoskin *(Marketing And Sales Director)*, Alex Kypriotis *(Marketing And Sales Director)*
**Branches:** Philips Electronics Uk Ltd, Lower Rd, Sudbury, Suffolk CO10 7QS
**US SIC:** 3357, 3651, 8911
**UK SIC:** 22470, 34541, 83701
**Auditors:** KPMG LLP

---

**Bankers:** HSBC Bank plc (40-05-30)

| | 31-12-13 | 31-12-12 | 31-12-11 |
|---|---|---|---|
| TO | 788,000,000 | 750,900,000 | 750,500,000 |
| P/L | (4,000,000) | (5,600,000) | 15,500,000 |
| NW | (138,000,000) | (120,100,000) | (95,200,000) |
| WC | (145,000,000) | (137,200,000) | (157,600,000) |
| Emp. | 1,893 | 2,043 | 2,058 |

---

**DUNS 21-393-1071**
### Philips Research Uk
101 Science Park, Cambridge, Cambridgeshire CB4 0FY
**Tel:** 01223427500
**Web:** www.research.philips.com
**Estd:** 2008 Proprietorship
**Line of Business:** Research and laboratory based activities
**Proprietor:** Mrs B Pieka
**Responsibilities**
**Senior:** Hans Huiberts *(Department Head)*
**US SIC:** 7391   **UK SIC:** 94000
**Employees:** 48

---

**DUNS 23-676-0385**
### Phillip Andrews
George Street, Bath, Avon BA1 2QS
**Tel:** 01225-404445
**Web:** www.moles.co.uk
**VAT No:** 318759523 **Estd:** 1978 Proprietorship
**Line of Business:** Managed public houses and bars
**Proprietor:** P Andrews
**Branches:** Phillip Andrews, George Street, Bath, Avon BA1 2QS
**US SIC:** 5813, 7399
**UK SIC:** 66200, 83954
**Bankers:** Barclays Bank Plc (20-05-06)
**Employees:** 10

---

**DUNS 21-006-8300**
### Phillips 66 Ltd
*(Subsidiary of:* Phillips 66)
7th Floor, 200-202 Aldersgate Street, London EC1A 4HD
**Tel:** 02078-224-400
**Web:** www.phillips66.com
**Reg No:** 0529086 **Estd:** 1954 Private Limited Company
**Line of Business:** Oil refining and distribution.
**Export Sales:** £1.240E + 10
**Trading Style:** Burlington Resources
**Issued Capital:** £405,400
**Directors:** G S Taylor, P George, D R Blakemore, J R Stoll, M J Morrison, J C Mccall
**Co. Secretary:** Ms Elaine Price
**Responsibilities**
**Senior:** Gregory Goff *(Manager)*, Jimmy Nokes *(Manager)*, Michael Stokeld *(Manager)*, Richard Swallow *(Manager)*, Steven Theede *(Manager)*, Stefan Wulkan *(Marketing Manager)*
**Finance:** Tony Reddington *(Financial Director)*
**Marketing:** Stefan Wulkan *(Marketing Manager)*
**Health & Safety:** Russell Best *(Health & Safety Manager)*
**Branches:** Phillips 66 Ltd, 707 London Road, Glasgow, Lanarkshire G40 3AS
**US SIC:** 5171   **UK SIC:** 61200
**Auditors:** Ernst & Young LLP
**Bankers:** Bank Of America, Na (16-50-50)
Following financial data are in thousands

| | 31-12-13 | 31-12-12 | 31-12-11 |
|---|---|---|---|
| TO | 18,405,800 | 21,657,000 | 27,433,900 |
| P/L | 44,000 | 205,700 | 233,000 |
| NW | 2,692,700 | 2,831,900 | 1,717,300 |
| WC | 893,800 | 1,051,000 | 1,127,300 |
| Emp. | 1,009 | 1,019 | 996 |

---

**DUNS 71-902-3280**
### Phillips & Cohen Associates (Uk) Ltd
Building 5, Floor 9, Salford, Lancashire M5 3EF
**Tel:** 08456035591 **Fax:** 016-1877-5504
**Web:** www.phillips-cohen.co.uk
**Reg No:** 5284353 **Estd:** 2006 Private Limited Company
**Line of Business:** Financial intermediation not elsewhere classified
**Issued Capital:** £100
**Directors:** A Cohen, H Enders, M Phillips
**Co. Secretary:** Mathew Phillips
**Responsibilities**
**Sales:** Tim Webb *(Sales Director)*
**Operations:** Nick Cherry *(Site Director)*
**US SIC:** 6111   **UK SIC:** 81501
**Bankers:** HSBC Bank plc (40-20-14)

| | 31-12-13 | 31-12-12 | 31-12-11 |
|---|---|---|---|
| TA | 1,866,873 | 1,591,431 | 931,251 |
| P/L | 1,502,572 | N/A | N/A |
| NW | 504,165 | (647,796) | (1,430,581) |
| WC | 398,855 | 225,465 | (149,823) |

---

**DUNS 22-210-2282**
### Phillips Auctioneers Ltd
7 Howick Place, London SW1P 1BB
**Tel:** 020-7318-4010 **Fax:** 02073184011
**Web:** www.phillipsdepury.com
**Reg No:** 4228373 **Estd:** 2003 Private Limited Company
**Line of Business:** Auctioneers and valuers
**Issued Capital:** £63,636,354
**Directors:** F S Dombernowsky, S Cleary, E J Dolman
**Co. Secretary:** Alexander Payne
**Responsibilities**
**Senior:** Michael Mcginnis *(Director)*, Simon Pury *(Chairman)*, Finn Schouenborg Dombernowsky *(Managing Director)*
**US SIC:** 7399   **UK SIC:** 83954
**Auditors:** Grant Thornton UK LLP

| | 31-12-13 | 31-12-12 | 31-12-11 |
|---|---|---|---|
| TO | 14,504,000 | 18,406,000 | 11,612,000 |
| P/L | (5,405,000) | (2,767,000) | (7,976,000) |
| NW | (57,695,000) | (52,290,000) | (51,573,000) |
| WC | (59,784,000) | (54,703,000) | (53,983,000) |
| Emp. | 93 | 81 | 75 |

---

**DUNS 73-461-8549**
### Phillips (Autos) Ltd
Unit 17 Ashford Road Stour Valley, Industrial Estate, Canterbury, Kent CT4 7HF
**Tel:** 01227-732700
**Web:** www.eastkentaudi.co.uk
**Reg No:** 2912552 **VAT No:** 619367711
**Estd:** 2000 Private Limited Company
**Line of Business:** Sale of new motor vehicles
**Trading Style:** East Kent Audi
**Issued Capital:** £1
**Managing Director:** B D Phillips
**Co. Secretary:** Ms Judy Jeanes
**Responsibilities**
**Marketing:** Janet Crawford *(Marketing Coordinator)*
**Sales:** Keith Batters *(Sales Manager)*
**Branches:** Phillips (Autos) Ltd, Stour Valley Business Pk Ashford Rd, Canterbury, Kent CT4 7HF
**US SIC:** 5511, 7539
**UK SIC:** 65100, 67100
**Auditors:** Spain Brothers
**Bankers:** National Westminster Bank Plc (60-60-08)

| | 30-06-14 | 30-06-13 | 30-06-12 |
|---|---|---|---|
| TA | 303,169 | 295,564 | 313,427 |
| NW | 274,378 | 281,556 | 307,380 |
| WC | 202,306 | 184,846 | 193,512 |

---

**DUNS 53-634-5184**
### Phillips Funeral Plans Ltd
*(Subsidiary of:* Dignity Plc)
Parchment House, 9 Victoria Road, Harpenden, Hertfordshire AL5 4EB
**Tel:** 01582-461100
**Web:** www.phillipsfunerals.co.uk
**Reg No:** 3439290 **Estd:** 1998 Private Limited Company
**Line of Business:** Monumental masons
**Issued Capital:** £50,000
**Directors:** A R Davies, M K Mccollum, S L Whittern
**Co. Secretary:** Richard Portman
**US SIC:** 7261   **UK SIC:** 98902
**Auditors:** PricewaterhouseCoopers LLP

| | 27-12-13 | 28-12-12 | 30-12-11 |
|---|---|---|---|
| TA | 34,401 | 34,401 | 34,401 |
| NW | 34,401 | 34,401 | 34,401 |

---

**DUNS 23-523-7849**
### Philpots Manor School Ltd
West Hoathly Road, East Grinstead, West Sussex RH19 4NF
**Web:** www.philpotsmanorschool.co.uk
**Reg No:** 0773122 **Estd:** 1963 Private Limited Company
**Line of Business:** Schools (special)
**Issued Capital:** £100
**Directors:** Mrs S J Ogilvie, S Ogilvie, Ms L M Churnside, R F Penticost
**Co. Secretary:** Ms Maria Velterop
**Responsibilities**
**Admin:** Jill Roberts *(Administration)*
**IT:** Roy Church *(Senior IT Executive)*
**Health & Safety:** Angela Burton *(Health & Safety Manager)*
**US SIC:** 8299   **UK SIC:** 93300
**Auditors:** Wood Branson Dickinson

| | 31-08-13 | 31-08-12 | 31-08-11 |
|---|---|---|---|
| TO | N/A | N/A | 2,480,224 |
| P/L | N/A | N/A | (70,779) |
| NW | 356,662 | 352,756 | 538,638 |
| WC | (688,863) | (767,182) | (581,590) |

---

**DUNS 29-674-9161**
### Philpotts Ltd
*(Subsidiary of:* Philpotts (Holdings) Ltd)
9 Pioneer Court, Darlington, County Durham DL1 4WD
**Tel:** 01412489080
**Web:** www.philpotts.co.uk
**Reg No:** 2001192 **Estd:** 1985 Private Limited Company

**Line of Business:** Retail sale in non-specialised stores with food, beverages or tobacco predominating
**Issued Capital:** £987
**Directors:** P E May, Ms L C Brook
**Co. Secretary:** Christopher Marsh
**Responsibilities**
**Senior:** Kevin Caven *(Operations Director)*, Richard Tonks *(Manager)*
**Branches:** Philpotts Ltd, Abbots House, Butcher Row, Shrewsbury, Shropshire SY1 1UW
**US SIC:** 5411 **UK SIC:** 64100
**Auditors:** Pennington Williams
**Bankers:** HSBC Bank plc (40-30-15)

| | 30-06-13 | 30-06-12 | 30-06-11 |
|---|---|---|---|
| TO | 10,014,000 | 10,059,000 | 9,967,000 |
| P/L | 710,000 | 609,000 | 415,000 |
| NW | 5,102,000 | 4,649,000 | 4,331,000 |
| WC | 1,975,000 | 1,773,000 | 1,085,000 |
| Emp. | 260 | 266 | 292 |

DUNS 29-143-3399 Exp

## Phipps & Co Ltd

Mathon Court, West Malvern Road, Mathon, Malvern, Worcestershire WR13 5NZ
**Tel:** 01684892242
**Web:** www.phippsaccountants.co.uk
**Reg No:** 1704113 **Estd:** 1983 Private Limited Company
**Line of Business:** Financial intermediation not elsewhere classified
**Issued Capital:** £100,200
**Directors:** Ms A R Neve, Ms M M Phipps, Ms H B Marsden, S L Phipps, C L Phipps
**Co. Secretary:** Mrs Dawn Harford
**Responsibilities**
**Senior:** Colin Phipps *(Manager)*
**US SIC:** 6111 **UK SIC:** 81501
**Auditors:** Hacker Young
**Bankers:** Barclays Bank Plc (20-84-41)

| | 31-03-14 | 31-03-13 | 31-03-12 |
|---|---|---|---|
| TA | 48,047,218 | 60,471,523 | 54,839,426 |
| P/L | 3,966,094 | 4,890,985 | 3,597,798 |
| NW | 24,047,095 | 23,081,690 | 24,152,791 |
| WC | 12,738,447 | 11,971,192 | 9,115,824 |
| Emp. | 304 | 283 | 285 |

DUNS 23-546-2475 Imp

## Phlexglobal Ltd

(**Subsidiary of:** Bridgepoint Advisers Group Ltd)
Mandeville House, 62 The Broadway, Amersham, Buckinghamshire HP7 0HJ
**Tel:** 01494-720420
**Web:** www.phlexglobal.com
**Reg No:** 3544670 **Estd:** 1998 Private Limited Company
**Line of Business:** Labour recruitment and provision of personnel
**Export Sales:** £10,884,633
**Issued Capital:** £170
**Directors:** Ms K Roy, P J Mcnaney
**Co. Secretary:** Ms Stella Donoghue
**Responsibilities**
**Senior:** Nicola Murgatroyd *(Manager)*
**US SIC:** 7399 **UK SIC:** 83954
**Auditors:** Unknown Auditor

| | 31-12-13 | 31-12-12 | 31-12-11 |
|---|---|---|---|
| TO | 15,253,129 | 13,434,828 | 9,264,888 |
| P/L | 4,077,232 | 2,876,255 | 1,253,333 |
| NW | 9,244,596 | 5,837,712 | 3,444,381 |
| WC | 8,318,172 | 5,023,708 | 2,878,114 |
| Emp. | 238 | 236 | 190 |

DUNS 21-034-6098

## Phls Middlesbrough Area Lab

Public Health Laboratory, Marton Road, Middlesbrough, Cleveland TS4 3RZ
**Web:** www.mbro.ac.uk
**Line of Business:** Microbiology laboratory
**US SIC:** 8249 **UK SIC:** 93300
**Employees:** 600

DUNS 21-661-7375

## Phmetrika Ltd

8 William Savage Way, Smethwick, West Midlands B66 4SQ
**Tel:** 01215652633
**Reg No:** 7172617 **Estd:** 2010 Private Company Limited By Guarantee
**Line of Business:** Research and experimental development on social sciences and humanities
**Directors:** Dr A O Uthman, Mrs R Uthman
**Co. Secretary:** Mrs Rashidah Uthman
**US SIC:** 8922 **UK SIC:** 94000

| | 31-03-14 | 31-03-13 |
|---|---|---|
| TO | 40,450 | 36,300 |
| P/L | 6,413 | 9,480 |

DUNS 22-780-8441

## Phn Enterprises Ltd

Brook Road, Oveross Industrial Estate, Ross-On-Wye, Herefordshire HR9 7QG
**Tel:** 01989568800
**Web:** www.uk-select.com
**Reg No:** 1216688 **Estd:** 1992 Private Limited Company
**Line of Business:** Maintenance and repair of motor vehicles
**Trading Style:** Peter Nash Accident Repair Centre
**Issued Capital:** £33,000
**Directors:** D P Rollings, Mrs J Rollings
**Co. Secretary:** Ms Joanne Rollings
**US SIC:** 7539 **UK SIC:** 67100
**Auditors:** Bartlett Kershaw Trott
**Bankers:** Lloyds TSB Bank plc (30-95-72)

| | 31-12-13 | 31-12-12 | 31-12-11 |
|---|---|---|---|
| TA | 1,441,942 | 1,414,651 | 1,019,691 |
| NW | 167,847 | 149,811 | 131,241 |
| WC | (87,664) | (86,276) | (96,191) |

DUNS 21-276-4197

## Phoenix

Golden Cross, 220 Chester Street, Aston, Birmingham, West Midlands B6 4AH
**Tel:** 0121-3802000
**Web:** www.phoenix.co.uk
**Estd:** 2013 Proprietorship
**Line of Business:** Computer systems and software (sales)
**Proprietor:** R Mann
**Responsibilities**
**Senior:** Tony Glanelli *(Operations Director)*, Mike Osborne *(Manager)*
**HR:** Jay Mcness *(Human Resources Manager)*
**US SIC:** 7379 **UK SIC:** 83940
**Employees:** 50

DUNS 64-071-3699

## Phoenix Administration Services Ltd

Springfield Lodge, Colchester Road, Springfield, Chelmsford, Essex CM2 5PW
**Tel:** 01245-398950 **Fax:** 01245398951
**Web:** www.phoenixadmin.co.uk
**Reg No:** 3466852 **Estd:** 1997 Private Limited Company
**Line of Business:** Secretarial and translation activities
**Issued Capital:** £459,526
**Directors:** A C Deptford, R W Leedham, Mrs D Jones, P Foley-Brickley, D C Tibble, D W Munting, M G Quirke
**Co. Secretary:** Duncan Hayes
**Responsibilities**
**Operations:** Martin Toole *(Production and Operations Mana)*
**US SIC:** 7399 **UK SIC:** 83954
**Auditors:** Taylor Viney & Marlow
**Bankers:** The Royal Bank Of Scotland Plc (16-00-32)

| | 30-09-13 | 30-09-12 | 30-09-11 |
|---|---|---|---|
| TO | 5,502,250 | 5,034,766 | 4,489,653 |
| P/L | (94,080) | (600,481) | (953,403) |
| NW | 967,067 | 884,833 | 1,540,522 |
| WC | 1,389,741 | 1,276,037 | 1,925,837 |
| Emp. | 48 | 60 | 56 |

DUNS 21-929-9155

## Phoenix Agency Services Ltd

The Green Man 355 Bromley Road, London SE6 2RP
**Tel:** 02082902700
**Reg No:** 8436155 **Estd:** 2013 Private Limited Company
**Line of Business:** Other construction work involving special trades
**Issued Capital:** £5,000
**Directors:** K C Donnelly, P Bloss, A Hall, Ms J Daby, D W Cummins, Ms P A Fordham Mbe, S Howlett, A E Harmer
**Co. Secretary:** Kevin Kelly
**Responsibilities**
**Senior:** Patricia Crawford *(Director)*, Margaret Mccarthy *(Director)*, Denise Newsam *(Director)*, Christopher Starke *(Director)*
**US SIC:** 1799 **UK SIC:** 50000

| | 31-03-14 |
|---|---|
| TO | 1,663,000 |
| P/L | 6,000 |
| NW | (328,000) |
| WC | 130,000 |
| Emp. | 51 |

DUNS 73-564-5843 Imp

## Phoenix Business Solutions (Uk) Ltd

Ibex House 42-47 Minories, London EC3N 1DY
**Tel:** 020-7680-4450 **Fax:** 02076804460
**Web:** www.phoenixbs.com
**Reg No:** 4826350 **Estd:** 2003 Private Limited Company
**Line of Business:** Management and business consultants
**Export Sales:** £2,708,830
**Issued Capital:** £81
**Directors:** M D Crocker, R Burch, D P Boswell, L Tomlinson
**Co. Secretary:** Roger Pickett
**US SIC:** 7399 **UK SIC:** 83954
**Bankers:** Barclays Bank Plc (20-54-30)

| | 31-07-13 | 31-07-12 | 31-07-11 |
|---|---|---|---|
| TO | 10,625,905 | N/A | N/A |
| P/L | (28,138) | N/A | N/A |
| NW | (133,917) | 106,338 | 119,072 |
| WC | (175,687) | 65,539 | 52,503 |
| Emp. | 63 | N/A | N/A |

DUNS 38-584-3677

## The Phoenix Car Company Ltd

Linwood Road, Phoenix Retail Park, Paisley, Renfrewshire PA1 2AB
**Tel:** 01418495000
**Web:** www.phoenixcars.co.uk
**Reg No:** 0173815SC **Estd:** 1997 Private Limited Company
**Line of Business:** Sale of new motor vehicles
**Trading Style:** Phoenix Mitsubishi
**Issued Capital:** £81,000
**Directors:** C M Johnston, J Mcguire, Mrs D A Hubner, R C Smith
**Responsibilities**
**Senior:** Eleanor Britten *(Manager)*
**Branches:** The Phoenix Car Company Ltd, 491 Aikenhead Road, Glasgow, Lanarkshire G42 0PW
**US SIC:** 5511, 5521, 6711
**UK SIC:** 65100, 83962
**Auditors:** ASE Audit LLP
**Bankers:** Bank Of Scotland (80-07-48)

| | 31-01-14 | 31-01-13 | 31-01-12 |
|---|---|---|---|
| TO | 134,375,431 | 126,931,201 | 143,334,180 |
| P/L | (208,750) | (833,004) | (795,427) |
| NW | 319,517 | 458,243 | 2,229,148 |
| WC | 500,780 | (8,929,700) | (3,650,202) |
| Emp. | 357 | 378 | 416 |

DUNS 34-758-7847

## Phoenix Care Cornwall Ltd

Barn A Hendra, Penzance, Cornwall TR20 8UD
**Tel:** 01736-360197 **Fax:** 01736-360581
**Web:** www.phoenixcarecornwall.com
**Reg No:** 5560068 **Estd:** 2006 Private Limited Company
**Line of Business:** Home care service providers
**Issued Capital:** £100
**Director:** Ms C M Pearce
**Co. Secretary:** Philip Pearce
**US SIC:** 8811 **UK SIC:** 99000

| | 30-09-13 | 30-09-12 | 30-09-11 |
|---|---|---|---|
| TA | 180,974 | 167,966 | 171,739 |
| NW | 32,048 | 31,181 | 12,214 |
| WC | 30,538 | 29,197 | 10,439 |

DUNS 21-557-4521

## Phoenix Care Partners

Broadway House, 2 Haygate Road, Wellington, Telford, Shropshire TF1 1QA
**Tel:** 01952-641753
**Estd:** 2011 Partnership
**Line of Business:** Home care service providers
**Partners:** J Bane, J Christy
**US SIC:** 8091 **UK SIC:** 95200
**Employees:** 100

DUNS 34-626-8530

## Phoenix Class Ltd

13 Rothersthorpe Avenue, Rothersthorpe Avenue Industrial Estate, Northampton, Northamptonshire NN4 8JH
**Tel:** 01604652828
**Web:** www.phoenixclass.net
**Reg No:** 5433196 **VAT No:** 770684309
**Estd:** 2005 Private Limited Company
**Line of Business:** Taxis and private hire vehicles
**Issued Capital:** £120
**Directors:** I R Paige, J L Seaman, D Seaman
**US SIC:** 4121, 7512
**UK SIC:** 72200, 84801

| | 30-04-14 | 30-04-13 | 30-04-12 |
|---|---|---|---|
| TA | 479,984 | 492,319 | 323,566 |
| NW | (23,453) | (40,012) | (78,192) |
| WC | (55,880) | (47,917) | (27,170) |

DUNS 21-558-0153

## Phoenix Community Housing Association

Wren Court, 15 London Road, Bromley, Kent BR1 1DE
**Tel:** 08442-642800
**Web:** www.phoenixcommunityhousing.org
**Line of Business:** Committee managed organisations
**Principals:** P Fordham *(Chairman)*, C Starke *(Financial)*, J Ripley, D Cummins, K Donnelly, J Shortt, A Hall, Ms D St Claire North
**Co. Secretary:** Ms Shirley Muchlow
**Responsibilities**
**Senior:** Denis Costelloe *(Principal)*, Pat Crawford *(Principal)*, Jonathan Kenney *(Principal)*, Christopher Lawal *(Principal)*, Walter McCann *(Principal)*, Margaret McCarthy *(Principal)*, Shirley Mucklow *(Principal)*, Ron Stockbridge *(Principal)*
**US SIC:** 8699 **UK SIC:** 96902
**Auditors:** Trowers & Hamlins

| | 31-03-12 | 31-03-11 | 31-03-09 |
|---|---|---|---|
| TO | 29,716,000 | 27,960,000 | 29,412,000 |
| P/L | 4,618,000 | 8,640,000 | 4,938,000 |
| NW | 19,198,000 | 17,607,000 | 4,516,000 |
| WC | (21,659,000) | (18,347,000) | 6,046,000 |
| Emp. | 134 | 123 | 103 |

DUNS 23-330-1261

## Phoenix Community Transport

Unit 2-3 Block E, Penmaen Industrial Estate, Pontllanfraith, Blackwood, Gwent NP12 2DQ
**Tel:** 01495222187
**Web:** www.phoenixct.co.uk
**Reg No:** 5012285 **VAT No:** 850941913
**Estd:** 2008 Private Company Limited By Guarantee
**Line of Business:** Other scheduled passenger land transport not elsewhere classified
**Directors:** G Evans, K D Cegielski
**Co. Secretary:** Mervyn Jones
**Branches:** Phoenix Community Transport, Unit 2-3, Penmaen Industrial Estate, Blackwood, Gwent NP12 2DQ
**US SIC:** 4119 **UK SIC:** 72200
**Auditors:** ATB Training & Consultancy Services Ltd

| | 31-01-14 | 31-01-13 | 31-01-12 |
|---|---|---|---|
| TO | 400,848 | 479,564 | 472,173 |
| P/L | (5,994) | (1,749) | (30,508) |
| NW | 113,546 | 119,540 | 121,289 |
| WC | 15,045 | 12,789 | 36,429 |

DUNS 22-140-7922

## Phoenix (Cumbria) Ltd

Hallwood Road, Workington, Cumbria CA14 4JR
**Tel:** 01900605100 **Fax:** 01900605700
**Web:** www.phoenixchimneys.co.uk
**Reg No:** 4159642 **Estd:** 2001 Private Limited Company
**Line of Business:** Tyre dealers
**Trading Style:** Gate Tyres
**Issued Capital:** £1,000
**Directors:** G G Thompson, R D Gate
**Co. Secretary:** Ms Diana Gate
**Responsibilities**
**Senior:** Katie-Ann Gate *(Facilities Manager)*
**Facilities:** Katie-Ann Gate *(Facilities Manager)*
**US SIC:** 5531 **UK SIC:** 65100

| | 31-03-14 | 31-03-13 | 31-03-12 |
|---|---|---|---|
| TO | 9,074,187 | 9,529,460 | 9,847,585 |
| P/L | 442,982 | 663,339 | 621,543 |
| NW | 2,261,247 | 2,148,143 | 1,737,672 |
| WC | 1,673,265 | 1,852,641 | 1,469,880 |
| Emp. | 55 | 56 | 55 |

DUNS 23-091-5258

## Phoenix Dental Castings Ltd

Unit 1, The Alpha Centre, Osprey Road, Exeter, Devon EX2 7LH
**Web:** www.phoenix-dental.co.uk
**Reg No:** 2879196 **Estd:** 1987 Private Limited Company
**Line of Business:** Dental equipment suppliers
**Export Sales:** £14,132
**Issued Capital:** £10,000
**Principals:** D Smith *(Managing)*, M Rasaiah
**Co. Secretary:** David Smith
**US SIC:** 3841 **UK SIC:** 37201
**Auditors:** J T Stapleton & Co
**Bankers:** National Westminster Bank Plc (60-17-21)

| | 31-12-13 | 31-12-12 | 31-12-11 |
|---|---|---|---|
| TO | 1,781,698 | 1,994,006 | 2,022,300 |
| P/L | (72,733) | (691) | (37,824) |
| NW | 408,429 | 468,589 | 473,703 |
| WC | 135,776 | 149,937 | 215,498 |
| Emp. | 48 | 50 | 53 |

DUNS 23-459-0131 Imp

## Phoenix Door Panels Ltd

(**Subsidiary of:** Masco Corporation)
West Newlands Industrial Estate, Somersham, Huntingdon, Cambridgeshire PE28 3EB
**Tel:** 01487740469
**Web:** www.phoenixdoorpanels.co.uk
**Reg No:** 2803027 **Estd:** 1993 Private Limited Company
**Line of Business:** Other manufacturing not elsewhere classified
**Issued Capital:** £124
**Principals:** N Peck *(Managing)*, W Devine, L D Gillett
**Responsibilities**
**Senior:** Tracy Peck *(Manager)*
**US SIC:** 3999, 3079
**UK SIC:** 49590, 48360
**Auditors:** George Hay
**Bankers:** National Westminster Bank Plc (60-11-30)

| | 31-12-13 | 30-01-13 | 31-12-12 |
|---|---|---|---|
| TO | 11,032,561 | 8,989,591 | 9,411,523 |
| P/L | 931,435 | 588,489 | 455,707 |
| NW | 2,300,983 | 1,352,588 | 1,077,777 |
| WC | 2,032,184 | 1,101,096 | 838,490 |
| Emp. | 106 | 96 | 88 |

DUNS 73-520-2942
### Phoenix Drivers Ltd
12 Enterprise Way, Pinchbeck, Spalding, Lincolnshire PE11 3YR
**Web:** www.lgvdrivingjobsspalding.co.uk
**Reg No:** 4783083 **Estd:** 2003 Private Limited Company
**Line of Business:** Driver hire agencies
**Issued Capital:** £1
**Director:** G C Brown
**Co. Secretary:** Ms Elizabeth Brown
**US SIC:** 4789, 7349
**UK SIC:** 77002, 92300

| | 30-06-14 | 30-06-13 | 30-06-12 |
|---|---|---|---|
| TA | 591,143 | 560,975 | 563,447 |
| NW | 524,188 | 494,137 | 503,478 |
| WC | 267,703 | 236,985 | 247,037 |

DUNS 21-607-8238 **Imp-Exp**
### Phoenix Engineering Company Ltd
(**Subsidiary of:** Jennings Industries Ltd)
Combe Street, Chard, Somerset TA20 1JE
**Tel:** 0146-063531 **Fax:** 01460-67388
**Web:** www.phoenixeng.co.uk
**Reg No:** 0086564 **VAT No:** 185753624
**Estd:** 1905 Private Limited Company
**Line of Business:** Construction of roads
**Export Markets:** Worldwide
**Issued Capital:** £9,452
**Directors:** S C Jennings, T P Jennings, Mrs B R Jennings
**Co. Secretary:** Thomas Jennings
**Responsibilities**
**Senior:** Paul Gidley *(Spares Manager)*
**US SIC:** 1611 **UK SIC:** 50200
**Auditors:** Albert Goodman LLP
**Bankers:** Lloyds TSB Bank plc (30-92-40)

| | 30-09-13 | 01-10-12 | 30-09-11 |
|---|---|---|---|
| TA | 5,254,909 | 5,871,683 | 4,799,708 |
| NW | 4,750,896 | 4,366,853 | 4,132,588 |
| WC | 4,685,480 | 4,271,310 | 4,055,423 |

DUNS 23-328-2453
### Phoenix Enterprises
Little Bassetts Farm, Magpie Lane, Brentwood, Essex CM13 3EA
**Tel:** 08707358464
**Web:** www.phoenixent.org.uk
**VAT No:** 820665537 **Estd:** 2003 Partnership
**Line of Business:** Security guard services
**Partners:** Mrs M Atkinson, J Atkinson
**US SIC:** 7393 **UK SIC:** 83954
**Bankers:** Lloyds TSB Bank plc (30-90-80)
**Employees:** 80

DUNS 23-575-0325
### Phoenix Enterprises (Rotherham)
18 High Street, Rotherham, South Yorkshire S60 1PP
**Tel:** 01709820208
**Web:** www.phoenixent.org.uk
**Reg No:** 3572996 **Estd:** 1998 Private Company Limited By Guarantee
**Line of Business:** Employment and recruitment companies and consultants
**Directors:** P Butters, D C Bliss, J O Sparrow, Mrs A L Ogley, P J Little
**Co. Secretary:** Mrs Michelle Cooper
**Responsibilities**
**Senior:** Diane Greenwood *(Manager)*
**Branches:** Phoenix Enterprises (Rotherham), Hayfield House, Devonshire Street, Chesterfield, Derbyshire S41 7ST
**US SIC:** 7392 **UK SIC:** 83951
**Auditors:** Hart Shaw LLP

| | 31-03-14 | 31-03-13 | 31-03-12 |
|---|---|---|---|
| TO | 1,955,689 | 1,719,488 | 1,389,064 |
| P/L | 59,861 | (81,524) | (267,539) |
| NW | 2,285,426 | 2,250,870 | 2,672,273 |
| WC | 236,372 | 274,967 | 386,188 |
| Emp. | 79 | 80 | 76 |

DUNS 29-127-9958
### Phoenix Futures
Asra House, 1 Long Lane, London SE1 4PG
**Tel:** 02072-349-740
**Web:** www.phoenix-futures.org.uk
**Reg No:** 1626869 **Estd:** 1970 Private Company Limited By Guarantee
**Line of Business:** Adult and other education not elsewhere classified
**Directors:** Ms A Hooper, Dr K Z Dar, Dr M J Kelleher, J W Cook, Ms S B Ellenby, Ms S A Thewlis, Dr M T Ewart, G Statham
**Co. Secretary:** George Lambis
**Responsibilities**
**Senior:** Emily Finch *(Director)*, Gavin Ollier *(Supported Housing Coordinator)*
**Branches:** Phoenix Futures, Storth Oaks, 229 Graham Road, Sheffield, South Yorkshire S10 3GS
**US SIC:** 8249, 8091, 8321
**UK SIC:** 93300, 95200, 96111
**Auditors:** Nexia Smith & Williamson
**Bankers:** National Westminster Bank Plc (50-30-20)

| | 31-03-14 | 31-03-13 | 31-03-12 |
|---|---|---|---|
| TO | 27,322,000 | 23,081,253 | 22,903,708 |
| P/L | 5,424,000 | 1,299,232 | 1,671,205 |
| NW | 12,431,000 | 7,006,748 | 5,707,516 |
| WC | 5,679,000 | 4,969,981 | 3,695,954 |
| Emp. | 548 | 560 | 592 |

DUNS 21-811-4078
### The Phoenix Health Centre
Phoenix Health Centre, Parkfield Road, Wolverhampton, West Midlands WV4 6ED
**Tel:** 01902444112
**Estd:** 2004
**Line of Business:** Health centres
**US SIC:** 8062 **UK SIC:** 95100
**Employees:** 63

DUNS 21-803-5947 **Imp**
### Phoenix Healthcare Distribution Ltd
(**Subsidiary of:** Phoenix Pharmahandel Gmbh & Co Kg)
Rivington Road, Runcorn, Cheshire WA7 3DJ
**Fax:** 01928-750750
**Web:** www.myp-i-n.co.uk
**Reg No:** 0129370 **VAT No:** 109898228
**Estd:** 2008 Private Limited Company
**Line of Business:** Distribution service providers
**Export Sales:** £32,044,000
**Issued Capital:** £3,363,937
**Directors:** K R Hudson, J D Meader, J S Hollins, T R Panke, P J Smith
**Co. Secretary:** Michael Blakeman
**Responsibilities**
**Senior:** Kenny Black *(Manager)*, David Heron *(General Manager)*
**Sales:** Stefan Pflug *(Managing Director, Wholesale)*
**Branches:** Phoenix Healthcare Distribution Ltd, Unit 4, Hams Hall Distribution Park, Birmingham, West Midlands B46 1DA
**US SIC:** 4712 **UK SIC:** 77002
**Auditors:** Ernst & Young LLP
**Following financial data are in thousands**

| | 31-01-14 | 31-01-13 | 31-01-12 |
|---|---|---|---|
| TO | 972,034 | 983,828 | 1,029,165 |
| P/L | 32,707 | 30,102 | 26,139 |
| NW | 167,116 | 140,528 | 115,422 |
| WC | 153,031 | 124,871 | 99,126 |
| Emp. | 1,571 | 1,641 | 1,653 |

DUNS 23-493-6573
### Phoenix Healthcare Ltd
(**Subsidiary of:** Newco A 13 Ltd)
Warren Lodge, Warren Lane, Finchampstead, Wokingham, Berkshire RG40 4HR
**Tel:** 01189733989
**Web:** www.foresthc.com
**Reg No:** 2820998 **Estd:** 1976 Private Limited Company
**Line of Business:** Other human health activities
**Trading Style:** Warren Lodge
**Issued Capital:** £350,000
**Director:** P Musgrave
**Co. Secretary:** Colin Haig
**US SIC:** 8091 **UK SIC:** 95200
**Auditors:** Piper Thompson
**Bankers:** National Westminster Bank Plc (01-00-61)

| | 31-12-13 | 31-12-12 | 31-12-11 |
|---|---|---|---|
| TO | 1,995,921 | 1,786,950 | 1,417,535 |
| P/L | 601,777 | 673,288 | 561,169 |
| NW | 10,671,742 | 10,069,965 | 9,396,677 |
| WC | 2,444,187 | 1,814,446 | 1,229,585 |
| Emp. | 60 | 50 | 38 |

DUNS 28-987-1253
### Phoenix Hotels Ltd
1-8 Kensington Gardens Square, London W2 4BH
**Tel:** 02072292494 **Fax:** 020-7727-1419
**Web:** www.bestwestern.co.uk
**Reg No:** 1805904 **Estd:** 1984 Private Limited Company
**Line of Business:** Hotels and motels without restaurant
**Trading Style:** Phoenix Hotel
**Issued Capital:** £600,000
**Principals:** B D Bhundia *(Managing)*, M D Bhundia, D B Bhundia
**Co. Secretary:** Prakash Bhundia
**Responsibilities**
**Senior:** Joie De Vivre *(General Manager)*, Mary Donelan *(Manager)*
**US SIC:** 7011 **UK SIC:** 66500
**Auditors:** KPMG LLP
**Bankers:** National Westminster Bank Plc (60-02-08)

| | 30-06-14 | 30-06-13 | 30-06-12 |
|---|---|---|---|
| TA | 46,439,604 | 34,129,408 | 33,641,440 |
| NW | 38,969,754 | 26,632,767 | 26,177,822 |
| WC | 7,321,926 | 7,168,930 | 6,892,252 |

DUNS 29-767-5779
### Phoenix House Live-in World Ltd
The Green Man, 355 Bromley Road, London SE6 2RP
**Tel:** 08000285700
**Web:** http://phoenixch.org.uk
**Reg No:** 2030544 **Estd:** 1969 Private Limited Company
**Line of Business:** Other human health activities
**Issued Capital:** £100
**Directors:** Phoenix House Limited, Ms K Biggs
**Co. Secretary:** George Lambis
**Responsibilities**
**HR:** Pria Rai *(Director of People Services &)*
**Facilities:** Andrea Lowman *(Director of Property and New B)*
**US SIC:** 8091 **UK SIC:** 95200

| | 31-03-14 | 31-03-13 | 31-03-12 |
|---|---|---|---|
| TO | 100 | 100 | 100 |
| NW | 100 | 100 | 100 |

DUNS 21-926-4017 **Imp**
### Phoenix International Freight Services Ltd
(**Subsidiary of:** C.H. Robinson Worldwide Inc.)
Unit 21 Willow Road, Derby, Derbyshire DE74 2NP
**Tel:** 01332850331 **Fax:** 01332-817-360
**Web:** www.portakabin.co.uk
**Reg No:** 1447025 **VAT No:** 309703268
**Estd:** 1979 Private Limited Company
**Line of Business:** Air conditioning contractors
**Export Sales:** £4,052,862
**Trading Style:** Phoenix International Freight Services Limited
**Issued Capital:** £24,000
**Directors:** S D Rambaud, A J Polley, J W Wang, E R Sanchez
**Co. Secretary:** David Goddon
**Responsibilities**
**Senior:** Julie Luckett *(Computer Director)*, Jeff West *(General Manager)*
**Marketing:** Sharon Mitchell *(Human Resources Officer)*
**IT:** Julie Luckett *(Computer Director)*
**HR:** Sharon Mitchell *(Human Resources Officer)*
**Facilities:** Peter Raven *(Facilities Manager)*
**Fleet:** Peter Raven *(Facilities Manager)*
**Branches:** Phoenix International Freight Services Ltd, Richmond House, Avonmouth Way, Bristol, Avon BS11 8DE
**US SIC:** 1711, 4411, 4226
**UK SIC:** 50300, 74001, 77003
**Auditors:** Grant Thornton UK LLP
**Bankers:** National Westminster Bank Plc (60-13-23)

| | 31-12-13 | 30-06-12 | 30-12-11 |
|---|---|---|---|
| TO | 14,590,792 | 15,402,725 | 15,094,911 |
| P/L | (137,979) | 379,460 | 280,273 |
| NW | 1,280,525 | 1,401,317 | 1,139,955 |
| WC | 1,147,236 | 1,174,681 | 1,031,092 |
| Emp. | 70 | 75 | 78 |

DUNS 64-080-8796 **Imp-Exp**
### Phoenix It Group Plc
Technology House, Hunsbury Hill Avenue, Northampton, Northamptonshire NN4 8QS
**Tel:** 01604-769000 **Fax:** 01604764323
**Web:** www.phoenixitgroup.com
**Reg No:** 3476115 **Estd:** 1997 Public Limited Company
**Line of Business:** Computer repair and maintenance services
**Issued Capital:** £753,879
**Directors:** Ms E J Aikman, D N Garman, S W Vaughan, R F Taylor, P M Bertram
**Co. Secretary:** Dirk Toulmin-Van Sittert
**Responsibilities**
**Senior:** Reeta Stokes *(Manager)*
**Marketing:** Vanessa Armstrong *(Head of Marketing)*
**IT:** Chris Almand *(IT Manager)*
**Facilities:** Dave Braithwaite *(Facilities Manager)*
**Branches:** Phoenix It Group Plc, Furnace Hill, Chesterfield, Derbyshire S45 9NF
**US SIC:** 6711, 7379
**UK SIC:** 83962, 83940
**Auditors:** PricewaterhouseCoopers LLP
**Bankers:** The Royal Bank Of Scotland Plc (16-25-27)

| | 31-03-14 | 31-03-13 | 31-03-12 |
|---|---|---|---|
| TO | 233,400,000 | 270,600,000 | 264,600,000 |
| P/L | (29,200,000) | (58,800,000) | 3,800,000 |
| NW | (44,500,000) | (53,900,000) | (39,400,000) |
| WC | (5,900,000) | (11,000,000) | (2,900,000) |
| Emp. | 2,344 | 2,265 | 2,521 |

DUNS 29-657-2456
### Phoenix It Managed Services Ltd
(**Subsidiary of:** Phoenix It Group Plc)
9 The Lakes, Northampton, Northamptonshire NN4 7HD
**Fax:** 08701218302
**Web:** www.servo.co.uk
**Reg No:** 1983540 **Estd:** 1986 Private Limited Company
**Line of Business:** Data processing
**Export Sales:** £1,772,000
**Trading Style:** Icm
**Issued Capital:** £6,176,500
**Directors:** S W Vaughan, Mrs E J Aikman
**Co. Secretary:** Dirk Toulmin-Van Sittert
**Responsibilities**
**Senior:** Reeta Stokes *(Manager)*
**HR:** Richard McDonald *(Training Manager)*
**Branches:** Phoenix It Managed Services Ltd, Unit 1 Wessex Road, Bourne End, Buckinghamshire SL8 5DT
**US SIC:** 7374, 7399
**UK SIC:** 83940, 83954
**Auditors:** Deloitte LLP
**Bankers:** The Royal Bank Of Scotland Plc (16-25-27)

| | 31-03-14 | 31-03-13 | 31-03-12 |
|---|---|---|---|
| TO | 66,240,000 | 83,693,000 | 87,493,000 |
| P/L | 250,000 | (36,274,000) | 4,859,000 |
| NW | (28,358,000) | (28,463,000) | (4,761,000) |
| WC | (37,176,000) | (36,845,000) | (20,111,000) |
| Emp. | 303 | 394 | 471 |

DUNS 21-926-5154
### Phoenix It Services Ltd
(**Subsidiary of:** Phoenix It Group Plc)
Lakeside House The Lakes, Bedford Road, Northampton, Northamptonshire NN4 7HD
**Tel:** 08448 630 000 **Fax:** 08448 630 002
**Web:** www.phoenix.co.uk
**Reg No:** 1466217 **VAT No:** 408586039
**Estd:** 1979 Private Limited Company
**Line of Business:** Other computer related activities
**Trading Style:** Phoenix
**Issued Capital:** £1,000,000
**Directors:** Ms E J Aikman, S W Vaughan, J Craig
**Co. Secretary:** Dirk Toulmin-Van Sittert
**Branches:** Phoenix It Services Ltd, 18 Horatius Way, Silver Wing Industrial Estate, Croydon, Surrey CR0 4RU
**US SIC:** 7379 **UK SIC:** 83940
**Auditors:** PricewaterhouseCoopers LLP
**Bankers:** National Westminster Bank Plc (56-00-60)

| | 31-03-14 | 31-03-13 | 31-03-12 |
|---|---|---|---|
| TO | 125,680,000 | 128,589,000 | 135,269,000 |
| P/L | (20,619,000) | 11,308,000 | 5,587,000 |
| NW | 6,435,000 | 7,375,000 | 9,568,000 |
| WC | 5,925,000 | 8,743,000 | 16,917,000 |
| Emp. | 1,814 | 1,606 | 1,714 |

DUNS 21-817-0653
### Phoenix Learning & Care Holdings Ltd
First Floor Rolle Quay, Barnstaple, Devon EX31 1JE
**Tel:** 01271379006
**Reg No:** 7899184 **Estd:** 2012 Private Limited Company
**Line of Business:** Management activities of holding companies
**Issued Capital:** £100,000
**Directors:** M Buckingham, F H Delbaere, D M Sherratt, K G Burley, M Parker
**Co. Secretary:** Francois Delbaere
**US SIC:** 6711 **UK SIC:** 83962

| | 31-08-13 | 31-08-12 |
|---|---|---|
| TO | 6,541,324 | 2,218,616 |
| P/L | (506,841) | (257,033) |
| NW | (4,903,196) | (4,605,643) |
| WC | (6,089,208) | (4,325,470) |
| Emp. | 232 | 200 |

DUNS 77-534-5440
### Phoenix Leisure Management Ltd
Thurston Drive, Kettering, Northamptonshire NN15 6PB
**Tel:** 01536414141
**Web:** www.ketteringconference.co.uk
**Reg No:** 2992507 **Estd:** 1994 Private Limited Company
**Line of Business:** Operation of sports arenas and stadiums
**Trading Style:** Lakeside Bar
**Issued Capital:** £79,000
**Directors:** D A Atkinson, Dr E G Schute
**Responsibilities**
**Marketing:** Samantha Nimmo *(Sales & Marketing Manager)*
**Sales:** Samantha Nimmo *(Sales & Marketing Manager)*
**HR:** Helen Ploughman *(Duty Manager)*
**Facilities:** Chris Chettle *(Operations Manager)*
**Purchasing:** Helen Ploughman *(Duty Manager)*

**US SIC:** 7941, 7911
**UK SIC:** 97911, 97913
**Auditors:** Bewers Turner & Co Ltd
**Bankers:** National Westminster Bank Plc (60-14-03)

| | 31-03-14 | 31-03-13 | 31-03-12 |
|---|---|---|---|
| TA | 10,295,571 | 9,894,228 | 9,851,384 |
| NW | 6,118,722 | 5,902,872 | 5,724,367 |
| WC | 261,565 | 178,115 | 104,342 |

DUNS 21-022-7260
## Phoenix Life Assurance Ltd
(**Subsidiary of:** Phoenix Life Holdings Ltd)
Peterborough Business Park, Peterborough, Cambridgeshire PE2 6FY
**Tel:** 01733470470 **Fax:** 01733472300
**Web:** www.pearl.co.uk
**Reg No:** 0001419 **Estd:** 1864 Private Limited Company
**Line of Business:** Life assurance services
**Issued Capital:** £342,109,474
**Directors:** A W Snow, W R Treen, M D Ross, J P Evans, A B Davidson, S Mohammed, M N Urmston, A Moss
**Co. Secretary:**
Pearl Group Secretariat Services
**Responsibilities**
**Senior:** Tricia Marchant *(Site Manager)*
**Branches:** Phoenix Life Assurance Ltd, Unit 10 Beacontree Plaza, Gillette Way, Reading, Berkshire RG2 0BS
**US SIC:** 6311 **UK SIC:** 82002
**Auditors:** Ernst & Young LLP
**Following financial data are in thousands**

| | 31-12-13 | 31-12-12 | 31-12-11 |
|---|---|---|---|
| TO | 387,000 | 537,000 | 346,000 |
| P/L | 145,000 | 196,000 | (18,000) |
| NW | 1,058,000 | 1,166,000 | 1,011,000 |
| WC | 782,000 | 12,621,000 | (17,451,000) |

DUNS 77-103-3073
## Phoenix Life Insurance Services Ltd
(**Subsidiary of:** Phoenix Life Holdings Ltd)
Po Box 30, Liverpool, Merseyside L69 3HS
**Tel:** 01512393000 **Fax:** 0151-239-3515
**Web:** www.phoenixlifegroup.co.uk
**Reg No:** 2680269 **Estd:** 1992 Private Limited Company
**Line of Business:** Other business activities not elsewhere classified
**Issued Capital:** £1,000
**Directors:** A Moss, A Kassimiotis
**Co. Secretary:**
Pearl Group Secretariat Services
**Responsibilities**
**Senior:** Keith Greenfield *(Manager)*
**Branches:** Phoenix Life Insurance Services Ltd, 248 Hoylake Rd, Wirral, Merseyside CH46 6AD
**US SIC:** 7399 **UK SIC:** 83954
**Auditors:** Ernst & Young LLP
**Employees:** 2,500

DUNS 22-708-6667
## Phoenix Life Ltd
(**Subsidiary of:** Phoenix Life Holdings Ltd)
Po Box 401, Liverpool, Merseyside L69 3TW
**Fax:** 01564-828822
**Web:** www.phoenixlifegroup.co.uk
**Reg No:** 1016269 **Estd:** 1960 Private Limited Company
**Line of Business:** Life insurance
**Trading Style:** Phoenix Life
**Issued Capital:** £69,087,572
**Directors:** S C True, A Moss, M Dale, H E Osmond, A B Davidson, A W Snow, M N Urmston, S Mohammed
**Co. Secretary:**
Pearl Group Secretariat Services
**Responsibilities**
**Senior:** Edward Hawkes *(Director)*, Michael Merrick *(Manager)*
**Branches:** Phoenix Life Ltd, 50 Bothwell Street, Glasgow, Lanarkshire G2 6NU
**US SIC:** 6311, 6371
**UK SIC:** 82002
**Auditors:** Ernst & Young LLP
**Bankers:** National Westminster Bank Plc (54-21-38)
**Following financial data are in thousands**

| | 31-12-13 | 31-12-12 | 31-12-11 |
|---|---|---|---|
| TO | 947,000 | N/A | 5,311,000 |
| P/L | 237,000 | 275,000 | 627,000 |
| NW | 734,000 | 771,000 | 785,000 |
| WC | (28,177,000) | 15,015,000 | (47,780,000) |
| Emp. | N/A | 3,000 | 8 |

DUNS 21-599-2554
## Phoenix Mazda
Linwood Road, Phoenix Retail Park, Paisley, Renfrewshire PA1 2AB
**Tel:** 01418495072
**Web:** www.phoenix-mazda.co.uk
**Estd:** 2002
**Line of Business:** New & Used Motor Vehicle Dealers
**Responsibilities**
**Senior:** Kelvin Illingsworth *(Manager)*, Peter Mustard *(Dealer Principal)*
**US SIC:** 5511 **UK SIC:** 65100
**Employees:** 100

DUNS 21-023-1080 Exp
## Phoenix Me Ltd
(**Subsidiary of:** Phoenix Electrical (Holdings) Ltd)
Cityside House, 40 Adler Street, London E1 1EE
**Tel:** 020-7422-1900 **Fax:** 02074221999
**Web:** www.phoenixme.co.uk
**Reg No:** 0255476 **Estd:** 1931 Private Limited Company
**Line of Business:** Electrical contractors and electricians
**Issued Capital:** £5,022,000
**Directors:** S Crane, C Mint, L Compton
**Co. Secretary:** Nigel Swanson
**Responsibilities**
**IT:** Mike Fanthome *(IT Manager)*
**HR:** Patricia Bristow *(Personnel Manager)*
**US SIC:** 1731, 1796
**UK SIC:** 50300, 50400
**Auditors:** hjs
**Bankers:** The Royal Bank Of Scotland Plc (15-10-00)

| | 30-09-13 | 30-09-12 | 30-09-11 |
|---|---|---|---|
| TO | 62,597,000 | 52,032,000 | 44,377,000 |
| P/L | 1,257,000 | 853,000 | 909,000 |
| NW | 8,362,000 | 7,010,000 | 6,393,000 |
| WC | 8,241,000 | 6,129,000 | 6,004,000 |
| Emp. | 153 | 148 | 155 |

DUNS 23-605-8900
## Phoenix Medical Supplies Ltd
(**Subsidiary of:** Phoenix Pharmahandel Gmbh & Co Kg)
Rivington Road, Whitehouse Industrial Estate, Runcorn, Cheshire WA7 3DJ
**Fax:** 01928-750750
**Web:** www.phoenixmedical.co.uk
**Reg No:** 3603234 **Estd:** 1998 Private Limited Company
**Line of Business:** Medical equipment leasing and rental
**Issued Capital:** £25,861,200
**Directors:** K J Black, T R Panke, P J Smith, K R Hudson, F Grobe-Natrop, S Herfeld, H K Fisher, O T Windholz
**Co. Secretary:** Michael Blakeman
**Responsibilities**
**Senior:** Henry Iberl *(Manager)*, Stefan Pflug *(Manager)*
**Branches:** Phoenix Medical Supplies Ltd, 140 Park Avenue, Wrexham, Clwyd LL12 7AN
**US SIC:** 5122, 6711
**UK SIC:** 61800, 83962
**Auditors:** Ernst & Young LLP

| | 31-01-14 | 31-01-13 | 31-01-12 |
|---|---|---|---|
| TA | 445,285,000 | 456,043,000 | 495,696,000 |
| P/L | 8,495,000 | 9,768,000 | 32,449,000 |
| NW | 169,185,000 | 192,647,000 | 213,269,000 |
| WC | 106,219,000 | 149,386,000 | 202,276,000 |
| Emp. | 142 | 129 | 85 |

DUNS 42-439-5242
## Phoenix Natural Gas Ltd
(**Subsidiary of:** Carmel Capital Ii Sarl)
197 Airport Road West, Belfast BT3 9ED
**Tel:** 0845 455 5555 **Fax:** 02890555500
**Web:** www.phoenixnaturalgas.com
**Reg No:** 0032809NI **Estd:** 1992 Private Limited Company
**Line of Business:** Manufacture of gas
**Issued Capital:** £54,681,891
**Directors:** A J Pollock, D G Russell, P J Ritson, W F Mckinstry, B Ambrose
**Co. Secretary:** William Mc Kinstry
**Responsibilities**
**Senior:** Richard Fulton *(Director)*
**Finance:** Michael MacKinstry *(Group Finance Director)*
**Marketing:** Nicola Faulkner *(Marketing Manager)*
**Sales:** Eamon Mee *(Sales Executive)*
**HR:** Claire McCay *(Personnel Manager)*
**Operations:** Ryan Love *(Network Operations Manager - L)*
**Fleet:** Joanne Quinn *(Manager)*
**US SIC:** 4925 **UK SIC:** 25670
**Auditors:** KPMG
**Bankers:** Northern Bank Ltd (95-00-01)

| | 31-12-13 | 31-12-12 | 31-12-11 |
|---|---|---|---|
| TO | 54,382,000 | 45,112,000 | 39,177,000 |
| P/L | 5,053,000 | (571,000) | (1,951,000) |
| NW | 102,200,000 | (93,102,000) | (97,061,000) |
| WC | (136,773,000) | (280,540,000) | (273,581,000) |
| Emp. | 117 | 121 | 118 |

DUNS 21-101-6366
## Phoenix Parker Holdings Ltd
Viaduct Works Canon Street, Leicester, Leicester, Leicestershire LE4 6GH
**Tel:** 08707505022
**Web:** www.phoenixtransworld.com
**Reg No:** 6450198 **Estd:** 2007 Private Limited Company
**Line of Business:** Management activities of production holding companies
**Export Sales:** £27,484,000
**Issued Capital:** £50,000
**Directors:** B L Dalby, G B Dalby
**Co. Secretary:** Glyn Wheeler
**US SIC:** 6711 **UK SIC:** 83962

| | 31-12-13 | 31-12-12 | 31-12-11 |
|---|---|---|---|
| TO | 38,115,000 | 27,626,000 | 29,949,717 |
| P/L | 7,307,000 | 2,505,000 | 5,369,233 |
| NW | 22,907,000 | 18,169,000 | 16,549,873 |
| WC | 13,788,000 | 9,400,000 | 7,087,923 |
| Emp. | 168 | 181 | 220 |

DUNS 22-076-3689
## The Phoenix Partnership (Leeds) Ltd
(**Subsidiary of:** Tpp Finance Ltd)
Mill House, Troy Road, Horsforth, Leeds, West Yorkshire LS18 5TN
**Tel:** 01132-050080 **Fax:** 01132050081
**Web:** www.tpp-uk.com
**Reg No:** 4077829 **Estd:** 2000 Private Limited Company
**Line of Business:** Computer software (development)
**Issued Capital:** £1,000
**Director:** F X Hester
**US SIC:** 7379 **UK SIC:** 83940

| | 31-03-14 | 31-03-13 | 31-03-12 |
|---|---|---|---|
| TO | 30,972,167 | 26,524,250 | 24,561,635 |
| P/L | 7,131,425 | 8,411,694 | 11,555,960 |
| NW | 20,830,772 | 15,270,711 | 8,794,129 |
| WC | 12,508,145 | 10,122,338 | 7,575,256 |
| Emp. | 240 | 208 | 148 |

DUNS 29-679-5248
## Phoenix Precision Ltd
Crompton Road, Glenrothes, Fife KY6 2SF
**Tel:** 01592-772077
**Web:** www.phoenixprecision.com
**Reg No:** 0098188SC **Estd:** 1986 Private Limited Company
**Line of Business:** Sheet metal fabricators
**Issued Capital:** £55,398
**Directors:** C G Brodie, Ms L J Smith, J Moffat
**Co. Secretary:**
Purple Venture Secretaries Limit
**US SIC:** 3469 **UK SIC:** 31200
**Auditors:** Morris & Young
**Bankers:** Bank Of Scotland (80-08-09)

| | 31-12-13 | 31-12-12 | 31-12-11 |
|---|---|---|---|
| TA | 2,092,338 | 2,220,258 | 2,369,377 |
| NW | 240,675 | 101,558 | 204,375 |
| WC | (238,865) | (223,101) | (13,736) |

DUNS 21-772-7772
## The Phoenix Primary School
Leinster Road, Basildon, Essex SS15 5NQ
**Tel:** 01268543664
**Web:** www.phoenix-pri.essex.sch.uk
**Estd:** 2011 Proprietorship
**Line of Business:** General secondary education
**Proprietor:** Mrs M Butchers
**Responsibilities**
**Senior:** Tracy Ahern *(Head Teacher)*
**US SIC:** 8211 **UK SIC:** 93200
**Employees:** 90

DUNS 77-950-4187
## Phoenix Protective Services Ltd
Unit 3 Apex Court, Spalding, Lincolnshire PE11 3UL
**Tel:** 01775724170
**Web:** www.kingdomsecurity.co.uk
**Reg No:** 5919777 **Estd:** 2002 Private Limited Company
**Line of Business:** Security activities
**Issued Capital:** £100
**Director:** D R Lockie
**Co. Secretary:** Mrs Sheila Lockie
**US SIC:** 7393 **UK SIC:** 83954

| | 30-09-13 | 30-09-12 | 30-09-11 |
|---|---|---|---|
| TA | 337,116 | 219,903 | 402,948 |
| NW | 24,669 | 2,659 | 126,112 |
| WC | 45,584 | 17,306 | 113,940 |

DUNS 42-413-8316
## Phoenix Resourcing Services (Holdings) Ltd
1 Alie Street, London E1 8DE
**Tel:** 084-5888-7788 **Fax:** 02075535699
**Web:** www.prsjobs.com
**Reg No:** 4401459 **Estd:** 2002 Private Limited Company
**Line of Business:** Management activities of service trades holding companies
**Issued Capital:** £122
**Directors:** R A Snarey, M A Oldfield, M B Evans
**Co. Secretary:** Malcolm Bell
**Responsibilities**
**Senior:** Jim Hine *(Manager)*, Sam Skelton *(Manager)*
**Purchasing:** Tanya Finnegan *(Buyer)*
**US SIC:** 7399 **UK SIC:** 83954
**Auditors:** HLB Vantis Audit PLC

| | 30-06-13 | 30-06-12 | 30-06-11 |
|---|---|---|---|
| TO | 22,749,432 | 16,960,662 | 17,262,788 |
| P/L | 1,141,135 | 487,498 | 883,064 |
| NW | 2,802,620 | 2,179,007 | 1,947,414 |
| WC | 2,833,940 | 2,194,731 | 1,965,180 |
| Emp. | 682 | 595 | 531 |

DUNS 64-254-5941
## Phoenix School
49 Bow Road, Bow, London E3 2AD
**Tel:** 020-8980-4740
**Web:** www.phoenix.towerhamlets.sch.uk
**Estd:** 1953
**Line of Business:** Schools (special)
**Director:** S Harris
**Responsibilities**
**Senior:** Jaqueline Brathwaite *(Head Teacher)*
**US SIC:** 8299 **UK SIC:** 93300
**Employees:** 46

DUNS 21-146-7301
## Phoenix Security (Essex) Ltd
Jubilee House, The Drive, Great Warley, Brentwood, Essex CM13 3FR
**Fax:** 01277 811496
**Web:** www.phoenixsecurity.uk.com
**Reg No:** 6769045 **VAT No:** 973385286
**Estd:** 2011 Private Limited Company
**Line of Business:** Security activities
**Issued Capital:** £1
**Director:** L Atkinson
**US SIC:** 7393 **UK SIC:** 83954
**Auditors:** Barry Clayden & Co

| | 31-12-13 | 31-12-12 | 31-12-11 |
|---|---|---|---|
| TA | 951,553 | 722,444 | 529,248 |
| NW | 230,612 | 191,051 | 116,459 |
| WC | 198,150 | 188,228 | 112,696 |

DUNS 55-048-4075
## Phoenix Sports & Social Club
Pavilion Lane, Brinsworth, Rotherham, South Yorkshire S60 5PA
**Tel:** 01709-363788
**Web:** www.phoenixssc.co.uk
**Estd:** 2002 Proprietorship
**Line of Business:** Operation of other sports arenas and stadiums not elsewhere classified
**Proprietor:** A White
**Branches:** Pavilion Lane, Brinsworth, Rotherham, South Yorkshire S60 5PA
**US SIC:** 7999 **UK SIC:** 97913
**Employees:** 50

DUNS 23-554-3415
## Phoenix Steel Ltd
12 Station Road, Hebburn, Tyne and Wear NE31 1BD
**Tel:** 0191-428-1999
**Web:** www.phoenixsteel.co.uk
**Reg No:** 3552674 **VAT No:** 708910727
**Estd:** 1998 Private Limited Company
**Line of Business:** Wholesale of metals and ores
**Issued Capital:** £138,275
**Principals:** J Mullen *(Managing)*, V Conroy
**Co. Secretary:** Ian Fuesdale
**Branches:** Phoenix Steel Ltd, Skerne Road, Hartlepool, Cleveland TS24 0RH
**US SIC:** 5051, 8911
**UK SIC:** 61200, 83701
**Auditors:** T.K. Kimti Ltd
**Bankers:** Lloyds TSB Bank plc (30-93-71)

| | 31-03-13 | 31-03-12 | 31-03-11 |
|---|---|---|---|
| TO | 7,728,448 | N/A | N/A |
| P/L | 201,511 | N/A | N/A |
| NW | 2,901,731 | 2,852,466 | 2,783,949 |
| WC | 2,569,403 | 2,452,678 | 2,426,016 |
| Emp. | 46 | N/A | N/A |

DUNS 22-511-0824 Imp-Exp
## Phoenix Surveying Equipment Ltd
(**Subsidiary of:** Brandon Hire Group Holdings Ltd)
Unit 4 Armstrong Court, Armstrong Way, Yate, Bristol, Avon BS37 5NG
**Tel:** 01454-312560
**Web:** www.brandontoolhire.co.uk
**Reg No:** 1336159 **VAT No:** 302607402
**Estd:** 1977 Private Limited Company
**Line of Business:** Plant and tool hire
**Issued Capital:** £14,000
**Directors:** A J Partridge, T V Smith, Ms S M Cummings
**Responsibilities**
**Senior:** Christopher Steel *(Manager)*
**Branches:** Phoenix Surveying Equipment Ltd, Leigham Business Units, Unit 4, Exeter, Devon EX2 8HY
**US SIC:** 3832, 7394, 7399
**UK SIC:** 37320, 84000, 83954

**Bankers:** Lloyds TSB Bank plc (30-16-11)

| | 31-12-13 | 31-12-12 | 31-12-11 |
|---|---|---|---|
| TO | 5,500,000 | 5,581,000 | 4,999,000 |
| P/L | 308,000 | 69,000 | 800,000 |
| NW | 1,042,000 | 752,000 | 660,000 |
| WC | (865,000) | (1,088,000) | (508,000) |
| Emp. | 52 | 54 | N/A |

DUNS 21-880-4460
## Phoenix Taxis & Minicoaches
Albion Way, Blyth, Northumberland NE24 5BW
**Tel:** 01912377777
**Estd:** 2012
**Line of Business:** Taxis and private hire vehicles
**Proprietor:** H Hurst
**US SIC:** 4121 **UK SIC:** 72200
**Employees:** 130

DUNS 21-774-7408
## Phoenix Vauxhall
Waterside Way, London SW17 0HB
**Tel:** 02086059393
**Web:** www.phoenixvauxhall.co.uk
**Estd:** 2002
**Line of Business:** Car dealers (new & used)
**Responsibilities**
**Senior:** Bob Quirk (Manager)
**US SIC:** 5511 **UK SIC:** 65100
**Employees:** 87

DUNS 21-213-9224 **Imp-Exp**
## Phoenox Textiles Ltd
Spring Grove Mills, Spring Grove, Huddersfield, West Yorkshire HD8 9HH
**Tel:** 01484-863227
**Web:** www.phoenox.co.uk
**Reg No:** 0528027 **VAT No:** 183370657
**Estd:** 1953 Private Limited Company
**Line of Business:** Manufacturers of carpets and rugs
**Export Sales:** £237,657
**Trading Style:** Dalesman Rug Co
**Issued Capital:** £18,528
**Principals:** C E Mosley (Managing), A C Mosley (Managing), S M Hirst (Financial), Mrs N E Mosley, Mrs E A Mosley, Mrs B M Mosley
**Responsibilities**
**Senior:** Tim Adair (Works Manager)
**Facilities:** Tim Adair (Works Manager)
**Branches:** Phoenox Textiles Ltd, Wood St Mills, Huddersfield, West Yorkshire HD8 9JS
**US SIC:** 2279 **UK SIC:** 43852
**Auditors:** Kubinski
**Bankers:** HSBC Bank plc (40-36-08)

| | 31-12-13 | 31-12-12 | 31-12-11 |
|---|---|---|---|
| TO | 6,938,701 | N/A | N/A |
| P/L | 1,159,896 | N/A | N/A |
| NW | 7,324,276 | 5,255,042 | 4,497,077 |
| WC | 3,714,343 | 3,709,547 | 3,172,429 |
| Emp. | 70 | N/A | N/A |

DUNS 21-583-3607
## The Phoneix Centre
Driving Test Centre, Newtown Road, Newbury, Berkshire RG14 7EB
**Web:** www.westberks.gov.uk
**Estd:** 2011 Proprietorship
**Line of Business:** Day and care centres
**Proprietor:** Mrs D Davies
**US SIC:** 8321 **UK SIC:** 96111
**Employees:** 50

DUNS 50-391-9417
## Phonepayplus Ltd
Clove Building, 4 Maguire Street, London SE1 2NQ
**Tel:** 02079407474 **Fax:** 020-7940-7456
**Web:** www.phonepayplus.org.uk
**Reg No:** 2398515 **Estd:** 1989 Private Company Limited By Guarantee
**Line of Business:** Telecommunications
**Trading Style:** Icstis
**Directors:** H S Webber, Mrs R C Sawtell, A J Pinder, H C Griffiths, K C Brown, P M Hinchliffe, S J Ricketts
**Co. Secretary:** Neil Hardwick
**Responsibilities**
**Senior:** Joanne Prowse (Acting CEO)
**Marketing:** Sarah Icken (Press Officer)
**US SIC:** 4899 **UK SIC:** 79020
**Auditors:** Littlejohn Frazer
**Bankers:** HSBC Bank plc (40-02-31)

| | 31-03-14 | 31-03-13 | 31-03-12 |
|---|---|---|---|
| TO | 5,864,638 | 5,077,624 | 4,411,850 |
| P/L | 8,759 | 8,976 | 8,119 |
| WC | 2,248,454 | 2,158,357 | 1,485,966 |
| Emp. | 64 | 62 | 60 |

DUNS 29-009-8417
## Phonographic Performance Ltd
1 Upper James Street, London W1F 9DE
**Tel:** 02075341444
**Web:** www.ppluk.com
**Reg No:** 0288046 **Estd:** 2010 Private Company Limited By Guarantee

**Line of Business:** Publishing of sound recordings
**Export Sales:** £34,572,000
**Trading Style:** P P L
**Directors:** C M Hunt, Ms C G Payne, P J Leathem, R C Armstrong, J F Smith, J French, J H Radice, F J Nevrkla
**Co. Secretary:** David Harmsworth
**Responsibilities**
**Senior:** Phylicia Chong (Manager), John Dobinson (Director), Christine Geissmar (Operations Director), Antony Kal (Manager), Jonathan Morrish (Director of PR and Communicati), Gerald Newson (Director), Laurence Oxenbury (Director of International), Vicki Pomphrey (Facilities Manager), Adrian Sear (Director), Peter Stack (Director)
**Finance:** Christian Barton (Financial Planning Manager)
**Marketing:** Fiona Haycock (Events & Marketing Manager), Jonathan Morrish (Director of PR and Communicati)
**Sales:** Shula Kerr (Head of Business Projects)
**IT:** Mark Douglas (Chief Technology Officer), Barry Reynolds (Head of IT Services)
**HR:** Janice Davies (Human Resources Director)
**Health & Safety:** Vicki Pomphrey (Facilities Manager)
**Facilities:** Christelle Charles-Morrell (Facilities), Vicki Pomphrey (Facilities Manager)
**Operations:** Tony Clark (Licensing Director), Rob Fish (Project Manager), Christine Geissmar (Operations Director)
**Engineering:** Sacha Fernando (Television Licencing Executive), Aman Khullar (Head of Television Licencing)
**Branches:** Phonographic Performance Ltd, 14-22 Ganton St, London W1F 7QY
**US SIC:** 3652 **UK SIC:** 34520
**Auditors:** PricewaterhouseCoopers LLP
**Bankers:** HSBC Bank plc (40-07-07)

| | 31-12-13 | 31-12-12 | 31-12-11 |
|---|---|---|---|
| TO | 176,893,000 | 170,759,000 | 153,516,000 |
| P/L | 152,194,000 | 146,573,000 | 130,829,000 |
| NW | (4,493,000) | (3,063,000) | (4,150,000) |
| WC | (8,275,000) | (7,494,000) | (9,324,000) |
| Emp. | 283 | 264 | 264 |

DUNS 23-113-6680
## Phoretix International Ltd
(Subsidiary of: Nonlinear 1d Ltd)
Keel House, Garth Heads, Newcastle-Upon-Tyne, Tyne and Wear NE1 2JE
**Tel:** 01912302121
**Reg No:** 2760697 **Estd:** 1992 Private Limited Company
**Line of Business:** Computer software (development)
**Issued Capital:** £110
**Managing Director:** W M Dracup
**Co. Secretary:** Duncan Barrie
**US SIC:** 7379, 7374
**UK SIC:** 83940

| | 30-09-13 | 30-09-12 | 30-09-11 |
|---|---|---|---|
| TA | 110 | 110 | 110 |
| NW | 110 | 110 | 110 |

DUNS 22-513-5433 **Imp-Exp**
## Photo Corporation (U K) Ltd
Unit G1, Harrowden Road, Brackmills Industrial Estate, Northampton, Northamptonshire NN4 7EB
**Tel:** 01604463000
**Web:** www.photocorp.com
**Reg No:** 1349085 **VAT No:** 296463026
**Estd:** 1978 Private Limited Company
**Line of Business:** Photographic activities not elsewhere classified
**Export Markets:** Europe
**Export Sales:** £323,588
**Trading Style:** Portrait Place
**Issued Capital:** £100
**Principals:** P C Watt (Managing), Ms B Fisher
**Co. Secretary:** Mrs Bernadette Fisher
**Responsibilities**
**Senior:** Martyn Dimmock (Warehouse Manager), Kay Richards (European General Manager)
**HR:** Kasenya Goodhead (Training Manager)
**Branches:** Photo Corporation (U K) Ltd, High Street, Sutton, Surrey SM1 1DU
**US SIC:** 7333, 7395
**UK SIC:** 83953, 49300
**Auditors:** Shipleys LLP
**Bankers:** National Westminster Bank Plc (60-06-03)

| | 31-07-13 | 31-07-12 | 31-07-11 |
|---|---|---|---|
| TO | 15,673,886 | 17,228,174 | 18,476,651 |
| P/L | (581,777) | 1,316,888 | 782,566 |
| NW | 913,669 | 1,714,070 | 790,739 |
| WC | 649,261 | 1,167,933 | (189,562) |
| Emp. | 575 | 580 | 598 |

DUNS 21-634-6205 **Imp-Exp**
## Photo-Me International Plc
Church Road, Bookham, Leatherhead, Surrey KT23 3EU
**Web:** www.photo-me.co.uk
**Reg No:** 0735438 **Estd:** 1958 Public Limited Company
**Line of Business:** Manufacture of photographic and cinematographic equipment
**Export Markets:** Europe; The Americas; Asia
**Trading Style:** Photo-Me
**Issued Capital:** £1,854,907
**Directors:** J M Denis, E J Olympitis, J H Lewis, Ms F R Coutaz-Replan, S P Crasnianski, Y Apeloig
**Co. Secretary:** Delmo Mansi
**Responsibilities**
**Marketing:** Nicola Cubitt (Marketing Director), Francois De Freitas (Sales & Marketing Manager)
**Sales:** Francois De Freitas (Sales & Marketing Manager), Steve Merrikin (Business Development Manager)
**IT:** Rick Dearman (Computer Manager), Tom Simons (Technical Support Manager)
**HR:** Tom Simons (Technical Support Manager)
**Facilities:** Danny Foley (Facilities Manager)
**Operations:** Olivier Gimpel (Chief Operating Officer)
**Branches:** Photo-Me International Plc, Isleworth Business Complex, Unit 10, Isleworth, Middlesex TW7 6NL
**US SIC:** 8999 **UK SIC:** 83954
**Auditors:** KPMG LLP
**Bankers:** Lloyds TSB Bank plc (30-00-02)

| | 30-04-14 | 30-04-13 | 30-04-12 |
|---|---|---|---|
| TO | 186,598,000 | 195,590,000 | 207,841,000 |
| P/L | 30,093,000 | 24,306,000 | 20,140,000 |
| NW | 87,427,000 | 80,446,000 | 76,987,000 |
| WC | 41,120,000 | 38,267,000 | 36,536,000 |
| Emp. | 1,110 | 1,106 | 1,128 |

DUNS 23-916-0844 **Imp**
## Photobox Ltd
(Subsidiary of: 230 Third Avenue)
Bridge House, 63-65 North Wharf Road, London W2 1LA
**Tel:** 02070874600
**Web:** www.photobox.co.uk
**Reg No:** 3906401 **Estd:** 2009 Private Limited Company
**Line of Business:** Photographic processing
**Export Sales:** £6,072,000
**Issued Capital:** £65,662
**Principals:** M W Chapman (Managing), A R Burns, S Laurent
**Co. Secretary:** Alan Burns
**Responsibilities**
**Marketing:** Lorraine Merritt (Marketing Manager)
**Admin:** Mayi Macalou (Office Administrator)
**IT:** Graham Obson (Computer Manager)
**HR:** Karine Moncer (Human Resources Manager)
**Health & Safety:** Mayi Macalou (Office Administrator)
**US SIC:** 7333, 7374
**UK SIC:** 83953, 83940
**Auditors:** Ernst & Young LLP
**Bankers:** National Westminster Bank Plc (60-00-08)

| | 30-04-14 | 30-04-13 | 30-04-12 |
|---|---|---|---|
| TO | 50,602,000 | 41,578,000 | 43,244,215 |
| P/L | 1,845,000 | 1,786,000 | 5,035,649 |
| NW | 10,230,000 | 7,974,000 | 5,240,963 |
| WC | 8,047,000 | 6,027,000 | 3,621,676 |
| Emp. | 310 | 230 | 190 |

DUNS 57-840-6605
## The Photographers' Gallery (Enterprises) Ltd
(Subsidiary of: The Photographers' Gallery Ltd)
16 Ramillies Street, London W1F 7LW
**Tel:** 02070879300
**Web:** www.photonet.org.uk
**Reg No:** 2893731 **Estd:** 1994 Private Limited Company
**Line of Business:** Retail sale in commercial art galleries
**Issued Capital:** £100
**Directors:** Ms S B Rogers, A M Haigh
**Co. Secretary:** Andrew Gault
**Responsibilities**
**Senior:** John Buckle (Manager of bookshop), Eva Eicker (Curator (Deutsche B*rse Photog), Karen Mcquaid (Curator), Brian Pomery (Chairman)
**Finance:** Terence Eytle (Finance Manager)
**Marketing:** Daniel Campbell Blight (Blog Editor), Elena Holtham (Head of Visitor Relations), Inbal Mizrahi (Press Manager), Natasha Plowright (Director of Communications), Katrina Sluis (Curator (Digital Programme))

**Sales:** Lynne Arnold (Development Officer), Gemma Barnett (Print Sales Manager), Alexandra Bukojemsky (Development Coordinator), Francesca Filippini Pinto (Head of Development), Anthony Hartley (Print Sales Manager), Anstice Oakeshott (Print Sales Coordinator), Shodor Uddin (Print Sales Coordinator)
**Admin:** Bindi Vora (Assistant to Director)
**Operations:** Jason Welling (Senior Gallery Manager)
**US SIC:** 5999 **UK SIC:** 65600
**Bankers:** National Westminster Bank Plc (50-42-28)

| | 31-03-14 | 31-03-13 | 31-03-12 |
|---|---|---|---|
| TO | N/A | N/A | 556,162 |
| P/L | N/A | N/A | 71,294 |
| NW | 10,506 | 10,506 | 10,506 |
| WC | 10,506 | 10,506 | 10,506 |

DUNS 29-234-9859
## Photolink Creative Group Ltd
(Subsidiary of: Walt & Co Ltd)
Old School House, Thirsk Street, Manchester M12 6PN
**Tel:** 01612777030 **Fax:** 0161-274-3326
**Web:** www.photolinkstudios.co.uk
**Reg No:** 1211027 **VAT No:** 150220232
**Estd:** 2013 Private Limited Company
**Line of Business:** Photographic studios
**Trading Style:** Photolink
**Issued Capital:** £100
**Principals:** D Walter (Managing), Ms J Riley, J Whalley
**Co. Secretary:** David Walter
**Responsibilities**
**Admin:** Alison Jackson (Office Manager)
**IT:** Paul Casey (IT Manager)
**Health & Safety:** John MacDonald (Facilities Manager)
**Facilities:** John MacDonald (Facilities Manager)
**Operations:** Alison Jackson (Office Manager)
**Branches:** London
**US SIC:** 7333, 7311
**UK SIC:** 83953, 83800
**Auditors:** Lomas & Co
**Bankers:** The Royal Bank Of Scotland Plc (16-25-14)

| | 30-11-13 | 30-11-12 | 30-11-11 |
|---|---|---|---|
| TO | 11,127,683 | 12,959,876 | 14,264,695 |
| P/L | 356,886 | 45,297 | 197,004 |
| NW | 742,171 | 600,385 | 577,805 |
| WC | 2,524,901 | 1,914,185 | 1,842,468 |
| Emp. | 91 | 89 | 104 |

DUNS 29-182-2476 **Imp**
## Photolox Ltd
1 Drum Mains Park, Cumbernauld, Glasgow, Lanarkshire G68 9LD
**Tel:** 01413339444 **Fax:** 08455195001
**Web:** www.loxleycolour.com
**Reg No:** 0081970SC **VAT No:** 397984759
**Estd:** 2011 Private Limited Company
**Line of Business:** Portrait photographic activities
**Trading Style:** Loxley Colour Labs, Loxley Colour
**Issued Capital:** £30,002
**Directors:** I W Loxley, Ms S Loxley
**Co. Secretary:** Morton Fraser Secretaries Limite
**Responsibilities**
**Senior:** Paul McKendrick (Lab Manager)
**Marketing:** Ashley Morrison (Marketing Manager)
**Sales:** Emma Strachan (Business Development Manager)
**IT:** Shaun Ferry (IT Manager)
**HR:** Hazel Edment (HR Manager)
**Facilities:** Paul McKendrick (Lab Manager)
**Branches:** Photolox Ltd, Loxley Colour, 1 Drum Mains Park, Glasgow, Lanarkshire G68 9LD
**US SIC:** 7221, 7333
**UK SIC:** 98901, 83953
**Auditors:** Finlaysons
**Bankers:** Clydesdale Bank Plc (82-68-28)

| | 31-01-14 | 31-01-13 | 31-01-12 |
|---|---|---|---|
| TO | 6,679,980 | 6,556,780 | 6,377,461 |
| P/L | 554,427 | 460,568 | 884,371 |
| NW | 3,265,272 | 2,979,900 | 2,913,343 |
| WC | 878,843 | 1,032,448 | 866,247 |
| Emp. | 103 | 92 | 88 |

DUNS 21-952-1262
## Photonstar Led Group Plc
Unit 8 Westlink, Belbins Business Park, Romsey, Hampshire SO51 7JF
**Tel:** 02381 230 381
**Web:** www.photonstarled.com
**Reg No:** 6133765 **Estd:** 2007 Public Limited Company
**Line of Business:** Manufacture of lighting equipment and electric lamps
**Export Sales:** £1,286,000
**Issued Capital:** £11,242,476
**Directors:** Dr A W Nelson, M E Zoorob, J S Mckenzie, J D Freeman, P A Marshall
**Co. Secretary:** Cfo Solutions Limited

**Responsibilities**
**Senior:** Russell Banks *(Director)*
**US SIC:** 3648 **UK SIC:** 34702
**Auditors:** BDO LLP
**Bankers:** Barclays Bank Plc (20-97-09)

| | 31-12-13 | 31-12-12 | 31-12-11 |
|---|---|---|---|
| TO | 9,423,000 | 8,701,000 | 6,061,000 |
| P/L | (728,000) | (836,000) | (1,105,000) |
| NW | 1,118,000 | 2,038,000 | 1,541,000 |
| WC | 690,000 | 1,479,000 | 1,068,000 |
| Emp. | 121 | 107 | 64 |

DUNS 49-312-6700 **Imp-Exp**

## Photronics (U K) Ltd

(**Subsidiary of:** Photronics Inc.)
1 Technology Drive, Bridgend, Mid Glamorgan CF31 3LU
**Tel:** 01656662171
**Web:** www.photronics.com
**Reg No:** 3121018 **VAT No:** 674593296
**Estd:** 1995 Private Limited Company
**Line of Business:** Manufacturers of electronic equipment and components
**Issued Capital:** £100
**Directors:** Ms R E Burr, S T Smith
**Co. Secretary:** Richelle Burr
**US SIC:** 3679, 3629
**UK SIC:** 34542, 34350
**Auditors:** Deloitte & Touche
**Bankers:** National Westminster Bank Plc (01-08-81)

| | 03-11-13 | 28-10-12 | 30-11-11 |
|---|---|---|---|
| TO | 23,140,427 | 22,962,483 | 26,959,695 |
| P/L | 2,939,385 | 4,198,402 | 6,341,167 |
| NW | 2,625,348 | 3,667,476 | 6,883,171 |
| WC | 1,637,862 | 2,669,372 | 6,225,361 |
| Emp. | 106 | 105 | 103 |

DUNS 23-819-1063

## Phs Compliance Ltd

(**Subsidiary of:** Phs Group Holdings Ltd)
Compliance House, Warrington, Cheshire WA3 3GR
**Tel:** 01942-290888 **Fax:** 01942-290889
**Web:** www.phscompliance.co.uk
**Reg No:** 3811260 **Estd:** 2003 Private Limited Company
**Line of Business:** Other business activities not elsewhere classified
**Trading Style:** Phs Compliance
**Issued Capital:** £2
**Directors:** S A Woods, J A Tydeman
**Co. Secretary:** David Finlayson
**Responsibilities**
**Senior:** Greg Bowen *(Finance Director)*, Kerry Nopley *(Customer Service Manager)*
**Finance:** Greg Bowen *(Finance Director)*, Jamie Costello *(Head of Key Accounts)*
**Marketing:** Vanessa Hatton *(Marketing Manager)*
**Sales:** Shaun Caddick *(Sales Director)*, Dan Childs *(Head of Sales)*
**HR:** Helen Gardner *(HR Manager)*, Yvonne Higgins *(Personnel Manager)*
**Health & Safety:** Yvonne Higgins *(Personnel Manager)*
**US SIC:** 7399 **UK SIC:** 83954
**Auditors:** PricewaterhouseCoopers LLP

| | 31-03-14 | 31-03-13 | 31-03-12 |
|---|---|---|---|
| TO | 34,345,000 | 33,894,000 | 30,449,000 |
| P/L | (2,009,000) | 4,551,000 | 2,510,000 |
| NW | 2,426,000 | 406,000 | (3,045,000) |
| WC | 2,317,000 | 201,000 | (3,455,000) |
| Emp. | 581 | 568 | 573 |

DUNS 22-412-5976

## Phs Greenleaf

Pick Hill, Waltham Abbey, Essex EN9 3LE
**Tel:** 01992761000
**Web:** www.phsgreenleaf.co.uk
**Estd:** 1998 Proprietorship
**Line of Business:** Landscape contractors
**Proprietor:** M Dickinson
**US SIC:** 0729 **UK SIC:** 01003
**Employees:** 50

DUNS 34-595-7372

## Phs Group Holdings Ltd

Block B, Western Industrial Estate, Lon-Y-Llyn, Caerphilly, Mid Glamorgan CF83 1XH
**Tel:** 02920 809209
**Web:** www.phs.co.uk
**Reg No:** 5402951 **Estd:** 2005 Private Limited Company
**Line of Business:** Management activities of holding companies
**Issued Capital:** £8,000,000
**Directors:** J S Arnell, G Prestia, S D Simpson, S A Woods
**Co. Secretary:** David Finlayson
**Responsibilities**
**Senior:** Gareth Rhys Williams *(Director Ceo)*
**US SIC:** 6711, 7399
**UK SIC:** 83962, 83954
**Auditors:** PricewaterhouseCoopers LLP

| | 31-03-14 | 31-03-13 | 31-03-12 |
|---|---|---|---|
| TO | 416,147,000 | 418,376,000 | 419,128,000 |
| P/L | (812,120,000) | (120,747,000) | (25,310,000) |
| NW | (1,474,579,000) | (1,384,166,000) | (1,311,869,000) |
| WC | (935,387,000) | (6,629,000) | (1,737,000) |
| Emp. | 5,203 | 5,076 | 5,049 |

DUNS 34-576-9231 **Exp**

## Phs Group Ltd

(**Subsidiary of:** Phs Group Holdings Ltd)
Block B, Western Industrial Estate, Lon-Y-Llyn, Caerphilly, Mid Glamorgan CF83 1XH
**Tel:** 02920851000 **Fax:** 08000731333
**Web:** www.phs.co.uk
**Reg No:** 5384799 **VAT No:** 542951438
**Estd:** 1998 Private Limited Company
**Line of Business:** Representative office
**Issued Capital:** £50,000
**Directors:** M R Pacitti, P J Williamson, C R Kemball, C G Oldroyd, J A Tydeman, S A Woods
**Co. Secretary:** David Finlayson
**Responsibilities**
**Senior:** Peter Cohen *(Chief Executive)*, Gareth Rhys Williams *(Chief Executive Officer)*
**Marketing:** Ruth O'Donoghue *(PR & Social Media Manager)*, Stuart Price *(Sales & Marketing Manager)*
**Sales:** Stuart Price *(Sales & Marketing Manager)*
**IT:** Roland Amos *(IT Manager)*, Nikita Dicker *(IT Manager)*, Ian Featherstone *(Chief Information Officer)*, John Lott *(Computer Operations Manager)*
**Operations:** Kathryn Wood *(Operations Manager)*
**Fleet:** Nigel Bannister *(Transport Manager)*
**Branches:** Phs Group Ltd, Ansley Hall Drive Birch Coppice Business Park, Tamworth, Staffordshire B78 1SQ
**US SIC:** 7399, 4959
**UK SIC:** 83954, 92110
**Auditors:** PricewaterhouseCoopers LLP
**Bankers:** National Westminster Bank Plc (52-10-40)

| | 31-03-14 | 31-03-13 | 31-03-12 |
|---|---|---|---|
| TO | 416,147,000 | 418,376,000 | 419,128,000 |
| P/L | (718,568,000) | (42,624,000) | 40,744,000 |
| NW | (1,107,294,000) | (1,107,545,000) | (1,109,372,000) |
| WC | (1,192,305,000) | (260,242,000) | (260,649,000) |
| Emp. | 5,203 | 5,076 | 5,049 |

DUNS 22-102-3562

## Phsc Plc

The Old Church, Aylesford, Kent ME20 7PR
**Web:** www.phsc.co.uk
**Reg No:** 4121793 **Estd:** 2000 Public Limited Company
**Line of Business:** Business and management consultancy activities not elsewhere classified
**Issued Capital:** £1,060,635
**Directors:** S King, M J Miller, G N Webb, Mrs N C Coote, S King
**Co. Secretary:** Mrs Lorraine Young
**Responsibilities**
**Finance:** Amanda Allen *(Finance Manager)*, Amanda Pound *(Group Accounts Admisitrator)*
**Admin:** Karen Fallows *(Administrator)*
**HR:** Karen Fallows *(Administrator)*
**US SIC:** 7392 **UK SIC:** 83951
**Auditors:** Horwath Clark Whitehill LLP

| | 31-03-14 | 31-03-13 | 31-03-12 |
|---|---|---|---|
| TO | 7,594,281 | 5,791,359 | 4,434,307 |
| P/L | 654,850 | 519,828 | 407,151 |
| NW | 1,831,228 | 990,073 | 2,055,119 |
| WC | 1,203,330 | 679,195 | 1,355,939 |
| Emp. | 84 | 85 | 70 |

DUNS 77-121-6009

## Phusion Im Ltd

14 Colmans Nook, Billingham, Cleveland TS23 4EG
**Tel:** 01642-373000
**Web:** www.pearson-harper.com
**Reg No:** 2694092 **VAT No:** 613542956
**Estd:** 1992 Private Limited Company
**Line of Business:** Image processing services
**Trading Style:** Westbury Filtermation Limited
**Issued Capital:** £100
**Principals:** S J Pearson *(Managing)*, B H Jobling, M T Pellew
**Co. Secretary:** Mrs Alexandra Hayward
**Responsibilities**
**Senior:** Alex Haywood *(Manager)*
**Health & Safety:** Steve Milbourne *(Health & Safety Officer)*
**US SIC:** 3579 **UK SIC:** 33010
**Auditors:** UNW LLP
**Bankers:** Chelsea Building Society (08-60-72)

| | 31-12-13 | 31-12-12 | 31-12-11 |
|---|---|---|---|
| TO | 5,819,136 | 5,031,573 | N/A |
| P/L | 697,832 | 594,027 | N/A |
| NW | 1,472,047 | 907,966 | 1,404,790 |
| WC | 851,146 | 1,019,142 | 1,242,191 |

DUNS 29-006-8345

## Phyllis Court Members Club Ltd

Meadow Farm, Marlow Road, Henley-On-Thames, Oxfordshire RG9 3AA
**Tel:** 01491-570500
**Web:** www.phylliscourt.co.uk
**Reg No:** 0088274 **VAT No:** 199191613
**Estd:** 1937 Private Limited Company
**Line of Business:** Conference centres and facilities
**Issued Capital:** £3,109
**Directors:** D E Young, R Brown, Dr P R Read, Professor A Jones, Mrs S M Van Der Veen, Mrs P M Christmas, J B Hardman, B M Jackson
**Co. Secretary:** Gary Panter
**Responsibilities**
**Senior:** Victoria Eaton *(Senior Sales Executive)*, Frank Fielding *(Manager)*, Patricia Mackenzie *(Manager)*, Geoffrey Probert *(Manager)*
**Sales:** Victoria Eaton *(Senior Sales Executive)*
**US SIC:** 8699, 7011
**UK SIC:** 96902, 66500
**Auditors:** Horwath Clark Whitehill
**Bankers:** National Westminster Bank Plc (60-10-35)

| | 31-12-13 | 31-12-12 | 31-12-11 |
|---|---|---|---|
| TO | 4,282,844 | 4,370,852 | 4,219,046 |
| P/L | 1,173,993 | 377,276 | 394,165 |
| NW | 5,416,197 | 4,260,775 | 3,916,004 |
| WC | 2,036,348 | 1,291,547 | 1,054,220 |
| Emp. | 109 | 109 | 110 |

DUNS 29-050-2921

## Phyllis Tuckwell Memorial Hospice Ltd

Waverley Lane, Farnham, Surrey GU9 8BL
**Tel:** 01252729400
**Web:** www.phyllistuckwellhospice.org.uk
**Reg No:** 1063033 **Estd:** 1979 Private Company Limited By Guarantee
**Line of Business:** Other human health activities
**Directors:** Dr D Eyre-Brook, I R Trotter, K J Kent, Mrs H Franklin, M Maher, Ms V Holdford, Professor M Bailey, Mrs F Campion-Smith
**Responsibilities**
**Senior:** Sarah Brocklebank *(Chief Executive)*, Alan Brooks *(Director)*, David Eyre-brook *(Director)*
**Branches:** Phyllis Tuckwell Memorial Hospice Ltd, 163 Ash Hill Road, Aldershot, Hampshire GU12 5DW
**US SIC:** 8091, 8062
**UK SIC:** 95200, 95100
**Auditors:** Menzies
**Bankers:** Barclays Bank Plc (20-31-06)

| | 31-03-14 | 31-03-13 | 31-03-12 |
|---|---|---|---|
| TO | 7,748,169 | 6,119,163 | 6,517,655 |
| P/L | 1,130,047 | (52,195) | 677,475 |
| NW | 17,105,409 | 15,537,821 | 14,689,606 |
| WC | 3,888,898 | 3,328,429 | 4,188,737 |
| Emp. | 139 | 133 | 123 |

DUNS 21-589-5940

## Physical and Theorethical Chemist

Physical Chemistry Laboratory, South Parks Road, Oxford, Oxfordshire OX1 3QZ
**Web:** www.ox.ac.uk
**Estd:** 2011
**Line of Business:** Chemists consulting
**Trading Style:** Oxford Collage
**Responsibilities**
**IT:** Karl Harrision *(IT Manager)*
**US SIC:** 5912 **UK SIC:** 64300
**Employees:** 100

DUNS 73-256-9780

## Physio World Ltd

Unit 6, The Pavilions, Cranmore Drive, Solihull, West Midlands B90 4SB
**Tel:** 01213742531
**Web:** http://physioworld.net
**Reg No:** 4530716 **Estd:** 2002 Private Limited Company
**Line of Business:** Medical practice activities
**Issued Capital:** £200
**Directors:** N Delaney, B V Rowe, K Doyle, Ms P Parr, R J Squire
**Co. Secretary:** Nicholas Delaney
**US SIC:** 8011 **UK SIC:** 95300

| | 31-05-13 | 31-05-12 | 31-05-11 |
|---|---|---|---|
| TO | 11,000,903 | 8,234,157 | 988,225 |
| P/L | 1,973,388 | 2,642,981 | 298,111 |
| NW | 4,193,162 | 2,663,112 | 704,264 |
| WC | 3,420,207 | 2,271,798 | 523,589 |
| Emp. | 213 | N/A | N/A |

DUNS 21-877-0470

## Pia Jewellery Direct Ltd

Unit 29-30, Monument Business Park, Warpsgrove Lane, Oxford, Oxfordshire OX44 7RW
**Tel:** 01865891044
**Reg No:** 8111999 **Estd:** 2012 Private Limited Company
**Line of Business:** Retail sale via mail order house
**Issued Capital:** £1
**Directors:** Ms S A Volkers, J R Beale, J Osborn
**Co. Secretary:** Francis Mckee
**US SIC:** 5961 **UK SIC:** 65600

| | 31-01-14 | 31-01-13 |
|---|---|---|
| TO | 11,559,207 | 11,966,062 |
| P/L | 211,740 | 206,307 |
| NW | 1,391,439 | 1,239,310 |
| WC | 1,179,352 | 707,077 |
| Emp. | 110 | 116 |

DUNS 28-961-0404

## Pianoforte Supplies Ltd

(**Subsidiary of:** Ci Holdings Limited)
Simplex Works, Ashton Road, Roade, Roade, Northampton, Northamptonshire NN7 2LG
**Tel:** 01604862441
**Web:** www.psluk.co.uk
**Reg No:** 1680544 **VAT No:** 294189125
**Estd:** 1932 Private Limited Company
**Line of Business:** Manufacturers of vehicle components
**Issued Capital:** £2
**Directors:** R W Cripps, D J Cochrane
**US SIC:** 3714, 3079, 3499
**UK SIC:** 35300, 48360, 31694
**Auditors:** Littlejohn LLP

| | 31-12-13 | 31-12-12 | 31-12-11 |
|---|---|---|---|
| TA | 43,031 | 173,722 | 146,561 |
| P/L | (96,953) | (159,105) | (187,890) |
| NW | (14,278,330) | (14,181,377) | (14,022,272) |
| WC | (14,278,330) | (14,181,377) | (14,022,272) |

DUNS 21-714-2157

## Picador Plc

Portsmouth Road, Southampton, Hampshire SO19 9RP
**Tel:** 023-8044-9232 **Fax:** 023-8068-5299
**Web:** www.picadorplc.co.uk
**Reg No:** 0774599 **VAT No:** 188495011
**Estd:** 1963 Public Limited Company
**Line of Business:** Car dealers (new & used)
**Issued Capital:** £1,610,000
**Principals:** L H Jacobs *(Chairman)*, G M Jacobs *(Managing)*, R J Oakeley *(Marketing)*
**Co. Secretary:** Neal Cruse
**Responsibilities**
**Senior:** Matthew Mountford *(Parts Manager)*
**Sales:** P Skuste *(Sales Manager)*
**Purchasing:** Wendy Laidlaw *(Sales Administrator)*
**Branches:** Picador Plc, Easton Lane Business Park, Easton Lane, Winchester, Hampshire SO23 7RQ
**US SIC:** 5511, 5521, 5531
**UK SIC:** 65100
**Auditors:** Fiander Tovell & Co
**Bankers:** Lloyds TSB Bank plc (30-99-87)

| | 31-03-14 | 31-03-13 | 31-03-12 |
|---|---|---|---|
| TO | 38,766,728 | 37,981,965 | 36,813,895 |
| P/L | 473,201 | 274,549 | 179,725 |
| NW | 4,072,224 | 3,719,713 | 3,550,083 |
| WC | 582,236 | 664,719 | 520,159 |
| Emp. | 125 | 124 | 134 |

DUNS 77-442-6282

## Picard Ltd

All Hallows Drive, Maltby, Rotherham, South Yorkshire S66 8NL
**Tel:** 01709812808
**Web:** www.picard.co.uk
**Reg No:** 2952271 **Estd:** 1996 Private Limited Company
**Line of Business:** Nursing homes
**Trading Style:** Layden Court Nursing Home
**Issued Capital:** £99
**Managing Director:** N C Maclean
**Co. Secretary:** Donald Maclean
**Responsibilities**
**Senior:** Jane Ridge *(Manager)*
**US SIC:** 8051 **UK SIC:** 95100
**Bankers:** National Westminster Bank Plc (55-81-56)

| | 31-05-14 | 31-05-13 | 31-05-12 |
|---|---|---|---|
| TA | 2,982,627 | 2,954,035 | 2,949,275 |
| NW | 2,033,800 | 1,889,288 | 1,749,526 |
| WC | 114,339 | 86,245 | 61,385 |

DUNS 21-778-5304

## Piccadilly Cars

Manchester College, Princess House, 105-107 Princess Street, Manchester M1 6DD
**Tel:** 01612360909
**Estd:** 2011 Proprietorship
**Line of Business:** Taxis and private hire vehicles
**Proprietor:** F Chaudry
**Responsibilities**
**Senior:** Frank Chaudry *(Proprietor)*
**US SIC:** 4121 **UK SIC:** 72200
**Employees:** 60

DUNS 76-497-0950 **Exp**

## Piccadilly Greetings Group Ltd

(**Subsidiary of:** Floret Holdings Limited)
4 Horizon Point, Swallowdale Lane, Hemel Hempstead, Hertfordshire HP2 7FZ
**Tel:** 01442215500
**Web:** www.piccadillygreetings.co.uk
**Reg No:** 2567156 **VAT No:** 586906684
**Estd:** 1990 Private Limited Company

**Line of Business:** Printing not elsewhere classified
**Trading Style:** Optimus Publications
**Issued Capital:** £100
**Principals:** J Kaneria *(Managing)*, S Snow *(Managing)*, K J Kaneria, D Kaneria
**Co. Secretary:** Jitesh Kaneria
**US SIC:** 2752 **UK SIC:** 47544
**Auditors:** Haines Watts
**Bankers:** Allied Irish Bank (gb) (23-84-83)

| | 31-12-13 | 31-12-12 | 31-12-11 |
|---|---|---|---|
| TA | 4,157,710 | 4,246,332 | 4,391,747 |
| NW | 3,506,593 | 3,427,692 | 3,396,623 |
| WC | 1,019,932 | 998,986 | 1,012,917 |

DUNS 34-648-2912
## Piccadilly Motors Ltd
Bradford Road, Wakefield, West Yorkshire WF1 2AH
**Tel:** 01924290220 **Fax:** 01924-291774
**Web:** www.piccadillymotors.co.uk
**Reg No:** 2773411 **VAT No:** 590986975
**Estd:** 1992 Private Limited Company
**Line of Business:** Car dealers (new & used)
**Issued Capital:** £36,000
**Principals:** S S Watts *(Managing)*, S C Hall
**Co. Secretary:** Simon Watts
**Responsibilities**
**Senior:** Chris Clapham *(Parts Manager)*, Mick Hargreaves *(Dealer Principal)*
**Marketing:** Julie Tomlinson *(Sales & Marketing Manager)*
**Sales:** Julie Tomlinson *(Sales & Marketing Manager)*
**HR:** Mick Hargreaves *(Dealer Principal)*
**Health & Safety:** Mick Hargreaves *(Dealer Principal)*
**Facilities:** Mick Hargreaves *(Dealer Principal)*
**Operations:** Mick Hargreaves *(Dealer Principal)*
**Branches:** Piccadilly Motors Ltd, Boroughbridge Road, Knaresborough, North Yorkshire HG5 0LZ
**US SIC:** 5511, 5521, 7539
**UK SIC:** 65100, 67100
**Auditors:** Fullertons
**Bankers:** Yorkshire Bank Plc (05-09-64)

| | 30-04-14 | 30-04-13 | 30-04-12 |
|---|---|---|---|
| TO | 33,196,050 | 31,733,294 | 29,120,142 |
| P/L | 1,330,417 | 1,310,386 | 788,542 |
| NW | 8,093,570 | 7,280,658 | 6,496,777 |
| WC | 3,743,223 | 3,115,260 | 3,653,353 |
| Emp. | 82 | 80 | 83 |

DUNS 21-041-7493
## Piccadilly Theatre
16 Denman Street, London W1D 7DY
**Tel:** 020-7478-8800
**Web:** www.atgtickets.com
**Estd:** 1928 Partnership
**Line of Business:** Theatres & concert halls
**Partners:** R Miller, F Hoyle
**Responsibilities**
**Senior:** Jason Bourley *(Manager)*, Jay Bourley *(Manager)*
**US SIC:** 7911 **UK SIC:** 97913
**Employees:** 60

DUNS 22-666-7764
## Pick Everard
Halford House, Charles Street, Leicester, Leicestershire LE1 1HA
**Web:** www.pickeverard.co.uk
**VAT No:** 114498565 **Estd:** 1866 Partnership
**Line of Business:** Engineers (consulting)
**Trading Style:** Pick Everard
**Partners:** A P Almond, A Donaldson, D C Green, M Colby, J R Beverley Burton, D M Nisbet, D Brunton, Ms J I Griffin-Shaw
**Responsibilities**
**Senior:** Allan Cowie *(Manager)*, Paul Darlow *(Manager)*, Ian Goodwin *(Manager)*
**Marketing:** Chris Trivett *(Marketing Manager)*
**Admin:** Donald Johnston *(Assistant Director)*, Doug Soutar *(Assistant Director)*
**Engineering:** John Simkin *(Manager)*
**Branches:** Pick Everard, Weaver House, 9 Looms Lane, Bury St. Edmunds, Suffolk IP33 1HE
**US SIC:** 8911 **UK SIC:** 83701
**Bankers:** National Westminster Bank Plc (60-60-06)
**Employees:** 425

DUNS 21-709-3947 **Imp-Exp**
## Pickering Electronics Ltd
Stephenson Road, Clacton-On-Sea, Essex CO15 4NL
**Tel:** 01255-428141 **Fax:** 01255-475058
**Web:** www.pickeringrelay.com
**Reg No:** 0857509 **VAT No:** 103536604
**Estd:** 1965 Private Limited Company
**Line of Business:** Manufacturers of electronic equipment and components
**Export Markets:** Worldwide
**Issued Capital:** £11,000
**Principals:** J K Moore *(Managing)*, K T Moore, G Dale
**Co. Secretary:** Ms Daisy Moore
**Responsibilities**
**Sales:** Klaas Jansma *(Sales Manager)*
**HR:** Jan Boggas *(Human Resources Manager)*
**Purchasing:** Julie Benson *(Purchasing Manager)*
**Engineering:** Steve Oldfield *(Production Manager)*
**US SIC:** 3679 **UK SIC:** 34542
**Auditors:** Landon Seamer & Co
**Bankers:** Barclays Bank Plc (20-22-67)

| | 30-06-13 | 30-06-12 | 30-06-11 |
|---|---|---|---|
| TO | 4,682,609 | 4,702,312 | N/A |
| P/L | 589,058 | 355,273 | N/A |
| NW | 3,229,459 | 2,668,170 | 2,265,646 |
| WC | 2,782,243 | 2,318,720 | 1,911,941 |
| Emp. | 147 | 146 | N/A |

DUNS 29-047-6456 **Imp**
## Pickering Interfaces Ltd
Stephenson Road, Gorse Lane Industrial Estate, Clacton-On-Sea, Essex CO15 4NL
**Tel:** 01255687900
**Web:** www.pickeringtest.com
**Reg No:** 1029133 **VAT No:** 418403372
**Estd:** 1971 Private Limited Company
**Line of Business:** Manufacture of telegraph and telephone apparatus and equipment
**Trading Style:** Pickering Interfaces Ltd
**Issued Capital:** £100
**Principals:** K T Moore *(Managing)*, I J Johnston, J K Moore
**Co. Secretary:** Ms Daisy Moore
**Responsibilities**
**IT:** Alan Hume *(Software Engineering Manager)*, Kerry White *(IT Manager)*
**US SIC:** 3661 **UK SIC:** 34410
**Auditors:** Landon Seamer & Co
**Bankers:** Barclays Bank Plc (20-22-67)

| | 31-12-13 | 31-12-12 | 31-12-11 |
|---|---|---|---|
| TO | 10,257,161 | 8,184,340 | 12,520,240 |
| P/L | 1,611,803 | 359,357 | 2,852,525 |
| NW | 6,805,631 | 5,211,226 | 4,856,739 |
| WC | 5,626,061 | 4,186,940 | 4,415,759 |
| Emp. | 133 | 121 | 100 |

DUNS 73-767-9964
## Pickfords Ltd
Unit 10 Laxcon Close Drury Way, Industrial Estate, London NW10 0TG
**Tel:** 02031882100 **Fax:** 0208-646-8320
**Web:** www.pickfords.co.uk
**Reg No:** 5025126 **Estd:** 2004 Private Limited Company
**Line of Business:** Removals and storage activities (domestic)
**Issued Capital:** £1
**Directors:** T P Romer, Y Mehta
**Co. Secretary:** Peter Gower
**Branches:** Pickfords Ltd, Wheatsheaf Wharf, Hythe Street, Dartford, Kent DA1 1BN
**US SIC:** 7399, 4226
**UK SIC:** 83954, 77003

| | 30-09-14 | 30-09-13 | 30-09-12 |
|---|---|---|---|
| TA | 1 | 1 | 1 |
| NW | 1 | 1 | 1 |

DUNS 21-836-2857
## Pickfords Move Management Ltd
(**Subsidiary of:** Pickfords Corporation Limited)
Unit 10 Laxcon Close Drury Way, Industrial Estate, London NW10 0TG
**Tel:** 02031882655
**Web:** www.pickfords.com
**Reg No:** 8044368 **Estd:** 2012 Private Limited Company
**Line of Business:** Storage and warehousing
**Export Sales:** £26,138,350
**Issued Capital:** £1,000,002
**Directors:** R J Start, T P Romer, Y Mehta, M Taylor
**Co. Secretary:** Peter Gower
**US SIC:** 4226 **UK SIC:** 77003
**Auditors:** Deloitte LLP

| | 30-09-13 | 30-09-12 |
|---|---|---|
| TO | 58,124,047 | N/A |
| P/L | 1,605,392 | N/A |
| NW | 2,206,708 | 2 |
| WC | 1,640,820 | N/A |
| Emp. | 731 | N/A |

DUNS 21-343-9180
## Pickles
20 Great Suffolk Street, London SE1 0UG
**Tel:** 020-7261-0966
**Estd:** 2002 Partnership
**Line of Business:** Take-away food shops
**Partners:** R Burgardi, Mrs E A1lan
**Responsibilities**
**Senior:** Ellen A lan *(Partner)*, R Brogarde *(Manager)*
**US SIC:** 5812 **UK SIC:** 66110
**Employees:** 66

DUNS 73-369-0288
## Pickstock Telford Ltd
Mile Oak Industrial Estate, Maesbury Road, Oswestry, Shropshire SY10 8GA
**Tel:** 01691662320
**Reg No:** 4642496 **Estd:** 2003 Private Limited Company
**Line of Business:** Production of meat and poultry meat products
**Export Sales:** £33,684,094
**Issued Capital:** £3
**Directors:** E Schottl, G V Pickstock, Ms D Pickstock, D G Mcdonald
**US SIC:** 2013 **UK SIC:** 41223

| | 31-03-14 | 31-03-13 | 31-03-12 |
|---|---|---|---|
| TO | 48,762,757 | 59,237,734 | 62,276,460 |
| P/L | 2,047,196 | 2,948,979 | 3,841,123 |
| NW | 12,846,272 | 11,339,561 | 9,153,232 |
| WC | 4,928,609 | 9,899,650 | 8,311,563 |
| Emp. | 83 | 64 | 60 |

DUNS 71-904-5903
## Pico Technology (Holdings) Ltd
James House, Marlborough Road, Eaton Socon, St Neots, Cambridgeshire PE19 8YP
**Web:** www.picotech.com
**Reg No:** 5286537 **Estd:** 1991 Private Limited Company
**Line of Business:** Manufacture of electronic instruments and appliances for measuring, checking, testing, navigating and other purposes, except industrial process control equipment
**Export Sales:** £8,862,409
**Issued Capital:** £1,000
**Directors:** A D Tong, G A Roderick, Mrs C Tong
**Co. Secretary:** Mrs Jane Percy
**Responsibilities**
**Sales:** Kieran Winstanley *(Distribution Sales Manager)*
**US SIC:** 3829, 1389
**UK SIC:** 37100, 13000

| | 30-06-14 | 30-06-13 | 30-06-12 |
|---|---|---|---|
| TO | 12,468,981 | 11,267,632 | 9,671,423 |
| P/L | 2,130,745 | 2,059,232 | 1,555,682 |
| NW | 6,422,700 | 5,126,817 | 3,850,914 |
| WC | 4,363,794 | 3,736,019 | 2,793,834 |
| Emp. | 93 | 88 | 57 |

DUNS 29-097-7743
## Picow Electrical Engineering Ltd
(**Subsidiary of:** Picow Engineering Group Ltd.)
1 Station House, Lowlands Road, Runcorn, Cheshire WA7 5TQ
**Tel:** 01928-567337
**Web:** www.picow.co.uk
**Reg No:** 1466425 **Estd:** 1979 Private Limited Company
**Line of Business:** Electrical contractors and electricians
**Issued Capital:** £1,000
**Directors:** D K Allen, D Cartwright, M E James, T A Allen
**Co. Secretary:** Trevor Allen
**Responsibilities**
**Senior:** Christopher Martindale *(Manager)*
**IT:** Andrew Ray *(Senior IT Executive)*
**Engineering:** Dave Cafferty *(Mechanical Director)*
**US SIC:** 1731 **UK SIC:** 50300
**Auditors:** Voisey & Co

| | 31-12-13 | 31-12-12 | 31-12-11 |
|---|---|---|---|
| TO | 8,320,054 | 6,370,953 | 8,700,123 |
| P/L | 727,456 | 385,284 | 953,286 |
| NW | 861,069 | 507,527 | 507,155 |
| WC | 846,569 | 469,725 | 444,404 |
| Emp. | 89 | 95 | 96 |

DUNS 29-083-7947
## The Picross Precision Engineering Co Ltd
16-18 Lister Road, Eastbourne, East Sussex BN23 6PU
**Tel:** 01323-507322
**Web:** www.picross-eng.com
**Reg No:** 1380671 **VAT No:** 315654561
**Estd:** 1978 Private Limited Company
**Line of Business:** Precision engineers
**Export Sales:** £93,451
**Issued Capital:** £100
**Managing Director:** D P Patfield
**Co. Secretary:** Mrs Lydia Patfield
**Responsibilities**
**Health & Safety:** Terri Taylor *(Health & Safety Officer)*
**Operations:** Terri Taylor *(Health & Safety Officer)*
**US SIC:** 3423 **UK SIC:** 31612
**Auditors:** Baker Tilly Tax & Accounting Ltd
**Bankers:** Barclays Bank Plc (20-23-97)

| | 31-03-14 | 31-03-13 | 31-03-12 |
|---|---|---|---|
| TO | 3,115,034 | 3,381,452 | 3,867,872 |
| P/L | (35,223) | (115,671) | 52,611 |
| NW | 1,055,871 | 1,069,786 | 1,172,774 |
| WC | 218,005 | 212,888 | 276,084 |

DUNS 57-830-3422 **Imp-Exp**
## Picsolve International Ltd
(**Subsidiary of:** Scream 1 Ltd)
Unit 9 Victoria Way, Derby, Derbyshire DE24 8AN
**Tel:** 01332220012 **Fax:** 01332270741
**Web:** www.picsolve.biz
**Reg No:** 2888552 **VAT No:** 616814145
**Estd:** 1994 Private Limited Company
**Line of Business:** Photographers (commercial)
**Export Markets:** E U & U.S.A.
**Export Sales:** £5,332,693
**Issued Capital:** £1,042
**Directors:** M S Aspinall, J D Kelisky, C J Tenwick
**Responsibilities**
**Senior:** Stephen Findlay *(Manager)*, Sebastian Mckinlay *(Manager)*
**US SIC:** 7333, 7996
**UK SIC:** 83953, 97913
**Auditors:** Deloitte LLP
**Bankers:** National Westminster Bank Plc (60-15-49)

| | 28-02-14 | 28-02-13 | 29-02-12 |
|---|---|---|---|
| TO | 21,372,997 | 18,860,640 | 18,064,795 |
| P/L | (1,766,232) | (1,127,477) | (109,763) |
| NW | 3,857,458 | 5,500,599 | 6,616,895 |
| WC | 480,189 | 3,061,503 | 4,742,856 |
| Emp. | 426 | 326 | 324 |

DUNS 21-210-5733
## Picton Court Nursing & Residential Home
Picton Court Care Home, 200 West Road, Porthcawl, Mid Glamorgan CF36 3RT
**Tel:** 01656784363
**Web:** www.hendre.org.uk
**Estd:** 1988 Partnership
**Line of Business:** Nursing homes
**Partners:** Mrs S Watkins, E Watkins
**Responsibilities**
**Senior:** Alex Chivers *(CEO, Managing Director)*, Mary Richard *(Manager)*
**US SIC:** 8051 **UK SIC:** 95100
**Employees:** 90

DUNS 23-219-2336
## Pictons Solicitors
28 Dunstable Road, Luton, Bedfordshire LU1 1DY
**Tel:** 01582870870
**Web:** www.pictons.co.uk
**VAT No:** 208131405 **Estd:** 1968 Partnership
**Line of Business:** Solicitors
**Trading Style:** Pictons Solicitors
**Partners:** R Talbot, D Fagan, G Sampson, C Brown, S Ryan
**Responsibilities**
**Senior:** Siobhan Rooney *(Partner)*, Sukhdeep Saini *(Managing Partner)*, Anil Virji *(Partner)*
**Sales:** Jacqueline Webb *(Head of Commercial)*
**Branches:** Pictons Solicitors, 24 The Avenue, Watford, Hertfordshire WD17 4NR
**US SIC:** 8111 **UK SIC:** 83500
**Employees:** 60

DUNS 28-945-8457
## Picturedrome Theatres Ltd
5 D'Abernon Close, Esher, Surrey KT10 8PT
**Tel:** 01249652498
**Reg No:** 1602127 **Estd:** 1994 Private Limited Company
**Line of Business:** Motion picture and video distribution
**Issued Capital:** £2
**Managing Director:** P Walker
**Co. Secretary:** Ms Jane Sumner
**Branches:** Picturedrome Theatres Ltd, Marshfield Road, Chippenham, Wiltshire SN15 1JR
**US SIC:** 7829 **UK SIC:** 97112
**Auditors:** Lindford & Co
**Bankers:** HSBC Bank plc (40-05-27)

| | 31-12-13 | 31-12-12 | 31-12-11 |
|---|---|---|---|
| TA | 1,206,015 | 1,310,009 | 930,764 |
| NW | 1,144,826 | 1,174,028 | 885,500 |
| WC | 487,843 | 510,072 | 513,612 |

DUNS 50-039-4911 **Imp**
## Picturehouse Cinemas Ltd
(**Subsidiary of:** Cineworld Group Plc)
The Coach House, Church Lane, Witnesham, Ipswich, Suffolk IP6 9JD
**Tel:** 01473-785026
**Web:** www.picturehouses.co.uk
**Reg No:** 2310403 **Estd:** 1988 Private Limited Company
**Line of Business:** Cinemas
**Issued Capital:** £155
**Directors:** V G Jervis, Ms C Binns, P Bowcock, Ms L M Goleby, Mrs C A Brookmyre, I Greidinger, M J Greidinger
**Co. Secretary:** Richard Ray

**Responsibilities**
**Senior:** Alastair Oatey *(Manager)*, Stephen Wiener *(Manager)*
**Branches:** Picturehouse Cinemas Ltd, 57-58 Walton Street, Oxford, Oxfordshire OX2 6AE
**US SIC:** 7832 **UK SIC:** 97113
**Auditors:** KPMG Audit PLC
**Bankers:** Barclays Bank Plc (20-78-98)

| | 26-12-13 | 31-12-12 | 31-12-11 |
|---|---|---|---|
| TO | 12,880,590 | 10,031,968 | 18,238,410 |
| P/L | 1,152,194 | 1,594,634 | 1,714,642 |
| NW | (2,401,096) | (2,777,231) | 10,518,973 |
| WC | (16,112,239) | (13,190,270) | (2,961,960) |
| Emp. | 252 | 213 | 466 |

DUNS 73-364-9698 Exp
### Pie Minister Ltd
Charlton Road, Bristol, Avon BS10 6NF
**Tel:** 01179504563 **Fax:** 01179429373
**Web:** www.pieminister.co.uk
**Reg No:** 4638465 **Estd:** 2009 Private Limited Company
**Line of Business:** Manufacture of other food products not elsewhere classified
**Export Markets:** Ireland
**Issued Capital:** £4,191
**Directors:** T R Hogg, J D Simon, S C Turner
**Co. Secretary:** Gonzalo Trujillo
**Responsibilities**
**Marketing:** Sophie Trecourt *(Sales and Marketing Manager)*
**Sales:** Emma Thorn *(Sales Manager)*, Sophie Trecourt *(Sales and Marketing Manager)*
**Purchasing:** Thomas Hamonet *(Purchasing Manager)*
**Branches:** Pie Minister Ltd, Glass Arcade St Nicholas Market, St Nicholas Street, Bristol, Avon BS1 1LJ
**US SIC:** 2099, 5462
**UK SIC:** 42399, 64100
**Bankers:** HSBC Bank plc (40-14-13)

| | 31-03-14 | 31-03-13 | 31-03-12 |
|---|---|---|---|
| TO | 7,598,335 | 8,955,515 | 8,312,731 |
| P/L | (108,768) | 572,619 | (66,417) |
| NW | 1,169,534 | 1,258,326 | 896,581 |
| WC | 658,202 | 900,551 | 644,756 |
| Emp. | 147 | 154 | 153 |

DUNS 21-548-0539
### Pield Heath House School
Pield Heath Road, Uxbridge, Middlesex UB8 3NW
**Tel:** 01895-258507
**Web:** www.pieldheathschool.org.uk
**Estd:** 2002 Proprietorship
**Line of Business:** Other adult and other education not elsewhere classified
**Proprietor:** J Rose
**US SIC:** 8299 **UK SIC:** 93300
**Employees:** 60

DUNS 29-038-9485
### Pier Amusements Felixstowe Ltd
Regal House, Manwick Road, Felixstowe, Suffolk IP11 2DQ
**Tel:** 01394284680 **Fax:** 01394-284231
**Reg No:** 0901003 **Estd:** 1967 Private Limited Company
**Line of Business:** Amusement park activities
**Trading Style:** Felixstowe Pier, The Silver Slipper
**Issued Capital:** £1,000
**Principals:** J S Threadwell *(Managing)*, Mrs G L Threadwell, D J Threadwell
**Co. Secretary:** Ms Deborah Woodmansee
**Responsibilities**
**Senior:** Barry Williment *(Manager)*
**Branches:** Pier Amusements Felixstowe Ltd, Regal House, Undercliff Road West, Felixstowe, Suffolk IP11 2AB
**US SIC:** 7996 **UK SIC:** 97913
**Auditors:** P R Adams & Co
**Bankers:** HSBC Bank plc (40-21-06)

| | 31-03-14 | 31-03-13 | 31-03-12 |
|---|---|---|---|
| TO | N/A | 1,803,849 | 2,017,304 |
| P/L | N/A | (618,172) | 5,292 |
| NW | 1,331,083 | 544,614 | 1,380,754 |
| WC | (797,013) | (1,028,879) | (1,440,885) |
| Emp. | N/A | 58 | 61 |

DUNS 33-989-0071
### Pier House Hotel
Harbour Front, Charlestown Road, St Austell, Cornwall PL25 3NJ
**Tel:** 01726-67955
**Web:** www.pierhousehotel.com
**Estd:** 1989 Proprietorship
**Line of Business:** Hotels
**Proprietor:** G Morcom
**US SIC:** 7011 **UK SIC:** 66500
**Employees:** 60

DUNS 23-801-0578
### Pier House Hotel (Charlestown) Ltd.
45 Charlestown Road, St Austell, Cornwall PL25 3NJ
**Tel:** 0172663322
**Web:** www.pierhousehotel.com
**Reg No:** 3793676 **Estd:** 1999 Private Limited Company
**Line of Business:** Licensed restaurants
**Issued Capital:** £1,000
**Director:** R G Morcom
**Co. Secretary:** Mrs Constance Morcom
**Responsibilities**
**Senior:** Danny Goudge *(Proprietor)*
**US SIC:** 5812 **UK SIC:** 66110

| | 30-04-14 | 30-04-13 | 30-04-12 |
|---|---|---|---|
| TA | 1,791,824 | 1,669,238 | 1,615,299 |
| NW | 1,425,762 | 1,358,108 | 1,270,740 |
| WC | 1,110,211 | 1,029,209 | 928,052 |

DUNS 42-372-8919
### Pierce C. A. Ltd
(**Subsidiary of:** 05107560 Ltd)
Mentor House, Blackburn, Lancashire BB1 6AY
**Tel:** 01254-688100 **Fax:** 0125-453122
**Web:** www.pierce.co.uk
**Reg No:** 4360541 **Estd:** 2002 Private Limited Company
**Line of Business:** Accounting and auditing activities
**Issued Capital:** £645,000
**Directors:** J D Green, N T Hussain, G G Boyes, B A Smith, M Maden-Wilkinson
**Co. Secretary:** Paul Warren
**Responsibilities**
**Admin:** Mary-Lou Duggan *(Office Manager)*
**HR:** Mary-Lou Duggan *(Office Manager)*
**Health & Safety:** Mary-Lou Duggan *(Office Manager)*
**US SIC:** 8931 **UK SIC:** 83600

| | 31-05-13 | 31-05-12 | 31-05-11 |
|---|---|---|---|
| TA | 2,117,563 | 2,430,579 | 2,398,999 |
| NW | 680,411 | 688,241 | 682,614 |
| WC | 572,885 | 601,096 | 639,664 |

DUNS 21-190-9478 Imp
### Pieroth Ltd
(**Subsidiary of:** Wiv Wein International Ag)
Dallow Road, Luton, Bedfordshire LU1 1UR
**Tel:** 01582405011
**Web:** www.pieroth.com
**Reg No:** 0698603 **Estd:** 1961 Private Limited Company
**Line of Business:** Wholesalers of beer and spirits
**Issued Capital:** £750,000
**Directors:** H W Falk, D H Samuel, Miss A J Cox
**Co. Secretary:** Ernst Bocker
**Responsibilities**
**Senior:** Marc Fronte *(Manager)*
**Branches:** Pieroth Ltd, Unit 1, Adair Way, Hebburn, Tyne and Wear NE31 2HG
**US SIC:** 5182 **UK SIC:** 61700
**Auditors:** Ernst & Young LLP
**Bankers:** Barclays Bank Plc (20-53-30)

| | 31-12-13 | 31-12-12 | 31-12-11 |
|---|---|---|---|
| TO | 13,994,234 | 14,383,884 | 14,633,709 |
| P/L | 171,556 | 527,373 | 257,115 |
| NW | 4,018,034 | 3,903,690 | 3,516,548 |
| WC | 2,278,244 | 2,105,205 | 1,679,486 |
| Emp. | 276 | 285 | 299 |

DUNS 73-496-9608
### Piers Meadows Recruitment Ltd
111 Wardour Street, London W1F 0UH
**Tel:** 02072-920730 **Fax:** 02077364527
**Web:** www.piersmeadows.co.uk
**Reg No:** 4760233 **Estd:** 2003 Private Limited Company
**Line of Business:** Employment and recruitment companies and consultants
**Issued Capital:** £1
**Director:** P R Meadows
**Co. Secretary:** Ms Michelle Meadows
**US SIC:** 7361 **UK SIC:** 83954

| | 31-03-14 | 31-03-13 | 31-03-12 |
|---|---|---|---|
| TO | 16,110,626 | 12,123,525 | N/A |
| P/L | 1,307,206 | 954,316 | N/A |
| NW | 1,587,289 | 1,003,224 | 628,011 |
| WC | 1,573,821 | 993,559 | 615,198 |
| Emp. | 98 | 65 | N/A |

DUNS 53-619-1653
### Pii Group Ltd
Atley Way, North Nelson Industrial Estate, Cramlington, Northumberland NE23 1WW
**Tel:** 0191-247-3200
**Web:** www.geoilandgas.com
**Reg No:** 3424318 **Estd:** 1997 Private Limited Company
**Line of Business:** Other service activities not elsewhere classified
**Issued Capital:** £11,253,067
**Directors:** B Worrell, S R Al-Muhannadi, M M Al-Mahmoud, B C Palmer, L Simonelli, A S Al-Sulaiti
**Co. Secretary:** John Hamilton
**Responsibilities**
**Senior:** Adam Bathgate *(Technical Manager)*, Marco Paparoni *(Financial Director)*
**Finance:** Marco Paparoni *(Financial Director)*
**IT:** Adam Bathgate *(Technical Manager)*
**US SIC:** 8999, 7349
**UK SIC:** 83954, 92300
**Auditors:** KPMG Audit PLC

| | 31-12-13 | 31-12-12 | 31-12-11 |
|---|---|---|---|
| TO | 84,383,000 | 80,782,000 | 68,781,000 |
| P/L | 7,348,000 | 412,000 | (841,000) |
| NW | 34,281,000 | 30,838,000 | 37,701,000 |
| WC | 20,648,000 | 21,720,000 | 22,859,000 |
| Emp. | 500 | 514 | 489 |

DUNS 21-787-6574
### Pike Textile Display
Unit 4 46 Sandall Road, Wisbech, Cambridgeshire PE13 2RS
**Tel:** 01945461361
**Web:** www.pike-textiles.com
**Estd:** 2011 Proprietorship
**Line of Business:** Pattern books
**Proprietor:** J Allen
**US SIC:** 2649 **UK SIC:** 47280
**Employees:** 150

DUNS 21-586-6485
### Pikes Lane Primary School
Gibraltar Street, Bolton, Lancashire BL3 5HU
**Web:** www.pikes-lane.bolton.sch.uk
**Estd:** 1998 Proprietorship
**Line of Business:** Primary education
**Proprietor:** Mrs L Flanagan
**Responsibilities**
**Senior:** Louise Mcardle *(Head Teacher)*
**US SIC:** 8211 **UK SIC:** 93200
**Employees:** 50

DUNS 28-999-3594
### Pikrevni Investments Ltd
Loch Monzievaird Chalets, Crieff, Perthshire PH7 4JR
**Tel:** 01764-652635 **Fax:** 01436860203
**Reg No:** 0042307SC **Estd:** 1970 Private Limited Company
**Line of Business:** Tourist information offices
**Trading Style:** The Lodge on Loch Lomond Hotel
**Issued Capital:** £20,000
**Directors:** S N Colquhoun, Mrs A I Colquhoun, A A Colquhoun
**Co. Secretary:** Mrs Elizabeth Colquhoun
**US SIC:** 7999 **UK SIC:** 97913
**Auditors:** The Kelvin Partnership

| | 30-09-13 | 30-09-12 | 30-09-11 |
|---|---|---|---|
| TO | 4,332,705 | 4,570,303 | 4,500,829 |
| P/L | (88,943) | 89,504 | 177,796 |
| NW | 3,057,351 | 1,006,816 | 998,746 |
| WC | (681,386) | (382,704) | (459,321) |
| Emp. | 136 | 135 | 133 |

DUNS 77-936-2789
### Piksel Ltd
(**Subsidiary of:** Piksel Inc.)
Innovation Close, York, North Yorkshire YO26 5ZD
**Tel:** 01904 438 000 **Fax:** 01904 435 450
**Web:** www.ioko.com
**Reg No:** 3048367 **VAT No:** 656244331
**Estd:** 1995 Private Limited Company
**Line of Business:** Computer support & services
**Export Sales:** £9,194,159
**Trading Style:** Kit Digital
**Issued Capital:** £10,534
**Directors:** F Hamaide, A Rodriguez
**Responsibilities**
**Senior:** Scott Sahadi *(Chief Executive, USA)*
**Finance:** Allan Dunn *(Financial Director)*
**Marketing:** Nicola Paisey *(Sales & Marketing manager)*
**Sales:** Nicola Paisey *(Sales & Marketing manager)*
**Branches:** Piksel Ltd, 17C Curzon St, London W1J 5HU
**US SIC:** 7379, 7374
**UK SIC:** 83940
**Auditors:** Garbutt & Elliott LLP
**Bankers:** HSBC Bank plc (40-47-31)

| | 31-12-13 | 31-12-12 | 31-12-11 |
|---|---|---|---|
| TO | 29,637,989 | 29,684,020 | 57,463,679 |
| P/L | 16,048 | 481,821 | 8,949,041 |
| NW | 23,390,913 | 22,764,529 | 22,565,078 |
| WC | 22,042,958 | 21,821,712 | 21,143,204 |
| Emp. | 251 | 252 | 316 |

DUNS 34-728-1730
### Pilgrim Foodservice Ltd
Marsh Lane, Boston, Lincolnshire PE21 7SJ
**Tel:** 01205312700 **Fax:** 01205-312701
**Web:** www.pilgrimfoods.co.uk
**Reg No:** 5526538 **VAT No:** 866046900
**Estd:** 2005 Private Limited Company
**Line of Business:** Frozen foods (wholesale)
**Issued Capital:** £10,943,233
**Principals:** P J Bateman *(Managing)*, C J Bateman, S R Eagle, P Parker
**Co. Secretary:** Charles Bateman
**US SIC:** 5149 **UK SIC:** 61700
**Bankers:** Lloyds TSB Bank plc (30-91-04)

| | 30-04-14 | 30-04-13 | 30-04-12 |
|---|---|---|---|
| TO | 24,278,601 | 20,527,721 | 18,920,847 |
| P/L | 664,075 | 439,636 | 529,410 |
| NW | (6,239,714) | (7,107,200) | (7,882,690) |
| WC | (699,045) | (52,716) | 282,830 |
| Emp. | 139 | 124 | 121 |

DUNS 50-689-6422
### Pilgrim Homes
35-36 Egremont Place, Brighton, East Sussex BN2 0GB
**Web:** www.pilgrimhomes.org.uk
**Estd:** 1905
**Line of Business:** Charities and charitable organisations
**Director:** P Tervet
**Responsibilities**
**Senior:** Anne Gower *(Manager)*
**US SIC:** 8699, 6732
**UK SIC:** 96902, 83100
**Auditors:** Jacob Cavenagh & Skeet
**Turnover:** £7,491,620

DUNS 21-579-0568
### The Pilgrim School
Warwick Crescent, Borstal, Rochester, Kent ME1 3LF
**Tel:** 01634335959
**Web:** www.thepilgrimschool.co.uk
**Estd:** 2011 Proprietorship
**Line of Business:** General secondary education
**Proprietor:** Mrs Taylor
**US SIC:** 8211 **UK SIC:** 93200
**Employees:** 250

DUNS 21-589-9899
### Pilgrim Systems Ltd
Commercial Quay, Dock Place, Edinburgh, Midlothian EH6 6LL
**Tel:** 01315559700
**Web:** www.elite.com
**Reg No:** 0066475SC **Estd:** 1978 Private Limited Company
**Line of Business:** Computer software sales
**Directors:** P Thorn, Ms H E Campbell, D M Mitchley
**Co. Secretary:** Ms Susan Jenner
**Responsibilities**
**Senior:** Robin Boyle *(Manager)*, James Cummings *(Manager)*
**Finance:** Michael McCloskey *(Financial Director)*
**Marketing:** Katy Aird *(Office Manager)*
**Sales:** James Cummings *(Manager)*
**Admin:** Katy Aird *(Office Manager)*
**HR:** Katy Aird *(Office Manager)*
**Health & Safety:** Michael McCloskey *(Financial Director)*
**Facilities:** Katy Aird *(Office Manager)*
**Operations:** James Cummings *(Manager)*
**Branches:** Pilgrim Systems Ltd, Commercial Quay, 96 Dock Place, Edinburgh, Midlothian EH6 6LL
**US SIC:** 7379 **UK SIC:** 83940
**Auditors:** Whitelaw Wells
**Bankers:** Bank Of Scotland (80-05-17)
**Employees:** 49
**Total Assets:** £2,973,755

DUNS 21-661-3741
### Pilgrims' Friend Society
175 Tower Bridge Road, London SE1 2AL
**Web:** www.pilgrimsfriend.org.uk
**Reg No:** 7169875 **Estd:** 2010 Private Company Limited By Guarantee
**Line of Business:** Life insurance
**Directors:** Ms J A Mclaren, A J Hare, A J Symonds, B R Jarvis, R W Thurgood, A R Copeman, R B Turnbull, J Edwards
**Co. Secretary:** Geoffrey Norris
**Responsibilities**
**Senior:** Peter Fullarton *(Chief Executive)*
**US SIC:** 7399, 8321
**UK SIC:** 83954, 96111
**Bankers:** Lloyds TSB Bank plc (30-15-97)

| | 31-03-14 | 31-03-13 | 31-03-12 |
|---|---|---|---|
| TO | 12,640,000 | 13,176,000 | 14,598,000 |
| P/L | (141,000) | 1,713,000 | 4,244,000 |
| NW | 31,735,000 | 35,129,000 | 33,400,000 |
| WC | 3,881,000 | 3,325,000 | 6,633,000 |
| Emp. | 308 | 332 | 318 |

DUNS 23-532-2075
### Pilgrims Group Ltd
The Links, Bridge Court, Woking, Surrey GU21 4NS
**Tel:** 08707570180 **Fax:** 0870-757-0181
**Web:** www.pilgrimsgroup.com
**Reg No:** 3531080 **VAT No:** 720885331
**Estd:** 1998 Private Limited Company

**Line of Business:** Safety advisers and technicians
**Issued Capital:** £65,000
**Directors:** D Freear, W E Freear
**Co. Secretary:** Ms Sarah Freear
**US SIC:** 8911 **UK SIC:** 83701
**Auditors:** McPherson's

| | 30-11-13 | 30-11-12 | 30-11-11 |
|---|---|---|---|
| TO | 29,039,033 | 27,977,070 | 24,304,177 |
| P/L | 1,394,415 | 1,974,420 | 2,034,815 |
| NW | 7,547,285 | 6,483,576 | 5,157,746 |
| WC | 6,853,848 | 6,587,299 | 5,109,596 |
| Emp. | 503 | 419 | 331 |

DUNS 21-034-3434
## Pilgrims Hospice
Ramsgate Road, Margate, Kent CT9 4AD
**Tel:** 01843-233920
**Web:** www.pilgrimshospice.org
**Estd:** 1992
**Line of Business:** Hospices
**Proprietor:** J Thomson
**Responsibilities**
**Senior:** Carla Jones *(Manager)*, Tori Mahoney *(Interim Hospice Manager)*
**IT:** Collin James *(Senior IT Executive)*
**HR:** Helen Bennett *(Director of HR)*
**US SIC:** 8091 **UK SIC:** 95200
**Employees:** 50

DUNS 29-674-1770
## Pilgrims Hospices in East Kent
Plender House, 56 London Road, Canterbury, Kent CT2 8JA
**Web:** www.pilgrimshospice.org
**Reg No:** 2000560 **Estd:** 1978 Private Limited Company
**Line of Business:** Other human health activities
**Directors:** Dr R N Mcwilliams, S H Perks, A J Hogarth, R J Davis, Dr A Dhiman, Mrs L Selman, Mrs P M King, M S August
**Co. Secretary:** Peter Simpson
**Responsibilities**
**Senior:** Steve Auty *(Chief Executive)*
**Finance:** Audrey Spain *(Accounts Manager)*
**Marketing:** Susan Booth *(Fundraising Manager)*
**IT:** Audrey Spain *(Accounts Manager)*
**Branches:** Pilgrims Hospices In East Kent, 22 Ashford Road, Tenterden, Kent TN30 6QU
**US SIC:** 8091 **UK SIC:** 95200
**Auditors:** Larkings

| | 31-03-14 | 31-03-13 | 31-03-12 |
|---|---|---|---|
| TO | 12,572,000 | 11,959,000 | 11,415,000 |
| P/L | (1,322,000) | (789,000) | 88,000 |
| NW | 20,528,000 | 21,676,000 | 21,801,000 |
| WC | 615,000 | 383,000 | 520,000 |
| Emp. | 273 | 270 | 243 |

DUNS 21-733-7823
## Pilgrims Ltd
**(Subsidiary of:** Oise Holdings Ltd)
4-6 Orange Street, Canterbury, Kent CT1 2JA
**Tel:** 01227762111
**Web:** www.pilgrims.co.uk
**Reg No:** 1272781 **VAT No:** 202880878
**Estd:** 1976 Private Limited Company
**Line of Business:** Language schools
**Issued Capital:** £5,000
**Director:** T Gins
**Co. Secretary:** Diamond College Limited
**Responsibilities**
**Senior:** Sarah Bowles *(Manager)*, Mandy Briggs *(Senior Manager)*, Grant Webber *(Principal)*, Lizzie Wojtkowska *(Centre Manager)*, Jim Wright *(Head Of Teacher Training)*
**HR:** Leah Luke *(Head of Recruitment)*
**Branches:** Pilgrims Ltd, Unit 2, 4-6 Orange Street, Canterbury, Kent CT1 2JA
**US SIC:** 8249 **UK SIC:** 93300
**Auditors:** Lakin Clark
**Bankers:** Barclays Bank Plc (20-17-92)

| | 31-12-13 | 31-12-12 | 31-12-11 |
|---|---|---|---|
| TA | 5,000 | 5,000 | 5,000 |
| NW | 5,000 | 5,000 | 5,000 |

DUNS 22-278-1226
## The Pilgrims' School
3 The Close, Winchester, Hampshire SO23 9LT
**Web:** www.thepilgrims-school.co.uk
**Reg No:** 4296085 **Estd:** 2001 Private Unlimited Company
**Line of Business:** Schools (independent)
**Directors:** Professor J Carter, J E Atwell, J E Hynam, Doctor H Harvey, Mrs M Chin-Wolf, J G Pringle, R I White, S M Wallace
**Co. Secretary:** Martin Kelly
**Responsibilities**
**Senior:** Jeremy Griffith *(Headmaster)*, Jennifer Hobbs *(Director)*, Peter Padmore *(Manager)*, Fiona Rainsbury *(Director)*, Anthony Revell *(Manager)*, Caspar Ridley *(Director)*, Paddy Watson *(Head Teacher)*
**US SIC:** 8211 **UK SIC:** 93200

**Bankers:** Girobank Plc (72-00-00)

| | 31-08-14 | 31-08-13 | 31-08-12 |
|---|---|---|---|
| TO | 3,973,512 | 3,939,222 | 3,772,026 |
| P/L | 75,175 | 140,707 | (101,504) |
| NW | 3,166,627 | 3,091,452 | 2,950,745 |
| WC | 337,456 | 470,959 | (1,141,584) |
| Emp. | 94 | 99 | 99 |

DUNS 50-023-0636 **Imp-Exp**
## Pilkington A G R (U K) Ltd
**(Subsidiary of:** Nippon Sheet Glass Company Limited)
7 Old Forge Drive, Redditch, Worcestershire B98 7AU
**Web:** www.pilkington.com
**Reg No:** 2303036 **Estd:** 1988 Private Limited Company
**Line of Business:** Windscreen replacement and repair services
**Export Markets:** E U
**Trading Style:** Pilkington Automotive
**Issued Capital:** £1
**Director:** Miss J A Brown
**Co. Secretary:** Iain Smith
**Responsibilities**
**Senior:** Andrea Manley *(Human Resources Manager)*
**Finance:** Tony Fradgely *(Senior Finance Administrator)*
**HR:** Andrea Manley *(Human Resources Manager)*
**Purchasing:** Colin Whitehead *(Purchasing Manager)*
**Branches:** "Triplex Replacement Service", Main Rd, Queenborough
**US SIC:** 5531 **UK SIC:** 65100
**Bankers:** Barclays Bank Plc (20-74-45)

| | 31-03-14 |
|---|---|
| TA | 1 |
| NW | 1 |

DUNS 22-840-3077
## Pilkington Ag Ltd
**(Subsidiary of:** Nippon Sheet Glass Company Limited)
Maple Road, Barnsley, South Yorkshire S75 3DL
**Tel:** 01226-356500 **Fax:** 01226356510
**Web:** www.pilkington.com
**Reg No:** 2025098 **VAT No:** 419491728
**Estd:** 1986 Private Limited Company
**Line of Business:** Double glazing suppliers
**Issued Capital:** £20,000
**Director:** Miss J A Brown
**Co. Secretary:** Iain Smith
**Responsibilities**
**Health & Safety:** Dean Ingram *(Quality Manager)*
**Operations:** Dean Ingram *(Quality Manager)*
**US SIC:** 1721 **UK SIC:** 50400
**Auditors:** Ernst & Young LLP
**Bankers:** Barclays Bank Plc (20-04-50)

| | 31-03-14 | 31-03-13 | 31-03-12 |
|---|---|---|---|
| TA | 1 | N/A | 1,065,000 |
| P/L | | 13,000 | 16,000 |
| NW | 1 | N/A | 1,065,000 |

DUNS 21-319-3857 **Imp-Exp**
## Pilkington United Kingdom Ltd
**(Subsidiary of:** Nippon Sheet Glass Company Limited)
European Technical Centre, Hall Lane, Lathom, Ormskirk, Lancashire L40 5UF
**Tel:** 01744-692-000
**Web:** www.pilkington.com
**Reg No:** 1417048 **Estd:** 1979 Private Limited Company
**Line of Business:** Manufacturers of glass vessels and products
**Export Markets:** E U; Middle East; U S A; S America; Africa; S & S E Asia; Australasia; Canada
**Export Sales:** £18,300,000
**Issued Capital:** £179,978,392
**Directors:** B J Pilling, G Charlton, A D Mcdowell, N J Ellison, M A Buckley
**Co. Secretary:** Iain Smith
**Branches:** Pilkington United Kingdom Ltd, 10 Granada Industrial Estate, Oldbury, West Midlands B69 4LH
**US SIC:** 3211, 3231
**UK SIC:** 24710, 24791
**Auditors:** Ernst & Young LLP

| | 31-03-14 | 31-03-13 | 31-03-12 |
|---|---|---|---|
| TO | 172,100,000 | 204,100,000 | 262,600,000 |
| P/L | (44,000,000) | (69,900,000) | (16,300,000) |
| NW | 51,600,000 | 100,900,000 | 169,100,000 |
| WC | 31,000,000 | 50,000,000 | 63,600,000 |
| Emp. | 1,288 | 1,539 | 1,817 |

DUNS 23-792-0462
## Pill Box Chemists Ltd
190 Studfall Avenue, Corby, Northamptonshire NN17 1LJ
**Tel:** 01536262434
**Web:** www.pillboxonline.co.uk
**Reg No:** 3784836 **VAT No:** 733515741
**Estd:** 2002 Private Limited Company

**Line of Business:** Mobility equipment
**Issued Capital:** £1,000
**Director:** D S Virdee
**Co. Secretary:** Harminder Virdee
**US SIC:** 3799, 5912
**UK SIC:** 36502, 64300
**Auditors:** Menzies LLP
**Bankers:** National Westminster Bank Plc (60-30-30)

| | 30-06-13 | 30-06-12 | 30-06-11 |
|---|---|---|---|
| TO | 19,097,455 | 18,850,275 | 16,124,093 |
| P/L | (4,621) | 59,041 | (216,330) |
| NW | (5,922,551) | (5,602,193) | (6,879,486) |
| WC | (235,468) | (540,550) | (1,200,546) |
| Emp. | 160 | 152 | 142 |

DUNS 21-205-1577
## Pillar Galvanizing Ltd
**(Subsidiary of:** B.E. Wedge Holdings Ltd)
Green Lane, Heywood, Lancashire OL10 2DY
**Tel:** 01706-366191
**Web:** www.wedge-galv.co.uk
**Reg No:** 0447722 **Estd:** 1948 Private Limited Company
**Line of Business:** Treatment and coating of metals
**Issued Capital:** £2,540,000
**Directors:** J D Parsons, J F Woolridge
**Co. Secretary:** Mrs Dawn Graham
**Branches:** Pillar Galvanizing Ltd, Whitehead Works, Newport, Gwent NP20 2NF
**US SIC:** 3398 **UK SIC:** 31380
**Auditors:** Baker Tilly
**Bankers:** National Westminster Bank Plc (56-00-36)

| | 31-03-14 | 31-03-13 | 31-03-12 |
|---|---|---|---|
| TA | 2,540,000 | 2,540,000 | 2,540,000 |
| NW | 2,540,000 | 2,540,000 | 2,540,000 |

DUNS 21-745-5724 **Imp-Exp**
## Piller Uk Ltd
**(Subsidiary of:** Langley Holdings P L C)
Phoenix Way, Cirencester, Gloucestershire GL7 1RY
**Tel:** 01285-657721
**Web:** www.piller.com
**Reg No:** 1234302 **VAT No:** 286102565
**Estd:** 1975 Private Limited Company
**Line of Business:** Power transmission equipment
**Export Markets:** Worldwide
**Issued Capital:** £2,000
**Directors:** A C Dyke, K D Breen
**Responsibilities**
**Health & Safety:** Mark Bignell *(Health & Safety Manager)*
**Branches:** Piller Uk Ltd, Caledonian Ho, Tatton St, Knutsford, Cheshire WA16 6AG
**US SIC:** 3568 **UK SIC:** 32613
**Auditors:** Nexia Smith & Williamson
**Bankers:** Lloyds TSB Bank plc (30-92-06)

| | 31-12-13 | 31-12-12 | 31-12-11 |
|---|---|---|---|
| TO | 18,455,129 | 20,515,305 | 11,500,817 |
| P/L | 5,543,327 | 6,224,539 | 3,559,548 |
| NW | 8,041,143 | 7,739,924 | 5,914,178 |
| WC | 7,612,335 | 7,949,410 | 5,860,367 |
| Emp. | 54 | 53 | 52 |

DUNS 21-723-8476
## Pilling Motor Group Ltd
28 Rucklers Lane, King's Langley, Hertfordshire WD4 8AU
**Tel:** 01923265118 **Fax:** 01442-240658
**Web:** www.pillingmotorgroup.com
**Reg No:** 0993353 **Estd:** 1965 Private Limited Company
**Line of Business:** Sale of new motor vehicles
**Issued Capital:** £250,000
**Principals:** C G Pilling *(Managing)*, K J Pilling
**Co. Secretary:** Carl Pilling
**Responsibilities**
**Senior:** Kay Pilling *(Dealer Principal)*
**Finance:** Mike Drew *(Financial Director)*
**Branches:** Pilling Motor Group Ltd, 1 Barnsdale Drive, Milton Keynes, Buckinghamshire MK4 4DD
**US SIC:** 5511, 5521, 5531
**UK SIC:** 65100
**Auditors:** Grant Thornton
**Bankers:** Barclays Bank Plc (20-03-18)

| | 31-12-13 | 31-12-12 | 31-12-11 |
|---|---|---|---|
| TO | N/A | 3,945,188 | 26,705,346 |
| P/L | N/A | (354,521) | (323,554) |
| NW | 1,204,152 | 1,576,316 | 2,770,837 |
| WC | (15,965) | (720,960) | (1,646,790) |
| Emp. | N/A | 21 | 99 |

DUNS 21-566-3594
## The Pilton Story
Pilton Street, Barnstaple, Devon EX31 1PQ
**Tel:** 01271342188
**Web:** www.piltonhouse.co.uk
**Estd:** 1949 Partnership
**Line of Business:** Residential care establishments
**Partner:** Mrs G Rodgers

**Responsibilities**
**Senior:** S Dumford *(Manager)*, Simone Dunford *(Home Manager)*, Louise Thomas *(General Manager)*
**US SIC:** 8321 **UK SIC:** 96111
**Employees:** 48

DUNS 76-838-2723
## Pimco Europe Ltd
**(Subsidiary of:** Allianz Se)
11 Baker Street, London W1U 3AH
**Fax:** 02036401007
**Web:** http://europe.pimco.com
**Reg No:** 2604517 **Estd:** 1991 Private Limited Company
**Line of Business:** Fund management activities
**Issued Capital:** £495,035
**Directors:** M C Amey, Ms L Arnold, E S Ravano, L W Jacobs, R P Blute, R A Kyprianou, D C Flattum, D M Hodge
**Co. Secretary:** Thomas Rice
**Responsibilities**
**Senior:** Andrew Balls *(Manager)*, William Benz *(Director)*, Greg Gibbons *(Office Manager)*
**US SIC:** 6371 **UK SIC:** 82002
**Auditors:** KPMG LLP

| | 31-12-13 | 31-12-12 | 31-12-11 |
|---|---|---|---|
| TO | 405,788,000 | 346,993,000 | 278,319,000 |
| P/L | 82,610,000 | 35,283,000 | 28,019,000 |
| NW | 169,833,000 | 105,712,000 | 82,779,000 |
| WC | 159,873,000 | 94,353,000 | 78,430,000 |
| Emp. | 285 | 285 | 231 |

DUNS 50-441-3550
## Pims Europe Ltd
**(Subsidiary of:** Mz Holding Ag)
1st Floor, 15 Basinghall Street, London EC2V 5BR
**Tel:** 02076281155 **Fax:** 020-7776-2828
**Web:** www.mailk-mzsg.ch
**Reg No:** 2429277 **VAT No:** 497531801
**Estd:** 1990 Private Limited Company
**Line of Business:** Business and management consultancy activities not elsewhere classified
**Issued Capital:** £213,674
**Directors:** F Malik, Dr. P Farschtschian, Dr. O Malik
**US SIC:** 7392, 6711
**UK SIC:** 83951, 83962
**Auditors:** Berley Chartered Accountants
**Bankers:** Lloyds TSB Bank plc (30-93-23)

| | 31-12-13 | 31-12-12 | 31-12-11 |
|---|---|---|---|
| TA | 288,267 | 269,578 | 271,872 |
| NW | 264,924 | 264,574 | 256,287 |
| WC | 264,924 | 264,574 | 256,287 |

DUNS 29-116-0893 **Imp-Exp**
## Pims Pumps Ltd
**(Subsidiary of:** Xylem Inc.)
106 Hawley Lane, Farnborough, Hampshire GU14 8JE
**Tel:** 01252-513366 **Fax:** 01252-516404
**Web:** www.pimsgroup.co.uk
**Reg No:** 1564082 **Estd:** 1981 Private Limited Company
**Line of Business:** Other manufacturing not elsewhere classified
**Export Markets:** Africa, W Europe
**Issued Capital:** £10,000
**Directors:** Mrs K L Pay, Mrs M L Sowter, R Grund
**Co. Secretary:** Mrs Melanie Sowter
**Branches:** Aldershot
**US SIC:** 3999, 7699
**UK SIC:** 49590, 67303
**Auditors:** BDO Stoy Hayward
**Bankers:** Barclays Bank Plc (20-16-99)

| | 31-07-13 | 30-04-12 | 30-07-11 |
|---|---|---|---|
| TO | 8,702,216 | 7,053,185 | 7,225,677 |
| P/L | (1,740,080) | (195,461) | (99,702) |
| NW | 1,224,699 | 2,559,509 | 2,754,645 |
| WC | 1,191,541 | 2,516,361 | 2,698,205 |
| Emp. | 135 | 132 | 142 |

DUNS 73-966-4758
## Pinacl Solutions Uk Ltd.
**(Subsidiary of:** Perseus L.L.C.)
Carlton Court, St Asaph Business Park, St Asaph, Clwyd LL17 0JG
**Web:** www.pinnaclesolutions.com
**Reg No:** 5217343 **VAT No:** 862823705
**Estd:** 2004 Private Limited Company
**Line of Business:** Telecommunication networks
**Issued Capital:** £3,140,295
**Directors:** R J Bardwell, G N Andrews, Mrs S M Davies, Mrs L Rockliffe, J H Firth
**Co. Secretary:** Mrs Leanne Rockliffe
**Responsibilities**
**Senior:** Leanne Henry *(Manager)*
**US SIC:** 7379, 4899
**UK SIC:** 83940, 79020
**Auditors:** Baker Tilly UK Audit LLP

**Bankers:** Barclays Bank Plc (20-53-30)

| | 31-03-14 | 31-03-13 | 31-03-12 |
|---|---|---|---|
| TO | 10,009,872 | 13,315,559 | 10,232,758 |
| P/L | (898,260) | (178,420) | 18,875 |
| NW | (290,301) | 173,898 | (305,394) |
| WC | 755,807 | 1,402,078 | 282,057 |
| Emp. | 96 | 100 | 102 |

DUNS 73-942-6653

## Pinden Ltd

**(Subsidiary of:** Watch It Come Down Ltd)
Greet St Green Road, Mile End Green, Dartford, Kent DA2 8EB
**Tel:** 01474707827 **Fax:** 01474-709973
**Web:** www.pindenltd.co.uk
**Reg No:** 5195416 **Estd:** 2002 Private Limited Company
**Line of Business:** Skip hire
**Issued Capital:** £100
**Principals:** T M Bishop *(Managing)*, S M Bishop, T J Bishop, S E Bishop
**Responsibilities**
**Senior:** Paul Elcombe *(Transport Manager)*
**US SIC:** 7394, 4953
**UK SIC:** 84000, 92110
**Auditors:** Creaseys LLP

| | 30-09-13 | 30-09-12 | 30-09-11 |
|---|---|---|---|
| TO | 9,537,253 | 9,403,899 | 9,207,815 |
| P/L | 210,587 | 11,693 | 130,652 |
| NW | 1,649,395 | 1,800,931 | 1,809,429 |
| WC | 223,856 | 662,065 | (2,701,125) |
| Emp. | 76 | 67 | 65 |

DUNS 21-041-5491

## Pine Ridge Golf Club

Old Bisley Road, Frimley, Camberley, Surrey GU16 9NX
**Tel:** 01276675444
**Web:** www.pineridgegolf.co.uk
**Estd:** 1990 Proprietorship
**Line of Business:** Golf clubs
**Proprietor:** B Chard
**Responsibilities**
**Marketing:** Eleanor Kelso *(Sales & Marketing Coordinator)*
**Sales:** Eleanor Kelso *(Sales & Marketing Coordinator)*
**US SIC:** 7999 **UK SIC:** 97913
**Employees:** 60

DUNS 23-568-0852

## Pineapple Pub Co Ltd

Honey Bee House, Droitwich, Worcestershire WR9 7LP
**Tel:** 01299851620
**Web:** www.pineapplepublishing.co.uk
**Reg No:** 3566259 **Estd:** 1998 Private Limited Company
**Line of Business:** Buying and selling of own real estate
**Issued Capital:** £1,006,287
**Director:** C N O'Rourke
**Co. Secretary:** Ms Sheena O'Rourke
**Branches:** Pineapple Pub Co Ltd, Bromsgrove Road, Stourbridge, West Midlands DY9 9PY
**US SIC:** 6531, 6519
**UK SIC:** 83400, 85000
**Auditors:** Pannell Kerr Forster
**Bankers:** National Westminster Bank Plc (52-21-27)

| | 30-04-14 | 30-04-13 | 30-04-12 |
|---|---|---|---|
| TA | 2,098,762 | 2,058,397 | 1,773,513 |
| NW | 1,464,800 | 1,520,501 | 1,519,409 |
| WC | (88,267) | (9,966) | (126,596) |

DUNS 34-799-6720

## Pinebird Ventures Ltd

121-125 Church Road, Addlestone, Surrey KT15 1SH
**Tel:** 01932849023
**Web:** www.fermoylenursinghome.com
**Reg No:** 2787736 **Estd:** 1984 Private Limited Company
**Line of Business:** Healthcare companies
**Trading Style:** Fermoyle House Nursing Home
**Issued Capital:** £1,000
**Director:** G E Samuel
**Co. Secretary:** Peter Stoakley
**Responsibilities**
**Senior:** Angela Partridge *(Manager)*
**US SIC:** 8051 **UK SIC:** 95100
**Auditors:** R J Cooper & Co

| | 30-06-14 | 30-06-13 | 30-06-12 |
|---|---|---|---|
| TA | 2,033,569 | 1,940,646 | 1,907,593 |
| NW | 1,369,328 | 1,286,161 | 1,232,720 |
| WC | (324,127) | (242,976) | (254,238) |

DUNS 39-777-0926 **Imp-Exp**

## Pinebridge Investments Europe Ltd

6th Floor, London EC3A 8AA
**Tel:** 02073986000 **Fax:** 02079547001
**Web:** www.pinebridge.com
**Reg No:** 2200753 **Estd:** 1987 Private Limited Company
**Line of Business:** Financial intermediation not elsewhere classified
**Export Markets:** Europe and U.S.A.
**Issued Capital:** £200,005
**Directors:** G R Hornig, A A King, K G Schuster, Ms C V Wade
**Co. Secretary:** Iain Hamilton
**Responsibilities**
**Senior:** Amanda Caffin *(Manager)*
**Admin:** Karly Weston *(Office Manager)*
**Facilities:** Alan Havard *(Maintenance Coordinator)*
**US SIC:** 6111, 6724
**UK SIC:** 81501, 81502
**Auditors:** PricewaterhouseCoopers LLP
**Bankers:** Barclays Bank Plc (20-00-00)

| | 31-12-13 | 31-12-12 | 31-12-11 |
|---|---|---|---|
| TA | 41,063,695 | 20,040,700 | 22,656,913 |
| P/L | 2,633,253 | (8,515,959) | (9,919,942) |
| NW | 28,596,424 | 8,741,249 | 8,852,113 |
| WC | 14,059,922 | 8,238,932 | 8,219,762 |
| Emp. | 64 | 72 | 79 |

DUNS 76-674-5806

## Pinelog Ltd

**(Subsidiary of:** Pinelog Group Ltd)
Riverside Business Park, Buxton Road, Bakewell, Derbyshire DE45 1GS
**Fax:** 01629814481
**Web:** www.pinelog.co.uk
**Reg No:** 2587185 **VAT No:** 593449891
**Estd:** 1973 Private Limited Company
**Line of Business:** Other manufacturing not elsewhere classified
**Issued Capital:** £1,034,960
**Principals:** J H Grayson *(Chairman)*, P S Daly *(Financial)*, C P Insley, R Langham, K Cooper, N M Grayson, Miss L F Grayson
**Co. Secretary:** Craig Insley
**Branches:** Pinelog Ltd, Northney Marina Club, Northney Marina, Hayling Island, Hampshire PO11 0NH
**US SIC:** 3999, 3441
**UK SIC:** 49590, 32042
**Auditors:** PricewaterhouseCoopers LLP
**Bankers:** Lloyds TSB Bank plc (30-94-43)

| | 03-11-13 | 28-10-12 | 30-11-11 |
|---|---|---|---|
| TO | 9,678,000 | 6,359,000 | 6,246,000 |
| P/L | 23,000 | (336,000) | (318,000) |
| NW | 665,000 | 651,000 | 924,000 |
| WC | 298,000 | 229,000 | 436,000 |
| Emp. | 75 | 76 | 80 |

DUNS 21-605-4623

## The Pines

The Pines, 104 West Hill, West Hill, London SW15 2UQ
**Tel:** 02088771951
**Web:** www.thepines.com
**Estd:** 2011 Proprietorship
**Line of Business:** Medical nursing home activities
**Proprietor:** Miss S Kolbe
**Responsibilities**
**Senior:** Debra Mcdonald *(Manager)*
**US SIC:** 8051 **UK SIC:** 95100
**Employees:** 68

DUNS 22-615-2395

## Pines Hotel

Burlington Road, Swanage, Dorset BH19 1LU
**Tel:** 01929-425211
**Web:** www.pineshotel.co.uk
**Estd:** 1969 Partnership
**Line of Business:** Hotels and motels without restaurant
**Partners:** P J Puddelpa, T J Puddelpa, B J Puddelpa, Ms M Puddelpa
**Responsibilities**
**Senior:** John Puddepha *(Proprietor)*
**US SIC:** 7011 **UK SIC:** 66500
**Bankers:** National Westminster Bank Plc (56-00-35)
**Employees:** 46

DUNS 23-565-0082

## Pines Hotel (Chorley) Ltd

**(Subsidiary of:** Bettercount Ltd)
570 Preston Road, Chorley, Lancashire PR6 7EB
**Tel:** 01772338551
**Web:** www.thepineshotel.co.uk
**Reg No:** 0748540 **Estd:** 1963 Private Limited Company
**Line of Business:** Hotels
**Trading Style:** Pines Hotel
**Issued Capital:** £4,000
**Managing Director:** Ms C B Duffin
**Co. Secretary:** Ms Constance Duffin
**Responsibilities**
**Finance:** Rick Huxley *(Operations Manager)*
**IT:** Rick Huxley *(Operations Manager)*
**HR:** Rick Huxley *(Operations Manager)*
**Health & Safety:** Rick Huxley *(Operations Manager)*
**US SIC:** 7011 **UK SIC:** 66500
**Auditors:** Abrams Ashton

**Bankers:** The Royal Bank Of Scotland Plc (16-29-23)

| | 30-09-13 | 30-09-12 | 30-09-11 |
|---|---|---|---|
| TA | 2,727,730 | 2,823,141 | 2,915,763 |
| NW | 353,713 | 491,440 | 650,270 |
| WC | 169,674 | 311,403 | 174,593 |

DUNS 64-264-7861

## The Pines Nursing Home

Furze Hill, Hove, East Sussex BN3 1PA
**Tel:** 01273-820275
**Web:** www.gracewell.co.uk
**Estd:** 1987
**Line of Business:** Nursing homes
**Proprietor:** Mrs J Weir
**Responsibilities**
**Senior:** Debra Mcdonald *(Manager)*
**US SIC:** 8051 **UK SIC:** 95100
**Employees:** 50

DUNS 21-780-5775

## Pinewood

96 Manford Way, Chigwell, Essex IG7 4DA
**Tel:** 02085008499
**Web:** www.sanctuary-care.co.uk
**Estd:** 1985 Proprietorship
**Line of Business:** Residential care establishments
**Proprietor:** Ms D Drown
**US SIC:** 8321 **UK SIC:** 96111
**Employees:** 65

DUNS 21-471-2197

## Pinewood Nursing Home

Cot Lane, Chidham, Chichester, West Sussex PO18 8ST
**Tel:** 01243-572480
**Web:** www.pinewoodnursinghome.co.uk
**Estd:** 1985 Proprietorship
**Line of Business:** Clinics private
**Proprietors:** Mrs D Marsh, Mrs D Marsh
**Responsibilities**
**Senior:** Lawrence Marsh *(Partner)*
**US SIC:** 8051 **UK SIC:** 95100
**Employees:** 55

DUNS 23-181-3184

## Pinewood School

Bourton, Swindon, Wiltshire SN6 8HZ
**Tel:** 01793-782205
**Web:** www.pinewoodschool.co.uk
**Estd:** 1875
**Line of Business:** Schools (independent)
**Trading Style:** Pinewood School
**Director:** J Croysdale
**Responsibilities**
**Senior:** Philip Hoyland *(Principal)*, Robin Thornhill *(Manager)*
**Finance:** Nicky McAvoy *(Bursar)*
**Marketing:** Emily Morley-Fletcher *(Head of Marketing)*
**Sales:** Nicky McAvoy *(Bursar)*
**Admin:** Janey Nelson *(School Secretary)*
**IT:** Mark Forsyth *(Head of IT)*, Laura Johnson *(Head of IT)*
**HR:** Nicky McAvoy *(Bursar)*
**Health & Safety:** Nicky McAvoy *(Bursar)*
**Facilities:** Gary Vaughan *(Estates Manager)*
**Branches:** Pinewood School, Pinewood School, Swindon, Wiltshire SN6 8HZ
**US SIC:** 8211 **UK SIC:** 93200
**Employees:** 80

DUNS 23-898-8161

## Pinewood Shepperton Plc

Pinewood Road, Iver, Buckinghamshire SL0 0NH
**Tel:** 01753651700
**Web:** www.pinewoodgroup.com
**Reg No:** 3889552 **Estd:** 1999 Public Limited Company
**Line of Business:** Motion picture production on film or video
**Export Sales:** £1,100,000
**Issued Capital:** £4,940,993
**Directors:** I P Dunleavy, N D Smith, S Underwood, M I Grade, N Lees, A M Smith, C J Naisby, Ms R C Prior
**Co. Secretary:** Andrew Smith
**Responsibilities**
**Senior:** Paul Darbyshire *(Broadcast Director)*, Patrick Garner *(Manager)*
**Sales:** Beryl Earl *(Sales Executive)*, Sarah Mcgettigan *(Sales Executive)*, Robert Norris *(Commercial Director)*, Jules Robinson *(Head of Business Development)*, Noel Tovey *(Sales Director)*
**IT:** Darren Woolfsen *(Senior IT Executive)*
**Facilities:** James Bryant *(Property Services and Faciliti)*
**Operations:** Peter Hicks *(Operations Director)*
**US SIC:** 7819 **UK SIC:** 97111
**Auditors:** Deloitte LLP

**Bankers:** The Royal Bank Of Scotland Plc (15-19-99)

| | 31-03-14 | 31-03-13 | 31-03-12 |
|---|---|---|---|
| TO | 64,058,000 | 55,642,000 | 62,991,000 |
| P/L | 3,592,000 | 1,319,000 | (1,891,000) |
| NW | 79,108,000 | 74,465,000 | 67,453,000 |
| WC | (11,439,000) | (12,818,000) | (6,581,000) |
| Emp. | 213 | 200 | 206 |

DUNS 23-544-4317

## Pinewood Technologies Plc

**(Subsidiary of:** Pendragon Plc)
2960 Trident Court, Birmingham, West, Midlands B37 7YN
**Tel:** 0121-697-6600
**Web:** www.pinewood.co.uk
**Reg No:** 3542925 **Estd:** 1955 Public Limited Company
**Line of Business:** Other software consultancy and supply
**Issued Capital:** £50,000
**Directors:** T G Finn, Pendragon Management Services Li, T P Holden, M S Casha
**Co. Secretary:** Ms Hilary Sykes
**Responsibilities**
**Senior:** Nevel Briggs *(Manager)*
**Purchasing:** Tim Barney *(Purchasing Manager)*
**US SIC:** 7379 **UK SIC:** 83940
**Auditors:** KPMG Audit PLC

| | 31-12-13 | 31-12-12 | 31-12-11 |
|---|---|---|---|
| TO | 20,123,000 | 19,862,000 | 19,454,000 |
| P/L | 9,030,000 | 8,823,000 | 8,060,000 |
| NW | 18,208,000 | 11,373,000 | 14,793,000 |
| WC | 17,026,000 | 10,255,000 | 13,452,000 |
| Emp. | 143 | 141 | 146 |

DUNS 21-775-1560

## Pinfold Health Centre

The Pinfold, Walsall, West Midlands WS3 3JP
**Tel:** 01922775500
**Estd:** 1999 Proprietorship
**Line of Business:** Doctors
**Proprietor:** Mrs K Williams
**US SIC:** 8011 **UK SIC:** 95300
**Employees:** 120

DUNS 21-030-9155

## Pinfold Street Jmi School

Pinfold St Extension, Wednesbury, West Midlands WS10 8PU
**Tel:** 0121-568-6366
**Web:** www.myportal.walsallcs.com
**Estd:** 1938 Proprietorship
**Line of Business:** Schools (local authority)
**Proprietor:** I Hankinson
**Responsibilities**
**Senior:** Sally-Ann Sinclair *(Head Teacher)*
**US SIC:** 8211 **UK SIC:** 93200
**Employees:** 50

DUNS 45-827-4032

## Pinford End Ltd

Pinford End Farmhouse, Bury St Edmunds, Suffolk IP29 5NU
**Tel:** 01284388874
**Web:** www.pinfordendhouse-suffolk.co.uk
**Reg No:** 3180502 **Estd:** 1996 Private Limited Company
**Line of Business:** Nursing homes
**Issued Capital:** £446,000
**Directors:** R D Chandler, Mrs T E Chandler
**Co. Secretary:** Karl Hunnibell
**Branches:** Pinford End Ltd, Pinford End Bull Lane, Bury St Edmunds, Bury St. Edmunds, Suffolk IP29 5NU
**US SIC:** 8051 **UK SIC:** 95100
**Auditors:** John W Pack
**Bankers:** Lloyds TSB Bank plc (30-91-49)

| | 31-10-13 | 31-10-12 | 31-10-11 |
|---|---|---|---|
| TA | 911,045 | 934,185 | 960,481 |
| NW | 212,012 | 183,112 | 162,253 |
| WC | (184,382) | (191,854) | (190,978) |

DUNS 21-912-2298 **Imp-Exp**

## Ping Europe Ltd

Corringham Road, Gainsborough, Lincolnshire DN21 1XZ
**Tel:** 01427-615405
**Web:** www.ping.com
**Reg No:** 1129505 **Estd:** 1973 Private Limited Company
**Line of Business:** Golf equipment
**Export Markets:** Europe
**Export Sales:** £27,182,459
**Trading Style:** Ping Europe
**Issued Capital:** £789
**Principals:** J J Clark *(Managing)*, Ms N L Solheim, K L Solheim, J A Solheim, A D Solheim
**Responsibilities**
**Marketing:** Dave Fanning *(Senior Marketing Executive)*
**Sales:** Steve Carter *(Sales Manager)*
**HR:** Nick Dear *(Human Resources Manager)*
**Health & Safety:** Nick Dear *(Human Resources Manager)*

**Facilities:** Nick Dear (*Human Resources Manager*)
**Operations:** Nick Dear (*Human Resources Manager*)
**Purchasing:** Michelle Wearing (*Purchasing Manager*)
**US SIC:** 3949, 5199, 5661
**UK SIC:** 49420, 61900, 64600
**Auditors:** Wilshaw & Ellis
**Bankers:** Lloyds TSB Bank plc (30-93-41)

|     | 31-12-13 | 31-12-12 | 31-12-11 |
|-----|----------|----------|----------|
| TO  | 50,991,519 | 55,481,517 | 54,374,239 |
| P/L | 814,041 | 2,458,222 | 1,953,795 |
| NW  | 20,497,356 | 19,894,882 | 18,739,443 |
| WC  | 13,510,281 | 12,547,401 | 13,165,455 |
| Emp.| 234 | 226 | 210 |

**DUNS 21-618-0248**
## Ping Pong Dim Sum
Belvedere Road Southbank Centre, London SE1 8XX
**Tel:** 02079604160
**Web:** www.pingpongdimsum.com
**Estd:** 2011
**Line of Business:** Restaurant - chinese
**US SIC:** 5812  **UK SIC:** 66110
**Employees:** 80

**DUNS 73-872-2276**
## Ping Pong Ltd
Unit 3f Standard Industrial Estate, Henley Road, London E16 2ES
**Tel:** 020-7473-3546 **Fax:** 02075409374
**Web:** www.pingpongdimsum.com
**Reg No:** 5126756  **Estd:** 2004 Private Limited Company
**Line of Business:** Restaurant - chinese
**Issued Capital:** £4,325
**Directors:** I Sagiryan, T P Thorpe, A Sagiryan
**Co. Secretary:** David Venus & Company Llp
**Responsibilities**
**Senior:** Chris Charalmbous (*Manager*)
**US SIC:** 5812  **UK SIC:** 66110
**Auditors:** Baker Tilly UK Audit LLP

|     | 30-03-14 | 31-03-13 | 25-03-12 |
|-----|----------|----------|----------|
| TO  | 13,924,810 | 14,419,418 | 15,608,849 |
| P/L | (1,487,000) | (295,606) | (1,814,960) |
| NW  | 5,027,490 | 6,356,212 | 6,596,092 |
| WC  | 475,988 | 160,384 | (1,309,631) |
| Emp.| 347 | 377 | 417 |

**DUNS 21-233-1082**
## Ping Pong Restaurant
44 Great Marlborough Street, London W1F 7JL
**Tel:** 02078516969
**Web:** www.pingpongdimsum.com
**Estd:** 2005 Proprietorship
**Line of Business:** Restaurant - chinese
**Proprietor:** Miss M Carpenter
**Responsibilities**
**Senior:** Francesco Volpe (*General Manager*)
**US SIC:** 5812  **UK SIC:** 66110
**Employees:** 53

**DUNS 21-160-1047**
## Pingle School
Coronation Street, Swadlincote, Derbyshire DE11 0QA
**Tel:** 01283-216837
**Web:** www.pingle.derbyshire.sch.uk
**Estd:** 1965
**Line of Business:** Schools (local authority)
**Director:** Mrs S Tabberer
**Responsibilities**
**Senior:** Vivien Sharples (*Head Teacher*)
**US SIC:** 8211  **UK SIC:** 93200
**Employees:** 197

**DUNS 42-436-0563**                                    Imp
## Pinguin Foods Uk Ltd
(**Subsidiary of:** Greenyard Foods Nv)
Scania Way, King's Lynn, Norfolk PE30 4LR
**Tel:** 01553-696250 **Fax:** 01553-696296
**Web:** www.pinguinfoods.com
**Reg No:** 4423715  **Estd:** 2002 Private Limited Company
**Line of Business:** Frozen food processors and distributors
**Export Sales:** £2,424,000
**Trading Style:** Pinguin Foods
**Issued Capital:** £16,161,414
**Directors:** Kofa Bvba, Haluvan Bvba, N S Terry
**Co. Secretary:** Arjan Buschman
**Responsibilities**
**Senior:** Stephen D'haene (*Manager*), Herwig Dejonghe (*Director*), Peter Denolf (*Manager*), Peter Ohms (*Operations Director*), Neil Winner (*Factory Manager*), IT: Rebecca King (*IT Manager*), Peter Ohms (*Operations Director*)
**Health & Safety:** Rob Ironmonger (*Health & Safety Manager*)
**Facilities:** Paul Spurrell (*Engineering Manager*)
**Operations:** Avis Baden (*Quality Assurance Manager*), Neil Winner (*Factory Manager*)

**Engineering:** Paul Spurrell (*Engineering Manager*)
**US SIC:** 5149, 7399
**UK SIC:** 61700, 83954
**Auditors:** Deloitte LLP
**Bankers:** Fortis Bank London Bch (formerly Generale Bk) (40-52-62)

|     | 31-03-14 | 31-03-13 | 31-03-12 |
|-----|----------|----------|----------|
| TO  | 98,035,000 | 101,361,000 | 126,760,000 |
| P/L | 786,000 | (4,536,000) | (9,818,000) |
| NW  | 4,016,000 | 3,174,000 | 7,709,000 |
| WC  | (18,318,000) | (6,234,000) | (1,783,000) |
| Emp.| 238 | 239 | 260 |

**DUNS 21-724-7259**
## Pinhoe Pre-School
Harrington Lane, Exeter, Devon EX4 8PE
**Tel:** 01392466878
**Web:** www.pinhoepre-school.co.uk
**Reg No:** 7616550  **Estd:** 1998 Private Company Limited By Guarantee
**Line of Business:** Pre school education
**Director:** G Henkus
**Co. Secretary:** Mrs Rachel Holland
**Responsibilities**
**Senior:** Amanda Cattell (*Manager*)
**US SIC:** 8211  **UK SIC:** 93200
**Bankers:** Lloyds TSB Bank plc (30-12-21)

|     | 31-08-13 | 31-08-12 |
|-----|----------|----------|
| TO  | 191,685 | 181,592 |
| P/L | 13,596 | 22,687 |
| NW  | 112,578 | 98,982 |
| WC  | 80,271 | 94,023 |

**DUNS 21-314-3761**
## Pinington Ltd
Aldrens Lane, Lancaster, Lancashire LA1 2DE
**Tel:** 01524-599770 **Fax:** 01524599771
**Web:** www.pinington.co.uk
**Reg No:** 1503477  **VAT No:** 334914554
**Estd:** 1948 Private Limited Company
**Line of Business:** Building construction contractors
**Issued Capital:** £40,132
**Directors:** T Pinington, N Pinington, S W Black
**Co. Secretary:** John Ayrton
**US SIC:** 1799, 1522, 1731, 1711
**UK SIC:** 50000, 50100, 50300
**Auditors:** Scott & Wilkinson LLP
**Bankers:** National Westminster Bank Plc (01-54-90)

|     | 31-12-13 | 31-12-12 | 31-12-11 |
|-----|----------|----------|----------|
| TO  | 8,245,316 | 6,945,420 | N/A |
| P/L | 231,485 | 205,697 | N/A |
| NW  | 313,164 | 317,919 | 304,698 |
| WC  | 31,688 | 296 | (34,955) |

**DUNS 29-574-8099**
## The Pink Corporation Ltd
11 London Road, Portsmouth, Hampshire PO2 0BQ
**Fax:** 02392783178
**Reg No:** 1936608  **Estd:** 1991 Private Limited Company
**Line of Business:** Labour recruitment and provision of personnel
**Issued Capital:** £65
**Director:** Ms C Thraves
**Co. Secretary:** Howard Thraves
**US SIC:** 7361  **UK SIC:** 83954
**Auditors:** Menzies
**Bankers:** National Westminster Bank Plc (56-00-64)

|     | 31-12-13 | 31-12-12 | 31-12-11 |
|-----|----------|----------|----------|
| TO  | 6,623 | 83,467 | 149,135 |
| P/L | 5,550 | (15,918) | (27,703) |
| NW  | (13,846) | (19,396) | (3,478) |
| WC  | (13,846) | (19,396) | (3,478) |

**DUNS 23-447-6856**
## Pink Home Loans
Shire House, Birmingham Road, Lichfield, Staffordshire WS14 9BW
**Web:** www.pink.uk.net
**Estd:** 2010 Proprietorship
**Line of Business:** Representative office
**Proprietor:** B Devine
**Responsibilities**
**Senior:** Mark Graves (*Sales Director*)
**Finance:** Lisa Hurley (*Finance Director*)
**Sales:** Mark Graves (*Sales Director*)
**Admin:** Shereen Shanahan (*Office Manager*)
**Health & Safety:** Shereen Shanahan (*Office Manager*)
**Facilities:** Shereen Shanahan (*Office Manager*)
**Purchasing:** Shereen Shanahan (*Office Manager*)
**US SIC:** 6111  **UK SIC:** 81501
**Employees:** 60

**DUNS 21-808-3340**
## Pink Ladies Yorkshire
Unit 2, The Business Centre, Bow Bridge Close, Rotherham, South Yorkshire S60 1BY
**Tel:** 01709375499
**Web:** www.pinkladyclean.co.uk
**Estd:** 2012
**Line of Business:** Cleaning activities not elsewhere classified
**Responsibilities**
**Senior:** John Chidlaw (*Sales Director*)
**Sales:** John Chidlaw (*Sales Director*)
**US SIC:** 7349  **UK SIC:** 92300
**Employees:** 50

**DUNS 73-478-5657**
## The Pink Link (Holdings) Ltd
Lower Crosland, Huddersfield, West Yorkshire HD4 7DQ
**Reg No:** 4742437  **Estd:** 2003 Private Limited Company
**Line of Business:** Management activities of holding companies
**Issued Capital:** £1,000
**Director:** R M Allen
**Co. Secretary:** Miss Vicki Davenport
**US SIC:** 6711  **UK SIC:** 83962

|     | 30-09-14 | 30-09-13 | 30-09-12 |
|-----|----------|----------|----------|
| TA  | 2,282,786 | 3,379,187 | 3,379,187 |
| NW  | 2,057,786 | 2,746,587 | 2,746,587 |

**DUNS 23-703-1492**
## Pinkstone Cars Ltd
(**Subsidiary of:** Pinkstone Retail Ltd)
The Britannia Stadium, Stanley Matthews Way, Stoke-On-Trent, Staffordshire ST4 4EG
**Tel:** 01782-599111 **Fax:** 01782-317666
**Web:** www.askaprice.com
**Reg No:** 3698373  **Estd:** 1983 Private Limited Company
**Line of Business:** Sale of new motor vehicles
**Trading Style:** Pinkstones Toyota
**Issued Capital:** £335,000
**Directors:** C J Loach, S N Pinkstone
**Co. Secretary:** Neil Pinkstone
**Responsibilities**
**Senior:** Giles Broomhall (*Centre Principal*)
**Marketing:** Giles Broomhall (*Centre Principal*)
**Sales:** Giles Broomhall (*Centre Principal*)
**Purchasing:** Giles Broomhall (*Centre Principal*)
**US SIC:** 5511, 7539
**UK SIC:** 65100, 67100
**Auditors:** Baker Tilly

|     | 31-12-13 | 31-12-12 | 31-12-11 |
|-----|----------|----------|----------|
| TO  | 28,365,334 | 26,285,829 | 23,499,543 |
| P/L | 755,391 | 699,455 | 484,371 |
| NW  | 3,228,958 | 2,907,514 | 2,620,019 |
| WC  | 637,860 | 493,896 | 366,390 |
| Emp.| 77 | 78 | 74 |

**DUNS 21-152-0574**
## Pinnacle Advantage Ltd
(**Subsidiary of:** Accomplished Accountancy & Taxation Llp)
Unit 1 Woodcock House, Waters Edge Business Park, Modwen Road, Salford, Lancashire M5 3EZ
**Tel:** 01618760333 **Fax:** 08707386389
**Web:** www.pinnacle.eu.com
**Reg No:** 6809998  **Estd:** 2009 Private Limited Company
**Line of Business:** Accounting activities
**Export Sales:** £354,029
**Issued Capital:** £110
**Directors:** R A Trew, L Negus-Hill, S J Breen
**Responsibilities**
**Senior:** Matthew Tyson (*Manager*)
**US SIC:** 8931  **UK SIC:** 83600

|     | 31-03-14 | 31-03-13 | 31-03-12 |
|-----|----------|----------|----------|
| TO  | 93,586,388 | 50,494,946 | N/A |
| P/L | 281,351 | 875,857 | N/A |
| NW  | 508,720 | 546,660 | 60,592 |
| WC  | (565,898) | (476,987) | (873,306) |
| Emp.| 1,101 | 531 | N/A |

**DUNS 22-057-7600**
## Pinnacle Care Ltd
Coalpitt Lane, Wolston Grange, Rugby, Warwickshire CV23 9HJ
**Tel:** 02476540935
**Web:** www.pinnaclecare.co.uk
**Reg No:** 4059677  **Estd:** 1986 Private Limited Company
**Line of Business:** Non-charitable social work activities with accommodation
**Issued Capital:** £2
**Director:** Ms V Bowen
**Co. Secretary:** Alan Dytham
**Responsibilities**
**Senior:** Amber Bond (*General Manager*)
**Branches:** Pinnacle Care Ltd, Wolston Grange Coalpit Lane, Rugby, Warwickshire CV23 9HH
**US SIC:** 8321  **UK SIC:** 96111

**Auditors:** C.H. Ivens & Co

|     | 31-08-13 | 31-08-12 | 31-08-11 |
|-----|----------|----------|----------|
| TO  | 3,738,044 | 3,625,078 | 3,404,125 |
| P/L | 523,886 | 525,803 | 612,203 |
| NW  | 2,166,847 | 1,884,386 | 1,628,886 |
| WC  | (610,216) | (575,856) | (541,749) |
| Emp.| 140 | 143 | 124 |

**DUNS 45-865-8069**
## Pinnacle Consulting Engineers Ltd
Pinnacle House, 3 Meridian Way, Meridian Business Park, Norwich, Norfolk NR7 0TA
**Tel:** 01603703068 **Fax:** 01603702015
**Web:** www.adviceyoucanbuildon.com
**Reg No:** 3208361  **Estd:** 1996 Private Limited Company
**Line of Business:** Building construction contractors
**Issued Capital:** £744
**Directors:** A J Dye, J Mayer, C J Bailey, M Byatt, E F Coupe, D J Meigh, S Dickerson
**Branches:** Pinnacle Consulting Engineers Ltd, 21-22 Berkeley Square, Bristol, Avon BS8 1HP
**US SIC:** 1522  **UK SIC:** 50100
**Auditors:** Larking Gowen
**Bankers:** Bank Of Scotland (12-09-25)

|     | 31-03-14 | 31-03-13 | 31-03-12 |
|-----|----------|----------|----------|
| TA  | 2,810,011 | 2,269,614 | 3,242,648 |
| NW  | 1,349,808 | 933,091 | 1,394,942 |
| WC  | 729,367 | 157,596 | 309,111 |

**DUNS 22-708-4050**
## Pinnacle Insurance Plc
(**Subsidiary of:** Bnp Paribas)
Pinnacle House, Stangate Crescent, Borehamwood, Hertfordshire WD6 2XX
**Tel:** 02082079100 **Fax:** 02083270298
**Web:** www.cardiffpinnacle.com
**Reg No:** 1007798  **Estd:** 1971 Public Limited Company
**Line of Business:** Insurance services
**Issued Capital:** £126,557,050
**Directors:** Bnp Paribas Cardif, N D Rochez, Cardif Assurance-Vie, P J Box, Cardif Assurances Risques Divers, A M Wigg, P E Glen, G Binet
**Co. Secretary:** Matthew Lorimer
**Responsibilities**
**Senior:** Natalie Atkinson (*Manager*)
**Branches:** Pinnacle Insurance Plc, Horizon One, Studio Way, Borehamwood, Hertfordshire WD6 5WH
**US SIC:** 6411, 6399
**UK SIC:** 83200, 82001
**Auditors:** Deloitte LLP
**Bankers:** The Royal Bank Of Scotland Plc (16-00-35)

|     | 31-12-13 | 31-12-12 | 31-12-11 |
|-----|----------|----------|----------|
| TO  | 180,861,000 | 144,999,000 | 146,377,000 |
| P/L | 2,606,000 | 2,059,000 | 3,493,000 |
| NW  | 180,958,000 | 179,649,000 | 177,446,000 |
| WC  | 28,179,000 | 526,000 | (12,005,000) |
| Emp.| N/A | 377 | 394 |

**DUNS 73-755-3912**
## Pinnacle International Freight Holdings Ltd
C Mortimer Road, Narborough, Leicester, Leicestershire LE19 2GA
**Tel:** 08456216111 **Fax:** 0116-286-7928
**Web:** www.pif.co.uk
**Reg No:** 5012885  **Estd:** 2004 Private Limited Company
**Line of Business:** Management activities of holding companies
**Issued Capital:** £100
**Director:** P S Burrell
**Co. Secretary:** Nathan Burrell
**Branches:** Pinnacle International Freight Holdings Ltd, The Red Ho, 360 Cranford La, Hayes, Middlesex UB3 5HD
**US SIC:** 6711  **UK SIC:** 83962

|     | 31-12-13 | 31-12-12 | 31-12-11 |
|-----|----------|----------|----------|
| TO  | 18,611,559 | 21,507,019 | 16,682,172 |
| P/L | 1,530,465 | 1,826,195 | 987,632 |
| NW  | 2,897,984 | 2,085,312 | 674,635 |
| WC  | 1,579,281 | 897,586 | 590,515 |
| Emp.| 49 | 45 | 43 |

**DUNS 50-426-6057**
## Pinnacle Office Equipment Ltd
(**Subsidiary of:** Solartravel Ltd)
Fairway House, Cardiff, South Glamorgan CF3 0LT
**Tel:** 02920363738
**Web:** www.pinnaclecos.co.uk
**Reg No:** 2418829  **VAT No:** 535171949
**Estd:** 1989 Private Limited Company
**Line of Business:** Wholesale of other office machinery and equipment
**Issued Capital:** £200
**Principals:** I Ryley (*Managing*), D A Stewart, S E Richards, C R Hamilton
**Co. Secretary:** Mrs Lisa Ryley
**Responsibilities**
**Senior:** Sharn Jones (*Manager*)
**US SIC:** 2599, 5199
**UK SIC:** 46720, 61900
**Auditors:** KTS

**Bankers:** National Westminster Bank Plc (56-00-41)

| | 30-04-14 | 30-04-13 | 30-04-12 |
|---|---|---|---|
| TA | 2,060,187 | 2,342,283 | 2,395,189 |
| NW | 519,223 | 1,022,780 | 1,039,869 |
| WC | (4,918) | 236,701 | 254,397 |

DUNS 22-222-8632

## Pinnacle Regeneration Group Ltd

(**Subsidiary of:** Greenmark Enterprises Limited)
1st Floor, London EC1M 3HN
**Tel:** 02070172000 **Fax:** 02070172599
**Web:** www.pinnacle-regen.com
**Reg No:** 4240859 **Estd:** 2001 Public Limited Company
**Line of Business:** Management of real estate on a fee or contract basis
**Trading Style:** Pinnacle Regeneration Group Ltd
**Issued Capital:** £2,400,468
**Directors:** R P Margree, S S Lee, P M Lloyd, R T Rann, G A Blott, Spring Master Limited, Ms P A Elliott
**Co. Secretary:** Michael Penny
**Responsibilities**
**Senior:** Neil Euesden *(Manager)*, Connie Mitchell-Innes *(Senior Finance Administrator)*
**Finance:** Connie Mitchell-Innes *(Senior Finance Administrator)*
**Admin:** Vicki Davis *(Administrator)*, Kathy McAneney *(Personal Assistant)*
**US SIC:** 6531 **UK SIC:** 83400
**Auditors:** PricewaterhouseCoopers LLP

| | 31-03-14 | 31-03-13 | 31-03-12 |
|---|---|---|---|
| TO | 75,796,000 | 67,174,000 | 58,357,000 |
| P/L | 1,857,000 | 1,470,000 | 1,852,000 |
| NW | 19,541,000 | 16,650,000 | 18,942,000 |
| WC | 9,707,000 | 7,469,000 | 17,587,000 |
| Emp. | 2,261 | 2,149 | 2,098 |

DUNS 71-877-2952

## Pinnacle Technology Group Plc

Brooke House, Northampton, Northamptonshire NN4 7YD
**Tel:** 08454333222 **Fax:** 0845-4334-333
**Web:** www.pinnacletelecomgroup.co.uk
**Reg No:** 5259846 **Estd:** 1998 Public Limited Company
**Line of Business:** Telecom services
**Trading Style:** Pinnacle Telecom
**Issued Capital:** £2,211,474
**Directors:** N B Scallan, Dr J E Dodd, Dr T J Black
**Co. Secretary:** Wjm Secretaries Limited
**Responsibilities**
**Senior:** Alan Bonner *(Manager)*
**US SIC:** 4899 **UK SIC:** 79020
**Auditors:** Grant Thornton UK LLP
**Bankers:** HSBC Bank plc (40-35-04)

| | 30-09-13 | 30-09-12 | 30-09-11 |
|---|---|---|---|
| TO | 10,138,681 | 12,710,446 | 8,522,079 |
| P/L | (2,439,262) | (1,115,558) | (117,316) |
| NW | (106,121) | (1,520,619) | 545,327 |
| WC | (324,824) | (1,873,807) | 10,117 |
| Emp. | 65 | 65 | 27 |

DUNS 51-032-5392

## Pinnacle Telecom (Wales) Ltd

(**Subsidiary of:** Extrasource Ltd)
Fairway House Links Business Park, Fortran Road, St Mellons, Cardiff, South Glamorgan CF3 0LT
**Tel:** 02920365200
**Web:** www.pinnacle-group.co.uk
**Reg No:** 3296134 **Estd:** 1999 Private Limited Company
**Line of Business:** Telecommunications
**Issued Capital:** £100
**Director:** D A Stewart
**US SIC:** 4899 **UK SIC:** 79020
**Auditors:** KTS Owens Thomas Ltd

| | 30-04-14 | 30-04-13 | 30-04-12 |
|---|---|---|---|
| TA | 1,585,315 | 1,337,401 | 1,387,167 |
| NW | 808,010 | 677,625 | 767,223 |
| WC | 764,144 | 630,136 | 703,597 |

DUNS 28-990-4815

## Pinnacle Workwear Management Ltd

24 Cliveland Street, Birmingham, West Midlands B19 3SH
**Tel:** 01213592613
**Web:** www.pinnacleltd.net
**Reg No:** 1819385 **Estd:** 1984 Private Limited Company
**Line of Business:** Manufacture of other wearing apparel and accessories not elsewhere classified
**Issued Capital:** £10,000
**Principals:** M A Jackson *(Managing)*, Mrs F Jackson
**Co. Secretary:** Mark Jackson
**Branches:** Pinnacle Workwear Management Ltd, 24 Cliveland Street, Birmingham, West Midlands B19 3SH
**US SIC:** 2389, 6519
**UK SIC:** 45393, 85000
**Auditors:** Rochesters
**Bankers:** National Westminster Bank Plc (60-02-35)

| | 30-09-13 | 30-09-12 | 30-09-11 |
|---|---|---|---|
| TA | 132,275 | 152,489 | 142,634 |
| NW | 25,915 | 25,201 | 23,264 |
| WC | 32,500 | 35,776 | 9,403 |

DUNS 21-729-8116

## Pinner View Motors Ltd

333 Pinner Road, Harrow, Middlesex HA1 4JR
**Tel:** 02084274444
**Web:** www.northernmotors.co.uk
**Reg No:** 0563696 **Estd:** 1956 Private Limited Company
**Line of Business:** Car dealers (new & used)
**Trading Style:** Northern Motors Harrow
**Issued Capital:** £70
**Directors:** Ms P M Beavis, Mrs D A Beavis
**Co. Secretary:** Michael Beavis
**Branches:** Pinner View Motors Ltd, Burnt Oak Broadway, Edgware, Middlesex HA8 5AG
**US SIC:** 5511, 7539
**UK SIC:** 65100, 67100
**Auditors:** Cyril Flood
**Bankers:** Lloyds TSB Bank plc (30-93-92)

| | 31-12-13 | 31-12-12 | 31-12-11 |
|---|---|---|---|
| TO | 19,922,278 | 17,270,221 | 17,227,922 |
| P/L | 53,031 | (384,460) | (108,983) |
| NW | 2,781,474 | 2,804,863 | 3,217,348 |
| WC | 1,882,946 | 1,891,066 | 2,277,594 |
| Emp. | 82 | 94 | 95 |

DUNS 67-216-1015

## Pinney Talfourd Llp

52 Station Road, Upminster, Essex RM14 2SU
**Tel:** 01708229444
**Web:** www.pinneytalfourd.co.uk
**Reg No:** 0324736OC **Estd:** 1900 Private Limited Company
**Line of Business:** Solicitors
**Responsibilities**
**Senior:** Kristian Croad *(Partner)*, Catherine Loadman *(Partner)*, Germaine Mccauley *(Partner)*
**Branches:** Pinney Talfourd Llp, 39-41 High Street, Brentwood, Essex CM14 4RH
**US SIC:** 8111 **UK SIC:** 83500

| | 30-04-14 | 30-04-13 | 30-04-12 |
|---|---|---|---|
| TA | 2,236,432 | 1,630,908 | 1,403,819 |
| NW | 700,001 | 220,180 | 217,770 |
| WC | 1,564,653 | 861,753 | 622,022 |

DUNS 21-601-6201

## Pinneys Scotland

Stapleton Road, Annan, Dumfriesshire DG12 6RX
**Tel:** 01461204071
**Web:** www.pinneysscotland.com
**Estd:** 2011
**Line of Business:** Manufacturers of food products
**Responsibilities**
**Senior:** Grant Mcfadyean *(Manager)*
**Operations:** Ally Scaife *(Technical, Production Manager)*
**US SIC:** 2099 **UK SIC:** 42399
**Employees:** 655

DUNS 22-185-8157

## Pinocchio's Childrens Nurseries Ltd

School Green, Lasswade, Midlothian EH18 1NB
**Fax:** 0131-454-0926
**Web:** www.pinocchiosnursery.co.uk
**Reg No:** 0218455SC **Estd:** 1997 Private Limited Company
**Line of Business:** Primary education
**Issued Capital:** £2
**Director:** S Koulis
**Co. Secretary:** Lewissa Koulis
**Responsibilities**
**Senior:** Shirley Dickson *(Manager)*
**US SIC:** 8211 **UK SIC:** 93200

| | 31-01-14 | 31-01-13 | 31-01-12 |
|---|---|---|---|
| TA | 353,758 | 589,634 | 278,316 |
| NW | 256,574 | 434,930 | 134,755 |
| WC | 39,655 | 212,689 | (69,961) |

DUNS 22-262-0747

## Pinsent Masons

1 Park Row, Leeds, West Yorkshire LS1 5AB
**Tel:** 01132445000 **Fax:** 01132-448000
**Web:** www.pinsentmasons.com
**Reg No:** 4280058 **Estd:** 2001 Private Limited Company
**Line of Business:** Solicitors
**Director:** Pinsent Masons Director Ltd
**Co. Secretary:** Pinsent Masons Secretarial Ltd
**Responsibilities**
**Senior:** Catherine Hemsworth *(Partner)*
**Finance:** Jay Birch *(Finance)*
**US SIC:** 8111 **UK SIC:** 83500
**Employees:** 400

DUNS 21-102-3394

## Pinsent Masons Llp

30 Crown Place, Earl Street, London EC2A 4ES
**Tel:** 02074904000
**Web:** www.pinsentmasons.com
**Reg No:** 0333653OC **VAT No:** 109530585
**Estd:** 1999
**Line of Business:** Solicitors
**Responsibilities**
**Senior:** Theresa Adamson *(Senior Associate)*, Alan Aisbett *(Partner - Projects and Interna)*, Ewan Alexander *(Partner)*, Fiona Alexander *(Senior Associate)*, Dawn Allen *(Senior Associate)*, Shirley Allen *(Partner)*, Graham Alty *(Non-designated Limited Liabili)*, Paul Amiss *(Partner)*, Kenneth Chong *(Partner)*, Christopher Chong *(Partner)*, Nina Choudhury *(Senior Associate)*, John Christian *(Partner)*, William Christopher *(Partner)*, Sarah Clayton *(Partner)*, Lee Clifford *(Senior Associate)*, Virginie Colaiuta *(Partner)*, Allyson Colby *(Senior Associate)*, Anthony Anderson *(Non-designated Limited Liabili)*, Mark Collingwood *(Partner)*, Stacey Collins *(Senior Associate)*, Simon Colvin *(Partner)*, Craig Connal *(Partner)*, Roger Connon *(Partner)*, Iain Connor *(Partner)*, Vincent Connor *(Partner)*, Angela Cooling *(Executive)*, Sadie Andrew *(Senior Associate)*, Vicky Cooper *(Senior Associate)*, Helen Corden *(Legal Director)*, Philip Corfield-Smith *(Senior Associate)*, Jim Cormack *(Partner)*, Deirdre Cormican *(Senior Associate)*, Steven Cottee *(Partner)*, James Cran *(Legal Director)*, Laura Crilly *(Senior Associate)*, Suzannah Crookes *(Senior Associate)*, Siobhan Cross *(Partner)*, Susan Andrews *(Partner)*, Damian Crosse *(Partner)*, Vicky Cumming *(Senior Associate)*, Richard Daffern *(Partner)*, Tim Dale *(Senior Associate)*, Richard Dartnell *(Senior Associate)*, Marc Dautlich *(Partner)*, Vanessa Davey *(Senior Associate)*, Karen Davidson *(Legal Director)*, Katharine Davies *(Partner)*, Heidi Archibald *(Senior Associate)*, Gregg Davison *(Partner)*, Reg Day *(Manager)*, Zoe De Courcy Arbiser *(Senior Associate)*, Matthew De Ferrars *(Partner)*, Shirley De Roche *(Property & Facilities Director)*, Leah De Vries *(Senior Associate)*, Ian Deakin *(Senior Associate)*, Dev Desai *(Senior Associate)*, Kevin Devanny *(Partner)*, Kirsty Ayre *(Non-designated Limited Liabili)*, Martin Devine *(Legal Director)*, Didar Dhillon *(Senior Associate)*, Alan Diamond *(Partner)*, Richard Dickman *(Legal Director)*, Gayle Ditchburn *(Senior Associate)*, Nicholas Dobson *(Partner)*, Pamela Doherty *(Senior Associate)*, Tim Dolan *(Partner)*, Suggen Dosanjh *(Senior Associate)*, Katie Douglas *(Legal Director)*, Rachel Dulberg *(Senior Associate)*, James Earl *(Senior Associate)*, Tom Eastwood *(Legal Director)*, Mike Edge *(Partner)*, Adrian Elliott *(Partner)*, Joanne Ellis *(Partner)*, Sean Elson *(Senior Associate)*, Jennifer Ballantyne *(Partner)*, James Elwen *(Senior Associate)*, Jane Emslie *(Senior Associate)*, Martin Ewan *(Partner)*, Lesley-Anne Faichnie *(Senior Associate)*, Ben Fairhead *(Senior Associate)*, Alan Farkas *(Partner)*, Gavin Farquhar *(Partner)*, Kate Featherstone *(Senior Associate)*, Peter Feehan *(Partner)*, Camilla Balleny *(Partner)*, Michael Fenn *(Partner)*, Kate Fergusson *(Manager)*, Audrey Ferrie *(Legal Director)*, Tom Ferrier *(Partner)*, Roger Fink *(Partner - Private Equity)*, Dale Fischer *(Partner)*, Jon Fischer *(Partner)*, Jody Fitchet *(Vice Chair)*, Sarah Banatvala *(Senior Associate)*, Sarah Flinn *(Senior Associate)*, Emma Flower *(Legal Director)*, Akshai Fofaria *(Partner)*, Anne-Laure Fonade *(Partner)*, Alicia Foo *(Partner)*, Jonathan Fortnam *(Partner, Local Office)*, Barry Francis *(Partner)*, Clare Francis *(Senior Associate)*, Gillian Frew *(Partner)*, Anne-Marie Friel *(Senior Associate)*, Louise Fullwood *(Legal Director)*, Hughes Gareth *(Partner)*, Shelagh Gaskill *(Partner)*, Jennifer Gee *(Senior Associate)*, Adrian Barlow *(Non-designated Limited Liabili)*, Bjorn Gehle *(Partner)*, Jacob Ghanty *(Partner)*, Iain Gilbey *(Partner)*, Sue Gilchrist *(Senior Associate)*, Howard Gill *(Partner)*, Suzanne Gill *(Partner)*, Paul Gillen *(Senior Associate)*, George Gillham *(Legal Director)*, Joanne Gillies *(Partner)*, Claudia Gizejewski *(Senior Associate)*, Rebecca Glover *(Senior Associate)*, Victoria Goddard *(Partner)*, Matthew Godfrey-Faussett *(Partner)*, Philip Goldsborough *(Partner)*, Hayley Goldstone *(Senior Associate)*, Edward Goodwyn *(Partner)*, Drysdale Graham *(Partner)*, Judith Greaves *(Partner)*, William Greig *(Partner)*, Tom Barton *(Senior Associate)*, Kristian Grice *(Senior Associate)*, Melanie Grimmitt *(Partner - Projects and Constru)*, Juliet Haldane *(Legal Director)*, Ajoy Halder *(Senior Associate)*, Chris Hallam *(Partner)*, Jason Hambury *(Partner)*, Katharine Hardie *(Partner)*, Michelle Beaumont *(Senior Associate)*, Keith Hartley *(Partner, International Constru)*, Simon Harvey *(Partner)*, Paul Haswell *(Senior Associate)*, Vanessa Heap *(Partner)*, Jillian Bechelli *(Senior Associate)*, Matthew Heaton *(Partner)*, Neil Hehir *(Legal Director)*, Catherine Hemsworth *(Legal Director)*, Kirsteen Henderson *(Senior Associate)*, Julie Herriott *(Legal Director)*, Matthew Heywood *(Senior Associate)*, Aileen Hill *(Senior Associate)*, Simon Hobday *(Partner)*, Neil Hogg *(Partner)*, Brooke Holden *(Senior Associate)*, Sam Beckett *(Partner)*, Louise Holden *(Senior Associate)*, Fraser Hopkins *(Senior Associate)*, Andrew Hornigold *(Partner)*, Simon Horsfield *(Partner)*, Janet Hoskin *(Partner)*, Sean Houlihan *(Legal Director)*, Justine Howard *(Legal Director)*, Alison Hubbard *(Partner)*, Sue Beech *(Partner)*, Ian Huddleston *(Partner)*, Claire Hughes *(Partner)*, Karen Hunt *(Legal Director)*, Jayne Hussey *(Partner)*, Rob Hutchings *(Partner)*, Ian Hyde *(Partner)*, Chen Ikeogu *(Senior Associate)*, Belinda Bell *(Senior Associate)*, Peter Instone *(Partner)*, David Isaac *(Partner - Head of Advanced Man)*, Shy Jackson *(Partner)*, Lynette Jacobs *(Partner)*, Jonathan Jeffries *(Partner)*, Mark Job *(Partner)*, Tom Johnson *(Partner)*, Scott Johnston *(Senior Associate)*, Lizanne Jones *(Senior Associate)*, Rupert Bent *(Legal Director)*, Sadhbh Kavanagh *(Senior Associate)*, Steve Keall *(Manager)*, Maria Kell *(Senior Associate)*, Michelle Kershaw *(Legal Director)*, Sachin Kerur *(Partner)*, Farook Khan *(Partner)*, Kultar Khangura *(Partner)*, Annie Kilvington *(Partner)*, Christopher Berkeley *(Partner)*, Vincent King *(Partner)*, Jonathan Kirkwood *(Legal Director)*, Jason Kirwin *(Legal Director)*, Rona Kostulin *(Senior Associate)*, Russell Kostulin *(Senior Associate)*, Rainer Kreifels *(Partner)*, James Ladner *(Senior Associate)*, Shourav Lahiri *(Partner)*, Simon Laight *(Partner)*, Pamela Laird *(Senior Associate)*, Michael Lakin *(Senior Associate)*, Richard Laudy *(Partner)*, Tom Leman *(Partner)*, Keith Levene *(Legal Director)*, Stephen Levy *(Partner)*, Arwen Berry *(Senior Associate)*, Kening Li *(Partner)*, Michelle Li *(Senior Associate)*, Simon Lightman *(Senior Associate)*, David Linacre *(Executive)*, Richard Linton *(Partner)*, Nicole Livesey *(Senior Associate)*, Samantha Livesey *(Partner)*, Shona Logie *(Senior Associate)*, Alastair Lomax *(Legal Director)*, Phil Berwick *(Manager)*, James Long *(Senior Associate)*, Guy Lougher *(Partner)*, Arthur Lovitt *(Partner)*, Jenny Luo *(Senior Associate)*, Ian Lyall *(Partner)*, Iain Macaulay *(Partner)*, Fiona Macgregor *(Senior Associate)*, Elaine Macgregor *(Senior Associate)*, Mohan Bhaskaran *(Partner)*, John Maciver *(Partner)*, Murdo Maclean *(Partner)*, Iain Macphail *(Partner)*, Craig Macphee *(Senior Associate)*, Julia Maguire *(Partner)*, Jennifer Malcolm *(Senior Associate)*, Frances Mallender *(Senior Associate)*, Bhaljinder Mander *(Senior Associate)*, Francesca Mangini *(Senior Associate)*, Jayson Marks *(Senior Associate)*, Indradeep Bhattacharya *(Senior Associate)*, Federica Marra *(Senior Associate)*, Andrew Masterson *(Partner)*, Ross Mc Dowall *(Legal Director)*, Ian Mc Kie *(Legal Director)*, James McBurney *(Legal Director)*, Ann McCarthy *(Senior Associate)*, Dawson McConkey *(Partner)*, Susan Biddle *(Partner)*, Powan McDaid *(Senior Associate)*, David McIlwaine *(Partner)*, Pamela McKerrall *(Senior Associate)*, Paul McQuillan *(Legal Director)*, Euan McVicar *(Partner)*, Serena Mcallister *(Senior Associate)*, Paul Mcbride *(Partner)*, Barry Mccaig *(Partner)*, Mark Mccall *(Legal Director)*, Robert Mccallough *(Partner)*, Scott Mccallum *(Senior Associate)*, Ray Mccann *(Manager)*, Ian Mccarlie *(Partner)*, Chris Mcgarvey *(Legal Director)*, Sinead Mcgrath *(Partner)*, Andrea Mcilroy-Rose *(Partner)*, Lynsey Mckenzie *(Senior Associate)*, Christine Mclintock *(Owner)*, Fraser Mcmillan *(Partner)*, Margaret Mcneil *(Senior Associate)*, Stuart Mcneill *(Senior Associate)*, Alastair Meeks *(Partner)*, Tracey Menzies *(Partner)*, Victoria Miller *(Legal Director)*, Carolyn Miller *(Legal Director)*, Luke Miotte *(Legal Director)*, Elaine Moffat *(Senior Associate)*, Robert Moir *(Partner)*, Sophie Black *(Senior Associate)*, Chris Mordue *(Partner)*, Craig Morrison *(Senior Associate)*, Pauline Munro *(Legal Director)*, Russell Munro *(Partner)*, Stuart Neilson *(Partner)*, Nicola Black *(Manager)*, Diane Nicol *(Partner - Head of Employment)*, Wendy Nicolson *(Legal Director)*, Brandon Nolan *(Partner)*, Stefan Paciorek *(Partner)*, William Park *(Senior Associate)*, Graham Pierce *(Partner)*, Michael Pulford *(Partner)*, Adrienne Quin *(Legal Director)*, Jonathan Reardon *(Partner)*, Georgina Reynard *(Senior Associate)*, Jim Richards *(Partner)*, Jonathan Riley *(Partner)*, Alexis Roberts *(Partner)*, Catherine Robins *(Partner)*, Samantha Rollason *(Partner)*, Peter Blackmore *(Partner)*, Alastair Ross *(Manager)*, Derek Roth-Biester *(Senior Associate)*, Bob Ruddiman *(Partner Head Of Energy And Nat)*, Carsten Rumberg *(Partner)*, Sara Sawicki *(Partner)*, Thilo

Schneider (*Senior Associate*), Clive Seddon (*Partner - Head of TMT & Sourci*), Angela Bleasdale (*Senior Associate*), Ciara Seymour (*Legal Director*), Alan Sheeley (*Senior Associate*), Lucy Shurwood (*Legal Director*), Arun Singh (*Partner*), Julian Sladdin (*Legal Director*), Richard Slaven (*Partner, International Ligitat*), Jenny Block (*Partner*), Vikki Smith (*Personal Assistant*), Ruth Smith (*Partner*), Ishbel Smith (*Senior Associate*), William Soileau (*Legal Director*), Daniel Tain (*Partner*), Lauren Taylor (*Manager*), Irene Thorne (*Manager*), Nigel Blundell (*Partner*), Stephen Tobin (*Partner*), Chen Toh (*Senior Associate*), Kate Turner (*Legal Director*), Patrick Twist (*Partner*), John Tyerman (*Partner*), Geoff Tyler (*Partner*), Kenny Valentine (*Senior Associate, Partner*), Kim Walker (*Partner*), Stuart Walsh (*Partner*), Selwyn Blyth (*Non-designated Limited Liabili*), Vivien Welsh (*Senior Associate*), Iona Whitaker (*Partner*), Jamie White (*Partner*), Rodney Whyte (*Partner*), Rob Wilkins (*Partner*), Robbie Wishart (*Senior Associate*), Kevin Boa (*Partner*), Rachel Wood (*Head of Knowledge Management*), Karl Woolley (*Partner*), John Yeap (*Partner*), Sarah Bond (*Senior Associate*), Russell Booker (*Partner*), Nicola Borthwick (*Senior Associate*), Yuri Botiuk (*Partner*), Deborah Bould (*Partner*), Emily Bourne (*Senior Associate*), Anne Bowden (*Partner*), Christina Bowyer (*Senior Associate*), Hayley Boxall (*Senior Associate*), Sam Boyling (*Partner*), Hannah Brader (*Partner*), Nicola Bradfield (*Senior Associate*), Anthony Bradley (*Partner*), Kevin Bridges (*Partner*), Conor Brindley (*Senior Associate*), Alice Broadfield (*Partner*), Kate Brock (*Senior Associate*), Jonathan Brocklehurst (*Partner*), Bill Broughton (*Partner*), Hugh Bruce-Watt (*Partner*), Andrew Brydon (*Senior Associate*), Katherine Brydon (*Partner*), Nicola Buchanan (*Senior Associate*), Nicola Bumpus (*Senior Associate*), Anthony Bunch (*Partner*), Seona Burnett (*Partner*), Lucy Bushell (*Senior Associate*), Iain Butler (*Senior Associate*), Stuart Cairns (*Partner*), Alistair Calvert (*Senior Associate*), Phillip Capper (*Partner*), Stewart Carlile (*Senior Associate*), Anna Cartledge (*Associate in the planning team*), Tom Cartwright (*Legal Director*), Alan Cassels (*Legal Director*), Jacquetta Castle (*Partner*), Caroline Catto (*Senior Associate*), Rosalie Chadwick (*Partner*), Alan Chan (*Senior Associate*), Kiran Chand (*Senior Associate*), Helen Chang (*Partner*), Jeremy Chang (*Legal Director*)
**Finance:** Charlotte Beckett (*Director of Finance*), Alison Brightmore (*Banking and Finance Assistant*), John Cleland (*Partner and Head of Banking an*), Vincent Gray (*Account Manager*), Andy Normington (*Finance Manager*), Joanne Robinson (*Manchester Banking Team Execut*), Matthew Rowbotham (*Senior Associate, Tax*), Suzanne Wingate (*Head of Finance*)
**Marketing:** Fred Banning (*Head of Public Relations*), Katie Dawson (*Development Manager*), Lisa-Marie Ferla (*Journalist*), Joe Glavina (*Media Consultant*), Matthew Magee (*Editor*)
**Sales:** Rachael Boswell (*Business Development Executive*), Geraint Evans (*Business Development Manager*), Liz Heathfield (*Business Development Manager*), Natalie Loughran (*Business Development Manager*), Joanne Morton (*Associate, Commercial Litigati*), Sue Murdoch (*Business Development Manager*), Andy Peat (*Director of Communications and*)
**Admin:** Linda Archibald (*Personal Assistant*), Sue Burney (*Personal Assistant*), Alida Dow (*Personal Assistant*), Louise Forster (*Legal Director*), Mandy Freeman (*Personal Assistant*), Helen Gill (*Administration*), Jane Harold (*Personal Assistant*), Leanne Hart (*Personal Assistant*), Louise Hart (*Personal Assistant*), Linda Henderson (*Personal Assistant*), Jacquie Hibbert (*Personal Assistant*), Janine Holt (*Legal PA*), Wendy Hyde (*Personal Assistant*), Douglas Keighley (*Advisor*), Sarah Kennedy (*Personal Assistant*), Lisa Lavinier (*Personal Assistant*), Katie Laws (*Public Relations Manager*), Lynne Lines (*Personal Assistant*), Shelley Lunn (*Personal Assistant*), Dee Martin (*Secretary*), Clare McKenna (*Personal Assistant*), Nicola McLintock (*Personal Assistant*), Kay Menzies (*Senior Associate PA*), May Montgomery (*Personal Assistant*), Emily Moon (*Personal Assistant*), Jennie Newton (*Legal Director*), Laura Over (*Managing Director PA*), Tiffany Paday (*Personal Assistant*), Jackie Powell (*Personal Assistant*), Louise Quinton (*Personal Assistant*), Doreen Scott (*Managing Director PA*), Sarah Sheehan (*Secretary*), Dawn Slater (*Administrator*), Julie Smyth (*Personal Assistant*), Mark Surguy (*Legal Director*), Kelly Tymburski (*Personal Assistant*), Joshua Van Raalte (*Advisor*), Diane Wade (*Personal Assistant*)
**IT:** Roger Gomes (*Computer Manager*), Daniel McNamara (*IT Manager*)

**HR:** Lorraine Christie (*Training Manager*), Hayley Dalton (*Training Coordinator*), Trish Embley (*National Client Trainer*), Karen Fentem (*Head of Human Resources*), Nicola Hart (*Head of Education*), Joan Hartwell (*Training Manager*), Spencer Hibbert (*Manager*), Deborah Mccormack (*Head of Training and Developme*), Diane Nicol (*Partner - Head of Employment*)
**Health & Safety:** Jonathan Cowlan (*Health and Safety Senior Manag*)
**Facilities:** Paul Bardens (*Maintenance Manager*), Adrian Barlow (*Non-designated Limited Liabili*), James Crookes (*Property Services and Faciliti*), Shirley De Roche (*Property & Facilities Director*), Judith Leggat (*Facilities Manager*)
**Operations:** Vicky Athersmith (*Production and Operations Mana*), Robin Baillie (*Senior Associate, Projects Gro*), Tara Layman (*Project Manager*), Michelle Nelson (*Partner, Projects and Internat*)
**Engineering:** Liz Hinchliffe (*Technical Manager*), Lucy Hurndall (*Engineer*)
**Branches:** Pinsent Masons Llp, 30 Crown Place, London EC2A 4ES
**US SIC:** 8111 **UK SIC:** 83500
**Auditors:** Deloitte LLP
**Bankers:** The Royal Bank Of Scotland Plc (15-00-00)

|  | 30-04-14 | 30-04-13 | 30-04-12 |
|---|---|---|---|
| TO | 323,525,000 | 305,669,000 | 220,494,000 |
| P/L | 90,348,000 | 87,326,000 | 62,814,000 |
| NW | 78,712,000 | 76,217,000 | 61,761,000 |
| WC | 113,347,000 | 121,599,000 | 94,608,000 |
| Emp. | 2,324 | 2,195 | 1,454 |

**DUNS 64-250-0599**
## Pinto Potts
Manor Park Chambers, 304 High Street, Aldershot, Hampshire GU12 4LT
**Tel:** 01252361200
**Web:** www.pintopotts.co.uk
**Estd:** 1987 Proprietorship
**Line of Business:** Solicitors
**Proprietor:** D Pinto
**Responsibilities**
**Senior:** Laura McCulloch (*Partner*), Nick Parr (*Partner*), David Potts (*Senior Partner*), Kevin Valler (*Partner*)
**Admin:** Terry Honeker (*Office Manager*)
**IT:** Glenn Farr (*IT Manager*)
**Branches:** Pinto Potts, 242 Fleet Rd, Oatsheaf Parade, Fleet, Hampshire GU51 4BX
**US SIC:** 8111 **UK SIC:** 83500
**Employees:** 80

**DUNS 21-231-5138**
## Pinxton Manor Nursing Home
Church St West, Pinxton, Nottingham, Nottinghamshire NG16 6PX
**Tel:** 01773-819191
**Web:** www.monarchhealthcare.co.uk
**Proprietorship**
**Line of Business:** Clinics private
**Proprietor:** Mrs S Akbar
**Responsibilities**
**Senior:** Yvonne Dziurman (*Manager*)
**US SIC:** 8051 **UK SIC:** 95100
**Employees:** 50

**DUNS 77-513-0339**
## Piolax Ltd.
(**Subsidiary of:** Piolax Inc.)
Shorten Brook Drive, Altham Business Par, Altham, Accrington, Lancashire BB5 5YH
**Tel:** 01282684000 **Fax:** 01282-684001
**Web:** www.piolax.co.uk
**Reg No:** 2984670 **Estd:** 1994 Private Limited Company
**Line of Business:** Manufacturers of car accessories
**Export Sales:** £7,910,680
**Issued Capital:** £10,000,000
**Directors:** S Sato, P England, Y Kimura
**Co. Secretary:** Andrew Cornwall
**Responsibilities**
**Senior:** T Ymeyama (*Manager*)
**HR:** Cheryl Barker (*Human Resources Manager*)
**Facilities:** Wayne Hackett (*Maintenance Manager*)
**US SIC:** 3714 **UK SIC:** 35300
**Auditors:** Ernst & Young LLP
**Bankers:** National Westminster Bank Plc (01-01-35)

|  | 31-12-13 | 31-12-12 | 31-12-11 |
|---|---|---|---|
| TO | 17,042,405 | 15,107,343 | 13,239,363 |
| P/L | 1,964,653 | 1,568,359 | 1,491,418 |
| NW | 11,705,854 | 11,175,594 | 10,457,293 |
| WC | 8,788,433 | 8,247,609 | 7,489,760 |
| Emp. | 77 | 72 | 65 |

**DUNS 21-097-4507**   Exp
## Pioneer Concrete Holdings Ltd
(**Subsidiary of:** Hanson Australia (Holdings) Proprietary Limited)
Stoneleigh House, Frome, Somerset BA11 2HB
**Tel:** 02084233066 **Fax:** 020-8423-3845
**Web:** www.pioneerconcrete.com
**Reg No:** 0741624 **Estd:** 1962 Private Limited Company
**Line of Business:** Management activities of other non-financial holding companies not elsewhere classified
**Trading Style:** Hanson Aggregates
**Issued Capital:** £1,887,244
**Directors:** R C Dowley, D J Clarke, E A Gretton, N A Benning-Prince
**Co. Secretary:** Roger Tyson
**US SIC:** 6711, 3273
**UK SIC:** 83962, 24360
**Auditors:** Ernst & Young LLP
**Bankers:** Barclays Bank Plc (20-03-53)

|  | 31-12-13 | 31-12-12 | 31-12-11 |
|---|---|---|---|
| TA | 126,969,000 | 127,275,000 | 127,275,000 |
| NW | 116,431,000 | 116,431,000 | 116,431,000 |
| WC | 109,784,000 | 109,784,000 | 109,784,000 |

**DUNS 39-887-6409**   Imp-Exp
## Pioneer Europe Ltd
(**Subsidiary of:** Continental American Corporation)
9 Stortford Hall Industrial Park, Dunmow Road, Bishops Stortford, Hertfordshire CM23 5GZ
**Tel:** 01279-501090 **Fax:** 01279-501091
**Web:** www.qualetex.com
**Reg No:** 2227318 **VAT No:** 523074768
**Estd:** 1988 Private Limited Company
**Line of Business:** Balloons novelty
**Export Markets:** France; Germany; Italy; South Africa
**Export Sales:** £5,882,207
**Issued Capital:** £1,000
**Principals:** Ms L Devlin (*Managing*), Ms E H Vlamis, T A Vlamis, T J Vlamis, Mrs M T Gransbury
**Co. Secretary:** Mrs Carmen Shivers
**Responsibilities**
**Senior:** Stephen Cundick (*Operations Manager*), Carmen Stillwell (*Office Manager*)
**Marketing:** Rozane Barnard (*Sales & Marketing Manager*)
**Sales:** Rozane Barnard (*Sales & Marketing Manager*)
**Admin:** Carmen Stillwell (*Office Manager*)
**HR:** Carmen Stillwell (*Office Manager*)
**Health & Safety:** Stephen Cundick (*Operations Manager*)
**Facilities:** Stephen Cundick (*Operations Manager*)
**Operations:** Carmen Stillwell (*Office Manager*)
**Engineering:** Stephen Cundick (*Operations Manager*)
**Branches:** Pioneer Europe Ltd, Nelson Trading Estate, Unit 5, London SW19 3BL
**US SIC:** 3069 **UK SIC:** 48123
**Auditors:** Baker Tilly
**Bankers:** National Westminster Bank Plc (50-00-00)

|  | 31-12-13 | 31-12-12 | 31-12-11 |
|---|---|---|---|
| TO | 13,484,956 | 12,937,049 | 12,585,300 |
| P/L | 505,829 | (267,376) | 668,189 |
| NW | 3,957,775 | 3,577,086 | 3,793,642 |
| WC | 3,696,929 | 3,352,016 | 3,552,568 |
| Emp. | 84 | 81 | 81 |

**DUNS 23-590-4919**   Imp-Exp
## Pioneer Film & Television Productions Ltd
(**Subsidiary of:** Dmwsl 660 Ltd)
32 Galena Road, London W6 0LT
**Tel:** 020-8748-0888
**Web:** www.pioneertv.com
**Reg No:** 2289176 **VAT No:** 495466986
**Estd:** 1988 Private Limited Company
**Line of Business:** Film production services and studios
**Export Markets:** U S A
**Export Sales:** £9,364,000
**Trading Style:** Pioneer Productions
**Issued Capital:** £80
**Directors:** S Carter, W A Rees, J E Willis, Ms K A Mclure, O G Jones, J Foulser, Ms J Roberts
**Co. Secretary:** Ms Sara Bond
**US SIC:** 7819, 4833
**UK SIC:** 97111, 97411
**Auditors:** Mercer & Hole
**Bankers:** Barclays Bank Plc (20-27-48)

|  | 30-09-13 | 30-09-12 | 30-09-11 |
|---|---|---|---|
| TO | 11,386,000 | 12,803,000 | 8,485,000 |
| P/L | 644,000 | 989,000 | 582,000 |
| NW | 2,950,000 | 2,797,000 | 2,461,000 |
| WC | 2,893,000 | 2,728,000 | 2,388,000 |
| Emp. | 57 | 51 | 31 |

**DUNS 21-026-7084**   Imp-Exp
## Pioneer G B Ltd
(**Subsidiary of:** Pioneer Corporation)
Pioneer House, Hollybush Hill, Stoke Poges, Slough, Berkshire SL2 4QP
**Tel:** 01753789789
**Web:** www.pioneer.co.uk
**Reg No:** 0512829 **Estd:** 1952 Private Limited Company
**Line of Business:** Wholesale of electrical household appliances and radio and television goods
**Export Markets:** Belgium
**Issued Capital:** £6,094,700
**Directors:** N Bukawa, J Nagahata
**Co. Secretary:** Ms Anita Wilkinson
**Responsibilities**
**Marketing:** Heidi Johnson-Cash (*Marketing Director*)
**IT:** David Hay (*IT Manager*)
**US SIC:** 5064 **UK SIC:** 61500
**Auditors:** Deloitte LLP
**Bankers:** National Westminster Bank Plc (60-22-10)

|  | 31-03-14 | 31-03-13 | 31-03-12 |
|---|---|---|---|
| TO | 33,756,000 | 30,698,000 | 25,472,000 |
| P/L | 422,000 | (386,000) | (860,000) |
| NW | 30,186,000 | 30,921,000 | 33,374,000 |
| WC | 33,024,000 | 30,528,000 | 31,736,000 |
| Emp. | 40 | 47 | 44 |

**DUNS 22-905-6189**   Imp-Exp
## Pioneer Oil Tools Ltd
Sir William Smith Road, Kirkton Industrial Estate, Arbroath, Angus DD11 3RD
**Fax:** 01241-871037
**Web:** www.pioneeroiltools.com
**Reg No:** 0083996SC **VAT No:** 384614142
**Estd:** 1983 Private Limited Company
**Line of Business:** Oil and gas exploration services
**Export Markets:** countries worldwide
**Issued Capital:** £24,672
**Principals:** F A Peterson (*Managing*), Ms P J Mcgill, D W Brown, Ms I A Peterson, T Y Mcgill, Ms M S Brown
**Co. Secretary:** Mrs Rosie Hill
**Responsibilities**
**Facilities:** Neil Patterson (*Foreman*)
**US SIC:** 1389 **UK SIC:** 13000
**Auditors:** Ernst & Young
**Bankers:** Clydesdale Bank Plc (82-61-09)

|  | 30-04-14 | 30-04-13 | 30-04-12 |
|---|---|---|---|
| TA | 6,589,171 | 6,386,620 | 5,742,974 |
| NW | 6,127,161 | 5,772,122 | 5,076,983 |
| WC | 4,787,433 | 4,304,491 | 4,302,507 |

**DUNS 29-018-7251**
## Pioneer Theatres Ltd
Theatre Square, London E15 1BN
**Tel:** 02085340310
**Web:** www.pioneertheatre.org
**Reg No:** 0556251 **VAT No:** 248934327
**Estd:** 1955 Private Company Limited By Guarantee
**Line of Business:** Theatres & concert halls
**Trading Style:** Theatre Royal Stratford East
**Directors:** Ms J C Melville, Ms S A Banks, Ms H Province, A J Cowan, D M Joseph, Ms C A Lake, P O'Leary, M O Eboda
**Responsibilities**
**Senior:** Rosemary Evans (*Director*), Paul O' Leary (*Director*), Mark Pritchard (*Director*), Sabine Vinck (*Director*)
**US SIC:** 7911 **UK SIC:** 97913
**Auditors:** Jon Catty & Co
**Bankers:** National Westminster Bank Plc (60-20-36)

|  | 31-03-14 | 31-03-13 | 31-03-12 |
|---|---|---|---|
| TO | 3,263,362 | 3,281,022 | 2,510,429 |
| P/L | (51,950) | 307,568 | (327,608) |
| NW | 92,304 | 144,254 | (163,314) |
| WC | 58,932 | 30,276 | (207,931) |
| Emp. | 95 | N/A | 70 |

**DUNS 42-433-2166**
## Pioneer Welding Co (2002) Ltd
Pioneer Business Park, Princes Road, Ramsgate, Kent CT11 7RX
**Web:** www.pioneer-welding.co.uk
**Reg No:** 4420866 **Estd:** 2002 Private Limited Company
**Line of Business:** Sheet metal fabrication equipment
**Issued Capital:** £102
**Director:** P J Yates
**Co. Secretary:** Michael Yates
**Responsibilities**
**IT:** David Munday (*Technical Manager*)
**Facilities:** David Munday (*Technical Manager*)
**Engineering:** David Munday (*Technical Manager*)
**US SIC:** 3542, 3499, 3559, 8911
**UK SIC:** 32212, 31694, 32863, 83701
**Auditors:** Philip Gambrill & Co

**Bankers:** National Westminster Bank Plc (60-14-05)

| | 30-06-13 | 30-06-12 | 30-06-11 |
|---|---|---|---|
| TA | 1,725,250 | 1,143,200 | 1,106,815 |
| NW | 1,038,334 | 827,769 | 848,804 |
| WC | 915,679 | 695,563 | 711,572 |

DUNS 77-019-7713

## Pioneer Willment Concrete Ltd

(**Subsidiary of:** Hanson Australia (Holdings) Proprietary Limited)
Scanmoor House 56 60, Northolt Road, Harrow, Middlesex HA2 0DW
**Tel:** 02082694900 **Fax:** 020-8423-6699
**Reg No:** 2664004 **Estd:** 1963 Private Limited Company
**Line of Business:** Management activities of holding companies
**Issued Capital:** £10,000
**Directors:** D J Clarke, E A Gretton, N A Benning-Prince, R C Dowley
**Co. Secretary:** Roger Tyson
**Branches:** Pioneer Willment Concrete Ltd, 21 Wintersells Road, West Byfleet, Surrey KT14 7LF
**US SIC:** 6711 **UK SIC:** 83962
**Bankers:** Barclays Bank Plc (20-03-53)

| | 31-12-13 | 31-12-12 | 31-12-11 |
|---|---|---|---|
| TA | 10,000 | 10,000 | 10,000 |
| NW | 10,000 | 10,000 | 10,000 |

DUNS 64-096-2643

## Pioneering Care Partnership

Carers Way, Newton Aycliffe, County Durham DL5 4SF
**Tel:** 01325321234
**Web:** www.pcp.uk.net
**Reg No:** 3491237 **Estd:** 1998 Private Unlimited Company
**Line of Business:** Other letting of own property
**Directors:** Mrs A Dinsdale, P G Davison, Ms I M Evans, B Knevitt, S J Howarth, Mrs H Brewster, Ms B Davidson, E M Fordham
**Co. Secretary:** Mrs Andria Murphy
**Responsibilities**
**Senior:** Agnes Armstrong *(Manager)*, Michael Dalton *(Director)*, Carol Gaskarth *(Chief Executive Officer)*
**Branches:** Pioneering Care Partnership, Carers Way, Newton Aycliffe, County Durham DL5 4SE
**US SIC:** 8999 **UK SIC:** 83954
**Auditors:** Slade & Cooper
**Bankers:** Unity Trust Bank Plc (08-60-01)

| | 31-03-14 | 31-03-13 | 31-03-12 |
|---|---|---|---|
| TO | 2,281,951 | 1,490,676 | 1,581,912 |
| P/L | 238,972 | (25,378) | (38,235) |
| NW | 995,480 | 756,508 | 781,886 |
| WC | 822,485 | 565,985 | 562,857 |
| Emp. | 79 | 50 | 42 |

DUNS 21-967-9243

## Pioneering Independence Ltd

7 Darklake View, Estover, Plymouth, Devon PL6 7TL
**Tel:** 01752696274 **Fax:** 01752-261728
**Web:** www.emtillprojects.co.uk
**Reg No:** 6149765 **Estd:** 2007 Private Limited Company
**Line of Business:** Other human health activities
**Issued Capital:** £1
**Directors:** P Mcdonald, S P Cook, Ms C A Barrett, Mrs J E Fowler Dimond, K P Roberts
**US SIC:** 8091 **UK SIC:** 95200

| | 31-03-14 | 31-03-13 | 31-03-12 |
|---|---|---|---|
| TA | 488,636 | 597,572 | 451,328 |
| NW | 381,936 | 420,429 | 324,405 |
| WC | 357,271 | 398,396 | 294,352 |

DUNS 73-715-6802

## Pioneers Uk Ministries

Bawtry Hall, South Parade, Bawtry, Doncaster, South Yorkshire DN10 6JH
**Tel:** 01302-710750
**Web:** www.pioneers-uk.org
**Reg No:** 2917955 **Estd:** 1994 Private Company Limited By Guarantee
**Line of Business:** Religious organisations and places of worship
**Directors:** D R Maddock, Reverend C N Mellor, Dr J R Hickson, P J Maddock, Ms C J Register
**Co. Secretary:** David Ware
**Responsibilities**
**Senior:** Martin Kavanagh *(Manager)*, Elizabeth Swain *(Manager)*, Karen Woodburn *(Manager)*
**US SIC:** 8661 **UK SIC:** 96600
**Auditors:** Mazars Neville Russell
**Bankers:** National Westminster Bank Plc (60-02-50)

| | 31-12-13 | 31-12-12 | 31-12-11 |
|---|---|---|---|
| TO | 1,086,434 | 949,527 | 1,243,014 |
| P/L | (103,737) | (375,172) | 266,810 |
| NW | 1,644,304 | 1,737,116 | 2,104,159 |
| WC | 140,989 | 351,803 | 761,054 |
| Emp. | 50 | 37 | 43 |

DUNS 22-769-1060 **Exp**

## Pipe Supports Ltd

(**Subsidiary of:** Hill & Smith Holdings Plc)
Unit 22 West Stone, Berry Hill Industrial Estate, Droitwich, Worcestershire WR9 9AS
**Tel:** 01905-795-500 **Fax:** 01905-794-126
**Web:** www.pipesupports.com
**Reg No:** 0926644 **VAT No:** 589508974
**Estd:** 1968 Private Limited Company
**Line of Business:** Manufacturers of pipeline
**Export Sales:** £10,388,000
**Issued Capital:** £1,177,000
**Directors:** D W Muir, D G Burns, S J Barry, M Pegler, D P Chapman
**Co. Secretary:** Charles Henderson
**US SIC:** 3317, 3494
**UK SIC:** 22200, 32880
**Auditors:** KPMG Audit PLC
**Bankers:** HSBC Bank plc (40-46-35)

| | 31-12-13 | 31-12-12 | 31-12-11 |
|---|---|---|---|
| TO | 12,395,000 | 14,543,000 | 19,415,000 |
| P/L | (1,547,000) | 483,000 | 634,000 |
| NW | 2,570,000 | 3,935,000 | 3,753,000 |
| WC | 442,000 | 2,147,000 | 1,847,000 |
| Emp. | 79 | 70 | 68 |

DUNS 51-988-1986 **Imp-Exp**

## Pipehawk Plc

Manor Park, 4 Church Hill, Aldershot, Hampshire GU12 4JU
**Tel:** 01252338959
**Web:** www.pipehawk.com
**Reg No:** 3995041 **VAT No:** 742686606
**Estd:** 2000 Public Limited Company
**Line of Business:** Other business activities not elsewhere classified
**Export Markets:** E C and Worldwide
**Export Sales:** £53,000
**Issued Capital:** £330,205
**Directors:** G G Watt, R M Macdonnell
**Co. Secretary:** Robert Tallentire
**Responsibilities**
**Senior:** Nick Field *(Manager)*
**US SIC:** 7399 **UK SIC:** 83954
**Auditors:** Crowe Clark Whitehill LLP

| | 30-06-14 | 30-06-13 | 30-06-12 |
|---|---|---|---|
| TO | 5,111,000 | 5,224,000 | 3,342,000 |
| P/L | (622,000) | (1,966,000) | (70,000) |
| NW | (3,560,000) | (3,037,000) | (3,453,000) |
| WC | 211,000 | 741,000 | 381,000 |
| Emp. | 70 | 65 | 61 |

DUNS 22-506-2389 **Imp-Exp**

## Pipeline Induction Heat Ltd

(**Subsidiary of:** Stanley Black & Decker Inc.)
Trans Britannia Industrial Estate, Farrington Road, Burnley, Lancashire BB11 5SW
**Tel:** 01282855000
**Web:** www.crc-evans.com
**Reg No:** 1478556 **VAT No:** 916247424
**Estd:** 1980 Private Limited Company
**Line of Business:** Manufacturers of pipeline
**Export Markets:** Worldwide
**Trading Style:** P I H
**Issued Capital:** £600
**Directors:** Ms S Stubbs, M R Smiley, T P Davison, A R Wynne-Hughes, A K Sood
**Co. Secretary:** Steven Costello
**Responsibilities**
**Senior:** Malcolm Carey *(Manager)*, Calvin Evans *(President)*, Scott Gifford *(Works Manager)*, Fred Hayhurst *(Manager)*
**Sales:** John Fahey *(Sales Manager)*
**Facilities:** Scott Gifford *(Works Manager)*, Robbie Griffin *(Facilities Manager)*
**Operations:** Damian Daykin *(Engineering Director)*, John Fahey *(Sales Manager)*
**Engineering:** Damian Daykin *(Engineering Director)*
**US SIC:** 4619, 3542
**UK SIC:** 72601, 32212
**Auditors:** UHY Hacker Young Manchester LLP
**Bankers:** Lloyds TSB Bank plc (30-90-87)

| | 31-12-13 | 31-12-12 | 31-12-11 |
|---|---|---|---|
| TO | 36,699,271 | 30,455,578 | 26,280,151 |
| P/L | 3,050,731 | 1,024,172 | 2,286,404 |
| NW | 14,796,519 | 11,956,822 | 11,740,382 |
| WC | 5,761,409 | 6,198,129 | 7,729,038 |
| Emp. | 130 | 91 | 92 |

DUNS 21-781-5657

## Piper Court Care Home

Sycamore Way, Stockton-On-Tees, Cleveland TS19 8FR
**Web:** www.schealthcare.co.uk
**Estd:** 2011
**Line of Business:** Medical nursing home activities
**Responsibilities**
**Senior:** Angela Healey *(Manager)*, V Tunney *(Manager)*
**US SIC:** 8051 **UK SIC:** 95100
**Employees:** 55

DUNS 21-580-6821

## Piper Hill High School

Firbank Road, Manchester M23 2YS
**Tel:** 01614363009
**Web:** www.piperhillschool.co.uk
**Estd:** 2006 Proprietorship
**Line of Business:** Schools (special)
**Proprietor:** Mrs L Jones
**US SIC:** 8299 **UK SIC:** 93300
**Employees:** 75

DUNS 21-968-5752

## Piper Smith Watton Llp

29 Great Peter Street, London SW1P 3LW
**Tel:** 02072229900 **Fax:** 020-7828-8008
**Web:** www.pswlaw.co.uk
**Reg No:** 0326659OC **Estd:** 2006 Private Limited Company
**Line of Business:** Solicitors
**Responsibilities**
**Senior:** Stojan Essex *(Non-designated Limited Liabili)*, Ian Insley *(Non-designated Limited Liabili)*, Ian Skuse *(Non-designated Limited Liabili)*, Richard Twyman *(Non-designated Limited Liabili)*
**Finance:** Zoe Jones *(Accounts Manager)*
**Marketing:** Trisha Hart *(Marketing Manager)*
**HR:** Trisha Hart *(Marketing Manager)*
**Health & Safety:** Chris Pottichry *(Health & Safety Officer)*
**US SIC:** 8111 **UK SIC:** 83500

| | 30-04-14 | 30-04-13 | 30-04-12 |
|---|---|---|---|
| TA | 3,348,951 | 2,843,520 | 2,325,044 |
| NW | 624,000 | 920,000 | 920,000 |
| WC | 2,343,632 | 1,849,583 | 1,115,827 |

DUNS 73-715-0433

## Piperdam Golf & Leisure Resort Ltd

Fowlis, Dundee, Angus DD2 5LP
**Tel:** 01382581374 **Fax:** 01382-581102
**Web:** www.piperdam.com
**Reg No:** 0150138SC **Estd:** 1994 Private Limited Company
**Line of Business:** Golf clubs
**Issued Capital:** £286,670
**Principals:** P Mulholland *(Managing)*, B R Linton
**Co. Secretary:** Ms Lynda Mulholland
**Responsibilities**
**Senior:** Phillip Mullholland *(CEO, Managing Director)*
**Marketing:** Claire Mcnally *(Senior Marketing Executive)*
**US SIC:** 7999, 5812, 5813
**UK SIC:** 97913, 66110, 66200

| | 30-06-14 | 30-06-13 | 30-06-12 |
|---|---|---|---|
| TO | 4,588,362 | 4,185,159 | 3,888,701 |
| P/L | 673,401 | 627,517 | 390,157 |
| NW | 2,386,218 | 1,874,353 | 1,422,437 |
| WC | (3,196,691) | (2,217,597) | (2,284,647) |
| Emp. | 102 | 97 | 88 |

DUNS 22-625-0769

## Pipers Corner School

Great Kingshill, High Wycombe, High Wycombe, Buckinghamshire HP15 6LP
**Tel:** 01494719850 **Fax:** 0149719806
**Web:** www.piperscorner.co.uk
**Reg No:** 0504032 **Estd:** 1945 Private Company Limited By Guarantee
**Line of Business:** Schools (independent)
**Directors:** Lady G P Allison, Professor B Mogford, Mrs E J Carrighan, A Cannon, H B Roberts, Ms H F Morton, Mrs J B Ingram, Mrs J E Smith
**Co. Secretary:** Peter Forrester
**Responsibilities**
**Senior:** Bernice Boyton Corbett *(Chairman)*, Alison Buckinghamshire *(Chairman of the Board and Dire)*, Brian Callaghan *(Director)*, Marcus Harborne *(Director)*, John Phimester *(Director)*, Philip Wayne *(Director)*
**US SIC:** 8211 **UK SIC:** 93200
**Auditors:** Seymour Taylor
**Bankers:** Barclays Bank Plc (20-40-71)

| | 31-07-14 | 31-07-13 | 31-07-12 |
|---|---|---|---|
| TO | 8,244,723 | 7,873,357 | 7,531,447 |
| P/L | 680,391 | 500,952 | 528,307 |
| NW | 11,406,676 | 10,726,285 | 10,225,333 |
| WC | 2,072,563 | 1,856,557 | 1,222,606 |
| Emp. | 116 | 113 | 112 |

DUNS 21-193-5650

## The Pipers Tryst

30-34 Mcphater Street, Glasgow, Lanarkshire G4 0HW
**Tel:** 01413535551
**Web:** www.thepipingcentre.co.uk
**Estd:** 1996 Proprietorship
**Line of Business:** Hotels
**Proprietor:** B Ivory
**Responsibilities**
**Senior:** Roddy Macleod *(Manager)*
**US SIC:** 7011, 2329
**UK SIC:** 66500, 45350
**Employees:** 150

DUNS 21-771-7546

## Piper's Vale Community Primary School

Raeburn Road, Ipswich, Suffolk IP3 0EW
**Tel:** 01473320413
**Web:** www.pipersvale.suffolk.sch.uk
**Estd:** 2001 Proprietorship
**Line of Business:** Schools (local authority)
**Proprietor:** Mrs S Wright
**Responsibilities**
**Senior:** Paul Arch *(Head Teacher)*
**US SIC:** 8211 **UK SIC:** 93200
**Employees:** 50

DUNS 21-166-4892

## Pipework Ltd

11 Lansdowne Road, Chadderton, Oldham, Lancashire OL9 9EG
**Tel:** 01616334879
**Reg No:** 6920032 **Estd:** 2009 Private Limited Company
**Line of Business:** Civil engineers
**Issued Capital:** £100
**Directors:** G H Vallely, M P Vallely, T M Vallely, Ms L A Vallely
**US SIC:** 8911 **UK SIC:** 83701

| | 31-05-13 | 31-05-12 | 31-05-11 |
|---|---|---|---|
| TA | 170,667 | 100 | 100 |
| NW | 12,032 | 100 | 100 |
| WC | 2,185 | N/A | N/A |

DUNS 77-953-2498

## Pipex Communications Services Ltd

(**Subsidiary of:** Talktalk Telecom Group Plc)
Carlton House 27a Carlton Drive, London SW15 2BS
**Tel:** 08712225550 **Fax:** 020-8957-1100
**Web:** www.pipex.co.uk
**Reg No:** 3059016 **Estd:** 1995 Private Limited Company
**Line of Business:** Telecommunications
**Trading Style:** Xo Communications
**Issued Capital:** £128
**Directors:** T S Morris, I W Torrens
**Co. Secretary:** Tim Morris
**US SIC:** 4899, 8999
**UK SIC:** 79020, 83954
**Auditors:** Deloitte LLP
**Bankers:** HSBC Bank plc (40-05-01)

| | 31-03-14 | 31-03-13 | 31-03-12 |
|---|---|---|---|
| TO | 21,000 | 71,000 | 93,000 |
| P/L | 16,000 | 70,000 | 91,000 |
| NW | N/A | (7,138,000) | (7,208,000) |
| WC | N/A | (7,138,000) | (7,208,000) |

DUNS 21-724-3712

## Pipex Px Ltd

Pipex House, Devon Enterprise Facility, Plymouth, Devon PL6 7BP
**Tel:** 01752581200
**Reg No:** 7613569 **Estd:** 2011 Private Limited Company
**Line of Business:** Other manufacturing not elsewhere classified
**Export Sales:** £2,637,466
**Issued Capital:** £1
**Directors:** T H Smith, G W Stait, A W Smith (Mbe), W J Murphy, T P Byrne
**Co. Secretary:**
Curzon Corporate Secretaries Lim
**Responsibilities**
**Senior:** Jeffrey Ince *(Director)*
**US SIC:** 3999 **UK SIC:** 49590

| | 30-09-13 | 30-09-12 | 30-09-11 |
|---|---|---|---|
| TO | 12,043,404 | N/A | N/A |
| P/L | 967,820 | N/A | N/A |
| NW | 2,822,493 | 1 | 1 |
| WC | 859,273 | N/A | N/A |
| Emp. | 133 | N/A | N/A |

DUNS 34-560-9965 **Imp-Exp**

## Piramal Healthcare Uk Ltd

(**Subsidiary of:** Piramal Enterprises Limited)
Whalton Road, Morpeth, Northumberland NE61 3YA
**Tel:** 01670-562400 **Fax:** 01670-562401
**Web:** www.piramalpharmasolutions.com
**Reg No:** 5370591 **VAT No:** 873640703
**Estd:** 2005 Private Limited Company
**Line of Business:** Other business activities not elsewhere classified
**Export Sales:** £50,426,962
**Issued Capital:** £17,672,501
**Directors:** N Piramal, A Walker, A Piramal
**Co. Secretary:** Rajesh Laddha
**Responsibilities**
**Senior:** Narayanaswamy Santhanam *(Manager)*
**HR:** Lesley Whittle *(Human Resources Manager)*
**Engineering:** Richard Packer *(Production Manager)*
**Branches:** Piramal Healthcare Uk Ltd, Earls Rd, Grangemouth, Stirlingshire FK3 8XG
**US SIC:** 7399 **UK SIC:** 83954
**Auditors:** KNAV UK Ltd

**Bankers:** HSBC Bank plc (40-27-15)

| | 31-12-13 | 31-12-12 | 31-12-11 |
|---|---|---|---|
| TO | 58,562,347 | 65,023,183 | 57,765,871 |
| P/L | (352,006) | 4,864,248 | 1,817,994 |
| NW | 22,622,074 | 23,582,101 | 19,529,225 |
| WC | 4,441,997 | 11,157,635 | 11,181,032 |
| Emp. | 442 | 428 | 418 |

DUNS 21-067-4777

## Pirate Petes

Clarence Pier, Southsea, Hampshire PO5 3AA
**Tel:** 023-9286-4789
**Estd:** 1990 Proprietorship
**Line of Business:** Children's activity playcentres
**Proprietor:** Mrs J Norman
**Responsibilities**
**Senior:** Jill Norman *(Proprietor)*
**US SIC:** 8699 **UK SIC:** 96902
**Employees:** 51

DUNS 22-655-7676 **Exp**

## The Pirbright Institute

Pirbright Laboratory Ash Road, Pirbright, Surrey, Woking, Surrey GU24 0NF
**Tel:** 01483232441
**Web:** www.pirbright.ac.uk
**Reg No:** 0559784 **VAT No:** 491452831
**Estd:** 1956 Private Company Limited By Guarantee
**Line of Business:** Research and laboratory based activities
**Export Markets:** North America, E U, others
**Directors:** Dr T Kanellos, Dr V L Mayatt, Professor J R Stephenson, Professor D J Rowlands, Sir B Ross, Dr A Craig, R Louth, Professor Q A Mckellar
**Co. Secretary:** Richard Shaw
**Responsibilities**
**Senior:** Mike Samuel *(Director)*
**Health & Safety:** Chrisitine Jones *(Health & Safety Manager)*
**Branches:** The Pirbright Institute, Ogston Building West, Mains Rd, Edinburgh, Midlothian EH9 3JF
**US SIC:** 7391 **UK SIC:** 94000
**Auditors:** Baker Tilly
**Bankers:** HSBC Bank plc (40-34-12)

| | 31-03-14 | 31-03-13 | 31-03-12 |
|---|---|---|---|
| TO | 61,553,000 | 82,994,000 | 60,920,000 |
| P/L | 9,048,000 | 35,956,000 | 9,237,000 |
| NW | 267,945,000 | 258,914,000 | 222,934,000 |
| WC | 36,256,000 | 36,890,000 | 38,100,000 |
| Emp. | 376 | 355 | 322 |

DUNS 76-953-9198 **Exp**

## Pirelli U K Tyres Ltd

**(Subsidiary of:** Pirelli & Co. Spa)
Derby Road, Stretton, Burton-On-Trent, Staffordshire DE13 0BH
**Tel:** 01283-525252 **Fax:** 01283-525565
**Web:** www.pirelli.com
**Reg No:** 2622111 **VAT No:** 125231020
**Estd:** 1991 Private Limited Company
**Line of Business:** Manufacturers and distributors of tyres
**Export Markets:** worldwide
**Export Sales:** £132,859,000
**Trading Style:** Pirelli Tyres
**Issued Capital:** £85,000,000
**Principals:** D A Sandivasci *(Managing)*, G Andrews, A L Panizzari, D A Deambrogio, P G Sierra
**Co. Secretary:** Charanjit Sagoo
**Branches:** Pirelli U K Tyres Ltd, 199 High St, Egham, Surrey TW20 9PG
**US SIC:** 3011, 5531
**UK SIC:** 48110, 65100
**Auditors:** Ernst & Young LLP

| | 31-12-13 | 31-12-12 | 31-12-11 |
|---|---|---|---|
| TO | 342,527,000 | 329,625,000 | 329,667,000 |
| P/L | 14,723,000 | 16,787,000 | 10,227,000 |
| NW | 79,290,000 | 75,017,000 | 73,872,000 |
| WC | 89,500,000 | 88,644,000 | 85,424,000 |
| Emp. | 1,139 | 1,116 | 1,110 |

DUNS 50-021-8870 **Imp-Exp**

## Pirtek (U K) Ltd

**(Subsidiary of:** New Super Selector Sarl)
Unit 35 Acton Park Industrial Estate, London W3 7QE
**Tel:** 020-8749-8444 **Fax:** 020-8749-8333
**Web:** www.pirtek.co.uk
**Reg No:** 2301810 **VAT No:** 495492790
**Estd:** 1988 Private Limited Company
**Line of Business:** Other business activities not elsewhere classified
**Export Markets:** European Union (E U)
**Export Sales:** £702,006
**Trading Style:** Pirtek Uk Limited
**Issued Capital:** £100
**Directors:** P J Dunlop, M R Wilton, A L Wiggins, A J Richards, K Hardy, Dr K Roberts
**Co. Secretary:** Adrian Richards
**Responsibilities**
**Senior:** Rupi Gill *(Office Manager)*
**Admin:** Rupi Gill *(Office Manager)*
**HR:** Rupi Gill *(Office Manager)*
**Facilities:** Rupi Gill *(Office Manager)*
**Branches:** Pirtek (U K) Ltd, Unit 8, Mill Road, Newtownabbey, Co Antrim BT36 7EE
**US SIC:** 7399 **UK SIC:** 83954
**Auditors:** BDO LLP
**Bankers:** The Royal Bank Of Scotland Plc (16-00-19)

| | 31-03-14 | 31-03-13 | 31-03-12 |
|---|---|---|---|
| TO | 16,835,677 | 15,693,488 | 14,076,853 |
| P/L | 5,158,104 | 4,533,528 | 3,022,496 |
| NW | 18,945,567 | 13,859,804 | 9,362,773 |
| WC | 18,490,914 | 13,612,368 | 9,086,544 |
| Emp. | 66 | 67 | 58 |

DUNS 39-886-9974

## Pirton Grange Ltd

**(Subsidiary of:** Embrace Group Ltd)
The Grange, Worcester Road, Pirton, Pirton, Worcester, Worcestershire WR8 9EF
**Tel:** 01905828239 **Fax:** 01905820963
**Web:** www.embracegroup.co.uk
**Reg No:** 2227206 **Estd:** 1989 Private Limited Company
**Line of Business:** Social work activities with accommodation
**Trading Style:** Embrace
**Issued Capital:** £52,382
**Directors:** D L Manson, Ms P L Lee
**Responsibilities**
**Senior:** Abigail Katsande *(General Manager)*
**US SIC:** 8321 **UK SIC:** 96111
**Auditors:** Heath Oliver
**Bankers:** National Westminster Bank Plc (60-09-02)

| | 30-06-14 | 30-06-13 | 31-06-11 |
|---|---|---|---|
| TA | 50,968 | 50,968 | 50,968 |
| NW | 50,968 | 50,968 | 50,968 |

DUNS 21-616-5951 **Imp-Exp**

## Pisani Plc

**(Subsidiary of:** Pisani (Holdings) Ltd)
Plane Tree Crescent, Feltham, Middlesex TW13 7AL
**Tel:** 020 8917 3350
**Web:** www.pisanigroup.com
**Reg No:** 0335887 **VAT No:** 538802823
**Estd:** 1938 Public Limited Company
**Line of Business:** Wholesale of wood, construction materials and sanitary equipment
**Export Markets:** Worldwide; Republic of Ireland
**Trading Style:** Frank England, Pisani Patrick Land
**Issued Capital:** £6,000,000
**Directors:** C J Sakellarios, Ms M E Mogia
**Co. Secretary:** Roger Billins
**Responsibilities**
**Senior:** David Kilpatrick *(Manager)*, Nicholas Telfer *(Manager)*
**Operations:** David Medlam *(Operations Manager)*
**Branches:** Pisani Plc, Bellmoor Quarry, Retford, Nottinghamshire DN22 8SG
**US SIC:** 5039, 1799
**UK SIC:** 61300, 50000
**Auditors:** Day, Smith & Hunter
**Bankers:** National Westminster Bank Plc (60-04-04)

| | 31-12-13 | 30-06-13 | 31-12-11 |
|---|---|---|---|
| TO | 3,549,696 | 19,979,305 | 16,727,186 |
| P/L | (815,766) | 2,043,458 | (1,135,220) |
| NW | 7,702,324 | 8,641,669 | 9,101,346 |
| WC | 6,871,429 | 8,042,931 | 8,515,775 |
| Emp. | 53 | 81 | 104 |

DUNS 21-810-2865

## Pisces Paper Co

Unit 1 Park Lane Business Park, Park Lane, Kirkby-In-Ashfield, Sutton-In-Ashfield, Nottinghamshire NG17 9GU
**Tel:** 08442570390
**Web:** www.pisces-art.co.uk
**Estd:** 2012
**Line of Business:** Other retail sale in specialised stores not elsewhere classified
**Responsibilities**
**Senior:** David Hook *(Manager)*
**US SIC:** 5199 **UK SIC:** 61900
**Employees:** 350

DUNS 50-554-1052 **Imp**

## Pitacs Ltd

Bradbourne Point, Bradbourne Drive, Tilbrook, Milton Keynes, Buckinghamshire MK7 8AT
**Tel:** 01908 271155 **Fax:** 01908 640017
**Web:** www.pitacs.com
**Reg No:** 2505544 **VAT No:** 544771526
**Estd:** 1990 Private Limited Company
**Line of Business:** Other wholesale
**Export Sales:** £292,292
**Issued Capital:** £20,000
**Director:** S Kalender
**Co. Secretary:** Levent Aci
**Responsibilities**
**Senior:** Pratul Shah *(Finance controller)*
**Finance:** Pratul Shah *(Finance controller)*
**US SIC:** 5199 **UK SIC:** 61900
**Auditors:** Guner Associates
**Bankers:** National Westminster Bank Plc (53-70-11)

| | 31-05-14 | 31-05-13 | 31-05-12 |
|---|---|---|---|
| TO | 21,959,917 | 18,702,365 | 16,881,246 |
| P/L | 721,469 | 54,032 | 613,776 |
| NW | 6,685,748 | 6,175,616 | 6,133,485 |
| WC | 6,398,958 | 5,884,745 | 5,824,536 |
| Emp. | 55 | 46 | 36 |

DUNS 21-385-4871

## Pitbauchlie House Hotel

47 Aberdour Road, Inverkeithing, Fife KY11 4PB
**Tel:** 01383-722282
**Web:** www.pitbauchlie.com
**Estd:** 1969 Partnership
**Line of Business:** Hotels
**Partners:** F Mair, S Solley, Ms M Solley, I Solley
**Responsibilities**
**Senior:** Ann Muir *(CEO, Managing Director)*
**US SIC:** 7011 **UK SIC:** 66500
**Employees:** 100

DUNS 21-319-2193

## Pitcairn Lodge

Skene, Westhill, Aberdeenshire AB32 6XT
**Tel:** 01224742888
**Web:** www.embracegroup.co.uk
**Estd:** 1998 Proprietorship
**Line of Business:** Medical nursing home activities
**Proprietor:** Ms I Mecdiermid
**Responsibilities**
**Senior:** Glynis Scott *(Home Manager)*
**Admin:** A Geldhart *(Administrator)*
**US SIC:** 8051 **UK SIC:** 95100
**Employees:** 54

DUNS 77-922-7292

## Pitchmastic Pmb Ltd

**(Subsidiary of:** Rpm International Inc.)
Royds Works, Attercliffe Road, Sheffield, South Yorkshire S4 7WZ
**Tel:** 0114-270-0100
**Web:** www.pitchmasticpmb.co.uk
**Reg No:** 5825725 **Estd:** 2006 Private Limited Company
**Line of Business:** Construction of domestic buildings
**Export Sales:** £4,698,425
**Issued Capital:** £1,000
**Directors:** Mrs K Hewitson, R A Rice, N R Simpson, N Bennett, E W Moore, A J Pike, D P Reif
**US SIC:** 1522 **UK SIC:** 50100
**Auditors:** Ernst & Young LLP
**Bankers:** National Westminster Bank Plc (55-61-11)

| | 31-05-14 | 31-05-13 | 31-05-12 |
|---|---|---|---|
| TO | 9,781,725 | 12,279,467 | 10,294,611 |
| P/L | 816,299 | 2,322,539 | 1,488,235 |
| NW | 2,642,716 | 7,507,116 | 5,772,034 |
| WC | 1,777,370 | 8,355,886 | 6,645,649 |
| Emp. | 52 | 46 | 48 |

DUNS 29-023-4186

## Pitcliffe Properties Ltd

**(Subsidiary of:** Pitcliffe (Holdings) Ltd)
183 Paradise Shopping Precinct, Paradise Fold, Bradford, West Yorkshire BD7 2SB
**Tel:** 01274521410
**Web:** www.ourproperty.co.uk
**Reg No:** 0642490 **VAT No:** 651771921
**Estd:** 1983 Private Limited Company
**Line of Business:** Property developers
**Issued Capital:** £20
**Principals:** G Blyth *(Chairman and Managing)*, D Blyth, Ms B Blyth
**Responsibilities**
**Senior:** Alexandra Blyth *(Manager)*, Florence Wilkinson *(Manager)*
**US SIC:** 6552 **UK SIC:** 85000
**Auditors:** Firth Parish
**Bankers:** Yorkshire Bank Plc (05-03-13)

| | 31-03-14 | 31-03-13 | 31-03-12 |
|---|---|---|---|
| TA | 11,660,637 | 10,795,670 | 10,779,050 |
| NW | 10,891,778 | 9,831,367 | 9,560,013 |
| WC | 806,472 | 559,010 | 358,821 |

DUNS 21-213-6332

## Pitlair House

Bow Of Fife, Cupar, Fife KY15 5RF
**Tel:** 01337-831159
**Web:** www.pitlairhouse.co.uk
**Estd:** 1996 Proprietorship
**Line of Business:** Nursing homes
**Proprietor:** Mrs J J Mcintosh
**Responsibilities**
**Senior:** Janetta McIntosh *(Proprietor)*, Valerie Ramkin *(General Manager)*
**US SIC:** 8051 **UK SIC:** 95100
**Bankers:** Bank Of Scotland (80-08-09)
**Employees:** 64

DUNS 28-998-5277

## Pitlochry Festival Theatre

Pitlochry Festival Theatre, Pitlochry, Perthshire PH16 5DR
**Tel:** 01796484626
**Web:** www.pitlochry.org.uk
**Reg No:** 0029243SC **Estd:** 1951 Private Company Limited By Guarantee
**Line of Business:** Licensed restaurants
**Directors:** A C Liddell, M V Taylor, Professor N C Kuenssberg Obe, J L Kellas, D R Mitchell, G Love, R J Sweetman, M D Dale
**Co. Secretary:** J & H Mitchell Ws
**Responsibilities**
**Senior:** Hamish Buchan *(Director)*, Giles Conisbee *(Head Of Marketing)*, John Durnin *(Chief Executive Officer)*, Mary Marquis Mbe *(Manager)*, Malcolm Mciver O B E *(Manager)*, Gail Pallin *(Director)*, Christopher Pighills *(Manager)*, Heather Stuart *(Director)*, Barbara Vaughan Obe *(Director)*
**Marketing:** Giles Conisbee *(Head Of Marketing)*
**US SIC:** 5812, 8999, 7922
**UK SIC:** 66110, 83954, 97412
**Auditors:** Moir Wood & Co
**Bankers:** Bank Of Scotland (80-09-41)

| | 31-03-14 | 31-03-13 | 31-03-12 |
|---|---|---|---|
| TO | 3,943,405 | 3,591,041 | 3,675,772 |
| P/L | (120,997) | (118,183) | (191,600) |
| NW | 5,162,801 | 5,283,798 | 5,401,981 |
| WC | (235,882) | (103,142) | (14,405) |
| Emp. | 106 | 105 | 105 |

DUNS 21-591-3897

## Pitmans People

16 Hanover Square, London W1S 1HT
**Tel:** 08701605800
**Web:** www.pitmanspeople.com
**Estd:** 2011
**Line of Business:** Labour recruitment and provision of personnel
**Proprietor:** O Pitman
**US SIC:** 7361 **UK SIC:** 83954
**Employees:** 100

DUNS 21-615-6695 **Exp**

## Pitney Bowes Ltd

**(Subsidiary of:** Pitney Bowes Inc.)
The Pinnacles, Po Box 6570, Harlow, Essex CM19 5BD
**Tel:** 08444992992 **Fax:** 01279449622
**Web:** www.pitneyworks.co.uk
**Reg No:** 0182037 **VAT No:** 213329300
**Estd:** 1922 Private Limited Company
**Line of Business:** Office furniture and equipment suppliers
**Export Sales:** £66,759,000
**Issued Capital:** £62,500,002
**Directors:** J L Coupland, D Denney, R Spielberger, I Davidson, P F Jelly
**Co. Secretary:** Gerard Willsher
**Responsibilities**
**Sales:** Daniel Hindman *(Sales Director)*
**IT:** Zowie Kazim *(Technical Manager)*
**Engineering:** Zowie Kazim *(Technical Manager)*
**Branches:** Pitney Bowes Ltd, Septimus Buildings, Unit 6, Bristol, Avon BS14 0BN
**US SIC:** 2599, 5081
**UK SIC:** 46720, 61490
**Auditors:** PricewaterhouseCoopers LLP
**Bankers:** Barclays Bank Plc (20-36-98)

| | 31-12-13 | 31-12-12 | 31-12-11 |
|---|---|---|---|
| TO | 195,716,000 | 206,858,000 | 213,278,000 |
| P/L | (6,550,000) | (9,126,000) | (9,857,000) |
| NW | 15,324,000 | 16,059,000 | 29,765,000 |
| WC | 37,942,000 | 48,782,000 | 56,268,000 |
| Emp. | 1,391 | 1,774 | 1,692 |

DUNS 22-583-6907

## Pitney Bowes Software Europe Ltd

**(Subsidiary of:** Pitney Bowes Inc.)
6 Hercules Way, Leavesden, Watford, Hertfordshire WD25 7GS
**Tel:** 08444992728 **Fax:** 01923-279101
**Web:** www.pbinsight.com
**Reg No:** 1977325 **VAT No:** 421544089
**Estd:** 1994 Private Limited Company
**Line of Business:** Hardware consultancy
**Trading Style:** Pitney Bowes Software Europe Ltd
**Issued Capital:** £8,281,642
**Director:** T Barber
**Co. Secretary:** Gerard Willsher
**US SIC:** 7379, 5065
**UK SIC:** 83940, 61500
**Auditors:** PricewaterhouseCoopers LLP
**Bankers:** National Westminster Bank Plc (56-00-20)

| | 31-12-13 | 31-12-12 | 31-12-11 |
|---|---|---|---|
| TO | 16,971,000 | 17,248,000 | 15,456,000 |
| P/L | 5,171,000 | (13,162,000) | 2,476,000 |
| NW | 11,842,000 | 6,025,000 | 17,154,000 |
| WC | 2,528,000 | (3,183,000) | (7,809,000) |
| Emp. | 69 | 79 | 96 |

DUNS 36-797-2684
## Pitreavie (Dunfermline) Golf Club
Queensferry Road, Dunfermline, Fife KY11 8PR
**Web:** www.pitreaviegolfclub.co.uk
**Estd:** 1922
**Line of Business:** Golf clubs
**Responsibilities**
**Senior:** Cathy Kobiela *(Club Secretary)*
**US SIC:** 7999 **UK SIC:** 97913
**Employees:** 420

DUNS 21-582-0440 **Imp-Exp**
## Pitreavie Property Co Ltd
(**Subsidiary of:** Abbey Road Lp)
Pitreavie Business Park, Dunfermline, Fife KY11 8UL
**Tel:** 01383-621505 **Fax:** 01383-620262
**Web:** www.sherring.com
**Reg No:** 0044851SC **VAT No:** 502767062
**Estd:** 1964 Private Limited Company
**Line of Business:** Other letting of own property
**Export Markets:** E C, Middle East, Africa, Far East
**Trading Style:** Shering Weighing
**Issued Capital:** £21,900
**Director:** J M Wilkie
**Co. Secretary:** Keith Murodch
**Responsibilities**
**Senior:** Sally Senior *(Manager)*
**US SIC:** 6519 **UK SIC:** 85000
**Auditors:** Mazars Neville Russell
**Bankers:** Lloyds Tsb Scotland Plc (87-70-01)

| | 31-03-14 | 31-03-13 | 31-03-12 |
|---|---|---|---|
| TA | 1,919,220 | 1,857,805 | 1,792,521 |
| NW | 1,869,889 | 1,806,402 | 1,744,710 |
| WC | 569,889 | 506,402 | 444,710 |

DUNS 21-636-7219 **Imp-Exp**
## Pittards Public Limited Company.
Sherborne Road, Yeovil, Somerset BA21 5BA
**Tel:** 01935-474-321 **Fax:** 01935-427-145
**Web:** www.pittards.com
**Reg No:** 0102384 **VAT No:** 186700843
**Estd:** 1826 Public Limited Company
**Line of Business:** Manufacture of luggage, handbags and the like, saddlery and harness
**Export Sales:** £32,435,000
**Trading Style:** Pittards Public Limited Company
**Issued Capital:** £4,631,019
**Directors:** S D Boyd, J G Holmstrom, G P Davis, R H Hankey
**Co. Secretary:** Ms Jill Williams
**Responsibilities**
**Senior:** Louise Cretton *(Non-Executive Director)*, Jon Loxston *(Production Director)*
**Marketing:** Debbie Burton *(Marketing Director)*
**Facilities:** Tim Copland *(Works Engineer)*
**Engineering:** Jon Loxston *(Production Director)*
**US SIC:** 3161 **UK SIC:** 44201
**Auditors:** Baker Tilly UK Audit LLP
**Bankers:** National Westminster Bank Plc (60-01-01)

| | 31-12-13 | 31-12-12 | 31-12-11 |
|---|---|---|---|
| TO | 35,813,000 | 37,029,000 | 38,194,000 |
| P/L | 1,712,000 | 300,000 | 2,758,000 |
| NW | 16,574,000 | 15,495,000 | 15,750,000 |
| WC | 10,874,000 | 9,017,000 | 7,502,000 |
| Emp. | 1,318 | 1,205 | 1,182 |

DUNS 22-550-6732
## Pitter Commercials Ltd
Botley Road, West End, Southampton, Hampshire SO30 3HA
**Tel:** 023-8047-7125
**Web:** www.pitter.co.uk
**Reg No:** 1317083 **VAT No:** 293572724
**Estd:** 1977 Private Limited Company
**Line of Business:** Sale of new motor vehicles
**Issued Capital:** £1,000
**Principals:** C J Pitter *(Managing)*, M J Pitter *(Managing)*, S M Pitter
**Co. Secretary:** Michael Pitter
**US SIC:** 5511, 7539, 5531
**UK SIC:** 65100, 67100
**Auditors:** Matthews Mist & Co
**Bankers:** Lloyds TSB Bank plc (30-97-80)

| | 31-12-13 | 31-12-12 | 31-12-11 |
|---|---|---|---|
| TO | 8,101,202 | 7,777,596 | N/A |
| P/L | 227,569 | 248,112 | N/A |
| NW | 2,492,666 | 2,464,002 | 385,552 |
| WC | 1,301,580 | 1,089,015 | 127,203 |
| Emp. | 55 | 61 | N/A |

DUNS 21-354-4690
## Pittville Grant Maintained Comprehensive School
Albert Road, Cheltenham, Gloucestershire GL52 3JD
**Tel:** 01242-524787
**Web:** www.pittville.gloucs.sch.uk
**Line of Business:** General secondary education
**Responsibilities**
**Senior:** Richard Gilpin *(Head Teacher)*
**Finance:** Sabran Lintern-Mole *(Bursar)*
**Facilities:** Sabran Lintern-Mole *(Bursar)*
**US SIC:** 8211 **UK SIC:** 93200
**Employees:** 50

DUNS 21-928-7646
## Pizza Express Ltd
(**Subsidiary of:** Hony Capital (Beijing) Co. Ltd.)
Hunton House, Highbridge Industrial Estate, Oxford Roa, Uxbridge, Middlesex UB8 1LX
**Tel:** 01895263263 **Fax:** 02089604792
**Web:** www.pizzaexpress.com
**Reg No:** 1404552 **Estd:** 1965 Private Limited Company
**Line of Business:** Licensed restaurants
**Trading Style:** Pizza Express
**Issued Capital:** £7,178,835
**Directors:** A D Pellington, R P Hodgson
**Co. Secretary:** Andrew Pellington
**Responsibilities**
**Senior:** Jackie Freeman *(Manager)*
**Branches:** Pizza Express Ltd, Pizza Express, 82 Clifton Street, Lytham St. Annes, Lancashire FY8 5EN
**US SIC:** 7399, 5812
**UK SIC:** 83954, 66110
**Auditors:** PricewaterhouseCoopers LLP
**Bankers:** HSBC Bank plc (40-05-27)

| | 30-06-13 | 01-07-12 | 26-06-11 |
|---|---|---|---|
| TA | 541,892,000 | 475,716,000 | 408,246,000 |
| P/L | 2,049,000 | 2,670,000 | 725,000 |
| NW | 103,570,000 | 102,027,000 | 100,087,000 |
| WC | 102,640,000 | 101,071,000 | 99,099,000 |

DUNS 49-130-6049
## Pizza Gogo Ltd
45 New Road, Gravesend, Kent DA11 0AB
**Tel:** 01474-532000 **Fax:** 01474-567779
**Web:** www.pizzagogo.co.uk
**Reg No:** 3104628 **Estd:** 1995 Private Limited Company
**Line of Business:** Pizza suppliers
**Trading Style:** Medhi
**Issued Capital:** £1,600
**Director:** H Aminnia
**Co. Secretary:** Hamid Haghighat
**Responsibilities**
**Senior:** Shafi Shaida *(Manager)*, Khan Totakhyl *(Proprietor)*
**Branches:** Pizza Gogo Ltd, 11 Bridge Street, Hemel Hempstead, Hertfordshire HP1 1EG
**US SIC:** 5812 **UK SIC:** 66110
**Auditors:** Templetons (UK) Ltd
**Bankers:** National Westminster Bank Plc (60-24-23)

| | 31-05-14 | 31-05-13 | 31-05-12 |
|---|---|---|---|
| TO | 20,272,479 | 16,343,880 | 15,215,144 |
| P/L | 753,623 | 829,780 | 838,057 |
| NW | 6,209,196 | 5,579,221 | 4,934,534 |
| WC | 1,615,656 | 1,859,152 | 1,549,658 |
| Emp. | 71 | 62 | 56 |

DUNS 21-523-8309
## Pizza House
12-14 Newbegin, Hornsea, North Humberside HU18 1AG
**Estd:** 2002 Proprietorship
**Line of Business:** Fast food delivery
**Proprietor:** A Arvis
**US SIC:** 5812 **UK SIC:** 66110
**Employees:** 99

DUNS 21-616-3744
## Pizza Hut Delivery
Unit 7 Ground Floor Colman Parade, Southbury Road, Enfield, Middlesex EN1 1YY
**Tel:** 02083660606
**Web:** www.pizzahut.co.uk
**Estd:** 1993
**Line of Business:** Fast food delivery
**Responsibilities**
**Senior:** Mazan Syed *(Manager)*
**US SIC:** 5812 **UK SIC:** 66110
**Employees:** 47

DUNS 21-580-1074
## Pizza Hut Uk
Great Portwood Street, Stockport, Cheshire SK1 2ED
**Tel:** 01614777252
**Web:** www.pizzahut.co.uk
**Estd:** 2005 Partnership
**Line of Business:** Restaurant - pizza
**Partners:** A Swali, Ms L Mcguinness
**Responsibilities**
**Senior:** L McGuinness *(Partner)*
**US SIC:** 5812 **UK SIC:** 66110
**Employees:** 50

DUNS 21-157-0031
## Pizza Hut (U.K.) Ltd
(**Subsidiary of:** Rutland Fund Ii L.P.)
1 Maxwell Road Imperial Place, Borehamwood, Hertfordshire WD6 1JN
**Tel:** 020-8732-9000 **Fax:** 020-8732-9001
**Web:** www.pizzahut.co.uk
**Reg No:** 1072921 **Estd:** 1972 Private Limited Company
**Line of Business:** Licensed restaurants
**Issued Capital:** £71,505,000
**Directors:** Mrs K E Austin, H G Birts, A R Walker, J T Hofma, M W Spencer
**Co. Secretary:** Mrs Maria Watkins
**Responsibilities**
**Senior:** Natalia Barsegiyan *(Manager)*
**Marketing:** Amy Ashken *(Digital Marketing Manager)*
**Branches:** Pizza Hut (U.k.) Ltd, 1-3 Ecclesall Road, Berkeley Precinct, Sheffield, South Yorkshire S11 8PN
**US SIC:** 7399, 5812
**UK SIC:** 83954, 66110
**Auditors:** KPMG LLP
**Bankers:** HSBC Bank plc (40-01-06)

| | 01-12-13 | 02-12-12 | 04-12-11 |
|---|---|---|---|
| TO | 230,106,000 | 268,692,000 | 330,959,000 |
| P/L | (968,000) | 1,329,000 | (24,178,000) |
| NW | 42,085,000 | 53,452,000 | 31,407,000 |
| WC | (6,971,000) | 3,083,000 | (40,903,000) |
| Emp. | 9,343 | 12,408 | 13,670 |

DUNS 21-225-2890
## Pizza on the Park
11-13 Knightsbridge, London SW1X 7LY
**Web:** www.pizzaonthepark.co.uk
**Estd:** 1971
**Line of Business:** Licensed restaurants
**US SIC:** 5812 **UK SIC:** 66110
**Employees:** 89

DUNS 23-946-6803
## Pj Care Ltd
(**Subsidiary of:** P J Care Holdings Ltd)
153 Sherwood Drive, Milton Keynes, Buckinghamshire MK3 6RT
**Tel:** 08702416527
**Web:** www.pjcare.co.uk
**Reg No:** 3936122 **VAT No:** 927379387
**Estd:** 2000 Private Limited Company
**Line of Business:** Social work activities with accommodation
**Issued Capital:** £34,444
**Directors:** M P Butler, J Van Zyl, Ms J Flawn, P Flawn
**Branches:** Pj Care Ltd, Faraday Drive, Milton Keynes, Buckinghamshire MK5 7FY
**US SIC:** 8321 **UK SIC:** 96111
**Auditors:** Mercer & Hole
**Bankers:** Barclays Bank Plc (20-57-40)

| | 31-03-14 | 31-03-13 | 31-03-12 |
|---|---|---|---|
| TO | 10,727,038 | 7,629,523 | 5,753,192 |
| P/L | (695,017) | (331,747) | 1,036,504 |
| NW | 9,162,414 | 9,756,996 | 6,721,312 |
| WC | 1,279,284 | 1,895,644 | 1,846,310 |
| Emp. | 388 | 216 | 126 |

DUNS 34-995-9952
## Pj Installations (Southern) Ltd
20 Harriotts Lane, Ashtead, Surrey KT21 2QH
**Tel:** 01372276122
**Web:** www.pjinstallations.com
**Reg No:** 5790905 **Estd:** 2006 Private Limited Company
**Line of Business:** Installation of ventilation
**Issued Capital:** £100
**Director:** P Selway
**Co. Secretary:** Ms Lisa Privett
**Responsibilities**
**Senior:** Tina Selway *(Manager)*
**US SIC:** 8911 **UK SIC:** 83701

| | 30-04-14 | 30-04-13 | 30-04-12 |
|---|---|---|---|
| TA | 265,552 | 187,179 | 290,228 |
| NW | 102,772 | 68,126 | 122,671 |
| WC | 100,523 | 54,861 | 98,770 |

DUNS 45-848-5430
## P.J. Livesey Holdings Ltd
Holden Mill, Blackburn Road, Bolton, Lancashire BL1 7LS
**Tel:** 01204592443 **Fax:** 01618488671
**Web:** www.pjlivesey.co.uk
**Reg No:** 3195231 **Estd:** 2006 Private Limited Company
**Line of Business:** Construction of domestic buildings
**Issued Capital:** £100
**Principals:** P J Livesey *(Managing)*, J W Allcock *(Financial)*, J N Woodmansee, Ms G A Livesey, P G Richardson, R Brocklehurst
**Co. Secretary:** Mrs Dorothea Livesey
**Responsibilities**
**Senior:** Georgina Livesey-Daniels *(Director)*
**US SIC:** 1522, 6552
**UK SIC:** 50100, 85000
**Auditors:** Ainsworths
**Bankers:** National Westminster Bank Plc (01-05-31)

| | 30-06-14 | 30-06-13 | 30-06-12 |
|---|---|---|---|
| TO | 42,697,422 | 28,344,604 | 33,523,473 |
| P/L | 1,851,012 | 1,256,918 | (1,020,049) |
| NW | 29,880,612 | 28,029,600 | 26,772,682 |
| WC | 26,070,271 | 24,443,214 | 23,650,133 |
| Emp. | 105 | 108 | 104 |

DUNS 45-817-8415
## P.J. Livesey Living Space Ltd
(**Subsidiary of:** P.J. Livesey Holdings Ltd)
Ashburton Park, Beacon Road, Manchester M17 1AF
**Tel:** 0161-873-7878 **Fax:** 01618488671
**Web:** www.pjlivesey-group.co.uk
**Reg No:** 3175509 **VAT No:** 673557796
**Estd:** 1982 Private Limited Company
**Line of Business:** Construction of domestic buildings
**Issued Capital:** £2
**Principals:** P J Livesey *(Managing)*, J W Allcock *(Financial)*, P G Richardson, Ms G A Livesey, R Brocklehurst, J N Woodmansee
**Co. Secretary:** Mrs Dorothea Livesey
**US SIC:** 1522 **UK SIC:** 50100
**Auditors:** Ainsworths Ltd
**Bankers:** National Westminster Bank Plc (01-05-31)

| | 30-06-14 | 30-06-13 | 30-06-12 |
|---|---|---|---|
| TO | 6,236,281 | 3,940,698 | 4,262,591 |
| P/L | (1,960,524) | 211,718 | 405,696 |
| NW | (512,230) | 1,448,294 | 1,236,576 |
| WC | (1,049,878) | 910,646 | 698,928 |

DUNS 22-776-0212
## P.J. Nicholls Ltd
The Motor House, Pershore Terrace, Pinvin, Pershore, Worcestershire WR10 2DR
**Tel:** 01386-555555
**Web:** www.pjnicholls.com
**Reg No:** 1777064 **VAT No:** 396191909
**Estd:** 1983 Private Limited Company
**Line of Business:** Car dealers (new & used)
**Issued Capital:** £100,000
**Principals:** P J Nicholls *(Managing)*, T R Nicholls, A M Nicholls
**Co. Secretary:** Mrs Susan Nicholls
**Branches:** P.j. Nicholls Ltd, Ashchurch Road, Tewkesbury, Gloucestershire GL20 8DT
**US SIC:** 5511, 7539
**UK SIC:** 65100, 67100
**Auditors:** Kendall Wadley LLP
**Bankers:** National Westminster Bank Plc (01-05-48)

| | 31-12-13 | 31-12-12 | 31-12-11 |
|---|---|---|---|
| TO | 32,937,943 | 26,599,280 | 23,135,725 |
| P/L | 470,483 | 242,145 | 44,448 |
| NW | 1,071,900 | 913,960 | 832,233 |
| WC | (398,680) | (513,938) | (613,052) |
| Emp. | 63 | 67 | 69 |

DUNS 52-561-5423
## P.J. Rhodes Ltd
Yardley Road, Birmingham, West Midlands B27 6EF
**Tel:** 01217063829 **Fax:** 0121-706-9152
**Web:** www.pjrhodes.co.uk
**Reg No:** 3247363 **Estd:** 1993 Private Limited Company
**Line of Business:** Car body repairers
**Issued Capital:** £100
**Directors:** T M Monaghan, D E Taylor
**Responsibilities**
**Finance:** Jayne Monaghan *(Finance Director)*
**US SIC:** 7539 **UK SIC:** 67100
**Auditors:** Haslehursts Ltd

| | 30-04-14 | 30-04-13 | 31-04-12 |
|---|---|---|---|
| TA | 1,682,103 | 1,148,824 | 1,168,954 |
| NW | 232,717 | 226,342 | 577,896 |
| WC | 121,896 | (117,455) | 338,828 |

DUNS 22-660-0120
## P.J. Thory Ltd
Eldernell Lane Coates Whittlesey, Peterborough, Cambridgeshire PE7 2DD
**Tel:** 01733840328
**Web:** www.pjthory.co.uk
**Reg No:** 1280198 **Estd:** 1942 Private Limited Company
**Line of Business:** Other supporting land transport activities
**Issued Capital:** £21,060
**Directors:** J P Thory, T D Thory
**Co. Secretary:** Ms June Thory
**Responsibilities**
**Senior:** Martin Ash *(General Manager)*, Danny Knight *(General Manager)*
**Sales:** Martin Ash *(General Manager)*
**HR:** Dave Dyke *(Health & Safety Manager)*
**Health & Safety:** Dave Dyke *(Health & Safety Manager)*
**Facilities:** Mark Agger *(Workshop Foreman)*

**Fleet:** Malcolm Agger (*Transport Manager*)
**Engineering:** Martin Ash (*General Manager*)
**US SIC:** 4789 **UK SIC:** 77002
**Auditors:** Whiting & Partners
**Bankers:** HSBC Bank plc (40-36-15)

|  | 31-03-14 | 31-03-13 | 31-03-12 |
|---|---|---|---|
| TO | 13,477,896 | 8,664,887 | 7,814,236 |
| P/L | 484,547 | 84,070 | 37,126 |
| NW | 3,811,519 | 3,404,538 | 3,305,915 |
| WC | 1,167,671 | 1,002,818 | 1,021,392 |
| Emp. | 89 | 65 | 68 |

DUNS 73-549-1115
## Pja Carpentry Ltd
Heddings Farm, The Lane, Wyboston, Bedford, Bedfordshire MK44 3AS
**Tel:** 01480-216787 **Fax:** 01767-601320
**Web:** www.pacarpentrylimited.co.uk
**Reg No:** 4811295 **Estd:** 2010 Private Limited Company
**Line of Business:** Carpenters
**Issued Capital:** £1
**Directors:** P J Albone, P Cross
**Responsibilities**
**Finance:** Anita Palumbo (*Accounts Manager*)
**US SIC:** 2431, 1761
**UK SIC:** 46300, 50400
**Auditors:** Cloke & Co

|  | 31-05-14 | 31-05-13 | 31-05-12 |
|---|---|---|---|
| TA | 428,246 | 490,912 | 456,820 |
| NW | 56,287 | 55,122 | 61,782 |
| WC | 37,427 | 33,576 | 47,481 |

DUNS 21-293-2313
## P.J.H. Group Ltd
(**Subsidiary of:** Globe Union Industrial Corp.)
Alder House, Slackey Brow, Kearsley, Bolton, Lancashire BL4 8SL
**Tel:** 01204-707070 **Fax:** 01204573140
**Web:** www.pjhgroup.com
**Reg No:** 1056008 **VAT No:** 145724661
**Estd:** 1972 Private Limited Company
**Line of Business:** Bathroom planners and furnishers
**Trading Style:** Hopkinsons, Fourways, Apple Kitchens
**Issued Capital:** £7,500,000
**Directors:** Y Chou, J D Shaw, K Yen, S Ouyoung, A Yates, K J Powell
**Co. Secretary:** Jason Shaw
**Responsibilities**
**Senior:** John Nobrega (*Operations Director*)
**Finance:** Nick Dalfen (*Chief Accountant*), Mark Errington (*Financial Director*)
**Marketing:** Sally Hough (*Sales & Marketing Manager*), Nathalie Vandecraen (*Sales & Marketing Director*)
**Sales:** Sally Hough (*Sales & Marketing Manager*), Stephen Johnstone (*Sales Director*), Nathalie Vandecraen (*Sales & Marketing Director*)
**IT:** Graham Allcroft (*Non-PC Systems Manager*), Andrew Baron (*Computer Operations Manager*), Robert Gilkey (*IT Manager*), John Nobrega (*Operations Director*)
**HR:** Jason Witton (*Training Manager*)
**Health & Safety:** Sarah Christian (*Health & Safety Officer*)
**Facilities:** John Nobrega (*Operations Director*)
**Operations:** Sarah Christian (*Health & Safety Officer*)
**Purchasing:** Rob Higgins (*Purchasing Director*)
**Branches:** P.j.h. Group Ltd, Radcliffe Moor Road, Bradley Fold Trading Estate, Bradley Fold, Bolton, Lancashire BL2 6RT
**US SIC:** 4712, 5199
**UK SIC:** 77002, 61900
**Auditors:** Ernst & Young LLP
**Bankers:** HSBC Bank plc (40-29-08)

|  | 31-12-13 | 31-12-12 | 31-12-11 |
|---|---|---|---|
| TO | 117,381,000 | 124,919,000 | 140,494,000 |
| P/L | 15,000 | 2,094,000 | 2,731,000 |
| NW | 50,765,000 | 51,203,000 | 49,765,000 |
| WC | 52,400,000 | 50,559,000 | 51,631,000 |
| Emp. | 576 | 662 | 735 |

DUNS 21-636-6088 **Exp**
## P.J.Hare Ltd
Havyatt Road, Bristol, Avon BS40 5AE
**Web:** www.harepress.co.uk
**Reg No:** 0465757 **VAT No:** 130019625
**Estd:** 1947 Private Limited Company
**Line of Business:** Manufacturers and distributiors of press tools and jigs
**Export Markets:** W Europe, Middle East, U S A, Australasia, Canada
**Issued Capital:** £102,500
**Principals:** K J Baston (*Managing*), M J Hare (*Managing*), Sir R P Williams, Ms C M Hare, S R Lock, Ms E A Hare, Ms A L Bennett, Ms P L Hare
**Co. Secretary:** Gwsp Secretaries Ltd

**Responsibilities**
**Senior:** Kenneth Crago (*Director & Chairman*), Penelope Hare (*Director*), Diana Hare (*Director*), William Hare (*Operations Director*), Nicola Hare (*Director*), Victoria Hare (*Director*)
**HR:** Steve Borrett (*Manufacturing Manager*)
**Facilities:** Steve Borrett (*Manufacturing Manager*)
**Purchasing:** Steve Borrett (*Manufacturing Manager*)
**Branches:** P.j.hare Ltd, 4 Mackenzie Way, Kingsditch Trad Est, Cheltenham, Gloucestershire GL51 9TX
**US SIC:** 3542 **UK SIC:** 32212
**Auditors:** Gordon Wood Scott & Partners
**Bankers:** National Westminster Bank Plc (60-23-23)

|  | 31-03-14 | 31-03-13 | 31-03-12 |
|---|---|---|---|
| TA | 2,011,016 | 2,070,999 | 2,091,289 |
| NW | 1,369,526 | 1,442,828 | 1,459,941 |
| WC | 1,004,002 | 1,047,456 | 1,031,038 |

DUNS 77-122-1611
## P.K. & I.F. Cobley Ltd
Rear Of Gees Garage, Morris's Yard, Leicester Road, Lutterworth, Leicestershire LE17 4NJ
**Tel:** 01455282111
**Web:** www.cobleytransport.co.uk
**Reg No:** 2694624 **VAT No:** 620142987
**Estd:** 1986 Private Limited Company
**Line of Business:** Freight transport by road not elsewhere classified
**Trading Style:** Cobley Transport
**Issued Capital:** £110
**Directors:** P K Cobley, I F Cobley
**US SIC:** 4213 **UK SIC:** 72300
**Auditors:** Simpson & Co
**Bankers:** National Westminster Bank Plc (60-13-30)

|  | 31-03-14 | 31-03-13 | 31-03-12 |
|---|---|---|---|
| TO | 8,157,835 | 7,714,036 | 7,965,901 |
| P/L | 808,389 | 232,312 | 177,593 |
| NW | 2,170,409 | 1,658,607 | 1,537,870 |
| WC | 1,154,575 | 360,732 | 377,189 |
| Emp. | 107 | 104 | 103 |

DUNS 21-624-2705
## Pk Food Concepts Ltd.
Milber Trading Estate, Newton Abbot, Devon TQ12 4SG
**Tel:** 08004587898
**Web:** www.pkfoodconcepts.co.uk
**Reg No:** 7043579 **Estd:** 2009 Private Limited Company
**Line of Business:** Management activities of holding companies
**Issued Capital:** £89,800
**Directors:** G Truman, A Raoux, P Kingsley-Bates, I M Rick
**US SIC:** 6711 **UK SIC:** 83962
**Bankers:** HSBC Bank plc (40-34-31)

|  | 30-06-14 | 30-06-13 | 30-06-12 |
|---|---|---|---|
| TO | 18,510,007 | 16,526,394 | 14,074,459 |
| P/L | (81,093) | 190,970 | (690,437) |
| NW | (9,031,826) | (9,547,712) | (10,229,176) |
| WC | (299,857) | 70,385 | (1,001,182) |
| Emp. | 209 | 173 | 175 |

DUNS 42-347-1275
## P.K. Murphy Construction Ltd
(**Subsidiary of:** Termon Holdings Ltd)
91 Sluggan Road, Dungannon, Co Tyrone BT70 2UP
**Tel:** 028-8775-8848 **Fax:** 028-8775-9699
**Web:** www.pkmurphy.co.uk
**Reg No:** 0030737NI **VAT No:** 390833242
**Estd:** 1996 Private Limited Company
**Line of Business:** Building construction contractors
**Issued Capital:** £20,000
**Director:** P K Murphy
**Co. Secretary:** Mrs Rosaleen Murphy
**US SIC:** 1522 **UK SIC:** 50100
**Auditors:** Cavanagh Kelly
**Bankers:** The Bank Of Ireland (90-48-51)

|  | 31-03-14 | 31-03-13 | 31-03-12 |
|---|---|---|---|
| TO | 15,676,032 | 20,894,854 | N/A |
| P/L | 984,162 | 2,976,772 | 3,256,709 |
| NW | 1,502,651 | 16,599,348 | 14,589,833 |
| WC | 1,188,801 | 16,051,493 | 14,035,414 |
| Emp. | 71 | 89 | 95 |

DUNS 42-408-6218
## Pkf Cooper Parry Llp
3 Centro Place, Pride Park, Derby, Derbyshire DE24 8RF
**Tel:** 01332 295544
**Web:** www.cooperparry.com
**Reg No:** 0301728OC **VAT No:** 117566168
**Estd:** 1850
**Line of Business:** Audit services

**Responsibilities**
**Senior:** Sarah Axe (*Partner*), Jonathan Bryant (*Partner*), Adrian Cheatham (*Designated Limited Liability P*), Alison Fovargue (*Designated Limited Liability P*), Andrew Geer (*Designated Limited Liability P*), Andrew Honarmand (*Designated Limited Liability P*), Daniel Parker (*Designated Limited Liability P*), Mark Pashley (*Designated Limited Liability P*), Andrew Timms (*Designated Limited Liability P*)
**Branches:** Pkf Cooper Parry Llp, Tax Department, 26 The Ropewalk, Nottingham, Nottinghamshire NG1 5DW
**US SIC:** 8931, 8999
**UK SIC:** 83600, 83954
**Auditors:** Buzzacott LLP

|  | 30-04-14 | 30-04-13 | 30-04-12 |
|---|---|---|---|
| TO | 15,931,135 | 15,625,284 | 15,748,436 |
| P/L | 377,791 | 190,358 | 32,323 |
| WC | 2,141,205 | 1,913,622 | 2,439,642 |
| Emp. | 182 | 172 | 169 |

DUNS 23-351-3006
## Pkf (Isle of Man) Ltd
Po Box 16, Analyst House, 20-26 Peel Road, Douglas, Douglas, Isle of Man IM99 1AP
**Fax:** 01624-652001
**Web:** www.westiom.com
**Reg No:** 0100479M **Estd:** 1886 Private Limited Company
**Line of Business:** Accounting and auditing activities
**Directors:** J Scott, J Nugent, P Dearden, D Drewell, P Seaward, J Cryer
**Responsibilities**
**Senior:** Charles Crossley (*Manager*)
**Admin:** Harry Bamber (*Office Manager*)
**HR:** Steve Hull (*Human Resources Manager*)
**Health & Safety:** Steve Hull (*Human Resources Manager*)
**Facilities:** Harry Bamber (*Office Manager*)
**US SIC:** 8931 **UK SIC:** 83600
**Employees:** 75

DUNS 21-149-3781
## Pkf Littlejohn Llp
1 Westferry Circus, London E14 4HA
**Web:** www.littlejohnllp.com
**Reg No:** 0342572OC **Estd:** 2009
**Line of Business:** Accounting activities
**Responsibilities**
**Senior:** Neil Coulson (*Non-designated Limited Liabili*), Cheryl Court (*Non-designated Limited Liabili*), Claire Giltrow (*Marketing Manager*), Stephen Goderski (*Non-designated Limited Liabili*), Alan Knapp (*Non-designated Limited Liabili*), Christopher Riley (*Non-designated Limited Liabili*), Alistair Roberts (*Non-designated Limited Liabili*), Julian Rummins (*Non-designated Limited Liabili*), Alison Sheridan (*Non-designated Limited Liabili*), Ian Singer (*Non-designated Limited Liabili*), James Sleight (*Non-designated Limited Liabili*)
**US SIC:** 8931 **UK SIC:** 83600
**Auditors:** Price Bailey LLP
**Bankers:** HSBC Bank plc (40-02-31)

|  | 31-05-13 | 31-05-12 | 31-05-11 |
|---|---|---|---|
| TO | 15,770,342 | 16,219,513 | 16,409,995 |
| P/L | 3,552,927 | 4,228,644 | 3,586,885 |
| NW | 1,403,424 | 1,129,877 | 776,462 |
| WC | 2,167,810 | 2,531,597 | 1,925,403 |
| Emp. | 139 | 140 | 135 |

DUNS 29-489-8671
## Pkl Group Ltd
(**Subsidiary of:** Countrywide Group Plc)
22-23 Widegate Street, London E1 7HP
**Tel:** 02076501700 **Fax:** 020-7430-0938
**Web:** www.pkl.co.uk
**Reg No:** 1853210 **VAT No:** 238695224
**Estd:** 1984 Private Limited Company
**Line of Business:** Holding company, for subsidiaries engaged as property managers and developers
**Trading Style:** John D Wood
**Issued Capital:** £951,000
**Directors:** G R Williams, J Clarke, D R Green
**Co. Secretary:** Oakwood Corporate Secretary Limi
**Branches:** Pkl Group Ltd, Lincoln House, 296-302 High Holborn, London WC1V 7JH
**US SIC:** 6531 **UK SIC:** 83400
**Bankers:** The Royal Bank Of Scotland Plc (16-00-16)

|  | 31-12-13 | 31-12-12 | 31-12-11 |
|---|---|---|---|
| TA | 951,000 | 951,000 | 951,000 |
| NW | 951,000 | 951,000 | 951,000 |

DUNS 50-037-8625 **Exp**
## Pkl Group (Uk) Ltd
(**Subsidiary of:** Pkl Intermediate Ltd)
Malvern View Business Park, Stella Way, Bishops Cleeve, Cheltenham, Gloucestershire GL52 7DQ
**Tel:** 08458404242
**Web:** www.pkl.co.uk
**Reg No:** 2308713 **VAT No:** 650825930

**Estd:** 1988 Private Limited Company
**Line of Business:** Renting of other machinery and equipment not elsewhere classified
**Export Markets:** Rest of world
**Export Sales:** £1,705,000
**Trading Style:** Pkl Group (Uk)
**Issued Capital:** £200
**Directors:** P R Joy, P F Schad, L A Vines, C J Irving
**Co. Secretary:** William Perry
**Responsibilities**
**Senior:** jay king (*Warehouse Manager*)
**IT:** edward godden (*IT Manager*)
**Branches:** Pkl Group (Uk) Ltd, Malvern View Business Park, Stella Way, Bishops Cleeve, Cheltenham, Gloucestershire GL52 7DQ
**US SIC:** 7394 **UK SIC:** 84000
**Auditors:** Hazlewoods LLP
**Bankers:** Bank Of Scotland (12-12-82)

|  | 30-04-14 | 30-04-13 | 30-04-12 |
|---|---|---|---|
| TO | 10,260,000 | 22,233,000 | 17,804,000 |
| P/L | 822,000 | 2,509,000 | 4,235,000 |
| NW | 21,484,000 | 20,914,000 | 19,125,000 |
| WC | 18,164,000 | 17,391,000 | 9,746,000 |
| Emp. | 84 | 99 | 87 |

DUNS 71-890-3144
## Pkr Technologies Ltd
(**Subsidiary of:** Pkr Ltd)
74-80 Camden Street, London NW1 0EG
**Tel:** 02073833697
**Web:** www.pkr.com
**Reg No:** 5272650 **Estd:** 2004 Private Limited Company
**Line of Business:** Secretarial and translation activities
**Export Sales:** £14,965,000
**Issued Capital:** £5,480
**Directors:** J E San, P J Brotherton
**Co. Secretary:** Leon Walters
**Responsibilities**
**Finance:** Greg Gera (*Senior Payment Executive*), Jean-Pierre Houareau (*Chief Financial Officer*), Marianna Katerusha (*Payments Executive*)
**US SIC:** 7339 **UK SIC:** 83954
**Bankers:** Coutts & Co (18-00-02)

|  | 31-12-12 | 31-12-11 | 31-12-10 |
|---|---|---|---|
| TO | 14,966,000 | 14,029,259 | 12,013,972 |
| P/L | (100,000) | 133,103 | 950,032 |
| NW | 1,970,000 | 191,962 | 2,844,557 |
| WC | 1,424,000 | (768,176) | 1,844,868 |
| Emp. | 135 | 126 | 118 |

DUNS 21-607-1099
## Place Court
Camps Road, Haverhill, Suffolk CB9 8HF
**Tel:** 03333218607
**Web:** www.careuk.com
**Estd:** 1967
**Line of Business:** Children's homes
**Proprietor:** Mrs R Abbink
**Responsibilities**
**Senior:** Karen Curle (*Manager*)
**US SIC:** 8321 **UK SIC:** 96111
**Employees:** 50

DUNS 21-759-1975
## Place Farm Community Primary School
Camps Road, Haverhill, Suffolk CB9 8HF
**Tel:** 01440 702836
**Web:** www.placefarm.suffolk.sch.uk
**Estd:** 1988 Proprietorship
**Line of Business:** Schools (local authority)
**Proprietor:** Mrs M Vigar
**US SIC:** 8211 **UK SIC:** 93200
**Employees:** 50

DUNS 50-376-6065
## Place Restaurants Ltd
(**Subsidiary of:** Panther Partners Ltd)
199a Kensington Church Street, London W8 7LX
**Tel:** 02072436626 **Fax:** 02072436627
**Web:** www.kensingtonplace-restaurant.co.uk
**Reg No:** 2385711 **Estd:** 1987 Private Limited Company
**Line of Business:** Wholesale of other food including fish, crustaceans and molluscs
**Trading Style:** Launceston Place Restaurant, Kensington Place Restaurant
**Issued Capital:** £1,579
**Directors:** D A Gunewardena, T C Harris, D M Loewi
**Responsibilities**
**Senior:** Frederick Linford (*Manager*), William McKechnie (*Restaurant Manager*), C Westall (*Manager*)
**Marketing:** Nikki Harris (*Marketing Manager*)
**HR:** William McKechnie (*Restaurant Manager*)
**Facilities:** William McKechnie (*Restaurant Manager*)
**Branches:** "Kensington Place", 201 Kensington Church St, London. Tel 0171-727-3184

**US SIC:** 5146 **UK SIC:** 61700
**Auditors:** Lewis Golden & Co
**Bankers:** Bank Of Scotland (12-11-03)

| | 31-03-14 | 31-03-13 | 31-03-12 |
|---|---|---|---|
| TO | 3,969,000 | 3,693,000 | 3,676,000 |
| P/L | (165,000) | (262,000) | (395,000) |
| NW | (500,000) | (364,000) | (159,000) |
| WC | (338,000) | (99,000) | 33,000 |
| Emp. | 69 | 69 | 73 |

DUNS 57-042-9795
## PIACE2BE
13-14 Angel Gate, London EC1V 2PT
**Tel:** 020-7923-5500
**Web:** www.place2be.org.uk
**Reg No:** 2876150 **Estd:** 1993
**Line of Business:** Primary education
**Directors:** Mrs S E Hill, The Hon R A Rayne, W A Russell, Miss E M Lecointe, B M Refson, Professor D F Rose, S J Dorrell, A J Levy
**Co. Secretary:** Nicholas Herod
**Responsibilities**
**Senior:** Laura Atherley *(Director)*, Lorna Bown *(trustee)*, Elizabeth Drummond *(Director)*, William Fowle *(Director)*, Robert Jezzard *(Director)*, Howard Long *(Manager)*, Timothy Smart *(Manager)*, Louise St Aldwyn *(Director)*, Caroline Twisleton Wykeham Fiennes *(Manager)*
**US SIC:** 8211, 8091
**UK SIC:** 93200, 95200
**Auditors:** MGR Audit Ltd
**Bankers:** Lloyds TSB Bank plc (30-96-38)

| | 31-03-14 | 31-03-13 | 31-03-12 |
|---|---|---|---|
| TO | 9,277,000 | 7,384,000 | 7,403,000 |
| P/L | 105,000 | (291,000) | 448,000 |
| NW | 4,207,000 | 4,102,000 | 4,376,000 |
| WC | 3,365,000 | 3,266,000 | 3,544,000 |
| Emp. | 209 | 178 | 176 |

DUNS 23-306-3895
## The Placement Group (Uk) Ltd
**(Subsidiary of:** The Placement Group (Holdings) Plc)
Wellington House, Trust Road, Waltham Cross, Hertfordshire EN8 7HF
**Tel:** 0845-130-6130 **Fax:** 08451309130
**Web:** www.justphysio.co.uk
**Reg No:** 4688077 **Estd:** 2002 Private Limited Company
**Line of Business:** Other human health activities
**Issued Capital:** £75,000
**Directors:** E C Simpson, S Porter
**US SIC:** 8091 **UK SIC:** 95200
**Auditors:** Raffingers Stuart

| | 31-12-13 | 31-12-12 | 31-12-11 |
|---|---|---|---|
| TO | 25,508,547 | 20,839,503 | 12,781,726 |
| P/L | 612,073 | 856,423 | 498,455 |
| NW | 853,134 | 570,322 | 766,808 |
| WC | (1,622,012) | 61,594 | 628,789 |
| Emp. | 47 | 46 | 42 |

DUNS 23-783-9571
## Places for People Group Ltd
4 The Pavilions, Ashton-On-Ribble, Preston, Lancashire PR2 2YB
**Tel:** 01772897200
**Web:** www.placesforpeople.co.uk
**Reg No:** 3777037 **Estd:** 1999 Private Company Limited By Guarantee
**Line of Business:** Housing associations societies trusts & co-operatives
**Directors:** D Cowans, J L Seet, Dr C L Garner, J S Lloyd, D J Shaw, Miss M V Parsons, N P Hopkins, C R Phillips
**Co. Secretary:** Christopher Martin
**Responsibilities**
**Senior:** Steven Binks *(Manager)*, Kieran Keane *(Director)*, Ehsan Mani *(Director)*, Garry Watson *(Manager)*
**Branches:** Places For People Group Ltd, Jack Harrison Court, Margaret Street, Hull, North Humberside HU3 1SH
**US SIC:** 8321 **UK SIC:** 96111
**Auditors:** KPMG LLP
**Bankers:** The Co-Operative Bank Plc (08-90-15)

| | 31-03-14 | 31-03-13 | 31-03-12 |
|---|---|---|---|
| TO | 485,416,000 | 380,086,000 | 369,457,000 |
| P/L | 28,228,000 | 17,071,000 | 17,390,000 |
| NW | 246,017,000 | 211,912,000 | 261,138,000 |
| WC | 104,123,000 | (102,097,000) | 162,045,000 |
| Emp. | 4,786 | 2,855 | 2,430 |

DUNS 23-209-0373
## Places for People Individual Support Ltd
18 Craven Drive, South Rings Business Park, Bamber Bridge, Preston, Lancashire PR5 6BZ
**Tel:** 01772666000 **Fax:** 01772666201
**Web:** www.placesforpeople.co.uk
**Reg No:** 0020014IP **Estd:** 2013 Friendly Society
**Line of Business:** Housing associations societies trusts & co-operatives
**Director:** D Cowans
**Branches:** Places For People Individual Support Limited, Noel Street, Nottingham, Nottinghamshire NG7 6AJ
**US SIC:** 8321 **UK SIC:** 96111

**Auditors:** KPMG LLP
**Bankers:** The Co-Operative Bank Plc (08-90-15)

| | 31-03-12 | 31-03-11 | 31-03-10 |
|---|---|---|---|
| TO | 44,973,000 | 45,275,000 | 40,689,000 |
| P/L | 6,025,000 | 5,167,000 | 5,349,000 |
| NW | 119,284,000 | 110,835,000 | 107,001,000 |
| WC | (2,126,000) | (2,948,000) | (1,738,000) |
| Emp. | 502 | 463 | 421 |

DUNS 29-665-0286
## Places for People Landscapes Ltd
**(Subsidiary of:** Places for People Group Ltd)
Westwood Nurseries, Pippin Street, Chorley, Lancashire PR6 8ND
**Tel:** 01772336647
**Web:** www.placesforpeople.co.uk
**Reg No:** 1991227 **VAT No:** 401269781
**Estd:** 1986 Private Limited Company
**Line of Business:** Forestry and logging related service activities
**Trading Style:** Places for People Landscapes Ltd
**Issued Capital:** £305,467
**Directors:** S Soin, D Cowans
**Co. Secretary:** Christopher Martin
**Responsibilities**
**Senior:** Joanne Tonge *(Administration Officer)*
**Health & Safety:** Pamela Fawcett *(Health & Safety Officer)*
**Branches:** Places For People Landscapes Ltd, 157 North Wing, Bradford, West Yorkshire BD3 0EL
**US SIC:** 0851 **UK SIC:** 02000
**Auditors:** KPMG LLP
**Bankers:** The Co-Operative Bank Plc (08-90-15)

| | 31-03-14 | 31-03-13 | 31-03-12 |
|---|---|---|---|
| TO | 3,077,000 | 2,875,000 | 3,172,000 |
| P/L | 172,000 | 2,000 | 109,000 |
| NW | 1,229,000 | 1,098,000 | 1,098,000 |
| WC | 857,000 | 905,000 | 910,000 |
| Emp. | 73 | 77 | 73 |

DUNS 21-920-3214
## Places for People Leisure Ltd
305 Gray's Inn Road, London WC1X 8QR
**Reg No:** 8363432 **Estd:** 2013 Private Company Limited By Guarantee
**Line of Business:** Operation of sports arenas and stadiums
**Directors:** D Cowans, C P Martin, C R Phillips
**Co. Secretary:** Christopher Martin
**US SIC:** 7941 **UK SIC:** 97911
**Bankers:** Lloyds TSB Bank plc (30-00-02)

| | 31-03-14 |
|---|---|
| TO | 80,479,000 |
| P/L | 549,000 |
| NW | 313,000 |
| WC | (3,946,000) |
| Emp. | 1,094 |

DUNS 50-434-3724
## Places for People Scotland - Care & Support Ltd
11 Harewood Road, Edinburgh, Midlothian EH16 4NT
**Tel:** 01316594702
**Web:** www.placesforpeople.co.uk
**Reg No:** 0120135SC **Estd:** 1989 Private Limited Company
**Line of Business:** Social work activities without accommodation
**Directors:** I M Stevenson, R C Lyall, Ms J Brown, Ms J V Scott, Ms E Haddow, S K Loh, Ms V E Freir, Ms L J Warren
**Co. Secretary:** Ms Rhona Murray
**Responsibilities**
**Senior:** Glenda Watt *(Director)*
**Branches:** Places For People Scotland - Care & Support Ltd, 51 Craigmount Brae, Edinburgh, Midlothian EH12 8XE
**US SIC:** 8321 **UK SIC:** 96111
**Bankers:** Bank Of Scotland (80-02-24)

| | 31-03-14 | 31-03-13 | 31-03-12 |
|---|---|---|---|
| TO | 6,557,000 | 4,683,000 | 4,386,000 |
| P/L | 1,462,000 | 490,000 | 235,000 |
| NW | 4,687,000 | 3,225,000 | 2,735,000 |
| WC | 3,320,000 | 3,167,000 | 2,676,000 |
| Emp. | 165 | 131 | 132 |

DUNS 64-108-7697
## The Plan Group Ltd
854 Orion House, Brighton Road, Purley, Surrey CR8 2BH
**Tel:** 08700660026
**Web:** www.planinsurance.co.uk
**Reg No:** 4108942 **Estd:** 2000 Private Limited Company
**Line of Business:** Non-life insurance
**Trading Style:** Plan Insurance
**Issued Capital:** £100
**Directors:** N D Beresford, P Georgiades, R Georgiades, N Cole, D Dove, G Georgiades, S Georgiades
**Co. Secretary:** Mrs Gail Georgiades
**US SIC:** 6399, 6411
**UK SIC:** 82001, 83200

**Auditors:** Haines Watts

| | 31-10-13 | 31-10-12 | 31-10-11 |
|---|---|---|---|
| TA | 3,873,680 | 3,240,426 | 2,691,418 |
| NW | 1,906,489 | 1,172,053 | 595,544 |
| WC | 1,790,848 | 1,076,028 | 526,370 |

DUNS 22-730-9507
## Plan International (U K)
5-7 Cranwood Street, London EC1V 9LH
**Tel:** 02074829777 **Fax:** 02072539989
**Web:** www.plan-uk.org
**Reg No:** 1364201 **Estd:** 1978 Private Company Limited By Guarantee
**Line of Business:** Charities and charitable organisations
**Directors:** Mrs A J Sector, Ms J H Pareskeva, L J Ward, T C Hoegh, Ms J French, Mrs H M Burgess, R G Laing, Mrs C F Imbert
**Co. Secretary:** Ms Kristen Morgan
**Responsibilities**
**Senior:** Peter Drissell *(Manager)*, Javaid Khan *(Director)*, Spencer Mchugh *(Director)*, Surina Narula *(Board Member)*, Omolara Oyesanya *(Director)*, Andrew Rogerson *(Director)*
**HR:** Angela Beerman *(Human Resources Director)*
**Health & Safety:** Angela Beerman *(Human Resources Director)*
**Purchasing:** Rino Sudibyo *(Procurement And Logistics Spec)*
**US SIC:** 8699 **UK SIC:** 96902
**Auditors:** PricewaterhouseCoopers LLP
**Bankers:** National Westminster Bank Plc (56-00-27)

| | 30-06-14 | 30-06-13 | 30-06-12 |
|---|---|---|---|
| TO | 63,170,000 | 52,949,000 | 54,248,000 |
| P/L | (309,000) | (2,306,000) | (1,304,000) |
| NW | 9,410,000 | 9,719,000 | 12,025,000 |
| WC | 7,695,000 | 8,620,000 | 10,125,000 |
| Emp. | 163 | 172 | 170 |

DUNS 77-587-9851
## Plan Ltd
**(Subsidiary of:** Plan International (U K))
Dukes Court Block A, Woking, Surrey GU21 5BH
**Tel:** 01483755155 **Fax:** 01483-756505
**Web:** www.plan-international.org
**Reg No:** 3001663 **Estd:** 1994 Private Limited Company
**Line of Business:** Other service activities not elsewhere classified
**Trading Style:** Plan International
**Issued Capital:** £1
**Directors:** N C Chapman, Ms A Firth, Ms P Innes
**Co. Secretary:** Miss Tara Camm
**Responsibilities**
**Senior:** Tjipke Bergsma *(Deputy CEO)*
**Marketing:** Jorn Johansen *(Director of Global Communicati)*
**IT:** Mark Banbury *(Chief Information Officer)*, Jaime Bowden *(Network, Security Manager)*
**US SIC:** 8999, 6732
**UK SIC:** 83954, 83100
**Auditors:** PricewaterhouseCoopers

| | 30-06-14 | 30-06-13 | 30-06-12 |
|---|---|---|---|
| TO | 26,797,000 | 28,317,000 | 21,086,000 |
| P/L | (462,000) | 977,000 | 519,000 |
| NW | (4,641,000) | (4,514,000) | 923,000 |
| WC | (6,875,000) | (5,634,000) | (4,607,000) |
| Emp. | 196 | 173 | 138 |

DUNS 50-485-5859
## Plan-Net Plc
Hamilton House, 1 Temple Avenue, London EC4Y 0HA
**Tel:** 020-7353-4313
**Web:** www.plan-net.co.uk
**Reg No:** 2459337 **Estd:** 1990 Public Limited Company
**Line of Business:** Computer consumables suppliers
**Issued Capital:** £50,000
**Directors:** A N Polley, Mrs D Caputo, P J Canavan, Mrs K Cave, R A Forkan
**Co. Secretary:** Jeremy Cave
**Responsibilities**
**Finance:** David McVittie *(Head of Accounts)*
**Sales:** Darren Fletcher *(Account Manager)*
**HR:** Catherine Amaro *(Human Resources Manager)*
**Health & Safety:** Catherine Amaro *(Human Resources Manager)*
**US SIC:** 7379 **UK SIC:** 83940
**Auditors:** Janelle Lankester

| | 31-12-13 | 31-12-12 | 31-12-11 |
|---|---|---|---|
| TO | 10,972,862 | 10,820,134 | 10,027,542 |
| P/L | 681,287 | 435,752 | 408,260 |
| NW | 1,556,748 | 1,239,770 | 1,165,989 |
| WC | 1,443,909 | 1,099,645 | 1,043,359 |
| Emp. | 162 | 149 | 149 |

DUNS 22-004-8578 **Imp-Exp**
## Pland Stainless Ltd
**(Subsidiary of:** Pland Group Holdings Ltd)
Ring Road, Lower Wortley, Lower Wortley, Leeds, West Yorkshire LS12 6AA
**Tel:** 01132-634184 **Fax:** 01132-310560
**Web:** www.plandstainless.co.uk
**Reg No:** 4008116 **Estd:** 2000 Private Limited Company
**Line of Business:** Steel fabricators
**Export Sales:** £189,165
**Trading Style:** Associated Metal
**Issued Capital:** £100,000
**Directors:** I Hodgson, S Duree
**Co. Secretary:** Ian Hodgson
**US SIC:** 3325, 3499
**UK SIC:** 31110, 31694
**Auditors:** Wheawill & Sudworth
**Bankers:** HSBC Bank plc (40-25-10)

| | 31-07-13 | 31-07-12 | 31-07-11 |
|---|---|---|---|
| TO | 3,637,781 | 4,466,927 | 4,444,360 |
| P/L | 113,622 | 294,251 | 316,450 |
| NW | 3,318,585 | 3,222,304 | 2,987,547 |
| WC | 3,208,482 | 3,071,443 | 2,872,183 |
| Emp. | 57 | 61 | 63 |

DUNS 21-001-3918 **Imp**
## Plandent Ltd
Unit 6 Argyle Way Trading Estate, Stevenage, Hertfordshire SG1 2AF
**Tel:** 08000279599 **Fax:** 01438 750901
**Web:** www.plandent.co.uk
**Reg No:** 0443223 **VAT No:** 421412113
**Estd:** 1829 Private Limited Company
**Line of Business:** Other wholesale
**Export Sales:** £803,000
**Trading Style:** Claudius Ash
**Issued Capital:** £1,710,102
**Principals:** K H Kyostila *(President)*, T O Lokki, A K Pitkanen, R K Schmidt, J G Stockley, V B Makela
**Co. Secretary:** Roland Schmidt
**Branches:** Plandent Ltd, Edgbaston House, 3 Duchess Place, Birmingham, West Midlands B16 8NH
**US SIC:** 5199, 5963, 8999
**UK SIC:** 61900, 65600, 83954
**Auditors:** Chantrey Vellacott DFK LLP
**Bankers:** Bank Of Scotland (80-20-00)

| | 31-01-14 | 31-01-13 | 30-01-12 |
|---|---|---|---|
| TO | 11,818,000 | 8,696,000 | 14,615,000 |
| P/L | (2,216,000) | (2,139,000) | (63,000) |
| NW | (6,290,000) | (4,074,000) | (1,935,000) |
| WC | (1,697,000) | 688,000 | 2,766,000 |
| Emp. | 81 | 81 | 87 |

DUNS 21-733-1381
## Plane Handling Ltd
**(Subsidiary of:** Government of Dubai)
Units 1 & 2, Staines, Middlesex TW19 7LN
**Tel:** 02088932279
**Web:** www.dnata.co.uk
**Reg No:** 7680474 **Estd:** 2011 Private Limited Company
**Line of Business:** Cargo handling
**Trading Style:** Dnata
**Issued Capital:** £1
**Directors:** R S Angus, R S Marino
**Responsibilities**
**Senior:** Alex Doisneau *(General Manager - Cargo)*, Stacey Shortall *(General Manager - UK Regions &)*, Steve Szalay *(General Manager - Ground Servi)*
**Finance:** Nick Hewitt *(Financial Controller)*, Jason Slade *(Account Handler - Ground)*, Lisa Utley *(Accounts Manager - Cargo)*
**Sales:** Mohammed Akhlaq *(Business Development Director)*, Colin Blush *(Cargo Business Manager)*, Gary Greenwood *(Senior Commercial Manager)*
**Admin:** Sarag Varndell *(Personal Assistant to CEO)*
**HR:** Len Wells *(HR Director)*
**Fleet:** Colin Blush *(Cargo Business Manager)*, Alex Doisneau *(General Manager - Cargo)*
**US SIC:** 4712 **UK SIC:** 77002

| | 31-03-14 | 31-03-13 | 31-03-12 |
|---|---|---|---|
| TA | 1 | 1 | 1,000 |
| NW | 1 | 1 | 1,000 |

DUNS 21-733-4937
## Planer Products Ltd
**(Subsidiary of:** Planer Plc)
110 Windmill Road, Sunbury-On-Thames, Middlesex TW16 7HD
**Fax:** 01932-781151
**Web:** www.planer.com
**Reg No:** 1116458 **Estd:** 1973 Private Limited Company
**Line of Business:** Manufacture of other special purpose machinery not elsewhere classified
**Trading Style:** Planer Plc
**Issued Capital:** £1,000
**Principals:** V G Planer *(Chairman)*, P Lakra, Dr G Planer
**Co. Secretary:** Douglas Burr

**US SIC:** 3559 **UK SIC:** 32863

| | 31-05-14 | 31-05-13 | 31-05-12 |
|---|---|---|---|
| TA | 1,000 | 1,000 | 1,000 |
| NW | 1,000 | 1,000 | 1,000 |

DUNS 21-599-2919 Imp

## Planet Hollywood

60 Haymarket, London SW1Y 4QX
**Tel:** 02070248461
**Web:** www.planethollywoodlondon.com
**Estd:** 2011 Proprietorship
**Line of Business:** Restaurants
**Proprietor:** P Croding
**Responsibilities**
**Senior:** Robert Darl *(Owner)*
**US SIC:** 5812 **UK SIC:** 66110
**Employees:** 120

DUNS 21-607-1103

## Planet Ice

Worting Road Basingstoke Ice Rink, West Ham Leisure Park, Basingstoke, Hampshire RG22 6PE
**Tel:** 01256355266
**Web:** www.planet-ice.co.uk
**Estd:** 1996
**Line of Business:** Other sporting activities not elsewhere classified
**Proprietor:** R Boprey
**Responsibilities**
**Senior:** Rebecca Chambers *(Manager)*
**US SIC:** 7999 **UK SIC:** 97913
**Employees:** 72

DUNS 23-834-4605

## Planet Organic Ltd

42 Westbourne Grove, London W2 5SH
**Tel:** 02072217171 **Fax:** 02077279408
**Web:** www.planetorganic.com
**Reg No:** 3826282 **VAT No:** 740238652
**Estd:** 1999 Private Limited Company
**Line of Business:** Representative office
**Issued Capital:** £2,562,968
**Principals:** Ms R J Elliott *(Managing)*, A K Smith, P J Marsh, D E Krantz, C C Fenn, B K Elliott
**Co. Secretary:** Eric Adatia
**Responsibilities**
**HR:** Elizabeth Cowper *(Human Resources Manager)*
**Health & Safety:** Guy Curlewis *(Store Manager)*
**Facilities:** Guy Curlewis *(Store Manager)*
**Branches:** Planet Organic Ltd, 22 Torrington Place, London WC1E 7HP
**US SIC:** 5431, 5423, 5499
**UK SIC:** 64100
**Auditors:** Smith & Williamson
**Bankers:** Lloyds TSB Bank plc (30-90-59)

| | 31-08-14 | 31-08-13 | 31-08-12 |
|---|---|---|---|
| TO | 20,781,931 | 17,239,058 | 14,883,989 |
| P/L | 389,048 | 438,967 | (178,167) |
| NW | 1,493,417 | 1,012,065 | (166,431) |
| WC | 262,244 | 120,949 | (1,302,401) |
| Emp. | 235 | 192 | 203 |

DUNS 21-925-1522

## Planet Platforms (Holdings) Ltd

Brunel Road, Wakefield 41 Industrial Estate, Wakefield, West Yorkshire WF2 0XG
**Tel:** 01924824470 **Fax:** 01924267090
**Web:** www.planetplatform.co.uk
**Reg No:** 6114976 **Estd:** 2007 Private Limited Company
**Line of Business:** Holding companies management activities
**Issued Capital:** £45,000
**Directors:** P Pemberton, T J Pemberton
**Co. Secretary:** Gregory Armitage
**US SIC:** 6711 **UK SIC:** 83962
**Bankers:** Barclays Bank Plc (20-04-50)

| | 31-03-14 | 31-03-13 | 31-03-12 |
|---|---|---|---|
| TO | 3,533,674 | 3,792,285 | 5,357,963 |
| P/L | 181,661 | 235,219 | 357,482 |
| NW | 2,159,435 | 1,960,025 | 1,780,290 |
| WC | 1,148,894 | 1,004,743 | 907,976 |

DUNS 21-112-5412 Imp

## Planet X Ltd

6 Ignite, Magna Way, Rotherham, South Yorkshire S60 1FD
**Tel:** 01709386666 **Fax:** 01709252382
**Web:** www.planet-x-bikes.com
**Reg No:** 6535324 **Estd:** 2008 Private Limited Company
**Line of Business:** Manufacture of bicycles
**Export Sales:** £3,350,119
**Issued Capital:** £312
**Directors:** C Potter, D A Loughran
**Responsibilities**
**Senior:** David Hanney *(Chief Executive Officer)*, Jules Swindells *(Manager)*
**Sales:** Ian Cammish *(Sales Executive)*
**Operations:** Jules Swindells *(Manager)*
**US SIC:** 3751 **UK SIC:** 36330

**Bankers:** Leopold Joseph And Sons Ltd (40-52-26)

| | 31-03-13 | 31-03-12 | 31-03-11 |
|---|---|---|---|
| TO | 12,818,118 | N/A | N/A |
| P/L | 1,733,273 | N/A | N/A |
| NW | 2,983,371 | 1,505,925 | 624,323 |
| WC | 2,689,062 | 1,190,063 | 403,663 |
| Emp. | 50 | N/A | N/A |

DUNS 53-650-8351

## Planetridge Ltd

**(Subsidiary of:** Flatoffice Ltd)
North House, North Street, Glenrothes, Fife KY7 5NA
**Tel:** 01382322515
**Web:** www.queenshotel-dundee.com
**Reg No:** 0180052SC **Estd:** 1997 Private Limited Company
**Line of Business:** Hotels
**Issued Capital:** £240,000
**Director:** A G Sneddon
**Co. Secretary:** Findlay & Company
**US SIC:** 7011 **UK SIC:** 66500
**Auditors:** Findlay & Co

| | 30-09-14 | 30-09-13 | 30-09-12 |
|---|---|---|---|
| TA | 1,900,761 | 1,916,070 | 1,911,520 |
| NW | 679,191 | 591,438 | 453,873 |
| WC | 714,855 | 186,999 | 114,936 |

DUNS 21-391-8365

## The Planning Inspectorate

Temple Quay House, 2 The Square, Temple Quay, Bristol, Avon BS1 6PN
**Web:** www.planningportal.gov.uk
**Estd:** 2011
**Line of Business:** Central government
**Proprietor:** M Pitt
**Responsibilities**
**Senior:** Laurence Wood *(Estates Team Manager)*
**Finance:** Shelley Bryant *(Financial Director)*
**Marketing:** Aled Herbert *(Publishing & Communications Ma)*
**Sales:** Stuart Mockford *(Corporate Development Manager)*
**Admin:** Baljeet Bennett *(Administration Manager)*
**IT:** Phil Theobald *(Technical Manager)*
**Health & Safety:** Laurence Wood *(Estates Team Manager)*
**Facilities:** Laurence Wood *(Estates Team Manager)*
**Operations:** Ben Linscott *(Director, Planning)*
**Purchasing:** Julie Oakes *(Procurement Officer)*
**US SIC:** 9121 **UK SIC:** 91110
**Employees:** 800

DUNS 22-113-4054 Imp

## Plant & Consumable Services Ltd

**(Subsidiary of:** Scap Holdings Ltd)
Unit 9b Pond End Willow Farm Business, Park, Derby, Derbyshire DE74 2UB
**Fax:** 01332-813301
**Web:** www.pax.uk.com
**Reg No:** 4132575 **Estd:** 1900 Private Limited Company
**Line of Business:** Engineers merchants
**Issued Capital:** £126,250
**Director:** C Eccleshall
**Co. Secretary:** Mark Evans
**Responsibilities**
**Senior:** Darren Bramhill *(Manager)*, David Homes *(Manager)*, John Pinkney *(Manager)*
**US SIC:** 2844, 7394
**UK SIC:** 25820, 84000
**Auditors:** Smith Cooper LLP
**Bankers:** HSBC Bank plc (40-19-15)

| | 31-03-14 | 31-03-13 | 31-03-12 |
|---|---|---|---|
| TO | 25,527,599 | 24,563,873 | 20,132,736 |
| P/L | 2,254,059 | 1,970,698 | 1,532,131 |
| NW | 7,884,072 | 6,648,154 | 5,533,617 |
| WC | 7,950,906 | 1,231,175 | 865,502 |
| Emp. | 82 | 87 | 102 |

DUNS 21-811-9741 Imp-Exp

## Plant & Safety Inspection Services Ltd

**(Subsidiary of:** Lloyds British Group Ltd)
Atlas House, 4-6 Belwell Lane, Four Oaks, Sutton Coldfield, West Midlands B74 4AB
**Fax:** 08701-975599
**Web:** www.lloydsbritishtesting.com
**Reg No:** 0065554 **VAT No:** 555220071
**Estd:** 1900 Private Limited Company
**Line of Business:** Other service activities not elsewhere classified
**Export Markets:** Middle East, E U
**Issued Capital:** £310,000
**Director:** R J Rabone
**Co. Secretary:** Ian White
**Branches:** Plant & Safety Inspection Services Ltd, Site Department Dock Street, Middlesbrough, Cleveland TS2 1AD
**US SIC:** 8999 **UK SIC:** 83954

**Bankers:** Merita Bank Ltd (40-50-43)

| | 31-12-13 | 31-12-12 | 31-12-11 |
|---|---|---|---|
| TA | 310,000 | 310,000 | 310,000 |
| NW | 310,000 | 310,000 | 310,000 |

DUNS 76-851-1008

## Plant & Site Services Ltd

**(Subsidiary of:** Ashtead Group Plc)
Beech Industrial Estate, St Albans, Hertfordshire AL3 6PQ
**Tel:** 01727-898678 **Fax:** 01727898679
**Web:** www.aplant.com
**Reg No:** 2606655 **VAT No:** 600329978
**Estd:** 1991 Private Limited Company
**Line of Business:** Renting of other machinery and equipment not elsewhere classified
**Issued Capital:** £6,450
**Directors:** M R Pratt, S S Dhaiwal, R D Thomas
**Co. Secretary:** Eric Watkins
**Responsibilities**
**Senior:** Peter Hammill *(Manager)*, Robert Hannibal *(Branch Manager)*, Daniela Moloney *(Manager)*, Dave Sperring *(Site Manager)*
**US SIC:** 7394 **UK SIC:** 84000
**Auditors:** Mercer & Hole
**Bankers:** Barclays Bank Plc (20-74-09)

| | 30-09-13 | 30-09-12 | 30-09-11 |
|---|---|---|---|
| TO | 6,417,000 | 8,479,000 | 7,941,643 |
| P/L | 524,000 | 392,000 | 915,592 |
| NW | 5,093,000 | 4,660,000 | 4,277,063 |
| WC | N/A | 1,821,000 | 1,490,552 |
| Emp. | 48 | 66 | 61 |

DUNS 21-909-2277

## Plant Installations (Coventry) Ltd

Crondal Road Exhall, Coventry, West Midlands CV7 9NH
**Tel:** 024-7636-0421
**Web:** www.plantinstallations.co.uk
**Reg No:** 0966319 **VAT No:** 272801368
**Estd:** 1969 Private Limited Company
**Line of Business:** Removals and storage activities (domestic)
**Trading Style:** P I C
**Issued Capital:** £46
**Principals:** C N Cullinane *(Managing)*, Mrs C A Cullinane, S C Cullinane
**Co. Secretary:** Mark Cullinane
**Responsibilities**
**Senior:** Brian Woodruffe *(Manager)*
**US SIC:** 4214 **UK SIC:** 72300
**Auditors:** Chaplin Hall & Co
**Bankers:** Barclays Bank Plc (20-23-55)

| | 30-11-13 | 30-11-12 | 30-11-11 |
|---|---|---|---|
| TA | 1,702,121 | 2,043,560 | 1,785,758 |
| NW | 824,574 | 1,538,391 | 1,433,720 |
| WC | 941,537 | 1,320,377 | 1,174,763 |

DUNS 23-771-4717

## Plant Raisers 2005 Ltd

Thorpe Road, Howden, Goole, North Humberside DN14 7PB
**Tel:** 01430-432200
**Web:** www.plantraisers.co.uk
**Reg No:** 3764847 **Estd:** 1999 Private Limited Company
**Line of Business:** Growing of vegetables, horticultural specialities and nursery products
**Issued Capital:** £43,500
**Directors:** R W Roberts, C L Van Dijk
**Co. Secretary:** Michael Kendall
**Responsibilities**
**Senior:** Nick Deham *(Manager)*
**US SIC:** 0161 **UK SIC:** 01001

| | 30-09-13 | 30-09-12 | 30-09-11 |
|---|---|---|---|
| TA | 1,388,818 | 1,347,374 | 1,318,223 |
| NW | 740,868 | 530,514 | 405,375 |
| WC | 12,612 | (237,721) | N/A |

DUNS 21-880-1977

## Plant Sciences

Downing Street, Cambridge, Cambridgeshire CB2 3EA
**Web:** www.plantsci.cam.ac.uk
**Estd:** 2012
**Line of Business:** Research and laboratory based activities
**Responsibilities**
**Senior:** Catherine Butler *(Department Administrator)*
**US SIC:** 7391 **UK SIC:** 94000
**Employees:** 120

DUNS 34-708-4068

## Plantec Holdings Ltd

Sumner House St Thomas's Road, Chorley, Lancashire PR7 1HP
**Tel:** 08445888066
**Web:** www.plantecholdings.co.uk
**Reg No:** 5512544 **Estd:** 2005 Private Limited Company
**Line of Business:** Management activities of holding companies
**Issued Capital:** £187,500
**Director:** R M Holcroft
**Co. Secretary:** Michael Astley
**Branches:** Plantec Holdings Ltd, Rear Of 161-165, Bispham Road, Southport, Merseyside PR9 7BL
**US SIC:** 6711 **UK SIC:** 83962
**Bankers:** Yorkshire Bank Plc (05-05-55)

| | 31-03-13 | 31-03-12 | 31-03-11 |
|---|---|---|---|
| TO | 6,651,702 | 8,243,069 | 7,875,552 |
| P/L | (702,735) | 620,572 | (653,618) |
| NW | 980,617 | 1,228,150 | 1,065,093 |
| WC | 38,281 | 32,565 | 113,296 |
| Emp. | 103 | 118 | 133 |

DUNS 77-856-1845

## Planters Garden Centre Ltd

Woodland Farm, Tamworth, Staffordshire B78 2EY
**Tel:** 01827251511 **Fax:** 01827-262440
**Web:** www.plantersgc.com
**Reg No:** 3034099 **VAT No:** 486692291
**Estd:** 1995 Private Limited Company
**Line of Business:** Garden centres
**Trading Style:** Garden King
**Issued Capital:** £1,000
**Managing Director:** G G Ingram
**Co. Secretary:** Ms Christine Ingram
**Branches:** Planters Garden Centre Ltd, 31 Bell Street, Wigston, Leicestershire LE18 1AD
**US SIC:** 5999 **UK SIC:** 65600
**Auditors:** Philip Barnes & Co Ltd

| | 31-12-13 | 31-12-12 | 31-12-11 |
|---|---|---|---|
| TO | 8,322,317 | 7,850,638 | 8,012,623 |
| P/L | 362,541 | 429,342 | 445,232 |
| NW | 2,271,343 | 2,010,902 | 1,699,036 |
| WC | 720,507 | 531,700 | 583,381 |
| Emp. | 184 | 183 | 190 |

DUNS 50-346-0495 Imp

## Plantiflor Ltd

Enterprise Way, Spalding, Lincolnshire PE11 3YR
**Tel:** 01775-715450
**Web:** www.bakker.co.uk
**Reg No:** 2366169 **Estd:** 1989 Private Limited Company
**Line of Business:** Retail sale via mail order house
**Trading Style:** Bakker-Holland
**Issued Capital:** £10,000
**Directors:** A P Nind, M L Van Diemen
**Co. Secretary:** Michael Van Diemen
**Responsibilities**
**Senior:** Denise Cooper *(Warehouse Manager)*
**Marketing:** David Chisnall *(Sales & Marketing Manager)*
**Sales:** David Chisnall *(Sales & Marketing Manager)*
**Facilities:** Denise Cooper *(Warehouse Manager)*
**Purchasing:** David Chisnall *(Sales & Marketing Manager)*
**Branches:** Plantiflor Ltd, Po Box 222, Spalding, Lincolnshire PE12 6EN
**US SIC:** 5961, 7399
**UK SIC:** 65600, 83954
**Auditors:** Moore Thompson
**Bankers:** Barclays Bank Plc (20-80-78)

| | 31-12-13 | 31-12-12 | 31-12-11 |
|---|---|---|---|
| TA | 1,379,444 | 868,514 | 957,072 |
| NW | 10,000 | 10,000 | 10,000 |
| WC | (82,266) | (30,543) | (34,801) |

DUNS 29-158-2823 Imp-Exp

## Plantronics Ltd

**(Subsidiary of:** Plantronics International Ltd)
Binknoll Lane Interface Business Park, Swindon, Wiltshire SN4 8QQ
**Tel:** 0800410014 **Fax:** 01793-848853
**Web:** www.plantronics.com
**Reg No:** 1773891 **Estd:** 1984 Private Limited Company
**Line of Business:** Other business activities not elsewhere classified
**Issued Capital:** £100
**Directors:** G K Tyrrell, R R Frankfort, M Bezemer, Ms P J Strayer, R R Pickard
**Co. Secretary:** Marten Bezemer
**Responsibilities**
**Marketing:** Penny Hoile *(Digital Marketing Manager)*, Clare Tibbitts *(Head of Marketing and Inside S)*
**Sales:** Clare Tibbitts *(Head of Marketing and Inside S)*
**Branches:** Plantronics Ltd, The Meads Business Centre, Ashworth Rd, Swindon, Wiltshire SN5 7YJ
**US SIC:** 7399, 3661
**UK SIC:** 83954, 34410
**Auditors:** PricewaterhouseCoopers LLP
**Bankers:** HSBC Bank plc (40-43-34)

| | 29-03-14 | 30-03-13 | 31-03-12 |
|---|---|---|---|
| TO | 17,634,653 | 15,397,887 | 14,575,630 |
| P/L | 693,722 | 539,192 | 1,268,974 |
| NW | 6,352,934 | 5,809,540 | 5,306,869 |
| WC | 2,610,666 | 2,080,793 | 1,796,680 |
| Emp. | 97 | 100 | 93 |

DUNS 22-851-7447
## Plantscene Ltd
(**Subsidiary of:** The Barton Grange Group Ltd)
746-768 Garstang Road, Barton, Preston, Lancashire PR3 5AA
**Tel:** 01772862551
**Web:** www.bartongrangehotel.co.uk
**Reg No:** 1585852 **Estd:** 1958 Private Limited Company
**Line of Business:** Hotels
**Trading Style:** Barton Grange Garden Centre (Woodford)
**Issued Capital:** £100
**Director:** E G Topping
**Co. Secretary:** Robert Dixon
**Responsibilities**
**Senior:** Eloic Montagnier *(General Manager)*, Stephen Panter *(General Manager)*, Daniel Rich *(General Manager)*
**US SIC:** 7011 **UK SIC:** 66500
**Auditors:** THR
**Bankers:** Barclays Bank Plc (20-69-85)

| | 31-01-14 | 31-01-13 | 31-01-12 |
|---|---|---|---|
| TA | 100 | 100 | 100 |
| NW | 100 | 100 | 100 |

DUNS 21-784-4121
## Plas Coch Holiday Home Park
Llanfair Pg, Llanfair Pg, Llanfairpwllgwyngyll, Gwynedd LL61 6EJ
**Tel:** 01248711920
**Web:** www.plascochholidayhomes.co.uk
**Estd:** 1967 Partnership
**Line of Business:** Holidays (self catering)
**Partners:** S Mcintyre, A Mcintyre
**Responsibilities**
**Senior:** Dean Styger *(Manager)*
**US SIC:** 7021 **UK SIC:** 66500
**Employees:** 60

DUNS 28-891-9137
## Plas Coch Holiday Homes Ltd
Station Road, Talacre, Holywell, Clwyd CH8 9RD
**Tel:** 01524831182
**Web:** www.hill-brothers.co.uk
**Reg No:** 1288058 **Estd:** 1976 Private Limited Company
**Line of Business:** Sale of new motor vehicles
**Trading Style:** New Pines Caravan Holiday Home & Leisure Park, Talacre Beach Caravan & Leisure Park, Tan Rallt Caravan Park, Bryntyg Holiday Home Park
**Issued Capital:** £41,502
**Principals:** J G Mcallister *(Managing)*, E V Mcallister
**Co. Secretary:** Carl Styger
**Branches:** Plas Coch Holiday Homes Ltd, Llanrug, Caernarfon, Gwynedd LL55 4RF
**US SIC:** 5511, 7021
**UK SIC:** 65100, 66500
**Auditors:** Grant Thornton
**Bankers:** Barclays Bank Plc (20-25-76)

| | 31-01-14 | 31-01-13 | 31-01-12 |
|---|---|---|---|
| TO | 9,822,000 | 8,636,000 | 13,040,000 |
| P/L | 1,471,000 | 606,000 | (3,679,000) |
| NW | 21,101,000 | 20,788,000 | 22,273,000 |
| WC | (1,777,000) | (2,266,000) | (4,556,000) |
| Emp. | 72 | 70 | 111 |

DUNS 55-070-5875
## Plas Morfa Residential Home
Mostyn Road, Holywell, Clwyd CH8 7EJ
**Tel:** 01352714500
**Estd:** 1990 Proprietorship
**Line of Business:** Nursing homes
**Proprietor:** Mrs J Mclean
**Responsibilities**
**Senior:** Andrea Dermott *(Proprietor)*, Joan McLean *(Proprietor)*
**US SIC:** 8051 **UK SIC:** 95100
**Employees:** 75

DUNS 42-428-6870
## Plas Talgarth Leisure Club
Talgarth, Pennal, Machynlleth, Powys SY20 9JY
**Tel:** 01654791631
**Web:** www.mcdonalds-resorts.co.uk
**Estd:** 2009 Proprietorship
**Line of Business:** Timeshare operations
**Proprietor:** R Hall
**Responsibilities**
**Senior:** Christopher Ainsworth *(General Manager)*, I Fullard *(General Manager)*, Susan Fullard *(General Manager)*, ROBERT HALL *(Proprietor)*
**US SIC:** 7021 **UK SIC:** 66500
**Employees:** 50

DUNS 50-537-5717
## Plas-Tech Thermoforming Ltd
(**Subsidiary of:** Poly Plastics Ltd)
Heyford Catfoss Industrial Estate, Catfoss Lane, Brandesburton, Driffield, North Humberside YO25 8EJ
**Tel:** 01964-544544
**Web:** www.plas-tech.co.uk
**Reg No:** 2495369 **VAT No:** 500931584
**Estd:** 1990 Private Limited Company
**Line of Business:** Manufacture of plastics in primary forms
**Issued Capital:** £1,000
**Principals:** J R Rial *(Managing)*, J A Jarvis
**Co. Secretary:** Ms Victoria Rial
**Responsibilities**
**Finance:** Betty Topham *(Finance Director)*
**US SIC:** 2821 **UK SIC:** 25140
**Auditors:** Graybrowne
**Bankers:** HSBC Bank plc (40-24-31)

| | 31-12-13 | 31-12-12 | 31-12-11 |
|---|---|---|---|
| TA | 2,735,328 | 2,465,592 | 2,219,755 |
| NW | 1,052,766 | 1,061,274 | 1,180,828 |
| WC | 396,404 | 408,930 | 500,764 |

DUNS 21-207-1000
## Plas Y Bryn E M I Nursing Home
31 Tan Y Bryn Road, Colwyn Bay, Clwyd LL28 4AD
**Tel:** 01492544117
**Web:** www.careathomewales.co.uk
**Estd:** 1989 Partnership
**Line of Business:** Nursing homes
**Partners:** G Roberts, Mrs P Roberts
**Responsibilities**
**Senior:** Ged Fitzpatrick *(Senior IT Executive)*
**Finance:** Daniel Fitzpatrick *(Senior Finance Administrator)*
**IT:** Ged Fitzpatrick *(Senior IT Executive)*
**US SIC:** 8051 **UK SIC:** 95100
**Employees:** 50

DUNS 21-208-4391
## Plas Y Bryn Nursing Home
Thornhill Road, Cwmgwili, Llanelli, Dyfed SA14 6PT
**Tel:** 01269844454
**Web:** www.comfortcarehomes.com
**Estd:** 1989 Partnership
**Line of Business:** Nursing homes
**Partners:** Mrs J Miles, Mrs J Harris
**Responsibilities**
**Senior:** Helen Corcoran *(Manager)*, June Harries *(Director)*, Celia Harries *(Home Manager)*, Julie Hurst *(Manager)*
**Branches:** Plas Y Bryn Nursing Home, Marine Drive, Colwyn Bay, Clwyd LL28 4HS
**US SIC:** 8051, 6732
**UK SIC:** 95100, 83100
**Bankers:** Barclays Bank Plc (20-51-32)
**Employees:** 55

DUNS 21-098-6755
## Plasgeller Care Home Ltd
2 Intermediate Road, Brynmawr, Ebbw Vale, Gwent NP23 4SF
**Tel:** 01495314907 **Fax:** 01495-314905
**Web:** www.carehome.co.uk
**Reg No:** 6427338 **Estd:** 2008 Private Limited Company
**Line of Business:** Social work activities with accommodation
**Trading Style:** Glanbury Care Home, Plasgeller Care Home, Brynwood Care Home
**Issued Capital:** £100
**Directors:** J Shah, S Joshi
**Co. Secretary:** Mrs Jyoti Joshi
**Responsibilities**
**Senior:** Helen Beecham *(Manager)*
**US SIC:** 8321 **UK SIC:** 96111
**Bankers:** The Royal Bank Of Scotland Plc (16-18-18)

| | 31-03-14 | 31-03-13 | 31-03-12 |
|---|---|---|---|
| TA | 1,334,437 | 1,342,175 | 1,328,556 |
| NW | 400,291 | 396,702 | 400,157 |
| WC | (237,571) | (261,439) | (280,660) |

DUNS 39-950-0842
## Plasman (Laminate Products) Ltd
Marquis St Plasman Industrial Centre, Manchester M19 3JH
**Tel:** 01612240101 **Fax:** 0161-224-9961
**Web:** www.plasman.co.uk
**Reg No:** 2256242 **VAT No:** 519726816
**Estd:** 1948 Private Limited Company
**Line of Business:** Flooring materials
**Issued Capital:** £5,544
**Principals:** R S Moss *(Managing)*, R S Sherratt *(Managing)*, H Chipman
**Co. Secretary:** Mrs Anna Balszan
**Responsibilities**
**Senior:** Kenneth Ashdown *(Manager)*
**IT:** Lisa Lynham *(Computer Manager)*
**Purchasing:** John Witkowski *(Purchasing Manager)*
**Branches:** Plasman (Laminate Products) Ltd, Unit 18 Ashbrooke Pk, Leeds, West Yorkshire LS11 5SF
**US SIC:** 5072 **UK SIC:** 61500
**Auditors:** Hurst & Co Accountants LLP
**Bankers:** Lloyds TSB Bank plc (30-95-42)

| | 31-03-14 | 31-03-13 | 31-03-12 |
|---|---|---|---|
| TO | N/A | N/A | 7,363,670 |
| P/L | N/A | N/A | 23,724 |
| NW | 261,721 | 236,449 | 373,501 |
| WC | (820,578) | (775,103) | (651,663) |

DUNS 21-216-5054
## Plasmor Ltd
Womersley Road, Knottingley, West Yorkshire WF11 0DN
**Tel:** 01977673221 **Fax:** 01977-607071
**Web:** www.plasmor.co.uk
**Reg No:** 0642173 **Estd:** 1959 Private Limited Company
**Line of Business:** Manufacture of concrete products for construction purposes
**Trading Style:** Plasmor Ltd
**Issued Capital:** £384,000
**Principals:** J A Slater *(Managing)*, Ms P E Slater, J Swain, J R Marshall, N Marwood
**Co. Secretary:** Noil Marwood
**Responsibilities**
**Senior:** Yasmin Smith *(Manager)*
**Branches:** Plasmor Ltd, Wick Lane, London E3 2TB
**US SIC:** 3271, 3281
**UK SIC:** 24370, 24503
**Auditors:** Garbutt & Elliott Ltd
**Bankers:** Lloyds TSB Bank plc (30-92-68)

| | 31-08-14 | 31-08-13 | 31-08-12 |
|---|---|---|---|
| TO | 58,654,643 | 47,205,318 | 46,302,486 |
| P/L | 4,665,348 | 311,339 | 100,255 |
| NW | 38,178,856 | 34,936,008 | 34,782,915 |
| WC | 18,781,421 | 17,746,990 | 16,568,514 |
| Emp. | 351 | 322 | 326 |

DUNS 76-622-5379
## Plasser Railway Machinery (Great Britain) Ltd
(**Subsidiary of:** Plasser & Theurer Beteiligungs- Und Finanzierungs-)
Manor Road, London W13 0PP
**Tel:** 01892853375
**Web:** www.plasser.co.uk
**Reg No:** 2578474 **Estd:** 1991 Private Limited Company
**Line of Business:** Manufacture of other transport equipment not elsewhere classified
**Issued Capital:** £1,000
**Director:** H Pilgerstorfer
**Co. Secretary:** Ms Anne Yeo
**Responsibilities**
**Senior:** Brenda Ennison *(Human Resources Manager)*, Herbert Pilgerstorser *(Chief Executive Officer)*, Maike Scherer *(Marketing Director)*
**HR:** Brenda Emerson *(Human Resources Manager)*, Brenda Ennison *(Human Resources Manager)*
**US SIC:** 3799 **UK SIC:** 36502
**Bankers:** Lloyds TSB Bank plc (30-98-71)

| | 31-12-13 | 31-12-12 | 31-12-11 |
|---|---|---|---|
| TA | 1,000 | 10,000 | 1,000,000 |
| NW | 1,000 | 10,000 | 1,000,000 |

DUNS 21-035-8032 **Exp**
## Plasser Uk Ltd
(**Subsidiary of:** Plasser & Theurer Beteiligungs- Und Finanzierungs-)
Manor Road, London W13 0PP
**Tel:** 02089913085
**Web:** www.plasser.co.uk
**Reg No:** 0652432 **VAT No:** 538796681
**Estd:** 1960 Private Limited Company
**Line of Business:** General mechanical engineering
**Export Sales:** £1,106,000
**Issued Capital:** £3,000,000
**Principals:** J Theurer *(Chairman)*, H Pilgerstorfer *(Managing)*, A L Yeo
**Co. Secretary:** Ms Anne Yeo
**Responsibilities**
**Marketing:** Angela Lowe *(Marketing Director)*
**IT:** B Isaac *(IT Manager)*
**HR:** Andrea Storey *(Human Resources Manager)*
**Facilities:** Steve Walden *(Mechanical Charge Hand)*
**Operations:** Katja Kusmicz *(Production Manager)*
**Engineering:** Katja Kusmicz *(Production Manager)*, Steve Walden *(Mechanical Charge Hand)*
**US SIC:** 7399, 4712
**UK SIC:** 83954, 77002
**Auditors:** RSM Robson Rhodes
**Bankers:** Lloyds TSB Bank plc (30-98-71)

| | 31-12-13 | 31-12-12 | 31-12-11 |
|---|---|---|---|
| TO | 13,065,000 | 13,904,000 | 12,196,000 |
| P/L | 688,000 | 1,032,000 | 2,885,000 |
| NW | 11,806,000 | 12,635,000 | 11,357,000 |
| WC | 10,922,000 | 10,433,000 | 9,786,000 |
| Emp. | 60 | 55 | 71 |

DUNS 49-388-5396 **Imp**
## Plastech Group Ltd
Queensway Industrial Estate Fullerton, Road, Glenrothes, Fife KY7 5PY
**Tel:** 01592752212 **Fax:** 01592-610315
**Web:** www.plastechgroup.com
**Reg No:** 0162078SC **VAT No:** 774606703
**Estd:** 1995 Private Limited Company
**Line of Business:** Manufacturers of packaging materials
**Issued Capital:** £275,000
**Directors:** Mrs C L Stirling, T Stirling, M Preston
**Responsibilities**
**Marketing:** Joe Stirling *(Sales & Marketing Manager)*
**Sales:** Joe Stirling *(Sales & Marketing Manager)*
**Operations:** Joe Stirling *(Sales & Marketing Manager)*
**Engineering:** Steve Leask *(Engineering Manager)*
**US SIC:** 2654 **UK SIC:** 47280
**Auditors:** Tenon Audit Ltd
**Bankers:** Clydesdale Bank Plc (82-45-05)

| | 31-03-14 | 31-12-12 | 31-03-11 |
|---|---|---|---|
| TA | 2,594,881 | 2,016,130 | 2,166,266 |
| NW | 1,430,605 | 959,524 | 985,435 |
| WC | 1,007,691 | 295,314 | 302,426 |

DUNS 23-569-5140 **Imp**
## Plastek U K Ltd
(**Subsidiary of:** Plastek Industries Inc.)
Crown Farm Way, Forest Town, Mansfield, Nottinghamshire NG19 0FT
**Web:** www.plastekuk.com
**Reg No:** 3567624 **VAT No:** 716398216
**Estd:** 1998 Private Limited Company
**Line of Business:** Plastic injection moulding
**Export Sales:** £7,904,265
**Issued Capital:** £1,675,000
**Directors:** J J Prischak, D J Prischak, D J Prischak
**Co. Secretary:** Michael Dzurik
**Responsibilities**
**IT:** Mark Fewkes *(IT Manager)*
**US SIC:** 3999 **UK SIC:** 49590
**Auditors:** PricewaterhouseCoopers LLP
**Bankers:** National Westminster Bank Plc (60-14-03)

| | 31-12-13 | 31-12-12 | 31-12-11 |
|---|---|---|---|
| TO | 20,671,129 | 18,937,527 | 15,122,489 |
| P/L | 1,536,486 | 2,073,681 | 1,853,618 |
| NW | 12,559,758 | 11,619,249 | 8,199,610 |
| WC | 5,351,797 | 4,423,480 | 3,613,771 |
| Emp. | 116 | 97 | 86 |

DUNS 21-635-4282 **Imp-Exp**
## Plastic Extruders Ltd
Russell Gardens, Wickford, Essex SS11 8DN
**Tel:** 01268571116
**Web:** www.plastex.co.uk
**Reg No:** 0745566 **VAT No:** 250287962
**Estd:** 1962 Private Limited Company
**Line of Business:** Manufacture of other plastic products
**Export Markets:** U S A, Canada, E U, South Africa, Korea, Middle East, Far East
**Trading Style:** Plastex
**Issued Capital:** £666,600
**Principals:** D E O'Sullivan *(Managing)*, P L O'Sullivan *(Sales)*
**Co. Secretary:** Ms Doreen Thomas
**US SIC:** 3079, 2271
**UK SIC:** 48360, 43841
**Auditors:** Clay Ratnage Strevens & Hills
**Bankers:** Barclays Bank Plc (20-04-96)

| | 30-03-14 | 31-03-13 | 05-03-12 |
|---|---|---|---|
| TO | 10,758,481 | 10,195,268 | 12,469,838 |
| P/L | 815,518 | 775,563 | 1,144,301 |
| NW | 6,076,732 | 6,311,798 | 5,860,043 |
| WC | 4,197,947 | 4,052,144 | 3,822,198 |
| Emp. | 79 | 81 | 65 |

DUNS 50-511-8059
## Plastic Formers Management Ltd
Unit 1, Crown Point South Industrial Park, King Street, Manchester M34 6PF
**Tel:** 01613207200 **Fax:** 01613350109
**Web:** www.plasticformers.co.uk
**Reg No:** 2479665 **Estd:** 1990 Private Limited Company
**Line of Business:** Other letting of own property
**Issued Capital:** £300,003
**Principals:** S W Jepson *(Managing)*, D S Jepson, Ms A C Rhodes
**Co. Secretary:** Leslie Cornwell
**US SIC:** 6519 **UK SIC:** 85000
**Auditors:** Madisons

**Bankers:** National Westminster Bank Plc (01-05-31)

| | 30-06-14 | 30-06-13 | 30-06-12 |
|---|---|---|---|
| TO | N/A | N/A | 382,064 |
| P/L | N/A | N/A | 331,291 |
| NW | 3,525,237 | 3,456,759 | 3,372,922 |
| WC | (495,326) | (415,268) | (416,572) |

DUNS 21-580-3024 **Exp**

## Plastic Mouldings Ltd

**(Subsidiary of:** Plastics Industries Ltd)
4 Ailsa Road, Irvine, Ayrshire KA12 8LP
**Tel:** 01294-278091
**Web:** www.plasticmouldings.com
**Reg No:** 0772753 **VAT No:** 428101288
**Estd:** 1963 Private Limited Company
**Line of Business:** Suppliers of plastics and plastic products
**Export Markets:** Scandinavia
**Issued Capital:** £396,570
**Director:** W T Houston
**Co. Secretary:** Mrs Nancy Ballintyne
**Responsibilities**
**Marketing:** Paula Aitken *(Sales & Marketing Manager)*
**Sales:** Paula Aitken *(Sales & Marketing Manager)*
**Health & Safety:** Robert Barclay *(Health & Safety Officer)*
**Facilities:** Les Coulter *(Maintenance Manager)*
**Purchasing:** Ian Spears *(Buyer)*
**Engineering:** Les Coulter *(Maintenance Manager)*, MIchael Mcqueen *(Production Manager)*
**US SIC:** 2821, 3031
**UK SIC:** 25140, 48123
**Auditors:** The Hansen Co
**Bankers:** Clydesdale Bank Plc (82-65-22)

| | 31-12-13 | 31-12-12 | 31-12-11 |
|---|---|---|---|
| TA | 1,076,314 | 1,218,758 | 1,004,078 |
| NW | 349,233 | 403,236 | 344,774 |
| WC | 231,400 | 285,114 | 216,199 |

DUNS 54-429-4945

## Plastic Omnium Automotive Ltd

**(Subsidiary of:** Burelle)
Westminster Industrial Estate, Measham, Swadlincote, Derbyshire DE12 7DS
**Tel:** 01530-273849 **Fax:** 01530-273863
**Web:** www.plasticomnium.com
**Reg No:** 3275572 **VAT No:** 741934819
**Estd:** 1988 Private Limited Company
**Line of Business:** Manufacture of plastics in primary forms
**Export Sales:** £1,298,000
**Trading Style:** Plastic Omnium
**Issued Capital:** £18,000,000
**Directors:** J M Szczerba, P Le Garrec
**Co. Secretary:** Brian O'Sullivan
**Responsibilities**
**Senior:** Mark Cornet *(President & CEO - Americas)*
**Branches:** Plastic Omnium Automotive Ltd, Faraday Avenue, Hams Hall Distribution Park, Birmingham, West Midlands B46 1AL
**US SIC:** 2821 **UK SIC:** 25140
**Auditors:** Mazars LLP
**Bankers:** Societe Generale (23-63-91)

| | 31-12-13 | 31-12-12 | 31-12-11 |
|---|---|---|---|
| TO | 170,989,000 | 130,597,000 | 125,099,000 |
| P/L | 9,606,000 | 3,811,000 | 4,660,000 |
| NW | 15,176,000 | 7,835,000 | 6,400,000 |
| WC | (16,000,000) | (23,596,000) | (7,585,000) |
| Emp. | 462 | 410 | 345 |

DUNS 37-871-7565

## Plastic Plate Ltd

**(Subsidiary of:** Paintbox Group Ltd)
Cherwell Iv, Middleton Close, Banbury, Oxfordshire OX16 4RS
**Tel:** 01295277227
**Web:** www.identisys.co.uk
**Reg No:** 3304854 **Estd:** 1997 Private Limited Company
**Line of Business:** Other manufacturing not elsewhere classified
**Issued Capital:** £37,500
**Director:** J G Sharp
**Co. Secretary:** Philip London
**US SIC:** 3999 **UK SIC:** 49590
**Auditors:** HLB Kidsons
**Employees:** 100

DUNS 23-724-2628 **Imp**

## The Plastic Surgeon Ltd

**(Subsidiary of:** The Plastic Surgeon Holdings Ltd)
Blue Water House, Pottery Road, Bovey Tracey, Newton Abbot, Devon TQ13 9DS
**Tel:** 01626-837770 **Fax:** 08451430000
**Web:** www.plastic-surgeon.co.uk
**Reg No:** 3718897 **VAT No:** 631086755
**Estd:** 1997 Private Limited Company
**Line of Business:** Other construction work involving special trades
**Issued Capital:** £11,317
**Directors:** T S Ross, R D Mouser
**Co. Secretary:** Trevor Harreld
**Responsibilities**
**Marketing:** Cathy Bailey *(Marketing Manager)*
**Admin:** Daniel Snell *(Network Administrator)*
**IT:** Daniel Snell *(Network Administrator)*
**Health & Safety:** Ross Gardner *(IT Manager)*
**US SIC:** 1799, 2599
**UK SIC:** 50000, 46720
**Auditors:** Francis Clark
**Bankers:** Barclays Bank Plc (20-30-47)

| | 31-10-13 | 31-10-12 | 31-10-11 |
|---|---|---|---|
| TA | 1,779,575 | 1,502,125 | 1,294,379 |
| NW | 354,798 | 274,441 | 9,707 |
| WC | 615,486 | 542,279 | 444,686 |

DUNS 73-963-6392

## Plastic Surgery Partners Holdings Ltd

Parkway House, Palatine Road, Manchester M22 4DB
**Tel:** 0800622222
**Web:** www.surgicare.co.uk
**Reg No:** 5214750 **Estd:** 2004 Private Limited Company
**Line of Business:** Medical practice activities
**Issued Capital:** £800
**Director:** P G Gollop
**US SIC:** 8011 **UK SIC:** 95300
**Employees:** 50

DUNS 29-493-1944 **Imp-Exp**

## Plastica Ltd

**(Subsidiary of:** Napier Holdings Ltd)
Perimeter House, Napier Road, St Leonards-On-Sea, East Sussex TN38 9NY
**Tel:** 01424-857857 **Fax:** 01424-857858
**Web:** www.plasticapools.net
**Reg No:** 1856576 **VAT No:** 790749290
**Estd:** 1972 Private Limited Company
**Line of Business:** Construction of water projects
**Export Markets:** European Union (E U); E Europe
**Trading Style:** Plastica Ltd
**Issued Capital:** £25,000
**Principals:** E H Campbell Salmon *(Managing)*, I A Warne, A P Adlington
**Co. Secretary:** Edward Campbell Salmon
**Responsibilities**
**Facilities:** Richard Gay *(Facilities Manager)*
**Operations:** Clare Crouch *(Production Director)*
**Engineering:** Clare Crouch *(Production Director)*
**US SIC:** 1629 **UK SIC:** 50000
**Auditors:** Baker Tilly UK Audit LLP
**Bankers:** National Westminster Bank Plc (60-10-15)

| | 31-12-13 | 31-12-12 | 31-12-11 |
|---|---|---|---|
| TO | 6,151,949 | 6,189,798 | 7,007,697 |
| P/L | 1,640 | 133,390 | 147,696 |
| NW | 3,129,952 | 3,124,630 | 3,033,839 |
| WC | 2,011,769 | 2,526,535 | 2,377,332 |
| Emp. | 72 | 75 | 78 |

DUNS 29-495-4631 **Imp-Exp**

## Plastico Ltd

**(Subsidiary of:** D.Green & Co.(Stoke Newington) Ltd)
Plastico House, Mitcham, Surrey CR4 4DA
**Tel:** 020-8646-0456 **Fax:** 020-8646-5440
**Web:** www.plastico.co.uk
**Reg No:** 1858859 **VAT No:** 407484252
**Estd:** 1984 Private Limited Company
**Line of Business:** Catering equipment
**Export Markets:** Worldwide
**Export Sales:** £2,197,849
**Issued Capital:** £501,000
**Principals:** Mrs E J Wiggins *(Chairman)*, Ms C A Wiggins
**Co. Secretary:** Mrs Eileen Wiggins
**Responsibilities**
**HR:** Amanda Knight *(Human Resources Manager)*
**Engineering:** Barry Punyer *(Works Manager)*
**US SIC:** 3551, 5199
**UK SIC:** 32441, 61900
**Auditors:** Mazars Neville Russell
**Bankers:** Barclays Bank Plc (20-77-67)

| | 31-03-14 | 31-03-13 | 31-03-12 |
|---|---|---|---|
| TO | 12,578,304 | 12,416,345 | 13,224,474 |
| P/L | (76,726) | 46,180 | 194,812 |
| NW | 1,685,565 | 1,777,788 | 1,739,510 |
| WC | 901,065 | 1,061,493 | 1,048,512 |
| Emp. | 80 | 80 | 82 |

DUNS 23-459-8498

## Plasticom Ltd

Hilton Road, Ashford, Kent TN23 1EW
**Tel:** 01233-621601 **Fax:** 01233-622169
**Web:** www.ukplasticmouldings.co.uk
**Reg No:** 2813653 **Estd:** 1993 Private Limited Company
**Line of Business:** Manufacture of other plastic products
**Trading Style:** D G Mortimers Ashford Mouldings
**Issued Capital:** £58,800
**Chairman:** E Simmonds
**Co. Secretary:** Mrs Sonia Froglia Simmonds
**Responsibilities**
**Senior:** Naz Zaman *(Production Manager)*
**Finance:** Sonia Simmonds *(Financial Director)*
**Facilities:** Ken Fuller *(Engineering Manager)*
**Purchasing:** Naz Zaman *(Production Manager)*
**Engineering:** Ken Fuller *(Engineering Manager)*, Naz Zaman *(Production Manager)*
**US SIC:** 3079 **UK SIC:** 48360
**Auditors:** Beresfords

| | 30-09-13 | 30-09-12 | 30-09-11 |
|---|---|---|---|
| TA | 3,607,958 | 3,677,061 | 1,235,777 |
| NW | 214,598 | 201,282 | 472,452 |
| WC | (45,753) | (43,332) | 504,946 |

DUNS 21-321-6112 **Exp**

## Plasticon Uk Ltd

**(Subsidiary of:** Welna Holding B.V.)
44c Stockholm Road, Hull, North Humberside HU7 0XW
**Web:** www.plasticoneurope.com
**Reg No:** 1118219 **VAT No:** 475461134
**Estd:** 1877 Private Limited Company
**Line of Business:** Manufacturers of plastic products
**Export Sales:** £2,155,287
**Issued Capital:** £1,000
**Directors:** T Berger, M Reilly
**Co. Secretary:** Ian Fisher
**Responsibilities**
**Marketing:** K Shadlock *(Commercial Manager)*
**Sales:** K Shadlock *(Commercial Manager)*
**Branches:** Plasticon Uk Ltd, 7 Dunlop Way, Scunthorpe, South Humberside DN16 3RN
**US SIC:** 2821 **UK SIC:** 25140
**Auditors:** Sowerby FRS LLP
**Bankers:** National Westminster Bank Plc (60-02-23)

| | 30-06-13 | 30-06-12 | 30-06-11 |
|---|---|---|---|
| TO | 9,642,004 | 9,554,249 | 8,142,381 |
| P/L | (822,384) | (519,639) | (534,920) |
| NW | 787,732 | 1,610,116 | 2,129,754 |
| WC | (560,071) | 270,281 | 1,512,398 |
| Emp. | 94 | 91 | 83 |

DUNS 21-016-5034

## Plastics Capital Plc

Room 1.1, London Heliport, Bridges Court Road, London SW11 3BE
**Tel:** 02079780574 **Fax:** 02073268457
**Web:** www.plasticscapital.com
**Reg No:** 6387173 **VAT No:** 918533119
**Estd:** 2007 Public Limited Company
**Line of Business:** Manufacture of other plastic products
**Export Sales:** £18,974,000
**Issued Capital:** £275,425
**Directors:** K O Butler-Wheelhouse, R C Vessey, A J Walker, F J Rahmatallah
**Co. Secretary:** Nicholas Ball
**US SIC:** 3079 **UK SIC:** 48360
**Auditors:** KPMG Audit PLC
**Bankers:** The Royal Bank Of Scotland Plc (15-00-00)

| | 31-03-14 | 31-03-13 | 31-03-12 |
|---|---|---|---|
| TO | 32,456,000 | 31,407,000 | 32,096,000 |
| P/L | 1,035,000 | 1,140,000 | 1,499,000 |
| NW | 2,359,000 | 109,000 | (1,923,000) |
| WC | 4,054,000 | 2,367,000 | 2,314,000 |
| Emp. | 312 | 302 | 306 |

DUNS 21-902-4486 **Imp-Exp**

## Plasticum Norwich Ltd.

Stanford Tuck Road, North Walsham, Norfolk NR28 0TY
**Tel:** 01692404488 **Fax:** 01692404373
**Web:** www.wppg.com
**Reg No:** 0964668 **Estd:** 1969 Private Limited Company
**Line of Business:** Manufacture of other plastic products
**Export Sales:** £1,548,948
**Issued Capital:** £5,850
**Director:** R Zeevat
**Co. Secretary:** Paul De Padova
**Responsibilities**
**Senior:** Cornelis Van Der Meer *(Manager)*
**Facilities:** Enzo de Luca *(Production Manager)*
**Purchasing:** Irene Appleford *(Unclassified)*, Mark Burrage *(Logistics Manager)*
**Fleet:** Mark Burrage *(Logistics Manager)*
**Engineering:** Enzo de Luca *(Production Manager)*
**US SIC:** 3079 **UK SIC:** 48360
**Auditors:** Ernst & Young
**Bankers:** Lloyds TSB Bank plc (30-96-17)

| | 31-12-13 | 31-12-12 | 31-12-11 |
|---|---|---|---|
| TO | 10,440,844 | 10,978,658 | 11,081,763 |
| P/L | (529,511) | (429,483) | (88,219) |
| NW | 2,785,724 | 3,543,859 | 3,973,342 |
| WC | (1,551,580) | (982,686) | (443,081) |
| Emp. | 71 | 81 | 71 |

DUNS 21-170-6314

## Plastique Group Ltd

Gladstone House, 77-79 High Street, Egham, Surrey TW20 9HY
**Tel:** 01159681938
**Web:** www.plastique.eu
**Reg No:** 6951808 **Estd:** 2009 Private Limited Company
**Line of Business:** Management activities of holding companies
**Export Sales:** £16,229,326
**Issued Capital:** £904
**Directors:** J Lowe, G M Percy, R C Pope, P S Rigler, T S Drew
**Co. Secretary:** John Lowe
**US SIC:** 6711 **UK SIC:** 83962

| | 31-12-13 | 31-12-12 | 31-12-11 |
|---|---|---|---|
| TO | 24,263,658 | 20,922,461 | 22,001,677 |
| P/L | 1,007,373 | 483,040 | 1,087,177 |
| NW | 2,694,712 | 1,977,146 | 1,441,318 |
| WC | (2,586) | (446,028) | 512,821 |
| Emp. | 166 | 160 | 148 |

DUNS 21-751-7937 **Imp-Exp**

## Plastique Ltd

**(Subsidiary of:** Plastique Group Ltd)
Unit 17-18 Decimus Park, Kingstanding Way, Tunbridge Wells, Kent TN2 3GP
**Tel:** 01892-543211 **Fax:** 01892-616713
**Web:** www.plastique.eu
**Reg No:** 1407990 **VAT No:** 445011547
**Estd:** 1979 Private Limited Company
**Line of Business:** Manufacture of other plastic products
**Export Markets:** W Europe
**Export Sales:** £3,602,762
**Issued Capital:** £60,000
**Principals:** P S Rigler *(Sales)*, T Drew, Miss A E Belamine
**Co. Secretary:** John Lowe
**Branches:** Plastique Ltd, Daniels Way, Nottingham, Nottinghamshire NG15 7LL
**US SIC:** 3999 **UK SIC:** 49590
**Auditors:** Wilkins Kennedy LLP
**Bankers:** HSBC Bank plc (40-44-37)

| | 31-12-13 | 31-12-12 | 31-12-11 |
|---|---|---|---|
| TO | 11,637,094 | 9,988,660 | 9,582,771 |
| P/L | 369,453 | (211,330) | (44,908) |
| NW | 1,929,697 | 1,907,673 | 2,080,243 |
| WC | 707,671 | 757,535 | 987,264 |
| Emp. | 90 | 89 | 87 |

DUNS 21-708-4579

## The Platanos Trust

Clapham Road, London SW9 0AL
**Tel:** 02077336156
**Web:** www.platanoscollege.com
**Reg No:** 7492094 **Estd:** 1970
**Line of Business:** General secondary education
**Directors:** H Whyte, Mrs A Domingo, A T Alabi
**Responsibilities**
**Senior:** Emanuel Afotey *(School Business Manager)*, Michelle Ferguson *(Deputy Head Teacher)*, Mike Rush *(Deputy Head Teacher)*, Judette Tapper *(Head Teacher)*, Teresa Williams *(Assistant Head Teacher)*
**US SIC:** 8211 **UK SIC:** 93200
**Bankers:** HSBC Bank plc (40-01-22)

| | 31-08-14 | 31-08-13 | 31-08-12 |
|---|---|---|---|
| TO | 10,552,172 | 8,794,599 | 8,661,235 |
| P/L | 227,640 | (634,232) | (704,784) |
| NW | 26,842,017 | 26,940,377 | 27,525,609 |
| WC | 200,282 | 522,240 | 559,287 |
| Emp. | 114 | 115 | 115 |

DUNS 21-388-2961

## Plateau Restaurant

Fourth Floor Canada Square, London E14 5ER
**Tel:** 020-77157100
**Web:** www.plateau-restaurant.co.uk
**Estd:** 2011
**Line of Business:** Licensed restaurants
**Proprietor:** J Jones
**Responsibilities**
**Facilities:** Hamed Khalil *(Maintenance Manager)*
**US SIC:** 5812 **UK SIC:** 66110
**Employees:** 64

DUNS 21-580-5650

## Platform Home Loans

P O Box 237, Plymouth, Devon PL1 1WG
**Tel:** 01752236555
**Estd:** 2011
**Line of Business:** Security brokers & dealers
**US SIC:** 6111 **UK SIC:** 81501
**Employees:** 400

DUNS 34-982-3604

## Platform Securities Holdings Ltd

**(Subsidiary of:** Toronto-Dominion Bank The)
Exchange Court, Duncombe Street, Leeds, West Yorkshire LS1 4AX
**Tel:** 01133462739
**Reg No:** 5777728 **Estd:** 2006 Private Limited Company
**Line of Business:** Financial services
**Issued Capital:** £7,281,994
**Directors:** I J Welch, N A Reynolds, K Woolley, G S Close, B W Jennings, J M Robinson, Viscountess C J Mackintosh, A W Elliott
**Co. Secretary:** David Mott
**Responsibilities**
**Senior:** Femi Sobo-Allen *(Manager)*
**US SIC:** 6111 **UK SIC:** 81501

| | 31-12-13 | 31-10-12 | 31-12-11 |
|---|---|---|---|
| TA | 15,364,815 | 12,000,000 | 12,021,145 |
| NW | 15,353,135 | 11,961,912 | 11,986,649 |
| WC | N/A | N/A | 1,101 |

DUNS 23-279-7840

## Platform Securities Llp

Canterbury House, 85 Newhall Street, Birmingham, West Midlands B3 1LH
**Tel:** 01212330336 **Fax:** 01216050909
**Web:** www.omxsecurities.com
**Reg No:** 0301316OC **Estd:** 2002 Limited Partnership
**Line of Business:** Security brokers and dealers
**Trading Style:** Omx Securities Llp
**US SIC:** 6111 **UK SIC:** 81501

| | 31-12-13 | 31-10-12 | 31-12-11 |
|---|---|---|---|
| TA | 44,501,000 | 45,843,000 | 340,265,000 |
| P/L | (1,970,000) | 15,000 | 75,000 |
| NW | 6,552,000 | 6,447,000 | 6,420,000 |
| WC | 6,757,000 | 6,652,000 | 6,623,000 |

DUNS 21-207-9532

## Platinium Heathcare

North View Lodge, Sunderland, Tyne and Wear SR5 3AF
**Web:** www.schealthcare.co.uk
**Estd:** 1999 Proprietorship
**Line of Business:** Rest and retirement homes
**Proprietor:** Mrs L Bell
**Responsibilities**
**Senior:** Wendy Dowson *(Home Manager)*
**US SIC:** 8321 **UK SIC:** 96111
**Employees:** 60

DUNS 21-601-6389

## Platinum

8 Meridian Business Park, North Bradley, Trowbridge, Wiltshire BA14 0BJ
**Tel:** 01225759500
**Web:** www.platinumnissan.co.uk
**Estd:** 2011 Proprietorship
**Line of Business:** Car dealers (new & used)
**Proprietor:** L Ball
**Responsibilities**
**Senior:** Richard Pulsford *(General Manager)*
**US SIC:** 5511 **UK SIC:** 65100
**Employees:** 50

DUNS 53-604-8226

## Platinum 2000 Ltd

**(Subsidiary of:** The Platinum Group (2003) Ltd)
6 Farley Hill, Luton, Bedfordshire LU1 5HQ
**Tel:** 01582402908
**Web:** www.theplatinumgroup.co.uk
**Reg No:** 3410056 **Estd:** 1997 Private Limited Company
**Line of Business:** Other non-store retail sale
**Issued Capital:** £100
**Director:** G L Rush
**Co. Secretary:** Maurice Duncan
**US SIC:** 5963 **UK SIC:** 65600
**Auditors:** Robert W Belcher

| | 28-02-14 | 28-02-13 | 28-02-12 |
|---|---|---|---|
| TA | 1,310 | 940 | 700 |
| NW | 100 | 100 | 100 |
| WC | 100 | 100 | 100 |

DUNS 42-409-5540 **Imp**

## Platinum Batteries (Europe) Ltd

**(Subsidiary of:** Taybrodale Group Ltd)
Platinum House, Bailey Road, Trafford Park, Manchester M17 1SA
**Tel:** 08450639999 **Fax:** 08450638888
**Web:** www.ukbatteries.co.uk
**Reg No:** 4397197 **Estd:** 2002 Private Limited Company
**Line of Business:** Battery suppliers
**Export Sales:** £2,573,784
**Issued Capital:** £200
**Directors:** M S Walton, M C Perkin, S D Taylor, N J Warren, K F Halliwell, S Dale, J M Richards, C Taylor
**Co. Secretary:** Ms Kirsty Mcewan
**US SIC:** 3692 **UK SIC:** 34321
**Auditors:** Wilds Ltd
**Bankers:** National Westminster Bank Plc (01-30-99)

| | 30-04-14 | 30-04-13 | 30-04-12 |
|---|---|---|---|
| TO | 36,007,067 | 34,383,693 | 32,794,562 |
| P/L | 2,301,195 | 2,439,760 | 1,811,728 |
| NW | 5,824,887 | 5,018,561 | 3,995,103 |
| WC | 5,628,270 | 4,804,593 | 3,808,207 |
| Emp. | 144 | 134 | 130 |

DUNS 50-964-3110

## Platinum Computer Solutions Ltd

10 Fraser Road, Priory Business Park, Bedford, Bedfordshire MK44 3WH
**Tel:** 01234832520
**Web:** www.platinum-connect.com
**Reg No:** 3294769 **Estd:** 1996 Private Limited Company
**Line of Business:** It consultants
**Issued Capital:** £1,000
**Principals:** S Foster *(Managing)*, S P Jackman
**Co. Secretary:** Ms Deborah Foster
**Responsibilities**
**HR:** Mandy Pryke *(Human Resources Manager)*
**Branches:** Platinum Computer Solutions Ltd, 10 Abbey Court, Priory Business Park, Bedford, Bedfordshire MK44 3WH
**US SIC:** 7379 **UK SIC:** 83940
**Auditors:** GB Accounting Solutions Ltd
**Bankers:** Lloyds TSB Bank plc (30-90-66)

| | 31-12-13 | 31-12-12 | 31-12-11 |
|---|---|---|---|
| TA | 1,393,343 | 1,036,099 | 1,071,696 |
| NW | 14,291 | 15,288 | 55,521 |
| WC | 11,501 | 11,786 | 66,123 |

DUNS 21-199-5105

## Platinum Facilities & Maintenance Services Ltd

3rd Floor, 1 Alie Street, London E1 8DE
**Tel:** 02079-775650 **Fax:** 02079775679
**Web:** www.pfms.co.uk
**Reg No:** 0936149 **VAT No:** 830243270
**Estd:** 1968 Private Limited Company
**Line of Business:** Property maintenance services
**Trading Style:** Platinum Facilities & Maintenance Services Ltd
**Issued Capital:** £100,000
**Directors:** G L Cardinal, M J Frost
**Co. Secretary:** Roger Feast
**Responsibilities**
**Sales:** Paul Samuels *(Account Manager)*
**Admin:** Nikki Hartnoll *(Senior administrator)*
**Health & Safety:** Richard Hayter *(Health and Safety Manager)*
**Engineering:** Frank Webster *(Operations and Technical Direc)*
**US SIC:** 1799, 1711, 7399
**UK SIC:** 50000, 50300, 83954
**Auditors:** Lambert Chapman LLP
**Bankers:** National Westminster Bank Plc (60-05-13)

| | 30-09-13 | 30-09-12 | 30-09-11 |
|---|---|---|---|
| TO | 10,049,232 | 10,540,520 | 8,943,384 |
| P/L | 918,064 | 1,039,155 | 601,198 |
| NW | 1,532,661 | 1,374,223 | 1,296,406 |
| WC | 1,113,696 | 943,030 | 785,358 |
| Emp. | 85 | 86 | 79 |

DUNS 34-706-7121

## Platinum Home Care (South Coast) Ltd

Cawley Place 15 Cawley Road, Chichester, West Sussex PO19 1UZ
**Tel:** 01243-605675
**Web:** www.platinumhomecare.co.uk
**Reg No:** 5510839 **Estd:** 2005 Private Limited Company
**Line of Business:** Other human health activities
**Issued Capital:** £1,000
**Directors:** Ms E M Greenwood, Ms M D Somner, S G Somner
**Co. Secretary:** Stephen Somner
**US SIC:** 8091 **UK SIC:** 95200

| | 31-08-13 | 31-08-12 | 31-08-11 |
|---|---|---|---|
| TA | 121,928 | 77,085 | 73,818 |
| NW | 1,848 | (6,069) | (18,901) |
| WC | 1,856 | (545) | (11,915) |

DUNS 21-230-8900

## Platinum Motor Group

16/17 The Causeway, Chippenham, Wiltshire SN15 3DA
**Tel:** 01249654321
**Web:** www.platinummotorgroup.co.uk
**Estd:** 1956 Proprietorship
**Line of Business:** Motor Vehicle Dealers ( New & Used)
**Proprietor:** G Gillian
**US SIC:** 5511 **UK SIC:** 65100
**Employees:** 50

DUNS 73-375-9257

## Platinum One Hotels Ltd

37 Wick Lane, Christchurch, Dorset BH23 1HU
**Tel:** 01202-475111 **Fax:** 01202-490111
**Web:** www.thecaptainsclubhotel.com
**Reg No:** 4649411 **Estd:** 2005 Private Limited Company
**Line of Business:** Hotels
**Trading Style:** Captains Club Hotel
**Issued Capital:** £150
**Directors:** C M Bradfield, Ms S Ross, R J Wilson, T C Lloyd, Ms R J Morgan
**US SIC:** 7011 **UK SIC:** 66500

| | 31-03-14 | 31-03-13 | 31-03-12 |
|---|---|---|---|
| TO | 3,523,373 | 3,486,130 | 3,708,002 |
| P/L | 80,521 | 32,287 | 77,634 |
| NW | 684,042 | 603,521 | 571,234 |
| WC | (772,907) | (831,581) | (907,741) |
| Emp. | 80 | 83 | 85 |

DUNS 67-138-3284

## Platinum Personnel Solutions (Uk) Ltd

King Georges Avenue, Leiston, Suffolk IP16 4US
**Tel:** 01728-833880
**Web:** www.platinumpersonnelukltd.co.uk
**Reg No:** 5997144 **VAT No:** 900467841
**Estd:** 2006 Private Limited Company
**Line of Business:** Labour recruitment and provision of personnel
**Issued Capital:** £4
**Directors:** C A Brooks, Mrs K K Brooks
**Co. Secretary:** Ms Katrina Brooks
**US SIC:** 7361 **UK SIC:** 83954

| | 30-11-14 | 30-11-13 | 30-11-12 |
|---|---|---|---|
| TA | 399,632 | 317,092 | 207,532 |
| NW | 161,657 | 110,182 | 123,534 |
| WC | 190,203 | 159,920 | 123,564 |

DUNS 45-826-5485 **Imp**

## Platinum Stairlifts Ltd

**(Subsidiary of:** Platinum Rails Holdings Ltd)
Unit 10 The Crossings, Cross Hills Business Park, Cross Hills, Keighley, West Yorkshire BD20 7BW
**Tel:** 01535631177 **Fax:** 01535-631188
**Web:** www.platinumstairlifts.com
**Reg No:** 3179671 **VAT No:** 708456130
**Estd:** 1998 Private Limited Company
**Line of Business:** Manufacture of other fabricated metal products not elsewhere classified
**Trading Style:** Platinum Stairlifts.
**Issued Capital:** £100
**Directors:** Ms L Frear, L Wells, R Blacka
**Co. Secretary:** Timothy Frear
**Responsibilities**
**Finance:** Denise Frear *(Operations Director)*
**IT:** Denise Frear *(Operations Director)*
**HR:** Denise Frear *(Operations Director)*
**US SIC:** 3499 **UK SIC:** 31694
**Auditors:** Wheawill & Sudworth
**Bankers:** National Westminster Bank Plc (54-21-00)

| | 31-03-14 | 31-03-13 | 31-03-12 |
|---|---|---|---|
| TO | 10,019,064 | 7,712,384 | N/A |
| P/L | 976,281 | 738,274 | N/A |
| NW | 1,566,038 | 1,188,320 | 1,249,773 |
| WC | 1,110,513 | 883,645 | 613,047 |
| Emp. | 89 | 72 | N/A |

DUNS 21-601-0327

## Platinum Training

Dudley House, Stone Street, Dudley, West Midlands DY1 1NS
**Tel:** 01384231645
**Web:** www.platinumtraining.co.uk
**Estd:** 2002 Partnership
**Line of Business:** Activities of private training providers
**Partners:** Mrs C Bremner, M Bremner
**US SIC:** 8299 **UK SIC:** 93300
**Employees:** 60

DUNS 21-805-0870 **Imp**

## Platnauer Group Ltd

Nuvo House, Austin Way, Hampstead Industrial Estate, Birmingham, West Midlands B42 1DU
**Tel:** 0121 357 4267 **Fax:** 0121 357 5900
**Web:** www.rplatnauer.co.uk
**Reg No:** 0596246 **Estd:** 1957 Private Limited Company
**Line of Business:** Manufacture of jewellery and related articles not elsewhere classified
**Issued Capital:** £221,052
**Principals:** P L Platnauer *(Managing)*, Mrs S L Platnauer, M Newell, H A Whittall
**Co. Secretary:** Graham Phipp
**Responsibilities**
**Senior:** J Platnauer *(Manager)*
**US SIC:** 3911, 6711
**UK SIC:** 49101, 83962
**Auditors:** Baker Tilly UK Audit LLP
**Bankers:** Lloyds TSB Bank plc (30-00-03)

| | 31-03-14 | 31-03-13 | 31-03-12 |
|---|---|---|---|
| TO | 47,445,695 | 107,006,048 | 121,528,550 |
| P/L | (1,632,949) | (2,148,627) | 528,217 |
| NW | 7,771,855 | 9,065,727 | 9,873,409 |
| WC | 1,904,621 | 3,363,731 | 6,303,363 |
| Emp. | 56 | 48 | 42 |

DUNS 21-274-3306 **Imp-Exp**

## Platt & Hill Ltd

Belgrave Mill, Fitton Hill Road, Oldham, Lancashire OL8 2LZ
**Tel:** 0161-621-4400
**Web:** www.phfillings.co.uk
**Reg No:** 0060275 **VAT No:** 306366763
**Estd:** 1899 Private Limited Company
**Line of Business:** Foam products (rubber and plastic)
**Export Markets:** Western Europe; U S A; South Africa
**Issued Capital:** £99,250
**Principals:** D S Hill *(Sales)*, N R Hill, A D Hill, J R Platt, J P Platt
**Co. Secretary:** Ms Michelle Iwanowytsch
**Responsibilities**
**Facilities:** Kevin Greaves *(Chief Engineer)*
**Purchasing:** Claire Yelen-Hey *(Purchasing Manager)*
**Engineering:** Kevin Greaves *(Chief Engineer)*
**Branches:** Platt & Hill Ltd, Belgrave Mill, Fitton Hill Road, Oldham, Lancashire OL8 2LZ
**US SIC:** 3079, 2517
**UK SIC:** 48360, 46714
**Auditors:** Wrigley Partington

| | 31-12-13 | 31-12-12 | 31-12-11 |
|---|---|---|---|
| TO | 9,666,892 | 9,505,308 | 9,396,245 |
| P/L | 234,091 | 170,359 | 236,481 |
| NW | 820,046 | 866,212 | 921,805 |
| WC | 143,516 | 136,384 | 197,896 |
| Emp. | 122 | 129 | 131 |

DUNS 21-114-5337

## Platt Bridge Consortium Llp

Rivington Avenue, Platt Bridge, Wigan, Lancashire WN2 5NG
**Tel:** 01942482300
**Reg No:** 0336081OC **Estd:** 2008 Private Limited Company
**Line of Business:** General medical and surgical hospitals
**US SIC:** 8062 **UK SIC:** 95100

| | 30-09-13 | 30-09-12 | 30-09-11 |
|---|---|---|---|
| TA | 754,246 | 942,493 | 866,277 |
| WC | 409,629 | 565,773 | 474,397 |

DUNS 21-621-5053

## Platts Motor Co Ltd

60 West Street, Marlow, Buckinghamshire SL7 2NJ
**Tel:** 01628890909
**Web:** www.platts.co.uk
**Reg No:** 0550585 **VAT No:** 207534675
**Estd:** 1927 Private Limited Company
**Line of Business:** Car dealers (new & used)
**Trading Style:** Platts of Marlow
**Issued Capital:** £160,000
**Principals:** B J Platt *(Managing)*, Mrs J S Brookes, A E Platt
**Co. Secretary:** Timothy Platt
**Responsibilities**
**Senior:** Jim Attwood *(Manager)*
**Finance:** Diane Head *(Accounts Manager)*
**IT:** Diane Head *(Accounts Manager)*
**Branches:** Platts Motor Co Ltd, London Road, Chippenham, Wiltshire SN15 3AZ
**US SIC:** 5511, 5521, 7539
**UK SIC:** 65100, 67100
**Auditors:** Grant Thornton UK LLP
**Bankers:** National Westminster Bank Plc (60-14-12)

| | 31-12-13 | 31-12-12 | 31-12-11 |
|---|---|---|---|
| TO | 15,642,421 | 13,796,545 | 14,046,486 |
| P/L | 320,552 | 144,520 | (292,044) |
| NW | 3,127,632 | 2,873,572 | 1,595,146 |
| WC | (338,305) | (679,078) | (757,839) |
| Emp. | 61 | 61 | 69 |

DUNS 21-824-2606

## Platts (U.K.) Ltd

The Mcgraw-Hill Companies, 20 Canada Square, London E14 5LH
**Tel:** 01270580716 **Fax:** 0120 7176 6111
**Web:** www.platts-uk.com
**Reg No:** 7953373 **Estd:** 2012 Private Limited Company
**Line of Business:** Other business activities not elsewhere classified
**Export Sales:** £69,993,000
**Issued Capital:** £387,950,423
**Directors:** K Wise, D R Pearce, P J Sansom
**Co. Secretary:** Ms Catherine Shelley
**US SIC:** 7399 **UK SIC:** 83954

| | 31-12-13 | 31-12-12 |
|---|---|---|
| TO | 70,419,000 | 65,747,000 |
| P/L | 23,769,000 | 35,220,000 |
| NW | 25,769,000 | 25,021,000 |
| WC | 25,711,000 | 24,896,000 |
| Emp. | 274 | 229 |

DUNS 73-845-9994

## Plaxton Ltd

(**Subsidiary of:** Alexander Dennis Ltd)
Cayton Low Road, Scarborough, North Yorkshire YO11 3BY
**Tel:** 01723581500 **Fax:** 01723-581479
**Web:** www.plaxtonlimited.co.uk
**Reg No:** 5101150 **VAT No:** 836666490
**Estd:** 2004 Private Limited Company
**Line of Business:** Manufacturers of vans and trucks
**Issued Capital:** £10,000
**Directors:** M Stewart, C Robertson
**Responsibilities**
**Finance:** Debbie Hatchett *(Finance Manager)*
**Marketing:** Andrew Warrender *(Senior Marketing Executive)*
**IT:** Dan Duckfield *(IT Manager)*
**HR:** Andrew Spivey *(Human Resources Manager)*
**Facilities:** Walter Schneider *(Site Maintenance Manager)*
**Branches:** Plaxton Ltd, Ryton Road, Sheffield, South Yorkshire S25 4DL
**US SIC:** 3711 **UK SIC:** 35101
**Auditors:** KPMG LLP

| | 31-12-13 | 31-12-12 | 31-12-11 |
|---|---|---|---|
| TA | 1,742,000 | 1,742,000 | 1,742,000 |
| NW | 1,742,000 | 1,742,000 | 1,742,000 |

DUNS 23-354-0322

## Play Ltd

(**Subsidiary of:** Rakuten Inc.)
Sovereign House, Vision Park, Chivers Way, Histon, Cambridge, Cambridgeshire CB24 9BZ
**Tel:** 08081311311 **Fax:** 01223 484001
**Web:** www.play.com
**Reg No:** 0086716J **Estd:** 2003 Private Limited Company
**Line of Business:** Mail order houses
**Trading Style:** Webworks
**Issued Capital:** £1
**US SIC:** 5961 **UK SIC:** 65600
**Employees:** 200

DUNS 77-117-7052

## Playboy Club London Ltd

(**Subsidiary of:** Caesars Entertainment Corporation)
14 Old Park Lane, London W1K 1ND
**Tel:** 020-7491-8586
**Web:** www.playboyclublondon.com
**Reg No:** 2690210 **Estd:** 1992 Private Limited Company
**Line of Business:** Gambling and betting activities
**Issued Capital:** £2
**Directors:** Ms A G Oswald, R A Ramm, G W Loveman, M Rothwell
**Co. Secretary:** Michael Cohen
**Responsibilities**
**Senior:** Michael Silberling *(Manager)*
**Branches:** Playboy Club London Ltd, 10 Brick St, London W1J 7HQ
**US SIC:** 7999 **UK SIC:** 97913
**Auditors:** PricewaterhouseCoopers
**Bankers:** National Westminster Bank Plc (56-00-25)

| | 31-12-13 | 31-12-12 | 31-12-11 |
|---|---|---|---|
| TO | 35,401,000 | 28,883,000 | 29,285,000 |
| P/L | (3,033,000) | (3,210,000) | 1,068,000 |
| NW | (9,666,000) | (6,633,000) | (3,423,000) |
| WC | (15,611,000) | (13,461,000) | (10,918,000) |
| Emp. | 223 | 226 | 208 |

DUNS 50-415-3024

## Playboy T V U K Ltd

(**Subsidiary of:** Icon Acquisition Holdings L.P.)
The Atrium, 1 Harefield Road, Uxbridge, Middlesex UB8 1PH
**Tel:** 02085817000
**Web:** www.playboyplus.com
**Reg No:** 2412178 **VAT No:** 545971412
**Estd:** 1989 Private Limited Company
**Line of Business:** Television activities
**Issued Capital:** £40,000
**Directors:** C Pachler, M W Palmer, J A Reader
**Co. Secretary:** Jordan Cosec Limited
**Responsibilities**
**Senior:** Thomas Flores *(Manager)*, Ruel Smith *(Manager)*, Jeremy Yates *(Manager)*
**US SIC:** 4833 **UK SIC:** 97411
**Bankers:** National Westminster Bank Plc (56-00-27)

| | 31-12-13 | 31-12-12 | 31-12-11 |
|---|---|---|---|
| TA | 1,797,000 | 1,797,000 | 1,782,000 |
| NW | 1,741,000 | 1,762,000 | 1,782,000 |
| WC | 1,741,000 | 1,762,000 | N/A |

DUNS 21-242-4717 **Imp**

## Playdale Playgrounds Ltd

Haverthwaite, Ulverston, Cumbria LA12 8AE
**Tel:** 01539-531561
**Web:** www.playdale.co.uk
**Reg No:** 0525615 **VAT No:** 155625362
**Estd:** 1953 Private Limited Company
**Line of Business:** Manufacture of sports goods
**Export Sales:** £563,906
**Issued Capital:** £5,000
**Managing Director:** J A Croasdale
**Co. Secretary:** Ms Gillian Croasdale
**Responsibilities**
**Senior:** Andrew Fullard *(Sales & Marketing Manager)*, Barry Leahey *(Senior Sales Executive)*
**Marketing:** Rachal Beach *(Sales & Marketing)*, Andrew Fullard *(Sales & Marketing Manager)*, Kimberley Hill *(Sales & Marketing Manager)*
**Sales:** Rachal Beach *(Sales & Marketing)*, Andrew Fullard *(Sales & Marketing Manager)*, Kimberley Hill *(Sales & Marketing Manager)*, Barry Leahey *(Senior Sales Executive)*
**HR:** Julia Nicholson *(Human Resources Manager)*
**Engineering:** Tony Postlethwaite *(Production Manager)*
**Branches:** Playdale Playgrounds Ltd, Mansfield Road, Sheffield, South Yorkshire S26 5PQ
**US SIC:** 3999, 3499
**UK SIC:** 49590, 31694
**Auditors:** Lonsdale & Partners
**Bankers:** Barclays Bank Plc (20-04-68)

| | 31-12-13 | 31-12-12 | 31-12-11 |
|---|---|---|---|
| TO | 11,000,653 | 10,142,293 | 12,956,295 |
| P/L | 51,852 | 76,616 | 508,482 |
| NW | 1,138,565 | 1,193,665 | 1,228,029 |
| WC | 917,615 | 1,048,531 | 1,023,420 |
| Emp. | 120 | 119 | 125 |

DUNS 21-620-4349

## Players Sports Bar

125-127 West Street, Sheffield, South Yorkshire S1 4ER
**Tel:** 01142767665
**Web:** www.playersbars.com
**Estd:** 2010 Proprietorship
**Line of Business:** Wine bars
**Proprietor:** N Sutton
**Responsibilities**
**Senior:** Gordon Codona *(Proprietor)*
**US SIC:** 5813 **UK SIC:** 66200
**Employees:** 70

DUNS 23-800-1270

## Playforce Ltd

(**Subsidiary of:** Newincco 1224 Ltd)
1 Pegasus Way, Bowerhill, Melksham, Wiltshire SN12 6TR
**Tel:** 01225-792060 **Fax:** 01225-792080
**Web:** www.playforce.co.uk
**Reg No:** 3792761 **Estd:** 1999 Private Limited Company
**Line of Business:** Other building installation
**Export Sales:** £40,238
**Issued Capital:** £100
**Directors:** T E Lacey, Dr C A Macadam, S J Black, S J Cashmore, S J Abley, Ms D J Houghton
**Co. Secretary:** Ms Deborah Houghton
**Responsibilities**
**Senior:** Louise Cole *(Internal Sales Manager)*
**Sales:** Melanie Blackhan *(Internal Sales Manager)*, Sam Flatman *(Field Sales Manager)*
**US SIC:** 1796 **UK SIC:** 50400
**Auditors:** Target Consulting Ltd
**Bankers:** HSBC Bank plc (40-14-13)

| | 31-12-13 | 31-12-12 | 31-12-11 |
|---|---|---|---|
| TO | 8,451,935 | 8,887,465 | 8,047,870 |
| P/L | (35,909) | 294,839 | 167,962 |
| NW | 2,688,315 | 2,713,858 | 2,402,847 |
| WC | 2,568,627 | 2,546,013 | 2,217,408 |
| Emp. | 54 | 52 | 49 |

DUNS 21-864-5176

## Playnation Ltd

(**Subsidiary of:** Ensco 962 Ltd)
Unit 17 Berkeley Court, Manor Park, Runcorn, Cheshire WA7 1TQ
**Tel:** 01925260200
**Reg No:** 8258418 **Estd:** 2012 Private Limited Company
**Line of Business:** Gambling and betting activities
**Issued Capital:** £1
**Directors:** A D Hodges, R J Hyde, E Doherty, M Chapman
**US SIC:** 7999 **UK SIC:** 97913

| | 15-03-14 |
|---|---|
| TO | 31,189,000 |
| P/L | 2,625,000 |
| NW | (4,684,000) |
| WC | (723,000) |
| Emp. | 714 |

DUNS 23-293-1043

## Playtech Plc

2nd Floor St George's Court, Upper Church Street, Douglas, Isle of Man IM1 1EE
**Tel:** 01624645999 **Fax:** 01624-645-955
**Web:** www.playtech.com
**Reg No:** 0008505M **Estd:** 1999 Private Limited Company
**Line of Business:** Software suppliers to the online gaming industry
**Principals:** G Emodi *(Financial)*, G Emodi *(Financial)*, G Emodi *(Financial)*, T Hall, T Hall, T Hall, S Barak, M Weizer
**Co. Secretary:** Jonathan Lockyer
**Responsibilities**
**Senior:** Avigur Zmora *(Non Executive Member)*
**Finance:** Ron Hoffman *(Chief Financial Officer)*
**US SIC:** 5065 **UK SIC:** 61500
**Employees:** 750

DUNS 73-955-2920

## Playworks Ltd

49 Park Road North, Urmston, Manchester M41 5AT
**Tel:** 0161-748-9400
**Web:** www.playworks-manchester.co.uk
**Reg No:** 5207555 **Estd:** 2004 Private Limited Company
**Line of Business:** After school care
**Issued Capital:** £1,429
**Director:** S J Walker
**Responsibilities**
**Senior:** Shirin Bunting *(Manager)*, Karl Frankland *(Proprietor)*
**US SIC:** 5812 **UK SIC:** 66110
**Bankers:** Lloyds TSB Bank plc (30-00-00)

| | 31-12-13 | 31-12-12 | 31-12-11 |
|---|---|---|---|
| TO | 1,615,282 | 3,070,057 | 3,116,260 |
| P/L | (96,574) | (302,606) | (672,090) |
| NW | (536,540) | (453,768) | (150,307) |
| WC | (1,068,767) | (743,821) | (697,428) |
| Emp. | N/A | 71 | 79 |

DUNS 34-876-8441

## Plaza Cars (Birmingham) Ltd

510 Slade Road, Birmingham, West Midlands B23 7JE
**Tel:** 01213821111 **Fax:** 0121-377-8823
**Web:** www.plaza-travel.co.uk
**Reg No:** 2820460 **Estd:** 1983 Private Limited Company
**Line of Business:** Taxis
**Issued Capital:** £2
**Director:** Ms J Taylor
**Co. Secretary:** Ms Lorraine Banks
**US SIC:** 4121 **UK SIC:** 72200
**Auditors:** Brown & Co

| | 31-05-13 | 31-05-12 | 31-05-11 |
|---|---|---|---|
| TA | 162,698 | 277,323 | 263,577 |
| NW | 10,297 | 37,348 | 33,976 |
| WC | (55,706) | (70,586) | (76,917) |

DUNS 42-404-9133

## Plaza Investments Ltd

Anchor Lane, Ingoldmells, Skegness, Lincolnshire PE25 1LX
**Tel:** 01754872149
**Reg No:** 4392601 **Estd:** 2002 Private Limited Company
**Line of Business:** Amusement park activities
**Issued Capital:** £1
**Director:** F W Bell
**Co. Secretary:** Miss Rachel Scarborough
**US SIC:** 7996 **UK SIC:** 97913

| | 31-10-14 | 31-10-13 | 31-10-12 |
|---|---|---|---|
| TO | 3,025,350 | 2,769,139 | 3,165,446 |
| P/L | 286,534 | 93,056 | 95,519 |
| NW | 330,141 | 97,452 | (519,607) |
| WC | (458,194) | 558,684 | (483,848) |
| Emp. | 68 | 69 | 66 |

DUNS 22-529-7092 **Imp**

## Plb Group Ltd

Dorset House, High Street, East Grinstead, West Sussex RH19 3DE
**Tel:** 01342-318-282 **Fax:** 01342-314-023
**Web:** www.plb.co.uk
**Reg No:** 1655729 **VAT No:** 381701364
**Estd:** 2012 Private Limited Company
**Line of Business:** Importers of beer, wine and spirits
**Trading Style:** Private Liquor Brands
**Issued Capital:** £200,000
**Directors:** J S Kowszun, J Osborne, J C Newton, M P Saunders
**Responsibilities**
**Senior:** James Burtson *(Business Development Director)*, Jeffrey Fredericks *(Chairman)*, Robin Kinahan *(Wholesale Area Manager)*
**Finance:** Robin Waters *(Finance Director)*
**Marketing:** Louisa Hollow *(Marketing/ Communications Execu)*, Adam Wyartt *(Brand Manager)*
**Sales:** James Burtson *(Business Development Director)*, Dominic Conway *(Sales Director)*, Joanna Cugley *(Buying Coordinator)*, Kate Faiweather *(New Business Development Manag)*, Paul Meihuizen *(Regional Buying Director- Worl)*
**Admin:** Linda Rees *(Office Manager)*
**HR:** Linda Rees *(Office Manager)*
**Health & Safety:** Linda Rees *(Office Manager)*
**Facilities:** Linda Rees *(Office Manager)*
**Operations:** Sophia Shaw *(Quality Assurance Assistant)*, Stephen Walder *(Technical Director)*
**Purchasing:** Debbie Savage *(Purchase Ledger)*
**Engineering:** Sarah Gurteen *(Technical Manager)*, Sarah Woodman *(Technical Manager)*
**US SIC:** 5149 **UK SIC:** 61700
**Auditors:** Grant Thornton UK LLP
**Bankers:** Barclays Bank Plc (20-23-97)

| | 31-08-14 | 31-08-13 | 31-08-12 |
|---|---|---|---|
| TO | 120,653,000 | 125,014,000 | 141,714,823 |
| P/L | 648,000 | 474,000 | 479,751 |
| NW | 4,694,000 | 4,269,000 | 4,093,838 |
| WC | 4,177,000 | 3,938,000 | 3,758,664 |
| Emp. | 92 | 90 | 72 |

DUNS 21-452-8879

## Plean Precast Ltd

President Kennedy Drive, Stirling, Stirlingshire FK7 8AX
**Tel:** 01786-812221
**Web:** www.plean-precast.co.uk
**Reg No:** 0044731SC **VAT No:** 260285079
**Estd:** 1967 Private Limited Company
**Line of Business:** Other manufacturing not elsewhere classified
**Issued Capital:** £41,500
**Director:** J G Bell
**Co. Secretary:** Neil Macgregor
**Responsibilities**
**Senior:** Laurie MacKrell *(Works Manager)*
**Engineering:** Laurie MacKrell *(Works Manager)*
**US SIC:** 3999, 5251
**UK SIC:** 49590, 64800
**Auditors:** Crichton Stringer
**Bankers:** Bank Of Scotland (80-06-74)

| | 30-06-13 | 30-06-12 | 30-06-11 |
|---|---|---|---|
| TO | 5,021,535 | 4,763,399 | 4,631,621 |
| P/L | 214,502 | (118,033) | 314,456 |
| NW | 16,728,850 | 16,564,460 | 16,694,742 |
| WC | 15,392,451 | 15,196,627 | 15,364,823 |
| Emp. | 106 | 106 | 72 |

DUNS 49-744-3663

## The Pleasance Theatre Festival

Carpenters Mews, North Road, London N7 9EF
**Tel:** 02076091800
**Web:** www.pleasance.co.uk
**Estd:** 1995 Proprietorship
**Line of Business:** Development and selling of real estate
**Proprietor:** J Faulkner
**Responsibilities**
**Senior:** Anthony Alderson *(Manager)*
**Branches:** The Pleasance Theatre Trust, 60 Pleasance, Edinburgh, Midlothian EH8 9TJ
**US SIC:** 8999 **UK SIC:** 83954
**Employees:** 70

DUNS 23-674-5373 **Imp**

## Please Hold (Uk) Ltd

Oakland House, Manchester M16 0PQ
**Tel:** 01618772253 **Fax:** 0161-872-5670
**Web:** www.phmg.com
**Reg No:** 3669221 **VAT No:** 720710869
**Estd:** 1998 Private Limited Company
**Line of Business:** Other computer related activities
**Trading Style:** P H Media Group
**Issued Capital:** £9,000
**Director:** G L Reed
**Co. Secretary:** Christopher Berisford
**Responsibilities**
**Senior:** Jason Daye *(Operations Manager)*
**HR:** Jason Daye *(Operations Manager)*
**Health & Safety:** Jason Daye *(Operations Manager)*
**Facilities:** Jason Daye *(Operations Manager)*
**US SIC:** 7379 **UK SIC:** 83940
**Auditors:** TFD Dunhams
**Bankers:** National Westminster Bank Plc (60-40-08)

| | 31-12-13 | 31-12-12 | 31-12-11 |
|---|---|---|---|
| TO | 11,136,974 | 8,063,946 | 5,753,553 |
| P/L | 1,620,980 | 916,632 | 573,315 |
| NW | 3,582,553 | 2,358,235 | 1,084,403 |
| WC | 3,211,546 | 2,242,446 | 947,439 |
| Emp. | 162 | 133 | 98 |

DUNS 76-276-8117

## Pleasure & Leisure Corporation Plc

Pleasure Beach, South Beach Parade, Great Yarmouth, Norfolk NR30 3EH
**Tel:** 01493-844585
**Web:** www.pleasure-beach.co.uk
**Reg No:** 2543667 **Estd:** 1957 Public Limited Company
**Line of Business:** Amusement park activities
**Trading Style:** Pleasure Beach
**Issued Capital:** £4,246,902
**Principals:** A T Jones *(Managing)*, J J Jones, G W Peak, Ms J E Jones, A J Jones, Mrs E J Peak
**Co. Secretary:** Ms Amanda Jones
**Responsibilities**
**Marketing:** Owen Branch *(Senior Marketing Executive)*, Richard Hardy *(Marketing Manager)*
**HR:** Lorraine Fuller *(Training Manager)*, Nigel Thurston *(Personnel Manager)*
**Purchasing:** Janet Houston *(Buyer)*
**US SIC:** 7996, 5813
**UK SIC:** 97913, 66200
**Auditors:** Robinson Knott & Co
**Bankers:** Barclays Bank Plc (20-99-21)

| | 31-03-14 | 31-03-13 | 31-03-12 |
|---|---|---|---|
| TO | 2,560,113 | 2,586,104 | 2,741,540 |
| P/L | (64,403) | (138,958) | (36,343) |
| NW | 6,733,592 | 6,797,995 | 6,936,953 |
| WC | (813,120) | (1,069,382) | (853,153) |
| Emp. | 92 | 93 | 93 |

DUNS 22-669-2523 **Imp**

## Pleasure Beach Amusements (Skegness) Ltd

(**Subsidiary of:** Pleasure Beach Holdings Ltd)
Grand Parade, Skegness, Lincolnshire PE25 2UQ
**Tel:** 01754-763697 **Fax:** 01754-611010
**Web:** www.pleasurebeach.skegness.co.uk
**Reg No:** 0838474 **VAT No:** 128134193
**Estd:** 1965 Private Limited Company
**Line of Business:** Operation of theme parks
**Issued Capital:** £70,000
**Managing Director:** J A Botton
**Co. Secretary:** Ms Marie Botton
**US SIC:** 7996, 7999
**UK SIC:** 97913
**Auditors:** Richard Anthony & Co
**Bankers:** Barclays Bank Plc (20-62-68)

| | 31-03-14 | 31-03-13 | 31-03-12 |
|---|---|---|---|
| TA | 2,763,210 | 2,930,956 | 3,228,603 |
| NW | 1,134,439 | 1,101,802 | 1,267,833 |
| WC | (638,480) | (767,294) | (620,074) |

DUNS 36-794-3800

## Pleasure Beach Arena

525 Ocean Boulevard, Promenade, Blackpool, Lancashire FY4 1EZ
**Tel:** 01253341707
**Web:** www.icearenablackpool.com
**Estd:** 1985 Proprietorship
**Line of Business:** Other sporting activities not elsewhere classified
**Proprietor:** J Thompson
**US SIC:** 7999 **UK SIC:** 97913
**Employees:** 1,600

DUNS 23-980-9515

## Pleasurewood Hills Ltd

Leisure Way, Lowestoft, Suffolk NR32 5DZ
**Tel:** 01502-586000 **Fax:** 01502567393
**Web:** www.pleasurewoodhills.com
**Reg No:** 3969399 **Estd:** 2000 Private Limited Company
**Line of Business:** Fair and amusement park activities
**Issued Capital:** £2,307,671
**Director:** L Bruloy
**Co. Secretary:** Laurent Bruloy
**Responsibilities**
**Senior:** Alexis Camelin *(Manager)*, Liam Holmes *(Technical, Production Manager)*, Alexis Temlin *(General Manager)*
**Engineering:** Liam Holmes *(Technical, Production Manager)*
**US SIC:** 7996 **UK SIC:** 97913
**Auditors:** PricewaterhouseCoopers LLP

| | 30-09-13 | 30-09-12 | 31-09-12 |
|---|---|---|---|
| TO | 2,796,083 | 2,431,667 | 2,828,128 |
| P/L | (497,707) | 67,222 | (660,480) |
| NW | 1,422,858 | 1,920,565 | 1,853,343 |
| WC | (1,263,704) | (789,404) | (903,377) |
| Emp. | 105 | N/A | 115 |

DUNS 21-694-0171 **Imp-Exp**

## Pledge Office Chairs Ltd

Millstream Works, Mill Road, Leighton Buzzard, Bedfordshire LU7 1BA
**Tel:** 01525-376181 **Fax:** 01525-382392
**Web:** www.pledgechairs.com
**Reg No:** 0979183 **VAT No:** 197654705
**Estd:** 1970 Private Limited Company
**Line of Business:** Wholesale of other office machinery and equipment
**Export Markets:** Far East & Middle East.
**Export Sales:** £155,530
**Issued Capital:** £50,000
**Principals:** D E Carter *(Managing)*, C Ioannou *(Financial)*, Ms K A Carter, S D Carter, M Mugford, S J Russell
**Co. Secretary:** Ms Doreen Carter
**Responsibilities**
**Senior:** Beverley Pledger *(Office Manager)*
**IT:** Bernie Clap *(IT Manager)*
**US SIC:** 5081 **UK SIC:** 61490
**Auditors:** Gittins Mulderrig
**Bankers:** National Westminster Bank Plc (52-21-27)

| | 31-05-14 | 31-05-13 | 31-05-12 |
|---|---|---|---|
| TO | 11,439,487 | 9,802,513 | 9,920,279 |
| P/L | 777,167 | 222,743 | 271,606 |
| NW | 11,292,780 | 10,682,445 | 10,472,210 |
| WC | 5,813,700 | 5,150,280 | 4,919,801 |
| Emp. | 150 | 143 | 137 |

DUNS 21-288-2815

## Pleroma Investments Ltd

(**Subsidiary of:** Pleroma (U K) Ltd)
Stock Lane, Langford, Bristol, Avon BS40 5ES
**Tel:** 01934-852751 **Fax:** 01934-853017
**Web:** www.pleromainvestment.com
**Reg No:** 0503007 **VAT No:** 181613375
**Estd:** 1951 Private Limited Company
**Line of Business:** Mushroom growers.
**Trading Style:** Monaghan Middlebrook
**Issued Capital:** £19,500,000
**Director:** R C Wilson
**Co. Secretary:** Philip Wilson
**Branches:** Pleroma Investments Ltd, Gravel Hill Lane, Goole, North Humberside DN14 0JD
**US SIC:** 0182 **UK SIC:** 01002
**Auditors:** KPMG
**Bankers:** National Westminster Bank Plc (60-23-32)
**Employees:** 1,124
**Turnover:** £237,000

DUNS 22-753-0748

## Pleroma Ltd

(**Subsidiary of:** Monaghan Middlebrook Mushrooms Ltd)
227 Battleford Road, Dungannon, Co Tyrone BT71 7NN
**Tel:** 028-3754-9846 **Fax:** 028-3754-9846
**Web:** www.pleroma.com
**Reg No:** 0009068NI **Estd:** 1972 Private Limited Company
**Line of Business:** Mushroom growers
**Issued Capital:** £75,000
**Directors:** P D Wilson, R C Wilson, P T Wilson, J Stanley
**Co. Secretary:** Philip Wilson
**US SIC:** 0161 **UK SIC:** 01001
**Auditors:** KPMG
**Bankers:** The Bank Of Ireland (90-20-47)

| | 31-12-12 | 31-12-11 | 31-12-10 |
|---|---|---|---|
| TO | 4,714,000 | 4,455,000 | 5,105,000 |
| P/L | 440,000 | 279,000 | 227,000 |
| NW | 1,511,000 | 1,075,000 | 796,000 |
| WC | 907,000 | 364,000 | 298,000 |
| Emp. | 106 | 84 | 92 |

DUNS 22-110-3620 **Imp**

## Plessey Semiconductors Ltd

(**Subsidiary of:** Plessey Jersey Ltd)
Tamerton Road, Woolwell, Plymouth, Devon PL6 7BQ
**Fax:** 01752-693-200
**Web:** www.plesseysemiconductors.co.uk
**Reg No:** 4129612 **VAT No:** 787351393
**Estd:** 2002 Private Limited Company
**Line of Business:** Manufacturers of semiconductors
**Export Sales:** £6,522,000
**Issued Capital:** £1
**Principals:** C S Bailey *(Managing)*, M Le Goff
**Responsibilities**
**Finance:** Iain Silvester *(Chief Finance Officer)*
**Purchasing:** Bob Whightman *(Purchasing Manager)*
**Branches:** Plessey Semiconductors Ltd, Delta Business Park, Swindon SN5 7XE Great Western Way
**US SIC:** 3999 **UK SIC:** 49590
**Auditors:** Francis Clark LLP

| | 31-12-13 | 31-12-12 | 31-12-11 |
|---|---|---|---|
| TO | 6,747,000 | 7,886,000 | 10,612,000 |
| P/L | (11,456,000) | (10,081,000) | (1,734,000) |
| NW | (7,790,000) | 2,623,000 | (2,296,000) |
| WC | (986,000) | 2,639,000 | (2,728,000) |
| Emp. | 153 | 159 | 162 |

DUNS 21-153-3256

## Plevin Holdings Ltd

Cheshire Street, Mossley, Ashton-Under-Lyne, Lancashire OL5 9NG
**Tel:** 01457838444
**Web:** www.plevin.co.uk
**Reg No:** 6819727 **Estd:** 2009 Private Limited Company
**Line of Business:** Management activities of holding companies
**Trading Style:** Ar Plevin &Sons
**Issued Capital:** £11,190
**Director:** J Plevin
**US SIC:** 6711 **UK SIC:** 83962
**Auditors:** KPMG LLP
**Bankers:** National Westminster Bank Plc (60-13-04)

| | 28-02-13 | 29-02-12 | 28-02-11 |
|---|---|---|---|
| TO | 19,525,000 | 18,160,000 | 18,009,313 |
| P/L | 1,000 | 341,000 | 53,544 |
| NW | 3,283,000 | 3,528,000 | 3,075,105 |
| WC | (2,662,000) | (1,678,000) | (1,654,377) |
| Emp. | 149 | 148 | 139 |

DUNS 50-028-3403 **Imp-Exp**

## Plextek Ltd

London Road, Great Chesterford, Saffron Walden, Essex CB10 1NY
**Tel:** 01799533200
**Web:** www.plextek.co.uk
**Reg No:** 2305889 **VAT No:** 532218867
**Estd:** 1988 Private Limited Company
**Line of Business:** Engineering design activities for industrial process and production
**Export Markets:** Worldwide
**Export Sales:** £3,756,923
**Issued Capital:** £3,840
**Principals:** Dr C R Smithers *(Managing)*, T Jackson *(Managing)*, I A Murphy
**Co. Secretary:** David Cox
**Responsibilities**
**Finance:** Penny Longland *(Senior Finance Administrator)*
**Marketing:** Tim Phipps *(Marketing Manager)*
**Sales:** Andrew Ashby *(New Business Development Manag)*
**IT:** Bill Garland *(Non-PC Systems Manager)*
**HR:** Janice Nicoll *(Human Resources Manager)*
**Health & Safety:** Gary Howard *(Health & Safety Officer)*
**Facilities:** Malcolm Germany *(Facilities Manager)*
**Engineering:** Tom Ross *(Engineering Director)*
**US SIC:** 8911 **UK SIC:** 83701
**Auditors:** PricewaterhouseCoopers LLP
**Bankers:** Barclays Bank Plc (20-17-19)

| | 31-03-13 | 31-03-12 | 31-03-11 |
|---|---|---|---|
| TO | 16,779,499 | 21,170,365 | 28,846,029 |
| P/L | 75,956 | 840,935 | 682,991 |
| NW | 3,165,612 | 3,953,463 | 3,008,758 |
| WC | (532,663) | 1,018,919 | (2,533,709) |
| Emp. | 113 | 129 | 117 |

DUNS 57-001-7335 **Imp-Exp**

## Plexus Corp (Uk) Ltd

(**Subsidiary of:** Plexus Corp.)
Pinnaclehill Industrial Estate, Kelso, Roxburghshire TD5 8XX
**Tel:** 01573-223601
**Web:** www.plexus.com
**Reg No:** 0146948SC **VAT No:** 634817526
**Estd:** 2000 Private Limited Company
**Line of Business:** Manufacturers of electronic equipment and components
**Export Markets:** Europe
**Export Sales:** £24,575,000
**Issued Capital:** £19,504,798
**Directors:** R Darroch, A Ninivaggi, P J Jermain, D Kerr
**Co. Secretary:** Ms Laura Middlemass
**Responsibilities**
**Senior:** George Setton *(Manager)*, Frank Zycinski *(General Manager)*
**US SIC:** 3679 **UK SIC:** 34542
**Auditors:** PricewaterhouseCoopers LLP
**Bankers:** Bank Of Scotland (80-16-57)

| | 28-09-13 | 29-09-12 | 01-09-11 |
|---|---|---|---|
| TO | 52,833,000 | 38,274,000 | 47,145,000 |
| P/L | (1,305,000) | (23,000) | 191,000 |
| NW | 39,334,000 | 39,990,000 | 39,657,000 |
| WC | 49,706,000 | 36,194,000 | 30,168,000 |
| Emp. | 466 | 358 | 375 |

DUNS 76-348-5166

## Plexus Cotton Ltd

20 Chapel Street, Liverpool, Merseyside L3 9AG
**Web:** www.plexus-cotton.com
**Reg No:** 2548312 **VAT No:** 548636900
**Estd:** 1990 Private Limited Company
**Line of Business:** Textile merchants
**Principals:** N P Earlam *(Managing)*, P M Egli, C J Harman, D Crausaz, C S Burns
**Co. Secretary:** Mrs Ann Adlington
**Responsibilities**
**Senior:** Jean Derossis *(Manager)*, Laurence Kirby *(Financial Director)*, Peter Salcedo *(Business Systems Manager)*
**Admin:** Andy Holden *(Senior System Administrator)*, Simon Mchattie *(Administration Manager)*
**IT:** Andy Holden *(Senior System Administrator)*
**US SIC:** 7399, 5133
**UK SIC:** 83954, 61600
**Auditors:** PricewaterhouseCoopers LLP
**Bankers:** Lloyds TSB Bank plc (30-95-11)
**Employees:** 3,416
**Turnover:** £396,244,000

DUNS 89-671-9796

## Plexus Holdings Plc

Thames House, Portsmouth Road, Esher, Surrey KT10 9AD
**Tel:** 020 7795 6890
**Web:** www.plexusplc.com
**Reg No:** 3322928 **Estd:** 1997 Private Limited Company
**Line of Business:** Management activities of holding companies
**Export Sales:** £17,132,000
**Issued Capital:** £827,467
**Directors:** C Jones, G E Thompson, R F Adair, C F Hendrie, B H Van Bilderbeek, G P Stevens, C Fraser, J J Thrall
**Co. Secretary:** Douglas Armour
**US SIC:** 6711 **UK SIC:** 83962
**Auditors:** Crowe Clark Whitehill LLP

| | 30-06-14 | 30-06-13 | 30-06-12 |
|---|---|---|---|
| TO | 27,024,000 | 25,566,000 | 19,706,000 |
| P/L | 5,375,000 | 4,269,000 | 3,088,000 |
| NW | 23,383,000 | 17,741,000 | 15,368,000 |
| WC | 12,407,000 | 8,028,000 | 9,690,000 |
| Emp. | 142 | 129 | 101 |

DUNS 77-935-6609

## Plm Dollar Group Ltd

The Heliport, Dalcross, Inverness, Inverness-Shire IV2 7XB
**Web:** www.pdghelicopters.com
**Reg No:** 0157532SC **Estd:** 1995 Private Limited Company
**Line of Business:** Goods delivery services
**Export Sales:** £2,017,502
**Trading Style:** P D G Helicopter
**Issued Capital:** £1,403,101
**Directors:** R Waddams, M Gardner, R Hill
**Co. Secretary:** Jerry Francis
**Responsibilities**
**Senior:** Alasdair Laing *(Director)*, Timothy Laing *(Director)*, Moira Murphy *(Centre Manager)*
**Operations:** Ian Innes *(Agricultural Operations Manage)*
**Fleet:** Stephen Dean *(AS355 / AS365 Line Pilot)*, Roger Griffiths *(Twin Squirrel Pilot)*
**Branches:** Plm Dollar Group Ltd, Ministry Of Defence Butec, Kyle, Ross-Shire IV40 8AJ
**US SIC:** 4213 **UK SIC:** 72300
**Auditors:** MacKenzie Kerr Ltd
**Bankers:** Bank Of Scotland (80-91-26)

| | 30-09-14 | 30-09-13 | 30-09-12 |
|---|---|---|---|
| TO | 15,619,535 | 15,505,605 | 14,419,434 |
| P/L | 3,281,113 | 3,004,345 | 1,888,896 |
| NW | 9,996,391 | 7,525,515 | 5,187,080 |
| WC | 1,827,280 | 1,653,691 | 1,351,349 |
| Emp. | 88 | 87 | 89 |

DUNS 54-852-6698

## The Ploughman

North Deeside Road, Peterculter, Aberdeenshire AB14 0QN
**Tel:** 01224-733365
**Web:** www.arealpub.co.uk
**Estd:** 1983 Proprietorship
**Line of Business:** Public house
**Proprietor:** G White
**Responsibilities**
**Senior:** Graeme Wight *(Proprietor)*
**US SIC:** 5813 **UK SIC:** 66200
**Employees:** 49

DUNS 21-098-9052

## Plowman Craven Ltd

Lea River House, Harpenden, Hertfordshire AL5 5EQ
**Tel:** 08453451584
**Web:** www.plowmancraven.co.uk
**Reg No:** 6429056 **Estd:** 1976 Private Limited Company
**Line of Business:** Engineering related scientific and technical consulting activities
**Export Sales:** £243,230
**Issued Capital:** £1
**Directors:** M F Donald, M D Howells, M D Swan, A G Molloy, P K Folwell, D R Norris, H S Mighell, D P De Laszlo
**Co. Secretary:** Howard Mighell
**Responsibilities**
**Finance:** Michelle Bourne *(Financial Accountant)*
**Branches:** Plowman Craven Ltd, 33A Clerkenwell Green, London EC1R 0DU
**US SIC:** 7399 **UK SIC:** 83954

| | 31-12-13 | 31-12-12 | 31-12-11 |
|---|---|---|---|
| TO | 10,987,443 | 8,903,113 | 8,169,020 |
| P/L | 1,373,529 | 667,333 | 696,632 |
| NW | (442,973) | (1,654,272) | 1,123,038 |
| WC | 255,831 | (156,535) | 733,320 |
| Emp. | 122 | 117 | 105 |

DUNS 21-171-2361
## Plp Architecture Ltd
2 Seething Lane, London EC3N 4AT
**Tel:** 02030063900
**Web:** www.plparchitecture.com
**Reg No:** 6956582 **Estd:** 2009 Private Limited Company
**Line of Business:** Architectural activities
**Export Sales:** £3,838,905
**Issued Capital:** £1
**Directors:** L Polisano, D M Leventhal
**Co. Secretary:** Anthony Plaw
**US SIC:** 8911 **UK SIC:** 83701
**Auditors:** Grant Thornton UK LLP

| | 31-12-13 | 31-12-12 | 31-12-11 |
|---|---|---|---|
| TO | 12,334,892 | 10,764,754 | 12,647,144 |
| P/L | 1,124,245 | 1,540,282 | 1,423,251 |
| NW | (162,429) | (1,265,680) | (2,729,906) |
| WC | (150,379) | (726,381) | (71,597) |
| Emp. | 108 | 100 | 90 |

DUNS 21-819-8481
## Plt Ownership Group Ltd
6a Longs Business Centre, 232 Fakenham Road, Norwich, Norfolk NR8 6QW
**Tel:** 01603216948
**Reg No:** 7920295 **Estd:** 2013 Private Limited Company
**Line of Business:** Secretarial and translation activities
**Issued Capital:** £99
**Director:** K L Thurston
**Co. Secretary:** Graham Eaglesham
**US SIC:** 7339 **UK SIC:** 83954

| | 31-03-13 |
|---|---|
| TA | 99 |
| NW | 99 |

DUNS 21-619-0254
## Plug
1 Rockingham Gate, Sheffield, South Yorkshire S1 4JD
**Tel:** 01142762676
**Web:** www.the-plug.com
**Proprietorship**
**Line of Business:** Alcoholic drink establishments
**Proprietor:** Mrs J Armitage
**US SIC:** 5813, 5812
**UK SIC:** 66200, 66110
**Employees:** 100

DUNS 50-030-1163
## Plum Recruitment Ltd
Brassey House, New Zealand Avenue, Walton-On-Thames, Surrey KT12 1QD
**Tel:** 01932-231233 **Fax:** 01932-241552
**Web:** www.plum-personnel.co.uk
**Reg No:** 2307709 **Estd:** 1988 Private Limited Company
**Line of Business:** Employment and recruitment companies and consultants
**Trading Style:** Plum Personnel
**Issued Capital:** £1,000
**Director:** P J Sumner
**Co. Secretary:** Ms Patricia Taylor
**Responsibilities**
**Senior:** Carole Gray *(Manager)*, Rosalind Robertson *(Manager)*
**US SIC:** 7361 **UK SIC:** 83954
**Auditors:** H W Fisher & Co Ltd
**Bankers:** HSBC Bank plc (40-43-04)

| | 31-03-14 | 31-03-13 | 31-03-12 |
|---|---|---|---|
| TA | 191,239 | 212,928 | 252,617 |
| NW | 121,712 | 164,214 | 125,681 |
| WC | 116,579 | 162,280 | 122,973 |

DUNS 64-074-4103
## Plumbcity Ltd
Unit 7 Commerce Way, Colchester, Essex CO2 8HX
**Tel:** 01206790550 **Fax:** 01206870201
**Web:** www.plumbcity.com
**Reg No:** 4477777 **VAT No:** 802565642
**Estd:** 2003 Private Limited Company
**Line of Business:** Plumbers merchants
**Trading Style:** Plumbclick
**Issued Capital:** £75,000
**Principals:** S J Wimbledon *(Managing)*, G F Eldred, P F Manby
**Responsibilities**
**Sales:** Tim Reynolds *(Commercial Manager)*
**Branches:** Plumbcity Ltd, 43 Roundtree Way, Norwich, Norfolk NR7 8SG
**US SIC:** 7399, 5961
**UK SIC:** 83954, 65600
**Bankers:** HSBC Bank plc (40-18-04)

| | 31-12-13 | 31-12-12 | 31-12-11 |
|---|---|---|---|
| TO | 19,925,682 | 17,789,360 | 16,538,769 |
| P/L | 2,404,297 | 1,900,969 | 1,723,818 |
| NW | 6,851,574 | 5,906,516 | 4,762,422 |
| WC | 6,304,163 | 5,341,054 | 4,209,146 |
| Emp. | 74 | 73 | 69 |

DUNS 21-043-0630
## Plumbing and Drainage Merchants
302 Drumoyne Road, Glasgow, Lanarkshire G51 4DX
**Web:** www.pdmltd.co.uk
**Estd:** 2006 Proprietorship
**Line of Business:** Plumbers merchants
**Proprietor:** J Goudie
**Responsibilities**
**Senior:** Brian Gault *(Manager)*
**US SIC:** 5074 **UK SIC:** 61300
**Employees:** 112

DUNS 21-309-6704 **Imp**
## Plumbs Ltd
Brookhouse Mill, Old Lancaster Lane, Preston, Lancashire PR1 7PZ
**Tel:** 01772838301 **Fax:** 01772838453
**Web:** www.plumbscovers.co.uk
**Reg No:** 1113238 **VAT No:** 154552174
**Estd:** 1973 Private Limited Company
**Line of Business:** Upholstering
**Trading Style:** Plumbs Mail Order, Plumbs Home Consultancy Service, Classic Covers
**Issued Capital:** £23,000
**Principals:** G G Plumb *(Chairman)*, Mrs L K Hindle *(Marketing)*, Ms S L Page, J R Page, M Harrison, C M Wontner-Smith
**Co. Secretary:** Martin Harrison
**Responsibilities**
**Senior:** Richard Gatley *(Financial Manager)*
**Finance:** Richard Gatley *(Financial Manager)*
**Marketing:** Alison Mason *(Product Marketing Manager)*, Janet Russell *(Marketing Manager)*
**Health & Safety:** George Blackburn *(Health & Safety Manager)*
**Operations:** Terry Lloyd *(Production Control Manager)*
**US SIC:** 2599 **UK SIC:** 46720
**Auditors:** Grant Thornton UK LLP
**Bankers:** HSBC Bank plc (40-37-25)

| | 31-12-13 | 31-12-12 | 31-12-11 |
|---|---|---|---|
| TO | 27,278,412 | 27,773,130 | 26,206,533 |
| P/L | 252,705 | 246,542 | 407,185 |
| NW | 1,315,800 | 766,828 | 934,611 |
| WC | 1,285,912 | 1,454,569 | 1,479,378 |
| Emp. | 343 | 320 | 312 |

DUNS 77-027-7077
## Plumbstop Ltd
Unit 9, Alder Hills Industrial Estate, Alder Hills, Poole, Dorset BH12 4AR
**Tel:** 01202732000 **Fax:** 01285-650055
**Web:** www.plumbstop.co.uk
**Reg No:** 2666030 **VAT No:** 576250823
**Estd:** 2012 Private Limited Company
**Line of Business:** Plumbers merchants
**Issued Capital:** £75
**Principals:** P M Fitzcharles *(Managing)*, D N Chappell, K C Parker, D J Tucker
**Responsibilities**
**Senior:** Mark Woodford *(Branch Manager)*
**Branches:** Plumbstop Ltd, Love Lane, The Rutherford Centre, Cirencester, Gloucestershire GL7 1YG
**US SIC:** 5074 **UK SIC:** 61300
**Auditors:** Taylors
**Bankers:** HSBC Bank plc (40-17-25)

| | 31-12-13 | 31-12-12 | 31-12-11 |
|---|---|---|---|
| TO | 13,805,269 | 11,501,463 | 7,974,617 |
| P/L | 535,196 | 367,186 | 160,836 |
| NW | 923,624 | 796,271 | 623,111 |
| WC | 734,882 | 630,015 | 477,157 |
| Emp. | 64 | 59 | N/A |

DUNS 73-980-7134
## Plumbstore (Plumbing + Heating Supplies) Ltd.
Unit 2 Alderston Way, Righead Industrial Estate, Bellshill, Lanarkshire ML4 3LT
**Tel:** 01698744107 **Fax:** 01698-744104
**Web:** www.plumbstores.co.uk
**Reg No:** 0273404SC **Estd:** 2004 Private Limited Company
**Line of Business:** Plumbers merchants
**Issued Capital:** £557,000
**Directors:** T A Todd, F J Stevenson
**Co. Secretary:** Robert Frew
**US SIC:** 5074 **UK SIC:** 61300
**Bankers:** Clydesdale Bank Plc (82-69-07)

| | 31-12-13 | 31-12-12 | 31-12-11 |
|---|---|---|---|
| TO | 15,881,515 | 15,807,463 | 16,947,936 |
| P/L | 191,492 | 111,818 | 61,307 |
| NW | 2,157,623 | 2,132,436 | 2,063,140 |
| WC | 1,801,363 | 1,699,737 | 1,520,712 |
| Emp. | 70 | 72 | 78 |

DUNS 21-755-4993
## Plume School
Fambridge Road, Maldon, Essex CM9 6AB
**Tel:** 01621854681
**Web:** www.plume.essex.sch.uk
**Reg No:** 7849731 **Estd:** 2011 Private Company Limited By Guarantee
**Line of Business:** General secondary education
**Directors:** P D Nagle, A J Almond, J R Everard, D M Stephenson, Mrs J C Sims, Mrs J M Binder, Mrs R C Mahoney, Mrs Y M Chick
**Responsibilities**
**Senior:** Rachael Barbrook *(Director)*, Mark Howell *(Director)*, Gillian Mckinnell *(Director)*, Christopher Pond *(Director)*, Clive Purdy *(Director)*, Debra Thomas *(Director)*
**US SIC:** 8211 **UK SIC:** 93200
**Bankers:** Lloyds TSB Bank plc (30-25-34)

| | 31-08-14 | 31-08-13 | 31-08-12 |
|---|---|---|---|
| TO | 11,212,045 | 12,116,853 | 34,141,895 |
| P/L | (348,150) | 906,179 | 26,565,533 |
| NW | 24,716,562 | 24,750,712 | 24,007,533 |
| WC | 1,229,229 | 1,443,049 | 930,444 |
| Emp. | 259 | 212 | 213 |

DUNS 22-654-8329
## Plumline Bespoke Joinery Ltd
171 Hucknall Road Sherwood, Nottingham, Nottinghamshire NG5 1SD
**Tel:** 01159-629444 **Fax:** 01159-691213
**Web:** www.plumline.co.uk
**Reg No:** 1545984 **Estd:** 1981 Private Limited Company
**Line of Business:** Manufacture of other office and shop furniture
**Issued Capital:** £132
**Principals:** D L Beasley *(Sales)*, R D Beasley, S C Beasley
**Responsibilities**
**Admin:** Claudette Brown *(Office Manager)*
**US SIC:** 2599 **UK SIC:** 46720
**Auditors:** Smith Cooper Nottingham
**Bankers:** National Westminster Bank Plc (56-00-61)

| | 31-12-13 | 31-12-12 | 30-12-12 |
|---|---|---|---|
| TA | 1,138,854 | 880,537 | 738,534 |
| NW | 120,671 | 76,315 | (15,993) |
| WC | (6,151) | (7,776) | (102,177) |

DUNS 21-154-9295
## Plumpton College
Ditchling Road, Plumpton, Lewes, East Sussex BN7 3AE
**Tel:** 01273890454
**Web:** www.plumpton.ac.uk
**Estd:** 2011
**Line of Business:** Colleges (higher education)
**Director:** J Brookham
**Responsibilities**
**Senior:** Emma Cook *(Manager)*, Louisa Devismes *(Senior Manager)*, Vicky Stevens *(Manager)*, Becky Taylor *(Senior Manager)*
**Finance:** Nick Lech *(CFO)*, Valerie Wilkinson *(Financial Director)*
**Marketing:** Jo Cowderoy *(Wineskills Project Coordinator)*, Sean Dexter *(Marketing Officer)*
**Sales:** Don Cranfield *(Sales Manager)*
**Admin:** Hannah Berry *(Office Manager)*, Valerie Raynor *(PA to the Principal)*
**IT:** Sam Howe *(Computer Manager)*
**HR:** Jenny Baer *(Human Resources Manager)*, Don Cranfield *(Sales Manager)*, Julia Hadden *(HR manager)*
**Facilities:** Geoff Gregory *(Resources Director)*
**Operations:** Sean Dexter *(Marketing Officer)*
**Branches:** Plumpton College, Ivyland Farm, Netherfield Road, Battle, East Sussex TN33 9QB
**US SIC:** 8221, 8249
**UK SIC:** 93100, 93300
**Employees:** 200

DUNS 21-579-0479
## Plumstead Manor School
Old Mill Road, London SE18 1QF
**Tel:** 020-32603333
**Web:** www.plumsteadmanor.com
**Estd:** 1986
**Line of Business:** Schools
**Trading Style:** Plumstead Manor / Negus School
**Responsibilities**
**Senior:** Rachel Archer *(Premises Manager)*, Alida Burdett *(Head of Sixth Form)*, Sue Flanigan *(Head Teacher)*, Douglas Greg *(Interim Head Teacher)*, Julie Porrison *(Proprietor)*
**Finance:** Barbara McBrien *(Bursar)*
**Admin:** Sylvia Heather *(Office Manager)*
**IT:** Barbara McBrien *(Bursar)*
**HR:** Janet Tarling *(Human Resources Officer)*, Caroline Wilshaw *(Deputy Headmaster)*
**Health & Safety:** Pip Newnham *(Health & Safety Officer)*
**Facilities:** Rachel Archer *(Premises Manager)*
**Purchasing:** Barbara McBrien *(Bursar)*
**US SIC:** 8211 **UK SIC:** 93200

DUNS 21-706-0591
## Plus Dane (Cheshire) Housing Association Ltd
Shepherds Mill, Worrall Street, Congleton, Cheshire CW12 1DT
**Tel:** 08001692988
**Web:** www.dane-housing.co.uk
**Reg No:** 0030489IP **Estd:** 2008 Friendly Society
**Line of Business:** Housing associations societies trusts & co-operatives
**US SIC:** 8321 **UK SIC:** 96111
**Bankers:** National Westminster Bank Plc (60-06-10)
**Turnover:** £18,605,000

DUNS 36-515-1310
## Plus Dane Housing Group Ltd
Baltimore Buildings, 13-15 Rodney Street, Liverpool, Merseyside L1 9EF
**Tel:** 01517-080674
**Web:** www.neighbourhoodinvestor.com
**Reg No:** 0029480IP **Estd:** 1994
**Line of Business:** Associations
**Trading Style:** Neighbourhood Investor
**Principals:** P Shaw *(Managing)*, Ms C Griffiths *(Managing)*, Ms J Phillips *(Managing)*, G Murden *(Managing)*, M Doran *(Managing)*, K Perry
**Responsibilities**
**Senior:** Alison Carey *(Manager)*, Paul Cropper *(Manager)*, James Downey *(Manager)*, Danielle Sharp *(Communications Manager)*
**Marketing:** Janet Cresswell *(?Campaigns Manager)*, Clare Feeney *(Communications Officer)*, Elizabeth Miller *(Marketing and Events Officer)*
**IT:** Ann Foy *(IT Manager)*
**HR:** Clare Maudsley *(Training Manager)*, Ian Meller *(Human Resources Manager)*
**Health & Safety:** Ian Meller *(Human Resources Manager)*
**Facilities:** Dawn Stackhouse *(Facilities Manager)*
**Operations:** Stephen Mcnicholas *(Operations Manager)*, Jeff O' Carroll *(Neighbourhood Engagement Officer)*, Hayley Pover *(Support Officer)*
**US SIC:** 8321 **UK SIC:** 96111
**Auditors:** Grant Thornton UK LLP
**Bankers:** National Westminster Bank Plc (01-05-15)

| | 31-03-12 | 31-03-11 | 31-03-10 |
|---|---|---|---|
| TO | 57,354,000 | 55,177,000 | 52,416,000 |
| P/L | 3,092,000 | 2,757,000 | 2,184,000 |
| NW | 8,039,000 | 6,962,000 | (6,598,000) |
| WC | 3,808,000 | 3,376,000 | 6,625,000 |
| Emp. | 518 | 523 | 482 |

DUNS 42-350-6620
## Plus (Forth Valley) Ltd
Broadleys Road Springkerse Industrial, Estate, Stirling, Stirlingshire FK7 7ST
**Tel:** 01786450086
**Web:** www.plus-stirling.org.uk
**Reg No:** 0226225SC **Estd:** 2001 Private Limited Company
**Line of Business:** Disability services
**Trading Style:** Plus Stirling
**Directors:** Ms J Livingstone, Mrs R F Campbell, P W Dumbleton, Ms J E Davidson, Mrs M A Palmer, S W Urquhart, J M Gill, R J Macrae
**Co. Secretary:** Mrs Susan Fullerton
**Responsibilities**
**Senior:** Khlayre Cairney *(Director)*, Irene Cavanagh *(Manager)*, Paul Dimeo *(Director)*, Ann Finlayson *(Director)*, Lesley-Anne Livesey *(Director)*
**US SIC:** 8321 **UK SIC:** 96111
**Auditors:** Macfarlane Gray
**Bankers:** Bank Of Scotland (80-91-29)

| | 31-03-14 | 31-03-13 | 31-03-12 |
|---|---|---|---|
| TO | 457,472 | 403,949 | 420,334 |
| P/L | (32,759) | (17,033) | 43,123 |
| NW | 231,116 | 263,875 | 280,908 |
| WC | 216,741 | 245,796 | 276,238 |
| Emp. | 49 | 59 | 54 |

DUNS 29-458-9890
## Plus One Services Ltd
**(Subsidiary of:** Hood Group Ltd**)**
1st Floor Maitland House, Warrior Square, Southend-On-Sea, Essex SS1 2AA
**Tel:** 01702-443668 **Fax:** 03453453801
**Web:** www.plusoneservices.com
**Reg No:** 1709711 **Estd:** 1983 Private Limited Company
**Line of Business:** Insurance - household
**Issued Capital:** £10,000
**Directors:** S A Hood, R Gildie, P R Firkins, Miss S M Milbourne, J M Wallis
**Co. Secretary:** Simon Drew
**US SIC:** 6399 **UK SIC:** 82001
**Auditors:** Wilkins Kennedy

**Bankers:** Lloyds TSB Bank plc (30-97-84)

| | 31-12-13 | 31-12-12 | 31-12-11 |
|---|---|---|---|
| TO | 7,129,579 | 7,032,217 | 6,918,981 |
| P/L | 550,493 | 409,016 | 477,343 |
| NW | 1,062,360 | 621,262 | 545,282 |
| WC | 632,573 | 65,272 | 31,001 |
| Emp. | 164 | 169 | 179 |

DUNS 34-745-6303

## Plus (Providence Linc United Services)

6 Belmont Hill, London SE13 5BD
**Tel:** 020-8297-1250
**Web:** www.plus-services.org
**Reg No:** 2782712 **Estd:** 1993 Private Limited Company
**Line of Business:** Charities and charitable organisations
**Directors:** Ms B Borysik, Mrs D Traquair, P Mould, D I Dannreuther, Ms E Janko Mulcahy, Mrs S K Eyres, J T Wallington
**Co. Secretary:** Ms Sally Pennington
**Responsibilities**
**Senior:** Peter Van Berckel (Manager)
**US SIC:** 8299 **UK SIC:** 93300
**Bankers:** HSBC Bank plc (40-02-05)

| | 31-03-14 | 31-03-13 | 31-03-12 |
|---|---|---|---|
| TO | 4,065,192 | 4,174,155 | 4,261,685 |
| P/L | (57,743) | (118,372) | 61,870 |
| NW | 5,683,148 | 5,578,792 | 5,321,104 |
| WC | 1,461,299 | 1,503,947 | 3,159,327 |
| Emp. | 195 | 199 | 182 |

DUNS 21-095-9531

## Pluscrates Ltd

(**Subsidiary of:** The Rental Group (London) Ltd)
Unit 9 Carey Way Towers Business Park, Wembley, Middlesex HA9 0LQ
**Tel:** 02089000321 **Fax:** 02089030188
**Web:** www.pluscrate.com
**Reg No:** 6406174 **VAT No:** 926186409
**Estd:** 2007 Private Limited Company
**Line of Business:** Storage systems
**Trading Style:** Pluscrates Ltd
**Issued Capital:** £100,000
**Director:** N S Mcguigan
**Co. Secretary:** Ms Helen Mcguigan
**Responsibilities**
**Senior:** Heather Miles (Business Manager)
**US SIC:** 2599 **UK SIC:** 46720
**Auditors:** Graham Keeble Partnership LLP

| | 30-06-14 | 30-06-13 | 30-06-12 |
|---|---|---|---|
| TA | 3,164,948 | 2,902,943 | 2,801,067 |
| NW | (105,058) | (223,659) | (413,954) |
| WC | (201,374) | (13,358) | (71,903) |

DUNS 37-971-1773

## Plusnet Plc

(**Subsidiary of:** Bt Group Plc)
Internet House, 8 Furnival Road, Victoria Quays, Sheffield, South Yorkshire S4 7YA
**Tel:** 01142200000 **Fax:** 01142200088
**Web:** www.plus.net
**Reg No:** 3279013 **Estd:** 1996 Public Limited Company
**Line of Business:** Other computer related activities
**Issued Capital:** £60,687
**Directors:** M J Davies, A J Baker, R Barzegar, J Petter
**Co. Secretary:**
Newgate Street Secretaries Limit
**Responsibilities**
**Senior:** Samantha Booth (Manager), Clare Sadlier (Manager), Anthony Vollmer (Manager), Henry Vollmer (Manager)
**US SIC:** 7379 **UK SIC:** 83940
**Auditors:** PricewaterhouseCoopers LLP
**Bankers:** HSBC Bank plc (40-41-07)

| | 31-03-14 | 31-03-13 | 31-03-12 |
|---|---|---|---|
| TO | 178,850,000 | 140,649,000 | 113,408,000 |
| P/L | 25,237,000 | 28,363,000 | 17,567,000 |
| NW | 40,903,000 | 25,028,000 | 3,528,000 |
| WC | 23,993,000 | 16,225,000 | (4,470,000) |
| Emp. | 873 | 732 | 608 |

DUNS 73-918-3361

## The Pluss Organisation

Yeoford Way, Marsh Barton Trading Estate, Exeter, Devon EX2 8LB
**Tel:** 01392204144
**Web:** www.pluss.org.uk
**Reg No:** 5171613 **Estd:** 2004 Private Company Limited By Guarantee
**Line of Business:** Hospital equipment
**Directors:** M E Aspinall, S Darling, P J Brock, Mrs C M Lawrence, M L Davies, S T Hawkins, S W Graham, B C Hughes
**Co. Secretary:** Paul James
**Responsibilities**
**Senior:** Lorraine Parker (Director), Jim Payne (Board Member), Cynthia Stocks (Director)
**Branches:** The Pluss Organisation, Unit 2, Aspen Way, Paignton, Devon TQ4 7QR
**US SIC:** 5199, 8999
**UK SIC:** 61900, 83954
**Auditors:** Francis Clark Chartered Accountants

**Bankers:** Barclays Bank Plc (20-05-74)

| | 31-03-14 | 31-03-13 | 31-03-12 |
|---|---|---|---|
| TO | 27,813,000 | 27,428,000 | 27,427,000 |
| P/L | 2,250,000 | (173,000) | 835,000 |
| NW | 1,326,000 | 583,000 | 213,000 |
| WC | 999,000 | 991,000 | 1,193,000 |
| Emp. | 633 | 594 | 580 |

DUNS 73-315-4475     Imp

## Pluswipes Ltd

(**Subsidiary of:** Professional Disposables Inc.)
Pywell Road, Corby, Northamptonshire NN17 5XJ
**Web:** www.pluswipes.co.uk
**Reg No:** 4589210 **Estd:** 2002 Private Limited Company
**Line of Business:** Manufacture of soap and detergents
**Export Sales:** £1,680,557
**Issued Capital:** £5,000
**Directors:** A J Culkin, A T Lockley, M L Teasdale Brown, D Cowell, M A Staton
**Co. Secretary:** David Cowell
**Responsibilities**
**Senior:** Tanya Teasdale Brown (Human Resources Manager)
**Finance:** Tanya Teasdale Brown (Human Resources Manager)
**HR:** Tanya Teasdale Brown (Human Resources Manager)
**US SIC:** 2841, 2647
**UK SIC:** 25810, 47220

| | 31-12-13 | 31-03-13 | 31-12-12 |
|---|---|---|---|
| TO | 7,251,726 | 10,687,936 | 9,963,499 |
| P/L | 329,830 | 1,138,117 | 868,594 |
| NW | 1,867,282 | 2,139,608 | 1,403,723 |
| WC | 1,164,504 | 1,723,736 | 1,198,816 |
| Emp. | 67 | 63 | 53 |

DUNS 29-103-9840

## Plymouth Age Concern

Elspeth Sitters House, 1 Hoegate Street, Plymouth, Devon PL1 2JB
**Tel:** 01752665424
**Web:** www.thefinishingtouchlimited.co.uk
**Reg No:** 1499927 **Estd:** 2005 Private Limited Company
**Line of Business:** Social work activities with accommodation
**Directors:** Mrs L M Wheeler, Professor S Asthana, Ms M Mcclarey, Ms L J Swain, Mrs S M Williams, M J Rose, Miss C H Bailey, Ms M Y Quinlan
**Co. Secretary:** Mrs Barbara Duffy
**Responsibilities**
**Senior:** Simon Arthurs (Director), Sheila Down (Manager)
**Branches:** Plymouth Age Concern, Elspeth Sitters House, Hoegate Street, Barbican, Plymouth, Devon PL1 2JB
**US SIC:** 8321 **UK SIC:** 96111
**Auditors:** Parkhurst Hill

| | 31-03-14 | 31-03-13 | 31-03-12 |
|---|---|---|---|
| TO | 2,009,421 | 2,194,319 | 2,154,593 |
| P/L | (33,536) | 65,866 | (199,372) |
| NW | 5,178,516 | 5,110,710 | 4,823,145 |
| WC | 389,964 | 344,863 | 182,597 |
| Emp. | 137 | 156 | 153 |

DUNS 21-691-0794

## Plymouth & South West Co-Operative Society Ltd

Holyoake House, Manchester M60 0AS
**Fax:** 01752303259
**Web:** www.uk.coop
**Reg No:** 0019007IP **VAT No:** 143543482
**Estd:** 1840 Friendly Society
**Line of Business:** Convenience stores
**Trading Style:** Co-Operatives Uk
**Principals:** D F Pidsley (Chairman), G H Townsend, B Dure, J W Wright, V R Nosworthy, K R Ferris, Mrs C Pearse, Mrs B Errington
**Co. Secretary:** D Fletcher
**Responsibilities**
**Senior:** Lisa Brierley (HR Business Partner), Jane John (Branch Manager), Louisa Westlake (Manager)
**Finance:** Philip Holmes (Head of Finance & Shared Servi)
**Facilities:** Kika Strong (Facilities Manager)
**Branches:** Plymouth & South West Co-Operative Society Ltd, 49-50 Southside Street, Plymouth, Devon PL1 2LD
**US SIC:** 5411, 5912
**UK SIC:** 64100, 64300
**Auditors:** PricewaterhouseCoopers LLP
**Bankers:** The Co-Operative Bank Plc (08-90-21)
**Employees:** 2,244
**Turnover:** £151,440,000

DUNS 22-553-3991

## Plymouth Business School

Drake Circus, Plymouth, Devon PL4 8AA
**Tel:** 01752232800
**Web:** www.plymouth.ac.uk
**Estd:** 2002 Proprietorship
**Line of Business:** Colleges (higher education)

**Directors:** Dr J C Cannon, Dr C Booth, R G Barker, Dr R F Robbins
**Branches:** 3 Portland Villas Plymouth Devon.
**US SIC:** 8221 **UK SIC:** 93100
**Employees:** 136

DUNS 22-551-5691

## Plymouth City Airport Ltd

(**Subsidiary of:** Sutton Harbour Holdings Plc)
North Quay House, North Quay, Plymouth, Devon PL4 0RA
**Tel:** 01752204090
**Web:** www.plymouthairport.com
**Reg No:** 1213405 **Estd:** 1931 Private Limited Company
**Line of Business:** Other supporting air transport activities
**Issued Capital:** £339,100
**Directors:** G S Miller, J W Schofield
**Co. Secretary:** Ms Natasha Gadsdon
**Branches:** St. Mawgan, Newquay
**US SIC:** 4582 **UK SIC:** 76400
**Auditors:** Grant Thornton
**Bankers:** Barclays Bank Plc (20-68-10)

| | 31-03-14 | 31-03-13 | 31-03-12 |
|---|---|---|---|
| TO | 488,000 | 412,000 | 1,156,000 |
| P/L | 220,000 | 121,000 | (432,000) |
| NW | 7,755,000 | 7,528,000 | 6,134,000 |
| WC | 7,573,000 | 7,353,000 | (34,000) |
| Emp. | N/A | N/A | 05 |

DUNS 23-641-6095     Imp

## Plymouth City Council

Civic Centre, Armada Way, Plymouth, Devon PL1 2AA
**Tel:** 01752668000
**Web:** www.plymouth.gov.uk
**VAT No:** 144675845 **Estd:** 1998
**Line of Business:** Adult education locations
**Trading Style:** Plymbridge Nursery School Children Centre, Mount Tamar School
**Directors:** Ms A Stone, D Shephard
**Responsibilities**
**Senior:** Tracey Lee (CEO), Gwyn Price (Board Member), David Shepperd (Head of Legal Dept)
**Finance:** Malcom Coe (Assistant Director for Finance), Davin Draffan (Assistant Director for Economi)
**Admin:** Ian McPhearson (Customer Services Manager)
**HR:** Sue Blackman (Training Manager), Mark Grimley (Assistant Director for HR and), Jean Jasper (Teacher), Jill Martin (Human Resources Manager), Tracy Shepherd (Training Officer)
**Operations:** Ian McPhearson (Customer Services Manager)
**Fleet:** Shona McGregor (Fleet Manager)
**Branches:** Plymouth City Council, 21 Boniface Lane, Plymouth, Devon PL5 3AG
**US SIC:** 9121 **UK SIC:** 91110
**Employees:** 2,000

DUNS 23-920-9229

## Plymouth College Enterprises Ltd

(**Subsidiary of:** Plymouth College)
Ford Park, Plymouth, Devon PL4 6RN
**Tel:** 01752203300
**Web:** www.plymouthcollege.com
**Reg No:** 3911069 **Estd:** 2000 Private Limited Company
**Line of Business:** Manufacture of workwear
**Issued Capital:** £100
**Directors:** Dr S J Wormleighton, D Woodgate, Mrs C Evans
**Co. Secretary:** David Baylis
**US SIC:** 7399 **UK SIC:** 83954

| | 31-08-13 | 31-08-12 | 31-08-11 |
|---|---|---|---|
| TO | 71,879 | 70,651 | 51,070 |
| P/L | 1,886 | 9,686 | 738 |
| NW | 63,474 | 61,938 | 54,152 |
| WC | 42,414 | 33,336 | 34,220 |

DUNS 42-319-2350     Imp

## Plymouth College of Art

Tavistock Place, Plymouth, Devon PL4 8AT
**Tel:** 01752-203434
**Web:** www.pcad.ac.uk
**Estd:** 1993
**Line of Business:** Technical and vocational secondary education
**Principals:** Ms K Hagen (Financial), M W Brindley
**Responsibilities**
**Senior:** Andrew Brewerton (Principal), Hari Sparkes (Executive), Lynne Staley-Brookes (Principal), Louise Thom (Executive)
**Admin:** Tim Bolton (Administrator), Janet Sturges (Registrar)
**IT:** Perry Middleton (Senior IT Executive)
**Operations:** Philip Purse (Production and Operations Mana)
**US SIC:** 8249 **UK SIC:** 93300
**Bankers:** Barclays Bank Plc (20-68-10)
**Employees:** 250

DUNS 21-775-1856

## Plymouth College Preparatory School

Craigie Drive, Plymouth, Devon PL1 3JL
**Tel:** 01752201352
**Web:** www.plymouthcollege.com
**Estd:** 2011 Proprietorship
**Line of Business:** Schools (independent)
**Proprietor:** C Gatherer
**US SIC:** 8211 **UK SIC:** 93200
**Employees:** 55

DUNS 21-558-5500

## Plymouth Community Homes Ltd

Princess Court, Plymouth, Devon PL1 2EX
**Tel:** 08006943101
**Web:** www.plymouthcommunityhomes.co.uk
**Reg No:** 0030637I **VAT No:** 945760005
**Estd:** 2009 Friendly Society
**Line of Business:** Building surveyors
**Principals:** N Jackson (Financial), M Snell, G Martin, Ms S Shaw, C Turner
**Responsibilities**
**Senior:** Greg Starkey (Regional Director)
**US SIC:** 6399, 6732
**UK SIC:** 82001, 83100
**Auditors:** KPMG LLP
**Bankers:** National Westminster Bank Plc (56-00-63)
**Employees:** 550
**Turnover:** £74,317,000

DUNS 76-854-6574

## Plymouth Guild

Buckwell Street, Plymouth, Devon PL1 2DA
**Web:** www.plymouthguild.org.uk
**Reg No:** 2610208 **Estd:** 1991 Private Limited Company
**Line of Business:** Counselling & advice services
**Trading Style:** Hearing & Sight Centre
**Directors:** Ms M Hammett, Mrs K L Bourke, Mrs M J Paine, M Lincoln, Ms J K Leverton, Dr D G Croot, E M Fowell, Ms S E Rodgers
**Co. Secretary:** George Plenderleith
**Responsibilities**
**Senior:** John Biggs (Director), Gregory Chambers (Manager), Claire Hill (Manager), Nicholas Holman (Manager)
**IT:** George Dale (Head of IT)
**US SIC:** 8321 **UK SIC:** 96111
**Auditors:** Geoffrey L Hohnson & Co
**Bankers:** Barclays Bank Plc (20-68-10)

| | 31-03-14 | 31-03-13 | 31-03-12 |
|---|---|---|---|
| TO | 1,632,061 | 1,048,011 | 942,684 |
| P/L | 69,551 | (16,021) | 120,670 |
| NW | 1,078,259 | 986,085 | 975,075 |
| WC | 81,310 | 35,544 | 431,976 |
| Emp. | 68 | 64 | 50 |

DUNS 21-775-7506

## Plymouth High School for Girls

St Lawrence Road, Plymouth, Devon PL4 6HT
**Tel:** 01752208308
**Web:** www.phsg.org
**Estd:** 2000 Partnership
**Line of Business:** Schools (local authority)
**Partners:** Mrs M Utton, Mrs S Martin
**Responsibilities**
**Finance:** Paul Renyard (Business Manager), Samantha Turner (Finance and Personnel Administ)
**IT:** Raymond Baish (Technology Technician), Wayne Dodgen (ICT Technician), Cletus Moisob (Senior IT Executive)
**HR:** Samantha Turner (Finance and Personnel Administ)
**US SIC:** 8211 **UK SIC:** 93200
**Employees:** 110

DUNS 42-319-7300

## Plymouth Hospitals N H S Trust

Derriford Hospital, Derriford Road, Plymouth, Devon PL6 8DH
**Tel:** 01752202082
**Web:** www.plymouthhospitals.org.uk
**VAT No:** 654936600 **Estd:** 1994
**Line of Business:** Leisure centres
**Issued Capital:** £1
**Principals:** P Bull (Chairman), P Roberts, P Burroughs, Ms M Schwarz, L Paschalides, I Douglas, Ms K Grimshaw
**Responsibilities**
**Senior:** Paul Philips (General Manager)
**Branches:** Plymouth Hospitals N H S Trust, Devon P C T, Tavistock Clinic, Tavistock, Devon PL19 8BX
**US SIC:** 8062 **UK SIC:** 95100
**Bankers:** Barclays Bank Plc (20-68-10)
**Employees:** 6,000

DUNS 22-159-9108 **Imp**

### Plymouth Marine Laboratory

Prospect Place, Plymouth, Devon PL1 3DH
**Web:** www.pml.ac.uk
**Reg No:** 4178503 **Estd:** 1988 Private Limited Company
**Line of Business:** Research and experimental development on natural sciences and engineering
**Directors:** Mrs J E Timberlake, Professor B B Ward, A Dixon, C T Lewis, Lord A Berkeley, Sir J M Burnell-Nugent, S P Sherrard, Professor T D Jickells
**Co. Secretary:** Ms Beverly Tremain
**Responsibilities**
**Senior:** Graeme Hart *(Director)*, Ralph Rayner *(Director)*, Claude Roy *(Trustee)*, Stephen de Mora *(Ceo)*
**Finance:** David Loynes *(Finance Coordinator)*
**Marketing:** Thecla Keizer *(Head of Marketing)*
**Admin:** Christine Fice *(Office Manager)*
**IT:** Kerry Hoskin *(Network, Security Manager)*
**HR:** Jennifer Weeks *(Human Resources Manager)*
**Purchasing:** David Loynes *(Finance Coordinator)*
**US SIC:** 7391 **UK SIC:** 94000
**Auditors:** Ernst & Young LLP
**Bankers:** HSBC Bank plc (40-36-22)

| | 31-03-14 | 31-03-13 | 31-03-12 |
|---|---|---|---|
| TO | 10,897,024 | 11,274,063 | 11,297,456 |
| P/L | 206,582 | 511,643 | 305,903 |
| NW | 6,626,415 | 5,748,173 | 5,029,011 |
| WC | (59,733) | 228,023 | (363,294) |
| Emp. | 170 | 166 | 153 |

DUNS 49-495-4688

### Plymouth Science Park Ltd

Tamar Science Park, Davy Road, Derriford, Plymouth, Devon PL6 8BX
**Tel:** 01752-772200 **Fax:** 01752-772227
**Web:** www.plymouthsciencepark.com
**Reg No:** 3157625 **Estd:** 1995 Private Company Limited By Guarantee
**Line of Business:** Other letting of own property
**Trading Style:** Plymouth Science Park
**Directors:** D J Heard, C Jenkins, D Draffan, Mrs S N Jones, I G Pearce, T Evans, S J Chamberlain, J K Acornley
**Co. Secretary:** Ian Pearce
**Responsibilities**
**Senior:** Julian Beer *(Director)*, Nigel Halford *(Chief Executive)*, Nina Sariaka *(Operations Director)*
**US SIC:** 6519, 7399
**UK SIC:** 85000, 83954
**Auditors:** Francis Clark
**Bankers:** HSBC Bank plc (40-36-22)

| | 31-03-14 | 31-03-13 | 31-03-12 |
|---|---|---|---|
| TO | 1,598,644 | 1,709,875 | 1,600,773 |
| P/L | 161,076 | 374,935 | 257,441 |
| NW | 11,387,147 | 11,873,570 | 10,937,973 |
| WC | 1,182,751 | 1,104,268 | 787,059 |

DUNS 21-717-0501

### Plymstock School

Church Road, Plymstock, Plymouth, Devon PL9 9AZ
**Tel:** 01752402679
**Web:** www.plymstockschool.org.uk
**Reg No:** 7557886 **Estd:** 2011 Private Company Limited By Guarantee
**Line of Business:** Schools (local authority)
**Directors:** Mrs V G Gregory, K J Bunt, Mrs H R Massey-Clamp, Mrs B Schulz-Golder, Mrs J Williams, J R Wright, Mrs S Everson, Mrs J Rickard
**Co. Secretary:** Ms Julia Crookston
**Responsibilities**
**Senior:** Jane Blonden *(Director)*, Stephen Capers *(Director)*, Vivien Pengelly *(Director)*, Sandie Woodford *(Director)*
**US SIC:** 8211 **UK SIC:** 93200
**Bankers:** Lloyds TSB Bank plc (30-94-58)

| | 31-08-14 | 31-08-13 | 31-08-12 |
|---|---|---|---|
| TO | 8,755,755 | 10,238,504 | 40,447,439 |
| P/L | (332,368) | 1,264,639 | 27,898,389 |
| NW | 27,892,661 | 28,533,028 | 27,350,389 |
| WC | 2,107,183 | 2,195,990 | 1,199,750 |
| Emp. | 185 | 198 | 194 |

DUNS 76-944-8598

### Plyvine Catering Ltd

Unit 7 Pedmore Road Pedmore Road, Industrial Estate, Brierley Hill, West Midlands DY5 1TJ
**Tel:** 01384-263178 **Fax:** 01384-482230
**Web:** www.plyvinecatering.co.uk
**Reg No:** 1532914 **Estd:** 1980 Private Limited Company
**Line of Business:** Wedding services
**Issued Capital:** £104
**Principals:** P C Matthews *(Managing)*, Ms S Cowling *(Financial)*, H P Matthews
**Co. Secretary:** Stuart Matthews
**Responsibilities**
**Senior:** Ann Hickman *(Manager)*, Stan Matthews *(Functions Director)*
**Branches:** Plyvine Catering Ltd, Worcester City Museum & Library, Foregate Street, Worcester, Worcestershire WR1 1DT
**US SIC:** 5812 **UK SIC:** 66110
**Auditors:** Guy & Co
**Bankers:** Yorkshire Bank Plc (05-09-83)

| | 31-03-14 | 31-03-13 | 31-03-12 |
|---|---|---|---|
| TA | 335,655 | 415,170 | 461,627 |
| NW | 195,067 | 215,094 | 257,669 |
| WC | (1,618) | 11,090 | 63,875 |

DUNS 22-652-5186

### P.M. Harris Ltd

**(Subsidiary of:** Fb 53 Ltd)
P.M Harris Ltd, Ashbourne, Derbyshire DE6 3DH
**Tel:** 01335331910 **Fax:** 01283-821211
**Reg No:** 1538942 **VAT No:** 295385121
**Estd:** 1975 Private Limited Company
**Line of Business:** Civil engineers
**Issued Capital:** £56,000
**Principals:** P M Harris *(Managing)*, S J Mountford, K Norris
**Co. Secretary:** Paul Harris
**US SIC:** 8911, 7394
**UK SIC:** 83701, 84000
**Auditors:** Smith Cooper
**Bankers:** Barclays Bank Plc (20-63-25)

| | 30-06-13 | 30-06-12 | 30-06-11 |
|---|---|---|---|
| TO | 12,930,483 | 10,046,237 | 7,479,675 |
| P/L | 531,759 | 428,968 | 361,684 |
| NW | 2,488,067 | 2,066,948 | 1,834,771 |
| WC | 1,361,175 | 1,127,304 | 270,751 |
| Emp. | 70 | 66 | 63 |

DUNS 21-868-6625

### Pm Pressings Ltd

18 Carlyon Road, Atherstone, Warwickshire CV9 1LQ
**Tel:** 01827716381
**Reg No:** 8290006 **Estd:** 2012 Private Limited Company
**Line of Business:** General mechanical engineering
**Issued Capital:** £1
**Directors:** M Carter, A Robinson
**US SIC:** 3999 **UK SIC:** 49590

| | 31-12-13 |
|---|---|
| TA | 2,841,174 |
| NW | 897,230 |

DUNS 23-574-0847 **Exp**

### Pm Project Services Ltd

**(Subsidiary of:** Project Management Holdings Limited)
Cosford Lane, Rugby, Warwickshire CV21 1QN
**Tel:** 01217676700
**Web:** www.pmgroup-global.com
**Reg No:** 3572078 **Estd:** 1997 Private Limited Company
**Line of Business:** Engineering design activities for industrial process and production
**Export Sales:** £4,456,532
**Issued Capital:** £1,000
**Directors:** P G Farrelly, D Murphy, J C O'Connell, A C Rayner, L Westman
**Co. Secretary:** Lee Watkins
**Responsibilities**
**Senior:** Ian Hart *(Manager)*
**Branches:** Pm Project Services Ltd, Fusion 2 Parkway, Solent Business Pk, Fareham, Hampshire PO15 7AB
**US SIC:** 8911 **UK SIC:** 83701
**Auditors:** KPMG
**Bankers:** The Bank Of Ireland (30-10-27)

| | 31-12-13 | 31-12-12 | 31-12-11 |
|---|---|---|---|
| TO | 33,198,636 | 17,102,973 | 17,636,811 |
| P/L | 813,918 | 769,139 | 525,144 |
| NW | 1,936,296 | 1,325,948 | 749,059 |
| WC | 1,728,752 | 1,318,819 | 943,710 |
| Emp. | 94 | 68 | 64 |

DUNS 22-076-3440

### Pm Rees & Sons 2000 Ltd

Unit 6, Barry, South Glamorgan CF63 3RF
**Tel:** 01446-743131 **Fax:** 01446-720133
**Web:** www.pmrees.com
**Reg No:** 4077804 **Estd:** 2000 Private Limited Company
**Line of Business:** Road haulage and transport services
**Issued Capital:** £100
**Director:** P Rees
**Co. Secretary:** Mrs Penelope Rees
**Responsibilities**
**Senior:** Christian Murphy *(Site Manager)*, Brian Nichols *(Manager)*
**Finance:** Patricia Murphy *(Finance Manager)*
**Operations:** Tim Cummings *(Traffic Operator)*
**Fleet:** Sean Davies *(Logistical & Financial Analyst)*
**US SIC:** 4789, 4213
**UK SIC:** 77002, 72300
**Auditors:** Linghams

| | 30-09-14 | 30-09-13 | 30-09-12 |
|---|---|---|---|
| TA | 3,270,005 | 3,011,426 | 2,972,159 |
| NW | 1,740,670 | 1,627,882 | 1,570,836 |
| WC | 286,617 | 249,859 | 203,936 |

DUNS 29-045-8561

### Pma Radiators Ltd

Waterside Road, Leicester, Leicestershire LE5 1TL
**Tel:** 01162-461808
**Web:** www.pmagroup.co.uk
**Reg No:** 1004150 **Estd:** 1971 Private Limited Company
**Line of Business:** Manufacture of parts and accessories for motor vehicles and their engines
**Issued Capital:** £1,600
**Director:** P I Westwood
**Co. Secretary:** Michael Westwood
**US SIC:** 3714 **UK SIC:** 35300
**Bankers:** HSBC Bank plc (40-43-39)

| | 31-08-14 | 31-08-13 | 31-08-12 |
|---|---|---|---|
| TA | 3,066 | 3,066 | 3,066 |
| NW | 771 | 771 | 771 |
| WC | 771 | 771 | 771 |

DUNS 23-841-3343

### Pma Solutions Ltd

14 Nightingale Close, Epsom, Surrey KT19 7EH
**Tel:** 01372-739990
**Web:** www.pmasolutions.co.uk
**Reg No:** 3832973 **Estd:** 1999 Private Limited Company
**Line of Business:** Other business activities not elsewhere classified
**Issued Capital:** £1,000
**Director:** P Pankhania
**Co. Secretary:** Ms Urmila Pankhania
**US SIC:** 7399 **UK SIC:** 83954

| | 31-01-14 | 31-01-13 | 31-01-12 |
|---|---|---|---|
| TA | 22,144 | 15,818 | 17,402 |
| NW | 393 | 409 | 2,617 |
| WC | 302 | 308 | 2,505 |

DUNS 22-559-4597

### P.M.C. Construction & Development Services Ltd

106 Queens Road, Portsmouth, Hampshire PO2 7NE
**Tel:** 02392-696025
**Web:** www.pmcconstruction.co.uk
**Reg No:** 1675790 **VAT No:** 339391041
**Estd:** 1982 Private Limited Company
**Line of Business:** Construction of domestic buildings
**Issued Capital:** £10,000
**Managing Director:** P J Mcgee
**Co. Secretary:** Mrs Mary Mcgee
**Branches:** P.m.c. Construction & Development Services Ltd, Unit 8, Alphage Rd, Gosport, Hampshire PO12 4DU
**US SIC:** 1522 **UK SIC:** 50100
**Auditors:** Menzies
**Bankers:** Lloyds TSB Bank plc (30-96-11)

| | 31-10-14 | 31-10-13 | 31-10-12 |
|---|---|---|---|
| TO | 35,060,146 | 25,587,414 | 21,071,026 |
| P/L | 508,059 | 602,448 | 497,145 |
| NW | 3,786,527 | 3,170,998 | 2,758,766 |
| WC | 2,248,605 | 2,302,689 | 2,009,213 |
| Emp. | 50 | 46 | 41 |

DUNS 21-810-3133

### P.M.D. Group Ltd

Broad Lane, Coventry, Cv5 7ay, Coventry, West Midlands CV5 7AY
**Tel:** 02476466691
**Web:** www.pmdgroup.co.uk
**Reg No:** 0589981 **Estd:** 1955 Private Limited Company
**Line of Business:** Management activities of holding companies
**Export Sales:** £657,413
**Issued Capital:** £4,100
**Principals:** A M Naylor *(Managing)*, Ms C A Blake, B J Fisher
**Co. Secretary:** Ms Sheila Fisher
**US SIC:** 6711 **UK SIC:** 83962
**Auditors:** Baker Tilly
**Bankers:** National Westminster Bank Plc (56-00-45)

| | 31-12-13 | 31-12-12 | 31-12-11 |
|---|---|---|---|
| TO | 8,730,413 | 9,553,898 | 8,135,153 |
| P/L | 185,803 | 259,300 | 297,741 |
| NW | 3,055,982 | 2,995,660 | 2,816,093 |
| WC | 1,399,108 | 1,356,075 | 1,305,277 |
| Emp. | 87 | 82 | 80 |

DUNS 23-502-8722

### P.M.F. Roofcraft Ltd

Warwick House, 116 Palmerston Road, Buckhurst Hill, Essex IG9 5LQ
**Tel:** 02085056898 **Fax:** 02085064738
**Web:** www.pmfroofcraft.co.uk
**Reg No:** 3502216 **Estd:** 1998 Private Limited Company
**Line of Business:** Roofing contracting services
**Issued Capital:** £100
**Directors:** M Dent, P M Flood, M A Rippe
**Co. Secretary:** Ms Nancy Flood
**US SIC:** 1761 **UK SIC:** 50400
**Bankers:** Lloyds TSB Bank plc (30-92-58)

| | 31-03-14 | 31-03-13 | 31-03-12 |
|---|---|---|---|
| TA | 171,676 | 25,134 | 56,544 |
| NW | (29,400) | (41,028) | (74,470) |
| WC | (48,178) | (41,028) | (74,470) |

DUNS 21-827-0532

### Pmgc Technology Group Ltd

4 Station Court, Old Station Road, Solihull, West Midlands B92 0HA
**Tel:** 020-7287-9928
**Web:** www.pmgroupuk.com
**Reg No:** 7974624 **Estd:** 2012 Private Limited Company
**Line of Business:** Telecommunications
**Issued Capital:** £101,000
**Director:** S S Cheema
**Co. Secretary:** Shehzada Cheema
**Responsibilities**
**Senior:** Jason Yeomans *(Manager)*
**US SIC:** 4899, 7374
**UK SIC:** 79020, 83940

| | 31-05-14 | 31-05-13 |
|---|---|---|
| TO | 10,940,814 | 11,024,313 |
| P/L | (2,100,681) | (1,407,799) |
| NW | (8,735,664) | (7,098,750) |
| WC | (7,543,101) | (5,000,136) |
| Emp. | 70 | 72 |

DUNS 42-425-6415

### Pmhl Realisations Ltd

**(Subsidiary of:** Deckers Hospitality Group Ltd)
Unit E-F, Lynroyle Way Royle Pennine Trading, Estate, Rochdale, Lancashire OL11 3EX
**Tel:** 01484642368
**Web:** www.thedeckersgroup.com
**Reg No:** 4413206 **Estd:** 2002 Private Limited Company
**Line of Business:** Hotels
**Issued Capital:** £1,000
**Director:** C Brierley
**Responsibilities**
**Senior:** Victoria Brierley *(Manager)*
**US SIC:** 7011, 5812
**UK SIC:** 66500, 66110
**Bankers:** Lloyds TSB Bank plc (30-95-42)

| | 31-03-13 | 31-03-12 | 31-03-11 |
|---|---|---|---|
| TA | 322,000 | 322,000 | 322,000 |
| NW | 322,000 | 322,000 | 322,000 |

DUNS 34-595-1396 **Exp**

### Pmp-Forward Ltd

6 Dewar Close, Fareham, Hampshire PO15 5UB
**Tel:** 01489557771 **Fax:** 01489557772
**Web:** www.pmp-forward.co.uk
**Reg No:** 2739196 **VAT No:** 568734984
**Estd:** 1992 Private Limited Company
**Line of Business:** Road haulage and transport services
**Export Markets:** Europe
**Issued Capital:** £126
**Directors:** S J Ward, Mrs R Lumb, J A Buckley, L J Emery
**Co. Secretary:** Ms Rebecca Lumb
**US SIC:** 4789, 4213
**UK SIC:** 77002, 72300
**Auditors:** David Earley & Co
**Bankers:** Barclays Bank Plc (20-79-25)

| | 30-09-14 | 30-09-13 | 30-09-12 |
|---|---|---|---|
| TO | 8,708,175 | 8,849,588 | 9,490,053 |
| P/L | 183,628 | 40,285 | 46,812 |
| NW | 1,930,132 | 1,833,270 | 1,836,629 |
| WC | (757,094) | (594,276) | (525,144) |
| Emp. | 62 | 61 | 67 |

DUNS 22-812-8740

### P.M.S. Diecasting Ltd

Unit 10 Braithwell Way, Rotherham, South Yorkshire S66 8QY
**Tel:** 01709701901 **Fax:** 01709 700833
**Web:** www.pmsdiecasting.co.uk
**Reg No:** 1359427 **VAT No:** 763801721
**Estd:** 2000 Private Limited Company
**Line of Business:** Die casting equipment and services
**Issued Capital:** £147,247
**Directors:** G W Panter, H D Facey
**Co. Secretary:** Richard Fry
**US SIC:** 3559 **UK SIC:** 32863
**Auditors:** Hollis & Co Ltd

| | 31-12-13 | 31-12-12 | 31-12-11 |
|---|---|---|---|
| TA | 3,014,364 | 2,718,974 | 2,682,636 |
| NW | 1,139,541 | 1,104,347 | 920,204 |
| WC | 406,976 | 575,110 | 365,090 |

DUNS 29-642-8063 **Exp**

### Pms International Holdings Plc

**(Subsidiary of:** Karussel Holdings Ltd)
International House, Cricketers Way, Basildon, Essex SS13 1ST
**Web:** www.pmsinternational.com
**Reg No:** 1969212 **Estd:** 1985 Public Limited Company

**Line of Business:** Wholesale of other household goods not elsewhere classified
**Export Markets:** Europe
**Export Sales:** £4,960,000
**Issued Capital:** £142,857
**Principals:** P W Beverley *(Managing)*, B N Beverley, T Goding, R J Crowe
**Co. Secretary:** Mark Benson
**US SIC:** 5199, 3944
**UK SIC:** 61900, 49410
**Auditors:** Mazars LLP
**Bankers:** The Hongkong And Shanghai Banking Corporation Ltd (40-48-69)

| | 30-11-13 | 01-12-12 | 03-11-11 |
|---|---|---|---|
| TO | 41,337,000 | 44,976,000 | 40,931,000 |
| P/L | 610,000 | 1,346,000 | 1,238,000 |
| NW | 16,234,000 | 15,678,000 | 14,445,000 |
| WC | 14,337,000 | 13,780,000 | 12,615,000 |
| Emp. | 262 | 263 | 261 |

DUNS 21-914-5992
## P.N. Sharpe Ltd
**(Subsidiary of:** White Arches Caravans Ltd)
Wellingborough Road, Rushden, Northamptonshire NN10 6AY
**Tel:** 01933-353818 **Fax:** 01933-410252
**Web:** www.sharpe1.com
**Reg No:** 1132276 **VAT No:** 550770938
**Estd:** 1972 Private Limited Company
**Line of Business:** Caravan dealers
**Trading Style:** White-Arches
**Issued Capital:** £260,000
**Principals:** S N Sharpe *(Sales)*, N P White, Mrs D Sharpe, Mrs J K White
**Branches:** P.n. Sharpe Ltd, 168 High Street, Milton Keynes, Buckinghamshire MK11 1AW
**US SIC:** 5511, 5531
**UK SIC:** 65100
**Auditors:** Moore Stephens
**Bankers:** Yorkshire Bank Plc (05-05-42)

| | 30-09-13 | 30-09-12 | 30-09-11 |
|---|---|---|---|
| TO | N/A | N/A | 2,720,261 |
| P/L | 486,546 | 459,421 | 343,978 |
| NW | 1,891,350 | 1,920,547 | 2,231,506 |
| WC | 1,746,765 | 1,961,480 | 2,452,695 |
| Emp. | 71 | 74 | 75 |

DUNS 21-276-7305
## P.N.Daly Ltd
Charles Lane, Rochdale, Lancashire OL16 3PA
**Tel:** 01706-659701 **Fax:** 01706-860756
**Web:** www.pndaly.co.uk
**Reg No:** 0871763 **VAT No:** 148227463
**Estd:** 1966 Private Limited Company
**Line of Business:** Civil engineers
**Issued Capital:** £671
**Principals:** P N Daly *(Chairman and Managing)*, Ms F A Daly, N D Price, P J Daly, C P Foynes, F P Daly
**Co. Secretary:** Ms Jennifer Daly
**Responsibilities**
**Senior:** Pj Daly *(General Manager)*
**HR:** Pj Daly *(General Manager)*
**Facilities:** Pj Daly *(General Manager)*
**Engineering:** Pj Daly *(General Manager)*
**Branches:** P.n.daly Ltd, Dennis House, 4 Hawley Rd, Hinckley, Leicestershire LE10 0PR
**US SIC:** 8911 **UK SIC:** 83701
**Auditors:** RSM Tenon Audit Ltd
**Bankers:** National Westminster Bank Plc (01-07-44)

| | 30-09-13 | 30-09-12 | 30-09-11 |
|---|---|---|---|
| TO | 24,267,621 | 22,501,245 | 24,007,332 |
| P/L | 1,214,890 | 1,034,245 | 1,059,761 |
| NW | 11,477,151 | 10,502,531 | 9,645,843 |
| WC | 11,170,860 | 10,431,606 | 9,752,125 |
| Emp. | 363 | 290 | 284 |

DUNS 21-239-3540 **Imp-Exp**
## Pneumatic Components Ltd
**(Subsidiary of:** Indus Holding Ag)
Holbrook Rise, Holbrook Industrial Estate, Sheffield, South Yorkshire S20 3GE
**Web:** www.pclairtechnology.com
**Reg No:** 0341813 **VAT No:** 172720768
**Estd:** 2014 Private Limited Company
**Line of Business:** Tyre production machinery and equipment
**Export Markets:** Worldwide
**Export Sales:** £4,858,780
**Trading Style:** P C L
**Issued Capital:** £2,300,000
**Principals:** I S Mccreadie *(Managing)*, S M Shorter, M C Mccaughey, T H Kutschinski, K Brix, P T Mccall
**Co. Secretary:** Ian Mccreadie
**Responsibilities**
**Senior:** Darren Pearson *(Production Manager)*
**IT:** Robert Poyton *(IT Manager)*
**Engineering:** Darren Pearson *(Production Manager)*
**US SIC:** 3559, 3714
**UK SIC:** 32863, 35300
**Auditors:** PricewaterhouseCoopers LLP
**Bankers:** The Royal Bank Of Scotland Plc (15-20-25)

| | 31-12-13 | 31-12-12 | 31-12-11 |
|---|---|---|---|
| TO | 10,333,911 | 9,556,063 | 9,500,431 |
| P/L | 1,615,490 | 1,004,852 | 2,105,083 |
| NW | 3,937,969 | 3,209,296 | 2,919,905 |
| WC | 2,729,253 | 1,940,729 | 1,549,384 |
| Emp. | 80 | 82 | 82 |

DUNS 21-934-8483
## Pneumatrol Ltd
West End Business Park, West End Business Park, Accrington, Lancashire BB5 4WZ
**Tel:** 01254872277
**Web:** www.pneumatrol.com
**Reg No:** 8473515 **Estd:** 2013 Private Limited Company
**Line of Business:** Manufacturers of valves
**Issued Capital:** £100
**Directors:** T H Salvesen, R M Mackean, A M Nash, J C Dummer
**US SIC:** 3494, 3629, 3519
**UK SIC:** 32880, 34350, 32811

| | 31-03-14 |
|---|---|
| TA | 1,926,419 |
| NW | 378,925 |
| WC | 94,401 |

DUNS 64-098-9104 **Exp**
## Pnj Engineering Ltd
Unit 30 Kinwarton Farm Road, Arden Forest Industrial Estate, Alcester, Warwickshire B49 6EH
**Tel:** 01789-768600
**Web:** www.pnjengineering.co.uk
**Reg No:** 4502414 **Estd:** 2002 Private Limited Company
**Line of Business:** Manufacture of other fabricated metal products not elsewhere classified
**Issued Capital:** £650,000
**Director:** J S Moberley
**Co. Secretary:** Nicholas Moberley
**Responsibilities**
**Marketing:** James Noberley *(Joint Managing Director)*
**Sales:** James Noberley *(Joint Managing Director)*
**US SIC:** 3499, 3469
**UK SIC:** 31694, 31200
**Auditors:** Guest Wilson Chartered Accountants

| | 31-12-13 | 31-12-12 | 31-12-11 |
|---|---|---|---|
| TA | 2,556,613 | 2,210,474 | 2,556,407 |
| NW | 746,579 | 668,884 | 815,593 |
| WC | 392,005 | 133,676 | 380,123 |

DUNS 29-193-6920 **Imp-Exp**
## Pobjoy Mint Ltd
**(Subsidiary of:** Derek Pobjoy Investments Ltd)
Kingswood Park, Bonsor Drive, Tadworth, Surrey KT20 6AY
**Tel:** 01737818181
**Web:** www.pobjoy.com
**Reg No:** 0509935 **VAT No:** 673116640
**Estd:** 1960 Private Limited Company
**Line of Business:** Coins and medals
**Export Markets:** Far East; E Europe; Japan
**Issued Capital:** £5,000
**Principals:** D C Pobjoy *(Chairman)*, T C Pobjoy *(Managing)*
**Co. Secretary:** Timothy Warner
**Responsibilities**
**Senior:** Gill Westbrook *(Sales Manager)*
**Marketing:** Gill Westbrook *(Sales Manager)*
**Sales:** Gill Westbrook *(Sales Manager)*
**US SIC:** 5941 **UK SIC:** 65400
**Auditors:** Williams & Co
**Bankers:** Barclays Bank Plc (20-36-47)

| | 31-12-13 | 31-12-12 | 31-12-11 |
|---|---|---|---|
| TA | 1,569,258 | 1,154,633 | 1,234,253 |
| NW | (1,946,641) | (1,455,903) | (1,406,490) |
| WC | (2,102,187) | (1,636,622) | (1,621,099) |

DUNS 21-821-1118
## Pochin's Ltd
Brooks Lane, Middlewich, Cheshire CW10 0JQ
**Web:** www.pochins.plc.uk
**Reg No:** 0300573 **VAT No:** 279434227
**Estd:** 1935 Private Limited Company
**Line of Business:** Buying and selling of own real estate
**Issued Capital:** £5,200,000
**Directors:** Mrs S E Nicholson, N K Rawlings, J C Pochin, R Fildes, J W Nicholson
**Co. Secretary:** Nigel Rawlings
**US SIC:** 6531, 6519
**UK SIC:** 83400, 85000
**Auditors:** PricewaterhouseCoopers LLP
**Bankers:** Girobank Plc (72-00-00)

| | 31-05-14 | 31-05-13 | 31-05-12 |
|---|---|---|---|
| TO | 62,151,000 | 77,958,000 | 71,601,000 |
| P/L | (4,320,000) | (6,718,000) | (1,108,000) |
| NW | 7,521,000 | 12,540,000 | 19,285,000 |
| WC | (24,013,000) | (16,096,000) | (15,117,000) |
| Emp. | 146 | 158 | 267 |

DUNS 21-403-5037
## Pocklington Pots
8-10 George Street, Pocklington, York, North Yorkshire YO42 2DF
**Tel:** 01759448320
**Web:** www.pockboilers.co.uk
**Estd:** 1970 Proprietorship
**Line of Business:** Public sector hospital activities, including nhs trusts
**Proprietor:** Mrs M Wilson
**Responsibilities**
**Senior:** Caroline Playfair *(Manager)*
**US SIC:** 8062 **UK SIC:** 95100
**Bankers:** Alliance & Leicester Plc (72-60-00)
**Employees:** 70

DUNS 29-673-3892
## Pocklington School Enterprises Ltd
West Green, Pocklington, York, North Yorkshire YO42 2NJ
**Tel:** 01759-321200 **Fax:** 01759-306366
**Web:** www.pocklingtonschool.com
**Reg No:** 1999738 **Estd:** 1999 Private Limited Company
**Line of Business:** Renting of other machinery and equipment not elsewhere classified
**Issued Capital:** £100
**Directors:** C M Oughtred, M E Ronan, Mrs S M Oughtred
**Co. Secretary:** Paul Bennett
**US SIC:** 7394, 5699
**UK SIC:** 84000, 64500
**Auditors:** Horwath Pulleyn Heselton
**Bankers:** National Westminster Bank Plc (56-00-63)

| | 31-08-14 | 31-08-13 | 31-08-12 |
|---|---|---|---|
| TO | 59,186 | 54,553 | 34,317 |
| P/L | 25 | (15,000) | N/A |
| NW | 14,820 | 14,795 | 29,795 |
| WC | 14,820 | 14,795 | 29,795 |

DUNS 21-010-0238
## Pod-Trak Ltd
Unit 8 Wadsworth Road Fleetway Business, Park, Greenford, Middlesex UB6 7LD
**Tel:** 02089 980010 **Fax:** 02082 000050
**Web:** www.pod-trak.com
**Reg No:** 6337165 **VAT No:** 885753273
**Estd:** 2007 Private Limited Company
**Line of Business:** Public works contractors
**Issued Capital:** £1
**Director:** P O'Donnell
**Co. Secretary:** Mrs Brenda O'Donnell
**US SIC:** 1799 **UK SIC:** 50000

| | 31-08-13 | 31-08-12 | 31-08-11 |
|---|---|---|---|
| TA | 4,178,963 | 2,664,585 | 1,731,401 |
| NW | 2,169,392 | 1,221,492 | 544,210 |
| WC | 1,438,049 | 1,126,169 | 534,780 |

DUNS 76-852-7756
## Poeticgem Ltd
**(Subsidiary of:** House of Pearl Fashions Limited)
Unit 4 The Trident Centre, Watford, Hertfordshire WD24 4JH
**Tel:** 01923-249497 **Fax:** 01923-249498
**Web:** www.houseofpearl.com
**Reg No:** 2608346 **VAT No:** 523409173
**Estd:** 1991 Private Limited Company
**Line of Business:** Manufacturers of clothing accessories
**Export Sales:** £24,037,499
**Issued Capital:** £50,000
**Directors:** Mrs P Seth, A Banaik
**Co. Secretary:** Krishna Kanodia
**Responsibilities**
**Senior:** Omprakash Makam *(Manager)*, Graeme Scoot *(General Manager)*, Tony Tudor *(General Manager)*
**Branches:** Poeticgem Ltd, Northfeild Indstl Est Northfield Drive, Milton Keynes, Buckinghamshire MK15 0DA
**US SIC:** 2389, 5136
**UK SIC:** 45393, 61600
**Auditors:** UHY Hacker Young LLP
**Bankers:** The Royal Bank Of Scotland Plc (16-33-45)

| | 31-03-14 | 31-03-13 | 31-03-12 |
|---|---|---|---|
| TO | 34,811,257 | 48,766,375 | 23,867,712 |
| P/L | 505,029 | 663,629 | 757,843 |
| NW | 4,611,871 | 3,916,658 | 7,089,555 |
| WC | 157,988 | (234,603) | 1,013,714 |
| Emp. | 118 | 115 | 115 |

DUNS 22-033-9050 **Imp**
## Poeton Holdings Ltd
Eastern Avenue, Gloucester, Gloucestershire GL4 3DN
**Tel:** 01452-300-500 **Fax:** 01452-500-400
**Web:** www.poeton.co.uk
**Reg No:** 4036407 **Estd:** 2000 Private Limited Company
**Line of Business:** Other financial intermediation not elsewhere classified
**Issued Capital:** £9,000
**Directors:** A R Poeton, B N Poeton, Mrs R Poeton
**Co. Secretary:** David Bignell
**US SIC:** 6711 **UK SIC:** 83962
**Auditors:** Kingscott Dix Ltd
**Bankers:** Barclays Bank Plc (20-33-83)

| | 31-12-13 | 31-12-12 | 31-12-11 |
|---|---|---|---|
| TO | 9,394,845 | 8,336,640 | 6,243,897 |
| P/L | 1,269,862 | 1,088,036 | 608,241 |
| NW | 1,822,813 | 1,211,797 | 881,143 |
| WC | 1,190,593 | 1,089,695 | 963,495 |
| Emp. | 163 | 152 | 125 |

DUNS 89-672-0786
## Pohwer
Hertlands House, Primett Road, Stevenage, Hertfordshire SG1 3EE
**Tel:** 01438 727192 **Fax:** 03004562365
**Web:** www.pohwer.net
**Reg No:** 3323040 **Estd:** 1996 Private Limited Company
**Line of Business:** Other human health activities
**Trading Style:** Pohwer Advoncy Agency
**Directors:** R A Carter, J P Godfrey, Ms L P Wilkin, L P Hutchings, S M Kumara-Moorthy, Mrs A Patel, G S Gibbs, P J Aylett
**Co. Secretary:** Geoffrey Gibbs
**Responsibilities**
**Senior:** Shashikant Bavishi *(Manager)*, Gary Blaker *(Manager)*, Nicholas Goss *(Director)*, Valerie Harrison *(Chief Executive)*, Riaz Khan *(Manager)*
**Branches:** Pohwer, Greyfriars, Ware, Hertfordshire SG12 0XW
**US SIC:** 8091 **UK SIC:** 95200
**Auditors:** Deloitte LLP
**Bankers:** Lloyds TSB Bank plc (30-97-25)

| | 31-03-14 | 31-03-13 | 31-03-12 |
|---|---|---|---|
| TO | 8,611,996 | 9,819,164 | 8,056,782 |
| P/L | 68,840 | 92,808 | 4,455 |
| NW | 834,445 | 772,438 | 757,632 |
| WC | 794,843 | 691,592 | 617,941 |
| Emp. | 208 | 243 | 207 |

DUNS 39-906-1605
## Pointbid Plc
3rd Floor, Metropolitan House, Station Road, Cheadle, Cheshire SK8 7AZ
**Tel:** 01614851033
**Web:** www.pointbidplc.com
**Reg No:** 2231266 **VAT No:** 511511502
**Estd:** 1988 Public Limited Company
**Line of Business:** Storage and warehousing
**Issued Capital:** £97,742
**Directors:** R A Cook, M Linney, S J Linney
**Co. Secretary:** Edward Rodriguez
**Branches:** Pointbid Plc, 16A Duck Lees Lane, Enfield, Middlesex EN3 7SS
**US SIC:** 4226 **UK SIC:** 77003
**Auditors:** SPW
**Bankers:** HSBC Bank plc (40-20-23)

| | 31-01-14 | 31-01-13 | 02-01-12 |
|---|---|---|---|
| TO | 7,870,803 | 7,937,966 | 6,314,886 |
| P/L | 289,472 | (756,863) | (711,515) |
| NW | 4,326,799 | 4,020,462 | 11,660,458 |
| WC | (93,955) | 678,687 | 1,507,715 |
| Emp. | 90 | 95 | N/A |

DUNS 21-584-7864 **Imp**
## Pointer Ltd
65 North Wallace Street, Glasgow, Lanarkshire G4 0DT
**Tel:** 01415 642500
**Web:** www.pointer.co.uk
**Reg No:** 0047359SC **VAT No:** 552180462
**Estd:** 1970 Private Limited Company
**Line of Business:** Installation of electrical wiring and fittings
**Export Sales:** £2,022,104
**Trading Style:** Pointer
**Issued Capital:** £250,000
**Principals:** R M Rowan *(Chairman)*, R A Rowan
**Co. Secretary:** Alexander Urquhart
**Responsibilities**
**Senior:** Ilan Aisic *(Owner and Chief Executive Offi)*
**Marketing:** Andy Kirby *(Marketing Manager)*
**Sales:** John MacAskill *(Head of Business Development)*
**HR:** Carol Harkins *(Human Resources Manager)*
**Fleet:** Carol Harkins *(Human Resources Manager)*
**Branches:** Pointer Ltd, Unit 10-11 Howley Park Business Village, Pullan Way, Morley, Leeds, West Yorkshire LS27 0BZ
**US SIC:** 7399, 8999
**UK SIC:** 83954
**Auditors:** BDO Stoy Hayward LLP
**Bankers:** Bank Of Scotland (80-07-48)

| | 30-06-13 | 30-06-12 | 31-06-11 |
|---|---|---|---|
| TO | 18,073,742 | 18,767,509 | 15,953,603 |
| P/L | (170,803) | 9,867 | (110,602) |
| NW | 90,657 | 263,240 | 348,863 |
| WC | (648,924) | (532,727) | (509,013) |
| Emp. | 208 | 212 | 226 |

DUNS 21-629-9093

## Pointer Pet Products Ltd

(**Subsidiary of:** Wholesome Pet Care Holdings Ltd)
Unit E Chesterton Business Centre, Chesterton Court, Eastwood Trading Estate, Rotherham, South Yorkshire S65 1SJ
**Tel:** 01709-820569 **Fax:** 01709837415
**Web:** www.pointerpetfoods.co.uk
**Reg No:** 7087314 **Estd:** 2009 Private Limited Company
**Line of Business:** Animal feed and pet foods
**Export Sales:** £895,000
**Issued Capital:** £225,000
**Directors:** T Matlock, D T Davies, A H Richards, R B Davies, M R Poff, Miss H S Thorne, J G Davies, G P Clarke
**Co. Secretary:**
Jordan Company Secretaries Limit
**Responsibilities**
**Senior:** Juan Garsallo *(Manager)*, Nicholas Whitley *(Manager)*
**US SIC:** 2047 **UK SIC:** 42221

| | 30-06-13 | 30-06-12 | 31-06-11 |
|---|---|---|---|
| TO | 4,474,000 | 2,348,000 | N/A |
| P/L | (544,000) | (529,000) | N/A |
| NW | 191,000 | 202,000 | (725,521) |
| WC | (311,000) | (291,000) | (413,046) |

DUNS 42-368-4013

## Pointon York Sipp Solutions Ltd

(**Subsidiary of:** Pointon York Group Ltd)
Unit P, Welland Industrial Estate, Valley Way, Market Harborough, Leicestershire LE16 7PS
**Tel:** 01858-419300
**Web:** www.pointonyork.co.uk
**Reg No:** 4356056 **Estd:** 2002 Private Limited Company
**Line of Business:** Pension funding
**Issued Capital:** £850,000
**Directors:** Ms M J Beaver, G N Pointon
**Co. Secretary:** Peter Collins
**Responsibilities**
**Senior:** Steven Clews *(Manager)*, Joanne French *(Manager)*
**US SIC:** 6371 **UK SIC:** 82002

| | 31-03-14 | 31-03-13 | 31-03-12 |
|---|---|---|---|
| TO | 2,651,845 | 3,115,755 | 3,213,786 |
| P/L | 186,236 | 1,037,066 | 488,137 |
| NW | 1,608,624 | 1,640,293 | 1,033,603 |
| WC | 1,063,441 | 1,017,587 | 326,218 |
| Emp. | 58 | 63 | 61 |

DUNS 21-672-9536

## Poker At the Pub Ltd

Sanderum House, 38 Oakley Road, Chinnor, Oxfordshire OX39 4TW
**Tel:** 08435235246 **Fax:** 08443571871
**Web:** www.pokeratthepub.co.uk
**Reg No:** 7252490 **Estd:** 2010 Private Limited Company
**Line of Business:** Live theatrical presentation
**Issued Capital:** £2
**Director:** M R Conneely
**US SIC:** 7922 **UK SIC:** 97412

| | 31-05-13 | 31-05-12 | 31-05-11 |
|---|---|---|---|
| TA | 480 | 2,440 | 4,600 |
| NW | (10,910) | (5,854) | (1,837) |
| WC | (11,140) | (7,678) | (4,836) |

DUNS 21-674-1270

## Polam Hall Darlington Ltd

Grange Road, Darlington, County Durham DL1 5PA
**Tel:** 01325463383
**Web:** www.polamhall.com
**Reg No:** 7261538 **Estd:** 2010 Private Company Limited By Guarantee
**Line of Business:** Schools (independent)
**Directors:** Ms N J Dobson, Dr M M Carr, N J Millar, Ms M P Atkins, Dr N J Wright, Ms C L Curran, Mrs S C Pelham
**Co. Secretary:** Christopher Pratt
**US SIC:** 8211 **UK SIC:** 93200

| | 31-08-13 | 31-08-12 |
|---|---|---|
| TO | 3,450,604 | 6,671,828 |
| P/L | 137,521 | 3,873,058 |
| NW | 4,010,579 | 3,873,058 |
| WC | (705,735) | (726,373) |
| Emp. | 69 | 73 |

DUNS 29-160-5806 **Imp-Exp**

## Polamco Ltd

Unit C, Weston Lock Retail Park, Lower Bristol Road, Bath, Avon BA2 1EP
**Tel:** 01225-322500 **Fax:** 01225425940
**Web:** www.polamco.com
**Reg No:** 1784597 **VAT No:** 398862674
**Estd:** 1976 Private Limited Company
**Line of Business:** Manufacture of other electrical equipment not elsewhere classified
**Export Markets:** European Union (E U); Worldwide
**Export Sales:** £5,706,145
**Issued Capital:** £9,304
**Directors:** A D Polson, S C Cooper, D W Sites, H G Barksdale
**Responsibilities**
**Sales:** Debbie Colley *(Accounts, Production)*
**Operations:** Debbie Colley *(Accounts, Production)*, Sophie Jennings *(Production Manager)*, Ralf Styles *(Engineer)*
**Purchasing:** Kevin Hiscock *(Procurement Officer)*
**Engineering:** Debbie Colley *(Accounts, Production)*, Sophie Jennings *(Production Manager)*
**US SIC:** 3629 **UK SIC:** 34350
**Auditors:** Richardson Groves
**Bankers:** Lloyds TSB Bank plc (30-90-54)

| | 31-05-14 | 31-05-13 | 31-05-12 |
|---|---|---|---|
| TO | 11,880,473 | 11,966,041 | 10,149,691 |
| P/L | 516,238 | 933,549 | 389,771 |
| NW | 4,902,286 | 4,519,693 | 3,846,588 |
| WC | 3,328,581 | 3,100,172 | 2,621,795 |
| Emp. | 151 | 144 | 136 |

DUNS 22-217-3630

## Polar Capital Holdings Plc.

4 Matthew Parker Street, London SW1H 9NP
**Tel:** 02072272700
**Web:** www.polarcapital.co.uk
**Reg No:** 4235369 **Estd:** 2001 Public Limited Company
**Line of Business:** Financial intermediation not elsewhere classified
**Export Sales:** £82,594,000
**Issued Capital:** £2,062,799
**Directors:** J B Mansell, T H Bartlam, H G Aldous, G V Bumeder, J M Cayzer Colvin, M W Thomas, B J Ashford-Russell, T J Woolley
**Co. Secretary:** Neil Taylor
**Responsibilities**
**Senior:** Daniel Mahony *(Partner)*, Ben Rogoff *(Joint Manager)*
**IT:** Mike Catlin *(Senior IT Executive)*
**US SIC:** 6111, 6711
**UK SIC:** 81501, 83962
**Auditors:** Ernst & Young LLP
**Bankers:** HSBC Bank plc (40-05-15)

| | 31-03-14 | 31-03-13 | 31-03-12 |
|---|---|---|---|
| TA | 108,848,000 | 73,627,000 | 56,596,000 |
| P/L | 32,799,000 | 15,348,000 | 9,616,000 |
| NW | 74,170,000 | 53,763,000 | 46,058,000 |
| WC | 66,825,000 | 49,562,000 | 18,056,000 |
| Emp. | 92 | 83 | 72 |

DUNS 21-170-4403

## Polar Ford

Canal Road, Bradford, West Yorkshire BD1 4SR
**Tel:** 01274756250
**Web:** www.polarford.co.uk
**Estd:** 2002 Proprietorship
**Line of Business:** Garage related services
**Proprietor:** P Byrne
**Responsibilities**
**Senior:** Matthew Kent *(After Sales Manager)*, Mark Knapton *(Manager)*, Alison Sutcliffe *(Dealership Secretary)*
**Finance:** Richard Whittacer *(Finance Director)*
**Marketing:** Wendy Racher *(Marketing Manager)*
**Sales:** Maureen Mcevoy *(Sales Manager)*, Moreen Mcvoy *(Sales Manager)*
**Admin:** Doreen Ball *(Office Manager)*
**IT:** Alice Sutclisse *(Network, Security Manager)*
**HR:** Alison Sutcliffe *(Dealership Secretary)*
**Health & Safety:** Matthew Kent *(After Sales Manager)*
**Facilities:** Matthew Kent *(After Sales Manager)*
**Operations:** Matthew Kent *(After Sales Manager)*
**Purchasing:** Alison Sutcliffe *(Dealership Secretary)*
**US SIC:** 5511 **UK SIC:** 65100
**Employees:** 100

DUNS 21-586-6607

## Polar Ford Retail

Wakefield Road, Barnsley, South Yorkshire S71 1NF
**Tel:** 01226732732
**Web:** www.ford.co.uk
**Estd:** 2011 Proprietorship
**Line of Business:** Car dealers (new & used)
**Proprietor:** I Wilson
**US SIC:** 5511 **UK SIC:** 65100
**Employees:** 100

DUNS 21-586-6606

## Polar Ford St Helens

Sherdley Road, St Helens, Merseyside WA9 5AD
**Tel:** 08448745305
**Web:** www.polarford.co.uk
**Estd:** 2011 Partnership
**Line of Business:** Car dealers (new & used)
**Partners:** G Greenway, G Woods
**Responsibilities**
**Finance:** Steve Grace *(Finance Controller)*
**US SIC:** 5511 **UK SIC:** 65100
**Employees:** 70

DUNS 22-814-0596

## Polar (N.E.) Ltd

Stephenson Court, Skippers Lane, Middlesbrough, Cleveland TS6 6UT
**Tel:** 01642-440844
**Web:** www.polarne.co.uk
**Reg No:** 1740670 **VAT No:** 391853816
**Estd:** 1983 Private Limited Company
**Line of Business:** Manufacturers of window frames
**Trading Style:** Polar Windows N E
**Issued Capital:** £588
**Principals:** A W Baxter *(Managing)*, J P Wilson, R Hill, T J Wade
**Co. Secretary:** Richard Dunn
**Responsibilities**
**HR:** Steven Rushforth *(Human Resources Manager)*
**US SIC:** 3442 **UK SIC:** 31420
**Auditors:** Barrowcliff Hamer & Co
**Bankers:** National Westminster Bank Plc (55-61-00)

| | 31-10-13 | 31-10-12 | 31-10-11 |
|---|---|---|---|
| TA | 1,727,370 | 1,985,391 | 1,561,910 |
| NW | 754,268 | 515,869 | 139,674 |
| WC | 695,424 | 477,922 | 94,645 |

DUNS 49-492-8690

## Polar Speed Distribution Ltd

8 Chartmoor Road, Leighton Buzzard, Bedfordshire LU7 4WG
**Tel:** 01525-217666
**Web:** www.polarspeed.co.uk
**Reg No:** 3155092 **VAT No:** 849745765
**Estd:** 1996 Private Limited Company
**Line of Business:** Pharmaceutical suppliers and wholesalers
**Issued Capital:** £18,298
**Directors:** Ms C J Miller, R A Holmes, H M Mensing
**Responsibilities**
**Senior:** Mumtaz Cheshire *(Manager)*, Alan Cheshire *(Manager)*
**Finance:** Mumtaz Cheshire *(Manager)*
**IT:** Kane Aston *(Head of IT)*
**Branches:** Polar Speed Distribution Ltd, Unit 8, Chartmoor Road, Leighton Buzzard, Bedfordshire LU7 4WG
**US SIC:** 5122, 4213
**UK SIC:** 61800, 72300
**Auditors:** Mazars LLP
**Bankers:** Barclays Bank Plc (20-29-77)

| | 31-03-14 | 31-03-13 | 31-03-12 |
|---|---|---|---|
| TO | 16,945,950 | 15,006,733 | 19,616,726 |
| P/L | 188,373 | 346,274 | 1,001,530 |
| NW | 2,757,437 | 2,614,602 | 2,367,519 |
| WC | 1,458,026 | 1,440,284 | 1,446,320 |
| Emp. | 199 | 193 | 181 |

DUNS 67-223-2063

## Polaroid Eyewear Ltd

The Polaroid Building, Vale Of Leven Industrial Estate, Dumbarton, Dunbartonshire G82 3PW
**Tel:** 01389714000
**Web:** www.polaroideyewear.co.uk
**Reg No:** 0313609SC **Estd:** 2006 Private Limited Company
**Line of Business:** Manufacture of optical precision instruments
**Issued Capital:** £1
**Directors:** P Sheerin, G S Ogle, Ms W Hamilton
**Co. Secretary:** Maclay Murray & Spens Llp
**US SIC:** 7399 **UK SIC:** 83954
**Auditors:** Grant Thornton UK LLP
**Bankers:** The Chase Manhattan Bank (60-91-41)

| | 31-12-13 | 31-12-12 | 31-12-11 |
|---|---|---|---|
| TO | 19,899,903 | 11,819,707 | 6,593,538 |
| P/L | 407,609 | (546,135) | 164,429 |
| NW | 4,050,902 | 3,765,413 | 4,146,939 |
| WC | 6,073,671 | 5,131,007 | 4,951,338 |
| Emp. | 130 | 119 | 118 |

DUNS 21-749-7783 **Imp-Exp**

## Polaron Manufacturing Ltd

(**Subsidiary of:** Cooper Controls (U.K.) Ltd)
Usk House, Lakeside, Cwmbran, Gwent NP44 3HD
**Tel:** 01633-838088
**Web:** www.zero88.com
**Reg No:** 1078182 **VAT No:** 227206976
**Estd:** 1972 Private Limited Company
**Line of Business:** Manufacture of lighting equipment and electric lamps
**Export Markets:** Worldwide
**Trading Style:** Zero 88
**Issued Capital:** £45,000
**Directors:** R J Davies, M G Bunker, S Sparrow
**Co. Secretary:** Abogado Nominees Limited
**Responsibilities**
**Senior:** Terrance Helz *(Manager)*
**US SIC:** 3648 **UK SIC:** 34702
**Auditors:** Blueprint Audit Ltd
**Bankers:** Barclays Bank Plc (20-53-30)

| | 31-12-13 | 31-12-12 | 31-12-11 |
|---|---|---|---|
| NW | (778,159) | (778,159) | (778,159) |

DUNS 22-872-9810 **Imp-Exp**

## Polartech Ltd

(**Subsidiary of:** Newmarket Corporation)
Nash Road, Manchester M17 1SX
**Tel:** 0161-876-5673 **Fax:** 0161-872-1922
**Web:** www.aftonchemical.com
**Reg No:** 1757293 **VAT No:** 401910304
**Estd:** 1983 Private Limited Company
**Line of Business:** Manufacturers of chemicals
**Export Markets:** International
**Issued Capital:** £737,500
**Directors:** M J Croft, D R Ellis, M A Lewis
**Responsibilities**
**Senior:** Peter Baumberger *(Manager)*, David Woodland *(Manager)*
**Finance:** Wendy O'Brien *(Financial Coordinator)*
**US SIC:** 2899, 8999
**UK SIC:** 25670, 83954
**Auditors:** PricewaterhouseCoopers LLP

| | 31-12-13 | 31-12-12 | 31-12-11 |
|---|---|---|---|
| TO | N/A | N/A | 2,867,772 |
| P/L | N/A | N/A | 3,824,858 |
| NW | 6,674,498 | 6,674,498 | 6,674,498 |

DUNS 21-211-6920

## Poldhu Care Homes

Poldhu Cove, Mullion, Helston, Cornwall TR12 7JB
**Tel:** 01326-240977
**Web:** www.swallowcourt.com
**Estd:** 2002 Partnership
**Line of Business:** Nursing homes
**Partners:** Mrs C Alliton, Mrs T Howard
**Responsibilities**
**Senior:** Christina Allerton *(Manager)*
**US SIC:** 8051, 6732
**UK SIC:** 95100, 83100
**Employees:** 63

DUNS 21-875-0267

## Pole to Win Europe Ltd

6th Floor, One Lampton Road, Hounslow, Middlesex TW3 1JB
**Tel:** 02086077900
**Web:** www.poletowineurope.com
**Reg No:** 8337264 **Estd:** 2012 Private Limited Company
**Line of Business:** Other business activities not elsewhere classified
**Issued Capital:** £1,500,000
**Directors:** M Suzuki, N Konishi, T Tachibana, T Tachibana
**Co. Secretary:** Masaru Harada
**US SIC:** 7399 **UK SIC:** 83954

| | 31-12-13 |
|---|---|
| TO | 4,933,621 |
| P/L | (63,215) |
| NW | 2,995,037 |
| WC | 2,566,908 |
| Emp. | 186 |

DUNS 21-810-7181

## Polestar Applied Solutions

Willow Drive, Annesley, Nottingham, Nottinghamshire NG15 0DP
**Tel:** 01623727500
**Web:** www.polestar-group.com
**Estd:** 1987
**Line of Business:** Direct mail service providers
**US SIC:** 7319 **UK SIC:** 83800
**Employees:** 125

DUNS 21-719-2887

## Polestar Print Holdings Ltd

(**Subsidiary of:** Sun Capital Partners Inc.)
1 Apex Business Centre, Boscombe Road, Dunstable, Bedfordshire LU5 4SB
**Tel:** 01924 829811 **Fax:** 01924 821608
**Web:** www.polestar-group.com
**Reg No:** 7574981 **Estd:** 2011 Private Limited Company
**Line of Business:** Management activities of holding companies
**Export Sales:** £8,800,000
**Issued Capital:** £20,029,090
**Directors:** P Andreou, A J Goodwin, B A Hibbert, P D Johnston
**Co. Secretary:** Alan Goodwin
**US SIC:** 6711 **UK SIC:** 83962
**Auditors:** KPMG LLP
**Bankers:** The Royal Bank Of Scotland Plc (16-71-67)

| | 30-09-13 | 30-09-12 | 30-09-11 |
|---|---|---|---|
| TO | 238,900,000 | 216,800,000 | 103,200,000 |
| P/L | (9,300,000) | (4,400,000) | (8,600,000) |
| NW | 2,800,000 | 2,800,000 | 5,100,000 |
| WC | (7,100,000) | (10,600,000) | (19,000,000) |
| Emp. | 1,847 | 1,663 | 2,101 |

DUNS 34-876-7737 **Imp**

## Polestar Uk Print Ltd

(**Subsidiary of:** Sun Capital Partners Inc.)
1 Apex Business Park, Dunstable, Bedfordshire LU5 4SB
**Tel:** 01582-678900 **Fax:** 01582-678901
**Web:** www.polestar-group.com
**Reg No:** 5674948 **Estd:** 2006 Private Limited Company
**Line of Business:** Printers general
**Export Sales:** £6,400,000
**Issued Capital:** £282,419,001
**Directors:** B A Hibbert, P D Johnston, P Andreou
**Co. Secretary:** Alan Goodwin
**Responsibilities**
**Senior:** Marie Baldwin *(Office Manager)*
**Branches:** Polestar Uk Print Ltd, 501 Dewsbury Road, Leeds, West Yorkshire LS11 5LL
**US SIC:** 2752 **UK SIC:** 47544
**Auditors:** KPMG LLP
**Bankers:** Lloyds TSB Bank plc (30-00-02)

| | 30-09-13 | 30-09-12 | 30-09-11 |
|---|---|---|---|
| TO | 192,800,000 | 216,600,000 | 233,100,000 |
| P/L | (6,100,000) | (12,500,000) | (70,600,000) |
| NW | 7,500,000 | 1,800,000 | 9,200,000 |
| WC | 3,100,000 | (11,300,000) | (19,200,000) |
| Emp. | 1,372 | 1,660 | 2,362 |

DUNS 21-771-1296

## Polestar Wheatons

Hennock Road North, Marsh Barton Trading Estate, Exeter, Devon EX2 8RP
**Tel:** 01392420222
**Web:** www.polestar-group.com
**Estd:** 2010 Proprietorship
**Line of Business:** Lithographic printers
**Proprietor:** A Lee
**US SIC:** 2752 **UK SIC:** 47544
**Employees:** 135

DUNS 29-039-0970

## Polesworth Garage Ltd

Grendon Road, Polesworth, Tamworth, Staffordshire B78 1HA
**Tel:** 01827-895125 **Fax:** 01827-893797
**Web:** www.polesworth-garage.com
**Reg No:** 0903691 **VAT No:** 109917552
**Estd:** 1967 Private Limited Company
**Line of Business:** Car dealers (new & used)
**Issued Capital:** £200,000
**Principals:** W R Newbold *(Chairman and Managing)*, M R Newbold *(Managing)*
**Co. Secretary:** Andrew Marven
**Responsibilities**
**Senior:** Martin William *(Manager)*
**US SIC:** 5511, 5521
**UK SIC:** 65100
**Auditors:** Philip Barnes & Co Ltd
**Bankers:** Lloyds TSB Bank plc (30-96-20)

| | 31-12-13 | 31-12-12 | 31-12-11 |
|---|---|---|---|
| TO | 17,968,235 | 17,967,091 | 17,427,659 |
| P/L | 682,337 | 1,132,108 | 503,143 |
| NW | 5,375,173 | 4,897,084 | 3,988,875 |
| WC | 3,078,021 | 3,387,154 | 2,484,505 |
| Emp. | 64 | 64 | 64 |

DUNS 76-870-6491

## Polesworth Group Homes Ltd

Laurel End, Laurel Avenue, Tamworth, Staffordshire B78 1LT
**Tel:** 01827896124
**Web:** www.polesworthhomes.co.uk
**Reg No:** 2614194 **Estd:** 1991 Private Company Limited By Guarantee
**Line of Business:** Other human health activities
**Directors:** Doctor S A Barratt, W G Wilkinson, Doctor S A Barratt, G A Irons, D R Lockwood, F D Price, A Wilson
**Co. Secretary:** Mrs Clare Forbes
**Responsibilities**
**Senior:** Valerie Boucher *(Chief Executive)*, Peter Boucher *(Manager)*, Leigh-Anne Smith *(Chief Executive Officer)*
**Branches:** Polesworth Group Homes Ltd, Laurel End, Laurel Avenue, Tamworth, Staffordshire B78 1LT
**US SIC:** 8091 **UK SIC:** 95200
**Auditors:** Burgis & Bullock
**Bankers:** HSBC Bank plc (40-08-35)

| | 31-03-14 | 31-03-13 | 31-03-12 |
|---|---|---|---|
| TO | 2,747,857 | 2,711,462 | 2,405,145 |
| P/L | 82,411 | 317,079 | 144,278 |
| NW | 3,042,287 | 2,944,321 | 2,607,312 |
| WC | 888,254 | 799,557 | 462,784 |
| Emp. | 115 | 107 | 103 |

DUNS 29-165-5710 **Imp**

## Polhill Garden Centre Ltd

London Road, Halstead, Sevenoaks, Kent TN14 7AD
**Tel:** 01959-534212 **Fax:** 01959-532777
**Web:** www.polhill.co.uk
**Reg No:** 1807258 **VAT No:** 209956727
**Estd:** 1984 Private Limited Company
**Line of Business:** Garden centres
**Trading Style:** Coton Green Centre
**Issued Capital:** £659,550
**Directors:** R G Wood, M R Novell, H C Novell, P A Bensted, S Mccabe, Mrs A M Novell
**Co. Secretary:** David Novell
**Responsibilities**
**Senior:** Paul Dye *(Manager)*, Daniel Hume *(Manager)*
**US SIC:** 5999 **UK SIC:** 65600
**Auditors:** Gilbert Allen & Co
**Bankers:** Barclays Bank Plc (20-24-61)

| | 31-12-13 | 30-12-12 | 25-12-11 |
|---|---|---|---|
| TO | 10,634,470 | 10,606,205 | 11,003,761 |
| P/L | 458,477 | 685,846 | 687,734 |
| NW | 2,204,444 | 2,525,521 | 2,761,567 |
| WC | 407,609 | 713,765 | 347,954 |
| Emp. | 185 | 181 | 180 |

DUNS 42-472-7613

## Poli Restaurants Ltd

9 Station Street, Kibworth, Leicester, Leicestershire LE8 0LN
**Tel:** 01162-796260
**Web:** www.firenze.co.uk
**Reg No:** 4460371 **Estd:** 2002 Private Limited Company
**Line of Business:** Restaurant - italian
**Issued Capital:** £2
**Director:** L M Poli
**Co. Secretary:** Ms Sarah Poli
**US SIC:** 5812 **UK SIC:** 66110

| | 31-12-13 | 31-12-12 | 31-12-11 |
|---|---|---|---|
| TA | 3,500 | 65,039 | 121,142 |
| NW | (102,467) | (120,149) | (41,838) |
| WC | (102,467) | (140,881) | (108,915) |

DUNS 23-293-0284

## Police Federation of England & Wales

Federation House, Highbury Drive, Leatherhead, Surrey KT22 7UY
**Tel:** 01372352000 **Fax:** 02083-902249
**Web:** www.polfed.org
**Estd:** 1919 Incorporate By Act Of Parliament
**Line of Business:** Public security, law and order activities
**Principals:** J Berry *(Chairman)*, B Fenlon, J Francis, E Hanrahan
**Responsibilities**
**Senior:** Steve William *(Chairman)*
**Finance:** Helen Gee *(Treasurer)*, Martyn Mordecai *(Treasurer)*
**Marketing:** Metin Enver *(Head of Communications)*
**HR:** Samantha Corner *(Human Resources Manager)*
**Facilities:** Samantha Corner *(Human Resources Manager)*
**US SIC:** 7399, 9221
**UK SIC:** 83954, 91300
**Auditors:** George Hay & Company
**Employees:** 70
**Turnover:** £15,975,814

DUNS 23-126-5443

## Police Information Technology Organisation

Peel Centre, Aerodrome Road, London NW9 5JE
**Tel:** 02083581636 **Fax:** 02083581644
**Web:** www.npia.police.uk
**Estd:** 1997 Incorporate By Act Of Parliament
**Line of Business:** Driving schools
**Trading Style:** Pito
**Chairman:** Sir T Morris
**US SIC:** 9221 **UK SIC:** 91300
**Employees:** 300

DUNS 21-231-4078

## Police Lochgilphead Strathclyde Police Police Stations

Police Station, Lochnell Street, Lochgilphead, Argyll PA31 8JJ
**Tel:** 01546702200
**Web:** www.strathclydepolice.co.uk
**Proprietorship**
**Line of Business:** Police forces
**US SIC:** 9221 **UK SIC:** 91300
**Employees:** 70

DUNS 23-213-3751

## Police Mutual Assurance Society Ltd

Alexandra House, Queen Street, Lichfield, Staffordshire WS13 6QS
**Tel:** 01543414191
**Web:** www.pmas.co.uk
**Reg No:** 0000727IP **Estd:** 1920 Friendly Society
**Line of Business:** Life assurance services
**Principals:** Sir D O'Dowd *(President)*, M J Foster *(Chairman)*
**Responsibilities**
**Senior:** Rachel Kirwan *(Manager)*, David Middleton *(Manager)*, Hazel Moss *(Manager)*
**Admin:** Diane Maddox *(Personnel Manager)*
**HR:** Diane Maddox *(Personnel Manager)*
**Facilities:** E Pinson *(Maintenance Manager)*
**US SIC:** 6111 **UK SIC:** 81501
**Auditors:** Ernst & Young
**Bankers:** Lloyds TSB Bank plc (30-00-02)
**Employees:** 175

DUNS 21-782-3054

## Police National Cbrn Centre

Leamington Road, Ryton On Dunsmore, Kenilworth, Warwickshire CV8 3EN
**Tel:** 02476516333
**Estd:** 2011 Proprietorship
**Line of Business:** Training services
**Proprietor:** D Edwards
**US SIC:** 8299 **UK SIC:** 93300
**Employees:** 50

DUNS 23-157-3986

## Police Rehabilitation & Retraining Trust-the

100 Belfast Road, Holywood, Co Down BT18 9QY
**Tel:** 02890427788
**Web:** www.prrt.org
**Reg No:** 0035737NI **Estd:** 1999 Private Company Limited By Guarantee
**Line of Business:** Other human health activities
**Directors:** J M Stewart, S Hamill, M Lindsay, D A Mcclurg, R E Walker
**Co. Secretary:** Norman Hanna
**Responsibilities**
**Senior:** Shean Dewar *(Health & Safety Officer)*, Terence Spence *(Director)*
**Health & Safety:** Shean Dewar *(Health & Safety Officer)*
**Facilities:** Shean Dewar *(Health & Safety Officer)*
**US SIC:** 8091, 8321
**UK SIC:** 95200, 96111
**Auditors:** BDO Northern Ireland
**Bankers:** First Trust Bank (aib Group (uk) Plc) (93-80-92)

| | 31-03-14 | 31-03-13 | 31-03-12 |
|---|---|---|---|
| TO | 2,700,256 | 3,194,459 | N/A |
| P/L | (197,480) | 102,405 | N/A |
| NW | 1,121,580 | 1,330,655 | 1,246,696 |
| WC | 53,331 | 212,164 | 21,653 |
| Emp. | 58 | 62 | N/A |

DUNS 23-707-9876

## Police Rehabilitation Centre

Flint House, Reading Road, Goring, Reading, Berkshire RG8 0LL
**Tel:** 01491874499
**Web:** www.flinthouse.co.uk
**Estd:** 2002
**Line of Business:** Police forces
**Trading Style:** Police Rehabilitation Centre
**Principals:** Sir P Condon *(President)*, A C Gill *(Chairman)*, Q Elizabeth Ii
**Responsibilities**
**Senior:** Queen Elizabeth II *(Principal)*, Lyndon Filer *(Chief Executive)*, Tom Mcauslin *(Chief Executive Officer)*
**Finance:** Lyndon Filer *(Chief Executive)*
**HR:** Nicola Day *(Personnel Manager)*
**Purchasing:** Nicola Day *(Personnel Manager)*
**US SIC:** 8699, 6732
**UK SIC:** 96902, 83100
**Auditors:** Moores Rowland
**Bankers:** Barclays Bank Plc (20-71-03)
**Employees:** 130

DUNS 23-820-1164

## Police Scotland

Police Headquarters, Old Perth Road, Inverness, Inverness-Shire IV2 3SY
**Tel:** 01463715555
**Web:** www.scotland.police.uk
**Estd:** 1975 Incorporate By Act Of Parliament
**Line of Business:** Public security, law and order activities
**Trading Style:** Police Scotland
**Directors:** W A Robertson, Ms E Stuart
**Branches:** Police Scotland, Area Command Office, Burnett Road, Inverness, Inverness-Shire IV1 1RL
**US SIC:** 7399, 9221
**UK SIC:** 83954, 91300
**Bankers:** The Royal Bank Of Scotland Plc (83-23-10)
**Employees:** 400

DUNS 22-747-0796

## Police Service of Northern Ireland

103 Kingsway, Dunmurry, Belfast BT17 9NS
**Tel:** 0845 600 8000 **Fax:** 02891888729
**Web:** www.psni.police.uk
**Estd:** 2010 Incorporate By Act Of Parliament
**Line of Business:** Public security, law and order activities
**Trading Style:** Psni
**Director:** R Hanigan
**Responsibilities**
**Senior:** Matt Baggort *(Chief Constable)*
**Branches:** Police Service Of Northern Ireland, 14 Castlewellan Road, Banbridge, Co Down BT32 4AX
**US SIC:** 9221 **UK SIC:** 91300
**Employees:** 400

DUNS 21-581-6493

## Police Southend Essex Police Service Desks

Southend-On-Sea Police Station, Victoria Avenue, Southend-On-Sea, Essex SS2 6ES
**Tel:** 01702431212
**Web:** www.essex.police.uk
**Estd:** 2011 Proprietorship
**Line of Business:** Crime prevention
**Proprietor:** Barker Mccardle
**US SIC:** 9221 **UK SIC:** 91300
**Employees:** 4,504

DUNS 55-076-7941

## The Policy Shop

46-47 Queens Road, Coventry, West Midlands CV1 3EH
**Tel:** 02476508090
**Estd:** 1993 Partnership
**Line of Business:** Insurance companies and agents
**Partners:** S Byrne, Mrs S Byrne
**US SIC:** 6311 **UK SIC:** 82002
**Employees:** 70

DUNS 42-411-3335

## The Policy Shop Insurance Services Ltd

46-47 Queens Road, Coventry, West Midlands CV1 3EH
**Tel:** 08000644404
**Web:** www.thepolicyshop.co.uk
**Reg No:** 4398937 **Estd:** 2002 Private Limited Company
**Line of Business:** Non-life insurance
**Issued Capital:** £152
**Directors:** A M Briscoe, Ms S E Byrne, D Ansell
**Co. Secretary:** Sean Byrne
**Responsibilities**
**Senior:** Neil Muldoon *(Manager)*
**US SIC:** 6399 **UK SIC:** 82001

| | 30-04-14 | 30-04-13 | 30-04-12 |
|---|---|---|---|
| TA | 2,310,037 | 1,953,752 | 1,944,617 |
| NW | 250,210 | 103,969 | 147,648 |
| WC | 207,876 | 51,323 | 79,632 |

DUNS 77-962-6282

## Policybest Ltd

(**Subsidiary of:** Genghis Topco Ltd)
Vale Works, Brighton, East Sussex BN41 1GD
**Tel:** 01273416727 **Fax:** 01273-701666
**Web:** www.cpacarparts.co.uk
**Reg No:** 3065895 **VAT No:** 665247811
**Estd:** 1995 Private Limited Company
**Line of Business:** Sale of motor vehicle parts and accessories
**Trading Style:** Car Parts and Accessories, C P A
**Issued Capital:** £123,500
**Directors:** M J Rourke, M J Block, J Austin, M E Murray, S N Best, P C Sephton, S W Lyall-Cottle, G W Spellins
**Co. Secretary:** Keith Anderson
**Responsibilities**
**IT:** N Farley *(Stock Manager)*
**Branches:** Policybest Ltd, 3 Nightingale Road, Horsham, West Sussex RH12 2NW
**US SIC:** 5531 **UK SIC:** 65100
**Auditors:** Carpenter Box LLP
**Bankers:** Lloyds TSB Bank plc (30-99-93)

| | 31-10-13 | 31-10-12 | 31-10-11 |
|---|---|---|---|
| TO | 10,701,993 | 10,062,632 | 10,941,946 |
| P/L | 348,589 | 755,444 | 322,104 |
| NW | 1,581,534 | 1,344,373 | 780,676 |
| WC | 1,156,631 | 818,060 | 289,574 |
| Emp. | 135 | 129 | 132 |

DUNS 34-778-8841

## Policyfast Ltd

Unit 5 Vantage Park, Washingley Road, Huntingdon, Cambridgeshire PE29 6SR
**Tel:** 08003081081
**Web:** www.policyfast.co.uk
**Reg No:** 5579631 **Estd:** 2005 Private Limited Company
**Line of Business:** Activities auxiliary to insurance and pension funding
**Issued Capital:** £85,654
**Directors:** K M Sinclair, M Taylor, J S Hooper, J R Barringer, N Taylor, R M Darling, M A Coverdale
**US SIC:** 6411 **UK SIC:** 83200
**Auditors:** Wilkins Kennedy LLP

**Bankers:** Barclays Bank Plc (20-17-19)

| | 31-03-14 | 31-03-13 | 31-03-12 |
|---|---|---|---|
| TO | 4,396,056 | 4,163,286 | 3,771,346 |
| P/L | 410,672 | 691,667 | 707,646 |
| NW | 1,209,697 | 274,515 | (311,303) |
| WC | 482,371 | 342,975 | (266,914) |
| Emp. | 61 | 70 | 65 |

DUNS 67-212-1761
## Polish & Eastern European Christian Family Centre Ltd
3rd Floor Harringay Irish Centre, Pretoria Road, London N17 8DX
**Tel:** 020-8365-9090
**Web:** www.peec.org.uk
**Reg No:** 6020288 **Estd:** 2007 Private Company Limited By Guarantee
**Line of Business:** Charities and charitable organisations
**Directors:** D A Jai-Persad, E K Gruca, Ms M Wrona, Ms W Banach, Ms A M Kowalska
**Co. Secretary:** Ms Malgorzata Shannon
**Responsibilities**
**Senior:** Gosia Shannon *(Manager)*
**US SIC:** 8699 **UK SIC:** 96902

| | 31-12-13 | 31-12-12 | 31-12-11 |
|---|---|---|---|
| TO | N/A | 58,774 | 60,222 |
| P/L | N/A | 3,881 | (3,220) |
| NW | 487 | 3,206 | (10) |
| WC | N/A | 2,119 | (1,862) |
| Emp. | N/A | 8 | 9 |

DUNS 21-042-8820
## Polish Bakeries
272 Abbeydale Road, Wembley, Middlesex HA0 1TW
**Tel:** 02089986077
**Web:** www.thepolishbakery.co.uk
**Estd:** 2005 Proprietorship
**Line of Business:** Bakers shops
**Proprietor:** M Toorley
**Responsibilities**
**Senior:** Maciek Piotrowski *(Manager)*
**US SIC:** 5462 **UK SIC:** 64100
**Employees:** 60

DUNS 21-163-1296
## Polish Ex-Combatants Association Ltd
238-246 King Street, London W6 0RF
**Tel:** 020-8741-1911
**Web:** www.polish.zzn.com
**Reg No:** 0421916 **Estd:** 1946 Private Company Limited By Guarantee
**Line of Business:** Licensed clubs
**Directors:** C Maryszczak, Ms B Orlowska, E Szymczak, A Siemiernik
**Co. Secretary:** Antoni Siemiernik
**Responsibilities**
**Senior:** Boleslaw Dobski *(Manager)*, Zygmunt Kedzierski *(Manager)*
**Branches:** Polish Ex-Combatants Association Ltd, 27 Tentercroft St, Lincoln, Lincolnshire LN5 7DB
**US SIC:** 5813 **UK SIC:** 66200
**Auditors:** Horwath Clark Whitehill
**Bankers:** The Royal Bank Of Scotland Plc (16-00-82)

| | 31-03-14 | 31-03-13 | 31-03-12 |
|---|---|---|---|
| TA | 2,680,046 | 2,398,745 | 2,719,758 |
| NW | 1,164,832 | 1,120,939 | 1,353,188 |
| WC | 1,828,961 | 353,311 | 652,232 |

DUNS 23-208-3121
## Polish Housing Society Ltd
Penrhos Home, Pwllheli, Gwynedd LL53 7HN
**Tel:** 01758612731
**Web:** www.polishhousingsociety.co.uk
**Reg No:** 0013517IP **Estd:** 1944 Friendly Society
**Line of Business:** Sheltered housing accommodation
**Responsibilities**
**Senior:** Michal Drewenski *(Manager)*
**HR:** Sophie Griffiths *(Personnel Manager)*
**US SIC:** 8321 **UK SIC:** 96111
**Employees:** 80

DUNS 55-043-6885
## Polkyth Leisure Centre
Carlyon Road, St Austell, Cornwall PL25 4DB
**Web:** www.polkythleisure.co.uk
**Estd:** 1976 Proprietorship
**Line of Business:** Leisure centres
**Proprietor:** S Dixon
**Responsibilities**
**Senior:** Annette Trethewey *(Practice Manager)*
**US SIC:** 8011 **UK SIC:** 95300
**Employees:** 100

DUNS 53-578-3922
## Pollard House
68 Pollard Lane, Bradford, West Yorkshire BD2 4RW
**Tel:** 01274636208
**Web:** www.pollardhouse.co.uk
**Estd:** 1984 Proprietorship
**Line of Business:** Non-charitable social work activities with accommodation
**Proprietor:** Dr M U Ahmed
**Responsibilities**
**Senior:** Michael Kainth *(Proprietor)*
**US SIC:** 8321 **UK SIC:** 96111
**Employees:** 55

DUNS 21-204-3780
## Pollard Mansfield & Co Ltd
**(Subsidiary of:** Mansfield Pollard (Holdings) Ltd)
Edward House, Parry Lane, Bradford, West Yorkshire BD4 8TL
**Web:** www.mansfieldpollard.co.uk
**Reg No:** 0135633 **VAT No:** 179331739
**Estd:** 1866 Private Limited Company
**Line of Business:** Plumbing
**Issued Capital:** £263,458
**Principals:** R A Pollard *(Managing)*, M E Brown *(Sales)*, P J Dresser, Ms J Z Robinson, Miss A J Howgate
**Co. Secretary:** Miss Allison Howgate
**Responsibilities**
**IT:** Neil Etherington *(IT Manager)*, Chris Strangeway *(Engineering Director)*
**HR:** Denise White *(Human Resources Manager)*
**Facilities:** Chris Strangeway *(Engineering Director)*
**Operations:** John Cusic *(Ventilation Department Coordin)*
**Purchasing:** Julie Humphries *(Purchase Ledger Controller)*
**Engineering:** Chris Strangeway *(Engineering Director)*
**US SIC:** 1711, 8911, 3629
**UK SIC:** 50300, 83701, 34350
**Auditors:** Firth Parish
**Bankers:** National Westminster Bank Plc (56-00-36)

| | 31-07-13 | 31-07-12 | 31-07-11 |
|---|---|---|---|
| TO | 12,892,267 | 11,324,456 | 12,234,648 |
| P/L | 428,767 | 386,242 | 355,263 |
| NW | 2,912,171 | 2,610,752 | 2,363,052 |
| WC | 2,866,427 | 2,766,296 | 2,727,608 |
| Emp. | 145 | 135 | 136 |

DUNS 22-931-8399 **Exp**
## Pollock Lifts Ltd
**(Subsidiary of:** John Pollock Designs for Disabled Ltd)
Unit 1 Sloefield Drive, Carrickfergus, Co Antrim BT38 8GX
**Tel:** 02893 368167 **Fax:** 02893 367846
**Web:** www.pollocklifts.co.uk
**Reg No:** 0018971NI **Estd:** 1985 Private Limited Company
**Line of Business:** Manufacture of lifting and handling equipment
**Export Markets:** Republic of Ireland
**Trading Style:** Pollock Lifts
**Issued Capital:** £9,250
**Director:** S T Graham
**Co. Secretary:** Gary Mcconville
**US SIC:** 3534 **UK SIC:** 32553
**Auditors:** Flannigan Edmonds Bannon
**Bankers:** The Bank Of Ireland (90-22-74)

| | 30-06-13 | 30-06-12 | 30-06-11 |
|---|---|---|---|
| TO | 9,984,825 | 8,820,224 | 7,817,140 |
| P/L | 245,769 | 200,546 | 193,760 |
| NW | 2,046,474 | 1,812,632 | 1,579,054 |
| WC | 1,422,559 | 1,168,497 | 972,357 |
| Emp. | 97 | 95 | 83 |

DUNS 21-443-8285
## Pollock Orr & Company Ltd
**(Subsidiary of:** Romanes Media Ltd)
2 Crawfurd Street, Greenock, Renfrewshire PA15 1LH
**Tel:** 01475-726511 **Fax:** 01475-783734
**Web:** www.greenocktelegraph.co.uk
**Reg No:** 0026973SC **Estd:** 2006 Private Limited Company
**Line of Business:** Publishing of newspapers
**Trading Style:** Greenock Telegraph, Ayrshire Weekly Press
**Issued Capital:** £90,030
**Directors:** G J Faulds, C J Allwood, G T Morrison
**Co. Secretary:** Graham Faulds
**Responsibilities**
**Senior:** Alan McClelland *(Works Engineer)*
**Sales:** Angela Simpson *(Advertising Manager)*
**IT:** Steven Cleisham *(IT Manager)*
**Health & Safety:** Alan McClelland *(Works Engineer)*
**Facilities:** Alan McClelland *(Works Engineer)*
**Engineering:** John Burrow *(Production Manager)*, Alan McClelland *(Works Engineer)*
**Branches:** Orr, Pollock & Company Ltd, 6 Glasgow Rd, Paisley, Renfrewshire PA1 3QA
**US SIC:** 2711 **UK SIC:** 47512
**Auditors:** Ernst & Young LLP
**Bankers:** Bank Of Scotland (80-91-25)
**Employees:** 70

DUNS 21-580-6118
## Pollock (Scotrans) Ltd
10 Blackburn Road, Bathgate, West Lothian EH48 2EY
**Tel:** 01506676333 **Fax:** 08707877997
**Web:** www.pollock.co.uk
**Reg No:** 0053751SC **Estd:** 1973 Private Limited Company
**Line of Business:** Road haulage and transport services
**Issued Capital:** £500,000
**Principals:** I Pollock *(Managing)*, Ms C G Pollock, H Mulvey, S G Pollock, F Pollock, M Jackson
**Co. Secretary:** Hbjgw Secretarial Limited
**Responsibilities**
**HR:** Phil Henderson *(Human Resources Manager)*
**Branches:** Pollock (Scotrans) Ltd, Royal Elizabeth Yard, Dalmeny, Kirkliston, West Lothian EH29 9EN
**US SIC:** 4789, 4226
**UK SIC:** 77002, 77003
**Auditors:** Frick & Co
**Bankers:** The Royal Bank Of Scotland Plc (83-19-04)

| | 24-08-13 | 25-08-12 | 27-08-11 |
|---|---|---|---|
| TO | 21,760,899 | 19,494,735 | 18,284,678 |
| P/L | 420,387 | 76,756 | (103,113) |
| NW | 4,199,532 | 4,006,236 | 4,096,316 |
| WC | (1,262,117) | (595,660) | (617,627) |
| Emp. | 214 | 204 | 190 |

DUNS 21-777-5911
## Pollok Fire Station
Leverside Crescent, Glasgow, Lanarkshire G53 5JY
**Tel:** 01418824872
**Estd:** 1963
**Line of Business:** Fire stations
**Responsibilities**
**Senior:** Callum Orr *(Station Commander)*
**US SIC:** 9224 **UK SIC:** 91400
**Employees:** 60

DUNS 36-797-3039
## The Pollok Golf Club
90 Barrhead Road, Glasgow, Lanarkshire G43 1BG
**Tel:** 01416321080
**Web:** www.pollokgolf.com
**Estd:** 2006
**Line of Business:** Golf clubs
**Principals:** I G Cumming, D Morgan, D Morgan
**Responsibilities**
**Senior:** Donald Mckeller *(Manager)*
**US SIC:** 7999 **UK SIC:** 97913
**Employees:** 50

DUNS 21-775-3174
## Polmadie Fire Station
Polmadie Fire Station, 560 Calder Street, Glasgow, Lanarkshire G42 0PA
**Tel:** 01414235752
**Web:** www.firescotland.gov.uk
**Estd:** 2011 Proprietorship
**Line of Business:** Fire stations
**Proprietor:** D Boyd
**Responsibilities**
**Senior:** Gregor Mcpherson *(Station Commander)*
**US SIC:** 9224 **UK SIC:** 91400
**Employees:** 84

DUNS 21-770-8626
## Poltons Family Centre
Poltons, Vale View Road, Dover, Kent CT17 9NR
**Estd:** 1994 Proprietorship
**Line of Business:** Adoption and fostering services
**Proprietor:** Mrs L Bennetts
**US SIC:** 8321 **UK SIC:** 96111
**Employees:** 60

DUNS 21-696-0070 **Imp-Exp**
## Polybags Ltd
1-1a Lyon Way, Greenford, Middlesex UB6 0BN
**Tel:** 020-8575-8200 **Fax:** 020-8578-2247
**Web:** www.polybagsbulksales.co.uk
**Reg No:** 0698834 **VAT No:** 226504973
**Estd:** 1961 Private Limited Company
**Line of Business:** Polythene sheeting supplies
**Export Markets:** E U
**Export Sales:** £954,973
**Issued Capital:** £950
**Principals:** J W Davies *(Managing)*, J H Lomax, Ms J C Copley, Ms S M Arbuthnott
**Co. Secretary:** Geoffrey Davies
**Responsibilities**
**Senior:** Darren Perry *(General Manager)*
**HR:** Darren Perry *(General Manager)*, Darren Relf *(Human Resources Manager)*
**Health & Safety:** Darren Perry *(General Manager)*
**Facilities:** Darren Perry *(General Manager)*
**Operations:** Darren Perry *(General Manager)*
**US SIC:** 3079 **UK SIC:** 48360
**Auditors:** Chapman Worth LLP
**Bankers:** Barclays Bank Plc (20-73-53)

| | 30-11-13 | 30-11-12 | 30-11-11 |
|---|---|---|---|
| TO | 11,870,179 | 10,907,661 | 10,472,520 |
| P/L | 357,849 | 311,475 | 303,255 |
| NW | 4,148,502 | 3,918,946 | 3,686,977 |
| WC | 2,773,586 | 2,530,945 | 2,339,912 |
| Emp. | 65 | 67 | 60 |

DUNS 76-701-7478
## Polycastle Ltd
12 Cooke Road, Lowestoft, Suffolk NR33 7NA
**Tel:** 01502-501036 **Fax:** 01502-501036
**Web:** www.polycastle.co.uk
**Reg No:** 2592957 **Estd:** 1991 Private Limited Company
**Line of Business:** Painting and glazing
**Issued Capital:** £2
**Managing Directors:** G R Catchpole, C I Catchpole
**Co. Secretary:** Glenn Catchpole
**Responsibilities**
**Senior:** Richard Eglington *(Proprietor)*
**Marketing:** Lee Godbold *(Sales Manager)*
**Sales:** Lee Godbold *(Sales Manager)*
**US SIC:** 1721 **UK SIC:** 50400

| | 31-01-14 | 31-01-13 | 31-01-12 |
|---|---|---|---|
| TA | 129,575 | 127,932 | 231,673 |
| NW | 39,005 | (40,471) | 39,021 |
| WC | 34,755 | (47,140) | 32,291 |

DUNS 23-731-8725 **Imp**
## Polycom (United Kingdom) Ltd.
**(Subsidiary of:** Polycom Europe Coöperatief U.A.)
270 Bath Road, Slough, Berkshire SL1 4DX
**Tel:** 01753723000 **Fax:** 01753-723010
**Web:** www.polycom.com
**Reg No:** 3726386 **Estd:** 1999 Private Limited Company
**Line of Business:** Video conferencing
**Issued Capital:** £2
**Directors:** Ms L J Durr, S M Darwish
**Co. Secretary:** Bartus De Vries
**Responsibilities**
**Senior:** Keith Hayden *(Sales Manager)*, Lizzie Sherwin *(Facilities Manager)*
**Sales:** Keith Hayden *(Sales Manager)*
**IT:** Karl Lovelock *(Vice President of Information)*
**US SIC:** 4899 **UK SIC:** 79020
**Auditors:** PricewaterhouseCoopers LLP

| | 31-12-13 | 31-12-12 | 31-12-11 |
|---|---|---|---|
| TO | 44,098,293 | 41,971,563 | 42,024,522 |
| P/L | 1,994,719 | 1,272,965 | 1,903,450 |
| NW | 23,264,651 | 19,525,088 | 15,981,691 |
| WC | 35,719,243 | 28,115,681 | 21,403,431 |
| Emp. | 246 | 255 | 269 |

DUNS 52-022-2274
## Polycon Ltd
**(Subsidiary of:** British Polythene Industries Plc)
96 Port Glasgow Road, Greenock, Renfrewshire PA15 2RP
**Tel:** 01314782395
**Reg No:** 0176578SC **Estd:** 1997 Private Limited Company
**Line of Business:** Manufacture of other plastic products
**Issued Capital:** £2
**Directors:** D G Duthie, British Polythene Limited
**Co. Secretary:** Ms Hilary Kane
**US SIC:** 3079, 3412
**UK SIC:** 48360, 31642
**Bankers:** Clydesdale Bank Plc (82-65-06)

| | 31-12-13 | 31-12-12 | 31-12-11 |
|---|---|---|---|
| NW | (2,299,675) | (2,299,675) | (2,299,675) |

DUNS 22-610-7761 **Imp-Exp**
## Polyformes Ltd
**(Subsidiary of:** Xpe Ltd)
Cherrycourt Way, Leighton Buzzard, Bedfordshire LU7 4UH
**Tel:** 01525-852444
**Web:** www.polyformes.co.uk
**Reg No:** 1296564 **Estd:** 1978 Private Limited Company
**Line of Business:** Manufacturers of moulded rubber and plastics
**Export Markets:** Germany, France, Holland
**Export Sales:** £881,008
**Issued Capital:** £35,000

**Principals:** P Henrick *(Chairman)*, I S Rumsey, R R Belger, C M Tarling
**Co. Secretary:** Neville Joseph
**Responsibilities**
**Senior:** Tim Bryans *(Head of Marketing)*
**Finance:** Karen McLean *(Financial Manager)*
**Marketing:** Tim Bryans *(Head of Marketing)*
**Branches:** Polyformes Ltd, Chiltern HousE,81 High Street North, Dunstable, Bedfordshire LU6 1JJ
**US SIC:** 3999 **UK SIC:** 49590
**Auditors:** Leigh, Sorene & Lawson
**Bankers:** National Westminster Bank Plc (60-07-08)

| | 31-12-13 | 31-12-12 | 31-12-11 |
|---|---|---|---|
| TO | 7,269,714 | 9,182,602 | 8,189,878 |
| P/L | 214,907 | 775,747 | 404,690 |
| NW | 2,292,104 | 2,133,244 | 1,700,321 |
| WC | 1,221,087 | 1,166,343 | 92,584 |
| Emp. | 74 | 85 | 85 |

DUNS 21-771-0288
## Polyframe Norwich
Unit 4, Atlas Works, Norwich Road, Norwich, Norfolk NR9 5SN
**Tel:** 01603879581
**Web:** www.polyframetrade.co.uk
**Estd:** 2011 Proprietorship
**Line of Business:** Manufacturers of window frames
**Proprietor:** D Eagle
**US SIC:** 3442 **UK SIC:** 31420
**Employees:** 50

DUNS 22-163-4533
## Polyframe (Trade) Ltd
**(Subsidiary of:** Polyframe Holdings Ltd)
Mile Thorn Works, Gibbet Street, Halifax, West Yorkshire HX1 4JR
**Tel:** 01422-330460 **Fax:** 01422-383292
**Web:** http://polyframetrade.co.uk
**Reg No:** 4181990 **Estd:** 1901 Private Limited Company
**Line of Business:** Manufacturers of domestic doors
**Issued Capital:** £100
**Directors:** P Dyson, C I Watson, M B Buckley, R J Lee, Mrs K M Buckley, J Riordan
**Co. Secretary:** Ms Patricia Earley
**Responsibilities**
**HR:** Jayne Thompson *(Human Resources Manager)*
**Health & Safety:** Jayne Thompson *(Human Resources Manager)*
**Facilities:** Robert Higgins *(Maintenance Manager)*
**Engineering:** Robert Higgins *(Maintenance Manager)*
**US SIC:** 2431 **UK SIC:** 46300
**Bankers:** HSBC Bank plc (40-23-05)

| | 31-10-13 | 31-10-12 | 31-10-11 |
|---|---|---|---|
| TO | 20,336,986 | 16,907,922 | 17,756,564 |
| P/L | 1,005,823 | 716,481 | 563,563 |
| NW | 793,617 | 582,767 | 530,490 |
| WC | 580,773 | 381,419 | 191,242 |
| Emp. | 199 | 187 | 197 |

DUNS 21-160-3667
## Polyglobe Ltd
**(Subsidiary of:** Cleverkey Ltd)
13 Grosvenor Gardens, London SW1W 0BD
**Tel:** 02078282425 **Fax:** 02078283332
**Web:** www.polyglobe-group.com
**Reg No:** 0484213 **VAT No:** 240155992
**Estd:** 1950 Private Limited Company
**Line of Business:** Other tourist assistance activities not elsewhere classified
**Trading Style:** British Hotel Reservation Centre, The Corporate Team, The Polyglobe Group
**Issued Capital:** £1,000
**Principals:** A G Kingsnorth *(Managing)*, E Beale
**Co. Secretary:** Suri Amarasinghe
**Responsibilities**
**Finance:** Monika Kubiczek *(Finance Manager)*
**Marketing:** Erwin Bostos *(Marketing Manager)*
**IT:** Jas Jandhu *(IT Manager)*
**Branches:** Polyglobe Ltd, Terminal Three, Arrivals, Hounslow, Middlesex TW6 1NB
**US SIC:** 7399, 8999
**UK SIC:** 83954
**Auditors:** Saffery Champness
**Bankers:** Barclays Bank Plc (20-32-29)

| | 30-11-13 | 30-11-12 | 30-11-11 |
|---|---|---|---|
| TO | 15,264,181 | 14,229,704 | 11,177,107 |
| P/L | 106,234 | 358,642 | 114,377 |
| NW | 2,046,356 | 1,012,045 | 323,403 |
| WC | (1,847,576) | (1,873,730) | (2,813,946) |
| Emp. | 89 | 101 | 96 |

DUNS 49-286-0812 **Imp**
## Polymark (G B) Ltd
14 Sopwith Way Drayton Fields, Daventry, Northamptonshire NN11 8PB
**Tel:** 01327308600 **Fax:** 01327-308610
**Web:** www.polymark.co.uk
**Reg No:** 3119261 **Estd:** 1995 Private Limited Company
**Line of Business:** Manufacture of lifting and handling equipment
**Trading Style:** Polymark Laundry Systems, Polymark Franklin
**Issued Capital:** £500,000
**Directors:** I Elliott, D W Rutland
**Co. Secretary:** James Clementson
**US SIC:** 3534, 3552
**UK SIC:** 32553, 32300
**Auditors:** Shipleys LLP
**Bankers:** National Westminster Bank Plc (60-50-06)

| | 31-03-14 | 31-03-13 | 31-03-12 |
|---|---|---|---|
| TA | 2,417,291 | 2,308,424 | 2,044,122 |
| NW | 1,118,095 | 1,038,853 | 929,166 |
| WC | 907,555 | 848,081 | 801,956 |

DUNS 28-828-5372 **Imp-Exp**
## Polymer Holdings Ltd
**(Subsidiary of:** Polymer N3 Ltd)
Unit 1 Spurryhillock Industrial Estate, Broomhill Road, Stonehaven, Kincardineshire AB39 2NH
**Tel:** 01569-766226 **Fax:** 01569-766419
**Web:** www.tubetec.co.uk
**Reg No:** 0089577SC **VAT No:** 498366287
**Estd:** 1987 Private Limited Company
**Line of Business:** Manufacturers of rubber products
**Export Sales:** £20,132,066
**Trading Style:** Rubber Engineering Services, Tubetec
**Issued Capital:** £272,280
**Principals:** G K Speirs *(Managing)*, Miss L J Speirs, Miss K M Speirs
**Co. Secretary:** Derek Stephen
**Responsibilities**
**Facilities:** Len Strange *(Facilities Manager)*
**Branches:** Polymer Holdings Ltd, 23-41 Willowdale Place, Aberdeen, Aberdeenshire AB24 5AQ
**US SIC:** 3069, 3079, 3317
**UK SIC:** 48123, 48360, 22200
**Auditors:** Simpson Forsyth
**Bankers:** The Royal Bank Of Scotland Plc (83-15-31)

| | 30-06-13 | 30-06-12 | 30-06-11 |
|---|---|---|---|
| TO | 27,853,411 | 26,210,488 | 22,756,945 |
| P/L | 8,576,131 | 5,363,276 | 6,834,729 |
| NW | 4,291,767 | 34,172,399 | 30,495,211 |
| WC | 3,636,533 | 11,551,619 | 6,931,358 |
| Emp. | 74 | 70 | 72 |

DUNS 22-985-6638 **Imp**
## Polymer Laboratories Ltd
Unit 1 Essex Road, Church Stretton, Shropshire SY6 6AX
**Web:** www.polymerlabs.com
**Line of Business:** Research & Development Laboratories
**US SIC:** 7391 **UK SIC:** 94000
**Employees:** 125

DUNS 22-012-3082 **Imp**
## Polymer Logistics (Uk) Ltd
**(Subsidiary of:** Polymer Logistics N.V.)
The Draw Bridge, Dudley, West Midlands DY1 4RD
**Tel:** 08452000001 **Fax:** 01384245750
**Web:** www.polymerlogistics.com
**Reg No:** 4015336 **Estd:** 2000 Private Limited Company
**Line of Business:** Activities of other transport agencies
**Issued Capital:** £3
**Directors:** M Mizrahy, G Feiner, A J Dale
**Co. Secretary:** Mrs Danit Cohen
**Responsibilities**
**Senior:** Dana Gerner *(Manager)*, Zvi Yemini *(Owner)*
**US SIC:** 7399 **UK SIC:** 83954
**Bankers:** Bank Leumi (uk) Plc (30-14-95)

| | 31-12-13 | 31-12-12 | 31-12-11 |
|---|---|---|---|
| TO | 10,297,292 | 12,007,484 | 10,720,399 |
| P/L | 114,906 | 76,606 | 619,498 |
| NW | 6,161,676 | 6,075,527 | 6,009,964 |
| WC | 1,976,179 | 1,305,355 | 2,044,558 |
| Emp. | 47 | 49 | 34 |

DUNS 21-326-0904 **Exp**
## Polypipe Ltd
**(Subsidiary of:** Pipe Luxembourg Sarl)
Broomhouse Lane, Doncaster, South Yorkshire DN12 1ES
**Tel:** 01709-770-000 **Fax:** 01709-770-001
**Web:** www.polypipe.com
**Reg No:** 1099323 **VAT No:** 590679887
**Estd:** 1973 Private Limited Company
**Line of Business:** Pipes and fittings
**Export Sales:** £17,400,000
**Trading Style:** Polypipe Group
**Issued Capital:** £1,000,000
**Directors:** D G Hall, P Rice
**Co. Secretary:** Peter Shepherd
**Responsibilities**
**Senior:** Tom Flint *(Factory Manager)*, Steve Holder *(Maintenance Coordinator)*, Cameron McLellan *(Deputy Managing Director)*, Richard Waiton *(Transport Manager)*
**Finance:** Jackie Becker *(Human Resources Manager)*, Brian Healey *(Financial Director)*
**Admin:** Gill Jowers *(Personal Assistant)*
**HR:** Jackie Becker *(Human Resources Manager)*
**Facilities:** Steve Holder *(Maintenance Coordinator)*
**Fleet:** S Nevins *(Transport Manager)*, Richard Waiton *(Transport Manager)*
**Engineering:** Steve Holder *(Maintenance Coordinator)*
**Branches:** Polypipe Ltd, 2410 London Road, Glasgow, Lanarkshire G32 8XZ
**US SIC:** 3317 **UK SIC:** 22200
**Auditors:** Deloitte LLP

| | 31-12-13 | 31-12-12 | 31-12-11 |
|---|---|---|---|
| TO | 232,700,000 | 215,700,000 | 212,300,000 |
| P/L | 36,400,000 | 32,000,000 | 8,400,000 |
| NW | 56,400,000 | 25,100,000 | 19,500,000 |
| WC | 53,700,000 | 39,400,000 | 23,100,000 |
| Emp. | 1,794 | 1,690 | 1,714 |

DUNS 23-694-2632 **Exp**
## Polypipe Terrain Holdings Ltd
**(Subsidiary of:** Pipe Luxembourg Sarl)
338 New Hythe Lane, Larkfield, Aylesford, Kent ME20 6RZ
**Tel:** 01622795200
**Web:** www.polypipe.com
**Reg No:** 3689125 **Estd:** 1998 Private Limited Company
**Line of Business:** Manufacture upvc plastic plumbing pipe & drainage products div ho part of honeywell control systems
**Issued Capital:** £16,000,000
**Director:** D G Hall
**Co. Secretary:** Peter Shepherd
**Responsibilities**
**Finance:** Lee Dawes *(Financial Manager)*
**HR:** Lisa Hatton *(Human Resources Manager)*
**Health & Safety:** Richard True *(Quality Control Manager)*
**Engineering:** Van Williams *(Production Manager)*
**US SIC:** 3079, 3261
**UK SIC:** 48360, 24892
**Auditors:** Deloitte LLP
**Bankers:** National Westminster Bank Plc (53-61-55)

| | 31-12-13 | 31-12-12 | 31-12-11 |
|---|---|---|---|
| TA | 12,472,000 | 12,472,000 | 12,472,000 |
| NW | 12,472,000 | 12,472,000 | 12,472,000 |

DUNS 22-933-2572 **Exp**
## Polypipe (Ulster) Ltd
**(Subsidiary of:** Polypipe Building Products Ltd)
Dromore Road, Donaghcloney, Craigavon, Co Armagh BT66 7HL
**Tel:** 028-3888-1270 **Fax:** 028-3888-2344
**Web:** www.polypipe.co.uk
**Reg No:** 0016612NI **Estd:** 1985 Private Limited Company
**Line of Business:** Manufacturers of pipeline
**Export Markets:** Republic of Ireland
**Issued Capital:** £100
**Director:** D G Hall
**Co. Secretary:** Peter Shepherd
**Responsibilities**
**Senior:** Henry White *(Manager)*
**Finance:** Brian Galbraith *(Finance Manager)*
**Marketing:** Harry Sheilds *(Sales & Marketing Director)*
**Sales:** Harry Sheilds *(Sales & Marketing Director)*
**IT:** Brian Galbraith *(Finance Manager)*
**HR:** Brian Galbraith *(Finance Manager)*
**Facilities:** Kenneth Forsythe *(Production Director)*
**Operations:** Harry Sheilds *(Sales & Marketing Director)*
**Purchasing:** Kenneth Forsythe *(Production Director)*
**Engineering:** Kenneth Forsythe *(Production Director)*
**US SIC:** 3317 **UK SIC:** 22200
**Auditors:** KPMG
**Bankers:** Northern Bank Ltd (95-03-71)

| | 31-12-13 | 31-12-12 | 31-12-11 |
|---|---|---|---|
| TA | 19,677,000 | 19,677,000 | 19,677,000 |
| NW | 19,677,000 | 19,677,000 | 19,677,000 |

DUNS 39-995-7109
## Polyprint Mailing Films Ltd
Mackintosh Road, Rackheath Industrial Estate, Rackheath, Norwich, Norfolk NR13 6LJ
**Tel:** 01603-721807
**Web:** www.polyprint.co.uk
**Reg No:** 2283792 **VAT No:** 525209661
**Estd:** 1988 Private Limited Company
**Line of Business:** Manufacture of plastic packing goods
**Issued Capital:** £202
**Managing Director:** J J Neville
**Co. Secretary:** Mrs Catherine Clayton
**Responsibilities**
**Senior:** Clive Royal *(Transport Manager)*
**Fleet:** Clive Royal *(Transport Manager)*
**US SIC:** 3079 **UK SIC:** 48360
**Auditors:** John W Mills & Co
**Bankers:** Lloyds TSB Bank plc (30-96-16)

| | 31-10-14 | 31-10-13 | 31-10-12 |
|---|---|---|---|
| TO | 8,002,974 | 8,115,734 | 7,653,680 |
| P/L | 271,451 | 103,759 | 28,102 |
| NW | 1,375,421 | 1,011,262 | 1,347,463 |
| WC | (1,315,265) | (987,347) | (689,344) |
| Emp. | 61 | 58 | 52 |

DUNS 77-117-8183
## Polystar Plastics Ltd
Peel House, Peel Street, Southampton, Hampshire SO14 5QT
**Tel:** 02380 232153
**Web:** www.polystar.co.uk
**Reg No:** 2690339 **VAT No:** 631655446
**Estd:** 1992 Private Limited Company
**Line of Business:** Manufacture of plastics in primary forms
**Issued Capital:** £10,000
**Principals:** J Talwar *(Managing)*, Ms R Talwar, S Talwar
**Co. Secretary:** Mrs Sukhwinder Talwar
**Responsibilities**
**Senior:** Philip Bassett *(Production Manager)*, Alan Freeman *(IT Manager)*
**Finance:** Sue Talwar *(Joint Managing Director)*
**Sales:** Alan Freeman *(IT Manager)*
**IT:** Alan Freeman *(IT Manager)*, Sue Talwar *(Joint Managing Director)*
**Health & Safety:** Sue Talwar *(Joint Managing Director)*
**Facilities:** Philip Bassett *(Production Manager)*
**Operations:** Jason Mcfeat *(Production Manager)*
**Purchasing:** Shamshad Shafique *(Purchasing Manager)*
**Engineering:** Philip Bassett *(Production Manager)*
**US SIC:** 3079 **UK SIC:** 48360
**Auditors:** James Cowper LLP
**Bankers:** National Westminster Bank Plc (60-20-03)

| | 31-07-14 | 31-07-13 | 31-07-12 |
|---|---|---|---|
| TO | 19,005,481 | 16,197,981 | 14,948,418 |
| P/L | 2,093,985 | 1,938,585 | 918,994 |
| NW | 4,403,215 | 3,185,916 | 2,130,304 |
| WC | 3,694,006 | 2,603,793 | 1,739,424 |
| Emp. | 95 | 84 | 84 |

DUNS 23-906-5977
## Polytank Ltd
**(Subsidiary of:** Polytank Group Ltd)
Po Box 850, Preston, Lancashire PR3 9BT
**Tel:** 01772-632850
**Web:** www.polytank.co.uk
**Reg No:** 3897197 **Estd:** 1999 Private Limited Company
**Line of Business:** Manufacture of other plastic products
**Issued Capital:** £2
**Principals:** J G Fidler *(Managing)*, J B Fidler
**Co. Secretary:** Sean Mchugh
**US SIC:** 3079 **UK SIC:** 48360

| | 30-09-13 | 30-09-12 | 30-09-11 |
|---|---|---|---|
| TA | 2 | 2 | 2 |
| NW | 2 | 2 | 2 |

DUNS 22-023-4046
## Polytec Car Styling Bromyard Ltd
**(Subsidiary of:** Polytec Holding Ag)
Unit 10, Bromyard, Herefordshire HR7 4NS
**Tel:** 01885-483000
**Web:** www.polytec-holden.com
**Reg No:** 4026072 **Estd:** 2000 Private Limited Company
**Line of Business:** Manufacturers of plastic products
**Export Sales:** £5,387,820
**Trading Style:** Polytec Group
**Issued Capital:** £100
**Directors:** M Huemer, N Munster
**Co. Secretary:** Michael Collinson
**Responsibilities**
**Senior:** Geoff McGladdery *(Manager)*, Shayne Probert *(Warehouse Manager)*
**Marketing:** Gareth Anderson *(Sales & Marketing Manager)*
**Sales:** Gareth Anderson *(Sales & Marketing Manager)*
**Health & Safety:** Julia Hill *(Environmental Coordinator)*
**Facilities:** Damian Connelly *(Maintenance Manager)*
**Operations:** Julia Hill *(Environmental Coordinator)*
**US SIC:** 2821, 3714
**UK SIC:** 25140, 35300

**Auditors:** Grant Thornton UK LLP

| | 31-12-13 | 31-12-12 | 31-12-11 |
|---|---|---|---|
| TO | 26,479,536 | 25,976,943 | 23,282,497 |
| P/L | 1,016,242 | 1,431,035 | 774,054 |
| NW | 3,727,804 | 3,715,556 | 2,658,466 |
| WC | 3,034,029 | 3,376,151 | 2,573,630 |
| Emp. | 298 | 322 | 311 |

DUNS 23-524-6568
## Polytec Personnel Ltd
Orwell House, Cowley Road, Cambridge, Cambridgeshire CB4 0PP
**Tel:** 01223-423267
**Web:** www.polytec.co.uk
**Reg No:** 1781726 **VAT No:** 388736784
**Estd:** 1984 Private Limited Company
**Line of Business:** Employment and recruitment companies and consultants
**Issued Capital:** £9,400
**Director:** Ms C A Ward
**Co. Secretary:** Kevin Young
**Responsibilities**
**Senior:** Esme Young *(Manager)*
**US SIC:** 7361 **UK SIC:** 83954
**Auditors:** Price Bailey
**Bankers:** Barclays Bank Plc (20-17-35)

| | 31-03-14 | 31-03-13 | 31-03-12 |
|---|---|---|---|
| TA | 842,809 | 720,867 | 729,917 |
| NW | 450,065 | 363,407 | 284,998 |
| WC | 438,784 | 356,576 | 280,526 |

DUNS 34-694-2878
## Polyteck Building Services Ltd
143 Loman Street, Whitechapel, London E1 8EY
**Tel:** 07817529034
**Web:** www.polyteck.co.uk
**Reg No:** 5498728 **Estd:** 2005 Private Limited Company
**Line of Business:** Installation of electrical wiring and fittings
**Trading Style:** Polyteck Group
**Issued Capital:** £100
**Directors:** J Polycarpou, C Polycarpou
**Co. Secretary:** Lefki Polycarpou
**US SIC:** 1731, 1711, 1799, 6531
**UK SIC:** 50300, 50000, 83400
**Auditors:** Lee & Associates (1993) Ltd

| | 31-12-13 | 31-12-12 | 31-12-11 |
|---|---|---|---|
| TO | 11,837,274 | 13,083,164 | 10,230,240 |
| P/L | 105,221 | 117,151 | 317,277 |
| NW | 704,370 | 630,847 | 532,620 |
| WC | 206,703 | 208,571 | 121,641 |
| Emp. | 67 | 64 | 59 |

DUNS 45-848-1512
## Pomeroy It Solutions Uk Ltd
Mercury Park, Wycombe Lane, Wooburn Green, High Wycombe, Buckinghamshire HP10 0HH
**Tel:** 01628-642000
**Web:** www.pomeroy.com
**Reg No:** 3194841 **VAT No:** 681083631
**Estd:** 1996 Private Limited Company
**Line of Business:** Other computer related activities
**Export Sales:** £1,353,717
**Trading Style:** O A O T
**Issued Capital:** £1,000
**Director:** C J Propst
**Co. Secretary:** Paul Yeomans
**Responsibilities**
**Finance:** David Tipton *(Financial Director)*
**Branches:** Pomeroy It Solutions Uk Ltd, 467 Malton Avenue, Slough, Berkshire SL1 4QU
**US SIC:** 7379 **UK SIC:** 83940
**Auditors:** Grenfell James
**Bankers:** Barclays Bank Plc (20-67-59)

| | 31-12-13 | 31-12-12 | 31-12-11 |
|---|---|---|---|
| TO | 12,832,404 | 12,455,644 | 10,520,186 |
| P/L | 1,374,971 | 1,951,004 | 1,275,430 |
| NW | 6,651,189 | 5,648,516 | 4,282,349 |
| WC | 6,638,683 | 5,627,861 | 4,266,976 |
| Emp. | 237 | 235 | 225 |

DUNS 34-588-8606
## Pomphrey of Sittingbourne Ltd
London Road, Sittingbourne, Kent ME9 9AQ
**Tel:** 01795-476222 **Fax:** 01795478209
**Web:** www.pomphreys.co.uk
**Reg No:** 2732980 **VAT No:** 572121273
**Estd:** 1992 Private Limited Company
**Line of Business:** Car dealers (new & used)
**Issued Capital:** £670
**Principals:** D S Pomphrey *(Managing)*, Ms E M Pomphrey
**Responsibilities**
**HR:** Kevin Belsey *(Human Resources Manager)*
**Health & Safety:** Kevin Belsey *(Human Resources Manager)*
**Branches:** Pomphrey Of Sittingbourne Ltd, Unit 38-42, Tribune Drive, Sittingbourne, Kent ME10 2PG
**US SIC:** 5511, 5521, 5531
**UK SIC:** 65100
**Auditors:** Grant Thornton

**Bankers:** The Royal Bank Of Scotland Plc (16-24-64)

| | 30-04-14 | 30-04-13 | 31-04-11 |
|---|---|---|---|
| TO | 2,731,751 | 14,801,715 | 12,510,271 |
| P/L | (45,332) | (71,747) | (165,931) |
| NW | 211,826 | 257,158 | 344,905 |
| WC | 211,826 | 257,158 | (137,507) |
| Emp. | 10 | 56 | 56 |

DUNS 22-937-7650
## Pond Park Stores & Filling Station
95 Pond Park Road, Lisburn, Co Antrim BT28 3RF
**Tel:** 02892601149
**Estd:** 2012 Proprietorship
**Line of Business:** Retail sale of automotive fuel
**US SIC:** 5541 **UK SIC:** 65200
**Employees:** 88

DUNS 21-742-0561 **Imp-Exp**
## Ponders End Investments Plc
Tradewinds House, Waltham Cross, Hertfordshire EN8 7UD
**Tel:** 01992650700 **Fax:** 01992-650800
**Web:** www.pei-plc.co.uk
**Reg No:** 1461903 **Estd:** 1973 Public Limited Company
**Line of Business:** Other letting of own property
**Export Markets:** Western Europe
**Export Sales:** £14,320,459
**Trading Style:** Ponders Cash and Carry, Cardin Golf, Polo Golf, Elite Superstores
**Issued Capital:** £50,000
**Principals:** S B Cole *(Managing)*, C Wallis
**Co. Secretary:** Mrs Frances Cole
**Responsibilities**
**Senior:** Graeme Sands *(Manager)*
**Branches:** Ponders End Investments Plc, 10 Fairfax Centre, Kidlington, Oxfordshire OX5 2PA
**US SIC:** 6519, 5611
**UK SIC:** 85000, 64500
**Auditors:** Gorrie Whltson
**Bankers:** Singer & Friedlander Ltd (60-01-56)

| | 30-06-14 | 30-06-13 | 30-06-12 |
|---|---|---|---|
| TO | 29,226,188 | 32,070,859 | 24,708,274 |
| P/L | 2,515,794 | 2,951,074 | 2,339,280 |
| NW | 19,573,171 | 18,902,387 | 17,488,860 |
| WC | 8,215,243 | 8,215,037 | 7,549,195 |
| Emp. | 78 | 78 | 95 |

DUNS 21-607-1117
## Pondsmead Residential & Nursing Home
Shepton Road, Bath, Avon BA3 5HT
**Tel:** 01749841111
**Web:** www.mimosahealthcare.com
**Estd:** 2000
**Line of Business:** Residential care establishments
**Proprietor:** Ms S Dutch
**Responsibilities**
**Senior:** Keran Kahan *(Home Manager)*
**US SIC:** 8091 **UK SIC:** 95200
**Employees:** 90

DUNS 21-773-1656
## Pontins
Barkby Avenue Central Beach, Prestatyn, Clwyd LL19 7LA
**Tel:** 01745855681
**Web:** www.pontins.co.uk
**Estd:** 2011 Proprietorship
**Line of Business:** Amusement park activities
**Proprietor:** C Sandals
**Responsibilities**
**Senior:** Stewart White *(Manager)*
**US SIC:** 7996 **UK SIC:** 97913
**Employees:** 100

DUNS 29-454-4978
## Ponti's Retail Ltd
(**Subsidiary of:** Ponti's Group Ltd)
17-21 Wenlock Road, London N1 7SL
**Tel:** 020-7250-1414
**Web:** www.pontis.co.uk
**Reg No:** 1683075 **VAT No:** 480940045
**Estd:** 1982 Private Limited Company
**Line of Business:** Licensed restaurants
**Trading Style:** Ponti''s Retail Limited
**Issued Capital:** £161,926
**Director:** S M Ispani
**Responsibilities**
**Senior:** Luca Leoncini *(Logistics Manager)*, Mike Ralf *(Financial director)*
**Finance:** Mike Ralf *(Financial director)*
**IT:** Matt Judd *(IT Manager)*
**Purchasing:** Gabriella Bassi *(Buyer)*
**Fleet:** Luca Leoncini *(Logistics Manager)*
**Branches:** Ponti's Retail Limited, 6 Eldon Street, London EC2M 7LS
**US SIC:** 5812 **UK SIC:** 66110

**Auditors:** Phillips Ell & Gross

| | 26-01-14 | 27-01-13 | 29-01-12 |
|---|---|---|---|
| TO | 12,700,073 | 13,328,176 | 15,867,174 |
| P/L | (2,307,947) | 358,061 | (2,171,764) |
| NW | (1,327,419) | 910,810 | 2,987,014 |
| WC | (856,056) | (722,816) | (5,192,102) |
| Emp. | 220 | 284 | 286 |

DUNS 21-814-3808
## Pontrilas Sawmills Ltd
(**Subsidiary of:** Pontrilas Group Ltd)
Pontrilas, Hereford, Herefordshire HR2 0BE
**Tel:** 01981240444 **Fax:** 01981-240748
**Web:** www.pontrilastimber.co.uk
**Reg No:** 0457573 **VAT No:** 134359961
**Estd:** 1948 Private Limited Company
**Line of Business:** Builders merchants
**Issued Capital:** £10,000
**Principals:** J J Hickman *(Chairman)*, E B Hilton, Ms S A Poynton, D Mills, J J Poynton, B W Pugh, Ms V S Hickman
**Responsibilities**
**Senior:** Edward Hickman *(Manager)*
**Health & Safety:** Reg Sayce *(Health & Safety Officer)*, Sara Withers *(Health & Safety Officer)*
**Facilities:** Phil Hulbert *(Production Manager)*
**Engineering:** Phil Hulbert *(Production Manager)*
**US SIC:** 5072 **UK SIC:** 61500
**Auditors:** Grant Thornton UK LLP
**Bankers:** HSBC Bank plc (40-16-18)

| | 31-07-14 | 31-07-13 | 31-07-12 |
|---|---|---|---|
| TO | 34,648,347 | 24,835,292 | 23,432,574 |
| P/L | 2,994,741 | 1,635,017 | 1,574,292 |
| NW | 10,897,251 | 9,185,337 | 8,089,037 |
| WC | 2,565,792 | 2,987,248 | 2,818,487 |
| Emp. | 221 | 199 | 197 |

DUNS 21-605-9065
## Pontypridd High School
Cilfynydd, Pontypridd, Mid Glamorgan CF37 4SF
**Tel:** 01443486133
**Web:** www.comprehensivehightskhool.co.uk
**Estd:** 1990
**Line of Business:** Schools (local authority)
**Proprietor:** H Cripps
**Responsibilities**
**Finance:** Claire Cook *(Senior Finance Administrator)*
**IT:** Gareth Baldwin *(Senior IT Executive)*
**US SIC:** 8211 **UK SIC:** 93200
**Employees:** 106

DUNS 21-879-9303
## Pool Innovation Centre
Trevenson Road, Pool, Redruth, Cornwall TR15 3PL
**Web:** www.poolinnovationcentre.co.uk
**Estd:** 2012
**Line of Business:** Serviced office facilities
**Responsibilities**
**Senior:** Richard Scutt *(Manager)*
**US SIC:** 7339 **UK SIC:** 83954
**Employees:** 160

DUNS 21-781-6181
## Poole Adult Social Services
Civic Centre Annexe, Park Road, Poole, Dorset BH15 2RT
**Tel:** 01202633600
**Web:** www.boroughofpoole.com
**Estd:** 2011
**Line of Business:** The dss
**Responsibilities**
**Senior:** Stephanie Mulrooney *(Team Manager)*
**Admin:** Karen-Ann Bruce *(Administrative Manager)*
**US SIC:** 8321 **UK SIC:** 96111
**Employees:** 100

DUNS 21-065-7966
## Poole Alcock & Co
240-246 Edleston Road, Crewe, Cheshire CW2 7EH
**Tel:** 01270-256665
**Web:** www.poolealcock.co.uk
**Proprietorship**
**Line of Business:** Solicitors
**Proprietor:** D Gaut
**Branches:** Poole Alcock & Co, 6 Middlewich Road, Sandbach, Cheshire CW11 1DL
**US SIC:** 8111 **UK SIC:** 83500
**Employees:** 150

DUNS 22-552-5591
## Poole Arts Trust Ltd
21 Kingland Road, Poole, Dorset BH15 1UG
**Tel:** 08700668701 **Fax:** 0870-066-8076
**Web:** www.lighthousepoole.co.uk
**Reg No:** 1368325 **Estd:** 1979 Private Company Limited By Guarantee
**Line of Business:** Art centres

**Directors:** D Pratley, A B Blackstock, Ms D Blanche, Professor O Lieberman, Ms T M Peters, M Lovibond, B Reeves, M Powell
**Co. Secretary:** Peter Wilson
**Responsibilities**
**Senior:** Sally Crawford *(Director)*, Amir Sadeh *(Director)*, John Sorton *(Manager)*, Chris Sparkhall *(Director)*, Sylvia Webster *(Director)*
**US SIC:** 7911 **UK SIC:** 97913
**Auditors:** RSM Tenon Audit Ltd
**Bankers:** Barclays Bank Plc (20-68-79)

| | 31-03-14 | 31-03-13 | 31-03-12 |
|---|---|---|---|
| TO | 3,708,967 | 3,717,526 | 3,669,441 |
| P/L | (398,368) | (410,556) | (291,638) |
| NW | 3,635,018 | 4,033,386 | 4,443,942 |
| WC | (22,496) | (54,408) | (87,827) |
| Emp. | 96 | 53 | 28 |

DUNS 21-224-7591
## Poole Audi
582-600 Ringwood Road, Poole, Dorset BH12 4LY
**Tel:** 01202-775050
**Web:** www.pooleaudi.co.uk
**Estd:** 1995
**Line of Business:** Car dealers (new & used)
**Proprietor:** D Kelly
**Responsibilities**
**Finance:** Gail Ninnim *(Accountant)*
**IT:** Gail Ninnim *(Accountant)*
**HR:** Rachel Rendell *(Personnel Manager)*
**US SIC:** 5511 **UK SIC:** 65100
**Employees:** 90

DUNS 21-731-2587
## Poole Grammar School
Gravel Hill, Poole, Dorset BH17 9JU
**Web:** www.poolegrammar.com
**Reg No:** 7666111 **Estd:** 2011 Private Company Limited By Guarantee
**Line of Business:** Schools (local authority)
**Directors:** Ms M H Holmes-Evans, Dr S A Eccles, J C Pullen, F M French, J K Rana, N J Bichard, A C Falck, M J Daniels
**Co. Secretary:** Jonathan Stiby
**Responsibilities**
**Senior:** Robert Bufton *(Director)*, Nathan Chase *(Director)*, Alexander Clarke *(Principal)*, Susan Gouveia *(Director)*, Michael Pidgley *(Director)*, Kenneth Power *(Director)*, Jane Risness *(Director)*, Anita Steel *(Director)*
**US SIC:** 8211 **UK SIC:** 93200
**Bankers:** HSBC Bank plc (40-37-36)

| | 31-08-14 | 31-08-13 | 31-08-12 |
|---|---|---|---|
| TO | 6,725,019 | 5,822,457 | 20,117,572 |
| P/L | 156,529 | (302,224) | 13,452,339 |
| NW | 12,427,644 | 12,586,115 | 12,901,339 |
| WC | 426,683 | 4,262 | 257,355 |
| Emp. | 123 | 113 | 112 |

DUNS 22-557-6263 **Imp**
## Poole Harbour Commissioners
Harbour Office, 20 New Quay Road, Poole, Dorset BH15 4AF
**Tel:** 01202440200 **Fax:** 01202440219
**Web:** www.portofpoole.co.uk
**Estd:** 1995 Incorporate By Act Of Parliament
**Line of Business:** Other supporting water transport activities
**Directors:** I Roberts, R Appleton, Captain J Barton
**Responsibilities**
**Senior:** Grant Mowlam *(Manager)*
**Health & Safety:** Dave Laut *(Health and Safety Officer)*
**Operations:** Clive Lane *(Port Manager)*
**US SIC:** 4469, 6732
**UK SIC:** 76300, 83100
**Auditors:** Grant Thornton UK LLP
**Bankers:** National Westminster Bank Plc (54-30-03)

| | 31-03-12 | 31-03-11 |
|---|---|---|
| TO | 9,078,000 | 8,965,000 |
| P/L | 712,000 | 904,000 |
| NW | 12,455,000 | 12,596,000 |
| WC | (112,000) | 718,000 |
| Emp. | 111 | 104 |

DUNS 21-777-3616
## Poole High School
Wimborne Road, Poole, Dorset BH15 2BW
**Tel:** 01202666988
**Web:** www.poolehigh.poole.sch.uk
**Estd:** 2011 Partnership
**Line of Business:** Schools (local authority)
**Partners:** C Lewis, C Lewis
**Responsibilities**
**Senior:** Fan Heafield *(Head Teacher)*
**IT:** Paul Thynne *(ICT Manager)*
**US SIC:** 8211 **UK SIC:** 93200
**Employees:** 150

DUNS 54-864-5050 **Imp**

## Poole Hospital Nhs Foundation Trust

**(Subsidiary of:** Department of Health)
Longfleet Road, Poole, Dorset BH15 2JB
**Web:** www.poole.nhs.uk
**Estd:** 2011
**Line of Business:** Nhs clinics
**Issued Capital:** £1
**Principals:** P Harvey *(Chairman)*, P James *(Personnel)*, J Filochowski, Ms S Sutherland, G Spencer, D Moores, C Cunningham, J Knowles
**Responsibilities**
**Senior:** Penny Scott *(Senior Speech And Language The)*
**Branches:** Poole Hospital Nhs Foundation Trust, Longfleet Road, Poole, Dorset BH15 2JB
**US SIC:** 8062 **UK SIC:** 95100
**Auditors:** Deloitte LLP

| | 31-03-14 | 31-03-13 | 31-03-12 |
|---|---|---|---|
| TO | 210,640,000 | 202,421,000 | 178,941,000 |
| P/L | (487,000) | (8,444,000) | 116,000 |
| NW | 108,596,000 | 103,302,000 | 103,559,000 |
| WC | (1,135,000) | 377,000 | 1,807,000 |
| Emp. | 2,942 | 3,108 | 3,048 |

DUNS 21-878-1589

## Poole Hospital Nhs Foundation Trust Charitable Fund

Poole Hospital Nhs Foundation Trust, Longfleet Road, Poole, Dorset BH15 2JB
**Web:** www.poole.nhs.uk
**Estd:** 1996
**Line of Business:** Educational, religious & charitable trusts
**Responsibilities**
**Senior:** Christopher Bown *(Trustee)*
**US SIC:** 6732 **UK SIC:** 83100
**Employees:** 4,200

DUNS 73-768-8437

## Poole Housing Partnership Ltd

28-30 Wimborne Road, Poole, Dorset BH15 2BU
**Tel:** 01202-264444
**Web:** www.yourphp.org.uk
**Reg No:** 5025994 **Estd:** 1994 Private Limited Company
**Line of Business:** Management of real estate on a fee or contract basis
**Directors:** Ms S Hobbs, C P Matthews, Mrs S E Carpenter, L C Knight, Ms C C Elliott, Ms A M Keogh, Ms D E Mclaughlin, I M Potter
**Co. Secretary:** Miss Jacqueline Barton
**Responsibilities**
**Senior:** Stephen Dunhill *(Director)*, Robert Dustan *(Director)*, Joan Gordon *(Director)*, Adele Kitson *(Director)*, Joe Logan *(Chief Executive)*, Peter Woodroffe *(Director)*
**Branches:** Poole Housing Partnership Ltd, Goathorn Clo, Poole, Dorset BH16 5AD
**US SIC:** 6531 **UK SIC:** 83400
**Bankers:** Barclays Bank Plc (20-68-79)

| | 31-03-14 | 31-03-13 | 31-03-12 |
|---|---|---|---|
| TO | 8,579,230 | 8,496,001 | 7,927,062 |
| P/L | (205,386) | 231,567 | 32,857 |
| NW | (1,178,808) | 119,501 | (887,198) |
| WC | 1,284,041 | 1,297,420 | 872,975 |
| Emp. | 106 | 102 | 102 |

DUNS 73-476-5246 **Imp**

## Poole Lighting Ltd

**(Subsidiary of:** Genesis 1:3 Ltd)
9 Cabot Lane, Poole, Dorset BH17 7BY
**Tel:** 01202690945
**Web:** www.poolelighting.com
**Reg No:** 4740426 **Estd:** 1985 Private Limited Company
**Line of Business:** Lighting contractors
**Issued Capital:** £1,000
**Directors:** J Schimmel, Mrs E Maslo
**Co. Secretary:** Meyer Maslo
**Responsibilities**
**Senior:** Trevor Hodder *(Manager)*, Michael Mansfield *(Operations Director)*, Abraham Schimmel *(Manager)*
**Marketing:** Trevor Hodder *(Manager)*
**Sales:** Trevor Hodder *(Manager)*
**HR:** Michael Mansfield *(Operations Director)*
**Facilities:** Michael Mansfield *(Operations Director)*
**US SIC:** 5719 **UK SIC:** 64700
**Auditors:** Beechams LLP

| | 31-12-13 | 31-12-12 | 31-12-11 |
|---|---|---|---|
| TO | 24,564,845 | 26,821,488 | 20,806,111 |
| P/L | 2,058,896 | 1,161,777 | 1,965,068 |
| NW | 9,368,367 | 7,580,138 | 5,912,660 |
| WC | 6,477,879 | 4,824,786 | 3,421,186 |
| Emp. | 130 | 150 | 115 |

DUNS 77-963-6232

## Poole Stadium Ltd

**(Subsidiary of:** Toklon Ltd)
Wimborne Road, Poole, Dorset BH15 2BP
**Tel:** 01202-677449
**Web:** www.stadiauk.com
**Reg No:** 3066878 **Estd:** 1995 Private Limited Company
**Line of Business:** Operation of other sports arenas and stadiums not elsewhere classified
**Issued Capital:** £1,000
**Director:** C Osborne
**Co. Secretary:** Stephen Hayward
**Responsibilities**
**Senior:** Marlene Todd *(Catering Manager)*
**Health & Safety:** Dave Pheby *(Health & Safety Manager)*
**Purchasing:** Marlene Todd *(Catering Manager)*
**Branches:** Poole Stadium Ltd, Wimborne Road, Poole, Dorset BH15 2BP
**US SIC:** 7999 **UK SIC:** 97913
**Auditors:** Grant Thornton
**Bankers:** Lloyds TSB Bank plc (30-00-01)

| | 31-12-13 | 31-12-12 | 31-12-11 |
|---|---|---|---|
| TO | 2,482,000 | 2,482,000 | 2,346,000 |
| P/L | 168,000 | 178,000 | 20,000 |
| NW | (326,000) | (494,000) | (672,000) |
| WC | (2,045,000) | (2,312,000) | (2,636,000) |
| Emp. | 76 | 84 | 81 |

DUNS 63-458-6408

## Poole Townsend

Palace Building, Main Street, Grange-Over-Sands, Cumbria LA11 6AB
**Tel:** 01539533316
**Web:** www.pooletownsend.co.uk
**Estd:** 1897 Partnership
**Line of Business:** Estate agents
**Partners:** J Poole, L Bayles, T Robert, Mrs J Copeland, Mrs L Pine, M Oates, A Dunn, D Dawson
**Responsibilities**
**Senior:** Martin Brownsord *(Valuer)*, Derek Pearce *(Partner)*, Susan Pine *(Partner)*
**Finance:** Marie Woodward *(Financial Advisor)*
**Sales:** Susan Danz *(Sales Progressor)*
**Branches:** Poole Townsend, Poole Townsend, 66 Market Street, Dalton-In-Furness, Cumbria LA15 8AA
**US SIC:** 8111, 6531
**UK SIC:** 83500, 83400
**Employees:** 70

DUNS 64-079-7874

## Poolearth Ltd

71-73 Hyde Park Road, Plymouth, Devon PL3 4JN
**Tel:** 01752-663216 **Fax:** 01752517403
**Web:** www.poolearth.com
**Reg No:** 3475069 **Estd:** 1997 Private Limited Company
**Line of Business:** Chemists dispensing
**Issued Capital:** £150
**Directors:** R Blatchford, R C Kirk, Ms S Retallick
**Co. Secretary:** Ronald Kirk
**US SIC:** 5912, 5999
**UK SIC:** 64300, 65600

| | 28-02-14 | 28-02-13 | 29-02-12 |
|---|---|---|---|
| TO | 7,437,416 | 7,246,612 | 7,166,722 |
| P/L | 89,237 | 154,399 | 75,509 |
| NW | (2,086,769) | (1,656,909) | (2,116,979) |
| WC | (73,101) | (184,736) | (217,104) |
| Emp. | 45 | 51 | 36 |

DUNS 50-459-6867

## Poolia Uk Ltd

**(Subsidiary of:** Staffing 360 Solutions Ltd)
18 King William Street, London EC4N 7BP
**Tel:** 02074641551
**Web:** www.poolia.co.uk
**Reg No:** 2442269 **VAT No:** 539201164
**Estd:** 1990 Private Limited Company
**Line of Business:** Employment and recruitment companies and consultants
**Issued Capital:** £10,000
**Director:** M A Olsson
**Responsibilities**
**Senior:** Timothy Hedger *(Manager)*, Dag Sundstr m *(Director)*
**Branches:** Poolia Uk Ltd, 15 York Pl, Edinburgh, Midlothian EH1 3EB
**US SIC:** 7361 **UK SIC:** 83954
**Auditors:** Deloitte LLP
**Bankers:** National Westminster Bank Plc (56-00-27)

| | 31-12-13 | 31-12-12 | 31-12-11 |
|---|---|---|---|
| TO | 3,804,925 | 7,167,376 | 10,797,452 |
| P/L | (338,405) | (141,782) | (247,348) |
| NW | (1,281,623) | (943,217) | (801,436) |
| WC | (1,285,930) | (952,993) | (815,029) |
| Emp. | 97 | 156 | 218 |

DUNS 22-855-2758

## Pools Co Ltd

**(Subsidiary of:** Sportech Plc)
Newton Court, Liverpool, Merseyside L13 1EJ
**Tel:** 01512883500 **Fax:** 0151-525-1889
**Web:** www.poolre.co.uk
**Reg No:** 0630845 **Estd:** 1959 Private Limited Company
**Line of Business:** Other service activities not elsewhere classified
**Issued Capital:** £80,000
**Directors:** C W Lynn, C Byrne, Miss N Mccabe
**Branches:** Pools Co Ltd, 222-228 Maybank Road, London E18 1ET
**US SIC:** 8999 **UK SIC:** 83954
**Auditors:** PricewaterhouseCoopers
**Bankers:** Barclays Bank Plc (20-51-01)

| | 31-12-13 | 31-12-12 | 31-12-11 |
|---|---|---|---|
| TA | 80,000 | 80,000 | 80,000 |
| NW | 80,000 | 80,000 | 80,000 |

DUNS 23-154-5468

## Poolside Cafe

Pudsey House, Market Place, Pudsey, West Yorkshire LS28 7BE
**Tel:** 01133367686
**Web:** www.leeds.gov.uk
**Estd:** 1987 Proprietorship
**Line of Business:** Other sporting activities not elsewhere classified
**Proprietor:** Mrs S Mayman
**US SIC:** 7999 **UK SIC:** 97913
**Employees:** 60

DUNS 21-033-9427

## Poor Servants of the Mother of God

Maryfield Convent Mount Angelus Road, Roehampton, London SW15 4JA
**Tel:** 02087884351
**Web:** www.poorservants.org.uk
**Estd:** 1926 Partnership
**Line of Business:** Religious organisations and places of worship
**Partners:** J Cunnane, B O'Shea, M Forrest, Ms S Goble
**Responsibilities**
**Senior:** Mary Whelan *(Sister)*
**US SIC:** 8661 **UK SIC:** 96600
**Employees:** 300

DUNS 21-310-2606

## The Popinjay Hotel

Popinjay Hotel, Rosebank, Carluke, Lanarkshire ML8 5QB
**Tel:** 01555-860441
**Web:** www.popinjayhotel.com
**Estd:** 1970 Proprietorship
**Line of Business:** Hotels
**Proprietor:** B Spence
**Responsibilities**
**Senior:** Denise Gregory *(General Manager)*, Colin McWhinnie *(Manager)*
**Health & Safety:** Denise Gregory *(General Manager)*
**US SIC:** 7011, 5812
**UK SIC:** 66500, 66110
**Employees:** 50

DUNS 34-821-3489

## Poplar 2000

**(Subsidiary of:** Macquarie Group Limited)
Cliff Lane, Lymm, Cheshire WA13 0SP
**Tel:** 01925757777
**Web:** www.motohospitality.com
**Reg No:** 2798288 **Estd:** 2011 Private Limited Company
**Line of Business:** Motorway services
**Trading Style:** Poplar 2000 Lymm Services
**Issued Capital:** £7,920,000
**Director:** T C Moss
**Co. Secretary:** Robert Prynn
**Responsibilities**
**Senior:** John Wilkie *(Manager)*
**US SIC:** 5812 **UK SIC:** 66110
**Auditors:** Deloitte & Touche LLP
**Bankers:** Bank Of Scotland (12-17-40)

| | 31-12-13 | 31-12-12 | 31-12-11 |
|---|---|---|---|
| TA | 13,661,000 | 13,661,000 | 13,661,000 |
| NW | 13,661,000 | 13,661,000 | 13,661,000 |

DUNS 53-659-9012

## Poplar Harca (Refurbishment) Ltd

**(Subsidiary of:** Poplar Housing & Regeneration Community Associatio)
167a East India Dock Road, London E14 0EA
**Tel:** 08000351991
**Web:** www.poplarharca.co.uk
**Reg No:** 3464996 **Estd:** 1999 Private Limited Company
**Line of Business:** Development and selling of real estate
**Trading Style:** Poplar Harca (Refurbishment) Ltd
**Issued Capital:** £2
**Directors:** C T Woolard, N F Hunt, Mrs B S Conroy
**Co. Secretary:** Stephen Stride
**Responsibilities**
**Senior:** Andrea Baker *(Director of Housing)*, Shiria Khatun *(Manager)*, Andrew Mahoney *(Manager)*, Millicent Muganyi *(Manager)*, Ben Wilson *(Manager)*
**Finance:** Neville Reid *(Financial Manager)*, Kevin Wright *(Director of Technical Resource)*
**Marketing:** Helen New *(Marketing Manager)*
**Sales:** Helen New *(Marketing Manager)*
**IT:** David Ieak *(IT Manager)*
**HR:** Babu Bhattacherjee *(Director of Communities and Ne)*
**Facilities:** Andrea Baker *(Director of Housing)*
**Engineering:** Kevin Wright *(Director of Technical Resource)*
**Branches:** Poplar Harca (Refurbishment) Ltd, Flat 25/A, Limborough House, Thomas Road, London E14 7AW
**US SIC:** 6552 **UK SIC:** 85000

| | 31-03-14 | 31-03-13 | 31-03-12 |
|---|---|---|---|
| TO | 1,457,009 | N/A | N/A |
| NW | 73 | 73 | 73 |
| WC | 73 | N/A | N/A |

DUNS 52-563-6411

## Poplar Housing & Regeneration Community Association Ltd

167a East India Dock Road, London E14 0EA
**Tel:** 02075100500
**Web:** www.poplarharca.co.uk
**Reg No:** 3249344 **Estd:** 1996 Private Company Limited By Guarantee
**Line of Business:** Other letting of own property
**Directors:** Ms J M Ellis, Ms B S Conroy, M W Rowe, D Mehta, P Rathinasabarathy, A M Ahmed, Reverend J Olanipekun, J Norman
**Co. Secretary:** Stephen Stride
**Responsibilities**
**Senior:** Juliana Ben Salem *(Director)*, Katherine Maciejewski *(Director)*, Andrew Mahoney *(Director)*, Tanya Martin *(Director)*, Sumaia Mashal *(Director)*, Helen New *(Manager)*, Simon Turek *(Director)*, Colin Woollard *(Director)*
**Branches:** Poplar Housing & Regeneration Community Association Ltd, Aberfeldy Street, London E14 0NU
**US SIC:** 6519, 8999
**UK SIC:** 85000, 83954
**Auditors:** KPMG

| | 31-03-14 | 31-03-13 | 31-03-12 |
|---|---|---|---|
| TO | 47,520,000 | 46,596,000 | 41,001,000 |
| P/L | 344,000 | 1,862,000 | 1,945,000 |
| NW | 23,678,000 | 23,355,000 | 21,094,000 |
| WC | 5,057,000 | 424,000 | 12,759,000 |
| Emp. | 307 | 302 | 289 |

DUNS 22-849-5297 **Imp**

## Poplar Nurseries Ltd

**(Subsidiary of:** Poplar Nurseries (Holdings) Ltd)
Coggeshall Road, Marks Tey, Marks Tey, Colchester, Essex CO6 1HR
**Tel:** 01206-210374 **Fax:** 01206211783
**Web:** www.poplarnurseries.co.uk
**Reg No:** 0469113 **Estd:** 1948 Private Limited Company
**Line of Business:** Garden centres
**Issued Capital:** £3,400
**Principals:** M A Cowan *(Managing)*, M C Cowan
**Co. Secretary:** Mrs Mandy Cowan
**Responsibilities**
**Senior:** Stewart Burle *(Manager)*
**US SIC:** 5999 **UK SIC:** 65600
**Auditors:** Griffin Chapman
**Bankers:** HSBC Bank plc (40-18-51)

| | 31-01-14 | 31-01-13 | 31-01-12 |
|---|---|---|---|
| TA | 1,394,236 | 1,414,556 | 1,330,752 |
| NW | 625,569 | 519,482 | 467,993 |
| WC | 8,693 | (64,699) | (186,455) |

DUNS 53-555-7672

## The Poplar Tree Co

Lower Lulham Farm, Lulham, Madley, Hereford, Herefordshire HR2 9JJ
**Web:** www.poplartree.co.uk
**Estd:** 1992 Partnership
**Line of Business:** Forestry advisers
**Partners:** H A Snell, G Snell
**US SIC:** 0851 **UK SIC:** 02000
**Employees:** 100

**DUNS 21-582-4364**
### The Poplars Care Home
Rolleston Road, Burton-On-Trent,
Staffordshire DE13 0JT
**Tel:** 01283562842
**Estd:** 2011 Proprietorship
**Line of Business:** Nursing homes
**Proprietor:** Mrs D Watson
**US SIC:** 8051  **UK SIC:** 95100
**Employees:** 49

**DUNS 21-150-8762**
### Poplars County Primary School
St Margarets Road, Lowestoft, Suffolk NR32
4HN
**Tel:** 01502565757
**Web:** www.poplarssuffolk.sch
**Estd:** 1997
**Line of Business:** Primary education
**Trading Style:** Poplars County Primary
School
**Partners:** Miss H Ann, Miss S Mcewan
**Responsibilities**
**Senior:** L Holzer (Head teacher), Suzanne
McEwan (Partner), Ian Sneddon (Joint Head
Teacher)
**Finance:** Jennifer Bullard (Bursar)
**Marketing:** Jennifer Bullard (Bursar)
**Health & Safety:** Nicola Gilroy (Health &
Safety Officer)
**Facilities:** Richard Woolnough (Caretaker)
**US SIC:** 8211  **UK SIC:** 93200
**Employees:** 60

**DUNS 29-651-7238**
### The Poplars Hotel Co. Ltd
(**Subsidiary of:** Ranu Ltd)
Wanborough House, Stratton Road,
Swindon, Wiltshire SN4 0AA
**Tel:** 01793-790774 **Fax:** 01793-790878
**Web:** www.poplars-nursery.co.uk
**Reg No:** 1977916  **Estd:** 1986 Private
Limited Company
**Line of Business:** Primary education
**Trading Style:** Poplars Day Care Nursery
**Issued Capital:** £427,523
**Managing Director:** R Kumar
**Co. Secretary:** Ms Nisha Kumar
**Responsibilities**
**Senior:** Rosaleen Monk (Child Care
Manager)
**US SIC:** 8211  **UK SIC:** 93200
**Auditors:** Morris Owen
**Bankers:** Lloyds TSB Bank plc (30-97-41)

|  | 31-03-14 | 31-03-13 | 31-03-12 |
|---|---|---|---|
| TA | 897,546 | 872,097 | 901,864 |
| NW | 729,063 | 693,979 | 666,539 |
| WC | (13,469) | (73,369) | (94,460) |

**DUNS 23-242-8800**
### The Poplars Ltd
66 South Road, Smethwick, West Midlands
B67 7BP
**Tel:** 0121-558-0962
**Web:** www.carltoncaregroup.co.uk
**Reg No:** 4160329  **Estd:** 1901 Private
Limited Company
**Line of Business:** Other human health
activities
**Issued Capital:** £100
**Director:** Ms S M Curry
**Co. Secretary:** Dr Robert Curry
**Responsibilities**
**Senior:** Antony Billingham (Manager)
**US SIC:** 8091  **UK SIC:** 95200

|  | 31-03-14 | 31-03-13 | 31-03-12 |
|---|---|---|---|
| TA | 910,285 | 937,444 | 998,498 |
| NW | 701,563 | 716,973 | 760,510 |
| WC | 633,044 | 651,796 | 729,739 |

**DUNS 23-693-3342**
### Poplars Nursery Garden Centre Ltd
Harlington Road, Dunstable, Bedfordshire
LU5 6HE
**Tel:** 01525872017
**Web:** www.poplars.co.uk
**Reg No:** 3688204  **Estd:** 1998 Private
Limited Company
**Line of Business:** Garden centres
**Issued Capital:** £1,180
**Directors:** Ms B Little, D J Little, J C Little
**Co. Secretary:** Ms Zoe Goodhand
**US SIC:** 5999  **UK SIC:** 65600
**Auditors:** Miller & Co
**Bankers:** National Westminster Bank Plc
(60-07-08)

|  | 28-02-14 | 28-02-13 | 29-02-12 |
|---|---|---|---|
| TO | 3,983,253 | 3,975,797 | 4,497,751 |
| P/L | 383,886 | 235,577 | 330,542 |
| NW | 4,073,656 | 3,866,711 | 3,692,793 |
| WC | 150,566 | 79,443 | 32,212 |
| Emp. | 111 | 115 | 123 |

**DUNS 64-254-6436**
### Poplars Nursing Home
158 Tonbridge Road, Maidstone, Kent ME16
8SU
**Tel:** 01622752872
**Web:** www.foresthc.com
**Estd:** 1996 Partnership
**Line of Business:** Nursing homes
**Partners:** S Dubowitz, M Kaplan
**Responsibilities**
**Senior:** Marion Harford (General Manager)
**Finance:** Marion Harford (General Manager)
**HR:** Marion Harford (General Manager)
**US SIC:** 8321  **UK SIC:** 96111
**Employees:** 103

**DUNS 42-354-1945**
### Poppies
6 Beech Road, Durham, County Durham
DH1 5JE
**Web:** www.poppiesdurham.co.uk
**Estd:** 1987 Proprietorship
**Line of Business:** Cleaning contracting
domestic
**Proprietor:** Mrs E Richardson
**US SIC:** 7349  **UK SIC:** 92300
**Bankers:** Barclays Bank Plc (20-27-41)
**Employees:** 50

**DUNS 34-608-3798**
### Poppies WI & S Ltd
71 Burscough Street, Ormskirk, Lancashire
L39 2EL
**Web:** www.poppies-wls.co.uk
**Reg No:** 5415230  **Estd:** 1996 Private
Limited Company
**Line of Business:** Cleaning contracting
domestic
**Issued Capital:** £10
**Director:** C J Wootton
**Co. Secretary:** Robert Piper
**US SIC:** 7349  **UK SIC:** 92300

|  | 31-03-14 | 31-03-13 | 31-03-12 |
|---|---|---|---|
| TA | 390,783 | 310,736 | 227,682 |
| NW | 305,772 | 222,310 | 140,567 |
| WC | 299,841 | 214,652 | 130,501 |

**DUNS 21-775-9097**
### Poppleton Road Primary School
Poppleton Road, York, North Yorkshire YO26
4UP
**Tel:** 01904553388
**Web:** www.poppletonroadprimary.co.uk
**Estd:** 1999 Proprietorship
**Line of Business:** Schools (local authority)
**Proprietor:** Mrs D Glover
**Responsibilities**
**Finance:** Kate Mawson (Senior Finance
Administrator)
**Admin:** Kate Mawson (Senior Finance
Administrator)
**IT:** Chris Pallister (Senior IT Executive)
**Purchasing:** Celia Galloway (Purchasing
Manager)
**US SIC:** 8211  **UK SIC:** 93200
**Employees:** 50

**DUNS 67-234-3407**
### The Poppy Room Ltd
9c Church Street, Troon, Ayrshire KA10 6AU
**Tel:** 01292318750
**Reg No:** 0315133SC  **Estd:** 2007 Private
Limited Company
**Line of Business:** Coffee shops
**Issued Capital:** £2
**Directors:** Mrs I G Mccullough,
Ms G Cameron
**Responsibilities**
**Senior:** Pamela Allison (Proprietor)
**US SIC:** 5812  **UK SIC:** 66110

|  | 31-01-14 | 31-01-13 | 31-01-12 |
|---|---|---|---|
| TA | 2,687 | 2,754 | 2,675 |
| NW | (24,933) | (24,794) | (23,183) |
| WC | (24,933) | (24,961) | (23,517) |

**DUNS 21-782-7699**
### Populas Data Solutions
Cragside House, Heaton Road, Newcastle-
Upon-Tyne, Tyne and Wear NE6 1SE
**Tel:** 01912650525
**Web:** www.populusdatasolutions.co.uk
**Estd:** 2011 Proprietorship
**Line of Business:** Market research
organisations
**Proprietor:** Mrs C Shill
**US SIC:** 7392  **UK SIC:** 83951
**Employees:** 200

**DUNS 39-666-7560**          **Imp**
### Populous Ltd
(**Subsidiary of:** Populous International
Holdings Inc.)
Blades Court, Deodar Road, West Hill,
London SW15 2NU
**Tel:** 020-8874-7666 **Fax:** 02088747470
**Web:** http://populous.com
**Reg No:** 2133361  **Estd:** 1925 Private
Limited Company
**Line of Business:** Architectural activities
**Issued Capital:** £50,000
**Principals:** R K Sheard (Managing),
B S Vickery, C D Lee, M R Trice,
N C Reynolds
**Co. Secretary:** Francis Henderson
**Responsibilities**
**Senior:** Catherine Sheard (Manager)
**Engineering:** Damon Lavelle (Principal),
Alicia Nahmad (Senior Design Manager),
Tim Reeves (Senior Associate)
**US SIC:** 8911, 7399
**UK SIC:** 83701, 83954
**Auditors:** Deloitte & Touche LLP
**Bankers:** National Westminster Bank Plc
(60-03-23)

|  | 31-12-13 | 31-12-12 | 31-12-11 |
|---|---|---|---|
| TO | 17,917,116 | 16,484,350 | 19,019,516 |
| P/L | 280,473 | 173,404 | 948,484 |
| NW | 3,104,149 | 3,165,724 | 3,694,881 |
| WC | 2,780,174 | 2,894,639 | 3,331,157 |
| Emp. | 125 | 125 | 158 |

**DUNS 21-616-0575**
### Porcelanosa
850 Europa Boulevard, Westbrook,
Warrington, Cheshire WA5 7ZR
**Web:** www.porcelanosa.co.uk
**Estd:** 2011 Partnership
**Line of Business:** Diy shops
**Partners:** M Dunleavey, M Dunleavy,
Mrs K Martin
**Responsibilities**
**Senior:** G Haughan (Proprietor)
**US SIC:** 5251  **UK SIC:** 64800
**Employees:** 50

**DUNS 49-387-5603**
### Porcelanosa (South East) Ltd
(**Subsidiary of:** Porcelanosa U.K. Ltd)
Units 1-6 Otterspool Way, Watford,
Hertfordshire WD25 8HL
**Tel:** 08444818950 **Fax:** 08708110304
**Web:** www.porcelanosa.com
**Reg No:** 3134596  **VAT No:** 668153316
**Estd:** 2007 Private Limited Company
**Line of Business:** Tile wholesalers and
suppliers
**Issued Capital:** £1,000
**Directors:** S Segarra, I Vazquez
**Co. Secretary:** Ms Natalia Vazquez Souto
**Responsibilities**
**Senior:** Juan Bodi (Manager), Miguel
Guillamon (Manager)
**IT:** Dave Fullerton (IT Manager)
**Branches:** Porcelanosa (South East) Ltd,
Unit B Newbridge Industrial Estate,
Cliftonhall Road, Newbridge, Midlothian
EH28 8PJ
**US SIC:** 5039  **UK SIC:** 61300
**Auditors:** Grant Thornton UK LLP
**Bankers:** Banco De Sabadell (60-92-70)

|  | 31-12-13 | 31-12-12 | 31-12-11 |
|---|---|---|---|
| TO | 27,440,000 | 23,311,000 | 21,181,000 |
| P/L | (2,844,000) | (3,412,000) | (3,781,000) |
| NW | 374,000 | 218,000 | 205,000 |
| WC | (1,752,000) | (2,143,000) | (2,010,000) |
| Emp. | 142 | 143 | 147 |

**DUNS 49-115-9794**
### Porcelanosa U.K. Ltd
Unit 3, Otterspool Way, Watford,
Hertfordshire WD25 8HL
**Tel:** 01923831867
**Web:** www.porcelanosa.co.uk
**Reg No:** 3098577  **Estd:** 1995 Private
Limited Company
**Line of Business:** Wholesale of wood,
construction materials and sanitary
equipment
**Issued Capital:** £102,000,000
**Director:** M Colonques
**Co. Secretary:** Ms Natalia Vazquez Souto
**US SIC:** 7399  **UK SIC:** 83954
**Auditors:** Grant Thornton
**Bankers:** Banco Do Brasil Sa (40-50-47)

|  | 31-12-13 | 31-12-12 | 31-12-11 |
|---|---|---|---|
| TO | 72,209,000 | 3,034,000 | 2,999,000 |
| P/L | (8,696,000) | 228,000 | 187,000 |
| NW | 100,140,000 | 101,772,000 | 101,943,000 |
| WC | 2,746,000 | 109,000 | 2,919,000 |
| Emp. | 391 | 1 | N/A |

**DUNS 29-384-7406**
### Porchlight
18-19 Watling Street, Canterbury, Kent CT1
2UA
**Web:** www.porchlight.org.uk
**Reg No:** 1157482  **Estd:** 1974 Private
Company Limited By Guarantee

**Line of Business:** Other tourist or short-stay
accommodation
**Directors:** G Miller, H Cohn, C J Wright,
A Croucher, Ms P A Unwin, S Chapman,
A J Pieterse, R A Porter
**Co. Secretary:** Michael Barrett
**Responsibilities**
**Senior:** Graeme Bosley (Support worker),
Jennifer Bough (Director), Tamsin Chayne
(Personal Assistant), Celia Glynn-Williams
(Director), Susan Hornibrook (Director),
Arnab Sanyal (Manager), Anna Stevens
(Manager), Keith Wren (Manager)
**Finance:** Catherine Keen (Financial
Director)
**Marketing:** Lisa Oeder (Commercial
Manager)
**Admin:** Jayne Nottage (Office Manager)
**HR:** Charles Elford (Human Resources
Manager)
**Health & Safety:** Charles Elford (Human
Resources Manager)
**Purchasing:** Catherine Keen (Financial
Director)
**Branches:** Porchlight, High Point Business
Vill, Henwood Rd, Ashford, Kent TN24 8DH
**US SIC:** 7021  **UK SIC:** 66500
**Auditors:** Finn-Kelcey & Chapman
**Bankers:** Lloyds TSB Bank plc (30-91-60)

|  | 31-03-14 | 31-03-13 | 31-03-12 |
|---|---|---|---|
| TO | 6,053,939 | 5,735,087 | 4,677,302 |
| P/L | (152,892) | 344,383 | 304,584 |
| NW | 1,644,151 | 1,797,043 | 1,452,660 |
| WC | 1,388,987 | 1,557,828 | 1,222,499 |
| Emp. | 179 | 148 | 127 |

**DUNS 67-139-5932**
### Pork Farms Ltd
(**Subsidiary of:** Eliot Luxembourg Holdco
Sarl)
Dunsil Drive, Nottingham, Nottinghamshire
NG2 1LU
**Tel:** 01159866541
**Web:** www.porkfarmsltd.com
**Reg No:** 5998346  **VAT No:** 897391264
**Estd:** 2006 Private Limited Company
**Line of Business:** Manufacturers and
suppliers of pies
**Issued Capital:** £1,160
**Directors:** K Mcgill, G J Voyle, G P Rutter,
M A Hodson, C Peters
**Co. Secretary:** Graham Rutter
**Responsibilities**
**Senior:** Sean Stewart (Manager)
**Branches:** Pork Farms Ltd, Maer Lane,
Market Drayton, Shropshire TF9 3AL
**US SIC:** 2099, 2013
**UK SIC:** 42399, 41223
**Auditors:** KPMG LLP
**Bankers:** Barclays Bank Plc (20-26-46)

|  | 29-03-14 | 30-03-13 | 31-03-12 |
|---|---|---|---|
| TO | 152,581,000 | 152,128,000 | 145,412,000 |
| P/L | (12,248,000) | (12,780,000) | (12,799,000) |
| NW | (107,060,000) | (92,302,000) | (84,069,000) |
| WC | (2,747,000) | 8,730,000 | 3,505,000 |
| Emp. | 1,412 | 1,439 | 1,384 |

**DUNS 21-023-4365**
### Porn & Dunwoody (Lifts) Ltd
(**Subsidiary of:** United Technologies
Corporation)
Express House, 100 Rolt Street, London SE8
5NN
**Tel:** 020-7919-9800 **Fax:** 02079199801
**Web:** www.pders-lifts.co.uk
**Reg No:** 0502884  **Estd:** 1951 Private
Limited Company
**Line of Business:** Other building installation
**Trading Style:** P D E R S
**Issued Capital:** £5,000
**Directors:** E F Smith, C B Idczak, R S Kullar
**Co. Secretary:** Mrs Caroline Kirk
**Responsibilities**
**Senior:** James Laurence (Manager)
**US SIC:** 1796, 7699
**UK SIC:** 50400, 67303
**Bankers:** Barclays Bank Plc (20-00-00)

|  | 30-11-13 | 30-11-12 | 30-11-11 |
|---|---|---|---|
| TA | 5,000 | 5,000 | 5,000 |
| NW | 5,000 | 5,000 | 5,000 |

**DUNS 21-721-9484**          **Imp-Exp**
### Porsche Cars Great Britain Ltd
(**Subsidiary of:** Volkswagen Ag)
Bath Road, Reading, Berkshire RG31 7SE
**Tel:** 01189303666
**Web:** www.porsche.com
**Reg No:** 0861097  **VAT No:** 222241222
**Estd:** 1965 Private Limited Company
**Line of Business:** Sale of new motor
vehicles
**Export Markets:** E U
**Export Sales:** £1,405,000
**Trading Style:** Porsche Cars Great Britain
Ltd
**Issued Capital:** £5,240,000
**Directors:** C N Craft, Doctor M Piech,
H Gerrmann, M S Mueller, B Maier,
Dr W Porsche, L Meschke
**Co. Secretary:** Bernard Moloney

**Responsibilities**
**Senior:** Rhona Andrews *(Finance Manager)*, Klaus Berning *(Manager)*, Felix Braeutigam *(Director)*, Christian Offermann *(Manager)*, Geoffrey Turral *(General Manager)*
**Finance:** Rhona Andrews *(Finance Manager)*
**Marketing:** Geoffrey Turral *(General Manager)*
**IT:** Geoffrey Turral *(General Manager)*
**US SIC:** 5511 **UK SIC:** 65100
**Auditors:** Ernst & Young LLP
**Bankers:** Barclays Bank Plc (20-71-03)

| | 31-12-13 | 31-12-12 | 31-12-11 |
|---|---|---|---|
| TO | 449,741,000 | 451,321,000 | 364,707,585 |
| P/L | 18,833,000 | 22,118,000 | 23,926,936 |
| NW | 57,890,000 | 45,271,000 | 65,265,960 |
| WC | 17,156,000 | 3,643,000 | 26,725,678 |
| Emp. | 107 | 102 | 102 |

DUNS 21-229-4246
## Porsche Centre
68-70 High Street, London E15 2NE
**Tel:** 020-85199999
**Web:** www.porsche.com
**Estd:** 1994
**Line of Business:** Car dealers (new & used)
**Proprietor:** T Harmon Wilson
**Responsibilities**
**Senior:** Ivan Howell *(Dealer Principal)*
**US SIC:** 5511 **UK SIC:** 65100
**Employees:** 100

DUNS 21-391-9222
## Porsche Centre Glasgow
9 Rocep Way, Renfrew, Renfrewshire PA4 8XT
**Tel:** 01419431155
**Web:** www.porche.co.uk
**Estd:** 1991 Proprietorship
**Line of Business:** Car dealers (new & used)
**Proprietor:** P Farrell
**US SIC:** 7539 **UK SIC:** 67100
**Employees:** 70

DUNS 21-618-9027
## Porsche Retail Group Ltd
(**Subsidiary of:** Volkswagen Ag)
Bath Road, Reading, Berkshire RG31 7SG
**Tel:** 0118-930-3911
**Web:** www.porsche.co.uk
**Reg No:** 0220221 **VAT No:** 479410133
**Estd:** 1927 Private Limited Company
**Line of Business:** Car dealers (new & used)
**Trading Style:** Porsche Centre Reading
**Issued Capital:** £5,800,000
**Directors:** H Gerrmann, C N Craft
**Co. Secretary:** Bernard Moloney
**Responsibilities**
**Senior:** Steven Layne *(Dealer Principal)*, Geoffrey Turral *(Manager)*
**IT:** Tim Newbury *(Head of IT)*
**Branches:** Porsche Retail Group Ltd, 931 Great West Road, Brentford, Middlesex TW8 9DU
**US SIC:** 5511, 7539
**UK SIC:** 65100, 67100
**Auditors:** Ernst & Young LLP
**Bankers:** Barclays Bank Plc (20-71-03)

| | 31-12-13 | 31-12-12 | 31-12-11 |
|---|---|---|---|
| TO | 196,928,000 | 183,904,000 | 161,143,267 |
| P/L | 1,348,000 | 457,000 | 793,933 |
| NW | 7,140,000 | 8,114,000 | 7,795,235 |
| WC | 6,268,000 | 6,379,000 | 6,488,742 |
| Emp. | 258 | 264 | 260 |

DUNS 21-587-3751
## Port-Er
Wonford Road Lister Close, Exeter, Devon EX2 4DU
**Tel:** 08458509808
**Estd:** 2011 Proprietorship
**Line of Business:** Charities and charitable organisations
**Proprietor:** Mrs D Corrick
**US SIC:** 8699 **UK SIC:** 96902
**Employees:** 200

DUNS 73-821-8945
## Port Express Ltd
Sub-Station Road, Felixstowe, Suffolk IP11 3JB
**Tel:** 01394675545 **Fax:** 01394675764
**Web:** www.port-express.com
**Reg No:** 5077834 **Estd:** 2004 Private Limited Company
**Line of Business:** Other supporting land transport activities
**Issued Capital:** £51,000
**Directors:** K G Stevens, K S Dawson, A R Nichols
**Co. Secretary:** John Stubbings
**US SIC:** 4789 **UK SIC:** 77002

| | 31-12-13 | 31-12-12 | 31-12-11 |
|---|---|---|---|
| TO | 8,205,148 | 7,786,050 | N/A |
| P/L | 300,209 | 399,856 | N/A |
| NW | 1,412,696 | 1,266,284 | 1,014,622 |
| WC | (90,858) | (3,645) | (110,352) |
| Emp. | 65 | 60 | N/A |

DUNS 22-615-1157
## Port Gaverne Hotel
Port Gaverne, Port Isaac, Cornwall PL29 3SQ
**Web:** www.portgavernehotel.co.uk
**VAT No:** 143647367 **Estd:** 1968 Proprietorship
**Line of Business:** Hotels
**Proprietor:** Mrs F P Ross
**Responsibilities**
**Senior:** Ian Brodey *(Head Chef)*, Graham Sylvester *(Proprietor)*
**US SIC:** 7011 **UK SIC:** 66500
**Bankers:** Barclays Bank Plc (20-90-56)
**Employees:** 49

DUNS 23-193-9294
## Port Lethen Medical Centre
Portlethen Medical Centre, Aberdeen, Aberdeenshire AB12 4QP
**Tel:** 01224-780223
**Web:** www.portlethenmedical.co.uk
**Proprietorship**
**Line of Business:** Doctors
**Proprietor:** Mrs L King
**US SIC:** 8011 **UK SIC:** 95300
**Employees:** 60

DUNS 77-741-7148
## Port of Dundee Ltd
(**Subsidiary of:** Deutsche Bank Ag)
Port Office, Stannergate Road, Dundee, Angus DD1 3LU
**Tel:** 01382224121
**Web:** www.forthports.co.uk
**Reg No:** 0155442SC **Estd:** 1995 Private Limited Company
**Line of Business:** Cargo handling
**Issued Capital:** £8,000,000
**Directors:** S R Paterson, C G Hammond
**Co. Secretary:** Ms Pamela Smyth
**Responsibilities**
**Senior:** Matt North *(Port Manager)*
**US SIC:** 4712 **UK SIC:** 77002
**Auditors:** PricewaterhouseCoopers LLP
**Bankers:** Bank Of Scotland (80-73-31)

| | 31-12-13 | 31-12-12 | 31-12-11 |
|---|---|---|---|
| TO | 9,522,000 | 8,973,000 | 8,345,000 |
| P/L | 4,150,000 | 1,928,000 | 2,796,000 |
| NW | 16,132,000 | 17,893,000 | 21,559,000 |
| WC | (57,000) | 2,988,000 | 5,825,000 |
| Emp. | 46 | 48 | 49 |

DUNS 22-596-9534
## Port of Leith Housing Association Ltd
108 Constitution Street, Edinburgh, Midlothian EH6 6AZ
**Tel:** 0131-554-0403
**Web:** www.polha.co.uk
**Reg No:** 0001844SC **Estd:** 1982
**Line of Business:** Housing associations societies trusts & co-operatives
**Principals:** W Penman *(Chairman)*, S Mohanjit *(Managing)*, R Dalgleish, Ms C B Reid, A Mcdonald, D C Mckay, T M Nichol, Ms M Clarke
**Co. Secretary:** Singh Mohanjit
**Responsibilities**
**Senior:** Robin Arthur *(Director)*, Alister McDonald *(Director)*, Douglas McKay *(Director)*, Margaret Rennie *(Director)*, Francis Wood *(Director)*
**US SIC:** 8321 **UK SIC:** 96111
**Auditors:** Chiene & Tait
**Bankers:** Bank Of Scotland (80-02-32)
**Employees:** 60
**Turnover:** £10,353,849

DUNS 21-156-5635
## Port of London Authority
Bakers Hall, 7 Harp Lane, London EC3R 6LB
**Tel:** 01474562200 **Fax:** 020-774-7999
**Web:** www.pla.co.uk
**Estd:** 1908 Incorporate By Act Of Parliament
**Line of Business:** Operation of habours and ports
**Principals:** R L Everitt, A B Richardson, B Chapman, D Cartlidge
**Responsibilities**
**Admin:** Sam Broome *(Secretary To Corporate Affairs)*
**HR:** Gary Holdforth *(HR Manager)*
**Branches:** Port of London Authority, London River House, Royal Pier Road, Gravesend, Kent DA12 2BG
**US SIC:** 4469 **UK SIC:** 76300
**Auditors:** Ernst & Young LLP

| | 31-12-12 | 31-12-11 | 31-12-10 |
|---|---|---|---|
| TO | 45,786,000 | 45,947,000 | 43,763,000 |
| P/L | 6,396,000 | 5,999,000 | 5,988,000 |
| NW | (18,009,000) | 13,404,000 | 42,408,000 |
| WC | 52,386,000 | 53,831,000 | 51,190,000 |
| Emp. | 364 | 359 | 344 |

DUNS 57-042-8334
## Port of London Tilbury Ltd
(**Subsidiary of:** Deutsche Bank Ag)
Leslie Ford House, Tilbury, Essex RM18 7EH
**Tel:** 01375-852200
**Web:** www.forthports.co.uk
**Reg No:** 2876001 **Estd:** 1991 Private Limited Company
**Line of Business:** Operation of habours and ports
**Issued Capital:** £2
**Directors:** C G Hammond, S R Paterson
**Co. Secretary:** Ms Pamela Smyth
**Responsibilities**
**Senior:** Andy Darlington *(Purchasing Manager)*
**Finance:** Jerry Gledhill *(Finance Manager)*
**Sales:** Steve Lyons *(Asset Manager)*
**HR:** Bill Carver *(Personnel Manager)*, Nadine Clarke *(Training Coordinator)*, Linda Stone *(Purchasing Department)*
**Health & Safety:** Tim Bridle *(Health & Safety Officer)*
**Facilities:** Gary Vincent *(Facilities Coordinator)*
**US SIC:** 4469 **UK SIC:** 76300

| | 31-12-13 | 31-12-12 | 31-12-11 |
|---|---|---|---|
| TA | 2 | 2 | 2 |
| NW | 2 | 2 | 2 |

DUNS 23-890-7088
## Port of Ness Harbour Ltd
Port Administration Building, Graven, Mossbank, Shetland ZE2 9QR
**Tel:** 01806244200
**Web:** www.shetland.gov.uk
**Reg No:** 0201756SC **Estd:** 1999 Private Limited Company
**Line of Business:** Activities of other membership organisations not elsewhere classified
**Directors:** J M Gunn, A Smith
**Co. Secretary:** John Gunn
**Responsibilities**
**Senior:** Colin Reeves *(Harbour Master)*
**US SIC:** 8699 **UK SIC:** 96902

| | 30-11-13 | 30-11-12 | 30-11-11 |
|---|---|---|---|
| TO | N/A | 7,010 | N/A |
| P/L | N/A | (4,734) | N/A |
| NW | 125,661 | 125,861 | 130,595 |
| WC | 4,737 | 829 | 1,455 |

DUNS 76-980-3172
## Port of Sheerness Ltd
(**Subsidiary of:** Tokenhouse Ltd)
Archway House, Sheerness Docks, Sheerness, Kent ME12 1RS
**Tel:** 01795596596 **Fax:** 01795-660093
**Web:** http://peelports.com
**Reg No:** 2639118 **Estd:** 1991 Private Limited Company
**Line of Business:** Freight sea and coastal water transport
**Issued Capital:** £500,000
**Directors:** T E Allison, I G Charnock, G Parkinson, S Underwood, G E Hodgson, J Whittaker, M Whitworth
**Co. Secretary:** Ms Caroline Marrison Gill
**Responsibilities**
**Senior:** Michelle Newton *(Manager)*, Mike Sutton *(Depot Manager)*
**Finance:** Graeme Charnock *(Chief Financial Officer)*
**Operations:** Russell Bird *(Dredging Manager)*, Pauline Pardoe *(Conservancy Executive)*
**US SIC:** 4411 **UK SIC:** 74001
**Auditors:** PricewaterhouseCoopers LLP
**Bankers:** National Westminster Bank Plc (60-19-04)

| | 31-03-14 | 31-03-13 | 31-03-12 |
|---|---|---|---|
| TO | 32,400,000 | 40,345,000 | 45,436,000 |
| P/L | 8,400,000 | 14,300,000 | 17,087,000 |
| NW | 30,300,000 | 35,437,000 | 36,924,000 |
| WC | (8,900,000) | (1,042,000) | 2,698,000 |
| Emp. | 181 | 204 | 213 |

DUNS 77-008-6817
## Port of Tilbury London Ltd
(**Subsidiary of:** Deutsche Bank Ag)
Leslie Ford House, Tilbury, Essex RM18 7EH
**Tel:** 01375852369
**Web:** www.londoncruiseterminal.com
**Reg No:** 2659118 **VAT No:** 583270042
**Estd:** 1992 Private Limited Company
**Line of Business:** Other supporting water transport activities
**Trading Style:** Fouth Ports
**Issued Capital:** £109,759,758
**Principals:** P D Glading *(Managing)*, S R Paterson, C G Hammond
**Co. Secretary:** Ms Pamela Smyth
**Responsibilities**
**HR:** Bill Carver *(Personnel Manager)*, Nadine Clarke *(Training Coordinator)*
**Health & Safety:** Tim Bridle *(Health & Safety Officer)*
**Facilities:** Gary Vincent *(Facilities Coordinator)*
**Purchasing:** Andy Darlington *(Purchasing Manager)*
**Branches:** Port Of Tilbury London Ltd, Leslie Ford House, Tilbury, Essex RM18 7EH
**US SIC:** 4469 **UK SIC:** 76300
**Auditors:** PricewaterhouseCoopers LLP
**Bankers:** National Westminster Bank Plc (60-09-11)

| | 31-12-13 | 31-12-12 | 31-12-11 |
|---|---|---|---|
| TO | 88,448,000 | 86,220,000 | 80,421,000 |
| P/L | 65,176,000 | 40,272,000 | 23,339,000 |
| NW | 307,135,000 | 314,959,000 | 266,162,000 |
| WC | 12,659,000 | 30,246,000 | 2,500,000 |
| Emp. | 466 | 457 | 487 |

DUNS 22-787-9350 **Imp**
## Port of Tyne Authority
Maritime House, Tyne Dock, South Shields, Tyne and Wear NE34 9PT
**Tel:** 0191-455-2671 **Fax:** 0191-455-4687
**Web:** www.portoftyne.co.uk
**VAT No:** 176442549 **Estd:** 1968 Incorporate By Act Of Parliament
**Line of Business:** Operation of habours and ports
**Principals:** Dr J Hudson *(Financial)*, B Reeve *(Technical)*, A Moffet
**Responsibilities**
**Senior:** Alasdair Kerr *(Commercial Director)*, Tracey Younger *(Warehouse Manager)*
**Sales:** Alasdair Kerr *(Commercial Director)*
**IT:** Ian Blake *(IT Manager)*
**HR:** Geoff Gillon *(Human Resources Director)*
**Facilities:** Andy Kahn *(Estates Manager)*, David Profit *(Clerk of Works)*
**Purchasing:** Heather Coltman *(Purchasing Manager)*
**Branches:** Port Of Tyne Authority, Ferry Terminal, Albert Edward Dock, North Shields, Tyne and Wear NE29 6EE
**US SIC:** 4469 **UK SIC:** 76300
**Auditors:** Ernst & Young LLP
**Bankers:** Barclays Bank Plc (20-59-42)

| | 31-12-12 | 31-12-11 | 31-12-10 |
|---|---|---|---|
| TO | 63,006,000 | 59,172,000 | 45,552,000 |
| P/L | 11,923,000 | 8,953,000 | 4,400,000 |
| NW | 105,106,000 | 99,119,000 | 98,798,000 |
| WC | (82,000) | 3,300,000 | 3,152,000 |
| Emp. | 462 | 446 | 448 |

DUNS 22-930-5289
## Port Regis School Ltd
Motcombe, Shaftesbury, Dorset SP7 9QA
**Tel:** 01747857800 **Fax:** 01747857836
**Web:** www.portregis.com
**Reg No:** 0440436 **Estd:** 1947 Private Company Limited By Guarantee
**Line of Business:** Schools (independent)
**Directors:** Ms C F Macdonald, Ms B S Oppenheim, C J Holloway, Mrs D E Watkins, N G Over, I A Grey, A O Cumine, G White
**Co. Secretary:** Mrs Nicola Miller
**Responsibilities**
**Senior:** Craig Considine *(Director)*, Frances Da Cunha *(Manager)*, Rokeya Dangor *(Manager)*, Benedict Dunhill *(Head Teacher)*, Stephen Edlmann *(Director)*, William Gething *(Director)*, Nicholas Gooch *(Director)*, Oliver Hawkins *(Director)*, Judy Williamson *(Director)*
**Finance:** Nikki Miller *(Bursar)*
**Marketing:** Henrietta Thorpe *(Marketing Manager)*
**HR:** Benedict Dunhill *(Head Teacher)*
**Health & Safety:** Nikki Miller *(Bursar)*
**Facilities:** Kevin Binns *(Estates Bursar)*
**US SIC:** 8211 **UK SIC:** 93200
**Auditors:** Haysmacintyre
**Bankers:** National Westminster Bank Plc (51-81-01)

| | 31-08-14 | 31-08-13 | 31-08-12 |
|---|---|---|---|
| TO | 6,581,232 | 6,793,568 | 6,978,531 |
| P/L | (194,536) | (160,620) | (143,241) |
| NW | 8,727,438 | 8,921,974 | 9,082,594 |
| WC | (365,727) | (417,302) | (372,121) |
| Emp. | 214 | 244 | 254 |

DUNS 22-171-4913
## Port Vale Fc Community Trust
43-45 Trinity Street, Hanley, Stoke-On-Trent, Staffordshire ST1 5LQ
**Tel:** 01782655832
**Web:** www.port-vale.co.uk
**Reg No:** 4189865 **Estd:** 2003 Private Company Limited By Guarantee
**Line of Business:** Other sporting activities not elsewhere classified
**Directors:** J P Nixon, G Bullock, P A Williams
**Co. Secretary:** Peter Williams
**Responsibilities**
**Senior:** Andrew Belfield *(Director)*, Perry Deakin *(Chief Executive)*, Norman Smurthwaite *(Manager)*
**US SIC:** 7999 **UK SIC:** 97913
**Bankers:** Barclays Bank Plc (20-36-43)

| | 31-03-13 | 31-03-12 | 31-03-11 |
|---|---|---|---|
| TO | 146,781 | 135,955 | 152,972 |
| P/L | 1,389 | (2,006) | 71,820 |
| NW | 10,814 | 222,097 | 224,103 |
| WC | 9,420 | 7,785 | (1,071) |

DUNS 34-543-2012

## Porta Communications Plc

Sky Light City Tower, London EC2V 5DE
**Tel:** 02076806500 **Fax:** 02076806510
**Web:** www.portacommunications.plc.uk
**Reg No:** 5353387 **Estd:** 2013 Public Limited Company
**Line of Business:** Public relations consultants
**Export Sales:** £3,171,947
**Issued Capital:** £10,891,396
**Directors:** B J Blasdale, G Golembiewski, R J Mckeeve, A L Morton, D Wright
**Co. Secretary:** Eugene Golembiewski
**Responsibilities**
**Admin:** Perri Dopson *(Executive Assistant)*
**US SIC:** 7392 **UK SIC:** 83951
**Auditors:** Nexia Smith & Williamson
**Bankers:** Coutts & Co (18-00-02)

| | 31-12-13 | 31-12-12 | 31-12-11 |
|---|---|---|---|
| TO | 24,441,290 | 8,384,625 | 1,025,407 |
| P/L | (3,062,027) | (4,627,532) | (1,570,909) |
| NW | (3,593,591) | (6,518,738) | 145,729 |
| WC | (89,662) | (4,915,137) | 886,419 |
| Emp. | 121 | 78 | 15 |

DUNS 23-534-3170

## Portable Foods Manufacturing Co Ltd

(**Subsidiary of:** Kellogg Company)
11 Caputhall Road, Deans Industrial Estate, Deans, Livingston, West Lothian EH54 8AS
**Tel:** 01506-413311 **Fax:** 01506413388
**Reg No:** 3533251 **Estd:** 1998 Private Limited Company
**Line of Business:** Manufacturers of food products
**Issued Capital:** £100,000
**Directors:** T W Mcknight, Ms J A Ayres-Smith, G P Maguire
**Co. Secretary:** Eversecretary Limited
**Responsibilities**
**Senior:** Benjamin Goodman *(Manager)*, Murgo Macleod *(Managor)*
**US SIC:** 2099 **UK SIC:** 42399
**Auditors:** PricewaterhouseCoopers LLP

| | 28-12-13 | 29-12-12 | 31-12-11 |
|---|---|---|---|
| TO | 19,947,000 | 19,628,000 | 19,273,000 |
| P/L | 1,385,000 | 1,655,000 | 1,661,000 |
| NW | 5,901,000 | 4,753,000 | 4,182,000 |
| WC | (4,480,000) | (7,958,000) | (11,433,000) |
| Emp. | 170 | 173 | 172 |

DUNS 21-094-3572

## Portadown Health Centre

Tavanagh Avenue, Portadown, Craigavon, Co Armagh BT62 3BU
**Tel:** 02838334400
**Web:** www.portadownhealthcentre.co.uk
**Estd:** 1994 Partnership
**Line of Business:** Nhs clinics
**Partners:** Dr F Goode, Dr J Mcconnell, Dr W Burnett, Dr D Grey
**Responsibilities**
**Senior:** Elinor Hamilton *(CEO, Managing Director)*, Caroline Jefferies *(Facilities Manager)*, J McConnell *(Partner)*, Julie Mcneal *(Senior Customer Services Execu)*
**Facilities:** Caroline Jefferies *(Facilities Manager)*
**US SIC:** 8062 **UK SIC:** 95100
**Employees:** 200

DUNS 21-245-0274 Exp

## Portakabin Ltd

(**Subsidiary of:** Shepherd Building Group Ltd)
New Lane, Huntington, York, North Yorkshire YO32 9PT
**Tel:** 01904-611655
**Web:** www.portakabin.co.uk
**Reg No:** 0685303 **VAT No:** 551855234
**Estd:** 1961 Private Limited Company
**Line of Business:** Erection of roof covering and frames
**Export Sales:** £60,738,000
**Trading Style:** Portakabin Ltd, Aircare
**Issued Capital:** £1,000,000
**Directors:** J M Collins, Mrs A C Stainton, C L Brown, J Guenard, B D Shaw, S W Ambler, D P Carter, N Runkee
**Co. Secretary:** Philip Clarke
**Responsibilities**
**Senior:** Richard Billingworth *(General Manager of production)*, Ian MacKenzie *(Director of Engineering)*
**Sales:** Lisa Hodgson *(Sales Manager)*
**IT:** Charles Bornello *(IT Manager)*, Paul Chamley *(Senior IT Executive)*
**Engineering:** Ian MacKenzie *(Director of Engineering)*
**Branches:** Portakabin Ltd, Nottingham Road, Beeston, Nottingham, Nottinghamshire NG9 6DP
**US SIC:** 3441, 3999, 7394
**UK SIC:** 32042, 49590, 84000

**Auditors:** KPMG LLP

| | 30-06-14 | 30-06-13 | 30-06-12 |
|---|---|---|---|
| TO | 218,940,000 | 185,408,000 | 174,255,000 |
| P/L | 29,516,000 | 22,559,000 | 23,924,000 |
| NW | 164,287,000 | 163,490,000 | 144,198,000 |
| WC | 47,104,000 | 53,866,000 | 40,919,000 |
| Emp. | 1,497 | 1,391 | 1,351 |

DUNS 34-911-3063

## The Portal Partnership Ltd

3 Bracknell Beeches, Old Bracknell Lane West, Bracknell, Berkshire RG12 7BW
**Tel:** 01344-386000 **Fax:** 01344-386001
**Web:** www.portalpartnership.com
**Reg No:** 5708371 **Estd:** 2006 Private Limited Company
**Line of Business:** Hardware consultancy
**Export Sales:** £179,050
**Issued Capital:** £519,530
**Directors:** N Birtles, S Kelly, J Bradshaw, G A Appleton, S J Conroy, S F Rogers, P C West, J C Lindley
**Responsibilities**
**Senior:** Brijinder Arjuna *(Director)*, Tony Egerton *(Sales & Marketing Director)*, Probal Sil *(Director)*
**Marketing:** Tony Egerton *(Sales & Marketing Director)*
**Sales:** Tony Egerton *(Sales & Marketing Director)*
**HR:** Sue Spanswick *(Human Resources Manager)*
**Health & Safety:** Sue Spanswick *(Human Resources Manager)*
**US SIC:** 7379 **UK SIC:** 83940
**Auditors:** Grant Thornton UK LLP

| | 31-03-14 | 31-03-13 | 31-03-12 |
|---|---|---|---|
| TO | 16,234,248 | 14,911,608 | 21,290,186 |
| P/L | (650,579) | (256,922) | 410,802 |
| NW | 327,672 | 1,062,101 | 1,297,681 |
| WC | 134,364 | 945,989 | 1,183,112 |
| Emp. | 61 | 61 | 58 |

DUNS 21-579-5800

## Portal Security

95 Marton Drive, Blackpool, Lancashire FY4 3EU
**Tel:** 08452098148
**Web:** www.portalsecurity.co.uk
**Estd:** 2011 Partnership
**Line of Business:** Security and related activities
**Partners:** S Swallow, J Thomas
**Responsibilities**
**Senior:** Nathan Williams *(General Manager)*
**US SIC:** 7393 **UK SIC:** 83954
**Employees:** 170

DUNS 21-624-7619

## Portchester Microtools Ltd

(**Subsidiary of:** P.M.T. (Metal Craft) Ltd)
Bilton Way, Portsmouth, Hampshire PO3 5FH
**Tel:** 023-9265-8000
**Web:** www.pmtltd.co.uk
**Reg No:** 0724391 **VAT No:** 107394767
**Estd:** 1932 Private Limited Company
**Line of Business:** Manufacture of basic iron and steel and of ferro-alloys
**Issued Capital:** £5,526
**Managing Director:** B H Wragg
**Co. Secretary:** Ms Annette Wragg
**US SIC:** 3325, 3499 **UK SIC:** 31110, 31694
**Bankers:** HSBC Bank plc (40-37-17)

| | 30-04-14 | 30-04-13 | 30-04-12 |
|---|---|---|---|
| TA | 66,780 | 81,406 | 97,947 |
| NW | 21,309 | 25,939 | 35,048 |
| WC | 47,709 | 47,031 | 47,619 |

DUNS 21-223-2263

## Porter Dodson

The Close, Church Path, Yeovil, Somerset BA20 1HH
**Web:** www.porterdodson.co.uk
**Estd:** 1997 Partnership
**Line of Business:** Solicitors
**Partners:** T Rose, R Fox, M Pitt, R Baker, Ms S Clarke, R Beatson, Ms J Perrins, D Perratt
**Responsibilities**
**Marketing:** Paula Whitehead *(Marketing Manager)*
**Admin:** Deborah Carrington *(Human Resources Manager)*
**HR:** Deborah Carrington *(Human Resources Manager)*
**Health & Safety:** Deborah Carrington *(Human Resources Manager)*
**Purchasing:** Deborah Carrington *(Human Resources Manager)*
**Branches:** Porter Dodson, Quad, Blackbrook Park Avenue, Taunton, Somerset TA1 2PX
**US SIC:** 8111 **UK SIC:** 83500
**Employees:** 150

DUNS 21-573-5846

## Porter Matthews & Marsden Chartered Accountants

Greenbank Technology Park, Challenge Way, Blackburn, Lancashire BB1 5QB
**Tel:** 01254679131
**Web:** www.pmm.co.uk
**Estd:** 2009 Partnership
**Line of Business:** Accounting activities
**Partners:** B C Marsden, Mrs D L Eatough, J N Stirrup, M G Battersby, D P Bradley, D M Lyon, S M Anderson, R A Ainscough
**Responsibilities**
**Senior:** Jim Akrill *(Partner & Managing Director)*, Tony Brierley *(Partner & Managing Director)*, Jackie Fisher *(Partner)*, David Gorton *(General Practice Partner)*
**Finance:** Tracy Dunston *(Credit Controller)*, Gillian Ibbotson *(Payroll Manager)*, Antony Keen *(Finance Manager)*, Julie Mason *(Payroll Services Manager)*
**Marketing:** Claire Jewsbury *(Marketing Manager)*
**Sales:** Sarah Alpe *(Business Services Senior)*, Sarah Clancey *(Business Services Team)*, Claire Furnival *(Corporate Services Team)*, Peter Oddie *(Rural Business Services Manage)*, Delyth Oxford *(Business Services Manager)*, Danielle Wright *(Business Services Assistant Ma)*
**Admin:** Glad Ashworth *(Receptionist)*, Lorraine Cade *(Secretary)*, Allison Hall *(Receptionist)*, Gillian Perris *(Administrator)*, Anne Ramsden *(Company Secretarial Administra)*, Linda Whitfield *(Receptionist)*
**Branches:** Porter Matthews & Marsden Chartered Accountants, 83 Bank Parade, Burnley, Lancashire BB11 1UG
**US SIC:** 8931, 7392
**UK SIC:** 83600, 83951
**Bankers:** HSBC Bank plc (40-12-04)
**Employees:** 65

DUNS 23-662-5450

## Porterbrook Maintenance Ltd

(**Subsidiary of:** Porterbrook Rail Finance Ltd)
Ivatt House, The Point, Pinnacle Way, Pride Park, Derby, Derbyshire DE24 8ZS
**Fax:** 01332 285051
**Web:** www.porterbrook.co.uk
**Reg No:** 3657463 **VAT No:** 927439496
**Estd:** 1998 Private Limited Company
**Line of Business:** Transport via railways
**Issued Capital:** £54,393
**Directors:** A C White, K R Howard, P A Francis, W J Day
**Co. Secretary:** Stephen Mcgurk
**Responsibilities**
**Senior:** Timothy Gilbert *(Engin Director)*
**US SIC:** 4011 **UK SIC:** 71000
**Auditors:** Deloitte LLP
**Bankers:** Lloyds TSB Bank plc (30-92-59)

| | 31-12-13 | 31-12-12 | 31-12-11 |
|---|---|---|---|
| TO | 62,845,000 | 65,964,000 | 59,712,000 |
| P/L | 5,061,000 | 4,699,000 | 4,495,000 |
| NW | 58,060,000 | 53,497,000 | 49,735,000 |
| WC | (4,636,000) | (3,923,000) | (141,000) |
| Emp. | 58 | 57 | 58 |

DUNS 21-777-3601

## Portfield Special School

Parley Lane, Christchurch, Dorset BH23 6BP
**Tel:** 01202573808
**Web:** www.autismwessex.org.uk
**Estd:** 2004 Proprietorship
**Line of Business:** Schools (special)
**Proprietor:** Mrs J Rodgers
**Responsibilities**
**Senior:** Tyler Collins *(Head Teacher)*
**US SIC:** 8299 **UK SIC:** 93300
**Employees:** 150

DUNS 23-824-6461

## Portfolio Catering Ltd.

49 North Fort Street, Edinburgh, Midlothian EH6 4HJ
**Tel:** 0131-555-2229 **Fax:** 01315558460
**Web:** www.heritageportfolio.co.uk
**Reg No:** 0198522SC **Estd:** 2002 Private Limited Company
**Line of Business:** Caterers
**Trading Style:** Heritage Portfolio
**Issued Capital:** £2
**Directors:** H K Monavar, A R Dishington, K B King, C S Verros, I D'Annunzio Green
**Co. Secretary:** Keith King
**Responsibilities**
**Senior:** Ian D'Annunzio-Green *(Executive Director)*
**Sales:** Kirsty Hepburn *(Business Development Manager)*
**US SIC:** 5812 **UK SIC:** 66110
**Auditors:** HBJ Gateley Wareing
**Bankers:** Bank Of Scotland (80-11-05)

| | 31-12-13 | 31-12-12 | 31-12-11 |
|---|---|---|---|
| TA | 2 | 2 | 2 |
| NW | 2 | 2 | 2 |

DUNS 34-890-3766

## Portfolio Design Group International Ltd

8-11 Grosvenor Court, Foregate Street, Chester, Cheshire CH1 1HG
**Tel:** 01244317999
**Reg No:** 2827417 **Estd:** 1993 Private Limited Company
**Line of Business:** Life Insurance
**Trading Style:** Surrenderlink
**Issued Capital:** £458,325
**Directors:** C P Sands, D W Roxburgh, J A Murphy, M Semple
**Co. Secretary:** John Murphy
**US SIC:** 6311 **UK SIC:** 82002
**Auditors:** Ernst & Young
**Bankers:** National Westminster Bank Plc (60-00-01)

| | 31-12-13 | 31-12-12 | 31-12-11 |
|---|---|---|---|
| TO | 3,780,099 | 6,111,239 | 5,450,681 |
| P/L | 45,276 | (386,652) | (599,041) |
| NW | 6,313,271 | 6,442,713 | 6,881,966 |
| WC | 4,063,399 | 5,919,069 | 5,647,775 |
| Emp. | 64 | 71 | 79 |

DUNS 21-557-2860

## Porthaven Care Homes Llp

Gatehouse Road, Aylesbury, Buckinghamshire HP19 8EH
**Tel:** 01296438000 **Fax:** 01296483432
**Reg No:** 0348553OC **Estd:** 2009 Private Limited Company
**Line of Business:** Medical nursing home activities
**Responsibilities**
**Senior:** Shaun Caravan *(Home Manager)*, Chee Jap *(Non-designated Limited Liabili)*
**US SIC:** 8999 **UK SIC:** 83954

| | 31-03-14 | 31-03-13 | 31-03-12 |
|---|---|---|---|
| TO | 9,236,734 | 7,232,795 | 4,126,631 |
| P/L | 539,676 | (631,495) | (1,387,848) |
| NW | 540,677 | (630,494) | (1,386,847) |
| WC | 822,685 | 361,819 | 420,524 |
| Emp. | 307 | 266 | 166 |

DUNS 21-732-7736

## Porthaven Group Holdings Ltd

271 Regent Street, London W1B 2ES
**Tel:** 02033005767
**Web:** www.hydroponics.eu
**Reg No:** 7677720 **Estd:** 2003 Private Limited Company
**Line of Business:** Management activities of holding companies
**Issued Capital:** £988
**Directors:** J Storey, N M Morgan, R W Devlin, J R Thomas
**Co. Secretary:** Sean Kime
**US SIC:** 6711 **UK SIC:** 83962

| | 31-03-14 | 31-03-13 | 31-03-12 |
|---|---|---|---|
| TO | 10,819,779 | 7,261,763 | 2,284,590 |
| P/L | (6,268,910) | (5,729,007) | (3,226,089) |
| NW | (4,071,292) | (6,170,160) | (2,763,817) |
| WC | (3,044,429) | (6,860,716) | 539,014 |
| Emp. | 392 | 291 | 174 |

DUNS 54-821-5458

## Porthminster Beach Townside Shop

Porthminster Beach, St Ives, Cornwall TR26 2EB
**Tel:** 01736795352
**Web:** www.porthminstercafe.co.uk
**Estd:** 1991 Partnership
**Line of Business:** Take-away food shops
**Partners:** D Fox, W Walker, T Simons, R Simons
**US SIC:** 5812 **UK SIC:** 66110
**Bankers:** HSBC Bank plc (40-40-08)
**Employees:** 60

DUNS 21-748-0482

## Porthminster Hotel Company Ltd

(**Subsidiary of:** Nicolas James Hotels Ltd)
The Terrace, St Ives, Cornwall TR26 2BN
**Tel:** 01736-795221
**Web:** www.porthminster-hotel.co.uk
**Reg No:** 0038487 **VAT No:** 131685278
**Estd:** 1893 Private Limited Company
**Line of Business:** Hotels
**Issued Capital:** £100,000
**Directors:** R A Jones, D Robbins
**Co. Secretary:** Stuart Bateman
**Responsibilities**
**Senior:** Peter Holgate *(Manager)*, Ben Young *(Manager)*
**US SIC:** 7011, 7399
**UK SIC:** 66500, 83954
**Auditors:** Walker Moyle
**Bankers:** Barclays Bank Plc (20-67-19)

| | 31-12-12 | 31-12-11 | 31-12-10 |
|---|---|---|---|
| TO | 2,441,268 | N/A | N/A |
| P/L | 10,146 | N/A | N/A |
| NW | 3,766,754 | 2,051,160 | 2,087,006 |
| WC | 1,279,336 | (399,103) | 436,587 |
| Emp. | 64 | N/A | N/A |

DUNS 21-725-5645
## Porthvan Enterprises Ltd
73 Loggans Road, Loggans, Hayle, Cornwall TR27 5BH
**Tel:** 0800317713 **Fax:** 01736-754523
**Web:** www.stivesbay.co.uk
**Reg No:** 0725654 **Estd:** 1962 Private Limited Company
**Line of Business:** Holiday parks and camps
**Trading Style:** St. Ives Bay Holiday Park
**Issued Capital:** £34,100
**Directors:** R M Harvey, Mrs S L Morris, Mrs A M Harvey, R T Harvey, C T Harvey, Mrs A E Harvey
**Co. Secretary:** Ms Anne Harvey
**Responsibilities**
**Facilities:** Dale Johnson *(Facilities Manager)*
**US SIC:** 7021 **UK SIC:** 66500
**Auditors:** Whitaker Redfearn Pappin
**Bankers:** Lloyds TSB Bank plc (30-13-88)

| | 31-03-14 | 31-03-13 | 31-03-12 |
|---|---|---|---|
| TO | 3,900,304 | 4,086,246 | 3,908,930 |
| P/L | 459,469 | 289,267 | 431,784 |
| NW | 3,120,711 | 2,761,212 | 2,533,802 |
| WC | (1,859,820) | (1,872,200) | (2,375,567) |
| Emp. | 64 | 67 | 64 |

DUNS 21-153-3542
## Portigon Ag
(**Subsidiary of:** Land Nordrhein-Westfalen)
Woolgate Exchange, 25 Basinghall Street, London EC2V 5HA
**Tel:** 020-7020-2000
**Web:** www.westlb.co.uk
**Reg No:** 0007772FC **Estd:** 1973 Foreign Company
**Line of Business:** Banks and financial institutions
**Trading Style:** West Lb Ag
**Principals:** Ms F Neuber *(Chairman)*, Doctor R Holdijk, Dr W A Prautzsch, Dr K W Franzmeyer, Dr P Stemper, Dr. D Kalus Leister, Dr J Ringel, S Dreesbach
**Responsibilities**
**Senior:** Wolfgan Burda *(Director)*, Dieter Falke *(Director)*, Axel Kollar *(Director)*, Klaus Lester *(Director)*, Hans Offen *(Director)*, Hans Sattelle *(Director)*, Jurgen Sengera *(Director)*
**US SIC:** 6012, 6111
**UK SIC:** 81402, 81501
**Bankers:** National Westminster Bank Plc (50-00-00)

DUNS 21-807-3792
## Portland Apartments
Unit E Zetland House, 5-25 Scrutton Street, London EC2A 4HJ
**Tel:** 08442251961
**Web:** www.portlandbrown.com
**Estd:** 2012
**Line of Business:** Hotels
**Responsibilities**
**Senior:** Sean Harris *(Digital Marketing Manager)*
**US SIC:** 7011 **UK SIC:** 66500
**Employees:** 60

DUNS 29-013-0590
## Portland College
Nottingham Road, Mansfield, Nottinghamshire NG18 4TJ
**Tel:** 01623-499111
**Web:** www.portland.ac.uk
**Reg No:** 0408340 **VAT No:** 117767547
**Estd:** 1950 Private Company Limited By Guarantee
**Line of Business:** Adult and other education not elsewhere classified
**Principals:** Professor C O'Brien *(Chairman)*, K Dennis, T Vasishta, Mrs A J Thomas, G W Hulse, Ms P Richards, M Khera, Mrs H K Atwal
**Responsibilities**
**Senior:** James Aleander *(Director)*, Mark Dale *(Principal)*, Heather Downey *(Manager)*, Alan Earnshaw *(Director)*, Alan Hopwood *(Manager)*
**Marketing:** Janet Tomblin *(Marketing & Communications Man)*
**IT:** Tony Beastall *(IT Manager)*
**HR:** Lisa Emmerson *(Human Resources Manager)*
**Health & Safety:** Keith Northridge *(Health & Safety Officer)*
**Facilities:** Keith Northridge *(Health & Safety Officer)*
**Operations:** Tony Beastall *(IT Manager)*
**US SIC:** 8249 **UK SIC:** 93300
**Auditors:** Cooper-Parry
**Bankers:** Lloyds TSB Bank plc (30-96-18)

| | 31-08-13 | 31-08-12 | 31-08-11 |
|---|---|---|---|
| TO | 10,793,606 | 9,361,182 | 9,210,464 |
| P/L | 548,896 | (87,148) | 237,764 |
| NW | 14,158,890 | 12,824,662 | 14,131,591 |
| WC | 4,531,476 | 3,494,761 | 3,297,928 |
| Emp. | 323 | 297 | 283 |

DUNS 21-395-6487
## Portland House
25 Belvidere Road, Shrewsbury, Shropshire SY2 5LS
**Tel:** 01743270070
**Web:** www.capitalcaregroup.co.uk
**Estd:** 2003 Proprietorship
**Line of Business:** Nursing homes
**Proprietor:** Ms M Griffith
**US SIC:** 8051 **UK SIC:** 95100
**Employees:** 100

DUNS 21-820-5235
## The Portland Laundry Company(Mansfield)Ltd
Nottingham Road, Mansfield, Nottinghamshire NG18 1BW
**Tel:** 01623627834
**Web:** www.imperiallaundry.co.uk
**Reg No:** 0143980 **VAT No:** 116556080
**Estd:** 1906 Private Limited Company
**Line of Business:** Washing and dry cleaning of textile and fur products
**Trading Style:** Imperial Laundry & Cleaners, Imperial Workwear
**Issued Capital:** £25,180
**Directors:** W E Hill, R M Hill, Ms A J Cormack
**Co. Secretary:** Robert Hill
**US SIC:** 7219 **UK SIC:** 98110
**Auditors:** Hewitt Card
**Bankers:** Lloyds TSB Bank plc (30-95-43)

| | 30-06-14 | 30-06-13 | 30-06-12 |
|---|---|---|---|
| TO | N/A | N/A | 4,088,563 |
| P/L | N/A | N/A | 145,906 |
| NW | 1,792,291 | 1,855,980 | 1,858,143 |
| WC | (152,219) | 39,261 | (85,988) |
| Emp. | N/A | N/A | 131 |

DUNS 22-176-6384
## Portland P R Ltd
(**Subsidiary of:** Omnicom Group Inc.)
1 Red Lion Court, London EC4A 3EB
**Tel:** 02078420123 **Fax:** 020-7842-0145
**Web:** www.portlandpr.co.uk
**Reg No:** 4195041 **Estd:** 2001 Private Limited Company
**Line of Business:** Other business activities not elsewhere classified
**Directors:** T N Allan, P D Trueman
**Co. Secretary:** Ms Sally-Ann Bray
**US SIC:** 7399 **UK SIC:** 83954
**Auditors:** Grunberg & Co Ltd

| | 31-12-13 | 31-12-12 | 31-12-11 |
|---|---|---|---|
| TO | 11,667,505 | 10,014,174 | 6,055,196 |
| P/L | 2,918,346 | 2,212,365 | 1,204,460 |
| NW | 4,634,172 | 3,919,655 | 2,193,584 |
| WC | 4,349,168 | 3,723,801 | 2,003,050 |
| Emp. | 96 | 82 | 75 |

DUNS 73-461-3284
## Portland Stone Firms Ltd
99 Easton Street, Portland, Dorset DT5 1BP
**Tel:** 01305820331
**Web:** www.stonefirms.com
**Reg No:** 2912016 **Estd:** 1994 Private Limited Company
**Line of Business:** Stonemasons
**Issued Capital:** £511,000
**Directors:** G G Smith, M Stewkesbury
**Co. Secretary:** Miss Emma Smith
**US SIC:** 1799, 3271
**UK SIC:** 50000, 24370

| | 31-03-14 | 31-03-13 | 31-03-12 |
|---|---|---|---|
| TO | 3,675,951 | N/A | N/A |
| P/L | 634,936 | N/A | N/A |
| NW | 4,375,913 | 4,936,156 | 4,412,949 |
| WC | 1,796,165 | 2,566,688 | 3,113,459 |
| Emp. | 51 | N/A | N/A |

DUNS 22-847-5489
## The Portland Thistle Hotel
3-5 Portland Street, Manchester M1 6DP
**Tel:** 01612283400
**Web:** www.thistle.com
**Estd:** 2003 Proprietorship
**Line of Business:** Hotels and motels without restaurant
**Proprietor:** I Corner
**Responsibilities**
**Finance:** Asif Chhibda *(Financial Controller)*
**IT:** Asif Chhibda *(Financial Controller)*
**Purchasing:** Asif Chhibda *(Financial Controller)*
**US SIC:** 7011, 6531
**UK SIC:** 66500, 83400
**Employees:** 50

DUNS 21-778-3072
## The Portman Early Childhood Centre
12-18 Salisbury Street, London NW8 8DE
**Tel:** 02076415436
**Web:** www.lgfl.net
**Estd:** 2003 Proprietorship
**Line of Business:** Nursery schools
**Proprietor:** Ms J White
**US SIC:** 8211 **UK SIC:** 93200
**Employees:** 50

DUNS 21-142-3619
## Portman Healthcare Ltd
6 Pittville Lawn, Cheltenham, Gloucestershire GL52 2BD
**Tel:** 01242-225-225
**Web:** www.pittvillelawn.co.uk
**Reg No:** 6740579 **Estd:** 2008 Private Limited Company
**Line of Business:** Other human health activities
**Trading Style:** Pittville Lawn Dental Practice
**Issued Capital:** £930,510
**Directors:** C M Lucas, Dr M Hamburger, Dr R P Ingledew, R B Waley-Cohen, S B Waley-Cohen, D J Milne
**Co. Secretary:** Darren Milne
**Responsibilities**
**Senior:** Brett Lefkowitz *(Director)*, Martin Terespolsky *(Director)*
**Branches:** Portman Healthcare Ltd, 6 Pittville Lawn, Cheltenham, Gloucestershire GL52 2BD
**US SIC:** 8091 **UK SIC:** 95200
**Auditors:** Deloitte LLP

| | 30-09-13 | 30-09-12 | 30-09-11 |
|---|---|---|---|
| TO | 12,414,001 | 9,930,263 | 6,375,676 |
| P/L | (181,710) | (696,644) | (1,092,962) |
| NW | (9,278,190) | (8,917,400) | (7,181,251) |
| WC | (488,591) | (296,603) | 147,834 |
| Emp. | 127 | 99 | 75 |

DUNS 21-735-7961
## Portman Insurance Ltd
(**Subsidiary of:** Axa Direction Juridique Centrale)
136-140 Fenchurch Street, London EC3M 6BL
**Tel:** 02077026600 **Fax:** 02077026929
**Web:** www.axa.co.uk
**Reg No:** 0145491 **Estd:** 1916 Private Limited Company
**Line of Business:** Insurance - commercial
**Trading Style:** Axa Corporate Solutions
**Issued Capital:** £126,300,000
**Directors:** J G Byrne, C De Linares, S Villeroy De Galhau, Ms K Le Duc
**Co. Secretary:** Lindsay Francis
**Responsibilities**
**Admin:** Jody Jones *(Personal Assistant to Commerci)*
**Branches:** Portman Insurance Ltd, Brooke Lawrance House, Civic Drive, 2ND Floor, Ipswich, Suffolk IP1 2AN
**US SIC:** 6399 **UK SIC:** 82001
**Auditors:** Mazars LLP

| | 31-12-13 | 31-12-12 | 31-12-11 |
|---|---|---|---|
| TO | 290,000 | 120,000 | 795,000 |
| P/L | 5,937,000 | 14,639,000 | 15,639,000 |
| NW | 85,315,000 | 80,297,000 | 69,787,000 |
| WC | 2,758,000 | 32,000 | (18,390,000) |

DUNS 34-836-6980
## Portman Lodge Ltd.
Hollies Farm, Sluice Road, Denver, Downham Market, Norfolk PE38 0EG
**Web:** www.portmanlodge.co.uk
**Reg No:** 2802788 **VAT No:** 626046454
**Estd:** 1993 Private Limited Company
**Line of Business:** Printing not elsewhere classified
**Issued Capital:** £100
**Managing Director:** H H Jaffe
**Co. Secretary:** Mrs Wendy Jaffe
**US SIC:** 2752 **UK SIC:** 47544
**Auditors:** Freedman Stuart
**Bankers:** HSBC Bank plc (40-19-25)

| | 31-03-14 | 31-03-13 | 31-03-12 |
|---|---|---|---|
| TA | 19,050 | 17,319 | 14,144 |
| NW | 3,169 | (1,333) | (5,008) |
| WC | 3,168 | (1,334) | (5,009) |

DUNS 21-190-9593
## Portman Travel Ltd
(**Subsidiary of:** New Super Selector Sarl)
57 Guildford Street, Chertsey, Surrey KT16 9AY
**Tel:** 01698262701
**Web:** www.portmantravel.com
**Reg No:** 0620104 **VAT No:** 440590759
**Estd:** 1959 Private Limited Company
**Line of Business:** Travel agency activities
**Issued Capital:** £2,000,200
**Directors:** O D Jones, M E Aldridge, D L Cohen, M J Hare, A C Parkes, Ms D Murphy, S D Allen
**Co. Secretary:** David Canavan
**Responsibilities**
**Senior:** Graeme Cunningham *(Assistant Head Of Finance)*
**Finance:** Richard Allardice *(Senior VP Finance)*, Graeme Cunningham *(Assistant Head Of Finance)*
**Sales:** Stephen Woodward *(Senior VP Global Account Manag)*
**IT:** James Baldwin *(Senior VP Technology)*, Tom Galloway *(Computer Manager)*
**Branches:** Portman Travel Ltd, 3700 Parkway, Fareham, Hampshire PO15 7AW
**US SIC:** 4722 **UK SIC:** 77001
**Auditors:** Ernst & Young LLP
**Bankers:** Clydesdale Bank Plc (82-04-03)

| | 31-12-13 | 31-12-12 | 31-12-11 |
|---|---|---|---|
| TO | 252,790,000 | 250,421,000 | 260,483,000 |
| P/L | 2,211,000 | 3,853,000 | 4,484,000 |
| NW | 4,025,000 | 4,591,000 | 4,407,000 |
| WC | 7,947,000 | 13,571,000 | 13,607,000 |
| Emp. | 448 | 452 | 466 |

DUNS 29-016-3823
## Portman Travel Solutions Ltd
(**Subsidiary of:** New Super Selector Sarl)
107 Canon Street, London EC4N 5AF
**Tel:** 02072556555 **Fax:** 020-7255-6555
**Reg No:** 0506440 **VAT No:** 615764626
**Estd:** 1948 Private Limited Company
**Line of Business:** Travel agency activities
**Issued Capital:** £100,000
**Directors:** S D Allen, Ms D Murphy, A C Parkes, M J Hare
**Co. Secretary:** David Canavan
**Branches:** Portman Travel Solutions Ltd, 6 Caer St, Swansea, West Glamorgan SA1 3PP
**US SIC:** 4722, 4712
**UK SIC:** 77001, 77002
**Auditors:** Ernst & Young LLP
**Bankers:** Lloyds TSB Bank plc (30-91-63)

| | 30-09-13 | 30-09-12 | 30-09-11 |
|---|---|---|---|
| TA | 16,000 | 16,000 | 16,000 |
| NW | 16,000 | 16,000 | 16,000 |

DUNS 21-830-0234
## Portmeirion Group Plc
London Road, Stoke-On-Trent, Staffordshire ST4 7QQ
**Tel:** 01782744721
**Web:** www.portmeirion.co.uk
**Reg No:** 0124842 **Estd:** 1912 Public Limited Company
**Line of Business:** Potteries
**Export Sales:** £42,860,000
**Trading Style:** Portmeirion Group Uk Ltd
**Issued Capital:** £548,608
**Directors:** P E Atherton, L F Bryan, Lady B Judge, R J Steele, J C Kong
**Co. Secretary:** Brett Phillips
**Responsibilities**
**Senior:** Barbara Thomas Judge *(Non-Executive Director)*
**Marketing:** Michael Haynes *(Sales and Marketing Director)*
**Sales:** Michael Haynes *(Sales and Marketing Director)*
**Health & Safety:** Gordon Lomax *(Health & Safety Officer)*
**Facilities:** Reg Booth *(Works Manager)*
**Operations:** Gordon Lomax *(Health & Safety Officer)*
**Branches:** Portmeirion Group Plc, London Rd, Stoke-On-Trent, Staffordshire ST4 7QE
**US SIC:** 6711 **UK SIC:** 83962
**Auditors:** Mazars LLP
**Bankers:** HSBC Bank plc (40-23-07)

| | 31-12-13 | 31-12-12 | 31-12-11 |
|---|---|---|---|
| TO | 58,295,000 | 55,525,000 | 53,610,000 |
| P/L | 7,009,000 | 6,750,000 | 6,330,000 |
| NW | 30,082,000 | 25,256,000 | 22,617,000 |
| WC | 21,201,000 | 22,046,000 | 19,115,000 |
| Emp. | 578 | 587 | 579 |

DUNS 22-767-6251 **Imp**
## Portmeirion Ltd
The Hotel Portmeirion, Penrhyndeudraeth, Gwynedd LL48 6ER
**Tel:** 01766770000 **Fax:** 01766770300
**Web:** www.portmeirion-village.com
**Reg No:** 0217358 **VAT No:** 159512258
**Estd:** 1926 Private Limited Company
**Line of Business:** Chocolate fountains
**Trading Style:** The Hotel Portmeirion, Cascell Deldrath
**Issued Capital:** £6,000
**Principals:** R Llywelyn *(Managing)*, D H Jones, J C Wallace, Ms R C Garden, I W Roberts, P W Garden, Miss M A Cooper, Ms C A Cooper-Willis
**Co. Secretary:** Ian Roberts
**Responsibilities**
**Senior:** Dylan Hughes *(Operations Manager)*, Robert Llywelyn *(Managing Director)*, Sian Llywelyn *(Managing Director of Shops)*
**Marketing:** Robert Llywelyn *(Managing Director)*
**Sales:** Robert Llywelyn *(Managing Director)*, Delyth Wyre *(Sales Manager)*
**Facilities:** Meurig Jones *(Property Manager)*, Gwynedd Roberts *(Gardens & Buildings Manager)*
**Operations:** Dylan Hughes *(Operations Manager)*, Robert Llywelyn *(Managing Director)*
**Purchasing:** Dylan Hughes *(Operations Manager)*
**US SIC:** 7011, 7999
**UK SIC:** 66500, 97913
**Auditors:** Conways

**Bankers:** HSBC Bank plc (40-37-13)

| | 31-01-14 | 31-01-13 | 31-01-12 |
|---|---|---|---|
| TO | 6,259,939 | 5,966,364 | 6,396,142 |
| P/L | 26,341 | 20,188 | 220,190 |
| NW | 1,996,701 | 1,996,362 | 1,988,613 |
| WC | (835,815) | (642,372) | (828,026) |
| Emp. | 180 | 183 | 190 |

DUNS 76-851-6155
## Portola Packaging Ltd
(**Subsidiary of:** Portola Ltd)
3 Carriage Drive, Doncaster, South Yorkshire DN4 5NT
**Tel:** 01302552400 **Fax:** 01302365541
**Web:** www.portola.eu.com
**Reg No:** 2607146 **VAT No:** 605413965
**Estd:** 1991 Private Limited Company
**Line of Business:** Manufacturers of plastic products
**Export Sales:** £9,143,000
**Issued Capital:** £2,000,000
**Directors:** G Heighington, R Kirkland
**Co. Secretary:** Philip Crawley
**Responsibilities**
**Senior:** Paul Dovey *(Operations Manager)*, Glenn Heighindton *(CEO, Managing Director)*, Glen Heighton *(Manager)*
**Marketing:** Ray Bruwen *(Marketing Manager)*
**IT:** Mark Strzala *(IT Manager)*
**HR:** Andrea Mullen *(Human Resources Manager)*
**Health & Safety:** Graham Dykes *(Health & Safety Officer)*
**Facilities:** Max Bytheway *(Engineering Process Manager)*
**Operations:** Paul Dovey *(Operations Manager)*
**Engineering:** Max Bytheway *(Engineering Process Manager)*
**US SIC:** 2821 **UK SIC:** 25140
**Auditors:** PricewaterhouseCoopers LLP

| | 31-08-13 | 31-08-12 | 31-08-11 |
|---|---|---|---|
| TO | 23,452,000 | 23,545,000 | 25,694,000 |
| P/L | 2,306,000 | 278,000 | 3,363,000 |
| NW | 13,996,000 | 13,070,000 | 12,938,000 |
| WC | 12,432,000 | 11,152,000 | 12,542,000 |
| Emp. | 135 | 137 | 141 |

DUNS 23-086-1069
## Portora Royal School
1 Lough Shore Road, Enniskillen, Co Fermanagh BT74 5HD
**Tel:** 028-6632-2658
**Web:** www.portoraroyal.co.uk
**Estd:** 2002
**Line of Business:** Schools (local authority)
**Principals:** R A Jackson *(Chairman)*, S Morrow
**Co. Secretary:** Hjw Logan
**Responsibilities**
**Senior:** Neil Morton *(Head Teacher)*
**Finance:** Alison Stronge *(Bursar)*
**Marketing:** Alison Stronge *(Bursar)*
**IT:** Aiden Corrigan *(IT Manager)*
**Health & Safety:** Alison Stronge *(Bursar)*
**Facilities:** Alison Stronge *(Bursar)*
**Operations:** Alison Stronge *(Bursar)*
**Purchasing:** Alison Stronge *(Bursar)*
**US SIC:** 8211 **UK SIC:** 93200
**Auditors:** Cooper Molloy O'Reilly Ltd
**Employees:** 50
**Turnover:** £2,487,349

DUNS 29-654-3358 **Exp**
## Portrait Software International Ltd
(**Subsidiary of:** Pitney Bowes Inc.)
39 Melville Street, Edinburgh, Midlothian EH3 7JF
**Tel:** 01312204491
**Web:** www.portraitsoftware.com
**Reg No:** 1980596 **VAT No:** 438139539
**Estd:** 1986 Private Limited Company
**Line of Business:** Other software consultancy and supply
**Export Markets:** New Zealand; France; Spain; Republic Of Ireland
**Issued Capital:** £1,000
**Directors:** G R Willsher, M Monahan, T Barber
**Co. Secretary:** Gerard Willsher
**US SIC:** 7379 **UK SIC:** 83940
**Auditors:** Deloitte & Touche LLP
**Bankers:** National Westminster Bank Plc (60-10-35)

| | 31-12-13 | 31-12-12 | 31-12-11 |
|---|---|---|---|
| TO | 6,817,000 | 7,316,000 | 11,246,000 |
| P/L | (3,176,000) | (2,208,000) | 1,341,000 |
| NW | 7,281,000 | 9,349,000 | 13,467,000 |
| WC | 6,736,000 | 8,924,000 | 16,227,000 |
| Emp. | 73 | 90 | 84 |

DUNS 21-732-0871
## Portslade Aldridge Community Academy Trust
Upper School, Chalky Road, Brighton, East Sussex BN41 2WS
**Tel:** 01273416300
**Web:** www.paca.uk.com
**Reg No:** 7672441 **Estd:** 1993 Private Company Limited By Guarantee
**Line of Business:** General secondary education
**Directors:** R M Aldridge, Mrs H Wilson-Fletcher, Ms Z Atkins, Ms J Haviland, P Currie, Ms R J Turner, S Thompson, Mrs C A Howe
**Co. Secretary:** Miss Rachael Brailsford
**Responsibilities**
**Senior:** Denise D'Souza *(Director)*, Mark Deacon *(Head Teacher)*, Sarah Jennings *(Director)*, Marc Pinter Krainer *(Director)*
**US SIC:** 8211 **UK SIC:** 93200

| | 31-08-13 | 31-08-12 |
|---|---|---|
| TO | 6,351,000 | 5,941,000 |
| P/L | 272,000 | (107,000) |
| NW | 2,424,000 | (300,000) |
| WC | 20,000 | 57,000 |
| Emp. | 113 | 130 |

DUNS 28-838-1478
## Portsmouth Aviation Holdings Ltd
Airport Service Road, Portsmouth, Hampshire PO3 5PF
**Tel:** 023-9266-2251 **Fax:** 023-9267-3690
**Web:** www.portav.co.uk
**Reg No:** 0476872 **Estd:** 1950 Private Limited Company
**Line of Business:** Manufacture of tools
**Export Sales:** £560,394
**Issued Capital:** £2,569
**Principals:** S P Escott *(Managing)*, G M Dickson *(Financial)*, W C Turner, C Webb
**Co. Secretary:** Andrew Hall
**Responsibilities**
**Senior:** Russell Tidbury *(Manager)*
**US SIC:** 3423, 3499
**UK SIC:** 31612, 31694
**Auditors:** Baker Tilly UK Audit LLP
**Bankers:** National Westminster Bank Plc (56-00-64)

| | 31-12-13 | 31-12-12 | 31-12-11 |
|---|---|---|---|
| TO | 23,439,662 | 13,539,004 | 17,804,734 |
| P/L | 2,546,408 | 462,249 | 2,499,372 |
| NW | 13,225,425 | 11,250,587 | 10,813,161 |
| WC | 8,350,497 | 7,394,935 | 7,128,021 |
| Emp. | 131 | 106 | 108 |

DUNS 21-118-3082
## Portsmouth City Council
City Council, Portsmouth, Hampshire PO1 2BG
**Web:** www.portsmouth.gov.uk
**VAT No:** 108365672 **Estd:** 1900
**Line of Business:** Local government
**Directors:** D Williams, J A Morgan, Ms V Lane
**Responsibilities**
**Senior:** Dave Battcock *(Manager)*, Gerald Jackson *(Council Leader)*
**Branches:** Portsmouth City Council, The Norrish Central Library, Guildhall Square, Portsmouth, Hampshire PO1 2DX
**US SIC:** 9121 **UK SIC:** 91110
**Bankers:** The Co-Operative Bank Plc (08-90-81)
**Employees:** 2,000

DUNS 77-139-0721
## Portsmouth College
Tangier Road, Portsmouth, Hampshire PO3 6PZ
**Tel:** 023-9266-7521 **Fax:** 023-9234-4363
**Web:** www.portsmouth-college.ac.uk
**Reg No:** 2703114 **Estd:** 1992 Private Limited Company
**Line of Business:** General secondary education
**Trading Style:** Portsmouth College
**Directors:** S D Frampton, N Mcmonagle
**Co. Secretary:** Peter Rudd
**Responsibilities**
**Senior:** Kevin Grieve *(Vice Principal)*
**Admin:** Kim Bogard *(Admissions Secretary)*
**IT:** Brian Chivers *(IT Manager)*, Steve Hatton *(Head of IT)*, Anthony Jankowski *(Head of IT)*
**HR:** Julia Clark *(Human Resources Manager)*, Oona Taylor *(Career Development Manager)*
**Health & Safety:** Evelyn Grant *(Health & Safety Officer)*
**Facilities:** Terry Ashdown *(Facilities Manager)*, Eamonn Ford *(Senior Caretaker)*
**Engineering:** Marie Elverson *(Technical Engineer)*
**US SIC:** 8211 **UK SIC:** 93200
**Employees:** 150

DUNS 21-230-9581
## Portsmouth Combined Court Centre
Courts Of Justice, Winston Churchill Avenue, Portsmouth, Hampshire PO1 2EB
**Tel:** 02392893000
**Web:** www.justice.gov.uk
**Estd:** 2002 Proprietorship
**Line of Business:** Courts
**Proprietor:** Mrs H Williams
**Responsibilities**
**Senior:** Eve Miller *(Courts Manager)*
**Health & Safety:** Jeanette Martin *(Health & Safety Officer)*
**US SIC:** 9211 **UK SIC:** 91200
**Employees:** 100

DUNS 21-811-5979
## Portsmouth Craft & Manufacturing Industries
85 Northern Road, Portsmouth, Hampshire PO6 3AH
**Tel:** 02392322800
**Web:** www.portsmouthcitycouncil.co.uk
**Estd:** 1988
**Line of Business:** Sign and nameplate suppliers
**Responsibilities**
**Senior:** Derek Christie *(Manager)*
**US SIC:** 2599 **UK SIC:** 46720
**Employees:** 50

DUNS 21-778-9856
## Portsmouth Ferry Port
Whale Island Way, Portsmouth, Hampshire PO2 8EB
**Tel:** 02392297391
**Web:** www.portsmouth-port.co.uk
**Estd:** 1972 Proprietorship
**Line of Business:** Other supporting water transport activities
**Proprietor:** M Putman
**US SIC:** 4469 **UK SIC:** 76300
**Employees:** 100

DUNS 52-034-5331
## The Portsmouth Grammar School
High Street, Portsmouth, Hampshire PO1 2LN
**Tel:** 02392364219
**Web:** www.pgs.org.uk
**Reg No:** 3401010 **Estd:** 1997 Private Company Limited By Guarantee
**Line of Business:** Creches
**Trading Style:** The Portsmouth Grammar School
**Directors:** Dr M C Grossel, P Lodder, J Rigby, C Pelling, Ms A Stanford, Mrs F J Boulton, D C Brindley, Ms M Scott
**Co. Secretary:** Donald Kent
**Responsibilities**
**Senior:** Kathy Bishop *(Director)*, Michael Coffin *(Director)*, Peter Hopkinson *(Head Teacher)*, Brian Larkman *(Director)*, Simon Lemieux *(Executive)*, Michael Pipes *(Director)*
**Sales:** Melanie Bushell *(Development Director)*
**IT:** Peter Galliver *(Head of Applications)*
**US SIC:** 8211 **UK SIC:** 93200
**Auditors:** Grant Thornton
**Bankers:** Lloyds TSB Bank plc (30-93-04)

| | 31-08-13 | 31-08-12 | 31-08-11 |
|---|---|---|---|
| TO | 18,817,141 | 17,811,036 | 17,763,990 |
| P/L | 1,906,788 | 1,006,540 | 1,110,817 |
| NW | 16,052,393 | 14,062,699 | 12,980,005 |
| WC | 3,779,660 | 2,417,365 | 1,831,567 |
| Emp. | 348 | 339 | 338 |

DUNS 21-715-6454
## The Portsmouth Harbour Ferry Co Ltd
(**Subsidiary of:** Falkland Islands Holdings Plc)
Business Station, South Street, Gosport, Hampshire PO12 1EP
**Tel:** 02392511895
**Web:** www.gosportferry.co.uk
**Reg No:** 0018751 **VAT No:** 381060966
**Estd:** 1883 Private Limited Company
**Line of Business:** Passenger sea and coastal water transport
**Trading Style:** Gosport Ferry
**Issued Capital:** £230,000
**Directors:** K D Edwards, M S Killingley, J L Foster, Ms C M Waters, E L Rowland
**Co. Secretary:** Mrs Christine Waters
**US SIC:** 4712 **UK SIC:** 77002
**Auditors:** KPMG Audit PLC
**Bankers:** Barclays Bank Plc (20-69-34)

| | 31-03-14 | 31-03-13 | 31-03-12 |
|---|---|---|---|
| TA | 6,011,000 | 4,431,000 | 4,650,000 |
| P/L | 541,000 | 256,000 | 886,000 |
| NW | 1,061,000 | 945,000 | 1,037,000 |
| WC | (2,741,000) | (892,000) | (464,000) |

DUNS 23-219-2294
## Portsmouth Hospitals Nhs Trust
Southwick Hill Road, Portsmouth, Hampshire PO6 3LY
**Tel:** 023 9228 6000
**Web:** www.porthosp.nhs.uk
**Estd:** 1991
**Line of Business:** Other human health activities
**Issued Capital:** £1
**Principals:** D Rhind *(Chairman)*, R Toole *(Financial)*, D Eccles *(Personnel)*, G Zaki, Ms U Ward, Ms M Macisaac, D Bailey, M Nellthorp
**Responsibilities**
**Senior:** Elizabeth Conway *(Non-Executive Director)*, Brett Gill *(Non-Executive Director)*, Jayne Jempson *(Manager)*, Maggie MacIsaac *(Chief Executive Officer)*
**IT:** Christopher Tite *(Head of ICT)*
**HR:** Liz Ellcome *(HR Manager)*
**Branches:** Portsmouth Hospitals Nhs Trust, Blackfriars Close, Southsea, Hampshire PO5 4NJ
**US SIC:** 8091 **UK SIC:** 95200
**Bankers:** National Westminster Bank Plc (56-00-64)
**Employees:** 5,500

DUNS 76-922-4270
## Portsmouth Naval Base Property Trust
19 College Road, H M Naval Base, Portsmouth, Hampshire PO1 3LJ
**Tel:** 023-9282-0921
**Web:** www.pnbpropertytrust.org
**Reg No:** 1959490 **Estd:** 1985 Private Company Limited By Guarantee
**Line of Business:** Preservation of historical sites and buildings
**Principals:** R T Bishop *(Managing)*, R P Ching, D E Butters, M J Ridley, E O Parry, Rear Admiral N E Rankin, M Cohen, L M Mason
**Co. Secretary:** Peter Goodship
**Responsibilities**
**Senior:** Theresa Hall *(Board Member)*, Patrick Holmes *(Director)*, Philip Marriott *(Director)*, Timothy Roberton *(Manager)*, Hugh Siegle *(Director)*, Linda Symes *(Director)*
**Facilities:** Tim Vincent *(Property Manager)*
**US SIC:** 8411 **UK SIC:** 97700
**Auditors:** PricewaterhouseCoopers
**Bankers:** The Royal Bank Of Scotland Plc (16-28-24)

| | 31-03-14 | 31-03-13 | 31-03-12 |
|---|---|---|---|
| TO | 4,373,802 | 2,527,770 | 2,475,269 |
| P/L | 1,065,129 | (469,092) | (698,504) |
| NW | 15,250,799 | 14,014,947 | 14,430,366 |
| WC | 737,041 | (190,365) | (128,897) |
| Emp. | 49 | 71 | 57 |

DUNS 29-391-8652
## Portsmouth Publishing & Printing Ltd
(**Subsidiary of:** Johnston Press Plc)
The News Centre, Portsmouth, Hampshire PO2 9SX
**Tel:** 023-9266-4488 **Fax:** 0239267777
**Web:** www.portsmouth.co.uk
**Reg No:** 1248289 **Estd:** 1987 Private Limited Company
**Line of Business:** Newspapers publishing
**Trading Style:** Sports Mail, Portsmouth News, Chichester Observer, West Sussex Gazette
**Issued Capital:** £150,000
**Directors:** G T Fearon, D J King, A G Highfield
**Co. Secretary:** Peter Mccall
**Responsibilities**
**Senior:** Carl Dimmock *(Manager)*
**Finance:** Craig Fisher *(Financial Director)*
**Branches:** Portsmouth Publishing & Printing Ltd, Unicorn House, 8 Eastgate Square, Chichester, West Sussex PO19 1JN
**US SIC:** 2731, 2752
**UK SIC:** 47532, 47544
**Auditors:** Deloitte LLP
**Bankers:** Lloyds TSB Bank plc (30-96-11)

| | 28-12-13 | 29-12-12 | 31-12-11 |
|---|---|---|---|
| TO | 6,352,000 | 6,431,000 | 7,255,000 |
| NW | 24,504,000 | 24,504,000 | 24,504,000 |
| WC | N/A | 24,504,000 | N/A |
| Emp. | 222 | 192 | 239 |

DUNS 23-686-4901
## Portsmouth Royal Maritime Club Ltd
Queen Street, Portsmouth, Hampshire PO1 3HH
**Tel:** 023-9282-4231
**Web:** www.homeclub.fsnet.co.uk
**Reg No:** 3681448 **Estd:** 1998 Private Limited Company
**Line of Business:** Hotels
**Issued Capital:** £2

**Directors:** D M Nesbit, Mrs J E Hopkins, Ms P Howse, D A Smith, D J Fowler, I A Carruthers
**Co. Secretary:** John Alderson
**US SIC:** 7011 **UK SIC:** 66500
**Auditors:** Grant Thornton

|     | 31-12-13 | 31-12-12 | 31-12-11 |
|-----|----------|----------|----------|
| TA  | 121,245  | 64,349   | 82,142   |
| NW  | 2        | 2        | 2        |
| WC  | 1,752    | 2,247    | 7,357    |

DUNS 21-137-3669
## Portsmouth Surgical Holdings Ltd
44 New Lane, Havant, Hampshire PO9 2NF
**Tel:** 02392499922
**Web:** www.portsmouthsurgicalequipment.co.uk
**Reg No:** 6701356 **Estd:** 2008 Private Limited Company
**Line of Business:** Management activities of holding companies
**Export Sales:** £1,590,867
**Trading Style:** Portsmouth Surgical Equipment Ltd
**Issued Capital:** £110
**Director:** G Schofield
**Co. Secretary:** Guy Schofield
**Responsibilities**
**Senior:** Ivor Schofield (Chairman)
**US SIC:** 6711 **UK SIC:** 03902

|      | 30-09-13   | 30-09-12   | 30-09-11  |
|------|------------|------------|-----------|
| TO   | 10,132,908 | 9,554,860  | 8,549,296 |
| P/L  | 2,824,528  | 2,243,295  | 2,175,572 |
| NW   | 15,324,667 | 13,348,876 | 11,889,480|
| WC   | 13,168,428 | 11,555,149 | 9,997,865 |
| Emp. | 51         | 52         | 49        |

DUNS 50-597-7421
## Portsmouth Water Ltd
(Subsidiary of: South Downs Capital Ltd)
West Street, Havant, Hampshire PO9 1LG
**Tel:** 02392499666 **Fax:** 023-9245-3632
**Web:** www.portsmouthwater.co.uk
**Reg No:** 2536455 **VAT No:** 615375835
**Estd:** 2012 Public Limited Company
**Line of Business:** Water companies
**Issued Capital:** £1,077,434
**Principals:** N Smith (Financial), M Kirk, M Johnson, Mrs H Benjamin, R C Porteous
**Co. Secretary:** Christopher Hardyman
**Responsibilities**
**Senior:** Barry Ashcroft (PC Manager)
**Branches:** Portsmouth Water Ltd, Main Rd, Chichester, West Sussex PO18 8EW
**US SIC:** 4941 **UK SIC:** 17000
**Auditors:** Saffery Champness
**Bankers:** Lloyds TSB Bank plc (30-93-97)

|      | 31-03-14    | 31-03-13    | 31-03-12    |
|------|-------------|-------------|-------------|
| TO   | 37,109,000  | 36,282,000  | 36,665,000  |
| P/L  | 1,329,000   | 3,117,000   | 2,650,000   |
| NW   | 66,011,000  | 64,780,000  | 63,880,000  |
| WC   | (7,309,000) | (9,216,000) | (5,867,000) |
| Emp. | 238         | 232         | 223         |

DUNS 36-810-7900
## Portstewart Golf Club
117 Strand Road, Portstewart, Co Londonderry BT55 7PG
**Tel:** 028-7083-2015
**Web:** www.portstewartgc.co.uk
**Estd:** 1906
**Line of Business:** Golf clubs
**Chairman:** M Moss
**Co. Secretary:** Richard Small
**Responsibilities**
**Admin:** Wendy McGrotty (Administrator)
**Branches:** Portstewart Golf Club, 117 Strand Road, Portstewart, Co Londonderry BT55 7PG
**US SIC:** 7999 **UK SIC:** 97913
**Employees:** 48

DUNS 22-753-0797                                    Imp-Exp
## Portview Fit-Out Ltd
(Subsidiary of: Portview Holdings Ltd)
46 Florenceville Avenue, Belfast BT7 3GZ
**Tel:** 02890644765 **Fax:** 02890-641330
**Web:** www.portview.co.uk
**Reg No:** 0010862NI **VAT No:** 286430936
**Estd:** 1975 Private Limited Company
**Line of Business:** Shopfitting contractors
**Export Markets:** UK & Ireland
**Issued Capital:** £100,000
**Directors:** P Scullion, M Sean
**Co. Secretary:** Simon Campbell
**Branches:** Portview Fit-Out Ltd, Walworth Enterprise Centre, Duke Close, West Way, Andover, Hampshire SP10 5AP
**US SIC:** 1799 **UK SIC:** 50000
**Auditors:** Grant Thornton UK LLP
**Bankers:** Northern Bank Ltd (95-01-06)

|      | 30-11-13   | 30-11-12   | 30-11-11   |
|------|------------|------------|------------|
| TO   | 32,838,995 | 23,520,163 | 23,723,637 |
| P/L  | 9,999      | 9,999      | 393,758    |
| NW   | 2,171,472  | 2,177,127  | 2,181,334  |
| WC   | 1,529,790  | 1,516,887  | 2,052,233  |
| Emp. | 61         | 57         | 53         |

DUNS 21-614-9413
## Portway Inn
Joule Road, Andover, Hampshire SP10 3UX
**Tel:** 01264321920
**Web:** www.brewersfayre.co.uk
**Estd:** 2011
**Line of Business:** Managed public houses and bars
**Responsibilities**
**Senior:** Laurence Adewusi (General Manager), Daniel Brakenbury (Manager)
**US SIC:** 5813 **UK SIC:** 66200
**Employees:** 60

DUNS 39-929-1616                                    Imp
## Portwest Clothing Ltd
(Subsidiary of: Mayo Workwear Ltd)
Fields End Business Park, Thurnscoe, Rotherham, South Yorkshire S63 0JF
**Tel:** 01709-894575 **Fax:** 01709-880830
**Web:** www.portwest.biz
**Reg No:** 2243347 **VAT No:** 511352982
**Estd:** 1988 Private Limited Company
**Line of Business:** Manufacture of workwear
**Issued Capital:** £50,000
**Principals:** H Hughes (Managing), C Hughes (Financial), D Crowley
**Co. Secretary:** Owen Hughes
**US SIC:** 2328 **UK SIC:** 45340
**Auditors:** HW (Leeds) LLP
**Bankers:** Allied Irish Bank (gb) (23-84-02)

|      | 28-02-14   | 28-02-13   | 29-02-12   |
|------|------------|------------|------------|
| TO   | 33,313,958 | 30,427,801 | 28,976,948 |
| P/L  | 999,420    | 916,896    | 895,409    |
| NW   | 8,352,756  | 7,547,774  | 6,883,208  |
| WC   | 4,434,146  | 4,109,432  | 3,699,707  |
| Emp. | 111        | 90         | 84         |

DUNS 29-038-1847                                    Imp-Exp
## Porvair Filtration Group Ltd
(Subsidiary of: Porvair Plc)
1 Concorde Close, Fareham, Hampshire PO15 5RT
**Fax:** 01489864399
**Web:** www.porvairfiltration.com
**Reg No:** 0888596 **VAT No:** 806638224
**Estd:** 2012 Private Limited Company
**Line of Business:** Manufacture of other special purpose machinery not elsewhere classified
**Export Markets:** E U
**Export Sales:** £21,208,000
**Trading Style:** Microfiltrex, Porvair Technology, Filters for Industry
**Issued Capital:** £18,207,720
**Directors:** T M Liddell, I Stirling, C P Tyler, B D Stocks, S Wells, D M Mellor, I S Boxall, D Amey
**Co. Secretary:** Dr Simon Rodgers
**Branches:** Porvair Filtration Group Ltd, 22 Dawkins Rd, Poole, Dorset BH15 4JD
**US SIC:** 3559 **UK SIC:** 32863
**Auditors:** PricewaterhouseCoopers LLP
**Bankers:** Barclays Bank Plc (20-46-65)

|      | 30-11-13   | 30-11-12   | 30-11-11   |
|------|------------|------------|------------|
| TO   | 36,920,000 | 33,783,000 | 30,022,000 |
| P/L  | 5,037,000  | 4,246,000  | 3,120,000  |
| NW   | 21,826,000 | 21,841,000 | 20,932,000 |
| WC   | 14,179,000 | 13,671,000 | 13,150,000 |
| Emp. | 322        | 313        | 298        |

DUNS 22-656-4755                                    Exp
## Porvair Plc
7 Regis Place, King's Lynn, Norfolk PE30 2JN
**Fax:** 01553-765599
**Web:** www.porvair.com
**Reg No:** 1661935 **Estd:** 1988 Public Limited Company
**Line of Business:** Manufacture of basic pharmaceutical products
**Export Markets:** Europe, Americas , Asia, Australasia, Africa
**Export Sales:** £66,495,000
**Issued Capital:** £852,251
**Directors:** B D Stocks, Dr K Rajagopal, C L Matthews, P D Dean
**Co. Secretary:** Christopher Tyler
**US SIC:** 2834, 3269, 3499, 3832
**UK SIC:** 25700, 24894, 31694, 37320
**Auditors:** PricewaterhouseCoopers LLP
**Bankers:** Barclays Bank Plc (20-46-65)

|      | 30-11-13   | 30-11-12   | 30-11-11   |
|------|------------|------------|------------|
| TO   | 84,267,000 | 76,455,000 | 68,090,000 |
| P/L  | 7,848,000  | 6,299,000  | 4,513,000  |
| NW   | 5,145,000  | 5,191,000  | 5,021,000  |
| WC   | 11,925,000 | 13,309,000 | 12,017,000 |
| Emp. | 611        | 563        | 526        |

DUNS 29-929-6897
## Positive Action Publications Ltd
(Subsidiary of: Amneh Developments Ltd)
Thorpe House, Kelleythorpe Industrial Estate, Kellythorpe, Driffield, North Humberside YO25 9DJ
**Tel:** 01377241724
**Web:** www.positiveaction.co.uk
**Reg No:** 2098311 **VAT No:** 390137363

**Estd:** 1987 Private Limited Company
**Line of Business:** Newspapers publishing
**Issued Capital:** £100
**Managing Director:** N E Horrox
**Co. Secretary:** Ms Anne Smith
**Responsibilities**
**Marketing:** Alison Burdass (Marketing Manager)
**US SIC:** 2731 **UK SIC:** 47532
**Auditors:** The CBA Partnership

|      | 31-03-14 | 31-03-13 | 31-03-12 |
|------|----------|----------|----------|
| TA   | 551,430  | 532,311  | 401,572  |
| NW   | 383,657  | 342,350  | 214,249  |
| WC   | 365,485  | 324,595  | 202,263  |

DUNS 23-228-0529
## Positive Futures: Achieving Dreams. Transforming Lives.
2b Park Drive, Bangor, Co Down BT20 4JZ
**Tel:** 028-9147-5720 **Fax:** 028-9414-7521
**Web:** www.positive-futures.net
**Reg No:** 0029849NI **Estd:** 1995 Private Company Limited By Guarantee
**Line of Business:** Charitable social work activities without accommodation
**Trading Style:** Bangor Supported Living Services
**Directors:** Mrs H Mark, Mrs M Somerville, Ms A Clydesdale, P F Shaw, M S May, D M Mcmillen, Ms K J Kendall, Mrs M B Bryce
**Co. Secretary:** Mrs Dawn Morrow
**Responsibilities**
**Senior:** Agnes Lunny (Chief Executive), Laurence Taggart (Director)
**Branches:** Positive Futures: Achieving Dreams. Transforming Lives., Creative Ideas Fashions, 5 Oldtown Street, Cookstown, Co Tyrone BT80 8EE
**US SIC:** 6732 **UK SIC:** 83100
**Auditors:** ASM Horwath (A) Ltd
**Bankers:** Northern Bank Ltd (95-02-52)

|      | 31-03-14  | 31-03-13  | 31-03-12  |
|------|-----------|-----------|-----------|
| TO   | 7,213,169 | 6,871,182 | 6,470,096 |
| P/L  | 120,976   | 46,760    | 232,832   |
| NW   | 2,799,280 | 2,623,631 | 2,550,011 |
| WC   | 562,372   | 845,103   | 1,335,800 |
| Emp. | 386       | 368       | 360       |

DUNS 21-601-6574
## Positive Pathways
Positive Pathways Limited, Park Business Centre, Hastingwood Industrial Park, Birmingham, West Midlands B24 9QR
**Web:** www.pospath.com
**Estd:** 2011 Proprietorship
**Line of Business:** Residential care establishments
**Proprietor:** K Epps
**US SIC:** 7399 **UK SIC:** 83954
**Employees:** 60

DUNS 76-436-9997
## Positive Steps Oldham
80 Union Street, Oldham, Lancashire OL1 1DJ
**Tel:** 01616219400 **Fax:** 01616219301
**Web:** www.positivestepsoldham.org.uk
**Reg No:** 2563094 **Estd:** 1990 Private Limited Company
**Line of Business:** Career information services
**Trading Style:** Positive Steps Oldham
**Directors:** Mrs V C Devenport, Ms H J Roberts, B J Keay, A Chadderton, Miss A G Freeman, Mrs S M Dixon, D Williamson, Ms E J Wrigglesworth
**Co. Secretary:** Ms Janet Richardson
**Responsibilities**
**Senior:** Alison Driver (Finance Director), Julie Edmondson (Director), Joseph Fitzpatrick (Manager), Kay Knox (Manager), Brian Lord (Manager), Colin McLaren (Manager), tim mitchell (Manager)
**Finance:** Alison Driver (Finance Director)
**IT:** Paul Wooding (Network, Security Manager)
**US SIC:** 7361, 8249
**UK SIC:** 83954, 93300
**Auditors:** Wrigley Partington
**Bankers:** Barclays Bank Plc (20-64-12)

|      | 31-03-14    | 31-03-13    | 31-03-12  |
|------|-------------|-------------|-----------|
| TO   | 7,494,241   | 6,628,421   | 8,747,744 |
| P/L  | (168,929)   | 127,814     | 38,460    |
| NW   | (2,459,123) | (2,196,194) | (716,100) |
| WC   | 1,166,431   | 938,974     | 847,422   |
| Emp. | 204         | 177         | 189       |

DUNS 21-721-2570                                    Imp
## Possum Ltd
(Subsidiary of: Eamont Holdings Ltd)
Unit 8 Farmbrough Close, Aylesbury, Buckinghamshire HP20 1DQ
**Fax:** 01296394349
**Web:** www.possum.co.uk
**Reg No:** 0711047 **VAT No:** 194764028
**Estd:** 1961 Private Limited Company
**Line of Business:** Manufacturers and distributiors of electronic components
**Export Sales:** £211,123

**Trading Style:** Palantype, Electronic Controls, Possum
**Issued Capital:** £130,000
**Principals:** P I Robinson (Managing), D B Scott
**Co. Secretary:** David Scott
**Responsibilities**
**Senior:** Sara Gibson (Manager Director), Richard Stepniewski (Operations Director)
**Health & Safety:** Mike Byrnes (Stock Controller Manager)
**Facilities:** Richard Stepniewski (Operations Director)
**Purchasing:** Mike Byrnes (Stock Controller Manager)
**Engineering:** Richard Stepniewski (Operations Director)
**Branches:** Possum Ltd, Unit 8, Farmbrough Close, Aylesbury, Buckinghamshire HP20 1DQ
**US SIC:** 3679 **UK SIC:** 34542
**Auditors:** Grant Thornton UK LLP
**Bankers:** HSBC Bank plc (40-08-39)

|      | 31-03-14  | 31-03-13  | 31-03-12  |
|------|-----------|-----------|-----------|
| TO   | 4,703,699 | 4,573,755 | 4,465,144 |
| P/L  | 861,055   | 816,940   | 506,990   |
| NW   | 4,069,638 | 3,609,050 | 3,160,687 |
| WC   | 3,341,257 | 2,612,099 | 2,863,772 |
| Emp. | 52        | 51        | 57        |

DUNS 21-224-1628
## The Post House Coventry
Hinckley Road, Walsgrave On Sowe, Coventry, West Midlands CV2 2HP
**Tel:** 08719429021
**Proprietorship**
**Line of Business:** Rooming And Boarding Houses
**Proprietor:** S Pateman
**US SIC:** 7021 **UK SIC:** 66500
**Employees:** 100

DUNS 22-812-5530
## The Post Office Fellowship of Remembrance C.I.C
Dumbleton Hall, Dumbleton, Evesham, Worcestershire WR11 7TS
**Tel:** 01386-881240
**Web:** www.dumbletonhall.co.uk
**Reg No:** 0288977 **Estd:** 1934 Private Company Limited By Guarantee
**Line of Business:** Hotels
**Trading Style:** Classic Hotels
**Directors:** E W Dudley, M R Grafton, P C Mason, A G Beasley, T Daffurn, M C Bunn, Mrs D J Terry, Ms J G Cole
**Co. Secretary:** Simon Kelly
**Responsibilities**
**Senior:** Gavin Dron (Duty Manager)
**Branches:** The Post Office Fellowship Of Remembrance C.i.c, Dumbleton, Evesham, Worcestershire WR11 7TS
**US SIC:** 7011 **UK SIC:** 66500
**Auditors:** Qed Partnership
**Bankers:** The Co-Operative Bank Plc (08-90-00)

|      | 31-03-14  | 31-03-13  | 31-03-12  |
|------|-----------|-----------|-----------|
| TO   | 3,347,363 | 3,155,061 | 3,109,461 |
| P/L  | 34,602    | 2,810     | 16,478    |
| NW   | 4,490,167 | 4,479,952 | 4,490,255 |
| WC   | (697,214) | (801,257) | (779,050) |
| Emp. | 101       | 108       | 111       |

DUNS 73-895-4259
## Postal Choices Ltd
(Subsidiary of: Postal Choices Holdings Ltd)
7 & 8 Gordano Court, Serbert Close, Portishead, Bristol, Avon BS20 7FS
**Tel:** 01275801000
**Web:** www.onepost.co.uk
**Reg No:** 5149376 **Estd:** 2004 Private Limited Company
**Line of Business:** National post activities
**Trading Style:** Onepost
**Issued Capital:** £113,750
**Directors:** L A Harris, Ms S Bishop, M A Plant, Ms J P Reynolds, G J Cooper, S A Roberts
**Co. Secretary:** Ms Suzanne Bishop
**Responsibilities**
**Marketing:** Luan Wise (Marketing Manager)
**US SIC:** 4311 **UK SIC:** 79010
**Auditors:** BJCA Ltd

|      | 30-06-14   | 30-06-13   | 30-06-12   |
|------|------------|------------|------------|
| TO   | 63,476,108 | 49,609,225 | 57,427,951 |
| P/L  | 801,057    | 903,841    | 637,661    |
| NW   | 1,561,017  | 1,093,647  | 524,019    |
| WC   | 1,244,146  | 796,438    | 138,063    |
| Emp. | 65         | 47         | 49         |

DUNS 23-254-6221
## Postal Services Commission
6 Hercules Road, London SE1 7DU
**Tel:** 02075932100
**Web:** www.postcomm.gov.uk
**Partnership**
**Line of Business:** Post offices
**Trading Style:** Post Com
**Partner:** T Brown
**US SIC:** 8699 **UK SIC:** 96902
**Employees:** 60

DUNS 22-073-4334
## Postal Services Holding Co Ltd
100 Victoria Embankment, London EC4Y 0HQ
**Tel:** 020-7250-2888 **Fax:** 020-7250-2632
**Web:** www.royalmailgroup.com
**Reg No:** 4074919 **Estd:** 2000 Private Limited Company
**Line of Business:** Post offices
**Issued Capital:** £50,006
**Directors:** R S Lowe, M F Russell, Ms R E Elliot
**Co. Secretary:** Alwen Lyons
**Responsibilities**
**Senior:** Moira Green *(CEO)*, Nick Horler *(Non-Executive Director)*, Jonathan Millidge *(Manager)*, Les Owen *(Non-Executive Director)*, Margaret Prosser *(Non-Executive Director)*, Paula Vennels *(Managing Director, Post Office)*
**Marketing:** Natasha Ayivor *(PR Manager - Stamps)*, Harshna Brahmbhatt *(Corporate PR Manager)*, James Eadie *(Public Relations Director)*, Neil McCrae *(Deputy Director Communications)*, Virginia Nanan *(Digital Marketing Executive an)*, Mish Tullar *(Media Relations Director)*
**Admin:** Rachel Butterworth *(Executive Assistant)*
**IT:** Catherine Doran *(Chief Information Officer)*
**HR:** Dale Haddon *(Human Resources Director)*, Jonathan Millidge *(Manager)*
**Operations:** Sue Whalley *(Chief Operating Officer)*
**Branches:** Postal Services Holding Co Ltd, Skegness Delivery Office, Roman Bank, Skegness, Lincolnshire PE25 2AA
**US SIC:** 4311, 6711
**UK SIC:** 79010, 83962
**Auditors:** Ernst & Young LLP
**Bankers:** Girobank Plc (72-00-00)
**Following financial data are in thousands**

| | 30-03-14 | 31-03-13 | 25-03-12 |
|---|---|---|---|
| TO | 1,179,000 | 10,103,000 | 9,532,000 |
| P/L | 158,000 | 575,000 | 263,000 |
| NW | 2,110,000 | 2,612,000 | (1,593,000) |
| WC | 1,912,000 | 962,000 | (79,000) |
| Emp. | 7,787 | 175,134 | 177,323 |

DUNS 73-601-5681
## Postcode Lottery Ltd
(**Subsidiary of:** Novamedia Holding B.V.)
72 George Street, Edinburgh, Midlothian EH2 3BX
**Tel:** 01315548794
**Web:** www.postcodelottery.co.uk
**Reg No:** 4862732 **Estd:** 2003 Private Limited Company
**Line of Business:** Fund raising services charitable and non charitable
**Issued Capital:** £10,000
**Director:** B J Poelmann
**Co. Secretary:** Rudolf Esser
**Responsibilities**
**Senior:** Daniel Higgs *(Manager)*
**US SIC:** 8321 **UK SIC:** 96111

| | 31-12-13 | 31-12-12 | 31-12-11 |
|---|---|---|---|
| TO | 16,650,859 | N/A | N/A |
| P/L | (78,203) | N/A | N/A |
| NW | (5,777,747) | (5,699,544) | (3,650,961) |
| WC | (6,654,125) | (6,060,251) | (3,985,008) |
| Emp. | 89 | N/A | N/A |

DUNS 21-912-3171
## Poste Hotels Ltd
(**Subsidiary of:** Poste Holdings Ltd)
High Street, St Martins, Stamford, Lincolnshire PE9 2LB
**Tel:** 01780-750750 **Fax:** 01780-750701
**Web:** www.georgehotelofstamford.com
**Reg No:** 0942008 **VAT No:** 638630133
**Estd:** 1964 Private Limited Company
**Line of Business:** Hotels
**Issued Capital:** £300,000
**Principals:** L O Hoskins *(Chairman and Managing)*, A M Hoskins, Ms A A Hoskins, I Vannocci, Ms E J Casey, M O Hoskins
**Co. Secretary:** David Landry
**US SIC:** 7011, 5812
**UK SIC:** 66500, 66110
**Auditors:** Mazars LLP
**Bankers:** National Westminster Bank Plc (60-80-09)

| | 31-10-13 | 31-10-12 | 31-10-11 |
|---|---|---|---|
| TO | 6,443,152 | 6,142,068 | 6,089,440 |
| P/L | 341,684 | 434,234 | (74,012) |
| NW | 12,683,809 | 12,405,560 | 12,075,298 |
| WC | 2,595,933 | 2,530,674 | 2,679,235 |
| Emp. | 166 | 153 | 139 |

DUNS 73-361-1706
## Postlethwaite Construction Ltd
Unit 24a Brampton Road, Longtown, Carlisle, Cumbria CA6 5TR
**Tel:** 01228-792769 **Fax:** 01228792939
**Web:** www.posbuild.co.uk
**Reg No:** 4634696 **Estd:** 2009 Private Limited Company
**Line of Business:** Building construction contractors
**Issued Capital:** £1,000
**Director:** G Postlethwaite
**Co. Secretary:** Kate Clode
**US SIC:** 1522 **UK SIC:** 50100
**Auditors:** Saint & Co

| | 31-12-13 | 31-12-12 | 31-12-11 |
|---|---|---|---|
| TA | 791,782 | 595,330 | 687,848 |
| NW | 381,681 | 251,060 | 230,157 |
| WC | 111,455 | (62,427) | (131,927) |

DUNS 22-018-8853 Imp
## Posturite (Uk) Ltd
The Mill, Berwick, Polegate, East Sussex BN26 6SZ
**Tel:** 01323874200
**Web:** www.posturite.co.uk
**Reg No:** 4021721 **Estd:** 2000 Private Limited Company
**Line of Business:** Ergonomics
**Issued Capital:** £2
**Director:** I G Fletcher Price
**Responsibilities**
**Senior:** Chris Hollely *(Regional Manager)*
**Finance:** Mike Fleming *(Head of Finance)*
**Sales:** Antony Burns *(Account Manager)*, Sue Greenham *(Account Manager)*, Jamie Hall *(Sales Manager)*, Craig Medhurst *(Account Manager)*, James Moxon *(Account Manager)*, Charles Webster *(Account Manager)*
**US SIC:** 5961 **UK SIC:** 65600

| | 30-06-13 | 30-06-12 | 30-06-11 |
|---|---|---|---|
| TA | 2 | 2 | 2 |
| NW | 2 | 2 | 2 |

DUNS 51-565-2878
## Potensial Ltd
68 Grange Road West, Birkenhead, Merseyside CH41 4DB
**Tel:** 01516511716
**Web:** www.potensial.co.uk
**Reg No:** 5846789 **Estd:** 2002 Private Limited Company
**Line of Business:** Residential care establishments
**Issued Capital:** £1,100
**Directors:** Ms N J Stadames, Ms R Farragher, T G Arnold
**Co. Secretary:** John Farragher
**Responsibilities**
**Senior:** Adele Matthews *(Manager)*
**Admin:** Ann Francis *(Administrator)*
**US SIC:** 8321 **UK SIC:** 96111

| | 31-03-14 | 31-03-13 | 31-03-12 |
|---|---|---|---|
| TO | 14,550,345 | 14,460,634 | 14,676,504 |
| P/L | (736,877) | 531,880 | 6,886 |
| NW | 4,059,265 | 4,246,988 | 3,460,777 |
| WC | 983,622 | (567,759) | 154,697 |
| Emp. | 624 | 625 | 677 |

DUNS 22-146-2141
## Potensis Holdings Ltd
Albert House 111-117, Victoria Street, Bristol, Avon BS1 6AX
**Tel:** 08448000681 **Fax:** 01179-272722
**Web:** www.potensis.com
**Reg No:** 4165038 **Estd:** 2001 Private Limited Company
**Line of Business:** Management activities of holding companies
**Issued Capital:** £100
**Directors:** J J Sullivan, Mrs B H Sullivan
**Co. Secretary:** Tony Hornik
**US SIC:** 6711 **UK SIC:** 83962

| | 29-12-13 | 31-12-12 | 25-12-11 |
|---|---|---|---|
| TO | 14,381,193 | 9,006,015 | 7,584,676 |
| P/L | 1,848,320 | 227,374 | 323,416 |
| NW | 4,001,023 | 2,161,417 | 1,744,381 |
| WC | 3,360,546 | 1,478,935 | 1,350,724 |
| Emp. | 56 | 35 | 34 |

DUNS 21-810-8326
## Potter Bars Station Cars
56 Darkes Lane, Potters Bar, Hertfordshire EN6 2HW
**Tel:** 01992878372
**Web:** www.pottersbarstationcars.co.uk
**Estd:** 2009
**Line of Business:** Locksmiths
**Proprietor:** J Tyers
**US SIC:** 4121 **UK SIC:** 72200
**Employees:** 92

DUNS 34-763-1504
## Potter Clarkson Llp
Belgrave Centre, Talbot Street, Nottingham, Nottinghamshire NG1 5GG
**Tel:** 01159552211
**Web:** www.potterclarkson.com
**Reg No:** 0315197OC **Estd:** 2005
**Line of Business:** Activities of patent and copyright agents
**Responsibilities**
**Senior:** Andrew Argyle *(Practice Director)*, Charlotte Crowhurst *(Non-designated Limited Liabili)*, Ian Dee *(Non-designated Limited Liabili)*, Mark Didmon *(Non-designated Limited Liabili)*, Sanjay Kapur *(Non-designated Limited Liabili)*, Stephen Mcneeney *(Non-designated Limited Liabili)*, Gareth Probert *(Non-designated Limited Liabili)*, Jane Wainwright *(Non-designated Limited Liabili)*
**US SIC:** 7399 **UK SIC:** 83954
**Auditors:** Hobsons
**Bankers:** The Royal Bank Of Scotland Plc (16-26-32)

| | 31-12-13 | 31-12-12 | 31-12-11 |
|---|---|---|---|
| TO | 23,403,100 | 22,716,987 | 23,543,962 |
| P/L | 915,499 | 6,771,206 | 777,480 |
| NW | 2,288,801 | 4,185,028 | 2,067,963 |
| WC | 3,533,980 | 3,734,412 | 3,621,757 |
| Emp. | 144 | 133 | 143 |

DUNS 21-304-7954
## The Potter Group (Holdings) Plc
Melmerby Industrial Estate, Melmerby Green Lane, Ripon, North Yorkshire HG4 5HP
**Tel:** 01765-640495
**Web:** www.pottergroup.co.uk
**Reg No:** 1300030 **Estd:** 1968 Public Limited Company
**Line of Business:** Other storage and warehousing not elsewhere classified
**Trading Style:** Potter Logistics
**Issued Capital:** £600,000
**Principals:** C D Potter *(Chairman)*, Mrs M A Potter, M G Lamb, I J Buntain
**Co. Secretary:** Kenneth Watson
**Responsibilities**
**Marketing:** Kirsty Mackenzie *(Marketing Manager)*
**Branches:** The Potter Group (Holdings) Plc, Queen Adelaide, Ely, Cambridgeshire CB7 4UB
**US SIC:** 4226 **UK SIC:** 77003
**Auditors:** Broadhead Peel Rhodes
**Bankers:** HSBC Bank plc (40-44-12)

| | 30-04-14 | 30-04-13 | 30-04-12 |
|---|---|---|---|
| TO | 24,722,291 | 22,882,173 | 15,153,063 |
| P/L | 1,731,818 | 1,123,401 | 1,035,857 |
| NW | 33,244,846 | 32,061,475 | 33,256,333 |
| WC | (1,462,930) | (2,568,061) | (919,588) |
| Emp. | 298 | 290 | 217 |

DUNS 22-983-0450
## Potter Raper Partnership
Duncan House, Burnhill Road, Beckenham, Kent BR3 3LA
**Tel:** 02086-583538
**Web:** www.prp.gb.com
**VAT No:** 205564871 **Estd:** 1970 Partnership
**Line of Business:** Chartered Surveyors
**Partners:** P Bass, S Daniels, G Potter, A Wells, R Humphrey, P Denny, R Dicker, J Parker
**Responsibilities**
**Senior:** Paul Skelly *(Partner)*
**Marketing:** Lucie Dicker *(Marketing Manager)*
**Branches:** Potter Raper Partnership, Julco House, 26-28 Great Portland Street, London W1W 8QT
**US SIC:** 8911 **UK SIC:** 83701
**Bankers:** Lloyds TSB Bank plc (30-92-16)
**Employees:** 137

DUNS 21-201-0243 Imp-Exp
## Potters-Ballotini Ltd
(**Subsidiary of:** The Carlyle Group L P)
Pontefract Road, Barnsley, South Yorkshire S71 1HJ
**Tel:** 01226704500
**Web:** www.potters-worldwide.com
**Reg No:** 0591872 **VAT No:** 518092939
**Estd:** 1957 Private Limited Company
**Line of Business:** Recycling
**Export Markets:** Rest Of Europe (68%) Middle Eastern States (1%) and others (2%)
**Export Sales:** £9,045,000
**Trading Style:** P B L, Potters Hollow Spheres
**Issued Capital:** £650,681
**Directors:** S Randolph, W J Sichko
**Co. Secretary:** Richard Tall
**Responsibilities**
**Senior:** Ray Jackson *(Plant Manager)*, Warwick Mayall *(Manager)*, S Moyer *(Vice President)*
**Sales:** P Curdy *(Sales Manager)*
**IT:** D Mendes *(IT Manager)*
**Branches:** Potters-Ballotini Ltd, Darlington Road, Bishop Auckland, County Durham DL14 9PR
**US SIC:** 3031 **UK SIC:** 48123
**Auditors:** PricewaterhouseCoopers LLP
**Bankers:** HSBC Bank plc (40-09-12)

| | 31-12-13 | 31-12-12 | 31-12-11 |
|---|---|---|---|
| TO | 14,705,000 | 11,792,000 | 10,591,000 |
| P/L | (963,000) | (1,136,000) | (569,000) |
| NW | 2,901,000 | 606,000 | 1,877,000 |
| WC | (125,000) | (2,656,000) | (1,068,000) |
| Emp. | 59 | 56 | 54 |

DUNS 21-775-5708
## Potters Bar Radio Cars
Station Forecourt, Darkes Lane, Potters Bar, Hertfordshire EN6 1AJ
**Estd:** 2002
**Line of Business:** Taxis and private hire vehicles
**US SIC:** 4121 **UK SIC:** 72200
**Employees:** 87

DUNS 21-779-4781
## Potters Heron Hotel
Winchester Road, Ampfield, Romsey, Hampshire SO51 9ZF
**Tel:** 02380277800
**Web:** www.pebblehotels.com
**Estd:** 1972 Proprietorship
**Line of Business:** Hotels
**Proprietor:** Miss K Garland
**Responsibilities**
**Senior:** Ludo Merleix *(General Manager)*, Frank Postel *(General Manager)*
**US SIC:** 7011 **UK SIC:** 66500
**Employees:** 60

DUNS 37-756-0271
## Potters International Hotel
1 Fleet Road, Aldershot, Hampshire GU11 2ET
**Tel:** 01252344000
**Web:** www.pottersinthotel.com
**Estd:** 1992 Proprietorship
**Line of Business:** Hotels
**Proprietor:** R Potter
**Responsibilities**
**Senior:** Ian Bonner *(Sales & Marketing Manager)*, Karen Goodey *(Wages Clerk)*, Brabara Leech *(General Manager)*
**Finance:** Karen Goodey *(Wages Clerk)*
**Branches:** Potters International Hotel, 1 Fleet Road, Aldershot, Hampshire GU11 2ET
**US SIC:** 7011 **UK SIC:** 66500
**Employees:** 150

DUNS 21-915-7831
## Potter's Leisure Ltd.
Coast Road, Hopton, Great Yarmouth, Norfolk NR31 9BX
**Tel:** 03333207418
**Web:** www.pottersholidays.com
**Reg No:** 0453567 **VAT No:** 105340812
**Estd:** 2010 Private Limited Company
**Line of Business:** Holiday parks and camps
**Trading Style:** Potters
**Issued Capital:** £4,656,450
**Directors:** Ms J M Potter, J H Potter, Miss S J Potter
**Responsibilities**
**Marketing:** Mike Scott *(Sales and Marketing Director)*
**Sales:** Mike Scott *(Sales and Marketing Director)*
**HR:** Beverley Read *(Human Resources Manager)*
**Health & Safety:** Beverley Read *(Human Resources Manager)*
**US SIC:** 7021 **UK SIC:** 66500
**Auditors:** Hebbleth Waites
**Bankers:** Barclays Bank Plc (20-99-21)

| | 31-12-13 | 31-12-12 | 31-12-11 |
|---|---|---|---|
| TO | 20,397,959 | 19,701,747 | 18,694,617 |
| P/L | 518,945 | 375,034 | 564,264 |
| NW | 14,930,830 | 14,528,462 | 14,235,532 |
| WC | (3,076,238) | (8,130,581) | (8,353,349) |
| Emp. | 528 | 514 | 505 |

DUNS 21-539-5141
## Potterspury Lodge School
Potterspury Lodge, Towcester, Northamptonshire NN12 7LL
**Tel:** 01908-542912
**Web:** www.potterspurylodge.co.uk
**Estd:** 1964
**Line of Business:** Schools (special)
**Director:** Ms G Lietz
**Responsibilities**
**Senior:** Nicholas Avis *(Trustee)*, Sarah Buckland *(Manager)*, Jacqueline Lawson *(Manager)*, Gretel Lietz *(Trustee)*, Oliver Low *(Manager)*, Andrew Manton *(Manager)*, Andrew Tyrer *(Manager)*
**US SIC:** 8299 **UK SIC:** 93300
**Employees:** 53

DUNS 21-820-3078
## Pottery Primary School
Kilburn Road, Belper, Derbyshire DE56 1HA
**Tel:** 01773-823383
**Web:** www.pottery.derbyshire.sch.uk
**Estd:** 2002 Proprietorship
**Line of Business:** Schools (local authority)
**Proprietor:** Mrs G Hutton
**US SIC:** 8211 **UK SIC:** 93200
**Employees:** 75

DUNS 21-240-4073 **Imp**

## Potts Print (Uk) Ltd

Atlas House, Nelson Park, Cramlington, Northumberland NE23 1WG
**Tel:** 0845-375-1875 **Fax:** 01670735451
**Web:** www.potts.co.uk
**Reg No:** 0536326 **Estd:** 1954 Private Limited Company
**Line of Business:** Printing not elsewhere classified
**Issued Capital:** £1,316
**Directors:** K Brown, M W Devine, Mrs C V Armstrong, R S Johnson, R Curtis, I R White, J Conway, Mrs S Tobin
**Co. Secretary:** Mrs Stephanie Tobin
**Responsibilities**
**Senior:** Iain Mcdougal *(Director)*, Keith Mchugh *(Director)*, Carla Reeves *(Corporate Services Director)*, Michael Sandford-Couch *(Director)*, Daniel Tobin *(Director)*
**Marketing:** Laurie Cansfield *(Corporate Communications Manag)*
**Admin:** Carla Reeves *(Corporate Services Director)*
**HR:** Carla Reeves *(Corporate Services Director)*
**Health & Safety:** Carla Reeves *(Corporate Services Director)*
**US SIC:** 2752 **UK SIC:** 47544
**Auditors:** Hawdon Bell & Co
**Bankers:** Barclays Bank Plc (20-62-09)

| | 31-12-13 | 31-12-12 | 31-12-11 |
|---|---|---|---|
| TO | 13,743,634 | 14,733,168 | 14,332,930 |
| P/L | 800,713 | 784,773 | 527,795 |
| NW | 2,135,797 | 1,726,545 | 1,395,764 |
| WC | (867,400) | (1,134,141) | (1,340,409) |
| Emp. | 151 | 164 | 160 |

DUNS 77-267-5120

## Poundfield Products Ltd

(**Subsidiary of:** Poundfield Products (Holdings) Ltd)
Grove Farm, Creeting St Peter, Ipswich, Suffolk IP6 8QG
**Tel:** 01449-723150
**Web:** www.poundfield.com
**Reg No:** 2714196 **VAT No:** 571388714
**Estd:** 1992 Private Limited Company
**Line of Business:** Other manufacturing not elsewhere classified
**Issued Capital:** £63,568
**Directors:** J P Alston, M Moss, M H Jardine
**Responsibilities**
**Senior:** George Franks *(Chairman)*, Martin Snowling *(Financial Director)*
**Finance:** Martin Snowling *(Financial Director)*
**Marketing:** Rory Faulkner *(Marketing Manager)*
**Sales:** Jane Aldous *(Sales Manager)*, Rory Faulkner *(Marketing Manager)*, Chris Skippins *(Sales Manager)*
**US SIC:** 3271 **UK SIC:** 24370
**Auditors:** Ensors
**Bankers:** Barclays Bank Plc (20-44-51)

| | 31-12-13 | 31-12-12 | 31-12-11 |
|---|---|---|---|
| TO | 5,692,963 | 6,837,341 | 5,551,335 |
| P/L | (193,592) | (222,521) | (32,206) |
| NW | 1,635,546 | 1,782,365 | 2,113,629 |
| WC | (446,386) | (86,440) | 37,928 |
| Emp. | 49 | 66 | 57 |

DUNS 21-216-8389

## Poundstretcher Ltd

(**Subsidiary of:** Crown Crest Group Ltd)
Unit 5 Baglan Bay Retail Park, Port Talbot, West Glamorgan SA12 6NR
**Tel:** 01639822846 **Fax:** 01484-441717
**Web:** www.poundstretcher.co.uk
**Reg No:** 0553014 **VAT No:** 482067833
**Estd:** 2011 Private Limited Company
**Line of Business:** Other retail sale in non-specialised stores
**Issued Capital:** £15,800,000
**Directors:** T A Shattock, M E Morrison, X Y Pan, A A Tayub, R G Ellis
**Co. Secretary:** Martin Collinson
**Branches:** Poundstretcher Ltd, 14-20 High Street, Galashiels, Selkirkshire TD1 1SD
**US SIC:** 5399 **UK SIC:** 65600
**Auditors:** PKF (UK) LLP

| | 31-03-14 | 31-03-13 | 31-03-12 |
|---|---|---|---|
| TO | 395,360,000 | 367,984,000 | 348,446,000 |
| P/L | 1,347,000 | (3,685,000) | 1,585,000 |
| NW | (3,361,000) | (4,708,000) | (1,023,000) |
| WC | (8,522,000) | (12,730,000) | (6,883,000) |
| Emp. | 6,200 | 6,003 | 5,647 |

DUNS 23-623-2377

## Poundworld Retail Ltd

Axis 62, Foxbridge Way, Normanton, West Yorkshire WF6 1TN
**Tel:** 01924-420-260 **Fax:** 01924688061
**Web:** http://poundworld.net
**Reg No:** 2215564 **VAT No:** 500171217
**Estd:** 1973 Private Limited Company
**Line of Business:** Other retail sale in non-specialised stores
**Export Sales:** £2,398,000
**Trading Style:** Poundworld, Itp Imports, Discount Uk
**Issued Capital:** £80,000
**Managing Director:** C Edwards
**Co. Secretary:** Laurence Edwards
**Responsibilities**
**Senior:** Mohammed Atef *(Manager)*
**Finance:** Avais Ahmed *(Finance Director)*
**Branches:** Poundworld Retail Ltd, Unit F8, 1-3 Flottergate Mall, Grimsby, South Humberside DN31 1QX
**US SIC:** 5399, 5699
**UK SIC:** 65600, 64500
**Auditors:** KPMG LLP
**Bankers:** Bank Of Scotland (80-05-14)

| | 31-03-14 | 31-03-13 | 31-03-12 |
|---|---|---|---|
| TO | 345,259,000 | 293,787,000 | 206,482,000 |
| P/L | 5,002,000 | 1,892,000 | 2,849,000 |
| NW | 11,498,000 | 8,527,000 | 7,693,000 |
| WC | 2,943,000 | (1,829,000) | (9,121,000) |
| Emp. | 4,475 | 4,305 | 3,428 |

DUNS 21-150-1721 **Imp**

## Poupart Ltd

(**Subsidiary of:** Fletcher Bay Group Ltd)
Turnford Place, Great Cambridge Road, Turnford, Broxbourne, Hertfordshire EN10 6NH
**Tel:** 01992443333 **Fax:** 01992-450915
**Web:** www.poupart.co.uk
**Reg No:** 0310358 **VAT No:** 237113587
**Estd:** 2012 Private Limited Company
**Line of Business:** Food import and exporters and agents
**Trading Style:** Berry World, Poupart Citrus, Poupart Imports
**Issued Capital:** £1,600,000
**Principals:** L S Olins *(Managing)*, A L Olins, A M Culley, A J Barnes, J M Olins, M C Hancock, M E Butlin, R C Dawson
**Branches:** Poupart Ltd, Baltimore St, Manchester M40 5AL
**US SIC:** 5149 **UK SIC:** 61700
**Auditors:** KPMG LLP
**Bankers:** The Royal Bank Of Scotland Plc (16-01-01)

| | 31-12-13 | 31-12-12 | 31-12-11 |
|---|---|---|---|
| TO | 327,436,000 | 294,556,000 | 295,433,000 |
| P/L | 5,766,000 | 4,785,000 | 5,385,000 |
| NW | 11,532,000 | 8,907,000 | 7,618,000 |
| WC | 14,562,000 | 9,003,000 | 8,564,000 |
| Emp. | 183 | 161 | 146 |

DUNS 21-158-9593 **Imp-Exp**

## Pourshins Ltd

(**Subsidiary of:** Gategroup Holding Ag)
The Lodge, Harmondsworth Lane, Harmondsworth, West Drayton, Middlesex UB7 0AB
**Tel:** 02089-175777
**Web:** www.pourshins.com
**Reg No:** 1576522 **VAT No:** 918572889
**Estd:** 1981 Private Limited Company
**Line of Business:** Storage and warehousing
**Issued Capital:** £7,311,750
**Directors:** A Langdale, S P Corr, J D Janow, R Van Dijk
**Co. Secretary:** Andrew Langdale
**Responsibilities**
**Senior:** Rufus Powell *(Financial Director)*
**Finance:** Rufus Powell *(Financial Director)*
**Admin:** S Eglesfield *(Office Manager)*
**Health & Safety:** S Eglesfield *(Office Manager)*
**Purchasing:** S Eglesfield *(Office Manager)*
**US SIC:** 4226, 5812
**UK SIC:** 77003, 66110
**Auditors:** PricewaterhouseCoopers LLP

| | 31-12-13 | 31-12-12 | 31-12-11 |
|---|---|---|---|
| TO | 100,129,000 | 90,503,000 | 79,087,000 |
| P/L | 1,384,000 | 2,098,000 | 2,160,000 |
| NW | 5,377,000 | 4,414,000 | 2,804,000 |
| WC | 4,938,000 | 4,409,000 | 2,798,000 |
| Emp. | 61 | 54 | 34 |

DUNS 21-818-1121 **Imp**

## Povoas Packaging Ltd

Stoke Albany Road, Kettering, Northamptonshire NN14 2SR
**Tel:** 01536-761155 **Fax:** 01536-764790
**Web:** www.povoas.co.uk
**Reg No:** 0529777 **VAT No:** 120107931
**Estd:** 1954 Private Limited Company
**Line of Business:** Manufacture of machinery for food, beverage and tobacco processing
**Export Sales:** £53,000
**Issued Capital:** £46,326
**Directors:** J M Kendall, Ms M R Brewin, A J Kendall, S J Povoas
**Co. Secretary:** Jonathan Kendall
**Responsibilities**
**Sales:** Joanne Daniels *(Sales Administrator)*
**Admin:** Joanne Daniels *(Sales Administrator)*, Christine Gosling *(Office Manager)*
**IT:** Christine Gosling *(Office Manager)*
**US SIC:** 3551 **UK SIC:** 32441
**Auditors:** Cooper Parry LLP
**Bankers:** Barclays Bank Plc (20-49-08)

| | 31-10-13 | 31-10-12 | 31-10-11 |
|---|---|---|---|
| TO | 20,794,000 | 19,764,000 | 20,683,000 |
| P/L | 1,353,000 | 1,048,000 | 856,000 |
| NW | 6,363,000 | 5,380,000 | 4,897,000 |
| WC | 2,658,000 | 2,342,000 | 2,065,000 |
| Emp. | 127 | 131 | 136 |

DUNS 21-741-9042 **Imp**

## Powakaddy International Ltd

Eurolink Industrial Centre, Sittingbourne, Kent ME10 3RN
**Tel:** 01795473555
**Web:** www.powakaddy.com
**Reg No:** 7747629 **Estd:** 1986 Private Limited Company
**Line of Business:** Manufacture of sports goods
**Issued Capital:** £9,000
**Directors:** J C Degraft-Johnson, D I Catford
**Responsibilities**
**Finance:** Michelle Harvey *(Financial controller)*
**US SIC:** 3949 **UK SIC:** 49420

| | 31-12-13 | 31-12-12 |
|---|---|---|
| TO | 7,693,508 | 2,570,842 |
| P/L | 68,860 | (750,513) |
| NW | (1,046,945) | (1,106,284) |
| WC | 1,428,403 | 1,541,397 |
| Emp. | 46 | 69 |

DUNS 39-908-3146 **Imp-Exp**

## Powder Systems Ltd

(**Subsidiary of:** Cobco 892 Ltd)
Estuary Business Park, Liverpool, Merseyside L24 8RG
**Tel:** 0151-448-7700 **Fax:** 0151-448-7702
**Web:** www.powdersystems.com
**Reg No:** 2233044 **VAT No:** 482813531
**Estd:** 1988 Private Limited Company
**Line of Business:** Manufacturers and suppliers of industrial machinery
**Issued Capital:** £76,627
**Principals:** M Pitcher *(Managing)*, Ms A Pitcher
**Co. Secretary:** Ms Karen Pitcher
**Responsibilities**
**Senior:** Barry O'Gorman *(Manager)*, Terry Welsh *(Goods In Manager)*
**Sales:** Terry Welsh *(Goods In Manager)*
**IT:** Ron Benson *(IT Manager)*
**Health & Safety:** Jayne Sloan *(Quality Assurance Manager)*
**Operations:** Jayne Sloan *(Quality Assurance Manager)*
**Engineering:** Ken Knowles *(Engineering Manager)*
**US SIC:** 3559, 3534
**UK SIC:** 32863, 32553
**Auditors:** Grant Thornton UK LLP
**Bankers:** Barclays Bank Plc (20-91-48)

| | 31-03-14 | 31-03-13 | 31-03-12 |
|---|---|---|---|
| TO | N/A | N/A | 5,580,060 |
| P/L | N/A | N/A | 82,649 |
| NW | 862,403 | 320,816 | 1,084,360 |
| WC | 793,779 | 260,111 | 1,013,703 |
| Emp. | N/A | N/A | 60 |

DUNS 39-936-4405

## Powdertech Ltd

Murdock Road, Bicester, Oxfordshire OX26 4PP
**Web:** www.powdertech.co.uk
**Reg No:** 2249909 **Estd:** 1984 Private Limited Company
**Line of Business:** Management activities of holding companies
**Issued Capital:** £10,000
**Managing Director:** M P Green
**Co. Secretary:** Ms Harriet Duckworth
**Branches:** Powdertech Ltd, 5 Cockerell Road, Corby, Northamptonshire NN17 5DU
**US SIC:** 6711 **UK SIC:** 83962
**Auditors:** Grant Thornton UK LLP
**Bankers:** Barclays Bank Plc (20-20-15)

| | 31-08-13 | 31-08-12 | 31-08-11 |
|---|---|---|---|
| TA | 739,751 | 459,118 | 470,721 |
| NW | 396,897 | 329,860 | 357,343 |
| WC | 68,733 | 302,468 | 346,137 |

DUNS 22-774-6872 **Exp**

## Powell & Harber (Precision Engineers) Ltd

Brickfields Road, Worcester, Worcestershire WR4 9WN
**Tel:** 01905-731717
**Web:** www.powell-harber.co.uk
**Reg No:** 1425350 **Estd:** 1979 Private Limited Company
**Line of Business:** Manufacture of other plastic products
**Export Markets:** Germany
**Issued Capital:** £100
**Directors:** R G Mcdonald, Mrs D Mcdonald
**Responsibilities**
**Senior:** William Harber *(Director)*, Lynda Harber *(Director)*
**Sales:** William Harber *(Director)*
**Branches:** Unit 3, Checketts La Indstl Est, Worcester
**US SIC:** 3079, 3423
**UK SIC:** 48360, 31612
**Auditors:** John Yelland & Co
**Bankers:** HSBC Bank plc (40-43-17)

| | 28-02-14 | 28-02-13 | 29-02-12 |
|---|---|---|---|
| TA | 2,525,163 | 2,479,038 | 2,494,253 |
| NW | 2,020,106 | 1,864,342 | 1,834,189 |
| WC | 1,490,755 | 1,303,291 | 1,258,852 |

DUNS 23-382-4002

## Powell Dobson

Charterhouse, Cardiff, South Glamorgan CF3 0LT
**Tel:** 029-2079-9699
**Web:** www.powelldobson.com
**VAT No:** 136491560 **Estd:** 1988 Partnership
**Line of Business:** Architects
**Partners:** T Percival, H Wainwright, D Dobson, G Davis
**Responsibilities**
**Senior:** Ann-marie Smale *(Manager)*, Jeffery Tucker *(Manager)*
**Marketing:** Darryl Rothwell *(Marketing Manager)*
**IT:** Ian Norman *(Senior IT Executive)*
**Branches:** Powell Dobson, 10J Shed, Kings Road, Swansea, West Glamorgan SA1 8PL
**US SIC:** 8911 **UK SIC:** 83701
**Bankers:** National Westminster Bank Plc (56-00-41)
**Employees:** 70

DUNS 23-863-2587

## Powell Engineering U K Ltd

Belton Road, Sandtoft, Doncaster, South Yorkshire DN8 5SX
**Tel:** 01724-712904 **Fax:** 01724712587
**Web:** www.poweng.net
**Reg No:** 3854782 **Estd:** 1999 Private Limited Company
**Line of Business:** Engineering services
**Issued Capital:** £2
**Directors:** R B Powell, A D Powell
**Co. Secretary:** Ainsley Powell
**Responsibilities**
**Senior:** Hazel Fims *(Office Manager)*, Jane Irani *(Manager)*, Carol Prendercast *(Office Manager)*
**Admin:** Hazel Barrass *(Office Manager)*, Carol Prendercast *(Office Manager)*
**US SIC:** 8911 **UK SIC:** 83701
**Auditors:** Royston Parkin Ltd

| | 31-10-13 | 31-10-12 | 31-10-11 |
|---|---|---|---|
| TO | 9,193,088 | 6,059,672 | N/A |
| P/L | 756,159 | 429,785 | N/A |
| NW | 1,617,740 | 2,158,033 | 1,992,345 |
| WC | 2,817,557 | 2,280,452 | 2,207,319 |
| Emp. | 81 | 69 | N/A |

DUNS 21-304-3227 **Exp**

## Powell Plastics Ltd

(**Subsidiary of:** One Fifty One Plc)
No 1 Whitehall Riverside, Leeds, West Yorkshire LS1 4BN
**Tel:** 01132452244 **Fax:** 08435570011
**Web:** www.straight.co.uk
**Reg No:** 1024015 **Estd:** 1971 Private Limited Company
**Line of Business:** Manufacture of other plastic products
**Trading Style:** Straight Plc
**Issued Capital:** £20,200
**Directors:** P Dalton, A Walsh, P R Murdoch
**Co. Secretary:** Ms Susan Holburn
**Responsibilities**
**Senior:** Mark Halford *(Manager)*, James Mellor *(Financial Director)*
**Engineering:** Douglas Forest *(Engineering Manager)*
**US SIC:** 3999 **UK SIC:** 49590

| | 31-12-13 | 31-12-12 | 31-12-11 |
|---|---|---|---|
| TA | 20,200 | 20,200 | 20,200 |
| NW | 20,200 | 20,200 | 20,200 |

DUNS 22-723-6742

## Powell Spencer Partners

290 Kilburn High Road, London NW6 2DD
**Tel:** 02076248888
**Web:** www.psplaw.co.uk
**Estd:** 2000 Partnership
**Line of Business:** Solicitors
**Trading Style:** Powell Spencer & Partners
**Partners:** C W Magrath, D K Greig Powell, R C Spencer
**US SIC:** 8111 **UK SIC:** 83500
**Bankers:** The Co-Operative Bank Plc (08-90-78)
**Employees:** 50

DUNS 34-659-3549 **Imp-Exp**

## Powell (Uk) Ltd

(**Subsidiary of:** Powell Industries International B.V.)
Ripley Road, Bradford, West Yorkshire BD4 7EH
**Tel:** 01274-734221
**Web:** www.switchgear.co.uk
**Reg No:** 5464765 **VAT No:** 859733572
**Estd:** 2005 Private Limited Company

**Line of Business:** Manufacture of telegraph and telephone apparatus and equipment
**Export Sales:** £6,457,000
**Trading Style:** Powell
**Issued Capital:** £100
**Directors:** M J Galley, Ms E L Howell
**Co. Secretary:** Don Madison
**Responsibilities**
**Senior:** Patrick McDonald *(Manager)*
**Finance:** Phil Powdrill *(Financial Director)*
**Facilities:** Jason Whomack *(Maintenance Manager)*
**Engineering:** Jason Whomack *(Maintenance Manager)*
**Branches:** Powell (Uk) Ltd, M W B Business Exchange, 2 Gayton Road, Harrow, Middlesex HA1 2XU
**US SIC:** 3661, 3629
**UK SIC:** 34410, 34350
**Auditors:** PricewaterhouseCoopers LLP
**Bankers:** HSBC Bank plc (40-27-15)

| | 30-09-14 | 30-09-13 | 30-09-12 |
|---|---|---|---|
| TO | 24,340,000 | 21,725,000 | 27,281,000 |
| P/L | 1,524,000 | (1,484,000) | 219,000 |
| NW | 9,386,000 | 7,821,000 | 9,070,000 |
| WC | 6,526,000 | 4,909,000 | 6,021,000 |
| Emp. | 207 | 256 | 288 |

DUNS 45-840-4159
## Powells Bus Co Ltd
Unit 26 Hellaby Industrial, Rotherham, South Yorkshire S66 8HN
**Tel:** 01709-702220
**Web:** www.powellsbus.co.uk
**Reg No:** 3190618 **Estd:** 1996 Private Limited Company
**Line of Business:** Other scheduled passenger land transport not elsewhere classified
**Issued Capital:** £125
**Directors:** Ms P Powell, J S Powell, I S Powell
**Co. Secretary:** Ms Jane Powell
**US SIC:** 4141 **UK SIC:** 72102
**Auditors:** Andertons Liversidge & Co
**Bankers:** The Royal Bank Of Scotland Plc (16-34-22)

| | 30-06-14 | 30-06-13 | 30-06-12 |
|---|---|---|---|
| TA | 532,127 | 554,550 | 538,331 |
| NW | 194,425 | 186,134 | 152,627 |
| WC | 143,890 | 139,655 | 90,843 |

DUNS 73-340-4284
## Powells Group Ltd
Unit 2-3, Mylen Business Centre, Beckett Road, Andover, Hampshire SP10 3HR
**Tel:** 01264366298
**Web:** www.powells.biz
**Reg No:** 4614165 **Estd:** 2002 Private Limited Company
**Line of Business:** Other building installation
**Export Sales:** £301,641
**Issued Capital:** £1,000
**Director:** G R Wells
**Co. Secretary:** Graham Turner
**US SIC:** 1796 **UK SIC:** 50400
**Bankers:** National Westminster Bank Plc (53-70-32)

| | 30-06-13 | 30-06-12 | 30-06-11 |
|---|---|---|---|
| TO | 29,203,341 | 29,475,747 | 39,242,348 |
| P/L | 451,116 | 133,553 | 258,769 |
| NW | 1,955,976 | 1,843,300 | 1,833,258 |
| WC | 1,733,016 | 1,573,922 | 1,540,395 |
| Emp. | 60 | 66 | 69 |

DUNS 77-442-1861 Imp-Exp
## Power Control Ltd
A E C Power Control Ltd, Sheffield, South Yorkshire S21 4HL
**Tel:** 01246-431-431
**Web:** www.borri.co.uk
**Reg No:** 0152126SC **VAT No:** 617477126
**Estd:** 1994 Private Limited Company
**Line of Business:** Production of electricity
**Export Sales:** £683,983
**Trading Style:** Borri
**Issued Capital:** £4,506
**Principals:** M D Rea *(Managing)*, I Tucker, M S Trolley
**Responsibilities**
**Senior:** Brian Tucker *(Financial Director)*
**Finance:** Brian Tucker *(Financial Director)*
**US SIC:** 5065, 7379
**UK SIC:** 61500, 83940
**Auditors:** White Hart Associates (London) Ltd
**Bankers:** Bank Of Scotland (80-11-60)

| | 31-12-13 | 31-12-12 | 31-12-11 |
|---|---|---|---|
| TO | 8,828,331 | 7,697,998 | 6,380,400 |
| P/L | 1,265,999 | 1,112,184 | 1,057,978 |
| NW | 1,496,713 | 1,303,992 | 1,081,808 |
| WC | 735,520 | 651,725 | 401,189 |
| Emp. | 57 | N/A | N/A |

DUNS 23-828-3654
## Power Efficiency Ltd
(**Subsidiary of:** Gdf Suez)
10th Floor, Marlowe House, 109 Station Road, Sidcup, Kent DA15 7BH
**Tel:** 02082696100
**Web:** www.powerefficiency.co.uk
**Reg No:** 3820315 **Estd:** 1999 Private Limited Company
**Line of Business:** Business and management consultancy activities not elsewhere classified
**Issued Capital:** £100
**Directors:** R J Blumberger, P E Rawson
**Responsibilities**
**Senior:** Melanie Allan *(Manager)*, Julius Brinkworth *(Energy Projects Director)*, Bobby Collinson *(Commercial Director)*, John Field *(Manager)*, Gary Harper *(Manager)*, Richard Puttman *(Manager)*, Carl Roberts *(New Business Development Direc)*, Simone Tudor *(Manager)*
**Marketing:** Bobby Collinson *(Commercial Director)*
**Sales:** Carl Roberts *(New Business Development Direc)*
**US SIC:** 7392, 8911
**UK SIC:** 83951, 83701
**Auditors:** Deloitte LLP
**Bankers:** The Royal Bank Of Scotland Plc (16-32-45)

| | 31-12-13 | 31-12-12 | 31-12-11 |
|---|---|---|---|
| TO | 8,712,000 | 9,082,000 | 6,899,000 |
| P/L | 55,000 | 1,256,000 | 879,000 |
| NW | 3,560,000 | 3,142,000 | 2,234,000 |
| WC | 3,306,000 | 2,708,000 | 1,876,000 |
| Emp. | 71 | 83 | 51 |

DUNS 22-523-8542 Exp
## Power Electrics (Bristol) Ltd
Unit 4, Abergarw Enterprise Centre, Abergarw Trading Estate, Bridgend, Mid Glamorgan CF32 9LW
**Tel:** 01656726050 **Fax:** 01179-479701
**Web:** www.powerelectrics.com
**Reg No:** 0776704 **VAT No:** 139124282
**Estd:** 1963 Private Limited Company
**Line of Business:** Renting of other machinery and equipment not elsewhere classified
**Export Markets:** Nigeria; Gambia; Middle East
**Export Sales:** £520,638
**Issued Capital:** £2,050
**Principals:** A J Pullin *(Managing)*, A P Jenkins *(Financial)*, J R Pullin, A P Jenkins
**Responsibilities**
**Senior:** Steve Summers *(Manager)*
**US SIC:** 7394, 5065
**UK SIC:** 84000, 61500
**Auditors:** RSM Bentley Jennison
**Bankers:** HSBC Bank plc (40-14-20)

| | 31-03-14 | 31-03-13 | 31-03-12 |
|---|---|---|---|
| TO | 23,393,808 | 23,110,500 | 21,482,339 |
| P/L | 1,797,493 | 1,668,933 | 1,033,492 |
| NW | 9,163,273 | 8,501,234 | 7,564,718 |
| WC | 271,387 | 485,634 | (24,280) |
| Emp. | 184 | 177 | 158 |

DUNS 22-289-7014
## Power Europe (Doncaster) Ltd
(**Subsidiary of:** Deutsche Post Ag)
Meridian South, Leicester, Leicestershire LE19 1WY
**Tel:** 01455555150 **Fax:** 01483-406444
**Reg No:** 4307693 **Estd:** 1997 Private Limited Company
**Line of Business:** Storage and warehousing
**Issued Capital:** £2
**Directors:** P F Watts, K R Smith
**Co. Secretary:** Exel Secretarial Services Limite
**US SIC:** 4226 **UK SIC:** 77003
**Auditors:** Ernst & Young LLP

| | 31-12-13 | 31-12-12 | 31-12-11 |
|---|---|---|---|
| TO | 7,172,000 | 7,815,000 | 7,323,000 |
| P/L | 589,000 | 442,000 | 877,000 |
| NW | 589,000 | 442,000 | 877,000 |
| WC | 589,000 | 442,000 | 877,000 |

DUNS 21-308-6168 Imp-Exp
## Power Health Products Ltd
Pocklington Industrial Estate, York, North Yorkshire YO42 1NR
**Tel:** 01759302595
**Web:** www.powerhealth.co.uk
**Reg No:** 1041196 **VAT No:** 169860908
**Estd:** 1972 Private Limited Company
**Line of Business:** Holding companies management activities
**Export Markets:** W Europe; W Indies
**Export Sales:** £984,627
**Trading Style:** Power Health
**Issued Capital:** £10,500
**Principals:** M D Mciver *(Chairman and Managing)*, Ms V C Mciver *(Managing)*, Miss H E Whilesmith, Miss C Brookshaw, Mrs A C Mciver
**Co. Secretary:** Mrs Gail Morgan
**Responsibilities**
**Marketing:** Jenny Baillie *(Marketing Manager)*
**Sales:** Terry Wylde *(Sales Manager)*
**US SIC:** 2099, 5122
**UK SIC:** 42399, 61800
**Auditors:** Finnie & Co
**Bankers:** Lloyds TSB Bank plc (30-95-48)

| | 30-04-14 | 30-04-13 | 30-04-12 |
|---|---|---|---|
| TO | 3,692,345 | 3,446,970 | 2,978,518 |
| P/L | 728,655 | 408,604 | 154,518 |
| NW | 2,242,555 | 1,547,536 | 1,216,626 |
| WC | 1,123,156 | 768,261 | 426,494 |
| Emp. | 59 | 57 | 55 |

DUNS 21-715-3793
## The Power Industrial Group Ltd
(**Subsidiary of:** Lloyds Banking Group Plc)
One Eleven Edmund Street, Birmingham, West Midlands B3 2HJ
**Tel:** 01332819550
**Web:** www.powerindustrial.com
**Reg No:** 7545141 **Estd:** 2011 Private Limited Company
**Line of Business:** Management activities of other non-financial holding companies not elsewhere classified
**Issued Capital:** £364,444
**Directors:** D N Hayle, C D Watson, C J Thomas, J Garner, J Callcott, P J Douglas
**US SIC:** 6711 **UK SIC:** 83962
**Auditors:** KPMG LLP

| | 31-12-13 | 30-09-12 | 30-12-11 |
|---|---|---|---|
| TO | 58,570,000 | 42,773,000 | N/A |
| P/L | (11,278,000) | 379,000 | N/A |
| NW | (17,143,000) | (14,431,000) | 1 |
| WC | (3,608,000) | 739,000 | N/A |
| Emp. | 255 | 319 | N/A |

DUNS 39-229-0995 Exp
## Power Jacks Ltd
Balmacassie Drive, Balmacassie Commercial Park, Ellon, Aberdeenshire AB41 8BX
**Tel:** 01358285100 **Fax:** 01346 519737
**Web:** www.powerjacks.com
**Reg No:** 0103849SC **VAT No:** 470955817
**Estd:** 1903 Private Limited Company
**Line of Business:** Lifting equipment
**Issued Capital:** £50,000
**Principals:** B C Bultitude *(Managing)*, C Mcgill, Mrs J Bultitude, J M Mccarthy, A J Greig, W B Hamper, Ms A M Bultitude, K D Mackie
**Co. Secretary:** Craig Mcgill
**US SIC:** 3542, 3561
**UK SIC:** 32212, 32870
**Auditors:** Johnston Carmichael
**Bankers:** The Royal Bank Of Scotland Plc (83-49-40)

| | 31-03-13 | 31-03-12 | 31-03-11 |
|---|---|---|---|
| TO | 13,098,301 | 4,656,378 | 5,118,326 |
| P/L | 1,461,451 | (955,149) | (215,914) |
| NW | 4,789,291 | 2,919,801 | 5,451,870 |
| WC | (1,479,370) | (2,519,755) | 1,736,598 |
| Emp. | 69 | 66 | 67 |

DUNS 23-830-6760
## Power Leisure Bookmakers Ltd
(**Subsidiary of:** Paddy Power Plc)
6 Hibernia Street, Holywood, Co Down BT18 9JE
**Tel:** 02890586762 **Fax:** 020-7089-9746
**Web:** www.paddypower.com
**Reg No:** 3822566 **VAT No:** 779069571
**Estd:** 2003 Private Limited Company
**Line of Business:** Gambling and betting activities
**Trading Style:** Paddy Power
**Issued Capital:** £1
**Directors:** A Mccue, C Mccarthy, J Massey
**Responsibilities**
**Senior:** Shaun Mccord *(District Manager)*
**Branches:** Power Leisure Bookmakers Ltd, 2 Coldharbour Lane, London SE5 9PR
**US SIC:** 7999 **UK SIC:** 97913
**Auditors:** KPMG
**Bankers:** Allied Irish Bank (gb) (23-83-94)

| | 31-12-13 | 31-12-12 | 31-12-11 |
|---|---|---|---|
| TO | 710,012,563 | 530,320,049 | 433,941,818 |
| P/L | (11,150,507) | (3,182,038) | 11,335,590 |
| NW | (50,513,719) | (39,676,872) | (39,592,273) |
| WC | (124,286,579) | (88,552,757) | (79,983,610) |
| Emp. | 2,511 | 2,014 | 1,577 |

DUNS 73-652-9137
## Power on Connections Ltd
(**Subsidiary of:** Brookfield Infrastructure Partners L.P.)
Dovecote Court, Potters Marston Hall, Stanton Lane, Potters Marston, Leicester, Leicestershire LE9 3JR
**Tel:** 01455-274-882 **Fax:** 01455-274-906
**Web:** www.poweronconnections.co.uk
**Reg No:** 4912774 **Estd:** 2003 Private Limited Company
**Line of Business:** Independent electricity connections provider
**Issued Capital:** £187,500
**Directors:** D J Corney, C E Linsdell, R S Theobald
**Co. Secretary:** Christopher Mumford
**Responsibilities**
**Senior:** Andy Cross *(Manager)*
**Health & Safety:** Jenny Walker *(Health & Safety Officer)*
**Operations:** Paul Wragg *(Operations Manager)*
**Branches:** Power On Connections Ltd, Ladfordfields Industrial Park, Stafford, Staffordshire ST18 9QE
**US SIC:** 1731 **UK SIC:** 50300
**Auditors:** Deloitte LLP

| | 31-12-13 | 31-12-12 | 31-12-11 |
|---|---|---|---|
| TO | 37,549,292 | 32,976,827 | 21,566,625 |
| P/L | 1,260,689 | 1,261,072 | 852,627 |
| NW | 4,662,113 | 3,761,278 | 2,839,061 |
| WC | 3,613,484 | 2,837,095 | 2,123,404 |
| Emp. | 150 | 127 | 119 |

DUNS 22-775-1179 Imp
## Power Panels Electrical Systems Ltd
Landywood Green, Walsall, West Midlands WS6 7QX
**Tel:** 01922419109 **Fax:** 01922418181
**Web:** www.powerpanels.uk.com
**Reg No:** 1398551 **Estd:** 1978 Private Limited Company
**Line of Business:** Assembling and wiring
**Export Sales:** £658,790
**Issued Capital:** £10,000
**Principals:** D W Fox *(Chairman and Managing)*, A Hague
**Co. Secretary:** Ms Susan Fox
**Responsibilities**
**Senior:** Frank Cox *(Warehouse Manager)*
**Operations:** Frank Cox *(Warehouse Manager)*
**Purchasing:** Sara Bowden *(Purchasing Manager)*
**Engineering:** sean Cayley *(Engineering Manager)*
**US SIC:** 1731 **UK SIC:** 50300
**Auditors:** Muras Baker Jones
**Bankers:** Lloyds TSB Bank plc (30-99-06)

| | 31-01-14 | 31-01-13 | 31-01-12 |
|---|---|---|---|
| TO | 15,598,064 | 15,074,996 | 21,083,219 |
| P/L | 252,367 | (20,668) | 489,486 |
| NW | 3,348,919 | 3,098,114 | 3,053,027 |
| WC | 1,801,539 | 1,355,776 | 1,053,678 |
| Emp. | 167 | 199 | 233 |

DUNS 42-340-4883 Imp-Exp
## Power Plastics Ltd
Station Road, Thirsk, North Yorkshire YO7 1PZ
**Tel:** 01845525503 **Fax:** 01845-525485
**Web:** www.powerplastics.biz
**Reg No:** 4328236 **Estd:** 2001 Private Limited Company
**Line of Business:** Polythene sheeting supplies
**Issued Capital:** £34,000
**Directors:** A J Beetles, J A Fawcett, S J Price
**Co. Secretary:** Ms Karen Stead
**Responsibilities**
**Senior:** Phil Sellers *(Technical Manager)*
**Finance:** Pauline Walker *(Accounts Manager)*
**IT:** Lyn MacAulay *(Computer Manager)*, Phil Sellers *(Technical Manager)*
**Engineering:** Phil Sellers *(Technical Manager)*
**US SIC:** 2821, 2394
**UK SIC:** 25140, 45560

| | 31-03-14 | 31-03-13 | 31-03-12 |
|---|---|---|---|
| TA | 1,965,554 | 1,686,632 | 1,430,520 |
| NW | 761,250 | 731,592 | 613,896 |
| WC | 479,924 | 530,162 | 441,604 |

DUNS 76-985-6287
## Power Tecnique Ltd
Unit 4 Concorde Close, Fareham, Hampshire PO15 5RT
**Tel:** 01489-560700
**Web:** www.powertecnique.com
**Reg No:** 2643516 **Estd:** 1991 Private Limited Company
**Line of Business:** Sales and servicing of generators
**Export Sales:** £745,353
**Issued Capital:** £56,000
**Directors:** P J Chai-Tsai, D E Pearce, Dr J M Blackman, T J Pettifor
**Co. Secretary:** Dr James Blackman
**Responsibilities**
**Marketing:** Owen McIntyre *(Head of Marketing)*
**IT:** Alan Blair *(Head of IT)*
**US SIC:** 3621 **UK SIC:** 34201
**Auditors:** Spofforths LLP

| | 30-09-13 | 30-09-12 | 30-09-11 |
|---|---|---|---|
| TO | 7,866,644 | 8,877,970 | 7,616,906 |
| P/L | 596,196 | 556,365 | 7,363 |
| NW | 63,022 | (480,333) | (972,071) |
| WC | 36,446 | 115,777 | 236,416 |
| Emp. | 57 | 48 | 51 |

DUNS 21-826-1907 **Imp-Exp**

## Power Torque Engineering Ltd

27 Herald Way, Binley Industrial Estate, Binley Industrial Estate, Coventry, West Midlands CV3 2RQ
**Tel:** 02476635757 **Fax:** 024-7663-5878
**Web:** www.powertorque.co.uk
**Reg No:** 0217422 **VAT No:** 272517361
**Estd:** 1919 Private Limited Company
**Line of Business:** Manufacture of engines and turbines, except aircraft, vehicle and cycle engines
**Export Markets:** Poland, Germany, Italy, U S A, Holland, South America
**Export Sales:** £1,472,744
**Issued Capital:** £83,333
**Principals:** J Varney *(Chairman)*, A Varney *(Managing)*, N Haycock, D Varney, P Varney, J Townley
**Branches:** Power Torque Engineering Ltd, Hinckley Rd, Nuneaton, Warwickshire CV11 6LF
**US SIC:** 3519 **UK SIC:** 32811
**Auditors:** Daferns
**Bankers:** National Westminster Bank Plc (54-41-00)

| | 30-04-14 | 30-04-13 | 30-04-12 |
|---|---|---|---|
| TO | 12,145,220 | 12,377,518 | 11,857,616 |
| P/L | 509,980 | 901,504 | 506,783 |
| NW | 5,270,166 | 4,805,923 | 4,427,577 |
| WC | 3,510,535 | 3,237,271 | 2,428,073 |
| Emp. | 56 | 56 | 63 |

DUNS 23-786-0361 **Exp**

## Power Utilities (Holdings) Ltd

Queen Street, Premier Business Park, Walsall, West Midlands WS2 9QE
**Tel:** 01922-720561
**Web:** www.metaltechnique.com
**Reg No:** 3779053 **Estd:** 1999 Private Limited Company
**Line of Business:** Management activities of holding companies
**Export Sales:** £2,341,944
**Trading Style:** Power Utilities Group, Filterserve Aercon, Toolmarque, Metal Technique
**Issued Capital:** £12,322
**Director:** J N Gardner
**Co. Secretary:** Alexander Attwater
**Responsibilities**
**HR:** Alan Rimell *(Quality Manager)*
**Health & Safety:** Alan Rimell *(Quality Manager)*
**US SIC:** 6711 **UK SIC:** 83962
**Auditors:** BDO LLP

| | 31-12-13 | 31-12-12 | 31-12-11 |
|---|---|---|---|
| TO | 7,931,628 | 7,644,957 | 7,031,487 |
| P/L | 237,834 | 227,548 | 237,427 |
| NW | 3,345,301 | 3,151,271 | 3,263,668 |
| WC | 2,271,849 | 2,062,627 | 2,252,320 |
| Emp. | 50 | 49 | 48 |

DUNS 57-746-5958 **Imp**

## Powerball Ltd

(**Subsidiary of:** Leisuredyne Ltd)
Unit 7 Eastern Road Elliott Industrial, Park, Aldershot, Hampshire GU12 4TF
**Tel:** 01252-408550
**Web:** www.powerball.com
**Reg No:** 2885577 **Estd:** 1994 Private Limited Company
**Line of Business:** Other service activities not elsewhere classified
**Issued Capital:** £1,350,000
**Co. Secretary:** John Brudenell-Bruce
**Branches:** Powerball Ltd, The Turnpike, Turnpike Cl, Grantham, Lincolnshire NG31 7XU
**US SIC:** 8999, 7379
**UK SIC:** 83954, 83940
**Auditors:** Anson Gowing
**Bankers:** Barclays Bank Plc (20-61-82)

| | 31-01-13 | 31-01-12 | 31-01-11 |
|---|---|---|---|
| TA | 647,582 | 631,680 | 735,092 |
| NW | 185,221 | 276,540 | 324,646 |
| WC | 185,221 | 276,540 | 324,646 |

DUNS 29-105-7883 **Exp**

## Powerday P L C

Crossan House, 28-31 Hythe Road, London NW10 6RS
**Tel:** 02089604646 **Fax:** 020 8960 3110
**Web:** www.powerday.co.uk
**Reg No:** 1509382 **VAT No:** 340439377
**Estd:** 1980 Public Limited Company
**Line of Business:** Collection and treatment of other waste
**Issued Capital:** £50,100
**Principals:** M R Crossan *(Managing)*, M L Bensted, J J Naughton
**Co. Secretary:** Michael Crossan
**Responsibilities**
**HR:** Fred Cogger *(Operations Manager)*
**US SIC:** 4953 **UK SIC:** 92110
**Auditors:** Brebners
**Bankers:** Allied Irish Bank (gb) (23-84-00)

| | 31-07-14 | 31-07-13 | 31-07-12 |
|---|---|---|---|
| TO | 41,683,166 | 37,295,831 | 31,204,922 |
| P/L | 3,853,522 | 7,110,177 | 6,050,309 |
| NW | 29,736,247 | 26,037,039 | 20,963,720 |
| WC | 33,413,451 | 10,942,777 | 8,025,035 |
| Emp. | 173 | 119 | 112 |

DUNS 21-607-3116

## Powerfield

Lyme Building Westmere Drive, Crewe Business Park, Crewe, Cheshire CW1 6ZD
**Tel:** 01270411500
**Web:** www.specialistengines.com
**Estd:** 2003
**Line of Business:** Military equipment dealers
**Proprietor:** P Kettle
**US SIC:** 5999 **UK SIC:** 65600
**Employees:** 87

DUNS 23-876-5965

## Powerleague Fives Ltd

(**Subsidiary of:** Coimbra Ltd)
Anchor Grounds, Blackhall Street, Paisley, Renfrewshire PA1 1TD
**Tel:** 0141-887-7758
**Web:** www.powerleague.co.uk
**Reg No:** 3867954 **Estd:** 1995 Private Limited Company
**Line of Business:** Sports clubs
**Export Sales:** £380,000
**Issued Capital:** £27,200
**Director:** S Tracey
**Co. Secretary:** Mrs Sheena Beckwith
**Responsibilities**
**Senior:** Jordan Mcgarvie *(Senior Manager)*, Jill Penman *(Sales & Marketing Manager)*
**Marketing:** Jill Penman *(Sales & Marketing Manager)*
**Sales:** Gillian Alexander *(Sales Director)*, Jill Penman *(Sales & Marketing Manager)*
**IT:** Kenny Green *(IT Manager)*
**Branches:** Powerleague Fives Ltd, Powerleague Group Ltd, 10 Westbank Street, Edinburgh, Midlothian EH15 1DR
**US SIC:** 7941, 6552
**UK SIC:** 97911, 85000
**Auditors:** Ernst & Young LLP
**Bankers:** Bank Of Scotland (80-29-10)

| | 28-12-13 | 29-12-12 | 31-12-11 |
|---|---|---|---|
| TO | 29,756,000 | 28,313,000 | 29,097,000 |
| P/L | (717,000) | (3,691,000) | (4,522,000) |
| NW | (14,060,000) | (15,331,000) | (10,734,000) |
| WC | 1,229,000 | (575,000) | 1,913,000 |
| Emp. | 793 | 617 | 634 |

DUNS 34-576-9645

## Powerleague Group Ltd

(**Subsidiary of:** Coimbra Ltd)
31 Pursley Road, Mill Hill, London NW7 2BB
**Tel:** 02082011200 **Fax:** 02089068408
**Web:** www.powerleague.co.uk
**Reg No:** 5384840 **Estd:** 1998 Private Limited Company
**Line of Business:** Other sporting activities not elsewhere classified
**Export Sales:** £380,000
**Issued Capital:** £8,182,000
**Directors:** N J Hargreaves, J B Gordon, S E Law, K Breslauer, A W Hill, S Tracey
**Co. Secretary:** Mrs Sheena Beckwith
**Responsibilities**
**Senior:** Paul Orchard-Lisle *(Manager)*, Ruth Rensburg *(Manager)*
**Branches:** Powerleague Group Ltd, Aldenham Road, Bushey, Hertfordshire WD23 2TY
**US SIC:** 7999 **UK SIC:** 97913
**Auditors:** Ernst & Young LLP
**Bankers:** HSBC Bank plc (40-22-47)

| | 28-12-13 | 29-12-12 | 31-12-11 |
|---|---|---|---|
| TO | 29,756,000 | 28,313,000 | 29,097,000 |
| P/L | (661,000) | (3,635,000) | (4,468,000) |
| NW | (2,931,000) | (4,197,000) | 344,000 |
| WC | 1,216,000 | (574,000) | 2,369,000 |
| Emp. | 797 | 621 | 638 |

DUNS 58-068-8521

## Powermann Ltd

(**Subsidiary of:** Schneider Electric Sa)
204 Cavendish Place, Birchwood, Warrington, Cheshire WA3 6WU
**Tel:** 01925845900
**Web:** www.schneider-electric.com
**Reg No:** 2905620 **Estd:** 1990 Private Limited Company
**Line of Business:** Manufacturers of electrical switchgear
**Trading Style:** Schneider Electric Ltd
**Issued Capital:** £2
**Directors:** T Lambeth, Mrs C A Sands
**Co. Secretary:** Invensys Secretaries Limited
**Responsibilities**
**Senior:** James Huntley *(General Manager)*, Thomas Lavin *(Services Director)*, Philippe Samama *(Manager)*, Maurice Williams *(Manager)*
**US SIC:** 8911 **UK SIC:** 83701

| | 31-12-13 | 31-12-12 | 31-12-11 |
|---|---|---|---|
| TA | 2,000 | 2,000 | 2,000 |
| NW | 2,000 | 2,000 | 2,000 |

DUNS 73-851-1521 **Imp**

## Powerperfector Ltd

(**Subsidiary of:** Powerperfector Group Ltd)
1-10 Praed Mews, London W2 1QY
**Tel:** 02072626004 **Fax:** 084-560-14724
**Web:** www.powerperfector.com
**Reg No:** 5106220 **VAT No:** 840679507
**Estd:** 2004 Private Limited Company
**Line of Business:** Energy conservation consultants
**Export Sales:** £4,110,218
**Issued Capital:** £48,803
**Directors:** Mrs T S Robertson-Lambert, A Robertson, M J Robertson-Lambert
**Responsibilities**
**Senior:** Jamie Buchanan *(Chief Executive Officer)*
**US SIC:** 7392 **UK SIC:** 83951
**Auditors:** Horwath Clark Whitehill LLP

| | 31-03-13 | 31-03-12 | 31-03-11 |
|---|---|---|---|
| TO | 21,334,682 | 23,479,605 | 32,702,647 |
| P/L | (3,182,340) | (1,179,104) | 1,895,029 |
| NW | (6,363,102) | (4,682,462) | 9,173,161 |
| WC | (141,359) | 4,261,754 | 8,977,698 |
| Emp. | 77 | 83 | 85 |

DUNS 21-734-7046

## Powersystems U K Ltd

Unit 1 Badminton Road Trading Estate, Bristol, Avon BS37 5GG
**Web:** www.powersystemsuk.co.uk
**Reg No:** 1534161 **VAT No:** 140646780
**Estd:** 1980 Private Limited Company
**Line of Business:** Engineers (general)
**Issued Capital:** £5,000
**Directors:** C A Jenkins, D C Earby, S J Wilsmore
**Co. Secretary:** Eirwyn Thomas
**Responsibilities**
**Health & Safety:** Nick Coles *(Health & Safety Manager)*
**Operations:** Mark Tanner *(Project Engineer)*
**Branches:** Powersystems U K Ltd, Unit 8, Castle St, Stafford, Staffordshire ST16 2TB
**US SIC:** 8911 **UK SIC:** 83701
**Auditors:** Burton Sweet
**Bankers:** National Westminster Bank Plc (55-61-38)

| | 31-12-13 | 31-12-12 | 31-12-11 |
|---|---|---|---|
| TO | 34,439,721 | 23,729,844 | 15,002,132 |
| P/L | 5,674,905 | 2,932,511 | 1,334,450 |
| NW | 11,160,795 | 7,202,283 | 5,196,485 |
| WC | 9,828,345 | 5,988,394 | 4,168,025 |
| Emp. | 70 | 59 | 50 |

DUNS 50-445-1196 **Exp**

## Powertherm Contract Services Ltd.

52 Orgreave Drive, Sheffield, South Yorkshire S13 9NR
**Tel:** 01142-889119
**Web:** www.powerthermcontracts.co.uk
**Reg No:** 2432954 **VAT No:** 533879314
**Estd:** 1989 Private Limited Company
**Line of Business:** Insulation installers
**Export Markets:** China
**Issued Capital:** £334
**Principals:** C Ashton *(Technical)*, P A Ashton, M A Ashton
**Co. Secretary:** George Cottrill
**Responsibilities**
**Finance:** David Binstead *(Accounts Manager)*
**US SIC:** 1742 **UK SIC:** 50400
**Auditors:** Kay Johnson Gee
**Bankers:** National Westminster Bank Plc (01-02-02)

| | 31-10-13 | 31-10-12 | 31-10-11 |
|---|---|---|---|
| TO | 7,333,587 | N/A | N/A |
| P/L | 491,532 | N/A | N/A |
| NW | 898,226 | 606,678 | 472,337 |
| WC | 652,718 | 484,579 | 348,427 |
| Emp. | 107 | N/A | N/A |

DUNS 21-671-6183 **Imp-Exp**

## Powrmatic Ltd

(**Subsidiary of:** Stamm International Inc)
Hort Bridge, Ilminster, Somerset TA19 9PS
**Tel:** 0146-053535
**Web:** www.powrmatic.co.uk
**Reg No:** 0657482 **VAT No:** 291040779
**Estd:** 1960 Private Limited Company
**Line of Business:** Ventilation systems
**Export Markets:** European Union (E U); Middle East
**Export Sales:** £1,840,521
**Trading Style:** Powrmatic Ltd
**Issued Capital:** £1,753
**Principals:** A Stamm *(Chairman)*, P A Brompton, Ms M Skony Stamm
**Co. Secretary:** Arthur Stamm
**Responsibilities**
**Facilities:** Mike Newbury *(Facilities Manager)*
**Branches:** Powrmatic Ltd, High Street, Grantham, Lincolnshire NG33 4HW
**US SIC:** 3585, 3441
**UK SIC:** 32841, 32042
**Auditors:** KPMG
**Bankers:** Barclays Bank Plc (20-99-40)

| | 30-06-14 | 30-06-13 | 30-06-12 |
|---|---|---|---|
| TO | 10,482,673 | 9,614,069 | 8,663,925 |
| P/L | 831,145 | 616,235 | 207,052 |
| NW | 5,280,228 | 5,742,478 | 5,130,999 |
| WC | 3,777,950 | 4,315,585 | 3,848,125 |
| Emp. | 96 | 93 | 97 |

DUNS 23-508-4241

## Powys County Council

County Hall, Llandrindod Wells, Powys LD1 5LG
**Tel:** 08456027030
**Web:** www.powys.gov.uk
**Estd:** 1996
**Line of Business:** Local government
**Trading Style:** Childrens & Families & Lifelong Learning Difficulties, Heart of Wales Line
**Director:** J Tonge
**Responsibilities**
**Senior:** Julie Nicholas-Humphreys *(Line Manager)*
**Finance:** Geoff Petty *(County Treasurer)*
**IT:** Nick Philpott *(Computer Manager)*
**Health & Safety:** Steve Cadwallader-Jones *(Head of Health & Safety)*, Bridget Farrington *(Area Road Safety Officer)*
**Facilities:** Terry Flynn *(Affordable Housing Officer)*
**Operations:** Rob Beardall *(Production and Operations Mana)*
**Fleet:** Anne Wozencraft *(Principal Officer, School Tran)*
**Branches:** Powys County Council, Rhayader Leisure Centre, North Street, Rhayader, Powys LD6 5BU
**US SIC:** 9121 **UK SIC:** 91110
**Bankers:** HSBC Bank plc (40-30-05)
**Employees:** 480

DUNS 23-599-8655

## Powys Healthcare N H S Trust

(**Subsidiary of:** The Wales Office)
Mansion House, Bronllys, Brecon, Powys LD3 0LS
**Web:** www.powyslhb.wales.nhs.uk
**Estd:** 1986
**Line of Business:** Representative office
**Issued Capital:** £1
**Directors:** A Coffey, M Woodford
**Responsibilities**
**Senior:** Bob Hudson *(Chief Executive)*
**Branches:** Powys Healthcare N H S Trust, 5 Lion Street, Brecon, Powys LD3 7AU
**US SIC:** 7399 **UK SIC:** 83954
**Employees:** 2,200

DUNS 76-559-9758 **Exp**

## Poyry Management Consulting (Uk) Ltd

(**Subsidiary of:** Pöyry Oyj)
King Charles House, Park End Street, Oxford, Oxfordshire OX1 1JD
**Web:** www.poyry.com
**Reg No:** 2573801 **Estd:** 2005 Private Limited Company
**Line of Business:** Management and business consultants
**Export Sales:** £8,846,000
**Issued Capital:** £162,350
**Principals:** A A Morris *(Managing)*, J T Sairanen, M Brown, P Hare
**Co. Secretary:** Tmf Corporate Administration Ser
**Responsibilities**
**Senior:** Larry Londo *(President)*, Wendy Warrick *(Business Manager)*
**Sales:** Wendy Warrick *(Business Manager)*
**Admin:** Wendy Warrick *(Business Manager)*
**IT:** Rakesh Baryia *(Uk Service Delivery Manager)*, Sanjay Tinani *(IT Manager)*
**HR:** Wendy Warrick *(Business Manager)*
**Health & Safety:** Wendy Warrick *(Business Manager)*
**Facilities:** Wendy Warrick *(Business Manager)*
**Operations:** Paul Oberleitner *(Head of Hydropower Plants Depa)*
**Engineering:** Brian Borin *(Senior Mechanical Engineer)*
**US SIC:** 7392 **UK SIC:** 83951
**Auditors:** KPMG LLP
**Bankers:** Lloyds TSB Bank plc (30-96-35)

| | 31-12-13 | 31-12-12 | 31-12-11 |
|---|---|---|---|
| TO | 16,255,546 | 15,629,592 | 12,041,934 |
| P/L | 2,029,788 | 2,356,549 | 1,788,541 |
| NW | 4,337,115 | 3,725,226 | 2,005,077 |
| WC | 4,116,770 | 3,278,877 | 1,325,041 |
| Emp. | 109 | 97 | 69 |

DUNS 21-033-9434

## Pozition

135-141 George Street, Hull, North Humberside HU1 3BN
**Tel:** 01482323643
**Web:** www.pozition.co.uk
**Proprietorship**
**Line of Business:** Managed public houses and bars
**Responsibilities**
**Senior:** Carole Bratley *(Financial Controller)*
**US SIC:** 5813, 5812
**UK SIC:** 66200, 66110
**Employees:** 50

DUNS 36-490-2283

## Pozzoni Design Group

Woodville House, 2 Woodville Road, Altrincham, Cheshire WA14 2FH
**Web:** www.pozzoni.co.uk
**Estd:** 1973 Partnership
**Line of Business:** Architects
**Principals:** D Hughes *(Partner)*, P Pozzoni
**Responsibilities**
**Marketing:** Kerry Fairhurst *(Marketing Manager)*
**HR:** Jane Mahon *(Human Resources Manager)*
**US SIC:** 8911 **UK SIC:** 83701
**Employees:** 60

DUNS 21-201-5663

## Ppg Architectural Coatings Uk Ltd

(**Subsidiary of:** Ppg Industries Inc.)
Huddersfield Road, Birstall, Batley, West Yorkshire WF17 9XA
**Tel:** 01924-354-000 **Fax:** 0128082142
**Web:** www.ppg.com
**Reg No:** 0436135 **Estd:** 1977 Private Limited Company
**Line of Business:** Manufacture of paints, varnishes and similar coatings, printing ink and mastics
**Issued Capital:** £350,000
**Directors:** M J Hollingworth, S Pocock, G Roebuck, P Lafford, P Dowie, J P Metcalf, R Hemingway, V O'Sullivan
**Co. Secretary:** Ms Claire Sherwood
**Responsibilities**
**Senior:** Matthew Baines *(Senior Marketing Executive)*, P Evan *(Manager)*, Greg Molymeux *(Manager)*, Felicity Parry *(Director)*
**Finance:** Felicity Parry *(Director)*
**Marketing:** Matthew Baines *(Senior Marketing Executive)*, Kelly Quaramby *(Senior Marketing Manager)*
**Branches:** Ppg Architectural Coatings Uk Ltd, A1-A3, Unit A1, Newcastle Upon Tyne, Tyne and Wear NE2 1AH
**US SIC:** 2851 **UK SIC:** 25510
**Auditors:** PricewaterhouseCoopers LLP
**Bankers:** Lloyds TSB Bank plc (30-00-05)

| | 31-12-13 | 31-12-12 | 31-12-11 |
|---|---|---|---|
| TO | 200,650,000 | 196,244,000 | 181,495,000 |
| P/L | 1,853,000 | 5,684,000 | 1,507,000 |
| NW | 103,440,000 | 92,421,000 | 87,288,000 |
| WC | 87,405,000 | 63,983,000 | 58,566,000 |
| Emp. | 1,454 | 1,544 | 1,689 |

DUNS 39-030-7635 **Imp**

## Ppg Industries (Uk) Ltd

(**Subsidiary of:** Ppg Industries Inc.)
Needham Road, Stowmarket, Suffolk IP14 2AD
**Tel:** 01449613161 **Fax:** 01449-677161
**Web:** www.ppg.com
**Reg No:** 2110620 **VAT No:** 559013248
**Estd:** 1950 Private Limited Company
**Line of Business:** Manufacture of paints, varnishes and similar coatings
**Export Sales:** £50,411,000
**Trading Style:** Ppg
**Issued Capital:** £65,000,000
**Directors:** Ms S Clarkson, M S Broome, C R Turner, G Davies, J K Ramsey, P Dowie, B K Stewart
**Co. Secretary:** Pinsent Masons Secretarial Limit
**Responsibilities**
**Senior:** Richard Cawthorpe *(Manager)*, Michael Clews *(Financial Manager)*, Richard Denison *(General Manager - UK and Irela)*, Craig Osbourne *(Warehouse Manager)*, Pedro Perez *(Site Manager)*, David Vigus *(Manager)*
**Finance:** Michael Clews *(Financial Manager)*
**Sales:** David Vigus *(Manager)*
**IT:** Katie Squirrel *(Head of IT)*
**HR:** Lisa Santillo *(Human Resources Manager)*
**Health & Safety:** Andrew Coxhead *(Health & Safety Officer)*
**Facilities:** Pedro Perez *(Site Manager)*
**Purchasing:** Kevin Wejknis *(Purchasing Manager)*
**Engineering:** Pedro Perez *(Site Manager)*, Mick Pugh *(Maintenance Manager)*, Clyde Stanford *(Production Manager)*
**Branches:** Ppg Industries (Uk) Ltd, West Wing Trigate 210-222, Hagley Road West, Oldbury, West Midlands B68 0NP
**US SIC:** 2851, 7399
**UK SIC:** 25510, 83954
**Auditors:** Deloitte LLP
**Bankers:** HSBC Bank plc (40-11-18)

| | 31-12-13 | 31-12-12 | 31-12-11 |
|---|---|---|---|
| TO | 149,516,000 | 151,350,000 | 149,573,000 |
| P/L | 1,158,000 | 3,308,000 | 4,634,000 |
| NW | (13,008,000) | (6,515,000) | 2,815,000 |
| WC | (8,471,000) | 17,919,000 | 22,442,000 |
| Emp. | 900 | 910 | 899 |

DUNS 34-860-3957

## Ppi Claimline Ltd

(**Subsidiary of:** Consumer Champion Group Ltd)
1 Olympic Way, Wembley, Middlesex HA9 0NP
**Tel:** 02076248353
**Web:** www.ppiclaimline.com
**Reg No:** 5659020 **Estd:** 2005 Private Limited Company
**Line of Business:** Other business activities not elsewhere classified
**Trading Style:** Ppi Claimline Limited
**Issued Capital:** £1,000,134
**Directors:** J E Scarth, S K Astley-Stone
**Co. Secretary:** James Scarth
**Responsibilities**
**Senior:** Kristi Flax *(Manager)*, James Kafton *(Manager)*, John Merry *(Manager)*, Samantha Porteous *(Manager)*
**US SIC:** 7399 **UK SIC:** 83954

| | 31-12-13 | 31-12-12 | 31-12-11 |
|---|---|---|---|
| TO | 12,245,000 | 15,976,000 | 3,286,000 |
| P/L | 1,822,000 | (1,744,000) | (1,507,000) |
| NW | (450,000) | (2,343,000) | (599,000) |
| WC | (546,000) | (2,520,000) | (700,000) |
| Emp. | 148 | 151 | 30 |

DUNS 50-694-8603

## Ppiaf

Linden House, 55 South Bar Street, Banbury, Oxfordshire OX16 9AB
**Tel:** 01295-752240
**Web:** www.adoptionuk.org
**VAT No:** 795034217 **Estd:** 2004 Proprietorship
**Line of Business:** Non-charitable social work activities without accommodation
**Director:** J Pearce
**Responsibilities**
**Admin:** Louise Beswick *(Administrator)*
**Branches:** Adoption Uk, 25 Randals Town Rd, Antrim, Co Antrim BT41 4LD
**US SIC:** 8321 **UK SIC:** 96111
**Employees:** 50

DUNS 22-249-5421

## Ppl Ww Holdings Ltd

(**Subsidiary of:** Ppl Corporation)
Avonbank, Bristol, Avon BS2 0TB
**Tel:** 01179-332000
**Web:** www.westernpower.co.uk
**Reg No:** 4267536 **Estd:** 1989 Private Limited Company
**Line of Business:** Management activities of holding companies
**Trading Style:** Western Power Distribution Private Limited Company
**Issued Capital:** £55,017,007
**Directors:** R A Symons, V Sorgi, P Swift, R L Klingensmith, M F Wilten, D C Oosthuizen, S K Breininger, A J Torok
**Co. Secretary:** Ms Sally Jones
**Responsibilities**
**IT:** Roger Smale *(Senior Support Manager)*
**Operations:** Bev Escott *(Compliance Manager)*
**US SIC:** 6711 **UK SIC:** 83962

| | 31-03-14 | 31-03-13 | 31-03-12 |
|---|---|---|---|
| TO | 677,700,000 | 609,600,000 | 570,100,000 |
| P/L | 308,700,000 | 297,900,000 | 282,300,000 |
| NW | 762,300,000 | 552,700,000 | 489,300,000 |
| WC | 5,300,000 | 19,200,000 | 24,700,000 |
| Emp. | 2,579 | 2,634 | 2,582 |

DUNS 77-541-4196

## P.P.S. Electrical Ltd

(**Subsidiary of:** Renew Holdings Plc.)
187-191 Duke Street, Barrow-In-Furness, Cumbria LA14 1XS
**Tel:** 01229-433838
**Web:** http://ppselectrical.co.uk
**Reg No:** 2996150 **Estd:** 1994 Private Limited Company
**Line of Business:** Electrical engineers
**Trading Style:** P.P.S. Electrical Ltd
**Issued Capital:** £50
**Directors:** P Scott, N P Houghton, J P Mcbain, Renew Corporate Director Limited
**Co. Secretary:** Renew Nominees Limited
**US SIC:** 8911 **UK SIC:** 83701
**Auditors:** RSM Robson Rhodes LLP
**Bankers:** Barclays Bank Plc (20-59-42)

| | 30-09-14 | 30-09-13 | 30-09-12 |
|---|---|---|---|
| TO | 22,480,000 | 14,904,000 | 10,667,000 |
| P/L | 1,392,000 | 450,000 | (131,000) |
| NW | 2,729,000 | 1,335,000 | 924,000 |
| WC | 2,646,000 | 1,212,000 | 755,000 |
| Emp. | 199 | 168 | 147 |

DUNS 50-472-2562

## Pps (Local & Regional) Ltd

(**Subsidiary of:** Pps Group Ltd)
Langham House, 302-308 Regent Street, London W1B 3AT
**Tel:** 02075291700
**Web:** www.localism.co.uk
**Reg No:** 2451155 **Estd:** 1989 Private Limited Company
**Line of Business:** Public relations consultants
**Trading Style:** P P S
**Issued Capital:** £50,500
**Directors:** S K Byfield, G J Golembiewski, D E Wright
**Branches:** Pps (Local & Regional) Ltd, Hanover House, Manchester M1 4SD
**US SIC:** 7392 **UK SIC:** 83951
**Auditors:** Magee Gammon Corporate Ltd

| | 30-04-14 | 30-04-13 | 30-04-12 |
|---|---|---|---|
| TO | 5,281,172 | 4,730,474 | 5,374,694 |
| P/L | 788,277 | 130,896 | 476,853 |
| NW | 2,631,348 | 2,427,591 | 2,430,309 |
| WC | 2,438,842 | 2,215,365 | 2,221,770 |

DUNS 21-102-7273 **Imp**

## Pq Silicas Uk Ltd

4 Liverpool Road, Warrington, Cheshire WA5 1AQ
**Tel:** 01925416100
**Reg No:** 6458647 **Estd:** 2007 Private Limited Company
**Line of Business:** Manufacture of other chemical products not elsewhere classified
**Export Sales:** £50,069,000
**Issued Capital:** £44,578,066
**Director:** A F Mcilroy
**Co. Secretary:** William Sichko
**US SIC:** 2899 **UK SIC:** 25670
**Auditors:** PricewaterhouseCoopers LLP
**Bankers:** Barclays Bank Plc (20-00-00)

| | 31-12-13 | 31-12-12 | 31-12-11 |
|---|---|---|---|
| TO | 65,359,000 | 59,195,000 | 64,001,000 |
| P/L | 5,874,000 | 1,443,000 | (1,719,000) |
| NW | 14,801,000 | 11,154,000 | (6,728,000) |
| WC | 21,216,000 | 15,604,000 | 11,990,000 |
| Emp. | 240 | 247 | 249 |

DUNS 73-354-9617

## Pr Books Ltd

2 Mealbank Mill Industrial Estat, Kendal, Cumbria LA8 9DL
**Tel:** 01539733332
**Web:** www.lakelandbooks.com
**Reg No:** 4628539 **Estd:** 2003 Private Limited Company
**Line of Business:** Book retailers
**Export Sales:** £1,354,527
**Issued Capital:** £100
**Directors:** M Farrar, P Farrar
**Co. Secretary:** Mrs Ruth Farrar
**Responsibilities**
**Senior:** Lisa Wridley *(Manager)*
**US SIC:** 5942, 5199
**UK SIC:** 65300, 61900
**Auditors:** CLB Coopers
**Bankers:** Svenska Handelsbanken Ab (publ) (40-51-62)

| | 31-01-14 | 31-01-13 | 31-01-12 |
|---|---|---|---|
| TO | 6,587,432 | 7,434,227 | 7,579,678 |
| P/L | 43,588 | 141,333 | 177,352 |
| NW | 1,637,368 | 1,595,866 | 1,599,943 |
| WC | 1,759,514 | 2,066,782 | 2,021,360 |
| Emp. | 116 | 116 | 112 |

DUNS 28-990-2801

## Pr Entertainments Ltd

5 Hill Rise, Richmond, Surrey TW10 6UQ
**Tel:** 020-8332-7388
**Web:** www.barestilo.co.uk
**Reg No:** 1818658 **Estd:** 1984 Private Limited Company
**Line of Business:** Restaurants
**Issued Capital:** £1,000
**Principals:** D T Charalambous *(Managing)*, Ms C Whelan
**Co. Secretary:** Mrs Christine Page
**Responsibilities**
**Admin:** Kelly Hollands *(Office Manager)*
**Branches:** Pr Entertainments Ltd, 5 Hill Rise, Richmond, Surrey TW10 6UQ
**US SIC:** 7399, 5813
**UK SIC:** 83954, 66200
**Auditors:** Hawkins Scott
**Bankers:** The Bank Of Ireland (30-11-55)

| | 31-05-13 | 31-05-12 | 31-05-11 |
|---|---|---|---|
| TO | 8,137,816 | 8,415,262 | 8,319,352 |
| P/L | (159,283) | 59,963 | (27,754) |
| NW | 2,380,095 | 2,271,805 | 2,319,793 |
| WC | (206,225) | (1,300,464) | (1,532,436) |
| Emp. | 186 | 175 | 206 |

DUNS 22-710-3686 **Exp**

## Pr Newswire Europe Ltd

(**Subsidiary of:** Maypond Ltd)
209-215 Blackfriars Road, London SE1 8NL
**Tel:** 020-7490-8111 **Fax:** 02074545331
**Web:** www.prnewswire.co.uk
**Reg No:** 1543272 **VAT No:** 480860826
**Estd:** 1981 Private Limited Company
**Line of Business:** Management activities of holding companies
**Issued Capital:** £2,229,874
**Directors:** Crosswall Nominees Limited, C H Gregson, K Burgess, Ms L Ashworth, P O Page, B L Leask, Unm Investments Limited
**Co. Secretary:** Crosswall Nominees Limited
**Responsibilities**
**Marketing:** Imogen Powell *(Marketing Manager)*
**US SIC:** 6711 **UK SIC:** 83962
**Auditors:** Ernst & Young LLP
**Bankers:** Lloyds TSB Bank plc (30-00-04)

| | 31-12-13 | 31-12-12 | 31-12-11 |
|---|---|---|---|
| TO | 21,734,000 | 20,975,000 | 19,650,000 |
| P/L | 2,818,000 | 4,575,000 | 1,217,000 |
| NW | 90,921,000 | 88,050,000 | 83,288,000 |
| WC | 88,744,000 | 85,536,000 | 80,365,000 |
| Emp. | 176 | 173 | 163 |

DUNS 49-486-3830

## P.R. Offshore Services Ltd

5a Barnards Way Quay View Business Park, Lowestoft, Suffolk NR32 2HD
**Tel:** 01502532530 **Fax:** 01502532539
**Web:** www.proffshoreservices.com
**Reg No:** 3151258 **Estd:** 1995 Private Limited Company
**Line of Business:** Labour recruitment and provision of personnel
**Issued Capital:** £3,000
**Principals:** Mrs P J Reid *(Managing)*, P R Reid, Ms J Y Beales
**Co. Secretary:** Patrick Utting
**Responsibilities**
**Finance:** Claire Clements *(Accounts Assistant)*, Lisa Page *(Accounts Assistant)*
**HR:** Marie Owen *(Recruitment Consultant)*, Steph Strowger *(Recruitment Assistant)*
**US SIC:** 7361 **UK SIC:** 83954
**Auditors:** Bloomfield & Co
**Bankers:** HSBC Bank plc (40-30-28)

| | 31-03-14 | 31-03-13 | 31-03-12 |
|---|---|---|---|
| TO | 15,050,012 | 14,900,763 | N/A |
| P/L | 787,799 | 1,012,688 | N/A |
| NW | 2,203,860 | 1,897,654 | 1,412,978 |
| WC | 1,952,252 | 1,656,369 | 1,213,161 |
| Emp. | 53 | 45 | N/A |

DUNS 21-815-9060

## Pra U.K. Holding Pty Ltd

C/O 7side Secretarial Limited, 14-18 City Road, Cardiff, South Glamorgan CF24 3DL
**Tel:** 01563556411
**Web:** www.portfoliorecovery.co.uk
**Reg No:** 7890150 **Estd:** 2011 Private Limited Company
**Line of Business:** Activities auxiliary to financial intermediation not elsewhere classified
**Issued Capital:** £200
**Directors:** Ms M R Hall, Ms J Scott
**Co. Secretary:** 7side Secretarial Limited
**US SIC:** 6111 **UK SIC:** 81501

| | 31-12-13 | 31-12-12 |
|---|---|---|
| TA | 45,204,000 | 42,843,000 |
| P/L | (3,255,000) | (2,772,000) |
| NW | (21,696,000) | (21,711,000) |
| WC | (10,171,000) | (6,197,000) |
| Emp. | 230 | 184 |

DUNS 21-865-5378

## Pra U.K. Management Services Ltd

14-18 City Road, Cardiff, South Glamorgan CF24 3DL
**Tel:** 01563556430
**Web:** www.mackenziehall.co.uk
**Reg No:** 8266212 **Estd:** 2012 Private Limited Company
**Line of Business:** Credit reporting and collection agency activities
**Issued Capital:** £1
**Directors:** Ms M F Link, N A Petrovich, Ms M R Hall, M J Petit
**Co. Secretary:** 7side Secretarial Limited
**US SIC:** 7399 **UK SIC:** 83954

| | 31-12-13 |
|---|---|
| TO | 5,653,924 |
| NW | (48,326) |
| WC | (913,401) |
| Emp. | 230 |

DUNS 22-722-5513 **Imp-Exp**

## Practical Action

The Schumacher Centre, Bourton, Rugby, Warwickshire CV23 9QZ
**Tel:** 01926-634400
**Web:** www.practicalaction.org
**Reg No:** 0871954 **VAT No:** 241515492
**Estd:** 1966 Private Company Limited By Guarantee

**Line of Business:** Social work activities without accommodation
**Trading Style:** Practical Action
**Directors:** Ms V Walford, I Khan, Ms H Molyneux, P L Turner, R N Saxby-Soffe, Dr M E Chadwick, D N Haslam, J A Walker
**Co. Secretary:** Mrs Patricia Adey
**Responsibilities**
**Senior:** Mahmood Hassan *(Trustee)*, Brenda Lipson *(Director)*, Ruth Mcneil *(Trustee)*, Toby Milner *(Proprietor)*, Paul Smith Lomas *(International Director)*
**Finance:** Mark Woodbridge *(Finance Director)*
**Marketing:** Clare Tawney *(Editor)*
**Operations:** Veena Khaleque *(Bangladesh Director)*
**US SIC:** 8321 **UK SIC:** 96111
**Auditors:** Horwath Clark Whitehill LLP
**Bankers:** Barclays Bank Plc (20-73-48)

| | 31-03-14 | 31-03-13 | 31-03-12 |
|---|---|---|---|
| TO | 30,252,000 | 26,237,000 | 30,871,000 |
| P/L | 2,428,000 | (1,280,000) | 1,148,000 |
| NW | 9,524,000 | 6,983,000 | 8,551,000 |
| WC | 4,531,000 | 2,519,000 | 3,381,000 |
| Emp. | 661 | 696 | 706 |

DUNS 34-888-1330
## The Practice (Group) Ltd
Bell Lane Office Village, Amersham, Buckinghamshire HP6 6FA
**Tel:** 01494690999
**Web:** www.thepracticeplc.com
**Reg No:** 5685937 **Estd:** 1988 Private Limited Company
**Line of Business:** Management activities of holding companies
**Issued Capital:** £2,451,267
**Directors:** R Hastings, Dr A Kadirgamar, A Johnson, A S Chan, B F Macfarlane, A D Black, Dr J D Rose, Sir W H Wells
**Co. Secretary:** Mrs Francine Godrich
**Responsibilities**
**Senior:** Wendy Kepetzis *(Proprietor)*
**Sales:** Justin Annett *(Sales Director)*
**Operations:** Jane Feierabend *(Operations Director)*
**US SIC:** 6711 **UK SIC:** 83962
**Auditors:** Nexia Smith & Williamson

| | 31-03-14 | 31-03-13 | 31-03-12 |
|---|---|---|---|
| TO | 28,522,144 | 33,742,018 | 35,554,711 |
| P/L | (736,362) | (2,652,685) | (5,814,581) |
| NW | (5,295,275) | (356,934) | 1,285,767 |
| WC | (4,555,920) | (2,400,152) | (3,938,226) |
| Emp. | 538 | 843 | 650 |

DUNS 34-661-9823
## Practice Plan Group (Holdings) Ltd
**(Subsidiary of:** Wesleyan Assurance Society)
Cambrian Works Gobowen Road, Oswestry, Shropshire SY11 1HS
**Tel:** 01691684120
**Web:** www.practiceplan.co.uk
**Reg No:** 5467316 **Estd:** 2005 Private Limited Company
**Line of Business:** Management activities of holding companies
**Issued Capital:** £2,838,476
**Directors:** J A Cawrey, A R Jessup, N K Jones, Ms Z E Denison, A J Darcy
**Co. Secretary:** Ms Zoe Denison
**US SIC:** 6711 **UK SIC:** 83962

| | 30-06-13 | 30-06-12 | 30-06-11 |
|---|---|---|---|
| TO | 7,314,432 | 7,201,395 | 7,479,655 |
| P/L | 3,195,438 | 2,754,966 | 3,305,337 |
| NW | (3,023,976) | (6,747,777) | (6,852,540) |
| WC | (2,519,878) | (5,751,761) | (5,690,018) |
| Emp. | 83 | 78 | 72 |

DUNS 21-113-9476
## The Practice Surgeries Ltd
Rose House, Bell Lane Office Village, Amersham, Buckinghamshire HP6 6FA
**Tel:** 01494690950
**Reg No:** 6545745 **Estd:** 2008 Private Limited Company
**Line of Business:** Medical practice activities
**Directors:** B F Macfarlane, Dr J D Rose, A Johnson, R Hastings, Ms C J Brinkley
**Co. Secretary:** Mrs Francine Godrich
**US SIC:** 8011 **UK SIC:** 95300

| | 31-03-14 | 31-03-13 | 31-03-12 |
|---|---|---|---|
| TO | 14,681,701 | 16,489,495 | 16,524,542 |
| P/L | 4,030,289 | (1,107,895) | (2,899,778) |
| NW | (523,362) | (4,557,845) | (3,454,144) |
| WC | (442,049) | (3,742,233) | (2,809,041) |
| Emp. | 270 | 402 | 232 |

DUNS 21-771-6127
## Practice Web
Bridge House 48-52, Baldwin Street, Bristol, Avon BS1 1QB
**Tel:** 01179158639
**Web:** www.practiceweb.co.uk
**Estd:** 2011
**Line of Business:** Computer software (development)
**US SIC:** 7379 **UK SIC:** 83940
**Employees:** 100

DUNS 21-785-8993
## Practicus
1 Temple Back, Bristol, Avon BS1 6FL
**Tel:** 01179221777
**Web:** www.practicus.co.uk
**Estd:** 2011 Proprietorship
**Line of Business:** Employment and recruitment companies and consultants
**Proprietor:** J Luckhurst
**Responsibilities**
**Senior:** Tom Bright *(Manager)*, Dave Wilcock *(Manager)*
**US SIC:** 7361 **UK SIC:** 83954
**Employees:** 70

DUNS 73-792-0913
## Practicus Ltd
Riverside Barns, Henley-On-Thames, Oxfordshire RG9 3DB
**Tel:** 01491-577122 **Fax:** 01491-579930
**Web:** www.practicus.co.uk
**Reg No:** 5048716 **VAT No:** 831564434
**Estd:** 2004 Private Limited Company
**Line of Business:** Management and business consultants
**Export Sales:** £5,402,000
**Issued Capital:** £270
**Directors:** P Wandless, D A Tolhurst, Mrs A Sheen, J W Luckhurst, S Bendall, D Bardoe-Pout, B A Kershaw
**Co. Secretary:** Rupert Hunte
**Responsibilities**
**Sales:** Lalit Kumar *(Commercial Manager)*
**US SIC:** 7392 **UK SIC:** 83951
**Auditors:** Grant Thornton UK LLP

| | 31-12-13 | 31-12-12 | 31-12-11 |
|---|---|---|---|
| TO | 40,538,000 | 36,733,000 | 30,587,000 |
| P/L | 430,000 | 1,009,000 | 483,000 |
| NW | (261,000) | 423,000 | (333,000) |
| WC | (711,000) | (29,000) | (546,000) |
| Emp. | 82 | 69 | 51 |

DUNS 21-103-1696
## Practitioner Services Ltd
1 North Esplanade West, Aberdeen, Aberdeenshire AB11 5QF
**Tel:** 01224358400
**Web:** www.practitionerservices.co.uk
**Reg No:** 6462053 **Estd:** 2008 Private Limited Company
**Line of Business:** Regulation of the activities of agencies that provide health care, education, cultural services and other social services excluding social security
**Issued Capital:** £1
**Director:** R P Baron
**Co. Secretary:** Giuseppe Marino
**Responsibilities**
**Senior:** Iain Young *(Operations Manager)*
**US SIC:** 7399 **UK SIC:** 83954

| | 31-12-12 | 31-12-11 |
|---|---|---|
| TA | 1,283 | 17,368 |
| NW | 114 | 8,228 |
| WC | 1 | 8,096 |

DUNS 37-848-5940 **Imp**
## Prada Retail U K Ltd
**(Subsidiary of:** Ludo Sa)
65 Curzon Street, London W1J 8PE
**Tel:** 02073992030
**Web:** www.prada.com
**Reg No:** 3299599 **Estd:** 1997 Private Limited Company
**Line of Business:** Retail sale of clothing
**Export Sales:** £2,138,455
**Issued Capital:** £5,000,000
**Directors:** S A Sutter, C Mazzi, Ms A D Lupas
**Responsibilities**
**Senior:** Sebastian Suhl *(Manager)*
**Branches:** Prada Retail U K Ltd, 16-18 Bond Street, London E15 1LT
**US SIC:** 5699 **UK SIC:** 64500
**Auditors:** Deloitte & Touche LLP

| | 31-01-14 | 31-01-13 | 31-01-12 |
|---|---|---|---|
| TO | 155,845,043 | 137,792,297 | 100,293,831 |
| P/L | 12,093,573 | 8,601,841 | 4,939,643 |
| NW | 23,807,030 | 14,686,928 | 8,914,005 |
| WC | 5,176,453 | (7,439,947) | (10,045,936) |
| Emp. | 415 | 360 | 271 |

DUNS 23-793-3846
## Pradera-A M Plc
**(Subsidiary of:** Tmf Trust Company (Asia) Limited)
60 New Broad Street, London EC2M 1JJ
**Tel:** 02075395432 **Fax:** 020-7504-8425
**Web:** www.pradera.com
**Reg No:** 3786152 **Estd:** 1999 Public Limited Company
**Line of Business:** Investment companies and vehicles
**Trading Style:** Pradera-A M Public Limited Company
**Issued Capital:** £850,300
**Directors:** C J Campbell, P J Whight, J R Bury
**Co. Secretary:** Ms Jenny Murley
**Responsibilities**
**Senior:** Neil Varnham *(Manager)*
**Finance:** Simon Cairns *(Fund Director)*, Scott Quinn *(Finance Director Europe)*
**US SIC:** 6371 **UK SIC:** 82002
**Auditors:** Deloitte & Touhce

| | 31-12-13 | 31-12-12 | 31-12-11 |
|---|---|---|---|
| TO | 14,662,014 | 13,787,295 | 15,870,055 |
| P/L | 2,252,497 | 4,215,425 | 4,867,620 |
| NW | 4,034,417 | 5,879,897 | 3,484,963 |
| WC | 3,404,157 | 5,349,020 | 2,825,102 |
| Emp. | 70 | 69 | 66 |

DUNS 21-161-1740
## Pradera Group Ltd
**(Subsidiary of:** Tmf Trust Company (Asia) Limited)
4th Floor Eldon House, 2-3 Eldon Street, London EC2M 7LS
**Tel:** 02074226550
**Web:** www.cadena.co.uk
**Reg No:** 6879270 **Estd:** 2006 Private Limited Company
**Line of Business:** Estate management services
**Issued Capital:** £1,000
**Directors:** Miss Y Beirne, C J Campbell, P J Whight
**Co. Secretary:** Miss Yvonne Beirne
**US SIC:** 6711 **UK SIC:** 83962

| | 31-12-13 | 31-12-12 | 31 12 11 |
|---|---|---|---|
| TO | 15,669,998 | 1,879,716 | 2,186,769 |
| P/L | 872,313 | (317,147) | 474,177 |
| NW | 4,056,518 | 2,634,329 | 2,951,476 |
| WC | 3,426,148 | 1,532,772 | 1,652,598 |
| Emp. | 78 | 6 | 8 |

DUNS 34-949-6120
## Praesepe Ltd
**(Subsidiary of:** Casino Merkur Spielothek Gmbh)
1a Seebeck House, Seebeck Place, Knowlhill, Milton Keynes, Buckinghamshire MK5 8FR
**Tel:** 08455215072
**Web:** www.praesepe.com
**Reg No:** 5745526 **Estd:** 2006 Private Limited Company
**Line of Business:** Casinos
**Issued Capital:** £25,347,988
**Directors:** B Evans, A J Hall, N S Harding
**Co. Secretary:** Emw Secretaries Limited
**US SIC:** 6111 **UK SIC:** 81501
**Auditors:** BDO LLP
**Bankers:** Barclays Bank Plc (20-00-00)

| | 31-12-13 | 30-12-12 | 25-12-11 |
|---|---|---|---|
| TA | 48,041,000 | 48,848,000 | 91,535,000 |
| P/L | N/A | (1,421,000) | (35,000) |
| NW | 47,077,000 | 47,077,000 | (19,376,000) |
| WC | 18,880,000 | 18,773,000 | (3,430,000) |
| Emp. | N/A | 4 | 975 |

DUNS 76-672-7408
## Praisecover Ltd
219 Hamstel Road, Southend-On-Sea, Essex SS2 4LB
**Tel:** 01702615838 **Fax:** 01702-466160
**Web:** www.kipmcgrath.co.uk
**Reg No:** 2586945 **Estd:** 1991 Private Limited Company
**Line of Business:** Taxi operation
**Issued Capital:** £100
**Directors:** D R Burch, D R Burch
**Co. Secretary:** John Holliday
**Responsibilities**
**Senior:** Andre Burch *(Director)*, Nicole O'shea *(Manager)*, Olga Preston *(Manager)*
**US SIC:** 4121 **UK SIC:** 72200
**Auditors:** The Mudd Partnership
**Bankers:** Lloyds TSB Bank plc (30-97-84)

| | 31-03-14 | 31-03-13 | 31-03-12 |
|---|---|---|---|
| TA | 343,125 | 321,044 | 380,623 |
| NW | (262,727) | (221,820) | (122,442) |
| WC | (338,625) | (448,916) | (418,370) |

DUNS 50-335-1397
## Pramacare
Unit 1 Sterte Avenue West Holes Bay Park, Poole, Dorset BH15 2AA
**Tel:** 01202-207300 **Fax:** 01202684255
**Web:** www.pramacare.co.uk
**Reg No:** 2359751 **Estd:** 1982 Private Limited Company
**Line of Business:** Home care service providers
**Trading Style:** Pramacare, Prama Shops
**Directors:** Ms L M Everett, T P Sharp, J H Simmons, Dr A J Morris, Mrs D M Tudor-Thomas, A J Binnington
**Co. Secretary:** Alan Murray
**Responsibilities**
**Senior:** Peter Malpas *(Manager)*, Jeff Russell *(Chief Executive Officer)*, David Tibbs *(Manager)*
**Branches:** Pramacare, 35 Vicarage Rd, Verwood, Dorset BH31 6DR
**US SIC:** 8091, 8321
**UK SIC:** 95200, 96111
**Auditors:** Princecroft Redman
**Bankers:** Barclays Bank Plc (20-96-96)

| | 31-03-14 | 31-03-13 | 31-03-12 |
|---|---|---|---|
| TO | 3,301,814 | 3,313,776 | 3,102,989 |
| P/L | 3,266 | (67,282) | 83,652 |
| NW | 1,177,145 | 1,163,436 | 1,204,761 |
| WC | (8,406) | 71,556 | 374,839 |
| Emp. | 282 | 301 | 299 |

DUNS 73-999-1607
## Pramerica (Gp) Ltd
**(Subsidiary of:** Prudential Financial Inc.)
Grand Building, 1-3 Strand, London WC2N 5HR
**Tel:** 02077662400
**Web:** www.pramerica.co.uk
**Reg No:** 5249549 **Estd:** 2004 Private Limited Company
**Line of Business:** Management activities of other non-financial holding companies not elsewhere classified
**Issued Capital:** £3,001
**Directors:** R Amabile, A H Radkiewicz, K M Shah, P M Barrett
**Co. Secretary:** Stephen Davies
**Responsibilities**
**Senior:** Eric Adler *(Chief Executive Officer)*
**US SIC:** 6711 **UK SIC:** 83962

| | 31-12-13 | 31-12-12 | 31-12-11 |
|---|---|---|---|
| TO | 2,000 | 3,067,191 | 1,406,516 |
| P/L | 2,037 | 6,960 | 6,311 |
| NW | 35,592 | 33,555 | 26,595 |
| WC | N/A | N/A | 23,595 |

DUNS 21-816-2675
## Prancers Boogie No 1 Ltd
**(Subsidiary of:** Ab Skf)
Wisbech Road, King's Lynn, Norfolk PE30 5JX
**Tel:** 01553767677
**Web:** www.cooperbearings.com
**Reg No:** 0201222 **Estd:** 1924 Private Limited Company
**Line of Business:** Manufacturers of bearings
**Issued Capital:** £5,157,833
**Directors:** I C Ross, Ms S L Smith, P Jeppesen, Ms D Crane
**Co. Secretary:** Ian Ross
**Responsibilities**
**Senior:** James O'Leary *(Ceo)*
**US SIC:** 3568 **UK SIC:** 32613
**Bankers:** Lloyds TSB Bank plc (30-94-75)

| | 31-12-13 | 31-12-12 | 31-12-11 |
|---|---|---|---|
| TA | 24,820,000 | 24,820,000 | 24,820,000 |
| NW | 24,820,000 | 24,820,000 | 24,820,000 |

DUNS 34-643-6095 **Imp**
## Prasco Uk Ltd
Unit 4 Alpha Court, Capitol Park, Thorne, Doncaster, South Yorkshire DN8 5TZ
**Tel:** 01302844300 **Fax:** 01302849728
**Web:** www.panelsandlamps.co.uk
**Reg No:** 5449383 **Estd:** 2005 Private Limited Company
**Line of Business:** Car accessories and parts
**Trading Style:** Panels & Lamps
**Issued Capital:** £400,000
**Principals:** K D Waugh *(Managing)*, D Egan
**Co. Secretary:** Darren Egan
**US SIC:** 5531 **UK SIC:** 65100
**Auditors:** Drury & Co
**Bankers:** National Westminster Bank Plc (60-06-39)

| | 31-12-13 | 31-12-12 | 31-12-11 |
|---|---|---|---|
| TO | 7,188,185 | N/A | N/A |
| P/L | 166,096 | N/A | N/A |
| NW | 792,223 | 702,509 | 701,273 |
| WC | 195,541 | 157,198 | 439,755 |
| Emp. | 65 | N/A | N/A |

DUNS 21-163-9101
## Praten Ltd
Holbrook House, 72 Bank Street, Knightrider Street, Maidstone, Kent ME14 1SN
**Web:** www.pratenstore.com
**Reg No:** 6900214 **Estd:** 2009 Private Limited Company
**Line of Business:** Retail sale via mail order house
**Issued Capital:** £1
**Director:** Hummesh Ltd
**Co. Secretary:** Andrew Okri
**US SIC:** 5961 **UK SIC:** 65600

| | 23-09-13 | 30-09-12 | 30-09-11 |
|---|---|---|---|
| TA | 23,997 | 43,967 | 58,287 |
| NW | 3,672 | 11,472 | 31,415 |
| WC | N/A | (9,922) | 31,415 |

DUNS 29-973-7205
## Prater Ltd
**(Subsidiary of:** Lindner Group Kg)
Perrywood Business Park Honeycro, Redhill, Surrey RH1 5JQ
**Tel:** 01737-772-331 **Fax:** 01737-766-021
**Web:** www.prater.co.uk
**Reg No:** 2107097 **VAT No:** 863149414
**Estd:** 1983 Private Limited Company
**Line of Business:** Roofing contracting services
**Issued Capital:** £97,887

**Principals:** M E Prater *(Managing)*, A L Birkbeck *(Managing)*, P J Wood, R Unwin, D J Galavan, G D Hamblett, A J Newman, H Weileder
**Co. Secretary:** Richard Davies
**Responsibilities**
**Senior:** Susan Prater *(Manager)*
**Branches:** Prater Limited, Gloucester Rd, Cheltenham, Gloucestershire GL51 8BQ
**US SIC:** 1761, 1799
**UK SIC:** 50400, 50000
**Auditors:** MHA MacIntyre Hudson
**Bankers:** Barclays Bank Plc (20-49-76)

| | 31-12-13 | 31-12-12 | 31-12-11 |
|---|---|---|---|
| TO | 83,265,963 | 77,868,998 | 65,440,793 |
| P/L | 3,753,188 | 2,669,628 | 2,887,871 |
| NW | 10,138,878 | 7,975,665 | 8,717,997 |
| WC | 8,583,117 | 6,384,509 | 6,975,564 |
| Emp. | 324 | 280 | 273 |

DUNS 34-812-0858　Imp
## Pravins Ltd
Chancellors House, 3 Brampton Lane, London NW4 4AB
**Tel:** 020-8359-9900
**Web:** www.pravins.co.uk
**Reg No:** 2792406 **Estd:** 1969 Private Limited Company
**Line of Business:** Retail sale of jewellery, clocks and watches
**Issued Capital:** £100,000
**Directors:** S Shah, H Shah
**Co. Secretary:** Rima Shah
**Branches:** Pravins Ltd, 221 Regent St, London W1B 4NJ
**US SIC:** 5944 **UK SIC:** 65400
**Auditors:** Ferguson Maidment & Co
**Bankers:** National Westminster Bank Plc (56-00-41)

| | 30-06-14 | 30-06-13 | 30-06-12 |
|---|---|---|---|
| TO | 6,536,644 | 5,370,883 | 5,128,548 |
| P/L | (212,108) | (131,548) | 209,258 |
| NW | 2,511,784 | 2,723,892 | 2,857,631 |
| WC | 1,646,761 | 1,633,072 | 2,379,996 |
| Emp. | 76 | 59 | 53 |

DUNS 50-424-4732　Imp-Exp
## Praxair Surface Technologies Ltd
*(Subsidiary of:* Praxair Inc.*)*
Drakes Way, Swindon, Wiltshire SN3 3HX
**Tel:** 01793-512555
**Web:** www.praxair.com
**Reg No:** 2416734 **VAT No:** 535615054
**Estd:** 1989 Private Limited Company
**Line of Business:** Coating companies
**Export Markets:** Rest of the World.
**Export Sales:** £8,541,000
**Issued Capital:** £5,500,000
**Directors:** V Slenders, R J Ward, D H Yankowsi, S Cast, A Draper, J Winterburn, P Luthi
**Co. Secretary:** Richard Ward
**Responsibilities**
**Senior:** John Estruch *(Manager)*, Mark Gruninger *(Manager)*, Edubrdo Menezes *(Manager)*, Alejandro Pena *(Manager)*
**Marketing:** Len Hills *(Sales & Marketing Manager)*
**Sales:** Len Hills *(Sales & Marketing Manager)*
**IT:** Jan Elliott *(Computer Manager)*
**Health & Safety:** Glenn Cordery *(Health & Safety Officer)*
**Facilities:** Glenn Cordery *(Health & Safety Officer)*
**Operations:** Glenn Cordery *(Health & Safety Officer)*, Len Hills *(Sales & Marketing Manager)*
**Branches:** Praxair Surface Technologies Ltd, 2 Oldmixon Crescent, Weston-Super-Mare, Avon BS24 9AX
**US SIC:** 2891 **UK SIC:** 25620
**Auditors:** PricewaterhouseCoopers LLP
**Bankers:** Bank Of America, Na (30-16-35)

| | 31-12-13 | 31-12-12 | 31-12-11 |
|---|---|---|---|
| TO | 39,587,000 | 39,393,000 | 36,429,000 |
| P/L | 5,506,000 | 5,640,000 | 2,011,000 |
| NW | 12,043,000 | 10,504,000 | 3,566,000 |
| WC | 736,000 | 4,017,000 | 4,326,000 |
| Emp. | 337 | 329 | 324 |

DUNS 23-264-2199
## Praxis Care
27-31 Lisburn Road, Belfast BT9 7AA
**Tel:** 028-9023-4555
**Web:** www.praxiscaregroup.org.uk
**Reg No:** 0017623NI **Estd:** 1981 Private Company Limited By Guarantee
**Line of Business:** Social work activities
**Directors:** Miss A S Vance, Dr O E Shanks, K S Brundle, Dr C Kennedy, J L Barrons, V Malone, Mrs C P Moore, J Mcgregor
**Co. Secretary:** Nevin Ringland
**Responsibilities**
**Senior:** Etta Eid-Jennings *(Manager)*, Francis Mcferran *(Director)*
**IT:** Jamie McDonald *(Head of IT)*
**HR:** Paul Leitch *(Human Resources Manager)*
**Branches:** Praxis Care, Kilmorey House, 3 Arthur Street, Newry, Co Down BT34 1HR

**US SIC:** 7399, 8091, 8321
**UK SIC:** 83954, 95200, 96111
**Auditors:** Moore Stephens
**Bankers:** First Trust Bank (aib Group (uk) Plc) (93-84-24)

| | 31-03-14 | 31-03-13 | 31-03-12 |
|---|---|---|---|
| TO | 27,987,472 | 27,147,195 | 27,159,286 |
| P/L | 104,445 | 364,536 | 1,140,734 |
| NW | 8,318,720 | 8,254,092 | 7,885,633 |
| WC | (878,414) | (993,872) | 2,895,865 |
| Emp. | 1,002 | 961 | 1,147 |

DUNS 67-215-9985
## Prco Holdings Ltd
36 Grosvenor Gardens, London SW1W 0EB
**Tel:** 020-7259-1110
**Web:** www.prco.com
**Reg No:** 6023843 **Estd:** 2006 Private Limited Company
**Line of Business:** Sale or leasing activities of advertising space or time
**Issued Capital:** £5,030
**Director:** R G Lyle
**Co. Secretary:** Mark Prior
**Responsibilities**
**Senior:** Melanie Cutcliffe *(Manager)*, Emily Lewis *(MD Real estate)*
**Marketing:** Andy Whiteside *(Director of Digital communicat)*
**Sales:** Celia Welham *(Account Manager)*
**Admin:** Lucy Gallagah *(Office Manager)*
**US SIC:** 7319 **UK SIC:** 83800
**Auditors:** KPMG LLP

| | 31-12-13 | 31-12-12 | 31 12 11 |
|---|---|---|---|
| TO | 8,613,258 | 8,857,685 | 9,040,608 |
| P/L | 648,789 | 676,654 | 1,662,078 |
| NW | 1,859,514 | 2,228,665 | 2,240,037 |
| WC | 2,517,248 | 3,076,266 | 3,310,950 |
| Emp. | 98 | 104 | 95 |

DUNS 21-225-3113
## Pre Hotel Out & Out Restaurants
Redbourn Road, St Albans, Hertfordshire AL3 6JZ
**Tel:** 01727-855259
**Web:** www.crowncarveries.co.uk
**Estd:** 2002 Proprietorship
**Line of Business:** Public house
**Proprietor:** J Kidby
**Responsibilities**
**Senior:** Mark Gale *(General Manager)*
**US SIC:** 5813 **UK SIC:** 66200
**Employees:** 46

DUNS 21-907-3319　Imp-Exp
## Pre-Met Ltd
*(Subsidiary of:* Direct File Ltd*)*
Studley Road, Redditch, Worcestershire B98 7HJ
**Tel:** 01527-510535
**Web:** www.pre-met.com
**Reg No:** 1110007 **Estd:** 1948 Private Limited Company
**Line of Business:** Metal spinners
**Export Sales:** £2,259,061
**Issued Capital:** £10,000
**Directors:** S B Haynes, K W Tonkin
**Co. Secretary:** Timothy Pomlett
**Responsibilities**
**Sales:** Joe Mulla *(Commercial Manager)*
**US SIC:** 3499, 3423
**UK SIC:** 31694, 31612
**Auditors:** Reeves & Co LLP
**Bankers:** HSBC Bank plc (40-16-11)

| | 31-08-13 | 31-08-12 | 31-08-11 |
|---|---|---|---|
| TO | 4,175,713 | 4,519,944 | 6,082,796 |
| P/L | 137,407 | 101,985 | 295,360 |
| NW | 709,506 | 616,748 | 615,886 |
| WC | 555,285 | 489,951 | 488,001 |
| Emp. | N/A | 54 | 55 |

DUNS 73-265-2099
## Pre-School Learning Alliance
The Fitzpatrick Building, 188 York Way, London N7 9AD
**Tel:** 020-7697-2500
**Web:** www.pre-school.org.uk
**Reg No:** 4539003 **Estd:** 1963 Private Company Limited By Guarantee
**Line of Business:** Primary education
**Directors:** G Mcmillan, Mrs L J Pendred, Mrs D M Aldridge, Mrs L J Maidment, D F Gilbert, Mrs S Ross, Mrs V Chadwick, R P Smith
**Co. Secretary:** Mrs Katharine Heeps
**Branches:** Pre-School Learning Alliance, Pinehurst Common Room, The Circle, Swindon, Wiltshire SN2 1RB
**US SIC:** 8211, 8221, 8321
**UK SIC:** 93200, 93100, 96111
**Auditors:** Crowe Clark Whitehill LLP
**Bankers:** National Westminster Bank Plc (50-00-00)

| | 31-03-14 | 31-03-13 | 31-03-12 |
|---|---|---|---|
| TO | 36,110,000 | 36,732,000 | 37,845,000 |
| P/L | 208,000 | 682,000 | 492,000 |
| NW | 11,003,000 | 10,774,000 | 10,033,000 |
| WC | 8,296,000 | 8,180,000 | 7,423,000 |
| Emp. | 1,383 | 1,430 | 1,509 |

DUNS 34-595-2832
## Precedent Communications Ltd
1st Floor, The Courtyard Build, 11 Curtain Raod, London EC2A 3LT
**Tel:** 020-7426-8900
**Web:** www.precedent.co.uk
**Reg No:** 2739347 **Estd:** 1992 Private Limited Company
**Line of Business:** Hardware consultancy
**Issued Capital:** £20,001
**Principals:** P E Hoskins *(Managing)*, Mrs J Williams, J Downes, N A Davis, H S Bhamra, Mrs S L Hoskins
**Co. Secretary:** Trevor Jones
**Responsibilities**
**Senior:** Mark Sherwin *(Global Commercial Director)*
**Marketing:** Rose Naylor *(Marketing officer)*
**Sales:** Mark Sherwin *(Global Commercial Director)*
**Operations:** Nikki D' Ambrosio *(Production and Operations Mana)*
**US SIC:** 7379 **UK SIC:** 83940
**Bankers:** HSBC Bank plc (40-18-35)

| | 31-03-13 | 31-03-12 | 31-03-11 |
|---|---|---|---|
| TA | 3,345,905 | 2,981,190 | 2,923,057 |
| NW | 1,461,763 | 968,498 | 688,311 |
| WC | 1,194,493 | 740,732 | 470,175 |

DUNS 23-341-2993
## Precesision Technologie
I ichfieldd Road Industrial Estat, Tamworth, Staffordshire B79 7UL
**Tel:** 01827-54371
**Web:** www.ptiltd.co.uk
**Proprietorship**
**Line of Business:** Precision engineers
**Proprietor:** B Penfield
**US SIC:** 8911 **UK SIC:** 83701
**Employees:** 80

DUNS 77-501-5589
## Precious Homes Ltd
*(Subsidiary of:* Cupio Healthcare Ltd*)*
5-11 Green Lanes, London N13 4TN
**Tel:** 020-8826-4343 **Fax:** 02088886251
**Web:** www.precious-homes.co.uk
**Reg No:** 2981404 **Estd:** 1994 Private Limited Company
**Line of Business:** Home care service providers
**Issued Capital:** £1,136
**Director:** M G Dhanak
**Co. Secretary:** Girdharlal Dhanak
**Branches:** Precious Homes Ltd, 93 Burgoyne Road, London N4 1AB
**US SIC:** 8091, 8321
**UK SIC:** 95200, 96111
**Auditors:** H W Fisher & Co
**Bankers:** Lloyds TSB Bank plc (30-00-09)

| | 30-06-13 | 30-06-12 | 28-06-11 |
|---|---|---|---|
| TO | 6,713,736 | 7,750,279 | 4,096,362 |
| P/L | 875,188 | 2,380,963 | 941,443 |
| NW | 7,473,935 | 6,914,585 | 4,964,417 |
| WC | 3,945,695 | 3,326,708 | 1,702,752 |
| Emp. | 255 | 188 | 103 |

DUNS 52-556-1569　Imp
## Precise Component Manufacture Ltd
Unit 2, Fenland Business Centre, Longhill Road, March, Cambridgeshire PE15 0BL
**Tel:** 01354-650781 **Fax:** 01354-650782
**Web:** www.pcml.net
**Reg No:** 3244862 **Estd:** 1996 Private Limited Company
**Line of Business:** Other engineering activities
**Issued Capital:** £100
**Directors:** A G Goates, K Miller, G A Goates
**Co. Secretary:** Ms Diane Miller
**Responsibilities**
**Marketing:** Harvey Richards *(Marketing Manager)*
**HR:** Sharon Goates *(Human Resources Manager)*
**Facilities:** Sharon Goates *(Human Resources Manager)*
**US SIC:** 8911 **UK SIC:** 83701
**Bankers:** HSBC Bank plc (40-32-18)

| | 30-09-13 | 30-09-12 | 30-09-11 |
|---|---|---|---|
| TA | 3,462,766 | 3,030,008 | 2,893,727 |
| NW | 2,817,181 | 2,472,211 | 2,066,679 |
| WC | 2,066,191 | 1,665,018 | 1,222,890 |

DUNS 52-562-1686
## Precise Media Monitoring Ltd
*(Subsidiary of:* Wpp Plc*)*
3 Royal Mint Court, London EC3N 4QN
**Tel:** 02072644788 **Fax:** 020 3301 4491
**Web:** www.precise.co.uk
**Reg No:** 3247942 **Estd:** 1996 Private Limited Company
**Line of Business:** Public relations consultants
**Export Sales:** £1,249,000
**Issued Capital:** £40,000

**Directors:** K M Fawcus, A R Prime, M Holroyd, P Low
**Co. Secretary:** Wpp Group (Nominees) Limited
**Responsibilities**
**Marketing:** Juliette Murray *(Marketing Manager)*
**IT:** Jason Barber *(Head of IT)*
**HR:** Farrella Ryan-Coker *(Human Resources Manager)*
**US SIC:** 7319 **UK SIC:** 83800
**Auditors:** KPMG LLP
**Bankers:** The Royal Bank Of Scotland Plc (16-00-11)

| | 30-09-13 | 30-09-12 | 30-09-11 |
|---|---|---|---|
| TO | 28,742,000 | 26,513,000 | 25,936,000 |
| P/L | 5,620,000 | 5,155,000 | 5,022,000 |
| NW | 11,924,000 | 7,423,000 | 3,042,000 |
| WC | 9,299,000 | 4,463,000 | 128,000 |
| Emp. | 416 | 412 | 369 |

DUNS 23-660-3051
## Precision Aerospace Fasteners Ltd
Blackwell Drive, Braintree, Essex CM7 2QJ
**Tel:** 01376340000
**Web:** www.pace-ltd.co.uk
**Reg No:** 3655271 **VAT No:** 466101664
**Estd:** 1994 Private Limited Company
**Line of Business:** Other manufacturing not elsewhere classified
**Issued Capital:** £2
**Director:** J Green
**Co. Secretary:** Richard Mullan
**US SIC:** 3999 **UK SIC:** 49590

| | 31-10-13 | 31-10-12 | 31-10-11 |
|---|---|---|---|
| TA | 2 | 2 | 2 |
| NW | 2 | 2 | 2 |

DUNS 21-909-9207　Imp-Exp
## Precision Chains Ltd
*(Subsidiary of:* Boycast Ltd*)*
Clee Road, Dudley, West Midlands DY2 0YG
**Tel:** 01384-455455
**Web:** www.precision-chains.com
**Reg No:** 0709436 **VAT No:** 277800537
**Estd:** 1957 Private Limited Company
**Line of Business:** Manufacturers of chains
**Export Markets:** E U and Worldwide
**Issued Capital:** £22,500
**Managing Director:** Ms J M Gorton
**Co. Secretary:** Neil Dayman
**Responsibilities**
**HR:** Melvyn Jones *(Quality Manager)*
**Branches:** Precision Chains Ltd, Oakdale Trading Estate, Ham Lane, Kingswinford, West Midlands DY6 7JH
**US SIC:** 3568, 3534
**UK SIC:** 32613, 32553

| | 28-02-14 | 28-02-13 | 28-02-12 |
|---|---|---|---|
| TA | 2,036,147 | 2,234,170 | 2,278,516 |
| NW | 1,125,265 | 1,042,492 | 995,026 |
| WC | 935,075 | 860,499 | 823,269 |

DUNS 23-832-3583
## Precision Dental Laboratories Group Ltd
Rivermead, Pipers Way, Thatcham, Berkshire RG19 4EP
**Tel:** 01635294200
**Web:** www.precisiondentalstudio.co.uk
**Reg No:** 3824228 **Estd:** 1999 Private Limited Company
**Line of Business:** Manufacture of medical and surgical equipment and orthopaedic appliances
**Issued Capital:** £2,148
**Directors:** C P Kay, M S Patel, D Hogg, C Nepute, R Stock
**Co. Secretary:** John Alflatt
**US SIC:** 3841 **UK SIC:** 37201
**Bankers:** National Westminster Bank Plc (60-11-13)

| | 30-09-13 | 30-09-12 | 30-09-11 |
|---|---|---|---|
| TA | 2,439,081 | 2,530,590 | 2,754,719 |
| NW | 1,006,105 | 715,170 | 474,078 |
| WC | 786,252 | 795,552 | 901,208 |

DUNS 34-649-4326
## Precision Engineering Plastics (Holdings) Ltd
Triumph Trading Estate Tariff Road, London N17 0EB
**Web:** www.pep-ltd.co.uk
**Reg No:** 5455025 **Estd:** 1986 Private Limited Company
**Line of Business:** Plastic injection moulding
**Issued Capital:** £11,136
**Managing Director:** V Marino
**Co. Secretary:** Padraic Doheny
**Responsibilities**
**Finance:** Tracy Lewingdon *(Accounts Manager)*
**US SIC:** 3079 **UK SIC:** 48360

**Auditors:** Mountsides Ltd

| | 31-12-13 | 31-12-12 | 31-12-11 |
|---|---|---|---|
| TO | 5,871,165 | 4,797,178 | N/A |
| P/L | 1,022,623 | 514,684 | 11,341 |
| NW | 2,816,339 | 2,125,027 | 17,541 |
| WC | 835,532 | 921,935 | (1,329,275) |
| Emp. | 101 | 105 | N/A |

DUNS 22-286-4014 **Imp**

## Precision Hydraulic Cylinders (Uk) Ltd

(**Subsidiary of:** Precision Hydraulic Cylinders Inc.)
Bassington Avenue, Cramlington, Northumberland NE23 8AG
**Tel:** 01670707203 **Fax:** 01670707204
**Web:** www.phc-uk.com
**Reg No:** 4304337 **VAT No:** 780518617
**Estd:** 1967 Private Limited Company
**Line of Business:** Manufacturers of hydraulic equipment
**Export Sales:** £7,367,173
**Issued Capital:** £1,400,001
**Directors:** G Macdonald, C S Barclay
**Co. Secretary:** Gordon Macdonald
**Responsibilities**
**Senior:** Jennifer Sibbald-Wall *(General Manager)*
**IT:** Steve Cowen *(Senior IT Executive)*
**Purchasing:** John Cairns *(Purchasing Manager)*
**US SIC:** 3563, 7999
**UK SIC:** 32831, 97913
**Auditors:** Grant Thornton UK LLP
**Bankers:** Barclays Bank Plc (20-58-17)

| | 31-01-14 | 31-01-13 | 31-01-12 |
|---|---|---|---|
| TO | 11,671,600 | 10,664,309 | 12,265,858 |
| P/L | 159,528 | (187,889) | 338,619 |
| NW | 2,578,276 | 2,286,006 | 2,433,895 |
| WC | 743,084 | 698,585 | 862,417 |
| Emp. | 79 | 72 | 68 |

DUNS 23-109-1856 **Exp**

## Precision Industrial Services Ltd

Unit 28 Mclean Road Campsie Industrial, Estate, Londonderry, Co Londonderry BT47 3XX
**Tel:** 02871860135
**Web:** www.precisiongroup.co.uk
**Reg No:** 0035996NI **VAT No:** 349757012
**Estd:** 1999 Private Limited Company
**Line of Business:** Commercial premises cleaning
**Export Markets:** Republic of Ireland
**Issued Capital:** £10,000
**Directors:** C Mccauley, Mrs C E Mcfadden, D Officer, J G Mcfadden, K M Williams, D J Morrison, J R Stewart
**Co. Secretary:** Kevin Williams
**Branches:** Precision Industrial Services Ltd, Unit 45, City Business Park, Belfast, Belfast BT17 9HY
**US SIC:** 7349, 7341
**UK SIC:** 92300
**Auditors:** Moore Stephens Bradley McDaid
**Bankers:** Ulster Bank Ltd (98-09-85)

| | 31-12-13 | 31-12-12 | 31-12-11 |
|---|---|---|---|
| TO | 7,399,601 | 8,623,330 | 8,871,744 |
| P/L | 242,652 | (75,355) | 419,366 |
| NW | 1,474,748 | 1,257,136 | 1,351,192 |
| WC | 992,973 | 910,325 | 747,351 |
| Emp. | 248 | 280 | 277 |

DUNS 45-871-1736 **Imp**

## Precision Lift Services Ltd

(**Subsidiary of:** P L S Holdings Ltd)
Unit 10 Upminster Trading Park, Warley Street, Upminster, Essex RM14 3PJ
**Tel:** 01708 250800 **Fax:** 01708 250400
**Web:** www.precisionlifts.co.uk
**Reg No:** 3213600 **Estd:** 1996 Private Limited Company
**Line of Business:** Lifts (maintenance and repair)
**Issued Capital:** £150,000
**Directors:** G S More, Ms D L More
**Responsibilities**
**Senior:** Vernon Foley *(Financial Director)*, Clifford Pace *(Technical Director)*
**Finance:** Jill Fayers *(Accountant)*, Vernon Foley *(Financial Director)*
**IT:** Clifford Pace *(Technical Director)*
**HR:** Clifford Pace *(Technical Director)*
**Health & Safety:** Clifford Pace *(Technical Director)*
**Facilities:** Jill Fayers *(Accountant)*
**US SIC:** 3534, 1799
**UK SIC:** 32553, 50000
**Auditors:** The Baker Clarke Partnership Ltd

| | 31-08-13 | 31-03-13 | 31-08-12 |
|---|---|---|---|
| TO | 4,111,937 | 9,759,856 | 10,659,344 |
| P/L | 379,294 | 131,224 | (41,236) |
| NW | 452,644 | 454,704 | 377,882 |
| WC | 543,443 | 529,273 | 508,729 |
| Emp. | 104 | 99 | 97 |

DUNS 77-944-6504

## Precision Manufacturing Solutions Ltd

Wonastow Road, East Industrial Estate, Monmouth, Gwent NP25 5JB
**Tel:** 01600710100
**Web:** www.pel-ltd.co.uk
**Reg No:** 5914204 **Estd:** 2006 Private Limited Company
**Line of Business:** Management activities of holding companies
**Export Sales:** £3,247,413
**Issued Capital:** £80,000
**Directors:** M A Jones, D R James, R N Mills
**Co. Secretary:** Ian Davies
**US SIC:** 6711 **UK SIC:** 83962
**Bankers:** HSBC Bank plc (40-33-11)

| | 31-05-14 | 31-05-13 | 31-05-12 |
|---|---|---|---|
| TO | 6,900,208 | 6,281,104 | 6,612,197 |
| P/L | 966,168 | 771,061 | 479,954 |
| NW | 1,575,890 | 1,119,429 | 694,643 |
| WC | 1,485,849 | 1,016,979 | 565,532 |
| Emp. | 188 | 189 | 186 |

DUNS 22-859-4941 **Imp-Exp**

## Precision Polymer Engineering Ltd

(**Subsidiary of:** Idex Corporation)
Greenbank Road, Blackburn, Lancashire BB1 3EA
**Tel:** 01254295400
**Web:** www.prepol.com
**Reg No:** 1476647 **VAT No:** 792427014
**Estd:** 1974 Private Limited Company
**Line of Business:** Other manufacturing not elsewhere classified
**Export Markets:** Europe; U S A
**Export Sales:** £27,951,177
**Trading Style:** Ppe, Prepol
**Issued Capital:** £5,506,862
**Directors:** P D Taylor, E C Gillyon, E D Ashleman
**Responsibilities**
**Senior:** Paolo Benedetto *(Director Finance)*, Brett Hogarth *(Operations Manager)*, Donna Maskell *(Marketing Director)*
**Marketing:** Donna Maskell *(Marketing Director)*
**US SIC:** 3999 **UK SIC:** 49590
**Auditors:** Deloitte LLP
**Bankers:** Lloyds TSB Bank plc (30-90-87)

| | 31-12-13 | 31-12-12 | 31-12-11 |
|---|---|---|---|
| TO | 33,760,654 | 30,852,122 | 30,250,002 |
| P/L | 10,482,900 | 9,303,359 | 8,325,832 |
| NW | 15,226,809 | 26,251,379 | 14,081,898 |
| WC | 11,205,078 | 22,278,758 | 9,853,661 |
| Emp. | 262 | 253 | 253 |

DUNS 22-707-8193 **Imp-Exp**

## Precision Printing Co. Ltd

47 Thames Road, Barking, Essex IG11 0HQ
**Tel:** 08456-064001 **Fax:** 08456-064002
**Web:** www.precisionprinting.co.uk
**Reg No:** 1466899 **VAT No:** 342044886
**Estd:** 1979 Private Limited Company
**Line of Business:** Printing not elsewhere classified
**Issued Capital:** £20,000
**Principals:** C D Cooper *(Chairman and Managing)*, G I Peeling *(Managing)*, E A Steward, P B Mason, S A Roucaute, A Skarpellis, Ms G Cooper
**Co. Secretary:** Ms Margaret Howell
**Responsibilities**
**Senior:** Kevin Pearman *(General Manager)*
**HR:** Keith Middleton *(Human Resources Manager)*
**US SIC:** 2752 **UK SIC:** 47544
**Auditors:** Arram Berlyn Gardner
**Bankers:** Barclays Bank Plc (20-67-59)

| | 31-12-13 | 31-12-12 | 31-12-11 |
|---|---|---|---|
| TO | 13,591,357 | 13,204,548 | 13,878,280 |
| P/L | 606,736 | 60,132 | 112,892 |
| NW | 1,428,611 | 933,933 | 893,059 |
| WC | (838,758) | (875,412) | (707,315) |
| Emp. | 114 | 125 | 136 |

DUNS 21-228-9102

## Precision Printing Plates Ltd

Philips Park Road, Manchester M11 3FU
**Web:** www.ppp-digital.co.uk
**Reg No:** 0698704 **Estd:** 1961 Private Limited Company
**Line of Business:** Printing production equipment and machinery
**Issued Capital:** £150,000
**Managing Director:** C Swift
**Co. Secretary:** Nigel Smith
**US SIC:** 8911 **UK SIC:** 83701
**Bankers:** National Westminster Bank Plc (01-10-01)

| | 31-08-13 | 31-08-12 | 31-08-11 |
|---|---|---|---|
| TA | 3,021,422 | 2,837,992 | 3,163,396 |
| NW | 198,757 | 229,745 | 229,536 |
| WC | (275,034) | (225,690) | (314,997) |

DUNS 29-558-5541

## Precision Tooling Services Ltd

(**Subsidiary of:** J & L Corrigan Ltd)
Prestwick Airport, Prestwick, Ayrshire KA9 2SB
**Tel:** 01292-678479
**Web:** www.precision-tooling.co.uk
**Reg No:** 0093877SC **VAT No:** 428249341
**Estd:** 1985 Private Limited Company
**Line of Business:** Manufacturers of machine tools
**Issued Capital:** £10,000
**Director:** J Corrigan
**Co. Secretary:** Allan Brese
**US SIC:** 3542 **UK SIC:** 32212
**Auditors:** John Kerr & Company

| | 31-10-13 | 31-10-12 | 31-10-11 |
|---|---|---|---|
| TO | 3,058,225 | 3,044,340 | 2,375,492 |
| P/L | 212,443 | 372,975 | 156,961 |
| NW | 1,433,054 | 1,379,561 | 744,056 |
| WC | 349,708 | 228,010 | (59,066) |

DUNS 21-907-6379 **Imp-Exp**

## Precispark Ltd

Chapel Street, Leicester, Leicestershire LE7 1GN
**Tel:** 01162607911
**Web:** www.preci-spark.co.uk
**Reg No:** 0661746 **VAT No:** 399860968
**Estd:** 1960 Private Limited Company
**Line of Business:** Representative office
**Export Markets:** Europe North U S A & Far East
**Export Sales:** £11,752,404
**Issued Capital:** £50,000
**Principals:** R G Jones *(Chairman)*, G D Jones *(Managing)*, V H Jones *(Managing)*, D W Jones *(Managing)*, W H Jones, M H Jones
**Co. Secretary:** Mrs Dorothy Jones
**Responsibilities**
**Health & Safety:** Kelvin Manship *(Maintenance Engineer)*
**Facilities:** Kelvin Manship *(Maintenance Engineer)*
**Operations:** Kelvin Manship *(Maintenance Engineer)*
**Branches:** Precispark Ltd, Falcon Street, Loughborough, Leicestershire LE11 1EH
**US SIC:** 7399, 3398
**UK SIC:** 83954, 31380
**Auditors:** Wagstaffs
**Bankers:** Lloyds TSB Bank plc (30-98-08)

| | 31-12-13 | 31-12-12 | 31-12-11 |
|---|---|---|---|
| TO | 34,580,663 | 37,417,327 | 52,433,248 |
| P/L | 1,261,459 | 1,124,181 | 1,469,394 |
| NW | 12,465,476 | 11,780,161 | 10,703,749 |
| WC | 5,920,407 | 3,898,792 | 1,520,969 |
| Emp. | 437 | 430 | 438 |

DUNS 23-913-8584 **Imp-Exp**

## Preconomy Ltd

Unit 3, Orchard Way, Sutton-In-Ashfield, Nottinghamshire NG17 1JU
**Tel:** 01623554211 **Fax:** 01623-514057
**Web:** www.preconomy.com
**Reg No:** 3904224 **VAT No:** 745351532
**Estd:** 2000 Private Limited Company
**Line of Business:** Manufacture of tools
**Export Markets:** Angola,India,Italy
**Trading Style:** Preconomy Led
**Issued Capital:** £6,874,921
**Principals:** P J Wilson Ramsay *(Managing)*, N A Giles
**Co. Secretary:** Paul Wilson Ramsay
**Responsibilities**
**Finance:** Paul Ramsay *(Finance Director)*
**Facilities:** Dave Chapman *(shop floor manager)*
**US SIC:** 3423 **UK SIC:** 31612
**Auditors:** Godkin & Co Ltd
**Bankers:** National Westminster Bank Plc (55-61-17)

| | 31-12-13 | 31-12-12 | 31-12-11 |
|---|---|---|---|
| TO | N/A | N/A | 3,581,557 |
| P/L | N/A | N/A | 91,904 |
| NW | 774,283 | 515,003 | 377,440 |
| WC | 457,547 | 275,182 | 199,553 |
| Emp. | N/A | N/A | 52 |

DUNS 21-600-4440 **Imp-Exp**

## Preformed Line Products (Great Britain) Ltd

(**Subsidiary of:** Preformed Line Products Company)
East Portway, Andover, Hampshire SP10 3LH
**Tel:** 01264-366234
**Web:** www.preformed-gb.com
**Reg No:** 0578922 **Estd:** 1957 Private Limited Company
**Line of Business:** Manufacturers cable and wire equipment
**Export Markets:** Export.
**Export Sales:** £3,632,106
**Issued Capital:** £1,500,000
**Directors:** S W Carley, R G Ruhlman, J A Bentley, M J Spayes, W H Haag
**Co. Secretary:** Trevor Rowcliffe

**Responsibilities**
**Senior:** John Coppella *(Distribution Manager)*
**US SIC:** 3357 **UK SIC:** 22470
**Auditors:** PricewaterhouseCoopers
**Bankers:** Barclays Bank Plc (20-02-25)

| | 31-12-13 | 31-12-12 | 31-12-11 |
|---|---|---|---|
| TO | 12,721,220 | 17,389,355 | 9,993,084 |
| P/L | 2,688,169 | 3,868,401 | 1,249,854 |
| NW | 4,648,665 | 5,154,384 | 4,243,983 |
| WC | 3,072,731 | 3,988,170 | 3,541,618 |
| Emp. | 111 | 115 | 99 |

DUNS 39-029-0997 **Imp-Exp**

## Premaberg Holdings Ltd

22-24 High Street, Halstead, Essex CO9 2AP
**Tel:** 01787475651
**Reg No:** 2108858 **Estd:** 1987 Private Limited Company
**Line of Business:** Management activities of holding companies
**Issued Capital:** £41,400
**Principals:** K A Beverley *(Chairman and Managing)*, G J Wadley
**US SIC:** 6711, 3531
**UK SIC:** 83962, 32541
**Auditors:** Ernst & Young LLP
**Bankers:** National Westminster Bank Plc (60-09-29)

| | 31-12-13 | 31-12-12 | 31-12-11 |
|---|---|---|---|
| TO | 3,679,769 | 3,435,611 | 3,747,555 |
| P/L | 333,794 | 5,762 | 354,387 |
| NW | 2,881,542 | 2,714,050 | 2,767,350 |
| WC | 3,022,142 | 2,837,844 | 2,874,000 |
| Emp. | 61 | 59 | 58 |

DUNS 45-890-4075 **Imp-Exp**

## Premdor Crosby Ltd

(**Subsidiary of:** Premdor U.K. Holdings Ltd)
Huddersfield Road, Barnsley, South Yorkshire S75 5NP
**Tel:** 08442090008 **Fax:** 01226-388808
**Web:** www.premdor.co.uk
**Reg No:** 3227274 **VAT No:** 678898536
**Estd:** 1996 Private Limited Company
**Line of Business:** Manufacturers of domestic doors
**Export Sales:** £248,000
**Issued Capital:** £21,001,000
**Director:** M Armstrong
**Co. Secretary:** Ms Rose Murphy
**Responsibilities**
**Senior:** Mick Love *(Plant Manager)*, Aidan Mincher *(Financial Director)*
**Finance:** Aidan Mincher *(Financial Director)*
**IT:** Mike Farrant *(IT Manager)*
**HR:** Beth Richardson *(Human Resources Manager)*
**Purchasing:** Jason Carpenter *(Purchasing Manager)*
**Branches:** Premdor Crosby Ltd, Bristol Road, Bridgwater, Somerset TA6 4AJ
**US SIC:** 2431 **UK SIC:** 46300
**Auditors:** Deloitte LLP
**Bankers:** National Westminster Bank Plc (60-60-05)

| | 28-12-13 | 29-12-12 | 31-12-11 |
|---|---|---|---|
| TO | 59,609,000 | 56,587,000 | 55,059,000 |
| P/L | 4,337,000 | 784,000 | (1,850,000) |
| NW | (4,667,000) | (9,741,000) | (9,539,000) |
| WC | (16,201,000) | (23,507,000) | (23,897,000) |
| Emp. | 397 | 374 | 375 |

DUNS 73-646-3428

## Premex Group Ltd

(**Subsidiary of:** Examworks Uk Ltd)
Premex House, Futura Park, Horwich, Bolton, Lancashire BL6 6SX
**Tel:** 01204478300
**Reg No:** 4906284 **Estd:** 2003 Private Limited Company
**Line of Business:** Other human health activities
**Issued Capital:** £39,216
**Directors:** I D Hill, R E Perlman, J K Price, S Margolis, D Fowler
**Co. Secretary:** Miss Caroline Russell
**US SIC:** 8091 **UK SIC:** 95200
**Auditors:** Deloitte LLP
**Bankers:** Lloyds TSB Bank plc (30-12-05)

| | 31-12-13 | 31-12-12 | 31-12-11 |
|---|---|---|---|
| TO | 79,666,000 | 73,146,273 | 63,503,088 |
| P/L | 10,132,000 | 8,014,811 | 4,421,916 |
| NW | 14,617,000 | 10,475,267 | 4,296,112 |
| WC | 15,833,000 | 9,469,877 | 3,041,259 |
| Emp. | 394 | 380 | 343 |

DUNS 21-706-7519

## The Premier Academy Ltd

The Premier Academy Limited Saffron, Street, Milton Keynes, Buckinghamshire MK2 3AH
**Tel:** 01908376236
**Web:** www.tpamk.co.uk
**Reg No:** 7324340 **Estd:** 2010 Private Limited Company
**Line of Business:** Primary education
**Directors:** C P Marsh, P F Ayres, M J Klein, L Robinson, Ms A Stepney, Mrs D V Farquharson, S W Harrison, Mrs M D West
**Co. Secretary:** Ms Michelle Reeve

**Responsibilities**
**Senior:** Angela Kennedy *(Director)*, June Mason *(Director)*
**US SIC:** 8211 **UK SIC:** 93200

| | 31-08-14 | 31-08-13 | 31-08-12 |
|---|---|---|---|
| TO | 2,649,155 | 2,525,728 | 3,109,863 |
| P/L | 366,661 | 330,166 | 928,940 |
| NW | 4,334,939 | 4,173,278 | 3,918,112 |
| WC | 553,698 | 240,659 | 339,634 |
| Emp. | 77 | 66 | 63 |

DUNS 29-557-9296

## Premier Asphalt Ltd

Hanson Road, Liverpool, Merseyside L9 7JN
**Tel:** 01515240033
**Web:** www.premierasphalt.com
**Reg No:** 1922245 **VAT No:** 414716760
**Estd:** 1985 Private Limited Company
**Line of Business:** Road surfacers
**Issued Capital:** £1,114
**Principals:** P Winskill *(Managing)*, S Winskill, S Harrison Smith, A Deans, P A Winskill, J Baker
**Co. Secretary:** Paul Winskill
**Responsibilities**
**Finance:** Michelle Gregory *(Credit Controller)*
**US SIC:** 1611 **UK SIC:** 50200
**Auditors:** Champion Accountants LLP
**Bankers:** HSBC Bank plc (40-12-26)

| | 31-03-14 | 31-03-13 | 31-03-12 |
|---|---|---|---|
| TO | 15,734,571 | 14,460,987 | 13,395,318 |
| P/L | 1,045,316 | 121,993 | 282,855 |
| NW | 2,237,261 | 1,446,001 | 1,684,954 |
| WC | 1,887,187 | 1,121,539 | 1,440,856 |
| Emp. | 66 | 58 | 64 |

DUNS 21-006-1444

## Premier Asset Management Group Ltd

**(Subsidiary of:** Electra Private Equity Partners 2006 Scottish L.P.)
1 High St Eastgate Court, Guildford, Surrey GU1 3DE
**Tel:** 01483306090
**Web:** www.theconbriofunds.co.uk
**Reg No:** 6306664 **Estd:** 2007 Private Limited Company
**Line of Business:** Financial intermediation not elsewhere classified
**Export Sales:** £583,000
**Issued Capital:** £37,369,262
**Directors:** M P O'Shea, M A Vogel, P D Tobias, L A Wiseman
**Co. Secretary:** Neil Macpherson
**US SIC:** 6111 **UK SIC:** 81501
**Bankers:** Lloyds TSB Bank plc (30-00-02)

| | 30-09-14 | 30-09-13 | 30-09-12 |
|---|---|---|---|
| TA | 82,866,000 | 68,268,281 | 76,381,813 |
| P/L | (4,174,000) | (7,819,365) | (7,860,338) |
| NW | (48,640,000) | (50,891,671) | (48,386,242) |
| WC | 421,000 | 2,959,281 | 2,839,522 |
| Emp. | 82 | 83 | 86 |

DUNS 21-722-3338

## Premier Autocentres Ltd

184-214 Blackfen Road, Sidcup, Kent DA15 8PT
**Tel:** 02088500066 **Fax:** 020-8850-0858
**Web:** www.123premier.com
**Reg No:** 0916352 **Estd:** 1967 Private Limited Company
**Line of Business:** Sale of new motor vehicles
**Issued Capital:** £99,088
**Principals:** B P Stone *(Managing)*, M J Rudd, M C Leathwood
**Co. Secretary:** Ms Eliane Stone
**US SIC:** 5511 **UK SIC:** 65100
**Auditors:** Trevor Jones & Co
**Bankers:** HSBC Bank plc (40-42-01)

| | 31-12-13 | 31-12-12 | 31-12-11 |
|---|---|---|---|
| TO | 13,778,808 | 13,183,591 | 11,267,406 |
| P/L | 403,996 | 348,449 | 95,269 |
| NW | 2,029,467 | 1,715,109 | 1,493,806 |
| WC | 657,307 | 421,734 | 274,945 |
| Emp. | 47 | 45 | 46 |

DUNS 77-153-1241

## Premier Automotive Ltd

145 Birch Lane, Dukinfield, Cheshire SK16 5AP
**Tel:** 01613302089 **Fax:** 0161-330-6577
**Web:** www.premier-car.co.uk
**Reg No:** 2706646 **VAT No:** 606353850
**Estd:** 1992 Private Limited Company
**Line of Business:** Sale of new motor vehicles
**Issued Capital:** £100
**Directors:** N P Bird, Miss L J Bird, D J Bird
**Co. Secretary:** Ronald Bird
**Responsibilities**
**Admin:** Bev Hopwood *(Administrator)*
**IT:** Bev Hopwood *(Administrator)*
**HR:** Bev Hopwood *(Administrator)*
**Health & Safety:** Bev Hopwood *(Administrator)*
**Purchasing:** Bev Hopwood *(Administrator)*
**US SIC:** 5511, 5521
**UK SIC:** 65100
**Auditors:** ECP

**Bankers:** National Westminster Bank Plc (60-20-21)

| | 31-05-14 | 31-05-13 | 31-05-12 |
|---|---|---|---|
| TO | 22,282,128 | 19,404,701 | 15,148,619 |
| P/L | 333,607 | 260,889 | 187,917 |
| NW | 1,473,548 | 1,304,973 | 1,238,405 |
| WC | 386,844 | 331,959 | 208,631 |
| Emp. | 46 | 46 | 35 |

DUNS 21-579-5403

## Premier Bakerys Ireland

Apollo Road, Belfast BT12 6LP
**Tel:** 02890388555
**Web:** www.premierfoods.co.uk
**Estd:** 1967 Proprietorship
**Line of Business:** Bakers and confectioners supplies
**Proprietor:** P Simpson
**Responsibilities**
**Senior:** Timothy Roddy *(Senior Site Manufacturing Mana)*
**US SIC:** 2051 **UK SIC:** 41960
**Employees:** 400

DUNS 77-116-8408 **Imp-Exp**

## Premier Cables Ltd

**(Subsidiary of:** Premier Cables Holdings Ltd)
Premier House, Dunstable, Bedfordshire LU5 4TP
**Tel:** 01582-665-050 **Fax:** 01582-665-060
**Web:** www.premiercables.com
**Reg No:** 2689345 **VAT No:** 581872312
**Estd:** 1992 Private Limited Company
**Line of Business:** Wholesale of hardware, plumbing and heating equipment and supplies
**Export Markets:** Republic of Ireland; Germany
**Export Sales:** £1,791,450
**Issued Capital:** £100,000
**Directors:** R Weinstein, J Weinstein, A Hopkins
**Co. Secretary:** Jeffrey Weinstein
**Branches:** Premier Cables Ltd, Templeton Business Centre, Building 5, Glasgow, Lanarkshire G40 1DA
**US SIC:** 5074 **UK SIC:** 61300
**Auditors:** Gerald Edelman
**Bankers:** Barclays Bank Plc (20-53-30)

| | 31-12-13 | 31-12-12 | 31-12-11 |
|---|---|---|---|
| TO | 28,898,671 | 29,546,437 | 26,721,400 |
| P/L | 1,650,832 | 1,574,866 | 1,136,203 |
| NW | 5,931,661 | 4,669,416 | 3,545,354 |
| WC | 5,833,391 | 4,563,337 | 3,415,009 |
| Emp. | 46 | 44 | 33 |

DUNS 34-641-6548

## Premier Care (Cumbria) Ltd

Premier House, Union Street, Pendlebury, Manchester M27 4HL
**Tel:** 01539622900 **Fax:** 01539-621710
**Web:** www.cobblecountry.co.uk
**Reg No:** 2768988 **Estd:** 1992 Private Limited Company
**Line of Business:** Other human health activities
**Trading Style:** Beamsmoor Care At Home
**Issued Capital:** £1,000
**Directors:** J P Regan, D Mcguinn, Mrs M A Regan
**Co. Secretary:** Mrs Michelle Regan
**Responsibilities**
**Senior:** Ruth Close *(Manager)*
**Branches:** Beckcliff Ltd, Beamsmoor Care At Home, 123 Highgate, Kendal, Cumbria LA9 4EN
**US SIC:** 8091 **UK SIC:** 95200
**Auditors:** Robertshaw & Myers

| | 30-04-14 | 30-04-13 | 30-04-12 |
|---|---|---|---|
| TA | 222,356 | 227,604 | 371,966 |
| NW | 62,421 | 43,864 | 193,074 |
| WC | 85,403 | 38,396 | 215,953 |

DUNS 21-012-9533

## Premier Care (Dorset) Ltd

Peartree Business Centre, Wimborne, Dorset BH21 7PT
**Tel:** 01202870032
**Web:** www.premiercaredorset.org.uk
**Reg No:** 6359687 **Estd:** 2010 Private Limited Company
**Line of Business:** Other human health activities
**Issued Capital:** £100
**Director:** Mrs C M De Jong
**Co. Secretary:** Kleis De Jong
**Responsibilities**
**Senior:** Christine Jong *(Manager)*
**US SIC:** 8091 **UK SIC:** 95200

| | 30-09-13 | 30-09-12 | 30-09-11 |
|---|---|---|---|
| TA | 262,090 | 207,666 | 200,946 |
| NW | 110,514 | 61,027 | 80,803 |
| WC | 104,695 | 53,180 | 74,427 |

DUNS 21-330-5550

## Premier Cleaning Services

Premier House, 45 Victoria Avenue, Sowerby, Thirsk, North Yorkshire YO7 1QX
**Tel:** 01845527111
**Web:** www.premierclean.co.uk
**Estd:** 2002 Partnership
**Line of Business:** Commercial premises cleaning
**Partners:** S Pickersgill, A Liddle, S Pickersgill
**Responsibilities**
**Senior:** Stephen Pickersgill *(Partner)*
**Branches:** Premier Cleaning Services, 11 Hull Sq, Salford, Lancashire M3 6FW
**US SIC:** 7349 **UK SIC:** 92300
**Employees:** 200

DUNS 23-579-3291 **Imp**

## Premier Components U.K. Ltd

**(Subsidiary of:** Premier European Group Ltd)
Campden Road, Stratford-Upon-Avon, Warwickshire CV37 8QR
**Tel:** 01789720061 **Fax:** 01789-722429
**Web:** www.premiercore.com
**Reg No:** 3577119 **VAT No:** 696034513
**Estd:** 1998 Private Limited Company
**Line of Business:** Vehicle salvage dealers
**Export Sales:** £5,523,243
**Trading Style:** Premier Components U.K. Limited
**Issued Capital:** £1,000
**Principals:** M S Garrison *(Managing)*, T Kowalski, M Edwards
**Co. Secretary:** Mrs Lisa Garrison
**Responsibilities**
**Senior:** Danny Edwards *(Manager)*
**US SIC:** 5093 **UK SIC:** 62200
**Auditors:** Walker Thompson

| | 30-06-13 | 30-06-12 | 30-06-11 |
|---|---|---|---|
| TO | 8,497,297 | N/A | N/A |
| P/L | 1,396,352 | N/A | N/A |
| NW | 3,101,451 | 2,008,835 | 1,422,628 |
| WC | 2,742,609 | 1,830,862 | 1,205,465 |
| Emp. | 50 | N/A | N/A |

DUNS 34-835-3355

## Premier Contract Cleaning Ltd

97 Broad Oaks, Attercliffe, Sheffield, South Yorkshire S9 3HH
**Tel:** 01142-449686 **Fax:** 01143449697
**Web:** www.premiercontractcleaning.co.uk
**Reg No:** 5634573 **Estd:** 2007 Private Limited Company
**Line of Business:** Cleaning contracting commercial
**Issued Capital:** £2
**Director:** S Slinn
**Co. Secretary:** Mrs Anne Slinn
**US SIC:** 7349 **UK SIC:** 92300

| | 31-12-13 | 31-12-12 | 31-12-11 |
|---|---|---|---|
| TA | 424,506 | 379,254 | 344,910 |
| NW | 38,163 | 34,215 | 21,455 |
| WC | (26,026) | (19,548) | (20,882) |

DUNS 23-505-5048

## Premier Contract Supplies Ltd

Unit 3, Eelmoor Road, Farnborough, Hampshire GU14 7QN
**Tel:** 01252-544411
**Web:** www.premiercontractsupplies.co.uk
**Reg No:** 3504742 **Estd:** 1998 Private Limited Company
**Line of Business:** Bathroom fixtures and fittings
**Issued Capital:** £100,000
**Principals:** V C Caldicot *(Managing)*, P J Caldicott, R W Beckman, I R Tuson
**Co. Secretary:** Ms Valerie Caldicott
**Responsibilities**
**Senior:** Mark Balls *(Manager)*
**US SIC:** 3499 **UK SIC:** 31694
**Auditors:** Soteriou Banerji

| | 31-03-14 | 31-03-13 | 31-03-12 |
|---|---|---|---|
| TO | 16,324,492 | 13,018,065 | 12,263,361 |
| P/L | 564,128 | 467,590 | 562,343 |
| NW | 1,394,717 | 962,533 | 701,776 |
| WC | (26,941) | (60,676) | (416,944) |
| Emp. | 54 | 46 | 45 |

DUNS 67-211-7657

## Premier Direct Marketing Ltd

Flathouse Quay, Portsmouth, Hampshire PO2 7SP
**Tel:** 023 9275 6301 **Fax:** 023 9275 1851
**Web:** www.premierdm.co.uk
**Reg No:** 6041698 **VAT No:** 897478736
**Estd:** 2007 Private Limited Company
**Line of Business:** Wholesale of fruit and vegetables
**Trading Style:** Premier Dm, Premierdm, Pdm
**Issued Capital:** £50,000
**Directors:** J T Hilliard, S J Turnbull, T Hilliard, R Hickson, J M Tanner
**Co. Secretary:** Jeffrey Hilliard

**Responsibilities**
**Senior:** Stuart Ballinger *(Manager)*, Stuart Buchanan *(Manager)*, Terry Cogdell *(Manager)*, James Hulse *(Non-Executive Director)*
**Sales:** David Flinders *(Sales Director)*
**Operations:** Nigel Bellenger *(Operations Director)*
**Purchasing:** Terry Cogdell *(Manager)*
**US SIC:** 5148 **UK SIC:** 61700
**Auditors:** Crouch Chapman

| | 02-06-13 | 27-05-12 | 31-06-11 |
|---|---|---|---|
| TO | 11,102,879 | 9,162,405 | 9,776,753 |
| P/L | 229,066 | 188,292 | 210,699 |
| NW | (102,925) | (290,456) | (437,421) |
| WC | 317,637 | 142,331 | (5,950) |
| Emp. | 46 | 43 | 36 |

DUNS 23-649-7520 **Imp**

## Premier Drapers Ltd

Unit 1, Premier House, 28 Linden Street, Leicester, Leicestershire LE5 5EE
**Tel:** 01162-490043
**Web:** www.premierdrapers.co.uk
**Reg No:** 3644955 **Estd:** 1998 Private Limited Company
**Line of Business:** Manufacturers of clothing and fabrics
**Issued Capital:** £100
**Director:** H K Ali
**Co. Secretary:** Mrs Ghazala Ali
**US SIC:** 2389 **UK SIC:** 45393
**Auditors:** Smith Hannah

| | 30-11-13 | 30-11-12 | 30-11-11 |
|---|---|---|---|
| TA | 3,688,724 | 1,746,945 | 1,718,943 |
| NW | 835,822 | 708,404 | 554,120 |
| WC | 315,652 | 451,163 | 353,569 |

DUNS 29-277-8354 **Imp-Exp**

## Premier Educational Supplies Ltd

**(Subsidiary of:** Findel P.L.C.)
Hyde Building, Ashton Road, Hyde, Cheshire SK14 4SH
**Tel:** 01613662900 **Fax:** 08003672009
**Web:** www.premier-education.co.uk
**Reg No:** 1543837 **Estd:** 1981 Private Limited Company
**Line of Business:** Retail sale via mail order house
**Export Markets:** Worldwide
**Trading Style:** Hope Education, Galt Educational, Gatt Pre-School Essentials
**Issued Capital:** £201,000
**Directors:** P B Maudsley, T J Kowalski, R W Siddle
**Co. Secretary:** Mark Ashcroft
**US SIC:** 5961 **UK SIC:** 65600
**Bankers:** HSBC Bank plc (40-15-31)

| | 28-03-14 | 29-03-13 | 30-03-12 |
|---|---|---|---|
| TA | 205,004 | 205,004 | 205,004 |
| NW | 5,004 | 5,004 | 5,004 |
| WC | 5,004 | 5,004 | 5,004 |

DUNS 73-298-3700

## Premier Entertainment Ltd

**(Subsidiary of:** Catwise Ltd.)
Maniland House 12, Court Parade East Lane, Wembley, Middlesex HA0 3HU
**Tel:** 01684298974
**Reg No:** 4572231 **Estd:** 2002 Private Limited Company
**Line of Business:** Telecommunications
**Issued Capital:** £100
**Directors:** J K Patel, J Patel, K R Scott
**Co. Secretary:** Stephen Martin
**US SIC:** 4899 **UK SIC:** 79020
**Bankers:** The Royal Bank Of Scotland Plc (16-00-83)

| | 31-12-13 | 31-12-12 | 31-12-11 |
|---|---|---|---|
| TO | 1,314,181 | 1,507,962 | 1,925,533 |
| P/L | 438,686 | 367,871 | 462,768 |
| NW | (1,881,526) | (2,320,212) | (2,688,083) |
| WC | (1,881,526) | (2,320,212) | (2,688,083) |
| Emp. | N/A | N/A | 52 |

DUNS 21-217-3561 **Imp-Exp**

## Premier Farnell Plc

150 Armley Road, Leeds, West Yorkshire LS12 2QQ
**Tel:** 08701298608 **Fax:** 08701298610
**Web:** www.premierfarnell.com
**Reg No:** 0876412 **VAT No:** 169680322
**Estd:** 1966 Public Limited Company
**Line of Business:** Management activities of holding companies
**Export Sales:** £733,300,000
**Issued Capital:** £22,498,220
**Directors:** L Bain, P N Withers, T Reddin, A J Dougal, P J Ventress, M A Whiteling, Miss V F Gooding
**Co. Secretary:** Steven Webb
**Responsibilities**
**Senior:** Lawrence Bain *(Chief Executive Officer)*, Garriet Green *(Chief Executive Officer)*
**Admin:** Sandy Han *(Personal Assistant)*
**IT:** Daniel Stead *(IT Buyer and Commercial Analys)*
**Operations:** Sam Pettman *(Head of Marketing Operations)*

**Purchasing:** Justin Willoughby *(EMCO Supplier Segment Manager)*
**Engineering:** Paul Creaby *(EAPAC UNIX Engineering Team Le)*
**Branches:** Premier Farnell Plc, Premier House, 36-48 Queen Street, Horsham, West Sussex RH13 5AD
**US SIC:** 6711 **UK SIC:** 83962
**Auditors:** PricewaterhouseCoopers LLP
**Bankers:** HSBC Bank plc (40-13-15)

| | 02-02-14 | 03-02-13 | 31-02-12 |
|---|---|---|---|
| TO | 968,000,000 | 952,000,000 | 973,100,000 |
| P/L | 74,800,000 | 70,600,000 | 104,600,000 |
| NW | 3,400,000 | (1,100,000) | 6,600,000 |
| WC | 279,600,000 | 246,900,000 | 343,900,000 |
| Emp. | 4,507 | 4,464 | 4,459 |

DUNS 67-218-2045
## Premier Fleet Management & Contract Hire Ltd
Masters House, 107 Hammersmith Road, London W14 0QH
**Tel:** 01484-688000
**Reg No:** 6025920 **Estd:** 1999 Private Limited Company
**Line of Business:** Holding companies management activities
**Issued Capital:** £10
**Directors:** J G Bateson, S J Staton, Ms S J Roff
**US SIC:** 6711, 7399
**UK SIC:** 83962, 83954

| | 31-12-13 | 31-12-12 | 31-12-11 |
|---|---|---|---|
| TO | 25,082,431 | 24,520,645 | 23,494,106 |
| P/L | (453,164) | (111,407) | 144,066 |
| NW | (6,026,429) | (6,006,836) | (6,367,006) |
| WC | 7,526,333 | 8,646,727 | 5,018,048 |
| Emp. | 116 | 116 | 112 |

DUNS 21-024-2244
## Premier Foods Group Ltd
(**Subsidiary of:** Premier Foods Plc)
Building Ct3 Centrium, Griffiths Way, St Albans, Hertfordshire AL1 2RE
**Tel:** 01727-815-850 **Fax:** 01727-815-982
**Web:** www.premierfoods.co.uk
**Reg No:** 0281728 **VAT No:** 421612005
**Estd:** 1933 Private Limited Company
**Line of Business:** Production of meat and poultry meat products
**Issued Capital:** £105,186
**Directors:** G J Darby, G K Hunter, D N Leggett, A J Mcdonald, A R Whitehouse, J Hepburn, M R Hughes, A S Murray
**Co. Secretary:** Simon Wilbraham
**Responsibilities**
**Senior:** Ian Deste *(Director of Sales)*
**Branches:** Premier Foods Group Ltd, 110 Reeds Lane, Wirral, Merseyside CH46 1PR
**US SIC:** 2013, 2041, 2051, 2099
**UK SIC:** 41223, 41600, 41960, 42399
**Auditors:** PricewaterhouseCoopers LLP
**Following financial data are in thousands**

| | 31-12-13 | 31-12-12 | 31-12-11 |
|---|---|---|---|
| TO | 1,509,944 | 1,734,935 | 2,156,482 |
| P/L | 133,293 | (118,158) | (66,110) |
| NW | (491,099) | (671,877) | (802,803) |
| WC | 2,476,661 | 3,014,513 | 2,670,939 |
| Emp. | 8,016 | 9,327 | 13,111 |

DUNS 21-008-9252
## Premier Forest Group Ltd
Alexandra Dock South Way, Newport, Gwent NP20 2PQ
**Tel:** 01633254422
**Reg No:** 6328322 **Estd:** 2007 Private Limited Company
**Line of Business:** Management activities of holding companies
**Export Sales:** £30,642,953
**Issued Capital:** £349,998
**Directors:** T E Edgell, P W Morgan, N J Williams, D J Howells, J L Antoniazzi
**Co. Secretary:** Peter Morgan
**US SIC:** 6711 **UK SIC:** 83962
**Bankers:** HSBC Bank plc (40-16-13)

| | 30-04-14 | 30-04-13 | 30-04-12 |
|---|---|---|---|
| TO | 76,687,569 | 70,576,802 | 60,044,804 |
| P/L | 1,249,593 | 4,171,564 | 1,843,416 |
| NW | 8,024,642 | 6,698,229 | 3,206,308 |
| WC | 437,385 | 4,086,377 | 1,218,807 |
| Emp. | 151 | 116 | 48 |

DUNS 42-411-2501
## Premier Fruits (Covent Garden) Ltd
D144 Covent Garden Market, London SW8 5JJ
**Tel:** 02077209012
**Web:** www.premierfruits.com
**Reg No:** 4398850 **Estd:** 2002 Private Limited Company
**Line of Business:** Catering food and drink suppliers
**Issued Capital:** £200,000
**Directors:** B Grant, P P Wearne, J M Tanner, J M Tanner, M Gregory, R Hickson, D Purcell
**Co. Secretary:** Roger Garber
**US SIC:** 5149 **UK SIC:** 61700
**Auditors:** Crouch Chapman
**Bankers:** Barclays Bank Plc (20-46-73)

| | 06-04-14 | 05-04-13 | 01-04-12 |
|---|---|---|---|
| TO | 38,316,202 | 28,491,267 | 32,051,392 |
| P/L | 795,602 | 291,886 | 234,378 |
| NW | 2,339,798 | 2,367,567 | 2,022,112 |
| WC | 1,983 | 1,943,446 | 575,582 |
| Emp. | 161 | 57 | 143 |

DUNS 23-881-9176
## Premier Galvanizing Ltd
Unit 25, Stoneferry Park, Foster Street, Hull, North Humberside HU8 8BT
**Tel:** 01482325425 **Fax:** 01482327229
**Web:** www.bollhoff-armstrong.co.uk
**Reg No:** 3873106 **VAT No:** 738160824
**Estd:** 1999 Private Limited Company
**Line of Business:** Treatment and coating of metals
**Issued Capital:** £48,000
**Directors:** T Cavill, Ms A Payne, E Cavill
**Co. Secretary:** Gary Hainsworth
**Responsibilities**
**Senior:** Leigh Burgoyne *(Manager)*
**Branches:** Premier Galvanizing Ltd, Darwin Road, Willowbrook East Industrial Estate, Corby, Northamptonshire NN17 5XZ
**US SIC:** 3398 **UK SIC:** 31380
**Auditors:** Smailes Goldie & Co

| | 31-03-14 | 31-03-13 | 31-03-12 |
|---|---|---|---|
| TO | 7,818,871 | 6,888,017 | 6,538,287 |
| P/L | 1,515,905 | 1,630,873 | 1,360,066 |
| NW | 2,820,575 | 3,701,918 | 2,465,560 |
| WC | 1,860,957 | 2,946,581 | 2,134,139 |
| Emp. | 53 | 51 | 52 |

DUNS 29-068-6807
## Premier Garage (Leek) Ltd
Sneyd Street, Leek, Staffordshire ST13 5HP
**Tel:** 01538398900 **Fax:** 01538398913
**Web:** www.premiergarage.co.uk
**Reg No:** 1274314 **VAT No:** 280562655
**Estd:** 1991 Private Limited Company
**Line of Business:** Sale of new motor vehicles
**Trading Style:** Premier Garage
**Issued Capital:** £100
**Principals:** W R Barker *(Managing)*, Mrs K J Barker
**Co. Secretary:** William Barker
**Responsibilities**
**Senior:** Terry Gallagher *(Manager)*
**Branches:** Premier Garage (Leek) Ltd, Norbury Garage, Sneyd Street, Leek, Staffordshire ST13 5HP
**US SIC:** 5511, 5521, 5531
**UK SIC:** 65100
**Auditors:** KPMG
**Bankers:** National Westminster Bank Plc (01-05-02)

| | 31-03-14 | 31-03-13 | 31-03-12 |
|---|---|---|---|
| TA | 877,406 | 962,013 | 965,818 |
| NW | 124,570 | 96,914 | 69,431 |
| WC | 71,638 | 40,464 | 100,015 |

DUNS 22-131-2171 **Imp**
## Premier Global Ltd
Unit 2, Trowbridge, Wiltshire BA14 8RH
**Tel:** 08451909091
**Web:** www.premierglobal.co.uk
**Reg No:** 4150192 **Estd:** 1999 Private Limited Company
**Line of Business:** Holding companies management activities
**Trading Style:** Premier Training & Development
**Issued Capital:** £130,883
**Directors:** G Sebasky, J Moulton, Mrs D L Stuart, W Aliber, J M Heywood
**Co. Secretary:** Jonathan Heywood
**Responsibilities**
**Senior:** Norman Basson *(Founder & Non-Executive Direct)*, Lucy Jackson *(Centre Manager)*
**Finance:** Philip Rogis *(Finance Manager)*
**Marketing:** Julian Berriman *(Research and Development Direc)*
**IT:** Simon Norton *(Network, Security Manager)*
**HR:** Bill Platt *(Executive)*, Ben Roughton *(Executive)*
**Facilities:** Malcolm Oakey *(Manager)*
**Operations:** Dave Christophi *(Operations Director)*, Malcolm Oakey *(Manager)*
**Branches:** Premier Global Ltd, Badgers Bottom, Lodge Rd, Reading, Berkshire RG10 0SG
**US SIC:** 6711 **UK SIC:** 83962
**Auditors:** Monahans

| | 31-08-13 | 31-08-12 | 31-08-11 |
|---|---|---|---|
| TO | 10,883,730 | 10,468,337 | 9,927,918 |
| P/L | 3,115,651 | 1,668,844 | 1,045,093 |
| NW | 2,498,565 | 1,826,537 | 1,234,739 |
| WC | 2,259,583 | 1,947,864 | 420,180 |
| Emp. | 127 | 130 | 135 |

DUNS 73-870-8259
## The Premier Group (Coventry) Ltd
Brindley Road, Bayton Road Industrial Estate, Coventry, West Midlands CV7 9EP
**Tel:** 01305260606
**Web:** www.bromfordindustries.co.uk
**Reg No:** 5125384 **Estd:** 1977 Private Limited Company
**Line of Business:** Management activities of production holding companies
**Export Sales:** £2,851,905
**Issued Capital:** £157,010
**Director:** D P Meagher
**Co. Secretary:** John Jackson
**Responsibilities**
**Senior:** Paul Gillmore *(Manager)*, David Mardel *(General Manager)*, Michael Vousden *(Manager)*
**US SIC:** 6711 **UK SIC:** 83962

| | 31-03-14 | 31-03-13 | 31-03-12 |
|---|---|---|---|
| TO | 14,575,401 | 11,887,295 | 7,228,279 |
| P/L | 2,356,014 | 421,781 | 387,466 |
| NW | 4,250,438 | 2,675,299 | 2,625,070 |
| WC | 1,185,271 | 172,048 | (259,058) |
| Emp. | 173 | 166 | 140 |

DUNS 21-409-1418
## Premier Highcourt Roofing
Unit 2 Inbox Selfstore, Yaxley, Peterborough, Cambridgeshire PE7 3NA
**Tel:** 01733286797
**Web:** www.townandcountyroofing.co.uk
**Estd:** 2010 Proprietorship
**Line of Business:** Roofing contracting services
**Proprietor:** P Webb
**US SIC:** 1761 **UK SIC:** 50400
**Employees:** 58

DUNS 22-681-6601
## Premier Holidays Ltd
82 Westbrook Centre, Cambridge, Cambridgeshire CB4 1YG
**Tel:** 01223-516516 **Fax:** 01223516615
**Web:** www.premierholidays.co.uk
**Reg No:** 1791598 **Estd:** 1984 Private Limited Company
**Line of Business:** Activities of travel organisers
**Trading Style:** Premier Holidays America, Premier Holidays Asia, Premier Channel Island Holidays, Everymann Holidays Most Faraway Holidays
**Issued Capital:** £750,000
**Principals:** R L Sargent *(Managing)*, P S Andrews *(Financial)*, Miss S J Smith, Ms S Earnshaw, Mrs R A Willis
**Co. Secretary:** Ms Susan Earnshaw
**Responsibilities**
**Senior:** Lynda Tanguy *(Manager)*
**Marketing:** Joanne Cook *(Product Manager)*, Debbie Goffin *(Business Manager)*
**Sales:** Debbie Goffin *(Business Manager)*
**HR:** Debbie Goffin *(Business Manager)*, Helen Hallworth *(Human Resources Manager)*
**Facilities:** Helen Hallworth *(Human Resources Manager)*
**Branches:** Premier Holidays Ltd, 61 High Street, Newmarket, Suffolk CB8 8NA
**US SIC:** 4722 **UK SIC:** 77001
**Auditors:** Deloitte LLP
**Bankers:** Lloyds TSB Bank plc (30-91-56)

| | 30-09-14 | 30-09-13 | 30-09-12 |
|---|---|---|---|
| TO | 45,403,617 | 43,883,347 | 38,683,882 |
| P/L | 1,228,094 | 1,004,449 | 667,637 |
| NW | 3,237,541 | 2,780,996 | 2,516,370 |
| WC | 2,988,361 | 2,485,694 | 2,268,503 |
| Emp. | 110 | 111 | 104 |

DUNS 22-295-3528
## Premier Home Logistics Ltd
(**Subsidiary of:** Laura Ashley Holdings Plc)
Premier House, Coalville, Leicestershire LE67 1TA
**Tel:** 08448157115 **Fax:** 01530516263
**Web:** www.premier-logisticsuk.co.uk
**Reg No:** 4313286 **Estd:** 2002 Private Limited Company
**Line of Business:** Freight forwarders
**Issued Capital:** £100,000
**Directors:** S T Anglim, K C Ng
**Co. Secretary:** Ms Alison Fraser
**Responsibilities**
**Senior:** Kein Ho *(Manager)*, Kai Teo *(Manager)*
**US SIC:** 4213, 4226, 4789
**UK SIC:** 72300, 77003, 77002
**Auditors:** Chantrey Vellacott DFK LLP
**Bankers:** The Royal Bank Of Scotland Plc (15-00-00)

| | 25-01-14 | 26-01-13 | 28-01-12 |
|---|---|---|---|
| TO | 9,776,511 | 8,985,501 | N/A |
| P/L | 824,315 | 882,120 | 807,030 |
| NW | 739,659 | 108,401 | 437,528 |
| WC | 516,789 | (13,423) | 359,806 |
| Emp. | 260 | 250 | 220 |

DUNS 73-628-5904
## Premier Homecare Ltd
67 Stoke Hill, Bristol, Avon BS9 1EP
**Tel:** 01179592013
**Web:** www.premier-homecare.com
**Reg No:** 4889020 **Estd:** 2009 Private Limited Company
**Line of Business:** Home care service providers
**Trading Style:** Duport Associates Ltd
**Issued Capital:** £2
**Directors:** S J Swindwells, Ms J P Tunnicliffe
**Co. Secretary:** Simon Swindells
**Responsibilities**
**Senior:** Judith Honeycliffe *(Proprietor)*
**US SIC:** 8091 **UK SIC:** 95200
**Bankers:** HSBC Bank plc (40-14-24)

| | 31-03-14 | 31-03-13 | 31-03-12 |
|---|---|---|---|
| TA | 456,129 | 545,487 | 673,670 |
| NW | 52,603 | (47,352) | (135,403) |
| WC | 6,416 | (74,455) | (162,674) |

DUNS 23-703-5969 **Imp-Exp**
## Premier Housewares
55 Jordanvale Avenue, Glasgow, Lanarkshire G14 0QP
**Tel:** 0141-579-2000
**Web:** www.premierhousewares.co.uk
**VAT No:** 481458232 **Estd:** 1989 Partnership
**Line of Business:** Manufacture of other furniture
**Export Markets:** Europe
**Trading Style:** L T C Distributors
**Partners:** A Mobarik, R Mobarik, S Mobarik
**Responsibilities**
**Senior:** Safana Mobarik *(Manager)*, Awais Mobarik *(Manager)*
**Finance:** Saleem Yusif *(Financial Director)*
**Marketing:** Lorna Jameson *(Head of Marketing)*
**Purchasing:** Wimon Paton *(Purchasing Manager)*
**US SIC:** 2517, 5199
**UK SIC:** 46714, 61900
**Bankers:** Clydesdale Bank Plc (82-20-00)
**Employees:** 100

DUNS 21-844-6507
## Premier Hytemp Topco Ltd
Newbridge Industrial Estate, Newbridge, Midlothian EH28 8PJ
**Tel:** 01313334140
**Web:** www.murray-metals.co.uk
**Reg No:** 0426384SC **Estd:** 1985 Private Limited Company
**Line of Business:** Management activities of holding companies
**Export Sales:** £20,155,000
**Issued Capital:** £9,050
**Directors:** T Hatt, M Mcbride, C M Mcpherson, D G Bennett, W J Gold
**Co. Secretary:** William Gold
**US SIC:** 6711 **UK SIC:** 83962

| | 30-09-13 |
|---|---|
| TO | 31,208,000 |
| P/L | (3,187,000) |
| NW | (4,574,000) |
| WC | 14,836,000 |
| Emp. | 219 |

DUNS 21-034-3399
## Premier Inn
Arlington Square, Wokingham Road, Bracknell, Berkshire RG42 1NA
**Tel:** 08715278132
**Web:** www.premierinn.com
**Proprietorship**
**Line of Business:** Hotels
**Proprietor:** L Futcher
**Responsibilities**
**Senior:** Daniel Hedges *(General Manager)*
**US SIC:** 7011 **UK SIC:** 66500
**Employees:** 94

DUNS 21-599-7440
## The Premier Inn
Thanet Way, Whitstable, Kent CT5 3DB
**Tel:** 08715279162
**Web:** www.premierinn.com
**Estd:** 1981
**Line of Business:** Hotels
**US SIC:** 7011, 7399
**UK SIC:** 66500, 83954
**Employees:** 60

DUNS 21-601-0881
## Premier Inn & Beefeater
Baglan Road, Baglan, Port Talbot, West Glamorgan SA12 8ES
**Tel:** 01639813017
**Web:** www.beefeatergrill.co.uk
**Estd:** 1992 Proprietorship
**Line of Business:** Restaurant - american
**Proprietor:** D Evans
**US SIC:** 5812 **UK SIC:** 66110
**Employees:** 75

DUNS 22-204-2082
## Premier It Group Ltd
**(Subsidiary of:** Escalla Ltd)
Ergon House, Horseferry Road, London SW1P 2AL
**Tel:** 020-7837-2690 **Fax:** 02072782113
**Web:** www.premierit.com
**Reg No:** 4222390 **VAT No:** 581125848
**Estd:** 2001 Private Limited Company
**Line of Business:** Training centres
**Issued Capital:** £3,245
**Director:** I West
**Co. Secretary:** Miss Jane Bodley-Scott
**Responsibilities**
**Senior:** Edward Arnett *(Manager)*, Mathew O'Connell *(Manager)*, Matt Rosenquist *(Product Manager)*, Juliette Skinner *(Group Marketing Manager)*
**Finance:** Claire McCready *(Finance Manager)*
**US SIC:** 8299 **UK SIC:** 93300

| | 30-04-14 | 30-04-13 | 30-04-12 |
|---|---|---|---|
| TA | 2,754,759 | 2,484,828 | 2,205,448 |
| NW | 967,207 | 909,551 | 560,247 |
| WC | 1,793,155 | 1,553,933 | 1,207,217 |

DUNS 73-386-9882
## Premier Kitchens & Bedrooms Ltd
Unit 14/15, Kingfisher Business Park, London Road, Bedford, Bedfordshire MK42 0NY
**Tel:** 08000929493
**Web:** www.premierkitchenaccessones.co.uk
**Reg No:** 4660448 **Estd:** 2003 Private Limited Company
**Line of Business:** Joinery installation
**Issued Capital:** £1,000
**Director:** I C Forsythe
**Co. Secretary:** Alison Forsythe
**US SIC:** 7399, 5719
**UK SIC:** 83954, 64700

| | 31-12-13 | 31-12-12 | 31-12-11 |
|---|---|---|---|
| TO | 7,241,663 | 6,710,160 | 6,799,812 |
| P/L | 207,333 | 84,757 | 104,074 |
| NW | 648,549 | 417,661 | 1,679,149 |
| WC | (1,298,084) | (1,359,380) | (1,143,837) |
| Emp. | 69 | 87 | 57 |

DUNS 21-041-2700
## Premier Lease & Loan Services
32 Queen Square, Bristol, Avon BS1 4ND
**Tel:** 08448094765
**Web:** www.plls.com
**Estd:** 1991 Proprietorship
**Line of Business:** Insurance - commercial
**Partners:** Mrs S Mcbride, Miss H Lomax, Miss A Greaves, J Bartlett, Miss S Mccatrhy
**Responsibilities**
**Senior:** S McBride *(Partner)*, S McCatrhy *(Partner)*
**US SIC:** 6111 **UK SIC:** 81501
**Employees:** 50

DUNS 34-720-8824
## Premier Marinas Holdings Ltd
**(Subsidiary of:** Premier Marinas Jersey Holdings Ltd)
Head Office Swanwick Marina, Southampton, Hampshire SO31 1ZL
**Tel:** 01489884080
**Web:** www.premiermarinas.com
**Reg No:** 5524490 **Estd:** 2005 Private Limited Company
**Line of Business:** Management activities of holding companies
**Issued Capital:** £9,856,305
**Directors:** N Patel, P D Tebbit, H Platt, R Boissier, J W Brown, J Jaap
**US SIC:** 6711, 7999
**UK SIC:** 83962, 97913
**Auditors:** Deloitte LLP
**Bankers:** HSBC Bank plc (40-00-00)

| | 30-03-14 | 31-03-13 | 01-03-12 |
|---|---|---|---|
| TO | 24,658,000 | 24,565,000 | 24,918,000 |
| P/L | (360,000) | 2,814,000 | 356,000 |
| NW | 6,912,000 | 7,252,000 | 4,901,000 |
| WC | 3,306,000 | 6,182,000 | 5,605,000 |
| Emp. | 146 | 143 | 144 |

DUNS 77-490-1706 **Exp**
## Premier Marinas Ltd
**(Subsidiary of:** Premier Marinas Jersey Holdings Ltd)
Swanwick Marina, Swanwick Shore, Swanwick, Southampton, Hampshire SO31 1ZL
**Tel:** 01489884081 **Fax:** 01489579073
**Web:** www.premiermarineinsurance.co.uk
**Reg No:** 2973858 **Estd:** 2011 Private Limited Company
**Line of Business:** Other construction work involving special trades
**Issued Capital:** £100
**Directors:** J M Cervenka, H Platt, J W Brown, G A Collins, N Patel, R Boissier, P H Bradshaw, P D Tebbit
**Responsibilities**
**Senior:** Glyn Davis *(Site Manager)*, Andy Osman *(General Manager)*
**HR:** Tracey Jefkins *(Personnel Manager)*
**Health & Safety:** Russell Asser *(Facilities Manager)*
**Facilities:** Russell Asser *(Facilities Manager)*
**Branches:** Premier Marinas Ltd, Swanwick, Southampton, Hampshire SO31 1ZL
**US SIC:** 1799, 7999
**UK SIC:** 50000, 97913
**Auditors:** Deloitte & Touche LLP
**Bankers:** HSBC Bank plc (40-03-28)

| | 30-03-14 | 31-03-13 | 01-03-12 |
|---|---|---|---|
| TO | 24,658,000 | 24,565,000 | 24,918,000 |
| P/L | 3,718,000 | 6,149,000 | 3,580,000 |
| NW | 19,885,000 | 20,135,000 | 18,272,000 |
| WC | 2,667,000 | 5,590,000 | 5,675,000 |
| Emp. | 146 | 143 | 144 |

DUNS 42-470-2777
## Premier Moves Ltd
1 Ardra Road, London N9 0BD
**Tel:** 02089762100 **Fax:** 020-8805-9955
**Web:** www.premiermoves.net
**Reg No:** 3250579 **Estd:** 1996 Private Limited Company
**Line of Business:** Removals industrial and business
**Issued Capital:** £3,400
**Directors:** D C Russinger, P Oram
**Co. Secretary:** Jeremy Marks
**Responsibilities**
**Health & Safety:** Sharon Stephens *(Health & Safety Officer)*
**US SIC:** 4214 **UK SIC:** 72300
**Auditors:** GKP Ltd

| | 31-03-14 | 31-03-13 | 31-03-12 |
|---|---|---|---|
| TO | 13,479,200 | 13,483,211 | 17,485,129 |
| P/L | 433,237 | 404,887 | 647,541 |
| NW | 1,649,059 | 1,765,783 | 2,010,777 |
| WC | 1,270,016 | 1,399,693 | 1,525,674 |
| Emp. | 175 | 186 | 211 |

DUNS 50-470-0006
## Premier Nursing Homes Ltd
**(Subsidiary of:** Custodes Topco Ltd)
Braidwood Road, Middlesbrough, Cleveland TS6 0HA
**Tel:** 01642-456222
**Web:** www.premiernursing.co.uk
**Reg No:** 2448895 **Estd:** 1993 Private Limited Company
**Line of Business:** Social work activities with accommodation
**Issued Capital:** £160,000
**Directors:** P A Warren, Ms M Ramsey, D H Evans
**Co. Secretary:** Dominic Evans
**Responsibilities**
**Senior:** Tracey Godfrey *(Care Home Manager)*, John Logan *(Care Home Manager)*, Stephen Pereira *(Director)*, Susan Tregonning *(Care Home Manager)*
**Finance:** John Logan *(Care Home Manager)*, Stephen Pereira *(Director)*, Susan Tregonning *(Care Home Manager)*
**HR:** John Logan *(Care Home Manager)*, Susan Tregonning *(Care Home Manager)*
**Health & Safety:** John Logan *(Care Home Manager)*, Susan Tregonning *(Care Home Manager)*
**Facilities:** John Logan *(Care Home Manager)*, Susan Tregonning *(Care Home Manager)*
**Branches:** Premier Nursing Homes Ltd, Willowdene Nursing Home, Victoria Road West, Hebburn, Tyne and Wear NE31 1LR
**US SIC:** 8321 **UK SIC:** 96111
**Auditors:** Jewitts
**Bankers:** National Westminster Bank Plc (60-06-33)

| | 31-12-13 | 31-12-12 | 31-12-11 |
|---|---|---|---|
| TO | 6,906,379 | 7,005,159 | 7,171,961 |
| P/L | (239,781) | 324,550 | 434,606 |
| NW | 5,722,586 | 9,286,190 | 8,941,636 |
| WC | (3,586,926) | (531,367) | (412,942) |
| Emp. | 326 | 325 | 319 |

DUNS 51-570-4042
## Premier Nursing Ltd
2 Arun Street, Arundel, West Sussex BN18 9DL
**Tel:** 01903883882
**Web:** www.premier-nursing.co.uk
**Reg No:** 5851764 **Estd:** 2010 Private Limited Company
**Line of Business:** Nursing agencies
**Issued Capital:** £100
**Director:** Ms C Wilson
**Co. Secretary:** Ms Penelope Aschan
**US SIC:** 8091 **UK SIC:** 95200

| | 30-09-14 | 30-09-13 | 30-09-12 |
|---|---|---|---|
| TA | 60,273 | 49,166 | 50,205 |
| NW | 10,435 | 13,101 | 18,774 |
| WC | 8,273 | 10,558 | 15,782 |

DUNS 23-875-5362
## Premier Occupational Healthcare Ltd
**(Subsidiary of:** People Asset Management Ltd)
Palmyra Square Chambers 13-15, Springfield Street, Warrington, Cheshire WA1 1BB
**Tel:** 01303298100
**Web:** www.premierohc.co.uk
**Reg No:** 3866894 **VAT No:** 837118034
**Estd:** 1999 Private Limited Company
**Line of Business:** Healthcare companies
**Issued Capital:** £515
**Directors:** J D Murphy, Ms J P Fairburn
**Co. Secretary:** Ms Jane Fairburn
**Responsibilities**
**Senior:** Timothy Ablett *(Manager)*, Trevor Chrismas *(Manager)*, Peter Dingle *(Manager)*, Sheila Fernandes *(Manager)*, Patrick Leroy *(Manager)*
**US SIC:** 8091 **UK SIC:** 95200
**Auditors:** Reeves & Co LLP
**Bankers:** The Royal Bank Of Scotland Plc (16-19-70)

| | 31-12-13 | 31-05-13 | 31-12-12 |
|---|---|---|---|
| TO | N/A | N/A | 2,584,800 |
| P/L | N/A | N/A | 9,057 |
| NW | 154,804 | (272,354) | (167,063) |
| WC | 154,804 | (286,609) | 34,154 |

DUNS 64-095-7796
## Premier Oil Plc
23 Lower Belgrave Street, London SW1W 0NR
**Tel:** 020 7730 1111 **Fax:** 020 7730 4696
**Web:** www.premier-oil.com
**Reg No:** 0234781SC **Estd:** 2002 Public Limited Company
**Line of Business:** Management activities of holding companies
**Directors:** A G Lodge, N Hawkings, M W Welton, Dr S A Bamford, Ms I J Hinkley, R A Rose, R A Allan, J Darby
**Co. Secretary:** Stephen Huddle
**Responsibilities**
**Senior:** Anthony Durrant *(Director)*, Michel Romieu *(Director)*
**US SIC:** 6711 **UK SIC:** 83962
**Auditors:** Deloitte LLP
**Employees:** 732
**Turnover:** £1,501,000,000

DUNS 23-677-5388 **Imp**
## Premier Paper Group Ltd
**(Subsidiary of:** G. C. Paper Ltd)
Midpoint Park, Sutton Coldfield, West Midlands B76 1AF
**Fax:** 01213133508
**Web:** www.paper.co.uk
**Reg No:** 3672117 **Estd:** 1998 Private Limited Company
**Line of Business:** Paper merchants
**Trading Style:** Premier Beswick
**Issued Capital:** £100,000
**Directors:** C Candler, G Griffiths
**Co. Secretary:** Simon Taylor
**Responsibilities**
**Marketing:** Paddy Byrne *(Corporate Social Responsibilit)*
**IT:** Dave Wilding *(IT Manager)*
**Health & Safety:** Pat Helyer *(?Health & Safety coordinator &)*
**Facilities:** Pat Helyer *(?Health & Safety coordinator &)*
**Branches:** Premier Paper Group Ltd, Premier House, Romford, Essex RM3 8SP
**US SIC:** 5199 **UK SIC:** 61900
**Auditors:** PKF (UK) LLP

| | 31-12-13 | 31-12-12 | 31-12-11 |
|---|---|---|---|
| TO | 144,720,000 | 152,301,000 | 155,445,000 |
| P/L | 4,747,000 | 5,201,000 | 6,030,000 |
| NW | 19,933,000 | 18,283,000 | 19,097,000 |
| WC | 18,631,000 | 17,647,000 | 18,232,000 |
| Emp. | 350 | 343 | 346 |

DUNS 21-180-2614
## Premier Parking Solutions Holdings Ltd
Minerva House, Orchard Way, Torquay, Devon TQ2 7FA
**Tel:** 01803-202020
**Web:** www.khlaw.co.uk
**Reg No:** 7025958 **Estd:** 2009 Private Limited Company
**Line of Business:** Holding companies management activities
**Issued Capital:** £505,264
**Directors:** B Douglass, R F Cox
**Responsibilities**
**Health & Safety:** Colin Brooking *(Practice Manager)*
**US SIC:** 6711 **UK SIC:** 83962

| | 31-03-14 | 31-03-13 | 31-03-12 |
|---|---|---|---|
| TA | 916,073 | 916,073 | 967,050 |
| NW | 591,014 | 591,014 | 516,013 |

DUNS 73-419-4629
## Premier Pensions Management Ltd
Corinthian House, 17 Lansdowne Road, Croydon, Surrey CR0 2BX
**Tel:** 02086-635800 **Fax:** 02086-635811
**Web:** www.premiercompanies.co.uk
**Reg No:** 4692580 **Estd:** 2003 Private Limited Company
**Line of Business:** Management and business consultants
**Issued Capital:** £18,500
**Directors:** A Aird, M C Thompson, I Gutteridge, P J Smith, P D Couchman, Ms J M Williams
**Co. Secretary:** David Smith
**Responsibilities**
**Senior:** Denise Morton *(General Manager)*
**US SIC:** 6371 **UK SIC:** 82002
**Auditors:** Mazars LLP

| | 31-12-13 | 31-12-12 | 31-12-11 |
|---|---|---|---|
| TO | 8,508,227 | 8,006,810 | 6,747,029 |
| P/L | 693,421 | 910,720 | 975,501 |
| NW | 1,860,108 | 1,728,674 | 1,407,899 |
| WC | 1,861,550 | 1,997,125 | 1,500,451 |
| Emp. | 82 | 65 | N/A |

DUNS 23-171-2209 **Exp**
## Premier Plc
Premier House, Braintree Road, Ruislip, Middlesex HA4 0EJ
**Tel:** 01323301157 **Fax:** 020-8624-5678
**Web:** www.premlerdec.com
**Reg No:** 2216895 **Estd:** 1988 Public Limited Company
**Line of Business:** Management activities of holding companies
**Export Markets:** Worldwide
**Export Sales:** £3,698,889
**Trading Style:** Premier
**Issued Capital:** £60,000
**Principals:** J S Athwal *(Managing)*, V Mahtani, J K Athwal, H L Mahtani
**Co. Secretary:** Michael Sancto
**Responsibilities**
**Senior:** David Moors *(Store Manager)*
**Sales:** Barry Harms *(Sales Account Manager - South)*, Rolf Hunt *(Sales Manager)*
**US SIC:** 6711, 5199
**UK SIC:** 83962, 61900
**Auditors:** Barnes Roffe LLP
**Bankers:** Lloyds TSB Bank plc (30-95-89)

| | 30-06-14 | 30-06-13 | 30-06-12 |
|---|---|---|---|
| TO | 31,511,981 | 25,840,863 | 24,003,851 |
| P/L | 2,297,362 | 1,310,358 | 1,222,629 |
| NW | 6,481,457 | 6,402,090 | 6,237,663 |
| WC | 2,661,767 | 2,305,984 | 2,186,468 |
| Emp. | 78 | 80 | 80 |

DUNS 29-390-6921
## Premier Portfolio Managers Ltd
**(Subsidiary of:** Electra Private Equity Partners 2006 Scottish L.P.)
1 Eastgate Court, High Street, Guildford, Surrey GU1 3DE
**Tel:** 01483400423 **Fax:** 01483-300845
**Web:** www.premierfunds.co.uk
**Reg No:** 1235867 **VAT No:** 243104900
**Estd:** 1984 Private Limited Company
**Line of Business:** Financial intermediation not elsewhere classified
**Issued Capital:** £105,252
**Directors:** S G Wilson, M A Friend, M P O'Shea, M J Hammond
**Co. Secretary:** Neil Macpherson
**Branches:** Premier Portfolio Managers Ltd, Eastgate Court High Street, Guildford, Surrey GU1 3DE
**US SIC:** 6111 **UK SIC:** 81501
**Auditors:** RSM Robson Rhodes
**Bankers:** Bank Of Scotland (12-01-03)

| | 30-09-14 | 30-09-13 | 30-09-12 |
|---|---|---|---|
| TA | 45,461,000 | 22,187,000 | 22,807,000 |
| P/L | 3,291,000 | 2,613,000 | 3,453,000 |
| NW | 12,251,000 | 9,098,000 | 6,485,000 |
| WC | 12,251,000 | 9,098,000 | 6,485,000 |
| Emp. | 82 | 83 | 86 |

DUNS 23-724-6905 **Imp**
## Premier Precision Engineering Ltd
**(Subsidiary of:** Premier Ina Holdings Ltd)
Unit 10 Rolling Mill Road, Jarrow, Tyne and Wear NE32 3DP
**Tel:** 01914-282295
**Web:** www.premier-engineering.com
**Reg No:** 2973516 **Estd:** 1994 Private Limited Company
**Line of Business:** Precision engineers
**Issued Capital:** £100
**Directors:** N A Bargewell, I Cassidy, A Robson
**Co. Secretary:** Ian Cassidy
**Responsibilities**
**Health & Safety:** Harry Herbert *(Health & Safety Officer)*
**US SIC:** 8911 **UK SIC:** 83701

**Bankers:** Barclays Bank Plc (20-80-47)

| | 31-10-13 | 31-10-12 | 31-10-11 |
|---|---|---|---|
| TO | 7,914,336 | 7,812,187 | 7,378,019 |
| P/L | 1,192,746 | 1,272,493 | 1,402,492 |
| NW | 2,454,994 | 2,638,465 | 2,098,311 |
| WC | 1,380,255 | 1,637,508 | 1,197,207 |
| Emp. | 73 | 68 | 64 |

DUNS 28-966-3841

## Premier Public Relations Ltd
91 Berwick Street, London W1F 0NE
**Tel:** 020-7292-8330 **Fax:** 020-7734-2024
**Web:** www.premierpr.com
**Reg No:** 1707417 **VAT No:** 480752633
**Estd:** 1983 Private Limited Company
**Line of Business:** Public relations consultants
**Export Sales:** £115,335
**Trading Style:** Premier
**Issued Capital:** £130
**Directors:** Ms A E Muller, D M Willing
**Co. Secretary:** John Reiss
**US SIC:** 7392 **UK SIC:** 83951
**Auditors:** Chantrey Vellacott DFK LLP

| | 30-09-14 | 30-09-13 | 30-09-12 |
|---|---|---|---|
| TO | 15,157,806 | 17,853,024 | 16,456,645 |
| P/L | (705,652) | (1,327,111) | (40,176) |
| NW | (2,815,220) | (2,502,386) | (1,258,284) |
| WC | (2,697,671) | (3,315,249) | (1,107,922) |
| Emp. | 187 | 194 | 148 |

DUNS 29-072-0514

## The Premier Pump & Tank Co Ltd
Upper Bourne End Lane, Hemel Hempstead, Hertfordshire HP1 2UJ
**Tel:** 01442-872296
**Web:** www.premiergroup.org.uk
**Reg No:** 2075865 **Estd:** 1986 Private Limited Company
**Line of Business:** Petrol pump maintenance services
**Export Sales:** £1,036,615
**Trading Style:** The Premier Group, The Premier Group of Companies
**Issued Capital:** £45,000
**Principals:** K L Owen (Managing), A K Olive, S J Trimmer, S Evans, G Owen
**Co. Secretary:** Kenneth Owen
**Responsibilities**
**Senior:** Barrie Robinson (Manager)
**Finance:** Sandie Hamilton (Head of Human Resources)
**HR:** Sandie Hamilton (Head of Human Resources)
**Branches:** The Premier Pump & Tank Co Ltd, Daybrook St, Nottingham, Nottinghamshire NG5 2HD
**US SIC:** 3563, 1799
**UK SIC:** 32831, 50000
**Auditors:** H W
**Bankers:** National Westminster Bank Plc (60-10-33)

| | 30-09-13 | 30-09-12 | 30-09-11 |
|---|---|---|---|
| TO | 15,261,268 | 13,449,409 | 9,441,551 |
| P/L | 126,897 | 414,230 | 113,634 |
| NW | 1,395,767 | 1,212,622 | 856,695 |
| WC | 1,149,069 | 1,199,501 | 835,966 |
| Emp. | 157 | 132 | 121 |

DUNS 34-840-1196

## Premier Research Germany Ltd
(**Subsidiary of:** Indigo Capital V L.P.)
Rubra Two, Fishponds Road Mulberry Business Park, Wokingham, Berkshire RG41 2GY
**Tel:** 01189-364000
**Web:** www.premierresearch.com
**Reg No:** 5639273 **Estd:** 2005 Private Limited Company
**Line of Business:** Research and experimental development on natural sciences and engineering
**Export Sales:** £2,725,000
**Trading Style:** Premier Research Ltd
**Issued Capital:** £1
**Directors:** Ms J M Emmett, A C Nicholson, L J Reynders
**Responsibilities**
**Senior:** Christopher Codeanne (Manager)
**Finance:** Christopher Codeanne (Manager)
**US SIC:** 7391 **UK SIC:** 94000

| | 31-12-13 | 31-12-12 | 31-12-11 |
|---|---|---|---|
| TO | 5,263,000 | 5,567,000 | 8,433,000 |
| P/L | (8,451,000) | (4,954,000) | (8,718,000) |
| NW | (26,911,000) | (18,199,000) | (13,278,000) |
| WC | (26,984,000) | (18,281,000) | (13,356,000) |
| Emp. | 82 | 89 | 83 |

DUNS 22-047-3867

## Premier Retail Ltd
(**Subsidiary of:** Premier Global Ltd)
1 Willowside Park, Canal Road, Trowbridge, Wiltshire BA14 8RH
**Tel:** 01225777426 **Fax:** 01225-353580
**Reg No:** 4049612 **Estd:** 1999 Private Limited Company
**Line of Business:** Retailers of fitness equipment & therapy equipment
**Issued Capital:** £100

---

**Director:** Mrs D L Stuart
**US SIC:** 5941 **UK SIC:** 65400

| | 31-08-13 | 31-08-12 | 31-08-11 |
|---|---|---|---|
| TA | 100 | 100 | 100 |
| NW | 100 | 100 | 100 |

DUNS 36-534-3490

## Premier Scaffolding Services Ltd
Unit 10 Waggonway Road Industrial Estate, Wagonway Road, Hebburn, Tyne and Wear NE31 1SP
**Tel:** 0191-483-9991
**Web:** www.premierscaffoldinghebburn.co.uk
**Reg No:** 3290578 **Estd:** 1996 Private Limited Company
**Line of Business:** Scaffolds and work platform erectors
**Issued Capital:** £100
**Managing Director:** N R Tatum
**Co. Secretary:** Mrs Carol Tatum
**Responsibilities**
**Senior:** Joanne Boyer (Manager), Tony Gowland (Contracts Manager)
**Finance:** Carol Howe (Manager), Deborah Tatum (Manager), Paula Watson (Accounts)
**IT:** Carol Howe (Manager), Deborah Tatum (Manager)
**US SIC:** 7394 **UK SIC:** 84000
**Bankers:** Barclays Bank Plc (20-80-47)

| | 30-11-13 | 30-11-12 | 30-11-11 |
|---|---|---|---|
| TA | 934,480 | 787,689 | 674,012 |
| NW | 348,585 | 283,647 | 247,959 |
| WC | 26,146 | (5,647) | (70,764) |

DUNS 73-723-3023　　　　　　　　　Exp

## Premier Sheet Metal (Coventry) Ltd
(**Subsidiary of:** The Premier Group (Coventry) Ltd)
Brindley Road North, Coventry, West Midlands CV7 9EP
**Tel:** 024-7636-2886
**Web:** http://premier-group.co
**Reg No:** 2920513 **VAT No:** 646812130
**Estd:** 1994 Private Limited Company
**Line of Business:** Sheet metal fabricators
**Export Markets:** European Union (E U); Scandinavia
**Export Sales:** £2,851,905
**Issued Capital:** £100
**Directors:** W Woolford, G Halton, D P Meagher
**Co. Secretary:** John Jackson
**Responsibilities**
**Marketing:** John Campton (Sales & Marketing Manager)
**Sales:** John Campton (Sales & Marketing Manager)
**US SIC:** 3469, 8911
**UK SIC:** 31200, 83701
**Auditors:** Baker Tilly
**Bankers:** Lloyds TSB Bank plc (30-00-03)

| | 31-03-14 | 31-03-13 | 31-03-12 |
|---|---|---|---|
| TO | 14,575,401 | 11,887,295 | 7,208,619 |
| P/L | 2,350,753 | 374,502 | 364,243 |
| NW | 4,035,023 | 2,459,525 | 2,562,420 |
| WC | 1,497,422 | 329,478 | 354,447 |
| Emp. | 173 | 166 | 140 |

DUNS 21-385-8396

## Premier Sports Group
Jubilee Suite, Telford Road, Bicester, Oxfordshire OX26 4LD
**Tel:** 08452641152
**Web:** www.premiersportsgroup.co.uk
**Estd:** 2008 Proprietorship
**Line of Business:** Sports coaching
**Partners:** J Merritt, J Gardner
**US SIC:** 7999 **UK SIC:** 97913
**Employees:** 70

DUNS 21-033-2605

## Premier Stamping
Station Street, Cradley Heath, West Midlands B64 6AJ
**Tel:** 01384-353100
**Web:** www.premierstampings.co.uk
**Proprietorship**
**Line of Business:** Blacksmiths
**Proprietor:** A Thomas
**US SIC:** 3469 **UK SIC:** 31200
**Employees:** 85

DUNS 34-842-9937

## Premier Support Services Ltd
4-5 Western Court, Birmingham, West Midlands B9 4AN
**Tel:** 08450555444
**Web:** www.premiergroupservices.co.uk
**Reg No:** 2806257 **Estd:** 2012 Private Limited Company
**Line of Business:** Cleaning contracting commercial
**Issued Capital:** £100
**Directors:** Ms T A Taylor, N Sleep, A Walker, S G Hughes, P G Taylor
**Co. Secretary:** Ms Tracey Taylor

---

**Branches:** Premier Cleaning Services Ltd, 23 Modwen Road, Sandpiper Quays, Salford, M5 3EZ Manchester
**US SIC:** 7393 **UK SIC:** 83954
**Auditors:** Lindley & Co

| | 30-09-13 | 30-09-12 | 30-09-11 |
|---|---|---|---|
| TO | 14,427,918 | 15,315,660 | N/A |
| P/L | 443,430 | 179,684 | N/A |
| NW | 716,572 | 636,168 | 759,696 |
| WC | 133,468 | 128,292 | 379,230 |
| Emp. | 1,201 | 1,216 | N/A |

DUNS 29-873-7115　　　　　　　　　Imp

## Premier Tax Free (U K) Ltd
(**Subsidiary of:** Fintrax Group Holdings Ltd)
Fintrax House, Station Road North, Merstham, Redhill, Surrey RH1 3ED
**Tel:** 01737-644922 **Fax:** 01737-648570
**Web:** www.premiertaxfree.com
**Reg No:** 2076853 **Estd:** 1986 Private Limited Company
**Line of Business:** Tax consultancy
**Issued Capital:** £795,000
**Directors:** P C Flanagan, P G Faherty
**Co. Secretary:** Christopher Parkin
**Responsibilities**
**Marketing:** Claire McLaughlin (Marketing Manager)
**US SIC:** 7399 **UK SIC:** 83954
**Auditors:** Baker Tilly UK Audit LLP
**Bankers:** Allied Irish Bank (gb) (23-84-81)

| | 31-12-13 | 31-12-12 | 31-12-11 |
|---|---|---|---|
| TO | 22,340,660 | 17,710,854 | 13,170,453 |
| P/L | 1,364,798 | 1,955,452 | 1,790,397 |
| NW | 5,549,593 | 4,330,618 | 2,853,453 |
| WC | 5,329,153 | 4,033,720 | 2,771,211 |
| Emp. | 56 | 52 | 39 |

DUNS 21-600-4056

## Premier Taxis
3 Bull Green, Halifax, West Yorkshire HX1 5AB
**Tel:** 01422323232
**Estd:** 1997 Proprietorship
**Line of Business:** Taxi operation
**Proprietor:** A Iqbal
**Responsibilities**
**Senior:** Shaid Yamin (Manager)
**US SIC:** 4121 **UK SIC:** 72200
**Employees:** 50

DUNS 21-136-9282　　　　　　　　　Imp

## Premier Tech Aqua Ltd
(**Subsidiary of:** Gestion Bernard Bélanger Ltée)
2 Whitehouse Way, South West Industrial Estate, Peterlee, County Durham SR8 2RA
**Tel:** 0870-264-0004 **Fax:** 0870-264-0005
**Web:** www.conderproducts.com
**Reg No:** 6698049 **VAT No:** 927592292
**Estd:** 2008 Private Limited Company
**Line of Business:** Manufacture of other plastic products
**Trading Style:** Conder Products Limited
**Issued Capital:** £750,000
**Directors:** S Wray, M Noel, D Buckley, H Ouellet, J Belanger
**Co. Secretary:** Martin Noel
**Responsibilities**
**Senior:** Patrick Buckley (Manager)
**Sales:** Tadhg Buckley (Business Development Manager)
**US SIC:** 3079 **UK SIC:** 48360
**Auditors:** Thos. Goodall & Son

| | 28-02-14 | 31-03-13 | 31-02-12 |
|---|---|---|---|
| TO | 6,336,947 | 8,573,640 | 9,691,333 |
| P/L | (429,049) | (164,219) | 10,562 |
| NW | (389,527) | 3,545 | 133,707 |
| WC | 671,152 | 486,845 | 528,951 |
| Emp. | 84 | 94 | 117 |

DUNS 77-142-8240

## Premier Trade Frames Ltd
(**Subsidiary of:** Masco Corporation)
Premier House, Caerphilly, Mid Glamorgan CF83 1BQ
**Tel:** 02920881200
**Web:** www.premier-trade.co.uk
**Reg No:** 2703952 **Estd:** 1992 Private Limited Company
**Line of Business:** Window frame sales and service
**Issued Capital:** £100
**Directors:** W Devine, L D Gillett, K Gorton
**Co. Secretary:**
　Pinsent Masons Secretarial Limit
**Responsibilities**
**Senior:** Steven Fifer (Manager)
**Finance:** Mark Shather (Finance Director)
**IT:** Matthew Dowsett (Network Manager)
**Health & Safety:** Andrew Parsells (Health & Safety Officer)
**Operations:** Andrew Parsells (Health & Safety Officer)
**Purchasing:** Mark Berrow (Purchasing Manager)
**Branches:** Premier Trade Frames Ltd, Unit 2B Brook Lane Indust Estate, Westbury, Wiltshire BA13 4EP
**US SIC:** 3442 **UK SIC:** 31420

---

**Auditors:** Deloitte & Touche
**Bankers:** Barclays Bank Plc (20-10-26)

| | 31-12-13 | 31-12-12 | 31-12-11 |
|---|---|---|---|
| TO | N/A | N/A | 20,141,194 |
| P/L | N/A | N/A | (33,772) |
| NW | 5,006,533 | 5,006,533 | 5,006,533 |
| Emp. | N/A | N/A | 240 |

DUNS 21-228-3848

## Premier Trave Inn
Pearce Way, Salisbury, Wiltshire SP1 3YU
**Tel:** 08701977225
**Web:** www.premierinn.com
**Estd:** 2007 Proprietorship
**Line of Business:** Hotels and motels without restaurant
**US SIC:** 7011 **UK SIC:** 66500
**Employees:** 55

DUNS 21-892-0320

## Premier Travel Agency Ltd
29 Sidney Street, Cambridge, Cambridgeshire CB2 3HW
**Tel:** 01223500007
**Web:** www.premier-travel.co.uk
**Reg No:** 0786323 **VAT No:** 637045934
**Estd:** 1963 Private Limited Company
**Line of Business:** Activities of travel agencies
**Trading Style:** Premier Travel, Premier Holidays
**Issued Capital:** £100,000
**Principals:** R L Sargent (Managing), P S Andrews, Mrs R A Willis, Mrs S J Smith, P A Waters
**Co. Secretary:** Ms Rachael Willis
**Responsibilities**
**Senior:** Gregory Mould (Manager), Sue White (Manager)
**Finance:** Gregory Mould (Manager)
**HR:** Victoria Dowsett (Human Resources Coordinator)
**Health & Safety:** Gregory Mould (Manager)
**Facilities:** Gregory Mould (Manager)
**Branches:** Premier Travel Agency Limited, Premier Travel Agency Ltd, 10 Rose Crescent, Cambridge, Cambridgeshire CB2 3LL
**US SIC:** 4722 **UK SIC:** 77001
**Auditors:** Deloitte LLP
**Bankers:** Lloyds TSB Bank plc (30-91-56)

| | 30-09-14 | 30-09-13 | 30-09-12 |
|---|---|---|---|
| TA | 2,718,576 | 2,816,029 | 2,780,010 |
| NW | 400,053 | 365,827 | 333,317 |
| WC | 198,202 | 281,244 | 262,569 |

DUNS 21-863-9883

## Premier Travel Inn
West Portway Industrial Estate, Joule Road, Andover, Hampshire SP10 3UX
**Tel:** 08715278020
**Web:** www.premierinn.com
**Estd:** 2010 Proprietorship
**Line of Business:** Hotels
**Proprietor:** J Frost
**Responsibilities**
**Senior:** Karen Fowle (Operations Manager)
**US SIC:** 7011 **UK SIC:** 66500
**Employees:** 50

DUNS 21-224-4431

## Premier Travel Inn & Restaurant
Cambridge Road, Harlow, Essex CM20 2EP
**Tel:** 08715278488
**Web:** www.premierinn.com
**Estd:** 1983
**Line of Business:** Hotels
**Proprietor:** Ms T Munn
**Responsibilities**
**HR:** Maria Symons (Human Resources Manager)
**Health & Safety:** Maria Symons (Human Resources Manager)
**US SIC:** 7011 **UK SIC:** 66500
**Employees:** 70

DUNS 21-230-4473

## Premier Travel Inn Warrington
1430 Park Boulevard, Warrington, Cheshire WA1 1PR
**Tel:** 08715279126
**Web:** www.premierinn.com
**Estd:** 2002
**Line of Business:** Hotels
**Proprietor:** P Lawrence
**Responsibilities**
**Senior:** Sean Kelley (General Manager)
**US SIC:** 7999 **UK SIC:** 97913
**Employees:** 60

DUNS 29-119-6376 Imp-Exp

## Premier Vanguard Ltd

(**Subsidiary of:** Midas Paper Converters Ltd)
Concorde House, Stewart Close, Bradford, West Yorkshire BD2 2EE
**Tel:** 08452229000
**Web:** www.premvan.com
**Reg No:** 1583045 **VAT No:** 362076266
**Estd:** 1981 Private Limited Company
**Line of Business:** Cash register accessories and services
**Export Markets:** Worldwide
**Issued Capital:** £10,000
**Principals:** R J Kirkham *(Managing)*, J P Clemie *(Managing)*, D W Deluca, C J Deluca, Ms L V Clemie, Ms R L Deluca, Ms J M Kirkham, Ms M A Deluca
**Co. Secretary:** Robert Kirkham
**Responsibilities**
**Senior:** Philip Parkes *(Branch Manager)*
**Marketing:** Ann Petty *(Sales & Marketing Manager)*
**Sales:** Ann Petty *(Sales & Marketing Manager)*
**Purchasing:** Heather Pawsey *(Purchasing Manager)*
**Branches:** Premier Vanguard Ltd, 49 Downside Road, Sutton, Surrey SM2 5HR
**US SIC:** 3579 **UK SIC:** 33010
**Auditors:** Hollings Crowe Storr & Co
**Bankers:** HSBC Bank plc (40-27-15)

| | 30-09-13 | 30-09-12 | 30-09-11 |
|---|---|---|---|
| TO | 14,383,090 | 13,669,510 | 14,178,663 |
| P/L | 1,344,475 | 1,333,669 | 1,307,200 |
| NW | 4,394,592 | 3,853,124 | 3,237,739 |
| WC | 3,377,560 | 2,783,802 | 2,133,760 |
| Emp. | 74 | 70 | 73 |

DUNS 21-986-5362

## Premier Veterinary Group Ltd

32-34 Zetland Road, Bristol, Avon BS6 7AB
**Tel:** 01179445111
**Web:** www.premierveterinarygroup.com
**Reg No:** 6167939 **Estd:** 2007 Private Limited Company
**Line of Business:** Veterinary activities
**Issued Capital:** £3,238,646
**Director:** D S Tonner
**Co. Secretary:** Daniel Smith
**US SIC:** 0741 **UK SIC:** 95601
**Auditors:** BDO LLP
**Bankers:** National Westminster Bank Plc (55-50-15)

| | 30-09-13 | 30-09-12 | 30-09-11 |
|---|---|---|---|
| TO | 7,436,978 | 8,215,491 | N/A |
| P/L | (796,669) | (929,389) | N/A |
| NW | (1,820,020) | (872,183) | 1,810,701 |
| WC | (2,297,594) | (1,195,351) | 553,892 |
| Emp. | 167 | 126 | N/A |

DUNS 73-885-2925

## Premier Work Support Ltd

(**Subsidiary of:** Premier Work Support Holdings Ltd)
Quadrant Chambers, Quadrant Arcade, Romford, Essex RM1 3EH
**Tel:** 01708-753713 **Fax:** 01708732819
**Web:** www.premierworksupport.co.uk
**Reg No:** 5139457 **Estd:** 2004 Private Limited Company
**Line of Business:** Labour recruitment and provision of personnel
**Issued Capital:** £179
**Directors:** D Liebman, Non-Executive Directors Limited, I Green
**Co. Secretary:** Joseph Green
**US SIC:** 7361 **UK SIC:** 83954

| | 30-09-13 | 30-09-12 | 30-09-11 |
|---|---|---|---|
| TO | 20,081,960 | 15,761,709 | 15,519,202 |
| P/L | 197,853 | 126,946 | 161,065 |
| NW | 871,296 | 721,395 | 622,741 |
| WC | 831,324 | 672,847 | 574,574 |
| Emp. | 53 | 52 | 43 |

DUNS 71-866-3185

## Premierchoice Ltd

3-5 Algores Way, Wisbech, Cambridgeshire PE13 2TQ
**Tel:** 01945589595
**Web:** www.premierchoice.co.uk
**Reg No:** 5250342 **Estd:** 2004 Private Limited Company
**Line of Business:** Manufacture of soft furnishings
**Issued Capital:** £152,188
**Directors:** R Bluck, Mrs L Hustler, J Anderson, R J Lloyd-Davies, L J Anderson, S Davis, Mrs H M Anderson
**Co. Secretary:** Walter Cook
**US SIC:** 2391 **UK SIC:** 45550

| | 31-12-13 | 31-12-12 | 31-12-11 |
|---|---|---|---|
| TA | 3,101,016 | 2,888,457 | 2,657,425 |
| NW | 2,426,080 | 2,263,378 | 2,162,977 |
| WC | 811,484 | 620,512 | 580,586 |

DUNS 42-349-4959

## Premiere Conferencing (U K) Ltd

(**Subsidiary of:** Pgi Worldwide Sarl)
17 Godliman Street, London EC4V 5BD
**Tel:** 020-7618-1930 **Fax:** 020-7618-1970
**Web:** www.pgi.com
**Reg No:** 4337199 **Estd:** 2001 Private Limited Company
**Line of Business:** Telecommunications
**Issued Capital:** £1
**Directors:** D R Fairtlough, T P Schrafft, J D Stone
**Co. Secretary:** Scott Leonard
**Responsibilities**
**Senior:** Tarenn Teller *(Office Manager)*
**Branches:** Premiere Conferencing (U K) Ltd, Apollo House, Eboracum Way, York, North Yorkshire YO31 7RE
**US SIC:** 4899 **UK SIC:** 79020
**Auditors:** Ernst & Young
**Bankers:** Allied Irish Bank (gb) (23-84-82)

| | 31-12-13 | 31-12-12 | 31-12-11 |
|---|---|---|---|
| TO | 7,923,626 | 5,104,136 | 4,320,833 |
| P/L | 57,165 | 626,489 | 546,615 |
| NW | 48,291 | 138,146 | 472,366 |
| WC | (297,327) | (1,268,020) | (944,211) |
| Emp. | 67 | 66 | 56 |

DUNS 73-704-7808

## Premiere Employment Group Ltd

(**Subsidiary of:** Cordant Group Plc)
7th Floor Blackfriars House, 1 Parsonage, Manchester M3 2JA
**Fax:** 01612112807
**Web:** www.premierepeople.com
**Reg No:** 4963501 **Estd:** 2003 Private Limited Company
**Line of Business:** Employment and recruitment companies and consultants
**Export Sales:** £6,444,220
**Trading Style:** Premiere People
**Issued Capital:** £650,000
**Directors:** P L Ullmann, J R Ullmann, S W Kirkpatrick
**Co. Secretary:** Alan Connor
**Branches:** Premiere Employment Group Ltd, 129 High Street, Bromsgrove, Worcestershire B61 8AE
**US SIC:** 7361 **UK SIC:** 83954
**Auditors:** Deloitte LLP
**Bankers:** The Co-Operative Bank Plc (08-90-00)

| | 30-06-13 | 30-06-12 | 30-06-11 |
|---|---|---|---|
| TO | 66,307,152 | 63,855,246 | 53,632,765 |
| P/L | 1,299,162 | 613,349 | 645,649 |
| NW | 2,368,434 | 1,340,058 | 858,701 |
| WC | 2,560,628 | 1,645,126 | 993,413 |
| Emp. | 3,955 | 3,488 | 3,050 |

DUNS 21-608-3949 Imp-Exp

## The Premiere Polish Company Ltd

Oakley Gardens, Bouncers Lane, Cheltenham, Gloucestershire GL52 5JD
**Tel:** 01242-537150 **Fax:** 01242-528445
**Web:** www.premierproducts.co.uk
**Reg No:** 0199037 **VAT No:** 274176740
**Estd:** 1924 Private Limited Company
**Line of Business:** Manufacture of soap and detergents
**Export Markets:** W Europe, Middle East, S & S E Asia
**Export Sales:** £841,797
**Trading Style:** Premiere Products
**Issued Capital:** £1,366,701
**Directors:** R G Lawson-Lee, D A Berry, Doctor K J Barnes, P Brown
**Co. Secretary:** Roger Lawson-Lee
**Responsibilities**
**Senior:** Steven Hammond *(Logistics Manager)*
**Finance:** Mike Cartwright *(Finance Director)*
**Marketing:** Matt Burtinshaw *(Marketing Manager)*, Layton Smith *(Marketing Manager)*
**IT:** Chris Wasley *(IT Manager)*
**HR:** Matthew Baines *(Training Manager)*
**Health & Safety:** Andrew Butterfield *(Chemist)*
**Operations:** Andrew Butterfield *(Chemist)*, Tom Childs *(Production Manager)*
**Purchasing:** Matt Burtinshaw *(Marketing Manager)*, Layton Smith *(Marketing Manager)*
**Fleet:** Steven Hammond *(Logistics Manager)*
**Engineering:** Tom Childs *(Production Manager)*
**US SIC:** 2841, 2842
**UK SIC:** 25810, 25990
**Auditors:** Grant Thornton U K LLP
**Bankers:** National Westminster Bank Plc (60-05-16)

| | 30-06-13 | 31-12-12 | 31-06-11 |
|---|---|---|---|
| TO | 6,665,930 | 14,031,159 | 15,071,582 |
| P/L | (885,085) | (377,453) | (101,946) |
| NW | (470,388) | 1,563,258 | 4,147,979 |
| WC | 1,274,186 | 1,452,702 | 1,935,938 |
| Emp. | 114 | 146 | 161 |

DUNS 21-708-5356 Exp

## Premierfirst Vehicle Rental Holdings Ltd

(**Subsidiary of:** Eurazeo)
Beasley Court, Warwick Place, Uxbridge, Middlesex UB8 1PE
**Tel:** 01293513031 **Fax:** 0990-666460
**Reg No:** 0915008 **VAT No:** 572442639
**Estd:** 1967 Private Limited Company
**Line of Business:** Management activities of holding companies
**Export Markets:** Europe & Worldwide
**Issued Capital:** £77,228,629
**Directors:** G N Smith, K S Mccall
**Branches:** Premierfirst Vehicle Rental Holdings Ltd, Olympic Ho, Manchester Airport, Manchester M90 1QX
**US SIC:** 6711 **UK SIC:** 83962
**Auditors:** Ernst & Young LLP
**Bankers:** National Westminster Bank Plc (56-00-55)

| | 31-12-13 | 31-12-12 | 31-12-11 |
|---|---|---|---|
| TA | 185,592,000 | 176,628,000 | 215,148,000 |
| P/L | 9,007,000 | 5,321,000 | 3,289,000 |
| NW | 158,616,000 | 149,398,000 | 146,190,000 |
| WC | (9,009,000) | (18,227,000) | (21,435,000) |

DUNS 23-853-4734

## Premium Choice Ltd

(**Subsidiary of:** Mers Ins Ltd)
406 Fort Dunlop, Birmingham, West Midlands B24 9FD
**Tel:** 08450737410
**Web:** www.premiumchoice.co.uk
**Reg No:** 3845329 **Estd:** 1999 Private Limited Company
**Line of Business:** Insurance - car and automotive
**Issued Capital:** £771,364
**Directors:** R Dornan, M Woods
**Responsibilities**
**Senior:** Jay Bayliss *(Customer Service Manager)*
**US SIC:** 6399, 6411
**UK SIC:** 82001, 83200
**Auditors:** Langard Lifford Hall Ltd
**Bankers:** Barclays Bank Plc (20-08-44)

| | 31-12-13 | 31-12-12 | 31-12-11 |
|---|---|---|---|
| TO | 11,594,684 | 10,284,520 | 7,796,990 |
| P/L | 246,328 | 804,858 | 660,247 |
| NW | 1,736,984 | 1,523,628 | 903,626 |
| WC | 1,312,185 | 1,185,786 | 845,381 |
| Emp. | 243 | 205 | 161 |

DUNS 29-691-6794 Exp

## Premium Credit Ltd

(**Subsidiary of:** Mizzen Mezzco Ltd)
60 East Street, Epsom, Surrey KT17 1HB
**Tel:** 0844-736-9836 **Fax:** 01372-748-811
**Web:** www.premium-credit.co.uk
**Reg No:** 2015200 **Estd:** 1986 Private Limited Company
**Line of Business:** Credit granting by non-deposit taking finance houses and other specialist consumer credit grantors
**Issued Capital:** £10,000
**Directors:** M S Hollander, A S Doman, C E Roche, A D Cohen, L C Powers-Freeling, J Reeve
**Co. Secretary:** Jasan Fitzpatrick
**Responsibilities**
**Senior:** Hohn Reeve *(Director)*
**Finance:** Jenny Johnson *(Chief Accounting Officer)*
**Sales:** Cristian Jackson *(National Sales Manager)*
**US SIC:** 6111 **UK SIC:** 81501
**Auditors:** PricewaterhouseCoopers LLP
**Bankers:** National Westminster Bank Plc (56-00-27)
**Following financial data are in thousands**

| | 31-12-13 | 31-12-12 | 31-12-11 |
|---|---|---|---|
| TA | 1,341,222 | 1,237,670 | 1,180,797 |
| P/L | 36,882 | 31,730 | 55,884 |
| NW | 142,527 | 141,737 | 118,148 |
| WC | 541,475 | 140,499 | 116,543 |
| Emp. | 337 | 321 | 333 |

DUNS 64-091-7589

## Premium Dining Restaurants & Pubs Ltd

(**Subsidiary of:** G.K. Holdings No.1 Ltd)
175 Hampton Road, Twickenham, Middlesex TW2 5NG
**Tel:** 02082556222
**Web:** www.lochfyneseafoodandgrill.co.uk
**Reg No:** 0181811SC **Estd:** 2003 Private Limited Company
**Line of Business:** Restaurant - seafood
**Issued Capital:** £839,600
**Directors:** J P Webster, S F Jebson, K D Davis, R Anand
**Co. Secretary:** Mrs Lindsay Keswick
**Responsibilities**
**Senior:** Gosia Cwiakla *(Manager)*, Matthew Fearn *(Manager)*
**Branches:** Premium Dining Restaurants & Pubs Ltd, 20 Market Place, Henley-On-Thames, Oxfordshire RG9 2AH
**US SIC:** 5812 **UK SIC:** 66110

**Auditors:** Ernst & Young LLP
**Bankers:** The Royal Bank Of Scotland Plc (83-23-07)

| | 04-05-14 | 28-04-13 | 29-05-12 |
|---|---|---|---|
| TO | 47,846,775 | 45,558,261 | 46,508,472 |
| P/L | 1,663,399 | 332,497 | 414,826 |
| NW | 9,088,415 | 7,831,732 | 8,002,890 |
| WC | (13,735,142) | (16,177,579) | (16,952,081) |
| Emp. | 1,164 | 1,110 | 1,234 |

DUNS 77-539-0941

## Premium Foods Ltd

Premium Restaurants, 4 Market Street, Hebden Bridge, West Yorkshire HX7 6AA
**Tel:** 01422846844 **Fax:** 01422-348269
**Web:** www.premierfoods.co.uk
**Reg No:** 2994865 **Estd:** 1994 Private Limited Company
**Line of Business:** Restaurants
**Trading Style:** McDonalds
**Issued Capital:** £100
**Director:** P G Singh
**Co. Secretary:** Mrs Christiane Singh
**Responsibilities**
**Senior:** Joe Calvert-Smith *(General Manager)*
**Branches:** Premium Foods Ltd, 22-24 Old Market, Halifax, West Yorkshire HX1 1TN
**US SIC:** 5812 **UK SIC:** 66110
**Auditors:** Townends
**Bankers:** The Royal Bank Of Scotland Plc (16-23-37)

| | 31-12-13 | 31-12-12 | 31-12-11 |
|---|---|---|---|
| TA | 402,390 | 401,715 | 401,481 |
| NW | 453,586 | 407,205 | 461,481 |
| WC | (7,932) | (54,303) | N/A |

DUNS 23-809-7674

## Premium Healthcare Ltd

(**Subsidiary of:** Hythe Care Homes Ltd)
Philbeach House, Tanners Hill, Hythe, Kent CT21 5UQ
**Tel:** 01303262421
**Web:** www.hythecare.com
**Reg No:** 3802128 **Estd:** 2011 Private Limited Company
**Line of Business:** Non-charitable social work activities with accommodation
**Issued Capital:** £1,000
**Directors:** P M Barker, R A Barnes
**Co. Secretary:** Ms Helen Barnes
**Responsibilities**
**Senior:** Karen Way *(Home Manager)*
**Branches:** Premium Healthcare Ltd, 46 Bartholomew Lane, Hythe, Kent CT21 4BX
**US SIC:** 8321 **UK SIC:** 96111
**Auditors:** Gary Sargeant & Co

| | 31-03-14 | 31-03-13 | 31-03-12 |
|---|---|---|---|
| TA | 1,006,733 | 965,850 | 940,214 |
| NW | 371,331 | 362,522 | 421,555 |
| WC | 210,280 | 197,762 | 290,701 |

DUNS 77-909-6192

## Premium Restaurants Ltd

Townends Financial Consultants, 6 Carlisle Street, Goole, North Humberside DN14 5DU
**Tel:** 01132456106
**Web:** www.premiumrestaurants.co.uk
**Reg No:** 5812953 **Estd:** 2006 Private Limited Company
**Line of Business:** Unlicensed restaurants and cafes
**Issued Capital:** £922,922
**Directors:** P G Singh, T Kelly, J Park
**Co. Secretary:** Ms Christiane Singh
**Branches:** Premium Restaurants Ltd, Rooley Lane, Bradford, West Yorkshire BD4 7SR
**US SIC:** 5812 **UK SIC:** 66110
**Bankers:** The Royal Bank Of Scotland Plc (16-08-05)

| | 31-12-13 | 31-12-12 | 31-12-11 |
|---|---|---|---|
| TO | 47,527,397 | 43,998,080 | 41,205,499 |
| P/L | 937,940 | 866,196 | 885,995 |
| NW | 515,288 | 401,568 | 110,192 |
| WC | (1,434,853) | (1,725,746) | (889,483) |
| Emp. | 1,756 | 1,698 | 1,623 |

DUNS 39-907-2206 Imp

## Premium Timber Products Ltd

Premium House, Axbridge, Somerset BS26 2JU
**Tel:** 01179163100 **Fax:** 01179-163149
**Web:** www.osdl.co.uk
**Reg No:** 2232367 **VAT No:** 520077679
**Estd:** 1988 Private Limited Company
**Line of Business:** Timber merchants
**Issued Capital:** £220,610
**Principals:** C J Gardner *(Managing)*, C A Westley *(Managing)*, D C Speck
**Co. Secretary:** Mrs Elaine Gardner
**Responsibilities**
**Senior:** Cameron Gardner *(Manager)*, Teresa Page *(Manager)*
**Branches:** Premium Timber Products Ltd, Meltham Mills, Holmfirth, West Yorkshire HD9 4DS
**US SIC:** 5072 **UK SIC:** 61500
**Auditors:** Deloitte & Touche LLP

**Bankers:** National Westminster Bank Plc (56-00-05)

| | 31-12-13 | 31-12-12 | 31-12-11 |
|---|---|---|---|
| TO | 24,737,986 | 25,504,128 | 29,806,119 |
| P/L | 1,231,685 | 1,369,959 | 1,607,531 |
| NW | 6,446,411 | 5,881,287 | 5,300,011 |
| WC | 4,933,249 | 4,555,108 | 4,110,592 |
| Emp. | 56 | 54 | 60 |

DUNS 73-786-6108
## Premiumstar Ltd
(**Subsidiary of:** Yes Money Ltd)
Cradoc House, Heol Y Llyfrau Aberkenfig, Bridgend, Mid Glamorgan CF32 9PL
**Tel:** 01633712712
**Web:** www.bb4uk.com
**Reg No:** 5043176 **Estd:** 2004 Private Limited Company
**Line of Business:** Call centre activities
**Issued Capital:** £750
**Directors:** D A Cowdery, Mrs J Chorlton
**Co. Secretary:** Stephen Francis
**US SIC:** 7399 **UK SIC:** 83954

| | 31-10-13 | 31-10-12 | 31-10-11 |
|---|---|---|---|
| TO | 8,009,840 | 8,753,056 | 10,355,337 |
| P/L | 308,292 | 810,208 | 1,597,668 |
| NW | 885,545 | 647,971 | 1,482,579 |
| WC | 870,356 | 621,952 | 1,466,823 |
| Emp. | 381 | 392 | 413 |

DUNS 29-623-7241
## Prentice Furniture Manufacturers Ltd
Brent, Tame Valley Industrial Estate, Wilnecote, Tamworth, Staffordshire B77 5DF
**Tel:** 01827287387
**Web:** www.prentice.co.uk
**Reg No:** 1950212 **VAT No:** 425472358
**Estd:** 1985 Private Limited Company
**Line of Business:** Furniture for home and office
**Trading Style:** P F M
**Issued Capital:** £1,005
**Principals:** D B Prentice *(Managing)*, Mrs J Pritchett *(Financial)*, P Pritchett
**Co. Secretary:** Mrs Caroline Prentice
**Responsibilities**
**Senior:** Thomas Prentice *(Production Director)*
**IT:** Andrew Cattell *(IT Manager)*
**Health & Safety:** Thomas Prentice *(Production Director)*
**Facilities:** Ken Brailsford *(Maintenance Manager)*
**Engineering:** Ken Brailsford *(Maintenance Manager)*, Thomas Prentice *(Production Director)*
**Branches:** Prentice Furniture Manufacturers Ltd, 5-6 Brent, Tame Valley Industrial Estate, Tamworth, Staffordshire B77 5DF
**US SIC:** 2599 **UK SIC:** 46720
**Auditors:** Tomkinson Teal
**Bankers:** National Westminster Bank Plc (54-21-13)

| | 30-09-13 | 30-09-12 | 30-09-11 |
|---|---|---|---|
| TA | 1,758,212 | 1,716,563 | 1,665,622 |
| NW | 1,255,638 | 1,203,713 | 1,139,588 |
| WC | 910,556 | 794,514 | 696,256 |

DUNS 22-925-7340
## Prentice Properties Ltd
(**Subsidiary of:** Prentice Estates Ltd)
20 Armagh Road, Portadown, Craigavon, Co Armagh BT62 3DP
**Tel:** 02838353377
**Reg No:** 0010098NI **Estd:** 1974 Private Limited Company
**Line of Business:** Estate agents
**Issued Capital:** £50,000
**Director:** Mrs M N Prentice
**Co. Secretary:** Albert Prentice
**US SIC:** 6531 **UK SIC:** 83400
**Auditors:** FitchCampbell
**Employees:** 150

DUNS 21-732-1510
## Prenton High School for Girls
Hesketh Avenue, Birkenhead, Merseyside CH42 6RR
**Tel:** 01515150238
**Web:** www.prentonhighschool.co.uk
**Reg No:** 7672980 **Estd:** 2011 Private Company Limited By Guarantee
**Line of Business:** General secondary education
**Directors:** E Harrison, J P Roper, Ms L Ayling, Mrs A L Winter, P Sandman, Mrs K Y Podmore, Mrs L Smith, Ms J M Sloane
**Responsibilities**
**Senior:** Paula Condliffe-Hughes *(Director)*, Lynda Eaton *(Director)*, Christopher Pierce *(Director)*
**US SIC:** 8211 **UK SIC:** 93200
**Bankers:** Lloyds TSB Bank plc (30-15-52)

| | 31-08-13 | 31-08-12 |
|---|---|---|
| TO | 4,550,000 | 5,127,000 |
| P/L | 420,000 | (251,000) |
| NW | 107,000 | (354,000) |
| WC | 1,042,000 | 809,000 |
| Emp. | 81 | 77 |

DUNS 85-614-7579
## Preparation for Life Ltd
65 Brutus Road, Newcastle, Staffordshire ST5 7QE
**Tel:** 01782-563329
**Web:** www.preparationforlife.com
**Reg No:** 6251264 **Estd:** 1997 Private Limited Company
**Line of Business:** Business and management consultancy activities not elsewhere classified
**Issued Capital:** £1,000
**Director:** R P Banfield
**Co. Secretary:** Charles Malacaso
**Responsibilities**
**Senior:** Lawrie Green *(Chairman)*, Moyinoluwa Ogedengbe *(Country Director)*
**Finance:** Shahkar Iqbal *(Group Finance Manager)*, Kashif Rizwan *(Financial Director)*
**Marketing:** Andrew Coyle *(Sales and Marketing Director)*
**Sales:** Andrew Coyle *(Sales and Marketing Director)*
**Operations:** Haris Shams *(Director of Operations)*
**US SIC:** 7392 **UK SIC:** 83951
**Employees:** 80

DUNS 53-641-3511 **Imp-Exp**
## The Preparation Group Ltd
Preparation House, Deacon Road, Lincoln, Lincolnshire LN2 4JB
**Tel:** 01522561460 **Fax:** 01522 561467
**Web:** www.ppcgroup.co.uk
**Reg No:** 3446892 **Estd:** 1997 Private Limited Company
**Line of Business:** Management activities of holding companies
**Trading Style:** P P C
**Issued Capital:** £100
**Director:** P Igo
**Co. Secretary:** Ms Tracey Glew
**Responsibilities**
**Senior:** Sarah Frankish *(PA / Office Manager)*
**Sales:** Kate Walshaw *(Area Sales Manager)*
**Operations:** Rebecca Crowe *(Contract Manager)*
**US SIC:** 6711 **UK SIC:** 83962

| | 28-02-14 | 28-02-13 | 28-02-12 |
|---|---|---|---|
| TA | 522,704 | 509,856 | 540,317 |
| NW | 53,878 | 65,898 | 17,300 |
| WC | (2,662) | (27,154) | (51,762) |

DUNS 22-004-8248
## Prepay Technologies Ltd
(**Subsidiary of:** Edenred Italia Srl)
Floor 6, 3 Sheldon Square, Paddington, London W1U 8EW
**Tel:** 020-7034-4344
**Web:** www.prepaysolutions.com
**Reg No:** 4008083 **Estd:** 2000 Private Limited Company
**Line of Business:** Other business activities not elsewhere classified
**Trading Style:** Prepay Solutions
**Issued Capital:** £149,578
**Directors:** G M Comley, A J Dumurgier, R C Brash, Ms D C Doyle
**Co. Secretary:** Julian Brand
**Responsibilities**
**Senior:** Philippe Bertinchamps *(Manager)*, Marc Divay *(Director)*, Alfredo Gangotena *(Manager)*, Matthieu Troubl *(Director)*
**Admin:** Kimberly Wright *(Office Manager)*
**Facilities:** Kimberly Wright *(Office Manager)*
**Branches:** Prepay Technologies Ltd, Station Square, 4th Floor, Swindon, Wiltshire SN1 1GW
**US SIC:** 7399 **UK SIC:** 83954
**Auditors:** Deloitte LLP
**Bankers:** Barclays Bank Plc (27-99-00)

| | 31-12-13 | 31-12-12 | 31-12-11 |
|---|---|---|---|
| TO | 13,447,203 | 11,544,974 | 9,950,299 |
| P/L | (2,287,236) | (2,450,104) | (4,018,479) |
| NW | 8,883,869 | 7,150,278 | 5,578,029 |
| WC | 7,614,772 | 6,554,894 | 4,810,386 |
| Emp. | 132 | 106 | 100 |

DUNS 42-469-1058
## Preqin Ltd
(**Subsidiary of:** Preqin Holding Ltd)
Equitable House, 47 King Williams Street, London
**Tel:** 020 7645 8888 **Fax:** 087 0330 5892
**Reg No:** 4456744 **Estd:** 2002 Private Limited Company
**Line of Business:** Other publishing
**Export Sales:** £10,673,697
**Trading Style:** Www.Preqin.Com
**Issued Capital:** £93,314
**Director:** M K Hodgson
**Co. Secretary:** Alfred O'Hare
**US SIC:** 2741 **UK SIC:** 47541

**Auditors:** Baker Tilly UK Audit LLP

| | 31-12-13 | 31-12-12 | 31-12-11 |
|---|---|---|---|
| TO | 12,936,247 | 9,504,506 | 7,438,664 |
| P/L | 1,900,776 | 1,200,263 | 976,194 |
| NW | 1,681,814 | 1,348,050 | 320,095 |
| WC | 1,684,248 | 1,331,854 | 188,161 |
| Emp. | 112 | 92 | N/A |

DUNS 23-806-1217 **Imp**
## Presbar Diecastings Ltd
(**Subsidiary of:** Presbar Group Ltd)
Store Street, Manchester M1 2WD
**Tel:** 0161-273-4381
**Web:** www.presbar-diecastings.co.uk
**Reg No:** 3798597 **Estd:** 1993 Private Limited Company
**Line of Business:** Forging, pressing, stamping and roll forming of metal; powder metallurgy
**Export Sales:** £2,897,057
**Issued Capital:** £2
**Principals:** R J Wrinch *(Managing)*, R P Wrinch, S Bradley, M J Wilson, D Kitching, T H Tottey, W B Hughes, Ms C N Wrinch
**Co. Secretary:** Robert Wrinch
**Responsibilities**
**Senior:** Russell Kaye *(Sales Director)*, Melanie Wrinch *(Director)*
**Sales:** Russell Kaye *(Sales Director)*
**US SIC:** 3559 **UK SIC:** 32863
**Auditors:** Blueprint Audit Ltd

| | 31-10-13 | 31-10-12 | 31-10-11 |
|---|---|---|---|
| TO | 10,699,857 | 10,804,486 | 10,407,127 |
| P/L | (37,369) | 247,458 | 702,418 |
| NW | 1,798,456 | 1,817,369 | 1,569,911 |
| WC | 1,703,436 | 3,561,612 | 3,642,598 |
| Emp. | 158 | 160 | 164 |

DUNS 36-487-7741
## Presbyterian Church in Ireland
Unit 14 Fisherwick Place, Belfast BT1 6DU
**Tel:** 02890-322284
**Web:** www.presbyterianireland.org
**Estd:** 1642
**Line of Business:** Residential care establishments
**Responsibilities**
**Senior:** William Mccaughey *(Manager)*, Charlotte Stevenson *(Board Member)*
**Branches:** Presbyterian Church In Ireland, Ballybog Road, Belfast, Belfast BT17 9QT
**US SIC:** 8661 **UK SIC:** 96600
**Auditors:** Ernst & Young LLP
**Employees:** 446
**Turnover:** £28,256,733

DUNS 23-694-1647
## The Presbyterian Church of Wales
81 Merthyr Road, Cardiff, South Glamorgan CF14 1DD
**Tel:** 02920627465
**Web:** www.ebcpcw.org.uk
**Estd:** 1933
**Line of Business:** Places of worship
**Directors:** Rev J T Williams, E Richards, Rev G Roden, Rev R Bebb, I Hughes, M Davies, Rev D A Jones, Rev I Roberts
**Responsibilities**
**Senior:** Andy Britton *(Principal)*, Eleri Melhuish *(Office Manager)*, Merion Morris *(General Secretary)*
**Branches:** The Presbyterian Church Of Wales, Gwasg Pantycelyn, St. Davids Road, Caernarfon, Gwynedd LL55 1ER
**US SIC:** 8661 **UK SIC:** 96600
**Auditors:** PricewaterhouseCoopers LLP
**Employees:** 117
**Turnover:** £4,296,000

DUNS 42-471-1554
## Presbyterian Residential Trust Ltd
Assembly Buildings, 2-10 Fisherwick Place, Belfast BT1 6DW
**Tel:** 02890417234
**Web:** www.pcibsw.org
**Reg No:** 0006536NI **Estd:** 2011 Private Company Limited By Guarantee
**Line of Business:** Social work activities with accommodation
**Directors:** L Conway, Reverend T J Mccormick
**Co. Secretary:** Ms Linda Wray
**Branches:** Presbyterian Residential Trust Ltd, 25 Riverwood Vale, Bangor, Co Down BT20 4QE
**US SIC:** 8321 **UK SIC:** 96111
**Auditors:** Ernst & Young LLP

| | 31-12-13 | 31-12-12 | 31-12-11 |
|---|---|---|---|
| TA | 64 | 64 | 77 |

DUNS 23-230-9265
## Presciption Pricing Authority
Wakefield House, Borough Road, Wakefield, West Yorkshire WF1 3UB
**Tel:** 03003301349
**Web:** www.ppa.nhs.uk
**Estd:** 1950 Partnership
**Line of Business:** General (overall) public service activities
**Principals:** N Scholte, E Mcgeever *(Partner)*, Ms J Stringer *(Partner)*
**Responsibilities**
**Senior:** Edward McGeever *(Divisional Manager)*
**US SIC:** 9121, 7374
**UK SIC:** 91110, 83940
**Employees:** 300

DUNS 51-581-2142
## Prescott & Conran Ltd
5 Redchurch Street, London E2 7DJ
**Tel:** 02077499800
**Web:** www.prescottandconran.com
**Reg No:** 5862310 **Estd:** 2006 Private Limited Company
**Line of Business:** Development and selling of real estate
**Issued Capital:** £1,010
**Directors:** Lady V J Conran, Sir T O Conran, P P Prescott
**Responsibilities**
**Marketing:** Samantha Samuel *(Marketing Manager)*
**US SIC:** 7399, 7011
**UK SIC:** 83954, 66500
**Bankers:** National Westminster Bank Plc (60-04-04)

| | 30-06-13 | 30-06-12 | 30-06-11 |
|---|---|---|---|
| TO | 8,134,685 | 7,822,691 | 8,567,685 |
| P/L | (202,619) | (257,737) | (95,086) |
| NW | (2,324,799) | (2,124,151) | (1,868,385) |
| WC | (721,062) | 40,589 | 269,080 |
| Emp. | 168 | 168 | 170 |

DUNS 21-023-6287 **Imp**
## Prescott-Thomas Ltd
New Spitalfields Market, Sherrin Road, London E10 5SQ
**Tel:** 02085-589-550
**Web:** www.prescott-thomas.com
**Reg No:** 0600075 **VAT No:** 243709070
**Estd:** 1958 Private Limited Company
**Line of Business:** Non-specialised wholesale of food, beverages and tobacco
**Issued Capital:** £10,000
**Managing Director:** P R Thomas
**Co. Secretary:** Mrs Susan Thomas
**Responsibilities**
**Finance:** Sharon Garett *(Finance Manager)*
**US SIC:** 5149, 5147
**UK SIC:** 61700
**Auditors:** Brindley Millen Ltd
**Bankers:** Barclays Bank Plc (20-77-67)

| | 30-06-14 | 30-06-13 | 30-06-12 |
|---|---|---|---|
| TO | 10,641,263 | 11,109,734 | 9,632,478 |
| P/L | 339,405 | 71,509 | (168,002) |
| NW | 231,712 | 199,702 | 181,225 |
| WC | 211,102 | 172,223 | 156,030 |
| Emp. | 101 | 99 | 96 |

DUNS 21-878-5753
## Prescription Pre Payment Service
P O Box 854, Newcastle-Upon-Tyne, Tyne and Wear NE99 2DE
**Tel:** 03003301341
**Web:** www.nhsbsa.nhs.uk
**Estd:** 2012
**Line of Business:** Health authorities
**US SIC:** 8062 **UK SIC:** 95100
**Employees:** 78

DUNS 21-771-7273
## Presdales School
Hoe Lane, Ware, Hertfordshire SG12 9NX
**Tel:** 01920462210
**Web:** www.presdales.herts.sch.uk
**Estd:** 2002 Proprietorship
**Line of Business:** Schools (local authority)
**Proprietor:** Mrs J Robinson
**Responsibilities**
**Finance:** Margaret Stanley *(Finance Director)*
**IT:** Carla Bagwell *(Network Manager)*, Steve Newman *(Senior IT Executive)*
**US SIC:** 8211 **UK SIC:** 93200
**Employees:** 120

DUNS 21-830-5383
## Presentation Products Group Ltd
Dundee Road, Arbroath, Angus DD11 2PT
**Web:** www.giftpack.co.uk
**Reg No:** 0420144SC **Estd:** 2012 Private Limited Company
**Line of Business:** Management activities of holding companies
**Export Sales:** £6,098,000

**Issued Capital:** £4,310,000
**Directors:** Mrs L Conway, J J Conway
**Co. Secretary:** Mrs Laura Conway
**Responsibilities**
**Marketing:** William Ovens *(Sales and Marketing Director)*
**Sales:** William Ovens *(Sales and Marketing Director)*
**US SIC:** 6711 **UK SIC:** 83962
**Bankers:** HSBC Bank plc (40-01-25)

| | 28-02-14 | 28-02-13 |
|---|---|---|
| TO | 27,705,000 | 26,450,000 |
| P/L | 2,225,000 | (304,000) |
| NW | 2,067,000 | 95,000 |
| WC | 2,538,000 | 896,000 |
| Emp. | 147 | 202 |

DUNS 21-683-1666 **Imp**
## President Engineering Group Ltd
President Way, Sheffield, South Yorkshire S4 7UR
**Tel:** 01142240000
**Web:** www.pegl.co.uk
**Reg No:** 7332395 **Estd:** 2010 Private Limited Company
**Line of Business:** Manufacturers of valves
**Export Sales:** £16,713,000
**Issued Capital:** £250,000
**Directors:** Ms M Broadhead, M A Henley, Mrs M Cooper, J D Waddington, D M Bramwell
**US SIC:** 3494 **UK SIC:** 32880
**Bankers:** National Westminster Bank Plc (54-41-34)

| | 31-10-14 | 31-10-13 | 31-10-12 |
|---|---|---|---|
| TO | 18,567,000 | 21,175,000 | 19,579,000 |
| P/L | 1,609,000 | 1,777,000 | 2,209,000 |
| NW | 3,321,000 | 1,314,000 | 973,000 |
| WC | 4,928,000 | 3,689,000 | 3,548,000 |
| Emp. | 119 | 116 | 107 |

DUNS 21-678-0683
## Presido Group Ltd
Lock 90 Trumpet Street, Manchester M1 5LW
**Tel:** 01924204830
**Reg No:** 7291725 **Estd:** 2010 Private Limited Company
**Line of Business:** Holding companies management activities
**Issued Capital:** £100
**Directors:** A J Pugh, M W Gray
**US SIC:** 6711 **UK SIC:** 83962
**Auditors:** Sedulo Business Services Ltd

| | 31-12-13 | 31-12-12 | 31-12-11 |
|---|---|---|---|
| TO | 7,047,280 | 7,008,577 | 7,184,332 |
| P/L | (89,672) | 159,308 | 108,977 |
| NW | 56,593 | 661,627 | 586,417 |
| WC | (1,160,665) | (574,858) | (507,623) |
| Emp. | 80 | 98 | 126 |

DUNS 53-603-9464
## Press Data Ltd
20-22 East London Street, Edinburgh, Midlothian EH7 4BQ
**Tel:** 01315503350
**Web:** www.pressdata.co.uk
**Reg No:** 0177530SC **Estd:** 2011 Private Limited Company
**Line of Business:** Press cutting bureau
**Issued Capital:** £2
**Director:** Ms S Briley Ward
**Co. Secretary:** Jeremy Ward
**US SIC:** 7351, 7311
**UK SIC:** 83954, 83800

| | 31-07-13 | 31-07-12 | 31-07-11 |
|---|---|---|---|
| TA | 681,143 | 782,974 | 701,463 |
| NW | (63,006) | 11,065 | 44,930 |
| WC | (91,191) | (15,413) | 34,974 |

DUNS 34-823-6386 **Imp**
## Pressac Communications Ltd
145 Glaisdale Drive West, Nottingham, Nottinghamshire NG8 4GY
**Tel:** 01159365200
**Web:** www.presscomm.co.uk
**Reg No:** 5623170 **VAT No:** 873529786
**Estd:** 1997 Private Limited Company
**Line of Business:** Telecommunications
**Export Sales:** £1,558,983
**Issued Capital:** £10,520
**Directors:** P L Burbidge, C A Howell
**Responsibilities**
**Senior:** Garry Gillespie *(Financial Director)*
**Finance:** Garry Gillespie *(Financial Director)*
**IT:** Kieth Moks *(Senior IT Executive)*
**HR:** Janet Fuller *(Human Resources Manager)*, Jane Rowlins *(Human Resources Manager)*
**Health & Safety:** Janet Fuller *(Human Resources Manager)*
**Purchasing:** Andrew Caldwell *(Purchasing Manager)*
**Engineering:** Brian Astill *(Production Manager)*
**US SIC:** 4899 **UK SIC:** 79020

**Auditors:** The Rowleys Partnership Ltd

| | 31-12-13 | 31-12-12 | 31-12-11 |
|---|---|---|---|
| TO | 11,826,314 | 8,587,549 | 7,884,539 |
| P/L | 813,900 | 272,433 | 765,181 |
| NW | 2,836,851 | 2,193,357 | 2,131,291 |
| WC | 2,071,213 | 1,466,708 | 1,300,023 |
| Emp. | 49 | 57 | 62 |

DUNS 29-161-3735
## Pressbeau Ltd
Park Road, Stoke Poges, Slough, Berkshire SL2 4PJ
**Tel:** 01753-784200 **Fax:** 01753-642141
**Web:** www.pressbeau.co.uk
**Reg No:** 1787750 **Estd:** 1984 Private Limited Company
**Line of Business:** Non-charitable social work activities with accommodation
**Trading Style:** Pressbeau Ltd
**Issued Capital:** £30,000
**Directors:** Mrs R Saraogi, Mrs P L Saraogi
**Co. Secretary:** Sharad Saraogi
**Branches:** Pressbeau Ltd, Greathed Manor, Ford Manor Rd, Lingfield, Surrey RH7 6PA
**US SIC:** 8321 **UK SIC:** 96111
**Auditors:** SMS Abacus & Co Ltd

| | 30-06-13 | 30-06-12 | 30-06-11 |
|---|---|---|---|
| TO | 5,115,296 | 4,940,515 | 5,307,056 |
| P/L | 334,638 | 258,302 | 997,223 |
| NW | 4,160,447 | 3,925,259 | 3,725,139 |
| WC | 1,406,209 | 1,303,099 | 1,111,884 |
| Emp. | 240 | 242 | 242 |

DUNS 23-588-4728
## Pressed Steel Products Ltd
Unit 11 All Saints Industrial Estate, Darlington Road, Shildon, County Durham DL4 2RD
**Tel:** 01388770490 **Fax:** 01388-778068
**Web:** www.pspuk.com
**Reg No:** 3586104 **Estd:** 1998 Private Limited Company
**Line of Business:** Manufacture of other fabricated metal products not elsewhere classified
**Trading Style:** P S P
**Issued Capital:** £46,667
**Directors:** H Hindmarch, K A Abdul Razaq
**US SIC:** 3499 **UK SIC:** 31694
**Auditors:** Clive Owen & Co LLP
**Bankers:** National Westminster Bank Plc (51-70-43)

| | 31-12-13 | 31-12-12 | 31-12-11 |
|---|---|---|---|
| TO | 5,480,190 | N/A | N/A |
| P/L | 151,945 | N/A | N/A |
| NW | 1,078,476 | 1,322,033 | 1,297,676 |
| WC | 15,855 | 33,109 | 49,309 |
| Emp. | 57 | N/A | N/A |

DUNS 21-292-0250 **Imp-Exp**
## Presspart Manufacturing Ltd
(**Subsidiary of:** Heitkamp & Thumann Kg)
Whitebirk Estate, Blackburn, Lancashire BB1 5RF
**Tel:** 01254582233
**Web:** www.presspart.com
**Reg No:** 0995387 **Estd:** 1970 Private Limited Company
**Line of Business:** Precision engineers
**Export Markets:** Worldwide
**Export Sales:** £22,192,000
**Issued Capital:** £25,000
**Directors:** J N Hemy, H J Neugebauer, D J Biggs, G Clark, P Schmelzer
**Co. Secretary:** Dietmar Schmitz
**Responsibilities**
**Senior:** Colin Watling *(Consultant)*
**Health & Safety:** V Riding *(Health & Safety Officer)*
**Operations:** V Riding *(Health & Safety Officer)*
**Purchasing:** Sylvana Wildman *(Head of Buying)*
**US SIC:** 8911, 3411, 3499
**UK SIC:** 83701, 31641, 31694
**Auditors:** Saffery Champness
**Bankers:** The Royal Bank Of Scotland Plc (16-00-01)

| | 31-12-13 | 31-12-12 | 31-12-11 |
|---|---|---|---|
| TO | 25,192,000 | 25,578,000 | 28,261,000 |
| P/L | 2,560,000 | 3,065,000 | 3,864,000 |
| NW | 4,169,000 | 2,616,000 | 2,757,000 |
| WC | 1,058,000 | 305,000 | 383,000 |
| Emp. | 142 | 141 | 137 |

DUNS 21-953-5544 **Imp**
## Pressure Technologies Plc
Meadowhall Road, Sheffield, South Yorkshire S9 1BT
**Tel:** 01142-427500 **Fax:** 01142427501
**Web:** www.pressuretechnologies.co.uk
**Reg No:** 6135104 **Estd:** 2007 Public Limited Company
**Line of Business:** Manufacture of other fabricated metal products not elsewhere classified
**Export Sales:** £28,285,000
**Issued Capital:** £568,112
**Directors:** N A Macdonald, J T Hayward, A J Wilson, N F Luckett, P S Cammerman
**Co. Secretary:** Thomas Lister
**US SIC:** 3499 **UK SIC:** 31694
**Auditors:** Grant Thornton UK LLP

**Bankers:** Bank Of Scotland (12-18-68)

| | 27-09-14 | 28-09-13 | 29-09-12 |
|---|---|---|---|
| TO | 54,015,000 | 34,383,000 | 30,442,000 |
| P/L | 5,349,000 | 2,878,000 | 1,778,000 |
| NW | 22,488,000 | 14,279,000 | 12,613,000 |
| WC | 17,963,000 | 10,342,000 | 8,940,000 |
| Emp. | 245 | 191 | 178 |

DUNS 29-082-2923
## Prestar Cleaning Co Ltd
298 Devon Road, Luton, Bedfordshire LU2 0RZ
**Tel:** 01582736951
**Web:** www.prestarcleaningcoltdluton.co.uk
**Reg No:** 1369927 **Estd:** 1978 Private Limited Company
**Line of Business:** Traditional cleaning activities
**Issued Capital:** £4
**Managing Director:** N P Soderberg
**US SIC:** 7349, 1751
**UK SIC:** 92300, 50400
**Bankers:** Lloyds TSB Bank plc (30-95-28)

| | 31-05-13 | 31-05-12 | 31-05-11 |
|---|---|---|---|
| TA | 58,289 | 52,439 | 32,475 |
| NW | (25,592) | (23,893) | (9,706) |
| WC | (26,212) | (24,622) | (10,564) |

DUNS 23-038-7383
## Presteigne Ltd
(**Subsidiary of:** Avesco Group Plc)
Units 2 & 3, Manor Gate, Manor Royal, Crawley, West Sussex RH10 9SX
**Tel:** 01293651300
**Web:** www.presteigne.co.uk
**Reg No:** 2720446 **Estd:** 1992 Private Limited Company
**Line of Business:** Broadcasting services
**Export Sales:** £3,573,000
**Issued Capital:** £280,000
**Principals:** M Ransome *(Managing)*, J L Christmas
**Co. Secretary:** Nicholas Conn
**Responsibilities**
**Senior:** Lisa Eddowes *(General Manager)*
**Branches:** Presteigne Ltd, Cocks Crescent, New Malden, Surrey KT3 4TA
**US SIC:** 4833 **UK SIC:** 97411
**Auditors:** PricewaterhouseCoopers LLP
**Bankers:** HSBC Bank plc (40-20-34)

| | 30-09-13 | 30-09-12 | 30-09-11 |
|---|---|---|---|
| TO | 8,773,000 | 17,359,000 | 13,527,000 |
| P/L | (4,738,000) | (139,000) | (494,000) |
| NW | (3,757,000) | 1,015,000 | 1,471,000 |
| WC | (13,288,000) | (10,476,000) | (13,657,000) |
| Emp. | 58 | 61 | 62 |

DUNS 29-166-8226
## Prestige Car Hire Ltd
25 Kings Terrace, London NW1 0JP
**Tel:** 020-7629-9262
**Web:** www.tstcars.co.uk
**Reg No:** 1813048 **Estd:** 1993 Private Limited Company
**Line of Business:** Chauffeur driven car hire
**Issued Capital:** £2
**Directors:** S Atik, T Guler
**US SIC:** 4141 **UK SIC:** 72102

| | 02-05-14 | 02-05-13 | 02-05-12 |
|---|---|---|---|
| TA | 590,380 | 563,016 | 437,914 |
| NW | 58,851 | 38,562 | 31,543 |
| WC | (141,791) | (105,004) | (58,345) |

DUNS 34-889-7281
## Prestige Industrial Ltd
(**Subsidiary of:** Fluorocarbon Group Ltd)
Lilac Grove, Nottingham, Nottinghamshire NG9 1PF
**Fax:** 01159431177
**Web:** www.fbsprestige.com
**Reg No:** 2826812 **VAT No:** 732844429
**Estd:** 2002 Private Limited Company
**Line of Business:** Catering equipment
**Trading Style:** Fbs Prestige
**Issued Capital:** £5,350,002
**Directors:** L Boggild, T J Wells, Mrs A J Campbell, G Stewart, W M Sharp
**Co. Secretary:** Fergus Wells
**Responsibilities**
**Senior:** Mark Schinagl *(Operations Manager)*
**HR:** Paul Essex *(HR Advisor)*
**Operations:** Mark Schinagl *(Operations Manager)*
**Branches:** Prestige Industrial Ltd, Birley Vale Ave, Sheffield, South Yorkshire S12 2AX
**US SIC:** 3551 **UK SIC:** 32441
**Auditors:** Rothman Pantall & Co
**Bankers:** Lloyds TSB Bank plc (30-94-17)

| | 31-12-13 | 31-08-12 | 31-12-11 |
|---|---|---|---|
| TO | 14,618,855 | 11,178,327 | 10,475,648 |
| P/L | 794,218 | 593,857 | 275,045 |
| NW | 2,837,823 | 1,986,430 | 1,349,685 |
| WC | 4,018,439 | 2,563,065 | 2,459,643 |
| Emp. | 69 | 72 | 97 |

DUNS 23-076-2288
## Prestige Insurance
161 High Street, Hampton Hill, Hampton, Middlesex TW12 1NG
**Tel:** 02089393900
**Web:** www.quotesa.co.uk
**Estd:** 2002 Partnership
**Line of Business:** Insurance services
**Trading Style:** High Performance Prestige
**Partners:** S Mcpherson, A Allen, Ms P Allen
**Responsibilities**
**Senior:** Carol Davidson *(Manager)*
**US SIC:** 6411 **UK SIC:** 83200
**Employees:** 300

DUNS 77-125-9173
## Prestige Leisure U K Ltd
36 Firth Road, Houstoun Industrial Estate, Livingston, West Lothian EH54 5DJ
**Tel:** 08006521234 **Fax:** 08006521244
**Web:** www.prestigeleisure.com
**Reg No:** 2698261 **VAT No:** 579355882
**Estd:** 1992 Private Limited Company
**Line of Business:** Distribution service providers
**Issued Capital:** £100,000
**Director:** M R Jumani
**Responsibilities**
**IT:** Bart Lewandowski *(IT Manager)*
**Branches:** Prestige Leisure U K Ltd, 36 Firth Road, Livingston, West Lothian EH54 5DJ
**US SIC:** 5136 **UK SIC:** 61600
**Auditors:** Seymour King
**Bankers:** National Westminster Bank Plc (60-22-40)

| | 31-12-13 | 31-12-12 | 31-12-11 |
|---|---|---|---|
| TO | 19,125,588 | 17,599,779 | 17,659,650 |
| P/L | 1,284,782 | 1,372,658 | 1,956,945 |
| NW | 7,590,817 | 6,628,642 | 5,565,503 |
| WC | 5,584,346 | 6,120,709 | 5,498,324 |
| Emp. | 73 | 68 | 62 |

DUNS 34-889-7125 **Imp-Exp**
## Prestige Medical Ltd
(**Subsidiary of:** The National Industries Group)
East House, Duttons Way, Shadsworth Business Park, Blackburn, Lancashire BB1 2QR
**Tel:** 01254-682622 **Fax:** 01254-682606
**Web:** www.prestigemedical.co.uk
**Reg No:** 2826793 **VAT No:** 633707835
**Estd:** 1993 Private Limited Company
**Line of Business:** Manufacture of medical and surgical equipment and orthopaedic appliances
**Export Sales:** £1,781,018
**Issued Capital:** £6,500,002
**Directors:** I Starkey, Mrs J A Ramsdale, A M Rodger
**Responsibilities**
**Finance:** Julie Carbine *(Finance Manager)*
**Marketing:** Christine Bowness *(Sales & Marketing Manager)*
**Sales:** Christine Bowness *(Sales & Marketing Manager)*
**Engineering:** Jason Whalley *(Production Manager)*
**US SIC:** 3841 **UK SIC:** 37201
**Auditors:** Grant Thornton UK LLP

| | 30-11-13 | 30-11-12 | 30-11-11 |
|---|---|---|---|
| TO | 4,662,020 | 5,107,520 | 5,515,014 |
| P/L | (390,530) | (127,132) | (61,845) |
| NW | (945,502) | (602,811) | (677,544) |
| WC | 644,931 | 1,194,806 | 1,131,366 |
| Emp. | 58 | 61 | 64 |

DUNS 22-523-1687
## Prestige Nursing Ltd
Greenview House, 5 Manor Road, Wallington, Surrey SM6 0BW
**Tel:** 02082-547-500
**Web:** www.prestige-nursing.co.uk
**Reg No:** 1006953 **VAT No:** 792010451
**Estd:** 1945 Private Limited Company
**Line of Business:** Nursing agencies
**Trading Style:** Prestige Nursing + Care
**Issued Capital:** £10,000
**Directors:** R G Bruce, Ms C L Hunt, Mrs P Bruce, J P Bruce
**Co. Secretary:** Ms Diane Jared
**Responsibilities**
**Senior:** Michael Dooley *(Branch Manager)*
**Marketing:** Samina Zeab *(Marketing Manager)*
**Branches:** Prestige Nursing Ltd, Beckwith House, 1 Wellington Road North, Stockport, Cheshire SK4 1AF
**US SIC:** 8091, 7361, 6732, 8321
**UK SIC:** 95200, 83954, 83100, 96111
**Auditors:** Jacob Cavenagh & Skeet
**Bankers:** Barclays Bank Plc (20-24-61)

| | 31-12-13 | 31-12-12 | 31-12-11 |
|---|---|---|---|
| TO | 22,700,500 | 22,485,954 | 21,038,371 |
| P/L | 714,020 | 744,554 | 302,914 |
| NW | 2,295,959 | 1,861,647 | 1,484,451 |
| WC | 2,109,800 | 1,785,979 | 1,493,679 |
| Emp. | 162 | 157 | 159 |

DUNS 85-604-1244

## Prestige Park & Leisure Homes Ltd

(**Subsidiary of:** Prestige Developments Group Ltd)
Unit 4 Pytchley Lodge Road, Kettering, Northamptonshire NN15 6JQ
**Tel:** 01536-518513
**Web:** www.prestigeparkandleisurehomes.com
**Reg No:** 6241050 **Estd:** 2007 Private Limited Company
**Line of Business:** Mobile homes
**Trading Style:** Prestige Park & Leisure Homes Ltd
**Issued Capital:** £1,000
**Directors:** M I Todd, S Geranio, K A Hanger
**Co. Secretary:** Eric Jones
**US SIC:** 3799 **UK SIC:** 36502
**Auditors:** Grant Thornton UK LLP
**Bankers:** Barclays Bank Plc (20-45-77)

| | 31-03-14 | 31-03-13 | 31-03-12 |
|---|---|---|---|
| TO | 14,654,472 | 14,937,932 | 13,806,824 |
| P/L | 1,197,164 | 683,682 | 1,016,505 |
| NW | 1,875,106 | 1,471,228 | 1,158,557 |
| WC | 1,448,836 | 1,082,172 | 683,703 |
| Emp. | 137 | 131 | 118 |

DUNS 22-097-4344

## Prestige Recruitment Specialists Ltd

12 Bowlalley Lane, Town Centre, Hull, North Humberside HU1 1XR
**Tel:** 01482-212581 **Fax:** 01482-212880
**Web:** www.prestige-recruitment.com
**Reg No:** 4098721 **Estd:** 2000 Private Limited Company
**Line of Business:** Employment and recruitment companies and consultants
**Issued Capital:** £100
**Director:** N D Stabler
**Co. Secretary:** John Headspith
**US SIC:** 7361 **UK SIC:** 83954
**Auditors:** Sadofskys
**Bankers:** National Westminster Bank Plc (60-19-14)

| | 30-09-13 | 30-09-12 | 30-09-11 |
|---|---|---|---|
| TO | 20,746,506 | N/A | N/A |
| P/L | 545,855 | N/A | N/A |
| NW | 907,720 | 490,525 | 228,585 |
| WC | 830,126 | 406,677 | 117,526 |
| Emp. | 1,371 | N/A | N/A |

DUNS 21-036-5905

## Prestige Scotland

Viewforth House, 31 The Loan, South Queensferry, West Lothian EH30 9SD
**Tel:** 08003281373
**Web:** www.prestigescotland.co.uk
**Partnership**
**Line of Business:** Catering
**Trading Style:** Prestige Scotland
**Partners:** Mrs A Cawley, Miss J Reeves, Mrs K Burton, A Tilsley, G Leich
**Responsibilities**
**Senior:** Graham Box *(Manager)*, Karen Burton *(HR Manager)*, Austin Tilsley *(Regional Director)*
**Finance:** Joe King *(Regional Commercial Manager)*
**HR:** Karen Burton *(HR Manager)*, Nikki Smith *(Senior Staffing Coordinator)*
**US SIC:** 5812 **UK SIC:** 66110
**Employees:** 110

DUNS 42-358-1743

## Prestige Underwriting Services Ltd

(**Subsidiary of:** Prestige Insurance Holdings Ltd)
Lanyon Building, Belfast BT15 3HL
**Tel:** 08450777666
**Web:** www.prestigeunderwriting.co.uk
**Reg No:** 0031853NI **Estd:** 1997 Private Limited Company
**Line of Business:** Non-life insurance
**Trading Style:** Ensign
**Issued Capital:** £1
**Directors:** D W Murray, G H Storey, T Shaw, P R Hanna, Mrs J Davidson, Ms G King, Mrs E Fitzgerald, I S Bond
**Co. Secretary:** Gary Martin
**Responsibilities**
**Senior:** Joanna Davidson *(Senior Financial Executive)*, Eugene Hassan *(Director)*, William Matier *(Senior IT Executive)*
**Finance:** Joanna Davidson *(Senior Financial Executive)*, Gary McMurry *(Management Accountant)*
**IT:** William Matier *(Senior IT Executive)*
**HR:** Sarah Tomms *(Group Human Resources Manager)*
**Branches:** Prestige Underwriting Services Ltd, Lanyon Building, 10 North Derby Street, Belfast, Belfast BT15 3HL
**US SIC:** 6399 **UK SIC:** 82001
**Auditors:** Pricewaterhouse Coopers
**Bankers:** Ulster Bank Ltd (98-11-45)

| | 31-03-14 | 31-03-13 | 31-03-12 |
|---|---|---|---|
| TO | 16,161,000 | 17,845,000 | 23,812,000 |
| P/L | 1,000,000 | 884,000 | 2,867,000 |
| NW | 3,948,000 | 4,115,000 | 3,429,000 |
| WC | 1,529,000 | 3,295,000 | 2,062,000 |
| Emp. | 116 | 147 | 155 |

DUNS 39-821-2993 **Imp-Exp**

## Prestigious Textiles Ltd

4 Cross Lane, Westgate Hill Street, Bradford, West Yorkshire BD4 0SG
**Tel:** 01274-688448
**Web:** www.prestigious.co.uk
**Reg No:** 2219358 **Estd:** 1988 Private Limited Company
**Line of Business:** Textile merchants
**Export Sales:** £14,014,535
**Issued Capital:** £51
**Principals:** T Helliwell *(Chairman and Managing)*, A D Gautry *(Financial)*, G R Bateman, M S Helliwell
**Co. Secretary:** Ms Nicola Brumfit
**Responsibilities**
**Senior:** Nicola Brumsitt *(Marketing Manager)*
**Finance:** Nicola Brumsitt *(Marketing Manager)*
**Marketing:** Nicola Brumsitt *(Marketing Manager)*
**Admin:** Curtis Mitchell *(Office Manager)*
**IT:** Adam Throp *(Head of IT)*
**HR:** Curtis Mitchell *(Office Manager)*
**Operations:** Curtis Mitchell *(Office Manager)*
**US SIC:** 5133 **UK SIC:** 61600
**Auditors:** Firth Parish
**Bankers:** Barclays Bank Plc (20-36-98)

| | 31-08-13 | 31-08-12 | 31-08-11 |
|---|---|---|---|
| TO | 28,271,037 | 29,603,576 | 29,136,044 |
| P/L | 1,193,576 | 1,423,305 | 1,464,226 |
| NW | 11,630,273 | 10,945,345 | 10,103,599 |
| WC | 10,794,301 | 10,410,565 | 9,765,539 |
| Emp. | 112 | 107 | 105 |

DUNS 21-729-0873 **Imp**

## Prestolite Electric Ltd

(**Subsidiary of:** Prestolite Electric Llc)
Unit 48, Greenford, Middlesex UB6 8UP
**Tel:** 02082-311-000 **Fax:** 02085-759-575
**Web:** www.prestolite.com
**Reg No:** 1189048 **VAT No:** 448440540
**Estd:** 1974 Private Limited Company
**Line of Business:** Manufacturers of electric motors
**Export Sales:** £15,554,000
**Trading Style:** Prestolite Electric
**Issued Capital:** £10,322,675
**Directors:** D Chelminski, F L Gemesi, T Rom
**Co. Secretary:** Ms Beverley Hounslow
**Responsibilities**
**Senior:** Peter Corrigan *(Manager)*, Joseph Lefave *(Manager)*, Steven Tarr *(Manager)*, Benson Woo *(Manager)*
**Marketing:** Chris Birkby *(Marketing Manager)*
**Branches:** Prestolite Electric Ltd, Larden Rd, London W3 7DG
**US SIC:** 3621, 3629
**UK SIC:** 34201, 34350
**Auditors:** PricewaterhouseCoopers LLP
**Bankers:** National Westminster Bank Plc (60-05-16)

| | 31-12-13 | 31-12-12 | 31-12-11 |
|---|---|---|---|
| TO | 24,096,000 | 20,942,000 | 24,310,000 |
| P/L | 977,000 | (301,000) | (10,501,000) |
| NW | (14,193,000) | (15,690,000) | (11,927,000) |
| WC | 1,497,000 | 1,304,000 | 2,653,000 |
| Emp. | 115 | 118 | 120 |

DUNS 21-773-2434

## Preston Brook Table Table

Chester Road, Preston Brook, Runcorn, Cheshire WA7 3BA
**Tel:** 01928716829
**Web:** www.tabletable.co.uk
**Estd:** 2011 Proprietorship
**Line of Business:** Managed public houses and bars
**Proprietor:** J Hansom
**US SIC:** 5813 **UK SIC:** 66200
**Employees:** 80

DUNS 23-996-1360

## Preston College

St Vincents Road, Preston, Lancashire PR2 8UR
**Tel:** 01772225000
**Web:** www.preston.ac.uk
**Estd:** 1974
**Line of Business:** Colleges (higher education)
**Principals:** S Ingleson, S Crane, R A Hill, J D Owen, P Mcmellon
**Responsibilities**
**Senior:** Jacqueline Hughes *(Manager)*
**Finance:** Sarah Woolford *(Finance Director)*
**Admin:** Shirley Rhodes *(Administration Manager)*
**Purchasing:** Nizam Ismail *(Purchasing Manager)*
**Branches:** Preston College, Fenton Street, Lancaster, Lancashire LA1 1AA
**US SIC:** 8221 **UK SIC:** 93100
**Bankers:** HSBC Bank plc (40-26-19)
**Employees:** 900

DUNS 49-099-2146

## Preston Electrical Ltd

Faraday House, Foss Sike Lane, Sandhutton, Thirsk, North Yorkshire YO7 4RH
**Tel:** 01845-587500
**Web:** www.prestonelectrical.co.uk
**Reg No:** 3093633 **VAT No:** 418052081
**Estd:** 1995 Private Limited Company
**Line of Business:** Electrical contractors and electricians
**Issued Capital:** £100
**Managing Director:** C D Preston
**Co. Secretary:** Mrs Louise Preston
**Branches:** Preston Electrical Ltd, 8 Station Road, Huddersfield, West Yorkshire HD8 9AU
**US SIC:** 1731 **UK SIC:** 50300

| | 31-03-14 | 31-03-13 | 31-03-12 |
|---|---|---|---|
| TA | 1,618,381 | 1,400,239 | 1,432,533 |
| NW | 566,530 | 529,650 | 506,530 |
| WC | 483,280 | 444,943 | 411,513 |

DUNS 22-847-0555

## Preston Health Authority

Ground Floor, Preston Business Park, Preston, Lancashire PR2 8DY
**Tel:** 01772716921 **Fax:** 01772-711621
**Web:** www.blatchford.co.uk
**Incorporate By Act Of Parliament**
**Line of Business:** Nhs clinics
**Branches:** Preston Health Authority, Market St, Colne, Lancashire BB8 0LJ
**US SIC:** 8062, 8091, 8051, 8021, 8011
**UK SIC:** 95100, 95200, 95400, 95300
**Employees:** 147

DUNS 89-637-2067

## Preston Innovations Ltd

(**Subsidiary of:** W. C. Bradley Co.)
Unit 2, Highbridge Court, Stafford Park 1, Telford, Shropshire TF3 3BD
**Tel:** 01952-290520
**Web:** www.prestoninnovations.com
**Reg No:** 3318338 **Estd:** 1997 Private Limited Company
**Line of Business:** Manufacturers and distributions of fishing and angling equipment
**Issued Capital:** £100
**Directors:** Ms S E Oldham, W J Pontius, S S Parducci
**Responsibilities**
**Senior:** Sarah Phoenix *(Human Resources Manager)*
**HR:** Sarah Phoenix *(Human Resources Manager)*
**Purchasing:** Mark Elliot *(Purchasing Manager)*
**US SIC:** 3949, 5199
**UK SIC:** 49420, 61900
**Auditors:** Baker Tilly UK Audit LLP
**Bankers:** Lloyds TSB Bank plc (30-18-55)

| | 31-12-13 | 31-12-12 | 31-12-11 |
|---|---|---|---|
| TO | 14,491,052 | 13,178,168 | 12,687,146 |
| P/L | 1,251,541 | 1,002,425 | 1,638,076 |
| NW | 6,390,121 | 5,992,797 | 5,457,290 |
| WC | 5,431,177 | 5,076,047 | 4,649,668 |
| Emp. | 74 | 69 | 65 |

DUNS 21-164-8147

## Preston Lodge High School

Park View, Longniddry, East Lothian EH32 9QJ
**Tel:** 01875-811170
**Web:** www.prestonlodge.net
**Estd:** 2002 Partnership
**Line of Business:** Schools (local authority)
**Partner:** G Clark
**Responsibilities**
**Finance:** Helen Findlay *(School Business Manager)*
**US SIC:** 8211 **UK SIC:** 93200
**Employees:** 85

DUNS 21-529-0441

## Preston Magistrates Court

Oxford Street, Barrow-In-Furness, Cumbria LA14 5JD
**Tel:** 01772-208000
**Web:** www.gov.uk
**Estd:** 2012 Proprietorship
**Line of Business:** Courts
**Responsibilities**
**Senior:** Simon Leck *(Operations Manager)*
**US SIC:** 9211 **UK SIC:** 91200
**Employees:** 55

DUNS 23-501-5740

## The Preston North End Football Club Ltd

(**Subsidiary of:** Grovemoor Ltd)
Sir Tom Finney Way, Preston, Lancashire PR1 6RU
**Tel:** 08448561964
**Web:** www.pne.com
**Reg No:** 0039494 **Estd:** 1893 Private Limited Company
**Line of Business:** Sports clubs
**Issued Capital:** £289,284
**Directors:** A S Hughes, J C Kay, D Robinson
**Co. Secretary:** Kevin Abbott
**Responsibilities**
**Senior:** Ben Rhodes *(General Manager)*
**Branches:** The Preston North End Football Club Ltd, Shop 7 Hough La, Leyland, Lancashire PR25 2SB
**US SIC:** 7999 **UK SIC:** 97913
**Auditors:** KPMG Audit PLC
**Bankers:** The Royal Bank Of Scotland Plc (16-00-01)

| | 30-06-14 | 30-06-13 | 30-06-12 |
|---|---|---|---|
| TO | 4,689,000 | 4,508,000 | 3,257,000 |
| P/L | (1,310,000) | (2,178,000) | 29,283,000 |
| NW | (2,166,000) | (2,746,000) | (1,668,000) |
| WC | (2,166,000) | (2,097,000) | (1,398,000) |
| Emp. | 274 | 75 | 82 |

DUNS 29-126-8357

## Preston North End Plc

(**Subsidiary of:** Grovemoor Ltd)
Sir Tom Finney Way, Preston, Lancashire PR1 6RU
**Tel:** 08704421964
**Web:** www.pne.com
**Reg No:** 1621060 **Estd:** 1863 Private Limited Company
**Line of Business:** Other sporting activities not elsewhere classified
**Trading Style:** Preston North End F C
**Issued Capital:** £164,784
**Directors:** A S Hughes, D Robinson, J C Kay, D W Taylor
**Co. Secretary:** Kevin Abbott
**Responsibilities**
**Senior:** Paul Newsham *(Non-Executive Director)*
**US SIC:** 7999 **UK SIC:** 97913
**Auditors:** KPMG Audit PLC
**Bankers:** Barclays Bank Plc (20-69-85)

| | 30-06-14 | 30-06-13 | 30-06-12 |
|---|---|---|---|
| TO | 6,071,000 | 5,800,000 | 6,180,000 |
| P/L | 16,430,000 | (999,000) | 3,514,000 |
| NW | 31,471,000 | (3,186,000) | (11,308,000) |
| WC | (1,660,000) | (9,604,000) | (10,005,000) |
| Emp. | 103 | 105 | 114 |

DUNS 21-116-1200

## Preston Redman Llp

Hinton House, Hinton Road, Bournemouth, Dorset BH1 2EN
**Tel:** 01202-292424
**Web:** www.prestonredman.co.uk
**Reg No:** 0336479OC **Estd:** 2008 Private Limited Company
**Line of Business:** Solicitors
**Responsibilities**
**Senior:** Adrian Cooke *(Office Manager)*, Rebecca Kefford *(Non-designated Limited Liabili)*
**Admin:** Adrian Cooke *(Office Manager)*
**US SIC:** 8111 **UK SIC:** 83500

| | 31-05-14 | 31-05-13 | 31-05-12 |
|---|---|---|---|
| TO | 3,088,379 | 3,035,810 | 3,028,486 |
| WC | 1,120,708 | 1,026,656 | 1,020,305 |

DUNS 42-377-6988

## Preston School

Monks Dale, Yeovil, Somerset BA21 3JD
**Tel:** 01935413477
**Web:** www.1610.org.uk
**Estd:** 2012 Partnership
**Line of Business:** Schools (local authority)
**Partners:** T Bloxham, T Bloxhan
**Responsibilities**
**Senior:** Matt Harras *(Manager)*
**US SIC:** 7999 **UK SIC:** 97913
**Employees:** 150

DUNS 34-812-2300

## Preston Technology Management Centre Ltd

Marsh Lane, Preston, Lancashire PR1 8UQ
**Tel:** 01772-880729 **Fax:** 01772-880783
**Web:** www.prestontmp.co.uk
**Reg No:** 2792560 **Estd:** 1993 Private Limited Company
**Line of Business:** Other service activities not elsewhere classified
**Directors:** G Driver, T Martin, D S Borrow, Ms N D Penney, B Winlow, D J Mein, J P Gibson, D J Watts
**Co. Secretary:** Ian Young
**Responsibilities**
**Senior:** Timothy Ashton *(Manager)*, Gerard Fitzgerald *(Manager)*, Julie Mcnulty *(Centre Manager)*

**US SIC:** 8999 **UK SIC:** 83954
**Auditors:** Grant Thornton
**Bankers:** The Royal Bank Of Scotland Plc (16-28-33)

| | 31-03-13 | 31-03-12 |
|---|---|---|
| TA | N/A | 1,320 |
| P/L | 2,919 | (60) |
| NW | N/A | (2,919) |
| WC | N/A | (2,919) |

---

DUNS 28-998-8206
## Prestonfield House Hotel Ltd
**(Subsidiary of:** Pacific Shelf 636 Ltd)
Priestfield Road, Edinburgh, Midlothian EH16 5UT
**Tel:** 01316683346
**Web:** www.prestonfield.com
**Reg No:** 0034405SC **VAT No:** 300600827
**Estd:** 1959 Private Limited Company
**Line of Business:** Other tourist assistance activities not elsewhere classified
**Issued Capital:** £1,150,000
**Directors:** C C Stevenson, J Thomson
**Co. Secretary:** Jacquie Sutherland
**Responsibilities**
**Senior:** Alan Mcguiggan (General Manager)
**Finance:** Alan Mcguiggan (General Manager)
**Marketing:** Alan Mcguiggan (General Manager)
**Sales:** Alan Mcguiggan (General Manager)
**Health & Safety:** Stewart Adam (Risk Manager)
**Facilities:** Stewart Adam (Risk Manager)
**US SIC:** 7999 **UK SIC:** 97913
**Auditors:** Carters
**Bankers:** Clydesdale Bank Plc (82-62-34)

| | 31-03-14 | 31-03-13 | 31-03-12 |
|---|---|---|---|
| TO | 5,195,873 | 4,517,659 | 4,515,057 |
| P/L | 313,793 | 218,912 | 76,093 |
| NW | 1,150,822 | 905,729 | 411,817 |
| WC | (563,458) | (679,295) | (1,258,654) |
| Emp. | 134 | 124 | 73 |

---

DUNS 23-522-7951
## Prestoplan Ltd
**(Subsidiary of:** Taylor Wimpey Plc)
366 Walton Summit Centre Four Oaks Road, Preston, Lancashire PR5 8AP
**Tel:** 08706000077 **Fax:** 01772-627575
**Web:** www.prestoplan.co.uk
**Reg No:** 3521811 **Estd:** 1998 Private Limited Company
**Line of Business:** Erection of roof covering and frames
**Issued Capital:** £1
**Directors:** J B Gainham, M A Lonnon
**Co. Secretary:** Colin Clapham
**Responsibilities**
**Senior:** Ian Loughnane (Technical Director)
**Sales:** Andrew Acford (Sales Director)
**IT:** Ian Loughnane (Technical Director)
**Operations:** Ian Loughnane (Technical Director)
**Engineering:** Ian Loughnane (Technical Director)
**Branches:** Prestoplan Ltd, 77 West Broadway, Bristol, Avon BS9 4ST
**US SIC:** 1761, 5999
**UK SIC:** 50400, 65600
**Auditors:** Deloitte LLP
**Bankers:** Barclays Bank Plc (20-61-51)

| | 31-12-13 | 31-12-12 | 31-12-11 |
|---|---|---|---|
| TO | 19,556,000 | 14,871,000 | 20,082,000 |
| P/L | (2,579,000) | (3,575,000) | (2,300,000) |
| NW | (3,985,000) | (1,406,000) | 2,169,000 |
| WC | (3,985,000) | (1,574,000) | 1,771,000 |
| Emp. | 173 | 151 | 169 |

---

DUNS 39-735-4432
## Prestwich Plastering Ltd
**(Subsidiary of:** Hetta Holdings Ltd.)
Vanguard House Merchants Quay, Salford, Lancashire M50 3ST
**Tel:** 01618727982 **Fax:** 01618-727-976
**Web:** www.prestwichplastering.com
**Reg No:** 2177164 **VAT No:** 519076733
**Estd:** 1988 Private Limited Company
**Line of Business:** Plastering and related building services
**Issued Capital:** £101,000
**Managing Director:** O Hetta
**Co. Secretary:** Ms Nishma Shah
**Responsibilities**
**Senior:** Oz Hetta (Manager)
**US SIC:** 1799, 1751
**UK SIC:** 50000, 50400
**Auditors:** Allens Accountants Ltd
**Bankers:** Barclays Bank Plc (20-55-34)

| | 31-03-14 | 31-03-13 | 31-03-12 |
|---|---|---|---|
| TA | 1,580,000 | 1,430,778 | 1,836,746 |
| NW | 525,547 | 485,921 | 446,009 |
| WC | 490,819 | 420,331 | 350,585 |

---

DUNS 76-708-4726
## Prestwick Aviation Holdings Ltd
**(Subsidiary of:** Ts Prestwick Holdco Ltd)
Aviation House, Glasgow Prestwick Intnl Airport, Prestwick, Ayrshire KA9 2PL
**Tel:** 01292511000
**Reg No:** 0130620SC **Estd:** 1991 Private Limited Company
**Line of Business:** Other supporting air transport activities
**Issued Capital:** £59,000
**Directors:** G H Mcleod, A Miller, A G Sweenie, I W Cochrane
**US SIC:** 4582 **UK SIC:** 76400
**Auditors:** KPMG LLP
**Bankers:** The Royal Bank Of Scotland Plc (83-15-26)

| | 31-03-14 | 31-03-13 | 31-03-12 |
|---|---|---|---|
| TO | 11,796,000 | N/A | N/A |
| P/L | (4,605,000) | N/A | N/A |
| NW | 146,000 | 413,000 | 413,000 |
| WC | (4,654,000) | N/A | 413,000 |
| Emp. | 311 | N/A | N/A |

---

DUNS 29-490-8074    Imp
## Pret A Manger (Europe) Ltd
**(Subsidiary of:** Pam Group Ltd)
1 Hudson's Place, London SW1V 1PZ
**Tel:** 02078278000 **Fax:** 02074046787
**Web:** www.pret.com
**Reg No:** 1854213 **Estd:** 2000 Private Limited Company
**Line of Business:** Retail sale in non-specialised stores with food, beverages or tobacco predominating
**Issued Capital:** £20,000,000
**Directors:** N J Candler, A M Jones
**Co. Secretary:** Clive Schlee
**Responsibilities**
**Senior:** Petra Millar (General Manager)
**Finance:** Jon Temple (?UK Finance Director)
**Marketing:** Adam Humble (Marketing Executive), Victoria Mann (Marketing Executive), Mark Palmer (Marketing Director)
**IT:** Angel Boyd (Facilities & IT Manager), Andy Chalkin (IT Director)
**Facilities:** Angel Boyd (Facilities & IT Manager)
**Purchasing:** Sandy Collyer (Head of Food)
**Branches:** Pret A Manger (Europe) Ltd, 44 New Oxford Street, London WC1A 1ES
**US SIC:** 5411, 5499
**UK SIC:** 64100
**Auditors:** KPMG LLP
**Bankers:** Rabobank Internation (40-50-91)

| | 02-01-14 | 03-01-13 | 29-01-11 |
|---|---|---|---|
| TO | 404,140,000 | 360,015,000 | 316,926,000 |
| P/L | 41,157,000 | 40,187,000 | 34,643,000 |
| NW | 221,869,000 | 184,244,000 | 151,739,000 |
| WC | 75,329,000 | 72,465,000 | 58,118,000 |
| Emp. | 6,194 | 5,896 | 5,273 |

---

DUNS 22-102-9262
## Pret A Manger Holdings Ltd
**(Subsidiary of:** Pam Group Ltd)
1 Hudsons Place, London SW1V 1PZ
**Tel:** 02078278855
**Reg No:** 4122331 **Estd:** 2000 Private Limited Company
**Line of Business:** Retail sale in non-specialised stores with food, beverages or tobacco predominating
**Issued Capital:** £10,000
**Directors:** A M Jones, N J Candler
**Co. Secretary:** Clive Schlee
**Branches:** Pret A Manger Holdings Ltd, 54-62 Sauchiehall Street, Glasgow, Lanarkshire G2 3AH
**US SIC:** 5411, 6711
**UK SIC:** 64100, 83962
**Auditors:** KPMG LLP
**Bankers:** HSBC Bank plc (40-00-00)

| | 02-01-14 | 03-01-13 | 29-01-11 |
|---|---|---|---|
| TA | 158,135,000 | 158,135,000 | 158,135,000 |
| NW | 157,157,000 | 157,157,000 | 157,157,000 |
| WC | 410,000 | 410,000 | 410,000 |

---

DUNS 77-945-1793
## Pretty Green Ltd
Unit 16, Sutton's Business Park, Reading, Berkshire RG6 1AZ
**Tel:** 08455 392 109
**Web:** www.prettygreen.com
**Reg No:** 5914755 **VAT No:** 947726578
**Estd:** 2009 Private Limited Company
**Line of Business:** Retail sale of clothing
**Export Sales:** £929,063
**Issued Capital:** £1,260
**Directors:** S Rendell, A P Johnson, R Ralph
**Co. Secretary:** Simon Rendell
**Branches:** Pretty Green Limited, Mancor House, Bolsover House, Hucknall, Nottingham, Nottinghamshire NG15 7TZ
**US SIC:** 5699 **UK SIC:** 64500
**Auditors:** haysmacintyre

---

**Bankers:** HSBC Bank plc (40-05-30)

| | 30-09-13 | 30-09-12 | 30-09-11 |
|---|---|---|---|
| TO | 10,927,069 | 10,799,039 | N/A |
| P/L | (2,050,332) | (846,113) | N/A |
| NW | 1,269,770 | 2,470,305 | 1,323,064 |
| WC | 401,628 | 1,520,537 | 727,343 |
| Emp. | 117 | 83 | N/A |

---

DUNS 21-809-6964    Imp
## Pretty Legs Hosiery Ltd
**(Subsidiary of:** Pretty Legs Holdings Ltd)
Caldow House, Crescent Road, Lutterworth, Leicestershire LE17 4PE
**Web:** www.prettylegshosiery.com
**Reg No:** 0618464 **VAT No:** 114136807
**Estd:** 1959 Private Limited Company
**Line of Business:** Manufacturers and wholesalers hosiery
**Trading Style:** Pretty Legs, Nicola Jane, Pretty Essential
**Issued Capital:** £1,000
**Principals:** D Lawlor (Managing), S Barker
**Co. Secretary:** Richard Tudor
**Branches:** Pretty Legs Hosiery Ltd, Great Central Street, Leicester, Leicestershire LE1 4JT
**US SIC:** 2251 **UK SIC:** 43631
**Auditors:** BDO Stoy Hayward
**Bankers:** National Westminster Bank Plc (60-13-30)

| | 30-04-14 | 30-04-13 | 30-04-12 |
|---|---|---|---|
| TA | 2,622,921 | 2,175,568 | 2,063,258 |
| NW | 942,681 | 846,552 | 810,486 |
| WC | 624,458 | 579,300 | 588,703 |

---

DUNS 76-899-6423
## Pretty Polly Ltd
**(Subsidiary of:** Huit Holdings Limited)
Courtaulds, P O Box 54, Nottingham, Nottinghamshire NG5 1DH
**Tel:** 08447701222 **Fax:** 01623-444317
**Reg No:** 0213491 **VAT No:** 598345976
**Estd:** 1926 Private Limited Company
**Line of Business:** Hosiery manufacturers acting as agents on behalf of the parent company: Sara Lee Holdings U K PLC (Duns No: 28-936-9209).
**Issued Capital:** £51,400
**Director:** S M Llewellyn
**Co. Secretary:** Huit Holdings (Uk) Limited
**Branches:** Pretty Polly Ltd, Conduit St, London W1S 2GF
**US SIC:** 2341, 2252
**UK SIC:** 45362, 43631
**Employees:** 900

---

DUNS 49-483-4294
## Prevista Ltd
United House, North Road, London N7 9DP
**Tel:** 020-7609-4198
**Web:** www.prevista.co.uk
**Reg No:** 3148833 **VAT No:** 662503254
**Estd:** 1996 Private Limited Company
**Line of Business:** Business services
**Issued Capital:** £118
**Principals:** J Clements Smith (Managing), Ms S M Fey, Ms S M Fey, J Clements Smith, M F Johnson, B A Coultas
**Co. Secretary:** Andi Dollia
**Responsibilities**
**HR:** Tina Sahota (Human Resources Manager)
**Health & Safety:** Jim McLean (Health & Safety Officer)
**Operations:** Alsion Raphael (Senior Quality, Claims and Com), Faye Thomas (Project Director)
**Branches:** Prevista Ltd, The Business Box, 2 Oswin Rd, Brailsford Indstl Est, Braunstone, Leicester, Leicestershire LE3 1HR
**US SIC:** 7399, 7392
**UK SIC:** 83954, 83951
**Auditors:** haysmacintyre

| | 31-03-14 | 31-03-13 | 31-03-12 |
|---|---|---|---|
| TA | 3,168,488 | 2,714,617 | 1,881,971 |
| NW | 1,491,031 | 1,566,337 | 1,118,237 |
| WC | 1,471,616 | 1,505,904 | 1,039,992 |

---

DUNS 23-929-7653
## Prezzo Ltd
Johnston House, 8 Johnston Road, Woodford Green, Essex IG8 0XA
**Tel:** 08456-023-257 **Fax:** 02085-047-903
**Web:** www.prezzorestaurants.co.uk
**Reg No:** 3919682 **Estd:** 2011 Private Limited Company
**Line of Business:** Unlicensed restaurants and cafes
**Trading Style:** The Ultimate Burger, Immo, Chimichamga
**Issued Capital:** £11,457,697
**Directors:** M Gashi, K S Sehmi
**Co. Secretary:** Alan Millar
**Responsibilities**
**Senior:** Michael Carlton (Director), Jonathan Kaye (Director), John Lederer (Director)
**Marketing:** Christian Poole (Marketing Director)
**Admin:** Josie Mulkerrin (Assistant Office Manager)

---

**Branches:** Prezzo P L C, Prezzo, 67-69 The Broadway, Stanmore, Middlesex HA7 4DJ
**US SIC:** 7399 **UK SIC:** 83954
**Auditors:** BDO LLP

| | 29-12-13 | 30-12-12 | 01-12-12 |
|---|---|---|---|
| TO | 166,541,000 | 144,524,000 | 123,873,000 |
| P/L | 18,449,000 | 17,324,000 | 16,131,000 |
| NW | 105,802,000 | 90,195,000 | 77,247,000 |
| WC | (18,250,000) | (18,060,000) | (16,202,000) |
| Emp. | 3,285 | 2,896 | 2,510 |

---

DUNS 22-642-5551
## Prgx Uk Ltd
**(Subsidiary of:** Meridian Corporation Ltd)
731 Capability Green, Luton, Bedfordshire LU1 3LU
**Tel:** 01582395800 **Fax:** 01582-395850
**Web:** www.prgx.com
**Reg No:** 1478123 **VAT No:** 814364930
**Estd:** 1992 Private Limited Company
**Line of Business:** Accounting and auditing activities
**Issued Capital:** £210
**Director:** R E Stewart
**Co. Secretary:** Miss Tracey Field
**Responsibilities**
**Senior:** Oliver Cooper (Manager), Steve Kingston (Manager)
**IT:** Steven Sheridan (Data Centre Administrator)
**Facilities:** Steven Sheridan (Data Centre Administrator)
**Purchasing:** Steven Sheridan (Data Centre Administrator)
**Branches:** Prgx Uk Ltd, The Lodge, Aviation House, West Drayton, Middlesex UB7 0LQ
**US SIC:** 8931 **UK SIC:** 83600
**Auditors:** BDO LLP
**Bankers:** Lloyds TSB Bank plc (30-98-41)

| | 31-12-13 | 31-12-12 | 31-12-11 |
|---|---|---|---|
| TO | 16,038,222 | 19,693,940 | 22,674,752 |
| P/L | (2,104,995) | (948,950) | (392,966) |
| NW | 1,854,108 | 2,878,669 | 3,163,872 |
| WC | 1,238,238 | 2,658,277 | 3,593,059 |
| Emp. | 204 | 245 | 211 |

---

DUNS 21-667-1355
## Pri Association
5th Floor 25 Camperdown Street, London E1 8DZ
**Tel:** 02037143220
**Web:** www.unpri.org
**Reg No:** 7207947 **Estd:** 2010 Private Company Limited By Guarantee
**Line of Business:** Activities of other membership organisations not elsewhere classified
**Export Sales:** £3,790,979
**Directors:** Ms P Mathur, M Skancke, D P Russell, Mrs E Bos, D N Atkin, C Ailman
**Co. Secretary:** Bristows Secretarial Limited
**Responsibilities**
**HR:** Craig Ferguson (Hr Director)
**US SIC:** 8699 **UK SIC:** 96902

| | 31-03-14 | 31-03-13 | 31-03-12 |
|---|---|---|---|
| TO | 4,502,350 | 3,637,936 | 3,182,764 |
| P/L | 39,888 | 144,745 | 442,893 |
| NW | 1,563,570 | 1,524,713 | 1,258,676 |
| WC | 1,359,287 | 1,524,363 | 1,257,251 |

---

DUNS 21-800-3861    Imp-Exp
## Price & Buckland Ltd
Benneworth Close, Hucknall, Nottingham, Nottinghamshire NG15 6EL
**Tel:** 01159640827
**Web:** www.price-buckland.co.uk
**Reg No:** 0636587 **VAT No:** 117300025
**Estd:** 1959 Private Limited Company
**Line of Business:** Embroiderers
**Export Markets:** Germany, Scandanavia
**Issued Capital:** £76,700
**Principals:** G F Buckland (Managing), N J Buckland, A J Buckland, Ms G Phillips, Mrs S Creamer
**Co. Secretary:** Ms Stephanie Creamer Acma
**US SIC:** 2269 **UK SIC:** 43702
**Auditors:** RSM Tenon Audit Ltd
**Bankers:** Barclays Bank Plc (20-63-25)

| | 31-12-13 | 31-12-12 | 31-12-11 |
|---|---|---|---|
| TO | 8,103,122 | 8,502,995 | 8,318,385 |
| P/L | 540,202 | 719,276 | 535,931 |
| NW | 2,675,561 | 2,713,983 | 2,450,848 |
| WC | 2,242,697 | 2,330,952 | 2,108,338 |
| Emp. | 81 | 79 | 75 |

---

DUNS 37-795-1942
## Price & Myers
30 Newman Street, London W1T 1LT
**Web:** www.pricemyers.com
**Estd:** 1978 Partnership
**Line of Business:** Engineering related scientific and technical consulting activities
**Partners:** S Price, R Myers
**Responsibilities**
**Senior:** Paul Batty (Designated Limited Liability P), David Derby (Designated Limited Liability P), Ian Flewitt (Designated Limited Liability P), John Helyer (Designated Limited Liability P), Andy Toohey (Partner), Stephen Wickham (Designated Limited Liability P)

**Engineering:** James Engwall *(Engineer)*, Sarah Fawcus *(Engineer)*
**Branches:** Price & Myers, 1 Kayes Walk, Nottingham, Nottinghamshire NG1 1PY
**US SIC:** 8911 **UK SIC:** 83701
**Employees:** 100

DUNS 22-832-2681
### Price Bailey
260 Barnwell Road The Quorum, Cambridge, Cambridgeshire CB5 8RE
**Tel:** 01223-565035
**Web:** www.pricebailey.co.uk
**VAT No:** 213959257 **Estd:** 1938 Partnership
**Line of Business:** Accounting activities
**Partners:** C Long, S Everall, R Wolverson, G Bradley, N Mayhew, C Olley, D Robinson, P Crouch
**Responsibilities**
**Senior:** Lawrence Bailey *(Partner)*, Peter Bass *(Partner)*, Peter Gillman *(Managing Director)*, Michale Horwood *(Partner)*, Andrew Hulme *(Partner)*, Michael Nichols *(Partner)*, Nicholas Pollington *(Partner)*, John Riseborough *(Partner)*, Paul Storer *(Manager)*
**Branches:** Price Bailey, Richmond House, Broad Street, Ely, Cambridgeshire CB7 4AH
**US SIC:** 8931 **UK SIC:** 83600
**Bankers:** Lloyds TSB Bank plc (30-13-55)
**Employees:** 70

DUNS 73-835-0375
### Price Bailey Llp
Causeway House, 1 Dane Street, Bishops Stortford, Hertfordshire CM23 3BT
**Tel:** 01279755888
**Web:** www.pricebailey.co.uk
**Reg No:** 0307551OC **VAT No:** 213959257
**Estd:** 1938
**Line of Business:** Accounting and auditing activities
**Responsibilities**
**Senior:** Peter Gillman *(Partner)*, Nadia Khan *(Non-designated Limited Liabili)*, Ravindra Parmar *(Non-designated Limited Liabili)*, Anthony Pennison *(Non-designated Limited Liabili)*, Paul Pittman *(Non-designated Limited Liabili)*, Catherine Willshire *(Non-designated Limited Liabili)*
**Finance:** Jamie Gladstone *(Director of Finance)*
**Marketing:** Peter Gillman *(Partner)*
**HR:** Lucy Carpen *(Head of Human Resources)*
**Facilities:** Derek Drane *(Director of Facilities)*
**Branches:** Price Bailey Llp, 7th Floor, Dashwood House, Old Broad Street, London EC2M 1QS
**US SIC:** 8931 **UK SIC:** 83600
**Auditors:** Horwath Clark Whitehill LLP
**Bankers:** Lloyds TSB Bank plc (30-13-55)

| | 31-03-14 | 31-03-13 | 31-03-12 |
|---|---|---|---|
| TO | N/A | 20,428,000 | 19,288,000 |
| P/L | 594,000 | 627,000 | 1,202,000 |
| NW | 3,149,000 | 1,979,000 | 868,000 |
| WC | 2,072,000 | 3,650,000 | 3,314,000 |
| Emp. | 204 | 274 | 264 |

DUNS 57-063-6365
### Pricecheck Ltd
Alpha House, 646c Kingsbury Road, Kingsbury, London NW9 9HN
**Tel:** 01234211036 **Fax:** 020-7427-7060
**Web:** www.costcutter.com
**Reg No:** 2883308 **Estd:** 1993 Private Limited Company
**Line of Business:** Retail sale of fruit and vegetables
**Issued Capital:** £56,530
**Director:** H Safi
**Branches:** Pricecheck Ltd, 399-401 Kilburn High Road, London NW6 7QE
**US SIC:** 5431 **UK SIC:** 64100
**Auditors:** Frasers Audit Ltd

| | 31-01-14 | 31-01-13 | 31-01-12 |
|---|---|---|---|
| TA | 10,000 | 10,000 | 22,500 |
| NW | 10,000 | 10,000 | 10,000 |

DUNS 22-800-2606 **Imp-Exp**
### Pricecheck Toiletries Ltd
201 Upwell Street, Sheffield, South Yorkshire S4 8AL
**Tel:** 01142-440887 **Fax:** 01142-431530
**Web:** www.pricecheck.uk.com
**Reg No:** 1359451 **VAT No:** 308152385
**Estd:** 1978 Private Limited Company
**Line of Business:** Wholesale of perfume and cosmetics
**Export Markets:** E U
**Export Sales:** £12,149,103
**Issued Capital:** £820
**Principals:** M A Lythe *(Financial)*, J E Harrison, B J Corker, Mrs A J Lythe, Mrs D Harrison
**Co. Secretary:** Mark Lythe
**Responsibilities**
**Senior:** Mark Amos *(Warehouse Manager)*, Moira Lythe *(Manager)*, Charles Lythe *(Manager)*, Deborah Lythe *(Manager)*
**Marketing:** Deborah Lythe *(Manager)*
**Branches:** Pricecheck Toiletries Ltd, 14-18 Kingsgate, Doncaster, South Yorkshire DN1 3JZ
**US SIC:** 5122, 5199
**UK SIC:** 61800, 61900
**Auditors:** Grant Thornton UK LLP
**Bankers:** Lloyds TSB Bank plc (30-97-51)

| | 30-04-14 | 30-04-13 | 30-04-12 |
|---|---|---|---|
| TO | 39,818,247 | 41,129,218 | 34,532,681 |
| P/L | (532,341) | 970,129 | 691,453 |
| NW | 6,699,361 | 7,097,224 | 6,435,360 |
| WC | 6,181,269 | 6,544,374 | 5,671,402 |
| Emp. | 71 | 60 | 50 |

DUNS 23-023-6106
### Pricewaterhousecoopers Associates (N.I.) Ltd
(**Subsidiary of:** Pricewaterhousecoopers Llp)
Waterfront Plaza, 8 Laganbank Road, Belfast BT1 3LR
**Web:** www.pwc.com
**Reg No:** 0009326NI **Estd:** 1973 Private Limited Company
**Line of Business:** Accounting, book-keeping and auditing activities; tax consultancy
**Issued Capital:** £02
**Directors:** K Macallister, P Terrington, P Rooney
**Co. Secretary:** Kevin Macallister
**US SIC:** 8931 **UK SIC:** 83600

| | 30-06-13 | 30-06-12 | 30-06-11 |
|---|---|---|---|
| TA | 2 | 2 | 2 |
| NW | 2 | 2 | 2 |

DUNS 73-987-0207
### Pricewaterhousecoopers Ci Llp
Twenty Two Colomberie, St Helier, Jersey, Channel Islands JE2 6NA
**Tel:** 01534-838200 **Fax:** 01534-838201
**Web:** www.pwc.com
**Reg No:** 0309347OC **Estd:** 2004 Private Limited Company
**Line of Business:** Accounting activities
**Responsibilities**
**Senior:** Nicholas Vermeulen *(Non-designated Limited Liabili)*
**US SIC:** 8931 **UK SIC:** 83600
**Auditors:** Horwath Clark Whitehill LLP

| | 30-06-13 | 30-06-12 | 30-06-11 |
|---|---|---|---|
| TO | 33,095,000 | 32,869,000 | 28,238,000 |
| P/L | 11,025,000 | 13,060,000 | 12,010,000 |
| NW | 10,565,000 | 11,889,000 | 10,282,000 |
| WC | 8,994,000 | 11,647,000 | 9,611,000 |
| Emp. | 239 | 237 | 234 |

DUNS 77-919-0870
### Pricewaterhousecoopers Legal Llp
10-18 Union Street, London SE1 1SZ
**Tel:** 02072121616
**Web:** www.pwclegal.co.uk
**Reg No:** 0319841OC **Estd:** 2006 Private Limited Company
**Line of Business:** Solicitors
**Responsibilities**
**Senior:** Leon Falvell *(Chief Executive)*, Stuart Hatcher *(Non-designated Limited Liabili)*, Alistair Hogarth *(Non-designated Limited Liabili)*, Agnes Quashie *(Non-designated Limited Liabili)*
**HR:** Kiran Fondhi *(Human Resources Manager)*
**Health & Safety:** Lesley Davies *(Health & Safety Officer)*
**US SIC:** 8111, 8931
**UK SIC:** 83500, 83600
**Auditors:** Crowe Clark Whitehill LLP

| | 30-06-14 | 30-06-13 | 30-06-12 |
|---|---|---|---|
| TO | 42,217,000 | 40,524,000 | 32,775,000 |
| P/L | 8,593,000 | 9,188,000 | 11,164,000 |
| NW | 7,857,000 | 9,764,000 | 7,406,000 |
| WC | 15,118,000 | 15,670,000 | 12,470,000 |
| Emp. | 203 | 191 | 175 |

DUNS 73-336-7952
### Pricewaterhousecoopers Llp
1 Embankment Place, London WC2N 6RH
**Tel:** 02075-835-000
**Web:** www.pwctermsandconditions.co.uk
**Reg No:** 0303525OC **VAT No:** 243823957
**Estd:** 2002
**Line of Business:** Accounting and auditing activities
**Trading Style:** Pwc
**Principals:** R J Veysey, Z P Randeria, D A Saunders, Ms E L Schofield, J C Lloyd, W E Hunt, R D Collier-Keywood, K J Ellis
**Responsibilities**
**Senior:** Joanna Ahlstrom *(Non-designated Limited Liabili)*, Iain Alexander *(Non-designated Limited Liabili)*, Shamshad Ali *(Non-designated Limited Liabili)*, Stella Amiss *(Non-designated Limited Liabili)*, Marco Amitrano *(Non-designated Limited Liabili)*, Robert Boulding *(Non-designated Limited Liabili)*, Albertha Charles *(Non-designated Limited Liabili)*, Richard Cleary *(Non-designated Limited Liabili)*, Daniel Cole *(Non-designated Limited Liabili)*, Alfred Conner *(Non-designated Limited Liabili)*, Michael Cooch *(Non-designated Limited Liabili)*, Rebecca Cooke *(Non-designated Limited Liabili)*, Martin Cowie *(Non-designated Limited Liabili)*, Neil Mcbride *(Non-designated Limited Liabili)*, Philippe Norre *(Non-designated Limited Liabili)*
**Branches:** Pricewaterhousecoopers Llp, 141 Bothwell Street, Glasgow, Lanarkshire G2 7EQ
**US SIC:** 8931, 7392, 7399
**UK SIC:** 83600, 83951, 83954
**Auditors:** Crowe Clark Whitehill LLP

**Following financial data are in thousands**

| | 30-06-13 | 30-06-12 | 30-06-11 |
|---|---|---|---|
| TO | 2,689,000 | 2,621,000 | 2,461,000 |
| P/L | 748,000 | 736,000 | 667,000 |
| NW | 555,000 | 530,000 | 515,000 |
| WC | 384,000 | 346,000 | 405,000 |
| Emp. | 17,420 | 17,617 | 17,079 |

DUNS 23-509-6539
### Pride Catering Partnership Ltd
1c, Guildford, Surrey GU4 7WA
**Tel:** 01483575000 **Fax:** 01483-567880
**Web:** www.pridecatering.co.uk
**Reg No:** 3508876 **Estd:** 1998 Private Limited Company
**Line of Business:** Catering
**Issued Capital:** £1,000
**Directors:** R C Aldridge, Ms J Gilbert, T N Price
**Co. Secretary:**
Roffe Swayne Secretaries Limited
**Responsibilities**
**IT:** Lynn MacKey *(Head of IT)*
**Branches:** Pride Catering Partnership Ltd, Walnut Close, Bath Road, Thatcham, Berkshire RG18 3GF
**US SIC:** 5812 **UK SIC:** 66110
**Auditors:** McNaught & Co
**Bankers:** Barclays Bank Plc (20-29-90)

| | 31-03-14 | 31-03-13 | 31-03-12 |
|---|---|---|---|
| TA | 1,648,616 | 1,454,331 | 1,408,687 |
| NW | 648,771 | 572,599 | 548,219 |
| WC | 616,452 | 557,751 | 525,133 |

DUNS 22-297-5406
### Priden Engineering Ltd
(**Subsidiary of:** Priden (Uk) Ltd)
Algores Way, Wisbech, Cambridgeshire PE13 2TQ
**Tel:** 01945-588476
**Web:** www.priden.co.uk
**Reg No:** 4315304 **Estd:** 2001 Private Limited Company
**Line of Business:** Construction of civil engineering constructions
**Export Sales:** £1,002,053
**Issued Capital:** £3
**Directors:** M Horsley, A Fordham, K Walker
**Co. Secretary:** Stuart Warren
**US SIC:** 1622, 3551, 3713, 3799
**UK SIC:** 50200, 32441, 35201, 36502
**Bankers:** Barclays Bank Plc (20-97-34)

| | 31-03-13 | 31-03-12 | 31-03-11 |
|---|---|---|---|
| TO | 10,365,260 | 10,137,679 | 10,973,717 |
| P/L | 610,520 | 256,937 | 308,080 |
| NW | 883,610 | 696,172 | 642,365 |
| WC | 334,737 | 245,680 | 328,244 |
| Emp. | 89 | 90 | 76 |

DUNS 23-276-9109
### Pridie Brewster
St Andrews House, 18-20 St Andrew Street, London EC4A 3AG
**Tel:** 02072825900
**VAT No:** 232998432 **Estd:** 1914 Partnership
**Line of Business:** Accounting activities
**Partners:** C Ellis, C R Hammond, R Faulkner, S P Harrison, J Auber, Miss M S Lai, D Mead, P Linsell
**Responsibilities**
**Senior:** Roger Clement *(Partner)*, Michael Dobbin *(Partner)*, Newton Grant *(Partner)*, Christopher Lowry *(Partner)*, David Woodage *(Partner)*
**Branches:** Pridie Brewster, Manor Farm, Unit 2, Alresford, Hampshire SO24 0DF
**US SIC:** 8931 **UK SIC:** 83600
**Bankers:** The Royal Bank Of Scotland Plc (15-80-00)
**Employees:** 60

DUNS 21-784-2941
### Priesthorpe School
Priesthorpe Lane, Farsley, Farsley, Pudsey, West Yorkshire LS28 5SG
**Tel:** 01133368833
**Web:** www.priesthorpe.leeds.sch.uk
**Estd:** 2011 Proprietorship
**Line of Business:** Schools (local authority)
**Proprietor:** K Hall
**US SIC:** 8211 **UK SIC:** 93200
**Employees:** 173

DUNS 21-153-7886
### Priestley College
Loushers Lane, Warrington, Cheshire WA4 6RD
**Tel:** 01925-633591
**Web:** www.priestley.ac.uk
**Estd:** 1956
**Line of Business:** Sixth form colleges
**Director:** M Southworth
**Responsibilities**
**Marketing:** Nat Ashurst *(Marketing Director)*
**IT:** Craig Birtwell *(Computer Manager)*
**HR:** Caroline Ford *(Human Resources Officer)*
**Branches:** Priestley College, School House, Grammar School Rd, Warrington, Cheshire WA4 1JN
**US SIC:** 8221 **UK SIC:** 93100
**Employees:** 300

DUNS 73-641-9685
### Prima Cheese Ltd
13 Partnership Court Seaham Grange Food, Park, Seaham, County Durham SR7 0PX
**Tel:** 01915-210-101
**Web:** www.primacheese.co.uk
**Reg No:** 4902094 **Estd:** 2003 Private Limited Company
**Line of Business:** Wholesale of dairy produce, eggs and edible oils and fats
**Issued Capital:** £12
**Directors:** Mrs E A Benl, Mrs N Ebanks-Beni, N Noudoost-Beni
**Co. Secretary:** Behroz Beni
**Responsibilities**
**IT:** Farhad Fereosim *(IT & Graphics Manager)*
**US SIC:** 5143 **UK SIC:** 61700
**Auditors:** G.D. O'Hehir & Co Ltd

| | 31-03-14 | 31-03-13 | 31-03-12 |
|---|---|---|---|
| TO | 37,519,337 | 25,050,786 | 22,053,497 |
| P/L | 982,640 | 1,067,739 | 223,605 |
| NW | 1,561,655 | 872,017 | 210,692 |
| WC | 70,918 | (566,657) | (722,697) |
| Emp. | 59 | 50 | 44 |

DUNS 42-359-2906
### Prima Doors Ltd
Unit 8a, Newby Road Industrial Estate, Newby Road, Hazel Grove, Stockport, Cheshire SK7 5DA
**Tel:** 0161-487-3286 **Fax:** 0161-487-3285
**Web:** www.primadoors.co.uk
**Reg No:** 3191384 **Estd:** 1996 Private Limited Company
**Line of Business:** Doors & shutters retails and installers
**Trading Style:** Prima Doors Ltd
**Issued Capital:** £1,500
**Director:** S J Davies
**Co. Secretary:** Anthony Bruce
**Responsibilities**
**Health & Safety:** Paul D'Souza *(Production Manager)*
**Engineering:** Paul D'Souza *(Production Manager)*
**US SIC:** 1751 **UK SIC:** 50400
**Auditors:** Appletons
**Bankers:** The Royal Bank Of Scotland Plc (16-32-28)

| | 30-04-14 | 30-04-13 | 30-04-12 |
|---|---|---|---|
| TA | 2,455,479 | 2,356,281 | 2,184,395 |
| NW | 1,554,010 | 1,483,036 | 1,173,370 |
| WC | 1,354,821 | 1,275,026 | 945,144 |

DUNS 23-604-0304
### Prima Hotels Ltd
66 Leicester Road, Loughborough, Leicestershire LE12 8BB
**Tel:** 01509-415050
**Web:** www.primahotels.co.uk
**Reg No:** 3601346 **Estd:** 1998 Private Limited Company
**Line of Business:** Hotels
**Issued Capital:** £460,300
**Managing Director:** L S Walshe
**Co. Secretary:** Ms Sylvia Walshe
**US SIC:** 7011 **UK SIC:** 66500
**Auditors:** Pierce
**Bankers:** Allied Irish Bank (gb) (23-83-96)

| | 31-12-13 | 31-12-12 | 31-12-11 |
|---|---|---|---|
| TO | 7,866,754 | 3,226,577 | 3,293,226 |
| P/L | (373,539) | (85,603) | 11,742 |
| NW | 3,373,635 | 3,486,533 | 3,559,404 |
| WC | 230,946 | 655,704 | 2,307,337 |
| Emp. | 271 | 129 | 98 |

DUNS 34-606-1232
### Prima Service Ltd
The Old Malt House, Easole Street, Nonington, Dover, Kent CT15 4HF
**Tel:** 08456062607
**Web:** www.primaservice.co.uk
**Reg No:** 5413129 **Estd:** 2005 Private Limited Company
**Line of Business:** Manufacture of builders ware of plastic
**Trading Style:** Prima Service Limited
**Issued Capital:** £258
**Director:** D Halfpenny

**Co. Secretary:** Ms Sue Halfpenny
**Responsibilities**
**Senior:** Justin Halfpenny (Manager)
**US SIC:** 3079, 8999
**UK SIC:** 48360, 83954
**Auditors:** Burgess Hodgson

|     | 30-06-13 | 30-06-12 | 31-06-11 |
|-----|----------|----------|----------|
| TA  | 399,711  | 384,153  | 355,116  |
| NW  | 95,745   | 87,430   | 1,349    |
| WC  | 86,592   | 81,104   | (2,314)  |

DUNS 76-616-2127
## Prima Solutions Ltd
Loughborough Technology Park, Ashby Road, Loughborough, Leicestershire LE11 3NG
**Tel:** 01509-232200
**Web:** www.primasoloutions.co.uk
**Reg No:** 2576695 **VAT No:** 558523225
**Estd:** 1991 Private Limited Company
**Line of Business:** Computer software (development)
**Trading Style:** Prima Solutions Ltd
**Issued Capital:** £1,000
**Principals:** J F Norman (Managing), G C Bacon, M Burrell, S D Belcher, Mrs K F Jarram
**Co. Secretary:** John Norman
**Responsibilities**
**Senior:** Richard Dennett (Senior Sales Executive), Fiona Haldenby (Manager)
**Sales:** Richard Dennett (Senior Sales Executive)
**IT:** Paul Melton (Senior IT Executive)
**HR:** Fiona Haldenby (Manager)
**Branches:** Prima Solutions Ltd, Moray House 23 31, Great Titchfield Street, London W1W 7PA
**US SIC:** 7379 **UK SIC:** 83940
**Auditors:** KPMG LLP
**Bankers:** HSBC Bank plc (40-28-06)

|     | 31-05-13  | 31-05-12  | 31-05-11  |
|-----|-----------|-----------|-----------|
| TO  | 4,364,572 | 4,180,446 | 3,683,460 |
| P/L | 798,042   | 698,206   | 555,521   |
| NW  | 1,643,580 | 1,280,889 | 666,193   |
| WC  | 1,603,431 | 1,231,846 | 602,574   |
| Emp.| 48        | 45        | 42        |

DUNS 23-459-4042
## Prima Systems (South East) Ltd
The Old Malt House, Easole Street, Nonington, Dover, Kent CT15 4HF
**Tel:** 01304-842999
**Web:** www.primasystems.co.uk
**Reg No:** 2809612 **Estd:** 1993 Private Limited Company
**Line of Business:** Manufacture of builders ware of plastic
**Issued Capital:** £115
**Principals:** D Halfpenny (Chairman), D Halfpenny (Managing), R Halfpenny, Mrs M Halfpenny
**Co. Secretary:** Ms Sue Halfpenny
**Branches:** Prima Systems (South East) Ltd, 29-31 Park Road, Herne Bay, Kent CT6 5ST
**US SIC:** 1721, 8999, 3079
**UK SIC:** 50400, 83954, 48360
**Auditors:** Burgess Hodgson

|     | 30-06-13  | 30-06-12  | 30-06-11  |
|-----|-----------|-----------|-----------|
| TA  | 1,486,156 | 1,569,137 | 2,221,197 |
| NW  | 868,847   | 661,099   | 765,063   |
| WC  | 698,681   | 383,028   | 639,127   |

DUNS 77-012-3149
## Primaflow Ltd
(**Subsidiary of:** Mueller Industries Inc.)
Stargate Business Park, Birmingham, West Midlands B7 5SE
**Tel:** 01213274000
**Web:** www.muellerprimaflow.com
**Reg No:** 2662075 **VAT No:** 294684213
**Estd:** 2006 Private Limited Company
**Line of Business:** Wholesale of hardware, plumbing and heating equipment and supplies
**Export Sales:** £710,000
**Issued Capital:** £20,000
**Directors:** P J Tallentire, Ms P A Quinn, J Kenrick, A P Goodland
**Responsibilities**
**Marketing:** Steven Handley (Sales & Marketing Manager)
**Sales:** Steven Handley (Sales & Marketing Manager)
**HR:** J Magner (Human Resources Manager)
**Branches:** Primaflow Ltd, Capital Point, Unit F2, Cardiff, South Glamorgan CF3 2PY
**US SIC:** 5074 **UK SIC:** 61300
**Auditors:** Ernst & Young LLP
**Bankers:** HSBC Bank plc (40-37-36)

|     | 28-12-13   | 29-12-12   | 31-12-11   |
|-----|------------|------------|------------|
| TO  | 39,078,000 | 40,392,000 | 43,241,000 |
| P/L | 2,170,000  | 2,233,000  | 2,089,000  |
| NW  | 11,923,000 | 16,163,000 | 14,356,000 |
| WC  | 11,437,000 | 15,594,000 | 13,692,000 |
| Emp.| 137        | 138        | 141        |

DUNS 22-643-6996                    Exp
## Primagraphics Ltd
(**Subsidiary of:** Curtiss-Wright Corporation)
Cambridge House Unit 2 Focus 4, Fourth Avenue, Letchworth, Hertfordshire SG6 2TU
**Tel:** 01462 472555 **Fax:** 01462 472556
**Web:** www.cwcembedded.com
**Reg No:** 1631263 **VAT No:** 370393257
**Estd:** 1982 Private Limited Company
**Line of Business:** Computer services
**Export Markets:** Europe and U S A
**Export Sales:** £16,250,847
**Trading Style:** Curtiss Wright Controls
**Issued Capital:** £5,503,209
**Directors:** G D Roberts, M Liversidge, K T Rooney, K Evans, A E Symonds
**Co. Secretary:** Glenn Tynan
**Responsibilities**
**Senior:** Dan Haines (IPT Director)
**HR:** Lara Martin (Human Resources Manager)
**Health & Safety:** Lara Martin (Human Resources Manager)
**Branches:** Primagraphics Ltd, Hughenden Avenue, High Wycombe, Buckinghamshire HP13 5RE
**US SIC:** 7379, 5065
**UK SIC:** 83940, 61500
**Auditors:** Deloitte LLP
**Bankers:** Barclays Bank Plc (20-17-19)

|     | 31-12-13   | 31-12-12   | 31-12-11   |
|-----|------------|------------|------------|
| TO  | 21,122,657 | 29,924,177 | 33,661,703 |
| P/L | (1,776,891)| 4,552      | 4,525,113  |
| NW  | (8,580,573)| (8,844,839)| (8,003,585)|
| WC  | (9,357,669)| (10,261,484)| (8,785,003)|
| Emp.| 82         | 109        | 103        |

DUNS 29-014-4179
## Primark Stores Ltd
(**Subsidiary of:** Wittington Investments Ltd)
32 West Street, Reading, Berkshire RG1 1TZ
**Tel:** 01189606300 **Fax:** 01189-606301
**Web:** www.primark.co.uk
**Reg No:** 0453448 **VAT No:** 422160891
**Estd:** 1948 Private Limited Company
**Line of Business:** Fashion shops
**Issued Capital:** £50,000,000
**Directors:** B J Mansfield, J G Bason
**Co. Secretary:** Mrs Rosalyn Schofield
**Responsibilities**
**Senior:** Jill Brown (Facilities Manager), Archer Ryan (CEO, Managing Director), Olly Rzysko (Head of Primark.com)
**Health & Safety:** Jill Brown (Facilities Manager)
**Facilities:** Jill Brown (Facilities Manager)
**Branches:** Primark Stores Ltd, 143-149 153 Union Street, Aberdeen, Aberdeenshire AB11 6BH
**US SIC:** 5621, 5611, 5661
**UK SIC:** 64500, 64600
**Auditors:** KPMG
**Bankers:** Lloyds TSB Bank plc (30-95-67)

**Following financial data are in thousands**

|     | 14-09-13  | 15-09-12  | 17-09-11  |
|-----|-----------|-----------|-----------|
| TO  | 2,583,515 | 2,297,946 | 2,096,422 |
| P/L | 237,147   | 167,507   | 168,062   |
| NW  | 287,336   | 188,219   | 179,018   |
| WC  | (910,268) | (973,473) | (943,422) |
| Emp.| 29,753    | 27,065    | 25,575    |

DUNS 21-751-7814
## The Primary Academies Trust
Blackpool C Of E Primary School, Liverton, Newton Abbot, Devon TQ12 6JB
**Tel:** 0136472203 **Fax:** 01364-722-03
**Web:** admin@south-brent-primary.devon.sch.uk
**Reg No:** 7821367 **Estd:** 2011 Private Company Limited By Guarantee
**Line of Business:** Primary education
**Trading Style:** South Brent Community P.S. / Orchard Vale Community P.S., Sampford Peverel C of E P.S. / Hemyock Community P.S., Wilcombe Community P.S. / Newton Ferrers C of E Vc P.S., Chudley Knighton C of E Vc P.S. / Blackpool C of E Vc P.S.
**Directors:** Mrs J E Baker, Mrs H M Nicholls, Miss R L Diebner, H F Whittaker, G C Chown
**Co. Secretary:** Ms Emma Hunt
**Branches:** THE PRIMARY ACADEMIES TRUST: South Brent Community Primary School, Totnes Road, South Brent, TQ10 9JN, DEVON.
**US SIC:** 8211, 6732
**UK SIC:** 93200, 83100
**Auditors:** Francis Clark LLP
**Bankers:** Lloyds TSB Bank plc (30-92-16)

|     | 31-08-14   | 31-08-13   | 31-08-12   |
|-----|------------|------------|------------|
| TO  | 9,459,000  | 13,885,000 | 23,895,000 |
| P/L | 382,000    | 4,365,000  | 17,288,000 |
| NW  | 12,832,000 | 12,002,000 | 15,780,000 |
| WC  | 538,000    | 1,790,000  | 1,093,000  |
| Emp.| 194        | 208        | 192        |

DUNS 36-547-2666
## Primary Care Support Service
187 Ewell Road, Surbiton, Surrey KT6 6AU
**Tel:** 02083351400 **Fax:** 02083351401
**Web:** www.pca.nhs.uk
**Incorporate By Act Of Parliament**
**Line of Business:** Health authorities

**Responsibilities**
**Finance:** Malcolm Ralston (Financial Director)
**Marketing:** Paul Coppini (Operations Director)
**Sales:** Paul Coppini (Operations Director)
**HR:** Theresa Gomersall (Human Resources Coordinator)
**Health & Safety:** Teresa Cooper (Contracts Manager)
**Facilities:** Adam Banks (Facilities Manager)
**Operations:** Paul Coppini (Operations Director)
**Purchasing:** Paul Coppini (Operations Director)
**Branches:** Primary Care Support Service, 187 Ewell Road, Surrey KT6 6AU Surbiton
**US SIC:** 8091 **UK SIC:** 95200
**Employees:** 250

DUNS 73-303-2937
## Primary Care (Uk) Ltd.
Bedford Lodge, 14 Carnarvon Road, Clacton-On-Sea, Essex CO15 6PH
**Tel:** 01255224680 **Fax:** 01255224681
**Web:** www.primarycareuk.com
**Reg No:** 4577121 **Estd:** 2002 Private Limited Company
**Line of Business:** Nursing agencies
**Issued Capital:** £2,000
**Directors:** A Winning, P A Sealey
**Co. Secretary:** Philip Sealey
**Responsibilities**
**Senior:** Chelsey Burgess (Manager), Maria Sadler (Project Executive), Janice Windred (General Manager)
**Admin:** Chantelle Cannell (Administrative Assistant)
**Operations:** Kelly Gant (Production and Operations Mana), Lilian Hicks (Operations Manager), Maria Sadler (Project Executive)
**US SIC:** 8091 **UK SIC:** 95200

|     | 31-03-14  | 31-03-13 | 31-03-12 |
|-----|-----------|----------|----------|
| TA  | 1,046,699 | 778,991  | 738,166  |
| NW  | 911,090   | 704,077  | 668,828  |
| WC  | 867,637   | 654,930  | 652,497  |

DUNS 21-670-7224                    Imp-Exp
## Primary Fluid Power Ltd
(**Subsidiary of:** Flowtech Fluidpower Plc)
Caddick Road, Knowsley Business Park, Prescot, Merseyside L34 9HP
**Tel:** 01516-329-500
**Web:** www.primaryfp.co.uk
**Reg No:** 0926679 **VAT No:** 648543314
**Estd:** 1968 Private Limited Company
**Line of Business:** Manufacture of parts and accessories for motor vehicles and their engines
**Export Markets:** Europe, S Africa
**Export Sales:** £1,289,869
**Issued Capital:** £7,800,100
**Directors:** A Browne, S M Fennon, P A Mcgrady, S Merrie, B R Brooks
**Co. Secretary:** Jon Burke
**Responsibilities**
**Senior:** Carl Burgess (General Manager), Keith Lockley (Manager)
**Marketing:** Peter Broom (Project Manager), Kenneth Hearton (Business Manager), Steve Lupton (Business Manager)
**Sales:** Allan Pritchard (Business Development Manager)
**IT:** Dave Caveen (IT Coordinator), graham palfreyman (IT Coordinator)
**HR:** Bob Jones (Operations Manager), Maura Parker (Head of Human Resources)
**Operations:** Peter Broom (Project Manager), Bob Jones (Operations Manager)
**Engineering:** Peter Broom (Project Manager), Chris Occomore (Technical Engineer)
**Branches:** Primary Fluid Power Ltd, Caddick Road, Prescot, Merseyside L34 9HP
**US SIC:** 3999, 5199
**UK SIC:** 49590, 61900
**Auditors:** Wilson Henry LLP
**Bankers:** Barclays Bank Plc (20-51-01)

|     | 31-12-13   | 31-12-12   | 31-12-11   |
|-----|------------|------------|------------|
| TO  | 11,166,035 | 11,616,815 | 10,428,862 |
| P/L | 1,101,492  | 1,217,476  | 813,947    |
| NW  | 5,396,814  | 4,579,812  | 3,367,336  |
| WC  | 4,158,051  | 3,775,049  | 2,547,897  |
| Emp.| 60         | 62         | 61         |

DUNS 21-232-8464
## Primary Health Care
Primary House, Wargrave Road, Henley-On-Thames, Oxfordshire RG9 2LT
**Tel:** 01491413021
**Web:** www.primaryhealthcare.net
**Proprietorship**
**Line of Business:** Home care service providers
**Proprietor:** Ms B Harrison
**US SIC:** 8091 **UK SIC:** 95200
**Employees:** 75

DUNS 21-933-0115                    Imp-Exp
## Primasil Silicones Ltd
(**Subsidiary of:** Chase Products Ltd)
Kington Road Industrial Estate, Weobley, Hereford, Herefordshire HR4 8QU
**Web:** www.primasil.com
**Reg No:** 1357452 **Estd:** 1978 Private Limited Company
**Line of Business:** Manufacturers of silicones
**Export Markets:** E U
**Export Sales:** £3,353,908
**Issued Capital:** £55,000
**Directors:** S J Wheeler, A W Zarebski, Mrs S E Wheeler, M R Wheeler
**Co. Secretary:** Richard Frost
**Responsibilities**
**Senior:** Stanley Wheeler (Manager)
**US SIC:** 2822 **UK SIC:** 25150
**Auditors:** Thorne & Co
**Bankers:** National Westminster Bank Plc (54-30-51)

|     | 30-04-14   | 30-04-13  | 30-04-12  |
|-----|------------|-----------|-----------|
| TO  | 10,172,491 | 9,881,057 | 9,863,297 |
| P/L | 3,438      | 322,930   | 126,876   |
| NW  | 1,365,557  | 1,379,139 | 1,047,275 |
| WC  | 522,101    | 614,209   | 176,640   |
| Emp.| 113        | 108       | 107       |

DUNS 21-034-7689
## Primate Dixon Primary School
4 School Lane, Coalisland, Dungannon, Co Tyrone BT71 4NW
**Web:** www.primatedixon.coalisland.ni.sch.uk
**Estd:** 1996
**Line of Business:** Schools (local authority)
**Proprietor:** S Dillon
**US SIC:** 8211 **UK SIC:** 93200
**Employees:** 86

DUNS 77-453-1727
## Primayer Ltd
Primayer House, Forest Road Parklands Business Park, Waterlooville, Hampshire PO7 6XP
**Fax:** 023-9225-2235
**Web:** www.primayer.co.uk
**Reg No:** 2959100 **Estd:** 1996 Private Limited Company
**Line of Business:** Electronic equipment (assembly)
**Export Sales:** £4,072,311
**Issued Capital:** £116,000
**Directors:** R Ironmonger, C T Hathaway, M O Merican
**Co. Secretary:** Ms Linda Parkes
**Responsibilities**
**Senior:** Stephen France (Manager)
**Sales:** Kevin Brook (UK Sales Manager), Ian Greenwell (Sales)
**US SIC:** 3643 **UK SIC:** 34203
**Auditors:** Hacker Young
**Bankers:** National Westminster Bank Plc (56-00-64)

|     | 31-12-13  | 31-12-12  | 31-12-11  |
|-----|-----------|-----------|-----------|
| TO  | 6,330,851 | 6,010,175 | 7,679,782 |
| P/L | (20,521)  | (538,313) | 586,578   |
| NW  | 869,521   | 914,329   | 1,589,452 |
| WC  | 882,293   | 879,040   | 1,573,793 |
| Emp.| 60        | 66        | 61        |

DUNS 67-153-4543
## Prime Accountants Group Ltd
5-6 Argosy Court, Scimitar Way, Coventry, West Midlands CV3 4GA
**Tel:** 02476518555
**Web:** www.primeaccountants.co.uk
**Reg No:** 5992313 **Estd:** 2006 Private Limited Company
**Line of Business:** Book-keeping activities
**Issued Capital:** £425
**Directors:** K H Johns, M Davies, J A Osborne, L P Moore
**Co. Secretary:** Jamie Skelding
**US SIC:** 8931, 6711
**UK SIC:** 83600, 83962

|     | 31-12-13  | 31-12-12  | 31-12-11  |
|-----|-----------|-----------|-----------|
| TO  | 3,207,496 | 3,118,854 | 3,115,340 |
| P/L | 460,816   | 502,054   | 569,643   |
| NW  | (291,040) | (666,853) | (1,055,581)|
| WC  | 73,004    | (156,530) | (373,535) |
| Emp.| 46        | 53        | 61        |

DUNS 77-143-0089
## Prime Appointments Ltd
Christmas House, 98b Newland Street, Witham, Essex CM8 1AH
**Tel:** 01376-502999 **Fax:** 01376-502846
**Web:** www.prime-appointments.co.uk
**Reg No:** 2704145 **Estd:** 1992 Private Limited Company
**Line of Business:** Labour recruitment and provision of personnel
**Issued Capital:** £600
**Directors:** C Trenfield, Ms C Van Aalst, Mrs M Locke, D Locke, P Holmes
**Co. Secretary:** Mrs Robyn Holmes

## Column 1

**Responsibilities**
**Finance:** Jackie Downs (*Accounts Manager*), Sue Le Compte (*Accounts Manager*), Jackie Pawsey (*Finance & Accountancy Manager*)
**Marketing:** Maria Kelly (*prime-appointments.co.uk*)
**Sales:** Suzanne Coles (*Commercial & Office Consultant*), Jane Hilton (*Trainee Commercial & Office Co*), Sue Le Compte (*Accounts Manager*), Melanie Perks (*Commercial & Office Consultant*), Melanie Walls (*Sales Manager*)
**Admin:** Jamie Aiello (*Office Assistant*), Donna Maiden (*Secretary*)
**Engineering:** Ben Bridle (*Technical & Engineering Consul*), Dave Walters (*Technical & Engineering Contra*)
**US SIC:** 7361  **UK SIC:** 83954
**Auditors:** A S Coleman & Co
**Bankers:** HSBC Bank plc (40-47-05)

|    | 31-01-14 | 31-01-13 | 31-01-12 |
|----|----------|----------|----------|
| TA | 1,062,040 | 650,087 | 534,758 |
| NW | 434,895 | 192,030 | 89,632 |
| WC | 395,939 | 177,918 | 76,002 |

DUNS 22-281-2765
## Prime Care Community Services Ltd
(*Subsidiary of:* Prime Care Holdings Ltd)
Talland Parade, Seaford, East Sussex BN25 1PH
**Tel:** 01323-491975
**Web:** www.primecarecom
**Reg No:** 4299246  **VAT No:** 927387879
**Estd:** 2001 Private Limited Company
**Line of Business:** Home care service providers
**Issued Capital:** £500
**Directors:** Ms D J Upton, Circle Care And Support Limited
**Co. Secretary:** Ms Deborah Howes
**Responsibilities**
**Senior:** Nicola Allen (*Manager*), Andrew Ewers (*Financial Director*), Nicki Whitehead (*Manager*)
**Finance:** Andrew Ewers (*Financial Director*)
**Branches:** Prime Care Community Services Ltd, 125 Tarring Road, Worthing, West Sussex BN11 4HE
**US SIC:** 8091, 8321
**UK SIC:** 95200, 96111
**Auditors:** Finance Directors Ltd
**Bankers:** HSBC Bank plc (40-20-06)

|     | 31-03-14 | 31-03-13 | 31-03-12 |
|-----|----------|----------|----------|
| TO  | 5,159,000 | 4,839,312 | N/A |
| P/L | (342,000) | (612,131) | N/A |
| NW  | (4,091,000) | (3,749,086) | (3,136,955) |
| WC  | 272,000 | 168,082 | 256,430 |
| Emp. | 221 | N/A | N/A |

DUNS 23-300-8817
## Prime Care Nursing Home
62 Downs Grove, Basildon, Essex SS16 4QL
**Tel:** 01268-553222
**Web:** www.selecthealthcaregroup.co.uk
**Estd:** 1992
**Line of Business:** Nursing homes
**Proprietor:** V Sadza
**US SIC:** 8051  **UK SIC:** 95100
**Employees:** 66

DUNS 22-729-5730                          Imp
## Prime Focus London Plc
160 Great Portland Street, London W1W 5QA
**Tel:** 02072409700  **Fax:** 020-7494-0059
**Web:** www.primefocusworld.com
**Reg No:** 1694613  **VAT No:** 539293906
**Estd:** 1983 Public Limited Company
**Line of Business:** Motion picture production on film or video
**Export Sales:** £3,699,000
**Issued Capital:** £1,644,122
**Directors:** R Sankaranarayanan, S Venkatachalam
**Co. Secretary:** Derringtons Limited
**Responsibilities**
**Senior:** Rivkaran Chadha (*Non-Executive Director*), Anshul Doshi (*Exec VP & Global Head of Produ*), Martin Hobbs (*Senior Vice President Features*)
**Marketing:** Piers Hampton (*Producer and Supervisor*)
**HR:** Elaine Pearce (*HR Manager*)
**Operations:** Anshul Doshi (*Exec VP & Global Head of Produ*)
**Fleet:** Matthew Bristowe (*SVP Production*)
**US SIC:** 7819, 8999
**UK SIC:** 97111, 83954
**Auditors:** Shipleys LLP
**Bankers:** National Westminster Bank Plc (56-00-29)

|     | 31-03-13 | 31-03-12 | 31-03-11 |
|-----|----------|----------|----------|
| TO  | 19,866,000 | 31,230,000 | 30,608,000 |
| P/L | 72,000 | 984,000 | 3,910,000 |
| NW  | 6,433,000 | 7,176,000 | 6,873,000 |
| WC  | (4,973,000) | (7,086,000) | 964,000 |
| Emp. | 235 | 337 | 306 |

## Column 2

DUNS 23-874-4481
## Prime Focus Regeneration Group Ltd
86 Old Snow Hill, Birmingham, West Midlands B4 6GD
**Tel:** 01216546694  **Fax:** 0870-607-0370
**Web:** www.midlandheart.org.uk
**Reg No:** 3865806  **Estd:** 2012 Private Company Limited By Guarantee
**Line of Business:** Management activities of holding companies
**Trading Style:** Focus Housing Central, Focus Housing Midlands, Hamac Housing, Focus Pathways Recruitment
**Directors:** Mrs J A Zacheva, G W Harris, Ms R M Cooke, Ms S J Beamand, A J Foster, R A Lake
**Co. Secretary:** Andrew Foster
**Branches:** Prime Focus Regeneration Group Ltd, Rea Street, Birmingham, West Midlands B5 6BB
**US SIC:** 6711  **UK SIC:** 83962
**Auditors:** KPMG LLP
**Bankers:** Lloyds TSB Bank plc (30-00-01)

|    | 31-03-14 | 31-03-13 | 31-03-12 |
|----|----------|----------|----------|
| TO | 240,000 | 246,000 | 268,000 |
| NW | 4,120,000 | 4,120,000 | 4,120,000 |
| WC | 1,944,000 | 2,475,000 | 2,771,000 |

DUNS 21-702-1698
## Prime Hotels (Uk) Ltd
171 Knightsbridge, London SW7 1DW
**Tel:** 02071511010
**Web:** www.bulgarihotels.com
**Reg No:** 7468060  **Estd:** 2010 Private Limited Company
**Line of Business:** Hotels
**Trading Style:** Bulgari Hotel and Residences
**Issued Capital:** £1
**Directors:** Ms K A Lord, S Ercoli
**Co. Secretary:**
Capita Company Secretarial Servi
**Responsibilities**
**Senior:** Dali Feller (*Assistant Manager*), Kirsten Swallow (*Manager*)
**US SIC:** 7011, 5812
**UK SIC:** 66500, 66110
**Auditors:** PricewaterhouseCoopers LLP

|     | 31-12-13 | 31-12-12 | 31-12-11 |
|-----|----------|----------|----------|
| TO  | 28,267,894 | 15,171,895 | N/A |
| P/L | 1,153,805 | (2,147,521) | (1,421,961) |
| NW  | (1,945,821) | (3,569,481) | (1,421,960) |
| WC  | (2,087,339) | (3,569,481) | (1,421,960) |
| Emp. | 236 | N/A | N/A |

DUNS 34-713-7671
## Prime Life Ltd
(*Subsidiary of:* Dmwsl 532 Ltd)
Caernarvon House, 121 Knighton Church Road, Leicester, Leicestershire LE2 3JN
**Tel:** 01162-705678
**Web:** www.prime-life.co.uk
**Reg No:** 2779611  **Estd:** 1993 Private Limited Company
**Line of Business:** Representative office
**Issued Capital:** £206,878
**Principals:** P A Van Herrewege (*Managing*), B Dawson, Ms S J Camwell, J Wood, Ms R Hack
**Co. Secretary:** Miss Janet Hairsine
**Responsibilities**
**Senior:** Jay Hairsine (*Financial Director*), Peter Herrewege (*Chairman*)
**Finance:** Jay Hairsine (*Financial Director*)
**Facilities:** David Cheney (*Estates Director*)
**Branches:** Prime Life Ltd, 8 King Street, Market Rasen, Lincolnshire LN8 3BB
**US SIC:** 7399, 6732
**UK SIC:** 83954, 83100
**Auditors:** IBDO
**Bankers:** National Westminster Bank Plc (60-80-09)

|     | 31-03-14 | 31-03-13 | 31-03-12 |
|-----|----------|----------|----------|
| TO  | 45,058,000 | 44,113,000 | 41,144,000 |
| P/L | 6,886,000 | 9,985,000 | 8,935,000 |
| NW  | 48,063,000 | 93,490,000 | 86,110,000 |
| WC  | 10,547,000 | (302,000) | (2,612,000) |
| Emp. | 1,731 | 1,701 | 1,583 |

DUNS 23-646-9412
## The Prime Medical Group Ltd
Centurion House, 129 Deansgate, Manchester M3 3WR
**Tel:** 01618385380  **Fax:** 01565-752121
**Web:** www.premiermedicalgroup.com
**Reg No:** 3642172  **Estd:** 2011 Private Limited Company
**Line of Business:** Printers general
**Trading Style:** The Prime Medical Group Ltd
**Issued Capital:** £50
**Director:** Doctor G E Peterson
**Co. Secretary:** Ms Raquel Simpson
**Responsibilities**
**Senior:** Julie Osborn (*Clinic Manager*)
**Health & Safety:** Kathy Owen (*office manager*)
**US SIC:** 8051, 2721

## Column 3

**UK SIC:** 95100, 47522

|    | 30-11-13 | 30-11-12 | 30-11-11 |
|----|----------|----------|----------|
| TA | 50,234 | 50,234 | 50,234 |
| NW | 50,002 | 50,002 | 50,002 |
| WC | (230) | (230) | (230) |

DUNS 21-160-1059
## Prime Motor Factors Ltd.
1-19 Milton Avenue, Croydon, Surrey CR0 2BP
**Tel:** 02084064606  **Fax:** 02084064612
**Web:** www.groupauto.co.uk
**Reg No:** 1453002  **VAT No:** 574187023
**Estd:** 2010 Private Limited Company
**Line of Business:** Motor factors
**Issued Capital:** £100
**Directors:** A S Brown, J M Lafont
**Co. Secretary:** John Coombes
**Responsibilities**
**Senior:** Jim Mazza (*Managing Director, UK*)
**Branches:** Prime Motor Factors Ltd., 1078 Harrow Rd, London NW10 5NL
**US SIC:** 5531  **UK SIC:** 65100
**Auditors:** Deloitte LLP
**Bankers:** National Westminster Bank Plc (60-03-29)

|     | 31-12-13 | 31-12-12 | 31-12-11 |
|-----|----------|----------|----------|
| TO  | 6,242,703 | 6,353,476 | 7,224,510 |
| P/L | 571,347 | 286,351 | 897,449 |
| NW  | 982,126 | 1,125,792 | 1,446,757 |
| WC  | 902,181 | 1,013,439 | 1,298,548 |
| Emp. | 58 | 70 | 78 |

DUNS 29-462-7856                          Exp
## Prime People Plc
40a Dover Street, London W1S 4NW
**Tel:** 02074935689
**Web:** www.prime-people.co.uk
**Reg No:** 1729887  **VAT No:** 519144550
**Estd:** 1983 Public Limited Company
**Line of Business:** Amusement and gaming machines
**Export Markets:** Rest of the World
**Export Sales:** £3,010,000
**Trading Style:** Harper Craven, Breakthrough, Portfolio International, Sherwoods Personnel
**Issued Capital:** £1,206,650
**Directors:** P H Moore, S J Murphy, R J Macdonald, J H Lewis
**Co. Secretary:** Christopher Heayberd
**Responsibilities**
**Senior:** Jonathon Lovett (*Proprietor*)
**Marketing:** Nick Dereka (*Group Social Media Manager*)
**Branches:** Prime People Plc, Rocklands Place, Boreham Lane, Hailsham, East Sussex BN27 1RS
**US SIC:** 7996, 6711
**UK SIC:** 97913, 83962
**Auditors:** Crowe Clark Whitehill LLP
**Bankers:** Barclays Bank Plc (20-49-76)

|     | 31-03-14 | 31-03-13 | 31-03-12 |
|-----|----------|----------|----------|
| TO  | 14,442,000 | 13,038,000 | 12,652,000 |
| P/L | 1,045,000 | 783,000 | 948,000 |
| NW  | 4,654,000 | 4,314,000 | 4,125,000 |
| WC  | 4,341,000 | 4,022,000 | 3,928,000 |
| Emp. | 91 | 95 | 108 |

DUNS 21-778-7674
## Prime Products
Alexander House, Chartwell Drive, Wigston, Leicestershire LE18 2EZ
**Tel:** 01162882500
**Web:** www.limitwatches.co.uk
**Estd:** 2010 Proprietorship
**Line of Business:** Manufacturers of watches and clocks
**Proprietor:** D Merriman
**Responsibilities**
**IT:** Andrew Boothroyd (*IT Manager*)
**US SIC:** 3873  **UK SIC:** 37400
**Employees:** 100

DUNS 21-663-9198
## Prime Public Infrastructure Ltd
(*Subsidiary of:* Prime (Gb) Holdings Ltd)
Unit 5 The Triangle, Wild Wood Drive, Worcester, Worcestershire WR5 2QX
**Web:** www.primeplc.com
**Reg No:** 7183429  **Estd:** 2010 Private Limited Company
**Line of Business:** Subdividers & developers, not cemeteries
**Issued Capital:** £1
**Directors:** R H Laing, R G Williams, L D Chumbley
**US SIC:** 6552  **UK SIC:** 85000

|    | 31-12-13 | 31-12-12 | 31-12-11 |
|----|----------|----------|----------|
| TA | 1 | 1 | 1 |
| NW | 1 | 1 | 1 |

DUNS 76-984-5223
## Prime Time Recruitment Ltd
(*Subsidiary of:* Cordant Group Plc)
55-57 Sheep Street, Northampton, Northamptonshire NN1 2NE
**Tel:** 01604-602700  **Fax:** 01604-603968
**Web:** www.primetime.co.uk
**Reg No:** 2636670  **VAT No:** 581283139

## Column 4

**Estd:** 1992 Private Limited Company
**Line of Business:** Employment and recruitment companies and consultants
**Issued Capital:** £1,941,678
**Directors:** P L Ullmann, S W Kirkpatrick, J R Ullmann
**Co. Secretary:** Alan Connor
**Responsibilities**
**Senior:** Lorraine Percival (*Manager*)
**Branches:** Prime Time Recruitment Ltd, 18 Market Square, Northampton, Northamptonshire NN1 2DL
**US SIC:** 7361  **UK SIC:** 83954
**Auditors:** KPMG LLP
**Bankers:** HSBC Bank plc (40-02-07)

|     | 30-06-13 | 30-06-12 | 30-06-11 |
|-----|----------|----------|----------|
| TO  | 202,698,592 | 205,743,462 | 192,288,066 |
| P/L | 1,717,070 | 2,179,637 | 4,279,753 |
| NW  | 21,435,872 | 20,174,589 | 18,530,278 |
| WC  | 28,656,637 | 26,861,300 | 24,794,484 |
| Emp. | 13,897 | 15,076 | 14,026 |

DUNS 23-563-3778
## Primecare Support Ltd
Inverforth House 21-23, Princes Street, Dunstable, Bedfordshire LU6 3AS
**Tel:** 01582601501
**Web:** www.primecare.co.uk
**Reg No:** 3561590  **Estd:** 1995 Private Limited Company
**Line of Business:** Home care service providers
**Issued Capital:** £19,002
**Principals:** J P Drury (*Managing*), Ms J Drury, J F Drury
**Co. Secretary:** Ms Beverley Drury
**Responsibilities**
**Senior:** Claire Sloan (*Manager*)
**Branches:** Primecare Support Ltd, Manor Farm, Aylesbury, Buckinghamshire HP22 4QP
**US SIC:** 8091  **UK SIC:** 95200
**Auditors:** Holmes Peat Thorpe
**Bankers:** HSBC Bank plc (40-19-30)

|    | 31-03-14 | 31-03-13 | 31-03-12 |
|----|----------|----------|----------|
| TA | 954,241 | 688,887 | 570,173 |
| NW | 463,426 | 359,664 | 335,945 |
| WC | 675,986 | 547,456 | 447,100 |

DUNS 73-848-9363
## Primeco Ltd
19 The Terrace, Torquay, Devon TQ1 1BN
**Fax:** 01803-212006
**Web:** www.primeco.co.uk
**Reg No:** 5104042  **Estd:** 2004 Private Limited Company
**Line of Business:** Other letting of own property
**Issued Capital:** £1
**Director:** D Nugent
**Co. Secretary:** Ms Audrey Nugent
**Responsibilities**
**Senior:** Clinton Owen (*Accountant*)
**Finance:** Clinton Owen (*Accountant*)
**Branches:** Primeco Ltd, 76 Regent Street, Weston-Super-Mare, Avon BS23 1AA
**US SIC:** 6519  **UK SIC:** 85000

|     | 30-11-13 | 30-11-12 | 30-11-11 |
|-----|----------|----------|----------|
| TO  | N/A | N/A | 468,552 |
| P/L | N/A | N/A | 17,715 |
| NW  | (2,117,858) | (2,440,752) | (2,546,287) |
| WC  | (9,911,776) | (10,362,448) | (10,474,832) |
| Emp. | N/A | N/A | 5 |

DUNS 73-946-7384
## Primeflora Uk Ltd
(*Subsidiary of:* Dutch Flower Group B.V.)
Washway Road, Holbeach, Spalding, Lincolnshire PE12 8LT
**Tel:** 01406421600  **Fax:** 01406-425965
**Reg No:** 5199391  **Estd:** 2004 Private Limited Company
**Line of Business:** Wholesale of flowers and plants
**Trading Style:** Superflora
**Issued Capital:** £1,000
**Directors:** M Van Zijverden, B Rip
**Co. Secretary:** Nick Manoussakis
**Responsibilities**
**Senior:** Arnold Kloostra (*Manager*), Hendrik Salome (*Manager*)
**US SIC:** 5199  **UK SIC:** 61900
**Auditors:** Thain Wildbur

|    | 31-12-13 | 31-12-12 | 31-12-11 |
|----|----------|----------|----------|
| TA | 485,834 | 663,200 | 1,033,456 |
| NW | (61,449) | (134,626) | 37,484 |
| WC | 76,341 | 283,129 | 458,513 |

DUNS 21-808-5402
## Primelife Care
Stadia Technology Park Unit B, 60 Shirland Lane, Sheffield, South Yorkshire S9 3SP
**Tel:** 01143270515
**Web:** www.primelifecare.co.uk
**Estd:** 2012
**Line of Business:** Home care service providers

**Responsibilities**
**Senior:** Nancy Moomba *(Manager)*, Adedayo Ogunjimi *(Manager)*
**US SIC:** 8091 **UK SIC:** 95200
**Employees:** 50

DUNS 21-834-2949
## Primeserve Sme Ltd
**(Subsidiary of:** Primeserve Consulting Ltd)
2 Woodberry Grove, London N12 0DR
**Tel:** 02030868599
**Web:** www.primeservesme.co.uk
**Reg No:** 8029268 **Estd:** 2012 Private Limited Company
**Line of Business:** Financial management
**Trading Style:** Primeserve Consulting
**Issued Capital:** £1
**Director:** A Ajasin
**US SIC:** 7392 **UK SIC:** 83951

| | 31-08-13 |
|---|---|
| TA | 1 |
| NW | 1 |

DUNS 29-175-4653 **Exp**
## Primesight Ltd
**(Subsidiary of:** Bell Holdco Ltd)
The Met Building, London W1T 2BU
**Tel:** 020-7908-4300 **Fax:** 02079084399
**Web:** www.primesight.co.uk
**Reg No:** 1847728 **Estd:** 1984 Private Limited Company
**Line of Business:** Advertising activities not elsewhere classified
**Export Markets:** Worldwide
**Trading Style:** Primesight Aviation Media
**Issued Capital:** £1,046,759
**Directors:** P J Daniels, V Krishna, N A Patel, T J Dyer, T S Green, A T Long
**Co. Secretary:** Mrs Monica Mackinnon
**Responsibilities**
**Senior:** Keith Lammie *(Regional Director, Scotland)*, Michele Mckay *(Manager)*
**Finance:** Elsa Gad *(Credit Controller)*, James Loomes *(Accountant)*, Keith Simpson *(Financial Controller)*
**Marketing:** Katy Bennett *(Head of Estate Management)*, Louise Kirkham *(Head of Regional Planning)*, Mungo Knott *(Marketing and Insight Director)*
**Sales:** Lindsey Brown *(Sales Director)*, Colette Caine *(Account Manager)*, Charlie Carlsen *(Account Manager)*, Kevin Corbin *(Sales Manager)*, Steve De Castro *(Trading Account Director)*, Chris Forrester *(Commercial Director)*, Nigel Fung *(Business Director)*, Caroline George *(Sales Manager)*, Nina Iandoli *(Direct Sales Manager)*, Petra Kmoskova *(Sales Executive)*, Martin Mcginnis *(Business Director)*, Colette Newbury *(Trading Director)*, Caroline Perry *(District Sales Manager)*, Marisa Russo *(Account Manager)*, Owen Wrein *(Sales Manager)*
**IT:** Vinay Ladwa *(Media and Technology services)*, Neil Porter *(Senior IT Executive)*
**HR:** Kathryn Bean *(Human Resources Manager)*
**Operations:** Lorna Cahill *(Production and Operations Mana)*, Shirley Holland *(Production and Operations Mana)*, Allcla Hunter *(Production and Operations Mana)*, Julian Kindred *(Despatch Supervisor)*
**US SIC:** 7319 **UK SIC:** 83800
**Auditors:** PricewaterhouseCoopers LLP
**Bankers:** Barclays Bank Plc (20-05-74)

| | 31-12-13 | 31-12-12 | 31-12-11 |
|---|---|---|---|
| TO | 48,254,495 | 46,543,985 | 46,588,000 |
| P/L | (135,379) | 1,214,831 | 690,000 |
| NW | 13,574,781 | 13,207,664 | 11,774,000 |
| WC | 18,023,618 | 17,418,610 | 2,892,000 |
| Emp. | 129 | 127 | 137 |

DUNS 50-526-4291 **Imp-Exp**
## Primeur Ltd
Castlefields, Crossflatts, Bingley, West Yorkshire BD16 2AF
**Tel:** 01274518800 **Fax:** 01274551121
**Web:** www.primeur.co.uk
**Reg No:** 2484431 **Estd:** 1968 Private Limited Company
**Line of Business:** Import and export agents
**Export Markets:** Eire & Holland
**Export Sales:** £605,481
**Issued Capital:** £54,400
**Principals:** B J Minal *(Sales)*, J A Keighley, S Fearnley
**Co. Secretary:** Ian Brazier
**Responsibilities**
**Senior:** Bruce Philpott *(Warehouse Manager)*
**Finance:** Marie Sowden *(Finance Director)*
**HR:** Richard Cadman *(Human Resources Manager)*
**Operations:** Charlotte Keith *(Quality Manager)*
**US SIC:** 2392, 2499
**UK SIC:** 45550, 46500
**Auditors:** BDO LLP

**Bankers:** National Westminster Bank Plc (51-70-19)

| | 31-12-13 | 31-12-12 | 31-12-11 |
|---|---|---|---|
| TO | 15,070,530 | 15,528,503 | 23,825,211 |
| P/L | 249,247 | 299,183 | 659,874 |
| NW | 1,127,644 | 1,140,041 | 1,170,589 |
| WC | 842,674 | 944,388 | 935,824 |
| Emp. | 64 | 65 | 68 |

DUNS 52-020-3365 **Imp**
## Primex Plastics Ltd
**(Subsidiary of:** Icc Industries Inc.)
Beaumont Way, Aycliffe Business Park, Newton Aycliffe, County Durham DL5 6SN
**Web:** www.primexplasticslimited.com
**Reg No:** 3387047 **VAT No:** 708062060
**Estd:** 1997 Private Limited Company
**Line of Business:** Manufacture of other plastic products
**Export Sales:** £4,092,382
**Issued Capital:** £12,950,000
**Directors:** T R Schultz, M J Cramer
**Co. Secretary:** Blaise Sarcone
**Responsibilities**
**Senior:** Paul Falick *(Manager)*, Alen Pollitt *(business manager)*
**Sales:** Alen Pollitt *(business manager)*
**US SIC:** 5199 **UK SIC:** 61900
**Auditors:** Garbutt & Elliott LLP
**Bankers:** Chase Manhattan International Limited (40-52-06)

| | 31-12-13 | 31-12-12 | 31-12-11 |
|---|---|---|---|
| TO | 7,889,338 | 5,799,822 | 7,238,269 |
| P/L | (600,257) | (1,377,115) | (355,042) |
| NW | 2,519,647 | 3,127,404 | 4,512,019 |
| WC | 890,587 | 1,225,339 | 2,317,912 |
| Emp. | 48 | 43 | 39 |

DUNS 21-029-9796
## Primodome
Castlegarth Works, Masonic Lane, Thirsk, North Yorkshire YO7 1PS
**Tel:** 01845570707
**Web:** www.primodome.co.uk
**Line of Business:** Speciality design activities
**Trading Style:** Primodome
**US SIC:** 7399 **UK SIC:** 83954
**Employees:** 60

DUNS 29-771-7555 **Imp**
## Primopost Ltd
**(Subsidiary of:** Ryhall Ltd)
1 Staden Park, Staden Lane, Buxton, Derbyshire SK17 9RZ
**Tel:** 01298-79113 **Fax:** 01298-70435
**Web:** www.primopost.com
**Reg No:** 2034670 **VAT No:** 453201488
**Estd:** 1986 Private Limited Company
**Line of Business:** Manufacture of machinery for food, beverage and tobacco processing
**Trading Style:** Americk Primopost
**Issued Capital:** £47,914
**Directors:** M Hill, D P Dowling, P Doran
**Co. Secretary:** Anthony Hooton
**Responsibilities**
**Senior:** Barry Bearman *(Manager)*
**Marketing:** Alastair Bearman *(Sales & Marketing Director)*
**Sales:** Alastair Bearman *(Sales & Marketing Director)*, Stuart Bearman *(Sales Director)*
**US SIC:** 2654, 2752
**UK SIC:** 47280, 47544
**Auditors:** BDO LLP
**Bankers:** The Royal Bank Of Scotland Plc (16-15-17)

| | 31-12-13 | 31-12-12 | 31-12-11 |
|---|---|---|---|
| TO | 21,475,258 | 21,255,663 | 17,571,401 |
| P/L | 1,131,979 | 1,395,444 | 799,620 |
| NW | 4,277,675 | 3,376,198 | 2,304,877 |
| WC | 452,553 | (707,293) | (22,589) |
| Emp. | 114 | 102 | 91 |

DUNS 21-100-1549
## Primrose Hill Day Nursery Ltd
Phoebe Street, Salford, Lancashire M5 3PJ
**Tel:** 01619212400
**Web:** www.primrosehillprimary.co.uk
**Reg No:** 6438730 **Estd:** 2007 Private Company Limited By Guarantee
**Line of Business:** Schools (local authority)
**Directors:** Ms M L Midgley, Ms J Atkinson
**Responsibilities**
**Senior:** Gill Harding *(Head Teacher)*
**US SIC:** 8211 **UK SIC:** 93200

| | 31-12-13 | 31-12-12 | 31-12-11 |
|---|---|---|---|
| TA | 46,721 | 46,841 | 48,051 |
| NW | 41,223 | 41,343 | 42,553 |
| WC | 41,222 | 41,342 | 42,553 |

DUNS 21-607-3160
## Primrose Valley Holiday Park
Primrose Valley, Filey, North Yorkshire YO14 9RF
**Tel:** 01723516641
**Web:** www.primrosevalleyholidays.com
**Estd:** 2002 Proprietorship
**Line of Business:** Holidays (self catering)
**Proprietor:** D Eccles

**Responsibilities**
**Senior:** Neil Ankers *(General Manager)*
**US SIC:** 7033 **UK SIC:** 66701
**Employees:** 300

DUNS 50-702-4339
## Prince & Bates
193 Station Street, Burton-On-Trent, Staffordshire DE14 1BH
**Tel:** 01283-542482
**Web:** www.princeandbates.co.uk
**Estd:** 1980 Partnership
**Line of Business:** Retail sale by opticians
**Partners:** V Prince, N Sheffield, N Dash, M Nixon, B Bates, R Bates
**Branches:** Prince & Bates, 16 High Street, Swadlincote, Derbyshire DE11 8HY
**US SIC:** 5999 **UK SIC:** 65600
**Employees:** 47

DUNS 76-909-8617
## The Prince & Princess of Wales Hospice
67-73 Carlton Place, Glasgow, Lanarkshire G5 9TD
**Tel:** 0141-429-5599
**Web:** www.ppwh.org.uk
**Reg No:** 0084008SC **VAT No:** 552276933
**Estd:** 1983 Private Company Limited By Guarantee
**Line of Business:** Other human health activities
**Directors:** I Reid, R S Bowie, B T Nicholls, M Cromar, A Gillespie, A C Tomkins, S S Chowdhary, D K Hunter
**Co. Secretary:** William Somerville
**Responsibilities**
**Senior:** Rhona Bailey *(Chief Executive)*, Rhona Baillie *(Chief Executive Officer)*, Robert Booth *(Director)*, Douglas Hansell *(Director)*, Maureen Henderson *(Director)*, Steuart Howie *(Director)*, Ally Mclaws *(Director)*
**Sales:** Bobby Grant *(Retail Development Manager)*
**HR:** Lorna Kirkpatrick *(Human Resources Manager)*, Lorna MacIntyre *(Director of HR and Volunteer S)*
**Health & Safety:** Anne Hattie *(Facilities Manager)*
**Facilities:** Anne Hattie *(Facilities Manager)*
**Branches:** The Prince & Princess Of Wales Hospice, 28 Townhead, Glasgow, Lanarkshire G66 1NL
**US SIC:** 8091, 6732
**UK SIC:** 95200, 83100
**Auditors:** Wylie & Bisset
**Bankers:** Clydesdale Bank Plc (82-20-00)

| | 31-03-14 | 31-03-13 | 31-03-12 |
|---|---|---|---|
| TO | N/A | N/A | 5,210,070 |
| P/L | 1,009,837 | 1,005,190 | 437,021 |
| NW | 13,649,661 | 12,639,824 | 11,634,634 |
| WC | 3,322,684 | 4,188,474 | 3,110,776 |
| Emp. | 122 | 115 | 114 |

DUNS 21-371-7304
## Prince Bishops Shopping Centre
High Street, Durham, County Durham DH1 3UJ
**Tel:** 01913750416
**Web:** www.princebishops.co.uk
**Estd:** 1999
**Line of Business:** Shopping centres
**Trading Style:** Prince Bishops Shopping Centre Carpark
**Proprietor:** R Toynbee
**Responsibilities**
**Senior:** Richard Toynbee *(Centre Manager)*
**US SIC:** 7011 **UK SIC:** 66500
**Employees:** 1,000

DUNS 21-233-4948
## Prince Edward Duke of Kent Court
Kings Lane, Stisted, Braintree, Essex CM77 8AG
**Tel:** 01376345534
**Web:** www.rmbi.org.uk
**Estd:** 1999
**Line of Business:** Non-charitable social work activities with accommodation
**Proprietor:** Mrs L Baxtor
**US SIC:** 8321 **UK SIC:** 96111
**Employees:** 51

DUNS 21-724-3221
## Prince Evans Solicitors Llp
Craven House, London W5 2BS
**Web:** www.prince-evans.co.uk
**Reg No:** 0364187OC **Estd:** 1978
**Line of Business:** Solicitors
**Principals:** G M Smith, R J Jennings, A R Best, Cb Mediation Limited, P E Legal Services Limited, I F Barry

**Responsibilities**
**Senior:** Lee Davis *(Senior IT Executive)*, Thomas Lemon *(Designated Limited Liability P)*, Charles Neill *(Designated Limited Liability P)*
**Finance:** Lee Davis *(Senior IT Executive)*
**Sales:** Thomas Lemon *(Designated Limited Liability P)*
**IT:** Lee Davis *(Senior IT Executive)*
**US SIC:** 8111 **UK SIC:** 83500

| | 31-05-13 | 31-05-12 |
|---|---|---|
| TA | 1,927,351 | 2,243,132 |
| WC | 1,040,972 | 931,361 |

DUNS 77-540-2514
## Prince Hotels Ltd
Birmingham Road, Coventry, West Midlands CV5 9GR
**Tel:** 02476403835
**Web:** www.princehotels.com
**Reg No:** 2995507 **Estd:** 1994 Private Limited Company
**Line of Business:** Hotels
**Export Sales:** £3,734,619
**Issued Capital:** £100
**Director:** P M Nasser
**Co. Secretary:** Michael Stoneman
**Responsibilities**
**Operations:** Bruce Wade *(Group Operation Manager)*
**US SIC:** 7011 **UK SIC:** 66500
**Auditors:** BKR Haines Watts
**Bankers:** Lloyds TSB Bank plc (77-62-08)

| | 31-12-13 | 31-12-12 | 31-12-11 |
|---|---|---|---|
| TO | 7,169,714 | 6,588,783 | 7,443,572 |
| P/L | (360,859) | 510,609 | 91,300 |
| NW | 7,585,897 | 7,812,674 | 7,830,692 |
| WC | (390,667) | (45,090) | 1,654,910 |
| Emp. | 182 | 178 | 204 |

DUNS 21-229-7830
## Prince Michael of Kent Court
Stratford Road, Watford, Hertfordshire WD17 4DH
**Web:** www.rmbi.org.uk
**Estd:** 1994
**Line of Business:** Residential care establishments
**Partner:** L Fais
**Responsibilities**
**Senior:** Elizabeth Corbett *(Home Manager)*
**US SIC:** 8321 **UK SIC:** 96111
**Employees:** 80

DUNS 34-781-5255 **Imp**
## Prince Minerals Ltd
Duke Street, Stoke-On-Trent, Staffordshire ST4 3BL
**Tel:** 01782343000
**Web:** www.princeminerals.com
**Reg No:** 5582239 **Estd:** 2005 Private Limited Company
**Line of Business:** Manufacturers of dye
**Export Sales:** £24,480,000
**Issued Capital:** £900
**Directors:** K St Germaine, A W Weiss, J W Ropp, M P Gee, C R Cherry
**Co. Secretary:** Matthew Gee
**Responsibilities**
**Senior:** Joe Curl *(General Manager)*, Charlie Truelove *(Works Manager)*
**Marketing:** Martin Barber *(Commercial Manager)*
**Sales:** Joe Curl *(General Manager)*
**Health & Safety:** Julie Vaughan *(Health & Safety Officer)*
**Operations:** Martin Barber *(Commercial Manager)*, Julie Vaughan *(Health & Safety Officer)*
**Engineering:** Charlie Truelove *(Works Manager)*
**US SIC:** 2269, 3299
**UK SIC:** 43702, 24504
**Auditors:** PricewaterhouseCoopers LLP

| | 31-12-13 | 31-12-12 | 31-12-11 |
|---|---|---|---|
| TO | 36,847,000 | 27,006,000 | 32,635,000 |
| P/L | (1,200,000) | 2,544,000 | 1,983,000 |
| NW | 6,459,000 | 7,179,000 | 5,036,000 |
| WC | 11,136,000 | 4,245,000 | 4,778,000 |
| Emp. | 224 | 72 | 77 |

DUNS 55-056-9552
## Prince of Wales Court
Penylan Avenue, Porthcawl, Mid Glamorgan CF36 3LY
**Tel:** 01656-785311
**Web:** www.rmbi.org.uk
**Estd:** 1973
**Line of Business:** Residential care establishments
**Partners:** Mrs A Owen, Mrs A Owen Neill
**US SIC:** 8321 **UK SIC:** 96111
**Employees:** 130

DUNS 50-574-9861
## The Prince of Wales Theatre Ltd
(**Subsidiary of:** Cameron Mackintosh Ltd)
Coventry Street, London W1D 6AS
**Tel:** 08444825115
**Web:** www.princeofwalestheatrelondon.inf
**Reg No:** 2522756 **Estd:** 1990 Private Limited Company
**Line of Business:** Theatres & concert halls
**Issued Capital:** £100
**Directors:** R A Johnston, N D Allott, Sir C Mackintosh
**Co. Secretary:** Richard Knibb
**Responsibilities**
**Senior:** Jaime Nabeta *(General Manager)*
**US SIC:** 7911, 7999
**UK SIC:** 97913
**Auditors:** BDO Stoy Hayward LLP

| | 31-03-14 | 31-03-13 | 31-03-12 |
|---|---|---|---|
| TA | 100 | 100 | 100 |
| NW | 100 | 100 | 100 |

DUNS 21-769-9558
## Prince Philip Hospital
Bryngwyn Mawr, Dafen, Llanelli, Dyfed SA14 8QF
**Tel:** 01554756567
**Estd:** 2002
**Line of Business:** Hospitals
**US SIC:** 8062 **UK SIC:** 95100
**Employees:** 4,000

DUNS 21-229-2448
## Prince Regent Swimming Complex
North Road, Brighton, East Sussex BN1 1YA
**Tel:** 01273-685692
**Web:** www.freedom-leisure.co.uk
**Estd:** 1982 Proprietorship
**Line of Business:** Leisure centres
**Proprietor:** G Easten
**Responsibilities**
**Senior:** Jonathan Hodgkins *(Manager)*
**US SIC:** 7999 **UK SIC:** 97913
**Employees:** 50

DUNS 21-909-6351
## Princebuild Ltd.
(**Subsidiary of:** Princebuild Holdings Ltd)
Empson Road Fengate, Peterborough, Cambridgeshire PE1 5UP
**Tel:** 01733-561216
**Web:** www.princebuild.co.uk
**Reg No:** 1026522 **VAT No:** 330312517
**Estd:** 1971 Private Limited Company
**Line of Business:** Development and selling of real estate
**Issued Capital:** £15,000
**Principals:** S S Pudney *(Managing)*, D J Asplin *(Managing)*, M D Asplin, D J Asplin, M J Pudney, J M Pudney, J M Pudney
**Co. Secretary:** Stuart Pudney
**Responsibilities**
**Senior:** Barbara Mehew *(Human Resources Manager)*
**Finance:** Billie Stewart *(Accountant)*
**HR:** Barbara Mehew *(Human Resources Manager)*
**Branches:** Princebuild Ltd., 22 Quarry Park Close, Northampton, Northamptonshire NN3 6QB
**US SIC:** 6552, 1541
**UK SIC:** 85000, 50100
**Auditors:** Forrester Boyd
**Bankers:** Barclays Bank Plc (20-67-37)

| | 30-09-13 | 30-09-12 | 30-09-11 |
|---|---|---|---|
| TO | 41,977,412 | 33,010,686 | 27,362,082 |
| P/L | 1,412,318 | 1,054,854 | 1,415,859 |
| NW | 5,932,813 | 5,582,916 | 5,310,755 |
| WC | 3,638,133 | 3,277,637 | 2,744,018 |
| Emp. | 188 | 187 | 211 |

DUNS 73-774-0766
## Princecroft Willis Accountants Llp
Towngate House, 2-8 Parkstone Road, Poole, Dorset BH15 2PW
**Web:** www.princecroftwillis.co.uk
**Reg No:** 0306767OC **Estd:** 1999
**Line of Business:** Tax consultancy
**Trading Style:** Partnership
**Responsibilities**
**Senior:** Anne-Marie Gates *(Partner)*, Anthony Raymond *(Partner)*, Dan Tout *(Manager)*
**Finance:** John Caithness *(Business Tax Director)*, Gaynor Fisher *(Tax Team Manager)*, Tim Grant-Barnes *(Accounts Manager)*, Kate Neal *(Tax Team Manager)*, Linda Preece *(Technical Tax Director)*, Anthony Raymond *(Partner)*, Jessica Tubbs *(Accounts Team Manager)*, Neil Walpole *(Accounts Team Manager)*, Lisa Whitbread *(Corporate Tax Technical Manage)*
**Marketing:** Sam Chapman *(Director of Business Enterpris)*, Elaine Wilkins *(Marketing Manager)*
**Sales:** Sarah King *(Accounts Team Manager)*
**Admin:** Karen Maple *(Administrator)*
**HR:** Lindsey Drake *(HR Assistant)*
**US SIC:** 8931 **UK SIC:** 83600

| | 31-03-14 | 31-03-13 | 31-03-12 |
|---|---|---|---|
| TA | 2,216,713 | 2,312,544 | 2,453,925 |
| NW | (14,581) | (68,979) | (149,976) |
| WC | 934,080 | 679,168 | 514,609 |

DUNS 21-221-5800
## Princes Foods Ltd
(**Subsidiary of:** Mitsubishi Corporation)
6th Floor Royal Liver Building, Pier Head, Liverpool, Merseyside L3 1NX
**Tel:** 01512 369282
**Web:** www.princes.co.uk
**Reg No:** 0158330 **Estd:** 1919 Private Limited Company
**Line of Business:** Supermarkets
**Trading Style:** Princes Manufacturing, Princes International Foods, Princes Ltd
**Issued Capital:** £875,000
**Director:** K D Critchley
**Co. Secretary:** Manabu Oda
**Branches:** Princes Foods Ltd, Crabtree Manorway South, Belvedere, Kent DA17 6BB
**US SIC:** 5411, 2099
**UK SIC:** 64100, 42399

| | 31-03-14 | 31-03-13 | 31-03-12 |
|---|---|---|---|
| TA | 12,655,695 | 12,655,695 | 12,655,695 |
| NW | 7,547,005 | 7,547,005 | 7,547,005 |
| WC | 7,547,005 | 7,547,005 | 7,547,005 |

DUNS 50-150-6315 **Imp-Exp**
## Princes Ltd
(**Subsidiary of:** Mitsubishi Corporation)
Royal Liver Building, Pier Head, Liverpool, Merseyside L3 1NX
**Tel:** 01519667000 **Fax:** 01519 667 010
**Web:** www.princes.co.uk
**Reg No:** 2328824 **VAT No:** 319601958
**Estd:** 1900 Private Limited Company
**Line of Business:** Non-specialised wholesale of food, beverages and tobacco
**Export Sales:** £366,377,000
**Issued Capital:** £7,000,000
**Principals:** K D Critchley *(Financial)*, M W Easterbrook, K Ito, K Misu, H Hayashi, H Kobayashi, N Onuma, N J Spruyt
**Co. Secretary:** Manabu Oda
**Responsibilities**
**Senior:** Tetsuro Terada *(Manager)*
**IT:** N Crewe *(IT Director)*
**Facilities:** Janice Moores *(Facilities Manager)*
**Branches:** Princes Limited, West Yorkshire Industrial Estate, Toftshaw Lane, Bradford, West Yorkshire BD4 6TD
**US SIC:** 5149, 2086
**UK SIC:** 61700, 42831
**Auditors:** Deloitte LLP
**Bankers:** National Westminster Bank Plc (60-13-19)

**Following financial data are in thousands**

| | 31-03-14 | 31-03-13 | 31-03-12 |
|---|---|---|---|
| TO | 1,617,601 | 1,740,396 | 1,511,771 |
| P/L | 65,180 | 57,088 | 47,241 |
| NW | 176,619 | 160,466 | 135,300 |
| WC | 124,469 | 147,435 | 128,140 |
| Emp. | 4,724 | 4,629 | 4,166 |

DUNS 29-160-8883
## Prince's Mead School Trust
Worthy Park House, Worthy Park, Winchester, Hampshire SO21 1AN
**Tel:** 01962-888000
**Web:** http://princesmeadschool.org.uk
**Reg No:** 1785733 **Estd:** 1984 Private Limited Company
**Line of Business:** Schools (local authority)
**Trading Style:** Princes Mead School
**Directors:** B D Welch, R J Pertwee, N Hendriksen, Mrs P A Hauser, R J Putt, Mrs G Lewis, Mrs S J Annesley, A Mcmillan
**Co. Secretary:** Richard White
**Responsibilities**
**Senior:** Penelope Kirk *(Headmistress)*, Melanie Renwick *(Director)*
**Marketing:** Penelope Kirk *(Headmistress)*
**IT:** Wendy Jack *(IT Manager)*
**Purchasing:** Sue Graves *(Purchasing Manager)*
**US SIC:** 8211 **UK SIC:** 93200
**Auditors:** Derek Webster & Co
**Bankers:** National Westminster Bank Plc (55-81-26)

| | 31-08-13 | 31-08-12 | 31-08-11 |
|---|---|---|---|
| TO | 3,068,529 | 2,848,122 | 2,460,583 |
| P/L | 238,609 | 134,216 | 148,728 |
| NW | 3,098,674 | 2,860,065 | 2,726,852 |
| WC | 806,506 | 170,803 | 172,647 |
| Emp. | 62 | 59 | 47 |

DUNS 21-737-3105
## Princes Risborough School
Merton Road, Princes Risborough, Buckinghamshire HP27 0DT
**Tel:** 01844346147
**Web:** www.princesrisborough.bucks.sch.uk
**Reg No:** 7712579 **Estd:** 2012 Private Company Limited By Guarantee
**Line of Business:** Schools (foundation)
**Directors:** Miss P Hulse, Ms M J Antrobus, P G Chidgey, A Stoodley
**Co. Secretary:** Peter Clark
**US SIC:** 8211 **UK SIC:** 93200
**Bankers:** Lloyds TSB Bank plc (30-00-00)

| | 31-08-14 | 31-08-13 | 31-08-12 |
|---|---|---|---|
| TO | 7,803,302 | 6,135,594 | 17,466,111 |
| P/L | 1,726,957 | 400,827 | 11,755,115 |
| NW | 13,382,900 | 11,708,943 | 11,370,115 |
| WC | 861,317 | 240,017 | (65,016) |
| Emp. | 118 | 119 | 122 |

DUNS 50-005-5611
## Princes Soft Drinks Ltd
Weaverthorpe Road, Bradford, West Yorkshire BD4 9RQ
**Fax:** 01274717171
**Web:** www.princes.co.uk
**Reg No:** 2295092 **Estd:** 1868 Private Limited Company
**Line of Business:** Manufacturers of soft drinks
**Trading Style:** Princes Soft Drinks Ltd
**Issued Capital:** £2
**Director:** K D Critchley
**Co. Secretary:** Manabu Oda
**Responsibilities**
**Senior:** Julian Bolton *(Database Manager)*
**Branches:** Princes Soft Drinks Ltd, Unit 68-69, Portmanmoor Road Industrial Estate, Cardiff, South Glamorgan CF24 5PS
**US SIC:** 2086, 3079
**UK SIC:** 42831, 48360
**Bankers:** National Westminster Bank Plc (60-13-19)

| | 31-03-14 | 31-03-13 | 31-03-12 |
|---|---|---|---|
| TA | 13,725,807 | 13,725,807 | 13,725,807 |
| NW | 13,725,807 | 13,725,807 | 13,725,807 |

DUNS 22-988-8151
## The Princes Youth Business Trust
18 Park Square East, London NW1 4LH
**Tel:** 0800842842
**Web:** www.princes-trust.org.uk
**Estd:** 1999
**Line of Business:** Charities and charitable organisations
**Trading Style:** P Y B T, The Prince'S Trust
**Principals:** H R Of Wales *(President)*, M Mercieca *(Financial)*, Ms M Milburn, P Mimpriss, Ms R Thorne, Sir M Farrer
**Responsibilities**
**Senior:** H of Wales *(President)*
**Branches:** The Princes Youth Business Trust, Honeywood Rd, Dover, Kent CT16 3EH
**US SIC:** 8321 **UK SIC:** 96111
**Employees:** 700

DUNS 42-342-8044
## Princess Alexandra Hospital N H S Trust
Hamstel Road, Harlow, Essex CM20 1QX
**Tel:** 01279-444455
**Web:** www.pah.nhs.uk
**Estd:** 2002
**Line of Business:** Hospitals
**Issued Capital:** £1
**Principals:** G Coteman *(Chairman)*, C Pocklington, Dr S Dimmock, Ms Y Blucher, G Flack, A Farmer, D Leech, J Day
**Responsibilities**
**Senior:** Christopher Bown *(Interim Chief Executive Office)*, Christine Carrington *(Chairman)*, Tim Escudier *(Board Member)*, Liz Mazura *(Radiology Business Manager)*, Nicole Perry *(Manager)*, Elmo Thambapillai *(Executive)*
**Marketing:** Dorothy Bioletti *(Business Manager)*, Angela Boon *(Head of Communications)*, Rachael Holden *(Communications Assistant)*, Kirsty O' Callaghan *(Head of Communications)*, Patricia Spence *(Marketing Manager)*, Victoria Thatcher *(Publications Manager)*
**Admin:** Jane Abbotson *(Secretary)*, Denise Andrews *(Secretary)*, Katie Bridge *(Secretary)*, Sarah Byrne *(Secretary)*, Diane Coyle *(Secretary)*, Theresa D' Cruz *(Secretary)*, Chris Davidge *(Secretary)*, Christine Day *(Secretary)*, Carole Denton *(Secretary)*, Janet Etherington *(Secretary)*, Angela Gilchrist *(Secretary)*, Karen Goodchild *(Secretary)*, Amanda Gordon *(Secretary)*, Penny Griffiths *(Secretary)*, Beverley Hall *(Secretary)*, Michelle Harris *(Secretary)*, Anna Hayes *(Administrator)*, Helen Hind *(Secretary)*, Helen Holdsworth *(Secretary)*, Lyn Horne *(Secretary)*, Nikki Johnson *(Secretary)*, Julie Jordan *(Secretary)*, Barbara Lawrence *(Secretary)*, Denise Maynard *(Administrator)*, Stephanie Mead *(Secretary)*, Laura Pascoe *(Secretary)*, Chris Prandy *(Secretary)*, Catherine Ray *(Secretary)*, Teresa Skingley *(Secretary)*, Lyn Stanley *(Secretary)*, Fiona Tredgett *(Secretary)*, Julie Tuohy *(Secretary)*, Sheila Wardle *(Secretary)*, Kate Wilkinson *(Secretary)*, Sandy Williams *(Secretary)*
**IT:** Anthony Lundrigan *(IT Director)*
**HR:** Debbie Cubitt *(Nursing Training Manager)*, Karen Kingsmill *(Training Administrator)*, Simon Meddick *(Director, Operations)*
**Facilities:** Lyn Milbourn *(Facilities Manager)*
**Operations:** Bill Dickson *(Energy Manager)*, Jules Martin *(Chief Operating Officer)*
**Branches:** Princess Alexandra Hospital N H S Trust, Galen House, Fourth Avenue, Harlow, Essex CM20 1DW
**US SIC:** 8062 **UK SIC:** 95100
**Employees:** 1,700

DUNS 29-122-8708
## Princess Alice Hospice
West End Lane, Esher, Surrey KT10 8NA
**Tel:** 01372468811
**Web:** www.pah.org.uk
**Reg No:** 1599796 **Estd:** 1981 Private Company Limited By Guarantee
**Line of Business:** Miscellaneous health & allied services
**Directors:** Ms J T Hogg, Dr P A West, J N Woolf, P J Quest, I F Elder, Ms A M Duncan, Professor F M Ross, A J Mcintosh
**Co. Secretary:** Mrs Diane Rickwood
**Responsibilities**
**Senior:** Alice Formby *(Director)*, Jane Hargrave *(Director)*, Sean Hilton *(Director)*, Jeannine Nolan *(Director)*, Jonathan Perkins *(Director)*, David Prest *(Retail Director)*, Nicholas Ratsey *(Chief Executive)*, Christopher Roshier *(Director)*, Nicki Shaw *(Chief Executive)*
**Finance:** Nigel Seymour *(Director of Fundraising and Co)*
**Marketing:** David Prest *(Retail Director)*, Nigel Seymour *(Director of Fundraising and Co)*
**Sales:** David Prest *(Retail Director)*
**Admin:** Dee Scannell *(Head of Administration)*
**HR:** Deborah Easson *(Human Resources Manager)*
**Health & Safety:** Sarah Tullett *(Health & Safety Officer)*
**Branches:** Princess Alice Hospice, 100 Church Road, Ashford, Middlesex TW15 2PL
**US SIC:** 8091, 6732, 8321
**UK SIC:** 95200, 83100, 96111
**Auditors:** Mazars LLP
**Bankers:** Barclays Bank Plc (20-90-56)

| | 31-03-14 | 31-03-13 | 31-03-12 |
|---|---|---|---|
| TO | 14,782,180 | 12,477,549 | 12,054,262 |
| P/L | (105,171) | (290,957) | 93,764 |
| NW | 16,005,110 | 15,994,081 | 15,963,271 |
| WC | 1,751,342 | 2,618,902 | 2,447,188 |
| Emp. | 263 | 248 | 224 |

DUNS 55-056-6780
## Princess Christian Homes
Stafford Lake, Knaphill, Woking, Surrey GU21 2SJ
**Tel:** 01483488917
**Estd:** 2009 Proprietorship
**Line of Business:** Non-charitable social work activities with accommodation
**Proprietor:** M Taherian
**US SIC:** 8321 **UK SIC:** 96111
**Employees:** 60

DUNS 23-263-1341
## Princess Elisabeth Hospital
Rue Mignot, St Martin, Guernsey, Channel Islands GY4 6UU
**Tel:** 01481-725241 **Fax:** 01481-235341
**Web:** www.concretecentre.com
**Estd:** 2010 Incorporate By Act Of Parliament
**Line of Business:** Hospitals
**Directors:** M Dorey, J D Martell
**Responsibilities**
**Senior:** Malcolm Nutley *(Acting CEO)*
**Finance:** Jim Harley *(Financial Director)*
**Purchasing:** Stephanie Mahy *(Purchasing Manager)*
**Branches:** Princess Elisabeth Hospital, Bell House, Grand Bouet, Guernsey, Channel Islands GY1 2SB
**US SIC:** 8062 **UK SIC:** 95100
**Employees:** 3,000

DUNS 21-545-4252
## Princess Frederica C E Primary School
College Road, London NW10 5TP
**Tel:** 02089697756
**Web:** www.princessfrederica.brent.sch.uk
**Estd:** 1995

**Line of Business:** Primary education
**Proprietor:** Mrs S Nettey
**US SIC:** 8211 **UK SIC:** 93200
**Employees:** 60

DUNS 21-782-5085
## The Princess Grace Hospital
29-32 Devonshire Street, London W1G 6PU
**Tel:** 02079083602
**Web:** www.theprincessgracehospital.co.uk
**Estd:** 2011 Partnership
**Line of Business:** Clinics private
**Partners:** C Kennedy, A Omeara, Ms S Smith, R Likhani
**US SIC:** 8051 **UK SIC:** 95100
**Employees:** 300

DUNS 23-269-4133
## The Princess Helena College
School Lane, Hitchin, Hertfordshire SG4 7UE
**Tel:** 01462-432100
**Web:** www.princesshelenacollege.co.uk
**Estd:** 1799 Incorporate By Act Of Parliament
**Line of Business:** General secondary education
**Director:** Mrs A Hodgkiss
**Responsibilities**
**Senior:** Jo-Anne Duncan *(Principal)*
**Finance:** James Bentall *(Bursar)*
**IT:** Ben Stanton *(Computer Manager)*
**HR:** James Bentall *(Bursar)*
**Health & Safety:** James Bentall *(Bursar)*
**Facilities:** James Bentall *(Bursar)*
**US SIC:** 8211 **UK SIC:** 93200
**Employees:** 80

DUNS 21-412-1466
## Princess Lodge
17 Curie Avenue, Swindon, Wiltshire SN1 4GB
**Tel:** 01793-715420
**Web:** www.lifestylecare.co.uk
**Estd:** 2010 Proprietorship
**Line of Business:** Nursing homes
**Proprietor:** Miss A Martin
**Responsibilities**
**Senior:** Kate Pearson *(Home Manager)*
**US SIC:** 8051 **UK SIC:** 95100
**Employees:** 150

DUNS 23-268-1932
## Princess Louise Scottish Hospital
Erskine Hospital Estate, Bishopton, Renfrewshire PA7 5PU
**Tel:** 01418144626
**Web:** www.erskine.org
**Estd:** 2005
**Line of Business:** Garden centres
**Trading Style:** Erskine Hospital Furniture Workshops, Erskine Pine, Erskine Garden Centre
**Principals:** Colonel M F Gibson, W K Shepherd, I W Grimmond, A Robertson
**Responsibilities**
**Senior:** Iain Milligan *(Manager)*, Jamie Neill *(Commercial Director)*
**Branches:** Princess Louise Scottish Hospital, 147 Alexandra Pde, Dunoon, Argyll PA23 8AW
**US SIC:** 5999, 8091, 8299
**UK SIC:** 65600, 95200, 93300
**Bankers:** Clydesdale Bank Plc (82-48-08)
**Employees:** 700

DUNS 21-098-0089
## Princess Motor Yacht Sales Holdings Ltd
6 Athena Court, Tachbrook Park, Warwick, Warwickshire CV34 6RT
**Tel:** 01489557755
**Web:** www.my-princess.co.uk
**Reg No:** 6422135 **Estd:** 2007 Private Limited Company
**Line of Business:** Management activities of holding companies
**Export Sales:** £64,918,553
**Issued Capital:** £5,882,353
**Directors:** M H Whale, P W Whale, H W Whale
**Co. Secretary:** Keith Hampson
**US SIC:** 6711 **UK SIC:** 83962

| | 31-12-13 | 31-12-12 | 31-12-11 |
|---|---|---|---|
| TO | 83,131,921 | 90,839,540 | 71,670,970 |
| P/L | (2,249,439) | 327,131 | 227,518 |
| NW | 415,797 | 2,274,717 | 1,930,598 |
| WC | 705,371 | 2,710,014 | 2,631,422 |
| Emp. | 66 | 55 | 53 |

DUNS 52-535-8719
## Princess Productions Ltd
**(Subsidiary of:** Nc Shine Acquisition Ltd.)
Unit 316 Whiteleys Centre, Unit 316, Whiteleys Centre, Queensway, London W2 4YN
**Tel:** 020-7985-1985
**Web:** www.princesstv.com
**Reg No:** 3239469 **Estd:** 1996 Private Limited Company
**Line of Business:** Radio and television production services
**Export Sales:** £1,218,000
**Issued Capital:** £2
**Directors:** T Hincks, Ms S Turner Laing
**Responsibilities**
**Senior:** Henrietta Conrad *(Manager)*, Elisabeth Murdoch *(Manager)*, Sebastian Scott *(Manager)*
**Finance:** Sam Welstead *(Financial Manager)*
**Marketing:** Henrietta Conrad *(Manager)*
**Sales:** Henrietta Conrad *(Manager)*
**IT:** Chris Steven *(IT Manager)*, richard gale *(IT Manager)*
**Branches:** Princess Productions Ltd, Whiteleys Centre, Third Floor, London W2 4YN
**US SIC:** 4833 **UK SIC:** 97411
**Auditors:** Lewis Golden & Co
**Bankers:** The Royal Bank Of Scotland Plc (16-00-38)

| | 30-06-13 | 01-07-12 | 31-06-10 |
|---|---|---|---|
| TO | 32,799,000 | 52,275,000 | 24,979,000 |
| P/L | 854,000 | 1,633,000 | 2,064,000 |
| NW | 6,871,000 | 5,910,000 | 5,088,000 |
| WC | 5,675,000 | 4,513,000 | 3,828,000 |
| Emp. | 218 | 202 | 120 |

DUNS 21-227-0229
## Princess Royal Health Centre
Princess Royal Health Centre, Greenhead Road, Huddersfield, West Yorkshire HD1 4EW
**Tel:** 01484344000
**Web:** www.cht.nhs.uk
**Estd:** 2002 Proprietorship
**Line of Business:** Public sector hospital activities, including nhs trusts
**Proprietor:** T Lockwood
**US SIC:** 8062 **UK SIC:** 95100
**Employees:** 127

DUNS 21-223-9044
## Princess Royal Maternity Hospital
8-16 Alexandra Parade, Glasgow, Lanarkshire G31 2ER
**Tel:** 0141-2115400
**Web:** www.nhsgg.org.uk
**Estd:** 1905 Proprietorship
**Line of Business:** Public sector hospital activities, including nhs trusts
**Proprietor:** Mrs L Mcilrath
**Responsibilities**
**Senior:** Heather Dawes *(Clinical Services Manager)*
**Sales:** Heather Dawes *(Clinical Services Manager)*
**HR:** David Dall *(Human Resources Manager)*
**US SIC:** 8062 **UK SIC:** 95100
**Employees:** 116

DUNS 21-680-7669 **Imp-Exp**
## Princess Yachts International Plc
**(Subsidiary of:** The Renwick Group Plc)
Newport Street, Plymouth, Devon PL1 3QG
**Tel:** 01752-203888 **Fax:** 01752-203777
**Web:** www.princessyachts.com
**Reg No:** 0856633 **VAT No:** 927314623
**Estd:** 1965 Public Limited Company
**Line of Business:** Boatbuilders
**Trading Style:** Princess Yachts
**Issued Capital:** £16,190,000
**Principals:** D S King *(Managing)*, W D Green, I A Duffin, C J Gates, D Pyle
**Co. Secretary:** Russell Gale
**Responsibilities**
**Senior:** Jim Donovan *(Machine Shop Manager)*
**Marketing:** Nicola Basil *(Marketing Coordinator)*
**IT:** Anita Gruitt *(IT Director)*, Ben Saunders *(IT Manager)*
**HR:** Diane Ekland *(Training Director)*, Eugene Van Jaarsveldt *(Human Resources Manager)*
**Health & Safety:** Jim Donovan *(Machine Shop Manager)*, Dave Richardson *(Health & Safety Officer)*
**Engineering:** James Nieto *(Head of Global Quality Enginee)*, Alex Stevens *(Head of Engineering and Qualit)*
**US SIC:** 3732 **UK SIC:** 36102
**Auditors:** PricewaterhouseCoopers LLP
**Bankers:** National Westminster Bank Plc (56-00-49)

| | 31-12-13 | 31-12-12 | 31-12-11 |
|---|---|---|---|
| TO | 239,365,000 | 249,906,000 | 207,855,000 |
| P/L | 17,938,000 | 18,445,000 | 15,109,000 |
| NW | 121,448,000 | 106,412,000 | 90,773,000 |
| WC | 92,793,000 | 76,518,000 | 60,712,000 |
| Emp. | 2,018 | 2,056 | 1,911 |

DUNS 23-633-1112
## Princeton Hotels & Leisure Ltd
Birmingham Road, Allesley, Coventry, West Midlands CV5 9GT
**Tel:** 02476403272
**Web:** www.ichotelsgroup.com
**Reg No:** 0015614FC **VAT No:** 545237347
**Estd:** 1990
**Line of Business:** Hotels and motels without restaurant
**Trading Style:** Allesley Hotel
**Directors:** K Kassam, N N Bandali, M Bandali, S Darveshali
**Co. Secretary:** Aly Kassam
**Responsibilities**
**Finance:** Jeanette Drinkall *(Financial Controller)*
**Admin:** Leanne Ward *(Office Manager)*
**Facilities:** Brian Flynn *(Maintenance Manager)*
**Branches:** Princeton Hotels & Leisure Ltd, Gloucester Road, Cheltenham, Gloucestershire GL51 0SS
**US SIC:** 7011 **UK SIC:** 66500
**Bankers:** Barclays Bank Plc (20-03-53)

DUNS 21-779-3267
## Princeville Primary School
Willowfield Street, Bradford, West Yorkshire BD7 2AH
**Tel:** 01274573298
**Web:** www.princeville.bradford.sch.uk
**Estd:** 1907 Proprietorship
**Line of Business:** General secondary education
**Proprietor:** Mrs S Rawnsley
**Responsibilities**
**IT:** Janet Pullford *(IT Manager)*
**US SIC:** 8211 **UK SIC:** 93200
**Employees:** 90

DUNS 21-005-4076
## Princi Uk Ltd
5th Floor 85-86 Newman Street, London W1T 3EX
**Tel:** 02074788888
**Web:** www.princi.co.uk
**Reg No:** 6300882 **Estd:** 2007 Private Limited Company
**Line of Business:** Management activities of holding companies
**Issued Capital:** £1,000,002
**Directors:** O M Rivers, J M Sheridan, A T Yau, R Princi
**Co. Secretary:** Dario Kadiev
**Responsibilities**
**Senior:** Jale Erentok *(Manager)*
**US SIC:** 6711 **UK SIC:** 83962

| | 26-10-13 | 27-10-12 | 31-10-11 |
|---|---|---|---|
| TO | 4,512,978 | 3,933,566 | 3,473,383 |
| P/L | (130,436) | (385,578) | (327,702) |
| NW | (2,317,260) | (2,310,078) | (2,924,500) |
| WC | (895,474) | (941,723) | (552,791) |
| Emp. | 99 | 81 | 64 |

DUNS 50-427-6809
## Principal Catering Consultants Ltd
321 Upper Elmers End Road, Beckenham, Kent BR3 3QP
**Web:** www.fare-catering.com
**Reg No:** 2419830 **VAT No:** 523939822
**Estd:** 1989 Private Limited Company
**Line of Business:** Caterers
**Trading Style:** Principal & Fare
**Issued Capital:** £107
**Principals:** J P Durden *(Managing)*, R M Kinder
**Co. Secretary:** Ms Nicola Colbran
**Responsibilities**
**Sales:** Charlie Brookes *(Commercial Director)*
**Branches:** Principal Catering Consultants Ltd, 171 Union Street, London SE1 0LN
**US SIC:** 5812, 7399
**UK SIC:** 66110, 83954
**Auditors:** The Rees Partnership
**Bankers:** National Westminster Bank Plc (60-14-15)

| | 31-08-14 | 31-08-13 | 31-08-12 |
|---|---|---|---|
| TO | 10,521,788 | 8,442,356 | 7,458,253 |
| P/L | 276,405 | (28,873) | (19,270) |
| NW | 726,505 | 534,610 | 617,548 |
| WC | 864,916 | 386,027 | 540,023 |
| Emp. | 272 | 319 | 276 |

DUNS 23-828-0429 **Imp**
## Principal Global Investors (Europe) Ltd
10 Gresham Street, London EC2V 7JD
**Tel:** 020-7710-0220 **Fax:** 020-7920-0061
**Web:** www.principalglobal.com
**Reg No:** 3819986 **Estd:** 1999 Private Limited Company
**Line of Business:** Investment companies and vehicles
**Trading Style:** Principal Global Investors (Europe) Ltd
**Issued Capital:** £2,724,002
**Principals:** N C Lyster *(Managing)*, A M Dion, C J Henderson, G Thornton, Ms M L Hanrahan, K K West
**Co. Secretary:** Ms Ruth Clapton
**Responsibilities**
**Senior:** Susan Cohn *(Manager)*, Simon Hedger *(Manager)*, Barbara McKenzie *(Manager)*
**US SIC:** 6111, 6371
**UK SIC:** 81501, 82002
**Bankers:** HSBC Bank plc (40-07-31)

| | 31-12-13 | 31-12-12 | 31-12-11 |
|---|---|---|---|
| TA | 19,838,825 | 16,251,913 | 18,044,563 |
| P/L | 2,724,225 | 2,458,047 | 2,735,009 |
| NW | 14,227,009 | 11,021,652 | 10,877,685 |
| WC | 13,459,048 | 10,750,474 | 10,431,436 |
| Emp. | 56 | 56 | 50 |

DUNS 22-952-2958
## Principality Building Society
Po Box 89, Principality Buildings, Queen Street, Cardiff, South Glamorgan CF10 1UA
**Tel:** 08450450452
**Web:** www.principality.co.uk
**Estd:** 1860
**Line of Business:** Representative office
**Principals:** D John *(Chairman)*, W G Thomas *(Financial)*, Eurfyl ap Gwilym, BSc PhD, Deput, P L Griffiths, C A Jones, C Rowlands, Ms J Kenrick, L Davies
**Responsibilities**
**Senior:** Anita Copp *(Branch Manager)*, Gordon MacLean *(Non-Executive Director)*, Jodie Moxham *(Branch Manager)*, Kelly Williams *(Senior Branch Manager)*
**Finance:** Gareth Cocks *(Financial Crime Analyst)*, WIlliam Thomas *(Financial Director)*
**Marketing:** Christine Edwards *(Relations Manager)*, Kirstie Evans *(Marketing Manager)*, Melanie Ward *(Relations Manager)*
**Sales:** Keely Bridges *(Regional Sales Quality Coach)*, Lynne Landricombe *(Business Development Consultan)*, Richard Wales *(Senior Business Development Ma)*
**Admin:** Rachel Ford *(Administrator)*
**IT:** Andrew Hadland *(PC Manager)*
**Facilities:** Gary Benson *(Facilities Manager)*
**Operations:** WIlliam Thomas *(Financial Director)*
**Branches:** Principality Building Society, 93 Taff Street, Pontypridd, Mid Glamorgan CF37 4SL
**US SIC:** 6111 **UK SIC:** 81501
**Auditors:** Deloitte LLP
**Following financial data are in thousands**

| | 31-12-13 | 31-12-10 | 31-12-09 |
|---|---|---|---|
| TA | 7,058,100 | 6,262,100 | 6,218,900 |
| P/L | 28,700 | 30,800 | 14,300 |
| NW | 350,300 | 308,900 | 287,200 |
| WC | 2,077,500 | 481,800 | 460,500 |
| Emp. | 1,033 | 878 | 838 |

DUNS 51-996-7251
## Principality Ltd
**(Subsidiary of:** Principality Building Society)
Po Box 89, Principality Buildings, Queen Street, Cardiff, South Glamorgan CF10 1UA
**Tel:** 01495213958
**Web:** www.principality.co.uk
**Reg No:** 3363851 **Estd:** 1997 Private Limited Company
**Line of Business:** Financial intermediation not elsewhere classified
**Issued Capital:** £2
**Director:** G H Yorston
**Co. Secretary:** Michael Borrill
**Branches:** Principality Ltd, 39 High Street, Mold, Clwyd CH7 1BQ
**US SIC:** 6111, 6012
**UK SIC:** 81501, 81402

| | 31-12-13 | 31-12-12 | 31-12-11 |
|---|---|---|---|
| TA | 1 | 1 | 2 |
| NW | 1 | 1 | 2 |

DUNS 51-628-1719
## Principia: Partners in Health Ltd
165 Loughborough Road, Ruddington, Nottingham, Nottinghamshire NG11 6LQ
**Tel:** 01158837880
**Web:** www.rushcliffeccg.nhs.uk
**Reg No:** 5908067 **Estd:** 2006 Private Company Limited By Guarantee
**Line of Business:** Healthcare companies

**Directors:** Dr G W Derbyshire, J R Booth, Ms N Lilley
**Responsibilities**
**Senior:** Vicky Bailey (Chief Officer)
**US SIC:** 8091 **UK SIC:** 95200

| | 31-08-13 | 31-08-12 | 31-08-11 |
|---|---|---|---|
| TO | N/A | 301,026 | 341,125 |
| P/L | N/A | 251 | 1,456 |
| NW | 28,343 | 25,970 | 25,778 |
| WC | 28,343 | 25,970 | 25,778 |

DUNS 76-926-9242
## Principle Cleaning Services Ltd
(**Subsidiary of:** Principle Services Holdings Ltd)
Unit 6-7 Principle House, The Campsbourne, London N8 7PN
**Web:** www.principlecleaning.com
**Reg No:** 2333935 **Estd:** 1989 Private Limited Company
**Line of Business:** Cleaning activities not elsewhere classified
**Issued Capital:** £600,100
**Principals:** D P Cooke (Managing), B J Staines, M I Vesey, T Murphy, J Freeman, P J Smith
**Co. Secretary:** Ms Elizabeth Cooke
**Responsibilities**
**Senior:** Elizabeth Pippard (executive Director), Sarah Thompson (Financial Manager)
**Finance:** Sarah Thompson (Financial Manager)
**US SIC:** 7349 **UK SIC:** 92300
**Auditors:** Quinneys
**Bankers:** Lloyds TSB Bank plc (30-00-09)

| | 31-03-14 | 31-03-13 | 31-03-12 |
|---|---|---|---|
| TO | 22,135,419 | 19,580,257 | 18,498,502 |
| P/L | 882,620 | 229,404 | 317,108 |
| NW | 2,108,340 | 1,486,741 | 1,345,542 |
| WC | 1,882,952 | 1,250,856 | 1,093,190 |
| Emp. | 1,280 | 1,317 | 1,398 |

DUNS 77-930-5015
## Principle Holdings Ltd
C/O Principle Tandem Industrial Estate, Huddersfield, West Yorkshire HD5 0AN
**Tel:** 01484-430003
**Web:** www.principlemaintenance.co.uk
**Reg No:** 5833239 **Estd:** 2006 Private Limited Company
**Line of Business:** Management activities of holding companies
**Issued Capital:** £248,902
**Directors:** Mrs V J Woodings, R H Butterfield, D R Pitt, P Shilling, M J Deuschle
**Co. Secretary:** David Pitt
**US SIC:** 6711 **UK SIC:** 83962

| | 31-12-13 | 31-12-12 | 31-12-11 |
|---|---|---|---|
| TO | 60,025,060 | 44,531,457 | 54,310,514 |
| P/L | 4,797,434 | 1,082,346 | 2,479,665 |
| NW | 4,713,117 | 3,271,029 | 3,141,628 |
| WC | 2,058,126 | 1,416,367 | 1,651,517 |
| Emp. | 286 | 192 | 179 |

DUNS 29-657-2464
## Principles Communications Ltd
(**Subsidiary of:** Advertising Principles Holdings Ltd)
Devonshire Hall, Devonshire Avenue, Leeds, West Yorkshire LS8 1AW
**Tel:** 01132262222
**Web:** www.p-pr.co.uk
**Reg No:** 1983541 **Estd:** 1986 Private Limited Company
**Line of Business:** Advertising
**Export Sales:** £24,419
**Trading Style:** Advertising Principals
**Issued Capital:** £100,000
**Directors:** B May, M Curtis
**Co. Secretary:** Christopher Goodwin
**Responsibilities**
**Facilities:** Maya Zaremba (Group Office Coordinator)
**Branches:** Principles Communications Ltd, Brighton Grove, Manchester M14 5JT
**US SIC:** 7311, 7392
**UK SIC:** 83800, 83951
**Auditors:** Mazars
**Bankers:** Lloyds TSB Bank plc (30-00-05)

| | 31-03-14 | 31-03-13 | 31-03-12 |
|---|---|---|---|
| TO | 6,518,642 | 7,393,071 | 9,532,064 |
| P/L | (31,141) | 250,014 | (149,589) |
| NW | 1,099,279 | 1,158,179 | 965,292 |
| WC | 627,384 | 665,545 | 432,645 |
| Emp. | 51 | 53 | 64 |

DUNS 23-929-3033      Exp
## Pringle of Scotland Ltd
(**Subsidiary of:** Pringle Enterprises Ltd)
Glebe Mill, Hawick, Roxburghshire TD9 9QE
**Tel:** 01450360200
**Web:** www.pringlescotland.com
**Reg No:** 0203627SC **VAT No:** 743381924
**Estd:** 2000 Private Limited Company
**Line of Business:** Retail sale of clothing
**Trading Style:** Pringle of Scotland Ltd
**Issued Capital:** £84,000,000

**Directors:** T K Lau, J Fang, K H Fang, D Fang, A Wong
**Co. Secretary:** Maclay Murray & Spens Llp
**Responsibilities**
**Senior:** Ted Brindley (Warehouse Manager), Tracy Chapman (Financial Controller), Benoit Duverger (Manager), Mary Maccair (Manager)
**Finance:** Tracy Chapman (Financial Controller)
**IT:** robert innes (Computer Manager)
**HR:** anne gavin (Personnel Manager)
**Purchasing:** Ted Brindley (Warehouse Manager)
**Branches:** Pringle Of Scotland Ltd, 111-112 New Bond Street, London W1S 1DP
**US SIC:** 5699 **UK SIC:** 64500
**Auditors:** Deloitte LLP
**Bankers:** HSBC Bank plc (40-00-00)

| | 01-02-14 | 26-01-13 | 28-02-12 |
|---|---|---|---|
| TO | 5,408,000 | 5,917,000 | 8,527,000 |
| P/L | (4,110,000) | (6,350,000) | (9,566,000) |
| NW | 1,483,000 | 593,000 | 943,000 |
| WC | 377,000 | 849,000 | 1,895,000 |
| Emp. | 62 | 70 | 81 |

DUNS 73-274-9499      Imp
## Prinova Europe Ltd
(**Subsidiary of:** Prinova Holdings Llc)
10 Aldersgate Street, London EC1A 4HJ
**Tel:** 020-7466-5460 **Fax:** 020-7466-5461
**Web:** www.prinovaeurope.com
**Reg No:** 4548728 **Estd:** 2004 Private Limited Company
**Line of Business:** Chemicals distribution and wholesale
**Director:** D K Thorp
**Co. Secretary:** David York
**US SIC:** 5161, 7399
**UK SIC:** 61200, 83954
**Auditors:** Baker Tilly UK Audit LLP
**Bankers:** The Chase Manhattan Bank (60-92-42)
**Employees:** 40
**Turnover:** £165,501,000

DUNS 73-807-5162      Imp
## Prinovis Uk Ltd
(**Subsidiary of:** Prinovis Ltd. & Co. Kg)
4 Dakota Drive, Speke, Liverpool, Merseyside L24 8RJ
**Tel:** 01514-945-200 **Fax:** 01514-270-876
**Web:** www.prinovis.com
**Reg No:** 5063783 **VAT No:** 849758066
**Estd:** 2004 Private Limited Company
**Line of Business:** Printing not elsewhere classified
**Issued Capital:** £1
**Directors:** R Gray, Dr B Stausberg
**Co. Secretary:** Dentons Secretaries Limited
**US SIC:** 2752, 7333
**UK SIC:** 47544, 83953
**Auditors:** PricewaterhouseCoopers LLP

| | 31-12-13 | 31-12-12 | 31-12-11 |
|---|---|---|---|
| TO | 63,772,000 | 73,746,000 | 84,620,000 |
| P/L | (37,842,000) | (34,537,000) | 1,603,000 |
| NW | (75,365,000) | (35,869,000) | (1,281,000) |
| WC | 8,622,000 | 3,997,000 | 5,677,000 |
| Emp. | 375 | 408 | 444 |

DUNS 39-678-1023
## Print Direct 1987 Ltd
Unit 5-6, Castlehill, Horsfield Way, Stockport, Cheshire SK6 2SU
**Tel:** 0161-406-7232
**Web:** www.printdirectuk.com
**Reg No:** 2142347 **VAT No:** 473441742
**Estd:** 1987 Private Limited Company
**Line of Business:** Manufacturers of albums
**Issued Capital:** £100,000
**Director:** P Utting
**Co. Secretary:** Mrs Zoe Repman
**Responsibilities**
**Senior:** Bryan Bedson (Manager), Andy Muir (Buyer)
**Finance:** Christopher Haresnape (Finance Director)
**Purchasing:** Andy Muir (Buyer)
**US SIC:** 2752 **UK SIC:** 47544
**Bankers:** Barclays Bank Plc (20-55-34)

| | 31-12-13 | 31-12-12 | 31-12-11 |
|---|---|---|---|
| TA | 100,021 | 815,650 | 815,650 |
| NW | 100,021 | 100,021 | 100,021 |
| WC | N/A | 100,021 | 100,021 |

DUNS 21-412-0713
## Print Exchange
Maghull Business Centre, 1 Liverpool Road North, Liverpool, Merseyside L31 2HB
**Web:** www.printxchange.co.uk
**Estd:** 2010 Proprietorship
**Line of Business:** Marketing consultants
**Proprietor:** A Smith
**US SIC:** 7392 **UK SIC:** 83951
**Employees:** 100

DUNS 22-526-4654
## Print Express
Unit B, Stonefield Way, Ruislip, Middlesex HA4 0JS
**Tel:** 08445678228
**Web:** www.printexpress.co.uk
**VAT No:** 226235189 **Estd:** 1983 Partnership
**Line of Business:** Pre-press activities
**Trading Style:** Print Express Corporate
**Partners:** R M Daya, S Varghese
**Branches:** Print Express, 4 Sunnyside Terrace, London NW9 5DL
**US SIC:** 2794, 5942
**UK SIC:** 47545, 65300
**Employees:** 120

DUNS 23-660-5346
## The Print People Group Ltd
17-21 Tolwell Road, Leicester, Leicestershire LE4 1BR
**Tel:** 01162342600 **Fax:** 0116-234-2638
**Web:** www.taylorbloxham.co.uk
**Reg No:** 3655511 **Estd:** 1998 Private Limited Company
**Line of Business:** Printers general
**Export Sales:** £1,161,291
**Trading Style:** Taylor Bloxham Ltd
**Issued Capital:** £83,083
**Directors:** R C Lockwood, C P Bowen, Ms A J Sharpless, K Moss
**Co. Secretary:** David Berry
**Responsibilities**
**Marketing:** Lisa Haynes (Marketing Manager)
**Sales:** Neil Tracey (Sales Manager)
**IT:** Paul Munckton (IT Manager)
**US SIC:** 2752 **UK SIC:** 47544
**Bankers:** HSBC Bank plc (40-00-00)

| | 30-09-13 | 30-09-12 | 30-09-11 |
|---|---|---|---|
| TO | 23,847,742 | 24,571,781 | 24,740,373 |
| P/L | 10,783 | (175,565) | 282,786 |
| NW | 1,169,353 | 1,152,665 | 1,419,255 |
| WC | (1,779,834) | (1,809,637) | (1,944,472) |
| Emp. | 206 | 209 | 206 |

DUNS 21-313-9058
## Print Search Ltd
(**Subsidiary of:** D C B Group Ltd)
Westinghouse Road, Trafford Park, Manchester M17 1PJ
**Tel:** 01618728921 **Fax:** 0161-848-7323
**Web:** www.printsearch.co.uk
**Reg No:** 1116162 **Estd:** 1972 Private Limited Company
**Line of Business:** Printing not elsewhere classified
**Trading Style:** Aspen, Aspen Corporate
**Issued Capital:** £52,200
**Directors:** D C Beale, Miss V Farrell, Miss M H Steele
**Co. Secretary:** David Beale
**Responsibilities**
**Senior:** Andrew Large (Director)
**IT:** Brian Carratt (Computer Manager)
**Branches:** Print Search Ltd, Hilliard House Lester Way, Hithercroft Indust Estate, Wallingford, Oxfordshire OX10 9TA
**US SIC:** 2752 **UK SIC:** 47544
**Auditors:** TFD Dunhams
**Bankers:** HSBC Bank plc (40-43-20)

| | 31-03-14 | 31-03-13 | 31-03-12 |
|---|---|---|---|
| TO | 7,526,420 | 7,818,526 | N/A |
| P/L | (20,303) | 103,300 | N/A |
| NW | 444,805 | 385,109 | 396,446 |
| WC | 91,125 | 110,366 | 105,055 |
| Emp. | 40 | 47 | N/A |

DUNS 29-004-4700      Imp
## Printagraph Ltd
(**Subsidiary of:** Jasmine Holdings Ltd)
Hillview Road, Aberdeen, Aberdeenshire AB12 3HB
**Tel:** 01224-893900 **Fax:** 01224633033
**Web:** www.printagraph.co.uk
**Reg No:** 0082975SC **VAT No:** 384612932
**Estd:** 1983 Private Limited Company
**Line of Business:** Advertising related services
**Issued Capital:** £1,732
**Directors:** A M Hall, N F Stewart, D D Cowie, K A Adams
**Co. Secretary:** Daniel Cowie
**Responsibilities**
**Senior:** Keith Tait (Manager)
**US SIC:** 2752 **UK SIC:** 47544
**Auditors:** Ritson Smith
**Bankers:** Clydesdale Bank Plc (82-62-22)

| | 30-06-13 | 30-06-12 | 30-06-11 |
|---|---|---|---|
| TA | 2,830,593 | 2,609,130 | 2,514,347 |
| NW | 1,131,198 | 922,053 | 669,616 |
| WC | 472,549 | 212,440 | 98,763 |

DUNS 21-179-4385
## Printcraft Ltd
(**Subsidiary of:** Cf Topco Ltd)
Acorn Park Ndustrial Estate, Shipley, West Yorkshire BD17 7SW
**Tel:** 01274581313
**Reg No:** 7019834 **Estd:** 2009 Private Limited Company
**Line of Business:** Printing not elsewhere classified
**Issued Capital:** £1
**Directors:** D Bryant, C R Beck, R Hayes
**US SIC:** 2752 **UK SIC:** 47544
**Auditors:** KPMG LLP

| | 31-01-14 | 31-01-13 | 31-01-12 |
|---|---|---|---|
| TO | 16,689,000 | 15,014,000 | 12,811,000 |
| P/L | 2,429,000 | 1,922,000 | 795,000 |
| NW | 3,202,000 | 1,021,000 | (777,000) |
| WC | (2,613,000) | (4,281,000) | (6,059,000) |
| Emp. | 113 | 114 | 113 |

DUNS 21-558-9430
## Printexpress Co Uk
Unit 5 Stonefield Way, Stonefield Way, Ruislip, Middlesex HA4 0JS
**Tel:** 02088390854
**Web:** www.printexpress.co.uk
**Estd:** 2006 Proprietorship
**Line of Business:** Printers general
**Proprietor:** M Daya
**Responsibilities**
**Senior:** Mohammed Daya (Director)
**US SIC:** 2752 **UK SIC:** 47544
**Employees:** 100

DUNS 22-651-9817      Imp-Exp
## Prior Diesel Ltd
(**Subsidiary of:** Suretank Group Limited)
Easy 2, Millenium House, Great Yarmouth, Norfolk NR31 0NL
**Tel:** 01493-441383
**Web:** www.priordiesel.com
**Reg No:** 1499503 **VAT No:** 849748854
**Estd:** 1980 Private Limited Company
**Line of Business:** Manufacture of other special purpose machinery not elsewhere classified
**Export Markets:** worldwide
**Export Sales:** £3,382,381
**Issued Capital:** £100
**Principals:** A B Maclean (Managing), D Beirne, C E Conroy, J Fitzgerald, G A Maclean
**Co. Secretary:** Dermot Beirne
**Responsibilities**
**Facilities:** Matt Dack (Service Manager)
**US SIC:** 3559, 7539
**UK SIC:** 32863, 67100
**Auditors:** Lovewell Blake LLP
**Bankers:** Barclays Bank Plc (20-53-06)

| | 31-03-14 | 31-03-13 | 31-03-12 |
|---|---|---|---|
| TO | 14,093,255 | 15,177,884 | 11,358,026 |
| P/L | 906,663 | 669,231 | 81,119 |
| NW | 2,571,665 | 2,072,282 | 2,578,041 |
| WC | 2,145,718 | 1,668,126 | 1,864,050 |
| Emp. | 92 | 85 | 69 |

DUNS 22-605-1688
## Prior Park Educational Trust
Ralph Allen Drive, Bath, Avon BA2 5AH
**Tel:** 01225835353
**Web:** www.thepriorfoundation.co.uk
**Reg No:** 1521832 **Estd:** 1980 Private Company Limited By Guarantee
**Line of Business:** General secondary education
**Directors:** Ms M M Rae, J M Shinkwin, W M Mcloughlin, P G Vaughan-Fowler, Dr H B Costigane, A M King, J P Webster, Rear Admiral N J Raby
**Co. Secretary:** Anthony Mcniff
**Responsibilities**
**Senior:** Anthony Bury (Director), Simon Eliot (Director), Nancy Freeman (Director), James Murphy-O'connor (Head Teacher), Peter O'Donoghue (Director), Nicola Pearson (Director), Anne Shepherd (Director)
**Marketing:** Margaret Ruxton (Admissions Director)
**Admin:** Alison Garrett-Smith (Office Manager)
**IT:** Andy Haines (Senior IT Executive)
**HR:** Alison Garrett-Smith (Office Manager)
**Branches:** Prior Park Preparatory School, Cricklade, Swindon Wilts.
**US SIC:** 8211 **UK SIC:** 93200
**Auditors:** HLB Kidsons
**Bankers:** Barclays Bank Plc (20-05-06)

| | 31-08-14 | 31-08-13 | 31-08-12 |
|---|---|---|---|
| TO | 14,226,266 | 13,437,438 | 13,090,728 |
| P/L | 1,334,775 | 684,084 | 460,073 |
| NW | 13,586,747 | 12,251,972 | 11,567,888 |
| WC | 2,102,693 | 990,494 | 648,437 |
| Emp. | 334 | 332 | 334 |

DUNS 54-873-3005
## Prior Park Preparatory School
Manor House, Calcutt Street, Cricklade, Swindon, Wiltshire SN6 6BB
**Tel:** 01793-750275
**Web:** www.priorparkprep.com
**Estd:** 1994 Proprietorship
**Line of Business:** Schools (independent)
**Proprietor:** G Hobern
**Responsibilities**
**Senior:** Vaughan Jelley *(Deputy Head)*, Mark Pearce *(Principal)*
**Finance:** Julie Barclay *(Facilities Manager)*
**IT:** Sarah Paddock *(Head of IT)*
**HR:** Julie Barclay *(Facilities Manager)*
**Health & Safety:** Julie Barclay *(Facilities Manager)*
**Facilities:** Julie Barclay *(Facilities Manager)*
**Purchasing:** Julie Barclay *(Facilities Manager)*
**US SIC:** 8211 **UK SIC:** 93200
**Employees:** 200

DUNS 23-276-7330
## Prior Pursglove College
Church Walk, Guisborough, Cleveland TS14 6BU
**Tel:** 01287280800
**Web:** www.pursglove.ac.uk
**Estd:** 1993
**Line of Business:** Further education schools and colleges
**Principals:** T Stephenson *(Financial)*, S Whitehead
**Responsibilities**
**Senior:** Judy Burton *(Principal)*, Stephen Whitehead *(Partner)*
**Admin:** Liz Grove *(Clerk)*
**IT:** Mark Ayres-Russon *(IT Support)*, Bob Marshall *(Network Manager)*
**US SIC:** 8221 **UK SIC:** 93100
**Employees:** 160

DUNS 21-603-0825 **Imp-Exp**
## Prior Scientific Instruments Ltd
Unit 3-4 Fielding Industrial Estate, Cambridge, Cambridgeshire CB21 5ET
**Tel:** 01223-881711
**Web:** www.prior.com
**Reg No:** 0404087 **VAT No:** 215896439
**Estd:** 1920 Private Limited Company
**Line of Business:** Manufacture of electronic instruments and appliances for measuring, checking, testing, navigating and other purposes, except industrial process control equipment
**Export Markets:** U S A; Worldwide
**Export Sales:** £10,627,718
**Trading Style:** Prior Scientific Instruments
**Issued Capital:** £523,600
**Directors:** Dr M M Maintz, J F Fielding, S J Smith, S Jarvis, F F Fielding, M J Fielding, T Freda
**Co. Secretary:** Simon Smith
**Responsibilities**
**Senior:** Stephen Ling *(Production Director)*
**IT:** Stephen Winters *(IT Manager)*
**HR:** Andy Wierney *(Quality Manager)*
**Health & Safety:** Andy Wierney *(Quality Manager)*
**Facilities:** Stephen Ling *(Production Director)*
**Engineering:** Stephen Ling *(Production Director)*
**US SIC:** 3829 **UK SIC:** 37100
**Auditors:** KPMG LLP
**Bankers:** HSBC Bank plc (40-15-22)

| | 31-03-14 | 31-03-13 | 31-03-12 |
|---|---|---|---|
| TO | 13,213,951 | 12,944,664 | 12,321,051 |
| P/L | 1,265,545 | 1,402,332 | 1,057,320 |
| NW | 6,947,974 | 6,405,576 | 5,411,616 |
| WC | 5,276,700 | 4,907,998 | 4,191,118 |
| Emp. | 97 | 96 | 96 |

DUNS 54-919-0205
## Priority Area Playgroups
477 Stratford Road, Sparkhill, Birmingham, West Midlands B11 4LE
**Tel:** 01214648117
**Estd:** 1967 Proprietorship
**Line of Business:** Nursery schools
**Director:** Ms J Roche
**US SIC:** 8699, 6732
**UK SIC:** 96902, 83100
**Employees:** 62

DUNS 29-127-9313
## Priority Area Playgroups & Day Care Centres
117 Pershore Road, Birmingham, West Midlands B5 7NX
**Web:** www.priorityareaplaygroups.co.uk
**Reg No:** 1626517 **Estd:** 1982
**Line of Business:** Social work activities without accommodation
**Trading Style:** P A P
**Directors:** M J Brown, Mrs M G Henson, J A Devereux, Ms J M Culley
**Responsibilities**
**Senior:** Amy Brooks *(Director)*
**US SIC:** 7399 **UK SIC:** 83954
**Auditors:** Malcolm Willcox & Co
**Bankers:** Lloyds TSB Bank plc (30-00-06)

| | 31-03-14 | 31-03-13 | 31-03-12 |
|---|---|---|---|
| TO | 651,603 | 737,115 | 779,373 |
| P/L | (32,521) | (9,046) | 37,151 |
| NW | 258,452 | 290,973 | 300,019 |
| WC | 256,205 | 289,480 | 298,915 |
| Emp. | 53 | 54 | 60 |

DUNS 23-619-0281
## Priority Care Group Ltd
1 Logie Street, Dundee, Angus DD2 2QF
**Tel:** 01382631010
**Web:** www.priority-care.co.uk
**Reg No:** 0188546SC **Estd:** 1998 Private Limited Company
**Line of Business:** Social work activities with accommodation
**Trading Style:** Priority First Training
**Issued Capital:** £100
**Directors:** A J Prior, H Locherty, Mrs V R Gibson
**Co. Secretary:** Andrew Prior
**Branches:** Priority Care Group Ltd, 122 Harestane Road, Dundee, Angus DD3 0NY
**US SIC:** 8321 **UK SIC:** 96111
**Auditors:** Findlay & Co
**Bankers:** Bank Of Scotland (80-20-19)

| | 30-06-13 | 30-06-12 | 30-06-11 |
|---|---|---|---|
| TO | 6,544,470 | 5,710,896 | 4,835,605 |
| P/L | 456,983 | 60,819 | (9,099) |
| NW | 5,487,087 | 5,216,502 | 5,386,974 |
| WC | 398,328 | 115,588 | (370,148) |
| Emp. | 317 | 323 | 263 |

DUNS 21-097-7462
## Priority Care (Shropshire) Ltd
2 Vineyard Road, Wellington, Telford, Shropshire TF1 1HA
**Tel:** 01952290230
**Reg No:** 6419989 **Estd:** 2007 Private Limited Company
**Line of Business:** Home care service providers
**Issued Capital:** £2
**Director:** Ms S L Johnson
**Co. Secretary:** Ms Tracy Davies
**US SIC:** 8091 **UK SIC:** 95200

| | 31-03-14 | 31-03-13 | 31-03-12 |
|---|---|---|---|
| TA | 361,556 | 256,510 | 178,900 |
| NW | 260,381 | 182,403 | 113,062 |
| WC | 245,705 | 168,980 | 99,157 |

DUNS 53-631-7084
## Priority Freight Ltd
**(Subsidiary of:** Priority Freight Holdings Ltd)
6-7 White Cliffs Business Park Menzies, Road, Dover, Kent CT16 3NJ
**Tel:** 01304828111 **Fax:** 01304828112
**Web:** www.priorityfreight.co.uk
**Reg No:** 3436573 **Estd:** 1996 Private Limited Company
**Line of Business:** Goods delivery services
**Export Sales:** £8,075,792
**Issued Capital:** £1,000
**Directors:** P C Mercer, P V Williams, G S Williams
**Co. Secretary:** Neal Williams
**Responsibilities**
**Senior:** Edward Benbridge *(Transport Manager)*
**Fleet:** Edward Benbridge *(Transport Manager)*
**US SIC:** 4712 **UK SIC:** 77002
**Auditors:** Websters
**Bankers:** The Royal Bank Of Scotland Plc (16-15-20)

| | 30-09-13 | 30-09-12 | 30-09-11 |
|---|---|---|---|
| TO | 17,770,404 | 17,164,597 | 14,162,408 |
| P/L | 141,986 | 221,453 | 177,343 |
| NW | 1,934,382 | 1,941,387 | 1,836,840 |
| WC | 612,035 | 801,703 | 684,611 |
| Emp. | 68 | 58 | 58 |

DUNS 34-580-9701 **Imp-Exp**
## Priority Pass Ltd
**(Subsidiary of:** Parminder Ltd)
Po Box 120, Croydon, Surrey CR9 4NU
**Tel:** 020-8680-1338
**Web:** www.prioritypass.com
**Reg No:** 2728518 **Estd:** 1994 Private Limited Company
**Line of Business:** Activities of other membership organisations not elsewhere classified
**Export Markets:** Africa, Middle East and countries worldwide
**Export Sales:** £92,776,899
**Trading Style:** Lounge Pass
**Issued Capital:** £200,000
**Directors:** Ms S Burns, S J Pinches, C R Evans
**Co. Secretary:** Mark Hampton
**Responsibilities**
**Senior:** David Gooderson *(Manager)*
**Marketing:** Salma Siddiqui *(Marketing Executive)*
**Sales:** Charles Facey *(Operations Account Manager)*
**Admin:** Gareth Gilbert *(Administration Supervisor)*
**IT:** Alan Lamprell *(Lounge Data Support Executive)*
**Operations:** Charles Facey *(Operations Account Manager)*
**US SIC:** 8699 **UK SIC:** 96902
**Auditors:** Nyman Libson Paul
**Bankers:** Barclays Bank Plc (20-24-61)

| | 30-04-14 | 30-04-13 | 30-04-12 |
|---|---|---|---|
| TO | 119,644,983 | 107,649,175 | 90,614,785 |
| P/L | 11,454,492 | 6,631,200 | 9,925,194 |
| NW | 34,022,039 | 25,077,301 | 20,039,166 |
| WC | 33,180,581 | 24,945,947 | 19,510,036 |
| Emp. | 71 | 61 | 56 |

DUNS 77-958-8495
## Priority Plus Ltd
Koco Buildings, Arches Industrial Estate, Spon End, Coventry, West Midlands CV1 3JQ
**Tel:** 02477677135
**Web:** www.priorityplusnursing.co.uk
**Reg No:** 5927829 **Estd:** 2006 Private Limited Company
**Line of Business:** Nursing agencies
**Issued Capital:** £2
**Director:** Mrs C W Githu
**Co. Secretary:** Duncan Gachani
**US SIC:** 8091 **UK SIC:** 95200

| | 30-09-13 | 30-09-12 | 30-09-11 |
|---|---|---|---|
| TA | 37,076 | 28,927 | 13,705 |
| NW | 5,918 | 4,790 | (13,848) |
| WC | 4,939 | 3,566 | (14,688) |

DUNS 23-023-1628
## Prior's Court Foundation
Hermitage, Thatcham, Berkshire RG18 9NU
**Tel:** 01635-247202
**Web:** www.priorscourt.org.uk
**Reg No:** 3583324 **Estd:** 1998 Private Unlimited Company
**Line of Business:** Schools (special)
**Directors:** K A Bisset, Mrs S Duncan, A M Bateson, W H Smith, P R Williams, Ms B E Mcdiarmid, G A Bull, C D Nickolds
**Co. Secretary:** Robert Beckley
**Responsibilities**
**Senior:** Stephen Bajdala *(Chief Executive Officer)*, Stephen Bajdla'brown *(Manager)*, Patricia Howlin *(Manager)*, Margaret Shirman *(Director)*, Michael Stark *(Manager)*
**US SIC:** 8299 **UK SIC:** 93300
**Auditors:** Horwath Clark Whitehill
**Bankers:** Barclays Bank Plc (20-59-14)

| | 31-08-14 | 31-07-13 | 31-08-12 |
|---|---|---|---|
| TO | 17,489,392 | 14,007,814 | 12,006,587 |
| P/L | 1,201,557 | 543,111 | 781,515 |
| NW | 15,422,431 | 14,220,874 | 13,677,763 |
| WC | 401,881 | (856,960) | (566,749) |
| Emp. | 397 | 348 | 294 |

DUNS 76-914-5715
## The Prior's Field School Trust Ltd
Priorsfield Road, Hurtmore, Godalming, Surrey GU7 2RH
**Tel:** 01483-810551 **Fax:** 01483801180
**Web:** www.priorsfieldschool.com
**Reg No:** 0667700 **Estd:** 1902 Private Limited Company
**Line of Business:** General secondary education
**Directors:** Mrs I Restell, J R Macleod, Dr A M Jacob, A R Morris, Ms D C Colvin, R W Long, R P Green, R J Southey
**Co. Secretary:** Mrs Joanna Reckord
**Responsibilities**
**Senior:** Neale Andrews *(Director)*, Benjamin Burton Brown *(Governor)*, Angus Cater *(Governor)*, Paul Grinham *(Director)*, Gavin Haig *(Director)*, Ian Hinckley *(Director)*, Julie Rose Blade *(Head of School)*
**Finance:** Leonie Ranson *(Bursar)*
**Marketing:** Josie Cook *(Head of Admissions and Marketi)*, Celia Toms *(Marketing Assistant)*
**IT:** Chris Boulton *(Senior IT Executive)*
**US SIC:** 8211 **UK SIC:** 93200
**Auditors:** Roffe Swayne

| | 31-07-13 | 31-07-12 | 31-07-11 |
|---|---|---|---|
| TO | 7,833,224 | 7,141,088 | 6,653,289 |
| P/L | 561,239 | 440,815 | 500,123 |
| NW | 7,318,839 | 6,757,600 | 6,181,241 |
| WC | (136,073) | (231,807) | (104,560) |
| Emp. | 94 | 91 | 90 |

DUNS 21-779-3817
## The Priory City of Lincoln Academy
Skellingthorpe Road, Lincoln, Lincolnshire LN6 0EP
**Tel:** 01522882800
**Web:** www.priorycity.co.uk
**Estd:** 2011 Proprietorship
**Line of Business:** Schools (foundation)
**Proprietor:** P Ryland
**US SIC:** 8211 **UK SIC:** 93200
**Employees:** 200

DUNS 21-735-5235
## Priory Community School
Priory Community School, Queensway, Weston-Super-Mare, Avon BS22 6BP
**Tel:** 01934511411
**Web:** www.priory.n-somerset.sch.uk
**Reg No:** 7698707 **Estd:** 2011 Private Company Limited By Guarantee
**Line of Business:** General secondary education
**Directors:** Ms F L Waters, Ms F C Richings, P Hemming, G Rosenberg, Mrs E D Mckenzie, C J Cox, N B Tokelove, B L Sleeman
**Responsibilities**
**Senior:** Neville Coles *(Director)*, Kevin Rooke *(Director)*, Roderick Sibley *(Director)*
**US SIC:** 8211 **UK SIC:** 93200
**Bankers:** Lloyds TSB Bank plc (30-99-51)

| | 31-08-14 | 31-08-13 | 31-08-12 |
|---|---|---|---|
| TO | 7,167,147 | 9,037,412 | 17,180,220 |
| P/L | 321,198 | 2,432,266 | 10,604,291 |
| NW | 12,888,755 | 13,040,557 | 10,465,291 |
| WC | 888,682 | 1,588,844 | 764,930 |
| Emp. | 156 | 148 | 148 |

DUNS 21-771-8823
## Priory Court
Priory Road, Stamford, Lincolnshire PE9 2EU
**Web:** www.hc-one.co.uk
**Estd:** 1983 Proprietorship
**Line of Business:** Nursing homes
**Proprietor:** Mrs A Walters
**Responsibilities**
**Senior:** Julie Britten *(Home Manager)*
**US SIC:** 8051 **UK SIC:** 95100
**Employees:** 75

DUNS 85-608-0507
## Priory Education Services Ltd
**(Subsidiary of:** Advent International Corporation)
Stoneleigh House, Frome, Somerset BA11 2HB
**Tel:** 01373814615
**Web:** www.priorygroup.com
**Reg No:** 6244880 **VAT No:** 626524835
**Estd:** 2007 Private Limited Company
**Line of Business:** General secondary education
**Issued Capital:** £10,000
**Directors:** T Riall, J D Lock
**Co. Secretary:** David Hall
**Branches:** Priory Education Services Ltd, Bolton, Appleby-In-Westmorland, Cumbria CA16 6AJ
**US SIC:** 8211 **UK SIC:** 93200
**Auditors:** PricewaterhouseCoopers LLP
**Bankers:** The Royal Bank Of Scotland Plc (15-10-00)

| | 31-12-13 | 31-12-12 | 31-12-11 |
|---|---|---|---|
| TO | 83,517,000 | 91,623,000 | 94,276,000 |
| P/L | 612,000 | 13,141,000 | 11,840,000 |
| NW | (18,435,000) | (18,571,000) | (11,593,000) |
| WC | 3,934,000 | 6,813,000 | 14,648,000 |
| Emp. | 1,827 | 1,933 | 2,046 |

DUNS 33-974-2157
## Priory Farm
Priory Farm, Sandy Lane, South Nutfield, Redhill, Surrey RH1 4EJ
**Tel:** 01737823304
**Web:** www.prioryfarm.co.uk
**Estd:** 2009 Proprietorship
**Line of Business:** Farm shops
**Proprietor:** A Shinner
**Responsibilities**
**Senior:** Sue Chapman *(Senior Manager)*
**US SIC:** 5499 **UK SIC:** 64100
**Employees:** 70

DUNS 21-103-2843
## The Priory Federation of Academies
Cross Ocliff Hillt, Lincoln, Lincolnshire LN5 8PW
**Tel:** 01522882929
**Reg No:** 6462935 **Estd:** 2008 Private Company Limited By Guarantee
**Line of Business:** General secondary education
**Directors:** Mrs R C Kirk, F L Knowles, P T Murphy, S Milner, R Partington, H D Gee, D J Knowles, S Richardson
**Co. Secretary:** John Cawdell
**Responsibilities**
**Senior:** Deborah Harry *(Director)*, Peter Houten *(Director)*
**US SIC:** 8211, 8221
**UK SIC:** 93200, 93100
**Auditors:** Nicholsons

**Bankers:** Lloyds TSB Bank plc (77-16-01)

| | 31-08-14 | 31-08-13 | 31-08-12 |
|---|---|---|---|
| TO | 42,467,000 | 31,987,000 | 57,388,000 |
| P/L | 9,988,000 | 390,000 | 28,269,000 |
| NW | 107,661,000 | 99,132,000 | 98,448,000 |
| WC | 11,337,000 | 11,301,000 | 7,887,000 |
| Emp. | 616 | 672 | 590 |

DUNS 21-584-9755

## Priory Fields School

Astor Avenue, Dover, Kent CT17 0AR
**Tel:** 01304211543
**Web:** www.prioryfields.kent.sch.uk
**Estd:** 2011 Proprietorship
**Line of Business:** Schools (local authority)
**Proprietor:** Mrs A Figgins
**US SIC:** 8211 **UK SIC:** 93200
**Employees:** 50

DUNS 85-608-0317

## Priory Healthcare Ltd

(**Subsidiary of:** Advent International Corporation)
5th Floor 80 Hammersmith Road, London W14 8UD
**Tel:** 08452774679 **Fax:** 02076050911
**Web:** www.priorygroup.com
**Reg No:** 6244860 **Estd:** 2007 Private Limited Company
**Line of Business:** Hospital activities
**Trading Style:** Priory Group
**Issued Capital:** £10,000
**Directors:** T Riall, J D Lock
**Co. Secretary:** David Hall
**Responsibilities**
**Senior:** Trevor Torrington *(Manager)*
**Sales:** George Broke *(Business Development Manager)*, Loraine Mason *(Business Development Manager)*, Annie Meharg *(Director Sales and Digital)*, Chris Screech *(Group Business Development Dir)*
**IT:** Emma Dalton *(IT Analyst)*, Annie Meharg *(Director Sales and Digital)*
**Operations:** Matthew Franzidis *(Operations Director)*
**US SIC:** 8062 **UK SIC:** 95100
**Auditors:** PricewaterhouseCoopers LLP

| | 31-12-13 | 31-12-12 | 31-12-11 |
|---|---|---|---|
| TO | 100,533,000 | 89,629,000 | 85,906,000 |
| P/L | 4,439,000 | 3,496,000 | (2,549,000) |
| NW | (33,782,000) | (38,112,000) | (41,796,000) |
| WC | 780,000 | (969,000) | 9,150,000 |
| Emp. | 2,034 | 2,168 | 2,051 |

DUNS 23-210-3580

## The Priory Hospital

Hythe Road, Marchwood, Southampton, Hampshire SO40 4WU
**Tel:** 023-8084-0044
**Web:** www.prioryhospital.co.uk
**Estd:** 1987
**Line of Business:** Hospitals
**Principals:** A Robertson, A Tate, S Conway, G Evans *(Manager)*
**Responsibilities**
**Senior:** Izzy Nicholls *(Hospital Director)*, Jane Stone *(Hospital Director)*, jane elderfield *(hospital director)*
**Health & Safety:** Iain Price *(Facilities Manager)*
**Facilities:** Iain Price *(Facilities Manager)*
**US SIC:** 8062 **UK SIC:** 95100
**Employees:** 150

DUNS 21-783-1413

## Priory Hospital Roehampton

Priory Lane, London SW15 5JJ
**Tel:** 02088768261
**Web:** www.prioryhealthcare.com
**Estd:** 1900 Proprietorship
**Line of Business:** Hospitals
**Proprietor:** P Pritchard
**Responsibilities**
**Senior:** Alison Pleszak *(Manager)*
**US SIC:** 8062 **UK SIC:** 95100
**Employees:** 150

DUNS 45-839-1562

## Priory Hospitals Ltd

(**Subsidiary of:** Advent International Corporation)
Priory Manor, Rosemary Lane, Bartle, Preston, Lancashire PR4 0HB
**Tel:** 01772691122
**Web:** www.priorygroup.com
**Reg No:** 3189363 **VAT No:** 521697733
**Estd:** 1998 Private Limited Company
**Line of Business:** Hospitals
**Trading Style:** The Priory Group
**Issued Capital:** £2
**Director:** J D Lock
**Co. Secretary:** David Hall
**Branches:** Priory Hospitals Ltd, Priory Manor, Rosemary Lane, Preston, Lancashire PR4 0HB
**US SIC:** 6111, 8062
**UK SIC:** 81501, 95100

**Bankers:** The Royal Bank Of Scotland Plc (15-10-00)

| | 31-12-13 | 31-12-12 |
|---|---|---|
| TA | 2 | 2 |
| NW | 2 | 2 |

DUNS 22-777-2019

## The Priory Nursing Home

Spring Hill, Wellington, Telford, Shropshire TF1 3NA
**Tel:** 01952242535
**Estd:** 1987
**Line of Business:** Nursing homes
**Proprietor:** P Singh
**Responsibilities**
**Senior:** Terence Peach *(Partner)*
**Finance:** Sheena Turner *(Administrator Accounts)*
**US SIC:** 8051 **UK SIC:** 95100
**Employees:** 40

DUNS 21-526-2135

## Priory Paddocks Nursing Home

Priory Road, Saxmundham, Suffolk IP17 1SA
**Estd:** 1987 Partnership
**Line of Business:** Nursing homes
**Partners:** Miss M Lloyd, A Burgess
**US SIC:** 8051 **UK SIC:** 95100
**Employees:** 57

DUNS 21-739-5717

## Priory School

Mount Road, Bury St Edmunds, Suffolk IP32 7BH
**Tel:** 01284761934
**Web:** www.priory.suffolk.sch.uk
**Reg No:** 7729941 **Estd:** 1990 Private Company Limited By Guarantee
**Line of Business:** Schools (special)
**Directors:** L C Chapman, R J Inman, Mrs R M Varley, Mrs A J Byham, Ms B M Parker, M J Truman, B Routledge, S R Mableson
**Co. Secretary:** Ms Barbara Parker
**Responsibilities**
**Senior:** Michael Attwood *(Director)*, Sally Hogg *(Director)*, Roger Mackenzie *(Head Teacher)*
**US SIC:** 8299 **UK SIC:** 93300

| | 31-08-14 | 31-08-13 | 31-08-12 |
|---|---|---|---|
| TO | 2,487,990 | 2,442,278 | 7,208,757 |
| P/L | 38,024 | 153,012 | 5,102,483 |
| NW | 4,895,518 | 5,176,495 | 4,985,483 |
| WC | 286,918 | 259,791 | 310,158 |
| Emp. | 52 | 51 | 47 |

DUNS 29-824-2389

## Priory School Edgbaston Trustees Ltd

Sir Harrys Road, Birmingham, West Midlands B15 2UR
**Tel:** 0121-440-4103 **Fax:** 0121-440-3639
**Web:** www.prioryschool.net
**Reg No:** 2042309 **Estd:** 2006 Private Limited Company
**Line of Business:** General secondary education
**Directors:** P A Murphy, Miss E A Hayward, Mrs J Surman, S M Gilmore, K Bird, Dr R A Howard, J A Claughton, C J Beesley
**Co. Secretary:** Alan Purnell
**Responsibilities**
**Senior:** Rokesh Bhalla *(Director)*, Rosemary Chukwulobelu *(Director)*, Charles Cram *(Head Teacher)*, Jonathon Cramb *(Headmaster)*, Monica Matthews *(Director)*
**Finance:** Alan Stevenage *(Bursar)*
**Marketing:** Jonathon Cramb *(Headmaster)*
**IT:** Alison Shuttleworth *(Computer Manager)*
**Health & Safety:** Alan Stevenage *(Bursar)*
**US SIC:** 8211 **UK SIC:** 93200
**Auditors:** HLB Kidsons
**Bankers:** Barclays Bank Plc (20-07-82)

| | 31-08-13 | 31-08-12 | 31-08-11 |
|---|---|---|---|
| TO | 3,888,207 | 3,658,393 | 3,245,614 |
| P/L | 179,705 | 101,052 | 58,139 |
| NW | 556,009 | 376,304 | 275,252 |
| WC | (164,483) | (278,938) | (243,380) |
| Emp. | 116 | 100 | 103 |

DUNS 21-583-4671

## The Priory School Foundation

Tintagel Road, Orpington, Kent BR5 4LG
**Tel:** 01689819219
**Web:** www.priory.bromley.sch.uk
**Estd:** 2004 Proprietorship
**Line of Business:** General secondary education
**Proprietor:** N Waer
**US SIC:** 8211 **UK SIC:** 93200
**Employees:** 200

DUNS 23-255-4316

## Priory Ticehurst House

Ticehurst, Wadhurst, East Sussex TN5 7HU
**Tel:** 01580200391
**Web:** www.priorygroup.com
**Estd:** 2003 Partnership
**Line of Business:** Hospitals
**Partners:** M Timble, Ms A Hanham
**Responsibilities**
**Senior:** Sue Harms *(Manager)*, Roger Skipp *(Hospital Director)*
**HR:** Suzanne Ratcliffe *(Human Resources Manager)*
**Health & Safety:** Mike Pamphilon *(Health & Safety Manager)*
**Operations:** Suzanne Ratcliffe *(Human Resources Manager)*
**US SIC:** 8062 **UK SIC:** 95100
**Employees:** 180

DUNS 21-900-3357 **Imp**

## Priory Woodfield Engineering Ltd

Millbrook Works, Lower Horseley Fields, Wolverhampton, West Midlands WV1 3DZ
**Tel:** 01902351530 **Fax:** 01902-351290
**Web:** www.priorywoodfield.co.uk
**Reg No:** 0872582 **VAT No:** 100141555
**Estd:** 1966 Private Limited Company
**Line of Business:** Engineers (general)
**Export Sales:** £1,706,266
**Trading Style:** Freeflow Pipesystems, Advanced Services
**Issued Capital:** £6,003
**Managing Director:** A J Marshall
**Co. Secretary:** Mrs Belinda Marshall
**Responsibilities**
**Senior:** Dorothy Marshall *(Manager)*
**IT:** Tony Cresswell *(IT Manager)*
**Branches:** Priory Woodfield Engineering Ltd, Autobase Industrial Park, Tipton Road, Tividale, Oldbury, West Midlands B69 3HU
**US SIC:** 8911, 3499
**UK SIC:** 83701, 31694
**Auditors:** Wilkes Tranter & Co Ltd
**Bankers:** HSBC Bank plc (40-47-11)

| | 31-03-14 | 31-03-13 | 31-03-12 |
|---|---|---|---|
| TO | 9,479,256 | 9,920,839 | 11,014,323 |
| P/L | 1,350,585 | 1,541,612 | 718,946 |
| NW | 8,438,323 | 7,619,549 | 6,555,317 |
| WC | 8,195,916 | 7,403,634 | 6,425,233 |
| Emp. | 84 | 88 | 100 |

DUNS 50-367-4384

## Pripear One Ltd

(**Subsidiary of:** Safariworld Holdings Ltd)
Spring Grove, Bewdley, Worcestershire DY12 1LF
**Tel:** 01299-400700 **Fax:** 01299-404519
**Web:** www.wmsp.co.uk
**Reg No:** 2382409 **Estd:** 1990 Private Limited Company
**Line of Business:** Fair and amusement park activities
**Trading Style:** Safari Trading
**Issued Capital:** £1,000
**Principals:** D F Chorley *(Managing)*, D D Chorley, I Knezovich, J H Mcfadden
**Branches:** Pripear One Ltd, West Midland Safari Park, Spring Grove, Bewdley, Worcestershire DY12 1LF
**US SIC:** 7996 **UK SIC:** 97913
**Auditors:** Price Pearson
**Bankers:** The Co-Operative Bank Plc (08-90-01)

| | 31-03-14 | 31-03-13 | 31-03-12 |
|---|---|---|---|
| TA | 1,000 | 1,000 | 1,000 |
| NW | 1,000 | 1,000 | 1,000 |

DUNS 76-433-2722 **Exp**

## Prism Electronics Ltd

30 Burrel Road, St Ives, Cambridgeshire PE27 3NF
**Tel:** 01480-462225
**Web:** www.prism-electronics.com
**Reg No:** 2562215 **VAT No:** 551030102
**Estd:** 1982 Private Limited Company
**Line of Business:** Electronic equipment (assembly)
**Export Markets:** U S A
**Trading Style:** Prism Electronics Ltd
**Issued Capital:** £21,000
**Principals:** D J Aspinall *(Managing)*, R C Walton, D Dickin
**Co. Secretary:** Richard Vyse
**US SIC:** 3643, 3629
**UK SIC:** 34203, 34350
**Auditors:** Kinnaird Hill
**Bankers:** Barclays Bank Plc (20-53-30)

| | 30-09-13 | 30-09-12 | 30-09-11 |
|---|---|---|---|
| TA | 1,470,309 | 1,392,387 | 1,430,936 |
| NW | 1,066,133 | 1,065,314 | 1,080,676 |
| WC | 926,233 | 908,086 | 909,080 |

DUNS 73-734-3009

## Prism Uk Medical Ltd

(**Subsidiary of:** Prism Medical Ltd)
Unit 1, Snownest Court, Tir Llwyd Industrial Estate, Rhyl, Clwyd LL18 5JY
**Tel:** 08449802296 **Fax:** 08449802297
**Web:** www.prismmedical.co.uk
**Reg No:** 4992349 **Estd:** 2003 Private Limited Company
**Line of Business:** Manufacture of lifting and handling equipment
**Export Sales:** £1,526,145
**Issued Capital:** £852,918
**Directors:** S Meldrum, A J Walker
**Co. Secretary:** Alastair Walker
**Branches:** Prism Uk Medical Ltd, Newcombe Street, Elland, West Yorkshire HX5 0EG
**US SIC:** 3534, 2517
**UK SIC:** 32553, 46714
**Auditors:** Deloitte & Touche LLP
**Bankers:** HSBC Bank plc (40-27-15)

| | 30-11-13 | 30-11-12 | 30-11-11 |
|---|---|---|---|
| TO | 25,874,506 | 27,041,375 | 24,971,675 |
| P/L | 2,855,953 | 2,551,352 | 1,415,421 |
| NW | 6,887,723 | 5,960,486 | 4,157,234 |
| WC | 5,786,220 | 4,558,570 | 2,934,242 |
| Emp. | 294 | 297 | 292 |

DUNS 51-626-3246

## Prismo Road Markings Ltd

(**Subsidiary of:** Ennis Paint Inc.)
5 Chorley North Industrial Park Drumhead, Road, Chorley, Lancashire PR6 7BX
**Tel:** 01257-225100 **Fax:** 01257-224605
**Web:** www.ennisprismo.com
**Reg No:** 5906228 **VAT No:** 918478288
**Estd:** 1968 Private Limited Company
**Line of Business:** Construction of motorways, roads, railways, airfields and sports facilities
**Export Sales:** £15,812,987
**Trading Style:** Ennis Prismo Traffic Safety Solutions
**Issued Capital:** £1
**Directors:** D L Lang, J B Anderson, M L Soule, R S Vetter
**Co. Secretary:** Warren Anderson
**Branches:** Prismo Road Markings Ltd, 5 Chorley North Industrial Park, Drumhead Road, Chorley, Lancashire PR6 7BX
**US SIC:** 3999, 1611
**UK SIC:** 49590, 50200
**Auditors:** Ernst & Young LLP

| | 31-12-13 | 31-12-12 | 31-12-11 |
|---|---|---|---|
| TO | 31,346,561 | 28,284,534 | 32,776,278 |
| P/L | 939,831 | 8,100,381 | (4,765,941) |
| NW | (31,391) | (1,293,991) | (9,446,872) |
| WC | 2,337,892 | 871,703 | (7,807,891) |
| Emp. | 75 | 75 | 108 |

DUNS 77-022-2834 **Imp**

## Prismtech Ltd

(**Subsidiary of:** Prismtech Group Ltd)
Prismtech House, Fifth Avenue, Team Valley Trading Estate, Gateshead, Tyne and Wear NE11 0NG
**Tel:** 01914979900 **Fax:** 01914979900
**Web:** www.prismtech.com
**Reg No:** 2664365 **Estd:** 1991 Private Limited Company
**Line of Business:** Computer software (development)
**Issued Capital:** £5,778,808
**Principals:** K R Steele *(Managing)*, D C Cairns Of Finavon, S J Jennis
**Co. Secretary:** Philip Wright
**Responsibilities**
**Marketing:** Greg Shenton *(Senior Marketing Executive)*
**US SIC:** 7379 **UK SIC:** 83940
**Auditors:** Royce Peeling Green Ltd

| | 30-04-14 | 30-04-13 | 30-04-12 |
|---|---|---|---|
| TO | N/A | N/A | 3,851,331 |
| P/L | N/A | N/A | (280,963) |
| NW | 1,973,482 | 3,155,618 | 3,275,986 |
| WC | 717,210 | 2,389,758 | 2,560,748 |

DUNS 29-345-7222

## Prison Advice & Care Trust (P A C T)

Park Place, 12 Lawn Lane, London SW8 1UD
**Tel:** 020-7735-9535
**Web:** www.prisonadvice.org
**Reg No:** 0356443 **Estd:** 1898 Private Company Limited By Guarantee
**Line of Business:** Non-charitable social work activities without accommodation
**Trading Style:** P A C T
**Directors:** A Masters, F D Galliano, Mrs L A Van Der Hoeven, M Page, Ms L Miles, J W Dring, P Taylor, Ms M Hodgson
**Co. Secretary:** Andrew Keen Downs
**Responsibilities**
**Senior:** Stephanie Loney *(Office Manager)*, Wilfred Weeks *(Director)*
**Marketing:** Angela Grimes *(Head of Development)*
**Sales:** Angela Grimes *(Head of Development)*
**HR:** Chris Dunne *(Human Resources Advisor)*, Sophie Newman *(Human Resources Advisor)*
**Health & Safety:** Sophie Newman *(Human Resources Advisor)*
**Branches:** Prison Advice & Care Trust (P A C T), 254 Caledonian Rd, London N1 0NG
**US SIC:** 8321 **UK SIC:** 96111
**Auditors:** Tom Carolan & Co

**Bankers:** Allied Irish Bank (gb) (23-84-84)

| | 31-03-14 | 31-03-13 | 31-03-12 |
|---|---|---|---|
| TO | 3,614,000 | 2,897,886 | 3,036,995 |
| P/L | 299,000 | (26,298) | 69,075 |
| NW | 618,000 | 318,582 | 344,880 |
| WC | 614,000 | 301,726 | 327,520 |
| Emp. | 71 | 59 | 71 |

DUNS 22-072-1828

## Pristine Cleaning Services Ltd

Rosedale House, School Lane, Wolvey, Hinckley, Leicestershire LE10 3LH
**Tel:** 01455-220267
**Reg No:** 4073715 **Estd:** 2000 Private Limited Company
**Line of Business:** Cleaning contracting commercial
**Issued Capital:** £2
**Director:** P M Duffy
**Co. Secretary:** Ms May Cummings
**Responsibilities**
**Senior:** Mary Cummings *(Director)*
**US SIC:** 7349 **UK SIC:** 92300

| | 30-09-13 | 30-09-12 | 30-09-11 |
|---|---|---|---|
| TA | 241,023 | 202,986 | 180,250 |
| NW | 141,740 | 104,209 | 79,030 |
| WC | 113,240 | 82,043 | 51,012 |

DUNS 22-189-5373 **Imp**

## Pritchard Patent Product Co (2001) Ltd

Underleys, Beer, Seaton, Devon EX12 3NA
**Tel:** 0129-721542 **Fax:** 0129-720229
**Web:** www.peco-uk.com
**Reg No:** 4207727 **Estd:** 1946 Private Limited Company
**Line of Business:** Management activities of holding companies
**Export Sales:** £1,946,007
**Issued Capital:** £19,800
**Directors:** Ms C B Sargent, J H Robarts-Arnold, Ms H M Robarts Arnold, C P Noake, C M Pritchard
**Co. Secretary:** Christopher Noake
**US SIC:** 6711 **UK SIC:** 83962

| | 30-04-14 | 30-04-13 | 30-04-12 |
|---|---|---|---|
| TO | 9,205,330 | 8,899,028 | 8,299,770 |
| P/L | 1,167,444 | 937,464 | 820,222 |
| NW | 6,703,697 | 4,320,532 | 5,446,073 |
| WC | 6,581,637 | 6,157,470 | 5,488,490 |
| Emp. | 144 | 151 | 149 |

DUNS 57-006-7447

## Private & Commercial Finance Group Plc

Brandon House, 180 Borough High Street, London SE1 1LB
**Tel:** 02072222426
**Web:** www.pcfg.co.uk
**Reg No:** 2863246 **VAT No:** 629509516
**Estd:** 1993 Public Limited Company
**Line of Business:** Financial intermediation not elsewhere classified
**Trading Style:** Private & Commercial Finance Company, Private & Commercial Credit, P C F Equipment Leasing
**Issued Capital:** £2,636,558
**Principals:** A N Nelson *(Managing)*, S D Maybury *(Financial)*, D G Anthony, D J Morgan, N P Winks, Z R Kerse
**Co. Secretary:** Robert Murray
**Responsibilities**
**Finance:** Neil Ballam *(General Manager, Business Fina)*, Andrew Currie *(Head of Business and Broker De)*, Robert Hobbs *(Financial Controller)*
**IT:** Andrew Barber *(Information Systems Manager)*
**US SIC:** 6111, 7392
**UK SIC:** 81501, 83951
**Auditors:** Ernst & Young LLP
**Bankers:** Barclays Bank Plc (20-06-05)

| | 31-03-14 | 31-03-13 | 31-03-12 |
|---|---|---|---|
| TA | 93,108,000 | 84,947,000 | 89,448,000 |
| P/L | 1,245,000 | 829,000 | 761,000 |
| NW | 9,369,000 | 8,280,000 | 7,630,000 |
| WC | 26,958,000 | 28,522,000 | 34,971,000 |
| Emp. | 46 | 49 | 52 |

DUNS 64-109-1983

## The Private Health Partnership Ltd

Butterfiled Park, Shipley, West Yorkshire BD17 7HE
**Tel:** 01274588862
**Web:** www.php.co.uk
**Reg No:** 4512698 **Estd:** 2002 Private Limited Company
**Line of Business:** Activities auxiliary to insurance and pension funding
**Issued Capital:** £2,387
**Directors:** J M Dean, S H Scullion, Ms J E Lawson, P J Johnston
**Co. Secretary:** Ian Nash
**Responsibilities**
**Senior:** Christine Husbands *(Finance Director)*
**Finance:** Christine Husbands *(Finance Director)*
**HR:** Christine Husbands *(Finance Director)*, Sue Pearson *(Human Resources Manager)*
**US SIC:** 6411 **UK SIC:** 83200
**Auditors:** KPMG Audit PLC

| | 31-12-13 | 31-12-12 | 31-12-11 |
|---|---|---|---|
| TO | 4,797,079 | 4,605,818 | 4,631,537 |
| P/L | 635,700 | 902,523 | 1,020,052 |
| NW | 2,652,629 | 2,432,912 | 2,110,087 |
| WC | (15,101) | (650,339) | (913,109) |
| Emp. | 74 | 73 | 68 |

DUNS 29-659-4534

## Private Medicare Ltd

344 Chanterlands Avenue, Hull, North Humberside HU5 4DT
**Tel:** 01482307590
**Web:** www.wecareforyou.co.uk
**Reg No:** 1985662 **Estd:** 1962 Private Limited Company
**Line of Business:** Other human health activities
**Trading Style:** St. Mary's Nursing Home, Pickering Hall Nursing Home
**Issued Capital:** £10,002
**Principals:** Mrs V Bignell *(Managing)*, P Bignell
**Co. Secretary:** Timothy Bignell
**Branches:** 896 Hessle High Rd, Hull, Hull
**US SIC:** 8051 **UK SIC:** 95100
**Auditors:** Dutton Moore
**Bankers:** HSBC Bank plc (40-25-20)

| | 30-06-13 | 30-06-12 | 30-06-11 |
|---|---|---|---|
| TO | 3,190,698 | 3,199,476 | 3,162,898 |
| P/L | 629,024 | 400,460 | 614,833 |
| NW | 5,746,655 | 5,597,358 | 5,486,903 |
| WC | 383,760 | 230,779 | 225,063 |
| Emp. | 139 | 149 | 141 |

DUNS 21-130-5866

## Pro - Direct Group Ltd

Torre House Shaldon Road, Newton Abbot, Devon TQ12 4PQ
**Tel:** 08448264555
**Reg No:** 6646626 **Estd:** 2008 Private Limited Company
**Line of Business:** Management activities of holding companies
**Issued Capital:** £10,000
**Directors:** A J Lake, P J Hammond, M W Lake
**Co. Secretary:** Norman Lake
**US SIC:** 6711 **UK SIC:** 83962

| | 31-01-14 | 31-01-13 | 31-01-12 |
|---|---|---|---|
| TO | 55,323,974 | 43,536,236 | 36,225,673 |
| P/L | 6,452,868 | 4,818,840 | 4,558,809 |
| NW | 17,287,860 | 13,956,341 | 10,997,209 |
| WC | 15,196,120 | 12,071,267 | 9,467,946 |
| Emp. | 216 | 190 | 174 |

DUNS 67-148-0416

## Pro-Active Recruitment Services Ltd

78 York Street, London W1H 1DP
**Tel:** 02079-936049 **Fax:** 02076-254530
**Web:** www.pro-activerecruitment.co.uk
**Reg No:** 5987131 **VAT No:** 847004832
**Estd:** 2013 Private Limited Company
**Line of Business:** Labour recruitment and provision of personnel
**Issued Capital:** £100
**Directors:** Ms R Purim, E B Rubin, Mrs R Rubin
**Co. Secretary:** Elad Rubin
**Responsibilities**
**Senior:** Benjamin Reuben *(Manager)*
**US SIC:** 7361, 4142
**UK SIC:** 83954, 72102
**Bankers:** Lloyds TSB Bank plc (30-93-80)

| | 30-11-12 | 30-11-11 | 30-11-10 |
|---|---|---|---|
| TA | 1,015,688 | 606,475 | 918,208 |
| NW | 260,482 | 152,668 | 325,591 |
| WC | 250,524 | 151,412 | 323,915 |

DUNS 22-628-0972

## Pro Cam Cp Ltd

**(Subsidiary of:** Pro Cam Europe Ltd)
Saxon Way, Melbourn, Royston, Hertfordshire SG8 6DN
**Tel:** 01763261587
**Web:** www.procam.co.uk
**Reg No:** 1420577 **Estd:** 1979 Private Limited Company
**Line of Business:** Agricultural service activities; landscape gardening
**Issued Capital:** £37,528
**Principals:** A J White *(Chairman)*, C J Butt *(Managing)*, I D Beswick, J D Bianchi, D J Parish
**Co. Secretary:** Michael Andrews
**Branches:** Pro Cam Cp Ltd, Morley St Botolph, Wymondham, Norfolk NR18 9TN
**US SIC:** 0729 **UK SIC:** 01003
**Auditors:** RSM Tenon Audit Ltd
**Bankers:** HSBC Bank plc (40-16-08)

| | 30-06-13 | 30-06-12 | 30-06-11 |
|---|---|---|---|
| TO | 103,664,000 | 110,740,000 | 90,669,000 |
| P/L | 4,752,000 | 9,142,000 | 5,612,000 |
| NW | 15,628,000 | 16,652,000 | 11,779,000 |
| WC | 6,381,000 | 7,290,000 | 4,934,000 |
| Emp. | 182 | 170 | 160 |

DUNS 21-099-5918

## Pro Cam Europe Ltd

The Paddocks, Toft Road, Bourn, Cambridge, Cambridgeshire CB23 2TT
**Tel:** 07712323557 **Fax:** 01763-269676
**Web:** www.procam.co.uk
**Reg No:** 6434314 **VAT No:** 538304156
**Estd:** 2012 Private Limited Company
**Line of Business:** Farming (livestock)
**Export Sales:** £100,176,000
**Issued Capital:** £400,000
**Directors:** C J Butt, A J White, I D Beswick
**Co. Secretary:** David Parish
**Responsibilities**
**Senior:** Julie Symonds *(Proprietor)*
**US SIC:** 0751, 5399
**UK SIC:** 01003, 65600
**Bankers:** HSBC Bank plc (40-16-08)

| | 30-06-13 | 30-06-12 | 30-06-11 |
|---|---|---|---|
| TO | 207,546,000 | 192,083,000 | 175,102,000 |
| P/L | 6,200,000 | 7,748,000 | 7,390,000 |
| NW | 10,939,000 | 8,074,000 | 6,784,000 |
| WC | 11,201,000 | 8,853,000 | 8,845,000 |
| Emp. | 451 | 458 | 366 |

DUNS 34-779-9103

## Pro-Force Ltd

Nickle Farm, Canterbury, Kent CT4 7PE
**Tel:** 01227733880
**Web:** www.pro-force.co.uk
**Reg No:** 5580634 **Estd:** 2005 Private Limited Company
**Line of Business:** Employment and recruitment companies and consultants
**Issued Capital:** £1
**Director:** M J Jarrett
**Co. Secretary:** Ms Patricia Cox
**US SIC:** 7361 **UK SIC:** 83954

| | 31-03-14 | 31-03-13 | 31-03-12 |
|---|---|---|---|
| TO | 13,326,810 | 9,579,879 | 8,128,015 |
| P/L | 281,298 | (26,950) | 46,110 |
| NW | 55,559 | 36,095 | 181,887 |
| WC | (18,936) | (37,719) | 102,790 |
| Emp. | 882 | 579 | 468 |

DUNS 21-582-0578

## Pro Freight

Ackworth Road Hilsea, Portsmouth, Hampshire PO3 5JT
**Tel:** 02392448086
**Web:** www.profreight.co.uk
**Estd:** 2008 Proprietorship
**Line of Business:** Freight services
**Proprietor:** T Lee
**US SIC:** 4213 **UK SIC:** 72300
**Employees:** 200

DUNS 34-827-9639

## Pro Insurance Solutions Ltd

**(Subsidiary of:** Pro Global Insurance Solutions Plc)
193 Marsh Wall, London E14 9SG
**Tel:** 02070688000 **Fax:** 020-7623-3318
**Web:** www.pro-ltd.co.uk
**Reg No:** 2801404 **Estd:** 1993 Private Limited Company
**Line of Business:** Activities auxiliary to insurance and pension funding
**Trading Style:** P R O
**Issued Capital:** £250,002
**Directors:** R F Lawson, A P Niemczewski, J M Richards
**Co. Secretary:** Michael Dalzell
**Responsibilities**
**Sales:** Philip Heitlinger *(General Manager)*
**Facilities:** Philip Heitlinger *(General Manager)*
**Branches:** Pro Insurance Solutions Ltd, Southgate House, Gloucester, Gloucestershire GL1 1UB
**US SIC:** 6411, 7399
**UK SIC:** 83200, 83954
**Auditors:** PricewaterhouseCoopers LLP
**Bankers:** Barclays Bank Plc (20-00-00)

| | 31-12-13 | 31-12-12 | 31-12-11 |
|---|---|---|---|
| TO | 16,741,986 | 21,257,643 | 33,629,177 |
| P/L | 407,362 | 6,479 | 3,715,233 |
| NW | 3,039,715 | 2,600,788 | 4,643,783 |
| WC | 2,826,668 | 3,752,966 | 5,339,163 |
| Emp. | 193 | 245 | 238 |

DUNS 42-358-3749

## Pro Iv Ltd

**(Subsidiary of:** Kkr & Co. L.P.)
239 Thorpe Road Thorpe Park, Peterborough, Cambridgeshire PE3 6JY
**Tel:** 01733555777 **Fax:** 01480-494039
**Web:** www.ngahr.com
**Reg No:** 3170569 **Estd:** 2012 Private Limited Company
**Line of Business:** Employment and recruitment companies and consultants
**Trading Style:** Nga Human Resources
**Issued Capital:** £400,000
**Directors:** A B Al-Saleh, J R Stier
**Co. Secretary:** Daniel Schenck
**Responsibilities**
**Senior:** Alan Harling *(Manager)*
**Branches:** Pro Iv Ltd, Hellier Court, Unit 2, Brierley Hill, West Midlands DY5 1TA
**US SIC:** 8931 **UK SIC:** 83600
**Auditors:** KPMG Audit Plc

| | 30-04-14 | 30-04-13 | 30-04-12 |
|---|---|---|---|
| TA | 510,262 | 510,262 | 510,262 |
| NW | 510,262 | 510,262 | 510,262 |

DUNS 23-558-3973 **Exp**

## Pro-Pak Foods Ltd

**(Subsidiary of:** Andelsselskabet Tican A.M.B.A.)
Seven Street, York Road Business Park, Malton, North Yorkshire YO17 6YA
**Tel:** 01653-600170 **Fax:** 01653-696066
**Web:** www.pro-pakfoods.co.uk
**Reg No:** 3556653 **VAT No:** 598996139
**Estd:** 1998 Private Limited Company
**Line of Business:** Manufacturers of food products
**Export Markets:** Germany
**Trading Style:** Pro Cuisine
**Issued Capital:** £208,164
**Directors:** K Watson, J A Guest, J M Appleford
**Co. Secretary:** Mark Duckworth
**Responsibilities**
**Senior:** Anders Jensen *(Manager)*
**Engineering:** Martin Whitaker *(Engineering Manager)*
**US SIC:** 7399, 2099
**UK SIC:** 83954, 42399
**Auditors:** PricewaterhouseCoopers LLP
**Bankers:** HSBC Bank plc (40-31-08)

| | 29-09-13 | 30-09-12 | 02-09-11 |
|---|---|---|---|
| TO | 30,527,146 | 28,614,264 | 34,923,173 |
| P/L | (1,403,447) | (379,506) | 900,100 |
| NW | 5,299,729 | 6,348,890 | 6,641,415 |
| WC | 1,544,398 | 2,128,178 | 3,264,107 |
| Emp. | 314 | 306 | 284 |

DUNS 45-808-6170

## Pro-Tec Security Services Ltd

Strathcylde Business Centre, Motherwell, Lanarkshire ML1 4JB
**Tel:** 01698-733822 **Fax:** 01689832588
**Web:** www.securitypro-tec.co.uk
**Reg No:** 0163843SC **Estd:** 1996 Private Limited Company
**Line of Business:** Security activities
**Issued Capital:** £100
**Directors:** Mrs M C Mclean, C Mclean
**Co. Secretary:** Mrs Sandra Burrows
**Responsibilities**
**Senior:** Colin McClean *(Managing Director)*
**US SIC:** 7393 **UK SIC:** 83954
**Auditors:** Stevenson & Kyles
**Bankers:** Bank Of Scotland (80-05-63)

| | 28-02-14 | 28-02-13 | 29-02-12 |
|---|---|---|---|
| TA | 201,144 | 221,775 | 258,527 |
| NW | 23,880 | 29,970 | 34,456 |
| WC | 13,965 | 18,943 | 20,484 |

DUNS 21-028-4858

## Pro-Tect Uk

10 Allenbrook Road, Rosehill Industrial Estate, Carlisle, Cumbria CA1 2UT
**Web:** www.pro-tect.co.uk
**Estd:** 2003 Proprietorship
**Line of Business:** Detective Agencies & Protective Services
**Proprietor:** J Jeffrey
**US SIC:** 7393 **UK SIC:** 83954
**Employees:** 74

DUNS 21-964-8693

## Pro-Tect Uk Security & Training Ltd

10 Allenbrook Road, Rosehill Industrial Estate, Carlisle, Cumbria CA1 2UT
**Tel:** 08432891875 **Fax:** 08721150189
**Web:** www.pro-tect.co.uk
**Reg No:** 6146602 **VAT No:** 916590018
**Estd:** 2003 Private Limited Company
**Line of Business:** Security and related activities
**Issued Capital:** £2
**Director:** J L Jeffrey
**US SIC:** 7393 **UK SIC:** 83954
**Auditors:** Butler Accountancy Services Ltd

| | 31-03-14 | 31-03-13 | 31-03-12 |
|---|---|---|---|
| TA | 199,337 | 153,398 | 101,571 |
| NW | 61,105 | 633 | (3,917) |
| WC | 41,017 | (15,520) | (13,704) |

DUNS 23-979-7793 **Exp**

## Proact It Uk Ltd

**(Subsidiary of:** Proact It Group Ab)
Grayson House, Venture Way, Dunston Technology Park, Chesterfield, Derbyshire S41 8NE
**Tel:** 01246 266300 **Fax:** 01246 267587
**Web:** www.proact.co.uk
**Reg No:** 3968273 **VAT No:** 745741222
**Estd:** 2000 Private Limited Company
**Line of Business:** Other computer related activities
**Export Sales:** £1,742,083
**Trading Style:** Proact It Uk Ltd

**Issued Capital:** £13,379
**Directors:** H M Odman, J Hoholdt, J G Clark, J A Persson
**Responsibilities**
**Sales:** Dave Hallam *(Account Manager)*
**Branches:** Proact It Uk Ltd, 68 Lombard St, London EC3V 9LJ
**US SIC:** 7379 **UK SIC:** 83940
**Auditors:** BDO LLP

|  | 31-12-13 | 31-12-12 | 31-12-11 |
|---|---|---|---|
| TO | 54,811,862 | 51,254,786 | 32,918,620 |
| P/L | 1,172,465 | (150,048) | (1,142,660) |
| NW | 2,304,466 | 1,132,150 | 1,085,888 |
| WC | 629,877 | (2,161,304) | (2,284,478) |
| Emp. | 162 | 160 | 144 |

DUNS 45-832-1643
### Proactis Group Ltd
**(Subsidiary of:** Proactis Holdings Plc)
Riverview Court, Castle Gate, Wetherby, West Yorkshire LS22 6LE
**Tel:** 01937-545070 **Fax:** 01937-545071
**Web:** www.proactis.com
**Reg No:** 3182974 **VAT No:** 647516323
**Estd:** 1996 Private Limited Company
**Line of Business:** Other computer related activities
**Issued Capital:** £204,629
**Directors:** R D Jones, A J Aubrey, S A Mcdonough, R Potts
**Co. Secretary:** Timothy Sykes
**Responsibilities**
**Marketing:** Lorraine Sewell *(Marketing Manager)*, Charlotte Sutton *(Marketing Manager)*
**IT:** Kevin Chidlow *(Chief Technology Officer)*
**US SIC:** 7379 **UK SIC:** 83940
**Auditors:** KPMG Audit PLC
**Bankers:** HSBC Bank plc (40-47-31)

|  | 31-07-13 | 31-07-12 | 31-07-11 |
|---|---|---|---|
| TO | 7,047,416 | 6,612,401 | 5,593,223 |
| P/L | (408,284) | 318,444 | (279,501) |
| NW | 679,345 | 944,895 | 675,546 |
| WC | 632,992 | 888,154 | 613,503 |
| Emp. | 49 | 46 | 48 |

DUNS 23-815-0929
### Proactive Personnel Ltd
8-12 Limes Walk, Oakengates, Telford, Shropshire TF2 6EP
**Fax:** 01952-525253
**Web:** www.proactivepersonnel.net
**Reg No:** 3807344 **VAT No:** 754416037
**Estd:** 1999 Private Limited Company
**Line of Business:** Employment and recruitment companies and consultants
**Issued Capital:** £100
**Principals:** J M Glews *(Managing)*, P A Knight *(Financial)*, D R Watson, P S Lowrey, R M Wheeler, S C Mackintosh
**Co. Secretary:** Ms Louise Glews
**Branches:** Proactive Personnel Ltd, College Auto Centre, Kingstanding Rd, Birmingham, West Midlands B44 8AA
**US SIC:** 7361 **UK SIC:** 83954
**Auditors:** Caerwyn Jones Chartered Accountants
**Bankers:** Barclays Bank Plc (20-07-71)

|  | 31-12-13 | 31-12-12 | 31-12-11 |
|---|---|---|---|
| TO | 21,455,858 | 36,477,803 | 30,347,488 |
| P/L | 139,233 | (40,068) | 243,702 |
| NW | 488,559 | 381,694 | 543,660 |
| WC | 115,580 | (6,655) | 92,599 |
| Emp. | 850 | 1,001 | 935 |

DUNS 42-336-2552
### Proaktive Ltd
**(Subsidiary of:** Proaktive Risk Group Ltd)
Proaktive House, Sidings Court, Doncaster, South Yorkshire DN4 5NU
**Tel:** 01302-341344
**Web:** www.proaktive.co.uk
**Reg No:** 4323903 **Estd:** 1975 Private Limited Company
**Line of Business:** Activities auxiliary to insurance and pension funding
**Trading Style:** Proaktive
**Issued Capital:** £1
**Directors:** I Laycock, Ms B J Brown, A Morley, Mrs J Cooling, J Whiteley
**Co. Secretary:** Mrs Sara Casson
**US SIC:** 6411 **UK SIC:** 83200

|  | 31-12-13 | 31-12-12 | 31-12-11 |
|---|---|---|---|
| TA | 2,347,246 | 1,977,381 | 2,119,865 |
| NW | 541,774 | 531,269 | 462,012 |
| WC | 394,597 | 437,801 | 388,829 |

DUNS 23-318-1510                              Imp
### Proav Ltd
**(Subsidiary of:** Proav Holdings Ltd)
Proav House, Omega Way, Egham, Surrey TW20 8RD
**Tel:** 08458382200 **Fax:** 01784-487060
**Web:** www.proav.com
**Reg No:** 2681563 **VAT No:** 584513428
**Estd:** 1969 Private Limited Company
**Line of Business:** Manufacture of radio and electronic capital goods
**Export Sales:** £9,024,215
**Issued Capital:** £50,000

**Directors:** R J Brookes, Mrs L Brookes, Mrs F Hazell
**Responsibilities**
**Senior:** Jonathan Cunningham *(Regional Manager)*, Raymond Phillpot *(Manager)*
**IT:** Simon Eade *(Computer Manager)*
**US SIC:** 3662 **UK SIC:** 34430
**Auditors:** Menzies LLP
**Bankers:** Barclays Bank Plc (20-90-56)

|  | 31-03-14 | 31-03-13 | 31-03-12 |
|---|---|---|---|
| TO | 48,201,956 | 52,766,319 | 40,996,819 |
| P/L | 927,405 | 566,659 | 862,805 |
| NW | 1,840,070 | 1,758,904 | 1,755,839 |
| WC | (1,525,894) | 282,649 | 1,143,958 |
| Emp. | 233 | 199 | 180 |

DUNS 21-395-8498
### Probate Registry
Centralofts, Newcastle-Upon-Tyne, Tyne and Wear NE1 4AL
**Tel:** 0191-211-2170
**Web:** www.justice.gov.uk
**Estd:** 1985
**Line of Business:** Probate registries
**Proprietor:** M Burdon
**US SIC:** 8111 **UK SIC:** 83500
**Employees:** 60

DUNS 22-822-1859
### Probation Board for Northern Ireland
80-90 North Street, Belfast BT1 1LD
**Tel:** 02890262400
**Web:** www.pbni.org.uk
**Estd:** 1982
**Line of Business:** Probation services
**Proprietor:** N Rooney
**Responsibilities**
**Senior:** Cheryl Lamont *(Director of Probation)*, Lisa Maginnis *(Senior Communications Officer)*, Eithne McIlroy *(Assistant Director - Urban)*, Brian Mccaughey *(Director of Probation)*, Roisin Muldoon *(Assistant Director - Prisons)*
**Finance:** Maura Canavan *(Senior Finance Administrator)*, Catherine McCann *(Head of Finance)*
**Marketing:** Lisa Maginnis *(Senior Communications Officer)*, Gail McGreevy *(Head of Communications)*
**Sales:** Louise Cooper *(Head of Business Planning & De)*
**IT:** Brian McCutcheon *(Head of Information Technology)*, Ciaran Reilly *(PC Manager)*
**HR:** Gillian Robinson *(Head of Human Resources)*
**Branches:** Probation Board For Northern Ireland, Northern Telecom (Northern Ireland) Ltd, 123 Doagh Rd, Newtownabbey, Co Antrim BT36 6XA
**US SIC:** 9121 **UK SIC:** 91110
**Employees:** 55

DUNS 21-228-2940
### Probation Centre
Nelps Probation Centre, 277-289 High Road, Ilford, Essex IG1 1QQ
**Tel:** 02084788500
**Proprietorship**
**Line of Business:** Probation services
**Proprietor:** Mrs T Cramer
**US SIC:** 9121 **UK SIC:** 91110
**Employees:** 62

DUNS 21-772-0003
### Probation Hostel
13 The Crescent, Middlesbrough, Cleveland TS5 6SG
**Tel:** 01642826606
**Estd:** 2011 Proprietorship
**Line of Business:** Local government
**Proprietor:** P Smith
**Responsibilities**
**Senior:** Julie Alen *(Operations Manager)*
**Operations:** Dave Gavaghan *(Operations Manager)*
**US SIC:** 9121 **UK SIC:** 91110
**Employees:** 50

DUNS 21-802-1961
### Probation Service
108 Lowther Street, York, North Yorkshire YO31 7WD
**Tel:** 01904526000
**Estd:** 2011
**Line of Business:** Central Government
**US SIC:** 9111 **UK SIC:** 91110
**Employees:** 60

DUNS 21-462-5829
### The Probation Service
206 Derby Road, Nottingham, Nottinghamshire NG7 1NQ
**Tel:** 01158455100
**Estd:** 2003 Proprietorship
**Line of Business:** Probation services
**Proprietor:** Miss H Towlson

**Branches:** The Probation Service, Crosby House, 9-13 Elmfield Road, Bromley, Kent BR1 1LT
**US SIC:** 9121 **UK SIC:** 91110
**Employees:** 100

DUNS 22-852-5333
### Probelook Ltd
Moor Street, Bury, Lancashire BL9 5AQ
**Tel:** 0161-797-6424
**Reg No:** 1571488 **Estd:** 1981 Private Limited Company
**Line of Business:** The manufacture assembly and installation of high quality U P V C window frames and doors. Incorporating double glazed units in a variety of glass designs. Principally supplying to the commercial & domestic market.
**Branches:** t Stockport, Preston, Burnley, Warrington & Stoke and Scotland.
**US SIC:** 3079, 1751
**UK SIC:** 48360, 50400
**Bankers:** Lloyds TSB Bank plc (30-91-01)
**Employees:** 525

DUNS 28-876-9276                              Imp
### Probiotics International Ltd
**(Subsidiary of:** Lloyds Banking Group Plc)
Lopenhead, South Petherton, Somerset TA13 5JH
**Tel:** 01460243230 **Fax:** 01217 793 110
**Web:** www.protexin.com
**Reg No:** 1122942 **VAT No:** 651210581
**Estd:** 1999 Private Limited Company
**Line of Business:** Manufacture of other food products not elsewhere classified
**Export Sales:** £11,135,162
**Trading Style:** Protexin Healthcare, Protexin
**Issued Capital:** £103,438
**Directors:** Ms A A Lockington, T M Lewis, J R Sowler, T M Lewis
**Co. Secretary:** John Melling
**Responsibilities**
**Marketing:** Kate Rouse *(Marketing Manager)*
**US SIC:** 2099, 5499
**UK SIC:** 42399, 64100
**Auditors:** BWMacfarlane LLP
**Bankers:** National Westminster Bank Plc (60-15-29)

|  | 31-07-14 | 31-07-13 | 31-07-12 |
|---|---|---|---|
| TO | 19,300,023 | 15,382,157 | 13,534,959 |
| P/L | 3,714,070 | 2,422,445 | 1,792,098 |
| NW | 7,821,925 | 5,120,054 | 3,615,919 |
| WC | 5,227,351 | 2,970,789 | 1,479,117 |
| Emp. | 94 | 90 | 69 |

DUNS 76-999-0276
### Probrand Ltd
37-55 Camden Street, Birmingham, West Midlands B1 3BP
**Tel:** 01216051000 **Fax:** 01216056600
**Web:** www.probrand.co.uk
**Reg No:** 2653446 **VAT No:** 580401565
**Estd:** 1991 Private Limited Company
**Line of Business:** Computer systems and software (sales)
**Trading Style:** The It Index
**Issued Capital:** £100,000
**Principals:** P M Robbins *(Managing)*, S Tatlock, C P Griesbach
**Responsibilities**
**IT:** Mark Allbutt *(IT Technical Manager)*
**Branches:** Probrand Ltd, Suite 6B, 6th Floor, Trafford Plaza, Manchester M16 0LD
**US SIC:** 7379, 7374
**UK SIC:** 83940
**Auditors:** HW Chartered Accountants
**Bankers:** The Royal Bank Of Scotland Plc (16-13-19)

|  | 31-12-13 | 31-12-12 | 31-12-11 |
|---|---|---|---|
| TO | 40,765,251 | 37,835,986 | 36,570,547 |
| P/L | 546,940 | 548,441 | 329,235 |
| NW | 2,360,393 | 2,041,221 | 1,702,109 |
| WC | 464,882 | 315,536 | (111,535) |
| Emp. | 72 | 67 | 71 |

DUNS 23-523-7174                              Imp
### Probus Creative Housewares Ltd
**(Subsidiary of:** European Quality Housewares Limited)
Volante House, Cannock, Staffordshire WS11 0NH
**Tel:** 01922743586
**Web:** www.probusmayfair.co.uk
**Reg No:** 3522710 **Estd:** 2000 Private Limited Company
**Line of Business:** Household stores
**Issued Capital:** £2
**Directors:** A Facklemann, K G Ogrodnik, S Urosevic
**Responsibilities**
**Senior:** Adrian Stevens *(Manager)*, Ingo van den Broek *(Manager)*
**US SIC:** 5399 **UK SIC:** 65600

|  | 30-06-13 | 30-06-12 | 30-06-11 |
|---|---|---|---|
| TA | 1,100,260 | 1,137,196 | 831,530 |
| NW | (458,219) | (520,632) | (609,544) |
| WC | 11,257 | (24,973) | (112,981) |

DUNS 50-348-6888
### Procam Television Ltd
**(Subsidiary of:** Procam Television Holdings Ltd)
Unit 3, 104 Stewarts Road, London SW8 4UG
**Tel:** 020-7622-9888 **Fax:** 02074981580
**Web:** www.procam.tv
**Reg No:** 2370730 **Estd:** 1989 Private Limited Company
**Line of Business:** Renting of radios, televisions, video recorders and dvd players
**Issued Capital:** £1,288
**Directors:** J A Brennan, Ms H C Cardrick, P R Sargeant
**Co. Secretary:** Mh Secretaries Limited
**Responsibilities**
**Senior:** Callen Barton *(Manager)*
**US SIC:** 7394 **UK SIC:** 84000
**Bankers:** National Westminster Bank Plc (56-00-17)

|  | 31-12-13 | 31-12-12 | 31-12-11 |
|---|---|---|---|
| TO | 6,610,167 | 5,671,393 | N/A |
| P/L | 204,958 | 902,869 | N/A |
| NW | 3,312,489 | 3,219,426 | 2,617,475 |
| WC | (880,825) | (35,334) | 128,859 |

DUNS 52-571-6155                              Imp
### Procar International Ltd
Long Lane, Staines, Middlesex TW19 7AU
**Tel:** 01784-247407
**Web:** www.procar.co.uk
**Reg No:** 3255217 **Estd:** 1996 Private Limited Company
**Line of Business:** Storage and warehousing
**Issued Capital:** £2
**Director:** B J Sullivan
**Co. Secretary:** Ms Pamela Sullivan
**Responsibilities**
**Finance:** Kathy Rogers *(Manager)*
**US SIC:** 4226 **UK SIC:** 77003
**Auditors:** Civvals
**Bankers:** Lloyds TSB Bank plc (30-98-79)

|  | 30-04-14 | 30-04-13 | 30-04-12 |
|---|---|---|---|
| TO | 3,663,821 | N/A | N/A |
| P/L | 106,230 | N/A | N/A |
| NW | 396,865 | 406,863 | 405,790 |
| WC | 321,799 | 318,383 | 326,567 |

DUNS 77-707-1309
### Procare Building Services Ltd
Orient Centre, Greycaine Road, Watford, Hertfordshire WD24 7GP
**Tel:** 01923-200250
**Web:** www.procare.co.uk
**Reg No:** 3007751 **Estd:** 1995 Private Limited Company
**Line of Business:** Property maintenance services
**Trading Style:** Procare Building Services Ltd
**Issued Capital:** £2,330
**Directors:** D R Williams, M C Griffiths, B J Sutton, J C Miles, F Minaeian
**Co. Secretary:** Paul Reynolds
**Responsibilities**
**IT:** Jake Emberton *(Helpdesk Assistant)*
**Health & Safety:** Michelle Strohm *(Health, Safety and Environment)*
**US SIC:** 6552, 1541, 1796, 1799
**UK SIC:** 85000, 50100, 50400, 50000
**Auditors:** Hillier Hopkins LLP

|  | 30-06-13 | 30-06-12 | 30-06-11 |
|---|---|---|---|
| TO | 9,273,271 | 10,094,428 | 7,898,469 |
| P/L | 347,202 | 384,212 | (341,421) |
| NW | 1,193,805 | 988,378 | 721,246 |
| WC | 1,115,138 | 913,177 | 687,125 |
| Emp. | 71 | 72 | 79 |

DUNS 73-439-4963
### Procare Nursing Ltd
400 Cowbridge Road East, Cardiff, South Glamorgan CF5 1JJ
**Tel:** 02920258300 **Fax:** 02920258305
**Web:** www.procarenursing.co.uk
**Reg No:** 4690152 **Estd:** 2003 Private Limited Company
**Line of Business:** Other human health activities
**Issued Capital:** £1
**Director:** J A Drew
**Responsibilities**
**Finance:** Sharon Wise *(Finance Director)*
**US SIC:** 8321 **UK SIC:** 96111

|  | 31-03-14 | 31-03-13 | 31-03-12 |
|---|---|---|---|
| TA | 1 | 1 | 1 |
| NW | 1 | 1 | 1 |

DUNS 21-558-0711
### Proceeds of Crime Lawyers Association
3 Paper Buildings Inner Temple, London EC4Y 7EU
**Web:** www.pocla.co.uk
**Estd:** 2008
**Line of Business:** Lawyers association
**Principals:** A Mitchell Qc *(Chairman)*, M S Williams
**US SIC:** 8111 **UK SIC:** 83500
**Employees:** 300

DUNS 37-875-8304 Imp

## Process Systems Enterprise Ltd

6th Floor East 26-28 Hammersmith Grove, London W6 7HA
**Web:** www.psenterprise.com
**Reg No:** 3307708 **Estd:** 1997 Private Limited Company
**Line of Business:** Computer software (development)
**Export Sales:** £8,593,240
**Issued Capital:** £110,607
**Directors:** Professor K W Guy, R J Whitby Smith, Professor C C Pantelides, Professor E Pistikopoulos, B J Waldron, B G Mckenzie
**Co. Secretary:** Brian Mckenzie
**Responsibilities**
**Senior:** Christian Schulz *(Manager)*
**Admin:** Trudie Stroud *(Office Manager)*
**HR:** Lisa Collard *(Training Coordinator)*, Tim Harridge *(Training Coordinator)*, Trudie Stroud *(Office Manager)*
**Health & Safety:** Trudie Stroud *(Office Manager)*
**Facilities:** Trudie Stroud *(Office Manager)*
**Engineering:** Bart De Groot *(Applications Engineer)*, James Marriott *(Technical Engineerer)*, Zbigniew Urban *(Chief Technician)*
**US SIC:** 7379 **UK SIC:** 83940
**Auditors:** Grant Thornton UK LLP

| | 31-12-13 | 31-12-12 | 31-12-11 |
|---|---|---|---|
| TO | 10,711,381 | 8,953,071 | 6,868,643 |
| P/L | (66,635) | (96,948) | (264,593) |
| NW | 2,608,985 | 2,097,738 | 1,148,884 |
| WC | 2,396,763 | 1,870,822 | 1,350,889 |
| Emp. | 105 | 83 | N/A |

DUNS 39-346-9572 Imp-Exp

## Processflows (Uk) Ltd

(**Subsidiary of:** Avanquest Software Avanquest Blue Squad Bvrp Softw)
Sheridan House, 40-43 Jewry Street, Winchester, Hampshire SO23 8RY
**Tel:** 01962-835000
**Web:** www.processflows.co.uk
**Reg No:** 2120661 **VAT No:** 631997605
**Estd:** 1987 Private Limited Company
**Line of Business:** Other computer related activities
**Export Markets:** Worldwide
**Export Sales:** £164,000
**Issued Capital:** £88,000
**Directors:** C J Thompson, T D Bonnefoi, G Reddie, Avanquest Software Sa, B M Vanryb
**Co. Secretary:** Peter Doyle
**Responsibilities**
**Senior:** Simon Bates *(Finance Manager)*, Roger Politis *(Manager)*, Malcolm Wilkes *(Manager)*
**Finance:** Simon Bates *(Finance Manager)*, Emma-Louise Young *(Accountant)*
**Marketing:** Lyn Fairall *(Marketing Manager)*
**IT:** John Freckelton *(It Manager)*
**HR:** Dawn Osborne *(Human Resources Manager)*
**Health & Safety:** Dawn Osborne *(Human Resources Manager)*
**US SIC:** 7399 **UK SIC:** 83954
**Auditors:** Nexia Smith & Williamson
**Bankers:** Lloyds TSB Bank plc (77-25-15)

| | 30-06-13 | 30-06-12 | 30-06-11 |
|---|---|---|---|
| TO | 13,496,000 | 15,445,000 | 15,661,000 |
| P/L | 886,000 | 463,000 | (156,000) |
| NW | (442,000) | (814,000) | (1,386,000) |
| WC | (781,000) | (1,006,000) | (1,086,000) |
| Emp. | 120 | 105 | 83 |

DUNS 39-740-0995

## Proclean Cleaning Services Ltd

Unit 23 Holmbush Industrial Estate, Midhurst, West Sussex GU29 9HX
**Web:** www.proclean.co.uk
**Reg No:** 2181348 **VAT No:** 397668770
**Estd:** 1987 Private Limited Company
**Line of Business:** Cleaning contracting commercial
**Issued Capital:** £13,600
**Principals:** A D Balchin *(Managing)*, D A Balchin, Mrs M E Balchin
**Co. Secretary:** Andrew Balchin
**US SIC:** 7349 **UK SIC:** 92300
**Auditors:** Tropman & Co Ltd
**Bankers:** Barclays Bank Plc (20-20-62)

| | 31-10-13 | 31-10-12 | 31-10-11 |
|---|---|---|---|
| TA | 213,240 | 278,232 | 257,846 |
| NW | 77,542 | 58,966 | 61,140 |
| WC | 67,088 | 49,867 | 50,885 |

DUNS 34-886-4245

## Proco (Holdings) Ltd

9 Parkway Close, Sheffield, South Yorkshire S9 4WJ
**Tel:** 01142-728888 **Fax:** 01142-502949
**Web:** www.proco.com
**Reg No:** 5684302 **Estd:** 2006 Private Limited Company
**Line of Business:** Management activities of holding companies
**Issued Capital:** £688,000
**Directors:** M J Schofield, M J Bailey
**Co. Secretary:** Ms Kathryn Bailey
**US SIC:** 6711 **UK SIC:** 83962

| | 30-06-14 | 30-06-13 | 30-06-12 |
|---|---|---|---|
| TO | 10,520,787 | 10,672,877 | 10,782,148 |
| P/L | 600,007 | 506,366 | 403,602 |
| NW | 2,329,921 | 2,012,661 | 1,343,678 |
| WC | 1,214,333 | 1,003,153 | 538,078 |
| Emp. | 125 | 139 | 123 |

DUNS 67-217-7396

## Proco Nw Ltd

Prescott Street, Wigan, Lancashire WN6 7DD
**Tel:** 01942488500 **Fax:** 01942488501
**Web:** www.proconw.co.uk
**Reg No:** 6047511 **Estd:** 2012 Private Company Limited By Guarantee
**Line of Business:** Training services
**Directors:** S F Lenagan, J A Johnson, Mrs C Halford, A P Lenagan, D J Tully, I F Lenagan, T Barton
**Co. Secretary:** David Tully
**Responsibilities**
**Senior:** Carol Dodgson *(Manager)*, Nigel Hansford *(Director)*, Elaine Walsh *(Chief Executive)*, Debra Woodruff *(Manager)*
**Health & Safety:** Craig Horrocks *(Health & Safety Officer)*
**US SIC:** 8299 **UK SIC:** 93300
**Auditors:** Hurst & Co Accountants LLP
**Bankers:** The Co-Operative Bank Plc (08-90-00)

| | 31-07-13 | 31-07-12 | 31-07-11 |
|---|---|---|---|
| TO | N/A | 2,373,296 | 2,186,687 |
| P/L | N/A | 93,301 | 123,168 |
| NW | 214,774 | 135,125 | 280,575 |
| WC | 539,316 | 354,225 | 282,040 |
| Emp. | N/A | 60 | 57 |

DUNS 42-373-6474

## Procomm Site Services Ltd

(**Subsidiary of:** Portchester Equity Ltd)
P O Box 1949, Wilton, Redcar, Cleveland TS10 4YG
**Tel:** 01642463888
**Web:** www.procommsiteservices.co.uk
**Reg No:** 4361255 **VAT No:** 991295187
**Estd:** 2007 Private Limited Company
**Line of Business:** Portable buildings
**Issued Capital:** £100,000
**Directors:** D C Harbord, D A Homer, N L Wood, W Kellie, P Beckett, S J Smith, M E Thistlethwayte, B J Cranny
**Co. Secretary:** Nicholas Wood
**Responsibilities**
**Senior:** Robin Thistlethwayte *(Director)*
**Branches:** Procomm Site Services Ltd, Lyncastle Road, Barleycastle Lane, Appleton, Warrington, Cheshire WA4 4SN
**US SIC:** 1761 **UK SIC:** 50400
**Auditors:** BDO LLP
**Bankers:** Barclays Bank Plc (20-66-97)

| | 30-09-13 | 30-09-12 | 30-09-11 |
|---|---|---|---|
| TO | 10,939,891 | 8,105,807 | 8,567,339 |
| P/L | 1,340,507 | 971,326 | 1,174,744 |
| NW | 5,823,845 | 5,051,543 | 4,640,223 |
| WC | (2,438,084) | (2,876,094) | (2,902,589) |
| Emp. | 71 | 65 | 59 |

DUNS 21-129-6062 Imp

## Procook Ltd

3 Io Centre, Hurricane Road, Gloucester Business Park, Brockworth, Gloucester, Gloucestershire GL3 4AQ
**Tel:** 03301001010
**Web:** www.procook.co.uk
**Reg No:** 6639057 **Estd:** 2008 Private Limited Company
**Line of Business:** Representative office
**Export Sales:** £618,161
**Issued Capital:** £100
**Directors:** D P O'Neill, Mrs S J O'Neill
**US SIC:** 5021, 5719
**UK SIC:** 61500, 64700

| | 30-03-14 | 31-03-13 | 01-03-12 |
|---|---|---|---|
| TO | 13,139,380 | 11,169,746 | N/A |
| P/L | 796,076 | 971,248 | N/A |
| NW | 1,338,860 | 1,168,487 | 988,353 |
| WC | 828,352 | 627,065 | 866,501 |
| Emp. | 124 | 160 | N/A |

DUNS 36-523-6215

## Procter & Gamble (L & Cp) Ltd

(**Subsidiary of:** The Procter & Gamble Company)
Hedley Avenue, Grays, Essex RM20 4AL
**Tel:** 01375395000
**Reg No:** 3288185 **Estd:** 1996 Private Limited Company
**Line of Business:** Other service activities not elsewhere classified
**Issued Capital:** £50,002
**Directors:** T Moody, Ms R J Hughes, B D Young, Ms H M Tucker, G Branda, Ms G C Huse
**Co. Secretary:** Anthony Appleton
**Responsibilities**
**Senior:** Huw Waters *(Director)*
**US SIC:** 8999 **UK SIC:** 83954
**Auditors:** Deloitte LLP
**Bankers:** HSBC Bank plc (40-37-37)

| | 30-06-13 | 30-06-12 | 30-06-11 |
|---|---|---|---|
| TA | 154,494,000 | 124,539,000 | 99,905,000 |
| P/L | 30,555,000 | 24,575,000 | 71,850,000 |
| NW | 151,695,000 | 122,205,000 | 98,337,000 |
| WC | 151,690,000 | 122,200,000 | 98,332,000 |

DUNS 49-043-6938

## Procter & Gamble Product Supply (U.K.) Ltd

(**Subsidiary of:** The Procter & Gamble Company)
The Heights, Brooklands, Weybridge, Surrey KT13 0XP
**Tel:** 01932-896-000 **Fax:** 01932-896-200
**Web:** www.pg.com
**Reg No:** 3074536 **VAT No:** 675491595
**Estd:** 1995 Private Limited Company
**Line of Business:** Manufacture of soap and detergents
**Trading Style:** Proctor & Gamble
**Issued Capital:** £70,101,000
**Directors:** Ms H M Tucker, G Branda, P Harrison, Ms K E Plumley, Ms S Martinelli, A J Appleton, E D Forsyth, B D Young
**Co. Secretary:** Anthony Appleton
**Responsibilities**
**Senior:** Marta Blyszczyk *(Director)*, Julian Harrington *(Manager)*, A McCarthy *(Manager)*, Philip Merrell *(Manager)*, Huw Waters *(Director)*
**Branches:** Procter & Gamble Product Supply (U.k.) Ltd, Trafford Park Road, Manchester M17 1NX
**US SIC:** 2841 **UK SIC:** 25810
**Auditors:** Deloitte LLP
**Bankers:** HSBC Bank plc (40-34-18)

| | 30-06-13 | 30-06-12 | 30-06-11 |
|---|---|---|---|
| TO | 200,682,000 | 201,420,000 | 202,980,000 |
| P/L | 28,455,000 | 29,182,000 | 27,272,000 |
| NW | 250,402,000 | 238,227,000 | 237,123,000 |
| WC | 70,916,000 | 54,659,000 | 36,553,000 |
| Emp. | 1,465 | 1,529 | 1,464 |

DUNS 37-973-9832

## Procter & Gamble Technical Centres Ltd

(**Subsidiary of:** The Procter & Gamble Company)
Rusham Park, Whitehall Lane, Egham, Surrey TW20 9NW
**Tel:** 01784474900
**Web:** www.pg.com
**Reg No:** 3281294 **Estd:** 1996 Private Limited Company
**Line of Business:** Technical testing and analysis
**Export Sales:** £226,038,000
**Trading Style:** London Innovation Centre (Egham), Procter & Gamble London Innovation Centre (Egham)
**Issued Capital:** £1,000,002
**Directors:** Ms H M Tucker, P H Masscheleyn, A Ewen, B D Young, C D Bragg
**Co. Secretary:** Anthony Appleton
**Responsibilities**
**Senior:** Anthony Appleby *(Manager)*, Sumit Bhasin *(Manager)*, Huw Waters *(Director)*
**Branches:** Procter & Gamble Technical Centres Ltd, Cobalt 12, Silver Fox Way, Cobalt Business Park, Newcastle-Upon-Tyne, Tyne and Wear NW27 0QW
**US SIC:** 7397, 7391
**UK SIC:** 83702, 94000
**Auditors:** Deloitte LLP
**Bankers:** HSBC Bank plc (40-34-18)

| | 30-06-13 | 30-06-12 | 30-06-11 |
|---|---|---|---|
| TO | 229,379,000 | 243,107,000 | 240,378,000 |
| P/L | 12,867,000 | 17,493,000 | 14,195,000 |
| NW | 118,018,000 | 112,998,000 | 123,334,000 |
| WC | 146,878,000 | 133,359,000 | 124,085,000 |
| Emp. | 1,337 | 1,476 | 1,500 |

DUNS 21-218-2406 Imp-Exp

## Procter Bros Ltd

1 Beaconsfield Court, Garforth, Leeds, West Yorkshire LS25 1QH
**Web:** www.procterbros.co.uk
**Reg No:** 0144614 **VAT No:** 168821829
**Estd:** 1916 Private Limited Company
**Line of Business:** Manufacture of concrete products for construction purposes
**Trading Style:** Procter Machine Guarding, Procter Caststone, Procter Concrete Products, Procter Fencing Systems
**Issued Capital:** £90,030
**Principals:** J C Procter *(Managing)*, G M Horsfall, H R Davies, J P Procter
**Co. Secretary:** Keith Kirwin
**Responsibilities**
**Senior:** Raheeda Inayat *(Manager)*, Tony Turner *(Manager)*
**Branches:** Procter Bros Ltd, Ninelands Lane, Leeds, West Yorkshire LS25 2BY
**US SIC:** 3271, 1796, 3272
**UK SIC:** 24370, 50400
**Auditors:** Ford Campbell Freedman LLP
**Bankers:** Lloyds TSB Bank plc (30-00-05)

| | 31-12-13 | 31-12-12 | 31-12-11 |
|---|---|---|---|
| TO | 14,055,447 | 16,412,985 | 16,330,000 |
| P/L | 11,432 | 237,729 | (325,576) |
| NW | (3,239,312) | (3,830,807) | (3,475,897) |
| WC | 739,120 | 986,958 | 839,491 |
| Emp. | 168 | 171 | 161 |

DUNS 21-581-0220

## Procter Caststone

Ash Lane, Garforth, Leeds, West Yorkshire LS25 2HQ
**Tel:** 01132863329
**Web:** www.caststoneuk.co.uk
**Estd:** 2011 Proprietorship
**Line of Business:** Concrete products
**Proprietor:** G Horsfall
**US SIC:** 3271 **UK SIC:** 24370
**Employees:** 50

DUNS 23-845-4602

## Procter Holdings Ltd

40 Hetherington Road, Shepperton, Middlesex TW17 0SP
**Web:** www.proctercleaning.co.uk
**Reg No:** 3837515 **Estd:** 1999 Private Limited Company
**Line of Business:** Cleaning contracting commercial
**Issued Capital:** £100
**Director:** A W Procter
**Co. Secretary:** Alan Procter
**US SIC:** 7349 **UK SIC:** 92300

| | 31-03-14 | 31-03-13 | 31-03-12 |
|---|---|---|---|
| TA | 686,398 | 680,568 | 649,086 |
| NW | 587,532 | 579,237 | 545,382 |
| WC | 384,672 | 368,576 | 339,188 |

DUNS 21-329-2147 Imp

## Proctor Paper & Board Ltd

Westland Square, Leeds, West Yorkshire LS11 5SS
**Tel:** 01132-774848
**Web:** www.proctors.biz
**Reg No:** 1460812 **VAT No:** 721264856
**Estd:** 1978 Private Limited Company
**Line of Business:** Wholesale of other intermediate products
**Issued Capital:** £90,600
**Principals:** R J Proctor *(Managing)*, J C Buchanan, M L Proctor, J H Proctor, Ms E F Proctor, Ms J Buchanan, Ms C L Proctor
**Co. Secretary:** Ms Rosemary Proctor
**Responsibilities**
**Senior:** Paul Hye *(Manager)*
**US SIC:** 5199 **UK SIC:** 61900
**Auditors:** Saffery Champness
**Bankers:** Yorkshire Bank Plc (05-00-58)

| | 28-02-14 | 28-02-13 | 29-02-12 |
|---|---|---|---|
| TO | 21,415,215 | 21,433,630 | 22,013,224 |
| P/L | 518,308 | 650,563 | 872,994 |
| NW | 2,151,428 | 2,120,568 | 2,408,358 |
| WC | 1,890,443 | 1,842,027 | 2,258,154 |
| Emp. | 46 | 45 | 46 |

DUNS 21-736-4942 Imp-Exp

## Procurri Uk Ltd

(**Subsidiary of:** Asvida Uk Ltd)
Unit O, Bankside, Love Lane, Cirencester, Gloucestershire GL7 1YG
**Tel:** 01285-642222 **Fax:** 01285644422
**Web:** www.tindirect.com
**Reg No:** 0644939 **VAT No:** 862642416
**Estd:** 1959 Private Limited Company
**Line of Business:** Manufacturers of pcs
**Export Sales:** £4,034,910
**Issued Capital:** £1,290,000
**Directors:** D J Gutteridge, M G Jordan
**Co. Secretary:** Pinsent Masons Secretarial Limit
**Responsibilities**
**IT:** Abbey Flint *(Senior IT Executive)*
**US SIC:** 3573, 5081
**UK SIC:** 33020, 61490
**Auditors:** Grant Thornton UK LLP
**Bankers:** Bank Of Scotland (12-05-77)

| | 31-12-13 | 31-05-13 | 31-12-12 |
|---|---|---|---|
| TO | 7,475,945 | 15,256,893 | 16,976,619 |
| P/L | 401,195 | 1,111,912 | 952,430 |
| NW | 6,021,065 | 5,619,749 | 4,666,833 |
| WC | 5,837,285 | 5,456,433 | 4,470,934 |
| Emp. | 74 | 66 | 71 |

DUNS 64-254-6741

## Proddow Mackay

The Cloisters, Sun Lane, Maidenhead, Berkshire SL6 7XW
**Web:** www.pm-law.co.uk
**Estd:** 1990 Partnership
**Line of Business:** Solicitors
**Partners:** D J Mackay, S K Proddow, Miss S Kaushall
**Responsibilities**
**Senior:** Proddow Mackay *(Partner)*, Simon Proddow *(director)*
**Health & Safety:** Simon Proddow *(director)*

**Branches:** Proddow Mackay, P M House, 250 Shepcote Lane, Sheffield, South Yorkshire S9 1TP
**US SIC:** 8111 **UK SIC:** 83500
**Employees:** 7

DUNS 34-650-3480
## Proddow Mackay Ltd
P M House, 250 Shepcote Lane, Sheffield, South Yorkshire S9 1TP
**Tel:** 01142965444 **Fax:** 01142-493440
**Web:** www.pm-law.co.uk
**Reg No:** 5455906 **Estd:** 1996 Private Limited Company
**Line of Business:** Solicitors
**Issued Capital:** £1,000
**Directors:** D J Mackay, R J Helsby, R S Mackay
**Co. Secretary:** Jonathan Bostock
**Responsibilities**
**Senior:** Sabya Kaushal *(Senior Partner)*
**US SIC:** 8111 **UK SIC:** 83500
**Auditors:** Hawsons

| | 31-05-13 | 31-05-12 | 31-05-11 |
|---|---|---|---|
| TA | 636,563 | 491,380 | 599,027 |
| NW | 69,170 | 58,656 | 45,549 |
| WC | 69,170 | 58,656 | 45,549 |

DUNS 23-650-1123 **Imp**
## Prodec Networks Ltd
**(Subsidiary of:** Barstone Ltd)
Unit 5 Chancerygate Business Centre, Ruscombe Park, Ruscombe, Reading, Berkshire RG10 9LT
**Tel:** 01189602504 **Fax:** 01344867774
**Web:** www.prodec.co.uk
**Reg No:** 3645275 **VAT No:** 918452903
**Estd:** 1998 Private Limited Company
**Line of Business:** Computer services
**Issued Capital:** £2,150
**Directors:** R G Barley, Ms C Billing
**Co. Secretary:** Gregory Stone
**US SIC:** 7379, 5399
**UK SIC:** 83940, 65600
**Auditors:** Saffery Champness
**Bankers:** National Westminster Bank Plc (60-17-21)

| | 30-04-14 | 30-04-13 | 30-04-12 |
|---|---|---|---|
| TO | 12,869,929 | 21,036,407 | 11,769,968 |
| P/L | (281,281) | 945,149 | 531,356 |
| NW | 1,423,511 | 1,650,142 | 959,285 |
| WC | 1,132,993 | 1,342,931 | 633,775 |
| Emp. | 45 | 52 | 55 |

DUNS 21-756-6315
## Prodene Hygiene Products Ltd
Meltham Mills, Huddersfield, West Yorkshire HD9 4FA
**Tel:** 01484854434
**Web:** www.prodenehygieneproductsltd.co.uk
**Reg No:** 7858403 **Estd:** 1987 Private Limited Company
**Line of Business:** Other wholesale
**Issued Capital:** £100
**Directors:** D Burkill, Ms D Storer, F E Beer
**US SIC:** 5199 **UK SIC:** 61900

| | 31-12-13 | 31-12-12 |
|---|---|---|
| TA | 100 | 100 |
| NW | 100 | 100 |

DUNS 21-167-9937
## Prodo Digital Marketing Ltd
Little Heath Road, Chester, Cheshire CH3 7DW
**Tel:** 08448 717272 **Fax:** 08707562838
**Web:** www.prodo.com
**Reg No:** 6931553 **Estd:** 1998 Private Limited Company
**Line of Business:** Marketing consultants
**Issued Capital:** £1
**Directors:** D R Adams, Mrs P C Adams
**Responsibilities**
**Senior:** Pippa Adams *(Manager)*
**HR:** Kerry Quayle *(HR Manager)*
**US SIC:** 7392 **UK SIC:** 83951

| | 31-12-13 | 31-12-12 | 30-12-11 |
|---|---|---|---|
| TA | 429,290 | 409,705 | 241,985 |
| NW | 147,407 | 4,775 | (122,382) |
| WC | 90,206 | (107,251) | (149,107) |

DUNS 52-572-1361 **Imp**
## Prodrive Automotive Technology (Europe) Ltd
**(Subsidiary of:** Hundred Percent Group Ltd)
Oldwich Lane East, Kenilworth, Warwickshire CV8 1NR
**Tel:** 01676536002 **Fax:** 01676536205
**Web:** www.prodrive.com
**Reg No:** 3255719 **VAT No:** 694209316
**Estd:** 1997 Private Limited Company
**Line of Business:** Other engineering activities
**Trading Style:** Prodrive Automotive Technology (Europe) Ltd
**Issued Capital:** £500,002
**Directors:** T Colchester, D Cartwright
**Co. Secretary:** Timothy Bailey
**Branches:** Prodrive Automotive Technology (Europe) Ltd, Precedent Dr, Milton Keynes, Buckinghamshire MK13 8PE
**US SIC:** 8911 **UK SIC:** 83701
**Auditors:** Ernst & Young LLP

| | 31-12-13 | 31-12-12 | 31-12-11 |
|---|---|---|---|
| TO | 13,250,000 | 20,356,000 | 17,798,000 |
| P/L | (545,000) | 364,000 | (1,172,000) |
| NW | (6,646,000) | (6,101,000) | (6,465,000) |
| WC | (4,243,000) | (4,322,000) | (5,537,000) |
| Emp. | 112 | 126 | 87 |

DUNS 21-744-1632
## Prodrive Composites Ltd
**(Subsidiary of:** Hundred Percent Group Ltd)
Acorn House, Acorn Way, Banbury, Oxfordshire OX16 3ER
**Tel:** 01295754000
**Reg No:** 7764727 **Estd:** 2011 Private Limited Company
**Line of Business:** Manufacture of parts and accessories for motor vehicles and their engines
**Issued Capital:** £1
**Directors:** T Colchester, D O Cartwright
**US SIC:** 3714 **UK SIC:** 35300

| | 31-12-13 | 31-12-12 | 31-12-11 |
|---|---|---|---|
| TO | 8,030,000 | 6,555,000 | N/A |
| P/L | (991,000) | 72,000 | N/A |
| NW | (1,048,000) | 62,000 | 1 |
| WC | (1,650,000) | (360,000) | N/A |
| Emp. | 98 | 99 | N/A |

DUNS 23-864-4582 **Exp**
## Prodrive (Holdings) Ltd
**(Subsidiary of:** Hundred Percent Group Ltd)
Acorn House, Acorn Way, Banbury, Oxfordshire OX16 3ER
**Tel:** 01295-273355
**Web:** www.prodrive.com
**Reg No:** 3855989 **Estd:** 1999 Private Limited Company
**Line of Business:** Management activities of holding companies
**Trading Style:** Prodrive
**Issued Capital:** £1,433,708
**Directors:** T Colchester, R Avsharian, Ms S M Scarf, Mrs K Richards
**Co. Secretary:** Timothy Bailey
**Responsibilities**
**Senior:** Andy Blackwell *(Warehouse Manager)*, Chris Englishby *(Warehouse Manager)*, Mahmoud Sayed *(Manager)*, Anthony Schulp *(Manager)*
**Engineering:** Paul Eastman *(Engineering Manager)*
**US SIC:** 6711 **UK SIC:** 83962
**Auditors:** Ernst & Young LLP

| | 31-12-13 | 31-12-12 | 31-12-11 |
|---|---|---|---|
| TO | 53,475,000 | 107,804,000 | 102,541,000 |
| P/L | (10,377,000) | 8,620,000 | (8,015,000) |
| NW | (14,843,000) | (6,415,000) | (5,010,000) |
| WC | (8,526,000) | 6,130,000 | 6,906,000 |
| Emp. | 452 | 593 | 593 |

DUNS 73-320-2936
## Produce World (Sutton Bridge) Ltd
**(Subsidiary of:** Russell Burgess Ltd)
Eastbank, Spalding, Lincolnshire PE12 9YB
**Tel:** 01406350528 **Fax:** 01406351091
**Web:** www.produceworld.co.uk
**Reg No:** 4594137 **Estd:** 2002 Private Limited Company
**Line of Business:** Potato merchants
**Trading Style:** Produce World Group
**Issued Capital:** £3,431,504
**Directors:** P Jones, D W Burgess
**Co. Secretary:** David Burgess
**Responsibilities**
**Senior:** Ian Batkin *(Manager)*, Katie Stark *(Operations Manager)*, Paul Tracey *(Procurement Director)*
**HR:** Ann Dobson *(Human Resources Manager)*
**Operations:** Katie Stark *(Operations Manager)*
**Purchasing:** Paul Tracey *(Procurement Director)*
**Branches:** Produce World (Sutton Bridge) Ltd, Eastbank, Wingland, Sutton Bridge, Spalding, Lincolnshire PE12 9YB
**US SIC:** 5148 **UK SIC:** 61700
**Auditors:** PricewaterhouseCoopers LLP
**Bankers:** Barclays Bank Plc (20-67-37)

| | 28-06-13 | 29-06-12 | 01-06-11 |
|---|---|---|---|
| TO | 40,957,000 | 33,917,000 | 41,115,000 |
| P/L | 960,000 | 1,059,000 | (1,261,000) |
| NW | 3,920,000 | 4,830,000 | 4,147,000 |
| WC | 358,000 | 1,046,000 | (32,000) |
| Emp. | 195 | 202 | 252 |

DUNS 77-490-1755
## Product Support Ltd
**(Subsidiary of:** Wincanton Plc)
152 Staplehurst Road, Sittingbourne, Kent ME10 1XS
**Tel:** 01795427242
**Web:** www.product-support.co.uk
**Reg No:** 2973863 **Estd:** 1965 Private Limited Company
**Line of Business:** Freight services
**Issued Capital:** £1,560,000
**Directors:** A M Colman, E M Born
**Co. Secretary:** Mrs Alison Dowling
**Branches:** Product Support Ltd, Cambridge Support Centre, Sandy, Bedfordshire SG19 3LB
**US SIC:** 2645, 3079
**UK SIC:** 47280, 48360

| | 31-03-14 | 31-03-13 | 31-03-12 |
|---|---|---|---|
| TA | 33,745,000 | 33,745,000 | 33,745,000 |
| NW | 33,745,000 | 33,745,000 | 33,745,000 |

DUNS 21-789-9290
## Production Glass
Unit K1-K4 Buckshaw Link, Ordnance Road, Buckshaw Village, Chorley, Lancashire PR7 7EL
**Tel:** 01772622444
**Web:** www.productionglassfibre.co.uk
**Estd:** 2011 Proprietorship
**Line of Business:** Manufacture of glass fibres
**Proprietor:** A Hill
**US SIC:** 7399 **UK SIC:** 83954
**Employees:** 70

DUNS 21-812-0720
## The Production House
42 Trinity Park, Calne, Wiltshire SN11 0QD
**Tel:** 07932740515
**Web:** www.theproductionhouse.co.uk
**Estd:** 2012
**Line of Business:** Corporate entertainment and hospitality
**Responsibilities**
**Senior:** Adam King *(Manager)*
**US SIC:** 7999 **UK SIC:** 97913
**Employees:** 100

DUNS 77-779-8570
## Production Resource Group (Europe) Ltd
**(Subsidiary of:** Production Resource Group Llc)
The Cofton Centre, Groveley Lane, Longbridge, Birmingham, West Midlands B31 4PT
**Tel:** 01217666400 **Fax:** 08454706401
**Web:** www.prg.com
**Reg No:** 3024622 **Estd:** 1995 Private Limited Company
**Line of Business:** Renting of radios, televisions, video recorders and dvd players
**Export Sales:** £10,393,152
**Issued Capital:** £1,118,889
**Director:** G Boyd
**Co. Secretary:** Richard Williams
**Responsibilities**
**Senior:** Robin Wain *(Senior Sales Executive)*
**Sales:** Robin Wain *(Senior Sales Executive)*
**Purchasing:** Mark Goslin *(Purchasing Manager)*
**US SIC:** 7394 **UK SIC:** 84000
**Auditors:** Bloomer Heaven
**Bankers:** HSBC Bank plc (40-11-18)

| | 31-12-13 | 31-12-12 | 31-12-11 |
|---|---|---|---|
| TO | 29,897,102 | 34,585,129 | 38,296,216 |
| P/L | (206,522) | (321,117) | (91,974) |
| NW | 4,085,994 | 4,041,887 | 4,110,744 |
| WC | 1,856,114 | (20,062) | 1,249,112 |
| Emp. | 186 | 206 | 193 |

DUNS 76-987-7804
## Prodware (Uk) Ltd
Waterfold Business Park, Bury, Lancashire BL9 7BR
**Tel:** 01617056000 **Fax:** 01617056001
**Web:** www.prodware.co.uk
**Reg No:** 2645947 **VAT No:** 561207859
**Estd:** 1991 Private Limited Company
**Line of Business:** Computer support & services
**Issued Capital:** £200
**Directors:** Prodware Sa, M C Cockings, A G Conrard
**Responsibilities**
**Sales:** Jamaine Campbell *(Sales Director)*
**US SIC:** 7379 **UK SIC:** 83940
**Auditors:** Alexander & Co
**Bankers:** National Westminster Bank Plc (01-10-01)

| | 31-12-13 | 31-12-12 | 31-12-11 |
|---|---|---|---|
| TO | 5,220,926 | 4,542,019 | 5,158,952 |
| P/L | 311,972 | (178,461) | 353,186 |
| NW | (304,452) | (622,426) | (507,674) |
| WC | (350,886) | (666,779) | (542,771) |
| Emp. | 46 | 45 | 38 |

DUNS 23-724-4173
## Profast Group Ltd
**(Subsidiary of:** Profast Holdings Ltd)
26-30 Rydalmere Street, Belfast BT12 6GF
**Tel:** 02890-243215 **Fax:** 028-9033-3301
**Web:** www.profast.co.uk
**Reg No:** 0029743NI **Estd:** 1995 Private Limited Company
**Line of Business:** Door and window furniture
**Issued Capital:** £112,903
**Directors:** P J Gregg, B Flynn, S I Taylor
**Co. Secretary:** Paul Grant
**Responsibilities**
**Purchasing:** Damian Conway *(Purchasing Manager)*
**US SIC:** 3442 **UK SIC:** 31420
**Auditors:** Goldblatt McGuigan
**Bankers:** Ulster Bank Ltd (98-00-17)

| | 31-12-13 | 31-12-12 | 31-12-11 |
|---|---|---|---|
| TO | 10,085,143 | 9,605,281 | 10,296,304 |
| P/L | 308,953 | (38,389) | 224,787 |
| NW | 1,002,391 | 887,573 | 990,272 |
| WC | 460,592 | 467,825 | 577,528 |
| Emp. | 55 | 55 | 58 |

DUNS 29-857-6695
## Professional Association for Childcare & Early Years
Royal Court, 81 Tweedy Road, Bromley, Kent BR1 1TG
**Tel:** 08458800044 **Fax:** 08458800043
**Web:** www.pacey.org.uk
**Reg No:** 2060964 **Estd:** 1986 Private Company Limited By Guarantee
**Line of Business:** Adult and other education not elsewhere classified
**Trading Style:** Pacey
**Directors:** Mrs E V Battersby, Mrs J S Comeau, Ms P E Tulloch, Ms S E Atkinson, H Adebiyi, C A Glennie, Mrs A J Calloway, Ms H D King
**Co. Secretary:** Mrs Jenny Edwards
**Responsibilities**
**Senior:** Nicola Alderson *(Manager)*, Liz Bayram *(Chief Executive)*, Jo-Anne Cullen *(Director)*, Susanna Dawson *(Chairman)*, Patricia Elliott *(Manager)*, Simon Ginns *(Business Development Director)*, Alison Lodge *(Director)*, Emma Moore *(Board Member)*, David Poulsom *(Board Member)*
**Finance:** Howard Bratter *(Head of Finance and Business S)*
**Branches:** Professional Association For Childcare & Early Years, 46 Farriers Close, Ipswich, Suffolk IP5 3SW
**US SIC:** 8249 **UK SIC:** 93300
**Auditors:** Connor Warin
**Bankers:** National Westminster Bank Plc (60-04-02)

| | 31-03-14 | 31-03-13 | 31-03-12 |
|---|---|---|---|
| TO | 7,739,961 | 10,222,013 | 11,241,287 |
| P/L | 305,356 | 194,535 | (513,740) |
| NW | 1,666,443 | 1,589,383 | 1,924,848 |
| WC | 1,597,646 | 971,572 | 450,398 |
| Emp. | 128 | 172 | 252 |

DUNS 23-709-5633 **Exp**
## Professional Data Management Services Ltd
Global House, Isle Of Man Business Park, Douglas, Douglas, Isle of Man IM2 2QZ
**Tel:** 01624664000 **Fax:** 01624825640
**Web:** www.pdms.com
**Reg No:** 0061568M **VAT No:** 001109941
**Estd:** 1999 Private Limited Company
**Line of Business:** Computer software (development)
**Export Markets:** U S A
**Trading Style:** P D M S
**Issued Capital:** £3,434
**Directors:** T J Nicholson, Dr P H Adcock, M P Bromwich, G H Milner, B Clark, Dr B J Mcgregor, C J Gledhill
**Responsibilities**
**Senior:** Bruce McGregor *(Director)*
**Finance:** Kerry Kelly *(Financial Controller)*
**Sales:** Andrew Cairns *(Head of Business Development)*, Gemma Webb *(Sales Process Manager)*
**HR:** Lauren Stewart *(Human Resources Manager)*
**US SIC:** 7379 **UK SIC:** 83940
**Auditors:** David Wilcock
**Bankers:** Barclays Bank Plc (20-26-74)

| | 31-03-13 | 31-03-12 | 31-03-11 |
|---|---|---|---|
| TO | 3,253,312 | 3,342,476 | 3,498,077 |
| P/L | (94,614) | 66,787 | 19,140 |
| NW | 1,287,000 | 1,221,101 | 1,162,841 |
| WC | 153,857 | 269,582 | 253,422 |

DUNS 29-497-8812 **Imp-Exp**
## The Professional Golfers' Association Ltd
The Belfry, Lichfield Road, Sutton Coldfield, West Midlands B76 9PT
**Tel:** 01675470333 **Fax:** 01675-477888
**Web:** www.pga.info
**Reg No:** 1861161 **Estd:** 1984 Private Company Limited By Guarantee
**Line of Business:** Sports clubs
**Trading Style:** P G A
**Directors:** D G Haines, D R Hart, L A Fickling, A White, G V Kavanagh, M A Heggie, D J Murchie, T Rouse
**Co. Secretary:** Alexander Jones
**Responsibilities**
**Senior:** James Christine *(Manager)*, Andrew Hanna *(Manager)*, Jack Lumb *(Manager)*, Philip Weaver *(Manager)*
**Marketing:** Robert Maxfield *(Commercial Director)*

**Sales:** Robert Maxfield (Commercial Director)
**Admin:** Derek Neal (Office Manager)
**Health & Safety:** Derek Neal (Office Manager)
**Facilities:** Derek Neal (Office Manager)
**Purchasing:** Derek Neal (Office Manager)
**Branches:** The Professional Golfers' Association Ltd, Lake View, Keswick, Cumbria CA12 4RG
**US SIC:** 7999 **UK SIC:** 97913
**Auditors:** PricewaterhouseCoopers LLP
**Bankers:** Lloyds TSB Bank plc (30-98-37)

|      | 31-12-13   | 31-12-12   | 31-12-11   |
|------|-----------|-----------|-----------|
| TO   | 12,469,000 | 11,852,000 | 12,169,000 |
| P/L  | (828,000)  | 844,000    | (456,000)  |
| NW   | 5,766,000  | 6,211,000  | 5,453,000  |
| WC   | 468,000    | 1,189,000  | 1,172,000  |
| Emp. | 130        | 125        | 125        |

DUNS 50-445-2889

## Professional Lighting & Sound Association Ltd

Unit 1, Redoubt House, 1b Edward Road, Eastbourne, East Sussex BN23 8AS
**Tel:** 01323524120 **Fax:** 01323524121
**Web:** www.plasa.org
**Reg No:** 2433137 **VAT No:** 550350966
**Estd:** 1989 Private Limited Company
**Line of Business:** Activities of business and employers organisations
**Trading Style:** Plasa
**Issued Capital:** £1,000
**Directors:** M Hawthorn, E Pagett, M J Griffiths
**Co. Secretary:** Shane Mcgreevy
**Responsibilities**
**Marketing:** Jen Barratt (Marketing Manager), Claire Beeson (Assistant Editor), Ilana Lawrence (Senior Marketing Executive)
**Admin:** Amanda Adler (PA to CEO)
**IT:** Oliver Kinne (IT Manager)
**Operations:** Sonja Walker (Production Manager)
**Engineering:** Ron Bonner (Technical Resources Manager)
**Branches:** Professional Lighting & Sound Association Ltd, 7 Highlight Ho, St Leonards Rd, Eastbourne, East Sussex BN21 3UH
**US SIC:** 8611, 8999
**UK SIC:** 96312, 83954
**Auditors:** Honey Barrett

|    | 31-12-13  | 31-12-12  | 31-12-11 |
|----|----------|----------|---------|
| TA | 1,154,346 | 1,037,868 | 949,919 |
| NW | 594,310   | 747,613   | 687,198 |
| WC | (64,985)  | 19,537    | (24,010) |

DUNS 22-283-8265

## Professional Supply Service Ltd

Lower Moddershall Farm, Mill Lane, Lower Moddershall, Moddershal, Stone, Staffordshire ST15 8TF
**Web:** www.professionalsupplyservice.co.uk
**Reg No:** 4301797 **Estd:** 2001 Private Limited Company
**Line of Business:** Employment and recruitment companies and consultants
**Issued Capital:** £5
**Director:** G Termine
**Co. Secretary:** Ms Margaret Termine
**Responsibilities**
**Senior:** Antonino Termine (Manager)
**US SIC:** 7361 **UK SIC:** 83954

|    | 31-12-13 | 31-12-12 | 31-12-11 |
|----|---------|---------|---------|
| TA | 5       | 5       | 5       |
| NW | 5       | 5       | 5       |

DUNS 23-985-9502

## Profile Security Group Ltd

374 Wandsworth Road, London SW8 4TD
**Tel:** 02074983511
**Web:** www.profilesecurity.co.uk
**Reg No:** 3974254 **Estd:** 1980 Private Limited Company
**Line of Business:** Security and related activities
**Issued Capital:** £204
**Directors:** Hon J A Forbes, Brigadier A Parker Bowles, A Prendergast
**Co. Secretary:** Dharmesh Parekh
**Responsibilities**
**IT:** Lawson Simpson (Chief Information Officer)
**Branches:** Profile Security Group Ltd, Suite A, 17 Bolton Rd, Reading, Berkshire RG2 0NH
**US SIC:** 7393, 7399
**UK SIC:** 83954
**Auditors:** Meadows & Co Ltd

|      | 30-09-13   | 30-09-12   | 30-09-11   |
|------|-----------|-----------|-----------|
| TO   | 25,507,451 | 27,598,364 | 23,854,000 |
| P/L  | 197,976    | 292,209    | 227,000    |
| NW   | 582,732    | 556,844    | 421,000    |
| WC   | 26,178     | 46,001     | 143,000    |
| Emp. | 1,048      | 1,126      | 990        |

DUNS 50-349-9774

## Profile Security Services Ltd

(Subsidiary of: Profile Security Group Ltd)
220 Easter Road, Edinburgh, Midlothian EH6 8LE
**Tel:** 01315-547-527
**Web:** www.profilesecurity.co.uk
**Reg No:** 2371997 **VAT No:** 524688716
**Estd:** 1974 Private Limited Company
**Line of Business:** Security activities
**Issued Capital:** £100
**Principals:** A Prendergast (Managing), A A Troughton, Hon J A Forbes, Brigadier A Parker Bowles, M Mcgowan Scanlon
**Co. Secretary:** Dharmesh Parekh
**Responsibilities**
**Senior:** Graham Stirling (Regional Manager)
**Branches:** Profile Security Services Ltd, Bouncers Lane, Cheltenham, Gloucestershire GL52 5JB
**US SIC:** 7393 **UK SIC:** 83954
**Auditors:** Meadows & Co Ltd
**Bankers:** The Royal Bank Of Scotland Plc (83-49-40)

|      | 30-09-13   | 30-09-12   | 30-09-11   |
|------|-----------|-----------|-----------|
| TO   | 25,412,743 | 27,462,543 | 23,716,543 |
| P/L  | 318,368    | 359,787    | 303,238    |
| NW   | 880,557    | 743,996    | 561,015    |
| WC   | 372,197    | 274,997    | 304,606    |
| Emp. | 1,048      | 1,126      | 987        |

DUNS 73-454-5093

## Proflex Ltd

Hch House Horton Road, Colnbrook, Slough, Berkshire SL3 0AT
**Tel:** 01753689946
**Web:** www.proflexgroup.com
**Reg No:** 4718765 **Estd:** 2003 Private Limited Company
**Line of Business:** Cargo handling
**Issued Capital:** £1,000
**Director:** G G Collacott
**Co. Secretary:** Lee Collacott
**US SIC:** 4712 **UK SIC:** 77002

|    | 31-05-14  | 31-05-13  | 31-05-12  |
|----|----------|----------|----------|
| TA | 1,255,515 | 1,211,301 | 1,173,547 |
| NW | 990,750   | 914,468   | 807,134   |
| WC | 970,171   | 890,890   | 776,726   |

DUNS 23-526-9730

## Progility Plc

4th Floor, London EC4A 1BW
**Tel:** 02073-714-444
**Web:** www.ilxgroup.com
**Reg No:** 3525870 **VAT No:** 718825412
**Estd:** 1998 Public Limited Company
**Line of Business:** Computer training
**Issued Capital:** £3,993,338
**Directors:** M J Higgins, J J Mcintosh, P R Lever, W M Bos, J F Caterer, D J Stewart
**Co. Secretary:** John Mcintosh
**Responsibilities**
**Senior:** Paul Virik (Non-Executive Director)
**Marketing:** Debbie Sharples (Marketing Manager)
**Admin:** Sanela Jordamovic (Office Manager)
**Branches:** Progility Plc, Theale Lakes Business Pk, Moulden Way, Sulhamstead, Reading, Berkshire RG7 4GB
**US SIC:** 8299, 7392
**UK SIC:** 93300, 83951
**Auditors:** Grant Thornton UK LLP
**Bankers:** Barclays Bank Plc (20-00-00)

|      | 30-06-14   | 30-06-13   | 31-06-12   |
|------|-----------|-----------|-----------|
| TO   | 38,786,000 | 16,992,000 | 13,473,000 |
| P/L  | (325,000)  | (1,650,000) | 647,000   |
| NW   | (4,831,000) | (2,940,000) | (3,116,000) |
| WC   | (2,143,000) | (2,851,000) | (3,282,000) |
| Emp. | 213        | 79         | 87         |

DUNS 77-784-1701     Exp

## Program Planning Professionals Ltd

(Subsidiary of: Alten)
Lutidine House, 3-5 Crutched Friars, London EC3N 2HT
**Tel:** 02074620100
**Web:** www.pcubed.com
**Reg No:** 3025947 **Estd:** 1995 Private Limited Company
**Line of Business:** Project management services
**Export Sales:** £5,730,292
**Trading Style:** Pcubed
**Issued Capital:** £4
**Directors:** J D Sheffield, A B Flande, J Soula
**Co. Secretary:** Nicholas Crook
**Responsibilities**
**Senior:** Richard Siddle (Manager)
**IT:** Chris Cobb (IT Technical Architect)
**US SIC:** 7392 **UK SIC:** 83951
**Auditors:** Menzies LLP

**Bankers:** The Royal Bank Of Scotland Plc (16-33-24)

|      | 31-12-13   | 31-12-12   | 31-12-11   |
|------|-----------|-----------|-----------|
| TO   | 22,036,327 | 24,089,611 | 15,005,087 |
| P/L  | (835,357)  | 3,461,918  | 705,223    |
| NW   | 11,320,655 | 11,679,297 | 8,832,246  |
| WC   | 9,388,053  | 9,882,321  | 8,167,652  |
| Emp. | 164        | 174        | 133        |

DUNS 45-800-8091

## Progress Care & Education Ltd

(Subsidiary of: Progress Care (Holdings) Ltd)
Centurion House Leyland Business Park, Preston, Lancashire PR25 3GR
**Tel:** 01772623333
**Web:** www.progressschool.co.uk
**Reg No:** 3162312 **Estd:** 1996 Private Limited Company
**Line of Business:** Adult and other education not elsewhere classified
**Trading Style:** Progress Adult Care Limited
**Issued Capital:** £1
**Director:** M J Calvert
**Co. Secretary:** Ms Margaret Calvert
**Branches:** Progress Care & Education Ltd, Pear Tree Street, Preston, Lancashire PR5 6EZ
**US SIC:** 8249, 8321
**UK SIC:** 93300, 96111
**Auditors:** Horwath Clark Whitehill
**Bankers:** The Royal Bank Of Scotland Plc (16-23-31)

|    | 31-03-14  | 31-03-13  | 31-03-12  |
|----|----------|----------|----------|
| TA | 1,362,097 | 1,229,619 | 1,152,020 |
| NW | 771,892   | 553,268   | 460,560   |
| WC | 494,267   | 270,003   | 170,239   |

DUNS 23-276-9914

## Progress Care Housing Asssociation Ltd

Warwick House, Kilnhouse Lane, Lytham St Annes, Lancashire FY8 3DU
**Fax:** 01253642001
**Web:** www.progressgroup.org.uk
**Reg No:** 0028761IP **Estd:** 1998 Private Limited Company
**Line of Business:** Housing associations societies trusts & co-operatives
**Trading Style:** New Progress
**Principals:** A Argile (Chairman), A Argile (Chairman), E Bennett, E Bennett, W Counsell, E C Woodcock, S M Hall, J O'Neill
**Responsibilities**
**Senior:** R Bulloch (Designated Limited Liability P), P Whiteside (Designated Limited Liability P)
**US SIC:** 8321, 6732
**UK SIC:** 96111, 83100
**Bankers:** Barclays Bank Plc (20-82-18)

|      | 31-03-12   | 31-03-11   | 31-03-10   |
|------|-----------|-----------|-----------|
| TO   | 30,967,000 | 28,509,000 | 24,336,000 |
| P/L  | 4,169,000  | 2,496,000  | 1,592,000  |
| NW   | 48,136,000 | 39,951,000 | 36,500,000 |
| WC   | 3,604,000  | (1,704,000) | (248,000) |
| Emp. | 70         | 65         | 67         |

DUNS 21-735-5320

## Progress Cleaning Services (Whiteplume) Ltd

Unit 16 Solent Industrial Estate, Shamblehurst Lane South, Hedge End, Southampton, Hampshire SO30 2FQ
**Tel:** 02380225181
**Web:** www.progresscleaningservices.co.uk
**Reg No:** 0868367 **VAT No:** 188419423
**Estd:** 1966 Private Limited Company
**Line of Business:** Cleaning activities not elsewhere classified
**Issued Capital:** £4,299
**Director:** I D Robson
**Co. Secretary:** Kevin Robson
**US SIC:** 7349 **UK SIC:** 92300
**Auditors:** Leonard Gold Chartered Accountants
**Bankers:** Lloyds TSB Bank plc (30-99-20)

|    | 31-03-14 | 31-03-13 | 31-03-12 |
|----|---------|---------|---------|
| TA | 767,612  | 716,236  | 784,702  |
| NW | 401,083  | 392,558  | 404,376  |
| WC | 128,248  | 62,762   | 86,323   |

DUNS 23-209-8165

## Progress Housing Group Ltd

Sumner House, 21 King Street Leyland, Preston, Lancashire PR25 2LW
**Web:** www.progressgroup.org.uk
**Reg No:** 0028685IP **Estd:** 1998 Incorporate By Act Of Parliament
**Line of Business:** Housing associations societies trusts & co-operatives
**Trading Style:** New Fylde Housing Association
**Issued Capital:** £20
**Principals:** S Miller (Chairman), G Davies, V Jackson, C Struthers, Mrs F Smith, J Kazer, C Kushner, T Harrison

**Responsibilities**
**Senior:** Edna Caunce (Manager), Dorothy Foster (Partner), Adrian Jeffs (Designated Limited Liability P), Bryan Jones (Manager), Bernie Keenan (Executive Director (Housing, C), Tony Kelly (Designated Limited Liability P), Des Procter (Manager), Phyllis Whiteside (Manager)
**Finance:** Debbie Atherton (Operations Director (Finance)), Andy Spear (Financial Director)
**Marketing:** Tim Frier (Head of Marketing)
**Sales:** Eric Tamanis (Executive Director, Business D)
**HR:** Andy Spear (Financial Director)
**Facilities:** Philomena Cunningham (Operations Director (Progress), Bernie Keenan (Executive Director (Housing, C), Gary Melia (Operations Director, Housing,), Sue Whitham (Head of Housing Support)
**Operations:** Vicki Appleton (Operations Director (Developme), Debbie Atherton (Operations Director (Finance)), Tammy Bradley (Operations Director), Philomena Cunningham (Operations Director (Progress), Lynn Hurrell (Operations Director (Property), Gary Melia (Operations Director, Housing)
**Branches:** Progress Housing Group Ltd, 18 Welsby Rd, Leyland, Lancashire PR25 1JA
**US SIC:** 6531 **UK SIC:** 83400
**Auditors:** Beever and Struthers
**Bankers:** Barclays Bank Plc (20-82-18)

|      | 31-03-12    | 31-03-11    | 31-03-10    |
|------|------------|------------|------------|
| TO   | 59,803,000  | 55,840,000  | 51,211,000  |
| P/L  | 9,484,000   | 6,688,000   | 3,374,000   |
| NW   | 170,208,000 | 160,020,000 | 123,099,000 |
| WC   | 1,090,000   | (1,622,000) | 580,000     |
| Emp. | 486         | 459         | 457         |

DUNS 39-929-7621     Exp

## Progress Software Ltd

(Subsidiary of: Progress Software Corporation)
3rd Floor 3 Arlington Square Downshire, Way, Bracknell, Berkshire RG12 1WA
**Tel:** 01344360444 **Fax:** 01344 386301
**Web:** www.progress.com
**Reg No:** 2243974 **VAT No:** 491547717
**Estd:** 1988 Private Limited Company
**Line of Business:** Other software consultancy and supply
**Export Markets:** E U
**Export Sales:** £2,142,000
**Issued Capital:** £2
**Directors:** B Flanagan, S H Faberman, S H Faberman
**Responsibilities**
**Senior:** Barbera Ainsworth (Facilities Manager)
**Branches:** Progress Software Ltd, Craigie Hall, 6 Rowan Rd, Glasgow, Lanarkshire G41 5BS
**US SIC:** 7379 **UK SIC:** 83940
**Auditors:** Deloitte LLP
**Bankers:** Barclays Bank Plc (20-05-00)

|      | 30-11-13   | 30-11-12   | 30-11-11   |
|------|-----------|-----------|-----------|
| TO   | 22,686,000 | 30,090,000 | 39,662,000 |
| P/L  | 5,647,000  | 103,000    | 73,000     |
| NW   | 6,161,000  | 64,000     | (1,257,000) |
| WC   | 6,029,000  | (521,000)  | (1,916,000) |
| Emp. | 63         | 108        | 124        |

DUNS 23-282-9924

## Progress Supported Housing Ltd

Progress House, Lancashire Enterprise Business Park, Preston, Lancashire PR26 6TZ
**Tel:** 01772642113 **Fax:** 01772-450602
**Web:** www.progressgroup.org.uk
**Reg No:** 0029245R **Estd:** 2001 Private Limited Company
**Line of Business:** Housing associations societies trusts & co-operatives
**US SIC:** 8321 **UK SIC:** 96111
**Employees:** 150

DUNS 23-980-6883

## Progress Vehicle Management Ltd

Unit 13, Progress Business Park, Progress Way, Croydon, Surrey CR0 4XD
**Tel:** 020-8760-0714 **Fax:** 02086811220
**Web:** www.progressvehiclemanagement.co.uk
**Reg No:** 3969191 **Estd:** 2007 Private Limited Company
**Line of Business:** Accident administration & management services
**Issued Capital:** £1,000
**Directors:** G Mason, B P Keating, C D Hill
**Co. Secretary:** Richard Keys
**Responsibilities**
**Senior:** Mark Boret (Shareholder)
**IT:** Matt Ryland (Head of IT)
**US SIC:** 7539 **UK SIC:** 67100

|    | 30-06-13  | 30-06-12  | 30-06-11  |
|----|----------|----------|----------|
| TA | 3,091,659 | 2,815,902 | 3,164,933 |
| NW | 1,561,215 | 1,442,407 | 1,342,991 |
| WC | 1,221,946 | 903,875   | 338,559   |

DUNS 23-626-7829
## Progressive Building Society
Progressive House, 33-37 Wellington Place, Belfast BT1 6HH
**Tel:** 02890-244-926
**Web:** www.theprogressive.com
**Reg No:** 0000011D **Estd:** 1914
**Line of Business:** Building societies.
**Principals:** W Webb *(Managing)*, Mrs D Armstrong, Dr J Smyth, S Towe, J Hunt, I Doherty, D N Templeton, T H Quin
**Responsibilities**
**Senior:** Darina Armstrong *(Financial Director)*, Sidney Towe *(Head of Operations)*
**Finance:** Darina Armstrong *(Financial Director)*
**Marketing:** Louise Loughran *(Marketing Executive)*, Sidney Towe *(Head of Operations)*
**Sales:** Sidney Towe *(Head of Operations)*
**Admin:** Christine Hammel *(PA)*
**Health & Safety:** Diane Huey *(Head of Premises)*
**Facilities:** Diane Huey *(Head of Premises)*
**Operations:** Sidney Towe *(Head of Operations)*
**Purchasing:** Sidney Towe *(Head of Operations)*
**Branches:** PROGRESSIVE BUILDING SOCIETY: 11 Donegall Square South, Belfast, BT1 5JE, CO. ANTRIM.
**US SIC:** 6111 **UK SIC:** 81501
**Auditors:** Deloitte LLP
**Bankers:** The Bank Of Ireland (90-21-27)
**Employees:** 82

DUNS 73-461-2096
## Progressive Care (Derbyshire) Ltd
**(Subsidiary of:** Gdma Group Ltd)
Buxton Road, Leek, Staffordshire ST13 6NF
**Tel:** 01538386523
**Web:** www.progressivecare.co.uk
**Reg No:** 2911895 **Estd:** 1995 Private Limited Company
**Line of Business:** Other human health activities
**Trading Style:** Lily Bank Nursing Home
**Issued Capital:** £100
**Director:** S Ali
**Branches:** Progressive Care (Derbyshire) Ltd, Abbey Court Care Home, Buxton Road, Leek, Staffordshire ST13 6NF
**US SIC:** 8091, 8321
**UK SIC:** 95200, 96111
**Auditors:** Hawson Jefferies
**Bankers:** The Bank Of Ireland (30-14-58)

| | 31-08-13 | 31-08-12 | 31-08-11 |
|---|---|---|---|
| TA | 6,036,902 | 4,699,379 | 4,800,668 |
| NW | 1,638,599 | 697,844 | 1,098,050 |
| WC | (329,061) | (45,710) | 276,686 |

DUNS 23-935-5584
## Progressive Digital Media Group Plc
John Carpenter House, John Carpenter Street, London EC4Y 0AN
**Tel:** 0207 936 6400
**Web:** www.progressivedigitalmedia.com
**Reg No:** 3925319 **Estd:** 1999 Public Limited Company
**Line of Business:** Management activities of holding companies
**Export Sales:** £38,269,000
**Trading Style:** Affiliatefuture, Tmnmedia
**Issued Capital:** £153,184
**Principals:** M Danson *(Chairman)*, S J Pyper, B A Cragg, K S Van Musschenbroek, M T Danson, M Freebairn, P M Harkness
**Co. Secretary:** Stephen Bradley
**US SIC:** 6711, 7399
**UK SIC:** 83962, 83954
**Auditors:** Grant Thornton UK LLP
**Bankers:** Barclays Bank Plc (20-65-82)

| | 31-12-13 | 31-12-12 | 31-12-11 |
|---|---|---|---|
| TO | 57,306,000 | 53,902,000 | 54,353,000 |
| P/L | 7,148,000 | 4,291,000 | (7,948,000) |
| NW | 7,188,000 | 93,000 | (29,773,000) |
| WC | 10,892,000 | 3,155,000 | (11,369,000) |
| Emp. | 918 | 863 | 920 |

DUNS 21-783-6389
## Progressive Media Group
Progressive House, 2 Maidstone Road, Sidcup, Kent DA14 5HZ
**Tel:** 02082697700
**Web:** www.progressivemediagroup.com
**Estd:** 2007 Partnership
**Line of Business:** Publishers
**Partners:** S Pyper, Mrs J Chard
**Responsibilities**
**Senior:** Mike Donson *(CEO, Managing Director)*
**HR:** Christine Denning *(Human Resources Manager)*
**US SIC:** 2731 **UK SIC:** 47532
**Employees:** 100

DUNS 85-619-4261
## Progressive Recruiting Ltd
3-5 Rathbone Place, London W1T 1HJ
**Tel:** 02074695255 **Fax:** 02074695256
**Web:** www.progressiverecruitment.com
**Reg No:** 6212736 **Estd:** 1990 Private Limited Company
**Line of Business:** Sale or leasing activities of advertising space or time
**Trading Style:** Sthree
**Issued Capital:** £1
**Director:** S J Pyper
**Responsibilities**
**Senior:** Lawrence Doe *(Manager)*
**HR:** James Winfield *(Senior Oil and Gas Recruitment)*
**US SIC:** 7319 **UK SIC:** 83800

| | 31-12-13 | 31-12-12 | 31-12-11 |
|---|---|---|---|
| TA | 263,652 | 100 | 1 |
| NW | (145,162) | 100 | 1 |
| WC | (186,451) | N/A | N/A |

DUNS 21-305-7565 **Imp-Exp**
## Progressive Safety Footwear & Clothing Ltd
101 Worthing Road, Sheffield, South Yorkshire S9 3JN
**Tel:** 01142738349 **Fax:** 0114-275-2452
**Web:** www.psf.co.uk
**Reg No:** 0688039 **VAT No:** 173389535
**Estd:** 1961 Private Limited Company
**Line of Business:** Distribution service providers
**Export Markets:** Middle East
**Export Sales:** £20,142
**Issued Capital:** £8,000
**Managing Director:** H J Topham
**Co. Secretary:** Mrs Rosemary Topham
**Responsibilities**
**Senior:** Barry Kittle *(Manager)*
**Sales:** Hazel Walker *(Customer Services Manager)*
**Operations:** Hazel Walker *(Customer Services Manager)*
**Branches:** Progressive Safety Footwear & Clothing Ltd, Unit C1, George Henry Rd, Tipton, West Midlands DY4 7BU
**US SIC:** 4712, 5661
**UK SIC:** 77002, 64600
**Auditors:** John Clarke & Co
**Bankers:** HSBC Bank plc (40-41-08)

| | 30-04-14 | 30-04-13 | 30-04-12 |
|---|---|---|---|
| TO | 10,498,662 | 11,079,555 | 11,255,011 |
| P/L | 156,254 | 214,121 | 223,576 |
| NW | 3,020,568 | 2,881,215 | 2,773,041 |
| WC | 2,137,878 | 1,959,750 | 1,850,721 |
| Emp. | 62 | 63 | 64 |

DUNS 21-752-9676
## Prohire Plc
**(Subsidiary of:** Pgch Ltd)
React House, Spedding Road, Fenton Industrial Estate, Stoke-On-Trent, Staffordshire ST4 2ST
**Tel:** 08708-501200 **Fax:** 08708501201
**Web:** www.prohire.plc.uk
**Reg No:** 1388495 **Estd:** 1978 Public Limited Company
**Line of Business:** Fleet management
**Issued Capital:** £50,000
**Directors:** P R Jacques, P D Hassall, A P Morley, D Barlow, D B Barlow
**Responsibilities**
**Finance:** Laura Hughes *(Financial Controller)*
**Admin:** Laura Rushton *(Administration Manager)*
**IT:** Jim McAlinden *(IT Manager)*
**HR:** Arlene Shearer *(Training & Compliance Manager)*
**Operations:** Mick Steele *(Operations Manager)*
**Engineering:** Paul Fewkes *(Fleet Engineer)*
**Branches:** Prohire Plc, Richmond Ho, Sproughton Rd, Ipswich, Suffolk IP1 5AN
**US SIC:** 7399, 7513
**UK SIC:** 83954, 84802
**Auditors:** Deloitte LLP
**Bankers:** HSBC Bank plc (40-17-46)

| | 31-03-14 | 31-03-13 | 31-03-12 |
|---|---|---|---|
| TO | 22,651,441 | 18,784,705 | 19,122,029 |
| P/L | 1,413,185 | 872,058 | 1,497,636 |
| NW | 12,101,628 | 11,002,416 | 10,112,704 |
| WC | 12,872,090 | 12,902,974 | 9,456,863 |
| Emp. | 47 | 51 | 42 |

DUNS 23-492-8109
## Project Centre Ltd
**(Subsidiary of:** Aac Capital Partners Holding B.V.)
Level 4, Westgate House, London W5 1YY
**Tel:** 02074218222 **Fax:** 02074218199
**Web:** www.theprojectcentre.com
**Reg No:** 2625312 **VAT No:** 573314056
**Estd:** 1992 Private Limited Company
**Line of Business:** Other business activities not elsewhere classified
**Issued Capital:** £2
**Principals:** M Raisbeck *(Managing)*, Dr A H Palser, H Robinson
**Co. Secretary:** Sunil Shah
**Responsibilities**
**Senior:** Mark Raisebeck *(Managing Director)*, Neil Wisher *(Director of Transport)*
**Finance:** Rosemary Crampton *(Financial Controller)*
**Fleet:** Neil Wisher *(Director of Transport)*
**Engineering:** Clive Chapman *(Director Of Engineering)*, David Moores *(Technical Director)*
**US SIC:** 7399 **UK SIC:** 83954
**Auditors:** Deloitte LLP
**Bankers:** National Westminster Bank Plc (60-00-01)

| | 31-12-13 | 31-12-12 | 31-12-11 |
|---|---|---|---|
| TO | 5,774,000 | 5,835,000 | 7,199,000 |
| P/L | 150,000 | 593,000 | 951,000 |
| NW | 5,040,000 | 4,895,000 | 4,196,000 |
| WC | 4,863,000 | 4,644,000 | 3,898,000 |
| Emp. | 58 | 58 | 64 |

DUNS 22-816-4133
## Project North East
Turners Building 7-15, Pink Lane, Newcastle-Upon-Tyne, Tyne and Wear NE1 5DW
**Tel:** 01912616009
**Web:** www.pne.org
**Reg No:** 1715761 **VAT No:** 436290745
**Estd:** 1980 Private Company Limited By Guarantee
**Line of Business:** Architectural and engineering activities and related technical consultancy
**Trading Style:** Design Works
**Directors:** N R Clark, A C Jones, J P Strawinski, Mrs C Pilling, D T Mitchell, J H Oswald, T R Smith, Ms D Cranswick
**Responsibilities**
**Senior:** Neville Martin *(Director)*, Stephen Renals *(Manager)*, Caroline Talbot *(Manager)*
**Branches:** Project North East, William Street, Gateshead, Tyne and Wear NE10 0JP
**US SIC:** 7399 **UK SIC:** 83954
**Auditors:** PricewaterhouseCoopers LLP
**Bankers:** National Westminster Bank Plc (54-10-31)

| | 31-12-13 | 31-12-12 | 31-12-11 |
|---|---|---|---|
| TO | N/A | 1,513,675 | 1,735,393 |
| P/L | N/A | 31,462 | (140,727) |
| NW | 1,756,141 | 1,583,494 | 1,552,434 |
| WC | 1,602,348 | 1,426,653 | 1,386,397 |
| Emp. | N/A | 42 | 40 |

DUNS 23-645-5767
## Project One Consulting Ltd
5 The Clock Tower, Manor Lane, Holmes Chapel, Crewe, Cheshire CW4 8DJ
**Tel:** 01477-544462 **Fax:** 01477-544460
**Web:** www.projectone.com
**Reg No:** 3640772 **Estd:** 1998 Private Limited Company
**Line of Business:** Business and management consultancy activities not elsewhere classified
**Trading Style:** Project One
**Issued Capital:** £410
**Directors:** P E Clark, T P Holland, N A Finnie, I Hellens, P S Fennell
**Co. Secretary:** Mrs Janet Hellens
**Responsibilities**
**Senior:** Sandra Wells *(Manager)*
**US SIC:** 7392, 7379
**UK SIC:** 83951, 83940
**Auditors:** Baker Tilly UK Audit LLP

| | 31-12-13 | 31-12-12 | 31-12-11 |
|---|---|---|---|
| TO | 21,466,676 | 18,106,476 | 16,119,434 |
| P/L | 2,460,736 | 1,781,310 | 1,951,238 |
| NW | 3,517,918 | 1,644,900 | 2,180,208 |
| WC | 3,425,501 | 1,522,515 | 2,079,501 |
| Emp. | 91 | 80 | 71 |

DUNS 77-796-6052
## Project People Ltd
**(Subsidiary of:** Capital Investments and Holdings Limited)
Whitefriars, Lewins Mead, Bristol, Avon BS1 2NT
**Tel:** 01179-087000 **Fax:** 01179-254676
**Web:** www.projectpeople.com
**Reg No:** 3027453 **Estd:** 1995 Private Limited Company
**Line of Business:** Employment agencies
**Export Sales:** £8,342,569
**Issued Capital:** £50,000
**Director:** P J Koria
**Co. Secretary:**
Velocity Company Secretarial Ser
**Branches:** Project People Ltd, 150 Minories, London EC3N 1LS
**US SIC:** 7361, 7399
**UK SIC:** 83954
**Auditors:** Baker Tilly UK Audit LLP

| | 30-04-14 | 30-04-13 | 30-04-12 |
|---|---|---|---|
| TO | 119,179,563 | 115,508,241 | 114,040,059 |
| P/L | 1,005,436 | 1,073,678 | 1,231,009 |
| NW | 5,992,229 | 5,917,499 | 6,727,470 |
| WC | 5,673,509 | 5,524,743 | 5,130,103 |
| Emp. | 116 | 125 | 158 |

DUNS 23-830-8444
## Project Sloane Ltd
**(Subsidiary of:** Onward Holdings Co. Ltd.)
Unit 11, The Piper Centre, 50 Carnwath Road, London SW6 3JX
**Tel:** 02077362522
**Reg No:** 3822739 **Estd:** 1999 Private Limited Company
**Line of Business:** Other retail sale in non-specialised stores
**Trading Style:** Joseph Ltd
**Issued Capital:** £20,000,000
**Directors:** N Shimamura, A J Franklin, F Pene, H Takagi, T Shiraishi
**Co. Secretary:** Ms Catherine Palmer
**Branches:** Project Sloane Ltd, The Piper Centre, Unit 11, London SW6 3JX
**US SIC:** 5399 **UK SIC:** 65600
**Auditors:** Deloitte & Touche LLP
**Bankers:** Barclays Bank Plc (20-29-37)

| | 30-11-13 | 30-11-12 | 30-11-11 |
|---|---|---|---|
| TO | 70,613,174 | 66,935,274 | 68,178,174 |
| P/L | 3,369,270 | (36,595,459) | (1,637,107) |
| NW | (2,511,538) | (11,472,939) | (7,133,774) |
| WC | (25,781,504) | (31,664,418) | (27,511,346) |
| Emp. | 446 | 430 | 444 |

DUNS 21-686-5931 **Imp-Exp**
## Project Sugar Ltd
**(Subsidiary of:** Smiths Group Plc)
Venture House, Bone Lane, Newbury, Berkshire RG14 5SH
**Tel:** 01635-42363
**Web:** www.processequipmentspx.com
**Reg No:** 0032872 **VAT No:** 362550953
**Estd:** 1790 Private Limited Company
**Line of Business:** Architectural woodwork
**Export Markets:** Worldwide
**Trading Style:** Plenty Mirlees Pumps
**Issued Capital:** £2,300,000
**Directors:** R J Paddison, D H Tallentire
**Co. Secretary:** Adam Powell
**Branches:** Project Sugar Ltd, Unit 1 Pinfold Rd, Thurmaston, Leicester, Leicestershire LE4 8AT
**US SIC:** 8911 **UK SIC:** 83701
**Auditors:** PricewaterhouseCoopers LLP
**Bankers:** Barclays Bank Plc (20-67-59)

| | 31-07-13 | 31-07-12 | 31-07-11 |
|---|---|---|---|
| TA | 2,300,000 | 2,300,000 | 2,300,000 |
| NW | 2,300,000 | 2,300,000 | 2,300,000 |

DUNS 21-099-6618
## Project Tristar Ltd
7 Horton Industrial Park, Horton Road, West Drayton, West Drayton, Middlesex UB7 8JD
**Tel:** 01895433433 **Fax:** 01895446606
**Web:** www.viasat.se
**Reg No:** 6434912 **Estd:** 2007 Private Limited Company
**Line of Business:** Television and radio station operators
**Export Sales:** £14,855,000
**Issued Capital:** £840,800
**Directors:** M J Fogarty, A J Nash, D P De Beer, Ms J E Vinson
**Co. Secretary:** Andrew Hohne
**Responsibilities**
**Senior:** Hans Albrecht *(President)*, Marc Zagar *(Manager)*
**US SIC:** 4833, 7361
**UK SIC:** 97411, 83954
**Auditors:** KPMG LLP
**Bankers:** Barclays Bank Plc (20-71-06)

| | 31-05-13 | 31-05-12 | 31-05-11 |
|---|---|---|---|
| TO | 45,448,000 | 42,269,000 | 37,414,000 |
| P/L | 1,734,000 | 1,352,000 | 372,000 |
| NW | (3,066,000) | (4,628,000) | (4,247,000) |
| WC | (497,000) | (295,000) | 146,000 |
| Emp. | 580 | 617 | 655 |

DUNS 49-075-7093
## Projen Ltd
17 Rochester Row, London SW1P 1QT
**Tel:** 01928752500 **Fax:** 01606-871133
**Web:** www.projen.co.uk
**Reg No:** 3085241 **Estd:** 1995 Private Limited Company
**Line of Business:** Engineering, Architectural & Surveying Services
**Issued Capital:** £71,203
**Directors:** Capita Corporate Director Limite, D J Greenspan, R M Marchant, S J Birchall
**Co. Secretary:**
Capita Group Secretary Limited
**Responsibilities**
**Senior:** Martin Seabrook *(Manager)*
**Finance:** Marcus Royal *(Financial Director)*
**IT:** John Poppitt *(IT Manager)*
**HR:** Pauline Yeomans *(Personnel Manager)*
**Health & Safety:** Lyndon Workman *(Health & Safety Officer)*
**Facilities:** Mark Warrington *(Procurement Manager)*
**Purchasing:** Mark Warrington *(Procurement Manager)*
**US SIC:** 8911 **UK SIC:** 83701
**Auditors:** RSM Tenon Audit Ltd

**Bankers:** National Westminster Bank Plc (60-15-29)

| | 30-04-14 | 30-04-13 | 30-04-12 |
|---|---|---|---|
| TO | 10,163,000 | 12,907,000 | 13,440,000 |
| P/L | 584,000 | 619,000 | 604,000 |
| NW | 2,246,000 | 1,802,000 | 1,333,000 |
| WC | 2,110,000 | 1,621,000 | 1,127,000 |
| Emp. | 61 | 60 | 56 |

DUNS 73-281-2768

## Proline Corporation Ltd

14 Carraway Road, Liverpool, Merseyside L11 0EE
**Tel:** 01515481976 **Fax:** 01515481977
**Web:** www.prolinecorp.co.uk
**Reg No:** 4555028 **Estd:** 2002 Private Limited Company
**Line of Business:** Manufacturers of food products
**Issued Capital:** £100
**Directors:** P T Cogill, M Barnfather
**Co. Secretary:** Simon Barnfather
**Responsibilities**
**Finance:** Ruth London *(Accounts Manager)*
**US SIC:** 2099 **UK SIC:** 42399

| | 31-03-14 | 31-03-13 | 31-03-12 |
|---|---|---|---|
| TA | 4,434,327 | 2,585,029 | 3,692,039 |
| NW | 2,033,048 | 1,007,700 | 2,325,624 |
| WC | 1,868,409 | 828,468 | 2,183,703 |

DUNS 52-012-8034

## Prolinx Ltd

View Farm Barn, Windmill Hill, Great Milton, Oxford, Oxfordshire OX44 7NW
**Web:** www.prolinx.co.uk
**Reg No:** 3379531 **Estd:** 1997 Private Limited Company
**Line of Business:** Miscellaneous computer services
**Issued Capital:** £100
**Principals:** A J Weller *(Managing)*, G Styles
**Co. Secretary:** Michael Wheeler
**US SIC:** 7379, 7374
**UK SIC:** 83940
**Auditors:** Blackstone Franks Smith & Co
**Bankers:** Barclays Bank Plc (20-85-73)

| | 31-12-13 | 30-09-12 | 30-12-11 |
|---|---|---|---|
| TO | 16,201,101 | 16,323,269 | 17,756,669 |
| P/L | 81,766 | 1,143,599 | 2,206,135 |
| NW | 3,953,847 | 4,849,326 | 4,964,914 |
| WC | 1,967,105 | 2,592,234 | 2,876,437 |
| Emp. | 83 | 88 | 79 |

DUNS 39-872-9111

## Promanex (Civils & Industrial Services) Ltd

(**Subsidiary of:** Costain Group Plc)
Queens Road, Immingham, South Humberside DN40 1QR
**Tel:** 01469-574888 **Fax:** 01469-574224
**Web:** www.costain.com
**Reg No:** 2224393 **VAT No:** 455644921
**Estd:** 1968 Private Limited Company
**Line of Business:** Civil engineers
**Trading Style:** Costain
**Issued Capital:** £10,000
**Directors:** M D Hunter, D G James
**Co. Secretary:** Ms Tracey Wood
**Responsibilities**
**Senior:** Geoffrey Hunter *(Operations Director)*
**Finance:** Ben Howard *(Senior Finance Administrator)*
**Marketing:** Geoff Dunderdale *(Senior Marketing Executive)*
**HR:** Ross Mcfarlane *(Health & Safety Manager)*
**Health & Safety:** Ross Mcfarlane *(Health & Safety Manager)*
**US SIC:** 8911, 7349
**UK SIC:** 83701, 92300
**Auditors:** Duncan & Toplis
**Bankers:** Barclays Bank Plc (20-35-27)

| | 31-12-13 | 31-12-12 | 31-12-11 |
|---|---|---|---|
| TO | 11,276,190 | 9,281,950 | 15,791,615 |
| P/L | (1,569,066) | (519,170) | 273,747 |
| NW | 363,333 | 1,596,119 | 2,004,180 |
| WC | (375,403) | 682,407 | 1,290,035 |
| Emp. | 233 | 221 | 267 |

DUNS 29-312-7973

## Promart Manufacturing Ltd

(**Subsidiary of:** Promart Holdings (Uk) Ltd)
Caddick Road, Knowsley Business Park, Prescot, Merseyside L34 9HP
**Tel:** 0151-547-4666
**Web:** www.promart.co.uk
**Reg No:** 1751832 **VAT No:** 387409613
**Estd:** 1985 Private Limited Company
**Line of Business:** Catering equipment
**Trading Style:** Promart
**Issued Capital:** £10,000
**Principals:** A J Davies *(Managing)*, A Tarbuck, I P Hulse, Ms E Davies
**Co. Secretary:** Alan Davies
**US SIC:** 3551 **UK SIC:** 32441
**Auditors:** Campbell Woolley LLP

**Bankers:** HSBC Bank plc (40-37-21)

| | 31-12-13 | 31-12-12 | 31-12-11 |
|---|---|---|---|
| TA | 2,077,802 | 1,629,481 | 1,830,178 |
| NW | 1,377,033 | 1,023,909 | 981,483 |
| WC | 1,377,033 | 1,023,909 | 981,483 |

DUNS 42-413-6906 **Imp**

## Promat Glasgow Ltd

(**Subsidiary of:** Etex Sa)
Germiston Works, 348 Petershill Road Springburn, Glasgow, Lanarkshire G21 4AU
**Tel:** 01415586144 **Fax:** 01344-381301
**Web:** www.capepalsil.com
**Reg No:** 4401299 **VAT No:** 798758241
**Estd:** 1958 Private Limited Company
**Line of Business:** Manufacture of other products of wood
**Export Sales:** £11,435,000
**Issued Capital:** £6,500,000
**Directors:** N C Vanden Abeele, K C Sharp, I A Heijster, J D Stevenson
**Co. Secretary:** Neil Stopford
**Responsibilities**
**Senior:** Paul Van Oyen *(Manager)*
**Branches:** Promat Glasgow Ltd, Glasgow District Council, Petershill Road, Glasgow, Lanarkshire G21 4AA
**US SIC:** 2499, 3272
**UK SIC:** 46500, 24370
**Auditors:** KPMG Audit PLC
**Bankers:** Lloyds TSB Bank plc (30-12-18)

| | 31-12-13 | 31-12-12 | 31-12-11 |
|---|---|---|---|
| TO | 13,130,000 | 12,809,000 | 14,004,000 |
| P/L | (129,000) | 117,000 | 864,000 |
| NW | 6,827,000 | 6,944,000 | 6,829,000 |
| WC | 4,456,000 | 3,274,000 | 2,908,000 |
| Emp. | 87 | 91 | 94 |

DUNS 22-695-2893 **Imp-Exp**

## Promat Uk Ltd

(**Subsidiary of:** Etex Sa)
8 Sterling Centre, Bracknell, Berkshire RG12 2TD
**Tel:** 01344-381300 **Fax:** 01344-381301
**Web:** www.promat.co.uk
**Reg No:** 1785071 **VAT No:** 599657847
**Estd:** 1958 Private Limited Company
**Line of Business:** Manufacture of plaster products for construction purposes
**Export Sales:** £6,407,000
**Issued Capital:** £5,300,000
**Directors:** I A Heijster, K C Sharp, J D Stevenson, N C Vanden Abeele
**Co. Secretary:** Neil Stopford
**Responsibilities**
**Senior:** Yves Kerkhof *(Manager)*, Axel Scheidt *(Manager)*
**Marketing:** Adrian Clark *(Sales and Marketing Director)*
**Sales:** Jason Challenger *(Area Sales Manager)*, Adrian Clark *(Sales and Marketing Director)*, Ian Cowley *(Business Development Director)*, Andy Flint *(Business Development Manager -)*, Iwona Lipinska *(Marine Area Sales Manager)*, Erik Spillemaeckers *(Manager)*, Sam de Ville *(Area Sales Manager)*
**Health & Safety:** Nigel Morrey *(Health & Safety Officer)*
**Engineering:** Stephen Cristoforo *(Engineering Manager)*, Nigel Morrey *(Health & Safety Officer)*
**Branches:** Promat Uk Ltd, Victoria Works, Bonsall Street, Blackburn, Lancashire BB2 4DD
**US SIC:** 3275, 3272
**UK SIC:** 24370
**Auditors:** Ernst & Young LLP
**Bankers:** Lloyds TSB Bank plc (30-13-55)

| | 31-12-13 | 31-12-12 | 31-12-11 |
|---|---|---|---|
| TO | 27,254,000 | 29,749,000 | 27,192,000 |
| P/L | (612,000) | (49,000) | 1,683,000 |
| NW | 10,566,000 | 12,817,000 | 13,140,000 |
| WC | 10,344,000 | 11,237,000 | 9,287,000 |
| Emp. | 95 | 90 | 98 |

DUNS 21-005-9609

## Promatic Group Ltd

Station Works, Hooton Road, Hooton, Ellesmere Port, Cheshire CH66 7NF
**Tel:** 0151-327-2220
**Web:** www.promatic.co.uk
**Reg No:** 6305236 **Estd:** 2007 Private Limited Company
**Line of Business:** Manufacture of other special purpose machinery not elsewhere classified
**Export Sales:** £7,630,688
**Issued Capital:** £97,600
**Directors:** J D Moses, B Jardine, J L Goodhart
**Co. Secretary:** John Lamb
**Responsibilities**
**Senior:** Richard Daly *(Director On Board)*
**Health & Safety:** Martin Sambrook *(Health & Safety Officer)*

**US SIC:** 3559 **UK SIC:** 32863

| | 31-12-13 | 31-12-12 | 31-12-11 |
|---|---|---|---|
| TO | 9,579,208 | 8,938,074 | 8,187,010 |
| P/L | 282,557 | 460,918 | 263,234 |
| NW | (2,946,471) | (3,314,361) | (3,918,297) |
| WC | (3,363,401) | (2,676,810) | 1,041,423 |
| Emp. | 73 | 68 | 68 |

DUNS 21-102-3124 **Imp**

## Promedics Orthopaedics Ltd

(**Subsidiary of:** Yorkmarsh Ltd)
Gareloch Road Devol Industrial Estate, Port Glasgow, Renfrewshire PA14 5XH
**Tel:** 01475-746400 **Fax:** 01475746401
**Web:** www.promedics.co.uk
**Reg No:** 6455477 **VAT No:** 927148511
**Estd:** 2008 Private Limited Company
**Line of Business:** Manufacture of medical and surgical equipment and orthopaedic appliances
**Issued Capital:** £1,136,844
**Directors:** J C Wakefield, J C Wakefield
**Co. Secretary:** David Baxendale
**Responsibilities**
**Senior:** Martin McLeod *(Marketing Manager)*, Sheena Pritchard *(Financial Manager)*
**Finance:** Carol Leech *(Marketing Manager)*, Sheena Pritchard *(Financial Manager)*
**Marketing:** Chris McLaughlan *(Marketing Manager)*, Martin McLeod *(Marketing Manager)*
**Sales:** Glen Kiernan *(Sales Manager)*
**HR:** Lisa Harvey *(Human Resources Manager)*, Sheena Pritchard *(Financial Manager)*
**US SIC:** 3841, 3999
**UK SIC:** 37201, 49590
**Bankers:** National Westminster Bank Plc (60-08-46)

| | 31-03-14 | 31-03-13 | 31-03-12 |
|---|---|---|---|
| TO | 9,323,129 | 8,141,795 | 7,892,514 |
| P/L | 916,995 | 866,210 | 861,266 |
| NW | 3,535,987 | 3,210,426 | 2,953,690 |
| WC | 3,171,356 | 2,831,022 | 2,564,059 |
| Emp. | 125 | 123 | 127 |

DUNS 55-056-6939

## The Promenade Rest Home

10-12 Promenade, Southport, Merseyside PR8 1QY
**Web:** www.promenadecarehome.co.uk
**Estd:** 1978
**Line of Business:** Residential care establishments
**US SIC:** 8321 **UK SIC:** 96111
**Employees:** 50

DUNS 73-584-8819 **Imp**

## Promens Packaging Ltd

(**Subsidiary of:** Promens Hf.)
Halfway Cottage, Ellough Road, Beccles, Suffolk NR34 7TG
**Tel:** 01502718400 **Fax:** 01502718450
**Web:** www.promens.com
**Reg No:** 4846267 **VAT No:** 887131208
**Estd:** 2003 Private Limited Company
**Line of Business:** Manufacturers of plastic products
**Export Sales:** £7,252,000
**Issued Capital:** £9,301,000
**Directors:** J O Sigurdsson, A Platt
**Co. Secretary:** David Learner
**Responsibilities**
**Marketing:** Andy Salisbury *(Sales & Marketing Manager)*
**Sales:** Andy Salisbury *(Sales & Marketing Manager)*
**US SIC:** 2821 **UK SIC:** 25140
**Auditors:** KPMG LLP

| | 31-12-13 | 31-12-12 | 31-12-11 |
|---|---|---|---|
| TO | 65,529,000 | 68,862,000 | 71,240,000 |
| P/L | (1,012,000) | 2,775,000 | 3,028,000 |
| NW | 15,217,000 | 16,205,000 | 14,151,000 |
| WC | 15,161,000 | 16,611,000 | 14,262,000 |
| Emp. | 312 | 328 | 321 |

DUNS 50-335-0472 **Imp-Exp**

## Promethean (Holdings) Ltd

(**Subsidiary of:** Promethean World Plc)
Promethean House, Lower Philips Road, Whitebirk Industrial Estate, Blackburn, Lancashire BB1 5TH
**Web:** www.prometheanworld.com
**Reg No:** 2359658 **VAT No:** 572259918
**Estd:** 1989 Private Limited Company
**Line of Business:** Management activities of holding companies
**Export Markets:** Worldwide
**Issued Capital:** £2,601,719
**Directors:** Ms W Baker, J Marshall, I A Baxter
**Co. Secretary:** Ms Wendy Baker
**Responsibilities**
**Senior:** Jean Charlier *(Chief Executive)*
**US SIC:** 6711, 7379
**UK SIC:** 83962, 83940
**Auditors:** KPMG LLP

**Bankers:** Lloyds TSB Bank plc (30-90-87)

| | 31-12-13 | 31-12-12 | 31-12-11 |
|---|---|---|---|
| TA | 27,094,000 | 27,094,000 | 27,279,000 |
| P/L | N/A | (163,000) | 7,062,000 |
| NW | 7,100,000 | 7,100,000 | 7,263,000 |
| WC | 2,494,000 | 2,494,000 | 762,000 |
| Emp. | N/A | 2 | 2 |

DUNS 21-647-0117 **Exp**

## Promethean Uk Ltd

Promethean House, Lower Philips Road, Whitebirk Industrial Estate, Blackburn, Lancashire BB1 5TH
**Tel:** 0870-241-3194
**Web:** www.prometaean.co.uk
**Proprietorship**
**Line of Business:** Computer systems and software (sales)
**Responsibilities**
**IT:** Jeff Hewson *(Technical Manager)*
**Operations:** Jeff Hewson *(Technical Manager)*
**US SIC:** 2648 **UK SIC:** 47231
**Employees:** 300

DUNS 21-633-9840

## Promethean World Plc

Lower Philips Road, Whitebirk Industrial Estate, Blackburn, Lancashire BB1 5TH
**Web:** www.prometheanworld.com
**Reg No:** 7118000 **Estd:** 2010 Public Limited Company
**Line of Business:** Management activities of holding companies
**Export Sales:** £128,507,000
**Issued Capital:** £20,000,000
**Directors:** I A Baxter, Ms J Verses, J Marshall, Ms J Yeaney, G E Howe, P E Rowley, Lord D T Puttnam
**Co. Secretary:** Ms Wendy Baker
**Responsibilities**
**Senior:** Majeed Sharaf *(Senior Vice President)*, Ken Uhlig *(Senior Vice President, People)*
**Marketing:** Alistair Hayward *(Head of UK & Ireland)*, Lupita Knittel *(Senior Vice President, Global)*
**IT:** Steve Benfield *(President, Solutions Division)*, Morten Brante *(Senior Vice President, Service)*, Jeff Hewson *(Senior IT Executive)*, Darren Murrey *(Chief Information Officer)*
**Engineering:** David Pallant *(Design Engineer)*
**US SIC:** 6711, 6111
**UK SIC:** 83962, 81501
**Auditors:** KPMG Audit PLC
**Bankers:** Lloyds TSB Bank plc (30-16-79)

| | 31-12-13 | 31-12-12 | 31-12-11 |
|---|---|---|---|
| TA | 82,149,000 | 86,916,000 | 259,466,000 |
| P/L | (6,706,000) | (165,430,000) | 16,095,000 |
| NW | 36,794,000 | 37,986,000 | 58,838,000 |
| WC | 21,412,000 | 21,940,000 | 43,824,000 |
| Emp. | 686 | 868 | 885 |

DUNS 73-560-9294

## Promise Solutions Ltd

Fullard House Neachells Lane, Wolverhampton, West Midlands WV11 3QG
**Tel:** 01902585054
**Web:** www.promisesolutions.co.uk
**Reg No:** 4822774 **Estd:** 2003 Private Limited Company
**Line of Business:** Charities and charitable organisations
**Issued Capital:** £1,000
**Directors:** D F Roberts, S C Walker, Ms D M Round
**Responsibilities**
**Senior:** Dave Hydon *(Contact Centre Manager)*
**US SIC:** 6111 **UK SIC:** 81501

| | 30-06-13 | 30-06-12 | 30-06-11 |
|---|---|---|---|
| TA | 305,827 | 237,024 | 276,200 |
| NW | (508,145) | (779,836) | (555,212) |
| WC | 230,306 | 116,799 | 122,294 |

DUNS 45-855-5620

## The Propaganda Agency Ltd

(**Subsidiary of:** Access 13 Ltd)
2 The Calls, Leeds, West Yorkshire LS2 7JU
**Tel:** 01132372888
**Web:** www.propaganda.co.uk
**Reg No:** 3201640 **Estd:** 1992 Private Limited Company
**Line of Business:** Marketing consultants
**Issued Capital:** £10,134
**Directors:** C Harrold, J M Kynaston, B S Cameron, R J Mcmurrough, Ms L Kynaston, J A Horberry
**Responsibilities**
**Senior:** Kirsty Birks *(Manager)*, Nicki Casey *(Executive)*
**Marketing:** Kirsty Birks *(Manager)*
**Sales:** Claire Anderson *(Account Director)*, Sara Azar *(Sales Manager)*
**US SIC:** 7319, 7311
**UK SIC:** 83800
**Auditors:** Bissell & Brown

**Bankers:** Lloyds TSB Bank plc (30-94-43)

| | 30-04-14 | 30-04-13 | 30-04-12 |
|---|---|---|---|
| TA | 6,034,756 | 6,190,049 | 5,963,428 |
| NW | 4,537,619 | 4,523,236 | 4,209,395 |
| WC | 4,427,964 | 4,513,994 | 4,296,504 |

DUNS 22-639-4823 Imp-Exp

## Propak Sheet Metal Ltd

Unit 1 Gunnelswood Industrial Estate, Stevenage, Hertfordshire SG1 2BH
**Fax:** 01438-740298
**Web:** www.propak.co.uk
**Reg No:** 1328169 **VAT No:** 322244694
**Estd:** 1977 Private Limited Company
**Line of Business:** Engineers (general)
**Export Markets:** Europe
**Export Sales:** £92,900
**Issued Capital:** £50,000
**Principals:** B F Bennett *(Managing)*, A Child, P A Deamer, A D Hughes
**Responsibilities**
**Health & Safety:** Bob Blows *(Health & Safety Officer)*
**Facilities:** Steve Glennon *(Facilities Manager)*
**US SIC:** 3469 **UK SIC:** 31200
**Auditors:** Ernst & Young
**Bankers:** Lloyds TSB Bank plc (30-98-08)

| | 31-08-14 | 31-08-13 | 31-08-12 |
|---|---|---|---|
| TO | 7,609,577 | 9,191,450 | 9,407,748 |
| P/L | 603,785 | 263,248 | 551,027 |
| NW | 3,034,740 | 3,018,875 | 3,127,951 |
| WC | 3,187,021 | 3,063,699 | 3,295,552 |
| Emp. | 98 | 114 | 112 |

DUNS 21-875-4020

## The Propeller Academy Trust

Abingdon And Witney College, Wootton Road, Abingdon, Oxfordshire OX14 1GG
**Tel:** 01235555512
**Web:** www.kingfisher.oxon.sch.uk
**Reg No:** 8340120 **Estd:** 2012 Private Company Limited By Guarantee
**Line of Business:** Adult and other education not elsewhere classified
**Directors:** S Jackson, Mrs S Coneboy, B M Taylor, T A Stock, Mrs P A Hudson, J J Rideout, Miss T M Kelly, P Mcconaghy
**Responsibilities**
**Senior:** Karyn Buck *(Director)*
**US SIC:** 8249 **UK SIC:** 93300
**Bankers:** Lloyds TSB Bank plc (30-10-04)

| | 31-08-14 | 31-08-13 |
|---|---|---|
| TO | 3,633,937 | 14,638,669 |
| P/L | 45,987 | 12,734,064 |
| NW | 12,290,052 | 12,547,064 |
| WC | 623,196 | 452,632 |
| Emp. | 87 | 110 |

DUNS 34-977-0094

## Propeller Marketing Ltd

18 Main Road, Old Dalby, Melton Mowbray, Leicestershire LE14 3LR
**Web:** www.propellermarketing.co.uk
**Reg No:** 5772409 **Estd:** 2006 Private Limited Company
**Line of Business:** Marketing consultants
**Issued Capital:** £1
**Directors:** Mrs M H Sallis, J R Sallis
**Co. Secretary:** James Sallis
**US SIC:** 7392 **UK SIC:** 83951
**Bankers:** HSBC Bank plc (40-32-14)

| | 30-04-14 | 30-04-13 | 30-04-12 |
|---|---|---|---|
| TA | 21,326 | 7,040 | 17,341 |
| NW | 3,444 | 119 | 414 |
| WC | 2,900 | (609) | (1,529) |

DUNS 23-797-0483

## Proper Cornish Ltd

Western House, 9 Lucknow Road, Bodmin, Cornwall PL31 1EZ
**Tel:** 0120878712
**Web:** www.propercornish.co.uk
**Reg No:** 3789756 **VAT No:** 737243530
**Estd:** 1990 Private Limited Company
**Line of Business:** Other business activities not elsewhere classified
**Trading Style:** Proper Cornish
**Issued Capital:** £15,000
**Principals:** P R Ugalde *(Managing)*, P B Saunders, G S Allen, M H Muncey, C I Pauling, D M Jeffs
**Co. Secretary:** Mrs Yvonne Hollyoak
**US SIC:** 7399, 2051
**UK SIC:** 83954, 41960
**Auditors:** Francis Clark LLP

| | 31-12-13 | 31-12-12 | 31-12-11 |
|---|---|---|---|
| TO | 13,337,416 | 13,398,848 | 16,413,573 |
| P/L | 133,451 | 170,943 | 131,841 |
| NW | 1,126,239 | 1,016,033 | 1,150,251 |
| WC | (359,445) | (723,772) | (735,077) |
| Emp. | 224 | 208 | 244 |

DUNS 64-115-3627 Imp

## Proper Job Superstores Ltd

Unit 1 Heathcharts, Weston-Super-Mare, Avon BS24 9AY
**Tel:** 01278238422 **Fax:** 01934 641 567
**Web:** www.properjob.biz
**Reg No:** 4518696 **Estd:** 2012 Private Limited Company
**Line of Business:** Hardware
**Trading Style:** Proper Job
**Issued Capital:** £100
**Director:** P C Tilley
**Co. Secretary:** Raymond Tilley
**Responsibilities**
**Senior:** Michelle Cleverley *(Store Manager)*, Ross Wells *(Store Manager)*
**Branches:** Proper Job Superstores Limited, 1 Warrington Road, Bristol, Avon BS4 5AQ
**US SIC:** 3499 **UK SIC:** 31694
**Auditors:** Dunkley's

| | 30-04-14 | 30-04-13 | 30-04-12 |
|---|---|---|---|
| TO | 9,366,965 | 8,184,103 | 7,109,704 |
| P/L | 763,317 | 366,638 | 532,348 |
| NW | 2,750,701 | 2,185,214 | 1,944,198 |
| WC | 1,622,836 | 1,132,582 | 964,289 |
| Emp. | 125 | 108 | 98 |

DUNS 23-904-2919

## Proper Music Group Ltd

C/O Myrus Smith, Norman House 8 Burnell Road, Sutton, Surrey SM1 4BW
**Tel:** 02086765100
**Web:** www.propermusicpublishing.com
**Reg No:** 3894953 **Estd:** 1999 Private Limited Company
**Line of Business:** Other entertainment activities not elsewhere classified
**Issued Capital:** £950
**Director:** M S Mills
**Co. Secretary:** Mrs Miriam Mills
**US SIC:** 7999 **UK SIC:** 97913
**Auditors:** Myrus Smith
**Bankers:** Allied Irish Bank (gb) (23-84-86)

| | 31-03-14 | 31-03-13 | 31-03-12 |
|---|---|---|---|
| TO | 19,595,217 | 27,473,246 | 26,685,810 |
| P/L | 109,979 | 160,402 | 140,053 |
| NW | 1,690,592 | 1,687,626 | 1,670,449 |
| WC | 727,258 | 675,678 | 757,996 |
| Emp. | 130 | 133 | 107 |

DUNS 23-448-8880

## The Property Business Group Ltd

2 East Point, High Street, Sevenoaks, Kent TN15 0EG
**Tel:** 01732763660
**Reg No:** 2807233 **Estd:** 1993 Private Limited Company
**Line of Business:** Financial intermediation not elsewhere classified
**Issued Capital:** £13,325
**Directors:** D C Whittaker, S W Whittaker
**Co. Secretary:** Simon Whittaker
**US SIC:** 6111 **UK SIC:** 81501
**Auditors:** Barnes Roffe
**Bankers:** Barclays Bank Plc (20-67-59)

| | 31-12-13 | 31-12-12 | 31-12-11 |
|---|---|---|---|
| TA | 566,435 | 563,459 | 563,459 |
| NW | 419,250 | 419,250 | 419,250 |
| WC | (88,555) | (88,555) | (88,555) |

DUNS 42-442-4005

## Property Care (Complete Maintenance) Ltd

120 Brize Norton Road, Minster Lovell, Witney, Oxfordshire OX29 0SQ
**Tel:** 01993775511
**Web:** www.propertycareltd.co.uk
**Reg No:** 4430064 **Estd:** 2002 Private Limited Company
**Line of Business:** Property maintenance services
**Issued Capital:** £4
**Directors:** B S Nobbs, D I Beesley
**Co. Secretary:** Ms Angela Nobbs
**Responsibilities**
**Senior:** Paul Haydon *(Financial Controller)*
**US SIC:** 1799 **UK SIC:** 50000
**Auditors:** Fiscalis Management Ltd

| | 31-10-13 | 31-10-12 | 31-10-11 |
|---|---|---|---|
| TA | 1,626,043 | 1,424,746 | 1,241,199 |
| NW | 668,123 | 537,185 | 228,946 |
| WC | 431,318 | 348,434 | 47,794 |

DUNS 22-389-3640

## Property Cleaning & Maintenance

25 Buckingham Road, Shoreham-By-Sea, West Sussex BN43 5UA
**Web:** www.upml.co.uk
**Estd:** 1994 Proprietorship
**Line of Business:** Cleaning contracting commercial
**Proprietor:** M Ingram
**US SIC:** 7349 **UK SIC:** 92300
**Employees:** 50

DUNS 21-713-6179

## Property Consortium (Holdings) Ltd

Blackdown House, Culmhead Business Centre, Taunton, Somerset TA3 7DY
**Tel:** 08704441424
**Reg No:** 7531688 **Estd:** 2011 Private Limited Company
**Line of Business:** Management activities of holding companies
**Issued Capital:** £1,000
**Directors:** J Hyams, M J Brady, A C Tarrant
**US SIC:** 6711 **UK SIC:** 83962
**Bankers:** HSBC Bank plc (40-44-04)

| | 31-05-14 | 31-05-13 | 31-05-12 |
|---|---|---|---|
| TO | 21,247,462 | 14,172,526 | 10,581,614 |
| P/L | 2,000,434 | 1,233,249 | 371,056 |
| NW | 2,819,425 | 1,839,064 | 1,304,400 |
| WC | 2,472,842 | 1,550,526 | 1,050,094 |
| Emp. | 120 | 88 | 90 |

DUNS 45-806-1777

## Property Consortium U K Ltd

Blackdown House, Culmhead Business Centre, Culmhead, Taunton, Somerset TA3 7DY
**Tel:** 08452504400 **Fax:** 08452504401
**Web:** www.propertyconsortium.co.uk
**Reg No:** 3164160 **VAT No:** 662023859
**Estd:** 1996 Private Limited Company
**Line of Business:** Other construction work involving special trades
**Issued Capital:** £3
**Principals:** J Hyams *(Managing)*, M J Brady, A Tarrant
**Co. Secretary:** Jeremy Hyams
**US SIC:** 1799, 6411
**UK SIC:** 50000, 83200
**Auditors:** Albert Goodman LLP
**Bankers:** HSBC Bank plc (40-31-06)

| | 31 05 14 | 31 05 13 | 31 05 12 |
|---|---|---|---|
| TO | 17,637,126 | 12,044,259 | 8,799,607 |
| P/L | 1,118,162 | 492,271 | 37,678 |
| NW | 2,700,119 | 1,847,939 | 1,475,058 |
| WC | 2,537,387 | 1,709,198 | 1,316,641 |
| Emp. | 118 | 86 | 88 |

DUNS 23-720-6339

## Property Management Services (Ni) Ltd

**(Subsidiary of:** Golf Holdings Limited)
3 Duncrue Place, Belfast BT3 9BU
**Tel:** 02890754036
**Web:** www.propertyservicesplus.co.uk
**Reg No:** 0012481NI **Estd:** 1978 Private Limited Company
**Line of Business:** Comestics & beauty products retailer
**Trading Style:** City Belfast Warehousing, Shop 4 You
**Issued Capital:** £2
**Directors:** P M Hunt, J O Hunt, P M Hunt, J O Hunt, R J Davis, J P Hunt, R J Davis, P M Hunt
**Co. Secretary:** William Wilson
**Responsibilities**
**Senior:** Rasa Stontuviene *(Proprietor)*
**Branches:** Property Management Services (Ni) Ltd, 1A Pond Park Road, Lisburn, Co Antrim BT28 3LE
**US SIC:** 5999, 5399
**UK SIC:** 65600
**Auditors:** James P Convey & Co
**Bankers:** Ulster Bank Ltd (98-30-01)

| | 31-12-13 | 31-12-12 | 31-12-11 |
|---|---|---|---|
| TO | 44,995,013 | 45,706,166 | 45,981,791 |
| P/L | 531,471 | 481,680 | (728,483) |
| NW | 5,671,282 | 4,660,972 | 4,082,353 |
| WC | (22,043,912) | (22,180,993) | (22,299,496) |
| Emp. | 422 | 425 | 422 |

DUNS 21-052-6216

## Property Portfolio (No 15) Ltd

**(Subsidiary of:** Steinhoff International Holdings Ltd)
Unit G1 Crossley Retail Park, Carpet Trades Way, Kidderminster, Worcestershire DY11 6DY
**Tel:** 01562515330 **Fax:** 01708-869462
**Web:** www.harveys4furniture.co.uk
**Reg No:** 0884341 **Estd:** 1964 Private Limited Company
**Line of Business:** Furniture retail outlets
**Trading Style:** Harveys
**Issued Capital:** £100,000
**Director:** S Reents
**Responsibilities**
**Finance:** Trudi James *(Head of Finance)*
**Purchasing:** Graham MacDonald *(Purchasing Director)*
**Branches:** Property Portfolio (No 15) Ltd, Darlington Retail Park, Yarm Road, Darlington, County Durham DL1 4PU
**US SIC:** 5719 **UK SIC:** 64700
**Bankers:** Barclays Bank Plc (20-67-59)

| | 30-06-13 | 30-06-12 | 25-06-11 |
|---|---|---|---|
| NW | (46,746,000) | (46,746,000) | (46,746,000) |

DUNS 50-322-4800

## Property Portfolio (No 8) Ltd

**(Subsidiary of:** Steinhoff International Holdings Ltd)
Unit 1a, Accrington, Lancashire BB5 6NJ
**Tel:** 08456781800 **Fax:** 01254-770290
**Web:** www.sleepmasters.co.uk
**Reg No:** 2347258 **VAT No:** 525515654
**Estd:** 1903 Private Limited Company
**Line of Business:** Manufacture of mattresses
**Issued Capital:** £1
**Director:** S Reents
**Responsibilities**
**Senior:** Mark Cort *(Chief Buyer)*
**IT:** Andy Bolton *(Computer Manager)*
**HR:** Noel Jolly *(Human Resources Manager)*
**Health & Safety:** Paul Eckersall *(Health & Safety Officer)*
**Facilities:** Mark Cort *(Chief Buyer)*
**Purchasing:** Mark Cort *(Chief Buyer)*
**Branches:** Property Portfolio (No 8) Ltd, 24 The Sandlings, Ipswich, Suffolk IP3 9SN
**US SIC:** 2515 **UK SIC:** 46715
**Bankers:** HSBC Bank plc (40-15-17)

| | 30-06-13 | 30-06-12 | 25-06-11 |
|---|---|---|---|
| TA | 1 | 50,000 | 50,000 |
| NW | 1 | 50,000 | 50,000 |

DUNS 23-546-9785

## Property Renaissance Ltd

28 Kirkgate, Silsden, Keighley, West Yorkshire BD20 0AL
**Web:** www.titanickspa.co.uk
**Reg No:** 3545454 **Estd:** 1998 Private Limited Company
**Line of Business:** Property developers
**Issued Capital:** £100
**Directors:** D N Wilkinson, W R Burton, Dr D J Oates
**Co. Secretary:** Mrs Eileen Harrison
**US SIC:** 6552, 7299
**UK SIC:** 85000, 98902
**Bankers:** National Westminster Bank Plc (53-61-30)

| | 31-12-13 | 31-12-12 | 31-12-11 |
|---|---|---|---|
| TO | 4,013,414 | 3,628,126 | 3,496,683 |
| P/L | 422,080 | 268,528 | 665,533 |
| NW | 1,893,370 | 1,573,005 | 1,375,292 |
| WC | 293,764 | 178,736 | 77,010 |
| Emp. | 112 | 108 | 101 |

DUNS 29-178-4155

## Property Repair Network Ltd

**(Subsidiary of:** Veitchi (Holdings) Ltd)
12 Bouverie Street, Rutherglen, Glasgow, Lanarkshire G73 2RX
**Tel:** 01416132480 **Fax:** 0141-613-2489
**Web:** www.veitchi.com
**Reg No:** 0048563SC **Estd:** 2001 Private Limited Company
**Line of Business:** Insurance services
**Trading Style:** Property Repair Network Ltd
**Issued Capital:** £110
**Directors:** G T Duncan, J J Preston
**Co. Secretary:** James Stewart
**Responsibilities**
**Senior:** Alistair Rattray *(Manager)*
**Branches:** Property Repair Network Ltd, Unit 5, Rutherford Square, Livingston, West Lothian EH54 9BU
**US SIC:** 6411 **UK SIC:** 83200
**Auditors:** Geoghegan & Co

| | 30-11-13 | 30-11-12 | 30-11-11 |
|---|---|---|---|
| TA | 902,729 | 1,149,013 | 617,816 |
| NW | 303,304 | 311,739 | 316,113 |
| WC | 283,459 | 285,319 | 301,498 |

DUNS 23-614-4080

## Property Tectonics Ltd

Heywood Hall, Bolton Road, Manchester M27 8UX
**Tel:** 0161-794-9977
**Web:** www.property-tectonics.co.uk
**Reg No:** 3611608 **Estd:** 1987 Private Limited Company
**Line of Business:** Building consultants and advisors
**Trading Style:** Property Tectonics Ltd
**Issued Capital:** £620,784
**Principals:** T Mole *(Managing)*, A R Matthias, I K Haywood, Miss K J Young, Ms E M Brady
**Co. Secretary:** Miss Kathryn Young
**Responsibilities**
**Senior:** Philip Beswick *(Manager)*, David Bracegirdle *(Manager)*
**US SIC:** 8911 **UK SIC:** 83701
**Auditors:** Stafford & Co
**Bankers:** National Westminster Bank Plc (60-16-19)

| | 31-03-14 | 31-03-13 | 31-03-12 |
|---|---|---|---|
| TA | 1,119,310 | 1,102,542 | 1,268,045 |
| NW | 662,376 | 640,722 | 743,430 |
| WC | 620,140 | 588,049 | 671,449 |

DUNS 50-445-1014

## Prophet Plc

Unit 1 Villiers Court, Coventry, West Midlands CV5 9RG
**Tel:** 01676-525555 **Fax:** 01676-525556
**Web:** www.prophet.com
**Reg No:** 2432936 **Estd:** 1990 Public Limited Company
**Line of Business:** Computer software sales
**Export Sales:** £2,484,903
**Issued Capital:** £50,400
**Principals:** M R Peachey *(Managing)*, P Walker *(Technical)*, P A Seekins, T B Peachey, S P Wade
**Co. Secretary:** Mark Peachey

**Responsibilities**
**Finance:** Rebecca Begley *(Accounts Administrator)*
**US SIC:** 7379, 5081
**UK SIC:** 83940, 61490
**Auditors:** Littlestone Martin Glenton
**Bankers:** Lloyds TSB Bank plc (30-10-52)

| | 31-12-13 | 31-12-12 | 31-12-11 |
|---|---|---|---|
| TO | 5,758,594 | 5,796,171 | 5,135,668 |
| P/L | 709,438 | 735,275 | 925,448 |
| NW | 4,143,445 | 3,474,139 | 2,672,474 |
| WC | 2,947,728 | 2,419,076 | 1,656,545 |
| Emp. | 91 | 85 | 77 |

DUNS 22-760-9484
## Prophets Garage Ltd
**(Subsidiary of:** Penske Automotive Group Inc.)
120 Highlands Road, Shirley, Solihull, West Midlands B90 4NU
**Tel:** 0121-733-3444 **Fax:** 0121-733-1444
**Web:** www.sytnersolihullbmw.co.uk
**Reg No:** 1630936 **Estd:** 1982 Private Limited Company
**Line of Business:** Car dealers (used)
**Issued Capital:** £50,000
**Directors:** A Collinson, G E Nieuwenhuys
**Co. Secretary:** Adam Collinson
**Responsibilities**
**Senior:** Luke Phillips *(General Mmanager)*
**US SIC:** 5521 **UK SIC:** 65100
**Auditors:** KPMG Audit PLC
**Bankers:** National Westminster Bank Plc (60-80-09)

| | 31-12-13 | 31-12-12 | 31-12-11 |
|---|---|---|---|
| TA | 50,000 | 50,000 | 50,000 |
| NW | 50,000 | 50,000 | 50,000 |

DUNS 49-141-0171 Imp
## Prophotonix Ltd
**(Subsidiary of:** Stocker Yale (Uk) Ltd)
Sparrow Lane, Bishops Stortford, Hertfordshire CM22 7BA
**Fax:** 01279717171
**Web:** www.photonic-products.com
**Reg No:** 3110900 **Estd:** 1995 Private Limited Company
**Line of Business:** Manufacturers and distributors of electronic components
**Export Sales:** £5,275,136
**Issued Capital:** £200
**Directors:** T Losik, J Lane
**Co. Secretary:** Mrs Tina Lea
**Responsibilities**
**Senior:** Mark Blodgett *(Manager)*, Marianne Molleur *(Vice President of Human Resour)*, Simon Stanley *(Regional Managing Director)*
**IT:** Pete Gottlieb *(Head of IT)*
**HR:** Marianne Molleur *(Vice President of Human Resour)*
**Health & Safety:** Mike Foster *(operations director)*
**Purchasing:** Mike Foster *(operations director)*
**US SIC:** 3679, 5065
**UK SIC:** 34542, 61500
**Auditors:** Baker Tilly UK Audit LLP
**Bankers:** Barclays Bank Plc (20-36-98)

| | 31-12-13 | 31-12-12 | 31-12-11 |
|---|---|---|---|
| TO | 6,768,154 | 4,974,871 | 5,287,103 |
| P/L | (131,689) | (777,056) | 204,449 |
| NW | (197,686) | (65,997) | 711,082 |
| WC | (304,431) | (217,415) | 548,421 |
| Emp. | 46 | 52 | 45 |

DUNS 76-722-6368
## Proportion London Ltd
**(Subsidiary of:** Brightstar Capital (Proportion) Ltd)
Galatix House, 9 Dallington Street, London EC1V 0LN
**Tel:** 020-7251-6943
**Web:** www.proportionlondon.com
**Reg No:** 2597122 **Estd:** 1991 Private Limited Company
**Line of Business:** Manufacturers general
**Export Sales:** £2,290,303
**Trading Style:** Siegel & Stockman
**Issued Capital:** £833
**Directors:** R N Taylor, R H Mcpherson, M A Henderson, Ms T K Reynolds, Ms A M D'Marco, T J Billings
**Co. Secretary:** Thomas Billings
**Responsibilities**
**Senior:** Peter Ferstendik *(CEO)*
**US SIC:** 7399, 3999
**UK SIC:** 83954, 49590
**Auditors:** Blackstone Franks
**Bankers:** National Westminster Bank Plc (60-22-23)

| | 31-12-13 | 31-12-12 | 31-12-11 |
|---|---|---|---|
| TO | 7,591,037 | 8,770,035 | 5,840,866 |
| P/L | 1,875,344 | 2,300,923 | 1,195,653 |
| NW | 6,678,070 | 5,215,552 | 3,501,673 |
| WC | 6,030,065 | 4,510,602 | 2,991,949 |
| Emp. | 75 | 78 | 66 |

DUNS 21-683-5447
## Proquest Uk Holdings Ltd
**(Subsidiary of:** Proquest European Holdings Ltd)
The Quorum, Barnwell Road, Cambridge, Cambridgeshire CB5 8SW
**Tel:** 01223-215512
**Web:** www.proquest.co.uk
**Reg No:** 0934268 **VAT No:** 775406609
**Estd:** 1968 Private Limited Company
**Line of Business:** Management activities of other non-financial holding companies not elsewhere classified
**Trading Style:** Proquest Information & Learning
**Director:** J P Allen
**Co. Secretary:** Ms Larisa Avner Trainor
**Responsibilities**
**Marketing:** Casey Ward *(Senior Marketing)*
**US SIC:** 7399 **UK SIC:** 83954
**Auditors:** RSM Tenon Audit Ltd
**Bankers:** Bank Of America, Na (30-16-35)

| | 31-12-12 | 31- -11 |
|---|---|---|
| TO | 38,361,000 | 41,650,000 |
| P/L | 4,022,000 | 2,276,000 |
| NW | 16,775,000 | 18,291,000 |
| WC | 15,583,000 | 17,513,000 |
| Emp. | 282 | 296 |

DUNS 64-100-7224 Imp
## Proseal U K Ltd
Factory 1-2 Adlington Industrial Estate, Unit 10, Adlington, Macclesfield, Cheshire SK10 4NL
**Tel:** 01625-856600
**Web:** www.prosealuk.co.uk
**Reg No:** 3493138 **Estd:** 2003 Private Limited Company
**Line of Business:** Restaurant and hotel equipment
**Export Sales:** £7,258,885
**Issued Capital:** £120
**Managing Director:** R J Hargreaves
**Co. Secretary:** Stephen Malone
**US SIC:** 3551 **UK SIC:** 32441
**Auditors:** Bennett Verby
**Bankers:** Lloyds TSB Bank plc (77-67-08)

| | 31-01-14 | 31-01-13 | 31-01-12 |
|---|---|---|---|
| TO | 23,549,619 | 20,189,358 | 16,584,579 |
| P/L | 4,456,139 | 6,197,704 | 4,813,212 |
| NW | 18,550,622 | 17,369,186 | 12,768,906 |
| WC | 12,447,881 | 12,167,144 | 7,807,255 |
| Emp. | 191 | 152 | 135 |

DUNS 67-148-3147 Imp
## Proseat Llp
Site A Stakehill Industrial Estate, Touchet Hall Road, Middleton, Manchester M24 2SJ
**Tel:** 01616542500 **Fax:** 01616554433
**Web:** www.proseat.de
**Reg No:** 0323646OC **Estd:** 1996 Private Limited Company
**Line of Business:** Manufacture of parts and accessories for motor vehicles and their engines
**Export Sales:** £203,000
**Responsibilities**
**Senior:** Richard Harry *(Business Unit Manager)*
**US SIC:** 3714, 7399
**UK SIC:** 35300, 83954
**Auditors:** Deloitte LLP
**Bankers:** Kredietbank Nv (16-54-87)

| | 31-12-13 | 31-12-12 | 31-12-11 |
|---|---|---|---|
| TO | 24,469,000 | 23,937,000 | 29,501,000 |
| P/L | (345,000) | 18,000 | 1,613,000 |
| NW | 2,205,000 | (1,050,000) | (1,434,000) |
| WC | 7,687,000 | 7,359,000 | 6,225,000 |
| Emp. | 155 | 164 | 183 |

DUNS 50-480-1481 Imp
## Proserv Uk Ltd
Proserv House, Prospect Road, Westhill, Aberdeenshire AB32 6FJ
**Tel:** 01224-737-000
**Web:** www.proserv.com
**Reg No:** 0122029SC **VAT No:** 553016765
**Estd:** 1989 Private Limited Company
**Line of Business:** Renting of other machinery and equipment not elsewhere classified
**Issued Capital:** £1,000
**Directors:** D M Larssen, D T Lamont
**Co. Secretary:** Davis Larssen
**Responsibilities**
**Senior:** Erik Brodahl *(Manager)*, Gordon Downey *(Quality Assurance Manager)*, Christian Eriksson *(Manager)*, Stephanie Freeman *(Financial Controller)*, Phil Hunt *(General Manager)*
**Finance:** Eric Chapman *(Financial Controller)*, Stephanie Freeman *(Financial Controller)*
**Marketing:** Phil Hunt *(General Manager)*
**Sales:** Phil Hunt *(General Manager)*
**IT:** Eric Chapman *(Financial Controller)*, Mike Dalgarno *(Engineering Manager)*
**Health & Safety:** Edward Matthews *(Quality Assurance Manager)*
**Facilities:** Edward Matthews *(Quality Assurance Manager)*
**Operations:** Mike Dalgarno *(Engineering Manager)*, Edward Matthews *(Quality Assurance Manager)*, David Mcwilliams *(Engineering Manager)*
**Engineering:** Mike Dalgarno *(Engineering Manager)*
**Branches:** Proserv Uk Ltd, Unit 1 Empress, Walker Riverside, NE6 3NW Newcastle Upon Tyne
**US SIC:** 7394, 1311
**UK SIC:** 84000, 13000
**Auditors:** Ernst & Young LLP

| | 31-12-13 | 31-12-12 | 31-12-11 |
|---|---|---|---|
| TO | 54,759,000 | 17,092,000 | 14,596,082 |
| P/L | 8,083,000 | 1,427,000 | 947,030 |
| NW | 9,847,000 | 4,910,000 | 3,398,044 |
| WC | 44,621,000 | 10,039,000 | 5,004,471 |
| Emp. | 639 | 158 | 120 |

DUNS 21-008-0760 Imp
## Proskauer Rose (Uk) Llp
10 Bishops Square, London E1 6EG
**Tel:** 02075390600
**Web:** www.proskauer.com
**Reg No:** 0330064OC **Estd:** 1907 Private Limited Company
**Line of Business:** Legal services
**Responsibilities**
**Senior:** Roberto Bruno *(Non-designated Limited Liabili)*, Hazel Miller *(Non-designated Limited Liabili)*, Katherine Mulhern *(Designated Limited Liability P)*, Daniel Ornstein *(Non-designated Limited Liabili)*, Oliver Rochman *(Non-designated Limited Liabili)*
**US SIC:** 8111 **UK SIC:** 83500
**Bankers:** Barclays Bank Plc (20-00-00)

| | 31-10-13 | 31-10-12 | 31-10-11 |
|---|---|---|---|
| TA | 5,785,703 | 5,163,982 | 2,848,810 |
| NW | (19,252,549) | (20,692,170) | (11,920,657) |
| WC | 3,814,231 | 2,032,908 | 1,450,001 |

DUNS 73-367-1296
## Proskills Uk
85b Milton Road, Abingdon, Oxfordshire OX14 4BX
**Tel:** 01235833844
**Web:** www.proskills.co.uk
**Reg No:** 4640647 **VAT No:** 864641113
**Estd:** 2006 Private Company Limited By Guarantee
**Line of Business:** Activities of private training providers
**Trading Style:** National Skills Academy
**Directors:** J Ledger, Mrs J A Bazeley, I P Aspley, Mrs S J Wright, P F Latham
**Co. Secretary:** David Marett
**Responsibilities**
**Senior:** Terry Watts *(Chief Executive)*
**US SIC:** 7399, 8249
**UK SIC:** 83954, 93300

| | 31-03-14 | 31-03-13 | 31-03-12 |
|---|---|---|---|
| TO | 918,061 | 919,597 | N/A |
| P/L | (195,258) | (57,645) | N/A |
| NW | 511,256 | 737,346 | 794,991 |
| WC | 496,151 | 719,024 | 685,732 |
| Emp. | 13 | N/A | N/A |

DUNS 73-367-5644
## Prosource.It (Uk) Ltd.
Hilldowntree, Aberdeen, Aberdeenshire AB12 5YL
**Fax:** 01224-876643
**Web:** www.prosource.it
**Reg No:** 0242550SC **Estd:** 2003 Private Limited Company
**Line of Business:** Other computer related activities
**Export Sales:** £20,341,546
**Issued Capital:** £11,599
**Directors:** S C Proctor, S R Houston, A Cowie, C I Adams
**Co. Secretary:** Stephen Mackie
**Responsibilities**
**Senior:** Anuj Sikka *(General Manager)*
**IT:** Erin Brown *(IT Services)*, Emma Durrand *(IT Services)*, Craig Howie *(IT Services)*, Barry Lagerman *(IT)*, Danny Simpson *(IT Services)*
**US SIC:** 7379 **UK SIC:** 83940
**Auditors:** Acumen Accountants & Advisors Ltd
**Bankers:** Clydesdale Bank Plc (82-64-12)

| | 30-06-13 | 30-06-12 | 30-06-11 |
|---|---|---|---|
| TO | 44,536,749 | 30,389,271 | 24,510,619 |
| P/L | 6,992,586 | 3,258,387 | 3,515,853 |
| NW | 3,413,442 | 1,525,260 | 1,984,042 |
| WC | 3,538,614 | 2,000,392 | 2,139,774 |
| Emp. | 399 | 273 | 180 |

DUNS 77-000-1022
## Prospec Court Systems Ltd
Canklow Meadows Industrial Estate, West Bawtry Road, Rotherham, South Yorkshire S60 2XL
**Tel:** 01709377147 **Fax:** 01709-375239
**Reg No:** 2654999 **Estd:** 1991 Private Limited Company
**Line of Business:** Other construction work involving special trades
**Issued Capital:** £5,000
**Director:** R Mitchell
**Co. Secretary:** Jonathan Watkin
**Responsibilities**
**Senior:** Jérôme Bourquard *(Director)*, Brice Clavel *(Director)*, Olivier Estèves *(Director)*
**Branches:** Prospec Court Systems Ltd, 10 Manor Way, Bristol, Avon BS8 3UY
**US SIC:** 1799 **UK SIC:** 50000

| | 31-03-14 | 31-03-13 | 31-03-11 |
|---|---|---|---|
| TA | 5,000 | 5,000 | 5,000 |
| NW | 5,000 | 5,000 | 5,000 |

DUNS 22-533-8995
## Prospect
New Prospect House, London SE1 7NN
**Tel:** 02079026600
**Web:** www.prospect.org.uk
**Estd:** 2001
**Line of Business:** Trade unions
**Principals:** N Titchen *(President)*, D Pelly, Ms D Mcguire, C Marshall, A Gray, D Hudd, L Manasseh, M Clancy
**Co. Secretary:** Paul Noone
**Responsibilities**
**Senior:** Denise McGuire *(Vice President)*
**Marketing:** Sue Ferns *(Director of Communications & R)*
**Branches:** Prospect, Unit 4 Midland Court, Central Park, Lutterworth, Leicestershire LE17 4PN
**US SIC:** 8631 **UK SIC:** 96313
**Auditors:** H W Fisher & Company
**Bankers:** Unity Trust Bank Plc (08-60-01)
**Employees:** 65
**Turnover:** £12,995,000

DUNS 33-944-1099
## Prospect Business Centre
Prospect Street, Huddersfield, West Yorkshire HD1 2NU
**Estd:** 2002 Proprietorship
**Line of Business:** Secretarial services
**Proprietor:** M Jones
**Responsibilities**
**Senior:** Sheila Silverman *(Office Manager)*
**US SIC:** 7392 **UK SIC:** 83951
**Employees:** 150

DUNS 29-160-9337
## Prospect Coaches (West) Ltd
81 High Street, Lye, Stourbridge, West Midlands DY9 8NG
**Web:** www.prospectcoaches.co.uk
**Reg No:** 1785956 **Estd:** 1984 Private Limited Company
**Line of Business:** Coach and bus hire
**Issued Capital:** £200
**Director:** R A Hadley
**Co. Secretary:** Geoffrey Watts
**US SIC:** 4119 **UK SIC:** 72200
**Auditors:** Chartwells Accountants Ltd

| | 31-03-14 | 31-03-13 | 31-03-12 |
|---|---|---|---|
| TA | 2,071,992 | 2,149,792 | 2,150,303 |
| NW | 928,194 | 835,549 | 727,636 |
| WC | 8,384 | (108,921) | (173,908) |

DUNS 29-103-0369
## Prospect Hospice Ltd
Moormead Road, Wroughton, Swindon, Wiltshire SN4 9BY
**Tel:** 01793-813355
**Web:** www.prospect-hospice.net
**Reg No:** 1494909 **Estd:** 1980 Private Company Limited By Guarantee
**Line of Business:** Hospices
**Directors:** D P Maurice, C Bassett, Mrs A H Gillibrand, Dr L Whittam, Dr F Baskett, Mrs S E Pycroft, Mrs C Hallatt, D Barrand
**Co. Secretary:** Mrs Kim Austen
**Responsibilities**
**Senior:** Peter Alberry *(Director)*, Kim Austin *(Financial Director)*, Mandy Casavant *(Director)*, Douglas Looman *(Director)*, Penny Tidbury *(Director)*, Timothy Willis *(Director)*
**Finance:** Kim Austin *(Financial Director)*
**IT:** Reginald Ebanks *(IT Manager)*
**Branches:** Prospect Hospice Ltd, 26 Regent St, Swindon, Wiltshire SN1 1JL
**US SIC:** 8091 **UK SIC:** 95200
**Auditors:** Monahans
**Bankers:** HSBC Bank plc (40-43-35)

| | 31-03-14 | 31-03-13 | 31-03-12 |
|---|---|---|---|
| TO | 7,380,000 | 7,830,000 | 6,278,654 |
| P/L | 1,096,000 | 5,975,000 | 106,145 |
| NW | 9,083,000 | 7,860,000 | 5,696,123 |
| WC | 3,042,000 | 3,567,000 | 1,670,714 |
| Emp. | 135 | 127 | 116 |

DUNS 54-426-5879
## Prospect House (Malpas) Ltd
High Street, Malpas, Cheshire SY14 8NR
**Tel:** 01948-860011
**Web:** www.prospecthousemalpas.co.uk
**Reg No:** 3272727 **Estd:** 1988 Private Limited Company
**Line of Business:** Medical nursing home activities
**Issued Capital:** £2
**Director:** Ms C D Howell

**Co. Secretary:** Peter Howell
**US SIC:** 8051 **UK SIC:** 95100
**Auditors:** Bright Grahame Murray
**Bankers:** National Westminster Bank Plc (55-81-16)

| | 31-03-14 | 31-03-13 | 31-03-12 |
|---|---|---|---|
| TA | 2,544,427 | 2,243,489 | 2,298,865 |
| NW | 2,335,596 | 1,985,868 | 1,753,101 |
| WC | 133,446 | (154,804) | (429,097) |

DUNS 39-977-8653
## Prospect House School
(**Subsidiary of:** House Schools Group)
75 Putney Hill, London SW15 3NT
**Tel:** 02087800456
**Web:** www.prospecths.org.uk
**Reg No:** 2274105 **Estd:** 1988 Private Limited Company
**Line of Business:** Primary education
**Issued Capital:** £290,000
**Directors:** C P Rentoul, J A Rentoul
**Co. Secretary:** Anthony Rentoul
**Responsibilities**
**Senior:** Dianne Barratt *(Headmistress)*
**IT:** Victoria Jordan *(ICT Officer)*
**Facilities:** John Jonas *(Facilities Manager)*
**US SIC:** 8211 **UK SIC:** 93200
**Auditors:** Oxley & Co
**Employees:** 50

DUNS 23-022-6230
## Prospect Housing Association Ltd
Hethersett Centre, Redhill, Surrey RH1 4DG
**Web:** www.prospecthousing.org.uk
**Reg No:** 0026618IP **Estd:** 1989
**Line of Business:** Housing associations societies trusts & co-operatives
**Trading Style:** Prospect Housing Support Services
**Principals:** G Wadsworth *(Chairman)*, D Claridge, D Parker, S Hicks, A Wood, K O'Rahilly, R Hellyer, S Gosling
**Co. Secretary:** Ms D Tosler
**Responsibilities**
**Senior:** L Kong *(Designated Limited Liability P)*, K O' Rahilly *(Manager)*, Deborah Tosler *(Chief Executive)*
**Branches:** Prospect Housing Association Ltd, 33 Blanford Rd, Reigate, Surrey RH2 7DP
**US SIC:** 8321 **UK SIC:** 96111
**Auditors:** PKF (UK) LLP
**Employees:** 113
**Turnover:** £7,494,000

DUNS 21-319-6459
## Prospect Private Nursing Home
3 Old Galgorm Road, Ballymena, Co Antrim BT42 1AL
**Tel:** 028-2564-5813
**Web:** www.prospectnursinghome.co.uk
**Estd:** 1991 Proprietorship
**Line of Business:** Nursing homes
**Proprietor:** T G Mcmullen
**Responsibilities**
**Senior:** Lisa Ross *(Home manager)*
**Admin:** Lisa Ross *(Home manager)*
**US SIC:** 8051 **UK SIC:** 95100
**Employees:** 70

DUNS 21-580-1159
## Prospect Training & Recruitment
Unit C4, Brunel Court, Gloucester, Gloucestershire GL2 2AL
**Tel:** 01452886888
**Web:** www.prospect-training.org.uk
**Estd:** 2005 Partnership
**Line of Business:** Training providers
**Partners:** D Evans, D Pinnell
**Responsibilities**
**Senior:** Louise Pinnell *(Manager)*
**US SIC:** 8299 **UK SIC:** 93300
**Employees:** 50

DUNS 55-057-7035
## Prospects
Abbeydale Ground Floor, 24 Trinity Square, Llandudno, Gwynedd LL30 2RH
**Tel:** 01492878152
**Web:** www.prospects.org.uk
**Estd:** 1995 Proprietorship
**Line of Business:** Disability services
**Partner:** D Bond
**Responsibilities**
**Senior:** Tina James *(Practice Manager)*
**Branches:** Prospects, Ballybot House, 28 Corn Market, Newry, Co Down BT35 8BG
**US SIC:** 8699, 6732
**UK SIC:** 96902, 83100
**Bankers:** Lloyds TSB Bank plc (30-13-30)
**Employees:** 50

DUNS 37-873-3190
## Prospects for People With Learning Disabilities
69 Honey End Lane, Reading, Berkshire RG30 4EL
**Web:** www.prospects.org.uk
**Reg No:** 3305658 **Estd:** 1997 Private Company Limited By Guarantee
**Line of Business:** Social work activities without accommodation
**Trading Style:** Prospects
**Directors:** Lord D T Curry, M J Ledden, R I Wilson, Ms S Stephen, T Cordrey, D Polley, Ms E Tilly, G R Worsfold
**Co. Secretary:** Geoffrey Wilson
**Responsibilities**
**Senior:** Graham Beckett *(Manager)*, Steve Crowthers *(Human Resource Director)*, Mark Featherstone *(Director)*, Helen Preece *(Director Finance)*
**Finance:** Helen Preece *(Director Finance)*
**Admin:** Jennifer Brickwell *(Administration)*, Teresa Cutmore *(Administration)*, Christine Mackie *(Administration)*
**HR:** Steve Crowthers *(Human Resource Director)*
**Operations:** Mike Howard *(Director of Operations)*, Esther Kuganja *(Production Manager)*
**Fleet:** Caroline Buyu *(Transport Manager)*
**Branches:** Prospects For People With Learning Disabilities, 40 The Avenue, Bournemouth, Dorset BH9 2UW
**US SIC:** 7399 **UK SIC:** 83954
**Auditors:** Cansdales
**Bankers:** Lloyds TSB Bank plc (30-25-02)

| | 31-03-14 | 31-03-13 | 31-03-12 |
|---|---|---|---|
| TO | 12,424,189 | 11,184,920 | 10,362,608 |
| P/L | 149,755 | (429,656) | (272,887) |
| NW | 3,541,989 | 3,342,806 | 3,914,175 |
| WC | 885,445 | 406,984 | 1,322,884 |
| Emp. | 319 | 1,007 | 323 |

DUNS 73-792-5669
## Prospects for Young People Ltd
Ash Road South, Wrexham, Clwyd LL13 9UG
**Tel:** 01978313777
**Web:** http://prospectscare.co.uk
**Reg No:** 2927657 **Estd:** 1994 Private Limited Company
**Line of Business:** Representative office
**Issued Capital:** £50,000
**Managing Directors:** C J Edwards, S J Elliott
**Co. Secretary:** Christopher Edwards
**Branches:** Prospects For Young People Ltd, Pentresaeson Hall Brymbo Rd, Wrexham, Clwyd LL11 5UA
**US SIC:** 7399, 8999
**UK SIC:** 83954
**Auditors:** PKF
**Bankers:** Barclays Bank Plc (20-25-69)

| | 30-06-14 | 30-06-13 | 30-06-12 |
|---|---|---|---|
| TA | 3,472,869 | 3,115,647 | 2,887,375 |
| NW | 1,418,672 | 1,296,723 | 1,151,619 |
| WC | (344,080) | (427,964) | (814,017) |

DUNS 28-864-5849
## Prospects Learning Foundation Ltd
Upper College Building, Southchurch Boulevard, Southend-On-Sea, Essex SS2 4XA
**Tel:** 01702415500
**Web:** www.prospectscollege.com
**Reg No:** 0949411 **VAT No:** 420633881
**Estd:** 2002 Private Company Limited By Guarantee
**Line of Business:** Further education schools and colleges
**Trading Style:** Prospects
**Directors:** N R Bates, B Clark, Ms T Carter, L T Steel
**Co. Secretary:** Alistair Grocock
**Responsibilities**
**Senior:** Janet Hodges *(non executive Director)*, Roy Newham *(Manager)*
**Branches:** Prospects Learning Foundation Ltd, 83 Vanguard Way, Southend-On-Sea, Essex SS3 9QY
**US SIC:** 8299 **UK SIC:** 93300
**Auditors:** Rickard Keen
**Bankers:** National Westminster Bank Plc (55-50-28)

| | 31-07-13 | 31-07-12 | 31-07-11 |
|---|---|---|---|
| TO | 7,585,494 | 8,834,119 | 7,152,145 |
| P/L | 165,165 | 2,233,659 | (932,147) |
| NW | 24,129,553 | 23,966,649 | 21,732,990 |
| WC | 364,254 | 1,061,127 | 511,962 |
| Emp. | 115 | 108 | 119 |

DUNS 23-732-0205
## Prospects Services
(**Subsidiary of:** Prospects Group 2011 Ltd)
19 Elmfield Road, Bromley, Kent BR1 1LT
**Tel:** 02083-151500 **Fax:** 02083151549
**Web:** www.prospects.co.uk
**Reg No:** 3042176 **Estd:** 1996 Private Unlimited Company
**Line of Business:** Training providers
**Directors:** Ms A R Williams, J N Bell, Mrs B P Cabras, K M Beerling, P Mcgee, B Rowbotham, T J Simpson, M L Iley
**Co. Secretary:** Miss Catherine Trevorrow
**Responsibilities**
**Senior:** Raymond Auvray *(Chief Executive)*, John Gaskin *(Manager)*, Peter Heaviside *(Manager)*, Carol Lee *(PA to Chief Executive)*, Vincent McDonnell *(Manager)*, Vincent Mcdonald *(Manager)*
**Marketing:** Stephanie Brain *(Digital Marketing Manager)*
**Health & Safety:** Bill Lockwood *(Health & Safety Officer)*
**Facilities:** Dapo Williams *(Facilities Manager)*
**Operations:** Victoria Blakeman *(Director of Offender Managemen)*, Kalpana Patel *(Programme Director)*, John Theedom *(Interim Director - Early Years)*
**Branches:** Prospects Services, 19 Elmfield Road, Bromley, Kent BR1 1LT
**US SIC:** 8299, 8211
**UK SIC:** 93300, 93200
**Auditors:** Grant Thornton UK LLP
**Bankers:** Barclays Bank Plc (20-06-72)

| | 31-03-14 | 31-03-13 | 31-03-12 |
|---|---|---|---|
| TO | 76,241,000 | 64,021,000 | 71,904,000 |
| P/L | 1,714,000 | 2,860,000 | 2,897,000 |
| NW | (9,033,000) | (5,913,000) | (11,251,000) |
| WC | 1,610,000 | 1,070,000 | 1,308,000 |
| Emp. | 1,210 | 1,108 | 1,157 |

DUNS 34-697-3709
## Prospects Training International Ltd
(**Subsidiary of:** Geason Holdings Ltd)
The Art House, 752-756 Argyle Street, Glasgow, Lanarkshire G3 8UJ
**Tel:** 01412485755
**Reg No:** 0287175SC **Estd:** 2005 Private Limited Company
**Line of Business:** Activities of private training providers
**Issued Capital:** £100
**Directors:** I G Kilpatrick, M Atkinson, I G Kilpatrick
**US SIC:** 7399 **UK SIC:** 83954
**Bankers:** The Royal Bank Of Scotland Plc (83-00-40)

| | 30-11-13 | 30-11-12 | 30-11-11 |
|---|---|---|---|
| TA | 848,626 | 901,911 | 460,935 |
| NW | 294,850 | 327,219 | 29,680 |
| WC | 273,026 | 301,751 | 18,293 |

DUNS 29-073-6586 **Imp-Exp**
## Prosper (2006) Ltd
(**Subsidiary of:** Sas Flovima)
67 Third Avenue, Pensnett Trading Estate, Brierley Hill, West Midlands DY6 7FA
**Tel:** 01384-400321
**Web:** www.midsteelgroup.com
**Reg No:** 1314153 **VAT No:** 547437031
**Estd:** 1983 Private Limited Company
**Line of Business:** Manufacturers of bolts and fixings
**Export Markets:** Middle East
**Issued Capital:** £20,000
**Principals:** M G Boulter *(Managing)*, Ms K I Charbonnier, H A Charbonnier
**Co. Secretary:** Timothy Rogers
**US SIC:** 3452 **UK SIC:** 31371
**Auditors:** Dafferns LLP
**Bankers:** Barclays Bank Plc (20-27-17)

| | 30-06-13 | 30-06-12 | 30-06-11 |
|---|---|---|---|
| TA | 22,129 | 22,129 | 22,129 |
| NW | 22,129 | 22,129 | 22,129 |

DUNS 76-999-4815
## Prostate Cancer Uk
Fourth Floor, London SE1 2QN
**Tel:** 02033107000
**Web:** http://prostatecanceruk.org
**Reg No:** 2653887 **Estd:** 1991 Private Company Limited By Guarantee
**Line of Business:** Retail sale of other second-hand goods in stores
**Trading Style:** The Prostate Cancer Charity
**Directors:** Dr C H Adams, H F Richardson, R F Kelly, Ms S J Thorne, C Smith, Professor J Waxman, Professor R S Kirby, L L Racke
**Co. Secretary:** Mrs Angela Culhane
**Responsibilities**
**Senior:** Mark Britnell *(Director)*, Alfred Forster *(Trustee)*, Sharon Fraser *(Trustee)*, Ruth Holdaway *(Operations Director)*, David Pretty *(Director)*

**Marketing:** Ellie Brooke *(Senior Media & PR Officer)*, Emma Fielder *(Media and PR Manager)*, Mary Frampton *(Media Relations Manager)*, Vivienne Francis *(Communications Director)*, Alistair Haw *(Head of Media and PR)*
**Health & Safety:** Angela Jura *(Head of Central Services)*
**Facilities:** Angela Jura *(Head of Central Services)*
**US SIC:** 7399, 8922, 8091, 8321
**UK SIC:** 83954, 94000, 95200, 96111
**Auditors:** MHA MacIntyre Hudson
**Bankers:** Barclays Bank Plc (20-01-89)

| | 31-03-14 | 31-03-13 | 31-03-12 |
|---|---|---|---|
| TO | 31,125,000 | 29,377,000 | 23,330,000 |
| P/L | (10,028,000) | 8,683,000 | 12,879,000 |
| NW | 23,218,000 | 33,246,000 | 24,534,000 |
| WC | 36,849,000 | 36,265,000 | 26,065,000 |
| Emp. | 185 | 139 | 102 |

DUNS 49-433-3511
## Protaform Holdings Ltd
(**Subsidiary of:** Whitemoor Manufacturing Ltd)
Orchard Works, 76 Arthur Street, Redditch, Worcestershire B98 8LJ
**Tel:** 01527-517500 **Fax:** 01527-502373
**Web:** www.protaform.com
**Reg No:** 3144318 **VAT No:** 661547820
**Estd:** 1973 Private Limited Company
**Line of Business:** Management of real estate on a fee or contract basis
**Issued Capital:** £50,000
**Managing Director:** G D Fagg
**Co. Secretary:** Paul Taylor
**Responsibilities**
**Senior:** David Buggins *(Manager)*
**Marketing:** Graham Allison *(Sales Manager)*
**Sales:** Graham Allison *(Sales Manager)*
**US SIC:** 6531, 6711
**UK SIC:** 83400, 83962
**Auditors:** Guest Wilson
**Bankers:** National Westminster Bank Plc (54-30-35)

| | 31-03-14 | 31-03-13 | 31-03-12 |
|---|---|---|---|
| TA | 2,185,410 | 2,134,641 | 2,101,569 |
| NW | 546,004 | 756,202 | 893,437 |
| WC | (541,641) | (395,929) | (481,628) |

DUNS 73-957-4460
## Protea Technology International Ltd
71 Faulkland View, Peasedown St John, Bath, Avon BA2 8TP
**Tel:** 01761-432164
**Reg No:** 5208646 **Estd:** 2004 Private Limited Company
**Line of Business:** Other business activities not elsewhere classified
**Issued Capital:** £2
**Director:** R B Sharples
**Co. Secretary:** Ms Joan Sharples
**US SIC:** 7399 **UK SIC:** 83954

| | 31-08-13 | 31-08-12 | 31-08-11 |
|---|---|---|---|
| TA | 2 | 2 | 2 |
| NW | 2 | 2 | 2 |

DUNS 21-143-9660 **Imp**
## Protean Electric Ltd
Silvertree Unit 10b, Coxbridge Business Park, Alton Road, Farnham, Surrey GU10 5EH
**Tel:** 01252-741-800
**Web:** www.proteanelectric.com
**Reg No:** 6747884 **Estd:** 2008 Private Limited Company
**Line of Business:** Research and experimental development on natural sciences and engineering
**Issued Capital:** £8,629,975
**Co. Secretary:** Nicholas Rich
**Responsibilities**
**Senior:** Robert Purcell *(Manager)*
**Engineering:** Mark Potter *(Principal Engineer)*
**US SIC:** 7391 **UK SIC:** 94000
**Auditors:** Deloitte LLP
**Bankers:** HSBC Bank plc (40-05-30)

| | 31-12-13 | 31-12-12 | 31-12-11 |
|---|---|---|---|
| TO | 122,774 | 479,318 | 465,966 |
| P/L | (12,387,094) | (13,598,197) | (13,398,261) |
| NW | (7,805,906) | (4,606,559) | (4,146,962) |
| WC | 3,848,485 | 618,349 | 747,427 |
| Emp. | 52 | 60 | 62 |

DUNS 29-821-1566 **Imp-Exp**
## Protec Fire & Security Group Ltd
Protec House, Churchill Way, Nelson, Lancashire BB9 6RT
**Web:** www.protec.co.uk
**Reg No:** 2039210 **VAT No:** 444844924
**Estd:** 1986 Private Limited Company
**Line of Business:** Wholesale of radio and television goods; wholesale of electrical household appliances not elsewhere classified
**Export Markets:** Republic of Ireland; Europe
**Export Sales:** £17,443,414

**Trading Style:** Protec Fire Protection Plc
**Issued Capital:** £50,000
**Chairman:** B Russell
**Co. Secretary:** Thomas Fairnie
**Responsibilities**
**IT:** Vinod Varkey (IT Manager), Luke Vaughan (IT Support)
**HR:** Zoe Richardson (Human Resources Manager)
**Operations:** Robert Cash (Project Manager), Dermot McArdle (Production Director), Damian Parker (Operations Manager)
**Engineering:** Dermot McArdle (Production Director), Aimmee Simpson (Engineer)
**Branches:** Protec Fire & Security Group Ltd, 25 Hackett Way, Fareham Enterprise Centre, Fareham, Hampshire PO14 1TH
**US SIC:** 5064, 5065
**UK SIC:** 61500
**Auditors:** KPMG LLP
**Bankers:** Barclays Bank Plc (20-15-70)

|     | 31-08-13 | 31-08-12 | 31-08-11 |
|-----|----------|----------|----------|
| TO  | 81,672,091 | 77,943,070 | 74,145,272 |
| P/L | 11,686,959 | 11,403,839 | 11,649,821 |
| NW  | 50,996,218 | 49,572,019 | 43,342,317 |
| WC  | 43,062,880 | 44,037,644 | 38,811,801 |
| Emp.| 965 | 891 | 865 |

DUNS 23-602-3425
## Protectagroup Ltd
Motaquote House, Dinas Isaf Industrial Estate, Tonypandy, Mid Glamorgan CF40 1NY
**Tel:** 01443-420700
**Web:** www.protectagrp.com
**Reg No:** 3599653 **Estd:** 1999 Private Limited Company
**Line of Business:** Non-life insurance
**Issued Capital:** £8,804,710
**Directors:** A D Lyons, S Egan
**Co. Secretary:** Ms Jennifer Owens
**Responsibilities**
**Senior:** Samuel Clark (Manager), Nigel Lombard (Manager), Kenneth Powell (Manager)
**US SIC:** 6399 **UK SIC:** 82001
**Auditors:** KTS Owens Thomas Ltd

|     | 31-12-13 | 31-12-12 | 31-12-11 |
|-----|----------|----------|----------|
| TO  | N/A | 5,524,655 | 9,575,814 |
| P/L | N/A | 15,570,994 | 1,276,465 |
| NW  | 9,009,042 | 9,009,042 | 7,653,372 |
| WC  | 9,008,942 | 9,008,942 | 7,792,224 |
| Emp.| N/A | 123 | 143 |

DUNS 50-046-5810     Imp
## Protective Packaging Ltd
(**Subsidiary of:** Betronics Ltd)
Dane Road Industrial Estate, Dane Road, Sale, Sale, Cheshire M33 7BH
**Tel:** 0161-976-2006
**Web:** www.protpack.com
**Reg No:** 2312465 **VAT No:** 519596993
**Estd:** 1988 Private Limited Company
**Line of Business:** Packaging equipment
**Issued Capital:** £5,000
**Principals:** S Jolly (Managing), C G Lewis
**Co. Secretary:** James Law
**Responsibilities**
**Senior:** John Mollyneux (Joint Managing Director)
**IT:** Andy Thompson (IT Manager)
**Health & Safety:** John Mollyneux (Joint Managing Director)
**US SIC:** 2654, 5199
**UK SIC:** 47280, 61900
**Auditors:** Ernst & Young LLP
**Bankers:** The Royal Bank Of Scotland Plc (16-12-11)

|     | 31-12-13 | 31-12-12 | 31-12-11 |
|-----|----------|----------|----------|
| TO  | 10,398,575 | 10,295,527 | 10,905,618 |
| P/L | 3,463,455 | 3,302,649 | 3,474,767 |
| NW  | 2,672,426 | 2,511,721 | 2,326,986 |
| WC  | 2,561,693 | 2,393,975 | 2,188,179 |
| Emp.| 62 | 62 | 64 |

DUNS 21-785-6622
## Protektor
Systems House Hoo Farm Industria, Worcester Road, Kidderminster, Worcestershire DY11 7RA
**Tel:** 01562515200
**Web:** www.protector.com
**Estd:** 1978 Proprietorship
**Line of Business:** Builders merchants
**Proprietor:** P Broadfield
**Responsibilities**
**Senior:** Thomas Maisch (Manager), Julie Whitehouse (Manager)
**Sales:** Christopher Mossey (Sales Director)
**US SIC:** 5072 **UK SIC:** 61500
**Employees:** 50

DUNS 53-659-1589     Imp-Exp
## Protherics Uk Ltd
Blaenwaun, Ffostrasol, Llandysul, Dyfed SA44 5JT
**Tel:** 01239-851122
**Web:** www.btgplc.com
**Reg No:** 3464264 **VAT No:** 692373019
**Estd:** 1997 Private Limited Company

**Line of Business:** Manufacture of basic pharmaceutical products
**Export Sales:** £22,210,000
**Trading Style:** Btg
**Issued Capital:** £8,132,321
**Directors:** Dr P L Makin, R K Soderstrom
**Co. Secretary:** Lygia Jones
**Responsibilities**
**Senior:** Peter Maddox (Manager)
**Finance:** Sam Jenkinson (Financial Controller), Duncan Kennedy (Group Director of Finance)
**IT:** Darren Topham (IT Manager)
**HR:** Yvonne Rogers (Head of Human Resources)
**Health & Safety:** D Sylvester (Engineering Manager)
**Facilities:** D Sylvester (Engineering Manager)
**Engineering:** Anthony Higham (Head of Manufacturing and Supp), D Sylvester (Engineering Manager)
**US SIC:** 2834 **UK SIC:** 25700
**Auditors:** KPMG Audit PLC
**Bankers:** Lloyds TSB Bank plc (30-91-65)

|     | 31-03-14 | 31-03-13 | 31-03-12 |
|-----|----------|----------|----------|
| TO  | 25,674,000 | 29,795,000 | 27,007,000 |
| P/L | 3,528,000 | 2,641,000 | (504,000) |
| NW  | 25,436,000 | 22,282,000 | 19,871,000 |
| WC  | 22,188,000 | 25,848,000 | 24,038,000 |
| Emp.| 112 | 118 | 121 |

DUNS 21-671-8940
## Protim Services Ltd
Monmouth House, 4 Monmouth Place, Bath, Avon BA1 2AT
**Tel:** 01225447960 **Fax:** 02085693143
**Web:** www.protimservicesltd.co.uk
**Reg No:** 0713374 **Estd:** 1962 Private Limited Company
**Line of Business:** Building services
**Issued Capital:** £1,075,100
**Principals:** D Marshall (Managing), M H Freeman
**Co. Secretary:** Mrs Petrina Pooley
**Branches:** Protim Services Ltd, Central Park, Unit 109, Bristol, Avon BS14 9BZ
**US SIC:** 1622, 1799
**UK SIC:** 50200, 50000
**Bankers:** National Westminster Bank Plc (60-00-01)
**Employees:** 125

DUNS 77-886-8091     Exp
## Protim Solignum Ltd
(**Subsidiary of:** Koppers Holdings Inc.)
Fieldhouse Lane Thames Industrial Estate, Marlow, Buckinghamshire SL7 1LS
**Tel:** 01628-486644 **Fax:** 01628-476757
**Web:** www.osmose-europe.com
**Reg No:** 3037845 **VAT No:** 651239742
**Estd:** 1995 Private Limited Company
**Line of Business:** Manufacturers of chemicals
**Export Sales:** £7,689,000
**Trading Style:** Osmose
**Issued Capital:** £2,020,001
**Directors:** S Jepson, P A Goydan, I Mcconnell, S R Lacy, L M Ball Jr
**Responsibilities**
**Senior:** Gordon Ewbank (Manager), Matthew Hempson (Business Development Director)
**Sales:** Matthew Hempson (Business Development Director)
**IT:** Ryan Harley (IT Manager)
**HR:** Ryan Harley (IT Manager)
**Health & Safety:** Peter Wynn (Health & Safety Officer)
**Branches:** Protim Solignum Ltd, Sawmills, Scotts Common, Checkendon, Reading, Berkshire RG8 0TH
**US SIC:** 2899 **UK SIC:** 25670
**Auditors:** PricewaterhouseCoopers LLP
**Bankers:** National Westminster Bank Plc (60-21-40)

|     | 31-12-13 | 31-12-12 | 31-12-11 |
|-----|----------|----------|----------|
| TO  | 17,275,000 | 17,337,000 | 16,188,000 |
| P/L | (306,000) | (475,000) | (1,158,000) |
| NW  | 8,686,000 | 8,418,000 | 8,563,000 |
| WC  | 6,731,000 | 6,253,000 | 6,241,000 |
| Emp.| 59 | 60 | 63 |

DUNS 21-362-6274
## Protiviti Consulting
Grand Buildings, 1-3 Strand, London WC2N 5AB
**Tel:** 020-79308808
**Web:** www.protiviti.com
**Estd:** 2001 Proprietorship
**Line of Business:** Management and business consultants
**Proprietor:** J Wyatt
**Responsibilities**
**Senior:** Johnathan Wyatt (Managing Director)
**US SIC:** 7392 **UK SIC:** 83951
**Employees:** 70

DUNS 34-556-3527     Imp
## Proto Labs Ltd
(**Subsidiary of:** Proto Labs Inc.)
Halesfield 8, Telford, Shropshire TF7 4QN
**Tel:** 01952683047 **Fax:** 01952-683048
**Web:** www.protolabs.co.uk
**Reg No:** 5366160 **VAT No:** 863756682
**Estd:** 2005 Private Limited Company
**Line of Business:** Manufacture of other plastic products
**Export Sales:** £13,853,720
**Trading Style:** Protomold, First Cut Prototype
**Issued Capital:** £485,002
**Directors:** L T Ball, J B Tumelty, D P Hennessey, D I Ferriday, L J Lukis
**Co. Secretary:** Bradley Cleveland
**Responsibilities**
**Senior:** Jane Hemmings (Sales Manager), Steven Walrond (Proprietor)
**US SIC:** 3079, 3999
**UK SIC:** 48360, 49590
**Auditors:** RSM Tenon Audit Ltd

|     | 31-12-13 | 31-12-12 | 31-12-11 |
|-----|----------|----------|----------|
| TO  | 20,109,747 | 14,201,471 | 12,140,541 |
| P/L | 4,491,295 | 2,202,673 | 1,511,358 |
| NW  | 9,521,376 | 5,331,999 | 2,830,755 |
| WC  | 6,347,044 | 2,732,733 | 1,158,609 |
| Emp.| 175 | 152 | 107 |

DUNS 73-783-6684
## Protocol Education Ltd
(**Subsidiary of:** Arthur Bidco Ltd)
247 Tottenham Court Road, London W1T 7QW
**Tel:** 02082530860 **Fax:** 02032-197-711
**Web:** www.protocol-education.com
**Reg No:** 2926583 **VAT No:** 779994039
**Estd:** 1994 Private Limited Company
**Line of Business:** Labour recruitment and provision of personnel
**Issued Capital:** £853
**Principals:** S F Lawrence (Managing), Ms P Swain, J N Roback, J V Bowman
**Co. Secretary:** Jonathan Roback
**Responsibilities**
**Senior:** K O'reilly (Manager)
**Marketing:** Scott Owen (Senior Marketing Executive)
**Branches:** Protocol Education Limited, Cobham House, Highfield Road North, Dartford, Kent DA1 2JJ
**US SIC:** 7361 **UK SIC:** 83954
**Auditors:** KPMG LLP

|     | 30-11-13 | 30-11-12 | 30-11-11 |
|-----|----------|----------|----------|
| TO  | 58,428,000 | 66,733,000 | 43,912,000 |
| P/L | 7,456,000 | 6,151,000 | 3,620,000 |
| NW  | 14,759,000 | 8,941,000 | 27,840,000 |
| WC  | 14,216,000 | 8,465,000 | 27,415,000 |
| Emp.| 210 | 187 | 181 |

DUNS 77-707-2299
## Protocol National Ltd
(**Subsidiary of:** Protocol Associates Nv)
The Point, Nottingham, Nottinghamshire NG2 7QW
**Tel:** 01159111100 **Fax:** 01159111205
**Web:** www.paladinsolutions.co.uk
**Reg No:** 3007851 **Estd:** 1995 Private Limited Company
**Line of Business:** Business and management consultancy activities not elsewhere classified
**Issued Capital:** £4,000,002
**Directors:** D L Wilkinson, S A Graham, Ms V H Cruickshank, D L Wilkinson, I M Sackree, D C Lewis
**Co. Secretary:** Michael Kelly
**Responsibilities**
**Senior:** Phillip Harrison (Chief Executive), Lee Tombs (Director)
**US SIC:** 7392, 8931
**UK SIC:** 83951, 83600
**Auditors:** PricewaterhouseCoopers
**Bankers:** National Westminster Bank Plc (56-00-61)

|     | 30-09-13 | 30-06-12 | 30-09-11 |
|-----|----------|----------|----------|
| TO  | 33,875,000 | 32,456,000 | 36,494,000 |
| P/L | 1,528,000 | 1,642,000 | 2,431,000 |
| NW  | 6,613,000 | 5,157,000 | 35,057,000 |
| WC  | 6,425,000 | 5,105,000 | 34,988,000 |
| Emp.| 87 | 90 | 107 |

DUNS 21-031-7505
## The Protorial Office
St Marys Passage, Cambridge, Cambridgeshire CB2 3PQ
**Proprietorship**
**Line of Business:** First-degree level higher education
**Proprietor:** Ms A Richard
**US SIC:** 8221 **UK SIC:** 93100
**Employees:** 1,000

DUNS 22-859-6755
## Protours Isle of Man Ltd
Ballasalla Airport Garage, Douglas Road, Ballasalla, Douglas, Isle of Man IM9 2AN
**Tel:** 01624822611 **Fax:** 01624-675656
**Web:** www.tours.co.im
**Reg No:** 0021637M **Estd:** 1969 Private Limited Company
**Line of Business:** Tour operators
**Responsibilities**
**Senior:** Roy Lightfoot (Manager), David Midghall (Manager)
**Fleet:** Roy Lightfoot (Manager)
**US SIC:** 4119 **UK SIC:** 72200
**Employees:** 62

DUNS 34-601-2730
## Protrade Ltd
(**Subsidiary of:** D.I.P.T. Holdings Ltd)
Unit 2 Riverside Road, Derby, Derbyshire DE24 8HY
**Tel:** 01332680120
**Web:** www.protrade.co.uk
**Reg No:** 5408392 **Estd:** 2005 Private Limited Company
**Line of Business:** Tool suppliers
**Issued Capital:** £1,000
**Directors:** C K Sanders, R B Sanders
**Co. Secretary:** Simon Lovatt
**Responsibilities**
**HR:** Sandra Rooney (Human Resources Manager)
**Health & Safety:** Neil Dawson (Quality Manager)
**Purchasing:** Tony Lambert (Purchasing Manager)
**Fleet:** Tony Lambert (Purchasing Manager)
**US SIC:** 5084, 7394
**UK SIC:** 61490, 84000
**Auditors:** Clear & Lane

|     | 31-12-13 | 31-12-12 | 31-12-11 |
|-----|----------|----------|----------|
| TA  | 629,708 | 574,367 | 641,967 |
| NW  | 43,120 | 14,995 | (27,842) |
| WC  | 18,073 | (55,980) | (100,174) |

DUNS 23-261-4789
## Prova
17 Doman Road, Camberley, Surrey GU15 3DF
**Tel:** 01276-678870
**Web:** www.exova.com
**Estd:** 1993 Proprietorship
**Line of Business:** Research and laboratory based activities
**Proprietor:** J Rennie
**Responsibilities**
**Senior:** Moyra Brookes (General Manager), Suzanne Measures (Manager)
**US SIC:** 7391 **UK SIC:** 94000
**Employees:** 50

DUNS 21-162-3093
## Provenance Inns Ltd
4 Wharfe Mews Cliffe Terrace, Wetherby, West Yorkshire LS22 6LX
**Tel:** 01347821506
**Web:** www.provenanceinns.com
**Reg No:** 6887888 **Estd:** 2009 Private Limited Company
**Line of Business:** Hotels
**Issued Capital:** £100
**Directors:** C J Blundell, M D Ibbotson
**US SIC:** 7011, 5813
**UK SIC:** 66500, 66200

|     | 31-08-13 | 31-08-12 | 31-08-11 |
|-----|----------|----------|----------|
| TO  | 2,641,251 | N/A | N/A |
| P/L | (264,933) | N/A | N/A |
| NW  | (1,121,860) | (872,261) | (434,593) |
| WC  | (6,085,651) | (5,328,549) | (2,658,196) |
| Emp.| 92 | N/A | N/A |

DUNS 52-568-7224
## Provend Group Ltd
(**Subsidiary of:** Staunton Luxco Sca)
Apollo House, Odyssey Business Park, West End Road, Ruislip, Middlesex HA4 6QD
**Tel:** 02036970620
**Web:** www.pelicanrouge.co.uk
**Reg No:** 3253929 **Estd:** 1991 Private Limited Company
**Line of Business:** Canteens and catering
**Trading Style:** Pelican Rouge
**Issued Capital:** £172,800
**Directors:** D H Abrahams, K P Geysels
**Responsibilities**
**IT:** Nigel Hunter (Information Technology Operati)
**Branches:** Provend Group Ltd, Enterprise Industrial Estate, Unit A3, Brighton, East Sussex BN1 8AF
**US SIC:** 5812 **UK SIC:** 66110
**Auditors:** PricewaterhouseCoopers LLP
**Bankers:** Bank Of Scotland (12-01-03)

|     | 31-03-14 | 31-03-13 | 01-03-12 |
|-----|----------|----------|----------|
| TA  | 37,894,000 | 37,894,000 | 37,894,000 |
| P/L | N/A | N/A | (303,000) |
| NW  | 19,553,000 | 19,553,000 | 19,553,000 |
| WC  | (6,568,000) | (6,568,000) | (6,568,000) |

DUNS 21-681-5461

## Provide Community Interest Co

St Peters Hospital, Spital Road, Maldon, Essex CM9 6EG
**Tel:** 01621725323
**Web:** www.cecs.org.uk
**Reg No:** 7320006 **Estd:** 2010 Private Limited Company
**Line of Business:** Other human health activities
**Trading Style:** Central Essex Community Services C.I.C
**Issued Capital:** £529
**Directors:** D J Louis, P B Richards, Ms V F Walden, D Royce, Ms R E Emmett, J M Willis, Ms R White, Mrs J M Hentley
**Co. Secretary:** Philip Richards
**Responsibilities**
**Senior:** John Niland *(Director)*, Anne Pearson *(Manager)*, Paul Spowage *(Manager)*
**US SIC:** 8091 **UK SIC:** 95200
**Bankers:** Lloyds TSB Bank plc (30-96-38)

| | 31-03-14 | 31-03-13 | 31-03-12 |
|---|---|---|---|
| TO | 55,471,096 | 54,100,521 | 48,339,131 |
| P/L | 1,299,052 | 1,641,397 | 1,106,880 |
| NW | 3,091,019 | 1,927,435 | 562,153 |
| WC | 2,346,430 | 2,049,992 | 806,405 |
| Emp. | 1,200 | 1,194 | 1,157 |

DUNS 21-224-0836

## Providence Court

Providence Way, Providence Way, Baldock, Hertfordshire SG7 6TT
**Tel:** 01462-490870
**Web:** www.quantumcare.co.uk
**Estd:** 1995
**Line of Business:** Children's homes
**Proprietor:** Mrs J Beaumont
**Responsibilities**
**Senior:** Maria Ball *(Chief Executive Officer)*, Jackie Beaumont *(Home Manager)*, Karen Parker *(Manager)*
**HR:** Wanda Spooner *(Director of Human Resources)*
**Health & Safety:** Katrina Faulkner *(Health & Safety Officer)*
**US SIC:** 8321 **UK SIC:** 96111
**Employees:** 48

DUNS 21-558-7724

## Providence Row Housing Association

458 Bethnal Green Road, London E2 0EA
**Tel:** 02079207300
**Web:** www.providencerow.org.uk
**Reg No:** 0019322IP **Estd:** 1970
**Line of Business:** Housing associations societies trusts & co-operatives
**Principals:** G Holloway *(Chairman)*, N Brittain, M Rennie, Ms C Yanetski, L A Kina, Ms E Crowther, J Boyde, A J Bartlett
**Responsibilities**
**Senior:** May Dominic *(Director)*, Geoffrey Piejus *(Director)*, Lynne Vickery *(Director)*
**US SIC:** 8699 **UK SIC:** 96902
**Bankers:** HSBC Bank plc (40-00-04)

| | 31-03-12 | 31-03-11 | 31-03-10 |
|---|---|---|---|
| TO | 8,310,000 | 8,877,000 | 8,420,000 |
| P/L | 495,000 | 280,000 | 337,000 |
| NW | 3,636,000 | 3,066,000 | 2,786,000 |
| WC | 2,092,000 | 804,000 | 357,000 |
| Emp. | 110 | 127 | 126 |

DUNS 21-205-3557

## Provident Financial Plc

No 1, Godwin Street, Bradford, West Yorkshire BD1 2SU
**Web:** www.providentfinancial.com
**Reg No:** 0668987 **VAT No:** 180555952
**Estd:** 1960 Public Limited Company
**Line of Business:** Financial intermediation not elsewhere classified
**Trading Style:** Provident Personal Credit, Greenwood Personal Credit, Provident Management Services
**Issued Capital:** £28,634,794
**Directors:** M J Le May, Ms M Wolstenholme, A C Fisher, S W Sinclair, Ms A M Halsey, P S Crook, R W Anderson
**Co. Secretary:** Kenneth Mullen
**US SIC:** 6111, 7399
**UK SIC:** 81501, 83954
**Auditors:** Deloitte LLP
**Bankers:** Barclays Bank Plc (20-11-81)
**Following financial data are in thousands**

| | 31-12-13 | 31-12-12 | 31-12-11 |
|---|---|---|---|
| TA | 1,810,200 | 1,686,500 | 1,478,400 |
| P/L | 182,400 | 196,700 | 162,100 |
| NW | 408,700 | 365,900 | 311,200 |
| WC | 1,443,600 | 1,248,300 | 1,172,100 |
| Emp. | 3,833 | 3,786 | 3,713 |

DUNS 21-003-4344 Exp

## Provident Personal Credit Ltd

**(Subsidiary of:** Provident Financial Plc**)**
1 Godwin Street, Bradford, West Yorkshire BD1 2SU
**Tel:** 08004096654 **Fax:** 01274-736185
**Web:** www.providentpersonalcredit.com
**Reg No:** 0146091 **Estd:** 1996 Private Limited Company
**Line of Business:** Credit granting by non-deposit taking finance houses and other specialist consumer credit grantors
**Export Markets:** Eire
**Issued Capital:** £71,844,095
**Directors:** P A Mclelland, T R Anson, Ms S M Dickins, S D Shaw, Ms S A Lawrence, H K Patel, M Stevens, A J Parkinson
**Co. Secretary:** Miss Emma Versluys
**Responsibilities**
**Senior:** Jonathan Gillespie *(Director)*
**Branches:** Provident Personal Credit Ltd, Unit 1-2, East Street, Prescot, Merseyside L34 5RR
**US SIC:** 6111 **UK SIC:** 81501
**Auditors:** PricewaterhouseCoopers
**Bankers:** Barclays Bank Plc (20-11-81)

| | 31-12-13 | 31-12-12 | 31-12-11 |
|---|---|---|---|
| TA | 870,200,000 | 985,900,000 | 985,800,000 |
| P/L | 68,000,000 | 108,200,000 | 95,000,000 |
| NW | 154,600,000 | 186,300,000 | 163,400,000 |
| WC | 79,700,000 | 94,700,000 | 280,000,000 |
| Emp. | 2,009 | 2,140 | 2,194 |

DUNS 23-556-5327

## Providor Ltd

4 Studlands Park Avenue Albion Court, Newmarket, Suffolk CB8 7XA
**Tel:** 01223652410
**Web:** www.providor.co.uk
**Reg No:** 3554820 **Estd:** 2010 Private Limited Company
**Line of Business:** Measuring instruments and appliances
**Issued Capital:** £200
**Directors:** P Wharrier, Ms A J Warrier, J Hall
**Co. Secretary:** Mrs Amanda Wharrier
**Responsibilities**
**Senior:** Phil Warrior *(Manager)*
**US SIC:** 3829, 3499
**UK SIC:** 37100, 31694
**Auditors:** HSA & Co

| | 31-05-14 | 31-05-13 | 31-05-12 |
|---|---|---|---|
| TO | 9,015,526 | 5,927,276 | N/A |
| P/L | 1,341,478 | 471,023 | N/A |
| NW | 1,007,318 | 427,158 | 239,748 |
| WC | 687,596 | 171,356 | 60,378 |
| Emp. | 106 | 95 | N/A |

DUNS 21-923-6163 Imp-Exp

## Provimi Ltd

**(Subsidiary of:** Cargill International Luxembourg 3 Sarl**)**
S C A Mill, Dalton Airfield, Dalton, Thirsk, North Yorkshire YO7 3HE
**Tel:** 01845-578125
**Web:** www.scanutec.com
**Reg No:** 1262691 **VAT No:** 289237417
**Estd:** 1976 Private Limited Company
**Line of Business:** Manufacture of prepared feeds for farm animals
**Export Markets:** E U, Middle East
**Export Sales:** £14,784,078
**Issued Capital:** £5,000,550
**Directors:** Ms G M Brown, M R Douglas, D Hordijk
**Co. Secretary:** Robin Thurston
**Responsibilities**
**Operations:** Adam Blackburn *(Production Manager)*, Fraser Hill *(Production Manager)*
**Branches:** Provimi Ltd, Eastern Avenue, Lichfield, Staffordshire WS13 7SE
**US SIC:** 2048 **UK SIC:** 42210
**Auditors:** Deloitte LLP
**Bankers:** Barclays Bank Plc (20-55-34)

| | 31-05-14 | 31-05-13 | 31-05-12 |
|---|---|---|---|
| TO | 46,917,172 | 44,529,697 | 54,748,201 |
| P/L | (743,703) | 522,599 | (1,100,277) |
| NW | 4,000,322 | 4,825,609 | 3,034,638 |
| WC | 2,194,988 | 3,518,726 | 3,463,851 |
| Emp. | 137 | 131 | 126 |

DUNS 67-209-9173 Imp

## Prowell Ltd

**(Subsidiary of:** Prowell Gmbh**)**
Pioneer Business Park, North Road, Ellesmere Port, Cheshire CH65 1AQ
**Tel:** 01513-574230 **Fax:** 01513574239
**Reg No:** 6018149 **VAT No:** 894523882
**Estd:** 2006 Private Limited Company
**Line of Business:** Manufacturers of paper and cardboard
**Trading Style:** Prowell Limited
**Issued Capital:** £6,510,000
**Directors:** K J Heindl, F G Gumbinger
**Co. Secretary:** Pinsent Masons Secretarial Limit
**Responsibilities**
**Senior:** Luke Banks *(Production Manager)*
**Operations:** Luke Banks *(Production Manager)*
**US SIC:** 2631 **UK SIC:** 47017
**Auditors:** Blick Rothenberg
**Bankers:** Bayerische Vereinsbank Ag (30-10-61)

| | 31-12-13 | 31-12-12 | 31-12-11 |
|---|---|---|---|
| TO | 43,020,786 | 40,586,323 | 41,081,818 |
| P/L | 921,342 | 2,677,721 | 1,332,901 |
| NW | 6,123,194 | 5,493,441 | 2,878,604 |
| WC | 9,679,942 | 7,928,646 | (889,419) |
| Emp. | 64 | 61 | 64 |

DUNS 21-102-7042

## Proxama Plc

St James' Mill, Norwich, Norfolk NR3 1TN
**Tel:** 01603 760 060
**Web:** www.proxama.com
**Reg No:** 6458458 **Estd:** 2007 Public Limited Company
**Line of Business:** Business services
**Export Sales:** £412,685
**Issued Capital:** £230,801
**Directors:** M Woods, M L Quitmann, G D Breeze, J Kennedy, Dr N R Garner, D J Bailey
**Co. Secretary:** Cargil Management Services Limit
**Responsibilities**
**Senior:** Adrianus Van Breda *(Director)*
**Finance:** Adrianus Van Breda *(Director)*
**Branches:** Proxama Plc, City Tower, 18th FlooR,40 Basinghall Street, London EC2V 5DE
**US SIC:** 7379 **UK SIC:** 83940
**Auditors:** Grant Thornton UK LLP

| | 31-12-13 | 31-12-12 | 31-12-11 |
|---|---|---|---|
| TO | 813,380 | N/A | N/A |
| P/L | (5,412,512) | (200,325) | (175,250) |
| NW | 6,946,859 | 1,315,320 | 3,000,464 |
| WC | 7,353,942 | 1,315,320 | 3,000,464 |
| Emp. | 57 | 3 | 3 |

DUNS 73-327-4778

## Proximo Ltd

**(Subsidiary of:** Proximo Holdings Ltd**)**
Park House, 37 Lower Bridge Street, Chester, Cheshire CH1 1RS
**Tel:** 08707770266 **Fax:** 0870-777-0265
**Web:** www.proximo.co.uk
**Reg No:** 4601376 **Estd:** 2002 Private Limited Company
**Line of Business:** Other scheduled passenger land transport not elsewhere classified
**Issued Capital:** £2,436,518
**Directors:** P Fairhurst, P Twilley, S Mullen, S Vare, Mrs E M Chadwick
**Co. Secretary:** Ms Eliane Chadwick
**US SIC:** 4119, 6111
**UK SIC:** 72200, 81501

| | 30-06-13 | 30-06-12 | 30-06-11 |
|---|---|---|---|
| TA | 9,155,319 | 8,774,656 | 9,164,399 |
| P/L | 860,906 | 569,537 | 1,224,661 |
| NW | 4,186,446 | 3,432,478 | 2,925,935 |
| WC | 2,594,529 | 2,233,583 | 1,601,019 |
| Emp. | 92 | 85 | 88 |

DUNS 21-710-0123

## Prp Architects Llp

Ferry Works, Summer Road, Thames Ditton, Surrey KT7 0QJ
**Tel:** 020-8339-3600
**Web:** www.prparchitects.co.uk
**Reg No:** 0361169OC **Estd:** 1964
**Line of Business:** Architects
**Export Sales:** £1,998,724
**Principals:** N T Griffiths, B S Chawla, Ms A M Nicholson, R H Battersby, B A Kilpatrick, A J Weir, R Harvey, M S Baptista
**Responsibilities**
**Senior:** Justin Bannister *(Associate)*, Ian Bott *(Associate Director)*, Jennifer Buterchi *(Care Homes Director)*, Frances Chaplin *(Non-designated Limited Liabili)*, Nigel Collier *(Non-designated Limited Liabili)*, Peter Dodds *(Non-designated Limited Liabili)*, Stephen Hynds *(Non-designated Limited Liabili)*, Simon Kaufman *(Non-designated Limited Liabili)*, Graham Locke *(Non-designated Limited Liabili)*, Viru Vadgama *(Non-designated Limited Liabili)*, Andrew Von Bradsky *(Non-designated Limited Liabili)*
**US SIC:** 8911, 7399
**UK SIC:** 83701, 83954

| | 31-03-14 | 31-03-13 | 31-03-12 |
|---|---|---|---|
| TO | 21,940,374 | 19,869,119 | 17,130,740 |
| P/L | 5,093,371 | 1,275,997 | 444,501 |
| NW | 1,927,311 | 1,217,652 | 444,501 |
| WC | 3,165,923 | 2,278,727 | 1,597,086 |
| Emp. | 239 | 273 | 217 |

DUNS 73-797-9856

## P.R.P. Training Ltd

13 Melville Street, Pembroke Dock, Dyfed SA72 6XS
**Tel:** 01646-623780 **Fax:** 01646623781
**Web:** www.prp-training.co.uk
**Reg No:** 2929263 **Estd:** 2007 Private Limited Company
**Line of Business:** Training providers
**Issued Capital:** £90
**Directors:** Mrs C Barley, M Roberts
**Responsibilities**
**Senior:** Shirley Laugharne *(Manager)*, Tracy Owen *(Manager)*
**Marketing:** David Klass *(Marketing Manager)*
**US SIC:** 8299, 8321
**UK SIC:** 93300, 96111
**Auditors:** Evens & Co Ltd
**Bankers:** HSBC Bank plc (40-33-04)

| | 31-07-13 | 31-07-12 | 31-07-11 |
|---|---|---|---|
| TA | 2,552,391 | 2,451,463 | 2,452,692 |
| NW | 2,293,281 | 2,207,383 | 2,108,847 |
| WC | 1,980,892 | 1,890,285 | 1,754,394 |

DUNS 21-911-8908

## Pruce Newman Pipework Ltd

Ayton Road, Wymondham, Norfolk NR18 0QJ
**Tel:** 01953605123 **Fax:** 01953-601115
**Web:** www.prucenewman.co.uk
**Reg No:** 1111151 **VAT No:** 247387922
**Estd:** 1970 Private Limited Company
**Line of Business:** Other building installation
**Trading Style:** Ayton Fabrication
**Issued Capital:** £110,100
**Principals:** B N Edwards *(Managing)*, T W Moorse, Ms S D Pruce, A J Pruce, G B Newman, B Newman
**Responsibilities**
**Senior:** Jamie Key *(Manager)*, Charles Smalley *(Manager)*, John Tanner *(Works Manager)*
**HR:** Dave Todd *(Human Resources Manager)*
**Branches:** Pruce Newman Pipework Ltd, Suite 5 Riverside House, Lower Southend Road, Wickford, Essex SS11 8BB
**US SIC:** 1796 **UK SIC:** 50400
**Auditors:** Hamilton Brading
**Bankers:** National Westminster Bank Plc (60-24-52)

| | 31-05-14 | 31-05-13 | 31-05-12 |
|---|---|---|---|
| TO | 8,129,085 | 10,373,958 | 7,726,754 |
| P/L | 165,957 | 347,426 | 77,710 |
| NW | 1,886,079 | 1,952,182 | 1,714,318 |
| WC | 971,853 | 1,034,887 | 847,287 |
| Emp. | 103 | 114 | 90 |

DUNS 21-023-8671

## The Prudential Assurance Company Ltd

**(Subsidiary of:** Prudential Plc**)**
12 Arthur Street, London EC4R 9AQ
**Tel:** 0800 000 000
**Web:** www.pru.co.uk
**Reg No:** 0015454 **Estd:** 1848 Private Limited Company
**Line of Business:** Life assurance services
**Trading Style:** Prudential
**Issued Capital:** £100
**Directors:** Ms W Au, T C Thiam, Ms J Hunt, N A Nicandrou, H A Hussain, M J Yardley
**Co. Secretary:** Ms Susan Windridge
**Responsibilities**
**HR:** Nicky Thompson *(Training Manager)*
**Branches:** The Prudential Assurance Company Ltd, Unit 50 Management Suite, George Street, Oldham, Lancashire OL1 1HD
**US SIC:** 6311, 6399
**UK SIC:** 82002, 82001
**Auditors:** KPMG Audit PLC
**Bankers:** HSBC Bank plc (40-03-28)
**Following financial data are in thousands**

| | 31-12-13 | 31-12-12 | 31-12-11 |
|---|---|---|---|
| TO | 6,635,000 | 13,021,000 | 13,195,000 |
| P/L | 227,000 | 459,000 | 480,000 |
| NW | 4,787,000 | 4,567,000 | 3,978,000 |
| WC | 12,873,000 | (1,334,000) | 1,091,000 |
| Emp. | 1,110 | 940 | 865 |

DUNS 21-162-8409

## Prudential Plc

Governors House, 5 Laurence Pountney Hill, London EC4R 0HH
**Tel:** 02072207588 **Fax:** 02075483725
**Web:** www.prudential.co.uk
**Reg No:** 1397169 **Estd:** 1978 Public Limited Company
**Line of Business:** Management activities of holding companies
**Issued Capital:** £127,963,717
**Directors:** The Hon P J Remnant, H J Davies, A D Schroeder, P V Manduca, N A Nicandrou, Lord A Turnbull, M G Mclintock, Ms J Hunt
**Co. Secretary:** Alan Porter
**Responsibilities**
**Senior:** Pierre Bouee *(Director)*, Miles Celic *(Director of Group Public Affai)*, Alexander Johnston *(Director)*, Matt Lilley *(Chief Executive Officer)*, Kaikhushru Nargolwala *(Director)*, Anthony Nightingale *(Director)*, Barry Stowe *(Director)*, Elisabeth Wenusch *(Managing Director, Deputy Grou)*
**Finance:** Heather Doig *(Rewards Analyst)*, Elisabeth Wenusch *(Managing Director, Deputy Grou)*, Lisa Young-Harry *(Head of Pensions and Benefits)*

**Marketing:** Miles Celic *(Director of Group Public Affai)*, Lynn Newton *(Media Relations Officer)*, Jonathan Oliver *(Media Relations Director)*
**Sales:** Jim Cheshire *(Head of Process Improvement)*
**Admin:** Paulette King *(Personal Assistant)*
**HR:** Peter Goerke *(Human Resources Director)*, Cathy Lewis *(HR Director UK & Europe)*
**Branches:** Prudential Plc, 121 Kings Road, Reading, Berkshire RG1 3ES
**US SIC:** 6711, 6411
**UK SIC:** 83962, 83200
**Auditors:** KPMG Audit PLC
**Bankers:** HSBC Bank plc (40-03-28)

**Following financial data are in thousands**

| | 31-12-13 | 31-12-12 | 31-12-11 |
|---|---|---|---|
| TO | 29,844,000 | 29,404,000 | 25,277,000 |
| P/L | 2,082,000 | 3,188,000 | 1,926,000 |
| NW | 2,645,000 | 4,367,000 | 2,316,000 |
| WC | 332,000 | (271,342,000) | (181,947,000) |
| Emp. | 22,186 | 27,619 | 25,414 |

DUNS 29-500-0681

## Prudential Property Investments Ltd

(**Subsidiary of:** Prudential Plc)
City Place House, 55 Basinghall Street, London EC2V 5DU
**Tel:** 02075486600 **Fax:** 020-7548-6999
**Web:** www.sovereigncentral.co.uk
**Reg No:** 1863304 **Estd:** 1984 Private Limited Company
**Line of Business:** Property developers
**Issued Capital:** £14,523,280
**Directors:** M&G Real Estate Limited, M A Towns, C M Perkins
**Co. Secretary:**
M&G Management Services Limited
**Branches:** Prudential Property Investments Ltd, Unit 22, Kingsway, Gateshead, Tyne and Wear NE11 0SR
**US SIC:** 6552 **UK SIC:** 85000
**Auditors:** KPMG Audit PLC

| | 31-12-13 | 31-12-12 | 31-12-11 |
|---|---|---|---|
| TA | 8,771,008 | 8,737,863 | 8,743,681 |
| P/L | 15,371 | 22,293 | 11,152 |
| NW | (7,148,785) | (7,161,862) | (7,136,678) |
| WC | (14,240,277) | 246,155 | 234,057 |

DUNS 21-756-1717

## Prudential Regulation Authority

8 Lothbury, London EC2R 7HH
**Tel:** 02920614678
**Web:** www.fshandbook.info
**Reg No:** 7854923 **Estd:** 2011 Private Limited Company
**Line of Business:** General (overall) public service activities
**Issued Capital:** £1
**Directors:** Ms S L Boss, A J Bailey, C D Randell, M J Carney, M Wheatley, J M Yallop, N T Shafik, I C Cornish
**Co. Secretary:** John Footman
**Responsibilities**
**Senior:** Jonathan Cunliffe *(Director)*
**US SIC:** 9121 **UK SIC:** 91110

| | 28-02-14 | 28-02-13 |
|---|---|---|
| TO | 202,542,000 | N/A |
| P/L | 78,000 | N/A |
| NW | (15,948,000) | N/A |
| WC | (24,561,000) | N/A |
| Emp. | 1,038 | N/A |

DUNS 29-872-2216

## Prv Engineering Ltd

(**Subsidiary of:** Transit Engineering Ltd)
Pegasus House, Polo Grounds, New Inn, Pontypool, Gwent NP4 0TW
**Tel:** 01495769697 **Fax:** 01495-769776
**Web:** www.prv-engineering.co.uk
**Reg No:** 2075421 **VAT No:** 927173220
**Estd:** 1986 Private Limited Company
**Line of Business:** Other engineering activities
**Issued Capital:** £2
**Directors:** C Day, S K Jones, L A Williams, M A Olerenshaw
**Co. Secretary:** Mrs Gaynor Flook
**US SIC:** 8911 **UK SIC:** 83701
**Auditors:** KTS Owens Thomas Ltd
**Bankers:** HSBC Bank plc (40-16-13)

| | 31-12-13 | 31-12-12 | 31-12-11 |
|---|---|---|---|
| TA | 4,438,395 | 4,151,849 | 3,749,267 |
| NW | 2,071,291 | 2,115,093 | 1,980,130 |
| WC | 1,545,187 | 1,511,582 | 1,546,599 |

DUNS 21-111-4823

## Pryers Solicitors Llp

13 The Stonebow, York, North Yorkshire YO1 7NP
**Tel:** 01904556600 **Fax:** 01904556601
**Web:** www.pryers-solicitors.co.uk
**Reg No:** 0335469OC **Estd:** 2008 Private Limited Company
**Line of Business:** Solicitors
**US SIC:** 8111 **UK SIC:** 83500

**Bankers:** Barclays Bank Plc (20-82-18)

| | 30-04-14 | 30-04-13 | 30-04-12 |
|---|---|---|---|
| TO | 5,141,836 | 4,239,595 | N/A |
| P/L | 1,476,180 | 748,733 | N/A |
| WC | 3,245,914 | 2,566,438 | 2,629,447 |
| Emp. | 53 | 55 | N/A |

DUNS 21-032-2474

## Pryke Dr R

Winyates Way, Redditch, Worcestershire B98 0NR
**Web:** www.winyateshc.co.uk
**Line of Business:** Doctors
**Responsibilities**
**Senior:** Julie Ingram *(Practice Manager)*
**US SIC:** 8011 **UK SIC:** 95300
**Employees:** 50

DUNS 21-233-3915

## Prymrose Hill Care Home

Thames Road, Huntingdon, Cambridgeshire PE29 1QW
**Tel:** 01480-450099
**Web:** www.abbeyhealthcare.org.uk
**Estd:** 2003 Proprietorship
**Line of Business:** Residential care establishments
**Proprietor:** Mrs L Martinez
**Responsibilities**
**Senior:** Yvonne Duffy *(Home Manager)*, Harold Pink *(Manager)*
**US SIC:** 8321, 7231
**UK SIC:** 96111, 98200
**Employees:** 52

DUNS 22-675-8381

## Pryors Cars

3 Mereland Road, Didcot, Oxfordshire OX11 8AP
**Web:** www.pryors.co.uk
**Estd:** 1955 Partnership
**Line of Business:** Taxis
**Partners:** Miss C Pryor, D Pryor
**Responsibilities**
**IT:** Terry White *(Senior IT Executive)*
**US SIC:** 4121 **UK SIC:** 72200
**Employees:** 114

DUNS 22-607-6719 **Imp**

## Prysmian Cables & Systems Ltd

(**Subsidiary of:** Prysmian Spa)
Chickenhall Lane, Eastleigh, Hampshire SO50 6YU
**Tel:** 023 8029 5555 **Fax:** 02380295437
**Web:** www.prysmiangroup.com
**Reg No:** 0958507 **VAT No:** 188509226
**Estd:** 1969 Private Limited Company
**Line of Business:** Manufacturers cable and wire equipment
**Export Sales:** £150,412,000
**Issued Capital:** £45,292,120
**Directors:** P R Atkinson, F I Romeo, L Caserta
**Co. Secretary:** Colin Briggs
**Responsibilities**
**Senior:** Bob Morrison *(Manager)*
**Marketing:** Julie Mould *(Marketing Manager)*
**Sales:** Toby Collins *(Sales Director)*, Ken Halford *(Business Development Manager)*, Graham Spraggs *(Business Development Manager)*, Chris Towle *(Sales Manager)*
**IT:** Andy Carton *(IT Manager)*
**Branches:** Prysmian Cables & Systems Ltd, Robslee Drive, Glasgow, Lanarkshire G46 7UB
**US SIC:** 3357, 5065
**UK SIC:** 22470, 61500
**Auditors:** PricewaterhouseCoopers LLP
**Bankers:** HSBC Bank plc (40-42-18)

| | 31-12-13 | 31-12-12 | 31-12-11 |
|---|---|---|---|
| TO | 486,598,000 | 501,849,000 | 425,595,000 |
| P/L | 5,448,000 | 786,000 | 17,572,000 |
| NW | 58,948,000 | 57,417,000 | 91,439,000 |
| WC | 22,017,000 | 2,653,000 | 13,311,000 |
| Emp. | 1,042 | 1,097 | 986 |

DUNS 21-878-3548

## Ps 99

2 North Road, Lee Mill Industrial Estate, Ivybridge, Devon PL21 9GN
**Tel:** 01752 395533
**Web:** www.ps99.co.uk
**Estd:** 1994 Proprietorship
**Line of Business:** Construction of commercial buildings
**Proprietor:** P Scrivener
**US SIC:** 1541 **UK SIC:** 50100
**Employees:** 53

DUNS 23-545-7137 **Imp-Exp**

## Psa Parts Ltd

2 Prince Georges Road, Colliers Wood, London SW19 2PX
**Tel:** 02086-856300 **Fax:** 02086-856310
**Web:** www.psaparts.co.uk
**Reg No:** 3544196 **Estd:** 1988 Private Limited Company

**Line of Business:** Manufacturers of pcs
**Export Sales:** £6,936,498
**Issued Capital:** £810
**Directors:** J E Mcbrien, J P Mcbrien, D Haskins
**Co. Secretary:** Peter Mcbrien
**Responsibilities**
**Senior:** Nick Walsh *(Sales Manager)*
**Finance:** Christy Shanker *(Accounts Manager)*
**US SIC:** 3573 **UK SIC:** 33020
**Auditors:** Hartley Fowler LLP

| | 31-05-13 | 31-05-12 | 31-05-11 |
|---|---|---|---|
| TO | 17,775,663 | 15,668,451 | 14,424,844 |
| P/L | 1,535,727 | 1,958,676 | 2,008,258 |
| NW | 5,242,168 | 4,025,235 | 2,550,141 |
| WC | 2,852,354 | 1,894,619 | 2,443,272 |
| Emp. | 58 | 56 | 47 |

DUNS 21-731-4326

## Psco Group Ltd

Unit B, 1-3 Acre Road, Reading, Berkshire RG2 0SU
**Tel:** 01183723300
**Web:** www.psco.co.uk
**Reg No:** 7667390 **Estd:** 2011 Private Limited Company
**Line of Business:** Hire and rental of television goods
**Export Sales:** £502,076
**Issued Capital:** £208,002
**Director:** S M Holmes
**Co. Secretary:** Nicholas Harding
**US SIC:** 3662 **UK SIC:** 34430

| | 30-06-13 | 30-06-12 |
|---|---|---|
| TO | 11,564,187 | 11,658,470 |
| P/L | 636,755 | 496,659 |
| NW | 1,204,215 | 1,145,456 |
| WC | 960,612 | 1,085,392 |
| Emp. | 54 | 49 |

DUNS 77-000-0438 **Exp**

## Psd Group Ltd

21 Perrymount Road, Haywards Heath, West Sussex RH16 3TP
**Fax:** 01293 802 001
**Web:** www.psdgroup.com
**Reg No:** 2654935 **Estd:** 1996 Private Limited Company
**Line of Business:** Employment and recruitment companies and consultants
**Issued Capital:** £781,750
**Directors:** Ms F M Robinson, P J Hearn, I D Moss
**Co. Secretary:** Ian Moss
**Responsibilities**
**Senior:** Gail Danvers *(Manager)*, Gillian Oakes *(Manager)*
**HR:** Alison French *(Human Resources Manager)*
**Health & Safety:** Zoe Child *(Facilities Manager)*, Hugh Willoubhy *(Facilities Manager)*
**Facilities:** Zoe Child *(Facilities Manager)*, Hugh Willoubhy *(Facilities Manager)*
**US SIC:** 7361 **UK SIC:** 83954
**Auditors:** Grant Thornton UK LLP
**Bankers:** The Royal Bank Of Scotland Plc (15-10-00)

| | 31-12-13 | 31-12-12 | 31-12-11 |
|---|---|---|---|
| TO | 57,989,000 | 60,612,000 | 58,926,000 |
| P/L | 2,643,000 | 1,957,000 | 3,592,000 |
| NW | 11,456,000 | 10,521,000 | 10,771,000 |
| WC | 10,589,000 | 9,476,000 | 10,258,000 |
| Emp. | 245 | 262 | 259 |

DUNS 34-565-2544

## Psigma Investment Management Ltd

(**Subsidiary of:** Punter Southall Group Ltd)
11 Strand, London WC2N 5HR
**Web:** www.psigma.com
**Reg No:** 5374633 **Estd:** 2005 Private Limited Company
**Line of Business:** Fund management activities
**Issued Capital:** £1,106,000
**Directors:** J A Samuels, J C Howard-Smith, K J Mckelvey
**Co. Secretary:** Ian Nash
**US SIC:** 6371 **UK SIC:** 82002
**Auditors:** BDO LLP

| | 31-12-13 | 31-12-12 | 31-12-11 |
|---|---|---|---|
| TO | 18,046,295 | 15,576,895 | 14,392,469 |
| P/L | 2,122,806 | 2,980,506 | 2,887,762 |
| NW | 4,670,921 | 6,002,988 | 8,184,910 |
| WC | 5,182,958 | 6,065,025 | 8,184,910 |
| Emp. | 64 | 59 | 54 |

DUNS 73-388-1911

## Psl Energy Services Ltd

(**Subsidiary of:** Halliburton Company)
Halliburton House, Pitmedden Road, Dyce, Dyce, Aberdeen, Aberdeenshire AB21 0DP
**Tel:** 01224776000
**Reg No:** 0243706SC **Estd:** 2003 Private Limited Company
**Line of Business:** Oil and gas exploration services
**Issued Capital:** £9,120,129
**Directors:** M Betts, D A Johnston

**Co. Secretary:** Scot Clifton
**Branches:** Psl Energy Services Ltd, Marine Support Base, 266 Southtown Road, Great Yarmouth, Norfolk NR31 0JJ
**US SIC:** 1389 **UK SIC:** 13000
**Bankers:** Bank Of Scotland (80-05-14)

| | 31-12-13 | 31-12-12 | 31-12-11 |
|---|---|---|---|
| TO | 12,324,000 | 13,405,000 | 10,609,000 |
| P/L | 3,099,000 | 3,873,000 | 2,687,000 |
| NW | 115,713,000 | 113,072,000 | 110,436,000 |
| WC | 107,700,000 | 104,701,000 | 102,463,000 |
| Emp. | 69 | 62 | 61 |

DUNS 29-162-9020 **Imp**

## The Psl Group Ltd

Quayside Park, Maldon, Essex CM9 5FA
**Fax:** 01621-852173
**Web:** www.pslgroup.net
**Reg No:** 1794983 **VAT No:** 570487130
**Estd:** 1984 Private Limited Company
**Line of Business:** Freight transport by road not elsewhere classified
**Trading Style:** P S L Freight, Skantrans
**Issued Capital:** £78,327
**Principals:** J E King *(Managing)*, P E Dawson *(Commercial)*, B E Dawson
**Co. Secretary:** Brian Benton
**Branches:** The Psl Group Ltd, Carrington First, Manchester Road, Manchester M31 4NW
**US SIC:** 4213, 4712
**UK SIC:** 72300, 77002
**Auditors:** KPMG
**Bankers:** Barclays Bank Plc (20-65-82)

| | 31-03-14 | 31-03-13 | 31-03-12 |
|---|---|---|---|
| TO | 23,912,000 | 21,609,000 | 22,368,000 |
| P/L | 839,000 | 708,000 | 1,012,000 |
| NW | 787,000 | 726,000 | 934,000 |
| WC | 822,000 | 674,000 | 851,000 |
| Emp. | 104 | 103 | 96 |

DUNS 21-909-8274 **Exp**

## P.S.L. International Ltd

(**Subsidiary of:** The Weir Group Plc)
4 Waters Edge Business Park, Salford, Lancashire M5 3EZ
**Tel:** 01618764066
**Web:** www.psl-international.co.uk
**Reg No:** 0971289 **VAT No:** 128165080
**Estd:** 1970 Private Limited Company
**Line of Business:** Manufacture of pumps
**Export Markets:** U S A, Western Europe, Middle East
**Trading Style:** Weir Ing. Sevices
**Issued Capital:** £535,770
**Directors:** K A Ruddock, C F Morgan
**Co. Secretary:** Walter Clark
**Responsibilities**
**Senior:** Stuart Mann *(Service centre manager)*, Frances Mccaw *(Manager)*, Catherine Stead *(Manager)*
**US SIC:** 3561 **UK SIC:** 32870
**Auditors:** Ernst & Young
**Bankers:** Lloyds TSB Bank plc (30-00-04)

| | 03-01-14 | 28-12-12 | 30-01-11 |
|---|---|---|---|
| TA | 1,521,000 | 1,521,000 | 1,521,000 |
| NW | 1,521,000 | 1,521,000 | 1,521,000 |

DUNS 34-887-0346

## Psl Purchasing Ltd

First Floor Walton House, 11-13 Parade, Leamington Spa, Warwickshire CV32 4DG
**Tel:** 01926315111
**Web:** www.psl-uk.co.uk
**Reg No:** 2824094 **Estd:** 1993 Private Limited Company
**Line of Business:** Canteens and catering
**Export Sales:** £679,135
**Issued Capital:** £100
**Directors:** I A Shenkman, P A Hipps
**Co. Secretary:** Simon Newth
**US SIC:** 5812 **UK SIC:** 66110
**Auditors:** Garside & Co

| | 30-04-14 | 30-04-13 | 30-04-12 |
|---|---|---|---|
| TO | 8,560,785 | 7,907,605 | 7,491,877 |
| P/L | 1,359,393 | 1,471,244 | 1,628,476 |
| NW | 1,608,152 | 1,302,160 | 1,782,059 |
| WC | 1,405,604 | 1,093,470 | 1,633,020 |
| Emp. | 73 | 63 | 62 |

DUNS 21-627-9729 **Imp-Exp**

## Psm International Fasteners Ltd

(**Subsidiary of:** Psm Investments Ltd)
Ferry Lane, Pembroke Dock, Pembroke, Dyfed SA71 4RE
**Tel:** 01646 683501 **Fax:** 01646 687251
**Web:** www.bas-components.co.uk
**Reg No:** 0375564 **VAT No:** 443111986
**Estd:** 1942 Private Limited Company
**Line of Business:** Manufacturers of bolts and fixings
**Export Markets:** Worldwide
**Export Sales:** £7,634,000
**Issued Capital:** £1,188,347
**Directors:** K H Chan, S F Thomas, D Creese
**Co. Secretary:** Darren Creese
**Branches:** Psm International Fasteners Ltd, Ferry Lane, Pembroke, Dyfed SA71 4RE
**US SIC:** 3452, 3999

**UK SIC:** 31371, 49590
**Auditors:** PricewaterhouseCoopers LLP
**Bankers:** HSBC Bank plc (40-40-32)

| | 31-12-13 | 31-12-12 | 31-12-11 |
|---|---|---|---|
| TO | 11,286,000 | 10,790,000 | 8,423,000 |
| P/L | 612,000 | 481,000 | 60,000 |
| NW | 2,436,000 | 2,110,000 | 2,193,000 |
| WC | 4,304,000 | 3,818,000 | 3,772,000 |
| Emp. | 55 | 59 | 49 |

DUNS 50-000-2977 Imp

## Psm International Holdings Ltd

(**Subsidiary of:** Psm Investments Ltd)
Psm Ferry Lane, Barton Industrial Estate, Pembroke, Dyfed SA71 4RE
**Tel:** 01902407370 **Fax:** 0 1646 687251
**Web:** www.psminternational.com
**Reg No:** 2290856 **Estd:** 1988 Private Limited Company
**Line of Business:** Holding companies management activities
**Issued Capital:** £16,580,931
**Directors:** K H Chan, A G Gremlin, D Creese, S F Thomas, M Mok
**Co. Secretary:** Darren Creese
**US SIC:** 6711 **UK SIC:** 83962
**Auditors:** PricewaterhouseCoopers LLP

| | 31-12-13 | 31-12-12 | 31-12-11 |
|---|---|---|---|
| TA | 24,974,000 | 25,781,000 | 26,147,029 |
| P/L | 2,646,000 | 3,063,000 | 2,769,596 |
| NW | 15,662,000 | 16,484,000 | 16,763,570 |
| WC | 1,606,000 | 3,285,000 | 3,315,368 |

DUNS 51-615-1359

## Psp Group Ltd

P S P House, Hung Road, Bristol, Avon BS11 9XJ
**Tel:** 01179-822919 **Fax:** 0870-286-2535
**Web:** www.pspgroup.uk.com
**Reg No:** 5895304 **Estd:** 2006 Private Limited Company
**Line of Business:** Other service activities not elsewhere classified
**Issued Capital:** £5,000,000
**Directors:** S Dewani, P Dewani
**US SIC:** 8999 **UK SIC:** 83954
**Auditors:** Dunkley"s

| | 31-01-13 | 31-01-12 | 31-01-11 |
|---|---|---|---|
| TO | 11,285,372 | 10,739,476 | 10,554,276 |
| P/L | (1,040,469) | 224,078 | 615,898 |
| NW | 16,773,177 | 3,433,646 | 3,209,565 |
| WC | 16,905,849 | 2,013,851 | 1,630,935 |
| Emp. | 514 | 502 | 478 |

DUNS 21-795-5044

## Psp Healthcare

Styles Hill, Frome, Somerset BA11 5JR
**Tel:** 01373473113
**Estd:** 2011
**Line of Business:** Nursing Homes
**US SIC:** 8051 **UK SIC:** 95100
**Employees:** 59

DUNS 77-959-2815

## Psp Publishing Ltd

Craighall House, 58 High Craighall Road, Glasgow, Lanarkshire G4 9UD
**Tel:** 01413532222 **Fax:** 01413323839
**Web:** www.psppublishing.com
**Reg No:** 0158316SC **Estd:** 1995 Private Limited Company
**Line of Business:** Publishing of books
**Issued Capital:** £6,380
**Directors:** M J Wemyss, P Grant, W G Thomson
**Co. Secretary:** Thomas Lovering
**Responsibilities**
**IT:** Greig McLachlan *(IT Manager)*
**US SIC:** 2731, 2721
**UK SIC:** 47532, 47522
**Auditors:** Scott-Moncrieff
**Bankers:** Bank Of Scotland (80-07-15)

| | 31-12-13 | 31-12-12 | 31-12-11 |
|---|---|---|---|
| TA | 1,289,988 | 889,488 | 1,157,585 |
| NW | 471,113 | 145,301 | 268,247 |
| WC | 352,042 | 48,041 | 178,226 |

DUNS 22-863-1487

## Pss (Uk)

18-24 Seel Street, Liverpool, Merseyside L1 4BE
**Tel:** 01517025555
**Web:** www.pss.org.uk
**Reg No:** 0214077 **Estd:** 1926 Private Company Limited By Guarantee
**Line of Business:** Charities and charitable organisations
**Trading Style:** P S S
**Directors:** Ms V A Jackson, E R Aitken, M E Rathbone, Ms A A Jones, Ms S L Proffitt, G J Manning, D W Shortall, J A Kellaway
**Co. Secretary:** Mrs Jane Evans
**Responsibilities**
**Senior:** Hilary Berg *(Director)*, Victoria Bolton *(Manager)*, Eileen Johnson *(Manager)*
**Branches:** Pss (Uk), 160 Lawrence Rd, Liverpool, Merseyside L15 3HA
**US SIC:** 8321 **UK SIC:** 96111

**Auditors:** Grant Thornton UK LLP
**Bankers:** Barclays Bank Plc (20-51-01)

| | 31-03-14 | 31-03-13 | 31-03-12 |
|---|---|---|---|
| TO | 14,749,795 | 13,949,288 | 14,423,704 |
| P/L | 550,162 | 94,759 | 172,899 |
| NW | 5,914,849 | 5,381,238 | 5,061,312 |
| WC | 910,715 | 868,625 | 661,388 |
| Emp. | 398 | 400 | 418 |

DUNS 21-135-5311 Imp

## Psv Glass Llp

16 Hillbottom Road, Sands Industrial Estate, High Wycombe, Buckinghamshire HP12 4HJ
**Tel:** 01494 533131 **Fax:** 01494 462675
**Web:** www.psvglass.com
**Reg No:** 0339796OC **VAT No:** 398530806
**Estd:** 1988 Private Limited Company
**Line of Business:** Glass engravers and decorators
**Responsibilities**
**Senior:** Philip Powell *(Non-designated Limited Liabili)*
**IT:** Chris Harbour *(?ITand Communications Manager)*
**US SIC:** 3231, 5039
**UK SIC:** 24791, 61300
**Auditors:** Charterhouse (Accountants) LLP

| | 31-01-13 | 31-01-12 | 31-01-11 |
|---|---|---|---|
| TO | 13,714,474 | 13,380,826 | 13,696,969 |
| P/L | 1,444,837 | 871,592 | 1,541,801 |
| NW | 7,633,455 | 7,545,096 | 7,097,277 |
| WC | 2,698,810 | 3,068,949 | 3,006,204 |
| Emp. | 84 | 95 | 101 |

DUNS 67-247-8963

## Psychology Solutions Partnership Llp

3 Ashley Park Street Andrews, Bristol, Avon BS6 5DX
**Tel:** 08450774088
**Web:** www.psychologysolutions.co.uk
**Reg No:** 0327113OC **Estd:** 2007 Private Limited Company
**Line of Business:** Psychologists
**US SIC:** 8091, 7399
**UK SIC:** 95200, 83954

| | 30-04-14 | 30-04-13 | 30-04-12 |
|---|---|---|---|
| TA | 125,763 | 150,238 | 128,530 |
| WC | 92,041 | 132,437 | 117,666 |

DUNS 50-028-7982

## P.T. (Holdings) Ltd

Western Avenue, Western Docks, Southampton, Hampshire SO15 0HH
**Tel:** 02380736800
**Web:** www.ptcontractors.co.uk
**Reg No:** 2306363 **Estd:** 1988 Private Limited Company
**Line of Business:** Management activities of construction holding companies
**Issued Capital:** £28,000
**Principals:** P M Trant *(Managing)*, P N Trant
**Co. Secretary:** John Primrose
**Responsibilities**
**Senior:** Alan Vallee *(General Manager)*
**US SIC:** 6711, 1522
**UK SIC:** 83962, 50100
**Auditors:** Fiander Tovell LLP
**Bankers:** Lloyds TSB Bank plc (30-90-34)

| | 31-10-13 | 31-10-12 | 31-10-11 |
|---|---|---|---|
| TO | 7,358,376 | 8,093,925 | 8,247,462 |
| P/L | 21,680 | 20,168 | (7,885) |
| NW | 759,523 | 737,843 | 717,675 |
| WC | (642,100) | (600,044) | (551,498) |
| Emp. | 62 | 54 | 76 |

DUNS 21-675-6124

## Ptarmigan Media Holdings Ltd

1st Floor Mill House, 8 Mill Street, London SE1 2BA
**Tel:** 02072310014
**Reg No:** 7272948 **Estd:** 2010 Private Limited Company
**Line of Business:** Advertising
**Export Sales:** £8,216,000
**Issued Capital:** £25,000
**Directors:** Ms E S Wiggin, D P Wiggin
**Responsibilities**
**Senior:** Leon Samuels *(Financial controller)*
**US SIC:** 7311 **UK SIC:** 83800

| | 31-12-13 | 31-12-12 | 31-12-11 |
|---|---|---|---|
| TO | 58,567,000 | 54,781,000 | 73,929,000 |
| P/L | 1,482,000 | 1,383,000 | 6,478,000 |
| NW | 5,047,000 | 4,704,000 | 4,367,000 |
| WC | 5,867,000 | 5,374,000 | 4,765,000 |
| Emp. | 52 | 46 | 34 |

DUNS 21-629-7274

## Pts Consulting Partners Llp

Pts House, London EC2M 7PR
**Tel:** 02075396200
**Web:** http://ptsconsulting.com
**Reg No:** 0350348OC **Estd:** 2009
**Line of Business:** General management consultancy activities
**Responsibilities**
**Senior:** Kevin Barry *(Non-designated Limited Liabili)*, Kevin Brownell *(Non-designated Limited Liabili)*, Craig Fenton *(Non-designated Limited Liabili)*, Roger Hutchinson *(Non-designated Limited Liabili)*, Giles Korner *(Non-designated Limited Liabili)*, Barry Lewington *(Non-designated Limited Liabili)*, John Mccomish *(Non-designated Limited Liabili)*, Emma Melling *(Non-designated Limited Liabili)*, Roger Myers *(Non-designated Limited Liabili)*, Kevin Riches *(Non-Executive Director)*, Kuldip Sandhu *(Non-designated Limited Liabili)*, Gareth Storey *(Non-designated Limited Liabili)*, Gregory Sutton *(Non-designated Limited Liabili)*
**Sales:** John Mccomish *(Non-designated Limited Liabili)*
**Purchasing:** Chris Charles *(Procurement Specialist)*
**US SIC:** 7392 **UK SIC:** 83951

| | 31-03-14 | 31-03-13 | 31-03-12 |
|---|---|---|---|
| TO | 7,948,059 | 9,717,639 | 5,511,908 |
| P/L | (536,261) | 1,504,964 | 334,560 |
| NW | 1,523,892 | 2,010,154 | 468,565 |
| WC | (346,074) | 1,385,365 | 516,793 |
| Emp. | 72 | 65 | 49 |

DUNS 39-821-3744

## Pts Group Ltd

(**Subsidiary of:** Travis Perkins Plc)
Fleet House, Lee Circle, Leicester, Leicestershire LE1 3QQ
**Tel:** 01162567145 **Fax:** 01788527799
**Web:** www.ptsplumbing.co.uk
**Reg No:** 2219435 **Estd:** 1984 Private Limited Company
**Line of Business:** Agents involved in the sale of timber and building materials
**Trading Style:** B S S Group
**Issued Capital:** £4,984,897
**Directors:** M D Parker, J P Carter, M R Meech, R D Proctor, Ms C Kavanagh, Ms S Greatorex, N Bell, A D Buffin
**Co. Secretary:**
Tpg Management Services Limited
**Responsibilities**
**Senior:** Andy Brook *(Area Director)*, Geoff Leeson *(Branch Manager)*, Rachel Mcintyre *(Customer Service Manager)*
**Sales:** Maxine Goldstone *(Sales Executive)*
**Branches:** Pts Group Ltd, Unit 2, Lagrange, Tamworth, Staffordshire B79 7XD
**US SIC:** 5072, 5074
**UK SIC:** 61500, 61300
**Auditors:** Deloitte LLP
**Bankers:** Lloyds TSB Bank plc (30-15-53)

**Following financial data are in thousands**

| | 31-12-13 | 31-12-12 | 31-12-11 |
|---|---|---|---|
| TO | 1,433,900 | 1,341,500 | 1,428,200 |
| P/L | 14,900 | 293,600 | 51,700 |
| NW | 411,200 | 411,800 | 81,000 |
| WC | 458,100 | 434,800 | 100,300 |
| Emp. | 4,106 | 4,466 | 4,906 |

DUNS 52-528-0269

## Ptsg Access and Safety Ltd

(**Subsidiary of:** Premier Technical Services Group Ltd)
13-14 Flemming Court, Castleford, West Yorkshire WF10 5HW
**Tel:** 01977-668-771
**Web:** www.ptsg.co.uk
**Reg No:** 3233894 **VAT No:** 670755713
**Estd:** 1996 Private Limited Company
**Line of Business:** Construction machinery manufacturers
**Trading Style:** National Cradle Maintenance
**Issued Capital:** £250,000
**Directors:** J R Foley, A J Coates, P W Teasdale
**Co. Secretary:** Adam Coates
**US SIC:** 3531, 8911, 5199
**UK SIC:** 32541, 83701, 61900
**Auditors:** Armstrong Watson
**Bankers:** HSBC Bank plc (40-11-18)

| | 31-12-13 | 31-12-12 | 31-12-11 |
|---|---|---|---|
| TO | 9,421,813 | 9,168,599 | 7,463,617 |
| P/L | 2,424,563 | 2,369,740 | 556,333 |
| NW | (155,647) | 2,312,378 | 1,239,623 |
| WC | 3,050,921 | 1,872,361 | 869,871 |
| Emp. | 89 | 75 | 70 |

DUNS 50-558-4920 Imp

## P.T.T. Design Ltd

Bleachers Yard, Radford Road, New Basford, Nottingham, Nottinghamshire NG7 7EF
**Tel:** 01159-420014
**Web:** www.pttdesign.com
**Reg No:** 2509708 **VAT No:** 568215819
**Estd:** 1988 Private Limited Company
**Line of Business:** Office furniture and equipment suppliers
**Issued Capital:** £16,667
**Principals:** S D Howkins *(Managing)*, A Moscatelli
**Co. Secretary:** Mark Howkins
**Responsibilities**
**Finance:** Louise Hallam *(Finance Manager)*
**Purchasing:** Mark Epton *(Estimator)*
**US SIC:** 2599 **UK SIC:** 46720
**Auditors:** R.E. George

| | 31-03-14 | 31-03-13 | 31-03-12 |
|---|---|---|---|
| TA | 2,110,761 | 2,866,248 | 3,156,642 |
| NW | 617,384 | 637,981 | 669,863 |
| WC | 132,376 | 177,903 | 212,592 |

DUNS 29-886-3366

## Pub Market Ltd

(**Subsidiary of:** Stradling Holdings Ltd)
Market Chmbrs, Market Street, Pontypridd, Mid Glamorgan CF37 2SP
**Tel:** 01443409077
**Reg No:** 2089245 **Estd:** 1987 Private Limited Company
**Line of Business:** Bars
**Issued Capital:** £750,000
**Directors:** N S John, J H Phillips, N S John
**Co. Secretary:** David John
**US SIC:** 5813 **UK SIC:** 66200
**Auditors:** Alan Newland & Co

| | 31-12-13 | 31-12-12 | 31-12-11 |
|---|---|---|---|
| TO | 1,326,329 | 1,282,976 | 1,449,469 |
| P/L | 38,143 | 50,543 | 162,302 |
| NW | 455,752 | 441,831 | 372,029 |
| WC | (2,159,677) | (2,193,024) | (2,474,173) |
| Emp. | 46 | 50 | 53 |

DUNS 42-393-9230

## Public & Commercial Services

160 Falcon Road, London SW11 2l N
**Tel:** 02079242727
**Web:** www.pcs.org.uk
**Estd:** 1999
**Line of Business:** Trade unions
**Principals:** Ms J Godrich *(President)*, D Newlyn *(Financial)*
**Co. Secretary:** Mark Serwotka
**Responsibilities**
**Senior:** Pav Alam *(Executive)*, John Baldock *(Chairman)*, John Beanland *(Member)*, Paul Bemrose *(Executive)*, Barry Bentham *(Executive)*, Simon Boniface *(Executive)*, Nigel Buller *(Chairman)*, Martin Cavanagh *(Executive)*, Danny Clarke *(Executive)*, Catherine Craig *(Executive)*, Cecile Day *(Member)*, Geoff Delissen *(Member)*, Geoff Dexter *(Executive)*, Stuart Dunn *(Executive)*, Diane Ebanks *(Executive)*, Alexis Edwards *(Member)*, Rachel Edwards *(Chairman)*, Matthew Garland *(Member)*, Jeremy Gautrey *(Aviation Group Secretary)*, Pete Gillum *(Executive)*, Kim Hendry *(Executive)*, Pauline Henry *(Member)*, Kevin Herns *(Technical Officer)*, Jason Hogg *(Executive)*, Yewande Ipaye *(Member)*, Michael Kavanagh *(Group President)*, Elizabeth Kearns *(Executive)*, Kate Ling *(Vice Chair)*, Fiona Low *(Office Manager)*, Dave Lunn *(Group Vice President)*, Fiona Mclatchie *(Executive)*, John Medhurst *(Executive)*, Sue Mossman *(Executive)*, Niraj Patel *(Member)*, Mike Quirk *(Board Member)*, Imogen Radford *(Executive)*, Eric Rothery *(Member)*, Jim Shannon *(Executive)*, Ann Stephenson *(Chairman)*, Jim Stringer *(Executive)*, John Thornton *(Administrator)*, Kevin Tolmie *(Member)*, Kit Tsang *(Member)*, Dave Vickers *(Board Member)*, Kevin Watkins *(Board Member)*, Keith Westbury *(Board Member)*, Hugo Wilson *(Group Executive Committee Memb)*, Adam Wissen *(Executive)*, Stuart Woodfine *(Board Member)*, Gordon Woollard *(President)*
**Finance:** Dean Fisher *(Treasurer)*, Nick Ling *(Treasurer)*, Scott Rudd *(Treasurer)*, Sue Schofield *(Treasurer)*
**Marketing:** Tracy Edwards *(Editor)*, David Greenall *(Editor)*, Kevin Herns *(Technical Officer)*, Richard Simcox *(National Press Officer)*, Andy Stuart *(Editor)*
**Admin:** Jan Baxter *(Secretary)*, Maureen Birrell *(Group Secretary)*, Rob Bowers *(Group Secretary)*, Dave Burke *(Assistant Secretary)*, Matt Burrows *(Assistant Secretary -DSA)*, Mike Chew *(Administrator)*, Jacqueline Cormack *(Assistant Secretary)*, Lorna Cox *(Administrator)*, Jon Dews *(Secretary)*, Joe Hartley *(Administrator)*, Joel Heyes *(Administrator)*, Kay Hinde *(Group Secretary)*, Jude Jackson *(Group Assistant Secretary)*, Naeem Manzur *(Admin Assistant, Courses and E)*, Elaine Matthews *(Group Secretary)*, Annette Mayers *(Administrator)*, Neil Mortson *(Administrator)*, Naliny Neeladoo *(Administrator)*, Jacqui Nichols *(Assistant Secretary)*, Julie Wade *(Group Secretary)*, Stuart Whigham *(Personal Assistant)*
**IT:** Kevin Herns *(Technical Officer)*, Quentin Hogg *(Senior Information Officer)*
**HR:** Marcus Ford *(Training Director)*
**Operations:** Helen Batty *(Production and Operations Mana)*, Molly Moyo *(Projects Manager)*
**Purchasing:** Kevin Herns *(Technical Officer)*
**Branches:** Public & Commercial Services, 20 Union Street, Edinburgh, Midlothian EH1 3LR
**US SIC:** 8631 **UK SIC:** 96313
**Auditors:** BDO Stoy Hayward
**Employees:** 150
**Turnover:** £32,032,657

DUNS 21-784-0770
### Public Bier Halles
9 Gordon Street, Glasgow, Lanarkshire G1 3PL
**Tel:** 01412486487
**Estd:** 1999 Proprietorship
**Line of Business:** Public house
**Proprietor:** A Mccoll
**Responsibilities**
**Senior:** Liz Mcdowall *(Manager)*
**US SIC:** 5813 **UK SIC:** 66200
**Employees:** 50

DUNS 22-536-0320
### Public Health England
Wellington House, 133-155 Waterloo Road, London SE1 8UG
**Tel:** 02079724610 **Fax:** 020-7811-7750
**Web:** www.dh.gov.uk
**Estd:** 2013 Incorporate By Act Of Parliament
**Line of Business:** Other human health activities
**Trading Style:** Phe
**Principals:** D Heymann *(Chairman)*, M Brodie *(Financial)*, A Sienkiewicz, Ms V Bennett, T Vickers Byrne, J Newton, Dr C Mccartney, J Marron
**Responsibilities**
**Senior:** Maggie Bishop *(Manager)*, Kevin Fenton *(Director)*, Richard Gleave *(Director)*, Liz Harnett *(Manager)*, Christine McCartney *(Director)*, Duncan Selbie *(Chief Executive Officer)*
**IT:** Andrew Whitcombe *(Project Manager)*
**Branches:** Public Health England, Ysbyty Glan Clwyd, Rhuddlan Rd, Bodelwyddan, Rhyl, Clwyd LL18 5UJ
**US SIC:** 8091 **UK SIC:** 95200
**Auditors:** Deloitte LLP
**Following financial data are in thousands**

| | 31-03-14 |
|---|---|
| TO | 231,557 |
| P/L | (3,498,281) |
| NW | 1,100,368 |
| WC | 175,282 |
| Emp. | 5,196 |

DUNS 21-335-8227
### Public Health Laboratory
Singleton Hospital, Sketty Lane, Sketty, Swansea, West Glamorgan SA2 8QA
**Tel:** 01792-285055
**Estd:** 1989 Proprietorship
**Line of Business:** Research and laboratory based activities
**Proprietor:** Dr P Thomas
**US SIC:** 7391 **UK SIC:** 94000
**Employees:** 55

DUNS 21-558-9473
### Public Health Wales Nhs Trust
Unit 1 Charnwood Court, Heol Billingsley, Parc Nantgarw, Nantgarw, Cardiff, South Glamorgan CF15 7QZ
**Tel:** 01443824172
**Web:** www.publichealthwales.org
**Estd:** 2014
**Line of Business:** Hospitals
**Responsibilities**
**Senior:** Julie Bishop *(Regional Director)*, Gary Dowling *(Finance Assistant)*, Bob Hudson *(Ceo)*
**Finance:** Gary Dowling *(Finance Assistant)*
**US SIC:** 6732 **UK SIC:** 83100
**Bankers:** National Westminster Bank Plc (56-00-41)
**Employees:** 1,100

DUNS 39-742-4268
### Public Ltd
Railway Court, Doncaster, South Yorkshire DN4 5FB
**Tel:** 01302-730303
**Web:** www.openatpublic.com
**Reg No:** 2164345 **VAT No:** 477035730
**Estd:** 1987 Private Limited Company
**Line of Business:** Advertising agency services
**Issued Capital:** £10,100
**Principals:** P A Green *(Managing)*, S P Ridgeway
**Co. Secretary:** Mrs Cheryl Green
**US SIC:** 7392, 7399
**UK SIC:** 83951, 83954
**Auditors:** Jonathan S White & Co
**Bankers:** Yorkshire Bank Plc (05-07-62)

| | 30-09-13 | 30-09-12 | 30-09-11 |
|---|---|---|---|
| TO | N/A | N/A | 6,551,022 |
| P/L | N/A | N/A | 365,181 |
| NW | 618,281 | 838,270 | 899,594 |
| WC | 436,965 | 630,892 | 683,984 |
| Emp. | N/A | N/A | 45 |

DUNS 21-172-9196
### Public Power Solutions Ltd
(**Subsidiary of:** Swindon Borough Council)
Cheney House, Darby Close, Cheney Manor Industrial Estate, Swindon, Wiltshire SN2 2PN
**Tel:** 01793616427 **Fax:** 01793431175
**Web:** www.swindon.gov.uk
**Reg No:** 6969563 **Estd:** 1995 Private Limited Company
**Line of Business:** Collection and treatment of other waste
**Issued Capital:** £100
**Directors:** P W Watts, J E Owen, O Donachie, B T Brannan, G J Perkins, P W Heath
**Co. Secretary:** Mrs Cheryl Sloan
**Responsibilities**
**Senior:** Mark Barnet *(Housing Manager)*
**US SIC:** 4953, 8911
**UK SIC:** 92110, 83701
**Bankers:** The Co-Operative Bank Plc (08-90-41)

| | 31-03-14 | 31-03-13 | 31-03-12 |
|---|---|---|---|
| TO | 35,228,000 | 52,895,000 | 60,045,000 |
| P/L | (606,000) | 95,000 | 358,000 |
| NW | 10,000 | 244,000 | 153,000 |
| WC | 942,000 | 2,579,000 | 1,279,000 |
| Emp. | 335 | 585 | 573 |

DUNS 21-812-4387
### Public Prosecution Service
58 Upper Arthur Street, Belfast BT1 4GJ
**Tel:** 028 90542444
**Web:** www.ppsni.gov.uk
**Estd:** 2012
**Line of Business:** Legal svcs
**Trading Style:** Pps Ni
**Responsibilities**
**IT:** Owen Crilly *(Senior IT Executive)*
**Branches:** Public Prosecution Service, Omagh Chambers, Townhall Square, Omagh, Co Tyrone BT78 1BL
**US SIC:** 7999, 8111
**UK SIC:** 97913, 83500
**Employees:** 560

DUNS 21-470-4681
### Public Record Office of Northern Ireland
2 Titanic Boulevard, Belfast BT3 9HQ
**Tel:** 02890534800
**Web:** www.proni.gov.uk
**Estd:** 2002 Proprietorship
**Line of Business:** Preparation of wills
**Proprietor:** H Stanley
**Responsibilities**
**Senior:** Sandra Ireland *(Senior Manager)*
**US SIC:** 9121 **UK SIC:** 91110
**Employees:** 80

DUNS 73-856-5493
### Public Restaurant Partner Ltd
(**Subsidiary of:** Company of Cooks Ltd.)
Kenwood West Lodge, Hampstead Lane, London NW3 7JR
**Tel:** 020-8341-5384 **Fax:** 02083482643
**Web:** www.companyofcooks.com
**Reg No:** 5111519 **VAT No:** 848797745
**Estd:** 2004 Private Limited Company
**Line of Business:** Licensed restaurants
**Trading Style:** Company of Cooks
**Issued Capital:** £200
**Director:** M Lucy
**Co. Secretary:** Colin Lees
**Branches:** Public Restaurant Partner Ltd, The Restaurant, Royal Horticultural Society Gardens, Woking, Surrey GU23 6QA
**US SIC:** 5812 **UK SIC:** 66110
**Auditors:** Goodman Jones LLP
**Bankers:** Coutts & Co (18-00-02)

| | 29-09-13 | 30-04-12 | 30-09-11 |
|---|---|---|---|
| TO | 46,072,251 | 31,604,679 | 30,206,327 |
| P/L | 766,614 | 457,305 | (993,797) |
| NW | (258,827) | (587,320) | (763,395) |
| WC | (3,501,950) | (3,980,219) | (3,513,570) |
| Emp. | 558 | 563 | 669 |

DUNS 39-755-9949
### Public Service Broadcasting Trust Ltd
7a Calpe House, St Thomas Street, Winchester, Hampshire SO23 9HE
**Fax:** 023-8033-5050
**Web:** www.psbt.co.uk
**Reg No:** 2194957 **VAT No:** 631743451
**Estd:** 1988 Private Company Limited By Guarantee
**Line of Business:** Television activities
**Directors:** S G Cross, N J Eldred, S P Pomeroy, Ms J Mccloskey, R Stephenson, B S Lister, Ms R Wrigley, J J Hopkins
**Co. Secretary:** Ms Margo Horsley
**Responsibilities**
**Senior:** Jay Mercer *(Trustee)*
**US SIC:** 4833 **UK SIC:** 97411
**Auditors:** Sheen Stickland LLP
**Bankers:** National Westminster Bank Plc (56-00-68)

| | 31-03-14 | 31-03-13 | 31-03-12 |
|---|---|---|---|
| TO | 3,070,151 | 2,089,104 | 519,986 |
| P/L | (103,300) | 109,791 | (105,795) |
| NW | 17,538 | 120,838 | 11,047 |
| WC | 17,538 | 120,838 | 11,047 |
| Emp. | 78 | 51 | 14 |

DUNS 21-706-5137
### Public Services Department
Po Box 30, Guernsey, Channel Islands GY1 3AS
**Web:** www.gov.gg
**Estd:** 2011
**Line of Business:** Delivers a diverse range of services to Guernsey.
**Trading Style:** Guernsey Water, Guernsey Harbours, Guernsey Airport, Central Services States Works
**Principals:** A Lewis, A Redhead, C Le Ray, N Dorey, P Gill, Ms C Brown
**Branches:** Public Services Department - Guernsey Water, Po Box 30, Brickfield House, GY1 3AS St Andrew
**US SIC:** 9121 **UK SIC:** 91110
**Employees:** 600

DUNS 21-706-1322
### Public Services Ombudsman for Wales
1 Old Field Road, Pencoed, Bridgend, Mid Glamorgan CF35 5LJ
**Tel:** 01656641150
**Web:** www.ombudsman-wales.org.uk
**Estd:** 2005 Proprietorship
**Line of Business:** Consumer organisations
**Proprietor:** P Tyndall
**Responsibilities**
**Senior:** A Peat *(Manager)*
**US SIC:** 8699 **UK SIC:** 96902
**Employees:** 50

DUNS 21-584-0537
### Publicis Blueprint
Oxford House, 76 Oxford Street, London W1D 1BS
**Tel:** 02078303979
**Web:** www.publicis-blueprint.co.uk
**Estd:** 2011 Proprietorship
**Line of Business:** Newspapers publishing
**Proprietor:** Miss J Richards
**Responsibilities**
**Marketing:** Kim Armstrong *(Insight Manager)*
**US SIC:** 2711 **UK SIC:** 47512
**Employees:** 60

DUNS 21-198-6385 **Exp**
### Publicis Healthcare Communications Group Ltd
(**Subsidiary of:** Publicis Groupe S.A.)
Pembroke Building, Avonmore Road Kensington Village, London W14 8DG
**Tel:** 02071734000
**Web:** www.publicishealthcare.com
**Reg No:** 1072087 **VAT No:** 547817607
**Estd:** 1952 Private Limited Company
**Line of Business:** Advertising related services
**Export Markets:** W Europe
**Export Sales:** £13,127,000
**Trading Style:** A D A, Advertising & Design Association, Publicis Life Brands Resolute
**Issued Capital:** £139,510
**Directors:** A P Kuchel, Ms N G Le Bos, N Colucci
**Co. Secretary:** Raj Basran
**Responsibilities**
**Facilities:** Neil Jennings *(Facilities Manager)*
**US SIC:** 7311 **UK SIC:** 83800
**Auditors:** Mazars LLP
**Bankers:** National Westminster Bank Plc (60-40-04)

| | 31-12-13 | 31-12-12 | 31-12-11 |
|---|---|---|---|
| TO | 18,389,000 | 19,494,000 | 18,879,000 |
| P/L | 9,472,000 | (6,000) | (479,000) |
| NW | (1,073,000) | (8,306,000) | (5,665,000) |
| WC | (188,099,000) | (91,258,000) | (4,459,000) |
| Emp. | 154 | 138 | 146 |

DUNS 21-878-7454
### Publicist Chemistry
82 Baker Street, London W1U 6AE
**Tel:** 02079357744
**Web:** www.publicischemistry.com
**Estd:** 2012
**Line of Business:** Advertising Agencies
**US SIC:** 7311 **UK SIC:** 83800
**Employees:** 600

DUNS 21-641-4664
### Publishing Technology Plc
8100 Alec Issigonis Way, Oxford Business Park North, Oxford, Oxfordshire OX4 2HU
**Tel:** 01865397800 **Fax:** 01865-397801
**Web:** www.publishingtechnology.com
**Reg No:** 0837205 **VAT No:** 134709471
**Estd:** 1965 Public Limited Company
**Line of Business:** Other software consultancy and supply
**Export Sales:** £9,288,000
**Issued Capital:** £841,361
**Directors:** M A Rowse, M P Cairns, M C Rose
**Co. Secretary:** Alan Moug
**Responsibilities**
**Senior:** George Lossius *(Manager)*
**Sales:** Randy Petway *(Executive Vice President, Stra)*
**Admin:** Marie Parkinson *(Office Manager)*
**IT:** Gary Bowman *(IT Director)*
**Health & Safety:** Marie Parkinson *(Office Manager)*
**Facilities:** Marie Parkinson *(Office Manager)*
**Operations:** Jay Tetelbaum *(Chief Operating Officer, Vista)*
**Purchasing:** Marie Parkinson *(Office Manager)*
**Branches:** Publishing Technology Plc, Accurist House, 44 Baker St, London W1U 7AL
**US SIC:** 7379, 7319
**UK SIC:** 83940, 83800
**Auditors:** Grant Thornton UK LLP
**Bankers:** Barclays Bank Plc (20-01-09)

| | 31-12-13 | 31-12-12 | 31-12-11 |
|---|---|---|---|
| TO | 16,471,000 | 16,136,000 | 14,879,000 |
| P/L | 665,000 | 283,000 | (183,000) |
| NW | (4,182,000) | (5,006,000) | (5,493,000) |
| WC | (3,237,000) | (3,786,000) | (4,308,000) |
| Emp. | 176 | 170 | 163 |

DUNS 37-875-5003
### Puckrup Hall Hotel Ltd
(**Subsidiary of:** Hilton Worldwide Holdings Inc.)
Puckrup, Tewkesbury, Gloucestershire GL20 6EL
**Tel:** 01684296200 **Fax:** 01684-850788
**Web:** www.tewkesbury.hilton.com
**Reg No:** 3307736 **Estd:** 1997 Private Limited Company
**Line of Business:** Hotels
**Issued Capital:** £1
**Directors:** J Tynan, B Wilson, H Uk Corporate Director Limited, J O Percival, S Beasley, H M Enayetullah, O Lifschitz, S R Vincent
**Co. Secretary:** Hlt Secretary Limited
**Responsibilities**
**Facilities:** Malcolm Teesdale *(Maintenance Manager)*
**US SIC:** 7011 **UK SIC:** 66500
**Auditors:** Ernst & Young LLP

| | 31-12-13 | 31-12-12 | 31-12-11 |
|---|---|---|---|
| TO | 4,992,866 | 4,555,317 | 4,606,117 |
| P/L | (1,707,281) | (1,760,469) | (1,352,435) |
| NW | (1,451,660) | 348,769 | 2,204,587 |
| WC | (1,451,660) | 348,769 | 2,204,587 |

DUNS 21-774-9805
### Pudsey Police Station
Pudsey Police Station, Dawsons Corner, Stanningley, Pudsey, West Yorkshire LS28 5TA
**Tel:** 01132414999
**Web:** www.westyorkshire.police.uk
**Estd:** 2011 Proprietorship
**Line of Business:** Police forces
**Proprietor:** M Bownass
**US SIC:** 9221 **UK SIC:** 91300
**Employees:** 150

DUNS 77-508-6044
### Puffin Investments Ltd
Withybush Trading Estate, Withybush Road, Haverfordwest, Dyfed SA62 4BS
**Fax:** 01437767319
**Web:** www.puffinproduce.com
**Reg No:** 2982454 **Estd:** 1986 Private Limited Company
**Line of Business:** Management activities of holding companies
**Issued Capital:** £120,338
**Directors:** J E Morris, P J Scale, R Hayman
**US SIC:** 6711, 5148
**UK SIC:** 83962, 61700
**Auditors:** Ashmole & Co

| | 30-06-13 | 30-06-12 | 30-06-11 |
|---|---|---|---|
| TO | 12,354,441 | 9,134,685 | 11,661,596 |
| P/L | 600,773 | 368,249 | 359,526 |
| NW | 1,702,511 | 3,089,008 | 1,563,531 |
| WC | (872,304) | (181,215) | 1,041,982 |
| Emp. | 77 | 68 | 55 |

DUNS 22-950-1457 **Imp**
### Puig Uk Ltd
(**Subsidiary of:** Puig Sl)
Grafton House, London W1F 9HR
**Tel:** 02074994420 **Fax:** 020-7494-6260
**Web:** www.puig.com
**Reg No:** 1087743 **VAT No:** 216935553
**Estd:** 1972 Private Limited Company
**Line of Business:** Suppliers and wholesalers of pefume
**Issued Capital:** £2,001,000

**Directors:** J Bach Kutschruetter, F H Billaud, J Albiol
**Responsibilities**
**Marketing:** Simon Tuplin *(Marketing Director)*
**Purchasing:** Dilsha Lathia *(Visual Merchandiser)*, Alix Watson *(Merchandising Coordinator)*
**Branches:** Puig Uk Ltd, 21 Cork St, London W1S 3LZ
**US SIC:** 2844 **UK SIC:** 25820
**Auditors:** Ernst & Young LLP
**Bankers:** Lloyds TSB Bank plc (30-98-62)

| | 31-12-13 | 31-12-12 | 31-12-11 |
|---|---|---|---|
| TO | 76,816,000 | 72,510,000 | 69,870,000 |
| P/L | 7,991,000 | 10,254,000 | 13,296,000 |
| NW | 453,000 | 2,732,000 | 14,692,000 |
| WC | (11,000) | 2,021,000 | 14,130,000 |
| Emp. | 172 | 179 | 178 |

DUNS 22-257-4753 **Imp**

## Pukka Herbs Ltd

8 Axis, Hawkfield Way, Bristol, Avon BS14 0BY
**Tel:** 01179-640944 **Fax:** 01179-640804
**Web:** www.pukkaherbs.com
**Reg No:** 4275539 **Estd:** 2001 Private Limited Company
**Line of Business:** Herbs and spices suppliers and retailers
**Export Sales:** £6,404,515
**Issued Capital:** £100
**Director:** S F Pole
**Co. Secretary:** Timothy Westwell
**Responsibilities**
**Senior:** Gilbert Williams *(Manager)*
**Marketing:** Liam Tullberg *(Marketing Director)*
**IT:** Tony Pottrell *(IT Manager)*
**US SIC:** 5499, 5431, 5148
**UK SIC:** 64100, 61700

| | 31-08-13 | 31-08-12 | 31-08-11 |
|---|---|---|---|
| TO | 12,977,162 | N/A | 6,669,243 |
| P/L | 340,829 | N/A | 196,760 |
| NW | 658,179 | 460,885 | 430,612 |
| WC | 503,226 | 283,742 | 344,361 |
| Emp. | 54 | N/A | 35 |

DUNS 21-913-2735

## Pukka Pies Ltd

The Halfcroft, Leicester, Leicestershire LE7 1LD
**Tel:** 01162644004
**Web:** www.pukkapies.co.uk
**Reg No:** 1008747 **VAT No:** 113755287
**Estd:** 1962 Private Limited Company
**Line of Business:** Steel fabricators
**Export Sales:** £389,633
**Trading Style:** Pukka Pies Ltd
**Issued Capital:** £50,000
**Principals:** T D Storer *(Managing)*, A J Storer *(Managing)*, Ms V C Storer
**Co. Secretary:** Andrew Storer
**Responsibilities**
**Senior:** Robert Church *(Factory Manager)*, Jason Inserra *(Manager)*, Russell Vines *(Warehouse Manager)*
**Finance:** Antonio Inserra *(Finance Director)*
**HR:** Kerry Dickens *(Personnel Officer)*, Kerry Jarvis *(Personnel Officer)*
**Health & Safety:** Bridget Coignec *(Quality Assurance Manager)*
**Facilities:** Simon Kemp *(Engineering Manager)*
**Operations:** Bridget Coignec *(Quality Assurance Manager)*, Kerry Dickens *(Personnel Officer)*
**Fleet:** Russell Vines *(Warehouse Manager)*
**Engineering:** Simon Kemp *(Engineering Manager)*
**Branches:** Pukka Pies Ltd, 33-43 Aldwarke Road, Rotherham, South Yorkshire S62 6BZ
**US SIC:** 1622 **UK SIC:** 50200
**Auditors:** Robert Whowell & Partners
**Bankers:** National Westminster Bank Plc (54-21-50)

| | 26-05-14 | 27-05-13 | 28-05-12 |
|---|---|---|---|
| TO | 43,913,254 | 40,296,708 | 40,125,524 |
| P/L | 4,416,110 | 3,638,457 | 3,743,021 |
| NW | 29,702,190 | 26,929,707 | 26,716,410 |
| WC | 12,125,736 | 10,250,757 | 8,526,341 |
| Emp. | 298 | 286 | 277 |

DUNS 21-096-8652

## Pulborough Medical Group

Spiro Close, Pulborough, West Sussex RH20 1FG
**Tel:** 01798872815
**Web:** www.pmgdoctors.co.uk
**Estd:** 2009 Partnership
**Line of Business:** Doctors
**Partners:** Dr M Shillingford, Dr P Hard
**Responsibilities**
**Senior:** Peter Hard *(Partner)*
**US SIC:** 8062 **UK SIC:** 95100
**Employees:** 60

DUNS 51-613-0015

## Pull & Bear Uk Ltd

(**Subsidiary of:** Pontegadea Inversiones Sl)
Unit 4 1 Victoria Square, Belfast BT1 4QG
**Tel:** 02890316160
**Reg No:** 5893279 **Estd:** 2006 Private Limited Company
**Line of Business:** Retail sale of clothing
**Issued Capital:** £4,500,000
**Directors:** A A Vasserot, P D Rivas, J M Romay De La Colina
**Co. Secretary:** Athenaeum Secretaries Limited
**Branches:** Pull & Bear Uk Ltd, Westfield Shopping Centre, Ariel Way, London W12 7SL
**US SIC:** 5699, 5661
**UK SIC:** 64500, 64600
**Auditors:** KPMG LLP

| | 31-01-14 | 31-01-13 | 31-01-12 |
|---|---|---|---|
| TO | 15,559,000 | 13,508,000 | 11,930,000 |
| P/L | 441,000 | 314,000 | (191,000) |
| NW | 4,031,000 | 3,729,000 | 3,499,000 |
| WC | 1,547,000 | 1,351,000 | 118,000 |
| Emp. | 143 | 96 | 97 |

DUNS 21-580-1161

## Pullen Brickwork

The Old Dairy Fronebridge Farm, Bristol, Avon BS37 6LU
**Estd:** 2011 Proprietorship
**Line of Business:** Bricklayers
**Proprietor:** A Pullen
**US SIC:** 1799 **UK SIC:** 50000
**Employees:** 70

DUNS 29-011-1772

## Pullins (Bakers) Ltd

27-29 High Street, Bristol, Avon BS49 4JD
**Tel:** 01934-832135 **Fax:** 01934-876503
**Web:** www.pullinsbakers.co.uk
**Reg No:** 0344817 **VAT No:** 130310441
**Estd:** 1925 Private Limited Company
**Line of Business:** Manufacture of bread; manufacture of fresh pastry goods and cakes
**Trading Style:** Pullins (Bakers) Ltd
**Issued Capital:** £1,860
**Principals:** T J Pullin *(Managing)*, M D Pullin, Ms S A Pullin, Ms A M Pullin
**Co. Secretary:** Trevor Pullin
**Branches:** Pullins (Bakers) Ltd, 27-29 High Street, Bristol, Avon BS49 4JD
**US SIC:** 5462 **UK SIC:** 64100
**Auditors:** Whyatt Pakeman Partners
**Bankers:** Lloyds TSB Bank plc (30-99-51)

| | 30-09-13 | 30-09-12 | 30-09-11 |
|---|---|---|---|
| TA | 1,107,495 | 937,821 | 933,462 |
| NW | 564,548 | 406,144 | 321,957 |
| WC | 245,129 | 119,357 | 65,909 |

DUNS 21-731-7379 **Imp-Exp**

## Pullmaflex U.K. Ltd

(**Subsidiary of:** Leggett & Platt Incorporated)
Parc Amanwy Ffordd Y Rhyd, Ammanford, Dyfed SA18 3ER
**Tel:** 01269592301 **Fax:** 01269-593262
**Reg No:** 0361006 **VAT No:** 125006713
**Estd:** 1949 Private Limited Company
**Line of Business:** Manufacture of wire products
**Export Markets:** E U
**Export Sales:** £8,751,179
**Issued Capital:** £51,000
**Directors:** J D Crusa, R Konig, K Beerly, S L Koch
**Co. Secretary:** Ms Sonia Smith
**Responsibilities**
**Facilities:** Dorian Jones *(Facilities Coordinator)*
**Purchasing:** Sharon Rees *(Materials Controller)*
**Branches:** Pullmaflex U.k. Ltd, Po Box 7237, Tadley, Hampshire RG26 4XB
**US SIC:** 3496, 3799
**UK SIC:** 31694, 36502
**Auditors:** PricewaterhouseCoopers LLP
**Bankers:** National Westminster Bank Plc (55-61-20)

| | 31-12-13 | 31-12-12 | 31-12-11 |
|---|---|---|---|
| TO | 11,335,748 | 11,088,895 | 12,838,460 |
| P/L | 665,830 | 891,288 | 1,168,077 |
| NW | 3,666,474 | 2,316,731 | 2,026,836 |
| WC | 4,272,378 | 3,963,787 | 3,241,481 |
| Emp. | 65 | 72 | 62 |

DUNS 21-029-3385

## Pullman Fleet Services

Middlebank House, Middle Bank, Doncaster, South Yorkshire DN4 5PF
**Tel:** 08704282050
**Web:** www.pullmanfleet.co.uk
**Proprietorship**
**Line of Business:** Commercial vehicle servicing repairs parts & accessories
**Proprietor:** V Strafford
**US SIC:** 7539 **UK SIC:** 67100
**Employees:** 170

DUNS 50-019-8452

## Pullman Premier Leisure Ltd

12-18 Dorchester Road, Weymouth, Dorset DT4 7JU
**Tel:** 01305-764000 **Fax:** 01305-764022
**Web:** www.bestwestern.co.uk
**Reg No:** 2300438 **Estd:** 1993 Private Limited Company
**Line of Business:** Management of real estate on a fee or contract basis
**Trading Style:** Hotel Rambrandt
**Issued Capital:** £281,325
**Directors:** P D Shaw, B Lister, J R Tate, K Jones, Mrs S J Roper
**Co. Secretary:** Graham Roper
**Responsibilities**
**Senior:** Maffimo Menin *(General Manager)*
**US SIC:** 6531 **UK SIC:** 83400
**Auditors:** Coyne Butterworth & Chalmers
**Bankers:** Lloyds TSB Bank plc (30-99-56)

| | 31-03-14 | 31-03-13 | 31-03-12 |
|---|---|---|---|
| TO | 4,211,676 | 4,115,314 | 4,025,666 |
| P/L | 262,577 | 127,122 | 104,760 |
| NW | 2,289,229 | 402,483 | 288,299 |
| WC | (1,122,494) | (1,214,310) | (1,119,816) |
| Emp. | 130 | 136 | 142 |

DUNS 39-740-4955

## Pullmanor Ltd

(**Subsidiary of:** Redwing of London Llp)
10 Dylan Road, London SE24 0HL
**Tel:** 020-7733-1124 **Fax:** 020-7733-5194
**Web:** www.redwing-coaches.co.uk
**Reg No:** 2170011 **VAT No:** 452364554
**Estd:** 1977 Private Limited Company
**Line of Business:** Other passenger land transport
**Trading Style:** Redwing Coaches
**Issued Capital:** £100,000
**Directors:** P D Hockley, N L Taylor
**Responsibilities**
**Senior:** Matthew Barbrook *(Manager)*
**Sales:** Jenny Bonner *(Sales and Reservations Manager)*
**Branches:** Pullmanor Ltd, 35 Pensbury Place, London SW8 4TR
**US SIC:** 4141 **UK SIC:** 72102
**Auditors:** Findlay Wetherfield Scott & Co
**Bankers:** National Westminster Bank Plc (60-40-05)

| | 31-08-13 | 31-08-12 | 31-08-11 |
|---|---|---|---|
| TO | 6,488,676 | 6,569,148 | 6,919,826 |
| P/L | 612,177 | (1,848,936) | (146,197) |
| NW | 212,483 | (111,468) | 1,348,887 |
| WC | (110,510) | (2,839,847) | (4,233,306) |
| Emp. | 84 | 90 | 94 |

DUNS 23-628-9281

## Pulsant Ltd

(**Subsidiary of:** Oh Pearl Bidco Ltd)
Cadogan House, Rose Kiln Lane, Reading, Berkshire RG2 0HP
**Tel:** 08451199933 **Fax:** 08702523699
**Web:** www.dedipower.com
**Reg No:** 3625971 **Estd:** 1998 Private Limited Company
**Line of Business:** Other computer related activities
**Issued Capital:** £9,899
**Directors:** M I Howling, N Shaw, G G Mackenzie
**Co. Secretary:** Graeme Mackenzie
**US SIC:** 7379 **UK SIC:** 83940
**Auditors:** Deloitte LLP
**Bankers:** National Westminster Bank Plc (60-24-21)

| | 31-12-13 | 31-12-12 | 31-12-11 |
|---|---|---|---|
| TO | 12,940,571 | 10,683,540 | 10,185,074 |
| P/L | 1,799,158 | 1,723,590 | (284,500) |
| NW | 3,982,740 | 3,029,209 | 1,818,392 |
| WC | (703,897) | 142,970 | (106,203) |
| Emp. | 63 | 54 | 49 |

DUNS 21-693-7625

## Pulsant Topco Ltd

(**Subsidiary of:** Oh Pearl Bidco Ltd)
Cadogan House Rose Kiln Lane, Reading, Berkshire RG2 0HP
**Tel:** 08451199900
**Reg No:** 7403360 **Estd:** 2010 Private Limited Company
**Line of Business:** Other business activities not elsewhere classified
**Issued Capital:** £6,548,949
**Directors:** M I Howling, M K Lovell, R Davies, G G Mackenzie, N Shaw
**US SIC:** 7399 **UK SIC:** 83954
**Bankers:** Lloyds TSB Bank plc (30-96-29)

| | 31-12-13 | 31-12-12 | 31-12-11 |
|---|---|---|---|
| TO | 43,729,000 | 30,433,000 | 20,181,000 |
| P/L | (6,710,000) | (3,865,000) | (2,831,000) |
| NW | (66,468,000) | (65,886,000) | (53,806,000) |
| WC | (448,000) | 4,605,000 | 3,478,000 |
| Emp. | 172 | 132 | 123 |

DUNS 21-908-7665 **Imp-Exp**

## Pulsar Light of Cambridge Ltd

Unit 3 Norman Way Coldhams Business Park, Cambridge, Cambridgeshire CB1 3LH
**Tel:** 01223-403500 **Fax:** 01223-403501
**Web:** www.pulsarlight.com
**Reg No:** 1300636 **VAT No:** 215159481
**Estd:** 1978 Private Limited Company
**Line of Business:** Manufacturers of lighting equipment
**Export Markets:** U.S.A, Canada, France
**Issued Capital:** £216
**Directors:** A Hilbert, B D Pohl, B J Dalton-Brockwell
**Responsibilities**
**Senior:** Blaise Dalgon-Brockwell *(Financial Controller)*
**Finance:** Blaise Dalgon-Brockwell *(Financial Controller)*
**US SIC:** 3648 **UK SIC:** 34702
**Auditors:** CKL Partnership Ltd
**Bankers:** National Westminster Bank Plc (52-10-46)

| | 31-12-13 | 31-12-12 | 31-12-11 |
|---|---|---|---|
| TA | 2,212,327 | 2,183,713 | 2,345,528 |
| NW | 483,269 | 1,306,221 | 1,727,576 |
| WC | 1,018,059 | 1,256,236 | 1,417,437 |

DUNS 21-369-5705

## Pulse Advertising

Ludgate House, 245 Blackfriars Road, London SE1 9UY
**Tel:** 02079218102
**Web:** www.ubm.com
**Estd:** 1989 Proprietorship
**Line of Business:** Advertising agency services
**Proprietor:** Mrs G Keys
**US SIC:** 7319 **UK SIC:** 83800
**Employees:** 200

DUNS 71-877-6938

## Pulse Films Ltd

17 Hanbury Street, London E1 6QR
**Fax:** 0844-310-4834
**Web:** www.pulsefilms.com
**Reg No:** 5260268 **Estd:** 2012 Private Limited Company
**Line of Business:** Tv and film producers and directors
**Export Sales:** £1,080,438
**Issued Capital:** £1,439
**Directors:** R T Styles, T Benski, A C Driscoll
**Co. Secretary:** Ms Marisa Clifford
**US SIC:** 7379 **UK SIC:** 83940
**Auditors:** Baker Tilly UK Audit LLP

| | 31-10-13 | 31-10-12 | 31-10-11 |
|---|---|---|---|
| TO | 21,608,761 | 10,719,793 | 14,108,457 |
| P/L | 1,148,658 | (1,174,478) | 850,498 |
| NW | 1,437,339 | 483,070 | 1,126,122 |
| WC | 1,798,087 | 1,005,958 | 1,055,907 |
| Emp. | 53 | 46 | 32 |

DUNS 42-366-3744 **Imp**

## Pulse Fitness Ltd

(**Subsidiary of:** Pulse Fitness Holdings Ltd)
Radnor Park Industrial Estate, Greenfield Road, Congleton, Cheshire CW12 4TW
**Tel:** 01260-294-600
**Web:** www.pulsefitness.com
**Reg No:** 4354059 **VAT No:** 785413509
**Estd:** 1902 Private Limited Company
**Line of Business:** Other business activities not elsewhere classified
**Export Sales:** £1,645,169
**Issued Capital:** £500,002
**Directors:** C P Johnson, D M Johnson
**Co. Secretary:** John Hodd
**Responsibilities**
**Sales:** Richard Sheen *(Sales Manager)*
**IT:** Aron Nassim *(Director of Projects)*
**Engineering:** Aron Nassim *(Director of Projects)*
**US SIC:** 7399, 5941
**UK SIC:** 83954, 65400
**Auditors:** Cowgill Holloway LLP
**Bankers:** The Co-Operative Bank Plc (08-90-00)

| | 31-12-13 | 31-12-12 | 31-12-11 |
|---|---|---|---|
| TO | 13,057,101 | 12,080,375 | 15,287,926 |
| P/L | 327,259 | 358,817 | 115,233 |
| NW | (124,211) | 273,851 | 113,705 |
| WC | (353,963) | 259,530 | 175,321 |
| Emp. | 84 | 84 | 83 |

DUNS 49-493-7956

## Pulse Healthcare Ltd

(**Subsidiary of:** Pulse Staffing Ltd)
Turnford Place, Great Cambridge Road, Turnford, Broxbourne, Hertfordshire EN10 6NH
**Fax:** 01992474901
**Web:** www.pulsejobs.com
**Reg No:** 3156103 **VAT No:** 676285493
**Estd:** 1996 Private Limited Company
**Line of Business:** Employment and recruitment companies and consultants
**Export Sales:** £268,000
**Issued Capital:** £2,202,316

**Directors:** R P Macmillan, R Mcbride
**Co. Secretary:** Richard Mcbride
**Branches:** Pulse Healthcare Ltd, & 14 Victoria Street, Kingsgate Parade, London SW1E 6SH
**US SIC:** 7361 **UK SIC:** 83954
**Auditors:** Ernst & Young LLP
**Bankers:** HSBC Bank plc (40-14-13)

|       | 31-12-13    | 31-12-12    | 31-12-11    |
|-------|-------------|-------------|-------------|
| TO    | 204,741,000 | 166,246,000 | 145,567,000 |
| P/L   | 17,136,000  | 12,863,000  | 3,736,000   |
| NW    | 32,035,000  | 30,289,000  | 18,311,000  |
| WC    | 45,520,000  | 43,316,000  | 30,817,000  |
| Emp.  | 628         | 507         | 407         |

---

DUNS 21-008-2485     Imp

## Pulse Home Products (Holdings) Ltd

(**Subsidiary of:** Holmes Products (Far East) Ltd)
Vine Mill, Holden Fold Lane, Oldham, Lancashire OL2 5LN
**Tel:** 0161-652-1211
**Web:** www.jarden.com
**Reg No:** 6322952 **Estd:** 2007 Private Limited Company
**Line of Business:** Distribution service providers
**Trading Style:** Jarden
**Issued Capital:** £2,000,000
**Directors:** R T Sansone, J E Capps, J E Capps
**Co. Secretary:** Quayseco Limited
**Responsibilities**
**Senior:** Deborah Gough (*Manager*), Mark Weems (*Financial Director*)
**Finance:** Mark Weems (*Financial Director*)
**Marketing:** Ross Beagrie (*Marketing Manager*), Peter Nightingale (*Marketing Director*)
**IT:** Martin Bird (*IT Director*)
**Facilities:** Mick Garlick (*Facilities Manager*)
**US SIC:** 4712, 5732
**UK SIC:** 77002, 64800
**Auditors:** PricewaterhouseCoopers LLP

|       | 31-12-13   | 31-03-13  | 31-12-12     |
|-------|------------|-----------|--------------|
| TO    | N/A        | N/A       | 65,265,000   |
| P/L   | N/A        | N/A       | (7,812,000)  |
| NW    | 2,000,000  | 2,000,000 | (43,787,000) |
| WC    | N/A        | N/A       | 17,502,000   |
| Emp.  | N/A        | N/A       | 136          |

---

DUNS 21-164-0160

## Pulse Umbrella Ltd

(**Subsidiary of:** The Pulse Umbrella Group Ltd)
Peakview, King Edward Street, Macclesfield, Cheshire SK10 1AQ
**Tel:** 08453055405
**Web:** www.pulseumbrella.com
**Reg No:** 6900984 **Estd:** 2009 Private Limited Company
**Line of Business:** Other business activities not elsewhere classified
**Issued Capital:** £80
**Director:** C J Futcher
**US SIC:** 8931 **UK SIC:** 83600

|       | 31-03-14  | 31-03-13  | 31-03-12   |
|-------|-----------|-----------|------------|
| TO    | 7,808,041 | 8,741,388 | 9,543,049  |
| P/L   | (257,233) | 958,892   | (19,906)   |
| NW    | (129,990) | 127,243   | (831,649)  |
| WC    | 42,165    | 327,308   | (537,125)  |
| Emp.  | 273       | 311       | 311        |

---

DUNS 23-717-9127     Imp

## Puma United Kingdom Ltd

(**Subsidiary of:** Financiere Pinault)
Barnett Wood Lane Challenge Court, Leatherhead, Surrey KT22 7LW
**Web:** www.puma.com
**Reg No:** 3712972 **Estd:** 1999 Private Limited Company
**Line of Business:** Wholesale of clothing and footwear
**Export Sales:** £14,360,000
**Issued Capital:** £6,500,000
**Directors:** P Spencer, M J Laemmermann, S J Venediger, V Bondi
**Co. Secretary:** Simon Venediger
**Responsibilities**
**Senior:** Stefano Caroti (*Chief Commercial Officer*)
**Marketing:** Ruth How (*Head of Sports Marketing*)
**Sales:** Stefano Caroti (*Chief Commercial Officer*)
**IT:** Dave Butler (*IT Manager*)
**Branches:** Puma United Kingdom Ltd, Unit 54 Mcarthur Glen Great Western Designer Outlet Village, Swindon, Wiltshire SN2 2DY
**US SIC:** 5136, 2339
**UK SIC:** 61600, 45330
**Auditors:** PricewaterhouseCoopers LLP
**Bankers:** HSBC Bank plc (40-05-30)

|       | 31-12-13   | 31-12-12     | 31-12-11    |
|-------|------------|--------------|-------------|
| TO    | 98,525,000 | 81,929,000   | 98,805,000  |
| P/L   | 247,000    | (23,839,000) | 278,000     |
| NW    | 11,822,000 | 11,708,000   | 34,950,000  |
| WC    | 9,853,000  | 10,060,000   | 34,676,000  |
| Emp.  | 218        | 229          | 233         |

---

DUNS 21-929-8366

## The Pump Group Ltd

(**Subsidiary of:** Inflexion Private Equity Partners Llp)
Apex Way, Hailsham, East Sussex BN27 3WA
**Tel:** 01323848846
**Web:** www.pumpgroup.co.uk
**Reg No:** 6119948 **Estd:** 2007 Private Limited Company
**Line of Business:** Management activities of holding companies
**Export Sales:** £18,166,000
**Issued Capital:** £1,125
**Directors:** I Stuart, A W Thompson, C C Thompson, H D Middleton
**Co. Secretary:** Christian Hamilton
**US SIC:** 6711 **UK SIC:** 83962
**Bankers:** Lloyds TSB Bank plc (30-00-02)

|       | 31-12-13    | 31-12-12     | 31-12-11     |
|-------|-------------|--------------|--------------|
| TO    | 28,018,000  | 27,026,000   | 25,747,000   |
| P/L   | 4,795,000   | 3,955,000    | 2,955,000    |
| NW    | (6,857,000) | (11,689,000) | (15,704,000) |
| WC    | 9,213,000   | 6,369,000    | 5,186,000    |
| Emp.  | 91          | 88           | 89           |

---

DUNS 21-233-9010

## Pump Room

Pump Room, Stall Street, Bath, Avon BA1 1LZ
**Tel:** 01225-444477
**Web:** www.searcys.co.uk
**Estd:** 2004 Proprietorship
**Line of Business:** Restaurant - english
**Proprietor:** G Plumb
**Responsibilities**
**Senior:** Stephen Clews (*General Manager*), Graham Plumb (*General Manager*)
**Marketing:** Patricia Dunlop (*Marketing Manager*)
**Health & Safety:** Stephen Clews (*General Manager*)
**Facilities:** Tom Byrne (*Facilities Manager*)
**Operations:** Stephen Clews (*General Manager*)
**US SIC:** 5812 **UK SIC:** 66110
**Employees:** 99

---

DUNS 22-768-2903

## Pump Supplies Ltd

Llewellyns Quay Dock, Port Talbot, West Glamorgan SA13 1RF
**Tel:** 01639895815
**Web:** www.pumpsupplies.co.uk
**Reg No:** 1628083 **VAT No:** 357773021
**Estd:** 1993 Private Limited Company
**Line of Business:** Pumps sales and servicing
**Export Sales:** £306,814
**Issued Capital:** £5,000
**Principals:** A V John (*Managing*), B C Jones
**Co. Secretary:** Ms Mair John
**Responsibilities**
**Senior:** Alan John (*Manager*)
**Branches:** Pump Supplies Ltd, Old Airfield Farm, Unit 1, Gloucester, Gloucestershire GL2 7NG
**US SIC:** 5084, 7394
**UK SIC:** 61490, 84000
**Auditors:** Haines Watts
**Bankers:** Lloyds TSB Bank plc (30-96-82)

|       | 31-07-13   | 30-04-12   | 30-07-11   |
|-------|------------|------------|------------|
| TO    | 18,949,028 | 13,140,997 | 10,935,823 |
| P/L   | 1,354,730  | 1,302,989  | 579,937    |
| NW    | 6,902,507  | 6,399,833  | 5,408,597  |
| WC    | 4,215,099  | 3,285,822  | 2,621,255  |
| Emp.  | 62         | 62         | 55         |

---

DUNS 23-226-3962

## Punch Robson

35 Albert Road, Middlesbrough, Cleveland TS1 1NU
**Web:** www.punchrobson.co.uk
**Estd:** 1890 Partnership
**Line of Business:** Solicitors
**Partners:** P Walker, A Mottram
**Responsibilities**
**Senior:** Marie Heeley (*Practice Manager*)
**Finance:** Geoff Cruickshank (*Financial Controller*)
**IT:** Chris Caley (*Computer Manager*)
**HR:** Marie Heeley (*Practice Manager*)
**Health & Safety:** Marie Heeley (*Practice Manager*)
**Facilities:** Marie Heeley (*Practice Manager*)
**Purchasing:** Marie Heeley (*Practice Manager*)
**Branches:** Punch Robson, Hampton Ho, Falcon Ct, Stockton-On-Tees, Cleveland TS18 3TS
**US SIC:** 8111 **UK SIC:** 83500
**Employees:** 50

---

DUNS 29-532-0592

## Punch Taverns (Ib) Ltd

(**Subsidiary of:** Punch Taverns Plc)
The Firs, Whitchurch, Aylesbury, Buckinghamshire HP22 4TH
**Tel:** 01442822287 **Fax:** 01296-640070
**Reg No:** 1899248 **Estd:** 1985 Private Limited Company
**Line of Business:** Bars
**Issued Capital:** £78,338,150
**Directors:** S P Dando, E M Bashforth
**Co. Secretary:** Ms Francesca Appleby
**Branches:** Punch Taverns (Ib) Ltd, 156 Cromford Rd, Nottingham, Nottinghamshire NG16 4EX
**US SIC:** 5813, 6531
**UK SIC:** 66200, 83400
**Bankers:** Lloyds TSB Bank plc (30-90-73)

|     | 17-08-13   | 18-08-12   | 20-08-11   |
|-----|------------|------------|------------|
| TA  | 93,477,000 | 93,477,000 | 93,477,000 |
| NW  | 38,008,000 | 38,008,000 | 38,008,000 |
| WC  | 16,522,000 | N/A        | 16,522,000 |

---

DUNS 23-513-4272

## Punch Taverns Intermediate Holdings Ltd

(**Subsidiary of:** Punch Taverns Plc)
Trent House, Fradley Park, Fradley Park, Lichfield, Staffordshire WS13 8RZ
**Tel:** 01543444100 **Fax:** 01543-443502
**Reg No:** 3512600 **Estd:** 1998 Private Limited Company
**Line of Business:** Public house management services
**Trading Style:** Punch Pub Companies
**Issued Capital:** £609,023
**Directors:** S P Dando, E M Bashforth, N R Griffiths
**Co. Secretary:** Ms Francesca Appleby
**Branches:** Punch Taverns Intermediate Holdings Ltd, Chequers End, Hemel Hempstead, Hertfordshire HP2 6HH
**US SIC:** 5813 **UK SIC:** 66200
**Auditors:** Ernst & Young
*Following financial data are in thousands*

|     | 17-08-13  | 18-08-12  | 20-08-11  |
|-----|-----------|-----------|-----------|
| TA  | 2,140,860 | 2,140,860 | 2,140,860 |
| NW  | 1,944,327 | 1,944,327 | 1,944,327 |
| WC  | N/A       | N/A       | 1,944,327 |

---

DUNS 23-758-9218

## Punch Taverns Plc

Jubilee House, Second Avenue, Centrum One Hundred, Burton-On-Trent, Staffordshire DE14 2WF
**Tel:** 01283501600 **Fax:** 01283-501601
**Web:** www.punchtaverns.com
**Reg No:** 3752645 **Estd:** 1999 Public Limited Company
**Line of Business:** Management activities of holding companies
**Issued Capital:** £318,409
**Directors:** S R Billingham, J S Allkins, I Dyson, Dr A J Porter, S P Dando
**Co. Secretary:** Edward Bashforth
**Responsibilities**
**HR:** Karen Caddick (*Human Resources Director*)
**Branches:** Punch Taverns Plc, 49 Woodhouse Lane, Wigan, Lancashire WN6 7LN
**US SIC:** 6711, 5813
**UK SIC:** 83962, 66200
**Auditors:** KPMG Audit PLC
**Bankers:** Barclays Bank Plc (20-07-71)

|       | 23-08-14    | 17-08-13    | 18-08-12    |
|-------|-------------|-------------|-------------|
| TO    | 448,100,000 | 457,600,000 | 491,700,000 |
| P/L   | (240,200,000) | 17,000,000 | 52,400,000 |
| NW    | 100,400,000 | 113,200,000 | 21,300,000  |
| WC    | 201,900,000 | 214,700,000 | 75,400,000  |
| Emp.  | 425         | 451         | 458         |

---

DUNS 22-169-1558

## Punch Taverns (Pmt) Ltd

(**Subsidiary of:** Punch Taverns Plc)
Greenbank, Hartlepool, Cleveland TS24 7QS
**Tel:** 01283840254
**Reg No:** 4187608 **Estd:** 2001 Private Limited Company
**Line of Business:** Management of real estate on a fee or contract basis
**Issued Capital:** £1
**Directors:** S P Dando, E M Bashforth, N R Griffiths
**Co. Secretary:** Ms Francesca Appleby
**Branches:** Punch Taverns (Pmt) Ltd, 26 Bridge St, Tranent, East Lothian EH33 1AG
**US SIC:** 6531 **UK SIC:** 83400
**Auditors:** Ernst & Young LLP

|     | 17-08-13    | 18-08-12    | 20-08-11    |
|-----|-------------|-------------|-------------|
| TA  | 21,050,000  | 21,050,000  | 21,050,000  |
| NW  | (4,508,000) | (4,508,000) | (4,753,000) |
| WC  | N/A         | N/A         | 8,323,000   |

---

DUNS 21-807-7576

## Punch Taverns (Rh) Ltd

(**Subsidiary of:** Punch Taverns Plc)
107 Station Street, Burton-On-Trent, Staffordshire DE14 1BZ
**Tel:** 01902843614
**Reg No:** 0124723 **Estd:** 1912 Private Limited Company
**Line of Business:** Intermediate holding company for a group engaged as public house and off-licence proprietors.
**Trading Style:** Fox & Hounds Inn
**Issued Capital:** £50,000,000
**Directors:** S P Dando, E M Bashforth
**Co. Secretary:** Ms Francesca Appleby
**Branches:** Punch Taverns (Rh) Ltd, 100-102 Gidlow Lane, Wigan, Lancashire WN6 7DY
**US SIC:** 6711, 5813
**UK SIC:** 83962, 66200
**Bankers:** HSBC Bank plc (40-15-20)
*Following financial data are in thousands*

|     | 17-08-13  | 18-08-12  | 20-08-11  |
|-----|-----------|-----------|-----------|
| TA  | 2,430,800 | 2,430,800 | 2,430,800 |
| P/L | N/A       | 50        | N/A       |
| NW  | 1,749,237 | 1,749,237 | 1,749,187 |
| WC  | N/A       | N/A       | (676,350) |

---

DUNS 34-986-1281     Imp

## Punjab National Bank (International) Ltd

160 Belgrave Road, Leicester, Leicestershire LE4 5AU
**Tel:** 01162661960
**Web:** www.pnbinternational.co.uk
**Reg No:** 5781326 **Estd:** 2006 Private Limited Company
**Line of Business:** Banks and financial institutions
**Directors:** Mrs S Bali, K R Kamath, M G Mccaig, D Hopton, M S Nayak, B S Passi
**Co. Secretary:** Bhupinder Passi
**Responsibilities**
**Senior:** Arya Gupta (*Assistant General Manager*), Pendarell Kent (*Manager*), Mukesh Khurana (*Manager*), Paresh Mashru (*Manager*)
**HR:** Payal Khanna (*Human Resources Manager*)
**Branches:** Punjab National Bank (International) Ltd, 90 South Road, Southall, Middlesex UB1 1RD
**US SIC:** 6012 **UK SIC:** 81402
**Auditors:** KPMG Audit PLC
**Employees:** 62
**Turnover:** £82,426,000

---

DUNS 21-455-5906     Imp-Exp

## Punjana Ltd

2 Carnforth Street, Belfast BT5 4QA
**Tel:** 028-9045-0631 **Fax:** 028-9045-3261
**Web:** www.punjana.com
**Reg No:** 0003724NI **VAT No:** 251748356
**Estd:** 1896 Private Limited Company
**Line of Business:** Cash and carry wholesalers
**Export Markets:** Republic of Ireland
**Issued Capital:** £540,792
**Directors:** J H Thompson, L R Skinner, Ms R F Thompson, Ms B E Thompson, D J Thompson, G W Kane
**Co. Secretary:** Graeme Kane
**Responsibilities**
**Senior:** Kane Graeme William Peter (*Manager*), Christine McCluney (*Factory Manager*)
**HR:** Christine McCluney (*Factory Manager*)
**Health & Safety:** Christine McCluney (*Factory Manager*)
**Facilities:** Christine McCluney (*Factory Manager*)
**Operations:** Greg Earl (*Operations Manager*), Christine McCluney (*Factory Manager*)
**Engineering:** Christine McCluney (*Factory Manager*)
**US SIC:** 5149, 5921
**UK SIC:** 61700, 64200
**Auditors:** PricewaterhouseCoopers
**Bankers:** Ulster Bank Ltd (98-00-10)

|       | 31-08-14  | 31-08-13   | 31-08-12   |
|-------|-----------|------------|------------|
| TO    | 9,374,438 | 10,002,285 | 10,687,910 |
| P/L   | 407,641   | (291,309)  | 736,045    |
| NW    | 3,064,585 | 3,501,059  | 4,115,316  |
| WC    | 1,032,595 | 333,874    | 764,618    |
| Emp.  | 47        | 47         | 47         |

---

DUNS 21-645-6751

## Punter Southall

Albion, Fishponds Road, Wokingham, Berkshire RG41 2QE
**Web:** www.psitl.com
**Estd:** 1993 Proprietorship
**Line of Business:** Pensions administrators

**Responsibilities**
**Senior:** Elizabeth Battams (Manager), John Batting (Chief Executive), Edwin Bruce-Gardner (Principal), Ann Geer (Trustee secretary), Wayne Phelan (Manager), Stuart Southall (Manager), Kathy Trusler (Trustees)
**US SIC:** 6411  **UK SIC:** 83200
**Employees:** 82

**DUNS 22-095-5517**
## Punter Southall Group Ltd
11 Strand, London WC2N 5HR
**Web:** www.pshpc.com
**Reg No:** 4096788  **Estd:** 2012 Private Limited Company
**Line of Business:** Actuaries
**Export Sales:** £4,794,153
**Issued Capital:** £196,859
**Directors:** L Van Der Walt, J D Punter, A S Du Plessis, K J Mckelvey, J A Samuels, C C Bannister, Ms S M Curtis
**Co. Secretary:** Ian Nash
**Responsibilities**
**Senior:** John Batting (Manager), David Cule (Manager)
**Branches:** Punter Southall Group Ltd, 7 Castle Street, 2 South Charlotte Street, Edinburgh, Midlothian EH2 4AW
**US SIC:** 6711  **UK SIC:** 83962
**Auditors:** BDO LLP

|     | 31-12-13 | 31-12-12 | 31-12-11 |
|-----|----------|----------|----------|
| TO  | 118,482,550 | 105,310,175 | 94,278,102 |
| P/L | 7,060,074 | 6,399,280 | 6,183,860 |
| NW  | (24,382,124) | 12,165,254 | 10,509,256 |
| WC  | 16,790,997 | 6,387,415 | 17,122,973 |
| Emp. | 879 | 816 | 736 |

**DUNS 73-611-7537**
## Pupil Parent Partnership Ltd
27 Pear Tree Street, London EC1V 3AG
**Tel:** 08454506014 **Fax:** 02088255757
**Web:** www.theppp.org.uk
**Reg No:** 4872659  **Estd:** 2003 Private Company Limited By Guarantee
**Line of Business:** General secondary education
**Directors:** C R Wright, B A Noble, Mrs T Pepper
**Co. Secretary:** Daniel Jansen
**US SIC:** 8211  **UK SIC:** 93200

|     | 31-08-13 | 31-08-12 | 31-08-11 |
|-----|----------|----------|----------|
| TO  | 1,739,988 | 2,563,764 | 3,111,096 |
| P/L | (213,061) | (23,801) | (17,774) |
| NW  | 433,696 | 646,878 | 670,725 |
| WC  | 313,353 | 495,153 | 505,607 |

**DUNS 21-394-4995**
## Pupil Support Service
Park Walk, London SW10 0AY
Proprietorship
**Line of Business:** Misc Schools & Educational Services
**US SIC:** 8299  **UK SIC:** 93300
**Employees:** 85

**DUNS 21-725-1545**                                    **Imp-Exp**
## Puratos Ltd
(Subsidiary of: Coprem Nv)
Buckingham Industrial Estate, Buckingham, Buckinghamshire MK18 1XT
**Tel:** 01280-822860 **Fax:** 01280-822857
**Web:** www.puratos.co.uk
**Reg No:** 0949175  **VAT No:** 208271775
**Estd:** 1969 Private Limited Company
**Line of Business:** Manufacturers of food products
**Export Markets:** Belgium; Denmark; France
**Export Sales:** £1,061,059
**Issued Capital:** £1,670,000
**Directors:** L K Kruit, P H Sanders, J B Lewis, E Van Belle
**Responsibilities**
**Senior:** Raymond Bouvy (Manager), Peter Deriemaeker (Global Markets Director), Dan Oakley (Manager), Bertrand Vanthournout (Manager)
**Marketing:** Peter Deriemaeker (Global Markets Director)
**Sales:** Peter Deriemaeker (Global Markets Director)
**IT:** Michel Demanet (IT Director), Neil Wayne (IT Manager)
**HR:** Jane Duthie (Personnel Officer)
**Health & Safety:** Phill Devanport (Engineering Manager), Mark Livingston (Engineering Manager)
**Operations:** Phill Devanport (Engineering Manager), Mark Livingston (Engineering Manager)
**Engineering:** Nick Bristow (Production Manager), Phill Devanport (Engineering Manager), Mark Livingston (Engineering Manager)
**Branches:** 12 Tatton Ct, Grange Indstl Est, Warrington
**US SIC:** 2099  **UK SIC:** 42399
**Auditors:** Deloitte LLP

**Bankers:** The Royal Bank Of Scotland Plc (16-10-15)

|     | 31-12-13 | 31-12-12 | 31-12-11 |
|-----|----------|----------|----------|
| TO  | 24,544,231 | 27,878,914 | 25,578,156 |
| P/L | 969,027 | 1,368,706 | 1,427,513 |
| NW  | 2,394,959 | 2,699,370 | 2,719,277 |
| WC  | 1,289,274 | 1,806,531 | 1,725,564 |
| Emp. | 67 | 77 | 69 |

**DUNS 23-635-6705**
## Purbeck District Council
Westport House, Worgret Road, Wareham, Dorset BH20 4PP
**Tel:** 01929556561
**Web:** www.dorsetforyou.com
**VAT No:** 187283429  **Estd:** 2010
**Line of Business:** Local government
**Principals:** R Anderson (Chairman), P Croft
**Responsibilities**
**Senior:** Steve Boyt (Chairman), Simon Burditt (Executive), Margaret Cheetham (Executive), Chris Frampton (Executive), Holly Lagden (Executive), Sylvia Leonard (Executive), Steven Mackenzie (Chief Executive), Jon Maidman (Planning Officer), Phil Mcstraw (General Manager - Central Serv), Neil Randall (Chairman), Alison Turnock (Manager)
**Finance:** Sue Eady (Treasurer), Sue Joyce (Head of Finance)
**Marketing:** Claire Lodge (Communications Officer)
**Admin:** Peter Aston (Principal Administrator), Leigh Johnson (Administrator), Lida Mutton (Administration Officer and Off), Rob Roriston (Senior Office Administrator), Rachael Shefford (Assistant)
**IT:** Diane Bemand (Project Executive), Paul Gammon (IT Manager)
**Health & Safety:** Alfred Agbonlahor (Health & Safety Officer), Karen Jaggs (Health and Safety Executive)
**Operations:** Alex Clothier (Project Development Officer), Bridget Downton (General Manager Planning), Ros Drane (Planning Manager), Marilyn Latcham (Production and Operations Mana)
**Fleet:** Cllr Quinn (Executive)
**Engineering:** Naomi Heys (Admin and Technical Officer), Philip Payne (Planning Officer)
**Branches:** Purbeck District Council, Worgret Road, Wareham, Dorset BH20 4PH
**US SIC:** 9121, 8091, 7392
**UK SIC:** 91110, 95200, 83951
**Employees:** 140

**DUNS 21-772-0273**
## Purbeck School
Worgret Road, Wareham, Dorset BH20 4PF
**Tel:** 01929550077
**Web:** www.purbeck.dorset.sch.uk
**Estd:** 2011 Proprietorship
**Line of Business:** Schools (local authority)
**Proprietor:** R Holman
**Responsibilities**
**Senior:** Leanne Symonds (Head Teacher)
**Finance:** Sarah Cuff (Business Manager)
**Marketing:** Sarah Cuff (Business Manager)
**Admin:** Anne Rowan (PA to Head Teacher)
**IT:** James Bray (Network, Security Manager), Richard Forgan (ICT Network Technician)
**US SIC:** 8211  **UK SIC:** 93200
**Employees:** 150

**DUNS 23-082-9033**
## Purbrook Park School
Park Avenue, Waterlooville, Hampshire PO7 5DS
**Tel:** 023-9237-0351
**Web:** www.purbrook.hants.sch.uk
**Estd:** 1917
**Line of Business:** Schools (local authority)
**Director:** M Dopson
**Responsibilities**
**Senior:** Paul Foxley (Head Teacher)
**IT:** Bradley Elmes (IT Technician)
**US SIC:** 8211  **UK SIC:** 93200
**Employees:** 100

**DUNS 34-765-6030**
## Purcell Miller Tritton Llp
3 Colegate, Norwich, Norfolk NR3 1BN
**Tel:** 01603-674444
**Web:** www.purcelluk.com
**Reg No:** 0315259OC  **Estd:** 1995
**Line of Business:** Architectural activities
**Export Sales:** £1,650,868
**Trading Style:** Purcell
**Responsibilities**
**Senior:** David Bissonnet (Non-designated Limited Liabili), James Coath (Non-designated Limited Liabili), Christopher Cotton (Non-designated Limited Liabili), David Pendery (Non-designated Limited Liabili), Richard Putnam (Non-designated Limited Liabili), Martin Stancliffe (Non-designated Limited Liabili), Nigel Sunter (Non-designated Limited Liabili), Alasdair Travers (Non-designated Limited Liabili)

**Finance:** Kate Balchem (Financial Manager)
**Branches:** Purcell Miller Tritton Llp, 16 Rutland Square, Edinburgh, Midlothian EH1 2BB
**US SIC:** 8911  **UK SIC:** 83701
**Auditors:** Larking Gowen

|     | 30-04-14 | 30-04-13 | 30-04-12 |
|-----|----------|----------|----------|
| TO  | 14,355,373 | 11,423,274 | 11,087,100 |
| P/L | 2,214,498 | 961,379 | 899,312 |
| NW  | 2,102,003 | 889,428 | 838,936 |
| WC  | 3,172,045 | 2,112,658 | 2,132,447 |
| Emp. | 192 | 180 | 172 |

**DUNS 76-900-0803**
## The Purcell School
Aldenham Road, Bushey, Hertfordshire WD23 2TS
**Tel:** 01923-331100
**Web:** www.purcell-school.org
**Reg No:** 0759327  **Estd:** 1963 Private Company Limited By Guarantee
**Line of Business:** Schools of music
**Directors:** Mrs J C Nicholls, M E Racz, Professor T J Blinko, J C Fowler, G P Van De Geest, Ms J A Agutter, C E Beer, Dr X H Cross
**Co. Secretary:** Ms Aideen Mcnamara
**Responsibilities**
**Senior:** Stephen Benson (Director), Janice Graham (Director), Jean Macgregor (Director), Hugh Saunders (Manager), Joanna Van Heyningen (Director)
**US SIC:** 8299  **UK SIC:** 93300
**Auditors:** Horwath Clark Whitehill
**Bankers:** The Bank Of Ireland (30-16-07)

|     | 31-08-13 | 31-08-12 | 31-08-11 |
|-----|----------|----------|----------|
| TO  | 5,313,234 | 5,423,376 | 5,604,888 |
| P/L | 64,441 | (9,377) | 445,261 |
| NW  | 12,195,087 | 12,130,646 | 12,140,023 |
| WC  | (504,490) | (118,681) | 935,846 |
| Emp. | 89 | 91 | 100 |

**DUNS 49-089-1124**
## Purchase Direct Ltd
1 Falcon Way, Shire Park, Welwyn Garden City, Hertfordshire AL7 1TW
**Fax:** 0845-408-1201
**Web:** www.purchase-direct.co.uk
**Reg No:** 3090591  **Estd:** 1995 Private Limited Company
**Line of Business:** Management and business consultants
**Issued Capital:** £50
**Managing Director:** R L Ashley
**Co. Secretary:** Ian Hicks
**Responsibilities**
**Marketing:** Dawn Langlais (Business Development Manager)
**IT:** Dawn Langlais (Business Development Manager)
**HR:** Dawn Langlais (Business Development Manager)
**Health & Safety:** Dawn Langlais (Business Development Manager)
**Facilities:** Dawn Langlais (Business Development Manager)
**US SIC:** 7392  **UK SIC:** 83951
**Auditors:** Barr & Associates

|     | 31-08-13 | 31-08-12 | 31-08-11 |
|-----|----------|----------|----------|
| TA  | 1,270,627 | 887,703 | 995,598 |
| NW  | 526,557 | 378,087 | 250,658 |
| WC  | 513,720 | 359,067 | 241,314 |

**DUNS 34-511-4545**
## Purchase Group Ltd
(Subsidiary of: Wates Group Ltd)
Unit 8 Reaymer Close, Bloxwich, Walsall, West Midlands WS2 7QZ
**Tel:** 01922407111 **Fax:** 01922473666
**Web:** www.purchasegroup.co.uk
**Reg No:** 5322443  **Estd:** 2004 Private Limited Company
**Line of Business:** Management activities of holding companies
**Issued Capital:** £400,000
**Directors:** J P Howell, S J Togwell, A O Davies, A H Hobart, D H Davies
**Co. Secretary:** David Davies
**US SIC:** 6711  **UK SIC:** 83962
**Auditors:** Grant Thornton UK LLP
**Bankers:** Bank Of Scotland (12-01-03)

|     | 31-12-13 | 31-12-12 | 31-12-11 |
|-----|----------|----------|----------|
| TO  | 26,073,644 | 35,221,692 | 27,077,234 |
| P/L | 626,466 | 1,740,077 | 2,021,531 |
| NW  | 3,864,523 | 3,836,054 | 2,480,971 |
| WC  | 3,770,401 | 3,110,310 | 2,036,904 |
| Emp. | 151 | 153 | 120 |

**DUNS 29-171-0176**
## Purdy Contracts Ltd
(Subsidiary of: Purdy Holdings Ltd)
Brooklyn Lodge, Mott Street, Chingford, London E4 7RW
**Tel:** 019-9270-3410 **Fax:** 019-9270-3411
**Web:** www.purdycontracts.co.uk
**Reg No:** 1830283  **VAT No:** 396562114
**Estd:** 1984 Private Limited Company
**Line of Business:** Heating system consultants
**Issued Capital:** £150

**Principals:** J R Horlock (Managing), L Venebles, G S Bruce
**Co. Secretary:** John Horlock
**Responsibilities**
**Senior:** Dennis Pickett (Purchasing Manager)
**Health & Safety:** Clive Hornsby (Operations Manager)
**Purchasing:** Dennis Pickett (Purchasing Manager)
**Fleet:** Alison Temple (Transport Manager)
**Branches:** Purdy Contracts Ltd, 207 High Street, Waltham Cross, Hertfordshire EN8 7AY
**US SIC:** 1799, 1731
**UK SIC:** 50000, 50300
**Auditors:** Kingston Smith LLP
**Bankers:** National Westminster Bank Plc (55-70-49)

|     | 31-12-13 | 31-12-12 | 31-12-11 |
|-----|----------|----------|----------|
| TO  | 15,843,320 | 14,736,051 | 14,498,332 |
| P/L | 1,108,669 | 1,499,265 | 1,450,089 |
| NW  | 9,458,154 | 8,677,762 | 7,520,784 |
| WC  | 9,059,481 | 8,329,661 | 7,220,070 |
| Emp. | 165 | 148 | 153 |

**DUNS 36-535-6851**
## Pure-Air Building Services Ltd
Units 1-7 Fulwood Industrial Estate, Fulwood Road South, Sutton-In-Ashfield, Nottinghamshire NG17 2JZ
**Tel:** 01623-741-004
**Web:** www.pure-air.co.uk
**Reg No:** 5910578  **VAT No:** 890472796
**Estd:** 2006 Private Limited Company
**Line of Business:** Plumbing
**Trading Style:** Pure-Air
**Issued Capital:** £100
**Director:** D Williams
**Responsibilities**
**Senior:** Keiran Brown (Director)
**US SIC:** 1711, 1731, 3499
**UK SIC:** 50300, 31694
**Auditors:** Elkingtons Accountants Ltd
**Bankers:** National Westminster Bank Plc (60-14-03)

|     | 31-08-13 | 31-08-12 | 31-08-11 |
|-----|----------|----------|----------|
| TA  | 1,907,719 | 1,322,154 | 881,202 |
| NW  | 342,581 | 238,064 | 98,073 |
| WC  | 15,875 | 2,133 | 75,217 |

**DUNS 64-077-8754**                                    **Imp**
## Pure Collection Ltd
Mowbray House, Mowbray Square, Harrogate, North Yorkshire HG1 5AU
**Tel:** 08448481030 **Fax:** 0870-225-5788
**Web:** www.purecollection.com
**Reg No:** 4481224  **Estd:** 2002 Private Limited Company
**Line of Business:** Mail order houses
**Issued Capital:** £800,101
**Directors:** A N Holdsworth, N B Falkingham
**Co. Secretary:** Miss Alys Strudwick
**Responsibilities**
**Marketing:** Katy Smith (Marketing Manager)
**Branches:** Pure Collection Ltd, 58 High Street, Tunbridge Wells, Kent TN1 1XF
**US SIC:** 5961  **UK SIC:** 65600
**Auditors:** Iredale & Co
**Bankers:** HSBC Bank plc (40-23-12)

|     | 31-08-13 | 31-08-12 | 31-08-11 |
|-----|----------|----------|----------|
| TO  | 30,759,015 | 27,857,457 | 24,155,312 |
| P/L | 729,803 | 690,389 | 502,185 |
| NW  | 2,165,543 | 1,449,562 | 932,015 |
| WC  | 1,231,096 | 708,939 | 532,242 |
| Emp. | 164 | 174 | 152 |

**DUNS 42-400-0391**
## Pure Creative Ltd
(Subsidiary of: Equity Solutions & Partners Ltd)
Building 1000 Kings Reach, Stockport, Cheshire SK4 2HG
**Tel:** 01618319722
**Web:** www.pure-creative.com
**Reg No:** 4387745  **Estd:** 2002 Private Limited Company
**Line of Business:** Speciality design activities
**Issued Capital:** £10
**Directors:** M Dwan, Ms A Sarginson, R J Miller
**Co. Secretary:** North Consulting Limited
**US SIC:** 7399  **UK SIC:** 83954

|     | 30-04-13 | 30-04-12 | 30-04-11 |
|-----|----------|----------|----------|
| TA  | 42,403 | 76,110 | 35,443 |
| NW  | (53,455) | (65,608) | (25,002) |
| WC  | (56,071) | (71,596) | (33,625) |

**DUNS 21-136-1131**
## Pure Gym Ltd
(Subsidiary of: Gym Topco Ltd)
Town Centre House, Merrion Centre, Leeds, West Yorkshire LS2 8LY
**Web:** www.puregym.com
**Reg No:** 6690189  **Estd:** 2006 Private Limited Company
**Line of Business:** Other sporting activities not elsewhere classified
**Issued Capital:** £5,260,686
**Directors:** A Bellamy, J De Bruin, P R Mcgrath, P W Roberts

**Co. Secretary:** Adam Bellamy
**Responsibilities**
**Senior:** Angela Crawshaw *(Property Director)*
**US SIC:** 7999 **UK SIC:** 97913
**Auditors:** PricewaterhouseCoopers LLP
**Bankers:** Barclays Bank Plc (20-06-05)

| | 31-12-13 | 28-02-13 | 29-12-12 |
|---|---|---|---|
| TO | 39,933,000 | 30,636,192 | 16,828,920 |
| P/L | 2,158,000 | 552,024 | 1,201,381 |
| NW | 8,206,000 | 7,697,200 | 7,186,100 |
| WC | (3,142,000) | (7,001,715) | (345,139) |
| Emp. | 150 | 107 | 61 |

DUNS 73-990-7769
## Pure Innovations Ltd
Sanderling Building, Bird Hall Lane, Stockport, Cheshire SK3 0RF
**Tel:** 01614745900 **Fax:** 0161-491-3717
**Web:** www.pureinnovations.co.uk
**Reg No:** 5241249 **Estd:** 1994 Private Company Limited By Guarantee
**Line of Business:** Day and care centres
**Directors:** J R Morgan, D Lennie, Ms L Lunn, Mrs J M Lancaster
**Co. Secretary:** Ian Taylor
**Responsibilities**
**Senior:** Louise Parrott-Bates *(Chief Operating Officer)*
**US SIC:** 8321 **UK SIC:** 96111
**Bankers:** The Co-Operative Bank Plc (08-90-24)

| | 31-03-14 | 31-03-13 | 31-03-12 |
|---|---|---|---|
| TO | 6,939,408 | 6,401,808 | 5,696,600 |
| P/L | (92,012) | 346,670 | 58,659 |
| NW | 606,065 | 533,112 | 953,950 |
| WC | 2,192,041 | 2,407,419 | 2,042,836 |
| Emp. | 199 | 189 | 187 |

DUNS 73-858-7695
## Pure Leisure Group Ltd
South Lakeland House, Yealand Redmayne, Carnforth, Lancashire LA5 9RN
**Tel:** 01524-781918
**Web:** www.pureleisuregroup.com
**Reg No:** 5113719 **Estd:** 1994 Private Limited Company
**Line of Business:** Other sporting activities not elsewhere classified
**Export Sales:** £10,811,000
**Trading Style:** Pure Leisure Group Ltd
**Issued Capital:** £100
**Directors:** N B Wimpenny, P Rossiter, M D Morphet, T J White
**Co. Secretary:** Paul Rossiter
**Responsibilities**
**Senior:** Bruce Casely *(Manager)*, Malcolm Hill *(Manager)*, Sara Ion *(Manager)*, John Morphet *(Proprietor)*, Gary Pitt *(Manager)*, Christopher Royle *(Manager)*
**US SIC:** 7399 **UK SIC:** 83954

| | 31-01-14 | 31-01-13 | 31-01-12 |
|---|---|---|---|
| TO | 26,649,000 | 26,708,000 | 37,730,000 |
| P/L | (10,881,000) | (3,455,000) | (365,000) |
| NW | 33,071,000 | 45,837,000 | 50,053,000 |
| WC | 3,159,000 | 7,437,000 | 24,579,000 |
| Emp. | 417 | 398 | 419 |

DUNS 21-443-9036 Imp-Exp
## Pure Malt Products Ltd
Whittinghame Drive, Haddington, East Lothian EH41 4BD
**Tel:** 01620-824696
**Web:** www.puremalt.com
**Reg No:** 0039605SC **VAT No:** 300544118
**Estd:** 1963 Private Limited Company
**Line of Business:** Manufacturers of food products
**Export Markets:** W Europe, U S A, Japan, Australia.
**Export Sales:** £6,165,102
**Issued Capital:** £84,750
**Principals:** B K Turner *(Chairman and Managing)*, P C Williams, T S Thomson
**Co. Secretary:** Raymond Paterson
**Responsibilities**
**Senior:** David Benger *(Head Brewer)*, Laura Gornall *(Head Brewer)*
**IT:** Laura Gornall *(Head Brewer)*
**Health & Safety:** Laura Gornall *(Head Brewer)*
**Operations:** Laura Gornall *(Head Brewer)*
**US SIC:** 2099, 2041
**UK SIC:** 42399, 41600
**Auditors:** Chiene & Tait CA
**Bankers:** Bank Of Scotland (80-08-23)

| | 31-03-14 | 31-03-13 | 31-03-12 |
|---|---|---|---|
| TO | 11,106,169 | 11,608,402 | 12,438,194 |
| P/L | 368,349 | 401,598 | 726,735 |
| NW | 5,736,900 | 5,371,726 | 4,982,976 |
| WC | 1,886,571 | 1,531,976 | 1,059,085 |
| Emp. | 61 | 64 | 62 |

DUNS 23-804-9279
## Pure Recruitment Group Ltd
2nd Floor 107 Queen Victoria Street, London EC2V 6DN
**Tel:** 020-7429-4400 **Fax:** 02072576501
**Web:** www.puresearch.com
**Reg No:** 3797452 **Estd:** 2005 Private Limited Company
**Line of Business:** Employment and recruitment companies and consultants
**Export Sales:** £3,727,672
**Trading Style:** Pure Search
**Issued Capital:** £12,794
**Directors:** C D Nelson, Mrs L H Ferguson, C S Ferguson, Mrs D Nelson
**Co. Secretary:** Malcolm Entwistle
**Responsibilities**
**Senior:** Kate Ingram *(Executive Consultant)*, C Neslon *(Manager)*, Barrie Sanderson *(Manager)*
**US SIC:** 7361 **UK SIC:** 83954
**Auditors:** HW Fisher & Co
**Bankers:** National Westminster Bank Plc (01-10-01)

| | 31-12-13 | 31-12-12 | 31-12-11 |
|---|---|---|---|
| TO | 14,141,991 | 12,880,472 | N/A |
| P/L | 1,471,465 | 679,240 | N/A |
| NW | 2,344,972 | 1,495,240 | 1,331,247 |
| WC | 2,296,825 | 1,492,111 | 1,319,267 |
| Emp. | 92 | 88 | N/A |

DUNS 64-093-5479
## Pure Resourcing Solutions Ltd
The Workspace Pioneer Court, Cambridge, Cambridgeshire CB24 9PT
**Tel:** 01223209888 **Fax:** 01223-232000
**Web:** www.prs.uk.com
**Reg No:** 4497007 **Estd:** 2002 Private Limited Company
**Line of Business:** Labour recruitment and provision of personnel
**Trading Style:** Pure Resourcing Solutions Ltd
**Issued Capital:** £100
**Directors:** Ms L J Walters, I P Walters
**Co. Secretary:** Ms Gillian Buchanan
**US SIC:** 7361 **UK SIC:** 83954
**Auditors:** Lakin Rose Ltd

| | 30-06-13 | 01-07-12 | 26-06-11 |
|---|---|---|---|
| TO | 10,395,693 | N/A | N/A |
| P/L | 735,464 | N/A | N/A |
| NW | 1,255,483 | 1,035,684 | 1,616,460 |
| WC | 1,172,976 | 928,910 | 1,521,731 |
| Emp. | 51 | N/A | N/A |

DUNS 23-802-7846
## Pure Synergy Group Ltd
Thornley House Carrington Business Park, Manchester Road, Manchester M31 4DD
**Tel:** 01617766340
**Web:** www.synergytechnology.co.uk
**Reg No:** 3795301 **Estd:** 1999 Private Limited Company
**Line of Business:** Computer support & services
**Issued Capital:** £24,891
**Director:** A B Poole
**Responsibilities**
**Senior:** Bronwen Wilkinson *(Manager)*
**US SIC:** 7379 **UK SIC:** 83940

| | 31-12-13 | 31-12-12 | 31-12-11 |
|---|---|---|---|
| TO | N/A | N/A | 2,318,078 |
| P/L | N/A | N/A | (99,240) |
| NW | (10,717) | (50,737) | (85,472) |
| WC | (279,700) | (293,696) | (265,056) |

DUNS 56-937-7278 Imp
## Pure Technology Ltd
290 Centennial Park, Borehamwood, Hertfordshire WD6 3SU
**Tel:** 02087329612 **Fax:** 02087 329 602
**Web:** www.puretech.co.uk
**Reg No:** 2837240 **Estd:** 1993 Private Limited Company
**Line of Business:** Retail sale by opticians
**Issued Capital:** £1,081,189
**Director:** S Kraitt
**Co. Secretary:** Ms Jacqueline Crofton
**Responsibilities**
**Senior:** Jamie Holoran *(Manager)*
**Branches:** Pure Technology Ltd, 22 Store St, London WC1E 7DF
**US SIC:** 5999 **UK SIC:** 65600
**Auditors:** Montpelier Audit Ltd

| | 31-08-13 | 31-08-12 | 31-08-11 |
|---|---|---|---|
| TO | 6,718,827 | 8,293,590 | 8,825,295 |
| P/L | (2,121,500) | (407,304) | 4,709 |
| NW | 1,941,675 | 4,018,267 | 4,413,608 |
| WC | 1,632,790 | 3,560,243 | 3,995,904 |
| Emp. | 76 | 97 | 104 |

DUNS 71-907-2469
## Pure Wafer Plc
Central Business Park Mill Brook Drive, Swansea, West Glamorgan SA7 0AB
**Web:** www.purewafer.com
**Reg No:** 5289130 **Estd:** 2004 Public Limited Company
**Line of Business:** Management activities of holding companies
**Directors:** S D Boyd, G W Winters, K Baker, D R Howells, P D Dolan, H M Lewis, Dr E Ap Gwilym, P G Harrington
**Co. Secretary:** Huw Lewis
**US SIC:** 6711 **UK SIC:** 83962
**Auditors:** Deloitte LLP
**Bankers:** The Royal Bank Of Scotland Plc (16-15-21)
**Employees:** 228
**Turnover:** £35,940,000

DUNS 21-741-5421
## Pureprint Group Ltd
**(Subsidiary of:** East Sussex Press Ltd)
Bellbrook Park, Uckfield, East Sussex TN22 1PL
**Tel:** 01825768811
**Web:** www.pureprint.com
**Reg No:** 1493898 **VAT No:** 350858051
**Estd:** 1989 Private Limited Company
**Line of Business:** Printing not elsewhere classified
**Export Sales:** £1,923,547
**Trading Style:** Pureprint Group
**Issued Capital:** £100,000
**Directors:** M W Handford, R W Owers, R Osborne, Ms B M Massey
**Co. Secretary:** Ian Brown
**Responsibilities**
**Senior:** Richard Osbourne *(Managing Director)*
**US SIC:** 2752, 2753
**UK SIC:** 47544, 47545
**Auditors:** Simmons Gainsford LLP
**Bankers:** Barclays Bank Plc (20-49-76)

| | 31-12-13 | 31-08-12 | 31-12-11 |
|---|---|---|---|
| TO | 37,584,176 | 25,560,699 | 21,771,532 |
| P/L | 528,838 | 704,712 | 563,742 |
| NW | 2,304,760 | 1,936,735 | 1,408,507 |
| WC | (778,041) | (469,144) | (320,250) |
| Emp. | 214 | 188 | 175 |

DUNS 23-260-3402
## Purepromoter Ltd
**(Subsidiary of:** Sep Iv Lp)
New England House, New England Street, Brighton, East Sussex BN1 4GH
**Tel:** 01273647870 **Fax:** 08707-657227
**Web:** www.pure360community.co.uk
**Reg No:** 4266410 **Estd:** 2008 Private Limited Company
**Line of Business:** Marketing consultants
**Export Sales:** £522,398
**Trading Style:** Purepromoter Limited
**Issued Capital:** £465
**Directors:** G Beveridge, S G Dawson
**Responsibilities**
**Senior:** Marc Munier *(Commercial Director)*
**US SIC:** 7392, 7374
**UK SIC:** 83951, 83940
**Auditors:** Macintyre Hudson LLP

| | 31-03-14 | 31-03-13 | 31-03-12 |
|---|---|---|---|
| TO | 7,500,377 | N/A | N/A |
| P/L | 20,881 | N/A | N/A |
| NW | 2,441,791 | 3,074,931 | 2,332,034 |
| WC | 2,095,180 | 2,662,410 | 1,858,524 |
| Emp. | 113 | N/A | N/A |

DUNS 23-609-3196
## Purico Ltd
**(Subsidiary of:** Clary Limited)
Environment House, 6 Union Road, Nottingham, Nottinghamshire NG3 1FH
**Tel:** 01159013000
**Reg No:** 3606531 **Estd:** 1998 Private Limited Company
**Line of Business:** Management activities of holding companies
**Export Sales:** £43,665,000
**Issued Capital:** £2
**Directors:** R Mochor, A Puri
**Co. Secretary:** M M Secretariat Limited
**US SIC:** 6711 **UK SIC:** 83962
**Auditors:** PKF (UK) LLP

| | 31-12-13 | 31-12-12 | 31-12-11 |
|---|---|---|---|
| TO | 44,320,000 | 45,814,000 | 38,421,000 |
| P/L | 1,617,000 | 1,019,000 | 67,000 |
| NW | 7,366,000 | 7,112,000 | 7,062,000 |
| WC | 7,726,000 | 5,831,000 | 6,419,000 |
| Emp. | 733 | 687 | 631 |

DUNS 22-632-8383 Imp
## Purite Ltd
**(Subsidiary of:** Suez Environnement Company)
Bandet Way, Thame, Oxfordshire OX9 3SJ
**Tel:** 01844-217141
**Web:** www.purite.com
**Reg No:** 1464412 **VAT No:** 537208743
**Estd:** 1979 Private Limited Company
**Line of Business:** Water treatment services
**Export Sales:** £801,660
**Issued Capital:** £100
**Directors:** J A Boulton, D T Reeve
**Co. Secretary:** Liano Lucherini
**Responsibilities**
**Senior:** Samuel Benoudiz *(Manager)*, Gilles Cotte *(Manager)*, B Stother *(Manager)*
**Sales:** Paul Fowler *(Export Sales Engineer)*
**US SIC:** 4941, 3542
**UK SIC:** 17000, 32212
**Auditors:** MacIntyre Hudson
**Bankers:** Girobank Plc (72-00-00)

| | 31-12-13 | 31-12-12 | 31-12-11 |
|---|---|---|---|
| TO | 6,038,113 | 7,239,102 | 5,029,433 |
| P/L | (20,653) | 86,456 | (428,137) |
| NW | (26,489) | (83,458) | (202,019) |
| WC | 339,443 | 224,002 | 70,956 |
| Emp. | 52 | 54 | 54 |

DUNS 21-832-8748 Imp
## Purity Soft Drinks Ltd
**(Subsidiary of:** Jb Drinks Holdings Ltd)
Douglas House, Wednesbury, West Midlands WS10 0BU
**Tel:** 0121-505-7585 **Fax:** 0121-505-2010
**Web:** www.puritysoftdrinks.co.uk
**Reg No:** 0358349 **Estd:** 1938 Private Limited Company
**Line of Business:** Manufacturers of soft drinks
**Export Sales:** £3,068,547
**Issued Capital:** £1,000
**Directors:** T M Lister, J C Evans, G S Nield, D J Bell
**Responsibilities**
**Senior:** Barbara Cox *(Manager)*, Michael Mann *(Manager)*, Stuart Nalley *(Operations Director)*
**Operations:** Stuart Nalley *(Operations Director)*
**US SIC:** 2086 **UK SIC:** 42831
**Auditors:** Nicklin LLP
**Bankers:** HSBC Bank plc (40-19-02)

| | 28-03-14 | 31-03-13 | 31-03-12 |
|---|---|---|---|
| TO | 15,767,738 | 16,428,948 | 16,126,175 |
| P/L | (259,101) | 548,634 | 943,576 |
| NW | 3,327,791 | 3,497,694 | 3,110,762 |
| WC | 848,276 | 1,363,612 | 1,604,931 |
| Emp. | 69 | 71 | 66 |

DUNS 21-228-8365
## Purley Community Health Clinic
62 Whytecliffe Road North, Purley, Surrey CR8 2AR
**Tel:** 02087142777
**Estd:** 1996 Proprietorship
**Line of Business:** Public sector hospital activities, including nhs trusts
**Proprietor:** Mrs M Colston
**US SIC:** 8062 **UK SIC:** 95100
**Employees:** 60

DUNS 29-044-8042
## Purley Park Trust Ltd
21 Huckleberry Close, Purley On Thames, Reading, Berkshire RG8 8EH
**Tel:** 01189439462
**Web:** www.purleyparktrust.org
**Reg No:** 0989820 **Estd:** 2012 Private Company Limited By Guarantee
**Line of Business:** Rest and retirement homes
**Trading Style:** Acorn House
**Directors:** Mrs K S Robinson, Ms J Farr, L D Jones, J Armitage, C D Trickey, S Barstow
**Co. Secretary:** Lawrence Grady
**Responsibilities**
**Senior:** Di Earl *(Home Manager)*
**HR:** Rachel Keeling *(Operations Manager)*
**Health & Safety:** Rachel Keeling *(Operations Manager)*
**US SIC:** 8321 **UK SIC:** 96111
**Auditors:** BDO Stoy Hayward
**Bankers:** National Westminster Bank Plc (54-21-28)

| | 31-03-14 | 31-03-13 | 31-03-12 |
|---|---|---|---|
| TO | 3,207,830 | 2,979,968 | 2,752,226 |
| P/L | 114,039 | 98,720 | (24,732) |
| NW | 341,123 | 227,084 | 128,364 |
| WC | 277,594 | 200,080 | 116,852 |
| Emp. | 120 | 114 | 103 |

DUNS 34-889-6635
## Purple Balm Ltd
Unit 8 Orchard Court, Heron Road, Sowton Industrial Estate, Exeter, Devon EX2 7LL
**Tel:** 01392-350010 **Fax:** 01392-363221
**Web:** www.purplebalm.co.uk
**Reg No:** 5687417 **Estd:** 2006 Private Limited Company
**Line of Business:** Labour recruitment and provision of personnel
**Issued Capital:** £94
**Directors:** Miss C A Sawer, Miss A L Greenaway, E G Beard
**Co. Secretary:** Miss Christine Sawer
**Responsibilities**
**Senior:** Michelle Barnes *(Manager)*, Jeanie Lister *(Manager)*, Hazel Proctor *(Manager)*
**US SIC:** 7361 **UK SIC:** 83954

| | 30-06-13 | 30-06-12 | 30-06-11 |
|---|---|---|---|
| TO | N/A | 1,103,785 | 1,094,979 |
| P/L | N/A | 31,815 | 37,596 |
| NW | (264,770) | (219,976) | (251,791) |
| WC | (1,561) | 22,041 | (116) |

DUNS 50-316-5797
## Purple Parking Ltd
Brent Road, Southall, Middlesex UB2 5LE
**Tel:** 02088138130 **Fax:** 02085746514
**Web:** www.purpleparking.com
**Reg No:** 2341479 **Estd:** 1989 Private Limited Company
**Line of Business:** Other storage and warehousing not elsewhere classified
**Issued Capital:** £375,002

**Directors:** A J Waters, O J Inwards, P E Shaw
**Co. Secretary:** Mark Hinge
**Responsibilities**
**Facilities:** Tony Church *(Facilities Manager)*
**US SIC:** 4226 **UK SIC:** 77003
**Auditors:** BDO LLP

| | 31-03-14 | 31-03-13 | 31-03-12 |
|---|---|---|---|
| TO | 20,165,909 | 18,808,514 | 16,747,113 |
| P/L | 907,276 | 5,633,124 | 5,177,073 |
| NW | (6,028,500) | (6,395,775) | (7,787,575) |
| WC | (493,844) | (1,378,722) | (2,058,998) |
| Emp. | 322 | 408 | 496 |

DUNS 21-151-4013
## Purple Surgical Holdings Ltd
2 Chestnut House, Radlett, Hertfordshire WD7 9AD
**Tel:** 01923839307 **Fax:** 020-8349-1962
**Web:** www.purplesurgical.com
**Reg No:** 1110380 **Estd:** 1973 Private Limited Company
**Line of Business:** Management activities of holding companies
**Export Sales:** £5,236,488
**Trading Style:** Purple Surgical Holdings Limited
**Issued Capital:** £22,980
**Directors:** Ms J E Sharpe, R Sharpe
**Co. Secretary:** Philip Franklin
**Branches:** Purple Surgical Holdings Ltd, Cliff Rd, Ipswich, Suffolk IP3 0AY
**US SIC:** 6711, 5199
**UK SIC:** 83962, 61900
**Auditors:** Landan Morley
**Bankers:** National Westminster Bank Plc (60-08-20)

| | 30-06-13 | 30-06-12 | 30-06-11 |
|---|---|---|---|
| TO | 13,357,112 | 12,509,328 | 11,591,300 |
| P/L | 1,359,045 | 1,254,750 | 798,869 |
| NW | 4,652,884 | 3,823,197 | 3,058,115 |
| WC | 3,603,039 | 3,397,397 | 2,458,248 |
| Emp. | 114 | 111 | 113 |

DUNS 36-814-1396
## Pursglove Centre
Church Walk, Guisborough, Cleveland TS14 6BU
**Tel:** 01287280260
**Estd:** 1995 Partnership
**Line of Business:** Leisure and recreation centre
**Trading Style:** Pursglove Centre
**US SIC:** 7999 **UK SIC:** 97913
**Employees:** 200

DUNS 21-773-3119
## Putney High School
35-37 Putney Hill, London SW15 6BH
**Tel:** 02087886523
**Web:** www.gdst.net
**Estd:** 1992 Proprietorship
**Line of Business:** Schools (independent)
**Proprietor:** Dr D Lodge
**US SIC:** 8211 **UK SIC:** 93200
**Employees:** 150

DUNS 21-811-0642
## Putney Rspca Animal Hospital
Putney Animal Hospital, 6 Clarendon Drive, London SW15 1AA
**Tel:** 03001230716
**Web:** www.rspca.org.uk
**Estd:** 2011
**Line of Business:** Animal welfare and care organisations
**Responsibilities**
**Senior:** Angela Grigg *(Manager)*
**US SIC:** 8699 **UK SIC:** 96902
**Employees:** 55

DUNS 64-256-1534
## Putterills of Hertfordshire
15a High Street, Welwyn, Hertfordshire AL6 9EE
**Tel:** 01438-717701
**Web:** www.putterills.co.uk
**Estd:** 1991 Proprietorship
**Line of Business:** Real Estate Agents And Managers
**Proprietor:** A Putterill
**Branches:** Putterills Of Hertfordshire, 135 London Rd, Knebworth, Hertfordshire SG3 6JE
**US SIC:** 6531 **UK SIC:** 83400
**Bankers:** Barclays Bank Plc (20-92-54)
**Employees:** 60

DUNS 21-152-9185 **Imp-Exp**
## Puzzler Media Ltd
(**Subsidiary of:** Puzzler Media Holdings Ltd)
Stonecroft, 69 Station Road, Redhill, Surrey RH1 1EY
**Web:** www.puzzler.com
**Reg No:** 1136669 **VAT No:** 654080839
**Estd:** 1973 Private Limited Company
**Line of Business:** Newspapers publishing
**Export Sales:** £578,625
**Issued Capital:** £1,063,988
**Directors:** D H Thomson, A F Thomson, N D Flockhart, R P Daly, E Watson, C H Thomson
**Responsibilities**
**Senior:** Lindsey Milton *(Office Manager)*
**Finance:** Guy Gibbons *(Financial Director)*
**Admin:** Lindsey Milton *(Office Manager)*
**HR:** Lindsey Milton *(Office Manager)*
**Health & Safety:** Vince Edwards *(Facilities Coordinator)*
**Facilities:** Vince Edwards *(Facilities Coordinator)*
**Purchasing:** Lindsey Milton *(Office Manager)*
**Engineering:** Pam Bains *(Production Manager)*
**US SIC:** 2731, 7372
**UK SIC:** 47532, 83940
**Auditors:** Henderson Loggie
**Bankers:** Bank Of Scotland (80-11-00)

| | 31-03-14 | 31-03-13 | 31-03-12 |
|---|---|---|---|
| TO | 17,097,840 | 19,855,813 | 22,114,000 |
| P/L | 3,271,589 | 5,364,067 | 6,289,000 |
| NW | 49,076,489 | 46,493,162 | 42,350,000 |
| WC | 48,925,410 | 46,327,286 | 42,172,000 |
| Emp. | 74 | 75 | 76 |

DUNS 67-211-2661
## Pv Crystalox Solar Plc
Brook House, High Street, Abingdon, Oxfordshire OX14 4QQ
**Tel:** 01235-437-160 **Fax:** 01235437199
**Web:** www.pvcrystalox.com
**Reg No:** 6019466 **Estd:** 1982 Public Limited Company
**Line of Business:** Management activities of holding companies
**Issued Capital:** £59,582,555
**Directors:** J K Sleeman, I A Dorrity, M D Parker
**Co. Secretary:** Matthew Wethey
**Responsibilities**
**Senior:** Maarten Henderson *(Non-Executive Director)*
**Finance:** Peter Finnegan *(Chief Financial Officer)*
**Operations:** Hubert Aulich *(Executive Director, German Ope)*
**US SIC:** 6711, 3629
**UK SIC:** 83962, 34350
**Auditors:** PricewaterhouseCoopers LLP
**Bankers:** National Westminster Bank Plc (60-17-21)

| | 31-12-13 | 31-12-12 | 31-12-11 |
|---|---|---|---|
| TO | 62,276,000 | 37,865,000 | 183,048,000 |
| P/L | 5,776,000 | (90,563,000) | (58,364,000) |
| NW | 50,854,000 | 77,436,000 | 208,024,000 |
| WC | 48,303,000 | 77,010,000 | 91,732,000 |
| Emp. | 194 | 311 | 385 |

DUNS 37-800-0871 **Imp-Exp**
## P.W. Hall Ltd
Woodilee Industrial Estate, Lenzie, Kirkintilloch, Glasgow, Lanarkshire G66 3UR
**Tel:** 0141-776-2384 **Fax:** 0141-776-2382
**Web:** www.pwhall.co.uk
**Reg No:** 0170917SC **Estd:** 1996 Private Limited Company
**Line of Business:** Manufacturers of plastic products
**Export Markets:** Europe
**Export Sales:** £5,608,877
**Issued Capital:** £100
**Directors:** I R Mccallum, G R Mccallum
**Co. Secretary:** Blair Syme
**Responsibilities**
**Senior:** Ian Colston *(Works Manager)*
**US SIC:** 2821, 2819
**UK SIC:** 25140, 25110
**Auditors:** PricewaterhouseCoopers
**Bankers:** Bank Of Scotland (80-07-48)

| | 31-12-13 | 31-12-12 | 31-12-11 |
|---|---|---|---|
| TO | 10,372,991 | 9,980,571 | 10,518,421 |
| P/L | 325,198 | 114,056 | 351,505 |
| NW | 3,816,339 | 3,604,370 | 3,446,630 |
| WC | 1,829,615 | 1,539,826 | 1,319,282 |
| Emp. | 56 | 55 | 57 |

DUNS 21-319-8609
## P.W.Greenhalgh & Co.Ltd
(**Subsidiary of:** P. W. Greenhalgh Holdings Ltd)
Newhey Bleach And Dye Works, Rochdale, Lancashire OL16 3TH
**Tel:** 01706-847911
**Web:** www.pwgreenhalgh.com
**Reg No:** 0199153 **VAT No:** 145116983
**Estd:** 1924 Private Limited Company
**Line of Business:** Finishing of textiles
**Export Sales:** £561,987
**Trading Style:** Pwg
**Issued Capital:** £20,100
**Principals:** A B Greenhalgh *(Managing)*, S R Greenhalgh
**Co. Secretary:** Andrew Greenhalgh
**Responsibilities**
**Senior:** Ben Greenhalgh *(Senior IT Executive)*
**Finance:** Tim Malkin *(Senior Finance Administrator)*
**IT:** Ben Greenhalgh *(Senior IT Executive)*
**US SIC:** 2269 **UK SIC:** 43702
**Auditors:** Baker Tilly UK Audit LLP
**Bankers:** The Co-Operative Bank Plc (08-90-52)

| | 31-12-13 | 31-12-12 | 31-12-11 |
|---|---|---|---|
| TO | 7,350,531 | 7,040,759 | 7,388,733 |
| P/L | (37,489) | (99,682) | (21,728) |
| NW | 1,777,363 | 2,085,452 | 2,447,134 |
| WC | 1,757,572 | 1,765,739 | 1,849,541 |
| Emp. | 87 | 89 | 95 |

DUNS 34-890-7544
## Pwp Building Services Ltd
The Oaks, Moor Road, Nottingham, Nottinghamshire NG6 8TU
**Tel:** 01159-647780 **Fax:** 01159555534
**Web:** www.pwpltd.co.uk
**Reg No:** 2827817 **Estd:** 1993 Private Limited Company
**Line of Business:** Installation of electrical wiring and fittings
**Export Sales:** £258,871
**Issued Capital:** £75
**Directors:** D B England, I Jarvis, R J Sowter, T P Holt, R Sweet
**Co. Secretary:** Nigel Richardson
**US SIC:** 1731, 1522
**UK SIC:** 50300, 50100
**Auditors:** Hobsons
**Bankers:** Yorkshire Bank Plc (05-08-41)

| | 30-09-14 | 30-09-13 | 30-09-12 |
|---|---|---|---|
| TO | 25,637,234 | 14,559,960 | 9,681,450 |
| P/L | 4,148,148 | 1,457,039 | 385,215 |
| NW | 5,494,802 | 2,265,987 | 1,895,559 |
| WC | 5,275,658 | 2,069,564 | 1,752,388 |
| Emp. | 143 | 116 | 104 |

DUNS 21-740-4098
## Pwr Events Holdings Ltd
Queen Anne House, 15 Thames Street, Hampton, Middlesex TW12 2EW
**Tel:** 02082419818
**Reg No:** 7736361 **Estd:** 2011 Private Limited Company
**Line of Business:** Management activities of holding companies
**Issued Capital:** £303
**Directors:** J D Rogers, J Wells, G P Popper
**US SIC:** 6711 **UK SIC:** 83962

| | 30-11-13 | 30-11-12 |
|---|---|---|
| TO | 20,974,566 | 15,256,563 |
| P/L | 2,756,535 | 2,810,536 |
| NW | 5,065,680 | 3,012,643 |
| WC | 2,480,247 | 480,434 |
| Emp. | 97 | 76 |

DUNS 39-809-9952 **Imp**
## Pws Distributors Ltd
Po Box 20, Newton Aycliffe, County Durham DL5 6XJ
**Tel:** 01325-505555
**Web:** www.pws.co.uk
**Reg No:** 2214406 **Estd:** 1990 Private Limited Company
**Line of Business:** Plant dealers
**Export Sales:** £123,434
**Issued Capital:** £6,640
**Directors:** J A Lennon, M W Stephenson, J B Whisker, P A Elenor
**Co. Secretary:** Jonathan Whisker
**Responsibilities**
**Senior:** Robert Cowen *(Manager)*
**Finance:** Robert Cowen *(Manager)*
**Marketing:** Andrew Langford *(Marketing Manager)*
**Sales:** Vicky Wilson *(Sales Manager)*
**IT:** Robert Cowen *(Manager)*
**Operations:** Andrew Langford *(Marketing Manager)*
**US SIC:** 2599 **UK SIC:** 46720
**Auditors:** KPMG LLP
**Bankers:** Barclays Bank Plc (20-25-29)

| | 30-04-14 | 31-10-13 | 30-04-12 |
|---|---|---|---|
| TO | 26,581,086 | 80,117,100 | 49,383,067 |
| P/L | 2,240,637 | 4,858,875 | 3,185,087 |
| NW | 18,581,150 | 21,275,122 | 17,572,464 |
| WC | 11,577,428 | 13,993,829 | 9,868,129 |
| Emp. | 258 | 283 | 270 |

DUNS 21-006-4636
## Px Group Ltd
Px House, Westpoint Road, Stockton-On-Tees, Cleveland TS17 6BF
**Tel:** 01642-623000
**Web:** www.pxlimited.com
**Reg No:** 6309132 **Estd:** 2002 Private Limited Company
**Line of Business:** Management and business consultants
**Export Sales:** £1,620,554
**Issued Capital:** £167
**Directors:** D J Salkeld, T J Underdown, Dr M R Green, C J Picotte, I Clifford
**Co. Secretary:** Px Appointments Limited
**Responsibilities**
**IT:** Dean Anderson *(IT Manager)*
**US SIC:** 6711 **UK SIC:** 83962

| | 31-03-14 | 31-03-13 | 31-03-12 |
|---|---|---|---|
| TO | 77,094,017 | 80,333,502 | 63,221,211 |
| P/L | 2,197,274 | 2,717,382 | 1,780,717 |
| NW | 6,879,203 | 10,421,818 | 7,095,946 |
| WC | 5,542,102 | 9,176,958 | 6,890,251 |
| Emp. | 253 | 286 | 285 |

DUNS 51-576-6801
## Pxp Holdings Ltd
The Station, Sandy, Bedfordshire SG19 3HB
**Tel:** 01767-651218 **Fax:** 01767651928
**Web:** www.pinewood-structures.co.uk
**Reg No:** 5857936 **Estd:** 2006 Private Limited Company
**Line of Business:** Management activities of production holding companies
**Trading Style:** Pinewood Structures
**Issued Capital:** £12,405,785
**Directors:** J D Gregory, M J Meyer, G Arnold
**Co. Secretary:** Anthony Vallely
**US SIC:** 6711 **UK SIC:** 83962
**Auditors:** WMT
**Bankers:** Bristol And West Plc (57-14-62)

| | 31-12-13 | 31-12-12 | 31-12-11 |
|---|---|---|---|
| TO | 7,667,046 | 8,107,382 | 14,378,389 |
| P/L | (355,972) | (1,554,028) | (1,862,954) |
| NW | (282,657) | (41,553) | (9,401,835) |
| WC | (93,625) | 145,175 | 258,041 |
| Emp. | 55 | 68 | 97 |

DUNS 39-232-6161 **Imp**
## Pxp Solutions Ltd
(**Subsidiary of:** Tc Invest Ag)
The Cornmill, Roydon Road, Stanstead Abbotts, Ware, Hertfordshire SG12 8XL
**Tel:** 08442094370 **Fax:** 08442094371
**Web:** www.servebase.com
**Reg No:** 2117319 **Estd:** 1987 Private Limited Company
**Line of Business:** Hardware consultancy
**Trading Style:** Pxp
**Issued Capital:** £100
**Directors:** R R Steytler, J Bennett, E W Chandler, J G Leigh
**Co. Secretary:** Robert Hoskin
**Responsibilities**
**Senior:** Franko Delbasso *(Chief Executive)*
**Finance:** Hitten Patel *(Head of Finance)*
**Marketing:** Melissa Law *(Product Marketing Director)*, Lisa Middleton *(Marketing Executive)*
**IT:** Graham Zwart *(Purchasing Manager)*
**Purchasing:** Graham Zwart *(Purchasing Manager)*
**US SIC:** 7379 **UK SIC:** 83940
**Auditors:** Nexia Smith & Williamson
**Bankers:** Lloyds TSB Bank plc (30-99-86)

| | 31-03-14 | 31-03-13 | 31-03-12 |
|---|---|---|---|
| TA | 1,224,662 | 1,373,381 | 2,157,674 |
| NW | (1,197,301) | (474,529) | 13,357 |
| WC | 356,767 | 396,129 | 931,651 |

DUNS 21-260-8285
## Pye Motors Ltd
Ovangle Road, Morecambe, Lancashire LA3 3PF
**Tel:** 01524-598598
**Web:** www.pyemotors.co.uk
**Reg No:** 0204727 **VAT No:** 153686543
**Estd:** 1925 Private Limited Company
**Line of Business:** Car dealers (new & used)
**Issued Capital:** £30,800
**Principals:** N Payne *(Managing)*, D L Pye *(Managing)*, J M Pye, Ms H J Morley Pye, A Payne
**Responsibilities**
**Senior:** Ian Bainbridge *(Parts Controller)*, Helen Pye *(Manager)*
**Sales:** Kevin Hannah *(Sales Manager)*
**HR:** Cathryn Roberts *(Human Resources Manager)*
**Purchasing:** Ian Bainbridge *(Parts Controller)*
**Branches:** Pye Motors Ltd, James Freel Close, Barrow-In-Furness, Cumbria LA14 2NW
**US SIC:** 5511, 5521
**UK SIC:** 65100
**Auditors:** RSM Tenon Audit Ltd
**Bankers:** National Westminster Bank Plc (01-54-90)

| | 31-12-13 | 31-12-12 | 31-12-11 |
|---|---|---|---|
| TO | 31,423,078 | 28,505,115 | 27,125,073 |
| P/L | 697,384 | 42,873 | 44,327 |
| NW | 2,073,325 | 1,689,255 | 1,777,182 |
| WC | (516,700) | (631,017) | (921,953) |
| Emp. | 115 | 114 | 115 |

DUNS 56-987-1288 **Imp**
## Pylones Uk Ltd
Octopus, London W1F 7DQ
**Tel:** 020-7287-3916 **Fax:** 020-7287-2206
**Web:** www.octopusshop.co.uk
**Reg No:** 2854436 **VAT No:** 653611742
**Estd:** 1993 Private Limited Company
**Line of Business:** Fashion accessories
**Trading Style:** Pylones
**Issued Capital:** £120,100
**Director:** Mrs A King
**Co. Secretary:** Ms Lena Guillemet

**Responsibilities**
**Senior:** Sara Ali *(Finance Assistant)*, Allison King *(Finance Director)*
**Finance:** Sara Ali *(Finance Assistant)*, Allison King *(Finance Director)*
**Branches:** Pylones Uk Ltd, 7 Queens Arcade, Leeds, West Yorkshire LS1 6LF
**US SIC:** 5621 **UK SIC:** 64500
**Auditors:** Perrys
**Bankers:** Lloyds TSB Bank plc (30-94-81)

| | 31-12-13 | 31-12-12 | 31-12-11 |
|---|---|---|---|
| TO | 6,335,459 | 6,644,684 | 7,184,266 |
| P/L | 453,540 | 378,338 | (351,277) |
| NW | 388,329 | (29,034) | (407,372) |
| WC | 246,850 | (160,518) | (683,240) |
| Emp. | 73 | 69 | 98 |

DUNS 21-744-8810
## Pyments of Campden Ltd
Old Station Yard, Station Road, Chipping Campden, Gloucestershire GL55 6LB
**Tel:** 01386840233
**Web:** www.pymentsbuilders.com
**Reg No:** 1448950 **VAT No:** 327165560
**Estd:** 1979 Private Limited Company
**Line of Business:** Builders
**Issued Capital:** £40,260
**Principals:** R V Brundle *(Managing)*, Mrs G A Brundle
**Co. Secretary:** Reid & Co Professional Services
**Branches:** Pyments Of Campden Ltd, Beaufort House, 4 Mansell Street, Stratford-Upon-Avon, Warwickshire CV37 6NZ
**US SIC:** 1522 **UK SIC:** 50100
**Auditors:** J Tonna & Co

| | 31-12-13 | 31-12-12 | 31-12-11 |
|---|---|---|---|
| TA | 1,415,175 | 1,361,379 | 1,373,843 |
| NW | (12,418) | 52,817 | 51,847 |
| WC | (205,613) | (153,207) | (174,736) |

DUNS 77-536-4680
## Pyramid Builders Ltd
38a Fourth Way, Wembley, Middlesex HA9 0LH
**Tel:** 02084-598880 **Fax:** 02084-598881
**Web:** www.pyramidbuildersltd.co.uk
**Reg No:** 2993516 **VAT No:** 544640056
**Estd:** 1986 Private Limited Company
**Line of Business:** Other building installation
**Issued Capital:** £100
**Director:** L Clear
**US SIC:** 1796 **UK SIC:** 50400
**Auditors:** Evans Mockler Ltd

| | 31-12-13 | 31-12-12 | 31-12-11 |
|---|---|---|---|
| TA | 4,830,447 | 3,858,325 | 3,749,650 |
| NW | 1,982,568 | 1,867,412 | 1,852,087 |
| WC | 3,789,041 | 2,932,569 | 2,355,748 |

DUNS 29-761-7342 Imp
## Pyramid Display Materials Ltd
(**Subsidiary of:** Cubic Holdings Ltd)
Unit 5 Clarence Avenue Westpoint, Enterprise Park, Manchester M17 1QS
**Tel:** 0161-872-5666
**Web:** www.pyramid-display.co.uk
**Reg No:** 2024809 **VAT No:** 437665226
**Estd:** 2002 Private Limited Company
**Line of Business:** Manufacturers and suppliers of pvc based products
**Export Sales:** £76,510
**Issued Capital:** £234,504
**Directors:** C Doherty, D Morgan, P L Madsen, A F Murphy, P G Edwards, G Cummings
**Co. Secretary:** Ms Tracey Morgan
**Branches:** Pyramid Display Materials Ltd, Birmingham Depot, Unit 15, Birmingham, West Midlands B8 1AB
**US SIC:** 3079, 5084
**UK SIC:** 48360, 61490
**Auditors:** Kubinski

| | 30-06-14 | 30-06-13 | 30-06-12 |
|---|---|---|---|
| TO | 28,376,042 | 25,091,190 | 24,094,868 |
| P/L | 1,105,958 | 801,698 | 846,913 |
| NW | 3,084,330 | 2,468,865 | 1,831,910 |
| WC | 1,022,371 | 902,773 | 546,436 |
| Emp. | 85 | 83 | 80 |

DUNS 34-770-5548
## Pyramids International Ltd
Suite 6 Heath Court, Birmingham, West Midlands B10 0JS
**Tel:** 08450090964 **Fax:** 08712562422
**Web:** www.pyramids-group.com
**Reg No:** 5571479 **Estd:** 2005 Private Limited Company
**Line of Business:** Wholesale of computers, computer peripheral equipment and software
**Issued Capital:** £100
**Director:** A B El-Fiky
**US SIC:** 5081, 5065
**UK SIC:** 61490, 61500

| | 31-03-14 | 31-03-13 | 31-03-12 |
|---|---|---|---|
| TA | 2,345,024 | 307,263 | 415,631 |
| NW | 136,903 | 86,859 | 97,680 |
| WC | 1,332,524 | N/A | 138,192 |

DUNS 21-920-3817 Imp-Exp
## Pyranha Mouldings Ltd
Unit 1 Premier Point, Aston Lane South, Whitehouse Industrial Estate, Runcorn, Cheshire WA7 3GG
**Tel:** 01928716666
**Web:** www.pyranha.com
**Reg No:** 1157125 **VAT No:** 152994928
**Estd:** 1971 Private Limited Company
**Line of Business:** Boatbuilders
**Export Markets:** France, Germany, Italy & U S A
**Trading Style:** Kayaks North West
**Issued Capital:** £21,704
**Principals:** G J Mackereth *(Managing)*, P H Mackereth *(Technical)*
**Co. Secretary:** Graham Mackereth
**Responsibilities**
**Senior:** Maurice Mackereth *(Manager)*
**US SIC:** 3079 **UK SIC:** 48360
**Auditors:** Haslam Tunstall
**Bankers:** Barclays Bank Plc (20-91-48)

| | 31-12-13 | 31-12-12 | 31-12-11 |
|---|---|---|---|
| TA | 3,207,501 | 3,048,405 | 3,547,764 |
| NW | 1,437,962 | 1,346,670 | 1,270,074 |
| WC | 929,724 | 891,964 | 952,078 |

DUNS 22-950-2794 Imp-Exp
## Pyroban Ltd
(**Subsidiary of:** Caterpillar Inc.)
Endeavour Works, 59 Dolphin Road, Shoreham-By-Sea, West Sussex BN43 6QG
**Tel:** 01273456800 **Fax:** 01273-465313
**Web:** www.pyroban.com
**Reg No:** 1390808 **Estd:** 1978 Private Limited Company
**Line of Business:** Fire protection consultants and engineers
**Export Markets:** Worldwide
**Export Sales:** £16,435,000
**Issued Capital:** £201,875
**Directors:** M D Cleaver, N J Burroughs
**Co. Secretary:** Mrs Janette Nicholls
**Responsibilities**
**Senior:** John Balkema *(General Manager)*, Nigel Tester *(Production Development Manager)*
**Marketing:** Malcolm Davis *(Sales & Marketing Director)*
**Sales:** Malcolm Davis *(Sales & Marketing Director)*
**IT:** Steve Noakes *(IT Manager)*
**Health & Safety:** Matthew Shirkie *(Health & Safety Officer)*
**Purchasing:** Mike Phelan *(Buyer)*
**Engineering:** Steve Noakes *(IT Manager)*, Nigel Tester *(Production Development Manager)*, Dave Waring *(Divisional Engineering Manager)*
**US SIC:** 3549, 3823
**UK SIC:** 32212, 37100
**Auditors:** Grant Thornton
**Bankers:** Barclays Bank Plc (20-12-75)

| | 31-12-13 | 31-12-12 | 31-12-11 |
|---|---|---|---|
| TO | 25,011,000 | 25,721,000 | 10,167,000 |
| P/L | 1,002,000 | 1,769,000 | (75,000) |
| NW | 9,133,000 | 8,396,000 | 7,225,000 |
| WC | 7,472,000 | 7,911,000 | 7,284,000 |
| Emp. | 164 | 182 | 196 |

DUNS 21-003-1803 Imp-Exp
## Pyrotek Engineering Materials Ltd
(**Subsidiary of:** Pyrotek Incorporated)
Garamonde Drive, Wymbush, Milton Keynes, Buckinghamshire MK8 8LN
**Tel:** 01908-561155 **Fax:** 01908-560473
**Web:** www.pyrotek.info
**Reg No:** 0269400 **VAT No:** 226505186
**Estd:** 1983 Private Limited Company
**Line of Business:** Cladding and insulation materials
**Export Markets:** E U, Middle East, Africa
**Export Sales:** £14,429,177
**Issued Capital:** £50,000
**Directors:** M B Vicent, M Roy, M Loose, A G Roy
**Co. Secretary:** Miss Anita Hollis
**Responsibilities**
**Senior:** Nigel Clear *(Senior Sales Executive)*
**Finance:** James Ball *(Joint Managing Director)*
**Sales:** Nigel Clear *(Senior Sales Executive)*
**IT:** Gareth Smith *(Senior IT Executive)*
**Branches:** Pyrotek Engineering Materials Ltd, Lee Bank Business Cntr, Unit 14B, 55 Holloway Head, Birmingham, West Midlands B1 1HP
**US SIC:** 3079 **UK SIC:** 48360
**Auditors:** BDO LLP
**Bankers:** Barclays Bank Plc (20-92-60)

| | 30-06-14 | 30-06-13 | 30-06-12 |
|---|---|---|---|
| TO | 16,223,826 | 14,689,136 | 15,245,535 |
| P/L | 1,420,246 | 746,736 | 832,028 |
| NW | 5,506,589 | 4,842,484 | 3,911,842 |
| WC | 3,924,847 | 3,405,758 | 2,771,998 |
| Emp. | 67 | 65 | 66 |

DUNS 73-974-7483 Imp
## Pyser-S G I Group Ltd
Fircroft Way, Edenbridge, Kent TN8 6HA
**Web:** www.pyser-sgi.com
**Reg No:** 2946375 **Estd:** 1994 Private Limited Company
**Line of Business:** Management activities of production holding companies
**Issued Capital:** £92,000
**Principals:** M J Wimsey *(Managing)*, B J Brown
**Co. Secretary:** Jeremy Smith
**US SIC:** 6711 **UK SIC:** 83962
**Auditors:** Horwath Clark Whitehill LLP
**Bankers:** Barclays Bank Plc (20-82-94)

| | 31-03-14 | 31-03-13 | 31-03-12 |
|---|---|---|---|
| TO | 8,918,229 | 7,675,052 | 12,087,267 |
| P/L | 1,746,722 | 444,778 | 2,572,152 |
| NW | 7,797,200 | 7,920,872 | 7,180,467 |
| WC | 6,556,771 | 6,746,661 | 6,418,408 |
| Emp. | 69 | 69 | 68 |

DUNS 21-724-7690 Imp
## Pz Cussons Beauty Llp
14 Upper St Martins Lane, London N1 0PQ
**Tel:** 02072572447
**Web:** www.pzcussonsbeauty.com
**Reg No:** 0364213OC **Estd:** 2011
**Line of Business:** Representative office
**Responsibilities**
**Senior:** Michelle Feeney *(Chief Executive Officer)*
**Marketing:** Nicola Francis *(Assistant Brand Manager)*
**US SIC:** 5199 **UK SIC:** 61900

| | 31-05-13 | 31-05-12 |
|---|---|---|
| TO | 62,408,000 | 54,970,000 |
| P/L | 8,319,000 | 6,757,000 |
| NW | (45,834,000) | (54,153,000) |
| WC | (44,959,000) | (54,854,000) |
| Emp. | 330 | 327 |

DUNS 21-228-7650
## Pz Cussons Plc
Manchester Business Park, Manchester M22 5TG
**Tel:** 01614-351-000 **Fax:** 01614-918-191
**Web:** www.pzcussons.com
**Reg No:** 0019457 **Estd:** 1963 Public Limited Company
**Line of Business:** Representative office
**Export Sales:** £672,600,000
**Issued Capital:** £4,287,250
**Directors:** Professor J A Arnold, R J Harvey, N Edozien, C Davis, Ms C L Silver, Mrs H Owers, G A Kanellis, B H Leigh
**Co. Secretary:** Simon Plant
**Responsibilities**
**Senior:** Denise Hayton *(Executive)*, John Pantelireis *(Supply Chain Director)*, Sam Plant *(Corporate Services Legal Direc)*
**Marketing:** Nina Shabanzadeh *(Communications Manager)*
**Sales:** Alex Huggon *(Business Development Manager)*, Chris Kirton *(Business Development Manager)*, Scott Marmo *(Business Development Manager)*, Awie Newell *(Commercial Director)*
**Admin:** Natalie O'Brien *(Executive Assistant)*
**HR:** Rachel Tyler *(Human Resources Manager)*
**Purchasing:** David Head *(Senior Purchasing & Contracts)*, Tony Payne *(Purchasing Manager)*
**US SIC:** 3999, 2841
**UK SIC:** 49590, 25810
**Auditors:** PricewaterhouseCoopers LLP
**Bankers:** Barclays Bank Plc (20-55-34)

| | 31-05-14 | 31-05-13 | 31-05-12 |
|---|---|---|---|
| TO | 861,400,000 | 883,200,000 | 858,900,000 |
| P/L | 123,700,000 | 94,800,000 | 48,500,000 |
| NW | 196,300,000 | 232,000,000 | 209,900,000 |
| WC | 133,800,000 | 160,600,000 | 70,900,000 |
| Emp. | 5,779 | 6,125 | 7,336 |

DUNS 21-223-9149 Imp
## Pz Cussons (Uk) Ltd
(**Subsidiary of:** Pz Cussons Plc)
Cussons House, Bird Hall Lane, Stockport, Cheshire SK3 0XN
**Tel:** 01614918000
**Web:** www.imperial-leather.com
**Reg No:** 0748096 **VAT No:** 145242292
**Estd:** 1879 Private Limited Company
**Line of Business:** Manufacture of perfumes and toilet preparations
**Issued Capital:** £7,000,000
**Directors:** J Lang, N J Craigie, F Yeomans, B H Leigh, S P Plant
**Co. Secretary:** Martyn Campbell
**Branches:** Pz Cussons (Uk) Ltd, 84 Brook St, London W1K 5EH
**US SIC:** 3999 **UK SIC:** 49590
**Auditors:** Deloitte & Touche LLP
**Bankers:** The Royal Bank Of Scotland Plc (16-00-01)

| | 31-05-13 | 31-05-12 | 31-05-11 |
|---|---|---|---|
| TO | 129,509,000 | 130,421,000 | 137,740,000 |
| P/L | 18,439,000 | 37,644,000 | 13,732,000 |
| NW | 41,826,000 | 36,873,000 | 41,767,000 |
| WC | 11,836,000 | 6,481,000 | 10,160,000 |
| Emp. | 244 | 234 | 255 |

# Q

DUNS 29-546-2881 Imp
## Q Associates Ltd
Langley Business Court, Worlds End, Beedon, Newbury, Berkshire RG20 8RY
**Tel:** 01635-248181 **Fax:** 01635244301
**Web:** www.qassociates.co.uk
**Reg No:** 1913004 **VAT No:** 363374153
**Estd:** 1985 Private Limited Company
**Line of Business:** Computer systems and software (sales)
**Export Sales:** £302,071
**Issued Capital:** £460
**Principals:** D M Cue *(Sales)*, J E Hawkins, A F Rigby, A C Griffiths
**Co. Secretary:** Neville Hopkins
**Responsibilities**
**Senior:** Dave Simmons *(Warehouse Controller)*
**Marketing:** Ben Gomez *(Social Business Manager)*
**Sales:** Nigel Horsell *(Business Development Manager)*, Gary Rawlins *(Sales Manager)*
**Admin:** Jane Sampson *(Office Manager)*
**IT:** Jim Fullarton *(IT Manager)*
**Facilities:** Jane Sampson *(Office Manager)*
**Operations:** Jane Sampson *(Office Manager)*
**US SIC:** 7379 **UK SIC:** 83940
**Auditors:** Grant Thornton UK LLP
**Bankers:** Lloyds TSB Bank plc (30-95-89)

| | 31-03-14 | 31-03-13 | 31-03-12 |
|---|---|---|---|
| TO | 29,051,228 | 35,390,739 | 29,364,792 |
| P/L | 922,851 | (171,460) | (1,745,643) |
| NW | 932,623 | 210,934 | 382,394 |
| WC | 696,505 | (100,513) | (111,525) |
| Emp. | 60 | 61 | 66 |

DUNS 73-309-0752
## Q C D Ltd
(**Subsidiary of:** Qcd Enterprises Ltd)
Unit B55, Gosport, Hampshire PO12 3UL
**Tel:** 023-9252-6888
**Web:** www.qcdlimited.co.uk
**Reg No:** 4582844 **Estd:** 2002 Private Limited Company
**Line of Business:** Precision engineers
**Issued Capital:** £100
**Director:** S Lindsell
**Co. Secretary:** Ms Madeleine Lindsell
**US SIC:** 8911, 3559
**UK SIC:** 83701, 32863
**Auditors:** Arthur Daniels & Co

| | 31-10-13 | 31-10-12 | 31-10-11 |
|---|---|---|---|
| TA | 398,435 | 350,982 | 294,988 |
| NW | 193,172 | 200,074 | 166,908 |
| WC | 47,521 | 61,750 | 59,229 |

DUNS 21-527-7489
## Q Care & Special Care
2b Sandy Lane, Prestatyn, Clwyd LL19 7SG
**Tel:** 01745851310
**Web:** www.qcare.co.uk
**Estd:** 1993 Partnership
**Line of Business:** Home care service providers
**Principals:** G Goodwin, Mrs S Day *(Partner)*, Miss A Kelly *(Partner)*
**US SIC:** 8091 **UK SIC:** 95200
**Employees:** 49

DUNS 57-056-3635
## Q Care Ltd
69 Bethcar Street, Ebbw Vale, Gwent NP23 6HW
**Tel:** 01495300160
**Web:** www.qcare.co.uk
**Reg No:** 2881343 **Estd:** 1993 Private Limited Company
**Line of Business:** Home care service providers
**Issued Capital:** £111,429
**Directors:** Ms J Whittal Williams, P Gregory, E B Whittal-Williams, T Dainty
**Co. Secretary:** Adrian Whittal Williams
**Responsibilities**
**Senior:** Phillip Gregory *(Managing Director)*, Ellis Williams *(Manager)*
**Finance:** Phillip Gregory *(Managing Director)*
**Marketing:** Laura Danter *(Sales & Marketing Manager)*, Christopher Gregory *(Marketing Director)*
**Sales:** Laura Danter *(Sales & Marketing Manager)*
**Health & Safety:** Howard Pinney *(Health & Safety Officer)*
**Branches:** Q Care Ltd, 5 Church Street, Newent, Gloucestershire GL18 1PU
**US SIC:** 7399 **UK SIC:** 83954

**Auditors:** Baker Tilly UK Audit LLP

| | 30-12-13 | 30-12-12 | 29-12-11 |
|---|---|---|---|
| TO | 6,894,982 | N/A | N/A |
| P/L | (42,320) | N/A | N/A |
| NW | 248,896 | 339,894 | 207,031 |
| WC | 200,269 | 248,124 | 99,671 |
| Emp. | 547 | N/A | N/A |

DUNS 29-050-7003
## Q Crane & Plant Hire Ltd
(**Subsidiary of:** Q Crane Hire Ltd)
1 Stampstone Street, Oldham, Lancashire OL1 3PW
**Tel:** 0161-620-2115
**Web:** www.qplanthire.co.uk
**Reg No:** 1068623 **VAT No:** 562410762
**Estd:** 1972 Private Limited Company
**Line of Business:** Plant hire and leasing
**Issued Capital:** £10,000
**Principals:** J Quinn *(Managing)*, A Quinn, M Gregory, R N Cotton
**Co. Secretary:** Ms Jeanette Quinn
**Responsibilities**
**Admin:** Tracy Scollon *(Administrator)*
**Purchasing:** Wendy Pinerney *(Purchasing Co- ordinator)*
**US SIC:** 7394 **UK SIC:** 84000
**Auditors:** Allens
**Bankers:** Lloyds TSB Bank plc (30-96-26)

| | 31-08-14 | 31-08-13 | 31-08-12 |
|---|---|---|---|
| TA | 6,744,480 | 6,548,316 | 6,879,092 |
| NW | 3,660,784 | 3,004,088 | 2,204,690 |
| WC | (276,000) | (626,095) | (1,212,679) |

DUNS 21-113-9640
## Q Dental Care Ltd
(**Subsidiary of:** Dh Dental Holdings Ltd)
Europa House Europa Trading Esta, Stoneclough Road, Manchester M26 1GG
**Tel:** 01179605900
**Web:** www.bristolorthodontics.com
**Reg No:** 6545882 **Estd:** 2008 Private Limited Company
**Line of Business:** Dental practice activities
**Issued Capital:** £100
**Directors:** Dr S R Williams, W H Robson, J M Bedford, D J Hills
**Co. Secretary:** William Robson
**Branches:** Q Dental Care Ltd, 63 Sketty Road, Swansea, West Glamorgan SA2 0EN
**US SIC:** 8021 **UK SIC:** 95400
**Auditors:** Taylor Roberts

| | 31-03-14 | 31-03-13 | 31-03-12 |
|---|---|---|---|
| TO | 8,233,837 | 6,982,989 | N/A |
| P/L | 1,543,648 | 575,524 | N/A |
| NW | (1,464,849) | (3,107,068) | (3,949,458) |
| WC | (2,475,522) | (64,150) | (180,930) |
| Emp. | 101 | 102 | N/A |

DUNS 29-934-7575
## Q Despatch (West) Ltd
2 Ella Mews, Hampstead, London NW3 2NH
**Tel:** 020-7424-9559 **Fax:** 020-7424-0862
**Web:** www.qdespatch.com
**Reg No:** 2103438 **VAT No:** 460736839
**Estd:** 1987 Private Limited Company
**Line of Business:** Passenger Car Company
**Issued Capital:** £2
**Managing Director:** Mrs A Pavlou
**Co. Secretary:** Nicky Pavlou
**Responsibilities**
**Senior:** Nyck Pavlou *(Senior Director)*
**US SIC:** 4119, 4212
**UK SIC:** 72200, 72300
**Bankers:** National Westminster Bank Plc (60-04-24)

| | 31-03-14 | 31-03-13 | 31-03-12 |
|---|---|---|---|
| TA | 1,142,735 | 863,440 | 762,886 |
| NW | 267,695 | 137,040 | 113,487 |
| WC | 252,750 | 117,113 | 89,244 |

DUNS 39-710-4001
## Q E D International (U K) Ltd
(**Subsidiary of:** Qed International Ltd)
Hareness House, Hareness Road, Aberdeen, Aberdeenshire AB12 3LE
**Tel:** 01224589773 **Fax:** 01224-589772
**Web:** www.qedi.co.uk
**Reg No:** 0106477SC **Estd:** 1987 Private Limited Company
**Line of Business:** Other business activities not elsewhere classified
**Issued Capital:** £100
**Directors:** A J Johnstone, G B Sleigh, C R Fleming
**Co. Secretary:** Christopher Fidler
**Responsibilities**
**Senior:** Martyn Canham *(General Director and Co-Founde)*
**US SIC:** 7399 **UK SIC:** 83954
**Auditors:** Baker Tilly UK Audit LLP

| | 31-12-13 | 31-12-12 | 31-12-11 |
|---|---|---|---|
| TO | 54,130,000 | 23,669,000 | 20,992,000 |
| P/L | 503,000 | (82,000) | (578,000) |
| NW | 1,138,000 | (355,000) | (1,167,000) |
| WC | 8,408,000 | 5,596,000 | 3,115,000 |
| Emp. | 55 | 36 | 26 |

DUNS 77-949-6751
## Q E D Scaffolding Ltd
Lock Street, St Helens, Merseyside WA9 1HS
**Tel:** 01744-751117
**Web:** www.qedscaffolding.com
**Reg No:** 3055531 **VAT No:** 643871127
**Estd:** 1995 Private Limited Company
**Line of Business:** Other service activities not elsewhere classified
**Issued Capital:** £2
**Principals:** B W Eades *(Managing)*, M Ward
**Co. Secretary:** Ms Lynn Eades
**Responsibilities**
**Senior:** Karen Bennett *(Manager)*
**IT:** Christine Kenny *(Network, Security Manager)*
**US SIC:** 8999 **UK SIC:** 83954
**Auditors:** Alexander Myerson & Co

| | 31-03-14 | 31-03-13 | 31-03-12 |
|---|---|---|---|
| TO | 3,537,098 | 3,296,202 | 3,242,701 |
| P/L | 22,701 | 37,639 | 14,403 |
| NW | 3,511,260 | 4,540,760 | 4,630,860 |
| WC | (1,034,625) | (683,578) | (723,556) |
| Emp. | 84 | 99 | 96 |

DUNS 73-410-5500
## Q Hotels Ltd
(**Subsidiary of:** Qhotels Group Limited)
Wellington House, 5 Bruntcliffe Road Cliffe Park Way, Leeds, West Yorkshire LS27 0RY
**Tel:** 01132052880 **Fax:** 01132-898955
**Web:** www.qhotels.co.uk
**Reg No:** 4683806 **Estd:** 2005 Private Limited Company
**Line of Business:** Management activities of holding companies
**Trading Style:** Forest Pines Golf & Country Club Hotel
**Issued Capital:** £4,348,572
**Director:** M E Purtill
**Co. Secretary:** Ian Goulding
**Responsibilities**
**HR:** Nicola Roskell *(Human Resources Manager)*
**Facilities:** Stacey Heslop *(Customer Relations Manager)*
**Operations:** Stacey Heslop *(Customer Relations Manager)*
**Branches:** Q Hotels Ltd, Ermine Street, Brigg, South Humberside DN20 0AQ
**US SIC:** 6711 **UK SIC:** 83962
**Auditors:** KPMG LLP
**Bankers:** Barclays Bank Plc (20-00-50)

| | 29-12-13 | 31-12-12 | 01-12-12 |
|---|---|---|---|
| TA | 567,063,000 | 539,486,000 | 523,926,000 |
| P/L | (14,304,000) | (5,388,000) | (36,612,000) |
| NW | 76,281,000 | 83,834,000 | 84,817,000 |
| WC | 291,167,000 | (73,933,000) | (69,903,000) |

DUNS 21-607-3245
## Q M P
Timmis Road, Stourbridge, West Midlands DY9 7BQ
**Tel:** 01384899800
**Web:** www.qmp.uk.com
**Estd:** 2004 Partnership
**Line of Business:** Fabricated metal products
**Partner:** P Drury
**Responsibilities**
**Marketing:** Brad Webster *(Sales & Marketing Manager)*
**Sales:** Brad Webster *(Sales & Marketing Manager)*
**HR:** Yvonne Partridge *(Human Resources Manager)*
**US SIC:** 3441 **UK SIC:** 32042
**Employees:** 70

DUNS 23-571-1538
## Q-Park Ltd
(**Subsidiary of:** Q Park N.V.)
72 Merrion Street, Leeds, West Yorkshire LS2 8LW
**Tel:** 08704420104 **Fax:** 01132-384206
**Web:** www.q-park.co.uk
**Reg No:** 1721817 **VAT No:** 417939617
**Estd:** 2011 Private Limited Company
**Line of Business:** Other letting of own property
**Trading Style:** Carminder 2
**Issued Capital:** £20,000,000
**Directors:** A J Bidder, S M Ellis
**Co. Secretary:** Stephen Ellis
**Responsibilities**
**Senior:** Paul Trew *(Manager)*
**Marketing:** Becky Maynard *(Marketing and PR Assistant)*
**Branches:** Q-Park Ltd, Flat 1, 7 Cumberland Street, London SW1V 4LS
**US SIC:** 6519 **UK SIC:** 85000
**Auditors:** Ernst & Young LLP
**Bankers:** Lloyds TSB Bank plc (30-00-05)

| | 31-12-13 | 31-12-12 | 31-12-11 |
|---|---|---|---|
| TO | 53,103,680 | 50,498,741 | 39,499,450 |
| P/L | (11,922,083) | (3,360,945) | (8,116,063) |
| NW | (20,889,157) | (8,618,992) | (6,469,198) |
| WC | 15,553,459 | 2,309,013 | 4,574,898 |
| Emp. | 275 | 270 | 253 |

DUNS 23-222-4154
## Q102 Fm Ltd
(**Subsidiary of:** Northern Media Group Ltd)
Woodside Industrial Estate, Ballymena, Co Antrim BT42 4QJ
**Tel:** 02825648777 **Fax:** 02825648778
**Web:** www.q102.fm
**Reg No:** 0027412NI **Estd:** 1993 Private Limited Company
**Line of Business:** Radio and television production services
**Issued Capital:** £1
**Directors:** D J Fitzpatrick, T Collins, J D Taylor, J Kilclooney, R F Walshe, P O'Dwyer, J J Fitzpatrick
**Co. Secretary:** Robert Walshe
**Responsibilities**
**Senior:** Padraig O' Dwyer *(Director)*
**Branches:** Q102 Fm Ltd, Flat 1-2, 60 Belmore Street, Enniskillen, Co Fermanagh BT74 6AA
**US SIC:** 4833 **UK SIC:** 97411
**Auditors:** Carlin MC Laughlin & Co
**Bankers:** First Trust Bank (aib Group (uk) Plc) (93-80-25)

| | 31-12-13 | 31-12-12 | 31-12-11 |
|---|---|---|---|
| TA | 1 | 1 | 1 |
| NW | 1 | 1 | 1 |

DUNS 85-619-0793
## Qa-Iq Holdings Ltd
(**Subsidiary of:** The Bregal Fund Ii L.P.)
Rath House, 55-65 Uxbridge Road, Slough, Berkshire SL1 1SG
**Tel:** 08450747839 **Fax:** 08450747840
**Web:** www.qa.com
**Reg No:** 6255402 **Estd:** 2007 Private Limited Company
**Line of Business:** Management activities of holding companies
**Issued Capital:** £17,150
**Directors:** H D Thomas, S Martin, W R Macpherson, C J Martin, E A Lazarus
**Co. Secretary:** Ian Johnson
**Responsibilities**
**IT:** Adrian Jakeman *(Head of Microsoft Technology T)*
**HR:** Adrian Jakeman *(Head of Microsoft Technology T)*
**US SIC:** 6711, 8299
**UK SIC:** 83962, 93300
**Auditors:** Deloitte LLP

| | 30-05-14 | 31-05-13 | 27-05-12 |
|---|---|---|---|
| TO | N/A | N/A | 111,211,017 |
| P/L | (15) | 2,047 | 1,299,628 |
| NW | (1,348,984) | (1,348,969) | (72,577,483) |
| WC | (1,390,985) | (1,390,970) | 38,748,435 |
| Emp. | N/A | N/A | 747 |

DUNS 50-416-2785
## Qa Ltd
(**Subsidiary of:** The Bregal Fund Ii L.P.)
Gelderd Trading Estate, West Vale, Leeds, West Yorkshire LS12 6BD
**Tel:** 08450559501 **Fax:** 01132346888
**Web:** www.qa.com
**Reg No:** 2413137 **Estd:** 1989 Private Limited Company
**Line of Business:** Business and management consultancy activities not elsewhere classified
**Issued Capital:** £1,510
**Directors:** H D Thomas, S Martin, W R Macpherson, C J Martin
**Co. Secretary:** Ian Johnson
**Responsibilities**
**Senior:** Owen Mills *(Sales Manager)*
**Finance:** Sue Tetley *(Financial Director)*
**Branches:** Qa Ltd, Witan Court, 294 Witan Gate West, Milton Keynes, Buckinghamshire MK9 1EJ
**US SIC:** 7392 **UK SIC:** 83951
**Auditors:** Deloitte LLP
**Bankers:** Barclays Bank Plc (20-55-34)

| | 30-05-14 | 31-05-13 | 27-05-12 |
|---|---|---|---|
| TO | 117,575,837 | 112,564,345 | 104,953,789 |
| P/L | 20,650,407 | 17,457,963 | 12,901,388 |
| NW | 48,425,355 | 28,841,919 | 12,785,131 |
| WC | 70,043,451 | 47,459,891 | 33,557,782 |
| Emp. | 809 | 782 | 716 |

DUNS 21-327-4897 **Imp-Exp**
## Q.A. (Weld Tech) Ltd
2a Bowes Road, Middlesbrough, Cleveland TS2 1LU
**Tel:** 01642222831
**Web:** www.qaweldtech.co.uk
**Reg No:** 1479089 **VAT No:** 329245747
**Estd:** 1980 Private Limited Company
**Line of Business:** Fabricators
**Export Markets:** Europe
**Issued Capital:** £50,000
**Principals:** C P Tighe *(Managing)*, P M Langley, R L Knowles
**Co. Secretary:** Paul Langley
**US SIC:** 5084 **UK SIC:** 61490
**Auditors:** Chipchase Manners & Co

**Bankers:** HSBC Bank plc (40-33-01)

| | 28-02-14 | 28-02-13 | 28-02-12 |
|---|---|---|---|
| TO | 8,118,770 | 5,913,603 | 5,766,211 |
| P/L | 444,982 | 104,571 | (186,161) |
| NW | 2,158,955 | 1,802,434 | 1,778,473 |
| WC | 1,275,677 | 1,151,659 | 1,212,481 |
| Emp. | 75 | 60 | 62 |

DUNS 21-052-1670 **Imp**
## Qantas Airways Ltd
(**Subsidiary of:** Qantas Airways Limited)
Qantas House, 395-399 King Street, London W6 9NJ
**Tel:** 08457747767 **Fax:** 02088460563
**Web:** www.qantas.com
**Reg No:** 0004096FC **Estd:** 1934 Foreign Company
**Line of Business:** Airlines
**Directors:** T J Kennedy, G A Hounsell, A J Joyce, Ms J C Hey, R L Clifford, R R Goodmanson, C G Storrie, A J Joyce
**Co. Secretary:** Ms Cassandra Hamlin
**Responsibilities**
**Senior:** Agnes Borkowski, Maxine Brenner *(Director)*, Peter Crosgrove *(Director)*, Patricia Cross-Meadow *(Director)*, William Meaney *(Director)*, John Schubert *(Director)*, James Strong *(Director)*
**Marketing:** Malcolm Trevor *(Marketing Manager)*
**HR:** Georgia Blackburn *(Human Resources Manager)*
**Health & Safety:** Peter Cherrill *(Property Manager)*
**Facilities:** Peter Cherrill *(Property Manager)*
**US SIC:** 4511 **UK SIC:** 75000

DUNS 34-805-9940
## Qas Copak Ltd
Mitchelston Drive, Kirkcaldy, Fife KY1 3NF
**Tel:** 01592-653743 **Fax:** 01592656716
**Web:** www.qascopak.co.uk
**Reg No:** 0142714SC **VAT No:** 607531848
**Estd:** 1995 Private Limited Company
**Line of Business:** Packagers
**Issued Capital:** £60,000
**Principals:** B J Kemp *(Managing)*, D Page
**Co. Secretary:** Garry Gilfillan
**Responsibilities**
**Senior:** Ronald Forsyth *(Financial Director)*
**Finance:** Michele Cowan *(Finance Manager)*, Ronald Forsyth *(Financial Director)*
**Admin:** Diane Farmer *(Administrator)*, Craig Mckenna *(Administrator)*, Nicola Merrifield *(Administrator)*, Carla Thomson *(Administrator)*
**Branches:** Qas Copak Ltd, Whm Warehouse, Burnbrae Drive, Linwood, Paisley, Renfrewshire PA3 3BW
**US SIC:** 7399 **UK SIC:** 83954
**Auditors:** Carters
**Bankers:** National Westminster Bank Plc (60-30-20)

| | 05-01-14 | 30-12-12 | 01-01-12 |
|---|---|---|---|
| TO | 8,356,542 | 8,985,112 | 7,455,742 |
| P/L | 436,792 | 585,210 | 577,808 |
| NW | 1,424,242 | 1,192,275 | 803,574 |
| WC | 893,344 | 718,611 | 813,279 |
| Emp. | 302 | 306 | 286 |

DUNS 76-983-3385
## Qbe European Operations Plc
(**Subsidiary of:** Qbe Insurance Group Limited)
Plantation Place, 30 Fenchurch Street, London EC3M 3BD
**Tel:** 08456061234 **Fax:** 020-7680-1962
**Web:** www.qbe.com
**Reg No:** 2641728 **Estd:** 1991 Public Limited Company
**Line of Business:** Management activities of holding companies
**Issued Capital:** £2,621,258,104
**Directors:** D J Winkett, J D Neal, P A Dodridge, T C Ingram, R V Pryce
**Co. Secretary:** Ms Sharon Boland
**US SIC:** 6711, 6399
**UK SIC:** 83962, 82001
**Auditors:** PricewaterhouseCoopers LLP
**Following financial data are in thousands**

| | 31-12-13 | 31-12-12 | 31-12-11 |
|---|---|---|---|
| TO | 2,299,350 | 2,109,586 | 1,966,793 |
| P/L | 71,907 | 173,701 | 83,191 |
| NW | 1,600,221 | 1,266,591 | 1,496,859 |
| WC | 9,779,381 | 522,787 | (57,850) |
| Emp. | 2,810 | 2,836 | 2,722 |

DUNS 29-378-8212
## Qbe European Services Ltd
(**Subsidiary of:** Qbe Insurance Group Limited)
Mill Court, Mill Street, Stafford, Staffordshire ST16 2AX
**Tel:** 08456090326 **Fax:** 08456090320
**Web:** www.qbeeurope.com
**Reg No:** 1064228 **Estd:** 1972 Private Limited Company
**Line of Business:** Insurance - other
**Trading Style:** M B P Insurance
**Issued Capital:** £100

**Directors:** I D Beckerson, D E Cooney, D J Winkett
**Co. Secretary:** Ms Sharon Boland
**Responsibilities**
**Admin:** Elaine Dodd *(Team Secretary)*
**US SIC:** 6399 **UK SIC:** 82001
**Auditors:** Ernst & Young LLP
**Bankers:** Barclays Bank Plc (20-81-00)

| | 31-12-13 | 31-12-12 | 31-12-11 |
|---|---|---|---|
| TO | 314,366 | 316,909 | 349,991 |
| P/L | 22,689 | 15,476 | 23,013 |
| NW | 254,932 | 237,716 | 240,789 |
| WC | 254,932 | 237,716 | 240,789 |

DUNS 22-138-5813
### Qc Data Uk Ltd
(**Subsidiary of:** Qc Communications Inc.)
Salisbury House, London Wall, London EC2M 5PS
**Tel:** 01159-415800
**Web:** www.qcdata.com
**Reg No:** 4157553 **VAT No:** 780411839
**Estd:** 2001 Private Limited Company
**Line of Business:** Data communication systems
**Trading Style:** Qc Data Uk Limited
**Issued Capital:** £100
**Directors:** M L Pfeiffer, Dr M F Balm, I J Wainwright
**Co. Secretary:** D & A Nominees Limited
**US SIC:** 8911 **UK SIC:** 83701
**Auditors:** KPMG LLP
**Bankers:** Lloyds TSB Bank plc (30-00-09)

| | 31-12-13 | 31-12-12 | 31-12-11 |
|---|---|---|---|
| TO | 6,966,828 | 5,131,944 | N/A |
| P/L | 774,765 | 253,436 | N/A |
| NW | 1,356,153 | 761,613 | 571,437 |
| WC | 1,334,771 | 748,366 | 556,536 |

DUNS 34-816-6638
### Q.C. Supplies Ltd
(**Subsidiary of:** Westcoast (Holdings) Ltd)
1 Quarry Road, Halifax, West Yorkshire HX3 5LL
**Tel:** 01422444666 **Fax:** 01422-444555
**Web:** www.cartridgepoint.com
**Reg No:** 2796130 **VAT No:** 567066714
**Estd:** 1993 Private Limited Company
**Line of Business:** Computer stationery
**Export Sales:** £3,187,321
**Issued Capital:** £21,707
**Principals:** J R Crabtree *(Managing)*, S J Madhani
**Responsibilities**
**Senior:** James Hepworth *(Warehouse Manager)*
**Admin:** Eric Hamer *(Administrator)*
**Facilities:** James Hepworth *(Warehouse Manager)*
**Branches:** Q.c. Supplies Ltd, Oaklife House 32 Church Street, Rickmansworth, Hertfordshire WD3 1DJ
**US SIC:** 3811 **UK SIC:** 37100
**Auditors:** Grant Thornton UK LLP
**Bankers:** National Westminster Bank Plc (53-61-07)

| | 31-03-14 | 31-03-13 | 31-03-12 |
|---|---|---|---|
| TO | 33,531,736 | 44,743,909 | 60,253,934 |
| P/L | (1,542,282) | (138,600) | 111,932 |
| NW | (211,368) | 1,140,806 | 1,285,356 |
| WC | (457,480) | 183,899 | 169,355 |
| Emp. | 134 | 163 | 170 |

DUNS 73-949-9924
### Qcc Information Security Ltd
(**Subsidiary of:** Blackthorn Technologies Ltd)
6th Floor Ergon House, Horseferry Road, London SW1P 2AL
**Tel:** 02030562800
**Web:** www.blackthorn.com
**Reg No:** 5202631 **Estd:** 2004 Private Limited Company
**Line of Business:** Security activities
**Issued Capital:** £1,153
**Director:** S Mathers
**Responsibilities**
**Senior:** Harry Beker *(Manager)*, Philip Drake *(Manager)*, Neil Hare Brown *(Manager)*, Andy Vickers *(Manager)*
**US SIC:** 7393 **UK SIC:** 83954
**Auditors:** Morgan Cameron Ltd

| | 31-03-14 | 31-03-13 | 31-03-12 |
|---|---|---|---|
| TO | N/A | 910,049 | 2,198,050 |
| P/L | (10,863) | 480,805 | (377,390) |
| NW | N/A | 10,863 | (469,942) |
| WC | N/A | 10,863 | (159,960) |

DUNS 39-738-1898
### Qdell Ltd
91 Station Road, West Drayton, Middlesex UB7 7LT
**Tel:** 01895444333 **Fax:** 01895-449961
**Web:** www.qdelllhr.co.uk
**Reg No:** 2179405 **Estd:** 1987 Private Limited Company
**Line of Business:** Courier activities other than national post activities
**Issued Capital:** £5,000
**Director:** I F Dickinson
**Co. Secretary:** Ingwe Services Limited
**US SIC:** 4311 **UK SIC:** 79010
**Auditors:** Koshal Associates
**Bankers:** Barclays Bank Plc (20-38-83)

| | 31-01-14 | 31-01-13 | 31-01-12 |
|---|---|---|---|
| TA | 734,471 | 578,289 | 615,618 |
| NW | 394,174 | 359,703 | 357,303 |
| WC | 354,659 | 329,919 | 310,975 |

DUNS 77-754-4834
### Qdos Entertainment Ltd
Qdos House, Queen Margarets Road, Scarborough, North Yorkshire YO11 2YH
**Tel:** 01723500038
**Web:** www.qdosentertainment.co.uk
**Reg No:** 3017503 **Estd:** 1990 Private Limited Company
**Line of Business:** Management activities of other non-financial holding companies not elsewhere classified
**Trading Style:** Qdos Entertainment Ltd
**Issued Capital:** £43,050
**Directors:** N J Thomas, P Parnaby
**Co. Secretary:** Mrs Sandra Thomas
**Responsibilities**
**Senior:** Philip Dale *(Manager)*
**Admin:** Mary Sellars *(Administrator)*
**US SIC:** 6711 **UK SIC:** 83962
**Auditors:** Croucher Needham Audit LLP
**Bankers:** National Westminster Bank Plc (54-41-24)

| | 31-03-14 | 31-03-13 | 31-03-12 |
|---|---|---|---|
| TO | 66,621,907 | 62,930,037 | 54,759,678 |
| P/L | 1,098,869 | 946,585 | 777,039 |
| NW | (145,612) | (238,643) | 608,446 |
| WC | (12,751,895) | (12,329,837) | (10,804,537) |
| Emp. | 1,086 | 960 | 900 |

DUNS 67-154-4885
### Qdos Holdings Ltd
Qdos Court, Rossendale Road, Leicester, Leicestershire LE9 7LY
**Tel:** 01455850000
**Web:** www.qdosconsulting.com
**Reg No:** 6012812 **Estd:** 2006 Private Limited Company
**Line of Business:** Activities auxiliary to insurance and pension funding
**Issued Capital:** £3,414
**Directors:** A A Gordon, P R Willcocks, A D Horton, S J Greenwell
**Responsibilities**
**Senior:** Ruppert Chapman *(Chief Executive Officer)*
**US SIC:** 6411 **UK SIC:** 83200
**Bankers:** Lloyds TSB Bank plc (30-96-20)

| | 30-09-13 | 30-09-12 | 30-09-11 |
|---|---|---|---|
| TO | 5,784,668 | 4,324,044 | N/A |
| P/L | 1,006,615 | 953,495 | N/A |
| NW | 1,051,387 | 747,738 | 1,050 |
| WC | 774,484 | 614,393 | 1,050 |
| Emp. | 90 | 88 | N/A |

DUNS 21-717-6261
### Qe Academy Trust
Upper School Western Road, Crediton, Devon EX17 3LU
**Web:** www.queenelizabeths.devon.sch.uk
**Reg No:** 7562194 **Estd:** 2011 Private Company Limited By Guarantee
**Line of Business:** General secondary education
**Directors:** R J Poole, D G Brenton, Mrs G E Poulton, Mrs B Gilbert, Dr H R Anderson, N A Way, Miss M Kempson, Mrs T S Hornett
**Co. Secretary:** Mrs Ann Fursdon
**Responsibilities**
**Senior:** Demitri Coryton *(Governor)*, Nigel Guthrie *(Director)*, Deborah Leighton Plom *(Director)*, David Morey *(Director)*, Mary Quicke *(Director)*, Marilyn Rickard *(Director)*, Peter Salmond *(Director)*
**US SIC:** 8211 **UK SIC:** 93200
**Bankers:** Lloyds TSB Bank plc (30-93-14)

| | 31-08-14 | 31-08-13 | 31-08-12 |
|---|---|---|---|
| TO | 9,762,605 | 9,699,560 | 35,300,498 |
| P/L | (84,171) | (397,681) | 21,253,686 |
| NW | 19,472,834 | 19,895,005 | 20,416,686 |
| WC | 624,902 | 244,171 | 300,234 |
| Emp. | 183 | 193 | 199 |

DUNS 21-041-3830
### Qedisconsulting
Tower House, 10 Southampton Street, Covent Garden, London WC2E 7HA
**Web:** www.qedis.com
**Estd:** 2003
**Line of Business:** Management and business consultants
**Responsibilities**
**Senior:** Paramjit Uppal *(Chief Executive Officer)*
**US SIC:** 7392 **UK SIC:** 83951
**Employees:** 93

DUNS 34-827-7856 **Imp**
### Qfh Ltd
Alma Park Road, Grantham, Lincolnshire NG31 9SE
**Tel:** 01476-514800 **Fax:** 0147673678
**Web:** www.qfc.co.uk
**Reg No:** 2801219 **VAT No:** 118885436
**Estd:** 1993 Private Limited Company
**Line of Business:** Manufacture of other furniture
**Issued Capital:** £1,023,210
**Managing Director:** V W Goldberg
**Co. Secretary:** David Bramwell
**US SIC:** 2517 **UK SIC:** 46714
**Auditors:** KPMG
**Bankers:** HSBC Bank plc (40-22-19)

| | 31-12-13 | 31-12-12 | 31-12-11 |
|---|---|---|---|
| TO | 34,348,000 | 23,235,000 | 23,793,000 |
| P/L | (779,000) | 17,000 | 841,000 |
| NW | 1,769,000 | 2,805,000 | 2,884,000 |
| WC | (244,000) | 673,000 | 1,379,000 |
| Emp. | 269 | 205 | 202 |

DUNS 22-226-2011
### Qfsl Cleaning Uk Ltd
(**Subsidiary of:** Uni-Flo Services Ltd)
47 Hutton Close, Washington, Tyne and Wear NE38 0AH
**Tel:** 01914 178125
**Web:** www.qfslgroup.com
**Reg No:** 4244104 **Estd:** 2001 Private Limited Company
**Line of Business:** Facilities management services
**Issued Capital:** £200
**Director:** S D Burrluck
**Responsibilities**
**Senior:** Michael Ilderton *(Manager)*, Richard Strauthan *(HR & Operations)*
**Finance:** Richard Strauthan *(HR & Operations)*
**US SIC:** 7399 **UK SIC:** 83954
**Auditors:** Inspire Chartered Accountants

| | 30-06-13 | 30-06-12 | 30-06-11 |
|---|---|---|---|
| TA | 534,936 | 436,415 | 373,010 |
| NW | 175,906 | 111,022 | 72,666 |
| WC | 158,260 | 82,216 | 41,885 |

DUNS 56-993-7188 **Imp**
### Qiagen Ltd
(**Subsidiary of:** Qiagen N.V.)
Skelton House, Lloyd Street North, Manchester M15 6SH
**Tel:** 0808 234 3665 **Fax:** 0808 234 3918
**Web:** www.qiagen.com
**Reg No:** 2858916 **VAT No:** 644373238
**Estd:** 1993 Private Limited Company
**Line of Business:** Other human health activities
**Issued Capital:** £105,002
**Directors:** R Sackers, Mrs N Bramwell, P M Schatz
**Co. Secretary:** John Riley
**Responsibilities**
**Senior:** Kelly Campbell *(Manager)*, Philip Sefton *(Manager)*
**Facilities:** Tracey Pollock *(Business Administrator)*
**US SIC:** 8091 **UK SIC:** 95200
**Auditors:** Grant Thornton UK LLP
**Bankers:** Lloyds TSB Bank plc (30-92-70)

| | 31-12-13 | 31-12-12 | 31-12-11 |
|---|---|---|---|
| TO | 35,987,859 | 33,094,975 | 31,608,437 |
| P/L | 216,412 | (207,150) | 2,620,165 |
| NW | 7,051,882 | 7,427,266 | 7,732,601 |
| WC | 5,800,403 | 6,113,326 | 6,349,169 |
| Emp. | 96 | 112 | 109 |

DUNS 73-313-1788
### Qinetiq Group Plc
Old Ively Road Cody Technology Park, Farnborough, Hampshire GU14 0LX
**Tel:** 08700100942
**Web:** www.qinetiq.com
**Reg No:** 4586941 **Estd:** 2002 Public Limited Company
**Line of Business:** Management activities of holding companies
**Export Sales:** £612,600,000
**Issued Capital:** £6,604,765
**Directors:** Sir J M Burnell-Nugent, P C Murray, M W Elliott, Mrs S J Searle, I Mason, J M Harper, D A Mellors
**Co. Secretary:** Jon Messent
**Responsibilities**
**Senior:** Miles Adcock *(Managing Director, Training)*, Jon Bayliss *(Senior Manager)*, Gaz Borland *(Managing Director, Air)*, Andy Brierley *(Managing Director- Shared Serv)*, Bob Connor *(Manager)*, Steve Franklin *(Manager)*, Trevor Martin *(Board Member)*, Neville Salkeld *(Managing Director, Strategy)*, Stuart Winter *(Manager)*
**Marketing:** Ronald Findlayson *(Strategic Business Director, D)*
**Admin:** Marion Stewart *(PA to Marketing Director)*
**HR:** Miles Adcock *(Managing Director, Training)*
**Operations:** Mike Kennedy *(Joint Capabilites Team Leader)*, Colin Podmore *(Production and Operations Mana)*, Jocelyn Smith *(Operations Manager)*
**Branches:** Qinetiq Group Plc, Douglas Pier, Cairndow, Argyll PA24 8AE
**US SIC:** 6711 **UK SIC:** 83962
**Auditors:** KPMG LLP
**Bankers:** Lloyds TSB Bank plc (30-00-00)

**Following financial data are in thousands**

| | 31-03-14 | 31-03-13 | 31-03-12 |
|---|---|---|---|
| TO | 1,191,400 | 1,327,800 | 1,469,600 |
| P/L | 4,100 | (137,000) | 331,600 |
| NW | 192,500 | 90,200 | 8,200 |
| WC | 160,500 | 67,500 | (38,300) |
| Emp. | 9,134 | 9,772 | 10,180 |

DUNS 21-681-4210 **Imp-Exp**
### Qioptiq Ltd
(**Subsidiary of:** Qioptiq Sarl)
Glascoed Road, St Asaph, Clwyd LL17 0LL
**Tel:** 01745588000 **Fax:** 01745-584-258
**Web:** www.qioptiq.co.uk
**Reg No:** 0876004 **Estd:** 1965 Private Limited Company
**Line of Business:** Manufacture of photographic and cinematographic equipment
**Export Markets:** EU, Non EU, North America, Africa, Australia, Other, Sales to other group companies
**Export Sales:** £36,219,000
**Issued Capital:** £22,521,142
**Directors:** M A Rees, D A Nislick, J V Rao, S D Shaw
**Co. Secretary:** Richard Groves
**Responsibilities**
**Health & Safety:** Ian McGregor *(Health & Safety Advisor)*
**Branches:** Qioptiq Ltd, Unit 2 Kinmel Park, Rhyl, Clwyd LL18 5TY
**US SIC:** 3861, 3811, 3832
**UK SIC:** 37330, 37100, 37320
**Auditors:** PricewaterhouseCoopers LLP
**Bankers:** National Westminster Bank Plc (60-17-30)

| | 29-12-13 | 31-12-12 | 31-12-11 |
|---|---|---|---|
| TO | 86,390,000 | 90,070,000 | 110,110,000 |
| P/L | 10,533,000 | 13,684,000 | 18,424,000 |
| NW | 34,245,000 | 26,559,000 | 26,842,000 |
| WC | 28,317,000 | 19,198,000 | 18,463,000 |
| Emp. | 465 | 489 | 520 |

DUNS 29-496-9829
### Q.K. Cold Stores (Marston) Ltd
(**Subsidiary of:** Q.K. (Holdings) Ltd)
Toll Bar Road, Marston, Grantham, Lincolnshire NG32 2HT
**Fax:** 01400-259310
**Web:** www.qkcoldstores.co.uk
**Reg No:** 1860326 **VAT No:** 416233676
**Estd:** 1984 Private Limited Company
**Line of Business:** Cold storage
**Trading Style:** Q.K. Cold Stores (Marston) Ltd
**Issued Capital:** £10,000
**Principals:** P Queally *(Managing)*, J Queally, R Beckett
**Co. Secretary:** Neil Joyce
**Responsibilities**
**Senior:** Brent Richardson *(Cold Store Manager)*
**Finance:** Suzanne Dawson *(Accountant)*
**Marketing:** Darryl Swain *(Commercial Manager)*
**Sales:** Darryl Swain *(Commercial Manager)*
**HR:** Ray Catton *(Health & Safety Officer)*, Suzanne Dawson *(Accountant)*
**Health & Safety:** Ray Catton *(Health & Safety Officer)*
**Operations:** Darryl Swain *(Commercial Manager)*
**US SIC:** 4226 **UK SIC:** 77003
**Auditors:** Duncan & Toplis
**Bankers:** HSBC Bank plc (40-22-19)

| | 31-12-13 | 31-12-12 | 31-12-11 |
|---|---|---|---|
| TO | 5,848,418 | 5,512,034 | 5,343,847 |
| P/L | 391,345 | 240,562 | 339,644 |
| NW | 2,401,654 | 2,118,154 | 1,948,494 |
| WC | 277,186 | 1,638,112 | 1,465,014 |
| Emp. | 59 | 56 | 52 |

DUNS 71-910-6903
### Qliktech Uk Ltd
(**Subsidiary of:** Qlik Technologies Inc.)
Villiers House, Leamington Spa, Warwickshire CV32 5PR
**Tel:** 01926458888
**Web:** www.qlik.com
**Reg No:** 5292408 **VAT No:** 855380312
**Estd:** 2004 Private Limited Company
**Line of Business:** Computer software sales
**Export Sales:** £2,301,386
**Issued Capital:** £1
**Directors:** L H Bjork, A W Bligh, Ms D M Cleary Lofton, S T Farrington, T J Maccarrick
**Co. Secretary:** Michal Eisenberg
**Branches:** Qliktech Uk Ltd, Villiers House, Clarnedon Avenue, Leamington Spa, Warwickshire CV32 5PR
**US SIC:** 7379 **UK SIC:** 83940

**Auditors:** Ernst & Young LLP
**Bankers:** HSBC Bank plc (40-27-06)

| | 31-12-13 | 31-12-12 | 31-12-11 |
|---|---|---|---|
| TO | 29,154,944 | 25,487,563 | 20,241,612 |
| P/L | 724,651 | 314,179 | 298,331 |
| NW | 7,099,109 | 3,334,674 | 1,373,947 |
| WC | 6,084,993 | 1,980,679 | 1,064,326 |
| Emp. | 234 | 201 | 128 |

DUNS 77-482-2175

## Qls - Quality Liaison Services Ltd

8 Roydon Road, Diss, Norfolk IP22 4LN
**Tel:** 01379-650651
**Web:** www.qls-automotive.com
**Reg No:** 2970064 **VAT No:** 638126144
**Estd:** 1997 Private Limited Company
**Line of Business:** Other service activities not elsewhere classified
**Issued Capital:** £100
**Principals:** M C Bowen *(Managing)*, I Coleman, C L Grater
**Co. Secretary:** Philip Sinclair
**Responsibilities**
**Senior:** Trevor Carrick *(Project Executive/ Engineer)*
**Operations:** Trevor Carrick *(Project Executive/Engineer)*
**Engineering:** Terry Brady *(Technical Director)*, Paddy Herbert *(Engineer)*
**Branches:** Qls - Quality Liaison Services Ltd, Unit S20, Wood La, Hastingwood Indstl Pk, Erdington, Birmingham, West Midlands B24 9QR
**US SIC:** 8999 **UK SIC:** 83954
**Bankers:** Barclays Bank Plc (20-74-05)

| | 31-03-14 | 31-03-13 | 31-03-12 |
|---|---|---|---|
| TA | 1,912,548 | 1,889,565 | 1,649,888 |
| NW | 1,580,161 | 1,459,165 | 1,369,982 |
| WC | 1,549,957 | 1,425,427 | 1,327,746 |

DUNS 21-658-9993

## Qmetric Group Ltd

**(Subsidiary of:** Primary Group Limited)
32-38 Dukes Place, London EC3A 7LP
**Tel:** 08454751415
**Web:** http://qmetric.co.uk
**Reg No:** 7151701 **Estd:** 2010 Private Limited Company
**Line of Business:** Insurance - other
**Issued Capital:** £3,333,333
**Directors:** Mrs E J Bannister, P R Carter, P J Hubbard, A D Deacon, P S Gildersleeves, A M Blowers
**Co. Secretary:** Paul Gildersleeves
**US SIC:** 6399 **UK SIC:** 82001
**Bankers:** Barclays Bank Plc (20-00-50)

| | 31-03-14 | 31-03-13 | 31-03-12 |
|---|---|---|---|
| TO | 11,368,000 | 5,660,000 | 775,000 |
| P/L | (9,134,000) | (6,799,000) | (4,608,000) |
| NW | 2,138,000 | 1,552,000 | (2,231,000) |
| WC | 4,155,000 | 1,081,000 | 308,000 |
| Emp. | 161 | 111 | 58 |

DUNS 21-632-3113

## Qmh Ltd

Queen's Court, Romford, Essex RM1 3NG
**Tel:** 01708-730522
**Web:** www.qmh-hotels.com
**Reg No:** 0416937 **Estd:** 1946 Private Limited Company
**Line of Business:** Management activities of holding companies
**Export Sales:** £77,800,000
**Trading Style:** Holiday Inn Luton, Cheltenham Chase Hotel
**Issued Capital:** £9,670,469
**Directors:** M P Jenkinson, B Kisakurek, D Frauman, N M Zilkha, Ms J Butler, G P Cassou, V B Schwartz
**Co. Secretary:** Ms Sally Coughlan
**Responsibilities**
**Senior:** Heather Allsop *(Manager)*, Veronique Menard *(Manager)*, Kathryn Ogden *(Manager)*, Irwin Reike *(Chief Executive)*, simon teasdale *(regional director)*
**HR:** Moira Laird *(HR Director)*
**Purchasing:** Cindy Walters *(Purchasing Director)*
**Branches:** Qmh Ltd, Mansfield Road, Nottingham, Nottinghamshire NG5 2BT
**US SIC:** 6711 **UK SIC:** 83962
**Auditors:** PricewaterhouseCoopers LLP
**Bankers:** Barclays Bank Plc (20-72-89)

| | 31-12-13 | 31-12-12 | 31-12-11 |
|---|---|---|---|
| TO | 154,700,000 | 229,900,000 | 254,700,000 |
| P/L | (23,800,000) | (66,000,000) | (42,000,000) |
| NW | (39,500,000) | (24,100,000) | 93,400,000 |
| WC | (131,800,000) | (335,000,000) | 2,200,000 |
| Emp. | 1,171 | 3,298 | 3,255 |

DUNS 56-987-4696

## Qms International Plc

**(Subsidiary of:** Monza Ltd)
Muspole Court, 21-23 Muspole Street, Norwich, Norfolk NR3 1DJ
**Tel:** 01603-630345 **Fax:** 01603-630405
**Web:** www.qmsuk.com
**Reg No:** 2854810 **Estd:** 1993 Public Limited Company
**Line of Business:** Business and management consultancy activities not elsewhere classified
**Issued Capital:** £50,050
**Principals:** P B Gamble *(Managing)*, Ms T A Hale
**Co. Secretary:** Ms Theresa Hale
**US SIC:** 7399 **UK SIC:** 83954
**Auditors:** Rostrons

| | 31-12-13 | 31-12-12 | 31-12-11 |
|---|---|---|---|
| TO | 5,603,425 | 4,960,532 | 4,890,654 |
| P/L | 1,525,220 | (2,871,817) | 821,224 |
| NW | (1,617,103) | (2,550,796) | 511,730 |
| WC | (1,419,877) | (1,813,679) | (2,339,676) |
| Emp. | 63 | 59 | 58 |

DUNS 56-961-8622

## Q.N. Hotels Ltd

The Swan Centre, Eastleigh, Hampshire SO50 5SF
**Tel:** 08712240240 **Fax:** 02085020854
**Web:** www.qnhgroup.com
**Reg No:** 2850880 **VAT No:** 627924613
**Estd:** 1993 Private Limited Company
**Line of Business:** Motion picture projection
**Trading Style:** Holiday Inn Garden Court Sandy, Holiday Inn Newport
**Issued Capital:** £1,000,000
**Director:** A Ahmed
**Co. Secretary:** Qamar Ahmed
**Responsibilities**
**Senior:** Nabeel Ahmed *(Manager)*, Stuart Mackie *(General Manager)*
**US SIC:** 7832 **UK SIC:** 97113
**Auditors:** Clayton Stark & Co
**Bankers:** Lloyds TSB Bank plc (30-90-38)

| | 31-12-12 | 31-12-11 | 31-12-10 |
|---|---|---|---|
| TO | 7,854,087 | 7,828,666 | 7,849,162 |
| P/L | (1,654,295) | (1,811,590) | (1,420,996) |
| NW | 5,204,263 | 6,855,835 | 8,374,578 |
| WC | (3,366,426) | (2,285,098) | (1,261,395) |
| Emp. | 312 | 276 | 281 |

DUNS 73-556-0620

## Qrs Ltd

The Stable House, 2d Priory Street, Hertford, Hertfordshire SG14 1XX
**Web:** www.qrs-research.co.uk
**Reg No:** 4818003 **VAT No:** 818149713
**Estd:** 2003 Private Limited Company
**Line of Business:** Employment and recruitment companies and consultants
**Issued Capital:** £300
**Director:** G Foxall
**Co. Secretary:** Mrs Rebecca Wood
**Responsibilities**
**Senior:** Kathy Tomlin *(Manager)*
**Admin:** Joanna Garratley *(Office Manager)*
**Branches:** Qrs Ltd, Malthouse Road, Tipton, West Midlands DY4 9AE
**US SIC:** 7361 **UK SIC:** 83954
**Auditors:** Philip Barnes & Co Ltd

| | 31-12-13 | 31-12-12 | 31-12-11 |
|---|---|---|---|
| TA | 475,871 | 818,773 | 514,665 |
| NW | 9,712 | (29,889) | 2,953 |
| WC | 5,885 | (34,837) | (4,857) |

DUNS 21-559-1961

## Qtec International

42 Albyn Place, Aberdeen, Aberdeenshire AB10 1YN
**Tel:** 08452130272
**Web:** www.qtec-energy.com
**Estd:** 2010 Proprietorship
**Line of Business:** Oil and gas exploration services
**Proprietor:** D Crosby
**Responsibilities**
**Senior:** Robbie Gordon *(Finance Director)*, William Walkinshaw *(General Manager)*
**Finance:** Robbie Gordon *(Finance Director)*
**US SIC:** 1389 **UK SIC:** 13000
**Employees:** 100

DUNS 76-672-5238

## Qtr Services Ltd

**(Subsidiary of:** S.B.G. Training & Developments Ltd)
14 Barnsley Road, South Elmsall, Pontefract, West Yorkshire WF9 2SE
**Tel:** 01977645645
**Web:** www.ukfiretraining.com
**Reg No:** 2586722 **Estd:** 1992 Private Limited Company
**Line of Business:** Labour recruitment and provision of personnel
**Issued Capital:** £33,673
**Principals:** A Vodden *(Chairman)*, I A Potter, G Talbot, J Coldwell, M Davies, M Hanley
**Co. Secretary:** John Thacker
**US SIC:** 7361, 8999
**UK SIC:** 83954
**Auditors:** Bailey Parkin & Co
**Bankers:** HSBC Bank plc (40-09-12)

| | 31-03-14 | 31-03-13 | 31-03-12 |
|---|---|---|---|
| TO | N/A | N/A | 35,780 |
| P/L | N/A | N/A | (44,175) |
| NW | 88,685 | 89,761 | 91,929 |
| WC | 7,767 | 7,661 | 8,637 |

DUNS 22-524-4227

## Qtr Transport Ltd

Cardiff Road, Reading, Berkshire RG1 8HD
**Tel:** 01189185900 **Fax:** 01189-185999
**Web:** www.qtrtransport.co.uk
**Reg No:** 1303208 **VAT No:** 314485366
**Estd:** 1977 Private Limited Company
**Line of Business:** Road haulage and transport services
**Export Sales:** £16,494
**Issued Capital:** £12
**Principals:** P A White *(Managing)*, T Smith
**Co. Secretary:** Mrs Sally White
**Responsibilities**
**Senior:** Derek Collings *(Manager)*
**Branches:** Qtr Transport Ltd, 66 Headley Road, Reading, Berkshire RG5 4JE
**US SIC:** 4712 **UK SIC:** 77002
**Auditors:** Hurst Morrison Thomson
**Bankers:** Lloyds TSB Bank plc (30-91-11)

| | 31-12-13 | 31-12-12 | 31-12-11 |
|---|---|---|---|
| TO | 10,262,631 | 9,748,147 | 8,509,600 |
| P/L | 318,568 | 216,532 | 286,865 |
| NW | 2,796,386 | 2,599,433 | 2,256,238 |
| WC | (140,926) | (132,923) | (92,001) |
| Emp. | 125 | 114 | 99 |

DUNS 21-131-4650 **Imp**

## Qts Rail Ltd

Unit 2, South Preston Office Village, Cuerden Way, Preston, Lancashire PR5 6BL
**Tel:** 01772696616
**Web:** www.qtsgroup.com
**Reg No:** 0346110SC **Estd:** 2008 Private Limited Company
**Line of Business:** Civil engineers
**Issued Capital:** £20
**Directors:** A Mcleish, B Mcleish, G J Dawes
**Co. Secretary:** Jamie Lewis
**Responsibilities**
**Senior:** Justine Hall *(Office Manager)*, Bruno Martin *(Project Director)*
**US SIC:** 8911 **UK SIC:** 83701
**Auditors:** William Duncan & Co
**Bankers:** Clydesdale Bank Plc (82-62-05)

| | 31-03-14 | 31-03-13 | 31-03-12 |
|---|---|---|---|
| TO | 65,223,206 | 27,735,163 | 24,097,034 |
| P/L | 6,529,495 | 3,061,666 | 2,024,321 |
| NW | 9,574,641 | 6,763,524 | 4,582,152 |
| WC | 1,718,055 | 528,011 | 337,603 |
| Emp. | 131 | 81 | 65 |

DUNS 21-677-8686

## Quacquarelli Symonds Consulting Ltd

**(Subsidiary of:** Qs Quacquarellisymonds Ltd)
1 Tranley Mews, Fleet Road, London NW3 2DG
**Fax:** 02072847201
**Web:** www.qs.com
**Reg No:** 7290156 **Estd:** 2010 Private Limited Company
**Line of Business:** Education services
**Issued Capital:** £100
**Director:** N Quacquarelli
**Co. Secretary:** Don Broodie
**Responsibilities**
**Senior:** Jamila Miller *(Manager)*, John Molony *(Manager)*, Benjamin Sowter *(Manager)*
**Admin:** Mel Shurmer *(Office Manager)*
**US SIC:** 8299 **UK SIC:** 93300
**Auditors:** Johnson Smith & Co Ltd
**Bankers:** HSBC Bank plc (40-02-03)

| | 31-12-13 | 31-12-12 | 31-12-11 |
|---|---|---|---|
| TA | 61,540 | 61,970 | 362,597 |
| NW | (134,703) | (131,748) | 212,065 |
| WC | (134,703) | (131,803) | 211,954 |

DUNS 71-910-3678

## Quadrangle Group Llp

Butlers Wharf Building, 36 Shad Thames, London SE1 2YE
**Web:** www.quadrangle.com
**Reg No:** 0310092OC **Estd:** 2004
**Line of Business:** Market research organisations
**Trading Style:** Quadrangle Research Group Ltd
**US SIC:** 7392 **UK SIC:** 83951

| | 31-12-13 | 31-12-12 | 31-12-11 |
|---|---|---|---|
| TA | 188,271 | 188,090 | 2,208,082 |
| NW | 970 | N/A | (80,976) |
| WC | 173,241 | 970 | 56,128 |

DUNS 42-355-3721

## Quadrant Group Ltd

Victoria Gardens, Burgess Hill, West Sussex RH15 9NB
**Tel:** 01444-246226
**Reg No:** 4343035 **Estd:** 2001 Private Limited Company
**Line of Business:** Management activities of holding companies
**Export Sales:** £8,745,701
**Trading Style:** Quadrant Systems Limited
**Issued Capital:** £1,658,101
**Directors:** T J Morley, J Sandiford, M V Male, S J Williams, D J Coghlan
**Co. Secretary:** Timothy Morley
**Responsibilities**
**Senior:** Stewart Rose *(Manager)*
**US SIC:** 6711 **UK SIC:** 83962

| | 31-05-13 | 31-05-12 | 31-05-11 |
|---|---|---|---|
| TO | 12,325,221 | 8,242,100 | 5,331,636 |
| P/L | 1,342,163 | 1,088,848 | (240,390) |
| NW | 458,781 | (1,321,779) | (2,324,168) |
| WC | 1,295,371 | (1,157,358) | (2,157,839) |
| Emp. | 154 | 53 | 45 |

DUNS 21-779-5982

## Quadrant Subscriptions Services

Rockwood House, 9-16 Perrymount Road, Haywards Heath, West Sussex RH16 3DH
**Tel:** 01444475600
**Web:** www.airbusonline.com
**Estd:** 2011
**Line of Business:** Publishing of newspapers
**Responsibilities**
**Senior:** Stuart Lacey *(Manager)*
**Marketing:** Diane Lewis *(Senior Marketing Executive)*
**Sales:** Dave Appleton *(Fulfilment Services)*
**HR:** Pippa Tickell *(Recruitment Officer)*
**US SIC:** 2711 **UK SIC:** 47512
**Employees:** 500

DUNS 21-589-8318

## Quadratek Ltd

Quadratek House, 1 Farnham Road The Drive, Guildford, Surrey GU2 7QF
**Web:** www.quadratek.net
**Line of Business:** Labour recruitment and provision of personnel
**US SIC:** 8999 **UK SIC:** 83954
**Employees:** 50

DUNS 77-141-2418

## Quadro Services Ltd

3 Eastboro Fields, Hemdale Business Park, Nuneaton, Warwickshire CV11 6GL
**Tel:** 024-7640-0400 **Fax:** 024-7640-0444
**Web:** www.quadroprecast.com
**Reg No:** 2703715 **VAT No:** 585050342
**Estd:** 1992 Private Limited Company
**Line of Business:** Building of complete constructions or parts thereof; civil engineering
**Issued Capital:** £200
**Directors:** N P Hutchison, C J Wright, B J Bosworth
**Co. Secretary:** Paul Beebe
**US SIC:** 1541 **UK SIC:** 50100
**Auditors:** Paul Carvell
**Bankers:** Lloyds TSB Bank plc (30-96-20)

| | 30-06-14 | 30-06-13 | 30-06-12 |
|---|---|---|---|
| TA | 941,329 | 912,234 | 1,331,266 |
| NW | 443,696 | 570,657 | 887,108 |
| WC | 370,829 | 473,501 | 783,694 |

DUNS 21-586-6766

## Quadron Services

Holland Park Nursery, Holland Park, London W8 6LU
**Tel:** 02073716619
**Web:** www.quadronservices.co.uk
**Estd:** 2002 Proprietorship
**Line of Business:** Horticultural consultants
**Proprietor:** C Ivil
**Responsibilities**
**Senior:** Ben Binnell *(Contracts Manager)*
**US SIC:** 0729 **UK SIC:** 01003
**Employees:** 65

DUNS 34-849-3883

## Quadron Services Ltd

**(Subsidiary of:** Pfeiffer Holdings Ltd)
Quadron House, Mendip Road, Weston-Super-Mare, Avon BS23 3HB
**Tel:** 01934-614444 **Fax:** 01934-614440
**Web:** www.quadronservices.co.uk
**Reg No:** 2810263 **Estd:** 1993 Private Limited Company
**Line of Business:** Representative office
**Issued Capital:** £55,100
**Directors:** Mrs J Daughtry, M C Martin, G Poulter, Miss J Moore, C Ivil
**Co. Secretary:** Mrs Claire Darby
**Responsibilities**
**Senior:** Joanne Balls *(Manager)*, Ian Carpenter *(Manager)*
**Admin:** Abdinasir Halane *(Administration Manager)*
**Health & Safety:** Ben Binnell *(Senior Contract Manager)*, Steve McKenna *(Contracts Manager)*
**Purchasing:** Ben Binnell *(Senior Contract Manager)*
**Branches:** Quadron Services Ltd, The Depot, Wilmott Lane, Gosport, Hampshire PO12 3RY
**US SIC:** 8999 **UK SIC:** 83954
**Auditors:** Baker Tilly UK Audit LLP

**Bankers:** The Royal Bank Of Scotland Plc (15-10-00)

| | 31-03-14 | 31-03-13 | 31-03-12 |
|---|---|---|---|
| TO | 28,669,000 | 25,382,000 | 27,527,000 |
| P/L | 1,309,000 | 1,547,000 | 1,334,000 |
| NW | 8,088,000 | 7,334,000 | 6,103,000 |
| WC | 4,623,000 | 3,945,000 | 3,299,000 |
| Emp. | 762 | 687 | 731 |

DUNS 73-485-5633

## Quaggy Development Trust

Childers Street, London SE8 5NU
**Tel:** 02084659785
**Web:** www.quaggydevelopmenttrust.org
**Reg No:** 4749158 **Estd:** 2004 Private Company Limited By Guarantee
**Line of Business:** Activities of other membership organisations not elsewhere classified
**Directors:** Ms M E Stenhouse, S C Riley, Mrs G R Crowley, T Donnelly, Ms S J Mckee, Miss N F Delap
**Responsibilities**
**Senior:** Dawn Jacavou *(Trust Manager)*
**US SIC:** 8699, 8321
**UK SIC:** 96902, 96111
**Auditors:** Spofforths
**Bankers:** The Co-Operative Bank Plc (08-92-50)

| | 31-03-14 | 31-03-13 | 31-03-12 |
|---|---|---|---|
| TO | 1,161,483 | 1,044,688 | 1,073,395 |
| P/L | 16,627 | (22,758) | 41,416 |
| NW | 1,071,936 | 990,360 | 1,013,118 |
| WC | 722,410 | 701,960 | 733,938 |
| Emp. | 47 | 46 | 43 |

DUNS 29-546-9191

## Quailfalcon Ltd

Unit 4 5, Charfleets Road, Canvey Island, Essex SS8 0PQ
**Tel:** 01268681612 **Fax:** 08708701058
**Web:** www.duration.co.uk
**Reg No:** 1913793 **VAT No:** 545958986
**Estd:** 1985 Private Limited Company
**Line of Business:** Other manufacturing not elsewhere classified
**Trading Style:** Duration Windows
**Issued Capital:** £100
**Directors:** G M Chelton, Mrs J G Chelton
**Co. Secretary:** Dennis Mitchell
**Responsibilities**
**Purchasing:** Dirk Campling *(Buyer)*
**US SIC:** 3442 **UK SIC:** 31420
**Auditors:** HLB Kidsons
**Bankers:** Barclays Bank Plc (20-70-93)

| | 31-12-13 | 31-12-12 | 31-12-11 |
|---|---|---|---|
| TO | 10,207,769 | 9,691,280 | 9,921,340 |
| P/L | 416,749 | 348,765 | 509,102 |
| NW | 1,943,836 | 1,657,711 | 1,503,161 |
| WC | 1,335,465 | 1,496,334 | 1,339,212 |
| Emp. | 78 | 79 | 79 |

DUNS 29-040-3278

## Quaker Housing Trust

Friends House, 173-177 Euston Road, London NW1 2BJ
**Tel:** 02076631030
**Web:** www.quaker.org.uk
**Reg No:** 0924311 **Estd:** 1967 Private Limited Company
**Line of Business:** Financial intermediation not elsewhere classified
**Trading Style:** Villages Society of Friends
**Directors:** Ms J M Brierley, T J Yeomans, J M Smith, D Cummings, A S Keith, Ms K L Parker, R H Williamson, R H Williams
**Co. Secretary:** Ms Paula Harvey
**Responsibilities**
**Senior:** Christina Birch *(Director)*, Alison Crane *(Director)*, George Gledhill *(Director)*
**Branches:** Quaker Housing Trust, The Nook, Skipton, North Yorkshire BD23 4AE
**US SIC:** 6111 **UK SIC:** 81501
**Bankers:** Girobank Plc (72-16-00)

| | 31-12-13 | 31-12-12 | 31-12-11 |
|---|---|---|---|
| TA | 1,226,385 | 1,122,969 | 1,279,100 |
| P/L | 94,130 | (159,782) | (125,135) |
| NW | 1,191,503 | 1,094,102 | 1,245,253 |
| WC | 1,171,201 | 1,082,071 | 922,352 |

DUNS 21-174-4637

## Qualasept Pharmaxo Holdings Ltd

A15 Fiveways Light Industrial Estate, Corsham, Wiltshire SN13 9RG
**Reg No:** 6981369 **Estd:** 2009 Private Limited Company
**Line of Business:** Management activities of holding companies
**Export Sales:** £13,106
**Issued Capital:** £80
**Directors:** C D Watt, Ms M Watt, R Wastnage
**US SIC:** 6711 **UK SIC:** 83962

| | 30-04-14 | 30-04-13 | 30-04-12 |
|---|---|---|---|
| TO | 30,605,444 | 15,857,894 | 11,285,267 |
| P/L | 2,047,430 | 1,181,028 | 455,197 |
| NW | 2,002,755 | 2,518,455 | 1,955,519 |
| WC | 1,505,099 | 1,918,857 | 1,305,235 |
| Emp. | 77 | 87 | 83 |

DUNS 23-931-1215

## Qualcomm (Uk) Ltd

**(Subsidiary of:** Qualcomm Global Trading Pte. Ltd.)
566 Chiswick High Road, London W4 5YE
**Tel:** 02089964100 **Fax:** 020-8237-7170
**Web:** www.qualcomm.com
**Reg No:** 3921033 **Estd:** 1985 Private Limited Company
**Line of Business:** Research and experimental development on natural sciences and engineering
**Issued Capital:** £2,500,990
**Directors:** S Mehta, F Mccabe
**Co. Secretary:** Jordan Company Secretaries Limit
**Responsibilities**
**Operations:** Stuart Strickland *(Director of Location Strategy)*
**Engineering:** Alex Dent *(Staff Engineer)*
**Branches:** Qualcomm (Uk) Ltd, Spectrum Point, Farnborough, Hampshire GU14 7LS
**US SIC:** 7391 **UK SIC:** 94000
**Auditors:** PricewaterhouseCoopers LLP

| | 29-09-13 | 30-09-12 | 25-09-11 |
|---|---|---|---|
| TO | 41,700,582 | 34,042,362 | 28,968,990 |
| P/L | 7,961,166 | 3,057,542 | 2,352,302 |
| NW | 36,776,622 | 26,478,048 | 20,669,928 |
| WC | 30,380,193 | 22,393,430 | 16,889,057 |
| Emp. | 186 | 180 | 159 |

DUNS 54-896-9005

## Qualifications & Curriculum Authority

53-55 Butts Road, Earlsdon Park, Coventry, West Midlands CV1 3BH
**Tel:** 03003033010
**Web:** www.qca.org.uk
**Estd:** 1997
**Line of Business:** Administration of the state and the economic and social policy of the community
**Trading Style:** Q C A
**Principals:** D Cadbury *(Chairman)*, Dr N Tate, Sir W Stubes
**Branches:** Qualifications & Curriculum Authority, 6 Murray Street, Belfast, Belfast BT1 6DN
**US SIC:** 9121 **UK SIC:** 91110
**Employees:** 300

DUNS 23-940-2261

## Qualitest Software Testing Ltd

2440 The Quadrant, Aztec West, Almondsbury, Bristol, Avon BS32 4AQ
**Tel:** 08458-696070 **Fax:** 01199-511959
**Web:** www.tcl.eu.com
**Reg No:** 3929849 **Estd:** 2000 Private Limited Company
**Line of Business:** It consultants
**Trading Style:** T C L
**Issued Capital:** £241
**Directors:** D V Cotterell, A Zylberman, U Einan, C D White, Ms T M Prosser
**Co. Secretary:** Ms Philippa Fresch
**Responsibilities**
**Senior:** Stewart Noakes *(Chief Executive Officer)*
**US SIC:** 7379 **UK SIC:** 83940
**Auditors:** PricewaterhouseCoopers LLP

| | 31-12-13 | 31-12-12 | 29-12-12 |
|---|---|---|---|
| TO | 5,892,403 | 4,077,665 | 4,595,922 |
| P/L | (125,954) | 159,731 | 164,019 |
| NW | 206,857 | 334,741 | 214,246 |
| WC | 198,929 | 330,295 | 213,231 |

DUNS 76-388-7445 Imp

## Qualitex Supplies Ltd

3a & 3b, Aylesford, Kent ME20 7SP
**Tel:** 01622790011 **Fax:** 01622790022
**Web:** www.qualitex.co.uk
**Reg No:** 2555629 **VAT No:** 573562032
**Estd:** 1991 Private Limited Company
**Line of Business:** Plumbers merchants
**Issued Capital:** £50,000
**Principals:** D E Andrews *(Managing)*, Mrs C Andrews
**Co. Secretary:** Duncan Andrews
**Responsibilities**
**Finance:** Val Smith *(Financial Director)*
**Branches:** Qualitex Supplies Ltd, Young Place Kelvin Industrial Es Colvilles Road, Glasgow, Lanarkshire G75 0TD
**US SIC:** 5072 **UK SIC:** 61500
**Auditors:** haysmacintyre
**Bankers:** The Royal Bank Of Scotland Plc (16-24-64)

| | 31-12-13 | 31-12-12 | 31-12-11 |
|---|---|---|---|
| TO | 10,720,136 | 12,146,870 | 13,326,000 |
| P/L | (284,511) | (298,166) | (290,019) |
| NW | 927,926 | 1,212,437 | 1,510,603 |
| WC | 924,051 | 1,213,274 | 1,547,207 |
| Emp. | 67 | 77 | 85 |

DUNS 23-528-1131

## Qualiti (Burnley) Ltd

**(Subsidiary of:** Qualiti Burnley Holdings Ltd)
Talbot Street, Burnley, Lancashire BB10 2JY
**Tel:** 01282-830042 **Fax:** 01282459848
**Web:** www.qualiti.co.uk
**Reg No:** 3527006 **Estd:** 1998 Private Limited Company
**Line of Business:** Activities of other transport agencies
**Trading Style:** Qualiti (Burnley) Limited
**Issued Capital:** £450,675
**Director:** M J Tedham
**Responsibilities**
**Senior:** Elizabeth Rawstron *(Manager)*, Rosemary Scott *(Production Manager)*
**Health & Safety:** Peter Simms *(Laboratory Manager)*
**Operations:** Peter Simms *(Laboratory Manager)*
**Engineering:** Rosemary Scott *(Production Manager)*
**US SIC:** 7399 **UK SIC:** 83954
**Auditors:** Porter Matthews & Marsden
**Bankers:** HSBC Bank plc (40-15-17)

| | 31-05-13 | 31-05-12 | 31-05-11 |
|---|---|---|---|
| TA | 3,640,890 | 3,403,567 | 3,168,056 |
| NW | 2,825,784 | 2,518,748 | 2,196,664 |
| WC | 2,330,921 | 1,944,396 | 1,539,306 |

DUNS 21-602-2726

## Quality Assurance

321 Avebury Boulevard, Milton Keynes, Buckinghamshire MK9 2FZ
**Tel:** 01908546335
**Web:** www.icaew.co.uk
**Estd:** 1998 Partnership
**Line of Business:** Accounting activities
**Partners:** G Ruddock, N Macdonald, P Burton, J Hobbs, P Simkins
**US SIC:** 8931 **UK SIC:** 83600
**Employees:** 50

DUNS 89-679-3692

## The Quality Assurance Agency for Higher Education

10-11 Carlton House Terrace, London SW1Y 5AH
**Fax:** 01452-557070
**Web:** www.qaa.ac.uk
**Reg No:** 3344784 **Estd:** 1997 Private Company Limited By Guarantee
**Line of Business:** Universities, colleges, prof. schools
**Directors:** Ms J E Hull, Professor P Winn, Professor J Carter, Professor J P Grattan, Professor P Wend, J L Prichard, C R Jelley, J R Tredwell
**Co. Secretary:** Douglas Blackstock
**Responsibilities**
**Senior:** Christopher Banks *(Director)*, Grace Burton *(Director)*, Antony Chapman *(Board Member)*, William Haywood *(Manager)*, Beverley Hunt *(Manager)*, Vinny Karadia *(Facilities Manager)*, Anthony McClaran *(Chief Executive)*, Denise Mcalister *(Director)*, Timothy Mcintyre-Bhatty *(Director)*, Rowena Pelik *(Director of QAA Scotland)*, Alexander Pool *(Board Member)*, Jennifer Rees *(Manager)*, Andrew Summers *(Manager)*, Robin Vaughan *(Manager)*
**Finance:** Liz Rosser *(Chief Financial Officer)*
**Marketing:** Janet Bohrer *(Development Officer)*, Richard Jarman *(Director of Public Engagement)*
**IT:** Steven Boylett *(Network Manager)*
**Health & Safety:** Vinny Karadia *(Facilities Manager)*
**Facilities:** Vinny Karadia *(Facilities Manager)*
**Operations:** Dawn Blackwood *(Project Officer)*, Sam Emanuel *(Project Officer)*
**Purchasing:** Vinny Karadia *(Facilities Manager)*
**Branches:** The Quality Assurance Agency For Higher Education, Lee Ho, 6A Highfield Rd, Birmingham, West Midlands B15 3ED
**US SIC:** 8221, 8249, 7392
**UK SIC:** 93100, 93300, 83951
**Auditors:** Mazars Neville Russell
**Bankers:** Barclays Bank Plc (20-33-83)

| | 31-07-13 | 31-07-12 | 31-07-11 |
|---|---|---|---|
| TO | 13,614,426 | 14,028,737 | 12,266,448 |
| P/L | 321,775 | 723,001 | 5,622 |
| NW | 4,861,649 | 4,482,242 | 3,759,241 |
| WC | 966,966 | 3,886,365 | 3,273,271 |
| Emp. | 156 | 135 | 128 |

DUNS 42-338-9837

## Quality Assured Property Maintenance Ltd

Utilities House, 40 North Ellen Street, Dundee, Angus DD3 7DH
**Tel:** 01382-346666 **Fax:** 01382-204185
**Web:** www.qapm.co.uk
**Reg No:** 0225578SC **Estd:** 2001 Private Limited Company
**Line of Business:** Specialised building trade contractors
**Issued Capital:** £75
**Directors:** N D Campbell, D Murray
**Co. Secretary:** Robert Ward
**US SIC:** 1799 **UK SIC:** 50000
**Auditors:** Findlay & Co
**Bankers:** The Royal Bank Of Scotland Plc (83-50-00)

| | 31-10-13 | 31-10-12 | 31-10-11 |
|---|---|---|---|
| TA | 730,398 | 577,071 | 603,465 |
| NW | 351,891 | 270,096 | 219,221 |
| WC | 284,749 | 237,548 | 210,947 |

DUNS 21-066-5776

## Quality Care

5 Dorset St Derwent View, Derby, Derbyshire DE21 6BE
**Tel:** 01332-616162
**Web:** www.qualitycare-em.co.uk
**Estd:** 2006 Proprietorship
**Line of Business:** Rest and retirement homes
**Proprietor:** L Flinn
**Responsibilities**
**Senior:** Julie Allen *(Manager)*, Amy Goodall *(Registers Manager)*
**US SIC:** 8321 **UK SIC:** 96111
**Employees:** 60

DUNS 73-378-0121

## Quality Care (Em) Ltd

20 Alfreton Road, Sutton-In-Ashfield, Nottinghamshire NG17 1FW
**Tel:** 01623512850
**Web:** www.qualitycare-em.co.uk
**Reg No:** 4651403 **Estd:** 2003 Private Limited Company
**Line of Business:** Residential care establishments
**Issued Capital:** £200
**Directors:** H Nathudkhan, Mrs T C Nathudkhan, Mrs S K Atwal, D P Smith, C J Holder
**Co. Secretary:** Hardev Atwal
**Responsibilities**
**Senior:** Russell Currie *(Home Manager)*
**US SIC:** 8321 **UK SIC:** 96111

| | 31-12-12 | 31-12-11 | 31-12-10 |
|---|---|---|---|
| TO | 6,071,545 | 6,959,373 | 5,236,206 |
| P/L | (1,239,690) | 578,183 | 638,115 |
| NW | 2,102,929 | 8,967,114 | 8,372,476 |
| WC | (403,804) | (349,705) | 72,773 |
| Emp. | 290 | 287 | 281 |

DUNS 21-103-4374

## Quality Care Group Ltd

Forest Brow, 63 Forest Road, Liss, Hampshire GU33 7BL
**Tel:** 01730893342
**Web:** www.southgategroup.co.uk
**Reg No:** 6464150 **Estd:** 2008 Private Limited Company
**Line of Business:** Business services
**Issued Capital:** £1,172
**Directors:** Mrs B E Hardman, J K Grimes, Mrs M J Watson, J W Hardman, B M Lambert, B D Maynard, G Murry, Ms P A Harris
**Co. Secretary:** Lester Aldridge Company Secretar
**Responsibilities**
**Senior:** Marese Pitman *(Director)*
**US SIC:** 8321 **UK SIC:** 96111
**Bankers:** Girobank Plc (72-01-00)

| | 30-09-13 | 30-09-12 | 30-09-11 |
|---|---|---|---|
| TO | 4,041,145 | 3,761,161 | 3,773,113 |
| P/L | 500,430 | 427,113 | 463,749 |
| NW | 2,000,459 | 1,745,078 | 1,477,563 |
| WC | (214,569) | (175,412) | (184,976) |
| Emp. | 158 | 158 | 164 |

DUNS 21-471-7147

## Quality Care Nursing Home

Glan Rhos, Brynsiencyn, Llanfairpwllgwyngyll, Gwynedd LL61 6TZ
**Tel:** 01248-430607
**Estd:** 1989 Partnership
**Line of Business:** Medical nursing home activities
**Partners:** Ms K Ombler, D Ombler, Ms H Ombler
**US SIC:** 8051 **UK SIC:** 95100
**Bankers:** Barclays Bank Plc (20-35-47)
**Employees:** 60

DUNS 21-631-3209

## Quality Care Resources Ltd

Madelvic House, Granton Park Avenue, Edinburgh, Midlothian EH5 1HS
**Tel:** 01315522271 **Fax:** 01319991924
**Web:** www.qualitycareresources.co.uk
**Reg No:** 0369777SC **Estd:** 2007 Private Limited Company
**Line of Business:** Home care and help services
**Issued Capital:** £1
**Director:** B Masiye
**US SIC:** 8811 **UK SIC:** 99000

| | 31-12-13 | 31-12-12 | 31-12-11 |
|---|---|---|---|
| TO | N/A | N/A | 260,200 |
| P/L | N/A | N/A | 20,292 |
| NW | 30,900 | 32,129 | N/A |
| WC | 35,137 | 36,986 | 49,737 |

DUNS 21-875-0651

### Quality Castings (Slough) Ltd

(**Subsidiary of:** Saxham Investments Ltd)
Northern Way, Bury St Edmunds, Suffolk IP32 6NW
**Tel:** 01284755941 **Fax:** 01284-761770
**Web:** www.qualitycastings.co.uk
**Reg No:** 0634519 **Estd:** 1959 Private Limited Company
**Line of Business:** Die casting equipment and services
**Trading Style:** Quality Castings (Slough) Ltd
**Issued Capital:** £250,000
**Principals:** P E Tarrant *(Chairman and Managing)*, Ms P A Honeyman, K N Bonsor
**Co. Secretary:** Ms Margaret Tarrant
**Responsibilities**
**Senior:** Martin Cleverdon *(Financial Director)*, Keith Honeyman *(Manager)*
**Finance:** Martin Cleverdon *(Financial Director)*
**Branches:** Quality Castings (Slough) Ltd, 22 De Moram Grove, Solihull, West Midlands B92 0PZ
**US SIC:** 3559 **UK SIC:** 32863
**Auditors:** Morley & Scott
**Bankers:** National Westminster Bank Plc (60-04-16)

| | 31-08-14 | 31-08-13 | 31-08-12 |
|---|---|---|---|
| TA | 2,232,712 | 2,282,398 | 2,469,560 |
| NW | 406,414 | 491,973 | 484,616 |
| WC | 765,994 | 819,503 | 903,799 |

DUNS 42-331-9961

### Quality Cleaning Services (Northern) Ltd

14 Woodland Road, Darlington, County Durham DL3 7PL
**Tel:** 01325-367770
**Web:** www.qcs.me.uk
**Reg No:** 3134741 **Estd:** 1995 Private Limited Company
**Line of Business:** Traditional cleaning activities
**Trading Style:** Quality Cleaning Services
**Issued Capital:** £100
**Principals:** Ms G Millington *(Managing)*, Ms Y Budgen
**Co. Secretary:** John Budgen
**US SIC:** 7349 **UK SIC:** 92300
**Bankers:** HSBC Bank plc (40-35-03)

| | 31-03-14 | 31-03-13 | 31-03-12 |
|---|---|---|---|
| TA | 241,911 | 252,463 | 274,933 |
| NW | 160,874 | 174,806 | 190,596 |
| WC | 152,216 | 164,451 | 178,322 |

DUNS 23-339-6782

### Quality Cleaning Uk Ltd

The Beeches, Rhodyate Lane Cleeve, Bristol, Avon BS49 4NT
**Tel:** 01934-830248 **Fax:** 01934835117
**Web:** www.topqualitycleaners.co.uk
**Reg No:** 4340765 **Estd:** 1994 Private Limited Company
**Line of Business:** Cleaning activities not elsewhere classified
**Issued Capital:** £2
**Director:** Ms M D Kew
**Co. Secretary:** Geoffrey Kew
**US SIC:** 7349 **UK SIC:** 92300

| | 31-12-13 | 31-12-12 | 31-12-11 |
|---|---|---|---|
| TA | 17,458 | 22,671 | 16,598 |
| NW | 252 | 503 | 7,114 |
| WC | (1,615) | (2,706) | 2,216 |

DUNS 21-589-7652

### Quality Decking

The Woodyard, Epping Road, Epping, Essex CM16 6TT
**Tel:** 01992561103
**Web:** www.hoppings.co.uk
**Estd:** 2011
**Line of Business:** Decking
**US SIC:** 5251 **UK SIC:** 64800
**Employees:** 60

DUNS 76-896-3373 **Imp**

### Quality Electrical Supplies & Technology Ltd

Victoria House, Victoria Works Industrial Estate, Burnley, Lancashire BB11 5EF
**Tel:** 01282-838000 **Fax:** 01282-452121
**Web:** www.questelectrical.co.uk
**Reg No:** 2616061 **VAT No:** 525561940
**Estd:** 1995 Private Limited Company
**Line of Business:** Electrical wholesalers
**Trading Style:** Quest Electrical
**Issued Capital:** £2,466
**Director:** A P Davies
**Co. Secretary:** Ian Briggs
**Responsibilities**
**Senior:** Sean Holly *(Manager)*
**Finance:** Laura Douding *(Finance Director)*
**Health & Safety:** Callum Antrobus *(Purchasing Assistant)*
**Purchasing:** Callum Antrobus *(Purchasing Assistant)*, K Hindsley *(Purchasing Manager)*
**US SIC:** 5074, 5065
**UK SIC:** 61300, 61500
**Bankers:** HSBC Bank plc (40-11-18)

| | 28-02-14 | 31-08-12 | 31-02-11 |
|---|---|---|---|
| TA | 1,436,882 | 1,234,728 | 1,344,066 |
| NW | 508,895 | 423,635 | 386,285 |
| WC | 163,064 | 96,283 | 65,370 |

DUNS 21-400-5423 **Imp**

### Quality Food Products (Aberdeen) Ltd

Unit 11 Craigshaw Drive, Aberdeen, Aberdeenshire AB12 3BE
**Tel:** 01224870400
**Web:** www.qfoods.co.uk
**Reg No:** 0046323SC **VAT No:** 266305952
**Estd:** 1969 Private Limited Company
**Line of Business:** Wholesale of meat and meat products
**Export Sales:** £2,523,000
**Issued Capital:** £120,000
**Principals:** G Rataj *(Managing)*, M T Rataj, K A Rataj
**Co. Secretary:** Mrs Fiona Scott
**Responsibilities**
**Senior:** Michelle Christie *(Accountant)*, Robert Guild *(Accountant)*, Barry Johnston *(Accountant)*, Stuart Shaw *(Despatch Manager)*
**Finance:** Michelle Christie *(Accountant)*, Robert Guild *(Accountant)*
**IT:** Michelle Christie *(Accountant)*, Robert Guild *(Accountant)*, David McIntosh *(Technical Manager)*
**Health & Safety:** David McIntosh *(Technical Manager)*
**Operations:** David McIntosh *(Technical Manager)*
**Engineering:** David McIntosh *(Technical Manager)*
**Branches:** Nairn
**US SIC:** 5147, 5423
**UK SIC:** 61700, 64100
**Auditors:** Deloitte & Touche
**Bankers:** Bank Of Scotland (80-05-11)

| | 30-08-13 | 31-08-12 | 26-08-11 |
|---|---|---|---|
| TO | 34,525,628 | 34,233,925 | 32,707,417 |
| P/L | 373,221 | 2,723,743 | 2,080,552 |
| NW | 6,541,449 | 6,243,316 | 4,439,564 |
| WC | 4,363,338 | 4,407,029 | 2,588,801 |
| Emp. | 75 | 71 | 63 |

DUNS 77-749-3925

### Quality Heating Services Ltd

Marlborough, 9 Spurlands End Road, High Wycombe, Buckinghamshire HP15 6HY
**Tel:** 01494 795000 **Fax:** 01494 795001
**Web:** www.quality-heating.co.uk
**Reg No:** 3014826 **VAT No:** 604085467
**Estd:** 1995 Private Limited Company
**Line of Business:** Central heating systems (installation and servicing)
**Issued Capital:** £100,000
**Directors:** I Craig, S C Attersall, P J O'Brien, P Tillotson, M B Kissane
**Co. Secretary:** Ms Karen Tillotson
**US SIC:** 1711 **UK SIC:** 50300
**Auditors:** J.B. Klein & Partners
**Bankers:** Barclays Bank Plc (20-40-71)

| | 31-03-13 | 31-03-12 | 31-03-11 |
|---|---|---|---|
| TO | 5,953,092 | 8,941,749 | 8,217,975 |
| P/L | 264,346 | 361,459 | 330,739 |
| NW | 665,928 | 649,606 | 396,753 |
| WC | 563,789 | 506,564 | 174,348 |
| Emp. | 58 | 74 | 85 |

DUNS 73-800-2604

### Quality Home Care (Barnsley) Ltd

G M Wilson, Unit 4, Great Cliffe Court, Dodworth Business Park, Barnsley, South Yorkshire S75 3SP
**Tel:** 01226249577
**Web:** www.quality-homecare.co.uk
**Reg No:** 5056629 **Estd:** 2004 Private Limited Company
**Line of Business:** Other human health activities
**Issued Capital:** £100
**Director:** A Dryden
**Co. Secretary:** Ms Pauline Dryden
**US SIC:** 8091, 8321
**UK SIC:** 95200, 96111

| | 31-03-14 | 31-03-13 | 31-03-12 |
|---|---|---|---|
| TA | 272,504 | 237,156 | 270,394 |
| NW | 17,887 | 5,213 | 5,319 |
| WC | 12,866 | (565) | 1,582 |

DUNS 21-392-0615

### Quality Homecare

402 The Ridge, Hastings, East Sussex TN34 2RR
**Tel:** 01424-754739
**Web:** www.a1qhc.com
**Estd:** 2001
**Line of Business:** Home care service providers
**Proprietor:** Ms Z Reid
**US SIC:** 8091 **UK SIC:** 95200
**Employees:** 100

DUNS 21-226-0420

### Quality Hotel

Cliff Road, Plymouth, Devon PL1 3DL
**Tel:** 01752507800
**Web:** www.quality-hotel-plymouth.com
**Estd:** 2002 Proprietorship
**Line of Business:** Hotels
**Proprietor:** Miss M Stanaway
**US SIC:** 7011, 6531
**UK SIC:** 66500, 83400
**Employees:** 83

DUNS 22-966-7530 **Imp-Exp**

### Quality Hydraulic Power Ltd

(**Subsidiary of:** Hydac International Gmbh)
Taylor House, Minerva Avenue, Chester West Employment Park, Chester, Cheshire CH1 4QL
**Tel:** 01244-393500 **Fax:** 01244393501
**Web:** www.qhp.co.uk
**Reg No:** 2131010 **VAT No:** 454058059
**Estd:** 1987 Private Limited Company
**Line of Business:** Engineers (general)
**Export Markets:** Norway, Sweden, India, Germany, U S A & South Africa.
**Export Sales:** £11,205,433
**Trading Style:** Q H P, Wingate Hydraulics
**Issued Capital:** £1,111
**Directors:** Dr W H Dieter, K G Brownlee, J H Pratt, R Bowden, J Cartwright
**Responsibilities**
**Health & Safety:** Phil Mcevoy *(Quality Manager)*
**US SIC:** 8911, 3692
**UK SIC:** 83701, 34321
**Auditors:** B M Howarth
**Bankers:** Lloyds TSB Bank plc (30-91-92)

| | 31-12-13 | 31-12-12 | 31-12-11 |
|---|---|---|---|
| TO | 16,239,758 | 13,169,007 | 12,168,598 |
| P/L | 3,043,435 | 1,652,621 | 937,435 |
| NW | 5,928,292 | 3,585,479 | 2,329,692 |
| WC | 5,495,059 | 3,185,212 | 1,953,599 |
| Emp. | 75 | 68 | 63 |

DUNS 29-167-9512 **Imp**

### Quality Industries Ltd

(**Subsidiary of:** Wrexon Ltd)
Unit C, Telford, Shropshire TF3 3BN
**Tel:** 01952-292166
**Web:** www.qivansystems.co.uk
**Reg No:** 1817981 **VAT No:** 404190489
**Estd:** 1984 Private Limited Company
**Line of Business:** Manufacture of tanks, reservoirs and containers of metal
**Trading Style:** Q I Van Systems
**Issued Capital:** £140
**Principals:** R Preece *(Managing)*, L Stonier
**Co. Secretary:** Mrs Lynda Preece
**US SIC:** 3443, 3499, 3799, 3999
**UK SIC:** 32051, 31694, 36502, 49590
**Auditors:** Clewleys Ltd
**Bankers:** Yorkshire Bank Plc (05-09-43)

| | 30-06-13 | 30-06-12 | 30-06-11 |
|---|---|---|---|
| TO | N/A | 7,454,322 | N/A |
| P/L | N/A | 449,684 | N/A |
| NW | 1,334,953 | 1,195,516 | 862,867 |
| WC | 740,478 | 623,152 | 288,865 |
| Emp. | N/A | 73 | N/A |

DUNS 89-652-2950

### Quality Office Supplies Ltd

Anchor Lane, Bilston, West Midlands WV14 9NE
**Tel:** 01902884688 **Fax:** 01902-880577
**Web:** www.qualityofficesupplies.co.uk
**Reg No:** 3320229 **VAT No:** 687840971
**Estd:** 1997 Private Limited Company
**Line of Business:** Commercial stationery supplies
**Issued Capital:** £100
**Managing Director:** E J Barnshaw
**Co. Secretary:** Jonathan Khan
**Branches:** Quality Office Supplies Ltd, Barns Court, Unit 55, Crawley, West Sussex RH10 4HQ
**US SIC:** 5942, 5199
**UK SIC:** 65300, 61900
**Auditors:** Wilkes Tranter & Co Ltd
**Bankers:** HSBC Bank plc (40-46-35)

| | 31-03-14 | 31-03-13 | 31-03-12 |
|---|---|---|---|
| TO | 18,224,472 | 13,395,232 | 8,346,846 |
| P/L | 107,330 | 31,187 | 285,030 |
| NW | 306,836 | 378,998 | 498,984 |
| WC | 258,643 | 107,878 | 74,163 |
| Emp. | 136 | 100 | 50 |

DUNS 21-628-7530

### Quality Plated Products Ltd

Shady Lane Great Barr, Birmingham, West Midlands B44 9ER
**Web:** www.qppltd.co.uk
**Reg No:** 7078314 **Estd:** 2009 Private Limited Company
**Line of Business:** Manufacture of other plastic products
**Trading Style:** Quality Plated Plastics
**Issued Capital:** £100
**Directors:** J W Timmins, M E Davis, Mrs K M Shakeshaft, S Taylor
**US SIC:** 3079 **UK SIC:** 48360
**Auditors:** Parker Business Development Ltd

| | 30-09-13 | 30-09-12 | 30-09-11 |
|---|---|---|---|
| TA | 2,396,362 | 1,699,706 | 1,616,488 |
| NW | 441,265 | 209,575 | 60,663 |
| WC | 264,201 | 71,229 | (45,733) |

DUNS 23-647-5922

### Qualitycall Centre Ltd

7a High Street, Gosport, Hampshire PO12 1BX
**Tel:** 023-9271-4100
**Web:** www.healthspan.co.uk
**Reg No:** 3642847 **Estd:** 1998 Private Limited Company
**Line of Business:** Call centres
**Issued Capital:** £2
**Director:** D S Coates
**Co. Secretary:** Graham Case
**Responsibilities**
**Senior:** Lorna Dalton *(Manager)*, Caroline Newell *(Call Centre Manager)*
**US SIC:** 7399 **UK SIC:** 83954
**Auditors:** Chandlers Ltd

| | 31-12-13 | 31-12-12 | 31-12-11 |
|---|---|---|---|
| TO | 3,447,053 | 4,679,092 | 4,870,263 |
| P/L | 27,215 | 113,187 | 106,239 |
| NW | 387,447 | 365,470 | 277,185 |
| WC | 266,606 | 214,617 | 107,865 |
| Emp. | 108 | 105 | 110 |

DUNS 77-950-1154

### Qualitycourse Ltd

Rational House, Manchester M3 3BN
**Tel:** 01422 349423 **Fax:** 01422365606
**Web:** www.resource-transline.co.uk
**Reg No:** 3055907 **VAT No:** 588941671
**Estd:** 1995 Private Limited Company
**Line of Business:** Labour recruitment and provision of personnel
**Trading Style:** Resource Recruitment, Transline Resource
**Issued Capital:** £100
**Directors:** Miss J Hardy, M Elms, C N Beasley, P M Beasley, J M Taylor
**Co. Secretary:** Ms Sandra Beasley
**Branches:** Qualitycourse Ltd, 1 King Cross St, Carlton Pl, Halifax, West Yorkshire HX1 2SB
**US SIC:** 7361 **UK SIC:** 83954
**Auditors:** Grant Thornton UK LLP
**Bankers:** National Westminster Bank Plc (60-08-46)

| | 31-12-13 | 31-12-12 | 31-12-11 |
|---|---|---|---|
| TO | 110,103,000 | 70,823,630 | 54,349,415 |
| P/L | 1,687,000 | 1,324,213 | 1,089,941 |
| NW | 3,839,000 | 3,048,256 | 1,850,362 |
| WC | 2,285,000 | 1,564,151 | 1,094,354 |
| Emp. | 6,972 | 3,957 | 3,044 |

DUNS 21-916-6980 **Imp-Exp**

### Qualtex Uk Ltd

(**Subsidiary of:** Cph Qtech Ltd)
National Distribution Centre, Manchester M34 2SX
**Tel:** 01613 202 660 **Fax:** 01613 202 666
**Web:** www.qualtexuk.com
**Reg No:** 0708974 **VAT No:** 157372452
**Estd:** 1961 Private Limited Company
**Line of Business:** Wholesale of other household goods not elsewhere classified
**Export Markets:** Australia; South Africa & Eire
**Issued Capital:** £1,500
**Directors:** Mrs C Hulme, Ms T L Norman, P Hulme
**Co. Secretary:** Mrs Caroline Hulme
**Responsibilities**
**Senior:** Jill Blackwell *(Manager)*, Susan Hulme *(Manager)*
**Sales:** Andy Cutler *(Internal Sales Operator)*
**Branches:** Qualtex Uk Limited, Qualtex North East, Unit 5B Drum Industrial Estate, Chester-Le-Street, DH2 1SS County Durham
**US SIC:** 5199, 5732
**UK SIC:** 61900, 64800
**Auditors:** Moss & Williamson Ltd
**Bankers:** National Westminster Bank Plc (01-01-75)

| | 31-12-13 | 31-12-12 | 31-12-11 |
|---|---|---|---|
| TO | 18,936,573 | 17,060,096 | 15,173,112 |
| P/L | 1,254,170 | 1,101,011 | 1,027,119 |
| NW | 5,706,393 | 4,709,453 | 3,897,684 |
| WC | 7,024,107 | 6,539,189 | 5,971,221 |
| Emp. | 104 | 95 | 80 |

DUNS 22-661-3495 **Imp**

### Qualvis Packaging Ltd

(**Subsidiary of:** Qualvis Print & Packaging Ltd)
854 Melton Road, Thurmaston, Leicester, Leicestershire LE4 8BT
**Tel:** 01162602220 **Fax:** 01162-601066
**Web:** www.qualvis.co.uk
**Reg No:** 1615940 **VAT No:** 371752544
**Estd:** 1982 Private Limited Company
**Line of Business:** Folding paperboard box manufacturers
**Issued Capital:** £1,000
**Director:** J A Short

**Responsibilities**
**Senior:** John Glassbrook *(Production Director)*
**Facilities:** David Swann *(Engineering Manager)*
**Operations:** Kris Freer *(Laboratory Manager)*
**Purchasing:** Kris Freer *(Laboratory Manager)*
**Engineering:** John Glassbrook *(Production Director)*
**Branches:** 854 Melton Rd, Thurmaston, Leicester
**US SIC:** 2651, 3999
**UK SIC:** 47253, 49590
**Auditors:** KPMG LLP
**Bankers:** The Royal Bank Of Scotland Plc (16-26-32)

| | 31-01-14 | 31-01-13 | 31-01-12 |
|---|---|---|---|
| TO | 9,622,793 | 9,390,193 | 11,247,879 |
| P/L | 283,923 | (296,774) | 146,123 |
| NW | 268,679 | 31,547 | 290,505 |
| WC | N/A | 447,850 | 694,506 |
| Emp. | 78 | 92 | 94 |

DUNS 57-870-7895
## Quanta Holdings Ltd
8-10 The Moors, Worcester, Worcestershire WR1 3EE
**Tel:** 08000185597
**Web:** www.quanta.co.uk
**Reg No:** 2902622 **Estd:** 1994 Private Limited Company
**Line of Business:** Holding companies management activities
**Issued Capital:** £900
**Managing Director:** J H Ward
**Co. Secretary:** Ms Jane Ward
**Responsibilities**
**Marketing:** Adam Montgomery *(Development & Training Manager)*
**HR:** Adam Montgomery *(Development & Training Manager)*
**Branches:** Quanta Holdings Ltd, 66 Leman Street, London E1 8EU
**US SIC:** 6711 **UK SIC:** 83962
**Auditors:** PKF

| | 28-02-14 | 28-02-13 | 28-02-12 |
|---|---|---|---|
| TA | 762,612 | 770,832 | 779,045 |
| NW | 567,045 | 561,168 | 432,825 |
| WC | (186,438) | (177,289) | (299,386) |

DUNS 21-702-8048
## Quantel Holdings Ltd
31 Turnpike Road, Newbury, Berkshire RG14 2NX
**Tel:** 0163548222
**Web:** www.quantel.com
**Reg No:** 7472957 **Estd:** 2010 Private Limited Company
**Line of Business:** Management activities of holding companies
**Issued Capital:** £104,900
**Directors:** P G Martin, D C Eales, M Mulligan, S J Owen, R J Cross, S D Rogers, K P Leggett, R Rowe
**Co. Secretary:** Ian Cooper
**Responsibilities**
**Senior:** Guy Eaton *(Director)*
**US SIC:** 6711 **UK SIC:** 83962
**Auditors:** Ernst & Young LLP

| | 31-12-13 | 31-12-12 | 30-12-11 |
|---|---|---|---|
| TO | 40,677,000 | 46,233,000 | 25,572,000 |
| P/L | 2,925,000 | (4,708,000) | 4,300,000 |
| NW | (14,479,000) | (14,802,000) | (6,312,000) |
| WC | 26,028,000 | 27,360,000 | 28,231,000 |
| Emp. | 236 | 235 | 231 |

DUNS 21-008-9238
## Quanticate Ltd
Bevan House, 9-11 Bancroft Court, Hitchin, Hertfordshire SG5 1LH
**Tel:** 01462-440084 **Fax:** 01462-440086
**Web:** www.quanticate.com
**Reg No:** 6328308 **Estd:** 2007 Private Limited Company
**Line of Business:** Research and laboratory based activities
**Export Sales:** £5,812,919
**Issued Capital:** £1,000
**Directors:** J R Mcdermott, Doctor D S Chapple, D Underwood
**Co. Secretary:** Giorgio Jones
**Responsibilities**
**Senior:** Lucy Harrigan *(Office Manager)*
**IT:** Ian Bunton *(IS Specialist)*
**US SIC:** 7391 **UK SIC:** 94000

| | 31-12-13 | 31-12-12 | 31-12-11 |
|---|---|---|---|
| TO | 10,966,705 | 11,061,284 | 11,798,859 |
| P/L | 296,486 | 422,346 | 740,883 |
| NW | 4,295,459 | 4,662,397 | 5,142,688 |
| WC | 4,084,686 | 4,463,365 | 4,852,378 |
| Emp. | 177 | 194 | 208 |

DUNS 23-459-5619
## Quantiq Technology Ltd
7 St Martins Place, London WC2N 4HA
**Tel:** 02074511200
**Web:** www.quantiq.com
**Reg No:** 2601751 **Estd:** 1991 Private Limited Company
**Line of Business:** Computer consumables suppliers
**Export Sales:** £4,702,775
**Issued Capital:** £140,000
**Directors:** S A Fenton, M D Wolf, J V Martin
**Co. Secretary:** Derek Walton
**Responsibilities**
**Senior:** Duane Bell *(Manager)*, David Kempski *(Manager)*, Christina Wegrzynski *(HR Director)*
**IT:** Mohsin Syed *(Dynamics AX Support Consultant)*
**US SIC:** 7379 **UK SIC:** 83940
**Auditors:** Rouse Audit LLP

| | 29-12-13 | 30-12-12 | 01-12-12 |
|---|---|---|---|
| TO | 11,191,024 | 14,418,485 | 15,343,211 |
| P/L | 914,959 | 708,036 | 673,262 |
| NW | (3,405,606) | (4,320,565) | (5,028,586) |
| WC | (3,436,351) | (4,366,150) | (5,059,838) |
| Emp. | 78 | 94 | 90 |

DUNS 23-633-7333
## Quantum Care Ltd
4 Silver Court, Watchmead, Welwyn Garden City, Hertfordshire AL7 1TS
**Tel:** 01707393293
**Web:** www.quantumcare.co.uk
**Reg No:** 0027608IP **VAT No:** 640094952
**Estd:** 1992 Friendly Society
**Line of Business:** Social work activities with accommodation
**Trading Style:** Quantum Care Ltd
**Principals:** D Goodall *(Chairman)*, Ms N Coulter, Dr E Thompson, Ms D Crook, I Barber, B Mills, Ms D Scivyer, Ms E Richardson
**Co. Secretary:** David Brown
**Responsibilities**
**Senior:** Maria Ball *(Chief Executive Officer)*, Dennis Bignell *(Principal)*, Liz Cook *(Manager)*, Brenda Hooper *(Director)*, Geoffrey Williamson *(Director)*
**Finance:** Caroline Bates *(Director of Finance & Faciliti)*
**HR:** Wanda Spooner *(Human Resources Director)*
**Facilities:** Caroline Bates *(Director of Finance & Faciliti)*
**Operations:** Jeannie Conder *(Senior Regional Manager)*, Julie Davey *(Regional Manager)*, Debbie Green *(Regional Manager)*, Siven Vencatasawmy *(Regional Manager)*
**Branches:** Quantum Care Ltd, Dellwood Field Way, Rickmansworth, Hertfordshire WD3 7EJ
**US SIC:** 7399, 6732
**UK SIC:** 83954, 83100
**Bankers:** National Westminster Bank Plc (60-10-39)
**Employees:** 1,485

DUNS 39-911-2556
## Quantum Claims Compensation Specialists Ltd
70 Carden Place, Aberdeen, Aberdeenshire AB10 1UL
**Tel:** 01224641111 **Fax:** 01224-621773
**Web:** www.quantumclaims.com
**Reg No:** 0110105SC **VAT No:** 498189182
**Estd:** 2012 Private Limited Company
**Line of Business:** Activities auxiliary to insurance and pension funding
**Trading Style:** Quantum Compensation Specialists
**Issued Capital:** £102,000
**Principals:** F H Lefevre *(Chairman)*, G A Clark *(Managing)*, P M Lefevre, J W Symon
**Co. Secretary:** Lefevre Litigation
**Branches:** Quantum Claims Compensation Specialists Ltd, 1 Tomnahurich Street, Inverness, Inverness-Shire IV3 5DA
**US SIC:** 7399, 8111
**UK SIC:** 83954, 83500
**Auditors:** Norman Gray & Co
**Bankers:** The Royal Bank Of Scotland Plc (83-15-31)

| | 30-04-14 | 30-04-13 | 30-04-12 |
|---|---|---|---|
| TO | 3,492,796 | 3,663,052 | 3,768,347 |
| P/L | 247,246 | 457,174 | 270,002 |
| NW | 3,743,587 | 3,563,613 | 3,227,284 |
| WC | 597,645 | 747,887 | 717,329 |
| Emp. | 51 | 56 | 56 |

DUNS 23-829-0311
## Quantum Leap Health & Fitness Ltd
**(Subsidiary of:** Tts Equity Ltd)
13 Sherwood Street, London W1F 7BR
**Tel:** 020-7439-6333 **Fax:** 02075342828
**Web:** www.thethirdspace.com
**Reg No:** 3820940 **Estd:** 1999 Private Limited Company
**Line of Business:** Operation of other sports arenas and stadiums not elsewhere classified
**Trading Style:** Third Space
**Issued Capital:** £1
**Directors:** I C Mahoney, J Penny, S Gandhi
**Responsibilities**
**Senior:** Eric Asher *(G P)*
**US SIC:** 7999 **UK SIC:** 97913
**Auditors:** Moore Stephens LLP
**Bankers:** Lloyds TSB Bank plc (30-15-57)

| | 30-09-13 | 30-09-12 | 30-09-11 |
|---|---|---|---|
| TO | 6,093,143 | 5,492,980 | 4,537,247 |
| P/L | (942,349) | (3,357,781) | (1,541,705) |
| NW | (872,551) | (4,755,202) | (1,397,421) |
| WC | (3,361,139) | (6,857,948) | (3,566,575) |
| Emp. | 85 | 86 | 82 |

DUNS 23-376-5986
## Quantum Pharmaceutical Ltd
**(Subsidiary of:** Hamsard 3149 Ltd)
Hobson Industrial Estate, Hobson, Newcastle-Upon-Tyne, Tyne and Wear NE16 6EA
**Tel:** 01207279400 **Fax:** 08000439378
**Web:** www.quantumpharma.co.uk
**Reg No:** 5240304 **Estd:** 2004 Private Limited Company
**Line of Business:** Pharmaceutical suppliers and wholesalers
**Issued Capital:** £1,005
**Directors:** B J Fisher, A J Scaife, D A Sanson, M J Such, A P Matthews
**Co. Secretary:** Martin Such
**US SIC:** 2834 **UK SIC:** 25700
**Auditors:** KPMG LLP

| | 31-01-14 | 31-01-13 | 31-01-12 |
|---|---|---|---|
| TO | 40,990,000 | 35,199,000 | 33,371,000 |
| P/L | 8,112,000 | 6,780,000 | 8,973,000 |
| NW | 16,751,000 | 11,327,000 | 10,109,000 |
| WC | (10,212,000) | (8,852,000) | 2,680,000 |
| Emp. | 251 | 217 | 215 |

DUNS 22-055-6653
## Quantum Profile Systems Ltd
Salmon Fields, Royton, Oldham, Lancashire OL2 6JG
**Tel:** 0161-627-4222 **Fax:** 0161-627-4333
**Web:** www.quantum-ps.co.uk
**Reg No:** 4057656 **Estd:** 1970 Private Limited Company
**Line of Business:** Plastic extruders
**Issued Capital:** £200,000
**Directors:** J A Brogdon, W J Hughes, J H Newsome
**Co. Secretary:** Clive Bowen
**Responsibilities**
**Senior:** Simon Crossley *(Operations Manager)*, Steve Keane *(Sales Manager)*
**IT:** Bruno Figueiredo *(?IT Systems Manager)*
**Health & Safety:** Simon Crossley *(Operations Manager)*
**Operations:** Simon Crossley *(Operations Manager)*
**US SIC:** 3079 **UK SIC:** 48360
**Auditors:** Booth Ainsworth LLP
**Bankers:** The Royal Bank Of Scotland Plc (16-00-01)

| | 31-12-13 | 31-12-12 | 31-12-11 |
|---|---|---|---|
| TO | 8,669,688 | 7,430,750 | N/A |
| P/L | 201,741 | 231,218 | N/A |
| NW | 311,063 | 133,122 | (53,800) |
| WC | (146,883) | (292,235) | (287,513) |
| Emp. | N/A | 63 | N/A |

DUNS 22-118-4695 **Imp-Exp**
## Quantum Storage U K Ltd
**(Subsidiary of:** Quantum Corporation)
3 Bracknell Beeches, Old Bracknell Lane West, Bracknell, Berkshire RG12 7BW
**Tel:** 01344353500 **Fax:** 01344-353510
**Web:** www.quantum.com
**Reg No:** 4137529 **VAT No:** 770617818
**Estd:** 2001 Private Limited Company
**Line of Business:** Data storage solutions
**Issued Capital:** £25,000
**Director:** J Gacek
**Co. Secretary:** Shawn Hall
**Responsibilities**
**Senior:** Christo Conidaris *(Manager)*, Ewan Johnston *(U K V P Sales)*
**Finance:** Katarina Catalano *(Financial Manager)*
**Sales:** Ewan Johnston *(U K V P Sales)*
**Admin:** Heather Lee *(Office Manager)*, Caroline Shillcock *(Facilities Manager)*
**Facilities:** Caroline Shillcock *(Facilities Manager)*
**Operations:** Jim Mudd *(SVP, Operations)*
**Engineering:** Don Martella *(SVP, Engineering)*
**US SIC:** 7374 **UK SIC:** 83940
**Auditors:** Newman & Partners
**Bankers:** National Westminster Bank Plc (60-24-21)

| | 31-03-14 | 31-03-13 | 31-03-12 |
|---|---|---|---|
| TO | 8,211,762 | 10,158,798 | 10,148,461 |
| P/L | 210,055 | (57,473) | 438,472 |
| NW | 2,422,741 | 2,276,075 | 2,329,199 |
| WC | 2,282,236 | 2,059,751 | 2,023,696 |
| Emp. | 78 | 93 | 103 |

DUNS 23-668-6221
## Quantum Technology Marketing Group Ltd
Abbey Square, Reading, Berkshire RG1 3BE
**Tel:** 01189-022500 **Fax:** 01189-022501
**Web:** www.quantummarketing-group.com
**Reg No:** 3663452 **Estd:** 1998 Private Limited Company
**Line of Business:** Business and management consultancy activities not elsewhere classified
**Trading Style:** Quantum Marketing
**Issued Capital:** £125
**Directors:** M Dale, G N Haley, J Claricoates
**Co. Secretary:** Carl Taylor
**Responsibilities**
**Senior:** Niaz Rahmani *(Manager)*
**US SIC:** 7399, 7999
**UK SIC:** 83954, 97913
**Auditors:** PricewaterhouseCoopers LLP
**Bankers:** Lloyds TSB Bank plc (30-91-31)

| | 31-12-13 | 31-12-12 | 31-12-11 |
|---|---|---|---|
| TO | N/A | N/A | 6,025,345 |
| P/L | N/A | N/A | (328,571) |
| NW | (577,894) | (387,073) | (414,878) |
| WC | (616,750) | (395,069) | (177,068) |
| Emp. | N/A | N/A | 111 |

DUNS 21-124-5761
## Quantum Windows
11 Causeway Road, Earlstrees Industrial Estate, Corby, Northamptonshire NN17 4DU
**Web:** www.quantumwindows.co.uk
**Estd:** 1992 Partnership
**Line of Business:** Manufacturers of window frames
**Trading Style:** Quantum Windows Ltd
**Partners:** A Britton, C Ashman
**Responsibilities**
**Finance:** Heather Hudson *(Office Manager)*
**Admin:** Heather Hudson *(Office Manager)*
**HR:** Heather Hudson *(Office Manager)*
**Engineering:** Tom Hall *(Services Engineer)*
**US SIC:** 3442 **UK SIC:** 31420
**Employees:** 100

DUNS 77-112-1167
## The Quarr Group Ltd
Flagship House, Reading Road North, Fleet, Hampshire GU51 4WD
**Tel:** 01252616100 **Fax:** 01252 819992
**Web:** www.thequanticgroup.com
**Reg No:** 2688985 **VAT No:** 582949193
**Estd:** 1992 Private Limited Company
**Line of Business:** Management activities of other non-financial holding companies not elsewhere classified
**Trading Style:** Pabulum, N-Viro
**Issued Capital:** £108,238
**Principals:** C C Howells *(Managing)*, G J Pengelly, M J Russell, Ms D J Harvey
**Co. Secretary:** Christopher Howells
**Responsibilities**
**Senior:** Corin Bowyer-Crombie *(Group Operations manager)*
**US SIC:** 6711 **UK SIC:** 83962
**Auditors:** taylorcocks
**Bankers:** HSBC Bank plc (40-34-26)

| | 30-04-14 | 30-04-13 | 30-04-12 |
|---|---|---|---|
| TO | 69,569,974 | 67,231,929 | 55,153,834 |
| P/L | 115,576 | 1,920,885 | 1,708,585 |
| NW | 2,123,740 | 2,842,677 | 2,413,765 |
| WC | 353,722 | 1,460,422 | 1,352,499 |
| Emp. | 2,760 | 2,791 | 2,582 |

DUNS 22-903-2743
## Quarriers
Quarriers Village, Bridge of Weir, Renfrewshire PA11 3SX
**Tel:** 01505612224
**Web:** www.quarriers.org.uk
**Reg No:** 0014361SC **VAT No:** 263500975
**Estd:** 1871 Private Company Limited By Guarantee
**Line of Business:** Charities and charitable organisations
**Directors:** Miss P C Cunningham, Mrs S A Gillies, D J Watt, Miss A Dougan, D A Adams, Mrs A Welsh, T A Scholes, Mrs T Godman
**Co. Secretary:** Christopher Harwood
**Responsibilities**
**Senior:** Alice Drife *(Chief Executive Officer)*, William Harkness *(Trustee)*, Eddie Jones *(Manager)*, David Macrobert *(Trustee)*, Ian Matson *(Trustee)*, Donald Mcrae *(Director)*, Roger Mills *(Trustee)*, Linda Nisbet *(Manager)*, Bill Scott *(Board Member)*, Angus Skinner *(Trustee)*
**Finance:** Niall MacPherson *(Director for Finance and Corpo)*
**Marketing:** Carol Eden *(Head of Marketing & Communicat)*
**HR:** Elaine Cowan *(Staff Development Officer)*, Karen Croan *(Human Resources Director)*
**Operations:** Heather Weir *(Project Manager)*
**Branches:** Quarriers, 46 Towpath Road, Trowbridge, Wiltshire BA14 7QD

**US SIC:** 6732, 8321
**UK SIC:** 83100, 96111
**Auditors:** Deloitte & Touche LLP
**Bankers:** Bank Of Scotland (80-05-82)

| | 31-03-14 | 31-03-13 | 31-03-12 |
|---|---|---|---|
| TO | 43,709,000 | 45,633,000 | 43,490,000 |
| P/L | 706,000 | 3,684,000 | 1,460,000 |
| NW | 15,561,000 | 13,668,000 | 8,940,000 |
| WC | 1,535,000 | 812,000 | 318,000 |
| Emp. | 2,001 | 1,950 | 1,985 |

DUNS 21-122-1450
## Quarry Bank Mill & Styal Estate
Quarry Bank Mill, Quarry Bank Road, Styal, Wilmslow, Cheshire SK9 4LA
**Tel:** 01625445846
**Web:** www.nationaltrust.org.uk
**Estd:** 1974
**Line of Business:** Caterers
**Proprietor:** D Thomas
**Responsibilities**
**Senior:** Jenny Haley *(Manager)*, Elenor Underhill *(General Manager)*
**Finance:** Elenor Underhill *(General Manager)*
**Marketing:** Rosalind Stone *(Marketing Manager)*
**US SIC:** 5812 **UK SIC:** 66110
**Employees:** 50

DUNS 23-534-8443
## Quarry Court Holdings Ltd
(**Subsidiary of:** Westcoast (Holdings) Ltd)
1 Quarry Court, Beacon Hill Road, Halifax, West Yorkshire HX3 6AQ
**Tel:** 01422-444561 **Fax:** 01422444571
**Reg No:** 3533628 **Estd:** 1998 Private Limited Company
**Line of Business:** Other business activities not elsewhere classified
**Export Sales:** £3,299,457
**Trading Style:** Q C Supplies
**Issued Capital:** £21,707
**Directors:** J R Crabtree, S J Madhani
**Responsibilities**
**Senior:** Robert Clavering *(Manager)*
**Branches:** Quarry Court Holdings Ltd, Atrium House, Callendar Road, Falkirk, Stirlingshire FK1 1XR
**US SIC:** 7399 **UK SIC:** 83954
**Auditors:** Grant Thornton
**Bankers:** National Westminster Bank Plc (53-61-07)

| | 31-03-14 | 31-03-13 | 31-03-12 |
|---|---|---|---|
| TO | 33,566,001 | 44,767,237 | 61,109,382 |
| P/L | (1,547,744) | (137,842) | 112,046 |
| NW | (211,363) | 1,146,468 | 1,290,434 |
| WC | (457,473) | 189,564 | 174,434 |
| Emp. | 134 | 163 | 170 |

DUNS 21-223-7658
## Quarry Hall Nursing Home
Newport Road, St Mellons, Cardiff, South Glamorgan CF3 5TW
**Web:** www.hc-one.co.uk
**Estd:** 1995
**Line of Business:** Non-charitable social work activities with accommodation
**Proprietor:** Mrs H Randle
**US SIC:** 8321 **UK SIC:** 96111
**Employees:** 94

DUNS 21-783-4008
## Quarter Jack Surgery
Rodways Corner, Wimborne, Dorset BH21 1AP
**Tel:** 01202843626
**Web:** www.quarterjacksurgery.co.uk
**Estd:** 2002
**Line of Business:** Doctors
**Responsibilities**
**Senior:** Sue Richards *(Practice Manager)*, Jenny Smith *(Deputy Practice Manager)*
**US SIC:** 8011 **UK SIC:** 95300
**Employees:** 50

DUNS 22-141-0363
## Quartix Ltd
(**Subsidiary of:** Quartix Holdings Plc)
Ladywell House, Newtown, Powys SY16 1PR
**Tel:** 01686621999 **Fax:** 01686-628774
**Web:** www.quartix.net
**Reg No:** 4159907 **Estd:** 2001 Private Limited Company
**Line of Business:** Database development services
**Export Sales:** £593,108
**Issued Capital:** £202,000
**Directors:** P D Brown, A M Kirk, A J Walters, W A Hibbert
**Co. Secretary:** David Bridge
**Responsibilities**
**Sales:** Sean Maher *(Sales Manager)*
**Branches:** Quartix Ltd, Wellington House, East Road, Cambridge, Cambridgeshire CB1 1BH
**US SIC:** 3799, 7374
**UK SIC:** 36502, 83940
**Auditors:** Grant Thornton UK LLP

| | 31-12-13 | 31-12-12 | 31-12-11 |
|---|---|---|---|
| TO | 13,180,172 | 8,289,546 | N/A |
| P/L | 4,826,045 | 2,894,576 | N/A |
| NW | 5,357,051 | 4,850,248 | 3,240,725 |
| WC | 5,283,387 | 4,728,697 | 3,251,297 |
| Emp. | 60 | 45 | N/A |

DUNS 22-798-9761
## The Quarto Group Inc
(**Subsidiary of:** Quarto Group Inc)
B S G House, 226 City Road, London EC1V 2TT
**Tel:** 02077009000 **Fax:** 020-7253-4437
**Web:** www.quarto.com
**Reg No:** 0013814FC **Estd:** 1986 Foreign Company
**Line of Business:** Book publishers
**Principals:** L Orbach *(Chairman and Managing)*, M Mousley *(Financial)*, M E Leaver, G Banks, P E Waine, Ms L Collins, P M Campbell, A Slavin
**Responsibilities**
**Senior:** George Tai *(Director)*
**Branches:** The Old Brewery 6 Brundell Street London N7 9BH
**US SIC:** 6711 **UK SIC:** 83962
**Bankers:** National Westminster Bank Plc (56-00-27)

DUNS 21-153-9259 Exp
## Quarto Publishing P L C
(**Subsidiary of:** Quarto Group Inc)
6 Blundell Street, London N7 9BH
**Tel:** 020-7700-6700 **Fax:** 020-7700-4191
**Web:** www.quarto.com
**Reg No:** 1252863 **VAT No:** 341128295
**Estd:** 1972 Public Limited Company
**Line of Business:** Publishing of books
**Export Markets:** N America, E U, Australasia, etc.
**Export Sales:** £31,436,000
**Trading Style:** Quintessence Editions, Quantum Books, Quarto, Q E D
**Issued Capital:** £100,000
**Directors:** M E Leaver, R Morley, Ms M J Clinch
**Co. Secretary:** Michael Mousley
**Responsibilities**
**Senior:** michael clarke *(group director)*
**Branches:** Quarto Publishing P L C, B S G House, 226 City Rd, London EC1V 2TT
**US SIC:** 2731 **UK SIC:** 47532
**Auditors:** Grant Thornton UK LLP
**Bankers:** National Westminster Bank Plc (56-00-29)

| | 31-12-13 | 31-12-12 | 31-12-11 |
|---|---|---|---|
| TO | 44,074,000 | 44,580,000 | 41,943,000 |
| P/L | 815,000 | 435,000 | 2,806,000 |
| NW | 11,201,000 | 11,031,000 | 11,569,000 |
| WC | 60,596,000 | 66,402,000 | 32,241,000 |
| Emp. | 207 | 197 | 171 |

DUNS 45-895-2090
## Quartz Electrical & Mechanical Services Ltd
Riverside, Low Green, Middlesbrough, Cleveland TS9 6NN
**Tel:** 01642-244411
**Web:** www.quartzelec.com
**Reg No:** 3229302 **Estd:** 1996 Private Limited Company
**Line of Business:** Electrical contractors and electricians
**Issued Capital:** £144,333
**Directors:** L Mcdermott, G Kendall, J G Orpen, S Wainwright, A Learmonth
**Responsibilities**
**Senior:** Graham Allenden *(Estimator)*, Garry Orpen *(Manager)*
**Finance:** Garry Orpen *(Manager)*
**Marketing:** Garry Orpen *(Manager)*
**Sales:** Garry Orpen *(Manager)*
**IT:** Garry Orpen *(Manager)*
**Facilities:** Garry Orpen *(Manager)*
**Branches:** Quartz Electrical & Mechanical Services Ltd, Unit 4, Strawberry Lane, Willenhall, West Midlands WV13 3RS
**US SIC:** 1731 **UK SIC:** 50300
**Auditors:** Keith Thomas Associates
**Bankers:** Barclays Bank Plc (20-82-18)

| | 31-12-13 | 31-12-12 | 31-12-11 |
|---|---|---|---|
| TO | N/A | N/A | 6,802,814 |
| P/L | N/A | N/A | 2,003 |
| NW | 500,042 | 473,707 | 449,994 |
| WC | 486,269 | 460,454 | 344,010 |
| Emp. | N/A | N/A | 74 |

DUNS 29-888-5781 Imp
## Quartz Technical Services Ltd
Stokes Industrial Park, Merrylees Road, Desford, Leicester, Leicestershire LE9 9FE
**Tel:** 01455-824646
**Web:** www.quartz-tsl.com
**Reg No:** 2091568 **VAT No:** 424693637
**Estd:** 1987 Private Limited Company
**Line of Business:** Printed and integrated circuit services
**Issued Capital:** £100
**Principals:** B A Mousley *(Managing)*, P S Mousley
**Co. Secretary:** Neil Mousley
**US SIC:** 3679 **UK SIC:** 34542
**Auditors:** Robert Whowell & Partners
**Bankers:** The Co-Operative Bank Plc (08-90-77)

| | 30-04-14 | 30-04-13 | 30-04-12 |
|---|---|---|---|
| TO | N/A | N/A | 2,900,840 |
| P/L | N/A | N/A | 112,763 |
| NW | 381,471 | 260,613 | 194,133 |
| WC | 339,522 | 210,716 | 143,823 |

DUNS 67-211-6464
## Quartzinvest Ltd
Leicester Road, Rugby, Warwickshire CV21 1BD
**Tel:** 01788-512512
**Web:** www.quartzelec.com
**Reg No:** 6019739 **Estd:** 2006 Private Limited Company
**Line of Business:** Car and commercial vehicle repairs
**Export Sales:** £8,756,000
**Issued Capital:** £750,000
**Directors:** D R Laval, D M Whyte, R J Annable, B Morris, R H Regan, D R Graham, D C Buse, T J Langhorn
**Co. Secretary:** Kenneth Wanless
**US SIC:** 1731 **UK SIC:** 50300

| | 30-09-14 | 30-09-13 | 30-09-12 |
|---|---|---|---|
| TO | 60,771,000 | 55,891,000 | 51,231,000 |
| P/L | 1,428,000 | (283,000) | 2,528,000 |
| NW | 14,509,000 | 14,887,000 | 17,207,000 |
| WC | 5,038,000 | 6,372,000 | 4,018,000 |
| Emp. | 592 | 541 | 513 |

DUNS 56-994-0299
## Quartzsite Medical Ltd
29 Gay Street, Bath, Avon BA1 2NT
**Tel:** 01225336100 **Fax:** 01225-448676
**Reg No:** 2859214 **Estd:** 1993 Private Limited Company
**Line of Business:** Electrical products (sales)
**Issued Capital:** £2
**Director:** Mrs S J Child
**Co. Secretary:** Nicholas Child
**US SIC:** 5732, 5999
**UK SIC:** 64800, 65600

| | 30-09-14 | 30-09-13 | 30-09-12 |
|---|---|---|---|
| TA | 1,032 | 1,032 | 1,032 |
| NW | 1,032 | 1,032 | 1,032 |

DUNS 22-771-7626
## Quartzteam Ltd
(**Subsidiary of:** Quartzinvest Ltd)
Swansea Business Park, Swansea, West Glamorgan SA5 4HF
**Tel:** 01792560980
**Reg No:** 1595603 **Estd:** 1981 Private Limited Company
**Line of Business:** Window cleaning
**Trading Style:** Teamseed
**Issued Capital:** £10,000
**Director:** D R Laval
**Co. Secretary:** Kenneth Wanless
**Branches:** Quartzteam Ltd, 51 York Street, Aberdeen, Aberdeenshire AB11 5DP
**US SIC:** 7349 **UK SIC:** 92300

| | 30-09-14 | 30-09-13 | 30-09-12 |
|---|---|---|---|
| TA | 10,000 | 10,000 | 10,000 |
| NW | 10,000 | 10,000 | 10,000 |

DUNS 50-393-9100 Imp
## Quattro Plant Ltd
(**Subsidiary of:** Arkose Investments Ltd)
Greenway Court, Canning Road, London E15 3ND
**Tel:** 02085196165
**Web:** www.quattroplant.co.uk
**Reg No:** 2400439 **Estd:** 1989 Private Limited Company
**Line of Business:** Plant and tool hire
**Issued Capital:** £628,593
**Principals:** J J Murphy *(Managing)*, A Richardson
**Responsibilities**
**Senior:** David Calle *(CEO & Finance Director)*
**Finance:** David Calle *(CEO & Finance Director)*
**Branches:** Quattro Plant Ltd, Martinfield Business Centre, Martinfield, Welwyn Garden City, Hertfordshire AL7 1HG
**US SIC:** 7394 **UK SIC:** 84000
**Auditors:** Accura Partners LLP
**Bankers:** The Bank Of Ireland (30-11-70)

| | 30-11-13 | 30-11-12 | 30-11-11 |
|---|---|---|---|
| TO | 40,009,906 | 36,781,107 | 32,259,579 |
| P/L | 3,300,065 | 3,634,136 | (1,065,355) |
| NW | 7,139,798 | 4,550,876 | 1,732,604 |
| WC | 8,150,818 | (663,940) | (3,183,053) |
| Emp. | 130 | 127 | 155 |

DUNS 34-603-4747
## Quattro (U K) Ltd
Regency Street, London NW10 6NR
**Tel:** 020-8838-2648 **Fax:** 020-8838-2741
**Web:** www.quattroukltd.co.uk
**Reg No:** 2744918 **VAT No:** 578649081
**Estd:** 1999 Private Limited Company
**Line of Business:** Road haulage and transport services
**Issued Capital:** £25,000
**Managing Directors:** T H James, E O'Loughlin
**Co. Secretary:** Thomas James
**Responsibilities**
**Senior:** Eamon O'laughlin *(Director)*
**Admin:** Marie Colgan *(Office Manager)*
**IT:** Marie Colgan *(Office Manager)*
**HR:** Robert Duddy *(Safety Officer)*
**Health & Safety:** Robert Duddy *(Safety Officer)*
**Purchasing:** Christine O'Neil *(Purchasing Manager)*
**Branches:** Quattro (U K) Ltd, 30 Great George Street, Preston, Lancashire PR1 1TJ
**US SIC:** 4789, 7394
**UK SIC:** 77002, 84000
**Auditors:** McCormack & Associates
**Bankers:** Allied Irish Bank (gb) (23-83-94)

| | 31-12-13 | 31-12-12 | 31-12-11 |
|---|---|---|---|
| TO | 19,646,716 | 18,061,109 | 18,150,917 |
| P/L | 303,623 | 301,333 | 263,250 |
| NW | 3,182,862 | 2,957,834 | 2,737,420 |
| WC | 2,369,900 | 2,185,278 | 2,346,093 |
| Emp. | 123 | 120 | 113 |

DUNS 50-574-9242
## Quattroleisure Ltd
(**Subsidiary of:** L A Dowl (Warrington) Ltd)
Moorgate House, King Street, Newton Abbot, Devon TQ12 2LG
**Tel:** 01925639222
**Web:** www.labowl.co.uk
**Reg No:** 2522221 **VAT No:** 534968995
**Estd:** 1991 Private Limited Company
**Line of Business:** Bars
**Trading Style:** L A Bowl
**Issued Capital:** £10,000
**Directors:** L V Howle, B D Waggett, D M Thornton
**Branches:** Quattroleisure Ltd, 10-15 Chetham Ct, Warrington, Cheshire WA2 8RF
**US SIC:** 5813, 7941, 7999
**UK SIC:** 66200, 97911, 97913
**Auditors:** Peplows
**Bankers:** Barclays Bank Plc (20-60-88)

| | 31-08-13 | 31-08-12 | 31-08-11 |
|---|---|---|---|
| TA | 343,366 | 468,768 | 553,292 |
| NW | 57,134 | 91,085 | 42,679 |
| WC | (161,474) | (209,821) | (310,327) |

DUNS 23-772-0086
## Quay Accounting Ltd
Unit 4 Coy Pond Business Park, Ingworth Road, Poole, Dorset BH12 1JY
**Tel:** 01202753100 **Fax:** 01202-753105
**Web:** www.clearskyaccounting.co.uk
**Reg No:** 3765395 **Estd:** 1999 Private Limited Company
**Line of Business:** Representative office
**Issued Capital:** £1,500
**Managing Director:** D J Strike
**US SIC:** 7399 **UK SIC:** 83954

| | 31-07-13 | 31-07-12 | 31-07-11 |
|---|---|---|---|
| TA | 64,030 | 118,030 | 226,577 |
| NW | 32,809 | 86,809 | 141,862 |
| WC | 32,809 | 86,809 | 223,697 |

DUNS 29-380-8069
## Quay Marinas Ltd
(**Subsidiary of:** Quay Marinas Holdings Ltd)
Newfoundland Way, Bristol, Avon BS20 7DF
**Tel:** 01275841941 **Fax:** 01275-841189
**Web:** www.quaymarinas.com
**Reg No:** 1094247 **VAT No:** 827079411
**Estd:** 1973 Private Limited Company
**Line of Business:** Marinas
**Issued Capital:** £60,000
**Directors:** A T Yates, P K Rye, S N Haigh
**Co. Secretary:** Paul Rye
**Responsibilities**
**Senior:** Keith Berry *(Marina Manager)*
**Branches:** Quay Marinas Ltd, The Docks, Bristol, Avon BS20 7DF
**US SIC:** 7999, 6552
**UK SIC:** 97913, 85000
**Auditors:** Baker Tilly
**Bankers:** Lloyds TSB Bank plc (30-00-01)

| | 31-03-14 | 31-03-13 | 31-03-12 |
|---|---|---|---|
| TO | 5,912,174 | 5,705,980 | 6,087,628 |
| P/L | 337,665 | 256,070 | 327,699 |
| NW | 5,027,120 | 4,725,988 | 4,533,580 |
| WC | (350,216) | (524,066) | (283,525) |
| Emp. | 69 | 68 | 71 |

DUNS 34-588-5057 Imp-Exp
## Quay Minerals Ltd
(**Subsidiary of:** Luossavaara-Kiirunavaara Ab)
Flixborough Industrial Estate, Scunthorpe, South Humberside DN15 8SG
**Tel:** 01724277411 **Fax:** 01724-866405
**Web:** http://lkabminerals.com
**Reg No:** 2732626 **VAT No:** 419398810
**Estd:** 1985 Private Limited Company
**Line of Business:** Manufacture of refractory ceramic products

**Export Markets:** Europe, Scandinavia
**Trading Style:** Lkab Minerals Ltd
**Issued Capital:** £904,000
**Director:** M A Franey
**Co. Secretary:** Ms Jane Potts
**US SIC:** 3269 **UK SIC:** 24894
**Bankers:** HSBC Bank plc (40-05-30)

| | 31-12-13 | 31-12-12 | 31-12-11 |
|---|---|---|---|
| TA | 1,000,000 | 1,000,000 | 1,000,000 |
| P/L | N/A | 138,748 | N/A |
| NW | 1,000,000 | 1,000,000 | 1,000,000 |
| Emp. | N/A | 1 | N/A |

DUNS 21-031-9498
## The Quays Swimming & Diving Complex
27 Harbour Parade, Southampton, Hampshire SO15 1BA
**Tel:** 02380720900
**Web:** www.activenation.org.uk
**Proprietorship**
**Line of Business:** Leisure centres
**Proprietor:** C Swift
**Responsibilities**
**Senior:** Bob Paton *(President)*, Matt Wale *(Facility Manager)*
**US SIC:** 7999 **UK SIC:** 97913
**Employees:** 100

DUNS 21-778-4141
## Quayside Leisure Centre
Rope Walk, Kingsbridge, Devon TQ7 1HH
**Tel:** 01548857100
**Web:** www.toneleisure.com
**Estd:** 1985 Proprietorship
**Line of Business:** Other sporting activities not elsewhere classified
**Proprietor:** M Green
**US SIC:** 7999 **UK SIC:** 97913
**Employees:** 70

DUNS 23-693-3151
## Quayside Sportswear Ltd
(**Subsidiary of:** Quayside 2012 Ltd)
Unit 9 Wheel Forge Way, Trafford Park, Manchester M17 1EH
**Tel:** 01618720677
**Web:** www.quaysidegroup.com
**Reg No:** 3688185 **Estd:** 1995 Private Limited Company
**Line of Business:** Manufacture of sports goods
**Issued Capital:** £200
**Director:** M D Conway
**Responsibilities**
**Senior:** Debra Hutchings *(Manager)*
**US SIC:** 3949 **UK SIC:** 49420
**Auditors:** Brody, Lee, Kershaw & Co.

| | 31-12-13 | 31-12-12 | 31-12-11 |
|---|---|---|---|
| TA | 361 | 361 | 361 |
| NW | 361 | 361 | 361 |

DUNS 29-295-8923 **Exp**
## Qube Global Software Ltd
(**Subsidiary of:** E C S (Holdings) Ltd)
9 King Street, London EC2V 8EA
**Tel:** 02077263200 **Fax:** 020-7977-9301
**Web:** www.qubeglobal.com
**Reg No:** 1656218 **Estd:** 1982 Private Limited Company
**Line of Business:** Other software consultancy and supply
**Export Markets:** E U
**Trading Style:** Qube Global Software
**Issued Capital:** £100
**Directors:** J Cuppello, B S Lerner, C Lerner
**Co. Secretary:** David Makins
**Responsibilities**
**Senior:** Daniel Cooke *(IT Manager)*, Seronne Romian *(Health & Safety Officer)*
**Marketing:** Mike Bennett *(Developmental Director)*, James Lavery *(Head of Marketing)*
**Sales:** Jacqui Adams *(Commercial and HR Manager)*
**Admin:** Seronne Romian *(Health & Safety Officer)*
**IT:** Daniel Cooke *(IT Manager)*
**HR:** Jacqui Adams *(Commercial and HR Manager)*
**Health & Safety:** Seronne Romian *(Health & Safety Officer)*
**Facilities:** Seronne Romian *(Health & Safety Officer)*
**Operations:** Jane Addey *(Operations Director)*
**Branches:** Qube Global Software Ltd, Westgate House, 25 Westgate, Sleaford, Lincolnshire NG34 7RJ
**US SIC:** 7379 **UK SIC:** 83940
**Auditors:** Wilder Coe

| | 28-02-14 | 28-02-13 | 29-02-12 |
|---|---|---|---|
| TO | 16,577,767 | 15,129,207 | 14,299,241 |
| P/L | 3,842,158 | 3,985,336 | 3,339,567 |
| NW | 12,847,766 | 11,582,933 | 10,175,952 |
| WC | 7,899,755 | 7,054,520 | 9,739,116 |
| Emp. | 171 | 156 | 155 |

DUNS 57-829-0470
## Qube Qualifications & Development Ltd
(**Subsidiary of:** Consumer Marketing Systems & Services Ltd)
7 Milton Park, Milton, Abingdon, Oxfordshire OX14 4RR
**Fax:** 01491824233
**Web:** www.qube-learning.co.uk
**Reg No:** 2887289 **Estd:** 2011 Private Limited Company
**Line of Business:** Training services
**Trading Style:** Qube Learning
**Issued Capital:** £186,875
**Directors:** E J Williams, G S Whichello
**Co. Secretary:**
Consumer Marketing Systems And S
**Responsibilities**
**Sales:** Sam Zalcman *(Commercial Director)*
**Branches:** Qube Qualifications & Development Ltd, Fillebrook Ho, 24 Fillebrook Ave, Enfield, Middlesex EN1 3BB
**US SIC:** 8299 **UK SIC:** 93300
**Auditors:** Oury Clark

| | 31-07-13 | 31-07-12 | 31-07-11 |
|---|---|---|---|
| TO | 7,274,170 | 7,070,636 | N/A |
| P/L | 216,107 | 495,065 | N/A |
| NW | 2,121,571 | 1,954,015 | 1,583,801 |
| WC | 2,121,571 | 2,018,082 | 1,583,801 |
| Emp. | 106 | 92 | N/A |

DUNS 52-021-0147
## Queen Alexandra College
Court Oak Road, Birmingham, West Midlands B17 9AB
**Tel:** 0121-428-5050 **Fax:** 0121-428-5048
**Web:** www.qac.ac.uk
**Reg No:** 3387540 **Estd:** 1929 Private Limited Company
**Line of Business:** Charity shops
**Directors:** I W Richards, Dr D C Mitchell, D J Corney, Professor J E Penny, C J Bradshaw, M Wedderburn, Dr A Green, Miss R K Ginday
**Co. Secretary:** Mrs Alison Lydon
**Responsibilities**
**Senior:** Catherine Cadbury *(Director)*, Heather Darby *(Executive)*, Andy Dennehy *(Director of Residential Servic)*, Sherv Garcha *(Head of DWP Programmes)*, Alan Hamer *(Director of Supported and Comm)*, David Heeley *(Director)*, John Hilbourne *(Governor)*, William Houle *(Director)*, Stephen Mccall *(Governor)*, Amanda Mcgeever *(Director)*, M Nickless *(Resource Manager)*
**Sales:** Sarah Adderley *(External Relations Manager)*
**IT:** M Nickless *(Resource Manager)*
**HR:** Angela Litchfield *(Human Resources Manager)*, Vicky Waldron *(Director of HR & Estates)*
**Health & Safety:** I Issott *(Vice Principal)*, Angela Litchfield *(Human Resources Manager)*
**Purchasing:** I Issott *(Vice Principal)*
**US SIC:** 8321, 8249
**UK SIC:** 96111, 93300
**Auditors:** Felton & Co

| | 31-08-13 | 31-08-12 | 31-08-11 |
|---|---|---|---|
| TO | 10,517,214 | 8,007,653 | 7,724,729 |
| P/L | 1,601,554 | 114,599 | 464,368 |
| NW | 9,699,071 | 7,922,097 | 7,773,372 |
| WC | 24,813 | 5,687 | 1,602,196 |
| Emp. | 212 | 200 | 174 |

DUNS 49-740-7122
## Queen Alexandra Cottage Homes
557 Seaside, Eastbourne, East Sussex BN23 6NE
**Tel:** 01323739689
**Web:** www.qach.co.uk
**Estd:** 1906
**Line of Business:** Nursing homes
**Proprietor:** I Stuart
**US SIC:** 8051 **UK SIC:** 95100
**Employees:** 60

DUNS 23-651-3631
## The Queen Alexandra Hospital Home
Gifford House, Worthing, West Sussex BN11 4LJ
**Tel:** 01903213458 **Fax:** 01903219151
**Web:** www.qahh.org.uk
**Reg No:** 3646570 **Estd:** 1998 Private Company Limited By Guarantee
**Line of Business:** Nursing homes
**Directors:** Mrs J N Annis, C W Pile, Commander D Habershon, M A Walker, J D Williams, C P Field, G R Jordan, Mrs R Taylor
**Co. Secretary:** David Hood
**Responsibilities**
**Senior:** Ian Eady *(Chairman of the Board)*, Selina Geddes *(Manager)*, John Paxman *(CEO)*, Richard Thornely *(Manager)*, Valerie Walker *(Head of Nursing)*
**Finance:** Jane Pescott *(Head of Fundraising)*
**Branches:** The Queen Alexandra Hospital Home, 19 Rowlands Rd, Worthing, West Sussex BN11 3JJ
**US SIC:** 8051, 6732
**UK SIC:** 95100, 83100
**Auditors:** Carpenter Box LLP
**Bankers:** Barclays Bank Plc (20-98-74)

| | 31-12-13 | 31-12-12 | 31-12-11 |
|---|---|---|---|
| TO | 4,514,355 | 3,847,346 | 4,080,957 |
| P/L | 18,301 | (587,816) | (171,472) |
| NW | 9,685,932 | 9,433,589 | 9,843,992 |
| WC | 550,629 | 37,917 | 110,740 |
| Emp. | 127 | 124 | 118 |

DUNS 21-879-9159
## Queen Alexandra Sixth Form College
Hawkeys Lane, North Shields, Tyne and Wear NE29 9BZ
**Tel:** 01912295123
**Web:** www.queenalex.co.uk
**Estd:** 1974
**Line of Business:** Further education schools and colleges
**Responsibilities**
**Senior:** Denise Bolton *(Head Teacher)*, Janette Donjon *(Manager)*
**US SIC:** 8221 **UK SIC:** 93100
**Employees:** 100

DUNS 23-261-5141
## Queen Annes School
6 Henley Road, Caversham, Reading, Berkshire RG4 6DX
**Tel:** 01189187300
**Web:** www.qas.org.uk
**Estd:** 2002 Proprietorship
**Line of Business:** Schools (independent)
**Proprietor:** Mrs J Harrington
**Responsibilities**
**Marketing:** Elizabeth Geake *(Marketing Manager)*, Aileen Kane *(Marketing Manager)*
**Sales:** Jane Gallie *(Registrar)*
**IT:** Areti Bizior *(IT Coordinator)*, Anthony Lennard *(IT Coordinator)*
**HR:** Judith Tremayne *(Human Resources Manager)*
**Operations:** Jane Gallie *(Registrar)*
**US SIC:** 8211 **UK SIC:** 93200
**Employees:** 79

DUNS 21-597-5532
## Queen Boudica Primary School
Cowper Crescent, Colchester, Essex CO4 5XT
**Web:** www.qbps.essex.sch.uk
**Estd:** 2011 Proprietorship
**Line of Business:** Schools (local authority)
**Proprietor:** C Duncan
**US SIC:** 8211 **UK SIC:** 93200
**Employees:** 50

DUNS 22-812-1109
## Queen Elizabeth Grammar School
154 Northgate, Wakefield, West Yorkshire WF1 3QX
**Tel:** 01924-373943
**Web:** www.wgsf.org.uk
**Estd:** 1901
**Line of Business:** Schools (independent)
**Trading Style:** Queen Elizabeth Grammar School, Q E G S
**Directors:** R P Mardling, R C Hemsley, M M Bisset
**Responsibilities**
**Senior:** Louise Gray *(Principal)*, Douglas Metcalfe *(Manager)*, Jim Palin *(Senior IT Executive)*, E Settle *(Chairman)*, Patricia Stark *(Manager)*, Dennis Wheatley *(Manager)*
**IT:** Anthony Ferguson *(Computer Manager)*, Jim Palin *(Senior IT Executive)*
**HR:** Anette Casey *(Human Resources Manager)*
**Facilities:** David Butterfield *(Estates Manager)*
**Branches:** Queen Elizabeth Grammar School, West Park Road, Blackburn, Lancashire BB2 6DF
**US SIC:** 8211 **UK SIC:** 93200
**Bankers:** Lloyds TSB Bank plc (30-99-01)
**Employees:** 200

DUNS 21-775-7613
## Queen Elizabeth High School
Llansteffan Road, Carmarthen, Dyfed SA31 3NL
**Tel:** 01267245300
**Web:** www.qehs.carms.sch.uk
**Estd:** 2005 Proprietorship
**Line of Business:** Schools (local authority)
**Proprietor:** T Daye
**Responsibilities**
**Senior:** Pete Spencer *(Head Teacher)*
**US SIC:** 8211 **UK SIC:** 93200
**Employees:** 200

DUNS 54-864-4368
## The Queen Elizabeth Hospital King's Lynn Nhs Foundation Trust
Gayton Road, King's Lynn, Norfolk PE30 4ET
**Tel:** 01553-613-613
**Web:** www.redcross.org.uk
**Estd:** 2013
**Line of Business:** Charities and charitable organisations
**Issued Capital:** £1
**Principals:** K Gordon *(Chairman)*, N Vaughan, Ms J Robinson, S Green, S Haney, N Harrison, J Hillier, S Haney
**Responsibilities**
**Senior:** Patrisa Wright *(CEO)*
**Finance:** David Stonehouse *(Finance Director)*
**Sales:** Barbara Cummings *(Director of Planning & Perform)*
**Operations:** Dorothy Hosein *(Chief Operating Officer)*
**Branches:** The Queen Elizabeth Hospital King's Lynn Nhs Foundation Trust, Queen Elizabeth Hospital, Gayton Road, King's Lynn, Norfolk PE30 4ET
**US SIC:** 8062 **UK SIC:** 95100
**Auditors:** KPMG LLP

| | 31-03-14 | 31-03-13 | 31-03-12 |
|---|---|---|---|
| TO | 153,061,000 | 153,620,000 | 152,382,000 |
| P/L | (12,850,000) | (865,000) | 1,050,000 |
| NW | 66,421,000 | 69,922,000 | 68,256,000 |
| WC | (8,128,000) | (1,240,000) | 2,083,000 |
| Emp. | 2,680 | 2,659 | 2,721 |

DUNS 22-845-2843 **Imp**
## Queen Elizabeth Ii Conference Centre
The Conference Centre, Broad Sanctuary, London SW1P 3EE
**Tel:** 02072225000 **Fax:** 02077984200
**Web:** www.qeiicc.co.uk
**Estd:** 1989 Incorporate By Act Of Parliament
**Line of Business:** Letting of conference and exhibition centres
**Trading Style:** The Queen Elisbeth the 2nd Conference Centre
**Director:** M Buck
**Responsibilities**
**Senior:** Sue Etherington *(Commercial Director)*
**Finance:** Becky Hoffman *(Revenue and Commercial Manager)*
**Marketing:** Sue Etherington *(Commercial Director)*
**Sales:** Jamie Ades *(Account Manager)*, Tony Brinsden *(Account Manager)*, Sue Etherington *(Commercial Director)*, Becky Hoffman *(Revenue and Commercial Manager)*
**IT:** Ravi Choudhry *(Senior ICT Engineer)*, Alan Suppaya *(ICT Manager)*
**US SIC:** 7399, 6519
**UK SIC:** 83954, 85000
**Employees:** 52

DUNS 21-775-0054
## Queen Elizabeth Ii Silver Jubilee School
Comptons Lane, Horsham, West Sussex RH13 5NW
**Tel:** 01403266215
**Web:** www.queenelizabeth2.w-sussex.sch.uk
**Estd:** 1977 Proprietorship
**Line of Business:** Schools (special)
**Proprietor:** Mrs L Dyer
**US SIC:** 8299 **UK SIC:** 93300
**Employees:** 70

DUNS 23-082-9025
## Queen Elizabeth School
Witherley Road, Atherstone, Warwickshire CV9 1LZ
**Tel:** 01827-712477
**Web:** www.queenelizabeth.warwickshire.sch.uk
**Estd:** 1958
**Line of Business:** Schools (local authority)
**Director:** M H Gillard
**Responsibilities**
**Senior:** Tony Wilmott *(Principal)*
**US SIC:** 8211 **UK SIC:** 93200
**Employees:** 90

**DUNS 21-698-3191**
## Queen Elizabeth School Kirkby Lonsdale
Kirkby Lonsdale Road, Carnforth, Lancashire LA6 2NZ
**Tel:** 01524271275
**Web:** www.queenelizabeth.cumbria.sch.uk
**Reg No:** 7438425 **Estd:** 1992 Private Company Limited By Guarantee
**Line of Business:** General secondary education
**Directors:** Mrs D K Harkness, Ms E H Shuttleworth, S A Nelson, Mrs M M Cunningham, M Day, C Clarke, S D Holmes, Dr R J Shepherd
**Co. Secretary:** Ms Angela Johnson
**Responsibilities**
**Senior:** Roger Bingham (Director), Stephen Dent (Director), Thomas Felix (Director), Philip Howden (Director), Walter Lawrenson (Director), Fenner Pearson (Director), Tyrone Power (Director), Daniel Tomlinson (Director)
**US SIC:** 8211 **UK SIC:** 93200

|     | 31-08-14 | 31-08-13 | 31-08-12 |
|-----|----------|----------|----------|
| TO | 8,280,470 | 9,358,677 | 8,977,805 |
| P/L | (612,963) | (223,190) | 486,638 |
| NW | 12,833,373 | 13,886,070 | 14,056,456 |
| WC | 1,380,192 | 1,561,041 | 1,740,803 |
| Emp. | 164 | 166 | 170 |

**DUNS 23-086-2232**
## Queen Elizabeth Sixth Form College
Vane Terrace, Darlington, County Durham DL3 7AU
**Tel:** 01325-461315
**Web:** www.qeliz.ac.uk
**Estd:** 2002
**Line of Business:** Post-graduate level higher education
**Director:** D Heaton
**Responsibilities**
**Senior:** Tim Fisher (Vice Principal)
**US SIC:** 8221 **UK SIC:** 93100
**Employees:** 200

**DUNS 22-523-2453**
## Queen Elizabeth's Foundation for Disabled People
Leatherhead Court, Woodlands Road, Leatherhead, Surrey KT22 0BN
**Web:** www.qef.org.uk
**Reg No:** 0892013 **VAT No:** 210009341
**Estd:** 1935 Private Company Limited By Guarantee
**Line of Business:** Activities of private training providers
**Trading Style:** Q E F Q E F Independent Living Services, Q E F Mobility Services, Q E F Neuro Rehabilitation Services, Q E F Vocational Services
**Directors:** Ms E E Dunweber, E J Denning, J G Wates, R H Douglas, M Dent, Ms L Scotcher, P D Gordon, F Myers
**Co. Secretary:** Gary Allcott
**Responsibilities**
**Senior:** Garry Billing (Director of Vocational Service), Edward Gates (Director), Frances Glanusk (Director), Bevil Granville (Director), David Hypher (Director), Charles Style (Director), Maxine Taylor (Director)
**Marketing:** Jan Podsiadly (Head of Communications & Marke)
**Purchasing:** Ashley Fifield (Purchasing Manager)
**Branches:** Queen Elizabeth's Foundation For Disabled People, Queen Elizabeth Mobility Services, 1 Metcalfe Avenue, Carshalton, Surrey SM5 4AW
**US SIC:** 8299 **UK SIC:** 93300
**Auditors:** PricewaterhouseCoopers LLP
**Bankers:** National Westminster Bank Plc (56-00-33)

|     | 31-03-14 | 31-03-13 | 31-03-12 |
|-----|----------|----------|----------|
| TO | 12,592,000 | 11,546,000 | 12,058,000 |
| P/L | (391,000) | (406,000) | 4,340,000 |
| NW | (1,212,000) | (7,253,000) | (3,387,000) |
| WC | 7,383,000 | 8,279,000 | 8,131,000 |
| Emp. | 251 | 244 | 239 |

**DUNS 23-083-1658**
## Queen Elizabeth's Grammar School
Station Road, Alford, Lincolnshire LN13 9HY
**Tel:** 01507-462403
**Web:** www.qegs.co.uk
**Estd:** 2010
**Line of Business:** General secondary education
**Director:** Miss A Francis
**US SIC:** 8211 **UK SIC:** 93200
**Employees:** 85

**DUNS 21-853-5423**
## Queen Elizabeth's Grammar School Horncastle
Queen Elizabeth's Grammar School, West Street, Horncastle, Lincolnshire LN9 5AD
**Tel:** 01507522465
**Reg No:** 8175402 **Estd:** 1913 Private Company Limited By Guarantee
**Line of Business:** General secondary education
**Directors:** J J Finley, J S Pearson, Ms H Payne, C J Waters, A Hurrell, A Bourn, M Roberts, M J Cherry
**Responsibilities**
**Senior:** Paul Brewster (Director), Mandy Elmer (Director), Liana Fox (Director), Jenny Humphreys (Director), Jason Kwee (Director), Gurdip Samra (Director), Kirsty Spence (Director), Kay Wingate (Director)
**US SIC:** 8211 **UK SIC:** 93200
**Auditors:** Streets Audit LLP
**Bankers:** Lloyds TSB Bank plc (30-94-39)

|     | 31-08-14 | 31-08-13 |
|-----|----------|----------|
| TO | 5,123,919 | 15,903,680 |
| P/L | 130,143 | 10,736,481 |
| NW | 10,709,112 | 10,777,197 |
| WC | 983,936 | 820,032 |
| Emp. | 100 | 102 |

**DUNS 49-723-3106**
## Queen Elizabeth's Hospital
Berkeley Place, Bristol, Avon BS8 1JX
**Tel:** 01179303040
**Web:** www.qehbristol.co.uk
**Estd:** 2004
**Line of Business:** Schools (independent)
**Trading Style:** Queen Elizabeth's Hospital School
**Director:** S Holliday
**Responsibilities**
**Senior:** Gerald Bird (Manager), Sallie Blanks (Manager), Jonathan Eyles (Manager), Gillian Rowcliffe (Manager), Charles Russell-Smith (Manager), Merle Shutt (Manager), Nicholas Tyrrell (Manager)
**Marketing:** John Colley (Development Manager)
**Branches:** Queen Elizabeth's Hospital, Queen Elizabeth Hospital, Lodge, Bristol, Avon BS8 1DN
**US SIC:** 8211 **UK SIC:** 93200
**Employees:** 136

**DUNS 23-635-7778**
## Queen Elizabeth's School
Hillbutts, Hillbutts, Wimborne, Dorset BH21 4DT
**Tel:** 01202-885233
**Web:** www.qe.dorset.sch.uk
**Estd:** 2012
**Line of Business:** Schools (local authority)
**Directors:** S Tong, C Buckle
**Responsibilities**
**Senior:** Martin Mcleman (Head Teacher), Andy Puttock (Head Teacher), A Puttock (Head Teacher)
**US SIC:** 8211 **UK SIC:** 93200
**Bankers:** National Westminster Bank Plc (60-24-43)
**Employees:** 180

**DUNS 21-685-6249**
## Queen Elizabeth's School Barnet
Queens Road, Barnet, Hertfordshire EN5 4DQ
**Tel:** 02084414646
**Web:** www.nd2.co.uk
**Reg No:** 7351253 **Estd:** 2010 Private Company Limited By Guarantee
**Line of Business:** Schools (foundation)
**Directors:** K R Cooper, A N Gaskell, B R Martin
**Co. Secretary:** Ms Emine Aghdiran
**US SIC:** 8211 **UK SIC:** 93200
**Bankers:** National Westminster Bank Plc (51-61-34)

|     | 31-08-14 | 31-08-13 | 31-08-12 |
|-----|----------|----------|----------|
| TO | 9,827,000 | 8,288,000 | 7,951,000 |
| P/L | 1,618,000 | 584,000 | 426,000 |
| NW | 23,373,000 | 22,031,000 | 21,522,000 |
| WC | 1,110,000 | 1,013,000 | 1,096,000 |
| Emp. | 122 | 125 | 127 |

**DUNS 76-560-0127**
## Queen Ethelburga's College Ltd
(Subsidiary of: Foxlow Ltd)
Thorpe Underwood Estate, Thorpe Underwood, York, North Yorkshire YO26 9SS
**Tel:** 01423333300 **Fax:** 08707423310
**Web:** www.qe.org
**Reg No:** 2573843 **Estd:** 1912 Private Limited Company
**Line of Business:** General secondary education
**Issued Capital:** £100

**Principals:** B R Martin (Managing), Mrs E Martin, F D Martin, C J Hall, Miss A K Martin
**Co. Secretary:** Christopher Hall
**Responsibilities**
**Senior:** Steven Jandrell (Head Teacher)
**IT:** David Millington (Internet Manager), Mark Nichols (IT assistant)
**US SIC:** 8211 **UK SIC:** 93200
**Auditors:** Watson Wood & Buckle
**Bankers:** Lloyds TSB Bank plc (77-71-01)

|     | 31-08-13 | 31-08-12 | 31-08-11 |
|-----|----------|----------|----------|
| TO | 11,514,693 | 9,716,452 | 22,832,107 |
| P/L | 251,774 | 741,279 | 1,445,272 |
| NW | 532,216 | 481,124 | 373,046 |
| WC | (2,552,079) | (2,072,897) | (5,801,462) |
| Emp. | 152 | 118 | 314 |

**DUNS 23-932-8248**
## Queen Hotel
City Road, Chester, Cheshire CH1 3AH
**Tel:** 01244-305000
**Web:** www.bestwestern.co.uk
**Estd:** 2009 Partnership
**Line of Business:** Hotels
**Trading Style:** Best Western Premier Queen Hotel
**Partners:** J Britton, S Williams, Ms S Preston
**Responsibilities**
**Marketing:** Caroline Voce (Marketing Manager)
**Sales:** Caroline Botd (Senior Sales Executive), Caroline Voce (Marketing Manager)
**US SIC:** 7011 **UK SIC:** 66500
**Employees:** 80

**DUNS 21-702-7860**
## The Queen Katherine School Multi Academy Trust
Appleby Road, Kendal, Cumbria LA9 6PJ
**Tel:** 01539743900
**Web:** www.queenkatherine.org
**Reg No:** 7472799 **Estd:** 2010 Private Company Limited By Guarantee
**Line of Business:** Schools (foundation)
**Directors:** Mrs H T Dixon, R J Moore, P C Townley, G P Roscoe, S J Parkman, Mrs E A Curl, J D Richardson, Ms E A Moffatt
**Co. Secretary:** Michael Walby
**US SIC:** 8211 **UK SIC:** 93200
**Bankers:** Yorkshire Bank Plc (05-05-40)

|     | 31-08-14 | 31-08-13 | 31-08-12 |
|-----|----------|----------|----------|
| TO | 8,107,886 | 10,661,019 | 8,998,201 |
| P/L | (820,606) | 1,647,094 | 1,203,970 |
| NW | 8,622,139 | 9,787,745 | 8,056,651 |
| WC | 1,190,813 | 1,596,224 | 1,331,306 |
| Emp. | 155 | 158 | 152 |

**DUNS 28-997-7761**    **Imp**
## Queen Margaret University Edinburgh
Queen Margaret University Drive, Musselburgh, Midlothian EH21 6UU
**Tel:** 01314740000 **Fax:** 0131-317-3902
**Web:** www.qmu.ac.uk
**Reg No:** 0007335SC **Estd:** 2002 Private Company Limited By Guarantee
**Line of Business:** First-degree level higher education
**Directors:** Ms M O'Connor, R H Rae, Ms L Mcpherson, Dr L Irvine, Mrs S Williams, J B Leggat, Professor G D Caie, C W Cathcart
**Co. Secretary:** Mrs Irene Hynd
**Responsibilities**
**Senior:** Keir Bloomer (Director), Fergus Boden (Director), James Bradshaw (Director), Avril Brown (Senior Manager), Robert Cormack (Director), Johnathan Elmer (Director), Anthony Falconer (Director), Alan Gilloran (Director), Simon Girdler (General Manager), Anna Gregor (Director), Trevor Laffin (Tourism, Hospitality and Event), Jacqueline Macdonald (Director), Miller Mclean (Director), Judith Sischy (Director)
**Finance:** Alasdair Black (Head of Finance), Fiona Chisholm (Finance Officer), Malcolm Cutt (Financial Controller), Michelle Donaldson (Systems Accountant), Jackie Harris (Finance Officer), Karen Inglis (Finance Office Manager), Linda Murray (Finance Officer), Carol-Anne Wightman (Assistant Accountant)
**Marketing:** Kerry Browne (Digital Marketing Manager), Jacquie L'Etang (Professor of Public Relations), Joanna Murray (Marketing Officer), Jon Perkins (Press and PR officer), Magda Pieczka (Reader Public Relations), Miranda Stevens-Clay (Marketing Assistant)
**Admin:** Sheila Adamson (Registry Officer, Quality Enha), Stacey Barnes (Administrator), Virag Hamori (Administrator), Hester Lean (Administrator), Paula Mcclellan (Administrator), Morag Thomson (Administrator)
**IT:** Dave Graham (IT Manager), Evelyn Marshall (MIS Manager), Mark Percival (Programme Leader), Christine Raffaelli (Programme Leader)

**HR:** Fiona Boyle (HR Executive), Beth Campbell (HR Partner), Hannah Carruthers (HR Partner), Dee Denholm (Head of Human Resources), Angela Gentle (HR Partner), Kate Hunter (Instructor)
**Facilities:** Steve Watson (Maintenance Manager)
**Operations:** Sheila Adamson (Registry Officer, Quality Enha), Stuart Burnside (Leisure Services Attendant), Malcolm Cutt (Financial Controller), Sarah Macdonald (Leisure Services Manager), Dawn Martin (Registrar (Quality Enhancement)
**Purchasing:** Malcolm Cutt (Financial Controller)
**Engineering:** Phil Bowbanks (Technician), Ricky McKenzie (Master Carpenter)
**US SIC:** 8221 **UK SIC:** 93100
**Auditors:** KPMG LLP

|     | 31-07-13 | 31-07-12 | 31-07-11 |
|-----|----------|----------|----------|
| TO | 34,843,000 | 34,346,000 | 34,041,000 |
| P/L | 1,472,000 | 1,536,000 | (159,000) |
| NW | 40,848,000 | 27,905,000 | 30,173,000 |
| WC | (38,883,000) | (42,040,000) | (45,712,000) |
| Emp. | 397 | 406 | 411 |

**DUNS 29-686-9654**
## Queen Margaret's School York Ltd
Escrick Park, York, North Yorkshire YO19 6EU
**Tel:** 01904720261
**Web:** www.queenmargarets.org.uk
**Reg No:** 2010493 **Estd:** 1986 Private Company Limited By Guarantee
**Line of Business:** Schools (independent)
**Directors:** Mrs C M Gooder, T S Kettlewell, Mrs E M Carnegie-Brown, N F Corner, F A Scott, N T Lambert, Professor D Parker, Ms E C Pearson
**Responsibilities**
**Senior:** David Maddan (Director), Michael Oakley (Director), Katherine Preston (Director), Rachael Rutland (Director), Paul Silverwood (Head Teacher)
**US SIC:** 8211 **UK SIC:** 93200
**Auditors:** PricewaterhouseCoopers
**Bankers:** Yorkshire Bank Plc (05-09-94)

|     | 31-08-14 | 31-08-13 | 31-08-12 |
|-----|----------|----------|----------|
| TO | 9,279,000 | 8,378,000 | 7,618,000 |
| P/L | 421,000 | 5,000 | (488,000) |
| NW | 5,775,000 | 5,354,000 | 5,349,000 |
| WC | (2,880,000) | (3,586,000) | (3,485,000) |
| Emp. | 161 | 154 | 145 |

**DUNS 23-182-2839**
## Queen Mary University of London
Mile End Road, London E1 4NS
**Tel:** 02078825555 **Fax:** 02089806533
**Web:** www.qmul.ac.uk
**Reg No:** 0000710RC **VAT No:** 248837911
**Estd:** 2011 Incorporate By Act Of Parliament
**Line of Business:** University
**Director:** S Gaskell
**Responsibilities**
**Senior:** Andrew Keeble (Financial Director), Jeremy Kilburn (Vice-Principal & Executive Dea)
**Finance:** Andrew Keeble (Financial Director)
**Branches:** Queen Mary University of London, Queen Mary University of London, 327 Mile End Road, London E1 4NS
**US SIC:** 8221 **UK SIC:** 93100
**Auditors:** KPMG LLP
**Employees:** 6,000
**Turnover:** £174,744,000

**DUNS 21-842-6202**
## Queen Mary University of London Students' Union
Bookshop, 329 Mile End Road, London E1 4NT
**Tel:** 02078828030
**Web:** www.qmsu.org
**Reg No:** 8092471 **Estd:** 2012 Private Company Limited By Guarantee
**Line of Business:** Charities and charitable organisations
**Directors:** S M Rowles, A Jawad, Ms K J Brindley-Macro, F V Mcclure, Ms C Mantzalos, Ms M Asim, O M Osilaja, E Moses
**Co. Secretary:** Mrs Prudence Slater
**Responsibilities**
**Senior:** Charlotte Evans (Director), Benjamin Gray (Director), Mika Schr der (Director), Mike Wojcik (Chief Executive Officer)
**Admin:** Tanya Choudhury (Administration Manager)
**US SIC:** 8699 **UK SIC:** 96902

|     | 31-07-13 |
|-----|----------|
| TO | 6,252,252 |
| P/L | 576,406 |
| NW | 583,498 |
| WC | (121,229) |
| Emp. | 269 |

DUNS 21-771-3834
## Queen Mary's
7 Hollington Park Road, St Leonards-On-Sea, East Sussex TN38 0SE
**Tel:** 01424728800
**Web:** www.galleoncare.com
**Estd:** 2006 Proprietorship
**Line of Business:** Nursing homes
**Proprietor:** Ms A Crousse
**Responsibilities**
**Senior:** Tara Cross (Home Manager)
**US SIC:** 8051 **UK SIC:** 95100
**Employees:** 100

DUNS 23-635-6812
## Queen Mary's College
Cliddesden Road, Basingstoke, Hampshire RG21 3HF
**Tel:** 01256417500
**Web:** www.qmc.ac.uk
**Estd:** 1972
**Line of Business:** Further education schools and colleges
**Director:** S Sheedy
**Responsibilities**
**Senior:** Ali Foss (Staff Development Director)
**Finance:** Sue Eele (Financial Controller)
**Marketing:** B Cornish (Marketing Manager), Carolyn Kirby (Marketing Manager), Erivan White (Director of Schools abd Admiss)
**HR:** Ali Foss (Staff Development Director)
**Facilities:** Nigel Westcombe (Premises Coordinator)
**Branches:** Queen Mary's College, Cliddesden Road, Basingstoke, Hampshire RG21 3HF
**US SIC:** 7999 **UK SIC:** 97913
**Bankers:** Lloyds TSB Bank plc (30-90-53)
**Employees:** 200

DUNS 21-150-9414
## Queen Mary's Grammar School
Sutton Road, Walsall, West Midlands WS1 2PG
**Tel:** 01922-720696
**Web:** www.qmgs.walsall.sch.uk
**Estd:** 1995
**Line of Business:** General secondary education
**Director:** S Holtam
**Responsibilities**
**Senior:** Timothy Swain (Head Teacher)
**US SIC:** 8211 **UK SIC:** 93200
**Employees:** 85

DUNS 23-083-1641
## Queen Mary's High School
Upper Forster Street, Walsall, West Midlands WS4 2AE
**Tel:** 01922-721013
**Web:** www.qmhs.org.uk
**Estd:** 1997
**Line of Business:** Schools (foundation)
**Director:** Mrs A Denny
**US SIC:** 8211 **UK SIC:** 93200
**Employees:** 80

DUNS 21-724-0338
## Queen Mary's High School (Walsall)
26 Birmingham Road, Walsall, West Midlands WS1 2LZ
**Tel:** 01922720027
**Web:** www.qmhs.org.uk
**Reg No:** 7611345 **Estd:** 2011 Private Company Limited By Guarantee
**Line of Business:** General secondary education
**Directors:** Mrs S J Jones, Miss R E Hearsey, Mrs R A Martin, Mrs G Binder, K Whitehead, A E Bruton, V M Fairbank, Mrs L K Daniels
**Co. Secretary:** Graham Underwood
**Responsibilities**
**Senior:** Abigail Gracie (Director), Timothy Normanton (Director)
**US SIC:** 8211 **UK SIC:** 93200
**Bankers:** Lloyds TSB Bank plc (30-00-00)

| | 31-08-14 | 31-08-13 | 31-08-12 |
|---|---|---|---|
| TO | 4,071,838 | 4,552,503 | 9,572,087 |
| P/L | (138,569) | (118,536) | 4,043,225 |
| NW | 3,859,120 | 3,808,689 | 3,911,225 |
| WC | 355,353 | 390,871 | 378,508 |
| Emp. | 73 | 77 | 98 |

DUNS 21-880-1380
## Queen Mother Hospital for Small Animals
Hawkshead Lane, North Mymms, Hatfield, Hertfordshire AL9 7TA
**Tel:** 01707666333
**Web:** www.rvc.ac.uk
**Estd:** 2012
**Line of Business:** Veterinary activities

**Responsibilities**
**Senior:** Graham Milligan (Manager)
**US SIC:** 0741 **UK SIC:** 95601
**Employees:** 1,000

DUNS 28-997-8561
## Queen of the South Football Club Ltd
76-94 Terregles Street, Dumfries, Dumfriesshire DG2 9BA
**Tel:** 01387-254853
**Web:** www.qosfc.com
**Reg No:** 0012085SC **Estd:** 1919 Private Limited Company
**Line of Business:** Sports clubs
**Trading Style:** Queen of the South Football Club Ltd
**Issued Capital:** £7,500
**Directors:** M A Blount, W J Hewitson
**Co. Secretary:** Craig Paterson
**Responsibilities**
**Senior:** Thomas Harkness (Manager)
**Finance:** Thomas Harkness (Manager)
**Sales:** Mark Mcminn (Commercial Manager)
**US SIC:** 7999 **UK SIC:** 97913
**Auditors:** Carson & Trotter
**Bankers:** Clydesdale Bank Plc (82-62-12)

| | 31-05-14 | 31-05-13 | 31-05-12 |
|---|---|---|---|
| TA | 1,463,484 | 1,059,651 | 916,139 |
| NW | 718,215 | 663,162 | (79,413) |
| WC | 48,333 | 76,112 | (224,593) |

DUNS 21-383-8837
## Queen Square Chambers
56 Queen Square, Bristol, Avon BS1 4PR
**Tel:** 01179276493
**Web:** www.queensquarechambers.co.uk
**Estd:** 1999 Proprietorship
**Line of Business:** Barristers
**Proprietor:** S Freeman
**US SIC:** 8111 **UK SIC:** 83500
**Employees:** 50

DUNS 53-611-8631
## Queen Theatrical Productions Ltd
(Subsidiary of: Queen Productions Ltd)
4 Gees Court, St Christophers Place, London W1U 1JD
**Tel:** 01494766799 **Fax:** 01628-520374
**Web:** www.schoolswillrockyou.com
**Reg No:** 3417105 **Estd:** 1997 Private Limited Company
**Line of Business:** Performing arts management and promotion
**Issued Capital:** £2
**Directors:** B H May, R M Taylor
**Co. Secretary:** Robert Lee
**US SIC:** 8999 **UK SIC:** 83954
**Bankers:** Coutts & Co (18-00-02)

| | 30-09-13 | 30-09-12 | 30-09-11 |
|---|---|---|---|
| TO | 14,339,811 | 14,417,505 | 16,204,380 |
| P/L | 123,900 | 266,767 | 324,655 |
| NW | 173,206 | 331,981 | 286,635 |
| WC | 173,206 | 331,981 | 286,635 |
| Emp. | 105 | 105 | 105 |

DUNS 29-006-2629
## The Queen's Club Ltd
(Subsidiary of: Qc Holdings Ltd)
Palliser Road, London W14 9EQ
**Tel:** 02073863425
**Web:** www.queensclub.co.uk
**Reg No:** 0023072 **VAT No:** 226804664
**Estd:** 1886 Private Limited Company
**Line of Business:** Sports clubs
**Issued Capital:** £2,563,820
**Directors:** S M Raphael, Miss A L Watson, Ms A J Sater, Mrs L P Engstrom, P F Begg, Miss K Phillips, D J Tarsh, J Acheson-Grey
**Co. Secretary:** Parthviraj Dhanoa
**Responsibilities**
**Senior:** Toby Foxcroft (Manager), Simon Mansfield (Director), Nick Pateras (Manager)
**IT:** Eilish Gartlan (IT Manager)
**Branches:** The Queen's Club Ltd, Palliser Road, London W14 9EQ
**US SIC:** 7999 **UK SIC:** 97913
**Auditors:** Arthur Andersen
**Bankers:** Lloyds TSB Bank plc (30-94-65)

| | 30-09-13 | 30-09-12 | 30-09-11 |
|---|---|---|---|
| TO | 10,030,067 | 9,878,572 | 9,498,774 |
| P/L | 1,564,491 | 1,160,686 | 711,791 |
| NW | 53,901,926 | 51,766,267 | 50,613,951 |
| WC | 9,828,945 | 7,772,734 | 7,683,578 |
| Emp. | 91 | 88 | 101 |

DUNS 22-775-1476
## Queens' College Cambridge
Silver Street, Cambridge, Cambridgeshire CB3 9ES
**Web:** www.queens.cam.ac.uk
**Reg No:** 0000422RC **VAT No:** 273249744
**Estd:** 1836
**Line of Business:** First-degree level higher education

**Trading Style:** Queens' College, N A C Events & Exibitions, National Rural Enterprise Centre
**Principals:** B Ross (Marketing), C Runge, Dr M Ducker
**Co. Secretary:** James Johnson
**Responsibilities**
**Admin:** Tim Shorey (Catering and Conference Direct)
**Operations:** Tim Shorey (Catering and Conference Direct)
**US SIC:** 8221 **UK SIC:** 93100
**Auditors:** Peters Elworthy & Moore
**Bankers:** HSBC Bank plc (40-02-06)

| | 30-06-13 | 30-06-11 | 31-06-08 |
|---|---|---|---|
| TO | 10,539,523 | 9,085,301 | 8,632,171 |
| P/L | 321,998 | 58,448 | (315,297) |
| NW | 75,212,753 | 70,219,725 | 5,180,283 |
| WC | 199,550 | (200,567) | (977,308) |
| Emp. | 134 | 156 | 205 |

DUNS 36-480-3432
## Queens College London
43-49 Harley Street, London W1G 8BT
**Tel:** 020-7291-7000
**Web:** www.qcl.org.uk
**Estd:** 2002 Proprietorship
**Line of Business:** Further education schools and colleges
**Proprietor:** Miss M Connell
**Responsibilities**
**Senior:** Frances Ramsey (Principal)
**US SIC:** 8211, 8221
**UK SIC:** 93200, 93100
**Employees:** 67

DUNS 42-398-4033
## Queen's College Taunton Foundation
Trull Road, Taunton, Somerset TA1 4QS
**Tel:** 01823272559 **Fax:** 01823351207
**Web:** www.queenscollege.org.uk
**Reg No:** 4386063 **Estd:** 2002 Private Company Limited By Guarantee
**Line of Business:** Banks and financial institutions
**Trading Style:** Queen''s College
**Directors:** Mrs H J Broderick, M G Davenport, C J Alcock, Mrs D C Carlson, T H Lang, J D Jones, Mrs T J Khodabandehloo, G Bisson
**Co. Secretary:** Miss Karen Murray
**Responsibilities**
**Senior:** Benjamin Elford (Director), Charlotte Mcleod (Director)
**Admin:** Sarah Frost (Admissions Officer)
**US SIC:** 8211 **UK SIC:** 93200
**Bankers:** HSBC Bank plc (40-44-04)

| | 31-08-13 | 31-08-12 | 31-08-11 |
|---|---|---|---|
| TO | 16,655 | 52,458 | 11,234 |
| P/L | 903 | 17,103 | 8,068 |
| NW | 59,104 | 55,816 | 37,929 |
| WC | 46,489 | 45,586 | 37,929 |

DUNS 21-771-0392
## Queen's Croft School
Birmingham Road, Lichfield, Staffordshire WS13 6PJ
**Tel:** 01543510669
**Web:** www.queenscroft.staffs.sch.uk
**Estd:** 1982 Proprietorship
**Line of Business:** General secondary education
**Proprietor:** J Edwards
**US SIC:** 8211 **UK SIC:** 93200
**Employees:** 50

DUNS 23-782-6276
## Queens Cross Housing Association
45 Firhill Road, Glasgow, Lanarkshire G20 7BE
**Tel:** 0141-945-3003 **Fax:** 0141-945-2429
**Web:** www.queenscrossha.org.uk
**Reg No:** 0001860IP **Estd:** 1976 Friendly Society
**Line of Business:** Non-charitable social work activities with accommodation
**Principals:** D Reffin (Chairman), H Malik, F English, D Donaghue, B Maan, J Mccafferty, Ms M Fyfe, J Andrews
**Co. Secretary:** Ms Emily Devers
**Responsibilities**
**Senior:** Winifred Canning (Director), Hugh Carroll (Director), Richard Hair (Director), Eric Jacobs (Director), Frank McCabe (Chief Executive), James McCafferty (Director), Elizabeth Murphy (Director), Mohammed Razaq (Director), Paul Rydquist (Chief Executive)
**Marketing:** Margaret Brannan (Communications Manager)
**HR:** Paula Brownlee (Personnel Manager)
**Facilities:** Fin McElhinney (Director of Housing Services)
**US SIC:** 8321 **UK SIC:** 96111
**Auditors:** Greenhill & Co
**Bankers:** Clydesdale Bank Plc (82-64-34)
**Employees:** 131
**Turnover:** £9,222,301

DUNS 21-064-2612
## Queens Head Hotel
38 Market Place, Bishop Auckland, County Durham DL14 7NX
**Tel:** 01388603477
**Web:** www.infotel.co.uk
**Estd:** 1990 Proprietorship
**Line of Business:** Hotels
**Proprietor:** Ms S Shaw
**US SIC:** 7011, 5812
**UK SIC:** 66500, 66110
**Bankers:** Barclays Bank Plc (20-09-44)
**Employees:** 48

DUNS 21-232-0193
## Queens Hospital
Rom Valley Way, Romford, Essex RM7 0AG
**Web:** www.bhrhospitals.nhs.uk
**Estd:** 2011 Proprietorship
**Line of Business:** Hospitals
**Proprietor:** J Goulston
**Responsibilities**
**Senior:** Averil Dongworth (Chief Executive)
**HR:** Jan Cripps (Human Resources Manager)
**US SIC:** 8062 **UK SIC:** 95100
**Employees:** 2,500

DUNS 21-614-4328
## Queens Hotel
City Square, Leeds, West Yorkshire LS1 1PJ
**Tel:** 01132431323
**Web:** www.qhotels.co.uk
**Estd:** 2003 Partnership
**Line of Business:** Hotels
**Partners:** S Perkins, M Platt, D Kambouris, D Kanarens, Ms E Kambouris, M Magrane, S Lawson
**Responsibilities**
**Senior:** Paul Priest (Director of Sales)
**Marketing:** Paul Priest (Director of Sales)
**Sales:** Paul Priest (Director of Sales)
**US SIC:** 7011 **UK SIC:** 66500
**Employees:** 300

DUNS 21-614-8849
## The Queens Hotel
Meyrick Road, Bournemouth, Dorset BH1 3DL
**Tel:** 01202554415
**Web:** www.queenshotelbournemouth.com
**Estd:** 2002 Partnership
**Line of Business:** Hotels
**Partners:** P Smith, D Young, A Young, D Marsh, D Burr, Mrs A Young, A Stevens
**US SIC:** 7011 **UK SIC:** 66500
**Employees:** 50

DUNS 29-008-7352
## Queen's Hotels (Penzance) Ltd
Promenade, Penzance, Cornwall TR18 4HG
**Tel:** 01736362371 **Fax:** 01736-350033
**Web:** www.queens-hotel.com
**Reg No:** 0229205 **VAT No:** 337026277
**Estd:** 1928 Private Limited Company
**Line of Business:** Hotels and motels without restaurant
**Trading Style:** The Queen's Hotel
**Issued Capital:** £61,000
**Principals:** A F Holman (Managing), Ms L J Leiworthy, Ms E W Holman
**Co. Secretary:** Anthony Holman
**Responsibilities**
**Senior:** Nicole Thomas (Front of House Manager)
**Finance:** Tracey Leah (Accounts Manager)
**Marketing:** Philip Aston (Marketing Manager)
**IT:** Tracey Leah (Accounts Manager)
**HR:** Lucinda Holman (General Manager)
**Health & Safety:** Lucinda Holman (General Manager)
**Facilities:** Mervin Rosewarne (Maintenance Manager)
**US SIC:** 7011 **UK SIC:** 66500
**Auditors:** Walker Moyle
**Bankers:** Barclays Bank Plc (20-67-19)

| | 30-11-13 | 30-11-12 | 30-11-11 |
|---|---|---|---|
| TA | 1,062,541 | 1,058,958 | 1,083,378 |
| NW | 333,205 | 450,434 | 450,298 |
| WC | (272,809) | (111,561) | (60,716) |

DUNS 21-038-8076
## Queens Lodge Nursing Home
Haslingden Road, Blackburn, Lancashire BB2 3HQ
**Tel:** 01254-681805
**Web:** www.queenslodge.co.uk
**Partnership**
**Line of Business:** Residential care establishments
**Partners:** Mrs M Thatcher, Mrs M Satcher, Miss L Wilkins
**US SIC:** 8321 **UK SIC:** 96111
**Employees:** 100

DUNS 21-772-2159

## Queen's Nursing Home

34 Ardayre Road, Prestwick, Ayrshire KA9 1QL
**Tel:** 01292470501
**Web:** www.europeancare.net
**Estd:** 1984 Partnership
**Line of Business:** Nursing homes
**Partners:** Mrs R Murphy, Mrs R Murphy
**Responsibilities**
**Senior:** Tracy Barker (Manager), Ree Murphy (CEO, Managing Director), Michelle Sommerville (Manager)
**US SIC:** 8051 **UK SIC:** 95100
**Employees:** 50

DUNS 21-849-6949

## Queens Park Community School Academy Trust

Queens Park Community School, Aylestone Avenue, London NW6 7BQ
**Tel:** 02084381700
**Web:** www.qpcs.brent.sch.uk
**Reg No:** 8146138 **Estd:** 2012 Private Company Limited By Guarantee
**Line of Business:** General secondary education
**Directors:** M Riddick, N Hale, Ms D S Griffiths, Ms R George, Ms G Self, Ms A Lester, M C Beard, T S York
**Co. Secretary:** Sebastian Mansfield-Steer
**Responsibilities**
**Senior:** Camilla Child (Director), Janet Gordon (Director), Michael Hulme (Director), Bryan Stark (Director)
**US SIC:** 8211 **UK SIC:** 93200
**Bankers:** Barclays Bank Plc (20-00-50)

| | 31-08-14 | 31-08-13 |
|---|---|---|
| TO | 10,751,000 | 72,146,000 |
| P/L | 861,000 | 62,904,000 |
| NW | 62,982,000 | 62,131,000 |
| WC | 979,000 | 1,407,000 |
| Emp. | 175 | 184 |

DUNS 21-621-2919

## Queens Park Sports Centre

Boythorpe Road, Chesterfield, Derbyshire S40 2ND
**Tel:** 01246345555
**Web:** www.chesterfield.gov.uk
**Estd:** 2002 Proprietorship
**Line of Business:** Other sporting activities not elsewhere classified
**Proprietor:** D Butler
**US SIC:** 7999 **UK SIC:** 97913
**Employees:** 20

DUNS 21-170-2373

## The Queen's School

City Walls Road, Chester, Cheshire CH1 2NN
**Tel:** 01244312078
**Web:** www.queens.cheshire.sch.uk
**Estd:** 2005 Proprietorship
**Line of Business:** Schools (independent)
**Proprietor:** Mrs C Buckley
**Responsibilities**
**Senior:** Mair Kelly (Bursar)
**Finance:** Mair Kelly (Bursar), Louise Rushforth (Financial Administrator)
**Marketing:** Mair Kelly (Bursar)
**Sales:** Mair Kelly (Bursar)
**Admin:** Patricia Brooks (Administration Manager), Mair Kelly (Bursar)
**IT:** Damien McKeown (Head of IT)
**HR:** Mair Kelly (Bursar)
**Health & Safety:** Mair Kelly (Bursar)
**Facilities:** Mair Kelly (Bursar)
**Purchasing:** Mair Kelly (Bursar)
**US SIC:** 8211 **UK SIC:** 93200
**Employees:** 175

DUNS 77-129-0343

## Queens Staith Leisure Ltd

Moorside Farm Lordsmoor Lane, Strensall, York, North Yorkshire YO32 5XF
**Tel:** 01904-491665
**Reg No:** 2700420 **Estd:** 1992 Private Limited Company
**Line of Business:** Hotels
**Issued Capital:** £9,000
**Directors:** P D Smith, L A Smith
**Co. Secretary:** Craig Smith
**US SIC:** 7011 **UK SIC:** 66500
**Bankers:** Cater Allen Ltd (16-51-69)

| | 30-04-14 | 30-04-13 | 30-04-12 |
|---|---|---|---|
| TO | 3,908,293 | 3,625,179 | 2,882,795 |
| P/L | 888,988 | 264,795 | 473,430 |
| NW | 5,609,053 | 4,907,178 | 4,689,173 |
| WC | (2,361,338) | (1,731,641) | (1,823,362) |
| Emp. | 112 | 110 | 86 |

DUNS 22-934-1789 **Imp**

## Queen's University Belfast

University Road, Belfast BT7 1NN
**Tel:** 02890 245133 **Fax:** 02890667023
**Web:** www.qub.ac.uk
**VAT No:** 254799511 **Estd:** 1845 Incorporate By Act Of Parliament
**Line of Business:** Universities, colleges, prof. schools
**Trading Style:** Queen''s University Belfast
**Principals:** S P Prente, C Gibson, W N Bennet, P J Gregson, Sir D Fell (Manager), Mrs R Johnston (Manager), J P O'Kane (Manager), Lady B Mclaughlin (Manager)
**Responsibilities**
**Senior:** Brenda McLaughlin (Manager)
**Finance:** Sharon Nicholl (Finance Manager), Caroline Norman (Financial Services)
**Marketing:** Andrea Fordham (Marketing Officer), Peter McConkey (Marketing Manager)
**IT:** Helen Browne (IT Systems & Services), Graham Norman (IT Support)
**Branches:** Queen's University Belfast, 5 Rugby Road, Belfast, Belfast BT7 1PS
**US SIC:** 8221, 7339
**UK SIC:** 93100, 83954
**Auditors:** PricewaterhouseCoopersLLP
**Bankers:** Northern Bank Ltd (95-01-49)
**Employees:** 4,000
**Turnover:** £293,668,000

DUNS 21-783-5298

## Queens University Belfast School of Chemistry

David Keir Building, Belfast BT9 5AB
**Tel:** 02890975418
**Web:** www.ch.qub.ac.uk
**Estd:** 2011 Proprietorship
**Line of Business:** University
**Proprietor:** Mrs F Mulligan
**US SIC:** 8221 **UK SIC:** 93100
**Employees:** 100

DUNS 21-589-7711

## Queensborough Motors

151 Kyle Street, Glasgow, Lanarkshire G4 0DS
**Tel:** 01415529000
**Web:** www.skoda.co.uk
**Estd:** 1926 Partnership
**Line of Business:** Sale of new motor vehicles
**Trading Style:** Henry''s for Skoda
**Partners:** J T Henry, Mrs E M Henry, G M Henry, Ms P Henry
**Responsibilities**
**Senior:** Alec Henry (Owner)
**Branches:** 106 Clarence Dr, Glasgow G12.
**US SIC:** 5511, 7539
**UK SIC:** 65100, 67100
**Employees:** 55

DUNS 21-150-9448

## Queensbury School

Langdale Road, Dunstable, Bedfordshire LU6 3BU
**Tel:** 01582-601241
**Web:** www.queensburyacademy.com
**Estd:** 2002
**Line of Business:** Schools (foundation)
**Directors:** R Clayton, Ms A Lancaster
**Responsibilities**
**Senior:** Oliver Button (Principal), Nigel Hill (Head Teacher)
**Finance:** Heather Harris (Finance Manager)
**US SIC:** 8211 **UK SIC:** 93200
**Employees:** 150

DUNS 23-830-2504 **Exp**

## Queensbury Shelters Ltd

Fitzherbert Road, Farlington, Portsmouth, Hampshire PO6 1SE
**Tel:** 023-9221-0052
**Web:** www.queensburyshelters.co.uk
**Reg No:** 3822195 **Estd:** 1999 Private Limited Company
**Line of Business:** Public works contractors
**Export Sales:** £51,517
**Issued Capital:** £100
**Directors:** D C Mundy, G Wilson, C I Heayberd
**Co. Secretary:** Robert Pilch
**Responsibilities**
**Senior:** Steve Gee (Factory Manager)
**Health & Safety:** Rob Serjent (Health & Safety Officer)
**Facilities:** Steve Gee (Factory Manager)
**Operations:** Steve Gee (Factory Manager)
**Fleet:** Steve Gee (Factory Manager)
**Engineering:** Steve Gee (Factory Manager)
**Branches:** Queensbury Shelters Ltd, Design & Manufacturing Division, Robinson Ho, Millbrook, Southampton, Hampshire SO15 0LG
**US SIC:** 1799, 2599, 3442

UK SIC: 50000, 46720, 31420
**Auditors:** Horwath Clark Whitehill
**Bankers:** Barclays Bank Plc (20-49-76)

| | 31-12-13 | 31-12-12 | 31-12-11 |
|---|---|---|---|
| TO | 6,315,953 | 6,644,878 | 7,445,367 |
| P/L | 435,826 | 139,771 | (367,648) |
| NW | 1,948,472 | 1,601,604 | 1,444,461 |
| WC | 654,587 | 261,037 | 22,122 |
| Emp. | 72 | 82 | 89 |

DUNS 29-933-6958

## Queenscourt Hospice

Town Lane, Southport, Merseyside PR8 6RE
**Tel:** 01704544645
**Web:** www.queenscourt.org.uk
**Reg No:** 2102320 **Estd:** 1988 Private Limited Company
**Line of Business:** Hospices
**Directors:** C D Leather, K C Mitchell, Ms G Fox, J A Woods, Doctor D J Unwin, T Fairclough, P A Downham, Ms Y Burns
**Co. Secretary:** Mrs Jane Royds
**Responsibilities**
**Senior:** John Gaine (Director), Richard Jacklin (Trustee), Sue Lovelock (Manager), Colin Ryan (Director), Margaret Tarpey (Director), Ann Throp (General Manager)
**Finance:** Walter Tait (Financial Manager)
**HR:** Cath Baldry (Principal Nurse)
**Health & Safety:** Cath Baldry (Principal Nurse)
**Facilities:** Ann Throp (General Manager)
**Operations:** Ann Throp (General Manager)
**Purchasing:** Ann Throp (General Manager)
**US SIC:** 8091 **UK SIC:** 95200
**Auditors:** Champion Accountants LLP
**Bankers:** National Westminster Bank Plc (60-20-11)

| | 31-03-14 | 31-03-13 | 31-03-12 |
|---|---|---|---|
| TO | 3,816,948 | 3,275,223 | 4,168,369 |
| P/L | (287,738) | (397,098) | 752,163 |
| NW | 12,605,061 | 12,573,822 | 11,925,661 |
| WC | 1,360,133 | 1,624,593 | 2,497,130 |
| Emp. | 138 | 129 | 124 |

DUNS 39-790-1588

## Queensferry Hotels Ltd

69-74 Bruntsfield Place, Edinburgh, Midlothian EH10 4HH
**Tel:** 01316228163 **Fax:** 0131-229-5634
**Web:** www.bisquebar.com
**Reg No:** 0108130SC **VAT No:** 502715088
**Estd:** 2011 Private Limited Company
**Line of Business:** Wine bars
**Trading Style:** Keavil House Hotel, The Brunsfield Hotel, Park Hotel
**Issued Capital:** £1,150,499
**Directors:** P H Gwyn, R H Imrie
**Co. Secretary:** Charnisay Gwyn
**Responsibilities**
**Senior:** Daniel Tomescu (Restaurant Manager)
**Branches:** Queensferry Hotels Ltd, Glendevon Farm, Crossford, Dunfermline, Fife KY11 3HQ
**US SIC:** 5813 **UK SIC:** 66200
**Auditors:** Blueprint
**Bankers:** Bank Of Scotland (80-20-00)

| | 30-04-14 | 30-04-13 | 30-04-12 |
|---|---|---|---|
| TO | 3,014,189 | 2,720,883 | 2,753,952 |
| P/L | 369,222 | 240,753 | 263,225 |
| NW | 5,334,910 | 5,050,763 | 4,856,733 |
| WC | (80,866) | (256,070) | (1,113,930) |
| Emp. | 72 | 72 | 72 |

DUNS 21-776-2295

## Queensferry Primary School

Burgess Road, South Queensferry, West Lothian EH30 9NX
**Tel:** 01313311349
**Web:** www.queensferry-pri.edin.sch.uk
**Estd:** 1991 Proprietorship
**Line of Business:** Schools (local authority)
**Proprietor:** Mrs K Macgregor
**US SIC:** 8211 **UK SIC:** 93200
**Employees:** 50

DUNS 29-128-9866

## Queensgate Centre Association Ltd

Centre Management Office, Queensgate Centre, Peterborough, Cambridgeshire PE1 1NT
**Tel:** 01733-311666
**Web:** www.queensgate-shopping.co.uk
**Reg No:** 1632036 **Estd:** 1982 Private Limited Company
**Line of Business:** Shopping centres
**Trading Style:** Queensgate Shopping Centre
**Directors:** C Burton, Ms C Rogers, P Marsden, Ms P Negus, M Savage, S F Wrench, W Clarke, J Ashley Webb
**Co. Secretary:** Ms Heather Lemmon
**Responsibilities**
**Senior:** Laura Bonner (Manager), Sam Eastwood (Centre Director), Frank Grant (Assistant Director), Sarah Hockley (Director), Roger Hutchins (Manager), Johanna Wilson (Manager)
**Finance:** Frank Grant (Assistant Director)

**Marketing:** Laura Briers (Marketing Coordinator), Phil Drinkwater (Marketing Manager), Laura Sayer (Marketing Manager)
**Sales:** Julie Steels (Retail Liaison Manager)
**Admin:** Jackie Risk (Systems & Administration Manag)
**IT:** Joanne Beedle (Systems Manager), Frank Grant (Assistant Director), Gayle Lobozzo (IT Manager)
**HR:** Jackie Risk (Systems & Administration Manag)
**Health & Safety:** Frank Grant (Assistant Director)
**Facilities:** Frank Grant (Assistant Director)
**Operations:** Frank Grant (Assistant Director)
**Purchasing:** Jackie Risk (Systems & Administration Manag)
**US SIC:** 5399 **UK SIC:** 65600
**Auditors:** Rawlinsons
**Bankers:** National Westminster Bank Plc (54-21-38)

| | 31-03-14 | 31-03-13 | 31-03-12 |
|---|---|---|---|
| TA | 95,400 | 120,910 | 188,987 |
| NW | 61,640 | 79,416 | 97,405 |
| WC | 61,630 | 79,406 | 97,395 |

DUNS 21-331-8731

## Queensmead School

Queens Walk, Ruislip. Middlesex HA4 0LS
**Tel:** 02088456266
**Web:** www.queensmeadschool.org.uk
**Estd:** 2002 Proprietorship
**Line of Business:** Schools (local authority)
**Proprietor:** N Mclaughlin
**Responsibilities**
**Senior:** Rhona Johnston (Head Teacher), N McLaughlin (Proprietor)
**US SIC:** 8211 **UK SIC:** 93200
**Employees:** 82

DUNS 76-999-5648

## Queensway Restaurants Ltd

1 Brandon Parade South, Motherwell, Lanarkshire ML1 1RB
**Tel:** 01698276055
**Reg No:** 0134500SC **Estd:** 1991 Private Limited Company
**Line of Business:** Unlicensed restaurants and cafes
**Trading Style:** McDonalds
**Issued Capital:** £101
**Co. Secretary:** Patrick Mckenna
**Branches:** Queensway Restaurants Ltd, Airdrie Retail Park, Unit 10, Airdrie, Lanarkshire ML6 9JB
**US SIC:** 5812 **UK SIC:** 66110
**Auditors:** WDM Associates
**Bankers:** The Royal Bank Of Scotland Plc (83-07-06)

| | 31-12-13 | 31-12-12 | 31-12-11 |
|---|---|---|---|
| TA | 52 | 228 | 80,728 |
| NW | (74,948) | (74,948) | 5,552 |
| WC | (74,948) | (74,424) | 6,076 |

DUNS 21-156-7073

## Queenswell Junior School

Sweets Way, London N20 0NQ
**Tel:** 020-8445-2056
**Web:** www.queenswelljunior.co.uk
**Estd:** 1950
**Line of Business:** Language schools
**Proprietor:** S Clayton
**US SIC:** 8211 **UK SIC:** 93200
**Employees:** 65

DUNS 39-819-2609 **Imp-Exp**

## Queenswood Natural Foods Ltd

Bristol Road, Bridgwater, Somerset TA6 4AW
**Tel:** 01278-423440
**Web:** www.queenswoodfoods.co.uk
**Reg No:** 2218336 **VAT No:** 336635056
**Estd:** 1976 Private Limited Company
**Line of Business:** Health food retailers
**Export Markets:** Portugal; Hong Kong
**Export Sales:** £1,167,095
**Issued Capital:** £100
**Directors:** R C Hunt, M J Douch, M D Norris
**Co. Secretary:** Melvyn Norris
**Responsibilities**
**Senior:** Peter Burke (General Manager), Roger Cooze (Managing Director), Gillian Cooze (Manager)
**HR:** Peter Burke (General Manager)
**Health & Safety:** Peter Burke (General Manager)
**Facilities:** Peter Burke (General Manager)
**US SIC:** 5499 **UK SIC:** 64100
**Auditors:** A C Mole & Sons
**Bankers:** Barclays Bank Plc (20-85-26)

| | 30-06-14 | 30-06-13 | 30-06-12 |
|---|---|---|---|
| TO | 14,962,753 | 14,319,619 | 13,191,681 |
| P/L | 372,317 | 274,583 | 308,082 |
| NW | 1,104,341 | 810,854 | 601,773 |
| WC | 611,167 | 363,192 | 340,128 |
| Emp. | 89 | 88 | 86 |

DUNS 29-006-3908
## Queenswood School Ltd
Shepherds Way, Brookmans Park, Hatfield, Hertfordshire AL9 6NS
**Tel:** 01707-602500
**Web:** www.queenswood.org
**Reg No:** 0040561 **Estd:** 1894 Private Limited Company
**Line of Business:** General secondary education
**Issued Capital:** £23
**Directors:** Mrs J Sotiriou, A D Poppleton, Professor Q A Mckellar, Ms P M Wrinch, H J De Sausmarez, Rev T A Swindell, T C Garnham, R A Baines
**Co. Secretary:** Ian Williams
**Responsibilities**
**Senior:** Pauline Edgar *(Principal)*, Sheila Langley *(Vice President)*, Victoria Neale *(Director)*, Angela Rawlinson *(Manager)*, Edmund Sautter *(Director)*
**Facilities:** Graham Waddingham *(Maintenance Manager)*
**Fleet:** Daphne Walton *(Boarding Assistant)*
**US SIC:** 8211 **UK SIC:** 93200
**Auditors:** Saffery Champness
**Bankers:** HSBC Bank plc (40-02-06)

| | 31-08-13 | 31-08-12 | 31-08-11 |
|---|---|---|---|
| TO | 9,425,196 | 9,863,941 | 9,966,247 |
| P/L | (679,864) | (179,371) | (485,392) |
| NW | 15,229,463 | 15,812,249 | 9,627,241 |
| WC | (2,388,125) | (1,812,192) | (1,770,820) |
| Emp. | 186 | 188 | 188 |

DUNS 23-763-7892
## Queenwood Golf Club Ltd
Stonehill Road, Chertsey, Surrey KT16 0QD
**Tel:** 01932454500
**Web:** www.queenwood.co.uk
**Reg No:** 3757421 **Estd:** 1999 Private Limited Company
**Line of Business:** Golf clubs
**Issued Capital:** £402
**Directors:** L Churchill Green, F D Green, D O Haythe, G Tvedt
**Co. Secretary:** Gerard Ivers
**Responsibilities**
**Senior:** Cameron Mcmillan *(Manager)*
**Branches:** Queenwood Golf Club Ltd, Stonehill Road, Chertsey, Surrey KT16 0AQ
**US SIC:** 7911 **UK SIC:** 97913
**Auditors:** S H Landes & Co
**Bankers:** National Westminster Bank Plc (56-00-27)

| | 31-12-13 | 31-12-12 | 31-12-11 |
|---|---|---|---|
| TO | 4,285,530 | 4,240,272 | 4,043,612 |
| P/L | (493,239) | (343,215) | (662,574) |
| NW | 16,533,444 | 18,301,830 | 18,163,683 |
| WC | 2,993,899 | 2,747,792 | 2,261,570 |
| Emp. | 68 | 68 | 66 |

DUNS 23-113-4680
## Quennevais Ltd
Bonita, Le Mont A Lane Brune, St Brelade, Jersey, Channel Islands JE3 8FL
**Tel:** 01534497000
**Web:** www.lesormesjersey.co.uk
**Reg No:** 0003881J **Estd:** 1969 Private Limited Company
**Line of Business:** Other sporting activities not elsewhere classified
**Trading Style:** Les Ormes Golf & Leisure Club, Les Ormes
**Issued Capital:** £1,012
**US SIC:** 7999 **UK SIC:** 97913
**Bankers:** HSBC Bank plc (40-25-34)
**Employees:** 66

DUNS 34-631-3302
## Quercus Publishing Ltd
55 Baker Street, 7th Floor, South Block, London W1U 8EW
**Tel:** 02072917200 **Fax:** 02072917201
**Web:** www.quercusbooks.co.uk
**Reg No:** 5437517 **Estd:** 2005 Private Limited Company
**Line of Business:** Book publishers
**Export Sales:** £4,882,000
**Issued Capital:** £164,365
**Directors:** P De Cacqueray, T M Hely-Hutchinson, J Hodder-Williams
**Co. Secretary:** Pierre De Cacqueray
**US SIC:** 2731 **UK SIC:** 47532
**Auditors:** Crowe Clark Whitehill LLP
**Bankers:** The Bank Of Ireland (30-16-07)

| | 31-12-13 | 31-12-12 | 31-12-11 |
|---|---|---|---|
| TO | 20,716,000 | 20,429,000 | 24,759,000 |
| P/L | (2,845,000) | 1,367,000 | 5,876,000 |
| NW | 9,959,000 | 13,188,000 | 13,182,000 |
| WC | 9,419,000 | 12,648,000 | 12,597,000 |
| Emp. | 77 | 68 | 54 |

DUNS 21-676-3887
## The Quest Academy - Coloma Trust
Farnborough Avenue, South Croydon, Surrey CR2 8HD
**Tel:** 02086578935
**Web:** www.thequestacademy.org.uk
**Reg No:** 7278887 **Estd:** 2010 Private Company Limited By Guarantee
**Line of Business:** General secondary education
**Directors:** Ms C P Waring, Mrs L Stotesbury, Mrs K S Nelson, A G Crofts, R J Huggett, B A Noble, P G Burley, F A Wright
**Responsibilities**
**Senior:** Camille Denton *(Director)*, Mary Griffin *(Director)*, Janet Marshall *(Director)*, Maureen Martin *(Director)*, Agnes O'Shea *(Director)*, Helen Pollard *(Director)*
**US SIC:** 8211 **UK SIC:** 93200
**Bankers:** Barclays Bank Plc (20-24-61)

| | 31-08-14 | 31-08-13 | 31-08-12 |
|---|---|---|---|
| TO | 4,624,000 | 3,780,000 | 4,267,000 |
| P/L | 898,000 | (308,000) | (2,000) |
| NW | (205,000) | (1,057,000) | (740,000) |
| WC | 63,000 | (48,000) | 5,000 |
| Emp. | 56 | 55 | 63 |

DUNS 23-758-4144 **Imp**
## Quest Diagnostics Ltd
**(Subsidiary of:** Quest Diagnostics Incorporated)
Unit B1, Parkway Trading Estate, Cranford Lane, Hounslow, Middlesex TW5 9QA
**Tel:** 02083773300 **Fax:** 02083773304
**Web:** www.questdiagnostics.com
**Reg No:** 3752194 **Estd:** 1999 Private Limited Company
**Line of Business:** Research and laboratory based activities
**Issued Capital:** £10
**Directors:** Ms T E Ahwieh, Dr. P R Berry, S A Calamari, Ms T D Cinco-Abela, Ms N P Thurlow
**Co. Secretary:** Ms Jacqueline Hunkler
**Branches:** Quest Diagnostics Ltd, 10 Upper Wimpole Street, London W1G 6LL
**US SIC:** 7391 **UK SIC:** 94000
**Auditors:** PricewaterhouseCoopers LLP
**Bankers:** HSBC Bank plc (40-00-00)

| | 31-12-13 | 31-12-12 | 31-12-11 |
|---|---|---|---|
| TO | 40,644,000 | 50,879,000 | 65,905,000 |
| P/L | 8,321,000 | 4,374,000 | 2,814,000 |
| NW | 25,169,000 | 19,189,000 | 13,428,000 |
| WC | 25,511,000 | 19,751,000 | 14,315,000 |
| Emp. | 218 | 336 | 370 |

DUNS 21-730-6053
## Quest Global Engineering Ltd
**(Subsidiary of:** Quest Global Services Pte. Ltd.)
Unit 1 Winterstoke Road, Weston-Super-Mare, Avon BS24 9AB
**Tel:** 01934421500
**Web:** http://engineering.quest-global.com
**Reg No:** 7661210 **Estd:** 2011 Private Limited Company
**Line of Business:** Speciality design activities
**Export Sales:** £10,422,000
**Issued Capital:** £1,500,000
**Directors:** R K Shreemal, R H Harvey, T P Jones
**Responsibilities**
**Senior:** Matthew Blay *(Manager)*
**HR:** Melanie Sharp *(HR Manager)*
**US SIC:** 7399 **UK SIC:** 83954
**Auditors:** Ernst & Young LLP

| | 31-03-14 | 31-03-13 | 31-03-12 |
|---|---|---|---|
| TO | 18,510,000 | 16,646 | 4,906,000 |
| P/L | (594,000) | (5,195) | (445,000) |
| NW | (5,098,000) | (4,552) | 1,055,000 |
| WC | (2,545,000) | (1,603) | 3,520,000 |
| Emp. | 172 | 211 | 168 |

DUNS 21-420-6064
## Quest Software
9 Bridewell Place, London EC4V 6AW
**Tel:** 020-78222700
**Web:** www.quest.com
**Line of Business:** Office equipment servicing
**Responsibilities**
**Senior:** Kelin Norlin *(Manager)*
**US SIC:** 7379 **UK SIC:** 83940
**Employees:** 120

DUNS 50-587-7738 **Imp-Exp**
## Quest Vitamins Ltd
**(Subsidiary of:** Farmoza Limited)
8 Venture Way, Birmingham, West Midlands B7 4AP
**Tel:** 0121-359-0056 **Fax:** 0121-359-0313
**Web:** www.questvitamins.co.uk
**Reg No:** 2530437 **VAT No:** 555097424
**Estd:** 1983 Private Limited Company
**Line of Business:** Health food retailers
**Export Markets:** E U, Middle East, Far East
**Export Sales:** £2,198,809
**Issued Capital:** £973,452
**Principals:** Dr A G Hassam *(Managing)*, M A Hassam, N B Dainty, Dr Z Hassam
**Co. Secretary:** Neil Dainty
**Responsibilities**
**Senior:** Paul Holderness *(Warehouse Manager)*, Eamonn Regan *(Manager)*
**Marketing:** Toni Hibbert *(Marketing Manager)*, Sanjeet Sohal *(Sales & Marketing Assistant Ma)*
**Sales:** Sanjeet Sohal *(Sales & Marketing Assistant Ma)*
**IT:** Jag Mahal *(IT Manager)*
**Fleet:** Paul Holderness *(Warehouse Manager)*
**US SIC:** 2099, 2834
**UK SIC:** 42399, 25700
**Auditors:** PKF
**Bankers:** Lloyds TSB Bank plc (30-00-03)

| | 31-12-13 | 31-12-12 | 31-12-11 |
|---|---|---|---|
| TO | 6,268,113 | 5,807,495 | 5,772,908 |
| P/L | 201,720 | 165,315 | 82,994 |
| NW | 1,279,585 | 1,017,994 | 810,337 |
| WC | 514,958 | 399,553 | 50,983 |
| Emp. | 56 | 56 | 59 |

DUNS 73-338-9907
## Questgates Ltd
7 The Wharf, Bridge Street, Birmingham, West Midlands B1 2JS
**Tel:** 08450709500 **Fax:** 01423524969
**Web:** www.questgates.co.uk
**Reg No:** 4612407 **Estd:** 2002 Private Limited Company
**Line of Business:** Activities auxiliary to insurance and pension funding
**Issued Capital:** £1,437,000
**Directors:** P Thurston, A N Steward, A Dobson, P M Tinsley, R Macpherson, G Laker, C D Hall
**Co. Secretary:** Peter Thurston
**Responsibilities**
**Senior:** Ross MacPherson *(Director)*, Mark Purvis *(Associate Director)*, Kevin Terry *(Associate Director & Divisiona)*
**Finance:** Greg Bannister *(Technical Claims Manager)*
**IT:** Greg Bannister *(Technical Claims Manager)*, Russell Woodward-Clarke *(IT Manager)*
**Branches:** Questgates Ltd, 10 Sandyford Place, Glasgow, Lanarkshire G3 7NB
**US SIC:** 6411 **UK SIC:** 83200
**Auditors:** Clarke Nicklin LLP

| | 30-06-13 | 30-06-12 | 30-06-11 |
|---|---|---|---|
| TO | 10,981,698 | 9,830,675 | 9,860,537 |
| P/L | 850,925 | 744,912 | 725,249 |
| NW | 4,284,419 | 3,617,961 | 3,043,537 |
| WC | 4,064,842 | 3,415,535 | 2,860,454 |
| Emp. | 149 | 138 | 130 |

DUNS 39-982-7914 **Imp-Exp**
## Questionmark Computing Ltd
4th Floor Hill House, London N19 5NA
**Tel:** 020-7263-7575
**Web:** www.questionmark.com
**Reg No:** 2278553 **VAT No:** 511112911
**Estd:** 1986 Private Limited Company
**Line of Business:** Computer systems and software (sales)
**Export Markets:** E C and other countries worldwide.
**Export Sales:** £6,636,305
**Issued Capital:** £169
**Principals:** J Kleeman *(Managing)*, E R Shepherd, P S Roberts
**Co. Secretary:** John Kleeman
**Responsibilities**
**Marketing:** Brian Macnamara *(Sales & Marketing Manager)*
**Sales:** Brian Macnamara *(Sales & Marketing Manager)*, Che Osbourne *(Vp Sales)*
**US SIC:** 7379 **UK SIC:** 83940
**Auditors:** Grant Thornton UK LLP
**Bankers:** HSBC Bank plc (40-05-16)

| | 31-12-13 | 31-12-12 | 31-12-11 |
|---|---|---|---|
| TO | 7,692,021 | 7,716,445 | 7,476,434 |
| P/L | 84,684 | 226,011 | (448,142) |
| NW | (1,179,776) | (228,053) | (291,104) |
| WC | (1,625,531) | (676,375) | (720,240) |
| Emp. | 96 | 93 | 94 |

DUNS 50-743-3621
## The Quetzal Project
Bridge Works, Knighton Fields Road West, Macaulay Street, Leicester, Leicestershire LE2 7NJ
**Tel:** 01162533383
**Estd:** 1990
**Line of Business:** Registered charity supporting women who have been sexually abused
**Chairman:** Ms M Munton
**US SIC:** 8699, 8321
**UK SIC:** 96902, 96111
**Employees:** 50

DUNS 71-871-9532
## Quick Slide Ltd
**(Subsidiary of:** Audasi Holdings Ltd)
Unit 15, Heaton Industrial Park, Bradford Road, Brighouse, West Yorkshire HD6 4BW
**Tel:** 08445610623 **Fax:** 08445 610624
**Web:** www.quickslide.co.uk
**Reg No:** 5254717 **VAT No:** 859760177
**Estd:** 2004 Private Limited Company
**Line of Business:** Film processing
**Trading Style:** Quick Slide Ltd
**Issued Capital:** £1
**Directors:** B T Weber, T G Swallow, A C Barraclough
**Responsibilities**
**Senior:** Audrey Weber *(Commercial Director)*
**Sales:** Audrey Weber *(Commercial Director)*
**Operations:** Mick Madigan *(Operations Director)*
**US SIC:** 3999 **UK SIC:** 49590
**Auditors:** Clough & Co LLP
**Bankers:** National Westminster Bank Plc (53-61-07)

| | 31-05-14 | 31-05-13 | 31-05-12 |
|---|---|---|---|
| TO | 9,761,695 | 7,486,838 | 7,489,374 |
| P/L | 142,849 | 9,193 | 81,528 |
| NW | 733,343 | 610,170 | 607,872 |
| WC | 299,315 | 139,050 | 164,736 |
| Emp. | 93 | 71 | 62 |

DUNS 23-932-8532
## Quicklight Ltd
Unit 3 3a Crown House, Crown Yard, Station Road, Thatcham, Berkshire RG19 4JE
**Tel:** 01635861684 **Fax:** 01635872168
**Web:** www.quicklight.co.uk
**Reg No:** 3922706 **Estd:** 1994 Private Limited Company
**Line of Business:** Lighting contractors
**Issued Capital:** £800
**Directors:** Ms N C Honey, R W Moss, A Galbraith, J Moss, Ms B Cole, R Mccabe
**Co. Secretary:** Andrew Cole
**Responsibilities**
**Senior:** Delila Cocklebum *(Quicklight Contact)*
**Branches:** Quicklight Ltd, Unit 3 3A Crown House, Crown Yard, Station Road, Thatcham, Berkshire RG19 4JE
**US SIC:** 1731, 8911
**UK SIC:** 50300, 83701

| | 30-06-13 | 30-06-12 | 30-06-11 |
|---|---|---|---|
| TO | 6,881,383 | 6,699,534 | N/A |
| P/L | 587,821 | 801,798 | N/A |
| NW | 267,513 | 174,245 | 313,430 |
| WC | (282,163) | (259,579) | (357,795) |
| Emp. | 98 | N/A | N/A |

DUNS 29-421-1552
## Quicks Car Supermarkets Ltd
**(Subsidiary of:** Pendragon Plc)
Newcastle Road, Stoke-On-Trent, Staffordshire ST4 6PQ
**Tel:** 08453-459701 **Fax:** 01782-624830
**Web:** www.quicks.co.uk
**Reg No:** 1482233 **Estd:** 1980 Private Limited Company
**Line of Business:** Car dealers (used)
**Trading Style:** Quicks
**Issued Capital:** £1,500,000
**Directors:**
Pendragon Management Services Li, T P Holden, T G Finn, M S Casha
**Co. Secretary:** Ms Hilary Sykes
**Responsibilities**
**Senior:** Don Beardmore *(Store Manager)*, Robert Lackie *(dealer principle)*
**Branches:** Quicks Car Supermarkets Ltd, 9 St. Georges Way, Leicester, Leicestershire LE1 1SP
**US SIC:** 5521 **UK SIC:** 65100
**Auditors:** KPMG Audit PLC
**Bankers:** Barclays Bank Plc (20-07-71)

| | 31-12-13 | 31-12-12 | 31-12-11 |
|---|---|---|---|
| TO | 51,561,000 | 50,751,000 | 47,531,000 |
| P/L | (2,782,000) | (4,128,000) | (4,800,000) |
| NW | 851,000 | (1,431,000) | (577,000) |
| WC | 128,000 | (2,242,000) | (1,499,000) |
| Emp. | 213 | 203 | 175 |

DUNS 29-687-9067 **Exp**
## Quidnunc Group Ltd
The Shoe Factory, 26-28 Paddenswick Road, London W6 0UA
**Tel:** 01817417117
**Web:** www.abreckner.com
**Reg No:** 2011524 **VAT No:** 538687295
**Estd:** 1985 Private Limited Company
**Line of Business:** Hardware consultancy
**Export Markets:** France; Switzerland
**Principals:** L E Holt *(Managing)*, Ms D N Hudson
**US SIC:** 7379 **UK SIC:** 83940
**Auditors:** Unknown Auditor
**Bankers:** Barclays Bank Plc (20-35-90)
**Employees:** 128

DUNS 23-814-1027

## Quill Construction Ltd

38 Brook Road, Rayleigh, Essex SS6 7XJ
**Tel:** 01268-776952 **Fax:** 01268779072
**Web:** www.quillconstruction.co.uk
**Reg No:** 3806388 **Estd:** 2008 Private Limited Company
**Line of Business:** Other construction work involving special trades
**Issued Capital:** £100
**Principals:** D Johnston *(Managing)*, R Johnston, G R Montague, R King
**Co. Secretary:** Ms Sharon Johnston
**US SIC:** 1799 **UK SIC:** 50000
**Auditors:** Tish Press & Co

| | 31-03-14 | 31-03-13 | 31-03-12 |
|---|---|---|---|
| TA | 1,329,010 | 1,046,199 | 1,205,791 |
| NW | 916,495 | 875,376 | 924,673 |
| WC | 708,192 | 684,713 | 754,728 |

DUNS 22-862-9127

## Quill Pinpoint Ltd

Barclay House, 35 Whitworth Street West, Manchester M1 5NG
**Tel:** 01612362910
**Web:** www.quill.co.uk
**Reg No:** 1348976 **VAT No:** 298823010
**Estd:** 1977 Private Limited Company
**Line of Business:** Other software consultancy and supply
**Issued Capital:** £20,999
**Principals:** A J Landes *(Chairman and Managing)*, Mrs M E Hadfield, R Salt, P Dye, J G Bryan, Miss H Fisher
**Branches:** Quill Pinpoint Ltd, First Floor, Liverpool Digital, Edge Lane, Liverpool, Merseyside L7 9NJ
**US SIC:** 7379, 8931
**UK SIC:** 83940, 83600
**Bankers:** The Royal Bank Of Scotland Plc (16-00-02)

| | 31-03-14 | 31-03-13 | 31-03-12 |
|---|---|---|---|
| TA | 2,471,051 | 2,004,896 | 2,020,077 |
| NW | 726,366 | 476,714 | 267,124 |
| WC | 542,237 | 282,132 | 149,216 |

DUNS 49-433-4899

## The Quilted Camel Ltd

36 Sandhill, Newcastle-Upon-Tyne, Tyne and Wear NE1 3JF
**Tel:** 01912211885
**Web:** www.quiltedcamel.com
**Reg No:** 3144445 **Estd:** 2010 Private Limited Company
**Line of Business:** Bars
**Trading Style:** Mushroom Bar
**Issued Capital:** £100
**Director:** Miss S B Cook
**Co. Secretary:** Oliver Vaulkhard
**Responsibilities**
**Senior:** Sarah Bowens *(Manager)*
**US SIC:** 5813 **UK SIC:** 66200
**Auditors:** R M T
**Bankers:** Lloyds TSB Bank plc (30-93-71)

| | 30-04-14 | 30-04-13 | 30-04-12 |
|---|---|---|---|
| TO | 1,396,492 | 1,429,685 | 1,512,254 |
| P/L | 143,506 | 150,389 | 141,956 |
| NW | 747,872 | 2,045,682 | 2,008,852 |
| WC | (179,001) | (131,021) | 215,906 |

DUNS 21-864-3833

## Quilter Cheviot Holdings Ltd

One Kingsway, London WC2B 6AN
**Tel:** 02071504000
**Web:** www.quiltercheviot.com
**Reg No:** 8257448 **Estd:** 2012 Private Limited Company
**Line of Business:** Financial intermediation not elsewhere classified
**Issued Capital:** £1
**Directors:** M N Black, M Duncan, S N Green, C M Meares, M H Baines, M I Macleod
**US SIC:** 6111 **UK SIC:** 81501
**Following financial data are in thousands**

| | 31-12-13 | 31-12-12 |
|---|---|---|
| TA | 1,061,115 | 5,901 |
| P/L | 18,983 | N/A |
| NW | 65,613 | N/A |
| WC | 69,638 | N/A |
| Emp. | 515 | N/A |

DUNS 23-804-9295

## Quilter Uk Investment Funds Icvc

St Helens, 1 Undershaft, London EC3A 8BB
**Tel:** 02076626200
**Reg No:** 0000034 **Estd:** 1999 Private Limited Company
**Line of Business:** Holding companies nec
**Issued Capital:** £16,952
**Director:** Quilter Fund Management Ltd
**US SIC:** 6711 **UK SIC:** 83962
**Employees:** 57
**Turnover:** £67,310,000

DUNS 23-859-5842

## Quindell Business Process Services (Uk) Ltd

**(Subsidiary of:** Quindell Plc)
Idemnity House, Sir Frank Whittle Way, Blackpool, Lancashire FY4 2FB
**Tel:** 08445713333 **Fax:** 08707010514
**Web:** www.aiautomotive.co.uk
**Reg No:** 3851175 **Estd:** 1999 Private Limited Company
**Line of Business:** Maintenance and repair of motor vehicles
**Issued Capital:** £2
**Directors:** R M Fielding, L Moorse, N D Allen
**Co. Secretary:** Edward Walker
**US SIC:** 7539, 7321, 7399
**UK SIC:** 67100, 83954
**Auditors:** Grant Thornton UK LLP
**Bankers:** HSBC Bank plc (40-31-24)

| | 31-12-13 | 31-12-12 | 30-12-11 |
|---|---|---|---|
| TO | 80,039,000 | 119,989,000 | 117,621,000 |
| P/L | 1,668,000 | 85,000 | 3,429,000 |
| NW | 4,992,000 | 6,637,000 | 6,426,000 |
| WC | 6,515,000 | 8,250,000 | 1,864,000 |
| Emp. | 552 | 434 | 469 |

DUNS 21-821-3902

## Quindell Legal Services Ltd

**(Subsidiary of:** Quindell Plc)
Dempster Building, Atlantic Way, Brunswick Business Park, Liverpool, Merseyside L3 4UU
**Tel:** 01512369594
**Reg No:** 7931918 **Estd:** 2012 Private Limited Company
**Line of Business:** Solicitors
**Issued Capital:** £17,530,000
**Directors:** Mrs J Harrison, R C Thomson, R M Fielding, R J Mares, L Moorse
**Co. Secretary:** Edward Walker
**US SIC:** 8111 **UK SIC:** 83500
**Bankers:** The Royal Bank Of Scotland Plc (16-29-25)

| | 31-12-13 | 31-12-12 |
|---|---|---|
| TO | 146,198,000 | 349,000 |
| P/L | 53,697,000 | (9,000) |
| NW | 82,821,000 | (6,574,000) |
| WC | 131,242,000 | (4,991,000) |
| Emp. | 824 | 382 |

DUNS 34-740-3714

## Quindell Plc

Quindell Court1 Barnes Wallis Road, Segensworth, Fareham, Hampshire PO15 5UA
**Tel:** 01489-864-200 **Fax:** 01489-864-251
**Web:** www.quindell.com
**Reg No:** 5542221 **Estd:** 2005 Public Limited Company
**Line of Business:** It consultants
**Export Sales:** £58,555,000
**Trading Style:** Quindell
**Issued Capital:** £41,375,188
**Directors:** R M Fielding, R P Burrow, D S Currie, R G Cooling, L Moorse, R S Bright
**Co. Secretary:** Edward Walker
**Responsibilities**
**Senior:** Anthony Bowers *(Manager)*
**Finance:** Claire Plunkett *(Finance Director)*
**US SIC:** 7379, 7372
**UK SIC:** 83940
**Auditors:** KPMG LLP
**Bankers:** HSBC Bank plc (40-05-20)

| | 31-12-13 | 31-12-12 | 31-12-11 |
|---|---|---|---|
| TO | 380,131,000 | 137,558,000 | 13,707,000 |
| P/L | 107,046,000 | 41,241,000 | 4,065,000 |
| NW | 372,492,000 | 110,818,000 | 3,388,000 |
| WC | 330,690,000 | 116,807,000 | 8,674,000 |
| Emp. | 2,412 | 597 | 139 |

DUNS 22-002-0874

## Quinn (London) Ltd

**(Subsidiary of:** Quinn Investment Holdings (London) Ltd)
Dome House, 8 Hartley Avenue, London NW7 2HX
**Tel:** 02082381950 **Fax:** 02082381951
**Web:** www.quinnlondon.co.uk
**Reg No:** 4005400 **Estd:** 2000 Private Limited Company
**Line of Business:** Building construction contractors
**Issued Capital:** £5,000
**Directors:** P Mgrath, P W Clement, S A Quinn, M Devon, R Broadfield
**Co. Secretary:** Ms Marian Quinn
**US SIC:** 1522, 1541
**UK SIC:** 50100
**Auditors:** Clay Ratnage Daffin & Co Ltd
**Bankers:** Allied Irish Bank (gb) (23-84-88)

| | 31-05-13 | 31-05-12 | 31-05-11 |
|---|---|---|---|
| TO | 44,683,934 | 37,094,094 | 21,456,828 |
| P/L | 628,720 | 942,663 | 595,418 |
| NW | 5,299,718 | 4,831,506 | 4,142,720 |
| WC | 5,163,008 | 4,668,346 | 4,077,081 |
| Emp. | 118 | 104 | 95 |

DUNS 54-429-6346

## Quinn Ltd

**(Subsidiary of:** Wm Quinn Group Ltd)
Waterside Mill, Texas Street, Ashton-Under-Lyne, Lancashire OL6 6UJ
**Tel:** 01613 396678 **Fax:** 01612 768165
**Web:** www.wmquinngroup.co.uk
**Reg No:** 3275716 **VAT No:** 639060439
**Estd:** 1996 Private Limited Company
**Line of Business:** Other business activities not elsewhere classified
**Issued Capital:** £2
**Directors:** G K Morris, M Quinn
**Co. Secretary:** Ms Suzanne Kettleton
**US SIC:** 7399 **UK SIC:** 83954
**Auditors:** Unknown

| | 30-10-13 | 30-10-12 | 31-10-11 |
|---|---|---|---|
| TA | 1,991,035 | 1,766,879 | 1,343,629 |
| NW | 97,197 | 80,323 | 76,711 |
| WC | (614,902) | (242,656) | (187,334) |

DUNS 34-637-3814 Imp

## Quinshield Ltd

Unit 27-28, Ammanford, Dyfed SA18 3SJ
**Tel:** 01269-832220 **Fax:** 01269-832221
**Web:** www.quinshield.com
**Reg No:** 2767033 **VAT No:** 558059024
**Estd:** 1993 Private Limited Company
**Line of Business:** Erection of roof covering and frames
**Issued Capital:** £50,004
**Principals:** Dr D J Jenkins *(Managing)*, D W Jenkins *(Managing)*, D Jenkins, I E Bellamy, J E Bellamy
**Co. Secretary:** Dr David Jenkins
**US SIC:** 1761, 1799
**UK SIC:** 50400, 50000
**Auditors:** Hammond & Davies
**Bankers:** Bank Of Wales Plc (12-23-07)

| | 31-12-13 | 31-12-12 | 31-12-11 |
|---|---|---|---|
| TO | 5,803,451 | N/A | N/A |
| P/L | 325,775 | N/A | N/A |
| NW | 3,395,324 | 3,136,438 | 2,531,185 |
| WC | 3,034,766 | 2,804,079 | 2,266,156 |
| Emp. | 98 | N/A | N/A |

DUNS 22-622-6868 Imp-Exp

## Quinta Raddison Ltd

High Lift Villas, Skye Hall Hill, Boxted, Colchester, Essex CO4 5TD
**Web:** www.quintaraddison.co.uk
**Reg No:** 1566906 **VAT No:** 368541428
**Estd:** 1981 Private Limited Company
**Line of Business:** Import and export agents
**Export Markets:** countries worldwide
**Export Sales:** £24,484,269
**Issued Capital:** £76
**Principals:** A J Muir *(Managing)*, S P Urwin, D S Linscott
**Co. Secretary:** Ms Susan Muir
**US SIC:** 4712, 5084
**UK SIC:** 77002, 61490
**Auditors:** Haines Watts
**Bankers:** Barclays Bank Plc (20-22-67)

| | 31-12-13 | 31-12-12 | 31-12-11 |
|---|---|---|---|
| TO | 24,484,269 | 21,693,156 | 18,424,632 |
| P/L | 2,034,518 | 2,115,935 | 1,546,849 |
| NW | 5,717,215 | 4,414,980 | 3,002,348 |
| WC | 5,259,122 | 3,970,831 | 2,771,284 |
| Emp. | 50 | 45 | 34 |

DUNS 77-122-4771 Exp

## Quintain Estates & Development Plc

43-45 Portman Square, London W1H 6LY
**Tel:** 02032192200 **Fax:** 02032192280
**Web:** www.quintain-estates.com
**Reg No:** 2694983 **VAT No:** 606015287
**Estd:** 1992 Public Limited Company
**Line of Business:** Development and selling of real estate
**Export Markets:** Rest of world
**Issued Capital:** £130,245,344
**Directors:** C Bell, Sir P J Dixon, The Honourable C W Cayzer, Ms R C Kerslake, S T Laffin, M D James, N J Kempner, R J Stearn
**Co. Secretary:** Ms Sandra Odell
**Responsibilities**
**Marketing:** Cressida Curtis *(Marketing Manager)*
**Sales:** Ben Giddens *(Commercial Development Directo)*
**IT:** Warren Mc Meeking *(Systems Administrator)*
**HR:** Sally Brown *(Human Resources Manager)*
**Health & Safety:** Stephen Daniels *(Health & Safety Officer)*
**Branches:** Quintain Estates & Development Plc, Empire Way, Wembley, Middlesex HA9 0EF
**US SIC:** 6552, 6531, 6711
**UK SIC:** 85000, 83400, 83962
**Auditors:** KPMG Audit PLC

| | 31-03-14 | 31-03-13 | 31-03-12 |
|---|---|---|---|
| TO | 32,600,000 | 52,100,000 | 45,400,000 |
| P/L | 4,700,000 | (50,400,000) | (43,500,000) |
| NW | 589,400,000 | 531,400,000 | 564,200,000 |
| WC | 158,100,000 | (13,300,000) | (67,600,000) |
| Emp. | 122 | 199 | 267 |

DUNS 73-650-9196

## Quintain (Holdings) Ltd

**(Subsidiary of:** Quintain Estates & Development Plc)
43-45 Portman Square, London W1H 6LY
**Web:** www.quintain-estates.com
**Reg No:** 4910856 **Estd:** 2003 Private Limited Company
**Line of Business:** Building services
**Issued Capital:** £150,267,000
**Directors:** R J Stearn, M D James
**Co. Secretary:** Ms Sandra Odell
**US SIC:** 6552, 6531
**UK SIC:** 85000, 83400

| | 30-06-14 | 30-06-13 | 30-06-12 |
|---|---|---|---|
| TA | 150,267,000 | 150,267,000 | 150,267,000 |
| NW | 150,267,000 | 150,267,000 | 150,267,000 |

DUNS 21-163-7195

## Quintessential Finance Group Ltd

Cottage Street Mill, Cottage Street, Macclesfield, Cheshire SK11 8DZ
**Tel:** 01625505464
**Web:** www.quintessentialfinancegroup.com
**Reg No:** 6898873 **Estd:** 2009 Private Limited Company
**Line of Business:** Financial intermediation not elsewhere classified
**Issued Capital:** £1,000
**Directors:** M C Ransom, P J Naden, G Cox, R A Taylor
**Co. Secretary:** Julian Lord
**US SIC:** 6111 **UK SIC:** 81501

| | 31-03-13 | 31-03-12 | 31-03-11 |
|---|---|---|---|
| TA | 9,223,207 | 4,150,837 | 133,519 |
| P/L | 3,449,196 | 1,380,701 | N/A |
| NW | 2,435,174 | 1,015,977 | (6,544) |
| WC | 3,057,545 | 1,052,267 | (51,383) |
| Emp. | 74 | 55 | N/A |

DUNS 23-888-0079 Imp

## Quintessentially (U K) Ltd

29 Portland Place, London W1B 1QB
**Tel:** 08453884329 **Fax:** 02075800988
**Web:** www.quintessentially.com
**Reg No:** 3879072 **Estd:** 1999 Private Limited Company
**Line of Business:** Other service activities not elsewhere classified
**Trading Style:** Quintessentially (U K) Ltd
**Issued Capital:** £13,857
**Directors:** A L Brooke, I M Birns, B W Elliot, B W Elliot, A T Simpson
**Co. Secretary:** Paul Drummond
**Responsibilities**
**Marketing:** Guido Hakkenberg *(Member Benefits Manager - Glob)*
**Sales:** David Zarzecki *(head of new business)*
**Operations:** Elizabeth McIntosh *(Global Operations & Customer S)*
**US SIC:** 8999, 7374
**UK SIC:** 83954, 83940
**Auditors:** Ivan Sopher & Co
**Bankers:** The Royal Bank Of Scotland Plc (16-00-33)

| | 30-04-13 | 30-04-12 | 30-04-11 |
|---|---|---|---|
| TO | 16,269,032 | 13,429,880 | 13,474,082 |
| P/L | 3,050,469 | (691,813) | 1,315,419 |
| NW | 3,642,126 | 2,500,225 | 3,201,092 |
| WC | 3,542,009 | 2,357,941 | 2,580,273 |
| Emp. | 211 | 247 | 183 |

DUNS 77-774-9441 Exp

## Quintiles Ltd

**(Subsidiary of:** Quintiles Transnational Holdings Inc.)
500 Brook Drive, Reading, Berkshire RG2 6UU
**Tel:** 01184508000
**Web:** www.quintiles.com
**Reg No:** 3022416 **Estd:** 2009 Private Limited Company
**Line of Business:** Research and experimental development on natural sciences and engineering
**Trading Style:** Quintiles Drug Research Unit
**Issued Capital:** £77,438,348
**Directors:** A Macdonald, J Goodacre, K J Turland
**Responsibilities**
**HR:** S Priest *(Personnel Director)*
**Branches:** Quintiles Ltd, Glengorse, Battle, East Sussex TN33 0TX
**US SIC:** 7391 **UK SIC:** 94000
**Auditors:** PricewaterhouseCoopers LLP

| | 31-12-13 | 31-12-12 | 31-12-11 |
|---|---|---|---|
| TO | 564,809,000 | 563,941,000 | 518,953,000 |
| P/L | 82,300,000 | 77,769,000 | 44,882,000 |
| NW | 77,091,000 | 171,329,000 | 126,152,000 |
| WC | 62,406,000 | 155,555,000 | 112,451,000 |
| Emp. | 2,039 | 1,960 | 1,851 |

DUNS 21-862-2355

## Quinto Crane & Plant Ltd

Anson Road Norwich Airport Industrial, Estate, Norwich, Norfolk NR6 6EH
**Web:** www.quinto.co.uk
**Reg No:** 0875008 **VAT No:** 304751480

**Estd:** 1977 Private Limited Company
**Line of Business:** Renting of construction and civil engineering machinery and equipment
**Issued Capital:** £31,500
**Directors:** O W Arnold, Mrs H R Arnold
**Responsibilities**
**Senior:** Des Coe *(Depot Manager)*, Colin Henson *(Manager)*, Nigel Kiddle *(Manager)*
**Branches:** Quinto Crane & Plant Ltd, Admiralty Road, Great Yarmouth, Norfolk NR30 3DY
**US SIC:** 7394, 7513
**UK SIC:** 84000, 84802
**Auditors:** Lovewell Blake
**Bankers:** HSBC Bank plc (40-35-09)

| | 31-12-13 | 31-12-12 | 31-12-11 |
|---|---|---|---|
| TO | 7,760,532 | 7,096,392 | 6,957,162 |
| P/L | (138,827) | (123,498) | (238,371) |
| NW | 3,188,095 | 3,244,531 | 2,487,276 |
| WC | 272,764 | 370,525 | 240,238 |
| Emp. | 130 | 130 | 129 |

DUNS 42-315-6454
## Quinton House School
The Hall, Upton Lane, Upton, Northampton, Northamptonshire NN5 4UX
**Web:** www.quintonhouseschool.co.uk
**Estd:** 1947 Partnership
**Line of Business:** Schools (independent)
**Principals:** Mrs S Griffiths *(Financial)*, Mrs P Griffiths *(Partner)*, G Griffiths *(Partner)*
**Responsibilities**
**Senior:** John Ing *(Head Teacher)*, Nicki Sparrow *(Business Manager)*
**Finance:** Nicki Sparrow *(Business Manager)*
**Sales:** Nicki Sparrow *(Business Manager)*
**IT:** Cathy Grove *(Head of IT)*
**HR:** Nicki Sparrow *(Business Manager)*
**Health & Safety:** Shaun Pape *(Health & Safety Officer)*
**Facilities:** Nicki Sparrow *(Business Manager)*
**US SIC:** 8211 **UK SIC:** 93200
**Employees:** 50

DUNS 22-606-7825 **Imp**
## Quirepace Ltd
Unit 6, Gosport, Hampshire PO12 8XU
**Web:** www.quirepace.co.uk
**Reg No:** 1748970 **VAT No:** 381077941
**Estd:** 1983 Private Limited Company
**Line of Business:** Pneumatic systems and equipment
**Issued Capital:** £10,000
**Principals:** D Alexander *(Managing)*, A P Johnson *(Sales)*, Ms R M Mauchline, L S Jury
**Co. Secretary:** Martin Chewter
**Responsibilities**
**Senior:** Rose Montiel *(Production Director)*
**Finance:** Martin Tutor *(Financial Director)*
**Marketing:** Zoe Raval *(Marketing Manager)*
**IT:** Eddie Shawyer *(Manager)*
**HR:** Wendy Ravall *(Human Resources Manager)*
**Facilities:** Barry Mackrell *(Chief Engineer)*
**Operations:** Barry Mackrell *(Chief Engineer)*
**Purchasing:** Mark Pampion *(Buyer)*
**Fleet:** Rose Montiel *(Production Director)*
**Engineering:** Barry Mackrell *(Chief Engineer)*, Rose Montiel *(Production Director)*
**US SIC:** 3563, 3999
**UK SIC:** 32831, 49590
**Auditors:** Compass Accountants Ltd
**Bankers:** Barclays Bank Plc (20-79-25)

| | 30-09-13 | 30-09-12 | 30-09-11 |
|---|---|---|---|
| TO | 7,745,850 | 7,553,252 | 7,843,870 |
| P/L | 542,434 | 563,056 | 589,273 |
| NW | 3,022,141 | 2,797,345 | 2,565,231 |
| WC | 2,796,849 | 2,560,999 | 2,303,745 |
| Emp. | 104 | 110 | 115 |

DUNS 23-573-1098 **Imp**
## Quiss Technology Plc
Unit 7 Claymore, Tamworth, Staffordshire B77 5DQ
**Web:** www.quiss.co.uk
**Reg No:** 2248732 **VAT No:** 505207191
**Estd:** 1988 Public Limited Company
**Line of Business:** Hardware consultancy
**Issued Capital:** £100,000
**Directors:** C Taylor, I Harrison, A Michael, Ms S Bull
**Co. Secretary:** Ms Joanne Ward
**Branches:** Quiss Technology Plc, Congress House, 14 Lyon Road, Harrow, Middlesex HA1 2EN
**US SIC:** 7379 **UK SIC:** 83940
**Auditors:** Cartwrights
**Bankers:** Barclays Bank Plc (20-92-60)

| | 31-05-14 | 31-05-13 | 31-05-12 |
|---|---|---|---|
| TO | 6,461,125 | 5,852,046 | 4,785,671 |
| P/L | 84,160 | 172,725 | 126,386 |
| NW | 1,803,430 | 1,649,504 | 1,616,374 |
| WC | (199,720) | 38,162 | 312,587 |

DUNS 23-267-0575
## Quixant Plc
100 High Street, Balsham, Cambridge, Cambridgeshire CB21 4EP
**Tel:** 01223892696 **Fax:** 01223892401
**Web:** www.quixant.com
**Reg No:** 4316977 **Estd:** 2012 Public Limited Company
**Line of Business:** Computer support & services
**Directors:** G C Van Zwanenberg, Ms A C Preddy, M J Peagram, N C Jarmany, G P Mullins, C T Lin
**Co. Secretary:** Alan Milne
**Responsibilities**
**Senior:** Jon Jayal *(General Manager)*
**US SIC:** 3944 **UK SIC:** 49410
**Auditors:** KPMG LLP
**Employees:** 4
**Turnover:** £24,235,000

DUNS 51-596-0172
## Quo Vadis Trust
Unit 12 Kent House Lane Gardner, Industrial Estate, Beckenham, Kent BR3 1QZ
**Tel:** 020-8778-4546 **Fax:** 020-8776-7191
**Web:** www.qvt.org.uk
**Reg No:** 5876659 **Estd:** 2003 Private Company Limited By Guarantee
**Line of Business:** Youth hostels and mountain refuges
**Directors:** Dr W Onyeama, A A Rodriguez, Mrs I Poyntz, Ms J Simkins, E Strudwick, S Osazuwa, W J Puddicombe, S Dellar
**Co. Secretary:** John O'Sullivan
**Responsibilities**
**Senior:** Zena Everett *(Director)*, Arnold Sami *(Manager)*
**US SIC:** 7021 **UK SIC:** 66500
**Auditors:** Knox Cropper
**Bankers:** The Co-Operative Bank Plc (08-92-04)

| | 31-03-14 | 31-03-13 | 31-03-12 |
|---|---|---|---|
| TO | 2,916,105 | 2,442,411 | 2,407,251 |
| P/L | 136,167 | 17,902 | (148,109) |
| NW | 603,391 | 509,169 | 491,267 |
| WC | 189,068 | 147,511 | 448,996 |
| Emp. | 66 | 53 | 58 |

DUNS 21-819-4877
## Quod Planning Services Ltd
2nd Floor Ingeni Building, 17 Broadwick Street, London W1F 0AX
**Tel:** 02035971000
**Web:** www.quod.com
**Reg No:** 7917483 **Estd:** 2012 Private Limited Company
**Line of Business:** Planning consultants
**Issued Capital:** £2
**Directors:** B Ford, T Rainbird
**US SIC:** 8911 **UK SIC:** 83701

| | 31-01-14 | 31-01-13 |
|---|---|---|
| TA | 2 | 2 |
| NW | 2 | 2 |

DUNS 49-084-5674
## Quorn Country Foods Ltd
(**Subsidiary of:** Fqf Holdings Ltd)
Quorn House, Comet Way, Coalville, Leicestershire LE67 3FS
**Tel:** 01530-830180
**Web:** www.foodconnections.co.uk
**Reg No:** 3089071 **Estd:** 1995 Private Limited Company
**Line of Business:** Manufacturers of biscuits
**Trading Style:** Food Connections
**Issued Capital:** £50,000
**Principals:** G J York *(Managing)*, Ms C J Haggis, Ms P R Broughton, D J Ralph, P J Haggis
**Co. Secretary:** Dean Spray
**US SIC:** 2052 **UK SIC:** 41970
**Auditors:** Clear & Lane
**Bankers:** Bank Of Scotland (12-08-81)

| | 30-09-13 | 30-09-12 | 30-09-11 |
|---|---|---|---|
| TA | 2,813,546 | 2,693,137 | 2,990,876 |
| NW | 1,824,167 | 1,744,079 | 1,642,752 |
| WC | 1,180,244 | 1,093,994 | 1,432,241 |

DUNS 21-697-9772
## Quorn Foods Ltd
(**Subsidiary of:** Exponent Private Equity Partners Ii Lp)
Station Road, Middlesbrough, Cleveland TS9 7AB
**Tel:** 08456029000
**Web:** www.quorn.co.uk
**Reg No:** 7435839 **Estd:** 2010 Private Limited Company
**Line of Business:** Manufacturers of food products
**Export Sales:** £30,223,000
**Issued Capital:** £10,369
**Directors:** S R Davidson, C M Graham, C R Sharpe, G J Knight, K F Brennan, M S Lofnes, P J Monk
**Co. Secretary:** Martin Lofnes
**US SIC:** 2099 **UK SIC:** 42399

| | 31-12-13 | 31-12-12 | 31-12-11 |
|---|---|---|---|
| TO | 140,941,000 | 131,578,000 | 110,177,000 |
| P/L | (14,256,000) | (13,536,000) | (13,578,000) |
| NW | (148,964,000) | (139,748,000) | (131,805,000) |
| WC | 32,864,000 | 26,406,000 | 27,375,000 |
| Emp. | 591 | 618 | 594 |

DUNS 21-435-2424
## Quorn Grange Hotel
88 Wood Lane, Quorn, Loughborough, Leicestershire LE12 8DB
**Tel:** 01509416763
**Web:** www.quorngrangehotel.co.uk
**Estd:** 1979
**Line of Business:** Pre school education
**Proprietor:** G Bland
**US SIC:** 7011 **UK SIC:** 66500
**Employees:** 50

DUNS 21-132-3953
## Quotemetoday.Co.Uk Llp
Unit 3 Boorman Way Ground Floor Estuary, View Business Park, Whitstable, Kent CT5 3SE
**Tel:** 08432274323 **Fax:** 08452913442
**Web:** www.quotemetoday.co.uk
**Reg No:** 0339071OC **Estd:** 2002 Private Limited Company
**Line of Business:** Insurance brokers
**Responsibilities**
**Senior:** Emma Bostock *(Marketing Manager)*
**Marketing:** Mike Denby *(Marketing Manager)*
**US SIC:** 6411 **UK SIC:** 83200
**Auditors:** Beresfords

| | 31-08-13 | 31-08-12 | 31-08-11 |
|---|---|---|---|
| TA | 2,144,267 | 1,823,704 | 2,313,120 |
| NW | (404,195) | (404,195) | (404,195) |
| WC | 4,489 | 3,414 | 83,510 |

DUNS 42-414-3899
## Quothquan Farms Ltd
Quothquan Law Farm, Biggar, Lanarkshire ML12 6NU
**Web:** www.quothquanfarms.co.uk
**Reg No:** 0031798NI **Estd:** 1980 Private Limited Company
**Line of Business:** Dairy produce merchants
**Issued Capital:** £100
**Directors:** B Hewitt, G Hewitt
**Co. Secretary:** Geoffrey Hewitt
**Responsibilities**
**Finance:** Janice Hewitt *(Finance Director)*, Debbie Oakes *(Finance Manager)*
**Operations:** Norman Gilvear *(Production Manager)*
**Fleet:** Bob Mooney *(Transport Manager)*
**Engineering:** Norman Gilvear *(Production Manager)*
**US SIC:** 0241 **UK SIC:** 01001
**Bankers:** Clydesdale Bank Plc (82-66-03)

| | 28-02-14 | 28-02-13 | 31-02-12 |
|---|---|---|---|
| TO | 8,605,769 | 7,078,716 | 7,178,231 |
| P/L | (231,901) | 151,643 | (641,494) |
| NW | (543,927) | (308,054) | (535,647) |
| WC | (784,929) | (553,885) | (1,015,095) |
| Emp. | 53 | 50 | 54 |

DUNS 21-584-9273
## Quotient Bioresearch
The Old Glassworks, Nettlefold Road, Cardiff, South Glamorgan CF24 5JQ
**Tel:** 02920474900
**Web:** www.quotientbioresearch.com
**Estd:** 2011 Proprietorship
**Line of Business:** Pharmaceutical suppliers and wholesalers
**Proprietor:** Ms J Poole
**US SIC:** 5122 **UK SIC:** 61800
**Employees:** 100

DUNS 23-080-7554
## Qvc
(**Subsidiary of:** Q V C Britain)
Chiswick Park, 566 Chiswick High Road, London W4 5XU
**Tel:** 02088115600 **Fax:** 020-7705-5601
**Web:** www.qvc.co.uk
**Reg No:** 2807164 **VAT No:** 723095447
**Estd:** 1993 Private Unlimited Company
**Line of Business:** Home shopping
**Issued Capital:** £5
**Directors:** M A George, S Hofmann
**Co. Secretary:** Lawrence Hayes
**Responsibilities**
**Finance:** John Devlin *(Finance Director)*
**HR:** Frank Robinson *(Human Resources Manager)*
**Branches:** Qvc, Media and Commerce Centre, Building 8 Chiswick Park, 566 Chiswick High Road, London W4 5XU
**US SIC:** 5961, 4833
**UK SIC:** 65600, 97411
**Auditors:** KPMG LLP
**Bankers:** HSBC Bank plc (40-03-05)

| | 31-12-13 | 31-12-12 | 31-12-11 |
|---|---|---|---|
| TO | 418,636,000 | 403,716,000 | 390,941,000 |
| P/L | 35,904,000 | 28,280,000 | 33,237,000 |
| NW | 88,242,000 | 84,781,000 | 66,006,000 |
| WC | 27,205,000 | 19,995,000 | 2,119,000 |
| Emp. | 1,515 | 1,626 | 1,649 |

DUNS 73-800-1283
## Qvc Britain I Ltd
(**Subsidiary of:** Starz)
Building 8 Chiswick Park, 566 Chiswick High Road, London W4 5XU
**Tel:** 02077055600 **Fax:** 02077055601
**Web:** www.qvcuk.com
**Reg No:** 5056490 **Estd:** 2004 Private Limited Company
**Line of Business:** Mail order houses
**Issued Capital:** £10
**Director:** M A George
**Co. Secretary:** Lawrence Hayes
**US SIC:** 5961 **UK SIC:** 65600
**Auditors:** KPMG LLP

| | 31-12-13 | 31-12-12 | 31-12-11 |
|---|---|---|---|
| TA | 49,171,000 | 49,171,000 | 49,172,000 |
| P/L | 6,000,000 | 1,999,000 | 2,000,000 |
| NW | 48,927,000 | 48,927,000 | 48,928,000 |
| WC | (199,000) | (199,000) | (198,000) |

DUNS 77-492-1415
## Qvs Electrical Wholesale Ltd
Unit 1 New House Farm, Antlands Lane, Shipley Bridge, Horley, Surrey RH6 9TF
**Tel:** 01342302244
**Web:** www.qvsdirect.com
**Reg No:** 2975861 **Estd:** 2004 Private Limited Company
**Line of Business:** Electrical wholesalers
**Issued Capital:** £270
**Managing Director:** P C Brain
**Co. Secretary:** Michael Duggan
**Branches:** Qvs Electrical Wholesale Ltd, Saxon Works, Olive Road, Hove, East Sussex BN3 5LE
**US SIC:** 5074, 5732
**UK SIC:** 61300, 64800
**Auditors:** Auker Hutton
**Bankers:** HSBC Bank plc (40-16-28)

| | 31-03-14 | 31-03-13 | 31-03-12 |
|---|---|---|---|
| TO | 12,141,134 | 11,861,975 | 11,495,449 |
| P/L | 366,562 | 193,689 | 189,054 |
| NW | 1,504,246 | 1,450,559 | 1,297,671 |
| WC | 1,453,807 | 1,387,629 | 1,229,639 |
| Emp. | 101 | 108 | 101 |

DUNS 51-573-5673
## Qw Security Ltd
8-9 Enterprise House, Thomlinson Road, Hartlepool, Cleveland TS25 1NS
**Tel:** 01429-268768
**Web:** www.qwsecurity.co.uk
**Reg No:** 5854868 **Estd:** 2006 Private Limited Company
**Line of Business:** Security and related activities
**Issued Capital:** £1,000
**Directors:** B H Irving, J C Walker, I M Morl
**Responsibilities**
**Senior:** Dennis McClelland *(Sales Manager)*
**US SIC:** 7393 **UK SIC:** 83954

| | 31-12-13 | 31-12-12 | 31-12-11 |
|---|---|---|---|
| TA | 608,073 | 609,000 | 844,126 |
| NW | 45,765 | 68,000 | 104,417 |
| WC | 24,799 | 37,000 | 54,013 |

DUNS 21-973-0137
## Qwerk Ltd
Mark Road, Hemel Hempstead, Hertfordshire HP2 7DN
**Tel:** 0870-900-4311 **Fax:** 0870-900-4313
**Web:** www.qwerk.biz
**Reg No:** 6154824 **Estd:** 2000 Private Limited Company
**Line of Business:** Other artistic and literary creation and interpretation
**Issued Capital:** £60
**Director:** C R Dann
**Co. Secretary:** Ian Crawford
**US SIC:** 8999 **UK SIC:** 83954

| | 31-03-14 | 31-03-13 | 31-03-12 |
|---|---|---|---|
| TA | 1,540,037 | 1,039,845 | 976,252 |
| NW | 711,502 | 607,755 | 467,223 |
| WC | 120,919 | 37,701 | (72,379) |

# R

DUNS 21-762-1241
## R A & C P Haddock
1 Bourne Court, Bristol, Avon
**Tel:** 07836-584944
**Estd:** 1980 Partnership
**Line of Business:** Farming (livestock)
**US SIC:** 0279 **UK SIC:** 01001
**Employees:** 60

## DUNS 21-054-2044
### R A & D H Bradley
Westfield Farm, Sherburn, Malton, North Yorkshire YO17 8EW
**Tel:** 01944710672
**Estd:** 1994 Partnership
**Line of Business:** General Farms Primarily Livestock
**Partners:** R A Bradley, D H Bradley
**US SIC:** 0291 **UK SIC:** 01001
**Bankers:** HSBC Bank plc (40-40-22)
**Employees:** 72

## DUNS 21-065-8782
### R A Clement Associates
Argyll Square, Oban, Argyll PA34 4AZ
**Web:** www.raclement.co.uk
**Estd:** 1977 Partnership
**Line of Business:** Accounting activities
**Partners:** Mrs F Mcglynn, G Anderson, J Macgregor, D Mudie
**Responsibilities**
**Senior:** Duncan Grout (Partner), John MacGregor (Partner), Andy Newiss (Partner)
**Branches:** R A Clement Associates, Po Box 1, Isle Of Mull, Islands PA64 6WZ
**US SIC:** 8931 **UK SIC:** 83600
**Bankers:** Clydesdale Bank Plc (82-67-04)
**Employees:** 50

## DUNS 21-395-9118
### R A F C T E
Douglas Bader House, Horcott Hill, Cirencester, Gloucestershire GL7 4RB
**Web:** www.airtattoo.com
**Proprietorship**
**Line of Business:** Charities and charitable organisations
**Proprietor:** T Price
**Responsibilities**
**Senior:** Timothy Prince (Chief Executive)
**US SIC:** 8699 **UK SIC:** 96902
**Employees:** 48

## DUNS 23-254-1420
### R A F Museum Enterprices
Cosford, Shifnal, Shropshire TF11 8UP
**Tel:** 01902-376200
**Web:** www.rafmuseum.org.uk
**Estd:** 1974 Proprietorship
**Line of Business:** Activities of other membership organisations not elsewhere classified
**Principals:** N Branagh (Chairman), J Francis, A Medhurst (Proprietor)
**US SIC:** 8699, 8999
**UK SIC:** 96902, 83954
**Employees:** 60

## DUNS 21-183-0364
### R A O B Social Club
7 St James Street, King's Lynn, Norfolk PE30 5DA
**Tel:** 01553-762725
**Estd:** 1984
**Line of Business:** Clubs social and associations
**Principals:** B Mason, P Leider
**US SIC:** 8699 **UK SIC:** 96902
**Employees:** 500

## DUNS 23-670-8939
### R A Rossborough Ltd
(**Subsidiary of:** Rossborough Holdings Limited)
41-43 Lane Motte Street, St Helier, Jersey, Channel Islands JE2 4SZ
**Tel:** 01534-500500 **Fax:** 01534-767806
**Web:** www.rossborough.co.uk
**Reg No:** 0000287J **Estd:** 1936 Private Limited Company
**Line of Business:** Financial advisors head office with 2 sites
**Trading Style:** Rossboroughs
**Issued Capital:** £5,000
**Principals:** J W Gollop (Chairman and Managing), I D Smith (Financial), K J Gollop, Ms P M Gollop
**Responsibilities**
**Senior:** Clive De La Cour (CEO, Managing Director), Steve Warner (Manager)
**US SIC:** 6711, 6111, 6411, 6531
**UK SIC:** 83962, 81501, 83200, 83400
**Employees:** 140

## DUNS 23-626-8061
### R A Shield Holdings Ltd
Troon Industrial Area, 191 Barkby Road, Leicester, Leicestershire LE4 9HX
**Web:** www.shieldeng.co.uk
**Reg No:** 3623882 **Estd:** 1998 Private Limited Company
**Line of Business:** Manufacture of engines and turbines, except aircraft, vehicle and cycle engines

**Export Sales:** £8,189,502
**Trading Style:** Shield Group
**Issued Capital:** £33,779
**Directors:** J Cooper, C R Shield
**Co. Secretary:** Mrs Susan Shield
**US SIC:** 3519 **UK SIC:** 32811
**Auditors:** Thomas May & Co

|     | 31-10-13 | 31-10-12 | 31-10-11 |
|-----|----------|----------|----------|
| TO  | 64,343,348 | 71,665,331 | 75,990,774 |
| P/L | 556,796 | 3,932,158 | 7,880,557 |
| NW  | 38,655,553 | 37,510,411 | 34,962,127 |
| WC  | 12,625,565 | 8,769,742 | 10,477,728 |
| Emp.| 458 | 493 | 465 |

## DUNS 73-455-5746
### R & A Group Services Ltd
Beach House, St Andrews, Fife KY16 9JA
**Tel:** 01334460000 **Fax:** 01334-460001
**Web:** www.r&a.org
**Reg No:** 0247048SC **Estd:** 2003 Private Limited Company
**Line of Business:** Other business activities not elsewhere classified
**Issued Capital:** £500
**Directors:** D I Turner, M N Donaldson, C L Edginton
**Co. Secretary:** John Murray
**Responsibilities**
**Senior:** Mark Dobell (Manager), Johnny Hamilton (Manager)
**Finance:** Jim McKane (Accountant)
**US SIC:** 7399 **UK SIC:** 83954
**Auditors:** Ernst & Young LLP
**Bankers:** The Royal Bank Of Scotland Plc (83-26-28)

|     | 31-12-13 | 31-12-12 | 31-12-11 |
|-----|----------|----------|----------|
| TO  | 11,784,000 | 12,759,000 | 10,493,000 |
| P/L | 782,000 | 1,862,000 | 871,000 |
| NW  | 5,224,000 | 3,478,000 | 1,886,000 |
| WC  | 1,712,000 | 1,463,000 | 2,105,000 |
| Emp.| 136 | 127 | 124 |

## DUNS 21-680-3221
### R & B Star(Electrical Wholesalers) Ltd
13-14 Kennet Road Thames Road, Dartford, Kent DA1 4SD
**Tel:** 01322555125
**Web:** www.rbstar.co.uk
**Reg No:** 0693828 **VAT No:** 205702010
**Estd:** 1960 Private Limited Company
**Line of Business:** Plumbing & heating equipment wholesalers
**Issued Capital:** £28,000
**Principals:** R W Robertson (Managing), A J Robertson, M A Mitchell, P Finnis, G J Robertson
**Responsibilities**
**Senior:** Stuart Burbridge (Warehouse Manager), Vicky Pearce (Manager)
**Facilities:** Stuart Burbridge (Warehouse Manager)
**Purchasing:** Cas Mitchell (Buyer)
**Branches:** R & B Star(Electrical Wholesalers) Ltd, Unit 10, Jerrard Street, London SE13 7SH
**US SIC:** 5074, 5039
**UK SIC:** 61300
**Auditors:** Jones & Co
**Bankers:** National Westminster Bank Plc (60-06-33)

|     | 30-09-13 | 31-05-12 | 31-09-11 |
|-----|----------|----------|----------|
| TO  | 14,728,535 | 11,004,515 | 10,437,648 |
| P/L | (89,620) | 56,998 | 61,377 |
| NW  | 1,231,877 | 1,471,497 | 1,449,661 |
| WC  | 38,307 | (425,284) | (316,136) |
| Emp.| 59 | 57 | 55 |

## DUNS 21-919-6268
### R & C Williams Ltd
(**Subsidiary of:** R+c Williams (Holdings) Ltd)
Spaghetti Junction, Birmingham, West Midlands B24 8NP
**Tel:** 0121-326-9696 **Fax:** 0121-328-3171
**Web:** www.randcwilliams.ltd.uk
**Reg No:** 1857915 **Estd:** 1968 Private Limited Company
**Line of Business:** Civil engineers
**Issued Capital:** £97,825
**Principals:** C J Williams (Managing), N D Drew (Financial), D P Braybrooke
**Co. Secretary:** Charles Williams
**Responsibilities**
**Sales:** Arron Roberts (Assistant Contracts Manager)
**Admin:** Aileen Bicknell (Office Manager)
**IT:** Ian Yardley (Logistics Manager)
**HR:** Ian Yardley (Logistics Manager)
**Health & Safety:** Ian Yardley (Logistics Manager)
**Operations:** Ian Yardley (Logistics Manager)
**Fleet:** Ian Yardley (Logistics Manager)
**US SIC:** 8911, 1622
**UK SIC:** 83701, 50200
**Auditors:** Howell Davies Ltd

**Bankers:** National Westminster Bank Plc (60-21-08)

|     | 30-09-13 | 01-10-12 | 31-09-11 |
|-----|----------|----------|----------|
| TO  | N/A | N/A | 6,472,400 |
| P/L | N/A | N/A | 247,559 |
| NW  | 1,257,609 | 1,314,210 | 1,411,419 |
| WC  | 1,106,740 | 1,127,883 | 1,190,281 |
| Emp.| N/A | N/A | 58 |

## DUNS 50-532-1968     Imp-Exp
### R & D Systems Europe Ltd.
(**Subsidiary of:** Bio-Techne Corporation)
19 Barton Lane, Abingdon, Oxfordshire OX14 3NB
**Tel:** 01235-529449
**Web:** www.rndsystems.com
**Reg No:** 2490104 **VAT No:** 630531673
**Estd:** 1991 Private Limited Company
**Line of Business:** Pest control
**Export Markets:** E U, USA, Japan & Rest of the World
**Export Sales:** £34,101,000
**Issued Capital:** £680,000
**Directors:** Ms K Backes, C R Kummeth
**Co. Secretary:** Ms Ruth Bright
**Responsibilities**
**Senior:** Thomas Oland (Manager)
**Finance:** Wazeem Labal (Financial Director)
**HR:** Gina Darling (Human Resources Manager)
**US SIC:** 2899, 5122
**UK SIC:** 25670, 61800
**Auditors:** KPMG LLP
**Bankers:** Barclays Bank Plc (20-65-18)

|     | 30-06-13 | 30-06-12 | 30-06-11 |
|-----|----------|----------|----------|
| TO  | 45,208,000 | 42,319,000 | 41,613,000 |
| P/L | 18,783,000 | 17,295,000 | 18,980,000 |
| NW  | 79,313,000 | 84,415,000 | 71,382,000 |
| WC  | (4,787,000) | 206,000 | 6,970,000 |
| Emp.| 55 | 59 | 59 |

## DUNS 29-502-9144     Imp-Exp
### R & D Tool & Engineering Ltd
(**Subsidiary of:** R & D Tool & Engineering Co.)
Hamilton Road, Sutton-In-Ashfield, Nottinghamshire NG17 5LD
**Tel:** 01623-556287
**Web:** www.rdleverage.com
**Reg No:** 1866185 **VAT No:** 419833726
**Estd:** 1984 Private Limited Company
**Line of Business:** Manufacturers of tools
**Export Markets:** U S A; S Africa; France; Belgium; Spain; Italy; Republic of Ireland
**Export Sales:** £2,561,722
**Issued Capital:** £50,000
**Principals:** A L Tolley (Managing), T White, W T Riley
**Co. Secretary:** Shaun Ennis
**Responsibilities**
**IT:** Mike Peat (IT Manager)
**Health & Safety:** Belinda Stacey (Health & Safety Officer)
**US SIC:** 3423, 3079
**UK SIC:** 31612, 48360
**Auditors:** Grant Thornton
**Bankers:** National Westminster Bank Plc (60-80-09)

|     | 31-12-13 | 31-12-12 | 31-12-11 |
|-----|----------|----------|----------|
| TO  | 4,729,027 | 5,044,179 | 6,250,978 |
| P/L | 75,434 | 437,314 | 969,221 |
| NW  | 2,065,083 | 1,871,376 | 1,540,569 |
| WC  | 11,592 | (234,595) | (562,066) |
| Emp.| 72 | 75 | 75 |

## DUNS 22-851-9682     Imp
### R. & E. Bamford Ltd
Globe Mill, 17 Midge Hall Lane, Midge Hall, Preston, Lancashire PR26 6TN
**Tel:** 01772456300 **Fax:** 01772456302
**Web:** www.bamfords.co.uk
**Reg No:** 1993923 **VAT No:** 153538758
**Estd:** 1986 Private Limited Company
**Line of Business:** Manufacture of prepared pet foods
**Issued Capital:** £401,845
**Managing Directors:** P Bamford, A Bamford
**Co. Secretary:** Mrs Joan Bullen
**Responsibilities**
**Senior:** Phillip Bamford (Managing Director)
**IT:** Richard Fare (IT Assistant)
**Facilities:** Marc Jackson (Warehouse Manager)
**Branches:** The Mill, Marloop, Bretherton, Preston
**US SIC:** 2047, 5153
**UK SIC:** 42221, 61100
**Auditors:** Cameron Valentine Ltd
**Bankers:** The Royal Bank Of Scotland Plc (16-27-22)

|     | 05-04-14 | 05-04-13 | 05-04-12 |
|-----|----------|----------|----------|
| TO  | N/A | N/A | 7,846,503 |
| P/L | N/A | N/A | 46,547 |
| NW  | 1,382,053 | 1,241,117 | 1,100,583 |
| WC  | 645,939 | 428,403 | 320,866 |

## DUNS 51-756-5636
### R & G Christie
Myreton Of Claverhouse Farm, Dundee, Angus DD3 0PY
**Tel:** 01382-825593
**Web:** www.christiesstrawberries.co.uk
**Estd:** 1970 Partnership
**Line of Business:** Farming (arable)
**Partners:** R Christie, Mrs I Christie, Mrs H Christie, G Christie
**US SIC:** 0119 **UK SIC:** 01001
**Employees:** 70

## DUNS 73-401-1799
### R & J (Builders Hardware) Ltd
Croft Head Road, Whitebirk Industrial Estate, Blackburn, Lancashire BB1 5TB
**Tel:** 01254-52525 **Fax:** 01254-665510
**Web:** www.randjbuildershardware.co.uk
**Reg No:** 4674519 **Estd:** 1971 Private Limited Company
**Line of Business:** Hardware and ironmongers merchants
**Issued Capital:** £2,625
**Director:** M R Bury
**Co. Secretary:** Mrs Susan Bury
**Responsibilities**
**Senior:** David Ayrton (Chief Executive), Rodney Bradley (Manager)
**Sales:** David Ayrton (Chief Executive)
**Health & Safety:** David Ayrton (Chief Executive)
**US SIC:** 5072 **UK SIC:** 61500
**Auditors:** Egan Roberts Ltd

|     | 31-12-13 | 31-12-12 | 31-12-11 |
|-----|----------|----------|----------|
| TO  | 10,579,874 | 10,460,097 | 10,069,185 |
| P/L | 929,564 | 732,303 | 808,271 |
| NW  | 4,180,175 | 3,744,899 | 3,380,336 |
| WC  | 3,140,502 | 2,966,898 | 2,587,824 |
| Emp.| 81 | 74 | 74 |

## DUNS 23-158-0320
### R & J Foods Ltd
47 Queen Street, Ballymoney, Co Antrim BT53 6JD
**Tel:** 02827669055 **Fax:** 02827669055
**Web:** www.rjfoodsflapjack.com
**Reg No:** 0035741NI **Estd:** 1999 Private Limited Company
**Line of Business:** Other retail sale in non-specialised stores
**Issued Capital:** £1
**Directors:** R Henderson, J Henderson
**Co. Secretary:** Richard Henderson
**US SIC:** 5399, 5431
**UK SIC:** 65600, 64100
**Bankers:** Northern Bank Ltd (95-02-77)

|     | 31-01-14 | 31-01-13 | 31-01-12 |
|-----|----------|----------|----------|
| TO  | 10,236,868 | 9,516,096 | 9,339,880 |
| P/L | 178,400 | (135,435) | 87,270 |
| NW  | 913,022 | 861,984 | 1,373,492 |
| WC  | 17,933 | 84,117 | 716,598 |
| Emp.| 90 | 101 | 103 |

## DUNS 23-645-4401
### R & J Simpson Ltd
(**Subsidiary of:** R J S (Scotland) Ltd)
27 Sinclair Road, Aberdeen, Aberdeenshire AB11 9PL
**Tel:** 01224-894043
**Reg No:** 0090710SC **Estd:** 1975 Private Limited Company
**Line of Business:** Road haulage and transport services
**Issued Capital:** £17,500
**Directors:** R Simpson, Mrs G C Simpson, N Stephen
**Co. Secretary:** Raymond Simpson, Senior
**Responsibilities**
**Senior:** Norman Stephens (Transport Manager)
**Health & Safety:** Norman Stephens (Transport Manager)
**Fleet:** Norman Stephens (Transport Manager)
**US SIC:** 4789 **UK SIC:** 77002
**Auditors:** James Milne & Co

|     | 31-12-13 | 31-12-12 | 31-12-11 |
|-----|----------|----------|----------|
| TA  | 1,445,914 | 1,201,394 | 1,141,540 |
| NW  | 981,672 | 914,937 | 885,762 |
| WC  | 552,505 | 561,140 | 444,909 |

## DUNS 34-590-3264     Imp-Exp
### R & K Drysdale Ltd
(**Subsidiary of:** R & K Drysdale (Holdings) Ltd)
Old Cambus Quarry, Cockburnspath, Berwickshire TD13 5YS
**Tel:** 01368-830448 **Fax:** 01368-830561
**Web:** www.rkdrysdale.co.uk
**Reg No:** 0139487SC **Estd:** 1992 Private Limited Company
**Line of Business:** Fruit and vegetable (producers)
**Export Markets:** Germany
**Issued Capital:** £1,000,000
**Principals:** C S Keenan (Managing), C R Fleet, S L Edwards
**Co. Secretary:** Gavin Simpson

**Responsibilities**
**Senior:** Kim Drysdale *(Manager)*, Charles Ross *(Manager)*
**US SIC:** 2099, 2033
**UK SIC:** 42399, 41473
**Auditors:** KPMG
**Bankers:** The Royal Bank Of Scotland Plc (83-15-28)

| | 30-06-13 | 30-06-12 | 30-06-11 |
|---|---|---|---|
| TO | 21,816,155 | 17,408,227 | 16,409,129 |
| P/L | 660,560 | 791,170 | 405,043 |
| NW | 7,308,282 | 6,700,982 | 6,093,800 |
| WC | 3,538,497 | 3,067,970 | 3,946,385 |
| Emp. | 170 | 249 | 142 |

DUNS 21-737-2333 Imp
## R. & M. Clarkson Ltd
(**Subsidiary of:** Clarkson Safety Services (Holdings) Ltd)
3 The Knowes, Kelso, Roxburghshire TD5 7BH
**Tel:** 01573228669
**Web:** www.clarksonsafety.com
**Reg No:** 1176505 **VAT No:** 219442173
**Estd:** 1974 Private Limited Company
**Line of Business:** Manufacture of electricity distribution and control apparatus
**Issued Capital:** £525
**Director:** N Shrubsole
**Responsibilities**
**Senior:** Philippe L yer *(Director)*
**US SIC:** 3643, 1796
**UK SIC:** 34203, 50400
**Bankers:** Lloyds TSB Bank plc (30-91-72)

| | 31-12-13 | 31-03-13 | 31-12-12 |
|---|---|---|---|
| TO | 4,632,988 | N/A | N/A |
| P/L | 599,099 | N/A | N/A |
| NW | 1,414,097 | 971,791 | 1,080,777 |
| WC | 1,317,594 | 807,043 | 897,152 |

DUNS 39-884-7962 Imp
## R & M Electrical Group Ltd
Unit 10, Milford Haven, Dyfed SA73 1SE
**Tel:** 01646601879 **Fax:** 023-8043-4067
**Web:** www.rm-electrical.com
**Reg No:** 2218034 **VAT No:** 458620923
**Estd:** 1987 Private Limited Company
**Line of Business:** Wholesale of hardware, plumbing and heating equipment and supplies
**Issued Capital:** £8,641
**Principals:** B A Robinson *(Managing)*, R J Sherin *(Managing)*, A L Baggott, A M Chandler, Ms C A Robinson, T Coomer, R I Hayes
**Co. Secretary:** William Crook
**Responsibilities**
**IT:** Mark Stones *(Computer Manager)*
**HR:** Rachael Wilson *(Human Resources Manager)*
**Health & Safety:** Rachael Wilson *(Human Resources Manager)*
**Facilities:** Neil Sherin *(Facilities Coordinator)*
**Branches:** R & M Electrical Group Ltd, Unit 5, 4C Mead Street, Bristol, Avon BS3 4RP
**US SIC:** 3629, 5021, 5199
**UK SIC:** 34350, 61500, 61900
**Auditors:** Fiander Tovell LLP
**Bankers:** HSBC Bank plc (40-42-18)

| | 30-04-14 | 30-04-13 | 30-04-12 |
|---|---|---|---|
| TO | 51,426,939 | 48,728,908 | 61,688,043 |
| P/L | 1,958,715 | 2,928,190 | 2,041,973 |
| NW | 7,600,849 | 7,377,096 | 5,958,833 |
| WC | 5,546,508 | 4,109,378 | 2,886,420 |
| Emp. | 168 | 153 | 149 |

DUNS 21-588-6532
## R. & M. Engineering Ltd
Steven Road, Huntly, Aberdeenshire AB54 8SX
**Tel:** 01466-793286 **Fax:** 01466-792157
**Web:** www.rm-engineering.co.uk
**Reg No:** 0070205SC **VAT No:** 297238713
**Estd:** 1979 Private Limited Company
**Line of Business:** Steel fabricators
**Issued Capital:** £15,000
**Principals:** R H Mackay *(Managing)*, A Mclean, D Penman, R N Mackay, A Mclean
**Co. Secretary:** Burness Paull Llp
**Responsibilities**
**Senior:** Alan McLean *(Data Communications Manager)*
**IT:** Alan McLean *(Data Communications Manager)*
**HR:** Brian Law *(Human Resources Manager)*
**Branches:** R. & M. Engineering Ltd, Cairnie Ho, Prince Charles Wharf, Dundee, Angus DD1 3NA
**US SIC:** 1622, 3545
**UK SIC:** 50200, 32223
**Auditors:** Johnston Carmichael
**Bankers:** Bank Of Scotland (80-08-33)

| | 31-12-13 | 31-12-12 | 31-12-11 |
|---|---|---|---|
| TO | 15,009,352 | 13,776,376 | 8,081,758 |
| P/L | 4,386,625 | 1,774,596 | (77,944) |
| NW | 5,401,462 | 2,041,481 | 704,091 |
| WC | 4,995,034 | 1,876,534 | 523,169 |
| Emp. | 72 | 65 | 63 |

DUNS 23-720-7105 Imp
## R & M Greenkeepers & Skip Hire
Unit 1 Forest Park Industrial, Pomeroy, Pomeroy, Dungannon, Co Tyrone BT70 3DR
**Tel:** 02887758465
**Estd:** 1986 Partnership
**Line of Business:** Skip hire
**Partners:** Mrs M Smyth, R Smyth
**US SIC:** 1799, 7394
**UK SIC:** 50000, 84000
**Bankers:** Ulster Bank Ltd (98-05-80)
**Employees:** 55

DUNS 73-452-3678
## R & M Williams (Holdings) Ltd
Williams House, West Point Industrial Estate, Penarth Road, Cardiff, South Glamorgan CF11 8JQ
**Tel:** 02920350800 **Fax:** 08456347378
**Web:** www.randmwilliams.co.uk
**Reg No:** 4716632 **Estd:** 2003 Private Limited Company
**Line of Business:** Management activities of construction holding companies
**Issued Capital:** £2,400,000
**Director:** M J Williams
**Co. Secretary:** Ms Diane Evans
**US SIC:** 6711 **UK SIC:** 83962

| | 31-01-14 | 30-11-12 | 30-01-11 |
|---|---|---|---|
| TO | 42,993,298 | 34,300,653 | 31,751,353 |
| P/L | (124,207) | 862,193 | 1,235,427 |
| NW | 5,558,879 | 5,734,024 | 5,560,267 |
| WC | 4,834,262 | 4,919,255 | 4,993,042 |
| Emp. | 164 | 193 | 179 |

DUNS 21-768-6416
## R & R C Bond
Albany House, Stevenage, Hertfordshire SG1 4PX
**Tel:** 01438730590
**Web:** www.bond.co.uk
**Estd:** 2011 Proprietorship
**Line of Business:** Wholesale suppliers of tyres
**Proprietor:** L Shepherd
**Responsibilities**
**Senior:** Roger Cooper *(Manager)*, Leon Shepherd *(Manager)*
**Finance:** Ian Fergison *(Finance Controller)*
**US SIC:** 5531 **UK SIC:** 65100
**Employees:** 70

DUNS 22-543-0123 Exp
## R. & R. Coaches Ltd
Bishopstrow Road, Warminster, Wiltshire BA12 9HQ
**Tel:** 01985213503
**Web:** www.beelinecoaches.co.uk
**Reg No:** 1004803 **Estd:** 1971 Private Limited Company
**Line of Business:** Coach and bus hire
**Trading Style:** Beeline Coaches
**Issued Capital:** £1,000
**Principals:** R G Hayball *(Managing)*, M N Hayball *(Financial)*, A D Hayball, Ms R Hayball
**Responsibilities**
**Senior:** Noel Ennis *(Transport Manager)*
**Fleet:** Noel Ennis *(Transport Manager)*
**US SIC:** 4119 **UK SIC:** 72200
**Auditors:** Martin Baber
**Bankers:** National Westminster Bank Plc (55-70-31)

| | 31-03-14 | 31-03-13 | 31-03-12 |
|---|---|---|---|
| TA | 1,472,591 | 1,388,803 | 1,342,597 |
| NW | 977,827 | 985,920 | 1,006,711 |
| WC | 546,317 | 595,333 | 552,907 |

DUNS 28-828-0746
## R & R Construction (Scotland) Ltd
(**Subsidiary of:** Macrocom 1028 Ltd)
197 Firpark Street, Glasgow, Lanarkshire G31 2HR
**Tel:** 01415566168 **Fax:** 0141-556-6215
**Web:** www.rrscot.co.uk
**Reg No:** 0087495SC **VAT No:** 383053459
**Estd:** 1983 Private Limited Company
**Line of Business:** Construction of commercial buildings
**Issued Capital:** £1,000
**Principals:** G A Russell *(Managing)*, S A Garrow *(Financial)*, R C Purdue, R Dodds
**Co. Secretary:** Mrs Anne Russell
**US SIC:** 1541 **UK SIC:** 50100
**Auditors:** Grant Thorntont U K LLP
**Bankers:** Bank Of Scotland (80-09-29)

| | 30-04-14 | 30-04-13 | 30-04-12 |
|---|---|---|---|
| TO | 7,787,104 | 7,246,043 | 8,894,452 |
| P/L | 447,167 | 798,011 | 844,706 |
| NW | 2,745,753 | 2,547,265 | 6,836,571 |
| WC | 2,761,725 | 2,695,179 | 6,577,696 |
| Emp. | 71 | 76 | 87 |

DUNS 77-937-5948
## R & R Electrical Services Ltd
13-14 Hurricane Way Hurricane Close, Wickford, Essex SS11 8YR
**Tel:** 01268-560881 **Fax:** 01268-560882
**Web:** http://rrgroupservices.com
**Reg No:** 3049680 **Estd:** 1989 Private Limited Company
**Line of Business:** Electrical contractors and electricians
**Issued Capital:** £100
**Directors:** R G Smith, R G Franklin
**Co. Secretary:** Caroline Smith
**Branches:** R & R Electrical Services Ltd, Unit 4, Technology Road, Poole, Dorset BH17 7FH
**US SIC:** 1731 **UK SIC:** 50300
**Auditors:** K P Doherty

| | 30-04-13 | 30-04-12 | 30-04-11 |
|---|---|---|---|
| TO | 13,992,827 | 14,107,838 | 9,845,251 |
| P/L | 296,254 | 288,986 | 315,848 |
| NW | 439,385 | 392,040 | 379,808 |
| WC | 152,578 | 124,035 | 126,699 |
| Emp. | 182 | 188 | N/A |

DUNS 34-777-2068
## R & R Frontline Services Ltd
Sandy Lane, Oxford, Oxfordshire OX4 6LJ
**Tel:** 01865712222
**Web:** www.randrfrontlineservices.co.uk
**Reg No:** 5578009 **Estd:** 2008 Private Limited Company
**Line of Business:** Security activities
**Issued Capital:** £100
**Director:** R Powell
**US SIC:** 7393 **UK SIC:** 83954

| | 31-01-14 | 31-01-13 | 31-01-12 |
|---|---|---|---|
| TA | 419,799 | 493,589 | 424,307 |
| NW | (4,511) | (8,123) | 31,149 |
| WC | (25,892) | (28,687) | 8,436 |

DUNS 22-808-1279 Imp
## R & R Group Services Ltd
R&R House, Normandy Lane, Stratton Business Park, Biggleswade, Bedfordshire SG18 8QB
**Tel:** 0845-600-4750 **Fax:** 0845-600-4751
**Web:** www.randrplc.com
**Reg No:** 1517855 **VAT No:** 335203982
**Estd:** 1980 Private Limited Company
**Line of Business:** Hardware consultancy
**Trading Style:** R & R Computers
**Issued Capital:** £50,000
**Principals:** S M Hodges *(Managing)*, Mrs J R Hodges
**Co. Secretary:** Stephen Hodges
**Responsibilities**
**Sales:** Andy Kempster *(Sales Manager)*
**Engineering:** Darren Philcox *(Engineering Manager)*
**Branches:** R & R Group Services Ltd, Unit 15, De Havilland Way, Witney, Oxfordshire OX29 0YG
**US SIC:** 7379, 5732
**UK SIC:** 83940, 64800
**Auditors:** Unknown
**Bankers:** National Westminster Bank Plc (60-13-08)

| | 31-03-14 | 31-03-13 | 31-03-12 |
|---|---|---|---|
| TO | N/A | N/A | 4,380,070 |
| P/L | N/A | N/A | (25) |
| NW | 336,874 | 293,153 | 206,845 |
| WC | 535,617 | 505,863 | 400,300 |
| Emp. | N/A | N/A | 59 |

DUNS 34-982-6011
## R & R Ice Cream Plc
(**Subsidiary of:** Riviera Topco Ltd)
Plews Way, Leeming Bar Industrial Estate, Northallerton, North Yorkshire DL7 9UL
**Tel:** 01677-423397
**Web:** www.rr-icecream.eu
**Reg No:** 5777981 **Estd:** 2006 Public Limited Company
**Line of Business:** Manufacture of ice cream
**Export Sales:** £410,910,000
**Issued Capital:** £50,886,374
**Director:** I Najafi
**Co. Secretary:** Andrew Finneran
**Responsibilities**
**Senior:** Phillip Griffin *(Manager)*
**Marketing:** Phillip Griffin *(Manager)*
**US SIC:** 2024 **UK SIC:** 42130
**Auditors:** KPMG LLP

| | 31-12-13 | 31-12-12 | 31-12-11 |
|---|---|---|---|
| TO | 593,501,000 | 490,608,000 | 419,761,000 |
| P/L | (42,272,000) | (14,745,000) | (22,889,000) |
| NW | (451,412,000) | (342,944,000) | (316,565,000) |
| WC | 21,945,000 | 80,890,000 | 106,431,000 |
| Emp. | 3,057 | 2,659 | 2,332 |

DUNS 21-312-9356 Imp
## R & R.C.Bond (Wholesale) Ltd
Halifax Way, York, North Yorkshire YO42 1NR
**Tel:** 08448440112
**Web:** www.bondint.co.uk
**Reg No:** 1024495 **VAT No:** 166846230
**Estd:** 1971 Private Limited Company
**Line of Business:** Sale of motor vehicle parts and accessories
**Export Sales:** £2,070,736
**Trading Style:** Bond International
**Issued Capital:** £1,000
**Principals:** R C Bond *(Managing)*, L Lanham Bond, C S Bond, G R Bond, R T Croft, M I Bond, W S Hardy, G J Martin
**Co. Secretary:** Ian Serginson
**Responsibilities**
**Senior:** Margaret Bond *(Director)*
**Admin:** Kevin Pickering *(Office Manager)*
**HR:** Kevin Pickering *(Office Manager)*
**Branches:** R & R.c.bond (Wholesale) Ltd, Albany, Wedgewood Way, Stevenage, Hertfordshire SG1 4QT
**US SIC:** 5531 **UK SIC:** 65100
**Auditors:** Baker Tilly
**Bankers:** National Westminster Bank Plc (56-00-70)

| | 31-12-13 | 31-12-12 | 31-12-11 |
|---|---|---|---|
| TO | 110,290,399 | 95,075,738 | 99,950,623 |
| P/L | 1,162,981 | (581,545) | 1,642,169 |
| NW | 8,521,349 | 7,670,354 | 8,129,678 |
| WC | 5,102,543 | 4,023,023 | 4,358,870 |
| Emp. | 219 | 209 | 213 |

DUNS 23-113-5336
## R & S Plant Ltd
24a Lenzimill Road, Cumbernauld
**Tel:** 01236736723
**Reg No:** 0148955FC **Estd:** 1994
**Line of Business:** Renting of Other Machinery and Equipment Not Elsewhere Classified
**Director:** R Docherty
**Co. Secretary:** Mrs Sandra Docherty
**US SIC:** 7394 **UK SIC:** 84000

DUNS 23-730-8846
## R B Associates
P O Box 31, Radlett, Hertfordshire WD7 8BW
**Estd:** 1981 Proprietorship
**Line of Business:** Promotion consultants (sales)
**Proprietor:** R H Beck
**US SIC:** 7319 **UK SIC:** 83800
**Employees:** 200

DUNS 34-772-3723
## R B B Economics Llp
199 Bishopsgate, London EC2M 3TY
**Tel:** 020-7421-2410
**Web:** www.rbbecon.com
**Reg No:** 0315356OC **Estd:** 2002 Proprietorship
**Line of Business:** Management and business consultants
**Export Sales:** £18,127,488
**Principals:** Mrs E Martine *(Proprietor)*, S R Baker, D J Ridyard, S L Bishop, A N Majumdar, B Durand, P J Van Der Veer, D Gore
**Responsibilities**
**Senior:** Coral Fernandez *(Manager)*, Bojana Ignjatovic *(Non-designated Limited Liabili)*, Andrea Lofaro *(Non-designated Limited Liabili)*, Richard Murgatroyd *(Non-designated Limited Liabili)*, Francesco Rosati *(Partner)*, Matthijs Visser *(Non-designated Limited Liabili)*
**Purchasing:** Francesco Rosati *(Partner)*
**US SIC:** 7392 **UK SIC:** 83951
**Bankers:** The Royal Bank Of Scotland Plc (16-08-05)

| | 31-03-14 | 31-03-13 | 31-03-12 |
|---|---|---|---|
| TO | 24,832,175 | 23,265,549 | 21,815,475 |
| P/L | 136,093 | 39,828 | 620,891 |
| WC | 12,948,434 | 12,931,855 | 11,613,572 |
| Emp. | 79 | 65 | 64 |

DUNS 21-585-1253
## R B Distributors
Fourth Way, Bristol, Avon BS11 8TB
**Tel:** 08451462604
**Web:** www.rbdistributors.co.uk
**Estd:** 2011
**Line of Business:** Distribution service providers
**Responsibilities**
**Senior:** Tony Mercer *(Sales Manager)*
**US SIC:** 4712 **UK SIC:** 77002
**Employees:** 100

DUNS 42-437-6759
## R B Emerson Group Ltd
8a Coopers Way, Southend-On-Sea, Essex SS2 5TE
**Tel:** 01702461999 **Fax:** 01702-462001
**Web:** www.emersons.uk.com
**Reg No:** 4425301 **Estd:** 1912 Private Limited Company
**Line of Business:** Management activities of construction holding companies
**Trading Style:** R B Emerson Group Ltd
**Issued Capital:** £77,320
**Directors:** M F Adams, M H Maddocks
**Co. Secretary:** Andrew Casey
**US SIC:** 6711, 1731

**UK SIC:** 83962, 50300
**Bankers:** National Westminster Bank Plc (60-09-24)

| | 31-03-14 | 31-03-13 | 31-03-12 |
|---|---|---|---|
| TO | 12,214,574 | 13,221,560 | 12,669,709 |
| P/L | 727,459 | 515,806 | 395,128 |
| NW | 3,478,885 | 2,984,309 | 2,591,961 |
| WC | 3,436,066 | 2,958,812 | 2,553,218 |
| Emp. | 97 | 81 | 88 |

DUNS 21-583-5610
## R B Grant Electrical Contractors
Office 17, Myregormie Place, Kirkcaldy, Fife KY1 3NA
**Tel:** 01592654553
**Web:** www.rbgrant.co.uk
**Estd:** 1974 Proprietorship
**Line of Business:** Electrical contractors and electricians
**Proprietor:** R Grant
**US SIC:** 1731 **UK SIC:** 50300
**Employees:** 50

DUNS 23-689-7120
## R C Moorhouse & Co
Protection House 16 17 East Parade, Leeds, West Yorkshire LS1 2BR
**Web:** www.hlwkeeblehawson.co.uk
**Estd:** 1898 Partnership
**Line of Business:** Solicitors
**Trading Style:** Keeble Hawson
**Partners:** W D Simpson, M G Moorhouse, J M Pickard, R A Brown, C Ward
**Branches:** 16-17 East Pde, Leeds
**US SIC:** 7392 **UK SIC:** 83951
**Employees:** 60

DUNS 77-612-1915
## R. Collard Ltd
**(Subsidiary of:** Collard Group Ltd)
Unit 4, Eversley Haulage Park, Brickhouse Hill, Hook, Hampshire RG27 0PZ
**Tel:** 01252844816
**Web:** www.rcollard.com
**Reg No:** 3002310 **Estd:** 1994 Private Limited Company
**Line of Business:** Skip hire
**Issued Capital:** £1
**Director:** R J Collard
**Co. Secretary:** John White
**Responsibilities**
**Senior:** Deborah Bradbury *(Manager)*
**Sales:** Philip East *(Contract Manager)*
**US SIC:** 1795, 4213
**UK SIC:** 50000, 72300
**Auditors:** Menzies LLP

| | 31-12-13 | 31-12-12 | 31-12-11 |
|---|---|---|---|
| TO | 15,759,808 | 16,223,948 | 14,929,650 |
| P/L | 1,041,805 | 717,803 | 704,711 |
| NW | 3,583,801 | 3,563,926 | 3,570,586 |
| WC | 3,008,057 | 2,909,483 | 2,945,911 |
| Emp. | 129 | 129 | 118 |

DUNS 63-468-8717
## R D Carter Colchester
5 Grange Way, Colchester, Essex CO2 8JA
**Web:** www.rgcarter-construction.co.uk
**Estd:** 1987 Partnership
**Line of Business:** Building construction contractors
**Directors:** M D Carter, M J Carter
**US SIC:** 1522 **UK SIC:** 50100
**Employees:** 114

DUNS 21-391-7661
## R D S Healthcare
Wyvis House Care Home, Station Road, Dingwall, Ross-Shire IV15 9FF
**Tel:** 01349866464
**Web:** www.rdshealthcare.co.uk
**Estd:** 2009 Proprietorship
**Line of Business:** Medical nursing home activities
**Proprietor:** Mrs J Chohan
**US SIC:** 8051 **UK SIC:** 95100
**Employees:** 50

DUNS 50-498-3164 **Imp**
## R. Delamore Ltd
**(Subsidiary of:** Delamore Holdings Ltd)
Station Road, Wisbech Saint Mary, Wisbech, Cambridgeshire PE13 4RY
**Tel:** 01945410411
**Web:** www.delamore.co.uk
**Reg No:** 2466472 **Estd:** 1990 Private Limited Company
**Line of Business:** Nurserymen
**Export Sales:** £327,880
**Issued Capital:** £100,000
**Directors:** W M Eady, J E Banton, P Murray, F Hudepohl, C J Finlay
**Responsibilities**
**Senior:** James Molden *(Manager)*
**Sales:** Steve Marriot *(Sales Coordinator)*
**US SIC:** 5199 **UK SIC:** 61900
**Auditors:** Saffery Champness

**Bankers:** National Westminster Bank Plc (60-04-23)

| | 31-05-14 | 30-11-12 | 30-05-11 |
|---|---|---|---|
| TO | 10,953,878 | 7,176,639 | 9,428,915 |
| P/L | (442,667) | (833,956) | 589,171 |
| NW | 1,430,405 | 1,399,797 | 2,008,992 |
| WC | 1,814,133 | 45,288 | 716,627 |
| Emp. | 105 | 105 | 83 |

DUNS 21-401-3377
## R Drummond (Carriers) Ltd
1 Bathgate Road, Armadale, Bathgate, West Lothian EH48 2PE
**Tel:** 01501-730221 **Fax:** 01501-732981
**Web:** www.drummond-distribution.co.uk
**Reg No:** 0084702SC **VAT No:** 268787881
**Estd:** 1927 Private Limited Company
**Line of Business:** Road haulage and transport services
**Trading Style:** Drummond Distribution, Drummond Carriers
**Issued Capital:** £9,999
**Directors:** R Drummond, J B Drummond, R Drummond, D J Burns
**Co. Secretary:** Walter Sneddon
**Branches:** R Drummond (Carriers) Ltd, 25 Berth, Windmill Croft Quay, Glasgow, Lanarkshire G5 8AT
**US SIC:** 4789 **UK SIC:** 77002
**Auditors:** I A Stewart & Co
**Bankers:** Clydesdale Bank Plc (82-68-30)

| | 30-09-13 | 30-09-12 | 30-09-11 |
|---|---|---|---|
| TO | 6,709,614 | 6,329,032 | 5,713,084 |
| P/L | 174,180 | 173,830 | 75,590 |
| NW | 4,039,571 | 3,917,369 | 3,784,356 |
| WC | 895,114 | 875,455 | 879,460 |
| Emp. | 109 | 103 | 95 |

DUNS 23-305-0256
## R. Dunham (Uk) Ltd
Aston House, 28-30 Thames Road, Barking, Essex IG11 0HZ
**Tel:** 020-8709-1700
**Web:** www.r-dunham.co.uk
**Reg No:** 4552613 **VAT No:** 247052768
**Estd:** 2002 Private Limited Company
**Line of Business:** Electrical contractors and electricians
**Issued Capital:** £10,000
**Director:** S Richardson
**Co. Secretary:** Mark Dunham
**Responsibilities**
**Senior:** David Jacques *(Manager)*, Dave Jakes *(Joint Managing Director)*
**US SIC:** 1731 **UK SIC:** 50300
**Auditors:** McMillan Rose & Co Ltd

| | 31-12-13 | 31-12-12 | 31-12-11 |
|---|---|---|---|
| TA | 1,364,428 | 1,340,076 | 1,522,656 |
| NW | (345,189) | (801,150) | (887,704) |
| WC | (628,740) | (834,789) | (861,730) |

DUNS 42-388-3128
## R Durtnell & Sons (Holdings) Ltd
Rectory Lane, Brasted, Westerham, Kent TN16 1JR
**Tel:** 01959-564105
**Web:** www.durtnell.co.uk
**Reg No:** 4375916 **Estd:** 2002 Private Limited Company
**Line of Business:** Holding companies management activities
**Issued Capital:** £20,009
**Director:** J A Durtnell
**Co. Secretary:** Simon Routh
**Responsibilities**
**Senior:** Matthew Hale *(Manager)*
**US SIC:** 1541 **UK SIC:** 50100

| | 31-12-13 | 31-12-12 | 31-12-11 |
|---|---|---|---|
| TO | 33,949,504 | 41,497,121 | 36,318,058 |
| P/L | 233,201 | 145,099 | (135,854) |
| NW | 1,823,957 | 1,597,176 | 1,549,238 |
| WC | (544,234) | (583,534) | (619,993) |
| Emp. | 93 | 129 | 137 |

DUNS 34-820-9750
## R E Buildings Ltd
Spout House, Bay Horse, Lancaster, Lancashire LA2 9DE
**Tel:** 01524-792247 **Fax:** 01524-791890
**Web:** www.dureble.co.uk
**Reg No:** 2797885 **VAT No:** 534368928
**Estd:** 1982 Private Limited Company
**Line of Business:** Agents involved in the sale of agricultural raw materials, live animals, textile raw materials and semi-finished goods
**Issued Capital:** £100
**Principals:** K J Ronson *(Managing)*, R Escolme
**Responsibilities**
**Senior:** Hazel Ronson *(Manager)*, Isabelle Thomas *(P A To The Director)*
**Admin:** Isabelle Thomas *(P A To The Director)*
**US SIC:** 5159, 3441
**UK SIC:** 61100, 32042
**Auditors:** Towers & Gornall

| | 31-12-13 | 31-12-12 | 31-12-11 |
|---|---|---|---|
| TA | 1,863,005 | 1,728,681 | 1,515,432 |
| NW | 722,952 | 669,299 | 470,136 |
| WC | (123,390) | (167,483) | (380,145) |

DUNS 21-590-2861
## The R E R Group
Crown House 22 Lynch Hill Lane, Slough, Berkshire SL2 2QL
**Tel:** 08453102435
**Web:** www.rer-group.co.uk
**Estd:** 2011
**Line of Business:** Management of real estate on a fee or contract basis
**US SIC:** 7399 **UK SIC:** 83954
**Employees:** 100

DUNS 21-780-6112
## R F D
1-5 Beaufort Road, Birkenhead, Merseyside CH41 1HQ
**Tel:** 01516709009
**Web:** www.survitecgroup.com
**Estd:** 1950 Partnership
**Line of Business:** Safety equipment suppliers
**Partners:** D Baxter, P Brown
**Responsibilities**
**Senior:** Nick Mulhall *(Manager)*
**US SIC:** 5999 **UK SIC:** 65600
**Employees:** 230

DUNS 21-393-6218
## R F K
27-33 Bethnal Green Road, London E1 6LA
**Web:** www.rfkarchitects.co.uk
**Estd:** 2003 Proprietorship
**Line of Business:** Architectural activities
**Proprietor:** A Farlie
**US SIC:** 8911 **UK SIC:** 83701
**Employees:** 132

DUNS 77-932-9775
## R F L (Governing Body) Ltd
Red Hall, Red Hall Lane, Leeds, West Yorkshire LS17 8NB
**Tel:** 08444777113 **Fax:** 08444770013
**Web:** www.therfl.co.uk
**Reg No:** 5835638 **Estd:** 2006 Private Company Limited By Guarantee
**Line of Business:** Other sporting activities not elsewhere classified
**Directors:** S H Johnson, R W Stott, B R Barwick, R W Rimmer, N J Wood, Mrs C Morrow
**Co. Secretary:** Mrs Susan Allan
**Responsibilities**
**IT:** Adam England *(?ICT Support and Projects Mana)*
**US SIC:** 7999 **UK SIC:** 97913

| | 31-12-13 | 31-12-12 | 31-12-11 |
|---|---|---|---|
| TO | 34,809,805 | 21,845,895 | 27,042,589 |
| P/L | 172,151 | 62,275 | 97,496 |
| NW | 1,488,798 | 1,414,456 | 1,762,064 |
| WC | (1,688,151) | (1,966,867) | (1,809,848) |
| Emp. | 167 | 204 | 208 |

DUNS 39-970-4196
## R G Bassett & Sons Ltd
Transport House, Stone Road, Tittensor, Stoke-On-Trent, Staffordshire ST12 9HD
**Web:** www.bassett-group.co.uk
**Reg No:** 2269632 **Estd:** 1988 Private Limited Company
**Line of Business:** Road haulage and transport services
**Issued Capital:** £30,002
**Directors:** L J Bassett, M A Bassett, Ms A C Bassett
**Co. Secretary:** Leonard Bassett
**Responsibilities**
**Senior:** Martin Leann *(Senior IT Executive)*
**Finance:** Martin Leann *(Senior IT Executive)*
**IT:** Martin Leann *(Senior IT Executive)*
**US SIC:** 4789, 8299
**UK SIC:** 77002, 93300
**Auditors:** A Wood & Co
**Bankers:** National Westminster Bank Plc (01-05-27)

| | 31-03-14 | 31-03-13 | 31-03-12 |
|---|---|---|---|
| TO | 8,136,205 | 7,823,695 | 7,890,113 |
| P/L | 420,813 | 87,317 | 225,729 |
| NW | 3,021,722 | 2,678,694 | 2,608,726 |
| WC | 1,537,626 | 1,085,406 | 798,062 |
| Emp. | 98 | 101 | 101 |

DUNS 21-811-6960
## R. G. Carter Holdings Ltd
**(Subsidiary of:** Rg Carter Group Ltd)
9-11 Drayton High Road, Norwich, Norfolk NR8 6AH
**Tel:** 01603867268
**Web:** www.rgcarter-construction.co.uk
**Reg No:** 0925049 **VAT No:** 353205484
**Estd:** 1967 Private Limited Company
**Line of Business:** Building construction contractors
**Issued Capital:** £241,806
**Principals:** R G Carter *(Chairman and Managing)*, A N Duckworth Chad, D Carter, D J Coventry, J G Carter, R E Carter, D J Coventry, J R Barclay
**Co. Secretary:** Gerald Daniels

**Responsibilities**
**IT:** James Harvey *(Senior IT Executive)*
**Branches:** R. G. Carter Holdings Ltd, 9-11 Drayton High Rd, Norwich, Norfolk NR8 6AH
**US SIC:** 6711 **UK SIC:** 83962
**Auditors:** Baker Tilly UK Audit LLP
**Bankers:** Barclays Bank Plc (20-62-53)

| | 31-12-13 | 31-12-12 | 31-12-11 |
|---|---|---|---|
| TA | 61,649,617 | 58,558,414 | 70,990,648 |
| NW | 40,118,202 | 46,844,956 | 41,202,279 |
| WC | 34,805,245 | 32,350,617 | 43,161,942 |

DUNS 73-505-6298
## R G Carter Ipswich Ltd
**(Subsidiary of:** Rg Carter Group Ltd)
9-11 Drayton High Road, Drayton, Norwich, Norfolk NR8 6AH
**Tel:** 01603867355
**Web:** www.rgcarter-construction.co.uk
**Reg No:** 4768800 **Estd:** 2003 Private Limited Company
**Line of Business:** Builders
**Trading Style:** R G Carter
**Issued Capital:** £100
**Directors:** S A Scott, S D Humphrey, A D Farrow, P A Jay, J D Wilson
**Co. Secretary:** Robert Alflatt
**Branches:** R G Carter Ipswich Ltd, Drayton House, 1 Belfry Road, Ipswich, Suffolk IP3 9UH
**US SIC:** 1522 **UK SIC:** 50100
**Auditors:** Baker Tilly UK Audit LLP

| | 31-12-13 | 31-12-12 | 31-12-11 |
|---|---|---|---|
| TO | 13,544,466 | 15,816,367 | 12,900,378 |
| P/L | 612,400 | 1,431,791 | 159,563 |
| NW | 1,943,577 | 2,253,820 | 1,175,446 |
| WC | 1,762,439 | 2,170,786 | 1,087,942 |
| Emp. | 47 | 50 | 53 |

DUNS 21-607-5457
## R G Falla Ltd
**(Subsidiary of:** Regent Group Ltd)
Bridge House, Garenne Park Rue De Lane Cache, St Sampson, Guernsey, Channel Islands GY2 4AF
**Tel:** 01481-256585 **Fax:** 01481-252318
**Web:** www.rgfalla.gg
**Reg No:** 0000431G **Estd:** 1949 Private Limited Company
**Line of Business:** Construction of domestic buildings
**Issued Capital:** £10,000
**Principals:** S J Falla *(Chairman)*, A J Hall *(Managing)*, P N Mckeary, D Cozens
**Responsibilities**
**Senior:** Vic Hall *(Chairperson)*, Patrick McKeary *(Director)*
**Marketing:** Graham Brook *(Sales & Marketing Manager)*
**Sales:** Graham Brook *(Sales & Marketing Manager)*
**Admin:** June Clayton *(Office Manager)*
**IT:** Graham Brook *(Sales & Marketing Manager)*
**HR:** June Clayton *(Office Manager)*
**US SIC:** 1522 **UK SIC:** 50100
**Bankers:** National Westminster Bank Plc (60-09-20)
**Employees:** 150

DUNS 21-580-9536
## R G I S Inventory Specialists
1631 Parkway, Whiteley, Fareham, Hampshire PO15 7AH
**Tel:** 01489589038
**Web:** www.rgis.com
**Estd:** 2011 Proprietorship
**Line of Business:** Stocktaking services
**Proprietor:** J Risebrow
**Responsibilities**
**Senior:** Nicola Ball *(Chief Executive Officer)*, Tony Ma *(District Manager)*, Daniel Worrall *(Area Manager)*
**US SIC:** 8931 **UK SIC:** 83600
**Employees:** 60

DUNS 42-317-4614
## R G Phillips & Son Ltd
Maori Lodge, Baubigny Road, St Sampson, Guernsey, Channel Islands GY2 4YQ
**Tel:** 01481722688
**Reg No:** 0016360G **Estd:** 1987 Private Limited Company
**Line of Business:** Construction of civil engineering constructions
**Principals:** R Phillips *(Managing)*, Ms M Phillips
**US SIC:** 1622, 1541
**UK SIC:** 50200, 50100
**Employees:** 50

DUNS 50-325-6810 **Imp**
## R G S Investments Ltd
**(Subsidiary of:** Fastwest Ltd)
1 Abingdon Road, Nuffield Industrial Estate, Poole, Dorset BH17 0UG
**Tel:** 01202-687220
**Reg No:** 2350517 **Estd:** 2010 Private Limited Company

**Line of Business:** Sheet metal fabrication equipment
**Trading Style:** R G Smith
**Issued Capital:** £1,000
**Co. Secretary:** Richard Taylor
**US SIC:** 3469 **UK SIC:** 31200
**Auditors:** JPP Accountants Ltd

| | 30-06-13 | 30-06-12 | 30-06-11 |
|---|---|---|---|
| TA | 1,038,089 | 1,134,862 | 991,721 |
| NW | 553,410 | 686,717 | 588,724 |
| WC | 576,979 | 496,725 | 376,321 |

DUNS 23-632-2848
## R H Bodyworks
A140 Ipswich Road, Brome, Eye, Suffolk IP23 8AW
**Web:** www.rhbodyworks.co.uk
**VAT No:** 571117461 **Estd:** 1968 Proprietorship
**Line of Business:** Car and commercial vehicle repairs
**Proprietor:** R Humphrey
**Responsibilities**
**Admin:** Martin Spilling *(Administrator)*
**Health & Safety:** Martin Spilling *(Administrator)*
**Branches:** R H Bodyworks, A140 Ipswich Road, Brome, Eye, Suffolk IP23 8AW
**US SIC:** 7539 **UK SIC:** 67100
**Bankers:** Barclays Bank Plc (20-26-34)
**Employees:** 160

DUNS 21-605-3430
## R H Joiners
36 Denholm Street, Greenock, Renfrewshire PA16 8RJ
**Tel:** 07857606619
**Estd:** 2011 Proprietorship
**Line of Business:** Manufacturers of central heating radiator cover
**Proprietor:** C Hall
**US SIC:** 2431 **UK SIC:** 46300
**Employees:** 220

DUNS 23-778-4413
## R H M Telecommunications Ltd
Goodridge House, Goodridge Avenue, Gloucester, Gloucestershire GL2 5EA
**Tel:** 08451366060
**Web:** www.rhmtelecom.com
**Reg No:** 3771726 **Estd:** 1995 Private Limited Company
**Line of Business:** Telecommunications
**Issued Capital:** £303
**Directors:** R J Head, M E Leach, Ms P R Henry, A Barrington, N C Dixon, N J Thomas
**Co. Secretary:** Mrs Evelyn Leach
**US SIC:** 4899 **UK SIC:** 79020
**Auditors:** Hazlewoods LLP

| | 30-06-13 | 30-06-12 | 30-06-11 |
|---|---|---|---|
| TA | 1,374,301 | 1,444,397 | 1,275,385 |
| NW | 505,253 | 433,327 | 211,176 |
| WC | 383,233 | 281,214 | 105,376 |

DUNS 22-849-5792
## R H Partnership Architects Ltd
94 Chesterton Road, Cambridge, Cambridgeshire CB4 1ER
**Tel:** 01223316309
**Web:** www.rhpartnership.co.uk
**Reg No:** 2071013 **VAT No:** 453307661
**Estd:** 1986 Private Limited Company
**Line of Business:** Architects
**Issued Capital:** £2,736
**Directors:** P Smith, K Myers, P Evans, R J Chudleigh, P Naylor, D Emond, D Ward, D Hills
**Co. Secretary:** David Hills
**Responsibilities**
**Senior:** Spencer Hatton *(Director)*, Lesley Tubb *(Manager)*
**Finance:** Lesley Tubb *(Manager)*
**Branches:** R H Partnership Architects Ltd, 70 Cowcross Street, London EC1M 6EJ
**US SIC:** 8911 **UK SIC:** 83701
**Auditors:** Ensors
**Bankers:** Lloyds TSB Bank plc (30-13-55)

| | 30-04-14 | 30-04-13 | 30-04-12 |
|---|---|---|---|
| TA | 2,333,506 | 2,217,111 | 1,817,770 |
| NW | 1,249,588 | 1,198,697 | 972,893 |
| WC | 1,221,914 | 1,166,277 | 1,035,006 |

DUNS 21-030-7141
## R Hillier
23 South Road, Englefield Green, Egham, Surrey TW20 0RL
**Tel:** 01784434592
**Estd:** 1999 Proprietorship
**Line of Business:** Builders
**US SIC:** 1522 **UK SIC:** 50100
**Employees:** 46

DUNS 22-700-7317 Exp
## R I B A Enterprises Ltd
**(Subsidiary of:** Royal Institute of British Architects)
The Old Post Office, Newcastle-Upon-Tyne, Tyne and Wear NE1 1RH
**Tel:** 08454569594 **Fax:** 01912325714
**Web:** www.ribaenterprises.com
**Reg No:** 0978271 **VAT No:** 232351891
**Estd:** 1970 Private Limited Company
**Line of Business:** Book publishers
**Export Markets:** Middle East, Africa & the West Indies.
**Trading Style:** R I B A Bookshop, N B S
**Issued Capital:** £1,317,450
**Principals:** C E Carr *(Chairman)*, Mrs H L Whitfield, B Beaumont, R P Waterhouse, P A Udall, A I Munro, Ms A A Van Hoorebeek, W D Smedley
**Co. Secretary:** Miss Irena Peel
**Responsibilities**
**Senior:** Dagmar Binsted *(Director)*, Paula Willmore *(Director)*
**Finance:** Geoffrey Denner *(Financial Director)*
**Admin:** Kate Briers *(Head of Executive Support)*, Jackie Brown *(Office Manager)*
**IT:** David Cun *(Computer Manager)*
**HR:** Joanne Morton *(Personnel Director)*
**Health & Safety:** Jackie Brown *(Office Manager)*
**Facilities:** Jackie Brown *(Office Manager)*
**Purchasing:** Jackie Brown *(Office Manager)*
**Branches:** R I B A Enterprises Ltd, Mansion House Chmbrs, The Close, Newcastle Upon Tyne, Tyne and Wear NE5 5DB
**US SIC:** 2731, 7372, 8911
**UK SIC:** 47532, 83940, 83701
**Auditors:** Sayer Vincent
**Bankers:** National Westminster Bank Plc (60-09-15)

| | 31-12-13 | 31-12-12 | 31-12-11 |
|---|---|---|---|
| TO | 20,470,035 | 19,515,847 | 19,251,969 |
| P/L | 2,415,694 | 2,418,599 | 2,567,947 |
| NW | 761,670 | 703,420 | 645,170 |
| WC | 457,297 | 676,825 | 956,313 |
| Emp. | 265 | 254 | 248 |

DUNS 29-755-9965
## R. J. & D. E. Billings Ltd
Gay Dawn Offices Pennis Lane, Longfield, Kent DA3 8LY
**Tel:** 01474573100
**Web:** www.rjdebillings.co.uk
**Reg No:** 2019068 **Estd:** 2012 Private Limited Company
**Line of Business:** Hotels
**Issued Capital:** £1,521,432
**Principals:** A J Billings *(Financial)*, C J Billings, R J Billings
**Co. Secretary:** Stephen Billings
**Branches:** R. J. & D. E. Billings Ltd, Maplescombe La, Farningham, Dartford, Kent DA4 0JY
**US SIC:** 7011, 6531
**UK SIC:** 66500, 83400
**Auditors:** Carly & Co
**Bankers:** Lloyds TSB Bank plc (30-93-61)

| | 31-12-13 | 31-12-12 | 31-12-11 |
|---|---|---|---|
| TA | 12,573,281 | 12,210,080 | 13,236,882 |
| NW | 1,288,773 | 1,619,035 | 2,002,388 |
| WC | (3,790,149) | (3,252,703) | (2,945,221) |

DUNS 53-560-9630
## R J Arguile & Son
Beacon View Farm, Finkell Street, Gringley-On-The-Hill, Doncaster, South Yorkshire DN10 4SF
**Estd:** 2002 Partnership
**Line of Business:** Farming (mixed)
**Partners:** R Arguile, Mrs E Arguile, J A Arguile
**US SIC:** 0291 **UK SIC:** 01001
**Bankers:** National Westminster Bank Plc (60-07-01)
**Employees:** 60

DUNS 64-074-3324
## R J B Stone Ltd
Unit 13, Ellerslie Square Industrial Estate, 11 Lyham Road, London SW2 5DZ
**Tel:** 02073460100
**Web:** www.rjbstone.com
**Reg No:** 3469752 **Estd:** 1997 Private Limited Company
**Line of Business:** Giftware wholesale
**Issued Capital:** £2
**Directors:** R J Stone, Ms A Stone, Ms P A Dabrowska
**Branches:** R J B Stone Ltd, Battersea Business Centre, Lavender Hill, London SW11 5QF
**US SIC:** 5719 **UK SIC:** 64700

| | 30-09-13 | 01-10-12 | 30-09-11 |
|---|---|---|---|
| TO | 8,317,871 | N/A | N/A |
| P/L | 1,003,639 | N/A | N/A |
| NW | 2,596,058 | 1,874,740 | 1,301,891 |
| WC | 2,367,100 | 1,713,699 | 1,174,034 |
| Emp. | 72 | N/A | N/A |

DUNS 21-781-6139
## R J C
Mews Place, The Street, Hatfield Peverel, Chelmsford, Essex CM3 2EH
**Tel:** 01245380870
**Web:** www.rjcuk.com
**Estd:** 2011
**Line of Business:** Building construction contractors
**Responsibilities**
**Marketing:** Mark Hiskey *(Senior Marketing Executive)*
**Health & Safety:** Mark Hiskey *(Senior Marketing Executive)*
**US SIC:** 1522 **UK SIC:** 50100
**Employees:** 100

DUNS 21-011-2934 Imp-Exp
## R J Fullwood & Bland Ltd
Grange Road, Ellesmere, Shropshire SY12 9DF
**Tel:** 01691-622391
**Web:** www.fullwood.com
**Reg No:** 0347190 **Estd:** 1938 Private Limited Company
**Line of Business:** Manufacture of other agricultural and forestry machinery
**Export Markets:** W Europe
**Issued Capital:** £916,949
**Directors:** R J Lancaster, V Phillips, K D Wharton, P J Lancaster, Joacchim Bvba
**Co. Secretary:** Spencer Davis
**Responsibilities**
**Sales:** Les Strickland *(Senior Sales Executive)*
**US SIC:** 3523, 0729
**UK SIC:** 32113, 01003
**Auditors:** Grant Thornton UK LLP
**Bankers:** National Westminster Bank Plc (55-50-05)

| | 31-12-13 | 31-12-12 | 31-12-11 |
|---|---|---|---|
| TO | 71,490,451 | 67,993,770 | 71,187,438 |
| P/L | 1,413,248 | 1,238,032 | 2,694,587 |
| NW | 16,762,930 | 16,511,245 | 16,023,501 |
| WC | 7,822,836 | 8,161,162 | 7,739,596 |
| Emp. | 601 | 586 | 586 |

DUNS 28-964-9097
## R. J. Sheen & Co. Ltd
1 Montpelier Avenue, Bexley, Kent DA5 3AP
**Tel:** 02083 035757 **Fax:** 01784247392
**Web:** www.rjsheen.com
**Reg No:** 1700214 **VAT No:** 412937849
**Estd:** 1983 Private Limited Company
**Line of Business:** Specialised building trade contractors
**Issued Capital:** £1,004
**Principals:** R J Sheen *(Managing)*, K F Mcdermott, M A Perry
**Co. Secretary:** Robert Sheen
**Responsibilities**
**Senior:** Kevin Mcdermott *(Manager)*
**Admin:** Sue Briley *(Office Manager)*
**HR:** Sue Briley *(Office Manager)*
**US SIC:** 1799 **UK SIC:** 50000
**Auditors:** Harrison Hill Castle & Co
**Bankers:** Barclays Bank Plc (20-14-33)

| | 28-02-14 | 28-02-13 | 28-02-12 |
|---|---|---|---|
| TA | 267,634 | 288,040 | 249,036 |
| NW | 22,568 | 110 | 19,543 |
| WC | (16,472) | (48,450) | (8,898) |

DUNS 53-647-0248
## R J Utility Services Ltd
Patterson Street, Blaydon-On-Tyne, Tyne and Wear NE21 5TZ
**Tel:** 01914143399 **Fax:** 0191-414-3400
**Web:** www.rjusl.co.uk
**Reg No:** 3452450 **Estd:** 1997 Private Limited Company
**Line of Business:** Pipework contractors
**Issued Capital:** £1,500
**Managing Director:** R T Henderson
**Co. Secretary:** Eamon Ohara
**Responsibilities**
**Senior:** Eamon O'hara *(Finance Director)*
**Finance:** Eamon O'hara *(Finance Director)*
**US SIC:** 1711 **UK SIC:** 50300
**Auditors:** Stephenson Coates
**Bankers:** Barclays Bank Plc (20-59-42)

| | 31-10-13 | 31-10-12 | 31-10-11 |
|---|---|---|---|
| TO | N/A | N/A | 5,639,498 |
| P/L | N/A | N/A | 200,332 |
| NW | 1,055,638 | 1,019,743 | 897,840 |
| WC | 945,715 | 926,801 | 856,028 |
| Emp. | N/A | N/A | 66 |

DUNS 34-837-5809
## R K Group Ltd
**(Subsidiary of:** The Kellan Group Plc)
Unit 10 Loughton Business Centre, Loughton, Essex IG10 3FL
**Tel:** 02085325959 **Fax:** 02085321923
**Web:** www.rkgrouplondon.com
**Reg No:** 2803672 **Estd:** 1993 Private Limited Company
**Line of Business:** Business and management consultancy activities not elsewhere classified
**Trading Style:** R K Group of Companies, R K Accountancy, Rk Supply Chain
**Issued Capital:** £97,594
**Directors:** R Kirpalani, A Reeves
**Co. Secretary:** Imco Secretary Limited
**Responsibilities**
**Senior:** Barry Hogal *(General Manager)*
**Branches:** R K Group Ltd, Faulkner House, Faulkner Street, Manchester M1 4DY
**US SIC:** 7392, 7361
**UK SIC:** 83951, 83954
**Auditors:** BDO Stoy Hayward LLP

| | 31-12-13 | 31-12-12 | 31-12-11 |
|---|---|---|---|
| TO | 4,049,174 | 4,834,691 | 6,627,170 |
| P/L | (586,924) | (1,089,832) | (150,042) |
| NW | (1,100,883) | (513,959) | 575,873 |
| WC | (1,100,887) | (513,963) | 554,312 |
| Emp. | 301 | 41 | 50 |

DUNS 28-851-3237
## R K Harrison Group Ltd
**(Subsidiary of:** R K Harrison Holdings Ltd)
One Whittington Avenue, London EC3V 1LE
**Fax:** 020 7456 9399
**Web:** www.rkhgroup.com
**Reg No:** 0725875 **VAT No:** 727885190
**Estd:** 1993 Private Limited Company
**Line of Business:** Activities auxiliary to insurance and pension funding
**Trading Style:** Penrose Ford, Rkh Group
**Issued Capital:** £26,659,464
**Directors:** P C Bridgwater, R C Snedden, J C Birkmire, A D Collins, A Tuffield, J M Thompson-Copsey
**Co. Secretary:** Andrew Moore
**Responsibilities**
**HR:** Katie Schreiber *(Human Resources Director)*
**Operations:** Jon Copsey *(Chief Operating Officer)*
**Branches:** R K Harrison Group Ltd, 52 Leadenhall Street, London EC3A 2BJ
**US SIC:** 6411 **UK SIC:** 83200
**Auditors:** Mazars LLP
**Bankers:** The Royal Bank Of Scotland Plc (15-20-25)

| | 30-06-13 | 30-06-12 | 30-06-11 |
|---|---|---|---|
| TO | 7,577,000 | 8,554,000 | 4,392,000 |
| P/L | 18,085,000 | 12,303,000 | 12,833,000 |
| NW | 54,308,000 | 49,750,000 | 48,578,000 |
| WC | 23,450,000 | 18,906,000 | 17,858,000 |
| Emp. | 120 | 100 | 84 |

DUNS 23-614-9386
## R K Harrison Holdings Ltd
Woodlands, Manton Lane, Bedford, Bedfordshire MK41 7LW
**Fax:** 02074569399
**Web:** www.rkhgroup.com
**Reg No:** 3612207 **Estd:** 1998 Private Limited Company
**Line of Business:** Activities auxiliary to insurance and pension funding
**Export Sales:** £85,859,000
**Issued Capital:** £3,569,757
**Directors:** J M Thompson-Copsey, A D Collins, A Tuffield, P C Bridgwater, J C Birkmire, R C Snedden
**Co. Secretary:** Andrew Moore
**Responsibilities**
**Senior:** Dominic Collins *(Chairman)*
**US SIC:** 6411 **UK SIC:** 83200
**Auditors:** Mazars LLP
**Bankers:** Lloyds TSB Bank plc (30-90-66)

| | 30-06-13 | 30-06-12 | 30-06-11 |
|---|---|---|---|
| TO | 115,459,000 | 92,900,000 | 76,588,000 |
| P/L | 22,717,000 | 15,791,000 | 12,268,000 |
| NW | 12,972,000 | 2,134,000 | 6,726,000 |
| WC | 38,074,000 | 23,329,000 | 26,495,000 |
| Emp. | 700 | 530 | 491 |

DUNS 21-139-8665
## R K Harrison Insurance Brokers Ltd
**(Subsidiary of:** R K Harrison Holdings Ltd)
1 Whittington Avenue, London EC3V 1LE
**Tel:** 01747820828
**Web:** www.tepfin.com
**Reg No:** 6720048 **Estd:** 2008 Private Limited Company
**Line of Business:** Activities auxiliary to insurance and pension funding
**Export Sales:** £58,037,000
**Issued Capital:** £50,000
**Directors:** N Coles, J M Thompson-Copsey, P C Bridgwater, S T Greener, A D Collins, B D Rugge-Price, N S Galletti, A Tuffield
**Co. Secretary:** Andrew Moore
**Responsibilities**
**Senior:** Paul Redgate *(Director)*
**US SIC:** 6411 **UK SIC:** 83200
**Bankers:** The Royal Bank Of Scotland Plc (16-10-60)

| | 30-06-13 | 30-06-12 | 30-06-11 |
|---|---|---|---|
| TO | 66,172,000 | 48,035,000 | 40,050,000 |
| P/L | 13,827,000 | 12,966,000 | 10,825,000 |
| NW | 13,914,000 | 12,412,000 | 9,660,000 |
| WC | 13,914,000 | N/A | 9,660,000 |
| Emp. | 289 | 167 | 124 |

DUNS 23-599-4878

## R L C Transport

20 Appleton Avenue, The Reddings, Cheltenham, Gloucestershire GL51 6TS
**Tel:** 01452-855666
**Web:** www.rlctransport.co.uk
**Estd:** 2002 Proprietorship
**Line of Business:** Road haulage and transport services
**Proprietor:** R L Cooper
**US SIC:** 4789, 4213
**UK SIC:** 77002, 72300
**Bankers:** Lloyds TSB Bank plc (77-27-32)
**Employees:** 66

DUNS 28-981-8700

## R. L. Davies & Son Ltd

Llys Derwen, Dolwen Road, Llysfaen, Colwyn Bay, Clwyd LL29 8SS
**Tel:** 01492517346 **Fax:** 01492-514118
**Web:** www.rldavies.co.uk
**Reg No:** 1783213 **VAT No:** 310053331
**Estd:** 1947 Private Limited Company
**Line of Business:** Builders
**Issued Capital:** £100,000
**Director:** G Davies
**Co. Secretary:** Olwen Evans
**Responsibilities**
**Senior:** Dave Belfield *(Construction Manager)*
**Finance:** Simon Broadhurst *(Financial Director)*
**US SIC:** 1522 **UK SIC:** 50100
**Auditors:** Sage & Co
**Bankers:** National Westminster Bank Plc (52-21-43)

| | 31-03-14 | 30-09-13 | 31-03-12 |
|---|---|---|---|
| TO | 5,160,852 | 14,449,286 | 11,237,168 |
| P/L | 153,636 | (577,965) | (520,062) |
| NW | 3,759,117 | 3,610,481 | 4,263,447 |
| WC | 3,706,143 | 3,552,829 | 4,160,650 |
| Emp. | 74 | 75 | 71 |

DUNS 23-532-0483

## R L E International Product Development Ltd

(**Subsidiary of:** Rle International Produktentwicklungsgesellschaft)
1 Endeavour Drive, Festival Leisure Park, Basildon, Essex SS14 3WF
**Tel:** 01268-247900
**Web:** www.rle-international.co.uk
**Reg No:** 3530918 **Estd:** 1998 Private Limited Company
**Line of Business:** Manufacture of motor vehicles
**Export Sales:** £772,482
**Issued Capital:** £400,000
**Directors:** N J Cushing, R Laufenberg, R P Rupa
**Co. Secretary:** Darren Gowland
**US SIC:** 3711 **UK SIC:** 35101
**Auditors:** PricewaterhouseCoopers
**Bankers:** Lloyds Tsb Scotland Plc (30-18-05)

| | 31-12-13 | 31-12-12 | 31-12-11 |
|---|---|---|---|
| TO | 15,434,913 | 14,159,642 | N/A |
| P/L | 448,950 | 820,994 | N/A |
| NW | 1,404,457 | 1,004,652 | 981,201 |
| WC | 1,314,786 | 893,253 | 917,097 |
| Emp. | 53 | 48 | N/A |

DUNS 49-076-5310 **Imp-Exp**

## R. L. Polk Uk Ltd

(**Subsidiary of:** Ihs Inc.)
Verulam Point, St Albans, Hertfordshire AL1 5HE
**Tel:** 01727845558
**Web:** www.polk.com
**Reg No:** 3086027 **Estd:** 1995 Private Limited Company
**Line of Business:** Marketing consultants
**Export Sales:** £1,524,258
**Issued Capital:** £21,796,057
**Directors:** S Dunlop, Mrs J K Chahal, S Lomholt-Thomsen
**Responsibilities**
**Senior:** Norman Marks *(Manager)*
**US SIC:** 7392 **UK SIC:** 83951
**Auditors:** BDO LLP
**Bankers:** HSBC Bank plc (40-02-31)

| | 30-11-13 | 31-03-13 | 31-11-12 |
|---|---|---|---|
| TO | 4,756,172 | 7,084,000 | 5,970,000 |
| P/L | 557,145 | 599,000 | (3,802,000) |
| NW | 8,663,096 | 8,106,000 | 7,454,000 |
| WC | 1,979,487 | 1,255,000 | 528,000 |
| Emp. | 51 | 52 | 49 |

DUNS 21-811-7751

## R M Education

Bellhaven House, Lark Way, Strathclyde Business Park, Bellshill, Lanarkshire ML4 3RB
**Tel:** 01698578000
**Web:** www.rm.com
**Estd:** 2012
**Line of Business:** Computer software (development)
**US SIC:** 7379 **UK SIC:** 83940
**Employees:** 100

DUNS 51-983-2963

## R M Hotels Ltd

(**Subsidiary of:** Neville & Griffin Ltd)
95a High Street, Slough, Berkshire SL1 7JZ
**Tel:** 01628-666928
**Reg No:** 3990206 **Estd:** 2000 Private Limited Company
**Line of Business:** Hotels
**Issued Capital:** £1,785,001
**Director:** C E Griffin
**Co. Secretary:** Brian Griffin
**Branches:** R M Hotels Ltd, Market Square, Buckingham, Buckinghamshire MK18 3AB
**US SIC:** 7011 **UK SIC:** 66500
**Auditors:** Oury Clark

| | 31-12-13 | 31-12-12 | 31-12-11 |
|---|---|---|---|
| TA | 263,864 | 451,235 | 2,228,401 |
| NW | 263,864 | 261,556 | 1,268,990 |
| WC | N/A | 261,556 | (899,226) |

DUNS 51-579-3136

## R M Solar Ltd

Unit 4 Gilcar Way, Wakefield Europort, Castleford, West Yorkshire WF10 5QS
**Tel:** 01924-224-282
**Web:** www.rmsolar.com
**Reg No:** 5860476 **Estd:** 2006 Private Limited Company
**Line of Business:** Manufacture of electronic valves and tubes and other electronic components
**Issued Capital:** £100
**Director:** R C Marsden
**US SIC:** 3999, 5084
**UK SIC:** 49590, 61490
**Auditors:** Bartfields (UK) Ltd
**Bankers:** Svenska Handelsbanken Ab (publ) (40-51-62)

| | 28-02-14 | 28-02-13 | 29-02-12 |
|---|---|---|---|
| TO | 17,196,446 | 15,423,501 | 14,559,378 |
| P/L | 844,182 | 626,788 | (24,724) |
| NW | 56,741 | (556,528) | (1,048,295) |
| WC | 1,074,541 | 1,446,279 | 1,259,914 |
| Emp. | 109 | 102 | 83 |

DUNS 50-323-9402

## R. McDowell Haulage & Distribution Ltd

Thunderbird Depot, Keighley, West Yorkshire BD21 4LW
**Tel:** 01535663941 **Fax:** 01535610657
**Web:** www.do-business.net
**Reg No:** 2348762 **Estd:** 1989 Private Limited Company
**Line of Business:** Road haulage and transport services
**Issued Capital:** £80,000
**Principals:** R H Mcdowell *(Managing)*, J C Balmforth, I Drybrough
**Co. Secretary:** Roger Mcdowell
**Responsibilities**
**Senior:** Ian Dryborough *(Health & Safety Manager)*
**Health & Safety:** Ian Dryborough *(Health & Safety Manager)*
**US SIC:** 4789 **UK SIC:** 77002
**Auditors:** Baty Casson Long
**Bankers:** Yorkshire Bank Plc (05-05-35)

| | 31-03-14 | 31-03-13 | 31-03-12 |
|---|---|---|---|
| TO | 12,452,792 | 12,061,392 | 12,237,492 |
| P/L | 314,600 | 295,918 | 422,041 |
| NW | 1,121,909 | 1,117,066 | 1,058,532 |
| WC | (1,130,299) | (1,156,003) | (1,055,729) |
| Emp. | 119 | 124 | 122 |

DUNS 23-683-7134

## R Moore

222 Newchurch Road, Bacup, Lancashire OL13 0TS
**Estd:** 2002 Proprietorship
**Line of Business:** Butchers
**Proprietor:** R Moore
**Responsibilities**
**Senior:** Ronald Moore *(Proprietor)*
**US SIC:** 5423 **UK SIC:** 64100
**Employees:** 49

DUNS 21-232-3290

## R Motson

Mile End Road Oaks Place, Colchester, Essex CO4 5XR
**Tel:** 01206-753209
**Estd:** 1994
**Line of Business:** Surgeons
**Partners:** R Motson, P Goddard
**US SIC:** 8062 **UK SIC:** 95100
**Employees:** 126

DUNS 21-209-3249

## R O Arnold Ltd

(**Subsidiary of:** Nutley-Goring Holdings Ltd)
Utopia Wheatley Hall Road, Doncaster, South Yorkshire DN2 4NY
**Tel:** 01302349231 **Fax:** 01302-730155
**Web:** www.roarnold.co.uk
**Reg No:** 0191363 **Estd:** 1923 Private Limited Company
**Line of Business:** Wholesale of hardware, plumbing and heating equipment and supplies
**Issued Capital:** £3,000
**Principals:** D R Gaylor *(Managing)*, G Baker
**Co. Secretary:** Cynitha Gaylor
**Responsibilities**
**Marketing:** Kevin Slater *(Sales & Marketing Manager)*
**Sales:** Kevin Slater *(Sales & Marketing Manager)*
**IT:** Lea Walters *(IT Manager)*
**Branches:** R.o.arnold,Ltd, D P S Motors, Station Road, Doncaster, South Yorkshire DN3 1HQ
**US SIC:** 5074 **UK SIC:** 61300
**Auditors:** Arthur Wigglesworth & Co
**Bankers:** HSBC Bank plc (40-19-20)

| | 31-12-13 | 31-12-12 | 31-12-11 |
|---|---|---|---|
| TO | 9,101,294 | 9,203,056 | 8,551,200 |
| P/L | 279,688 | 246,804 | 271,100 |
| NW | 2,973,785 | 2,773,657 | 2,576,173 |
| WC | 1,370,602 | 1,005,275 | 892,341 |
| Emp. | 54 | 62 | 63 |

DUNS 34-741-4539

## R Owton (Wholesale Butchers) Ltd

Chalcroft Farm, Burnetts Lane, West End, Southampton, Hampshire SO30 2HU
**Tel:** 02380692206 **Fax:** 02380602110
**Reg No:** 5543261 **Estd:** 2005 Private Limited Company
**Line of Business:** Meat wholesalers
**Issued Capital:** £200
**Directors:** Mrs S Owton, Mrs N D Owton, W M Owton
**Co. Secretary:** Simon Owton
**Responsibilities**
**Senior:** Robert Owton *(Manager)*
**US SIC:** 5147 **UK SIC:** 61700

| | 30-04-14 | 30-04-13 | 30-04-12 |
|---|---|---|---|
| TO | 16,123,983 | N/A | N/A |
| P/L | 312,335 | N/A | N/A |
| NW | 598,728 | 449,218 | 306,037 |
| WC | (5,044) | 25,867 | (2,133) |
| Emp. | 57 | N/A | N/A |

DUNS 37-874-3454

## R P A Architectural Consultants Ltd

51-53 Church Road, Ashford, Middlesex TW15 2TY
**Tel:** 01784-256579 **Fax:** 01784257940
**Web:** www.therpagroup.com
**Reg No:** 3306725 **Estd:** 1990 Private Limited Company
**Line of Business:** Architectural services
**Issued Capital:** £9,000
**Directors:** D Pratley, D M Rosborough
**Co. Secretary:** Kevin Walter
**Responsibilities**
**Senior:** James Breaks *(Associate Director of Design)*, Tony Gregory *(IT Manager)*
**Marketing:** Sasha Cuff *(Marketing Executive)*
**IT:** Tony Gregory *(IT Manager)*
**Engineering:** Darryl Beck *(Architectural Team Leader)*, Ketan Bhavsar *(Senior Architectural Technicia)*, Brandon Boyes *(Architectural Team Leader)*, Mark Cherrett *(Associate Director of Interior)*, Terry Cowan *(Architectural Team Leader)*, Lisa Eldridge *(Senior Architectural Technicia)*, Jamie Harvie *(Senior Architectural Technicia)*, Wes MacCabe *(Senior Architectural Technicia)*, Martin Playford *(Executive Technical Director)*
**US SIC:** 1799 **UK SIC:** 50000
**Auditors:** ASA & Co
**Bankers:** HSBC Bank plc (40-42-13)

| | 31-03-14 | 31-03-13 | 31-03-12 |
|---|---|---|---|
| TA | 1,558,191 | 1,703,647 | 1,759,406 |
| NW | 953,388 | 909,510 | 700,797 |
| WC | 840,896 | 763,249 | 562,753 |

DUNS 57-615-3290 **Exp**

## R P Adam Ltd

Arpal Works, Riverside Road, Selkirk, Selkirkshire TD7 5DU
**Tel:** 0175021586
**Web:** www.rpadam.co.uk
**Reg No:** 0148256SC **Estd:** 1994 Private Limited Company
**Line of Business:** Misc chemical/chemical preparation mfrs
**Export Sales:** £655,078
**Issued Capital:** £56,200
**Directors:** M Carroll, G F Adam, J Taylor, R H Leith, G M Adam
**Co. Secretary:** Sydney Farquharson
**Responsibilities**
**Senior:** Sidney Farquharson *(Senior Finance Administrator)*
**Finance:** Sidney Farquharson *(Senior Finance Administrator)*, Mike Henderson *(Accountant)*
**Marketing:** Max Adam *(Sales & Marketing Manager)*
**Sales:** Max Adam *(Sales & Marketing Manager)*
**HR:** Alison Gaddie *(Human Resources Manager)*, Gladys Skeldon *(Human Resources Manager)*
**US SIC:** 2899, 2842
**UK SIC:** 25670, 25990
**Auditors:** Grant Thornton UK LLP
**Bankers:** Barclays Bank Plc (20-33-70)

| | 30-06-13 | 30-06-12 | 30-06-11 |
|---|---|---|---|
| TO | 7,473,787 | 7,542,214 | 7,397,971 |
| P/L | 987,914 | 342,857 | 961,838 |
| NW | 1,300,474 | 658,811 | 1,088,957 |
| WC | 657,286 | 313,712 | 226,517 |
| Emp. | 67 | 73 | 74 |

DUNS 23-541-6059 **Exp**

## R P International Ltd

2nd Floor, 21 Garlick Hill, London EC4V 2AU
**Tel:** 0203-597-7150
**Web:** www.rpint.com
**Reg No:** 3540188 **VAT No:** 885510211
**Estd:** 1998 Private Limited Company
**Line of Business:** Other computer related activities
**Export Sales:** £21,772,000
**Issued Capital:** £62,103
**Principals:** S B Lovelace *(Chairman)*, J A Frankum *(Managing)*, D F Northey, S A Wilson, D C Higgins
**Responsibilities**
**Senior:** John Kobelt *(Client Partner)*
**Marketing:** Jessica Mayman *(Marketing Manager)*
**IT:** Jay Sidikki *(IT Manager)*
**HR:** Terry Hiscock *(Head of Talent Management)*
**US SIC:** 7379, 7399
**UK SIC:** 83940, 83954
**Auditors:** BDO LLP
**Bankers:** HSBC Bank plc (40-18-22)

| | 30-04-13 | 30-04-12 | 30-04-11 |
|---|---|---|---|
| TO | 22,152,000 | 20,888,000 | 18,204,000 |
| P/L | 660,000 | (287,000) | 387,000 |
| NW | 2,369,000 | 1,736,000 | 2,143,000 |
| WC | 2,234,000 | 1,548,000 | 1,933,000 |
| Emp. | 63 | 78 | 77 |

DUNS 76-971-7760

## R P L Transport Ltd

(**Subsidiary of:** Bedfords Holdings Ltd)
Unit 1 Fingle Drive, Milton Keynes, Buckinghamshire MK13 0ER
**Tel:** 01908-318383 **Fax:** 01908-318448
**Web:** www.rpltransport.co.uk
**Reg No:** 2633099 **VAT No:** 563785208
**Estd:** 1991 Private Limited Company
**Line of Business:** Road haulage and transport services
**Issued Capital:** £25,000
**Directors:** D R Webster, D I Storey, K S Pfadenhauer
**Co. Secretary:** David Storey
**Responsibilities**
**Senior:** Christine Lockett *(Manager)*, Ray Lockett *(Manager)*, Peter Locklett *(Manager)*
**Finance:** Helen Atkins *(Financial Director)*, Sarah Lockett *(Financial Director)*
**US SIC:** 4789, 4226
**UK SIC:** 77002, 77003
**Auditors:** Foxley Kingham
**Bankers:** Barclays Bank Plc (20-53-30)

| | 31-03-13 | 31-03-12 | 31-03-11 |
|---|---|---|---|
| TA | 3,080,139 | 3,183,630 | 3,157,291 |
| NW | 736,392 | 872,707 | 974,955 |
| WC | (608,124) | (537,468) | (312,447) |

DUNS 29-884-8508 **Exp**

## R P S Group Plc

20 Western Avenue, Milton Park, Abingdon, Oxfordshire OX14 4SH
**Tel:** 01235821888
**Web:** www.rpsgroup.com
**Reg No:** 2087786 **Estd:** 1970 Public Limited Company
**Line of Business:** Engineers (consulting)
**Export Markets:** Europe
**Export Sales:** £327,549,000
**Trading Style:** R P S Group
**Issued Capital:** £6,598,952
**Principals:** Dr A S Hearne *(Managing)*, Dr J P Williams, J H Bennett, Ms L E Charlton, Mrs T Graham, R L Miller-Bakewell, A Page, G R Young
**Co. Secretary:** Nicholas Rowe
**Responsibilities**
**Senior:** Nick Ball *(Operations Director)*, James Blanchard *(Managing Director, HSERM)*, Trevor Hoyle *(Divisional Managing Director,)*, Harry Land *(Non Executive Chairperson)*, Belinda Morgan *(Operations Director)*, Richard Mould *(Recruitment Director)*, John Pothecary *(Managing Director, EAME)*, Andy Young *(Commercial Director)*
**Marketing:** Ed Jankowski *(Director, Commercial and Gas)*, Andy Young *(Commercial Director)*
**Admin:** Eve Gillard *(Personal Assistant)*
**HR:** Neil Harbury *(Managing Director ? Training)*, Richard Mould *(Recruitment Director)*

**Operations:** Nick Ball (*Operations Director*), Simon Bicknell (*Project Manager - Site Investi*), Belinda Morgan (*Operations Director*)
**Engineering:** Corinna Demmar (*Technical Director*), Simon Zisman (*Technical Director*)
**Branches:** R P S Group Plc, Bridge Foot, 4C Eat Mill, Belper, Derbyshire DE56 2UA
**US SIC:** 8911 **UK SIC:** 83701
**Auditors:** Deloitte LLP
**Bankers:** Lloyds TSB Bank plc (30-96-24)

| | 31-12-13 | 31-12-12 | 31-12-11 |
|---|---|---|---|
| TO | 567,614,000 | 555,863,000 | 528,710,000 |
| P/L | 43,607,000 | 40,174,000 | 40,451,000 |
| NW | (3,241,000) | 45,374,000 | 35,338,000 |
| WC | 49,604,000 | 57,459,000 | 67,724,000 |
| Emp. | 4,306 | 4,507 | 4,686 |

DUNS 22-935-5540
## R P S Ireland Ltd
(**Subsidiary of:** R P S Group Plc)
Elmwood House, 74 Boucher Road, Belfast BT12 6RZ
**Fax:** 028 9066 8286
**Web:** www.rpsgroup.com
**Reg No:** 0020604NI **Estd:** 2012 Private Limited Company
**Line of Business:** Other engineering activities
**Export Sales:** £3,172,000
**Issued Capital:** £2
**Directors:** G R Young, Dr A S Hearne
**Co. Secretary:** Nicholas Rowe
**US SIC:** 8911 **UK SIC:** 83701
**Auditors:** Ernst & Young LLP

| | 31-12-13 | 31-12-12 | 31-12-11 |
|---|---|---|---|
| TO | 10,755,000 | 10,585,000 | 10,905,000 |
| P/L | 622,000 | 682,000 | 320,000 |
| NW | 1,947,000 | 1,718,000 | 1,593,000 |
| WC | 1,895,000 | 1,762,000 | 1,602,000 |
| Emp. | 159 | 152 | 155 |

DUNS 21-595-3950
## R P S Planning & Development
2420 The Quadrant, Aztec West, Almondsbury, Bristol, Avon BS32 4AQ
**Tel:** 01454 853000
**Web:** www.rpsgroup.com
**Estd:** 2011 Proprietorship
**Line of Business:** Architectural services
**Proprietor:** S Taylor
**US SIC:** 8911 **UK SIC:** 83701
**Employees:** 90

DUNS 53-568-5986
## R Pollard
Near Salter Syke, Skipton Old Road, Colne, Lancashire BB8 7EW
**Tel:** 01282 865364
**Partnership**
**Line of Business:** Livestock farming
**Partners:** R Pollard, Mrs E Pollard
**US SIC:** 0291 **UK SIC:** 01001
**Employees:** 64

DUNS 21-595-3953
## R R Donnelley
Booths Park 1, Chelford Road, Knutsford, Cheshire WA16 8GS
**Tel:** 02030475160
**Web:** www.rrd.com
**Estd:** 2003
**Line of Business:** Business information services
**Proprietor:** Ms C Lynch
**US SIC:** 7399 **UK SIC:** 83954
**Employees:** 88

DUNS 23-344-9656
## R R Donnelly
25 Copthall Avenue, London EC2R 7BP
**Tel:** 02030476200
**Web:** www.rrdonnelley.com
**Estd:** 1991 Proprietorship
**Line of Business:** Printing not elsewhere classified
**Proprietor:** N Hodson
**Responsibilities**
**Senior:** Jeremy Jenkins (*Vice President*)
**US SIC:** 7399 **UK SIC:** 83954
**Employees:** 70

DUNS 22-712-2793
## R. Raphael & Sons Plc
(**Subsidiary of:** Lenlyn Holdings P L C)
Walton Lodge, Walton Terrace, Aylesbury, Buckinghamshire HP21 7QY
**Web:** www.raphaelsbank.com
**Reg No:** 1288938 **Estd:** 1787 Public Limited Company
**Line of Business:** Banks and financial institutions
**Trading Style:** Raphaels Bank
**Issued Capital:** £13,600,000
**Directors:** M T Roberts, T E Johnson, A T Pooley, J H Tattersall, D Beale, R C Wells, J H Quitter, Ms A R Frost
**Co. Secretary:** Mrs Kerry Penfold

**Responsibilities**
**Senior:** Judith Beale (*Head Of Banking*), Andy Downes (*General Manager*)
**Sales:** Emily Baum (*Business Development Manager*)
**US SIC:** 6012 **UK SIC:** 81402
**Auditors:** KPMG Audit PLC

| | 28-02-14 | 28-02-13 | 29-02-12 |
|---|---|---|---|
| TA | 284,474,000 | 213,619,000 | 164,922,000 |
| P/L | 1,902,000 | 775,000 | 1,342,000 |
| NW | 22,169,000 | 22,603,000 | 22,337,000 |
| WC | 18,056,000 | 20,992,000 | 13,740,000 |
| Emp. | 71 | 84 | 79 |

DUNS 28-986-6485
## R S A Consulting Ltd
(**Subsidiary of:** Rsa (Holdings) Ltd)
The Melon Ground, Hatfield Park, Hatfield, Hertfordshire AL9 5NB
**Web:** www.pharmarecruit.com
**Reg No:** 1803896 **VAT No:** 404045304
**Estd:** 1984 Private Limited Company
**Line of Business:** Employment and recruitment companies and consultants
**Issued Capital:** £27,567
**Directors:** C R Molloy, N D Stephens, M A Ryans
**Co. Secretary:** Graham Kilbey
**Responsibilities**
**Senior:** Keith Hobson (*Manager*)
**US SIC:** 7361 **UK SIC:** 83954
**Auditors:** Hillier Hopkins LLP
**Bankers:** Barclays Bank Plc (20-67-59)

| | 31-12-13 | 31-08-12 | 31-12-11 |
|---|---|---|---|
| TO | 8,105,207 | 8,204,609 | N/A |
| P/L | (155,034) | (39,779) | N/A |
| NW | 729,133 | 939,766 | 1,075,087 |
| WC | 608,386 | 752,984 | 954,103 |

DUNS 21-828-4990                    Exp
## R S A Waterheating Ltd
(**Subsidiary of:** Stichting Aandelen Remeha)
Wednesbury One, Blackcountry New Road, Wednesbury, West Midlands WS10 7NZ
**Tel:** 0845-070-1055 **Fax:** 08450701059
**Web:** www.andrewswaterheaters.co.uk
**Reg No:** 0302628 **VAT No:** 562322757
**Estd:** 1935 Private Limited Company
**Line of Business:** Manufacture of other fabricated metal products not elsewhere classified
**Export Markets:** W Europe, Middle East, U S A, Australasia, S & S E Asia, Africa, S America, Canada.
**Trading Style:** Andrews Water Heaters, Range Cylinders
**Issued Capital:** £5,780,000
**Directors:** P T Moss, J Zwiers
**Co. Secretary:** Ms Karen Roberts
**Branches:** R S A Waterheating Ltd, New Era Wks, Mark St, Wakefield, West Yorkshire WF1 4EJ
**US SIC:** 3499 **UK SIC:** 31694
**Bankers:** Lloyds TSB Bank plc (30-95-42)

| | 31-12-13 | 31-12-12 | 31-12-11 |
|---|---|---|---|
| TA | 6,697,000 | 6,842,000 | 6,842,000 |
| P/L | 92,000 | N/A | 36,000 |
| NW | 5,932,000 | 5,840,000 | 5,840,000 |
| WC | 5,932,000 | 5,840,000 | 5,836,000 |

DUNS 21-219-8170                    Imp-Exp
## R S Clare & Co Ltd
8-14 Stanhope Street, Liverpool, Merseyside L8 5RQ
**Tel:** 0151-709-2902
**Web:** www.rsclare.com
**Reg No:** 0072349 **VAT No:** 163312689
**Estd:** 1902 Private Limited Company
**Line of Business:** Other treatment of petroleum products (excluding petrochemicals manufacture)
**Export Sales:** £9,617,192
**Issued Capital:** £250,000
**Principals:** R I Meadows (*Managing*), R S Higgin, N J Patterson, N L Biddle, S D Scott
**Co. Secretary:** Ms Geraldine Chapple
**Responsibilities**
**Senior:** Rosemary Heaney (*Manager*)
**Engineering:** John Hartley (*Engineering Manager*)
**Branches:** R.s.clare & Co.,Ltd, 9 Bernham Cres, Stonehaven, Kincardineshire AB39 2WQ
**US SIC:** 2999, 5171
**UK SIC:** 11150, 61200
**Auditors:** Grant Thornton UK LLP
**Bankers:** Barclays Bank Plc (20-51-01)

| | 31-12-13 | 31-12-12 | 31-12-11 |
|---|---|---|---|
| TO | 27,335,804 | 24,280,680 | 23,060,031 |
| P/L | 3,292,664 | 2,134,432 | 1,961,790 |
| NW | 9,726,754 | 7,956,073 | 7,352,345 |
| WC | 5,623,905 | 4,725,068 | 3,829,008 |
| Emp. | 145 | 149 | 139 |

DUNS 21-931-5629
## R S D Technology Ltd
134 Nantwich Road, Crewe, Cheshire CW2 6AX
**Tel:** 01270215910
**Web:** www.rsd.uk.com
**Reg No:** 0941818 **VAT No:** 279074133
**Estd:** 1966 Private Limited Company
**Line of Business:** Labour recruitment and provision of personnel
**Issued Capital:** £805,000
**Principals:** S H Bailey (*Financial*), R S Bailey, I S Bailey
**Co. Secretary:** Ms Gail Beard
**Branches:** R S D Technology Ltd, Kingsway Business Centre, Kingsway, Swansea, West Glamorgan SA5 4DL
**US SIC:** 7361 **UK SIC:** 83954
**Auditors:** Afford Astbury Bond
**Bankers:** National Westminster Bank Plc (60-06-23)

| | 31-12-13 | 31-12-12 | 31-12-11 |
|---|---|---|---|
| TO | 15,830,242 | 16,542,749 | 12,667,555 |
| P/L | 53,406 | 27,018 | 3,557 |
| NW | 1,039,160 | 994,760 | 968,141 |
| WC | 293,598 | 268,769 | 274,990 |
| Emp. | 492 | 498 | 459 |

DUNS 23-044-9019                    Exp
## R S M Castings Ltd
North Portway Close, Northampton, Northamptonshire NN3 8RQ
**Tel:** 01604-671333
**Web:** www.rsm-castings.co.uk
**Reg No:** 1184461 **VAT No:** 121853685
**Estd:** 1974 Private Limited Company
**Line of Business:** Production of alloys
**Export Markets:** Germany; Italy; U S A; Denmark
**Export Sales:** £3,646,934
**Trading Style:** R S M Castings Ltd
**Issued Capital:** £3,617
**Directors:** D Smith, B Jones, K Danns
**Responsibilities**
**Senior:** Margaret Frankland (*Manager*)
**US SIC:** 3325 **UK SIC:** 31110
**Auditors:** Moore Stephens
**Bankers:** Yorkshire Bank Plc (05-06-33)

| | 31-12-13 | 31-12-12 | 31-12-11 |
|---|---|---|---|
| TO | 8,242,267 | 7,554,883 | N/A |
| P/L | 133,955 | (178,009) | N/A |
| NW | 1,452,707 | 1,530,181 | 2,074,735 |
| WC | (263,734) | (339,762) | 244,069 |
| Emp. | 108 | 99 | N/A |

DUNS 21-595-3960
## R S M Tenon
Davidson House, The Forbury, Reading, Berkshire RG1 3EU
**Tel:** 01189530350
**Web:** www.bakertilly.co.uk
**Estd:** 2011 Proprietorship
**Line of Business:** Accounting activities
**Proprietor:** Ms C Telford
**Responsibilities**
**Senior:** Alison Sapford (*Proprietor*)
**US SIC:** 8931 **UK SIC:** 83600
**Employees:** 100

DUNS 21-916-7624
## R S Miller Roofing Ltd
(**Subsidiary of:** R.S. Miller Holdings Ltd)
Premier Partnership Estate, Leys Road, Brierley Hill, West Midlands DY5 3UP
**Tel:** 01384-571-144
**Web:** www.rsmiller.co.uk
**Reg No:** 1009892 **VAT No:** 100124554
**Estd:** 1971 Private Limited Company
**Line of Business:** Roofing contracting services
**Trading Style:** Midland Industrial Cladding
**Issued Capital:** £2,000
**Principals:** R S Miller (*Managing*), S J Green, N J Sadler, G J Little
**Co. Secretary:** Julian Ash
**Responsibilities**
**Senior:** Jay Ash (*Manager*)
**Finance:** Joanne Bayliss (*Credit Controller*), Tina Newton (*Accounts*)
**Marketing:** Sheila Miller (*Administrator*)
**Admin:** Sheila Miller (*Administrator*)
**HR:** Sheila Miller (*Administrator*)
**Branches:** R S Miller Roofing Ltd, Redroof Yard, Acton Gro, Nottingham, Nottinghamshire NG10 1FY
**US SIC:** 1761 **UK SIC:** 50400
**Auditors:** Wright & Co Partnership Ltd
**Bankers:** National Westminster Bank Plc (60-08-49)

| | 31-05-14 | 31-05-13 | 31-05-12 |
|---|---|---|---|
| TA | 2,790,508 | 2,447,168 | 2,225,451 |
| NW | 676,760 | 527,385 | 520,423 |
| WC | 499,733 | 369,900 | 284,854 |

DUNS 23-355-3861
## R S Motorhomes
Unit C Harworth Business Park, Blyth Road, Harworth, Doncaster, South Yorkshire DN11 8DB
**Tel:** 01302741710
**Web:** www.rsmotorhomes.com
**Estd:** 1989 Partnership
**Line of Business:** Manufacturers and dealers of caravans
**Partners:** A Rowe, M Rowe
**Responsibilities**
**Senior:** Mick Rowe (*Manager*)
**US SIC:** 3792 **UK SIC:** 35230
**Employees:** 50

DUNS 23-912-3768
## R. S. V. P. Call Centres Ltd
1 Heron Quay, London E14 4JA
**Tel:** 0800665400
**Web:** www.rsvp.co.uk
**Reg No:** 3902803 **Estd:** 1999 Private Limited Company
**Line of Business:** Call centre activities
**Issued Capital:** £50,000
**Directors:** R J Fitzjohn, M P Abernethy
**Co. Secretary:** Peter Diegeler
**US SIC:** 8999, 7399
**UK SIC:** 83954

| | 31-03-14 | 31-03-13 | 31-03-12 |
|---|---|---|---|
| TO | 8,332,572 | 7,210,573 | N/A |
| P/L | 1,801,159 | 1,913,994 | N/A |
| NW | (1,768,958) | (2,022,144) | 44,123 |
| WC | (2,574,242) | (2,686,350) | 44,123 |
| Emp. | 357 | 263 | N/A |

DUNS 50-025-9221
## R. Savage Plant Hire Co. Ltd
(**Subsidiary of:** Savage Plant Ltd)
222 St Margarets Road, Birmingham, West Midlands B8 2BG
**Web:** www.savageplanthire.co.uk
**Reg No:** 2304174 **Estd:** 1988 Private Limited Company
**Line of Business:** Plant hire and leasing
**Issued Capital:** £100
**Principals:** Mrs J Smith (*Managing*), P Savage (*Managing*), P J Mcnulty
**Co. Secretary:** Mrs Joy Smith
**Responsibilities**
**Senior:** Joy Savage (*Manager*)
**US SIC:** 7394 **UK SIC:** 84000
**Auditors:** Bentley Jennison
**Bankers:** HSBC Bank plc (40-11-37)

| | 31-12-13 | 31-12-12 | 31-12-11 |
|---|---|---|---|
| TA | 1,757,547 | 1,691,984 | 1,599,792 |
| NW | 1,109,636 | 1,022,063 | 910,854 |
| WC | (60,866) | (130,552) | (107,250) |

DUNS 21-812-6480
## R. Sinclair Transport Ltd
Unit 10 10-10a Davies Road, Evesham, Worcestershire WR11 1FN
**Web:** www.rsinclairtransport.com
**Reg No:** 1015925 **VAT No:** 274341169
**Estd:** 1971 Private Limited Company
**Line of Business:** Other supporting land transport activities
**Issued Capital:** £62,001
**Principals:** D A Sinclair (*Financial*), T Sinclair, S J Sinclair
**Co. Secretary:** Nigel Sinclair
**US SIC:** 4789, 4226
**UK SIC:** 77002, 77003
**Auditors:** Clement Rabjohns
**Bankers:** National Westminster Bank Plc (60-08-44)

| | 31-03-14 | 31-03-13 | 31-03-12 |
|---|---|---|---|
| TA | 3,351,893 | 3,221,234 | 3,177,906 |
| NW | 1,888,954 | 1,957,605 | 2,097,339 |
| WC | (274,525) | (162,577) | (298,199) |

DUNS 21-128-5775
## R Skinner & Sons
Car Showroom, Tafarnaubach Industrial Estate, Tafarnaubach, Tredegar, Gwent NP22 3AA
**Tel:** 01495-713400
**Web:** www.ronskinnerandsons.co.uk
**Estd:** 1966 Proprietorship
**Line of Business:** Sale of motor vehicles
**Proprietor:** R Skinner
**US SIC:** 5511, 7539, 5521
**UK SIC:** 65100, 67100
**Employees:** 50

DUNS 23-827-7060
## R Sons (Homes) Ltd
Orchard House Residential Care Home, 155 Barton Road, Kettering, Northamptonshire NN15 6RT
**Tel:** 01536485599 **Fax:** 01536-485599
**Reg No:** 3819684 **Estd:** 1999 Private Limited Company
**Line of Business:** Social work activities with accommodation
**Issued Capital:** £100
**Director:** A R Patel

**US SIC:** 8321  **UK SIC:** 96111

|     | 31-08-13 | 30-08-12 | 31-08-11 |
|-----|----------|----------|----------|
| TO  | N/A      | 1,505,743 | 1,453,546 |
| P/L | N/A      | 170,088  | 147,520  |
| NW  | (1,180,459) | 753,412 | 672,337 |
| WC  | 170,493  | (378,592) | (371,796) |
| Emp. | N/A     | 72       | 71       |

DUNS 21-277-9383                                         **Imp-Exp**

### R. Soper Ltd
Crownest Mill, Skipton Road, Barnoldswick, Lancashire BB18 5RH
**Tel:** 01282666000 **Fax:** 01282-666002
**Web:** www.rsoper.co.uk
**Reg No:** 0381472 **Estd:** 1922 Private Limited Company
**Line of Business:** Manufacture of soft furnishings
**Export Markets:** Finland; U S A
**Trading Style:** Sandown & Bourne
**Issued Capital:** £1,020
**Principals:** C R Soper (Managing), J Kidd, B D Soper
**Co. Secretary:** Jack Simpson
**Branches:** R. Soper Ltd, Fernbank House, Springwood Way, Tytherington Business Park, Macclesfield, Cheshire SK10 2XA
**US SIC:** 2391, 5133
**UK SIC:** 45550, 61600
**Auditors:** Whitehead & Howarth
**Bankers:** The Royal Bank Of Scotland Plc (16-28-33)

|     | 31-01-14 | 31-01-13 | 31-01-12 |
|-----|----------|----------|----------|
| TO  | 14,182,924 | 14,119,579 | 11,411,744 |
| P/L | 223,987  | 323,560  | 280,646  |
| NW  | 4,836,764 | 4,681,059 | 4,766,360 |
| WC  | 423,899  | (406,398) | (376,131) |
| Emp. | 129     | 168      | 178      |

DUNS 64-097-8904

### R Stratton (Knutsford) Ltd
(Subsidiary of: Penske Automotive Group Inc.)
Manchester Road, Knutsford, Cheshire WA16 0ST
**Tel:** 01565-632525
**Web:** www.guysalmon.knutsford.landrover.co.uk
**Reg No:** 3493567 **Estd:** 1998 Private Limited Company
**Line of Business:** Car dealers (new & used)
**Trading Style:** Guy Salmon Land Rover
**Issued Capital:** £2
**Directors:** G E Nieuwenhuys, A Collinson
**Co. Secretary:** Adam Collinson
**Responsibilities**
**Senior:** Jason Emanuell (Dealer Principal)
**Admin:** Julie Ripley (Administration Manager)
**Purchasing:** Julie Ripley (Administration Manager)
**US SIC:** 5511, 7539, 5531
**UK SIC:** 65100, 67100
**Auditors:** KPMG Audit PLC
**Bankers:** National Westminster Bank Plc (56-00-55)
**Employees:** 60

DUNS 21-580-1282

### R Stuart
The Docks, Methil, Leven, Fife KY8 3RE
**Tel:** 01333439333
**Estd:** 2011 Proprietorship
**Line of Business:** Bakers shops
**Proprietor:** A Stuart
**US SIC:** 5462  **UK SIC:** 64100
**Employees:** 150

DUNS 21-783-7977

### R T A Business Consultants
Telephone Exchange, Dunstable Place, Luton, Bedfordshire LU1 2QD
**Tel:** 01582480101
**Web:** www.rtabusinessesforsale.com
**Estd:** 2011
**Line of Business:** Business transfer agents
**US SIC:** 6211  **UK SIC:** 83100
**Employees:** 120

DUNS 23-588-0452                                         **Imp-Exp**

### R T I International Metals Ltd
(Subsidiary of: Rti International Metals Inc.)
Titan House, Trinity Road, Kingsbury Link, Piccadilly, Tamworth, Staffordshire B78 2EX
**Web:** www.rtiintl.com
**Reg No:** 3585661 **Estd:** 1998 Private Limited Company
**Line of Business:** Production of non ferrous metals
**Export Sales:** £24,397,671
**Issued Capital:** £151,000
**Director:** D Hall
**Co. Secretary:** Dawne Hickton
**Responsibilities**
**Senior:** Harry Klein (General Manager), Steve South (Operations Manager), Michael Wellham (Manager)
**Finance:** Peter Eccles (Accounts Manager)
**Sales:** Harry Klein (General Manager)
**IT:** Mandev Dass (It Controller)

**HR:** Samantha Hyde (Human Resources Manager)
**Health & Safety:** Steve South (Operations Manager)
**Facilities:** Steve South (Operations Manager)
**Operations:** Steve South (Operations Manager)
**Engineering:** Amar Iqbal (Engineering Manager)
**US SIC:** 3339, 8911
**UK SIC:** 22470, 83701
**Auditors:** Clements Keys
**Bankers:** Lloyds TSB Bank plc (30-98-44)

|     | 31-12-13 | 31-12-12 | 31-12-11 |
|-----|----------|----------|----------|
| TO  | 52,490,388 | 49,522,252 | 45,007,211 |
| P/L | 2,410,372 | 2,220,000 | 1,242,406 |
| NW  | 11,175,974 | 9,518,572 | 8,106,082 |
| WC  | 8,754,596 | 7,272,323 | 6,018,334 |
| Emp. | 49      | 52       | 52       |

DUNS 76-711-5173                                              **Imp**

### R-Tek Ltd.
(Subsidiary of: Kasai Kogyo Co. Ltd.)
Stephenson Road, Washington, Tyne and Wear NE37 3HR
**Tel:** 01914157000
**Web:** www.r-tek.co.uk
**Reg No:** 2594244 **VAT No:** 588107318
**Estd:** 1991 Private Limited Company
**Line of Business:** Manufacturers of car interiors
**Issued Capital:** £10,000,000
**Directors:** K Watanabe, P R Watson, F Fukuda
**Responsibilities**
**Senior:** Jacques Jaubert (Manager), Hideaki Matsuya (Manager), Glenda Minor (Manager), F Sukuda (Manager)
**Sales:** Jill Usher (Purchasing Manager)
**IT:** David Stook (Information Technology Systems)
**Purchasing:** Jill Usher (Purchasing Manager)
**Branches:** R-Tek Ltd., Unit 1 Triangle Business Pk, Merthyr Tydfil, Mid Glamorgan CF48 4TQ
**US SIC:** 3714  **UK SIC:** 35300
**Auditors:** Deloitte & Touche LLP
**Bankers:** The Sumitomo Bank, Ltd (40-51-25)

|     | 31-12-13 | 31-12-12 | 31-12-11 |
|-----|----------|----------|----------|
| TO  | 94,348,330 | 92,932,468 | 70,097,626 |
| P/L | 9,919,916 | 10,461,114 | 5,225,180 |
| NW  | 22,966,665 | 16,364,660 | 19,368,031 |
| WC  | 8,271,067 | 5,140,070 | 10,843,645 |
| Emp. | 621     | 628      | 531      |

DUNS 23-246-1970

### R Timperley & Partners
29 Main Street, Leeds, West Yorkshire LS25 1DS
**Web:** www.isonharrison.co.uk
**VAT No:** 169312163 **Estd:** 1993 Partnership
**Line of Business:** Solicitors
**Trading Style:** Ison Harrison Solicitors, Ison Harrison & Co, Harrison Bundey
**Partners:** J Wearing, S C Harrison, R Timperley, D Mackenzie
**Responsibilities**
**Senior:** Stacey Allen (Partner), Nancy Fairbairn (Partner), Dominic MacKenzie (Partner), Steve Neale (Partner), Evelyn Peacock (Partner)
**Finance:** Elaine Russell (Accounts Manager)
**Marketing:** Tim Arnott (Head of Marketing), Stuart Cretch (Marketing Coordinator), Anne-Marie O'Hagan (Personnel Manager)
**Sales:** Anne-Marie O'Hagan (Personnel Manager)
**Admin:** Gillian Ainsley (Office Manager), Pete Colley (Office Manager), Nigel Cowley (Office Manager)
**IT:** Adrian Barker (IT Manager)
**HR:** Anne-Marie O'Hagan (Personnel Manager)
**Health & Safety:** Anne-Marie O'Hagan (Personnel Manager)
**Facilities:** Paul Allinson (Facilities Manager)
**Purchasing:** David Bancroft (Head of Conveyancing & Remortg)
**Branches:** R Timperley & Partners, 219-223 Chapeltown Road, Leeds, West Yorkshire LS7 3DX
**US SIC:** 8111  **UK SIC:** 83500
**Bankers:** The Royal Bank Of Scotland Plc (16-23-37)
**Employees:** 7

DUNS 22-655-3857

### R. Turner (Haulage) Ltd
Isleham Road, Fordham, Ely, Cambridgeshire CB7 5NL
**Tel:** 01638720911 **Fax:** 01638-721214
**Web:** www.rturnerhaulage.com
**Reg No:** 1622477 **VAT No:** 370371565
**Estd:** 2002 Private Limited Company
**Line of Business:** Road haulage and transport services
**Issued Capital:** £10,000
**Managing Director:** R J Turner

**Co. Secretary:** Mrs Veronica Turner
**US SIC:** 4789  **UK SIC:** 77002
**Auditors:** Hodson Lewis
**Bankers:** Barclays Bank Plc (20-29-68)

|     | 31-03-14 | 31-03-13 | 31-03-12 |
|-----|----------|----------|----------|
| TO  | N/A      | 7,758,065 | N/A      |
| P/L | N/A      | 25,396   | N/A      |
| NW  | 1,931,720 | 1,834,170 | 1,809,111 |
| WC  | 299,867  | 448,514  | 731,580  |

DUNS 21-810-3253

### R U Craft
Brunel House, Brunel Road, Newton Abbot, Devon TQ12 4PU
**Tel:** 08448805853
**Web:** www.stitchcraftcreate.co.uk
**Estd:** 2012
**Line of Business:** Other retail sale in specialised stores not elsewhere classified
**Responsibilities**
**Senior:** James Woollam (Manager)
**US SIC:** 5199  **UK SIC:** 61900
**Employees:** 60

DUNS 22-678-4726

### R W Chenery
Wellesley Road, Tharston, Norwich, Norfolk NR15 2PD
**Tel:** 01379-741221
**Web:** www.chenerytravel.co.uk
**VAT No:** 104972279 **Estd:** 1947 Partnership
**Line of Business:** Renting of buses and coaches
**Trading Style:** R W Chenery
**Partners:** Mrs P C Garnham, J M Mcgraffin
**Responsibilities**
**Senior:** Peter Croxson (Transport Manager), Julia McGriffin (Operations Manager)
**Marketing:** Julia McGriffin (Operations Manager)
**Sales:** Julia McGriffin (Operations Manager)
**IT:** Julia McGriffin (Operations Manager)
**HR:** Julia McGriffin (Operations Manager)
**Health & Safety:** Julia McGriffin (Operations Manager)
**Facilities:** Jerry Scoggins (Workshop Manager)
**Fleet:** Peter Croxson (Transport Manager)
**Branches:** R W Chenery, 2 Spains Hall Road, Braintree, Essex CM7 4NG
**US SIC:** 4142  **UK SIC:** 72102
**Bankers:** Barclays Bank Plc (20-26-34)
**Employees:** 60

DUNS 21-660-9383

### R W L Products
Unit 1h Pegswood Industrial Estate, Pegswood, Morpeth, Northumberland NE61 6HZ
**Tel:** 01670505516
**Web:** www.rwlproducts.co.uk
**Estd:** 2003 Proprietorship
**Line of Business:** Hospitals
**Proprietor:** R Lillico
**US SIC:** 3534  **UK SIC:** 32553
**Bankers:** Barclays Bank Plc (20-00-50)
**Employees:** 107

DUNS 21-607-7164

### R W Randall Ltd
Po Box 154, Guernsey, Channel Islands GY1 3JG
**Tel:** 01481-720134 **Fax:** 01481-713233
**Web:** www.randallsbrewery.com
**Reg No:** 0000111G **Estd:** 1868 Private Limited Company
**Line of Business:** Brewers
**Trading Style:** Randall's Brewery
**Principals:** J M Randall (Managing), N R Scott (Financial), B Randall (Marketing), P J Randall
**Responsibilities**
**Senior:** Sarah Langlois (Operations Manager)
**Finance:** Guy Plummer (Financial Director)
**Facilities:** Guy Plummer (Financial Director)
**Branches:** R W Randall Ltd, St. Jacques, St. Peter Port, Guernsey, Channel Islands GY1 1SW
**US SIC:** 2082, 2085, 5182
**UK SIC:** 42702, 42402, 61700
**Bankers:** HSBC Bank plc (40-22-25)
**Employees:** 60

DUNS 36-547-8341

### R Wiseman Dairies
Ashmore Lake Way, Willenhall, West Midlands WV12 4LF
**Tel:** 03301230123
**Web:** www.wiseman-dairies.co.uk
**Estd:** 2010 Proprietorship
**Line of Business:** Dairy produce merchants
**Proprietor:** M Wood
**US SIC:** 5199  **UK SIC:** 61900
**Employees:** 230

DUNS 34-632-3897

### R2 International Ltd
9a 9b, Imperial Road, London SW6 2AG
**Tel:** 02071002312 **Fax:** 0870 490 6845
**Web:** www.r2international.com
**Reg No:** 5438530 **VAT No:** 867516194
**Estd:** 2005 Private Limited Company
**Line of Business:** Other software consultancy and supply
**Issued Capital:** £500
**Director:** U A Sheikh
**Co. Secretary:** Tariq Sheikh
**US SIC:** 7379  **UK SIC:** 83940

|     | 30-04-14 | 30-04-13 | 30-04-12 |
|-----|----------|----------|----------|
| TA  | 214,497  | 436,874  | 326,076  |
| NW  | 104,293  | 83,787   | 63,798   |
| WC  | 103,999  | 83,348   | 63,141   |

DUNS 21-618-5314                                         **Imp-Exp**

### R3 Polygon Uk Ltd.
(Subsidiary of: Muha Luxco Sarl)
7 Blackstone Road, Stukeley Meadows Industrial Estate, Huntingdon, Cambridgeshire PE29 6EE
**Tel:** 01480442327
**Web:** www.polygonrental.com
**Reg No:** 0402652 **VAT No:** 927238020
**Estd:** 1946 Private Limited Company
**Line of Business:** Plant hire and leasing
**Export Markets:** E U, Australia, Singapore, U S A
**Issued Capital:** £250,000
**Directors:** J A Sykes, E J Jansen, M S Norberg
**Co. Secretary:** Purmpal Taggar
**Branches:** R3 Polygon Uk Ltd., Unit 9, Aerodrome Way, Hounslow, Middlesex TW5 9QB
**US SIC:** 1799  **UK SIC:** 50000
**Auditors:** Ernst & Young LLP
**Bankers:** Svenska Handelsbanken Ab (publ) (40-51-62)

|     | 31-12-13 | 31-12-12 | 31-12-11 |
|-----|----------|----------|----------|
| TO  | 24,429,000 | 23,928,000 | 23,363,000 |
| P/L | 3,524,000 | 3,165,000 | 1,899,000 |
| NW  | 5,373,000 | 5,981,000 | 9,417,000 |
| WC  | 4,970,000 | 6,379,000 | 9,128,000 |
| Emp. | 241     | 221      | 213      |

DUNS 21-101-1162

### R3: Innovation & Solutions Ltd
Pond Hall Pond Hall Road, Hadleigh, Ipswich, Suffolk IP7 5PP
**Tel:** 01473384830
**Reg No:** 6446226 **Estd:** 2007 Private Limited Company
**Line of Business:** Activities auxiliary to insurance and pension funding
**Issued Capital:** £100
**Director:** R Williams
**Co. Secretary:** Robert Proudman
**US SIC:** 6411  **UK SIC:** 83200
**Bankers:** Bank Of Scotland (12-26-06)

|     | 31-12-13 | 31-12-12 | 31-12-11 |
|-----|----------|----------|----------|
| TO  | 12,615   | 43,862   | 710,515  |
| P/L | 12,615   | 978,638  | (579,682) |
| NW  | 12,715   | 100      | (978,636) |
| WC  | 12,715   | 100      | (994,811) |
| Emp. | N/A     | N/A      | 27       |

DUNS 29-767-4038

### R.A. Cowen & Partners (Financial Services) Ltd
Inbro House, Commercial Gate, Mansfield, Nottinghamshire NG18 1EU
**Tel:** 01623666123
**Web:** www.cowensifa.com
**Reg No:** 2030364 **Estd:** 1986 Private Limited Company
**Line of Business:** Financial intermediation not elsewhere classified
**Issued Capital:** £650
**Directors:** A Duckworth, Mrs C T Royle, S Kuchta, D Evanson
**Co. Secretary:** Miss Larysa Kuchta
**US SIC:** 6111, 6311
**UK SIC:** 81501, 82002
**Auditors:** Brooks Mayfield
**Bankers:** HSBC Bank plc (40-32-01)

|     | 31-03-14 | 31-03-13 | 31-03-12 |
|-----|----------|----------|----------|
| TA  | 83,839   | 57,412   | 40,443   |
| NW  | 39,970   | 10,984   | 13,840   |
| WC  | 31,082   | 1,749    | 5,030    |

DUNS 22-954-3004                                              **Exp**

### R.A. Homden Ltd
Brixton Way, Harlescott, Shrewsbury, Shropshire SY1 3LB
**Tel:** 01743450501
**Web:** www.salopdesign.co.uk
**Reg No:** 1362506 **Estd:** 1940 Private Limited Company
**Line of Business:** Management activities of holding companies
**Export Markets:** U S A, Belgium, Germany, Netherlands, Canada.
**Export Sales:** £1,077,347
**Trading Style:** Salop Design and Engineering
**Issued Capital:** £1,667,128

**Directors:** R L Homden, Mrs G M Homden, J S Homden
**Responsibilities**
**Operations:** Matt Bowker *(Production & Purchasing contro)*, Ben Ewels *(Manufacturing Manager)*, Chris Greenough *(Manager)*, Del Lees *(Quality Manager)*
**Fleet:** Andy Emmerson *(Logistics Manager)*
**Engineering:** Matt Bowker *(Production & Purchasing contro)*
**US SIC:** 6711, 3545
**UK SIC:** 83962, 32223
**Auditors:** Whittingham Riddell
**Bankers:** Barclays Bank Plc (20-77-85)

| | 31-03-14 | 31-03-13 | 31-03-12 |
|---|---|---|---|
| TO | 6,489,506 | 7,224,450 | 6,722,587 |
| P/L | 385,247 | 83,360 | 212,766 |
| NW | 7,446,434 | 7,154,898 | 7,414,582 |
| WC | 3,534,180 | 3,147,969 | 3,966,626 |
| Emp. | 61 | 67 | 60 |

DUNS 22-752-8452 **Imp-Exp**
## R.A. Irwin & Company Ltd
Bannside Mill, Craigavon, Co Armagh BT63 5AG
**Tel:** 028-3833-6215 **Fax:** 028-3835-0310
**Web:** www.ra-irwin.co.uk
**Reg No:** 0013665NI **VAT No:** 252492951
**Estd:** 1960 Private Limited Company
**Line of Business:** Manufacturers of textiles
**Export Markets:** Worldwide
**Issued Capital:** £812,220
**Directors:** S I Irwin, W H Irwin, F Knox, D Irwin, R A Irwin, R S Bingham
**Co. Secretary:** Mrs Dorothy Irwin
**Responsibilities**
**Senior:** Brian Wickie *(Manager)*, Alistair Wilson *(Despatch Manager)*
**Facilities:** Bobby Ruddell *(Maintenance Manager)*
**Operations:** Bobby Ruddell *(Maintenance Manager)*
**Engineering:** Bobby Ruddell *(Maintenance Manager)*
**Branches:** R.a. Irwin & Company Ltd, 90 Milltown Road, Craigavon, Co Armagh BT66 7NF
**US SIC:** 2392 **UK SIC:** 45550
**Auditors:** KPMG
**Bankers:** Northern Bank Ltd (95-03-71)

| | 30-09-13 | 30-09-12 | 30-09-11 |
|---|---|---|---|
| TO | 7,932,520 | 7,519,106 | 7,100,200 |
| P/L | 133,795 | (37,641) | 57,847 |
| NW | 9,350,722 | 9,384,419 | 9,595,268 |
| WC | 5,053,247 | 5,054,738 | 5,440,617 |
| Emp. | 83 | 83 | 85 |

DUNS 34-572-6269
## R.A. Meredith & Son (London) Ltd
Fretherne, Saul, Gloucester, Gloucestershire GL2 7JF
**Tel:** 01452740216 **Fax:** 01452-741405
**Web:** www.rameredith.com
**Reg No:** 2722515 **Estd:** 1992 Private Limited Company
**Line of Business:** Growing of vegetables, horticultural specialities and nursery products
**Trading Style:** R A Meredith & Son Nurseries Ltd
**Issued Capital:** £900
**Directors:** P Meredith, E R Meredith
**Co. Secretary:** Samuel Greaves
**US SIC:** 7399 **UK SIC:** 83954
**Auditors:** Giffiths Marshall

| | 31-12-13 | 31-12-12 | 31-12-11 |
|---|---|---|---|
| TA | 228,720 | 365,303 | 566,576 |
| NW | 16,030 | 86,397 | 69,102 |
| WC | 14,149 | 81,859 | 61,867 |

DUNS 28-960-7376 **Imp**
## R.A. Smart (Holdings) Ltd
Clough Bank, Bollington, Macclesfield, Cheshire SK10 5NZ
**Tel:** 01625576199
**Web:** www.rasmart.co.uk
**Reg No:** 1678885 **VAT No:** 431626569
**Estd:** 1982 Private Limited Company
**Line of Business:** Bookbinding
**Trading Style:** R A Smart Card & Machinery
**Issued Capital:** £2
**Managing Director:** R A Smart
**Co. Secretary:** Mrs Carole Smart
**Branches:** R.a. Smart (Holdings) Ltd, Unit F17 Coppull Enterprise Ctre, Mill La, Coppull, Chorley, Lancashire PR7 5BW
**US SIC:** 2789, 5081
**UK SIC:** 47545, 61490
**Bankers:** National Westminster Bank Plc (01-05-41)

| | 30-09-13 | 30-09-12 | 30-09-11 |
|---|---|---|---|
| TA | 2,857,834 | 2,958,131 | 2,248,744 |
| NW | 1,064,484 | 898,506 | 744,887 |
| WC | 502,288 | 380,900 | 270,078 |

DUNS 23-731-3056
## Rabobank Corporate Trustees I Ltd
**(Subsidiary of:** Rabo U K Group Holdings Unltd)
Thames Court, 1 Queenhithe, London EC4V 3RL
**Tel:** 02078093000
**Web:** https://www.rabobank.com
**Reg No:** 3725804 **Estd:** 1999 Private Limited Company
**Line of Business:** Banks and financial institutions
**Issued Capital:** £2
**Directors:** E Buck, K M Towers, Ms M K Parsons, D Mccoubrie, The Law Debenture Pension Trust
**Co. Secretary:** David Frame
**Responsibilities**
**Senior:** Maarten D' Haese *(Director)*
**Finance:** Maarten D' Haese *(Director)*
**US SIC:** 6012 **UK SIC:** 81402

| | 31-12-13 | 31-12-12 | 31-12-11 |
|---|---|---|---|
| TA | 2 | 2 | 2 |
| NW | 2 | 2 | 2 |
| WC | 2 | N/A | N/A |
| Emp. | 560 | N/A | N/A |

DUNS 21-224-1264
## Raby Estates
Office Square, Staindrop, Darlington, County Durham DL2 3NF
**Web:** www.rabycastle.com
**Estd:** 1973 Proprietorship
**Line of Business:** Estate management services
**Proprietor:** Lord H Barnard
**Responsibilities**
**Senior:** Harry Barnard *(Proprietor)*
**Branches:** Raby Estates, Estate Office, Telford, Shropshire TF6 5HL
**US SIC:** 6531 **UK SIC:** 83400
**Employees:** 80

DUNS 23-090-0813
## Rac Automotive Solutions
Stonebridge Trading Estate, Rowley Drive, Coventry, West Midlands CV3 4FG
**Tel:** 024-7663-9090
**Web:** www.solusarc.co.uk
**Line of Business:** Maintenance and repair of motor vehicles
**Trading Style:** Solus Accident and Repair Centre
**Responsibilities**
**Senior:** Andrew Diethrich *(General Manager)*
**US SIC:** 7399 **UK SIC:** 83954
**Employees:** 100

DUNS 21-581-0218
## Rac Commercial Assistance
Po Box 200, Brockhurst Crescent, Walsall, West Midlands WS5 4QZ
**Tel:** 0800591111
**Estd:** 2011 Proprietorship
**Line of Business:** Van and truck breakdown and recovery
**Proprietor:** Mrs J Cardew
**US SIC:** 7539 **UK SIC:** 67100
**Employees:** 500

DUNS 21-017-9453
## Rac Group Ltd
**(Subsidiary of:** Carlyle Europe Partners Iii L.P.)
5 Plumstead Road Sienna Mews, Norwich, Norfolk NR1 4LR
**Fax:** 01603683659
**Web:** www.racplc.co.uk
**Reg No:** 0229121 **Estd:** 1928 Private Limited Company
**Line of Business:** Management activities of holding companies
**Issued Capital:** £30,647,542
**Directors:** Ms D Cougill, R W Templeman, G M Wood, C K Woodhouse
**Co. Secretary:** Scott Morrison
**Branches:** Rac Group Ltd, Terminal Four, Fleet Ho, Hounslow, Middlesex TW6 3XZ
**US SIC:** 6711, 5511
**UK SIC:** 83962, 65100
**Auditors:** Ernst & Young LLP
**Bankers:** National Westminster Bank Plc (56-00-03)

| | 31-12-13 | 31-12-12 | 31-12-11 |
|---|---|---|---|
| TO | 486,000,000 | 457,000,000 | 271,000,000 |
| P/L | 125,000,000 | 119,000,000 | 386,000,000 |
| NW | (194,000,000) | (180,000,000) | 439,000,000 |
| WC | (196,000,000) | (166,000,000) | 5,000,000 |
| Emp. | 3,419 | 3,535 | N/A |

DUNS 21-223-1669
## Rac Insure Quotes Caravan Insurance
Wyresdale Road, Lancaster, Lancashire LA1 3JQ
**Tel:** 0800-678000
**Web:** www.rac.co.uk
**Proprietorship**
**Line of Business:** Insurance services
**Proprietor:** H Hessing
**US SIC:** 6411 **UK SIC:** 83200
**Employees:** 250

DUNS 22-501-2012
## Rac Motoring Services
**(Subsidiary of:** Carlyle Europe Partners Iii L.P.)
Rac House, Walsall, West Midlands WS5 4AW
**Tel:** 01922437000 **Fax:** 01922721019
**Web:** www.rac.co.uk
**Reg No:** 1424399 **Estd:** 1908 Private Unlimited Company
**Line of Business:** Car breakdown and recovery
**Issued Capital:** £29,596,002
**Directors:** R W Templeman, K Michael, Ms D Cougill, C K Woodhouse, G M Wood
**Co. Secretary:** Scott Morrison
**Branches:** Rac Motoring Services, Great Park Road, Bristol, Avon BS32 4QN
**US SIC:** 7539 **UK SIC:** 67100
**Auditors:** Ernst & Young LLP

| | 31-12-13 | 31-12-12 | 31-12-11 |
|---|---|---|---|
| TO | 422,000,000 | 397,000,000 | 388,000,000 |
| P/L | 83,000,000 | 117,000,000 | 86,000,000 |
| NW | 146,000,000 | 194,000,000 | 78,000,000 |
| WC | (133,000,000) | (74,000,000) | (148,000,000) |
| Emp. | 3,419 | 3,535 | 3,700 |

DUNS 73-761-7162 **Imp**
## Racal Acoustics Ltd
**(Subsidiary of:** Esterline Technologies Ltd)
Unit 2-4, Hailsham Drive Waverley Industrial, Estate, Harrow, Middlesex HA1 4TR
**Tel:** 02085 156200
**Web:** www.esterline.com
**Reg No:** 5019038 **Estd:** 2004 Private Limited Company
**Line of Business:** Manufacture of other electrical equipment not elsewhere classified
**Export Sales:** £11,850,000
**Trading Style:** Esterline
**Issued Capital:** £8,647,525
**Directors:** C C Reusser, F E Houston, R D George, K E Hartlage
**Co. Secretary:** Taylor Wessing Secretaries Limit
**Responsibilities**
**Senior:** david watton *(finance director)*
**Finance:** david watton *(finance director)*
**Marketing:** Stephanie Salguero *(Marketing Assistant)*
**US SIC:** 3629, 3662
**UK SIC:** 34350, 34430
**Auditors:** Ernst & Young LLP
**Bankers:** Barclays Bank Plc (20-00-00)

| | 25-10-13 | 26-10-12 | 28-10-11 |
|---|---|---|---|
| TO | 19,007,000 | 23,150,000 | 33,283,000 |
| P/L | 1,479,000 | 2,046,000 | 5,713,000 |
| NW | 52,164,000 | 50,073,000 | 47,599,000 |
| WC | 52,013,000 | 49,912,000 | 47,483,000 |
| Emp. | 124 | 150 | 164 |

DUNS 28-829-3673 **Imp**
## The Racecourse Association Ltd
Winkfield Road, Ascot, Berkshire SL5 7HX
**Tel:** 01344873536
**Web:** www.britishracecourses.org
**Reg No:** 0093447 **VAT No:** 233193971
**Estd:** 1907 Private Company Limited By Guarantee
**Line of Business:** Trade and business organisations
**Export Sales:** £5,910
**Directors:** I E Barlow, P G Masterson, J J Sanderson, C H Barnett, S L Bazalgette, Ms V A Kyles, A B Kelly
**Co. Secretary:** Stephen Atkin
**Responsibilities**
**Senior:** William Farnsworth *(Manager)*, Christopher Tetley *(Manager)*, Adam Waterworth *(Director)*
**Finance:** Lance Havell *(Financial Accountant)*
**US SIC:** 8611 **UK SIC:** 96312
**Auditors:** Feltons
**Bankers:** Barclays Bank Plc (20-02-53)

| | 31-12-13 | 31-12-12 | 31-12-11 |
|---|---|---|---|
| TO | 12,595,075 | 11,879,075 | 12,191,599 |
| P/L | 421,971 | (70,352) | (137,496) |
| NW | 2,154,572 | 1,262,565 | 1,563,813 |
| WC | 1,374,056 | 1,327,755 | 1,381,362 |
| Emp. | 93 | 94 | 100 |

DUNS 34-602-2148 **Imp**
## Racelogic Ltd
Unit 10 11 Swan Close Business Centre, Buckingham, Buckinghamshire MK18 7EP
**Tel:** 01280-823803
**Web:** www.racelogic.co.uk
**Reg No:** 2743719 **Estd:** 1992 Private Limited Company
**Line of Business:** Manufacturers of electronic equipment and components
**Export Sales:** £8,839,496
**Issued Capital:** £107
**Directors:** Mrs A J Clifton, G R Mackie, J A Thomas, H F Thuillier, C Smith, L M Speth, K Bursnall, I M Jones
**Co. Secretary:** Ms Melanie Marshall
**US SIC:** 3679 **UK SIC:** 34542
**Bankers:** Lloyds TSB Bank plc (30-91-39)

| | 30-09-13 | 30-09-12 | 30-09-11 |
|---|---|---|---|
| TO | 10,169,387 | 9,572,656 | N/A |
| P/L | 2,129,155 | 2,260,679 | N/A |
| NW | 4,224,154 | 3,420,278 | 2,407,789 |
| WC | 2,522,150 | 2,024,127 | 1,370,620 |
| Emp. | 61 | 52 | N/A |

DUNS 23-273-5951
## Rachel's Dairy Ltd
**(Subsidiary of:** B.S.A)
Unit 63, Llanon, Dyfed SY23 3JQ
**Tel:** 01970-625805
**Web:** www.rachelsorganic.co.uk
**Reg No:** 2545149 **VAT No:** 594009824
**Estd:** 1990 Private Limited Company
**Line of Business:** Dairies
**Issued Capital:** £50,000
**Directors:** V Metz, A Sharpe, M Ducre
**Co. Secretary:** David Venus & Company Llp
**Responsibilities**
**Senior:** Kerry Boyd *(Manager)*
**HR:** Shirley Mackintosh *(Human Resources Manager)*
**Health & Safety:** Tim Pink *(Health & Safety Manager)*
**Operations:** Tim Pink *(Health & Safety Manager)*
**US SIC:** 0241 **UK SIC:** 01001
**Auditors:** KPMG Audit PLC
**Bankers:** Barclays Bank Plc (20-00-00)

| | 31-12-13 | 31-12-12 | 31-12-11 |
|---|---|---|---|
| TO | 21,479,000 | 29,063,000 | 34,664,000 |
| P/L | 660,000 | 3,134,000 | (27,000) |
| NW | 3,328,000 | 3,048,000 | 5,439,000 |
| WC | (197,000) | (1,260,000) | 1,378,000 |
| Emp. | 116 | 140 | 152 |

DUNS 22-966-7886 **Imp-Exp**
## Racing Technology Norfolk Ltd
**(Subsidiary of:** Spc Holdings Ltd)
Ironside Way, Hingham, Norwich, Norfolk NR9 4LF
**Fax:** 01953-851239
**Web:** www.racingtechnologynorfolk.co.uk
**Reg No:** 2112444 **VAT No:** 451331679
**Estd:** 1998 Private Limited Company
**Line of Business:** Motor sport preparation
**Export Markets:** E U, Africa
**Trading Style:** R T N
**Issued Capital:** £3,250,000
**Directors:** A P Serruys, R Cubitt
**US SIC:** 3999, 3713, 7999
**UK SIC:** 49590, 35201, 97913
**Auditors:** Grant Thornton UK LLP
**Bankers:** Barclays Bank Plc (20-62-68)

| | 31-10-13 | 31-10-12 | 31-10-11 |
|---|---|---|---|
| TO | N/A | N/A | 1,871 |
| P/L | (898,500) | (17,052) | (7,436) |
| NW | (719,273) | 179,227 | (253,721) |
| WC | (719,273) | 179,227 | (253,721) |

DUNS 23-620-5357
## Rack Systems (Engineering) Ltd
52-56 Kirkby Mills Industrial Estate, Dove Way, York, North Yorkshire YO62 6QR
**Web:** www.racksystems.co.uk
**Reg No:** 2331441 **VAT No:** 500934183
**Estd:** 1988 Private Limited Company
**Line of Business:** Manufacture of metal structures and parts of structures
**Issued Capital:** £25,000
**Principals:** D Field *(Managing)*, R J Field *(Managing)*, M J Hutchinson, A C Campbell, Ms C W Field
**Co. Secretary:** Ms Carol Hammond
**US SIC:** 3441, 3398
**UK SIC:** 32042, 31380
**Auditors:** Daffern & Co
**Bankers:** Barclays Bank Plc (20-99-56)

| | 31-12-13 | 31-12-12 | 31-12-11 |
|---|---|---|---|
| TO | 6,885,733 | 6,392,311 | 5,357,836 |
| P/L | 835,532 | 337,505 | 388,500 |
| NW | 3,041,439 | 2,423,779 | 2,185,411 |
| WC | 1,858,029 | 1,437,284 | 1,224,885 |
| Emp. | 63 | 60 | 52 |

**DUNS 22-806-4143**

## Rackham Housefloors Ltd

Mill Street East, Dewsbury, West Yorkshire WF12 9TA
**Tel:** 01924455876
**Web:** www.rackhamhousefloors.co.uk
**Reg No:** 1471339 **VAT No:** 525881035
**Estd:** 1980 Private Limited Company
**Line of Business:** Manufacture of concrete products for construction purposes
**Issued Capital:** £3,336
**Principals:** P Moore *(Managing)*, R M Varley
**Co. Secretary:** Eps Secretaries Limited
**Responsibilities**
**Marketing:** Karen Waterhouse *(Marketing Manager)*
**HR:** Donna Crossingham *(Human Resources Manager)*
**Branches:** Rackham Housefloors Ltd, Ashfield Works, Withambrook Park Industrial Estate, Grantham, Lincolnshire NG31 9ST
**US SIC:** 3271, 3273
**UK SIC:** 24370, 24360
**Auditors:** Grant Thornton
**Bankers:** Lloyds TSB Bank plc (30-10-47)

|  | 31-12-13 | 31-12-12 | 31-12-11 |
|---|---|---|---|
| TO | 12,803,493 | 11,020,177 | 11,096,933 |
| P/L | 565,991 | 599,829 | 601,203 |
| NW | 4,327,003 | 4,009,182 | 3,802,461 |
| WC | 1,316,875 | 1,378,681 | 1,446,327 |
| Emp. | 74 | 69 | 67 |

**DUNS 73-445-3959**

## Rackline Ltd

Oaktree Lane, Stoke-On-Trent, Staffordshire ST7 1RX
**Tel:** 01782-777-666
**Web:** www.rackline.com
**Reg No:** 4697883 **Estd:** 1985 Private Limited Company
**Line of Business:** Racking systems suppliers and installers
**Issued Capital:** £2,655
**Principals:** L K Khan *(Managing)*, J M Hibbert, F P Doherty
**Co. Secretary:** Lindsay Khan
**Responsibilities**
**Senior:** Tracy Goodwin *(Manager)*, Brian Horan *(Manager)*, Gerard Keary *(Manager)*
**Finance:** Stephen Leicester *(Finance Director)*
**HR:** Stephen Leicester *(Finance Director)*
**Branches:** Rackline Ltd, 18 Sauchie Street, FK7 0QW Stirling
**US SIC:** 2599, 1799
**UK SIC:** 46720, 50000
**Auditors:** Mazars LLP
**Bankers:** HSBC Bank plc (40-31-24)

|  | 31-12-13 | 31-12-12 | 31-12-11 |
|---|---|---|---|
| TO | 7,667,121 | 7,375,303 | 8,597,145 |
| P/L | 66,210 | (159,986) | 397,315 |
| NW | (346,925) | (466,280) | (493,883) |
| WC | (525,598) | (636,977) | (312,747) |
| Emp. | 67 | 65 | 59 |

**DUNS 23-906-4194**　　　　　　**Imp**

## Rackspace Ltd

**(Subsidiary of:** Rackspace Benelux Coöperatie U.A.)
5 Millington Road, Hayes, Middlesex UB3 4AZ
**Tel:** 02087342600 **Fax:** 02088974719
**Web:** www.rackspace.co.uk
**Reg No:** 3897010 **Estd:** 1999 Private Limited Company
**Line of Business:** Data processing
**Export Sales:** £192,631,898
**Issued Capital:** £1,000
**Directors:** D Norfolk, K Pichler, W T Rhodes, Ms T E Lathe
**Co. Secretary:** Ms Tiffany Lathe
**Responsibilities**
**Finance:** Mark McCardle *(Director of Finance, Internati)*
**US SIC:** 7374 **UK SIC:** 83940
**Auditors:** KPMG LLP

|  | 31-12-13 | 31-12-12 | 31-12-11 |
|---|---|---|---|
| TO | 192,631,898 | 195,466,864 | 150,067,144 |
| P/L | 17,071,627 | 46,677,215 | 32,353,399 |
| NW | 93,213,405 | 84,106,499 | 63,604,590 |
| WC | (27,989,494) | (20,933,141) | (17,998,546) |
| Emp. | 953 | 842 | 672 |

**DUNS 85-617-8525**

## Racs Collective Ltd

Racs Group House, Three Horseshoes Walk, Warminster, Wiltshire BA12 9BT
**Tel:** 08456040571
**Web:** www.racsgroup.com
**Reg No:** 6254291 **Estd:** 2007 Private Limited Company
**Line of Business:** Payroll services
**Issued Capital:** £1,000
**Directors:** T W Hillier, M N Polden
**US SIC:** 8931 **UK SIC:** 83600

|  | 31-03-14 | 31-03-13 | 31-03-12 |
|---|---|---|---|
| TO | 67,975,866 | 48,205,648 | 26,905,073 |
| P/L | 641,275 | (56,711) | 110,697 |
| NW | 323,364 | (55,763) | 17,024 |
| WC | (602,579) | (996,762) | (59,421) |
| Emp. | 3,113 | 2,004 | 1,048 |

**DUNS 36-800-9726**

## Radcliffe-on-Trent Swimming Pool Association

Cropwell Road, Nottingham, Nottinghamshire NG12 2FQ
**Web:** www.rotspa.co.uk
**Estd:** 1970 Proprietorship
**Line of Business:** Operation of swimming pools
**Proprietor:** B Cannell
**Responsibilities**
**Senior:** Nigel Buck *(Chairman)*
**US SIC:** 7999 **UK SIC:** 97913
**Employees:** 90

**DUNS 77-919-1647**

## Radford Hmy Group Ltd

**(Subsidiary of:** Hmy International)
Hobson Industrial Estate Burnopfield, Hobson, Newcastle-Upon-Tyne, Tyne and Wear NE16 6EA
**Fax:** 01207-272-175
**Web:** www.ms50marketstalls.com
**Reg No:** 5822214 **VAT No:** 883248202
**Estd:** 2006 Private Limited Company
**Line of Business:** Manufacture of other office and shop furniture
**Export Sales:** £4,914,000
**Issued Capital:** £3,000,000
**Directors:** I G Marin Villamayor, S A Geekie, G Renault
**Co. Secretary:** Michael Scarr
**Responsibilities**
**Finance:** M McDonald *(Finance Director)*
**Marketing:** S Karty *(Sales & Marketing Manager)*
**Sales:** S Karty *(Sales & Marketing Manager)*
**HR:** Peter Turnbill *(Human Resources Manager)*, D Walterson *(Personnel Officer)*
**Engineering:** Greg Rickeby *(Engineering Manager)*
**US SIC:** 2599 **UK SIC:** 46720
**Auditors:** PricewaterhouseCoopers LLP

|  | 31-12-13 | 31-12-12 | 31-12-11 |
|---|---|---|---|
| TO | 37,163,000 | 36,957,000 | 36,296,000 |
| P/L | (1,620,000) | 42,000 | (242,000) |
| NW | 1,032,000 | 2,479,000 | 2,246,000 |
| WC | 1,834,000 | 3,197,000 | 2,624,000 |
| Emp. | 254 | 248 | 262 |

**DUNS 64-087-1349**

## Radian Group Ltd

Collins House, Bishopstoke Road, Eastleigh, Hampshire SO50 6AD
**Tel:** 03001231567 **Fax:** 023 8062 8390
**Web:** www.radian.co.uk
**Reg No:** 3482228 **Estd:** 2006 Private Company Limited By Guarantee
**Line of Business:** Activities of professional organisations
**Trading Style:** Radian Direct
**Directors:** Mrs M D Clarke, M P Collis, L Todd, Ms B U Phelps, S J Porter, C Hessey, Mrs C A Bode, O L Graham
**Co. Secretary:** Terry Walker
**Responsibilities**
**Senior:** Gina Small *(Director of Radian Support)*, Lynsey Todd *(Chief Executive Officer)*
**Finance:** Elizabeth Froude *(Financial Controller)*
**Marketing:** Jo Slawson *(Sales and Marketing)*
**Sales:** Sally Blackman *(Sales Manager)*, Nicola O' Rourke *(Head of Development South Team)*, Kim Russell *(Post Sales Officer)*, Jo Slawson *(Sales and Marketing)*
**Admin:** Maggie Reeve *(Personal Assistant)*
**IT:** Jonathan Crolla *(IT Manager)*, Tim Leather *(Head of IT)*, John McKechnie *(IT Manager)*
**Facilities:** Ralph Facey *(Director of Housing and Custom)*
**Operations:** Gavin Board *(Project Development Manager)*, Ross Bryant *(Project Manager)*, Rob Cummins *(Senior Project Manager)*, Isabelle Simon-Evans *(Director of Corporate Services)*
**Purchasing:** Zoe Bonnington *(Procurement Officer)*, Tim Willcocks *(Procurement Officer)*
**Branches:** Radian Group Ltd, 49 Cheviot Road, Slough, Berkshire SL3 8LA
**US SIC:** 8999 **UK SIC:** 83954
**Auditors:** Deloitte LLP
**Bankers:** Barclays Bank Plc (20-71-03)

|  | 31-03-14 | 31-03-13 | 31-03-12 |
|---|---|---|---|
| TO | 131,477,000 | 122,331,000 | 110,045,000 |
| P/L | 11,482,000 | 14,145,000 | 6,119,000 |
| NW | 123,246,000 | 111,271,000 | 107,887,000 |
| WC | 60,558,000 | 55,641,000 | 104,334,000 |
| Emp. | 1,092 | 1,083 | 1,196 |

**DUNS 22-530-6034**　　　　　　**Exp**

## Radiatron Holdings Ltd

**(Subsidiary of:** Acal Plc)
Alpha Way, Egham, Surrey TW20 8RZ
**Tel:** 01189029723 **Fax:** 01189-026095
**Web:** www.acal-radiatron.com
**Reg No:** 1707985 **Estd:** 1983 Private Limited Company
**Line of Business:** Management activities of holding companies
**Issued Capital:** £1,000,000
**Directors:** G P Shillinglaw, S M Gibbins
**Co. Secretary:** Gary Shillinglaw
**US SIC:** 6711, 5065
**UK SIC:** 83962, 61500
**Auditors:** Deloitte & Touche

|  | 31-03-14 | 31-03-13 | 31-03-12 |
|---|---|---|---|
| TA | 1,145,915 | 1,145,915 | 1,145,915 |
| NW | 1,000,002 | 1,000,002 | 1,000,002 |

**DUNS 37-876-7289**　　　　　　**Imp**

## Radical Motorsport Ltd

**(Subsidiary of:** Radical Sportscars Ltd)
24 Ivatt Way, Peterborough, Cambridgeshire PE3 7PG
**Tel:** 01733331616 **Fax:** 01733-264959
**Web:** www.radicalsportscars.com
**Reg No:** 3308491 **Estd:** 1997 Private Limited Company
**Line of Business:** Motor sport preparation
**Trading Style:** Radical Motor Sport
**Issued Capital:** £204
**Directors:** C Droop, P R Abbott, J M Osterloh
**Co. Secretary:** Philip Abbott
**Responsibilities**
**Senior:** Mick Hyde *(Joint Managing Director)*
**Purchasing:** David Pell *(Purchasing Manager)*
**Branches:** Radical Motorsport Ltd, 27 St. Davids Sq, Peterborough, Cambridgeshire PE1 5QA
**US SIC:** 7999 **UK SIC:** 97913
**Auditors:** Bulley Davey
**Bankers:** Barclays Bank Plc (20-67-37)

|  | 31-12-12 | 31-12-11 | 31-12-10 |
|---|---|---|---|
| TO | 17,388,026 | N/A | 14,131,378 |
| P/L | 597,061 | 1,179,226 | 1,147,277 |
| NW | 2,604,940 | 2,747,115 | 2,053,250 |
| WC | 2,272,931 | 2,468,405 | 1,786,825 |
| Emp. | 78 | 72 | 65 |

**DUNS 77-750-0927**

## Radical Services Ltd

Canal Wharf, Leeds, West Yorkshire LS5 3BT
**Tel:** 0113 265 3340 **Fax:** 0113 278 2486
**Web:** www.radicalservices.org.uk
**Reg No:** 3015008 **VAT No:** 654202463
**Estd:** 1997 Private Limited Company
**Line of Business:** Non-charitable social work activities without accommodation
**Issued Capital:** £10,202
**Directors:** L Guilherme, T Rodham
**Co. Secretary:** Thomas Rodham
**Responsibilities**
**Sales:** Karen Blanchard-Ellis *(Business Manager)*
**Branches:** Radical Services Ltd, 14 Moor View, Haltwhistle, Northumberland NE49 0LS
**US SIC:** 7399, 8999
**UK SIC:** 83954
**Auditors:** Montpelier Audit Ltd
**Bankers:** Clydesdale Bank Plc (82-60-32)

|  | 31-08-13 | 31-08-12 | 31-08-11 |
|---|---|---|---|
| TO | N/A | 2,545,114 | 1,794,635 |
| P/L | N/A | 356,461 | (92,456) |
| NW | 760,559 | 300,630 | 49,169 |
| WC | 244,080 | (161,132) | (553,710) |

**DUNS 21-693-0754**

## Radicon Transmission Uk Ltd

**(Subsidiary of:** Elecon Engineering Company Limited)
Unit J3, Lowfields Way, Lowfields Business Park, Elland, West Yorkshire HX5 9DA
**Tel:** 01484465800 **Fax:** 01484 465801
**Web:** www.radicon.com
**Reg No:** 7397993 **Estd:** 2010 Private Limited Company
**Line of Business:** Manufacture of bearings, gears, gearing and driving elements
**Export Sales:** £5,772,674
**Issued Capital:** £2,156,020
**Directors:** P Patel, P Amin, P Patel
**Responsibilities**
**Senior:** Chris Riley *(General Manager)*, Neville Vickery *(General Manager)*
**US SIC:** 3568 **UK SIC:** 32613
**Bankers:** Svenska Handelsbanken Ab (publ) (40-51-62)

|  | 31-03-14 | 31-03-13 | 31-03-12 |
|---|---|---|---|
| TO | 13,644,967 | 13,001,891 | 11,739,240 |
| P/L | (126,614) | (286,914) | (170,441) |
| NW | (2,108,124) | (2,204,149) | (2,139,874) |
| WC | 1,230,317 | (3,139,482) | (3,052,356) |
| Emp. | 72 | 66 | 62 |

**DUNS 64-146-4755**

## Radio Amateurs' Emergency Network

Far Cockcroft, Rishworth, Ripponden, Sowerby Bridge, West Yorkshire HX6 4SB
**Tel:** 03030401080
**Web:** www.raynet-uk.net
**Estd:** 2002 Partnership
**Line of Business:** Charities and charitable organisations
**Partners:** R Carroll, D Green, R Beever, P Williams, D Duff
**Responsibilities**
**Senior:** Cathy Clark *(Chairman)*
**US SIC:** 8699 **UK SIC:** 96902
**Employees:** 2,000

**DUNS 54-843-1576**

## Radio Cherwell

Old Road, Headington, Headington, Oxford, Oxfordshire OX3 7LJ
**Web:** www.radiocherwell.com
**Estd:** 1967 Proprietorship
**Line of Business:** Charities and charitable organisations
**Proprietor:** N Stockton
**US SIC:** 6732 **UK SIC:** 83100
**Employees:** 52

**DUNS 21-591-1141**

## Radio Humberside B B C

96-98 Victoria Street, Grimsby, South Humberside DN31 1BA
**Tel:** 01472256680
**Web:** www.bbc.co.uk
**Estd:** 2011
**Line of Business:** Radio and television production services
**Responsibilities**
**Senior:** Simon Pattern *(Station Editor)*
**US SIC:** 4833 **UK SIC:** 97411
**Employees:** 50

**DUNS 21-396-6571**

## Radio Leeds

2 St Peters Square, Leeds, West Yorkshire LS9 8AH
**Web:** www.bbc.co.uk
**Estd:** 2009 Proprietorship
**Line of Business:** Radio and television production services
**Proprietor:** A Evans
**Responsibilities**
**Senior:** Rozina Breen *(Manager)*
**US SIC:** 4833 **UK SIC:** 97411
**Employees:** 50

**DUNS 21-029-9607**

## Radio Lollipop

Royal Hospital For Sick Children, 9 Sciennes Road, Edinburgh, Midlothian EH9 1LF
**Tel:** 01316683097
**Web:** www.radiolollipop.org
**Line of Business:** Film Distribution Services
**Responsibilities**
**Senior:** Pete Linseell *(Chairman)*
**US SIC:** 7829 **UK SIC:** 97112
**Employees:** 50

**DUNS 73-427-0056**

## Radio North Angus Ltd

Arbroath Infirmary, Rosemount Road, Arbroath, Angus DD11 2AT
**Tel:** 01241-879660
**Web:** www.radionorthangus.co.uk
**Reg No:** 0245875SC **Estd:** 2003 Private Company Limited By Guarantee
**Line of Business:** Radio activities
**Directors:** Mrs B Reid, D Law, I T Clark, J Mcdougall, Mrs H Wallace
**Co. Secretary:** Malcolm Finlayson
**Responsibilities**
**Senior:** Eileen Brymer *(Manager)*, Michael McEwan *(Manager)*
**US SIC:** 4832 **UK SIC:** 97411
**Bankers:** The Royal Bank Of Scotland Plc (83-15-22)

|  | 31-03-14 | 31-03-13 | 31-03-12 |
|---|---|---|---|
| TO | 20,092 | 18,880 | 23,430 |
| P/L | 2,171 | 729 | (5,025) |
| NW | 29,064 | 26,893 | 26,414 |
| WC | 22,406 | 24,753 | 22,405 |
| Emp. | 56 | 56 | 49 |

**DUNS 28-851-4607**

## Radio Trent Ltd

**(Subsidiary of:** Global Radio Group Limited)
Chapel Quater, Nottingham, Nottinghamshire NG1 6HJ
**Tel:** 01158731500 **Fax:** 01158731569
**Web:** www.trentfm.co.uk
**Reg No:** 0728182 **Estd:** 1962 Private Limited Company
**Line of Business:** Radio activities
**Trading Style:** 96 Trent F M
**Issued Capital:** £547,607

**Directors:** R F Park, S G Miron, M D Connole
**Co. Secretary:** Clive Potterell
**US SIC:** 4832 **UK SIC:** 97411
**Auditors:** Deloitte & Touche LLP
**Bankers:** National Westminster Bank Plc (56-00-61)

| | 31-03-14 | 31-03-13 | 31-03-12 |
|---|---|---|---|
| TO | 5,924,000 | 5,828,000 | 5,856,000 |
| P/L | 768,000 | 426,000 | 734,000 |
| NW | 1,775,000 | 1,192,000 | 4,397,000 |

DUNS 21-735-2947 **Imp-Exp**

## Radiodetection Ltd

(**Subsidiary of:** Spx International Eg)
Western Drive, Bristol, Avon BS14 0AF
**Fax:** 01179-767775
**Web:** www.eecol.com
**Reg No:** 1334448 **VAT No:** 609576707
**Estd:** 1977 Private Limited Company
**Line of Business:** Other manufacturing not elsewhere classified
**Export Markets:** Canada, S & S E Asia, Middle East, Africa, E U, U S A
**Export Sales:** £30,843,000
**Issued Capital:** £261,751
**Directors:** J W Smeltser, M A Reilly, K P Lench
**Co. Secretary:** Kevin Lilly
**Branches:** Radiodetection Ltd, 36 Thornhill Rd, Keighley, West Yorkshire BD20 6TN
**US SIC:** 3999 **UK SIC:** 49590
**Auditors:** Deloitte LLP
**Bankers:** Bank Of Scotland (12-05-77)

| | 31-12-13 | 31-12-12 | 31-12-11 |
|---|---|---|---|
| TO | 44,030,000 | 39,078,000 | 34,667,000 |
| P/L | 10,089,000 | 13,908,000 | 9,529,000 |
| NW | 70,859,000 | 60,765,000 | 44,504,000 |
| WC | 67,960,000 | 57,724,000 | 41,377,000 |
| Emp. | 160 | 160 | 158 |

DUNS 76-689-4448 **Imp-Exp**

## Radiometer Ltd

Manor Court, Manor Royal, Crawley, West Sussex RH10 9FY
**Tel:** 01293-517599
**Web:** www.radiometer.co.uk
**Reg No:** 2590624 **Estd:** 1989 Private Limited Company
**Line of Business:** Manufacturers of medical equipment
**Issued Capital:** £650,000
**Directors:** L S Knudsen, L A Wallseth
**Responsibilities**
**Senior:** Mette Brink *(Manager)*, Claus Madsen *(Manager)*, Derek Stone *(Manager)*, David Tunley *(Manager)*
**HR:** Sarah burling *(Human Resources Manager)*
**US SIC:** 3841, 7399
**UK SIC:** 37201, 83954
**Auditors:** Grant Thornton UK LLP
**Bankers:** HSBC Bank plc (40-18-22)

| | 31-12-13 | 31-12-12 | 31-12-11 |
|---|---|---|---|
| TO | 15,111,000 | 13,928,000 | 12,728,000 |
| P/L | 716,000 | 859,000 | 985,000 |
| NW | 12,063,000 | 11,152,000 | 10,156,000 |
| WC | 10,566,000 | 9,469,000 | 8,267,000 |
| Emp. | 47 | 48 | 45 |

DUNS 21-390-5699

## Radis Community Care

55 Lichfield Road, Stafford, Staffordshire ST17 4LL
**Tel:** 01785-212421
**Web:** www.radis.co.uk
**Estd:** 2009 Proprietorship
**Line of Business:** Home care and help services
**Proprietor:** Ms S Grainger
**Responsibilities**
**Senior:** Heather Cave *(Manager)*, Claire Cooper *(Manager)*
**US SIC:** 8811 **UK SIC:** 99000
**Employees:** 50

DUNS 23-820-2910

## Radis Ltd

Mercia House, 15 Galena Close, Tamworth, Staffordshire B77 4AS
**Tel:** 03301008150
**Web:** www.radis.co.uk
**Reg No:** 3812402 **Estd:** 1999 Private Limited Company
**Line of Business:** Management activities of holding companies
**Trading Style:** Radis Community Care
**Issued Capital:** £126,316
**Directors:** D R Patel, D R Patel, S R Patel
**Co. Secretary:** Samirkumar Patel
**Branches:** Radis Ltd, 51 Ashbourne Road, Derby, Derbyshire DE22 3FS
**US SIC:** 6711 **UK SIC:** 83962
**Auditors:** Mercer & Hole

**Bankers:** The Royal Bank Of Scotland Plc (16-12-33)

| | 31-08-13 | 31-08-12 | 31-08-11 |
|---|---|---|---|
| TO | 21,950,885 | 21,825,158 | 21,158,095 |
| P/L | 386,541 | 458,493 | 693,579 |
| NW | 878,113 | 290,626 | (268,636) |
| WC | 1,175,815 | 838,906 | 202,534 |
| Emp. | 1,500 | 1,472 | 1,378 |

DUNS 21-771-4155

## Radisson Blu

Herald Way Pegasus Business Park, East Midlands Airport, Castle, Derby, Derbyshire DE74 2TU
**Web:** www.central-networks.co.uk
**Estd:** 2011 Proprietorship
**Line of Business:** Other tourist assistance activities not elsewhere classified
**Proprietor:** D Keane
**US SIC:** 7999 **UK SIC:** 97913
**Employees:** 150

DUNS 21-582-0509

## Radisson Blu Hotel

Marsh House, Marsh Street, Bristol, Avon BS1 4AQ
**Tel:** 01179349500
**Web:** www.radissonblu.co.uk
**Estd:** 2008 Proprietorship
**Line of Business:** Hotels
**Proprietor:** D Glover
**US SIC:** 7011 **UK SIC:** 66500
**Employees:** 50

DUNS 21-810-6559

## Radisson Hotel

Frankland Lane, Durham, County Durham DH1 5TA
**Tel:** 01913727200
**Web:** www.durham.radissonsas.com
**Estd:** 2012
**Line of Business:** Other tourist assistance activities not elsewhere classified
**US SIC:** 7999 **UK SIC:** 97913
**Employees:** 60

DUNS 21-864-8093

## Radius Payment Solutions Ltd

Euro Card Centre Herald Park, Herald Drive, Crewe, Cheshire CW1 6EG
**Tel:** 01270655600
**Web:** www.radiuspaymentsolutions.com
**Reg No:** 8260702 **Estd:** 2012 Private Limited Company
**Line of Business:** Wholesale of other fuels and related products
**Export Sales:** £247,228,000
**Issued Capital:** £100
**Directors:** K Sturtewagen, L J Everett, S Gent, R Price, D F Roberts, W S Holmes, R A Sciortino
**US SIC:** 5052 **UK SIC:** 61200
**Following financial data are in thousands**

| | 31-03-14 | 31-12-12 |
|---|---|---|
| TO | 1,582,594 | N/A |
| P/L | 27,615 | N/A |
| NW | 46,472 | 0 |
| WC | 21,445 | N/A |
| Emp. | 431 | N/A |

DUNS 22-937-4053 **Imp-Exp**

## Radius Plastics Ltd

(**Subsidiary of:** Radius Systems Holdings Ltd)
Scarva Road Industrial Estate, Banbridge, Co Down BT32 3QD
**Tel:** 028-4066-9999
**Web:** www.radius-systems.com
**Reg No:** 0013308NI **VAT No:** 496928279
**Estd:** 1988 Private Limited Company
**Line of Business:** Plastic extruders
**Export Markets:** Republic of Ireland, Europe
**Export Sales:** £13,020,000
**Trading Style:** Radius Systems
**Issued Capital:** £40,000
**Directors:** D Walsh, V Buyanovsky, M Gorilovskiy, A R Taylor, G Devine
**Co. Secretary:** David Walsh
**Responsibilities**
**Senior:** Stuart Godfrey *(Chief Executive Officer)*
**Marketing:** Sandra Davoust *(Sales & Marketing Coordinator)*
**Sales:** Sandra Davoust *(Sales & Marketing Coordinator)*
**Health & Safety:** Steven Douglas *(Quality Assurance Manager)*
**Operations:** Sandra Davoust *(Sales & Marketing Coordinator)*
**Purchasing:** Annita Hornby *(Purchasing Manager)*
**Branches:** Radius Plastics, 29 Lowfield Lane, St. Helens, Merseyside WA9 5TA
**US SIC:** 3079 **UK SIC:** 48360
**Auditors:** KPMG

**Bankers:** Northern Bank Ltd (95-01-22)

| | 31-12-13 | 31-03-13 | 31-12-12 |
|---|---|---|---|
| TO | 19,987,000 | 25,025,000 | 36,424,000 |
| P/L | 1,681,000 | 8,393,000 | 978,000 |
| NW | 4,954,000 | 2,822,000 | (6,228,000) |
| WC | 7,936,000 | 7,264,000 | 1,522,000 |
| Emp. | 120 | 120 | 123 |

DUNS 22-521-0285 **Imp-Exp**

## Radius Systems Ltd

(**Subsidiary of:** Radius Systems Holdings Ltd)
Radius House, Alfreton, Derbyshire DE55 2JJ
**Tel:** 01773811112 **Fax:** 01773812343
**Web:** www.radius-systems.com
**Reg No:** 1585669 **VAT No:** 168937312
**Estd:** 1981 Private Limited Company
**Line of Business:** Pipes and fittings
**Export Sales:** £16,407,000
**Trading Style:** Uponor International, Radius Systems
**Issued Capital:** £15,387,000
**Directors:** A R Taylor, V Buyanovsky, G Devine, M Gorilovskiy, D Walsh
**Co. Secretary:** David Walsh
**Responsibilities**
**Senior:** Stuart Godfrey *(Manager)*, Lawrence Richards *(Site Manager)*
**Marketing:** Vicky Melbourne *(Marketing Officer)*
**Sales:** Dave Macdonald *(Business Development Manager)*
**Admin:** Debra Wheeler *(Business Administrator)*
**IT:** Martin Fielder *(IT Manager)*
**Engineering:** Steve Kirk *(Engineering Projects Manager)*
**Branches:** Radius Systems Ltd, Heighington Lane, Newton Aycliffe, County Durham DL5 6AL
**US SIC:** 3317, 3494
**UK SIC:** 22200, 32880
**Auditors:** PricewaterhouseCoopers LLP
**Bankers:** Barclays Bank Plc (20-63-25)

| | 31-12-13 | 31-03-13 | 31-12-12 |
|---|---|---|---|
| TO | 64,398,000 | 86,179,000 | 133,495,000 |
| P/L | (1,139,000) | 19,248,000 | (19,988,000) |
| NW | 38,314,000 | 752,000 | (19,159,000) |
| WC | 19,535,000 | 21,536,000 | (37,132,000) |
| Emp. | 381 | 369 | 445 |

DUNS 73-722-0251

## Radius Trust Ltd

Grafham Grange, Grafham, Guildford, Surrey GU5 0LH
**Tel:** 01483-892214
**Web:** www.grafham-grange.co.uk
**Reg No:** 2919225 **Estd:** 1994 Private Limited Company
**Line of Business:** Primary education
**Directors:** Mrs M M Fisher, Ms A Livesley, K C Cowdery, M E Taylor, Mrs J A Scott, K G Noble, Dr A G Davidson, Dr A J Bailey
**Co. Secretary:** Alan Smith
**Responsibilities**
**Senior:** Susan Martin *(Manager)*, Lloyd Richards *(Manager)*
**US SIC:** 8211, 6732, 8321
**UK SIC:** 93200, 83100, 96111
**Bankers:** National Westminster Bank Plc (60-06-19)

| | 31-08-13 | 31-08-12 | 31-08-11 |
|---|---|---|---|
| TO | 5,605,915 | 6,810,173 | 4,798,883 |
| P/L | 525,463 | 592,593 | 450,325 |
| NW | 3,244,561 | 1,009,188 | 1,663,595 |
| WC | 932,837 | 496,237 | 524,276 |
| Emp. | 105 | 108 | 109 |

DUNS 23-758-3476

## Radius (Uk) Ltd

(**Subsidiary of:** Hg Investment Managers Ltd)
Whitefriars, Lewins Mead, Bristol, Avon BS1 2NT
**Tel:** 01179299661
**Web:** www.radiusworldwide.com
**Reg No:** 3752124 **VAT No:** 840252850
**Estd:** 1993 Private Limited Company
**Line of Business:** Other business activities not elsewhere classified
**Directors:** J O Fullman, J T Sullivan, L M Conley
**Responsibilities**
**Senior:** Shankaran Nair *(Manager)*
**Finance:** Timothy Loh *(Head of Tax Consulting/Client)*, Lee Sheehan *(Head of Tax)*
**Sales:** Gary Pavlik *(Director, Business Development)*
**IT:** Perry Roche *(IT Manager)*
**Operations:** Alan Mathers *(Operations Director)*
**US SIC:** 7399 **UK SIC:** 83954
**Auditors:** Griffiths Marshall
**Employees:** 20
**Turnover:** £25,679,019

DUNS 76-559-9907 **Exp**

## Radley & Co. Ltd

(**Subsidiary of:** Truly Spv 1 Ltd)
Greater London House, Mornington Crescent, London NW1 7QX
**Tel:** 01224630257 **Fax:** 020-7756-7911
**Web:** www.radleyandco.com
**Reg No:** 2573819 **Estd:** 1991 Private Limited Company
**Line of Business:** Management activities of holding companies
**Export Markets:** Eire, E U
**Issued Capital:** £67,550
**Directors:** O B Bower, P H Lenon, N J Vance, R C Best, Mrs N Halliday, X M Simonet, Mrs J M Worden, R L Tudor
**Co. Secretary:** Gregory Pratt
**Responsibilities**
**Senior:** Lowell Harder *(Director)*
**Admin:** Holly Redfern *(Office Coordinator)*
**Branches:** Radley & Co. Ltd, 15 Broadwalk, Dunstable, Bedfordshire LU5 4RH
**US SIC:** 6711 **UK SIC:** 83962
**Auditors:** Ernst & Young LLP
**Bankers:** National Westminster Bank Plc (60-01-35)

| | 30-04-14 | 30-04-13 | 30-04-12 |
|---|---|---|---|
| TO | 38,534,958 | 34,096,541 | 41,239,280 |
| P/L | 1,073,229 | (1,690,594) | (737,405) |
| NW | 16,746,407 | 15,932,196 | 17,316,322 |
| WC | 16,785,780 | 15,318,046 | 17,783,920 |
| Emp. | 202 | 191 | 166 |

DUNS 42-440-0521

## Radley College

Radley, Radley, Abingdon, Oxfordshire OX14 2HR
**Tel:** 01235543111
**Web:** www.radley.org.uk
**Reg No:** 0000611RC **Estd:** 1847 Proprietorship
**Line of Business:** Leisure centres
**Proprietor:** L Neweoo
**Responsibilities**
**Senior:** IAN BALDING *(Principal)*, LORD DINTON *(Principal)*, TOM DURIE *(Principal)*, MICHAEL HODGSON *(Principal)*, E MCKENDRICK *(Principal)*, Angus McPhail *(Principal)*, Andrew Mildmay Fanebishop Anthony *(Manager)*, DAVID PECK *(Principal)*, MARK RUSHTON *(Principal)*, THOMAS SEYMOUR *(Principal)*, Simon Whitworth *(Manager)*
**Admin:** Roger Shaw *(Director of Administration)*
**HR:** Sarah Ballard *(Human Resources Manager)*
**US SIC:** 8221 **UK SIC:** 93100

| | 31-07-12 |
|---|---|
| TO | 22,426,000 |
| P/L | 1,976,000 |
| NW | 52,030,000 |
| WC | (4,910,000) |
| Emp. | 366 |

DUNS 22-846-9052

## Radley Yeldar Ltd

24-27 Charlotte Road, London EC2A 3PB
**Tel:** 020-7033-0700 **Fax:** 020-7033-0800
**Web:** www.ry.com
**Reg No:** 2049294 **VAT No:** 446927416
**Estd:** 1986 Private Limited Company
**Line of Business:** Design consultants
**Issued Capital:** £8,269
**Managing Director:** C R Radley
**Responsibilities**
**Senior:** Andrew Gibbs *(Manager)*
**Finance:** Aaron Bell *(Accounts Manager)*, Andrew Gibbs *(Manager)*
**Marketing:** Clare Barker *(Project Manager)*, Michela Graci *(Marcomms Research Manager)*
**IT:** Tyrone Cato *(Computer Manager)*
**HR:** Aaron Bell *(Accounts Manager)*
**Health & Safety:** Aaron Bell *(Accounts Manager)*
**Facilities:** Aaron Bell *(Accounts Manager)*
**US SIC:** 8911 **UK SIC:** 83701
**Auditors:** RSM Tenon Audit Ltd
**Bankers:** Lloyds TSB Bank plc (30-95-74)

| | 31-12-13 | 31-12-12 | 31-12-11 |
|---|---|---|---|
| TO | 22,245,045 | 18,005,404 | 17,600,001 |
| P/L | 1,587,539 | 1,158,584 | 1,877,615 |
| NW | 2,408,119 | 1,232,036 | 3,661,147 |
| WC | 1,673,177 | 1,392,429 | 2,924,560 |
| Emp. | 153 | 140 | 130 |

DUNS 54-368-7206 **Imp-Exp**

## Radnor Hills Ltd

The Wain House Heartsease, Knighton, Powys LD7 1LU
**Tel:** 01547-530220
**Web:** www.radnorhills.co.uk
**Reg No:** 3258545 **Estd:** 1982 Private Limited Company
**Line of Business:** Wholesale of fruit and vegetable juices, mineral waters and soft drinks

**Export Markets:**
Belgium;Cyprus;Holland;Spain (including Spanish territories in North Africa with Ceuta and Melilla)
**Trading Style:** John Watkins & Son
**Issued Capital:** £100
**Director:** W W Watkins
**Co. Secretary:** Mrs Penelope Butler
**Responsibilities**
**Senior:** Lenor Mansfield (*Office Manager*)
**Admin:** Lenor Mansfield (*Office Manager*)
**US SIC:** 5149   **UK SIC:** 61700
**Bankers:** HSBC Bank plc (40-26-21)

|       | 31-05-14 | 31-05-13 | 31-05-12 |
|-------|----------|----------|----------|
| TA    | 100      | 100      | 100      |
| NW    | 100      | 100      | 100      |

DUNS 22-780-0091       **Exp**

## Radshape Sheet Metal Ltd
Shefford Road, Birmingham, West Midlands B6 4PL
**Tel:** 01212423323 **Fax:** 0121-242-3385
**Web:** www.radshape.co.uk
**Reg No:** 1248311 **Estd:** 1967 Private Limited Company
**Line of Business:** Manufacture of parts and accessories for motor vehicles and their engines
**Export Markets:** Austria; Netherlands
**Trading Style:** Radiator Shaping Services
**Issued Capital:** £13,400
**Principals:** W C Jones (*Managing*), J R Morrall (*Financial*), K M Chadwick, C H Dickinson
**Co. Secretary:** Stephen Morrall
**Responsibilities**
**Senior:** Malcolm Imms (*Warehouse Manager*), Lesley Tonks (*Manager*)
**US SIC:** 3714   **UK SIC:** 35300
**Auditors:** Felton & Co
**Bankers:** HSBC Bank plc (40-11-15)

|    | 31-03-14  | 31-03-13  | 31-03-12  |
|----|-----------|-----------|-----------|
| TA | 2,830,656 | 2,129,696 | 2,159,896 |
| NW | 1,120,720 | 1,168,158 | 1,123,294 |
| WC | 532,088   | 673,953   | 644,427   |

DUNS 21-722-9863

## Radstock Co-Operative Society Ltd
3 Wells Road, Bath, Avon BA3 3RQ
**Tel:** 01761432142 **Fax:** 01761-436187
**Web:** www.radstock-co-op.com
**Reg No:** 0001159IP **VAT No:** 138215480
**Estd:** 1868 Friendly Society
**Line of Business:** Activities of professional organisations
**Trading Style:** Radco Superstore
**Principals:** Miss A Wilson (*Chairman*), F Luke, G J Weeks, R C Inchley, C Dando, R Slade, E G Wilson, R A Perrett
**Co. Secretary:** Robert Slade
**Responsibilities**
**Senior:** Alan Bonner (*Chief Executive Officer*), Don Morris (*Chief Executive Officer*)
**Finance:** Annette Pellow (*Financial Controller*)
**IT:** Matthew Doughty (*IT Manager*)
**US SIC:** 7399   **UK SIC:** 83954
**Auditors:** PricewaterhouseCoopers LLP
**Bankers:** The Co-Operative Bank Plc (08-90-02)
**Employees:** 321
**Turnover:** £18,183,739

DUNS 21-677-5421       **Imp**

## Radwell International- Uk Ltd
(**Subsidiary of:** Radwell International Inc.)
Unit D, Dalewood Road, Lymedale Business Park, Newcastle, Staffordshire ST5 9QZ
**Tel:** 01782576800
**Web:** www.plccenter.co.uk
**Reg No:** 7287728 **Estd:** 2010 Private Limited Company
**Line of Business:** Other manufacturing not elsewhere classified
**Issued Capital:** £1
**Directors:** D Love, B Radwell, G Mitchell, T Radwell
**US SIC:** 3999   **UK SIC:** 49590

|      | 31-12-13  | 31-12-12  | 31-12-11  |
|------|-----------|-----------|-----------|
| TO   | 7,128,932 | N/A       | N/A       |
| P/L  | 629,211   | N/A       | N/A       |
| NW   | (34,190)  | (593,975) | (629,145) |
| WC   | 3,542,590 | 2,501,114 | 1,874,462 |
| Emp. | 53        | N/A       | N/A       |

DUNS 22-100-0008

## Radwise Ltd
36 Ballot Road, Irvine, Ayrshire KA12 0HW
**Tel:** 01294318375 **Fax:** 01294318373
**Web:** www.radwiselimited.co.uk
**Reg No:** 0213485SC **Estd:** 2000 Private Limited Company
**Line of Business:** Employment and recruitment companies and consultants
**Issued Capital:** £99
**Directors:** D Mcbride, I Anderson
**Co. Secretary:** Paul Allan

**US SIC:** 8911, 8091
**UK SIC:** 83701, 95200
**Auditors:** William Duncan & Co
**Bankers:** HSBC Bank plc (40-22-47)

|      | 31-01-14   | 31-01-13   | 31-01-12   |
|------|------------|------------|------------|
| TO   | 13,457,959 | 14,838,878 | 10,784,904 |
| P/L  | 1,422,533  | 1,912,611  | 771,008    |
| NW   | 2,651,679  | 2,338,253  | 1,223,264  |
| WC   | 2,635,366  | 2,331,704  | 1,217,094  |
| Emp. | 79         | 113        | 91         |

DUNS 28-827-9581

## Raeburn Brick Ltd
15 East Avenue, Glasgow, Lanarkshire G71 6LG
**Tel:** 01698-828888 **Fax:** 01698-824039
**Web:** www.raeburnbrick.co.uk
**Reg No:** 0086968SC **VAT No:** 383048056
**Estd:** 1984 Private Limited Company
**Line of Business:** Manufacture of bricks, tiles and construction products, in baked clay
**Issued Capital:** £500,000
**Managing Director:** D G Raeburn
**Co. Secretary:** James Raeburn
**Responsibilities**
**Senior:** Graham Legge (*Works Manager*)
**Health & Safety:** Graham Legge (*Works Manager*)
**Facilities:** Graham Legge (*Works Manager*)
**Engineering:** Graham Legge (*Works Manager*)
**US SIC:** 3251, 4213
**UK SIC:** 24100, 72300
**Auditors:** Bannerman Johnstone Maclay
**Bankers:** Bank Of Scotland (80-06-64)

|      | 31-03-14   | 31-03-13   | 31-03-12  |
|------|------------|------------|-----------|
| TO   | 12,319,958 | 12,066,304 | 9,697,337 |
| P/L  | 752,034    | 460,322    | (733,215) |
| NW   | 5,434,227  | 4,718,242  | 4,262,200 |
| WC   | 3,409,700  | 2,629,845  | 2,074,671 |
| Emp. | 177        | 150        | 147       |

DUNS 37-810-6546

## Raeburn Group Ltd
(**Subsidiary of:** Raeburn Energy Ltd)
Ruby House, 8 Ruby Place, Aberdeen, Aberdeenshire AB10 1QZ
**Tel:** 01224628700
**Web:** www.raeburn.com
**Reg No:** 0171037SC **VAT No:** 682914017
**Estd:** 1996 Private Limited Company
**Line of Business:** Nursing agencies
**Export Sales:** £1,164,198
**Trading Style:** Raeburn Technical
**Issued Capital:** £1
**Directors:** S G Rowbottom, Z Hussain
**Co. Secretary:** Clp Secretaries Limited
**Responsibilities**
**Senior:** S Bogle (*Joint Managing Director*)
**Finance:** S Bogle (*Joint Managing Director*)
**Health & Safety:** D McBain (*Joint Managing Director*)
**US SIC:** 7361, 8299
**UK SIC:** 83954, 93300
**Auditors:** Acumen Accountants & Advisers Ltd

|      | 31-05-13   | 31-05-12   | 31-05-11   |
|------|------------|------------|------------|
| TO   | 36,727,611 | 28,977,999 | 24,419,120 |
| P/L  | 961,576    | 542,502    | 185,715    |
| NW   | 2,404,294  | 1,935,221  | 1,811,233  |
| WC   | 2,385,469  | 1,911,539  | 1,769,557  |
| Emp. | 449        | 406        | 373        |

DUNS 50-412-1625

## Raemoir Garden Centre Ltd
Raemoir Road, Banchory, Kincardineshire AB31 4EJ
**Web:** www.raemoirgardencentre.co.uk
**Reg No:** 0119268SC **VAT No:** 552803058
**Estd:** 1989 Private Limited Company
**Line of Business:** Other retail sale in non-specialised stores
**Issued Capital:** £137,500
**Directors:** F F Mair, E Mair
**Co. Secretary:** Stewart & Watson
**Responsibilities**
**Senior:** Elliott Mair (*Managing Director*)
**US SIC:** 5399, 0161
**UK SIC:** 65600, 01001
**Auditors:** Williamson & Dunn

|      | 31-01-14  | 31-01-13  | 31-01-12  |
|------|-----------|-----------|-----------|
| TO   | 5,327,868 | 5,071,077 | 5,004,379 |
| P/L  | 365,610   | 143,699   | 239,237   |
| NW   | 1,637,934 | 1,434,555 | 1,332,283 |
| WC   | (575,602) | (706,763) | (703,015) |
| Emp. | 100       | 101       | 101       |

DUNS 21-070-6684

## Raf Croughton Mwr
Building 75, Croughton, Brackley, Northamptonshire NN13 5NQ
**Tel:** 01280708373
**Web:** www.shopmyexchange.com
**Estd:** 2011 Proprietorship
**Line of Business:** Petrol service stations
**Proprietor:** G Randa
**Responsibilities**
**Senior:** Ann Damon (*Manager*)
**US SIC:** 9711
**UK SIC:** 65600, 01001
**Employees:** 150

DUNS 21-888-2442

## Raf Ltd
Doshi Accountants Ltd, 6th Floor, Amp House, Croydon, Surrey CR0 2LX
**Tel:** 01347848261
**Reg No:** 6072427 **Estd:** 2007 Private Limited Company
**Line of Business:** Plumbers merchants
**Issued Capital:** £1
**Director:** M R Rajani
**Co. Secretary:** Ms Laila Rajani
**Responsibilities**
**Health & Safety:** Steve Tugby (*Health & Safety Officer*)
**US SIC:** 5074   **UK SIC:** 61300

|    | 31-03-14 | 31-03-13 | 31-03-12 |
|----|----------|----------|----------|
| TA | 15,113   | 19,061   | 15,312   |
| NW | 547      | 5,231    | 3,914    |
| WC | (3,023)  | 849      | 3,618    |

DUNS 21-600-9085

## Raf Station
Raf, Kinloss, Forres, Morayshire IV36 3UH
**Tel:** 01309672161
**Estd:** 2011
**Line of Business:** Defence activities
**US SIC:** 9711   **UK SIC:** 61300
**Employees:** 2,500

DUNS 29-755-0306       **Imp-Exp**

## Rafflecourt Ltd
Crossfield Road, Birmingham, West Midlands B33 9HP
**Tel:** 0121-683-2600
**Web:** www.carrtech.com
**Reg No:** 2018213 **VAT No:** 444609543
**Estd:** 1986 Private Limited Company
**Line of Business:** Metal finishing and polishing services
**Export Markets:** E U, worldwide
**Trading Style:** Carrtech
**Issued Capital:** £10,000
**Principals:** S W Carr (*Managing*), Mrs S Blackwell, A L Barnes, A P Carr
**Co. Secretary:** Ms Colleen Carr
**US SIC:** 3499   **UK SIC:** 31694
**Auditors:** Keith Whitaker & Co
**Bankers:** National Westminster Bank Plc (53-50-10)

|      | 31-07-13  | 31-07-12  | 31-07-11  |
|------|-----------|-----------|-----------|
| TA   | 2,734,106 | 2,291,941 | 1,836,124 |
| NW   | 1,430,541 | 1,069,736 | 821,750   |
| WC   | 373,401   | 110,369   | (83,898)  |

DUNS 21-580-4546

## Rag & Waste Textile
Unit 4f Towngate Business Centre, Lester Road, Little Hulton, Manchester M38 0PT
**Tel:** 01619752742
**Web:** www.swdclothing.co.uk
**Estd:** 2005 Proprietorship
**Line of Business:** Rag merchants
**Proprietor:** Mrs S Wood
**Responsibilities**
**Senior:** Suzanne Woods (*Managing Director*)
**US SIC:** 5093   **UK SIC:** 62200
**Employees:** 50

DUNS 23-782-9531

## Rag Collections Ltd
46-48 Portman Road, Reading, Berkshire RG30 1EA
**Tel:** 01189508912 **Fax:** 01189-508917
**Reg No:** 3776053 **Estd:** 1999 Private Limited Company
**Line of Business:** Rag merchants
**Export Sales:** £3,583,391
**Issued Capital:** £2
**Director:** R Ahmed
**Co. Secretary:** Mrs Shahida Ahmed
**Responsibilities**
**Senior:** Taskeen Ahmed (*Manager*)
**US SIC:** 5093, 3031
**UK SIC:** 62200, 48123
**Bankers:** National Westminster Bank Plc (01-08-15)

|      | 30-09-13   | 30-09-12   | 30-09-11   |
|------|------------|------------|------------|
| TO   | 12,356,520 | 14,223,686 | 15,250,316 |
| P/L  | (57,085)   | 877,807    | 426,641    |
| NW   | (65,847)   | 66,156     | (634,855)  |
| WC   | (172,283)  | (26,165)   | (858,027)  |
| Emp. | 78         | 77         | 103        |

DUNS 23-275-4697

## Ragley Hall
Alcester, Alcester, Alcester, Warwickshire B49 5NJ
**Tel:** 01789762090
**Web:** www.ragley.co.uk
**VAT No:** 589200132 **Estd:** 2010 Proprietorship
**Line of Business:** Places of interest
**Proprietor:** M Of Hertford
**Responsibilities**
**Senior:** Marquis of Hertford (*Proprietor*)
**Finance:** Teresa Banks (*Financial Manager*)
**IT:** Teresa Banks (*Financial Manager*)

**Operations:** Steven Lyon (*Property Manager*)
**US SIC:** 8411, 7999
**UK SIC:** 97700, 97913
**Bankers:** HSBC Bank plc (40-43-54)
**Employees:** 50

DUNS 73-894-2197       **Imp**

## Ragt Seeds Ltd
Grange Road, Ickleton, Saffron Walden, Essex CB10 1TA
**Web:** www.ragtsemences.com
**Reg No:** 5148203 **Estd:** 2004 Private Limited Company
**Line of Business:** Growing of cereals and other crops not elsewhere classified
**Export Sales:** £3,767,773
**Issued Capital:** £1,400,000
**Directors:** L R Bordas, L F Guerreiro, S P Gaste, S A Howell
**Co. Secretary:** Simon Howell
**Responsibilities**
**Senior:** Claude Tabel (*Manager*)
**US SIC:** 0119   **UK SIC:** 01001
**Auditors:** Deloitte LLP
**Bankers:** National Westminster Bank Plc (60-04-23)

|      | 30-06-14  | 30-06-13  | 30-06-12  |
|------|-----------|-----------|-----------|
| TO   | 8,537,410 | 7,502,555 | 6,853,915 |
| P/L  | 84,688    | (176,185) | (51,160)  |
| NW   | (71,167)  | (181,857) | (31,674)  |
| WC   | (625,578) | (605,706) | (279,512) |
| Emp. | 50        | 49        | 49        |

DUNS 21-170-5284

## Rahim Brothers Ltd
216-218 Mile End Road, London E1 4LJ
**Tel:** 020 7790 6220
**Web:** www.rahims.net
**Reg No:** 6951042 **Estd:** 2009 Private Limited Company
**Line of Business:** Wholesale of meat and meat products
**Issued Capital:** £100
**Directors:** S S Hussain, M J Hussain
**Co. Secretary:** Sharif Hussain
**US SIC:** 5147, 5143
**UK SIC:** 61700
**Auditors:** Appiatse & Associates

|      | 30-09-13   | 30-09-12   | 30-09-11 |
|------|------------|------------|----------|
| TO   | 22,200,303 | 16,948,484 | N/A      |
| P/L  | 199,868    | 131,553    | N/A      |
| NW   | 386,939    | 229,245    | 113,655  |
| WC   | 45,621     | 335,450    | 329,018  |
| Emp. | 70         | 60         | N/A      |

DUNS 21-808-0086

## Rahims
Atlas Wharf, Berkshire Road, London E9 5NB
**Tel:** 02089853335
**Web:** www.rahims.net
**Estd:** 2012
**Line of Business:** Cash and carry wholesalers
**US SIC:** 5199   **UK SIC:** 61900
**Employees:** 60

DUNS 21-155-7354       **Imp-Exp**

## Raicam Clutch Ltd
(**Subsidiary of:** Elisa Srl)
Driveline House, Tachbrook Road, Leamington Spa, Warwickshire CV31 3ER
**Tel:** 01926-473100 **Fax:** 01926473330
**Web:** www.raicamclutch.com
**Reg No:** 6837643 **VAT No:** 946983167
**Estd:** 2009 Private Limited Company
**Line of Business:** Manufacture of parts and accessories for motor vehicles and their engines
**Export Sales:** £6,122,576
**Issued Capital:** £3
**Directors:** G Gullo, M Di Sipio, Ms N Di Sipio
**Responsibilities**
**Senior:** Aldivano Ferrucci (*Manager*), Tony Hodgekins (*Plant Manager*), Aldivano Massimo (*Manager*), Adrian Rowland (*Manager*), Ian Tarver (*Plant Manager*)
**Sales:** Tom Hodgekins (*Sales Manager*)
**IT:** Jim Friar (*IT Manager*)
**HR:** Sonia Peterson (*Human Resources Advisor*)
**Health & Safety:** Richard Avery (*Facilities Manager*)
**Facilities:** Richard Avery (*Facilities Manager*)
**Operations:** Peter Hoeman (*Operations Manager*), Keith Homeins (*Operations Directors*), Ian Tarver (*Plant Manager*)
**Purchasing:** Tony Hodgekins (*Plant Manager*)
**US SIC:** 3714   **UK SIC:** 35300
**Bankers:** Bayerische Vereinsbank Ag (30-10-61)

|      | 31-12-13   | 31-12-12   | 31-12-11   |
|------|------------|------------|------------|
| TO   | 14,371,140 | 13,963,293 | 14,978,730 |
| P/L  | 855,712    | 351,180    | (584,806)  |
| NW   | 3,525,628  | 2,748,886  | 2,466,502  |
| WC   | 2,963,879  | 2,002,466  | 1,787,003  |
| Emp. | 123        | 120        | 157        |

DUNS 21-780-1796
## Raigmore Hospital
Old Perth Road, Inverness, Inverness-Shire IV2 5BE
**Tel:** 01463704000
**Web:** www.nhshighland.scot.nhs.uk
**Estd:** 2011 Proprietorship
**Line of Business:** Hospitals
**Proprietor:** G Coutts
**Responsibilities**
**Senior:** Richard Carey *(Chief Executive Officer)*
**Finance:** David Mcronald *(Finance Director)*
**IT:** Peter Light *(It Desktop Manager)*, Kathleen McFadyen *(IT Manager)*
**Purchasing:** John Bogle *(Purchasing Manager)*
**US SIC:** 8062 **UK SIC:** 95100
**Employees:** 3,500

DUNS 21-853-6377
## Rail Delivery Group Ltd
200-202 Aldersgate Street, London EC1A 4HD
**Tel:** 02078418069
**Web:** www.raildeliverygroup.com
**Reg No:** 8176197 **Estd:** 2012 Private Company Limited By Guarantee
**Line of Business:** Activities of other transport agencies
**Directors:** D Sutherland, D Finch, P J Plummer, A Thauvette, T T O'Toole, A E Collins, M M Carne, D A Brown
**Co. Secretary:** Christopher Yelland
**Responsibilities**
**Senior:** Edward Welsh *(Director Of Communications)*
**US SIC:** 4712 **UK SIC:** 77002

| | 31-03-14 | 31-08-13 |
|---|---|---|
| TO | 40,000 | 200,000 |
| P/L | (149,523) | 159,692 |
| NW | 8,135 | 127,754 |
| WC | 8,133 | 127,752 |

DUNS 51-649-1649
## Rail for London Ltd
**(Subsidiary of:** Greater London Authority)
Windsor House, 42 50 Victoria Street, London SW1H 0TL
**Tel:** 08001954040
**Reg No:** 5965930 **Estd:** 2006 Private Limited Company
**Line of Business:** Transport via railways
**Issued Capital:** £1
**Directors:** Mrs S A Atkins, G W Powell, Ms J Collis, H G Smith, A Pollins, D G Keep, M W Brown
**Co. Secretary:** Howard Carter
**US SIC:** 4011 **UK SIC:** 71000

| | 31-03-14 | 31-03-13 | 31-03-12 |
|---|---|---|---|
| TO | 160,900,000 | 133,000,000 | 102,567,000 |
| P/L | 100,000 | (100,000) | (19,000) |
| NW | 960,400,000 | 933,100,000 | 934,359,000 |
| WC | (24,800,000) | (42,200,000) | (29,951,000) |
| Emp. | 120 | 118 | 146 |

DUNS 77-946-2241
## Rail Gourmet U.K. Ltd
**(Subsidiary of:** S S P Group Plc)
169 Euston Road, London NW1 2AE
**Tel:** 02075298330 **Fax:** 020-7387-6934
**Web:** www.railgourmet.com
**Reg No:** 3052537 **VAT No:** 646674404
**Estd:** 1995 Private Limited Company
**Line of Business:** Take-away food shops
**Issued Capital:** £1
**Principals:** I B Mitchell *(Financial)*, M E Collins, J O Davies, L L Tait
**Co. Secretary:** Mrs Helen Byrne
**Responsibilities**
**Senior:** Kim Bircham *(Chief Executive)*
**US SIC:** 5812, 5499
**UK SIC:** 66110, 64100
**Auditors:** KPMG LLP
**Bankers:** Bank Of Scotland (80-11-00)

| | 30-09-13 | 30-09-12 | 30-09-11 |
|---|---|---|---|
| TO | 72,527,000 | 71,080,000 | 66,760,000 |
| P/L | 3,600,000 | 3,359,000 | 3,302,000 |
| NW | 29,371,000 | 28,704,000 | 28,064,000 |
| WC | 34,429,000 | 31,141,000 | 27,918,000 |
| Emp. | 1,242 | 1,231 | 1,282 |

DUNS 73-382-1966 **Imp**
## Rail Safety & Standards Board Ltd
2 Angel Square, London EC1V 1NY
**Tel:** 02031425300 **Fax:** 02031425301
**Web:** www.rssb.co.uk
**Reg No:** 4655675 **Estd:** 2003 Private Company Limited By Guarantee
**Line of Business:** Safety advisers and technicians
**Directors:** J N Candfield, A C Jack, G M Llewellyn, C V Fenton, C S Horton, A C Emery, S J Murphy, N J Mcdonald
**Co. Secretary:** Ms Elizabeth Fleming
**Responsibilities**
**Senior:** Anna Bradley *(Director)*, Iain Coucher *(Manager)*, Keith Heller *(Manager)*, Paul Kirk *(Director)*, Diana Lucas *(Corporate Communications Manag)*, George Profit *(Manager)*
**Finance:** Helen Goodman *(Director of Business Services)*
**Marketing:** Diana Lucas *(Corporate Communications Manag)*, Greg Morse *(Rail Editor, Right Track magaz)*
**IT:** Timothy Babalola *(Network, Security Manager)*
**Operations:** Gary Mewis *(Lead Operations Specialist)*, Gary Portsmouth *(Lead Operations Specialist)*
**Engineering:** Tom Lee *(Principal CCS Engineer)*
**US SIC:** 8911, 4789, 4712, 8611
**UK SIC:** 83701, 77002, 96312
**Auditors:** Grant Thornton UK LLP
**Bankers:** HSBC Bank plc (40-07-31)

| | 31-03-14 | 31-03-13 | 31-03-12 |
|---|---|---|---|
| TO | 36,175,000 | 33,295,000 | 31,682,000 |
| P/L | (2,341,000) | 2,867,000 | 4,252,000 |
| NW | 1,797,000 | 3,124,000 | 6,489,000 |
| WC | 12,161,000 | 13,283,000 | 10,350,000 |
| Emp. | 252 | 234 | 225 |

DUNS 64-089-4788
## Railscape Ltd
**(Subsidiary of:** Railscape Holdings Ltd)
15 Totman Crescent, Rayleigh, Essex SS6 7UY
**Tel:** 01268-777795 **Fax:** 01268777762
**Web:** www.railscape.com
**Reg No:** 3484561 **Estd:** 2013 Private Limited Company
**Line of Business:** Manufacture of metal structures and parts of structures
**Issued Capital:** £2
**Directors:** J Phipps, C Nicholls, M G Hayes
**Co. Secretary:** Ms Catherine Hayes
**US SIC:** 8999 **UK SIC:** 83954
**Bankers:** HSBC Bank plc (40-23-33)

| | 31-03-14 | 31-03-13 | 31-03-12 |
|---|---|---|---|
| TO | 7,947,503 | N/A | 3,940,426 |
| P/L | 678,869 | N/A | 166,960 |
| NW | 1,603,384 | 1,203,634 | 878,689 |
| WC | 1,163,115 | 784,926 | 558,688 |
| Emp. | 48 | N/A | N/A |

DUNS 22-608-8979 **Imp**
## Railston Ltd
**(Subsidiary of:** Railston Holdings Ltd)
Whitehill Lane, Swindon, Wiltshire SN4 7DB
**Tel:** 01793-848000 **Fax:** 01793-848014
**Web:** www.railston.co.uk
**Reg No:** 1767273 **VAT No:** 392057054
**Estd:** 1983 Private Limited Company
**Line of Business:** Shopfitting contractors
**Export Sales:** £4,976,985
**Issued Capital:** £15,200
**Directors:** G O'Sullivan, S Rumsey, A Fox
**Co. Secretary:** Geoffrey Owen
**Responsibilities**
**Senior:** Nick Slade *(Facilities Manager)*
**HR:** Tracey Hicks *(Human Resources Administrator)*
**Facilities:** Nick Slade *(Facilities Manager)*
**Purchasing:** Reg Prim *(Purchasing Manager)*
**Branches:** Railston Ltd, Unit 44, Paices Hill, Reading, Berkshire RG7 4PW
**US SIC:** 1796, 1751
**UK SIC:** 50400
**Auditors:** Robson Taylor
**Bankers:** National Westminster Bank Plc (60-05-41)

| | 31-12-13 | 31-12-12 | 31-12-11 |
|---|---|---|---|
| TO | 25,551,413 | 19,783,385 | 20,622,332 |
| P/L | 515,743 | 397,631 | 665,249 |
| NW | 5,354,319 | 5,228,216 | 5,501,261 |
| WC | 4,682,793 | 4,627,641 | 5,015,485 |
| Emp. | 81 | 72 | 69 |

DUNS 21-595-4069
## Railway Inn
120 Ashbourne Road, Cowers Lane, Belper, Derbyshire DE56 2LF
**Tel:** 01773550271
**Estd:** 2002 Proprietorship
**Line of Business:** Public house
**Proprietor:** Mrs E Geddes
**Responsibilities**
**Senior:** Michael Perry *(Licensee)*
**US SIC:** 5813 **UK SIC:** 66200
**Employees:** 46

DUNS 21-715-5798
## Railway Resistors Ltd
Unit 5, Jupiter House, Calleva Park, Reading, Berkshire RG7 8NN
**Tel:** 02035142801
**Web:** www.railway-resistors.com
**Reg No:** 7546651 **Estd:** 2011 Private Limited Company
**Line of Business:** Holding companies management activities
**Issued Capital:** £1,000
**Director:** Y Korduban
**Co. Secretary:** Oleg Korduban
**US SIC:** 6711 **UK SIC:** 83962

| | 28-02-14 | 28-02-13 | 29-02-12 |
|---|---|---|---|
| TA | 241,068 | 217,440 | 1,042,740 |
| NW | 38,300 | 4,000 | 101,000 |
| WC | 133,800 | N/A | 1,015,740 |

DUNS 67-223-9431 **Imp**
## Railway Vehicle Engineering Ltd
**(Subsidiary of:** Rvel Holdings Ltd)
Vehicles Workshop, R T C Business Park, London Road, Derby, Derbyshire DE24 8UP
**Tel:** 01332293035 **Fax:** 01332331210
**Web:** www.rvel.co.uk
**Reg No:** 6031483 **Estd:** 2006 Private Limited Company
**Line of Business:** Manufacture of railway and tramway locomotives and rolling stock
**Issued Capital:** £54,000
**Directors:** A Houghton, A T Lynch, P W Swallow, P A Ervin, P Riley, D M Rogers, S R Brennan Brown
**US SIC:** 3743 **UK SIC:** 36201
**Auditors:** Tomkinson Teal LLP

| | 31-12-13 | 31-12-12 | 31-12-11 |
|---|---|---|---|
| TA | 3,779,433 | 3,149,591 | 2,527,768 |
| P/L | 318,105 | N/A | N/A |
| NW | 2,002,661 | 1,230,376 | 1,189,199 |
| WC | 1,671,077 | 881,557 | 953,462 |
| Emp. | 78 | N/A | N/A |

DUNS 21-122-9094
## The Rainbow Centre (Marham)
Elm Road, Upper Marham, King's Lynn, Norfolk PE33 9NF
**Tel:** 01760446161
**Web:** www.rafmarham.co.uk
**Reg No:** 6580163 **Estd:** 2008 Private Company Limited By Guarantee
**Line of Business:** Primary education
**Trading Style:** The Rainbow Centre (Marham)
**Directors:** G D Williams, D A Smith, D C Shaw, Ms R L Wotton, N D Tomlin
**Co. Secretary:** Ms Dora Gent
**Responsibilities**
**Senior:** Stephen Dharamraj *(Manager)*, Dee Gent *(Manager)*
**US SIC:** 8211 **UK SIC:** 93200

| | 31-05-14 | 31-05-13 | 31-05-12 |
|---|---|---|---|
| TO | 1,275,731 | 721,979 | 1,181,069 |
| P/L | 61,226 | 15,166 | (34,405) |
| NW | 119,219 | 57,993 | 42,827 |
| WC | 119,219 | 57,993 | 42,827 |
| Emp. | 65 | 68 | 67 |

DUNS 39-821-8511
## Rainbow Home Shopping Ltd
Brook Street, Welshpool, Powys SY21 7NA
**Tel:** 01938554013
**Web:** www.grattan.co.uk
**Reg No:** 2219920 **Estd:** 1988 Private Limited Company
**Line of Business:** Mail order houses
**Trading Style:** Freemans and Grattan Holdings, Freemans, Look Again
**Issued Capital:** £2
**Director:** N L Moore
**Co. Secretary:** Andrew Lord
**Responsibilities**
**Senior:** Koert Tullenrs *(Chief Executive)*, James Varty *(Project Manager)*
**Marketing:** Alexandra Wood-Ives *(Marketing Manager)*
**Admin:** Wendy Sheffield *(Administrator)*
**IT:** Stewart McMillan *(IT Manager)*
**HR:** Daniela Marques *(Shared Services Manager)*
**Health & Safety:** Marilyn Noutch *(Health & Safety Officer)*
**Facilities:** Sarah Blackburn *(Facilities Manager)*
**Purchasing:** Sarah Blackburn *(Facilities Manager)*
**Branches:** Rainbow Home Shopping Ltd, Valentine Road, Lincoln, Lincolnshire LN6 7BH
**US SIC:** 5961 **UK SIC:** 65600

| | 01-03-14 | 02-03-13 | 03-03-12 |
|---|---|---|---|
| TA | 2 | 2 | 5,500,000 |
| NW | 2 | 2 | 324,596 |
| WC | N/A | N/A | 324,596 |

DUNS 21-395-7860
## Rainbow House
Ayrshire Central Hospital, Kilwinning Road, Irvine, Ayrshire KA12 8SS
**Tel:** 01294-323070
**Estd:** 1991
**Line of Business:** Non-charitable social work activities without accommodation
**Proprietor:** Mrs E Murray
**US SIC:** 8321 **UK SIC:** 96111
**Employees:** 50

DUNS 23-097-5653
## Rainbow International Hotel
Belgrave Road, Torquay, Devon TQ2 5HJ
**Tel:** 01803213232
**Web:** www.rainbow-hotel.co.uk
**Estd:** 1949 Partnership
**Line of Business:** Hotels
**Trading Style:** The Rainbow International Hotel, Raven Leisure
**Partners:** Mrs K V Simpson, R V Simpson
**Responsibilities**
**Senior:** Roger Hulstone *(General Manager)*, Marco Pasquale *(Proprietor)*
**Finance:** Julia Pugh *(Accountant)*
**Marketing:** Roger Hulstone *(General Manager)*
**Sales:** Roger Hulstone *(General Manager)*
**IT:** Roger Hulstone *(General Manager)*
**Facilities:** Tony Mitten *(Maintenance Manager)*
**Operations:** Roger Hulstone *(General Manager)*
**US SIC:** 7011 **UK SIC:** 66500
**Employees:** 85

DUNS 21-584-6986
## Rainbow Nursery
The Almner And Apos;s Priory Complex A, Chertsey, Surrey KT16 0BH
**Tel:** 01932-570888
**Web:** www.rainbownursery.com
**Estd:** 2010 Proprietorship
**Line of Business:** Nursery schools
**Proprietor:** P Kapila
**US SIC:** 8211 **UK SIC:** 93200
**Bankers:** National Westminster Bank Plc (60-07-33)
**Employees:** 76

DUNS 73-556-0518
## Rainbow Nursery Ltd
**(Subsidiary of:** Rainbow Nursery (2010) Ltd)
Pentland Park, Glenrothes, Fife KY6 2AL
**Tel:** 01592630126 **Fax:** 01592-630126
**Web:** www.rainbownursery.com
**Reg No:** 0149934SC **Estd:** 2001 Private Limited Company
**Line of Business:** Pre school education
**Issued Capital:** £100
**Directors:** I C Skinner, C Skinner
**Responsibilities**
**Senior:** Nikki Webster *(Manager)*
**Finance:** Audrey McFarlane *(Finance Director)*
**Branches:** Rainbow Nursery Ltd, Crawley Hospital, West Green Drive, Crawley, West Sussex RH11 7DH
**US SIC:** 8211 **UK SIC:** 93200
**Auditors:** Honeyman Fleming
**Bankers:** Clydesdale Bank Plc (82-66-01)

| | 30-11-13 | 30-11-12 | 30-11-11 |
|---|---|---|---|
| TA | 728,618 | 607,136 | 737,460 |
| NW | 525,865 | 434,921 | 542,224 |
| WC | 52,561 | (52,939) | 51,128 |

DUNS 23-717-1025
## Rainbow Private Nursery School Ltd
**(Subsidiary of:** Advenio (Yorkshire) Ltd)
London Road, Barkston Ash, Tadcaster, North Yorkshire LS24 9PW
**Tel:** 01937-557115
**Web:** www.rainbownurseryschool.co.uk
**Reg No:** 3711931 **Estd:** 1990 Private Limited Company
**Line of Business:** Primary education
**Issued Capital:** £2
**Director:** Ms H E Shields
**Co. Secretary:** Karl Shields
**Responsibilities**
**Senior:** Lisa Watson *(Manager)*
**US SIC:** 8211 **UK SIC:** 93200
**Auditors:** Child & Co
**Bankers:** The Royal Bank Of Scotland Plc (16-23-17)

| | 31-12-13 | 31-12-12 | 31-12-11 |
|---|---|---|---|
| TA | 1,008,582 | 961,987 | 910,630 |
| NW | 880,738 | 829,558 | 769,103 |
| WC | 741,867 | 705,040 | 644,176 |

DUNS 21-226-7687
## Rainbow Superstore
Rainbow Super Store, Great North Road, St Neots, Cambridgeshire PE19 8FT
**Tel:** 01480404484
**Estd:** 1991 Proprietorship
**Line of Business:** Convenience stores
**Proprietor:** M Gough
**US SIC:** 5411 **UK SIC:** 64100
**Employees:** 79

DUNS 21-595-4109
## Rainbow Telecom
Rainbow House, Maryland Industrial Estate, Newtownards, Co Down BT23 6BL
**Web:** www.rainbowtele.com
**Estd:** 2005 Partnership

**Line of Business:** Telecommunications
**Partners:** M Hamill, E Carson
**US SIC:** 4899 **UK SIC:** 79020
**Employees:** 50

DUNS 23-587-4935
## Rainbow Trust Children's Charity
6 Cleeve Court, Cleeve Road, Leatherhead, Surrey KT22 7UD
**Tel:** 01372363438
**Web:** www.rainbowtrust.org.uk
**Reg No:** 3585123 **Estd:** 2012 Private Unlimited Company
**Line of Business:** Social work activities without accommodation
**Directors:** Ms F M Smith, Ms C J Woollett, M V Cunningham, O H Stanley, G Tempest-Hay, Dr J M Rabbs, T B Bunting, M R Richardson
**Co. Secretary:** Michael Wainwright
**Responsibilities**
**Senior:** Simon Meller (Trustee), Geraldine Peacock (Trustee), Heather Wood (Chief Executive Officer)
**Branches:** Rainbow Trust Children's Charity, 1A Church Street, Southampton, Hampshire SO15 5LG
**US SIC:** 8321 **UK SIC:** 96111
**Auditors:** Hays Allan
**Bankers:** National Westminster Bank Plc (60-12-36)

|  | 30-06-14 | 30-06-13 | 30-06-12 |
|---|---|---|---|
| TO | 4,652,556 | 2,712,691 | 4,019,851 |
| P/L | (97,495) | 951 | (269,178) |
| NW | 1,989,231 | 2,050,544 | 1,910,131 |
| WC | 573,589 | 535,737 | 453,167 |
| Emp. | 90 | 84 | 82 |

DUNS 34-865-1597
## Raindrop Information Systems International Ltd
Queens House, 55-56 Lincoln's Inn Fields, London WC2A 3LJ
**Tel:** 02072698500 **Fax:** 02077341095
**Web:** www.manhattansoftware.co.uk
**Reg No:** 2817013 **Estd:** 1993 Private Limited Company
**Line of Business:** Computer software (development)
**Issued Capital:** £10,000
**Managing Director:** S Vatidis
**Responsibilities**
**Senior:** Iwona Wiseman (Manager)
**US SIC:** 7379, 7372
**UK SIC:** 83940
**Auditors:** E A Associates
**Bankers:** Barclays Bank Plc (20-05-75)

|  | 30-04-13 | 30-04-12 | 30-04-11 |
|---|---|---|---|
| TA | 959,379 | 946,369 | 936,235 |
| NW | 158,723 | 158,471 | 156,099 |
| WC | 1,660 | 1,408 | (964) |

DUNS 23-086-2117
## Raine's Foundation Secondary Upper School
Approach Road, London E2 9LY
**Tel:** 020-8981-1231
**Web:** www.rainesfoundation.org.uk
**Estd:** 1997
**Line of Business:** Schools (foundation)
**Director:** P Hollingman
**Responsibilities**
**Senior:** Graham Riggans (Senior Manager)
**US SIC:** 8211 **UK SIC:** 93200
**Employees:** 70

DUNS 23-229-6272
## Rainey Endowed School
79 Rainey Street, Magherafelt, Co Londonderry BT45 5DB
**Tel:** 02879632478
**Web:** www.raineyendowed.com
**Estd:** 1931
**Line of Business:** General secondary education
**Principals:** Dr H S Clark (Chairman), C E Flanaghan
**US SIC:** 8211 **UK SIC:** 93200
**Employees:** 100

DUNS 52-005-1269
## Rainford Group Ltd
Rainford House, Mill Lane, Rainford Industrial Estate, Rainford, St Helens, Merseyside WA11 8LS
**Tel:** 01744-889886 **Fax:** 01744-885612
**Web:** www.rainfordsolutions.com
**Reg No:** 3372015 **VAT No:** 860230948
**Estd:** 1997 Private Limited Company
**Line of Business:** Sheet metal fabricators
**Issued Capital:** £50,000
**Director:** S Blackburn
**Co. Secretary:** James Crawford
**Responsibilities**
**Senior:** Graham Bingley (Proprietor)

**Sales:** Jerome Fox (Business Development Manager), Peter O'Neale (Business Development Manager), Carl Pegnam (Internal Sales Manager)
**US SIC:** 6711, 3499
**UK SIC:** 83962, 31694
**Auditors:** Fairhurst
**Bankers:** HSBC Bank plc (40-35-29)

|  | 31-01-14 | 31-07-12 | 31-01-11 |
|---|---|---|---|
| TO | 12,936,183 | 6,727,504 | 7,322,246 |
| P/L | 521,529 | 376,635 | 204,187 |
| NW | 1,928,037 | 1,796,582 | 1,502,589 |
| WC | 969,336 | 626,655 | 337,298 |
| Emp. | 96 | 88 | 79 |

DUNS 73-308-5778
## Rainham Industrial Services Ltd
Rainham House, Grays, Essex RM20 3LH
**Tel:** 01708683483 **Fax:** 01708683490
**Web:** www.rainhamis.co.uk
**Reg No:** 4582381 **VAT No:** 805919710
**Estd:** 2002 Private Limited Company
**Line of Business:** Engineering design activities for industrial process and production
**Trading Style:** R I S
**Issued Capital:** £2,500
**Directors:** A M Rynston, T Mccarthy, C P Boocock, D P Hoskins, D Paget, T M Toulson, M Scaife
**Co. Secretary:** Jayasegaram Gnanasegaram
**Branches:** Rainham Industrial Services Ltd, Tilbury Power Station, Fort Road, Tilbury, Essex RM18 8UJ
**US SIC:** 7399, 1731, 1796, 7349
**UK SIC:** 83954, 50300, 50400, 92300
**Auditors:** Giess Wallis Crisp LLP
**Bankers:** Barclays Bank Plc (20-72-89)

|  | 31-12-13 | 31-12-12 | 31-12-11 |
|---|---|---|---|
| TO | 44,850,678 | 33,257,628 | 35,128,357 |
| P/L | 4,606,526 | 969,525 | 1,484,087 |
| NW | 4,721,667 | 1,437,299 | 1,136,635 |
| WC | 2,647,671 | 131,565 | (137,309) |
| Emp. | 309 | 39 | 45 |

DUNS 21-729-7424
## Rainham Mark Grammar School
Rainham Mark Grammar School, Pump Lane, Gillingham, Kent ME8 7AJ
**Tel:** 01634260209
**Web:** www.rainhammark.com
**Reg No:** 7654628 **Estd:** 2011 Private Company Limited By Guarantee
**Line of Business:** General secondary education
**Directors:** Ms R A Shillabeer, S J Decker, Ms E Jackson, Mrs M J Kirk, M L Campbell, N Carter, Dr M J Mcgibbon, N J Goodall
**Co. Secretary:** Ms Deborah Capelin
**Responsibilities**
**Senior:** Hari Aggarwal (Director), Barry Kemp (Director), Richard Meacham (Director), Jonathan O'Donnell (Director), Stephanie Smith (Director), Carol Wallis (Director), Terence Whittaker (Director)
**US SIC:** 8211 **UK SIC:** 93200
**Bankers:** Barclays Bank Plc (20-54-11)

|  | 31-08-14 | 31-08-13 | 31-08-12 |
|---|---|---|---|
| TO | 6,687,000 | 6,196,000 | 23,928,000 |
| P/L | (19,000) | (98,000) | 15,903,000 |
| NW | 15,700,000 | 15,552,000 | 15,687,000 |
| WC | 1,257,000 | 1,036,000 | 826,000 |
| Emp. | 102 | 104 | 109 |

DUNS 21-713-9062　　　　　　Imp-Exp
## Rainham Steel Co Ltd
(Subsidiary of: Rainham Steel Holdings Ltd)
Kathryn House, Manor Way, Rainham, Essex RM13 8RE
**Fax:** 01708559024
**Web:** www.rainhamsteel.co.uk
**Reg No:** 1093531 **VAT No:** 247209659
**Estd:** 1973 Private Limited Company
**Line of Business:** Wholesale of metals and ores
**Export Markets:** E U
**Export Sales:** £2,451,895
**Issued Capital:** £9,993
**Principals:** W J Ives (Chairman), Miss A M Chapman, Ms K F Ives, T Webb
**Co. Secretary:** Richard Carr
**Responsibilities**
**HR:** Pat Wisber (Human Resources Manager)
**Branches:** Rainham Steel Co Ltd, Mannaberg Way, Scunthorpe, South Humberside DN15 8XF
**US SIC:** 5051, 3441
**UK SIC:** 61200, 32042
**Auditors:** Kingston Smith LLP
**Bankers:** National Westminster Bank Plc (55-50-28)

|  | 31-03-14 | 31-03-13 | 31-03-12 |
|---|---|---|---|
| TO | 99,868,504 | 96,049,117 | 90,756,802 |
| P/L | 3,276,721 | 3,607,816 | 3,063,211 |
| NW | 34,764,436 | 32,315,689 | 29,651,714 |
| WC | 27,582,058 | 25,186,928 | 20,850,327 |
| Emp. | 158 | 147 | 135 |

DUNS 22-953-9739　　　　　　　　Exp
## Rainheath Ltd
North Hill Dishforth Airfield, Thirsk, North Yorkshire YO7 3DH
**Tel:** 01423-322706
**Web:** www.a-one.co.uk
**Reg No:** 0990307 **VAT No:** 170984244
**Estd:** 1975 Private Limited Company
**Line of Business:** Growing of cereals and other crops not elsewhere classified
**Export Markets:** E E C
**Export Sales:** £3,504,186
**Trading Style:** A1 Feed Supplement
**Issued Capital:** £7,682
**Directors:** Mrs J C Stephenson, A G Simpson Snr
**Co. Secretary:** Mrs Patricia Simpson
**Responsibilities**
**Senior:** Norman Gordon (Manager)
**Engineering:** Mike Windroff (Production Manager)
**Branches:** Rainheath Ltd, Lyster Road, Bootle, Merseyside L20 1AS
**US SIC:** 2047, 0291
**UK SIC:** 42221, 01001
**Auditors:** Dutton Moore
**Bankers:** Barclays Bank Plc (20-29-23)

|  | 30-11-13 | 30-11-12 | 30-11-11 |
|---|---|---|---|
| TO | 21,867,829 | 21,496,974 | 19,840,489 |
| P/L | (1,243,644) | (1,175,674) | (626,242) |
| NW | 12,909,638 | 14,141,707 | 14,375,872 |
| WC | 5,072,373 | 6,031,250 | 6,778,929 |
| Emp. | 93 | 87 | 74 |

DUNS 21-774-2740
## Rainsbrook Secure Training Centre
Onley Park, Rugby, Warwickshire CV23 8SY
**Tel:** 01788528800
**Web:** www.ofsted.gov.uk
**Estd:** 2011 Proprietorship
**Line of Business:** Training centres
**Proprietor:** V Raymond
**Responsibilities**
**Senior:** Phil Headley (Manager)
**US SIC:** 8299 **UK SIC:** 93300
**Employees:** 300

DUNS 28-821-6484
## Raith Rovers Football Club Ltd
Starks Park, Pratt Street, Kirkcaldy, Fife KY1 1SA
**Tel:** 01592263514 **Fax:** 01592-642833
**Web:** www.raithroversfc.com
**Reg No:** 0026287SC **VAT No:** 270751169
**Estd:** 1948 Private Limited Company
**Line of Business:** Operation of other sports arenas and stadiums not elsewhere classified
**Issued Capital:** £93,670
**Directors:** M Caira, Ms V L Mcdermid, J G Sim, A N Young, T I Morgan, D M Wann, T Phillips
**Co. Secretary:** Eric Drysdale
**Responsibilities**
**Senior:** Alex Condie (Manager), Turnbull Hutton (Manager), Bob Mullen (General Manager), David Somerville (Manager)
**Marketing:** Cliff Lumsden (Sales & Marketing Manager)
**Sales:** Cliff Lumsden (Sales & Marketing Manager)
**Health & Safety:** Alexander Latto (Health & Safety Officer), Craig Surgeon (Health & Safety Officer)
**Branches:** Raith Rovers Football Club Ltd, 18 Links Street, Kirkcaldy, Fife KY1 1QE
**US SIC:** 7999 **UK SIC:** 97913
**Auditors:** Unknown Auditor
**Bankers:** Clydesdale Bank Plc (82-62-19)

|  | 30-06-13 | 30-06-12 | 30-06-11 |
|---|---|---|---|
| TO | 1,043,681 | N/A | 1,151,430 |
| P/L | 81,350 | N/A | (162,424) |
| NW | (605,131) | (989,206) | (1,439,090) |
| WC | (291,356) | (359,941) | (309,990) |

DUNS 49-389-8738
## Raj & Knoll Ltd
79 Hythe Road, Ashford, Kent TN24 8PH
**Tel:** 01233-620788
**Web:** www.postoffice.co.uk
**Reg No:** 3136897 **Estd:** 1995 Private Limited Company
**Line of Business:** Other letting of own property
**Trading Style:** Hythe Road Post Office
**Issued Capital:** £100
**Director:** N G Patel
**Co. Secretary:** Mrs Amita Patel
**Responsibilities**
**Senior:** Puvanachandran Visvalingam (Proprietor)
**US SIC:** 6519, 8321, 8091
**UK SIC:** 85000, 96111, 95200
**Auditors:** M B Patel & Co

**Bankers:** Barclays Bank Plc (20-02-62)

|  | 31-03-14 | 31-03-13 | 31-03-12 |
|---|---|---|---|
| TO | 2,549,567 | 2,629,989 | N/A |
| P/L | 778,620 | 891,568 | N/A |
| NW | 3,940,647 | 3,400,945 | 2,747,323 |
| WC | 3,834,938 | 3,224,440 | 1,036,537 |
| Emp. | 65 | 57 | N/A |

DUNS 21-732-9606
## Rajani (Wholesale) Ltd
Maggs Lane, Fishponds, Clay Hill, Bristol, Avon BS5 7EW
**Tel:** 01179585401
**Web:** www.rajanis.co.uk
**Reg No:** 1625621 **VAT No:** 140135911
**Estd:** 1982 Private Limited Company
**Line of Business:** Departmental stores
**Trading Style:** Rajanis Superstore
**Issued Capital:** £100
**Managing Director:** R Rajani
**Co. Secretary:** Mrs Gita Rajani
**Branches:** Rajani (Wholesale) Ltd, 420-422 Stapleton Road, Bristol, Avon BS5 6NQ
**US SIC:** 5399, 5714
**UK SIC:** 65600, 64700
**Auditors:** John Bradley & Co
**Bankers:** Lloyds TSB Bank plc (30-98-06)

|  | 31-12-13 | 31-12-12 | 31-12-11 |
|---|---|---|---|
| TO | N/A | N/A | 4,076,192 |
| P/L | N/A | N/A | 440,429 |
| NW | 4,452,207 | 4,493,979 | 4,719,627 |
| WC | 1,375,642 | 1,716,768 | 1,861,273 |

DUNS 49-140-4380
## Rajapack Ltd
(Subsidiary of: Kcf)
Unit 1 Badgers Rise, Bedford, Bedfordshire MK43 0YL
**Tel:** 01525289720 **Fax:** 08005424429
**Web:** www.rajapack.co.uk
**Reg No:** 3110319 **VAT No:** 218214293
**Estd:** 2001 Private Limited Company
**Line of Business:** Wholesale of other intermediate products
**Issued Capital:** £500,100
**Directors:** V Terradot, Ms D Marcovici
**Co. Secretary:** Daniel Cohen
**Branches:** Rajapack Ltd, Portaferry Aquarium, Castle Street, Newtownards, Co Down BT22 1NZ
**US SIC:** 5199, 6711
**UK SIC:** 61900, 83962
**Auditors:** Buckland Steadman & Roberts
**Bankers:** National Westminster Bank Plc (54-21-25)

|  | 31-12-13 | 31-12-12 | 31-12-11 |
|---|---|---|---|
| TO | 14,748,713 | 14,951,284 | 14,913,593 |
| P/L | 304,474 | 1,008,266 | 1,421,698 |
| NW | 2,909,144 | 2,682,996 | 3,416,442 |
| WC | 2,250,116 | 1,856,555 | 2,610,383 |
| Emp. | 80 | 77 | 71 |

DUNS 77-123-5868
## Rajja Ltd
5 Dwellings Lane, Quinton, Birmingham, West Midlands B32 1RJ
**Tel:** 0121-421-6840
**Web:** www.rajjachemists.co.uk
**Reg No:** 2695981 **Estd:** 1987 Private Limited Company
**Line of Business:** Chemists dispensing
**Trading Style:** Rajja Chemists
**Issued Capital:** £1,000
**Directors:** K Rajja, S S Dhami, R A Street
**Co. Secretary:** Rajesh Basandrai
**Branches:** Rajja Ltd, Selcroft Avenue, Birmingham, West Midlands B32 2BX
**US SIC:** 5912 **UK SIC:** 64300
**Auditors:** Sethi & Sethi
**Bankers:** The Royal Bank Of Scotland Plc (16-34-31)

|  | 31-03-14 | 31-03-13 | 31-03-12 |
|---|---|---|---|
| TO | 16,571,684 | 17,429,412 | 18,208,379 |
| P/L | 721,386 | 737,349 | 853,024 |
| NW | (851,206) | (1,680,713) | 3,338,735 |
| WC | 115,905 | (380,330) | (380,156) |
| Emp. | 76 | 75 | 74 |

DUNS 73-873-6748　　　　　　　Imp
## Rakon Uk Ltd
(Subsidiary of: Rakon Limited)
Dowsett House, Sadler Road, Lincoln, Lincolnshire LN6 3RS
**Tel:** 01522883500 **Fax:** 01522-883535
**Web:** www.rakon.com
**Reg No:** 5128090 **Estd:** 2004 Private Limited Company
**Line of Business:** Manufacture of electronic valves and tubes and other electronic components
**Export Sales:** £21,680,000
**Issued Capital:** £2
**Directors:** B J Robinson, Dr. S Altug, Dr P C Davies, D P Robinson
**Responsibilities**
**Senior:** Duncan Jamieson (Store Manager), Alain Rougier (General Manager)
**Marketing:** Kevin McAloon (Head of Product Management), Andrew McCraith (Global Strategic Marketing & B)

**Sales:** Nick John *(Sales Manager)*, Hugh Tucker *(Global Sales General Manager)*
**IT:** Carl Inglis *(Computer Manager)*, Jan Ooijman *(Senior Applications Engineer)*
**HR:** June Wass *(Human Resources Manager)*
**Health & Safety:** Denis Weston *(Facilities Manager)*
**Facilities:** Denis Weston *(Facilities Manager)*
**Branches:** Rakon Uk Ltd, Station Road, Crewkerne, Somerset TA18 8AR
**US SIC:** 3679, 7399
**UK SIC:** 34542, 83954
**Auditors:** Grant Thornton UK LLP
**Bankers:** National Westminster Bank Plc (56-00-14)

| | 31-03-14 | 31-03-13 | 31-03-12 |
|---|---|---|---|
| TO | 22,946,000 | 25,637,000 | 28,580,000 |
| P/L | 2,191,000 | 3,291,000 | 5,679,000 |
| NW | 7,220,000 | 5,893,000 | 11,368,000 |
| WC | 5,654,000 | 3,906,000 | 9,427,000 |
| Emp. | 110 | 114 | 120 |

DUNS 50-376-7188 **Exp**

## Rakusen's Ltd

**(Subsidiary of:** Capmac Ltd)
Clayton Wood Rise, Leeds, West Yorkshire LS16 6QN
**Tel:** 01132-784821 **Fax:** 01132-784064
**Web:** www.rakusens.co.uk
**Reg No:** 2385824 **Estd:** 1984 Private Limited Company
**Line of Business:** Manufacture of rusks and biscuits; manufacture of preserved pastry goods and cakes
**Export Markets:** U S A, E U, Canada
**Issued Capital:** £100
**Principals:** D Macfarlane *(Managing)*, C A Pridmore *(Financial)*, G Knapton
**Co. Secretary:** Charles Pridmore
**Responsibilities**
**Senior:** Joanne Bowman *(Financial Director)*, A Pridmore *(Manager)*
**Finance:** Joanne Bowman *(Financial Director)*
**Marketing:** A Pridmore *(Manager)*
**Sales:** A Pridmore *(Manager)*
**IT:** Joanne Bowman *(Financial Director)*
**HR:** M Gazanayi *(Human Resources Manager)*
**Purchasing:** Joanne Bowman *(Financial Director)*
**US SIC:** 2052, 2033
**UK SIC:** 41970, 41473
**Auditors:** PricewaterhouseCoopers
**Bankers:** National Westminster Bank Plc (60-60-05)

| | 30-06-14 | 30-06-13 | 30-06-12 |
|---|---|---|---|
| TA | 2,261,000 | 2,340,000 | 2,617,000 |
| NW | 1,722,000 | 1,498,000 | 1,551,000 |
| WC | 743,000 | 480,000 | 503,000 |

DUNS 29-578-1835

## Ral Ltd

**(Subsidiary of:** European Gaming (Finance) Ltd)
Silbury Court, 368 Silbury Boulevard, Milton Keynes, Buckinghamshire MK9 2AF
**Tel:** 01908696100 **Fax:** 01908-393865
**Web:** www.sstd.rl.ac.uk
**Reg No:** 1940045 **Estd:** 1986 Private Limited Company
**Line of Business:** Gambling and betting activities
**Trading Style:** Talarius
**Issued Capital:** £5,000,000
**Directors:** N J O'Connell, Ms A E Tucker, P J Harvey, F Makryllos
**Branches:** Ral Ltd, 25 Friar Street, Reading, Berkshire RG1 1DP
**US SIC:** 7999 **UK SIC:** 97913
**Auditors:** KPMG Audit PLC
**Bankers:** Lloyds TSB Bank plc (30-00-01)

| | 08-06-13 | 09-06-12 | 11-06-11 |
|---|---|---|---|
| TO | 47,482,000 | 42,189,000 | 42,824,000 |
| P/L | (374,000) | (2,001,000) | (154,000) |
| NW | 14,986,000 | 15,299,000 | 17,215,000 |
| WC | (636,000) | (1,709,000) | (1,325,000) |
| Emp. | 1,044 | 982 | 910 |

DUNS 21-914-3849 **Imp-Exp**

## R.A.Labone & Co Ltd

Lower Middleton Street, Ilkeston, Derbyshire DE7 5TN
**Tel:** 01159-448800
**Web:** www.ralabone.co.uk
**Reg No:** 0833741 **VAT No:** 116868741
**Estd:** 1963 Private Limited Company
**Line of Business:** Metal spinners
**Export Markets:** European countries
**Export Sales:** £4,542,154
**Trading Style:** Labone Precision
**Issued Capital:** £100,000
**Principals:** A A Stiegler *(Chairman and Managing)*, C Young *(Managing)*, A K Roe, L J Roe, R B Goldthorpe, Ms A B Stiegler, Mrs R F Young
**Co. Secretary:** Ms Ruth Young
**Responsibilities**
**Sales:** Michael McDonald *(Sales Manager)*
**IT:** Mick Duffin *(IT Officer)*
**HR:** Louise Buck *(Human Resources Manager)*
**Health & Safety:** Angela Farrar *(Health & Safety Officer)*
**Operations:** Nigel Meakin *(Commercial Manager)*
**Purchasing:** Nigel Meakin *(Commercial Manager)*
**Branches:** R.a.labone & Co Ltd, Lower Middleton Street, Ilkeston, Derbyshire DE7 5TN
**US SIC:** 3499, 3079
**UK SIC:** 31694, 48360
**Auditors:** Cooper Parry LLP
**Bankers:** National Westminster Bank Plc (60-13-23)

| | 31-12-13 | 31-12-12 | 31-12-11 |
|---|---|---|---|
| TO | 21,641,363 | 19,971,261 | 18,167,124 |
| P/L | 822,871 | 557,691 | 799,330 |
| NW | 5,665,158 | 4,937,850 | 4,581,889 |
| WC | 2,966,933 | 2,388,996 | 2,157,992 |
| Emp. | 243 | 222 | 190 |

DUNS 28-903-2443 **Imp-Exp**

## Ralawise Ltd

Unit 112 Tenth Avenue, Deeside, Clwyd CH5 2UA
**Tel:** 01244-838300 **Fax:** 01244-289010
**Web:** www.ralawise.com
**Reg No:** 1362849 **VAT No:** 338228549
**Estd:** 1978 Private Limited Company
**Line of Business:** Leisure wear
**Export Sales:** £10,065,000
**Issued Capital:** £1,850,000
**Directors:** Mrs E V Batson, J P Batson, J P Batson
**Co. Secretary:** Mrs Edna Batson
**Responsibilities**
**Senior:** Nicola O'keefe *(Manager)*, Paul Shore *(Operations Manager)*
**IT:** Paul Shore *(Operations Manager)*
**Health & Safety:** Alistair McPherson *(Manager)*
**Operations:** Paul Shore *(Operations Manager)*
**Branches:** Ralawise Ltd, 30-31 Poplar Drive, Birmingham, West Midlands B6 7AD
**US SIC:** 5611 **UK SIC:** 64500
**Auditors:** Banks Sheridan
**Bankers:** National Westminster Bank Plc (60-23-05)

| | 31-12-13 | 31-12-12 | 31-12-11 |
|---|---|---|---|
| TO | 75,937,017 | 63,579,565 | 55,003,852 |
| P/L | 6,764,301 | 5,670,851 | 5,182,974 |
| NW | 23,913,458 | 19,321,123 | 15,520,270 |
| WC | 24,057,204 | 21,109,489 | 16,825,954 |
| Emp. | 333 | 264 | 216 |

DUNS 21-910-3330 **Imp-Exp**

## Raleigh Holdings Ltd

136 Church Street, Eastwood, Nottingham, Nottinghamshire NG16 3HT
**Tel:** 01773532651
**Web:** www.raleigh.co.uk
**Reg No:** 0076181 **VAT No:** 116649266
**Estd:** 1903 Private Limited Company
**Line of Business:** Wholesale of other household goods not elsewhere classified
**Export Markets:** E U and Rest of World
**Issued Capital:** £5,000,000
**Directors:** J M Blok, H H Sybesma, M A Gouldthorp, R J Takens
**Co. Secretary:** Alan Graham
**Branches:** Raleigh Holdings Ltd, Lenton Boulevard, Nottingham, Nottinghamshire NG7 2BY
**US SIC:** 5199 **UK SIC:** 61900
**Auditors:** BDO Stoy Hayward LLP
**Bankers:** HSBC Bank plc (40-35-18)

| | 31-12-13 | 30-09-12 | 30-12-11 |
|---|---|---|---|
| TO | 480,000 | 36,369,000 | 37,108,000 |
| P/L | 303,000 | 683,000 | 976,000 |
| NW | 3,884,000 | 2,568,000 | 3,005,000 |
| WC | (2,048,000) | 6,527,000 | 6,754,000 |
| Emp. | N/A | 149 | 158 |

DUNS 77-956-0507

## Raleigh International Trust

Third Floor, London SE1 7TJ
**Tel:** 02071831270 **Fax:** 020 7504 8094
**Web:** www.raleighinternational.org
**Reg No:** 3059479 **Estd:** 1995 Private Company Limited By Guarantee
**Line of Business:** Activities of travel organisers
**Directors:** J W Stacey, Miss A Jhanji, Ms M A Owusu-Gyamfi, Ms C F Woolf, Mrs P O'Hayer, R Spencer, Ms M R Staunton, Miss P C Mcgivern
**Co. Secretary:** Keith Mitchell
**Responsibilities**
**Senior:** Stacey Adams *(Chief Executive)*, Jeremy Fish *(Director)*, Amy Holmes *(Director)*, Leonie Martin *(Marketing and Recruitment Mana)*, Samuel Parker *(Director)*
**Finance:** Mari Espinar *(Management Accountant)*
**Marketing:** Brandon Charleston *(Training and Development Manag)*, Rachel Collinson *(Head of Sales and Marketing)*, Sally Ferguson *(Senior Development Manager)*, Britanny Glenn *(Development Officer)*, Leonie Martin *(Marketing and Recruitment Mana)*, Laura Woodward *(Corporate Communications and P)*
**Sales:** Rachel Collinson *(Head of Sales and Marketing)*, Adam Scott *(Corporate Account Executive)*
**Admin:** Mary Eva *(Human Resources Manager)*
**IT:** Terry Finnegan *(Database Officer)*
**HR:** Shaddy Bajelvand *(Alumni Manager)*, Hayley Burnell *(Trainer Facilitator)*, Ewelina Burzywoda *(Recruitment Manager)*, Brandon Charleston *(Training and Development Manag)*, Eddie Church *(Trainer)*, Mary Eva *(Human Resources Manager)*, Leonie Martin *(Marketing and Recruitment Mana)*
**Facilities:** Crawford Blagden *(Facilities Manager)*
**Branches:** Raleigh International Trust, 36 Saville Street West, North Shields, Tyne and Wear NE29 6QR
**US SIC:** 4722, 7999
**UK SIC:** 77001, 97913
**Auditors:** Kingston Smith LLP
**Bankers:** National Westminster Bank Plc (60-05-14)

| | 31-12-13 | 31-12-12 | 31-12-11 |
|---|---|---|---|
| TO | 6,049,030 | 4,100,282 | 3,346,290 |
| P/L | 67,112 | 128,809 | 18,457 |
| NW | 869,946 | 802,833 | 674,024 |
| WC | 640,481 | 575,061 | 619,353 |
| Emp. | 59 | 45 | 36 |

DUNS 63-458-6572

## Raleys Solicitors

Permanent Building, Regent Stree, Barnsley, South Yorkshire S70 2AF
**Tel:** 01226 211111
**Web:** www.raleys.co.uk
**Estd:** 1990 Partnership
**Line of Business:** Solicitors
**Partners:** I Fur, P Hollingworth, D Barber, Ms K Richards
**Responsibilities**
**Senior:** Mark Shannon Little *(Human Resources Director)*, John Welsh *(Partner)*
**Marketing:** Jim Gladman *(Partner)*, Kate Swinscoe *(Marketing & PR Manager)*
**IT:** Diane Wall *(Systems Analyst & Trainer)*
**HR:** Mark Shannon Little *(Human Resources Director)*, Diane Wall *(Systems Analyst & Trainer)*
**US SIC:** 8111 **UK SIC:** 83500
**Employees:** 100

DUNS 21-148-2137

## Ralli Llp

Brook House, 64-72 Spring Gardens, Manchester M2 2BQ
**Tel:** 01618326131 **Fax:** 0870-998-9100
**Web:** www.ralli.co.uk
**Reg No:** 0342354OC **Estd:** 2008 Private Limited Company
**Line of Business:** Solicitors
**Responsibilities**
**Marketing:** Robert Illidge *(Marketing Assistant)*
**Facilities:** Duncan Clegg *(Facilities Assistant)*
**US SIC:** 8111 **UK SIC:** 83500

| | 31-12-13 |
|---|---|
| TA | 1 |
| NW | 1 |

DUNS 39-904-6580 **Exp**

## Ralph Davies International Ltd

The Runnings, Cheltenham, Gloucestershire GL51 9NJ
**Tel:** 01242-236266
**Web:** www.ralphdavies.co.uk
**Reg No:** 2226625 **VAT No:** 484658693
**Estd:** 1969 Private Limited Company
**Line of Business:** Other supporting land transport activities
**Export Markets:** other EEC & Non EEC
**Issued Capital:** £2
**Principals:** R Davies *(Managing)*, Mrs J E Davies
**US SIC:** 4789 **UK SIC:** 77002
**Auditors:** Little & Co
**Bankers:** Barclays Bank Plc (20-20-15)

| | 30-09-13 | 01-10-12 | 30-09-11 |
|---|---|---|---|
| TO | 6,342,411 | N/A | N/A |
| P/L | 246,818 | N/A | N/A |
| NW | 1,929,207 | 1,734,565 | 1,761,425 |
| WC | 1,059,391 | 831,597 | 1,000,710 |
| Emp. | 59 | N/A | N/A |

DUNS 21-316-0989 **Exp**

## Ralph Ellerker (1795) Ltd

Angels Wing, Whitehouse Street, Leeds, West Yorkshire LS10 1AD
**Tel:** 01132-448393 **Fax:** 01132-421307
**Web:** www.unionindustries.co.uk
**Reg No:** 1206585 **Estd:** 1975 Private Limited Company
**Line of Business:** Manufacture of other fabricated metal products not elsewhere classified
**Export Markets:** Worldwide
**Export Sales:** £228,883
**Trading Style:** Union Industries
**Issued Capital:** £3,000
**Principals:** Ms C I Schofield *(Managing)*, P J Rodgers, A A Lane, A S Metcalfe, A P Hirst
**Co. Secretary:** Ms Christine Schofield
**Responsibilities**
**Senior:** Graham Bickerdike *(Manager)*
**Finance:** Elaine Harper *(Finance Director)*
**US SIC:** 3499, 3999
**UK SIC:** 31694, 49590
**Auditors:** Ernst & Young
**Bankers:** Lloyds TSB Bank plc (30-00-05)

| | 31-03-14 | 31-03-13 | 31-03-12 |
|---|---|---|---|
| TO | 4,894,077 | 5,124,949 | 5,257,561 |
| P/L | 131,999 | 407,998 | 483,776 |
| NW | 3,931,449 | 3,834,677 | 3,601,360 |
| WC | 2,015,890 | 1,953,403 | 1,723,098 |
| Emp. | 63 | 61 | 60 |

DUNS 21-804-4782 **Imp-Exp**

## Ralph Martindale & Company Ltd

Crocodile House, Strawberry Lane Strawberry Lane, Industrial Estate, Willenhall, West Midlands WV13 3RS
**Tel:** 01902-826826 **Fax:** 01902-826827
**Web:** www.ralphmartindale.co.uk
**Reg No:** 0065418 **VAT No:** 346318945
**Estd:** 1874 Private Limited Company
**Line of Business:** Management activities of holding companies
**Export Markets:** African Countries, including Ghana and Nigeria.
**Export Sales:** £14,734,422
**Issued Capital:** £3,886,788
**Principals:** M Kearney *(Chairman)*, M D Barrett, C D Melrose, N W Ensor, P R Holloway, A Tsepisis
**Co. Secretary:** Shaun Fox
**Responsibilities**
**Senior:** Richard Legiewicz *(Manager)*
**Branches:** Ralph Martindale & Company Ltd, Manfield Rd, Willenhall, West Midlands WV13 3RX
**US SIC:** 6711, 3423
**UK SIC:** 83962, 31612
**Auditors:** Baker Tilly UK Audit LLP
**Bankers:** Barclays Bank Plc (20-07-71)

| | 31-12-13 | 31-12-12 | 31-12-11 |
|---|---|---|---|
| TO | 14,892,916 | 18,589,877 | 20,937,688 |
| P/L | (116,768) | 1,709,802 | 1,953 |
| NW | 11,349,171 | 12,670,462 | 11,833,718 |
| WC | 3,707,031 | 4,664,799 | 3,952,260 |
| Emp. | 591 | 654 | 685 |

DUNS 64-139-2931

## Ralph Pearson

Unit 1 Linton Street, Bradford, West Yorkshire BD4 7EZ
**Tel:** 01274-733918
**Web:** www.ralphpearson.co.uk
**Estd:** 2010 Proprietorship
**Line of Business:** Meat wholesalers
**Proprietor:** R Pearson
**US SIC:** 5147 **UK SIC:** 61700
**Bankers:** Barclays Bank Plc (20-11-81)
**Employees:** 120

DUNS 39-968-7151

## Ralph Peters & Sons Ltd

Slush Puppy, 12-13 Lyon Way, Greenford, Middlesex UB6 0BN
**Tel:** 08007830065 **Fax:** 02085753611
**Web:** www.slushpuppy.co.uk
**Reg No:** 2268310 **Estd:** 1988 Private Limited Company
**Line of Business:** Other business activities not elsewhere classified
**Export Sales:** £909,439
**Issued Capital:** £50,002
**Directors:** Miss L Peters, M J Peters, R Peters
**US SIC:** 7399 **UK SIC:** 83954
**Auditors:** BFCA Ltd
**Bankers:** Barclays Bank Plc (20-00-00)

| | 31-12-13 | 31-12-12 | 31-12-11 |
|---|---|---|---|
| TO | 11,367,993 | 10,591,320 | 8,334,319 |
| P/L | 847,770 | 583,847 | 531,252 |
| NW | (715,542) | (1,565,130) | (2,107,085) |
| WC | (576,753) | (760,173) | (489,026) |
| Emp. | 70 | 72 | 60 |

DUNS 21-776-1270

## Ramada Bristol North the Grange Hotel

The Grange, Old Gloucester Roa, Northwoods, Winterbourne Winterbourne, Bristol, Avon BS36 1RP
**Tel:** 08448159063
**Web:** www.ramadajarvis.co.uk
**Estd:** 2011 Proprietorship
**Line of Business:** Hotels

**Proprietor:** M Kandemir
**US SIC:** 7011 **UK SIC:** 66500
**Employees:** 100

DUNS 21-614-4470
### Ramada Chester
Whitchurch Road, City Centre, Chester, Cheshire CH3 5QL
**Tel:** 01244332121
**Web:** www.ramada.com
**Estd:** 2011
**Line of Business:** Hotels
**Responsibilities**
**Senior:** Iain McGuigan *(General Manager)*
**Finance:** Richard Marks *(Senior Finance Administrator)*
**HR:** Sarah Hercules *(Human Resources Manager)*
**US SIC:** 7011 **UK SIC:** 66500
**Employees:** 100

DUNS 21-585-8414
### Ramada Encore
Invest Milton Keynes, 406 Midsummer Boulevard, Milton Keynes, Buckinghamshire MK9 2EA
**Tel:** 01908545500
**Web:** www.encoremiltonkeynes.co.uk
**Estd:** 2011 Proprietorship
**Line of Business:** Hotels
**Proprietor:** I Kose
**Responsibilities**
**Senior:** Garry Cruise *(General Manager)*
**US SIC:** 7011 **UK SIC:** 66500
**Employees:** 60

DUNS 21-771-2146
### Ramada Fairfield Manor Hotel Reservations
Shipton Road, Skelton, Skelton, York, North Yorkshire YO30 1XW
**Tel:** 01904670222
**Web:** www.booking.com
**Estd:** 2011 Proprietorship
**Line of Business:** Hotels
**Proprietor:** I Flemming
**US SIC:** 7011 **UK SIC:** 66500
**Employees:** 80

DUNS 21-222-4805
### Ramada Hatfield
St Albans Road West, Hatfield, Hertfordshire AL10 9RH
**Tel:** 01707252400
**Web:** www.ramadajarvis.co.uk
**Estd:** 2004 Proprietorship
**Line of Business:** Hotels
**Proprietor:** K Mcdonald
**Responsibilities**
**Senior:** Howard Dunn *(General Manager)*, Gavin Gones *(General Manager)*, Edward Holland *(General Manager)*
**Finance:** Fiona Bourke *(Financial Manager)*
**Admin:** Jeanette McKenna *(Administration Officer)*
**IT:** Jeanette McKenna *(Administration Officer)*
**HR:** Jeanette McKenna *(Administration Officer)*
**Health & Safety:** Sahala Chegwidden *(Operations Manager)*
**Facilities:** Mike Kennedy *(Maintenance Manager)*, Mike Riddles *(Maintenance Manager)*
**Operations:** Roberto Pereira *(Operations Manager)*
**US SIC:** 7011 **UK SIC:** 66500
**Employees:** 50

DUNS 21-231-0129
### Ramada Hotel
Habberley Road, Bewdley, Worcestershire DY12 1LA
**Tel:** 08448159033
**Web:** www.ramadajarvis.co.uk
**Estd:** 2001
**Line of Business:** Rooming and boarding houses
**Proprietor:** J Mccaskill
**Responsibilities**
**Senior:** John McCaskill *(Proprietor)*
**US SIC:** 7011 **UK SIC:** 66500
**Employees:** 57

DUNS 21-775-4913
### The Ramada Hotel
Penns Lane, Sutton Coldfield, West Midlands B76 1LH
**Tel:** 01213513111
**Web:** www.ramadasuttonhotel.co.uk
**Estd:** 2011 Proprietorship
**Line of Business:** Hotels
**Proprietor:** Ms C Stonebridge
**Responsibilities**
**Senior:** Fiona Lockyear *(General Manager)*
**Finance:** Stanlye Nichols *(Senior Finance Administrator)*
**IT:** Jonathan Riley *(Senior IT Executive)*
**HR:** Donna Kaylor *(Human Resources Manager)*
**US SIC:** 7011 **UK SIC:** 66500
**Employees:** 250

DUNS 21-031-4593
### Ramada Jarvis
Otley Road, Leeds, West Yorkshire LS16 8AG
**Web:** www.ramadajarvis.co.uk
**Proprietorship**
**Line of Business:** hotel with 118 bedrooms & conference facilities part of Jarvis Hotels
**Proprietor:** R Shearer
**Responsibilities**
**Senior:** Julia Douglas *(Restaurant Manager)*, Robert Shearer *(Head of Accounts)*
**Finance:** Robert Shearer *(Head of Accounts)*
**HR:** Heather Clark-Coates *(Human Resources Manager)*
**US SIC:** 7011 **UK SIC:** 66500
**Employees:** 100

DUNS 21-775-3523
### Ramada Leicester Hotel
Granby Street, Leicester, Leicestershire LE1 6ES
**Tel:** 08448159012
**Web:** www.mercure-leicester-city.com
**Estd:** 2011 Proprietorship
**Line of Business:** Hotels
**Proprietor:** J Conoghan
**US SIC:** 7011 **UK SIC:** 66500
**Employees:** 70

DUNS 21-772-9141
### Ramada Manchester Piccadilly Hotel Reservations
Portland Street, Manchester M1 4PH
**Tel:** 08448159024
**Web:** www.mercure.com
**Estd:** 2011 Proprietorship
**Line of Business:** Hotels
**Proprietor:** S Beach
**US SIC:** 7011 **UK SIC:** 66500
**Employees:** 150

DUNS 50-638-0661
### Ramada Park Hall Hotel
Park Drive, Wolverhampton, West Midlands WV4 5AJ
**Tel:** 01902349510
**Web:** www.ramadaparkhall.co.uk
**VAT No:** 695438486 **Estd:** 2012 Proprietorship
**Line of Business:** Other tourist assistance activities not elsewhere classified
**Proprietor:** S K Sharma
**Responsibilities**
**Senior:** James Jaypal *(General Manager)*
**US SIC:** 7011 **UK SIC:** 66500
**Bankers:** Yorkshire Bank Plc (05-09-83)
**Employees:** 53

DUNS 21-581-3368
### Ramada Plaza Gatwick
Tinsley Lane South, Three Bridges, Crawley, West Sussex RH10 8XH
**Tel:** 01293561186
**Web:** www.ramadajarvis.co.uk
**Estd:** 2011 Proprietorship
**Line of Business:** Hotels
**Proprietor:** T Fletcher
**Responsibilities**
**Senior:** Tony Flectcher *(General Manager)*
**US SIC:** 7011 **UK SIC:** 66500
**Employees:** 65

DUNS 21-584-8528
### Ramada Wetherby
Leeds Road, Wetherby, West Yorkshire LS22 5HE
**Tel:** 08448159067
**Web:** www.ramada.co.uk
**Estd:** 2011 Proprietorship
**Line of Business:** Other tourist assistance activities not elsewhere classified
**Proprietor:** Mrs K Sharpe
**US SIC:** 7999 **UK SIC:** 97913
**Employees:** 55

DUNS 22-802-0913
### Ramage Transport Ltd
New York Way, New York Industrial Park, Newcastle-Upon-Tyne, Tyne and Wear NE27 0QE
**Tel:** 01912573050 **Fax:** 01912961784
**Web:** www.relyonramage.co.uk
**Reg No:** 1830580 **VAT No:** 179267224
**Estd:** 1984 Private Limited Company
**Line of Business:** Road haulage and transport services
**Issued Capital:** £10,000
**Principals:** R R Ramage *(Managing)*, Mrs D A Ramage
**Co. Secretary:** Ms Denise Hodgson
**US SIC:** 4789 **UK SIC:** 77002
**Auditors:** Johnstons
**Bankers:** Barclays Bank Plc (20-59-42)

| | 31-12-13 | 31-12-12 | 31-12-11 |
|---|---|---|---|
| TO | 9,984,424 | 9,493,201 | 9,041,352 |
| P/L | 89,121 | 100,745 | 224,514 |
| NW | 2,227,503 | 2,189,305 | 2,162,350 |
| WC | 126,514 | 181,016 | (68,132) |
| Emp. | 121 | 124 | 108 |

DUNS 21-333-0389
### Rambla Nursing Home
374 Scalby Road, Scarborough, North Yorkshire YO12 6ED
**Tel:** 01723-500136
**Web:** www.completecarehomes.net
**Estd:** 1988 Partnership
**Line of Business:** Nursing homes
**Partners:** M Stephenson, D Stephenson
**Responsibilities**
**Senior:** Heather Mccausland *(Manager)*
**US SIC:** 8051 **UK SIC:** 95100
**Employees:** 48

DUNS 42-470-8837
### The Ramblers' Association
2nd Floor Camelford House, London SE1 7TW
**Tel:** 02073398500
**Web:** www.ramblers.org.uk
**Reg No:** 4458492 **Estd:** 1935 Private Company Limited By Guarantee
**Line of Business:** Associations
**Directors:** A Mannings, J M Kipling, M Church, Miss C A O'Byrne, J Lawson, D A Thomson, R A Peel, G Lewis
**Co. Secretary:** Miss Christine Grant
**Responsibilities**
**Senior:** Naseem Akhtar *(Director)*, Kate Ashbrook *(President)*, Moira Fraser *(Director)*, Des Garrahan *(Director)*, David Grosz *(Chairman)*, Richard May *(Director)*, Benedict Southworth *(Chief Executive Officer)*, Frank Syratt *(Chief Executive Officer)*, Richard Trueman *(Director)*
**Marketing:** Dominic Bates *(Editor)*, Maria Castellina *(Media Manager)*, Ellie Clewlow *(Press and Communications Offic)*
**IT:** Dave Humphrey *(Engineer)*
**HR:** Emma Rich *(HR Manager)*
**US SIC:** 8699 **UK SIC:** 96902
**Bankers:** Unity Trust Bank Plc (08-60-01)

| | 30-09-13 | 30-09-12 | 30-09-11 |
|---|---|---|---|
| TO | 8,120,000 | 7,699,000 | 8,152,117 |
| P/L | 470,000 | 345,000 | 699,833 |
| NW | 5,405,000 | 4,934,000 | 4,583,399 |
| WC | 4,084,000 | 3,648,000 | 3,505,907 |
| Emp. | 68 | 72 | 67 |

DUNS 21-734-4117
### Ramblers Holidays Group Ltd
Lemsford Mill Lemsford Village, Welwyn Garden City, Hertfordshire AL8 7TR
**Tel:** 01707331133
**Reg No:** 7690156 **Estd:** 2011 Private Company Limited By Guarantee
**Line of Business:** Travel agency activities
**Directors:** Ms A K Cotter, Ms C J Bonnick, P M Balchin, A G Lock, B C Southwell, Mrs S Brown, M J Duxbury, J R Cook
**Co. Secretary:** Anthony Lock
**Responsibilities**
**Senior:** Katharine Bensen *(Manager)*, Kathleen Cook *(Director)*, Theresa Milton *(Director)*, Gillian Welsman *(Director)*
**US SIC:** 4722 **UK SIC:** 77001

| | 31-10-14 | 31-10-13 | 31-10-12 |
|---|---|---|---|
| TO | 15,414,929 | 14,763,027 | 14,534,404 |
| P/L | 520,951 | 578,203 | 45,784 |
| NW | 10,530,854 | 10,118,518 | 9,683,173 |
| WC | 7,781,432 | 7,296,408 | 6,833,769 |
| Emp. | 57 | 52 | 51 |

DUNS 29-756-3744
### Ramboll Middle East Ltd
(**Subsidiary of:** Rambøll Fonden)
60 Newman Street, London W1T 3DA
**Fax:** 02073234645
**Web:** www.ramboll.co.uk
**Reg No:** 2019473 **Estd:** 1983 Private Limited Company
**Line of Business:** Engineering related scientific and technical consulting activities
**Issued Capital:** £100
**Directors:** R Beard, Y A Abidi, A K Pauling, J Soerensen, G B Evans, M Rosenvold
**Co. Secretary:** Andrew Thorp
**Responsibilities**
**Senior:** Flemming Pedersen *(Manager)*
**Branches:** Ramboll Middle East Ltd, Carlton House, Ringwood Road, Southampton, Hampshire SO40 7HT
**US SIC:** 8911 **UK SIC:** 83701
**Bankers:** Barclays Bank Plc (20-32-53)

| | 31-12-13 | 31-12-12 | 31-12-11 |
|---|---|---|---|
| TO | 17,158,000 | 14,360,000 | 8,138,299 |
| P/L | (5,873,000) | (1,218,000) | (3,184,851) |
| NW | 707,000 | 1,747,000 | (1,803,056) |
| WC | 634,000 | 1,677,000 | (1,804,917) |
| Emp. | 214 | 152 | 136 |

DUNS 73-438-6241
### Ramboll Oil & Gas Uk Ltd
(**Subsidiary of:** Rambøll Fonden)
1 Union Wynd, Aberdeen, Aberdeenshire AB10 1SL
**Tel:** 01224-652200
**Web:** www.altra.co.uk
**Reg No:** 0245357SC **Estd:** 2004 Private Limited Company
**Line of Business:** Engineers (consulting)
**Trading Style:** Apply Altra Limited
**Issued Capital:** £3,287,645
**Directors:** E Simonsen, L Krogh, J Rebsdorf-Gregersen
**Responsibilities**
**Senior:** Agnar Kongshaug *(Executive Director)*
**US SIC:** 8911 **UK SIC:** 83701
**Auditors:** Ernst & Young LLP
**Bankers:** The Royal Bank Of Scotland Plc (83-15-31)

| | 31-12-13 | 31-12-12 | 31-12-11 |
|---|---|---|---|
| TA | 1,499,000 | 2,921,000 | 2,483,000 |
| NW | (81,000) | 059,000 | 767,000 |
| WC | (461,000) | 406,000 | 456,000 |

DUNS 23-665-0953 **Imp**
### Ramboll Uk Ltd
(**Subsidiary of:** Rambøll Fonden)
240 Blackfriars Road, London SE1 8NW
**Fax:** 02073234645
**Web:** www.ramboll.co.uk
**Reg No:** 3659970 **Estd:** 2012 Private Limited Company
**Line of Business:** Engineers (consulting)
**Export Sales:** £12,245,000
**Issued Capital:** £23,900,002
**Directors:** L O Riemann, K Akselvoll, D J Harvey, M Rosenvold, S C Canadine, T J Dobbins, Mrs D J Beaven
**Co. Secretary:** Andrew Thorp
**Branches:** Ramboll Uk Ltd, Newton House, 457 Sauchiehall Street, Glasgow, Lanarkshire G2 3LG
**US SIC:** 8911 **UK SIC:** 83701
**Bankers:** Unibank A/s (40-48-78)

| | 31-12-13 | 31-12-12 | 31-12-11 |
|---|---|---|---|
| TO | 63,707,000 | 60,423,000 | 59,199,000 |
| P/L | 1,299,000 | (6,824,000) | (304,000) |
| NW | 13,718,000 | 11,695,000 | 15,031,000 |
| WC | 9,937,000 | 8,556,000 | 11,811,000 |
| Emp. | 949 | 809 | 1,006 |

DUNS 29-757-6167 **Imp-Exp**
### Ramco Tubular Services Ltd
(**Subsidiary of:** L D C Ii Lp)
Ramco Building, Badentoy Road, Badentoy Industrial Estate, Portlethen, Aberdeen, Aberdeenshire AB12 4YA
**Tel:** 01224782278
**Web:** www.ramcotubular.co.uk
**Reg No:** 0099251SC **Estd:** 1986 Private Limited Company
**Line of Business:** Blast cleaning
**Export Sales:** £623,419
**Issued Capital:** £3,000,000
**Directors:** R J Taylor, P W Mitchell, M Edward
**Co. Secretary:** Paul Mitchell
**Branches:** Ramco Tubular Services Ltd, Imperial Wks, Martyn St, Airdrie, Lanarkshire ML6 9AU
**US SIC:** 1799, 7699
**UK SIC:** 50000, 67303
**Auditors:** Deloitte LLP
**Bankers:** Clydesdale Bank Plc (82-69-27)

| | 31-12-13 | 31-12-12 | 31-12-11 |
|---|---|---|---|
| TO | 10,829,899 | 11,756,359 | 9,161,945 |
| P/L | 2,650,912 | 2,357,446 | 1,470,562 |
| NW | 28,354,655 | 19,240,881 | 14,779,113 |
| WC | 4,420,176 | 1,800,862 | 1,010,205 |
| Emp. | 87 | 78 | 72 |

DUNS 34-529-6268
### Ramcore Operations Ltd
(**Subsidiary of:** United Overseas Bank Limited)
Bath Road, West Drayton, Middlesex UB7 0DU
**Tel:** 01414194567
**Web:** www.encorederby.co.uk
**Reg No:** 5340129 **Estd:** 2005 Private Limited Company
**Line of Business:** Management activities of holding companies
**Issued Capital:** £100
**Directors:** K D Heininger, D Sedlmayer, P M Gaffney, P Voit
**Co. Secretary:**
Citco Management (Uk) Limited
**Branches:** Ramcore Operations Ltd, Locomotive Way, Derby, Derbyshire DE24 8PU

**US SIC:** 6711 **UK SIC:** 83962
**Bankers:** Bank Of Scotland (12-22-40)

| | 05-01-14 | 31-12-12 | 30-01-11 |
|---|---|---|---|
| TO | 7,645,982 | 8,916,882 | 7,194,085 |
| P/L | (262,470) | 16,613 | (1,180,621) |
| NW | (3,819,396) | (3,556,926) | 69,003 |
| WC | (1,120,339) | 288,155 | 174,090 |
| Emp. | 80 | 80 | 98 |

DUNS 22-200-9842 **Exp**

## Ramon Hygiene Products Ltd

(**Subsidiary of:** Ramon Holdings Ltd)
380 Thurmaston Boulevard, Leicester, Leicestershire LE4 9LE
**Tel:** 01162-761881
**Web:** www.ramonhygiene.co.uk
**Reg No:** 4219151 **Estd:** 2001 Private Limited Company
**Line of Business:** Cleaning materials and equipment
**Issued Capital:** £7,619
**Directors:** J Y Butler, S N Baldock, A Alinson, B S Davinson, M D Bartoszewicz, R D Flowers
**Co. Secretary:** Gordon Peters
**Responsibilities**
**Finance:** Shirley Griffiths *(Sales Ledger Control and Credi)*
**Marketing:** Sophie Hamilton *(Marketing Manager)*
**Sales:** Colin Cheetham *(Business Development Manager)*, Samantha Farmer *(Commercial Manager)*, Gordon Mcgregor *(Business Development Manager)*, Sandi Puri *(Business Development Manager)*
**Admin:** Carolyn Muggleton *(Office Manager and PA)*
**Health & Safety:** Clive Eager *(Quality Manager)*
**Operations:** Clive Eager *(Quality Manager)*, Samantha Farmer *(Commercial Manager)*, Patrick Staples *(Inventory Control)*
**US SIC:** 2647, 3991
**UK SIC:** 47220, 46630
**Auditors:** KPMG LLP

| | 31-03-14 | 31-03-13 | 31-03-12 |
|---|---|---|---|
| TA | 5,608,000 | 5,608,000 | 5,608,000 |
| NW | 3,416,000 | 3,416,000 | 3,416,000 |

DUNS 23-419-5746

## Ramore Restaurant Ltd

C/O Falconer Stewart, 248-266 Upper Newtownards Road, Belfast BT4 3EU
**Tel:** 02870824313
**Web:** www.ramorerestaurant.com
**Reg No:** 0019950NI **Estd:** 1986 Private Limited Company
**Line of Business:** Licensed restaurants
**Issued Capital:** £47,497
**Directors:** G Mcalpin, Ms J Mcalpin
**Co. Secretary:** James Falconer
**US SIC:** 5812 **UK SIC:** 66110

| | 31-03-14 | 31-03-13 | 31-03-12 |
|---|---|---|---|
| TO | 7,504,795 | 6,711,211 | 7,361,594 |
| P/L | 253,816 | 369,961 | 239,225 |
| NW | 4,470,147 | 4,638,676 | 4,417,770 |
| WC | (1,657,483) | (1,197,422) | (1,359,436) |
| Emp. | 186 | 151 | 146 |

DUNS 73-884-3924

## Ramos Healthcare Ltd

Batchworth House, Rickmansworth, Hertfordshire WD3 1JE
**Tel:** 01704532173
**Reg No:** 5138580 **Estd:** 2004 Private Limited Company
**Line of Business:** Other business activities not elsewhere classified
**Issued Capital:** £60
**Directors:** R Ramos, L Ramos
**Co. Secretary:** Jon Ramos
**US SIC:** 7399 **UK SIC:** 83954

| | 31-07-13 | 31-07-12 | 31-07-11 |
|---|---|---|---|
| TO | 1,973,928 | 2,091,515 | 1,887,388 |
| P/L | 253,184 | 311,021 | 241,726 |
| NW | 1,391,126 | 1,310,433 | 1,093,518 |
| WC | (591,814) | (525,606) | (529,925) |
| Emp. | 103 | 103 | 86 |

DUNS 56-993-8269

## Ramp Industries Ltd

(**Subsidiary of:** Featurepoint Ltd)
1-3 Garrett Road, Lynx Trading Estate, Yeovil, Somerset BA20 2TJ
**Tel:** 01935-427290 **Fax:** 01935-420753
**Web:** www.ramp.co.uk
**Reg No:** 2859030 **VAT No:** 850554234
**Estd:** 1990 Private Limited Company
**Line of Business:** Paint and coating sprayers
**Issued Capital:** £2
**Director:** M A Ham
**Co. Secretary:** Ms Michelle Ham
**Responsibilities**
**Finance:** Carole Champion *(Finance Director)*
**Admin:** Sarah Fifield *(Administration Manager)*
**US SIC:** 2891, 3545
**UK SIC:** 25620, 32223
**Auditors:** Davies Williams

**Bankers:** Bank Of Wales Plc (12-23-11)

| | 31-03-14 | 31-03-13 | 31-03-12 |
|---|---|---|---|
| TO | 3,294,598 | 2,898,770 | 3,353,442 |
| P/L | 349,623 | (1,761,173) | 126,130 |
| NW | 2,443,290 | 2,183,164 | 4,136,700 |
| WC | 1,978,878 | 1,896,610 | 3,802,014 |

DUNS 21-810-3334

## Ramsay & District Cottage Hospital

Cumberland Road, Ramsey, Douglas, Isle of Man IM8 3RH
**Tel:** 01624811811
**Web:** www.gov.im
**Estd:** 2012
**Line of Business:** General Medical And Surgical Hospitals
**Responsibilities**
**Senior:** Janet Grib *(Manager)*
**US SIC:** 8062 **UK SIC:** 95100
**Employees:** 150

DUNS 21-406-9486 **Imp-Exp**

## Ramsay & Sons (Forfar) Ltd

61 West High Street, Forfar, Angus DD8 1BG
**Web:** www.ramsayladders.co.uk
**Reg No:** 0024001SC **VAT No:** 269754896
**Estd:** 1771 Private Limited Company
**Line of Business:** Manufacturers of step ladders
**Trading Style:** Ramsay Ladders, Ramsay Access
**Issued Capital:** £13,650
**Director:** S R Lowson
**Co. Secretary:** Andrew Lowson
**Responsibilities**
**Senior:** Gordon Leith *(Warehouse Manager)*, Irene Lowson *(Manager)*
**Branches:** Ramsay & Sons (Forfar) Ltd, 11 Copley Hill Way, Leeds, West Yorkshire LS12 1HF
**US SIC:** 2499 **UK SIC:** 46500
**Auditors:** Bell & Co
**Bankers:** The Royal Bank Of Scotland Plc (83-20-13)

| | 31-12-13 | 31-12-12 | 31-12-11 |
|---|---|---|---|
| TO | N/A | N/A | 3,299,226 |
| P/L | N/A | N/A | 296,382 |
| NW | 3,162,956 | 3,445,594 | 3,491,995 |
| WC | 1,289,281 | 1,574,951 | 1,611,065 |
| Emp. | N/A | N/A | 49 |

DUNS 29-276-0683

## Ramsay Health Care Uk Operations Ltd

(**Subsidiary of:** Ramsay Health Care Limited)
1 Hassett Street, Bedford, Bedfordshire MK40 1HA
**Tel:** 01234273473
**Web:** www.ramsayhealth.co.uk
**Reg No:** 1532937 **VAT No:** 426505170
**Estd:** 1980 Private Limited Company
**Line of Business:** Hospital activities
**Trading Style:** Ramsay Health Care Uk
**Issued Capital:** £1,066,125
**Directors:** H Mehta, M F Page
**Co. Secretary:** Mehdi Erfan
**Responsibilities**
**Senior:** Tara Hastings *(Legal Director)*
**Admin:** Kayla Wood *(Executive PA)*
**HR:** Sarah Browne *(Human Resources Manager)*
**Branches:** Ramsay Health Care Uk Operations Ltd, Swallowscroft, Wensley Road, Reading, Berkshire RG1 6UZ
**US SIC:** 8062 **UK SIC:** 95100
**Auditors:** Ernst & Young LLP
**Bankers:** National Westminster Bank Plc (60-02-13)

| | 30-06-13 | 30-06-12 | 30-06-11 |
|---|---|---|---|
| TO | 357,671,000 | 356,110,000 | 345,431,000 |
| P/L | 7,522,000 | 8,931,000 | 15,636,000 |
| NW | 44,414,000 | 39,612,000 | 34,084,000 |
| WC | 41,264,000 | 26,759,000 | (2,694,000) |
| Emp. | 5,380 | 5,174 | 4,855 |

DUNS 21-812-2346

## Ramsay Neurological Services

High Wych Road, Sawbridgeworth, Hertfordshire CM21 0HH
**Tel:** 01279603870
**Web:** www.ramsayhealthcare.co.uk
**Estd:** 2012
**Line of Business:** Doctors
**US SIC:** 8011 **UK SIC:** 95300
**Employees:** 200

DUNS 29-868-9456

## Ramsay World Travel (Perth) Ltd

(**Subsidiary of:** Ramsay World Travel Ltd)
10-12 Crichton Street, Dundee, Angus DD1 3AJ
**Tel:** 08700857999 **Fax:** 01382-226861
**Web:** www.ramsayworldtravel.co.uk
**Reg No:** 0101882SC **Estd:** 1986 Private Limited Company
**Line of Business:** Travel agency activities
**Issued Capital:** £25,000
**Director:** J S Hughes
**Co. Secretary:** Colin Ramsay
**US SIC:** 4722 **UK SIC:** 77001

| | 31-10-13 | 31-10-12 | 31-10-11 |
|---|---|---|---|
| TA | 59,254 | 54,971 | 49,284 |
| NW | 15,000 | 15,000 | 15,000 |
| WC | 15,000 | 15,000 | 15,000 |

DUNS 52-001-2881

## Ramsbury Estates Ltd

Priory Farm, Axford, Marlborough, Wiltshire SN8 2HA
**Tel:** 01672-520647
**Web:** www.ramsburybrewery.com
**Reg No:** 3368361 **Estd:** 1997 Private Limited Company
**Line of Business:** Farming (arable)
**Issued Capital:** £3,369,368
**Director:** C S Persson
**Co. Secretary:** Ms Nancy Bignall
**Responsibilities**
**Senior:** Alistair Ewing *(Estates Manager)*
**Branches:** Ramsbury Estates Ltd, Axford, Marlborough, Wiltshire SN8 2HA
**US SIC:** 0119 **UK SIC:** 01001
**Auditors:** Bromhead & Co
**Bankers:** HSBC Bank plc (40-32-07)

| | 31-12-13 | 31-12-12 | 31-12-11 |
|---|---|---|---|
| TO | 6,437,483 | N/A | N/A |
| P/L | 258,070 | N/A | N/A |
| NW | 4,782,797 | 4,594,031 | 5,198,494 |
| WC | 322,918 | 95,333 | 786,244 |
| Emp. | 55 | N/A | N/A |

DUNS 29-772-1342

## Ramsden Holdings Ltd

361 Cleethorpe Road, Grimsby, South Humberside DN31 3BP
**Tel:** 01472-313100
**Web:** www.ramsdenssuperstore.co.uk
**Reg No:** 2035067 **Estd:** 1960 Private Limited Company
**Line of Business:** Departmental stores
**Export Sales:** £41,890,430
**Trading Style:** Ramsdens
**Issued Capital:** £12,000
**Managing Director:** D B Ramsden
**Co. Secretary:** Ms Louisa Metcalf
**Responsibilities**
**Senior:** David Christy *(Sales & Marketing Director)*
**Marketing:** David Christy *(Sales & Marketing Director)*
**Sales:** David Christy *(Sales & Marketing Director)*
**US SIC:** 5399 **UK SIC:** 65600
**Auditors:** McCrackens
**Bankers:** HSBC Bank plc (40-22-24)

| | 31-01-14 | 31-01-13 | 31-01-12 |
|---|---|---|---|
| TO | 101,530,589 | 100,862,126 | 105,262,461 |
| P/L | 2,804,517 | 1,721,668 | 1,554,687 |
| NW | 11,532,112 | 10,286,346 | 9,821,899 |
| WC | 7,656,843 | 5,412,218 | 4,861,146 |
| Emp. | 255 | 242 | 255 |

DUNS 77-932-9283

## Ramsdens Financial Ltd

Unit 16 The Parkway Centre, Coulby Newham, Middlesbrough, Cleveland TS8 0TJ
**Tel:** 01642577539
**Web:** www.ramsdensforcash.co.uk
**Reg No:** 3045495 **Estd:** 1995 Private Limited Company
**Line of Business:** Financial intermediation not elsewhere classified
**Issued Capital:** £996
**Directors:** A D Meehan, M Johnson, P Kenyon, J J Carr
**Co. Secretary:** Kevin Brown
**Responsibilities**
**Senior:** Mandy Williams *(Branch Manager)*
**Branches:** Ramsdens Financial Ltd, Ramsdens Jewellers, 19 Bede Precinct, Jarrow, Tyne and Wear NE32 3LW
**US SIC:** 6111, 6711
**UK SIC:** 81501, 83962
**Auditors:** M. Wasley Chapman & Co

| | 31-03-14 | 31-03-13 | 31-03-11 |
|---|---|---|---|
| TA | 31,965,981 | 37,342,960 | 26,155,008 |
| P/L | 1,063,022 | 9,194,119 | 8,260,187 |
| NW | 20,431,761 | 19,880,174 | 16,101,718 |
| WC | 18,047,265 | 20,653,149 | 14,442,045 |
| Emp. | 545 | 458 | 324 |

DUNS 34-849-4357

## Ramsdens Solicitors Llp

Oakley House, 1 Hungerford Road, Huddersfield, West Yorkshire HD3 3AL
**Tel:** 01484558066
**Web:** www.id30-test.co.uk
**Reg No:** 0316582OC **Estd:** 2005
**Line of Business:** Other legal activities not elsewhere classified
**Responsibilities**
**Senior:** Katie Butters *(Marketing Assistant)*, John Fryer *(Senior Partner)*, Mark Hepworth *(Non-designated Limited Liabili)*, Debbie Kaye *(Partner)*, Julia Lees *(Non-designated Limited Liabili)*, Jill Mccurdy *(Non-designated Limited Liabili)*, Malcolm Parkinson *(Non-designated Limited Liabili)*, Lynda Shackleton *(Non-designated Limited Liabili)*
**Marketing:** Katie Butters *(Marketing Assistant)*
**HR:** Claire Richardson *(Human Resources Manager)*
**US SIC:** 8111 **UK SIC:** 83500
**Bankers:** Barclays Bank Plc (20-43-04)

| | 30-04-14 | 30-04-13 | 30-04-12 |
|---|---|---|---|
| TO | 8,754,973 | 6,999,676 | N/A |
| P/L | N/A | 2,172,777 | N/A |
| WC | 1,801,642 | 1,096,518 | 1,051,679 |
| Emp. | 164 | 142 | N/A |

DUNS 21-361-0829

## Ramsey Abbey School

The Abbey, Ramsey, Huntingdon, Cambridgeshire PE26 1DH
**Tel:** 01487-813285
**Web:** www.ramseyabbey.cambs.sch.uk
**Proprietorship**
**Line of Business:** General secondary education
**Proprietor:** W Birks
**US SIC:** 8211 **UK SIC:** 93200
**Employees:** 103

DUNS 22-858-4363

## Ramsey Bakery Ltd

Station Road, Ramsey, Douglas, Isle of Man IM8 2LF
**Tel:** 01624647300 **Fax:** 01624-816221
**Web:** www.ramseybakery.com
**Reg No:** 0007736M **Estd:** 1975 Private Limited Company
**Line of Business:** Manufacture of bread; manufacture of fresh pastry goods and cakes
**Issued Capital:** £20,000
**Principals:** J C Duncan *(Managing)*, R A Jelski
**Co. Secretary:** Ms Olga Duncan
**Branches:** Ramsey Bakery Ltd, 5 Circular Road, Isle Of Man, Isle Of Man IM1 1AF
**US SIC:** 2051 **UK SIC:** 41960
**Bankers:** Isle Of Man Bank (55-91-00)
**Employees:** 80

DUNS 21-608-8091

## Ramsey Grammar School

Lezayre Road, Ramsey, Douglas, Isle of Man IM8 2RG
**Web:** www.ramseygrammarschool.im
**Estd:** 2010
**Line of Business:** Schools (local authority)
**Proprietor:** D Trace
**US SIC:** 8211 **UK SIC:** 93200
**Employees:** 70

DUNS 73-517-8621

## Ramsey Hill Garage Ltd

Rectory Lane, Ramsey, Harwich, Essex CO12 5HA
**Web:** www.iessex.co.uk
**Reg No:** 4780737 **Estd:** 2003 Private Limited Company
**Line of Business:** Garage related services
**Issued Capital:** £100
**Director:** C J Taylor
**Co. Secretary:** Richard Wood
**US SIC:** 7539 **UK SIC:** 67100

| | 31-10-13 | 31-10-12 | 31-10-11 |
|---|---|---|---|
| TA | 167,899 | 186,089 | 206,771 |
| NW | 109,200 | 131,465 | 121,858 |
| WC | 93,724 | 116,943 | 108,582 |

DUNS 23-635-6739

## The Ramsey School

Colne Road, Halstead, Essex CO9 2HR
**Web:** www.ramsey.essex.sch.uk
**Estd:** 1999
**Line of Business:** Schools (local authority)
**Directors:** Mrs G Nichols, W J Woodward
**Responsibilities**
**Senior:** Mike Murray *(Head Teacher)*
**US SIC:** 8211 **UK SIC:** 93200
**Employees:** 100

DUNS 21-609-4172
## Ramsey Town Commissioners
Town Hall, Parliament Square, Ramsey, Douglas, Isle of Man IM8 1RT
**Tel:** 01624-810100
**Web:** www.ramsey.gov.im
**Estd:** 2010 Proprietorship
**Line of Business:** Central government
**Responsibilities**
**Senior:** Peter Whiteway *(Chief Executive Officer)*
**Branches:** Ramsey Town Commissioners, Lezayre Estate, Isle Of Man, Isle Of Man IM8 2NL
**US SIC:** 9121 **UK SIC:** 91110
**Employees:** 51

DUNS 23-784-5149
## Ramshorn Ltd
Industrial Estate, Sinfin Lane, Derby, Derbyshire DE24 9GL
**Tel:** 01332-761361
**Web:** www.skipunits.com
**Reg No:** 3777568 **Estd:** 1999 Private Limited Company
**Line of Business:** Manufacture of tanks, reservoirs and containers of metal
**Issued Capital:** £2,369,999
**Directors:** R Wake, R M Stamps, D Singer, M Hampson, A P Powis, A J Muirhead
**Co. Secretary:** Richard Stamps
**US SIC:** 3443 **UK SIC:** 32051
**Auditors:** Smith Cooper

| | 31-05-14 | 31-05-13 | 31-05-12 |
|---|---|---|---|
| TO | 8,439,190 | 7,243,645 | 10,367,115 |
| P/L | 162,815 | (300,392) | (4,995) |
| NW | 2,002,209 | 1,804,218 | 1,904,517 |
| WC | 536,761 | 323,313 | 232,782 |
| Emp. | 71 | 78 | 86 |

DUNS 21-552-6380
## Ramside Golf Club
Carrville, Durham, Durham, County Durham DH1 1TD
**Tel:** 0191-386-9514
**Web:** www.ramsidehallhotel.co.uk
**Estd:** 1995 Partnership
**Line of Business:** Other sporting activities not elsewhere classified
**Partner:** R Smith
**Responsibilities**
**Senior:** Helen Roseberry *(Manager)*
**Operations:** Jonny Mould *(Golf Sales & Operations Manage)*
**US SIC:** 7999 **UK SIC:** 97913
**Employees:** 50

DUNS 21-006-8111
## Ramside Holdings Ltd
Carrville, Durham, County Durham DH1 1TD
**Tel:** 01913865282
**Web:** www.ramsidehallhotel.co.uk
**Reg No:** 6311789 **Estd:** 2007 Private Limited Company
**Line of Business:** Hotels
**Issued Capital:** £5,500
**Directors:** Mrs M E Adamson, J R Adamson
**Co. Secretary:** David Farrow
**US SIC:** 7011 **UK SIC:** 66500

| | 30-11-13 | 30-11-12 | 30-11-11 |
|---|---|---|---|
| TO | 17,320,633 | 15,979,877 | 15,937,052 |
| P/L | 2,999,488 | 759,192 | 614,323 |
| NW | 14,279,949 | 11,574,333 | 11,028,308 |
| WC | 276,602 | (820,743) | 899,593 |
| Emp. | 413 | 418 | 611 |

DUNS 50-147-2872
## Ranc Care Homes Ltd
**(Subsidiary of:** Ranc Holdings Ltd)
King George Place, Ilford, Essex IG2 7HU
**Tel:** 020-8554-5600 **Fax:** 020-8554-5944
**Web:** www.ranccare.co.uk
**Reg No:** 2325401 **Estd:** 1988 Private Limited Company
**Line of Business:** Residential care establishments
**Trading Style:** R C H
**Issued Capital:** £105,000
**Director:** R S Rai
**Co. Secretary:** Aneet Rai
**Responsibilities**
**Senior:** Rob Rai *(Manager)*
**Branches:** Ranc Care Homes Ltd, Hook Green Road, Gravesend, Kent DA13 9NQ
**US SIC:** 8321 **UK SIC:** 96111
**Auditors:** Haines Watts
**Bankers:** Barclays Bank Plc (20-77-67)

| | 31-03-14 | 31-03-13 | 31-03-12 |
|---|---|---|---|
| TO | 22,337,505 | 21,773,697 | 21,221,927 |
| P/L | 4,858,569 | 4,567,678 | 5,169,675 |
| NW | 51,115,555 | 47,305,730 | 43,760,854 |
| WC | 4,411,611 | 2,587,565 | 24,421 |
| Emp. | 786 | 819 | 559 |

DUNS 34-581-3547
## Rand Europe Community Interest Co
Westbrook Centre, Milton Road, Cambridge, Cambridgeshire CB4 1YG
**Tel:** 01223-353329
**Web:** www.rand.org
**Reg No:** 2728021 **Estd:** 1992 Private Limited Company
**Line of Business:** Research and experimental development on social sciences and humanities
**Export Sales:** £3,299,824
**Issued Capital:** £2
**Directors:** Dr J K Rubin, D Howarth, H J Pung, M Gowers, C P Ries, R Fallon, M D Rich, Professor F P Kelly
**Co. Secretary:** Mark Gowers
**Responsibilities**
**Senior:** Ian Mcewan *(Company Director)*
**US SIC:** 8922 **UK SIC:** 94000
**Auditors:** PricewaterhouseCoopers LLP
**Bankers:** National Westminster Bank Plc (52-10-46)

| | 30-09-13 | 30-09-12 | 30-09-11 |
|---|---|---|---|
| TO | 7,224,510 | 7,708,400 | 6,521,847 |
| P/L | (163,560) | (38,964) | (210,420) |
| NW | (514,331) | (350,771) | (311,807) |
| WC | 632,453 | 784,671 | 907,937 |
| Emp. | 89 | 76 | 70 |

DUNS 21-908-0835 **Imp-Exp**
## R.& J.M.Place Ltd
International Farm Camp, Church Road, Tunstead, Norwich, Norfolk NR12 8RQ
**Web:** www.placeuk.com
**Reg No:** 0537599 **VAT No:** 104951682
**Estd:** 1954 Private Limited Company
**Line of Business:** Management activities of other non-financial holding companies not elsewhere classified
**Issued Capital:** £18,001
**Principals:** J M Place *(Managing)*, T M Place *(Financial)*, Mrs C A Place, Mrs S A Place
**Co. Secretary:** James Starling
**Responsibilities**
**Marketing:** Chris Oaten *(Sales & Marketing Manager)*
**Sales:** Chris Oaten *(Sales & Marketing Manager)*
**HR:** Andy Shepherdson *(Operations Manager)*
**Health & Safety:** Joanne Chambers *(Health & Safety Advisor)*
**Facilities:** Marc Chambers *(Engineer)*
**Purchasing:** Andy Boud *(Purchasing Manager)*, Rachel Long *(Purchasing Manager)*
**Engineering:** Marc Chambers *(Engineer)*
**US SIC:** 6711, 7399, 5148
**UK SIC:** 83962, 83954, 61700
**Auditors:** Larking Gowen
**Bankers:** Barclays Bank Plc (20-99-21)

| | 31-01-14 | 31-01-13 | 31-01-12 |
|---|---|---|---|
| TO | 14,607,848 | 12,764,528 | 12,889,148 |
| P/L | 2,244,604 | 1,655,706 | 1,761,699 |
| NW | 9,582,422 | 9,375,117 | 8,130,690 |
| WC | 6,658,737 | 7,270,378 | 6,139,828 |
| Emp. | 371 | 334 | 312 |

DUNS 34-920-6771
## Randa Uk Ltd
**(Subsidiary of:** Randa Accessories Leather Goods Llc)
1 Red Place, London W1K 6PL
**Tel:** 01592-771777 **Fax:** 01592-631717
**Web:** www.randa.net
**Reg No:** 2835344 **Estd:** 1993 Private Limited Company
**Line of Business:** Manufacture of other wearing apparel and accessories not elsewhere classified
**Trading Style:** Woodstock Neckwear Ltd
**Issued Capital:** £2
**Director:** J O Spiegel
**Co. Secretary:** Purple Venture Secretaries Limit
**Responsibilities**
**Admin:** Shelly Brazier *(manager)*
**US SIC:** 2389, 5021, 3161
**UK SIC:** 45393, 61500, 44201
**Auditors:** Gerald Edelman
**Bankers:** The Royal Bank Of Scotland Plc (83-22-37)

| | 31-12-13 | 31-12-12 | 31-12-11 |
|---|---|---|---|
| TO | 8,800,345 | 7,185,152 | 3,884,483 |
| P/L | 531,260 | 318,758 | 218,680 |
| NW | 1,759,893 | 1,312,746 | 1,696,394 |
| WC | 1,705,139 | 1,237,651 | 1,602,393 |

DUNS 22-797-1645
## Randall & Payne
Chargrove House, Main Road, Shurdington, Cheltenham, Gloucestershire GL51 4GA
**Web:** www.randall-payne.co.uk
**VAT No:** 274232469 **Estd:** 1988 Partnership
**Line of Business:** Accounting activities
**Partners:** T Watkins, R Bailey, I Selwood, M A Anthony, F J Baker
**Branches:** Randall & Payne, 23 High St, Melksham, Wiltshire SN12 6JY
**US SIC:** 8931, 6211
**UK SIC:** 83600, 83100
**Bankers:** Lloyds TSB Bank plc (30-98-29)
**Employees:** 50

DUNS 23-661-4595
## Randall & Walsh Associates Ltd
339 York Town Road, Sandhurst, Berkshire GU47 0PX
**Tel:** 0845-1668491 **Fax:** 08451668492
**Web:** www.raw-group.com
**Reg No:** 3656434 **Estd:** 1998 Private Limited Company
**Line of Business:** Wholesale of other intermediate products
**Trading Style:** Raw Group
**Issued Capital:** £4,190
**Directors:** J Stainton, J C Randall
**Co. Secretary:** Peter Walsh
**Responsibilities**
**Operations:** Neil Stothert *(Operations Director)*
**Branches:** Randall & Walsh Associates Ltd, Claremont Ho, Church St, Malvern, Worcestershire WR14 2AJ
**US SIC:** 7399 **UK SIC:** 83954
**Auditors:** Cowgill Holloway LLP
**Bankers:** National Westminster Bank Plc (01-30-99)

| | 30-06-13 | 30-06-12 | 30-06-11 |
|---|---|---|---|
| TO | 9,531,582 | 9,686,342 | 9,567,769 |
| P/L | 195,295 | 579,532 | 359,584 |
| NW | 2,765,496 | 2,500,193 | 1,687,206 |
| WC | 2,157,941 | 1,545,548 | 1,516,884 |
| Emp. | 96 | 88 | 83 |

DUNS 49-043-8694 **Exp**
## Randall Parker Food Group Ltd
The Old Rectory, Banbury Lane, Cold Higham, Towcester, Northamptonshire NN12 8LR
**Web:** www.wsdepots.com
**Reg No:** 3074722 **Estd:** 1995 Private Limited Company
**Line of Business:** Wholesale of meat and meat products
**Export Sales:** £18,490,000
**Trading Style:** Blue Water Antigua, Weddel Swift Distributors
**Issued Capital:** £249,823
**Director:** R L Randall
**Co. Secretary:** David Brady
**Branches:** Randall Parker Food Group Ltd, Hickman Avenue, Wolverhampton, West Midlands WV1 2UA
**US SIC:** 8999, 5147
**UK SIC:** 83954, 61700
**Auditors:** PricewaterhouseCoopers LLP

| | 30-09-13 | 30-09-12 | 30-09-11 |
|---|---|---|---|
| TO | 184,224,000 | 291,899,000 | 274,842,000 |
| P/L | 1,381,000 | 1,501,000 | 1,698,000 |
| NW | 6,540,000 | 10,971,000 | 11,128,000 |
| WC | (6,551,000) | (6,950,000) | (6,479,000) |
| Emp. | 478 | 782 | 727 |

DUNS 64-080-3714
## Randalls (Holdings) Ltd
Monmouth House, Park Road, Abergavenny, Gwent NP7 5TT
**Tel:** 01873851656
**Reg No:** 3475627 **Estd:** 1997 Private Limited Company
**Line of Business:** Secretarial and translation activities
**Issued Capital:** £200
**Directors:** M Randall, Mrs M J Wood, R G Hardwick
**Co. Secretary:** Ms Cherie Randall
**US SIC:** 7339 **UK SIC:** 83954
**Bankers:** HSBC Bank plc (40-08-04)

| | 31-03-14 | 31-03-13 | 31-03-12 |
|---|---|---|---|
| TO | 15,934,232 | 14,373,993 | 15,272,388 |
| P/L | 617,391 | 153,513 | 512,236 |
| NW | 1,289,533 | 1,008,066 | 1,022,110 |
| WC | 314,396 | 76,946 | (10,389) |
| Emp. | 173 | 152 | 161 |

DUNS 21-743-4406 **Imp**
## Randalls Vautier Ltd
Po Box 43, Jersey, Channel Islands JE4 9NB
**Tel:** 01534836700 **Fax:** 01534-836701
**Web:** www.randallsjersey.com
**Reg No:** 0016595J **Estd:** 1823 Private Limited Company
**Line of Business:** Public house operator with 30 sites
**Principals:** Daresbury *(Chairman)*, D Le Quesne *(Managing)*, D Edwards *(Financial)*, H P Director, A Whitehead, R Denton, H Le Roux
**Responsibilities**
**Sales:** Andy Michalski *(Sales Manager)*
**IT:** Owen Carroll *(Computer Manager)*
**HR:** Gavin Reid *(Area Manager)*
**Health & Safety:** Adrian Follain *(Transport Manager)*
**Purchasing:** Andy Michalski *(Sales Manager)*
**Fleet:** Adrian Follain *(Transport Manager)*
**Branches:** Randalls Vautier Ltd, La Marquanderie Hill, St Brelade, Jersey, Channel Islands JE3 8EP
**US SIC:** 2084 **UK SIC:** 42611
**Bankers:** National Westminster Bank Plc (60-12-03)
**Employees:** 200

DUNS 21-746-4297
## R&B South East Ltd
Unit 7 Henwood Industrial Estate, Ashford, Kent TN24 8DH
**Tel:** 01233647019
**Reg No:** 7782012 **Estd:** 2011 Private Limited Company
**Line of Business:** Insurance - household
**Issued Capital:** £200
**Directors:** R Winstanley, R T Burgess
**US SIC:** 6711 **UK SIC:** 83962

| | 30-06-13 | 30-06-12 |
|---|---|---|
| TA | 122,112 | 62,162 |
| NW | 68,794 | 6,200 |
| WC | 68,594 | 6,000 |

DUNS 73-278-5220
## R&D Cleaning Services Ltd
Ashtenne Business Centre, Oxleasow Road, Redditch, Worcestershire B98 0RE
**Tel:** 01527830454
**Web:** www.rdcleaning.co.uk
**Reg No:** 4552235 **Estd:** 2008 Private Limited Company
**Line of Business:** Commercial premises cleaning
**Issued Capital:** £100
**Director:** R D White
**Co. Secretary:** Ms Diane White
**US SIC:** 7349 **UK SIC:** 92300
**Auditors:** Clive Shedd & Co

| | 31-10-13 | 31-10-12 | 31-10-11 |
|---|---|---|---|
| TA | 115,166 | 106,603 | 97,789 |
| NW | 13,488 | 259 | (821) |
| WC | (11,222) | (10,781) | (11,233) |

DUNS 21-791-2064
## Randells Peugeot
Cobridge Road, Stoke-On-Trent, Staffordshire ST1 5LG
**Tel:** 01782286333
**Web:** www.greenhouse.co.uk
**Estd:** 2011 Proprietorship
**Line of Business:** Garage related services
**Proprietor:** P Wade
**US SIC:** 5511 **UK SIC:** 65100
**Employees:** 61

DUNS 22-526-0553
## R&G
Lucas Green Nurseries, Lucas Green, West End, Woking, Surrey GU24 9LY
**Web:** www.rgherbs.com
**VAT No:** 212126031 **Estd:** 1963 Partnership
**Line of Business:** Herb growers
**Partners:** Ms J Prestwich, M Prestwich, W Prestwich
**Responsibilities**
**Finance:** Anita Blanks *(Accounts Manager)*
**IT:** Anita Blanks *(Accounts Manager)*
**HR:** Len Keyworth *(Human Resources Manager)*
**Health & Safety:** Len Keyworth *(Human Resources Manager)*
**US SIC:** 0179 **UK SIC:** 01002
**Bankers:** Lloyds TSB Bank plc (77-49-08)
**Employees:** 58

DUNS 21-902-5889
## Randles (Garages) Ltd
**(Subsidiary of:** Randles Ltd)
Cobridge Road, Stoke-On-Trent, Staffordshire ST1 5JQ
**Tel:** 01782917917
**Web:** www.randles.co.uk
**Reg No:** 0513858 **VAT No:** 279238323
**Estd:** 2012 Private Limited Company
**Line of Business:** Car dealers (new & used)
**Trading Style:** Randles (Suzuki)
**Issued Capital:** £2,942
**Directors:** N P Wood, R S Teatum, S Foweather
**Responsibilities**
**Senior:** Paul Lamare *(Director)*, Benjamin Perkin *(Director)*, David Willott *(Managing Director)*
**Marketing:** David Willott *(Managing Director)*
**Sales:** Dave Woolett *(Director Of Sales)*
**Health & Safety:** Kevin Brookes *(Health & Safety Officer)*
**Purchasing:** Claire Wade *(Administration Officer)*
**Branches:** Randles (Garages) Ltd, Deansgate Garage, Higherland, Newcastle, Staffordshire ST5 2HN
**US SIC:** 5511, 7539
**UK SIC:** 65100, 67100
**Auditors:** Baker Tilly UK Audit LLP

**Bankers:** The Royal Bank Of Scotland Plc (16-20-35)

| | 30-09-13 | 30-09-12 | 30-09-11 |
|---|---|---|---|
| TO | 30,631,067 | 31,257,523 | 32,846,233 |
| P/L | 230,533 | 127,648 | 242,636 |
| NW | 1,399,139 | 1,222,083 | 1,122,588 |
| WC | (199,826) | 112,027 | 293,872 |
| Emp. | 77 | 78 | 79 |

DUNS 39-969-5469

## Randolph Hill Nursing Homes Group Ltd

31 Dunedin Street, Edinburgh, Midlothian EH7 4JG
**Web:** www.randolphhill.com
**Reg No:** 0111827SC **Estd:** 1986 Private Limited Company
**Line of Business:** Medical nursing home activities
**Trading Style:** Randolph Hill Nursing Home
**Issued Capital:** £1,000,000
**Director:** Ms I H Neville
**Co. Secretary:** Peter Mccormick
**Responsibilities**
**Senior:** Carol Campbell *(Office Manager)*
**Admin:** Carol Campbell *(Office Manager)*
**US SIC:** 7399, 8091
**UK SIC:** 83954, 95200
**Auditors:** McFadden Associates Ltd
**Bankers:** The Bank Of Ireland (30-14-58)

| | 31-03-14 | 31-03-13 | 31-03-12 |
|---|---|---|---|
| TO | 12,345,494 | 11,847,158 | 10,951,922 |
| P/L | 1,350,386 | 1,207,194 | 808,801 |
| NW | 3,280,075 | 2,448,900 | (54,069) |
| WC | (1,212,252) | (1,697,867) | (1,984,334) |
| Emp. | 502 | 507 | 493 |

DUNS 21-605-3770

## Randolph Hotel

Beaumont Street, Oxford, Oxfordshire OX1 2LN
**Tel:** 01865256400
**Estd:** 2011
**Line of Business:** Other tourist assistance activities not elsewhere classified
**US SIC:** 7999 **UK SIC:** 97913
**Employees:** 56

DUNS 21-811-5472

## Randolph Wemyss Memorial Hospital

Wellesley Road, Buckhaven, Leven, Fife KY8 1HU
**Tel:** 01592712427
**Estd:** 2002
**Line of Business:** Hospitals
**Responsibilities**
**Senior:** Heather Fernie *(Manager)*
**US SIC:** 8062 **UK SIC:** 95100
**Employees:** 150

DUNS 21-197-7749 **Exp**

## The Random House Group Ltd

**(Subsidiary of:** Bertelsmann Uk Ltd)
20 Vauxhall Bridge Road, London SW1V 2SA
**Tel:** 020-7840-8400
**Web:** www.careersatrandom.co.uk
**Reg No:** 0954009 **Estd:** 1969 Private Limited Company
**Line of Business:** Book publishers
**Export Markets:** Worldwide
**Issued Capital:** £81,956,072
**Directors:** T D Weldon, M W Gardiner, B J Davies, M F Dohle
**Co. Secretary:** Mrs Helena Peacock
**Branches:** The Random House Group Ltd, St Lukes Close, Colchester, Essex CO4 0LZ
**US SIC:** 2731 **UK SIC:** 47532
**Auditors:** KPMG LLP
**Bankers:** Lloyds TSB Bank plc (30-00-02)

| | 31-12-13 | 31-12-12 | 31-12-11 |
|---|---|---|---|
| TO | 238,921,091 | 284,882,434 | 227,025,027 |
| P/L | 45,348,793 | 56,121,148 | 36,585,022 |
| NW | 194,592,918 | 111,738,242 | 111,325,449 |
| WC | (39,693,446) | 54,930,064 | 51,109,001 |
| Emp. | 688 | 659 | 633 |

DUNS 21-861-0724

## Randox Holdings Ltd

Ardmore 55 Diamond Road, Crumlin, Co Antrim BT29 4QY
**Tel:** 02894422413
**Reg No:** 0614690NI **Estd:** 2012 Private Limited Company
**Line of Business:** Dental technicians
**Issued Capital:** £1
**Directors:** R P Kelly, Dr S P Fitzgerald
**US SIC:** 2899 **UK SIC:** 25670

| | 31-12-13 | 31-12-12 |
|---|---|---|
| TO | 90,929,000 | 72,213,000 |
| P/L | 12,923,000 | 2,501,000 |
| NW | 24,054,000 | 15,006,000 |
| WC | 14,675,000 | 20,147,000 |
| Emp. | 989 | 905 |

DUNS 52-037-1311

## Randstad Education Ltd

**(Subsidiary of:** Randstad Luxembourg North America Sarl)
1st Floor Imperial Court, Laporte Way, Luton, Bedfordshire LU4 8SB
**Tel:** 01582811600
**Web:** www.randstad.co.uk
**Reg No:** 3403530 **Estd:** 1997 Private Limited Company
**Line of Business:** Employment and recruitment companies and consultants
**Issued Capital:** £50,000
**Directors:** J C Gietelink, M J Bull
**Responsibilities**
**Senior:** Lisa Headford *(Area Manager)*
**Branches:** Randstad Education Ltd, Randstad Education, Median House, Warrington, Cheshire WA1 1EY
**US SIC:** 6711 **UK SIC:** 83962
**Auditors:** PricewaterhouseCoopers LLP

| | 31-12-13 | 31-12-12 | 31-12-11 |
|---|---|---|---|
| TO | 51,098,000 | 43,680,000 | 45,750,000 |
| P/L | 4,287,000 | 4,131,000 | 3,686,000 |
| NW | 43,755,000 | 39,381,000 | 35,372,000 |
| WC | 43,767,000 | 39,453,000 | 35,423,000 |
| Emp. | 158 | 136 | 188 |

DUNS 50-379-9819

## Randstad Employment Bureau Ltd

**(Subsidiary of:** Randstad Luxembourg North America Sarl)
Regent Court, Laporte Way, Luton, Bedfordshire LU4 8SB
**Tel:** 01582544100
**Web:** www.randstad.co.uk
**Reg No:** 2389033 **VAT No:** 535564042
**Estd:** 1989 Private Limited Company
**Line of Business:** Employment and recruitment companies and consultants
**Issued Capital:** £3,810,000
**Directors:** M J Bull, J C Gietelink
**Responsibilities**
**Senior:** Lisa Gainsford *(Manager)*, Patrick Maloney *(Director For Education)*, Colin Reader *(Manager)*
**Branches:** Randstad Employment Bureau Ltd, Walcot Street, Bath, Avon BA1 5BJ
**US SIC:** 7361 **UK SIC:** 83954
**Auditors:** PricewaterhouseCoopers LLP
**Bankers:** Barclays Bank Plc (20-84-58)

| | 31-12-13 | 31-12-12 | 31-12-11 |
|---|---|---|---|
| TO | 196,739,000 | 232,406,000 | 289,343,000 |
| P/L | 57,000 | (6,563,000) | 4,400,000 |
| NW | (20,467,000) | (19,901,000) | (13,905,000) |
| WC | (31,414,000) | (33,170,000) | (28,099,000) |
| Emp. | 221 | 457 | 608 |

DUNS 21-735-4879

## Ranelagh Church of England School

Ranelagh Drive, Bracknell, Berkshire RG12 9DA
**Tel:** 01344421233
**Web:** www.ranelagh.bracknell-forest.sch.uk
**Reg No:** 7698406 **Estd:** 2011 Private Company Limited By Guarantee
**Line of Business:** Schools (local authority)
**Directors:** Mrs A Atkins, G G Joyner, M A Williams, M E Harris, Ms L V Hodkinson, R D Ireson, Mrs A C Mclean, Ms M J Lansley
**Responsibilities**
**Senior:** Mark Amos *(Director)*, Christopher Barrows Mbe *(Director)*, Jean Bettison *(Director)*, Michael Bovis *(Director)*, Kate Dossett *(Director)*, Andrew Felton *(Director)*, Patricia Harrop *(Director)*, David Tait *(Director)*, Harold Uffindell *(Director)*
**Finance:** Trisha Harrop *(Bursar)*
**US SIC:** 8211 **UK SIC:** 93200

| | 31-08-14 | 31-08-13 | 31-08-12 |
|---|---|---|---|
| TO | 6,095,220 | 5,725,361 | 19,590,575 |
| P/L | (394,858) | (536,585) | 13,576,093 |
| NW | 11,745,650 | 12,272,508 | 12,879,093 |
| WC | 377,333 | 435,556 | 693,567 |
| Emp. | 104 | 103 | 105 |

DUNS 21-580-4335

## Range

736 Sewall Highway, Coventry, West Midlands CV6 7JJ
**Tel:** 02476667309
**Web:** www.therange.co.uk
**Estd:** 2011 Proprietorship
**Line of Business:** Home improvement
**Proprietor:** J Noble
**US SIC:** 5399 **UK SIC:** 65600
**Employees:** 62

DUNS 21-620-9322

## The Range

Jockey Lane, Huntington, York, North Yorkshire YO32 9NE
**Tel:** 01904624326
**Web:** www.therange.co.uk
**Estd:** 2011
**Line of Business:** Departmental stores
**US SIC:** 5399 **UK SIC:** 65600
**Employees:** 200

DUNS 21-773-8585

## The Range Erdington

Unit A Ravenside Retail Park, Kingsbury Road, Erdington, Birmingham, West Midlands B24 9QB
**Tel:** 01213863269
**Web:** www.therange.co.uk
**Estd:** 2011
**Line of Business:** Departmental stores
**Responsibilities**
**Senior:** Mike Mittox *(Store Manager)*
**US SIC:** 5399 **UK SIC:** 65600
**Employees:** 100

DUNS 21-561-6894

## Range Home & Leisure

Avon Meads, St Philips Causeway, Bristol, Avon BS2 0SP
**Tel:** 0117-980-3883
**Web:** www.therange.co.uk
**Estd:** 2011 Proprietorship
**Line of Business:** Departmental stores
**Proprietor:** N Crossey
**US SIC:** 5399 **UK SIC:** 65600
**Employees:** 50

DUNS 21-391-0322

## The Range Home & Leisure

Northern Avenue, Northern Business Park, Andover, Hampshire SP10 4DU
**Tel:** 01264-369127
**Web:** www.therange.co.uk
**Estd:** 2006
**Line of Business:** Departmental stores
**Proprietor:** A Hardy
**Responsibilities**
**Senior:** Diane Brierley *(Store Manager)*
**US SIC:** 5399 **UK SIC:** 65600
**Employees:** 50

DUNS 21-812-1034

## The Range Home Leisure & Garden

Unit F Longwater Business Park, New Costessey, Norwich, Norfolk NR5 0JT
**Tel:** 01603742687
**Web:** www.therange.co.uk
**Estd:** 2012
**Line of Business:** Departmental stores
**Responsibilities**
**Senior:** Adam Newbold *(Manager)*
**US SIC:** 5399 **UK SIC:** 65600
**Employees:** 130

DUNS 21-708-8348

## The Range Superstore

230-234 Winchester Road, Shirley, Southampton, Hampshire SO16 6TL
**Tel:** 023-8077-5577
**Web:** www.therange.co.uk
**Estd:** 2003 Proprietorship
**Line of Business:** Departmental stores
**Proprietor:** C Dawson
**Responsibilities**
**Senior:** Shane Stewart *(Manager)*
**US SIC:** 5399 **UK SIC:** 65600
**Employees:** 20

DUNS 28-935-3153

## Ranger Industries Ltd

**(Subsidiary of:** Bpx Group Ltd)
124 Ross Walk, Leicester, Leicestershire LE4 5HA
**Tel:** 01162-999299
**Web:** www.rangercomputersystems.com
**Reg No:** 1550659 **Estd:** 2002 Private Limited Company
**Line of Business:** Computer systems and software (sales)
**Trading Style:** Ranger Computer Systems
**Issued Capital:** £100
**Principals:** W A Collins *(Managing)*, Mrs S M Collins, R W Collins, A G Collins
**Co. Secretary:** Roger Collins
**Responsibilities**
**Finance:** Diane Ryan *(Head of Accounts)*
**IT:** Adrian Davy *(Computer Manager)*
**US SIC:** 7379 **UK SIC:** 83940
**Auditors:** Thomas May & Co
**Bankers:** National Westminster Bank Plc (60-02-17)

| | 31-10-13 | 31-10-12 | 31-10-11 |
|---|---|---|---|
| TA | 402 | 402 | 401 |
| NW | (3,830) | (3,830) | (3,256) |
| WC | (3,830) | (3,830) | (3,256) |

DUNS 21-869-6023 **Imp**

## Rangers International Football Club Plc

Ibrox Stadium, 150 Edmiston Drive, Glasgow, Lanarkshire G51 2XD
**Tel:** 01415808500 **Fax:** 01415808580
**Web:** www.rangers.co.uk
**Reg No:** 0437060SC **Estd:** 2012 Public Limited Company
**Line of Business:** Other sporting activities not elsewhere classified
**Issued Capital:** £1
**Directors:** J Easdale, D Llambias, D Somers, B J Leach
**Co. Secretary:** Matthew Wood
**Responsibilities**
**Senior:** Mike Mcgill *(Non-Executive Director)*, Donald Muir *(Non-Executive Director)*
**US SIC:** 7999 **UK SIC:** 97913
**Auditors:** Deloitte LLP

| | 30-06-14 | 30-06-13 |
|---|---|---|
| TO | 25,230,000 | 19,107,000 |
| P/L | (8,024,000) | 1,258,000 |
| NW | 31,471,000 | 38,473,000 |
| WC | (7,155,000) | 1,391,000 |
| Emp. | 175 | 196 |

DUNS 49-426-1175 **Imp**

## The Rank Group Plc

Statesman House, Stafferton Way, Maidenhead, Berkshire SL6 1AY
**Tel:** 01628-504000
**Web:** www.rank.com
**Reg No:** 3140769 **Estd:** 1995 Public Limited Company
**Line of Business:** Representative office
**Export Sales:** £42,400,000
**Issued Capital:** £54,261,912
**Directors:** C A Jennings, H B Birch, Ms L S Wasmund, M I Burke, R F Kilmorey Pc, T J Scoble, O O'Donnell
**Co. Secretary:** Miss Frances Bingham
**Responsibilities**
**Senior:** Marc Cohen *(Associate Vice President)*, Ben Foster *(Manager)*, Bill Gannon *(Non-Executive Director)*, Graeme Hart *(Owner)*, Catherin Hickson *(Manager)*, Jorge Ibanez *(Manager)*, Glenda Mullany *(Board Member)*, Owen O' Donnell *(Director)*, Phil Urban *(Manager)*, Susan Waldock *(Human Resources Manager)*, Dan Waugh *(Director, Investor Relations)*
**Finance:** Paddy Gallagher *(Financial Director)*, Richard Playle *(Head of Finance)*
**Marketing:** Lesly Clifford *(?Head of Communications)*, Amy Culora *(Head of PR & Marcomms)*, Gary Dooley *(Development Director)*, Warren Tristram *(Head of Marketing)*
**Admin:** Karen Rush *(Secretary)*
**IT:** Stewart Cruickshank *(IT Director)*
**HR:** Gary Dooley *(Development Director)*, Meera Mehra *(Human Resources)*, Susan Waldock *(Human Resources Manager)*
**Health & Safety:** Brian Duffin *(Health & Safety Officer)*
**Facilities:** Christine Stanyon *(Facilities Manager)*
**Operations:** Enric Milan *(Operations Director)*, John Wiggins *(Senior Project Coordinator)*
**Purchasing:** Simonh Bishop *(Director of Acquisitions)*, Austen Bushrod *(Director, Purchasing)*
**Branches:** The Rank Group Plc, Excalibur Building, 77 Whitworth Street, Manchester M1 6EZ
**US SIC:** 7399 **UK SIC:** 83954
**Auditors:** Ernst & Young LLP

| | 30-06-14 | 30-06-13 | 30-06-12 |
|---|---|---|---|
| TO | 678,500,000 | 596,200,000 | 854,900,000 |
| P/L | 14,400,000 | 42,700,000 | 216,100,000 |
| NW | (147,900,000) | (150,600,000) | 74,300,000 |
| WC | (80,500,000) | (85,000,000) | (36,500,000) |
| Emp. | 10,909 | 9,642 | 9,262 |

DUNS 22-707-8466 **Exp**

## Rank Nemo (Dms) Ltd

**(Subsidiary of:** The Rank Group Plc)
Unit 11 Ealing Road Phoenix Park, Brentford, Middlesex TW8 9PL
**Tel:** 02087580519 **Fax:** 020-8232-7601
**Web:** www.benchmarxjoinery.co.uk
**Reg No:** 1534277 **Estd:** 1981 Private Limited Company
**Line of Business:** Kitchen planners and installers
**Export Markets:** Europe, U S A, Worldwide
**Trading Style:** Deluxe Media
**Issued Capital:** £16,000,000
**Directors:** C A Jennings, H B Birch
**Co. Secretary:**
The Rank Organisation Limited
**Responsibilities**
**Senior:** Adnan Godnal *(Manager)*, Daniel Reeves *(Branch Manager)*, Binnie Sandhu *(Branch Manager)*
**Branches:** Rank Nemo (Dms) Ltd, 6 Solar Way, Enfield, Middlesex EN3 7XY
**US SIC:** 7399 **UK SIC:** 83954

**Auditors:** PricewaterhouseCoopers LLP
**Bankers:** National Westminster Bank Plc (56-00-25)

| | 30-06-13 | 30-06-12 | 31-06-10 |
|---|---|---|---|
| TA | N/A | N/A | 130,000 |
| P/L | N/A | 70,000 | 202,000 |
| NW | (33,252,000) | (33,252,000) | (33,304,000) |
| WC | N/A | N/A | (33,304,000) |

DUNS 21-210-6038
## Rannoch Lodge Nursing Home
Rannoch Drive, Cumbernauld, Glasgow, Lanarkshire G67 4ES
**Tel:** 01236729273
**Web:** www.carechoice.co.uk
**Estd:** 1989 Partnership
**Line of Business:** Medical nursing home activities
**Trading Style:** Care Choice
**Partners:** S Green, Mrs I Green
**Responsibilities**
**Senior:** Audrey Johnston *(Matron)*
**Marketing:** Audrey Johnston *(Matron)*
**HR:** Audrey Johnston *(Matron)*
**Health & Safety:** Audrey Johnston *(Matron)*
**Facilities:** Audrey Johnston *(Matron)*
**US SIC:** 8051 **UK SIC:** 95100
**Employees:** 60

DUNS 21-722-6380
## Ranom Ltd
Old London Road, Wickford, Essex SS11 8UE
**Tel:** 01268561234
**Web:** www.thechichester.co.uk
**Reg No:** 0539575 **Estd:** 1954 Private Limited Company
**Line of Business:** Licensed restaurants
**Issued Capital:** £15,000
**Principals:** R F Harris *(Managing)*, T R Harris, R C Harris
**Co. Secretary:** Ms Anne Tyson
**US SIC:** 5812, 8999
**UK SIC:** 66110, 83954
**Auditors:** Culwick & Co

| | 31-12-13 | 31-12-12 | 31-12-11 |
|---|---|---|---|
| TA | 910,684 | 899,054 | 868,996 |
| NW | 725,859 | 678,831 | 654,562 |
| WC | 408,009 | 395,917 | 361,367 |

DUNS 29-225-5320 **Imp-Exp**
## Ransomes Jacobsen Ltd
**(Subsidiary of:** Textron Inc.)
West Road, Ransomes Industrial Estate, Ipswich, Suffolk IP3 9TT
**Tel:** 01473270000 **Fax:** 01473-276300
**Web:** www.ransomesjacobsen.com
**Reg No:** 1070731 **VAT No:** 103157907
**Estd:** 1789 Private Limited Company
**Line of Business:** Manufacturers of horticultural equipments
**Export Markets:** Worldwide
**Export Sales:** £38,020,000
**Issued Capital:** £21,500,100
**Directors:** D P Withers, A M Prickett
**Co. Secretary:** Eversecretary Limited
**Responsibilities**
**Senior:** Martin Cowgill *(Manager)*, Rupert Price *(Sales Director)*, Neil Yellop *(Despatch Manager)*
**Finance:** Richard Hall-Roberts *(Finance Director)*
**Sales:** Rupert Price *(Sales Director)*
**HR:** Jason King *(Training Manager)*
**Fleet:** Neil Yellop *(Despatch Manager)*
**Engineering:** Christain Clifford *(Engineering Manager)*
**Branches:** Ransomes Jacobsen Ltd, Unit 9, Oakney Wood Road, Selby, North Yorkshire YO8 8LZ
**US SIC:** 3523 **UK SIC:** 32113
**Auditors:** Ernst & Young LLP
**Bankers:** HSBC Bank plc (40-22-26)

| | 31-12-13 | 31-12-12 | 31-12-11 |
|---|---|---|---|
| TO | 68,047,000 | 69,562,000 | 63,133,000 |
| P/L | 1,121,000 | 1,523,000 | (114,000) |
| NW | 46,669,000 | 45,449,000 | 46,293,000 |
| WC | 28,361,000 | 27,217,000 | 28,127,000 |
| Emp. | 301 | 288 | 280 |

DUNS 21-595-4188
## Ranstad Care
107 Gray's Inn Road, London WC1X 8TZ
**Tel:** 02076111150
**Web:** www.reliancecare.com
**Estd:** 1981 Proprietorship
**Line of Business:** Labour recruitment and provision of personnel
**Proprietor:** R Smith
**US SIC:** 7361 **UK SIC:** 83954
**Employees:** 100

DUNS 21-226-3472
## Ranstead
Rutherford Road, Basingstoke, Hampshire RG24 8PD
**Tel:** 01256-364188
**Estd:** 2005 Proprietorship
**Line of Business:** Employment and recruitment companies and consultants
**Proprietor:** C Ndka
**US SIC:** 7361 **UK SIC:** 83954
**Employees:** 79

DUNS 73-890-2621
## Ranyard Charitable Trust
2b Brandram Road, London SE13 5EA
**Tel:** 02083181119
**Web:** www.ranyard.org
**Reg No:** 5144314 **Estd:** 2002 Private Company Limited By Guarantee
**Line of Business:** Nursing homes
**Directors:** R S Cunningham, N W Lines, Mrs M M Blake, Lady V W Stone Of Blackheath
**Co. Secretary:** Ms Elizabeth Warwick
**Responsibilities**
**Senior:** Elizabeth Jenkins *(Manager)*, Glenis Shaw *(Manager)*
**US SIC:** 8051 **UK SIC:** 95100
**Bankers:** HSBC Bank plc (40-18-30)

| | 31-03-14 | 31-03-13 | 31-03-12 |
|---|---|---|---|
| TO | 3,930,652 | 4,033,659 | 4,004,509 |
| P/L | 107,577 | 358,099 | 472,506 |
| NW | 1,781,011 | 1,670,776 | 1,299,260 |
| WC | 1,492,458 | 1,358,061 | 943,876 |
| Emp. | 145 | 141 | 132 |

DUNS 21-182-0589
## Raob Club & Institute
51 Wilton Street, Middlesbrough, Cleveland TS1 3QB
**Tel:** 01642860511
**Estd:** 1886
**Line of Business:** Licensed clubs
**Principals:** D Greenslade *(President)*, D Morgan
**Responsibilities**
**Senior:** John Corden *(Acting Secretary)*
**US SIC:** 5813 **UK SIC:** 66200
**Employees:** 30

DUNS 29-236-0773 **Imp-Exp**
## Rap Industries Ltd
Welbeck Way, Peterborough, Cambridgeshire PE2 7WH
**Tel:** 01733394941
**Web:** www.rapind.com
**Reg No:** 1225443 **VAT No:** 360009102
**Estd:** 1975 Private Limited Company
**Line of Business:** Manufacture of other electrical equipment not elsewhere classified
**Export Markets:** Netherlands
**Issued Capital:** £100
**Principals:** R Payn *(Managing)*, Ms C E Johnson, Mrs H A Payn
**Co. Secretary:** Roy Payn
**US SIC:** 2599 **UK SIC:** 46720
**Auditors:** BDO Stoy Hayward
**Bankers:** Barclays Bank Plc (20-67-37)

| | 31-10-13 | 31-10-12 | 31-10-11 |
|---|---|---|---|
| TA | 970,506 | 822,796 | 564,031 |
| NW | 611,127 | 432,888 | 297,297 |
| WC | 192,678 | 37,838 | (112,496) |

DUNS 21-772-7691
## Rape & Sexual Violence Project
Po Box 9558, Birmingham, West Midlands B4 7QE
**Tel:** 01216430301
**Web:** www.rsvporg.co.uk
**Estd:** 2011
**Line of Business:** Counselling & advice services
**Responsibilities**
**Senior:** Lisa Thompson *(Chief Executive)*
**US SIC:** 4899 **UK SIC:** 79020
**Employees:** 50

DUNS 21-880-3902
## Rape Crisis - South London Rasasc
Po Box 383, Croydon, Surrey CR9 2AW
**Web:** www.rasasc.org.uk
**Estd:** 2012
**Line of Business:** Telephone helpline services
**Responsibilities**
**Senior:** Yvonne Traynor *(Chief Executive)*
**US SIC:** 8321 **UK SIC:** 96111
**Employees:** 50

DUNS 71-872-5182
## Raphael Health Care Ltd
**(Subsidiary of:** Rhc Group (2012) Ltd)
Briar Hey, Mill Lane, Rainhill, Prescot, Merseyside L35 6NE
**Tel:** 01514307765
**Web:** www.raphaelhealthcare.org.uk
**Reg No:** 5255132 **Estd:** 2004 Private Limited Company
**Line of Business:** Other human health activities
**Issued Capital:** £10
**Directors:** A L Robinson, Mrs C J Thomson, J T Lamb
**Responsibilities**
**Senior:** Roderick Morris *(Financial Director)*
**Finance:** Roderick Morris *(Financial Director)*
**US SIC:** 8091 **UK SIC:** 95200
**Bankers:** The Bank Of Ireland (30-14-58)

| | 31-03-14 | 31-03-13 | 31-03-12 |
|---|---|---|---|
| TO | 8,164,817 | 7,885,063 | 7,624,333 |
| P/L | 1,625,836 | 992,227 | 193,768 |
| NW | 18,525,597 | 14,314,558 | 13,405,562 |
| WC | (600,536) | (813,979) | (1,247,451) |
| Emp. | 178 | 196 | 193 |

DUNS 22-630-4954
## The Raphael Medical Centre Ltd
Coldharbour Lane, Hildenborough, Tonbridge, Kent TN11 9LE
**Tel:** 01732-833924 **Fax:** 01732-838883
**Web:** www.raphaelmedicalcentre.co.uk
**Reg No:** 0568116 **Estd:** 1956 Private Limited Company
**Line of Business:** Other human health activities
**Issued Capital:** £435,000
**Managing Director:** G U Florschutz
**Co. Secretary:** Gerhard Florschutz
**Responsibilities**
**HR:** Ruth Langridge *(Personnel Coordinator)*
**Health & Safety:** Ruth Langridge *(Personnel Coordinator)*
**Branches:** The Raphael Medical Centre Ltd, Swanborough Dr, Brighton, East Sussex BN2 5PH
**US SIC:** 8091 **UK SIC:** 95200
**Auditors:** Wilkins Kennedy
**Bankers:** National Westminster Bank Plc (55-70-13)

| | 31-12-13 | 31-12-12 | 31-12-11 |
|---|---|---|---|
| TO | 10,247,227 | 8,576,024 | 7,488,295 |
| P/L | 368,830 | 32,889 | 81,864 |
| NW | 1,378,286 | 1,100,175 | 1,139,830 |
| WC | (1,174,777) | (8,703) | 6,409 |
| Emp. | 131 | 129 | 128 |

DUNS 22-601-4611 **Imp**
## Rapid Climate Control Ltd
**(Subsidiary of:** Rapid Climate Control Holdings Ltd)
Unit A Neptune Business Park, Dolphin Way, Purfleet, Essex RM19 1NZ
**Tel:** 02085984000 **Fax:** 02085038967
**Web:** www.rapidclimatecontrol.co.uk
**Reg No:** 1439934 **VAT No:** 918516804
**Estd:** 1979 Private Limited Company
**Line of Business:** Air conditioning equipment
**Issued Capital:** £20,000
**Directors:** N Payne, M J Payne
**Co. Secretary:** James Bellingham
**Branches:** Rapid Climate Control Ltd, Unit 8, Alston Road, Oldbury, West Midlands B69 2PP
**US SIC:** 3585, 5081
**UK SIC:** 32841, 61490
**Auditors:** McCabe Ford Williams
**Bankers:** Barclays Bank Plc (20-25-42)

| | 31-03-14 | 31-03-13 | 31-03-12 |
|---|---|---|---|
| TO | 9,144,347 | 8,163,108 | 7,135,442 |
| P/L | 314,725 | 66,862 | 389,126 |
| NW | 6,213,430 | 5,960,715 | 5,887,461 |
| WC | 5,511,887 | 5,009,469 | 4,836,428 |
| Emp. | 76 | 72 | 68 |

DUNS 22-631-8608 **Imp-Exp**
## Rapid Electronics Ltd
**(Subsidiary of:** Conrad Electronic Regensburg Gmbh & Co. Kg)
Severalls Hall, Severalls Lane, Colchester, Essex CO4 5JS
**Fax:** 01206-751188
**Web:** www.rapidonline.com
**Reg No:** 1509592 **VAT No:** 304175784
**Estd:** 1983 Private Limited Company
**Line of Business:** Manufacturers and distributors of electronic components
**Export Markets:** Worldwide
**Export Sales:** £1,053,246
**Trading Style:** Rapid
**Issued Capital:** £810,002
**Directors:** H P Ruban, J A Bell
**Responsibilities**
**Marketing:** Kelly Everett *(Marketing Manager)*
**Sales:** Ron McConnachie *(Office Manager)*
**Admin:** Ron McConnachie *(Office Manager)*
**HR:** Denise Bird *(Human Resources Manager)*
**Health & Safety:** Diane Farrow *(Finance Administrator)*
**US SIC:** 3679 **UK SIC:** 34542
**Auditors:** Baker Tilly UK Audit LLP
**Bankers:** HSBC Bank plc (40-18-51)

| | 31-12-13 | 31-10-12 | 31-12-11 |
|---|---|---|---|
| TO | 20,023,115 | 17,123,760 | 17,413,241 |
| P/L | 1,490,550 | 1,282,395 | 811,836 |
| NW | 5,854,513 | 4,715,609 | 3,790,652 |
| WC | 5,593,219 | 4,273,386 | 3,523,080 |
| Emp. | 133 | 138 | 142 |

DUNS 23-583-1463
## Rapid Frame Ltd
6 Landywood Enterprise Park, Holly Lane, Great Wyrley, Walsall, West Midlands WS6 6BD
**Tel:** 01922412333 **Fax:** 01922-412323
**Web:** www.rapidframe.co.uk
**Reg No:** 3580872 **Estd:** 1998 Private Limited Company
**Line of Business:** Manufacturers and suppliers of pvc based products
**Issued Capital:** £100
**Directors:** A D Young, Mrs C M Corcoran, M T Corcoran
**Co. Secretary:** Mrs Christie Corcoran
**Responsibilities**
**Finance:** Malcolm Owen *(Finance Director)*
**US SIC:** 3079, 5039
**UK SIC:** 48360, 61300
**Auditors:** Gravestock 7 Own Ltd

| | 30-11-13 | 30-11-12 | 30-11-11 |
|---|---|---|---|
| TA | 1,339,554 | 1,279,395 | 1,104,961 |
| NW | 343,976 | 194,177 | 117,066 |
| WC | 286,748 | 118,215 | 28,898 |

DUNS 29-665-9105 **Exp**
## Rapid Racking Ltd
**(Subsidiary of:** Manutan International)
Unit M3 Kemble Business Park, Cirencester, Gloucestershire GL7 6BQ
**Tel:** 01285686800 **Fax:** 01285686060
**Web:** www.rapidracking.com
**Reg No:** 1992143 **VAT No:** 728888959
**Estd:** 1986 Private Limited Company
**Line of Business:** Retail sale via mail order house
**Export Sales:** £340,529
**Issued Capital:** £679
**Directors:** P Brial, Ms B Auffrett, M Luddington, J Guichard
**Co. Secretary:** Pierre-Olivier Brial
**Responsibilities**
**Senior:** Yvonne Folliard *(Marketing Manager)*
**Health & Safety:** Andrew Moony *(Health & Safety Manager)*
**US SIC:** 5961, 5399
**UK SIC:** 65600
**Auditors:** PricewaterhouseCoopers LLP
**Bankers:** National Westminster Bank Plc (60-05-16)

| | 30-09-13 | 30-09-12 | 30-09-11 |
|---|---|---|---|
| TO | 17,314,232 | 17,866,059 | 16,955,607 |
| P/L | 1,292,089 | 2,020,933 | 1,723,153 |
| NW | 16,836,306 | 15,821,955 | 14,260,939 |
| WC | 16,526,579 | 15,400,312 | 13,916,221 |
| Emp. | 60 | 66 | 66 |

DUNS 77-746-2862
## Rapid Support Services Ltd
**(Subsidiary of:** Rss (Holdings) Ltd)
Rss House, Manchester M28 1NL
**Tel:** 01617908449 **Fax:** 01908225252
**Web:** www.rapidsupport.co.uk
**Reg No:** 3012870 **Estd:** 1995 Private Limited Company
**Line of Business:** Fire and associated damage restoration services
**Issued Capital:** £10,000
**Director:** A R Crompton
**Co. Secretary:** Ms Valerie Brown
**Branches:** Rapid Support Services Ltd, 39 Cambridge Street, Milton Keynes, Buckinghamshire MK12 5AE
**US SIC:** 1799, 1721
**UK SIC:** 50000, 50400
**Auditors:** Cowgill Holloway
**Bankers:** National Westminster Bank Plc (01-03-21)

| | 31-03-14 | 31-03-13 | 31-03-12 |
|---|---|---|---|
| TA | 1,638,781 | 1,520,221 | 1,283,866 |
| NW | 501,049 | 445,199 | 421,642 |
| WC | 416,729 | 349,155 | 356,614 |

DUNS 50-496-1012
## Rapidgrid Ltd
**(Subsidiary of:** Rapidgrid Holdings Ltd)
Y Graig, Aberdare, Mid Glamorgan CF44 9UP
**Tel:** 01685819280 **Fax:** 01685810102
**Web:** www.rapidgrid.co.uk
**Reg No:** 2464305 **VAT No:** 535227554
**Estd:** 2006 Private Limited Company
**Line of Business:** Groundwork contractors
**Issued Capital:** £200
**Director:** C Hughes
**Co. Secretary:** Grant Hughes
**Branches:** Rapidgrid Ltd, Ty Bruce Tybruce Rd, Aberdare, Mid Glamorgan CF44 9TD
**US SIC:** 1622 **UK SIC:** 50200
**Auditors:** Watts Gregory LLP
**Bankers:** National Westminster Bank Plc (52-21-26)

| | 30-04-14 | 30-04-13 | 30-04-12 |
|---|---|---|---|
| TO | 14,026,382 | 14,464,072 | 12,988,725 |
| P/L | 136,602 | 22,217 | 88,556 |
| NW | 839,214 | 737,661 | 695,948 |
| WC | 710,335 | 562,916 | 560,073 |
| Emp. | 105 | 116 | 99 |

DUNS 34-698-9846 **Imp**

## Rapidrop Global Ltd

Rutland Business Park, Newark Road, Peterborough, Cambridgeshire PE4 5SW
**Tel:** 01733-847-510 **Fax:** 01733-553-958
**Web:** www.rapidrop.com
**Reg No:** 5503278 **Estd:** 2005 Private Limited Company
**Line of Business:** Production and sale of fire fighting equipment
**Export Sales:** £6,203,999
**Issued Capital:** £30,100
**Directors:** M P Willimer, M Smith, S Kaushik, D P Gill, Ms T J Vernon, M A Curran, K S Plater
**US SIC:** 3559 **UK SIC:** 32863
**Auditors:** Price Bailey LLP

| | 31-12-13 | 31-12-12 | 31-12-11 |
|---|---|---|---|
| TO | 16,458,336 | 16,288,547 | 14,868,500 |
| P/L | 255,808 | 301,541 | 414,685 |
| NW | 3,251,473 | 3,013,407 | 2,772,938 |
| WC | 2,272,413 | 2,264,313 | 2,400,801 |
| Emp. | 65 | 60 | 55 |

DUNS 23-518-7593

## Rapier Design Group Ltd

4-6 Crane Mead Crane Mead Business Park, Ware, Hertfordshire SG12 9PW
**Tel:** 01920885100 **Fax:** 0870-900-7783
**Web:** www.rapiergroup.com
**Reg No:** 3517840 **Estd:** 2001 Private Limited Company
**Line of Business:** Exhibition services
**Trading Style:** Rapier Group
**Issued Capital:** £8,871
**Directors:** C Whittaker, P S Denny
**Co. Secretary:** Ms Helen Seaman
**Responsibilities**
**Marketing:** Stephanie Bloomfield *(Marketing Manager)*
**US SIC:** 6711, 7399
**UK SIC:** 83962, 83954
**Auditors:** Moore Stephens
**Bankers:** Coutts & Co (18-00-02)

| | 31-12-13 | 31-12-12 | 31-12-11 |
|---|---|---|---|
| TO | 10,409,699 | 19,091,706 | 20,595,384 |
| P/L | 540,446 | 248,796 | 552,627 |
| NW | 766,538 | 922,129 | 889,953 |
| WC | 33,120 | (8,273) | 9,140 |
| Emp. | 53 | 74 | 82 |

DUNS 50-352-2070

## Rapier Employment Ltd

Tannery Court, Stratton Way, Abingdon, Oxfordshire OX14 5TS
**Web:** www.rapieremployment.co.uk
**Reg No:** 2374214 **Estd:** 1989 Private Limited Company
**Line of Business:** Employment and recruitment companies and consultants
**Issued Capital:** £100
**Directors:** F H Townson, W Lourens
**Responsibilities**
**Senior:** Kellie Pether *(Manager)*, Stanley Street *(Manager)*
**Branches:** Rapier Employment Ltd, Tannery Court, Stratton Way, Abingdon, Oxfordshire OX14 5TS
**US SIC:** 7361 **UK SIC:** 83954
**Auditors:** Sowerbutts & Co Ltd
**Bankers:** Bank Of Scotland (12-18-05)

| | 30-06-13 | 30-06-12 | 30-06-11 |
|---|---|---|---|
| TO | 25,086,662 | 19,286,852 | 19,747,132 |
| P/L | 43,683 | 204,352 | 317,076 |
| NW | 602,238 | 864,249 | 867,268 |
| WC | 287,822 | 528,805 | 650,227 |
| Emp. | 47 | 929 | 1,033 |

DUNS 23-276-2294

## Rapier Security Services

Westford, Ramsden Park Road, Ramsden Bellhouse, Billericay, Essex CM11 1NR
**Web:** www.rapiersecurityltd.co.uk
**VAT No:** 546146737 **Estd:** 1990 Partnership
**Line of Business:** Security activities
**Partners:** P Hayward, J G Mair
**US SIC:** 7393 **UK SIC:** 83954
**Bankers:** National Westminster Bank Plc (60-09-43)
**Employees:** 50

DUNS 34-618-0375 **Imp**

## Rapiscan Systems Ltd

X Ray House, 8 Bonehurst Road, Redhill, Surrey RH1 5GG
**Tel:** 08707 774301 **Fax:** 08707 774302
**Web:** www.rapiscansystems.com
**Reg No:** 2755398 **VAT No:** 602558163
**Estd:** 1993 Private Limited Company
**Line of Business:** Installation of electrical wiring and fittings
**Export Sales:** £93,900,000
**Issued Capital:** £11,591,117
**Principals:** A Mehra *(Financial)*, T S Ghattaure, F Baldwin, P A Diamond, P C Williamson, M J Stas
**Co. Secretary:** Gravitas Company Secretarial Ser
**Responsibilities**
**Health & Safety:** Jola Mieczkowska *(Quality Assurance Manager)*
**Operations:** Jola Mieczkowska *(Quality Assurance Manager)*
**Branches:** Rapiscan Systems Ltd, Brook Indstl Est, Bullsbrook Rd, Hayes, Middlesex UB4 0JZ
**US SIC:** 7399 **UK SIC:** 83954
**Auditors:** Mazars LLP
**Bankers:** HSBC Bank plc (40-18-22)

| | 30-06-13 | 30-06-12 | 30-06-11 |
|---|---|---|---|
| TO | 118,492,000 | 81,561,000 | 61,320,000 |
| P/L | 22,057,000 | 8,473,000 | 3,793,000 |
| NW | 57,099,000 | 42,317,000 | 24,010,000 |
| WC | 56,383,000 | 40,922,000 | 22,827,000 |
| Emp. | 222 | 231 | 186 |

DUNS 39-712-3290

## Rapleys Consultants Ltd

Caledonian Exchange, 19a Canning Street, Edinburgh, Midlothian EH3 8EG
**Tel:** 08707776292 **Fax:** 020-7439-7678
**Web:** www.rapleys.co.uk
**Reg No:** 2162386 **Estd:** 2008 Private Limited Company
**Line of Business:** Commercial property agents
**Issued Capital:** £2
**Directors:** J C Banks, P J Blackford
**Co. Secretary:** Roderick Bishop
**Responsibilities**
**Senior:** Mark Coles *(Building Surveying Manager)*, Paul Styles *(Manager)*
**HR:** Sheila Coulman *(Human Resources Manager)*
**Health & Safety:** Sheila Coulman *(Human Resources Manager)*
**Purchasing:** Sheila Coulman *(Human Resources Manager)*
**Branches:** Rapleys Consultants Ltd, Godwin House, George Street, Huntingdon, Cambridgeshire PE29 3BD
**US SIC:** 6531 **UK SIC:** 83400

| | 30-04-14 | 30-04-13 | 30-04-12 |
|---|---|---|---|
| TO | 6,701,126 | 5,922,957 | 3,288,224 |
| P/L | 232,174 | 68,643 | 32,556 |
| NW | 167,486 | 2 | 2 |
| WC | 167,486 | 2 | 2 |
| Emp. | 103 | 97 | 97 |

DUNS 23-978-7844

## Rare Butchers of Distinction Ltd

Unit 28-29 Chiltonian Industrial Estate, Manor Lane, London SE12 0TX
**Tel:** 020-8852-8401
**Web:** www.rarebutchers.co.uk
**Reg No:** 3967297 **VAT No:** 757029124
**Estd:** 2000 Private Limited Company
**Line of Business:** Meat wholesalers
**Issued Capital:** £100
**Principals:** J J Preston *(Managing)*, Ms P B Reffold, N J Humphreys, D J Light
**Co. Secretary:** David House
**US SIC:** 5147 **UK SIC:** 61700
**Auditors:** Raffingers Stuart

| | 30-09-13 | 30-09-12 | 30-09-11 |
|---|---|---|---|
| TO | N/A | 12,332,862 | 11,879,624 |
| P/L | N/A | 79,466 | 294,298 |
| NW | (152,009) | 649,081 | 877,415 |
| WC | (359,439) | 443,513 | 788,128 |
| Emp. | N/A | 67 | 55 |

DUNS 73-938-4381

## Rascal Solutions Ltd

Sigma House, Northfield Drive, Milton Keynes, Buckinghamshire MK15 0DQ
**Tel:** 01908283900
**Web:** www.rascalsystems.com
**Reg No:** 5191277 **Estd:** 2004 Private Limited Company
**Line of Business:** Business services
**Issued Capital:** £20,000
**Directors:** J Bunting, Ms C Southon, Ms L Ryan, M J Kemble
**Co. Secretary:** Peter Kemble
**US SIC:** 7399 **UK SIC:** 83954
**Bankers:** HSBC Bank plc (40-33-33)

| | 31-08-13 | 31-08-12 | 31-08-11 |
|---|---|---|---|
| TO | 7,364,132 | N/A | N/A |
| P/L | 973,017 | N/A | N/A |
| NW | 686,510 | 152,614 | 411,873 |
| WC | 750,425 | 374,633 | 833,778 |
| Emp. | 61 | N/A | N/A |

DUNS 50-396-8174 **Imp**

## Rase Distribution Ltd

Wickenby Airfield, Wickenby, Lincoln, Lincolnshire LN3 5AX
**Tel:** 01673885083
**Web:** www.thruster.co.uk
**Reg No:** 2403313 **VAT No:** 613889904
**Estd:** 1995 Private Limited Company
**Line of Business:** Manufacturers and suppliers of aircrafts
**Issued Capital:** £100
**Directors:** G D Hill, D A Hill
**Co. Secretary:** Mrs Katherine Dame
**Responsibilities**
**Senior:** Gerald Cooper *(Partner)*, Russell Ingham *(Transport Manager)*, Ian Lovely *(General Manager)*
**Admin:** Zoe Martin *(Management PA/ Accounts)*
**Operations:** Ian Noon *(Company Operations Manager)*
**Fleet:** Dale Christie *(Warehouse Manager)*, Chris Fable *(Traffic Coordinator)*, Russell Ingham *(Transport Manager)*, Graham Pearce *(Traffic Coordinator)*, Wayne Rowett *(Transport Manager)*, Troy Steadman *(Traffic Coordinator)*
**Branches:** Rase Distribution Ltd, Horncastle Road, Bardney, Lincoln, Lincolnshire LN3 5SU
**US SIC:** 4213, 4226
**UK SIC:** 72300, 77003
**Auditors:** Streets Audit LLP
**Bankers:** Lloyds TSB Bank plc (30-95-05)

| | 31-01-14 | 31-01-13 | 31-01-12 |
|---|---|---|---|
| TO | 8,755,555 | 8,278,396 | 7,908,804 |
| P/L | 541,339 | 618,057 | 457,705 |
| NW | 2,581,105 | 2,232,406 | 1,772,939 |
| WC | 497,061 | 193,736 | (47,792) |
| Emp. | 96 | 109 | 97 |

DUNS 22-813-5075

## Rashcliffe Holdings Ltd

(**Subsidiary of:** Bulmer & Lumb Group Ltd)
Albert Street, Huddersfield, West Yorkshire HD1 3RP
**Tel:** 01484423231 **Fax:** 01484-438313
**Web:** www.bandlcleaningservices.co.uk
**Reg No:** 1542350 **Estd:** 1981 Private Limited Company
**Line of Business:** Textile weaving
**Issued Capital:** £700,000
**Directors:** W Waterhouse, D W Midgley
**Co. Secretary:** Matthew Whitehead
**US SIC:** 2269, 2231
**UK SIC:** 43702, 43103
**Auditors:** Wheawill & Sudworth
**Bankers:** Lloyds TSB Bank plc (30-94-43)

| | 30-09-13 | 30-09-12 | 30-09-11 |
|---|---|---|---|
| TA | 700,000 | 700,000 | 700,000 |
| NW | 700,000 | 700,000 | 700,000 |

DUNS 21-853-0912

## Rashwood Tyres Ltd

Barn Rashwood Hill, Rashwood, Droitwich, Worcestershire WR9 0BJ
**Tel:** 01527861379
**Reg No:** 8171923 **Estd:** 1955 Private Limited Company
**Line of Business:** Car accessories and parts
**Issued Capital:** £2
**Directors:** Ms A Swanson, R L Parkes
**Responsibilities**
**Senior:** Justine Carhill *(Manager)*
**US SIC:** 5531 **UK SIC:** 65100

| | 31-08-13 |
|---|---|
| TA | 28,898 |
| NW | 238 |
| WC | 238 |

DUNS 23-086-1507

## Rasrtick High School

Field Top Road, Brighouse, West Yorkshire HD6 3XB
**Tel:** 01484-710235
**Web:** www.rastrick.calderdale.sch.uk
**Estd:** 1987
**Line of Business:** Schools (foundation)
**Director:** P Clarke
**Responsibilities**
**Senior:** Helen Lennie *(CEO, Managing Director)*
**IT:** Chris Brookes *(Senior IT Executive)*
**US SIC:** 8211 **UK SIC:** 93200
**Employees:** 200

DUNS 23-138-0809

## Rastrick Educational Services Ltd

Ogden Lane, Brighouse, West Yorkshire HD6 3HF
**Tel:** 01484-400344
**Web:** www.rastrickschool.co.uk
**Reg No:** 2911219 **Estd:** 1994 Private Limited Company
**Line of Business:** Schools (independent)
**Trading Style:** Rastrick Preparatory & Nursery School
**Issued Capital:** £100
**Director:** Ms S A Vaughey
**Co. Secretary:** Miss Elizabeth Green
**US SIC:** 8211 **UK SIC:** 93200
**Auditors:** Geoffreyn Britton & Co

| | 31-08-13 | 31-08-12 | 31-08-11 |
|---|---|---|---|
| TA | 1,479,628 | 1,517,977 | 1,531,963 |
| NW | 523,332 | 533,195 | 500,493 |
| WC | (250,391) | (248,838) | (345,330) |

DUNS 21-689-5938 **Imp-Exp**

## The Ratcliff Group Ltd

Bessemer Road, Welwyn Garden City, Hertfordshire AL7 1ET
**Tel:** 01707-325571
**Web:** www.ratcliff.co.uk
**Reg No:** 0938100 **Estd:** 1968 Private Limited Company
**Line of Business:** Lifting equipment
**Export Markets:** Worldwide
**Export Sales:** £876,222
**Trading Style:** Palfinger
**Issued Capital:** £8,956
**Principals:** J E Ratcliff *(Chairman)*, R C Williams
**Co. Secretary:** Mark Ivinson
**Responsibilities**
**Senior:** Paul Addis *(Manager)*, Wayne Harmer *(Manager)*
**Operations:** David Agg *(Director, Engineering)*, Jez Green *(Operations Director)*
**Branches:** The Ratcliff Group Ltd, Lotherton Way, Leeds, West Yorkshire LS25 2JY
**US SIC:** 6711, 3534
**UK SIC:** 83962, 32553
**Auditors:** Cook & Partners Ltd
**Bankers:** National Westminster Bank Plc (60-23-07)

| | 31-12-13 | 31-12-12 | 31-12-11 |
|---|---|---|---|
| TO | 21,572,363 | 20,259,212 | 20,209,513 |
| P/L | 205,567 | (74,178) | (415,598) |
| NW | 11,253,959 | 5,246,754 | 7,754,705 |
| WC | 7,212,630 | 7,009,393 | 9,608,610 |
| Emp. | 268 | 274 | 274 |

DUNS 51-620-6849

## Ratcliffe College

Ratcliffe College, Fosse Way, Leicester, Leicestershire LE7 4SG
**Tel:** 01509-817000
**Web:** www.ratcliffecollege.com
**Reg No:** 5900743 **Estd:** 2006 Private Company Limited By Guarantee
**Line of Business:** General secondary education
**Directors:** A J Furlong, Rev P A Sainter, B E Cuddihy, B N Kennedy, J O'Reilly, C J Fuse, Mrs M Espinasse, R W Gamble
**US SIC:** 8211 **UK SIC:** 93200
**Bankers:** National Westminster Bank Plc (60-14-10)

| | 31-08-13 | 31-08-12 | 31-08-11 |
|---|---|---|---|
| TO | 9,110,956 | 8,816,692 | 8,312,677 |
| P/L | 614,872 | 518,643 | 422,247 |
| NW | 19,930,852 | 19,291,497 | 18,764,629 |
| WC | 1,251,088 | 611,367 | (36,743) |
| Emp. | 228 | 229 | 170 |

DUNS 23-759-0331

## Ratcliffe Financial Services Ltd

Wolseley House, Wolseley Terrace, Cheltenham, Gloucestershire GL50 1TH
**Tel:** 01242544544
**Web:** www.ratcliffes.co.uk
**Reg No:** 3752762 **Estd:** 1999 Private Limited Company
**Line of Business:** Financial intermediation not elsewhere classified
**Issued Capital:** £22,500
**Director:** Mrs J Uzzell
**Co. Secretary:** Miss Rachel Uzzell
**US SIC:** 6111 **UK SIC:** 81501

| | 30-04-14 | 30-04-13 | 30-04-12 |
|---|---|---|---|
| TA | 11,468 | 14,178 | 10,000 |
| NW | 9,344 | 6,215 | 5,356 |
| WC | 9,344 | 6,215 | 5,356 |

DUNS 34-738-4435

## Rated People Ltd

240 Blackfriars, Blackfriars Road, London SE1 8NW
**Tel:** 08702208811
**Web:** www.ratedpeople.com
**Reg No:** 5540422 **Estd:** 2005 Private Limited Company
**Line of Business:** Directories
**Issued Capital:** £1,770
**Directors:** K S Roberts, T J Parsons, Mrs C M Francis, R M Reid, A N Cox, C J Havemann, A W Skipwith
**Co. Secretary:** Timothy Parsons
**US SIC:** 2731 **UK SIC:** 47532
**Bankers:** The Royal Bank Of Scotland Plc (16-00-42)

| | 31-12-13 | 31-12-12 | 31-12-11 |
|---|---|---|---|
| TO | 12,120,522 | N/A | N/A |
| P/L | (4,992,760) | N/A | N/A |
| NW | (9,783,148) | (276,558) | 2,069,784 |
| WC | (6,813,473) | 1,161,482 | 1,987,017 |
| Emp. | 46 | N/A | N/A |

DUNS 22-706-0472 **Imp-Exp**

## Rathbone Brothers Plc

159 New Bond Street, London W1S 2UD
**Web:** www.rathbones.com
**Reg No:** 1000403 **Estd:** 1971 Public Limited Company
**Line of Business:** Financial intermediation not elsewhere classified

**Export Markets:** Switzerland, Europe, USA
**Issued Capital:** £2,311,689
**Directors:** Ms K A Matthews, J W Dean, P D Chavasse, M P Nicholls, R P Stockton, Ms S F Gentleman, P L Howell, D T Harrel
**Co. Secretary:** Richard Loader
**Responsibilities**
**Marketing:** Emily Morris *(Marketing Director)*, Jane Seymour *(Marketing Director)*
**Admin:** Mark McGahern *(Office Manager)*
**IT:** Muneer Alam *(Computer Manager)*
**HR:** Rosemary Lloyd *(Human Resources Manager)*
**Health & Safety:** Mark McGahern *(Office Manager)*
**Facilities:** Mark McGahern *(Office Manager)*
**Operations:** Mark McGahern *(Office Manager)*, Emily Morris *(Marketing Director)*, Jane Seymour *(Marketing Director)*
**Branches:** Rathbone Brothers Plc, Port Of Liverpool Building, Pier Head, Liverpool, Merseyside L3 1NW
**US SIC:** 6111 **UK SIC:** 81501
**Auditors:** KPMG Audit PLC
**Bankers:** Bank Of England (10-00-00)
**Following financial data are in thousands**

| | 31-12-13 | 31-12-12 | 31-12-11 |
|---|---|---|---|
| TA | 1,229,777 | 1,138,714 | 1,183,839 |
| P/L | 44,204 | 38,812 | 39,152 |
| NW | 146,031 | 132,070 | 97,809 |
| WC | 129,900 | 54,321 | 81,355 |
| Emp. | 833 | 789 | 746 |

DUNS 21-034-2188

## Rathbone Investment Management

28 St Andrew Square, Edinburgh, Midlothian EH2 1AF
**Web:** www.rathbones.com
**Estd:** 1999 Proprietorship
**Line of Business:** Investment consultants
**Proprietor:** J Henderson
**Responsibilities**
**Senior:** Carol MacIntyre *(Investment Director)*, David Macaulay *(Branch Director)*
**US SIC:** 6111 **UK SIC:** 81501
**Employees:** 52

DUNS 28-916-3826

## Rathbone Investment Management Ltd

(**Subsidiary of:** Rathbone Brothers Plc)
Port Of Liverpool Building, Pier Head, Liverpool, Merseyside L3 1NW
**Fax:** 0151-243-7001
**Web:** www.rathbones.com
**Reg No:** 1448919 **Estd:** 1979 Private Limited Company
**Line of Business:** Banks and financial institutions
**Trading Style:** Rathbone Investment Management
**Issued Capital:** £1,825,000
**Directors:** D T Harrel, Ms K A Matthews, P L Howell, R P Stockton, P D Chavasse, Ms S F Gentlemen, M P Nicholls, J W Dean
**Co. Secretary:** Richard Loader
**Responsibilities**
**Senior:** Timothy Bolton Carter *(Manager)*, Ian Buckley *(Manager)*, Julian Chillingworth *(Manager)*, Martin Lumber *(Group Health & Safety Officer)*
**Finance:** Yvonne Young *(Payroll Manager)*
**Marketing:** Eleanor McCormack *(Marketing Executive)*
**IT:** Mark Cummins *(IT Manager)*, Barry Darlow *(Group IT Manager)*
**HR:** Davina Coogan *(Training Manager)*, Joan Crawford *(Personnel Administrator)*, Elaine Grierson *(Senior Human Resources Manager)*
**Health & Safety:** Martin Lumber *(Group Health & Safety Officer)*
**Branches:** Rathbone Investment Management Ltd, 1 Northgate, Chichester, West Sussex PO19 1AT
**US SIC:** 6012 **UK SIC:** 81402
**Auditors:** KPMG Audit PLC
**Bankers:** Barclays Bank Plc (20-51-01)
**Following financial data are in thousands**

| | 31-12-13 | 31-12-12 | 31-12-11 |
|---|---|---|---|
| TA | 1,109,557 | 1,065,977 | 1,119,872 |
| P/L | 41,349 | 34,461 | 36,062 |
| NW | 101,388 | 68,682 | 52,607 |
| WC | 85,542 | 67,976 | 43,666 |
| Emp. | 720 | 673 | 639 |

DUNS 34-610-3182

## Rathbone Kear Ltd

(**Subsidiary of:** Wm Morrison Supermarkets P L C)
Claremont, Bulley Lane, Gloucester, Gloucestershire GL2 8AS
**Tel:** 01594845678
**Web:** www.rathbones-bakery.co.uk
**Reg No:** 5417123 **Estd:** 2005 Private Limited Company
**Line of Business:** Bakers and confectioners supplies
**Issued Capital:** £1,500,000
**Directors:** M Harrison, A Pleasance, J Lill
**Co. Secretary:** Mark Amsden
**US SIC:** 2051 **UK SIC:** 41960
**Auditors:** KPMG Audit PLC

| | 02-02-14 | 03-02-13 | 29-02-12 |
|---|---|---|---|
| TO | 51,882,000 | 62,664,000 | 61,691,000 |
| P/L | 1,272,000 | 3,669,000 | 9,708,000 |
| NW | 27,454,000 | 26,292,000 | 23,591,000 |
| WC | (878,000) | (500,000) | 8,862,000 |
| Emp. | 328 | 391 | 364 |

DUNS 21-752-9969

## Rathbone Training

4th Floor Churchgate House 56 Oxford, Street, Manchester M1 6EU
**Tel:** 01612365358
**Web:** www.rathboneuk.org
**Reg No:** 7830590 **Estd:** 2011 Private Company Limited By Guarantee
**Line of Business:** General secondary education
**Trading Style:** Rathbone
**Directors:** J P Docherty, J Martin, C Payne
**Branches:** RATHBONE TRAINING - 2nd and 3rd Floor, 2-4 Colton Street, Leicester, LE1 1QA.
**US SIC:** 8211, 8249
**UK SIC:** 93200, 93300
**Bankers:** HSBC Bank plc (40-00-00)

| | 31-07-13 | 31-07-12 |
|---|---|---|
| TO | 34,949,000 | 18,883,000 |
| P/L | 1,848,000 | (326,000) |
| NW | (6,981,000) | (11,522,000) |
| WC | 7,435,000 | 3,705,000 |
| Emp. | 549 | 652 |

DUNS 21-212-8701

## Ratheane Private Nursing Home

58a Mountsandel Road, Coleraine, Co Londonderry BT52 1JF
**Tel:** 02870344299
**Web:** www.macklingroup.com
**Estd:** 1990 Proprietorship
**Line of Business:** Nursing homes
**Proprietor:** B Macklin
**Responsibilities**
**Senior:** Joy Hynds *(Manager)*, Wendy McMaster *(Home Manager)*
**US SIC:** 8051 **UK SIC:** 95100
**Employees:** 75

DUNS 22-705-2461 **Imp**

## Rathern Ltd

(**Subsidiary of:** Tirupati Balaji Ltd)
4 Bryanston Street, London W1H 7BY
**Tel:** 020-7935-2361
**Web:** www.mostynhotel.co.uk
**Reg No:** 1581516 **VAT No:** 362444852
**Estd:** 1981 Private Limited Company
**Line of Business:** Hotels
**Trading Style:** Rathern Ltd
**Issued Capital:** £100,000
**Managing Director:** K R Patel
**Co. Secretary:** Mrs Sulochana Patel
**Responsibilities**
**Senior:** Sardia Kabore *(Front of House Manager)*, Anup Sarin *(General Manager)*
**Finance:** Janak Sampat *(Financial Controller)*
**Marketing:** Anup Sarin *(General Manager)*
**IT:** Janak Sampat *(Financial Controller)*, Vikrant Shah *(Senior IT Executive)*
**HR:** Sardia Kabore *(Front of House Manager)*, Janak Sampat *(Financial Controller)*
**Health & Safety:** Anup Sarin *(General Manager)*
**Facilities:** Anup Sarin *(General Manager)*
**Operations:** Sardia Kabore *(Front of House Manager)*
**Purchasing:** Janak Sampat *(Financial Controller)*
**US SIC:** 7011 **UK SIC:** 66500
**Auditors:** N S Amin & Co

| | 31-12-13 | 31-12-12 | 31-12-11 |
|---|---|---|---|
| TA | 21,569,354 | 22,681,145 | 23,663,833 |
| NW | 1,639,846 | 1,252,413 | 727,032 |
| WC | (1,433,411) | (1,096,125) | (612,044) |

DUNS 21-209-4374

## Rathfriland Manor

Rosconnor Terrace, Rathfriland, Newry, Co Down BT34 5DJ
**Tel:** 028-4063-8383
**Web:** www.manorhealthcare.org
**Estd:** 1989 Partnership
**Line of Business:** Nursing homes
**Partners:** Mrs Y O'Hare, P O'Hare
**Responsibilities**
**Senior:** Brenda Mcpolin *(Manager)*, Peter O' Hare *(Partner)*
**US SIC:** 8051 **UK SIC:** 95100
**Bankers:** Ulster Bank Ltd (98-13-60)
**Employees:** 50

DUNS 23-719-2257

## Rathmore Estates Ltd

556 Antrim Road, Newtownabbey, Co Antrim BT36 4RF
**Tel:** 028-9083-7441 **Fax:** 028-9034-2469
**Web:** www.vaughan-group.co.uk
**Reg No:** 0028289NI **VAT No:** 253265566
**Estd:** 1955 Private Limited Company
**Line of Business:** Mechanical engineering general
**Issued Capital:** £25,000
**Directors:** B P Vaughan, A J Vaughan, M J Vaughan
**Co. Secretary:** Gavin Vaughan
**Responsibilities**
**Senior:** James Vaughan *(Manager)*
**US SIC:** 6711, 1731
**UK SIC:** 83962, 50300
**Auditors:** McCreery Turkingston Stockman
**Bankers:** Northern Bank Ltd (95-00-33)

| | 31-03-14 | 31-03-13 | 31-03-12 |
|---|---|---|---|
| TO | 54,828,403 | 51,945,414 | 51,468,127 |
| P/L | (788,566) | 944,813 | 682,772 |
| NW | 5,163,241 | 9,637,178 | 9,397,068 |
| WC | 1,330,987 | 7,339,896 | 7,647,475 |
| Emp. | 311 | 282 | 248 |

DUNS 21-580-1248

## Rathore School

23 Martins Lane, Newry, Co Down BT35 8PJ
**Tel:** 02830261617
**Web:** www.rathoreschool.com
**Estd:** 2004 Proprietorship
**Line of Business:** Schools (special)
**Proprietor:** R Casody
**Responsibilities**
**Senior:** Raymond Cassidy *(Head Teacher)*
**US SIC:** 8299 **UK SIC:** 93300
**Employees:** 50

DUNS 77-513-4679

## Rautomead Holdings Ltd

Nobel Road, West Gourdie Industrial Estate, Dundee, Angus DD2 4UH
**Fax:** 01382622941
**Web:** www.rautomead.com
**Reg No:** 0153985SC **Estd:** 1994 Private Limited Company
**Line of Business:** Manufacture of other special purpose machinery not elsewhere classified
**Export Sales:** £5,214,590
**Issued Capital:** £48,674
**Principals:** M Nairn *(Managing)*, G B Wood *(Financial)*, M A Nairn
**Responsibilities**
**Senior:** Brian Frame *(Manager)*
**US SIC:** 3559, 3339
**UK SIC:** 32863, 22470
**Auditors:** KPMG
**Bankers:** Bank Of Scotland (80-73-31)

| | 30-06-13 | 30-06-12 | 30-06-11 |
|---|---|---|---|
| TO | 5,347,526 | 6,673,958 | 7,817,529 |
| P/L | (130,645) | 304,696 | 755,497 |
| NW | 3,126,991 | 3,189,085 | 2,326,364 |
| WC | 2,154,227 | 2,181,809 | 1,775,436 |
| Emp. | 53 | 52 | 46 |

DUNS 34-628-1053 **Imp**

## Raven Holdings Ltd

Building 66, Third Avenue, Brierley Hill, West Midlands DY6 7GA
**Tel:** 01384400240
**Reg No:** 5434371 **Estd:** 2005 Private Limited Company
**Line of Business:** Manufacture of other furniture
**Issued Capital:** £2,000
**Directors:** P E Bennett, G A Aston, D D Milligan
**Co. Secretary:** Timothy Yorke
**US SIC:** 2517 **UK SIC:** 46714

| | 31-12-13 | 31-12-12 | 31-12-11 |
|---|---|---|---|
| TO | 19,401,639 | 20,006,148 | 21,907,769 |
| P/L | 526,838 | 850,925 | 612,433 |
| NW | 967,711 | 868,406 | 598,796 |
| WC | 283,691 | 97,602 | (322,133) |
| Emp. | N/A | 247 | 250 |

DUNS 21-121-8639

## Raven Housing Trust Ltd

29 Linkfield Lane, Redhill, Surrey RH1 1SS
**Tel:** 01737272400
**Web:** www.ravenht.org.uk
**Reg No:** 0030070IP **Estd:** 2003 Friendly Society
**Line of Business:** Property developers
**Principals:** M Bennett *(Chairman)*, N Newman, J Higgs, C Thorne
**Responsibilities**
**Finance:** Mark Thrasher *(Finance Manager)*
**Marketing:** Jenny Rawlinson *(Communications Manager)*, Peter Trowbridge *(Development Manager)*
**IT:** Dawn Rhodes *(IT Manager)*
**US SIC:** 8321 **UK SIC:** 96111
**Auditors:** Nexia Smith & Williamson
**Employees:** 172
**Turnover:** £26,658,000

DUNS 21-141-3912

## Raven Uk Holdings Ltd

(**Subsidiary of:** Raven Antenna Systems Inc.)
The Pinnacle, 160 Midsummer Boulevard, Milton Keynes, Buckinghamshire MK9 1FF
**Tel:** 01282770000 **Fax:** 01282770022
**Web:** www.raven.co.uk
**Reg No:** 6731771 **Estd:** 2008 Private Limited Company
**Line of Business:** Fabricated metal products
**Trading Style:** Skywarer Global
**Issued Capital:** £1,000
**Directors:** J D Malloy, G Jones, M D Steele
**Co. Secretary:** David Mccourt
**Responsibilities**
**Senior:** Steve Beaumount *(President)*, Anthony Doe *(Site Manager)*
**US SIC:** 8911 **UK SIC:** 83701
**Auditors:** KPMG LLP

| | 31-12-12 | 31-12-11 | 31-12-10 |
|---|---|---|---|
| TO | 5,556,225 | 6,920,785 | 9,822,457 |
| P/L | (331,654) | (1,063,714) | (771,376) |
| NW | 646,571 | 1,008,636 | 2,087,744 |
| WC | (1,958,243) | (1,832,512) | (1,562,113) |
| Emp. | 75 | 94 | 125 |

DUNS 29-454-6924 **Imp-Exp**

## Ravendale Foods Ltd

Unit 2, Consett, County Durham DH8 7RN
**Tel:** 01207-581166
**Web:** www.ravendalefoods.co.uk
**Reg No:** 1684198 **VAT No:** 385910133
**Estd:** 1982 Private Limited Company
**Line of Business:** Butchers
**Export Markets:** Holland
**Issued Capital:** £5,000
**Managing Director:** R A Gray
**Co. Secretary:** Ms Brenda Gray
**Responsibilities**
**Finance:** Linda Stoker *(Senior Finance Administrator)*
**HR:** Liz Robson *(Human Resource Manager)*
**Branches:** Ravendale Foods Ltd, Broom Hill, Consett, County Durham DH8 6RY
**US SIC:** 5423 **UK SIC:** 64100
**Auditors:** Moore Thompson
**Bankers:** Barclays Bank Plc (20-17-35)

| | 31-12-13 | 31-12-12 | 31-12-11 |
|---|---|---|---|
| TO | 40,825,689 | 38,825,460 | 34,624,229 |
| P/L | 830,335 | 253,623 | 449,125 |
| NW | 2,290,625 | 1,810,774 | 1,649,177 |
| WC | 614,389 | 313,664 | 233,063 |
| Emp. | 100 | 112 | 107 |

DUNS 22-910-7925 **Imp**

## Ravenhill Ltd

Moycroft Industrial Estate, Elgin, Morayshire IV30 1XZ
**Tel:** 01343541121
**Web:** www.ravenhill.co.uk
**Reg No:** 0090191SC **VAT No:** 415847440
**Estd:** 1984 Private Limited Company
**Line of Business:** Agricultural machinery sales service and repair
**Issued Capital:** £105,000
**Principals:** F D Davidson *(Managing)*, J D Wills, S M Davidson
**Co. Secretary:** Ms Anne Bruce
**Responsibilities**
**Senior:** Les Finney *(Parts Manager)*, Charlie Singer *(Manager)*
**Finance:** Lance Davidson *(Financial Manager)*
**Sales:** Graham Mutch *(Agri Sales Manager)*
**Engineering:** Less Finnie *(Parts Manager)*
**Branches:** Ravenhill Ltd, Clifton Lodge, The Avenue, Peterhead, Aberdeenshire AB42 4NA
**US SIC:** 3523, 7539, 5531
**UK SIC:** 32113, 67100, 65100
**Auditors:** KPMG LLP
**Bankers:** The Royal Bank Of Scotland Plc (83-49-40)

| | 31-12-13 | 31-12-12 | 31-12-11 |
|---|---|---|---|
| TO | 39,910,750 | 42,123,259 | 43,677,642 |
| P/L | 1,158,679 | 510,643 | 881,255 |
| NW | 5,565,348 | 4,684,289 | 4,522,335 |
| WC | 2,547,618 | 3,826,249 | 19,198 |
| Emp. | 122 | 126 | 127 |

DUNS 21-469-9840

## Ravenhill Nursing Home

81 Shore Road, Greenisland, Carrickfergus, Co Antrim BT38 8TZ
**Web:** www.ravenhillpnh.co.uk
**Estd:** 1985 Proprietorship
**Line of Business:** Nursing homes
**Proprietor:** N Mcgranaghan
**Responsibilities**
**Senior:** L Barne *(Manager)*, Christine Kim *(Nursing Manager)*, N McGranaghan , *(Proprietor)*
**US SIC:** 8051 **UK SIC:** 95100
**Employees:** 47

DUNS 21-231-9533
## Ravenor Park Clinic
Taywood Road, Northolt, Middlesex UB5 6WL
**Tel:** 02033137500
**Web:** www.ealingcct.co.uk
**Proprietorship**
**Line of Business:** Nhs clinics
**Proprietor:** Ms C Seijas
**US SIC:** 8062 **UK SIC:** 95100
**Employees:** 100

DUNS 50-471-0112 **Imp**
## Ravensbourne Ltd
6 Penrose Way, London SE10 0EW
**Tel:** 02030403500 **Fax:** 02082930266
**Web:** www.ravensbourne.ac.uk
**Reg No:** 2449934 **Estd:** 1989 Private Limited Company
**Line of Business:** Business and management consultancy activities not elsewhere classified
**Trading Style:** Ravensbourne College
**Issued Capital:** £100
**Directors:** F S Burrill, Professor L S Drew
**Responsibilities**
**Senior:** Karen Fishman *(Manager)*, Graham Reed *(Manager)*
**Marketing:** Debbie Haynes *(Planning Manager)*, Pauline Taylor *(Broadcasting Industry Liaison)*
**Sales:** Claire Selby *(Commercial Relationships Manag)*, Janthia Taylor *(Director of postgraduate devel)*
**IT:** Tricia Mcmahon *(Information Services Support M)*
**Operations:** Ian Cownley *(Outreach Broadcasting Tutor)*, Rachel Green *(Director of Physical Resources)*
**US SIC:** 7392 **UK SIC:** 83951
**Auditors:** Deloitte & Touche

| | 31-07-14 | 31-07-13 | 31-07-12 |
|---|---|---|---|
| TO | 285,221 | 215,441 | 402,731 |
| P/L | N/A | 815 | 195 |
| NW | 1,742 | 1,742 | 927 |
| WC | 1,742 | 1,742 | 927 |

DUNS 21-121-3267
## The Ravensbourne School
Hayes Lane, Keston, Kent BR2 9EH
**Tel:** 02084-600083
**Web:** www.ravensbourne.bromley.sch.uk
**Estd:** 1988
**Line of Business:** Schools (local authority)
**Proprietor:** P Murphy
**Responsibilities**
**Finance:** Tina Futcher-Smith *(Chair of Finance committee)*, Cathy Whiting *(Business Manager)*
**Marketing:** Cathy Whiting *(Business Manager)*
**IT:** Andreas Schmitz *(Network Manager)*
**HR:** Cathy Whiting *(Business Manager)*
**Health & Safety:** Cathy Whiting *(Business Manager)*
**Facilities:** Andy Wightman *(Facilities Manager)*
**US SIC:** 8211 **UK SIC:** 93200
**Employees:** 100

DUNS 21-781-7841
## Ravenscourt Nursing Home
111-113 Station Lane, Hornchurch, Essex RM12 6HT
**Estd:** 1996 Proprietorship
**Line of Business:** Nursing homes
**Proprietor:** J Seevathean
**US SIC:** 8051 **UK SIC:** 95100
**Employees:** 50

DUNS 23-535-3922
## Ravenscourt Services Ltd
**(Subsidiary of:** Permira Advisers Llp)
26 Paddenswick Road, London W6 0UB
**Tel:** 02088462000 **Fax:** 02084620001
**Web:** www.liontv.co.uk
**Reg No:** 3534197 **Estd:** 1998 Private Limited Company
**Line of Business:** Television licence suppliers
**Trading Style:** Lion Television
**Issued Capital:** £2
**Directors:** Mrs V J Turton, J Mills, R Bradley, N I Catliff, N I Bright, S E Meer
**Co. Secretary:** Neil Bright
**Responsibilities**
**Senior:** Julian Burns *(Manager)*, John Pfeil *(Manager)*
**US SIC:** 4833 **UK SIC:** 97411
**Auditors:** KPMG

| | 31-08-13 | 31-08-12 | 31-08-11 |
|---|---|---|---|
| TO | 5,588,894 | 5,584,819 | 5,047,253 |
| P/L | 284,554 | 393,256 | (446,331) |
| NW | (495,989) | (764,992) | (1,155,858) |
| WC | (649,607) | (989,964) | (1,342,671) |
| Emp. | 53 | 53 | 55 |

DUNS 21-771-7518
## Ravenscroft Nursing & Residential Care Home
44 Hilperton Road, Trowbridge, Wiltshire BA14 7JQ
**Tel:** 01225752087
**Web:** www.larchwoodcare.co.uk
**Estd:** 1983 Proprietorship
**Line of Business:** Nursing homes
**Proprietor:** Miss J Rowland
**Responsibilities**
**Senior:** Philip Bale *(Manager)*, Caroline Orrell *(Manageress)*
**US SIC:** 8051 **UK SIC:** 95100
**Employees:** 52

DUNS 21-780-9208
## Ravensthorpe C of E Junior School
Myrtle Road, Dewsbury, West Yorkshire WF13 3AS
**Tel:** 01924326610
**Estd:** 1990 Proprietorship
**Line of Business:** Schools (local authority)
**Proprietor:** C Lockwood
**US SIC:** 8211 **UK SIC:** 93200
**Employees:** 60

DUNS 21-772-1763
## Ravenswood Primary School
Ravenswood Road, Newcastle-Upon-Tyne, Tyne and Wear NE6 5TU
**Tel:** 01912659599
**Web:** www.ravenswood.newcastle.sch.uk
**Estd:** 1964
**Line of Business:** Schools (local authority)
**Responsibilities**
**Senior:** Clive Maddison *(Head Teacher)*
**US SIC:** 8211 **UK SIC:** 93200
**Employees:** 50

DUNS 23-193-4915
## Ravenswood School
Oakley Road, Keston, Kent BR2 8HP
**Tel:** 01689-856050
**Web:** www.ravenswood.bromley.sch.uk
**Estd:** 1950
**Line of Business:** Schools (local authority)
**Director:** Dr G Berwick
**Branches:** Ravenswood School, Oakley Road, Bromley, Kent BR2 8HP
**US SIC:** 8211 **UK SIC:** 93200
**Employees:** 62

DUNS 34-992-1952
## Raventree Ltd
Unit Q1, Quadrant Distribution Centre, Quadrant Way, Gloucester, Gloucestershire GL2 2RN
**Tel:** 01452-886100
**Web:** www.premierekitchens.co.uk
**Reg No:** 5787195 **Estd:** 2006 Private Limited Company
**Line of Business:** Manufacture of other kitchen furniture
**Issued Capital:** £134
**Directors:** A J Markey, P F Markey
**Co. Secretary:** Gary Holt
**Responsibilities**
**Marketing:** Bernard Kent *(Head of Sales and Marketing)*
**Sales:** Bernard Kent *(Head of Sales and Marketing)*, Tom Veli *(Commercial Manager)*
**US SIC:** 2599 **UK SIC:** 46720

| | 28-03-14 | 29-03-13 | 30-03-12 |
|---|---|---|---|
| TO | 12,274,899 | 13,417,050 | 11,908,589 |
| P/L | 656,164 | 158,345 | (764,569) |
| NW | 3,055,735 | 2,458,097 | 2,299,752 |
| WC | 1,109,530 | 1,233,905 | 1,006,966 |
| Emp. | 128 | 128 | 146 |

DUNS 29-644-1280
## Ravenwood Hall Hotel Ltd
Rougham, Bury St Edmunds, Suffolk IP30 9JA
**Tel:** 01359-270345 **Fax:** 01359-270788
**Web:** www.ravenwoodhall.co.uk
**Reg No:** 1970451 **Estd:** 1985 Private Limited Company
**Line of Business:** Hotels
**Issued Capital:** £100
**Director:** D N Jarvis
**Co. Secretary:** Craig Jarvis
**Responsibilities**
**HR:** Sharon Banevicius *(General Manager)*
**Health & Safety:** Sharon Banevicius *(General Manager)*
**Facilities:** Sharon Banevicius *(General Manager)*
**Operations:** Sharon Banevicius *(General Manager)*
**US SIC:** 7011 **UK SIC:** 66500
**Auditors:** Grant Thornton

**Bankers:** Barclays Bank Plc (20-26-34)

| | 31-01-14 | 31-01-13 | 31-01-12 |
|---|---|---|---|
| TA | 1,803,475 | 2,012,832 | 1,855,578 |
| NW | 150,422 | 183,223 | (50,604) |
| WC | (370,494) | (508,242) | (418,674) |

DUNS 77-957-7956
## The Raw Shoe Co Ltd
Marlow House, Churchill Way, Fleckney, Leicester, Leicestershire LE8 8UD
**Tel:** 01162-402282 **Fax:** 01162404277
**Web:** www.rawshoes.co.uk
**Reg No:** 3061220 **Estd:** 1995 Private Limited Company
**Line of Business:** Retail sale of footwear
**Issued Capital:** £482,187
**Director:** G P Brown
**Co. Secretary:** Ms Katrina Wells
**Branches:** The Raw Shoe Co Ltd, 6 Feasegate, York, North Yorkshire YO1 8SQ
**US SIC:** 5661 **UK SIC:** 64600
**Auditors:** The Rowleys Partnership Ltd

| | 30-04-13 | 30-04-12 | 30-04-11 |
|---|---|---|---|
| TA | 246,343 | 377,214 | 590,967 |
| NW | (99,081) | 8,755 | 169,891 |
| WC | (179,271) | (69,926) | 84,189 |

DUNS 21-693-0917 **Imp**
## Rawle Gammon & Baker Holdings Ltd
Gammon House, Barnstaple, Devon EX31 1QN
**Tel:** 01271313000
**Web:** www.rgbltd.co.uk
**Reg No:** 0308273 **Estd:** 1850 Private Limited Company
**Line of Business:** Agents involved in the sale of timber and building materials
**Issued Capital:** £174,062
**Directors:** K P Fenlon, C J Worth, C W Smith, P J Turner, R W Isaac
**Co. Secretary:** Mrs Linda Allen
**Responsibilities**
**Marketing:** Laura Stroud *(Marketing Manager)*
**Purchasing:** Rod Norman *(Buyer)*
**Branches:** Rawle Gammon & Baker Holdings Ltd, 4B Aspen Way, Yelberton Industrial Estate, Paignton, Devon TQ4 7QR
**US SIC:** 5072 **UK SIC:** 61500
**Auditors:** Ernst & Young LLP
**Bankers:** The Royal Bank Of Scotland Plc (16-19-25)

| | 31-03-14 | 31-03-13 | 31-03-12 |
|---|---|---|---|
| TO | 47,711,692 | 42,389,388 | 38,608,576 |
| P/L | 1,597,523 | 737,462 | 1,560,365 |
| NW | 12,004,068 | 11,875,573 | 12,261,122 |
| WC | 8,852,481 | 7,801,352 | 7,754,046 |
| Emp. | 269 | 268 | 236 |

DUNS 22-741-7003
## Rawlinson & Hunter
6 New St Square, London EC4A 3AQ
**Tel:** 020-7842-2000
**Web:** www.rawlinson-hunter.com
**Estd:** 2008 Partnership
**Line of Business:** Accounting activities
**Principals:** R A Stockwell, B M Covell, K W Dent, Ms F Stephens *(Partner)*, D Cunningham *(Partner)*, C R Greene *(Partner)*, J C Kelly *(Partner)*, R Drennan *(Partner)*
**Responsibilities**
**Marketing:** Susan Carthew *(Human Resources Manager)*, Katie Griffin *(Marketing Coordinator)*
**HR:** Susan Carthew *(Human Resources Manager)*
**Branches:** Rawlinson & Hunter, Lower Mill, Kingston Road, Ewell, Epsom, Surrey KT17 2AE
**US SIC:** 8931 **UK SIC:** 83600
**Employees:** 120

DUNS 23-213-7216
## Rawlinson Hunter
P O Box 83, Jersey, Channel Islands JE4 8PW
**Tel:** 01534825322
**Web:** www.computershare.com
**Proprietorship**
**Line of Business:** Accounting activities
**US SIC:** 8931 **UK SIC:** 83600
**Employees:** 85

DUNS 21-391-3172
## Rawlinson Workwear
Unit D6, Dutton Road, Redwither Business Park, Wrexham, Clwyd LL13 9UL
**Tel:** 01978-363300
**Estd:** 2002
**Line of Business:** Protective clothing and workwear
**US SIC:** 2389 **UK SIC:** 45393
**Employees:** 50

DUNS 39-911-9395
## Rawlinsons Ltd
Ruthlyn House, 90 Lincoln Road, Peterborough, Cambridgeshire PE1 2SP
**Tel:** 01733-568321
**Web:** www.rawlinsons.co.uk
**Reg No:** 2236458 **Estd:** 1935 Private Limited Company
**Line of Business:** Accounting activities
**Issued Capital:** £700
**Directors:** G H Jones, Mrs T L Richardson, M A Jackson, A J Cox, C J Collier, K P Craig, Mrs J N Bloodworth
**Co. Secretary:** Colin Crowley
**Responsibilities**
**Sales:** Joanna Bacon *(Business Development Manager)*
**US SIC:** 8931 **UK SIC:** 83600

| | 30-06-13 | 30-06-12 | 30-06-11 |
|---|---|---|---|
| TA | 698,494 | 561,451 | 369,507 |
| NW | 622,471 | 502,481 | 308,565 |
| WC | (75,529) | 502,481 | 308,565 |

DUNS 34-941-5393
## Rawlison Butler Llp
Griffin House, 135 High Street, Crawley, West Sussex RH10 1DQ
**Tel:** 01293-527744
**Web:** www.rawlisonbutler.com
**Reg No:** 0318343OC **VAT No:** 209574255
**Estd:** 1865
**Line of Business:** Solicitors
**Responsibilities**
**Senior:** Stuart Evans *(Non-designated Limited Liabili)*, Barbara Matthews *(Partner)*, Mark O'Shea *(Non-designated Limited Liabili)*, Chris Strange *(Partner)*
**Sales:** Katherine Mcalister *(Solicitor, Commercial Disputes)*, Cassandra Mccarthy *(Solicitor, Commercial Disputes)*, Jodie Pearce *(Plot Sales Legal Executive)*
**Operations:** Dennis Emson *(Chief Operations Officer)*
**Branches:** Rawlison Butler Llp, Rawlison Butler, 15 Carfax, Horsham, West Sussex RH12 1DY
**US SIC:** 8111, 7392
**UK SIC:** 83500, 83951
**Auditors:** PKF (UK) LLP
**Bankers:** Barclays Bank Plc (20-23-97)

| | 31-03-14 | 31-03-13 | 31-03-12 |
|---|---|---|---|
| TO | 6,027,907 | 5,765,471 | 6,048,521 |
| P/L | 1,529,441 | 1,482,271 | 1,432,990 |
| NW | 1,529,441 | 1,482,271 | 1,432,990 |
| WC | 2,155,512 | 2,184,920 | 2,136,093 |
| Emp. | 68 | 77 | 78 |

DUNS 34-693-3570 **Imp-Exp**
## Rawlplug Ltd
**(Subsidiary of:** Amicus Poliniae Sp Z O O)
Rawlplug House, Thornliebank Industrial Estate Skibo, Drive, Glasgow, Lanarkshire G46 8DB
**Tel:** 01416 387 961 **Fax:** 01416 387 397
**Web:** www.rawlplug.co.uk
**Reg No:** 5497750 **VAT No:** 870399786
**Estd:** 2004 Private Limited Company
**Line of Business:** Fasteners and fixings
**Export Sales:** £320,636
**Issued Capital:** £11,500,000
**Director:** M Anderson
**Co. Secretary:** Sisec Limited
**Responsibilities**
**Senior:** Sebastian Tecza *(Manager)*
**Finance:** John Grove *(Finance Director)*
**Marketing:** Tom Waver *(Marketing Manager)*
**HR:** Barbara Little *(Human Resources Manager)*
**Purchasing:** Marcin Horczak *(Purchasing Manager)*
**US SIC:** 3452 **UK SIC:** 31371
**Auditors:** T.B. Dunn & Co
**Bankers:** Barclays Bank Plc (20-04-90)

| | 31-12-13 | 31-12-12 | 31-12-11 |
|---|---|---|---|
| TO | 10,493,167 | 9,039,062 | N/A |
| P/L | 462,937 | 462,172 | 7,066,177 |
| NW | 4,621,965 | 4,163,889 | 13,842,781 |
| WC | 2,868,009 | 2,346,557 | 11,946,025 |
| Emp. | 48 | 42 | 42 |

DUNS 21-812-1935
## Rawmarsh City Learning Centre
Monkwood Road, Rawmarsh, Rotherham, South Yorkshire S62 7GA
**Tel:** 01709523107
**Estd:** 2002
**Line of Business:** Educational training
**US SIC:** 8211 **UK SIC:** 93200
**Employees:** 111

DUNS 21-771-6228
## Rawthorpe Infant & Nursery School
Rawthorpe Lane, Huddersfield, West Yorkshire HD5 9NT
**Tel:** 01484226601
**Web:** www.nlconline.org.uk
**Estd:** 2002 Proprietorship
**Line of Business:** Nursery schools
**Proprietor:** Mrs J Rock
**Responsibilities**
**Senior:** Carrie Green *(Vice Principal)*
**US SIC:** 8211 **UK SIC:** 93200
**Employees:** 50

DUNS 21-778-4824
## Ray Allen
Stanhope Road, Ashford, Kent TN23 5RN
**Tel:** 01233620495
**Web:** www.kent.gov.uk
**Estd:** 1996 Proprietorship
**Line of Business:** Children's activity playcentres
**Proprietor:** Miss M Williams
**Responsibilities**
**Senior:** Monica Williams *(Manager)*
**US SIC:** 7999 **UK SIC:** 97913
**Employees:** 81

DUNS 29-644-8343
## Ray & Paul Carpets Ltd
3 Oxford Road, Peterborough, Cambridgeshire PE1 3BL
**Tel:** 01733-555843
**Web:** www.rayandpaul.tel
**Reg No:** 1971212 **Estd:** 1985 Private Limited Company
**Line of Business:** Retail sale of floor coverings
**Trading Style:** Ray & Paul Interiors
**Issued Capital:** £102
**Directors:** D C Noble, M J Shaw, P R Shaw
**Co. Secretary:** Mrs Kim Noble
**Branches:** Ray & Paul Carpets Ltd, 236-240 High Street, Cheltenham, Gloucestershire GL50 3HF
**US SIC:** 5713, 8999
**UK SIC:** 64700, 83954
**Auditors:** Gospel Hunt & Co
**Bankers:** Lloyds TSB Bank plc (77-72-16)

| | 31-03-14 | 31-03-13 | 31-03-12 |
|---|---|---|---|
| TA | 1,089,008 | 754,173 | 799,937 |
| NW | 435,070 | 485,200 | 495,551 |
| WC | 215,414 | 368,660 | 390,114 |

DUNS 77-613-5485
## Rayburn Holdings Ltd
Whitehouse Street, Walsall, West Midlands WS2 8HR
**Tel:** 01922625572
**Web:** www.rayburn.co.uk
**Reg No:** 3003332 **Estd:** 1995 Private Limited Company
**Line of Business:** Management activities of holding companies
**Issued Capital:** £50,002
**Directors:** Ms E D Griffiths, A M Griffiths, Mrs J A Shelley, C Parsonage, J Griffiths
**Co. Secretary:** Colin Parsonage
**US SIC:** 6711, 3079
**UK SIC:** 83962, 48360

| | 31-05-13 | 31-05-12 | 31-05-11 |
|---|---|---|---|
| TA | 566,582 | 308,237 | 328,791 |
| NW | 555,868 | 298,242 | 320,626 |
| WC | 278,165 | 16,174 | 34,193 |

DUNS 29-490-3687
## Rayburn Tours Ltd
**(Subsidiary of:** Rayburn Tours (Holdings) Ltd)
Rayburn House, 37 Brunel Parkway, Derby, Derbyshire DE24 8HR
**Tel:** 01332-347828
**Web:** www.rayburntours.com
**Reg No:** 1853736 **VAT No:** 411214810
**Estd:** 1984 Private Limited Company
**Line of Business:** Tour operators
**Issued Capital:** £50,000
**Principals:** Mrs B Boyden *(Chairman)*, Miss K Boyden, J T Boyden, Mrs L G James, J Boyden
**Co. Secretary:** Mrs Brenda Boyden
**US SIC:** 7999 **UK SIC:** 97913
**Auditors:** John W Mills & Co

| | 31-10-13 | 31-10-12 | 31-10-11 |
|---|---|---|---|
| TA | 4,149,392 | 3,254,000 | 3,237,724 |
| NW | 817,235 | 94,019 | 55,270 |
| WC | (366,986) | (515,188) | (597,176) |

DUNS 21-229-0183 **Imp-Exp**
## Rayburn Trading Co Ltd
**(Subsidiary of:** Jesem Holdings Ltd)
90 North Street, Manchester M8 8RA
**Fax:** 01612141327
**Web:** www.rayburntrading.co.uk
**Reg No:** 0588569 **Estd:** 2005 Private Limited Company
**Line of Business:** Health food retailers
**Issued Capital:** £4,165
**Principals:** M D Goldman *(Managing)*, H Goldman, R S Goldman, S Weiner
**Co. Secretary:** Tony Hobson
**Responsibilities**
**Health & Safety:** Andy Walker *(Health & Safety Manager)*
**Facilities:** Dave Cutayar *(Health & Safety Officer)*
**Branches:** Rayburn Trading Co Ltd, Porritt Street, Bury, Lancashire BL9 6HJ
**US SIC:** 2844, 5122
**UK SIC:** 25820, 61800
**Auditors:** Kay Johnson Gee
**Bankers:** Singer & Friedlander Ltd (16-52-18)

| | 31-08-13 | 31-08-12 | 31-08-11 |
|---|---|---|---|
| TO | 79,298,206 | 82,737,787 | 81,556,269 |
| P/L | 3,913,688 | 4,436,799 | 3,884,946 |
| NW | 23,997,976 | 21,043,229 | 17,727,561 |
| WC | 16,332,956 | 13,155,904 | 9,728,223 |
| Emp. | 170 | 174 | 170 |

DUNS 71-931-8987
## Raycare Ltd
69 Cranbourne Gardens, London NW11 0JB
**Tel:** 020-8455-1893
**Reg No:** 5312918 **Estd:** 2004 Private Limited Company
**Line of Business:** Other human health activities
**Issued Capital:** £100
**Managing Director:** R R Weiniger
**Co. Secretary:** Ms Sharon Weiniger
**US SIC:** 8091 **UK SIC:** 95200

| | 31-03-14 | 31-03-13 | 31-03-12 |
|---|---|---|---|
| TO | N/A | 2,078,045 | 2,040,393 |
| P/L | N/A | 244,901 | 358,416 |
| NW | 288,975 | 267,819 | 89,058 |
| WC | 317,925 | 430,101 | 355,318 |
| Emp. | N/A | 90 | 80 |

DUNS 34-580-3712 **Exp**
## Rayfern Ltd
**(Subsidiary of:** Rayfern Holdings Ltd)
Rayfern House, Newark Road, Peterborough, Cambridgeshire PE1 5DE
**Tel:** 01733-297500 **Fax:** 01733297500
**Web:** www.peme.co.uk
**Reg No:** 2727513 **VAT No:** 576756779
**Estd:** 1992 Private Limited Company
**Line of Business:** Installation of electrical wiring and fittings
**Export Markets:** U S A; European Union (E U)
**Export Sales:** £295,004
**Trading Style:** P E M E
**Issued Capital:** £156,038
**Directors:** P Jackson, B Barr, A J Maile, D J Martin, D G Bodart
**Co. Secretary:** Ian Morris
**Responsibilities**
**HR:** Karen Pike *(Human Resources Manager)*
**Purchasing:** Adam Beeton *(Purchasing Coordinator)*
**Branches:** Rayfern Ltd, 716 Banbury Avenue, Slough, Berkshire SL1 4LR
**US SIC:** 1731, 7397
**UK SIC:** 50300, 83702
**Auditors:** Grant Thornton
**Bankers:** Barclays Bank Plc (20-67-37)

| | 31-10-13 | 31-10-12 | 31-10-11 |
|---|---|---|---|
| TO | 12,168,246 | 12,021,328 | 11,015,303 |
| P/L | 439,243 | 687,582 | 622,152 |
| NW | 1,973,624 | 1,646,948 | 2,937,798 |
| WC | 1,906,099 | 1,550,598 | 3,039,849 |
| Emp. | 158 | 154 | 144 |

DUNS 73-304-6366
## Raymarine Uk Ltd
**(Subsidiary of:** Flir Systems Inc.)
Marine House, Cartwright Drive, Fareham, Hampshire PO15 5RJ
**Tel:** 01329-246-700 **Fax:** 01329246701
**Web:** www.raymarine.co.uk
**Reg No:** 4578449 **VAT No:** 615456443
**Estd:** 1974 Private Limited Company
**Line of Business:** Manufacture of electronic instruments and appliances for measuring, checking, testing, navigating and other purposes, except industrial process control equipment
**Trading Style:** Raymarine Inc
**Issued Capital:** £1
**Directors:** T A Surran, A L Trunzo
**Co. Secretary:** Mrs Joanne Dobbie
**Responsibilities**
**Senior:** Gr?ire Outters *(Director)*, Larry Rencken *(Vice President, Sales)*
**Marketing:** Derek Gilbert *(Relations Manager)*, Michelle Hildyard *(Marketing Manager)*
**Sales:** Larry Rencken *(Vice President, Sales)*, Michelle Salter *(Business Development Manager)*, Peter Wales *(Sales Manager, Eastern Europe,)*
**Branches:** Raymarine Uk Limited, Robinson Way, Anchorage Pk, Portsmouth, Hampshire PO6 5TD
**US SIC:** 3829 **UK SIC:** 37100
**Auditors:** KPMG LLP
**Bankers:** National Westminster Bank Plc (56-00-64)

| | 31-12-13 | 31-12-12 | 31-12-11 |
|---|---|---|---|
| TO | 17,542,000 | 19,810,000 | 28,148,000 |
| P/L | (19,342,000) | 3,152,000 | 2,162,000 |
| NW | 66,270,000 | 84,748,000 | 82,019,000 |
| WC | 2,114,000 | 491,000 | (3,533,000) |
| Emp. | 173 | 190 | 148 |

DUNS 29-878-8894
## Raymond Brown Construction Ltd
**(Subsidiary of:** Raymond Brown Group Ltd)
Innovation Centre, Bridgend, Mid Glamorgan CF31 3NA
**Tel:** 01425472241 **Fax:** 01656769975
**Web:** www.raymondbrowngroup.co.uk
**Reg No:** 2081940 **VAT No:** 504164971
**Estd:** 1987 Private Limited Company
**Line of Business:** Civil engineers
**Issued Capital:** £5,000
**Principals:** R G Isaac *(Managing)*, K White, M J Isaac, C C Craufurd, J K Currie, S J Harris, D T Wootton, G P Hardacre
**Co. Secretary:** Gregory Eaton
**Responsibilities**
**Senior:** Scott Best *(Plant Manager)*
**Finance:** Sharon Dyke *(Credit Controller)*
**Marketing:** John Canning *(Sales & Marketing Manager)*
**Sales:** John Canning *(Sales & Marketing Manager)*, Cath Waller *(Business Development Manager)*
**HR:** Lin Reed *(Human Resources Manager)*
**Health & Safety:** Nick Muir *(Health & Safety Manager)*
**Facilities:** Tim Waller *(Site Manager)*
**Operations:** John Canning *(Sales & Marketing Manager)*, Jamie Craufurd *(Quantity Surveyor)*, Andrew Eilbeck *(Project Manager)*
**Fleet:** Scott Best *(Plant Manager)*
**Branches:** Raymond Brown Construction Ltd ,Suite 3 Delta House,Laser Quay ,Culpepper Close,Medway City Estate,Rochester, ME2 4HUkent
**US SIC:** 1541, 1795
**UK SIC:** 50100, 50000
**Auditors:** Grant Thornton UK LLP
**Bankers:** The Royal Bank Of Scotland Plc (15-10-00)

| | 31-03-14 | 31-03-13 | 31-03-12 |
|---|---|---|---|
| TO | 47,062,000 | 40,826,000 | 45,388,000 |
| P/L | 1,309,000 | 1,250,000 | 1,708,000 |
| NW | 5,764,000 | 5,301,000 | 4,351,000 |
| WC | 5,117,000 | 4,646,000 | 3,594,000 |
| Emp. | 176 | 170 | 170 |

DUNS 21-657-1676
## Raymond Brown Group Ltd
160 Christchurch Road, Ringwood, Hampshire BH24 3AR
**Tel:** 01425472241
**Web:** www.raymondbrowngroup.co.uk
**Reg No:** 7137701 **Estd:** 2010 Private Limited Company
**Line of Business:** Management activities of holding companies
**Issued Capital:** £177
**Directors:** M J Isaac, R G Isaac, W I Lazarus, S J Harris, K White
**Co. Secretary:** Gregory Eaton
**US SIC:** 6711 **UK SIC:** 83962

| | 31-03-14 | 31-03-13 | 31-03-12 |
|---|---|---|---|
| TO | 85,504,000 | 73,120,000 | 72,844,000 |
| P/L | 1,650,000 | 690,000 | 1,381,000 |
| NW | (2,808,000) | (4,379,000) | (5,110,000) |
| WC | (7,112,000) | (7,043,000) | (7,773,000) |
| Emp. | 413 | 390 | 383 |

DUNS 23-786-6574 **Imp**
## Raymond James Investment Services Ltd
**(Subsidiary of:** Raymond James Financial Inc.)
77 Cornhill, London EC3V 3QQ
**Tel:** 02071513000 **Fax:** 02071513099
**Web:** www.rjis.co.uk
**Reg No:** 3779657 **Estd:** 1999 Private Limited Company
**Line of Business:** Investment consultants
**Issued Capital:** £5,402,923
**Directors:** R A Miller Iii, P D Moores
**Co. Secretary:** Nazibul Islam
**Responsibilities**
**Senior:** Leighton Bascom *(Branch Manager)*
**Branches:** Raymond James Investment Services Ltd, 31 Bridge St, Hitchin, Hertfordshire SG5 2DF
**US SIC:** 6111, 6211
**UK SIC:** 81501, 83100
**Auditors:** KPMG Audit PLC

| | 30-09-13 | 30-09-12 | 30-09-11 |
|---|---|---|---|
| TA | 6,891,550 | 6,764,604 | 5,441,300 |
| P/L | 234,591 | 17,479 | (826,688) |
| NW | 3,466,548 | 3,231,957 | 2,240,478 |
| WC | 1,846,757 | 2,111,544 | 1,451,701 |
| Emp. | 78 | 74 | 69 |

DUNS 21-090-8513
## Rayner & Sons Ltd
118-120 Garratt Lane, London SW18 4DR
**Tel:** 02088706000
**Web:** www.jraynerandsonsltd.co.uk
**Reg No:** 0543523 **VAT No:** 216427674
**Estd:** 1922 Private Limited Company
**Line of Business:** Renting of other machinery and equipment not elsewhere classified
**Issued Capital:** £3,000
**Principals:** G W Rayner *(Managing)*, R J Rayner, Mrs O L Rayner
**Co. Secretary:** Gordon Rayner
**Branches:** Rayner & Sons Ltd, 46 Randlesdown Rd, London SE6 3BT
**US SIC:** 7394, 2052
**UK SIC:** 84000, 41970
**Auditors:** J R Jewry & Co
**Bankers:** Barclays Bank Plc (20-90-69)

| | 31-01-14 | 31-01-13 | 31-01-12 |
|---|---|---|---|
| TA | 3,436,114 | 3,397,921 | 3,358,464 |
| NW | 3,415,739 | 3,366,083 | 3,327,986 |
| WC | 1,801,566 | 1,734,032 | 1,728,859 |

DUNS 22-985-0144
## Rayner Essex
Faulkner House, Victoria Street, St Albans, Hertfordshire AL1 3SE
**Tel:** 01727-833222
**Web:** www.rayneressex.com
**Estd:** 2001 Partnership
**Line of Business:** Accounting activities
**Trading Style:** Rayner Essex Chartered Accountants
**Partners:** C Walters, C W Goodkind
**Branches:** Rayner Essex, Faulkner House, Victoria Street, St. Albans, Hertfordshire AL1 3SE
**US SIC:** 8931 **UK SIC:** 83600
**Bankers:** National Westminster Bank Plc (60-18-11)
**Employees:** 70

DUNS 21-128-6577
## Rayner Essex Llp
Tavistock House South, London WC1H 9LG
**Tel:** 02073882641 **Fax:** 02073878969
**Web:** www.rayneressex.com
**Reg No:** 0338376OC **Estd:** 1970 Private Limited Company
**Line of Business:** Accounting activities
**Trading Style:** Rayner Essex Llp
**Responsibilities**
**Senior:** Lawrence Essex *(Partner)*, Clive Goodking *(Partner)*
**US SIC:** 8931 **UK SIC:** 83600

| | 30-09-13 | 30-09-12 | 30-09-11 |
|---|---|---|---|
| TO | 4,758,625 | 4,705,490 | 4,506,305 |
| NW | N/A | N/A | (83,165) |
| WC | 1,772,553 | 2,854,709 | 3,180,255 |
| Emp. | 69 | 69 | 71 |

DUNS 21-024-3259 **Imp-Exp**
## Rayner Surgical Group Ltd
Lowndes House, The Bury, Church Street, Chesham, Buckinghamshire HP5 1DJ
**Web:** www.rayner.com
**Reg No:** 0111927 **Estd:** 1910 Private Limited Company
**Line of Business:** Opticians ophthalmic
**Export Sales:** £15,959,000
**Issued Capital:** £824,357
**Directors:** N H De Coninck Smith, C E Dawes, T J Clover, T E Hobson, D Millington
**Co. Secretary:** Cepta Kelly
**Branches:** Rayner Surgical Group Ltd, 2 Wentworth Court, Church Street, Rotherham, South Yorkshire S61 4DX
**US SIC:** 6711, 5999
**UK SIC:** 83962, 65600
**Auditors:** Crowe Clark Whitehill LLP

| | 31-12-13 | 31-12-12 | 31-12-11 |
|---|---|---|---|
| TO | 43,820,000 | 45,653,000 | 49,473,000 |
| P/L | 1,340,000 | 5,390,000 | 7,186,000 |
| NW | 23,760,000 | 22,747,000 | 22,871,000 |
| WC | 14,864,000 | 14,895,000 | 14,814,000 |
| Emp. | 730 | 787 | 847 |

DUNS 23-547-8521
## Rayners Bakery Ltd
**(Subsidiary of:** Wildbeach Ltd)
12a Deer Park Road, Wimbledon, London SW19 3UQ
**Tel:** 02085436695
**Web:** www.bod.bak
**Reg No:** 3546318 **Estd:** 1998 Private Limited Company
**Line of Business:** Manufacture of bread; manufacture of fresh pastry goods and cakes
**Issued Capital:** £260,000
**Director:** P J Rayner
**Co. Secretary:** Ms Sheena Rayner
**US SIC:** 2051 **UK SIC:** 41960
**Auditors:** Wilson Sandford & Co

| | 29-03-14 | 29-03-13 | 29-03-12 |
|---|---|---|---|
| TA | 164 | 164 | 164 |
| NW | (315,975) | (315,975) | (315,975) |
| WC | (315,975) | (315,975) | (315,975) |

DUNS 39-963-7602
## Rayners (Extra Care Home) Ltd
Weedon Hill, Hyde Heath, Amersham, Buckinghamshire HP6 5UH
**Web:** www.careatrayners.co.uk
**Reg No:** 2263928 **Estd:** 1990 Private Limited Company
**Line of Business:** Non-charitable social work activities with accommodation
**Issued Capital:** £200
**Principals:** J I Matthews *(Managing)*, Mrs J M Matthews, Ms A J Gibbins, C J Matthews
**Co. Secretary:** James Matthews
**Responsibilities**
**HR:** Di Verrent *(Human Resources Manager)*
**US SIC:** 8321 **UK SIC:** 96111
**Auditors:** Chantrey Vellacott DFK
**Bankers:** National Westminster Bank Plc (60-01-15)

| | 30-09-13 | 30-09-12 | 30-09-11 |
|---|---|---|---|
| TO | 2,643,359 | 2,547,992 | 2,427,918 |
| P/L | 83,242 | 38,427 | 24,671 |
| NW | 2,642,372 | 2,586,379 | 2,416,010 |
| WC | (457,350) | (422,065) | (338,165) |
| Emp. | 78 | 76 | 73 |

DUNS 23-719-2112
## Raynor Foods Ltd
Farrow Road, Chelmsford, Essex CM1 3TH
**Tel:** 01245-353249 **Fax:** 01245-347889
**Web:** www.raynorfoods.co.uk
**Reg No:** 3713964 **VAT No:** 529311358
**Estd:** 1988 Private Limited Company
**Line of Business:** Manufacturers of food products
**Trading Style:** Raynors
**Issued Capital:** £104
**Principals:** A S Raynor *(Managing)*, Ms R A Raynor, C G Swaffin-Smith, A P Newland, Ms H A Bell, M A Raynor
**Co. Secretary:** Dr Andrew Twist
**Responsibilities**
**Marketing:** Heather Raynor *(Business Development Director)*
**Engineering:** aaron bratchley *(Production Manager)*
**US SIC:** 2099, 2052
**UK SIC:** 42399, 41970

| | 31-03-14 | 31-03-13 | 31-03-12 |
|---|---|---|---|
| TA | 1,560,180 | 1,496,088 | 1,191,810 |
| NW | 695,324 | 567,081 | 422,327 |
| WC | 392,976 | 265,157 | 171,122 |

DUNS 22-902-2157
## Raynor Roofing Ltd
**(Subsidiary of:** Raynor Holdings Ltd)
Craigmill House, Bridgefoot, Dundee, Angus DD3 0PH
**Web:** www.raynorgroup.co.uk
**Reg No:** 0073719SC **Estd:** 1986 Private Limited Company
**Line of Business:** Property maintenance services
**Issued Capital:** £20,250
**Principals:** R M Kelly *(Managing)*, B Donnelly
**Co. Secretary:** Ms Carla Kelly
**US SIC:** 1799 **UK SIC:** 50000
**Auditors:** W D Hall & Co
**Bankers:** The Royal Bank Of Scotland Plc (83-18-12)

| | 31-01-14 | 31-01-13 | 31-01-12 |
|---|---|---|---|
| TA | 1,104,574 | 1,060,728 | 1,043,684 |
| NW | 757,264 | 756,883 | 761,275 |
| WC | 729,393 | 727,707 | 720,613 |

DUNS 22-954-9837 Exp
## Rayovac (U K) Ltd
**(Subsidiary of:** Harbinger Group Inc.)
Unit 2a, Stephenson Road, Washington, Tyne and Wear NE37 3HW
**Tel:** 01914160441 **Fax:** 0191-417-8390
**Web:** www.spectrumbrands.com
**Reg No:** 1704133 **Estd:** 1983 Private Limited Company
**Line of Business:** Battery suppliers
**Export Markets:** Europe and other markets worldwide.
**Trading Style:** Rayovac (U K) Ltd
**Issued Capital:** £22,071,565
**Directors:** A D Streets, C Berry
**Co. Secretary:** Andrew Streets
**Responsibilities**
**Senior:** Claire Grant *(Human Resources Officer)*, Ian McCoy *(Warehouse Controller)*, Glen Rutherford *(Plant Manager)*
**Marketing:** Simon Farthing *(Marketing Manager)*
**HR:** Julia Potts *(Human Resources Officer)*
**Health & Safety:** Julia Potts *(Human Resources Officer)*
**Engineering:** Mark Ellison *(Production Manager)*
**Branches:** Rayovac (U K) Ltd, King Street, Maidstone, Kent ME14 1BG
**US SIC:** 3692 **UK SIC:** 34321
**Auditors:** KPMG LLP

**Bankers:** National Westminster Bank Plc (60-15-08)

| | 30-09-14 | 30-09-13 | 30-09-12 |
|---|---|---|---|
| TA | 73,373,000 | 70,032,000 | 66,690,000 |
| P/L | 3,341,000 | 3,342,000 | 3,351,000 |
| NW | 73,373,000 | 70,032,000 | 66,690,000 |

DUNS 21-280-0510
## Rayrigg Motors Ltd
**(Subsidiary of:** R.N.Smith Holdings Ltd)
Rayrigg Road, Windermere, Cumbria LA23 3DN
**Reg No:** 0750115 **Estd:** 1963 Private Limited Company
**Line of Business:** Sale of new motor vehicles
**Issued Capital:** £100
**Director:** D N Smith
**Co. Secretary:** Robert Smith
**Responsibilities**
**Senior:** Ann Spiby *(Manager)*
**US SIC:** 5511 **UK SIC:** 65100

| | 31-01-14 | 31-01-13 | 31-01-12 |
|---|---|---|---|
| TA | 2 | 2 | 2 |
| NW | 2 | 2 | 2 |

DUNS 28-856-7548
## The Raystede Centre for Animal Welfare Ltd
The Broyle, Ringmer, Lewes, East Sussex BN8 5AJ
**Tel:** 01825840252
**Web:** www.raystede.org
**Reg No:** 0816674 **Estd:** 1964 Private Company Limited By Guarantee
**Line of Business:** Animal welfare and care organisations
**Directors:** Dr J O'Neill, P J Vine-Hall, A D Zeal, R H Brown, M C Brown, J S Amies, M Wallwork, Ms M A Roberts
**Responsibilities**
**Senior:** Cyril Mann *(Manager)*
**Finance:** Brian Norton *(Financial Director)*
**Marketing:** Tracey Harris *(Marketing Manager)*
**IT:** Brian Norton *(Financial Director)*
**Branches:** The Raystede Centre For Animal Welfare Ltd, 27 Brighton Rd, Crawley, West Sussex RH10 6AE
**US SIC:** 0741, 8321
**UK SIC:** 95601, 96111
**Auditors:** Knill James
**Bankers:** Barclays Bank Plc (20-49-76)

| | 31-03-14 | 31-03-13 | 31-03-12 |
|---|---|---|---|
| TO | 1,821,045 | 2,088,311 | 1,556,194 |
| P/L | (543,264) | (128,568) | (528,761) |
| NW | 17,534,914 | 17,462,170 | 16,482,471 |
| WC | 1,440,527 | 1,452,120 | 1,374,756 |
| Emp. | 74 | 69 | 63 |

DUNS 34-730-5398 Imp
## Raytec Ltd
**(Subsidiary of:** Optex Company Limited)
Unit 3 Wansbeck Business Park, Rotary Parkway, Ashington, Northumberland NE63 8QW
**Tel:** 01670-520055 **Fax:** 01670819760
**Web:** www.raytecctv.com
**Reg No:** 5532798 **Estd:** 2006 Private Limited Company
**Line of Business:** Cctv & video equipment
**Export Sales:** £7,913,379
**Issued Capital:** £100
**Directors:** D J Coates, Doctor M E Wherrett, Y Kuroda, K Miyamoto, K Matsumoto, D Lambert, A G Whiting, T Kamimura
**Responsibilities**
**Senior:** Kenneth Bowman *(Technical Director)*, Shaun Cutler *(joint Managing director)*, Masakazu Nagano *(Director)*
**Finance:** Elaine Nordstrom *(Accounts Manager)*
**Marketing:** Declan Clark *(Marketing Executive)*, Catherine McElroy *(PR & Marketing Manager)*
**Sales:** Steve Devlin *(Sales Rep)*, Amy Sladdin *(Sales Executive)*
**Engineering:** Kenneth Bowman *(Technical Director)*
**US SIC:** 3651, 3662
**UK SIC:** 34541, 34430
**Auditors:** Murray & Lamb
**Bankers:** HSBC Bank plc (40-34-45)

| | 31-12-13 | 31-12-12 | 31-12-11 |
|---|---|---|---|
| TO | 11,595,283 | 11,494,637 | 10,732,194 |
| P/L | 2,237,744 | 2,235,925 | 2,156,405 |
| NW | 6,033,042 | 5,290,070 | 3,523,002 |
| WC | 5,043,018 | 4,320,133 | 3,374,340 |
| Emp. | 59 | 57 | 44 |

DUNS 21-753-3504 Imp-Exp
## Raytel Group Ltd
Raytel House, Cutlers Road, South Woodham Ferrers, Chelmsford, Essex CM3 5WA
**Tel:** 01245428300
**Web:** www.raytel.co.uk
**Reg No:** 1279536 **Estd:** 1980 Private Limited Company
**Line of Business:** Manufacture of electronic industrial process control equipment

**Issued Capital:** £610,000
**Principals:** R Lawrence *(Chairman and Managing)*, F T Hoare, D G Brookes
**Co. Secretary:** Mrs Eileen Biddle
**Responsibilities**
**Senior:** Roy Laurence *(Group Managing Director)*, Barry Mitchell *(Health & Safety Officer)*, Pam Stanton *(Shipping Manager)*
**IT:** Dave Coleman *(IT Manager)*
**HR:** Carol Wrigglesworth *(Personnel Coordinator)*
**Health & Safety:** Barry Mitchell *(Health & Safety Officer)*
**Operations:** Barry Mitchell *(Health & Safety Officer)*
**US SIC:** 3823, 6711
**UK SIC:** 37100, 83962
**Auditors:** BDO Stoy Hayward
**Bankers:** Barclays Bank Plc (20-04-96)

| | 30-06-14 | 30-06-13 | 30-06-12 |
|---|---|---|---|
| TO | 8,415,625 | 7,370,348 | 8,018,458 |
| P/L | 360,433 | 306,169 | 362,252 |
| NW | 2,108,852 | 1,815,543 | 1,573,870 |
| WC | 1,267,576 | 1,569,622 | 1,326,494 |
| Emp. | 56 | 58 | 59 |

DUNS 21-615-6158 Imp-Exp
## Raytheon Systems Ltd
**(Subsidiary of:** Raytheon United Kingdom Ltd)
The Pinnacles, Elizabeth Way, Harlow, Essex CM19 5BB
**Tel:** 01279 426862 **Fax:** 01279 410413
**Web:** www.raytheon.co.uk
**Reg No:** 0406809 **Estd:** 1946 Private Limited Company
**Line of Business:** Other manufacturing not elsewhere classified
**Export Markets:** worldwide
**Export Sales:** £233,255,000
**Issued Capital:** £359,711,780
**Directors:** R R Yuse, R M Delorge, Dr T W Lawrence, Mrs R L Rhoads, J D Harris Ii, J M Quinn, I R Stopps, R N Daniel
**Co. Secretary:** John Reilly
**Responsibilities**
**Senior:** Matthew Riddle *(Manager)*
**Fleet:** Brooke Hoskins *(Director Of Strategy And Gover)*
**Branches:** Raytheon Systems Ltd, The Pinnacles, Elizabeth Way, Harlow, Essex CM19 5BB
**US SIC:** 3999 **UK SIC:** 49590
**Auditors:** PricewaterhouseCoopers LLP
**Bankers:** Citibank Na (18-50-08)

| | 31-12-13 | 31-12-12 | 31-12-11 |
|---|---|---|---|
| TO | 386,320,000 | 261,581,000 | 300,010,000 |
| P/L | 76,734,000 | 27,546,000 | 332,452,000 |
| NW | 524,935,000 | 441,469,000 | 487,932,000 |
| WC | 313,183,000 | 255,205,000 | 305,432,000 |
| Emp. | 1,240 | 1,226 | 1,284 |

DUNS 21-316-2605 Imp-Exp
## Rayware Ltd
26-32 Spitfire Road, Triumph Trading Park, Speke Hall Road, Liverpool, Merseyside L24 9BF
**Tel:** 0151-486-1888 **Fax:** 0151-486-1467
**Web:** www.rayware.co.uk
**Reg No:** 1237389 **VAT No:** 166252268
**Estd:** 1975 Private Limited Company
**Line of Business:** China and glassware wholesalers
**Export Markets:** E U
**Trading Style:** I P H Direct, Islington Pottery
**Issued Capital:** £100
**Principals:** A E Endfield *(Financial)*, Hilton Trade Corporation Ltd
**Co. Secretary:** Christopher Mcdonough
**Responsibilities**
**Senior:** Robert Dale-Jones *(Manager)*
**Marketing:** Kate O'Neill *(Marketing Manager)*, Sarah Selzer *(Marketing, PR & Media Manager)*
**IT:** Ceri Wilde *(IT Manager)*
**US SIC:** 5199, 8999
**UK SIC:** 61900, 83954
**Auditors:** Grant Thornton UK LLP
**Bankers:** HSBC Bank plc (40-29-08)

| | 31-12-13 | 31-12-12 | 31-12-11 |
|---|---|---|---|
| TO | 29,453,246 | 27,032,325 | 27,475,742 |
| P/L | (37,737) | (41,767) | 8,068 |
| NW | 151,586 | (93,561) | 331,752 |
| WC | 1,498,493 | 1,253,536 | 1,653,902 |
| Emp. | 121 | 112 | 112 |

DUNS 21-558-4303 Imp
## Rb & W Corporation
12b Two Locks, Hurst Business Park, Brierley Hill, West Midlands DY5 1UU
**Tel:** 01384-400-936
**Web:** www.rbwmfg.com
**VAT No:** 944291217 **Estd:** 1966 Proprietorship
**Line of Business:** Agricultural shows
**US SIC:** 7399 **UK SIC:** 83954
**Employees:** 130

DUNS 53-654-9447
## R.B. Hilton Ltd
**(Subsidiary of:** Cape East Ec)
6-9 Stockley Park The Square, Uxbridge, Middlesex UB11 1ET
**Tel:** 01895595595
**Web:** www.hiltonpage.com
**Reg No:** 3460194 **Estd:** 1997 Private Limited Company
**Line of Business:** Business services
**Issued Capital:** £2
**Directors:** Mrs V A George, R F Allan
**Co. Secretary:** Richard Allan
**Responsibilities**
**Senior:** Gary Lowndes *(Director)*
**US SIC:** 7399 **UK SIC:** 83954
**Auditors:** PricewaterhouseCoopers LLP
**Bankers:** Barclays Bank Plc (20-00-00)

| | 31-12-13 | 31-12-12 | 31-12-11 |
|---|---|---|---|
| TO | 7,901,000 | 9,646,000 | 8,279,000 |
| P/L | 6,082,000 | 11,963,000 | 752,000 |
| NW | 5,990,000 | 5,166,000 | 4,840,000 |
| WC | 4,644,000 | 3,722,000 | 3,828,000 |
| Emp. | 385 | 596 | 578 |

DUNS 21-663-9223
## Rb Pharmaceuticals Ltd
**(Subsidiary of:** Reckitt Benckiser Group Plc)
103-105 Bath Road, Slough, Berkshire SL1 3UH
**Tel:** 08457697079
**Web:** www.rb.com
**Reg No:** 7183451 **Estd:** 2010 Private Limited Company
**Line of Business:** Manufacture of basic pharmaceutical products
**Export Sales:** £337,729,000
**Issued Capital:** £100,002
**Directors:** M W Crossley, S Sehgal, R M Jameson, A J Gawman
**Co. Secretary:** Ms Lola Emetulu
**US SIC:** 2834 **UK SIC:** 25700
**Auditors:** PricewaterhouseCoopers LLP

| | 31-12-13 | 31-12-12 | 31-12-11 |
|---|---|---|---|
| TO | 355,241,000 | 395,029,000 | 441,012,000 |
| P/L | (798,120,000) | 201,199,000 | 13,139,000 |
| NW | (222,281,000) | (428,228,000) | 9,657,000 |
| WC | (226,451,000) | (428,375,000) | 9,657,000 |
| Emp. | 210 | 247 | N/A |

DUNS 42-380-8166
## Rb Sport & Leisure Holdings Plc
Botley Road, West End, Southampton, Hampshire SO30 3XJ
**Tel:** 023-8047-2002
**Web:** www.gsbowl.com
**Reg No:** 4368413 **Estd:** 2002 Public Limited Company
**Line of Business:** Sports clubs
**Trading Style:** Rose Bowl Fitness and Squash
**Issued Capital:** £7,722,783
**Directors:** P M Trant, A N Williams, F I Janmohamed, R G Bransgrove, S J Robertson, B Smith
**Co. Secretary:** David Mann
**Responsibilities**
**Senior:** Christopher Egelstaff *(Director)*
**US SIC:** 7999 **UK SIC:** 97913
**Auditors:** HLB AV Audit plc
**Bankers:** Allied Irish Bank (gb) (23-91-39)

| | 31-12-13 | 31-12-12 | 31-12-11 |
|---|---|---|---|
| TO | 8,143,877 | 7,647,049 | 10,291,261 |
| P/L | 212,946 | (1,341,221) | (3,229,781) |
| NW | 4,537,490 | 4,263,738 | 5,577,511 |
| WC | (5,272,221) | (8,676,824) | (12,986,161) |
| Emp. | 61 | 71 | 82 |

DUNS 21-263-0693
## R.B.A.Moody Bros(Contractors) Ltd
Binks Close, Northallerton, North Yorkshire DL6 2YB
**Tel:** 01609-772207 **Fax:** 01609-779349
**Web:** www.moody-construction.co.uk
**Reg No:** 0516941 **VAT No:** 258097234
**Estd:** 1953 Private Limited Company
**Line of Business:** Development and selling of real estate
**Issued Capital:** £8,250
**Principals:** R D Moody *(Managing)*, J R Moody, Mrs M E Moody
**Co. Secretary:** Roy Moody
**Responsibilities**
**Health & Safety:** Angela Doran *(Health & Safety Officer)*
**US SIC:** 6552, 1541
**UK SIC:** 85000, 50100
**Auditors:** McGregors Corporate
**Bankers:** HSBC Bank plc (40-35-03)

| | 30-04-14 | 30-04-13 | 30-04-12 |
|---|---|---|---|
| TO | 5,812,621 | 3,693,884 | 3,677,351 |
| P/L | 352,242 | 31,087 | 146,851 |
| NW | 7,126,036 | 6,952,439 | 7,080,016 |
| WC | 5,593,848 | 5,410,046 | 5,503,655 |
| Emp. | 56 | 47 | 52 |

DUNS 21-192-2158 **Imp-Exp**

## Rbc Europe Ltd

(**Subsidiary of:** Royal Bank of Canada)
Riverbank House, 2 Swan Lane, London EC4R 3BF
**Tel:** 02076-534-000 **Fax:** 02070-927-900
**Web:** www.rbc.com
**Reg No:** 0995939 **VAT No:** 365345640
**Estd:** 1970 Private Limited Company
**Line of Business:** Banks
**Trading Style:** Royal Bank of Canada
**Issued Capital:** £501,960,584
**Directors:** R E Talbot, A D Mcgregor, Dr J E Roberts, G Hepworth, S R Krag, H J Samuel, Ms J R Fukakusa, J N Pettigrew
**Co. Secretary:** Jason Wright
**Responsibilities**
**Senior:** Mark Standish *(Manager)*
**US SIC:** 6012, 7399
**UK SIC:** 81402, 83954
**Auditors:** Deloitte LLP
**Bankers:** National Westminster Bank Plc (60-00-01)

**Following financial data are in thousands**

| | 31-10-13 | 31-10-12 | 31-10-11 |
|---|---|---|---|
| TA | 27,466,865 | 28,200,222 | 34,089,339 |
| P/L | (26,280) | (57,314) | (133,049) |
| NW | 914,334 | 942,427 | 977,565 |
| WC | 1,479,370 | 418,357 | (5,293,047) |
| Emp. | 617 | 599 | 559 |

DUNS 23-280-8733

## Rbc Trust Company (Guernsey) Ltd

Po Box 48 Canada Court, St Peter Port, Guernsey, Channel Islands GY1 4PW
**Tel:** 01481732600 **Fax:** 01481-728493
**Web:** www.rbcwminternational.com
**Reg No:** 0008028G **Estd:** 1979 Private Limited Company
**Line of Business:** Trustee company.
**Trading Style:** Abacus Financial Trustees
**Issued Capital:** £7
**Directors:** N J Crocker, Ms H Hunter, F Dearie, D C Jeffreys
**US SIC:** 6733 **UK SIC:** 83100
**Bankers:** National Westminster Bank Plc (60-09-20)
**Employees:** 300

DUNS 45-854-4129 **Imp**

## Rbf Comms. Services Ltd

(**Subsidiary of:** Alexstel Ltd)
Pontymister Industrial Estate, Risca, Newport, Gwent NP11 6NP
**Tel:** 01633-601081 **Fax:** 01633-619595
**Web:** www.rbfcomms.com
**Reg No:** 3200457 **VAT No:** 742048156
**Estd:** 1996 Private Limited Company
**Line of Business:** Telecom services
**Issued Capital:** £3
**Principals:** R Barton *(Managing)*, Ms S Barton, S A Barton
**Co. Secretary:** Ms Julie Jamieson
**Branches:** Rbf Comms. Services Ltd, Pontymister Industrial Estate, Risca, Risca, Newport, Gwent NP11 6NP
**US SIC:** 4899 **UK SIC:** 79020
**Auditors:** Guilfoyle Sage & Co
**Bankers:** HSBC Bank plc (40-38-49)

| | 30-09-13 | 30-09-12 | 30-09-11 |
|---|---|---|---|
| TA | 1,417,007 | 1,279,804 | 1,149,300 |
| NW | 475,768 | 598,490 | 662,454 |
| WC | 36,158 | 227,113 | 377,438 |

DUNS 54-890-6114

## R.B.F. Healthcare Ltd

(**Subsidiary of:** Rbf Industries Ltd)
55 Vanguard Way, Shoeburyness, Southend-On-Sea, Essex SS3 9QY
**Tel:** 01702527401
**Web:** www.rbfhealthcare.co.uk
**Reg No:** 3471890 **Estd:** 1997 Private Limited Company
**Line of Business:** Healthcare companies
**Issued Capital:** £1,000
**Co. Secretary:** David Howard
**US SIC:** 8091 **UK SIC:** 95200
**Bankers:** HSBC Bank plc (40-43-21)

| | 31-03-14 | 31-03-13 | 31-03-12 |
|---|---|---|---|
| TA | 1,000 | 1,000 | 1,000 |
| NW | 1,000 | 1,000 | 1,000 |

DUNS 21-279-6627

## R.Bland Ltd

Morton Road, Darlington, County Durham DL1 4PT
**Tel:** 01325-744960
**Web:** www.rblandltd.co.uk
**Reg No:** 0705164 **VAT No:** 258371735
**Estd:** 1961 Private Limited Company
**Line of Business:** Plumbing, heating & air cond contractors
**Issued Capital:** £502
**Managing Director:** P R Bland
**Co. Secretary:** Graham Bland
**Responsibilities**
**IT:** Gareth Bland *(IT Manager)*
**Branches:** R.bland Ltd, Bowesfield La, Stockton-On-Tees, Cleveland TS18 3EU
**US SIC:** 1711 **UK SIC:** 50300
**Auditors:** Chipchase Manners & Co
**Bankers:** Barclays Bank Plc (20-25-29)

| | 31-08-13 | 31-08-12 | 31-08-11 |
|---|---|---|---|
| TO | 6,700,925 | 7,185,741 | 6,672,441 |
| P/L | 911,132 | 643,545 | 315,612 |
| NW | 4,396,054 | 3,861,686 | 3,564,191 |
| WC | 3,822,362 | 3,265,911 | 2,910,059 |
| Emp. | 101 | 128 | 130 |

DUNS 49-383-2067

## Rbm Agricultural Ltd

Holme Road, Market Weighton, York, North Yorkshire YO43 3EW
**Tel:** 01430-872421
**Web:** www.rbmagricultural.co.uk
**Reg No:** 3130243 **Estd:** 1995 Private Limited Company
**Line of Business:** Agents involved in the sale of agricultural raw materials, live animals, textile raw materials and semi-finished goods
**Export Sales:** £1,915,581
**Issued Capital:** £20,000
**Principals:** A G Denner *(Managing)*, Mrs K E Denner
**Co. Secretary:** Adrian Denner
**Branches:** Rbm Agricultural Ltd, Clarborough Hall, Main Street, Retford, Nottinghamshire DN22 9NH
**US SIC:** 5159 **UK SIC:** 61100
**Auditors:** James B Kennedy & Co
**Bankers:** HSBC Bank plc (40-26-01)

| | 31-12-13 | 31-12-12 | 31-12-11 |
|---|---|---|---|
| TO | 36,344,146 | 37,564,395 | 34,961,775 |
| P/L | 1,073,319 | 958,747 | 786,829 |
| NW | 4,208,962 | 3,895,380 | 3,189,147 |
| WC | 1,337,090 | 1,053,023 | 1,361,961 |
| Emp. | 84 | 83 | 73 |

DUNS 21-227-9761

## Rbs Care Homes Foundation

4-6 St Lukes Road Matlock Terrace, Torquay, Devon TQ2 5NY
**Tel:** 01803400007
**Proprietorship**
**Line of Business:** Residential care establishments
**Proprietor:** Mrs J Middleton
**US SIC:** 8321 **UK SIC:** 96111
**Employees:** 50

DUNS 73-937-2415

## Rbs Hg (Uk) Ltd

(**Subsidiary of:** Hm Treasury)
250 Bishopsgate, London EC2M 4AA
**Tel:** 02076788000 **Fax:** 02076788245
**Web:** www.abnamro.com
**Reg No:** 2943784 **Estd:** 1994 Private Limited Company
**Line of Business:** Management activities of holding companies
**Trading Style:** Rbs
**Issued Capital:** £177,500,000
**Directors:** R J Lawrence, R A Horrocks
**Co. Secretary:**
Rbs Secretarial Services Limited
**Responsibilities**
**Senior:** Kathy Fernanders *(Manager)*, Simon Mould *(Director)*
**US SIC:** 6711, 6211
**UK SIC:** 83962, 83100
**Auditors:** Emst & Young LLP

| | 31-12-13 | 31-12-12 | 31-12-11 |
|---|---|---|---|
| TA | 41,366,000 | 45,670,000 | 57,199,000 |
| P/L | (4,304,000) | (11,529,000) | (5,719,000) |
| NW | 41,366,000 | 45,670,000 | 57,199,000 |

DUNS 22-526-8283

## Rbs Invoice Finance Ltd

(**Subsidiary of:** Hm Treasury)
Smith House, Feltham, Middlesex TW13 7QD
**Tel:** 08706000520 **Fax:** 02087513367
**Web:** www.rbsif.co.uk
**Reg No:** 0662221 **Estd:** 1960 Private Limited Company
**Line of Business:** Financial intermediation not elsewhere classified
**Issued Capital:** £1,000,000
**Directors:** A Holden, M J Morrin, A A Rankin
**Co. Secretary:**
Rbs Secretarial Services Limited
**Responsibilities**
**IT:** Andrew Gore *(Head of IT)*
**Branches:** Rbs Invoice Finance Ltd, 6th Floor, 1 Redcliff Street, Bristol, Avon BS1 6NP
**US SIC:** 6111 **UK SIC:** 81501
**Auditors:** Deloitte LLP
**Bankers:** National Westminster Bank Plc (60-08-46)

**Following financial data are in thousands**

| | 31-12-13 | 31-12-12 | 31-12-11 |
|---|---|---|---|
| TA | 4,330,250 | 4,239,417 | 3,968,008 |
| P/L | 126,279 | 113,689 | 114,317 |
| NW | 532 | (921) | 1,127 |
| WC | 325 | (116,403) | (155,289) |
| Emp. | 959 | 935 | 984 |

DUNS 77-119-1830

## Rbs Management Services (Uk) Ltd

(**Subsidiary of:** Hm Treasury)
A B N Amro Securities Uk Ltd, London EC2M 3XW
**Tel:** 02076781922
**Web:** www.rbs.co.uk
**Reg No:** 2691666 **Estd:** 1992 Private Limited Company
**Line of Business:** Other business activities not elsewhere classified
**Issued Capital:** £25,000
**Directors:** R A Horrocks, R J Lawrence, M Geslak
**Co. Secretary:**
Rbs Secretarial Services Limited
**Responsibilities**
**Senior:** Simon Mould *(Director)*
**US SIC:** 7399 **UK SIC:** 83954
**Auditors:** Deloitte LLP
**Bankers:** Lloyds TSB Bank plc (30-00-02)

| | 31-12-13 | 31-12-12 | 31-12-11 |
|---|---|---|---|
| TO | N/A | 46,013,000 | 208,441,000 |
| P/L | (1,411,000) | 30,980,000 | 113,990,000 |
| NW | 6,864,000 | 9,776,000 | 37,413,000 |
| WC | 6,864,000 | 9,776,000 | (91,153,000) |
| Emp. | N/A | 6 | 410 |

DUNS 23-759-2592

## Rbs Scaffolding Ltd

The Grove, Upper Northam Drive, Hedge End, Southampton, Hampshire SO30 4BG
**Tel:** 023-8047-1119
**Web:** www.rbsscaffolding.co.uk
**Reg No:** 3753002 **Estd:** 1987 Private Limited Company
**Line of Business:** Scaffolds and work platform erectors
**Issued Capital:** £100
**Directors:** R B Shaw, A T Willis, G A Kennett, Mrs D A Shaw
**Co. Secretary:** Ms Denise Shaw
**US SIC:** 7394 **UK SIC:** 84000
**Auditors:** Cooke & Co
**Bankers:** National Westminster Bank Plc (55-50-26)

| | 30-04-14 | 30-04-13 | 30-04-12 |
|---|---|---|---|
| TA | 2,152,791 | 2,097,413 | 1,762,803 |
| NW | 1,761,896 | 1,544,905 | 1,289,381 |
| WC | 705,602 | 723,086 | 667,181 |

DUNS 21-622-5763

## R.C. Austin Ltd

6 Courtenay Street, Newton Abbot, Devon TQ12 2DU
**Tel:** 01626-333-444 **Fax:** 01626-207-208
**Web:** www.austins-uk.com
**Reg No:** 0254274 **VAT No:** 140743588
**Estd:** 1924 Private Limited Company
**Line of Business:** Other retail sale in non-specialised stores
**Trading Style:** Austins Department Store
**Issued Capital:** £940
**Managing Director:** D C Austin
**Co. Secretary:** Ms Mary White
**Responsibilities**
**Senior:** Karen Berry *(Marketing Manager)*, Paul Maloney *(Warehouse Manager)*
**Finance:** Gill Podilchuck *(Accountant)*
**Marketing:** Trevor Boobyea *(Store Manager)*
**Sales:** Trevor Boobyea *(Store Manager)*
**Admin:** Gill Podilchuck *(Accountant)*
**IT:** Gill Podilchuck *(Accountant)*
**HR:** Trevor Boobyea *(Store Manager)*
**Health & Safety:** Trevor Boobyea *(Store Manager)*
**Facilities:** Paul Maloney *(Warehouse Manager)*
**Operations:** Trevor Boobyea *(Store Manager)*
**Purchasing:** Trevor Boobyea *(Store Manager)*
**Branches:** R.c. Austin Ltd, 10-12 Wolborough Street, Newton Abbot, Devon TQ12 1JJ
**US SIC:** 5399 **UK SIC:** 65600
**Auditors:** Beavis Morgan Audit Ltd
**Bankers:** Lloyds TSB Bank plc (30-96-06)

| | 01-02-14 | 26-01-13 | 29-02-12 |
|---|---|---|---|
| TO | 6,309,766 | 6,239,046 | 6,319,694 |
| P/L | 436,592 | 314,610 | 239,914 |
| NW | 5,670,181 | 5,325,095 | 5,108,764 |
| WC | 833,428 | 884,340 | 619,271 |
| Emp. | 145 | 143 | 153 |

DUNS 22-721-0481

## R.C. Cutting & Co. Ltd

10-12 Arcadia Avenue, Finchley, London N3 2JU
**Web:** www.rccutting.co.uk
**Reg No:** 0326209 **VAT No:** 231726482
**Estd:** 1879 Private Limited Company
**Line of Business:** Installation of electrical wiring and fittings
**Issued Capital:** £5,020
**Directors:** P T Cripps, M T Clarke
**Co. Secretary:** John Jolly
**Responsibilities**
**Senior:** David Bayford *(Manager)*, Roy Hiscock *(Manager)*
**Finance:** Roy Hiscock *(Manager)*
**Marketing:** Roy Hiscock *(Manager)*
**Sales:** Roy Hiscock *(Manager)*
**Facilities:** Roy Hiscock *(Manager)*
**US SIC:** 1731 **UK SIC:** 50300
**Auditors:** MacIntyre Hudson LLP
**Bankers:** National Westminster Bank Plc (50-30-03)

| | 31-12-13 | 31-12-12 | 31-12-11 |
|---|---|---|---|
| TO | 2,167,271 | N/A | N/A |
| P/L | 82,680 | N/A | N/A |
| NW | 1,054,204 | 991,381 | 1,098,904 |
| WC | 728,967 | 673,217 | 660,952 |

DUNS 28-975-0465

## R.C. Warren Packers Ltd

Unit C, Watford, Hertfordshire WD18 9TL
**Web:** www.giftwarren.com
**Reg No:** 1751747 **VAT No:** 354053964
**Estd:** 1983 Private Limited Company
**Line of Business:** Food packers
**Issued Capital:** £20,100
**Directors:** P R Cox, A Warren
**Co. Secretary:** Mrs Karen Trott
**Responsibilities**
**IT:** Carren Woodeck *(Network, Security Manager)*
**US SIC:** 7399 **UK SIC:** 83054
**Auditors:** Murra Young
**Bankers:** National Westminster Bank Plc (60-18-11)

| | 30-09-14 | 30-09-13 | 30-09-12 |
|---|---|---|---|
| TA | 380,689 | 507,276 | 522,649 |
| NW | 152,934 | 163,845 | 127,182 |
| WC | 108,813 | 103,468 | 184,627 |

DUNS 22-709-2418 **Imp-Exp**

## Rci Europe

(**Subsidiary of:** Wyndham Worldwide Corporation)
Kettering Parkway, Kettering, Northamptonshire NN15 6EY
**Tel:** 01536310101
**Web:** www.rci.com
**Reg No:** 1148410 **VAT No:** 217704768
**Estd:** 1973 Private Unlimited Company
**Line of Business:** Timeshare operations
**Trading Style:** R C I
**Issued Capital:** £69,126,000
**Directors:** A Liggins, P A Carter, S J Lowe
**Co. Secretary:** Henry Bankes
**Responsibilities**
**Senior:** Gregg Anderson *(Global Managing Director)*
**Sales:** Sarah Tracey *(Senior Sales Executive)*
**IT:** Jon Rodger *(Senior IT Executive)*
**HR:** Audrey Barnard *(Human Resources Manager)*
**Health & Safety:** John Beveridge *(Head of Facilities)*
**Facilities:** John Beveridge *(Head of Facilities)*
**US SIC:** 7021, 7399
**UK SIC:** 66500, 83954
**Auditors:** Deloitte & Touche LLP
**Bankers:** National Westminster Bank Plc (60-04-04)

| | 31-12-13 | 31-12-12 | 31-12-11 |
|---|---|---|---|
| TO | 50,185,696 | 50,468,531 | 51,999,064 |
| P/L | 7,873,961 | 4,678,672 | 31,611,313 |
| NW | 128,021,040 | 119,825,662 | 115,607,512 |
| WC | 37,046,733 | 31,409,191 | 28,028,814 |
| Emp. | 235 | 229 | 228 |

DUNS 37-851-5340

## Rci Financial Services Ltd

(**Subsidiary of:** Renault)
Egale House, 78 St Albans Road, Watford, Hertfordshire WD17 1AF
**Tel:** 08456001600 **Fax:** 01923-718203
**Web:** www.rcibanque.com
**Reg No:** 3302462 **Estd:** 1997 Private Limited Company
**Line of Business:** Car finance
**Issued Capital:** £106,400,000
**Directors:** Ms A Altemaire, S M Gowler, M J Banfield, P J Claude, A R Heaffey, P A Cabrier
**Co. Secretary:** Ms Suzette Shipton
**Responsibilities**
**Senior:** Eric Spielrein *(Director)*, Ruth Walkden *(Manager)*
**US SIC:** 6111 **UK SIC:** 81501
**Auditors:** Ernst & Young LLP
**Bankers:** National Westminster Bank Plc (60-17-32)

**Following financial data are in thousands**

| | 31-12-13 | 31-12-12 | 31-12-11 |
|---|---|---|---|
| TA | 2,059,590 | 1,647,473 | 1,446,763 |
| P/L | 58,346 | 41,904 | 31,918 |
| NW | 160,562 | 132,879 | 120,409 |
| WC | 1,161,075 | 984,423 | 831,874 |
| Emp. | 179 | 171 | 164 |

DUNS 73-362-2612
## Rcl Express Ltd
Lowfield Way, Lowfield Busns Park, Elland, West Yorkshire HX5 9DA
**Tel:** 01422327423
**Web:** www.rclexpress.co.uk
**Reg No:** 4635778 **Estd:** 2003 Private Limited Company
**Line of Business:** Freight transport by road not elsewhere classified
**Issued Capital:** £1,000
**Director:** R Lilley
**US SIC:** 4213 **UK SIC:** 72300

| | 30-06-14 | 30-06-13 | 30-06-12 |
|---|---|---|---|
| TA | 163,031 | 82,072 | 26,079 |
| NW | (26,746) | (14,756) | (7,471) |
| WC | (86,523) | (44,095) | (25,427) |

DUNS 39-345-5340
## Rcn Publishing Company Ltd
(**Subsidiary of:** The Royal College of Nursing of the United Kingdom)
The Heights, 59-65 Lowlands Road, Harrow, Middlesex HA1 3AW
**Tel:** 02084231066 **Fax:** 02088723195
**Web:** www.rcnpublishing.co.uk
**Reg No:** 2119155 **Estd:** 1987 Private Limited Company
**Line of Business:** Newspapers publishing
**Trading Style:** Nursing Standard
**Issued Capital:** £500,000
**Directors:** M J Richardson, Dr A Holloway, Ms C A Mcnamara, Dr M A Chamberlain, D Cooper, R Grant, Mrs K Fawcett
**Co. Secretary:** Mukund Kotecha
**Responsibilities**
**Senior:** Louise Daggett *(Administration Director)*, Andrew McGovern *(Non-Executive Director)*, Tony O'Rourke *(Commercial Director)*, Rhonda Oliver *(Manager)*
**Marketing:** Gary Bell *(Senior Editor)*, Sarah Harrison *(News Editor)*, Helen Sumner *(Marketing Manager)*, Christine Walker *(Editor)*
**Sales:** Neil Hobson *(Sales Manager)*, Andy Mccallum *(Sales Manager)*
**Admin:** Louise Daggett *(Administration Director)*
**IT:** Alex Oldfield *(Computer Manager)*
**HR:** Louise Daggett *(Administration Director)*
**Health & Safety:** Louise Daggett *(Administration Director)*
**Facilities:** Louise Daggett *(Administration Director)*
**Operations:** Louise Daggett *(Administration Director)*
**Purchasing:** Louise Daggett *(Administration Director)*
**US SIC:** 2711 **UK SIC:** 47512
**Auditors:** BDO Stoy Hayward
**Bankers:** National Westminster Bank Plc (60-40-02)

| | 31-12-13 | 31-12-12 | 31-12-12 |
|---|---|---|---|
| TO | 10,683,717 | 13,478,233 | 13,833,162 |
| P/L | 1,052,559 | 1,410,290 | 934,919 |
| NW | 3,505,274 | 3,947,419 | 3,554,229 |
| WC | 3,418,965 | 3,828,602 | 3,409,669 |
| Emp. | 86 | 86 | 88 |

DUNS 58-021-5655
## Rcp Parking Ltd
Grosvenor House, Norwich, Norfolk NR1 1NS
**Tel:** 01603-620720
**Web:** www.regionalcarparks.co.uk
**Reg No:** 2904876 **Estd:** 1994 Private Limited Company
**Line of Business:** Car parking and garaging services
**Trading Style:** Sekura-Byk
**Issued Capital:** £104
**Directors:** S Naghshineh, Ms S D Naghshineh, E G Cameron
**Co. Secretary:** Ardeshir Naghshineh
**Responsibilities**
**Senior:** Vanessa Fletcher *(Manager)*, Simon Legood *(Financial Manager)*
**Finance:** Vanessa Fletcher *(Manager)*, Simon Legood *(Financial Manager)*
**Branches:** Rcp Parking Ltd, Leisure World, Croft Road, Coventry, West Midlands CV1 3AZ
**US SIC:** 4226, 4789
**UK SIC:** 77003, 77002
**Auditors:** Adler Shine
**Bankers:** The Royal Bank Of Scotland Plc (16-26-30)

| | 31-03-14 | 31-03-13 | 31-03-12 |
|---|---|---|---|
| TO | 6,525,570 | 5,533,823 | 5,383,188 |
| P/L | 668,266 | 297,062 | (719,881) |
| NW | (88,515) | (723,531) | (1,089,111) |
| WC | (5,191,589) | (5,525,516) | (5,663,017) |
| Emp. | 62 | 56 | 58 |

DUNS 23-612-0510 Imp
## Rcs Logistics Ltd
Darwin Road, Willowbrook East Industrial Estate, Corby, Northamptonshire NN17 5XZ
**Tel:** 01536443900
**Web:** www.rcslogistics.co.uk
**Reg No:** 3609237 **Estd:** 1973 Private Limited Company
**Line of Business:** Other supporting land transport activities
**Export Sales:** £2,116,040
**Issued Capital:** £274,100
**Directors:** R J Robinson, P E Mitchell, S J Gray, S R Smith
**Responsibilities**
**Senior:** Darren Beaty *(Manager)*
**HR:** Maxine Harding-Wines *(HR Manager)*
**US SIC:** 4789, 4226
**UK SIC:** 77002, 77003
**Auditors:** Jacksons & Grimes Ltd
**Bankers:** National Westminster Bank Plc (60-06-11)

| | 31-12-13 | 31-12-12 | 31-12-11 |
|---|---|---|---|
| TO | 7,727,071 | 8,375,062 | 9,439,933 |
| P/L | 560,757 | 648,914 | 934,112 |
| NW | 1,669,592 | 1,350,625 | 1,007,715 |
| WC | 975,093 | 624,930 | 165,477 |
| Emp. | 114 | 136 | 150 |

DUNS 21-120-7809
## Rct Homes Ltd
Unit 1-2, Pennant House, Mill Street, Pontypridd, Mid Glamorgan CF37 2SW
**Tel:** 01443494400
**Web:** www.rcthomes.co.uk
**Reg No:** 0030261IP **Estd:** 2007
**Line of Business:** Housing associations and trust
**US SIC:** 6732, 7399
**UK SIC:** 83100, 83954
**Employees:** 350

DUNS 23-641-9235
## Rdf Group Plc
2 Bartholomews, Brighton, East Sussex BN1 1HG
**Tel:** 01273-200100 **Fax:** 01273200500
**Web:** www.rdfgroup.com
**Reg No:** 3637683 **Estd:** 1998 Public Limited Company
**Line of Business:** Employment and recruitment companies and consultants
**Trading Style:** Rdf Group Plc
**Issued Capital:** £208,000
**Directors:** A G Antoniades, Mrs E Buckley, M Watson
**Co. Secretary:** David Squair
**Responsibilities**
**Senior:** Jim Carr *(Chairman)*
**Finance:** Richard Beeforth *(Finance Director)*, Amy Fellows *(Financial Manager)*, Keith Molineux *(Financial Manager)*
**IT:** Jason Yeo *(Systems Administrator)*
**HR:** Josia Bullock *(HR Manager)*
**Branches:** Rdf Group Plc, Unit 5, Deer Park Avenue, Livingston, West Lothian EH54 8AF
**US SIC:** 7379 **UK SIC:** 83940
**Auditors:** Baker Tilly UK Audit LLP

| | 31-03-14 | 31-03-13 | 31-03-12 |
|---|---|---|---|
| TO | 27,617,000 | 25,942,000 | 24,808,000 |
| P/L | 1,009,000 | 1,101,000 | 728,000 |
| NW | 3,733,000 | 3,430,000 | 1,869,000 |
| WC | 3,233,000 | 2,780,000 | 1,590,000 |
| Emp. | 78 | 81 | 85 |

DUNS 21-041-4060
## Rdf Television
Regent House, Regent Street, Clifton, Bristol, Avon BS8 4HG
**Tel:** 01179707600
**Web:** www.rdftelevision.com
**Estd:** 2012
**Line of Business:** Motion picture production on film or video
**Responsibilities**
**Senior:** Tasha Roche *(Executive Assistant)*
**Admin:** Sarah Black *(Administrator)*
**US SIC:** 8999 **UK SIC:** 83954
**Employees:** 50

DUNS 85-601-6626
## Rdf Television Ltd
(**Subsidiary of:** B&D Holding Di Marco Drago E C. Sapa)
The Gloucester Building, Avonmore Road, London W14 8RF
**Tel:** 02070134000
**Web:** www.rdftelevision.com
**Reg No:** 6219647 **Estd:** 1999 Private Limited Company
**Line of Business:** Video production companies
**Export Sales:** £667,024
**Issued Capital:** £1
**Directors:** R W Henwood, J G Freeston, Ms S J Gregson
**Responsibilities**
**Senior:** Joely Fether *(Manager)*
**Facilities:** Moyra Simpson *(Head Of Facilities)*
**US SIC:** 7819 **UK SIC:** 97111
**Auditors:** Ernst & Young LLP
**Bankers:** National Westminster Bank Plc (57-00-00)

| | 31-12-13 | 31-12-12 | 31-12-11 |
|---|---|---|---|
| TO | 27,134,806 | 9,253,785 | 15,807,923 |
| P/L | 925,309 | (22,362) | 96,393 |
| NW | 964,365 | 39,056 | 61,418 |
| WC | 847,702 | (13,916) | (16,396) |
| Emp. | 48 | 32 | 34 |

DUNS 21-005-5903
## Rdl Corporation Ltd
Rdl House, Chertsey Road, Woking, Surrey GU21 5AD
**Tel:** 01483888999 **Fax:** 01483888998
**Web:** www.rdlcorp.com
**Reg No:** 6302328 **Estd:** 2007 Private Limited Company
**Line of Business:** Employment and recruitment companies and consultants
**Export Sales:** £11,204,377
**Issued Capital:** £105,000
**Directors:** I R Livingston, M J Walker, S G Britton, J N Gardner
**Co. Secretary:** James Gardner
**Responsibilities**
**Senior:** Justin Carpenter *(Manager)*
**Marketing:** Justin Carpenter *(Manager)*
**Sales:** Justin Carpenter *(Manager)*
**US SIC:** 7361, 7392
**UK SIC:** 83954, 83951

| | 31-12-13 | 31-12-12 | 31-12-11 |
|---|---|---|---|
| TO | 17,541,956 | 17,985,058 | 18,266,130 |
| P/L | (740,580) | (597,417) | (202,463) |
| NW | (4,370,575) | (4,281,373) | (4,308,604) |
| WC | 495,470 | 335,510 | 153,065 |
| Emp. | 63 | 76 | 72 |

DUNS 45-814-4631
## Rdl Scientific Ltd
13/29 City Business Centre, Winchester, Hampshire SO23 7TA
**Web:** www.rdlscientific.com
**Reg No:** 3172164 **Estd:** 1999 Private Limited Company
**Line of Business:** Employment service
**Issued Capital:** £2
**Director:** Ms S F Hill
**Co. Secretary:** William Hill
**US SIC:** 7361 **UK SIC:** 83954
**Auditors:** C P O Donnell & Co
**Bankers:** HSBC Bank plc (40-33-10)

| | 31-12-13 | 31-12-12 | 31-12-11 |
|---|---|---|---|
| TA | 642,761 | 650,828 | 733,284 |
| NW | 448,869 | 411,436 | 420,450 |
| WC | 319,629 | 282,196 | 291,210 |

DUNS 39-889-8825
## R.D.M. Electrical Services Ltd
Unit 6 Cambrian Court, Ferryboat Close, Swansea Enterprise Park, Swansea, West Glamorgan SA6 8PZ
**Tel:** 01792-701256 **Fax:** 01792-781705
**Web:** www.rdmelectrical.com
**Reg No:** 2229614 **VAT No:** 558116436
**Estd:** 1988 Private Limited Company
**Line of Business:** Electrical contractors and electricians
**Issued Capital:** £100
**Principals:** R D Moriarty *(Managing)*, S Pridmore
**Co. Secretary:** David Kieft
**Responsibilities**
**Admin:** Lesley Evans *(Administration Manager)*
**HR:** Lesley Evans *(Administration Manager)*
**US SIC:** 1731 **UK SIC:** 50300
**Auditors:** James & Uzzell Ltd
**Bankers:** Lloyds TSB Bank plc (30-93-53)

| | 31-03-14 | 31-03-13 | 31-03-12 |
|---|---|---|---|
| TA | 1,175,616 | 939,158 | 912,198 |
| NW | 302,763 | 240,182 | 293,440 |
| WC | 276,081 | 206,492 | 255,853 |

DUNS 21-780-6255
## Rdm Engineering
Stakehill Lane, Stakehill Middleton, Manchester M24 2RY
**Tel:** 01616439333
**Web:** www.rdmengineering.co.uk
**Estd:** 2003 Proprietorship
**Line of Business:** Industrial engineers
**Proprietor:** R Horidge
**US SIC:** 8911 **UK SIC:** 83701
**Employees:** 50

DUNS 21-018-2669 Imp-Exp
## Rdm (Uk) Ltd
147-165 Lynchford Road, Farnborough, Hampshire GU14 6HG
**Tel:** 01252400400 **Fax:** 01252-400001
**Web:** www.rdmengineering.co.uk
**Reg No:** 6400968 **VAT No:** 918803116
**Estd:** 2010 Private Limited Company
**Line of Business:** Cycle accessories
**Trading Style:** Infinity Motorcycles
**Issued Capital:** £100
**Directors:** D A Holloway, R S Puttick, D R Watkins, M Bray
**Responsibilities**
**Senior:** Ashley Bavastock *(Manager)*
**Branches:** Rdm (Uk) Ltd, Enchanted House, 46-50 Piccadilly, York, North Yorkshire YO1 9NX
**US SIC:** 3751, 5699
**UK SIC:** 36330, 64500
**Bankers:** HSBC Bank plc (40-00-00)

| | 31-12-13 | 31-12-12 | 31-12-11 |
|---|---|---|---|
| TO | 7,825,982 | 6,560,689 | N/A |
| P/L | 167,413 | 151,353 | N/A |
| NW | 335,915 | 352,695 | 316,766 |
| WC | 1,152,525 | 1,159,273 | 761,618 |
| Emp. | 80 | N/A | N/A |

DUNS 28-962-5998 Imp-Exp
## R.D.P. Electronics Ltd
Grove Street, Heath Town, Wolverhampton, West Midlands WV10 0PY
**Tel:** 01902-457512
**Web:** www.rdpe.com
**Reg No:** 1688591 **Estd:** 1966 Private Limited Company
**Line of Business:** Manufacturers of electronic equipment and components
**Export Markets:** Worldwide
**Issued Capital:** £1,000
**Managing Director:** P J Smith
**Co. Secretary:** Richard Garbett
**Responsibilities**
**Marketing:** Robin Guest *(Sales & Marketing Manager)*
**Sales:** Robin Guest *(Sales & Marketing Manager)*
**US SIC:** 3679 **UK SIC:** 34542
**Auditors:** Horwath Clark Whitehill
**Bankers:** Lloyds TSB Bank plc (30-99-83)

| | 30-06-14 | 30-06-13 | 30-06-12 |
|---|---|---|---|
| TA | 1,928,672 | 1,808,763 | 1,930,135 |
| NW | 1,480,296 | 1,442,641 | 1,440,355 |
| WC | 1,426,004 | 1,397,971 | 1,383,851 |

DUNS 23-979-2430
## Rds Software Group Ltd
(**Subsidiary of:** Rds Group Ltd)
Weir Bank Bray-On-Thames, Maidenhead, Berkshire SL6 2ED
**Tel:** 01628-783784
**Web:** www.rds-group.com
**Reg No:** 3967767 **Estd:** 2000 Private Limited Company
**Line of Business:** Other business activities not elsewhere classified
**Trading Style:** Rds Group
**Issued Capital:** £1,000
**Director:** B J Thompson
**Co. Secretary:** Rajan Sharma
**US SIC:** 7399 **UK SIC:** 83954
**Auditors:** Deloitte & Touche

| | 30-04-14 | 30-04-13 | 30-04-12 |
|---|---|---|---|
| TO | N/A | 4,105,035 | 6,445,728 |
| P/L | (5,517) | (1,794,621) | 10,645,371 |
| NW | 3,199,082 | 1,911,275 | 12,868,580 |
| WC | 3,192,472 | 1,850,916 | 11,482,270 |
| Emp. | N/A | 63 | 72 |

DUNS 77-127-2341
## R.D.Trading Ltd
(**Subsidiary of:** Computacenter Plc)
Tekhnicon House, Springwood Drive, Braintree, Essex CM7 2YN
**Tel:** 01376336400 **Fax:** 01376-515158
**Web:** www.rdc.co.uk
**Reg No:** 2699427 **VAT No:** 591712530
**Estd:** 2010 Private Limited Company
**Line of Business:** Computer services
**Export Sales:** £34,820,927
**Trading Style:** R D C
**Issued Capital:** £100
**Directors:** G P Tarpinian, P J Reilly
**Co. Secretary:** Gregory Tarpinian
**Responsibilities**
**Senior:** Stephen Benade *(Manager)*, Gerry Hackett *(Manager)*, Simon Woollatt *(Service Manager)*
**Finance:** Eloise Stephens *(Financial Officer)*
**Marketing:** Martin Series *(Sales & Marketing Director)*
**Sales:** Martin Series *(Sales & Marketing Director)*
**HR:** Claire Trundle *(Hr Executive)*
**Branches:** R.d.trading Ltd, 1 Freebourne Rd, Witham, Essex CM8 3UN
**US SIC:** 7379 **UK SIC:** 83940
**Auditors:** Edmund Carr LLP
**Bankers:** Barclays Bank Plc (20-19-95)

| | 31-12-13 | 31-12-12 | 31-12-11 |
|---|---|---|---|
| TO | 54,652,737 | 48,854,771 | 45,624,825 |
| P/L | 3,672,501 | 3,630,635 | 3,203,452 |
| NW | 12,512,028 | 9,684,190 | 6,954,373 |
| WC | 7,402,911 | 4,396,613 | 2,444,353 |
| Emp. | 255 | 228 | 207 |

**DUNS 29-509-7448**

## Re-Nu Electronics Ltd

(**Subsidiary of:** Re-Nu Electronics (Holdings) Ltd)
Unit H, Leicester, Leicestershire LE8 4GZ
**Tel:** 01162-642570
**Web:** www.renu-direct.co.uk
**Reg No:** 1872980 **Estd:** 2003 Private Limited Company
**Line of Business:** Television and radio goods servicing and maintenance
**Issued Capital:** £100
**Director:** C Mistry
**Co. Secretary:** Bhikhu Thanki
**Responsibilities**
**Senior:** Dave Mistry (Partner), Bic Thanki (CEO, Managing Director)
**Branches:** Re-Nu Electronics Ltd, Blaby Industrial Park, Winchester Avenue, Blaby, Leicester, Leicestershire LE8 4GZ
**US SIC:** 7629 **UK SIC:** 67301
**Auditors:** Richard Anthony & Co

|     | 31-03-14 | 31-03-13 | 31-03-12 |
|-----|----------|----------|----------|
| TA  | 443,631  | 530,890  | 423,884  |
| NW  | 104,137  | 84,080   | 45,858   |
| WC  | 34,949   | 5,717    | (49,304) |

**DUNS 21-130-5824**

## Re Tensator Holdings Ltd

Unit 7 Danbury Court, Linford Wood, Milton Keynes, Buckinghamshire MK14 6TS
**Tel:** 01908-684600
**Web:** www.tensator.com
**Reg No:** 6646591 **Estd:** 2008 Private Limited Company
**Line of Business:** Management activities of holding companies
**Directors:** K Langer, A R Mcpherson, P Parmentier, J Rufilanchas Gomez
**Co. Secretary:** Adrian Day
**Responsibilities**
**Finance:** Rachael Hawes (Financial Manager)
**US SIC:** 6711 **UK SIC:** 83962
**Bankers:** Lloyds TSB Bank plc (30-15-53)
**Employees:** 182
**Turnover:** £52,228,000

**DUNS 21-913-3378**           Imp-Exp

## R.E. Tricker Ltd

56-60 St Michaels Road, Northampton, Northamptonshire NN1 3JX
**Tel:** 01604630595 **Fax:** 01604624978
**Web:** www.trickers.com
**Reg No:** 1114160 **VAT No:** 284623639
**Estd:** 1973 Private Limited Company
**Line of Business:** Manufacturers of footwear
**Export Markets:** Europe, Canada, Australasia, Japan & U S A
**Issued Capital:** £5,000
**Principals:** E D Barltrop (Chairman), N D Barltrop (Managing), B Jones
**Co. Secretary:** Nicholas Barltrop
**Responsibilities**
**Marketing:** Ailsa Fleming (Marketing Manager)
**Sales:** Richard Gammidge (Director of Sales and Business), Roy Martyniak (Sales Director)
**Branches:** R.e. Tricker Ltd, 9 Abbey Green, Bath, Avon BA1 1NW
**US SIC:** 3149 **UK SIC:** 45100
**Auditors:** Jervis & Partners
**Bankers:** HSBC Bank plc (40-35-04)

|     | 31-12-13  | 31-12-12  | 31-12-11  |
|-----|-----------|-----------|-----------|
| TO  | 8,793,653 | 8,337,166 | 8,440,632 |
| P/L | 605,226   | 417,948   | 1,118,765 |
| NW  | 4,034,697 | 3,501,635 | 3,178,054 |
| WC  | 3,688,873 | 3,211,702 | 2,929,316 |
| Emp.| 106       | 104       | 96        |

**DUNS 21-025-4645**

## R.E.A. Trading Ltd

Nutmeg House, 60 Gainsford Street, London SE1 2NY
**Tel:** 02079406000 **Fax:** 020-7403-3232
**Reg No:** 0088367 **VAT No:** 243290674
**Estd:** 1906 Private Limited Company
**Line of Business:** Other wholesale
**Issued Capital:** £4,202,000
**Directors:** R M Robinow, J J Robinow
**Co. Secretary:** R.E.A. Services Limited
**US SIC:** 5199 **UK SIC:** 61900
**Auditors:** Arthur Andersen
**Bankers:** Lloyds TSB Bank plc (30-91-59)

|     | 31-12-13   | 31-12-12  | 31-12-11   |
|-----|------------|-----------|------------|
| TO  | 19,620,000 | 19,490,000| 15,047,000 |
| P/L | 3,873,000  | 3,732,000 | 4,713,000  |
| NW  | 10,944,000 | 9,710,000 | 9,179,000  |
| WC  | 5,905,000  | 4,672,000 | 4,063,000  |
| Emp.| 3,635      | 3,479     | 2,966      |

**DUNS 21-880-3099**

## Reablement Services North Team

Third Floor, Kings House, King Street, Bedworth, Warwickshire CV12 8LL
**Tel:** 02476754020
**Estd:** 2012

**Line of Business:** Home care service providers
**Responsibilities**
**Senior:** Lucille Chester (General Manager)
**US SIC:** 8091 **UK SIC:** 95200
**Employees:** 130

**DUNS 21-320-1007**           Imp-Exp

## Reabrook Ltd

(**Subsidiary of:** Trgom Ltd)
Rawdon Road, Moira, Swadlincote, Derbyshire DE12 6DA
**Tel:** 01283221044 **Fax:** 01283225731
**Web:** www.arrowchem.com
**Reg No:** 0804733 **Estd:** 1968 Private Limited Company
**Line of Business:** Traditional cleaning activities
**Export Sales:** £4,513,000
**Trading Style:** Arrow Cleaning & Hygiene Solutions, Nielsen, Enviro Clean
**Issued Capital:** £1,890,339
**Directors:** Mrs M E Brealey, Mrs S Y Watkins, A W Brealey
**Co. Secretary:** Malcolm Watkins
**Responsibilities**
**Senior:** Chris Grew (Warehouse Manager), Julian Hill (Manager), Anne Mcteague (Finance Manager)
**IT:** Martin Gallimore (IT Manager)
**HR:** Lynne Chapman (Human Resources Manager)
**Operations:** Lynne Chapman (Human Resources Manager)
**Branches:** Reabrook Ltd, 116 High St, Solihull, West Midlands B90 1JS
**US SIC:** 3999, 7399
**UK SIC:** 49590, 83954
**Auditors:** PricewaterhouseCoopers LLP

|     | 31-12-13   | 31-12-12   | 31-12-11   |
|-----|------------|------------|------------|
| TO  | 19,291,000 | 22,335,000 | 24,779,000 |
| P/L | 75,000     | 20,000     | 304,000    |
| NW  | 5,247,000  | 5,134,000  | 5,245,000  |
| WC  | 2,013,000  | 1,874,000  | 1,969,000  |
| Emp.| 200        | 220        | 235        |

**DUNS 21-841-7596**

## Reach Agency Ltd

238 Kelvin Street, Ashton-Under-Lyne, Lancashire OL7 0HZ
**Tel:** 08005427591
**Web:** www.reachagency.co.uk
**Reg No:** 8086002 **Estd:** 2012 Private Limited Company
**Line of Business:** Web site design and development
**Issued Capital:** £10
**Director:** J P Boon
**US SIC:** 7379 **UK SIC:** 83940

|     | 31-05-13 |
|-----|----------|
| TA  | 4,264    |
| NW  | 968      |
| WC  | (992)    |

**DUNS 21-000-4844**

## Reach Holdings Ltd

111 Chertsey Road, Woking, Surrey GU21 5BW
**Web:** www.reach.co.uk
**Reg No:** 6262884 **Estd:** 2007 Private Limited Company
**Line of Business:** Marketing consultants
**Export Sales:** £2,922,000
**Issued Capital:** £4,561
**Directors:** I J Glen, M P Smith, W Price, G P Macmanus
**Co. Secretary:** Peter Handscomb
**Responsibilities**
**Senior:** Roger Looker (Chairman)
**US SIC:** 6711 **UK SIC:** 83962

|     | 31-12-13    | 31-12-12    | 31-12-11    |
|-----|-------------|-------------|-------------|
| TO  | 48,704,000  | 50,878,000  | 37,365,000  |
| P/L | 1,860,000   | 1,880,000   | 1,479,000   |
| NW  | (21,418,000)| (24,971,000)| (28,127,000)|
| WC  | (6,428,000) | (5,183,000) | (5,061,000) |
| Emp.| 957         | 1,003       | 707         |

**DUNS 23-401-8302**

## Reach (Supported Living) Ltd

11 Devon Place, Newport, Gwent NP20 4NP
**Tel:** 01633-679899
**Web:** www.reach-support.co.uk
**Reg No:** 0029706IP **VAT No:** 790418615
**Estd:** 2004 Friendly Society
**Line of Business:** Disability services
**Trading Style:** Reach
**Director:** J Shelton
**Responsibilities**
**Senior:** Judith North (corporate director)
**US SIC:** 8321 **UK SIC:** 96111

|     | 31-03-13   |
|-----|------------|
| TO  | 12,134,000 |
| P/L | (96,000)   |
| NW  | 1,562,000  |
| WC  | 1,536,000  |
| Emp.| 392        |

**DUNS 21-835-8148**

## ReACH2 Ltd

Scientia Academy Mona Road, Burton-On-Trent, Staffordshire DE13 0UF
**Tel:** 07817474418
**Web:** www.reach2.org
**Reg No:** 8040828 **Estd:** 2012 Private Company Limited By Guarantee
**Line of Business:** Business and management consultancy activities not elsewhere classified
**Directors:** D Ashton, S A Tewes, Ms C M Walsh, P C Little, Prof J H West-Burnham, Dr L Askew, Mrs C S Paine, D D Rossdale
**Co. Secretary:** Lee Francis
**Responsibilities**
**Senior:** Steve Lancashire (Director)
**US SIC:** 8999 **UK SIC:** 83954

|     | 31-08-13   |
|-----|------------|
| TO  | 65,454,282 |
| P/L | 51,024,990 |
| NW  | 50,890,990 |
| WC  | 2,288,845  |
| Emp.| 436        |

**DUNS 34-577-8591**

## ReACH4ENTERTAINMENT Enterprises Plc

85a Wembley Hill Road, Wembley, Middlesex HA9 8BU
**Tel:** 02089001818
**Web:** www.firstartist.com
**Reg No:** 2725009 **VAT No:** 626117360
**Estd:** 1992 Public Limited Company
**Line of Business:** Sports management services
**Export Sales:** £39,746,000
**Issued Capital:** £1,872,370
**Directors:** D C Stoller, R M Ingham, M Yeoman
**Co. Secretary:** Cargil Management Services Limit
**Responsibilities**
**Senior:** Robert Baldock (Manager), Cheryl Coutts (Manager), William Fitzpatrick (Manager), David Noble (Manager)
**Marketing:** Julieanne Coutts (Manager)
**HR:** Julieanne Coutts (Manager)
**Health & Safety:** Julieanne Coutts (Manager)
**Facilities:** Julieanne Coutts (Manager)
**Branches:** ReaCH4ENtertainment Enterprises Plc, Kingsway Ho, Kingsway, Team Valley Trad Est, Gateshead, Tyne and Wear NE11 0HW
**US SIC:** 6711, 8999
**UK SIC:** 83962, 83954
**Auditors:** Baker Tilly UK Audit LLP
**Bankers:** Allied Irish Bank (gb) (23-84-82)

|     | 31-12-13    | 31-12-12    | 31-12-11    |
|-----|-------------|-------------|-------------|
| TO  | 75,749,000  | 69,326,000  | 78,198,000  |
| P/L | 308,000     | 162,000     | (2,952,000) |
| NW  | (17,155,000)| (18,177,000)| (19,696,000)|
| WC  | (1,537,000) | (1,272,000) | (3,770,000) |
| Emp.| 211         | 229         | 236         |

**DUNS 21-105-3427**

## Reachlocal Uk Ltd

(**Subsidiary of:** Reachlocal Europe B.V.)
2 Queen Caroline Street, London W6 9DX
**Tel:** 02030088778
**Web:** www.reachlocal.co.uk
**Reg No:** 6479111 **Estd:** 2008 Private Limited Company
**Line of Business:** Advertising
**Issued Capital:** £851
**Directors:** C Harris, F Ter Weeme
**Co. Secretary:** Norose Company Secretarial Servi
**Responsibilities**
**Senior:** John Laser (Chief Executive)
**Marketing:** Roger Burgess (Strategic Partnerships Manager)
**US SIC:** 7319 **UK SIC:** 83800

|     | 31-12-13    | 31-12-12    | 31-12-11    |
|-----|-------------|-------------|-------------|
| TO  | 28,804,989  | 25,458,010  | 17,438,157  |
| P/L | (140,786)   | (474,761)   | (963,789)   |
| NW  | (4,169,740) | (4,028,954) | (3,554,193) |
| WC  | (4,699,009) | (4,183,765) | (3,687,802) |
| Emp.| 132         | 130         | 107         |

**DUNS 53-620-6089**

## React Transport Services Ltd

11 Nettlehill Road, Livingston, West Lothian EH54 5PP
**Tel:** 01506443888 **Fax:** 01506-435138
**Web:** www.react-transport.co.uk
**Reg No:** 0178268SC **Estd:** 1996 Private Limited Company
**Line of Business:** Road haulage and transport services
**Issued Capital:** £10,000
**Director:** A C Duncan
**Co. Secretary:** Simon Platts
**Responsibilities**
**Admin:** Mandy Robertson (Office Manager)
**Operations:** Graeme Sword (Operations Manager)

**Branches:** React Transport Services Ltd, 16 Woodgate Way South, Glenrothes, Fife KY7 4PF
**US SIC:** 4789 **UK SIC:** 77002
**Auditors:** Blueprint Scotland

|     | 31-03-14  | 31-03-13  | 31-03-12  |
|-----|-----------|-----------|-----------|
| TA  | 2,029,391 | 1,729,025 | 1,440,708 |
| NW  | 192,149   | 106,182   | 92,371    |
| WC  | (234,795) | (233,269) | (124,851) |

**DUNS 38-784-7304**

## Read & Errington

Unit 5, Guild House, 221 Kincraig Road, Blackpool, Lancashire FY2 0PJ
**Tel:** 01253-359960
**Web:** www.read-errington.co.uk
**Estd:** 2005 Partnership
**Line of Business:** Plumbers
**Partners:** G R Read, A Errington
**Responsibilities**
**Senior:** Adam Farrar (Manager)
**US SIC:** 1799 **UK SIC:** 50000
**Employees:** 63

**DUNS 34-838-2628**

## Read Construction Group Ltd

Enterprise Centre Blast Road, Wrexham, Clwyd LL11 5BT
**Tel:** 01978-721950
**Reg No:** 5637448 **Estd:** 2005 Private Limited Company
**Line of Business:** Development and selling of real estate
**Issued Capital:** £1,200
**Director:** R D Heaton
**Co. Secretary:** Ms Linda Heaton
**Responsibilities**
**IT:** Andy Richards (Computer Manager)
**Health & Safety:** Rilo Rhys (Health & Safety Advisor)
**US SIC:** 6552 **UK SIC:** 85000

|     | 31-03-14   | 31-03-13   | 31-03-12   |
|-----|------------|------------|------------|
| TO  | 13,267,263 | 14,363,260 | 12,178,854 |
| P/L | 132,920    | 275,210    | 109,026    |
| NW  | 1,150,683  | 1,072,763  | 897,021    |
| WC  | 853,871    | 897,043    | 670,339    |
| Emp.| 54         | 60         | 62         |

**DUNS 77-453-3111**

## The Read Group Ltd

St Georges House, 15 Pembroke Road, Sevenoaks, Kent TN13 1XR
**Tel:** 01732-460000
**Web:** www.readgroupplc.com
**Reg No:** 2959244 **Estd:** 1991 Private Limited Company
**Line of Business:** Data storage solutions
**Trading Style:** Trg Strath
**Issued Capital:** £50,000
**Directors:** M S Roy, J Cano-Lopez
**Co. Secretary:** Mrs Joanna Mceachern
**Responsibilities**
**Senior:** Colin Lloyd (Manager)
**US SIC:** 7374 **UK SIC:** 83940
**Auditors:** Baker Tilly UK Audit LLP
**Bankers:** Lloyds TSB Bank plc (30-97-49)

|     | 31-12-13   | 31-12-12   | 31-12-11    |
|-----|------------|------------|-------------|
| TO  | 6,733,015  | 7,454,605  | 9,264,471   |
| P/L | (271,571)  | (898,814)  | 750,264     |
| NW  | (2,573,410)| (2,492,802)| (1,279,487) |
| WC  | (1,322,572)| (1,443,590)| (107,531)   |
| Emp.| 53         | 59         | 63          |

**DUNS 77-878-1203**

## Reader Offers Ltd

Lexden House, London Road, Colchester, Essex CO3 4DB
**Tel:** 01206790935 **Fax:** 01206-795247
**Web:** www.readeroffers.travel
**Reg No:** 3036965 **Estd:** 2012 Private Limited Company
**Line of Business:** Cruiselines
**Issued Capital:** £50,000
**Directors:** J R Dickinson, Mrs K Hall, N R Lingard
**Co. Secretary:** Melvin Childs
**Responsibilities**
**Senior:** Peter Beadles (Manager)
**US SIC:** 4452 **UK SIC:** 74002
**Auditors:** Thornton & Co

|     | 30-04-14   | 30-04-13   | 30-04-12   |
|-----|------------|------------|------------|
| TO  | 39,433,195 | 43,511,773 | 42,423,439 |
| P/L | 5,019,061  | 3,407,764  | 3,016,139  |
| NW  | 5,095,523  | 8,889,408  | 8,142,414  |
| WC  | 4,508,127  | 5,441,873  | 4,816,855  |
| Emp.| 111        | 103        | 109        |

**DUNS 21-125-5243**

## The Reader Organisation

Bute Street, Liverpool, Merseyside L5 3LA
**Tel:** 01512077207
**Web:** www.thereader.org.uk
**Reg No:** 6607389 **Estd:** 2008 Private Company Limited By Guarantee
**Line of Business:** Other adult and other education not elsewhere classified
**Directors:** Ms K Doran, S Mukherjee, G R Brand, S Barber, R N Phillips, J R Flamson, P M Davis, Mrs S J Rutherford
**Co. Secretary:** Mrs Ruth Scott-Williams

**Responsibilities**
**Senior:** Brian Denton *(Manager)*, Lindsey Dyer *(Director)*, Zoe Gilling *(Manager)*, Rosemary Hawley *(Director)*, Lawrence Holden *(Director)*
**US SIC:** 8299, 7392
**UK SIC:** 93300, 83951
**Bankers:** Alliance & Leicester Plc (72-50-00)

| | 31-03-14 | 31-03-13 | 31-03-12 |
|---|---|---|---|
| TO | 2,067,242 | 1,624,897 | 1,297,300 |
| P/L | 68,550 | 77,042 | 30,320 |
| NW | 467,457 | 398,907 | 321,865 |
| WC | 462,275 | 386,258 | 297,095 |
| Emp. | 80 | 58 | 41 |

DUNS 45-846-2108
## Readers Holdings Ltd
79 Place Road, Newport, Isle of Wight PO30 1JE
**Tel:** 01983-292131
**Web:** www.readersgroup.com
**Reg No:** 3192918 **Estd:** 1996 Private Limited Company
**Line of Business:** Management activities of other non-financial holding companies not elsewhere classified
**Issued Capital:** £469,485
**Directors:** Ms S J Massey, L E Reader, M W Reader
**Co. Secretary:** Ms Janet Snudden
**US SIC:** 7399, 5199
**UK SIC:** 83954, 61900
**Auditors:** BDO Stoy Hayward
**Employees:** 200

DUNS 29-643-9169
## Readibus
Cradock Road, Reading, Berkshire RG2 0JT
**Web:** www.readibus.co.uk
**Reg No:** 1970233 **Estd:** 1982 Private Company Limited By Guarantee
**Line of Business:** Other passenger land transport
**Trading Style:** Readibus Training Services
**Directors:** G W Grandison, Mrs R P Williams, G M Khan, Ms S F Beggs, Doctor S R Bowlby, D D Chopping, A Mattingley, Ms M E Turner
**Co. Secretary:** Trevor Bottomley
**Responsibilities**
**Senior:** Daniel Dennett *(Director)*, Ricky Duveen *(Director)*, Norman Gould *(Director)*, Steven Landau *(Director)*
**Admin:** Helen Whittock *(Office Manager)*
**US SIC:** 4141 **UK SIC:** 72102
**Auditors:** Horwath Clark Whitehill
**Bankers:** National Westminster Bank Plc (60-17-21)

| | 31-03-14 | 31-03-13 | 31-03-12 |
|---|---|---|---|
| TO | 1,245,707 | 1,318,710 | 1,261,938 |
| P/L | (50,890) | 56,626 | 82,528 |
| NW | 525,981 | 576,871 | 520,245 |
| WC | 271,022 | 282,419 | 306,193 |
| Emp. | 73 | 73 | 72 |

DUNS 36-533-2381
## Reading Blue Coat School
Holme Park, Sonning Lane, Reading, Berkshire RG4 6SU
**Tel:** 01189441005
**Web:** www.blue-coat.reading.sch.uk
**Reg No:** 4243510 **Estd:** 2001 Private Limited Company
**Line of Business:** Schools (independent)
**Directors:** Mrs L E Hague, Mrs E Morgan, Mrs F E Dawson, C A Hubbard, D J Few, D E Sillitoe, P A Smith, R W Norkett
**Co. Secretary:** Simon Jackson
**Responsibilities**
**Senior:** Clive Litten *(Director)*
**IT:** Paul Zambon *(Senior IT Executive)*
**US SIC:** 8211 **UK SIC:** 93200

| | 31-08-13 | 31-08-12 | 31-08-11 |
|---|---|---|---|
| TO | 9,967,387 | 9,102,811 | 8,446,731 |
| P/L | 893,995 | 942,431 | 672,791 |
| NW | 10,911,455 | 10,021,113 | 9,071,000 |
| WC | (569,438) | (1,072,329) | (702,417) |
| Emp. | 143 | 140 | 140 |

DUNS 21-127-1820 **Imp**
## Reading Borough Council
Civic Centre, Reading, Berkshire RG1 7AE
**Tel:** 01189373737
**Web:** www.reading.gov.uk
**Estd:** 1974
**Line of Business:** Administration of the state and the economic and social policy of the community
**Trading Style:** St Michael's Primary School
**Financial Directors:** D Peasley, P Innen
**Responsibilities**
**Senior:** Chris Branagan *(Spokesman)*, Geoff Chivers *(Chairman)*, Michael Coghlin *(Chief Executive)*, Polly English *(Senior Manager)*, Sally Monger *(Executive)*, Oscar Mortali *(Spokesman)*, Jo Stanbury *(Executive)*
**Finance:** David Breeze *(Planning Manager)*
**Marketing:** Sarah Bishton *(Spokeswoman)*, Chris Bloomfield *(Neighbourhood Regeneration Man)*, Debi Daniels *(Promotions Manager)*, David Legge *(Chief Communications Officer)*
**Admin:** Jan Sagoo *(Office Manager)*
**IT:** John Barnfield *(IT Manager)*, Tony Maynell *(Computer Operations Manager)*, Andrew Withey *(Business Change Manager-IT)*
**HR:** Anne Burton *(Head of Human Resources)*, James Hoggert *(Human Resources Manager)*
**Health & Safety:** Jo O' Connor *(Workplace Health Coordinator)*, Robin Pringle *(Health & Safety Officer)*
**Facilities:** Ivan Somerville *(Facilities Manager)*
**Operations:** Nick Burston *(Production and Operations Mana)*, Kevin Hollier *(Head of Environmental & Consum)*
**Fleet:** Ruth Leuillette *(Planning Manager)*
**Branches:** Reading Borough Council, Po Box 600, Reading, Berkshire RG1 7UA
**US SIC:** 9121 **UK SIC:** 91110
**Bankers:** The Co-Operative Bank Plc (08-90-16)
**Employees:** 6,000

DUNS 21-879-3570
## Reading Enterprise Centre
University Of Reading, Whiteknights Road, Reading, Berkshire RG6 6BU
**Tel:** 01189357300
**Estd:** 2012
**Line of Business:** Business and commerce centres
**Responsibilities**
**Senior:** David Gillham *(Manager)*, Cris Snitt *(Manager)*
**US SIC:** 8221 **UK SIC:** 93100
**Employees:** 200

DUNS 23-898-2883
## Reading Football Club (Holdings) P L C
Madejski Stadium, Reading, Berkshire RG2 0FL
**Tel:** 01189253844 **Fax:** 01189681101
**Web:** www.readingfc.co.uk
**Reg No:** 3889049 **VAT No:** 724458624
**Estd:** 1999 Public Limited Company
**Line of Business:** Sports clubs
**Issued Capital:** £2,233,367
**Directors:** Ms C A Morris, Miss H J Morris, Sir R J Madejski, I Smith, I M Wood Smith
**Co. Secretary:** Bryan Stabler
**Responsibilities**
**Senior:** Craig Guze *(Manager)*, Megan Kelly *(Manager)*
**HR:** Jackie Evans *(Human Resources Manager)*
**US SIC:** 7299, 6711
**UK SIC:** 98902, 83962
**Auditors:** Myers Clark
**Bankers:** HSBC Bank plc (40-16-33)

| | 30-06-14 | 30-06-13 | 30-06-12 |
|---|---|---|---|
| TO | 18,975,587 | 5,841,309 | 19,933,953 |
| P/L | (29,355,134) | (860,029) | (1,728,473) |
| NW | (32,628,804) | 830,635 | 1,536,070 |
| WC | (68,432,050) | (3,779,972) | (4,546,307) |
| Emp. | 528 | 118 | 541 |

DUNS 22-627-5824
## The Reading Football Club Ltd
Madejski Stadium, Reading, Berkshire RG2 0FL
**Tel:** 01189-681100 **Fax:** 01189-681101
**Web:** www.readingfc.co.uk
**Reg No:** 0053703 **VAT No:** 199429014
**Estd:** 1897 Private Limited Company
**Line of Business:** Sports clubs
**Issued Capital:** £750,000
**Principals:** Sir R J Madejski *(Chairman)*, S Thanakarnjanasuth, T Srisumrid, N Niruttinanon, I M Wood Smith, T Piamphongsarn, S Srivikorn, N Howe
**Co. Secretary:** Bryan Stabler
**Responsibilities**
**Health & Safety:** Ray Booth *(Stadium Manager)*
**Branches:** The Reading Football Club Ltd, Norfolk Rd, Reading, Berkshire RG30 2EF
**US SIC:** 7999 **UK SIC:** 97913
**Auditors:** Myers Clark
**Bankers:** HSBC Bank plc (40-16-33)

| | 30-06-14 | 30-06-13 | 30-06-12 |
|---|---|---|---|
| TO | 38,082,311 | 59,265,980 | 14,753,324 |
| P/L | (7,291,469) | (2,338,832) | (11,718,912) |
| NW | (34,837,787) | (31,677,761) | (23,802,146) |
| WC | (53,693,278) | (22,630,172) | (14,272,831) |
| Emp. | 410 | 428 | 367 |

DUNS 29-762-2425
## The Reading Foundation
Main House, Erleigh Road, Reading, Berkshire RG1 5LW
**Tel:** 01189-015600
**Web:** www.reading-school.co.uk
**Reg No:** 2025362 **Estd:** 1986 Private Company Limited By Guarantee
**Line of Business:** General secondary education
**Directors:** M Dawes, D R Fisher, I L Martin, Professor S Nortcliff, P J Szell, R Childs, R P Huggins, S Noori
**Co. Secretary:** Ian Judd
**Responsibilities**
**Senior:** Gary Butler *(Manager)*, Mary Chaplin *(Manager)*, Helen Cullura *(Director)*, Michael Maule *(Director)*, Ameet Phadnis *(Director)*
**US SIC:** 8211 **UK SIC:** 93200
**Auditors:** Ernest Francis
**Bankers:** National Westminster Bank Plc (60-17-21)

| | 31-07-14 | 31-07-13 | 31-07-12 |
|---|---|---|---|
| TO | 129,877 | 235,561 | 351,490 |
| P/L | 91,568 | 44,888 | (156,792) |
| NW | 3,747,588 | 3,515,129 | 3,754,543 |
| WC | 259,929 | 168,258 | 2,056,819 |

DUNS 23-738-1959
## Reading Girls School
Northumberland Avenue, Reading, Berkshire RG2 7PY
**Tel:** 01189861336
**Web:** www.readinggirlsschool.co.uk
**Estd:** 2002
**Line of Business:** Schools (local authority)
**Chairman:** A J Markham
**Responsibilities**
**Senior:** Vivien Angus *(Head Teacher)*
**US SIC:** 8211 **UK SIC:** 93200
**Employees:** 200

DUNS 37-972-7928 **Imp**
## Reading Room Ltd
65-66 Frith Street, London W1D 3JR
**Tel:** 02071732800
**Web:** www.readingroom.com
**Reg No:** 3280127 **VAT No:** 833043556
**Estd:** 1996 Private Limited Company
**Line of Business:** Web site design and development
**Export Sales:** £5,747,783
**Issued Capital:** £1,218
**Directors:** Ms S Vick, S M Usher, Ms M A Manning, D C Burgess, T Hempenstall, Ms J E Vinson
**Co. Secretary:** Adam Portlock
**Responsibilities**
**Senior:** Kristian Croucher *(Manager)*, Polly Willson *(Manager)*
**Sales:** Kristian Croucher *(Manager)*
**US SIC:** 7379 **UK SIC:** 83940
**Auditors:** H.W. Fisher & Co
**Bankers:** Coutts & Co (18-00-02)

| | 31-03-14 | 31-03-13 | 31-03-12 |
|---|---|---|---|
| TO | 13,839,852 | 15,084,107 | 13,100,941 |
| P/L | 221,885 | 212,137 | (97,757) |
| NW | 1,623,067 | 1,244,295 | 1,150,745 |
| WC | 1,327,171 | 898,016 | 836,283 |
| Emp. | 197 | 198 | 186 |

DUNS 29-361-0085
## Reading Scientific Services Ltd
(**Subsidiary of:** Chromium Suchex Llp)
Pepper Lane, Reading, Berkshire RG6 6LA
**Tel:** 01189-868541
**Web:** www.rssl.com
**Reg No:** 0741326 **Estd:** 1962 Private Limited Company
**Line of Business:** Research and experimental development on natural sciences and engineering
**Issued Capital:** £50,000
**Directors:** Ms J M George, A Gundle, Ms T J Gale
**Co. Secretary:** Cadbury Nominees Limited
**Responsibilities**
**Senior:** Robert Macnair *(Manager)*, Kay Spicer *(Manager)*
**Sales:** Mike Day *(Commercial Director)*, Karen Masters *(Commercial Operations Manager)*, Jane Staniforth *(Food Business Development Mana)*
**US SIC:** 7391 **UK SIC:** 94000
**Auditors:** Deloitte & Touche LLP
**Bankers:** Lloyds TSB Bank plc (30-00-02)

| | 31-12-13 | 29-12-12 | 31-12-11 |
|---|---|---|---|
| TO | 11,214,000 | 10,700,000 | 9,894,000 |
| P/L | 468,000 | (1,190,000) | 209,000 |
| NW | 6,394,000 | 5,852,000 | 7,408,000 |
| WC | (3,686,000) | (3,665,000) | (724,000) |
| Emp. | 299 | 229 | 281 |

DUNS 29-681-4957
## Reading Transport Ltd
(**Subsidiary of:** Reading Borough Council)
Great Knollys Street, Reading, Berkshire RG1 7HH
**Tel:** 01189-594000
**Web:** www.reading-buses.co.uk
**Reg No:** 2004963 **Estd:** 1986 Private Limited Company
**Line of Business:** Bus operators and stations
**Trading Style:** Reading Buses
**Issued Capital:** £3,974,000
**Directors:** Ms C D Anscombe, D C Sutton, Mrs J E Stanford-Beale, Mrs J T Gavaghan, Ms T Thomas, F Connolly, M A Townend, P Woodward
**Co. Secretary:** Norman Fryer-Saxby
**Responsibilities**
**Senior:** Daniel Downes *(Director)*, Keith Moffatt *(Director)*, Cony Pettit *(Director of Resources)*, Anthony Pettitt *(Director)*
**Branches:** Reading Transport Ltd, Bev & Geoffs Pitstop, Greenham Island, Newbury, Berkshire RG14 5SG
**US SIC:** 4119 **UK SIC:** 72200
**Auditors:** BDO LLP
**Bankers:** Girobank Plc (72-00-00)

| | 29-09-13 | 30-09-12 | 02-09-11 |
|---|---|---|---|
| TO | 26,537,000 | 26,201,000 | 24,408,000 |
| P/L | 411,000 | 203,000 | (855,000) |
| NW | (6,512,000) | (5,040,000) | (2,973,000) |
| WC | 2,234,000 | 1,394,000 | 880,000 |
| Emp. | 444 | 449 | 461 |

DUNS 21-121-1224
## Reading University Students' Union
P O Box 230, Whiteknights, Reading, Berkshire RG6 6AZ
**Web:** www.rusu.co.uk
**Estd:** 1927
**Line of Business:** Activities of other membership organisations not elsewhere classified
**Principals:** Ms S Pearman *(President)*, B Elger, P Jeffreys, Ms J Horne, D Campbell, Ms J Mobbs, Ms N Fox *(Manager)*, S Kelly *(Manager)*
**Responsibilities**
**Senior:** Richard Silcock *(Chief Executive)*, Cara Swift *(Vice President)*
**Marketing:** Christine Whitburn *(Marketing Manager)*
**US SIC:** 8699 **UK SIC:** 96902
**Employees:** 50

DUNS 22-752-7108 **Exp**
## Ready Egg Products Ltd
(**Subsidiary of:** Lough Erne Investments Ltd)
Dp1 Milltate, Lisnaskea, Enniskillen, Co Fermanagh BT92 0BN
**Tel:** 02867721345
**Web:** www.readyeggsproducts.com
**Reg No:** 0015561NI **VAT No:** 286845113
**Estd:** 1977 Private Limited Company
**Line of Business:** Farming of poultry
**Export Markets:** Europe
**Issued Capital:** £13,202
**Directors:** C E Crawford, G Caulfield, S Kerrigan, D F Charters, D F Charters
**Co. Secretary:** Colum Caughey
**US SIC:** 0259 **UK SIC:** 01001
**Auditors:** PricewaterhouseCoopers
**Bankers:** Ulster Bank Ltd (98-09-70)

| | 31-12-13 | 31-12-12 | 31-12-11 |
|---|---|---|---|
| TO | N/A | N/A | 5,015,672 |
| P/L | N/A | N/A | 848,827 |
| NW | 10,826,402 | 10,895,521 | 7,439,902 |
| WC | (4,202,554) | (4,240,361) | (2,909,435) |
| Emp. | N/A | N/A | 6 |

DUNS 34-736-8610
## Ready Foods Ltd
(**Subsidiary of:** Laf Holdings Ltd)
Unit 3 Cibyn Industrial Estate, Caernarfon, Gwynedd LL55 2BD
**Tel:** 01286-662910 **Fax:** 01286676719
**Web:** www.readyfoods.co.uk
**Reg No:** 5538853 **Estd:** 2005 Private Limited Company
**Line of Business:** Manufacturers of food products
**Export Sales:** £816,464
**Issued Capital:** £139,720
**Directors:** I R Thomas, S L Kynaston, A Williams
**Co. Secretary:** Stephen Wantling
**US SIC:** 2099, 3999
**UK SIC:** 42399, 49590
**Auditors:** DRE & Co

| | 31-03-14 | 31-03-13 | 31-03-12 |
|---|---|---|---|
| TO | 11,110,816 | 10,748,436 | 9,320,034 |
| P/L | 78,843 | 400,958 | 544,614 |
| NW | 892,219 | 850,900 | 564,378 |
| WC | (73,491) | (81,733) | (288,701) |
| Emp. | 71 | 62 | 55 |

DUNS 77-105-0283
## Readypower Engineering Ltd
Molly Millars Bridge, Wokingham, Berkshire RG41 2WY
**Tel:** 01189774901 **Fax:** 01189-774902
**Web:** www.readypower.com
**Reg No:** 2681963 **Estd:** 1992 Private Limited Company
**Line of Business:** Renting of construction and civil engineering machinery and equipment
**Issued Capital:** £100
**Director:** K L Mahoney-Veitch
**Co. Secretary:** Mrs Julie Mahoney

**Responsibilities**
**Senior:** Rick Frost (Manager), Russell Jack (Operations Director), Natalie Watson (Office Supervisor)
**Operations:** Russell Jack (Operations Director)
**Branches:** Readypower Engineering Ltd, Station Car Park, Station Road, Kings Langley, Hertfordshire WD4 8LF
**US SIC:** 7394 **UK SIC:** 84000
**Auditors:** Baker Tilly UK Audit LLP
**Bankers:** Barclays Bank Plc (20-35-90)

|  | 31-03-14 | 31-03-13 | 31-03-12 |
|---|---|---|---|
| TO | 22,012,578 | 14,279,002 | 11,157,381 |
| P/L | 4,827,855 | 1,503,558 | (636,078) |
| NW | 10,798,505 | 7,347,458 | 6,318,352 |
| WC | 3,897,515 | 270,037 | (356,157) |
| Emp. | 124 | 104 | 100 |

DUNS 21-042-2352
## The Real Adventure
Alexander House, James Street West, Bath, Avon BA1 2BT
**Tel:** 01225476100
**Web:** www.realadventure.co.uk
**Proprietorship**
**Line of Business:** Advertising agency services
**Proprietor:** S Dewhurst
**Responsibilities**
**IT:** Simon Eady (Head of IT)
**US SIC:** 7319 **UK SIC:** 83800
**Employees:** 70

DUNS 50-480-8957 **Exp**
## Real Asset Management Plc
(**Subsidiary of:** Real Asset Management Group Ltd)
Central Court, Knoll Rise, Orpington, Kent BR6 0JA
**Web:** www.realassetmgt.com
**Reg No:** 2454806 **VAT No:** 547875490
**Estd:** 1981 Public Limited Company
**Line of Business:** Computer software (development)
**Export Markets:** Germany
**Issued Capital:** £100,000
**Principals:** G K Snelgrove (Managing), R Shaw, M J Scholes, A M Perks
**Co. Secretary:** Stafford Fitch-Bunce
**Responsibilities**
**Finance:** Denise Pope (Accounts Assistant)
**Marketing:** Karen Conneeley (Marketing Manager)
**IT:** Bismark Appah (Software Developer)
**Facilities:** Angela Yearsley (Facilities Manager)
**US SIC:** 7379 **UK SIC:** 83940
**Auditors:** Barnes Roffe LLP
**Bankers:** The Royal Bank Of Scotland Plc (16-17-32)

|  | 31-12-13 | 31-12-12 | 31-12-11 |
|---|---|---|---|
| TO | 4,810,545 | 5,070,195 | 4,966,797 |
| P/L | (44,512) | 312,284 | 378,658 |
| NW | 1,255,919 | 1,450,431 | 1,222,165 |
| WC | 2,936,745 | 2,974,515 | 2,590,557 |
| Emp. | 63 | 63 | 59 |

DUNS 73-877-9375 **Imp**
## Real Digital International Ltd
2 Queensway, Croydon, Surrey CR0 4BD
**Tel:** 02086-037000 **Fax:** 02086-037099
**Web:** www.real-digital.co.uk
**Reg No:** 5132313 **Estd:** 2006 Private Limited Company
**Line of Business:** Printing not elsewhere classified
**Export Sales:** £1,276,533
**Issued Capital:** £1,237,000
**Directors:** D Laybourne, B Stephens, C J Godfrey, C J Tagg
**Co. Secretary:** Christopher Godfrey
**Responsibilities**
**Senior:** Peter Rivett (General Manager)
**US SIC:** 2752 **UK SIC:** 47544
**Auditors:** Grant Thornton UK LLP

|  | 31-12-13 | 31-12-12 | 31-12-11 |
|---|---|---|---|
| TO | 16,875,480 | 15,843,540 | 16,328,961 |
| P/L | 2,946,064 | 2,554,775 | 3,077,694 |
| NW | 6,832,542 | 6,115,375 | 4,920,840 |
| WC | (929,810) | (1,921,304) | (3,447,716) |
| Emp. | 136 | 132 | 131 |

DUNS 21-809-1805
## R.E.A.L Education
Sandhill Street, Worksop, Nottinghamshire S80 1SY
**Tel:** 01909532975
**Web:** www.real-education.org
**Estd:** 2012
**Line of Business:** Education services
**Responsibilities**
**Senior:** Zac Holland (Centre Manager)
**US SIC:** 8299 **UK SIC:** 93300
**Employees:** 70

DUNS 21-582-1851
## Real Foods (Wholesale Victuallers)
37 Broughton Street, Edinburgh, Midlothian EH1 3JU
**Web:** www.realfoods.co.uk
**Estd:** 1975 Partnership
**Line of Business:** Health food retailers
**Partners:** Ms S Martin, M Grimm-Foxen
**Responsibilities**
**Senior:** Michael Foxen (Manager)
**Branches:** Real Foods (Wholesale Victuallers), 14 Ashley Place, Edinburgh, Midlothian EH6 5PX
**US SIC:** 5499, 2834
**UK SIC:** 64100, 25700
**Bankers:** The Co-Operative Bank Plc (83-91-26)
**Employees:** 60

DUNS 73-392-4869
## Real Good Food Plc
229 Crown Street, Liverpool, Merseyside L8 7RF
**Fax:** 01517068201
**Web:** www.renshawnapier.co.uk
**Reg No:** 4666282 **Estd:** 2003 Public Limited Company
**Line of Business:** Manufacture of bread; manufacture of fresh pastry goods and cakes
**Trading Style:** Renshaw Napier
**Issued Capital:** £1,300,387
**Directors:** P G Ridgwell, P C Salter, C O Thomas, M J Mcdonough, J D'Unienville, P W Totte
**Co. Secretary:** David Newman
**Responsibilities**
**Sales:** Peter Hough (Group Sugar Sourcing and Busin)
**HR:** Heather Billington (Group HR Director)
**Operations:** Bill Harrower (Operations Director)
**Engineering:** Stuart Gallie (Engineering Manager), Gary Kramer (Sugar Technical Manager)
**Branches:** Real Good Food Plc, Renshaw Napier, Mead Court, Bristol, Avon BS35 3UW
**US SIC:** 2051, 2062
**UK SIC:** 41960, 42000
**Auditors:** Crowe Clark Whitehill LLP
**Bankers:** The Royal Bank Of Scotland Plc (16-29-25)

|  | 31-03-14 | 31-03-13 | 31-03-12 |
|---|---|---|---|
| TO | 272,576,000 | 265,754,000 | 305,529,000 |
| P/L | (1,536,000) | 6,260,000 | 4,360,000 |
| NW | 10,116,000 | 10,897,000 | 6,519,000 |
| WC | 1,536,000 | 7,320,000 | (688,000) |
| Emp. | 947 | 979 | 899 |

DUNS 73-658-7903
## The Real Greek Food Co Ltd
(**Subsidiary of:** The Fulham Shore Plc)
Suite C 1 Lindsey Street, London EC1A 9HP
**Tel:** 08454563598
**Web:** www.therealgreek.com
**Reg No:** 4918527 **Estd:** 2003 Private Limited Company
**Line of Business:** Licensed restaurants
**Issued Capital:** £43,086
**Directors:** N Mankarious, D Page
**US SIC:** 5812 **UK SIC:** 66110
**Auditors:** Baker Tilly

|  | 30-06-13 | 01-07-12 | 27-06-11 |
|---|---|---|---|
| TO | 7,763,000 | 8,816,000 | 6,022,000 |
| P/L | 485,000 | 180,000 | 49,000 |
| NW | 2,923,000 | 2,553,000 | (1,824,000) |
| WC | 427,000 | 160,000 | (838,000) |
| Emp. | 168 | 160 | 147 |

DUNS 37-761-5257
## Real Hair
6-8 Cale Street, London SW3 3QU
**Tel:** 02075890877
**Web:** www.realhair.co.uk
**Estd:** 1966 Proprietorship
**Line of Business:** Hairdressers (unisex)
**Proprietor:** R Dover
**Responsibilities**
**Senior:** Belle Cannan (Proprietor), Lisa-Marie Rowland (Manager)
**US SIC:** 7231 **UK SIC:** 98200
**Employees:** 60

DUNS 77-127-4255
## Real Life Options
David Wandless House, Knottingley Road A1 Business Park, Knottingley, West Yorkshire WF11 0BU
**Tel:** 01977781800 **Fax:** 01977-795361
**Web:** www.reallifeoptions.org
**Reg No:** 2699638 **Estd:** 1992 Private Company Limited By Guarantee
**Line of Business:** Social work activities with accommodation
**Directors:** Mrs A N Kirkby, D Wilkin, C A Myers, Mrs L P Hobbs, G J Collingham, B R Hutchinson, J Mcdonald
**Co. Secretary:** Mrs Azra Kirkby

**Branches:** Real Life Options, 90 Capel Gardens, Pinner, Middlesex HA5 5RD
**US SIC:** 8321 **UK SIC:** 96111
**Auditors:** Hansons
**Bankers:** National Westminster Bank Plc (55-70-23)

|  | 31-03-14 | 31-03-13 | 31-03-12 |
|---|---|---|---|
| TO | 39,350,938 | 38,018,192 | 33,625,642 |
| P/L | 717,155 | 868,309 | 867,878 |
| NW | 2,037,934 | 3,120,746 | 2,654,558 |
| WC | 281,728 | 1,379,919 | 1,217,252 |
| Emp. | 1,941 | 1,786 | 1,564 |

DUNS 21-601-0364
## Real Radio Wales
Ty-Nant Court, Morganstown, Cardiff, South Glamorgan CF15 8LW
**Tel:** 02920315100
**Web:** www.realradio.co.uk
**Estd:** 2000 Partnership
**Line of Business:** Television and radio station operators
**Partner:** T Dowling
**US SIC:** 4833 **UK SIC:** 97411
**Employees:** 50

DUNS 42-459-3015 **Imp**
## Real V N C Ltd
(**Subsidiary of:** Vnc Group Ltd)
Betjeman House, 104 Hills Road, Cambridge, Cambridgeshire CB2 1LQ
**Tel:** 01223310421 **Fax:** 01223-310411
**Web:** www.realvnc.com
**Reg No:** 4446945 **Estd:** 2002 Private Limited Company
**Line of Business:** Computer software (development)
**Export Sales:** £7,239,033
**Issued Capital:** £5,333
**Directors:** Dr A C Harter, Professor A Hopper, T J Richardson
**Co. Secretary:** Tom Mcguire
**Responsibilities**
**Senior:** Tom Blackie (Vice President)
**Operations:** Adam Byrne (Vice-President Strategic Allia)
**US SIC:** 7379, 7391
**UK SIC:** 83940, 94000
**Auditors:** Ernst & Young LLP
**Bankers:** Barclays Bank Plc (20-17-35)

|  | 31-12-13 | 31-12-12 | 31-12-11 |
|---|---|---|---|
| TO | 7,689,659 | 6,561,584 | 12,784,394 |
| P/L | 1,481,031 | 908,919 | 7,529,234 |
| NW | 13,627,976 | 12,135,805 | 10,497,012 |
| WC | 12,045,057 | 11,820,504 | 10,500,202 |
| Emp. | 82 | 80 | 69 |

DUNS 45-816-7939
## Real Yorkshire Pudding Co Ltd
(**Subsidiary of:** Rypc Holdings Ltd)
Coulman Road Industrial Estate, Doncaster, South Yorkshire DN8 5JS
**Tel:** 01405-815523
**Web:** www.realyorks.co.uk
**Reg No:** 3174495 **Estd:** 1996 Private Limited Company
**Line of Business:** Manufacturers of food products
**Export Sales:** £222,034
**Issued Capital:** £40
**Principals:** P J Holmes (Managing), C R Payne, M A Wood
**Co. Secretary:** Mark Wood
**US SIC:** 2099 **UK SIC:** 42399
**Auditors:** Jeffrey Price

|  | 31-03-14 | 31-03-13 | 31-03-12 |
|---|---|---|---|
| TO | 8,525,955 | 8,389,849 | 7,376,070 |
| P/L | 667,910 | 629,727 | 812,260 |
| NW | 2,341,937 | 1,879,127 | 1,536,124 |
| WC | 2,606,587 | 2,474,068 | 498,575 |
| Emp. | 116 | 113 | N/A |

DUNS 89-669-8602
## Realise Ltd
(**Subsidiary of:** St Ives Plc)
142 Commercial Street, Edinburgh, Midlothian EH6 6LB
**Tel:** 01314-766000
**Web:** www.realise.com
**Reg No:** 0172507SC **Estd:** 1997 Private Limited Company
**Line of Business:** Internet services
**Issued Capital:** £89,542
**Principals:** A P Murphy (Managing), P B Gray, P N Martell, Ms F M Proudler, M R Armitage, A Lamond
**Co. Secretary:** Philip Harris
**Responsibilities**
**Senior:** Nathan Fulwood (Business Development Director)
**Sales:** Nathan Fulwood (Business Development Director)
**US SIC:** 7379, 6711
**UK SIC:** 83940, 83962
**Auditors:** Springfords LLP

**Bankers:** Bank Of Scotland (80-02-34)

|  | 30-09-13 | 30-09-12 | 30-09-11 |
|---|---|---|---|
| TO | 9,274,837 | 7,857,241 | N/A |
| P/L | 2,645,860 | 1,598,991 | N/A |
| NW | 2,493,347 | 3,982,760 | 2,884,925 |
| WC | 2,289,304 | 3,847,315 | 2,743,166 |
| Emp. | 82 | 60 | N/A |

DUNS 23-908-5959 **Imp**
## Really Useful Products Ltd
(**Subsidiary of:** Shaman Investments Ltd)
Unit 2 Foxbridge Way, Normanton Industrial Estate, Normanton, West Yorkshire WF6 1TN
**Tel:** 01924-898477 **Fax:** 01924-898588
**Web:** www.reallyusefulproducts.co.uk
**Reg No:** 3899123 **VAT No:** 734663716
**Estd:** 1999 Private Limited Company
**Line of Business:** Manufacture of plastic packing goods
**Export Sales:** £19,562,271
**Issued Capital:** £3,000,000
**Directors:** M Pickles, M A Pickles, Ms K G Andersson, Mrs J H Walker
**Co. Secretary:** Marc Pickles
**Responsibilities**
**Senior:** Charlotte Haw (P A to Managing Director)
**IT:** Mark Mclean (Technical Engineer)
**Facilities:** Mark Mclean (Technical Engineer)
**Engineering:** Mark Mclean (Technical Engineer)
**Branches:** Really Useful Products Ltd, Unit 2, Foxbridge Way, Normanton, West Yorkshire WF6 1TN
**US SIC:** 3079 **UK SIC:** 48360
**Auditors:** RSM Bentley Jennison
**Bankers:** HSBC Bank plc (40-39-07)

|  | 31-05-14 | 31-05-13 | 31-05-12 |
|---|---|---|---|
| TO | 39,973,074 | 32,549,933 | 30,059,185 |
| P/L | 1,749,825 | 1,074,808 | 447,334 |
| NW | 5,826,771 | 4,546,240 | 3,564,042 |
| WC | (3,888,387) | (2,797,422) | (2,167,259) |
| Emp. | 232 | 225 | 188 |

DUNS 23-999-8300
## Really Useful Theatres Group Ltd
(**Subsidiary of:** Really Useful Investments Ltd)
65 Drury Lane, London WC2B 5SP
**Tel:** 08444124654
**Web:** www.reallyusefultheatres.co.uk
**Reg No:** 3987955 **Estd:** 2000 Private Limited Company
**Line of Business:** Operation of arts facilities
**Issued Capital:** £1,177
**Directors:** B D Chakraborty, M G Wordsworth, J Rees
**Co. Secretary:** Bishu Chakraborty
**US SIC:** 7911 **UK SIC:** 97913
**Auditors:** Deloitte LLP
**Bankers:** Bank Of Scotland (80-11-45)

|  | 29-06-14 | 30-06-13 | 01-06-12 |
|---|---|---|---|
| TO | 44,712,000 | 34,897,000 | 51,070,000 |
| P/L | (3,020,000) | (3,791,000) | 3,622,000 |
| NW | 81,315,000 | 83,940,000 | 86,361,000 |
| WC | 5,565,000 | 9,574,000 | 490,000 |
| Emp. | 184 | 184 | 222 |

DUNS 21-028-2885 **Imp**
## Really Useful Theatres Ltd
(**Subsidiary of:** Really Useful Investments Ltd)
19-22 Tower Street, London WC2H 9TW
**Tel:** 02072400880
**Web:** www.reallyuseful.com
**Reg No:** 0233200 **VAT No:** 238689608
**Estd:** 1928 Private Limited Company
**Line of Business:** Operation of arts facilities
**Issued Capital:** £22,000,000
**Directors:** B D Chakraborty, M G Wordsworth
**Co. Secretary:** Bishu Chakraborty
**Branches:** Really Useful Theatres Ltd, 29 Shaftesbury Ave, London W1D 7ES
**US SIC:** 7911 **UK SIC:** 97913
**Auditors:** Deloitte & Touche LLP
**Bankers:** HSBC Bank plc (40-05-27)

|  | 29-06-14 | 30-06-13 | 01-06-12 |
|---|---|---|---|
| TO | 43,660,000 | 43,273,000 | 36,679,000 |
| P/L | 4,240,000 | 4,581,000 | 3,331,000 |
| NW | 83,459,000 | 80,158,000 | 74,990,000 |
| WC | 78,751,000 | 75,522,000 | 70,344,000 |
| Emp. | 192 | 189 | 177 |

DUNS 21-034-0343
## Realm
Bridgford House, 1 Heyes Lane, Wilmslow, Cheshire SK9 7JP
**Web:** www.realm.ltd.uk
**Estd:** 1901
**Line of Business:** Estate management services
**Partners:** A Fyfe, D Mason, M Watts, I Watters, Ms C Finlay, C Brooks
**Responsibilities**
**Senior:** Christine Grace (Manager)
**US SIC:** 6531 **UK SIC:** 83400
**Employees:** 54

DUNS 39-923-8963
### Realm Construction Ltd
Thistle House, Cartmore Industrial Estate, Lochgelly, Fife KY5 8LL
**Tel:** 01592-782500 **Fax:** 01592-781908
**Web:** www.purvisgroup.co.uk
**Reg No:** 0110359SC **VAT No:** 502761962
**Estd:** 1988 Private Limited Company
**Line of Business:** Building construction contractors
**Issued Capital:** £211,000
**Principals:** R Purvis *(Managing)*, G Wight, C R Purvis
**Co. Secretary:** James Thomson
**US SIC:** 1522 **UK SIC:** 50100
**Auditors:** Carters Accountants LLP
**Bankers:** Clydesdale Bank Plc (82-45-05)

| | 31-08-13 | 31-08-12 | 31-08-11 |
|---|---|---|---|
| TO | 18,690,118 | 17,618,269 | 16,704,397 |
| P/L | 412,019 | 146,749 | 219,580 |
| NW | 3,858,370 | 3,502,115 | 3,369,969 |
| WC | 1,508,266 | 1,011,070 | 735,235 |
| Emp. | 119 | 121 | 115 |

DUNS 22-029-4339
### Realm Projects Ltd
**(Subsidiary of:** Titan Developments Ltd)
Millenium Business Park, Mansfield, Nottinghamshire NG19 7JY
**Tel:** 01623-655252
**Web:** www.realm-projects.com
**Reg No:** 4032010 **VAT No:** 746059027
**Estd:** 2007 Private Limited Company
**Line of Business:** Shopfitting contractors
**Issued Capital:** £4
**Director:** D M Renshaw
**Co. Secretary:** Graeme Blakey
**US SIC:** 1796, 1751
**UK SIC:** 50400
**Auditors:** tcp Chartered Accountants
**Bankers:** National Westminster Bank Plc (60-14-03)

| | 31-12-13 | 31-12-12 | 31-12-11 |
|---|---|---|---|
| TO | 6,929,541 | N/A | N/A |
| P/L | 881,746 | N/A | N/A |
| NW | 2,863,393 | 2,188,940 | 1,469,336 |
| WC | 2,703,266 | 2,082,009 | 1,449,940 |

DUNS 37-895-2162
### Realnetworks Ltd
**(Subsidiary of:** Realnetworks Inc.)
233 High Holborn, London WC1V 7DN
**Tel:** 020-7618-4000 **Fax:** 02072901201
**Web:** www.realnetworks.com
**Reg No:** 3312996 **Estd:** 1997 Private Limited Company
**Line of Business:** Advertising, radio, tv and other media
**Issued Capital:** £1,000
**Directors:** M J Eccles, K E Murphy
**Co. Secretary:** Abogado Nominees Limited
**Responsibilities**
**Senior:** Tracy Daw *(Manager)*, Mike Lunford *(President)*, Thomas Nielsen *(Chief Executive)*
**IT:** Rex Asare *(IT Manager)*, Rex Osaso-Asare *(IT Manager)*
**US SIC:** 7319 **UK SIC:** 83800
**Auditors:** The Norton Practice

| | 31-12-13 | 31-12-12 | 31-12-11 |
|---|---|---|---|
| TO | N/A | 4,688,146 | 5,756,907 |
| P/L | N/A | 247,991 | 196,982 |
| NW | 912,015 | 749,820 | 541,657 |
| WC | 900,225 | 722,311 | 507,010 |
| Emp. | N/A | 27 | 30 |

DUNS 21-120-2364
### Realstone (Holdings) Ltd
Bolehill Quarry, Bolehill, Wingerworth, Chesterfield, Derbyshire S42 6RG
**Tel:** 01246270244
**Web:** www.realstone.co.uk
**Reg No:** 6594206 **Estd:** 2008 Private Limited Company
**Line of Business:** Management activities of production holding companies
**Export Sales:** £363,456
**Issued Capital:** £250,000
**Directors:** S J Wright, J A Gregory, I H Kennedy, P S Bailey
**Co. Secretary:** Stephen Wright
**US SIC:** 6711 **UK SIC:** 83962
**Auditors:** PKF (UK) LLP

| | 31-12-13 | 31-12-12 | 31-12-11 |
|---|---|---|---|
| TO | 5,162,519 | 6,038,155 | 6,367,246 |
| P/L | (395,879) | (365,489) | (119,829) |
| NW | (1,772,473) | (1,690,694) | (1,437,064) |
| WC | 293,125 | 326,338 | 598,441 |
| Emp. | 60 | 60 | 65 |

DUNS 29-331-6071
### Realty Estates Ltd
25 Rochdale Road, Manchester M4 4HT
**Tel:** 01618329447 **Fax:** 01618320065
**Reg No:** 1841868 **Estd:** 1984 Private Limited Company
**Line of Business:** Property developers
**Issued Capital:** £100
**Managing Director:** Y Tishbi
**Co. Secretary:** Mrs Jaleh Tishbi
**Branches:** Realty Estates Ltd, Unit 6, Woolley Bridge Road, Glossop, Derbyshire SK13 2NS
**US SIC:** 6552, 6531, 6519
**UK SIC:** 85000, 83400
**Auditors:** Deloitte & Touche
**Bankers:** The Bank Of Ireland (30-14-74)

| | 30-09-13 | 30-09-12 | 30-09-11 |
|---|---|---|---|
| TO | 4,563,712 | 4,573,334 | 4,438,648 |
| P/L | 1,189,228 | (3,407,454) | (2,430,466) |
| NW | 31,586,930 | 31,899,891 | 32,866,929 |
| WC | (3,878,971) | (13,243,363) | 1,521,762 |
| Emp. | 50 | N/A | 46 |

DUNS 21-035-2773
### Reardonsmith Architects
Unit 10-13 The Leather Market, Weston Street, London SE1 3ER
**Tel:** 020-7378-6006
**Web:** www.reardonsmith.com
**Estd:** 1996
**Line of Business:** Architectural activities
**Proprietor:** P Reardon
**Responsibilities**
**Senior:** Condrad Smith *(Manager)*
**Health & Safety:** Wareen Binns *(Officer Manager)*
**US SIC:** 8911 **UK SIC:** 83701
**Employees:** 72

DUNS 76-615-9180
### Rearo Laminates Ltd
**(Subsidiary of:** Hamepark Holdings Ltd)
Loanbank Quadrant, Glasgow, Lanarkshire G51 3HZ
**Tel:** 0141-440-0800 **Fax:** 01414453342
**Web:** www.rearo.co.uk
**Reg No:** 0129568SC **VAT No:** 596701801
**Estd:** 1991 Private Limited Company
**Line of Business:** Manufacturers of veneer sheets
**Issued Capital:** £100
**Principals:** J Mercer *(Managing)*, J C Mercer, R G Mercer
**Co. Secretary:** Ms Cissie Mercer
**Branches:** Rearo Laminates Ltd, 28 Phoenix Rd, Washington, Tyne and Wear NE38 0AD
**US SIC:** 2435, 3999
**UK SIC:** 46201, 49590
**Auditors:** Williamson & Dunn
**Bankers:** Clydesdale Bank Plc (82-66-08)

| | 30-06-13 | 30-06-12 | 30-06-11 |
|---|---|---|---|
| TO | 7,323,191 | 7,062,695 | 7,481,716 |
| P/L | 375,848 | 32,764 | (244,143) |
| NW | 889,777 | 738,506 | 727,579 |
| WC | 675,982 | 179,175 | 44,816 |
| Emp. | 79 | 88 | 87 |

DUNS 22-621-5754
### Reassure Ltd
**(Subsidiary of:** Swiss Re Ag)
Windsor House, Ironmasters Way, Telford, Shropshire TF3 4NB
**Tel:** 01952292929 **Fax:** 08707-091111
**Web:** www.reassure.co.uk
**Reg No:** 0754167 **Estd:** 1963 Private Limited Company
**Line of Business:** Life assurance services
**Issued Capital:** £262,942,949
**Directors:** D J Baxter, M Eves, Professor J D Gallagher, M H Cuhls, R O Hudson, M F Swallow, R M Ratcliffe, R W Howe
**Co. Secretary:** Paul Shakespeare
**Responsibilities**
**Senior:** James Crotty *(Director)*, Michael Woodcock *(Director)*
**US SIC:** 6411, 6371
**UK SIC:** 83200, 82002
**Auditors:** PricewaterhouseCoopers LLP
**Bankers:** National Westminster Bank Plc (56-00-14)

**Following financial data are in thousands**

| | 31-12-13 | 31-12-12 | 31-12-11 |
|---|---|---|---|
| TO | 202,000 | 189,800 | 371,700 |
| P/L | 485,700 | 357,700 | 578,500 |
| NW | 1,140,800 | 1,091,800 | 1,275,300 |
| WC | (119,900) | (83,800) | (86,800) |

DUNS 21-155-8264
### Reassured Ltd
Wey Court West Union Road, Farnham, Surrey GU9 7PT
**Tel:** 08081682025
**Web:** www.re-assured.co.uk
**Reg No:** 6838409 **Estd:** 2009 Private Limited Company
**Line of Business:** Life insurance
**Issued Capital:** £100
**Director:** S L Marshall
**US SIC:** 6311 **UK SIC:** 82002

| | 31-01-14 | 31-01-13 | 31-01-12 |
|---|---|---|---|
| TO | 11,060,338 | N/A | N/A |
| P/L | 822,666 | N/A | N/A |
| NW | 651,346 | 23,102 | 16,338 |
| WC | 3,058,741 | (67,656) | (6,336) |
| Emp. | 73 | N/A | N/A |

DUNS 23-920-1366
### Reays Coaches Ltd
Syke Park, Wigton, Cumbria CA7 9NE
**Tel:** 01697-349999 **Fax:** 01697-349900
**Web:** www.reays.co.uk
**Reg No:** 3910309 **VAT No:** 843144443
**Estd:** 2006 Private Limited Company
**Line of Business:** Coach and bus hire
**Issued Capital:** £2
**Directors:** C W Reay, C J Bowness
**Co. Secretary:** Ms Nicola Reay
**US SIC:** 4119 **UK SIC:** 72200
**Auditors:** Butler Accountancy Services Ltd
**Bankers:** Clydesdale Bank Plc (82-70-24)

| | 31-08-13 | 31-08-12 | 31-08-11 |
|---|---|---|---|
| TO | 7,156,262 | 5,594,652 | 4,177,477 |
| P/L | 540,863 | 433,833 | 251,952 |
| NW | 1,162,430 | 774,692 | 613,624 |
| WC | (1,236,474) | (1,414,984) | (853,850) |
| Emp. | 124 | 107 | 95 |

DUNS 34-645-7815 **Imp**
### Rebellion Developments Ltd
Osney Mead, Oxford, Oxfordshire OX2 0ES
**Tel:** 01865792201
**Web:** www.rebellion.co.uk
**Reg No:** 2770940 **Estd:** 1992 Private Limited Company
**Line of Business:** Publishing of software
**Export Sales:** £132,202
**Issued Capital:** £1,000
**Directors:** C R Kingsley, A J Hurcombe, Dr P J Kingsley, J J Kingsley
**Co. Secretary:** Christopher Kingsley
**Responsibilities**
**Marketing:** Robbie Cooke *(Head of Marketing & PR)*, Kristien Wendt *(Marketing Manager)*
**US SIC:** 7372, 7379
**UK SIC:** 83940
**Auditors:** Neville Russell

| | 30-06-13 | 30-06-12 | 30-06-11 |
|---|---|---|---|
| TO | 12,311,822 | 7,843,050 | 9,124,280 |
| P/L | 982,707 | 154,133 | 156,618 |
| NW | 4,756,208 | 4,110,868 | 4,390,274 |
| WC | 4,694,018 | 4,098,197 | 4,221,440 |
| Emp. | 109 | 115 | 124 |

DUNS 50-376-7329 **Imp-Exp**
### Rebound Electronics (Uk) Ltd
**(Subsidiary of:** Rebound Technology Group Holdings Ltd)
2100 London Road Newbury Business Park, Newbury, Berkshire RG14 2PZ
**Tel:** 01635555999 **Fax:** 01635555998
**Web:** www.reboundeu.com
**Reg No:** 2385838 **VAT No:** 537464035
**Estd:** 1989 Private Limited Company
**Line of Business:** Manufacturers and distributors of electronic components
**Export Markets:** Europe; U S A; Far East
**Export Sales:** £24,917,555
**Issued Capital:** £20,000
**Directors:** N Raggett, A K Brown, S J Madley, S L Thake, Ms A Miller
**Co. Secretary:** Mrs Cecilia Taylor
**Responsibilities**
**Senior:** Colin Pease *(Operations Manager)*, Cif Taylor *(Human Resources Manager)*
**Admin:** Beckie Crump *(Office Manager)*
**IT:** Jeff Brind *(IT Manager)*
**HR:** Colin Pease *(Operations Manager)*, Cif Taylor *(Human Resources Manager)*
**Health & Safety:** Colin Pease *(Operations Manager)*
**Facilities:** Colin Pease *(Operations Manager)*
**Operations:** Colin Pease *(Operations Manager)*
**Branches:** Rebound Electronics (Uk) Ltd, Old Pill Fm Indust Est The Pill, Caldicot, Gwent NP26 5JH
**US SIC:** 3679 **UK SIC:** 34542
**Auditors:** KPMG LLP
**Bankers:** Barclays Bank Plc (20-36-98)

| | 31-12-13 | 31-12-12 | 31-12-11 |
|---|---|---|---|
| TO | 37,073,884 | 36,016,203 | 43,611,301 |
| P/L | 642,813 | 1,040,350 | 514,950 |
| NW | 3,055,654 | 3,310,835 | 2,489,919 |
| WC | 2,635,349 | 2,756,525 | 1,947,686 |
| Emp. | 85 | 99 | 108 |

DUNS 22-777-2340
### Recaf Equipment Ltd
**(Subsidiary of:** Recaf Holdings Ltd)
Unit 202 Pointon Way Stonebridge Cross, Business Park, Droitwich, Worcestershire WR9 0LW
**Fax:** 01905797564
**Web:** www.recaf.co.uk
**Reg No:** 1187727 **VAT No:** 299007530
**Estd:** 2008 Private Limited Company
**Line of Business:** Amusement and gaming machines
**Issued Capital:** £50,000
**Directors:** K B Turner, M A White
**Co. Secretary:** Mark White
**Responsibilities**
**Senior:** Brian Merriman *(Manager)*
**Finance:** John Byng *(Financial Controller)*
**Marketing:** Brian Merriman *(Manager)*
**Sales:** Brian Merriman *(Manager)*
**HR:** Glenda Brown *(Human Resources Manager)*
**Facilities:** Bob Hamblin *(General Manager)*
**Branches:** Recaf Equipment Ltd, Worcester Mail Centre, Wainwright Road, Worcester, Worcestershire WR4 9WW
**US SIC:** 3944, 5199
**UK SIC:** 49410, 61900
**Auditors:** John Sherwood & Co
**Bankers:** Barclays Bank Plc (20-98-61)

| | 30-04-13 | 30-04-12 | 30-04-11 |
|---|---|---|---|
| TA | 2,638,144 | 2,601,038 | 2,714,466 |
| NW | 878,984 | 888,380 | 844,231 |
| WC | (191,512) | (106,088) | (151,452) |

DUNS 28-898-3208 **Imp**
### Recall Ltd
**(Subsidiary of:** Brambles Limited)
Rotherwick House, 3 Thomas More Street, London E1W 1YZ
**Tel:** 02077096705 **Fax:** 01788542639
**Web:** www.recall.com
**Reg No:** 1331798 **Estd:** 2002 Private Limited Company
**Line of Business:** Data storage solutions
**Issued Capital:** £1,278,178
**Directors:** M Franklin, R G Glazier, U R Tatla
**Co. Secretary:** Imran Razak
**Responsibilities**
**Senior:** Christian Coenen *(Manager)*, Marcus Heap *(Director Sales And Marketing)*, Andrew Hussey *(Store Manager)*, Gabriel Pirona *(Manager)*
**Marketing:** Marcus Heap *(Director Sales And Marketing)*
**Sales:** Marcus Heap *(Director Sales And Marketing)*
**Operations:** Andrew Hussey *(Store Manager)*
**Branches:** Recall Ltd, 21 Kennet Road, Dartford, Kent DA1 4QN
**US SIC:** 4226 **UK SIC:** 77003
**Auditors:** PricewaterhouseCoopers LLP
**Bankers:** HSBC Bank plc (40-47-08)

| | 30-06-14 | 30-06-13 | 30-06-12 |
|---|---|---|---|
| TO | 21,840,663 | 21,929,900 | 23,776,086 |
| P/L | 3,538,538 | 1,075,859 | 747,497 |
| NW | 11,593,585 | 9,427,065 | 8,630,491 |
| WC | 5,507,437 | 3,944,252 | 3,151,472 |
| Emp. | 119 | 113 | 149 |

DUNS 21-853-4677 **Imp**
### Recipharm Ltd
**(Subsidiary of:** B&E Participation Ab)
Bardsley Vale Mills, Ashton-Under-Lyne, Lancashire OL7 9RR
**Tel:** 01613426000
**Web:** www.recipharm.com
**Reg No:** 8174784 **Estd:** 2012 Private Limited Company
**Line of Business:** Manufacture of basic pharmaceutical products
**Export Sales:** £5,307,000
**Issued Capital:** £1
**Directors:** M R Quick, T B Eldered
**Responsibilities**
**Senior:** Steve Dimmock *(General Manager)*
**US SIC:** 2834 **UK SIC:** 25700
**Bankers:** Lloyds TSB Bank plc (30-12-51)

| | 31-12-13 |
|---|---|
| TO | 20,857,000 |
| P/L | (147,000) |
| NW | (147,000) |
| WC | 5,576,000 |
| Emp. | 173 |

DUNS 22-025-0281
### Reckitt Benckiser Corporate Services Ltd
**(Subsidiary of:** Reckitt Benckiser Group Plc)
Wellcroft House, Wellcroft Road, Slough, Berkshire SL1 4AQ
**Tel:** 01753 506 800 **Fax:** 01753 217 899
**Web:** www.rb.com
**Reg No:** 4027682 **Estd:** 2000 Private Limited Company
**Line of Business:** Labour recruitment and provision of personnel
**Trading Style:** Air Wick / Calgon / Cillit Bang / Bonjela, Clearasil / Dettol / Durex / E45, Brasso / Finish / Disprin
**Issued Capital:** £75
**Directors:** S A Nash, Dr P N Clements, W R Mordan
**Co. Secretary:** Ms Christine Logan
**US SIC:** 7361 **UK SIC:** 83954
**Auditors:** PricewaterhouseCoopers LLP

**Following financial data are in thousands**

| | 31-12-13 | 31-12-12 | 31-12-11 |
|---|---|---|---|
| TO | 172,657 | 203,633 | 190,413 |
| P/L | (21,810) | (18,816) | 173,166 |
| NW | 1,836,358 | 1,841,097 | 1,848,224 |
| WC | 1,620,543 | 1,646,936 | 1,663,653 |
| Emp. | 388 | 586 | 523 |

DUNS 23-078-0363 **Exp**
## Reckitt Benckiser Healthcare International Ltd
(**Subsidiary of:** Grosvenor Square Holding B.V.)
D95 Building, Nottingham, Nottinghamshire NG90 1BS
**Tel:** 01159078523 **Fax:** 01159079616
**Web:** www.reckittbenckiser.com
**Reg No:** 2741587 **Estd:** 1992 Private Limited Company
**Line of Business:** Manufacturers of pharmaceutical products
**Export Sales:** £127,164,000
**Issued Capital:** £70,000,002
**Directors:** W R Mordan, S P Troote, Dr P N Clements, D N Walters
**Co. Secretary:** Ms Christine Logan
**Responsibilities**
**Senior:** Grant Allen *(Site Director)*
**Facilities:** Ben McClemens *(Facilities Manager)*
**Branches:** Reckitt Benckiser Healthcare International Ltd, P O Box 57, Central Pk, Lenton La, Nottingham, Nottinghamshire NG4 1HG
**US SIC:** 5122 **UK SIC:** 61800
**Auditors:** PricewaterhouseCoopers LLP
**Bankers:** National Westminster Bank Plc (60-80-09)

| | 31-12-13 | 31-12-12 | 31-12-11 |
|---|---|---|---|
| TO | 161,201,000 | 139,101,000 | 163,878,000 |
| P/L | 26,328,000 | 28,793,000 | 65,147,000 |
| NW | 214,722,000 | 195,032,000 | 173,783,000 |
| WC | 170,752,000 | 157,363,000 | 136,264,000 |
| Emp. | 699 | 595 | 568 |

DUNS 21-275-6134
## Reckitt Benckiser Healthcare (U K) Ltd
(**Subsidiary of:** Grosvenor Square Holding B.V.)
103-105 Bath Road, Slough, Berkshire SL1 3UH
**Tel:** 01753217800 **Fax:** 01753-217899
**Web:** www.reckittbenckiser.com
**Reg No:** 0261312 **Estd:** 1931 Private Limited Company
**Line of Business:** Manufacture of household and sanitary goods and of toilet requisites
**Export Sales:** £134,508,000
**Issued Capital:** £257,000,000
**Directors:** Dr P N Clements, W R Mordan, A Granena Aracil, D N Walters, S P Troote
**Co. Secretary:** Ms Christine Logan
**Branches:** Reckitt Benckiser Healthcare (U K) Ltd, Dansom Lane, Hull, North Humberside HU8 7DS
**US SIC:** 2647 **UK SIC:** 47220
**Auditors:** PricewaterhouseCoopers LLP
**Bankers:** HSBC Bank plc (40-25-20)
**Following financial data are in thousands**

| | 31-12-13 | 31-12-12 | 31-12-11 |
|---|---|---|---|
| TO | 784,851 | 761,904 | 1,168,254 |
| P/L | (69,640) | 866,786 | 314,773 |
| NW | 1,030,248 | 1,177,089 | (678,506) |
| WC | 671,694 | 834,149 | (994,065) |
| Emp. | 1,027 | 1,646 | 1,747 |

DUNS 21-148-8801
## Reco Trading Ltd
6 Station Road, St Neots, Cambridgeshire PE19 1AR
**Tel:** 01480401501
**Reg No:** 6785609 **Estd:** 2009 Private Limited Company
**Line of Business:** Management activities of other non-financial holding companies not elsewhere classified
**Export Sales:** £1,449,087
**Issued Capital:** £36,382
**Directors:** I F Ruston, M J Seymour, R A Ruston
**US SIC:** 6711 **UK SIC:** 83962
**Bankers:** Barclays Bank Plc (20-31-52)

| | 31-10-13 | 31-10-12 | 31-10-11 |
|---|---|---|---|
| TO | 14,487,211 | 16,849,799 | 16,168,822 |
| P/L | 167,461 | 459,882 | 431,162 |
| NW | 9,557,731 | 9,439,620 | 9,121,181 |
| WC | 6,120,405 | 7,137,890 | 8,326,160 |
| Emp. | 64 | 65 | 67 |

DUNS 29-648-3894
## Recol Ltd
Lodge Way, Lodge Farm Industrial Estate, Northampton, Northamptonshire NN5 7US
**Web:** www.recolengineering.co.uk
**Reg No:** 1974684 **VAT No:** 486004940
**Estd:** 1986 Private Limited Company
**Line of Business:** Sheet metal fabricators
**Trading Style:** Recol Engineering
**Issued Capital:** £1,000
**Managing Director:** R Guntrip
**Co. Secretary:** Mrs Janet Guntrip
**Responsibilities**
**Senior:** Michael Shane *(General Manager)*
**Branches:** Recol Ltd, Barn Way, Lodge Farm Indstl Est, Northampton, Northamptonshire NN5 7UW
**US SIC:** 3499 **UK SIC:** 31694
**Auditors:** A J Lewis
**Bankers:** Barclays Bank Plc (20-57-40)

| | 30-04-14 | 30-04-13 | 30-04-12 |
|---|---|---|---|
| TA | 3,261,482 | 3,255,205 | 2,361,150 |
| NW | 861,593 | 834,636 | 864,683 |
| WC | 48,026 | 274,812 | 185,943 |

DUNS 29-565-7282 **Exp**
## Record Plc
Morgan House, Madeira Walk, Windsor, Berkshire SL4 1EP
**Tel:** 01753-852222 **Fax:** 01753-852224
**Web:** www.recordcm.com
**Reg No:** 1927640 **Estd:** 1985 Public Limited Company
**Line of Business:** Financial intermediation not elsewhere classified
**Export Markets:** U S A, Europe, Middle East, Bermuda
**Issued Capital:** £55,345
**Principals:** N P Record *(Chairman)*, D A Wood-Collins, B F Noyen, Dr C A Schrauwers, L F Meier, D J Morrison, S P Cullen, A F Sykes
**Co. Secretary:** Ms Joanne Manning
**US SIC:** 6111, 7392
**UK SIC:** 81501, 83951
**Auditors:** Grant Thornton UK LLP
**Bankers:** Lloyds TSB Bank plc (30-97-73)

| | 31-03-14 | 31-03-13 | 31-03-12 |
|---|---|---|---|
| IA | 36,567,000 | 35,745,000 | 32,073,000 |
| P/L | 6,537,000 | 6,078,000 | 6,709,000 |
| NW | 28,506,000 | 27,679,000 | 25,213,000 |
| WC | 29,175,000 | 31,180,000 | 27,308,000 |
| Emp. | 66 | 64 | 68 |

DUNS 50-534-5777 **Imp**
## Record U.K. Ltd
(**Subsidiary of:** Agta Finance)
Garrion Business Park, Smith Avenue, Wishaw, Lanarkshire ML2 0RY
**Tel:** 01698376411 **Fax:** 01698376422
**Web:** www.recorduk.co.uk
**Reg No:** 0124392SC **Estd:** 1990 Private Limited Company
**Line of Business:** Specialised building trade contractors
**Issued Capital:** £2,000
**Directors:** S Riva, H Jouffroy, Dr H Plaut
**Co. Secretary:** Alexander Marshall
**Responsibilities**
**Senior:** Mark Barrie *(Manager)*, Thomas McAvoy *(Manager)*
**US SIC:** 2431 **UK SIC:** 46300
**Auditors:** KPMG LLP
**Bankers:** Bank Of Scotland (80-09-93)

| | 31-12-13 | 31-12-12 | 31-12-11 |
|---|---|---|---|
| TO | 16,181,762 | 16,046,989 | 15,485,434 |
| P/L | (99,999) | (635,865) | (1,003,863) |
| NW | (3,261,019) | (3,525,855) | (3,272,029) |
| WC | 1,052,110 | 679,039 | 796,324 |
| Emp. | 140 | 151 | 157 |

DUNS 22-001-4787
## Recover Me Ltd
Beaufort House, 7-8 Talavera Court, Moulton Park, Northampton, Northamptonshire NN3 6RW
**Tel:** 01604 496830
**Web:** www.autorescuelogistics.co.uk
**Reg No:** 8867330 **Estd:** 2014 Private Limited Company
**Line of Business:** Maintenance and repair of motor vehicles
**Directors:** R M Reames, Ms T Dabija, M Iqbal, H J Hodgkin, P A Beckerley
**US SIC:** 7539 **UK SIC:** 67100
**Employees:** 60

DUNS 22-064-4830
## Recresco Ltd
Lane End, Sutton-In-Ashfield, Nottinghamshire NG17 8AP
**Tel:** 01623-721006 **Fax:** 01623772044
**Web:** www.recresco.com
**Reg No:** 4066165 **VAT No:** 764399483
**Estd:** 1958 Private Limited Company
**Line of Business:** Recycling
**Export Sales:** £3,162,714
**Issued Capital:** £104
**Directors:** T Gent, S Gent, P J Hathaway, E Gent, P G Martin, S J Marjoram
**Co. Secretary:** Graham Gent
**Responsibilities**
**Senior:** Simon Etches *(Manager)*
**IT:** Stuart Yaxley *(IT Manager)*
**Branches:** Recresco Ltd, Herbert Walker Avenue, Southampton, Hampshire SO15 1HJ
**US SIC:** 3341 **UK SIC:** 22470
**Auditors:** RSM Tenon Audit Ltd

| | 30-09-13 | 30-09-12 | 30-09-11 |
|---|---|---|---|
| TO | 37,078,680 | 16,268,815 | 16,827,076 |
| P/L | 5,514,843 | 1,601,585 | 1,118,193 |
| NW | 6,921,154 | 3,186,100 | 2,278,775 |
| WC | (636,835) | (1,609,136) | 269,960 |
| Emp. | 146 | 127 | 128 |

DUNS 73-979-6022
## Recroot Ltd
2a Abbey Walk, Grimsby, South Humberside DN31 1NB
**Tel:** 01472351200
**Web:** www.recroot.net
**Reg No:** 5230309 **Estd:** 2010 Private Limited Company
**Line of Business:** Employment and recruitment companies and consultants
**Issued Capital:** £150,001
**Director:** J Marrs
**Co. Secretary:** Andrew Marrs
**Responsibilities**
**Senior:** Monika Walkowicz *(Office Manager)*
**Branches:** Recroot Ltd, Trinity House, Trinity Street, Colchester, Essex CO1 1JN
**US SIC:** 7361 **UK SIC:** 83954
**Bankers:** Barclays Bank Plc (20-85-93)

| | 30-09-13 | 30-09-12 | 30-09-11 |
|---|---|---|---|
| TO | 11,173,132 | 10,463,552 | N/A |
| P/L | 271,587 | 245,599 | N/A |
| NW | 440,130 | 379,640 | 117,618 |
| WC | 413,916 | 370,811 | 73,538 |
| Emp. | 876 | 712 | N/A |

DUNS 64-076-0302
## Recruitment Zone Ltd
Ratho Park, 88 Glasgow Road, Ratho Station, Newbridge, Midlothian EH28 8PP
**Tel:** 01313331555 **Fax:** 01313-332666
**Web:** www.rzgroup.co.uk
**Reg No:** 0180976SC **Estd:** 1997 Private Limited Company
**Line of Business:** Labour recruitment and provision of personnel
**Issued Capital:** £200
**Principals:** A R Barton *(Managing)*, D Bedford
**Co. Secretary:** Mrs Laura Barton
**Responsibilities**
**Operations:** Lisa Kwiecinska *(Operations Manager)*
**Branches:** Recruitment Zone Ltd, Ullswater Suite Paragon Business Park, Chorley New Road, Horwich, Bolton, Lancashire BL6 6HG
**US SIC:** 7361 **UK SIC:** 83954
**Auditors:** Donnellys
**Bankers:** National Westminster Bank Plc (01-03-21)

| | 31-12-13 | 31-12-12 | 31-12-11 |
|---|---|---|---|
| TO | 46,933,808 | 40,443,223 | 41,492,339 |
| P/L | 1,041,816 | 891,343 | 1,042,453 |
| NW | 2,963,309 | 2,385,693 | 1,840,944 |
| WC | 2,850,640 | 2,258,901 | 1,661,539 |
| Emp. | 88 | 101 | 109 |

DUNS 21-229-0290 **Imp-Exp**
## Rectella Ltd
Julian House, Manchester M32 0QY
**Tel:** 01618 662610 **Fax:** 01618 662620
**Web:** www.rectella.co.uk
**Reg No:** 0430344 **Estd:** 1947 Private Limited Company
**Line of Business:** Wholesale of textiles
**Export Markets:** countries worldwide.
**Trading Style:** Rectella Limited
**Issued Capital:** £118,122
**Principals:** C F Greibach *(Managing)*, A G Davis, A W Graham, J Greibach, F H Greibach
**Co. Secretary:** Ms Anne Greibach
**Responsibilities**
**Senior:** Peter Bolton *(Manager)*, Sue Wilson *(Manager)*
**IT:** Dave Muir *(IT Manager)*
**Branches:** Rectella Ltd, 27 Bell St, Wolverhampton, West Midlands WV1 3PT
**US SIC:** 5133, 5714, 6711
**UK SIC:** 61600, 64700, 83962
**Auditors:** Lopian Gross Barnett & Co
**Bankers:** Barclays Bank Plc (20-12-05)

| | 30-04-13 | 30-04-12 | 30-04-11 |
|---|---|---|---|
| TO | 16,201,653 | 19,460,154 | 20,452,427 |
| P/L | (464,559) | 388,449 | 182,005 |
| NW | 6,578,507 | 7,057,066 | 6,777,224 |
| WC | 5,675,744 | 6,507,864 | 6,337,673 |
| Emp. | 193 | 188 | 201 |

DUNS 21-620-5682 **Imp-Exp**
## Recticel Ltd
(**Subsidiary of:** Recticel Sa)
Bluebell Close, Clover Nook Industrial Park, Alfreton, Derbyshire DE55 4RD
**Tel:** 01773838000 **Fax:** 01773-835563
**Web:** www.recticel.co.uk
**Reg No:** 0665376 **VAT No:** 408706551
**Estd:** 1960 Private Limited Company
**Line of Business:** Foam products (rubber and plastic)
**Export Sales:** £2,483,000
**Trading Style:** Recticel Insulation Products
**Issued Capital:** £58,484,647
**Directors:** R Becker, P Warrant, M Clockaerts, D E Wilkinson
**Co. Secretary:** Paul Moss
**Responsibilities**
**Senior:** David Birkby *(Manager)*, Rik De Vos *(Director)*
**Branches:** Recticel Ltd, Mitchell Hey, Mills College Rd, Rochdale, Lancashire OL12 6AE
**US SIC:** 3079 **UK SIC:** 48360
**Auditors:** HLB Vantis Audit PLC
**Bankers:** HSBC Bank plc (40-35-18)

| | 31-12-13 | 31-12-12 | 31-12-11 |
|---|---|---|---|
| TO | 110,208,000 | 100,797,000 | 93,083,000 |
| P/L | (4,533,000) | (669,000) | (1,257,000) |
| NW | (142,000) | 12,057,000 | 12,726,000 |
| WC | (6,484,000) | (1,792,000) | (543,000) |
| Emp. | 629 | 570 | 568 |

DUNS 21-206-7453
## Rectory House Nursing Home
West Street, Sompting, Lancing, West Sussex BN15 0DA
**Tel:** 01903-750026
**Web:** www.caringhomes.org
**Estd:** 1989 Proprietorship
**Line of Business:** Nursing homes
**Principals:** A Revell, Ms D Revell *(Proprietor)*
**Responsibilities**
**Senior:** Sheila Sheriff *(Manager)*
**US SIC:** 8051 **UK SIC:** 95100
**Bankers:** National Westminster Bank Plc (60-03-32)
**Employees:** 63

DUNS 21-778-6937
## Rectory Lane Health Centre
Rectory Lane, Loughton, Essex IG10 3RU
**Tel:** 02082724600
**Estd:** 2011 Proprietorship
**Line of Business:** Public sector hospital activities, including nhs trusts
**Proprietor:** Ms O Mckay
**Responsibilities**
**Senior:** Hayley Freeth *(Clinical Lead)*, Obi McKay *(Proprietor)*
**US SIC:** 8062 **UK SIC:** 95100
**Employees:** 50

DUNS 34-865-3176
## Recycling Lives Holdings Ltd
Essex Street, Preston, Lancashire PR1 1QE
**Tel:** 01772654321
**Web:** www.recyclinglives.com
**Reg No:** 5664702 **Estd:** 2006 Private Limited Company
**Line of Business:** Management activities of holding companies
**Issued Capital:** £190
**Director:** S T Jackson
**Co. Secretary:** Paul Finnerty
**US SIC:** 6711 **UK SIC:** 83962
**Auditors:** KPMG LLP

| | 30-09-13 | 30-09-12 | 30-09-11 |
|---|---|---|---|
| TO | 22,403,265 | 22,922,912 | 23,445,656 |
| P/L | 361,607 | 1,114,984 | 1,197,966 |
| NW | 682,484 | 1,134,752 | 228,352 |
| WC | (5,067,947) | (2,652,996) | (2,046,878) |
| Emp. | 198 | 192 | 201 |

DUNS 22-070-8825
## The Recycling Partnership Ltd
(**Subsidiary of:** Cox Management Services Ltd)
Burleigh Oaks Farm, East Street, Turners Hill, Crawley, West Sussex RH10 4PZ
**Tel:** 01342-715456 **Fax:** 01342-716013
**Web:** www.recyclingpartnership.co.uk
**Reg No:** 4072350 **Estd:** 2004 Private Limited Company
**Line of Business:** Waste disposal
**Trading Style:** Cox Skips
**Issued Capital:** £100
**Director:** S Cox
**Co. Secretary:** Anthony Page
**US SIC:** 8911, 7399
**UK SIC:** 83701, 83954
**Auditors:** Clarkson Hyde LLP
**Bankers:** Barclays Bank Plc (20-24-61)

| | 31-03-14 | 31-03-13 | 31-03-12 |
|---|---|---|---|
| TO | N/A | 1,277,914 | 1,187,297 |
| P/L | N/A | 259,555 | 331,624 |
| NW | 6,806 | 187,595 | 218 |
| WC | 615,733 | (186,190) | (214,736) |

DUNS 21-679-3961
## Recycoal Holdings Ltd
Spinner Point, Lakeside Boulevard, Doncaster, South Yorkshire DN4 5PL
**Tel:** 01302539032 **Fax:** 01302379239
**Web:** www.recycoal.com
**Reg No:** 7301988 **Estd:** 2010 Private Limited Company
**Line of Business:** Quarries
**Trading Style:** Recycoal Holdings Ltd
**Issued Capital:** £3,250,001
**Directors:** S Beaumont, T J Allchurch, R M Frost, Ms C Piwnica
**Responsibilities**
**Senior:** Mario Frandino *(Manager)*
**Operations:** Mike Lenagh *(Group Operations Director)*
**US SIC:** 1499, 4959

UK SIC: 23960, 92110

|  | 30-06-13 | 01-07-12 | 03-06-11 |
|---|---|---|---|
| TO | 9,252,000 | 13,172,000 | 12,545,000 |
| P/L | (6,519,000) | (1,882,000) | 1,035,000 |
| NW | (4,285,000) | 2,512,000 | 3,946,000 |
| WC | (2,027,000) | (5,590,000) | (916,000) |
| Emp. | 120 | 83 | 66 |

DUNS 34-664-1785 **Imp**

## Red 5 (Retail) Ltd
Unit B Saxon Way, Priory Park West, Hessle, North Humberside HU13 9PB
Tel: 02079981804 Fax: 01977685596
Web: www.red5.co.uk
Reg No: 5469356 Estd: 2005 Private Limited Company
Line of Business: Other retail sale in specialised stores not elsewhere classified
Issued Capital: £200
Directors: P R Wilkinson, J Baron, C D Martinez, J D Elvidge
Co. Secretary: Martin Rushforth
US SIC: 5199, 5399
UK SIC: 61900, 65600

|  | 31-03-14 | 31-03-13 | 31-03-12 |
|---|---|---|---|
| TO | 15,764,814 | 13,785,547 | 12,477,731 |
| P/L | 668,646 | 328,445 | 89,097 |
| NW | 845,710 | 294,984 | 46,024 |
| WC | 29,982 | (520,201) | (834,620) |
| Emp. | 255 | 243 | 292 |

DUNS 21-676-7936

## Red Ant Design Ltd
(Subsidiary of: Red Ant Group Ltd)
The Pump House, Forstal Road, Aylesford, Kent ME20 7AH
Tel: 01622664333
Web: www.redantdesign.com
Reg No: 7282011 Estd: 2010 Private Limited Company
Line of Business: Graphic designers
Issued Capital: £1
Director: D J Mortimer
Responsibilities
Senior: Fiona Grundy (Office Manager)
US SIC: 7399 UK SIC: 83954

|  | 30-06-13 | 30-06-12 | 30-06-11 |
|---|---|---|---|
| TA | 1 | 1 | 1 |
| NW | 1 | 1 | 1 |

DUNS 21-585-5727

## Red Band Chemical Company; Ltd
(Subsidiary of: Clark & Company Raimes Ltd)
17-19 Smith's Place, Edinburgh, Midlothian EH6 8NU
Web: www.lindsayandgilmour.co.uk
Reg No: 0016876SC Estd: 1816 Private Limited Company
Line of Business: Representative office
Trading Style: Lindsay & Gilmour
Issued Capital: £1,250
Principals: C N Cumming (Managing), Mrs Y Williams, P C Galt, Mrs E Robertson, A C Cumming, A Roberts
Co. Secretary: Ms Moira O'Toole
Responsibilities
Senior: Norman Jess (Manager)
Branches: "Red Band" Chemical Company; Ltd, Lyndsey & Gilmour, 16 Central Avenue, Grangemouth, Stirlingshire FK3 8SD
US SIC: 5912 UK SIC: 64300
Auditors: Blueprint Audit Ltd
Bankers: Clydesdale Bank Plc (82-66-07)

|  | 31-12-13 | 31-12-12 | 31-12-11 |
|---|---|---|---|
| TO | 23,419,538 | N/A | 24,262,956 |
| P/L | 547,590 | 786,327 | 415,511 |
| NW | (117,147) | (585,654) | (989,418) |
| WC | 2,946,919 | 2,211,314 | 1,829,764 |
| Emp. | 159 | 141 | 142 |

DUNS 21-583-3665

## Red Bee Media
100 Brand Street, Glasgow, Lanarkshire G51 1DG
Tel: 01414194000
Web: www.redbeemedia.com
Estd: 2011 Proprietorship
Line of Business: Advertising, radio, tv and other media
Proprietor: Mrs V Maguire
Responsibilities
Senior: Juliet Gauthier (Office Manager)
US SIC: 7319 UK SIC: 83800
Employees: 50

DUNS 34-829-8030

## The Red Brick Road Ltd
(Subsidiary of: Trbr Ltd)
50-54 Beak Street, London W1F 9RN
Tel: 02075757600 Fax: 02075757633
Web: www.theredbrickroad.com
Reg No: 5629150 Estd: 1992 Private Limited Company
Line of Business: Advertising agency services
Export Sales: £1,222,024
Issued Capital: £2,760

Directors: D N Miller, R S Megson, B G Mitchell, M B Davis
Responsibilities
Sales: Luke Abbott (Social Media Account Director)
IT: Andy Murdoch (IT Manager)
US SIC: 7319 UK SIC: 83800

|  | 31-12-13 | 31-12-12 | 31-12-11 |
|---|---|---|---|
| TO | 10,183,531 | 26,611,552 | 35,760,045 |
| P/L | 575,316 | 3,426,919 | 101,560 |
| NW | 739,175 | 4,211,015 | 876,342 |
| WC | 714,170 | 3,792,879 | 726,158 |
| Emp. | 46 | 80 | 87 |

DUNS 34-805-6375 **Imp**

## Red Bull Co Ltd
155-171 Tooley Street, London SE1 2JP
Tel: 02031172000
Web: www.redbull.co.uk
Reg No: 2790349 Estd: 1993 Private Limited Company
Line of Business: Wholesale of fruit and vegetable juices, mineral waters and soft drinks
Export Sales: £23,089,087
Issued Capital: £1,000
Directors: D Mateschitz, R Maas Geesteranus, A Shaw, C Yoovidhya
Co. Secretary: Robert Maas Geesteranus
Responsibilities
Senior: Karl Sengstbratl (Manager), Nigel Trood (Manager)
HR: Lynda Connor (People Manager)
US SIC: 5149 UK SIC: 61700
Auditors: Ernst & Young LLP
Bankers: Lloyds TSB Bank plc (30-94-81)

|  | 31-12-13 | 31-12-12 | 31-12-11 |
|---|---|---|---|
| TO | 232,525,064 | 238,478,325 | 236,233,336 |
| P/L | 15,774,537 | 11,422,784 | 13,779,849 |
| NW | 20,108,222 | 20,346,215 | 24,229,632 |
| WC | 12,154,668 | 12,970,270 | 16,520,162 |
| Emp. | 230 | 188 | 181 |

DUNS 49-312-3145

## Red Bull Racing Ltd
(Subsidiary of: Red Bull Gmbh)
Building 1, Bradbourne Drive, Milton Keynes, Buckinghamshire MK7 8BJ
Tel: 01908-279700 Fax: 01908-279711
Web: www.redbullracing.com
Reg No: 3120645 Estd: 1995 Private Limited Company
Line of Business: Other sporting activities not elsewhere classified
Trading Style: Red Bull Technology
Issued Capital: £1,000,000
Directors: Dr H Marko, D Mateschitz, C E Horner
Co. Secretary: Laytons Secretaries Limited
Responsibilities
Marketing: Barbara Proske (Press Officer), Katie Tweedle (Communications Manager)
IT: Matt Cadieux (Chief Information Officer)
Engineering: Shawn Hetherington (Additive Manufacturing Enginee), Adrian Newey (Chief Technical Officer)
US SIC: 7999 UK SIC: 97913
Auditors: Ernst & Young LLP
Bankers: HSBC Bank plc (40-05-30)

|  | 31-12-13 | 31-12-12 | 31-12-11 |
|---|---|---|---|
| TO | 197,599,000 | 176,310,000 | 176,844,000 |
| P/L | 1,392,000 | 700,000 | 641,000 |
| NW | 5,319,000 | 4,277,000 | 3,577,000 |
| WC | (3,902,000) | (3,971,000) | (4,723,000) |
| Emp. | 57 | 55 | 52 |

DUNS 76-629-0829

## Red Circle Security Services (Europe) Ltd
10 Upper Tachbrook Street, London SW1V 1SH
Tel: 020-7233-6955 Fax: 02072336629
Reg No: 2580414 Estd: 1991 Private Limited Company
Line of Business: Security and related activities
Issued Capital: £100
Managing Director: B A Rana
Co. Secretary: Ms Veena Bahl
US SIC: 7393 UK SIC: 83954
Auditors: Shabbir & Co
Bankers: Barclays Bank Plc (20-47-34)

|  | 31-03-14 | 31-03-13 | 31-03-12 |
|---|---|---|---|
| TA | 299,064 | 303,277 | 320,836 |
| NW | 293,545 | 292,831 | 284,543 |
| WC | 290,288 | 289,203 | 281,208 |

DUNS 23-924-7237

## Red Commerce Ltd
1st Floor 51-55 Gresham Street, London EC2V 7EL
Tel: 020-7107-7600 Fax: 020-7107-7601
Web: www.redcommerce.com
Reg No: 3914762 VAT No: 872504522
Estd: 2000 Private Limited Company
Line of Business: Labour recruitment and provision of personnel
Export Sales: £58,144,000
Issued Capital: £50,000
Directors: A J Mcrae, A R Hunt, A R Duke, C D Mitchell

Co. Secretary: Craig Mitchell
Responsibilities
Senior: Richard Berbesie (Chief Executive Officer), Richard Vercesi (Manager)
Admin: Nicola Cash (Office Manager), Nicola Domb (Office Manager)
Facilities: Nicola Cash (Office Manager), Nicola Domb (Office Manager)
Branches: Red Commerce Ltd, 10 Parade Street, Penzance, Cornwall TR18 4BU
US SIC: 7361 UK SIC: 83954
Auditors: KPMG LLP

|  | 31-03-13 | 31-03-12 | 31-03-11 |
|---|---|---|---|
| TO | 67,660,000 | 78,142,000 | 62,130,450 |
| P/L | 3,750,000 | 5,920,000 | 5,210,075 |
| NW | 21,610,000 | 18,762,000 | 14,430,925 |
| WC | 20,906,000 | 18,383,000 | 14,135,678 |
| Emp. | 167 | 151 | 109 |

DUNS 73-509-5135 **Exp**

## The Red Consultancy Ltd
(Subsidiary of: Huntsworth Plc)
41-44 Great Windmill Street, London W1D 7NF
Tel: 020-7025-6500 Fax: 020-7025-6499
Web: www.redconsultancy.com
Reg No: 2913684 VAT No: 649273801
Estd: 1994 Private Limited Company
Line of Business: Public relations activities
Export Markets: Germany, France
Export Sales: £859,077
Issued Capital: £200
Directors: E H Staples, M E Park, Ms A J Duncan, Lord Chadlington, M Morgan, Ms I K Coney, G C Chapman, Ms E Morgan
Responsibilities
Senior: Perena Barrett (board Director), Andrea Donovan (Director), Rebecca Fergusson (Director), Jennifer Lees (Manager), Jono Marshall (Office Manager), Sophie Taylor-Roberts (Director), Paul Weigold (Financial Controller), Sally-Ann Withey (Director)
Finance: Paul Weigold (Financial Controller)
Admin: Dave Webster (Office Manager)
Health & Safety: Dave Webster (Office Manager)
Facilities: Dave Webster (Office Manager)
Operations: Dave Webster (Office Manager)
Purchasing: Dave Webster (Office Manager)
US SIC: 7392 UK SIC: 83951
Auditors: KPMG Audit Plc
Bankers: Lloyds TSB Bank plc (30-94-92)

|  | 31-12-13 | 31-12-12 | 31-12-11 |
|---|---|---|---|
| TO | 16,680,206 | 17,856,509 | 15,977,336 |
| P/L | 2,310,176 | 2,251,467 | 1,546,892 |
| NW | 921,262 | 787,855 | 567,317 |
| WC | 764,764 | 888,703 | 513,875 |
| Emp. | 131 | 141 | 135 |

DUNS 21-770-5654

## Red Deer
Joseph Locke Way, Crediton, Devon EX17 3FD
Web: www.reddeerpubcrediton.co.uk
Estd: 2011 Proprietorship
Line of Business: Restaurant - pub food
Proprietor: P Wright
US SIC: 5812 UK SIC: 66110
Employees: 50

DUNS 21-568-5919

## Red Dragon Sport
South Road, Bridgend Industrial Estate, Bridgend, Mid Glamorgan CF31 3PT
Tel: 01656652121
Web: www.reddragondarts.com
Estd: 1977 Proprietorship
Line of Business: Sports goods and equipment - mail order
Proprietor: J Blouck
Responsibilities
Senior: V Black (Manager), John Bluck (Manager)
US SIC: 5961 UK SIC: 65600
Employees: 70

DUNS 21-779-6359

## Red Driving School
Colemans Nook, Belasis Hall Technology Park, Billingham, Cleveland TS23 4EG
Web: www.reddrivingschool.com
Estd: 2011 Proprietorship
Line of Business: Training centres
Proprietor: Mrs P Wilson
Responsibilities
Senior: Tracy Garrod (Manager)
US SIC: 8299 UK SIC: 93300
Employees: 50

DUNS 71-906-4896

## Red Eagle Ltd
39 Bouverie Square, Folkestone, Kent CT20 1BA
Web: www.redeagle.jobs
Reg No: 5288420 VAT No: 855119911
Estd: 2003 Private Limited Company

Line of Business: Labour recruitment and provision of personnel
Issued Capital: £2
Directors: J Hodgson, W M Cotter
Co. Secretary: Wayne Hodgson
Responsibilities
Senior: Leigh Cripps (Industrial Manager), Jo-Anna Hodgson (Director)
Finance: Kellie Hocking (Finance Administrator)
Operations: Leigh Cripps (Industrial Manager), Gary Warlosz (Industrial Director)
US SIC: 7361 UK SIC: 83954
Bankers: The Royal Bank Of Scotland Plc (16-00-55)

|  | 31-12-13 | 31-12-12 | 31-12-11 |
|---|---|---|---|
| TO | 11,892,396 | 10,272,560 | 8,815,647 |
| P/L | 294,422 | 488,953 | 437,533 |
| NW | 204,329 | 203,004 | 167,436 |
| WC | 182,306 | 189,118 | 161,272 |
| Emp. | 1,508 | 775 | 583 |

DUNS 73-568-2192

## Red Embedded Holdings Ltd
The Waterfront, Salts Mill Road, Shipley, West Yorkshire BD17 7EZ
Web: www.redembedded.com
Reg No: 4829985 Estd: 2003 Private Limited Company
Line of Business: Electronic engineers
Issued Capital: £96
Directors: D J Longhorn, W T Hoath, D Taylor, R Mehra
Co. Secretary: Dr Stuart Griffin
US SIC: 8911, 6711
UK SIC: 83701, 83962

|  | 31-08-13 | 31-08-12 | 31-08-11 |
|---|---|---|---|
| TA | 1,452,788 | 1,454,229 | 1,454,336 |
| NW | 1,444,477 | 1,444,477 | 1,444,477 |
| WC | 1,444,186 | 1,444,186 | 1,444,177 |

DUNS 73-860-3047

## Red Funnel Group (Holdings) Ltd
(Subsidiary of: Infracapital Partners Lp)
12 Bugle Street, Southampton, Hampshire SO14 2JY
Tel: 0844-844-2699 Fax: 0844-844-2698
Web: www.redfunnel.co.uk
Reg No: 5115188 Estd: 2004 Private Limited Company
Line of Business: Management activities of holding companies
Issued Capital: £559,000
Directors: S K Nelson, M D Helmore, P R Winter, K A George
US SIC: 6711 UK SIC: 83962
Auditors: Grant Thornton UK LLP
Bankers: HSBC Bank plc (40-08-21)

|  | 31-12-13 | 31-12-12 | 31-12-11 |
|---|---|---|---|
| TA | 40,639,000 | 105,812,000 | 105,812,000 |
| P/L | 3,799,000 | N/A | (19,000) |
| NW | 40,562,000 | 40,563,000 | 40,563,000 |

DUNS 21-947-1110

## Red Gate Enterprises Ltd
Newnham House, Cambridge Business Park, Cowley Road, Cambridge, Cambridgeshire CB4 0WZ
Tel: 01223420397
Reg No: 8566599 Estd: 2013 Private Limited Company
Line of Business: Publishing of software
Export Sales: £27,113,234
Issued Capital: £1
Directors: Dr S D Galbraith, N G Davidson
Co. Secretary: Colin Oakman
US SIC: 7372 UK SIC: 83940
Bankers: National Westminster Bank Plc (52-10-46)

|  | 31-12-13 |
|---|---|
| TO | 31,715,503 |
| P/L | 5,951,804 |
| NW | (878,803) |
| WC | 2,728,429 |
| Emp. | 282 |

DUNS 23-866-0927

## Red Gate Software Ltd
(Subsidiary of: Red Gate Enterprises Ltd)
Newnham House, 12 Cambridge Business Park, Cowley Road, Cambridge, Cambridgeshire CB4 0WZ
Tel: 01223438500 Fax: 08700635117
Web: www.red-gate.com
Reg No: 3857576 Estd: 2008 Private Limited Company
Line of Business: Computer software (development)
Export Sales: £26,859,723
Trading Style: Red Gate Software Limited
Issued Capital: £1,168
Directors: S W Brown, A Platt, S D Galbraith, J Theron, N G Davidson, G Marlow
Co. Secretary: Colin Oakman
Responsibilities
Senior: Colin Millerchip (Product Manager)
Marketing: Sofie Westlake (Marketing Manager)

**Admin:** Simon Lye *(information systems engineer)*
**IT:** Simon Lye *(information systems engineer)*, Richard Mitchell *(?Project Manager)*
**Health & Safety:** Jaime Peart *(facilities manager)*
**Facilities:** Jaime Peart *(facilities manager)*
**Operations:** Colin Millerchip *(Product Manager)*
**Engineering:** Simon Lye *(information systems engineer)*
**US SIC:** 7379 **UK SIC:** 83940
**Auditors:** Peters Elworthy & Moore
**Bankers:** National Westminster Bank Plc (52-10-46)

| | 31-12-13 | 31-10-12 | 31-12-11 |
|---|---|---|---|
| TO | 31,446,042 | 26,437,375 | 23,615,544 |
| P/L | 6,865,504 | 3,093,755 | 3,923,285 |
| NW | 337,517 | 3,001,195 | 395,514 |
| WC | 2,529,324 | 4,612,139 | 2,800,163 |
| Emp. | 253 | 255 | 216 |

DUNS 21-795-9020
## Red Gates School
School House, Farnborough Avenue, South Croydon, Surrey CR2 8HD
**Web:** www.redgates.croydon.sch.uk
**Estd:** 2011 Proprietorship
**Line of Business:** Primary education
**Proprietor:** Mrs V Watkins
**Responsibilities**
**Senior:** Sue Beaman *(Head Teacher)*
**US SIC:** 8999 **UK SIC:** 83954
**Employees:** 90

DUNS 23-806-4195 **Imp**
## Red Hat U K Ltd
**(Subsidiary of:** Redhat Ltd)
200 Fowler Avenue, Farnborough, Hampshire GU14 7JP
**Tel:** 01252362700 **Fax:** 01252-548117
**Web:** www.redhat.com
**Reg No:** 3798903 **Estd:** 1999 Private Limited Company
**Line of Business:** Hardware consultancy
**Issued Capital:** £2
**Directors:** C E Peters Jr, M M O'Neill, M A Parson
**Co. Secretary:** Michael Cunningham
**Responsibilities**
**Senior:** Charles Peters *(Director)*
**Branches:** Red Hat U K Ltd, 64 Baker Street, London W1U 7GB
**US SIC:** 7379 **UK SIC:** 83940
**Auditors:** PricewaterhouseCoopers
**Bankers:** Barclays Bank Plc (20-38-81)

| | 28-02-14 | 28-02-13 | 29-02-12 |
|---|---|---|---|
| TO | 38,470,733 | 32,388,893 | 25,189,644 |
| P/L | 1,741,205 | 1,413,196 | 1,117,004 |
| NW | 12,069,318 | 7,682,088 | 4,349,680 |
| WC | 11,094,065 | 6,428,427 | 3,220,320 |
| Emp. | 295 | 251 | 217 |

DUNS 21-595-4296
## Red Hot World Buffet & Bar
8 Savoy Crescent, Milton Keynes, Buckinghamshire MK9 3PU
**Tel:** 01908609606
**Web:** www.redhot-worldbuffet.com
**Estd:** 2011 Proprietorship
**Line of Business:** Restaurants
**Proprietor:** R Singh
**US SIC:** 5812 **UK SIC:** 66110
**Employees:** 50

DUNS 21-114-0980
## Red Hotels Ltd
Bedruthan House Trenance, Mawgan Porth, Wadebridge, Cornwall PL27 7JU
**Tel:** 01637860860
**Reg No:** 6547005 **Estd:** 2008 Private Limited Company
**Line of Business:** Hotels and motels, with restaurant (unlicensed)
**Issued Capital:** £104,255
**Directors:** Mrs E Stratton, Ms R Whittington, Mrs D J Wakefield, J R Waghorn
**Co. Secretary:** Robert Waghorn
**US SIC:** 7011 **UK SIC:** 66500

| | 29-12-13 | 30-12-12 | 25-12-11 |
|---|---|---|---|
| TO | 9,049,165 | 8,630,792 | 8,261,020 |
| P/L | 321,917 | 233,673 | 487,525 |
| NW | 7,279,068 | 7,064,737 | 6,985,016 |
| WC | (2,071,509) | (1,665,030) | (434,052) |
| Emp. | 276 | 270 | 228 |

DUNS 29-929-9446
## The Red House Nursing Home Ltd
London Road, Canterbury, Kent CT2 8NB
**Fax:** 01227-462516
**Web:** www.theredhousenursinghome.co.uk
**Reg No:** 2098595 **Estd:** 1987 Private Limited Company
**Line of Business:** Clinics private
**Issued Capital:** £100
**Director:** Ms R M Morton
**Co. Secretary:** John Gichigi
**Responsibilities**
**Senior:** Alison D'lima *(Manager)*
**US SIC:** 8051 **UK SIC:** 95100

| | 31-03-14 | 31-03-13 | 31-03-12 |
|---|---|---|---|
| TA | 145,362 | 152,420 | 126,581 |
| NW | 36,439 | 30,329 | 25,627 |
| WC | (45,888) | (53,549) | (61,263) |

DUNS 76-942-4946
## Red House School Ltd
36 The Green, Norton, Stockton-On-Tees, Cleveland TS20 1DX
**Web:** www.redhouseschool.co.uk
**Reg No:** 0312473 **Estd:** 1929 Private Limited Company
**Line of Business:** Schools (foundation)
**Directors:** J Henning, Mrs K E Huddart, V A Bedi, Ms A L Mallen-Beadle, S J Asforth, M S Craggs, G Taylor, S D Wright
**Responsibilities**
**Senior:** Jim Bradley *(Manager)*, John Greenaway *(Director)*, Joanna Grylls *(Manager)*, Amar Rangan *(Director)*, Jennifer Readman *(Director)*, Alex Taylor *(Headmaster)*, Eric Whitehouse *(Manager)*
**Finance:** Lisa Dunn *(Bursar)*
**Marketing:** J Allinson *(Sales & Marketing Manager)*, Sarah Tomlinson *(Marketing Manager)*
**Sales:** J Allinson *(Sales & Marketing Manager)*
**Admin:** Heather Jefferson *(Headmaster's PA)*, Linda Ward *(Secretary)*
**HR:** Alex Taylor *(Headmaster)*
**Health & Safety:** Lisa Dunn *(Bursar)*
**Facilities:** Lisa Dunn *(Bursar)*
**US SIC:** 8211 **UK SIC:** 93200
**Auditors:** King Hope & Co
**Bankers:** The Royal Bank Of Scotland Plc (16-25-24)

| | 31-08-14 | 31-08-13 | 31-08-12 |
|---|---|---|---|
| TO | 4,025,400 | 3,962,706 | 3,651,676 |
| P/L | 369,279 | 352,157 | 106,004 |
| NW | 2,316,974 | 1,947,695 | 1,595,538 |
| WC | 241,762 | (72,306) | (2,936,444) |
| Emp. | 76 | 74 | 74 |

DUNS 73-950-1083
## Red Industries Ltd
**(Subsidiary of:** Red Industries Holdings Ltd)
Treatment Centre, Sneyd Hill, Stoke-On-Trent, Staffordshire ST6 2DZ
**Tel:** 01782824100
**Web:** www.redindustries.co.uk
**Reg No:** 5202754 **Estd:** 2004 Private Limited Company
**Line of Business:** Collection and treatment of other waste
**Issued Capital:** £1,000
**Directors:** Ms J Share, A Share, J M Clewes, D J Scott, T P Wilson
**Co. Secretary:** Alan Clapperton
**Branches:** Red Industries Ltd, Burnside Works, Lochgelly, Fife KY5 0UP
**US SIC:** 4953, 4959
**UK SIC:** 92110
**Auditors:** BDO LLP

| | 31-12-13 | 31-12-12 | 31-12-11 |
|---|---|---|---|
| TO | 6,669,305 | 7,022,543 | 7,142,886 |
| P/L | 148,689 | 314,198 | 352,869 |
| NW | 923,318 | 1,823,290 | 1,665,211 |
| WC | 751,824 | 1,621,334 | 1,610,991 |
| Emp. | 52 | 54 | 52 |

DUNS 21-761-9891
## Red Kite Community Housing Ltd
Windsor Court, Kingsmead Business Park, Frederick Place, High Wycombe, Buckinghamshire HP11 1JU
**Tel:** 01494-476-100
**Web:** www.redkitehousing.org.uk
**Reg No:** 0031322I **Estd:** 2011 Friendly Society
**Line of Business:** Community Services
**Director:** T Morrow
**US SIC:** 8699 **UK SIC:** 96902
**Employees:** 110

DUNS 34-668-6632 **Imp**
## Red Letter Days Ltd
77 Muswell Hill, London N10 3PJ
**Tel:** 08456408000 **Fax:** 0870-444-9004
**Web:** www.redletterdays.co.uk
**Reg No:** 5473745 **Estd:** 1989 Private Limited Company
**Line of Business:** Gift services
**Issued Capital:** £1,000
**Directors:** T Paphitis, T Paphitis, I M Childs, P D Jones, W N Alexander
**Co. Secretary:** Kypros Kyprianou
**Responsibilities**
**Senior:** Rachel Elnaugh *(Managing Director, Director)*
**Finance:** Mark Boyce *(Head of Finance)*
**Marketing:** Courtney Glymph *(Senior Communications Executiv)*, Joshna Patel *(Head of Online)*
**Sales:** Peter Dando *(Corporate Sales Manager)*, Rav Hayer *(Director of Business Developme)*, Tony Heather *(Sales Director)*
**Admin:** Rebecca Landey *(Corporate Administrator)*, Alison Pye *(Corporate Administrator)*
**HR:** Anne Guerin *(Human Resources Manager)*
**Health & Safety:** Anne Guerin *(Human Resources Manager)*
**US SIC:** 5999, 7399
**UK SIC:** 65600, 83954
**Bankers:** Barclays Bank Plc (20-71-03)

| | 31-12-13 | 31-12-12 | 31-12-11 |
|---|---|---|---|
| TO | 16,372,176 | 14,996,929 | 12,979,632 |
| P/L | 561,503 | 500,842 | 404,694 |
| NW | (8,549,379) | (9,121,028) | (9,632,016) |
| WC | (4,783,941) | (4,864,252) | (5,362,791) |
| Emp. | 81 | 91 | 87 |

DUNS 34-552-8850 **Imp-Exp**
## Red Lion 49 Ltd
**(Subsidiary of:** Solid State Logic Holdings Ltd)
25 Springhill Road, Kidlington, Oxfordshire OX5 1RU
**Tel:** 01865-842300
**Web:** www.solidstatelogic.com
**Reg No:** 5362730 **VAT No:** 862069123
**Estd:** 2005 Private Limited Company
**Line of Business:** Other manufacturing not elsewhere classified
**Export Sales:** £19,394,000
**Trading Style:** Red Lion 49 Ltd
**Issued Capital:** £3,023,479
**Directors:** P Plaskitt, Dr E Perez Gonzalez, S J Loach, D G Hearn, G R Rampton, A M David, M D Large
**Co. Secretary:** Mrs Sharon Probitts
**Responsibilities**
**Senior:** Dan Duffell *(Marketing Director)*
**Marketing:** Dan Duffell *(Marketing Director)*
**Sales:** Philippe Guerinet *(Sales Manager)*
**IT:** Marc Hendrickse *(IT Manager)*
**Health & Safety:** Austen Christer *(Health & Safety Officer)*
**US SIC:** 3999, 3679
**UK SIC:** 49590, 34542
**Auditors:** Deloitte LLP
**Bankers:** HSBC Bank plc (40-38-04)

| | 31-12-13 | 31-12-12 | 31-12-11 |
|---|---|---|---|
| TO | 20,877,000 | 19,628,000 | 20,141,000 |
| P/L | 595,000 | 149,000 | 45,000 |
| NW | 2,660,000 | 1,768,000 | 1,185,000 |
| WC | 2,374,000 | 1,511,000 | 1,145,000 |
| Emp. | 131 | 133 | 130 |

DUNS 21-227-6181
## Red Lion Big Steak Wacky Warehouse
164 Warrington Road, Penketh, Warrington, Cheshire WA5 2LZ
**Tel:** 01925-722185
**Web:** www.orchidgroup.co.uk
**Estd:** 1999 Proprietorship
**Line of Business:** Licensed restaurants
**Proprietor:** M Evans
**Responsibilities**
**Senior:** Marie Evans *(Manager)*, Rachael Worth *(Manager)*
**US SIC:** 5812 **UK SIC:** 66110
**Employees:** 46

DUNS 21-231-3396
## Red Lodge Residential Home
Hope Corner Lane, Taunton, Somerset TA2 7PB
**Tel:** 01823-286158
**Web:** www.notarohomes.co.uk
**Estd:** 2002 Proprietorship
**Line of Business:** Residential care establishments
**Proprietor:** M Parish
**Responsibilities**
**Senior:** Matthew Parrish *(Manager)*
**US SIC:** 8321, 7231
**UK SIC:** 96111, 98200
**Employees:** 65

DUNS 73-911-6940
## The Red Maids' School
Westbury Road, Westbury-On-Trym, Westbury-On-Trym, Bristol, Avon BS9 3AW
**Tel:** 01179-622641
**Web:** www.redmaids.bristol.sch.uk
**Reg No:** 5165135 **Estd:** 1985 Private Company Limited By Guarantee
**Line of Business:** Schools (independent)
**Directors:** J R Fox, Ms J A Macfarlane, Mrs M C Culligan, A C Hardwick, S P Ryan, M W Davies, D J Taylor, J M Whatmough
**Co. Secretary:** Peter Taylor
**Responsibilities**
**Senior:** Valerie Dixon *(Director)*, Andrew Hillman *(Director)*, John Hollingdale *(Chairman of Finance and Genera)*, Thelma Howell *(Director)*, Judith Pattison *(Director)*, Lucy Pollock *(Director)*
**Finance:** John Hollingdale *(Chairman of Finance and Genera)*
**Marketing:** Maxine Walter *(?Head of Marketing and Develop)*
**IT:** Sarah Dymond *(Head of IT)*
**US SIC:** 8211 **UK SIC:** 93200
**Bankers:** Lloyds TSB Bank plc (30-99-38)

| | 31-08-14 | 31-08-13 | 31-08-12 |
|---|---|---|---|
| TO | 6,930,645 | 6,618,649 | 6,111,323 |
| P/L | 700,986 | 368,098 | 219,440 |
| NW | 11,285,937 | 10,280,843 | 9,775,301 |
| WC | (767,226) | 297,825 | 76,923 |
| Emp. | 119 | 109 | 104 |

DUNS 77-116-7848
## Red Mail Ltd
Unit 1 Anchorage Point Industrial Estate, Anchor And Hope Lane, London SE7 7SQ
**Tel:** 02088589142
**Web:** www.cycplc.com
**Reg No:** 2689281 **Estd:** 1990 Private Limited Company
**Line of Business:** Couriers
**Trading Style:** C Y C Initial Logistics
**Issued Capital:** £80
**Principals:** A R Fry *(Managing)*, J E Sinclair, D Ali, N J Hayes, Ms H L Fry
**Co. Secretary:** Anthony Fry
**US SIC:** 4311 **UK SIC:** 79010
**Auditors:** Shipleys LLP
**Bankers:** National Westminster Bank Plc (56-00-31)

| | 31-03-13 | 31-03-12 | 31-03-11 |
|---|---|---|---|
| TO | 10,175,461 | N/A | N/A |
| P/L | 264,997 | N/A | N/A |
| NW | 1,292,868 | 1,076,293 | 1,326,320 |
| WC | 912,954 | 635,741 | 911,296 |
| Emp. | 63 | N/A | N/A |

DUNS 21-665-6650
## Red Poppy (Uk) Ltd
**(Subsidiary of:** Red Poppy (Gibraltar) Limited)
1a Dukesway Court Team Valley, Gateshead, Tyne and Wear NE11 0PJ
**Tel:** 01538-560-010
**Reg No:** 7196804 **Estd:** 2010 Private Limited Company
**Line of Business:** Holding companies management activities
**Issued Capital:** £80,000,000
**Directors:** D J Horrocks, I Imrie
**Co. Secretary:** Phillip Blain
**US SIC:** 6711 **UK SIC:** 83962
**Auditors:** PricewaterhouseCoopers LLP

| | 31-10-12 | 31-10-11 | 31-10-10 |
|---|---|---|---|
| TO | 102,884,000 | 94,354,000 | 112,175,000 |
| P/L | (7,880,000) | 15,452,000 | (510,000) |
| NW | (5,806,000) | 5,239,000 | 34,498,000 |
| WC | (18,425,000) | (43,852,000) | (27,076,000) |
| Emp. | 1,925 | 1,784 | 2,143 |

DUNS 21-612-4765
## The Red Room At Waterstone's
36 Garstang Road, Preston, Lancashire PR3 0TD
**Web:** www.waterstones.com
**Estd:** 2002
**Line of Business:** Book retailers
**Responsibilities**
**Senior:** Simon Bristowe *(Manager)*
**US SIC:** 5942 **UK SIC:** 65300
**Employees:** 100

DUNS 21-729-5705
## Red Stack Technology Ltd
Farr House, 27-30 Railway Street, Chelmsford, Essex CM1 1QS
**Tel:** 01245-200-510
**Web:** www.redstacktechnology.com
**Reg No:** 7653209 **Estd:** 2011 Private Limited Company
**Line of Business:** Other computer related activities
**Export Sales:** £253,787
**Issued Capital:** £500
**Directors:** J C Anthony, R C Cook, A B Louth
**US SIC:** 7379 **UK SIC:** 83940
**Auditors:** Hazlewoods LLP

| | 31-12-13 | 31-12-12 | 31-12-11 |
|---|---|---|---|
| TO | 12,085,094 | N/A | N/A |
| P/L | 20,075 | 117,542 | (35,475) |
| NW | (1,957,031) | 322,435 | 260,493 |
| WC | (1,336,824) | (1,150,866) | (666,793) |
| Emp. | 73 | N/A | N/A |

DUNS 50-513-2209
## Red Star Growers Ltd
Woodfield Farm, Broadway Road, Birlingham, Pershore, Worcestershire WR10 3AG
**Web:** www.redstargrowers.co.uk
**Reg No:** 2481083 **Estd:** 1987 Private Limited Company
**Line of Business:** Fruit and vegetable (producers)
**Issued Capital:** £5,003
**Principals:** C L Simms *(Managing)*, A L Hartley, G W Revill, G J Revill, Ms M J Bennett, W J Revill
**Co. Secretary:** Ms Teresa Wilson
**US SIC:** 0179, 0161
**UK SIC:** 01002, 01001
**Auditors:** Crowe Clark Whitehill LLP

**Bankers:** Lloyds TSB Bank plc (30-93-11)

| | 31-12-13 | 31-12-12 | 31-12-11 |
|---|---|---|---|
| TO | 7,742,002 | 7,607,336 | 8,825,968 |
| P/L | 552,750 | 184,158 | 575,865 |
| NW | 1,770,762 | 1,391,958 | 1,292,077 |
| WC | 1,182,159 | 892,744 | 800,879 |
| Emp. | 75 | 75 | 84 |

DUNS 49-146-1091 **Imp**

## Red Submarine Ltd

**(Subsidiary of:** Key Capital Partners Llp)
Kettlestring Lane, York, North Yorkshire YO30 4XF
**Tel:** 03303654444 **Fax:** 01904-898626
**Web:** www.gear4music.com
**Reg No:** 3113256 **VAT No:** 552033282
**Estd:** 1995 Private Limited Company
**Line of Business:** Retail sale of furniture, lighting equipment and household articles not elsewhere classified
**Trading Style:** Gear4music
**Issued Capital:** £57,692
**Directors:** C D Scott, A P Wass, G J Bevan
**Co. Secretary:** Christopher Scott
**US SIC:** 5719, 5963, 5732
**UK SIC:** 64700, 65600, 64800
**Auditors:** David Newton & Co Ltd

| | 28-02-14 | 28-02-13 | 29-02-12 |
|---|---|---|---|
| TO | 17,677,674 | 12,265,651 | 10,195,978 |
| P/L | 184,602 | 237,323 | 313,524 |
| NW | 1,423,213 | 1,200,634 | 979,796 |
| WC | 1,884,930 | 2,446,489 | 863,850 |
| Emp. | 74 | N/A | N/A |

DUNS 29-183 0263 **Imp**

## ReD24 Plc

The Coachhouse, Bill Hill Park, Wokingham, Berkshire RG40 5QT
**Tel:** 02077412091
**Web:** www.red24plc.com
**Reg No:** 0086069SC **Estd:** 1983 Public Limited Company
**Line of Business:** Management activities of other non-financial holding companies not elsewhere classified
**Export Sales:** £2,739,432
**Issued Capital:** £487,284
**Directors:** M S Worsley-Tonks, S A Richards, Ms L A Adlam
**Co. Secretary:** John Mocatta
**US SIC:** 6711, 6399
**UK SIC:** 83962, 82001
**Auditors:** Baker Tilly UK Audit LLP
**Bankers:** Lloyds TSB Bank plc (30-97-20)

| | 31-03-14 | 31-03-13 | 31-03-12 |
|---|---|---|---|
| TO | 5,886,707 | 6,503,265 | 5,819,328 |
| P/L | 854,905 | 940,104 | 863,093 |
| NW | 3,427,231 | 2,794,033 | 2,214,441 |
| WC | 2,507,709 | 2,203,463 | 1,973,799 |
| Emp. | 84 | 86 | 80 |

DUNS 45-882-5981

## Redactive Media Sales Ltd

17-18 Britton Street, London EC1M 5TP
**Tel:** 020-7880-6200
**Reg No:** 3220190 **Estd:** 1998 Private Limited Company
**Line of Business:** Sale or leasing activities of advertising space or time
**Trading Style:** Centurion Publishing Group
**Issued Capital:** £2
**Director:** B Grant
**Co. Secretary:** Stuart Edmundson
**US SIC:** 7319 **UK SIC:** 83800
**Auditors:** Simmons Gainsford LLP

| | 28-02-14 | 28-02-13 | 29-02-12 |
|---|---|---|---|
| TA | 3,203,377 | 2,735,570 | 2,045,626 |
| NW | 83,321 | 110,927 | 880,959 |
| WC | 83,321 | 110,927 | 880,959 |

DUNS 23-992-7320

## Redbridge College

Null, Romford, Essex RM6 4XT
**Tel:** 02085487400
**Web:** www.redbridge-college.ac.uk
**Estd:** 1993
**Line of Business:** Further education schools and colleges
**Director:** T Mcgrath
**Responsibilities**
**Senior:** Theresa Drowley *(Principal)*, Tony McGrath *(Principal)*, Alan Steward *(Warehouse Manager)*
**Finance:** Steve Hendy *(Accounts Manager)*
**Marketing:** Sarah Plater *(Marketing Manager)*
**IT:** Andy Adebo *(Computer Manager)*
**US SIC:** 8211 **UK SIC:** 93200
**Bankers:** National Westminster Bank Plc (60-50-09)
**Employees:** 300

DUNS 28-868-0739

## Redbridge Sports Centre Trust Ltd

Forest Road, Ilford, Essex IG6 3HD
**Tel:** 02084981000 **Fax:** 020-8498-1020
**Web:** www.rslonline.co.uk
**Reg No:** 1000490 **VAT No:** 246605755
**Estd:** 1971 Private Company Limited By Guarantee
**Line of Business:** Leisure centres
**Directors:** K S Leggate, C B Rippon, R C Littlewood, J C Fortescue, E W Brown, T Jameson, P H Fishenden, J G Hill
**Co. Secretary:** Ms Carolynne Spencer
**Responsibilities**
**Senior:** Richard Firmstone *(Director)*, Rasmita Gohil *(Director)*, Jane Kelloe *(Director)*, Joyce Ryan *(Director)*, Wendy Spencer *(Board Member)*, Wesley Streeting *(Director)*
**Admin:** Debbie O'Reilly *(Office Manager)*, Viv Westwood *(Office Manager)*
**HR:** Debbie O'Reilly *(Office Manager)*, Viv Westwood *(Office Manager)*
**Health & Safety:** Emma Reynolds *(Health & Safety Officer)*
**US SIC:** 7999 **UK SIC:** 97913
**Auditors:** The Hart Partnership
**Bankers:** Barclays Bank Plc (20-44-22)

| | 31-12-13 | 31-12-12 | 31-12-11 |
|---|---|---|---|
| TO | 2,022,560 | 1,761,878 | 1,715,926 |
| P/L | (99,952) | (289,604) | 10,017 |
| NW | 8,891,789 | 9,034,933 | 8,776,709 |
| WC | (116,748) | (336,705) | (1,456,028) |
| Emp. | 138 | 130 | 121 |

DUNS 73-509-2087

## Redburn Partners Llp

75 King William Street, London EC4N 7BE
**Tel:** 02070002020
**Web:** www.redburn.com
**Reg No:** 0304714OC **Estd:** 2003
**Line of Business:** Investment consultants
**Responsibilities**
**Senior:** Lance Burbidge *(Partner)*, Pascal Hautcoeur *(Partner)*, Neil Steer *(Partner)*
**Sales:** Max Casini *(Head of Equity Sales)*
**IT:** Peter Culver *(Information Technology Manager)*
**Operations:** Robin Thompson *(Head of Operations and Settlem)*
**US SIC:** 7399 **UK SIC:** 83954
**Bankers:** Bank Of Scotland (12-21-37)

| | 31-03-14 | 31-05-13 | 31-03-12 |
|---|---|---|---|
| TO | 64,793,130 | 58,777,117 | 58,386,147 |
| P/L | 20,502,142 | 18,364,691 | 17,645,368 |
| NW | 50,003 | 11,852,204 | 11,716,884 |
| WC | N/A | 22,875,537 | 19,464,921 |
| Emp. | 100 | 96 | 95 |

DUNS 21-867-4790

## Redcar Academy - A Community School for the Performing & Visua

Kirkleatham Lane, Redcar, Cleveland TS10 4AB
**Tel:** 01642289211
**Web:** www.redcaracademy.com
**Reg No:** 8281046 **Estd:** 1988 Private Company Limited By Guarantee
**Line of Business:** General secondary education
**Directors:** Ms S J George, Ms C Parker, D Gallagher, M Grainger, Ms L M Winter, S A Henman, Ms D A Mcfarlane, Ms T O'Neill
**Responsibilities**
**Senior:** Sally Hobday *(Manager)*, Rebecca Sill *(Manager)*
**US SIC:** 8211 **UK SIC:** 93200
**Bankers:** Lloyds TSB Bank plc (30-95-56)

| | 31-08-14 | 31-08-13 |
|---|---|---|
| TO | 4,835,000 | 11,649,000 |
| P/L | (139,000) | 7,509,000 |
| NW | 7,236,000 | 7,434,000 |
| WC | 328,000 | 327,000 |
| Emp. | 102 | 102 |

DUNS 23-985-4177

## Redcar & Cleveland Borough Council

Hensons Business Centre, Kirkleatham Street, Redcar, Cleveland TS10 1RE
**Tel:** 01642771500
**Web:** www.redcar-cleveland.gov.uk
**Estd:** 2012
**Line of Business:** Information services
**Principals:** T Todd *(Chairman)*, P Kirkman *(Financial)*, C Moore
**Responsibilities**
**Senior:** Heather Mclean *(Coordinator)*, Corinne Templeman *(Education Manager)*
**HR:** Pauline Kavanagh *(Human Resources Manager)*
**Branches:** Redcar & Cleveland Borough Council, Belmont House, Rectory Lane, Guisborough, Cleveland TS14 7FD
**US SIC:** 7399 **UK SIC:** 83954
**Bankers:** The Co-Operative Bank Plc (08-90-89)
**Employees:** 7,000

DUNS 21-746-0281

## Redcar & Cleveland Pct

Unit 5-6 Chaloner House, Bow St Centre North, Guisborough, Cleveland TS14 6PR
**Tel:** 01287634706
**Web:** www.caremark.co.uk
**Estd:** 2008
**Line of Business:** Home care service providers
**Principals:** B Gamble *(Chairman)*, N Nicholson *(Financial)*, Ms C Willis, Ms C Hunter, Dr B King, P Race, I Taylor, Ms V Fegan
**Responsibilities**
**Senior:** Charles Folkes *(Proprietor)*
**Branches:** Redcar & Cleveland Pct, Linthorpe Rd, Middlesbrough, Cleveland TS1 3QY
**US SIC:** 8091, 9121
**UK SIC:** 95200, 91110
**Employees:** 960

DUNS 21-693-6360

## Redcar Bulk Terminal Ltd

Steel House Trunk Road, Redcar, Cleveland TS10 5QW
**Reg No:** 7402297 **Estd:** 2010 Private Limited Company
**Line of Business:** Cargo handling
**Issued Capital:** £26,502,718
**Directors:** S J Putz, D Nicol, C J Louwrens, S A Mason, M Earl, J M Bolton
**Co. Secretary:** Chipchase Manners Nominees Limit
**US SIC:** 4712 **UK SIC:** 77002

| | 31-12-13 | 31-12-12 | 31-12-11 |
|---|---|---|---|
| TO | 28,739,000 | 17,468,000 | 12,692,000 |
| P/L | 9,780,000 | 343,000 | 128,000 |
| NW | 35,234,000 | 26,601,000 | 26,447,000 |
| WC | 12,095,000 | 861,000 | 1,710,000 |
| Emp. | 92 | 89 | 85 |

DUNS 21-204-5942 **Imp**

## Redcats (Brands) Ltd

**(Subsidiary of:** Financiere Pinault)
2 Holdsworth Street, Bradford, West Yorkshire BD1 4AH
**Tel:** 01274729544
**Web:** www.redcats.com
**Reg No:** 0110433 **Estd:** 1873 Private Limited Company
**Line of Business:** Retail sale via mail order house
**Issued Capital:** £45,000,100
**Directors:** Ms F S Deve, M Truluck, S Gallouj, P Kenworthy, Ms N C Balla
**Branches:** Redcats (Brands) Ltd, The Bargain St, 5 Horsefair, Pontefract, West Yorkshire WF8 1PP
**US SIC:** 5961 **UK SIC:** 65600
**Auditors:** Deloitte LLP
**Bankers:** Barclays Bank Plc (20-11-81)

| | 31-12-13 | 31-12-12 | 31-12-11 |
|---|---|---|---|
| TO | 45,058,000 | 54,405,000 | 52,930,000 |
| P/L | 4,388,000 | 621,000 | 39,000 |
| NW | 49,634,000 | 46,364,000 | 45,253,000 |
| WC | 45,697,000 | 41,808,000 | 42,276,000 |
| Emp. | 449 | 455 | 474 |

DUNS 23-013-2623

## Redcentric Communications Ltd

**(Subsidiary of:** Redcentric Plc)
80 Great Eastern Street, London EC2A 3RS
**Tel:** 08000380023 **Fax:** 08452000099
**Web:** www.redstone.co.uk
**Reg No:** 3021292 **Estd:** 1995 Private Limited Company
**Line of Business:** Aeronautical engineers
**Issued Capital:** £10,262,166
**Directors:** A C Weaver, T J Coleman
**Co. Secretary:** Miss Estelle Croft
**Branches:** Redcentric Communications Ltd, Beckwith Knowle, Central House, Harrogate, North Yorkshire HG3 1UF
**US SIC:** 8911 **UK SIC:** 83701
**Auditors:** PricewaterhouseCoopers LLP
**Bankers:** Barclays Bank Plc (20-03-80)

| | 31-03-14 | 31-03-13 | 31-03-12 |
|---|---|---|---|
| TA | N/A | 30,394,978 | 30,394,978 |
| P/L | 15,032,084 | N/A | N/A |
| NW | N/A | (15,032,084) | (15,032,084) |
| WC | N/A | (15,032,093) | (15,032,093) |
| Emp. | 2 | N/A | N/A |

DUNS 21-924-8238

## Redcentric Plc

Newton House, Cambridge Business Park, Cambridge, Cambridgeshire CB4 0WZ
**Tel:** 08450-341-111
**Web:** www.redcentricplc.com
**Reg No:** 8397584 **Estd:** 2013 Public Limited Company
**Line of Business:** Management activities of holding companies
**Directors:** A C Weaver, F S Fisher, D G Payne, C Cole, S R Puckett, T J Coleman
**Co. Secretary:** Timothy Coleman
**US SIC:** 6711 **UK SIC:** 83962
**Bankers:** Barclays Bank Plc (20-00-50)

| | 31-03-14 |
|---|---|
| TO | 58,323,000 |
| P/L | (2,562,000) |
| NW | (474,000) |
| WC | (894,000) |
| Emp. | 221 |

DUNS 21-032-1249

## Redcliffe Catering

Botanical Garden, Westbourne Road, Edgbaston, Birmingham, West Midlands B15 3TR
**Tel:** 0121-456-2244
**Web:** www.birminghambotanicalgardens.org.uk
**Estd:** 1986 Proprietorship
**Line of Business:** Catering food and drink suppliers
**Proprietor:** C Cook
**US SIC:** 6531 **UK SIC:** 83400
**Employees:** 400

DUNS 28-868-6322

## Redcliffe Hotel Ltd

4 Marine Drive, Paignton, Devon TQ3 2NL
**Tel:** 01803-526397
**Web:** www.redcliffehotel.co.uk
**Reg No:** 1008906 **VAT No:** 585425417
**Estd:** 1950 Private Limited Company
**Line of Business:** Hotels
**Issued Capital:** £1,000
**Principals:** S J Twigger *(Managing)*, D Twigger
**Co. Secretary:** Mrs Jean Twigger
**Responsibilities**
**Finance:** Marilyn Twigger *(Financial Controller)*
**Facilities:** Ron Harding *(Maintenance Manager)*
**US SIC:** 7011 **UK SIC:** 66500
**Auditors:** Bishop Fleming
**Bankers:** HSBC Bank plc (40-44-43)

| | 30-04-14 | 30-04-13 | 30-04-12 |
|---|---|---|---|
| TA | 2,094,990 | 1,974,870 | 1,941,763 |
| NW | 1,482,756 | 1,416,216 | 1,409,224 |
| WC | 37,626 | (28,231) | (197,270) |

DUNS 22-512-4353 **Exp**

## Redcliffe Ltd

**(Subsidiary of:** Redcliffe Holdings Ltd)
Clothier Road, Brislington, Bristol, Avon BS4 5PS
**Tel:** 01179-729400
**Web:** www.redcliffe.biz
**Reg No:** 1589034 **VAT No:** 664476602
**Estd:** 1937 Private Limited Company
**Line of Business:** Electrical testing services
**Export Markets:** W Europe; E & S E Asia; Australasia; U S A
**Issued Capital:** £125,000
**Director:** S R Parsons
**Responsibilities**
**Purchasing:** Kevin Wadsworth *(Materials Manager)*
**Engineering:** Daniel Hawkins *(Production Supervisor)*
**US SIC:** 1731, 7391
**UK SIC:** 50300, 94000
**Auditors:** KPMG
**Bankers:** Lloyds TSB Bank plc (30-00-01)

| | 30-09-13 | 30-09-12 | 30-09-11 |
|---|---|---|---|
| TA | 493 | 99,401 | 99,401 |
| NW | 493 | 99,401 | 99,401 |

DUNS 21-340-0659

## Redcliffe Sixth Form Centre

Dulverton House, Redcliff Hill, Bristol, Avon BS1 6RB
**Tel:** 0117-3532073
**Web:** www.smrt.bristol.sch.uk
**Estd:** 2003 Proprietorship
**Line of Business:** Further education schools and colleges
**Proprietor:** A Champion
**US SIC:** 8221 **UK SIC:** 93100
**Employees:** 150

DUNS 21-239-9062

## Redcourt-St Anselm's

7 Devonshire Place, Prenton, Merseyside CH43 1TX
**Tel:** 0151-652-5228
**Web:** www.redcourtstanselms.com
**Estd:** 1949 Proprietorship
**Line of Business:** Nursery schools
**Principals:** Christian Brothers *(Chairman)*, K Davey *(Proprietor)*
**US SIC:** 8211 **UK SIC:** 93200
**Employees:** 48

DUNS 49-311-6552

## Redde Plc

Pinesgate Lower Bristol Road, Bath, Avon BA2 3DP
**Tel:** 01225321000
**Web:** www.helphire.co.uk
**Reg No:** 3120010 **VAT No:** 682207047
**Estd:** 1995 Public Limited Company
**Line of Business:** Management activities of holding companies
**Trading Style:** Redde
**Issued Capital:** £16,567,383
**Directors:** Ms A Palmer-Baunack, M Mccafferty, S E Oakley, J L Davies, Ms A Palmer-Baunack, M Ward

**Co. Secretary:** Nicholas Tilley
**Responsibilities**
**Senior:** James Church (Manager), Alan Gilbert (Technical Director), Alistair Mathers (Non-Executive Director)
**Admin:** Michelle Brain (Executive Assistant)
**Operations:** Andy Langford (Manager)
**Engineering:** Alan Gilbert (Technical Director), Nick Litchfield (Manager)
**Branches:** Redde Plc, Pinesgate, Lower Bristol Road, Bath, Avon BA2 3DP
**US SIC:** 6711, 7399
**UK SIC:** 83962, 83954
**Auditors:** KPMG Audit PLC
**Bankers:** HSBC Bank plc (40-09-19)

| | 30-06-14 | 30-06-13 | 30-06-12 |
|---|---|---|---|
| TO | 197,419,000 | 204,767,000 | 224,309,000 |
| P/L | 10,518,000 | 32,426,000 | (6,254,000) |
| NW | 82,932,000 | 58,058,000 | (8,444,000) |
| WC | 66,777,000 | 50,808,000 | 24,792,000 |
| Emp. | 1,182 | 1,196 | 1,263 |

### DUNS 22-795-9483
## Reddie & Grose
12-16 Theobalds Road, London WC1X 8PL
**Tel:** 020-7242-0901
**Web:** www.reddie.co.uk
**VAT No:** 243908749 **Estd:** 1929 Partnership
**Line of Business:** Activities of patent and copyright agents
**Principals:** P A Smith, S J Goodman, S J Mohon, D S Jackson, J H Bass, Ms H R Wakerley (Partner), A J Robson (Partner), P A Brereton (Partner)
**Responsibilities**
**Senior:** Richard Abnett (Partner), Keith Geering (Partner), Linda Harland (Partner), Patrick Lloyd (Partner), Nicholas Marlow (Partner), J Vleck (Partner)
**US SIC:** 7399 **UK SIC:** 83954
**Bankers:** Lloyds TSB Bank plc (30-94-25)
**Employees:** 100

### DUNS 21-327-5584
## Reddiford School
38 Cecil Park, Pinner, Middlesex HA5 5HH
**Tel:** 020-8866-0660
**Web:** www.reddiford.co.uk
**Estd:** 1992 Proprietorship
**Line of Business:** Schools (independent)
**Proprietor:** Mrs J Batt
**Responsibilities**
**Senior:** Jean Batt (Principal)
**IT:** C Raddette (Computer Manager)
**US SIC:** 8211, 8299
**UK SIC:** 93200, 93300
**Employees:** 67

### DUNS 21-954-7960
## Reddiplex 2011 Ltd
The Furlong, Berry Hill Industrial Estate, Droitwich, Worcestershire WR9 9BG
**Tel:** 08451658234 **Fax:** 01905796662
**Web:** www.reddiplex.com
**Reg No:** 6136269 **Estd:** 1994 Private Limited Company
**Line of Business:** Manufacture of other plastic products
**Issued Capital:** £52,650
**Directors:** M W Morgan, C D Dawson, Ms L C Morgan
**Co. Secretary:** Ms Janet Dawson
**US SIC:** 3079 **UK SIC:** 48360

| | 30-04-14 | 30-04-13 | 30-04-12 |
|---|---|---|---|
| TO | 18,977,754 | 16,748,857 | 17,260,153 |
| P/L | 2,960,941 | 2,402,583 | 2,332,759 |
| NW | 16,621,813 | 14,907,731 | 13,513,475 |
| WC | 11,723,904 | 10,100,426 | 8,614,829 |
| Emp. | 137 | 129 | 138 |

### DUNS 73-741-3849 Imp-Exp
## Reddiplex Ltd
(**Subsidiary of:** Reddiplex 2011 Ltd)
The Furlong, Berry Hill Industrial Estate, Droitwich, Worcestershire WR9 9BG
**Tel:** 01905795432 **Fax:** 01905796662
**Web:** www.reddiplex.com
**Reg No:** 2922638 **VAT No:** 488055709
**Estd:** 1978 Private Limited Company
**Line of Business:** Plastic material & synthetic resin mfrs
**Export Markets:** Worldwide
**Issued Capital:** £58,600
**Directors:** O Boylan, C D Dawson, M W Morgan, Ms M Senatore, Ms L C Morgan, S Ryman
**Co. Secretary:** Ms Janet Dawson
**Responsibilities**
**Senior:** Christina Boot (Manager)
**Marketing:** Francisco Lancina (Marketing Director)
**HR:** D Thiltott (Buyer), M Yahia (Personnel Manager)
**Operations:** Andy Walsh (Quality Manager)
**US SIC:** 2821, 3079
**UK SIC:** 25140, 48360
**Auditors:** Andorran Ltd

**Bankers:** National Westminster Bank Plc (60-04-05)

| | 30-04-14 | 30-04-13 | 30-04-12 |
|---|---|---|---|
| TA | 2,276,127 | 2,225,075 | 2,164,482 |
| NW | 1,155,161 | 1,152,004 | 1,024,282 |
| WC | 1,146,254 | 1,143,097 | 1,015,375 |

### DUNS 23-641-7630
## Redditch Borough Council
Town Hall, Alcester Street, Redditch, Worcestershire B98 8AH
**Tel:** 01527-64252 **Fax:** 01527-65216
**Web:** www.redditchbc.gov.uk
**Estd:** 1974 Incorporate By Act Of Parliament
**Line of Business:** General (overall) public service activities
**Trading Style:** Pitcheroak Golf Club
**Directors:** C Smith, Ms D Colley, K J Tyers
**Responsibilities**
**Senior:** Kevin Dicks (Manager)
**HR:** Becky Barr (Head of Human Resources)
**Branches:** Redditch Borough Council, The South East Quadrant, Unit 1B, Redditch, Worcestershire B98 8AE
**US SIC:** 9121 **UK SIC:** 91110
**Bankers:** Barclays Bank Plc (20-71-45)
**Employees:** 450

### DUNS 23-734-5611 Imp
## Redeem Ltd
(**Subsidiary of:** Redeem Holdings Ltd)
Unit 9b, Pyramids Business Parks, Bathgate, West Lothian EH48 2EH
**Tel:** 01506633388 **Fax:** 013246789014
**Web:** www.redeemplc.com
**Reg No:** 0194216SC **Estd:** 1999 Private Limited Company
**Line of Business:** Retail sale of mobile telephones
**Export Sales:** £25,661,684
**Issued Capital:** £350,000
**Directors:** J S Carver, C A Svensson, M R Chambers, T K Bayley, C D Lovatt
**Co. Secretary:** Ms Angela Bayley
**Responsibilities**
**Senior:** Kurt Hopkins (Manager)
**Finance:** Robbie Hart (Financial Controller)
**Marketing:** Richard Mavers (Head of Client Marketing)
**HR:** Lisbeth Robertson (Human Resources Manager)
**Branches:** Redeem Ltd, 14 Winchester Ave, Denny, Stirlingshire FK6 6QE
**US SIC:** 5942, 7379
**UK SIC:** 65300, 83940
**Auditors:** Ernst & Young LLP
**Bankers:** HSBC Bank plc (40-22-47)

| | 31-03-14 | 31-03-13 | 31-03-12 |
|---|---|---|---|
| TO | 39,968,160 | 30,123,571 | 25,139,170 |
| P/L | 784,317 | 534,056 | 520,665 |
| NW | 1,335,624 | 727,058 | 1,065,952 |
| WC | 1,213,934 | 617,075 | 979,277 |
| Emp. | 94 | 95 | 106 |

### DUNS 21-782-5198
## Redeemer C of E Primary School
Jack Walker Way, Blackburn, Lancashire BB2 4JJ
**Tel:** 01254296409
**Web:** www.the-redeemer.org.uk
**Estd:** 2011 Proprietorship
**Line of Business:** Places of worship
**Proprietor:** Mrs A Ashworth-Taylor
**Responsibilities**
**Senior:** Sheila Fielding (Administrator)
**US SIC:** 8661 **UK SIC:** 96600
**Employees:** 50

### DUNS 21-681-0880
## Redefine Hotel Management Ltd
10th Floor The Mille, 1000 Great West Road, Brentford, Middlesex TW8 9DW
**Tel:** 02082329014 **Fax:** 02082329029
**Web:** www.redefineinternational.com
**Reg No:** 7316555 **Estd:** 2006 Private Limited Company
**Line of Business:** Management of real estate on a fee or contract basis
**Issued Capital:** £6,250
**Directors:** D Hart, S Campbell, H R Silva Pereira
**Co. Secretary:** Ms Paula Ross
**Responsibilities**
**Senior:** Stephen Carlin (Marketing Director), Stephen Enderle (Manager), Hans Enderle (Marketing Director), Lisa Hibberd (Manager)
**Marketing:** Stephen Carlin (Marketing Director), Hans Enderle (Marketing Director)
**US SIC:** 6531 **UK SIC:** 83400
**Bankers:** National Westminster Bank Plc (01-03-87)

| | 31-08-13 | 31-08-12 | 31-08-11 |
|---|---|---|---|
| TO | 23,163,383 | 23,142,652 | 9,474,182 |
| P/L | (338,931) | (273,895) | 89,480 |
| NW | 961,797 | 1,300,728 | 1,589,480 |
| WC | (2,420,240) | (1,899,456) | (999,568) |
| Emp. | 213 | 220 | 129 |

### DUNS 21-308-9972
## Redfern Travel Ltd
(**Subsidiary of:** A. I. T Travel Ltd)
Ait House, Bradford, West Yorkshire BD1 3AZ
**Tel:** 01274760600 **Fax:** 01274-760633
**Web:** www.redfern-travel.com
**Reg No:** 0488182 **VAT No:** 708374133
**Estd:** 1990 Private Limited Company
**Line of Business:** Travel agency activities
**Issued Capital:** £50,000
**Principals:** I C Wotton (Managing), G N Hopwood, M W Bowers, A S Shawe
**Co. Secretary:** Allan Webster
**Responsibilities**
**IT:** Mark Hirst (IT Manager)
**Branches:** Redfern Travel Ltd, 19 Queensgate, Bradford, West Yorkshire BD1 1RB
**US SIC:** 4722 **UK SIC:** 77001
**Auditors:** Garbutt & Elliott Ltd
**Bankers:** National Westminster Bank Plc (60-60-05)

| | 31-03-14 | 31-03-13 | 31-03-11 |
|---|---|---|---|
| TO | 202,514,150 | 140,558,126 | N/A |
| P/L | 2,586,466 | 702,514 | N/A |
| NW | 2,478,530 | 832,707 | 719,115 |
| WC | 1,462,979 | 1,514,188 | 823,585 |
| Emp. | 96 | 74 | N/A |

### DUNS 73-766-7563
## Redfield Property Co. Ltd.
Avonvale Road, Bristol, Avon BS5 9RG
**Tel:** 01173534320
**Web:** www.bristol.gov.uk
**Reg No:** 5023941 **Estd:** 2004 Private Limited Company
**Line of Business:** Development and selling of real estate
**Issued Capital:** £4
**Directors:** C M Cruse, Mrs P I Cruse
**Co. Secretary:** Peter Taylor
**Responsibilities**
**Senior:** Sharon Baker (Manager)
**US SIC:** 6552 **UK SIC:** 85000

| | 31-01-14 | 31-01-13 | 31-01-12 |
|---|---|---|---|
| TA | 788,040 | 865,271 | 651,585 |
| NW | 27,714 | (25,586) | (18,437) |
| WC | 196,513 | 279,715 | 143,428 |

### DUNS 22-552-3570
## Redfields Garden Nursery Ltd
Redfields Garden Centre Ltd, Fleet, Hampshire GU52 8UB
**Tel:** 01252627785
**Web:** www.redfieldsgardencentre.com
**Reg No:** 1296122 **VAT No:** 190078267
**Estd:** 1977 Private Limited Company
**Line of Business:** Other retail sale in specialised stores not elsewhere classified
**Issued Capital:** £104
**Principals:** M D Goater (Managing), R A Jones
**Co. Secretary:** Ms Anne Goater
**Responsibilities**
**Health & Safety:** Andy Webb (Facilities Manager)
**Facilities:** Andy Webb (Facilities Manager)
**US SIC:** 5999 **UK SIC:** 65600
**Auditors:** Wilkins Kennedy
**Bankers:** National Westminster Bank Plc (60-08-42)

| | 30-04-13 | 30-04-12 | 30-04-11 |
|---|---|---|---|
| TO | N/A | N/A | 1,063,577 |
| P/L | N/A | N/A | (304,932) |
| NW | 760,565 | 1,296,692 | 1,510,012 |
| WC | (954,573) | (1,471,113) | (1,145,199) |
| Emp. | N/A | N/A | 13 |

### DUNS 23-645-5791
## Redgate Properties Ltd
4 Little Borough, Brockham, Betchworth, Surrey RH3 7ND
**Tel:** 01737-843011
**Reg No:** 3640776 **Estd:** 1998 Private Limited Company
**Line of Business:** Tv and film producers and directors
**Issued Capital:** £10,000
**Director:** Lord J Clack Of Gerard'S Bromley
**Co. Secretary:** Lady Sally Clack Of Thulston
**Responsibilities**
**Senior:** Dora Clack Of Gerard'S Bromley (Accounts), Sally Thulston (Manager)
**Finance:** Dora Clack Of Gerard'S Bromley (Accounts)
**US SIC:** 7819 **UK SIC:** 97111
**Auditors:** Bullimores

| | 30-09-13 | 30-09-12 | 30-09-11 |
|---|---|---|---|
| TA | 27,895 | 29,081 | 30,801 |
| NW | (138,559) | (126,740) | (107,596) |
| WC | (141,306) | (130,089) | (111,782) |

### DUNS 21-203-3955 Exp
## Redhall Group Plc
1 Red Hall Court, Wakefield, West Yorkshire WF1 2UN
**Tel:** 01924-385386 **Fax:** 01924374548
**Web:** www.redhallgroup.co.uk
**Reg No:** 0263995 **Estd:** 1932 Public Limited Company
**Line of Business:** Manufacture of other fabricated metal products not elsewhere classified
**Export Markets:** Overseas
**Export Sales:** £10,331,000
**Trading Style:** Booth Industries, Oakland Elevators, C H B Fabrications
**Issued Capital:** £7,461,675
**Directors:** J D Brooke, P Brierley, C J Kelly, M J Everett, P B Hilling
**Co. Secretary:** Christopher Kelly
**Responsibilities**
**Senior:** Tony Goodenough (Managing Director, R Blackett), Laura Houghton (Group SHEQ Manager), Paul Kirk (Non-Executive Director), Christopher Lewis Jones (Group Financial Director), John O'Kane (Group Financial Director), Richard Shuttleworth (Chief Executive Officer)
**Finance:** Christopher Lewis Jones (Group Financial Director), John O'Kane (Group Financial Director)
**Health & Safety:** Laura Houghton (Group SHEQ Manager)
**Branches:** Redhall Group Plc, Stover Trading Estate, Millbrook Road, Yate, Bristol, Avon BS37 5PB
**US SIC:** 3499, 1799
**UK SIC:** 31694, 50000
**Auditors:** KPMG Audit PLC
**Bankers:** HSBC Bank plc (40-28-06)

| | 30-09-14 | 30-09-13 | 30-09-12 |
|---|---|---|---|
| TO | 103,180,000 | 113,082,000 | 116,771,000 |
| P/L | (5,765,000) | (9,781,000) | (4,653,000) |
| NW | (5,515,000) | (6,764,000) | 1,379,000 |
| WC | 4,768,000 | (3,096,000) | 12,226,000 |
| Emp. | 1,119 | 1,225 | 1,282 |

### DUNS 77-459-8411
## Redhill Analysts Ltd
(**Subsidiary of:** Redhill Hco Ltd)
Unit 1 Deanhouse Farm Church Lane, Dorking, Surrey RH5 5DL
**Tel:** 01306-631-820
**Web:** www.redhills.co.uk
**Reg No:** 2962375 **VAT No:** 725128841
**Estd:** 1994 Private Limited Company
**Line of Business:** Asbestos products & removal
**Trading Style:** Redhills
**Issued Capital:** £50,000
**Directors:** J W Walsh, Obs 24 Llp, L C Carter
**Co. Secretary:** Rjp Secretaries Limited
**Responsibilities**
**Senior:** Brian Giddings (Manager), Matt Griggs (Manager), Kieran Moon (Manager), Sean Nutley (CEO)
**Finance:** Brian Giddings (Manager)
**IT:** Brian Giddings (Manager)
**HR:** Brian Giddings (Manager)
**Branches:** Redhill Analysts Ltd, Links Court, Fortran Road, St Mellons, Cardiff, South Glamorgan CF3 0LT
**US SIC:** 1799, 7397
**UK SIC:** 50000, 83702
**Auditors:** PricewaterhouseCoopers LLP
**Bankers:** HSBC Bank plc (40-19-22)

| | 31-12-13 | 30-09-12 | 30-12-11 |
|---|---|---|---|
| TO | 18,135,000 | 9,651,000 | 7,869,000 |
| P/L | (1,304,000) | 931,000 | 971,000 |
| NW | 2,269,000 | 4,872,000 | 3,972,000 |
| WC | 7,077,000 | 1,684,000 | 1,058,000 |
| Emp. | 238 | 164 | 127 |

### DUNS 21-229-8912
## Redhill Court
229 London Road, Worcester, Worcestershire WR5 2JG
**Tel:** 01905-354000
**Web:** www.schousecare.co.uk
**Estd:** 1996 Proprietorship
**Line of Business:** Nursing homes
**Proprietor:** Ms S Heller
**Responsibilities**
**Senior:** Irene Herring (Branch Manager), Shirley Houghton (Home Manager)
**US SIC:** 8051 **UK SIC:** 95100
**Employees:** 80

### DUNS 73-645-0490
## Redholme Memory Care Ltd
11 Carnatic Road, Liverpool, Merseyside L18 8BY
**Tel:** 01517242016
**Reg No:** 4905065 **Estd:** 1988 Private Limited Company
**Line of Business:** Medical nursing home activities
**Issued Capital:** £1,000
**Directors:** Mrs A L Nicky, Mrs A C Hughes
**Co. Secretary:** Mrs Ann Mccann

**US SIC:** 8051 **UK SIC:** 95100

| | 31-12-13 | 31-12-12 | 31-12-11 |
|---|---|---|---|
| TA | 374,288 | 339,072 | 342,863 |
| NW | 116,362 | 21,727 | (38,579) |
| WC | (362) | (51,366) | (108,145) |

DUNS 21-530-7575

## Redhouse Nursing Home

11 Emlyns Street, Stamford, Lincolnshire PE9 1QP
**Estd:** 1989 Proprietorship
**Line of Business:** Clinics private
**Proprietor:** D Patel
**Responsibilities**
**Senior:** Dinesh Patel *(Proprietor)*
**US SIC:** 8051 **UK SIC:** 95100
**Employees:** 46

DUNS 73-446-0194

## Rediweld Holdings Ltd

5 High March, High March Industrial Estate, Daventry, Northamptonshire NN11 4QE
**Web:** www.rediweldtraffic.co.uk
**Reg No:** 4698687 **Estd:** 2003 Private Limited Company
**Line of Business:** Management activities of holding companies
**Export Sales:** £1,716,420
**Issued Capital:** £200,609
**Directors:** R D Mcdougall, D R How, R W Marsh
**Co. Secretary:** David Cartwright
**US SIC:** 6711 **UK SIC:** 83962
**Bankers:** Samuel Montagu & Company Ltd (40-05-50)

| | 31-12-13 | 31-12-12 | 31-12-11 |
|---|---|---|---|
| TO | 6,719,141 | 8,622,274 | 7,804,685 |
| P/L | 20,125 | 413,469 | 578,893 |
| NW | 3,267,769 | 3,299,621 | 3,095,264 |
| WC | 2,583,334 | 2,649,252 | 2,482,098 |
| Emp. | 86 | 85 | 85 |

DUNS 21-778-6863

## Redken

255 Hammersmith Road, London W6 8AZ
**Web:** www.loreal.com
**Estd:** 2000
**Line of Business:** Representative office
**Responsibilities**
**Senior:** P Tighe *(General Manager)*, Trevor Tighe *(General Manager)*
**US SIC:** 7399 **UK SIC:** 83954
**Employees:** 700

DUNS 28-828-8095

## The Redland High School for Girls

Redland Court Road, Bristol, Avon BS6 7EF
**Tel:** 01179245796
**Web:** www.redlandhigh.com
**Reg No:** 0038470 **Estd:** 1882 Private Limited Company
**Line of Business:** General secondary education
**Issued Capital:** £490
**Directors:** Ms S M Perry, Ms C Melvin, P J Breach, Dame E A Hoodless, M J Henry, Ms C Y Fleming, Ms P L Pyper, Dr J Shemilt
**Co. Secretary:** Benjamin Blackwood
**Responsibilities**
**Senior:** C Bateson *(Head Mistress)*
**US SIC:** 8211 **UK SIC:** 93200
**Auditors:** J & A W Sully & Co

| | 31-08-14 | 31-08-13 | 31-08-12 |
|---|---|---|---|
| TO | 4,560,119 | 4,163,728 | 3,917,019 |
| P/L | 18,194 | 32,933 | (81,773) |
| NW | 3,138,428 | 3,114,157 | 3,075,553 |
| WC | 100,506 | 95,449 | (27,850) |
| Emp. | 114 | 81 | 81 |

DUNS 21-158-5592

## Redmayne-Bentley Llp

9 Bond Court, Leeds, West Yorkshire LS1 2JZ
**Tel:** 01132436941 **Fax:** 01132-445516
**Web:** www.redmayne.co.uk
**Reg No:** 0344361OC **Estd:** 1875 Private Limited Company
**Line of Business:** Stockbrokers
**Responsibilities**
**Senior:** Mark Decker *(Non-designated Limited Liabili)*, Paul Lumley *(Branch Manager (York))*, Michelle Parkin *(Investment Manager)*, Georgina Summers *(Non-designated Limited Liabili)*
**US SIC:** 6211 **UK SIC:** 83100

| | 31-03-14 | 31-03-13 | 31-03-12 |
|---|---|---|---|
| TA | 84,143,467 | 70,386,401 | 69,274,024 |
| NW | 5,578,507 | 4,576,310 | 3,989,648 |
| WC | 8,591,000 | 7,079,000 | 6,682,000 |
| Emp. | 209 | 189 | 182 |

DUNS 21-689-0764 Exp

## Redmayne Engineering Ltd

**(Subsidiary of:** Redmayne Hgs Ltd)
Gordleton Industrial Estate, Hannah Way, Pennington, Lymington, Hampshire SO41 8JD
**Tel:** 01590682994
**Web:** www.redmayne-eng.co.uk
**Reg No:** 0745097 **VAT No:** 188294808
**Estd:** 1962 Private Limited Company
**Line of Business:** Precision engineers
**Export Markets:** Sweden
**Export Sales:** £413,474
**Trading Style:** Precision Engineers
**Issued Capital:** £213
**Principals:** G J Wickham *(Managing)*, S Batchelor, K Spurway, S R Finch
**Co. Secretary:** Ms Janice Wickham
**Responsibilities**
**Senior:** Peter Butt *(Manager)*
**Branches:** Redmayne Engineering Ltd, Unit 19, Greatbridge Road, Romsey, Hampshire SO51 0HR
**US SIC:** 8911 **UK SIC:** 83701
**Auditors:** Burnett Swayne
**Bankers:** HSBC Bank plc (40-42-18)

| | 31-01-14 | 31-01-13 | 31-01-12 |
|---|---|---|---|
| TO | 6,699,204 | 6,532,527 | 6,603,577 |
| P/L | 178,684 | 110,538 | 414,844 |
| NW | 2,924,080 | 2,813,992 | 2,682,856 |
| WC | 2,208,950 | 1,978,453 | 1,508,362 |
| Emp. | 86 | 85 | 81 |

DUNS 21-783-5777

## Redmill Nursing Homes

Lady Court, East Whitburn, Bathgate, West Lothian EH47 0PN
**Web:** www.hc-one.co.uk
**Estd:** 1995 Partnership
**Line of Business:** Nursing homes
**Partner:** Mrs E Hotchkiss
**US SIC:** 8051 **UK SIC:** 95100
**Employees:** 70

DUNS 22-902-9657

## Redpath Tyres Ltd

The Knowes, Kelso, Roxburghshire TD5 7BH
**Tel:** 01573-224929
**Web:** www.redpath-tyres.co.uk
**Reg No:** 0068083SC **VAT No:** 327404082
**Estd:** 1979 Private Limited Company
**Line of Business:** Tyre dealers
**Trading Style:** Newlife Tyres
**Issued Capital:** £10,000
**Directors:** N J Redpath, G Redpath
**Co. Secretary:** Ms Agnes Redpath
**Responsibilities**
**Senior:** Gary Burrows *(Manager)*
**Branches:** Redpath Tyres Ltd, Industrial Estate, Duns, Berwickshire TD11 3HS
**US SIC:** 5531 **UK SIC:** 65100
**Auditors:** Rennie Welch
**Bankers:** Bank Of Scotland (80-16-57)

| | 30-04-14 | 30-04-13 | 30-04-12 |
|---|---|---|---|
| TO | 10,428,528 | 9,895,123 | 9,382,436 |
| P/L | 326,610 | 293,352 | 567,417 |
| NW | 1,198,493 | 1,084,585 | 979,184 |
| WC | 884,800 | 781,875 | 771,532 |
| Emp. | 65 | 63 | 60 |

DUNS 23-940-0331

## Redr Uk

1 Great George Street, London SW1P 3AA
**Fax:** 02072333590
**Web:** www.redr.org.uk
**Reg No:** 3929653 **Estd:** 2000 Private Company Limited By Guarantee
**Line of Business:** Other service activities not elsewhere classified
**Trading Style:** Redr U K
**Directors:** Miss J Mills, P J Greeves, Miss S E Walters, A D Lamb, Ms J Smallman, G H French, Miss C P Lassen, I K Smout
**Co. Secretary:** Paul Orme
**Responsibilities**
**Senior:** Timothy Healing *(Director)*, Paul Sherlock *(Director)*
**US SIC:** 8999, 8299
**UK SIC:** 83954, 93300
**Auditors:** Sayer Vincent
**Bankers:** National Westminster Bank Plc (60-02-49)

| | 31-03-14 | 31-03-13 | 31-03-12 |
|---|---|---|---|
| TO | 5,485,677 | 5,034,335 | 4,252,945 |
| P/L | 223,752 | (89,468) | (83,634) |
| NW | 790,046 | 566,294 | 655,762 |
| WC | 763,788 | 529,672 | 605,791 |
| Emp. | 115 | 161 | 159 |

DUNS 21-773-9794

## Redridge Youth Offending Team

Station Road, Ilford, Essex IG6 1NB
**Tel:** 02087087800
**Estd:** 2011
**Line of Business:** Administration of the state and the economic and social policy of the community
**US SIC:** 9121 **UK SIC:** 91110
**Employees:** 50

DUNS 21-880-2923

## Redring Showers Uk

Newcombe House, Newcombe Way, Orton Southgate, Peterborough, Cambridgeshire PE2 6SE
**Tel:** 08443727761
**Web:** www.redring.co.uk
**Estd:** 2012
**Line of Business:** Manufacturers and suppliers of shower-baths
**Responsibilities**
**Senior:** Kevin Tolson *(Manager)*
**US SIC:** 3499 **UK SIC:** 31694
**Employees:** 220

DUNS 21-825-1718 Imp-Exp

## Redring Xpelair Group Ltd

**(Subsidiary of:** Glen Dimplex)
Morley Way, Peterborough, Cambridgeshire PE2 9JJ
**Tel:** 01733456789 **Fax:** 01733456727
**Web:** www.applied-energy.com
**Reg No:** 0306008 **VAT No:** 287131550
**Estd:** 1931 Private Limited Company
**Line of Business:** Manufacture of electric domestic appliances
**Export Markets:** E Europe, U S A, European Union (E U), Far East, Africa, Middle East
**Issued Capital:** £625,000
**Directors:** M Singh, N M Patel, M L Naughton, M Maher, S O'Driscoll
**Co. Secretary:** Michael Maher
**Responsibilities**
**Senior:** Darren Cannon *(Warehouse Manager)*
**US SIC:** 3639 **UK SIC:** 34600
**Auditors:** KPMG

| | 31-03-14 | 31-03-13 | 31-03-12 |
|---|---|---|---|
| TO | 29,894,000 | 32,625,000 | 31,659,000 |
| P/L | (202,000) | (865,000) | (666,000) |
| NW | 13,801,000 | 14,003,000 | 14,814,000 |
| WC | 10,201,000 | 9,764,000 | 9,953,000 |
| Emp. | 260 | 268 | 248 |

DUNS 34-608-8987

## Redrock Consulting Ltd

Pembroke House, 15 Pembroke Road, Clifton, Bristol, Avon BS8 3BA
**Tel:** 01173171300 **Fax:** 01179-707960
**Web:** www.redrockconsulting.co.uk
**Reg No:** 5415757 **Estd:** 2005 Private Limited Company
**Line of Business:** Employment and recruitment companies and consultants
**Issued Capital:** £10,085
**Directors:** P J Steer, D R Chapman, B M Curnock, G J Drever, B J Johnston
**Co. Secretary:** Dean Harte
**US SIC:** 7379, 7361
**UK SIC:** 83940, 83954

| | 31-12-13 | 31-12-12 | 31-12-11 |
|---|---|---|---|
| TO | 22,587,071 | 24,645,162 | 19,956,878 |
| P/L | 843,331 | 1,189,210 | 1,063,769 |
| NW | 2,024,777 | 1,592,849 | 1,008,434 |
| WC | 1,966,089 | 1,530,173 | 937,274 |
| Emp. | 49 | 46 | 37 |

DUNS 57-043-6865

## Redrow Plc

Redrow House, Deeside, Clwyd CH5 3RX
**Tel:** 01244520044 **Fax:** 01244-520580
**Web:** www.redrow.co.uk
**Reg No:** 2877315 **Estd:** 1993 Public Limited Company
**Line of Business:** Builders
**Issued Capital:** £36,979,994
**Principals:** S P Morgan *(Chairman)*, Sir M T Lyons, J F Tutte, Ms B M Richmond, A N Hewson, A D Hewitt, Mrs E A Peace, Mrs A D Hewitt
**Co. Secretary:** Graham Cope
**Responsibilities**
**Senior:** Nick Hewson *(Non-Executive Director and Cha)*, Matthew Pratt *(Regional Director, Midlands)*, Stuart Rowlands *(CEO / Managing Director)*
**Finance:** Nick Hewson *(Non-Executive Director and Cha)*
**Marketing:** Janine Lawton *(Sales & Marketing Administrato)*, Kim Peters *(Sales & Marketing Manager)*
**Sales:** Janine Lawton *(Sales & Marketing Administrato)*, Lesley Myers *(Area Sales Manager)*, Kim Peters *(Sales & Marketing Manager)*, Mary Timlin *(Sales Director)*, Tonia Tyler *(Area Sales Manager)*
**Admin:** Lynn Barnes *(Accounts Clerk)*, Sharon Warren *(Secretary)*
**Health & Safety:** David Bunyard *(Health and Safety Manager)*
**Engineering:** Paul Cromby *(Construction Manager)*, Peter Shergold *(Construction Director)*
**US SIC:** 1522, 1541
**UK SIC:** 50100
**Auditors:** PricewaterhouseCoopers LLP
**Bankers:** Barclays Bank Plc (20-18-15)

| | 30-06-14 | 30-06-13 | 30-06-12 |
|---|---|---|---|
| TO | 864,500,000 | 604,800,000 | 478,900,000 |
| P/L | 132,600,000 | 70,000,000 | 43,000,000 |
| NW | 693,700,000 | 607,300,000 | 559,700,000 |
| WC | 895,700,000 | 661,900,000 | 542,600,000 |
| Emp. | 1,245 | 1,061 | 967 |

DUNS 23-207-8717

## Redruth Royal British Legion Club Ltd

Penryn Street, Redruth, Cornwall TR15 2SP
**Tel:** 01209215743
**Reg No:** 0009383IP **Estd:** 2006 Friendly Society
**Line of Business:** Licensed clubs
**US SIC:** 5813 **UK SIC:** 66200
**Employees:** 100

DUNS 73-898-8166 Imp-Exp

## Redspeed International Ltd

Unit 21 26 Coppice Trading Estate, Kidderminster, Worcestershire DY11 7QY
**Tel:** 01562747137 **Fax:** 01562-747165
**Web:** www.redspeed-int.com
**Reg No:** 5152563 **VAT No:** 847118223
**Estd:** 2004 Private Limited Company
**Line of Business:** Technical testing and analysis
**Export Sales:** £5,983,546
**Issued Capital:** £426,667
**Director:** D Zaydman
**Co. Secretary:** Ms Kerri Mayson
**Responsibilities**
**Senior:** Robert Ryan *(Manager)*
**HR:** Helen Walford *(Human Resources Manager)*
**Health & Safety:** Helen Walford *(Human Resources Manager)*
**Facilities:** Simon Joyce *(Logistics Manager)*
**Purchasing:** Simon Joyce *(Logistics Manager)*
**Fleet:** Simon Joyce *(Logistics Manager)*
**US SIC:** 7397, 3629
**UK SIC:** 83702, 34350
**Auditors:** UHY Hacker Young

| | 31-12-13 | 31-12-12 | 31-12-11 |
|---|---|---|---|
| TO | 9,300,914 | 9,890,157 | 8,210,581 |
| P/L | 1,109,952 | 1,492,001 | 603,592 |
| NW | (1,991,423) | (2,377,377) | (3,136,395) |
| WC | (1,828,380) | (1,520,356) | (2,657,639) |
| Emp. | 81 | 80 | 80 |

DUNS 29-764-1276

## Redstone Converged Solutions Ltd

**(Subsidiary of:** Coms Plc)
160 Centennial Avenue, Centennial Park, Elstree, Borehamwood, Hertfordshire WD6 3SG
**Tel:** 08452-010-000 **Fax:** 01614-741-666
**Web:** www.redstone.co.uk
**Reg No:** 2027207 **Estd:** 1995 Private Limited Company
**Line of Business:** Hardware consultancy
**Export Sales:** £293,315
**Trading Style:** Redstone
**Issued Capital:** £900,000
**Directors:** B Loughrey, S Williams, D Breith, M Salter, Mrs S Alexander, P J Hallett
**Branches:** Redstone Converged Solutions Ltd, 40 Holborn Viaduct, London EC1N 2PB
**US SIC:** 7379, 7374
**UK SIC:** 83940
**Auditors:** PricewaterhouseCoopers LLP
**Bankers:** Barclays Bank Plc (20-00-50)

| | 31-03-13 | 31-03-12 | 31-03-11 |
|---|---|---|---|
| TO | 45,163,885 | 54,671,588 | 56,885,833 |
| P/L | 1,772,798 | 2,813,981 | (2,256,465) |
| NW | 14,923,052 | 13,007,413 | 9,162,472 |
| WC | 14,770,888 | 11,992,242 | 8,535,467 |
| Emp. | 314 | 364 | 448 |

DUNS 21-764-8537

## Redvers Centre

Redvers Road, Chatham, Kent ME4 5UU
**Tel:** 01634337333
**Estd:** 2011 Proprietorship
**Line of Business:** Non-charitable social work activities without accommodation
**Proprietor:** D Harper
**Responsibilities**
**Senior:** Daniel Harper *(Office Manager)*, Sandy Weaver *(Group Manager)*
**Admin:** Daniel Harper *(Office Manager)*
**US SIC:** 8321 **UK SIC:** 96111
**Employees:** 50

DUNS 28-853-0884

## Redwalls Care Services Ltd

Weaverham Road, Northwich, Cheshire CW8 2ND
**Tel:** 01606889339
**Web:** www.redwalls.net
**Reg No:** 0755609 **Estd:** 1986 Private Limited Company
**Line of Business:** Nursing homes
**Trading Style:** Redwall Nursing Home

**Issued Capital:** £500
**Director:** D R Walker
**Co. Secretary:** Ms Rhiannon Walker
**Responsibilities**
**Senior:** Carole Evans *(Manager)*
**US SIC:** 8051 **UK SIC:** 95100

| | 23-10-13 | 23-10-12 | 23-10-11 |
|---|---|---|---|
| TA | 2,320,448 | 2,387,421 | 2,307,743 |
| NW | 2,178,633 | 2,258,158 | 2,092,651 |
| WC | 480,225 | 548,939 | 371,873 |

DUNS 53-615-7480
## Redweb Ltd
Unit 35, Bournemouth, Dorset BH8 8EJ
**Tel:** 01202-779944
**Web:** www.redweb.com
**Reg No:** 3420895 **Estd:** 1997 Private Limited Company
**Line of Business:** Web site design and development
**Issued Capital:** £9,000
**Directors:** L A Platt, A H Henning
**Co. Secretary:** Andrew Henning
**Responsibilities**
**Senior:** Katie Street *(new business manager)*
**Marketing:** Dave Benham *(Client Services Director)*, Wayne Rowley *(Development Director)*
**Sales:** Sarah Groany *(Account Director)*, Katie Street *(new business manager)*
**IT:** Jeremy Blight *(Computer Manager)*
**HR:** Catherine Drennan *(Human Resources Manager)*
**Branches:** Redweb Ltd, 7 Rosebery Avenue, London EC1R 4SP
**US SIC:** 7379 **UK SIC:** 83940

| | 31-12-13 | 31-12-12 | 31-12-11 |
|---|---|---|---|
| TA | 1,876,151 | 1,846,419 | 1,594,373 |
| NW | 928,053 | 903,164 | 706,475 |
| WC | 669,921 | 666,934 | 442,468 |

DUNS 23-021-1075 Imp
## Redwings Horse Sanctuary
Hapton, Norwich, Norfolk NR15 1SP
**Tel:** 01508481000 **Fax:** 0870-458-1947
**Web:** www.redwings.co.uk
**Reg No:** 3524502 **Estd:** 1998 Private Company Limited By Guarantee
**Line of Business:** Animal welfare and care organisations
**Trading Style:** Redwings
**Directors:** Ms A G Polley, M R Little, P G Horrocks, S Clark, A E Fryer
**Co. Secretary:** Ms Lynn Cutress
**Responsibilities**
**Senior:** Lynn Cuttress *(Chief Executive)*
**Finance:** Gemma Carnell *(Fundraising Manager)*
**Marketing:** Gemma Carnell *(Fundraising Manager)*, Richard Ewles *(Marketing Manager)*, Nicola Markwell *(Press and Communications Manag)*
**Admin:** Charlotte Oliver *(Assistant to the CEO)*
**IT:** Richard Marden *(IT Manager)*
**Health & Safety:** Vikki Gordon *(Night Welfare and Security Man)*
**Facilities:** Lee Granville *(Maintenance Team Member)*
**Branches:** Redwings Horse Sanctuary, Hapton Hall, Norwich, Norfolk NR15 1SP
**US SIC:** 0214 **UK SIC:** 01001
**Auditors:** BDO Stoy Hayward
**Bankers:** National Westminster Bank Plc (60-15-31)

| | 31-12-13 | 31-12-12 | 31-12-11 |
|---|---|---|---|
| TO | 10,414,545 | 10,281,645 | 8,160,693 |
| P/L | 1,765,836 | 2,152,355 | 483,802 |
| NW | 29,134,050 | 27,251,955 | 25,065,949 |
| WC | 14,288,871 | 12,888,906 | 11,336,185 |
| Emp. | 257 | 243 | 223 |

DUNS 21-580-8676
## Redwood Birkhill Ltd
**(Subsidiary of:** Redwood Birkhill (Holdings) Ltd)
Suite B Dunsinane House, Kilspindie Road, Dunsinane Industrial Estate, Dundee, Angus DD2 3PW
**Tel:** 01382-815511
**Web:** www.redwoodleisure.co.uk
**Reg No:** 0061741SC **Estd:** 1977 Private Limited Company
**Line of Business:** Representative office
**Issued Capital:** £20,000
**Directors:** Ms M Whiting, G K Whiting
**Co. Secretary:** Burness Paull Llp
**Branches:** Redwood Birkhill Ltd, 96-98 Clepington Road, Dundee, Angus DD3 7SW
**US SIC:** 7399 **UK SIC:** 83954
**Auditors:** PricewaterhouseCoopers
**Bankers:** Bank Of Scotland (80-20-00)

| | 31-08-14 | 31-08-13 | 31-08-12 |
|---|---|---|---|
| TO | 3,427,000 | 6,433,000 | 6,392,000 |
| P/L | 405,000 | 733,000 | 617,000 |
| NW | 683,000 | 1,680,000 | 1,814,000 |
| WC | 324,000 | (6,483,000) | (6,457,000) |
| Emp. | 108 | 207 | 204 |

DUNS 64-093-2331
## Redwood Care Homes Ltd
11 Cherry Hill Road, Barnt Green, Birmingham, West Midlands B45 8LL
**Tel:** 01214477447
**Reg No:** 3488210 **Estd:** 1998 Private Limited Company
**Line of Business:** Non-charitable social work activities with accommodation
**Trading Style:** Abele View Residential Home
**Issued Capital:** £2,198
**Directors:** H D James, Mrs C S James
**Co. Secretary:** Miles Fidlin
**Responsibilities**
**Senior:** Glyndwr James *(Manager)*
**Branches:** Redwood Care Homes Ltd, Abele View, Roman Road, Stourbridge, West Midlands DY7 6PR
**US SIC:** 8321 **UK SIC:** 96111
**Auditors:** Haines Watts
**Bankers:** The Royal Bank Of Scotland Plc (16-00-06)

| | 30-06-14 | 30-06-13 | 30-06-12 |
|---|---|---|---|
| TO | 3,437,713 | 3,323,551 | 3,229,491 |
| P/L | 372,502 | 396,857 | 442,272 |
| NW | 1,766,345 | 1,619,553 | 1,581,128 |
| WC | 275,696 | 875,253 | 963,779 |
| Emp. | 151 | 125 | 127 |

DUNS 73-836-1039
## Redwood Health Care Ltd
Foresters Nursing Home, Walton Pool Lane, Clent, Stourbridge, West Midlands DY9 9RP
**Tel:** 01562883068
**Reg No:** 2933315 **Estd:** 1994 Private Limited Company
**Line of Business:** Other human health activities
**Issued Capital:** £50,000
**Principals:** H D James *(Managing)*, G F Rodgers, Mrs C S James, Ms J E Rodgers
**Co. Secretary:** Miles Fidlin
**Branches:** Redwood Health Care Ltd, 335A Stroud Road, Gloucester, Gloucestershire GL4 0BD
**US SIC:** 8091 **UK SIC:** 95200
**Auditors:** BKR Haines Watts
**Bankers:** Barclays Bank Plc (20-46-06)

| | 30-09-13 | 30-09-12 | 30-09-11 |
|---|---|---|---|
| TO | 6,805,494 | 6,860,681 | 6,681,106 |
| P/L | 1,578,585 | 538,313 | 403,427 |
| NW | 4,772,388 | 3,503,389 | 3,116,926 |
| WC | 1,235,206 | 36,103 | 43,189 |
| Emp. | 301 | 309 | 306 |

DUNS 50-133-3710
## Redwood Photographic Laboratories Ltd
Severalls Business Park, Colchester, Essex CO4 9XW
**Tel:** 01206-751241 **Fax:** 01206-855134
**Web:** www.redwoodphoto.com
**Reg No:** 2321439 **VAT No:** 341722087
**Estd:** 1988 Private Limited Company
**Line of Business:** Photographic processing
**Issued Capital:** £100,000
**Principals:** J A Williams *(Managing)*, Ms J K Chandler, Mrs A M Williams, J R Chandler
**Co. Secretary:** Mrs Julie Chandler
**Responsibilities**
**Senior:** Lynne Nolan *(Customer Care Director)*
**Admin:** Lesley Leach *(Administration Assistant)*
**HR:** Mark Winterbottom *(Health & Safety Officer)*
**Health & Safety:** Mark Winterbottom *(Health & Safety Officer)*
**Facilities:** Mark Winterbottom *(Health & Safety Officer)*
**Operations:** Mark Winterbottom *(Health & Safety Officer)*
**Branches:** Redwood Photographic Laboratories Ltd, 7 Brunel Ct, Brunel Way, Colchester, Essex CO4 9XP
**US SIC:** 7333 **UK SIC:** 83953
**Auditors:** Kneill & Co
**Bankers:** Barclays Bank Plc (20-22-67)

| | 31-12-13 | 31-12-12 | 31-12-11 |
|---|---|---|---|
| TA | 555,534 | 539,546 | 410,933 |
| NW | 260,125 | 305,495 | 245,453 |
| WC | 225,566 | 268,788 | 190,081 |

DUNS 42-344-3118 Imp-Exp
## Redwood Publishing Channel Islands Ltd
7 Street Martins Place, London WC2N 4HA
**Tel:** 02077-470700
**Web:** www.redwoodgroup.net
**Reg No:** 0018070FC **VAT No:** 629530139
**Estd:** 1994 Foreign Company
**Line of Business:** Publishing of newspapers
**Export Markets:** Europe; U S A
**Trading Style:** Redwood
**Directors:** C J Ward, K I Grainger, Ms J E Penney, Ms S J Cremer, R Park
**Co. Secretary:** Mrs Sally Bray
**Responsibilities**
**Senior:** Philip O'Connell *(Manager)*
**US SIC:** 2711 **UK SIC:** 47512
**Auditors:** KPMG Audit Plc
**Bankers:** HSBC Bank plc (40-02-50)

DUNS 57-830-7175 Imp
## Redwood Ttm Ltd
1 Paddock Road, West Pimbo, Skelmersdale, Lancashire WN8 9PL
**Tel:** 01695 553 830 **Fax:** 01695 455 601
**Web:** www.redwood-ttm.com
**Reg No:** 2879108 **VAT No:** 927301244
**Estd:** 1992 Private Limited Company
**Line of Business:** Manufacturers of textiles
**Export Sales:** £6,584,286
**Issued Capital:** £100,000
**Directors:** D Rose, Mrs M H Atherton, J A Atherton
**Co. Secretary:** Brian Atherton
**Responsibilities**
**Sales:** Zoe Flannery *(Sales Administrator)*
**Health & Safety:** Edward Ratsangham *(Group Technical Manager)*
**US SIC:** 2392 **UK SIC:** 45550
**Auditors:** Grant Thornton UK LLP
**Bankers:** Barclays Bank Plc (20-51-01)

| | 31-12-13 | 31-12-12 | 31-12-11 |
|---|---|---|---|
| TO | 26,868,093 | 27,652,955 | 25,838,567 |
| P/L | 1,696,859 | 1,808,803 | 1,724,242 |
| NW | 9,412,812 | 8,219,965 | 7,005,338 |
| WC | 6,574,139 | 5,595,125 | 4,696,816 |
| Emp. | 166 | 164 | 154 |

DUNS 21-487-4393
## Redwoods Nursing Home
Old Walled Garden, Teaninich, Alness, Ross-Shire IV17 0XB
**Tel:** 01349-884216
**Web:** www.meallmorelodge.co.uk
**Estd:** 1983 Partnership
**Line of Business:** Residential care establishments
**Partners:** J Hough, Mrs E Hough
**Responsibilities**
**Senior:** Gerald Hennessey *(Owner)*, Maragaret Rollo *(Home Manager)*, Margrette Rolough *(Manager)*
**US SIC:** 8321 **UK SIC:** 96111
**Employees:** 50

DUNS 21-580-0859
## Redworth House Nursing Home
Redworth House, Byerley Road, Shildon, County Durham DL4 1HQ
**Tel:** 01388777311
**Web:** www.bondcare.co.uk
**Estd:** 2003 Proprietorship
**Line of Business:** Nursing homes
**Proprietor:** Mrs L Small
**Responsibilities**
**Senior:** Joan Mcneil *(Home Manager)*
**US SIC:** 8051 **UK SIC:** 95100
**Employees:** 46

DUNS 50-345-1064
## Ree Distribution Ltd
**(Subsidiary of:** Canute Uk Ltd)
Crooklands Road, Ackenthwaite, Milnthorpe, Cumbria LA7 7LR
**Tel:** 01539-565477 **Fax:** 01539565466
**Web:** www.canute.com
**Reg No:** 2365268 **Estd:** 1983 Private Limited Company
**Line of Business:** Freight transport by road not elsewhere classified
**Issued Capital:** £50,000
**Directors:** S L Ely, N A Marshall, A P Marshall, Ms T Ablitt, G Marshall, Ms C Hurst, D Marshall, W Marshall
**US SIC:** 4213, 4226
**UK SIC:** 72300, 77003
**Auditors:** Horwath Clark Whitehill
**Bankers:** Barclays Bank Plc (20-45-28)
**Employees:** 104

DUNS 28-976-2775 Imp
## Reebok International Ltd
**(Subsidiary of:** Adidas Ag)
The Adidas Centre, Pepper Road, Stockport, Cheshire SK7 5SA
**Tel:** 08702-427300 **Fax:** 01524-580200
**Web:** www.reebok.co.uk
**Reg No:** 1757889 **VAT No:** 546415639
**Estd:** 1983 Private Limited Company
**Line of Business:** Retail sale of sports goods, games and toys, stamps and coins
**Issued Capital:** £2,862,563
**Directors:** M H O'Toole, M E O'Brien, Ms K Roseveare, Ms S Talbot, J T Warren
**Co. Secretary:** Melville Stephens
**Responsibilities**
**HR:** Michelle Armitage *(Operations Manager)*
**Branches:** Reebok International Ltd, Gretna Gateway Outlet Village, Unit 24, Gretna, Dumfriesshire DG16 5GG
**US SIC:** 5941, 7399
**UK SIC:** 65400, 83954
**Auditors:** KPMG Audit PLC
**Bankers:** Barclays Bank Plc (20-16-08)

| | 31-12-13 | 31-12-12 | 31-12-11 |
|---|---|---|---|
| TO | 130,970,000 | 120,390,000 | 125,233,000 |
| P/L | 8,124,000 | 26,430,000 | 48,471,000 |
| NW | 993,311,000 | 929,452,000 | 963,084,000 |
| WC | 442,582,000 | 415,557,000 | 417,805,000 |
| Emp. | 202 | 202 | 163 |

DUNS 21-726-5845
## Reece Group Ltd
Wincomblee Road Walker, Newcastle-Upon-Tyne, Tyne and Wear NE6 3QS
**Tel:** 01912348700
**Web:** www.reece-group.com
**Reg No:** 7630662 **Estd:** 2011 Private Limited Company
**Line of Business:** Management activities of holding companies
**Export Sales:** £46,952,000
**Issued Capital:** £100
**Directors:** Ms A D Reece, R D Anderton, P J Kite, J P Reece, R H Maudslay
**US SIC:** 6711 **UK SIC:** 83962
**Bankers:** Barclays Bank Plc (20-59-42)

| | 31-12-13 | 31-12-12 | 31-12-11 |
|---|---|---|---|
| TO | 82,861,000 | 92,536,000 | 211,695,000 |
| P/L | 8,910,000 | 31,393,000 | 61,532,000 |
| NW | 146,093,000 | 140,299,000 | 127,303,000 |
| WC | 128,953,000 | 135,896,000 | 121,647,000 |
| Emp. | 516 | 382 | 268 |

DUNS 34-777-0864
## Reed & Mackay Holdings Ltd
**(Subsidiary of:** Rtv Holdco Limited)
Nexus Place, 25 Farringdon Street, London EC4A 4AF
**Tel:** 02072463333
**Web:** www.reedmac.com
**Reg No:** 5577881 **Estd:** 2005 Private Limited Company
**Line of Business:** Travel agency activities
**Issued Capital:** £243,719
**Directors:** F A Stratford, A Hibbert, Ms A T Baumfield, M Everson
**Co. Secretary:** Frederick Stratford
**Responsibilities**
**Senior:** Richard Boardman *(Manager)*
**Marketing:** Lyndsey Atkins *(Marketing Manager)*
**Sales:** Tracey Baumfield *(Sales Director)*, Matthew Forbes *(Business Development Manager)*
**HR:** Victoria O'Rourke *(Head of HR)*
**US SIC:** 4722 **UK SIC:** 77001
**Auditors:** BDO LLP

| | 31-03-14 | 31-03-13 | 31-03-12 |
|---|---|---|---|
| TO | 25,845,000 | 23,521,000 | 21,548,000 |
| P/L | 6,900,000 | 5,481,000 | 4,359,000 |
| NW | 12,194,000 | 5,883,000 | 713,000 |
| WC | 19,534,000 | 12,975,000 | 7,669,000 |
| Emp. | 334 | 324 | 296 |

DUNS 21-315-4693
## Reed Boardall Cold Storage Ltd
**(Subsidiary of:** The Reed Boardall Group Ltd)
Bar Lane, Boroughbridge, York, North Yorkshire YO51 9NN
**Tel:** 01423-324537 **Fax:** 01423-324875
**Web:** www.reedboardall.co.uk
**Reg No:** 0995076 **Estd:** 1970 Private Limited Company
**Line of Business:** Cold storage
**Issued Capital:** £14,752
**Directors:** T W Cassells, J H Gill, K Boardall, A L Baldwin
**Co. Secretary:** Marcus Boardall
**Responsibilities**
**Senior:** Guy Reed *(Chairman of the Board and Dire)*
**Facilities:** Graham Fletcher *(Maintenance Manager)*
**Branches:** Reed Boardall Cold Storage Ltd, Darlington Road, Northallerton, North Yorkshire DL6 2XB
**US SIC:** 4226 **UK SIC:** 77003
**Auditors:** Grant Thornton
**Bankers:** HSBC Bank plc (40-23-12)

| | 31-03-14 | 31-03-13 | 31-03-12 |
|---|---|---|---|
| TO | 42,065,264 | 37,766,640 | 37,379,072 |
| P/L | 2,332,983 | 2,926,295 | 5,130,287 |
| NW | 31,741,617 | 30,533,786 | 29,056,716 |
| WC | 641,687 | 709,712 | 8,996,600 |
| Emp. | 317 | 294 | 273 |

DUNS 21-109-2724
## The Reed Boardall Group Ltd
The Reed Boardall Group, York, North Yorkshire YO51 9NN
**Tel:** 01423321300 **Fax:** 01423321314
**Web:** www.reedboardall.co.uk
**Reg No:** 6509923 **Estd:** 2008 Private Limited Company

Line of Business: Management activities of other non-financial holding companies not elsewhere classified
Issued Capital: £130,740
Director: K Boardall
Co. Secretary: Marcus Boardall
Responsibilities
Senior: Guy Reed (Manager)
Finance: Jaqueline Ray (Senior Financial Executive)
IT: Jon Wormald (IT Systems Analyst)
US SIC: 6711 UK SIC: 83962

|  | 31-03-14 | 31-03-13 | 31-03-12 |
| --- | --- | --- | --- |
| TO | 64,081,768 | 58,295,641 | 55,142,491 |
| P/L | 2,531,681 | 3,523,073 | 5,451,115 |
| NW | 50,768,154 | 49,034,197 | 46,876,894 |
| WC | 3,402,855 | 3,848,581 | 11,539,700 |
| Emp. | 726 | 671 | 621 |

**DUNS 29-530-2236**
### Reed Boardall Transport Ltd
(Subsidiary of: The Reed Boardall Group Ltd)
Bar Lane, Boroughbridge, York, North Yorkshire YO51 9NN
Tel: 01423321301 Fax: 01423322637
Web: www.reedboardall.co.uk
Reg No: 1897313 Estd: 1956 Private Limited Company
Line of Business: Activities of other transport agencies
Issued Capital: £100
Principals: T W Cassells (Managing), K Boardall, A L Baldwin, J H Gill
Co. Secretary: Marcus Boardall
Responsibilities
Senior: Leslie Kirby (Manager), Guy Reed (Manager)
US SIC: 4712, 4213
UK SIC: 77002, 72300
Auditors: Grant Thornton
Bankers: HSBC Bank plc (40-12-28)

|  | 31-03-14 | 31-03-13 | 31-03-12 |
| --- | --- | --- | --- |
| TO | 42,815,917 | 38,788,602 | 35,889,538 |
| P/L | 660,218 | 1,057,276 | 792,039 |
| NW | 4,799,155 | 4,306,401 | 3,512,479 |
| WC | 3,535,489 | 4,078,730 | 3,524,885 |
| Emp. | 394 | 364 | 335 |

**DUNS 21-052-3254**   Imp
### Reed Business Information Ltd
(Subsidiary of: Reed Elsevier (Uk) Ltd)
Quadrant House, The Quadrant, Sutton, Surrey SM2 5AS
Fax: 02086-524-043
Web: www.reedbusiness.com
Reg No: 0151537 VAT No: 235723565
Estd: 1918 Private Limited Company
Line of Business: Newspapers publishing
Export Sales: £121,860,000
Trading Style: Icis / Utility Week Week, New Scientist / Bankersaccuity, Railway Gazette International, Hairdressers Journal International
Issued Capital: £57,614,093
Directors: G M Roy, M V Kelsey, D J Feltham, J A O'Sullivan
Co. Secretary: Ian Glencross
Responsibilities
Senior: Jayne Lewis Orr (Publishing Director for HJ Mag), William Muttram (Manager)
Finance: Alison Stanworth (Group Chief Accountant)
Marketing: Julia Cahill (Deputy Editor - Book Reviewer), Jayne Lewis Orr (Publishing Director for HJ Mag), Laurence Mitchel (Marketing Director), Noel O'Reilly (Editor - Employers Law Magazin)
Sales: Sean Behan (Business Development Manager)
IT: Neil Argent (Director of Security & Complia)
HR: Nathan Carhill (Global Human Resources Manager)
Branches: Reed Business Information Ltd, National Agricultural Centre, Kenilworth, Warwickshire CV8 2LZ
US SIC: 2731, 7399
UK SIC: 47532, 83954
Auditors: Deloitte LLP
Bankers: National Westminster Bank Plc (60-00-01)

|  | 31-12-13 | 31-12-12 | 31-12-11 |
| --- | --- | --- | --- |
| TO | 232,983,000 | 222,605,000 | 202,966,000 |
| P/L | 73,769,000 | 119,294,000 | 24,800,000 |
| NW | 498,429,000 | 414,429,000 | 290,561,000 |
| WC | 468,359,000 | 385,264,000 | 233,579,000 |
| Emp. | 1,437 | 1,608 | 1,664 |

**DUNS 49-129-8782**
### Reed Educational & Professional Publishing Ltd
(Subsidiary of: Reed Elsevier (Uk) Ltd)
Jordan Hill Business Park, Banbury Road, Oxford, Oxfordshire OX2 8EJ
Tel: 01865-311366
Web: www.pearsoneducation.com
Reg No: 3104090 Estd: 1995 Private Limited Company
Line of Business: Book retailers

Trading Style: Harcourt Education
Issued Capital: £2
Directors: Re Directors No 2 Limited, Re Directors (No 1) Limited, A W Mcculloch, H A Udow
Co. Secretary: Re Secretaries Limited
Branches: Reed Educational & Professional Publishing Ltd, Halley Court Jordan Hill Business Park, Banbury Road, Oxford, Oxfordshire OX2 8TA
US SIC: 5942 UK SIC: 65300

|  | 31-12-13 | 31-12-12 | 31-12-11 |
| --- | --- | --- | --- |
| TA | 2 | 2 | 2 |
| NW | 2 | 2 | 2 |

**DUNS 21-024-4596**
### Reed Elsevier Plc
Grand Buildings 1 3, Strand, London WC2N 5JR
Tel: 020-7930-7077 Fax: 02071665799
Web: www.reedelsevier.com
Reg No: 0077536 Estd: 1903 Public Limited Company
Line of Business: Publishing of books
Export Sales: £5,050,000,000
Issued Capital: £181,301,555
Directors: N L Luff, W G Hauser, B Van Der Veer, Ms L A Hook, A Hennah, Ms L S Sanford, A J Habgood, R B Polet
Co. Secretary: Henry Udow
Responsibilities
Senior: Adrian Henneah (Non-Executive Director)
Branches: Reed Elsevier Plc, Windsor Court, Wood Street, East Grinstead, West Sussex RH19 1UZ
US SIC: 2731, 2721, 2741, 7372
UK SIC: 47532, 47522, 47541, 83940
Auditors: Deloitte LLP
Bankers: Lloyds TSB Bank plc (30-92-32)
Following financial data are in thousands

|  | 31-12-13 | 31-12-12 | 31-12-11 |
| --- | --- | --- | --- |
| TO | 6,035,000 | 6,116,000 | 6,002,000 |
| P/L | 1,196,000 | 1,187,000 | 948,000 |
| NW | (5,310,000) | (5,540,000) | (6,051,000) |
| WC | (2,017,000) | (1,384,000) | (1,832,000) |
| Emp. | 28,200 | N/A | 30,600 |

**DUNS 21-033-2383**   Exp
### Reed Exhibitions Ltd
(Subsidiary of: Reed Elsevier (Uk) Ltd)
Gateway House, Richmond, Surrey TW9 1DN
Tel: 02089107910 Fax: 02089107823
Web: www.reedexpo.com
Reg No: 0678540 VAT No: 232400420
Estd: 1960 Private Limited Company
Line of Business: Exhibition and trade fair organisers
Export Sales: £55,455,036
Issued Capital: £531,260
Directors: M J Rusbridge, A D Bowden, R J Mortimore, L Algoud, A T Fowles, Ms C L Cunningham, R C Rees
Co. Secretary: Ms Jacqueline Poole
Responsibilities
Senior: Chet Burchett (Regional President The America), Peter Forster (Manager), Lucy Gillam (Event Director), Justin Tadman (Manager), Sam Willoughby (Events Director)
Marketing: Alison Berends (Global Marketing & Communicati), Lucy Gillam (Event Director), Rebecca Hearn (Marketing Manager), Jonathan Heastie (Exhibition Director), Kate MacBeth (Global Marketing and Communica), Katie Morris (Marketing Manager), Orna O' Brien (Conference Manager), Sam Willoughby (Events Director)
Sales: Matt Colgan (Group Sales Manager), Kirsten Conlon (Key Account Manager), Adam Ford (Group Commercial Director), Nick Forster (Group Commercial Director), Dan Londero (Chief Sales Officer - Global H), Charlie Pace (Sales manager), Dijana Pejovic (International Sales Manager)
IT: Judith Patten (Project Director), Alexa Taylor (Salesforce Application Support)
Operations: Jennifer Booth (Group Operations Manager), Jessamy Marsden (Operations Manager)
Branches: Reed Exhibitions Ltd, Radcliffe House, Blenheim Court, Solihull, West Midlands B91 2BG
US SIC: 7999 UK SIC: 97913
Auditors: Deloitte LLP
Bankers: Nationwide Building Society (07-00-94)

|  | 31-12-13 | 31-12-12 | 31-12-11 |
| --- | --- | --- | --- |
| TO | 87,445,132 | 81,271,328 | 73,907,086 |
| P/L | 8,594,934 | 2,115,494 | 7,168,121 |
| NW | 29,609,847 | 19,323,527 | 21,162,383 |
| WC | (20,779,415) | (29,740,823) | (31,507,238) |
| Emp. | 385 | 342 | 349 |

**DUNS 29-859-3922**
### Reed Health Group No.1 Ltd
(Subsidiary of: Reed Global Limited)
Clocktower House, 287-289 Cranbrook Road, Ilford, Essex IG1 4UA
Tel: 020-8252-5000 Fax: 02082525001
Web: www.reedhealth.com
Reg No: 2062711 Estd: 1986 Private Limited Company
Line of Business: Labour recruitment and provision of personnel
Issued Capital: £100
Director: J A Reed
Co. Secretary: Ms Joan Edmunds
Branches: Reed Health Group NO.1 Ltd, The Charters, 102 New Street, Birmingham, West Midlands B2 4HQ
US SIC: 7361 UK SIC: 83954
Auditors: RSM Robson Rhodes
Bankers: HSBC Bank plc (40-06-30)

|  | 30-06-14 | 30-06-13 | 30-06-12 |
| --- | --- | --- | --- |
| TA | 100 | 100 | 100 |
| NW | 100 | 100 | 100 |

**DUNS 23-957-4713**
### Reed Learning Ltd
(Subsidiary of: Reed Global Limited)
9 Kingsway, London WC2B 6XF
Tel: 08001707777 Fax: 02073847221
Web: www.reedlearning.com
Reg No: 3946675 VAT No: 832778108
Estd: 2000 Private Limited Company
Line of Business: Activities of private training providers
Trading Style: Reed Training
Issued Capital: £66,047
Directors: J M Trangard, J A Reed, N C Bradley
Co. Secretary: Ms Joan Edmunds
Responsibilities
Senior: Jon Buttriss (Manager), Hugh Greenway (Manager)
Finance: Wayne Giddens (Financial Director)
Marketing: Louise Ogle (Marketing Manager)
HR: Emily Courtney (Human Resources Manager), Hugh Greenway (Manager)
Health & Safety: Emily Courtney (Human Resources Manager)
Branches: Reed Learning Ltd, Beam St, Nantwich, Cheshire CW5 5LJ
US SIC: 8299 UK SIC: 93300
Auditors: KPMG LLP
Bankers: Barclays Bank Plc (20-72-17)

|  | 30-06-13 | 30-06-12 | 30-06-11 |
| --- | --- | --- | --- |
| TO | 33,848,000 | 13,179,000 | 17,520,000 |
| P/L | 702,000 | (730,000) | 237,000 |
| NW | 3,353,000 | 2,808,000 | 3,362,000 |
| WC | 2,893,000 | 2,478,000 | 3,165,000 |
| Emp. | 55 | 79 | 91 |

**DUNS 23-928-6284**
### Reed Managed Services Ltd
(Subsidiary of: Reed Global Limited)
Blenheim Court, 19 George Street, Banbury, Oxfordshire OX16 5DP
Tel: 01295228060
Web: www.reed.co.uk
Reg No: 3918568 Estd: 2000 Private Limited Company
Line of Business: Employment and recruitment companies and consultants
Issued Capital: £66,047
Director: J A Reed
Co. Secretary: Ms Joan Edmunds
Branches: Reed Managed Services Ltd, 68 Lewisham High Street, London SE13 5JH
US SIC: 7361 UK SIC: 83954
Auditors: Deloitte LLP
Bankers: Barclays Bank Plc (20-29-90)

|  | 30-06-13 | 30-06-12 | 30-06-11 |
| --- | --- | --- | --- |
| TA | 3,979,000 | 4,023,000 | 4,156,000 |
| P/L | N/A | N/A | (120,000) |
| NW | 3,828,000 | 3,838,000 | 3,842,000 |
| WC | 3,828,000 | 3,838,000 | 4,147,000 |

**DUNS 28-865-6960**
### Reed Personnel Ltd
(Subsidiary of: Reed Global Limited)
69a Broadway, Bexleyheath, Kent DA6 7JN
Tel: 02083036398
Reg No: 0965669 Estd: 1969 Private Limited Company
Line of Business: Labour recruitment and provision of personnel
Issued Capital: £100
Director: J A Reed
Co. Secretary: Ms Joan Edmunds
US SIC: 7361 UK SIC: 83954
Auditors: RSM Robson Rhodes

|  | 30-06-14 | 30-06-13 | 30-06-12 |
| --- | --- | --- | --- |
| TA | 82,430 | 82,430 | 82,430 |
| NW | 82,430 | 82,430 | 82,430 |

**DUNS 29-502-2040**
### Reed Smith Corporate Services Ltd
(Subsidiary of: Reed Smith Llp)
Broadgate Tower, London EC2A 2RS
Tel: 020-7403-2900
Web: www.reedsmith.com
Reg No: 1865431 Estd: 1984 Private Limited Company
Line of Business: Business and management consultancy activities not elsewhere classified
Issued Capital: £4
Directors: D J Boutcher, J F Wilkinson, E S Miller, R R Montague-Jones, D J Rofe
Co. Secretary: Ms April Kenny
US SIC: 7392 UK SIC: 83951

|  | 31-12-13 | 31-12-12 | 31-12-11 |
| --- | --- | --- | --- |
| TA | 4 | 4 | 4 |
| NW | 4 | 4 | 4 |

**DUNS 73-349-8815**   Imp
### Reed Smith Llp
The Broadgate Tower, 20 Primrose Street, London EC2A 2RS
Tel: 020-3116-3000
Web: www.reedsmith.com
Reg No: 0303620OC Estd: 1920
Line of Business: Solicitors
Responsibilities
Senior: Marie Albertini (Non-designated Limited Liabili), Peter Alfandary (Partner), Alexander Andrews (Non-designated Limited Liabili), Ana Atallah (Non-designated Limited Liabili), Patrick Beale (Non-designated Limited Liabili), Giles Beale (Partner), Charles Bezzant (Partner), Gautam Bhattacharyya (Non-designated Limited Liabili), Richard Ceeney (Partner), Mark Connoley (Partner), Colleen Davies (Designated Limited Liability P), Mark Douglas (Partner), Jeff Drew (Partner), Kyriacos Evagora (Designated Limited Liability P), Robert Falkner (Partner), Sian Fellows (Partner), Lynne Freeman (Partner), Dale Gabbert (Partner), Graham Green (Partner), Richard Gunn (Partner), Jacqui Hatfield (Partner), Charles Hewetson (Partner), Marjorie Holmes (Partner), Thomas Ince (Partner), Robin Jeffcott (Partner), Andrew Jenkinson (Partner), Emma Lenthall (Partner), Nicola Maguire (Partner), Michael Maxtone-Smith (Partner), Harriet Morgan (Partner), Belinda Paisley (Designated Limited Liability P), Robert Parson (Partner), Scott Pearman (Partner), Carolyn Pepper (Partner), Richard Philipps (Partner), Gregor Pryor (Partner), Lawrence Radley (Partner), Laurence Rees (Partner), Karen Saxton (Manager), Nick Shaw (Partner), Richard Spafford (Partner), Nick Speed (Partner), Leon Stephenson (Partner), Richard Swinburne (Managing Partner), Peter Teare (Partner), Jimmy Theodorou (Partner), Charles Weller (Owner)
Finance: Nola Beirne (Vice Chair of the Financial In), David Duckhouse (Finance Director)
Admin: Fiona Bower (?Secretary), Nikki Douglas (Legal Secretary)
IT: Bavesh Amin (Systems & IT Manager), Tim Hyman (IT Director), Valarie O'Connell (IT Operations Manager)
Operations: Phil Page (Director Operations)
US SIC: 8111 UK SIC: 83500
Auditors: PricewaterhouseCoopers LLP
Bankers: Coutts & Co (18-00-09)

|  | 31-12-13 | 31-12-12 | 31-12-11 |
| --- | --- | --- | --- |
| TO | 145,195,131 | 135,833,682 | 115,457,251 |
| P/L | 58,484,750 | 55,815,900 | 38,748,968 |
| NW | 58,715,748 | 54,970,126 | 38,048,796 |
| WC | 74,676,522 | 74,017,802 | 56,218,262 |
| Emp. | 566 | 528 | 505 |

**DUNS 21-164-2883**
### Reed Specialist Recruitment Ltd
(Subsidiary of: Reed Global Limited)
Academy Court, 94 Chancery Lane, Strand, London WC2A 1DT
Tel: 020-7421-1640
Web: www.reed.co.uk
Reg No: 6903140 Estd: 2011 Private Limited Company
Line of Business: Employment and recruitment companies and consultants
Issued Capital: £2
Directors: N Marsh, R Post, I A Nicholas
Co. Secretary: Ms Joan Edmunds
Branches: Reed Specialist Recruitment Ltd, Unit 1 Time Square, Warrington, Cheshire WA1 2AR
US SIC: 7361 UK SIC: 83954
Auditors: KPMG LLP
Bankers: Barclays Bank Plc (20-72-17)

|  | 30-06-13 | 30-06-12 | 30-06-11 |
| --- | --- | --- | --- |
| TO | 833,318,000 | 785,377,000 | 761,397,000 |
| P/L | 1,450,000 | (2,380,000) | 758,000 |
| NW | 6,614,000 | (5,361,000) | (3,109,000) |
| WC | 14,985,000 | (9,338,000) | (6,162,000) |
| Emp. | 1,992 | 2,057 | 2,142 |

## DUNS 21-590-4171
### Reed Specialist Recrutiment
112-120 Coombe Lane, London SW20 0BA
**Tel:** 02082885065
**Web:** www.reed.co.uk
**Estd:** 2011
**Line of Business:** Representative office
**Responsibilities**
**Senior:** Anne Christie (Manager)
**US SIC:** 7361 **UK SIC:** 83954
**Employees:** 150

## DUNS 21-428-7592
### Reed Specialist Recruitment
Charles House 61-69, Derngate,
Northampton, Northamptonshire NN1 1UE
**Tel:** 01604885620
**Estd:** 2011
**Line of Business:** Employment and
recruitment companies and consultants
**Responsibilities**
**Senior:** Colette Burgess (Office Manager)
**US SIC:** 7361 **UK SIC:** 83954
**Employees:** 100

## DUNS 50-551-4927
### Reed's School Enterprises Ltd
Sandy Lane, Cobham, Surrey KT11 2ES
**Tel:** 01932869044 **Fax:** 01932869046
**Web:** www.reeds.surrey.sch.uk
**Reg No:** 2503013 **Estd:** 1990 Private
Limited Company
**Line of Business:** Schools (local authority)
**Issued Capital:** £850,459
**Directors:** M W Hoskins, A R Balls,
N D Taunt, Mrs L K Hurford,
Ms B O'Brien-Twohig, P R Kemp, R Stewart
**Co. Secretary:** Mrs Emma Stanger
**Responsibilities**
**Senior:** Ian Clapp (Director of Sport &
Activities)
**Marketing:** Richard Garrett (Development
Director)
**IT:** Dan Rayner (IT Manager)
**HR:** Sharmaine Matthews (Alumni Manager)
**US SIC:** 5941, 7999, 7941
**UK SIC:** 65400, 97913, 97911
**Auditors:** Schaverien & Co
**Bankers:** The Royal Bank Of Scotland Plc
(15-10-00)

| | 31-08-13 | 31-08-12 | 31-08-11 |
|---|---|---|---|
| TO | 152,375 | 182,219 | 172,812 |
| P/L | (27,020) | (18,205) | (16,861) |
| NW | 495,032 | 522,052 | 539,943 |
| WC | (56,626) | (46,668) | (60,831) |

## DUNS 21-746-6592
### Reef Subsea Uk Ltd
(**Subsidiary of:** Reef Subsea As)
Gac House Sabatier Close, Thornaby,
Stockton-On-Tees, Cleveland TS17 6EW
**Tel:** 01642704400
**Web:** www.reefsubsea.com
**Reg No:** 7783740 **Estd:** 2011 Private
Limited Company
**Line of Business:** Other building installation
**Issued Capital:** £2,000,100
**Directors:** D Macpherson, I R Coyard,
D J Lynch
**US SIC:** 1796 **UK SIC:** 50400
**Auditors:** Ernst & Young LLP

| | 31-12-13 | 31-12-12 |
|---|---|---|
| TO | 27,683,509 | 24,210,542 |
| P/L | (15,943,014) | (2,946,725) |
| NW | (16,221,401) | (236,839) |
| WC | (6,587,240) | (4,990,378) |
| Emp. | 52 | 20 |

## DUNS 23-563-3844
### Reel Cinemas Ltd
(**Subsidiary of:** Reel Cinemas (Europe) Ltd)
3r Construction & Property Development,
Ltd, Loughborough, Leicestershire LE11 3DL
**Web:** www.reelcinemas.co.uk
**Reg No:** 3561597 **Estd:** 1999 Private
Limited Company
**Line of Business:** Cinemas
**Issued Capital:** £3,000,000
**Directors:** S Suri, Mrs S Suri, N Suri, R Suri
**Co. Secretary:** Kailash Suri
**Responsibilities**
**Senior:** Liz Oxlade (Group Accountant)
**Finance:** Liz Oxlade (Group Accountant)
**US SIC:** 7832 **UK SIC:** 97113
**Auditors:** Clear & Lane
**Bankers:** Svenska Handelsbanken Ab (publ)
(40-53-59)

| | 31-12-13 | 31-12-12 | 30-12-12 |
|---|---|---|---|
| TO | 9,200,988 | 3,334,957 | 5,515,711 |
| P/L | (4,044) | 202,757 | 33,908 |
| NW | 3,110,803 | 2,890,927 | (287,844) |
| WC | (1,273,573) | 2,255,879 | (2,740,170) |
| Emp. | 223 | 143 | 144 |

## DUNS 77-761-7960
### Reel Ltd
(**Subsidiary of:** Geg (Holdings) Ltd)
Unit 2 Wellheads Cresent, Aberdeen,
Aberdeenshire AB21 7GA
**Tel:** 01224799000
**Web:** www.reelgroup.com
**Reg No:** 0155901SC **Estd:** 1995 Private
Limited Company
**Line of Business:** Technical testing and
analysis
**Export Sales:** £6,988,520
**Issued Capital:** £1,000
**Directors:** R J Macgregor, J D Macdonald
**Co. Secretary:** James Macdonald
**Responsibilities**
**Senior:** Alexander Mair (Manager), Russell
Ritchie (Manager)
**US SIC:** 7397, 7399
**UK SIC:** 83702, 83954
**Auditors:** Ernst & Young LLP
**Bankers:** Bank Of Scotland (80-05-11)

| | 31-03-14 | 31-03-13 | 31-03-12 |
|---|---|---|---|
| TO | 30,492,087 | 24,074,052 | 17,352,354 |
| P/L | 1,615,672 | 1,737,119 | 562,450 |
| NW | 6,245,591 | 5,043,738 | 3,789,456 |
| WC | 5,115,879 | 3,745,901 | 2,526,779 |
| Emp. | 128 | 102 | 86 |

## DUNS 22-916-1575      Imp-Exp
### Reel Service Ltd
(**Subsidiary of:** Asti Holdings Limited)
55 Nasmyth Road, Glenrothes, Fife KY6 2SD
**Tel:** 01592-773208 **Fax:** 01592-774696
**Web:** www.reelservice.com
**Reg No:** 0101979SC **VAT No:** 435716936
**Estd:** 1986 Private Limited Company
**Line of Business:** Manufacture of other
electrical equipment not elsewhere classified
**Export Markets:** E U, U S A, Far East &
Middle East
**Export Sales:** £1,034,423
**Issued Capital:** £29,412
**Principals:** J C Simpson (Managing),
K H Chee, T Lim Boon Liat
**Co. Secretary:** Rollos Law Llp
**Responsibilities**
**Senior:** Woo Kiong (Manager), Charles
Siang (Manager)
**IT:** Graham Birrell (Computer Manager)
**HR:** Vivienne Bern (Personnel Manager)
**Health & Safety:** Vivienne Bern (Personnel
Manager)
**Operations:** Vivienne Bern (Personnel
Manager), Janice Reekie (Technical,
Production Manager)
**Purchasing:** Shirley Kinnear (Purchasing
Manager)
**Engineering:** Carol Grant (Technical
Manager), Adam Reel (Engineering
Manager), Adam Rigby (Engineering
Manager)
**US SIC:** 3629 **UK SIC:** 34350
**Auditors:** Ernst & Young LLP
**Bankers:** Bank Of Scotland (80-08-09)

| | 31-12-13 | 31-12-12 | 31-12-11 |
|---|---|---|---|
| TO | 2,401,358 | 2,213,892 | 2,764,094 |
| P/L | 344,848 | 52,345 | 487,202 |
| NW | 1,254,679 | 988,907 | 961,964 |
| WC | 692,940 | 367,029 | 377,799 |
| Emp. | 54 | 55 | 55 |

## DUNS 77-932-2791
### Rees Bradley Hepburn Ltd
(**Subsidiary of:** Rbh Holdings Ltd)
Diddington Farm, Diddington Lane, Meriden,
Coventry, West Midlands CV7 7HQ
**Tel:** 01675-443939
**Web:** www.rbh.co.uk
**Reg No:** 3044820 **Estd:** 1995 Private
Limited Company
**Line of Business:** Advertising agency
services
**Trading Style:** Rees.Bradley.Hepburn
Limited
**Issued Capital:** £18,400
**Directors:** Ms D J Hepburn, T P Rees
**Co. Secretary:** James Hodges
**Responsibilities**
**Senior:** Rob Drewry (Managing Partner)
**Finance:** Chris Ramstedt (Financial Director)
**Marketing:** Angel Gibbons (Commercial
Director)
**US SIC:** 7319, 7399
**UK SIC:** 83800, 83954
**Auditors:** Baker Tilly UK Audit LLP
**Bankers:** Lloyds TSB Bank plc (30-99-06)

| | 31-12-13 | 31-12-12 | 31-12-11 |
|---|---|---|---|
| TO | N/A | 2,752,218 | 2,858,580 |
| P/L | N/A | 97,354 | 47,468 |
| NW | 446,801 | 427,808 | 359,844 |
| WC | 361,395 | 501,613 | 266,524 |
| Emp. | N/A | 44 | 41 |

## DUNS 21-107-3019
### Rees Leisure Ltd
18 The Central Precinct, Chandler's Ford,
Eastleigh, Hampshire SO53 2GB
**Tel:** 02380273657
**Reg No:** 6494697 **Estd:** 2008 Private
Limited Company
**Line of Business:** Management activities of
other non-financial holding companies not
elsewhere classified
**Issued Capital:** £10
**Director:** C D Rees
**Co. Secretary:** Ms Denise Sayers
**US SIC:** 6711 **UK SIC:** 83962

| | 31-03-14 | 28-02-13 | 29-03-12 |
|---|---|---|---|
| TA | 23,011 | 10 | 10 |
| NW | 6,848 | 10 | 10 |
| WC | 6,745 | N/A | N/A |

## DUNS 64-251-7304
### Rees Page
8-12 Waterloo Road, Wolverhampton, West
Midlands WV1 4BL
**Tel:** 01902577799
**Web:** www.valuemine.co.uk
**Estd:** 1960 Partnership
**Line of Business:** Solicitors
**Partners:** S Woodward, W Williams
**Responsibilities**
**Senior:** Andrew Lund (Senior Partner)
**Finance:** Andrew Lund (Senior Partner)
**Sales:** Peter Sills (Sales Manager), Adam
Whitehouse (Sales Manager)
**IT:** Anthony Hood (Computer Manager)
**Facilities:** Ian MacPherson (Senior Partner)
**Branches:** Rees Page, 8-12 Waterloo Road,
Wolverhampton, West Midlands WV1 4BL
**US SIC:** 8111 **UK SIC:** 83500
**Employees:** 60

## DUNS 23-679-5043
### Rees Pollock
35 New Bridge Street, London EC4V 6BW
**Tel:** 020-7778-7200
**Web:** www.reespollock.co.uk
**Estd:** 1991 Partnership
**Line of Business:** Book-keeping activities
**Partners:** T Howkins, J Moulsdale,
Ms C Kimberlin, S Rees, A Pollock
**Responsibilities**
**Senior:** Alex Macpherson (Partner), Phil
Vipond (Partner)
**Finance:** Daniel Edgson (Tax Manager),
Yvonne Goddard (Accountant)
**Sales:** Ewa Manias (Accounts Management
Manager), Leanne Norman (Accounts
Management Manager)
**Admin:** Renu Kapur (Office Manager)
**Facilities:** Renu Kapur (Office Manager)
**Purchasing:** Renu Kapur (Office Manager)
**US SIC:** 8931 **UK SIC:** 83600
**Bankers:** The Royal Bank Of Scotland Plc
(16-00-19)
**Employees:** 55

## DUNS 22-100-8530
### Reeve (Derby) Ltd
(**Subsidiary of:** Pentagon Motor Holdings
Ltd)
Pentagon Island, Nottingham Road, Derby,
Derbyshire DE21 6HB
**Tel:** 01332362661 **Fax:** 01332292736
**Web:** www.pentagon-vauxhall.co.uk
**Reg No:** 4120259 **Estd:** 1951 Private
Limited Company
**Line of Business:** Car dealers (new & used)
**Trading Style:** Pentagon Vauxhall
**Issued Capital:** £2,201,982
**Directors:** G P Hall,
Motors Directors Limited, T J Reeve
**Co. Secretary:** Motors Secretaries Limited
**Responsibilities**
**Senior:** Dave White (General Manager)
**US SIC:** 5511 **UK SIC:** 65100
**Auditors:** Grant Thornton U K LLP
**Bankers:** The Royal Bank Of Scotland Plc
(16-23-37)

| | 31-12-13 | 31-12-12 | 31-12-11 |
|---|---|---|---|
| TO | 323,094,000 | 281,424,000 | 341,443,000 |
| P/L | 1,488,000 | 1,786,000 | (2,252,000) |
| NW | 8,752,000 | 10,017,000 | 8,352,000 |
| WC | 2,712,000 | 2,973,000 | 1,603,000 |
| Emp. | 614 | 615 | 683 |

## DUNS 29-885-3805
### Reeve the Baker Ltd
Kingsway, Wilton, Salisbury, Wiltshire SP2
0AW
**Tel:** 01722-743272
**Web:** www.reevethebaker.co.uk
**Reg No:** 2088228 **VAT No:** 329999875
**Estd:** 1977 Private Limited Company
**Line of Business:** Representative office
**Issued Capital:** £300
**Principals:** R L Reeve (Managing),
G Reeve, Ms S J Reeve
**Co. Secretary:** Raymond Reeve
**Responsibilities**
**Senior:** Gary Reeves (Managing Director)

**Finance:** Robin Hackforth (Accountant)
**Marketing:** Julie Huxtable (Retail Manager)
**Sales:** Julie Huxtable (Retail Manager)
**HR:** Gary Reeves (Managing Director)
**Facilities:** Gary Reeves (Managing Director)
**Operations:** Gary Reeves (Managing
Director)
**Purchasing:** Gary Reeves (Managing
Director)
**Branches:** Reeve The Baker Ltd, 17 Market
Place, Warminster, Wiltshire BA12 9AY
**US SIC:** 5462 **UK SIC:** 64100
**Auditors:** Fawcetts
**Bankers:** Lloyds TSB Bank plc (30-97-41)

| | 30-09-13 | 30-09-12 | 30-09-11 |
|---|---|---|---|
| TA | 1,604,463 | 1,577,083 | 1,584,242 |
| NW | 803,371 | 903,324 | 987,586 |
| WC | (330,132) | (80,733) | (95,714) |

## DUNS 77-947-2984
### Reeves Oilfield Services Ltd
(**Subsidiary of:** Weatherford (G.B.) Llp)
East Leake, Loughborough, Leicestershire
LE12 6JX
**Tel:** 01159 457800
**Web:** www.waitherford.com
**Reg No:** 3053591 **Estd:** 1995 Private
Limited Company
**Line of Business:** Holding companies
management activities
**Issued Capital:** £781,250
**Directors:** E R Prentice, I Jones
**Co. Secretary:** Mrs Gemma Rose-Garvie
**Responsibilities**
**Senior:** Brian Moncur (Manager)
**US SIC:** 6711 **UK SIC:** 83962
**Auditors:** Ernst & Young LLP

| | 31-12-13 | 31-12-12 | 31-12-11 |
|---|---|---|---|
| TA | 19,693,000 | 19,699,000 | 20,311,000 |
| P/L | (313,000) | (68,000) | 24,000 |
| NW | 2,641,000 | 2,956,000 | 2,927,000 |
| WC | (10,628,000) | (10,305,000) | (10,334,000) |

## DUNS 29-341-6715      Imp
### Reeves Wireline Technologies Ltd
(**Subsidiary of:** Weatherford (G.B.) Llp)
East Leake, Loughborough, Leicestershire
LE12 6JX
**Tel:** 01159457880
**Web:** www.weatherford.com
**Reg No:** 0096365 **VAT No:** 735227734
**Estd:** 1908 Private Limited Company
**Line of Business:** Mineral oil refining
**Trading Style:** Reeves Wireline
**Issued Capital:** £9,834,140
**Principals:** I Jones (Managing),
M C Enstone, E R Prentice
**Co. Secretary:** Mrs Gemma Rose-Garvie
**US SIC:** 2911 **UK SIC:** 14010
**Auditors:** PricewaterhouseCoopers
**Bankers:** The Royal Bank Of Scotland Plc
(16-01-23)

| | 31-12-13 | 31-12-12 | 31-12-11 |
|---|---|---|---|
| TO | 26,031,000 | 33,779,000 | 29,609,000 |
| P/L | 1,557,000 | 4,818,000 | 3,790,000 |
| NW | 51,853,000 | 51,348,000 | 49,298,000 |
| WC | 53,429,000 | 57,608,000 | 54,956,000 |
| Emp. | 168 | 173 | 161 |

## DUNS 29-174-6964
### Refinery Marketing Communications Ltd
(**Subsidiary of:** Refinery Holdings Ltd)
Pittbrook House, 10 Pittbrook Street,
Manchester M12 6JX
**Tel:** 0161-273-5511
**Web:** www.refinerygroup.co.uk
**Reg No:** 1845011 **Estd:** 1984 Private
Limited Company
**Line of Business:** Other business activities
not elsewhere classified
**Issued Capital:** £1,000
**Principals:** N Papworth (Managing),
S J Barron, D J Pye, T N Barron,
P A Armitage, M Laffan, J S Bowler
**Co. Secretary:** Colin Bowers
**US SIC:** 7399, 7333
**UK SIC:** 83954, 83953
**Auditors:** McNamara Cosgrove & Co Ltd
**Bankers:** National Westminster Bank Plc
(01-10-01)

| | 31-10-13 | 31-10-12 | 31-10-11 |
|---|---|---|---|
| TA | 2,502,259 | 2,611,722 | 1,999,524 |
| NW | 1,230,553 | 1,270,138 | 966,722 |
| WC | 1,087,747 | 1,144,903 | 915,007 |

## DUNS 21-631-7334
### Reflect
Nicholas House, 3 Laurence Pountney Hill,
London EC4R 0BB
**Tel:** 020-7929-1999
**Web:** www.hydrogengroup.com
**Estd:** 2002 Proprietorship
**Line of Business:** Business consulting
**Proprietor:** T Smeaton
**US SIC:** 7392 **UK SIC:** 83951
**Employees:** 68

DUNS 21-260-6107 **Imp-Exp**

## Reflecting Roadstuds Ltd

Crown Works, Mill Lane, Halifax, West Yorkshire HX3 6TN
**Tel:** 01422-360208
**Web:** www.percyshawcatseyes.com
**Reg No:** 0298350 **VAT No:** 183479527
**Estd:** 1935 Private Limited Company
**Line of Business:** Manufacturers of road and highway equipment
**Export Markets:** Europe & Worldwide.
**Issued Capital:** £450
**Principals:** T Shaw *(Managing)*, W M Dunn, J P Horton, R A Saunderson
**Co. Secretary:** Michael Steele
**US SIC:** 3531 **UK SIC:** 32541
**Auditors:** Firth Parish
**Bankers:** National Westminster Bank Plc (60-09-27)

| | 31-03-14 | 31-03-13 | 31-03-12 |
|---|---|---|---|
| TA | 2,825,602 | 2,566,642 | 2,600,389 |
| NW | 2,738,322 | 2,473,848 | 2,501,674 |
| WC | 2,600,497 | 2,328,118 | 2,346,394 |

DUNS 21-595-4519

## Reflex

36-37 Broad Street, Birmingham, West Midlands B1 2DY
**Tel:** 01216430444
**Web:** www.reflex-bars.co.uk
**Estd:** 1997
**Line of Business:** Nightclub
**Proprietor:** N Clarke
**US SIC:** 5813 **UK SIC:** 66200
**Employees:** 46

DUNS 42-353-8557 **Imp**

## The Reflex Group Ltd

Vision House, Hamilton Way, Mansfield, Nottinghamshire NG18 5BU
**Tel:** 01623675000
**Web:** www.reflexlabels.co.uk
**Reg No:** 4341532 **Estd:** 2001 Private Limited Company
**Line of Business:** Manufacture of printed labels
**Issued Capital:** £80,001
**Directors:** I Kendall, Mrs C Kendall
**Co. Secretary:** Michael Turner
**Responsibilities**
**Senior:** Kevin Mitchell *(Manager)*
**US SIC:** 2648, 6519
**UK SIC:** 47231, 85000
**Auditors:** Tenon Audit Ltd
**Bankers:** HSBC Bank plc (40-35-18)

| | 28-02-14 | 28-02-13 | 29-02-12 |
|---|---|---|---|
| TO | 51,996,000 | 45,057,000 | 39,344,000 |
| P/L | 2,600,000 | 2,795,000 | 1,355,000 |
| NW | 6,837,000 | 5,577,000 | 3,468,000 |
| WC | (3,422,000) | (1,657,000) | (3,640,000) |
| Emp. | 391 | 301 | 286 |

DUNS 49-384-8097 **Imp**

## Reflex Ltd

**(Subsidiary of:** Reflex 2005 Ltd)
1 Bennet Road, Reading, Berkshire RG2 0QX
**Tel:** 01189313611 **Fax:** 01189-314439
**Web:** www.reflex.co.uk
**Reg No:** 3131814 **Estd:** 1995 Private Limited Company
**Line of Business:** Audio visual equipment
**Export Sales:** £41,958
**Issued Capital:** £800,001
**Directors:** R Dreesden, A W Brymer
**Co. Secretary:** William Jepps
**Branches:** Reflex Ltd, Bennet Court, Unit 1, Reading, Berkshire RG2 0QX
**US SIC:** 3662, 1799
**UK SIC:** 34430, 50000
**Auditors:** Hurst Morrison Thomson
**Bankers:** Lloyds TSB Bank plc (30-11-27)

| | 31-12-13 | 31-12-12 | 31-12-11 |
|---|---|---|---|
| TO | 13,778,189 | 12,026,240 | 12,117,914 |
| P/L | 591,949 | 437,552 | 502,286 |
| NW | 3,732,752 | 3,311,255 | 3,028,220 |
| WC | 3,596,478 | 3,243,079 | 2,977,554 |
| Emp. | 51 | 50 | 50 |

DUNS 22-635-8414 **Imp-Exp**

## Reflex&Allen Uk Ltd

**(Subsidiary of:** Finlite Srl)
Kinmel Park Industrial Estate Ab, Bodelwyddan, Bodelwyddan, Rhyl, Clwyd LL18 5TY
**Tel:** 01745-586300
**Web:** www.reflexallen.com
**Reg No:** 1626825 **VAT No:** 370173667
**Estd:** 1982 Private Limited Company
**Line of Business:** Motor factors
**Export Markets:** E U
**Export Sales:** £28,556,268
**Issued Capital:** £11,933
**Directors:** G Da Re, R Gibellini
**Responsibilities**
**Senior:** Maggie Dobbs *(Accounts Manager)*
**Sales:** Stephen Shore *(Sales Director)*
**Branches:** Reflex&allen Uk Ltd, Unit 1, Boston Place, Coventry, West Midlands CV6 5NN
**US SIC:** 5531, 3714
**UK SIC:** 65100, 35300
**Auditors:** Newman & Partners
**Bankers:** The Royal Bank Of Scotland Plc (16-16-33)

| | 31-12-13 | 31-12-12 | 31-12-11 |
|---|---|---|---|
| TO | 34,699,637 | 29,316,861 | 31,277,594 |
| P/L | 2,194,143 | 2,249,138 | 1,758,673 |
| NW | 16,665,293 | 14,689,823 | 12,546,178 |
| WC | 12,143,185 | 10,074,062 | 7,633,631 |
| Emp. | 186 | 176 | 151 |

DUNS 21-096-8604

## Reflexion Care Group Ltd

Black Birches, Hadnall, Shrewsbury, Shropshire SY4 3DH
**Tel:** 01939-210040 **Fax:** 01939210874
**Web:** www.newreflexions.co.uk
**Reg No:** 6413244 **VAT No:** 922026658
**Estd:** 2009 Private Limited Company
**Line of Business:** Individual & family social services
**Issued Capital:** £100
**Directors:** K A Harrington, R C Storey, G D Watson
**Co. Secretary:** Gary Parker
**US SIC:** 8321, 8091, 7999
**UK SIC:** 96111, 95200, 97913
**Auditors:** Dyke Yaxley Ltd

| | 31-03-14 | 31-03-13 | 31-03-12 |
|---|---|---|---|
| TA | 2,727,854 | 2,363,592 | 2,147,056 |
| NW | 855,568 | 551,281 | 501,637 |
| WC | (704,276) | 88,053 | 49,634 |

DUNS 22-538-3926

## The Reform Club

104-105 Pall Mall, London SW1Y 5EW
**Tel:** 020-7930-9374
**Web:** www.reformclub.com
**VAT No:** 238887702 **Estd:** 1836
**Line of Business:** Clubs social and associations
**Co. Secretary:** Michael Mckerchar
**Responsibilities**
**Senior:** Michael Corby *(Trustee)*, Marco Dasilva *(Manager)*, Terry Howard *(Food & Beverage Manager)*, Michael McKerchar *(Club Secretary)*, Jonathon Smith *(Trustee)*
**HR:** Maxine Clarke *(Human Resources Manager)*
**Health & Safety:** Ron Harley *(Chief Engineer)*
**Facilities:** Ron Harley *(Chief Engineer)*
**Engineering:** Ron Harley *(Chief Engineer)*
**US SIC:** 8699 **UK SIC:** 96902
**Auditors:** haysmacintyre
**Employees:** 100
**Turnover:** £2,012,395

DUNS 50-453-1559

## Reformation Ltd

Unit 9 Barton Marina, Barton Turns, Centrum One Hundred, Barton Under Needwood, Burton-On-Trent, Staffordshire DE13 8DZ
**Tel:** 01283722720 **Fax:** 01283-492511
**Web:** www.mgm-trading.com
**Reg No:** 2435840 **VAT No:** 558409710
**Estd:** 1989 Private Limited Company
**Line of Business:** Upholstering
**Issued Capital:** £106,100
**Principals:** G E Sloane *(Managing)*, E T Sloane
**Co. Secretary:** Ms Susan Sloane
**US SIC:** 7392 **UK SIC:** 83951
**Auditors:** D E K M
**Bankers:** HSBC Bank plc (40-15-20)

| | 30-06-13 | 30-06-12 | 30-06-11 |
|---|---|---|---|
| TA | 359,118 | 380,000 | 331,881 |
| NW | 21,231 | 26,940 | (127,767) |
| WC | (14,452) | (18,759) | (68,299) |

DUNS 21-591-4315

## Refracto Instrumentation

Unit B Chancel Close, Gloucester, Gloucestershire GL4 3SN
**Tel:** 08454682513
**Web:** www.refractoinstrumentation.com
**Estd:** 2011 Proprietorship
**Line of Business:** Surgical/medical Instrument Mfrs
**Proprietor:** P Ferry
**US SIC:** 3841 **UK SIC:** 37201
**Employees:** 120

DUNS 21-604-4222 **Imp-Exp**

## Refresco Gerber Uk Ltd

**(Subsidiary of:** Hanover Acceptances Ltd)
Express Park, Bristol Road, Bridgwater, Somerset TA6 4RN
**Fax:** 01278-441777
**Web:** www.gerberfoods.com
**Reg No:** 0161079 **Estd:** 1919 Private Limited Company
**Line of Business:** Fruit juice producers and merchants
**Export Markets:** Middle East; Far East; W Europe
**Export Sales:** £11,685,000
**Trading Style:** Gerber Emig
**Issued Capital:** £428,728
**Directors:** D J Saint, Refresco B.V., A C Duijzer, J H Roelofs
**Co. Secretary:** Pieter Van Meerteren
**Responsibilities**
**Senior:** Herman De Boer *(Non-PC Systems Manager)*, Richard Peak *(Financial Controller)*
**US SIC:** 5149 **UK SIC:** 61700
**Auditors:** Deloitte LLP

| | 25-12-13 | 25-12-12 | 25-12-11 |
|---|---|---|---|
| TO | 299,998,000 | 329,293,000 | 299,868,000 |
| P/L | (2,502,000) | 5,301,000 | 7,597,000 |
| NW | 44,024,000 | 40,984,000 | 36,552,000 |
| WC | 35,889,000 | 18,986,000 | 26,995,000 |
| Emp. | 871 | 838 | 863 |

DUNS 22-018-6410

## Refresco Ltd

**(Subsidiary of:** Refresco Gerber B.V.)
Belmont Industrial Estate, Durham, County Durham DH1 1ST
**Tel:** 0191-386-7111
**Web:** www.refresco.com
**Reg No:** 4021465 **Estd:** 2000 Private Limited Company
**Line of Business:** Manufacturers of soft drinks
**Trading Style:** Refresco Uk
**Issued Capital:** £120,000
**Director:** Refresco B.V.
**Co. Secretary:** Aart Duijzer
**Responsibilities**
**Senior:** Stephen Elder *(Manager)*, Norval Hughan *(Manager)*, Marnie-jane Millard *(Manager)*
**US SIC:** 2086 **UK SIC:** 42831
**Auditors:** PricewaterhouseCoopers LLP
**Bankers:** Fortis Bank London Bch (formerly Generale Bk) (40-52-62)

| | 31-12-13 | 31-12-12 | 31-12-11 |
|---|---|---|---|
| TO | 43,089,000 | 43,300,000 | 49,259,000 |
| P/L | (15,930,000) | (6,038,000) | (6,067,000) |
| NW | (26,068,000) | (9,763,000) | (3,729,000) |
| WC | (22,692,000) | (22,206,000) | (17,235,000) |
| Emp. | 96 | 105 | 137 |

DUNS 29-327-9345

## Refreshment Systems Ltd

31 Bolling Road, Bradford, West Yorkshire BD4 7HN
**Tel:** 01274750000
**Web:** www.refreshmentsystems.co.uk
**Reg No:** 1826322 **VAT No:** 606982321
**Estd:** 1984 Private Limited Company
**Line of Business:** Other service activities not elsewhere classified
**Trading Style:** Drinkup
**Issued Capital:** £10,108
**Principals:** W D Balmforth *(Managing)*, R A Balmforth, P P Shaw, Mrs M V Balmforth
**Co. Secretary:** Mrs Noreen Balmforth
**Responsibilities**
**IT:** Daniel Woolley *(Senior IT Executive)*
**Branches:** Refreshment Systems Ltd, 3 Innovation Way, Barnsley, South Yorkshire S75 1JL
**US SIC:** 8999, 5146
**UK SIC:** 83954, 61700
**Auditors:** BKR Haines Watts
**Bankers:** HSBC Bank plc (40-13-15)

| | 31-03-14 | 31-03-13 | 31-03-12 |
|---|---|---|---|
| TO | 9,413,268 | 9,950,949 | 9,059,549 |
| P/L | 615,682 | 544,517 | 373,629 |
| NW | 3,605,530 | 3,402,685 | 3,053,771 |
| WC | 1,986,442 | 1,857,899 | 1,856,678 |
| Emp. | 115 | 114 | 116 |

DUNS 29-410-6380

## Refuge

Refuge International House 1 Str, London E1W 1UN
**Tel:** 020-7395-7700
**Web:** www.refuge.org.uk
**Reg No:** 1412276 **Estd:** 1979 Private Limited Company
**Line of Business:** Other service activities not elsewhere classified
**Issued Capital:** £2
**Directors:** Ms R M Harding, Ms M Rae, Baroness H A Kennedy, Dame S Rimington, Mrs B J Vavalidis, Ms S Mckibbin, M De Silva, Ms D G Nelmes
**Co. Secretary:** Ms Sandra Horley
**Responsibilities**
**Senior:** Jane Keeper *(Director of Operations)*, Janice Panton *(Director)*
**HR:** Joanne Stewart *(Head of Human Resources)*
**Operations:** Jane Keeper *(Director of Operations)*
**US SIC:** 8999 **UK SIC:** 83954
**Auditors:** Sayers Butterworth
**Bankers:** HSBC Bank plc (40-02-13)

| | 31-03-14 | 31-03-13 | 31-03-12 |
|---|---|---|---|
| TO | 11,099,596 | 11,372,947 | 10,449,256 |
| P/L | 1,231,972 | 1,102,954 | 180,941 |
| NW | 5,034,828 | 3,802,856 | 2,699,902 |
| WC | 4,922,961 | 3,651,287 | 2,532,671 |
| Emp. | 169 | 173 | 169 |

DUNS 28-943-9929

## Refugee Action

The Victoria Charity Centre, 11 Belgrave Road, London SW1V 1RB
**Tel:** 08458942536
**Web:** www.worldfoodnight.org.uk
**Reg No:** 1593454 **Estd:** 1981 Private Limited Company
**Line of Business:** Social work activities without accommodation
**Directors:** C W Hodgetts, A Gregg, Miss S A Pfeil, C W Randall, Ms R Pendlebury, J P Lester, M Jalali, Mrs J J Meiklejohn
**Co. Secretary:** David Garratt
**Responsibilities**
**Senior:** Susan Cueva *(Director)*
**Branches:** Refugee Action, 2ND Floor China Ct Buldg, Ladywell Walk, Birmingham, West Midlands B5 4ST
**US SIC:** 8321, 7361
**UK SIC:** 96111, 83954
**Auditors:** MHA MacIntyre Hudson
**Bankers:** National Westminster Bank Plc (60-12-01)

| | 31-03-14 | 31-03-13 | 31-03-12 |
|---|---|---|---|
| TO | 20,240,000 | 17,655,000 | 16,455,000 |
| P/L | (81,000) | 47,000 | 223,000 |
| NW | 5,169,000 | 5,250,000 | 5,203,000 |
| WC | 5,017,000 | 4,907,000 | 4,725,000 |
| Emp. | 281 | 266 | 288 |

DUNS 73-296-9857 **Imp**

## Refulgent Ltd

Monkton Business Park, Hebburn, Tyne and Wear NE31 2JZ
**Tel:** 0191-423-7070 **Fax:** 0191-423-7071
**Web:** www.vmslimited.co.uk
**Reg No:** 4570825 **Estd:** 2002 Private Limited Company
**Line of Business:** Manufacture of lighting equipment and electric lamps
**Export Sales:** £46,041
**Issued Capital:** £5,932,740
**Director:** A J Duffield
**Co. Secretary:** Andrew Duffield
**Responsibilities**
**Senior:** Bill Hamilton *(Chief Executive Officer)*, Tony Isaacs *(Business Manager for Real)*, Jack Mcgrory *(Manager)*, Geoff Rogerson *(Business Manager)*
**Sales:** Glynn Hutton *(Sales Manager)*
**IT:** Andrew Ramsey *(Head of IT)*
**Engineering:** Gary Cadman *(Chief Engineer)*
**Branches:** Refulgent Ltd, Unit 22, Kingsway, Gateshead, Tyne and Wear NE11 0SR
**US SIC:** 3648 **UK SIC:** 34702
**Auditors:** KPMG LLP

| | 31-03-14 | 31-03-13 | 31-03-11 |
|---|---|---|---|
| TO | 12,630,101 | 10,102,700 | 10,517,790 |
| P/L | (3,219,752) | (2,043,477) | (1,937,422) |
| NW | 340,232 | 1,422,702 | 1,189,797 |
| WC | 485,862 | 1,433,898 | 1,095,278 |
| Emp. | 64 | 61 | 72 |

DUNS 21-296-9703

## Reg Greenwood (Tyres & Exhausts) Ltd

78 Knottingley Road, Pontefract, West Yorkshire WF8 2LB
**Tel:** 01977-702317 **Fax:** 01977-600337
**Web:** www.reggreenwood.co.uk
**Reg No:** 1592639 **Estd:** 1981 Private Limited Company
**Line of Business:** Exhaust centres
**Issued Capital:** £1,000
**Principals:** S K Clarke *(Managing)*, K Clarke *(Managing)*, Mrs A L Andrassy *(Financial)*
**Co. Secretary:** Mrs Jean Clarke
**US SIC:** 7539 **UK SIC:** 67100
**Auditors:** Jolliffe Cork
**Bankers:** Barclays Bank Plc (20-89-68)

| | 31-01-14 | 31-01-13 | 31-01-12 |
|---|---|---|---|
| TA | 823,803 | 701,318 | 936,296 |
| NW | 416,186 | 352,190 | 455,044 |
| WC | 398,084 | 329,875 | 431,100 |

DUNS 21-578-8001

## Reg Vardy (Aberdeen) Ltd

**(Subsidiary of:** Pendragon Plc)
Lang Stracht, Mascrick, Aberdeen, Aberdeenshire AB16 6LA
**Tel:** 01224666411 **Fax:** 01224-666428
**Web:** www.regvardy.com
**Reg No:** 0052978SC **Estd:** 1973 Private Limited Company
**Line of Business:** Sale of new motor vehicles
**Trading Style:** Vardy Reg Jaguar
**Issued Capital:** £2
**Directors:** T G Finn, T P Holden, M S Casha
**Co. Secretary:** Ms Hilary Sykes

**Branches:** Reg Vardy (Aberdeen) Ltd, 10 Greenwell Rd, Aberdeen, Aberdeenshire AB12 3AZ
**US SIC:** 5511 **UK SIC:** 65100
**Bankers:** Barclays Bank Plc (20-59-42)

| | 31-12-13 | 31-12-12 | 31-12-11 |
|---|---|---|---|
| TA | 2 | 2 | 2 |
| NW | 2 | 2 | 2 |

DUNS 21-213-3938
## Reg Vardy Ltd
**(Subsidiary of:** Pendragon Plc)
Riverside Farm, Tottle Road, Nottingham, Nottinghamshire NG2 1RT
**Tel:** 01159578000
**Web:** www.evanshalshaw.com
**Reg No:** 0611190 **Estd:** 1958 Private Limited Company
**Line of Business:** Sale of new motor vehicles
**Trading Style:** Evans Halshaw, Venture Land Rover, Bushbury Land Rover
**Issued Capital:** £5,641,326
**Directors:** M S Casha, T G Finn, T P Holden, Pendragon Management Services Li
**Co. Secretary:** Ms Hilary Sykes
**Branches:** Reg Vardy Ltd, Stoneygate Garage, Houghton Le Spring, Tyne and Wear DH4 4NJ
**US SIC:** 5511 **UK SIC:** 65100
**Auditors:** KPMG Audit PLC
**Bankers:** Barclays Bank Plc (20-59-42)

| | 31-12-13 | 31-12-12 | 31-12-11 |
|---|---|---|---|
| TO | 244,318,000 | 229,329,000 | 253,727,000 |
| P/L | 6,481,000 | 24,815,000 | 5,100,000 |
| NW | 104,173,000 | 99,234,000 | 99,855,000 |
| WC | 43,415,000 | 38,906,000 | 42,401,000 |
| Emp. | 454 | 481 | 528 |

DUNS 39-964-7403
## Reg Vardy (Mml) Ltd
**(Subsidiary of:** Pendragon Plc)
104 Gelderd Road, Leeds, West Yorkshire LS27 7ND
**Tel:** 01132902300 **Fax:** 01132-902309
**Reg No:** 0736438 **Estd:** 1996 Private Limited Company
**Line of Business:** Maintenance and repair of motor vehicles
**Issued Capital:** £2,398,000
**Directors:** T G Finn, M S Casha, T P Holden
**Co. Secretary:** Ms Hilary Sykes
**US SIC:** 7539 **UK SIC:** 67100
**Auditors:** KPMG Audit PLC

| | 31-12-13 | 31-12-12 | 31-12-11 |
|---|---|---|---|
| TO | 6,224,000 | 4,963,000 | 4,877,000 |
| P/L | 856,000 | 586,000 | 518,000 |
| NW | 4,137,000 | 3,492,000 | 3,059,000 |
| WC | 3,985,000 | 3,343,000 | 2,901,000 |
| Emp. | 78 | 70 | 65 |

DUNS 34-888-8314
## Reg Vardy (Tmh) Ltd
**(Subsidiary of:** Pendragon Plc)
Riverside Road, Sunderland, Tyne and Wear SR5 3JG
**Tel:** 08454091062
**Web:** www.evanshalshaw.com
**Reg No:** 2825899 **Estd:** 2004 Private Limited Company
**Line of Business:** Car dealers (new & used)
**Trading Style:** Evans Halshaw Nissan
**Issued Capital:** £1,000
**Directors:** M S Casha, T P Holden, T G Finn
**Co. Secretary:** Ms Hilary Sykes
**US SIC:** 6711, 5511
**UK SIC:** 83962, 65100
**Auditors:** Deloitte & Touche

| | 31-12-13 | 31-12-12 | 31-12-11 |
|---|---|---|---|
| TA | 609,993 | 609,993 | 609,993 |
| NW | 488,010 | 488,010 | 488,010 |

DUNS 22-629-4643 **Imp**
## Rega Research Ltd
6 The Forum, Southend-On-Sea, Essex SS2 5TE
**Tel:** 01702461982
**Web:** www.rega.co.uk
**Reg No:** 1118303 **Estd:** 1973 Private Limited Company
**Line of Business:** Sound recording apparatus and equipment
**Export Sales:** £6,473,832
**Issued Capital:** £1,250
**Managing Director:** R L Gandy
**Responsibilities**
**Sales:** Dave Brooks *(Commercial Director)*
**US SIC:** 3629 **UK SIC:** 34350
**Auditors:** Rickard Keen LLP

| | 30-06-14 | 30-06-13 | 30-06-12 |
|---|---|---|---|
| TO | 8,327,327 | 7,103,841 | 5,877,671 |
| P/L | 1,391,501 | 805,026 | 423,856 |
| NW | 4,224,499 | 3,068,016 | 2,385,107 |
| WC | 4,351,898 | 3,401,472 | 2,900,107 |
| Emp. | 86 | 78 | 68 |

DUNS 21-677-7814
## Regain Polymers Ltd
**(Subsidiary of:** Chamonix Ii Lp)
Allerton Bywater Business Park, Newton Lane, Castleford, West Yorkshire WF10 2AL
**Tel:** 01977604080
**Web:** www.regainpolymers.com
**Reg No:** 7289595 **Estd:** 2010 Private Limited Company
**Line of Business:** Manufacture of other plastic products
**Issued Capital:** £1,550,001
**Directors:** A J Hartley, M A Roberts, M J Dunn, M J Marron, S J Armstrong, S T Catling
**US SIC:** 3079 **UK SIC:** 48360

| | 31-12-13 | 31-12-12 | 31-12-11 |
|---|---|---|---|
| TO | 28,958,000 | 26,403,000 | 24,107,000 |
| P/L | (475,000) | (1,208,000) | 416,000 |
| NW | (2,475,000) | (2,067,000) | (981,000) |
| WC | (2,976,000) | (3,420,000) | (1,400,000) |
| Emp. | 114 | 104 | 94 |

DUNS 28-958-0177
## Regal Credit Consultants Ltd
Regal House, 18 High Street, Bagshot, Surrey GU19 5AA
**Tel:** 01276-470500 **Fax:** 01276-470503
**Web:** www.regalcredit.co.uk
**Reg No:** 1665165 **Estd:** 1983 Private Limited Company
**Line of Business:** Credit reporting and collection agency activities
**Issued Capital:** £1,052
**Principals:** R Spiteri *(Managing)*, R Spiteri, N P Rutzler
**Co. Secretary:** Ms Margaret Spiteri
**Responsibilities**
**Senior:** John Bisset *(Manager)*
**Admin:** Jenny Thatcher *(Administrator)*
**HR:** Anna Doherty *(Human Resources Manager)*
**Purchasing:** Jenny Thatcher *(Administrator)*
**US SIC:** 7321 **UK SIC:** 83954
**Auditors:** Leiwy Sherman & Co

| | 30-04-14 | 30-04-13 | 30-04-12 |
|---|---|---|---|
| TO | 1,927,732 | 2,018,106 | 2,622,532 |
| P/L | 95,783 | (24,206) | 215,586 |
| NW | 821,328 | 859,619 | 1,010,132 |
| WC | 693,485 | 696,651 | 844,537 |

DUNS 34-857-2538
## Regal Fish Supplies Ltd
Ardent Road, Barton-Upon-Humber, South Humberside DN18 5RN
**Tel:** 01652662100 **Fax:** 01652-634790
**Web:** www.regalfish.co.uk
**Reg No:** 2813471 **Estd:** 1993 Private Limited Company
**Line of Business:** Fishmongers and related services
**Issued Capital:** £200
**Directors:** T R Wheller, G D Sopp, G K Firth
**Co. Secretary:** David Porter
**Responsibilities**
**Senior:** Mike Brummitt *(General Manager)*, Chris Sopp *(Dock Manager)*
**Finance:** David Stagg *(Finance Manager)*
**Sales:** Keith Hudson *(Sales Manager)*
**IT:** Tim Canty *(ICt Support Development Office)*
**HR:** Janet Tabort *(Human Resources Manager)*
**Health & Safety:** Mike Brummitt *(General Manager)*
**Operations:** Keith Hudson *(Sales Manager)*
**Purchasing:** Chris Sopp *(Dock Manager)*
**US SIC:** 5146, 5963
**UK SIC:** 61700, 65600
**Auditors:** Martin Fish & Co

| | 23-05-14 | 24-05-13 | 18-05-12 |
|---|---|---|---|
| TO | 8,937,889 | 9,225,789 | 8,946,834 |
| P/L | 213,300 | 143,451 | 381,517 |
| NW | 475,217 | 317,115 | 210,465 |
| WC | (233,636) | (325,828) | (416,631) |
| Emp. | 100 | 100 | 99 |

DUNS 21-169-3980
## Regal Holiday Homes Ltd
Highfield Court, Tollgate, Chandler's Ford, Eastleigh, Hampshire SO53 3TY
**Tel:** 01929557850
**Web:** www.regalholidayhomes.com
**Reg No:** 6942267 **Estd:** 2009 Private Limited Company
**Line of Business:** Manufacture of bodies (coachwork) for motor vehicles (except caravans)
**Export Sales:** £178,528
**Issued Capital:** £212,500
**Directors:** E Jones, S Geranio, D M Ward, M J Clifford, N J Heslington, A Jones
**US SIC:** 3713, 3999
**UK SIC:** 35201, 49590
**Bankers:** National Westminster Bank Plc (54-30-03)

| | 30-09-13 | 30-09-12 | 30-09-11 |
|---|---|---|---|
| TO | 7,449,294 | 7,004,735 | N/A |
| P/L | 103,686 | (85,043) | N/A |
| NW | 182,723 | 132,631 | 259,545 |
| WC | 155,166 | (104,430) | 75,376 |
| Emp. | 72 | 72 | N/A |

DUNS 21-914-8871 **Imp-Exp**
## Regal Manufacturing Ltd
**(Subsidiary of:** Regal-Beloit Corporation)
Heapham Road Industrial Estate, Gainsborough, Lincolnshire DN21 1XU
**Tel:** 01427-614141
**Web:** www.regalmanufacturing.co.uk
**Reg No:** 0516559 **VAT No:** 129500583
**Estd:** 1976 Private Limited Company
**Line of Business:** Manufacture of insulated wire and cable
**Export Markets:** Canada; Thailand; U S A; European Union (E U)
**Export Sales:** £11,884,530
**Issued Capital:** £610,221
**Directors:** P C Underwood, C Hinrichs, M J Gliebe, Ms S C Sutton
**Co. Secretary:**
Gravitas Company Secretarial Ser
**US SIC:** 3357, 3629
**UK SIC:** 22470, 34350
**Auditors:** Duncan & Toplis
**Bankers:** National Westminster Bank Plc (52-41-46)

| | 31-12-13 | 31-12-12 | 31-12-11 |
|---|---|---|---|
| TO | 21,732,338 | 13,918,183 | 8,337,202 |
| P/L | 2,953,403 | 1,316,462 | 548,204 |
| NW | 2,655,957 | 1,668,588 | 1,710,264 |
| WC | 8,500,015 | 4,062,791 | 1,430,958 |
| Emp. | 95 | 81 | 85 |

DUNS 21-907-7773
## Regal Motors (Bilston) Ltd
Oxford Street, Bilston, West Midlands WV14 7DG
**Tel:** 01902353000
**Web:** www.regal-motors.co.uk
**Reg No:** 1067821 **VAT No:** 100548220
**Estd:** 2002 Private Limited Company
**Line of Business:** Car dealers (new & used)
**Issued Capital:** £100
**Principals:** Mrs J M Taylor *(Managing)*, P Jackson
**Co. Secretary:** Mrs Vera Jackson
**US SIC:** 7539 **UK SIC:** 67100
**Auditors:** Attwood & Co
**Bankers:** HSBC Bank plc (40-19-02)

| | 31-12-13 | 31-12-12 | 31-12-11 |
|---|---|---|---|
| TO | 14,072,543 | 13,685,624 | 12,491,110 |
| P/L | 205,982 | 105,242 | (132,289) |
| NW | 1,011,374 | 921,515 | 906,473 |
| WC | 397,647 | 256,904 | 245,534 |
| Emp. | 48 | 47 | 52 |

DUNS 42-474-8866
## Regal Petroleum Plc
16 Old Queen Street, London SW1H 9HP
**Tel:** 02034273550 **Fax:** 020-7408-9501
**Web:** www.regalpetroleum.co.uk
**Reg No:** 4462555 **Estd:** 1998 Private Limited Company
**Line of Business:** Petroleum product producers
**Directors:** A J Coates, Dr A M Graham, A Pertin, K N Henry, S Glazunov, O Tymofieiev
**Co. Secretary:** Christopher Phillips
**Responsibilities**
**Finance:** Robert Smyth *(Finance Director)*
**US SIC:** 2999 **UK SIC:** 11150
**Auditors:** Deloitte LLP
**Employees:** 8
**Turnover:** £36,737,000

DUNS 23-114-4668
## The Regal Sunderland Stadium
Newcastle Road, Sunderland, Tyne and Wear SR5 1RP
**Tel:** 0191-568-6200
**Web:** http://sunderlanddogs.com
**Estd:** 1988 Proprietorship
**Line of Business:** Stadiums and sports grounds
**Partners:** D Harding, I Spearing, D Lowrey, N Tinker, T Singer
**Responsibilities**
**Senior:** Joe O'Donnell *(Manager)*
**US SIC:** 7999 **UK SIC:** 97913
**Employees:** 114

DUNS 64-069-9567
## Regal Vehicle Rentals Ltd
Parkgate Road, Chester, Cheshire CH1 6RR
**Tel:** 01244852000
**Web:** www.regalrental.co.uk
**Reg No:** 3465480 **Estd:** 1997 Private Limited Company
**Line of Business:** Renting of automobiles
**Trading Style:** Regal Rentals
**Issued Capital:** £9,505
**Directors:** J H Frost, B Hastings, D H Fielding
**Branches:** Regal Vehicle Rentals Ltd, Parkgate Road, Chester, Cheshire CH1 6RR
**US SIC:** 7512 **UK SIC:** 84801

**Auditors:** McEwan Wallace

| | 31-03-14 | 31-03-13 | 31-03-12 |
|---|---|---|---|
| TO | 4,028,082 | 5,698,451 | 5,302,595 |
| P/L | 111,514 | 238,130 | 178,764 |
| NW | 1,153,548 | 1,141,884 | 1,005,546 |
| WC | (190,054) | (1,123,861) | (1,745,067) |
| Emp. | 81 | 100 | 104 |

DUNS 22-193-1053 **Imp**
## Regalead Ltd
Columbus House, Manchester M22 9AF
**Tel:** 01619461164 **Fax:** 0161-946-1033
**Web:** www.regalead.co.uk
**Reg No:** 4211244 **Estd:** 2001 Private Limited Company
**Line of Business:** Fabricated metal products
**Export Sales:** £3,281,505
**Issued Capital:** £5,340
**Directors:** J Whalley, D Baker, G Hubble, S J Clough, V H Cruise
**Co. Secretary:** Stephen Clough
**Responsibilities**
**Senior:** David Rabone *(Manager)*
**US SIC:** 3441 **UK SIC:** 32042
**Auditors:** Ford Campbell

| | 30-12-13 | 30-09-12 | 30-12-11 |
|---|---|---|---|
| TO | 13,262,171 | 9,603,290 | 8,491,748 |
| P/L | 400,401 | 211,204 | 313,428 |
| NW | 1,904,736 | 1,453,992 | 1,168,287 |
| WC | 1,639,141 | 1,259,033 | 1,256,026 |
| Emp. | 85 | 88 | 64 |

DUNS 21-991-9151
## Regard Holdings Ltd
Units 6 7 Princeton Mews, Kingston-Upon-Thames, Surrey KT2 6PT
**Tel:** 020-8255-4433
**Web:** www.regard.co.uk
**Reg No:** 6173337 **Estd:** 2007 Private Limited Company
**Line of Business:** Management activities of holding companies
**Issued Capital:** £102,465
**Directors:** M G Hawkes, Mrs S Foxall-Smith
**Responsibilities**
**Senior:** Karl Farragher *(Commercial Director)*, Fiona Hannah *(Manager)*, Bal Johal *(Manager)*
**Finance:** Matthew Boyd *(Management Accountant)*, Tania Bristow *(Revenue Accountant)*, Nick Martin *(Payroll Officer)*, Polly Riley *(Senior Payroll Officer)*, Zara White *(Financial Controller)*
**Sales:** Karl Farragher *(Commercial Director)*
**Admin:** Gemma Jones *(PA to Operations Director)*
**IT:** Skender Azemi *(Head of IT)*
**HR:** Lorraine Hicks *(HR Administrator)*, Louise Ridger *(HR Officer)*
**Operations:** Jan Cartmell *(Regional Director)*
**US SIC:** 6711 **UK SIC:** 83962
**Bankers:** Bank Of Scotland (80-20-19)

| | 21-03-14 | 22-03-13 | 30-03-12 |
|---|---|---|---|
| TO | 42,133,707 | 39,523,885 | 40,668,142 |
| P/L | (1,240,946) | (1,520,623) | (75,767) |
| NW | (15,519,728) | (13,865,457) | (13,279,557) |
| WC | (3,179) | (757,242) | (4,398,581) |
| Emp. | 1,479 | 1,408 | 1,398 |

DUNS 23-305-8143
## Regen Waste Ltd
**(Subsidiary of:** Regen Waste Holdings Ltd)
Unit 7 Shepherds Drive, Carnbane Industrial Estate, Newry, Co Down BT35 6JQ
**Tel:** 028 3026 5432 **Fax:** 028 3026 9898
**Web:** www.regenwaste.com
**Reg No:** 0044110NI **Estd:** 2004 Private Limited Company
**Line of Business:** Waste disposal
**Issued Capital:** £45,000
**Directors:** A Doherty, C Doherty, J Doherty
**Co. Secretary:** Aidan Doherty
**US SIC:** 4953, 5093, 3341
**UK SIC:** 92110, 62200, 22470
**Auditors:** FPM Accountants LLP

| | 31-12-13 | 31-12-12 | 31-12-11 |
|---|---|---|---|
| TO | 9,397,189 | 7,298,558 | 7,338,391 |
| P/L | 512,267 | 204,781 | 852,282 |
| NW | 5,244,029 | 4,825,382 | 4,668,780 |
| WC | 1,964,157 | 1,586,858 | 1,423,833 |
| Emp. | 126 | 115 | 95 |

DUNS 23-719-4956 **Imp-Exp**
## Regency Carpet Manufacturing Ltd
**(Subsidiary of:** Furlong Investments Ltd)
9 Balloo Avenue, Bangor, Co Down BT19 7QT
**Tel:** 02891270900 **Fax:** 02891 464825
**Web:** www.regencycarpet.co.uk
**Reg No:** 0028991NI **VAT No:** 653434049
**Estd:** 1994 Private Limited Company
**Line of Business:** Manufacture of other carpets and rugs
**Export Markets:** Republic of Ireland
**Issued Capital:** £13,020,000
**Directors:** M M O'Loghlen, N Furlong
**Co. Secretary:** Richard Clark
**Responsibilities**
**Senior:** Mike Wackett *(Manager)*

**US SIC:** 2279 **UK SIC:** 43852
**Auditors:** HSOC Consultants Ltd

| | 30-06-13 | 30-06-12 | 30-06-11 |
|---|---|---|---|
| TO | 46,089,587 | 50,412,395 | 43,440,281 |
| P/L | (134,871) | 1,531,109 | 542,615 |
| NW | 4,972,996 | 4,295,540 | (9,477,928) |
| WC | 5,957,469 | 9,881,551 | 8,187,476 |
| Emp. | 159 | 155 | 151 |

DUNS 21-009-8037
## Regency Cleaning (Halesowen) Ltd
86 Windsor Road, Halesowen, West Midlands B63 4BH
**Tel:** 0121-501-1783
**Reg No:** 6335434 **Estd:** 1972 Private Limited Company
**Line of Business:** Cleaning contracting commercial
**Issued Capital:** £800
**Directors:** Ms J A Ford, Ms T A Thompson, M Thompson
**Co. Secretary:** Graham Ford
**US SIC:** 7349 **UK SIC:** 92300

| | 31-08-14 | 31-08-13 | 31-08-12 |
|---|---|---|---|
| TA | 135,509 | 137,951 | 141,033 |
| NW | (49,887) | (58,301) | (64,596) |
| WC | (50,859) | (58,341) | (64,357) |

DUNS 22-239-2883
## Regency Cleaning Services Ltd
Graffix House, Newtown Business Park, Henley-On-Thames, Oxfordshire RG9 1HG
**Tel:** 01491-842942 **Fax:** 01491637868
**Web:** www.regencycleaning.co.uk
**Reg No:** 4257325 **Estd:** 2001 Private Limited Company
**Line of Business:** Cleaning contracting commercial
**Issued Capital:** £2
**Director:** D J Penny
**Co. Secretary:** Ms Sarah Penny
**Branches:** Regency Cleaning Services Ltd, 75 Wordsworth Road, Welling, Kent DA16 3NT
**US SIC:** 7349 **UK SIC:** 92300
**Auditors:** Robert J. Tucker & Co

| | 31-12-13 | 31-12-12 | 31-12-11 |
|---|---|---|---|
| TA | 831,055 | 708,479 | 744,691 |
| NW | 580,622 | 512,622 | 516,952 |
| WC | 577,382 | 512,622 | 516,952 |

DUNS 77-007-6875
## Regency Factors Plc
2 Regency Chambers, Jubilee Way, Bury, Lancashire BL9 0JW
**Tel:** 01612804000 **Fax:** 01617 614018
**Web:** www.regencyfactors.co.uk
**Reg No:** 2658006 **Estd:** 1991 Private Limited Company
**Line of Business:** Invoice discounting services
**Export Sales:** £6,002,889
**Issued Capital:** £1,600,004
**Directors:** M H Craft, P Ratcliffe, Mrs H S Craft, S Clague, P D Dusara, J Farrell
**Co. Secretary:** Jonathan Craft
**Responsibilities**
**Finance:** Sue Lam *(Financial Controller)*, Rebecca Ramsden *(Head of Trade Finance)*
**US SIC:** 8931 **UK SIC:** 83600
**Auditors:** Jackson Stephen LLP
**Bankers:** Yorkshire Bank Plc (05-09-33)

| | 31-01-14 | 31-01-13 | 31-01-12 |
|---|---|---|---|
| TO | 111,785,859 | 90,651,607 | 101,503,044 |
| P/L | 430,507 | 562,090 | 684,432 |
| NW | 3,349,545 | 3,345,236 | 3,239,695 |
| WC | 12,669,228 | 11,639,506 | 11,513,121 |
| Emp. | 50 | 51 | 53 |

DUNS 73-571-3229
## Regency Healthcare Ltd
The Laurels Nursing Home, Bankside Lane, Bacup, Lancashire OL13 8GT
**Tel:** 01706878389
**Web:** www.rhcl.co.uk
**Reg No:** 4833014 **Estd:** 2008 Private Limited Company
**Line of Business:** Nursing homes
**Issued Capital:** £1,002
**Director:** M F Chauhdry
**Co. Secretary:** Asif Alvi
**Responsibilities**
**Senior:** Bernie Brown *(Manager)*, Marie Harris *(Manager)*
**US SIC:** 8051 **UK SIC:** 95100
**Bankers:** National Westminster Bank Plc (60-18-11)

| | 28-02-14 | 28-02-13 | 29-02-12 |
|---|---|---|---|
| TO | 2,482,111 | 2,364,530 | 2,280,281 |
| P/L | 14,545 | 114,992 | 96,635 |
| NW | (28,216) | (139,018) | (222,139) |
| WC | (641,300) | (590,382) | (549,023) |
| Emp. | 159 | 155 | 155 |

DUNS 21-595-4564
## Regency High School Sports College
Carnforth Drive, Worcester, Worcestershire WR4 9JL
**Tel:** 01905454828
**Web:** www.regency.worcs.sch.uk
**Estd:** 1974
**Line of Business:** Schools (local authority)
**Proprietor:** F Steel
**US SIC:** 8211 **UK SIC:** 93200
**Employees:** 120

DUNS 42-414-2842
## Regency Hotel (Northern Ireland)
(**Subsidiary of:** Golf Holdings Limited)
13 Lower Crescent, Belfast BT7 1NR
**Tel:** 028-9032-3349 **Fax:** 02890326466
**Web:** www.regencyhotels.com
**Reg No:** 0006303NI **Estd:** 1981 Private Limited Company
**Line of Business:** Hotels
**Trading Style:** Cresent Tyne Height
**Issued Capital:** £18,000
**Directors:** R J Davis, J P Hunt, P M Hunt, P Hunt, J O Hunt, J O Hunt, P M Hunt, J P Hunt
**Co. Secretary:** William Wilson
**US SIC:** 7011, 5813
**UK SIC:** 66500, 66200
**Auditors:** James P Convery & Co
**Bankers:** First Trust Bank (aib Group (uk) Plc) (93-80-92)

| | 31-12-13 | 31-12-12 | 31-12-11 |
|---|---|---|---|
| TO | 10,107,736 | 10,290,222 | 10,028,397 |
| P/L | (641,947) | (1,064,325) | (482,742) |
| NW | 4,917,273 | 5,883,648 | 6,614,438 |
| WC | (14,746,121) | (14,557,808) | (14,868,043) |
| Emp. | 287 | 293 | 299 |

DUNS 55-080-9792
## Regency House
Parkes Lane, Tranch, Pontypool, Gwent NP4 6BA
**Tel:** 01495763597
**Estd:** 1999 Partnership
**Line of Business:** Rest and retirement homes
**Partners:** Mrs J Eagles, J Eagles
**US SIC:** 8321 **UK SIC:** 96111
**Employees:** 60

DUNS 64-262-3250
## Regency Nursing Home
13 St Helens Parade, Southsea, Hampshire PO4 0QJ
**Web:** www.regencynursinghome.co.uk
**Estd:** 1989 Partnership
**Line of Business:** Nursing homes
**Partners:** M Raven, Mrs J Raven
**Responsibilities**
**Senior:** Sen Bungaroo *(Proprietor)*
**US SIC:** 8051 **UK SIC:** 95100
**Employees:** 50

DUNS 22-108-4275
## Regency Security Services Ltd
Regency House Freeport Office, Braintree, Essex CM77 8YG
**Tel:** 01376528888
**Web:** www.regencysecurity.co.uk
**Reg No:** 4127718 **Estd:** 2000 Private Limited Company
**Line of Business:** Security and related activities
**Issued Capital:** £100
**Director:** G Powers
**Branches:** Regency Security Services Ltd, 205 Westbury La, Newport Pagnell, Buckinghamshire MK16 8RX
**US SIC:** 7393 **UK SIC:** 83954

| | 30-04-14 | 30-04-13 | 30-04-12 |
|---|---|---|---|
| TA | 508,212 | 508,215 | 511,405 |
| NW | 362,729 | 362,729 | 358,787 |
| WC | 362,729 | 362,729 | 358,787 |

DUNS 77-764-5912
## Regency Shipping Ltd
Unit 15 Trident Industrial Estate, Slough, Berkshire SL3 0AX
**Tel:** 01753287800
**Web:** www.rsllhr.co.uk
**Reg No:** 3020703 **VAT No:** 653644427
**Estd:** 1995 Private Limited Company
**Line of Business:** Activities of other transport agencies
**Issued Capital:** £67,000
**Directors:** D Singh, M H Vincent, S A Grief, N J Garratt, M J Hawkins, R W Maybey
**Co. Secretary:** London Law Secretarial Limited
**Responsibilities**
**IT:** Dave Cooper *(Head of IT)*
**US SIC:** 4712 **UK SIC:** 77002
**Auditors:** Atkinsons

**Bankers:** Barclays Bank Plc (20-38-83)

| | 31-03-14 | 31-03-13 | 31-03-12 |
|---|---|---|---|
| TO | 10,653,321 | 10,884,399 | 10,415,475 |
| P/L | 504,402 | 405,634 | 287,608 |
| NW | 1,614,174 | 1,442,027 | 1,337,887 |
| WC | 1,422,660 | 1,268,292 | 1,166,650 |
| Emp. | 60 | 50 | 46 |

DUNS 21-018-1520
## Regency Taxis
5 Comberton Terrace, Kidderminster, Worcestershire DY10 1QP
**Tel:** 0156266666
**Estd:** 1975 Proprietorship
**Line of Business:** Taxis and private hire vehicles
**Proprietor:** T Owen
**US SIC:** 4121, 7512
**UK SIC:** 72200, 84801
**Employees:** 70

DUNS 76-941-6751
## Regenersis (Glasgow) Ltd
(**Subsidiary of:** Regenersis Plc)
1 James Watt Avenue, Glenrothes, Fife KY7 4UA
**Tel:** 01592774704 **Fax:** 0141-812-1121
**Web:** www.regenersis.com
**Reg No:** 0112872SC **Estd:** 1988 Private Limited Company
**Line of Business:** Mobile phone repairs
**Issued Capital:** £1,000
**Director:** J Dhody
**Co. Secretary:** Lorraine Young Company Secretari
**Responsibilities**
**Senior:** Wayne Halliwell *(Chief Executive)*, Cameron Radford *(Manager)*, Sergio Tansini *(Chief Executive)*
**IT:** Tristian Borrer *(IT Manager)*
**HR:** Archie McLeish *(Health& Safety Officer)*
**US SIC:** 4899, 8999
**UK SIC:** 79020, 83954
**Auditors:** PricewaterhouseCoopers LLP
**Bankers:** The Royal Bank Of Scotland Plc (83-20-27)

| | 30-06-13 | 30-06-12 | 30-06-11 |
|---|---|---|---|
| TO | 21,821,000 | 29,799,000 | 26,121,134 |
| P/L | (795,000) | (3,464,000) | (179,784) |
| NW | (983,000) | (545,000) | 2,351,796 |
| WC | (1,135,000) | (591,000) | 1,209,361 |
| Emp. | 335 | 523 | 565 |

DUNS 21-751-7903 **Imp-Exp**
## Regenersis (Glenrothes) Ltd
(**Subsidiary of:** Regenersis Plc)
1 James Watt Avenue, Westwood Park, Glenrothes, Fife KY7 4UA
**Tel:** 01865 594070
**Web:** www.ratesrecovery.com
**Reg No:** 1319856 **VAT No:** 196192334
**Estd:** 2013 Private Limited Company
**Line of Business:** Manufacture of computers and other information processing equipment
**Export Markets:** U S A, E U
**Trading Style:** C R C
**Issued Capital:** £540,000
**Directors:** W P Hellewell, J A Krauthausen, J Dhody
**Co. Secretary:** Lorraine Young Company Secretari
**Branches:** Regenersis (Glenrothes) Ltd, 1 James Watt Avenue, Glenrothes, Fife KY7 4UA
**US SIC:** 3573 **UK SIC:** 33020
**Auditors:** KPMG Audit PLC
**Bankers:** Barclays Bank Plc (20-85-73)

| | 30-06-13 | 30-06-12 | 30-06-11 |
|---|---|---|---|
| TO | 27,134,000 | 18,846,000 | 17,787,000 |
| P/L | 5,138,000 | 972,000 | 1,937,000 |
| NW | (1,636,000) | 328,000 | 744,000 |
| WC | (2,225,000) | 333,000 | 110,000 |
| Emp. | 510 | 451 | 420 |

DUNS 73-858-8685
## Regenersis Plc
Kingfisher Way, Hichingbrooke Business Park, Huntingdon, Cambridgeshire PE29 6FN
**Tel:** 01480431431 **Fax:** 01865-471935
**Web:** www.regenesis.com
**Reg No:** 5113820 **Estd:** 2004 Public Limited Company
**Line of Business:** Call centres
**Issued Capital:** £994,308
**Directors:** R S Woodward, T A Russell, J Dhody, F Blin, M R Peacock
**Co. Secretary:** Lorraine Young Company Secretari
**Responsibilities**
**Senior:** Billy Goldsmith *(Site Manager)*, David Kelham *(Manager)*, Gary Stokes *(Chief Executive Officer)*
**Branches:** Regenersis Plc, 1 James Watt Avenue, Glenrothes, Fife KY7 4UA
**US SIC:** 7399, 6711
**UK SIC:** 83954, 83962
**Auditors:** KPMG Audit PLC

**Bankers:** Bank Of Scotland (12-20-10)

| | 30-06-14 | 30-06-13 | 30-06-12 |
|---|---|---|---|
| TO | 197,482,000 | 179,714,000 | 139,857,000 |
| P/L | 2,870,000 | 5,671,000 | 1,684,000 |
| NW | 19,573,000 | (5,631,000) | 2,362,000 |
| WC | 22,076,000 | 4,181,000 | 6,190,000 |
| Emp. | 4,212 | 2,681 | 2,401 |

DUNS 50-548-1713
## Regent Academy of Fine Arts Ltd
(**Subsidiary of:** Bsy Group Ltd)
6 John Street, London SE25 4UJ
**Tel:** 0800378281 **Fax:** 020-7430-8401
**Web:** www.royalacademy.org.uk
**Reg No:** 2502592 **Estd:** 1990 Private Limited Company
**Line of Business:** Publishing services
**Issued Capital:** £100
**Managing Director:** P Laniado
**Co. Secretary:** Andrew Scannell
**Branches:** Regent Academy Of Fine Arts Ltd, Stanhope Sq, Holsworthy, Devon EX22 6DS
**US SIC:** 2741 **UK SIC:** 47541
**Auditors:** BDO Stoy Hayward LLP
**Bankers:** National Westminster Bank Plc (56-00-29)

| | 31-12-13 | 31-12-12 | 31-12-11 |
|---|---|---|---|
| TA | 155,934 | 119,880 | 32,143 |
| NW | 5,508 | 4,937 | 2,896 |
| WC | 5,508 | 4,937 | 1,356 |

DUNS 21-001-3388
## Regent Automotive Ltd
The Hyde, Edgware Road, London NW9 6NW
**Tel:** 0202009797
**Web:** www.volvocarslondon.co.uk
**Reg No:** 6269592 **Estd:** 2007 Private Limited Company
**Line of Business:** Car dealers (new & used)
**Issued Capital:** £500,000
**Directors:** A Shackleton, J R Caney
**Co. Secretary:** Andrew Shackleton
**Responsibilities**
**Senior:** Tom Horna *(Dealer Principal)*, Tracey Perry *(Manager)*
**US SIC:** 5511, 5521
**UK SIC:** 65100

| | 31-12-13 | 31-12-12 | 31-12-11 |
|---|---|---|---|
| TO | 61,865,678 | 60,005,222 | 57,710,952 |
| P/L | 910,610 | 301,454 | 410,372 |
| NW | 2,281,302 | 1,916,571 | 1,699,850 |
| WC | (385,752) | (715,368) | (440,033) |
| Emp. | 193 | 198 | 165 |

DUNS 21-600-6784
## Regent Cambridge
119 Mill Road, Cambridge, Cambridgeshire CB1 2AZ
**Tel:** 01223312333
**Web:** www.regent.org.uk
**Estd:** 1984 Proprietorship
**Line of Business:** Technical and vocational secondary education
**Proprietor:** Ms N Albert
**Responsibilities**
**Senior:** Najah Hussain *(Principal)*
**US SIC:** 8249 **UK SIC:** 93300
**Employees:** 46

DUNS 21-124-2739
## Regent College
Regent Road, Leicester, Leicestershire LE1 7LW
**Tel:** 01162-554629
**Web:** www.regent-college.ac.uk
**Estd:** 1996 Partnership
**Line of Business:** Further education schools and colleges
**Trading Style:** Regent College
**Partner:** E Playfair
**Responsibilities**
**Finance:** Alan Staniforth *(Financial Manager)*
**Marketing:** Rhiannon Lloyd-Jones *(Marketing Manager)*
**Admin:** Lynn Murdoch *(Administration Manager)*
**IT:** Chris Swain *(IT Network Manager)*
**HR:** Rhiannon Lloyd-Jones *(Marketing Manager)*, Lynn Murdoch *(Administration Manager)*
**Health & Safety:** Alan Staniforth *(Financial Manager)*
**Purchasing:** Alan Staniforth *(Financial Manager)*
**US SIC:** 8221 **UK SIC:** 93100
**Employees:** 130

DUNS 77-964-7416

## Regent Electrical Sevenoaks Ltd

**(Subsidiary of:** White Strake Investments Ltd)
182-186 Risborough Lane, Folkestone, Kent CT20 3LX
**Tel:** 01303-271010 **Fax:** 01303-273839
**Web:** www.regentelectrical.com
**Reg No:** 5933557 **Estd:** 2006 Private Limited Company
**Line of Business:** Wholesale of radio and television goods; wholesale of electrical household appliances not elsewhere classified
**Trading Style:** Regent Electrical, Regent Electrical Distributors
**Issued Capital:** £200,000
**Directors:** P M Ford, G A Allen, S Charlton
**Co. Secretary:** Nicholas Ford
**US SIC:** 5064 **UK SIC:** 61500

| | 30-06-14 | 30-06-13 | 30-06-12 |
|---|---|---|---|
| TO | 646,629 | 684,148 | 670,707 |
| P/L | 22,658 | 48,972 | (8,462) |
| NW | 236,050 | 219,932 | 184,490 |
| WC | 236,050 | 219,072 | 242,577 |

DUNS 22-226-0502

## Regent Exhibitions Ltd

1st Floor The Agora, Hove, East Sussex BN3 3LN
**Tel:** 01273-227311 **Fax:** 01273227312
**Web:** www.imexexhibitions.com
**Reg No:** 4244004 **Estd:** 2001 Private Limited Company
**Line of Business:** Activities of exhibition and fair organisers
**Issued Capital:** £1,125,030
**Directors:** Mrs C A Bauer, A G Bloom, R A Bloom
**Co. Secretary:** Ms Joanna Frost Maidment
**Responsibilities**
**Senior:** David Broadus *(Database Manager)*
**Marketing:** Oliver Hone *(Marketing Director)*
**US SIC:** 7999 **UK SIC:** 97913

| | 31-12-13 | 31-12-12 | 31-12-11 |
|---|---|---|---|
| TO | 20,294,193 | 17,930,044 | 5,563,630 |
| P/L | 2,724,201 | 3,121,211 | 85,326 |
| NW | 6,810,535 | 6,420,947 | 4,132,772 |
| WC | 6,139,692 | 5,760,864 | 3,593,551 |
| Emp. | 51 | 49 | 49 |

DUNS 21-773-2303

## Regent Farm First School

Wansbeck Road South, Newcastle-Upon-Tyne, Tyne and Wear NE3 3PE
**Tel:** 01912852294
**Web:** www.regentfarmfirstschool.co.uk
**Estd:** 1973 Proprietorship
**Line of Business:** Schools (local authority)
**Proprietor:** Mrs D Ashcroft
**US SIC:** 8211 **UK SIC:** 93200
**Employees:** 51

DUNS 21-327-3329 **Imp**

## Regent Greeting Cards Ltd

Regent House, Dockfield Road, Shipley, West Yorkshire BD17 7SF
**Tel:** 01274580555 **Fax:** 01274580888
**Web:** www.regent-group.com
**Reg No:** 1513675 **Estd:** 1976 Private Limited Company
**Line of Business:** Printers general
**Trading Style:** Expression Factory, Regent Envelopes
**Issued Capital:** £225,000
**Principals:** T Regan *(Chairman)*, D M Regan *(Managing)*, A C Wells, A E Crankshaw, M J Cuthbertson
**Co. Secretary:** Ms Karen England
**Responsibilities**
**Senior:** Julian Robinson *(Manager)*
**HR:** Emma Armytage *(Human Resources Manager)*
**Health & Safety:** Emma Armytage *(Human Resources Manager)*
**Purchasing:** Sheron Parkin *(Production Manager)*
**Engineering:** Sheron Parkin *(Production Manager)*
**Branches:** Regent Greeting Cards Ltd, Regent House, Dockfield Rd, Shipley, West Yorkshire BD17 7SF
**US SIC:** 2648, 2752
**UK SIC:** 47231, 47544
**Auditors:** Ernst & Young LLP
**Bankers:** Lloyds TSB Bank plc (30-91-12)

| | 31-12-12 | 31-12-11 | 31-12-10 |
|---|---|---|---|
| TO | 10,917,653 | 12,481,681 | 12,497,409 |
| P/L | (965,441) | 17,267 | 35,779 |
| NW | 526,003 | 1,460,907 | 1,447,483 |
| WC | 1,779,644 | 661,374 | 583,211 |
| Emp. | 123 | 125 | 124 |

DUNS 21-781-1796

## Regent Hotel

Corran Esplanade, Oban, Argyll PA34 5PZ
**Tel:** 01631562341
**Web:** www.oxfordhotelsandinns.co.uk
**Estd:** 2011 Partnership
**Line of Business:** Hotels
**Partners:** D Fitzsimmons, A Whitlow
**Responsibilities**
**Senior:** Tommy Sutherland *(General Manager)*
**US SIC:** 7011 **UK SIC:** 66500
**Employees:** 50

DUNS 28-880-8777 **Exp**

## Regent Language Training Ltd

**(Subsidiary of:** Oise Holdings Ltd)
12 Buckingham Street, London WC2N 6DF
**Tel:** 020-7872-6620
**Web:** www.regentedinburgh.org.uk
**Reg No:** 1175684 **VAT No:** 242361586
**Estd:** 1974 Private Limited Company
**Line of Business:** Technical and vocational secondary education
**Export Markets:** Poland, Sweden, France
**Trading Style:** Regent London
**Issued Capital:** £1,000
**Director:** T Gins
**Co. Secretary:** Diamond College Limited
**Responsibilities**
**Senior:** Diego Amaya *(Office Manager)*, Janey Futerill *(Principal)*
**Admin:** Diego Amaya *(Office Manager)*
**Branches:** Regent Language Training Ltd, 12 Buckingham Street, London WC2N 6DF
**US SIC:** 8249 **UK SIC:** 93300
**Auditors:** Mazars
**Bankers:** Lloyds TSB Bank plc (30-98-71)

| | 31-12-13 | 31-12-12 | 31-12-11 |
|---|---|---|---|
| TA | 1,000 | 1,000 | 1,000 |
| NW | 1,000 | 1,000 | 1,000 |

DUNS 73-849-2763

## Regent Medical Ltd

**(Subsidiary of:** Investor Ab)
2 Omega Drive, Manchester M44 5BJ
**Tel:** 01616213900
**Reg No:** 5104407 **Estd:** 2004 Private Limited Company
**Line of Business:** Other human health activities
**Issued Capital:** £4,750,001
**Directors:** J A Brannan, R M Bennison, Ms M L Roy, S P Ternstrom
**Co. Secretary:** Christopher Stubbs
**US SIC:** 8091, 5199
**UK SIC:** 95200, 61900
**Auditors:** Deloitte & Touche LLP

| | 31-12-13 | 31-12-12 | 31-12-11 |
|---|---|---|---|
| TO | 43,151,000 | 42,889,000 | 48,395,000 |
| P/L | 19,773,000 | 15,823,000 | 26,586,000 |
| NW | 20,359,000 | 10,453,000 | 9,220,000 |
| WC | (71,621,000) | (30,840,000) | (32,361,000) |

DUNS 55-044-5928

## The Regent Motel

42 Cinque Ports Street, Rye, East Sussex TN31 7AN
**Web:** www.regentmotel.co.uk
**Estd:** 2002 Proprietorship
**Line of Business:** Hotels
**Responsibilities**
**Senior:** S Toby *(Proprietor)*
**US SIC:** 7011 **UK SIC:** 66500
**Bankers:** Lloyds TSB Bank plc (30-90-28)
**Employees:** 84

DUNS 29-664-4552

## Regent Office Care Ltd

**(Subsidiary of:** Figji)
Unit 7, Godalming, Surrey GU7 1XW
**Tel:** 08006781170 **Fax:** 02476 338626
**Web:** www.regentsamsic.com
**Reg No:** 1990614 **VAT No:** 415252873
**Estd:** 1986 Private Limited Company
**Line of Business:** Security activities
**Trading Style:** Regent Cleaning
**Issued Capital:** £834
**Directors:** Ms J D Kingsnorth, J Critchell, J King
**Responsibilities**
**Senior:** Patrick Dubos *(Manager)*, Gerard Jicquel *(Manager)*, Olivier Payen *(Director)*, Christian Roulleau *(Director)*, Gary Sheffield *(Manager)*
**Branches:** Regent Office Care Ltd, 7A Market St, Crediton, Devon EX17 2AJ
**US SIC:** 7393, 7341
**UK SIC:** 83954, 92300
**Auditors:** Nexia Smith & Williamson
**Bankers:** Lloyds TSB Bank plc (30-94-38)

| | 31-12-13 | 31-12-12 | 31-12-11 |
|---|---|---|---|
| TO | 24,551,300 | 25,446,656 | 30,950,313 |
| P/L | (197,644) | 32,095 | 961,176 |
| NW | (1,184,688) | (1,158,116) | (1,294,075) |
| WC | 319,522 | 188,843 | 277,178 |
| Emp. | 2,342 | 3,062 | 3,045 |

DUNS 21-414-4152

## Regent Place

41-43 Regent Road, Stoke-On-Trent, Staffordshire ST1 3BT
**Tel:** 01782263720
**Web:** www.richmondcaregroup.co.uk
**Estd:** 1990
**Line of Business:** Residential care establishments
**Proprietor:** D Vincent
**Responsibilities**
**Senior:** Donna Walklet *(Manager)*
**US SIC:** 8321 **UK SIC:** 96111
**Employees:** 47

DUNS 21-035-0934

## The Regent Shopping Centre

Regent Way, Hamilton, Lanarkshire ML3 7DZ
**Tel:** 01698285947
**Web:** www.regentcentre.co.uk
**Estd:** 1999 Proprietorship
**Line of Business:** Shopping centres
**Proprietor:** A Cameron
**Responsibilities**
**Senior:** Bill Reid *(Centre Manager)*
**US SIC:** 5399 **UK SIC:** 65600
**Employees:** 200

DUNS 21-387-2687

## The Regent Theatre

Stoke-On-Trent Theatres Ltd, Victoria Hall, Bagnall Street, Stoke-On-Trent, Staffordshire ST1 3AD
**Tel:** 01782213800
**Web:** www.ambassadortickets.com
**Proprietorship**
**Line of Business:** Theatres & concert halls
**Proprietor:** R Wingate
**US SIC:** 7911 **UK SIC:** 97913
**Employees:** 128

DUNS 64-096-5968

## Regents Contracting Ltd

Elms House, Church Road, Harold Wood, Romford, Essex RM3 0JU
**Tel:** 01708-384884
**Web:** www.regentscontracting.co.uk
**Reg No:** 3491529 **Estd:** 1998 Private Limited Company
**Line of Business:** Bricklayers
**Issued Capital:** £100
**Director:** M M Parrett
**Co. Secretary:** Beatons Accountants Ltd
**US SIC:** 1799 **UK SIC:** 50000

| | 28-02-14 | 28-02-13 | 28-02-12 |
|---|---|---|---|
| TA | 15,686 | 69,425 | 191,492 |
| NW | (39,928) | (16,356) | (39,118) |
| WC | N/A | (16,356) | (39,118) |

DUNS 21-804-3402

## Regents Park Clinic

121 Harley Street, London W1G 6AX
**Tel:** 08442570660
**Web:** www.doctorcall.co.uk
**Estd:** 2011
**Line of Business:** Clinics private
**Responsibilities**
**Senior:** Linda Cook *(Practice Manager)*
**US SIC:** 8051 **UK SIC:** 95100
**Employees:** 50

DUNS 29-030-4815

## Regent's Park Theatre Ltd

Open Air Theatre Inner Circle, London NW1 4NU
**Tel:** 08443753460 **Fax:** 02072241625
**Web:** www.openairtheatre.com
**Reg No:** 0759557 **Estd:** 1963 Private Limited Company
**Line of Business:** Artistic and literary creation and interpretation
**Issued Capital:** £6
**Directors:** R J Davis, Sir P Rogers, Dame J O Dench, J Reed, R F Noble, M R Wilkinson, Ms P A Ailion
**Co. Secretary:** William Village
**US SIC:** 7999, 8999
**UK SIC:** 97913, 83954
**Auditors:** HLB Kidsons
**Bankers:** Coutts & Co (18-00-02)

| | 31-12-13 | 31-12-12 | 31-12-11 |
|---|---|---|---|
| TO | 6,287,421 | 2,806,154 | 3,961,218 |
| P/L | 1,804,904 | (3,153,505) | 197,555 |
| NW | 2,115,085 | 310,181 | 3,463,687 |
| WC | 2,063,551 | 224,197 | 2,404,095 |
| Emp. | 54 | 49 | 51 |

DUNS 64-253-6460

## Regents Theological College

West Malvern Road, Malvern, Worcestershire WR14 4AY
**Tel:** 03453026758
**Web:** www.regents-tc.ac.uk
**Estd:** 1996
**Line of Business:** Further education schools and colleges
**Director:** Dr W Atkinson
**Responsibilities**
**Senior:** Nigel Tween *(Principal)*
**Finance:** Matt Hunter *(Finance Officer)*
**Admin:** Richard Allsopp *(Database Administrator)*, Katie Cameron *(Faculty Administrator)*, Judy Warrington *(PA to the Princioal)*
**Operations:** Andrew Cave *(Operations Director)*, Phil Hidderley *(Estates Manager)*, Rebekah Marshall *(Admissions & Operations Office)*
**Branches:** London Road, Nantwich, Cheshire CW5 6LW
**US SIC:** 8221 **UK SIC:** 93100
**Employees:** 61

DUNS 28-983-8922

## Regent's University London

Regents Park Inner Circle, London NW1 4NS
**Tel:** 02074877700 **Fax:** 02078777425
**Web:** www.regents.ac.uk
**Reg No:** 1791760 **Estd:** 2002 Private Company Limited By Guarantee
**Line of Business:** First-degree level higher education
**Directors:** Doctor C M Mcconnell, Ms C D Baume, I N Mehrtens, Ms S B Milne, L J Barrett, T J Weekenborg, Miss C A Richmond, A J Cooper
**Co. Secretary:** Ms Sinead Mcquillan
**Responsibilities**
**Senior:** Anne Cleveland *(Director)*, Marguerite Dennis *(Director)*, Matthias Feist *(Director)*, Dominic Laffy *(Director)*, Pamela Loch *(Director)*, Andrew Masheter *(Director)*, Elisa Nardi *(Director)*, Stephen Newstead *(Director)*, Murray Thomas *(Director)*
**Facilities:** Jim Dillon *(Facilities Manager)*
**US SIC:** 8221 **UK SIC:** 93100
**Auditors:** BDO LLP
**Bankers:** Barclays Bank Plc (20-65-82)

| | 31-07-14 | 31-07-13 | 31-07-12 |
|---|---|---|---|
| TO | 53,170,000 | 48,196,000 | 41,468,000 |
| P/L | (2,489,000) | 1,730,000 | 861,000 |
| NW | 17,776,000 | 20,189,000 | 18,135,000 |
| WC | 2,241,000 | 5,780,000 | 3,735,000 |
| Emp. | 584 | 526 | 443 |

DUNS 22-936-7149

## Reginald Hogg Holdings Ltd

Sounding Hill Quarry, Tobermore Road, Magherafelt, Co Londonderry BT45 5EJ
**Tel:** 028-7963-2364 **Fax:** 02879632834
**Reg No:** 0021328NI **Estd:** 1988 Private Limited Company
**Line of Business:** Management activities of holding companies
**Export Sales:** £625,496
**Issued Capital:** £27,002
**Directors:** Dr F W Hogg, R Hogg, S R Hogg, I F Hogg, R Hogg, J F Hogg
**Co. Secretary:** Dr Frederick Hogg
**US SIC:** 6711, 3272
**UK SIC:** 83962, 24370
**Auditors:** John Graves & Co
**Bankers:** Northern Bank Ltd (95-03-81)

| | 31-03-14 | 31-03-13 | 31-03-12 |
|---|---|---|---|
| TO | 12,803,441 | 11,353,870 | 15,705,640 |
| P/L | (276,051) | (1,240,722) | 70,359 |
| NW | 8,535,351 | 8,811,402 | 10,052,124 |
| WC | 6,010,080 | 6,452,356 | 7,622,705 |
| Emp. | 91 | 82 | 87 |

DUNS 21-211-7451

## Reginald Maude Ltd

Globe House, Miall Street, Halifax, West Yorkshire HX1 4AE
**Tel:** 01422252525
**Web:** www.rmltd.co.uk
**Reg No:** 0320694 **VAT No:** 183665631
**Estd:** 1936 Private Limited Company
**Line of Business:** Electrical contractors and electricians
**Issued Capital:** £2,280
**Principals:** M P Maude *(Chairman and Managing)*, D Cameron *(Managing)*, Ms A Wright *(Financial)*, M C Maude
**US SIC:** 1731 **UK SIC:** 50300
**Auditors:** Riley & Co Ltd
**Bankers:** Barclays Bank Plc (20-35-84)

| | 30-09-14 | 30-09-13 | 30-09-12 |
|---|---|---|---|
| TA | 1,085,124 | 936,587 | 1,074,861 |
| NW | 548,888 | 536,518 | 466,577 |
| WC | 375,560 | 351,120 | 283,428 |

DUNS 49-497-1997

## Reginson Engineering Ltd

Whitacre Road Industrial Estate, Nuneaton, Warwickshire CV11 6BX
**Tel:** 02476385807 **Fax:** 02476385981
**Web:** www.reginson.com
**Reg No:** 3159353 **VAT No:** 620324881
**Estd:** 1995 Private Limited Company
**Line of Business:** Other engineering activities
**Export Sales:** £2,195,618
**Issued Capital:** £1,000
**Director:** S J Hatch
**Co. Secretary:** Ms Christine Hatch
**Responsibilities**
**Operations:** Steve Cramphorn *(Operations Manager)*
**US SIC:** 8999 **UK SIC:** 83954
**Auditors:** Shah & Co

**Bankers:** National Westminster Bank Plc (54-21-13)

| | 30-11-13 | 30-11-12 | 30-11-11 |
|---|---|---|---|
| TO | 6,587,908 | 6,161,695 | N/A |
| P/L | 907,861 | 496,923 | N/A |
| NW | 2,790,514 | 2,178,309 | 1,849,767 |
| WC | 1,282,617 | 809,460 | 1,210,470 |
| Emp. | 81 | 76 | N/A |

DUNS 50-571-0715

## Regional Airports Ltd

Wellhouse Farm, Hook, Hampshire RG29 1TL
**Tel:** 01256862059 **Fax:** 01256862115
**Web:** www.regionalairportslimited.com
**Reg No:** 2519047 **Estd:** 1990 Private Limited Company
**Line of Business:** Other supporting air transport activities
**Issued Capital:** £88,500
**Directors:** W D Lowe, A R Walters, M B Del Mar, P Lonergan
**Co. Secretary:** Tmf Corporate Administration Ser
**Responsibilities**
**Senior:** Jenny Munroe *(MD)*
**US SIC:** 7399 **UK SIC:** 83954
**Auditors:** Smith & Williamson
**Bankers:** The Royal Bank Of Scotland Plc (15-10-00)

| | 31-03-14 | 31-03-13 | 31-03-12 |
|---|---|---|---|
| TO | 13,721,068 | 12,961,324 | 12,520,975 |
| P/L | 747,504 | 652,633 | 453,852 |
| NW | 17,807,670 | 17,671,023 | 17,953,073 |
| WC | 4,437,467 | 4,592,718 | 4,646,785 |
| Emp. | 98 | 100 | 89 |

DUNS 21-391-3198

## Regional Care Services

10 Pyle Street, Newport, Isle of Wight PO30 1JW
**Tel:** 01983530981
**Web:** www.carewatch.co.uk
**Estd:** 2006 Proprietorship
**Line of Business:** Home care and help services
**Proprietor:** Mrs M Bunce
**US SIC:** 2711 **UK SIC:** 47512
**Employees:** 125

DUNS 73-845-5745

## Regional Contract Services Ltd

Unit 6 1b Bethwin Road, London SE5 0SN
**Tel:** 02077083814
**Web:** www.regionalservices.co.uk
**Reg No:** 5100805 **Estd:** 2004 Private Limited Company
**Line of Business:** Cleaning contracting commercial
**Issued Capital:** £2
**Director:** M Jardim
**Co. Secretary:** William Proctor
**Responsibilities**
**Senior:** William Potter *(Manager)*
**US SIC:** 7349 **UK SIC:** 92300

| | 30-04-14 | 30-04-13 | 30-04-12 |
|---|---|---|---|
| TA | 682,242 | 623,719 | 601,417 |
| NW | (1,614) | (12,507) | (21,091) |
| WC | (96,305) | (106,828) | (114,092) |

DUNS 73-760-6462

## Regional Hearing Services Ltd

(**Subsidiary of:** Widex Holding A/S)
111-113 Fore Street, Saltash, Cornwall PL12 6AE
**Tel:** 01752840835
**Web:** www.regionalhearingservices.co.uk
**Reg No:** 5018028 **Estd:** 2006 Private Limited Company
**Line of Business:** Retail sale of hearing aids
**Issued Capital:** £200
**Directors:** A J Carmichael, J Jensen, C M Jensen, J Rekling, J Goudie
**Responsibilities**
**Senior:** A Carmicheal *(Manager)*, Jan-peter Rekling *(Director)*, Anders Westermann *(Manager)*
**US SIC:** 3841 **UK SIC:** 37201

| | 30-04-14 | 30-04-13 | 30-04-12 |
|---|---|---|---|
| TO | 13,788,865 | 12,604,151 | 9,126,617 |
| P/L | (1,487,561) | (8,057,555) | (1,100,426) |
| NW | (237,152) | (3,441,163) | (1,796,625) |
| WC | (709,244) | (1,259,518) | (752,100) |
| Emp. | 166 | 177 | 116 |

DUNS 64-738-4601

## Regional Training Unit C/O Balmoral High School

Blacks Road, Belfast BT10 0NB
**Tel:** 02890618121
**Web:** www.otuni.org
**Estd:** 1990
**Line of Business:** Education agencies and authorities
**Trading Style:** R T U
**Proprietor:** Dr T Hesketh
**US SIC:** 8299 **UK SIC:** 93300
**Employees:** 48

DUNS 76-837-5784

## Regis Uk Ltd

(**Subsidiary of:** Regis Corporation)
1st Floor - Lynchgate House, Coventry, West Midlands CV4 7EH
**Tel:** 024-7684-0300 **Fax:** 024-7684-0301
**Web:** www.regissalons.co.uk
**Reg No:** 2603786 **Estd:** 1991 Private Limited Company
**Line of Business:** Hairdressers (unisex)
**Issued Capital:** £1,000
**Directors:** Ms J Lang, E A Bakken
**Co. Secretary:** Michael Haringman
**Branches:** Regis Uk Ltd, 39 Monmouth Street, Bath, Avon BA1 2AN
**US SIC:** 7231 **UK SIC:** 98200
**Auditors:** Baker Tilly UK Audit LLP

| | 29-06-13 | 30-06-12 | 25-06-11 |
|---|---|---|---|
| TO | 76,882,000 | 83,541,000 | 89,041,000 |
| P/L | (2,594,000) | (735,000) | 2,123,000 |
| NW | 23,552,000 | 12,121,000 | 12,605,000 |
| WC | 17,654,000 | 4,185,000 | 5,140,000 |
| Emp. | 2,358 | 2,485 | 2,594 |

DUNS 54-863-5366

## Registers of Scotland

Meadowbank House, 153 London Road, Edinburgh, Midlothian EH8 7AU
**Tel:** 0845 607 0161
**Web:** www.ros.gov.uk
**Estd:** 2002
**Line of Business:** Births, marriage & deaths registration offices
**Managing Director:** F Mansen
**Responsibilities**
**Senior:** Stephen Dingle *(Non Executive Director)*, Jim Meldrum *(CEO)*
**Finance:** Allisson Chisholn *(Senior Finance Administrator)*
**Marketing:** Kenny Crawford *(Business Development Manager)*
**Sales:** Kenny Crawford *(Business Development Manager)*
**Admin:** Ruth Webster *(Communications Office Manager)*
**IT:** Keith Harkness *(Computer Operations Manager)*
**Health & Safety:** Alan Low *(Health & Safety Officer)*
**Branches:** Registers Of Scotland, 9 George Square, Glasgow, Lanarkshire G2 1DY
**US SIC:** 9121 **UK SIC:** 91110
**Employees:** 1,400

DUNS 21-589-7087

## Registration of Births Deaths & Civil Ceremonies

Invicta House, Maidstone, Kent ME14 1XX
**Tel:** 03000416262
**Web:** www.kent.gov.uk
**Estd:** 2011 Proprietorship
**Line of Business:** Library and archive activities
**Proprietor:** G Adey
**US SIC:** 8231 **UK SIC:** 97700
**Employees:** 200

DUNS 21-414-4204

## Registration of Births Deaths & Marriages

Penallta House, Tredomen Park, Ystrad Mynach, Hengoed, Mid Glamorgan CF82 7PG
**Tel:** 01443-863478
**Estd:** 2002
**Line of Business:** Births, marriage & deaths registration offices
**Responsibilities**
**Senior:** Della Mahoney *(Registrar)*
**US SIC:** 8231 **UK SIC:** 97700
**Employees:** 500

DUNS 23-944-1301

## Registration Transfers Ltd

Transfer House, 139 High St South, Dunstable, Bedfordshire LU6 3SS
**Fax:** 01582-607713
**Web:** www.regtransfers.co.uk
**Reg No:** 3933658 **Estd:** 2000 Private Limited Company
**Line of Business:** Retail sale via mail order house
**Issued Capital:** £1,000
**Director:** T B Brown
**Co. Secretary:** Paul Brown
**US SIC:** 5961 **UK SIC:** 65600
**Bankers:** Barclays Bank Plc (20-00-00)

| | 28-02-14 | 28-02-13 | 29-02-12 |
|---|---|---|---|
| TO | 31,675,964 | 31,062,318 | 32,140,823 |
| P/L | 2,879,498 | 1,552,929 | 2,771,636 |
| NW | 9,016,922 | 7,228,530 | 5,792,918 |
| WC | (2,511,756) | (3,633,764) | (2,206,296) |
| Emp. | 93 | 91 | 93 |

DUNS 21-070-7534

## Registry of Shipping and Seamen

Mca Cardiff Anchor Court, Keen Road, Cardiff, South Glamorgan CF24 5JW
**Tel:** 02920448800
**Proprietorship**
**Line of Business:** Legislative Bodies
**Proprietor:** Mrs C Bradshaw
**US SIC:** 9121 **UK SIC:** 91110
**Employees:** 50

DUNS 21-912-0748 **Imp**

## Regorco Ltd

(**Subsidiary of:** Chargill (Holdings) Ltd)
Walton Road, Drakelow, Burton-On-Trent, Staffordshire DE15 9UA
**Tel:** 01283-511115 **Fax:** 01283512233
**Web:** www.roger-bullivant.co.uk
**Reg No:** 1022309 **Estd:** 1971 Private Limited Company
**Line of Business:** Manufacture pilings & precast concrete building products & underpinning contractors group head office 11 sites
**Issued Capital:** £225,000
**Directors:** J E Brown, R Brown
**Co. Secretary:** Robert Brown
**Responsibilities**
**Finance:** Mike Harris *(Financial Director)*
**Health & Safety:** John Fawcett *(Health & Safety Officer)*
**Branches:** Regorco Ltd, First Floor, Unit 1, Wilks Avenue, Dartford, Kent DA1 1JS
**US SIC:** 1799 **UK SIC:** 50000
**Auditors:** H W
**Bankers:** National Westminster Bank Plc (60-02-35)

| | 31-10-11 |
|---|---|
| TO | 50,132,038 |
| P/L | 372,952 |
| Emp. | 556 |

DUNS 21-584-2508

## Regulatory Services Economic Development

Liberation Place, Jersey, Channel Islands JE1 1BB
**Tel:** 01534448120
**Web:** www.gov.je
**Estd:** 2011
**Line of Business:** General (overall) public service activities
**Proprietor:** Ms H Grimes
**US SIC:** 9121 **UK SIC:** 91110
**Employees:** 50

DUNS 23-287-2056

## Regus Business Services Ltd

(**Subsidiary of:** Regus Plc)
Regus House, Belfast BT1 3BW
**Tel:** 08708808484
**Web:** www.regus.co.uk
**Reg No:** 0042675NI **Estd:** 2010 Private Limited Company
**Line of Business:** Tour operators
**Issued Capital:** £100
**Directors:** Ms X Walters, P D Gibson, R Morris
**Responsibilities**
**Senior:** Paul Coyle *(Centre Manager)*
**US SIC:** 7999, 6531
**UK SIC:** 97913, 83400
**Auditors:** KPMG

| | 31-12-13 | 31-12-12 | 31-12-11 |
|---|---|---|---|
| TO | 2,976,000 | 3,195,000 | 5,776,000 |
| P/L | 129,000 | 169,000 | 305,000 |
| NW | 881,000 | 1,332,000 | 1,163,000 |
| WC | 623,000 | 1,002,000 | 890,000 |
| Emp. | 65 | 67 | 129 |

DUNS 21-697-7670

## Regus Group Services Ltd

(**Subsidiary of:** Regus Plc)
268 Bath Road, Slough, Berkshire SL1 4DX
**Web:** http://offices.regus.co.uk
**Reg No:** 7434265 **Estd:** 2010 Private Limited Company
**Line of Business:** Management of real estate on a fee or contract basis
**Issued Capital:** £1
**Directors:** T S Regan, R S Bertasi, R J Lobo, S J Wetherall
**US SIC:** 6531, 6711
**UK SIC:** 83400, 83962

| | 31-12-13 | 31-12-12 | 31-12-11 |
|---|---|---|---|
| TO | 55,645,000 | 42,365,000 | 29,987,000 |
| P/L | 4,246,000 | 5,472,000 | 153,000 |
| NW | 12,757,000 | 8,208,000 | 2,630,000 |
| WC | 9,849,000 | 5,985,000 | 872,000 |
| Emp. | 374 | 203 | 154 |

DUNS 34-617-7108

## Regus Management (Uk) Ltd

Princess House, Swansea, West Glamorgan SA1 3LW
**Tel:** 01792482482
**Web:** www.regus.co.uk
**Reg No:** 2755077 **Estd:** 1992 Private Limited Company
**Line of Business:** Other letting of own property
**Issued Capital:** £100
**Directors:** P D Gibson, R Morris
**US SIC:** 7399 **UK SIC:** 83954
**Auditors:** KPMG
**Bankers:** Lloyds TSB Bank plc (30-94-31)

| | 31-12-13 | 31-12-12 | 31-12-11 |
|---|---|---|---|
| TO | N/A | 25,197,000 | 30,679,000 |
| P/L | 7,305,000 | 2,700,000 | 2,303,000 |
| NW | 10,501,000 | 3,696,000 | 996,000 |
| WC | 10,314,000 | 3,391,000 | 813,000 |
| Emp. | 860 | 863 | 887 |

DUNS 21-558-1061

## Regus Plc

Exchange House, 494, Midsummer Boulevard, Milton Keynes, Buckinghamshire MK9 2EA
**Tel:** 08453003585
**Web:** www.regus.co.uk
**Reg No:** 0101523J **Estd:** 2006 Public Limited Company
**Line of Business:** Business and commerce centres
**Responsibilities**
**Senior:** Judith Bennett *(Centre Manager)*
**Branches:** Regus Plc, Regus House, Whitehill Way, Swindon, Wiltshire SN5 6QR
**US SIC:** 7392, 6531
**UK SIC:** 83951, 83400
**Auditors:** KPMG

**Following financial data are in thousands**

| | 31-12-12 | 31-12-11 | 31-12-10 |
|---|---|---|---|
| TO | 1,244,100 | 1,162,600 | 1,040,400 |
| P/L | 85,100 | 45,500 | 7,800 |
| NW | 163,500 | 157,400 | 154,900 |
| WC | (183,700) | (102,200) | (75,200) |
| Emp. | 7,138 | 6,452 | N/A |

DUNS 21-712-1287

## Rehab Jobfit Llp

Lombard House, 145 Great Charles St Queensway, Birmingham, West Midlands B3 3LP
**Tel:** 01212005900
**Web:** www.tbglearning.com
**Reg No:** 0361645OC **Estd:** 2011
**Line of Business:** Training providers
**US SIC:** 7361, 8299
**UK SIC:** 83954, 93300
**Bankers:** Barclays Bank Plc (20-07-71)

| | 31-12-13 | 31-12-12 | 31-12-11 |
|---|---|---|---|
| TO | 23,261,509 | 17,109,050 | 7,204,670 |
| P/L | 1,839,243 | 369,384 | 13,640 |
| NW | 31,098 | 383,024 | 13,640 |
| WC | (131,111) | 299,863 | (52,996) |

DUNS 49-095-0896

## Rehabilitation Education & Community Homes Ltd

Marcus Lee & Co, Gerrards Cross, Buckinghamshire SL9 8ES
**Tel:** 01753-888688
**Web:** www.reach-disabilitycare.co.uk
**Reg No:** 3092509 **Estd:** 1995 Private Limited Company
**Line of Business:** Other human health activities
**Issued Capital:** £50,000
**Director:** A Shams
**Co. Secretary:** Nasrin Saeedi-Faskhoudi
**Responsibilities**
**Marketing:** Suzie Holton *(Marketing Manager)*
**HR:** Julie Hall *(Personnel Manager)*
**Branches:** Rehabilitation Education & Community Homes Ltd, Stoke Pl, Stoke Grn, Stoke Poges, Slough, Berkshire SL2 4HT
**US SIC:** 8091 **UK SIC:** 95200
**Auditors:** MacIntyre Hudson LLP
**Bankers:** National Westminster Bank Plc (60-13-28)

| | 30-06-13 | 30-06-12 | 30-06-11 |
|---|---|---|---|
| TO | 4,551,579 | 4,385,006 | 4,149,153 |
| P/L | 955,517 | 951,528 | 1,128,708 |
| NW | 5,085,293 | 4,409,776 | 3,757,033 |
| WC | 836,098 | 746,097 | 144,157 |
| Emp. | 139 | 125 | 105 |

DUNS 76-420-7510

## Rehabilitation for Addicted Prisoners Trust

17-19 Oval Way, London SE11 5RR
**Tel:** 02037525560 **Fax:** 020-7820-3716
**Web:** www.rapt.org.uk
**Reg No:** 2560474 **Estd:** 1990 Private Limited Company
**Line of Business:** Counselling & advice services

**Directors:** Lady L Gibbings, Hon Mrs I A Laurent, Ms B Refson, Obe, P B Houghton, Dr M Wilks, J N Wates, Obe, The Hon D S Bernstein, J Mason
**Co. Secretary:** Miss Merlin Gaston
**Responsibilities**
**Senior:** Mike Trace *(Chief Executive Officer)*, John Wates Obe *(Director)*
**US SIC:** 8321 **UK SIC:** 96111
**Bankers:** National Westminster Bank Plc (51-50-14)

| | 31-03-14 | 31-03-13 | 31-03-12 |
|---|---|---|---|
| TO | 18,134,000 | 14,323,000 | 10,246,000 |
| P/L | 240,000 | 490,000 | 79,000 |
| NW | 2,916,000 | 2,719,000 | 2,233,000 |
| WC | 2,901,000 | 2,694,000 | 2,207,000 |
| Emp. | 463 | 349 | 310 |

DUNS 73-744-9079
## Rehabworks Ltd
**(Subsidiary of:** Alcumus Acquisitions Ltd)
Suffolk House, Bury St Edmunds, Suffolk IP33 1UZ
**Tel:** 01284-748340 **Fax:** 01284-748342
**Web:** www.rehabworks.co.uk
**Reg No:** 5002629 **Estd:** 1996 Private Limited Company
**Line of Business:** Other human health activities
**Trading Style:** Rehabworks Ltd
**Issued Capital:** £1,000
**Directors:** G J Kane, A D Holdcroft, M R Armour, S D Lambert
**Co. Secretary:** Andrew Holdcroft
**Responsibilities**
**Senior:** Andy Holdsworth *(Manager)*
**Finance:** Emma Pope *(Accountant)*
**Marketing:** Kate Dennehy *(Sales & Marketing Manager)*
**Sales:** Kate Dennehy *(Sales & Marketing Manager)*
**HR:** Julie Elsegood *(HR Manager)*
**US SIC:** 8091 **UK SIC:** 95200
**Auditors:** Grant Thornton UK LLP

| | 31-07-13 | 31-07-12 | 31-07-11 |
|---|---|---|---|
| TO | 6,571,108 | 5,269,700 | 3,857,440 |
| P/L | (1,638,635) | 17,475 | 85,279 |
| NW | 510,245 | 2,141,505 | 2,111,037 |
| WC | 296,810 | 1,982,894 | 1,915,750 |
| Emp. | 102 | N/A | N/A |

DUNS 21-628-9603 **Imp-Exp**
## Rehau Ltd
**(Subsidiary of:** Wagner Holding Ag)
Hill Court, Walford, Ross-On-Wye, Herefordshire HR9 5QN
**Tel:** 01989-762600
**Web:** www.rehau.co.uk
**Reg No:** 0722004 **VAT No:** 578184008
**Estd:** 1962 Private Limited Company
**Line of Business:** Representative office
**Export Sales:** £10,417,233
**Issued Capital:** £26,900,000
**Principals:** H E Wagner *(Chairman)*, C T Ware, M J Hitchin, M R Baker
**Co. Secretary:** Carlos Esteves
**Responsibilities**
**Senior:** Rudolf Hasert *(Manager)*, Erika White *(Manager)*
**Admin:** Paul Sabel *(Administration Manager)*, Jacquelyn Woodhouse *(PA to CEO (Martin Hitchin))*
**IT:** Shaun Williams *(IT Manager)*
**Health & Safety:** Richard Bladon *(Health & Safety Officer)*
**Facilities:** Ian Grifenthwaite *(Estates Manager)*
**Branches:** Rehau Ltd, Northbank Industrial Estate, Brinell Drive, Irlam, Manchester M44 5BL
**US SIC:** 1721 **UK SIC:** 50400
**Auditors:** PricewaterhouseCoopers LLP
**Bankers:** Barclays Bank Plc (20-78-58)

| | 31-12-13 | 31-12-12 | 31-12-11 |
|---|---|---|---|
| TO | 80,173,655 | 77,287,142 | 84,025,402 |
| P/L | (644,669) | (860,528) | (249,104) |
| NW | 13,339,196 | 13,332,161 | 15,283,836 |
| WC | 14,904,006 | 15,751,251 | 16,508,408 |
| Emp. | 460 | 497 | 520 |

DUNS 21-224-1764 **Imp**
## Reid Egan Stationery Co Ltd
Horsfield Way, Stockport, Cheshire SK6 2SU
**Web:** www.eganreid.co.uk
**Reg No:** 0593651 **VAT No:** 145602680
**Estd:** 1957 Private Limited Company
**Line of Business:** Commercial stationery supplies
**Trading Style:** Reid Egan Stationery Co Ltd
**Issued Capital:** £1,200
**Principals:** J Reid *(Chairman)*, A R Reid *(Managing)*, M J Reid *(Managing)*
**Co. Secretary:** Jack Reid
**Responsibilities**
**Finance:** Brent Derbyshire *(Financial Manager)*
**Purchasing:** Mike Lord *(Purchasing Manager)*
**US SIC:** 5942, 5199
**UK SIC:** 65300, 61900
**Auditors:** Wyatt Morris Golland & Co

**Bankers:** Barclays Bank Plc (20-82-14)

| | 31-03-14 | 31-03-13 | 31-03-12 |
|---|---|---|---|
| TO | 13,209,371 | 11,540,482 | 9,006,057 |
| P/L | 129,897 | 307,902 | 221,151 |
| NW | (215,711) | (305,531) | 673,896 |
| WC | (158,412) | (104,301) | 549,917 |
| Emp. | 82 | 74 | 59 |

DUNS 22-226-0080
## Reid Furniture (2014) Ltd
**(Subsidiary of:** Steinhoff International Holdings Ltd)
50 Dorchester Road, Lytchett Minster, Poole, Dorset BH16 6JE
**Tel:** 07739072003 **Fax:** 01708-630624
**Web:** www.jwcarpentryltd.com
**Reg No:** 4243961 **Estd:** 2010 Private Limited Company
**Line of Business:** Carpenters
**Trading Style:** The Kitchen Studio
**Issued Capital:** £100
**Director:** S Reents
**Responsibilities**
**Senior:** Johnathan White *(Manager)*
**Branches:** Reid Furniture (2014) Ltd, Unit 5 East Kent Retail Park Westwood R, Broadstairs, Kent CT10 2RQ
**US SIC:** 7399 **UK SIC:** 83954
**Auditors:** Deloitte & Touche LLP
**Bankers:** National Westminster Bank Plc (60-13-19)

| | 30-06-13 | 30-06-12 | 25-06-11 |
|---|---|---|---|
| NW | (5,121,000) | (5,121,000) | (5,121,000) |

DUNS 21-762-0914
## Reigate College
Castlefield Road, Reigate, Surrey RH2 0SD
**Tel:** 01737 221118
**Web:** www.reigate.ac.uk
**Estd:** 1974
**Line of Business:** Schools (local authority)
**US SIC:** 8211 **UK SIC:** 93200
**Employees:** 188

DUNS 57-844-3764
## Reilly Concrete Pumping Ltd
Old Premier Stone Yard, Station Road, St Helens, Merseyside WA9 3JG
**Tel:** 01744-819995
**Web:** www.reilly-concretepumping.com
**Reg No:** 2897319 **Estd:** 1994 Private Limited Company
**Line of Business:** Concrete pumping services
**Issued Capital:** £10,000
**Director:** B Reilly
**Co. Secretary:** Wayne Critchley
**US SIC:** 1622 **UK SIC:** 50200
**Auditors:** Joe Saldanha Co

| | 31-12-13 | 31-12-12 | 31-12-11 |
|---|---|---|---|
| TA | 5,436,018 | 3,928,810 | 3,917,373 |
| NW | 2,919,923 | 2,766,256 | 2,890,961 |
| WC | 1,054,839 | 1,016,554 | 565,412 |

DUNS 23-657-7453
## Reilly Holdings Ltd
Highfield Court, Tollgate, Chandler's Ford, Eastleigh, Hampshire SO53 3TY
**Tel:** 023-8062-9900
**Reg No:** 3652736 **Estd:** 1998 Private Limited Company
**Line of Business:** Construction of commercial buildings
**Issued Capital:** £45,000
**Directors:** D P Reilly, M J Reilly
**Co. Secretary:** John Reilly
**US SIC:** 1541 **UK SIC:** 50100
**Auditors:** Baker Tilly Audit Ltd
**Bankers:** The Bank Of Ireland (30-14-39)

| | 31-08-14 | 31-08-13 | 31-08-12 |
|---|---|---|---|
| TO | 59,507,558 | 46,216,555 | 43,952,858 |
| P/L | 3,370,252 | 3,471,731 | 1,808,311 |
| NW | 7,206,876 | 5,266,722 | 3,365,903 |
| WC | 6,007,033 | 3,967,399 | 2,535,255 |
| Emp. | 191 | 177 | 187 |

DUNS 23-697-5608
## Reiss (Holdings) Ltd
12 Eastbury Road, London E6 6LP
**Tel:** 02074739633 **Fax:** 0207 473 9639
**Web:** www.reiss.com
**Reg No:** 3692285 **Estd:** 1999 Private Limited Company
**Line of Business:** Management activities of other non-financial holding companies not elsewhere classified
**Export Sales:** £21,831,000
**Issued Capital:** £1,014,503
**Principals:** D A Reiss *(Managing)*, D Reiss, Ms D Reiss, A S Jacobs, A Jacobs
**Co. Secretary:** Steven Downes
**Branches:** Reiss (Holdings) Ltd, Princes House, 46-48 Stanley Street, Liverpool, Merseyside L1 6AL
**US SIC:** 7399, 5621
**UK SIC:** 83954, 64500
**Auditors:** Wilder Coe LLP

**Bankers:** Barclays Bank Plc (20-00-00)

| | 31-01-14 | 31-01-13 | 31-01-12 |
|---|---|---|---|
| TO | 115,936,000 | 106,097,000 | 100,022,000 |
| P/L | 2,878,000 | (6,177,000) | 3,019,000 |
| NW | 15,772,000 | 14,758,000 | 21,367,000 |
| WC | (4,775,000) | (8,794,000) | (4,848,000) |
| Emp. | 1,379 | 1,223 | 1,193 |

DUNS 77-000-4653
## Reiss Ltd
**(Subsidiary of:** Reiss (Holdings) Ltd)
12 Picton Place, London W1U 1BW
**Tel:** 02030-752-000 **Fax:** 02030-752-001
**Web:** www.reiss.co.uk
**Reg No:** 2655347 **VAT No:** 563052362
**Estd:** 2007 Private Limited Company
**Line of Business:** Representative office
**Export Sales:** £6,315,000
**Trading Style:** Reiss Online
**Issued Capital:** £265,810
**Principals:** D A Reiss *(Managing)*, A Jacobs, D Reiss, Ms D Reiss
**Co. Secretary:** Steven Downes
**Responsibilities**
**Senior:** Daniel O'shea *(Office Manager)*, Paul Petts *(Warehouse Manager)*
**IT:** Hugh Raeburn *(Chief Information Officer)*
**Facilities:** Larisa Stahic *(Facilities & Maintenance Coord)*
**Branches:** Reiss Ltd, 32A New Street, Birmingham, West Midlands B2 4RQ
**US SIC:** 5641, 2339
**UK SIC:** 64500, 45330
**Auditors:** Wilder Coe LLP
**Bankers:** Barclays Bank Plc (20-65-82)

| | 31-01-14 | 31-01-13 | 31-01-12 |
|---|---|---|---|
| TO | 98,281,000 | 91,960,000 | 91,060,000 |
| P/L | 3,557,000 | (4,798,000) | 3,644,000 |
| NW | 17,193,000 | 15,470,000 | 20,700,000 |
| WC | 1,019,000 | (1,905,000) | 588,000 |
| Emp. | 1,174 | 1,039 | 1,109 |

DUNS 21-586-6831
## Rejects
123 St Clair Street, Kirkcaldy, Fife KY1 2BS
**Tel:** 01592655955
**Web:** www.rejectsonline.com
**Estd:** 1978
**Line of Business:** Departmental stores
**Partners:** Mrs A M Cruickshank, Ms C Cruickshank, A Cruickshank, A Cruickshank
**Branches:** Rejects, 129 South St, St. Andrews, Fife KY16 9UN
**US SIC:** 5399, 5714, 5719
**UK SIC:** 65600, 64700
**Bankers:** Bank Of Scotland (80-16-84)
**Employees:** 51

DUNS 56-988-6757
## Rel Ltd
**(Subsidiary of:** Rbg Property Group Ltd)
Dale Road, Worthing, West Sussex BN11 2RU
**Tel:** 08451279331 **Fax:** 01323-740023
**Web:** www.rossetts.co.uk
**Reg No:** 2856048 **Estd:** 1993 Private Limited Company
**Line of Business:** Management activities of holding companies
**Trading Style:** Rossetts Commercials
**Issued Capital:** £100
**Managing Director:** R G Maxwell
**Co. Secretary:** Eddi Zoratti
**Branches:** Rel Ltd, Eastern Road, Aldershot, Hampshire GU12 4TD
**US SIC:** 6711, 7539
**UK SIC:** 83962, 67100
**Auditors:** Carpenter Box LLP
**Bankers:** National Westminster Bank Plc (60-30-09)

| | 31-12-13 | 31-12-12 | 31-12-11 |
|---|---|---|---|
| TA | 100 | 100 | 100 |
| NW | 100 | 100 | 100 |

DUNS 73-296-7703
## Relate Cymru
47 Walter Road, Swansea, West Glamorgan SA1 5PW
**Tel:** 01792480088
**Web:** www.relatecymru.org.uk
**Reg No:** 4570591 **Estd:** 2002 Private Company Limited By Guarantee
**Line of Business:** Counselling & advice services
**Directors:** R A Hoffman, J N Barry, Ms M P Bell, D R Evans, K Ingham, Ms N J Twigg, K Jones, Ms F G Fletcher
**Co. Secretary:** Richard Hoffman
**Responsibilities**
**Senior:** John Hill-Tout *(Manager)*
**US SIC:** 8321 **UK SIC:** 96111
**Bankers:** National Westminster Bank Plc (56-00-42)

| | 31-03-14 | 31-03-13 | 31-03-12 |
|---|---|---|---|
| TO | 919,575 | 846,191 | 878,531 |
| P/L | (29,676) | (56,677) | 42,406 |
| NW | 109,014 | 138,690 | 195,367 |
| WC | 106,362 | 133,114 | 194,400 |
| Emp. | 86 | 85 | 80 |

DUNS 73-722-4258
## Relate Derby & Southern Derbyshire
62 Friar Gate, Derby, Derbyshire DE1 1DJ
**Tel:** 01332-349177
**Web:** www.relatederby.org.uk
**Reg No:** 4980776 **Estd:** 2003 Private Company Limited By Guarantee
**Line of Business:** Counselling & advice services
**Directors:** P B Purnell, Mrs A Pearson, J W Watkin, K W Molyneux, Mrs S A Wilson, R Watson, Mrs P Morgan, A Worthy
**Co. Secretary:** Mrs Beverley Miller
**Responsibilities**
**Senior:** Jacqueline Storer *(Director)*
**US SIC:** 8321 **UK SIC:** 96111
**Bankers:** Cafcash Ltd (40-52-40)

| | 31-03-14 | 31-03-13 | 31-03-12 |
|---|---|---|---|
| TO | 628,357 | 634,900 | 648,449 |
| P/L | 83,829 | 161,740 | 112,974 |
| NW | 826,533 | 742,704 | 580,964 |
| WC | 706,533 | 622,410 | 460,168 |
| Emp. | 47 | 37 | 33 |

DUNS 23-959-8944
## Relate North East
West Lodge, West Crescent, Darlington, County Durham DL3 7PS
**Tel:** 01325461500
**Web:** www.relatenortheast.org.uk
**Reg No:** 3948938 **Estd:** 2000 Private Company Limited By Guarantee
**Line of Business:** Social work activities without accommodation
**Directors:** M J Hill, Mrs G M Kane, D S Simpson
**US SIC:** 8321 **UK SIC:** 96111
**Auditors:** Wm Fortune & Son
**Bankers:** Unity Trust Bank Plc (08-60-01)

| | 31-03-14 | 31-03-13 | 31-03-12 |
|---|---|---|---|
| TO | N/A | 281,712 | 280,075 |
| P/L | N/A | (7,999) | (11,452) |
| NW | 35,026 | 8,932 | 42,088 |
| WC | 162,746 | 19,001 | 40,994 |

DUNS 45-809-7201
## Relate North Essex & East Herts
47 Broomfield Road, Chelmsford, Essex CM1 1SY
**Tel:** 01245-258680
**Web:** www.relate-northessex.org
**Reg No:** 3167701 **Estd:** 1996 Private Limited Company
**Line of Business:** Counselling & advice services
**Directors:** I J Parkins, Ms S Padworth, P J Phelan, Ms S L Orrell, C Waud, Mrs S Steel, Ms J M Anslow
**Branches:** Relate North Essex & East Herts, 51 Watchouse Rd, Chelmsford, Essex CM2 8PU
**US SIC:** 8321 **UK SIC:** 96111
**Auditors:** CBHC LLP
**Bankers:** Barclays Bank Plc (20-19-95)

| | 31-03-14 | 31-03-13 | 31-03-12 |
|---|---|---|---|
| TO | 768,480 | 653,033 | 573,790 |
| P/L | 132,387 | 68,542 | 5,623 |
| NW | 355,018 | 222,631 | 154,089 |
| WC | 350,756 | 218,850 | 154,027 |
| Emp. | 43 | 54 | 52 |

DUNS 45-800-7382
## Relate Shropshire Herefordshire & North Staffordshire Ltd
The Roy Fletcher Centre, Shrewsbury, Shropshire SY1 1JE
**Tel:** 01743-344010
**Web:** www.relatesandh.org.uk
**Reg No:** 3162232 **Estd:** 1963 Private Limited Company
**Line of Business:** Social work activities without accommodation
**Directors:** J K Riley, Mrs S Frankfort, D Johnson, P S Bennett, R B Pemberton, A D Mitchell, R R Jervis, Ms C S Fitzmaurice
**Responsibilities**
**Senior:** Sian Beckett *(Director)*, Gordon Channon *(Finance Director)*, Morgan Clark *(Trustee)*, Linda Foley *(Retail Manager)*, Michael Hardiman *(Trustee)*, Mary Richey *(Director)*, Clive Shortman *(Trustee)*, Kayleigh Walker *(Trustee)*
**Finance:** Gordon Channon *(Finance Director)*
**Branches:** Relate Shropshire Herefordshire & North Staffordshire Ltd, 28 Claremont St, Shrewsbury, Shropshire SY1 1QG
**US SIC:** 8321 **UK SIC:** 96111
**Auditors:** Aston Gilbert & Squire
**Bankers:** Barclays Bank Plc (20-77-85)

| | 31-03-14 | 31-03-13 | 31-03-12 |
|---|---|---|---|
| TO | 974,659 | 821,823 | 675,612 |
| P/L | 2,822 | (1,637) | 12,695 |
| NW | 82,030 | 83,420 | 85,490 |
| WC | 70,010 | 64,735 | 66,793 |
| Emp. | 78 | 69 | 60 |

DUNS 33-994-7624
## Relaxation Centre
9 All Saints Road, Bristol, Avon BS8 2JG
**Web:** www.relaxationcentre.co.uk
**Estd:** 1993 Partnership
**Line of Business:** Suppliers of spas and whirlpool baths
**Partners:** R Hicks, C Hicks
**Responsibilities**
**Senior:** Bernadette Ryder *(Manager)*
**US SIC:** 5999, 7999, 8091
**UK SIC:** 65600, 97913, 95200
**Employees:** 100

DUNS 34-638-3029
## Relaxion (South Oxfordshire) Ltd
**(Subsidiary of:** Eco Master Fund Limited)
P O Box 5666, Bletchley, Milton Keynes, Buckinghamshire MK2 2WT
**Tel:** 01908377251 **Fax:** 01908-374094
**Web:** www.taichichuan.org.uk
**Reg No:** 2767973 **Estd:** 1992 Private Limited Company
**Line of Business:** Leisure centres and services, gyms and swimming pools.
**Trading Style:** Leisure Connection
**Issued Capital:** £1,000
**Directors:** J F Nicholls, I A Hendrie
**Co. Secretary:** Ian Hendrie
**Responsibilities**
**Senior:** Richard Still *(Manager)*
**Branches:** Relaxion (South Oxfordshire) Ltd, West Lindsey Leisure Centre, The Avenue, Gainsborough, Lincolnshire DN21 1EP
**US SIC:** 7999 **UK SIC:** 97913
**Bankers:** National Westminster Bank Plc (56-00-31)

| | 30-09-13 | 30-09-12 | 30-09-11 |
|---|---|---|---|
| TA | 1,000 | 1,000 | 1,000 |
| NW | 1,000 | 1,000 | 1,000 |

DUNS 50-443-8318
## Relay Engineering Ltd
**(Subsidiary of:** J. & J. Denholm Ltd)
S167 South Yard, Plymouth, Devon PL2 2BG
**Tel:** 01752606206 **Fax:** 0175256501
**Web:** www.relay-engineering.com
**Reg No:** 2431701 **VAT No:** 434431474
**Estd:** 1989 Private Limited Company
**Line of Business:** Electrical engineers
**Issued Capital:** £172,172
**Principals:** P M Fisher *(Managing)*, P D Clunie, A R Froud, M J Beveridge
**Co. Secretary:** Gregory Hanson
**US SIC:** 3441, 1731
**UK SIC:** 32042, 50300
**Auditors:** Deloitte LLP
**Bankers:** National Westminster Bank Plc (56-00-63)

| | 31-12-13 | 31-12-12 | 31-12-11 |
|---|---|---|---|
| TO | 12,051,797 | 11,862,725 | 10,653,783 |
| P/L | 3,744,575 | 2,623,269 | 1,754,363 |
| NW | 2,591,660 | 2,061,163 | 1,634,256 |
| WC | 1,928,025 | 3,714,490 | 2,022,160 |
| Emp. | 104 | 93 | 87 |

DUNS 21-730-3676 Imp
## Relay Technical Transport Ltd.
5 The Ridgeway, Iver, Buckinghamshire SL0 9HX
**Tel:** 01753-652457 **Fax:** 01753-652377
**Web:** www.relayeurope.co.uk
**Reg No:** 1314775 **VAT No:** 224760571
**Estd:** 1976 Private Limited Company
**Line of Business:** Other supporting land transport activities
**Issued Capital:** £5,900
**Sales Director:** J P Schulein
**Co. Secretary:** Hugh Reid
**Responsibilities**
**Finance:** Stuart Berry *(Facilities Manager)*
**IT:** Stuart Berry *(Facilities Manager)*
**HR:** Stuart Berry *(Facilities Manager)*
**Health & Safety:** Stuart Berry *(Facilities Manager)*
**Facilities:** Stuart Berry *(Facilities Manager)*
**Branches:** Relay Technical Transport Ltd., 1-3 Eagle Park Drive, Warrington, Cheshire WA2 8JA
**US SIC:** 4789, 4226
**UK SIC:** 77002, 77003
**Auditors:** Barnes Roffe LLP
**Bankers:** Barclays Bank Plc (20-38-83)

| | 31-03-14 | 31-03-13 | 31-03-12 |
|---|---|---|---|
| TO | 10,212,920 | 9,191,722 | 9,120,940 |
| P/L | 439,610 | 156,042 | 327,225 |
| NW | 2,111,422 | 1,832,362 | 1,714,480 |
| WC | 1,464,179 | 1,315,656 | 1,335,563 |
| Emp. | 164 | 156 | 143 |

DUNS 42-446-2104
## Reliable Contractors Ltd
301 Northdown Road, Margate, Kent CT9 3PA
**Tel:** 01843294546
**Web:** www.reliablecontractors.co.uk
**Reg No:** 4433925 **Estd:** 2002 Private Limited Company
**Line of Business:** Building construction contractors
**Issued Capital:** £100
**Director:** P Greene
**Co. Secretary:** Brian Greene
**US SIC:** 1522 **UK SIC:** 50100
**Bankers:** National Westminster Bank Plc (52-41-42)

| | 31-05-14 | 31-05-13 | 31-05-12 |
|---|---|---|---|
| TO | 18,511,643 | 11,764,470 | 7,983,402 |
| P/L | 1,743,569 | 1,036,495 | 363,076 |
| NW | 3,228,319 | 1,871,307 | 1,078,506 |
| WC | 3,222,694 | 1,867,128 | 1,078,506 |
| Emp. | 344 | 261 | 205 |

DUNS 28-895-3466 Exp
## Reliance Garage (Ryedale) Ltd
Seven Street, York Road Business Park, Malton, North Yorkshire YO17 6YA
**Tel:** 01653-693751 **Fax:** 01653-697914
**Web:** www.raychapmanmotors.co.uk
**Reg No:** 1313672 **Estd:** 1993 Private Limited Company
**Line of Business:** Car dealers (new & used)
**Export Markets:** Worldwide
**Trading Style:** Ray Chapman Motors
**Issued Capital:** £100
**Principals:** R Chapman *(Managing)*, D R Chapman
**Co. Secretary:** Ms Felicity Chapman
**Responsibilities**
**Senior:** Emma Clayton *(Manager)*
**Branches:** Reliance Garage (Ryedale) Ltd, Foss Island Rd, York, North Yorkshire YO26 6RA
**US SIC:** 5511 **UK SIC:** 65100
**Auditors:** Ashby Berry & Co
**Bankers:** Barclays Bank Plc (20-67-75)

| | 31-12-13 | 31-12-12 | 31-12-11 |
|---|---|---|---|
| TO | 32,064,629 | 31,582,899 | 32,448,792 |
| P/L | 594,973 | 416,897 | (20,685) |
| NW | 2,021,662 | 1,893,739 | 1,639,541 |
| WC | 290,277 | 163,172 | 41,565 |
| Emp. | 63 | 58 | 64 |

DUNS 21-808-9767
## Reliance High-Tech
Berkshire Place, Wharfedale Road, Wokingham, Berkshire RG41 5RD
**Tel:** 01189335730
**Estd:** 2012
**Line of Business:** Security and related activities
**Responsibilities**
**Senior:** Clive Hayton *(Chairman)*
**US SIC:** 7393 **UK SIC:** 83954
**Employees:** 170

DUNS 22-629-2324
## Reliance Mutual Insurance Society Ltd
Reliance House, Tunbridge Wells, Kent TN1 1RG
**Fax:** 01892-510676
**Web:** www.reliancemutual.co.uk
**Reg No:** 0491580 **Estd:** 1911 Private Company Limited By Guarantee
**Line of Business:** Life assurance services
**Directors:** O W Johnson, C K Mills, F B Sanjana, S N Creedon, Mrs S J O'Connor, C J Lerpiniere, N A Sherry, M Goodale
**Co. Secretary:** Anthony Field
**Responsibilities**
**Finance:** Tim Birse *(Senior Finance Administrator)*, Cara Whatford *(Financial Controller)*
**Marketing:** Barbara O' Driscoll *(Policy & Product Actuary)*
**Admin:** Tim Birse *(Senior Finance Administrator)*
**IT:** Damian Mccabe *(Network, Security Manager)*
**HR:** Clive Allison *(Head of Member Recruitment)*
**Operations:** Mark Holly *(Production Manager)*
**Branches:** Reliance Mutual Insurance Society Ltd, Overhouse Chambers, Wedgwood Pl, Stoke-On-Trent, Staffordshire ST6 4ED
**US SIC:** 6411 **UK SIC:** 83200
**Auditors:** Baker Tilly
**Bankers:** Barclays Bank Plc (20-88-13)

| | 31-12-13 | 31-12-12 | 31-12-11 |
|---|---|---|---|
| TO | 31,558,000 | 45,321,000 | 27,269,000 |
| P/L | 8,135,000 | 1,181,000 | (20,023,000) |
| NW | 100,674,000 | 95,799,000 | 85,145,000 |
| WC | 14,768,000 | 9,123,000 | 7,217,000 |
| Emp. | 93 | 83 | 76 |

DUNS 21-213-9398 Imp-Exp
## Reliance Precision Ltd
**(Subsidiary of:** Reliance Rg Ltd)
Rowley Mills, Penistone Road, Huddersfield, West Yorkshire HD8 0LE
**Tel:** 01484-601000
**Web:** www.reliance.co.uk
**Reg No:** 0171578 **VAT No:** 333759637
**Estd:** 1920 Private Limited Company
**Line of Business:** Other engineering activities
**Export Markets:** European Union (E U)
**Export Sales:** £9,426,614
**Issued Capital:** £906,987
**Principals:** S M Selka *(Chairman)*, Mrs E R Goldsztajn, A E Wright, W J Selka, Dr I Laidler, I D Walter, R W Dennis
**Responsibilities**
**Senior:** Robert Dundon *(Warehouse Manager)*, Jane Gibson *(Warehouse Manager)*
**IT:** Simon Sheard *(Computer System Manager)*
**HR:** Mick Hallam *(Training Manager)*, Judith O'Brien *(Human Resources Officer)*
**Operations:** William Barraclough *(Drawing Office Manager)*, Jon Plascot *(Quality Manager)*
**Purchasing:** Ken Jolly *(Purchasing Manager)*, Judith O'Brien *(Human Resources Officer)*
**Engineering:** Keith Rushwood *(Production Manager)*
**US SIC:** 8911, 3832, 3568, 3999
**UK SIC:** 83701, 37320, 32613, 49590
**Auditors:** BDO LLP
**Bankers:** HSBC Bank plc (40-25-10)

| | 31-03-14 | 31-03-13 | 31-03-12 |
|---|---|---|---|
| TO | 20,875,949 | 21,045,323 | 20,404,880 |
| P/L | 2,333,481 | 2,717,923 | 3,077,526 |
| NW | 14,586,877 | 13,114,371 | 11,141,969 |
| WC | 8,641,907 | 7,933,376 | 6,541,369 |
| Emp. | 237 | 231 | 217 |

DUNS 22-750-5385 Imp-Exp
## Reliance Worldwide Corporation (Uk) Ltd
**(Subsidiary of:** Malory Pty. Ltd.)
Worcester Road, Evesham, Worcestershire WR11 4RA
**Tel:** 01386712400 **Fax:** 01386-47028
**Web:** www.rwc.co.uk
**Reg No:** 1223637 **VAT No:** 112825986
**Estd:** 1975 Private Limited Company
**Line of Business:** Manufacturers of valves
**Export Markets:** European Union; Australia; New Zealand; S Africa; France; Germany; Italy; Czech Republic; Norway; Oman; Qatar
**Export Sales:** £1,682,326
**Trading Style:** R W C
**Issued Capital:** £5,000
**Directors:** J B Munz, P Munz
**Co. Secretary:** Dale Hudson
**Responsibilities**
**Senior:** John Kowalczyk *(Manager)*
**Finance:** Wayne Burman *(Financial Director)*
**Marketing:** Orion Johnson *(Marketing Coordinator)*
**Admin:** Sally Pearson *(Administration Manager)*
**HR:** Sally Pearson *(Administration Manager)*
**Facilities:** Sally Pearson *(Administration Manager)*
**US SIC:** 3494 **UK SIC:** 32880
**Auditors:** Ernst & Young LLP
**Bankers:** Lloyds TSB Bank plc (30-93-11)

| | 30-06-13 | 30-06-12 | 30-06-11 |
|---|---|---|---|
| TO | 17,547,215 | 17,686,416 | 18,338,199 |
| P/L | 631,969 | 1,006,315 | 1,623,616 |
| NW | 6,685,809 | 6,205,721 | 5,457,084 |
| WC | 7,176,001 | 5,339,789 | 8,939,432 |
| Emp. | 52 | 44 | 40 |

DUNS 64-072-8262
## Relief International-Uk
Development House, London EC2A 4LT
**Tel:** 02070650871
**Web:** www.ri-uk.org
**Reg No:** 4476247 **Estd:** 2002 Private Company Limited By Guarantee
**Line of Business:** Fund raising services charitable and non charitable
**Directors:** Ms A Barnes, Ms B A Simmonds, P K Levengood, G D Bell, R Cope
**Responsibilities**
**Senior:** Jamie Hall *(Executive Director)*
**HR:** Elia Maker *(Director of Human Resources)*
**US SIC:** 8321 **UK SIC:** 96111
**Bankers:** The Co-Operative Bank Plc (08-92-40)

| | 31-12-12 | 31- -11 |
|---|---|---|
| TO | 10,122,231 | 15,713,506 |
| P/L | 366,663 | (128,468) |
| NW | 442,251 | 75,588 |
| WC | 436,892 | 70,525 |
| Emp. | 621 | 590 |

DUNS 73-800-8601
## Relyon Cleaning Services Ltd
Resource Centre, Bristol, Avon BS10 6HZ
**Tel:** 01179505115 **Fax:** 01179-506611
**Web:** www.relyonservices.com
**Reg No:** 5057258 **Estd:** 2003 Private Limited Company
**Line of Business:** Cleaning contracting commercial
**Issued Capital:** £100
**Director:** K Boyle
**Co. Secretary:** Daniel Boyle
**US SIC:** 7349 **UK SIC:** 92300

| | 31-03-14 | 31-03-13 | 31-03-12 |
|---|---|---|---|
| TA | 100 | 100 | 100 |
| NW | 100 | 100 | 100 |

DUNS 73-800-8585
## Relyon Guarding & Security Services Ltd
Unit A7 Redham Works, Redham Lane, Pilning, Bristol, Avon BS35 4HQ
**Tel:** 01179505511 **Fax:** 01179-506611
**Web:** www.relyonservices.com
**Reg No:** 5057256 **Estd:** 2004 Private Limited Company
**Line of Business:** Cleaning contracting commercial
**Issued Capital:** £100
**Director:** K Boyle
**Co. Secretary:** Daniel Boyle
**US SIC:** 7393 **UK SIC:** 83954

| | 31-03-14 | 31-03-13 | 31-03-12 |
|---|---|---|---|
| TA | 473,349 | 466,710 | 470,630 |
| NW | 184,731 | 163,871 | 121,372 |
| WC | 153,502 | 145,650 | 99,297 |

DUNS 21-634-2402 Exp
## Relyon Ltd
**(Subsidiary of:** Steinhoff International Holdings Ltd)
Station Mills, Wellington, Somerset TA21 8NN
**Tel:** 01823667501
**Web:** www.relyon.co.uk
**Reg No:** 0470381 **Estd:** 1858 Private Limited Company
**Line of Business:** Manufacture of mattresses
**Export Sales:** £1,433,000
**Issued Capital:** £39,636
**Directors:** A J Murdoch, P J Dieperink, A C Chapman, P Little, D J Lambert, D I Wescomb
**Co. Secretary:** John Robins
**Responsibilities**
**Finance:** David Houghton *(Financial Director)*
**US SIC:** 2515, 2517
**UK SIC:** 46715, 46714
**Auditors:** Deloitte LLP
**Bankers:** National Westminster Bank Plc (60-23-05)

| | 30-06-13 | 30-06-12 | 30-06-11 |
|---|---|---|---|
| TO | 44,988,000 | 39,343,000 | 30,804,000 |
| P/L | 2,209,000 | 1,898,000 | 1,912,000 |
| NW | (1,042,000) | (2,772,000) | (4,200,000) |
| WC | 2,546,000 | 5,319,000 | 4,292,000 |
| Emp. | 436 | 429 | 410 |

DUNS 23-732-7408 Imp-Exp
## R.E.M. (Uk) Ltd
**(Subsidiary of:** Blazro Holdings Ltd)
Rear Of 40, Glenfield Road, Nelson, Lancashire BB9 8AP
**Web:** www.rem.co.uk
**Reg No:** 3094826 **VAT No:** 634133467
**Estd:** 1995 Private Limited Company
**Line of Business:** Hairdressers supplies
**Export Markets:** Belgium;France(including French Guyane;Norway
**Export Sales:** £1,033,167
**Issued Capital:** £30,000
**Directors:** M Roach, M Azam
**Co. Secretary:** Christopher Blakey
**US SIC:** 7231, 2599
**UK SIC:** 98200, 46720
**Auditors:** Unity
**Bankers:** National Westminster Bank Plc (01-67-14)

| | 30-09-14 | 30-09-13 | 30-09-12 |
|---|---|---|---|
| TO | 8,267,473 | 7,759,060 | 8,900,532 |
| P/L | 545,916 | 157,360 | 208,084 |
| NW | 1,906,986 | 1,640,334 | 1,602,456 |
| WC | 1,951,322 | 1,316,852 | 1,270,688 |
| Emp. | 83 | 82 | 89 |

DUNS 21-144-3579
## Rema Tip Top Holdings Uk Ltd
**(Subsidiary of:** Stahlgruber Otto Gruber Ag)
Westland Square, Leeds, West Yorkshire LS11 5XS
**Tel:** 01132-772-139 **Fax:** 01132-776-200
**Web:** www.rema-tiptop.co.uk
**Reg No:** 6750854 **Estd:** 2008 Private Limited Company
**Line of Business:** Management activities of other non-financial holding companies not elsewhere classified
**Export Sales:** £1,401,235
**Issued Capital:** £1,000,000
**Director:** M B Insley
**Co. Secretary:** Garry Mangham
**US SIC:** 6711 **UK SIC:** 83962
**Auditors:** Baker Tilly Audit Ltd

| | 31-12-13 | 31-12-12 | 31-12-11 |
|---|---|---|---|
| TO | 24,211,914 | 21,379,031 | N/A |
| P/L | 1,534,804 | 594,118 | N/A |
| NW | 8,035,757 | 6,873,939 | 1,000,000 |
| WC | 6,119,822 | 5,063,822 | N/A |
| Emp. | 143 | 156 | N/A |

DUNS 21-317-1440 **Imp**

## Rema Tip Top Industry Uk Ltd

**(Subsidiary of:** Stahlgruber Otto Gruber Ag)
Westland Square, Leeds, West Yorkshire LS11 5XS
**Tel:** 01132770044 **Fax:** 01132772139
**Web:** www.rema-tiptop.co.uk
**Reg No:** 1176719 **VAT No:** 182683145
**Estd:** 1971 Private Limited Company
**Line of Business:** Tyre production machinery and equipment
**Export Sales:** £1,104,315
**Issued Capital:** £116,666
**Directors:** M B Insley, A P West
**Co. Secretary:** Garry Mangham
**Responsibilities**
**Senior:** Annerose Schenk *(Manager)*
**Branches:** Rema Tip Top Industry Uk Ltd, Brealey Works, Station St, Doncaster, South Yorkshire DN10 4DD
**US SIC:** 3559 **UK SIC:** 32863
**Auditors:** RSM Tenon Audit Ltd
**Bankers:** Lloyds TSB Bank plc (30-92-68)

| | 31-12-13 | 31-12-12 | 31-12-11 |
|---|---|---|---|
| TO | 10,585,305 | 10,110,417 | 10,139,926 |
| P/L | 577,246 | 135,506 | 292,727 |
| NW | 877,067 | 658,782 | 562,919 |
| WC | (395,459) | (761,814) | (586,591) |
| Emp. | 93 | 96 | 101 |

DUNS 77-831-1845

## Remarc Technologies Ltd

**(Subsidiary of:** The Bregal Fund Ii L.P.)
Islington House, Brown Lane West, Leeds, West Yorkshire LS12 6BH
**Tel:** 01132346777 **Fax:** 08450747802
**Web:** www.remarc.co.uk
**Reg No:** 3032039 **VAT No:** 651465438
**Estd:** 1995 Private Limited Company
**Line of Business:** Training services
**Trading Style:** Qa
**Issued Capital:** £21,765
**Director:** W R Macpherson
**Co. Secretary:** Ian Johnson
**Responsibilities**
**Sales:** Jennie Marshall *(Head of Courseware Development)*
**HR:** Nova Ferguson *(Training Delivery Manager)*, Siobhan Merrion *(Learning Programme Manager)*
**Branches:** Remarc Technologies Ltd, Westminster House, 11 Portland Street, Manchester M1 3HU
**US SIC:** 8299, 8249
**UK SIC:** 93300
**Auditors:** Deloitte LLP
**Bankers:** National Westminster Bank Plc (60-24-30)

| | 30-05-14 | 31-05-13 | 27-05-12 |
|---|---|---|---|
| TA | 2,311,341 | 2,311,341 | 2,311,341 |
| P/L | N/A | N/A | (1,000) |
| NW | 2,291,341 | 2,291,341 | 2,291,341 |
| WC | 2,291,341 | 2,291,341 | 2,291,341 |

DUNS 49-109-0932

## Remarkable Group Ltd

The Pump House, Winchester, Hampshire SO23 9QG
**Tel:** 01962893893 **Fax:** 01962893893
**Web:** www.remarkablegroup.co.uk
**Reg No:** 3096503 **Estd:** 2014 Private Limited Company
**Line of Business:** Marketing consultants
**Issued Capital:** £141,646
**Principals:** J E Isaacson *(Managing)*, R M George, N J Tipple, J J Duncan, S P Pomeroy
**Responsibilities**
**Senior:** Christopher Wotton *(Manager)*
**Marketing:** Iman Khalif *(Relations Manager)*
**Sales:** Jo Hilder *(Business Development Manager)*, Matthew Trace *(Account Manager)*
**US SIC:** 7392, 7311
**UK SIC:** 83951, 83800
**Auditors:** Smith Acreman
**Bankers:** HSBC Bank plc (40-21-03)

| | 31-03-14 | 31-03-13 | 31-03-12 |
|---|---|---|---|
| TA | 1,100,470 | 832,594 | 1,152,656 |
| NW | 351,914 | 148,166 | 248,971 |
| WC | 375,218 | 151,081 | 247,947 |

DUNS 22-903-3824 **Imp**

## Rembrand Timber Ltd

**(Subsidiary of:** Low Holdings (Scotland) Ltd)
Shielhill Wood, Tealing, Dundee, Angus DD4 0PW
**Tel:** 01382323200 **Fax:** 01382323222
**Web:** www.rembrand-timber.com
**Reg No:** 0080045SC **VAT No:** 356382928
**Estd:** 1982 Private Limited Company
**Line of Business:** Timber merchants
**Issued Capital:** £300
**Directors:** S Mason, J Low, G E Low, G D Low
**Co. Secretary:** Steven Mason
**Branches:** Rembrand Timber Ltd, Unit 19, Ormlie Industrial Estate, Thurso, Caithness KW14 7QU
**US SIC:** 5072, 5039
**UK SIC:** 61500, 61300
**Auditors:** Henderson Loggie
**Bankers:** Clydesdale Bank Plc (82-44-04)

| | 30-09-13 | 30-09-12 | 30-09-11 |
|---|---|---|---|
| TO | 28,117,091 | 28,485,195 | 29,216,710 |
| P/L | 808,598 | 741,192 | 1,021,410 |
| NW | 11,819,236 | 11,181,701 | 10,641,579 |
| WC | 11,127,036 | 10,704,468 | 6,012,220 |
| Emp. | 180 | 170 | 169 |

DUNS 34-863-2415 **Imp**

## Rembrandt Hotel Ltd

11 Thurloe Place, London SW7 2RS
**Tel:** 02075898100 **Fax:** 020-7225-3363
**Web:** www.sarova.com
**Reg No:** 2815107 **Estd:** 1993 Private Limited Company
**Line of Business:** Hotels
**Issued Capital:** £100
**Principals:** A S Vohra *(Managing)*, S S Vohra, R S Vohra
**Co. Secretary:** Rajesh Vohra
**Responsibilities**
**Senior:** Virginia Barlow *(General Manager)*, Kenny Mcbean *(Food & Beverage Manager)*, Duncan Watson *(Deputy General Manager)*
**Finance:** Lisa Booth *(Financial Controller)*, Bipin Shah *(Senior Finance Administrator)*, Steve Turox *(Financial Controller)*
**Sales:** Kay Shelford *(Sales Manager)*
**Facilities:** Joseph Marques *(Facilities Manager)*
**Operations:** Virginia Barlow *(General Manager)*
**Branches:** Rembrandt Hotel Ltd, 11 Thurloe Place, London SW7 2RS
**US SIC:** 7011 **UK SIC:** 66500
**Auditors:** BDO LLP
**Bankers:** Barclays Bank Plc (20-32-29)

| | 30-06-14 | 30-06-13 | 30-06-12 |
|---|---|---|---|
| TO | 10,236,893 | 9,917,744 | 9,743,137 |
| P/L | 1,158,394 | 939,787 | 1,080,617 |
| NW | 7,414,102 | 6,609,940 | 5,855,661 |
| WC | 1,103,683 | 335,829 | 100,902 |
| Emp. | 117 | 117 | 114 |

DUNS 42-343-6752

## Remedi-Restorative Services

The Circle 33 Rockingham Lane, Sheffield, South Yorkshire S1 4FW
**Tel:** 01142536669 **Fax:** 01142-412796
**Web:** www.remediuk.org
**Reg No:** 4331410 **Estd:** 2001 Private Company Limited By Guarantee
**Line of Business:** Social work activities
**Directors:** Ms A Dews, Ms M A Payling, D Pidwell, Mrs J Coulthard, T Gee, Ms B A Cross, R D Unwin
**US SIC:** 8999 **UK SIC:** 83954
**Bankers:** HSBC Bank plc (40-41-08)

| | 31-03-14 | 31-03-13 | 31-03-12 |
|---|---|---|---|
| TO | 1,830,750 | 1,484,455 | 1,585,975 |
| P/L | 36,957 | (66,431) | 73,053 |
| NW | 461,708 | 424,751 | 491,182 |
| WC | 450,131 | 412,530 | 473,864 |
| Emp. | 115 | 63 | 61 |

DUNS 23-260-0853 **Imp**

## Remel Europe Ltd

**(Subsidiary of:** Erie U.K. Ltd)
Remel House, Dartford, Kent DA2 6PT
**Tel:** 01322295600
**Web:** www.remelinc.com
**Reg No:** 4245812 **Estd:** 2001 Private Limited Company
**Line of Business:** Research and laboratory based activities
**Trading Style:** Thermo Fisher
**Issued Capital:** £12,176
**Directors:** Ms L M Grant, Ms K R Wright, K N Wheeler
**Co. Secretary:** Oakwood Corporate Secretary Limi
**Responsibilities**
**Senior:** James Coley *(CEO, Managing Director)*, Nicola Ward *(Manager)*
**US SIC:** 2834, 3829
**UK SIC:** 25700, 37100
**Bankers:** Barclays Bank Plc (20-07-71)

| | 31-12-13 | 31-12-12 | 31-12-11 |
|---|---|---|---|
| TO | 13,334,000 | 12,598,000 | 12,460,000 |
| P/L | 1,180,000 | 435,000 | (1,588,000) |
| NW | 20,751,000 | 19,281,000 | 18,746,000 |
| WC | 18,685,000 | 16,575,000 | 15,038,000 |
| Emp. | 135 | 132 | 152 |

DUNS 37-851-8435

## The Remet Co Ltd

9a South Crescent, London E16 4TL
**Tel:** 02074760121 **Fax:** 020-7474-5809
**Web:** www.remetcompany.com
**Reg No:** 3302783 **VAT No:** 248443645
**Estd:** 1997 Private Limited Company
**Line of Business:** Wholesale of waste and scrap
**Export Sales:** £83,579,874
**Issued Capital:** £300
**Principals:** W Reid *(Managing)*, P J Brewer, S Cohen
**Co. Secretary:** Ms Rosalind Joseph
**Responsibilities**
**Senior:** J Ried *(Manager)*
**Admin:** Qian Lin *(Administration Manager)*
**US SIC:** 5093 **UK SIC:** 62200
**Auditors:** Dodd Harris
**Bankers:** HSBC Bank plc (40-06-30)

| | 30-06-14 | 30-06-13 | 30-06-12 |
|---|---|---|---|
| TO | 141,771,030 | 154,315,429 | 157,266,251 |
| P/L | 3,147,417 | 4,937,769 | 4,497,893 |
| NW | 27,650,074 | 25,720,562 | 22,437,105 |
| WC | 28,566,938 | 26,329,386 | 22,924,991 |
| Emp. | 93 | 84 | 76 |

DUNS 23-787-7894

## Remix Dry Mortar Ltd

**(Subsidiary of:** Remix International B.V.)
Newgate Lane, Fareham, Hampshire PO16 8SS
**Tel:** 01329-231200
**Web:** www.remixdrymortar.co.uk
**Reg No:** 3780780 **Estd:** 2008 Private Limited Company
**Line of Business:** Manufactures of mortars
**Issued Capital:** £1
**Director:** R M Reef
**Responsibilities**
**Senior:** Dave Rawson *(Manager)*
**Marketing:** Mark Leverson *(Commercial Manager)*
**Sales:** Mark Leverson *(Commercial Manager)*
**Engineering:** Rakesh Nar *(Technical Manager)*
**US SIC:** 3275 **UK SIC:** 24370

| | 31-12-13 | 31-12-12 | 31-12-11 |
|---|---|---|---|
| TO | 14,120,232 | 12,247,012 | 10,474,982 |
| P/L | 75,431 | (367,901) | 7,045 |
| NW | (1,132,671) | (1,208,102) | (840,201) |
| WC | (1,591,935) | (1,710,105) | (1,333,033) |
| Emp. | 64 | 56 | 50 |

DUNS 21-153-0662 **Imp-Exp**

## Remploy Ltd

Remploy House, 18c Rockingham Meridian East, Meridian Business Par, Leicester, Leicestershire LE19 1WZ
**Tel:** 0845-155-2700 **Fax:** 0845-155-2701
**Web:** www.remploy.co.uk
**Reg No:** 0394532 **VAT No:** 226502979
**Estd:** 1944 Private Company Limited By Guarantee
**Line of Business:** Manufacture of machinery for food, beverage and tobacco processing
**Directors:** A J Osmond, I Black, Mrs E M Carruthers, I S Russell, I Thornley, Mrs A R Owen
**Co. Secretary:** Ms Joanne Munns
**Responsibilities**
**Health & Safety:** David Wintle *(Health & Safety Officer)*
**Branches:** Remploy,Ltd, Knowsley Rd, St Helens, St. Helens, Merseyside WA10 4PX
**US SIC:** 3551, 2654, 2517, 7361
**UK SIC:** 32441, 47280, 46714, 83954
**Auditors:** Deloitte LLP

| | 31-03-14 | 31-03-13 | 31-03-12 |
|---|---|---|---|
| TO | 60,153,000 | 171,635,000 | 224,443,000 |
| P/L | 19,222,000 | (19,323,000) | 48,247,000 |
| NW | (236,842,000) | (339,065,000) | (257,953,000) |
| WC | (11,924,000) | (13,115,000) | (23,219,000) |
| Emp. | 1,711 | 2,927 | 4,129 |

DUNS 21-945-4833

## Rempower Ltd

**(Subsidiary of:** Arlington Securities Ltd)
79 Torrington Avenue, Tile Hill, Coventry, West Midlands CV4 9AQ
**Tel:** 02476462715
**Web:** www.remploy.co.uk
**Reg No:** 8554261 **Estd:** 2013 Private Limited Company
**Line of Business:** Manufacture of parts and accessories for motor vehicles and their engines
**Issued Capital:** £1
**Directors:** S Stott, D G Roberts, Professor K T Morley, M I Merryweather, M B Franckel
**Co. Secretary:** Adrian Kay
**US SIC:** 5531 **UK SIC:** 65100

| | 31-03-14 |
|---|---|
| TO | 18,236,000 |
| P/L | 1,793,000 |
| NW | (1,660,000) |
| WC | (680,000) |
| Emp. | 208 |

DUNS 53-612-0611 **Imp-Exp**

## Remsdaq Ltd

Parkway, Deeside Industrial Park, Deeside, Clwyd CH5 2NL
**Tel:** 01244 286495 **Fax:** 01244 286496
**Web:** www.remsdaq.com
**Reg No:** 3417251 **Estd:** 1973 Private Limited Company
**Line of Business:** Manufacture of electronic industrial process control equipment
**Export Sales:** £1,646,460
**Issued Capital:** £73,757
**Principals:** T J Breen *(Managing)*, R J Colston
**Co. Secretary:** Paul Napier
**Responsibilities**
**Senior:** Michael Lilley *(Production Manager)*
**Marketing:** Katie Wilson *(Marketing Coordinator)*
**Engineering:** William Cave *(Principal Software Engineer)*, Michael Lilley *(Production Manager)*
**US SIC:** 3823, 7393
**UK SIC:** 37100, 83954
**Auditors:** Baker Tilly UK Audit LLP
**Bankers:** Barclays Bank Plc (20-35-81)

| | 31-05-13 | 31-05-12 | 31-05-11 |
|---|---|---|---|
| TO | 11,931,261 | 16,715,569 | 21,488,296 |
| P/L | 1,115,930 | 1,362,547 | 1,243,522 |
| NW | 5,760,209 | 5,633,664 | 4,477,111 |
| WC | 4,077,658 | 4,594,397 | 2,949,320 |
| Emp. | 104 | 111 | 117 |

DUNS 38-561-3831 **Imp**

## Ren Ltd

223-231 Old Marylebone Road, London NW1 5QT
**Tel:** 020-7724-2900 **Fax:** 02077242678
**Web:** www.renskincare.com
**Reg No:** 3332668 **Estd:** 1997 Private Limited Company
**Line of Business:** Beauty products
**Issued Capital:** £200
**Directors:** Mrs C M Haydon, R M Calcraft
**Co. Secretary:** Antony Buck
**US SIC:** 2844, 5999
**UK SIC:** 25820, 65600
**Auditors:** Harris & Trotter LLP

| | 31-12-13 | 31-12-12 | 30-12-12 |
|---|---|---|---|
| TO | 11,000,963 | 5,614,401 | 9,144,920 |
| P/L | 1,226,540 | 796,556 | 622,263 |
| NW | 3,619,995 | 3,079,801 | 2,478,517 |
| WC | 3,454,503 | 3,002,419 | 2,384,359 |
| Emp. | 46 | 45 | 42 |

DUNS 77-955-8246

## Renaissance Capital Ltd

**(Subsidiary of:** Renaissance Financial Holdings Limited)
50 Bank Street, London E14 5NT
**Tel:** 02073-677777 **Fax:** 02073677778
**Web:** www.rencap.com
**Reg No:** 3059237 **Estd:** 1995 Private Limited Company
**Line of Business:** Merchants banks
**Directors:** M G Mccaig, A G Simone, M J Slatter, H A Main, J Mittlemann
**Co. Secretary:** Ms Natalia Semakova
**Responsibilities**
**Senior:** Dominic Bokor-Ingram *(Manager)*, Terry Leitao *(Manager)*, Paresh Mashru *(Manager)*, Lucien Moolenaar *(Manager)*, Natasha Powazka *(Reception Manager)*
**Finance:** David Nangle *(Head of Equity Research)*
**US SIC:** 6111, 7399
**UK SIC:** 81501, 83954
**Auditors:** Ernst & Young LLP
**Bankers:** The Chase Manhattan Bank (60-92-42)
**Employees:** 80

DUNS 23-649-2968

## Renaissance Care (Scotland) Ltd

**(Subsidiary of:** Dow Investments Plc)
Stuart House Eskmills Park, Station Road, Musselburgh, Midlothian EH21 7PB
**Tel:** 01316534100 **Fax:** 0131-653-6880
**Web:** www.renaisance-care.co.uk
**Reg No:** 0190022SC **Estd:** 2011 Private Limited Company
**Line of Business:** Human health activities
**Issued Capital:** £500,000
**Directors:** R D Kilgour, W D Mcleish, Ms C Docherty
**Responsibilities**
**Senior:** Elaine Murie *(Manager)*
**US SIC:** 7399 **UK SIC:** 83954
**Auditors:** Tenono Audit Ltd
**Bankers:** Bank Of Scotland (80-11-00)

| | 30-11-13 | 30-11-12 | 30-11-11 |
|---|---|---|---|
| TO | 2,662,295 | 2,823,820 | 2,776,284 |
| P/L | (12,154) | 250,561 | 204,927 |
| NW | 2,175,967 | 2,521,316 | 2,329,538 |
| WC | 808,035 | 587,688 | 832,559 |
| Emp. | 102 | 93 | 126 |

DUNS 22-243-6862

## Renaissance (Ecosse) Ltd

17 High Street, Queensferry, South Queensferry, West Lothian EH30 9PP
**Tel:** 08701181664
**Web:** www.renaissance-ecosse.co.uk
**Reg No:** 0221722SC **Estd:** 2003 Private Limited Company
**Line of Business:** Chocolate fountains
**Trading Style:** Orocco Pier Hotel
**Issued Capital:** £3
**Directors:** Ms E C Cooke, W G Manson
**Co. Secretary:** Peter Wilson
**US SIC:** 7011 **UK SIC:** 66500

**Auditors:** Stewart & Cumming Ltd

| | 30-09-13 | 30-09-12 | 30-09-11 |
|---|---|---|---|
| TO | 3,328,925 | 3,354,108 | 2,969,602 |
| P/L | 712,340 | 684,227 | 491,586 |
| NW | 1,952,233 | 1,611,822 | 1,298,145 |
| WC | (317,806) | (494,333) | (609,748) |
| Emp. | 66 | 63 | 61 |

DUNS 23-649-9716      Imp

## Renaissance Learning U K Ltd

(**Subsidiary of:** Renaissance Learning Inc.)
32 Harbour Exchange Square, London E14 9GE
**Tel:** 020-7184-4000 **Fax:** 020-7538-2625
**Web:** www.renlearn.co.uk
**Reg No:** 3645180 **Estd:** 1998 Private Limited Company
**Line of Business:** Computer software (development)
**Export Sales:** £239,083
**Issued Capital:** £200,000
**Directors:** D J Foch, A Thurber
**Co. Secretary:** Ms Mary Minch
**Responsibilities**
**Marketing:** Gareth Andrews (Marketing Manager)
**Health & Safety:** Steve Chatterton (Health & Safety Officer)
**US SIC:** 7379 **UK SIC:** 83940
**Auditors:** Nyman Libson Paul
**Bankers:** National Westminster Bank Plc (60-07-38)

| | 31-12-13 | 31-12-12 | 31-12-11 |
|---|---|---|---|
| TO | 5,493,157 | 4,043,093 | 3,389,328 |
| P/L | 129,054 | 91,401 | 110,558 |
| NW | 667,286 | 563,499 | 497,913 |
| WC | 695,791 | 616,462 | 521,307 |
| Emp. | 48 | 46 | 45 |

DUNS 34-608-9340

## Renaissance Pubs Ltd

71 Abbeville Road, London SW4 9JW
**Tel:** 02086731421 **Fax:** 02086752292
**Web:** www.renaissancepubs.co.uk
**Reg No:** 5415795 **VAT No:** 798963438
**Estd:** 2005 Private Limited Company
**Line of Business:** Retailers of beer, wine and spirits
**Trading Style:** The Abbeville
**Issued Capital:** £6
**Directors:** T Peake, M E Reynolds
**Co. Secretary:** Nicholas Fox
**Responsibilities**
**Senior:** Sajad Hussain (Proprietor)
**Branches:** Renaissance Pubs Ltd, 165 Stonhouse Street, London SW4 6BJ
**US SIC:** 5921 **UK SIC:** 64200

| | 31-03-14 | 31-03-13 | 31-03-12 |
|---|---|---|---|
| TO | 8,255,638 | 7,737,421 | 7,736,201 |
| P/L | 885,740 | 760,934 | 676,124 |
| NW | 580,770 | 451,663 | 388,724 |
| WC | (1,666,184) | (1,581,595) | (1,779,222) |
| Emp. | 189 | 117 | 101 |

DUNS 22-733-8548

## Renaissancere Syndicate Management Ltd

(**Subsidiary of:** Renaissancere Holdings Ltd)
125 Old Broad Street, London EC2N 1AR
**Tel:** 02072832646
**Web:** http://renre.com
**Reg No:** 1120384 **Estd:** 1973 Private Limited Company
**Line of Business:** Underwriting
**Issued Capital:** £10,900,000
**Directors:** G W Lynch, R A Curtis, Mrs P M Billingham, J R Hustler, D A Heatherly, H R Brennan, Miss K T Fox, R J Murphy
**Co. Secretary:** Mrs Julie Marshall
**Responsibilities**
**Senior:** Bruce Bills (Manager), Todd Fonner (Senior Vice President, Chief I), Daniel Malloy (Manager), Peter McLoughlin (Head of Claims), Conor Mcmenamin (Director), Norman Mintz (Manager), Jeffrey Park (Manager)
**Finance:** Jeffrey Kelly (Executive Vice President and C)
**Admin:** Peter Durhager (Executive Vice President and C)
**IT:** Rory French (IT Manager)
**Purchasing:** Clare Marshall (Purchasing Manager)
**US SIC:** 6411, 6399
**UK SIC:** 83200, 82001
**Auditors:** Littlijohn Frazer
**Bankers:** Coutts & Co (18-00-01)

| | 31-12-13 | 31-12-12 | 31-12-11 |
|---|---|---|---|
| TO | 18,483,629 | 17,396,189 | 14,524,680 |
| P/L | (3,806,891) | (2,011,455) | (1,597,107) |
| NW | 2,524,767 | 6,331,658 | 4,336,411 |
| WC | 2,607,058 | 6,010,712 | 3,458,451 |
| Emp. | 67 | 65 | 57 |

DUNS 51-601-8723

## Renal Services (Uk) Ltd

22a Ives Street, London SW3 2ND
**Tel:** 020-7581-3139 **Fax:** 020-7225-3885
**Web:** www.renalservices.com
**Reg No:** 5882395 **Estd:** 2006 Private Limited Company
**Line of Business:** Clinics private
**Issued Capital:** £1,556,207
**Directors:** Dr Y Mouzouris, J P Buckley, R C Pope, M S Maguire, H Westling, S Ciampolini
**Responsibilities**
**Senior:** Kathy Lloyd (Clinical Operations Manager), Diana Mortimer (Manager), Thomas Sackville (Manager)
**US SIC:** 8051 **UK SIC:** 95100
**Auditors:** Mercer & Hole

| | 31-03-14 | 31-03-13 | 31-03-12 |
|---|---|---|---|
| TO | 4,521,740 | 3,976,716 | 3,477,819 |
| P/L | 164,486 | 68,467 | (588,822) |
| NW | 366,467 | 235,474 | (47,429) |
| WC | (665,643) | (454,330) | (810,553) |

DUNS 21-224-6660

## Renault

107 Abbey Lane, Leicester, Leicestershire LE4 5QU
**Tel:** 01162801000
**Web:** www.renaultretail.co.uk
**Estd:** 1993 Proprietorship
**Line of Business:** Car dealers (new & used)
**Proprietor:** Mrs T Bennett
**Responsibilities**
**Senior:** Mark Whitaker (General Manager), mervyn hughs (general Manager)
**Finance:** Lisa Bonner (Accounts Manager)
**Marketing:** Annie Cooper (Sales & Marketing Manager)
**Sales:** Annie Cooper (Sales & Marketing Manager)
**IT:** Lisa Bonner (Accounts Manager)
**HR:** Mark Whitaker (General Manager)
**Health & Safety:** Joe Vaja (Service Manager)
**Facilities:** Joe Vaja (Service Manager)
**Purchasing:** Mark Whitaker (General Manager)
**US SIC:** 5511 **UK SIC:** 65100
**Employees:** 55

DUNS 21-370-2670

## Renault Birmingham

75-80 High Street, Bordesley, Birmingham, West Midlands B12 0LL
**Tel:** 0121-2527000
**Web:** www.renault.co.uk
**Estd:** 1990 Partnership
**Line of Business:** Car dealers (new & used)
**Partners:** C Layton, A Beach, R Davison, M Walker, I Rice
**US SIC:** 5511 **UK SIC:** 65100
**Employees:** 53

DUNS 49-338-2816

## Renault Institute of Quality Management Ltd

(**Subsidiary of:** Renault Consulting)
Rivers Office Park, Denham Way, Rickmansworth, Hertfordshire WD3 9YS
**Tel:** 01923-697-269
**Web:** www.rnconsulting.co.uk
**Reg No:** 3125199 **Estd:** 1995 Private Limited Company
**Line of Business:** Business and management consultancy activities
**Issued Capital:** £50,000
**Directors:** P Jombart, K A Ramirez, D J Payne, M A Crockett, F Aractingi, Mrs S E Johal
**Co. Secretary:** David Howells
**US SIC:** 7392, 8299
**UK SIC:** 83951, 93300
**Auditors:** Ernst & Young LLP
**Bankers:** Barclays Bank Plc (20-92-60)

| | 31-12-13 | 31-12-12 | 31-12-11 |
|---|---|---|---|
| TO | 4,292,127 | 4,079,476 | 4,071,404 |
| P/L | 298,352 | 293,947 | 201,084 |
| NW | 859,362 | 567,573 | 351,281 |
| WC | 952,836 | 730,065 | 659,819 |
| Emp. | 83 | 76 | 74 |

DUNS 21-227-5566

## Renault Liverpool

Sefton Street, Toxteth, Liverpool, Merseyside L8 6PZ
**Tel:** 01515528000
**Web:** www.renault.co.uk
**Estd:** 1992 Proprietorship
**Line of Business:** Car dealers (new & used)
**Proprietor:** N Jackson
**Responsibilities**
**Senior:** Steven Parsley (General Manager)
**Finance:** Mike Hancock (Accountant)
**Admin:** Pauline Murphy (Administration Manager)

**HR:** Pauline Murphy (Administration Manager)
**US SIC:** 5511 **UK SIC:** 65100
**Employees:** 50

DUNS 21-151-3452

## Renault Truck Commercials Ltd

(**Subsidiary of:** Ab Volvo)
Houghton Hall Park, Houghton Regis, Dunstable, Bedfordshire LU5 5FT
**Tel:** 01926475333 **Fax:** 01582-479456
**Web:** www.renault-trucks.co.uk
**Reg No:** 0290604 **Estd:** 1987 Private Limited Company
**Line of Business:** Sale of new motor vehicles
**Trading Style:** Renault Trucks
**Issued Capital:** £63,691,012
**Directors:** G Costa, C M Sharp, R E Ericsson
**Co. Secretary:** Simon Villanueva
**Responsibilities**
**Senior:** Pascal Bittner (Manager), Laurence Hildenbrand (Manager), Marc Martinez (Manager), Jean Mateos (Director and Company Secretary)
**Finance:** Laurence Hildenbrand (Manager), Jean Mateos (Director and Company Secretary)
**Sales:** Nigel Butler (Commercial Director)
**HR:** Barbara Dawson (Personnel Manager)
**Branches:** Renault Truck Commercials Ltd, Unit 43, South Hampshire Industrial Park, Southampton, Hampshire SO40 3SA
**US SIC:** 5511, 7539
**UK SIC:** 65100, 67100
**Auditors:** PricewaterhouseCoopers LLP
**Bankers:** HSBC Bank plc (40-05-23)

| | 31-12-13 | 31-12-12 | 31-12-11 |
|---|---|---|---|
| TO | 90,118,000 | 88,512,000 | 89,544,000 |
| P/L | 619,000 | 359,000 | (333,000) |
| NW | 16,676,000 | 15,929,000 | 15,425,000 |
| WC | 11,389,000 | 10,846,000 | 10,354,000 |
| Emp. | 208 | 196 | 219 |

DUNS 22-611-2498      Imp-Exp

## Renault Trucks U K Ltd

(**Subsidiary of:** Ab Volvo)
Houghton Hall Business Park, Dunstable, Bedfordshire LU5 5FT
**Tel:** 01582-471122 **Fax:** 01582479146
**Web:** www.renault-trucks.com
**Reg No:** 0321658 **Estd:** 1981 Private Limited Company
**Line of Business:** Sale of motor vehicles
**Export Markets:** Europe, Rest of the World
**Export Sales:** £6,204,000
**Issued Capital:** £54,832,680
**Directors:** B R Blin, R E Ericsson, G Costa
**Co. Secretary:** Simon Villanueva
**Responsibilities**
**Senior:** Nigel Butler (Sales Manager), Laurent Farman (Manager)
**Marketing:** Nigel Butler (Sales Manager)
**Sales:** Nigel Butler (Sales Manager)
**HR:** Barbara Dawson (Human Resources Manager)
**Health & Safety:** John Twitchen (Facilities Manager)
**Facilities:** John Twitchen (Facilities Manager)
**Purchasing:** John Twitchen (Facilities Manager)
**US SIC:** 5511, 5531
**UK SIC:** 65100
**Auditors:** PricewaterhouseCoopers LLP

| | 31-12-13 | 31-12-12 | 31-12-11 |
|---|---|---|---|
| TO | 184,508,000 | 162,687,000 | 182,587,000 |
| P/L | 1,211,000 | 649,000 | 1,263,000 |
| NW | 25,471,000 | 25,862,000 | 26,607,000 |
| WC | 60,553,000 | 51,500,000 | 42,027,000 |
| Emp. | 125 | 125 | 105 |

DUNS 21-024-6161      Imp

## Renault U.K. Ltd

(**Subsidiary of:** Renault)
Rivers Office Park, Maple Cross, Rickmansworth, Hertfordshire WD3 9YS
**Tel:** 01923-895-000 **Fax:** 01923-895-101
**Web:** www.renault.co.uk
**Reg No:** 0082932 **Estd:** 1904 Private Limited Company
**Line of Business:** Car importers
**Issued Capital:** £2,750,000
**Directors:** M A Crockett, J M Townsend, A Hebert, Ms S E Johal, K A Ramirez, S M Gowler, M Bordeanu, D J Payne
**Co. Secretary:** Imraan Esmail
**Responsibilities**
**Senior:** Roland Bouchara (Manager), Leonard Curran (Manager), Gilles Laroche (Manager), Jean Llobet (Financial Director), Philip York (Marketing Director)
**Finance:** Jean Llobet (Financial Director), Bob Miller (Finance Director)
**Marketing:** Louise O'Sullivan (Head of Marketing Communicatio), Philip York (Marketing Director)
**Admin:** Paula Jenkins (Office Manager)

**IT:** Mike Frost (Computer Director)
**Branches:** Renault U.k. Ltd, 270 Stratford Road, Solihull, West Midlands B90 3AD
**US SIC:** 5511 **UK SIC:** 65100
**Auditors:** Ernst & Young LLP
**Bankers:** Barclays Bank Plc (20-65-63)
Following financial data are in thousands

| | 31-12-13 | 31-12-12 | 31-12-11 |
|---|---|---|---|
| TO | 979,127 | 772,399 | 1,088,541 |
| P/L | 7,945 | 7,043 | (8,299) |
| NW | 50,373 | 45,894 | 39,451 |
| WC | 56,312 | 50,223 | 46,467 |
| Emp. | 165 | 183 | 219 |

DUNS 21-226-3038

## Renault Wolverhampton

2-24 Bilston Road, Wolverhampton, West Midlands WV2 2PT
**Tel:** 01902-439500
**Web:** www.renaultwolverhampton.co.uk
**Estd:** 1975 Proprietorship
**Line of Business:** Car dealers (new & used)
**Proprietor:** B Dennell
**US SIC:** 5511 **UK SIC:** 65100
**Employees:** 65

DUNS 50-567-6791

## Rendall & Rittner Ltd

(**Subsidiary of:** R & R Residential Management Ltd)
Portsoken House, 155-157 Minories, London EC3N 1LJ
**Web:** www.rendallandrittner.co.uk
**Reg No:** 2515428 **Estd:** 1990 Private Limited Company
**Line of Business:** Estate management services
**Issued Capital:** £7,000
**Principals:** D L Rendall (Managing), J W Rittner (Managing), R J Daver, Ms C Riva, W G Hammond, K J Marshall, S M Ellman
**Co. Secretary:** Duncan Rendall
**Responsibilities**
**Senior:** Matthew Kirk (Manager), Mark Lake (Manager), Matt Rittner (Manager)
**Branches:** Rendall & Rittner Ltd, 1 Watson Street, Manchester M3 4EE
**US SIC:** 6531 **UK SIC:** 83400
**Auditors:** Robinsons Consulting Ltd
**Bankers:** Robert Fleming & Co Ltd (16-57-10)

| | 30-06-13 | 30-06-12 | 30-06-11 |
|---|---|---|---|
| TO | 8,505,730 | 7,228,158 | N/A |
| P/L | 446,153 | 427,109 | N/A |
| NW | 1,440,103 | 1,260,413 | 1,123,151 |
| WC | 1,232,679 | 996,198 | 698,491 |
| Emp. | 155 | 127 | N/A |

DUNS 51-610-9191

## Rendcomb College

Abronhill, 36 22 Larch Road, Cumbernauld, Glasgow, Lanarkshire G67 3AZ
**Tel:** 01236733944
**Web:** www.rendcombsurgery.co.uk
**Reg No:** 5891198 **Estd:** 1920 Private Company Limited By Guarantee
**Line of Business:** Adult and other education not elsewhere classified
**Directors:** R D Lane, Major General P G Williams, R S Levinge, Ms L H Singer, S D Parsons, Mrs J R Gunner, H C Robinson, A Marchand
**Co. Secretary:** Mrs Eleanor Sharman
**Responsibilities**
**Senior:** Sara Arkle (Director), Edward Daniels (Director), Prudence Hornby (Director), Kate Jacques (Practice Manager), Imogen Ormerod (Director), Francis Richards (Director), Richard Wills (Director)
**US SIC:** 8249 **UK SIC:** 93300
**Bankers:** Lloyds TSB Bank plc (30-92-06)

| | 31-08-14 | 31-08-13 | 31-08-12 |
|---|---|---|---|
| TO | 6,749,986 | 6,577,625 | 6,025,580 |
| P/L | (19,838) | (141,881) | (98,911) |
| NW | 1,682,956 | 1,651,010 | 1,666,844 |
| WC | 263,478 | 271,830 | 402,474 |
| Emp. | 167 | 166 | 167 |

DUNS 21-452-4949

## The Rendevous Casino

The Kursaal, Eastern Esplanade, Southend-On-Sea, Essex SS1 2ZG
**Tel:** 01702-616000
**Web:** www.clublci.com
**Estd:** 2001 Proprietorship
**Line of Business:** Casinos
**Proprietor:** T Donnerly
**Responsibilities**
**Senior:** Johanna Johnson (Manager)
**Finance:** Kate Mizon (Administration Manager)
**Marketing:** Naomi Gross (Marketing Manager)
**Admin:** Kate Mizon (Administration Manager)
**Purchasing:** Julian Chesworth (General Manager)
**US SIC:** 7999 **UK SIC:** 97913
**Employees:** 100

DUNS 21-059-4067
## Rendezvous
Keighley Road, Skipton, North Yorkshire BD23 2TA
**Tel:** 01756700100
**Web:** www.rendezvous-skipton.com
**Proprietorship**
**Line of Business:** Hotels
**Proprietor:** M Wheading
**Responsibilities**
**Senior:** Malcolm Weaving *(Proprietor)*, Michael dudds *(Food & Beverage Manager)*
**Marketing:** Malcolm Weaving *(Proprietor)*
**HR:** Malcolm Weaving *(Proprietor)*
**Facilities:** Malcolm Weaving *(Proprietor)*
**Purchasing:** Malcolm Weaving *(Proprietor)*
**US SIC:** 6531 **UK SIC:** 83400
**Employees:** 50

DUNS 21-620-5204
## Rendezvous Casino
Brighton Marina, Brighton Marina, Brighton Marina Village, Brighton, East Sussex BN2 5UT
**Tel:** 01273936938
**Web:** www.rendezvouscasino.com
**Estd:** 2011
**Line of Business:** Casinos
**US SIC:** 7999 **UK SIC:** 97913
**Employees:** 100

DUNS 77-931-3787
## Renegade Pictures (Uk) Ltd
**(Subsidiary of:** Warner Bros. Television Production Uk Ltd)
Warner House 98 Theobald's Road, London WC1X 8WB
**Tel:** 02074493200
**Web:** www.renegadepictures.co.uk
**Reg No:** 5834060 **Estd:** 2006 Private Limited Company
**Line of Business:** Television broadcasting services
**Export Sales:** £4,207,446
**Issued Capital:** £100
**Directors:** A D Hayling, T W Downing, Ms A Y Cooke, J H Rowlands, Miss C E Hungate
**US SIC:** 4833, 7829
**UK SIC:** 97411, 97112
**Auditors:** Parkers
**Bankers:** Barclays Bank Plc (20-03-80)

| | 31-12-13 | 31-12-12 | 31-12-11 |
|---|---|---|---|
| TO | 12,082,089 | 12,285,349 | 12,612,127 |
| P/L | 1,042,323 | 977,363 | 1,399,553 |
| NW | 1,003,544 | 1,468,111 | 1,825,526 |
| WC | 1,407,375 | 563,168 | 1,737,084 |
| Emp. | 71 | 65 | 67 |

DUNS 21-719-5536
## Renelec Ltd
**(Subsidiary of:** Renelec Group Ltd)
Brownston House, New Park Street, Devizes, Wiltshire SN10 1DS
**Tel:** 01380726363 **Fax:** 01380-729255
**Web:** www.renelec.co.uk
**Reg No:** 1053189 **Estd:** 1972 Private Limited Company
**Line of Business:** Central heating systems (installation and servicing)
**Issued Capital:** £48,590
**Directors:** V R Couse, B G Crew, S J Couse, M A Rymes, A K Harper, J Skeen
**Co. Secretary:** Robert Kennedy
**US SIC:** 1711, 8911, 1731
**UK SIC:** 50300, 83701
**Auditors:** PKF
**Bankers:** National Westminster Bank Plc (52-30-27)

| | 30-09-13 | 30-09-12 | 30-09-11 |
|---|---|---|---|
| TO | 34,049,294 | 29,922,146 | 34,440,777 |
| P/L | 393,538 | 5,986 | (356,922) |
| NW | 4,256,670 | 3,957,579 | 4,031,826 |
| WC | 2,476,677 | 2,260,495 | 1,693,687 |
| Emp. | 223 | 216 | 230 |

DUNS 73-312-9600 **Imp-Exp**
## Renesas Electronics Europe Ltd
**(Subsidiary of:** Innovation Network Corporation of Japan)
2 Millboard Road Dukes Meadow, Bourne End, Buckinghamshire SL8 5FH
**Tel:** 01628585100 **Fax:** 01628643131
**Web:** www.renesas.com
**Reg No:** 4586709 **Estd:** 2003 Private Limited Company
**Line of Business:** Wholesale of other electronic parts and equipment
**Export Sales:** £767,950,000
**Issued Capital:** £78,149,470
**Directors:** H Suzuki, H Nitta, A Chikami, T Tanaka, G H Look
**Responsibilities**
**Senior:** John Gorrie *(Manager)*, Tsutomu Miki *(Manager)*, Shoji Oga *(Manager)*
**HR:** Hailey Hyde *(Human Resources Manager)*
**US SIC:** 5065 **UK SIC:** 61500
**Auditors:** Ernst & Young LLP

| | 31-03-14 | 31-03-13 | 31-03-12 |
|---|---|---|---|
| TO | 779,642,000 | 690,401,000 | 813,472,000 |
| P/L | 27,567,000 | 24,667,000 | 20,727,000 |
| NW | 87,699,000 | 64,043,000 | 62,067,000 |
| WC | 115,109,000 | 97,815,000 | 99,930,000 |
| Emp. | 700 | 783 | 805 |

DUNS 21-614-1440
## Renew Holdings Plc.
Yew Trees, Main Street North, Aberford, Leeds, West Yorkshire LS25 3AA
**Tel:** 01132814200
**Web:** www.renewholdings.com
**Reg No:** 0650447 **Estd:** 1960 Public Limited Company
**Line of Business:** Holding companies management activities
**Issued Capital:** £5,989,893
**Directors:** R J Harrison, J W Samuel, B W May, J M Bishop, D M Forbes
**Co. Secretary:** John Samuel
**Responsibilities**
**IT:** James Eastwood *(IT Manager)*
**HR:** Louise White *(Human Resources Director)*
**Branches:** Renew Holdings Plc., Fountain St, Leeds, West Yorkshire LS27 0AA
**US SIC:** 6711, 1522
**UK SIC:** 83962, 50100
**Auditors:** KPMG Audit PLC
**Bankers:** Barclays Bank Plc (20-02-06)

| | 30-09-14 | 30-09-13 | 30-09-12 |
|---|---|---|---|
| TO | 464,474,000 | 350,061,000 | 337,423,000 |
| P/L | 13,051,000 | 10,699,000 | 8,421,000 |
| NW | (47,182,000) | (26,684,000) | (20,274,000) |
| WC | (44,606,000) | (32,184,000) | (24,363,000) |
| Emp. | 2,706 | 2,006 | 1,890 |

DUNS 73-653-6090
## Renewable Energy Systems Holdings Ltd
Beaufort Court, Egg Farm Lane, King's Langley, Hertfordshire WD4 8LR
**Tel:** 01923 299 200 **Fax:** 01923 299 299
**Web:** www.res-group.com
**Reg No:** 4913497 **Estd:** 2003 Private Limited Company
**Line of Business:** Management activities of holding companies
**Export Sales:** £338,348,000
**Issued Capital:** £60,000,000
**Directors:** C Mcalpine, Dr G M Mcalpine, Dr I D Mays, D S Jenkins, M C Shelley, D C Joyce, D S Jenkins
**Co. Secretary:** Dominic Hearth
**Branches:** Renewable Energy Systems Holdings Ltd, Unit 7000, Gower Street, Glasgow, Lanarkshire G51 1PR
**US SIC:** 6711 **UK SIC:** 83962
**Auditors:** Deloitte LLP

| | 31-10-13 | 31-10-12 | 31-10-11 |
|---|---|---|---|
| TO | 452,977,000 | 449,113,000 | 748,908,000 |
| P/L | 144,577,000 | 529,000 | 37,561,000 |
| NW | 321,007,000 | 169,312,000 | 157,171,000 |
| WC | 190,548,000 | 55,321,000 | 64,401,000 |
| Emp. | 1,119 | 1,061 | 990 |

DUNS 29-511-4474
## Renewable Uk Association
Greencoat House, Francis Street, London SW1P 1DH
**Tel:** 02079013000
**Web:** www.renewableuk.com
**Reg No:** 1874667 **VAT No:** 432958530
**Estd:** 1984 Private Company Limited By Guarantee
**Line of Business:** Associations
**Directors:** D S Shaw, C D Egal, Ms R Ruffle, Dr R W Yemm, M A Knight, J A Brown, D A Crowther, M R Partridge
**Responsibilities**
**Senior:** Thomas Brostrøm *(Director)*, Zoe Keeton *(Director)*, Leonard Magrill *(Director)*, Maria Mccaffery *(Chief Executive)*, Lindsay Mcquade *(Director)*, Sarah Merrick *(Director)*
**Finance:** Shamiso Mushambi *(Finance Officer)*
**US SIC:** 8611 **UK SIC:** 96312
**Auditors:** Warneford Gibbs
**Bankers:** National Westminster Bank Plc (01-09-51)

| | 31-12-13 | 31-12-12 | 31-12-11 |
|---|---|---|---|
| TA | 6,793,802 | 6,398,874 | 6,658,178 |
| NW | 2,496,485 | 3,039,204 | 2,499,578 |
| WC | 2,412,082 | 2,923,978 | 2,369,893 |

DUNS 50-443-3707
## Renewal Leeds Ltd
Regent Street, Leeds, West Yorkshire LS2 7QN
**Fax:** 01133-912592
**Web:** www.renewleeds.co.uk
**Reg No:** 2431232 **Estd:** 1989 Private Company Limited By Guarantee
**Line of Business:** Activities of other membership organisations not elsewhere classified
**Directors:** M R Lobley, M W Copsey, A Taylor
**Co. Secretary:** Ali Akbor
**Branches:** Renewal Leeds Ltd, 190 Dewsbury Road, Leeds, West Yorkshire LS11 6PF
**US SIC:** 8999 **UK SIC:** 83954
**Auditors:** Moore & Smalley
**Bankers:** The Co-Operative Bank Plc (08-90-72)

| | 31-03-14 | 31-03-13 | 31-03-12 |
|---|---|---|---|
| TO | N/A | N/A | 1,549,677 |
| P/L | N/A | N/A | 934 |
| NW | (7,022) | 80,359 | 80,359 |
| WC | (7,022) | 80,359 | 80,359 |

DUNS 22-912-6511
## Renfrewshire Council
Renfrewshire House, Cotton Street, Paisley, Renfrewshire PA1 1LE
**Tel:** 03003000300
**Web:** www.renfrewshire.gov.uk
**VAT No:** 264909334 **Estd:** 2008
**Line of Business:** Property maintenance services
**Principals:** W Hughes *(Financial)*, I Snodgrass, N Morrow, B Forteath, Ms M Quinn, Ms S Duncan, H Hann, Ms S Rae
**Responsibilities**
**Senior:** Sandra Black *(Credit Controller)*, Mary Crearie *(Manager)*, Tom Scholes *(Chief Executive Officer)*
**Finance:** Sandra Black *(Credit Controller)*
**Marketing:** John McKenzie *(Marketing Manager)*
**IT:** Jackie Evans *(IT Manager)*
**Branches:** Renfrewshire Council, West Johnstone Shared Campus, Beith Road, Johnstone, Renfrewshire PA5 0BB
**US SIC:** 9121 **UK SIC:** 91110
**Bankers:** The Royal Bank Of Scotland Plc (83-46-00)
**Employees:** 100

DUNS 21-778-3254
## Renfrewshire Council Emergency Council House Repairs
Clark Street, Paisley, Renfrewshire PA3 1RX
**Tel:** 01416187998
**Estd:** 2011 Proprietorship
**Line of Business:** Property maintenance services
**Proprietor:** P Kind
**Responsibilities**
**IT:** Kevin Mullan *(IT manager)*
**US SIC:** 1799 **UK SIC:** 50000
**Employees:** 250

DUNS 73-346-3546
## Renfrewshire Leisure Trading Ltd
**(Subsidiary of:** Renfrewshire Leisure Limited)
Lagoon Leisure Centre, 11 Christie Street, Paisley, Renfrewshire PA1 1NB
**Tel:** 0300 300 0250
**Web:** www.renfrewshireleisure.com
**Reg No:** 0241310SC **VAT No:** 806119254
**Estd:** 2002 Private Limited Company
**Line of Business:** Catering
**Issued Capital:** £1
**Directors:** A S Russell, C Neill, J Roger
**Co. Secretary:** Ms Joyce Mckellar
**Responsibilities**
**Senior:** Joyce McKellar *(Chief Executive)*
**Marketing:** Tony Finn *(Senior Marketing Executive)*
**US SIC:** 5812 **UK SIC:** 66110
**Auditors:** Milne Craig
**Bankers:** Clydesdale Bank Plc (82-20-00)

| | 31-03-14 | 31-03-13 | 31-03-12 |
|---|---|---|---|
| TA | 5,976 | 6,849 | 6,349 |
| NW | 1 | 1 | 1 |
| WC | 1 | 1 | 1 |

DUNS 64-747-1242
## Renfrewshire Valuation Joint Board
The Robertson Centre, 16 Glasgow Road, Paisley, Renfrewshire PA1 3QF
**Tel:** 03003000150
**Web:** www.renfrewshire-vjb.gov.uk
**Estd:** 1997 Proprietorship
**Line of Business:** Assessors
**Proprietor:** S Carlton
**Responsibilities**
**Senior:** Shona Carlton *(Director)*, Alasdair Mactaggart *(Lands Valuation Assessor and E)*
**IT:** Cameron Hynd *(IT Support Officer)*
**Branches:** Renfrewshire Valuation Joint Board, 40 West Stewart Street, Greenock, Renfrewshire PA15 1YA
**US SIC:** 7397 **UK SIC:** 83702
**Employees:** 49

DUNS 21-722-6935 **Exp**
## Renishaw P L C
New Mills, Wotton-Under-Edge, Gloucestershire GL12 8JR
**Tel:** 01453 524524 **Fax:** 01453524401
**Web:** www.renishaw.com
**Reg No:** 1106260 **VAT No:** 422900581
**Estd:** 1973 Public Limited Company
**Line of Business:** Measurement, motion control, spectroscopy and precision machining
**Trading Style:** Renishaw Metrology, Renishaw Transducer Systems
**Issued Capital:** £14,557,709
**Principals:** Sir D R Mcmurtry *(Chairman)*, A C Roberts *(Financial)*, D J Deer, G Mcfarland, B R Taylor, Ms K L Durrant, Dr D Grant, D J Jeans
**Co. Secretary:** Ms Norma Tang
**Responsibilities**
**Senior:** Ellen Chesney *(Director)*, Terry Garthwaite *(Non-Executive Director)*
**Marketing:** Corrie Fearon *(Sales and Marketing Manager)*, Robin Weston *(Marketing Manager)*
**Sales:** Corrie Fearon *(Sales and Marketing Manager)*, Stewart Lane *(Group Business Development Man)*
**Facilities:** David Frankham *(Engineering Manager)*
**Operations:** Gareth Hankins *(Group Manufacturing Director)*
**Engineering:** Andy Forrest *(Group Engineering Software Ope)*, David Frankham *(Engineering Manager)*, Simon McAdam *(Technical Manager)*, Adrian Welsford *(Principal Engineer)*
**Branches:** Renishaw P L C, Wellington House, Bath Road, Stroud, Gloucestershire GL5 5EY
**US SIC:** 3829, 6711
**UK SIC:** 37100, 83962
**Auditors:** KPMG LLP

| | 30-06-14 | 30-06-13 | 30-06-12 |
|---|---|---|---|
| TO | 355,498,000 | 346,881,000 | 331,892,000 |
| P/L | 96,386,000 | 84,419,000 | 86,046,000 |
| NW | 296,268,000 | 221,910,000 | 188,733,000 |
| WC | 183,635,000 | 142,776,000 | 130,198,000 |
| Emp. | 3,345 | 3,092 | 2,765 |

DUNS 22-734-8505
## Renlon Ltd
**(Subsidiary of:** Renlon Holdings Ltd)
Renlon Limited, Mitcham, Surrey CR4 3TD
**Tel:** 020-8687-4000
**Web:** www.renlon.co.uk
**Reg No:** 1272413 **VAT No:** 468689766
**Estd:** 1976 Private Limited Company
**Line of Business:** Holding companies management activities
**Issued Capital:** £1,042,593
**Principals:** R Scibilia *(Managing)*, J G Eaton, P M Ashwood, P Seaton
**Co. Secretary:** Mrs Christine Carter
**US SIC:** 1742, 1799
**UK SIC:** 50400, 50000
**Auditors:** BDO Stoy Hayward
**Bankers:** Bank Of Scotland (12-11-03)

| | 30-04-14 | 30-04-13 | 30-04-12 |
|---|---|---|---|
| TA | 895,584 | 775,229 | 660,757 |
| NW | 478,276 | 284,246 | 173,268 |
| WC | 412,890 | 227,910 | 108,203 |

DUNS 21-878-5365
## Rennaiassance Care
58 Duddingston Road, Edinburgh, Midlothian EH15 1SG
**Tel:** 01316698551
**Estd:** 2011
**Line of Business:** Nursing homes
**Responsibilities**
**Senior:** Elaine Murie *(Manager)*, Ann Roy *(Manager)*
**US SIC:** 8051 **UK SIC:** 95100
**Employees:** 50

DUNS 21-708-0708
## Rennie Grove Hospice Care
Grove House, Waverley Road, St Albans, Hertfordshire AL3 5QX
**Tel:** 01727897552
**Web:** www.hospice10k.org
**Reg No:** 7479930 **Estd:** 2010 Private Limited Company
**Line of Business:** Hospices
**Directors:** Ms A C Sheppard, L M King, Professor S G Spiro, P C Murphy, E Coleridge Smith, Dr S L Cottam, Mrs J Fryer, Mrs J E Macleod
**Co. Secretary:** Mrs Jane Macleod
**Responsibilities**
**Senior:** David Parkins *(Manager)*, Alexandra Wainwright *(Director)*
**US SIC:** 8091 **UK SIC:** 95200
**Bankers:** Barclays Bank Plc (27-99-00)

| | 31-03-14 | 31-03-13 | 31-03-12 |
|---|---|---|---|
| TO | 6,994,008 | 6,212,089 | 5,850,354 |
| P/L | 461,830 | (201,734) | (434,693) |
| NW | 4,683,487 | 4,230,552 | 4,911,231 |
| WC | 985,823 | 567,264 | 1,322,335 |
| Emp. | 187 | 180 | 184 |

DUNS 21-052-2876 Imp-Exp

## Renolit Cramlington Ltd

**(Subsidiary of:** Jm Holding Gmbh & Co. Kgaa)
Station Road, Cramlington, Northumberland NE23 8AQ
**Tel:** 01670-718222
**Web:** www.renolit.com
**Reg No:** 0207104 **VAT No:** 436184644
**Estd:** 1925 Private Limited Company
**Line of Business:** Plastics - fabrics, film and sheet
**Export Sales:** £30,056,000
**Trading Style:** Cova
**Issued Capital:** £10,000,000
**Directors:** P P Winant, M T Kundel, Dr D Taylorson, S M Wilson
**Co. Secretary:** Simon Wilson
**Responsibilities**
**Senior:** Jozef Claerbout *(President)*, Dominique Clerbois *(Manager)*, Dave Hall *(Operations Manager)*
**Marketing:** Leeson Hughes *(Marketing Manager)*
**IT:** Alan Lawton *(Computer Manager)*, Martin Lott *(Technology Development Manager)*
**Facilities:** Joe Cocker *(Facilities Manager)*
**Operations:** Martin Lott *(Technology Development Manager)*
**Purchasing:** N Crete *(Purchasing Manager)*
**US SIC:** 2821 **UK SIC:** 25140
**Auditors:** Garbutt & Elliott LLP
**Bankers:** National Westminster Bank Plc (54-10-31)

| | 31-12-13 | 31-12-12 | 31-12-11 |
|---|---|---|---|
| TO | 62,587,000 | 57,911,000 | 60,662,000 |
| P/L | 5,524,000 | 3,852,000 | 5,477,000 |
| NW | 20,114,000 | 19,461,000 | 20,523,000 |
| WC | 7,867,000 | 8,078,000 | 9,092,000 |
| Emp. | 240 | 238 | 244 |

DUNS 21-290-1094

## Renown Engineering Ltd

**(Subsidiary of:** Renown Group Ltd)
Dudley Lane, Cramlington, Northumberland NE23 7RH
**Tel:** 01912500113 **Fax:** 0191-250-1980
**Web:** www.renownengineering.co.uk
**Reg No:** 0948075 **VAT No:** 454955121
**Estd:** 1969 Private Limited Company
**Line of Business:** Engineers (general)
**Export Sales:** £189,203
**Trading Style:** Renown Engineering Ltd
**Issued Capital:** £1,500,000
**Director:** J D Hamilton
**Co. Secretary:** Ms Katherine Hamilton
**US SIC:** 3499 **UK SIC:** 31694
**Auditors:** Ernst & Young LLP
**Bankers:** Barclays Bank Plc (20-23-81)

| | 31-12-13 | 31-12-12 | 31-12-11 |
|---|---|---|---|
| TO | 5,263,957 | 6,613,431 | 13,178,704 |
| P/L | (898,784) | (138,818) | 932,567 |
| NW | 3,715,201 | 4,528,922 | 4,486,583 |
| WC | 3,165,939 | 3,877,523 | 3,688,845 |
| Emp. | 86 | 97 | 100 |

DUNS 23-534-7171

## Renown Railway Training Services Ltd

Brookside Business Park, Cold Meece, Stone, Staffordshire ST15 0RZ
**Tel:** 01785764476
**Web:** www.renownrailway.co.uk
**Reg No:** 3533490 **Estd:** 1998 Private Limited Company
**Line of Business:** Training providers
**Issued Capital:** £2
**Director:** W T Smith
**Co. Secretary:** Patrick Mulvihill
**US SIC:** 8299 **UK SIC:** 93300
**Auditors:** Thomas, Wood & Co

| | 30-09-13 | 30-09-12 | 30-09-11 |
|---|---|---|---|
| TA | 291,063 | 371,599 | 197,012 |
| NW | 80,604 | 126,481 | 146,832 |
| WC | 80,603 | 126,480 | 146,831 |

DUNS 21-099-6594 Exp

## Renray Healthcare Ltd

**(Subsidiary of:** Renray Holdings Ltd)
Road Five, Winsford Industrial Estate, Winsford, Cheshire CW7 3RB
**Tel:** 01606595427
**Web:** www.renrayhealthcare.com
**Reg No:** 6434893 **Estd:** 2007 Private Limited Company
**Line of Business:** Manufacture of household textiles
**Issued Capital:** £3
**Directors:** G D Silman, Ms J A Dearden, J S Cartman
**Co. Secretary:** Keith Fairhurst
**Responsibilities**
**Finance:** Kevin Roe *(Finance Director)*
**Marketing:** Clare Shergold *(Marketing Manager)*

**US SIC:** 2392 **UK SIC:** 45550

| | 31-12-13 | 31-12-12 | 31-12-11 |
|---|---|---|---|
| TO | 13,052,167 | 12,846,777 | 11,301,759 |
| P/L | 433,303 | 410,720 | 508,938 |
| NW | 3,290,650 | 3,338,988 | 3,330,336 |
| WC | 2,762,693 | 2,964,594 | 2,883,613 |
| Emp. | 86 | 84 | 86 |

DUNS 73-705-2352

## Renrod Holdings Ltd

Union House, Union Street, Trowbridge, Wiltshire BA14 8RY
**Tel:** 01225756100
**Web:** www.renrodmg.co.uk
**Reg No:** 4963884 **Estd:** 2003 Private Limited Company
**Line of Business:** Management activities of holding companies
**Issued Capital:** £1,500,000
**Directors:** Ms O Shocklidge, R J Cuff, Ms R E Mccabe, J C Cuff, M Read
**Co. Secretary:** Ms Amanda Cuff
**US SIC:** 6711 **UK SIC:** 83962
**Bankers:** Lloyds TSB Bank plc (30-00-00)

| | 31-12-13 | 31-12-12 | 31-12-11 |
|---|---|---|---|
| TO | 116,430,254 | 109,382,944 | 96,506,206 |
| P/L | 1,451,215 | 1,329,598 | 791,859 |
| NW | 20,524,653 | 19,373,981 | 18,402,167 |
| WC | 2,145,330 | 1,308,473 | (4,094,514) |
| Emp. | 372 | 379 | 394 |

DUNS 21-032-2489

## Renshaw Napier Ltd

52 Clyde Street, Carluke, Lanarkshire ML8 5BD
**Tel:** 01555777900
**Web:** www.renshawnapier.co.uk
**Proprietorship**
**Line of Business:** Manufacture of other food products not elsewhere classified
**Proprietor:** Mrs D Lunt
**Responsibilities**
**Senior:** John Easton *(Factory Manager)*
**Health & Safety:** John Easton *(Factory Manager)*
**Facilities:** John Easton *(Factory Manager)*
**Purchasing:** Anne McKenna *(Purchasing Manager)*
**US SIC:** 3999 **UK SIC:** 49590
**Employees:** 80

DUNS 21-039-3017

## Rent It

Unit 4, Geoscan House, Denmore Road, Aberdeen, Aberdeenshire AB23 8JW
**Tel:** 08002985186
**Web:** www.rentit.biz
**Estd:** 1997 Proprietorship
**Line of Business:** Computer leasing
**Proprietor:** D Currie
**US SIC:** 7379, 7394
**UK SIC:** 83940, 84000
**Employees:** 50

DUNS 49-386-7238 Imp

## Rentair Ltd

**(Subsidiary of:** Centurion Acquisition Ltd)
Unit 6 Dyce Avenue, Aberdeen, Aberdeenshire AB21 0LQ
**Tel:** 01224 215400 **Fax:** 01224215438
**Web:** www.rentairoffshore.com
**Reg No:** 3133771 **Estd:** 1989 Private Limited Company
**Line of Business:** Air and other gas compressors
**Export Sales:** £9,178,000
**Trading Style:** Rentair Offshore
**Issued Capital:** £3,730,000
**Directors:** P J Stuart, K P White
**Co. Secretary:** Blackwood Partners Llp
**Responsibilities**
**Senior:** Leigh Ainsworth *(Chief Executive Officer)*, Alan Macleod *(Manager)*
**Marketing:** Iain Cass *(Sales & Marketing Director)*
**Sales:** Iain Cass *(Sales & Marketing Director)*
**Facilities:** Alan Leslie *(Facilities Manager)*
**Branches:** Rentair Ltd, Esso Refinery, Southampton, Hampshire SO45 1DY
**US SIC:** 3563 **UK SIC:** 32831
**Auditors:** PricewaterhouseCoopers LLP
**Bankers:** National Westminster Bank Plc (60-24-06)

| | 30-06-13 | 30-06-12 | 30-06-11 |
|---|---|---|---|
| TO | 19,501,000 | 17,784,000 | 15,144,000 |
| P/L | 4,515,000 | 4,043,000 | 4,110,000 |
| NW | 29,279,000 | 25,812,000 | 22,818,000 |
| WC | 3,252,000 | (1,057,000) | 3,400,000 |
| Emp. | 72 | 67 | 60 |

DUNS 21-909-6518 Imp-Exp

## Renthal Ltd

**(Subsidiary of:** Ldi Ltd. Llc)
Bredbury Park Way, Stockport, Cheshire SK6 2SN
**Tel:** 0161-406-6399 **Fax:** 0161-406-6440
**Web:** www.renthal.com
**Reg No:** 1224533 **VAT No:** 158842335
**Estd:** 1969 Private Limited Company
**Line of Business:** Manufacturers of motorcycles engines and component
**Export Markets:** Japan; U S A; Australia; Canada; South America
**Export Sales:** £9,285,000
**Issued Capital:** £5,280
**Principals:** T D Wade *(Financial)*, B M Etter, A W Ackerman, P J Watkins, R Whittal-Williams
**Co. Secretary:** Mrs Laura Birchall
**Responsibilities**
**Senior:** Anthony Brough *(Production Manager)*, Michael Mohacsi *(Manager)*, Henry Rosenthal *(Manager)*
**IT:** Adam Kirby *(IT Manager)*
**Health & Safety:** David Cartledge *(Health & Safety Officer)*
**Engineering:** Anthony Brough *(Production Manager)*, Michael Mohacsi *(Manager)*
**US SIC:** 3751 **UK SIC:** 36330
**Auditors:** Ernst & Young LLP
**Bankers:** Barclays Bank Plc (20-82-14)

| | 31-12-13 | 31-12-12 | 31-12-11 |
|---|---|---|---|
| TO | 11,851,000 | 10,824,000 | 10,888,000 |
| P/L | 750,000 | 206,000 | (193,000) |
| NW | 8,451,000 | 7,866,000 | 7,696,000 |
| WC | 6,688,000 | 6,031,000 | 6,553,000 |
| Emp. | 78 | 78 | 69 |

DUNS 34-585-6400

## Rentokil Initial Plc

Riverbank Meadows Business Park, Blackwater, Camberley, Surrey GU17 9AB
**Tel:** 01293858000 **Fax:** 01293858300
**Web:** www.rentokil-initial.com
**Reg No:** 5393279 **Estd:** 2005 Public Limited Company
**Line of Business:** Representative office
**Trading Style:** Rentokil Initial
**Issued Capital:** £18,148,310
**Directors:** R Burrows, Mrs A C Seymour-Jackson, P R Bamford, A M Ransom, Mrs J H Southern, J C Townsend, Dr J D Mcadam, A J Giles
**Co. Secretary:** Daragh Fagan
**Responsibilities**
**Senior:** Gareth Brown *(Manager)*, David McConnachie *(Manager)*
**Finance:** Stuart Ingall-Tombs *(Group Financial Controller)*
**Marketing:** Stewart Power *(Marketing and Strategy Directo)*
**IT:** Mark Purcell *(General Manager, Systems Devel)*
**Operations:** Terry O'Sullivan *(Project Manager)*
**Engineering:** Andy Brigham *(General Technical Manager)*, Andrew Carver *(Group Technology Manager)*
**Branches:** Rentokil Initial Plc, 81 St. Modwen Road, Plymouth, Devon PL6 8LH
**US SIC:** 7399, 8999, 6711
**UK SIC:** 83954, 83962
**Auditors:** KPMG LLP
**Bankers:** Samuel Montagu & Company Ltd (40-05-50)

**Following financial data are in thousands**

| | 31-12-13 | 31-12-12 | 31-12-11 |
|---|---|---|---|
| TO | 2,327,100 | 2,546,300 | 2,544,300 |
| P/L | 122,600 | 82,700 | (50,500) |
| NW | (657,100) | (607,900) | (500,100) |
| WC | (115,200) | (58,900) | (128,200) |
| Emp. | 53,508 | 59,519 | 66,470 |

DUNS 21-000-3505

## Rentokil Initial Services Ltd

**(Subsidiary of:** Rentokil Initial Plc)
Ground And Part 1st Floor, 2 City Place, Beehive Ring Road, Horley, Surrey RH6 0HA
**Tel:** 08002182205 **Fax:** 01293-858300
**Web:** www.rentokil.co.uk
**Reg No:** 0293397 **VAT No:** 190621474
**Estd:** 1904 Private Limited Company
**Line of Business:** Disinfecting and exterminating services
**Trading Style:** Rentokil Pest Control, Initial Washroom Solutions, Initial Vending
**Issued Capital:** £1,250,000
**Directors:** M Gillespie, P P Wood, J K Hampson
**Co. Secretary:** Ms Alexandra Laan
**Responsibilities**
**Senior:** Andy Ransom *(Ceo)*
**Marketing:** Malcolm Padley *(Head of Corporate Communicatio)*
**Facilities:** Paul Hales *(Facilities Manager)*
**Branches:** Rentokil Initial Services Ltd, Ronald Close, Woburn Road Indstrial Estate, Kempston, Bedford, Bedfordshire MK42 7SH
**US SIC:** 7399 **UK SIC:** 83954
**Auditors:** PricewaterhouseCoopers LLP
**Bankers:** HSBC Bank plc (40-02-17)

| | 31-12-13 | 31-12-12 | 31-12-11 |
|---|---|---|---|
| TO | 51,084,000 | 51,895,000 | 54,886,000 |
| P/L | 3,699,000 | 2,283,000 | (3,859,000) |
| NW | 22,270,000 | 21,633,000 | 17,170,000 |
| WC | 1,552,000 | 2,508,000 | (7,653,000) |
| Emp. | 857 | 895 | 958 |

DUNS 23-694-2244

## Rentsmart Ltd

**(Subsidiary of:** Thinksmart Europe Ltd)
7th Floor Oakland House, Manchester M16 0PQ
**Tel:** 01613332400 **Fax:** 01613332450
**Web:** www.rentsmart.co.uk
**Reg No:** 3689086 **Estd:** 1998 Private Limited Company
**Line of Business:** Other credit granting not elsewhere classified
**Issued Capital:** £2,750,000
**Directors:** J B Van Roon, F De Vicente, D E Twigg
**Co. Secretary:** Gary Halton
**Responsibilities**
**Senior:** Natale Montarello *(Owner)*
**Finance:** Kelly Jackson *(Head of Credit and Compliance)*
**Marketing:** Valeria Scialbini *(Marketing Coordinator)*
**Sales:** Mark Skehill *(Sales Director)*
**IT:** Barry Topham *(IT Director)*
**US SIC:** 6111 **UK SIC:** 81501

| | 30-06-14 | 31-12-13 | 31-06-12 |
|---|---|---|---|
| TA | 14,664,310 | 14,704,575 | 13,958,777 |
| P/L | 37,234 | 2,162,116 | 2,279,728 |
| NW | (5,456,918) | (5,564,734) | (5,998,983) |
| WC | 4,670,738 | 4,626,125 | (430,895) |
| Emp. | 67 | 66 | 61 |

DUNS 54-429-1958

## Renvac Scaffolding Ltd

Front Street, Gateshead, Tyne and Wear NE10 4HP
**Tel:** 01670828688 **Fax:** 01670-825640
**Web:** www.renvac-scaffolding.com
**Reg No:** 3275290 **VAT No:** 652180944
**Estd:** 1993 Private Limited Company
**Line of Business:** Scaffolds and work platform erectors
**Issued Capital:** £1,000
**Directors:** Ms D A Gridley, Mrs P Cavner
**Co. Secretary:** Richard Cavner
**Responsibilities**
**Senior:** Debra Halliburton *(Manager)*, Richard Kavanagh *(Manager)*
**Admin:** Lesley Randall *(Administrator)*
**HR:** Lesley Randall *(Administrator)*
**Facilities:** Richard Kavanagh *(Manager)*
**Purchasing:** Lesley Randall *(Administrator)*
**US SIC:** 7394, 1799
**UK SIC:** 84000, 50000
**Auditors:** AWS Accountancy Ltd
**Bankers:** National Westminster Bank Plc (60-03-55)

| | 31-01-14 | 31-01-13 | 31-01-12 |
|---|---|---|---|
| TA | 496,197 | 384,848 | 441,032 |
| NW | 151,643 | 167,232 | 166,565 |
| WC | 100,620 | 122,286 | 115,307 |

DUNS 23-909-1585 Imp

## Repairtech Ltd

Unit 4b, Westfield Road, Kineton Road Industrial Estate, Kineton Road Industrial, Southam, Warwickshire CV47 0JH
**Tel:** 01926-810030 **Fax:** 01926-810052
**Web:** www.repairtech.co.uk
**Reg No:** 3899678 **Estd:** 2000 Private Limited Company
**Line of Business:** Computer systems and software (sales)
**Issued Capital:** £1,000
**Director:** Ms R E Costello
**Co. Secretary:** Richard Costello
**US SIC:** 7379 **UK SIC:** 83940

| | 31-03-14 | 31-03-13 | 31-03-12 |
|---|---|---|---|
| TA | 669,802 | 596,229 | 652,882 |
| NW | 263,209 | 176,136 | 171,649 |
| WC | 162,098 | 122,137 | 122,683 |

DUNS 34-583-4527 Imp

## Repl International Ltd

R E P L House, Kingsdown Road, Swindon, Wiltshire SN25 6PB
**Tel:** 01793-821220 **Fax:** 01793-480922
**Web:** www.repl.com
**Reg No:** 2730556 **VAT No:** 578654974
**Estd:** 1999 Private Limited Company
**Line of Business:** Manufacturers cable and wire equipment
**Export Sales:** £17,565,815
**Trading Style:** Hi Power Correlation
**Issued Capital:** £379,300
**Directors:** G B Gardner, H R Patel, Mrs L Mehta, R H Patel
**Co. Secretary:** Amardeep Dhanoa
**Responsibilities**
**Senior:** Lyla Patel *(Manager)*
**Branches:** Repl International Ltd, Unit 2271 Dunbeath Road, Swindon, Wiltshire SN2 8EA
**US SIC:** 3357, 3629
**UK SIC:** 22470, 34350
**Auditors:** RSM Bentley Jennison

**Bankers:** National Westminster Bank Plc (54-41-19)

| | 31-03-14 | 31-03-13 | 31-03-12 |
|---|---|---|---|
| TO | 17,924,301 | 15,706,668 | 14,953,824 |
| P/L | 1,766,461 | 1,113,521 | 956,313 |
| NW | 4,899,777 | 4,276,130 | 3,968,961 |
| WC | 4,255,079 | 4,009,401 | 3,734,160 |
| Emp. | 109 | 102 | 59 |

DUNS 29-088-6613

## Replay Maintenance Ltd

(**Subsidiary of:** Lawrenco Rm Ltd)
Wesley House, Newark, Nottinghamshire NG24 2ER
**Fax:** 01636612860
**Web:** www.replaymaintenance.co.uk
**Reg No:** 1416487 **Estd:** 1979 Private Limited Company
**Line of Business:** Stadium developers and contractors
**Issued Capital:** £10,000
**Directors:** G Martin, R S Goss, N C Allen, C C Lawrence
**Co. Secretary:** Richard Hills
**US SIC:** 7999 **UK SIC:** 97913
**Auditors:** Deloitte & Touche

| | 31-12-13 | 31-12-12 | 31-12-11 |
|---|---|---|---|
| TA | 522,287 | 431,198 | 331,077 |
| NW | 229,945 | 170,235 | 124,096 |
| WC | 145,255 | 99,247 | 47,560 |

DUNS 21-948-2140

## Replicon Europe Ltd

(**Subsidiary of:** Replicon Corporation)
Hillswood Drive, Chertsey, Surrey KT16 0RS
**Tel:** 020-3514-5511
**Web:** www.replicon.com
**Reg No:** 8574979 **Estd:** 2013 Private Limited Company
**Line of Business:** Project management services
**Trading Style:** Replicon
**Issued Capital:** £100
**Director:** P Kinash
**US SIC:** 7392 **UK SIC:** 83951

| | 31-12-13 |
|---|---|
| TA | 142,558 |
| NW | 23,627 |
| WC | 22,737 |

DUNS 23-855-4039

## Reply Ltd

(**Subsidiary of:** Alika Srl)
38 Grosvenor Gardens, London SW1W 0EB
**Tel:** 0207 730 6000 **Fax:** 0207 259 8600
**Web:** www.replyltd.co.uk
**Reg No:** 3847202 **Estd:** 1999 Private Limited Company
**Line of Business:** Other computer related activities
**Export Sales:** £1,927,246
**Issued Capital:** £54,175
**Directors:** R Lodigiani, M Rizzante, Ms T Rizzante, Dr M W Wassel, Ms D Angelucci, F Rizzante
**Co. Secretary:** Temple Secretarial Limited
**US SIC:** 7379 **UK SIC:** 83940
**Auditors:** Ernst & Young LLP

| | 31-12-13 | 31-12-12 | 31-12-11 |
|---|---|---|---|
| TO | 27,602,411 | 15,039,849 | 12,439,834 |
| P/L | 2,782,558 | (3,472,684) | (1,382,426) |
| NW | (1,527,067) | (3,585,839) | (22,916) |
| WC | (21,000,351) | (13,236,546) | (4,473,299) |
| Emp. | 130 | 98 | 73 |

DUNS 42-454-3890

## Representative Body of the Church in Wales

39 Cathedral Road, Cardiff, South Glamorgan CF11 9XF
**Tel:** 02920-348200
**Web:** www.churchinwales.org.uk
**Reg No:** 0000432RC **Estd:** 1931
**Line of Business:** Social work activities
**Trading Style:** Representative Body of the Church in Wales
**Principals:** J Richfield, J Shirley, Ms D Clifton
**Responsibilities**
**Finance:** Louise Davis *(Head of Finance)*
**Facilities:** Alex Glanville *(Head of Property Services)*
**Branches:** Representative Body Of The Church In Wales, 58 Miskin St, Treorchy, Mid Glamorgan CF42 5LR
**US SIC:** 7399, 8661
**UK SIC:** 83954, 96600
**Auditors:** PricewaterhouseCoopers
**Bankers:** Lloyds TSB Bank plc (77-62-01)
**Employees:** 50
**Turnover:** £727,207

DUNS 21-734-2609 **Exp**

## Repropoint Ltd

15 Poole Road, Woking, Surrey GU21 6BB
**Fax:** 01483596291
**Web:** www.repropoint.com
**Reg No:** 1228936 **VAT No:** 689012614
**Estd:** 1975 Private Limited Company
**Line of Business:** Manufacture of paper stationery
**Export Markets:** U S A, Middle East
**Trading Style:** Repropoint
**Issued Capital:** £98,000
**Principals:** M J Webb *(Managing)*, D Bennett, S Hallett, O G Gosden
**Responsibilities**
**Senior:** Alistair Beswick *(Transport Manager)*, Alexander North *(Technical Director)*
**Marketing:** Alexander North *(Technical Director)*
**IT:** Alexander North *(Technical Director)*
**Facilities:** Alexander North *(Technical Director)*
**Fleet:** Alistair Beswick *(Transport Manager)*
**Branches:** Repropoint Ltd, 53 London Rd, Portsmouth, Hampshire PO2 0BH
**US SIC:** 2648, 5999
**UK SIC:** 47231, 65600
**Auditors:** Bristow Burrell
**Bankers:** HSBC Bank plc (40-47-08)

| | 31-10-13 | 31-10-12 | 31-10-11 |
|---|---|---|---|
| TA | 2,163,006 | 2,224,035 | 2,376,204 |
| NW | (196,982) | (261,256) | (143,070) |
| WC | (318,881) | (422,594) | (358,097) |

DUNS 28-956-8511

## Reproprint Ltd

15 Poole Road, Woking, Surrey GU21 6BB
**Web:** www.repropoint.com
**Reg No:** 1659441 **Estd:** 1982 Private Limited Company
**Line of Business:** Printing not elsewhere classified
**Trading Style:** Repropoint Ltd
**Issued Capital:** £100
**Director:** M J Webb
**Responsibilities**
**Senior:** Frank De Barro *(Service Manager)*, Jean Merricks *(Financial Director)*
**Marketing:** Douglas Creighton *(Area Sales Manager)*
**Sales:** Douglas Creighton *(Area Sales Manager)*
**US SIC:** 2752 **UK SIC:** 47544
**Auditors:** Bristow Burrell

| | 31-10-13 | 31-10-12 | 31-10-11 |
|---|---|---|---|
| TA | 100 | 100 | 100 |
| NW | 100 | 100 | 100 |

DUNS 28-861-8192

## The Repton School Shop Ltd

The Paddock, Repton, Derby, Derbyshire DE65 6SE
**Tel:** 01283-559323
**Web:** www.repton.org.uk
**Reg No:** 0905547 **Estd:** 1967 Private Limited Company
**Line of Business:** Other retail sale in non-specialised stores
**Issued Capital:** £12
**Directors:** C P Bilson, R A Holroyd
**Co. Secretary:** Ms Pauline Sharratt
**Responsibilities**
**Marketing:** Cathy Twigg *(Marketing Manager)*
**IT:** Aidan Cooke *(Head of IT)*
**HR:** Kerri Butts *(Human Resources Officer)*
**US SIC:** 5399 **UK SIC:** 65600
**Auditors:** Bates Weston

| | 31-08-13 | 31-08-12 | 31-08-11 |
|---|---|---|---|
| TA | 135,240 | 172,193 | 189,158 |
| NW | (30,104) | (29,366) | (32,713) |
| WC | 90,991 | 113,853 | (72,359) |

DUNS 23-773-7783

## Republic Media Ltd

7 Broadbent Close, Highgate Village, London N6 5JW
**Tel:** 02032130135
**Web:** www.republicmedia.net
**Reg No:** 3767121 **Estd:** 1999 Private Limited Company
**Line of Business:** Other entertainment activities not elsewhere classified
**Issued Capital:** £100
**Co. Secretary:** Miss Susan Harris
**US SIC:** 7999 **UK SIC:** 97913

| | 31-05-14 | 31-05-13 | 31-05-12 |
|---|---|---|---|
| TA | 41,100 | 56,176 | 35,325 |
| NW | (4,010) | 4,401 | (7,747) |
| WC | (4,263) | 8,262 | 314 |

DUNS 28-975-1604 **Exp**

## Repucom Uk & Ireland Ltd

(**Subsidiary of:** Rsmg Insights Coöperatief U.A.)
66 Porchester Road, London W2 6ET
**Tel:** 02072217040
**Web:** www.repucom.net
**Reg No:** 1752310 **VAT No:** 395200459
**Estd:** 1983 Private Limited Company
**Line of Business:** Market research and public opinion polling
**Export Sales:** £2,696,071
**Issued Capital:** £5,000
**Directors:** P M Smith, R Millott, D Townsend
**Co. Secretary:** Heshan Suriyabandara
**Responsibilities**
**Senior:** Heinz Abel *(Manager)*, John Bushell *(Manager)*, Charlie Dundas *(Manager)*, Francisco Saez *(Manager)*
**US SIC:** 7392, 7311
**UK SIC:** 83951, 83800
**Auditors:** Mazars LLP
**Bankers:** Barclays Bank Plc (20-73-53)

| | 31-12-13 | 31-12-12 | 31-12-11 |
|---|---|---|---|
| TO | 7,054,965 | N/A | 3,545,151 |
| P/L | 216,595 | N/A | 923,402 |
| NW | (343,374) | (620,471) | 104,529 |
| WC | (581,091) | (105,293) | (168,814) |
| Emp. | 61 | N/A | N/A |

DUNS 21-600-1988

## Resale Weekly

Unit 13 Bourne Court, Unity Trading Estate, Southend Road, Woodford Green, Essex IG8 8HD
**Tel:** 02084718221
**Estd:** 1975 Proprietorship
**Line of Business:** Newspapers publishing
**Partners:** D Moffat, Miss J Milligan
**US SIC:** 2711 **UK SIC:** 47512
**Employees:** 50

DUNS 57-853-2012 **Imp**

## Rescroft Ltd

20 Oxleasow Road, Redditch, Worcestershire B98 0RE
**Fax:** 01527-521301
**Web:** www.rescroft.com
**Reg No:** 2900615 **VAT No:** 641050582
**Estd:** 1994 Private Limited Company
**Line of Business:** Manufacturers of car accessories
**Issued Capital:** £100
**Principals:** A C Restall *(Managing)*, J Kimberley *(Technical)*, P Johnson
**Co. Secretary:** Ms Kay Restall
**Responsibilities**
**Marketing:** Phil Bushell *(Sales Supervisor)*
**Sales:** Phil Bushell *(Sales Supervisor)*, Lee Perry *(Technical Sales Manager)*
**IT:** Lee Perry *(Technical Sales Manager)*
**US SIC:** 3714 **UK SIC:** 35300
**Auditors:** Lowe McTernan
**Bankers:** Barclays Bank Plc (20-71-45)

| | 31-03-14 | 31-03-13 | 31-03-12 |
|---|---|---|---|
| TA | 3,200,395 | 3,115,720 | 2,964,519 |
| NW | 1,869,008 | 1,856,880 | 1,762,576 |
| WC | 1,203,541 | 1,164,817 | 1,001,663 |

DUNS 21-321-6153 **Exp**

## Resdev Ltd

Puma Floor House, Ainley Industrial Estate, Elland, West Yorkshire HX5 9JP
**Tel:** 01422-379131 **Fax:** 01422-370943
**Web:** www.resdev.co.uk
**Reg No:** 1392506 **Estd:** 1978 Private Limited Company
**Line of Business:** Manufacturers and wholesalers of floorcoverings
**Export Markets:** E U, Netherlands, Malaysia
**Export Sales:** £1,560,512
**Issued Capital:** £3,983
**Principals:** J C Wright *(Chairman and Managing)*, G S Parratt, D A Greenwood, M J Spowage, M D Spindley, Mrs J S Wright, N M Wright
**Co. Secretary:** Graham Parratt
**Responsibilities**
**Senior:** Andy Gledhill *(Works Manager)*
**Marketing:** Jill Coley *(Marketing Manager)*
**Sales:** Richard Coley *(Sales Manager)*
**IT:** Shane Doherty *(IT Director)*
**Facilities:** Andy Gledhill *(Works Manager)*
**Operations:** Paul Whittham *(Quality Manager)*
**Engineering:** Andy Gledhill *(Works Manager)*
**US SIC:** 2279, 2891
**UK SIC:** 43852, 25620
**Auditors:** Cooksons
**Bankers:** Barclays Bank Plc (20-35-84)

| | 30-09-14 | 30-09-13 | 30-09-12 |
|---|---|---|---|
| TO | 7,399,996 | 6,778,557 | 6,177,139 |
| P/L | 797,307 | 395,900 | 90,148 |
| NW | 1,587,947 | 1,329,321 | 993,538 |
| WC | 1,384,805 | 1,401,340 | 941,860 |
| Emp. | 43 | N/A | N/A |

DUNS 53-613-9413 **Imp**

## Research Instruments Ltd

Bickland Industrial Park, Falmouth, Cornwall TR11 4TA
**Tel:** 01326-372753
**Web:** www.research-instruments.com
**Reg No:** 3419143 **Estd:** 1997 Private Limited Company
**Line of Business:** Manufacturers of medical equipment
**Trading Style:** I V F, R I Uk
**Issued Capital:** £1,000
**Principals:** W R Brown *(Managing)*, J C Retallack
**Co. Secretary:** David Lansdowne
**Responsibilities**
**Purchasing:** Les Stockton *(Purchasing Manager)*
**US SIC:** 5122 **UK SIC:** 61800
**Auditors:** Bishop Fleming

| | 31-03-14 | 31-03-13 | 31-03-12 |
|---|---|---|---|
| TO | 8,817,128 | 7,769,192 | 6,482,232 |
| P/L | 1,554,217 | 1,334,866 | 973,462 |
| NW | 5,546,831 | 4,703,175 | 3,860,808 |
| WC | 4,491,971 | 3,901,532 | 3,071,520 |
| Emp. | 76 | 68 | 63 |

DUNS 23-986-8008 **Imp**

## Research Now Ltd

(**Subsidiary of:** Research Now Group Inc.)
160 Queen Victoria Street, London EC4V 4BF
**Tel:** 02070843000 **Fax:** 02079212401
**Web:** www.researchnow.co.uk
**Reg No:** 3975073 **Estd:** 2000 Private Limited Company
**Line of Business:** Market research organisations
**Issued Capital:** £395,661
**Directors:** S J Decosta, K Knapton
**Co. Secretary:** Nathan Runnicles
**Responsibilities**
**Senior:** Miles Worne *(Managing Director, EMEA)*
**Finance:** Brenda McGimpsey *(Head of Finance)*
**Marketing:** Laia Gallart *(Online Marketing Manager)*, Rowena Hay *(Digital Marketing Executive)*, Konstanze Just *(Marketing Manager)*, Craig Pagett *(Client Development)*, Alvaro Sanchez *(Online Marketing Manager)*
**Sales:** Chris Dubreuil *(Vice President Sales)*
**IT:** Kostas Vlassis *(Computer Manager)*
**HR:** Fiona Wynne *(Human Resources Manager)*
**Health & Safety:** Fiona Wynne *(Human Resources Manager)*
**US SIC:** 7392 **UK SIC:** 83951
**Auditors:** Ernst & Young LLP
**Bankers:** HSBC Bank plc (40-07-13)

| | 31-12-13 | 31-12-12 | 31-12-11 |
|---|---|---|---|
| TO | 31,522,000 | 30,022,000 | 29,460,000 |
| P/L | 7,896,000 | 4,469,000 | 4,375,000 |
| NW | (1,235,000) | 24,133,000 | 23,698,000 |
| WC | 6,589,000 | 15,093,000 | 10,695,000 |
| Emp. | 296 | 311 | 288 |

DUNS 51-982-9097

## The Research Partnership Ltd

Chester House, London SW6 3JW
**Tel:** 02080695000 **Fax:** 08455442095
**Web:** www.researchpartnership.com
**Reg No:** 3350410 **Estd:** 1997 Private Limited Company
**Line of Business:** Market research organisations
**Export Sales:** £15,318,464
**Issued Capital:** £101
**Director:** Ms M Assimakopoulos
**Co. Secretary:** Mark Jeffery
**Responsibilities**
**Senior:** Marc Yates *(Manager)*
**US SIC:** 7392 **UK SIC:** 83951
**Auditors:** Munslows
**Bankers:** National Westminster Bank Plc (60-17-31)

| | 30-04-13 | 30-04-12 | 30-04-11 |
|---|---|---|---|
| TO | 17,548,358 | 16,826,959 | 16,122,413 |
| P/L | 988,291 | 2,368,928 | 2,371,085 |
| NW | 5,841,570 | 5,588,981 | 4,344,730 |
| WC | 3,931,540 | 4,087,174 | 3,418,816 |
| Emp. | 97 | 75 | 67 |

DUNS 77-946-3053

## Research Sites Restoration Ltd

(**Subsidiary of:** Babcock International Group Plc)
Harwell Oxford, Didcot, Oxfordshire OX11 0DF
**Tel:** 01235432228 **Fax:** 01305202316
**Web:** www.research-sites.com
**Reg No:** 5915837 **Estd:** 2012 Private Limited Company
**Line of Business:** Nuclear engineers
**Issued Capital:** £1
**Directors:** Ms B D Grey, A T Staples, A J Wratten, K M Douglas, Dr R J Pentreath, R A Hardy, S H White, R G Thomas
**Co. Secretary:** Darren Bailey
**Responsibilities**
**Senior:** Stanley Gordelier *(Director)*
**Marketing:** Angela Vincent *(Communications Manager)*
**US SIC:** 8911 **UK SIC:** 83701
**Auditors:** PricewaterhouseCoopers LLP

| | 31-03-14 | 31-03-13 | 31-03-12 |
|---|---|---|---|
| TO | 82,051,000 | 74,428,000 | 69,544,000 |
| P/L | 357,000 | 387,000 | 346,000 |
| NW | 280,000 | 1,292,000 | 601,000 |
| WC | 4,597,000 | 7,140,000 | 3,547,000 |
| Emp. | 474 | 425 | 411 |

**DUNS 21-585-1250**
## Reservoir Group
1 Albyn Terrace, Aberdeen, Aberdeenshire AB10 1YP
**Tel:** 01224628970
**Web:** www.reservoir-group.com
**Estd:** 2011 Proprietorship
**Line of Business:** Oil and gas exploration services
**Proprietor:** C Hutcheon
**Responsibilities**
**Finance:** Rick Clark (Financial Director)
**US SIC:** 1389 **UK SIC:** 13000
**Employees:** 300

**DUNS 23-212-1454**
## The Residential Care Home
Care Home, Leigh, Sherborne, Dorset DT9 6HL
**Web:** www.theoldvicarage-leigh.com
**Estd:** 1984 Proprietorship
**Line of Business:** Residential care establishments
**Proprietor:** Mrs A Sinnott
**Responsibilities**
**Senior:** Natalie Adams (Manager)
**US SIC:** 8321 **UK SIC:** 96111
**Employees:** 60

**DUNS 21-751-5196**
## Resilient Plc
(Subsidiary of: Resilient (Holdings) Plc)
25-27 Shaftesbury Avenue, London W1D 7EQ
**Tel:** 02073067300
**Web:** www.resilientplc.com
**Reg No:** 1403177 **VAT No:** 645532731
**Estd:** 1978 Public Limited Company
**Line of Business:** Telecommunications
**Trading Style:** Smart Numbers
**Issued Capital:** £50,000
**Principals:** G D Paterson (Chairman and Managing), A P Lamb, J J Foley
**Co. Secretary:** Miss Felicity Noble
**Responsibilities**
**Senior:** Ann-Marie Walker (Manager)
**HR:** Zara Osborn (Head of HR)
**Operations:** Paul Cheslaw (VP Strategy), David Menniss (Head of Platform management), Guy Stringer (Head of Projects)
**US SIC:** 4899 **UK SIC:** 79020
**Auditors:** Elman Wall Ltd
**Bankers:** National Westminster Bank Plc (55-81-26)

| | 30-09-13 | 30-09-12 | 30-09-11 |
|---|---|---|---|
| TO | 12,231,530 | 8,460,233 | 7,097,563 |
| P/L | 1,671,055 | 793,236 | 589,487 |
| NW | 4,252,715 | 2,653,294 | 1,786,793 |
| WC | 2,845,414 | 907,063 | 999,909 |
| Emp. | 67 | 58 | 46 |

**DUNS 34-543-3754**
## Resimed Ltd
New Park, Stoke-On-Trent, Staffordshire ST4 8HN
**Tel:** 01782657583
**Web:** www.safeharbor.co.uk
**Reg No:** 5353570 **Estd:** 2005 Private Limited Company
**Line of Business:** Security and related activities
**Trading Style:** Safe Harbour
**Issued Capital:** £200
**Directors:** Ms S Klonin, P Morris, W Morris, Miss L Morris, W Morris Jnr, J Abadi
**Co. Secretary:** Mrs Caroline Foster
**Responsibilities**
**Senior:** Caroline Ankers (Manager)
**US SIC:** 7399 **UK SIC:** 83954
**Bankers:** National Westminster Bank Plc (01-05-27)

| | 31-10-13 | 31-10-12 | 31-10-11 |
|---|---|---|---|
| TO | 4,746,365 | 4,383,254 | 5,217,402 |
| P/L | 269,689 | 21,164 | 201,839 |
| NW | 1,670,278 | 1,521,472 | 1,528,298 |
| WC | (890,522) | (266,267) | (425,693) |
| Emp. | 249 | 213 | 215 |

**DUNS 57-007-0466** **Imp**
## Resmed (U K) Ltd
(Subsidiary of: Resmed Holdings Limited)
96 Milton Park, Abingdon, Oxfordshire OX14 4RY
**Tel:** 01235862997
**Web:** www.resmed.com
**Reg No:** 2863553 **VAT No:** 596479469
**Estd:** 1993 Private Limited Company
**Line of Business:** Hospital equipment
**Issued Capital:** £20,000
**Directors:** R W Sommerville, D B Pendarvis
**Co. Secretary:** Bryn Jones
**Responsibilities**
**Senior:** Paul Bruce (Manager), Andrew Huxter (Manager)
**US SIC:** 5199 **UK SIC:** 61900
**Auditors:** KPMG

**Bankers:** Barclays Bank Plc (20-65-21)

| | 30-06-14 | 30-06-13 | 30-06-12 |
|---|---|---|---|
| TO | 27,149,229 | 23,488,922 | 20,480,405 |
| P/L | 1,857,896 | 1,255,237 | 1,371,734 |
| NW | 15,764,971 | 13,825,196 | 12,353,101 |
| WC | 9,318,363 | 7,606,419 | 6,118,887 |
| Emp. | 82 | 79 | 73 |

**DUNS 49-389-1303**
## Resolute Management Services Ltd
London Underwriting Centre, 3 Minster Court, Mincing Lane, Ppp, London EC3R 7DD
**Tel:** 020-7342-2000
**Reg No:** 3136297 **Estd:** 1995 Private Limited Company
**Line of Business:** Financial intermediation not elsewhere classified
**Issued Capital:** £25,000
**Directors:** F N Krutter, S A Michael, J A Collins
**Co. Secretary:** Mrs Colleen Martin
**Responsibilities**
**HR:** Chris Llewellyn (Human Resources Manager)
**Health & Safety:** Sue Twist (Health & Safety Officer)
**Branches:** Resolute Management Services Ltd, Nelson House, 55-59 Victoria Rd, Farnborough, Hampshire GU14 7PA
**US SIC:** 6111 **UK SIC:** 81501
**Auditors:** PricewaterhouseCoopers
**Bankers:** Barclays Bank Plc (20-00-00)

| | 31-03-14 | 31-03-13 | 31-03-12 |
|---|---|---|---|
| TA | 8,249,264 | 8,716,523 | 13,526,315 |
| P/L | 500,000 | 500,000 | 500,000 |
| NW | 2,590,000 | 2,205,000 | 1,825,000 |
| WC | 3,590,000 | 3,205,000 | 2,825,000 |
| Emp. | 82 | 90 | 96 |

**DUNS 73-317-0919**
## Resource & Environmental Consultants (Asbestos) Ltd
(Subsidiary of: Concept Life Sciences (Environmental Consulting) L)
100 Barbirolli Square, Manchester M2 3AB
**Tel:** 01618742499
**Web:** www.recltd.co.uk
**Reg No:** 4590936 **Estd:** 2002 Private Limited Company
**Line of Business:** Engineering consultative and design activities
**Issued Capital:** £1
**Directors:** P Mccluskey, D Wood, A S Morgan, K A Moss
**Co. Secretary:** Paul Mccluskey
**US SIC:** 7399 **UK SIC:** 83954

| | 31-12-13 | 31-12-12 | 31-12-11 |
|---|---|---|---|
| TA | 3,620,990 | 3,730,929 | 2,974,810 |
| NW | 788,795 | 1,202,077 | 739,107 |
| WC | 571,139 | 994,709 | 564,439 |

**DUNS 22-011-9858** **Imp**
## Resource Data Management Ltd
80 Johnstone Avenue, Glasgow, Lanarkshire G52 4NZ
**Tel:** 0141-810-2828
**Web:** www.resourcedm.com
**Reg No:** 0208148SC **Estd:** 2000 Private Limited Company
**Line of Business:** Manufacture of electronic instruments and appliances for measuring, checking, testing, navigating and other purposes, except industrial process control equipment
**Export Sales:** £2,104,611
**Issued Capital:** £400,727
**Directors:** E Mirandola, A J Chandler, A J Mcbride
**Co. Secretary:** Gordon Mcbride
**Responsibilities**
**Senior:** Steven Nicoll (Sales Director)
**Sales:** Steven Nicoll (Sales Director)
**US SIC:** 3829, 7374
**UK SIC:** 37100, 83940
**Auditors:** Tenon Audit Ltd
**Bankers:** HSBC Bank plc (40-22-47)

| | 31-12-13 | 31-12-12 | 31-12-11 |
|---|---|---|---|
| TO | 9,721,578 | 10,029,001 | 10,087,661 |
| P/L | 1,690,635 | 1,921,869 | 2,139,297 |
| NW | 5,369,950 | 5,465,393 | 3,431,733 |
| WC | 4,355,024 | 5,043,914 | 3,117,805 |
| Emp. | 142 | 136 | 130 |

**DUNS 50-471-2852**
## Resource Development International Ltd
(Subsidiary of: Capella Education Company)
Midland Management Centre, 1a Brandon Lane, Coventry, West Midlands CV3 3RD
**Tel:** 024-7651-5700 **Fax:** 02476515701
**Web:** www.rdi.co.uk
**Reg No:** 2450180 **Estd:** 2013 Private Limited Company
**Line of Business:** Technical and vocational secondary education
**Trading Style:** R D I

**Issued Capital:** £120,481
**Directors:** S Polacek, Ms R Jackson, Professor C A Mahoney, Professor J K Fidler, Dr P Hallam
**US SIC:** 8249, 8221
**UK SIC:** 93300, 93100
**Auditors:** Ernst & Young LLP
**Bankers:** Barclays Bank Plc (20-23-55)

| | 31-10-13 | 31-10-12 | 31-10-11 |
|---|---|---|---|
| TO | 3,338,365 | 2,798,075 | 9,374,980 |
| P/L | (3,953,703) | (2,283,766) | (1,987,073) |
| NW | (7,182,499) | (3,228,796) | (1,909,826) |
| WC | (3,556,317) | (1,326,919) | (1,776,586) |
| Emp. | 81 | 72 | 87 |

**DUNS 34-603-2097**
## Resource Environmental Services Ltd
Sabre House, Bath Road, Midgham, Reading, Berkshire RG7 5UU
**Fax:** 01189-715920
**Reg No:** 2744696 **VAT No:** 591807612
**Estd:** 1992 Private Limited Company
**Line of Business:** Other construction work involving special trades
**Issued Capital:** £21,902
**Directors:** Mrs L Williamson, C S Hale, R J Blumberger
**Branches:** Resource Environmental Services Ltd, 120 Old Broad St, London EC2N 1AR
**US SIC:** 1799, 1731
**UK SIC:** 50000, 50300
**Bankers:** HSBC Bank plc (40-34-12)

| | 31-12-13 | 31-12-12 | 31-12-11 |
|---|---|---|---|
| NW | (89,000) | (89,000) | (89,000) |

**DUNS 77-868-5974**
## Resource Experience Ltd
(Subsidiary of: Field Marketing (Uk) Holdings Ltd)
Resouce House, Bracknell, Berkshire RG12 7FS
**Tel:** 01344418383 **Fax:** 0134-441-8384
**Web:** www.relfm.com
**Reg No:** 3035364 **Estd:** 1995 Private Limited Company
**Line of Business:** Marketing consultants
**Trading Style:** Resource Experience Limited
**Issued Capital:** £956
**Principals:** D Norbury (Managing), V Davies
**Co. Secretary:** Eoin Kane
**Responsibilities**
**Senior:** Peter Brook (Manager), Laurence Clube (Manager), Lacy Ray (Office Manager)
**US SIC:** 7392 **UK SIC:** 83951
**Auditors:** KPMG LLP

| | 30-06-13 | 30-06-12 | 30-06-11 |
|---|---|---|---|
| TO | 24,885,747 | 21,548,596 | 16,112,383 |
| P/L | 2,425,519 | 1,577,178 | 1,684,598 |
| NW | 4,734,757 | 2,721,259 | 1,975,622 |
| WC | 4,521,392 | 2,543,610 | 1,841,838 |
| Emp. | 462 | 393 | 306 |

**DUNS 77-043-6350**
## Resource Group Ltd
Teme House, Whittington Road, Whittington, Worcester, Worcestershire WR5 2RY
**Tel:** 08453752500 **Fax:** 08453 752501
**Web:** www.resourcegroup.co.uk
**Reg No:** 2667200 **VAT No:** 542896314
**Estd:** 1991 Private Limited Company
**Line of Business:** Labour recruitment and provision of personnel
**Issued Capital:** £72,020
**Directors:** J G Minihan, Ms J E Larkin, R E Hunter, R L Gott
**Co. Secretary:** John Larkin
**Responsibilities**
**Senior:** Adrian Leatherland (Sales Director), Georgina Neep (Group Marketing Executive)
**Marketing:** Georgina Neep (Group Marketing Executive)
**Sales:** Adrian Leatherland (Sales Director)
**Branches:** Resource Group Ltd, Teme House, Whittington Road, Worcester, Worcestershire WR5 2RY
**US SIC:** 7399, 7361
**UK SIC:** 83954
**Auditors:** Kenneth Morris Ltd

| | 31-12-13 | 31-12-12 | 31-12-11 |
|---|---|---|---|
| TO | 48,801,166 | 37,639,760 | 34,741,476 |
| P/L | 917,509 | (1,339,201) | 220,333 |
| NW | 5,225,810 | 4,486,949 | 6,077,001 |
| WC | 3,797,906 | 2,992,685 | 5,085,667 |
| Emp. | 211 | 278 | 354 |

**DUNS 21-728-3786**
## Resource (No.1) Ltd
Edgewater Business Park, 8 Edgewater Road, Belfast BT3 9JQ
**Tel:** 02890774799
**Reg No:** 0607563NI **Estd:** 2011 Private Limited Company
**Line of Business:** Management activities of holding companies
**Issued Capital:** £5
**Directors:** D J Seaton, Mrs D Donnelly, J King, R W Gray, R C Foran
**Co. Secretary:** John King

**US SIC:** 6711 **UK SIC:** 83962
**Auditors:** Ernst & Young LLP

| | 30-09-12 | 30-09-11 |
|---|---|---|
| TO | 78,473,000 | N/A |
| P/L | (1,602,000) | N/A |
| NW | (12,433,000) | (12,261,000) |
| WC | 1,022,000 | (625,000) |
| Emp. | 5,171 | N/A |

**DUNS 73-604-9573**
## Resource Print Solutions Ltd
Bath Lane, Leeds, West Yorkshire LS13 3AT
**Tel:** 01132-058300 **Fax:** 01132-058308
**Web:** www.resource-ps.co.uk
**Reg No:** 4865997 **Estd:** 2001 Private Limited Company
**Line of Business:** Printers general
**Issued Capital:** £421,058
**Directors:** P G Thompson, D Woodcock, A Choudry
**Co. Secretary:** Ms Joanne Thompson
**Responsibilities**
**Engineering:** Jon Wendell (Production Manager)
**US SIC:** 6711 **UK SIC:** 83962
**Auditors:** Brown Butler

| | 30-09-13 | 30-09-12 | 30-09-11 |
|---|---|---|---|
| TA | 1,633,621 | 1,633,832 | 1,634,231 |
| NW | 421,058 | 421,058 | 220,311 |
| WC | (1,212,494) | (1,212,494) | (1,413,241) |

**DUNS 28-949-0997**
## Resource Solutions Group P L C
First Floor, Clifton Down House, Bristol, Avon BS8 2NH
**Tel:** 01179150380
**Web:** www.resource-management.co.uk
**Reg No:** 1617971 **VAT No:** 357912724
**Estd:** 1982 Public Limited Company
**Line of Business:** Labour recruitment and provision of personnel
**Issued Capital:** £6,050,000
**Principals:** K W Dawe (Chairman), M W Griffiths, M A Beesley, Ms J P Dawe
**Co. Secretary:** Neil Pollinger
**US SIC:** 7361 **UK SIC:** 83954
**Auditors:** Robson Taylor LLP
**Bankers:** HSBC Bank plc (40-14-13)

| | 30-06-14 | 30-06-13 | 30-06-12 |
|---|---|---|---|
| TO | 176,174,000 | 157,563,000 | 164,015,141 |
| P/L | 7,367,000 | 6,354,000 | 6,072,247 |
| NW | 16,284,000 | 10,899,000 | 6,321,386 |
| WC | 21,492,000 | 16,018,000 | 19,781,285 |
| Emp. | 191 | 176 | 173 |

**DUNS 77-106-8921**
## Resourcebank Recruitment Ltd.
R B R House, Hawksworth Road, Central Park, Telford, Shropshire TF2 9TU
**Tel:** 01952-281900
**Web:** www.resourcebank.co.uk
**Reg No:** 2683801 **Estd:** 1992 Private Limited Company
**Line of Business:** Labour recruitment and provision of personnel
**Issued Capital:** £4,000
**Director:** R J Pearson
**Co. Secretary:** Ms Susan Kaufman
**Responsibilities**
**Senior:** Lee Hawkshaw (General Manager)
**Finance:** Lee Hawkshaw (General Manager)
**Health & Safety:** Lee Hawkshaw (General Manager)
**Facilities:** Amanda Charlesworth (Facilities Manager), Lee Hawkshaw (General Manager)
**Branches:** Resourcebank Recruitment Ltd., 1A Bell Street, Henley-On-Thames, Oxfordshire RG9 2BA
**US SIC:** 7361 **UK SIC:** 83954
**Auditors:** J G Rhodes

| | 30-04-14 | 30-04-13 | 30-04-12 |
|---|---|---|---|
| TA | 1,662,527 | 1,884,273 | 1,813,624 |
| NW | 537,427 | 523,794 | 482,473 |
| WC | 443,328 | 305,511 | 267,126 |

**DUNS 38-527-9278**
## Resources for Autism
858 Finchley Road, London NW11 6AB
**Tel:** 020-8458-3259
**Web:** www.resourcesforautism.org.uk
**Reg No:** 3326332 **Estd:** 1997 Private Limited Company
**Line of Business:** Disability services
**Directors:** C N Hunter Gordon, B A Linden, Dr V E Booth, Mrs J Ternent, Mrs D Montgomery, E J Stourton
**Co. Secretary:** Raymond Esdaile
**Responsibilities**
**Senior:** Liza Dresder (Manager), Christopher Gordon (Manager), David Plummer (Manager)
**US SIC:** 8321 **UK SIC:** 96111
**Auditors:** Lindeyer Francis Ferguson

**Bankers:** National Westminster Bank Plc (55-70-13)

| | 31-03-14 | 31-03-13 | 31-03-12 |
|---|---|---|---|
| TO | 1,566,518 | 1,358,822 | 1,536,857 |
| P/L | (83,570) | (154,166) | 281,253 |
| NW | 1,220,234 | 1,303,804 | 1,457,970 |
| WC | 408,787 | 475,344 | 649,452 |
| Emp. | 59 | 53 | 48 |

DUNS 22-512-3694 **Imp-Exp**

## Respirex International Ltd

Unit F Kingsfield Business Centre, Philanthropic Road, Redhill, Surrey RH1 4DP
**Tel:** 01737-778600 **Fax:** 01737-779441
**Web:** www.respirex.co.uk
**Reg No:** 0592506 **VAT No:** 367311750
**Estd:** 1957 Private Limited Company
**Line of Business:** Manufacture of workwear
**Export Markets:** Worldwide
**Export Sales:** £5,585,567
**Issued Capital:** £1,000
**Principals:** M B Simpson *(Managing)*, D G Mackie *(Sales)*
**Co. Secretary:** Mark Simpson
**Responsibilities**
**Senior:** Neil Crimp *(Design)*, Christopher Musgrove *(Manager)*, Dave Ralf *(Warehouse Manager)*
**Sales:** James Southwell *(Sales Manager)*, Jim Tomlin *(European Sales Manager)*
**Facilities:** Dave Ralf *(Warehouse Manager)*
**Purchasing:** Mark Stebbens *(Purchasing Manager)*
**US SIC:** 2328, 2329, 2339, 2389
**UK SIC:** 45340, 45350, 45330, 45393
**Auditors:** Peter Hodgson & Co
**Bankers:** HSBC Bank plc (40-20-24)

| | 30-09-13 | 30-09-12 | 30-09-11 |
|---|---|---|---|
| TO | 10,197,625 | 9,696,979 | 8,957,170 |
| P/L | 697,882 | 933,379 | 536,394 |
| NW | 7,859,108 | 7,077,413 | 6,280,232 |
| WC | 3,490,980 | 3,190,654 | 2,381,866 |
| Emp. | 101 | 95 | 102 |

DUNS 22-504-4106 **Imp-Exp**

## Respironics (Uk) Ltd.

(**Subsidiary of:** Koninklijke Philips N.V.)
Chichester Business Park Cityfields Way, Bognor Regis, West Sussex PO21 1FP
**Tel:** 08001300840
**Web:** www.healthcare.philips.com
**Reg No:** 1314118 **VAT No:** 194102578
**Estd:** 1977 Private Limited Company
**Line of Business:** Manufacture of electronic instruments and appliances for measuring, checking, testing, navigating and other purposes, except industrial process control equipment
**Export Markets:** U S A, W Europe
**Issued Capital:** £1,203,529
**Director:** H Vivash
**Co. Secretary:** Martin Armstrong
**US SIC:** 3829, 3841
**UK SIC:** 37100, 37201
**Auditors:** Ernst & Young LLP
**Bankers:** Lloyds TSB Bank plc (30-91-97)

| | 31-12-12 | 31-12-11 |
|---|---|---|
| TA | N/A | 21,869,000 |
| P/L | (21,869,000) | 1,049,000 |
| NW | N/A | 21,869,000 |

DUNS 21-393-1398

## Respond Services

Unit 16, Capitol Industrial Park, Capitol Way, London NW9 0EQ
**Tel:** 02083036300
**Proprietorship**
**Line of Business:** Miscellaneous electrical repair shops
**Proprietor:** P Casey
**US SIC:** 8211 **UK SIC:** 93200
**Employees:** 50

DUNS 73-693-7694 **Imp**

## Respondez Europe Ltd

(**Subsidiary of:** Delphi Automotive Plc)
Unit A, Brenda Road Sovereign Park, Hartlepool, Cleveland TS25 1NN
**Tel:** 01429241400
**Web:** www.respondez.co.uk
**Reg No:** 4952694 **Estd:** 2003 Private Limited Company
**Line of Business:** Call centre activities
**Trading Style:** Respondez
**Issued Capital:** £1,200,000
**Directors:** A Wadhwa, J N Patel
**Co. Secretary:** Sanjay Mutha
**Responsibilities**
**Senior:** Ricky Mehra *(Operations Manager)*
**US SIC:** 7399 **UK SIC:** 83954
**Auditors:** PSJ Alexander & Co

| | 31-03-14 | 31-03-13 | 31-03-12 |
|---|---|---|---|
| TO | 4,062,803 | 4,573,552 | 4,135,636 |
| P/L | (414,134) | (65,042) | (136,937) |
| NW | 282,811 | 643,037 | 619,693 |
| WC | 128,256 | 456,391 | 473,091 |
| Emp. | 121 | 133 | 126 |

DUNS 42-444-3005

## Response 2 Ltd

Telecom House, Station Road, Steeton, Keighley, West Yorkshire BD20 6RB
**Tel:** 01535290000 **Fax:** 01535-290008
**Web:** www.acornstairlifts.com
**Reg No:** 4431966 **Estd:** 2002 Private Limited Company
**Line of Business:** Manufacture of medical and surgical equipment and orthopaedic appliances
**Trading Style:** Acorn Stairlifts
**Issued Capital:** £1
**Director:** J S Jakes
**Co. Secretary:** David Belmont
**Responsibilities**
**Finance:** Zofia Garvey *(Senior Financial Executive)*
**Sales:** Jules Allen *(Senior Sales Executive)*
**US SIC:** 3841 **UK SIC:** 37201

| | 31-03-14 | 31-03-13 | 31-03-12 |
|---|---|---|---|
| TA | 1 | 1 | 1 |
| NW | 1 | 1 | 1 |

DUNS 49-382-0831

## Response Building Maintenance Services (Scotland) Ltd

Thistle House Caputhall Road, Deans Industrial Estate, Livingston, West Lothian EH54 8AS
**Tel:** 01506411555 **Fax:** 01506-414181
**Web:** www.responsebms.co.uk
**Reg No:** 0161832SC **Estd:** 1995 Private Limited Company
**Line of Business:** Other building completion
**Issued Capital:** £30,000
**Principals:** J D Mcleish *(Managing)*, S A Drummond
**Responsibilities**
**Admin:** Fiona Curtis *(Office Manager)*
**US SIC:** 1799, 1711
**UK SIC:** 50000, 50300
**Auditors:** Condie & Co
**Bankers:** Clydesdale Bank Plc (82-69-34)

| | 31-03-14 | 31-03-13 | 31-03-12 |
|---|---|---|---|
| TO | N/A | N/A | 7,095,580 |
| P/L | N/A | N/A | 10,686 |
| NW | 225,042 | 219,806 | 542,468 |
| WC | 54,572 | 15,039 | 336,272 |
| Emp. | N/A | N/A | 114 |

DUNS 76-631-6772

## Response (Building Rewarding Relationships) Ltd

(**Subsidiary of:** Kura (Cs) Ltd)
21 Tyndrum Street, Glasgow, Lanarkshire G4 0JY
**Tel:** 0141 272 1105 **Fax:** 0141 272 1666
**Web:** www.response-uk.co.uk
**Reg No:** 0129877SC **Estd:** 1991 Private Limited Company
**Line of Business:** Call centres
**Export Sales:** £538,631
**Trading Style:** R H L
**Issued Capital:** £852,770
**Directors:** A Harvey, B Bannantyne, Miss J Mcintosh, J Wordsworth-Goodram, M A Moughal
**Co. Secretary:** Ms Julie Mcintosh
**US SIC:** 7379 **UK SIC:** 83940
**Auditors:** Grant Thornton UK LLP
**Bankers:** Bank Of Scotland (80-11-30)

| | 30-06-14 | 30-06-13 | 30-06-12 |
|---|---|---|---|
| TO | 24,960,892 | 19,683,667 | 28,301,201 |
| P/L | 91,234 | 288,992 | 364,392 |
| NW | 2,887,866 | 5,928,557 | 5,888,374 |
| WC | 694,929 | 4,290,256 | 3,574,882 |
| Emp. | 1,180 | 929 | 1,308 |

DUNS 21-391-0070

## Response Engineering Solutions

3 Oakland Drive, Pentre, Mid Glamorgan CF41 7QW
**Tel:** 01685812666
**Web:** www.response-engineering.com
**Proprietorship**
**Line of Business:** Mechanical engineering general
**Proprietor:** G Tuck
**US SIC:** 8911 **UK SIC:** 83701
**Employees:** 50

DUNS 23-627-8052

## Response One Ltd

(**Subsidiary of:** St Ives Plc)
The Old Dairy, Melcombe Road, Bath, Avon BA2 3LR
**Tel:** 01225-480480
**Web:** www.responseone.co.uk
**Reg No:** 3624881 **Estd:** 1998 Private Limited Company
**Line of Business:** Advertising
**Export Sales:** £1,213,506
**Issued Capital:** £48,875
**Directors:** P B Gray, Ms A D Harris, Ms N G Thompson, S Huke, P J Sargeant, M R Armitage, D Coverdale
**Co. Secretary:** Philip Harris
**Responsibilities**
**Senior:** Amanda Ling *(Information Technology Directo)*, Rob McGowan *(Associate Director, Data and I)*, Matthew Oram *(Group Head)*
**Sales:** Nicholas Blake *(Account Manager)*
**IT:** Amanda Ling *(Information Technology Directo)*
**US SIC:** 7311 **UK SIC:** 83800
**Auditors:** Moore Stephens
**Bankers:** Barclays Bank Plc (20-05-06)

| | 02-08-13 | 27-07-12 | 31-08-11 |
|---|---|---|---|
| TO | 21,193,635 | 13,544,000 | 25,397,718 |
| P/L | 142,346 | 763,717 | 2,737,639 |
| NW | 3,294,020 | 5,008,119 | 4,270,357 |
| WC | 3,202,829 | 4,659,881 | 4,075,051 |
| Emp. | 70 | 69 | 65 |

DUNS 73-343-9116

## Responsive Engineering Ltd

(**Subsidiary of:** Reece Group Ltd)
Kingsway South, Team Valley Trading Estate, Gateshead, Tyne and Wear NE11 0SH
**Tel:** 01914973420 **Fax:** 0191-497-3401
**Web:** www.responsive-engineering.com
**Reg No:** 4617703 **Estd:** 1992 Private Limited Company
**Line of Business:** Specialised building trade contractors
**Export Sales:** £1,344,328
**Issued Capital:** £138,957
**Directors:** J P Reece, S N Simpson, R D Anderton, P J Kite
**Co. Secretary:** Philip Kite
**US SIC:** 8911, 3499
**UK SIC:** 83701, 31694
**Auditors:** unw LLP
**Bankers:** Lloyds TSB Bank plc (30-93-71)

| | 31-12-13 | 31-03-13 | 31-12-12 |
|---|---|---|---|
| TO | 11,189,321 | 15,330,924 | 13,142,887 |
| P/L | 454,674 | 4,522,910 | 1,391,765 |
| NW | 6,876,606 | 6,521,414 | 4,007,575 |
| WC | 6,850,883 | 3,242,840 | 1,762,748 |
| Emp. | 175 | 175 | 160 |

DUNS 22-073-6529 **Imp**

## Responsys Ltd

Thames Tower, Station Road, Reading, Berkshire RG1 1LX
**Tel:** 08450-940088
**Web:** www.responsys.com
**Reg No:** 4075156 **Estd:** 2000 Private Limited Company
**Line of Business:** Other business activities not elsewhere classified
**Export Sales:** £9,192,700
**Issued Capital:** £1,000
**Directors:** D J Hudson, Oracle Corporation Nominees Limi
**Branches:** Responsys, Ltd, Whittaker House, 2 Whittaker Avenue, Richmond, Surrey TW9 1EH
**US SIC:** 7399 **UK SIC:** 83954
**Auditors:** Clark Howes Auditing Solutions Ltd
**Bankers:** Lloyds TSB Bank plc (30-00-08)

| | 31-12-13 | 31-12-12 | 31-12-11 |
|---|---|---|---|
| TO | 9,192,700 | N/A | N/A |
| P/L | 114,975 | N/A | N/A |
| NW | 1,104,561 | 768,557 | 529,353 |
| WC | 846,238 | 632,643 | 383,996 |
| Emp. | 85 | N/A | N/A |

DUNS 21-249-7277

## Restaurant Bar & Grill Liverpool

1st Floor, India Building, Brunswick Street, Liverpool, Merseyside L2 0XH
**Tel:** 0151-2366703
**Web:** www.therestaurantbarandgrill.co.uk
**Proprietorship**
**Line of Business:** Restaurants
**Proprietor:** P Warden
**US SIC:** 5812 **UK SIC:** 66110
**Employees:** 50

DUNS 23-613-4446 **Imp**

## Restaurant Bar & Grill Ltd

(**Subsidiary of:** W2d2 Ltd)
Ridgefield House, 14 John Dalton Street, Manchester M2 6JR
**Tel:** 01618391999 **Fax:** 01618399622
**Web:** www.individualrestaurantcompanyplc.co.uk
**Reg No:** 3610858 **Estd:** 1998 Private Limited Company
**Line of Business:** Restaurant - pub food
**Issued Capital:** £1,014,286
**Directors:** V Lord, S J Walker
**Co. Secretary:** John Hammond
**Responsibilities**
**Marketing:** Emma Walker *(Senior Marketing Executive)*
**US SIC:** 5812 **UK SIC:** 66110
**Auditors:** Grant Thornton UK LLP
**Bankers:** Bank Of Scotland (12-12-85)

| | 31-03-14 | 31-03-13 | 31-03-12 |
|---|---|---|---|
| TO | 57,211,750 | 55,268,363 | 67,734,336 |
| P/L | 139,454 | (2,172,528) | 610,640 |
| NW | 736,594 | 812,054 | 2,594,013 |
| WC | (4,415,547) | (5,911,770) | (4,403,386) |
| Emp. | 1,225 | 1,398 | 1,396 |

DUNS 21-408-1846

## The Restaurant Group Plc

5 - 7 Marshalsea Road, London SE1 1EP
**Tel:** 02031175001 **Fax:** 08456-125011
**Web:** www.ccruk.com
**Reg No:** 0030343SC **Estd:** 1994 Public Limited Company
**Line of Business:** Representative office
**Issued Capital:** £56,422,661
**Directors:** A M Jackson, Ms S A Cowdry, S M Critoph, A Hughes, D P Breithaupt, S F Cloke
**Co. Secretary:** Stephen Critoph
**Responsibilities**
**Marketing:** V Rymond *(Advertising Manager)*
**Admin:** Pushpa Bhandari *(Administrator)*
**HR:** James Atherton *(Human Resources Director)*
**Branches:** The Restaurant Group Plc, 40-42 Parkway, London NW1 7AH
**US SIC:** 6711 **UK SIC:** 83962
**Auditors:** Deloitte LLP
**Bankers:** Barclays Bank Plc (20-00-00)

| | 29-12-13 | 30-12-12 | 01-12-12 |
|---|---|---|---|
| TO | 579,589,000 | 532,541,000 | 487,114,000 |
| P/L | 72,685,000 | 64,561,000 | 48,608,000 |
| NW | 189,532,000 | 157,415,000 | 130,849,000 |
| WC | (80,168,000) | (65,268,000) | (62,641,000) |
| Emp. | 12,295 | 11,664 | 10,572 |

DUNS 22-718-5907

## The Restaurant Group (Uk) Ltd

(**Subsidiary of:** The Restaurant Group Plc)
5-7 Marshalsea Road, London SE1 1EP
**Tel:** 02079396500 **Fax:** 084-5612-5011
**Web:** www.trgconcessions.co.uk
**Reg No:** 0894426 **Estd:** 1966 Private Limited Company
**Line of Business:** Licensed restaurants
**Trading Style:** Trg Concessions Frankie & Benny's, Blube Ckers Chiquito, Edwinns Brasserie Garfunkel's, Brunning and Price
**Issued Capital:** £3,437,461
**Directors:** D P Breithaupt, S M Critoph
**Co. Secretary:** Alex Small
**Branches:** The Restaurant Group (Uk) Ltd, 106 Queensway, London W2 3RR
**US SIC:** 7399, 5813
**UK SIC:** 83954, 66200
**Auditors:** BDO Stoy Hayward LLP
**Bankers:** Barclays Bank Plc (20-00-50)

| | 29-12-13 | 30-12-12 | 01-12-12 |
|---|---|---|---|
| TO | 446,787,000 | 416,107,000 | 376,438,000 |
| P/L | 64,724,000 | 58,701,000 | 48,796,000 |
| NW | 85,813,000 | 73,097,000 | 61,193,000 |
| WC | (55,212,000) | (38,173,000) | (32,163,000) |
| Emp. | 9,214 | 8,844 | 7,826 |

DUNS 36-480-6062

## Restaurant Services

Heasley Mill, South Molton, Devon EX36 3LF
**VAT No:** 540484552 **Estd:** 1990 Partnership
**Line of Business:** Eating Establishments
**Partners:** A Louis, Mrs D Bale
**US SIC:** 5812 **UK SIC:** 66110
**Employees:** 100

DUNS 21-000-6494

## Restaurants Etc Ltd

Old Barn House, 2 Wannions Close, Chesham, Buckinghamshire HP5 1YA
**Tel:** 08450055551
**Web:** www.restaurantsetcltd.com
**Reg No:** 6264158 **Estd:** 2007 Private Limited Company
**Line of Business:** Licensed restaurants
**Issued Capital:** £105
**Director:** M Hix
**Co. Secretary:** Ratnesh Bagdai
**US SIC:** 7399 **UK SIC:** 83954

| | 31-12-13 | 31-12-12 | 31-12-11 |
|---|---|---|---|
| TO | 13,952,208 | 13,677,095 | 8,655,720 |
| P/L | 1,060,411 | 158,649 | 637,173 |
| NW | 1,519,212 | 817,027 | 714,343 |
| WC | (688,456) | (918,668) | 220,719 |
| Emp. | 242 | 246 | 154 |

DUNS 21-032-6384

## Restful Homes Group

Milton Court Care Centre, Tunbridge Grove, Milton Keynes, Buckinghamshire MK7 6JD
**Tel:** 01908-699555
**Web:** www.restfulhomes.co.uk
**Proprietorship**
**Line of Business:** Residential care establishments
**Proprietor:** Mrs C Plant
**Responsibilities**
**Senior:** Cheryl Rolt *(Home Manager)*
**Finance:** Mark Ricket *(Finance Administrator)*

**Admin:** Mark Ricket *(Finance Administrator)*
**US SIC:** 8091 **UK SIC:** 95200
**Employees:** 95

DUNS 73-916-4064
## Restore Plc
66 Grosvenor Street, London W1K 3KL
**Tel:** 02074092420 **Fax:** 020 7868 8600
**Web:** www.restoreplc.com
**Reg No:** 5169780 **Estd:** 2004 Public Limited Company
**Line of Business:** Other business activities not elsewhere classified
**Issued Capital:** £8,740,025
**Directors:** J C Wilde, S J Davidson, Sir W H Wells, Ms S Baylay, C A Skinner, A T Councell
**Co. Secretary:** Ms Sarah Waudby
**US SIC:** 7399 **UK SIC:** 83954
**Auditors:** Baker Tilly UK Audit LLP
**Bankers:** Lloyds TSB Bank plc (30-00-02)

| | 31-12-13 | 31-12-12 | 31-12-11 |
|---|---|---|---|
| TO | 53,600,000 | 43,300,000 | 34,800,000 |
| P/L | 5,000,000 | 1,500,000 | 2,000,000 |
| NW | 5,200,000 | 3,600,000 | 1,200,000 |
| WC | 200,000 | 900,000 | 1,100,000 |
| Emp. | 550 | 565 | 536 |

DUNS 57-829-6402
## Result Group Ltd
Unit B4 Lowfields Close, Elland, West Yorkshire HX5 9DX
**Tel:** 01422 327000 **Fax:** 01422 370030
**Web:** www.rentalresult.com
**Reg No:** 2887881 **Estd:** 1994 Public Limited Company
**Line of Business:** Computer software (development)
**Trading Style:** Result Group Ltd
**Issued Capital:** £33,524
**Principals:** W D Robson *(Managing)*, J C Wakefield, Ms H J Sowerby
**Co. Secretary:** David Griffiths
**Responsibilities**
**Senior:** James Horsfall *(Manager)*
**IT:** Craig Richmond *(Software Development Director)*
**HR:** Dawn Ogden *(Human Resources Manager)*, Craig Richmond *(Software Development Director)*
**US SIC:** 7379, 6711
**UK SIC:** 83940, 83962
**Auditors:** Grant Thornton UK LLP
**Bankers:** Bank Of Scotland (12-08-95)

| | 31-12-13 | 31-12-12 | 31-12-11 |
|---|---|---|---|
| TO | 4,795,146 | 3,355,513 | 4,050,073 |
| P/L | (155,042) | (962,979) | (591,192) |
| NW | (4,161,805) | (3,976,745) | (2,786,795) |
| WC | (2,132,508) | (4,014,184) | (2,825,697) |
| Emp. | 71 | 65 | 64 |

DUNS 49-431-9239 **Imp**
## Retail Decisions Europe Ltd
**(Subsidiary of:** Aci Worldwide Inc.)
Red House, Cemetery Pales, Brookwood, Woking, Surrey GU24 0BL
**Tel:** 01483728700
**Web:** www.redworldwide.com
**Reg No:** 3142903 **Estd:** 1999 Private Limited Company
**Line of Business:** Data processing
**Export Sales:** £3,411,778
**Issued Capital:** £10,000
**Directors:** D P Byrnes, D G King, P Thomalla, S W Behrens, T F Rodriguez
**Co. Secretary:** Dennis Byrnes
**Responsibilities**
**Senior:** Neshia Batchasingh *(Manager)*, Carlyle Clump *(Manager)*, Clive Drysdale *(Manager)*, Fabio Giuseppetti *(Manager)*
**US SIC:** 7374 **UK SIC:** 83940
**Auditors:** PricewaterhouseCoopers LLP
**Bankers:** National Westminster Bank Plc (60-00-01)

| | 31-12-13 | 31-12-12 | 31-12-11 |
|---|---|---|---|
| TO | 15,599,204 | 13,965,446 | 12,017,923 |
| P/L | 3,669,193 | 1,205,756 | 3,200,031 |
| NW | 25,516,412 | 21,774,330 | 21,103,666 |
| WC | 23,585,470 | 19,104,221 | 18,407,897 |
| Emp. | 81 | 80 | 73 |

DUNS 73-321-9377
## Retail Furniture Ltd
**(Subsidiary of:** Retail Furniture Holdings Ltd)
Unit E, Telford, Shropshire TF7 4PL
**Tel:** 01952-587277 **Fax:** 01952201269
**Web:** www.retailfurniture.net
**Reg No:** 4595802 **Estd:** 2002 Private Limited Company
**Line of Business:** Manufacture of other office and shop furniture
**Issued Capital:** £2
**Director:** N Enefer
**Co. Secretary:** Kevin Bell
**Responsibilities**
**Admin:** Thereasa Farr *(Office Manager)*
**US SIC:** 2599 **UK SIC:** 46720

**Auditors:** Cheadles

| | 31-10-13 | 31-10-12 | 31-10-11 |
|---|---|---|---|
| TA | 1,042,649 | 1,168,310 | 1,223,802 |
| NW | 249,440 | 299,399 | 289,439 |
| WC | 282,929 | 299,399 | 289,439 |

DUNS 23-704-0774
## Retail Human Resources P L C
14 Bristol Gardens, London N6 4JH
**Tel:** 02074328888
**Web:** www.retailhumanresources.co.uk
**Reg No:** 3699291 **Estd:** 1999
**Line of Business:** Employment and recruitment companies and consultants
**Trading Style:** Adgrafix Advertising
**Issued Capital:** £56,125
**Directors:** G P Heather, Miss E E Burgess, P Burgess, J Burgess, M Flesch, A Tomkinson, R J Horwood
**Co. Secretary:** Rakesh Tailor
**Responsibilities**
**Senior:** Shelley Pinto *(Director)*
**Branches:** Retail Human Resources P L C, 14 Bristol Gardens, London W9 2JG
**US SIC:** 7361 **UK SIC:** 83954
**Auditors:** Sproull & Co

| | 30-06-14 | 30-06-13 | 30-06-12 |
|---|---|---|---|
| TO | 5,453,701 | 4,886,707 | 4,750,033 |
| P/L | 88,944 | 36,154 | (216,052) |
| NW | 1,618,743 | 1,631,537 | 1,708,369 |
| WC | 512,681 | 204,140 | 415,641 |
| Emp. | 115 | 92 | 83 |

DUNS 71-929-1762
## Retail Marketing Group Ltd
Hatch Farm, Mill Lane, Sindlesham, Wokingham, Berkshire RG41 5DF
**Tel:** 01189070490
**Web:** www.retailmarketing.co.uk
**Reg No:** 5310251 **Estd:** 2004 Private Limited Company
**Line of Business:** Marketing consultants
**Issued Capital:** £100
**Directors:** J Keleher, W J Richmond
**Co. Secretary:** Wren Accounting Limited
**US SIC:** 7392 **UK SIC:** 83951
**Auditors:** Roy Pinnock & Co LLP

| | 31-12-13 | 31-12-12 | 31-12-11 |
|---|---|---|---|
| TO | 10,828,257 | N/A | N/A |
| P/L | 989,516 | N/A | N/A |
| NW | 2,613,166 | 2,056,562 | 766,728 |
| WC | 2,247,768 | 1,810,653 | 654,582 |
| Emp. | 410 | N/A | N/A |

DUNS 21-938-5262
## Retail Merchant Group Ltd
Matrix House, 2 North Fourth Street, Milton Keynes, Buckinghamshire MK9 1NJ
**Tel:** 08452419960
**Web:** www.retailmerchantservices.co.uk
**Reg No:** 6257540 **Estd:** 2007 Private Limited Company
**Line of Business:** Retail sale of alcoholic and other beverages
**Export Sales:** £92,360
**Issued Capital:** £2,800,000
**Directors:** G D Poppleton, I G Pennick, I Robson, P Mcomish, M E Postle
**Co. Secretary:** Paul Mcomish
**US SIC:** 7399 **UK SIC:** 83954
**Bankers:** National Westminster Bank Plc (53-50-10)

| | 31-12-13 | 31-12-12 | 31-12-11 |
|---|---|---|---|
| TO | 10,773,901 | 7,916,313 | N/A |
| P/L | 1,858,034 | 385,360 | N/A |
| NW | (187,442) | (2,048,776) | (2,091,459) |
| WC | 609,882 | (217,618) | 1,234,651 |
| Emp. | 188 | 143 | N/A |

DUNS 29-007-3048
## The Retail Motor Industry Federation Ltd
201 Great Portland Street, London W1W 5AB
**Tel:** 01788576465 **Fax:** 020-7580-6376
**Web:** www.rmif.co.uk
**Reg No:** 0133095 **VAT No:** 354308268
**Estd:** 1997 Private Company Limited By Guarantee
**Line of Business:** Activities of business and employers organisations
**Directors:** P Johnson, Mrs B V Evans, K J Briggs, P A Hill, C B Madderson, M C Marshall, P Jones, A Lowe
**Co. Secretary:** Kevin Briggs
**Responsibilities**
**Senior:** Alec Murray *(Director)*, Colin Parlett *(Director)*
**Finance:** Kevin Waterman *(Financial Director)*
**Marketing:** Louise Wallis *(Marketing Manager)*
**Branches:** The Retail Motor Industry Federation Ltd, 201 Great Portland Street, London W1W 5AB
**US SIC:** 8611 **UK SIC:** 96312
**Auditors:** Kingston Smith

**Bankers:** Lloyds TSB Bank plc (30-93-68)

| | 31-12-13 | 31-12-12 | 31-12-11 |
|---|---|---|---|
| TO | 16,832,000 | 16,030,000 | 13,005,000 |
| P/L | (697,000) | 645,000 | (118,000) |
| NW | 18,206,000 | 18,485,000 | 17,764,000 |
| WC | (1,295,000) | (548,000) | (278,000) |
| Emp. | 246 | 197 | 190 |

DUNS 73-706-5354
## Retail Solutions (Holdings) Ltd
Hardings Chartered Certified Accountants, Newcastle, Staffordshire ST5 1DU
**Tel:** 01782-617868 **Fax:** 01782-712673
**Web:** www.retailsolutionsonline.com
**Reg No:** 4965155 **Estd:** 2003 Private Limited Company
**Line of Business:** Management activities of holding companies
**Export Sales:** £786,794
**Issued Capital:** £9,519
**Directors:** S Hinchliffe, S C Robinson, G A Phillips, S J Machin, I D Andrews, E P Byrnes
**Co. Secretary:** Ms Deborah Bufton
**Responsibilities**
**Senior:** Walter Latham *(Manager)*
**US SIC:** 6711 **UK SIC:** 83962

| | 31-12-13 | 31-12-12 | 31-12-11 |
|---|---|---|---|
| TO | 98,055,493 | 84,271,820 | 73,628,732 |
| P/L | 2,867,000 | 2,032,451 | 1,335,876 |
| NW | 7,182,476 | 5,238,518 | 3,903,045 |
| WC | 2,529,528 | 1,032,867 | (1,905,787) |
| Emp. | 2,840 | 2,157 | 1,533 |

DUNS 36-520-4010
## Retail Trust
Hammers Lane Marshall Estate, London NW7 4EE
**Tel:** 02083587225
**Web:** www.retailtrust.org.uk
**Reg No:** 4254201 **Estd:** 2001 Private Company Limited By Guarantee
**Line of Business:** Miscellaneous real property lessors
**Directors:** T Duddy, Mrs K A Payne, A Daramola-Martin, R H Newman, Ms A Darzins, L D Page, P R Clarke, N D Duxbury
**Co. Secretary:** David Kaye
**Branches:** Retail Trust, Crookfur Cottage Homes, Crookfur Road House, Newton Mearns, Glasgow, Lanarkshire G77 6JY
**US SIC:** 6519, 7392, 8321, 8999
**UK SIC:** 85000, 83951, 96111, 83954
**Auditors:** Baker Tilly UK Audit LLP
**Bankers:** National Westminster Bank Plc (60-14-27)

| | 30-04-14 | 30-04-13 | 30-04-12 |
|---|---|---|---|
| TO | 9,861,539 | 9,657,451 | 9,074,040 |
| P/L | 2,451,456 | 621,787 | 497,549 |
| NW | 33,565,081 | 28,261,903 | 28,864,533 |
| WC | 4,867,239 | 4,027,819 | 4,725,526 |
| Emp. | 145 | 152 | 148 |

DUNS 73-857-8231
## Retailmenot Uk Ltd
**(Subsidiary of:** Retailmenot Ltd)
6th Floor, 200 Grays Inn Road, London WC1X 8XZ
**Web:** www.vouchercodes.co.uk
**Reg No:** 5112833 **Estd:** 2004 Private Limited Company
**Line of Business:** Marketing consultants
**Export Sales:** £411,690
**Issued Capital:** £1,171
**Directors:** M D Lester, Ms C S Davenport, G C Cunningham
**Responsibilities**
**Senior:** Duncan Jennings *(Manager)*, Max Jennings *(Operations Director)*
**Operations:** Max Jennings *(Operations Director)*
**US SIC:** 7392 **UK SIC:** 83951
**Auditors:** Kingston Smith LLP

| | 31-12-13 | 31-12-12 | 31-12-11 |
|---|---|---|---|
| TO | 19,881,527 | 13,449,291 | 8,164,684 |
| P/L | 7,134,494 | 5,157,061 | 3,452,729 |
| NW | 8,324,545 | 4,426,951 | 2,951,606 |
| WC | 7,696,006 | 4,105,098 | 2,640,289 |
| Emp. | 88 | 62 | 41 |

DUNS 21-034-0633
## Retford Oaks Academy School
Babworth Road, Retford, Nottinghamshire DN22 7NJ
**Tel:** 01777-861-618
**Web:** www.retfordoaks-ac.org.uk
**Estd:** 2012
**Line of Business:** Schools (foundation)
**US SIC:** 8211 **UK SIC:** 93200
**Employees:** 100

DUNS 73-822-5023
## The Rethink Group Ltd
The Crane Building, 22 Lavington Street, London SE1 0NZ
**Tel:** 0161-214-7450 **Fax:** 0162147499
**Web:** www.rethink-recruitment.com
**Reg No:** 5078352 **VAT No:** 853991090
**Estd:** 2004 Private Limited Company

**Line of Business:** Employment service
**Export Sales:** £19,993,000
**Issued Capital:** £1,044,819
**Directors:** P M Crystal, B Felton, J A Kirkham, J Osullivan, S D Wright
**Co. Secretary:** Benjamin Felton
**Responsibilities**
**Senior:** Alan Darling *(?Energy Practice Manager)*, Deborah Davenport *(?Client Services Director)*
**US SIC:** 7361 **UK SIC:** 83954
**Auditors:** BDO LLP
**Bankers:** Bank Of Scotland (80-02-52)

| | 31-12-13 | 31-12-12 | 31-12-11 |
|---|---|---|---|
| TO | 111,693,000 | 91,201,000 | 78,898,000 |
| P/L | 830,000 | (755,000) | 2,529,000 |
| NW | 1,964,000 | 1,183,000 | 1,156,000 |
| WC | 1,566,000 | 675,000 | 1,046,000 |
| Emp. | 206 | 241 | 173 |

DUNS 21-245-4594
## Retired Nurses National Home
Riverside Avenue, Bournemouth, Dorset BH7 7EE
**Tel:** 01202396418
**Web:** www.rnnh.co.uk
**Estd:** 1974
**Line of Business:** Residential care establishments
**Co. Secretary:** Brian Newman
**Responsibilities**
**Senior:** Elaine Brace *(Home Manager)*, Alwyne Cross *(Manager)*, Jean Kelleway *(Manager)*, Margaret Lovett *(Manager)*, Eileen Richardson *(Manager)*, Margaret Sharkey *(Manager)*, Shirley Young *(Manager)*
**HR:** Elaine Brace *(Home Manager)*, Rosie Kuropka *(Head of Training)*
**Health & Safety:** Rosie Kuropka *(Head of Training)*
**Facilities:** Elaine Brace *(Home Manager)*
**US SIC:** 8321, 6732
**UK SIC:** 96111, 83100
**Bankers:** National Westminster Bank Plc (56-00-35)
**Employees:** 62

DUNS 76-906-4429
## Retirement Lease Housing Association
1 Pickford Street, Aldershot, Hampshire GU11 1TY
**Tel:** 01252-356000
**Web:** www.rlha.org.uk
**Reg No:** 0019730IP **Estd:** 1971 Friendly Society
**Line of Business:** Non-charitable social work activities with accommodation
**Principals:** E D Gould *(Chairman)*, Mrs C Stuart, S Gallop, P Haler, J Williams, A J Perkins, W M B Young
**Responsibilities**
**Senior:** Lorraine Collis *(Chief Executive Officer)*
**Finance:** Gary Newell *(Financial Controller)*
**Branches:** Retirement Lease Housing Association, Hillcroft, Petworth Road, Godalming, Surrey GU8 5LT
**US SIC:** 8321 **UK SIC:** 96111
**Bankers:** Coutts & Co (18-00-09)
**Employees:** 21
**Turnover:** £3,085,400

DUNS 34-525-1107
## Retirement Villages Group Ltd
**(Subsidiary of:** Romac Investments Ltd)
Kings Lodge, 28 Church Street, Epsom, Surrey KT17 4QB
**Tel:** 01372731888
**Web:** www.retirementvillages.co.uk
**Reg No:** 5335724 **Estd:** 2005 Private Limited Company
**Line of Business:** Management activities of holding companies
**Issued Capital:** £12,947,584
**Directors:** J P Puckering, Ms S D Burgess, D C Phillips, N Donaldson, P M Walsh, N F Welby
**Co. Secretary:** David Miller
**US SIC:** 6711 **UK SIC:** 83962
**Auditors:** BDO LLP

| | 31-03-14 | 31-03-13 | 31-03-12 |
|---|---|---|---|
| TO | 28,021,000 | 23,490,000 | 22,977,000 |
| P/L | (260,000) | (10,993,000) | (982,000) |
| NW | 26,174,000 | 20,335,000 | 25,790,000 |
| WC | 8,590,000 | 706,000 | (886,000) |
| Emp. | 641 | 619 | 577 |

DUNS 23-036-6226
## Retlan Manufacturing Ltd
116 Deer Park Road, Antrim, Co Antrim BT41 3SS
**Tel:** 02879-650765
**Web:** www.sdctrailers.com
**Reg No:** 0034211NI **Estd:** 1998 Private Limited Company
**Line of Business:** Manufacture of other transport equipment not elsewhere classified
**Trading Style:** Sdc Trailers Ltd

**Issued Capital:** £692,041
**Directors:** M F Cuskeran, C Mccauley, Ms J Donnelly, D Donnelly, J J Donnelly, E J Cushnahan
**Co. Secretary:** Darren Donnelly
**Branches:** Retlan Manufacturing Ltd, Common Road, Sutton-In-Ashfield, Nottinghamshire NG17 2JY
**US SIC:** 3799, 3715
**UK SIC:** 36502, 35220
**Auditors:** ASM (M) Ltd
**Bankers:** Northern Bank Ltd (95-03-81)

| | 31-03-14 | 31-03-13 | 31-03-12 |
|---|---|---|---|
| TO | 131,087,000 | 113,744,000 | 111,352,000 |
| P/L | 6,328,000 | 2,780,000 | 2,467,000 |
| NW | 23,942,000 | 19,155,000 | 19,066,000 |
| WC | 20,187,000 | 16,036,000 | 13,252,000 |
| Emp. | 665 | 600 | 582 |

DUNS 21-724-6354
## Retrac Productions Ltd
Unit 3-5, Swindon, Wiltshire SN2 8HB
**Web:** www.retrac-group.com
**Reg No:** 1080012 **VAT No:** 194854223
**Estd:** 1972 Private Limited Company
**Line of Business:** Precision engineers
**Trading Style:** Retrac Productions Ltd
**Issued Capital:** £60,810
**Principals:** J A Carter *(Managing)*, R A Carter, A J Carter, A J Carter
**Co. Secretary:** Ms Irene Carter
**Responsibilities**
**Senior:** John Howarth *(Works Director)*, Steve Murray *(Stores Coordinator)*
**Finance:** Jodie Jefferies-Clark *(Financial Director)*
**HR:** John Howarth *(Works Director)*
**Facilities:** John Howarth *(Works Director)*
**Engineering:** John Howarth *(Works Director)*
**US SIC:** 8911, 2499
**UK SIC:** 83701, 46500
**Auditors:** Morris Owen
**Bankers:** Lloyds TSB Bank plc (30-98-41)

| | 30-11-13 | 30-11-12 | 30-11-11 |
|---|---|---|---|
| TO | 4,996,010 | N/A | N/A |
| P/L | 673,108 | N/A | N/A |
| NW | 2,629,510 | 2,308,838 | 2,294,034 |
| WC | 1,222,491 | 926,040 | 1,193,511 |
| Emp. | 62 | N/A | N/A |

DUNS 21-098-3170
## Retrak
Metropolitan House, Cheadle, Cheshire SK8 7AZ
**Tel:** 01614856685
**Web:** www.retrak.org
**Reg No:** 6424507 **Estd:** 1998 Private Company Limited By Guarantee
**Line of Business:** Social work activities without accommodation
**Directors:** I B Pettigrew, Ms D R Brower Latz, D King, Ms D White, Ms V Floy, M Royal
**Co. Secretary:** Stephen Thomas
**Branches:** TIGERS CLUB PROJECT, Plot 245 Mengo Hill Road, Kampala, Uganda, Kampala
**US SIC:** 8321 **UK SIC:** 96111
**Auditors:** Baldwin Scofield & Co
**Bankers:** Cafcash Ltd (40-52-40)

| | 31-12-13 | 31-12-12 | 31-12-11 |
|---|---|---|---|
| TO | 1,248,955 | 943,409 | 1,106,387 |
| P/L | 46,708 | (12,737) | 155,220 |
| NW | 316,481 | 269,773 | 249,699 |
| WC | 136,814 | 91,013 | 90,164 |
| Emp. | 74 | 61 | 56 |

DUNS 23-277-3333
## The Retreat
Heslington Road, York, North Yorkshire YO10 5BW
**Tel:** 01904412551
**Web:** www.retreat-hospital.org
**Estd:** 1796
**Line of Business:** Mental health centres
**Trading Style:** The Retreat
**Directors:** Mrs J Mcaleese, J N Naish, S Haywood, J Eversely
**Responsibilities**
**Senior:** Peter Edley *(Manager)*, Roger Mattingly *(Manager)*, Stephen Redgate *(Manager)*, Kay Whittle *(Manager)*
**Marketing:** Louise Clarke *(Marketing Manager)*
**Health & Safety:** Martyn Ferguson *(Facilities Manager)*
**Facilities:** Martyn Ferguson *(Facilities Manager)*
**Operations:** Martyn Ferguson *(Facilities Manager)*, Maggie Scott *(Director of Operations)*
**Purchasing:** Brian Forshaw *(Purchasing Manager)*
**US SIC:** 8091 **UK SIC:** 95200
**Bankers:** HSBC Bank plc (40-47-31)
**Employees:** 311

DUNS 42-340-0303
## Retro Clothing Ltd
34 Pembridge Road, London W11 3HN
**Tel:** 020-7792-1715
**Web:** www.mgeshops.com
**Reg No:** 4327733 **Estd:** 2001 Private Limited Company
**Line of Business:** Retail of second-hand goods
**Trading Style:** Music and Goods Exchange
**Issued Capital:** £100
**Director:** Ms P M Cummings
**Co. Secretary:** John Goulden
**Responsibilities**
**Senior:** Brian Abraham *(Manager)*
**Branches:** Retro Clothing Ltd, Unit 3, Chester Road, Borehamwood, Hertfordshire WD6 1NA
**US SIC:** 2341 **UK SIC:** 45362
**Auditors:** HLB Vantis Audit Plc

| | 31-07-14 | 30-06-13 | 30-07-12 |
|---|---|---|---|
| TA | 1,349,711 | 926,422 | 987,676 |
| NW | 150,931 | 114,013 | 66,875 |
| WC | 119,567 | 92,260 | 45,925 |

DUNS 21-831-5599
## Retroscreen Virology Group Plc
Queen Mary Bioenterprises, Innovation Centre, 42 New Road, London E1 2AX
**Tel:** 02077561300
**Web:** www.retroscreen.com
**Reg No:** 8008725 **Estd:** 2012 Public Limited Company
**Line of Business:** Research and experimental development on natural sciences and engineering
**Issued Capital:** £2,048,846
**Directors:** Dr A M Fielding, G E Yeatman, Dr T J Nicholls, Ms K Denny, J F Winschel, D R Norwood, J W Ellertson
**Co. Secretary:** Graham Yeatman
**Responsibilities**
**Sales:** Ian Meikle *(Business Development Director)*
**HR:** Jelena Jovanovic *(Human Resources Manager)*
**US SIC:** 7391 **UK SIC:** 94000
**Auditors:** Baker Tilly UK Audit LLP

| | 31-12-13 | 31-12-12 |
|---|---|---|
| TO | 27,490,000 | 14,395,000 |
| P/L | (1,193,000) | (428,000) |
| NW | 41,778,000 | 16,336,000 |
| WC | 38,846,000 | 14,959,000 |
| Emp. | 273 | 123 |

DUNS 34-864-3164
## Rettie & Company Ltd
11 Wemyss Place, Edinburgh, Midlothian EH3 6DH
**Tel:** 0131-220-4160 **Fax:** 0131-220-4159
**Web:** www.rettie.co.uk
**Reg No:** 0144330SC **Estd:** 1993 Private Limited Company
**Line of Business:** Real estate agencies
**Issued Capital:** £1,090
**Directors:** C Hall, S J Rettie, Ms S M Rettie, M J Benson
**Co. Secretary:** David Gibson
**Responsibilities**
**Senior:** Will Scarlett *(Manager)*
**Sales:** Alastair Houlden *(Associate Director - Residenti)*, Stuart Montgomery *(Business Development Director)*
**Branches:** Rettie & Company Ltd, 1-3 India Street, Edinburgh, Midlothian EH3 6HA
**US SIC:** 6531 **UK SIC:** 83400
**Bankers:** Bank Of Scotland (80-11-05)

| | 30-04-14 | 30-04-13 | 30-04-12 |
|---|---|---|---|
| TO | 5,741,100 | 4,852,128 | 5,175,504 |
| P/L | 674,533 | 270,288 | 448,484 |
| NW | 2,136,652 | 2,029,868 | 1,922,150 |
| WC | 1,805,348 | 1,827,838 | 1,686,200 |
| Emp. | 107 | 112 | 104 |

DUNS 21-622-8437 Imp
## Rettig (Uk) Ltd
**(Subsidiary of:** Rettig Capital Oy Ab)
Eastern Avenue, Gateshead, Tyne and Wear NE11 0PG
**Tel:** 01914914466 **Fax:** 0191 491 7439
**Web:** www.rettigicc.com
**Reg No:** 0653648 **Estd:** 1960 Private Limited Company
**Line of Business:** Wholesale of hardware, plumbing and heating equipment and supplies
**Trading Style:** Myson
**Issued Capital:** £8,307,387
**Directors:** C Gasser, Mrs L Currie, B Lynch, K Mccauley, M Wright, T Olander
**Co. Secretary:** Gary Marshall
**Responsibilities**
**IT:** Ian Going *(IT Manager)*
**HR:** Helen Duke *(Human Resources Officer)*
**Facilities:** Ken Moffitt *(Engineering Manager)*
**Operations:** Ken Moffitt *(Engineering Manager)*
**Engineering:** Grant Lennon *(Production Manager)*, Ken Moffitt *(Engineering Manager)*
**Branches:** Rettig (Uk) Ltd, Rettig Park, Chester Le Street, County Durham DH2 1AB
**US SIC:** 5074 **UK SIC:** 61300
**Auditors:** KPMG LLP
**Bankers:** National Westminster Bank Plc (50-41-01)

| | 31-12-13 | 31-12-12 | 31-12-11 |
|---|---|---|---|
| TO | 65,832,000 | 65,302,000 | 69,584,000 |
| P/L | 630,000 | (911,000) | (347,000) |
| NW | 16,271,000 | 16,775,000 | 18,278,000 |
| WC | 11,071,000 | 9,276,000 | 11,238,000 |
| Emp. | 314 | 331 | 321 |

DUNS 73-452-6788
## Return on Investment Ltd.
**(Subsidiary of:** Njs Holdings Ltd)
Pepper House, Market Street, Nantwich, Cheshire CW5 5DQ
**Tel:** 08704605474 **Fax:** 01270-628135
**Web:** www.roiltd.co.uk
**Reg No:** 4716956 **Estd:** 1903 Private Limited Company
**Line of Business:** Marketing consultants
**Issued Capital:** £4
**Director:** N J Sandiford
**US SIC:** 7392, 7399
**UK SIC:** 83951, 83954

| | 31-03-14 | 31-03-13 | 31-03-12 |
|---|---|---|---|
| TA | 1,585,077 | 1,023,441 | 1,170,082 |
| NW | 406,800 | 425,008 | 379,344 |
| WC | 222,147 | 284,034 | 295,455 |

DUNS 22-082-8441
## Reuse Collections Ltd
**(Subsidiary of:** Parridale Pty. Limited)
49 Lidgate Crescent, Langthwaite Grange Industrial Estate, South Kirkby, Pontefract, West Yorkshire WF9 3NR
**Tel:** 01977608020
**Web:** www.berrymanglassrecycling.com
**Reg No:** 4084246 **VAT No:** 758535394
**Estd:** 2000 Private Limited Company
**Line of Business:** Collection and treatment of other waste
**Export Sales:** £1,881,732
**Trading Style:** Berryman
**Issued Capital:** £2
**Director:** A C Johnston
**Co. Secretary:** Andrew Stuart
**Responsibilities**
**Health & Safety:** Pat Duker *(Health & Safety Officer)*
**Branches:** Reuse Collections Limited, 73 Chequers La, Dagenham, Essex RM9 6QJ
**US SIC:** 4953, 3231
**UK SIC:** 92110, 24791
**Auditors:** Mitchells (UK) Ltd
**Bankers:** Bank Of Scotland (12-08-83)

| | 30-01-14 | 31-01-13 | 31-01-12 |
|---|---|---|---|
| TO | 36,301,667 | 29,586,499 | 13,532,586 |
| P/L | 2,654,344 | 1,059,438 | 191,154 |
| NW | 7,317,042 | 4,824,065 | 3,994,173 |
| WC | 2,370,637 | (1,296,657) | (1,790,151) |
| Emp. | 96 | 91 | 89 |

DUNS 23-580-5202
## Reuse Glass U K Ltd
**(Subsidiary of:** Parridale Pty. Limited)
Headlands Lane, Knottingley, West Yorkshire WF11 0HP
**Tel:** 01977-671777
**Reg No:** 3578299 **Estd:** 1999 Private Limited Company
**Line of Business:** Recycling
**Issued Capital:** £1,000,002
**Director:** A C Johnston
**Co. Secretary:** Andrew Stuart
**Responsibilities**
**Senior:** Jamie Brown *(Manager)*
**US SIC:** 3031 **UK SIC:** 48123
**Auditors:** Barber Harrison & Platt
**Bankers:** Bank Of Scotland (12-08-83)

| | 30-01-14 | 31-01-13 | 31-01-12 |
|---|---|---|---|
| TO | 39,933,822 | 31,447,808 | 14,492,701 |
| P/L | 2,016,439 | 1,158,429 | (366,144) |
| NW | 10,803,916 | 9,082,196 | 8,226,341 |
| WC | 5,186,348 | (2,224,387) | (3,377,639) |
| Emp. | 175 | 171 | 162 |

DUNS 21-024-6856
## Reuters Ltd
**(Subsidiary of:** Thomson Company Inc The)
The Reuters Building, South Colonnade Canary Wharf, London E14 5EP
**Tel:** 020-7250-1122 **Fax:** 02075425411
**Web:** www.thomsonreuters.com
**Reg No:** 0145516 **Estd:** 1916 Private Limited Company
**Line of Business:** Information services
**Trading Style:** Thomson Reuters
**Issued Capital:** £502,800
**Directors:** P D Moss, G Erol, Mrs H E Campbell, Ms P Hughes, D M Mitchley
**Co. Secretary:** Miss Carla O'Hanlon
**Responsibilities**
**Senior:** Trevor Blackmoore *(Manager)*
**Branches:** Reuters Ltd, Reuters Ltd, 30 South Colonnade, London E14 5EP
**US SIC:** 7399 **UK SIC:** 83954
**Auditors:** PricewaterhouseCoopers LLP
**Bankers:** Bank Of Scotland (12-01-03)

**Following financial data are in thousands**

| | 31-12-13 | 31-12-12 | 31-12-11 |
|---|---|---|---|
| TO | 1,582,000 | 1,706,000 | 1,812,000 |
| P/L | 118,000 | 105,000 | 81,000 |
| NW | 2,535,000 | 2,461,000 | 2,340,000 |
| WC | (2,947,000) | (3,049,000) | (3,155,000) |
| Emp. | 4,594 | 4,645 | 4,927 |

DUNS 23-077-4718
## Revenue Assurance Consulting Ltd
**(Subsidiary of:** Cilantro Luxembourg Sarl)
One Crown Square Church Street East, Woking, Surrey GU21 6HR
**Tel:** 0845-130-3593
**Web:** www.rasplc.com
**Reg No:** 3618259 **VAT No:** 722670936
**Estd:** 1998 Private Limited Company
**Line of Business:** Management and business consultants
**Issued Capital:** £100
**Directors:** A L Duggan, D L Cruddace, D C Humphreys
**Co. Secretary:** David Humphreys
**Responsibilities**
**Senior:** Liam O'sullivan *(Manager)*
**US SIC:** 7392 **UK SIC:** 83951
**Auditors:** Simmons Gainsford LLP
**Bankers:** National Westminster Bank Plc (60-03-12)

| | 30-04-13 | 30-04-12 | 30-04-11 |
|---|---|---|---|
| TO | N/A | N/A | 13,577,000 |
| P/L | N/A | N/A | 8,519,000 |
| NW | 3,543,000 | 21,043,000 | 24,139,000 |
| Emp. | N/A | N/A | 43 |

DUNS 76-663-0602
## Revisecatch Ltd
324 Kensal Road, London W10 5BZ
**Tel:** 02075651575
**Web:** www.ecourier.co.uk
**Reg No:** 2584802 **VAT No:** 577249206
**Estd:** 1988 Private Limited Company
**Line of Business:** Couriers
**Trading Style:** Courier Systems, Ecourier, National Film Transport (Nft)
**Issued Capital:** £2
**Directors:** I W Oliver, G J Howell, M I Fullick
**Co. Secretary:** Ms Brigitte Oliver
**Responsibilities**
**Senior:** Carl Truscott *(Joint Managing Director)*
**Facilities:** Carl Truscott *(Joint Managing Director)*
**US SIC:** 4213 **UK SIC:** 72300
**Auditors:** Leaman Mattei
**Bankers:** Lloyds TSB Bank plc (30-96-20)

| | 30-04-13 | 31-03-12 | 31-04-11 |
|---|---|---|---|
| TO | 16,215,097 | 8,439,538 | 8,244,049 |
| P/L | 464,943 | 84,464 | 55,963 |
| NW | 2,130,477 | 2,312,123 | 2,250,102 |
| WC | 1,787,709 | 2,154,861 | 2,051,933 |
| Emp. | 90 | 74 | 71 |

DUNS 23-441-7678
## Revital Health Place
The Colonade, 125 Buckingham Palace Road, London SW1W 9SH
**Tel:** 02079766615
**Web:** www.revital.com
**Estd:** 1992 Proprietorship
**Line of Business:** Health food retailers
**Proprietor:** R Vora
**US SIC:** 5499, 5912
**UK SIC:** 64100, 64300
**Employees:** 50

DUNS 76-539-1792
## Revital Ltd
Unit D3, Braintree Road Industrial Estate, Braintree Road, Ruislip, Middlesex HA4 0EJ
**Tel:** 02088454118
**Web:** www.revital.com
**Reg No:** 2570370 **Estd:** 2005 Private Limited Company
**Line of Business:** Health food retailers
**Export Sales:** £473,567
**Trading Style:** Revital Health Shop
**Issued Capital:** £50,000
**Director:** Mrs N Vora
**Co. Secretary:** Raj Vora
**Responsibilities**
**Senior:** Amit Jassal *(Manager)*, Ashish Raja *(Marketing Manager)*
**US SIC:** 5499 **UK SIC:** 64100
**Auditors:** Weston Kay
**Bankers:** Barclays Bank Plc (20-36-47)

| | 30-04-14 | 30-04-13 | 30-04-12 |
|---|---|---|---|
| TO | 11,126,214 | 10,295,531 | 10,012,080 |
| P/L | 92,725 | 78,995 | 301,429 |
| NW | 1,526,910 | 1,384,081 | 1,266,807 |
| WC | 1,197,363 | 255,693 | 259,403 |
| Emp. | 127 | 119 | 107 |

DUNS 29-826-1884
## Revitalise Respite Holidays
212 Business Design Centre, 52 Upper Street, London N1 0QH
**Tel:** 0303 303 0147 **Fax:** 020 7288 6899
**Web:** www.vitalise.org.uk
**Reg No:** 2044219 **Estd:** 1963 Private Company Limited By Guarantee
**Line of Business:** Individual & Family Social Services
**Trading Style:** Vitalise Jubilee Lodge, Vitalise Netley Waterside House, Vitalise Sandpipers, Vitalise Long Stay Care Services
**Directors:** G D Wright, M Sawhney, P T White, Dr F H Woodard, S J Law, M K Ashton, D N Robinson, R J Poxton
**Co. Secretary:** John Parker
**Responsibilities**
**Senior:** Linda Beaney *(Director)*, Chris Simmons *(Chief Executive)*
**Branches:** Revitalise Respite Holidays, Netley Waterside House, Abbey Hill, Southampton, Hampshire SO31 5FA
**US SIC:** 8321 **UK SIC:** 96111
**Auditors:** Sayer Vincent
**Bankers:** Lloyds TSB Bank plc (30-00-08)

| | 31-01-14 | 31-01-13 | 31-01-12 |
|---|---|---|---|
| TO | 7,724,000 | 7,252,000 | 7,832,000 |
| P/L | 1,000 | (3,199,000) | 114,000 |
| NW | 6,016,000 | 6,015,000 | 9,214,000 |
| WC | 1,518,000 | 2,165,000 | 2,542,000 |
| Emp. | 192 | 182 | 203 |

DUNS 21-921-9615
## Revlon International Corporation
**(Subsidiary of:** Revlon Inc.)
Greater London House, Hampstead Road, London NW1 7QX
**Tel:** 02073917400 **Fax:** 02072554635
**Web:** www.revlon.com
**Reg No:** 0004037FC **VAT No:** 135584752
**Estd:** 2010 Foreign Company
**Line of Business:** Representative office
**Trading Style:** Almay, Ultima Ii
**Principals:** M C Bergerac *(Chairman)*, R W Armstrong, I B Jay, J Burns, E K Zilkha, J London, W J Fox, S Levine
**Co. Secretary:** Wade Nicholls
**Responsibilities**
**Senior:** Paul Block *(Director)*, Irving Bottner *(Director)*, Howard Gittis *(Director)*, Lewis Glucksmann *(Director)*, Aileen Mehle *(Director)*, Ronald Perelman *(Director)*, Simon Rifkind *(Director)*, Edwin Whitehead *(Director)*
**Branches:** Revlon International Corporation, Fairfield Works Ewenny Rd, Maesteg, Mid Glamorgan CF34 9TU
**US SIC:** 2844 **UK SIC:** 25820
**Bankers:** Citibank Na (18-50-08)

DUNS 21-126-9878
## Revolution
Unit 2, The Plaza, 8 Fitzwilliam Street, Sheffield, South Yorkshire S1 4JB
**Tel:** 01142739469
**Web:** www.revolution-bars.co.uk
**Estd:** 2008 Proprietorship
**Line of Business:** Public house
**Proprietor:** J Hastings
**Responsibilities**
**Senior:** Ian Boyles *(General Manager)*
**Health & Safety:** Ian Boyles *(General Manager)*
**Facilities:** Ian Boyles *(General Manager)*
**US SIC:** 5813 **UK SIC:** 66200
**Employees:** 55

DUNS 21-390-5050
## Revolution Bar
3-6 Downing Street, Cambridge, Cambridgeshire CB2 3DS
**Tel:** 01223-364895
**Web:** www.revolution-bars.co.uk
**Estd:** 2009 Partnership
**Line of Business:** Managed public houses and bars
**Partners:** Mrs M Menesh, M Perry
**US SIC:** 5813, 5812
**UK SIC:** 66200, 66110
**Employees:** 55

DUNS 21-585-2643
## Revolution Health Club & Spa
O G H Hotel, 1 Ann's Place, St Peter Port, Guernsey, Channel Islands GY1 2NU
**Tel:** 01481738680
**Web:** www.theoghhotel.com
**Estd:** 2011 Proprietorship
**Line of Business:** Health clubs
**Proprietor:** C Toffanello
**Responsibilities**
**Senior:** Charlene Carter *(Health Manager)*
**US SIC:** 7299 **UK SIC:** 98902
**Employees:** 70

DUNS 23-992-9842
## Revolve Group Ltd
22-40 Tenter Road, Northampton, Northamptonshire NN3 6PZ
**Tel:** 01604497733
**Reg No:** 3981256 **Estd:** 2000 Private Limited Company
**Line of Business:** Holding companies management activities
**Export Sales:** £43,714,000
**Issued Capital:** £50,642
**Directors:** Dr J Hohenbuhel, M L Coles
**Co. Secretary:** Simon Wallington
**US SIC:** 6711 **UK SIC:** 83962
**Auditors:** RSM Tenon Audit Ltd

| | 31-12-13 | 31-12-12 | 31-12-11 |
|---|---|---|---|
| TO | 54,007,000 | 58,687,000 | 60,582,000 |
| P/L | (378,000) | 1,268,000 | 585,000 |
| NW | 2,848,000 | 3,282,000 | 2,368,000 |
| WC | 1,982,000 | 2,122,000 | 1,410,000 |
| Emp. | 132 | 138 | 132 |

DUNS 23-862-9575 **Imp**
## Revolve Technologies Ltd
**(Subsidiary of:** Nitec Ltd)
Prospect Way, Hutton, Hutton, Brentwood, Essex CM13 1XA
**Tel:** 01277-261400
**Web:** www.revolve.co.uk
**Reg No:** 3854474 **VAT No:** 927227419
**Estd:** 1999 Private Limited Company
**Line of Business:** Engineers (consulting)
**Trading Style:** Mountune Racing
**Issued Capital:** £1,000,000
**Directors:** A P Williams, A T Pell Johnson, J D Mitchell, D J Mountain, P J Turner
**Co. Secretary:** Andrew Williams
**Responsibilities**
**Senior:** Gary Robertson *(Manager)*
**Finance:** Elaine Paveley *(Accountant)*
**IT:** Paul Shordon *(ITAdministrator)*
**HR:** Andrea Hunneybel *(Human Resources Manager)*
**US SIC:** 8911, 7391
**UK SIC:** 83701, 94000
**Auditors:** Lakin Rose Ltd
**Bankers:** National Westminster Bank Plc (60-03-25)

| | 31-12-13 | 31-12-12 | 31-12-11 |
|---|---|---|---|
| TO | 7,881,203 | 7,138,163 | 5,756,755 |
| P/L | 489,748 | (961,736) | (306,591) |
| NW | 1,879,129 | 1,497,058 | 2,114,924 |
| WC | 1,516,099 | 1,252,895 | 1,820,945 |
| Emp. | 60 | 61 | 62 |

DUNS 49-312-5520 **Exp**
## The Revvo Castor Co Ltd
**(Subsidiary of:** Jones & Jones Corner Store)
Unit A Mulberry Court, Christchurch, Dorset BH23 1PS
**Tel:** 01202-484211
**Web:** www.revvo.co.uk
**Reg No:** 3120897 **Estd:** 1924 Private Limited Company
**Line of Business:** Manufacturers of wheels and castors
**Issued Capital:** £1,666,667
**Directors:** J A Smithies, D J Towell, T W Blashill, J Hinds, R W White
**Co. Secretary:** John Smithies
**Responsibilities**
**Senior:** A Damoo *(Manager)*, Caroline Dodds *(Manager)*, Graham Ellis-Dawe *(Business Manager)*, John Vresics *(Manager)*
**Sales:** B Dearman *(Sales Manager)*
**Operations:** Graham Dawe *(Technical, Production Manager)*
**Purchasing:** K Bellows *(Purchasing Manager)*
**US SIC:** 3999, 3499
**UK SIC:** 49590, 31694
**Auditors:** Ernst & Young
**Bankers:** National Westminster Bank Plc (60-04-30)

| | 31-12-13 | 31-12-12 | 31-12-11 |
|---|---|---|---|
| TA | 2,035,667 | 2,035,667 | 2,035,000 |
| NW | 2,035,667 | 2,035,667 | 2,035,000 |

DUNS 34-898-7574
## Reward Gateway (Uk) Ltd
**(Subsidiary of:** International Benefits Holdings Ltd)
90 Westbourne Grove, London W2 5RT
**Tel:** 020-7229-0349
**Web:** www.asperity.co.uk
**Reg No:** 5696250 **Estd:** 2006 Private Limited Company
**Line of Business:** Business services
**Export Sales:** £35,713
**Issued Capital:** £1,206
**Directors:** G Elliott, T P Lavery, J Gaunt, G R Farrow, R W Hurd-Wood
**Co. Secretary:** Squire Patton Boggs Secretarial
**Responsibilities**
**Senior:** Rizwan Kanval *(Manager)*, Sarah Millward *(Compliance Manager)*, Kristian Sibast *(Manager)*
**US SIC:** 7399 **UK SIC:** 83954

**Auditors:** PricewaterhouseCoopers LLP

| | 30-06-14 | 30-06-13 | 30-06-12 |
|---|---|---|---|
| TO | 145,354,019 | 123,045,528 | 117,897,093 |
| P/L | 6,612,926 | 4,443,399 | 2,261,349 |
| NW | 13,105,991 | 8,436,771 | 4,469,815 |
| WC | 13,016,985 | 7,347,582 | 3,500,941 |
| Emp. | 115 | 119 | 116 |

DUNS 53-615-9734
## Rewards Training Recruitment Consultancy Ltd
Belgrave House, Crawley, West Sussex RH10 1HU
**Tel:** 01293562651
**Web:** www.rewardstraining.co.uk
**Reg No:** 3421136 **Estd:** 1990 Private Limited Company
**Line of Business:** Business and management consultancy activities not elsewhere classified
**Trading Style:** M R Clark & Sons
**Issued Capital:** £12,502
**Directors:** Ms M Y Ward, M D Ward, D A Ayres, Mrs L Powell
**Co. Secretary:** Eric Smith
**Responsibilities**
**Finance:** Bill McLeod *(Financial Manager)*
**Marketing:** Sarah Easy *(Sales & Marketing Director)*
**Sales:** Sarah Easy *(Sales & Marketing Director)*
**HR:** Stephanie Gale *(Recruitment Officer)*
**Facilities:** Bill McLeod *(Financial Manager)*
**Branches:** Rewards Training Recruitment Consultancy Ltd, 15-17 South St. Andrew Street, Edinburgh, Midlothian EH2 2AU
**US SIC:** 7392, 7361, 8249
**UK SIC:** 83951, 83954, 93300
**Auditors:** Tyas & Co

| | 31-07-13 | 31-07-12 | 31-07-11 |
|---|---|---|---|
| TA | 444,944 | 368,488 | 485,734 |
| NW | 118,612 | 111,759 | 89,339 |
| WC | 17,088 | 21,059 | 21,638 |

DUNS 21-311-2469 **Imp-Exp**
## Rewinds & J. Windsor & Sons (Engineers) Ltd
81 Regent Road, Liverpool, Merseyside L5 9SY
**Tel:** 0151-207-2074
**Web:** www.rjweng.com
**Reg No:** 0603096 **VAT No:** 164073279
**Estd:** 1946 Private Limited Company
**Line of Business:** Manufacturers of electric motors
**Export Sales:** £37,983
**Issued Capital:** £5,252
**Principals:** J A Windsor *(Managing)*, M C Windsor *(Managing)*, L Windsor, Mrs S Windsor, L J Windsor
**Responsibilities**
**Senior:** A Windsor *(Manager)*, Ruth Windsor *(Manager)*
**Finance:** Howard Martin *(Manager)*
**Sales:** Graham Bellis *(Sales Manager)*
**Admin:** Howard Martin *(Manager)*
**IT:** Frank Whittle *(IT Manager)*
**Purchasing:** Howard Martin *(Manager)*
**Branches:** Rewinds & J. Windsor & Sons (Engineers) Ltd, Unit 7-8, Westfield Road, Wallasey, Merseyside CH44 7HX
**US SIC:** 3621, 3629
**UK SIC:** 34201, 34350
**Auditors:** Horner Downey & Co
**Bankers:** HSBC Bank plc (40-12-26)

| | 30-04-14 | 30-04-13 | 30-04-12 |
|---|---|---|---|
| TO | 6,653,832 | 6,178,637 | 6,731,744 |
| P/L | 40,012 | (173,636) | 25,463 |
| NW | 2,421,288 | 2,357,054 | 2,468,741 |
| WC | 1,721,826 | 1,599,875 | 1,785,998 |
| Emp. | 98 | 89 | 96 |

DUNS 28-833-6597 **Imp-Exp**
## Rex Bousfield Ltd
Holland Road, Oxted, Surrey RH8 9BD
**Tel:** 01883-717033 **Fax:** 01883-717890
**Web:** www.bousfield.com
**Reg No:** 0331922 **Estd:** 1937 Private Limited Company
**Line of Business:** Manufacturers of laminate
**Export Markets:** W Europe, Middle East, U S A
**Export Sales:** £880,619
**Issued Capital:** £122,500
**Directors:** R J Thompson, G P Fielding, B W Baldwyn, R G Smith, Mrs M Ellis, Mrs C A Bashford, J D Thompson
**Co. Secretary:** Ms Michelle Ellis
**Responsibilities**
**IT:** Hamish Brownlie *(Operations Director)*
**Health & Safety:** Hamish Brownlie *(Operations Director)*
**Facilities:** Hamish Brownlie *(Operations Director)*
**US SIC:** 2499 **UK SIC:** 46500
**Auditors:** Rushton Osborne & Co

**Bankers:** National Westminster Bank Plc (50-41-02)

| | 31-03-14 | 31-03-13 | 31-03-12 |
|---|---|---|---|
| TO | 14,042,689 | 15,038,692 | 16,453,702 |
| P/L | (1,198,954) | 28,602 | 150,990 |
| NW | 3,121,221 | 4,332,817 | 4,287,560 |
| WC | 718,066 | 1,890,480 | 1,911,634 |
| Emp. | 74 | 75 | 71 |

DUNS 34-850-1110
## Rex Develop Ltd
85 Town Gate, Mapplewell, Barnsley, South Yorkshire S75 6AS
**Tel:** 01226387085
**Reg No:** 5649017 **Estd:** 2005 Private Limited Company
**Line of Business:** Business services
**Issued Capital:** £1,000,000
**Directors:** S Dryden, T Dryden
**US SIC:** 7399 **UK SIC:** 83954

| | 31-12-13 | 31-12-12 | 31-12-11 |
|---|---|---|---|
| TO | 1,376,785 | 1,334,621 | N/A |
| P/L | 131,185 | 77,907 | N/A |
| NW | 349,626 | 255,838 | 200,807 |
| WC | (144,772) | 103,980 | 240,236 |
| Emp. | 79 | 77 | N/A |

DUNS 21-733-3571
## Rex Features (Holdings) Ltd
18 Vine Hill, London EC1R 5DZ
**Web:** www.rexfeatures.com
**Reg No:** 7682194 **Estd:** 2011 Private Limited Company
**Line of Business:** Photographic activities not elsewhere classified
**Export Sales:** £3,383,624
**Issued Capital:** £28,850
**Director:** L A Lawson
**Responsibilities**
**Senior:** Miguel Ferro *(Director)*, Nicola Pedroni *(Director)*, Luca Tassan *(Director)*
**US SIC:** 7333 **UK SIC:** 83953

| | 31-12-13 | 31-12-12 | 31-12-11 |
|---|---|---|---|
| TO | 10,630,830 | 10,528,125 | 4,826,996 |
| P/L | 1,554,873 | 1,268,977 | 521,557 |
| NW | (1,391,048) | (2,788,207) | (3,961,855) |
| WC | 812,578 | 1,388,991 | 1,051,515 |
| Emp. | 62 | 63 | 65 |

DUNS 22-705-2644 **Imp-Exp**
## Rex International Ltd
Unit 3-4, Allied Way, Warple Way, London W3 0RL
**Tel:** 020 8746 1700 **Fax:** 020 8746 2234
**Web:** www.rexinter.com
**Reg No:** 1578798 **VAT No:** 340661575
**Estd:** 1981 Private Limited Company
**Line of Business:** Wholesale of other household goods not elsewhere classified
**Export Markets:** E U, S America
**Export Sales:** £2,829,637
**Issued Capital:** £126,000
**Managing Directors:** M R Howe, E L Mirelman
**Co. Secretary:** Michael Howe
**Responsibilities**
**Senior:** Nigel Biggs *(Sales & Marketing Manager)*, Alan McLeod *(Warehouse Manager)*
**Marketing:** Nigel Biggs *(Sales & Marketing Manager)*
**Sales:** Nigel Biggs *(Sales & Marketing Manager)*
**HR:** Candy Smith *(Human Resources Manager)*
**Facilities:** Phil Baran *(Facilities Manager)*
**Branches:** London
**US SIC:** 3999 **UK SIC:** 49590
**Auditors:** Jones Fisher Downes
**Bankers:** Bank Of China (40-50-37)

| | 30-04-14 | 30-04-13 | 30-04-12 |
|---|---|---|---|
| TO | 11,925,366 | 9,855,015 | 13,902,438 |
| P/L | 1,565,687 | 3,216,179 | 1,959,287 |
| NW | 7,536,064 | 6,337,571 | 3,891,559 |
| WC | 7,468,931 | 6,267,413 | 3,838,494 |
| Emp. | 73 | 67 | 63 |

DUNS 21-580-7404
## Rexam Beverage Can
Maryland Road, Tongwell, Milton Keynes, Buckinghamshire MK15 8HF
**Tel:** 01908517600
**Web:** www.rexam.com
**Estd:** 2007 Proprietorship
**Line of Business:** Manufacturers of cans
**Proprietor:** B Neilson
**US SIC:** 3411 **UK SIC:** 31641
**Employees:** 50

DUNS 76-383-3043 **Exp**
## Rexam Beverage Can Europe Ltd
**(Subsidiary of:** Rexam Plc)
100 Capability Green, Luton, Chatham, Kent
**Tel:** 01582 408999 **Fax:** 01582 726065
**Web:** www.rexam.com
**Reg No:** 2554348 **Estd:** 1991 Private Limited Company
**Line of Business:** Other service activities not elsewhere classified
**Export Markets:** E U, India, Sweden

**Issued Capital:** £2
**Directors:** I P Percival, R J Peachey, P J Hocken
**Co. Secretary:** Alan Harber
**Responsibilities**
**Senior:** Nikki Rolfe *(Group Director, Human Resource)*, Tomas Sjolin *(Manager)*
**IT:** Ric Shortman *(Global Enterprise Architecture)*
**HR:** Nikki Rolfe *(Group Director, Human Resource)*
**Operations:** Linda Herrera *(Operational Risk Manager)*
**US SIC:** 8999 **UK SIC:** 83954
**Auditors:** PricewaterhouseCoopers LLP
**Bankers:** HSBC Bank plc (40-30-32)
**Following financial data are in thousands**

| | 31-12-13 | 31-12-12 | 31-12-11 |
|---|---|---|---|
| TO | 1,364,290 | 1,294,976 | 1,294,437 |
| P/L | 54,513 | 59,870 | 93,011 |
| NW | 49,395 | 49,391 | 40,017 |
| WC | 88,543 | 48,144 | 34,846 |
| Emp. | 165 | 170 | 187 |

DUNS 76-678-8020
## Rexel Senate Ltd
**(Subsidiary of:** Rexel)
W F Senate, Dagenham, Essex RM10 8SX
**Tel:** 02089842000
**Web:** www.rexelsenate.co.uk
**Reg No:** 2588733 **Estd:** 1899 Private Limited Company
**Line of Business:** Electrical wholesalers
**Trading Style:** Wf Senate, C S D Professional, Rexel Senate Electrical Supplies
**Issued Capital:** £413,505,002
**Directors:** M Ludwig, N M Croxson, H Laschkar
**Responsibilities**
**Marketing:** David Gwyer *(Commercial Director)*
**Branches:** Rexel Senate Ltd, 16 Bucklers Lane, St. Austell, Cornwall PL25 3JN
**US SIC:** 5074 **UK SIC:** 61300
**Auditors:** Ernst & Young LLP
**Bankers:** Barclays Bank Plc (20-35-90)

| | 31-12-13 | 31-12-12 | 31-12-11 |
|---|---|---|---|
| TO | N/A | 37,877,000 | 142,365,000 |
| P/L | N/A | (4,653,000) | 5,440,000 |
| NW | 384,212,000 | 384,212,000 | 32,303,000 |
| WC | (1,732,000) | (1,732,000) | 52,237,000 |
| Emp. | N/A | 502 | 573 |

DUNS 21-619-4324 **Imp-Exp**
## Rexel Uk Ltd
**(Subsidiary of:** Rexel)
12 Frederick Road, Birmingham, West Midlands B15 1JD
**Tel:** 01214559727 **Fax:** 020 8596 7281
**Web:** www.rexel.co.uk
**Reg No:** 0434724 **VAT No:** 614213680
**Estd:** 1947 Private Limited Company
**Line of Business:** Wholesale of hardware, plumbing and heating equipment and supplies
**Trading Style:** Rexel National / Parker Merchanting / Senate Electrical, Wf Electrical / Newey & Eyre / Denmans, Wilts Wholesale Electrical, Britsource International
**Issued Capital:** £246,679,885
**Directors:** H Laschkar, J C Hogan, M G Hauw, R J Gill, R S Provoost, B Smithers, N M Croxson
**Co. Secretary:** Toby Train
**Branches:** Rexel Uk Limited, Unit 20, Ben Nevis Drive, Fort William, Inverness-Shire PH33 6RU
**US SIC:** 5074 **UK SIC:** 61300
**Auditors:** Ernst & Young LLP
**Bankers:** Barclays Bank Plc (20-53-30)

| | 31-12-13 | 31-12-12 | 31-12-11 |
|---|---|---|---|
| TO | 808,482,000 | 810,538,000 | 652,124,000 |
| P/L | 5,494,000 | 29,996,000 | 10,754,000 |
| NW | 43,894,000 | 14,561,000 | 44,776,000 |
| WC | (37,785,000) | (20,948,000) | (34,987,000) |
| Emp. | 3,740 | 3,713 | 3,118 |

DUNS 34-911-8216 **Imp-Exp**
## Reydon Sports Plc
Unit 17 Easter Park, Lenton Lane, Nottingham, Nottinghamshire NG7 2PX
**Tel:** 01159002342 **Fax:** 01159-002343
**Web:** www.reydonsports.com
**Reg No:** 2833782 **VAT No:** 610612295
**Estd:** 1993 Public Limited Company
**Line of Business:** Sportswear wholesalers
**Export Markets:** European union and rest of the world
**Export Sales:** £1,477,541
**Issued Capital:** £598,508
**Principals:** F E Doherty *(Chairman)*, N J Carter *(Managing)*, Ms S J Doherty, R Vimpany, D C Sanderson, D A James
**Co. Secretary:** Richard Vimpany
**Responsibilities**
**Senior:** Jonathan Castledine *(Facilities Manager)*, David France *(Manager)*, Richard Hopkin *(Manager)*
**Facilities:** Jonathan Castledine *(Facilities Manager)*
**US SIC:** 5941 **UK SIC:** 65400

**Auditors:** Tenon Audit Ltd
**Bankers:** HSBC Bank plc (40-08-46)

| | 31-12-13 | 31-12-12 | 31-12-11 |
|---|---|---|---|
| TO | 10,466,019 | 12,152,830 | 13,318,225 |
| P/L | 18,251 | 231,767 | 550,424 |
| NW | 3,232,964 | 3,214,713 | 3,965,916 |
| WC | 3,457,863 | 3,572,516 | 3,895,336 |
| Emp. | 54 | 58 | 57 |

DUNS 84-691-2343
## Reynards Ltd
Greengate, Middleton, Manchester M24 1RU
**Tel:** 0161-653-7700
**Web:** www.reynards.com
**Reg No:** 6222871 **Estd:** 2007 Private Limited Company
**Line of Business:** Other wholesale
**Issued Capital:** £481,553
**Directors:** R L Perkins, R E Tindal, A K Reynard
**Co. Secretary:** Ms Julie Ward
**US SIC:** 5199 **UK SIC:** 61900
**Bankers:** Barclays Bank Plc (20-30-47)

| | 31-03-14 | 31-03-13 | 31-03-12 |
|---|---|---|---|
| TO | 15,419,893 | 15,198,776 | 15,374,144 |
| P/L | (3,786) | (91,607) | (214,908) |
| NW | 1,034,615 | 985,111 | 1,019,037 |
| WC | (423,759) | (401,892) | (401,236) |
| Emp. | 79 | 82 | 83 |

DUNS 23-882-7997
## Reynolds 2000 Ltd
Gibson Lane, Melton, North Ferriby, North Humberside HU14 3HH
**Tel:** 01482637373
**Web:** www.crreynolds.co.uk
**Reg No:** 3873947 **Estd:** 1999 Private Limited Company
**Line of Business:** Builders
**Issued Capital:** £30,000
**Director:** C R Reynolds
**Co. Secretary:** Ms Fiona Reynolds
**US SIC:** 6711, 7394
**UK SIC:** 83962, 84000
**Auditors:** Sadofskys
**Bankers:** National Westminster Bank Plc (56-00-06)

| | 30-06-13 | 30-06-12 | 30-06-11 |
|---|---|---|---|
| TO | 10,574,112 | 11,739,972 | 10,969,733 |
| P/L | 572,044 | 690,293 | 1,425,240 |
| NW | 6,426,024 | 6,536,332 | 6,061,742 |
| WC | 3,755,446 | 4,086,660 | 3,735,506 |
| Emp. | 57 | 59 | 60 |

DUNS 22-268-2754 **Imp**
## Reynolds & Reynolds Ltd
**(Subsidiary of:** Universal Computer Systems Inc.)
1200 Bristol Road South, Northfield, Birmingham, West Midlands B31 2RW
**Tel:** 01214832000
**Web:** www.reyrey.com
**Reg No:** 4286244 **Estd:** 2001 Private Limited Company
**Line of Business:** Computer bureau service providers
**Export Sales:** £1,816,000
**Trading Style:** Kalamazoo - Reynolds
**Issued Capital:** £18,943,551
**Directors:** C M Cooper, R M Nalley, R D Burnett, D S Agan, T W Jones, R T Brockman, N T Barras
**Co. Secretary:** Michael Moss
**Responsibilities**
**Marketing:** Howard Barnett *(Marketing Manager & CSR)*
**Sales:** George Clarke *(Sales Manager)*
**IT:** David Hiam *(Computer Manager)*
**HR:** Jennie Wilson *(Personnel Manager)*
**Purchasing:** Alison Franks *(Purchasing Manager)*
**US SIC:** 7379, 7374
**UK SIC:** 83940
**Auditors:** Ernst & Young LLP
**Bankers:** National Westminster Bank Plc (60-01-35)

| | 31-12-13 | 31-12-12 | 31-12-11 |
|---|---|---|---|
| TO | 19,685,000 | 14,283,000 | 14,818,000 |
| P/L | 2,647,000 | 1,097,000 | 1,407,000 |
| NW | 18,035,000 | 15,255,000 | 13,967,000 |
| WC | 16,511,000 | 13,517,000 | 12,159,000 |
| Emp. | 263 | 246 | 261 |

DUNS 77-446-6783
## Reynolds Catering Supplies Ltd
Britannia Road, Waltham Cross, Hertfordshire EN8 7RQ
**Tel:** 08453-106200 **Fax:** 0845-634-8100
**Web:** www.reynolds-cs.com
**Reg No:** 2955734 **VAT No:** 649428600
**Estd:** 1994 Private Limited Company
**Line of Business:** Wholesale of fruit and vegetables
**Issued Capital:** £5,000
**Principals:** A W Reynolds *(Managing)*, P J Collins, I P Booth, R I Smith, R A Calder, A D Austin
**Responsibilities**
**Senior:** Graham Shore *(Maintenance Manager)*
**Marketing:** Mike Thorpe *(Sales & Marketing Manager)*
**Sales:** Mike Thorpe *(Sales & Marketing Manager)*
**IT:** Jordan Hack *(IT Technician)*
**HR:** Sue Haydon *(Human Resources Advisor)*
**Facilities:** Graham Shore *(Maintenance Manager)*
**Branches:** Reynolds Catering Supplies Ltd, Unit 9G , Kingswood Indstl Est, Aldermoor Way, Longwell Green, Bristol, Avon BS30 7DA
**US SIC:** 5148 **UK SIC:** 61700
**Auditors:** BDO LLP
**Bankers:** Fortis Bank London Bch (formerly Generale Bk) (40-52-62)

| | 31-12-13 | 31-12-12 | 31-12-11 |
|---|---|---|---|
| TO | 178,512,000 | 156,415,000 | 147,561,000 |
| P/L | 2,825,000 | 1,375,000 | 1,033,000 |
| NW | 3,894,000 | 11,771,000 | 10,816,000 |
| WC | (5,273,000) | (3,223,000) | (3,641,000) |
| Emp. | 694 | 627 | 682 |

DUNS 23-746-8215
## Reynolds Logistics Uk Ltd
68 Argyle Street, Birkenhead, Merseyside CH41 6AF
**Reg No:** 3740926 **Estd:** 2002 Private Limited Company
**Line of Business:** Car and commercial vehicle repairs
**Issued Capital:** £100,000
**Directors:** J W Reynolds, A Reynolds
**Co. Secretary:** Declan Maxwell
**Responsibilities**
**Senior:** Christopher Dalton *(Manager)*, Rob Greenwood *(Operations Director)*
**US SIC:** 4789 **UK SIC:** 77002
**Auditors:** McEwan Wallace

| | 31-12-13 | 31-12-12 | 31-12-11 |
|---|---|---|---|
| TO | 10,587,418 | 10,243,157 | 10,809,280 |
| P/L | 140,341 | 81,129 | (45,625) |
| NW | 687,736 | 565,726 | 520,623 |
| WC | 467,224 | 443,446 | 240,886 |
| Emp. | 77 | 56 | 63 |

DUNS 21-603-3472
## Reynolds Ltd
27-31 High Street, Bognor Regis, West Sussex PO21 1RR
**Tel:** 01243871200
**Web:** www.reynoldsfurniture.co.uk
**Reg No:** 0461520 **VAT No:** 192712360
**Estd:** 1867 Private Limited Company
**Line of Business:** Furniture retail outlets
**Trading Style:** Reynolds Fine Furniture
**Issued Capital:** £42,661
**Principals:** N A Reynolds *(Chairman)*, J B Reynolds *(Managing)*, M Reynolds, D J Reynolds, S J Reynolds
**Co. Secretary:** Jean Reynolds
**Branches:** Reynolds Ltd, 1 London Rd, Bognor Regis, West Sussex PO21 1PQ
**US SIC:** 5719, 7261, 8999
**UK SIC:** 64700, 98902, 83954
**Auditors:** Hunt & Partners
**Bankers:** National Westminster Bank Plc (60-03-08)

| | 28-02-14 | 28-02-13 | 29-02-12 |
|---|---|---|---|
| TA | 4,336,694 | 3,709,128 | 3,217,690 |
| NW | 2,961,425 | 2,570,812 | 2,117,017 |
| WC | 79,167 | 393,423 | (5,677) |

DUNS 22-701-6755
## Reynolds Porter Chamberlain Llp
Tower Bridge House, St Katharines Way, London E1W 1AA
**Tel:** 020-3060-6000
**Web:** www.rpc.co.uk
**Reg No:** 0317402OC **Estd:** 2006
**Line of Business:** Solicitors
**Partners:** K Y Pollock, D G Haywood, R Gare, T C Brown, R Williams, C Jaycock, C J Russell, S G Kirkby
**Responsibilities**
**Senior:** A Aylmer *(Partner)*, Jeremy Barnes *(Partner)*, Nick Bird *(Partner)*, Sarah Blunn *(Partner)*, Oliver Bray *(Partner)*, Tim Bull *(Partner)*, C Byram *(Partner)*, Sarah Cassidy *(Partner Utilities And Waste)*, Paul Castellani *(Partner)*, David Cran *(Partner)*, Geraldine Elliott *(Partner)*, Ed Fitzgerald *(Head Of Marketing And Communic)*, Tim Fogarty *(Partner Real Estate)*, C Gardener *(Partner)*, Alex Hamer *(Partner, Policy)*, Thomas Hibbert *(Partner)*, W Hogarth *(Partner)*, Karen Howard *(Partner)*, Simon Laird *(Partner)*, Jaron Lewis *(Partner)*, Gwyneth Macaulay *(Partner)*, Stephen Malley *(Partner)*, Keith Mathieson *(Partner)*, Stephen Mayer *(Consultant)*, E Meerloo *(Partner)*, C Micklem *(Partner)*, Catherine Percy *(Partner)*, Katherine Rees *(Partner)*, Gavin Reese *(Partner Energy)*, Charles Suchett-Kaye *(Partner)*, Cath Thorpe *(Partner)*, A Toulson *(Partner)*, Vivien Tyrell *(Partner)*, A Ulm *(Partner)*, N le Roux *(Partner)*
**Finance:** Kathryn Greaves *(Chief Financial Officer)*
**Marketing:** Ed Fitzgerald *(Head Of Marketing And Communic)*
**HR:** Nicola Denegri *(Training Manager)*
**Facilities:** Tim Fogarty *(Partner Real Estate)*
**US SIC:** 8111 **UK SIC:** 83500
**Auditors:** Baker Tilly UK Audit LLP
**Bankers:** Coutts & Co (18-00-02)

| | 30-04-14 | 30-04-13 | 30-04-12 |
|---|---|---|---|
| TO | 84,284,961 | 81,685,084 | 67,353,684 |
| P/L | 21,338,244 | 25,625,160 | 23,679,485 |
| NW | 21,343,225 | 26,571,142 | 2,340,501 |
| WC | 32,738,414 | 39,470,419 | 27,042,820 |
| Emp. | 568 | 526 | 446 |

DUNS 23-806-9231
## Reynolds Recruitment Ltd
31 Eldon Road, Attenborough, Beeston, Nottingham, Nottinghamshire NG9 6DZ
**Tel:** 01159250747 **Fax:** 01159250550
**Web:** www.reynoldsrecruitment.com
**Reg No:** 2180367 **VAT No:** 416352372
**Estd:** 1987 Private Limited Company
**Line of Business:** Employment and recruitment companies and consultants
**Issued Capital:** £313
**Directors:** D J Painter, R S Harris
**US SIC:** 7361 **UK SIC:** 83954
**Auditors:** tcp chartered accountants
**Bankers:** National Westminster Bank Plc (60-15-17)

| | 31-12-13 | 31-12-12 | 31-12-11 |
|---|---|---|---|
| TA | 961,904 | 807,718 | 786,912 |
| NW | 34,253 | 8,988 | 3,491 |
| WC | (173,940) | (166,613) | (160,812) |

DUNS 22-637-1607
## Reyven Sportsfields Ltd
Greenhill Farm, Dunstable Road, Tilsworth, Leighton Buzzard, Bedfordshire LU7 9PU
**Tel:** 01525210714
**Reg No:** 1220529 **VAT No:** 198885869
**Estd:** 1975 Private Limited Company
**Line of Business:** Agricultural service activities; landscape gardening
**Issued Capital:** £1,000
**Principals:** R P Venn *(Managing)*, Mrs M R Venn, Mrs A M Reynolds
**Co. Secretary:** Stephen Venn
**US SIC:** 0729 **UK SIC:** 01003
**Auditors:** R.A. & D.A. Thompson

| | 30-09-14 | 31-03-13 | 31-09-12 |
|---|---|---|---|
| TA | 8,841 | 28,043 | 22,484 |
| NW | 5,711 | 25,355 | 21,538 |
| WC | 5,711 | 25,355 | 21,538 |

DUNS 52-572-0710
## Rezidor Hotel Manchester Ltd
**(Subsidiary of:** Rezidor Hospitality A/S)
Chicago Avenue, Manchester Airport, Manchester M90 3RA
**Tel:** 0161-490-5000 **Fax:** 0161-490-5100
**Web:** www.radissonblu.com
**Reg No:** 3255653 **Estd:** 1996 Private Limited Company
**Line of Business:** Hotels
**Trading Style:** Radisson S A S Portman Hotel, Radisson S A S Manchester Airport
**Issued Capital:** £1
**Directors:** K J Kleiven, S G Fondell, R J Moore
**Co. Secretary:** Kevin Greenwood
**Responsibilities**
**Senior:** C Boersma *(Manager)*, Jens Hallman *(General Manager)*, Suresh Raje-Urs *(Food & Beverage Manager)*, Marianne Ruhngaard *(Manager)*, Ian Rydin *(General Manager)*, Yilmaz Yildirinler *(CEO, Managing Director)*
**Finance:** Kevin Greenmott *(Senior Finance Administrator)*, N Reddington *(Finance Director)*
**Marketing:** Jane Carwardine-Wheeler *(Sales & Marketing Director)*
**Sales:** Jane Carwardine-Wheeler *(Sales & Marketing Director)*, Rachel Fitzpatrick *(Senior Sales Executive)*
**Branches:** Rezidor Hotel Manchester Ltd, Waltham Close, Stansted, Essex CM24 1PP
**US SIC:** 7011, 6531
**UK SIC:** 66500, 83400
**Auditors:** Deloitte LLP

| | 31-12-13 | 31-12-12 | 31-12-11 |
|---|---|---|---|
| TO | 14,242,000 | 14,261,000 | 13,548,000 |
| P/L | (1,340,000) | (786,000) | (826,000) |
| NW | 21,503,000 | 22,843,000 | 23,629,000 |
| WC | 15,683,000 | 21,468,000 | 22,851,000 |
| Emp. | 165 | 158 | 167 |

DUNS 50-136-1133
## Rezidor Hotels Uk Ltd
**(Subsidiary of:** Rezidor Hospitality A/S)
22 Portman Square, London W1H 7BG
**Tel:** 07718364945 **Fax:** 02072086001
**Web:** www.rezidor.com
**Reg No:** 2321986 **VAT No:** 538916116
**Estd:** 1988 Private Limited Company
**Line of Business:** Hotels
**Issued Capital:** £32,240,441
**Directors:** M J Farrell, S G Fondell, R J Moore, K J Kleiven
**Co. Secretary:** Kevin Greenwood

**Responsibilities**
**Senior:** Marianne Ruhngaard (*Legal Director*)
**Branches:** Rezidor Hotels Uk Ltd, 3 Cromac Place, Belfast, Belfast BT7 2JB
**US SIC:** 7011 **UK SIC:** 66500
**Auditors:** Deloitte LLP

|  | 31-12-13 | 31-12-12 | 31-12-11 |
|---|---|---|---|
| TO | 9,650,000 | 9,303,000 | 8,114,000 |
| P/L | (1,068,000) | (603,000) | (89,000) |
| NW | 60,076,000 | 61,144,000 | 61,747,000 |
| WC | 50,076,000 | 51,144,000 | 51,747,000 |
| Emp. | 76 | 63 | 45 |

DUNS 34-782-7321
## R.F. Holdings Ltd
38 Hall Lane, Walsall, West Midlands WS9 9AS
**Web:** www.rubbernek.co.uk
**Reg No:** 2786895 **Estd:** 1993 Private Limited Company
**Line of Business:** Management activities of other non-financial holding companies not elsewhere classified
**Issued Capital:** £100,002
**Director:** M P Creighton
**Co. Secretary:** Ms Lisa Guest
**US SIC:** 6711 **UK SIC:** 83962
**Auditors:** Bentley Jennison
**Bankers:** HSBC Bank plc (40-42-10)

|  | 30-04-14 | 30-04-13 | 30-04-12 |
|---|---|---|---|
| TO | 6,528,008 | 6,394,075 | 6,720,474 |
| P/L | 833,367 | 525,471 | 891,674 |
| NW | 4,796,819 | 4,336,449 | 4,152,089 |
| WC | 4,189,036 | 3,735,238 | 3,578,655 |
| Emp. | 67 | 77 | 81 |

DUNS 29-550-8659
## R.F.A. Manufacturing Ltd
(**Subsidiary of:** Ipo Wire Holdings Sa)
Whaley Road, Barugh Green, Barnsley, South Yorkshire S75 1HT
**Tel:** 01226-764425 **Fax:** 01226-767562
**Web:** www.rfa-tech.co.uk
**Reg No:** 1917680 **VAT No:** 391228941
**Estd:** 1985 Private Limited Company
**Line of Business:** Manufacture of concrete products for construction purposes
**Issued Capital:** £1,000
**Directors:** A J Fort, F Mesegue, L S Villares, M L Mckillop
**Co. Secretary:** Xavier Puig
**Responsibilities**
**Senior:** Francesco Rubio (*Manager*)
**US SIC:** 3271 **UK SIC:** 24370
**Auditors:** PricewaterhouseCoopers
**Bankers:** National Westminster Bank Plc (56-00-34)

|  | 31-12-13 | 31-12-12 | 31-12-11 |
|---|---|---|---|
| TA | 1,000 | 1,000 | 1,000 |
| NW | 1,000 | 1,000 | 1,000 |

DUNS 36-794-6068
## R.F.C Llandovery
Church Bank, Llandovery, Dyfed SA20 0DT
**Tel:** 01550-721110
**Web:** www.llandoveryrfc.co.uk
**Estd:** 2002
**Line of Business:** Misc Amusement & Recreation Services
**Proprietor:** H Davies
**US SIC:** 7999 **UK SIC:** 97913
**Employees:** 100

DUNS 54-424-1938
## Rfea Ltd
Mountbarrow House, 6-20 Elizabeth Street, London SW1W 9RB
**Tel:** 01142611312 **Fax:** 020-7839-0970
**Web:** www.rfea.org.uk
**Reg No:** 3270369 **Estd:** 1996 Private Company Limited By Guarantee
**Line of Business:** Ministry of defence
**Directors:** S E Golding, Brigadier D Godsal, A Mckay, Ms E G Cassidy, J D Stokoe, J Mill, Captain G R Peel, Major General A S Ritchie
**Co. Secretary:** Brigadier Stephen Gledhill
**Responsibilities**
**Senior:** Stuart Burdess (*Director*)
**Branches:** Rfea Ltd, 41 Church St, Sheffield, South Yorkshire S1 2GL
**US SIC:** 7361, 8699
**UK SIC:** 83954, 96902
**Auditors:** Chantrey Vellacott DFK LLP
**Bankers:** Coutts & Co (18-00-02)

|  | 30-09-13 | 30-09-12 | 30-09-11 |
|---|---|---|---|
| TO | 2,688,354 | 2,257,705 | 1,490,943 |
| P/L | 38,347 | 270,614 | 62,435 |
| NW | 2,063,427 | 1,963,974 | 1,583,202 |
| WC | 1,021,169 | 400,210 | 178,852 |
| Emp. | 68 | 54 | 37 |

DUNS 73-792-8531 **Imp**
## Rfmd (Uk) Ltd
(**Subsidiary of:** Rf Micro Devices (Holland) B.V.)
Heighinton Lane Business Park, Millennium Way, Newton Aycliffe, County Durham DL5 6JW
**Tel:** 01325-301111
**Web:** www.filtronic.co.uk
**Reg No:** 2927965 **Estd:** 2000 Private Limited Company
**Line of Business:** Manufacturers and distributiors of electronic components
**Export Sales:** £37,946,579
**Trading Style:** Compound Filtronics
**Issued Capital:** £489,975
**Directors:** R Bruggeworth, W A Priddy Jr
**Co. Secretary:** Ms Suzanne Rudy
**Responsibilities**
**Senior:** William Priddy (*Director*)
**US SIC:** 3679 **UK SIC:** 34542
**Auditors:** Ernst & Young LLP
**Bankers:** Barclays Bank Plc (20-11-81)

|  | 30-03-13 | 31-03-12 | 02-03-11 |
|---|---|---|---|
| TO | 39,727,619 | 32,109,764 | 47,003,143 |
| P/L | 11,508,442 | 6,731,412 | 14,653,591 |
| NW | 25,900,926 | 43,117,813 | 36,391,823 |
| WC | 27,194,664 | 41,152,332 | 34,912,017 |
| Emp. | 182 | 199 | 211 |

DUNS 36-510-9487
## R.G. Carter Construction Ltd
(**Subsidiary of:** Rg Carter Group Ltd)
30 Out Westgate, Bury St Edmunds, Suffolk IP33 3PA
**Tel:** 01284753355 **Fax:** 01284-753099
**Web:** www.rgcarter-construction.co.uk
**Reg No:** 3284871 **Estd:** 1921 Private Limited Company
**Line of Business:** Builders
**Issued Capital:** £100
**Directors:** J G Carter, P Smith, R E Carter, M Turner, G R Whistler, D Carter, S D Humphrey
**Co. Secretary:** Robert Alflatt
**Branches:** R.g. Carter Construction Ltd, 27 Yarmouth Road, Norwich, Norfolk NR7 0EE
**US SIC:** 1522 **UK SIC:** 50100
**Auditors:** Baker Tilly UK Audit LLP
**Bankers:** Barclays Bank Plc (20-62-53)

|  | 31-12-13 | 31-12-12 | 31-12-11 |
|---|---|---|---|
| TO | 238,781,000 | 212,134,000 | 220,647,000 |
| P/L | 3,048,000 | 4,134,000 | 4,296,000 |
| NW | 32,767,000 | 33,550,000 | 34,850,000 |
| WC | 24,980,000 | 27,182,000 | 28,781,000 |
| Emp. | 766 | 873 | 955 |

DUNS 51-626-1570
## Rg Carter Group Ltd
9-11 Drayton High Road, Drayton, Norwich, Norfolk NR8 6AH
**Tel:** 01842754086
**Web:** www.rgcarter-construction.co.uk
**Reg No:** 5906053 **Estd:** 2006 Private Limited Company
**Line of Business:** Management activities of construction holding companies
**Issued Capital:** £241,807
**Directors:** R G Carter, D J Coventry, R E Carter, A N Duckworth Chad, J R Barclay, D Carter, J G Carter
**Co. Secretary:** Gerald Daniels
**US SIC:** 6711 **UK SIC:** 83962
**Auditors:** Baker Tilly UK Audit LLP

|  | 31-12-13 | 31-12-12 | 31-12-11 |
|---|---|---|---|
| TO | 261,397,000 | 238,535,000 | 249,192,000 |
| P/L | 5,107,000 | 5,426,000 | 5,120,000 |
| NW | 105,040,000 | 100,942,000 | 100,167,000 |
| WC | 56,119,000 | 63,228,000 | 64,073,000 |
| Emp. | 1,094 | 1,208 | 1,298 |

DUNS 21-748-7941
## R.G. Spiller Ltd
(**Subsidiary of:** Howard Contractors Ltd)
Chard Business Park, Chard, Somerset TA20 1FB
**Tel:** 0146062881
**Web:** www.rgspiller.com
**Reg No:** 1539123 **VAT No:** 355454151
**Estd:** 1840 Private Limited Company
**Line of Business:** Building construction contractors
**Issued Capital:** £100,000
**Principals:** D R Howard (*Chairman and Managing*), A Howard
**Co. Secretary:** Ms Tracey Howard
**Responsibilities**
**Sales:** Lester Channing (*Account Manager*)
**Branches:** R.g. Spiller Ltd, Wessex Rd, Yeovil, Somerset BA21 3LS
**US SIC:** 1522, 1541
**UK SIC:** 50100
**Auditors:** Francis Clark
**Bankers:** Barclays Bank Plc (20-30-47)

|  | 31-12-13 | 31-12-12 | 31-12-11 |
|---|---|---|---|
| TO | 15,622,809 | 13,791,388 | 17,012,054 |
| P/L | 51,851 | 49,480 | 66,749 |
| NW | 664,570 | 612,719 | 563,239 |
| WC | 654,690 | 599,999 | 536,057 |
| Emp. | N/A | 69 | 68 |

DUNS 49-080-4895 **Imp**
## Rga Uk Services Ltd
(**Subsidiary of:** Reinsurance Group of America Incorporated)
16th Floor 5 Aldermanbury Square, London EC2V 7HR
**Tel:** 02077106700
**Web:** www.rgare.com
**Reg No:** 3086510 **Estd:** 1995 Private Limited Company
**Line of Business:** Life insurance
**Issued Capital:** £750,002
**Directors:** J A Galloway, G B Lane, S Wainwright
**Co. Secretary:** Ms Nameeta Biswas
**US SIC:** 6311 **UK SIC:** 82002

|  | 31-12-13 | 31-12-12 | 31-12-11 |
|---|---|---|---|
| TO | 17,990,000 | 15,407,100 | 12,029,700 |
| P/L | 917,900 | 686,800 | 852,200 |
| NW | 5,865,800 | 4,518,300 | 3,947,200 |
| WC | 5,424,300 | 3,985,700 | 3,314,900 |
| Emp. | 114 | 102 | 96 |

DUNS 22-284-8579
## Rga Underwriting Ltd
551 London Road, Isleworth, Middlesex TW7 4DS
**Tel:** 08007831626
**Web:** www.rentguard.co.uk
**Reg No:** 4302819 **Estd:** 2001 Private Limited Company
**Line of Business:** Financial services
**Issued Capital:** £115,789
**Directors:** J R Castell, Mrs X Cao, Ms Y Ota, S J Jones
**US SIC:** 6111, 6399
**UK SIC:** 81501, 82001
**Auditors:** Day, Smith & Hunter

|  | 31-12-13 | 31-12-12 | 31-12-11 |
|---|---|---|---|
| TA | 4,941,648 | 4,263,752 | 4,486,304 |
| P/L | 536,727 | 478,275 | 327,472 |
| NW | 1,297,870 | 1,002,745 | 541,008 |
| WC | 1,048,374 | 712,010 | 365,115 |
| Emp. | 67 | 71 | 85 |

DUNS 76-934-5802
## Rgcm Ltd
(**Subsidiary of:** Spritestore Ltd)
4 Abbey Wood Road, Kings Hill, West Malling, Kent ME19 4AB
**Tel:** 01732-526-850
**Web:** www.rg-group.co.uk
**Reg No:** 2477053 **VAT No:** 574011956
**Estd:** 1990 Private Limited Company
**Line of Business:** Construction of commercial buildings
**Trading Style:** Rg Group
**Issued Capital:** £1,000
**Principals:** J H Chadwick (*Managing*), T Puttick, J R Casey, S W Roe, M D Mullarkey, J C Noble, J A Kallend
**Co. Secretary:** Michael Steel
**Responsibilities**
**IT:** Rick Harper (*IT Manager*)
**HR:** Michelle Drew (*Human Resources Manager*), Mike Ridger (*Facilities Manager*)
**Health & Safety:** Mike Ridger (*Facilities Manager*)
**Facilities:** Mike Ridger (*Facilities Manager*)
**Branches:** Rgcm Limited, 4 York Pl, Leeds, West Yorkshire LS1 2DR
**US SIC:** 1541 **UK SIC:** 50100
**Auditors:** Simmons Gainsford LLP

|  | 31-12-13 | 31-12-12 | 31-12-11 |
|---|---|---|---|
| TO | 147,809,085 | 165,834,295 | 214,784,074 |
| P/L | 1,185,228 | 1,617,960 | 2,364,370 |
| NW | 7,351,937 | 7,176,006 | 6,151,938 |
| WC | 7,096,993 | 6,881,860 | 5,795,410 |
| Emp. | 124 | 139 | 171 |

DUNS 21-908-1445
## Rgf Logistics Ltd
Magnum House, Garretts Green Trading Estate, Valepits Road, Birmingham, West Midlands B33 0TD
**Tel:** 0121-783-1100
**Web:** www.rgflogistics.com
**Reg No:** 0958875 **Estd:** 1969 Private Limited Company
**Line of Business:** Road haulage and transport services
**Trading Style:** Richard Gary Ford
**Issued Capital:** £230,600
**Principals:** G R Ford (*Managing*), R G Ford (*Financial*), R C Bennett, Ms E A Newton, R B Pike, S H Share, Ms E A Ford
**Co. Secretary:** Geoffrey Ford
**Branches:** Rgf Logistics Ltd, Weldon Road, Corby, Northamptonshire NN17 5UE
**US SIC:** 4789 **UK SIC:** 77002
**Auditors:** Grant Thornton UK LLP
**Bankers:** Barclays Bank Plc (20-08-98)

|  | 31-08-13 | 31-08-12 | 31-08-11 |
|---|---|---|---|
| TO | 14,699,875 | 13,549,841 | 15,043,320 |
| P/L | 384,917 | 124,080 | 218,879 |
| NW | 1,254,033 | 971,633 | 882,415 |
| WC | 82,284 | 174,415 | 109,277 |
| Emp. | 138 | 125 | 152 |

DUNS 21-772-2436
## Rgis
308 Peel House, London Road, Morden, Surrey SM4 5BT
**Tel:** 02036421238
**Web:** www.rgisinv.com
**Estd:** 2011 Proprietorship
**Line of Business:** Stocktaking services
**Proprietor:** A Wise
**Responsibilities**
**Senior:** Hetal Patel (*Dristict Manager*)
**US SIC:** 8931 **UK SIC:** 83600
**Employees:** 75

DUNS 23-868-2004 **Imp**
## Rgis Inventory Specialists Ltd
(**Subsidiary of:** The Blackstone Group L P)
300 Trinity Park, Birmingham, West Midlands B37 7ES
**Tel:** 01926888882 **Fax:** 01926888883
**Web:** www.rgis.com
**Reg No:** 3859648 **Estd:** 1999 Private Limited Company
**Line of Business:** Representative office
**Issued Capital:** £50,000
**Directors:** A Chinoy, H H Krause
**Co. Secretary:** Ms Elise Cordier
**Responsibilities**
**Senior:** David Feidner (*Manager*), Peter Keenoy (*Manager*), Karen Page (*Sales Coordinator*)
**Finance:** Dawn Ashley (*Financial Director*), Maxine Roberts (*Finance Controller*)
**Sales:** Karen Page (*Sales Coordinator*)
**IT:** Justin Passmore (*Head of Information Systems*)
**HR:** Anne Simmonds (*Human Resources Manager*)
**Health & Safety:** Anne Simmonds (*Human Resources Manager*)
**Branches:** Rgis Inventory Specialists Ltd, 1A Katharine Street, Croydon, Surrey CR0 1NX
**US SIC:** 8931 **UK SIC:** 83600
**Auditors:** MRI Moores Rowland LLP

|  | 31-12-13 | 31-12-12 | 31-12-11 |
|---|---|---|---|
| TO | 21,944,991 | 18,748,488 | 16,725,521 |
| P/L | 779,801 | 1,764,059 | 1,713,584 |
| NW | 3,231,326 | 2,628,619 | 3,280,086 |
| WC | 2,885,848 | 2,349,026 | 3,077,236 |
| Emp. | 1,294 | 910 | 854 |

DUNS 73-484-9420
## Rgl Llp
8th Floor Dashwood House, 69 Old Broad Street, London EC2M 1QS
**Web:** www.rgl.com
**Reg No:** 0304572OC **VAT No:** 815022569
**Estd:** 2003
**Line of Business:** Technical testing and analysis
**Export Sales:** £4,888,133
**Trading Style:** Rgl Forensics
**US SIC:** 7399 **UK SIC:** 83954
**Auditors:** CBHC LLP

|  | 31-03-14 | 31-03-13 | 31-03-12 |
|---|---|---|---|
| TO | 9,450,159 | 9,133,753 | 8,762,814 |
| P/L | 1,235,914 | 1,451,346 | 1,243,858 |
| NW | 1,818,236 | 1,900,970 | 1,921,970 |
| WC | 3,729,695 | 3,795,239 | 3,708,433 |
| Emp. | 66 | 62 | 69 |

DUNS 21-208-8793 **Imp-Exp**
## R.Gledhill Ltd
Pingle Mill, Pingle Lane, Delph, Oldham, Lancashire OL3 5EX
**Tel:** 01457-874651 **Fax:** 01457-872428
**Web:** www.rgledhill.co.uk
**Reg No:** 0313566 **VAT No:** 145536563
**Estd:** 1935 Private Limited Company
**Line of Business:** Wholesale suppliers of yarn
**Export Markets:** Worldwide
**Issued Capital:** £1,000
**Principals:** P Gledhill (*Chairman*), B Gledhill (*Managing*), R Gledhill, J Gledhill
**Co. Secretary:** John Gledhill
**Responsibilities**
**Purchasing:** Howard Guant (*Purchasing Manager*)
**US SIC:** 2299 **UK SIC:** 43992
**Auditors:** Bostocks Boyce Welch
**Bankers:** National Westminster Bank Plc (01-08-99)

|  | 31-10-13 | 31-10-12 | 31-10-11 |
|---|---|---|---|
| TO | 7,923,420 | 7,561,260 | 6,358,791 |
| P/L | 643,636 | 584,008 | 133,225 |
| NW | 2,989,156 | 2,466,663 | 2,009,477 |
| WC | 1,610,197 | 1,396,847 | 1,334,390 |

DUNS 53-628-0100
## Rgs Cleaning Ltd
96 Hangingwater Road, Sheffield, South Yorkshire S11 7ER
**Tel:** 01142-630303
**Web:** www.rgscleaningltd.co.uk
**Reg No:** 3432909 **Estd:** 1997 Private Limited Company
**Line of Business:** Cleaning contracting commercial
**Issued Capital:** £2

**Principals:** R K Guise Smith *(Financial)*, O R Guise Smith, Ms C G Guise Smith
**Responsibilities**
**Senior:** Andrew Coupe *(Manager)*, Dianne Needham *(Manager)*
**US SIC:** 7349 **UK SIC:** 92300
**Auditors:** Webster & Co Ltd

| | 31-03-14 | 31-03-13 | 31-03-12 |
|---|---|---|---|
| TA | 345,954 | 345,815 | 321,549 |
| NW | 144,945 | 103,867 | 95,612 |
| WC | (17,338) | (37,987) | (34,044) |

DUNS 39-980-2321

## Rh Development (Property) Ltd

7a Colwick Quays Business Park, Road No 2, Colwick, Nottingham, Nottinghamshire NG4 2JY
**Tel:** 01159873988
**Reg No:** 2276251 **Estd:** 1988 Private Limited Company
**Line of Business:** Property developers
**Issued Capital:** £1,000,000
**Directors:** N A Baxter, P J Baxter
**Co. Secretary:** Nigel Baxter
**US SIC:** 6552 **UK SIC:** 85000
**Bankers:** Barclays Bank Plc (20-63-25)

| | 31-12-13 | 31-12-12 | 31-12-11 |
|---|---|---|---|
| TO | 15,264,000 | 1,968,556 | 1,375,970 |
| P/L | 498,000 | 60,891 | 263,152 |
| NW | 887,000 | 737,036 | 681,492 |
| WC | (3,455,000) | (4,040,641) | (3,713,359) |
| Emp. | 61 | 3 | 3 |

DUNS 21-894-1532 **Imp**

## The Rh Group Ltd

**(Subsidiary of:** Kühne Holding Ag)
Unit 4, Castlebridge Office Village, Castle Marina Road, Nottingham, Nottinghamshire NG7 1TP
**Tel:** 01159-438000 **Fax:** 01159-489090
**Web:** www.rhfreight.com
**Reg No:** 1035457 **VAT No:** 117406687
**Estd:** 1971 Private Limited Company
**Line of Business:** Road haulage and transport services
**Trading Style:** Rh Freight, Rh European Freight Network
**Issued Capital:** £600,000
**Directors:** T P Held, J Hedderwick, M Bennett
**Co. Secretary:** Robert Layton
**Responsibilities**
**Finance:** Amanda Guiblin *(Finance General Manager)*
**Branches:** The Rh Group Ltd, The Atlantic Terminal, Liverpool Intermodal Freeport Terminal, Bootle, Merseyside L20 1HA
**US SIC:** 4789, 4213
**UK SIC:** 77002, 72300
**Auditors:** Deloitte LLP
**Bankers:** Barclays Bank Plc (20-63-25)

| | 31-12-12 | 31-12-11 | 31-12-10 |
|---|---|---|---|
| TO | 135,865,000 | 19,963,000 | 133,827,000 |
| P/L | 8,836,000 | 551,000 | 4,555,000 |
| NW | 13,961,000 | 7,045,000 | 12,944,000 |
| WC | 3,618,000 | (7,194,000) | 1,349,000 |
| Emp. | 568 | 136 | 591 |

DUNS 21-751-1815 **Imp**

## R.H. Hall (Microwave) Ltd

Unit 1, Beacon Court, Pitstone Green Business Park, Quarry Roa, Leighton Buzzard, Bedfordshire LU7 9GY
**Tel:** 01296-663400 **Fax:** 01296663401
**Web:** www.rhhall.com
**Reg No:** 1361433 **VAT No:** 322212517
**Estd:** 1978 Private Limited Company
**Line of Business:** Manufacture of machinery for food, beverage and tobacco processing
**Export Sales:** £161,338
**Issued Capital:** £10,000
**Directors:** Mrs K L Hall, K Brearley
**Co. Secretary:** Raymond Hall
**Responsibilities**
**Health & Safety:** Ray Copper *(Health & Safety Officer)*
**Branches:** R.h. Hall (Microwave) Ltd, 17 St Johns Rd, Watford, Hertfordshire WD17 1PW
**US SIC:** 3551 **UK SIC:** 32441
**Auditors:** Wilkins Kennedy
**Bankers:** HSBC Bank plc (40-15-23)

| | 31-03-14 | 31-03-13 | 31-03-12 |
|---|---|---|---|
| TO | 11,468,242 | 10,188,706 | 10,274,206 |
| P/L | 488,822 | 475,183 | 354,801 |
| NW | 2,603,166 | 2,555,423 | 2,503,795 |
| WC | 1,177,697 | 1,016,095 | 966,052 |
| Emp. | 51 | 48 | 46 |

DUNS 57-892-1751

## R.H. Irving Construction Ltd

Borders Business Park, Carlisle, Cumbria CA6 5TD
**Tel:** 01228 792777
**Web:** www.rhi-construction.com
**Reg No:** 2903530 **VAT No:** 257209652
**Estd:** 2001 Private Limited Company
**Line of Business:** Groundwork contractors
**Issued Capital:** £5,179

**Principals:** B S Field *(Financial)*, Ms A M Dodd, J W Birkett, R W Grant, M A Moodycliffe
**Co. Secretary:** Richard Irving
**US SIC:** 1622 **UK SIC:** 50200
**Auditors:** Barrett & Co
**Bankers:** Barclays Bank Plc (20-18-47)

| | 28-02-14 | 28-02-13 | 29-02-12 |
|---|---|---|---|
| TA | 4,051,724 | 3,088,535 | 3,388,530 |
| NW | 2,183,530 | 2,047,923 | 1,883,980 |
| WC | 1,660,199 | 1,504,511 | 1,320,034 |

DUNS 42-464-6144

## R.H. Miller (Group) Ltd

Fordel Lauder Road, Dalkeith, Midlothian EH22 2PH
**Tel:** 0131-663-3046
**Web:** www.rhmiller.co.uk
**Reg No:** 0232276SC **Estd:** 2002 Private Limited Company
**Line of Business:** Retail sale of clothing
**Issued Capital:** £90,002
**Director:** R H Miller
**Co. Secretary:** Drummond Miller
**US SIC:** 5699, 5661
**UK SIC:** 64500, 64600
**Bankers:** Bank Of Scotland (80-20-00)

| | 31-01-14 | 31-01-13 | 31-01-12 |
|---|---|---|---|
| TO | 7,284,517 | 8,196,890 | 8,886,850 |
| P/L | (120,822) | (898) | 9,931 |
| NW | 587,762 | 702,915 | 710,642 |
| WC | (983,051) | (961,486) | (167,031) |
| Emp. | 46 | 50 | 44 |

DUNS 21-024-2137 **Imp**

## Rh Oldco Ltd

**(Subsidiary of:** Premier Foods Plc)
The Lord Rank Centre, High Wycombe, Buckinghamshire HP12 3QS
**Tel:** 08707281111 **Fax:** 01159536001
**Web:** www.rankhovis.co.uk
**Reg No:** 0062065 **VAT No:** 765350619
**Estd:** 1899 Private Limited Company
**Line of Business:** Flour & Grain Mill Product Mfrs
**Trading Style:** Fleming Howden
**Issued Capital:** £145,000,000
**Directors:** D N Leggett, A J Mcdonald
**Co. Secretary:** Simon Wilbraham
**Responsibilities**
**Admin:** Christine Webster *(Office Manager)*
**Branches:** Rh Oldco Ltd, Fish Dam Lane, Barnsley, South Yorkshire S71 3HF
**US SIC:** 2041 **UK SIC:** 41600

| | 31-12-13 | 31-12-12 | 31-12-11 |
|---|---|---|---|
| TA | 145,704,000 | 147,704,000 | 147,704,000 |
| NW | 145,000,000 | 145,000,000 | 145,000,000 |
| WC | 144,528,000 | 144,528,000 | 144,478,000 |

DUNS 21-912-2272 **Imp-Exp**

## R.H. Smith & Sons (Wigmakers) Ltd

Caldicott Drive, Gainsborough, Lincolnshire DN21 1FJ
**Tel:** 01427616831 **Fax:** 01427-617-190
**Web:** www.smiffys.com
**Reg No:** 1179968 **VAT No:** 129579528
**Estd:** 1894 Private Limited Company
**Line of Business:** Manufacturers and wholesalers of fancy goods
**Export Markets:** Canada; U S A
**Export Sales:** £18,570,764
**Trading Style:** Smiffy's
**Issued Capital:** £100
**Principals:** R Peckett *(Managing)*, Ms D Clugston, E Peckett
**Co. Secretary:** Mrs Geraldine Peckett
**Responsibilities**
**Senior:** Susan Barker *(Manager)*
**Sales:** H Corfield *(Sales Manager)*
**Branches:** R.h. Smith & Sons (Wigmakers) Ltd, 265 High St, Lincoln, Lincolnshire LN2 1HW
**US SIC:** 5199, 3961
**UK SIC:** 61900, 49103
**Auditors:** Hemming Vincent LLP
**Bankers:** HSBC Bank plc (40-22-01)

| | 31-12-13 | 31-12-12 | 31-12-11 |
|---|---|---|---|
| TO | 50,728,520 | 50,008,911 | 43,928,277 |
| P/L | 4,203,323 | 5,445,807 | 4,363,988 |
| NW | 11,629,666 | 10,088,781 | 8,328,867 |
| WC | 7,887,291 | 6,394,520 | 5,805,479 |
| Emp. | 238 | 242 | 232 |

DUNS 21-000-8413 **Imp**

## R.H.Amar & Co Ltd

Unit K, High Wycombe, Buckinghamshire HP12 3TF
**Tel:** 01494-530200
**Web:** www.rhamar.com
**Reg No:** 0497691 **VAT No:** 207557168
**Estd:** 1951 Private Limited Company
**Line of Business:** Other business activities not elsewhere classified
**Issued Capital:** £24,244
**Principals:** H R Amar *(Chairman and Managing)*, J S Lilleystone, T J Brady, J Heynen, P M Tuhrim, S D Fry, R E Amar
**Co. Secretary:** Ms Ruth Amar

**Responsibilities**
**Senior:** Maureen Amar *(Manager)*
**US SIC:** 5149 **UK SIC:** 61700
**Auditors:** Hacker Young
**Bankers:** Barclays Bank Plc (20-02-06)

| | 31-01-14 | 31-01-13 | 31-01-12 |
|---|---|---|---|
| TO | 56,529,494 | 54,739,206 | 67,540,405 |
| P/L | 1,410,510 | 818,150 | 1,259,888 |
| NW | 7,186,507 | 6,518,483 | 5,888,483 |
| WC | 7,084,486 | 6,441,104 | 5,787,519 |
| Emp. | 68 | 59 | 57 |

DUNS 21-728-6855 **Imp-Exp**

## R.Hamilton & Co. Ltd

Quarryfields Industrial Estate, Warminster, Wiltshire BA12 6LA
**Tel:** 01747-860088
**Web:** www.hamilton-litestat.com
**Reg No:** 0941624 **VAT No:** 222660784
**Estd:** 1968 Private Limited Company
**Line of Business:** Wholesale of hardware, plumbing and heating equipment and supplies
**Export Markets:** Worldwide
**Trading Style:** Hamilton Litestat Group
**Issued Capital:** £10,000
**Principals:** R Hamilton *(Managing)*, I Hamilton, R Haines, J R Berry, C P Savory
**Co. Secretary:** Mrs Alison Hamilton
**Responsibilities**
**Senior:** William Milne *(Manager)*
**Branches:** R.hamilton & Co. Ltd, 28-30 South Bank Business Centre, Ponton Rd, London SW8 5BL
**US SIC:** 5074, 3643
**UK SIC:** 61300, 34203
**Auditors:** Bentley Jennison
**Bankers:** Barclays Bank Plc (20-67-59)

| | 30-06-14 | 30-06-13 | 30-06-12 |
|---|---|---|---|
| TO | 10,429,806 | 9,949,036 | 9,458,078 |
| P/L | 44,611 | 269,678 | 200,322 |
| NW | 5,256,984 | 5,219,158 | 5,012,847 |
| WC | 4,672,974 | 4,534,965 | 4,236,474 |
| Emp. | 126 | 126 | 128 |

DUNS 42-412-6139 **Imp**

## R.Hannah & Sons Ltd

**(Subsidiary of:** Hannah Holdings Ltd)
Raymond House 4, Garnett Place Glebe Road, Skelmersdale, Lancashire WN8 9UB
**Tel:** 01695-51400
**Web:** www.hannahfoodservice.co.uk
**Reg No:** 4400237 **Estd:** 2002 Private Limited Company
**Line of Business:** Wholesale of meat and meat products
**Issued Capital:** £102
**Directors:** A P Whiteside, S Hannah
**Co. Secretary:** Gary Hannah
**US SIC:** 5147 **UK SIC:** 61700
**Auditors:** Edwards Veeder LLP

| | 31-03-14 | 31-03-13 | 31-03-12 |
|---|---|---|---|
| TO | 18,289,909 | 17,305,482 | 15,217,634 |
| P/L | 280,966 | 199,638 | 110,625 |
| NW | 1,434,193 | 1,269,065 | 1,187,040 |
| WC | (45,550) | (101,651) | (294,185) |
| Emp. | 62 | 61 | 51 |

DUNS 21-907-9431 **Imp**

## R.H.Claydon Ltd

Saxham Business Park, Little Saxham, Bury St Edmunds, Suffolk IP28 6RZ
**Tel:** 01284700748 **Fax:** 01284754833
**Web:** www.rhc.co.uk
**Reg No:** 0944192 **VAT No:** 102093424
**Estd:** 1953 Private Limited Company
**Line of Business:** Sale of motor vehicle parts and accessories
**Export Sales:** £95,641
**Issued Capital:** £657,522
**Principals:** R H Claydon *(Managing)*, C R Clements, J R Parker, Ms D A Claydon, J L Gilks, M H Claydon, Ms E I Beck
**Co. Secretary:** Jeremy Gilks
**Responsibilities**
**Marketing:** Jim Parker *(Marketing Manager)*
**IT:** Adrian Durrant *(IT Coordinator)*
**Purchasing:** Heidi Adamson *(Purchasing Controller)*
**Branches:** R.h.claydon Ltd, Unit 3, Carrongrove Road, Falkirk, Stirlingshire FK2 8NZ
**US SIC:** 5531 **UK SIC:** 65100
**Auditors:** Grant Thornton
**Bankers:** Barclays Bank Plc (20-16-12)

| | 31-12-13 | 31-12-12 | 31-12-11 |
|---|---|---|---|
| TO | 14,821,882 | 13,984,128 | 13,795,710 |
| P/L | 296,719 | 540,856 | 594,095 |
| NW | 6,233,177 | 6,120,706 | 5,845,823 |
| WC | 3,631,183 | 3,583,986 | 3,344,297 |
| Emp. | 53 | 51 | 54 |

DUNS 23-500-6517

## Rhead Group Ltd

**(Subsidiary of:** Rhead Group Holdings Ltd)
Suite 2 2 Merchants Place, River Street, Bolton, Lancashire BL2 1BX
**Tel:** 01204-380682
**Web:** www.rheadgroup.com
**Reg No:** 1890057 **VAT No:** 418754236
**Estd:** 2002 Private Limited Company

**Line of Business:** Quantity surveyors
**Export Sales:** £3,096,000
**Issued Capital:** £12,903
**Director:** N A Curry
**Responsibilities**
**Senior:** Christopher Barron *(Manager)*
**Branches:** Rhead Group Ltd, 2 Merchants Place, Suite 2, Bolton, Lancashire BL2 1BX
**US SIC:** 7397, 8911
**UK SIC:** 83702, 83701
**Auditors:** Murphy Salisbury
**Bankers:** Barclays Bank Plc (20-48-08)

| | 31-07-13 | 31-07-12 | 31-07-11 |
|---|---|---|---|
| TO | 47,508,000 | 41,187,000 | 32,676,000 |
| P/L | 5,652,000 | 5,313,000 | 4,490,000 |
| NW | 9,081,000 | 13,850,000 | 9,646,000 |
| WC | 8,178,000 | 13,351,000 | 9,210,000 |
| Emp. | 309 | 232 | 206 |

DUNS 29-582-8552

## Rhenus Hauser Midlands Ltd

**(Subsidiary of:** Rhenus Logistics Ltd)
Unit 1, Gallan Park, Watling Street, Cannock, Staffordshire WS11 0XG
**Tel:** 01543-501150 **Fax:** 01922418942
**Web:** www.rhenus.com
**Reg No:** 1944635 **Estd:** 2010 Private Limited Company
**Line of Business:** Airfreight forwarding services
**Issued Capital:** £1,000
**Directors:** G T Miller, D Williams
**Co. Secretary:** Richard Kennerley
**Responsibilities**
**Senior:** Darren Cater *(General Manager)*, Martin Cleary *(Manager)*
**US SIC:** 4511 **UK SIC:** 75000
**Auditors:** Deloitte & Touche

| | 31-12-13 | 31-12-12 | 31-12-11 |
|---|---|---|---|
| TA | 154,019 | 154,019 | 154,019 |
| NW | (19,231) | (19,231) | (19,231) |
| WC | (19,231) | (19,231) | (19,231) |

DUNS 21-785-4514

## Rhenus Logistics

Frodsh Bridge Lane, Frodsham, Cheshire WA6 7HZ
**Tel:** 01928736900
**Web:** www.de.rhenus.com
**Estd:** 2011 Proprietorship
**Line of Business:** Freight services
**Proprietor:** P Martin
**US SIC:** 4213 **UK SIC:** 72300
**Employees:** 17,000

DUNS 42-414-0007

## Rhenus Logistics Ltd

Unit 2 Westpoint Enterprise Park, Manchester M17 1QS
**Tel:** 0161-886-4200
**Web:** www.uk.rhenus.com
**Reg No:** 4401654 **VAT No:** 146892628
**Estd:** 2002 Private Limited Company
**Line of Business:** Freight transport by road not elsewhere classified
**Issued Capital:** £172,001
**Directors:** G T Miller, D Williams, T Bartz, R Kennerley
**Co. Secretary:** Richard Kennerley
**Responsibilities**
**Senior:** Uwe Oemmelen *(Manager)*
**Branches:** Rhenus Logistics Ltd, Unit 3 Hanging Wood Way, West 26 Indstl Est, Bradford, West Yorkshire BD19 4TS
**US SIC:** 4213 **UK SIC:** 72300
**Auditors:** CLB Coopers
**Bankers:** Lloyds TSB Bank plc (30-95-42)

| | 31-12-13 | 31-12-12 | 31-12-11 |
|---|---|---|---|
| TO | 53,581,408 | 52,267,035 | 52,048,910 |
| P/L | 639,273 | 1,857,820 | 1,852,928 |
| NW | 6,863,073 | 6,187,949 | 4,818,609 |
| WC | 1,886,433 | 1,445,040 | 1,253,721 |
| Emp. | 212 | 201 | 196 |

DUNS 50-501-0702 **Imp-Exp**

## Rhenus Lupprians Ltd

**(Subsidiary of:** Rhenus High Tech Uk Ltd)
Siren P H D Ltd, Ashford, Middlesex TW15 1AX
**Tel:** 01784422900
**Web:** www.lupprians.co.uk
**Reg No:** 2469124 **VAT No:** 538007554
**Estd:** 1990 Private Limited Company
**Line of Business:** Freight transport by road not elsewhere classified
**Export Markets:** E U
**Export Sales:** £2,900,291
**Issued Capital:** £100,003
**Directors:** J P Delport, G A Barrow, I Fowler
**US SIC:** 4213 **UK SIC:** 72300
**Auditors:** Menzies LLP
**Bankers:** HSBC Bank plc (40-32-19)

| | 31-03-14 | 31-03-13 | 31-03-12 |
|---|---|---|---|
| TO | 14,851,999 | 15,511,863 | 12,950,872 |
| P/L | (32,159) | (351,223) | 42,242 |
| NW | 1,346,992 | 1,529,450 | 1,816,745 |
| WC | 1,981,213 | (284,269) | 31,445 |
| Emp. | 189 | 224 | 175 |

DUNS 77-452-7170
## Rhetorik Ltd
**(Subsidiary of:** Arteva Europe Sarl)
Ascot House, Wokingham, Berkshire RG40 2NW
**Tel:** 01189898580
**Web:** www.rhetoriksolutions.co.uk
**Reg No:** 2958622 **Estd:** 2005 Private Limited Company
**Line of Business:** Marketing consultants
**Trading Style:** Rhetorik Solutions
**Issued Capital:** £9,000
**Directors:** M M Manassee, M Nicolelli
**Co. Secretary:** Mrs Rachel Stern
**Responsibilities**
**Senior:** Ian Beaumont *(CEO)*, Michael Brading *(Manager)*
**Finance:** Darren Quigley *(Financial Director)*
**Admin:** Geraldine Bridges *(Office Manager)*
**IT:** John Maister *(IT Manager)*
**HR:** Geraldine Bridges *(Office Manager)*
**Health & Safety:** Geraldine Bridges *(Office Manager)*
**Facilities:** Geraldine Bridges *(Office Manager)*
**Operations:** Geraldine Bridges *(Office Manager)*
**US SIC:** 7392 **UK SIC:** 83951
**Auditors:** David G. Simon & Co Ltd
**Bankers:** Lloyds TSB Bank plc (30-97-73)

| | 31-03-13 | 31-03-12 | 31-03-11 |
|---|---|---|---|
| TO | 1,873,812 | 2,326,760 | 1,664,988 |
| P/L | 382,989 | 495,147 | 52,546 |
| NW | 2,130,639 | 1,747,650 | 1,252,182 |
| WC | 2,115,641 | 1,727,396 | 1,228,749 |

DUNS 21-622-1457 **Imp**
## R.H.H. Franks (New Milton) Ltd
Gore Road Industrial Estate, New Milton, Hampshire BH25 6SA
**Tel:** 01425-614730 **Fax:** 01425616472
**Web:** www.rhhfranks.com
**Reg No:** 0690175 **Estd:** 1961 Private Limited Company
**Line of Business:** Manufacture of metal structures and parts of structures
**Issued Capital:** £2,000
**Principals:** J House *(Managing)*, Ms A J House, D J Goodfellow, S A Jones
**Co. Secretary:** John House
**Responsibilities**
**Purchasing:** Erica Garner *(Purchasing Manager)*
**US SIC:** 3441 **UK SIC:** 32042
**Auditors:** H.G. Field & Co
**Bankers:** National Westminster Bank Plc (60-15-04)

| | 28-02-14 | 28-02-13 | 29-02-12 |
|---|---|---|---|
| TA | 2,701,497 | 2,470,266 | 2,100,873 |
| NW | 1,115,653 | 1,071,844 | 922,314 |
| WC | 581,280 | 508,060 | 284,877 |

DUNS 22-756-0182 **Imp-Exp**
## Rhi Refractories Uk Ltd
**(Subsidiary of:** Rhi Ag)
Hillview Road, Bonnybridge, Stirlingshire FK4 2EH
**Tel:** 01324819400 **Fax:** 01419411925
**Web:** www.rhi-ag.com
**Reg No:** 0075200SC **VAT No:** 476940604
**Estd:** 1981 Private Limited Company
**Line of Business:** Carbon products
**Export Markets:** Export
**Export Sales:** £17,167,862
**Issued Capital:** £8,875,000
**Directors:** D Lawrie, F Buxbaum, R Steiner
**Co. Secretary:** Gerald Mcfadden
**Responsibilities**
**Marketing:** J Bauner *(Sales & Marketing Manager)*
**Sales:** J Bauner *(Sales & Marketing Manager)*
**IT:** K Lockhart *(IT Manager)*
**US SIC:** 2873, 3299
**UK SIC:** 25130, 24504
**Auditors:** Deloitte LLP
**Bankers:** Citibank Na (18-50-08)

| | 31-12-13 | 31-12-12 | 31-12-11 |
|---|---|---|---|
| TO | 19,048,151 | 25,138,865 | 30,902,212 |
| P/L | 1,385,155 | 217,675 | 819,327 |
| NW | 9,750,260 | 8,365,105 | 7,653,003 |
| WC | 5,591,655 | 5,429,343 | 10,033,744 |
| Emp. | 171 | 237 | 289 |

DUNS 23-792-5834
## Rhinefield House Hotel Ltd
**(Subsidiary of:** Alscot Sarl)
Rhinefield Road, Brockenhurst, Hampshire SO42 7QB
**Tel:** 08450727516 **Fax:** 01590-622800
**Web:** www.laterooms.com
**Reg No:** 3785381 **Estd:** 1999 Private Limited Company
**Line of Business:** Hotels
**Issued Capital:** £4,450,002
**Directors:** P S Fullerton, Ms J Hands, K Arkley
**Co. Secretary:**
Jordan Company Secretaries Limit

**Responsibilities**
**Senior:** Mark Dicks *(General Manager)*, Alec Howarth *(General Manager)*, Johnathon Owen *(General Manager)*
**HR:** Carole Donnelly *(Human Resources Manager)*
**US SIC:** 7011 **UK SIC:** 66500
**Auditors:** Ernst & Young

| | 28-11-13 | 29-11-12 | 24-11-11 |
|---|---|---|---|
| TO | 4,031,120 | 4,236,314 | 3,892,144 |
| P/L | (286,415) | (74,503) | (342,984) |
| NW | 4,429,812 | 4,716,227 | 4,790,730 |
| WC | (4,820,953) | (4,835,714) | (5,037,402) |
| Emp. | 59 | 62 | 62 |

DUNS 22-522-3668
## Rhinegold Publishing Ltd
Buckingham House, 20 Rugby Street, London WC1N 3QZ
**Tel:** 02073-331-733
**Web:** www.rhinegold.co.uk
**Reg No:** 1308794 **VAT No:** 242357180
**Estd:** 1978 Private Limited Company
**Line of Business:** Publishing of journals and periodicals
**Trading Style:** Classical Music/Singer, Music Teacher/ Piano, International Arts Manager
**Issued Capital:** £700
**Directors:** C G Morton, Dr D B Smith
**Responsibilities**
**Senior:** Amy Driscoll *(National Accounts Manager)*
**IT:** Neil Cording *(Head of Advertising)*
**Branches:** Rhinegold Publishing Ltd, Buckingham House, 20 Rugby Street, London WC1N 3QZ
**US SIC:** 2721 **UK SIC:** 47522
**Bankers:** Lloyds TSB Bank plc (30-00-04)

| | 31-03-14 | 31-03-13 | 31-03-12 |
|---|---|---|---|
| TA | 450,349 | 562,248 | 574,683 |
| NW | (1,048,070) | (1,082,705) | (1,113,482) |
| WC | (1,062,146) | (1,068,589) | (1,007,588) |

DUNS 21-748-5606
## Rhodes Foods Ltd
90 Walton Road, West Molesey, Surrey KT8 0DL
**Tel:** 02089796600
**Web:** www.superfishuk.co.uk
**Reg No:** 0995962 **VAT No:** 222852576
**Estd:** 1970 Private Limited Company
**Line of Business:** Fish and chip shops
**Trading Style:** Superfish
**Issued Capital:** £965
**Principals:** M F Rhodes *(Chairman and Managing)*, Ms J E Catmull, Mrs B Rhodes
**Co. Secretary:** Mrs Sally Taylor
**Branches:** Rhodes Foods Ltd, 9 Castle Parade, Ewell By Pass, Epsom, Surrey KT17 2PR
**US SIC:** 5812 **UK SIC:** 66110
**Auditors:** Hagley Knight
**Bankers:** Lloyds TSB Bank plc (30-98-62)

| | 31-03-14 | 31-03-13 | 31-03-12 |
|---|---|---|---|
| TA | 1,255,737 | 1,176,839 | 1,176,231 |
| NW | 850,689 | 776,913 | 815,351 |
| WC | 2,190 | (65,378) | (87,303) |

DUNS 21-819-3918
## Rhodes Technical Services Ltd
Yew Street, Stockport, Cheshire SK4 2JW
**Tel:** 01514 766667
**Web:** www.grouprhodes.com
**Reg No:** 7916872 **Estd:** 2012 Private Limited Company
**Line of Business:** Manufacture of other special purpose machinery not elsewhere classified
**Issued Capital:** £1
**Directors:** R Waring, C M Ridgway
**Co. Secretary:** Alastair Cooper
**US SIC:** 3559 **UK SIC:** 32863

| | 28-02-14 | 31-03-13 |
|---|---|---|
| TA | 14,390 | 1 |
| NW | 262 | 1 |
| WC | 262 | 1 |
| Emp. | N/A | 200 |

DUNS 22-213-3469
## Rhodi Ltd
1 Fishwick Park, Mercer Street, Preston, Lancashire PR1 4LZ
**Tel:** 01772-562288 **Fax:** 01772-562277
**Web:** www.rhodi.co.uk
**Reg No:** 4231479 **Estd:** 2001 Private Limited Company
**Line of Business:** Manufacturers of clothing and fabrics
**Issued Capital:** £300,002
**Directors:** R I Bux, I V Bux
**Co. Secretary:** Mrs Hamida Bux
**Responsibilities**
**Senior:** Asif Bux *(Manager)*, Firoz Bux *(Manager)*, Firoz Patel *(Manager)*
**US SIC:** 2389, 6711
**UK SIC:** 45393, 83962
**Auditors:** Hayes & Co

**Bankers:** National Westminster Bank Plc (01-67-14)

| | 30-09-13 | 30-09-12 | 30-09-11 |
|---|---|---|---|
| TO | 7,344,332 | 12,120,072 | 10,885,889 |
| P/L | 23,411 | 8,762 | (707,514) |
| NW | (373,392) | (391,930) | (397,693) |
| WC | (373,392) | (391,930) | (397,693) |
| Emp. | 66 | N/A | 47 |

DUNS 73-250-8739
## Rhokett Ltd
Courtlands, Turnden Road, Cranbrook, Kent TN17 2QL
**Web:** www.rhokett.co.uk
**Reg No:** 4524677 **VAT No:** 803722357
**Estd:** 2002 Private Limited Company
**Line of Business:** Manufacturers of food products
**Issued Capital:** £133
**Principals:** M R Dockett *(Managing)*, G Rhodes, P J Le Voir
**Co. Secretary:** Ms Gail Bartlett
**US SIC:** 2099 **UK SIC:** 42399
**Bankers:** HSBC Bank plc (40-08-32)

| | 30-09-13 | 30-09-12 | 30-09-11 |
|---|---|---|---|
| TO | 8,306,101 | 8,605,273 | N/A |
| P/L | 21,491 | 443,968 | N/A |
| NW | 1,067,856 | 938,612 | 611,612 |
| WC | 444,409 | 338,858 | 73,269 |
| Emp. | 85 | 82 | N/A |

DUNS 21-600-9751
## Rhondda Community Mental Health Team
Municipal Offices, Llewellyn Street, Pentre, Mid Glamorgan CF41 7BT
**Tel:** 01443424350
**Estd:** 1999 Proprietorship
**Line of Business:** Health authorities
**Proprietor:** Mrs A Lewis
**US SIC:** 8062 **UK SIC:** 95100
**Employees:** 70

DUNS 42-400-6245
## Rhondda Cynon Taff County Borough Council
The Pavilions, Cambrian Industrial Park, Clydach Vale, Tonypandy, Mid Glamorgan CF40 2XX
**Tel:** 01443424000
**Web:** www.rhondda-cynon-taf.gov.uk
**Estd:** 2012
**Line of Business:** Local government
**Trading Style:** Rhondda Cynon Taf C.B.C., Rhondda Cynon Taf Council
**Directors:** K Griffith, C Lee
**Responsibilities**
**Finance:** Steve Merritt *(Head Financial Services)*
**Health & Safety:** Gerwyn Hogben *(Health & Safety Officer)*
**Facilities:** Colin Atyeo *(General Manager)*
**Branches:** Rhondda Cynon Taff County Borough Council, Grawen St, Porth, Mid Glamorgan CF39 0BU
**US SIC:** 9121, 8091, 7399
**UK SIC:** 91110, 95200, 83954
**Bankers:** Barclays Bank Plc (20-68-76)
**Employees:** 14,000

DUNS 22-834-0501
## Rhondda Housing Association Ltd
9 Compton Road, Tonypandy, Mid Glamorgan CF40 1BE
**Tel:** 01443-424200 **Fax:** 01443-437366
**Web:** www.rhondda.org
**Reg No:** 0022527IP **Estd:** 1981 Friendly Society
**Line of Business:** Children's homes
**Trading Style:** Rhondda Housing Association
**Principals:** Mrs T Stirling *(Chairman)*, G Lewis, M Berry, J Kinsey, Ms S Holness, J Andrews, P Young, K Morgan
**Responsibilities**
**Senior:** Stephen Emery *(Director)*, Sian Tinsley *(Director)*, Janet Whiteman *(Director)*
**Marketing:** Ian Whitehill *(Human Resources Manager)*
**HR:** Ian Whitehill *(Human Resources Manager)*
**Health & Safety:** Ian Whitehill *(Human Resources Manager)*
**Facilities:** Ian Whitehill *(Human Resources Manager)*
**US SIC:** 8321 **UK SIC:** 96111
**Auditors:** HCWA Ltd
**Bankers:** Lloyds TSB Bank plc (30-96-72)
**Employees:** 61
**Turnover:** £7,148,000

DUNS 29-013-1226 **Imp**
## Rhone Products (U K) Ltd
**(Subsidiary of:** Patek Philippe Sa Geneve)
P O Box 860, Gerrards Cross, Buckinghamshire SL9 7SB
**Tel:** 01753-891348 **Fax:** 01753891495
**Reg No:** 0410287 **Estd:** 1946 Private Limited Company
**Line of Business:** Furniture wholesale
**Export Sales:** £3,892,629
**Issued Capital:** £500
**Directors:** T H Stern, C Peny
**Co. Secretary:** Andrew Hearn
**US SIC:** 5199 **UK SIC:** 61900
**Auditors:** David Morgan & Co

| | 31-01-14 | 31-01-13 | 31-01-12 |
|---|---|---|---|
| TO | 99,549,526 | 92,742,397 | 81,393,280 |
| P/L | 14,460,140 | 12,071,809 | 6,990,165 |
| NW | 39,525,170 | 28,200,230 | 18,863,554 |
| WC | 24,102,560 | 22,316,835 | 15,163,480 |
| Emp. | 52 | 46 | 42 |

DUNS 34-603-5442
## Rhopoint Holdings Ltd
Rhopoint House, Unit B Imberhorne Lane, East Grinstead, West Sussex RH19 1QZ
**Tel:** 01342330493
**Web:** www.rhopoint.com
**Reg No:** 5410572 **Estd:** 2005 Private Limited Company
**Line of Business:** Wholesale of other electronic parts and equipment
**Export Sales:** £4,526,483
**Issued Capital:** £1,000
**Directors:** A A Theodorou, J C Briggs, Mrs L J Briggs
**US SIC:** 5065 **UK SIC:** 61500

| | 31-03-14 | 31-03-13 | 31-03-12 |
|---|---|---|---|
| TO | 9,011,724 | 7,999,206 | N/A |
| P/L | 438,235 | 587,138 | N/A |
| NW | 448,561 | 360,957 | 344,824 |
| WC | 863,763 | 701,049 | 430,483 |
| Emp. | 66 | 60 | N/A |

DUNS 21-777-6984
## Rhubarb
Priestfield Road, Edinburgh, Midlothian EH16 5UT
**Tel:** 01312257800
**Web:** www.prestonfield.com
**Estd:** 2011 Proprietorship
**Line of Business:** Restaurant - english
**Proprietor:** M Rowley
**US SIC:** 7011 **UK SIC:** 66500
**Employees:** 100

DUNS 23-635-6387 **Imp**
## Rhubarb Food Design Ltd
**(Subsidiary of:** Briers Topco Ltd)
5-25 Burr Road, London SW18 4SQ
**Tel:** 02088123200 **Fax:** 020-8812-3201
**Web:** www.rhubarb.net
**Reg No:** 3632492 **Estd:** 1998 Private Limited Company
**Line of Business:** Caterers
**Issued Capital:** £10,959
**Directors:** Ms L K Beament, P Jacobse, Ms H Bowcy, R C Beharrell
**Co. Secretary:** Ms Laraine Beament
**Responsibilities**
**Senior:** Martin Clare *(Partner)*, Patrick Donaldson *(General Manager)*, Gregg Forte *(General Manager)*, Lucy Gemmill *(Partner)*, Dan Groat *(General Manager)*, Lance Lawry *(Manager)*, Chris Rettie *(General Manager)*
**Sales:** Aaron Whitelock *(Director of Business developme)*
**US SIC:** 5812 **UK SIC:** 66110
**Bankers:** Barclays Bank Plc (20-00-50)

| | 31-12-13 | 31-12-12 | 31-12-11 |
|---|---|---|---|
| TO | 29,576,189 | 29,691,212 | 27,130,913 |
| P/L | 1,216,468 | 968,457 | 713,704 |
| NW | 3,258,338 | 2,238,988 | 701,386 |
| WC | 1,155,415 | 323,140 | (580,960) |
| Emp. | 400 | 412 | 312 |

DUNS 64-099-5916
## Rhyal Engineering Ltd
8 Thornton Road Industrial Estate, Milford Haven, Dyfed SA73 2RA
**Tel:** 01646699191
**Web:** www.rhyalengineering.com
**Reg No:** 3495210 **Estd:** 1998 Private Limited Company
**Line of Business:** Mechanical engineering general
**Export Sales:** £3,070,337
**Issued Capital:** £25,000
**Managing Director:** R L Thomson
**Co. Secretary:** Ms Ruth Thomson
**Responsibilities**
**Sales:** Richard Nayler *(Sales Manager)*
**HR:** Trish Preen *(Human Resources Manager)*
**Operations:** Willie Findlay *(Quality Assurance Manager)*
**US SIC:** 8911 **UK SIC:** 83701

**Auditors:** Evens & Co Ltd

| | 31-01-14 | 31-01-13 | 31-01-12 |
|---|---|---|---|
| TO | 16,823,022 | 11,711,471 | 11,207,196 |
| P/L | 465,542 | 392,475 | 533,746 |
| NW | 1,994,722 | 1,996,729 | 2,168,454 |
| WC | 1,669,539 | 1,720,938 | 1,723,794 |
| Emp. | 152 | 100 | 130 |

DUNS 21-772-6369

## Rhyl College

Cefndy Road, Rhyl, Clwyd LL18 2HG
**Tel:** 01745354797
**Web:** www.llandrillo.ac.uk
**Estd:** 2011 Proprietorship
**Line of Business:** Further education schools and colleges
**Proprietor:** Mrs C Jones
**US SIC:** 8221 **UK SIC:** 93100
**Employees:** 200

DUNS 21-607-3745

## Rhyl High School

86 Grange Road, Rhyl, Clwyd LL18 4BY
**Tel:** 01745343533
**Web:** www.rhylhigh.denbighshire.sch.uk
**Estd:** 2011 Proprietorship
**Line of Business:** Schools (local authority)
**Proprietor:** Mrs C Armstead
**Responsibilities**
**Senior:** Claire Armis *(Head Teacher)*, Claire Armitstead *(Head Teacher)*, Juliet Peters *(Deputy Head Teacher)*
**HR:** Sharon Hughes *(HR Manager)*
**US SIC:** 8211 **UK SIC:** 93200
**Employees:** 144

DUNS 28-993-7914

## Rhymecare Ltd

(**Subsidiary of:** Cw Residential Plc)
Coombelands Lane, Pulborough, West Sussex RH20 1AG
**Tel:** 01798-874779
**Web:** www.allroundcare.co.uk
**Reg No:** 1834232 **Estd:** 1984 Private Limited Company
**Line of Business:** Other human health activities
**Issued Capital:** £220,937
**Directors:** Ms S M Wyatt, N M Wyatt
**Co. Secretary:** John Woolfenden
**US SIC:** 8091 **UK SIC:** 95200
**Auditors:** Grant Thornton
**Bankers:** Lloyds TSB Bank plc (30-12-05)

| | 31-12-13 | 31-12-12 | 31-12-11 |
|---|---|---|---|
| TO | 2,104,399 | 2,127,237 | 2,039,635 |
| P/L | 344,265 | 345,102 | 323,366 |
| NW | 4,692,005 | 2,695,039 | 2,447,535 |
| WC | 414,630 | 355,774 | 101,521 |
| Emp. | 64 | 67 | 65 |

DUNS 21-467-8430

## Rhys Davies

Unit 1 Autobase Industrial Estate, Tipton Road, Tividale, Oldbury, West Midlands B69 3HU
**Tel:** 0121-520-6300
**Web:** www.rhysdavies.co.uk
**Estd:** 2002 Proprietorship
**Line of Business:** Road haulage and transport services
**Proprietor:** A Stone
**US SIC:** 4789 **UK SIC:** 77002
**Employees:** 80

DUNS 28-968-4649

## Rhys Davies & Sons Ltd

(**Subsidiary of:** Rhys Davies Holdings Ltd)
Taffs Well, Cardiff, South Glamorgan CF15 7QR
**Tel:** 029-2081-0587 **Fax:** 029-2081-0717
**Web:** www.rhysdavies.co.uk
**Reg No:** 1718283 **Estd:** 1952 Private Limited Company
**Line of Business:** Freight transport by road not elsewhere classified
**Export Sales:** £1,210,397
**Trading Style:** Freight Logistics, Rhys Davies Forwarding
**Issued Capital:** £55
**Directors:** P D Hodgkiss, M C Richmond, S J Thomas
**Co. Secretary:** Stephen Thomas
**Responsibilities**
**Senior:** Steve Joyce *(General Manager)*
**Finance:** Cerianne Cullen *(Finance Manager)*
**Sales:** Steve Apsey *(Business Development Manager)*
**HR:** Pam White *(Human Resources Manager)*
**Branches:** Rhys Davies & Sons Ltd, Unit 5, Murraysgate Industrial Estate, Bathgate, West Lothian EH47 0LE
**US SIC:** 4213 **UK SIC:** 72300
**Auditors:** PricewaterhouseCoopers LLP
**Bankers:** National Westminster Bank Plc (54-30-01)

| | 31-08-14 | 31-08-13 | 31-08-12 |
|---|---|---|---|
| TO | 41,224,779 | 39,348,198 | 37,852,500 |
| P/L | 657,733 | 1,122,027 | 1,058,669 |
| NW | 8,106,333 | 7,654,744 | 6,938,690 |
| WC | 5,316,587 | 5,436,096 | 4,668,400 |
| Emp. | 463 | 442 | 443 |

DUNS 50-381-3586

## Rhys Davies Ltd

(**Subsidiary of:** Rhys Davies Holdings Ltd)
Unit 15 Industry Road, Barnsley, South Yorkshire S71 3PQ
**Tel:** 01226776700 **Fax:** 02920810717
**Web:** www.rhysdavies.co.uk
**Reg No:** 2390390 **Estd:** 2012 Private Limited Company
**Line of Business:** Road haulage and transport services
**Issued Capital:** £50,000
**Directors:** M C Richmond, P D Hodgkiss
**Co. Secretary:** Stephen Thomas
**US SIC:** 4789, 4213
**UK SIC:** 77002, 72300
**Auditors:** PricewaterhouseCoopers LLP
**Bankers:** National Westminster Bank Plc (54-30-01)

| | 31-08-13 | 31-08-12 | 31-08-10 |
|---|---|---|---|
| TA | 520,615 | 520,615 | 65,200 |
| NW | 65,200 | 65,200 | 65,200 |
| WC | (55,400) | (55,400) | N/A |

DUNS 23-714-1853

## Ri Blow Ltd

55a Portland Square, Sutton-In-Ashfield, Nottinghamshire NG17 1AZ
**Tel:** 01773862343
**Web:** www.diblow.co.uk
**Reg No:** 3709152 **Estd:** 1999 Private Limited Company
**Line of Business:** Retail sale by opticians
**Trading Style:** Di Blow
**Issued Capital:** £300,100
**Managing Director:** R I Blow
**Co. Secretary:** Ms Kathryn Blow
**US SIC:** 5999 **UK SIC:** 65600
**Auditors:** Colin J B Spinks & Co

| | 30-04-14 | 30-04-13 | 30-04-12 |
|---|---|---|---|
| TA | 1,387,382 | 1,385,687 | 1,674,554 |
| NW | 923,436 | 768,155 | 738,816 |
| WC | (112,151) | (177,965) | (105,493) |

DUNS 22-245-1796

## Ria Financial Services Ltd

(**Subsidiary of:** Euronet Worldwide Inc.)
75 Baker Street, London W1U 6RE
**Fax:** 02072244993
**Web:** www.riafinancial.com
**Reg No:** 4263192 **Estd:** 2001 Private Limited Company
**Line of Business:** Financial intermediation not elsewhere classified
**Issued Capital:** £3,951,000
**Directors:** Ms M D Gozalez Sepulveda, M Villena
**Co. Secretary:** Ms Marcela Gonzalez Sepulveda
**Branches:** Ria Financial Services Ltd, Glaisyers Solicitors Llp, 601 Stockport Road, Manchester M13 0RX
**US SIC:** 6111 **UK SIC:** 81501
**Auditors:** Oury Clark

| | 31-12-13 | 31-12-12 | 31-12-11 |
|---|---|---|---|
| TA | 5,615,077 | 5,417,511 | 7,199,887 |
| P/L | (1,094,202) | (1,063,575) | 436,422 |
| NW | 1,489,638 | 2,258,058 | (651,776) |
| WC | (571,336) | 90,794 | (3,075,564) |
| Emp. | 86 | 83 | 80 |

DUNS 23-336-7874

## Rialto Restaurants

Clowes House, 319 Bury New Road, Salford, Lancashire M7 2YN
**Web:** www.mcdonalds.co.uk
**Estd:** 2002 Proprietorship
**Line of Business:** Restaurant - american
**Trading Style:** Macdonalds
**US SIC:** 5812 **UK SIC:** 66110
**Bankers:** National Westminster Bank Plc (01-05-41)
**Employees:** 46

DUNS 21-925-5510 Imp-Exp

## R.I.B. - Koti Ltd

Unit 1-12 Industrial Estate, Church Bank, Llandovery, Dyfed SA20 0DT
**Tel:** 01550-720077 **Fax:** 01550-720911
**Web:** www.rib-uk.co.uk
**Reg No:** 1214442 **VAT No:** 124729568
**Estd:** 1975 Private Limited Company
**Line of Business:** Manufacture of brooms and brushes
**Export Markets:** Worldwide.
**Issued Capital:** £100,000
**Directors:** D G Johns, Mrs N L Van Kowen, M J Huybreckx
**Co. Secretary:** Andreas Bruhn
**Responsibilities**
**Senior:** Dieter Kullen *(Manager)*
**US SIC:** 3991 **UK SIC:** 46630
**Auditors:** Willis Jones

| | 31-12-13 | 31-03-13 | 31-12-12 |
|---|---|---|---|
| TA | 1,821,706 | 1,971,171 | 2,057,732 |
| P/L | N/A | N/A | 90,868 |
| NW | 1,485,547 | 1,428,105 | 1,407,528 |
| WC | 1,099,909 | 1,309,211 | 1,302,884 |
| Emp. | N/A | N/A | 53 |

DUNS 29-529-2072

## Ribble Farm Fare Ltd

Shay Lane Industrial Estate, Shay Lane, Longridge, Preston, Lancashire PR3 3BT
**Tel:** 01772782693 **Fax:** 01772-786076
**Web:** www.ribblefarmfare.co.uk
**Reg No:** 1896240 **Estd:** 1965 Private Limited Company
**Line of Business:** Retail sale of fruit and vegetables
**Trading Style:** Ribble Farm Fare Ltd
**Issued Capital:** £20,000
**Principals:** D Coulston *(Managing)*, I R Coulston, Ms G Coulston, R D Coulston
**Co. Secretary:** Ms Marina Goodman
**Responsibilities**
**HR:** Dominika Paruzel *(Training Officer)*
**Health & Safety:** Dominika Paruzel *(Training Officer)*
**US SIC:** 5431 **UK SIC:** 64100
**Auditors:** Brown & Lonsdale

| | 30-09-13 | 30-09-12 | 30-09-11 |
|---|---|---|---|
| TO | 8,381,508 | 7,390,315 | N/A |
| P/L | 8,996 | 234,373 | N/A |
| NW | 1,271,002 | 1,411,453 | 1,334,165 |
| WC | 457,757 | 645,352 | 562,592 |
| Emp. | 91 | 88 | N/A |

DUNS 21-233-4403 Imp

## Ribble Packaging Ltd

(**Subsidiary of:** Ribble Investments Ltd)
Greengate Street, Oldham, Lancashire OL4 1DF
**Tel:** 01612-849000
**Web:** www.ribble-pack.co.uk
**Reg No:** 0521820 **VAT No:** 589041123
**Estd:** 1953 Private Limited Company
**Line of Business:** Manufacture of cartons, boxes and cases of non-corrugated paper and paperboard
**Issued Capital:** £10,000
**Financial Director:** S Rector
**Co. Secretary:** Michael Kernaghan
**Responsibilities**
**Senior:** Brian Parkin *(IT Manager)*
**Marketing:** Brian Parkin *(IT Manager)*
**IT:** Brian Parkin *(IT Manager)*
**HR:** Samantha Barber *(Human Resources Manager)*
**Operations:** Brian Parkin *(IT Manager)*
**Purchasing:** Jeanette Horsfield *(Purchasing Manager)*
**US SIC:** 2651 **UK SIC:** 47253
**Auditors:** Royce Peeling Green Ltd
**Bankers:** HSBC Bank plc (40-47-26)

| | 31-12-13 | 31-12-12 | 31-12-11 |
|---|---|---|---|
| TO | 19,666,088 | 21,014,323 | 22,239,046 |
| P/L | (113,368) | 41,179 | 503,747 |
| NW | 4,764,482 | 4,838,618 | 4,780,360 |
| WC | 1,347,308 | 1,441,843 | 2,063,455 |
| Emp. | 141 | 143 | 141 |

DUNS 23-261-7894

## Ribble Valley Borough Council

Council Offices, Church Walk, Clitheroe, Lancashire BB7 2RA
**Tel:** 01200425111 **Fax:** 01200-414488
**Web:** www.ribblevalley.gov.uk
**Estd:** 1974 Incorporate By Act Of Parliament
**Line of Business:** Local government
**Principals:** M Scott *(Financial)*, D Morris, J Hunt
**Responsibilities**
**Senior:** Tom Bamber *(Sports Development Officer)*, Jane Horsfield *(Executive)*, Grace Whowell *(Senior Manager)*
**Admin:** Dawn Slater *(Benefits Manager)*
**HR:** Tracy Balko *(Health and Fitness Development)*
**Health & Safety:** Bill Alker *(Health and Safety Executive)*
**Facilities:** Colin Hirst *(?Head of Regeneration & Housin)*
**Operations:** Melissa Thorpe *(Project Executive)*
**Engineering:** Alan Coar *(Assistant Surveyor)*, Terry Longden *(Head of Engineering Services)*
**Branches:** Ribble Valley Borough Council, Showley Ct, Blackburn, Lancashire BB1 9HS
**US SIC:** 9121 **UK SIC:** 91110
**Bankers:** HSBC Bank plc (40-17-35)
**Employees:** 300

DUNS 21-847-8844

## Ribbon Academy Trust

The Ribbon Barnes Road, Seaham, County Durham SR7 9QR
**Tel:** 01915175900
**Web:** www.theribbonschool.co.uk
**Reg No:** 8132353 **Estd:** 2012 Private Company Limited By Guarantee
**Line of Business:** Primary education
**Directors:** S G Ball, M Morton, I Stephenson, Ms S Jolly, J Taylor, P A Scott, W G Burnett, Ms V Patchett
**Co. Secretary:** Prima Secretary Limited
**Responsibilities**
**Senior:** Louise Hall *(Director)*, Jeanette Lawson *(Director)*, Peter Mannion *(Director)*, Kate Mccarthy *(Director)*
**US SIC:** 8211 **UK SIC:** 93200
**Bankers:** Lloyds TSB Bank plc (30-98-34)

| | 31-08-14 | 31-08-13 |
|---|---|---|
| TO | 2,469,000 | 5,260,000 |
| P/L | 4,000 | 2,961,000 |
| NW | 2,943,000 | 2,813,000 |
| WC | 295,000 | 237,000 |
| Emp. | 68 | 55 |

DUNS 29-538-6635 Imp-Exp

## Ribbons Ltd

(**Subsidiary of:** Mandaco 502 Ltd)
Treorchy Industrial Estate, Treorchy, Mid Glamorgan CF42 6EJ
**Tel:** 01443-432473 **Fax:** 01443-437413
**Web:** www.ribbons.co.uk
**Reg No:** 1905537 **VAT No:** 417346260
**Estd:** 1985 Private Limited Company
**Line of Business:** Representative office
**Export Markets:** E U, North America
**Export Sales:** £945,144
**Issued Capital:** £100,040
**Directors:** G J Codrington, M J Porch, N J Codrington
**Co. Secretary:** David Edwards
**Responsibilities**
**Sales:** Paula Cockburn *(Sales Manager)*
**Admin:** Theresa Speller *(Office Manager)*
**HR:** Theresa Speller *(Office Manager)*
**Health & Safety:** Martin Bray *(Production Manager)*
**Facilities:** Martin Bray *(Production Manager)*
**Operations:** Martin Bray *(Production Manager)*
**Purchasing:** Leigh Rees *(Purchasing Manager)*
**Engineering:** Martin Bray *(Production Manager)*
**US SIC:** 2392, 2824
**UK SIC:** 45550, 26000
**Auditors:** Grant Thornton UK LLP
**Bankers:** The Royal Bank Of Scotland Plc (16-00-16)

| | 31-12-13 | 31-12-12 | 31-12-11 |
|---|---|---|---|
| TO | 3,482,938 | 3,376,148 | 3,622,450 |
| P/L | 3,968 | (163,513) | 29,350 |
| NW | 699,066 | 695,098 | 872,617 |
| WC | 622,952 | 601,870 | 752,868 |
| Emp. | 59 | 60 | 63 |

DUNS 28-956-5095

## Ribby Hall Management Co Ltd

(**Subsidiary of:** Dowbridge Ltd)
Ribby Road, Preston, Lancashire PR4 2PR
**Tel:** 01772687829
**Web:** www.ribbyhallequestriancentre.co.uk
**Reg No:** 1657629 **Estd:** 1995 Private Limited Company
**Line of Business:** Riding schools livery stables & equestrian centres
**Trading Style:** Ribby Hall Equestrian Center
**Issued Capital:** £14
**Directors:** P Harrison, M Partington, Ms D M Priestley, D A Jackson, R Spencer
**Co. Secretary:** John Atkinson
**Responsibilities**
**Senior:** Jason Ledden *(Manager)*, John Oakes *(Facilities Manager)*
**Marketing:** Kirsty Clarke *(Marketing Executive)*, Charlotte Gili-Ross *(Marketing Manager)*, Vicky Roberts *(Marketing & Design Coordinator)*
**Sales:** Diane Cottam *(Projects Manager)*
**HR:** Susan Houseman *(Human Resources Manager)*
**Facilities:** John Oakes *(Facilities Manager)*
**US SIC:** 7999, 7032
**UK SIC:** 97913, 66702
**Auditors:** Rawcliffe & Co
**Bankers:** National Westminster Bank Plc (01-04-84)

| | 31-03-14 | 31-03-13 | 31-03-12 |
|---|---|---|---|
| TO | 13,942 | 7,435 | N/A |
| NW | 14 | 14 | 14 |
| WC | (1,336) | (1,336) | (1,336) |

DUNS 51-562-7016

## Ribston Hall High School

Stroud Road, Gloucester, Gloucestershire GL1 5LE
**Tel:** 01452-382249
**Web:** www.ribstonhall.gloucs.sch.uk
**Estd:** 1922
**Line of Business:** Schools (local authority)
**Proprietor:** Mrs A Chong
**US SIC:** 8211, 8299
**UK SIC:** 93200, 93300
**Bankers:** Lloyds TSB Bank plc (30-93-48)
**Employees:** 102

DUNS 21-894-1094      **Imp**
## Rical Ltd
Tramway, Smethwick, West Midlands B66 1NY
**Fax:** 01215584239
**Web:** www.ricalltd.com
**Reg No:** 0088330 **VAT No:** 369541030
**Estd:** 1906 Private Limited Company
**Line of Business:** Casting of other non-ferrous metals
**Export Sales:** £7,375,000
**Issued Capital:** £348,057
**Director:** B P Head
**Co. Secretary:** Paul Marsh
**Responsibilities**
**Senior:** Andy Fogarty (General Manager)
**Branches:** Rical Ltd, Unit 10, Wayside, 7 Commerce Way, Lancing, West Sussex BN15 8SW
**US SIC:** 3369, 8911, 3496, 3499
**UK SIC:** 31120, 83701, 31694
**Auditors:** RSM Bentley Jennison
**Bankers:** Allied Irish Bank (gb) (23-83-93)

| | 31-08-13 | 31-08-12 | 31-08-11 |
|---|---|---|---|
| TO | 21,528,000 | 23,699,000 | 23,868,000 |
| P/L | 661,000 | 792,000 | 1,377,000 |
| NW | 10,663,000 | 5,381,000 | 7,175,000 |
| WC | 5,824,000 | 5,236,000 | 4,775,000 |
| Emp. | 297 | 325 | 333 |

DUNS 21-024-7268
## Ricardo Plc
Shoreham Technical Centre, Old Shoreham Road, Shoreham-By-Sea, West Sussex BN43 5FG
**Web:** www.ricardo.com
**Reg No:** 0222915 **Estd:** 1927 Public Limited Company
**Line of Business:** Management activities of holding companies
**Export Sales:** £138,800,000
**Trading Style:** Ricardo
**Issued Capital:** £12,995,108
**Directors:** D J Hall, Professor H Schoepf, I M Lee, D J Shemmans, T K Morgan, M W Garrett, P Gilchrist, I J Gibson
**Co. Secretary:** Ms Patricia Ryan
**Responsibilities**
**Marketing:** Scott Day (Marketing Manager), Ben Holst (Marketing Manager), Cynthia Tamraz (Marketing Specialist)
**Sales:** Roger Atkins (EVP Business Development), Tim Jameson (Business Development Manager)
**IT:** David Rich (System/Server Administrator)
**Health & Safety:** Johnnie Walker (Health & Safety Manager)
**Facilities:** Ben Pierce (General Purchasing Officer)
**Operations:** Nick Tebbutt (Project Director - Hybrid and), Roger Thornton (Global Product Group Director)
**Fleet:** Kieran Fribbens (Inventory & Warehousing)
**Engineering:** Paul Adlington (Principal Engineer), Andrew Atkins (Chief Engineer - Technology), Ed Bower (Principal Engineer), Will Drury (Senior Engineer), Jonathan Fennell (Senior Design Engineer), Philip Hore (Manager - Control and Electron), Jason March (Engineering Director), Roland Meister (Group chief engineer - hybrid), Paul Rivera (Chief Engineer & Hybrid and El), David Valantin (Chief Engineer), Eddie Wearing (Chief Engineer of Hybrid Elect), Jonathan Wheals (Chief Engineer Innovation), Corin Wren (Chief Engineer)
**Branches:** Ricardo Plc, Shoreham Technical Centre, Old Shoreham Road, Shoreham-By-Sea, West Sussex BN43 5FG
**US SIC:** 6711, 8911
**UK SIC:** 83962, 83701
**Auditors:** PricewaterhouseCoopers LLP
**Bankers:** HSBC Bank plc (40-18-22)

| | 30-06-14 | 30-06-13 | 30-06-12 |
|---|---|---|---|
| TO | 236,200,000 | 229,700,000 | 197,400,000 |
| P/L | 23,500,000 | 21,000,000 | 17,600,000 |
| NW | 65,800,000 | 58,400,000 | 67,700,000 |
| WC | 28,000,000 | 19,300,000 | 27,700,000 |
| Emp. | 2,075 | 1,974 | 1,679 |

DUNS 73-366-5256
## Riccall Carers Ltd
17 Escrick Business Park, York, North Yorkshire YO19 6FD
**Tel:** 01904-720700
**Web:** www.riccallcare.co.uk
**Reg No:** 4640010 **Estd:** 2003 Private Limited Company
**Line of Business:** Activities of households as employers of domestic staff
**Issued Capital:** £368
**Directors:** Ms G M Conroy, M J Richards
**Co. Secretary:** John Conroy
**Responsibilities**
**Senior:** Tony Conroy (Manager)
**US SIC:** 8811 **UK SIC:** 99000

| | 31-08-14 | 31-08-13 | 31-08-13 |
|---|---|---|---|
| TA | 487,628 | 481,795 | 603,862 |
| NW | 326,655 | 293,067 | 378,633 |
| WC | 168,805 | 171,866 | 290,059 |

DUNS 55-056-7432
## Riccall House Care Home
78 Main Street, Riccall, York, North Yorkshire YO19 6QD
**Web:** www.riccallhouse.co.uk
**Estd:** 2010 Partnership
**Line of Business:** Rest and retirement homes
**Partners:** Mrs G Conroy, J Conroy
**Responsibilities**
**Senior:** Diane Moughan (Manager)
**US SIC:** 8321 **UK SIC:** 96111
**Employees:** 55

DUNS 23-305-7970
## Rice's Supermarket Ltd
9 Victoria Street, Keady, Armagh, Co Armagh BT60 3SL
**Tel:** 02837539400 **Fax:** 028-3753-9444
**Reg No:** 0044086NI **Estd:** 1994 Private Limited Company
**Line of Business:** Supermarkets
**Issued Capital:** £326,710
**Directors:** C Rice, Ms A Mccreesh, Ms P Rice, P Rice
**Co. Secretary:** Ms Philomena Rice
**Responsibilities**
**Senior:** Mark Smylie (Manager)
**Branches:** Rice's Supermarket Ltd, 9 Victoria Street, Armagh, Co Armagh BT60 3SL
**US SIC:** 5411 **UK SIC:** 64100
**Bankers:** The Bank Of Ireland (90-22-90)

| | 30-09-13 | 30-09-12 | 30-09-11 |
|---|---|---|---|
| TA | 1,324,204 | 1,434,772 | 1,480,269 |
| NW | 577,787 | 521,691 | 592,167 |
| WC | 102,107 | 28,043 | 70,438 |

DUNS 29-175-4224      **Imp**
## Rich Products Ltd
(**Subsidiary of:** Rich Products Corporation)
Solent Gate, Unit 5 Speedfields Park, Fareham, Hampshire PO14 1TL
**Web:** www.rich.co.uk
**Reg No:** 1847615 **VAT No:** 409882618
**Estd:** 1945 Private Limited Company
**Line of Business:** Manufacturers of biscuits
**Export Sales:** £1,560,390
**Issued Capital:** £650,000
**Directors:** K Malchoff, R E Rich Junior, Ms M Kiener, W E Grieshober, D E Hunt, J W Segarra
**Co. Secretary:** Mrs Theresa Pickard
**Responsibilities**
**Senior:** Robert Rich (Director)
**HR:** Karen Relf (Human Resources Manager)
**Health & Safety:** Gemma Adkins (Health & Safety Officer)
**Facilities:** Alex Grieve (Maintenance Manager)
**Engineering:** Alex Grieve (Maintenance Manager)
**Branches:** Rich Products Ltd, Unit 71, Hartlebury Trading Estate, Kidderminster, Worcestershire DY10 4JB
**US SIC:** 2052 **UK SIC:** 41970
**Auditors:** Ernst & Young LLP
**Bankers:** National Westminster Bank Plc (60-10-43)

| | 29-12-13 | 30-12-12 | 01-12-12 |
|---|---|---|---|
| TO | 34,650,732 | 35,573,882 | 34,987,028 |
| P/L | 1,906,767 | 1,239,541 | 1,114,682 |
| NW | 6,627,837 | 5,165,350 | 4,240,809 |
| WC | 5,558,697 | 3,056,935 | 1,727,428 |
| Emp. | 267 | 244 | 272 |

DUNS 34-724-7160
## Richard Alan Group Ltd
Richard Alan House, Owl Lane, Shaw Cross Business Park, Dewsbury, West Yorkshire WF12 7RD
**Tel:** 01924-467040
**Web:** www.richardalan.co.uk
**Reg No:** 5528297 **Estd:** 2005 Private Limited Company
**Line of Business:** Other engineering activities
**Export Sales:** £304,642
**Issued Capital:** £1,500
**Director:** R P Johnson
**Co. Secretary:** Stuart Deakes
**US SIC:** 8911, 3325
**UK SIC:** 83701, 31110
**Bankers:** Yorkshire Bank Plc (05-03-03)

| | 30-04-14 | 30-04-13 | 30-04-12 |
|---|---|---|---|
| TO | 14,148,695 | 13,233,447 | 12,623,146 |
| P/L | 241,886 | 400,353 | 313,340 |
| NW | 1,492,312 | 1,313,826 | 1,185,102 |
| WC | (89,503) | (565,569) | (530,723) |
| Emp. | 171 | 166 | 156 |

DUNS 21-588-8330      **Imp**
## Richard Austin Alloys Ltd
31 Dunivaig Road, Glasgow, Lanarkshire G33 4TP
**Tel:** 0141-771-8391 **Fax:** 0141-771-9454
**Web:** www.raaltd.com
**Reg No:** 0074125SC **Estd:** 1981 Private Limited Company
**Line of Business:** Steel stockholders
**Issued Capital:** £22,093
**Principals:** S T Kelly (Chairman and Managing), J R Johnston, A J Mchale, G Higgins, A J Finlay, P Rawlinson, J Murdoch, L Hall
**Co. Secretary:** John Murdoch
**Branches:** Richard Austin Alloys Ltd, Bessemer Road, North Bank Ind Park Irlam, Manchester M44 5BF
**US SIC:** 5051 **UK SIC:** 61200
**Auditors:** Milne Craig
**Bankers:** Bank Of Scotland (80-20-00)

| | 31-03-14 | 31-03-13 | 31-03-12 |
|---|---|---|---|
| TO | 95,568,548 | 91,013,852 | 96,353,567 |
| P/L | 3,509,530 | 2,600,820 | 2,778,076 |
| NW | 14,142,047 | 13,386,917 | 11,929,625 |
| WC | 8,911,621 | 6,171,493 | 7,843,099 |
| Emp. | 183 | 169 | 166 |

DUNS 21-738-0241
## Richard Challoner School
Manor Drive North, New Malden, Surrey KT3 5PE
**Tel:** 02083305947
**Web:** www.richardchalloner.com
**Reg No:** 7718002 **Estd:** 2011 Private Company Limited By Guarantee
**Line of Business:** General secondary education
**Directors:** J C Malden, H A Staples, S P Binns, Mrs M B Turnpenny, M Osborn, Mrs M M Guntrip, D H Fraser, K W Hayden
**Co. Secretary:** Reginald Baker
**Responsibilities**
**Senior:** Valerie Bradnick (Governor), Thomas Cahill (Director), Nicola Cloudsdale (Director), Neil D'Aguiar (Director), Mark Draper (Director), Ernest Mcdonald (Director), Ellen O'Connell (Director), Hugh Perkins (Director), John Sabourin (Governor)
**Finance:** Sue Underwood (Senior Finance Administrator)
**IT:** Nick Carpenter (Network Manager), Mike Cloudsdale (Network, Security Manager), Neil Henderson (Head of IT)
**HR:** Clark Cahill (Human Resources Manager)
**US SIC:** 8211 **UK SIC:** 93200

| | 31-08-14 | 31-08-13 | 31-08-12 |
|---|---|---|---|
| TO | 8,184,039 | 7,362,226 | 7,381,634 |
| P/L | 489,608 | 636,337 | 68,753 |
| NW | 852,698 | 548,090 | (69,247) |
| WC | 18,083 | 255,406 | 91,239 |
| Emp. | 180 | 170 | 171 |

DUNS 23-636-1473
## Richard Cobden Primary School
Camden Street, London NW1 0LL
**Tel:** 020-7387-5909
**Web:** www.rcobden.camden.sch.uk
**Estd:** 2002
**Line of Business:** Primary education
**Directors:** Ms P Gouch, Ms P Chaplin, Ms B Crawley, J Shearman
**Responsibilities**
**Senior:** Kathy Bannon (Head Teacher)
**US SIC:** 8211 **UK SIC:** 93200
**Employees:** 70

DUNS 21-998-0047      **Imp**
## Richard Designs Ltd
Unit 1a, Lancaster Way Business Park, Ely, Cambridgeshire CB6 3NW
**Tel:** 01353-661600 **Fax:** 01353-662554
**Web:** www.richard-designs.com
**Reg No:** 6179288 **Estd:** 1987 Private Limited Company
**Line of Business:** Other service activities not elsewhere classified
**Issued Capital:** £200,000
**Directors:** Ms E V Dicks, W R Dicks, B R Allen, Ms L R Dicks, Ms E L Dicks, B B Dicks
**Co. Secretary:** Ms Elaine Dicks
**US SIC:** 8999 **UK SIC:** 83954
**Bankers:** Clydesdale Bank Plc (82-04-03)

| | 31-03-14 | 31-03-13 | 31-03-12 |
|---|---|---|---|
| TA | 1,381,260 | 1,984,694 | 1,819,498 |
| NW | 553,609 | 398,930 | 186,536 |
| WC | 751,854 | 622,703 | 491,741 |

DUNS 21-606-9020
## Richard Dunn Sports Centre
Rooley Avenue, Bradford, West Yorkshire BD6 1EZ
**Tel:** 01274307822
**Web:** www.bradford.gov.uk
**Estd:** 2011 Partnership
**Line of Business:** Leisure centres
**Partners:** A Bailey, M York
**Responsibilities**
**Senior:** Andrea Collingwood (Centre Manager)
**US SIC:** 7999 **UK SIC:** 97913
**Employees:** 150

DUNS 21-774-1919
## Richard Hale School
Hale Road, Hertford, Hertfordshire SG13 8EN
**Tel:** 01992583441
**Web:** www.richardhale.herts.sch.uk
**Estd:** 2011 Proprietorship
**Line of Business:** Schools (local authority)
**Proprietor:** S Neate
**Responsibilities**
**Senior:** David Boatman (Manager), Philip Camm (Manager), Stephen Goodair (Manager), Catherine Macleod (Manager), Michelle Rashford (Manager), Allan Tyrer (Manager)
**Admin:** Karren Dart (PA to Head Teacher)
**US SIC:** 8211 **UK SIC:** 93200
**Employees:** 150

DUNS 21-207-5436
## Richard Hardie Ltd
Trafford Road, Sunderland, Tyne and Wear SR5 2DA
**Tel:** 01915488811 **Fax:** 0191-548-5519
**Web:** www.richardhardie.co.uk
**Reg No:** 1055767 **VAT No:** 177500364
**Estd:** 1972 Private Limited Company
**Line of Business:** Car dealers (new & used)
**Trading Style:** Richard Hardie
**Issued Capital:** £5,000
**Principals:** R P Hardie (Managing), N R Hardie, Ms B Hardie
**Co. Secretary:** John Anderson
**Responsibilities**
**Senior:** David Banks (Manager), Jimmy Milner (Manager)
**Health & Safety:** George Baxter (Service Manager)
**Branches:** Richard Hardie Ltd, Lintonville Parkway, Ashington, Northumberland NE63 9JZ
**US SIC:** 5511, 5521, 5531
**UK SIC:** 65100
**Auditors:** Jennings Johnson
**Bankers:** National Westminster Bank Plc (60-15-08)

| | 31-12-13 | 31-12-12 | 31-12-11 |
|---|---|---|---|
| TO | 44,801,680 | 39,496,161 | 37,132,117 |
| P/L | 371,054 | 53,437 | 3,161 |
| NW | 3,126,153 | 2,906,915 | 3,214,794 |
| WC | 982,262 | 853,869 | 877,393 |
| Emp. | 105 | 105 | 106 |

DUNS 39-761-1005
## Richard Hardie (Stanley) Ltd
Newfield Garage, Grange Villa Road, Newfield, Chester-Le-Street, County Durham DH2 2SR
**Tel:** 01913865522 **Fax:** 01913705021
**Web:** www.richardhardie.co.uk
**Reg No:** 2198118 **Estd:** 1952 Private Limited Company
**Line of Business:** Sale of new motor vehicles
**Issued Capital:** £100
**Director:** R P Hardie
**Co. Secretary:** John Anderson
**Responsibilities**
**Admin:** Sue Dixon (Administration Manager)
**HR:** Sue Dixon (Administration Manager)
**Health & Safety:** Sue Dixon (Administration Manager)
**Facilities:** Sue Dixon (Administration Manager)
**Branches:** Richard Hardie (Stanley) Ltd, Richard Hardie Ltd, Trafford Road, Sunderland, Tyne and Wear SR5 2DA
**US SIC:** 5511 **UK SIC:** 65100
**Employees:** 50

DUNS 21-014-4226      **Imp-Exp**
## Richard Hochfeld Ltd
Orchard Place Farm, Comp Road, Wrotham Heath, Sevenoaks, Kent TN15 8LW
**Tel:** 01732-885566
**Web:** www.richardhochfeld.co.uk
**Reg No:** 0315760 **VAT No:** 245867623
**Estd:** 1936 Private Limited Company
**Line of Business:** Import and export agents
**Export Markets:** Worldwide
**Issued Capital:** £4,000
**Directors:** J L Jones, A C Guindi, A J Guindi
**Co. Secretary:** Colin Barber
**Responsibilities**
**Senior:** Louis Bellard (Manager)
**Health & Safety:** Nicola McBride (Health & Safety Officer)
**Branches:** Richard Hochfeld Ltd, Western Link, Faversham, Kent ME13 7TZ
**US SIC:** 5148 **UK SIC:** 61700
**Auditors:** Reeves & Co LLP
**Bankers:** Banco De Sabadell (60-92-70)

| | 30-06-14 | 30-06-13 | 30-06-12 |
|---|---|---|---|
| TO | 4,795,813 | 4,423,810 | 4,215,108 |
| P/L | 206,054 | 188,150 | 217,827 |
| NW | (5,703,250) | (4,680,088) | (4,649,999) |
| WC | 1,053,421 | 855,076 | 520,779 |
| Emp. | 47 | N/A | N/A |

DUNS 21-203-6222 **Imp-Exp**

## Richard Hough Ltd

Mill St Mill Hill, Bolton, Lancashire BL2 2AB
**Tel:** 01204-526562
**Web:** www.richardhough.co.uk
**Reg No:** 0101147 **VAT No:** 145502000
**Estd:** 1909 Private Limited Company
**Line of Business:** Other engineering activities
**Export Markets:** Worldwide
**Issued Capital:** £15,000
**Principals:** J O Ashton *(Chairman)*, A J Ashton, M J Hughes
**Co. Secretary:** James Ashton
**Responsibilities**
**Senior:** Douglas Swarbrick *(Works Manager)*
**Finance:** Emma Highton *(Account Manager)*
**Sales:** Lucy Ashton *(Sales Manager)*, Mike Urey *(Technical Sales Manager)*
**Health & Safety:** Douglas Swarbrick *(Works Manager)*
**Facilities:** Douglas Swarbrick *(Works Manager)*
**Operations:** Trish Eckersley *(Shipping Manager)*, Douglas Swarbrick *(Works Manager)*
**Engineering:** Douglas Swarbrick *(Works Manager)*
**Branches:** Richard Hough Ltd, Whalley Bank Trd Est, Blackburn, Lancashire BB2 1NR
**US SIC:** 8911, 2269
**UK SIC:** 83701, 43702
**Auditors:** Barlow Andrews
**Bankers:** National Westminster Bank Plc (01-30-99)

| | 31-12-13 | 31-12-12 | 31-12-11 |
|---|---|---|---|
| TA | 3,615,842 | 3,992,233 | 4,016,153 |
| NW | 2,184,066 | 2,481,243 | 2,445,472 |
| WC | 351,942 | 610,975 | 577,678 |

DUNS 23-801-5429

## Richard House Trading Co. Ltd.

Richard House Drive, London E16 3RG
**Tel:** 02075400226
**Web:** www.richardhouse.org.uk
**Reg No:** 3794127 **Estd:** 1999 Private Limited Company
**Line of Business:** Retail sale of other second-hand goods in stores
**Issued Capital:** £2
**Directors:** Mrs P K Handley, D J Lovelock, C G Skidmore
**Co. Secretary:** Peter Ellis
**US SIC:** 5931, 7399
**UK SIC:** 65400, 83954
**Bankers:** HSBC Bank plc (40-04-17)

| | 31-03-14 | 31-03-13 | 31-03-12 |
|---|---|---|---|
| TO | 489,905 | 457,495 | 476,805 |
| NW | 136 | 136 | 136 |
| WC | (29,523) | (37,862) | (41,974) |

DUNS 52-525-1476

## Richard House Trust

Richard House Drive, London E16 3RG
**Tel:** 020-7511-0222
**Web:** http://richardhouse.org.uk
**Reg No:** 3232837 **Estd:** 1996 Private Limited Company
**Line of Business:** Other human health activities
**Trading Style:** Richard House Childrens Hospice
**Directors:** M H Abdulrouf, Ms N Ukiah, A K Gordon, Ms K Mcnamara-Goodger, R S Knowles, Dr M Tan, Ms W J Pritchard, Q C Humberstone
**Co. Secretary:** Peter Ellis
**Responsibilities**
**Senior:** Jeremy Allgrove *(Trustee)*, Simon Gifford *(Treasurer)*, James Joly *(Director)*, Isaac Kaye *(Chairman)*, Jim Lawrie *(Trustee)*
**Finance:** Sam Chambers *(Financial Director)*, Simon Gifford *(Treasurer)*
**Marketing:** Niall Cooper *(Communications Director)*
**Sales:** Niall Cooper *(Communications Director)*
**IT:** Sam Chambers *(Financial Director)*
**HR:** Jemma Nash *(HR and Volunteering officer)*, Rachel Power *(Human Resources Manager)*
**Health & Safety:** Rachel Power *(Human Resources Manager)*
**Facilities:** Irene Chamberlain *(Facilities Coordinator)*
**Purchasing:** Sam Chambers *(Financial Director)*
**Branches:** Richard House Trust, 794 Green Lane, Dagenham, Essex RM8 1YT
**US SIC:** 8091, 6732
**UK SIC:** 95200, 83100
**Auditors:** Mazars Neville Russell
**Bankers:** HSBC Bank plc (40-04-17)

| | 31-03-14 | 31-03-13 | 31-03-12 |
|---|---|---|---|
| TO | 3,432,699 | 2,939,311 | 3,170,723 |
| P/L | (115,359) | (363,242) | (163,821) |
| NW | 5,934,748 | 6,050,107 | 6,413,349 |
| WC | 1,816,311 | 1,900,665 | 2,163,344 |
| Emp. | 66 | 66 | 66 |

DUNS 21-921-4681 **Imp**

## Richard H.Powell & Partners Ltd

1 Tollgate Close, Cardiff, South Glamorgan CF11 8UE
**Tel:** 02920232323
**Web:** www.powell.co.uk
**Reg No:** 1051190 **VAT No:** 135717761
**Estd:** 1972 Private Limited Company
**Line of Business:** Office furniture and equipment suppliers
**Export Sales:** £984,589
**Issued Capital:** £100
**Principals:** R H Powell *(Chairman and Managing)*, R H Powell, Ms A Powell, Dr C L Manning
**Co. Secretary:** Kevin Padfield
**Responsibilities**
**Senior:** Craig Powell *(Manager)*
**Marketing:** Craig Powell *(Manager)*
**Sales:** Craig Powell *(Manager)*
**Health & Safety:** Craig Powell *(Manager)*
**Facilities:** Craig Powell *(Manager)*
**US SIC:** 2599, 5081
**UK SIC:** 46720, 61490
**Auditors:** Watts Gregory
**Bankers:** Barclays Bank Plc (20-18-15)

| | 30-04-14 | 30-04-13 | 30-04-12 |
|---|---|---|---|
| TO | 7,748,616 | 7,227,415 | 7,729,457 |
| P/L | 316,937 | 292,816 | 238,636 |
| NW | 2,168,329 | 1,966,953 | 1,790,928 |
| WC | 1,611,281 | 1,584,423 | 1,366,746 |
| Emp. | 57 | 53 | 53 |

DUNS 54-902-1483

## Richard Huish College

South Road, Taunton, Somerset TA1 3DZ
**Tel:** 01823-320800
**Web:** www.huish.ac.uk
**Line of Business:** Sixth form education providers. charity reg no : 52959.
**Principals:** J White *(Chairman)*, Dr P Avery
**US SIC:** 8221, 8249
**UK SIC:** 93100, 93300
**Employees:** 120

DUNS 21-400-3659 **Imp**

## Richard Irvin & Sons Ltd

Irvin House, Hareness Road, Athen Industrial Estate, Aberdeen, Aberdeenshire AB12 3LE
**Tel:** 01224367000 **Fax:** 01224367002
**Web:** www.richard-irvin.co.uk
**Reg No:** 0096281 **Estd:** 1907 Private Limited Company
**Line of Business:** Installation of electrical wiring and fittings
**Issued Capital:** £922,813
**Directors:** Ms L A Cradock, G C Still, R J Emmerson, H J Stewart, W C Maclean, R Brannan, W H Lund
**Co. Secretary:** George Still
**Responsibilities**
**Senior:** Henry Lints *(Manager)*, David McGrath *(Manager)*, Joe Murdock *(Manager)*
**Finance:** Gary Crisp *(Major Contracts Director)*
**Sales:** Kevin Shinnie *(Commercial Director)*
**Operations:** Gary Crisp *(Major Contracts Director)*, Kevin McDonald *(Maintenance Coordinator)*
**Engineering:** George Dempster *(Electrical Manager, Building S)*, Colin Downie *(Domestic Gas Service Manager)*
**Branches:** Richard Irvin & Sons Ltd, 30 Tyock Industrial Estate, Elgin, Morayshire IV30 1XY
**US SIC:** 1731, 1711, 1796
**UK SIC:** 50300, 50400
**Auditors:** Anderson Anderson & Brown LLP
**Bankers:** The Royal Bank Of Scotland Plc (83-23-10)

| | 31-12-13 | 31-12-12 | 31-12-11 |
|---|---|---|---|
| TO | 38,670,000 | 45,130,000 | 44,093,000 |
| P/L | (3,138,000) | 332,000 | 517,000 |
| NW | 2,249,000 | 3,521,000 | 4,264,000 |
| WC | (21,000) | 2,974,000 | 3,432,000 |
| Emp. | 428 | 457 | 474 |

DUNS 34-602-8442

## Richard Jackson Ltd

**(Subsidiary of:** M T B G Ltd)
26 High Street, Hadleigh, Ipswich, Suffolk IP7 5AP
**Web:** www.richardjackson.uk.com
**Reg No:** 2744316 **Estd:** 1974 Private Limited Company
**Line of Business:** Engineers (consulting)
**Issued Capital:** £47,724
**Directors:** K R Tosh, R H Miall, M J Geddes, Mrs L A Butcher
**Co. Secretary:** Mrs Laura Butcher
**Responsibilities**
**Senior:** Brian Butcher *(Manager)*
**Marketing:** Natalie Dunn *(Human Resources Manager)*
**HR:** Natalie Dunn *(Human Resources Manager)*
**Health & Safety:** Brian Butcher *(Manager)*
**Facilities:** Natalie Dunn *(Human Resources Manager)*
**Branches:** Richard Jackson Ltd, Malvern House Meridian Gate 199 Marsh Wall, London E14 9YT
**US SIC:** 8911, 1751
**UK SIC:** 83701, 50400
**Auditors:** Walter Wright
**Bankers:** HSBC Bank plc (40-18-04)

| | 30-04-14 | 30-04-13 | 30-04-12 |
|---|---|---|---|
| TO | 4,250,808 | 3,662,360 | 3,083,547 |
| P/L | 377,331 | 266,982 | (95,048) |
| NW | 1,310,964 | 1,182,542 | 1,078,183 |
| WC | 1,546,319 | 1,374,895 | 1,226,258 |
| Emp. | 68 | 60 | 58 |

DUNS 21-958-8983

## Richard Kendall Estate Agent Ltd

66 Northgate, Wakefield, West Yorkshire WF1 3AP
**Tel:** 01924291294
**Web:** www.richardkendall.co.uk
**Reg No:** 8656163 **Estd:** 2013 Private Limited Company
**Line of Business:** Real estate agencies
**Issued Capital:** £1,000
**Directors:** Mrs J A Kendall, S J Kendall, Mrs C V Boswell, R Kendall
**US SIC:** 6531 **UK SIC:** 83400
**Employees:** 50

DUNS 21-233-2597

## Richard Preston & Son Ltd

Golden Lane, Northallerton, North Yorkshire DL6 3HX
**Tel:** 01642700243
**Web:** www.prestonofpotto.com
**Reg No:** 0967165 **VAT No:** 258102476
**Estd:** 1969 Private Limited Company
**Line of Business:** Road haulage and transport services
**Trading Style:** Prestons of Potto
**Issued Capital:** £5,000
**Principals:** D R Preston *(Managing)*, R H Preston *(Managing)*, Mrs A Preston
**Co. Secretary:** Richard Preston
**Responsibilities**
**Senior:** Martin Plummer *(Operations Manager)*
**Finance:** Stephen Deighton *(Financial Controller)*
**IT:** Stephen Deighton *(Financial Controller)*
**Facilities:** Stephen Deighton *(Financial Controller)*
**Fleet:** Martin Plummer *(Operations Manager)*
**Branches:** Richard Preston & Son Ltd, Unit 8, 9 Howard Road, St. Neots, Cambridgeshire PE19 8ET
**US SIC:** 4213, 4226
**UK SIC:** 72300, 77003
**Auditors:** Baines Goldston
**Bankers:** National Westminster Bank Plc (55-61-02)

| | 31-12-13 | 31-12-12 | 31-12-11 |
|---|---|---|---|
| TO | 18,855,643 | 19,507,257 | 21,037,845 |
| P/L | 9,873 | (237,964) | (197,619) |
| NW | 4,568,667 | 4,562,754 | 4,602,718 |
| WC | (208,521) | (292,443) | 6,736 |
| Emp. | 230 | 246 | 265 |

DUNS 67-243-5278

## Richard Read Holdings Ltd

Longhope Monmouth Road, Mitcheldean, Gloucestershire GL17 0QG
**Tel:** 01452830456
**Web:** www.richardread.com
**Reg No:** 6181300 **Estd:** 2007 Private Limited Company
**Line of Business:** Management activities of holding companies
**Issued Capital:** £26,750
**Directors:** Ms B S Herring, Mrs K Read, R P Read
**Co. Secretary:** Mrs Kay Read
**Responsibilities**
**Senior:** Mary Read *(Manager)*
**US SIC:** 6711, 5511
**UK SIC:** 83962, 65100
**Bankers:** Lloyds TSB Bank plc (30-93-48)

| | 30-04-14 | 30-04-13 | 30-04-12 |
|---|---|---|---|
| TO | 4,986,055 | 4,875,407 | 4,010,180 |
| P/L | 133,803 | 170,896 | 92,834 |
| NW | 3,689,288 | 3,580,934 | 3,429,640 |
| WC | (122,894) | (134,695) | (102,191) |
| Emp. | 77 | 68 | 55 |

DUNS 42-467-5093

## Richard Sanders Ltd

Northfield Avenue, Kettering, Northamptonshire NN16 9HU
**Tel:** 01536512221
**Web:** www.richardsanders.co.uk
**Reg No:** 4455141 **Estd:** 2002 Private Limited Company
**Line of Business:** Car dealers (new & used)
**Issued Capital:** £175,000
**Directors:** M R Sanders, R O Sanders, N O Sanders, Ms J D Sanders
**Co. Secretary:** White Rose Formations Limited
**Responsibilities**
**Finance:** Barry Hardwick *(Accountant)*
**IT:** Chris Golsby *(IT Manager)*
**Health & Safety:** Robert Elsey *(Service Manager)*
**Operations:** Robert Elsey *(Service Manager)*
**Branches:** Richard Sanders Ltd, Unit 3, Trafalgar Road, Kettering, Northamptonshire NN16 8DB
**US SIC:** 5511, 7539, 5531
**UK SIC:** 65100, 67100
**Bankers:** Bank Of Scotland (80-54-01)

| | 31-07-13 | 31-07-12 | 31-07-11 |
|---|---|---|---|
| TO | 36,674,736 | 28,998,820 | 27,391,206 |
| P/L | 916,438 | 235,092 | 521,451 |
| NW | 2,064,834 | 1,557,086 | 1,346,482 |
| WC | 385,356 | (13,485) | 391,851 |
| Emp. | 101 | 95 | 78 |

DUNS 22-278-8288

## Richard Wellock & Sons Ltd

Unit 4 Pendleside, Lomeshaye Business Village, Nelson, Lancashire BB9 6SH
**Tel:** 0844-4993-444 **Fax:** 0844-4993-555
**Web:** www.wellocks.com
**Reg No:** 1296795 **Estd:** 2001 Private Limited Company
**Line of Business:** Wholesale of fruit and vegetables
**Trading Style:** Wellocks
**Issued Capital:** £1,000
**Co. Secretary:** Alistair Wellock
**US SIC:** 5148, 5149
**UK SIC:** 61700
**Auditors:** Windle & Bowker Ltd

| | 31-10-13 | 31-10-12 | 31-10-11 |
|---|---|---|---|
| TO | 26,621,930 | 19,825,054 | 15,029,096 |
| P/L | 751,739 | 342,266 | 387,142 |
| NW | 551,864 | 311,968 | 90,970 |
| WC | (921,522) | (889,225) | (705,580) |
| Emp. | 185 | 137 | 108 |

DUNS 21-917-7573 **Imp-Exp**

## Richard Western Ltd

The Durbans, Apsey Green, Framlingham, Woodbridge, Suffolk IP13 9RP
**Tel:** 01728-723224 **Fax:** 01728-724291
**Web:** www.richard-western.co.uk
**Reg No:** 1296660 **VAT No:** 334122205
**Estd:** 1960 Private Limited Company
**Line of Business:** Agricultural machinery sales service and repair
**Export Markets:** Sudan, Nigeria, Sri Lanka, Trinidad, Ghana, France, Denmark,; Sweden; Estonia; Lithuania
**Issued Capital:** £1,000
**Principals:** R Western *(Chairman and Managing)*, A J Western, M J Murray
**Co. Secretary:** Malcolm Roberts
**US SIC:** 3559, 5083
**UK SIC:** 32863, 61490

| | 31-01-14 | 31-01-13 | 31-01-12 |
|---|---|---|---|
| TO | 6,053,544 | 6,881,054 | N/A |
| P/L | 86,283 | 60,842 | N/A |
| NW | 983,226 | 952,896 | 920,685 |
| WC | 490,083 | 755,773 | 641,361 |
| Emp. | 59 | 60 | N/A |

DUNS 21-219-2488

## Richard Whittaker Ltd

**(Subsidiary of:** Richard Whittaker Holdings Ltd)
Unit 1-3 Mayfield Centre, Mayfield Street Off Belfield Road, Rochdale, Lancashire OL16 2UZ
**Tel:** 01706341300
**Web:** www.richard-whittaker.com
**Reg No:** 0731811 **VAT No:** 146850552
**Estd:** 2010 Private Limited Company
**Line of Business:** Food packers
**Trading Style:** Brown James & Co
**Issued Capital:** £33,585
**Principals:** A Rigby *(Managing)*, T J Rigby, L Burrill
**Co. Secretary:** Daniel Magee
**Responsibilities**
**Marketing:** Paul Devenny *(Sales & Marketing Manager)*
**Sales:** Paul Devenny *(Sales & Marketing Manager)*
**HR:** Sue Rigby *(Quality Manager)*
**Health & Safety:** Sue Rigby *(Quality Manager)*
**US SIC:** 2819 **UK SIC:** 25110
**Auditors:** Mosley & Co
**Bankers:** HSBC Bank plc (40-39-01)

| | 31-05-13 | 31-05-12 | 31-05-11 |
|---|---|---|---|
| TO | 7,511,183 | 6,200,130 | N/A |
| P/L | 277,291 | (56,520) | N/A |
| NW | 963,361 | 743,107 | 791,462 |
| WC | 85,395 | (46,248) | (50,233) |
| Emp. | 90 | 80 | N/A |

DUNS 22-721-1018 **Imp-Exp**

## Richards & Appleby Ltd

(**Subsidiary of:** Richards & Appleby Holdings Ltd)
Unit 3 Heads Of The Valley Industrial, Estate, Rhymney, Tredegar, Gwent NP22 5RL
**Tel:** 01685-843384 **Fax:** 01685-842466
**Web:** www.richardsandappleby.co.uk
**Reg No:** 0937090 **VAT No:** 648491109
**Estd:** 1967 Private Limited Company
**Line of Business:** Other manufacturing not elsewhere classified
**Export Markets:** Belgium, France, Poland, Nigeria, Italy, Finland, Denmark, Australia
**Export Sales:** £1,308,231
**Trading Style:** Madison Cosmetics, Matty, Daniel Field, Richards & Appleby
**Issued Capital:** £51,000
**Principals:** M L Field *(Managing)*, D R Shah
**Co. Secretary:** Mitchell Field
**Branches:** Richards & Appleby Ltd, 139 Pembroke Road, London N10 2JE
**US SIC:** 3999 **UK SIC:** 49590
**Auditors:** Sinclairs
**Bankers:** National Westminster Bank Plc (60-24-23)

| | 31-03-14 | 31-03-13 | 31-03-12 |
|---|---|---|---|
| TO | 9,474,181 | 8,537,058 | 8,226,768 |
| P/L | 148,167 | 287,980 | 233,704 |
| NW | 3,249,630 | 3,117,022 | 2,908,971 |
| WC | 3,065,002 | 2,861,648 | 2,762,675 |
| Emp. | 105 | 105 | 112 |

DUNS 30 081 1108

## Richards Butler Ltd

(**Subsidiary of:** Reed Smith Llp)
Bradgate Tower, 20 Primrose Street, London EC2A 2RS
**Tel:** 02072476555
**Web:** www.reedsmith.com
**Reg No:** 2277157 **Estd:** 1988 Private Limited Company
**Line of Business:** Management activities of holding companies
**Issued Capital:** £2
**Directors:** D J Boutcher, J F Wilkinson
**Co. Secretary:** Reed Smith Corporate Services Li
**US SIC:** 6711 **UK SIC:** 83962

| | 31-12-13 | 31-12-12 | 31-12-11 |
|---|---|---|---|
| TA | 2 | 2 | 2 |
| NW | 2 | 2 | 2 |

DUNS 21-772-8196

## Richards Closed Circuit Television

Great Western Street, Wednesbury, West Midlands WS10 7LL
**Tel:** 01215674002
**Web:** www.richardscctv.com
**Estd:** 2007 Proprietorship
**Line of Business:** Cctv & video equipment
**Proprietor:** R Garbett
**US SIC:** 3651 **UK SIC:** 34541
**Employees:** 50

DUNS 21-601-1668

## Richardson & Partners Ltd

(**Subsidiary of:** Lexador Entreprises Ltd)
Suite 3.1 Marsh Wall, London E14 9TP
**Tel:** 020-7093-3637 **Fax:** 020-7093-3638
**Web:** www.chalegrove.co.uk
**Reg No:** 0690464 **Estd:** 2004 Private Limited Company
**Line of Business:** Construction of domestic buildings
**Trading Style:** Chalegrove
**Issued Capital:** £15,030
**Principals:** D J Richardson *(Managing)*, K Palmer
**Co. Secretary:** Anthony Bell
**Branches:** Richardson & Partners Ltd, 382-386 Edgware Road, London W2 1EB
**US SIC:** 1522 **UK SIC:** 50100
**Auditors:** Moore Stephens
**Bankers:** HSBC Bank plc (40-27-07)

| | 31-03-13 | 31-03-12 | 31-03-11 |
|---|---|---|---|
| TO | 1,774,610 | N/A | N/A |
| P/L | 24,393 | N/A | N/A |
| NW | 196,286 | 176,772 | 176,772 |
| WC | 196,286 | N/A | N/A |

DUNS 21-751-4729

## Richardson Hotels Holdings Ltd

65 Daisy Bank Road, Manchester M14 5QL
**Tel:** 01612562481
**Web:** www.richardsonhotels.co.uk
**Reg No:** 7818936 **Estd:** 2011 Private Limited Company
**Line of Business:** Other letting of own property
**Issued Capital:** £110,000
**Directors:** Mrs F V Richardson, E K Richardson, Mrs G Foster
**Co. Secretary:** Mrs Georgina Foster
**US SIC:** 6519, 6711
**UK SIC:** 85000, 83962

**Bankers:** The Royal Bank Of Scotland Plc (16-00-01)

| | 31-03-14 | 31-03-13 | 31-03-12 |
|---|---|---|---|
| TO | 11,007,026 | 10,580,949 | N/A |
| P/L | 220,973 | (116,185) | N/A |
| NW | 5,309,112 | 5,090,637 | 5,206,799 |
| WC | (1,375,741) | (3,689,547) | (862,352) |
| Emp. | 304 | 333 | N/A |

DUNS 21-243-2939

## Richardson Partnership for Care

144 Boughton Green Road, Northampton, Northamptonshire NN2 7AA
**Tel:** 01604791070
**Web:** www.careresidential.co.uk
**Estd:** 2011 Partnership
**Line of Business:** Residential care establishments
**Partners:** Mrs J Richardson, B Richardson
**Responsibilities**
**Senior:** Jacky Johnson *(Manager)*
**US SIC:** 8321 **UK SIC:** 96111
**Employees:** 100

DUNS 21-922-7766

## Richardson Retail Ltd

(**Subsidiary of:** The Richardsons Holding Group Ltd)
1 Earl Street, Northampton, Northamptonshire NN1 3AU
**Tel:** 01604-630666
**Web:** www.richardsonsevents.com
**Reg No:** 1023441 **Estd:** 1971 Private Limited Company
**Line of Business:** Dispensing chemists
**Issued Capital:** £4
**Principals:** C J Richardson *(Managing)*, M Sadrani, J T Richardson, J J Richardson
**Co. Secretary:** Colin Richardson
**Responsibilities**
**Senior:** Hamilton Richardson *(Manager)*
**Finance:** Ensa Sanderson *(Wages Clerk)*
**Branches:** Northampton
**US SIC:** 5912 **UK SIC:** 64300
**Auditors:** Macintyre Hudson
**Employees:** 250

DUNS 23-693-3615

## Richardson Roofing Holdings Ltd

Richardson House, Moor Lane, Staines, Middlesex TW19 6EQ
**Fax:** 01784465853
**Web:** www.richardson-roofing.com
**Reg No:** 3688448 **Estd:** 2001 Private Limited Company
**Line of Business:** Management activities of holding companies
**Trading Style:** Richardson Roofing International, Richardson Roofing Industrial, Richardson Roofing Hard Metals, Richardson Roofing Special Projects
**Issued Capital:** £100,000
**Directors:** S D Wright, G M Richardson
**Co. Secretary:** Ms Dawn Willmont
**US SIC:** 6711 **UK SIC:** 83962
**Auditors:** Goodman Jones
**Bankers:** Lloyds TSB Bank plc (30-93-68)

| | 31-08-13 | 31-08-12 | 31-08-11 |
|---|---|---|---|
| TO | 18,003,760 | 17,886,908 | 16,076,174 |
| P/L | 755,121 | 414,577 | 231,045 |
| NW | 3,481,226 | 3,148,311 | 2,955,792 |
| WC | 4,086,978 | 2,974,131 | 2,773,229 |
| Emp. | 48 | 48 | 49 |

DUNS 21-925-0990

## Richardsons Leisure Ltd

The Staithe, Stalham, Stalham, Norwich, Norfolk NR12 9BX
**Tel:** 01692581081 **Fax:** 01692-584005
**Web:** www.horning.com
**Reg No:** 0685774 **VAT No:** 765328019
**Estd:** 1961 Private Limited Company
**Line of Business:** Travel agency activities
**Trading Style:** Horning Pleasurecraft Ltd
**Issued Capital:** £886,002
**Principals:** R J Richardson *(Managing)*, R J Richardson, C J Richardson, C J Richardson, P J Richardson, Ms L J Richardson
**Co. Secretary:** Paul Richardson
**Branches:** Richardsons Leisure Ltd, Acle Bridge, Norwich, Norfolk NR13 3AS
**US SIC:** 3732, 7032, 5813, 7999
**UK SIC:** 36102, 66702, 66200, 97913
**Auditors:** PKF (UK) LLP
**Bankers:** Barclays Bank Plc (20-62-53)

| | 03-11-13 | 04-11-12 | 01-11-12 |
|---|---|---|---|
| TO | 15,647,198 | 13,731,897 | 8,937,435 |
| P/L | 806,649 | 1,822,648 | (33,807) |
| NW | 10,687,827 | 10,029,516 | 3,347,778 |
| WC | (5,430,055) | (5,134,757) | (6,141,349) |
| Emp. | 418 | 499 | 268 |

DUNS 21-209-8198

## Richardsons Ltd

(**Subsidiary of:** Richardsons (Holdings) Ltd)
Westgate, Driffield, North Humberside YO25 6SY
**Tel:** 01377252166
**Web:** www.richardson-ford.co.uk
**Reg No:** 0280806 **VAT No:** 167485427
**Estd:** 1918 Private Limited Company
**Line of Business:** Car dealers (new & used)
**Trading Style:** Richardsons Ford
**Issued Capital:** £47,773
**Principals:** P A Richardson *(Managing)*, S A Richardson
**Co. Secretary:** Paul Richardson
**Responsibilities**
**Finance:** Keith Atkin *(Accountant)*
**Branches:** Richardsons Ltd, 141-147 Hilderthorpe Road, Bridlington, North Humberside YO15 3HA
**US SIC:** 5511, 5521, 7539, 5531
**UK SIC:** 65100, 67100
**Auditors:** Firth Parish
**Bankers:** National Westminster Bank Plc (60-07-05)

| | 31-12-13 | 31-12-12 | 31-12-11 |
|---|---|---|---|
| TO | 13,197,289 | 11,589,525 | 10,016,611 |
| P/L | 110,535 | 81,825 | 23,303 |
| NW | 2,373,972 | 2,312,768 | 2,254,385 |
| WC | 716,970 | 700,354 | 640,018 |
| Emp. | 50 | 49 | 51 |

DUNS 73-573-3466

## Richbridge Ltd

(**Subsidiary of:** Woodford Group Plc)
Unit 6 Lockside Office Park, Lockside Road, Preston, Lancashire PR2 2YS
**Tel:** 01772733777
**Web:** www.rosyapplechildcare.com
**Reg No:** 4835009 **Estd:** 2003 Private Limited Company
**Line of Business:** Primary education
**Issued Capital:** £100
**Director:** A F Lochery
**Co. Secretary:** Jason Parkinson
**Responsibilities**
**Senior:** Sharon Alexander *(Manager)*
**US SIC:** 7399 **UK SIC:** 83954

| | 31-08-13 | 31-08-12 | 31-08-11 |
|---|---|---|---|
| TA | 103 | 103 | 103 |
| NW | 100 | 100 | 100 |
| WC | 97 | 97 | 97 |

DUNS 21-159-0963 **Imp-Exp**

## Richer Sounds Plc

Unit 3 4 Richer House, Hankey Place, London SE1 4BB
**Tel:** 02079402222
**Web:** www.richersounds.com
**Reg No:** 1402643 **VAT No:** 237678131
**Estd:** 1978 Public Limited Company
**Line of Business:** Manufacture of radio and electronic capital goods
**Export Markets:** Europe
**Issued Capital:** £50,000
**Principals:** J Richer *(Chairman)*, D B Robinson *(Managing)*
**Co. Secretary:** John Currier
**Branches:** Richer Sounds Plc, 77 London Road, Southampton, Hampshire SO15 2AA
**US SIC:** 3662, 3639
**UK SIC:** 34430, 34600
**Auditors:** Baker Tilly UK Audit LLP
**Bankers:** Barclays Bank Plc (20-80-57)

| | 03-05-14 | 04-05-13 | 28-05-12 |
|---|---|---|---|
| TO | 143,371,000 | 144,338,000 | 138,419,000 |
| P/L | 5,756,000 | 5,072,000 | 4,139,000 |
| NW | 21,841,000 | 17,606,000 | 13,891,000 |
| WC | 20,596,000 | 16,932,000 | 14,481,000 |
| Emp. | 494 | 471 | 460 |

DUNS 23-275-0872

## Richmond and Twinckenham Pct

Thames House, 180 High Street, Teddington, Middlesex TW11 8HU
**Web:** http://www.hrch.nhs.uk/#
**Estd:** 2002
**Line of Business:** Nhs clinics
**Trading Style:** Hounslow & Richmond Community Health Care, Hrch
**Issued Capital:** £1
**Principals:** Ms S Bates *(Chairman)*, I Maxwell *(Financial)*, Ms M Plant, Ms J Mager, J Thompson, Ms S Jenkins, Ms J Rutherford, J Simpson
**Responsibilities**
**Senior:** Charles Humphry *(Non-Executive Director)*, Stephen Swords *(Non Executive Member)*
**Branches:** Richmond and Twinckenham Pct, 70 Sheen La, London SW14 8LP
**US SIC:** 8062 **UK SIC:** 95100
**Employees:** 210

DUNS 39-691-7056

## Richmond Cabinet Co Ltd

(**Subsidiary of:** Extrapure Ltd)
Regent House, Waterside, Hadfield Industrial Estate, Hadfield, Glossop, Derbyshire SK13 1BS
**Tel:** 01457767000 **Fax:** 01457856073
**Web:** www.richmondcabinet.co.uk
**Reg No:** 2141717 **VAT No:** 927538494
**Estd:** 1987 Private Limited Company
**Line of Business:** Manufacturers of household furnishings
**Export Sales:** £28,342
**Issued Capital:** £100,000
**Directors:** M Wakeham, G Tootell, D A Fitton
**Co. Secretary:** Stuart Henderson
**Responsibilities**
**Sales:** Jerry Warhurst *(Commercial Manager)*
**Health & Safety:** Roy Fletcher *(Facilities Manager)*
**Facilities:** Roy Fletcher *(Facilities Manager)*
**Operations:** Roy Fletcher *(Facilities Manager)*
**Purchasing:** Gary Kinder *(Purchasing Manager)*
**US SIC:** 2517 **UK SIC:** 46714
**Auditors:** Tenon Audit Ltd
**Bankers:** Yorkshire Bank Plc (05-05-73)

| | 31-12-13 | 31-12-12 | 31-12-11 |
|---|---|---|---|
| TO | 18,001,480 | 13,905,091 | 13,812,205 |
| P/L | 84,270 | (177,918) | (567,119) |
| NW | 422,210 | 328,578 | 506,496 |
| WC | 789,633 | 1,293,200 | 1,388,663 |
| Emp. | 162 | 166 | 186 |

DUNS 21-589-2148

## Richmond Care Villages

South Street, Letcombe Regis, Wantage, Oxfordshire OX12 9JY
**Tel:** 01235773970
**Web:** www.richmond-villages.com
**Estd:** 2011
**Line of Business:** Residential care establishments
**Responsibilities**
**Senior:** Elisabeth Parker *(Village Manager)*
**US SIC:** 8321 **UK SIC:** 96111
**Employees:** 160

DUNS 77-485-3519

## Richmond Cars Ltd

Fitzherbert Road, Farlington, Portsmouth, Hampshire PO6 1RU
**Tel:** 023-9222-1441 **Fax:** 023-9220-0417
**Web:** www.richmondhyundai.co.uk
**Reg No:** 2971884 **Estd:** 1996 Private Limited Company
**Line of Business:** Sale of new motor vehicles
**Trading Style:** Richmond Hyundai
**Issued Capital:** £150,000
**Director:** M R Nobes
**Co. Secretary:** Ms Catherine Brown
**Responsibilities**
**Marketing:** Becky Nobes *(Marketing Manager)*
**US SIC:** 5511 **UK SIC:** 65100
**Auditors:** Harris Rule
**Bankers:** HSBC Bank plc (40-37-15)

| | 31-03-14 | 31-03-13 | 31-03-12 |
|---|---|---|---|
| TO | 47,043,751 | 39,475,265 | 28,021,505 |
| P/L | 680,057 | 446,788 | 183,893 |
| NW | 1,374,132 | 977,622 | 755,419 |
| WC | (783,249) | (791,351) | (1,110,009) |
| Emp. | 112 | 88 | 82 |

DUNS 23-829-0022

## Richmond Cars (Southampton) Ltd

66 70 Oxford Street, Southampton, Hampshire SO14 3DL
**Tel:** 01243583185 **Fax:** 01243584333
**Web:** www.richmondhyundai.co.uk
**Reg No:** 3820911 **Estd:** 1999 Private Limited Company
**Line of Business:** Sale of new motor vehicles
**Issued Capital:** £100
**Managing Director:** M R Nobes
**Co. Secretary:** Ms Catherine Brown
**US SIC:** 5511 **UK SIC:** 65100
**Bankers:** HSBC Bank plc (40-37-15)

| | 31-03-14 | 31-03-13 | 31-03-12 |
|---|---|---|---|
| TO | 21,832,615 | 18,153,177 | 16,246,392 |
| P/L | 396,898 | 177,340 | 52,593 |
| NW | 1,571,963 | 764,392 | 632,414 |
| WC | (11,061) | 35,305 | 343,083 |
| Emp. | 62 | 56 | 51 |

DUNS 77-165-5412
## Richmond Coventry Ltd
(**Subsidiary of:** The British United Provident Association Ltd)
Bede Village, Hospital Lane, Bedworth, Warwickshire CV12 0PB
**Tel:** 02476645544
**Web:** www.richmond-villages.com
**Reg No:** 2707797 **Estd:** 1992 Private Limited Company
**Line of Business:** Residential care establishments
**Trading Style:** Richmond Lodge Nursing Home
**Issued Capital:** £100
**Directors:** A J Cannon, J S Picken, K Moore
**Co. Secretary:** Bupa Secretaries Limited
**Responsibilities**
**Senior:** Sonia Tenniswood *(Relief Manager)*
**Finance:** Paddy Brice *(Finance Director)*, Jon Hather *(Finance Director)*
**Marketing:** David Reaves *(Marketing Manager)*
**US SIC:** 8321, 6732
**UK SIC:** 96111, 83100
**Auditors:** Jerrom Associates

| | 31-12-13 | 31-12-12 | 31-12-11 |
|---|---|---|---|
| TO | 3,640,000 | 3,869,000 | 4,073,000 |
| P/L | 806,000 | 649,000 | 675,000 |
| NW | 5,871,000 | 4,516,000 | 3,809,000 |
| WC | (657,000) | (1,933,000) | (2,524,000) |
| Emp. | 120 | 109 | 85 |

DUNS 23-650-6551
## Richmond Dairies Ltd
Fferm Fach, Blaen Y Coed, Carmarthen, Dyfed SA33 6ET
**Tel:** 01267-281294
**Reg No:** 3645860 **Estd:** 1998 Private Limited Company
**Line of Business:** Caterers mobile
**Issued Capital:** £5
**Director:** T Routley
**US SIC:** 5812 **UK SIC:** 66110
**Bankers:** Barclays Bank Plc (20-00-07)

| | 31-01-14 | 31-01-13 | 31-01-12 |
|---|---|---|---|
| TA | 18,599 | 17,322 | 17,749 |
| NW | 6,662 | 6,723 | 7,962 |
| WC | 5,112 | 5,745 | 6,671 |

DUNS 77-120-7347 Exp
## Richmond Events Ltd
St Leonards House, St Leonards Road, London SW14 7LY
**Tel:** 020-8487-2200
**Web:** www.richmondevents.com
**Reg No:** 2693237 **Estd:** 1992 Private Limited Company
**Line of Business:** Activities of exhibition and fair organisers
**Export Markets:** Rest of world
**Export Sales:** £3,505,000
**Issued Capital:** £100
**Principals:** M S Rayner *(Managing)*, J E Gorst, L G Quinn
**Co. Secretary:** Ms Sharon Bond
**Responsibilities**
**Senior:** Simon Churchill *(Sales Executive (IT Directors)*
**Marketing:** Susan Cartwright *(Office Manager)*, Rachel Langton *(Marketing Manager)*, Chris Wishart *(Web Developer)*
**Sales:** Simon Churchill *(Sales Executive (IT Directors)*, Andy Macey *(Head of Business Development)*
**Admin:** Susan Cartwright *(Office Manager)*
**IT:** Tom Keeley *(Network Manager)*
**HR:** Susan Cartwright *(Office Manager)*
**Health & Safety:** Susan Cartwright *(Office Manager)*
**Facilities:** Susan Cartwright *(Office Manager)*
**Operations:** Susan Cartwright *(Office Manager)*
**Purchasing:** Susan Cartwright *(Office Manager)*
**Engineering:** Susan Cartwright *(Office Manager)*
**US SIC:** 8999 **UK SIC:** 83954
**Auditors:** PricewaterhouseCoopers
**Bankers:** Bank Of Scotland (12-01-03)

| | 31-12-13 | 31-12-12 | 31-12-11 |
|---|---|---|---|
| TO | 9,361,000 | 8,971,000 | 8,570,000 |
| P/L | 325,000 | 473,000 | 268,000 |
| NW | (3,796,000) | (4,002,000) | (4,423,000) |
| WC | (3,712,000) | (3,808,000) | (5,710,000) |
| Emp. | 64 | 61 | 59 |

DUNS 28-847-5817
## The Richmond Fellowship
80 Holloway Road, London N7 8JG
**Tel:** 02076973300 **Fax:** 02076973301
**Web:** www.richmondfellowship.org.uk
**Reg No:** 0662712 **Estd:** 1959 Private Company Limited By Guarantee
**Line of Business:** Other human health activities
**Directors:** P F Corley, Dr M W Holland, A Powell, P J Molyneux, Ms A T Harper, Mrs B L Deacon-Hedges, Ms D French, G Bland
**Responsibilities**
**Senior:** Kate Beaumont *(Locality Manager)*, Derek Caren *(Director)*, Stephanie De La Haye *(Director)*, Edward Gatward *(Manager)*, Nigel Goldie *(Manager)*, Rajesh Lakhani *(Financial Director)*, Stuart Riggall *(Director of People and Organis)*
**Finance:** Paul Harrington *(Assistant Director of Planning)*, Rajesh Lakhani *(Financial Director)*
**HR:** Stuart Riggall *(Director of People and Organis)*
**Branches:** The Richmond Fellowship, 20 Davenport Road, Coventry, West Midlands CV5 6PY
**US SIC:** 8091, 8321
**UK SIC:** 95200, 96111
**Auditors:** Nexia Smith & Williamson
**Bankers:** The Co-Operative Bank Plc (08-02-28)

| | 31-03-14 | 31-03-13 | 30-03-12 |
|---|---|---|---|
| TO | 44,307,000 | 33,414,000 | 40,817,000 |
| P/L | 6,416,000 | 46,000 | 6,750,000 |
| NW | 35,242,000 | 28,790,000 | 28,726,000 |
| WC | 23,649,000 | 18,823,000 | 18,884,000 |
| Emp. | 1,141 | 916 | 981 |

DUNS 21-034-2399
## Richmond Fellowship Scotland
3 Buchanan Gate, Glasgow, Lanarkshire G33 6FB
**Tel:** 08450136300
**Web:** www.trfs.org.uk
**Estd:** 1993 Proprietorship
**Line of Business:** Activities of other membership organisations not elsewhere classified
**Responsibilities**
**Senior:** Jack Blake *(Board Member)*, Vincent Iles *(Executive Director- Central)*, George Welsh *(Executive Director- North)*
**IT:** Michael Marek *(IT Manager)*
**Health & Safety:** George Tominey *(Health & Safety Officer)*
**US SIC:** 8699 **UK SIC:** 96902
**Employees:** 60

DUNS 42-468-6855
## The Richmond Fellowship Scotland Ltd
26 Park Circus, Glasgow, Lanarkshire G3 6AP
**Tel:** 01413534050
**Web:** www.trfs.org.uk
**Reg No:** 0002450SP **Estd:** 1997 Private Limited Company
**Line of Business:** Charities and charitable organisations
**Issued Capital:** £9
**Principals:** J Fraser *(Chairman)*, A Smyth, P Tompkins, J Anderson, B Hutchison, N Buchan, Ms C Morrison, C Gibb
**Responsibilities**
**Senior:** Vince Iiles *(Executive Director)*
**Branches:** The Richmond Fellowship Scotland Limited, 171 Butterbiggins Road, Glasgow, Lanarkshire G42 7AS
**US SIC:** 6732 **UK SIC:** 83100
**Auditors:** Pannell Kerr Forster
**Employees:** 2,500

DUNS 73-979-6469
## Richmond Group Ltd
Nova Building, Bournemouth, Dorset BH2 5LT
**Tel:** 01202638555
**Web:** www.therichmondgroup.co.uk
**Reg No:** 5230353 **Estd:** 2014 Private Limited Company
**Line of Business:** Representative office
**Trading Style:** Amigo Loans
**Issued Capital:** £50,000
**Directors:** C I Jones, H L Cragoe, D R Coates, J Benamor, M A Robins, N S Beal
**Co. Secretary:** Nicholas Beal
**Responsibilities**
**Senior:** Trevor Frankiess *(Managing Director, Debt Line)*, Mourad Malki *(Manager)*
**Admin:** Catriona Patterson *(Manager)*
**Operations:** Amber Branch *(Project Manager)*, Vikki McCallum *(Operations Director)*
**US SIC:** 6111 **UK SIC:** 81501

| | 31-03-14 | 31-03-13 | 31-03-12 |
|---|---|---|---|
| TA | 241,302,365 | 196,216,700 | 168,027,000 |
| P/L | 43,495,934 | 32,842,386 | 40,762,000 |
| NW | 144,189,248 | 111,706,999 | 86,835,000 |
| WC | 139,886,202 | 185,799,979 | 157,691,000 |
| Emp. | 274 | 269 | 298 |

DUNS 21-121-1898
## The Richmond Hotel Ltd
L And Apos; L'Hyvreuse, St Peter Port, Guernsey, Channel Islands GY1 1UY
**Tel:** 01481-726221 **Fax:** 01481-728945
**Web:** www.dukeofrichmond.com
**Reg No:** 0000151G **Estd:** 1972 Private Limited Company
**Line of Business:** Hotels
**Trading Style:** The Duke of Richmond Hotel
**Responsibilities**
**Senior:** Lucas Laubscher *(Manager)*, James McMullen *(Restaurant Manager)*, Stephen Purtill *(Manager)*
**Finance:** Helen Lenkovska *(Financial Manager)*
**Marketing:** Stephen Purtill *(Manager)*
**Sales:** Stephen Purtill *(Manager)*
**IT:** Stephen Purtill *(Manager)*
**HR:** Stephen Purtill *(Manager)*
**Health & Safety:** Stephen Purtill *(Manager)*
**Purchasing:** Stephen Purtill *(Manager)*
**US SIC:** 7011, 5812
**UK SIC:** 66500, 66110
**Employees:** 50

DUNS 23-568-8934
## Richmond Housing Partnership Ltd
8 Waldegrave Road, Teddington, Teddington, Middlesex TW11 8GT
**Web:** www.rhp.org.uk
**Reg No:** 0030939IP **Estd:** 2010
**Line of Business:** RHP is a local housing company, registered with the Tenant Services Authority (TSA),it is a member of the National Housing Federation and a registered charity
**Trading Style:** Rhp
**Principals:** R Petty *(Chairman)*, R Dobbs *(Managing)*, Ms A Graham, Ms L Wallace, Ms S Smith, Ms C Hall, J Elleway, D Done
**Responsibilities**
**Senior:** Lynnette Rolph *(Senior Manager)*
**Admin:** Jenny Coppard *(PA to CEO)*
**IT:** Jonathan Creaser *(Head of ICT)*
**Facilities:** Tracey Elliott *(Retirement Housing Manager)*
**Branches:** Richmond Housing Partnership Limited, Woodville Road, Richmond, Surrey TW10 7QW
**US SIC:** 8399, 6531
**UK SIC:** 96111, 83400
**Auditors:** Grant Thornton UK LLP
**Bankers:** Barclays Bank Plc (20-03-80)

| | 31-03-12 | 31-03-11 | 31-03-10 |
|---|---|---|---|
| TO | 41,700,000 | 37,655,000 | 37,151,000 |
| P/L | 8,916,000 | 5,612,000 | 678,000 |
| NW | 33,239,000 | 16,058,000 | 7,502,000 |
| WC | 8,093,000 | (1,994,000) | (9,296,000) |
| Emp. | 237 | 233 | 240 |

DUNS 39-911-0113
## Richmond Medical Agency Ltd
(**Subsidiary of:** S.& T. Holdings Ltd)
157 Stanwell Road, Ashford, Middlesex TW15 3QN
**Tel:** 01784-422300
**Web:** www.rma-locums.co.uk
**Reg No:** 2235841 **Estd:** 1988 Private Limited Company
**Line of Business:** Labour recruitment and provision of personnel
**Issued Capital:** £100
**Principals:** Mrs S Tiagi *(Managing)*, P Tiagi, K Vengadasalam, A R Tiagi, Ms A Stevenson
**Co. Secretary:** Mrs Saroja Tiagi
**Responsibilities**
**Senior:** Anoushka-sudhira Tiagi *(Manager)*, Kumar Tiagi *(Manager)*
**US SIC:** 7361 **UK SIC:** 83954
**Auditors:** Robert James Partnership
**Bankers:** Barclays Bank Plc (20-41-41)

| | 31-03-14 | 31-03-13 | 31-03-12 |
|---|---|---|---|
| TA | 307,746 | 364,439 | 241,597 |
| NW | 97,893 | 80,584 | 53,674 |
| WC | 97,481 | 80,584 | 53,632 |

DUNS 77-523-4529
## Richmond Nantwich Ltd
(**Subsidiary of:** The British United Provident Association Ltd)
St Josephs Way Richmond Village, Nantwich, Cheshire CW5 6LZ
**Tel:** 01270-629080
**Web:** www.richmond-villages.com
**Reg No:** 2988901 **Estd:** 1996 Private Limited Company
**Line of Business:** Residential care establishments
**Issued Capital:** £2
**Directors:** A J Cannon, K Moore, J S Picken
**Co. Secretary:** Bupa Secretaries Limited
**Responsibilities**
**Senior:** Lynne Griffin *(Manager)*, Jon Hather *(Manager)*
**Admin:** Joanne Rowe *(Administrator)*
**US SIC:** 8321 **UK SIC:** 96111
**Auditors:** Moore Stephens
**Bankers:** The Bank Of Ireland (30-14-58)

| | 31-12-13 | 31-12-12 | 31-12-11 |
|---|---|---|---|
| TO | 2,403,000 | 2,498,000 | 2,387,000 |
| P/L | 532,000 | 843,000 | 758,000 |
| NW | 5,076,000 | 4,481,000 | 3,652,000 |
| WC | 5,070,000 | 4,204,000 | 3,482,000 |
| Emp. | 74 | 65 | 58 |

DUNS 22-192-8562
## Richmond Nursing Agency Ltd
The Avenue Delta Lakes Enterprise Centre, Llanelli, Dyfed SA15 2DR
**Tel:** 01554756148 **Fax:** 01554823149
**Web:** www.richmondnursing.co.uk
**Reg No:** 4210985 **Estd:** 2001 Private Limited Company
**Line of Business:** Nursing agencies
**Issued Capital:** £200
**Director:** A M Hearne
**Co. Secretary:** Anthony Davies
**US SIC:** 8091 **UK SIC:** 95200
**Auditors:** Charles & Co

| | 31-05-14 | 31-05-13 | 31-05-12 |
|---|---|---|---|
| TA | 680,422 | 353,010 | 234,211 |
| NW | 400,673 | 208,831 | 137,016 |
| WC | 397,913 | 205,139 | 132,406 |

DUNS 22-251-2662 Imp
## Richmond Pharmacology Ltd
Suite 18, 5th Floor, Victoria House, Aldershot, Hampshire GU11 1EJ
**Tel:** 02086645200
**Web:** www.richmondpharmacology.com
**Reg No:** 4269261 **Estd:** 2001 Private Limited Company
**Line of Business:** Technical testing and analysis
**Trading Style:** St George's Hospital Medical School
**Issued Capital:** £8,357
**Directors:** Dr U Lorch, Dr J Taubel
**Co. Secretary:** Dr Radivoj Arezina
**Responsibilities**
**Senior:** Jorge Taubel *(Managing Director)*
**Marketing:** Charlotte Gowling *(Marketing Manager)*
**IT:** Mark Simkin *(IT Manager)*
**HR:** Keith Berelowitz *(Human Resources Manager)*
**Health & Safety:** Maureen Symester *(Facilities Manager)*
**Facilities:** Maureen Symester *(Facilities Manager)*
**US SIC:** 7397, 7391
**UK SIC:** 83702, 94000
**Auditors:** Gilroy & Brookes

| | 31-12-13 | 31-12-12 | 31-12-11 |
|---|---|---|---|
| TO | 7,415,744 | 5,146,863 | 5,101,013 |
| P/L | 502,258 | 6,509 | (2,035,160) |
| NW | (422,993) | (925,251) | (931,760) |
| WC | (279,178) | (1,254,424) | (1,367,342) |
| Emp. | N/A | N/A | 83 |

DUNS 21-770-2473
## Richmond Primary School
Nursery Close, Sheerness, Kent ME12 2QT
**Tel:** 01795662891
**Web:** www.richmond.kent.sch.uk
**Estd:** 1970 Proprietorship
**Line of Business:** Schools (local authority)
**Proprietor:** Mrs M Smith
**Responsibilities**
**Senior:** Jacqui Lockwood *(Acting Principal)*
**US SIC:** 8211 **UK SIC:** 93200
**Employees:** 80

DUNS 21-772-5268
## Richmond Southampton
West Quay Road, Southampton, Hampshire SO15 1GY
**Tel:** 02380333435
**Web:** www.richmondhyundai.co.uk
**Estd:** 2001 Proprietorship
**Line of Business:** Car dealers (new & used)
**Proprietor:** M Nobes
**Responsibilities**
**Senior:** Alex Jackson *(General Manager)*
**US SIC:** 5511 **UK SIC:** 65100
**Employees:** 50

DUNS 21-093-6857
## The Richmond Surgery
Richmond Close, Fleet, Hampshire GU52 7US
**Tel:** 01252-811466
**Web:** www.richmondsurgeryfleet.com
**Estd:** 1978 Partnership
**Line of Business:** Doctors
**Partner:** Dr A Sharp
**Responsibilities**
**Senior:** Donna Brennan *(Practice Manager)*
**US SIC:** 8011 **UK SIC:** 95300
**Employees:** 60

DUNS 22-522-2587

## Richmond the American International University in London Inc

American International University In, London, Queens Road, Richmond, Surrey TW10 6JP
**Tel:** 02083329000
**Web:** www.richmond.ac.uk
**Reg No:** 0008955FC **Estd:** 1988
**Line of Business:** University
**Trading Style:** Richmond University
**Directors:** Ms W W Miller, Ms A Brookes, P R Williams, Dame M Richardson, Dr J Annette, J Michael, K M Everett, Professor W Durden
**Responsibilities**
**Senior:** Alan Hoffman *(Director)*, Ian Newbould *(Manager)*
**Branches:** 57 Albans Gro, Kensington, W8 5PN., London
**US SIC:** 8221 **UK SIC:** 93100
**Auditors:** Baker Tilly
**Bankers:** National Westminster Bank Plc (60-17-31)

DUNS 50-022-7731

## Richmond Theatre Management Ltd

The Little Green, Richmond, Surrey TW9 1QJ
**Tel:** 02083324500
**Web:** www.atgtickets.com
**Reg No:** 2302724 **Estd:** 2011 Private Limited Company
**Line of Business:** Theatrical presentation companies
**Issued Capital:** £450,002
**Director:** Ms R A Squire
**Co. Secretary:** Mrs Helen Enright
**Responsibilities**
**Senior:** Karin Gartzke *(Chief Executive)*, Kate Wrightson *(General Manager)*
**Marketing:** Alison Tracey *(Marketing Manager)*
**US SIC:** 7911 **UK SIC:** 97913
**Auditors:** BDO Stoy Hayward
**Bankers:** Barclays Bank Plc (20-72-17)

| | 30-04-14 | 30-04-13 | 30-04-12 |
|---|---|---|---|
| TA | 15,819 | 192,306 | 173,878 |
| P/L | (97) | 888,116 | 762,661 |
| NW | 5,520 | 5,617 | (881,073) |
| WC | 5,520 | 5,617 | (881,073) |

DUNS 22-741-1410

## Richmond-upon-Thames College

Egerton Road, Twickenham, Middlesex TW2 7SJ
**Tel:** 02086078000
**Web:** www.rutc.ac.uk
**Estd:** 1975
**Line of Business:** Further education schools and colleges
**Director:** Ms J Redfern
**Responsibilities**
**Senior:** David Ansell *(Principal)*, Robin Ghurbhurun *(Principal)*, Jean Goodeve *(Manager)*, Sue Lockett *(Estates Manager)*
**Finance:** Jackie Miles *(Head of Finance)*
**IT:** Judy May *(Head of IT)*
**HR:** Yvonne Glennon *(Personnel Coordinator)*, Clare Traloar *(Personnel Manager)*
**Facilities:** Sue Lockett *(Estates Manager)*
**Purchasing:** Sue Lockett *(Estates Manager)*
**US SIC:** 8221 **UK SIC:** 93100
**Employees:** 400

DUNS 21-442-4160

## Richmonds Plumbing & Heating Merchants Ltd

(**Subsidiary of:** Strathcairn Ltd)
15-25 Carnoustie Place, Glasgow, Lanarkshire G5 8PA
**Tel:** 0141-429-7441
**Web:** www.richmonds-phm.co.uk
**Reg No:** 0098337SC **VAT No:** 259692213
**Estd:** 1985 Private Limited Company
**Line of Business:** Plumbers merchants
**Issued Capital:** £128,000
**Principals:** W G Jackson *(Managing)*, R W Jackson, W A Millar
**Co. Secretary:** Ross Mcinroy
**Responsibilities**
**IT:** T Grierson *(IT Manager)*
**Branches:** Richmonds Plumbing & Heating Merchants Ltd, Block 21, Unit 1, Mallard Way, Bellshill, Lanarkshire ML4 3BF
**US SIC:** 5074 **UK SIC:** 61300
**Auditors:** Baker Tilly UK Audit LLP
**Bankers:** Bank Of Scotland (80-07-48)

| | 31-12-13 | 31-12-12 | 31-12-11 |
|---|---|---|---|
| TO | 6,405,586 | 6,027,856 | 7,161,735 |
| P/L | 115,545 | 102,560 | 285,527 |
| NW | 1,791,647 | 2,331,120 | 2,313,173 |
| WC | 1,595,911 | 1,525,772 | 1,570,417 |
| Emp. | 49 | 49 | 47 |

DUNS 23-618-4438

## Richmondshire District Council

Mercury House, Richmond, North Yorkshire DL10 4JX
**Tel:** 01748829100
**Web:** www.richmondshire.gov.uk
**Estd:** 1974
**Line of Business:** Local government
**Principals:** A Orchard *(Financial)*, G Beacall *(Commercial)*, H Tabiner, R Alderson
**Responsibilities**
**Senior:** Callum McKeon *(Resources Director)*
**Finance:** Claire Blackburn *(Finance Director)*, Callum McKeon *(Resources Director)*
**Health & Safety:** Cynthia Edwards *(Health & Safety Officer)*
**Branches:** Richmondshire District Council, Central Chambers, 4 Railway St, Leyburn, North Yorkshire DL8 5AY
**US SIC:** 9121 **UK SIC:** 91110
**Bankers:** Barclays Bank Plc (20-25-29)
**Employees:** 100

DUNS 23-518-1034

## Richoux Group Plc

5-8 Cochrane Mews, London NW8 6NY
**Tel:** 02074837000 **Fax:** 02074837001
**Web:** www.richouxgroup.co.uk
**Reg No:** 3517191 **Estd:** 1998 Public Limited Company
**Line of Business:** Restaurants
**Issued Capital:** £3,680,784
**Directors:** E J Standring, P A Shotter, S Diliberto, The Hon R A Rayne
**Co. Secretary:** Ms Susan Ludley
**Responsibilities**
**Senior:** James Rhodes *(Non-Executive Director)*
**US SIC:** 5812, 6711
**UK SIC:** 66110, 83962
**Auditors:** Rees Pollock
**Bankers:** National Westminster Bank Plc (60-00-01)

| | 29-12-13 | 30-12-12 | 25-12-11 |
|---|---|---|---|
| TO | 11,483,000 | 9,853,000 | 9,009,000 |
| P/L | 740,000 | 879,000 | (2,710,000) |
| NW | 7,686,000 | 6,917,000 | 4,009,000 |
| WC | 1,586,000 | 2,811,000 | 260,000 |
| Emp. | 271 | 217 | 235 |

DUNS 50-350-7147 **Exp**

## Rick Bestwick Ltd

(**Subsidiary of:** Beta (International) Ltd)
Park Road, Holmewood Industrial Park, Holmewood, Chesterfield, Derbyshire S42 5UY
**Tel:** 01246-854999
**Web:** www.rickbestwick.com
**Reg No:** 2372728 **VAT No:** 345833933
**Estd:** 1979 Private Limited Company
**Line of Business:** Storage and warehousing
**Issued Capital:** £200,000
**Directors:** K Hancock, P Charters
**Responsibilities**
**Senior:** Patrick Bestwick *(Joint Managing Director)*, Pamela Bestwick *(Joint Managing Director)*
**Finance:** Pamela Bestwick *(Joint Managing Director)*
**Sales:** Diane Nason *(Commercial Contracts Manager)*
**IT:** Pamela Bestwick *(Joint Managing Director)*
**Health & Safety:** Martin Tipper *(H&S and IT Systems Manager)*
**Operations:** Amanda Cogan *(Operations Director)*
**Engineering:** Ana Sanchez *(Technical Manager)*
**Branches:** Rick Bestwick Ltd, Tayview Industrial Estate, Friarton Road, Perth, Perthshire PH2 8DG
**US SIC:** 4226 **UK SIC:** 77003
**Auditors:** Walters Hawson Ltd
**Bankers:** National Westminster Bank Plc (60-40-09)

| | 31-12-13 | 31-12-12 | 30-12-11 |
|---|---|---|---|
| TO | 13,646,082 | 13,038,866 | 8,693,082 |
| P/L | 511,232 | 271,501 | 217,488 |
| NW | 5,613,253 | 4,980,256 | 4,552,695 |
| WC | 3,082,524 | (824,635) | (474,788) |
| Emp. | 112 | 100 | 82 |

DUNS 42-418-8824

## Rick White (Holdings) Ltd

Units 1, Ascot Road, Pershore, Worcestershire WR10 2JJ
**Tel:** 01386552200
**Web:** www.whitelogistics.co.uk
**Reg No:** 4406546 **Estd:** 2002 Private Limited Company
**Line of Business:** Management activities of holding companies
**Issued Capital:** £100
**Managing Director:** Mrs J M Stracey
**Co. Secretary:** Thomas Stracey
**US SIC:** 6711 **UK SIC:** 83962
**Bankers:** Barclays Bank Plc (20-98-61)

| | 30-04-14 | 30-04-13 | 30-04-12 |
|---|---|---|---|
| TO | 7,237,751 | 6,394,439 | 6,254,112 |
| P/L | 249,700 | 78,940 | 100,961 |
| NW | 2,451,557 | 2,256,197 | 2,192,992 |
| WC | 152,771 | 40,738 | (126,039) |
| Emp. | 97 | 89 | 82 |

DUNS 21-102-0353

## Ricker Restaurants (Holdings) Ltd

Bcl House, 2 Pavilion Business Park, Leeds, West Yorkshire LS12 6AJ
**Tel:** 02072295454
**Web:** www.rickerrestaurants.com
**Reg No:** 6453269 **Estd:** 2007 Private Limited Company
**Line of Business:** Management activities of other non-financial holding companies not elsewhere classified
**Issued Capital:** £1,000,000
**Director:** W R Ricker
**Co. Secretary:** Ms Annie Coles
**US SIC:** 6711 **UK SIC:** 83962

| | 31-12-13 | 31-12-12 | 31-12-11 |
|---|---|---|---|
| TO | 8,071,822 | 9,991,480 | 9,554,106 |
| P/L | 674,334 | 566,616 | 862,411 |
| NW | 2,673,995 | 1,780,771 | 2,229,418 |
| WC | 178,737 | 21,273 | (1,384,452) |
| Emp. | 156 | 192 | 201 |

DUNS 21-207-2714

## Rickerby Holdings Ltd

Currock Road, Carlisle, Cumbria CA2 4AU
**Tel:** 01228527521
**Web:** www.rickerby.net
**Reg No:** 0149685 **VAT No:** 256935427
**Estd:** 1918 Private Limited Company
**Line of Business:** Manufacture of other agricultural and forestry machinery
**Issued Capital:** £991,673
**Principals:** A D Rickerby *(Chairman)*, P R Rickerby *(Sales)*, N Platton, W M Rickerby
**Co. Secretary:** Neil Platton
**Responsibilities**
**Senior:** Ken Connelly *(Manager)*
**Sales:** Martyn Henderson *(Sales Manager)*
**Branches:** Rickerby Holdings Ltd, Wynyard Estate, Billingham, Cleveland TS22 5QJ
**US SIC:** 3523 **UK SIC:** 32113
**Auditors:** PricewaterhouseCoopers
**Bankers:** HSBC Bank plc (40-16-22)

| | 30-09-13 | 30-09-12 | 30-09-11 |
|---|---|---|---|
| TO | 46,014,983 | 47,243,445 | 44,336,804 |
| P/L | 963,396 | 834,744 | 1,060,038 |
| NW | 8,114,654 | 7,933,016 | 8,236,938 |
| WC | 5,488,169 | 5,228,459 | 5,704,151 |
| Emp. | 128 | 130 | 120 |

DUNS 21-000-1592

## Rickerbys Llp

Ellenborough House, Wellington Street, Cheltenham, Gloucestershire GL50 1YD
**Tel:** 01242224422 **Fax:** 01242518428
**Web:** www.hcrlaw.com
**Reg No:** 0328675OC **Estd:** 2007 Private Limited Company
**Line of Business:** Solicitors
**Responsibilities**
**Senior:** Phillipa Bruce Kerr *(Non-designated Limited Liabili)*, Anne Compton *(Managing Partner)*, Louise Crook *(Non-designated Limited Liabili)*, Carolyn Green *(Non-designated Limited Liabili)*, Mark Hartley *(Non-designated Limited Liabili)*, Jennifer Okafor *(Non-designated Limited Liabili)*, Alexander Taylor *(Non-designated Limited Liabili)*
**US SIC:** 8111 **UK SIC:** 83500
**Auditors:** Hazlewoods LLP
**Bankers:** Lloyds TSB Bank plc (30-91-87)

| | 31-03-14 | 31-03-13 | 31-03-12 |
|---|---|---|---|
| TO | N/A | 6,136,745 | 7,298,784 |
| WC | 240,933 | 1,489,761 | 2,435,245 |
| Emp. | N/A | N/A | 23 |

DUNS 21-164-8568

## Rickmansworth School

Scots Hill, Rickmansworth, Hertfordshire WD3 3AQ
**Tel:** 01923-773296
**Web:** www.rickmansworth.herts.sch.uk
**Estd:** 1953
**Line of Business:** Schools (foundation)
**Directors:** Dr S Burton, Mrs K Mendlessohn
**Responsibilities**
**Senior:** Stuart Adcock-Kersting *(Manager)*, Mahmooda Ausat *(Manager)*, Andrew Buddie *(Manager)*, Harvey Collyer *(Manager)*, John De Braux *(Manager)*, Brian Dorling *(Manager)*, Kevin Flanaghan *(Acting Head Teacher)*, Peter Harman *(Manager)*, Neeshat Hussein *(Manager)*, Ashley Lagrange *(Manager)*, Sarah Munn *(Manager)*, Elizabeth Pickford *(Manager)*, Wendy Rennoldson *(Manager)*, Tanya Sinclair *(Manager)*, David Wellings *(Manager)*, Hoss Youssefi *(Manager)*
**US SIC:** 8211 **UK SIC:** 93200
**Employees:** 130

DUNS 21-595-5151

## Ricoh

Cannon Park Way, Middlesbrough, Cleveland TS1 1AA
**Tel:** 01189833893
**Web:** www.ricoh.co.uk
**Estd:** 2002 Proprietorship
**Line of Business:** Manufacture of office machinery
**Proprietor:** Mrs K Ashby
**US SIC:** 3579 **UK SIC:** 33010
**Employees:** 100

DUNS 21-001-8018

## Ricoh Europe Holdings Plc

(**Subsidiary of:** Ricoh Company Ltd.)
20 Triton Street, London NW1 3BF
**Tel:** 020 7456 1145
**Web:** www.ricoh-europe.com
**Reg No:** 6273215 **Estd:** 2007 Public Limited Company
**Line of Business:** Management activities of holding companies
**Issued Capital:** £2,000,001
**Directors:** Y Yamashita, D Mills, H Osawa, I P Winham
**Co. Secretary:** Ms Nicola Downing
**US SIC:** 6711 **UK SIC:** 83962
**Auditors:** KPMG LLP

**Following financial data are in thousands**

| | 31-03-14 | 31-03-13 | 31-03-12 |
|---|---|---|---|
| TO | 3,087,900 | 3,010,100 | 3,116,600 |
| P/L | 139,200 | 139,400 | 123,100 |
| NW | 1,112,700 | 1,031,600 | 925,900 |
| WC | 699,800 | 1,011,100 | 977,200 |
| Emp. | 17,199 | 16,258 | 16,328 |

DUNS 29-240-3714

## Ricoh Uk Ltd

(**Subsidiary of:** Ricoh Company Ltd.)
800 Pavilion Drive, Northampton Business Park, Northampton, Northamptonshire NN4 7YL
**Tel:** 02082-614000
**Web:** www.ricoh.co.uk
**Reg No:** 1271033 **Estd:** 1980 Private Limited Company
**Line of Business:** Hardware consultancy
**Issued Capital:** £30,000,000
**Principals:** D Mills *(President)*, P J Keoghan *(Managing)*, R M Hewitt, I P Winham
**Co. Secretary:** Ms Nicola Downing
**Responsibilities**
**Senior:** Michelle Greenhalgh *(PA To Marketing Director)*, Shiro Sasaki *(Manager)*
**Marketing:** Michelle Greenhalgh *(PA To Marketing Director)*
**Branches:** Ricoh Uk Ltd, James House, 55 Welford Rd, Leicester, Leicestershire LE2 7AR
**US SIC:** 7379 **UK SIC:** 83940
**Auditors:** KPMG LLP
**Bankers:** National Westminster Bank Plc (50-00-00)

| | 31-03-14 | 31-03-13 | 31-03-12 |
|---|---|---|---|
| TO | 463,070,000 | 438,433,000 | 422,864,000 |
| P/L | 15,651,000 | 8,554,000 | 7,494,000 |
| NW | 66,613,000 | 49,553,000 | 41,668,000 |
| WC | 63,372,000 | 50,864,000 | 44,587,000 |
| Emp. | 2,565 | 2,589 | 2,696 |

DUNS 22-781-2989 **Imp**

## Ricoh Uk Products Ltd

(**Subsidiary of:** Ricoh Company Ltd.)
Priorslee, Priorslee, Telford, Shropshire TF2 9NS
**Tel:** 01952290090
**Web:** www.rplnet.co.uk
**Reg No:** 1763860 **VAT No:** 386301452
**Estd:** 2012 Private Limited Company
**Line of Business:** Printing production equipment and machinery
**Export Sales:** £381,381,000
**Trading Style:** Ricoh
**Issued Capital:** £5,500,000
**Directors:** T Tokura, T Webber, C Weaver
**Co. Secretary:** Roderick Baggott
**Responsibilities**
**Senior:** Andy Cowdell *(Logistics Manager)*, Keith Kerr *(Proprietor)*
**Facilities:** Stuart Bristow *(Maintenance Manager)*
**Operations:** Andy Whyle *(Environmental Officer)*
**Fleet:** Andy Cowdell *(Logistics Manager)*
**Engineering:** Matthew Garbett *(Engineering Manager)*
**Branches:** Ricoh Uk Products Limited, Ricoh Ho, 1 Plane Tree Crescent, Feltham, Middlesex TW13 7HG
**US SIC:** 3554, 3559
**UK SIC:** 32754, 32863
**Auditors:** KPMG LLP
**Bankers:** Barclays Bank Plc (20-85-46)

| | 31-03-14 | 31-03-13 | 31-03-12 |
|---|---|---|---|
| TO | 384,588,000 | 356,119,000 | 350,450,000 |
| P/L | 16,938,000 | 14,818,000 | 7,157,000 |
| NW | 101,715,000 | 92,648,000 | 85,777,000 |
| WC | 99,481,000 | 98,797,000 | 88,852,000 |
| Emp. | 717 | 715 | 759 |

DUNS 22-142-9397 **Imp**
## Ricor Ltd
(**Subsidiary of:** Ricor International Ltd)
Needles House, Birmingham Road, Studley, Warwickshire B80 7AS
**Tel:** 01527-857757 **Fax:** 01527-857224
**Web:** www.ricor.co.uk
**Reg No:** 4161766 **Estd:** 2001 Private Limited Company
**Line of Business:** Manufacture of other electrical equipment not elsewhere classified
**Export Sales:** £8,639,999
**Trading Style:** Fredboggs
**Issued Capital:** £500,000
**Directors:** J P Beary, K Johnson, C A Howell
**Co. Secretary:** Sean Collins
**Responsibilities**
**HR:** Tim Cummings *(Human Resources Manager)*
**Health & Safety:** Tim Cummings *(Human Resources Manager)*
**Purchasing:** Mandy Gillard *(Purchasing Manager)*
**US SIC:** 3629 **UK SIC:** 34350
**Auditors:** Law & Co

| | 31-03-14 | 29-03-13 | 30-03-12 |
|---|---|---|---|
| TO | 37,074,964 | 32,531,692 | 33,339,500 |
| P/L | 3,006,264 | 3,233,388 | 3,700,190 |
| NW | 7,548,245 | 7,122,494 | 6,519,355 |
| WC | 5,736,174 | 5,478,738 | 5,618,957 |
| Emp. | 204 | 201 | 197 |

DUNS 49-011-6746
## Rics International Ltd
(**Subsidiary of:** The Royal Institution of Chartered Surveyors)
Parliament Square, London SW1P 3BD
**Tel:** 02476868555
**Web:** www.rics.org
**Reg No:** 3072915 **Estd:** 1995 Private Limited Company
**Line of Business:** Other business activities not elsewhere classified
**Issued Capital:** £2
**Directors:** S Tompkins, M J Powell, M Walley
**Co. Secretary:** Rics Services Limited
**Responsibilities**
**Senior:** Stuart Allan *(Fellow)*, Paul Bagust *(Associate Director)*, Jeffrey Belk *(Fellow)*, Peter Bolton King *(Global Residential Director)*, Benjamin Bradford *(Board Member)*, Lee Chye *(Fellow)*, Alan Cripps *(Associate Director - Built Env)*, Richard Cullingworth *(Fellow)*, David Dalby *(Associate Director)*, Jim Drysdale *(Director - Middle East & Afric)*, Mark Gerold *(Chairman)*, Georgiana Hibberd *(Associate Director)*, Suzie Lynch *(Communications Director)*, Jamie Marsh *(Fellow)*, Anne-Marie Mills *(Manager)*, Richard Moxon *(Chairman)*, Tony Mulhall *(Associate Director)*, Anna Orcsik *(Regional Manager - Central & E)*, Martin Russell-Croucher *(Director of Sustainability and)*, Paul Syms *(Fellow)*
**Marketing:** Jeremy Blackburn *(UK Director of External Affair)*, Darrell Gorman *(Member Service Administrator)*, Ellie Irwin *(UK Media Relations Manager)*, Harriet Langton *(Member Services Manager)*, Hannah Leslie *(Conferences Marketing Executiv)*, Suzie Lynch *(Communications Director)*, Matt McDermott *(Sales & Marketing Director)*, Kate Owen *(Senior Press Officer)*, Zsolt Toth *(EU Affairs Officer)*
**Sales:** Liz Mackenzie *(National Account Manager)*, Matt McDermott *(Sales & Marketing Director)*
**Admin:** Audrey Chadwick *(Personal Assistant)*, Darrell Gorman *(Member Service Administrator)*, Rose Liddell *(PA to Chief Executive Officer)*, Rose Pile *(Personal Assistant)*
**Facilities:** Peter Bolton King *(Global Residential Director)*
**Operations:** Nathalie Bellanger *(Project Officer)*, Martin Russell-Croucher *(Director of Sustainability and)*
**Engineering:** Clare Andrews *(Chartered Surveyor)*, Stephen Anelay *(Chartered Surveyor)*, David Askham *(Chartered Surveyor)*, Nur Aziz *(Chartered Surveyor)*, Meryl Baker *(Chartered Surveyor)*, Rory Ballantyne *(Chartered Surveyor)*, Dominic Birkmyre *(Chartered Surveyor)*, Alan Muse *(Director of Construction)*, Rebecca Parry *(Chartered Surveyor)*, Charlie Paton *(Chartered Surveyor)*, Andrew Putland *(Chartered Surveyor)*, Sarah Rawlins *(Chartered Surveyor)*, Jeremy Rawlins *(Chartered Surveyor)*, Andrew Blackmrics *(Chartered Surveyor)*, Alistair Redler *(Chartered Surveyor)*, Doris Schumacher *(Chartered Surveyor)*, Ghislaine Seguin *(Chartered Surveyor)*, Jonathan Selby *(Chartered Surveyor)*, Geoffrey Shaw *(Chartered Surveyor)*, Martin Sheard *(Chartered Surveyor)*, David Blanchard *(Chartered Surveyor)*, Jerome Stewart *(Chartered Surveyor)*, Michael Stubbs *(Chartered Surveyor)*, Paul Taggart *(Chartered Surveyor)*, Joel Taller *(Chartered Surveyor)*, Sandy Thomson *(Chartered Surveyor)*, Paul Tombleson *(Chartered Surveyor)*, David Tropp *(Chartered Surveyor)*, Harry True *(Chartered Surveyor)*, Thomas Van Straubenzee *(Chartered Surveyor)*, Rachel Wakely *(Chartered Surveyor)*, Simon Walter *(Chartered Surveyor)*, Megan Walters *(Chartered Surveyor)*, Edward Weightman *(Chartered Surveyor)*, Louise Wheeler *(Chartered Surveyor)*, Asha Winterflood *(Chartered Surveyor)*, Neil Woolcock *(Chartered Surveyor)*, Danielle Yong *(Chartered Surveyor)*, Jessica Yonwin *(Chartered Surveyor)*, Adrian Bower *(Chartered Surveyor)*, Jack Cadell *(Chartered Surveyor)*, Camilla Calverley-Halford *(Chartered Surveyor)*, Adrian Camps *(Chartered Surveyor)*, Gurdip Chamba *(Chartered Surveyor)*, Timmy Chan *(Chartered Surveyor)*, Bela Chauhan *(Chartered Surveyor)*, Tom Chetwynd *(Chartered Surveyor)*, Colin Church *(Chartered Surveyor)*, Simon Coates *(Chartered Surveyor)*, Stan Colclough *(Chartered Surveyor)*, Neil Colver *(Chartered Surveyor)*, Ian Corker *(Chartered Surveyor)*, Kenelm Cornwall-Legh *(Chartered Surveyor)*, Julie Corrance *(Chartered Surveyor)*, Robin Curtis *(Chartered Surveyor)*, Michael Darroch *(Chartered Surveyor)*, Abigail Deakins *(Chartered Surveyor)*, Gillian Dibb *(Chartered Surveyor)*, Chris Doyle *(Chartered Surveyor)*, Nigel Dubben *(Chartered Surveyor)*, Petra Duffin *(Chartered Surveyor)*, Penny Duggleby *(Chartered Surveyor)*, Phill Edmondson *(Chartered Surveyor)*, Oliver Facer-Harrison *(Chartered Surveyor)*, Mohamad Faiz *(Chartered Surveyor)*, Roger Farrow *(Chartered Surveyor)*, Jeremy Ferris *(Chartered Surveyor)*, Roland Finch *(Chartered Surveyor)*, Andrew Foulds *(Chartered Surveyor)*, Terry Garnett *(Chartered Surveyor)*, Colin Garvin *(Chartered Surveyor)*, Frank Gillespie *(Chartered Surveyor)*, Joanne Glover *(Chartered Surveyor)*, Robin Goodchild *(Chartered Surveyor)*, Tom Goodley *(Chartered Surveyor)*, Peter Greenwood *(Chartered Surveyor)*, Shelley Griffith *(Chartered Surveyor)*, Ursula Hartenberger *(Global Head of Sustainability)*, David Hawke *(Chartered Surveyor)*, John Holtby *(Chartered Surveyor)*, Lars Huber *(Chartered Surveyor)*, Wayne Humphries *(Chartered Surveyor)*, Tunde Jagun *(Chartered Surveyor)*, Clare Kelly *(Chartered Surveyor)*, Denise Kent *(Chartered Surveyor)*, Michael Kenyon *(Chartered Surveyor)*, Tomasz Kozlowski *(Chartered Surveyor)*, Ryan Kuszek *(Chartered Surveyor)*, Bruce Laing *(Chartered Surveyor)*, Brian Lamden *(Chartered Surveyor)*, Michael Landers *(Chartered Surveyor)*, Jean Lane *(Chartered Surveyor)*, Mike Luscombe *(Chartered Surveyor)*, Julian Lyon *(Chartered Surveyor)*, Luke Mackenzie *(Chartered Surveyor)*, Alexandra Maclean *(Chartered Surveyor)*, James Maddocks *(Chartered Surveyor)*, Richard Mascall *(Chartered Surveyor)*, Phillip Mawby *(Chartered Surveyor)*, Ben McCarthy *(Chartered Surveyor)*, Kevin McCloud *(Chartered Surveyor)*, Jim McCluskey *(Chartered Surveyor)*, Agnieszka Miler *(Chartered Surveyor)*, Simon Moffat *(Chartered Surveyor)*, Nicholas Moldon *(Chartered Surveyor)*, Clare Montague *(Chartered Surveyor)*, Richard Moxon *(Chairman)*
**US SIC:** 7399, 8621
**UK SIC:** 83954, 96311
**Auditors:** Deloitte & Touche LLP

| | 31-07-13 | 31-07-12 | 31-07-11 |
|---|---|---|---|
| TO | 9,094,000 | 7,798,000 | 6,262,000 |
| P/L | 980,000 | 619,000 | 267,000 |
| NW | (4,995,000) | (5,774,000) | (6,161,000) |
| WC | (5,082,000) | (5,881,000) | (6,280,000) |
| Emp. | 106 | 83 | 75 |

DUNS 45-857-6261
## R.I.C.S. Services Ltd
(**Subsidiary of:** The Royal Institution of Chartered Surveyors)
Surveyor Court, Westwood Way, Westwood Business Park, Coventry, West Midlands CV4 8JE
**Tel:** 02476694757
**Web:** www.rics.org
**Reg No:** 3203697 **Estd:** 1996 Private Limited Company
**Line of Business:** Other engineering activities
**Issued Capital:** £2
**Directors:** Mrs V E Parylo, S Tompkins
**Co. Secretary:** Mrs Violetta Parylo
**Responsibilities**
**Senior:** Rosanna Roughley *(Manager)*
**US SIC:** 8911, 8621
**UK SIC:** 83701, 96311

| | 31-07-14 | 31-07-13 | 31-07-12 |
|---|---|---|---|
| TA | 2 | 2 | 2 |
| NW | 2 | 2 | 2 |

DUNS 21-838-1867
## Riddlesdown Collegiate
Riddlesdown Collegiate, Honister Heights, Purley, Surrey CR8 1EX
**Tel:** 02086685136
**Web:** www.riddlesdown.org
**Reg No:** 8058921 **Estd:** 2012 Private Company Limited By Guarantee
**Line of Business:** General secondary education
**Directors:** C P Hotham, P S Khan, Ms K S Myring, G H Smith, Ms E A Ash, A D Cameron, Ms S E Anderson, Ms W A Prichard-Smith
**Co. Secretary:** David Clarke
**US SIC:** 8211 **UK SIC:** 93200
**Bankers:** Lloyds TSB Bank plc (30-92-45)

| | 31-08-14 | 31-08-13 |
|---|---|---|
| TO | 12,951,270 | 37,629,467 |
| P/L | 1,876,853 | 22,094,496 |
| NW | 23,598,349 | 21,917,496 |
| WC | 1,037,899 | 1,547,924 |
| Emp. | 199 | 196 |

DUNS 34-819-8672
## Rider House Ltd
(**Subsidiary of:** Elder Holdings Ltd)
Rider House Stapenhill Road, Burton-On-Trent, Staffordshire DE15 9AE
**Tel:** 01283-512973
**Web:** www.elderhomes.co.uk
**Reg No:** 2796826 **Estd:** 1993 Private Limited Company
**Line of Business:** Residential care establishments
**Issued Capital:** £100
**Director:** D H Messenger
**Co. Secretary:** Richard Shore
**Branches:** Stapenhill Road, Burton-On-Trent, Staffordshire DE15 9AE
**US SIC:** 8321 **UK SIC:** 96111
**Auditors:** Ernst & Young
**Bankers:** Barclays Bank Plc (20-00-00)

| | 30-04-13 | 30-04-12 | 30-04-11 |
|---|---|---|---|
| TO | 1,046,272 | N/A | N/A |
| P/L | 100,698 | N/A | N/A |
| NW | 2,939,672 | 2,864,639 | 2,767,926 |
| WC | (27,930) | (97,528) | (269,362) |
| Emp. | 58 | N/A | N/A |

DUNS 21-025-3939
## Rider Hunt International
9 Carden Place, Aberdeen, Aberdeenshire AB10 1UR
**Tel:** 01224-650222
**Web:** www.rhi-group.com
**Estd:** 2005 Proprietorship
**Line of Business:** Quantity surveyors
**Proprietor:** D Lane
**Responsibilities**
**Senior:** Stewart Hayward *(Manager)*, Bill Sutherland *(Operations Manager)*
**Health & Safety:** Karin Mulle *(Health & Safety Officer)*
**US SIC:** 7397 **UK SIC:** 83702
**Employees:** 300

DUNS 50-027-3321
## Rider Hunt International Ltd
(**Subsidiary of:** Amec Foster Wheeler Plc)
The Guildway, Old Portsmouth Road, Artington, Guildford, Surrey GU3 1LR
**Fax:** 01483412090
**Web:** www.rhi-group.com
**Reg No:** 2305615 **Estd:** 1950 Private Limited Company
**Line of Business:** Quantity surveyors
**Issued Capital:** £9,000
**Directors:** J J Harrison, R V Reeves, J M Young
**Co. Secretary:** Christopher Fidler
**Responsibilities**
**Senior:** Stewart Hayward *(Operations Director UK & Europ)*
**Operations:** Stewart Hayward *(Operations Director UK & Europ)*, Marcus Wilson *(Operations Manager - Guildford)*
**Branches:** Rider Hunt International Ltd, Wilton Centre, Wilton Wks, Redcar, Cleveland TS10 4RF
**US SIC:** 7397, 8911
**UK SIC:** 83702, 83701
**Auditors:** Ernst & Young LLP

| | 31-12-13 | 31-12-12 | 31-12-11 |
|---|---|---|---|
| TO | 9,592,000 | 9,798,000 | 8,474,000 |
| P/L | 1,075,000 | 124,000 | 375,000 |
| NW | 1,791,000 | 3,701,000 | 3,526,000 |
| WC | 1,678,000 | 4,072,000 | 3,905,000 |
| Emp. | 47 | 51 | 46 |

DUNS 21-750-1563
## Rider Industrial & Specialist Cleaning
Windfall House, Strawgate Lane, Strawgate Lane, Stapleton, Darlington, County Durham DL2 2QW
**Web:** www.riderindustrialservices.co.uk
**Estd:** 2010 Proprietorship
**Line of Business:** Business and management consultancy activities not elsewhere classified
**Proprietor:** P Rider
**US SIC:** 7392, 1541
**UK SIC:** 83951, 50100
**Employees:** 140

DUNS 73-380-0564 **Exp**
## Rider Levett Bucknall Uk Ltd
Cathedral Court, Birmingham, West Midlands B3 2BH
**Tel:** 01215-031500
**Web:** www.bucknall.com
**Reg No:** 4653580 **Estd:** 2003 Private Limited Company
**Line of Business:** Surveyors and valuers
**Issued Capital:** £1,748,135
**Directors:** A J Reynolds, D Sheehy, A Catchpole, M Weaver, Ms A E Bentley
**Co. Secretary:** Stuart Stables
**Responsibilities**
**Senior:** Steve Aikman *(Managing Partner)*, Deryck Barton *(Managing Partner)*, Simon Kerton *(Managing Partner)*
**HR:** Louise North *(Human Resources Manager)*
**Branches:** Rider Levett Bucknall Uk Ltd, Old Shoreham Rd, Hove, East Sussex BN3 7BD
**US SIC:** 8911 **UK SIC:** 83701
**Auditors:** KPMG LLP

| | 30-04-14 | 30-04-13 | 30-04-12 |
|---|---|---|---|
| TO | 50,267,000 | 49,169,000 | 48,260,000 |
| P/L | 873,000 | 1,012,000 | 1,004,000 |
| NW | 5,003,000 | 4,583,000 | 4,197,000 |
| WC | 4,108,000 | 3,860,000 | 3,790,000 |
| Emp. | 330 | 342 | 350 |

DUNS 45-825-5106 **Imp**
## Riders for Health
Springhill Farm Harborough Road, Northampton, Northamptonshire NN6 9AA
**Tel:** 01604889570 **Fax:** 01604889595
**Web:** www.riders.org
**Reg No:** 3178605 **Estd:** 1989 Private Limited Company
**Line of Business:** Maintenance and repair of motor vehicles
**Directors:** G James, P R Hocking, Sir R W Miller, F Minoli, S C Male, Dr B M Margetts, Ms J Ryan, Ms R B Marvel
**Co. Secretary:** Ms Andrea Coleman
**Responsibilities**
**Senior:** Naa Addo *(Director)*, Barry Coleman *(Manager)*, Michael Mcculloch *(Manager)*, Binay Nagaraju *(Manager)*, Michael Shipster *(Director)*
**US SIC:** 7539, 5571
**UK SIC:** 67100, 65100
**Auditors:** Buzzacott
**Bankers:** HSBC Bank plc (40-19-07)

| | 31-12-13 | 31-12-12 | 31-12-11 |
|---|---|---|---|
| TO | 6,674,371 | 6,201,178 | 6,011,772 |
| P/L | (202,386) | (538,764) | 99,119 |
| NW | 1,118,526 | 1,268,214 | 1,989,051 |
| WC | 725,298 | 353,732 | 923,946 |
| Emp. | 419 | 389 | 390 |

DUNS 21-613-3553
## Riders Garages Ltd
Falmouth Marina, North Parade, Falmouth, Cornwall TR11 2TF
**Tel:** 01326213399 **Fax:** 01326312989
**Web:** www.riders.co.uk
**Reg No:** 0247027 **Estd:** 2011 Private Limited Company
**Line of Business:** Sale of used motor vehicles
**Trading Style:** Riders of Falmouth, Riders Garages
**Issued Capital:** £3,000
**Principals:** R G Sweet *(Managing)*, Ms S R Paddy
**Co. Secretary:** Mrs Stephanie Paddy
**Responsibilities**
**Senior:** Brett Willy *(Dealer Principal)*
**IT:** Ray Penhaul *(IT Manager)*
**Branches:** Riders Garages Ltd, Threemilestone Industrial Estate, Truro, Cornwall TR4 9LD
**US SIC:** 7399, 5521, 5531
**UK SIC:** 83954, 65100
**Auditors:** Kitchen & Brown
**Bankers:** Barclays Bank Plc (20-87-94)

| | 31-12-13 | 31-12-12 | 31-12-11 |
|---|---|---|---|
| TO | 22,311,000 | 21,535,000 | 38,124,000 |
| P/L | (393,000) | (1,436,000) | 2,146,000 |
| NW | 2,116,000 | 2,491,000 | 4,152,000 |
| WC | 83,000 | (413,000) | 1,121,000 |
| Emp. | 82 | 104 | 135 |

DUNS 22-100-2673 **Imp**
## Riders of Bridgwater Ltd.
Riders House, Wylds Road, Bridgwater, Somerset TA6 4DH
**Tel:** 01278-457652 **Fax:** 01278-453190
**Web:** www.ridersmotorcycles.com
**Reg No:** 4119701 **VAT No:** 357278913
**Estd:** 1976 Private Limited Company
**Line of Business:** Motor cycles & scooters
**Trading Style:** Riders Motorcycles

**Issued Capital:** £200
**Principals:** P S Jessopp *(Managing)*, Mrs S M Massey, Mrs A P Jessopp
**Co. Secretary:** Philip Jessopp
**US SIC:** 5571 **UK SIC:** 65100
**Auditors:** Chalmers & Co

| | 30-11-13 | 30-11-12 | 30-11-11 |
|---|---|---|---|
| TO | 13,027,321 | 12,091,653 | 13,512,301 |
| P/L | 114,204 | 100,744 | 155,891 |
| NW | 3,094,441 | 2,982,170 | 2,906,643 |
| WC | 1,496,791 | 1,223,772 | 1,191,475 |
| Emp. | 69 | 67 | 80 |

DUNS 73-992-7452 **Exp**
## Ridge and Partners Llp
The Cowyards, Woodstock, Oxfordshire OX20 1QR
**Tel:** 01993 815000
**Web:** www.ridge.co.uk
**Reg No:** 0309402OC **VAT No:** 892212231
**Estd:** 2004
**Line of Business:** property and construction consultancy
**Responsibilities**
**Senior:** Guy Austin *(Designated Limited Liability P)*, Jason Howard *(Partner)*, Noel Reid *(Partner)*, Michael Rumbelow *(Partner)*, David Steer *(Partner)*, Clive Woodford *(Designated Limited Liability P)*
**HR:** Bel Appleby *(Personnel Manager)*
**Health & Safety:** Bel Appleby *(Personnel Manager)*
**Operations:** Guy Austin *(Designated Limited Liability P)*
**Engineering:** Milka Kerridge *(Electrical Engineer)*
**Branches:** Ridge and Partners Llp, Partnership House, Winchester SO23 7RX Moorside Road
**US SIC:** 8911 **UK SIC:** 83701
**Auditors:** Critchleys LLP
**Bankers:** Barclays Bank Plc (20-71-74)

| | 31-12-13 | 31-12-12 | 31-12-11 |
|---|---|---|---|
| TO | 26,610,548 | 22,314,559 | 22,204,204 |
| P/L | 5,963,797 | (4,246) | 27,933 |
| NW | 5,804,210 | (170,167) | (571,673) |
| WC | 9,496,592 | 4,898,993 | 4,810,587 |
| Emp. | 259 | 241 | 238 |

DUNS 21-787-8763
## Ridge Hill League of Friends
Ridgehill, Brierley Hill Road, Stourbridge, West Midlands DY8 5ST
**Estd:** 1981
**Line of Business:** Charities and charitable organisations
**Principals:** R Childs, Mrs B Nock
**US SIC:** 6732 **UK SIC:** 83100
**Employees:** 140

DUNS 21-231-8952
## Ridge Lea Hospital
Moor Park, Quernmore Road, Lancaster, Lancashire LA1 3JR
**Tel:** 01524550500
**Web:** www.lancashirecare.nhs.uk
**Estd:** 2002 Partnership
**Line of Business:** Mental health centres
**Partners:** Mrs S Crutchley, Mrs P Watson
**Responsibilities**
**Senior:** Angie Gregory *(Operational Manager)*, Andrea Wilson *(Matron)*
**Purchasing:** Angie Gregory *(Operational Manager)*
**US SIC:** 8091 **UK SIC:** 95200
**Employees:** 107

DUNS 21-602-3711
## Ridge View School
Cage Green Road, Tonbridge, Kent TN10 4PT
**Tel:** 01732771384
**Web:** www.ridge-view.kent.sch.uk
**Estd:** 1991 Proprietorship
**Line of Business:** Schools (special)
**Proprietor:** Mrs J Tovey
**Responsibilities**
**Finance:** Leslie Chaning *(Senior Finance Administrator)*
**HR:** Leslie Chaning *(Senior Finance Administrator)*
**US SIC:** 8299 **UK SIC:** 93300
**Employees:** 60

DUNS 23-700-3868
## Ridgehill Housing Association Ltd
12 Elstree Way, Borehamwood, Hertfordshire WD6 1JE
**Tel:** 02082357000
**Web:** www.ridgehill.org
**Reg No:** 0027733IP **VAT No:** 644963408
**Estd:** 1994 Friendly Society
**Line of Business:** Housing associations societies trusts & co-operatives
**Principals:** G Lomax *(Chairman)*, H Chilemba *(Financial)*, R Watson, R Page, D Bearfield, L Moan
**Co. Secretary:** David Shimpe
**Branches:** Ridgehill Housing Association Ltd, 27 Monkswood Gardens, Borehamwood, Hertfordshire WD6 2FA
**US SIC:** 8321 **UK SIC:** 96111
**Auditors:** Deloitte & Touche LLP
**Bankers:** Lloyds TSB Bank plc (30-98-07)
**Employees:** 171
**Turnover:** £19,496,000

DUNS 21-775-8581
## Ridgehill Learning Disability Centre
Ridgehill, Brierley Hill Road, Stourbridge, West Midlands DY8 5ST
**Tel:** 01384323047
**Web:** www.bcpft.nhs.uk
**Estd:** 2011 Partnership
**Line of Business:** Disability services
**Partners:** Ms C Richardson, Mrs C Richardson, M Cooke
**Responsibilities**
**Senior:** Darinka Novak *(General Manager)*
**US SIC:** 8062 **UK SIC:** 95100
**Employees:** 140

DUNS 21-808-3855 **Imp**
## Ridgeon Group Ltd
Nuffield Road Trinity Hall Industrial, Estate, Cambridge, Cambridgeshire CB4 1TS
**Web:** www.ridgeons.co.uk
**Reg No:** 0253252 **Estd:** 1912 Private Limited Company
**Line of Business:** Builders merchants
**Issued Capital:** £640,948
**Directors:** D Sarti, F A Attwood, I C Northen, Mrs A L Rushforth, Ms A H Smith, M H Ridgeon, Ms A K Ridgeon, R P Baker-Bates
**Co. Secretary:** Gordon Ridgeon
**Responsibilities**
**Senior:** Alistair Brace *(General Manager)*, Martin Hurrell *(Area General Manager)*
**Marketing:** Nick Sims *(Group Commercial Director)*
**HR:** John Mortlock *(Training Manager)*
**Branches:** Ridgeon Group Ltd, Attleborough Road, Attleborough, Norfolk NR17 1UF
**US SIC:** 5072 **UK SIC:** 61500
**Auditors:** RSM Robson Rhodes LLP
**Bankers:** HSBC Bank plc (40-16-08)

| | 31-12-13 | 31-12-12 | 31-12-11 |
|---|---|---|---|
| TO | 123,305,000 | 111,841,000 | 105,675,000 |
| P/L | 3,714,000 | 2,530,000 | 1,893,000 |
| NW | 62,468,000 | 59,915,000 | 59,439,000 |
| WC | 20,933,000 | 19,431,000 | 20,552,000 |
| Emp. | 759 | 792 | 767 |

DUNS 50-424-6398 **Imp**
## Ridgeons Ltd
**(Subsidiary of:** Ridgeon Group Ltd)
Cambridge Road, St Neots, Cambridgeshire PE19 6SN
**Tel:** 01480214463 **Fax:** 01480405456
**Web:** www.ridgeons.co.uk
**Reg No:** 2416904 **VAT No:** 599604582
**Estd:** 2012 Private Limited Company
**Line of Business:** Builders merchants
**Issued Capital:** £100,000
**Principals:** D C Ridgeon *(Chairman and Managing)*, Ms A K Ridgeon, D Sarti, J Sam, F A Attwood, Mrs A L Rushforth, R P Baker-Bates, M H Ridgeon
**Co. Secretary:** Gordon Ridgeon
**Responsibilities**
**Senior:** Robbie Cannon *(Manager)*
**Finance:** Nick Sims *(Financial Director)*
**Sales:** Ian Hastings *(Sales Director)*
**IT:** Chris Greaves *(IT Director)*
**Facilities:** Ivor Muncey *(Maintenance Manager)*
**Purchasing:** Nigel Haslop *(Group Buyer)*
**Branches:** Ridgeons Ltd, Ridgeons Ltd, Peartree Road, Colchester, Essex CO3 0JW
**US SIC:** 5072, 5251
**UK SIC:** 61500, 64800
**Auditors:** BDO Stoy Hayward LLP
**Bankers:** HSBC Bank plc (40-16-08)

| | 31-12-13 | 31-12-12 | 31-12-11 |
|---|---|---|---|
| TO | 120,905,000 | 109,989,000 | 103,553,000 |
| P/L | 1,874,000 | (287,000) | (1,130,000) |
| NW | 25,210,000 | 23,543,000 | 24,460,000 |
| WC | 12,116,000 | 9,552,000 | 11,797,000 |
| Emp. | 745 | 658 | 633 |

DUNS 37-810-8005
## Ridgeway Garages (Newbury) Ltd
The Triangle, Newbury, Berkshire RG14 7HT
**Tel:** 01635264003 **Fax:** 01635569095
**Web:** www.ridgeway.co.uk
**Reg No:** 3297014 **Estd:** 1938 Private Limited Company
**Line of Business:** Car dealers (new & used)
**Trading Style:** Ridgeway Newbury
**Issued Capital:** £66,668
**Principals:** J F O'Hanlon *(Managing)*, D J Newman *(Managing)*, D S Taylor
**Co. Secretary:** Ms Katharine Newman
**Responsibilities**
**Senior:** John Head *(Manager)*, John Horsey *(Manager)*
**Admin:** Leanne Bowsher *(P.A. to the Chairman, CEO and)*
**IT:** Peter Jennings *(IT Manager)*
**Health & Safety:** Paul Lambert *(After Sales Manager)*
**Operations:** Paul Lambert *(After Sales Manager)*
**Branches:** Ridgeway Garages (Newbury) Ltd, Rose Kiln Lane, Reading, Berkshire RG2 0JZ
**US SIC:** 5511, 7539
**UK SIC:** 65100, 67100
**Auditors:** Grant Thornton
**Bankers:** National Westminster Bank Plc (60-14-55)

| | 31-12-13 | 31-12-12 | 31-12-11 |
|---|---|---|---|
| TO | 546,982,008 | 443,885,324 | 332,817,274 |
| P/L | 8,168,570 | 7,233,247 | 6,201,342 |
| NW | 30,577,716 | 24,960,985 | 21,060,887 |
| WC | 8,369,520 | 9,888,204 | 7,446,952 |
| Emp. | 1,085 | 1,010 | 823 |

DUNS 21-028-2643
## The Ridgeway Group
2 Oxford Road, Kidlington, Oxfordshire OX5 1AA
**Tel:** 01865566034
**Web:** www.oxford.audi.co.uk
**Estd:** 1999 Proprietorship
**Line of Business:** Sale of new motor vehicles
**Proprietor:** D Newman
**Responsibilities**
**Senior:** David Carde *(Dealer Principal)*, Alex Matschy *(Head Of Business)*, Dean Rolinski *(Parts Manager)*
**US SIC:** 5511 **UK SIC:** 65100
**Employees:** 50

DUNS 21-125-2887
## Ridgeway International Ltd
69 High Street, Wallingford, Oxfordshire OX10 0BX
**Web:** www.ridgewayinternational.com
**Reg No:** 1224746 **VAT No:** 614749723
**Estd:** 1975 Private Limited Company
**Line of Business:** Freight forwarders
**Issued Capital:** £5,070
**Principals:** C H Hawker *(Managing)*, E J Evelegh, K Flint, R G Williamson
**Co. Secretary:** Richard Garner
**Responsibilities**
**Senior:** Anthony Pearce *(Operations Manager)*
**IT:** Anthony Pearce *(Operations Manager)*
**Branches:** Ridgeway International Ltd, Cliff Jetty, Salt Lane Cliff, Rochester, Kent ME3 0XX
**US SIC:** 4712, 4411
**UK SIC:** 77002, 74001
**Auditors:** BDO LLP
**Bankers:** Lloyds TSB Bank plc (30-96-96)

| | 30-09-13 | 30-09-12 | 30-09-11 |
|---|---|---|---|
| TO | 12,829,561 | N/A | N/A |
| P/L | 2,668,012 | N/A | N/A |
| NW | 2,832,073 | 1,345,320 | 1,254,240 |
| WC | 2,757,593 | 1,270,359 | 1,210,145 |
| Emp. | 48 | N/A | N/A |

DUNS 21-778-8800
## The Ridgeway Primary School
Willow Gardens, Reading, Berkshire RG2 7EL
**Tel:** 01189015530
**Web:** www.theridgewayprimary.net
**Estd:** 1989 Proprietorship
**Line of Business:** Schools (local authority)
**Proprietor:** Miss S Hancock
**Responsibilities**
**Senior:** Madeleine Cosgrove *(Head Teacher)*
**Finance:** Louise Haynes *(Senior Finance Administrator)*
**Admin:** Sue Ambrose *(Secretary)*
**US SIC:** 8211 **UK SIC:** 93200
**Employees:** 50

DUNS 21-717-5021
## Ridgeway School
Moorland Road, Plymouth, Devon PL7 2RS
**Tel:** 01752338373 **Fax:** 01752331559
**Web:** www.ridgeway.plymouth.sch.uk
**Reg No:** 7561356 **Estd:** 1971 Private Company Limited By Guarantee
**Line of Business:** Schools (local authority)
**Directors:** Mrs R A Smith, Mrs R Boyask, P Hutchings, J E Didymus, A Harris, Mrs A Chapple, Mrs M Hall, Dr P G Barnwell
**Co. Secretary:** Mark Matthew
**Responsibilities**
**Senior:** Graham Blake-Lobb *(Manager)*, Patrick Maloney *(Manager)*, Alan Weekes *(Director)*
**US SIC:** 8211 **UK SIC:** 93200

| | 31-08-14 | 31-08-13 | 31-08-12 |
|---|---|---|---|
| TO | 5,730,959 | 6,495,457 | 22,631,757 |
| P/L | (231,244) | 125,913 | 13,665,627 |
| NW | 12,774,296 | 13,429,540 | 13,347,627 |
| WC | 1,090,448 | 979,583 | 834,331 |
| Emp. | 122 | 139 | 149 |

DUNS 21-734-6484
## The Ridgeway School Sixth Form College
Ridgeway School, Inverary Road, Swindon, Wiltshire SN4 9DJ
**Tel:** 01793813280
**Web:** www.ridgewayschool.com
**Reg No:** 7691947 **Estd:** 2011 Private Company Limited By Guarantee
**Line of Business:** General secondary education
**Directors:** Mrs R Cairns, S J James, M D Francis, Mrs J Davies, M R Pease, P C Bulman, R Gagan, Mrs S E Smith
**Responsibilities**
**Senior:** Arthur Amos *(Director)*, Andrew Capewell *(Director)*, Steven Colledge *(Director)*, Elizabeth Palfrey *(Director)*, James Povoas *(Director)*
**US SIC:** 8211 **UK SIC:** 93200
**Bankers:** Lloyds TSB Bank plc (30-18-86)

| | 31-08-14 | 31-08-13 | 31-08-12 |
|---|---|---|---|
| TO | 6,980,000 | 7,152,000 | 27,886,000 |
| P/L | (420,000) | (106,000) | 20,501,000 |
| NW | 19,583,000 | 20,304,000 | 20,391,000 |
| WC | 265,000 | 682,000 | 1,239,000 |
| Emp. | 195 | 207 | 207 |

DUNS 21-784-1045
## Ridgewood Community High School
Eastern Avenue, Burnley, Lancashire BB10 2AT
**Tel:** 01282682316
**Web:** www.ridgewood.lancs.sch.uk
**Estd:** 2011 Partnership
**Line of Business:** Schools (special)
**Partners:** Mrs F Entwistle, Mrs F Entwistle
**US SIC:** 8299 **UK SIC:** 93300
**Employees:** 80

DUNS 39-700-3393
## Riding Properties Ltd
The Riding Shopping Centre, Wakefield, West Yorkshire WF1 1DS
**Tel:** 01132574274
**Reg No:** 0958654 **Estd:** 1968 Private Limited Company
**Line of Business:** Other letting of own property
**Issued Capital:** £1,200
**Director:** Ms B S Gaunt
**Co. Secretary:** John Gaunt
**US SIC:** 6519 **UK SIC:** 85000
**Auditors:** Armstrong Watson
**Bankers:** HSBC Bank plc (40-24-32)

| | 31-07-13 | 31-07-12 | 31-07-11 |
|---|---|---|---|
| TA | 7,025,939 | 6,980,940 | 6,887,626 |
| NW | 6,872,784 | 6,828,192 | 6,703,313 |
| WC | 167,704 | 245,776 | 120,275 |

DUNS 21-151-1228
## The Ridings Federation of Academies Trust
High Street, Winterbourne, Bristol, Avon BS36 1JL
**Tel:** 01454252000
**Web:** www.trfwia.org.uk
**Reg No:** 6802948 **Estd:** 2009 Private Company Limited By Guarantee
**Line of Business:** Schools (foundation)
**Directors:** R J Westacott, A Lazarides, Mrs G M Cope, Dr J E Cook, C Smith, I A Butcher, P Moorhouse
**Co. Secretary:** Norman Duthie
**US SIC:** 8211 **UK SIC:** 93200
**Bankers:** National Westminster Bank Plc (01-00-61)

| | 31-08-14 | 31-08-13 | 31-08-12 |
|---|---|---|---|
| TO | 16,040,722 | 15,588,062 | 33,090,151 |
| P/L | (813,728) | (2,087,323) | 16,727,972 |
| NW | 29,468,766 | 30,401,495 | 32,050,817 |
| WC | 117,762 | 278,667 | 1,233,553 |
| Emp. | 322 | 321 | 304 |

DUNS 21-600-6480
## Ridley Arms
Stannington, Stannington, Stannington, Morpeth, Northumberland NE61 6EL
**Web:** www.ridleyarmsstannington.co.uk
**Estd:** 2000 Proprietorship
**Line of Business:** Managed public houses and bars
**Proprietor:** B Dixon
**Responsibilities**
**Senior:** Clair Potts *(Manager)*
**US SIC:** 5813 **UK SIC:** 66200
**Employees:** 40

DUNS 21-817-4951 **Imp-Exp**

## Rieke Packaging Systems Ltd

**(Subsidiary of:** Trimas Corporation)
44 Scudamore Road, Leicester, Leicestershire LE3 1UQ
**Tel:** 01162-331100
**Web:** www.riekepackaging.com
**Reg No:** 0291835 **VAT No:** 536283340
**Estd:** 1934 Private Limited Company
**Line of Business:** Manufacturers of packaging materials
**Export Markets:** E U, U S A
**Export Sales:** £12,229,000
**Trading Style:** Rieke Packaging System Englass
**Issued Capital:** £173,885
**Directors:** Ms L A Brooks, D M Wathen, M E Box, A M Zeffiro, J A Sherbin, J Bignall
**Responsibilities**
**IT:** Dean Hill *(IT Director)*
**HR:** Michaela Farthing *(Human Resources Manager)*
**Purchasing:** Daniel Wheeler *(Purchasing Manager)*
**US SIC:** 2654, 3999
**UK SIC:** 47280, 49590
**Auditors:** KPMG LLP
**Bankers:** Lloyds TSB Bank plc (30-94-97)

| | 31-12-13 | 31-12-12 | 31-12-11 |
|---|---|---|---|
| TO | 18,313,000 | 15,264,000 | 16,287,000 |
| P/L | 7,100,000 | 2,200,000 | 5,006,000 |
| NW | 8,126,000 | 12,841,000 | 14,259,000 |
| WC | 5,581,000 | 4,505,000 | 13,894,000 |
| Emp. | 72 | 78 | 83 |

DUNS 73-308-7113

## Riello Ups Ltd

**(Subsidiary of:** Recycling Pallets Srl)
Clywedog Road North Unit 50, Wrexham, Clwyd LL13 9XN
**Tel:** 01978729297 **Fax:** 01978-729290
**Web:** www.riello-ups.co.uk
**Reg No:** 4582458 **Estd:** 2003 Private Limited Company
**Line of Business:** Wind generation equipment and windmills
**Export Sales:** £597,668
**Trading Style:** Riello Ups
**Issued Capital:** £100,000
**Directors:** K R Wilson, F Passuello, R Facci
**Responsibilities**
**Senior:** Ennio Ambroso *(Manager)*
**IT:** Darryl Davies *(Sales Office Manager & IT Mana)*
**US SIC:** 4911 **UK SIC:** 16101
**Auditors:** RSM Tenon Audit Ltd

| | 31-12-13 | 31-12-12 | 31-12-11 |
|---|---|---|---|
| TO | 16,321,193 | 16,243,032 | 16,089,952 |
| P/L | 1,467,120 | 1,158,600 | 1,301,578 |
| NW | 5,082,703 | 4,634,894 | 3,639,875 |
| WC | 4,973,217 | 4,513,769 | 3,538,905 |
| Emp. | 49 | 48 | 41 |

DUNS 21-810-8219 **Imp**

## Rieter Automotive

Flush Mills, West Gate, Heckmondwike, West Yorkshire WF16 0EP
**Tel:** 08706066608
**Web:** www.rieter.com
**Estd:** 2012
**Line of Business:** Woven Carpet & Rug Manufacturers
**US SIC:** 2271 **UK SIC:** 43841
**Employees:** 350

DUNS 42-428-6727

## Rif Worldwide Plc

Unit 3 Radius Park Faggs Road, Feltham, Middlesex TW14 0NG
**Tel:** 02089 178850 **Fax:** 02089 178860
**Web:** www.rifworldwide.co.uk
**Reg No:** 4416179 **VAT No:** 799420384
**Estd:** 2007 Public Limited Company
**Line of Business:** Freight forwarders
**Issued Capital:** £50,500
**Directors:** M J Gilbert, S J Fox
**Co. Secretary:** Scott Sully
**Responsibilities**
**Finance:** Duncan Lebbern *(joint director)*
**Branches:** Rif Worldwide Plc, 16D Manchester International Office Centre, Styal Road, Manchester M22 5WB
**US SIC:** 4712 **UK SIC:** 77002
**Auditors:** Stiles & Co

| | 30-09-13 | 30-09-12 | 30-09-11 |
|---|---|---|---|
| TO | 14,431,804 | 13,719,104 | 13,729,191 |
| P/L | 782,165 | 690,680 | 768,757 |
| NW | 1,155,494 | 1,156,979 | 1,132,466 |
| WC | 1,101,604 | 1,136,837 | 1,121,149 |
| Emp. | 46 | 46 | 44 |

DUNS 21-167-6462

## Rifa Ltd

**(Subsidiary of:** Proav Holdings Ltd)
Asysco House, Omega Way, Egham, Surrey TW20 8RD
**Tel:** 01784487000
**Web:** www.rslav.com
**Reg No:** 6928886 **Estd:** 2009 Private Limited Company
**Line of Business:** Management activities of holding companies
**Export Sales:** £9,024,215
**Issued Capital:** £50,000
**Directors:** Mrs L Brookes, Mrs F Hazell, R J Brookes
**US SIC:** 6711 **UK SIC:** 83962

| | 31-03-14 | 31-03-13 | 31-03-12 |
|---|---|---|---|
| TO | 48,201,956 | 52,766,319 | 40,996,819 |
| P/L | 927,405 | 566,659 | 862,805 |
| NW | 1,840,070 | 1,758,904 | 1,755,839 |
| WC | (1,525,894) | 282,649 | 1,143,958 |
| Emp. | 233 | 199 | 180 |

DUNS 23-929-0377 **Imp**

## Rift & Co (Services) Ltd

**(Subsidiary of:** Rift & Co Ltd)
21 Old Street, Ashton-Under-Lyne, Lancashire OL6 6LA
**Tel:** 01613303876
**Web:** www.revolution-bars.co.uk
**Reg No:** 3918986 **Estd:** 2000 Private Limited Company
**Line of Business:** Retail sale of alcoholic and other beverages
**Issued Capital:** £1
**Directors:** A J Murray, C R Anderson
**US SIC:** 5921 **UK SIC:** 64200
**Bankers:** Bank Of Scotland (80-29-01)

| | 30-06-13 | 30-06-12 | 30-06-11 |
|---|---|---|---|
| TO | 111,619,000 | 106,090,000 | 94,899,000 |
| P/L | 1,649,000 | 6,196,000 | 5,303,000 |
| NW | 31,304,000 | 29,655,000 | 23,810,000 |
| WC | 31,623,000 | 32,006,000 | 31,156,000 |
| Emp. | 2,700 | 2,427 | 2,216 |

DUNS 73-252-4157

## Rig Medical Recruit Ltd

**(Subsidiary of:** Recruitment Investment Group Ltd)
South Tower, 26 Elmfield Road, Bromley, Kent BR1 1WA
**Tel:** 08453631187 **Fax:** 02082281349
**Web:** www.righealthcare.co.uk
**Reg No:** 4526207 **VAT No:** 928204724
**Estd:** 2009 Private Limited Company
**Line of Business:** Employment and recruitment companies and consultants
**Issued Capital:** £10,001
**Directors:** F C Kyriakos, B Lloyd, P Wareham, P P Flaherty
**Co. Secretary:** Stuart Goldup
**US SIC:** 7361 **UK SIC:** 83954
**Auditors:** Crane & Partners

| | 31-12-13 | 31-12-12 | 31-12-11 |
|---|---|---|---|
| TO | 20,271,927 | 14,986,957 | 14,524,965 |
| P/L | 317,697 | 122,970 | 20,896 |
| NW | 115,317 | 170,402 | 77,279 |
| WC | 93,328 | 167,844 | 75,003 |

DUNS 21-090-5436 **Imp**

## Rigby and Peller Ltd

**(Subsidiary of:** Ambo Holding Nv)
5 Portal Way Business Centre, London W3 6RT
**Tel:** 08450765545
**Web:** www.rigbyandpeller.co.uk
**Reg No:** 0707368 **VAT No:** 218198646
**Estd:** 1961 Private Limited Company
**Line of Business:** Lingerie retail
**Issued Capital:** £2,500
**Principals:** D H Kenton *(Managing)*, Mrs J S Kenton *(Financial)*, M Miller, Ebvba 4f, Herman Van De Velde Nv, D De Vos
**Responsibilities**
**Senior:** Dirk de Vos *(Director)*
**Marketing:** Caroline Noble *(Marketing & PR Manager)*
**Operations:** Dita Summerfield *(Operations Director)*
**US SIC:** 5714 **UK SIC:** 64700
**Auditors:** Ernst & Young LLP
**Bankers:** Barclays Bank Plc (20-06-05)

| | 31-12-13 | 31-12-12 | 31-12-11 |
|---|---|---|---|
| TO | 9,231,623 | 9,175,938 | 8,902,832 |
| P/L | (59,843) | 27,539 | (520,262) |
| NW | 1,348,346 | 1,587,323 | 1,660,016 |
| WC | 409,853 | 419,372 | 337,006 |
| Emp. | 96 | 84 | 112 |

DUNS 53-632-2217

## Rigby Group (Rg) Plc

James House, Warwick Road, Birmingham, West Midlands B11 2LE
**Tel:** 01217667000
**Web:** www.rigbygroupplc.com
**Reg No:** 3437118 **Estd:** 1997 Public Limited Company
**Line of Business:** Computer support & services
**Export Sales:** £984,676,000
**Issued Capital:** £6,178,095
**Directors:** H W Campion, Mrs P A Rigby, S P Rigby, J P Rigby, Sir P Rigby
**Co. Secretary:** Owen Williams
**US SIC:** 7379 **UK SIC:** 83940
**Auditors:** Deloitte LLP
**Bankers:** HSBC Bank plc (40-00-00)
**Following financial data are in thousands**

| | 31-03-14 | 31-03-13 | 31-03-12 |
|---|---|---|---|
| TO | 1,782,641 | 2,201,683 | 2,761,715 |
| P/L | 9,624 | 108,809 | 29,427 |
| NW | 221,947 | 258,146 | 146,898 |
| WC | 125,974 | 186,939 | 91,029 |
| Emp. | 5,573 | 4,904 | 5,094 |

DUNS 39-818-0810

## Rigg Construction (Southern) Ltd

Lancaster House, Lancaster Park Industrial Estate, Bowerhill, Melksham, Wiltshire SN12 6TT
**Tel:** 01225-705668
**Web:** www.riggconstruction.co.uk
**Reg No:** 2217116 **VAT No:** 452782532
**Estd:** 1988 Private Limited Company
**Line of Business:** Building construction contractors
**Issued Capital:** £100
**Principals:** P K Rigg *(Managing)*, Mrs D Tristram
**Co. Secretary:** Philip Rigg
**US SIC:** 1522, 1541, 1799
**UK SIC:** 50100, 50000
**Auditors:** O'Hara Wood Ltd
**Bankers:** National Westminster Bank Plc (52-21-30)

| | 31-12-13 | 31-12-12 | 31-12-11 |
|---|---|---|---|
| TA | 1,908,071 | 1,724,216 | 1,838,432 |
| NW | 691,467 | 652,445 | 666,513 |
| WC | (99,001) | (14,227) | (115,825) |

DUNS 23-713-4916

## The Right Car (Uk) Ltd

**(Subsidiary of:** Right Car Holdings (Uk) Ltd)
Clough Road, Hull, North Humberside HU6 7PL
**Tel:** 01482887577 **Fax:** 01482-679989
**Web:** www.rightcarford.co.uk
**Reg No:** 3708461 **Estd:** 1999 Private Limited Company
**Line of Business:** Sale of new motor vehicles
**Trading Style:** The Right Car (Uk) Ltd
**Issued Capital:** £70,000
**Managing Director:** S A Kamis
**Co. Secretary:** Mike Jackson
**Responsibilities**
**IT:** Mike Crosier *(IT Manager)*
**Health & Safety:** Shaun Coulson *(Health & Safety Officer)*
**Branches:** The Right Car (Uk) Ltd, Clough Road, Hull, North Humberside HU6 7PL
**US SIC:** 5511, 5521, 7539
**UK SIC:** 65100, 67100
**Auditors:** Ernst & Young
**Bankers:** National Westminster Bank Plc (60-02-23)

| | 31-05-13 | 31-05-12 | 31-05-11 |
|---|---|---|---|
| TO | 25,350,503 | 18,682,195 | 18,575,713 |
| P/L | 1,080,553 | 708,909 | 717,631 |
| NW | 3,159,388 | 2,763,309 | 2,341,969 |
| WC | 111,695 | 506,529 | 641,014 |
| Emp. | 94 | 74 | 77 |

DUNS 73-998-3026

## Right Care (Lancashire) Ltd

**(Subsidiary of:** Littleton Hall Ltd)
55 Hoole Road, Chester, Cheshire CH2 3NJ
**Tel:** 01282-424240 **Fax:** 01282835579
**Web:** www.homecareburnley.co.uk
**Reg No:** 5248664 **Estd:** 2007 Private Limited Company
**Line of Business:** Home care service providers
**Issued Capital:** £2
**Directors:** Mrs H R Wyatt, R O Wyatt
**US SIC:** 8091 **UK SIC:** 95200

| | 31-03-14 | 31-03-13 | 31-03-12 |
|---|---|---|---|
| TA | 638,430 | 743,745 | 748,743 |
| NW | 459,787 | 420,393 | 372,091 |
| WC | 429,651 | 408,426 | 380,573 |

DUNS 21-098-1745

## Right Choice Insurance Brokers Ltd

Bank Chambers, 180 Main Road, Romford, Essex RM2 5HX
**Tel:** 01708-380370
**Web:** www.rcib.co.uk
**Reg No:** 6423401 **Estd:** 2007 Private Limited Company
**Line of Business:** Insurance companies and agents
**Issued Capital:** £975
**Directors:** D J Joseph, R C Bignell
**Co. Secretary:** Michael Joseph
**US SIC:** 6399 **UK SIC:** 82001

| | 31-12-13 | 31-12-12 | 31-12-11 |
|---|---|---|---|
| TO | 5,868,489 | N/A | N/A |
| P/L | 3,077,036 | N/A | N/A |
| NW | 1,452,383 | 1,506,244 | 1,104,275 |
| WC | 1,283,790 | 1,419,460 | 1,067,709 |
| Emp. | 118 | N/A | N/A |

DUNS 21-163-8855

## Right Guard Security Uk Ltd

34 Simmonds Road, Wincheap Industrial Estate, Canterbury, Kent CT1 3RA
**Tel:** 01227464588
**Web:** www.rightguard.co.uk
**Reg No:** 6900006 **VAT No:** 982201727
**Estd:** 2009 Private Limited Company
**Line of Business:** Security and related activities
**Issued Capital:** £100
**Director:** A G Smith
**Co. Secretary:** Sameday Company Services Ltd
**US SIC:** 7393 **UK SIC:** 83954

| | 31-03-14 | 31-03-13 | 31-03-12 |
|---|---|---|---|
| TA | 426,526 | 363,316 | 303,818 |
| NW | 252,002 | 198,625 | 139,572 |
| WC | 193,896 | 131,530 | 63,717 |

DUNS 21-163-8002 **Exp**

## Right Management Ltd

**(Subsidiary of:** Manpowergroup Inc.)
75 King William Street, London EC4N 7BE
**Tel:** 020-7469-6660 **Fax:** 020-7469-6770
**Web:** www.right.com
**Reg No:** 1479160 **Estd:** 1908 Private Limited Company
**Line of Business:** Business and management consultancy activities not elsewhere classified
**Export Markets:** E U
**Issued Capital:** £100
**Directors:** R S Gorton, R Schaefer, J T Andringa, I C Symes
**Co. Secretary:** Ross Gorton
**Responsibilities**
**Finance:** Robert Creswell *(Financial Director)*
**Branches:** Right Management Ltd, Alteus House, 1 North Fourth Street, Milton Keynes, Buckinghamshire MK9 1NE
**US SIC:** 7392 **UK SIC:** 83951
**Auditors:** Deloitte & Touche LLP
**Bankers:** National Westminster Bank Plc (60-30-06)

| | 31-12-13 | 31-12-12 | 31-12-11 |
|---|---|---|---|
| TO | 29,551,000 | 27,646,000 | 26,831,000 |
| P/L | 4,091,000 | 1,023,000 | 938,000 |
| NW | 22,658,000 | 18,751,000 | 17,578,000 |
| WC | 22,868,000 | 19,381,000 | 18,209,000 |
| Emp. | 229 | 223 | 252 |

DUNS 23-280-0115

## Right Medicine Pharmacy Ltd

Unit 11 Fenlake Business Centre, Peterborough, Cambridgeshire PE1 5BQ
**Tel:** 01733 311349
**Web:** www.carehomemedicines.net
**Reg No:** 0228623SC **Estd:** 2012 Private Limited Company
**Line of Business:** Dispensing chemists
**Issued Capital:** £95
**Directors:** N J Wicks, J Burton
**Co. Secretary:** Michael Embrey
**Responsibilities**
**Senior:** Riaz Kauser *(Manager)*
**Branches:** Right Medicine Pharmacy Ltd, 71 Newton Church Road, Dalkeith, Midlothian EH22 1LX
**US SIC:** 5912, 5999
**UK SIC:** 64300, 65600
**Auditors:** Condie & Co
**Bankers:** National Westminster Bank Plc (53-61-30)

| | 28-02-14 | 28-02-13 | 29-02-12 |
|---|---|---|---|
| TO | 7,912,878 | 8,007,479 | 10,382,155 |
| P/L | 168,483 | 151,839 | 265,363 |
| NW | (1,168,697) | (1,371,446) | (1,636,492) |
| WC | 657,823 | (23,132) | (101,017) |
| Emp. | 79 | 78 | 72 |

DUNS 21-659-3445

## Right Security & Retail Skills Ltd

5th Floor, The Tower Building, 11 York Road, Waterloo, London SE1 7NX
**Tel:** 08458487074 **Fax:** 08458387374
**Web:** www.rightskills.co.uk
**Reg No:** 7154333 **Estd:** 2010 Private Limited Company
**Line of Business:** Hardware consultancy
**Issued Capital:** £2
**Directors:** S Ali, Ms M Adil
**US SIC:** 7379, 6111
**UK SIC:** 83940, 81501

| | 28-02-14 | 28-02-13 | 28-02-12 |
|---|---|---|---|
| TA | 497,663 | 50,663 | 2 |
| NW | (275,257) | 6,442 | 2 |
| WC | (290,856) | (13,056) | N/A |

DUNS 21-035-7910
## Right to Health
Crown House, Home Gardens, Dartford, Kent DA1 1DZ
**Tel:** 01322424605
**Web:** www.righttohealth.co.uk
**Estd:** 2010 Proprietorship
**Line of Business:** Health insurance services
**US SIC:** 6399 **UK SIC:** 82001
**Employees:** 50

DUNS 21-687-0890
## Rightio Ltd
66 Hagley Road, Birmingham, West Midlands B16 8PF
**Fax:** 01214107001
**Web:** www.tradetek.co.uk
**Reg No:** 7357774 **Estd:** 2000 Private Limited Company
**Line of Business:** Plumbers
**Issued Capital:** £100
**Directors:** K A Tulloch, C J Carswell
**Co. Secretary:** Christopher Carswell
**US SIC:** 1711 **UK SIC:** 50300

| | 30-09-13 | 30-09-12 | 30-09-11 |
|---|---|---|---|
| TA | 1,087,134 | 247,919 | 108,344 |
| NW | 51,850 | (51,303) | 17,405 |
| WC | 221,437 | (61,611) | 11,101 |

DUNS 51-990-9258
## Rightmove Group Ltd
(**Subsidiary of:** Rightmove Plc)
Grafton Court, Snowdon Drive, Winterhill, Milton Keynes, Buckinghamshire MK6 1AJ
**Tel:** 01908308500 **Fax:** 0845-330-2311
**Web:** www.rightmove.co.uk
**Reg No:** 3997679 **Estd:** 2000 Private Limited Company
**Line of Business:** Interactive broadcasting
**Issued Capital:** £1,294,000
**Directors:** Ms R Perriss, N J Mckittrick, P Brooks-Johnson
**Co. Secretary:** Mrs Jennifer Warburton
**Branches:** Rightmove Group Ltd, 157 Piccadilly, London W1J 9EA
**US SIC:** 7379, 7374
**UK SIC:** 83940
**Auditors:** KPMG Audit PLC

| | 31-12-13 | 31-12-12 | 31-12-11 |
|---|---|---|---|
| TO | 139,935,000 | 119,365,000 | 97,017,000 |
| P/L | 141,106,000 | 103,118,000 | 85,795,000 |
| NW | 43,129,000 | 62,839,000 | 157,605,000 |
| WC | 24,966,000 | 14,105,000 | 103,174,000 |
| Emp. | 346 | 325 | 290 |

DUNS 77-456-1419
## Rightstepcareers Ltd
Council House, Earl Street, Coventry, West Midlands CV1 5RR
**Tel:** 01926461600 **Fax:** 02476230165
**Web:** www.cswp.org.uk
**Reg No:** 2960454 **Estd:** 1994 Private Limited Company
**Line of Business:** Labour recruitment and provision of personnel
**Directors:** C Ridge, P A Deeley, A I Hardy, P A Tolley
**Co. Secretary:** Ms Linda Gilleard
**Branches:** Coventry Solihull & Warwickshire Partnership Ltd, 16 Smalley Pl, Kenilworth, Warwickshire CV8 1QG
**US SIC:** 7361 **UK SIC:** 83954
**Auditors:** HLB Kidsons

| | 31-03-14 | 31-03-13 | 31-03-12 |
|---|---|---|---|
| TO | N/A | N/A | 12,320,618 |
| P/L | 755,050 | 47,059 | 998,758 |
| NW | (11,876,612) | (14,601,455) | (10,708,144) |
| WC | 1,329,371 | 714,551 | 914,151 |
| Emp. | 173 | 177 | 199 |

DUNS 21-727-1011
## Rightster Ltd
(**Subsidiary of:** Rightster Group Plc)
1 Neal Street, Covent Garden, London WC2H 9QL
**Tel:** 02071-834-545
**Web:** www.rightster.com
**Reg No:** 7634543 **Estd:** 2011 Private Limited Company
**Line of Business:** Film distributors
**Issued Capital:** £3,347
**Directors:** M C Broughton, C S Muirhead, J A Barnett, P J Walker
**Co. Secretary:** Gerard Cranley
**Responsibilities**
**Senior:** Jez Coyle *(Solutions Delivery Director)*, Charl De Beer *(Manager)*
**Finance:** Niall Dore *(Group Chief Financial Officer)*, Dennis Muirhead *(Financial Director)*
**IT:** Jez Coyle *(Solutions Delivery Director)*, Steve Larson *(IT Manager)*
**US SIC:** 7829 **UK SIC:** 97112
**Auditors:** Rawlinson & Hunter

| | 31-12-13 | 31-03-12 |
|---|---|---|
| TO | 1,043,384 | 325,403 |
| P/L | (18,513,432) | (2,886,347) |
| NW | (5,271,645) | (1,883,014) |
| WC | (8,067,238) | (1,960,959) |
| Emp. | 106 | N/A |

DUNS 21-623-2112
## Rigid Charta Ltd
(**Subsidiary of:** Stichting Administratiekantoor Packaging Investmen)
Stoke Albany Road Desborough, Kettering, Northamptonshire NN14 2SR
**Tel:** 01536760266
**Web:** www.rigid.co.uk
**Reg No:** 7035324 **Estd:** 2009 Private Limited Company
**Line of Business:** Manufacture of paper and paperboard
**Issued Capital:** £100
**Directors:** L O Maynard, R J Coward
**Co. Secretary:** Lars Maynard
**US SIC:** 2631 **UK SIC:** 47017
**Bankers:** Barclays Bank Plc (20-17-19)

| | 31-12-13 | 31-12-12 | 31-12-11 |
|---|---|---|---|
| TO | N/A | 3,386,270 | 3,069,555 |
| P/L | N/A | 53,116 | (83,403) |
| NW | (783,002) | (763,220) | (814,645) |
| WC | (988,050) | (968,828) | (941,505) |
| Emp. | N/A | 30 | 26 |

DUNS 22-118-2954
## Rigisystems Ltd
(**Subsidiary of:** Rigisystems International Ltd)
Unit 62, Worcester, Worcestershire WR3 8ZJ
**Tel:** 01905 750 500 **Fax:** 01905 750 555
**Web:** www.rigisystems.org
**Reg No:** 4137351 **VAT No:** 632196152
**Estd:** 2001 Private Limited Company
**Line of Business:** Roofing contracting services
**Issued Capital:** £648,148
**Principals:** P Taylor *(Managing)*, G Rankin, M Walder, S C Neale, J R Williams
**Co. Secretary:** Simon Neale
**US SIC:** 1761 **UK SIC:** 50400
**Auditors:** Crowe Clark Whitehill LLP
**Bankers:** Bank Of Scotland (12-05-65)

| | 30-04-13 | 30-04-12 | 30-04-11 |
|---|---|---|---|
| TO | 16,254,159 | 19,095,527 | 18,975,317 |
| P/L | (58,165) | 612,333 | 851,449 |
| NW | 7,104,003 | 7,137,377 | 6,647,344 |
| WC | 6,805,271 | 6,796,900 | 6,244,929 |
| Emp. | 66 | 74 | 71 |

DUNS 21-005-2514
## Rigmar Services Ltd
Hareness Circle, Altens Industrial Estate, Aberdeen, Aberdeenshire AB12 3LY
**Tel:** 01224243000
**Web:** www.rigmar.co.uk
**Reg No:** 0327164SC **Estd:** 2007 Private Limited Company
**Line of Business:** Service activities incidental to oil and gas extraction excluding surveying
**Export Sales:** £934,912
**Issued Capital:** £123
**Directors:** G Macgregor, R Dalziel, K W Nelson
**Co. Secretary:** Burness Paull Llp
**US SIC:** 1389 **UK SIC:** 13000
**Bankers:** Clydesdale Bank Plc (82-40-00)

| | 31-12-13 | 31-12-12 | 31-12-11 |
|---|---|---|---|
| TO | 28,412,995 | 8,227,559 | N/A |
| P/L | 640,268 | 342,145 | N/A |
| NW | 1,247,176 | 606,522 | 475,856 |
| WC | 38,562 | (42,275) | 190,022 |
| Emp. | 69 | 41 | N/A |

DUNS 34-781-0330 Imp
## Rignet Uk Ltd
(**Subsidiary of:** Rignet Uk Holdings Ltd)
Nessco House Discovery Drive, Arnhall Business Park, Westhill, Aberdeenshire AB32 6FG
**Tel:** 01224-442100
**Web:** www.rig.net
**Reg No:** 0291250SC **Estd:** 2005 Private Limited Company
**Line of Business:** Telecom consultants
**Directors:** A J Byers, Ms S Watson, J Crenshaw, J Perez
**Co. Secretary:** Maclay Murray & Spens Llp
**US SIC:** 4899, 7394
**UK SIC:** 79020, 84000
**Auditors:** Johnston Carmichael LLP
**Employees:** 18
**Turnover:** £33,335,235

DUNS 23-693-4832
## Rikkyo School
Guildford Road, Rudgwick, Horsham, West Sussex RH12 3BE
**Tel:** 01403-822107
**Web:** www.rikkyo.w-sussex.sch.uk
**Estd:** 1972
**Line of Business:** General secondary education
**Chairman:** H Nagata
**Responsibilities**
**Senior:** Roger Munechika *(Head Teacher)*
**US SIC:** 8211 **UK SIC:** 93200
**Employees:** 100

DUNS 21-818-9348
## Rilmac Holdings Ltd
Crofton Drive, Allenby Road Industrial Estate, Lincoln, Lincolnshire LN3 4NJ
**Tel:** 01522781441
**Web:** www.rilmac.co.uk
**Reg No:** 0587816 **Estd:** 1954 Private Limited Company
**Line of Business:** Scaffolds and work platform erectors
**Issued Capital:** £2,200
**Principals:** P K Walker *(Managing)*, S A Baxter
**Co. Secretary:** Ms Nicola Walker
**Responsibilities**
**Senior:** Mick Quincey *(Director of Fabrication)*
**Marketing:** Dave Stephenson *(Sales & Marketing Manager)*
**Sales:** Dave Stephenson *(Sales & Marketing Manager)*
**Operations:** Terry Curry *(Director of Frabrication)*
**Engineering:** Mick Quincey *(Director of Fabrication)*
**Branches:** Rilmac Holdings Ltd, Crofton Drive, Lincoln, Lincolnshire LN3 4NJ
**US SIC:** 6711, 1799, 1731
**UK SIC:** 83962, 50000, 50300
**Auditors:** Streets & Co
**Bankers:** National Westminster Bank Plc (60-13-15)

| | 31-08-13 | 31-08-12 | 31-08-11 |
|---|---|---|---|
| TO | 15,912,342 | 16,086,636 | 17,474,130 |
| P/L | 57,365 | 483,913 | 639,037 |
| NW | 3,093,888 | 3,170,320 | 2,878,299 |
| WC | 577,970 | 596,678 | 361,634 |
| Emp. | 222 | 218 | 219 |

DUNS 21-914-4581
## Rilmac Insulation Ltd
(**Subsidiary of:** Rilmac Holdings Ltd)
Crofton Drive, Allenby Road Industrial Estate, Lincoln, Lincolnshire LN3 4NJ
**Tel:** 01522-531711
**Web:** www.rilmac.co.uk
**Reg No:** 1022984 **VAT No:** 365016272
**Estd:** 1954 Private Limited Company
**Line of Business:** Insulation installers
**Trading Style:** Rilmac Group
**Issued Capital:** £8,100
**Directors:** S R Finn, P K Walker, M A Woods, S A Baxter
**Co. Secretary:** Ms Nicola Walker
**Responsibilities**
**Senior:** Lee Hodgkins *(Area Manager)*
**US SIC:** 1742 **UK SIC:** 50400
**Auditors:** Streets Audit LLP
**Bankers:** National Westminster Bank Plc (60-13-15)

| | 31-08-13 | 31-08-12 | 31-08-11 |
|---|---|---|---|
| TA | 1,873,233 | 1,992,648 | 2,069,045 |
| NW | 125,682 | 114,688 | 104,155 |
| WC | (271,582) | (325,213) | (289,858) |

DUNS 42-465-6721
## R.I.M. Fabrications Ltd
East Leschangie, Kintore, Kintore, Inverurie, Aberdeenshire AB51 0XX
**Tel:** 01467-642582 **Fax:** 01467-642319
**Web:** www.rim.uk.com
**Reg No:** 0232360SC **Estd:** 1976 Private Limited Company
**Line of Business:** Steel fabricators
**Issued Capital:** £300,000
**Principals:** N R Mcdonald *(Managing)*, Ms F Booth
**Co. Secretary:** Lc Secretaries Limited
**Responsibilities**
**Senior:** Iain McDonald *(Manager)*, Roger McDonald *(Manager)*
**Finance:** Nancy McDonald *(Finance Director)*
**US SIC:** 1622, 1541, 1799
**UK SIC:** 50200, 50100, 50000
**Auditors:** Hall Morrice

| | 31-07-13 | 31-07-12 | 31-07-11 |
|---|---|---|---|
| TO | 9,973,340 | 13,615,600 | 13,710,172 |
| P/L | 28,988 | (700,630) | (649,375) |
| NW | 3,686,444 | 3,670,064 | 2,736,765 |
| WC | (890,815) | (1,150,504) | (477,631) |
| Emp. | 85 | 97 | 93 |

DUNS 29-870-4081 Exp
## Rim Plastics Technology Ltd
1 Wollaston Way, Burnt Mills Industrial Estate, Basildon, Essex SS13 1DJ
**Tel:** 01268729679 **Fax:** 01268-729031
**Web:** www.rimplas.co.uk
**Reg No:** 2073596 **VAT No:** 451918636
**Estd:** 1986 Private Limited Company
**Line of Business:** Manufacture of other plastic products
**Export Markets:** U S A
**Issued Capital:** £3,076
**Principals:** R K Whyte *(Managing)*, A Hills
**Responsibilities**
**Senior:** Ken Whyte *(Manager)*
**Finance:** Ken Whyte *(Manager)*
**Marketing:** Ken Whyte *(Manager)*
**Facilities:** Ken Whyte *(Manager)*
**US SIC:** 3079 **UK SIC:** 48360
**Auditors:** Edmund Carr
**Bankers:** National Westminster Bank Plc (56-00-47)

| | 31-12-13 | 31-12-12 | 31-12-11 |
|---|---|---|---|
| TO | 5,249,019 | 5,261,774 | N/A |
| P/L | 724,964 | 664,176 | N/A |
| NW | 2,883,970 | 2,383,787 | 1,973,887 |
| WC | 1,278,519 | 968,568 | 602,346 |
| Emp. | 66 | 58 | N/A |

DUNS 21-583-6460
## Rim Tec
Unit 2c & 3 Railway Sidings, Station Approach, Meopham, Gravesend, Kent DA13 0LT
**Tel:** 01474813919
**Web:** www.rimtecrefurbs.co.uk
**Estd:** 2011 Proprietorship
**Line of Business:** Garage related services
**Proprietor:** Mrs J Watts
**US SIC:** 7539 **UK SIC:** 67100
**Employees:** 62

DUNS 73-449-4151
## Rima Uk Ltd
(**Subsidiary of:** Rima Spa)
Unit 2 Rashs Green, Dereham, Norfolk NR19 1JG
**Tel:** 01362-697772
**Web:** www.rima-uk.com
**Reg No:** 4713781 **Estd:** 2003 Private Limited Company
**Line of Business:** Agricultural merchants
**Export Sales:** £2,737,072
**Issued Capital:** £162,400
**Principals:** A Monfardini *(Managing)*, R Faganelli, G Zonta, C Salvi
**Co. Secretary:** Miss Sarah Conti
**Responsibilities**
**Finance:** Anita Cook *(Accounts Manager)*
**US SIC:** 0729, 5199
**UK SIC:** 01003, 61900
**Auditors:** N.J. Smart & Co
**Bankers:** HSBC Bank plc (40-20-08)

| | 31-12-13 | 31-12-12 | 31-12-11 |
|---|---|---|---|
| TO | 3,851,061 | N/A | N/A |
| P/L | 630,343 | N/A | N/A |
| NW | 1,315,499 | 512,309 | 168,205 |
| WC | 563,643 | 434,744 | 184,433 |
| Emp. | 99 | N/A | N/A |

DUNS 23-863-9285 Imp
## Rimes Technologies Ltd
(**Subsidiary of:** Rimes Technologies Corporation)
1 Cornhill, London EC3V 3ND
**Tel:** 02077436040
**Web:** www.rimes.com
**Reg No:** 3855448 **Estd:** 2012 Private Limited Company
**Line of Business:** Data information services
**Export Sales:** £6,382,423
**Issued Capital:** £1,000
**Director:** F Mancuso
**Co. Secretary:** Christian Fauvelais
**US SIC:** 7399 **UK SIC:** 83954
**Auditors:** Sedley Richard Laurence Voulters
**Bankers:** Barclays Bank Plc (20-19-90)

| | 31-12-13 | 31-12-12 | 31-12-11 |
|---|---|---|---|
| TO | 16,072,026 | 13,488,333 | 11,950,231 |
| P/L | 2,183,001 | 2,264,575 | 1,739,329 |
| NW | 5,230,062 | 3,281,331 | 1,946,277 |
| WC | 4,914,448 | 3,049,785 | 1,483,335 |
| Emp. | 107 | 88 | 82 |

DUNS 22-669-2515 Imp-Exp
## Rimmer Bros. Ltd
Triumph House, Sleaford Road, Bracebridge Heath, Lincoln, Lincolnshire LN4 2NA
**Tel:** 01522-568000
**Web:** www.rimmerbros.co.uk
**Reg No:** 2155394 **VAT No:** 352847340
**Estd:** 1982 Private Limited Company
**Line of Business:** Maintenance and repair of motor vehicles
**Export Markets:** Worlwide
**Issued Capital:** £211,136
**Principals:** W H Rimmer *(Managing)*, C G Rimmer, Ms G L Rimmer
**Co. Secretary:** William Rimmer
**Responsibilities**
**IT:** Richard Caunt *(IT Manager)*
**US SIC:** 7539, 5531
**UK SIC:** 67100, 65100
**Auditors:** Bentley Jennison
**Bankers:** National Westminster Bank Plc (54-10-23)

| | 31-05-13 | 31-05-12 | 31-05-11 |
|---|---|---|---|
| TO | 10,673,597 | 10,283,235 | 9,202,316 |
| P/L | 945,277 | 915,340 | 295,358 |
| NW | 788,518 | 758,501 | 295,638 |
| WC | 449,270 | 964,887 | 534,866 |
| Emp. | 62 | 59 | 60 |

DUNS 54-858-6007
## Rimmers Taxis
2 Formby Bypass, Formby, Liverpool, Merseyside L37 8EH
**Tel:** 01704-831212
**Estd:** 1991 Proprietorship
**Line of Business:** Taxi operation
**Proprietor:** T Berry
**Responsibilities**
**Senior:** Dave Johnson *(Proprietor)*
**US SIC:** 4121, 7512
**UK SIC:** 72200, 84801
**Employees:** 47

DUNS 77-517-7082 Exp
## Rimor Ltd
(**Subsidiary of:** Lloyds Banking Group Plc)
Denmead Industrial Estate, Forest Road, Denmead, Waterlooville, Hampshire PO7 6TJ
**Tel:** 02392-264063
**Web:** www.rimor.co.uk
**Reg No:** 2987112 **Estd:** 1994 Private Limited Company
**Line of Business:** Engineers (general)
**Export Sales:** £1,399,006
**Issued Capital:** £210,308
**Directors:** P Mason, K P Fry, S M Bushby
**Co. Secretary:** Scott Bushby
**Responsibilities**
**Senior:** Geoffrey Mullis *(Manager)*, Glenn Musson *(Manager)*, Julie Riley *(Company Director)*, Christopher Riley *(Chief Executive Officer)*
**Purchasing:** Steve Tuffs *(Purchasing Manager)*
**US SIC:** 8911 **UK SIC:** 83701
**Auditors:** Grant Thornton UK LLP
**Bankers:** National Westminster Bank Plc (54-30-11)

| | 31-12-13 | 31-12-12 | 31-12-11 |
|---|---|---|---|
| TO | 18,428,973 | 14,208,070 | 11,985,429 |
| P/L | 2,181,532 | 1,755,065 | 669,959 |
| NW | 8,038,854 | 6,306,501 | 5,156,902 |
| WC | 6,935,058 | 4,455,833 | 2,731,824 |
| Emp. | 119 | 114 | 104 |

DUNS 50-690-3764
## Ring & Ride Coventry
Unit 10-11, Henley Industrial Park, Henley Road, Coventry, West Midlands CV2 1ST
**Tel:** 024-7660-2177
**Web:** www.wmsnt.org
**Estd:** 1989
**Line of Business:** Disability services
**US SIC:** 8699 **UK SIC:** 96902
**Employees:** 70

DUNS 21-782-2186
## Ring & Ride South Birmingham
Unit 2-4 Arden Park Arden Road, Rubery, Rednal, Birmingham, West Midlands B45 0JA
**Tel:** 01214539382
**Web:** www.ringandride.org
**Estd:** 2011 Proprietorship
**Line of Business:** Charities and charitable organisations
**Proprietor:** Mrs J Webb
**Responsibilities**
**Senior:** Jim Macguire *(Deputy Manager)*
**US SIC:** 8321 **UK SIC:** 96111
**Employees:** 90

DUNS 71-923-9480 Imp
## Ring Automotive Ltd
(**Subsidiary of:** Elysian Capital I Lp)
Volvox House, Gelderd Road, Leeds, West Yorkshire LS12 6NA
**Tel:** 01132132000 **Fax:** 01122-630475
**Web:** www.ringautomotive.co.uk
**Reg No:** 5305131 **Estd:** 2012 Private Limited Company
**Line of Business:** Car accessories and parts
**Export Sales:** £8,288,000
**Issued Capital:** £2,800,000
**Directors:** J F Skalski, Ms K N Hawkins, J M Hall
**Responsibilities**
**Senior:** Nick Cameron *(Senior Marketing Executive)*
**Marketing:** Nick Cameron *(Senior Marketing Executive)*
**US SIC:** 5531 **UK SIC:** 65100
**Auditors:** KPMG LLP

| | 30-09-13 | 30-09-12 | 30-09-11 |
|---|---|---|---|
| TO | 33,878,000 | 30,221,000 | 29,396,000 |
| P/L | 3,173,000 | 2,487,000 | 2,216,000 |
| NW | 7,576,000 | 7,618,000 | 6,258,000 |
| WC | 6,921,000 | 6,997,000 | 5,617,000 |
| Emp. | 124 | 121 | 119 |

DUNS 29-892-1966
## Ring Road Garage Ltd
Unit 5 Gawcott Road, Buckingham, Buckinghamshire MK18 1DR
**Tel:** 01280814741
**Web:** www.ringroadgarage.co.uk
**Reg No:** 2095240 **VAT No:** 460971534
**Estd:** 1977 Private Limited Company
**Line of Business:** Maintenance and repair of motor vehicles
**Issued Capital:** £100
**Principals:** S Chalmers *(Managing)*, Mrs N L Chalmers
**Responsibilities**
**Senior:** Harry Chalmers *(Manager)*
**US SIC:** 7539 **UK SIC:** 67100
**Auditors:** M Knights & Co Ltd
**Bankers:** Lloyds TSB Bank plc (30-91-39)

| | 31-07-13 | 31-07-12 | 31-07-11 |
|---|---|---|---|
| TA | 1,897,030 | 2,264,746 | 2,453,144 |
| NW | 1,452,872 | 1,841,586 | 2,163,724 |
| WC | 776,869 | 1,256,557 | 1,568,649 |

DUNS 73-403-7802 Imp
## RiNG2 Communications Ltd
Token House 11 12, London EC2R 7AS
**Tel:** 02036173180 **Fax:** 02070332766
**Web:** www.ring2.com
**Reg No:** 4677393 **Estd:** 2003 Private Limited Company
**Line of Business:** Telecommunications
**Export Sales:** £3,465,000
**Issued Capital:** £116,816
**Directors:** M Reynolds, A Scott, T M Hughes, S G Flavell, N R Goulet Wright, B Meftah
**Co. Secretary:** Robert Baugh
**US SIC:** 4899, 7392
**UK SIC:** 79020, 83951
**Auditors:** BDO LLP

| | 31-12-13 | 31-12-12 | 31-12-11 |
|---|---|---|---|
| TO | 6,049,000 | 4,940,000 | 4,225,000 |
| P/L | (2,273,000) | (2,301,000) | (503,000) |
| NW | (2,760,000) | (334,000) | (1,745,000) |
| WC | (1,260,000) | 243,000 | (1,888,000) |
| Emp. | 76 | 63 | 40 |

DUNS 37-851-4723
## Ringley Ltd
349 Royal College Street, Camden Town, London NW1 9QS
**Fax:** 02074281971
**Web:** www.ringley.co.uk
**Reg No:** 3302438 **Estd:** 1997 Private Limited Company
**Line of Business:** Engineering related scientific and technical consulting activities
**Trading Style:** Ringley Chartered Surveyors
**Issued Capital:** £100,000
**Principals:** Ms M A Bowring *(Managing)*, D J Field, D A Powell, A Chadwick, A M Pratt, M J Richardson
**Co. Secretary:** Ms Mary Bowring
**Responsibilities**
**Senior:** Mary-Anne Bowring *(Managing Director)*, Mehdi Mehra *(Chairman)*, Aron Schermaul *(Manager)*
**US SIC:** 7399 **UK SIC:** 83954
**Auditors:** Kounnis & Partners PLC
**Bankers:** Barclays Bank Plc (20-37-75)

| | 31-03-14 | 31-03-13 | 31-03-12 |
|---|---|---|---|
| TO | 1,717,601 | N/A | N/A |
| P/L | 19,649 | N/A | N/A |
| NW | 286,254 | 276,895 | 179,692 |
| WC | (267,173) | (227,761) | (280,081) |

DUNS 21-067-5234
## Ringrose Law
Norwich Union House, 7 St Peter At Arches, Lincoln, Lincolnshire LN2 1EA
**Tel:** 01522561020
**Web:** www.ringroselaw.co.uk
**Estd:** 2008 Proprietorship
**Line of Business:** Solicitors
**Proprietor:** R Georgeson
**Responsibilities**
**Senior:** Sally Hubbard *(Head Of Employment)*
**US SIC:** 8111 **UK SIC:** 83500
**Employees:** 130

DUNS 39-756-2232
## Ringtons Holdings Ltd
Algernon Road, Byker, Newcastle-Upon-Tyne, Tyne and Wear NE6 2YN
**Tel:** 0191-209-7030
**Web:** www.ringtons.co.uk
**Reg No:** 2195196 **Estd:** 1987 Private Limited Company
**Line of Business:** Tea processing
**Issued Capital:** £312,888
**Principals:** S M Smith *(Managing)*, C J Smith, P N Smith, Mrs J C Thompson, S M Smith, J D Smith
**Co. Secretary:** Peter Smith
**US SIC:** 2099 **UK SIC:** 42399
**Auditors:** PricewaterhouseCoopers
**Bankers:** Lloyds TSB Bank plc (30-91-50)

| | 30-06-13 | 30-06-12 | 30-06-11 |
|---|---|---|---|
| TO | 47,336,068 | 41,477,520 | 35,658,472 |
| P/L | 4,454,438 | 3,906,090 | 3,558,187 |
| NW | 43,751,411 | 40,926,504 | 38,752,730 |
| WC | 37,642,636 | 35,376,156 | 34,623,364 |
| Emp. | 505 | 483 | 460 |

DUNS 21-232-7993 Imp
## Ringtons Ltd
(**Subsidiary of:** Ringtons Holdings Ltd)
Algernon Road, Newcastle-Upon-Tyne, Tyne and Wear NE6 2YN
**Tel:** 08000522440
**Web:** www.ringtons.co.uk
**Reg No:** 0572008 **Estd:** 1907 Private Limited Company
**Line of Business:** Other non-store retail sale
**Issued Capital:** £142,444
**Principals:** P N Smith *(Chairman)*, S M Smith *(Managing)*, J R Malton, J D Smith, Mrs J C Thompson, C J Smith, S M Smith
**Co. Secretary:** Peter Smith
**Responsibilities**
**Senior:** Carl Moffett *(Financial Director)*
**Finance:** Carl Moffett *(Financial Director)*
**Marketing:** Suzanne Goldie *(Marketing Manager)*, Sarah Thompson *(Marketing Manager)*
**Sales:** John Malton *(Sales Director)*
**Admin:** Stephen Killinger *(Operations Director)*
**IT:** Jess Curley *(Computer Manager)*
**HR:** Liz Jackson *(Human Resources Manager)*, Judith Moffatt *(Human Resources Manager)*
**Health & Safety:** Carl Moffett *(Financial Director)*
**Facilities:** Stephen Killinger *(Operations Director)*
**Purchasing:** Sharon McManus *(Purchasing Coordinator)*
**Branches:** Ringtons Ltd, 245 Sprotbrough Road, Doncaster, South Yorkshire DN5 8BP
**US SIC:** 5963 **UK SIC:** 65600
**Auditors:** UNW LLP
**Bankers:** Lloyds TSB Bank plc (30-91-50)

| | 30-06-13 | 30-06-12 | 30-06-11 |
|---|---|---|---|
| TO | 46,211,255 | 39,950,690 | 34,207,598 |
| P/L | 3,074,256 | 2,945,668 | 1,762,394 |
| NW | 14,210,712 | 12,513,543 | 11,030,498 |
| WC | 6,765,436 | 5,280,100 | 3,905,195 |
| Emp. | 497 | 479 | 455 |

DUNS 23-503-7319
## Ringway Hotels Ltd
(**Subsidiary of:** Toureen Group Ltd)
Eltwood Lane, Manchester M90 4HL
**Tel:** 01614980333 **Fax:** 0161-498-0222
**Web:** www.bewleyshotels.com
**Reg No:** 3502987 **Estd:** 1998 Private Limited Company
**Line of Business:** Hotels
**Trading Style:** Bewleys Hotel
**Issued Capital:** £10,000
**Directors:** M Moran, T Moran, Ms K Moran, P K Power, D O'Doherty, T Moran, Ms T L Moran, W Mcgreal
**Co. Secretary:** Donal O' Doherty
**Responsibilities**
**Senior:** Sarah Curren *(Proprietor)*
**US SIC:** 7011 **UK SIC:** 66500
**Auditors:** PricewaterhouseCoopers

| | 31-12-13 | 31-01-13 | 31-12-12 |
|---|---|---|---|
| TA | 64,665,891 | 65,695,025 | 36,219,280 |
| P/L | 8,970,741 | 2,255,258 | 197,637 |
| NW | 41,031,703 | 29,121,709 | 18,576,316 |
| WC | 18,091,979 | 18,488,869 | (10,016,271) |
| Emp. | 152 | 139 | 133 |

DUNS 34-622-5626
## Ringway Infrastructure Services Ltd
(**Subsidiary of:** Vinci)
Albion House, Springfield Road, Horsham, West Sussex RH12 2RW
**Fax:** 01709871131
**Web:** www.ringway.co.uk
**Reg No:** 2756434 **Estd:** 1992 Private Limited Company
**Line of Business:** Construction of motorways, roads, railways, airfields and sports facilities
**Trading Style:** Ringway Group
**Issued Capital:** £5,200,000
**Directors:** G C Batut, R I Gillespie, W Taylor, J Nicholson, P C Horton, N Goddard, S A Wardrop, D N Binding
**Co. Secretary:** Ms Susan Lysionek
**Responsibilities**
**Senior:** Francois Amosse *(Financial Director)*
**Finance:** Francois Amosse *(Financial Director)*
**Marketing:** Tracey Elms *(Marketing Manager)*
**HR:** Kristine Pollock *(Group Personnel Manager)*
**Branches:** Ringway Infrastructure Services Ltd, Fromebridge, Gloucester, Gloucestershire GL2 7NJ
**US SIC:** 1611 **UK SIC:** 50200
**Auditors:** KPMG LLP
**Bankers:** National Westminster Bank Plc (60-11-17)

| | 31-12-13 | 31-12-12 | 31-12-11 |
|---|---|---|---|
| TO | 216,851,488 | 157,714,304 | 162,974,578 |
| P/L | (1,785,680) | (2,273,272) | 2,002,979 |
| NW | 12,409,393 | 14,209,233 | 15,449,979 |
| WC | 8,880,623 | 15,957,854 | 16,813,159 |
| Emp. | 1,506 | 1,194 | 905 |

DUNS 34-775-6632
## Ringway Jacobs Ltd
Albion House, 38 Springfield Road, Horsham, West Sussex RH12 2RW
**Tel:** 02075363652
**Web:** www.ringwayjacobs.co.uk
**Reg No:** 5576465 **Estd:** 2006 Private Limited Company
**Line of Business:** Construction of motorways, roads, railways, airfields and sports facilities
**Issued Capital:** £10,000
**Directors:** D N Binding, R S Duff, S A Wardrop, M I Notman, G C Batut, L Power, A A Seywright, W Taylor
**Co. Secretary:** Ms Susan Lysionek
**US SIC:** 1611, 7349
**UK SIC:** 50200, 92300
**Auditors:** Grant Thornton UK LLP
**Bankers:** National Westminster Bank Plc (60-11-17)

| | 31-12-13 | 31-12-12 | 31-12-11 |
|---|---|---|---|
| TO | 189,900,810 | 162,474,695 | 104,819,358 |
| P/L | 6,470,710 | 5,893,428 | 5,017,018 |
| NW | 6,321,409 | 5,453,206 | 4,054,390 |
| WC | 3,419,860 | 1,728,637 | 3,181,290 |
| Emp. | 970 | 842 | 552 |

DUNS 22-067-4530
## Ringwealth Ltd
International House, Chapel Hill, Huddersfield, West Yorkshire HD1 3EE
**Tel:** 01484540006
**Reg No:** 4069065 **Estd:** 2000 Private Limited Company
**Line of Business:** Other letting of own property
**Export Sales:** £4,522,243
**Issued Capital:** £427,092
**Directors:** D U Armitage, Mrs C E Armitage
**Co. Secretary:** David Armitage
**US SIC:** 6519 **UK SIC:** 85000
**Auditors:** KPMG LLP
**Bankers:** National Westminster Bank Plc (53-61-07)

| | 31-10-13 | 31-10-12 | 31-10-11 |
|---|---|---|---|
| TO | 5,491,303 | 5,963,519 | 7,049,873 |
| P/L | (87,014) | 160,247 | 70,391 |
| NW | 3,208,017 | 3,606,854 | 4,617,566 |
| WC | 456,333 | 486,281 | 532,272 |
| Emp. | 67 | 75 | 76 |

DUNS 21-796-0915
## Ringwood Brewery
138 Christchurch Road, Ringwood, Hampshire BH24 3AP
**Tel:** 01425471177
**Web:** www.ringwoodbrewery.co.uk
**Estd:** 1977
**Line of Business:** Manufacture of beer
**US SIC:** 2082 **UK SIC:** 42702
**Employees:** 48

DUNS 21-716-3437
## Ringwood School
Parsonage Barn Lane, Ringwood, Hampshire BH24 1SE
**Tel:** 01425475000 **Fax:** 01425473063
**Web:** www.ringwood.hants.sch.uk
**Reg No:** 7552519 **Estd:** 2011 Private Company Limited By Guarantee
**Line of Business:** General secondary education
**Directors:** Ms E S Fernandez Lee, D R Scott, Mrs J R Jones, S P Lee, M A Macario, T M Shortall, R A Southern, Ms C E Edwards
**Co. Secretary:** Ross Bowell
**Responsibilities**
**Senior:** Katherine Green *(Director)*, Margaret Groves *(Governor)*, Allison Jones *(Governor)*, Clare Pittman *(Director)*, Robert Woodrow *(Director)*
**US SIC:** 8211 **UK SIC:** 93200

| | 31-08-14 | 31-08-13 | 31-08-12 |
|---|---|---|---|
| TO | 9,327,799 | 8,589,205 | 37,802,097 |
| P/L | 209,631 | (358,820) | 25,383,432 |
| NW | 21,200,217 | 21,132,586 | 24,510,432 |
| WC | 760,560 | 486,513 | 1,002,023 |
| Emp. | 178 | 187 | 188 |

DUNS 21-149-2076

## Rinus Roofing Supplies Ltd

Unit 3, St Theodores Way, Bridgend, Mid Glamorgan CF32 9TZ
**Tel:** 01656722380
**Web:** www.rinusroofingsupplies.co.uk
**Reg No:** 6788061 **Estd:** 2009 Private Limited Company
**Line of Business:** Roofing materials
**Issued Capital:** £189,583
**Directors:** J R Watson, Ms S Heston-King, D M Proos
**Responsibilities**
**Senior:** Craig Harcombe *(Manager)*
**US SIC:** 3271 **UK SIC:** 24370

| | 30-06-13 | 30-06-12 | 30-06-11 |
|---|---|---|---|
| TO | 19,809,683 | N/A | N/A |
| P/L | (1,049,177) | N/A | N/A |
| NW | (3,109,050) | (2,259,577) | 175,344 |
| WC | 2,800,383 | 1,715,079 | (96,854) |
| Emp. | 86 | N/A | N/A |

DUNS 22-763-4854

## Rio Surfacing Ltd

**(Subsidiary of:** Rio (Holdings) Ltd)
50 Devon Street, Birmingham, West Midlands B7 4SL
**Tel:** 0121-359-5522 **Fax:** 01213598538
**Web:** www.riogroup.co.uk
**Reg No:** 1176777 **Estd:** 1974 Private Limited Company
**Line of Business:** Construction of motorways, roads, railways, airfields and sports facilities
**Trading Style:** Rio Surfacing Ltd
**Issued Capital:** £4,000
**Director:** M Wragg
**Co. Secretary:** Ian Deacon
**US SIC:** 1611 **UK SIC:** 50200
**Auditors:** Jerrom Associates
**Bankers:** National Westminster Bank Plc (60-06-37)

| | 31-05-14 | 31-05-13 | 31-05-12 |
|---|---|---|---|
| TA | 1,258,836 | 1,397,175 | 1,358,204 |
| NW | 705,901 | 676,676 | 673,008 |
| WC | 662,958 | 627,172 | 623,959 |

DUNS 21-727-2376 **Imp-Exp**

## Rio Tinto Mining & Exploration Ltd

**(Subsidiary of:** Rio Tinto Plc)
2 Eastbourne Terrace, London W2 6LG
**Tel:** 020 7781 1101 **Fax:** 01179-226358
**Web:** www.riotinto.com
**Reg No:** 1305702 **Estd:** 1977 Private Limited Company
**Line of Business:** Research and experimental development on natural sciences and engineering
**Export Markets:** Worldwide
**Directors:** G K Hodgkinson, S A Sullivan, J G Beswick, Dr K M Tainton
**Co. Secretary:** Ms Helen Day
**Responsibilities**
**Senior:** Gemma Aldridge *(Manager)*, Arnaud Brion *(Director)*, Kevin Fox *(Exploration Director)*
**US SIC:** 7391 **UK SIC:** 94000
**Auditors:** Grant Thornton UK LLP
**Bankers:** Barclays Bank Plc (20-87-94)
**Employees:** 108
**Turnover:** £10,633,000

DUNS 21-024-8928 **Exp**

## Rio Tinto Plc

2 Eastbourne Terrace, London W2 6LG
**Tel:** 020-7781-2000 **Fax:** 02077811856
**Web:** www.riotinto.com
**Reg No:** 0719885 **Estd:** 2008 Public Limited Company
**Line of Business:** Management activities of holding companies
**Directors:** R R Goodmanson, Lord J O Kerr Of Kinlochard, R E Brown, M C Fitzpatrick, Dr M E Clark, Mrs A M Lauvergeon, S M Walsh, P M Tellier
**Co. Secretary:** Vaughn Walton
**Responsibilities**
**Senior:** Barry Bloch *(Manager)*, Brett Clayton *(?Group Executive)*, Michael L'Estrange *(Director)*, Greg Lilleyman *(Group executive, Technology &)*
**Marketing:** Jean Chawapiwa-Pama *(Chairman)*, Robert Court *(?Global Head of External Affai)*, Brian Fall *(Consultant)*, Iltah Harri *(Chief Media Relations)*, Mitchell Inness *(Relations Manager)*, Laurent Odeh *(Marketing Director)*, Jacko Preyser *(GM Sales and Marketing)*, Houston Spencer *(Vice President of Communicatio)*, Anita Webster *(Relations Manager)*, Frank Webster *(Spokesperson)*
**Sales:** Holly Hawkins *(Business Development Manager)*, Jacko Preyser *(GM Sales and Marketing)*
**HR:** Magalie Jacob *(Recruitment Specialist)*
**Operations:** Stephane Leblanc *(Plant Manager)*, Mike Spreadborough *(General Manager)*
**Purchasing:** Tony Breault *(Purchasing Manager)*
**Engineering:** Natasha Haggard *(Process Engineer)*, Kay Williams *(Technical Manager)*
**Branches:** Rio Tinto Plc, Pengelly, Delabole, Cornwall PL33 9AZ
**US SIC:** 6711, 1099
**UK SIC:** 83962, 21000
**Auditors:** PricewaterhouseCoopers LLP
**Bankers:** HSBC Bank plc (40-05-30)
**Employees:** 67,930
**Turnover:** £5.117E+10

DUNS 21-627-3189

## Ripat Ltd

Archwood Ltd Whittington Road, Oswestry, Shropshire SY11 1HZ
**Tel:** 01691658444
**Web:** www.leyland-paints.co.uk
**Reg No:** 7067225 **Estd:** 2009 Private Limited Company
**Line of Business:** Holding companies management activities
**Export Sales:** £532,000
**Issued Capital:** £37,500
**Directors:** S Underhill, R H Burbidge
**Co. Secretary:** Richard Lincoln
**US SIC:** 6711 **UK SIC:** 83962
**Bankers:** National Westminster Bank Plc (55-50-05)

| | 28-09-13 | 29-09-12 | 01-09-11 |
|---|---|---|---|
| TO | 46,770,000 | 49,317,000 | 46,396,000 |
| P/L | 3,446,000 | 2,405,000 | 2,760,000 |
| NW | 36,436,000 | 39,617,000 | 39,017,000 |
| WC | 19,400,000 | 22,571,000 | 22,887,000 |
| Emp. | 377 | 412 | 353 |

DUNS 33-995-2087

## Ripley Castle

Ripley, Harrogate, North Yorkshire HG3 3AY
**Web:** www.ripleycastle.co.uk
**VAT No:** 343430092 **Estd:** 2002 Proprietorship
**Line of Business:** Places of interest
**Proprietor:** Sir T Ingleby
**Responsibilities**
**Senior:** Irene Freeman *(Operations Manager)*
**Finance:** Linda Hazlett *(Accounts Manager)*
**Facilities:** Linda Hazlett *(Accounts Manager)*
**Purchasing:** Donna Idle *(Retail Manager)*
**US SIC:** 8411 **UK SIC:** 97700
**Bankers:** National Westminster Bank Plc (55-61-02)
**Employees:** 100

DUNS 21-777-3557

## Ripley Community Hospital

Sandham Lane, Ripley, Derbyshire DE5 3HE
**Tel:** 01773743456
**Web:** www.nhs.uk
**Estd:** 2011 Proprietorship
**Line of Business:** Hospitals
**Proprietor:** Ms S Coope
**Responsibilities**
**Senior:** Sally Cooper *(Matron)*
**US SIC:** 8062 **UK SIC:** 95100
**Employees:** 105

DUNS 23-176-5843

## Ripley St. Thomas Church of England School

Ashton Road, Lancaster, Lancashire LA1 4RS
**Tel:** 01524-64496
**Web:** www.ripley.lancsngfl.ac.uk
**Estd:** 2004
**Line of Business:** Schools (local authority)
**Chairman:** Ms M Wallis
**Responsibilities**
**Senior:** Liz Nicholls *(Principal)*
**IT:** Ian Janes *(IS/IT Management)*
**US SIC:** 8211 **UK SIC:** 93200
**Employees:** 251

DUNS 21-024-8977 **Imp-Exp**

## Ripmax Ltd

**(Subsidiary of:** Ultimate Model Corporation Ltd)
241 Green Street, Enfield, Middlesex EN3 7SJ
**Web:** www.ripmax.com
**Reg No:** 0467046 **VAT No:** 220906885
**Estd:** 1949 Public Limited Company
**Line of Business:** Wholesale of other intermediate products
**Export Markets:** E U
**Trading Style:** Ripmax, Hobby Stores
**Issued Capital:** £50,000
**Directors:** P A Halman, M Wood, R A Hales, M Hull, N J Moss, G J Hales, J H Metcalf, C M Straus
**Co. Secretary:** Stephen Mussett
**Responsibilities**
**Senior:** Jack Jeffers *(Manager)*, Kenneth Morrissey *(Manager)*
**Sales:** Jon Wesley *(Sales Manager)*
**Branches:** Ripmax Ltd, Hamdon House, 2 Railway Street, Aylesbury, Buckinghamshire HP20 1QX
**US SIC:** 5941 **UK SIC:** 65400
**Auditors:** Mazars LLP
**Bankers:** Barclays Bank Plc (20-91-79)

| | 31-03-13 | 31-03-12 | 31-03-11 |
|---|---|---|---|
| TO | 7,339,113 | 7,895,977 | 8,928,726 |
| P/L | (213,175) | 26,578 | 58,135 |
| NW | 5,828,701 | 6,037,231 | 6,009,139 |
| WC | 5,217,098 | 5,611,523 | 5,869,005 |
| Emp. | 79 | 77 | 75 |

DUNS 22-800-7902 **Imp-Exp**

## Ripon Farm Services Ltd

Dallamires Lane, Ripon, North Yorkshire HG4 1TT
**Fax:** 01765604310
**Web:** www.riponfarmservices.com
**Reg No:** 1667383 **VAT No:** 372040191
**Estd:** 1982 Private Limited Company
**Line of Business:** Suppliers of
**Export Markets:** European Union (E U)
**Export Sales:** £598,763
**Trading Style:** Ripon Land Rover, T & J Calvert, Smith Bros
**Issued Capital:** £1,021,666
**Principals:** G Brown *(Managing)*, S A Hymas, P M Brown, N D Riley
**Co. Secretary:** Nicholas Riley
**Responsibilities**
**Senior:** William Houseman *(Manager)*, Maurice Hymas *(Manager)*
**Finance:** Maurice Hymas *(Manager)*
**Sales:** Brian Sowray *(Sales Manager)*
**IT:** Peter Hambling *(IT Manager)*
**Branches:** Ripon Farm Services Ltd, York Road, Tadcaster, North Yorkshire LS24 8EB
**US SIC:** 3523, 5521, 5531
**UK SIC:** 32113, 65100
**Auditors:** Wilson Braithwaite Scholey
**Bankers:** HSBC Bank plc (40-38-23)

| | 31-01-14 | 31-01-13 | 31-01-12 |
|---|---|---|---|
| TO | 87,273,434 | 76,494,269 | 73,265,370 |
| P/L | 707,085 | 922,593 | 1,033,269 |
| NW | 10,754,096 | 10,276,888 | 8,683,877 |
| WC | 6,590,777 | 7,605,668 | 6,633,911 |
| Emp. | 225 | 202 | 194 |

DUNS 28-829-0133

## The Ripon Race Company Ltd

The Racecourse, Boroughbridge Road, Ripon, North Yorkshire HG4 1UG
**Fax:** 01765698900
**Web:** www.ripon-races.co.uk
**Reg No:** 0061171 **VAT No:** 170550680
**Estd:** 1899 Private Limited Company
**Line of Business:** Operation of other sports arenas and stadiums not elsewhere classified
**Issued Capital:** £49,928
**Directors:** A M Hutchinson, C R Armstrong, J M Hutchinson, C N Clark, D J Wilmot-Smith, A T Wells
**Co. Secretary:** Andrew Hutchinson
**Branches:** The Ripon Race Company Ltd, Race Course House, Boroughbridge Road, Ripon, North Yorkshire HG4 1UG
**US SIC:** 7999 **UK SIC:** 97913
**Auditors:** Wilson Braithwatie Scholey
**Bankers:** HSBC Bank plc (40-38-23)

| | 31-03-14 | 31-03-13 | 31-03-12 |
|---|---|---|---|
| TA | 2,897,540 | 2,607,349 | 2,520,815 |
| NW | 1,222,779 | 1,069,413 | 926,855 |
| WC | 280,248 | 44,203 | 182,633 |

DUNS 21-315-7167 **Exp**

## Ripon Select Foods Ltd

Dallamires Way North, Ripon, North Yorkshire HG4 1TL
**Tel:** 01765-601711
**Web:** www.riponselectfoods.co.uk
**Reg No:** 1161649 **Estd:** 1975 Private Limited Company
**Line of Business:** Manufacture of other food products not elsewhere classified
**Export Markets:** Eire, Western Europe, Africa, Canada and Malta
**Export Sales:** £1,880,538
**Issued Capital:** £457,594
**Principals:** T H Wood *(Chairman and Managing)*, Mrs S P Cooper *(Financial)*, D Baines, T M Wood, J M Cooper
**Co. Secretary:** Anton Gordon
**Responsibilities**
**Sales:** Glenn Coldwell *(Sales Manager)*
**Admin:** Maggie Williams *(Administrator)*
**Health & Safety:** Maggie Williams *(Administrator)*
**US SIC:** 2099, 5149
**UK SIC:** 42399, 61700
**Auditors:** Clive Owen & Co
**Bankers:** Barclays Bank Plc (20-37-13)

| | 31-03-14 | 31-03-13 | 31-03-12 |
|---|---|---|---|
| TO | 29,699,884 | 26,971,283 | 22,634,131 |
| P/L | 1,033,502 | 763,387 | 474,123 |
| NW | 9,042,955 | 8,257,604 | 7,686,028 |
| WC | 3,050,175 | 3,147,222 | 2,632,696 |
| Emp. | 86 | 84 | 82 |

DUNS 23-879-8768

## Rippleffect Studio Ltd

**(Subsidiary of:** Trinity Mirror Plc)
5th Floor The Podium, Liverpool, Merseyside L3 9PP
**Tel:** 08458 038381 **Fax:** 08458 038382
**Web:** www.rippleffect.com
**Reg No:** 3871086 **VAT No:** 440356767
**Estd:** 1999 Private Limited Company
**Line of Business:** Web site design and development
**Issued Capital:** £100,650
**Directors:** S R Fox, T M Directors Limited, V L Vaghela
**Co. Secretary:** T M Secretaries Limited
**Responsibilities**
**Marketing:** Kirstie Buchanan *(Sales & Marketing Director)*
**Sales:** Kirstie Buchanan *(Sales & Marketing Director)*
**Branches:** Rippleffect Studio Ltd, Innovation Centre, 131 Mount Pleasant, Liverpool, Merseyside L3 5TF
**US SIC:** 7379, 7333, 7319
**UK SIC:** 83940, 83953, 83800
**Auditors:** Deloitte LLP

| | 29-12-13 | 30-12-12 | 01-12-12 |
|---|---|---|---|
| TO | 6,353,666 | 5,586,128 | 4,420,712 |
| P/L | 59,538 | 81,528 | (16,611) |
| NW | 1,113,253 | 1,070,417 | 1,013,912 |
| WC | 1,100,579 | 1,054,801 | 988,582 |
| Emp. | 75 | 67 | 62 |

DUNS 22-701-5206

## Rippleglen Ltd

**(Subsidiary of:** First Stop News Ltd)
York House, Pennine Way, Birmingham, West Midlands B8 1JW
**Fax:** 0121-322-2599
**Web:** www.rippleglen.co.uk
**Reg No:** 1415903 **VAT No:** 377586689
**Estd:** 1979 Private Limited Company
**Line of Business:** Retail sale of bread, cakes, flour confectionery and sugar confectionery
**Trading Style:** Arden News, Supernews, Mercury News
**Issued Capital:** £121,255
**Directors:** Ms C A Beverley, A R Hargreave, M J Colley, Ms L Jones
**Co. Secretary:** Peter Hyett
**Responsibilities**
**Senior:** Lorraine Jones *(Buying Director)*, Henry Medcalf *(Chairman)*
**Marketing:** Anthony Morgan *(Marketing Coordinator)*
**Admin:** Sharon Whitehouse *(Office Manager)*
**Operations:** Sharon Whitehouse *(Office Manager)*
**Purchasing:** Lorraine Jones *(Buying Director)*, Sharon Whitehouse *(Office Manager)*
**Branches:** Rippleglen Limited, 12 Kingfisher Square, Redditch, Worcestershire B97 4EQ
**US SIC:** 5462, 5942, 5921
**UK SIC:** 64100, 65300, 64200
**Auditors:** Mazars LLP
**Bankers:** Lloyds TSB Bank plc (30-00-03)

| | 26-07-14 | 27-07-13 | 28-07-12 |
|---|---|---|---|
| TO | 14,049,000 | 16,131,000 | 18,929,000 |
| P/L | 224,000 | 234,000 | (28,000) |
| NW | 541,000 | 407,000 | 6,000 |
| WC | (952,000) | (1,096,000) | (1,594,000) |
| Emp. | 119 | 133 | 150 |

DUNS 21-595-5184

## Risahighlight

Quayside Tower 252 260, Broad Street, Birmingham, West Midlands B1 2HF
**Tel:** 01216324936
**Web:** www.thehighlight.co.uk
**Estd:** 2011
**Line of Business:** Bars
**Proprietor:** J Bolton
**US SIC:** 5813 **UK SIC:** 66200
**Employees:** 50

DUNS 21-014-7784

## Risborough Carers Ltd

1 Chinnor Road, Thame, Oxfordshire OX9 3LN
**Tel:** 01844 212271 **Fax:** 01844 358190
**Web:** www.risboroughcarersltd.com
**Reg No:** 6373710 **Estd:** 2006 Private Limited Company
**Line of Business:** Activities of households as employers of domestic staff
**Issued Capital:** £100
**Director:** Ms J A Hill
**Co. Secretary:** Ms Stephanie Hill
**Responsibilities**
**Health & Safety:** Sally Fothergill *(Health & Safety Officer)*
**US SIC:** 8811 **UK SIC:** 99000

| | 30-11-14 | 30-11-13 | 30-11-12 |
|---|---|---|---|
| TA | 423,985 | 406,292 | 394,400 |
| NW | 306,266 | 256,136 | 237,364 |
| WC | 281,727 | 226,019 | 205,132 |

**DUNS 29-881-5044**    **Imp-Exp**

## Risco Group Uk Ltd

Commerce House, Manchester M24 2SS
**Tel:** 0161-655-5500
**Web:** www.riscogroup.com
**Reg No:** 2084510 **Estd:** 1987 Private
Limited Company
**Line of Business:** Wholesale of other
electronic parts and equipment
**Export Markets:** Worldwide
**Export Sales:** £689,000
**Issued Capital:** £2,900,000
**Directors:** S D Riley, J D Green, M Alkelai
**Co. Secretary:** Mrs Sally Whone
**Responsibilities**
**Senior:** Graham Bolton (CEO)
**Branches:** Risco Group Uk Ltd, Unit 4 City
Grove Est, Woodside Rd, Eastleigh,
Hampshire SO50 4ET
**US SIC:** 3643, 5199
**UK SIC:** 34203, 61900
**Auditors:** Ernst & Young LLP
**Bankers:** The Royal Bank Of Scotland Plc
(16-00-06)

| | 31-12-13 | 31-12-12 | 31-12-11 |
|---|---|---|---|
| TO | 15,009,000 | 14,387,000 | 13,529,000 |
| P/L | 487,000 | 554,000 | 402,000 |
| NW | 3,329,000 | 3,225,000 | 3,054,000 |
| WC | 3,159,000 | 3,062,000 | 3,049,000 |
| Emp. | 65 | 66 | 71 |

**DUNS 21-781-7687**

## The Riseborough

11-13 Branksome Wood Road,
Bournemouth, Dorset BH2 6BT
**Tel:** 01202318567
**Web:** www.fshc.co.uk
**Estd:** 1999 Proprietorship
**Line of Business:** Residential care
establishments
**Proprietor:** Mrs A Orsberry
**Responsibilities**
**Senior:** Suzanne Croft (Manager)
**US SIC:** 8321 **UK SIC:** 96111
**Employees:** 64

**DUNS 29-647-9454**

## Risedale Estates Ltd

Abbey Road, Barrow-In-Furness, Cumbria
LA14 5LE
**Tel:** 01229839669 **Fax:** 01229877867
**Web:** www.risedale-carehomes.co.uk
**Reg No:** 1974198 **Estd:** 1986 Private
Limited Company
**Line of Business:** Non-charitable social
work activities with accommodation
**Trading Style:** Risedale Retirement Home
**Issued Capital:** £100
**Principals:** C T Dent (Chairman), P A Fraser
(Managing), J G Edmond (Financial)
**Co. Secretary:** Mrs Barbara Hetherington
**Responsibilities**
**Senior:** Pam Harper (Manager), Paula Poole
(Home Manager), Barbara Redshaw
(Director of Nursing)
**HR:** Barbara Redshaw (Director of Nursing)
**Health & Safety:** Barbara Redshaw (Director
of Nursing)
**Purchasing:** Tracy Downward (Purchasing
Manager), Barbara Redshaw (Director of
Nursing)
**Branches:** Risedale Estates Ltd, Albert
Street, Barrow-In-Furness, Cumbria LA14
2JB
**US SIC:** 8321, 8091
**UK SIC:** 96111, 95200
**Auditors:** Ernst & Young
**Bankers:** Barclays Bank Plc (20-04-68)

| | 27-04-14 | 28-04-13 | 30-04-12 |
|---|---|---|---|
| TO | 10,746,110 | 9,972,791 | 9,903,548 |
| P/L | 717,254 | 821,631 | 966,155 |
| NW | 4,228,500 | 3,658,001 | 3,008,982 |
| WC | (1,737,289) | (1,608,197) | (1,830,428) |
| Emp. | 547 | 509 | 526 |

**DUNS 51-574-1556**

## Rishworth School

Rishworth, Sowerby Bridge, West Yorkshire
HX6 4QT
**Tel:** 01422-822217 **Fax:** 01422-820911
**Web:** www.rishworth-school.co.uk
**Reg No:** 5855479 **Estd:** 2006 Private
Company Limited By Guarantee
**Line of Business:** Primary education
**Directors:** Reverend T L Swinhoe,
G C Allan, Dr C A Brooks, T M Wheelwright,
A Gloag, J C Slim, W P Hodgson,
Ms M L Ringland
**Co. Secretary:** Ms Joanne Clague
**Responsibilities**
**Senior:** Dilys Whitaker (Director)
**Finance:** Michael Schofield (Bursar)
**Marketing:** Sharon Stamp (Marketing
Manager)
**HR:** Peter Seery (Deputy Head)
**US SIC:** 8211 **UK SIC:** 93200

**Bankers:** Lloyds TSB Bank plc (30-00-00)

| | 31-07-13 | 31-07-12 | 31-07-11 |
|---|---|---|---|
| TO | 5,482,471 | 5,566,904 | 6,113,257 |
| P/L | (258,888) | (255,877) | 216,602 |
| NW | 5,374,787 | 5,539,725 | 5,796,761 |
| WC | 618,441 | 896,857 | 1,044,717 |
| Emp. | N/A | 3 | N/A |

**DUNS 73-935-5050**

## The Risk Advisory Group (Holdings)Plc

Russell Square House 10 12, Russell
Square, London WC1B 5EH
**Tel:** 02075-780-000 **Fax:** 02075-787-855
**Web:** www.riskadvisory.net
**Reg No:** 5188468 **VAT No:** 881853390
**Estd:** 2004 Public Limited Company
**Line of Business:** Management activities of
holding companies
**Export Sales:** £12,886,000
**Trading Style:** Risk Advisory
**Issued Capital:** £728,824
**Directors:** Dr D Claridge, C S Rowley,
J A Smith, Miss L J Ferrar, O Babinov,
G J Wood, R D Prior, W F Waite
**Co. Secretary:** William Waite
**Responsibilities**
**Senior:** Toby Cotton (Financial Director),
Geraldine Davies (Director), Philip Keevil
(Manager), Nigel Turnbull (Manager)
**Finance:** Toby Cotton (Financial Director)
**Admin:** Mandy Parker (Office Manager)
**HR:** Mandy Parker (Office Manager)
**Health & Safety:** Mandy Parker (Office
Manager)
**Facilities:** Mandy Parker (Office Manager)
**US SIC:** 6711, 8111
**UK SIC:** 83962, 83500
**Auditors:** Baker Tilly UK Audit LLP

| | 31-12-13 | 31-12-12 | 31-12-11 |
|---|---|---|---|
| TO | 20,027,000 | 19,172,000 | 16,542,000 |
| P/L | 1,955,000 | 2,990,000 | 2,815,000 |
| NW | 7,187,000 | 7,631,000 | 7,376,000 |
| WC | 6,889,000 | 7,632,000 | 7,011,000 |
| Emp. | 106 | 104 | 95 |

**DUNS 28-934-0523**

## Risk Management Services (Chiltern) Ltd

(Subsidiary of: Risk Management Services
(Holdings) Ltd)
The Old Courthouse, Hughenden Road, High
Wycombe, Buckinghamshire HP13 5DT
**Tel:** 01494441805 **Fax:** 01494-452045
**Web:** www.riskmanagementsecurity.co.uk
**Reg No:** 1544192 **VAT No:** 442430384
**Estd:** 1976 Private Limited Company
**Line of Business:** Security activities
**Trading Style:** Risk Management Security
Services
**Issued Capital:** £110,000
**Directors:** J J Herring, G R Tilly, P M Smith
**Co. Secretary:** Ms Josephine Herring
**US SIC:** 7393 **UK SIC:** 83954
**Auditors:** Whitley Stimpson LLP
**Bankers:** Lloyds TSB Bank plc (30-95-36)

| | 31-03-14 | 31-03-13 | 31-03-12 |
|---|---|---|---|
| TO | N/A | N/A | 5,805,795 |
| P/L | N/A | N/A | 130,991 |
| NW | 943,975 | 902,105 | 894,998 |
| WC | 913,267 | 863,486 | 828,827 |
| Emp. | N/A | N/A | 211 |

**DUNS 21-710-1373**

## Riskalliance Direct Ltd

(Subsidiary of: Riskalliance Group Ltd)
2 Wagon Lane, Bingley, West Yorkshire
BD16 1LT
**Tel:** 01274565734
**Reg No:** 7505078 **Estd:** 2011 Private
Limited Company
**Line of Business:** Insurance - other
**Trading Style:** Riskalliance Group Ltd
**Issued Capital:** £100
**Directors:** S G Wilson, N G Klenk, A Lister,
S A Kaznowski
**US SIC:** 6399 **UK SIC:** 82001

| | 31-07-13 | 31-07-12 | 31-07-11 |
|---|---|---|---|
| TO | 2,381,705 | 2,140,443 | 987,861 |
| P/L | 177,421 | 64,477 | 155,493 |
| NW | 342,345 | 211,499 | 155,593 |
| WC | 335,109 | 203,570 | 151,016 |
| Emp. | 49 | 50 | 35 |

**DUNS 57-842-7775**

## Riskcare Ltd

25 Worship Street, London EC2A 2DX
**Tel:** 02076-143-600 **Fax:** 02076143601
**Web:** www.riskcare.com
**Reg No:** 2895746 **Estd:** 1994 Private
Limited Company
**Line of Business:** Financial advisers
(independent)
**Export Sales:** £1,369,167
**Issued Capital:** £161,022
**Principals:** C W Bray (Managing),
Ms H S Duffy, S R White
**Co. Secretary:** Ms Helen Duffy
**Responsibilities**
**Senior:** Richard Haddow (Manager),
Matthew Hayday (Manager)

**Sales:** Andy Ross (Head Of Sales Team)
**US SIC:** 7379, 7392
**UK SIC:** 83940, 83951
**Auditors:** PKF (UK) LLP
**Bankers:** Barclays Bank Plc (20-41-41)

| | 30-04-14 | 30-04-13 | 30-04-12 |
|---|---|---|---|
| TO | 9,779,761 | 9,983,564 | 11,765,083 |
| P/L | 128,878 | (421,750) | (408,451) |
| NW | 1,846,232 | 1,874,619 | 2,453,766 |
| WC | 1,516,245 | 1,443,684 | 1,918,907 |
| Emp. | 100 | 107 | 125 |

**DUNS 84-694-9704**

## Riskstop Group Ltd

The Pavilion, Botleigh Grange Business
Park, Southampton, Hampshire SO30 2AF
**Tel:** 01305215500
**Web:** www.riskstop.co.uk
**Reg No:** 6236118 **Estd:** 2007 Private
Limited Company
**Line of Business:** Activities auxiliary to
insurance and pension funding
**Issued Capital:** £4,109
**Directors:** T L Lillington, D Lillington,
V N Raywood, T R Smith
**Co. Secretary:** Trethowans Services Limited
**US SIC:** 6411 **UK SIC:** 83200

| | 31-12-13 | 30-06-12 | 30-12-11 |
|---|---|---|---|
| TO | 13,754,402 | 9,508,437 | 9,367,426 |
| P/L | 1,070,309 | 903,669 | 1,326,975 |
| NW | 1,700,320 | 1,772,503 | 1,611,762 |
| WC | 1,269,013 | 1,587,100 | 1,715,013 |
| Emp. | 98 | 96 | 84 |

**DUNS 64-118-0039**

## Risktec Solutions Ltd

(Subsidiary of: Technischer Überwachungs-
Verein Rheinland Berlin B)
Technology Centre, James Watt Avenue,
East Kilbride, Glasgow, Lanarkshire G75
0QD
**Tel:** 01355340200 **Fax:** 01925-611232
**Web:** www.risktec.co.uk
**Reg No:** 4118059 **Estd:** 2000 Private
Limited Company
**Line of Business:** Nuclear engineers
**Export Sales:** £10,344,104
**Issued Capital:** £92,585
**Directors:** A J Hoy, G R Dixon, G J Book,
Dr J M Llambias, S J Lewis, D A Bonsall,
N S Notis, G Davidson
**Co. Secretary:** Graham Wallace
**Responsibilities**
**Senior:** Gareth Ellor (Manager)
**US SIC:** 8911 **UK SIC:** 83701
**Auditors:** RSM Tenon Audit Ltd

| | 31-12-13 | 31-12-12 | 31-12-11 |
|---|---|---|---|
| TO | 28,520,951 | 23,654,630 | 17,193,593 |
| P/L | 4,864,844 | 3,952,818 | 3,509,000 |
| NW | 10,134,523 | 7,892,871 | 6,088,979 |
| WC | 10,459,913 | 7,994,836 | 6,054,226 |
| Emp. | 189 | 156 | 143 |

**DUNS 23-636-7520**    **Imp-Exp**

## Riso (U.K.) Ltd

(Subsidiary of: Riso Kagaku Corporation)
610 Centennial Avenue Centennial Park,
Borehamwood, Hertfordshire WD6 3TJ
**Tel:** 02082365800 **Fax:** 020-8236-5801
**Web:** www.riso.co.uk
**Reg No:** 2717706 **VAT No:** 578638578
**Estd:** 1992 Private Limited Company
**Line of Business:** Manufacture of computers
and other information processing equipment
**Export Markets:** Europe
**Export Sales:** £2,029,243
**Issued Capital:** £3,800,000
**Directors:** Y Takahashi, T Murakami,
K Harada
**Co. Secretary:** Stephen Root
**Responsibilities**
**Marketing:** Dale Pilfold (Marketing Manager)
**Branches:** Riso (U.k.) Ltd, Lowton Way,
Rotherham, South Yorkshire S66 8RY
**US SIC:** 3573 **UK SIC:** 33020
**Auditors:** KPMG LLP
**Bankers:** National Westminster Bank Plc
(50-41-10)

| | 31-03-14 | 31-03-13 | 31-03-12 |
|---|---|---|---|
| TO | 16,649,155 | 13,486,662 | 14,247,430 |
| P/L | 262,049 | (1,868,330) | (623,589) |
| NW | 335,019 | 72,970 | (82,669) |
| WC | 195,823 | (52,595) | 482,725 |
| Emp. | 61 | 55 | 54 |

**DUNS 22-851-3016**    **Imp-Exp**

## Risol Imports Ltd

Risol House, Mercury Way, Urmston,
Manchester M41 7RR
**Tel:** 01617491313 **Fax:** 01617491287
**Web:** www.regatta.com
**Reg No:** 0354803 **Estd:** 1939 Private
Limited Company
**Line of Business:** Management activities of
holding companies
**Export Markets:** Worldwide
**Trading Style:** Gegatta
**Issued Capital:** £5,409
**Principals:** K J Black (Managing),
N J Young, D M Holt, Mrs T H Black,
Ms J Black

**Co. Secretary:** David Holt
**Responsibilities**
**Senior:** Martyn Ifould (Manager)
**Branches:** Risol Imports Ltd, 22A Bexley
High Street, Bexley, Kent DA5 1AD
**US SIC:** 6711, 5136
**UK SIC:** 83962, 61600
**Auditors:** Deloitte & Touche
**Bankers:** HSBC Bank plc (40-35-26)

| | 31-01-14 | 31-01-13 | 31-01-12 |
|---|---|---|---|
| TO | 125,656,000 | 121,667,000 | 119,906,000 |
| P/L | 8,673,000 | 7,791,000 | 5,430,000 |
| NW | 42,287,000 | 36,717,000 | 30,980,000 |
| WC | 30,905,000 | 25,274,000 | 24,400,000 |
| Emp. | 537 | 503 | 534 |

**DUNS 21-682-9191**

## Ritchey Ltd

(Subsidiary of: Merko Acquisition Nv)
Fearby Road, Masham, Ripon, North
Yorkshire HG4 4ES
**Tel:** 01765689541
**Web:** www.ritchey.co.uk
**Reg No:** 7330611 **Estd:** 2010 Private
Limited Company
**Line of Business:** Business services
**Issued Capital:** £1
**Directors:** K D Parker, S C Ward, N S Myers,
J A Musgrave, G C Wambergue
**Co. Secretary:** Louis-Marie Allain
**Responsibilities**
**Senior:** Szymon Nowaczek (Marketing
Manager)
**US SIC:** 3079 **UK SIC:** 48360
**Auditors:** Deloitte LLP
**Bankers:** Barclays Bank Plc (20-04-48)

| | 31-12-13 | 31-12-12 | 31-12-11 |
|---|---|---|---|
| TO | 6,739,112 | 4,534,897 | 5,702,503 |
| P/L | 565,387 | 225,532 | 166,866 |
| NW | 704,020 | 252,771 | 3,633 |
| WC | 853,142 | 672,169 | 861,038 |
| Emp. | 58 | 59 | 68 |

**DUNS 21-730-3247**

## Ritec Decorators Ltd

109 Richmond Road, Thornton Heath, Surrey
CR7 7QF
**Tel:** 020-8684-4319
**Web:** www.ritecdecorators.co.uk
**Reg No:** 0952909 **Estd:** 1969 Private
Limited Company
**Line of Business:** Building of complete
constructions or parts thereof; civil
engineering
**Issued Capital:** £300
**Principals:** R J Murphy (Managing),
S C Smith, P J Murphy
**Co. Secretary:** Paul Murphy
**US SIC:** 1541, 1711, 1751, 1721
**UK SIC:** 50100, 50300, 50400
**Bankers:** HSBC Bank plc (40-35-01)

| | 30-09-13 | 30-09-12 | 30-09-11 |
|---|---|---|---|
| TA | 362,957 | 401,865 | 436,313 |
| NW | 33,472 | 76,919 | 101,348 |
| WC | 28,477 | 70,413 | 92,865 |

**DUNS 22-859-3927**    **Imp-Exp**

## Ritrama (U.K.) Ltd

(Subsidiary of: Rink Holding Srl)
Unit 2 Fifth Avenue, Dukinfield, Cheshire
SK16 4PP
**Tel:** 01617861700
**Web:** www.ritrama.com
**Reg No:** 1547937 **VAT No:** 359290525
**Estd:** 1981 Private Limited Company
**Line of Business:** Printers services and
supplies
**Export Markets:** Worldwide
**Export Sales:** £14,015,065
**Issued Capital:** £310,000
**Directors:** Dr M D Attwood, R Rink,
M L Evans, R Rink, L P Ward, T F Rink,
P L Burton
**Co. Secretary:** Peter Burton
**Responsibilities**
**Finance:** Anthony Mcmanus (Finance
Director)
**Engineering:** Ian Blackshaw (Engineering
Manager)
**US SIC:** 5081 **UK SIC:** 61490
**Auditors:** Deloitte LLP
**Bankers:** Barclays Bank Plc (20-16-08)

| | 31-12-13 | 31-12-12 | 31-12-11 |
|---|---|---|---|
| TO | 32,138,994 | 30,707,101 | 30,337,225 |
| P/L | 2,653,289 | 2,025,490 | 1,671,336 |
| NW | 5,972,834 | 5,749,107 | 4,534,157 |
| WC | 6,738,927 | 6,090,739 | 5,063,128 |
| Emp. | 68 | 69 | 88 |

**DUNS 22-988-6080**

## Ritson Smith

16 Carden Place, Aberdeen, Aberdeenshire
AB10 1FX
**Tel:** 01224-643311
**Web:** www.jcca.co.uk
**Estd:** 1909 Partnership
**Line of Business:** Accounting activities
**Trading Style:** Johnston Carmichael

**Principals:** A P Drury, I Smith, N Farherson (*Partner*), N Harper (*Partner*), C Edmond (*Partner*), I Baker (*Partner*), E Alexander (*Partner*), G Leadley (*Partner*)
**Responsibilities**
**Senior:** Niall Farquharson (*Manager*), John Laing (*Manager*)
**Branches:** Ritson Smith, 42 Market Street, Ellon, Aberdeenshire AB41 9JD
**US SIC:** 8931, 7399
**UK SIC:** 83600, 83954
**Bankers:** Bank Of Scotland (80-73-30)
**Employees:** 52

DUNS 22-845-3312
## Ritson Young
28 High Street, Nairn, Nairnshire IV12 4AU
**Web:** www.ritsonsca.com
**Estd:** 1909 Partnership
**Line of Business:** Accounting and auditing activities
**Partners:** J Yeoman, W L Young, W B Deans, A E Simpson, I Forsyth
**Branches:** Ritson Young, 27 Huntly Street, Inverness, Inverness-Shire IV3 5PR
**US SIC:** 8931 **UK SIC:** 83600
**Bankers:** Bank Of Scotland (80-06-66)
**Employees:** 80

DUNS 21-715-7700     Imp-Exp
## Rittal-C S M Ltd
(**Subsidiary of:** Rittal International Stiftung & Co. Kg)
Broadley Industrial Park, Plymouth, Devon PL6 7EZ
**Fax:** 01752-207625
**Web:** www.rittal.com
**Reg No:** 0858856 **VAT No:** 143060411
**Estd:** 1965 Private Limited Company
**Line of Business:** Manufacturers general
**Export Markets:** Worldwide
**Issued Capital:** £900,000
**Principals:** A P Courts (*Managing*), Dr. S Hobbs
**Co. Secretary:** Alan Courts
**Responsibilities**
**IT:** John Purchase (*Non-PC Systems Manager*)
**Operations:** Martin Hurrell (*Technical, Production Manager*)
**Engineering:** Paul Runnalls (*Production Engineer*)
**US SIC:** 3357 **UK SIC:** 22470
**Auditors:** KPMG LLP
**Bankers:** National Westminster Bank Plc (56-00-63)

| | 31-12-13 | 31-12-12 | 31-12-11 |
|---|---|---|---|
| TO | 59,759,000 | 64,075,000 | 72,024,000 |
| P/L | 4,313,000 | 5,571,000 | 6,979,000 |
| NW | 14,803,000 | 18,306,000 | 18,658,000 |
| WC | 10,403,000 | 10,649,000 | 11,753,000 |
| Emp. | 361 | 380 | 389 |

DUNS 23-838-5152
## Ritz Associates Ltd
62 Leeming Street, Mansfield, Nottinghamshire NG18 1NG
**Web:** www.andwhynot.co.uk
**Reg No:** 3830224 **Estd:** 2000 Private Limited Company
**Line of Business:** Public house
**Trading Style:** Andwhynot & the Late Lounge
**Issued Capital:** £130
**Director:** J Edwards
**Co. Secretary:** Paul Anderton
**Responsibilities**
**Senior:** Johnathan Edwards (*Proprietor*)
**Branches:** Ritz Associates Ltd, The Cheeky Monkey, 2 Handley Arcade, Mansfield, Nottinghamshire NG18 1NQ
**US SIC:** 5813 **UK SIC:** 66200
**Auditors:** Jon Jarvis & Associates
**Bankers:** Lloyds TSB Bank plc (77-22-28)

| | 31-01-14 | 31-01-13 | 31-01-12 |
|---|---|---|---|
| TA | 1,530,151 | 1,469,219 | 1,348,950 |
| NW | 945,352 | 855,874 | 807,120 |
| WC | 446,806 | 374,250 | 457,334 |

DUNS 38-548-2708     Imp
## The Ritz Hotel Casino Ltd
(**Subsidiary of:** B Uk Limited)
22 Arlington Street, London SW1A 1RD
**Tel:** 02074991818 **Fax:** 02074916028
**Web:** www.theritzclub.com
**Reg No:** 3329884 **Estd:** 1985 Private Limited Company
**Line of Business:** Gambling and betting activities
**Issued Capital:** £24,000,000
**Directors:** A M Love, M Seal, R G Marris, Ms S Kennedy, A S Barclay
**Co. Secretary:** Ms Alexa Brummer
**Responsibilities**
**Senior:** Lyndsey Barrett (*Manager*)
**Marketing:** Anne-Marie McGrath (*Marketing Manager*)
**HR:** Sharon Robinson (*Personnel Manager*)
**Health & Safety:** John Wootton (*Head of Security*)

**Facilities:** Jamie Harrison (*Facilities Manager*)
**Operations:** John Wootton (*Head of Security*)
**Branches:** The Ritz Hotel Casino Ltd, 150 Piccadilly, London W1J 9BS
**US SIC:** 7999 **UK SIC:** 97913
**Auditors:** PricewaterhouseCoopers LLP

| | 31-12-13 | 31-12-12 | 31-12-11 |
|---|---|---|---|
| TO | 31,999,000 | 21,542,000 | 14,615,000 |
| P/L | (12,708,000) | (3,333,000) | (2,577,000) |
| NW | (444,000) | (543,000) | 24,000 |
| WC | (4,303,000) | (4,073,000) | (3,773,000) |
| Emp. | 176 | 167 | 163 |

DUNS 21-024-9173
## The Ritz Hotel (London) Ltd
(**Subsidiary of:** B Uk Limited)
150 Piccadilly, London W1J 9BR
**Tel:** 020-7493-8181 **Fax:** 02073002245
**Web:** www.theritzhotel.co.uk
**Reg No:** 0064203 **Estd:** 2011 Private Limited Company
**Line of Business:** Hotels
**Trading Style:** The Ritz Hotel
**Issued Capital:** £1,000,000
**Directors:** A S Barclay, M Seal, R K Mowatt, H M Barclay, P L Peters, A M Love
**Responsibilities**
**Senior:** Stephen Boxall (*Managing Director*), Ruth Jones (*Marketing & Development Manage*)
**US SIC:** 7011, 6531
**UK SIC:** 66500, 83400
**Auditors:** PricewaterhouseCoopers LLP
**Bankers:** Bank Of Scotland (12-01-03)

| | 31-12-13 | 31-12-12 | 31-12-11 |
|---|---|---|---|
| TO | 36,515,000 | 35,421,000 | 32,270,000 |
| P/L | 9,595,000 | 8,892,000 | 6,014,000 |
| NW | 38,156,000 | 30,792,000 | 24,079,000 |
| WC | 43,998,000 | 36,704,000 | 29,391,000 |
| Emp. | 398 | 393 | 333 |

DUNS 21-150-5770
## Riva Foods Ltd
32 Copenhagen Road Sutton Fields, Industrial Estate, Hull, North Humberside HU7 0XQ
**Tel:** 01482-837285 **Fax:** 01482824323
**Web:** www.rivafoods.co.uk
**Reg No:** 6798694 **Estd:** 1996 Private Limited Company
**Line of Business:** Manufacture of other food products not elsewhere classified
**Issued Capital:** £97,500
**Directors:** Ms A Lowthorpe, P J Lempriere, F G Blake
**Co. Secretary:** Simon Lunt
**Responsibilities**
**Senior:** Stephen Lowthorpe (*Operations Manager*), Robin Southgate (*Manager*)
**IT:** Stephen Lowthorpe (*Operations Manager*)
**HR:** Denise Beacock (*Human Resources Manager*)
**Health & Safety:** Stephen Lowthorpe (*Operations Manager*)
**Engineering:** Stephen Lowthorpe (*Operations Manager*)
**US SIC:** 2099 **UK SIC:** 42399

| | 29-03-14 | 31-03-13 | 31-03-12 |
|---|---|---|---|
| TA | 1,370,271 | 1,540,075 | 1,535,125 |
| NW | 356,217 | 339,040 | 240,192 |
| WC | 59,710 | 58,486 | 21,762 |

DUNS 29-972-7198     Imp
## Rivalminster Ltd
57-59 Welbeck Street, London W1G 9BL
**Tel:** 02079354442
**Web:** www.holidayinn.com
**Reg No:** 2106051 **VAT No:** 524076658
**Estd:** 1987 Private Limited Company
**Line of Business:** Hotels
**Trading Style:** Holiday Inn
**Issued Capital:** £124
**Director:** P H Sehgal
**Co. Secretary:** Mrs Barbara Sehgal
**Responsibilities**
**Senior:** Jakane Boubker (*Food & Beverage Manager*), Kevin Fraser (*General Manager*), David Melrose (*General Manager*)
**Facilities:** David Melrose (*General Manager*)
**Branches:** Rivalminster Ltd, 11-17 Seymour St, London W1H 7JW
**US SIC:** 7011 **UK SIC:** 66500
**Auditors:** UHY Hacker Young LLP
**Bankers:** Lloyds TSB Bank plc (30-99-62)

| | 30-04-14 | 30-04-13 | 30-04-12 |
|---|---|---|---|
| TO | 10,442,599 | 9,796,132 | 9,546,284 |
| P/L | 662,446 | 229,283 | 476,753 |
| NW | 6,313,018 | 5,937,159 | 5,934,216 |
| WC | (2,214,972) | (2,058,488) | (1,511,368) |
| Emp. | 73 | 77 | 78 |

DUNS 22-208-4308
## Rivaoil (U.K.) Ltd
(**Subsidiary of:** Clivedon Sales Corporation)
21 Courthouse Road, Maidenhead, Berkshire SL6 6JE
**Tel:** 01628776022
**Web:** www.careuk.com
**Reg No:** 4226531 **Estd:** 2011 Private Limited Company
**Line of Business:** Non-charitable social work activities with accommodation
**Issued Capital:** £29,988
**Director:** E Duman
**Co. Secretary:** Victor Duman
**US SIC:** 8321 **UK SIC:** 96111

| | 31-12-13 | 31-12-12 | 31-12-11 |
|---|---|---|---|
| TA | 31,608 | 32,163 | 32,725 |
| NW | 31,107 | 31,663 | 32,225 |
| WC | 31,052 | 31,589 | 32,126 |

DUNS 52-007-9625     Exp
## Rivendell Europe Ltd
(**Subsidiary of:** Rivendell (Holdings) Ltd)
Wira Business Park, Ring Road, West Park, Leeds, West Yorkshire LS16 6EB
**Web:** www.rivendell-europe.com
**Reg No:** 3374815 **Estd:** 1997 Private Limited Company
**Line of Business:** Printers general
**Issued Capital:** £41,000
**Director:** A D Spowart
**Co. Secretary:** James Mcaulay
**Responsibilities**
**Senior:** Ivan Ferris (*Manager*)
**Health & Safety:** Tony Gamblin (*Production Manager*)
**Engineering:** Tony Gamblin (*Production Manager*)
**US SIC:** 2794, 2752
**UK SIC:** 47545, 47544
**Auditors:** KPMG LLP

| | 30-09-13 | 30-09-12 | 30-09-11 |
|---|---|---|---|
| TO | 3,646,426 | 3,535,156 | 3,692,939 |
| P/L | 22,359 | 84,557 | (191,363) |
| NW | 466,728 | 455,581 | 394,733 |
| WC | 195,063 | 204,268 | 148,440 |
| Emp. | 55 | 58 | 65 |

DUNS 29-510-2404
## Rivendell Nurseries Ltd
(**Subsidiary of:** Notcutts Group Ltd)
Mill Lane, Widnes, Cheshire WA8 3UU
**Tel:** 01514232638 **Fax:** 01514239348
**Web:** www.rivendellnursery.com
**Reg No:** 1873497 **Estd:** 1984 Private Limited Company
**Line of Business:** Other retail sale in specialised stores not elsewhere classified
**Issued Capital:** £1,275,000
**Directors:** I W Furniss, A M Staff
**Co. Secretary:** Ian Furniss
**US SIC:** 5999, 0161
**UK SIC:** 65600, 01001
**Auditors:** PricewaterhouseCoopers LLP

| | 28-02-14 | 28-02-13 | 29-02-12 |
|---|---|---|---|
| TA | 9,937,420 | 9,937,420 | 9,937,420 |
| NW | 9,937,420 | 9,937,420 | 9,937,420 |

DUNS 21-808-9868
## River Beach School
York Road, Littlehampton, West Sussex BN17 6EW
**Tel:** 01903725500
**Web:** www.learning.riverbeach.w-sussex.sch.uk
**Estd:** 2012
**Line of Business:** Schools (local authority)
**Responsibilities**
**Senior:** Judy Grevett (*Head Teacher*)
**US SIC:** 8211 **UK SIC:** 93200
**Employees:** 130

DUNS 29-971-7884
## The River Cafe Ltd
Thames Wharf, Rainville Road, London W6 9HA
**Tel:** 020-7386-4200
**Web:** www.rivercafe.co.uk
**Reg No:** 2105075 **VAT No:** 495125237
**Estd:** 1987 Private Limited Company
**Line of Business:** Restaurants
**Trading Style:** The River Cafe Ltd
**Issued Capital:** £575
**Managing Director:** Ms R Rogers
**Co. Secretary:** Lady Ruth Rogers
**Responsibilities**
**Senior:** Clemency Gray (*Manager*)
**Health & Safety:** Ian Heidi (*Health & Safety Officer*)
**US SIC:** 5812 **UK SIC:** 66110
**Auditors:** Lee Associates
**Bankers:** Samuel Montagu & Company Ltd (40-05-50)

| | 30-04-14 | 30-04-13 | 30-04-12 |
|---|---|---|---|
| TO | 6,363,907 | 5,789,535 | 5,490,029 |
| P/L | 309,210 | 233,490 | 521,556 |
| NW | 526,146 | 550,738 | 629,649 |
| WC | (237,025) | (608,379) | (684,958) |

DUNS 21-010-1505
## River Clyde Homes
Roxburgh House, 102-110 Roxburgh Street, Greenock, Renfrewshire PA15 4JT
**Tel:** 01475-788887
**Web:** www.riverclydehomes.org.uk
**Reg No:** 0329031SC **Estd:** 2007 Private Company Limited By Guarantee
**Line of Business:** Caterers
**Directors:** Mrs E Grant, S J Mccabe, A Duncan, A Henderson, C W Mceleny, R P Ahlfeld, C A Mcginn, W Dunlop
**Co. Secretary:** James Aird
**Responsibilities**
**Senior:** Katrina Anderson (*Director*), Joe Mcilwee (*Director*), Kevin Scarlett (*Chief Executive Officer*), Lynn Wassell (*Director*)
**US SIC:** 6531 **UK SIC:** 83400
**Auditors:** Baker Tilly UK Audit LLP
**Bankers:** The Royal Bank Of Scotland Plc (83-22-04)

| | 31-03-14 | 31-03-13 | 31-03-12 |
|---|---|---|---|
| TO | 25,105,000 | 24,508,000 | 25,487,000 |
| P/L | 5,612,000 | 3,045,000 | 4,871,000 |
| NW | 20,653,000 | 16,882,000 | 16,295,000 |
| WC | 16,838,000 | 14,477,000 | 18,976,000 |
| Emp. | 438 | 439 | 217 |

DUNS 23-864-8500
## The River Group Ltd
(**Subsidiary of:** Compass Delta Holdings Ltd)
1 Waterhouse Square, London EC1N 2ST
**Tel:** 02074207000 **Fax:** 020-7836-6646
**Web:** www.therivergroup.co.uk
**Reg No:** 3856348 **Estd:** 1999 Private Limited Company
**Line of Business:** Publishing of journals and periodicals
**Issued Capital:** £5,768
**Directors:** B A Hibbert, P D Johnston, Ms N Murphy
**Co. Secretary:** Keith Amess
**Responsibilities**
**Senior:** Jackie Garford (*Publishing Director*), Nigel Mackay (*Production Director*)
**Marketing:** Natalie Firth (*Publisher*), Alex Marks (*Strategy Director*)
**HR:** Samantha Richardson (*Human Resources Manager*)
**Operations:** Nigel Mackay (*Production Director*)
**US SIC:** 2721 **UK SIC:** 47522
**Auditors:** Shipleys LLP

| | 31-03-14 | 31-03-13 | 31-03-12 |
|---|---|---|---|
| TO | 17,204,740 | 18,206,759 | 14,776,696 |
| P/L | 1,089,310 | 253,239 | 341,140 |
| NW | 107,873 | (736,460) | (920,361) |
| WC | (529) | (827,441) | (534,887) |
| Emp. | 84 | 93 | 84 |

DUNS 73-799-7924
## River House Montessori School Ltd
Great Eastern Enterprise Centre, London E14 9XP
**Tel:** 020-7538-9886
**Web:** www.river-house.co.uk
**Reg No:** 2930209 **Estd:** 1994 Private Limited Company
**Line of Business:** Schools (independent)
**Issued Capital:** £209,000
**Directors:** K D Piper, Ms S J Greenwood
**Co. Secretary:** Ms Janet Pearson
**US SIC:** 8211 **UK SIC:** 93200

| | 30-06-13 | 30-06-12 | 30-06-11 |
|---|---|---|---|
| TO | 2,624,583 | N/A | N/A |
| P/L | (167,501) | N/A | N/A |
| NW | (163,418) | (14,874) | (204,975) |
| WC | 194,304 | 200,624 | 32,772 |

DUNS 21-157-2623     Imp
## River Island Clothing Co. Ltd
(**Subsidiary of:** Lfh International Limited)
Chelsea House, West Gate, London W5 1DR
**Tel:** 08448472584 **Fax:** 02089914523
**Web:** www.riverisland.com
**Reg No:** 0636095 **VAT No:** 227179454
**Estd:** 2007 Private Limited Company
**Line of Business:** Retail sale of other men's clothing
**Trading Style:** River Island
**Issued Capital:** £3,400,010
**Principals:** B J Lewis (*Managing*), C R Lewis (*Managing*), S Lewis, B Lewis, Mrs V J Lewis
**Co. Secretary:** Cavendish Square Secretarial
**Responsibilities**
**Marketing:** Angela Asiedua (*Marketing Executive*), Linda Imadojemun (*Marketing Officer*), Mary McClenahan (*Brand Marketing Manager*), Josie Roscop (*Marketing Director*)
**Facilities:** Jamie Davis (*Facilities Manager*)
**Branches:** River Island Clothing Co. Ltd, 470-482 Oxford Street, London W1C 1LA
**US SIC:** 5611, 5621
**UK SIC:** 64500
**Auditors:** BDO LLP

**Bankers:** Standard Chartered Bank
(60-91-04)

|     | 28-12-13 | 29-12-12 | 31-12-11 |
|-----|----------|----------|----------|
| TO  | 809,500,000 | 739,700,000 | 720,700,000 |
| P/L | 86,100,000 | 93,300,000 | 81,600,000 |
| NW  | 242,700,000 | 268,700,000 | 189,900,000 |
| WC  | 143,500,000 | 171,000,000 | 76,000,000 |
| Emp. | 10,393 | 1,266 | 10,213 |

DUNS 21-581-0013
### River Meadows Nursing Home
Edgebolton, Shawbury, Shrewsbury,
Shropshire SY4 4EL
**Tel:** 01939250700
**Web:** www.springcare.co.uk
**Estd:** 2011 Partnership
**Line of Business:** Nursing homes
**Partners:** Miss A Patterson, Mrs A Mcmullan
**Responsibilities**
**Senior:** Ann McMullan (Partner), Alison
Peake (CEO, Managing Director)
**US SIC:** 8051 **UK SIC:** 95100
**Employees:** 50

DUNS 21-879-4973
### River View Community Primary School
1 Wheaters Street, Salford, Lancashire M7
1QZ
**Tel:** 01619212670
**Web:** www.riverviewprimary.co.uk
**Estd:** 2012
**Line of Business:** Primary education
**Responsibilities**
**Senior:** Daniel Gauld (Head Teacher)
**US SIC:** 8211 **UK SIC:** 93200
**Employees:** 60

DUNS 21-209-4820
### River View Nursing Home
Styles Hill, Frome, Somerset BA11 5JR
**Tel:** 08702869464
**Estd:** 1988 Proprietorship
**Line of Business:** Nursing Homes
**Proprietor:** J Dalais
**Branches:** River View Nursing Home, 13
Grove Park Rd, Weston-Super-Mare, Avon
BS23 2LW
**US SIC:** 8051 **UK SIC:** 95100
**Employees:** 64

DUNS 23-112-2826
### Riverbank
Egerton Street, Warrington, Cheshire WA1
2DF
**Tel:** 01925-573772
**Estd:** 2003 Proprietorship
**Line of Business:** Nursing homes
**Proprietor:** Mrs I Marsden
**US SIC:** 8051 **UK SIC:** 95100
**Employees:** 146

DUNS 21-787-9207
### Riverbank Bar & Kitchen
Arkwright Street, Nottingham,
Nottinghamshire NG2 2GS
**Web:** www.riverbanknotts.co.uk
**Estd:** 2011 Proprietorship
**Line of Business:** Restaurant - english
**Proprietor:** G Manager
**Responsibilities**
**Senior:** David Hage (General Manager)
**US SIC:** 5812 **UK SIC:** 66110
**Employees:** 60

DUNS 22-122-4301
### Riverbank Care Ltd
The Warren, Cluden Road, Bideford, Devon
EX39 3QF
**Tel:** 01237-476932
**Web:** www.riverbankcare.co.uk
**Reg No:** 4141491 **Estd:** 2001 Private
Limited Company
**Line of Business:** Residential care
establishments
**Issued Capital:** £1,000
**Director:** R G Thisby
**Co. Secretary:** Mrs Jacqueline Thisby
**Responsibilities**
**Senior:** Laura Hobbs (Home Manager)
**US SIC:** 8051 **UK SIC:** 95100

|     | 31-03-14 | 31-03-13 | 31-03-12 |
|-----|----------|----------|----------|
| TA  | 134,412 | 187,400 | 206,360 |
| NW  | (53,655) | 30,598 | 60,965 |
| WC  | (134,179) | (50,010) | (1,006) |

DUNS 73-716-3498    **Imp**
### Riverbank Hotel Operator Ltd
18 Albert Embankment, London SE1 7TJ
**Tel:** 020-7958-8000 **Fax:** 020-7769-2400
**Web:** www.parkplaza.com
**Reg No:** 4974811 **Estd:** 2003 Private
Limited Company
**Line of Business:** Other tourist assistance
activities not elsewhere classified
**Trading Style:** Riverbank Park Plaza,
Carlson Hotels

**Issued Capital:** £1
**Directors:** C C Moravsky,
Euro Sea Hotels N V
**Co. Secretary:** Mrs Inbar Zilberman
**Responsibilities**
**Senior:** Greg Hegarty (General Manager),
Kirsten Lindenann (Operations Manager)
**Marketing:** Robert Henke (Vice President
Marketing and B), Dave Shilling (Senior
Marketing Executive)
**Sales:** Edwin Wijgergangs (Vice President
Sales and Distr)
**Admin:** Kamil Zajaczkowski (System
Administrator)
**IT:** Kamil Zajaczkowski (System
Administrator)
**Operations:** Andrew Swindells (Chief
Operations Officer)
**US SIC:** 7999 **UK SIC:** 97913
**Auditors:** Mazars LLP

|     | 31-12-13 | 31-12-12 | 31-12-11 |
|-----|----------|----------|----------|
| TO  | 27,111,000 | 27,105,000 | 26,073,000 |
| P/L | (609,000) | (861,000) | (1,390,000) |
| NW  | (10,781,000) | (10,172,000) | (9,311,000) |
| WC  | (10,781,000) | (10,172,000) | (9,311,000) |
| Emp. | 241 | 265 | 196 |

DUNS 73-834-9427    **Imp**
### Riverbed Technology Ltd
(Subsidiary of: Riverbed Technology Inc.)
One Thames Valley Wokingham Road, Level
2, Bracknell, Berkshire RG42 1NG
**Tel:** 01344 401900 **Fax:** 01344 401903
**Web:** www.riverbed.com
**Reg No:** 5090414 **Estd:** 2004 Private
Limited Company
**Line of Business:** Other computer related
activities
**Trading Style:** Riverbed
**Issued Capital:** £100
**Directors:** M J Palu, J M Kennelly
**Co. Secretary:** Abogado Nominees Limited
**Responsibilities**
**Senior:** Helen Dickens (Office Manager)
**Branches:** Riverbed Technology Ltd, The
Jeffreys Building Cowley Road, Cambridge,
Cambridgeshire CB4 0DS
**US SIC:** 7379 **UK SIC:** 83940
**Auditors:** Littlejohn LLP

|     | 31-12-13 | 31-12-12 | 31-12-11 |
|-----|----------|----------|----------|
| TO  | 25,205,758 | 24,728,201 | 19,770,102 |
| P/L | 1,162,141 | 10,840,911 | (49,658,358) |
| NW  | 6,630,141 | 5,098,282 | 14,791,541 |
| WC  | 6,092,577 | 4,777,553 | (30,942,134) |
| Emp. | 163 | 148 | 83 |

DUNS 50-582-2163
### Riverbryce Ltd
5 Greenbank Crescent, Bassett,
Southampton, Hampshire SO16 7FR
**Tel:** 023-8076-8130 **Fax:** 02380768130
**Reg No:** 2524934 **Estd:** 1990 Private
Limited Company
**Line of Business:** Telecommunications
**Issued Capital:** £100
**Director:** M M Cataldo
**Co. Secretary:** Pagona Cataldo
**US SIC:** 4899 **UK SIC:** 79020
**Auditors:** Underwood Barron
**Bankers:** HSBC Bank plc (40-42-21)

|     | 05-04-14 | 05-04-13 | 05-04-12 |
|-----|----------|----------|----------|
| TA  | 340,565 | 380,089 | 334,654 |
| NW  | 267,214 | 328,226 | 317,674 |
| WC  | 267,214 | 327,773 | 315,906 |

DUNS 23-737-2268
### Riverford Organic Farms Ltd
Wash Barn, Buckfastleigh, Devon TQ11 0JU
**Tel:** 01803762059
**Web:** www.riverford.co.uk
**Reg No:** 3731570 **Estd:** 1999 Private
Limited Company
**Line of Business:** Organic food production
and supply
**Trading Style:** Riverford Organic Vegtables
**Issued Capital:** £100
**Director:** W G Watson
**Co. Secretary:** Mrs Katherine Cameron
**Responsibilities**
**Finance:** Steve Tarr (Financial Director)
**Marketing:** Rachel Watson (Sales &
Marketing Manager)
**Sales:** Rachel Watson (Sales & Marketing
Manager)
**HR:** Charlotte Tickle (Human Resources
Manager)
**Health & Safety:** Charlotte Tickle (Human
Resources Manager)
**Facilities:** Jason Gipson (Facilities
Manager)
**Purchasing:** Luke King (Purchasing
Manager)
**Branches:** Riverford Organic Farms Ltd, 12
May Tree Close, Winchester, Hampshire
SO22 4JE
**US SIC:** 5499, 5148
**UK SIC:** 64100, 61700

**Auditors:** Francis Clark

|     | 03-05-14 | 04-05-13 | 05-05-12 |
|-----|----------|----------|----------|
| TO  | 44,392,960 | 41,045,981 | 37,096,235 |
| P/L | 1,383,435 | 1,098,536 | 1,351,532 |
| NW  | 6,557,333 | 5,617,476 | 5,190,323 |
| WC  | 1,341,443 | (77,476) | 169,470 |
| Emp. | 430 | 417 | 373 |

DUNS 21-620-0612
### The Riverfront @ Bfi Southbank
Belvedere Road, London SE1 8XT
**Tel:** 02079280808
**Web:** www.benugo.com
**Estd:** 2011
**Line of Business:** Restaurants
**Responsibilities**
**Senior:** Gian-Maria Baldassarre (General
Manager)
**US SIC:** 5812 **UK SIC:** 66110
**Employees:** 50

DUNS 22-547-9377
### Riverhaven Ltd
Estra House, Streatham Station Appr,
London SW16 6HW
**Tel:** 020-8672-4000 **Fax:** 020-8767-3522
**Web:** www.riverhavenltd.org.uk
**Reg No:** 0017932IP **Estd:** 1967 Friendly
Society
**Line of Business:** Residential Care
**Principals:** M R Cornwall-Jones (Chairman),
Ms J Chalk, J Collier, D Treanor,
Ms S Felton, Ms V Graham, T Gaden,
K Jenkins
**Responsibilities**
**Senior:** Audrey Dixon (Director), James
Macnamara (Director), Gwen Rymer
(Director), Bill Steele (Director), T Tuck
(Director)
**US SIC:** 8361 **UK SIC:** 96112
**Auditors:** KPMG
**Bankers:** Barclays Bank Plc (20-90-69)
**Employees:** 59

DUNS 45-827-2689
### Riverhead Commercial Services Ltd
(Subsidiary of: Park Leisure Marketing Ltd)
208 North Sea Lane, Grimsby, South
Humberside DN36 4ET
**Tel:** 01472-812666 **Fax:** 01472210227
**Web:** www.beachcomberholidaypark.co.uk
**Reg No:** 3180358 **Estd:** 1996 Private
Limited Company
**Line of Business:** Camping sites, including
caravan sites
**Issued Capital:** £100
**Directors:** M R Varley, R J Varley
**Co. Secretary:** Ian Appleyard
**US SIC:** 7033 **UK SIC:** 66701
**Auditors:** Nexia Audit Ltd
**Bankers:** Yorkshire Bank Plc (05-04-44)

|     | 31-12-13 | 31-12-12 | 31-12-11 |
|-----|----------|----------|----------|
| TA  | 2,690,033 | 2,765,791 | 2,762,167 |
| NW  | 1,541,328 | 1,479,086 | 1,404,334 |
| WC  | 314,705 | 204,142 | 122,010 |

DUNS 34-618-5846    **Exp**
### Riverlea Tractors Ltd
Riverlea Limited, Crymych, Dyfed SA41 3QX
**Fax:** 01239-831668
**Web:** www.riverlea.co.uk
**Reg No:** 2755953 **Estd:** 1971 Private
Limited Company
**Line of Business:** Wholesale of agricultural
machinery and accessories and implements,
including tractors
**Export Markets:** Eire
**Export Sales:** £265,660
**Issued Capital:** £472,500
**Director:** D A Hill
**Co. Secretary:** Mrs Gillian Hill
**Responsibilities**
**IT:** Chris Windship (IT Manager)
**Branches:** Riverlea Tractors Ltd, Riverlea
Tractors Ltd, Unit 30, Cowbridge, South
Glamorgan CF71 7PF
**US SIC:** 5083, 7519
**UK SIC:** 61490, 84804
**Auditors:** Tyssul Ll Jenkins
**Bankers:** National Westminster Bank Plc
(52-21-11)

|     | 30-09-14 | 30-09-13 | 30-09-12 |
|-----|----------|----------|----------|
| TO  | 25,339,693 | 24,582,868 | 23,796,563 |
| P/L | 562,401 | 367,078 | 418,789 |
| NW  | 2,977,002 | 2,541,370 | 2,258,972 |
| WC  | 1,779,768 | 1,348,503 | 1,038,788 |
| Emp. | 71 | 74 | 76 |

DUNS 21-597-1567
### Riverlee Care Home
Franklin Place, London SE13 7QT
**Tel:** 02086947140
**Web:** www.sanctuary-housing.co.uk
**Estd:** 2011
**Line of Business:** Nursing homes

**Responsibilities**
**Senior:** Rebecca Sowle (Manager)
**US SIC:** 8051 **UK SIC:** 95100
**Employees:** 94

DUNS 21-772-2402
### Rivermead Primary School
Loddon Bridge Road, Woodley, Reading,
Berkshire RG5 4BS
**Tel:** 01189690305
**Web:** www.rivermeadschool.org.uk
**Estd:** 1941 Proprietorship
**Line of Business:** Schools (local authority)
**Proprietor:** B Preble
**US SIC:** 8211 **UK SIC:** 93200
**Employees:** 60

DUNS 21-582-4461
### Rivers Agency
Hydebank, 4 Hospital Road, Belfast BT8 8JL
**Tel:** 02890253355
**Web:** www.dardni.gov.uk
**Estd:** 2011 Proprietorship
**Line of Business:** River authorities
**Proprietor:** J C Clarke
**US SIC:** 9121 **UK SIC:** 91110
**Employees:** 80

DUNS 21-772-1099
### Rivers Education Support Centre
Churchfields, Hertford, Hertfordshire SG13
8AE
**Tel:** 01992534841
**Estd:** 2011 Proprietorship
**Line of Business:** Adult and other education
not elsewhere classified
**Proprietor:** Mrs A Brown
**US SIC:** 8249 **UK SIC:** 93300
**Employees:** 50

DUNS 36-521-2807
### Rivers Hospital
High Wych Road, Sawbridgeworth,
Hertfordshire CM21 0HH
**Tel:** 01279600282
**Web:** www.rivers-hospital.co.uk
**Estd:** 1992 Proprietorship
**Line of Business:** Public sector hospital
activities, including nhs trusts
**Proprietor:** R Parson
**Responsibilities**
**Senior:** Amanda Foster (Supplies
Coordinator), Andrew Haysman (General
Manager)
**Marketing:** Nicola Thorp (Marketing
Manager)
**Facilities:** Issi Lekha (Facilities Manager)
**US SIC:** 8062 **UK SIC:** 95100
**Employees:** 300

DUNS 23-635-1243
### Riverside College Halton
Kingsway, Widnes, Cheshire WA8 7QQ
**Tel:** 01512572800
**Web:** www.riversidecollege.ac.uk
**VAT No:** 582288902 **Estd:** 1894
**Line of Business:** Further education schools
and colleges
**Trading Style:** Kingsway Campus
**Directors:** M D Jenkins, I Clinton
**Responsibilities**
**Senior:** Faisal Hashimi (Computer
Manager), Lyn Rhodes (Principal and
Chairman), Michael Sheehan (Principal)
**Finance:** Julie Holland (Head of Finance)
**IT:** Faisal Hashimi (Computer Manager)
**HR:** Neil Atherton (Learning Resources Team
Leader)
**Health & Safety:** Lee Walls (Head of
Estates)
**Facilities:** Lee Walls (Head of Estates)
**Branches:** Riverside College Halton,
Waterloo Community Centre, Waterloo
Road, Runcorn, Cheshire WA7 1JU
**US SIC:** 8221 **UK SIC:** 93100
**Bankers:** HSBC Bank plc (40-46-31)
**Employees:** 500

DUNS 21-580-3105
### Riverside Community Primary School
210 Poole Park Road, Plymouth, Devon PL5
1DD
**Tel:** 01752365297
**Web:** www.riversideprimary.net
**Estd:** 1956 Proprietorship
**Line of Business:** Schools (local authority)
**Proprietor:** B Jones
**US SIC:** 8211 **UK SIC:** 93200
**Employees:** 80

DUNS 21-781-8922
## Riverside Court
Salmoor Way, Maryport, Cumbria CA15 8AZ
**Tel:** 01900815323
**Web:** www.fshc.co.uk
**Estd:** 1994 Proprietorship
**Line of Business:** Nursing homes
**Proprietor:** Mrs J Eveleigh
**Responsibilities**
**Senior:** Colette Redhead *(Manager)*
**US SIC:** 8051 **UK SIC:** 95100
**Employees:** 60

DUNS 73-926-1480
## Riverside Garden Centre (Bristol) Ltd
Clift House Road, Bristol, Avon BS3 1RX
**Tel:** 01179667535 **Fax:** 01179-530411
**Web:** www.riversidegardencentre.com
**Reg No:** 5179239 **Estd:** 1985 Private Limited Company
**Line of Business:** Garden centres
**Issued Capital:** £121
**Directors:** Ms L L Carmichael, Miss L Finlayson, Mrs P A Biggs, G S Schofield, D Crossland, A T Avery
**Co. Secretary:** Stephen Shaw
**Responsibilities**
**Senior:** Deborah Buffery *(Manager)*, Joanne Hawkins *(Manager)*, Michael Tobin *(Manager)*
**US SIC:** 5999 **UK SIC:** 65600
**Bankers:** HSBC Bank plc (40-35-34)

| | 31-07-13 | 31-07-12 | 31-07-11 |
|---|---|---|---|
| TA | 757,333 | 747,641 | 769,451 |
| NW | 540,913 | 542,349 | 526,591 |
| WC | 315,529 | 322,757 | 301,286 |

DUNS 21-585-6502
## The Riverside Group Housing Association
Englishgate Plaza, Botchergate, Carlisle, Cumbria CA1 1RP
**Tel:** 08001693245
**Web:** www.riverside.org.uk
**Estd:** 2011 Proprietorship
**Line of Business:** Housing associations societies trusts & co-operatives
**Proprietor:** Mrs J Sutherland
**Responsibilities**
**Senior:** Anna Desmond *(Marketing Officer)*
**Marketing:** Anna Desmond *(Marketing Officer)*
**US SIC:** 8321 **UK SIC:** 96111
**Employees:** 250

DUNS 21-705-4974
## The Riverside Group Ltd
2 Estuary Boulevard, Speke, Liverpool, Merseyside L24 8RF
**Tel:** 08451127722 **Fax:** 08451127733
**Web:** www.riverside.org.uk
**Reg No:** 0030938IP **Estd:** 2006 Friendly Society
**Line of Business:** Housing associations societies trusts & co-operatives
**Principals:** P Brant *(Chairman)*, Mrs D Shackleton, M Steinberg, P Raw, Mrs S Jee, D Jepson, Mrs J Baggaley, Mrs A Jones
**Responsibilities**
**Senior:** Jo Kennefick *(Board Member)*, Carol Matthews *(CEO / Managing Director)*, Yashar Turgut *(Director)*
**Finance:** Andy Gladwin *(Senior Finance Director)*
**Admin:** R Clawson *(Director, Corporate Services)*
**US SIC:** 6531 **UK SIC:** 83400
**Auditors:** kPMG LLP
**Bankers:** National Westminster Bank Plc (50-30-20)

| | 31-03-12 | 31-03-11 | 31-03-10 |
|---|---|---|---|
| TO | 270,800,000 | 256,780,000 | 257,260,000 |
| P/L | 22,098,000 | 18,031,000 | 14,374,000 |
| NW | 236,992,000 | 221,391,000 | 193,965,000 |
| WC | 60,730,000 | 52,386,000 | 60,795,000 |
| Emp. | 2,464 | 2,354 | 2,333 |

DUNS 21-528-0871
## Riverside Healthcare Centre
Bridge Street, Selkirk, Selkirkshire TD7 5BU
**Tel:** 01750-22701
**Web:** www.kippenhouse.net
**Estd:** 1988 Partnership
**Line of Business:** Nursing homes
**Partners:** Mrs E Shubert, Miss T Canning
**Responsibilities**
**Senior:** Mary Armstrong *(Manager)*, Arthur McLean *(Joint Managing Director)*
**Marketing:** Arthur McLean *(Joint Managing Director)*
**IT:** Arthur McLean *(Joint Managing Director)*
**HR:** Arthur McLean *(Joint Managing Director)*
**Health & Safety:** Arthur McLean *(Joint Managing Director)*
**Facilities:** Arthur McLean *(Joint Managing Director)*
**Operations:** Sue Briggs *(Operations Manager)*
**Purchasing:** Arthur McLean *(Joint Managing Director)*
**US SIC:** 8051 **UK SIC:** 95100
**Employees:** 54

DUNS 29-545-5869
## Riverside Homes Ltd
56 Chorley New Road, Bolton, Lancashire BL1 4AP
**Tel:** 01204-394525 **Fax:** 01204377550
**Reg No:** 1912265 **Estd:** 1985 Private Limited Company
**Line of Business:** Nursing homes
**Issued Capital:** £321,585
**Managing Director:** M K Raja
**Co. Secretary:** Indumati Raja
**Branches:** Riverside Homes Ltd, 226-228 Wigan Road, Bolton, Lancashire BL3 5QE
**US SIC:** 8051 **UK SIC:** 95100
**Auditors:** Harold Sharp Son & Gresty

| | 30-06-13 | 30-06-12 | 30-06-11 |
|---|---|---|---|
| TA | 1,106,393 | 1,132,967 | 1,137,507 |
| NW | (196,823) | 54,171 | 94,825 |
| WC | (518,498) | (289,851) | (247,037) |

DUNS 73-753-6602
## Riverside Hotel Kendal Ltd
6 Station Road, Lancaster, Lancashire LA2 6HP
**Tel:** 01539732363
**Web:** www.riversidekendal.co.uk
**Reg No:** 5011182 **Estd:** 2004 Private Limited Company
**Line of Business:** Hotels
**Issued Capital:** £100
**Director:** Mrs M A Nicolson
**Co. Secretary:** Peter Denby
**Branches:** Riverside Hotel Kendal Ltd, Lound Road, Kendal, Cumbria LA9 7EQ
**US SIC:** 7011 **UK SIC:** 66500

| | 31-12-13 | 31-12-12 | 31-12-11 |
|---|---|---|---|
| TA | 1,861,790 | 1,857,079 | 1,806,492 |
| NW | 365,593 | 211,234 | 166,884 |
| WC | (363) | (45,367) | 6,248 |

DUNS 21-595-5285
## Riverside House
Riverside Drive, Aberdeen, Aberdeen, Aberdeenshire AB11 7LH
**Tel:** 01224213078
**Web:** www.lifeatnettlebed.co.uk
**Estd:** 1994
**Line of Business:** Property leasing
**Proprietor:** K Stirling
**US SIC:** 6531 **UK SIC:** 83400
**Employees:** 400

DUNS 28-913-0213 **Imp-Exp**
## Riverside Medical Packaging Co Ltd
Newmarket Drive, Derby, Derbyshire DE24 8SW
**Tel:** 01332755622 **Fax:** 01332757722
**Web:** www.riversidemedical.co.uk
**Reg No:** 1430113 **VAT No:** 331479362
**Estd:** 1983 Private Limited Company
**Line of Business:** Manufacture of medical and surgical equipment and orthopaedic appliances
**Export Markets:** Worldwide
**Export Sales:** £855,901
**Issued Capital:** £33,750
**Principals:** D N Shaw *(Managing)*, M W Roe, A Wade
**Co. Secretary:** David Shaw
**Responsibilities**
**Senior:** Neil Riddolls *(Sales Director)*
**Finance:** Beverley Jeffery *(Accounts Manager)*
**Sales:** Neil Riddolls *(Sales Director)*
**HR:** Beverley Jeffery *(Accounts Manager)*
**US SIC:** 3841, 7399
**UK SIC:** 37201, 83954
**Auditors:** Cooper Parry LLP
**Bankers:** National Westminster Bank Plc (01-02-66)

| | 31-12-13 | 31-12-12 | 31-12-11 |
|---|---|---|---|
| TO | 7,935,663 | 7,034,075 | 6,020,127 |
| P/L | 647,838 | 920,982 | 628,073 |
| NW | 2,951,391 | 2,781,527 | 2,145,144 |
| WC | 1,111,358 | 1,187,831 | 733,309 |
| Emp. | 136 | 115 | 99 |

DUNS 54-891-8556
## Riverside Motors Holdings Ltd
Marland House, 13 Huddersfield Road, Barnsley, South Yorkshire S70 2LW
**Tel:** 01302327108
**Web:** www.riversidemotors.co.uk
**Reg No:** 3445546 **Estd:** 1997 Private Limited Company
**Line of Business:** Management activities of holding companies
**Issued Capital:** £666
**Directors:** S Wright, M D Denton
**Co. Secretary:** Ms Christine Vasey
**US SIC:** 6711 **UK SIC:** 83962

| | 31-12-13 | 31-12-12 | 31-12-11 |
|---|---|---|---|
| TO | 51,148,635 | 45,250,008 | 45,260,127 |
| P/L | 1,219,244 | 910,542 | 1,426,068 |
| NW | 4,627,852 | 4,312,170 | 4,180,765 |
| WC | 2,118,409 | 1,764,370 | 1,643,145 |
| Emp. | 95 | 92 | 89 |

DUNS 57-044-0909
## Riverside Nursing Home Ltd
9 Church Street, Littleborough, Lancashire OL15 8DA
**Tel:** 01935812046
**Web:** www.riversidenursinghome.co.uk
**Reg No:** 2876914 **Estd:** 1993 Private Limited Company
**Line of Business:** Other tourist or short-stay accommodation
**Issued Capital:** £2
**Director:** F Pardhan
**Branches:** Riverside Nursing Home Ltd, Riverside House, Millburngate, Durham, County Durham DH1 4UD
**US SIC:** 7021 **UK SIC:** 66500
**Auditors:** Milsted Langdon

| | 30-04-14 | 30-04-13 | 30-04-12 |
|---|---|---|---|
| TA | 2,935,069 | 2,685,567 | 2,517,251 |
| NW | 2,688,481 | 2,488,099 | 2,285,007 |
| WC | 1,598,654 | 1,386,446 | 1,171,485 |

DUNS 21-776-4669
## Riverside Restaurant
Granta Place, Cambridge, Cambridgeshire CB2 1RU
**Web:** www.unicen.cam.ac.uk
**Estd:** 2011 Proprietorship
**Line of Business:** Restaurants
**Proprietor:** N White
**US SIC:** 5812 **UK SIC:** 66110
**Employees:** 100

DUNS 21-877-9278
## Riverside School
Main Road, Orpington, Kent BR5 3HS
**Tel:** 01689870519
**Web:** www.riversideschool.org.uk
**Estd:** 1976
**Line of Business:** Schools (special)
**Responsibilities**
**Senior:** Vivian Hinchcliffe *(Head Teacher)*, Steve Solomons *(Head Teacher)*
**US SIC:** 8299 **UK SIC:** 93300
**Employees:** 150

DUNS 21-600-6521
## Riverside View
Hutton Avenue, Darlington, County Durham DL1 2AQ
**Tel:** 01325488584
**Web:** www.fshc.co.uk
**Estd:** 2004 Proprietorship
**Line of Business:** Non-charitable social work activities with accommodation
**Proprietor:** Mrs L Beaumont
**US SIC:** 8321 **UK SIC:** 96111
**Employees:** 52

DUNS 23-209-0647
## Riversmead Housing Association
36 Ware Road, Hertford, Hertfordshire SG13 7HH
**Tel:** 01992-514514 **Fax:** 01992-514500
**Web:** www.riversmead.org.uk
**Reg No:** 0027918IP **Estd:** 1994 Friendly Society
**Line of Business:** Non-charitable social work activities with accommodation
**Principals:** H Banks *(Chairman)*, Ms J Evans, L Slight, V Townell, L Dutt, M Hargreaves, Ms A Dutt, Ms C Moules
**Responsibilities**
**Senior:** LUKE DUTT *(Director)*, ANNA DUTT *(Director)*, JANET EVANS *(Director)*, MICHAEL HARGREAVES *(Director)*, Steve Hemmings *(Chief Executive)*, Paul Huckstep *(Executive Director)*, CONNIE MOULES *(Director)*, LES SLIGHT *(Director)*, Debbie Saucede *(Office Manager)*, VAUGHAN TOWNELL *(Director)*
**Finance:** BARRY PARKER *(Treasurer)*
**Admin:** Wayne Donaldson *(Secretary)*
**US SIC:** 8321, 6519
**UK SIC:** 96111, 85000
**Bankers:** HSBC Bank plc (40-46-09)

| | 31-03-12 | 31-03-11 | 31-03-10 |
|---|---|---|---|
| TO | 21,913,314 | 18,861,110 | 17,072,654 |
| P/L | 3,737,231 | 3,138,934 | 2,512,001 |
| NW | 16,283,831 | 13,287,600 | 8,055,668 |
| WC | (1,732,265) | (1,685,260) | 518,592 |
| Emp. | 70 | 66 | 67 |

DUNS 50-553-8181
## Riverston Group Ltd
Eltham Road, London SE12 8UF
**Tel:** 02083184327 **Fax:** 020-8297-0514
**Web:** www.riverstonschool.co.uk
**Reg No:** 2505250 **Estd:** 1990 Private Limited Company
**Line of Business:** Schools (independent)
**Trading Style:** Riverston School
**Issued Capital:** £273,100
**Managing Director:** Professor D M Lewis
**Co. Secretary:** Ms Janina Lewis
**Responsibilities**
**Senior:** Sarah Salathiel *(Headmistress)*
**Finance:** Tracey Cook *(Bursar)*, Maria Mihoney *(Assistant Bursar)*
**Admin:** Mei Aldridge *(Headmistress PA)*
**IT:** Mel Mitchell *(IT Coordinator)*
**HR:** Tracey Cook *(Bursar)*
**Health & Safety:** Tracey Cook *(Bursar)*
**Facilities:** Stephen Scarlett *(Facilities Manager)*
**Purchasing:** Tracey Cook *(Bursar)*
**US SIC:** 8211 **UK SIC:** 93200
**Auditors:** Elman Wall
**Bankers:** National Westminster Bank Plc (60-04-02)

| | 31-08-14 | 31-08-13 | 31-08-12 |
|---|---|---|---|
| TO | 3,507,569 | 2,972,919 | 2,384,866 |
| P/L | 251,347 | 215,494 | (203,167) |
| NW | 3,624,503 | 3,480,875 | 3,369,221 |
| WC | (689,738) | (666,242) | (749,125) |
| Emp. | 87 | 75 | 71 |

DUNS 22-517-2055 **Imp**
## Riverstone Management Ltd
(**Subsidiary of:** Riverstone Holdings Ltd)
Park Gate, 161-163 Preston Road, Brighton, East Sussex BN1 6AU
**Tel:** 01273562345
**Web:** www.rsml.co.uk
**Reg No:** 1268308 **VAT No:** 452471554
**Estd:** 1982 Private Limited Company
**Line of Business:** Insurance services
**Trading Style:** Sphere Drake Insurance
**Issued Capital:** £100,000
**Directors:** M J Bannister, Ms L A Hemsley, F Henry, S C Roberts, L R Tanzer, N C Bentley, A C Tilley
**Co. Secretary:** Fraser Henry
**Branches:** Riverstone Management Ltd, Mint House, 2ND Floor, London E1 8AF
**US SIC:** 6411 **UK SIC:** 83200
**Auditors:** PricewaterhouseCoopers LLP
**Bankers:** The Royal Bank Of Scotland Plc (16-14-24)

| | 31-12-13 | 31-12-12 | 31-12-11 |
|---|---|---|---|
| TO | 21,218,000 | 12,246,000 | 11,966,000 |
| P/L | 35,000 | (8,000) | N/A |
| NW | 616,000 | 561,000 | 25,000 |
| WC | (1,863,000) | (1,339,000) | (1,771,000) |
| Emp. | 79 | 70 | 66 |

DUNS 21-600-6522
## Riversway Nursing Home
Crews Hole Road, Bristol, Avon BS5 8GG
**Web:** www.riverswaycare.com
**Estd:** 1997 Proprietorship
**Line of Business:** Nursing homes
**Proprietor:** K Nolan
**Responsibilities**
**Senior:** Gregory Grant *(Partner)*, Glen Grant *(Partner)*
**US SIC:** 8051 **UK SIC:** 95100
**Employees:** 100

DUNS 23-871-4344
## Riverway Foods Ltd.
(**Subsidiary of:** Riverway Investments Ltd)
Crown House, River Way, Harlow, Essex CM20 2DL
**Tel:** 01279 450999
**Web:** www.riverwayfoods.co.uk
**Reg No:** 3862803 **VAT No:** 740976901
**Estd:** 1999 Private Limited Company
**Line of Business:** Animal by-product processing
**Issued Capital:** £30,000
**Directors:** J W Crosby, S D Crosby
**Co. Secretary:** Stephen Crosby
**US SIC:** 2013 **UK SIC:** 41223
**Auditors:** Haslers

| | 30-03-14 | 31-03-13 | 01-03-12 |
|---|---|---|---|
| TO | 24,526,724 | 22,463,304 | 23,908,865 |
| P/L | 975,348 | 4,873 | 228,392 |
| NW | 1,448,912 | 589,384 | 1,231,395 |
| WC | (1,360,065) | (2,106,657) | (1,668,261) |
| Emp. | 136 | 116 | 89 |

DUNS 21-225-0486
## Riviera
Gabriels Wharf, 56 Upper Ground, London SE1 9PP
**Line of Business:** Licensed restaurants
**Responsibilities**
**Senior:** Justaf Bartoni *(Manager)*
**US SIC:** 5812 **UK SIC:** 66110
**Employees:** 49

DUNS 21-600-9916
## Riviera Hotel
Bowleaze Coveway, Weymouth, Dorset DT3 6PR
**Tel:** 01305836600
**Web:** www.rivierahotelweymouth.co.uk
**Estd:** 1999 Partnership
**Line of Business:** Hotels
**Partners:** A Merideth, J Wright
**Responsibilities**
**Senior:** Carol Rooke *(General Manager)*
**US SIC:** 7999 **UK SIC:** 97913
**Employees:** 70

DUNS 22-292-8496
## Riviera Leisure Ltd
(**Subsidiary of:** Riviera Leisure (Holdings) Ltd)
Unit 2, Therm Road, Hull, North Humberside HU8 7BF
**Tel:** 01482602988
**Reg No:** 4310848 **Estd:** 2001 Private Limited Company
**Line of Business:** Gambling and betting activities
**Issued Capital:** £1,000
**Directors:** C E Clark, W E Clark, Ms K O'Callaghan
**Branches:** Riviera Leisure Ltd, 9-11 Sicey Avenue, Sheffield, South Yorkshire S5 6NF
**US SIC:** 7999 **UK SIC:** 97913
**Bankers:** Bank Of Scotland (12-16-30)

| | 31-03-14 | 31-03-13 | 31-03-12 |
|---|---|---|---|
| TO | 2,470,160 | 2,847,482 | 2,974,827 |
| P/L | 322,396 | 288,233 | 121,715 |
| NW | 2,200,334 | 3,060,040 | 2,372,091 |
| WC | 1,017,555 | (545,729) | (552,791) |
| Emp. | 60 | 68 | 80 |

DUNS 53-651-4706
## Riviera Produce Ltd
14 Gwinear Road, Hayle, Cornwall TR27 5JQ
**Tel:** 01736-850960 **Fax:** 01736850968
**Web:** www.rivieraproduce.eu
**Reg No:** 3456808 **Estd:** 1997 Private Limited Company
**Line of Business:** Wholesalers of fruit and vegetable
**Issued Capital:** £300,002
**Director:** D J Simmons
**Co. Secretary:** Ms Suzanne Simmons
**Responsibilities**
**Marketing:** Matthew Wiggins *(Marketing Manager)*
**US SIC:** 5148 **UK SIC:** 61700
**Auditors:** Graham Smith

| | 30-09-13 | 30-09-12 | 30-09-11 |
|---|---|---|---|
| TA | 2,619,199 | 2,547,763 | 2,785,094 |
| NW | 1,448,331 | 1,273,986 | 1,186,618 |
| WC | 1,453,698 | 1,364,003 | 1,236,687 |

DUNS 29-506-0826
## Riviera Tours Ltd
(**Subsidiary of:** Riviera Tours (Holdings) Ltd)
328 Wetmore Road, Burton-On-Trent, Staffordshire DE14 1SP
**Tel:** 01283-742300 **Fax:** 01283742301
**Web:** www.rivieratravel.co.uk
**Reg No:** 1869298 **VAT No:** 411194292
**Estd:** 1984 Private Limited Company
**Line of Business:** Activities of travel agencies
**Trading Style:** Riviera Travel
**Issued Capital:** £50,000
**Principals:** M G Wright *(Managing)*, E Moore, D Clemson
**Responsibilities**
**Senior:** Claire Wright *(Manager)*
**US SIC:** 4722 **UK SIC:** 77001
**Auditors:** Bourne & Co
**Bankers:** Lloyds TSB Bank plc (30-91-47)

| | 30-11-13 | 30-11-12 | 30-11-11 |
|---|---|---|---|
| TO | 106,295,407 | 84,966,752 | 70,670,843 |
| P/L | 9,993,120 | 6,550,848 | 5,685,097 |
| NW | 14,324,148 | 11,566,174 | 9,587,576 |
| WC | 14,047,781 | 11,405,040 | 9,485,816 |
| Emp. | 84 | 73 | 70 |

DUNS 45-831-1610
## Rivington Biscuits Ltd
Ormside Close, Hindley Green, Wigan, Lancashire WN2 4HR
**Tel:** 01942-255959
**Web:** www.rivifoods.com
**Reg No:** 3182725 **Estd:** 1996 Private Limited Company
**Line of Business:** Manufacturers of biscuits
**Issued Capital:** £224,380
**Directors:** M R Van Der Zwan, O S De Lange
**Co. Secretary:** Tim Sanders
**Responsibilities**
**Senior:** Robbie Beckett *(Factory Manager)*, Tracie Jackson *(Administrator)*, Alistair Marsden *(Manager)*
**Marketing:** Alistair Marsden *(Manager)*
**Health & Safety:** Robbie Beckett *(Factory Manager)*
**Facilities:** Robbie Beckett *(Factory Manager)*
**US SIC:** 2052 **UK SIC:** 41970
**Auditors:** Alexander Knight & Co Ltd
**Bankers:** HSBC Bank plc (40-29-08)

| | 31-12-13 | 31-12-12 | 31-12-11 |
|---|---|---|---|
| TO | 16,109,760 | 13,759,583 | 10,246,291 |
| P/L | 122,051 | 62,701 | (703,129) |
| NW | 4,552,763 | 3,762,088 | 3,683,387 |
| WC | 2,681,812 | 2,860,874 | 3,500,712 |
| Emp. | 154 | 158 | 137 |

DUNS 21-584-9237
## Rivington Village Club
Horrobin Lane, Rivington, Bolton, Lancashire BL6 7SE
**Tel:** 01204691509
**Web:** www.rivingtonbowlingclub.co.uk
**Estd:** 2011 Proprietorship
**Line of Business:** Sports clubs
**Proprietor:** Mrs R Taylor
**US SIC:** 7999 **UK SIC:** 97913
**Employees:** 60

DUNS 28-962-1617 **Imp-Exp**
## Rivitswade Ltd
(**Subsidiary of:** Melidite Ltd)
Rivitswade House, 9 Ackworth Road Shawcross Industrial, Park, Portsmouth, Hampshire PO3 5HU
**Tel:** 023-9266-3336
**Web:** www.rivitswade.co.uk
**Reg No:** 1686194 **Estd:** 1982 Private Limited Company
**Line of Business:** Manufacture of other fabricated metal products not elsewhere classified
**Export Markets:** Middle East, Cyprus
**Issued Capital:** £100
**Principals:** R A Bernier *(Managing)*, Ms A Bernier
**Co. Secretary:** Mc Secretaries Limited
**Responsibilities**
**Senior:** Alan Erridge *(Financial Director)*, Malcolm Weston *(Operations Director)*
**Finance:** Alan Erridge *(Financial Director)*
**IT:** Malcolm Weston *(Operations Director)*
**HR:** Malcolm Weston *(Operations Director)*
**Engineering:** Malcolm Weston *(Operations Director)*
**Branches:** Rivitswade Ltd, Unit 1, Fareham Road, Gosport, Hampshire PO13 0BA
**US SIC:** 3499 **UK SIC:** 31694
**Auditors:** Grant Thornton
**Bankers:** Barclays Bank Plc (20-30-89)

| | 30-11-14 | 30-11-13 | 30-11-12 |
|---|---|---|---|
| TO | N/A | N/A | 3,839,085 |
| P/L | N/A | N/A | 181,672 |
| NW | 1,251,679 | 1,408,224 | 1,548,125 |
| WC | (19,362) | 29,431 | 126,916 |
| Emp. | N/A | N/A | 56 |

DUNS 22-269-9196
## Rivo Software Ltd
The Innovation Centre, Warwick Technology Park, Warwick, Warwickshire CV34 6UW
**Tel:** 01926622320
**Web:** www.rivosoftware.com
**Reg No:** 4287879 **Estd:** 2001 Private Limited Company
**Line of Business:** Computer software (development)
**Export Sales:** £516,456
**Issued Capital:** £1,151
**Directors:** S C Husk, P T Bullivant, D Hebel, M S Elias, H L Zidel
**Responsibilities**
**Senior:** Ken Baxter *(Manager)*, Matthew Duckhouse *(Manager)*, Simon Hook *(Manager)*
**Marketing:** Stacey Henson *(Marketing Manager)*
**Health & Safety:** Jo Warde *(account manager)*
**US SIC:** 7379 **UK SIC:** 83940
**Auditors:** Deloitte LLP

| | 31-12-13 | 31-12-12 | 31-12-11 |
|---|---|---|---|
| TO | 5,533,169 | N/A | N/A |
| P/L | (914,063) | N/A | N/A |
| NW | 1,657,226 | 1,184,689 | 522,292 |
| WC | 1,521,152 | 1,106,520 | 459,028 |
| Emp. | 55 | N/A | N/A |

DUNS 21-327-8435
## Rixonway Kitchens Ltd
(**Subsidiary of:** August Equity Llp)
Churwell Vale, Dewsbury, West Yorkshire WF12 7RD
**Tel:** 01924 431300
**Web:** www.rixonway.co.uk
**Reg No:** 1382317 **Estd:** 1978 Private Limited Company
**Line of Business:** Kitchen planners and installers
**Issued Capital:** £1,000
**Principals:** P P Rose *(Technical)*, B M Norman, D J Anderson, P Kane, A Ahmed, D A Carr
**Co. Secretary:** Keith Robinson
**Responsibilities**
**Senior:** Nicholas Greenall *(Operations Director)*
**Sales:** Julian Dudley *(Commercial Director)*
**Operations:** Nicholas Greenall *(Operations Director)*
**Purchasing:** Steven Hodgkiss *(Purchasing Manager)*
**Branches:** Rixonway Kitchens Ltd, Headway Business Park, Denby Dale Road, Wakefield, West Yorkshire WF2 7AZ
**US SIC:** 2599 **UK SIC:** 46720
**Auditors:** PKF (UK) LLP
**Bankers:** Yorkshire Bank Plc (05-01-06)

| | 28-02-14 | 28-02-13 | 29-02-12 |
|---|---|---|---|
| TO | 35,146,928 | 30,105,588 | 29,734,913 |
| P/L | 685,205 | 684,748 | 1,563,412 |
| NW | 17,559,386 | 16,982,909 | 16,459,467 |
| WC | 17,016,802 | 10,346,529 | 9,568,112 |
| Emp. | 469 | 472 | 453 |

DUNS 28-820-8960
## Riyad Bank
(**Subsidiary of:** Riyad Bank)
Riyad Bank House, 17b Curzon Street, London W1J 5HX
**Tel:** 020-7830-9000 **Fax:** 02074931134
**Reg No:** 0012256FC **Estd:** 1984 Foreign Company
**Line of Business:** Banks and financial institutions
**Directors:** N I Wehibi, F A Abaalkhail, A I Al-Hudaithi, K H Al-Nahas, M A Al-Afaleq, F A Al-Howaimel, R I Al-Rashed, A H Sharbatly
**Responsibilities**
**Senior:** Abdulla Al-Ayyadhi *(Director)*, Abdullah Al-Issa *(Director)*, Abdulaziz Al-Jarbou *(Director)*, Waleed Aleisa *(Director)*, Fahad Howaimel *(Manager)*, Abdullah Hudaithi *(Manager)*, Abdulaziz Jarbou *(Manager)*, Khaled Nahas *(Manager)*, Al Rashed *(Manager)*
**US SIC:** 6012 **UK SIC:** 81402
**Bankers:** HSBC Bank plc (40-05-15)

DUNS 21-910-8065 **Imp-Exp**
## R.J. Herbert Engineering Ltd
(**Subsidiary of:** R J Herbert Group Ltd)
Bank House Farm, Middle Drove, Marshland St James, Wisbech, Cambridgeshire PE14 8JT
**Tel:** 01945-430666
**Web:** www.herbertenvironmental.co.uk
**Reg No:** 1793875 **VAT No:** 106231518
**Estd:** 1958 Private Limited Company
**Line of Business:** Agricultural machinery sales service and repair
**Export Markets:** Worldwide
**Export Sales:** £6,607,771
**Trading Style:** Herbert
**Issued Capital:** £6,800
**Principals:** R J Herbert *(Managing)*, N J Herbert *(Managing)*, Mrs J E Savory
**Co. Secretary:** Georgina Herbert
**Responsibilities**
**Senior:** Nigel Goodrum *(Stores Manager)*, John Oram *(Accountant)*
**Finance:** John Oram *(Accountant)*
**HR:** Ken North *(Operations Manager)*, Mark Sinden *(Operations Manager)*
**Health & Safety:** Ken North *(Operations Manager)*, Mark Sinden *(Operations Manager)*
**Facilities:** Ken North *(Operations Manager)*, Mark Sinden *(Operations Manager)*
**Operations:** Nigel Goodrum *(Stores Manager)*, Ken North *(Operations Manager)*, Mark Sinden *(Operations Manager)*
**Purchasing:** Ken North *(Operations Manager)*
**Engineering:** Ken North *(Operations Manager)*, Mark Sinden *(Operations Manager)*
**US SIC:** 8911 **UK SIC:** 83701
**Auditors:** Wheelers
**Bankers:** Barclays Bank Plc (20-97-34)

| | 31-03-13 | 31-12-11 | 31-03-10 |
|---|---|---|---|
| TO | 19,347,154 | 16,520,534 | 12,006,357 |
| P/L | 825,266 | 258,566 | 149,450 |
| NW | 1,135,375 | 137,369 | 346,066 |
| WC | 1,360,046 | 89,144 | (73,406) |
| Emp. | 155 | 169 | 149 |

DUNS 21-441-6851
## R.J. McLeod (Contractors) Ltd
2411 London Road, Glasgow, Lanarkshire G32 8XT
**Tel:** 01417-642411
**Web:** www.rjmcleod.co.uk
**Reg No:** 0028565SC **VAT No:** 260283771
**Estd:** 1951 Private Limited Company
**Line of Business:** Representative office
**Issued Capital:** £472,375
**Principals:** B G Clark *(Managing)*, G S Clark *(Managing)*, N M Judd *(Financial)*, A R Osborne
**Responsibilities**
**Sales:** Jamie Corser *(Business Development Manager)*, Margarete O'Sriel *(Office Manager)*
**Admin:** Margarete O'Sriel *(Office Manager)*
**IT:** Darren Slupek *(IT Manager)*
**HR:** Margarete O'Sriel *(Office Manager)*
**Facilities:** Margarete O'Sriel *(Office Manager)*
**Branches:** R.j. Mcleod (Contractors) Ltd, Unit 4, Fodderty Way, Dingwall, Ross-Shire IV15 9XB
**US SIC:** 1611, 1622, 1541
**UK SIC:** 50200, 50100
**Auditors:** French Duncan LLP
**Bankers:** Bank Of Scotland (80-11-80)

| | 03-11-13 | 28-10-12 | 30-11-11 |
|---|---|---|---|
| TO | 84,359,159 | 83,337,266 | 65,782,774 |
| P/L | 6,478,806 | 5,141,696 | 6,219,690 |
| NW | 30,829,597 | 28,283,096 | 26,701,782 |
| WC | 22,858,772 | 20,531,418 | 19,811,111 |
| Emp. | 387 | 389 | 386 |

DUNS 21-282-1939
## R.J. Trevarthen
Roskrow Abattoir, Roskrow, Penryn, Cornwall TR10 9AP
**Tel:** 01326-377081
**Web:** www.rjtrevarthen.co.uk
**Estd:** 1984 Proprietorship
**Line of Business:** Wholesale of meat and meat products
**Proprietor:** R J Trevarthen
**Responsibilities**
**Senior:** M Mankee *(Manager)*
**US SIC:** 5147, 2013
**UK SIC:** 61700, 41223
**Employees:** 50

DUNS 56-949-7613
## R.J.D. Ltd.
(**Subsidiary of:** Rjd Quarries Ltd)
Cecil House, Foster Street, Harlow, Essex CM17 9HY
**Tel:** 01279-421456 **Fax:** 01279-422992
**Web:** www.pryor.co.uk
**Reg No:** 2842908 **Estd:** 1993 Private Limited Company
**Line of Business:** Waste disposal
**Issued Capital:** £2,000
**Directors:** R G Pryor, C J Pryor, D P Rees, A S Clark, D L Rees
**Responsibilities**
**Senior:** Allan Gifford *(Manager)*, Dave Parrack *(General Manager)*
**Admin:** Michelle Aley *(Accounts)*
**Branches:** R.j.d. Ltd., Tillingham Road, Southminster, Essex CM0 7DT
**US SIC:** 4953 **UK SIC:** 92110
**Auditors:** H E Godwin & Co

| | 30-06-14 | 30-06-13 | 30-06-12 |
|---|---|---|---|
| TA | 2,234,501 | 2,085,294 | 1,061,065 |
| NW | 191,006 | 190,823 | 150,399 |
| WC | 163,585 | 156,262 | 267,935 |

DUNS 77-750-2477
## R.J.H. Eccles Holdings Ltd
14 Chancel Way, Halesowen, West Midlands B62 8SE
**Tel:** 01215855908
**Web:** www.ecclestooling.co.uk
**Reg No:** 3015173 **Estd:** 1995 Private Limited Company
**Line of Business:** Management activities of holding companies
**Issued Capital:** £20,000
**Director:** R J Eccles
**Co. Secretary:** Ms Diane Eccles
**US SIC:** 6711, 7399
**UK SIC:** 83962, 83954
**Auditors:** Price Pearson

| | 30-04-14 | 30-04-13 | 30-04-12 |
|---|---|---|---|
| TO | N/A | 220,000 | N/A |
| P/L | N/A | 291,973 | N/A |
| NW | 1,109,760 | 1,107,634 | 1,102,428 |
| WC | (188,802) | (106,157) | (218,140) |
| Emp. | N/A | 2 | N/A |

DUNS 21-620-6045
## R.J.Stearn Ltd
(**Subsidiary of:** R.J.Stearn Holdings Ltd)
32 Vincent Avenue, Regent Business Park, Crownhill, Milton Keynes, Buckinghamshire MK8 0AB
**Tel:** 0845 034 6420 **Fax:** 0190 826 3310
**Web:** www.rjstearn.com
**Reg No:** 0390223 **VAT No:** 991238594
**Estd:** 1921 Private Limited Company
**Line of Business:** Installation of electrical wiring and fittings
**Issued Capital:** £3,000
**Principals:** R H Stearn *(Managing)*, J P Grant
**Co. Secretary:** Ms Janice Stearn
**Responsibilities**
**Admin:** Laura Ward *(Project Administrator)*
**US SIC:** 1731 **UK SIC:** 50300
**Bankers:** HSBC Bank plc (40-30-32)

| | 31-10-13 | 31-10-12 | 31-10-11 |
|---|---|---|---|
| TA | 2,392,618 | 2,355,086 | 2,475,887 |
| NW | 1,225,461 | 1,180,916 | 1,436,943 |
| WC | 1,022,761 | 1,150,512 | 1,374,640 |

DUNS 21-239-7178
## R.J.Stokes & Co. Ltd
Holbrook Industrial Estate, Sheffield, South Yorkshire S20 3RW
**Tel:** 01142512680
**Web:** www.stokestiles.co.uk
**Reg No:** 0190422 **VAT No:** 172677438
**Estd:** 1899 Private Limited Company
**Line of Business:** Manufacture of paints, varnishes and similar coatings, printing ink and mastics
**Trading Style:** Stokes Tiles, Stokes Paints, Advance Coatings, Pandel Tiles
**Issued Capital:** £40,899
**Principals:** R J Stokes *(Chairman and Managing)*, R C Stokes, T J Stokes
**Co. Secretary:** Richard Askham
**Responsibilities**
**Purchasing:** Kirsty Farrow *(Purchasing Manager)*
**Branches:** R.j.stokes & Co. Ltd, Little London Road, Sheffield, South Yorkshire S8 0UH
**US SIC:** 2851, 5199
**UK SIC:** 25510, 61900
**Auditors:** UHY Wingfield Slater
**Bankers:** National Westminster Bank Plc (54-41-48)

| | 31-12-13 | 31-12-12 | 31-12-11 |
|---|---|---|---|
| TO | 4,877,827 | 12,514,980 | 14,220,195 |
| P/L | (49,527) | 257,625 | 152,099 |
| NW | 9,961,482 | 9,970,971 | 9,718,137 |
| WC | 2,830,246 | 2,348,496 | 3,619,313 |
| Emp. | 54 | 118 | 138 |

DUNS 50-378-7798
## R.J.T. Excavations Ltd
Oxnam Road Industrial Estate, Jedburgh, Roxburghshire TD8 6LS
**Tel:** 01835-862367 **Fax:** 01835-863025
**Web:** www.rjtexcavations.co.uk
**Reg No:** 0118090SC **Estd:** 1989 Private Limited Company
**Line of Business:** Construction of civil engineering constructions
**Issued Capital:** £100
**Directors:** B White, A F Carr, J Smyth, G W Young
**Co. Secretary:** Alan Jackson
**Branches:** R.j.t. Excavations Ltd, Enterprise Centre, Unit 6, Loanhead, Midlothian EH20 9LZ
**US SIC:** 1795 **UK SIC:** 50000
**Auditors:** Messrs Paterson Reid
**Bankers:** Bank Of Scotland (80-16-48)

| | 31-05-13 | 31-05-12 | 31-05-11 |
|---|---|---|---|
| TO | 17,733,191 | 15,449,089 | 18,002,328 |
| P/L | 511,111 | 1,037,783 | (327,447) |
| NW | 2,787,293 | 2,285,401 | 1,000,298 |
| WC | (747,357) | (447,951) | (1,131,121) |
| Emp. | 95 | 64 | 77 |

DUNS 73-334-2609
## Rk Construction (Essex) Ltd
59 Gafzelle Drive, Canvey Island, Essex SS8 7LZ
**Tel:** 01268680241
**Reg No:** 4608064 **Estd:** 2002 Private Limited Company
**Line of Business:** Development and selling of real estate
**Issued Capital:** £1,000
**Director:** R C Knight
**Co. Secretary:** Ms Laura Holt
**US SIC:** 6552, 1799
**UK SIC:** 85000, 50000
**Auditors:** Maltel Services

| | 30-04-14 | 30-04-13 | 30-04-12 |
|---|---|---|---|
| TA | 100 | 100 | 100 |
| NW | 100 | 100 | 100 |

DUNS 22-695-7827
## Rkb Underwood Holdings Ltd
**(Subsidiary of:** Rkb Property Investments Ltd)
Tower Hill House, 13 New Road, Sandy, Bedfordshire SG19 1NX
**Tel:** 07897895511
**Reg No:** 0966942 **Estd:** 1969 Private Limited Company
**Line of Business:** Other letting of own property
**Issued Capital:** £18,336
**Managing Director:** B Underwood
**Co. Secretary:** Ms Judith Underwood
**US SIC:** 6519 **UK SIC:** 85000
**Auditors:** Horwath Wagstaff
**Bankers:** HSBC Bank plc (40-10-02)

| | 28-02-14 | 28-02-13 | 29-02-12 |
|---|---|---|---|
| TA | 462,826 | 473,944 | 480,372 |
| NW | 169,150 | 198,871 | 218,512 |
| WC | (205,469) | (175,040) | (155,399) |

DUNS 29-025-3392
## Rl Design Solutions Ltd
**(Subsidiary of:** Henderson Infrastructure Holdco Ltd)
Maxted House, Maxted Road, Hemel Hempstead Industrial Estate, Hemel Hempstead, Hertfordshire HP2 7DX
**Tel:** 01442220950 **Fax:** 01442-286650
**Web:** http://rldesignmfg.com
**Reg No:** 0675629 **Estd:** 1960 Private Limited Company
**Line of Business:** Consultancy service company. Design consultants, ground engineering, technical services and graphical surveying for the construction industry
**Trading Style:** Ltg Geotechnical & Enviromental
**Issued Capital:** £1,000,000
**Director:** Mrs M B Lewis
**Co. Secretary:** Ms Maria Lewis
**Responsibilities**
**Senior:** Roger Miller *(Manager)*
**US SIC:** 7392, 8911
**UK SIC:** 83951, 83701
**Auditors:** KPMG Audit Plc
**Bankers:** Clydesdale Bank Plc (82-43-03)

| | 31-12-13 | 31-12-12 | 31-12-11 |
|---|---|---|---|
| TA | 1,000,000 | 1,000,000 | 1,000,000 |
| NW | 1,000,000 | 1,000,000 | 1,000,000 |

DUNS 76-994-4885 **Imp**
## Rl La Ltd
**(Subsidiary of:** The Royal London Mutual Insurance Society Limited)
301 St Vincent Street, Glasgow, Lanarkshire G2 5HN
**Tel:** 0141-275-8000
**Web:** www.resolution.com
**Reg No:** 0134205SC **Estd:** 1991 Private Limited Company
**Line of Business:** Activities auxiliary to insurance and pension funding
**Issued Capital:** £149,062,335
**Directors:** M Lewis, A M Nixon, S C Mitchley
**Co. Secretary:**
Royal London Management Services
**US SIC:** 6411 **UK SIC:** 83200
**Employees:** 2,000

DUNS 45-800-6400 **Imp**
## R.L. Plastics Ltd
Britannia House, Dock Road, Birkenhead, Merseyside CH41 1DF
**Tel:** 0151-639-0002
**Web:** www.buybuckets.co.uk
**Reg No:** 3162133 **Estd:** 1996 Private Limited Company
**Line of Business:** Manufacturers of plastic products
**Trading Style:** H & O Plastics
**Issued Capital:** £1,000
**Directors:** Ms R Lavender, G Ocego
**Co. Secretary:** Robert Lavender
**US SIC:** 2821 **UK SIC:** 25140
**Auditors:** Whitnalls

| | 31-12-13 | 31-12-12 | 31-12-11 |
|---|---|---|---|
| TA | 658,027 | 605,712 | 568,463 |
| NW | 203,980 | 158,352 | 116,267 |
| WC | 52,876 | 8,423 | (24,311) |

DUNS 23-911-0583
## Rl Retail Services Ltd
**(Subsidiary of:** Acqui Polo C.V.)
Sentinel House, 46 Clarendon Road, Watford, Hertfordshire WD17 1HE
**Tel:** 01923475100
**Reg No:** 3901528 **Estd:** 1999 Private Limited Company
**Line of Business:** Business services
**Issued Capital:** £1
**Directors:** M R Kerschen, G C Van Raemdonck, J B Taylor, A A Fleri, C Lund
**Co. Secretary:** Abogado Nominees Limited
**Responsibilities**
**Senior:** Christopher Lund *(Director)*
**US SIC:** 7399 **UK SIC:** 83954
**Auditors:** Ernst & Young LLP

| | 29-03-14 | 30-03-13 | 31-03-12 |
|---|---|---|---|
| TO | 30,790,860 | 25,880,024 | 410,024,149 |
| P/L | 12,501,846 | 8,331,667 | 49,833,963 |
| NW | 17,747,074 | 19,976,508 | 110,074,036 |
| WC | 18,578,516 | 20,505,544 | 110,304,231 |
| Emp. | 1,468 | 1,391 | 1,245 |

DUNS 22-863-0885 **Imp**
## Rlc (Uk) Ltd
**(Subsidiary of:** Rlc Engineering Group Ltd)
Metcalf Drive, Altham, Accrington, Lancashire BB5 5AY
**Tel:** 01282-688500 **Fax:** 01282-688501
**Web:** www.rlc-callender.com
**Reg No:** 1195730 **VAT No:** 175511369
**Estd:** 1975 Private Limited Company
**Line of Business:** Aviation supplies
**Export Sales:** £33,378,204
**Trading Style:** Callender Aeropart
**Issued Capital:** £1,500,000
**Directors:** C P Harris, Ms S C Holt, G Chisnall, G R Menzies, D Nutton
**Co. Secretary:** Simon Comer
**Responsibilities**
**IT:** Gerard Swinson *(IT Manager)*
**Facilities:** Tony Butterworth *(Maintenance Manager)*
**US SIC:** 3721 **UK SIC:** 36400
**Auditors:** PKF (UK) LLP
**Bankers:** The Royal Bank Of Scotland Plc (16-11-14)

| | 31-05-13 | 31-05-12 | 31-05-11 |
|---|---|---|---|
| TO | 93,221,835 | 85,814,070 | 42,252,410 |
| P/L | 11,884,385 | 12,535,537 | 4,341,759 |
| NW | 26,783,252 | 21,181,216 | 5,985,774 |
| WC | 10,792,583 | 8,804,036 | 11,705,401 |
| Emp. | 547 | 552 | 302 |

DUNS 21-115-1287
## R.Lord & Co.(Newcastle) Ltd
337-343 Shields Road Byker Hill, Newcastle-Upon-Tyne, Tyne and Wear NE6 2UD
**Tel:** 01912240044 **Fax:** 0191-276-2566
**Web:** www.lordhire.co.uk
**Reg No:** 1014434 **VAT No:** 176957603
**Estd:** 2002 Private Limited Company
**Line of Business:** Renting of construction and civil engineering machinery and equipment
**Trading Style:** Lord Hire Centres
**Issued Capital:** £200,000
**Managing Director:** C J Rowley
**Responsibilities**
**Senior:** T Hodgekiss *(Partner)*
**Finance:** Peter O'Keith *(Accountant)*
**Sales:** Carl Bartlett *(Operations Manager)*
**IT:** Peter O'Keith *(Accountant)*, Steve Redhead *(Technical Manager)*
**HR:** Carl Bartlett *(Operations Manager)*
**Health & Safety:** Steve Redhead *(Technical Manager)*
**Facilities:** Carl Bartlett *(Operations Manager)*
**Fleet:** Carl Bartlett *(Operations Manager)*
**Branches:** R.lord & Co.(Newcastle) Ltd, Dragonville Industrial Park, Dragon Lane, Durham, County Durham DH1 2XH
**US SIC:** 7399, 7394
**UK SIC:** 83954, 84000
**Auditors:** PricewaterhouseCoopers
**Bankers:** HSBC Bank plc (40-34-18)

| | 30-04-14 | 30-04-13 | 30-04-12 |
|---|---|---|---|
| TA | 1,591,088 | 1,567,411 | 1,570,108 |
| NW | 809,903 | 845,321 | 919,593 |
| WC | 143,839 | 212,363 | 269,945 |

DUNS 71-877-1889
## Rm Books Ltd
**(Subsidiary of:** Rm Plc)
183 Milton Park, Milton, Abingdon, Oxfordshire OX14 4SE
**Tel:** 08709200200 **Fax:** 01235-826999
**Web:** www.rm.com
**Reg No:** 5259733 **Estd:** 2004 Private Limited Company
**Line of Business:** Computer systems and software (sales)
**Issued Capital:** £1
**Directors:** G Davidson-Shrine, I P Mcintosh
**Co. Secretary:** Gregory Davidson-Shrine
**US SIC:** 7379, 7374
**UK SIC:** 83940

| | 30-11-13 | 30-11-12 | 30-11-11 |
|---|---|---|---|
| TO | 7,000 | N/A | N/A |
| P/L | (1,869,000) | (887,000) | N/A |
| NW | (2,537,000) | (630,000) | 1 |
| WC | (2,537,000) | (630,000) | N/A |

DUNS 21-440-2950 **Imp-Exp**
## R.M. Easdale & Company Ltd
67 Washington Street, Glasgow, Lanarkshire G3 8BB
**Fax:** 0141043159
**Web:** www.rmeasdale.com
**Reg No:** 0035960SC **VAT No:** 259978089
**Estd:** 1960 Private Limited Company
**Line of Business:** Scrap metal dealers
**Export Markets:** Italy; Spain; Germany
**Issued Capital:** £103,500
**Principals:** W L Easdale *(Chairman and Managing)*, D K Stirrat, R M Easdale, J D Easdale
**Co. Secretary:** Graeme Watt
**Branches:** R.m. Easdale & Company Ltd, 7B Scottish Rd Services Dept, Irvine Rd, Kilmarnock, Ayrshire KA3 2RH
**US SIC:** 5093 **UK SIC:** 62200
**Auditors:** Bannerman Johnstone Maclay
**Bankers:** The Royal Bank Of Scotland Plc (83-52-00)

| | 31-12-13 | 31-12-12 | 31-12-11 |
|---|---|---|---|
| TO | 51,638,085 | 57,767,837 | 63,470,610 |
| P/L | 230,108 | 277,603 | 919,819 |
| NW | 3,757,570 | 3,596,920 | 3,387,247 |
| WC | 2,896,331 | 2,669,493 | 2,517,971 |
| Emp. | 63 | 61 | 56 |

DUNS 21-746-1060
## R.M. Penny (Plant Hire & Demolition) Ltd
Green Street, Ston Easton, Bath, Avon BA3 4BY
**Tel:** 01761-241387
**Web:** www.pennyplant.com
**Reg No:** 1195918 **VAT No:** 139950242
**Estd:** 1960 Private Limited Company
**Line of Business:** Renting of construction and civil engineering machinery and equipment
**Issued Capital:** £8,717
**Principals:** R M Penny *(Chairman and Managing)*, D J Pick, C N Penny
**Co. Secretary:** Mrs Catherine Penny
**US SIC:** 7394, 1799
**UK SIC:** 84000, 50000
**Auditors:** Moore Stephens
**Bankers:** Barclays Bank Plc (20-05-06)

| | 31-01-14 | 31-01-13 | 31-01-12 |
|---|---|---|---|
| TO | 8,541,745 | 6,667,414 | 6,753,218 |
| P/L | 576,523 | 59,779 | 283,657 |
| NW | 3,724,914 | 3,437,791 | 3,500,634 |
| WC | 637,289 | 788,786 | 987,089 |
| Emp. | 77 | 72 | 67 |

DUNS 22-670-5002 **Imp-Exp**
## Rm Plc
183 Park Drive, Milton, Abingdon, Oxfordshire OX14 4SE
**Tel:** 08450700300 **Fax:** 08450700400
**Web:** www.rm.com
**Reg No:** 1749877 **Estd:** 1983 Public Limited Company
**Line of Business:** Education services
**Trading Style:** Rm Education
**Issued Capital:** £1,870,309
**Directors:** I P Mcintosh, P N Martell, Ms D Mattar, J W Poulter, D J Brooks, Lord A Adonis
**Co. Secretary:** Gregory Davidson-Shrine
**Responsibilities**
**Senior:** Alistair Goulden *(General Manager)*, John Ingram *(Manager)*, Adonis Windeler *(Independent Non-Executive Dire)*
**Marketing:** Suzanne Kyle *(Head of Communications)*, Paul Ostridge *(Head of Implementation Service)*, Jodie Taylor *(Event Manager)*
**IT:** Paul Brears *(Principal Internet Development)*, Lisa Loyld *(IT Manager)*
**HR:** Angela Sherwood *(Human Resources Manager)*
**Health & Safety:** Jayne Heason *(Facilities Manager)*
**Facilities:** Jayne Heason *(Facilities Manager)*
**Operations:** Anna Pulisciano *(Head of Operations)*
**Branches:** Rm Plc, 209 Cowley Rd, Oxford, Oxfordshire OX4 1XE
**US SIC:** 6711 **UK SIC:** 83962
**Auditors:** KPMG Audi PLC
**Bankers:** Barclays Bank Plc (20-00-00)

| | 30-11-13 | 30-11-12 | 30-11-11 |
|---|---|---|---|
| TO | 261,759,000 | 288,688,000 | 350,785,000 |
| P/L | 9,435,000 | 8,389,000 | (23,380,000) |
| NW | 13,168,000 | 7,599,000 | 6,360,000 |
| WC | 23,074,000 | 20,006,000 | 26,028,000 |
| Emp. | 2,148 | 2,305 | 2,799 |

DUNS 21-232-5476
## R.Manners & Sons Ltd
Meadowfield, Ponteland, Newcastle-Upon-Tyne, Tyne and Wear NE20 9SF
**Tel:** 01661-823261 **Fax:** 01661-822516
**Web:** www.manners.co.uk
**Reg No:** 0532687 **VAT No:** 176283932
**Estd:** 1954 Private Limited Company
**Line of Business:** Wholesale of meat and meat products
**Issued Capital:** £3,528
**Principals:** I C Manners *(Chairman and Managing)*, A J Manners, Mrs J Manners
**Co. Secretary:** Ms Carol Lumsden
**Branches:** 4 in Newcastle-Upon-Tyne
**US SIC:** 5147 **UK SIC:** 61700
**Auditors:** Greaves West & Ayre
**Bankers:** HSBC Bank plc (40-37-37)

| | 31-03-14 | 31-03-13 | 31-03-12 |
|---|---|---|---|
| TO | 17,777,140 | 19,069,663 | 15,327,291 |
| P/L | 999,574 | 1,024,257 | 673,837 |
| NW | 3,569,518 | 2,877,878 | 2,158,052 |
| WC | 3,103,635 | 2,430,315 | 1,748,212 |
| Emp. | 75 | 77 | 86 |

DUNS 73-477-8678
## Rmb Automotive Ltd
Cygnet Drive, Stockton-On-Tees, Cleveland TS18 3DZ
**Tel:** 01642-667788 **Fax:** 01642808050
**Web:** www.rmbauto.co.uk
**Reg No:** 4741721 **VAT No:** 814097728
**Estd:** 2003 Private Limited Company
**Line of Business:** Sale of new motor vehicles
**Issued Capital:** £250,000
**Directors:** R Bennett, Ms M Bennett
**Co. Secretary:** Ms Sarah Waddington

**Branches:** RMB AUTOMOTIVE LTD, MCMULLEN RD, Darlington, DL1 1XP, COUNTY DURHAM.
**US SIC:** 5511 **UK SIC:** 65100
**Auditors:** Baines Jewitt

|  | 31-12-13 | 31-12-12 | 31-12-11 |
|---|---|---|---|
| TO | 45,059,972 | 40,377,526 | 37,625,126 |
| P/L | 603,914 | 324,502 | 291,656 |
| NW | 2,892,696 | 2,507,577 | 3,134,562 |
| WC | (2,774,138) | (2,650,905) | (2,821,831) |
| Emp. | 147 | 138 | 149 |

DUNS 21-007-6113    **Imp-Exp**

## R.M.Curtis & Co. Ltd
95 Camberwell Station Road, London SE5 9JJ
**Tel:** 020-7274-0717 **Fax:** 020-7737-1827
**Web:** www.rmcurtis.co.uk
**Reg No:** 0252966 **VAT No:** 235580854
**Estd:** 1850 Private Limited Company
**Line of Business:** Windscreen replacement and repair services
**Issued Capital:** £16,000
**Directors:** W H Porter, M Setterfield, P J Felix
**Co. Secretary:** Keith Smith
**US SIC:** 2099, 5199
**UK SIC:** 42399, 61900
**Auditors:** Dyer & Co
**Bankers:** HSBC Bank plc (40-02-31)

|  | 31-12-13 | 31-12-12 | 31-12-11 |
|---|---|---|---|
| TO | 53,971,301 | 46,249,945 | 39,614,185 |
| P/L | 369,625 | 325,978 | 283,721 |
| NW | 2,468,277 | 2,213,418 | 1,973,863 |
| WC | 2,095,180 | 1,679,554 | 1,574,025 |
| Emp. | 61 | 50 | 47 |

DUNS 21-020-3782    **Exp**

## Rmd Kwikform Ltd
(**Subsidiary of:** Interserve Plc)
Foundation House, Walsall, West Midlands WS9 8BW
**Tel:** 01922 743-743 **Fax:** 01922 743-400
**Web:** www.rmdkwikform.com
**Reg No:** 0301199 **Estd:** 1935 Private Limited Company
**Line of Business:** Shuttering and formwork
**Export Markets:** U S A, The Far East, Middle East & Europe.
**Export Sales:** £3,616,000
**Issued Capital:** £11,700,000
**Directors:** I M Hayes, I N Fryer, M J Pickard, M R Follett
**Co. Secretary:** Mark Pickard
**Responsibilities**
**Senior:** Andy Broom (Manager), Steven Dance (Divisional Managing Director), Allan Hannah (Manager), Graham Jacks (Manager)
**Purchasing:** Denise Richards (Procurement Manager)
**Branches:** Rmd Kwikform Limited, Unit C3, Penarth Road, Cardiff, South Glamorgan CF11 8JQ
**US SIC:** 7394 **UK SIC:** 84000
**Auditors:** Deloitte LLP
**Bankers:** HSBC Bank plc (40-11-04)

|  | 31-12-13 | 31-12-12 | 31-12-11 |
|---|---|---|---|
| TO | 22,179,000 | 19,446,000 | 19,385,000 |
| P/L | 3,292,000 | 450,000 | 1,307,000 |
| NW | 53,064,000 | 50,191,000 | 59,353,000 |
| WC | 42,867,000 | 40,397,000 | 49,848,000 |
| Emp. | 193 | 207 | 209 |

DUNS 22-024-7436

## R.M.F. Construction Services Ltd
2 Oughton Road, Highgate, Birmingham, West Midlands B12 0DF
**Tel:** 01217730043
**Web:** www.rmfconstruction.co.uk
**Reg No:** 4027393 **Estd:** 2000 Private Limited Company
**Line of Business:** Other building installation
**Issued Capital:** £100
**Director:** C Mcgee
**Co. Secretary:** Raphael Mcgee
**US SIC:** 1522 **UK SIC:** 50100
**Auditors:** N. Alam & Co

|  | 31-07-13 | 31-07-12 | 31-07-11 |
|---|---|---|---|
| TO | N/A | 2,106,053 | 1,531,124 |
| P/L | N/A | 28,198 | 11,712 |
| NW | 261,192 | 241,448 | 219,661 |
| WC | 238,670 | 225,051 | 198,990 |

DUNS 73-300-0686

## Rmg Client Services Ltd
(**Subsidiary of:** Places for People Group Ltd)
Rmg House Essex Road, Hoddesdon, Hertfordshire EN11 0DR
**Tel:** 03450024444
**Web:** www.rmgltd.co.uk
**Reg No:** 4573945 **Estd:** 2002 Private Limited Company
**Line of Business:** Estate management services
**Issued Capital:** £2
**Directors:** H Mcgeever, C R Phillips, A J Inglis, D Cowans
**Co. Secretary:** Christopher Martin

**US SIC:** 7361 **UK SIC:** 83954

|  | 31-03-14 | 31-12-12 | 31-03-11 |
|---|---|---|---|
| TA | 44 | 44 | 44 |
| NW | 44 | 44 | 44 |

DUNS 23-623-9166    **Imp-Exp**

## Rmg Networks Ltd
(**Subsidiary of:** Rmg Networks Holding Corporation)
1 Enterprise Way, Hemel Hempstead Industrial Estate, Hemel Hempstead, Hertfordshire HP2 7YJ
**Tel:** 01442-233222
**Web:** www.rmgnetworks.com
**Reg No:** 2542776 **VAT No:** 540296748
**Estd:** 1990 Private Limited Company
**Line of Business:** Telecommunications
**Export Sales:** £4,731,243
**Issued Capital:** £252,000
**Directors:** J Rabah, Mrs J Richings, L Buck, D Horgan
**Co. Secretary:** William Cole
**Branches:** Rmg Networks Ltd, Singleton Court Business Centre, Wonastow Road Industrial Estate West, Monmouth, Gwent NP25 5JA
**US SIC:** 7399 **UK SIC:** 83954
**Auditors:** Baker Tilly UK Audit LLP
**Bankers:** National Westminster Bank Plc (60-10-07)

|  | 31-12-13 | 31-01-13 | 31-12-12 |
|---|---|---|---|
| TO | 8,230,880 | 8,041,239 | 7,002,484 |
| P/L | 154,685 | 1,105,032 | 1,472,133 |
| NW | 2,822,255 | 2,706,549 | 1,874,133 |
| WC | 2,843,264 | 2,799,521 | 1,973,758 |
| Emp. | 48 | 41 | 36 |

DUNS 76-964-8114

## Rmg:Connect Ltd
(**Subsidiary of:** Wpp Plc)
1 Knightsbridge Green, London SW1X 7NW
**Tel:** 02076567310 **Fax:** 02083320522
**Web:** www.rmgconnect.com
**Reg No:** 2629696 **VAT No:** 584330537
**Estd:** 1991 Private Limited Company
**Line of Business:** Advertising
**Issued Capital:** £32,000
**Directors:** N S Yap, Ms S S Spensley
**Co. Secretary:** Peter Dipple
**Responsibilities**
**Senior:** M Chadman (Manager), Victoria Lynch-Robinson (Office Services Director)
**US SIC:** 7311 **UK SIC:** 83800
**Auditors:** Deloitte LLP
**Bankers:** National Westminster Bank Plc (60-40-05)

|  | 31-12-13 | 31-12-12 | 31-12-11 |
|---|---|---|---|
| TA | 462,842 | 462,842 | 462,842 |
| NW | 462,342 | 462,342 | 462,342 |
| WC | 462,342 | 462,342 | 462,342 |

DUNS 67-207-5991

## Rmh (Guildford) Ltd
Flat 5 6 Upper John Street, London W1F 9HB
**Tel:** 01383417149
**Reg No:** 6015825 **Estd:** 2006 Private Limited Company
**Line of Business:** Hotels
**Issued Capital:** £2,654,306
**Directors:** M N Steinberg, N J Roach, T S Cole, S R Collins
**Co. Secretary:** Stuart Bateman
**US SIC:** 7011 **UK SIC:** 66500
**Bankers:** Bank Of Scotland (12-05-65)

|  | 31-12-13 | 31-12-12 | 31-12-11 |
|---|---|---|---|
| TO | 8,243,346 | 13,108,679 | N/A |
| P/L | 208,990 | (1,035,494) | N/A |
| NW | 37,426 | (407,564) | 655,581 |
| WC | 1,529,416 | 823,114 | (602,351) |
| Emp. | 122 | 124 | N/A |

DUNS 76-951-3052    **Exp**

## The Rml Group Ltd
6-10 Whittle Close, Park Farm Industrial Estate, Wellingborough, Northamptonshire NN8 6TY
**Web:** www.rmlmallock.co.uk
**Reg No:** 2550671 **Estd:** 1994 Private Limited Company
**Line of Business:** Manufacture of motor vehicles
**Issued Capital:** £100
**Director:** A R Mallock
**Co. Secretary:** Ivor Howard
**Responsibilities**
**Facilities:** Dennis Dowsen (Works Manager)
**Operations:** Graham Norden (Chief Engineer)
**Engineering:** Graham Norden (Chief Engineer)
**US SIC:** 3711 **UK SIC:** 35101

|  | 31-10-13 | 31-10-12 | 31-10-11 |
|---|---|---|---|
| TA | 100 | 100 | 100 |
| NW | 100 | 100 | 100 |

DUNS 21-100-9705

## Rmo International Healthcare Llp
Saxon Business Park, Hanbury Road Stoke Prior, Bromsgrove, Worcestershire B60 4AD
**Tel:** 01527882080
**Web:** www.rmointernational.co.uk
**Reg No:** 0333350OC **Estd:** 2007 Private Limited Company
**Line of Business:** Employment and recruitment companies and consultants
**Responsibilities**
**Senior:** Petio Anguelov (Designated Limited Liability P), Christine Eales (Designated Limited Liability P), Matthew Fullelove (Designated Limited Liability P), Brian Gaskin (Designated Limited Liability P), Norman Goode (Designated Limited Liability P), Kevin Wright (Designated Limited Liability P)
**US SIC:** 8091 **UK SIC:** 95200

|  | 31-03-14 | 31-03-13 | 31-03-12 |
|---|---|---|---|
| TO | 8,072,887 | 7,917,041 | 7,916,520 |
| P/L | 956,394 | 934,991 | 922,984 |
| WC | (111,608) | (87,559) | (112,078) |
| Emp. | 134 | 120 | 116 |

DUNS 50-495-8448

## Rms Goole Ltd
(**Subsidiary of:** Rms Group Holdings Ltd)
Boothferry Terminal, Bridge Street, Goole, North Humberside DN14 5SS
**Web:** www.rms-humber.co.uk
**Reg No:** 2464026 **VAT No:** 518408839
**Estd:** 1995 Private Limited Company
**Line of Business:** Activities of other transport agencies
**Issued Capital:** £21,965
**Directors:** M Johnston, C J Tyler, M Kirby
**Co. Secretary:** David Johnson
**US SIC:** 4712 **UK SIC:** 77002
**Auditors:** Smailes Goldie
**Bankers:** HSBC Bank plc (40-24-36)

|  | 31-12-13 | 31-12-12 | 31-12-11 |
|---|---|---|---|
| TO | 11,405,305 | 11,344,272 | 12,302,845 |
| P/L | 1,453,838 | 1,936,084 | 1,600,024 |
| NW | 1,717,376 | 1,999,935 | 2,536,693 |
| WC | 1,051,684 | 1,316,580 | 1,936,849 |
| Emp. | 74 | 74 | 78 |

DUNS 73-713-6689

## Rms International Plc
International House, 66 Pendlebury Road, Pendlebury, Swinton, Manchester M27 4LY
**Tel:** 01617278182 **Fax:** 021-6356-8165
**Web:** www.rmsint.com
**Reg No:** 2915858 **Estd:** 1994 Public Limited Company
**Line of Business:** Management activities of holding companies
**Export Sales:** £13,292,000
**Issued Capital:** £66,180
**Directors:** Y L Abramson, T S Farber, J Hammond
**Responsibilities**
**Senior:** Ryan Farber (Manager)
**US SIC:** 6711, 5199
**UK SIC:** 83962, 61900
**Auditors:** Grant Thornton
**Bankers:** HSBC Bank plc (40-31-24)

|  | 31-12-13 | 31-12-12 | 31-12-11 |
|---|---|---|---|
| TO | 33,765,000 | 27,335,000 | 22,270,000 |
| P/L | 1,816,000 | 1,665,000 | 1,099,000 |
| NW | 2,704,000 | 1,417,000 | 191,000 |
| WC | 2,312,000 | (202,000) | (454,000) |
| Emp. | 100 | 98 | 88 |

DUNS 67-206-3810

## Rmt Accountants & Business Advisors Ltd
Gosforth Park Avenue, Newcastle-Upon-Tyne, Tyne and Wear NE12 8EG
**Tel:** 01912818816 **Fax:** 01912569501
**Web:** www.actas.co.uk
**Reg No:** 6036364 **Estd:** 2006 Private Limited Company
**Line of Business:** Accounting activities
**Issued Capital:** £10
**Directors:** S D Slater, A Andreasen, A A Josephs, Ms J M Pott, M A Pott
**Co. Secretary:** John Richards
**US SIC:** 8931 **UK SIC:** 83600

|  | 31-12-13 | 31-12-12 | 31-12-11 |
|---|---|---|---|
| TA | 3,248,507 | 3,244,580 | 3,677,272 |
| NW | (691,476) | (1,250,407) | (1,788,136) |
| WC | 56,433 | (435,199) | (364,404) |

DUNS 53-650-5944

## Rmt Technology Ltd
Unit 2, Gosforth Park Avenue, Newcastle-Upon-Tyne, Tyne and Wear NE12 8EG
**Tel:** 01912569550 **Fax:** 01912810530
**Web:** www.r-m-t.co.uk
**Reg No:** 3455946 **Estd:** 1997 Private Limited Company
**Line of Business:** Accounting and auditing activities
**Issued Capital:** £7
**Principals:** S D Slater (Financial), P W Holborow, A A Josephs, J Richards
**Co. Secretary:** Ms Maxine Pott

**US SIC:** 7379 **UK SIC:** 83940
**Auditors:** R M T

|  | 30-04-14 | 30-04-13 | 30-04-12 |
|---|---|---|---|
| TA | 7 | 14,079 | 19,426 |
| NW | 7 | 11,750 | 14,481 |
| WC | N/A | 11,750 | 14,481 |

DUNS 64-084-1289

## R.N. Wooler & Co (Holdings) Ltd
Florence House, 5 Spearhead Way, Lawkholme Lane, Keighley, West Yorkshire BD21 3LA
**Tel:** 01535-691699 **Fax:** 01535-691213
**Web:** www.rnwooler.co.uk
**Reg No:** 4487555 **Estd:** 2002 Private Limited Company
**Line of Business:** Construction of commercial buildings
**Issued Capital:** £1,000
**Directors:** R N Wooler, G D Wooler, A Wooler
**Co. Secretary:** Mrs Margaret Wooler
**US SIC:** 1541, 1522
**UK SIC:** 50100
**Bankers:** Barclays Bank Plc (20-45-14)

|  | 31-12-13 | 31-12-12 | 31-12-11 |
|---|---|---|---|
| TO | 33,397,368 | 28,918,958 | 20,191,869 |
| P/L | 776,039 | 1,065,733 | 1,192,065 |
| NW | 11,459,603 | 10,780,507 | 9,886,202 |
| WC | 1,699,195 | 2,005,504 | 4,651,143 |
| Emp. | 203 | 191 | 180 |

DUNS 21-250-8893

## Rnid
Poolemead Centre, Bath, Avon BA2 1RN
**Web:** www.actiononhearingloss.org.uk
**Estd:** 2012
**Line of Business:** Residential care establishments
**Trading Style:** Action on Hearing Loss
**Responsibilities**
**Health & Safety:** Derek Cantwell (Facilities Manager)
**Facilities:** Derek Cantwell (Facilities Manager)
**US SIC:** 8321 **UK SIC:** 96111
**Employees:** 200

DUNS 28-982-2140

## Rnli (Enterprises) Ltd
West Quay Road, Poole, Dorset BH15 1HZ
**Web:** www.rnli.org
**Reg No:** 1784500 **Estd:** 1984 Private Limited Company
**Line of Business:** Charities and charitable organisations
**Trading Style:** Royal National Lifeboat Institution
**Issued Capital:** £2
**Directors:** G Ireland, N R Palmer
**Co. Secretary:** Darren Spivey
**Responsibilities**
**Senior:** Paul Boissier (Chief Executive)
**Finance:** Mark Hallam (Financial Director)
**Sales:** Clare McDermott (Sales Director)
**IT:** Mark Hallam (Financial Director)
**Branches:** Rnli (Enterprises) Ltd, 8 Sunlea Ave, North Shields, Tyne and Wear NE30 3DS
**US SIC:** 7999 **UK SIC:** 97913
**Auditors:** Horwath Clark Whitehill LLP
**Bankers:** HSBC Bank plc (40-37-36)

|  | 31-12-13 | 31-12-12 | 31-12-11 |
|---|---|---|---|
| TO | 4,007,000 | 4,382,000 | 5,938,000 |

DUNS 71-909-8324

## Ro Trading Ltd
Graham House, 7 Wyllyotts Place, Potters Bar, Hertfordshire EN6 2JD
**Web:** www.rogroup.co.uk
**Reg No:** 5291694 **Estd:** 2004 Private Limited Company
**Line of Business:** Management activities of holding companies
**Issued Capital:** £2,078
**Directors:** R Woodman-Bailey, E T Rowlandson, D C Roberts, R G Rowlandson, Ms S M Younghusband
**Co. Secretary:** The Finance & Industrial Trust L
**US SIC:** 6711, 6552
**UK SIC:** 83962, 85000

|  | 31-03-14 | 31-03-13 | 31-03-12 |
|---|---|---|---|
| TO | 29,951,000 | 17,846,000 | 17,022,000 |
| P/L | (4,939,000) | (9,354,000) | 1,402,000 |
| NW | 69,568,000 | 59,933,000 | 60,167,000 |
| WC | 80,630,000 | 58,900,000 | 61,191,000 |
| Emp. | 574 | 549 | 551 |

DUNS 21-711-2275    **Exp**

## Roach Foods Ltd
(**Subsidiary of:** Tulip International (U K) Ltd)
Newtons Margate Industrial Estate, Bodmin, Cornwall PL31 1HF
**Tel:** 01208262600 **Fax:** 01208-262662
**Web:** www.tulipltd.co.uk
**Reg No:** 0663499 **VAT No:** 390583825
**Estd:** 1960 Private Limited Company

**Line of Business:** Bacon and ham production
**Export Markets:** Europe
**Trading Style:** Tulip Ltd
**Issued Capital:** £11,684,171
**Director:** C Thomas
**Co. Secretary:** Herluf Jensen
**Responsibilities**
**IT:** Phil Brotherwood *(IT Manager)*
**Branches:** Roach Foods Ltd, Newport Indstrial Estate, Launceston, Cornwall PL15 8EX
**US SIC:** 2013 **UK SIC:** 41223
**Bankers:** Unibank A/s (40-48-78)

| | 29-09-13 | 30-09-12 | 02-09-11 |
|---|---|---|---|
| TA | 139,000 | 139,000 | 139,000 |

DUNS 22-715-2915
## Road Haulage Association Ltd
Roadway House, Weybridge, Surrey KT13 9DZ
**Web:** www.rha.uk.net
**Reg No:** 0391886 **VAT No:** 232479364
**Estd:** 1944 Private Company Limited By Guarantee
**Line of Business:** Trade and business organisations
**Trading Style:** R H A
**Directors:** J A French, D C Bratt, A P Howard, Mrs C L O'Brien, A B Mcculla, R J Fry, W C Hockin, A W Jenkins
**Co. Secretary:** Cr Secretaries Limited
**Responsibilities**
**Senior:** Andrew Macrae *(Director)*
**Branches:** Road Haulage Association Ltd, 57 Ballyrussell Rd, Newtownards, Co Down BT23 5RG
**US SIC:** 8699 **UK SIC:** 96902
**Auditors:** MHA MacIntyre Hudson
**Bankers:** National Westminster Bank Plc (60-23-34)

| | 31-12-13 | 31-12-12 | 31-12-11 |
|---|---|---|---|
| TO | 8,124,397 | 7,135,682 | 6,399,536 |
| P/L | 538,096 | 442,173 | 780,476 |
| NW | 2,384,895 | 1,455,816 | 613,978 |
| WC | 1,181,034 | 1,304,732 | 871,596 |
| Emp. | 101 | 100 | 99 |

DUNS 21-932-4621
## Road Maintenance Services (Holdings) Ltd
Mowpen Brow, High Legh, Knutsford, Cheshire WA16 6NZ
**Web:** www.rms-ltd.com
**Reg No:** 0437756 **Estd:** 1947 Private Limited Company
**Line of Business:** Management activities of construction holding companies
**Issued Capital:** £5,759
**Directors:** J H Chorlton, G W Barlow, A P Holland
**Co. Secretary:** Stephen Barlow
**Responsibilities**
**Health & Safety:** Craig Charlesworth *(Health & Safety Officer)*
**US SIC:** 6711 **UK SIC:** 83962
**Auditors:** Tim R Anderson
**Bankers:** National Westminster Bank Plc (60-20-29)

| | 31-12-13 | 31-12-12 | 31-12-11 |
|---|---|---|---|
| TO | 29,557,572 | 21,638,333 | 23,048,371 |
| P/L | 2,055,610 | 1,009,267 | 1,160,155 |
| NW | 6,480,892 | 5,906,122 | 5,352,197 |
| WC | 3,595,741 | 3,508,734 | 3,429,393 |
| Emp. | 126 | 114 | 121 |

DUNS 34-526-2120
## Road Range Ltd
**(Subsidiary of:** Enza Group Ltd)
Rathbone Road, Wavertree, Liverpool, Merseyside L13 1BA
**Tel:** 0151-330-7000
**Web:** www.commercials.roadrange.co.uk
**Reg No:** 5336774 **Estd:** 2005 Private Limited Company
**Line of Business:** Sale of motor vehicles
**Export Sales:** £2,558,300
**Issued Capital:** £1,001,000
**Directors:** S C Fox, M P Jones, R C Reed, B A Kempson
**Co. Secretary:** Michael Jones
**Responsibilities**
**Senior:** Christopher Hodgkins *(Manager)*
**Finance:** Christopher Hodgkins *(Manager)*
**Sales:** Leanne Walsh *(Sales Manager)*
**US SIC:** 5511, 7539, 5531
**UK SIC:** 65100, 67100
**Auditors:** Langtons

| | 31-12-13 | 31-12-12 | 31-12-11 |
|---|---|---|---|
| TO | 55,347,896 | 36,184,373 | 27,893,757 |
| P/L | 603,829 | 448,760 | 47,605 |
| NW | 1,585,603 | 1,144,982 | 847,210 |
| WC | 555,238 | (95,383) | 322,997 |
| Emp. | 133 | 137 | 119 |

DUNS 23-838-3970
## Road Safety Contracts Ltd
102 Glen Road, Maghera, Co Londonderry BT46 5JG
**Web:** www.magherafelt.gov
**Reg No:** 0024282NI **Estd:** 1973 Private Limited Company
**Line of Business:** Collection and treatment of other waste
**Issued Capital:** £3
**Directors:** J Mchugh, E Mchugh, J Mchugh
**Co. Secretary:** Edward Mc Hugh
**Responsibilities**
**Finance:** Claire McGuiness *(Head of Finance)*
**IT:** Claire McGuiness *(Head of Finance)*
**US SIC:** 4953 **UK SIC:** 92110
**Auditors:** BDO Stoy Hayward
**Bankers:** Ulster Bank Ltd (98-10-60)

| | 30-04-14 | 30-04-13 | 30-04-12 |
|---|---|---|---|
| TO | 6,446,732 | 7,057,149 | 6,949,217 |
| P/L | 343,903 | 306,306 | 233,595 |
| NW | 2,656,906 | 2,354,990 | 2,038,695 |
| WC | 1,458,385 | 1,141,944 | 747,115 |
| Emp. | 79 | 82 | 90 |

DUNS 22-843-3819 Exp
## Road Tech Computer Systems Ltd
Shenley Hall, Rectory Lane, Shenley, Radlett, Hertfordshire WD7 9AN
**Tel:** 01923460000
**Web:** www.roadtech.co.uk
**Reg No:** 2017435 **VAT No:** 449358217
**Estd:** 1985 Private Limited Company
**Line of Business:** Publishing of software
**Export Markets:** Australia, Hungary, Holland and Eire
**Export Sales:** £28,535
**Trading Style:** Roadrunner, Techomaster
**Issued Capital:** £20,000
**Managing Director:** D A Beevor
**Co. Secretary:** Ms Bernadette Beevor
**Responsibilities**
**Finance:** Kim Swift *(Financial Manager)*
**IT:** David Rye *(Senior IT Executive)*
**HR:** Yvonne Rogers *(Human Resources Manager)*, Kim Swift *(Financial Manager)*
**Health & Safety:** Kim Swift *(Financial Manager)*
**Facilities:** Darren Cole *(General Manager)*
**US SIC:** 7379 **UK SIC:** 83940
**Auditors:** Hillier Hopkins
**Bankers:** National Westminster Bank Plc (60-00-08)

| | 30-04-14 | 30-04-13 | 30-04-12 |
|---|---|---|---|
| TO | 8,660,834 | 7,893,071 | 7,306,852 |
| P/L | 3,159,573 | 1,691,747 | 1,991,575 |
| NW | 6,954,209 | 4,148,550 | 2,522,073 |
| WC | 6,743,268 | 3,861,863 | 2,195,931 |
| Emp. | 61 | 60 | 60 |

DUNS 21-586-2715
## Road Trucks Ltd
Circular Road, Larne, Co Antrim BT40 3AE
**Tel:** 02828279611 **Fax:** 028-2826-0186
**Web:** www.roadtrucksscania.co.uk
**Reg No:** 0010084NI **VAT No:** 255905935
**Estd:** 1974 Private Limited Company
**Line of Business:** Sale of new motor vehicles
**Issued Capital:** £45,000
**Directors:** Ms S Russell, J Marks
**Co. Secretary:** Ms Stella Russell
**Responsibilities**
**HR:** Lorraine Healy *(Accounts Manager)*
**Health & Safety:** Sam Maxwell *(Parts Manager)*
**Branches:** Road Trucks Ltd, Gortrush Industrial Estate, Great Northern Road, Omagh, Co Tyrone BT78 5LU
**US SIC:** 5511, 7539, 5531
**UK SIC:** 65100, 67100
**Auditors:** Falconer Stewart
**Bankers:** Ulster Bank Ltd (98-02-70)

| | 31-12-13 | 31-12-12 | 31-12-11 |
|---|---|---|---|
| TO | 15,236,385 | 9,884,621 | 13,159,384 |
| P/L | 541,656 | 252,792 | 511,366 |
| NW | 6,240,823 | 5,820,271 | 5,608,991 |
| WC | 5,464,794 | 4,900,648 | 4,956,198 |
| Emp. | 46 | 43 | 45 |

DUNS 28-967-5084
## Roadchef Ltd
**(Subsidiary of:** Roadchef Bidco Ltd)
Roadchef House, Bettys Lane, Cannock, Staffordshire WS11 9UX
**Tel:** 01543496938 **Fax:** 01543272554
**Web:** www.roadchef.com
**Reg No:** 1713437 **Estd:** 1983 Private Limited Company
**Line of Business:** Maintenance and repair of motor vehicles
**Issued Capital:** £34,100,000
**Directors:** Dr I Mckay, S C Turl, R I Tindale, L Dafna
**Co. Secretary:** Michael Hedditch
**Responsibilities**
**Senior:** Barak Mashraki *(Manager)*
**Branches:** Roadchef Ltd, Durham Motorway Service Area, Tursdale Road, Bowburn, Durham, County Durham DH6 5NP
**US SIC:** 7539 **UK SIC:** 67100
**Auditors:** Ernst & Young LLP
**Bankers:** Barclays Bank Plc (20-65-82)

| | 31-12-13 | 01-01-13 | 03-12-12 |
|---|---|---|---|
| TO | 181,900,000 | 222,200,000 | 203,500,000 |
| P/L | (6,800,000) | (7,300,000) | (11,400,000) |
| NW | 229,100,000 | 227,400,000 | 207,900,000 |
| WC | 42,000,000 | 43,000,000 | 17,200,000 |
| Emp. | 2,775 | 2,499 | 2,181 |

DUNS 21-723-6892
## Roadchef Motorways Ltd
**(Subsidiary of:** Roadchef Bidco Ltd)
Norton Canes M S A, Cannock, Staffordshire WS11 9UX
**Tel:** 01543-272540 **Fax:** 01452-623333
**Web:** www.roadchef.com
**Reg No:** 1123082 **Estd:** 1972 Private Limited Company
**Line of Business:** Motorway services
**Issued Capital:** £1,045,000
**Directors:** R I Tindale, S C Turl, L Dafna, Dr I Mckay
**Co. Secretary:** Michael Hedditch
**Responsibilities**
**Finance:** Assaf Haiat *(Financial Director)*
**HR:** Tony D'souza *(Human Resources Director)*
**Health & Safety:** Tony D'souza *(Human Resources Director)*
**Branches:** Roadchef Motorways Ltd, Shroner Wood, Winchester, Hampshire SO21 1AG
**US SIC:** 5812, 7011
**UK SIC:** 66110, 66500
**Auditors:** Arthur Andersen
**Bankers:** Barclays Bank Plc (20-65-82)

| | 31-12-13 | 01-01-13 | 03-12-12 |
|---|---|---|---|
| TO | 120,936,000 | 148,213,000 | 135,393,000 |
| P/L | (1,328,000) | (157,000) | (2,680,000) |
| NW | 255,009,000 | 246,613,000 | 239,106,000 |
| WC | 142,244,000 | 171,830,000 | 164,469,000 |
| Emp. | 1,649 | 1,354 | 1,201 |

DUNS 39-998-7403
## Roadform Civil Engineering Co Ltd
Unit 32 Milber Trading Estate, Newton Abbot, Devon TQ12 4SG
**Tel:** 01626-331564
**Web:** www.roadform.co.uk
**Reg No:** 2287410 **VAT No:** 525046468
**Estd:** 1988 Private Limited Company
**Line of Business:** Builders
**Issued Capital:** £2
**Managing Director:** E N Potter
**Co. Secretary:** Wayne Voysey
**Responsibilities**
**Health & Safety:** Mark Shopland *(Health & Safety Officer)*
**US SIC:** 8911, 1799
**UK SIC:** 83701, 50000
**Auditors:** R.E. Stratford & Co
**Bankers:** Lloyds TSB Bank plc (30-96-06)

| | 31-10-13 | 31-10-12 | 31-10-11 |
|---|---|---|---|
| TO | 15,148,224 | 14,469,307 | 12,390,292 |
| P/L | 50,957 | 69,376 | 84,158 |
| NW | 3,767,274 | 3,727,175 | 3,773,276 |
| WC | 2,616,369 | 2,604,416 | 2,702,714 |
| Emp. | 168 | 148 | 158 |

DUNS 34-967-8529
## Roadlink Holdings Ltd
Strawberry Lane, Willenhall, West Midlands WV13 3RL
**Tel:** 01902606210
**Web:** www.roadlink-international.co.uk
**Reg No:** 5763355 **Estd:** 2006 Private Limited Company
**Line of Business:** Management activities of other non-financial holding companies not elsewhere classified
**Issued Capital:** £500,000
**Directors:** K N Sedgley, D G Sedgley
**Co. Secretary:** Ms Helen Arthur
**US SIC:** 7399 **UK SIC:** 83954

| | 31-03-14 | 31-03-13 | 31-03-12 |
|---|---|---|---|
| TO | 7,900,198 | 6,905,049 | N/A |
| P/L | 213,167 | (5,097) | N/A |
| NW | 2,152,090 | 1,980,351 | 1 |
| WC | 1,036,339 | 934,752 | N/A |
| Emp. | 70 | 68 | N/A |

DUNS 49-068-6060
## Roadside Group Ltd
64 Aylesbury Road, Aston Clinton, Aylesbury, Buckinghamshire HP22 5AH
**Tel:** 01740644875
**Web:** www.shell.com
**Reg No:** 3079092 **Estd:** 1995 Private Limited Company
**Line of Business:** Petrol service stations
**Trading Style:** Winyard Park Services Station
**Issued Capital:** £2
**Director:** V Ramakrishnan
**Co. Secretary:** Colin Fullerton
**Branches:** Roadside Group Ltd, Mandale Road, Thornaby, Stockton-On-Tees, Cleveland TS17 6AE
**US SIC:** 5541, 6552
**UK SIC:** 65200, 85000
**Auditors:** Ramsdens
**Bankers:** National Westminster Bank Plc (60-02-21)

| | 30-11-13 | 30-11-12 | 30-11-11 |
|---|---|---|---|
| TO | 58,449,619 | 60,855,837 | 56,758,113 |
| P/L | 985,974 | 721,226 | 911,546 |
| NW | 12,353,899 | 11,634,943 | 11,134,234 |
| WC | 135,917 | (533,451) | (475,983) |
| Emp. | 60 | 61 | 63 |

DUNS 22-925-2713
## Roadside Motors Ltd
71 Belfast Road, Lurgan, Craigavon, Co Armagh BT66 7JP
**Tel:** 02838323232 **Fax:** 02838321756
**Web:** www.roadsidemotors.com
**Reg No:** 0010431NI **VAT No:** 252105504
**Estd:** 1974 Private Limited Company
**Line of Business:** Car dealers (new & used)
**Issued Capital:** £7,833
**Director:** B C Hutchinson
**Co. Secretary:** William Hutchinson
**Branches:** Roadside Motors Ltd, 22 Market Place, Lisburn, Co Antrim BT28 1AN
**US SIC:** 5511 **UK SIC:** 65100
**Auditors:** Grant Thornton
**Bankers:** Northern Bank Ltd (95-02-46)

| | 30-09-13 | 30-09-12 | 30-09-11 |
|---|---|---|---|
| TO | 47,114,329 | 44,161,917 | 46,026,530 |
| P/L | 381,949 | 286,787 | 384,992 |
| NW | 5,782,291 | 5,481,657 | 5,268,910 |
| WC | 2,746,439 | 2,583,941 | 2,481,598 |
| Emp. | 126 | 138 | 134 |

DUNS 52-531-3474 Imp
## Roadtechs Europe Ltd
**(Subsidiary of:** Roadtechs Holdings Ltd)
Barondale Lane, Topcroft, Bungay, Suffolk NR35 2BE
**Tel:** 01508-536360
**Web:** www.roadtechs.net
**Reg No:** 3236016 **Estd:** 2000 Private Limited Company
**Line of Business:** Construction of roads
**Issued Capital:** £1,000
**Principals:** J S Lilley *(Managing)*, M A Prentice
**Co. Secretary:** Ms Tina Lilley
**Branches:** Roadtechs Europe Ltd, Park Rd, Crowborough, East Sussex TN6 2QT
**US SIC:** 1611 **UK SIC:** 50200
**Auditors:** Larking Gowen Ipswich Ltd
**Bankers:** HSBC Bank plc (40-35-09)

| | 31-03-14 | 31-03-13 | 31-03-12 |
|---|---|---|---|
| TO | N/A | 5,972,658 | 7,590,094 |
| P/L | N/A | (467,484) | 145,421 |
| NW | 1,288,913 | 1,312,403 | 1,585,759 |
| WC | 1,316,298 | 1,349,545 | 984,983 |
| Emp. | N/A | N/A | 68 |

DUNS 21-194-7296
## Roadways Container Logistics Ltd
**(Subsidiary of:** Aegeus Transport Ltd)
Capital Gate, Ilford, Essex IG6 3ES
**Tel:** 01827726500 **Fax:** 02087004952
**Web:** www.roadways.co.uk
**Reg No:** 0046913 **VAT No:** 942578494
**Estd:** 1997 Private Limited Company
**Line of Business:** Freight transport by road not elsewhere classified
**Issued Capital:** £664,782
**Director:** J H Williams
**Co. Secretary:** Alan Mcnicol
**Responsibilities**
**Senior:** Marc Wynne *(General Manager)*
**Finance:** David Fowle *(Financial Director)*
**IT:** Philip Wilkes *(Business Systems Manager)*
**HR:** Andy Frost *(Operations Manager)*
**Branches:** Roadways Container Logistics Ltd, 50 Erskine St, Birmingham, West Midlands B7 4RU
**US SIC:** 4213 **UK SIC:** 72300
**Auditors:** KPMG Audit PLC
**Bankers:** Barclays Bank Plc (20-00-00)

| | 28-12-13 | 29-12-12 | 31-12-11 |
|---|---|---|---|
| TO | 48,492,000 | 46,178,000 | 43,031,000 |
| P/L | 320,000 | 570,000 | 319,000 |
| NW | 16,278,000 | 16,392,000 | 16,136,000 |
| WC | 1,048,000 | 1,612,000 | 1,564,000 |
| Emp. | 398 | 432 | 428 |

DUNS 64-254-8028
## Roadwise
1 Interchange Park, Robinson Way, Portsmouth, Hampshire PO3 5QD
**Web:** www.roadwise-lgv.com
**Estd:** 1992 Proprietorship
**Line of Business:** Training providers
**Proprietor:** J Perry
**Branches:** Roadwise, 239 Goldsmith Avenue, Southsea, Hampshire PO4 0BS
**US SIC:** 8299 **UK SIC:** 93300
**Employees:** 48

DUNS 21-738-7372
## Roalco Ltd
Ardleigh House, Dedham Road, Ardleigh, Colchester, Essex CO7 7QA
**Tel:** 01206-231-700 **Fax:** 01206-231-800
**Web:** www.roalco.co.uk
**Reg No:** 1328878 **VAT No:** 312444887
**Estd:** 1977 Private Limited Company
**Line of Business:** Other building completion
**Issued Capital:** £100,000
**Principals:** A R Potter *(Managing)*, R W Potter
**Co. Secretary:** Adrian Cook
**Responsibilities**
**IT:** Kieran Chapman *(IT Manager)*
**Branches:** Roalco Ltd, 24 St. Faiths Lane, Norwich, Norfolk NR1 1NN
**US SIC:** 1799 **UK SIC:** 50000
**Auditors:** THP Ltd
**Bankers:** Barclays Bank Plc (20-22-67)

| | 31-12-13 | 31-12-12 | 31-12-11 |
|---|---|---|---|
| TO | 19,200,419 | 16,433,985 | 16,275,175 |
| P/L | 305,008 | (229,914) | 418,303 |
| NW | 1,501,577 | 1,377,039 | 1,637,083 |
| WC | 1,375,147 | 1,294,760 | 1,431,524 |
| Emp. | 260 | 249 | 236 |

DUNS 23-839-4774
## Roast Restaurants Ltd
Southwark Street, London SE1 1TL
**Tel:** 0845 031 7300 **Fax:** 0845 034 7301
**Web:** www.roast-restaurant.com
**Reg No:** 3831146 **Estd:** 1999 Private Limited Company
**Line of Business:** Restaurant - english
**Issued Capital:** £1,000
**Directors:** I Wahhab, B Joshi
**US SIC:** 5812 **UK SIC:** 66110

| | 31-08-13 | 31-08-12 | 31-08-11 |
|---|---|---|---|
| TA | 2,023,909 | 2,243,121 | 2,306,258 |
| NW | 51,231 | 46,611 | 106,731 |
| WC | (307,567) | (156,813) | 91,097 |

DUNS 21-602-4007
## Robartes Junior School
23 Barn Lane, Bodmin, Cornwall PL31 1LU
**Tel:** 0120872644
**Web:** www.robartesjunior.co.uk
**Estd:** 2001 Proprietorship
**Line of Business:** Schools (local authority)
**Proprietor:** E Murray
**US SIC:** 8211 **UK SIC:** 93200
**Employees:** 48

DUNS 21-605-3201
## Robert Bean Lodge
Pattens Lane, Rochester, Kent ME1 2QT
**Tel:** 01634831122
**Estd:** 2011 Proprietorship
**Line of Business:** Other human health activities
**Proprietor:** Mrs A Togwell
**US SIC:** 8091 **UK SIC:** 95200
**Employees:** 70

DUNS 42-485-1157
## Robert Bird & Partners Ltd
Level 2 47-51 Great Suffolk Street, London SE1 0BS
**Tel:** 02076332880
**Web:** www.robertbird.com
**Reg No:** 4472743 **Estd:** 2002 Private Limited Company
**Line of Business:** Urban planning and landscape architectural activities
**Export Sales:** £1,017,114
**Issued Capital:** £100
**Directors:** J G Beutel, J W Ward, D C Seel, R O Bird
**Co. Secretary:** Drew Foxcroft
**Responsibilities**
**Senior:** Christian Cuvelier *(Manager)*, Ross McDonald *(Manager)*, Terence Raggett *(Manager)*, Scott Wheeler *(Manager)*
**Admin:** Dawn Ward *(Administration Manager)*
**US SIC:** 8911 **UK SIC:** 83701

| | 30-06-14 | 30-06-13 | 30-06-12 |
|---|---|---|---|
| TO | 7,412,750 | 6,629,355 | 6,797,128 |
| P/L | 584,233 | 245,556 | 492,538 |
| NW | 1,733,946 | 1,292,989 | 1,133,163 |
| WC | 1,326,103 | 1,071,878 | 1,050,845 |
| Emp. | 61 | 55 | 66 |

DUNS 77-119-7548 Exp
## Robert Bosch Investment Ltd
**(Subsidiary of:** R O B E R T B O S C H S T I F T U N G Gesellschaft)
B B T Thermotechnology, Cotswold Way, Worcester, Worcestershire WR4 9SW
**Tel:** 03301239339 **Fax:** 01905754619
**Web:** www.rbvc.com
**Reg No:** 2692230 **Estd:** 1992 Private Limited Company
**Line of Business:** Management activities of holding companies
**Export Markets:** Belgium; Netherlands
**Export Sales:** £8,900,000
**Issued Capital:** £33,394,040
**Directors:** U Glock, T Bauer, R Drave
**Co. Secretary:** Ms Brigitte Malige
**US SIC:** 6711, 3433
**UK SIC:** 83962, 32041
**Auditors:** PricewaterhouseCoopers LLP
**Bankers:** Barclays Bank Plc (20-98-61)

| | 31-12-13 | 31-12-12 | 31-12-11 |
|---|---|---|---|
| TO | 434,500,000 | 371,200,000 | 366,700,000 |
| P/L | 66,100,000 | 55,600,000 | 47,000,000 |
| NW | 119,900,000 | 96,500,000 | 82,800,000 |
| WC | 115,200,000 | 83,400,000 | 65,900,000 |
| Emp. | 1,490 | 1,481 | 1,615 |

DUNS 21-101-0541 Imp
## Robert Bosch Ltd
**(Subsidiary of:** R O B E R T B O S C H S T I F T U N G Gesellschaft)
North Orbital Road Broadwater Park, Uxbridge, Middlesex UB9 5HJ
**Tel:** 01895834466
**Web:** www.bosch.co.uk
**Reg No:** 0013418SC **VAT No:** 196404153
**Estd:** 1994 Private Limited Company
**Line of Business:** Manufacture of other electrical equipment not elsewhere classified
**Export Sales:** £1,000
**Trading Style:** Bosch
**Issued Capital:** £21,300,000
**Directors:** Dr S T Hoffmann, J Burton, Dr K P Fouquet
**Co. Secretary:** Jonathan Burton
**Responsibilities**
**Senior:** Karen Bloodworth *(Manager)*, Rajesh Darji *(Divisional Director - Automoti)*, Marco Firminger *(Manager)*, Hans Klotz *(Manager)*, Detlef Konter *(Manager)*
**Marketing:** Robert Hesse *(VP Sales & Marketing)*, Mike Thomas *(Senior Marketing Executive)*
**Sales:** Robert Hesse *(VP Sales & Marketing)*
**HR:** Peter Macalik *(HR Manager)*
**Branches:** Robert Bosch Ltd, North Orbital Road, Broadwater Park, Uxbridge, Middlesex UB9 5HJ
**US SIC:** 3629, 7392, 5084
**UK SIC:** 34350, 83951, 61490
**Auditors:** PricewaterhouseCoopers LLP
**Bankers:** Barclays Bank Plc (20-89-16)

| | 31-12-13 | 31-12-12 | 31-12-11 |
|---|---|---|---|
| TO | 227,501,000 | 220,151,000 | 252,807,000 |
| P/L | 5,862,000 | 5,118,000 | 40,733,000 |
| NW | 24,075,000 | 73,718,000 | 98,228,000 |
| WC | 31,698,000 | 81,971,000 | 105,034,000 |
| Emp. | 550 | 520 | 732 |

DUNS 21-306-1195
## Robert Bowett (Ossett) Ltd
**(Subsidiary of:** Robert Bowett (Ossett Holdings) Ltd)
Low Road, Leeds, West Yorkshire LS10 1RB
**Tel:** 01132-776099 **Fax:** 01924-281005
**Reg No:** 1006783 **Estd:** 1971 Private Limited Company
**Line of Business:** New & used motor vehicle dealers
**Trading Style:** Bowett Robert Honda, Bowett Robert Daihatsu, Bowett Robert Superstore
**Issued Capital:** £25,000
**Chairman:** R G Bowett
**Responsibilities**
**Senior:** Andrew Bowett *(Manager)*
**US SIC:** 5511, 5521, 7539, 5531
**UK SIC:** 65100, 67100
**Auditors:** Thomas Coombs & Son
**Bankers:** National Westminster Bank Plc (51-61-35)

| | 30-06-13 | 31-12-11 | 31-06-10 |
|---|---|---|---|
| TA | 432,232 | 1,232,232 | 1,232,291 |
| P/L | N/A | (72) | 267 |
| NW | 432,146 | 1,232,146 | 1,232,218 |
| WC | 432,146 | 1,232,146 | 1,232,218 |

DUNS 21-607-1282 Imp-Exp
## Robert Brett & Sons Ltd
Ashford Road, Canterbury, Kent CT4 7PP
**Tel:** 01227-829000
**Web:** www.brett.co.uk
**Reg No:** 0227266 **Estd:** 1928 Private Limited Company
**Line of Business:** Holding companies nec
**Issued Capital:** £62,150
**Directors:** L Poston, H A Shaw, C P Jackson, W J Brett
**Co. Secretary:** John Gilbert
**Responsibilities**
**Senior:** Claire Dooley *(Administrator)*
**Marketing:** Jay Moyes *(IT Manager)*
**IT:** Jay Moyes *(IT Manager)*
**HR:** Deana Wheatley *(HR Manager)*
**Health & Safety:** Gavin Palmer *(Health & Safety Officer)*
**Facilities:** Clive Sherliker *(Estates Manager)*
**Purchasing:** Neville Parry *(Purchasing Manager)*
**Engineering:** Neil Amos *(Engineering & Surveying Manage)*
**Branches:** Robert Brett & Sons,Ltd, Ayletts Camp Warwick Lane, Rainham, Essex RM13 9EW
**US SIC:** 6711, 5039
**UK SIC:** 83962, 61300
**Auditors:** Moore Stephens LLP

| | 31-12-13 | 31-12-12 | 31-12-11 |
|---|---|---|---|
| TO | 151,010,000 | 134,434,000 | 150,520,000 |
| P/L | 434,000 | (3,573,000) | (4,837,000) |
| NW | 78,396,000 | 74,143,000 | 73,772,000 |
| WC | 7,526,000 | 3,532,000 | 6,302,000 |
| Emp. | 636 | 668 | 681 |

DUNS 21-773-1419
## Robert Bruce Middle School
Bedford Road, Kempston, Bedford, Bedfordshire MK42 8PU
**Tel:** 01234301222
**Web:** www.robertbruce.beds.sch.uk
**Estd:** 1991 Partnership
**Line of Business:** General secondary education
**Partners:** M Short, Mrs U Burn
**Responsibilities**
**Senior:** Karen D'angelo *(Head Teacher)*
**Finance:** Agnes Cunningham *(Senior Finance Administrator)*
**Admin:** Agnes Cunningham *(Senior Finance Administrator)*
**US SIC:** 8211 **UK SIC:** 93200
**Employees:** 70

DUNS 34-843-4325
## Robert Burns Ltd
**(Subsidiary of:** Vitrans Ltd.)
17 Youngs Road, East Mains Industrial Estate, East Mains Industrial Estate, Broxburn, West Lothian EH52 5LY
**Tel:** 01506856746
**Web:** www.robertburnsltd.co.uk
**Reg No:** 0143715SC **Estd:** 1986 Private Limited Company
**Line of Business:** Road haulage and transport services
**Issued Capital:** £10,000
**Principals:** R M Burns *(Managing)*, Mrs J M Burns
**Co. Secretary:** Mrs Julie Burns
**US SIC:** 4789 **UK SIC:** 77002
**Auditors:** Tindell, Grant & Co
**Bankers:** Bank Of Scotland (80-17-86)

| | 30-11-13 | 30-11-12 | 30-11-11 |
|---|---|---|---|
| TO | 10,732,748 | 10,077,566 | 10,503,448 |
| P/L | 1,230,341 | 1,147,385 | 1,523,509 |
| NW | 6,998,405 | 6,561,751 | 6,171,181 |
| WC | 4,429,944 | 4,113,284 | 3,870,831 |
| Emp. | 71 | 67 | 68 |

DUNS 21-771-1144
## Robert Clack School of Science Lower School
Green Lane, Dagenham, Essex RM8 1AL
**Tel:** 02082704222
**Web:** www.robertclack.co.uk
**Estd:** 2002 Proprietorship
**Line of Business:** Schools (local authority)
**Proprietor:** Sir P Grant
**US SIC:** 8211 **UK SIC:** 93200
**Employees:** 100

DUNS 21-625-4540
## Robert Cort & Son (Properties) Ltd
34 Britten Road Robert Cort Industrial, Estate, Reading, Berkshire RG2 0AU
**Tel:** 01189860248
**Web:** www.robertcort.co.uk
**Reg No:** 0097922 **VAT No:** 537509235
**Estd:** 1823 Private Limited Company
**Line of Business:** Commercial property agents
**Issued Capital:** £100,000
**Principals:** C J Ball *(Managing)*, Mrs A M Zographos
**Co. Secretary:** Laurence Cox
**Responsibilities**
**Senior:** Kalman Magyar *(Manager)*
**US SIC:** 6519 **UK SIC:** 85000
**Auditors:** HLB Kidsons
**Bankers:** National Westminster Bank Plc (60-17-21)

| | 31-12-13 | 31-12-12 | 31-12-11 |
|---|---|---|---|
| TA | 19,821,932 | 19,797,697 | 19,884,344 |
| NW | 18,582,854 | 19,092,604 | 18,217,382 |
| WC | 3,443,837 | 3,682,076 | 4,540,531 |

DUNS 21-154-9309 Imp
## Robert Cullen Ltd
10 Dalsholm Avenue, Glasgow, Lanarkshire G20 0TS
**Tel:** 01419452222 **Fax:** 0141 945 3567
**Web:** www.cullen.co.uk
**Reg No:** 0355707SC **VAT No:** 975453581
**Estd:** 2009 Private Limited Company
**Line of Business:** Manufacturers of boxes and cartons
**Export Sales:** £473,612
**Trading Style:** Cullen Packaging
**Issued Capital:** £2
**Directors:** R A Kelly, A Maitland, D R Macdonald, R D Macdonald
**Co. Secretary:** David Macdonald
**Responsibilities**
**IT:** Thomas Jardin *(Technical Manager)*
**Engineering:** Thomas Jardin *(Technical Manager)*
**US SIC:** 2651, 3999
**UK SIC:** 47253, 49590
**Bankers:** Allied Irish Bank (gb) (23-83-92)

| | 31-12-13 | 31-12-12 | 31-12-11 |
|---|---|---|---|
| TO | 12,982,891 | 12,499,400 | 11,629,427 |
| P/L | 559,453 | 566,334 | 613,729 |
| NW | 2,242,938 | 1,808,785 | 1,296,303 |
| WC | (412,947) | 547,875 | (696,640) |
| Emp. | 135 | 128 | 118 |

DUNS 21-231-9559
## Robert Darbishire Practice
Rusholme Health Centre, Walmer Street, Rusholme, Manchester M14 5NP
**Web:** www.rdp.org.uk
**Estd:** 1982 Proprietorship
**Line of Business:** Doctors
**Proprietor:** S Brunt
**US SIC:** 8011 **UK SIC:** 95300
**Employees:** 50

DUNS 21-275-3206 Imp
## Robert Duncan (Timber) Ltd
**(Subsidiary of:** Mh Southern (Holdings) Ltd)
Green Lane Sawmill, Gateshead, Tyne and Wear NE10 0JS
**Tel:** 01914698743
**Web:** www.robertduncan.co.uk
**Reg No:** 0452261 **VAT No:** 176135167
**Estd:** 1948 Private Limited Company
**Line of Business:** Saw milling and planing of wood, impregnation of wood
**Trading Style:** Treat Wood
**Issued Capital:** £250,125
**Principals:** R C Duncan *(Chairman and Managing)*, I M Macdonald
**Responsibilities**
**Engineering:** Brent Duncan *(Production Director)*
**Branches:** Robert Duncan (Timber) Ltd, 32-33 Brewsdale Road, Middlesbrough, Cleveland TS3 6LJ
**US SIC:** 2421 **UK SIC:** 46101
**Auditors:** Tenon Audit Limited
**Bankers:** Lloyds TSB Bank plc (30-93-71)
**Employees:** 80

DUNS 22-039-4949 Imp
## Robert Dyas Holdings Ltd
**(Subsidiary of:** Gladys Emmanuel Ltd)
Cleeve Court, Cleeve Road, Leatherhead, Surrey KT22 7SD
**Tel:** 01372361444
**Web:** www.robertdyas.co.uk
**Reg No:** 4041884 **Estd:** 2000 Private Limited Company
**Line of Business:** Hardware and ironmongers merchants
**Issued Capital:** £706,108
**Directors:** Mrs B Pearson, Ms S E Dover, K Kyprianou, T Paphitis
**Co. Secretary:** Ms Ann Mantz
**Responsibilities**
**Senior:** Geoff Brady *(Non Executive Chairman)*, Julia Jordan *(Manager)*, Bearne Pearson *(Director)*
**Marketing:** Dean Morris *(Marketing Manager)*
**IT:** Warren Woods *(IT Manager)*
**HR:** Catherine Collins *(Human Resources Manager)*
**Purchasing:** Paul McDermott *(Trading Manager)*
**Branches:** Robert Dyas Holdings Ltd, 40-42 Middle Street, Yeovil, Somerset BA20 1LX
**US SIC:** 5251, 5732
**UK SIC:** 64800
**Auditors:** KPMG LLP
**Bankers:** Lloyds TSB Bank plc (30-00-00)

| | 29-03-14 | 30-03-13 | 31-03-12 |
|---|---|---|---|
| TO | 124,209,000 | 114,374,000 | 105,911,000 |
| P/L | 5,087,000 | 3,152,000 | 186,000 |
| NW | 14,271,000 | 10,422,000 | 7,912,000 |
| WC | 10,796,000 | 7,838,000 | 5,003,000 |
| Emp. | 1,338 | 1,280 | 1,233 |

DUNS 21-403-3615
## Robert G Kinnaird
The Cross, Dalbeattie, Kirkcudbrightshire DG5 4HD
**Tel:** 01556-610279
**Estd:** 1970 Partnership
**Line of Business:** Grocers
**Partners:** R Kinnaird, J Kinnaird
**US SIC:** 5411, 5921
**UK SIC:** 64100, 64200
**Bankers:** Clydesdale Bank Plc (82-62-02)
**Employees:** 47

## DUNS 29-879-0775
### Robert Gibbs (Contracting) Co Ltd
Bridge Works, Rye Park Industrial Estate, Hoddesdon, Hertfordshire EN11 0EW
**Tel:** 01992-441585
**Web:** www.gibbsscrap.co.uk
**Reg No:** 2082145 **VAT No:** 214930286
**Estd:** 1986 Private Limited Company
**Line of Business:** Scrap metal dealers
**Export Sales:** £14,057,737
**Issued Capital:** £10,000
**Directors:** D Maskell, P A Batchelor, H V Jones
**Co. Secretary:** Barry Elvidge
**Responsibilities**
**HR:** Jamie King (Health & Safety Officer)
**Health & Safety:** Jamie King (Health & Safety Officer)
**US SIC:** 5093 **UK SIC:** 62200
**Auditors:** Davis Grant LLP
**Bankers:** Lloyds TSB Bank plc (30-00-09)

|      | 31-05-13   | 31-05-12   | 31-05-11   |
|------|-----------|-----------|-----------|
| TO   | 23,283,109 | 27,723,652 | 31,204,025 |
| P/L  | 1,038,764  | 3,377,231  | 3,762,388  |
| NW   | 11,703,787 | 11,210,254 | 9,820,392  |
| WC   | 9,058,520  | 8,244,065  | 6,784,094  |
| Emp. | 54         | 52         | 54         |

## DUNS 22-909-0741
### Robert Gordon University
Schoolhill, Aberdeen, Aberdeenshire AB10 7QD
**Tel:** 01224262000
**Web:** www.rgu.ac.uk
**Estd:** 1992 Incorporate By Act Of Parliament
**Line of Business:** University
**Responsibilities**
**Senior:** Dj Capaldi (President), M Collie (General Manager), L Haugh (Manager), G Lawie (Vice President), Stuart Mcdonald (Head Teacher)
**Marketing:** Ross Anderson (Communications Officer), Karen Barrett-Ayres (Marketing Officer), Kate Blake (Senior Marketing Executive), Sean Brosnan (Digital Marketing Officer), Anna Duthie (Communications Officer), Rachael Hayward (Marketing Officer), Stacey Horne (Communications Officer), Louise Mackie (B2B Marketing Officer), Jeannie Price (Marketing Officer), Jenny Rush (Communications Officer), Jonathan Shackleton (Head of Communications)
**Sales:** Stuart Rennie (Director Business Development)
**Admin:** Fernidand Vonprondzynski (Principal)
**Purchasing:** Leon Mouat (Procurement Adviser), Rod Strachan (Procurement Adviser)
**Branches:** Robert Gordon University, 60 Schoolhill, Aberdeen, Aberdeenshire AB10 1JQ
**US SIC:** 8299 **UK SIC:** 93300
**Auditors:** PricewaterhouseCoopers LLP
**Bankers:** The Royal Bank Of Scotland Plc (83-49-40)
**Employees:** 200
**Turnover:** £94,321,000

## DUNS 22-232-7343
### The Robert Gordon University - the Energy University Ltd
Schoolhill, Aberdeen, Aberdeenshire AB10 1FE
**Tel:** 01224646346 **Fax:** 01224-263000
**Web:** www.rgu.ac.uk
**Reg No:** 0221180SC **Estd:** 2001 Private Limited Company
**Line of Business:** Adult and other education not elsewhere classified
**Issued Capital:** £1
**Director:** M D Mccall
**Responsibilities**
**Senior:** Mike Pittilo (Principal), Bell Somerville (Head of Estates), Ferdinand Von Prondzynski (Principal)
**IT:** Andrew McCreath (Computer Services Director)
**HR:** Lydia Ross (Training Manager)
**US SIC:** 8249 **UK SIC:** 93300

|    | 31-07-14 | 31-07-13 | 31-07-12 |
|----|----------|----------|----------|
| TA | 1        | 1        | 1        |
| NW | 1        | 1        | 1        |

## DUNS 21-810-3147
### Robert Gough Centre
Aithernie Road, Leven, Fife KY8 4BU
**Tel:** 01334659357
**Estd:** 2012
**Line of Business:** The dss
**Responsibilities**
**Senior:** Paula Birks (Manager), Margaret Mcseveney (Manager)
**US SIC:** 8321 **UK SIC:** 96111
**Employees:** 50

## DUNS 29-884-2303 — Imp
### Robert Half Ltd
(**Subsidiary of:** Robert Half International Inc.)
Colmore Plaza, 20 Colmore Circus Queensway, Birmingham, West Midlands B4 6AT
**Tel:** 01217676100 **Fax:** 0121-782-4160
**Web:** www.roberthalf.co.uk
**Reg No:** 2087139 **Estd:** 1987 Private Limited Company
**Line of Business:** Employment and recruitment companies and consultants
**Trading Style:** Robert Half International
**Issued Capital:** £2,885,498
**Directors:** S M Hilton, M C Buckley
**Co. Secretary:** Andrew Plumbly
**Responsibilities**
**Senior:** Phil Sheridan (Manager), Matt Weston (Manager)
**Marketing:** Michelle Witman (Sales & Marketing Manager)
**Sales:** Michelle Witman (Sales & Marketing Manager)
**IT:** Tony Abbatrello (IT Manager)
**HR:** Vicky Milsom (Human Resources Manager)
**Health & Safety:** Simon Yates (Facilities Manager)
**Facilities:** Simon Yates (Facilities Manager)
**Branches:** Robert Half Ltd, 4 Greyfriars Rd, Coventry, West Midlands CV1 3RY
**US SIC:** 7361 **UK SIC:** 83954
**Auditors:** PricewaterhouseCoopers LLP
**Bankers:** National Westminster Bank Plc (60-02-35)

|      | 31-12-13   | 31-12-12   | 31-12-11   |
|------|-----------|-----------|-----------|
| TO   | 78,208,000 | 82,648,000 | 96,055,000 |
| P/L  | (131,000)  | 1,302,000  | (857,000)  |
| NW   | 15,579,000 | 14,932,000 | 13,476,000 |
| WC   | 15,442,000 | 14,300,000 | 12,758,000 |
| Emp. | 1,730      | 1,825      | 2,068      |

## DUNS 28-979-8340
### Robert Heath Heating Ltd
(**Subsidiary of:** Robert Heath Group Ltd)
Heath House, New Malden, Surrey KT3 4NN
**Tel:** 02083-366767 **Fax:** 02083-366777
**Web:** www.robertheath.co.uk
**Reg No:** 1773699 **VAT No:** 317787327
**Estd:** 1983 Private Limited Company
**Line of Business:** Central heating systems (installation and servicing)
**Issued Capital:** £1,000
**Principals:** R B Heath (Managing), F Corr, S Cocks, M Heath, R Foster, K L Ellmore
**Co. Secretary:** Mrs Jennifer Heath
**US SIC:** 1711 **UK SIC:** 50300
**Auditors:** Ward Williams
**Bankers:** National Westminster Bank Plc (60-24-28)

|      | 31-12-13   | 31-12-12   | 31-12-11   |
|------|-----------|-----------|-----------|
| TO   | 24,705,994 | 18,750,320 | 18,006,691 |
| P/L  | 539,532    | 303,443    | 1,069,929  |
| NW   | 2,217,491  | 2,185,035  | 2,199,493  |
| WC   | 719,899    | 703,691    | 806,342    |
| Emp. | 308        | 242        | 233        |

## DUNS 22-503-7795
### The Robert Hitchins Group Ltd
(**Subsidiary of:** Bay Group Limited)
The Manor, Boddington Lane, Boddington, Cheltenham, Gloucestershire GL51 0TJ
**Tel:** 01242-680694
**Web:** www.robert-hitchins-properties.co.uk
**Reg No:** 0678982 **Estd:** 1958 Private Limited Company
**Line of Business:** Development and selling of real estate
**Issued Capital:** £1,000,000
**Principals:** J C Hitchins (Managing), J J Dunley, D A Furst, S R Hitchins, J R Hitchins
**Co. Secretary:** Jonathan Dunley
**Responsibilities**
**Senior:** Helen Hawke (Manager of accounts and admin)
**Finance:** Helen Hawke (Manager of accounts and admin)
**Admin:** Mary Derrick (Department & Marketing Adminis), Helen Hawke (Manager of accounts and admin)
**Facilities:** Christopher Haslam (Property and Development Direc)
**Branches:** The Robert Hitchins Group Ltd, The Manor, Boddington Lane, Boddington, Cheltenham, Gloucestershire GL51 0TJ
**US SIC:** 6552, 1522
**UK SIC:** 85000, 50100
**Auditors:** Horwath Clark Whitehill
**Bankers:** Lloyds TSB Bank plc (30-93-48)

|      | 31-03-14   | 31-03-13   | 31-03-12    |
|------|-----------|-----------|------------|
| TO   | 19,180,498 | 21,648,512 | 22,531,240  |
| P/L  | 3,401,758  | 2,179,569  | 1,303,099   |
| NW   | 93,001,196 | 88,050,672 | 84,642,149  |
| WC   | 54,432,729 | 66,886,166 | 106,662,198 |
| Emp. | 62         | 64         | 62          |

## DUNS 21-198-2285 — Imp-Exp
### Robert Horne Group Ltd
(**Subsidiary of:** Paperlinx Limited)
Huntsman House, Mansion Close, Moulton Park, Northampton, Northamptonshire NN3 6RU
**Web:** www.paperlinx.com
**Reg No:** 0584756 **VAT No:** 235722176
**Estd:** 1957 Private Limited Company
**Line of Business:** Wholesale of other intermediate products
**Export Sales:** £5,166,000
**Trading Style:** Paperlinx, Robert Horne Commercial Print, Robert Horne Sign & Display
**Issued Capital:** £12,000,000
**Directors:** M Siwak, Mrs G Mccolm, J W Smallenbroek
**Co. Secretary:** Mrs Michelle Brightman
**Responsibilities**
**Senior:** Mark Armston (Group Financial Director), Adrian Brockhouse (Manager), Marc Jacobs (Director), Frank Moran (Director), Andy Vels Jensen (Manager)
**Finance:** Mark Armston (Group Financial Director), Gail McColm (Finance Director)
**Marketing:** Peter Crisp (Product Manager)
**Facilities:** Steve Carlin (Facilities Manager)
**Branches:** Robert Horne Group Ltd, Huntsman House, 40 Tameside Drive, Birmingham, West Midlands B35 7BD
**US SIC:** 5199, 5161
**UK SIC:** 61900, 61200
**Auditors:** KPMG LLP
**Bankers:** Barclays Bank Plc (20-00-00)

|      | 30-06-13     | 30-06-12    | 30-06-11    |
|------|-------------|-------------|-------------|
| TO   | 234,991,000  | 273,684,000 | 302,943,000 |
| P/L  | (6,306,000)  | (3,556,000) | 222,000     |
| NW   | 5,652,000    | 18,990,000  | 32,775,000  |
| WC   | 37,600,000   | 58,678,000  | 60,977,000  |
| Emp. | 552          | 763         | 725         |

## DUNS 53-641-0152
### Robert Hutchison Ltd
(**Subsidiary of:** Carr's Milling Industries Plc)
East Bridge, Kirkcaldy, Fife KY1 2SR
**Tel:** 01592-267191
**Web:** www.carrs-flourmills.co.uk
**Reg No:** 3446518 **Estd:** 1895 Private Limited Company
**Line of Business:** Mills and millers
**Trading Style:** Carrs Flour Hutchison''s Ltd
**Issued Capital:** £2
**Directors:** N Austin, T J Davies
**Co. Secretary:** Ms Katie Sinclair
**Responsibilities**
**Finance:** George Wishart (Finance Director)
**Sales:** Allan Burns (Sales Director)
**US SIC:** 2043 **UK SIC:** 42398
**Auditors:** PricewaterhouseCoopers LLP
**Bankers:** Bank Of Scotland (80-16-84)

|    | 31-08-13  | 01-09-12  | 03-08-11  |
|----|-----------|-----------|-----------|
| TA | 4,144,064 | 4,144,064 | 4,144,064 |
| NW | 4,144,064 | 4,144,064 | 4,144,064 |

## DUNS 23-686-9459
### The Robert Jones and Agnes Hunt Orthopaedic Hospital Nhs Foundation Trust
Gobowen, Oswestry, Shropshire SY10 7AG
**Tel:** 01691-404-000
**Web:** www.rjah.nhs.uk
**Estd:** 1993
**Line of Business:** Public sector hospital activities, including nhs trusts
**Trading Style:** R J A H Nhs Trust
**Issued Capital:** £1
**Principals:** R Burbage (Chairman), Mrs W Farrington (Financial), A Steadman, Ms R Harrison
**Responsibilities**
**Senior:** Wendy Farrington-Chadd (Chief Executive)
**Finance:** Wendy Farrington-Chadd (Chief Executive)
**Branches:** The Robert Jones and Agnes Hunt Orthopaedic Hospital Nhs Foundation Tr, G F Kempster & Son, The Oldport, Oswestry, Shropshire SY10 7JU
**US SIC:** 8062 **UK SIC:** 95100
**Auditors:** Deloitte LLP
**Bankers:** HSBC Bank plc (40-35-32)

|      | 31-03-14   | 31-03-13    | 31-03-12   |
|------|-----------|------------|-----------|
| TO   | 84,371,000 | 88,832,000  | 53,525,000 |
| P/L  | 1,628,000  | (2,596,000) | 1,042,000  |
| NW   | 56,214,000 | 51,485,000  | 52,053,000 |
| WC   | 6,311,000  | 2,575,000   | 1,841,000  |
| Emp. | 1,160      | 1,144       | 1,117      |

## DUNS 21-444-8714 — Imp-Exp
### Robert Laidlaw & Sons Ltd
(**Subsidiary of:** J.H. Clissold & Son Ltd)
17 Hangar Hill, Whitwell, Worksop, Nottinghamshire S80 4TB
**Tel:** 01909720696
**Web:** www.croftermachinery.co.uk
**Reg No:** 0026087SC **VAT No:** 296831514
**Estd:** 2011 Private Limited Company
**Line of Business:** Suppliers of

**Export Markets:** countries worldwide.
**Trading Style:** Scottish Crofter Weavers
**Issued Capital:** £817,000
**Co. Secretary:** Frank O'Reilly
**Responsibilities**
**Senior:** Richard Mallender (Proprietor)
**Branches:** Robert Laidlaw & Sons Ltd, Oldgate Mill, North Wing, Bradford, West Yorkshire BD3 0DH
**US SIC:** 3523 **UK SIC:** 32113
**Auditors:** KPMG Audit Plc
**Bankers:** Barclays Bank Plc (20-11-81)

|    | 31-12-13 | 31-12-12 | 31-12-11 |
|----|----------|----------|----------|
| TA | 143,947  | 143,947  | 143,947  |
| NW | 143,947  | 143,947  | 143,947  |

## DUNS 29-478-4574 — Imp
### Robert Lee Distribution Ltd
(**Subsidiary of:** Marchase Ltd)
Riverside Place, Lea Road, Waltham Abbey, Essex EN9 1AS
**Tel:** 01992-703220 **Fax:** 0800-376-5556
**Web:** www.rlee.co.uk
**Reg No:** 1812213 **VAT No:** 220424027
**Estd:** 1984 Private Limited Company
**Line of Business:** Wholesale of wood, construction materials and sanitary equipment
**Issued Capital:** £999
**Directors:** C T O'Reilly, D J Ground, C W Smith, T J Wayman, M S Earle, M R Earle
**Co. Secretary:** Robert Ellender
**US SIC:** 5039, 5074
**UK SIC:** 61300
**Auditors:** Price Bailey LLP
**Bankers:** Lloyds TSB Bank plc (30-94-17)

|      | 31-10-13   | 31-10-12   | 31-10-11   |
|------|-----------|-----------|-----------|
| TO   | 33,355,015 | 30,867,101 | 27,168,690 |
| P/L  | 1,347,108  | 1,338,437  | 1,543,570  |
| NW   | 11,198,624 | 10,165,421 | 9,162,719  |
| WC   | 10,077,141 | 9,059,601  | 8,323,336  |
| Emp. | 139        | 130        | 123        |

## DUNS 21-914-3203 — Exp
### Robert Lickley Holdings Ltd
Dormston Trading Estate, Burton Road, Dudley, West Midlands DY1 2UF
**Tel:** 01902880123 **Fax:** 01902-880019
**Web:** www.robertlickley.co.uk
**Reg No:** 1303146 **Estd:** 1977 Private Limited Company
**Line of Business:** Refractory materials
**Export Markets:** Worldwide
**Export Sales:** £643,508
**Issued Capital:** £1,400
**Principals:** B Bridgen (Managing), K J Winchurch, C R Clarke, R J Lickley
**Co. Secretary:** Mrs Mary Lickley
**US SIC:** 6711, 3299
**UK SIC:** 83962, 24504
**Auditors:** Bissell & Brown Ltd
**Bankers:** HSBC Bank plc (40-19-28)

|      | 31-08-13   | 31-08-12   | 31-08-11  |
|------|-----------|-----------|-----------|
| TO   | 11,438,646 | 10,231,948 | 9,823,000 |
| P/L  | 381,164    | 321,889    | 190,961   |
| NW   | 2,980,208  | 2,690,264  | 2,448,440 |
| WC   | 2,058,321  | 1,766,574  | 1,530,345 |
| Emp. | 62         | 61         | 52        |

## DUNS 21-776-5415
### Robert M Sayer Partnership
Broad Lane, Gilberdyke, Brough, North Humberside HU15 2TB
**Estd:** 2011 Proprietorship
**Line of Business:** Fruit and vegetable (producers)
**Proprietor:** T Shields
**US SIC:** 0179 **UK SIC:** 01002
**Employees:** 90

## DUNS 21-231-0791 — Imp-Exp
### Robert McBride Ltd
(**Subsidiary of:** McBride Plc)
Middleton Way, Middleton, Manchester M24 4DP
**Tel:** 01616539037
**Web:** www.mcbride.co.uk
**Reg No:** 0220175 **VAT No:** 606565732
**Estd:** 1927 Private Limited Company
**Line of Business:** Manufacturers of chemicals
**Export Sales:** £25,904,000
**Issued Capital:** £10,439,446
**Directors:** C S Mcintyre, D R Main, S F Barriskell
**Co. Secretary:** Mrs Carole Barnet
**Responsibilities**
**Senior:** Anthony Allot (Distribution Manager), Janice Massey (Personal Assistant), Timothy Seaman (Manager)
**Finance:** Anthony Barwise (Head of Finance)
**Marketing:** Andrew Leydon (Marketing Controller)
**IT:** Pauline Thornton (Operations Manager)
**HR:** Malcolm Allen (Personnel Director), Jane Cronin (Personnel Manager)
**Health & Safety:** Kevin Holland (Health & Safety Officer)
**Facilities:** Mark Loates (Chief Engineer)

**Operations:** Bert Dickinson (*Purchasing Manager*)
**Purchasing:** Bert Dickinson (*Purchasing Manager*)
**Engineering:** Mark Loates (*Chief Engineer*)
**Branches:** Robert Mcbride Ltd, Millshaw Park Drive, Leeds, West Yorkshire LS11 0LU
**US SIC:** 2899, 2842, 2844
**UK SIC:** 25670, 25990, 25820
**Auditors:** PricewaterhouseCoopers LLP
**Bankers:** Bank Of Scotland (80-20-00)

| | 30-06-13 | 30-06-12 | 30-06-11 |
|---|---|---|---|
| TO | 298,278,000 | 315,222,000 | 310,731,000 |
| P/L | 4,396,000 | 6,299,000 | (5,160,000) |
| NW | 35,960,000 | 37,728,000 | 32,429,000 |
| WC | (11,557,000) | (17,032,000) | (21,293,000) |
| Emp. | 1,775 | 1,986 | 2,177 |

DUNS 22-900-6382     **Exp**

## Robert Morton Dg Ltd

(**Subsidiary of:** Avingtrans Plc)
Boardman Road Boardman Industrial Estate, Swadlincote, Derbyshire DE11 9EN
**Tel:** 01283-550960
**Web:** www.rmdg.co.uk
**Reg No:** 0003755SC   **Estd:** 1932 Private Limited Company
**Line of Business:** Manufacture of aircraft and spacecraft
**Export Markets:** U S A, E U
**Trading Style:** R M D G Aerospace
**Issued Capital:** £10
**Directors:** M I Welburn, P Lee
**Co. Secretary:** Phillip Lee
**US SIC:** 3721, 8911
**UK SIC:** 36400, 83701
**Auditors:** Tenon Audit Ltd
**Bankers:** Bank Of Scotland (12-01-03)

| | 31-03-14 | 31-03-13 | 31-03-12 |
|---|---|---|---|
| TA | 10 | 10 | 10 |
| NW | 10 | 10 | 10 |

DUNS 23-859-9174

## Robert Owen Communities Housing

Unit C, Dart Marine Park, Steamer Quay Road, Totnes, Devon TQ9 5AL
**Tel:** 01803-868550 **Fax:** 01803-868560
**Web:** www.roc-uk.org
**Reg No:** 3851512   **Estd:** 1990 Private Company Limited By Guarantee
**Line of Business:** Non-charitable social work activities with accommodation
**Directors:** P Boys, D G Knowles, R K Heath, J R Graham
**Co. Secretary:** David Wilson
**US SIC:** 8321 **UK SIC:** 96111
**Auditors:** Sinclair Taylor & Martin

| | 31-03-14 | 31-03-13 | 31-03-12 |
|---|---|---|---|
| TO | 46,378 | 20,596 | 327,331 |
| P/L | 26,868 | 9,766 | 324,206 |
| NW | 360,840 | 333,972 | 324,206 |
| WC | 24,765 | 32,157 | 16,231 |

DUNS 21-222-7134

## Robert Owen Foundation

Laura House, Belmont Terrace, Totnes, Devon TQ9 5QB
**Tel:** 01803-866541
**Estd:** 2003 Proprietorship
**Line of Business:** Non-charitable social work activities with accommodation
**Proprietor:** Mrs T Timberlake
**Responsibilities**
**Senior:** Marie Broadhurst (*Manager*)
**US SIC:** 8321 **UK SIC:** 96111
**Employees:** 50

DUNS 85-598-5005

## Robert Owen Society for Learning and Social Economic Development Ltd

Robert Owen House, 18 Burgess Street, Leominster, Herefordshire HR6 8DE
**Tel:** 01568-615510
**Web:** www.robertowen.org
**Reg No:** 0029301R   **Estd:** 1982
**Line of Business:** Teacher training courses
**Branches:** Robert Owen Society For Learning and Social Economic Development Ltd, Rola Castlefields, Leominster, Leominster, Herefordshire HR6 8BG
**US SIC:** 9121, 8299
**UK SIC:** 91110, 93300
**Employees:** 181

DUNS 23-086-1820

## Robert Pattinson School

Moor Lane, North Hykeham, Lincoln, Lincolnshire LN6 9AF
**Tel:** 01522-882020
**Web:** www.rps.lincs.sch.uk
**Estd:** 1953
**Line of Business:** General secondary education
**Director:** S Macfarane

**Responsibilities**
**Senior:** Stuart Macfarane (*CEO, Managing Director*), Helen Renard (*Headmistress*)
**Finance:** Stella Bentley (*Bursar*)
**IT:** Mark Saywell (*IT Manager*)
**HR:** Anne Kotek (*Human Resources Coordinator*)
**Facilities:** Alan Otter (*Facilities Manager*)
**Purchasing:** Stella Bentley (*Bursar*)
**US SIC:** 8211 **UK SIC:** 93200
**Employees:** 150

DUNS 21-818-0941

## Robert Pochin Ltd

Pochin House, 2 Murrayfield Road, Braunstone, Leicester, Leicestershire LE3 1UW
**Tel:** 0116-232-7660
**Web:** www.pochin.com
**Reg No:** 0179511   **Estd:** 1861 Private Limited Company
**Line of Business:** Hardware
**Issued Capital:** £49,893
**Principals:** D R Pochin (*Managing*), S Froggatt, S Press
**Co. Secretary:** Glynn Barrington
**Responsibilities**
**Finance:** Linda Kirman (*Finance Manager*)
**Branches:** Robert Pochin Ltd, 7 Hawley Road, Hinckley, Leicestershire LE10 0PR
**US SIC:** 3499 **UK SIC:** 31694
**Auditors:** Cooper Parry LLP
**Bankers:** National Westminster Bank Plc (60-60-06)

| | 31-12-13 | 31-12-12 | 31-12-11 |
|---|---|---|---|
| TO | 14,428,324 | 12,752,879 | 12,277,049 |
| P/L | 658,497 | 977,818 | 270,050 |
| NW | 3,465,421 | 3,403,688 | 2,475,650 |
| WC | 661,046 | 374,784 | (150,429) |
| Emp. | 76 | 70 | 72 |

DUNS 21-641-0654

## Robert Price & Sons Ltd

Park Road, Abergavenny, Gwent NP7 5PF
**Tel:** 01873-858585
**Web:** www.robert-price.co.uk
**Reg No:** 0418758 **VAT No:** 134611790
**Estd:** 1946 Private Limited Company
**Line of Business:** Agents involved in the sale of timber and building materials
**Issued Capital:** £18,708
**Managing Director:** W A Godfrey
**Co. Secretary:** Ms Tessa Pike
**Responsibilities**
**Admin:** Diane Barrett (*Administration Manager*)
**IT:** Diane Barrett (*Administration Manager*)
**Facilities:** Llew Roper (*Property Manager*)
**Branches:** Robert Price & Sons Ltd, 145 Pontygwindy Road, Caerphilly, Mid Glamorgan CF83 3TD
**US SIC:** 5072, 5039
**UK SIC:** 61500, 61300
**Auditors:** Peacheys
**Bankers:** Lloyds TSB Bank plc (30-90-02)

| | 30-09-13 | 30-09-12 | 30-09-11 |
|---|---|---|---|
| TO | 25,737,473 | 25,703,699 | 27,721,108 |
| P/L | 487,620 | 329,686 | 1,530,588 |
| NW | 17,037,320 | 16,617,307 | 16,219,064 |
| WC | 14,582,532 | 14,352,782 | 15,158,776 |
| Emp. | 220 | 215 | 228 |

DUNS 22-905-5132

## Robert Purvis Plant Hire Ltd

Thistle House, Cartmore Industrial Estate, Lochgelly, Fife KY5 8LL
**Tel:** 01592780492 **Fax:** 01592-781908
**Web:** www.robertpurvisplanthire.co.uk
**Reg No:** 0071830SC **VAT No:** 345260666
**Estd:** 1980 Private Limited Company
**Line of Business:** Renting of construction and civil engineering machinery and equipment
**Trading Style:** Realm Constructions, Thistle Structures
**Issued Capital:** £137,000
**Principals:** R Purvis (*Chairman and Managing*), R M Garmory, Ms J J Hepburn, Ms L M Crookston, D M Smith
**Co. Secretary:** Craig Purvis
**US SIC:** 7399 **UK SIC:** 83954
**Auditors:** Carters
**Bankers:** The Royal Bank Of Scotland Plc (83-16-44)

| | 31-03-14 | 31-03-13 | 31-03-12 |
|---|---|---|---|
| TO | 14,929,452 | 17,774,320 | 17,408,092 |
| P/L | 1,009,486 | 484,862 | 234,253 |
| NW | 4,374,906 | 3,534,061 | 3,225,004 |
| WC | (3,920,156) | (3,518,216) | (3,032,289) |
| Emp. | 130 | 158 | 134 |

DUNS 21-233-7182     **Imp-Exp**

## Robert Scott & Sons Ltd

Oakview Mills, Manchester Road, Greenfield, Oldham, Lancashire OL3 7HG
**Web:** www.robert-scott.co.uk
**Reg No:** 1099088 **VAT No:** 148556635
**Estd:** 1973 Private Limited Company
**Line of Business:** Manufacture of other textiles not elsewhere classified
**Export Markets:** Western Europe

**Export Sales:** £2,311,741
**Trading Style:** Robert Scott & Sons Ltd
**Issued Capital:** £25,000
**Principals:** P R Scott (*Managing*), J A Scott (*Managing*), D P Scott, Ms M J Scott, M Smith, Mrs A K Scott, A M Scott, F Murphy
**Co. Secretary:** Angus Scott
**Responsibilities**
**Finance:** Tom Capper (*Accounts Manager - North of En*), Louise Kennedy (*Accounts Manager - West Coast*), Ceale Vance (*Accounts Manager - East Coast*), Catherine Watson (*Accounts Manager - Central Eng*), Judith Wight (*Senior Accounts Manager for Na*)
**US SIC:** 2299, 3079
**UK SIC:** 43992, 48360
**Auditors:** Wrigley Partington
**Bankers:** National Westminster Bank Plc (01-08-99)

| | 30-09-14 | 30-09-13 | 30-09-12 |
|---|---|---|---|
| TO | 45,621,205 | 45,288,323 | 40,591,462 |
| P/L | 7,562,608 | 4,993,698 | 4,305,738 |
| NW | 32,141,055 | 26,135,420 | 22,223,905 |
| WC | 26,306,667 | 20,201,585 | 16,491,784 |
| Emp. | 232 | 237 | 245 |

DUNS 21-028-4659     **Exp**

## Robert Stuart Ltd

10-11 Edinburgh Way, Harlow, Essex CM20 2DH
**Tel:** 01279-442931
**Web:** www.robertstuart.plc.uk
**Reg No:** 0398525 **VAT No:** 573190928
**Estd:** 1945 Private Limited Company
**Line of Business:** Manufacture of other fabricated metal products not elsewhere classified
**Export Markets:** E U
**Export Sales:** £259,309
**Issued Capital:** £300,000
**Directors:** Mrs S J Maxwell, T B Maxwell, H P Maxwell
**Co. Secretary:** John Hammett
**Responsibilities**
**Senior:** Lee Bruce (*Quality Manager*), Janette Button (*Manager*), Ian McDonald (*General Manager*)
**Finance:** Shaun Canfield (*Financial Director*)
**IT:** Paul Compton (*Technical Manager*)
**Health & Safety:** Paul Compton (*Technical Manager*)
**Facilities:** Cliff Richardson (*Maintenance Manager*)
**Operations:** Tony Browne (*Works Manager*), Lee Bruce (*Quality Manager*), Paul Compton (*Technical Manager*)
**Engineering:** Cliff Richardson (*Maintenance Manager*)
**US SIC:** 3398 **UK SIC:** 31380
**Auditors:** Gallagher & Brocklehurst
**Bankers:** The Royal Bank Of Scotland Plc (83-16-07)

| | 30-11-13 | 30-11-12 | 30-11-11 |
|---|---|---|---|
| TO | 4,395,072 | N/A | 3,848,845 |
| P/L | 234,688 | N/A | 32,702 |
| NW | 2,096,779 | 2,045,836 | 2,016,181 |
| WC | 1,250,631 | 1,183,752 | 1,092,189 |

DUNS 23-086-1812

## Robert the Napier

Third Avenue, Gillingham, Kent ME7 2LX
**Web:** www.robertnapier.org.uk
**Estd:** 1926
**Line of Business:** Further education schools and colleges
**Director:** R Moreton
**Responsibilities**
**IT:** Philip Trice (*ICT Network Administrator*)
**US SIC:** 8221 **UK SIC:** 93100
**Employees:** 122

DUNS 22-702-1029     **Imp-Exp**

## Robert W. Baird Group Ltd

(**Subsidiary of:** Baird Holding Company)
15 Finsbury Circus, London EC2M 7EB
**Tel:** 02074881212 **Fax:** 02074813911
**Web:** www.rwbaird.com
**Reg No:** 0863502   **Estd:** 1965 Private Limited Company
**Line of Business:** Banks and financial institutions
**Issued Capital:** £9,691,046
**Principals:** J A Fordham (*Managing*), P H Spencer, S G Booth, D Zarcone, P E Purcell, G F Hackmann, W W Mahler
**Co. Secretary:** Tmf Corporate Administration Ser
**Responsibilities**
**Senior:** Michael Proudlock (*Manager*), Leonard Rush (*Manager*)
**HR:** Alexia Constantinou (*Human Resources Director*)
**US SIC:** 6012 **UK SIC:** 81402
**Auditors:** Grant Thornton UK LLP

| | 31-12-13 | 31-12-12 | 31-12-11 |
|---|---|---|---|
| TA | 47,519,244 | 44,937,540 | 50,234,404 |
| P/L | 6,255,884 | 3,545,994 | 8,883,230 |
| NW | 31,820,342 | 33,118,193 | 30,103,241 |
| WC | 21,111,856 | 32,248,291 | 29,320,271 |
| Emp. | 90 | 88 | 79 |

DUNS 21-198-7698     **Imp-Exp**

## Robert Walker (Food Merchants) Ltd

3 Croydon Road, Keston, Kent BR2 6EA
**Tel:** 01689854911 **Fax:** 08708508224
**Web:** www.walkerschocolates.co.uk
**Reg No:** 1056042 **VAT No:** 206475471
**Estd:** 1972 Private Limited Company
**Line of Business:** Manufacture of cocoa and chocolate confectionery
**Export Markets:** countries worldwide
**Export Sales:** £6,180,437
**Trading Style:** Walkers Chocolate
**Issued Capital:** £100,000
**Principals:** R W Walker (*Chairman and Managing*), B M Tomlins (*Financial*), J Craig
**Co. Secretary:** Neil Rose
**Branches:** Robert Walker (Food Merchants) Ltd, Unit 8, Wested Lane, Swanley, Kent BR8 8TE
**US SIC:** 2066, 2065
**UK SIC:** 42141, 42142
**Auditors:** BDO Stoy Hayward LLP
**Bankers:** Barclays Bank Plc (20-57-06)

| | 31-01-14 | 31-01-13 | 31-01-12 |
|---|---|---|---|
| TO | 24,982,732 | 26,596,583 | 28,084,198 |
| P/L | 717,497 | 2,010,840 | 2,032,296 |
| NW | 22,154,774 | 21,579,262 | 19,964,451 |
| WC | 15,656,552 | 15,748,338 | 14,536,720 |
| Emp. | 114 | 118 | 128 |

DUNS 21-863-3667

## Robert Walker (Haulage) Ltd

(**Subsidiary of:** Robert Walker Haulage Holdings Ltd)
Hall Lane, Stockport, Cheshire SK6 1PR
**Tel:** 01614302618 **Fax:** 0161-430-3154
**Web:** www.rwalkers.co.uk
**Reg No:** 0598102   **Estd:** 1958 Private Limited Company
**Line of Business:** Freight transport by road not elsewhere classified
**Issued Capital:** £3,000
**Directors:** P Walker, N E Walker
**US SIC:** 4213 **UK SIC:** 72300
**Auditors:** Booth Ainsworth

| | 31-03-14 | 31-03-13 | 31-03-12 |
|---|---|---|---|
| TA | 2,046,097 | 2,295,828 | 2,576,941 |
| NW | 1,480,087 | 1,532,236 | 1,825,829 |
| WC | 944,022 | 938,905 | 1,149,396 |

DUNS 23-967-1972

## Robert Walters Plc

11 Slingsby Place, London WC2E 9AB
**Tel:** 02073793333 **Fax:** 02075098714
**Web:** www.robertwalters.com
**Reg No:** 3956083   **Estd:** 1986 Public Limited Company
**Line of Business:** Employment and recruitment companies and consultants
**Export Sales:** £361,985,000
**Trading Style:** Walters Robert Operation, Robert Walters
**Issued Capital:** £17,056,750
**Principals:** R C Walters (*Chairman*), Ms C Hui, A D Kemp, G P Daubeney, B D Mcarthur-Muscroft, P L Vandewalle
**Co. Secretary:** Alan Bannatyne
**Responsibilities**
**Senior:** Marshall Brown (*Senior Vice President*), Toby Fowlston (*Manager*), Susan Major (*Manager*), Mairead Spendiff (*Executive*)
**Finance:** Daniel Quint (*Finance Director*), Andrew Setchell (*Director of Accountancy, Treas*)
**Marketing:** Steven Coxall (*Senior Marketing Manager*), Tim Gilbert (*Director of Sales Marketing an*), Emma Lang (*Marketing Executive*), Faye Walshe (*Marketing Manager*), Caroline Watkin (*Head of Group Communications*)
**Sales:** Tim Gilbert (*Director of Sales Marketing an*)
**Admin:** Malcolm Heskins (*Office Manager*), Cara Wellman (*Personal Assistant*)
**IT:** Jp Browne (*Information Technology Consult*), Julian Munzu (*Services Desk Technician*)
**HR:** Colin Loth (*Director of Legal, HR and Secr*), Jon Mullin (*Recruitment Consultant*)
**Health & Safety:** Malcolm Heskins (*Office Manager*)
**Facilities:** Malcolm Heskins (*Office Manager*)
**Operations:** Lexi Lincke (*Head of Operational Projects*)
**Branches:** Robert Walters Plc, 1 Walnut Tree Close, Bishops Wharf, Guildford, Surrey GU1 4RA
**US SIC:** 7361 **UK SIC:** 83954
**Auditors:** Deloitte LLP
**Bankers:** HSBC Bank plc (40-01-06)

| | 31-12-13 | 31-12-12 | 31-12-11 |
|---|---|---|---|
| TO | 597,719,000 | 567,771,000 | 528,114,000 |
| P/L | 10,071,000 | 7,725,000 | 15,082,000 |
| NW | 64,365,000 | 62,041,000 | 60,950,000 |
| WC | 47,155,000 | 42,934,000 | 43,396,000 |
| Emp. | 2,273 | 2,193 | 1,934 |

DUNS 21-690-3930 Imp

## Robert Welch Designs Ltd

Lower High Street, Chipping Campden, Gloucestershire GL55 6DY
**Tel:** 01386840522
**Web:** www.robertwelch.com
**Reg No:** 0689103 **Estd:** 1966 Private Limited Company
**Line of Business:** Cutlery suppliers
**Export Sales:** £4,489,583
**Issued Capital:** £100
**Directors:** Ms A J Welch, A R Welch
**Co. Secretary:** Ms Alice Welch
**Responsibilities**
**Marketing:** Rod Oates *(Commercial Manager)*
**Sales:** Rod Oates *(Commercial Manager)*
**Health & Safety:** James Lindner *(Operations Manager)*
**Facilities:** James Lindner *(Operations Manager)*
**Branches:** Robert Welch Designs Ltd, Studio Shop, 19 Old Square, Warwick, Warwickshire CV34 4RU
**US SIC:** 5021, 7399
**UK SIC:** 61500, 83954
**Auditors:** P B Reast

| | 30-04-14 | 30-04-13 | 30-04-12 |
|---|---|---|---|
| TO | 11,215,420 | 10,363,663 | 10,468,971 |
| P/L | 258,093 | 439,175 | 744,228 |
| NW | 2,269,646 | 3,112,960 | 2,837,514 |
| WC | 2,992,481 | 3,327,403 | 2,613,900 |
| Emp. | 61 | 55 | 52 |

DUNS 57-854-2565

## Robert West Ltd

**(Subsidiary of:** Robert West Group Ltd)
Delta House, London SE1 1HR
**Tel:** 02079399916 **Fax:** 02079399909
**Web:** www.robertwest.co.uk
**Reg No:** 2901543 **Estd:** 1994 Private Limited Company
**Line of Business:** Other business activities not elsewhere classified
**Issued Capital:** £500
**Directors:** P E Pawsey, T M Williams
**Co. Secretary:** Jonathan Howard
**Responsibilities**
**Senior:** Mark Bellringer *(Associate Director)*
**US SIC:** 7399 **UK SIC:** 83954
**Auditors:** Kingston Smith
**Bankers:** HSBC Bank plc (40-18-22)

| | 30-06-13 | 30-06-12 | 30-06-11 |
|---|---|---|---|
| TA | 73,183 | 73,183 | 73,183 |
| NW | 1,417 | 1,417 | 1,417 |
| WC | (48,583) | (48,583) | (48,583) |

DUNS 22-902-5390 Imp

## Robert Wiseman & Sons Ltd

**(Subsidiary of:** Tm Dairy (Uk Holding) Sarl)
159 Glasgow Road, Glasgow, Lanarkshire G74 4PA
**Tel:** 01355247777 **Fax:** 01355246838
**Web:** www.muller-wiseman.co.uk
**Reg No:** 0087376SC **VAT No:** 262465555
**Estd:** 1948 Private Limited Company
**Line of Business:** Dairies
**Trading Style:** Robert Wiseman Dairies
**Issued Capital:** £740,518
**Directors:** C E Ravenhall, W D Laing, R K Kers, L Greenbury, A Mcinnes
**Co. Secretary:** Ms Maureen Burnside
**Responsibilities**
**Senior:** Julian Bell *(Director HR)*, David Clemenson *(Manager)*, Patrick Davenport *(Director of Trade)*, Jonathon Maxwell *(Manager)*, Scott Mcglashaian *(Site Manager)*
**IT:** David Clemenson *(Manager)*
**HR:** Julian Bell *(Director HR)*
**Branches:** Robert Wiseman & Sons Ltd, National Bee Supplies, 2 Okement Units, Okehampton, Devon EX20 1UB
**US SIC:** 0241 **UK SIC:** 01001
**Auditors:** Deloitte LLP
**Bankers:** Clydesdale Bank Plc (82-62-24)

| | 31-12-13 | 31-12-12 | 28-12-12 |
|---|---|---|---|
| TO | 485,165,000 | 880,555,000 | 779,779,000 |
| P/L | 147,789,000 | (4,180,000) | 10,886,000 |
| NW | 272,332,000 | 93,682,000 | 94,391,000 |
| WC | (53,599,000) | (106,021,000) | (71,765,000) |
| Emp. | 2,006 | 4,984 | 4,926 |

DUNS 56-976-6124

## Robert Wiseman Dairies Ltd

**(Subsidiary of:** Tm Dairy (Uk Holding) Sarl)
159 Glasgow Road, East Kilbride, Glasgow, Lanarkshire G74 4PA
**Tel:** 01355-244261 **Fax:** 01355-230352
**Web:** www.muller-wiseman.co.uk
**Reg No:** 0146494SC **Estd:** 1994 Private Limited Company
**Line of Business:** Dairies
**Trading Style:** Muller Wiseman Dairies
**Issued Capital:** £7,228,293
**Directors:** L Greenbury, C E Ravenhall, W D Laing, A Mcinnes
**Co. Secretary:** Ms Maureen Burnside
**Responsibilities**
**Senior:** Heiner Kamps *(Chairman)*, Theo Mueller *(Non-Executive Director)*
**Marketing:** Graeme Jack *(Communications Director)*
**HR:** Garry Frame *(Human Resources Manager)*
**Branches:** Robert Wiseman Dairies Ltd, Pensilva Industrial Estate, St Ive Road, Pensilva, Liskeard, Cornwall PL14 5RE
**US SIC:** 2026, 6711
**UK SIC:** 41301, 83962
**Auditors:** PricewaterhouseCoopers LLP
**Bankers:** Clydesdale Bank Plc (82-62-24)

| | 31-12-13 | 31-12-12 | 28-12-12 |
|---|---|---|---|
| TO | N/A | 880,555,000 | 779,779,000 |
| P/L | N/A | (7,126,000) | 7,551,000 |
| NW | 84,674,000 | 155,540,000 | 156,835,000 |
| WC | N/A | (51,075,000) | (17,438,000) |
| Emp. | N/A | 4,984 | 4,926 |

DUNS 28-971-7340

## Robert Woodhead Holdings Ltd

Edwinstow House, High Street, Edwinstow, Mansfield, Nottinghamshire NG21 9PR
**Tel:** 01623871101
**Reg No:** 1735075 **Estd:** 1983 Private Limited Company
**Line of Business:** Management activities of construction holding companies
**Issued Capital:** £100
**Director:** D P Woodhead
**Co. Secretary:** Ms Hilary Cheshire
**Responsibilities**
**Senior:** Craig Pygall *(Manager)*, Glenn Slater *(Manager)*
**US SIC:** 6711, 1522
**UK SIC:** 83962, 50100

| | 31-10-13 | 31-10-12 | 31-10-11 |
|---|---|---|---|
| TO | 21,637,196 | 18,598,566 | 11,474,166 |
| P/L | 427,874 | 554,493 | 137,453 |
| NW | 2,032,050 | 1,752,954 | 1,248,398 |
| WC | 1,134,214 | 1,267,699 | 1,118,568 |
| Emp. | 75 | 65 | 54 |

DUNS 76-630-0735

## Roberts & Cubbage Joinery Ltd

Unit 1-4, Orlando Works, Thynne Street, Bolton, Lancashire BL3 6DE
**Fax:** 01204365335
**Web:** www.windowplas.com
**Reg No:** 2580682 **Estd:** 1979 Private Limited Company
**Line of Business:** Conservatories
**Trading Style:** Windowplas
**Issued Capital:** £1,000
**Managing Directors:** K Cubbage, K Roberts
**Co. Secretary:** Kenneth Roberts
**US SIC:** 3442 **UK SIC:** 31420
**Auditors:** Metcalfe & Co
**Bankers:** The Royal Bank Of Scotland Plc (16-29-20)

| | 31-03-14 | 31-03-13 | 31-03-12 |
|---|---|---|---|
| TA | 717,543 | 695,142 | 711,398 |
| NW | 126,104 | 59,855 | 104,662 |
| WC | 77,690 | 14,054 | 53,884 |

DUNS 23-842-4571

## Roberts & Prowse (Swindon) Ltd

**(Subsidiary of:** Brill Holdings Ltd)
Dunbeath Road, Swindon, Wiltshire SN2 8EA
**Tel:** 01793-487807
**Web:** www.robertsandprowse.com
**Reg No:** 3834098 **Estd:** 1999 Private Limited Company
**Line of Business:** Plumbing
**Issued Capital:** £400
**Director:** M P Glover
**Co. Secretary:** Ms Marilyn Anderson Glover
**US SIC:** 1711, 1731
**UK SIC:** 50300
**Auditors:** Kirk Hills

| | 31-03-14 | 31-03-13 | 31-03-12 |
|---|---|---|---|
| TA | 2,562,939 | 1,546,133 | 1,333,033 |
| NW | 1,041,869 | 508,082 | 176,456 |
| WC | 1,061,843 | 559,126 | 209,575 |

DUNS 23-623-8929

## Roberts Brothers Taxis

14b High Street, Prestatyn, Clwyd LL19 9AF
**Tel:** 01745888444
**Web:** www.robertstaxisltd.co.uk
**VAT No:** 162608862 **Estd:** 1946 Proprietorship
**Line of Business:** Taxis and private hire vehicles
**Proprietor:** P Roberts
**US SIC:** 4121 **UK SIC:** 72200
**Bankers:** National Westminster Bank Plc (60-17-30)
**Employees:** 80

DUNS 23-636-7566

## Roberts Care Agency Ltd

1 Anchor Hill Creswell Corner, Woking, Surrey GU21 2JD
**Tel:** 01483-799138
**Web:** www.robertscareagency.co.uk
**Reg No:** 3633635 **Estd:** 1998 Private Limited Company
**Line of Business:** Other human health activities
**Issued Capital:** £2
**Director:** Ms V V Roberts
**Co. Secretary:** David Roberts
**US SIC:** 8091 **UK SIC:** 95200
**Bankers:** HSBC Bank plc (40-47-08)

| | 30-09-13 | 30-09-12 | 30-09-11 |
|---|---|---|---|
| TA | 211,011 | 225,080 | 173,237 |
| NW | 149,119 | 152,515 | 111,601 |
| WC | 139,511 | 145,676 | 102,779 |

DUNS 21-132-0360

## Roberts Limbrick Ltd

**(Subsidiary of:** Roberts Limbrick Holdings Ltd)
The Carriage Building, Bruton Way, Gloucester, Gloucestershire GL1 1DG
**Tel:** 03333405500 **Fax:** 03333 408920
**Web:** www.limbrick.com
**Reg No:** 6658029 **Estd:** 1987 Private Limited Company
**Line of Business:** Architectural activities
**Issued Capital:** £100,000
**Directors:** Mrs D Limbrick, A S Terry, J J Roberts, Mrs E E Roberts, D P Billingham, P W Newth, W Organ, S Limbrick
**Co. Secretary:** Mrs Elizabeth Thompson
**Responsibilities**
**Senior:** Philip Dryden *(Director)*, Paul Gooderson *(Director)*, Joseph Roberts *(Director)*, Aled Roberts *(Director)*
**US SIC:** 8911 **UK SIC:** 83701

| | 31-08-13 | 31-08-12 | 31-08-11 |
|---|---|---|---|
| TA | 3,022,903 | 1,932,490 | 2,217,503 |
| NW | 1,502,629 | 1,119,208 | 1,020,619 |
| WC | 1,502,629 | 1,119,208 | 710,619 |

DUNS 34-528-3134 Imp-Exp

## Roberts Mart (Holdings) Co Ltd

Thornes Farm Way, Leeds, West Yorkshire LS9 0AN
**Web:** www.roberts-mart.co.uk
**Reg No:** 5338875 **Estd:** 2005 Private Limited Company
**Line of Business:** Management activities of holding companies
**Export Markets:** Ireland
**Issued Capital:** £192,944
**Principals:** J Roberts *(Managing)*, B J Roberts, W P Roberts
**Co. Secretary:** Craig Worley
**US SIC:** 6711 **UK SIC:** 83962
**Bankers:** HSBC Bank plc (40-27-15)

| | 31-12-13 | 31-12-12 | 31-12-11 |
|---|---|---|---|
| TO | 25,419,651 | 24,656,928 | 22,579,502 |
| P/L | 851,313 | 1,209,829 | 466,921 |
| NW | 14,190,002 | 13,628,406 | 12,833,901 |
| WC | 4,521,593 | 3,651,320 | 3,081,133 |
| Emp. | 153 | 140 | 134 |

DUNS 73-261-2598

## Roberts Nationwide Support Services Ltd

Unit 9 Dukes Court, Wellington Street, Luton, Bedfordshire LU1 5AF
**Tel:** 01582876222
**Web:** www.roberts-nationwide.co.uk
**Reg No:** 4535054 **Estd:** 2002 Private Limited Company
**Line of Business:** Security activities
**Issued Capital:** £2
**Directors:** Mrs S Robert, R Dass
**US SIC:** 7393 **UK SIC:** 83954
**Auditors:** Neil Clark

| | 30-09-13 | 30-09-12 | 30-09-11 |
|---|---|---|---|
| TA | 519,028 | 466,264 | 544,354 |
| NW | 195,688 | 187,502 | 216,607 |
| WC | 178,939 | 178,716 | 210,115 |

DUNS 29-582-9956 Imp-Exp

## Roberts of Port Dinorwic Ltd

**(Subsidiary of:** Wynco Ltd)
Griffiths Crossing Industrial Estate, Caernarfon, Gwynedd LL55 1TS
**Tel:** 01286-676111
**Web:** www.roberts-wales.co.uk
**Reg No:** 1944778 **VAT No:** 905054746
**Estd:** 1985 Private Limited Company
**Line of Business:** Manufacturers of food products
**Export Markets:** U S A; Europe
**Issued Capital:** £200,000
**Directors:** Ms M Williams, G C Thomas
**Co. Secretary:** Ms Sara Roberts
**Responsibilities**
**HR:** Gareth Luke *(Human Resources Manager)*
**Operations:** Hedd Druce *(Operations Manager)*, Gareth Luke *(Human Resources Manager)*
**Branches:** Roberts Of Port Dinorwic Ltd, Caernarfon Road, Bangor, Gwynedd LL57 4SU
**US SIC:** 2099 **UK SIC:** 42399
**Auditors:** Grant Thornton UK LLP
**Bankers:** Lloyds TSB Bank plc (30-90-43)

| | 30-06-14 | 30-06-13 | 30-06-12 |
|---|---|---|---|
| TO | 10,181,057 | 8,967,341 | 8,065,067 |
| P/L | 51,674 | (50,900) | (155,286) |
| NW | 2,430,230 | 2,393,645 | 2,438,784 |
| WC | 1,657,340 | 1,629,648 | 1,649,805 |
| Emp. | 81 | 77 | 65 |

DUNS 21-784-4139

## Roberts Primary School

Robert Street, Dudley, West Midlands DY3 2AZ
**Web:** www.robertsprimary.org.uk
**Estd:** 1987 Proprietorship
**Line of Business:** Schools (local authority)
**Proprietor:** D Baker
**US SIC:** 8211 **UK SIC:** 93200
**Employees:** 103

DUNS 23-569-0935

## Robertson Facilities Management Ltd

**(Subsidiary of:** Robertson Group (Holdings) Ltd)
Robertson Farm Building, Inverness, Inverness Shire IV3 8NF
**Tel:** 01463-729866 **Fax:** 01463713421
**Web:** www.robertsonfm.co.uk
**Reg No:** 0185956SC **VAT No:** 893342404
**Estd:** 1986 Private Limited Company
**Line of Business:** Management of real estate on a fee or contract basis
**Issued Capital:** £100,000
**Directors:** S Roberts, W G Robertson, S J Kelly, I Gibson
**Co. Secretary:** Craig Robertson
**Responsibilities**
**Senior:** Stephen Curle *(Manager)*, Andy Grigor *(Regional Manager)*
**US SIC:** 6531, 1796
**UK SIC:** 83400, 50400
**Bankers:** The Royal Bank Of Scotland Plc (16-13-29)

| | 31-03-14 | 31-03-13 | 30-03-12 |
|---|---|---|---|
| TO | 36,330,000 | 29,574,000 | 27,058,000 |
| P/L | 2,741,000 | 2,057,000 | 1,993,000 |
| NW | 5,237,000 | 4,043,000 | 3,370,000 |
| WC | 4,987,000 | 3,875,000 | 3,224,000 |
| Emp. | 651 | 600 | 541 |

DUNS 21-579-3787

## Robertson Group Ltd

**(Subsidiary of:** Robertson Group (Holdings) Ltd)
10 Perimeter Road, Elgin, Morayshire IV30 6AE
**Tel:** 01343-548621 **Fax:** 01343-546265
**Web:** www.robertson.co.uk
**Reg No:** 0060077SC **Estd:** 1963 Private Limited Company
**Line of Business:** Building of complete constructions or parts thereof; civil engineering
**Trading Style:** Robertson Construction, Robertson Timber Products, Robertson Developments, Doric Precast Concrete
**Issued Capital:** £21,000
**Principals:** W G Robertson *(Managing)*, R E Bodnar-Horvath, I Clark, D W Shewan, Mrs H M Robertson, S Roberts
**Co. Secretary:** Ms Irene Wilson
**Responsibilities**
**Marketing:** Fraser Edgar *(Marketing Executive)*
**Sales:** John Meichan *(Sales Manager)*
**Purchasing:** Mike McBride *(Head Buyer)*
**Branches:** Robertson Group Ltd, Robertson House, The Castle Business Park, Stirling, Stirlingshire FK9 4TZ
**US SIC:** 7399 **UK SIC:** 83954
**Auditors:** KPMG LLP
**Bankers:** The Royal Bank Of Scotland Plc (83-20-06)

| | 31-03-14 | 31-03-13 | 30-03-12 |
|---|---|---|---|
| TO | 251,517,000 | 209,972,000 | 226,110,000 |
| P/L | 34,629,000 | (3,722,000) | 709,000 |
| NW | 62,772,000 | 30,645,000 | 34,892,000 |
| WC | 58,592,000 | (9,257,000) | 79,754,000 |
| Emp. | 1,219 | 1,132 | 1,064 |

DUNS 73-942-2400

## Robertson Homes Ltd

**(Subsidiary of:** Robertson Group (Holdings) Ltd)
Robertson House, The Castle Business Park, Stirling, Stirlingshire FK9 4TZ
**Tel:** 01786-431600 **Fax:** 01786-431620
**Web:** www.robertsonhomes.co.uk
**Reg No:** 0151825SC **Estd:** 1994 Private Limited Company
**Line of Business:** Development and selling of real estate
**Issued Capital:** £20,020,000

**Directors:** W G Robertson, S Roberts
**Co. Secretary:** Ms Irene Wilson
**Responsibilities**
**Sales:** Mary Grant (Sales Manager)
**HR:** Jacqueline Cassidy (HR Manager)
**Branches:** Robertson Homes Ltd, Robertson House, The Castle Business Park, Stirling, Stirlingshire FK9 4TZ
**US SIC:** 6552  **UK SIC:** 85000
**Auditors:** KPMG LLP
**Bankers:** The Royal Bank Of Scotland Plc (83-15-31)

|     | 31-03-14 | 31-03-13 | 30-03-12 |
|-----|----------|----------|----------|
| TO | 20,600,000 | 17,901,000 | 20,016,000 |
| P/L | (11,369,000) | (7,138,000) | 40,000 |
| NW | 2,791,000 | 13,310,000 | 19,819,000 |
| WC | 11,165,000 | 15,082,000 | 59,682,000 |
| Emp. | 51 | 49 | 57 |

DUNS 29-000-1809

## The Robertson Hotel Co (Denny) Ltd

(**Subsidiary of:** The Edinburgh Collection Ltd)
4 Parkfoot Street, Kilsyth, Glasgow, Lanarkshire G65 0SP
**Tel:** 01236-821649
**Web:** www.coachmanhotel.com
**Reg No:** 0053226SC  **Estd:** 1987 Private Limited Company
**Line of Business:** Hotels
**Trading Style:** The Coachman Hotel
**Issued Capital:** £80,001
**Directors:** S Kapoor, R Kapoor
**Co. Secretary:** Rakesh Kapoor
**US SIC:** 7011  **UK SIC:** 66500
**Auditors:** Barrie Scott & Co
**Bankers:** Bank Of Scotland (80-06-33)

|     | 31-12-13 | 31-12-12 | 31-12-11 |
|-----|----------|----------|----------|
| TA | 240,860 | 240,860 | 240,860 |
| NW | 80,463 | 80,463 | 80,463 |
| WC | 80,463 | 80,463 | 80,463 |

DUNS 21-442-4640                              Imp

## Robertson Outerwear Ltd

(**Subsidiary of:** The International Coat Co Ltd)
20-24 Telford Road, Lenziemill, Cumbernauld, Glasgow, Lanarkshire G67 2AX
**Tel:** 01236-722192  **Fax:** 01414-232828
**Web:** www.robertsonouterwear.com
**Reg No:** 0019133SC  **VAT No:** 259982887
**Estd:** 1936 Private Limited Company
**Line of Business:** Retail sale of clothing
**Issued Capital:** £10,000
**Principals:** H C Locke (Chairman), Ms M D Davidson (Managing), Mrs D A Hunter
**Co. Secretary:** Ms Deborah Hunter
**Branches:** Robertson Outerwear Ltd, Robertson Outerwear Ltd, 40 Gordon Street, Glasgow, Lanarkshire G1 3PU
**US SIC:** 5699  **UK SIC:** 64500
**Auditors:** Tenon Audit Ltd
**Bankers:** The Royal Bank Of Scotland Plc (83-07-06)

|     | 29-03-14 | 31-03-13 | 31-03-12 |
|-----|----------|----------|----------|
| TA | 608,453 | 602,129 | 568,274 |
| NW | 453,051 | 431,814 | 389,629 |
| WC | 397,656 | 365,192 | 318,415 |

DUNS 21-908-7368

## Robertson Roofing Ltd

Croft House, Solihull, West Midlands B93 0HL
**Tel:** 01564776278  **Fax:** 01564-779607
**Web:** www.robertsonroofing.com
**Reg No:** 0653926  **VAT No:** 111945391
**Estd:** 1960 Private Limited Company
**Line of Business:** Erection of roof covering and frames
**Issued Capital:** £10,100
**Principals:** J C Mulvey (Managing), M A Robertson, D N Wright
**Co. Secretary:** David Wright
**Responsibilities**
**Senior:** Maurice Ball (Manager)
**Branches:** Robertson Roofing Ltd, Park House, 12 High Street, Thornbury, Bristol, Avon BS35 2AQ
**US SIC:** 1761  **UK SIC:** 50400
**Auditors:** Michael Heaven & Associates Ltd
**Bankers:** HSBC Bank plc (40-19-34)

|     | 31-05-14 | 31-05-13 | 31-05-12 |
|-----|----------|----------|----------|
| TA | 2,806,604 | 3,080,803 | 3,253,435 |
| NW | 1,738,264 | 1,732,693 | 1,718,576 |
| WC | 1,364,203 | 1,266,337 | 1,252,658 |

DUNS 22-703-6787                              Exp

## Robertson Taylor Insurance Brokers Ltd

(**Subsidiary of:** Entertainment Insurance Partners Ltd)
America House, 2 America Square, London EC3N 2LU
**Tel:** 02075101234  **Fax:** 020-7510-1134
**Web:** www.robertson-taylor.com
**Reg No:** 1301462  **Estd:** 1977 Private Limited Company

**Line of Business:** Activities auxiliary to insurance and pension funding
**Export Markets:** Europe
**Export Sales:** £2,483,661
**Issued Capital:** £750,000
**Directors:** J B Davies, B B Knox, J Silcock, A I France, N Henry, J C Hunnisett, A D Chapman
**Responsibilities**
**Senior:** Franz Knoblauch (Manager)
**Marketing:** Laura Wellstead (Marketing Manager)
**Sales:** Paul Twomey (Marketing/Business Development)
**Admin:** Lisa rodgers (Office Manager)
**US SIC:** 6411  **UK SIC:** 83200
**Auditors:** Mazars LLP
**Bankers:** Barclays Bank Plc (20-78-98)

|     | 31-12-13 | 31-12-12 | 31-12-11 |
|-----|----------|----------|----------|
| TO | 6,714,940 | 6,496,964 | 5,243,720 |
| P/L | 531,268 | 443,873 | 539,845 |
| NW | 4,374,061 | 3,888,675 | 3,444,802 |
| WC | 4,117,664 | 3,792,979 | 3,330,753 |
| Emp. | 55 | 50 | 47 |

DUNS 77-696-5980                              Exp

## Robertson (Uk) Ltd

(**Subsidiary of:** Cgg)
Tyn Y Coed, Pentywyn Road, Llandudno, Gwynedd LL30 1SA
**Tel:** 01492-581811
**Web:** www.cgg.com
**Reg No:** 3006207  **Estd:** 1995 Private Limited Company
**Line of Business:** Research and experimental development on natural sciences and engineering
**Export Sales:** £18,273,000
**Trading Style:** Esso Care Laboratory, Wearcheck
**Issued Capital:** £1,204,000
**Directors:** A J Buckley, M E Weber, R I Thornton, D P Watson
**Co. Secretary:** Ms Samantha Boast
**Responsibilities**
**Senior:** Douglas Paton (Manager)
**Branches:** Robertson (Uk) Ltd, Horizon House, Azalea Drive, Swanley, Kent BR8 8JR
**US SIC:** 7391  **UK SIC:** 94000
**Auditors:** KPMG LLP
**Bankers:** Bank Of Scotland (12-09-19)

|     | 31-12-13 | 31-12-12 | 31-12-11 |
|-----|----------|----------|----------|
| TO | 21,130,000 | 19,718,000 | 19,975,000 |
| P/L | 4,777,000 | 4,699,000 | 4,204,000 |
| NW | 4,855,000 | 7,370,000 | 3,893,000 |
| WC | 4,146,000 | 6,607,000 | 3,295,000 |
| Emp. | 267 | 246 | 230 |

DUNS 22-512-5715                              Imp

## Robimatic Ltd

Sandall Stones Road, Kirk Sandall Industrial Estate, Doncaster, South Yorkshire DN3 1QR
**Tel:** 01302790790  **Fax:** 01302790088
**Web:** www.polypipe.com
**Reg No:** 1507994  **VAT No:** 449673894
**Estd:** 1980 Private Limited Company
**Line of Business:** Manufacture of plastics in primary forms
**Trading Style:** Robimatic Ltd
**Issued Capital:** £58,823
**Director:** D G Hall
**Co. Secretary:** Peter Shepherd
**Responsibilities**
**Senior:** Keir Littlewood (Manager), Andy Warchol (Manager)
**US SIC:** 2821, 5074
**UK SIC:** 25140, 61300
**Auditors:** Deloitte & Touche LLP
**Bankers:** Lloyds TSB Bank plc (30-91-44)

|     | 31-12-13 | 31-12-12 | 31-12-11 |
|-----|----------|----------|----------|
| TO | 12,098,000 | 11,283,000 | 10,960,000 |
| P/L | 1,059,000 | 953,000 | 1,019,000 |
| NW | 10,228,000 | 9,169,000 | 8,216,000 |
| WC | 9,783,000 | 8,765,000 | 7,851,000 |
| Emp. | 70 | 72 | 74 |

DUNS 39-930-9814

## Robin Concrete & Waste Disposal Ltd

(**Subsidiary of:** Rct Group Ltd)
Foster Street, Stoneferry Road, Hull, North Humberside HU8 8BT
**Tel:** 01482-585985
**Web:** www.robinconcrete.co.uk
**Reg No:** 2235332  **VAT No:** 347539330
**Estd:** 2012 Private Limited Company
**Line of Business:** Mortar ready mixed
**Issued Capital:** £100
**Managing Director:** J R Thornham
**Co. Secretary:** Ms Margaret Thornham
**US SIC:** 3273, 4213
**UK SIC:** 24360, 72300
**Auditors:** Smailes, Goldie & Co
**Bankers:** National Westminster Bank Plc (60-02-23)

|     | 30-04-14 | 30-04-13 | 30-04-12 |
|-----|----------|----------|----------|
| TA | 1,136,938 | 1,194,188 | 1,357,387 |
| NW | (507,501) | (622,788) | (179,783) |
| WC | (743,947) | (1,267,845) | (970,901) |

DUNS 21-036-9529

## Robin Hood Airport

Heyford House, First Avenue, Finningley, Doncaster, South Yorkshire DN9 3RH
**Tel:** 01302801010
**Web:** www.robinhoodairport.com
**Estd:** 2005
**Line of Business:** Airports
**Responsibilities**
**HR:** Diane Bunting (Human Resources Manager), Marie Le-Masney (Human Resources Manager)
**US SIC:** 4582  **UK SIC:** 76400
**Employees:** 600

DUNS 21-231-8280

## Robins & Day

141 Hersham Road, Walton-On-Thames, Surrey KT12 1RW
**Tel:** 01932797400
**Web:** www.peugeot.co.uk
**Estd:** 1973 Proprietorship
**Line of Business:** Car dealers (new & used)
**Proprietor:** Mrs A Tiffin
**Responsibilities**
**Senior:** Kevin Ambrose (Service Manager), Dito Lepore (General Manager)
**Finance:** Kim Anderson (Accountant)
**Operations:** Kevin Ambrose (Service Manager)
**US SIC:** 5511  **UK SIC:** 65100
**Employees:** 67

DUNS 21-395-3431

## Robins & Day Motors

332-340 Clapham Road, Stockwell, London SW9 9AJ
**Tel:** 02077205151
**Estd:** 1997 Proprietorship
**Line of Business:** Car dealers (new & used)
**Proprietor:** A Odonnell
**Responsibilities**
**Senior:** Nathan Butters (After Sales Manager), Alex O'Donnell (General Manager)
**Marketing:** Alex O'Donnell (General Manager)
**Sales:** Alex O'Donnell (General Manager)
**Health & Safety:** Nathan Butters (After Sales Manager)
**Operations:** Nathan Butters (After Sales Manager)
**Purchasing:** Alex O'Donnell (General Manager)
**US SIC:** 5511, 5521
**UK SIC:** 65100
**Employees:** 50

DUNS 23-792-2760

## Robins Close

Middle Green Road, Wellington, Somerset TA21 9NS
**Tel:** 01823662032
**Web:** www.carehome.co.uk
**Estd:** 1991
**Line of Business:** Residential care establishments
**Proprietor:** Miss M Ngomane
**Responsibilities**
**Senior:** Ann Bright (Manager), Andy Kirby (Manager)
**US SIC:** 8321, 6732
**UK SIC:** 96111, 83100
**Employees:** 56

DUNS 21-777-3508

## Robins Lane Community Primary School

Robins Lane, St Helens, Merseyside WA9 3NF
**Tel:** 01744678503
**Web:** http://webfronter.com
**Estd:** 1998 Proprietorship
**Line of Business:** Schools (local authority)
**Proprietor:** Mrs A Morten
**Responsibilities**
**Senior:** Lisa Howard (Head Teacher)
**US SIC:** 8211  **UK SIC:** 93200
**Employees:** 50

DUNS 21-227-2370

## Robins Respite Centre

Shinners Bridge, Dartington, Totnes, Devon TQ9 6JU
**Web:** www.lifeworks-uk.org
**Estd:** 1999 Proprietorship
**Line of Business:** Disability services
**Proprietor:** T Andrews
**US SIC:** 8321  **UK SIC:** 96111
**Employees:** 50

DUNS 21-863-2131                              Imp-Exp

## Robinson Brothers (Ryders Green) Ltd

Phoenix Street, West Bromwich, West Midlands B70 0AH
**Tel:** 0121-553-2451  **Fax:** 01215005183
**Web:** www.robinsonbrothers.ltd.uk
**Reg No:** 0041367  **VAT No:** 277885979
**Estd:** 1894 Private Limited Company
**Line of Business:** Management activities of production holding companies
**Export Markets:** Worldwide
**Export Sales:** £25,019,000
**Issued Capital:** £1,949,587
**Principals:** E R Greey (Chairman), M B Robinson, M A Austin, J C Robinson, E H Price
**Co. Secretary:** Graham Parker
**Responsibilities**
**Senior:** Adrian Hanrahan (Manager)
**US SIC:** 6711, 2869
**UK SIC:** 83962, 25120
**Auditors:** PricewaterhouseCoopers
**Bankers:** Barclays Bank Plc (20-93-15)

|     | 31-12-13 | 31-12-12 | 31-12-11 |
|-----|----------|----------|----------|
| TO | 35,640,000 | 31,981,000 | 30,472,000 |
| P/L | 1,686,000 | 1,337,000 | 848,000 |
| NW | 1,833,000 | 2,066,000 | 628,000 |
| WC | 9,467,000 | 9,090,000 | 7,237,000 |
| Emp. | 271 | 266 | 251 |

DUNS 36-513-4605

## Robinson College

Grange Road, Cambridge, Cambridgeshire CB3 9AN
**Web:** www.robinson.cam.ac.uk
**Estd:** 1984
**Line of Business:** First-degree level higher education
**Directors:** Prof A D Yates, Dr E Guild, P D Milloy
**US SIC:** 8221  **UK SIC:** 93100
**Auditors:** Peters Elworthy & Moore

|     | 30-06-13 | 30-06-12 | 30-06-11 |
|-----|----------|----------|----------|
| TO | 8,167,000 | 8,624,000 | 7,644,000 |
| P/L | (315,000) | 97,000 | 107,000 |
| NW | 75,521,000 | 74,197,000 | 30,433,000 |
| WC | 1,896,000 | 1,675,000 | 1,803,000 |
| Emp. | 181 | 183 | 181 |

DUNS 21-281-5781                              Exp

## Robinson Group Ltd

(**Subsidiary of:** European Metal Recycling Limited)
Robinson House, Whiteley Road, Blaydon-On-Tyne, Tyne and Wear NE21 5NJ
**Tel:** 01914143618
**Reg No:** 0707119  **VAT No:** 176920930
**Estd:** 1961 Private Limited Company
**Line of Business:** Wholesale of waste and scrap
**Export Markets:** U S A; Spain; Taiwan
**Issued Capital:** £3,804
**Directors:** C P Sheppard, R Sheppard, N A Stinson
**Co. Secretary:** Christopher Tinsley
**Branches:** Robinson Group Ltd, Thomlinson Rd, Hartlepool, Cleveland TS25 1NS
**US SIC:** 5093  **UK SIC:** 62200
**Bankers:** Barclays Bank Plc (20-59-42)

|     | 31-12-13 | 31-12-12 | 31-12-11 |
|-----|----------|----------|----------|
| TA | 16,357,382 | 16,357,382 | 16,357,382 |
| NW | 16,357,382 | 16,357,382 | 16,357,382 |

DUNS 42-429-1222

## Robinson Healthcare Holdings Ltd

(**Subsidiary of:** Robinson Healthcare Group Ltd)
Unit 3, Lawn Road, Carlton-In-Lindrick, Worksop, Nottinghamshire S81 9LB
**Tel:** 01909735000
**Web:** www.robinson.uk.com
**Reg No:** 4416668  **Estd:** 2002 Private Limited Company
**Line of Business:** Manufacture of homogenised food preparations and dietetic food
**Export Sales:** £2,073,000
**Trading Style:** Robinson Healthcare Holdings Ltd
**Issued Capital:** £18,000
**Directors:** G D Smith, L Thomasson, R A Hall, M Richardson, N Jeffrey
**Co. Secretary:** Mark Richardson
**US SIC:** 2654  **UK SIC:** 47280
**Auditors:** Tenon Audit Ltd
**Bankers:** Bank Of Scotland (12-09-26)

|     | 30-06-14 | 30-06-13 | 30-06-12 |
|-----|----------|----------|----------|
| TO | 20,956,000 | 21,157,000 | 21,400,000 |
| P/L | 1,223,000 | 1,123,000 | 950,000 |
| NW | 6,327,000 | 4,279,000 | 4,049,000 |
| WC | 3,963,000 | 4,722,000 | 4,195,000 |
| Emp. | 166 | 163 | 159 |

DUNS 22-414-5321
## Robinson Holidays
9 Harrison Road, Halifax, West Yorkshire HX1 2AF
**Tel:** 01422344087
**Estd:** 2000 Proprietorship
**Line of Business:** Miscellaneous business services
**Proprietor:** Miss G Holdsworth
**US SIC:** 6531 **UK SIC:** 83400
**Employees:** 163

DUNS 23-749-2801
## Robinson Keane Ltd
**(Subsidiary of:** The Kellan Group Plc)
Faulkner House, Faulkner Street, Manchester M1 4DY
**Tel:** 01619299105 **Fax:** 0161-929-1142
**Web:** www.rkaccountancy.co.uk
**Reg No:** 3743251 **Estd:** 2002 Private Limited Company
**Line of Business:** Employment and recruitment companies and consultants
**Issued Capital:** £2
**Director:** R Kirpalani
**Co. Secretary:** Imco Secretary Limited
**Responsibilities**
**Senior:** Jane Chantry *(Manager)*
**Finance:** J Crossley *(Financial Controller)*
**IT:** N Middlebrough *(IT Manager)*
**US SIC:** 7392, 7361
**UK SIC:** 83951, 83954
**Auditors:** Grant Thornton

| | 31-12-13 | 31-12-12 | 31-12-11 |
|---|---|---|---|
| TA | 2 | 2 | 2 |
| NW | 2 | 2 | 2 |

DUNS 73-979-2328
## Robinson Low Francis Llp
Marylebone House, 52-54 St John Street, London EC1M 4HF
**Web:** www.rlf.co.uk
**Reg No:** 0309255OC **VAT No:** 847632502
**Estd:** 1903
**Line of Business:** Quantity surveyors
**Trading Style:** Rlf
**Responsibilities**
**Senior:** Stephen Cheesman *(Non-designated Limited Liabili)*, Paul Chesworth *(Non-designated Limited Liabili)*, Christopher Greening *(Non-designated Limited Liabili)*, Neville Onan-Read *(Non-designated Limited Liabili)*
**Branches:** Robinson Low Francis Llp, 7th Floor West Wing, 54 Hagley Road, Birmingham, West Midlands B16 8PE
**US SIC:** 7397 **UK SIC:** 83702
**Auditors:** MHA MacIntyre Hudson
**Bankers:** Barclays Bank Plc (20-65-82)

| | 31-05-13 | 31-05-12 | 31-05-11 |
|---|---|---|---|
| TO | 10,207,204 | 9,083,048 | 9,793,054 |
| P/L | 1,280,221 | 702,368 | 701,526 |
| NW | 3,981,227 | 3,485,668 | 3,488,432 |
| WC | 4,433,894 | 3,880,300 | 3,813,963 |
| Emp. | 113 | 118 | 123 |

DUNS 21-579-7133
## Robinson Plastics Packaging
Brierley Park Close, Sutton-In-Ashfield, Nottinghamshire NG17 3FW
**Tel:** 01623550045
**Web:** www.r1pp.co.uk
**Estd:** 2002
**Line of Business:** Plastic injection moulding
**Responsibilities**
**Senior:** Steve Wakelin *(Manager)*
**US SIC:** 3079 **UK SIC:** 48360
**Employees:** 65

DUNS 21-809-2062 **Imp-Exp**
## Robinson Plc
Field House, Chesterfield, Derbyshire S40 1YJ
**Tel:** 01246389280
**Web:** www.robinsonpackaging.com
**Reg No:** 0039811 **VAT No:** 828269203
**Estd:** 1991 Public Limited Company
**Line of Business:** Manufacturers and suppliers of disbility equipment
**Export Markets:** Worldwide
**Export Sales:** £4,962,000
**Trading Style:** Robinson Plastic Packaging, Consumer Packaging, Rompa International
**Issued Capital:** £88,436
**Directors:** A J Formela, R J Clothier, C C Glossop
**Co. Secretary:** Charles Robinson
**Responsibilities**
**Senior:** David Birkby *(Manager)*
**Finance:** Jeremy Vaughan *(Financial Director)*
**Branches:** Robinson Plc, 122 West End Lane, London NW6 2LS
**US SIC:** 3799, 3079
**UK SIC:** 36502, 48360
**Auditors:** Deloitte LLP
**Bankers:** National Westminster Bank Plc (60-40-09)

| | 31-12-13 | 31-12-12 | 31-12-11 |
|---|---|---|---|
| TO | 23,329,000 | 21,171,000 | 21,516,000 |
| P/L | 3,693,000 | 2,818,000 | 2,672,000 |
| NW | 25,104,000 | 22,582,000 | 23,187,000 |
| WC | 9,433,000 | 5,056,000 | 3,331,000 |
| Emp. | 233 | 226 | 233 |

DUNS 23-217-3372
## Robinson Services Ltd
Rathenraw Industrial Estate, Antrim, Co Antrim BT41 2SJ
**Tel:** 02894429717
**Web:** www.robinson-services.com
**Reg No:** 0039582NI **Estd:** 2000 Private Limited Company
**Line of Business:** Laundries
**Trading Style:** Robinson Services Limited
**Issued Capital:** £10,000
**Director:** D J Robinson
**Co. Secretary:** James Robinson
**Responsibilities**
**Senior:** Lorriane Smith *(Manager)*
**US SIC:** 7219 **UK SIC:** 98110
**Auditors:** Osborne Glenn & Co
**Bankers:** The Bank Of Ireland (90-23-89)

| | 29-06-14 | 30-06-13 | 31-06-11 |
|---|---|---|---|
| TO | 14,770,841 | 19,849,718 | 11,380,285 |
| P/L | 354,917 | 51,629 | 430,806 |
| NW | 918,920 | 501,897 | 988,176 |
| WC | (1,004,653) | (1,292,416) | (728,710) |
| Emp. | 1,140 | 1,014 | 1,022 |

DUNS 21-690-5058
## Robinson Structures Ltd
**(Subsidiary of:** L.B.J. Ltd)
Wincanton Close, Derby, Derbyshire DE24 8NJ
**Tel:** 01332574711 **Fax:** 01332861401
**Web:** www.robinsons.com
**Reg No:** 7378233 **Estd:** 2010 Private Limited Company
**Line of Business:** Development and selling of real estate
**Issued Capital:** £1,501
**Directors:** M H Preece, A C Slack, I R Drozd, A D Robinson, S Robinson, E J Gregory, A E Robinson
**Co. Secretary:** Malcolm Preece
**Responsibilities**
**Finance:** Lydia Robinson *(Accounts Manager)*
**US SIC:** 6552 **UK SIC:** 85000
**Auditors:** Malcolm H. Preece & Co
**Bankers:** Barclays Bank Plc (20-25-85)

| | 30-09-13 | 30-09-12 | 30-09-11 |
|---|---|---|---|
| TO | N/A | 5,165,428 | 3,450 |
| P/L | N/A | 379,460 | 47 |
| NW | 639,746 | 453,801 | 39 |
| WC | 590,644 | 525,653 | 39 |

DUNS 21-173-7642
## Robinson Way Ltd
**(Subsidiary of:** Hoist Finance Ab (Publ))
Quays Reach Carolina Way, Salford, Lancashire M50 2ZY
**Tel:** 01619352100
**Web:** www.robinson-way.com
**Reg No:** 6976081 **Estd:** 1966 Private Limited Company
**Line of Business:** Debt collection agencies
**Issued Capital:** £1,225
**Directors:** L J Olsson, J M Winfield, N A Nathoo, L P Sardal
**Co. Secretary:** Daniel Taylor
**Responsibilities**
**Senior:** Graham Prosser *(Manager)*
**Sales:** John Freel *(Sales Director)*
**HR:** Angela Stephens *(Human Resources Coordinator)*
**US SIC:** 7321 **UK SIC:** 83954

| | 31-12-13 | 31-12-12 | 01-12-11 |
|---|---|---|---|
| TO | 11,120,694 | 21,476,821 | 19,611,391 |
| P/L | (1,613,375) | 3,195,331 | 2,527,244 |
| NW | 4,740,669 | 5,977,910 | 3,338,150 |
| WC | 4,508,623 | 7,035,069 | 38,372,464 |
| Emp. | 209 | 247 | 268 |

DUNS 21-739-4154 **Imp-Exp**
## Robinson Webster (Holdings) Ltd
**(Subsidiary of:** Kewsaw Ltd)
Meeks Road, Falkirk, Stirlingshire FK2 7EZ
**Tel:** 02070422777
**Web:** www.jigsaw-online.com
**Reg No:** 1069599 **VAT No:** 645483125
**Estd:** 1972 Private Limited Company
**Line of Business:** Other transport via railways
**Export Markets:** Rest of world
**Export Sales:** £575,000
**Trading Style:** Jigsaw
**Issued Capital:** £90,416
**Principals:** J G Robinson *(Managing)*, Ms K D Fuller, Ms B Robinson, R Gilmore, C S Atterton, P Ruis
**Co. Secretary:** Ms Rebecca Paul
**Responsibilities**
**Senior:** Kate Corpey *(Manager)*, Darryl Shergold *(Warehouse Manager)*
**Admin:** Tracey Caldrey *(Office Manager)*
**Health & Safety:** Tracey Caldrey *(Offico Manager)*
**Facilities:** Colin Bryant *(Property Estates Manager)*
**Branches:** Robinson Webster (Holdings) Ltd, 21-23 Bridlesmith Gate, Nottingham, Nottinghamshire NG1 2GR
**US SIC:** 4011, 5611
**UK SIC:** 71000, 64500
**Auditors:** PricewaterhouseCoopers LLP
**Bankers:** S G Hambros Bank & Trust (guernsey) Ltd (40-48-60)

| | 27-09-14 | 28-09-13 | 29-09-12 |
|---|---|---|---|
| TO | 71,056,000 | 64,230,000 | 60,214,000 |
| P/L | 819,000 | 1,510,000 | 1,454,000 |
| NW | 17,940,000 | 16,436,000 | 14,514,000 |
| WC | 12,717,000 | 12,898,000 | 10,743,000 |
| Emp. | 745 | 776 | 723 |

DUNS 21-908-3755
## Robinson-White Plastics Ltd
**(Subsidiary of:** Robinson Plc)
Lowmoor Road, Kirkby-In-Ashfield, Nottingham, Nottinghamshire NG17 7JU
**Tel:** 01623-752869
**Reg No:** 0984917 **Estd:** 1970 Private Limited Company
**Line of Business:** Injection Molders
**Issued Capital:** £40,000
**Directors:** C W Robinson, Dr J B Marx
**Co. Secretary:** John Raby
**US SIC:** 3079 **UK SIC:** 48360
**Employees:** 180

DUNS 21-111-0109 **Imp**
## Robinson Young Holdings Ltd
Ibson House, Eastern Way Industrial Estate, Bury St Edmunds, Suffolk IP32 7AB
**Tel:** 01284-766261
**Web:** www.robinsonyoung.co.uk
**Reg No:** 6524358 **Estd:** 2008 Private Limited Company
**Line of Business:** Management activities of holding companies
**Issued Capital:** £2
**Director:** M C Robinson
**Co. Secretary:** Michael Jones
**Responsibilities**
**Senior:** Kate Nash *(Sales Operations Director)*
**Sales:** Kate Nash *(Sales Operations Director)*
**Purchasing:** Liam Shore *(Buyer)*
**US SIC:** 6711 **UK SIC:** 83962

| | 31-12-13 | 31-12-12 | 31-12-11 |
|---|---|---|---|
| TO | 46,774,780 | 55,446,410 | 58,664,540 |
| P/L | 157,917 | 314,328 | 466,329 |
| NW | 348,622 | 196,805 | (49,453) |
| WC | 467,488 | 466,618 | 159,863 |
| Emp. | 80 | 98 | 111 |

DUNS 23-324-9247
## Robinson's
Cooil Road, Douglas, Isle of Man IM4 2AF
**Estd:** 1903 Partnership
**Line of Business:** Fruit & veg Wholesalers
**US SIC:** 5148 **UK SIC:** 61700
**Employees:** 150

DUNS 22-852-6018 **Imp**
## Robinsons Country Leisure Ltd
Unit 6, Wigan, Lancashire WN4 8DE
**Tel:** 01942771800
**Web:** www.robinsonsuk.com
**Reg No:** 1204722 **VAT No:** 439163833
**Estd:** 1867 Private Limited Company
**Line of Business:** Footwear retailers
**Issued Capital:** £100
**Principals:** E J Bentham *(Managing)*, Ms P J Bentham, M S Bentham, P J Bentham, D M Forsey, B J Leach
**Co. Secretary:** Cameron Olsen
**Responsibilities**
**Senior:** Jim Bentham *(Manager)*
**Marketing:** Mike Church *(IT Manager)*
**IT:** Mike Church *(IT Manager)*
**HR:** Chloe Foster *(Human Resources Administrator)*
**Operations:** Sharon Warland *(Call Centre Manager)*
**Branches:** Robinsons Country Leisure Ltd, Mill Lane, St Helens, St. Helens, Merseyside WA11 8LS
**US SIC:** 5948, 5961
**UK SIC:** 64600, 65600
**Auditors:** Satterthwaite Brooks & Pomfret LLP
**Bankers:** National Westminster Bank Plc (01-09-17)

| | 22-02-13 | 24-02-12 | 25-02-11 |
|---|---|---|---|
| TO | 12,737,425 | 13,043,384 | 13,159,759 |
| P/L | (515,213) | (633,783) | (38,997) |
| NW | 1,787,176 | 2,836,680 | 3,348,352 |
| WC | 1,412,671 | 1,577,578 | 2,117,880 |
| Emp. | 143 | 163 | 156 |

DUNS 21-609-4115
## Robinson's Fresh Foods
1 Midland Farm, Fenwick, Kilmarnock, Ayrshire KA3 6BY
**Tel:** 01560600415
**Web:** www.kabedesign.co.uk
**Estd:** 1982 Proprietorship
**Line of Business:** Design consultants
**Proprietor:** J Horsthuis
**US SIC:** 8911 **UK SIC:** 83701
**Employees:** 100

DUNS 21-229-1694
## Robinsons International Moving Group Ltd
Park Seventeen, Manchester M45 8FJ
**Tel:** 0161-766-8414 **Fax:** 01617679057
**Web:** www.robinsons-intl.com
**Reg No:** 0158027 **Estd:** 1919 Private Limited Company
**Line of Business:** Management activities of other non-financial holding companies not elsewhere classified
**Export Sales:** £10,285,159
**Trading Style:** Robinsons International Removals
**Issued Capital:** £164,792
**Principals:** P J Robinson *(Chairman and Managing)*, A J Robinson, Mrs P J Stevens, Ms C E Walker
**Co. Secretary:** Ms Pamela Lewis
**Branches:** Robinsons International Moving Group Ltd, Blackett Road, Darlington, County Durham DL1 2BJ
**US SIC:** 6711, 4213
**UK SIC:** 83962, 72300
**Auditors:** Baker Tilly
**Bankers:** Barclays Bank Plc (20-54-58)

| | 31-12-13 | 31-12-12 | 31-12-11 |
|---|---|---|---|
| TO | 14,422,551 | 14,064,749 | 14,917,750 |
| P/L | 248,775 | (34,991) | (7,419) |
| NW | 2,566,408 | 2,484,592 | 2,567,595 |
| WC | 1,379,998 | 1,250,715 | 1,207,554 |
| Emp. | 148 | 170 | 183 |

DUNS 22-919-1648 **Imp**
## Robinsons Ltd
Ballapaddag Farm, Cooil Road, Douglas, Douglas, Isle of Man IM4 2AF
**Tel:** 01624626908
**Web:** www.robinsonsflowers.im
**Reg No:** 0028900M **Estd:** 1880 Private Limited Company
**Line of Business:** Wholesalers of fruit and vegetable
**Trading Style:** Delifresh, Robinsons Fresh Foods
**Issued Capital:** £100
**Principals:** J E Horsthuis *(Managing)*, T Fox, A Horsthuis, J M Horstuis, J M Horsthuis, Mrs J M Horsthuis, M Horsthuis, M Horsthuis
**Co. Secretary:** Anthony Horsthuis
**Responsibilities**
**Senior:** Noel O'Reilley *(Marketing Manager)*, Tony Wilson-Spratt *(Operations Director)*
**Finance:** Tony Wilson-Spratt *(Operations Director)*
**Marketing:** Noel O'Reilley *(Marketing Manager)*
**HR:** Tony Wilson-Spratt *(Operations Director)*
**Health & Safety:** Noel O'Reilley *(Marketing Manager)*
**Facilities:** Tony Wilson-Spratt *(Operations Director)*
**US SIC:** 5999 **UK SIC:** 65600
**Bankers:** Isle Of Man Bank (55-91-00)
**Employees:** 150

DUNS 34-804-3766
## Robinsons Scotland Ltd
9 Theatre Court, London Road, Northwich, Cheshire CW9 5HB
**Tel:** 01606330227 **Fax:** 01606812259
**Web:** www.rbscotland.co.uk
**Reg No:** 0292348SC **Estd:** 2007 Private Limited Company
**Line of Business:** Agricultural buildings
**Issued Capital:** £1
**Directors:** R J Brown, H J Brown
**Co. Secretary:** Ms Sheila Brown
**Responsibilities**
**Senior:** Tony Astbury *(Manager)*
**US SIC:** 1541, 5039
**UK SIC:** 50100, 61300

| | 30-06-13 | 30-06-12 | 30-06-11 |
|---|---|---|---|
| TO | 12,441,679 | 11,578,834 | N/A |
| P/L | 118,650 | 103,512 | N/A |
| NW | 380,927 | 380,833 | 428,979 |
| WC | (664,438) | (593,235) | (377,895) |
| Emp. | 86 | 98 | N/A |

DUNS 77-517-6746
## Robinsons Soft Drinks Ltd
(Subsidiary of: Britvic Plc)
Carrow Works, Bracondale, Norwich, Norfolk NR1 2DD
**Tel:** 01603-632633
**Web:** www.britvic.co.uk
**Reg No:** 2987077 **Estd:** 1994 Private Limited Company
**Line of Business:** Bottlers
**Trading Style:** Britvic Barr
**Issued Capital:** £10,000,002
**Principals:** J M Gibney *(Financial)*, P S Litherland, Mrs A C Thomas, A D Spreadbury
**Co. Secretary:** Mrs Vanessa Lewis Camacho
**Responsibilities**
**Senior:** Jeremy Howard *(Manager)*, Dewi Price *(Manager)*
**Branches:** Robinsons Soft Drinks Ltd, Carrow Works, Bracondale, Norwich, Norfolk NR1 2DD
**US SIC:** 2086, 5149
**UK SIC:** 42831, 61700
**Auditors:** Ernst & Young LLP

|  | 29-09-13 | 30-09-12 | 02-09-11 |
|---|---|---|---|
| TA | 381,992,000 | 381,206,000 | 390,579,000 |
| P/L | 26,360,000 | 25,923,000 | 25,421,000 |
| NW | 152,262,000 | 182,171,000 | 152,699,000 |
| WC | (95,022,000) | (29,142,000) | (38,290,000) |

DUNS 23-055-0212
## Robinwood Activity Centre Ltd
School House, Jumps Road, Todmorden, Lancashire OL14 8HJ
**Tel:** 01706819149
**Web:** www.robinwood.co.uk
**Reg No:** 2844179 **Estd:** 1994 Private Limited Company
**Line of Business:** Outdoor leisure pursuit organisers and equipment
**Issued Capital:** £1,100
**Directors:** Ms J C Vasey, M G Vasey, Miss L R Vasey, I Goldsack
**Branches:** Robinwood Activity Centre Ltd, Barhaugh Hall, Kirkhaugh, Alston, Cumbria CA9 3NJ
**US SIC:** 8699 **UK SIC:** 96902
**Auditors:** Smith Partnership

|  | 31-12-13 | 31-12-12 | 31-12-11 |
|---|---|---|---|
| TO | 6,014,910 | 5,702,437 | 5,259,469 |
| P/L | 303,879 | 251,041 | 248,872 |
| NW | 1,242,392 | 1,020,447 | 845,098 |
| WC | (2,322,092) | (2,153,328) | (1,840,998) |
| Emp. | 183 | 185 | 171 |

DUNS 34-590-8719
## Robore Cuts Ltd
(Subsidiary of: Futureplus Ltd)
Unit 16, Mitcham, Surrey CR4 2AP
**Tel:** 020-8646-4466 **Fax:** 020-8646-4046
**Web:** www.robore.com
**Reg No:** 2735000 **VAT No:** 611883346
**Estd:** 1992 Private Limited Company
**Line of Business:** Construction of civil engineering constructions
**Issued Capital:** £2
**Director:** D Rickus
**Co. Secretary:** Paul Nattrass
**Responsibilities**
**Senior:** Francoise Desroches *(Accounts Executive)*
**Finance:** Francoise Desroches *(Accounts Executive)*, Pam Savage *(Accounts Manager)*
**Operations:** Colin Hibbert *(Operations Manager)*
**Fleet:** Ray Nunn *(Plant & Logistics Manager)*
**US SIC:** 1622 **UK SIC:** 50200
**Auditors:** Robert E Price & Co
**Bankers:** HSBC Bank plc (40-33-09)

|  | 30-06-13 | 30-06-12 | 30-06-11 |
|---|---|---|---|
| TO | 16,445,046 | 16,568,470 | 13,468,255 |
| P/L | 153,484 | 411,359 | 283,688 |
| NW | 5,333,779 | 5,250,009 | 4,940,829 |
| WC | 4,304,900 | 4,273,307 | 4,103,373 |
| Emp. | 157 | 156 | 160 |

DUNS 21-208-1025
## Roborough House
Tamerton Lane, Woolwell, Plymouth, Devon PL6 7BQ
**Tel:** 01752-700788
**Web:** www.roboroughhouse.com
**Estd:** 1990 Proprietorship
**Line of Business:** Nursing homes
**Proprietor:** Ms E Walters
**US SIC:** 8051 **UK SIC:** 95100
**Employees:** 55

DUNS 23-600-4532
## Robsons of Spalding Ltd
Hamlin Way, King's Lynn, Norfolk PE30 4NG
**Tel:** 01553-768501 **Fax:** 01553-819190
**Web:** www.robsons.tc
**Reg No:** 3597825 **Estd:** 1993 Private Limited Company
**Line of Business:** Road haulage and transport services

**Issued Capital:** £10,000
**Directors:** R G Baxter, T B Robson
**Co. Secretary:** Ian Robson
**Responsibilities**
**Senior:** Martyn Kemp *(Manager)*
**Facilities:** Martyn Kemp *(Manager)*
**Fleet:** Martyn Kemp *(Manager)*
**US SIC:** 4789 **UK SIC:** 77002
**Auditors:** Moore Thompson
**Bankers:** National Westminster Bank Plc (55-50-36)

|  | 31-07-14 | 31-07-13 | 31-07-12 |
|---|---|---|---|
| TO | 10,610,341 | 8,007,440 | 8,975,466 |
| P/L | 265,329 | 295,800 | 291,916 |
| NW | 3,642,455 | 3,548,983 | 3,315,851 |
| WC | 3,854,112 | 3,359,655 | 3,123,878 |
| Emp. | 76 | 74 | 86 |

DUNS 23-539-4983
## Roc Systems Consulting Ltd
(Subsidiary of: Roc Systems Holdings Ltd)
Hersham Place, 41-61 Molesey Road, Walton-On-Thames, Surrey KT12 4RZ
**Tel:** 01932213250 **Fax:** 01932213251
**Web:** www.roc-group.com
**Reg No:** 3538201 **VAT No:** 709084922
**Estd:** 1998 Private Limited Company
**Line of Business:** Computer consumables suppliers
**Issued Capital:** £10,100
**Directors:** C I Goodwin, J E James, J A Chilvers
**Co. Secretary:** Damian Williams
**Responsibilities**
**Senior:** Les Hayman *(Chairman)*, Tom James *(Manager)*
**IT:** Raymond Bader *(Project Manager)*
**Branches:** Roc Systems Consulting Ltd, 53 Cotswold Meadow, Witney, Oxfordshire OX28 5FA
**US SIC:** 7379 **UK SIC:** 83940
**Auditors:** Jackson Taylor

|  | 30-09-13 | 30-09-12 | 30-09-11 |
|---|---|---|---|
| TO | N/A | 4,226,601 | 4,236,888 |
| P/L | N/A | 391,061 | 57,359 |
| NW | 922,141 | 824,640 | 522,968 |
| WC | 910,377 | 810,621 | 508,959 |
| Emp. | N/A | 35 | 39 |

DUNS 34-638-2708    Imp
## Roca Ltd
(Subsidiary of: Roca Corporacion Empresarial Sa)
Samson Road, Coalville, Leicestershire LE67 3FP
**Tel:** 01530830080 **Fax:** 01530-830010
**Web:** www.roca-uk.com
**Reg No:** 2767941 **Estd:** 1992 Private Limited Company
**Line of Business:** Manufacture of taps and valves
**Export Sales:** £392,102
**Issued Capital:** £17,607,000
**Principals:** A T Dodds *(Managing)*, J Albos Barbarrosa, R Sidhu
**Co. Secretary:** Miguel Munar Saura
**Responsibilities**
**Senior:** Ramon Forrellad *(Manager)*, Miguel Saura *(Manager)*
**Marketing:** Georgina Spencer *(Sales & Marketing Manager)*
**Sales:** Georgina Spencer *(Sales & Marketing Manager)*
**IT:** Heena Kotecha *(Computer Manager)*
**US SIC:** 3494 **UK SIC:** 32880
**Auditors:** KPMG LLP
**Bankers:** Lloyds TSB Bank plc (30-92-15)

|  | 31-12-13 | 31-12-12 | 31-12-11 |
|---|---|---|---|
| TO | 34,854,828 | 33,542,584 | 27,241,069 |
| P/L | (2,659,186) | (1,978,820) | (1,246,132) |
| NW | 10,435,187 | 13,094,373 | 15,269,515 |
| WC | (2,729,022) | (383,984) | 1,280,925 |
| Emp. | 62 | 67 | 59 |

DUNS 29-531-3142
## Rocare Building Services Ltd
(Subsidiary of: Rocare Holdings Ltd)
Headlands Business Park, Salisbury Road, Blashford, Ringwood, Hampshire BH24 3PB
**Fax:** 01425-482026
**Web:** www.rocare.co.uk
**Reg No:** 1898466 **VAT No:** 393046349
**Estd:** 1985 Private Limited Company
**Line of Business:** Other building installation
**Issued Capital:** £125
**Principals:** A R Mcquin *(Managing)*, R C Mackintosh, A R Bennetts
**Co. Secretary:** Roy Mackintosh
**Responsibilities**
**Senior:** Tony Logan *(Warehouse Manager)*
**US SIC:** 1796, 1799
**UK SIC:** 50400, 50000
**Auditors:** Blueprint Audit Ltd

|  | 30-09-13 | 30-09-12 | 30-09-11 |
|---|---|---|---|
| TA | 1,679,613 | 1,851,632 | 1,885,682 |
| NW | 583,385 | 568,191 | 559,601 |
| WC | 341,288 | 330,115 | 315,480 |

DUNS 21-136-1263
## Rocca Ltd
307 Linton House, 164-180 Union Street, London SE1 0LH
**Tel:** 02870356030
**Web:** www.roccaonline.com
**Reg No:** 6690296 **Estd:** 2011 Private Limited Company
**Line of Business:** Licensed restaurants
**Issued Capital:** £242
**Directors:** D M Page, D J Sykes, N Mankarious, G M Mascoli, S Wasif, G M Jones
**Responsibilities**
**Senior:** Stephen Henry *(Manager)*
**US SIC:** 5812 **UK SIC:** 66110

|  | 27-04-14 | 30-04-13 | 30-04-12 |
|---|---|---|---|
| TO | 9,102,338 | 6,631,168 | N/A |
| P/L | 1,058,702 | 675,054 | N/A |
| NW | 3,595,162 | 2,755,030 | 3,545,474 |
| WC | (117,696) | 231,160 | N/A |
| Emp. | 192 | 135 | N/A |

DUNS 37-957-4155    Imp
## Rocco Forte & Family Ltd
70 Jermyn Street, London SW1Y 6NY
**Tel:** 02073212626 **Fax:** 020 7321 2424
**Web:** www.roccofortecollection.com
**Reg No:** 3277921 **Estd:** 1996 Private Limited Company
**Line of Business:** Hotels
**Export Sales:** £133,310,000
**Issued Capital:** £65,919,913
**Directors:** R G Mendoza, Mrs G M Alen-Buckley, D G Caldecott, D H Nelson, K Naffah, The Hon Mrs O M Sorrentino, Sir R G Forte, R Power
**Responsibilities**
**Senior:** Portia Forte *(Director)*, Aliai Forte *(Director)*, John Walker-Haworth *(Director)*
**US SIC:** 7011 **UK SIC:** 66500
**Auditors:** PKF (UK) LLP
**Bankers:** Bank Of Scotland (80-11-00)

|  | 30-04-13 | 30-04-12 | 30-04-11 |
|---|---|---|---|
| TO | 185,425,000 | 181,918,000 | 103,978,000 |
| P/L | 2,864,000 | (9,261,000) | (9,618,000) |
| NW | 60,203,000 | 60,920,000 | 14,020,000 |
| WC | (322,521,000) | (311,818,000) | (107,920,000) |
| Emp. | 2,280 | 2,255 | 1,308 |

DUNS 29-846-8570    Imp-Exp
## Roch Valley Ltd
Pennine Business Park, Heywood, Lancashire OL10 2TL
**Tel:** 01706362507 **Fax:** 01706-362525
**Web:** www.roch-valley.co.uk
**Reg No:** 2049641 **VAT No:** 145600001
**Estd:** 1967 Private Limited Company
**Line of Business:** Manufacture of sports goods
**Export Markets:** Worldwide
**Issued Capital:** £127,000
**Principals:** J Doughty *(Chairman)*, R Doughty *(Managing)*, D Doughty *(Marketing)*
**Co. Secretary:** Stephen Elvidge
**Responsibilities**
**Senior:** Karl Pearson *(Warehouse Manager)*
**IT:** Caroline Brooks *(Computer Manager)*
**Health & Safety:** Karl Pearson *(Warehouse Manager)*
**Facilities:** Karl Pearson *(Warehouse Manager)*
**Branches:** Roch Valley Ltd, Showstoppers, 59 Topping Street, Blackpool, Lancashire FY1 3AF
**US SIC:** 3949, 2339
**UK SIC:** 49420, 45330
**Auditors:** Wyatt Morris Golland & Co
**Bankers:** Barclays Bank Plc (20-72-67)

|  | 31-07-13 | 31-07-12 | 31-07-11 |
|---|---|---|---|
| TO | 5,864,579 | 5,816,145 | 5,636,738 |
| P/L | 775,353 | 544,987 | 553,741 |
| NW | 2,501,801 | 2,158,764 | 1,749,474 |
| WC | 747,860 | 411,526 | 16,370 |
| Emp. | 89 | 86 | 85 |

DUNS 22-867-2291
## The Rochdale Association Football Club Ltd
Sandy Lane, Spotland, Rochdale, Lancashire OL11 5DR
**Tel:** 01706-644648
**Web:** www.rochdaleafc.co.uk
**Reg No:** 0111019 **VAT No:** 146712469
**Estd:** 1908 Private Limited Company
**Line of Business:** Other sporting activities not elsewhere classified
**Trading Style:** Rochdale A F C
**Issued Capital:** £227,429
**Directors:** P A Hazlehurst, G F Rawlinson, C M Dunphy, A J Kelly, J Marsh, W H Goodwin
**Co. Secretary:** Colin Garlick
**Responsibilities**
**Senior:** Martin Macleod *(Manager)*
**Health & Safety:** ian weller *(H&S Officer)*
**US SIC:** 7999 **UK SIC:** 97913
**Auditors:** Tenon Audit Ltd

**Bankers:** Lloyds TSB Bank plc (77-01-11)

|  | 31-05-13 | 31-05-12 | 31-05-11 |
|---|---|---|---|
| TA | 1,239,981 | 1,792,201 | 1,639,229 |
| NW | 579,616 | 951,824 | 570,757 |
| WC | 185,260 | 549,976 | 160,872 |

DUNS 67-223-3322
## Rochdale Boroughwide Cultural Trust
1 Riverside Court Smith Street, Rochdale, Lancashire OL12 8NQ
**Tel:** 01706-926-232 **Fax:** 01706-926-232
**Web:** www.link4life.org
**Reg No:** 6052980 **Estd:** 2007 Private Company Limited By Guarantee
**Line of Business:** Art galleries and dealers
**Trading Style:** Link4life
**Directors:** R G Platt, M Sarwar, D J Crouch, S A Cooke, M C Holly, Mrs J A Emsley, S Griffiths, Ms A Taylor
**Co. Secretary:** David Weldon
**Responsibilities**
**Senior:** Katherine Budd *(Director)*, John Heywood *(Director)*, Miah Mohammed *(Director)*, Janine Partington *(Director)*, William Sheerin *(Director)*, Clinton Street *(Director)*
**Branches:** ROCHDALE BOROUGHWIDE CULTURAL TRUST - Touchstones Rochdale, The Esplanade, Rochdale, Lancs, OL16 1AQ.
**US SIC:** 7011, 8411, 7941, 7999
**UK SIC:** 97913, 97700, 97911
**Auditors:** Grant Thornton UK LLP
**Bankers:** The Co-Operative Bank Plc (08-90-00)

|  | 31-03-14 | 31-03-13 | 31-03-12 |
|---|---|---|---|
| TO | 10,636,314 | 9,978,043 | 9,612,634 |
| P/L | 304,156 | (370,454) | 332,648 |
| NW | (1,235,479) | (3,271,635) | (1,454,181) |
| WC | 788,370 | 342,444 | 686,509 |
| Emp. | 283 | 246 | 241 |

DUNS 36-799-8218
## Rochdale Council
The Esplanade, Rochdale, Lancashire OL16 1AB
**Tel:** 01706924797
**Web:** www.rochdale.gov.uk
**Estd:** 2012
**Line of Business:** Corporate entertainment and hospitality
**Trading Style:** Middleton & Rochdale City Learning Centre
**Principals:** R Alice, C W Lambert
**Responsibilities**
**Senior:** Dorothy Johnstone *(Events Manager)*
**Branches:** Rochdale Council, Kenyon Lane, Middleton, M24 2GT Manchester
**US SIC:** 9121 **UK SIC:** 91110
**Employees:** 700

DUNS 34-649-5765
## Rochdale Gateway Leisure Ltd
Gateway Centre, 2 Kenion Street, Rochdale, Lancashire OL16 1SN
**Tel:** 01706-515800
**Web:** www.gatewayleisure.org
**Reg No:** 2774692 **Estd:** 1992 Private Company Limited By Guarantee
**Line of Business:** Charities and charitable organisations
**Directors:** S Ellis, T Carr, Miss S T Burke, A P Collinson, J M Barlow
**Co. Secretary:** Andrew Tweedale
**Responsibilities**
**Senior:** Paula Lidbury *(Manager)*, Nancy Wood *(Chief Executive)*
**US SIC:** 8321 **UK SIC:** 96111
**Auditors:** Wyatt, Morris, Golland & Co
**Bankers:** National Westminster Bank Plc (01-07-44)

|  | 05-04-13 | 05-04-12 | 05-04-11 |
|---|---|---|---|
| TO | 1,197,040 | 1,131,506 | 1,090,983 |
| P/L | 176,770 | 186,100 | 84,010 |
| NW | 763,014 | 586,244 | 400,144 |
| WC | 639,763 | 475,319 | 312,858 |
| Emp. | 50 | 49 | 49 |

DUNS 21-231-3905
## Rochdale Infirmary
Whitehall Street, Rochdale, Lancashire OL12 0NB
**Tel:** 01616240420
**Web:** www.pat.nhs.uk
**Estd:** 2002 Proprietorship
**Line of Business:** Hospitals
**Proprietor:** Miss E Claybourn
**Responsibilities**
**Senior:** Eileen Claybourne *(Telecoms Manager)*
**HR:** Alison Brophy *(Divisional Human Resources Man)*
**Facilities:** Mike Wroe *(Estates Officer)*
**US SIC:** 8062 **UK SIC:** 95100
**Employees:** 2,000

DUNS 21-879-9285
## Rochdale Mbc
Environmental Management Headquarters, Green Lane, Heywood, Heywood, Lancashire OL10 2DY
**Tel:** 01706925700
**Web:** www.rochdale.gov.uk
**Estd:** 2012
**Line of Business:** Environmental consultants
**Responsibilities**
**Senior:** Mark Widdup *(Services Manager)*
**US SIC:** 8299 **UK SIC:** 93300
**Employees:** 60

DUNS 22-868-6317
## Rochdale Metropolitan Borough Council
1 Riverside Court, Rochdale, Lancashire OL12 8NQ
**Tel:** 01706-647474
**Web:** www.rochdale.gov.uk
**Estd:** 1974
**Line of Business:** Local government
**Directors:** R Ellis, Ms F W Done
**Responsibilities**
**IT:** Neville Johnson *(Operating Support Manager)*
**Branches:** Rochdale Metropolitan Borough Council, Town Hall, Rochdale, Lancashire OL16 9SB
**US SIC:** 9121 **UK SIC:** 91110
**Bankers:** National Westminster Bank Plc (01-07-44)
**Employees:** 700

DUNS 22-291-9560 **Imp**
## Rochdale Textile Supplies Ltd
**(Subsidiary of:** Rochdale Textile Supplies (Jersey) Ltd)
Adlington Works-Market Street, Chorley, Lancashire PR7 4HJ
**Tel:** 01257-480202
**Web:** www.pincroft.com
**Reg No:** 4309959 **Estd:** 2001 Private Limited Company
**Line of Business:** Management activities of holding companies
**Export Sales:** £55,179,000
**Trading Style:** Pincroft
**Issued Capital:** £951
**Directors:** J J Vareldzis, N Dowds, I Molyneux
**Co. Secretary:** Nigel Bate
**US SIC:** 6711 **UK SIC:** 83962

| | 30-11-13 | 30-11-12 | 30-11-11 |
|---|---|---|---|
| TO | 78,180,000 | 71,660,000 | 80,530,000 |
| P/L | 5,188,000 | 4,154,000 | 5,934,000 |
| NW | 31,474,000 | 27,313,000 | 23,972,000 |
| WC | 30,091,000 | 26,340,000 | 23,734,000 |
| Emp. | 230 | 202 | 203 |

DUNS 21-579-4363 **Imp-Exp**
## Roche Diagnostics Ltd
**(Subsidiary of:** Roche Holding Ag)
Charles Avenue, Burgess Hill, West Sussex RH15 9RY
**Tel:** 01444-256000 **Fax:** 01273-480266
**Web:** www.rocheuk.com
**Reg No:** 0571546 **VAT No:** 327215183
**Estd:** 1956 Private Limited Company
**Line of Business:** Other business activities not elsewhere classified
**Issued Capital:** £22,600,000
**Directors:** C S Parker, R F Fischer, J D Dallas
**Co. Secretary:** Richard Daniel
**Responsibilities**
**Senior:** Jan Boer *(Manager)*, Elmer Monster *(Manager)*
**HR:** K Hoile *(Human Resources Director)*
**US SIC:** 7399 **UK SIC:** 83954
**Auditors:** KPMG LLP

| | 31-12-13 | 31-12-12 | 31-12-11 |
|---|---|---|---|
| TO | 283,116,000 | 266,313,000 | 244,844,000 |
| P/L | 1,020,000 | 6,231,000 | 8,804,000 |
| NW | 50,318,000 | 49,968,000 | 45,572,000 |
| WC | 38,530,000 | 35,199,000 | 6,380,000 |
| Emp. | 550 | 533 | 512 |

DUNS 77-534-7511
## Roche Healthcare Ltd
Unit 1 Manor Court, Manor Mill Lane, Leeds, West Yorkshire LS11 8LQ
**Tel:** 01132-703355 **Fax:** 0113-270-3366
**Web:** www.rochehealthcare.co.uk
**Reg No:** 2992723 **Estd:** 1994 Private Limited Company
**Line of Business:** Nursing homes
**Issued Capital:** £3,119,101
**Director:** P J Roche
**Co. Secretary:** Mrs Colleen Roche
**Branches:** Roche Healthcare Ltd, Rectory Park Church Lane, Dewsbury, West Yorkshire WF12 0JZ
**US SIC:** 7399, 8051, 8321
**UK SIC:** 83954, 95100, 96111
**Auditors:** Richard Smedley Ltd
**Bankers:** National Westminster Bank Plc (60-60-05)

| | 31-07-13 | 31-07-12 | 31-07-11 |
|---|---|---|---|
| TO | 7,913,850 | 7,276,497 | 7,096,621 |
| P/L | 508,509 | 344,961 | 159,746 |
| NW | 6,471,680 | 6,194,467 | 5,889,640 |
| WC | 860,609 | (871,453) | (1,235,113) |
| Emp. | 370 | 357 | 345 |

DUNS 21-025-0734 **Imp**
## Roche Products Ltd
**(Subsidiary of:** Roche Holding Ag)
Hexagon Place, Welwyn Garden City, Hertfordshire AL7 1TW
**Tel:** 01707366000
**Web:** www.roche.co.uk
**Reg No:** 0100674 **Estd:** 1997 Private Limited Company
**Line of Business:** Manufacture of basic pharmaceutical products
**Export Sales:** £368,138,000
**Issued Capital:** £61,000,000
**Directors:** B C Kraehenmann, J D Dallas, T C Schilke, C S Parker
**Co. Secretary:** Richard Daniel
**Responsibilities**
**Senior:** Andreas Brabeck Letmathe *(Director of finance and corpor)*, Peter Hug *(Manager)*
**Finance:** Andreas Brabeck Letmathe *(Director of finance and corpor)*
**Branches:** Roche Products Ltd, 156 Fareham Rd, Gosport, Hampshire PO13 0AU
**US SIC:** 2834 **UK SIC:** 25700
**Auditors:** KPMG LLP

| | 31-12-13 | 31-12-12 | 31-12-11 |
|---|---|---|---|
| TO | 940,631,000 | 901,938,000 | 867,891,000 |
| P/L | 115,559,000 | 60,335,000 | 23,628,000 |
| NW | 160,870,000 | 100,684,000 | 111,935,000 |
| WC | 162,088,000 | 147,179,000 | 105,446,000 |
| Emp. | 1,407 | 1,375 | 1,294 |

DUNS 34-983-8636 **Imp**
## Rochester Medical Ltd
**(Subsidiary of:** C. R. Bard Inc.)
Unit 5 Commerce Way, Lancing, West Sussex BN15 8TA
**Tel:** 01903875055 **Fax:** 01903-875085
**Web:** www.rochestermedical.co.uk
**Reg No:** 5779226 **VAT No:** 883611803
**Estd:** 2006 Private Limited Company
**Line of Business:** Manufacturers of medical equipment
**Issued Capital:** £1
**Director:** J C Allsop
**Co. Secretary:** Nathan Royds-Jones
**Responsibilities**
**Senior:** Patrick Mcleod *(Manager)*, Hugh Mcleod *(Manager)*
**US SIC:** 3841 **UK SIC:** 37201
**Auditors:** RSM Tenon Audit Ltd
**Bankers:** Barclays Bank Plc (20-23-97)

| | 30-09-13 | 30-09-12 | 30-09-11 |
|---|---|---|---|
| TO | 16,654,653 | 13,405,575 | 11,390,042 |
| P/L | 1,867,837 | 1,347,202 | 39,743 |
| NW | 3,354,104 | 1,683,317 | 56,656 |
| WC | 8,337,331 | 6,722,512 | 5,306,155 |
| Emp. | 72 | 70 | 60 |

DUNS 23-776-4860
## Rochford Community Church Trust
The Freight House, Bradley Way, Rochford, Essex SS4 1BU
**Web:** www.rcc.co.uk
**Reg No:** 3769768 **Estd:** 1999 Private Company Limited By Guarantee
**Line of Business:** Places of worship
**Directors:** C D Porter, Ms S M Stokes, A Bater, D J Green, S G Halliwell, Ms S R Tyer
**Co. Secretary:** Andrew Bater
**Responsibilities**
**Senior:** Geoffrey Durham *(Manager)*, Michael Ewers *(Church Leader)*, Sheila Pethen *(Manager)*
**US SIC:** 8661 **UK SIC:** 96600

| | 31-03-14 | 31-03-13 | 31-03-12 |
|---|---|---|---|
| TA | 58,706 | 51,302 | 46,923 |
| NW | 56,510 | 51,302 | 46,923 |
| WC | 51,585 | N/A | N/A |

DUNS 38-782-8767
## Rochford District Council
3-19 South Street, Rochford, Essex SS4 1BW
**Tel:** 01702546366
**Web:** www.rochford.gov.uk
**Estd:** 2002
**Line of Business:** Local government
**Director:** P Warren
**Responsibilities**
**Senior:** Janet Cox *(Chairman)*, Amar Dave *(Chief Executive)*, Paul Gowers *(Executive)*, Tony Humphries *(Chairman)*, Linda Swinnerton *(Executive)*
**Finance:** Yvonne Woodward *(Head of Finance)*
**Marketing:** Andrew Lowing *(Community Planning Officer)*
**Admin:** John Honey *(Law Planning & Administration)*
**HR:** Janet Cox *(Chairman)*
**Fleet:** Shaun Scrutton *(Head of Planning and Transport)*
**Branches:** Rochford District Council, Main Road, Hockley, Essex SS5 4EH
**US SIC:** 9121 **UK SIC:** 91110
**Employees:** 230

DUNS 29-621-4877 **Imp-Exp**
## Rochling Engineering Plastics (Uk) Ltd
**(Subsidiary of:** Röchling Se & Co. Kg)
Waterwells Drive, Waterwells Business Park, Gloucester, Gloucestershire GL2 4AA
**Tel:** 01452727900 **Fax:** 01452-728056
**Web:** www.roechling-plastics.co.uk
**Reg No:** 1947990 **VAT No:** 419297034
**Estd:** 1985 Private Limited Company
**Line of Business:** Suppliers of plastics and plastic products
**Export Markets:** Middle East
**Export Sales:** £952,763
**Issued Capital:** £200,000
**Principals:** M S Knowles *(Managing)*, Dr J Brunswicker, L Bartels
**Co. Secretary:** Mrs Elizabeth Elliott
**Responsibilities**
**Senior:** Wilhelm Bolscher *(Manager)*
**Marketing:** Wilhelm Bolscher *(Manager)*
**Facilities:** Nigel Burford *(Maintenance Manager)*
**Engineering:** Jason Griffiths *(Production Manager)*
**US SIC:** 5161, 3079
**UK SIC:** 61200, 48360
**Auditors:** Shoesmiths
**Bankers:** HSBC Bank plc (40-38-07)

| | 31-12-13 | 31-12-12 | 31-12-11 |
|---|---|---|---|
| TO | 11,397,173 | 8,406,082 | 7,959,762 |
| P/L | 1,057,978 | 442,093 | 505,556 |
| NW | 5,286,221 | 4,490,572 | 4,156,808 |
| WC | 3,461,070 | 2,777,612 | 2,406,563 |
| Emp. | 73 | 66 | 60 |

DUNS 22-654-6448
## Rochmills Ltd
Burlington House, 369 Wellingborough Road, Northampton, Northamptonshire NN1 4EU
**Web:** www.rochmills.co.uk
**Reg No:** 1261231 **Estd:** 1976 Private Limited Company
**Line of Business:** Other letting of own property
**Trading Style:** Rochmills Group
**Issued Capital:** £1,556,196
**Principals:** J S Sehmi *(Managing)*, J S Gill, D R Ward
**Co. Secretary:** Mrs Sutinder Hanspaul
**Responsibilities**
**Finance:** Greig Smith *(finance director)*
**Branches:** Rochmills Ltd, 31 High St, Milton Keynes, Buckinghamshire MK17 8RB
**US SIC:** 6519, 7399, 6732, 8321
**UK SIC:** 85000, 83954, 83100, 96111
**Auditors:** Hawsons Chartered Accountants
**Bankers:** Lloyds TSB Bank plc (30-96-09)

| | 31-12-13 | 31-12-12 | 31-12-11 |
|---|---|---|---|
| TO | 5,805,250 | 5,485,373 | 5,535,914 |
| P/L | 955,167 | (1,645,721) | (997,171) |
| NW | 4,615,930 | 2,785,943 | 4,321,765 |
| WC | (426,268) | (339,866) | (598,413) |
| Emp. | 255 | 255 | 289 |

DUNS 73-934-3127
## Rochpack Group Ltd
Woodhams Road, Coventry, West Midlands CV3 4FX
**Tel:** 024-7651-1754 **Fax:** 024-7663-9717
**Web:** www.coventry-chemicals.com
**Reg No:** 2940920 **Estd:** 1994 Private Limited Company
**Line of Business:** Cleaning materials and equipment
**Trading Style:** Coventry Chemicals
**Issued Capital:** £100
**Managing Director:** D A Stewart
**Co. Secretary:** Ms Joan Stewart
**US SIC:** 5199 **UK SIC:** 61900
**Bankers:** The Royal Bank Of Scotland Plc (16-29-34)

| | 30-06-13 | 30-06-12 | 30-06-11 |
|---|---|---|---|
| TA | 405,503 | 401,674 | 402,221 |
| NW | 379,099 | 384,092 | 392,507 |
| WC | (22,230) | (17,237) | (8,822) |

DUNS 22-650-2391
## Rocialle Ltd
**(Subsidiary of:** Berendsen Plc)
Unit D Cwm Cynon Industrial Park, Mountain Ash, Mid Glamorgan CF45 4ER
**Tel:** 01443 471300 **Fax:** 01443 471301
**Web:** www.rocialle.com
**Reg No:** 1510162 **VAT No:** 599596349
**Estd:** 1977 Private Limited Company
**Line of Business:** Medical equipment leasing and rental
**Trading Style:** Unisurge International, Rocialle Inhealth, Berendsen Uk
**Issued Capital:** £10,000,000
**Directors:** K Quinn, D M Embleton, S R Finch
**Co. Secretary:** Nigel Hiorns
**Responsibilities**
**Senior:** Stephen Burt *(Manager)*
**Sales:** Tony Spencer-Smith *(National Sales Manager)*
**Facilities:** Adrian Dunleavy *(Facilities Manager)*
**Engineering:** Stuart McLellan *(Engineering Manager)*
**Branches:** Rocialle Ltd, Cwm Cynon Business Park, Mountain Ash, Mid Glamorgan CF45 4ER
**US SIC:** 3841, 5199
**UK SIC:** 37201, 61900
**Bankers:** HSBC Bank plc (40-16-13)

| | 31-12-13 | 31-12-12 | 31-12-11 |
|---|---|---|---|
| TA | 1 | 1 | 22,668,000 |
| NW | 1 | 1 | 22,668,000 |

DUNS 28-984-7626
## Rock & Alluvium Ltd
**(Subsidiary of:** Galliford Try Plc)
Bridge House, 27 Bridge Street, Leatherhead, Surrey KT22 8BL
**Tel:** 01372389333 **Fax:** 01372389339
**Web:** www.rockal.com
**Reg No:** 1795468 **VAT No:** 667532215
**Estd:** 1984 Private Limited Company
**Line of Business:** Other construction work involving special trades
**Issued Capital:** £100,120
**Directors:** K Gillespie, G Corden, D M Brockett, D M Ashton, M T Kemp
**Co. Secretary:** Galliford Try Secretariat Servic
**Responsibilities**
**Senior:** Stan Goddard *(Estimation Manager)*
**Finance:** Geoff Foreman *(Financial Director)*
**HR:** Andrew Hainge *(Head of Human Resources)*
**Branches:** Rock & Alluvium Ltd, Bridge House, 27 Bridge Street, Leatherhead, Surrey KT22 8BL
**US SIC:** 1799 **UK SIC:** 50000
**Auditors:** PricewaterhouseCoopers LLP
**Bankers:** Barclays Bank Plc (20-07-71)

| | 30-06-13 | 30-06-12 | 30-06-11 |
|---|---|---|---|
| TO | 16,333,000 | 13,660,000 | 13,818,000 |
| P/L | 99,000 | (660,000) | (287,000) |
| NW | 535,000 | 461,000 | 208,000 |
| WC | 73,000 | 40,000 | (217,000) |
| Emp. | 55 | 62 | 68 |

DUNS 21-303-5108 **Exp**
## Rock Chemicals Ltd
90 Priestley Street, Warrington, Cheshire WA5 1ST
**Tel:** 01925636191 **Fax:** 01925-632499
**Web:** www.rockoil.co.uk
**Reg No:** 0835494 **VAT No:** 152249870
**Estd:** 1928 Private Limited Company
**Line of Business:** Manufacturers of lubricating oils
**Export Markets:** U S A, New Zealand, Scandinavia, Far East, E U, Australia
**Export Sales:** £1,485,167
**Trading Style:** Rock Oil Company
**Issued Capital:** £120
**Principals:** C E Hewitt *(Managing)*, G E Hewitt
**Co. Secretary:** Ms Barbara Hewitt
**Responsibilities**
**Senior:** Gavin Hewitt *(Operations Director)*
**Facilities:** Brian Kneebone *(Maintenance Manager)*
**Purchasing:** Gavin Hewitt *(Operations Director)*
**Engineering:** Keith Dunne *(Production Manager)*, Gavin Hewitt *(Operations Director)*
**Branches:** Rock Chemicals Ltd, 9-10 Trentwood Indstl Est, Rowden Lane, Bradford-On-Avon, Wiltshire BA15 2AU
**US SIC:** 2999 **UK SIC:** 11150
**Auditors:** Chadwick LLP
**Bankers:** National Westminster Bank Plc (01-09-17)

| | 31-03-14 | 31-03-13 | 31-03-12 |
|---|---|---|---|
| TO | 21,292,840 | 18,150,580 | 19,611,803 |
| P/L | 1,415,375 | 584,680 | 376,159 |
| NW | 3,545,397 | 3,142,106 | 2,745,423 |
| WC | 2,274,306 | 1,868,888 | 1,569,967 |
| Emp. | 64 | 67 | 69 |

DUNS 64-109-4581
## Rock City Stage Crew Ltd
8 Darklake View, Estover, Plymouth, Devon PL6 7TL
**Tel:** 01752255933 **Fax:** 01752-202101
**Web:** www.rockcitycrew.co.uk
**Reg No:** 4512821 **Estd:** 1991 Private Limited Company
**Line of Business:** Employment and recruitment companies and consultants
**Issued Capital:** £400
**Principals:** T B Short *(Managing)*, D J Smith
**Co. Secretary:** Ms Sharon Short
**US SIC:** 7999, 7922
**UK SIC:** 97913, 97412

**Bankers:** National Westminster Bank Plc (01-09-51)

| | 31-12-13 | 31-12-12 | 31-12-11 |
|---|---|---|---|
| TA | 1,161,289 | 1,228,621 | 1,332,215 |
| NW | 838,448 | 781,555 | 719,303 |
| WC | 582,916 | 540,754 | 288,714 |

DUNS 21-239-9745

## Rock Merchanting Ltd

(**Subsidiary of:** Pulse Fitness Holdings Ltd)
The Bromley Centre, Congleton, Cheshire CW12 1PT
**Tel:** 07758911333
**Web:** www.recoverycheshire.co.uk
**Reg No:** 0644831 **Estd:** 1989 Private Limited Company
**Line of Business:** Manufacture of sports goods
**Trading Style:** Pulse Fitness
**Issued Capital:** £126,500
**Directors:** C P Johnson, D M Johnson
**Co. Secretary:** John Hodd
**Responsibilities**
**Senior:** Dave Poole *(Partner)*
**Health & Safety:** John Copeland *(Service Manager)*
**Facilities:** John Copeland *(Service Manager)*
**Branches:** Rock Merchanting Ltd, Herts Business Centre, Alexander Rd, London Colney, St. Albans, Hertfordshire AL2 1JG
**US SIC:** 3949 **UK SIC:** 49420
**Auditors:** Cowgill Holloway LLP
**Bankers:** Lloyds TSB Bank plc (30-94-28)

| | 31-12-13 | 31-12-12 | 31-12-11 |
|---|---|---|---|
| TO | 3,915,200 | 2,273,286 | 8,266,418 |
| P/L | 204,050 | 229,753 | 194,902 |
| NW | 1,715,456 | 1,705,567 | 1,675,583 |
| WC | (152,789) | (106,264) | (51,002) |
| Emp. | 182 | 147 | 94 |

DUNS 28-876-3477

## Rock (Nominees) Ltd

(**Subsidiary of:** Charles Stanley Group Plc)
Granville House, 25 Luke Street, London EC2A 4AR
**Tel:** 02071496000
**Web:** www.charles-stanley.co.uk
**Reg No:** 1115143 **Estd:** 1973 Private Limited Company
**Line of Business:** Financial intermediation not elsewhere classified
**Issued Capital:** £15
**Directors:** E M Clark, N M Anderson, P D Allen, Sir D H Howard, P A Abberley, M R Lilwall
**Co. Secretary:** Ms Julie Ung
**Responsibilities**
**Senior:** James Rawlingson *(Director)*
**US SIC:** 6111 **UK SIC:** 81501
**Auditors:** Saffery Champness

| | 31-03-14 | 31-03-13 | 31-03-12 |
|---|---|---|---|
| TA | 15 | 15 | 15 |
| NW | 15 | 15 | 15 |

DUNS 73-454-6299

## Rock Uk Adventure Centres Ltd

Frontier Centre Addington Road, Wellingborough, Northamptonshire NN9 5UH
**Tel:** 08448000222
**Web:** www.rockuk.org
**Reg No:** 4718891 **Estd:** 2003 Private Company Limited By Guarantee
**Line of Business:** Outdoor leisure pursuit organisers and equipment
**Directors:** Reverend D W Flanagan, Ms M Wooding Jones, A M Arnold, D W Adams, M P Stevens, A J Fraser, J P Heasman
**Responsibilities**
**Senior:** Andrew Butcher *(Director)*, Richard Suwell *(Centre Director)*
**US SIC:** 7999 **UK SIC:** 97913
**Bankers:** Lloyds TSB Bank plc (30-98-63)

| | 31-08-14 | 31-08-13 | 31-08-12 |
|---|---|---|---|
| TO | 3,371,038 | 3,048,566 | 4,628,807 |
| P/L | 522,550 | 493 | 202,424 |
| NW | 5,008,651 | 4,332,694 | 4,332,201 |
| WC | (209,650) | (55,102) | (986,151) |
| Emp. | 90 | 96 | 106 |

DUNS 23-208-2875

## Rockdale Housing Association Ltd

Rockdale Lodge, Rockdale Road, Sevenoaks, Kent TN13 1JT
**Tel:** 01732458762
**Web:** www.rockdale.org.uk
**Reg No:** 0013507IP **Estd:** 1948 Friendly Society
**Line of Business:** Non-charitable social work activities with accommodation
**Trading Style:** Rockdale House
**Principals:** M Thompsett *(Chairman)*, J Griffiths
**Responsibilities**
**Senior:** Jill Drake *(Operations Director)*, Jill Griffiths *(CEO, Managing Director)*, Jane Vaughan *(Manager)*
**IT:** Liz Austin *(IT Manager)*
**HR:** Jill Drake *(Operations Director)*
**US SIC:** 8321 **UK SIC:** 96111
**Auditors:** Creaseys
**Bankers:** National Westminster Bank Plc (60-19-02)
**Employees:** 65
**Turnover:** £1,975,484,000

DUNS 54-427-2677

## Rockdoor Ltd

(**Subsidiary of:** General All Purpose Plastics Group Ltd)
Partnership Way Shadsworth Industrial, Park, Blackburn, Lancashire BB1 2QP
**Tel:** 01254662999
**Web:** www.rockdoor.com
**Reg No:** 3273404 **Estd:** 1996 Private Limited Company
**Line of Business:** Manufacture of other plastic products
**Issued Capital:** £100
**Principals:** D L Chesney *(Managing)*, S M Brayshaw, S D Bird
**Co. Secretary:** Andrew Greensmith
**Responsibilities**
**Marketing:** Mark Simms *(Commercial Director)*
**Sales:** Mark Simms *(Commercial Director)*
**HR:** Mark Simms *(Commercial Director)*
**Health & Safety:** Mark Simms *(Commercial Director)*
**US SIC:** 3079 **UK SIC:** 48360
**Auditors:** Grant Thornton UK LLP
**Bankers:** Yorkshire Bank Plc (05-07-27)

| | 31-05-13 | 31-05-12 | 31-05-11 |
|---|---|---|---|
| TO | N/A | N/A | 7,947,921 |
| P/L | N/A | N/A | 3,111,573 |
| Emp. | N/A | N/A | 76 |

DUNS 77-127-3133

## Rocket Badge Co Ltd

1 Torriano Mews, London NW5 2RZ
**Tel:** 08452012588 **Fax:** 02074244041
**Web:** www.rocketbadge.co.uk
**Reg No:** 2699509 **Estd:** 1990 Private Limited Company
**Line of Business:** Corporate promotional products
**Issued Capital:** £2
**Director:** D Lyons
**Co. Secretary:** Leetrice Lyons
**Responsibilities**
**HR:** Andrew Greaves *(Human Resources Manager)*
**Health & Safety:** Andrew Greaves *(Human Resources Manager)*
**Facilities:** Andrew Greaves *(Human Resources Manager)*
**US SIC:** 3999 **UK SIC:** 49590
**Auditors:** Aaron Zimbler Associates

| | 31-03-14 | 31-03-13 | 31-03-12 |
|---|---|---|---|
| TA | 2 | 2 | 2 |
| NW | 2 | 2 | 2 |

DUNS 42-362-0843

## The Rocket Club Ltd

258 Broad Street, Birmingham, West Midlands B1 2HF
**Tel:** 01216434525 **Fax:** 0121-643-8086
**Web:** www.therocketclub.com
**Reg No:** 4349693 **Estd:** 2002 Private Limited Company
**Line of Business:** Nightclub
**Issued Capital:** £300
**Directors:** C A Dunkley, L Reddy
**Responsibilities**
**Senior:** Lisa Bates *(Manager)*, William Reddy *(Director)*
**US SIC:** 5813 **UK SIC:** 66200

| | 31-01-14 | 31-01-13 | 31-01-12 |
|---|---|---|---|
| TA | 300 | 300 | 300 |
| NW | 300 | 300 | 300 |

DUNS 54-431-3588 **Imp-Exp**

## Rocket Medical Plc

Imperial Way, Watford, Hertfordshire WD24 4XX
**Tel:** 01923239791
**Web:** www.rocketmedical.com
**Reg No:** 3276608 **Estd:** 1986 Public Limited Company
**Line of Business:** Manufacturers of medical equipment
**Export Sales:** £5,514,253
**Issued Capital:** £410,926
**Directors:** L Todd, S Hastings, R L Bernberg
**Co. Secretary:** Jeffrey Jackson
**Responsibilities**
**Senior:** Stephen Meredith *(Manager)*
**Branches:** Rocket Medical Plc, 2-4 Wear Industrial Estate, Sedling Road, Washington, Tyne and Wear NE38 9BZ
**US SIC:** 3841 **UK SIC:** 37201
**Auditors:** Cameron Baum Davis LLP

| | 31-03-14 | 31-03-13 | 31-03-12 |
|---|---|---|---|
| TO | 15,114,551 | 14,278,072 | 13,364,963 |
| P/L | 1,925,541 | 3,088,750 | 2,198,398 |
| NW | 7,220,191 | 7,856,192 | 6,524,678 |
| WC | 6,152,882 | 6,877,786 | 5,594,434 |
| Emp. | 145 | 143 | 147 |

DUNS 22-229-3701

## Rocket Software Uk Ltd

(**Subsidiary of:** Rocket Software (Holdings) Uk Ltd)
Innovation Centre, Gallows Hill, Warwick Technology Park, Warwick, Warwickshire CV34 6UW
**Tel:** 01926-482553 **Fax:** 01926-482521
**Web:** www.rocketsoftware.com
**Reg No:** 4247316 **Estd:** 2001 Private Limited Company
**Line of Business:** Other computer related activities
**Export Sales:** £10,323,121
**Issued Capital:** £12,790,939
**Directors:** K Thimble, M Jones, A Youniss
**Co. Secretary:**
D & A Secretarial Services Limit
**Responsibilities**
**Senior:** Brian Agle *(Manager)*, Johan Gedda *(Manager)*
**Branches:** Rocket Software Uk Ltd, 4 The Square, Stockley Park, UB11 1ET Uxbridge
**US SIC:** 7379 **UK SIC:** 83940
**Auditors:** PricewaterhouseCoopers LLP
**Bankers:** The Royal Bank Of Scotland Plc (16-08-05)

| | 31-12-13 | 31-12-12 | 31-12-11 |
|---|---|---|---|
| TO | 14,705,289 | 12,159,203 | 13,455,601 |
| P/L | (150,437) | 121,670 | 1,399,876 |
| NW | (2,801,096) | 6,130,758 | 3,956,329 |
| WC | (2,548,867) | 6,697,934 | 3,846,388 |
| Emp. | 63 | 59 | 55 |

DUNS 28-994-6121 **Imp**

## Rockford Components Ltd

Rockford House, Acer Road, Rendlesham, Woodbridge, Suffolk IP12 2GJ
**Tel:** 01394420800 **Fax:** 01394420820
**Web:** www.rockford.co.uk
**Reg No:** 1838700 **VAT No:** 637761217
**Estd:** 1984 Private Limited Company
**Line of Business:** Manufacturers of electronic equipment and components
**Export Sales:** £821,666
**Issued Capital:** £100
**Directors:** S D Hayter, J V Marks, B S Hayter, L A Betts, C Miller, P A Lion
**Co. Secretary:** Ms Patricia Marks
**Responsibilities**
**HR:** Victoria Atkins *(Human Resources Manager)*
**Branches:** Rockford Components Ltd, The New Barn, Odstock Rd, Salisbury, Wiltshire SP5 4NZ
**US SIC:** 3679 **UK SIC:** 34542
**Auditors:** Ballams
**Bankers:** Lloyds TSB Bank plc (30-99-85)

| | 30-06-13 | 30-06-12 | 30-06-11 |
|---|---|---|---|
| TO | 13,211,851 | 13,319,693 | 11,458,294 |
| P/L | 778,521 | 400,600 | 1,084,420 |
| NW | 2,031,266 | 1,537,661 | 1,342,308 |
| WC | 2,511,837 | 2,399,963 | 2,434,533 |
| Emp. | 274 | 219 | 225 |

DUNS 21-773-5921

## Rocking Horse

1 Ormskirk Road, Liverpool, Merseyside L9 5AD
**Tel:** 01515242602
**Web:** www.orchidgroup.co.uk
**Estd:** 2003 Proprietorship
**Line of Business:** Public house
**Proprietor:** Mrs S Baker
**US SIC:** 5813 **UK SIC:** 66200
**Employees:** 48

DUNS 21-604-8192

## Rocklands Special School

Purcell Avenue, Lichfield, Staffordshire WS13 7PH
**Tel:** 01543510760
**Web:** www.rocklands.staffs.sch.uk
**Estd:** 1996 Proprietorship
**Line of Business:** Schools (local authority)
**Proprietor:** A Dooley
**Responsibilities**
**Senior:** Sandra Swift *(Head Teacher)*
**US SIC:** 8211 **UK SIC:** 93200
**Employees:** 50

DUNS 21-035-5317

## Rockleypoint Beach Club

Napier Road, Poole, Dorset BH15 4LZ
**Tel:** 01202680691
**Web:** www.havenholidayhomes.co.uk
**Proprietorship**
**Line of Business:** Caravan parks
**Proprietor:** A Clarke
**US SIC:** 4469 **UK SIC:** 76300
**Employees:** 300

DUNS 51-655-9452

## Rockliffe Hall Ltd

(**Subsidiary of:** The Gibson o'Neill Company Ltd)
Hurworth Place, Darlington, County Durham DL2 2DU
**Web:** www.rockliffehall.com
**Reg No:** 5972297 **Estd:** 2006 Private Limited Company
**Line of Business:** Hotels
**Issued Capital:** £39,100,000
**Directors:** S Gibson, A W Brindle, J R Bloom
**Co. Secretary:** Jeremy Bloom
**Responsibilities**
**Marketing:** Wendy Benson *(Marketing Director)*, Katie Scott *(Marketing Coordinator)*
**US SIC:** 7011, 6531, 7299
**UK SIC:** 66500, 83400, 98902

| | 30-06-14 | 30-06-13 | 30-06-12 |
|---|---|---|---|
| TO | 9,729,000 | 8,908,000 | 8,434,000 |
| P/L | (1,441,000) | (1,572,000) | (3,962,000) |
| NW | 24,600,000 | 25,422,000 | 26,569,000 |
| WC | 5,019,000 | 5,108,000 | 5,070,000 |
| Emp. | 284 | 273 | 294 |

DUNS 77-783-9960 **Imp-Exp**

## Rockline Industries Ltd

(**Subsidiary of:** Rocklino Industries Inc.)
Heming Road, Redditch, Worcestershire B98 0DH
**Web:** www.rockline.co.uk
**Reg No:** 3025769 **VAT No:** 660758515
**Estd:** 1995 Private Limited Company
**Line of Business:** Wholesale of other household goods not elsewhere classified
**Export Markets:** Europe
**Export Sales:** £26,424,369
**Issued Capital:** £36,586,677
**Directors:** C Roush, R Rudolph
**Co. Secretary:** Simon Ellis
**US SIC:** 5199, 3842
**UK SIC:** 61900, 37203
**Auditors:** Nicklin LLP
**Bankers:** Barclays Bank Plc (20-27-17)

| | 30-06-14 | 30-06-13 | 30-06-12 |
|---|---|---|---|
| TO | 48,825,301 | 40,840,607 | 45,928,777 |
| P/L | (530,644) | (2,327,000) | (1,432,782) |
| NW | 1,878,577 | 520,669 | 831,678 |
| WC | 10,174,026 | 8,812,146 | 10,795,716 |
| Emp. | 263 | 292 | 310 |

DUNS 23-216-6009

## Rockmount Enterprises Ltd

27-28 Drumalig Road, Carryduff, Belfast BT8 8EQ
**Tel:** 028-9081-2279 **Fax:** 028-9081-5851
**Web:** www.rockmountgolfclub.com
**Reg No:** 0027715NI **Estd:** 1995 Private Limited Company
**Line of Business:** Golf clubs
**Trading Style:** Rockmount Golf Club
**Issued Capital:** £276,000
**Directors:** R Patterson, Ms D Patterson
**Co. Secretary:** Ms Diane Patterson
**Responsibilities**
**Finance:** Shirley Graham *(General Manager)*
**IT:** Shirley Graham *(General Manager)*
**HR:** Shirley Graham *(General Manager)*
**Health & Safety:** Shirley Graham *(General Manager)*
**Facilities:** Shirley Graham *(General Manager)*
**Purchasing:** Shirley Graham *(General Manager)*
**US SIC:** 7999 **UK SIC:** 97913
**Auditors:** David J Bennett & Co
**Bankers:** Northern Bank Ltd (95-01-31)

| | 31-08-13 | 31-08-12 | 31-08-11 |
|---|---|---|---|
| TA | 2,336,792 | 2,379,188 | 2,424,562 |
| NW | 1,197,308 | 1,203,177 | 1,186,740 |
| WC | (408,574) | (402,159) | (387,590) |

DUNS 23-086-1523

## Rockport Craigavad

15 Rockport Road, Holywood, Co Down BT18 0DD
**Tel:** 028-9042-8372
**Web:** www.rockportschool.com
**Estd:** 1967
**Line of Business:** Schools (local authority)
**Trading Style:** Rockport School
**Director:** Mrs H Tentland
**Responsibilities**
**Senior:** George Vance *(Principal)*
**Finance:** Sarah Parkinson *(Bursar)*
**Admin:** Christine Hamill *(Administrator)*
**Health & Safety:** George Vance *(Principal)*
**Facilities:** George Vance *(Principal)*
**Purchasing:** Sarah Parkinson *(Bursar)*
**US SIC:** 8211 **UK SIC:** 93200
**Employees:** 51

DUNS 21-132-6708 Imp

## Rocks & Co Productions Ltd

**(Subsidiary of:** Juwelo Tv Deutschland Gmbh)
Insight House, Blick Road, Heathcote Industrial Estate, Warwick, Warwickshire CV34 6TA
**Tel:** 01926440261
**Web:** www.rocksandco.com
**Reg No:** 6662909 **Estd:** 2008 Private Limited Company
**Line of Business:** Other motion picture and video production activities
**Issued Capital:** £10,000,000
**Directors:** R Northall, A S Jablonski
**US SIC:** 7819, 5963
**UK SIC:** 97111, 65600
**Auditors:** Malde & Co

| | 31-12-13 | 31-12-12 | 31-12-11 |
|---|---|---|---|
| TO | 9,985,429 | 10,257,658 | 10,054,202 |
| P/L | (632,209) | (1,165,237) | 345,772 |
| NW | 1,490,935 | 2,123,144 | 3,288,381 |
| WC | 1,472,803 | 2,223,949 | 3,199,720 |
| Emp. | 50 | 46 | 37 |

DUNS 21-136-5558

## Rockspring Hanover Feeder (General Partner) Ltd

**(Subsidiary of:** Rockspring Property Holdings Ltd)
166 Sloane Street, London SW1X 9QF
**Tel:** 02072356643
**Reg No:** 6695213 **Estd:** 2008 Private Limited Company
**Line of Business:** Business services
**Issued Capital:** £1
**Directors:** I E Baker, R A Gilchrist, F A Casero, H Elrington, J De Clercq, R Bains, S R Reid, E Craston
**Co. Secretary:** Andrew Grant Duff
**Responsibilities**
**Senior:** Frances Harnetty *(Director)*, Neal Shegog *(Director)*
**US SIC:** 7399 **UK SIC:** 83954

| | 31-03-14 | 31-03-13 | 31-03-12 |
|---|---|---|---|
| TA | 1 | 1 | 1 |
| NW | 1 | 1 | 1 |

DUNS 73-853-4978

## Rockspring Property Holdings Ltd

166 Sloane Street, London SW1X 9QF
**Tel:** 020-7761-3300
**Web:** www.rockspringpim.com
**Reg No:** 5108612 **Estd:** 2004 Private Limited Company
**Line of Business:** Management activities of holding companies
**Export Sales:** £14,486,806
**Issued Capital:** £37,501
**Directors:** R A Gilchrist, R Bains, S R Reid, B Phillips, F A Casero, P J Hampton, Ms K Dixon, E Craston
**Co. Secretary:** Ian Baker
**Responsibilities**
**Senior:** Frances Harnetty *(Director)*, Richard Plummer *(Director)*, Neal Shegog *(Director)*
**US SIC:** 6711 **UK SIC:** 83962

| | 31-03-14 | 31-03-13 | 31-03-12 |
|---|---|---|---|
| TO | 28,291,702 | 28,284,678 | 29,005,650 |
| P/L | 8,724,127 | 9,946,804 | 10,149,772 |
| NW | 3,741,349 | 5,418,949 | 185,283 |
| WC | 1,458,448 | 4,380,821 | 2,895,559 |
| Emp. | 79 | 78 | 78 |

DUNS 67-218-8893

## Rockstar Lincoln Ltd

**(Subsidiary of:** Take-Two Interactive Software Inc.)
Building F The Point, Lincoln, Lincolnshire LN6 3QZ
**Tel:** 01522-686-878
**Web:** www.rockstarlincoln.com
**Reg No:** 6026627 **Estd:** 2006 Private Limited Company
**Line of Business:** Other computer related activities
**Issued Capital:** £20
**Director:** R M Hajaj
**Co. Secretary:** Daniel Emerson
**US SIC:** 7379 **UK SIC:** 83940
**Auditors:** Ernst & Young LLP
**Bankers:** The Royal Bank Of Scotland Plc (83-00-81)

| | 31-03-14 | 31-03-13 | 31-03-12 |
|---|---|---|---|
| TO | 5,710,179 | 4,128,280 | 2,870,698 |
| P/L | 375,441 | 275,231 | 52,576 |
| NW | 401,625 | 143,033 | 610,510 |
| WC | 144,145 | 59,928 | 533,534 |
| Emp. | 179 | 129 | 95 |

DUNS 37-894-2007 Imp

## Rockstar North Ltd

**(Subsidiary of:** Take-Two Interactive Software Inc.)
Calton Square, 1 Greenside Row, Edinburgh, Midlothian EH1 3AP
**Tel:** 0131-524-7800
**Web:** www.rockstarnorth.com
**Reg No:** 3312220 **VAT No:** 761671127
**Estd:** 1997 Private Limited Company
**Line of Business:** Publishing of software
**Export Sales:** £32,252,221
**Issued Capital:** £1
**Director:** R M Hajaj
**Co. Secretary:** Daniel Emerson
**US SIC:** 7372 **UK SIC:** 83940
**Auditors:** Johnston & Co
**Bankers:** The Royal Bank Of Scotland Plc (83-00-81)

| | 31-03-14 | 31-03-13 | 31-03-12 |
|---|---|---|---|
| TO | 32,252,221 | 20,127,149 | 18,054,810 |
| P/L | 2,162,491 | 1,136,416 | (12,679,857) |
| NW | 2,036,375 | 761,519 | 5,556,136 |
| WC | 807,070 | 350,216 | 5,156,506 |
| Emp. | 356 | 318 | 269 |

DUNS 21-783-9910

## Rockwell Automation

Millennium House Campus 1, Balgownie Road, Bridge Of Don, Aberdeen, Aberdeenshire AB22 8GT
**Tel:** 01224227780
**Web:** www.oilandgas.rockwellautomation.com
**Estd:** 2011 Proprietorship
**Line of Business:** Manufacturers of aeronautical instrumentation
**Proprietor:** A Howard
**Responsibilities**
**Senior:** William Nicolson *(Manager)*, Tom Shannon *(Manager)*
**US SIC:** 3811 **UK SIC:** 37100
**Employees:** 70

DUNS 21-685-1022 Imp-Exp

## Rockwell Automation Ltd

**(Subsidiary of:** Industrial Control Services Group Ltd)
Pitfield, Kiln Farm, Milton Keynes, Buckinghamshire MK11 3DR
**Tel:** 01908838800 **Fax:** 01908-261-917
**Web:** www.rockwellautomation.com
**Reg No:** 0872110 **VAT No:** 463475235
**Estd:** 1969 Private Limited Company
**Line of Business:** Automation systems and controls
**Export Markets:** Australia, Middle East, Far East, Africa, Europe, Americas
**Export Sales:** £81,331,000
**Issued Capital:** £19,844,733
**Directors:** A K Suttle, K Maharaj, W Dennison, W J Quinn
**Responsibilities**
**Finance:** Mark Tarala *(Finance Director)*
**Marketing:** Josh Chambers *(Marketing Manager)*, Graham Mullins *(Marketing Manager)*
**HR:** Thomas Doyle *(Human Resources Manager)*
**Engineering:** Tom Compton *(Engineering Manager)*
**Branches:** Rockwell Automation Ltd, Westwing Millenium Balgowire Bridge Of Dawn, Aberdeen, Aberdeenshire AB22 8GT
**US SIC:** 3811, 3714
**UK SIC:** 37100, 35300
**Auditors:** Deloitte LLP
**Bankers:** National Westminster Bank Plc (60-00-01)

| | 30-09-13 | 30-09-12 | 30-09-11 |
|---|---|---|---|
| TO | 82,404,000 | 81,650,000 | 77,326,000 |
| P/L | 12,832,000 | 11,558,000 | 8,316,000 |
| NW | 10,363,000 | 2,551,000 | 18,989,000 |
| WC | 25,517,000 | 14,568,000 | 8,708,000 |
| Emp. | 805 | 720 | 656 |

DUNS 21-618-0885 Imp-Exp

## Rockwell Collins Uk Ltd

**(Subsidiary of:** Rockwell Collins Inc.)
Unit 21 Sutton Park Avenue Suttons, Business Park, Reading, Berkshire RG6 1AZ
**Tel:** 01189 359 000 **Fax:** 01189 359 355
**Web:** www.rockwellcollins.com
**Reg No:** 0543016 **Estd:** 1955 Private Limited Company
**Line of Business:** Other supporting air transport activities
**Export Markets:** Worldwide
**Export Sales:** £63,628,000
**Issued Capital:** £16,340,000
**Directors:** C Hazeel, D Jordan, V M Klopfenstein, C R Mahoney, I W Boyle, C Alber, R K Ortberg
**Co. Secretary:** Miss Helen Barton
**Responsibilities**
**Senior:** Bernard Loth *(Manager)*, Jane Middleton *(Manager)*
**Sales:** Alan Prowse *(Sales Director)*
**IT:** Robbie Birch *(Systems Consultant)*
**HR:** P Jellyman *(Training Manager)*
**Purchasing:** Anna Halls *(Purchasing Executive)*, Graham Snook *(Source Supply Manager)*
**Branches:** Rockwell Collins Uk Ltd, Edward Way, Burgess Hill, West Sussex RH15 9UE
**US SIC:** 4582, 9711
**UK SIC:** 76400
**Auditors:** Deloitte LLP
**Bankers:** Barclays Bank Plc (20-00-00)

| | 27-09-13 | 28-09-12 | 30-09-11 |
|---|---|---|---|
| TO | 84,511,000 | 92,572,000 | 84,817,000 |
| P/L | (3,933,000) | (3,046,000) | 3,503,000 |
| NW | 17,579,000 | (18,000) | (19,994,000) |
| WC | 10,515,000 | (4,931,000) | (25,599,000) |
| Emp. | 461 | 569 | 467 |

DUNS 53-609-9419 Imp-Exp

## Rockwell Solutions Ltd

Brunel Road, West Gourdie Industrial Estate, Dundee, Angus DD2 4TG
**Tel:** 01382-622-122
**Web:** www.rockwellsolutions.com
**Reg No:** 0177774SC **VAT No:** 694083410
**Estd:** 1997 Private Limited Company
**Line of Business:** Representative office
**Export Sales:** £2,077,931
**Issued Capital:** £50,000
**Directors:** Mrs R Okhai, A A Okhai
**Co. Secretary:** Zain Okhai
**Responsibilities**
**Finance:** Heather Ewing *(Finance Manager)*
**HR:** Brian Macdonald *(Personnel Officer)*
**Health & Safety:** Brian Macdonald *(Personnel Officer)*
**US SIC:** 7399, 2752
**UK SIC:** 83954, 47544
**Auditors:** Henderson Loggie
**Bankers:** The Royal Bank Of Scotland Plc (83-50-00)

| | 31-08-13 | 31-08-12 | 31-08-11 |
|---|---|---|---|
| TO | 10,330,237 | 9,833,337 | 12,692,041 |
| P/L | 743,999 | 341,971 | 717,412 |
| NW | 4,091,296 | 3,676,034 | 3,359,538 |
| WC | 730,796 | 611,044 | 556,719 |
| Emp. | 69 | 70 | 71 |

DUNS 21-113-6189 Imp-Exp

## Rockwool Ltd

**(Subsidiary of:** Rockwool International A/S)
Pencoed, Bridgend, Mid Glamorgan CF35 6NY
**Tel:** 08452412586
**Web:** www.rockwool.co.uk
**Reg No:** 0972252 **Estd:** 1970 Private Limited Company
**Line of Business:** Manufacturers general
**Trading Style:** Rockwool Firesafe Insulation
**Issued Capital:** £112,500,000
**Directors:** K Fedorovskiy, R W Perry, R Moss
**Co. Secretary:** Kirill Fedorovskiy
**Responsibilities**
**Senior:** Shayne Gilbert *(Facilities Manager)*, Thomas Helgard *(Manager)*
**Sales:** Andrew Champ *(Business Development Director)*
**Health & Safety:** Alan Clancy *(Facilities Manager)*
**Facilities:** Alan Clancy *(Facilities Manager)*
**Branches:** Rockwool, 4 Leazes Pk, Hexham, Northumberland NE46 3AX
**US SIC:** 1742, 1799
**UK SIC:** 50400, 50000
**Auditors:** Ernst & Young LLP
**Bankers:** HSBC Bank plc (40-13-23)

| | 31-12-13 | 31-12-12 | 31-12-11 |
|---|---|---|---|
| TO | 79,703,000 | 87,044,000 | 97,412,000 |
| P/L | (10,789,000) | (10,453,000) | (4,088,000) |
| NW | 48,114,000 | 56,532,000 | 23,705,000 |
| WC | 6,048,000 | 4,727,000 | 7,845,000 |
| Emp. | 443 | 447 | 429 |

DUNS 21-024-5978

## Rodale Press

Sovereign Park, Market Harborough, Leicestershire LE16 9EF
**Tel:** 01858-438851
**Web:** www.natmags.co.uk
**Estd:** 2010
**Line of Business:** Newspapers publishing
**Trading Style:** Tower Publishing
**Responsibilities**
**Senior:** Sarah Sharpe *(Manager)*
**US SIC:** 2711 **UK SIC:** 47512
**Employees:** 200

DUNS 21-390-5893

## Roddis House

Roddis House 4 12, Old Christchurch Road, Bournemouth, Dorset BH1 1LG
**Tel:** 01202-290311
**Estd:** 2009 Proprietorship
**Line of Business:** Estate management services
**Responsibilities**
**Senior:** Metal Sawyer *(Owner)*
**US SIC:** 6531 **UK SIC:** 83400
**Employees:** 120

DUNS 22-636-6672

## Roddy & Reid Construction Ltd

Rodreid House, Luton, Bedfordshire LU4 9LQ
**Tel:** 01582-592893
**Web:** www.roddyandreid.co.uk
**Reg No:** 1549493 **VAT No:** 366940227
**Estd:** 1981 Private Limited Company
**Line of Business:** Civil engineers
**Issued Capital:** £2,000
**Principals:** A Reid *(Managing)*, M Roddy, J V Reid
**Co. Secretary:** Alphonsus Reid
**Responsibilities**
**Admin:** Carol Kilham *(office manager)*
**US SIC:** 1541 **UK SIC:** 50100
**Auditors:** Brewer, Clark & Partners

| | 30-04-14 | 31-05-13 | 31-04-12 |
|---|---|---|---|
| TA | 1,216,020 | 891,601 | 838,096 |
| NW | 230,405 | 246,099 | 216,507 |
| WC | 151,805 | 152,820 | 119,568 |

DUNS 21-031-9950 Imp-Exp

## Rodenstock (U.K.) Ltd

**(Subsidiary of:** Bridgepoint Advisers Group Ltd)
Unit U Springhead Enterprise Park, Springhead Road, Northfleet, Gravesend, Kent DA11 8HJ
**Tel:** 01474-325555 **Fax:** 01474-325537
**Web:** www.rodenstock.co.uk
**Reg No:** 0266467 **VAT No:** 243639847
**Estd:** 1932 Private Limited Company
**Line of Business:** Manufacturers of optical products
**Export Sales:** £2,042
**Issued Capital:** £1,800,000
**Directors:** M D Goodwin, S E Schirmer, Dr M Kleer, O R Kastalio, Mrs J Ponter, N B Jensen
**Co. Secretary:** Michael Goodwin
**Responsibilities**
**Senior:** Olaf Gottgens *(Manager)*, Dietmar Rathbauer *(Manager)*
**IT:** Steve Beaty *(IT Manager)*
**Branches:** Rodenstock (U.k.) Ltd, Unit 2A Bridge Park Road, Leicester, Leicestershire LE4 8BL
**US SIC:** 3861, 5199
**UK SIC:** 37330, 61900
**Auditors:** Baker Tilly
**Bankers:** Barclays Bank Plc (20-00-00)

| | 31-12-13 | 31-12-12 | 31-12-11 |
|---|---|---|---|
| TO | 11,379,003 | 11,589,965 | 11,024,865 |
| P/L | 412,122 | 453,379 | 65,678 |
| NW | 394,739 | (185,287) | (73,648) |
| WC | 573,799 | 843,144 | 1,361,996 |
| Emp. | 97 | 121 | 145 |

DUNS 28-830-7184

## Rodericks Ltd

**(Subsidiary of:** Rodericks Dental Holdings Ltd)
28 Queensbridge, Rushmills, Northampton, Northamptonshire NN4 7BF
**Tel:** 01604-602491 **Fax:** 01604-602551
**Web:** www.rodericksdental.co.uk
**Reg No:** 0190237 **Estd:** 2005 Private Limited Company
**Line of Business:** Dental practice activities
**Issued Capital:** £129,836
**Directors:** L I Ross, Miss S E Gregory, C Clark, A Khetia, S A Brookes
**Co. Secretary:** Shalin Mehra
**Responsibilities**
**Senior:** Victoria Steed *(Financial Controller)*
**Finance:** Victoria Steed *(Financial Controller)*
**US SIC:** 8021 **UK SIC:** 95400
**Auditors:** Blue Cube Business Ltd
**Bankers:** National Westminster Bank Plc (60-02-35)

| | 31-03-14 | 31-05-13 | 31-03-12 |
|---|---|---|---|
| TO | 26,238,443 | 28,900,910 | 23,916,384 |
| P/L | 1,374,067 | 1,393,571 | 1,029,178 |
| NW | (851,207) | (768,171) | (2,131,584) |
| WC | 1,980,288 | (139,813) | (2,012,567) |
| Emp. | 483 | 466 | 411 |

DUNS 73-385-9552

## Rodger Griffiths Ltd

4 Brookside Gardens, Bishopswood, Bishops Wood, Stafford, Staffordshire ST19 9AL
**Tel:** 01785-840207
**Reg No:** 4659480 **Estd:** 2003 Private Limited Company
**Line of Business:** Specialised building trade contractors
**Issued Capital:** £2
**Director:** R Griffiths
**Co. Secretary:** Ms Claire Griffiths
**Responsibilities**
**Finance:** Claire Caddick *(Finance Director)*
**US SIC:** 1799 **UK SIC:** 50000

| | 31-03-14 | 31-03-13 | 31-03-12 |
|---|---|---|---|
| TA | 186,720 | 100,920 | 111,130 |
| NW | 40,546 | 16,092 | 4,956 |
| WC | 16,554 | 8,521 | (4,824) |

DUNS 50-328-1891

## Rodgers Leask Ltd

**(Subsidiary of:** Rodgers Leask Group Ltd)
49 Canal Street, Derby, Derbyshire DE1 2RJ
**Tel:** 01332285000
**Web:** www.rodgersleask.co.uk
**Reg No:** 2352923 **VAT No:** 508063073
**Estd:** 1989 Private Limited Company

**Line of Business:** Management activities of holding companies
**Issued Capital:** £80
**Directors:** L Pacey, G Stokes, A P Catmur, Ms S Hewish, P J Spencer, K Harvey, A W Leask
**Branches:** Rodgers Leask Ltd, Old House, Gorsey Lane, Birmingham, West Midlands B46 1JU
**US SIC:** 6711 **UK SIC:** 83962
**Auditors:** Bates Weston
**Bankers:** The Royal Bank Of Scotland Plc (16-18-18)

| | 31-07-14 | 31-07-13 | 31-07-12 |
|---|---|---|---|
| TA | 2,230,252 | 1,934,973 | 1,446,408 |
| NW | 279,977 | 260,437 | 214,017 |
| WC | 383,664 | 334,844 | 379,921 |

DUNS 28-936-7013
### Rodgers of Plymouth Ltd
Brixton Road Garage, Chittleburn Hill, Brixton, Plymouth, Devon PL8 2BL
**Tel:** 01752402623
**Web:** www.rodgersofplymouth.co.uk
**Reg No:** 1557586 **VAT No:** 381699505
**Estd:** 1981 Private Limited Company
**Line of Business:** Miscellaneous vehicle repair
**Issued Capital:** £39,996
**Principals:** A R Pugh *(Managing)*, R K Ackland, A Hext, N Broxham, J N Gruitt, R J Endicott
**Co. Secretary:** Richard Ackland
**Responsibilities**
**Senior:** Steven Worth *(Manager)*
**Branches:** Rodgers Of Plymouth Ltd, Ocean Quay, Unit 1, Plymouth, Devon PL1 4LL
**US SIC:** 7539, 5521, 5531
**UK SIC:** 67100, 65100
**Auditors:** Francis Clark
**Bankers:** HSBC Bank plc (40-36-22)

| | 31-12-13 | 31-12-12 | 31-12-11 |
|---|---|---|---|
| TO | 19,767,797 | 17,042,461 | 15,903,835 |
| P/L | 117,063 | 32,530 | 40,991 |
| NW | 1,298,476 | 1,265,567 | 1,250,013 |
| WC | (407,002) | (427,969) | (421,289) |
| Emp. | 91 | 95 | 100 |

DUNS 21-244-9995 Imp
### Rodgers of York Ltd
Monk Green, York, North Yorkshire YO61 1RY
**Tel:** 01904-610570 **Fax:** 01904-643240
**Web:** www.rodgersofyork.co.uk
**Reg No:** 0362284 **VAT No:** 170105706
**Estd:** 1940 Private Limited Company
**Line of Business:** Carpet and rug retailers
**Issued Capital:** £18,420
**Principals:** W F Browne *(Managing)*, J D Browne
**Co. Secretary:** Ms Susan Browne
**Branches:** Rodgers Of York Ltd, 47 Fossgate, York, North Yorkshire YO1 9TF
**US SIC:** 5714, 5719
**UK SIC:** 64700
**Auditors:** Barber Harrison & Platt
**Bankers:** Barclays Bank Plc (20-99-56)

| | 28-02-14 | 28-02-13 | 29-02-12 |
|---|---|---|---|
| TA | 4,186,938 | 3,658,388 | 3,674,706 |
| NW | 2,620,936 | 2,658,247 | 2,513,283 |
| WC | 498,803 | 457,199 | 237,158 |

DUNS 23-740-7262 Imp
### Rodial Ltd
(**Subsidiary of:** Starmark Holdings Ltd)
535 Kings Road, London SW10 0TZ
**Tel:** 020-7351-1720
**Web:** www.rodial.co.uk
**Reg No:** 3734993 **VAT No:** 766092704
**Estd:** 1999 Private Limited Company
**Line of Business:** Beauty products
**Issued Capital:** £2
**Directors:** E Hatzistefanis, Ms M Papageorgiou
**Co. Secretary:** Efstratios Hatzistefanis
**Responsibilities**
**Senior:** Hat Zistesinas *(Chief Executive Officer)*
**US SIC:** 2844 **UK SIC:** 25820
**Auditors:** Hamlyns LLP

| | 31-03-14 | 31-03-13 | 31-03-12 |
|---|---|---|---|
| TA | 4,471,596 | 3,214,403 | 2,397,125 |
| NW | 2,887,855 | 2,249,585 | 1,340,785 |
| WC | 2,756,996 | 2,207,105 | 1,296,168 |

DUNS 21-691-1586 Exp
### Rodmatic Holdings Ltd
(**Subsidiary of:** Rodmatic Ltd)
Battle Farm Trading Estate, 30 Portman Road, Reading, Berkshire RG30 1PD
**Tel:** 01189-596969
**Web:** www.rodmatic.co.uk
**Reg No:** 0758674 **Estd:** 1963 Private Limited Company
**Line of Business:** Precision engineers
**Export Markets:** Europe
**Issued Capital:** £1,051
**Principals:** B C Steatham *(Chairman)*, J R Todd, R Newborough
**Responsibilities**
**Sales:** Alan Iddenden *(Business Development Manager)*, Bob Todd *(Sales Manager)*
**US SIC:** 8911 **UK SIC:** 83701
**Auditors:** BDO Stoy Hayward
**Bankers:** National Westminster Bank Plc (60-24-20)

| | 30-06-14 | 30-06-13 | 30-06-12 |
|---|---|---|---|
| TA | 1,951 | 1,951 | 2,527,081 |
| NW | 1,951 | 1,951 | (460,792) |
| WC | N/A | N/A | (868,861) |

DUNS 28-993-4929 Imp
### Rodo Ltd
Lumb Lane, Droylsden, Manchester M43 7BU
**Tel:** 0161-371-6400
**Web:** www.rodo.co.uk
**Reg No:** 1832828 **VAT No:** 146386743
**Estd:** 1926 Private Limited Company
**Line of Business:** Painting and decorating merchants and suppliers
**Issued Capital:** £300,000
**Principals:** P W Brierley *(Managing)*, C G Thomason, J Brierley, D A Williamson
**Co. Secretary:** Peter Brierley
**Responsibilities**
**Senior:** Bill Briley *(Manager)*
**Marketing:** Gary Bent *(Marketing Controller)*
**Sales:** Geoff Winstanley *(National Account Manager)*
**Admin:** L McArthy *(Administration Supervisor)*
**Facilities:** Robert Ashelby *(Maintenance Manager)*
**US SIC:** 2389 **UK SIC:** 45393
**Auditors:** D A Williamson & Co
**Bankers:** HSBC Bank plc (40-08-33)

| | 31-03-14 | 31-03-13 | 31-03-12 |
|---|---|---|---|
| TO | 24,972,544 | 22,799,499 | 20,300,953 |
| P/L | 1,766,087 | 1,529,342 | 1,274,031 |
| NW | 14,068,773 | 13,070,592 | 12,163,428 |
| WC | 9,759,281 | 9,963,995 | 9,109,917 |
| Emp. | 94 | 95 | 92 |

DUNS 21-581-3351
### Rodwell Bayne Air Conditioning
Howard Chase Pipps Hill Industrial, Estate, Basildon, Essex SS14 3BD
**Web:** www.rodwell-bayne.com
**Estd:** 2011 Proprietorship
**Line of Business:** Air and other gas compressors
**Proprietor:** A Rodwell
**US SIC:** 3563 **UK SIC:** 32831
**Employees:** 50

DUNS 21-928-7448 Imp
### Roe Bros. & Co Ltd.
1 Fenlake Business Centre, Fengate, Peterborough, Cambridgeshire PE1 5BQ
**Tel:** 01733-358-821 **Fax:** 01733-555-260
**Web:** www.theroegroup.com
**Reg No:** 1564981 **VAT No:** 486509606
**Estd:** 1956 Private Limited Company
**Line of Business:** Steel fabricators
**Trading Style:** The Roe Group, Reinforcement Northern
**Issued Capital:** £126,000
**Principals:** J P Roe *(Chairman)*, Mrs J Robertson, C J Taylor
**Responsibilities**
**Senior:** Haydon Whitham *(Manager)*
**Finance:** Haydon Whitham *(Manager)*
**IT:** Tony Herbert *(IT Manager)*
**Branches:** Roe Bros. & Co Ltd., Albert Road, Edinburgh, Midlothian EH6 7DP
**US SIC:** 1622, 5039
**UK SIC:** 50200, 61300
**Auditors:** Wright Vigar Ltd
**Bankers:** National Westminster Bank Plc (54-21-38)

| | 31-12-13 | 31-12-12 | 31-12-11 |
|---|---|---|---|
| TO | 42,277,694 | 35,901,833 | 37,538,246 |
| P/L | 483,054 | 423,128 | 179,747 |
| NW | 3,584,555 | 3,155,621 | 3,046,464 |
| WC | 1,605,757 | 1,070,207 | 797,049 |
| Emp. | 136 | 124 | 126 |

DUNS 21-591-7522
### Roe Dry Lining
295 Drumsurn Road, Limavady, Co Londonderry BT49 0PX
**Web:** www.roedrylinings.com
**Estd:** 2002 Partnership
**Line of Business:** Ceilings (suspended)
**Partners:** K Mcgowan, J Mcgowan
**US SIC:** 1799 **UK SIC:** 50000
**Employees:** 70

DUNS 22-626-1691
### Roe Electronics Ltd
(**Subsidiary of:** Active Electronics Plc)
Albion House, Gordon Road, High Wycombe, Buckinghamshire HP13 6ET
**Reg No:** 1239629 **Estd:** 1978 Private Limited Company
**Line of Business:** Wholesale of other electronic parts and equipment
**Issued Capital:** £100
**Director:** P H Jones
**Co. Secretary:** Graham Ireland
**US SIC:** 5065 **UK SIC:** 61500
**Auditors:** Grant Thornton

| | 31-12-13 | 31-12-12 | 31-12-11 |
|---|---|---|---|
| TA | 1,078 | 1,078 | 1,078 |
| NW | 1,078 | 1,078 | 1,078 |

DUNS 23-222-5313
### Roe Green Junior School
Princes Avenue, London NW9 9JL
**Tel:** 020-8204-5221
**Web:** www.rgjs.brent.sch.uk
**Estd:** 1963
**Line of Business:** General secondary education
**Proprietor:** Ms M Loosemore
**Responsibilities**
**Senior:** Melissa Loosemore *(Head Teacher)*
**US SIC:** 8211 **UK SIC:** 93200
**Employees:** 56

DUNS 23-700-5835
### Roe Ltd
Enterprise Road, Westwood Industrial Estate, Margate, Kent Ct0 4ja, Margate, Kent CT9 4JA
**Tel:** 01843232888
**Web:** www.roeltd.co.uk
**Reg No:** 3695845 **Estd:** 1999 Private Limited Company
**Line of Business:** Construction of commercial buildings
**Trading Style:** Roe Ltd
**Issued Capital:** £300
**Directors:** Mrs M N Roe, D Roe, L Chilcott, I M Brownlee, Mrs T Roe, W P Roe
**Co. Secretary:** James Roe
**Responsibilities**
**Marketing:** Dave MacMillan *(Sales & Marketing Manager)*
**Sales:** Dave MacMillan *(Sales & Marketing Manager)*
**HR:** Jo Davidge *(Human Resources Manager)*
**Branches:** Roe Ltd, Unit J2, Westwood Industrial Estate, Margate, Kent CT9 4JS
**US SIC:** 1541, 1522
**UK SIC:** 50100
**Auditors:** McCabe Ford Williams
**Bankers:** HSBC Bank plc (40-38-02)

| | 30-04-14 | 30-04-13 | 30-04-12 |
|---|---|---|---|
| TO | 11,186,361 | 9,738,001 | 9,045,479 |
| P/L | 448,157 | 77,817 | 113,214 |
| NW | 2,206,907 | 2,040,814 | 1,995,288 |
| WC | 46,550 | 192,406 | (134,124) |
| Emp. | 97 | 92 | 88 |

DUNS 33-966-9939
### Roebucks Solicitors
7-8 Richmond Terrace, Blackburn, Lancashire BB1 7BD
**Tel:** 01254274000
**Web:** www.roebuckslaw.co.uk
**Estd:** 2001 Partnership
**Line of Business:** Solicitors
**Partners:** Ms D Hayden-Pawton, T Hoyle
**Responsibilities**
**Senior:** Robin Phoenix *(Managing Partner)*, Graeme Tootle *(Manager)*
**Branches:** Roebucks Solicitors, 34 High Street, Blackburn, Lancashire BB1 4LA
**US SIC:** 8111 **UK SIC:** 83500
**Employees:** 50

DUNS 73-724-0457
### Roedean School Enterprises Ltd
(**Subsidiary of:** Roedean School)
Roedean Way, Brighton, East Sussex BN2 5RQ
**Tel:** 01273-667500
**Web:** www.roedean.co.uk
**Reg No:** 2921272 **Estd:** 1994 Private Limited Company
**Line of Business:** General secondary education
**Issued Capital:** £1
**Directors:** Ms A Whitaker, R S Poffley
**Co. Secretary:** Richard Poffley
**Responsibilities**
**Senior:** Oliver Blond *(Head Teacher)*
**Finance:** Martin Lyne *(Accountant)*
**US SIC:** 8211, 6519
**UK SIC:** 93200, 85000
**Auditors:** Grant Thornton
**Bankers:** National Westminster Bank Plc (60-30-09)

| | 31-08-13 | 31-08-12 | 31-08-11 |
|---|---|---|---|
| TO | 321,131 | 294,430 | 318,483 |
| P/L | 160,967 | 136,145 | N/A |
| NW | 6,330 | 6,330 | 6,330 |
| WC | 6,330 | 6,330 | 4,815 |

DUNS 50-380-8552
### Roehampton Club Members Ltd
Roehampton Lane, London SW15 5LR
**Tel:** 020-8480-4200 **Fax:** 020-8480-4265
**Web:** www.roehamptonclub.co.uk
**Reg No:** 2389907 **Estd:** 1990 Private Limited Company
**Line of Business:** Clubs social and associations
**Issued Capital:** £3,313,750
**Directors:** Mrs E Dand, Ms M P Walker, C C Blackhurst, J W Bailey, M Newey, J C Roe, R A Scallon, R Storer
**Co. Secretary:** James May
**Responsibilities**
**Senior:** Robert Dickson *(Manager)*, Emile Fernandes *(Manager)*, Alan Giddins *(Director)*, Christopher Gotla *(Manager)*, Richard Major *(Director)*, Wendy Moss *(Manager)*
**Health & Safety:** Beverley Prior *(Health & Safety Manager)*
**Facilities:** norman Gibbs *(Head of Maintenance)*, Paul Swain *(Head of Maintenance)*
**US SIC:** 7999, 5812
**UK SIC:** 97913, 66110
**Auditors:** Pannell Kerr Forster

| | 31-12-13 | 31-12-12 | 31-12-11 |
|---|---|---|---|
| TO | 8,631,000 | 8,479,000 | 7,760,000 |
| P/L | 1,062,000 | 922,000 | (114,000) |
| NW | 10,097,000 | 9,033,000 | 8,080,000 |
| WC | (1,190,000) | (2,444,000) | (1,003,000) |
| Emp. | 92 | 92 | 103 |

DUNS 73-907-7365 Imp
### Roehampton University
Erasmus House, Roehampton Lane, London SW15 5PU
**Tel:** 02083923000
**Web:** www.roehampton.ac.uk
**Reg No:** 5161359 **Estd:** 2013 Private Company Limited By Guarantee
**Line of Business:** University
**Directors:** S B Newey, D J Lochtie, Ms C E Delmar, D G Deeks, Miss S Kelly, Dr P O'Prey, S J Ludlow, N G Brookes
**Co. Secretary:** Laurence Benson
**Responsibilities**
**Senior:** Susan Acheson *(Director)*, Robert Alexander *(Director)*, Gary Coates *(Manager)*, Roger Dawe *(Director)*, Terence Knight *(Manager)*, James Mckinney *(Director)*, Paul O' Prey *(Vice-Chancellor)*, June Tillman *(Manager)*, Matthew Trustman *(Partner)*
**Finance:** Irene Cooke *(Financial Coordinator)*
**Admin:** Sally Dell'Osa *(Secretary Administrator)*, Jenny Ilsley *(Administrator)*, Tracey Rowden *(Health Science Administrator)*, Judith Stevens *(Administrator)*
**HR:** Heidi Davies *(Head of Employee Relations)*, Davina Fernyhough *(HR Account Manager)*
**Facilities:** Tim Cozens *(Assistant Director of Faciliti)*
**US SIC:** 8221 **UK SIC:** 93100
**Bankers:** Barclays Bank Plc (20-03-80)

| | 31-07-14 | 31-07-13 | 31-07-12 |
|---|---|---|---|
| TO | 82,761,000 | 76,437,000 | 72,223,000 |
| P/L | 328,000 | 1,487,000 | 2,103,000 |
| NW | 10,510,000 | 19,821,000 | 13,349,000 |
| WC | 12,802,000 | 11,446,000 | 10,942,000 |
| Emp. | 988 | 958 | 917 |

DUNS 22-837-4492
### Roffe Swayne
Ashcombe Court, Woolsack Way, Godalming, Surrey GU7 1LQ
**Web:** www.roffeswayne.com
**Estd:** 1987 Partnership
**Line of Business:** Accounting activities
**Partners:** C R Baxter, J Saunders, J Fisher, R Marshman, Mrs S Ward, R W Edmonson, M S Leigh
**Responsibilities**
**Senior:** Sharon Ward *(Senior Partner)*, Linda Warner *(Manager)*
**Marketing:** Bev Waters *(Marketing Manager)*, Ann Whatley *(Marketing Manager)*
**IT:** Olie Warwick *(IT Manager)*
**HR:** Jane Steel *(Personnel Manager)*
**Branches:** Roffe Swayne, St James Ho, East St, Farnham, Surrey GU9 7TJ
**US SIC:** 8931 **UK SIC:** 83600
**Employees:** 70

DUNS 28-893-7949
### Roffes Transport Ltd
West Bank, Sutton Bridge, Spalding, Lincolnshire PE12 9QH
**Tel:** 01406-351111
**Reg No:** 1303593 **Estd:** 1977 Private Limited Company
**Line of Business:** Road haulage and transport services
**Issued Capital:** £52,000

**Managing Director:** T M Roffe
**Co. Secretary:** Ms Julie Roffe
**Responsibilities**
**Senior:** P Roffe *(Partner)*
**US SIC:** 4789 **UK SIC:** 77002
**Auditors:** Stephenson Smart
**Bankers:** Barclays Bank Plc (20-82-75)

| | 31-07-13 | 31-07-12 | 31-07-11 |
|---|---|---|---|
| TA | 3,012,505 | 2,632,097 | 2,501,116 |
| NW | 817,680 | 816,421 | 822,221 |
| WC | (455,810) | (309,649) | (239,609) |

DUNS 22-528-0742 Exp

## Roffey Park Institute Ltd

Forest Road, Colgate, Horsham, West Sussex RH12 4TB
**Tel:** 01293851644
**Web:** www.roffeypark.com
**Reg No:** 0923975 **VAT No:** 821797900
**Estd:** 1967 Private Company Limited By Guarantee
**Line of Business:** Sub-degree level higher education
**Export Markets:** Countries worldwide
**Trading Style:** Roffey Park Management Institute
**Directors:** Mrs C A Waters, P H Ling, P A Breckell, A Talbot, P Gallagher, M J Tiplady, C S Horton, Ms C M Waddington
**Co. Secretary:** Ms Amanda Humphrey
**Responsibilities**
**Senior:** Daniel Cloke *(Manager)*, Clara Freeman *(Manager)*, Sian Harrington *(Director)*, Alison Ritchie *(Director)*
**US SIC:** 8221 **UK SIC:** 93100
**Auditors:** Baker Tilly UK Audit LLP
**Bankers:** HSBC Bank plc (40-18-22)

| | 31-07-14 | 31-07-13 | 31-07-12 |
|---|---|---|---|
| TO | 7,435,972 | 6,800,800 | 5,506,735 |
| P/L | 499,419 | 511,894 | 63,814 |
| NW | 6,497,646 | 5,998,227 | 5,486,333 |
| WC | 214,912 | 255,725 | (34,324) |
| Emp. | 75 | 72 | 69 |

DUNS 64-081-9264 Imp-Exp

## Rofin-Sinar Uk Ltd.

(**Subsidiary of:** Rofin-Sinar Technologies Inc.)
York Way, Willerby, Hull, North Humberside HU10 6HD
**Web:** www.rofin-uk.com
**Reg No:** 3477444 **Estd:** 1997 Private Limited Company
**Line of Business:** Manufacturers general
**Issued Capital:** £589,200
**Principals:** K Lipton *(Managing)*, A J Chambers, R Jeynes, G Braun, N Avci, Professor D R Hall, J R Lee
**Co. Secretary:** Robert Mead
**Responsibilities**
**Senior:** David Mcqueen *(Operations Director)*
**Finance:** Mitch Mead *(Financial Director)*
**Health & Safety:** Jim Sharp *(Quality Manager)*
**Facilities:** Mitch Mead *(Financial Director)*
**Operations:** Tony Dudding *(Design Engineer)*, David Mcqueen *(Operations Director)*
**Branches:** Rofin-Sinar Uk Ltd., P.o. Box 27, Hinckley, Leicestershire LE10 0BF
**US SIC:** 3999 **UK SIC:** 49590
**Auditors:** Deloitte LLP

| | 30-09-14 | 30-09-13 | 30-09-12 |
|---|---|---|---|
| TO | 24,288,000 | 24,252,000 | 18,822,000 |
| P/L | 4,419,000 | 5,440,000 | 3,745,000 |
| NW | 17,319,000 | 15,269,000 | 11,046,000 |
| WC | 15,700,000 | 14,850,000 | 10,690,000 |
| Emp. | 124 | 118 | 110 |

DUNS 21-492-4891

## The Rogano Restaurant

11 Exchange Place, Glasgow, Lanarkshire G1 3AN
**Tel:** 0141-248-4055
**Web:** www.roganoglasgow.com
**Estd:** 1904 Proprietorship
**Line of Business:** Restaurant - seafood
**Proprietor:** I Smith
**US SIC:** 5812 **UK SIC:** 66110
**Employees:** 62

DUNS 21-099-6486

## Roger Dyson Ltd

Unit 18 Long Bank, Berry Hill Industrial Estate, Droitwich, Worcestershire WR9 9AN
**Tel:** 01905775808
**Web:** www.rogerdyson.com
**Reg No:** 6434803 **Estd:** 2007 Private Limited Company
**Line of Business:** Manufacture of other special purpose machinery not elsewhere classified
**Issued Capital:** £1
**Director:** R Dyson
**Co. Secretary:** Mrs Lorraine Keeley
**US SIC:** 3559 **UK SIC:** 32863

| | 31-01-14 | 31-01-13 | 31-01-12 |
|---|---|---|---|
| TA | 4,089,709 | 3,514,183 | 4,030,852 |
| NW | 1,201,001 | 976,685 | 916,607 |
| WC | 183,179 | (519,622) | (692,890) |

DUNS 34-611-2329

## Roger Preston & Partners Ltd

(**Subsidiary of:** Grontmij N.V.)
1 Bath Road, Maidenhead, Berkshire SL6 4AQ
**Tel:** 01628-623423 **Fax:** 01628-639860
**Web:** www.rpreston.com
**Reg No:** 2748664 **Estd:** 1992 Private Limited Company
**Line of Business:** Engineering services
**Trading Style:** Preston Roger & Partners
**Issued Capital:** £56
**Director:** J J Chubb
**Co. Secretary:** Miss Jennifer Hamilton
**US SIC:** 8911 **UK SIC:** 83701
**Auditors:** BSG Valentine

| | 31-12-13 | 31-12-12 | 31-12-11 |
|---|---|---|---|
| TO | N/A | N/A | 433,417 |
| P/L | N/A | N/A | (19,218) |
| NW | (32,366) | (32,366) | (32,366) |
| Emp. | N/A | N/A | 12 |

DUNS 22-670-7255 Imp-Exp

## Roger Skinner Ltd

The Mill, Stradbroke, Diss, Norfolk IP21 5HL
**Tel:** 01379384247
**Web:** www.skinnerspetfoods.co.uk
**Reg No:** 1272854 **VAT No:** 283547924
**Estd:** 1976 Private Limited Company
**Line of Business:** Animal feed and pet foods
**Export Markets:** Scandinavia
**Export Sales:** £664,277
**Issued Capital:** £2,002
**Principals:** R A Skinner *(Chairman and Managing)*, M R Peters, W Delamore, G J Panter, L R Phillips
**Co. Secretary:** Ms Wendy Skinner
**Responsibilities**
**Senior:** Mary Skinner *(Manager)*
**US SIC:** 2047 **UK SIC:** 42221
**Auditors:** PKF
**Bankers:** HSBC Bank plc (40-19-18)

| | 31-03-14 | 31-03-13 | 31-03-12 |
|---|---|---|---|
| TO | 12,572,215 | 10,742,334 | 9,063,550 |
| P/L | 1,849,076 | 1,312,431 | 721,678 |
| NW | 4,350,213 | 4,767,649 | 3,835,486 |
| WC | 1,796,188 | 2,411,676 | 1,649,081 |
| Emp. | 47 | 46 | 42 |

DUNS 22-782-2905

## Roger Thompson & Partners

Agincourt House 14 18 Newport Road, Cardiff, South Glamorgan CF24 0SW
**Tel:** 02920445300
**Web:** www.thompsons.co.uk
**Estd:** 1965 Partnership
**Line of Business:** Solicitors
**Partners:** M Antoniw, G R Bent, E Roth
**US SIC:** 8111 **UK SIC:** 83500
**Bankers:** National Westminster Bank Plc (56-00-41)
**Employees:** 50

DUNS 29-494-5498

## Roger Warnes Transport Ltd

Great Dunham Hall, Great Dunham, King's Lynn, Norfolk PE32 2LQ
**Tel:** 01328-701317
**Web:** www.rogerwarnestransport.co.uk
**Reg No:** 1857891 **Estd:** 1971 Private Limited Company
**Line of Business:** Road haulage and transport services
**Issued Capital:** £100
**Principals:** R G Warnes *(Managing)*, A M Wall, N R Alderton
**Co. Secretary:** Mrs Anita Warnes
**Branches:** Roger Warnes Transport Ltd, Station Rd, King's Lynn, Norfolk PE32 1EJ
**US SIC:** 4789 **UK SIC:** 77002
**Auditors:** Larking Gowen
**Bankers:** Barclays Bank Plc (20-28-20)

| | 30-04-14 | 30-04-13 | 30-04-12 |
|---|---|---|---|
| TO | 12,316,367 | 10,642,161 | 9,873,017 |
| P/L | 1,186,337 | 118,086 | 353,778 |
| NW | 4,959,067 | 4,143,159 | 4,152,759 |
| WC | 128,491 | (548,901) | 399,964 |
| Emp. | 9 | 85 | 86 |

DUNS 42-468-9149

## Rogers & Norton

5-7 Willow Lane, Norwich, Norfolk NR2 1EU
**Tel:** 01603-666001
**Web:** www.rogers-norton.co.uk
**Estd:** 1991 Partnership
**Line of Business:** Solicitors
**Partners:** M C Greig, M B Hambling, R W Etheridge, N G Norton, P N Kerridge, D A Laws, T S Nobbs, B W Faulkner
**Responsibilities**
**Senior:** Richard Etheridge *(senior partner)*, C Grooms *(Partner)*
**Finance:** Richard Aldridge *(finance manager)*
**HR:** Graham Knights *(practice manager)*
**Health & Safety:** Graham Knights *(practice manager)*
**US SIC:** 8111 **UK SIC:** 83500
**Employees:** 65

DUNS 29-891-9226

## Rogers Chapman U K Ltd

(**Subsidiary of:** Jones Lang Lasalle Inc)
22 Hanover Square, London W1S 1JA
**Fax:** 020-8759-5367
**Web:** www.joneslanglasalle.co.uk
**Reg No:** 2094942 **VAT No:** 636151551
**Estd:** 1987 Private Limited Company
**Line of Business:** Real estate agencies
**Issued Capital:** £339,425
**Director:** R Howling
**Co. Secretary:** Nicolas Taylor
**Branches:** Rogers Chapman U K Ltd, 30 Botolph La, London EC3R 8DE
**US SIC:** 6531 **UK SIC:** 83400
**Auditors:** KPMG Audit PLC
**Bankers:** Barclays Bank Plc (20-67-59)

| | 31-12-13 | 31-12-12 | 31-12-11 |
|---|---|---|---|
| TO | 570,028 | 570,028 | 570,028 |
| P/L | (535,410) | 836,640 | 860,601 |
| NW | 17,958,972 | 18,494,382 | 17,657,742 |
| WC | (71,606,809) | (71,071,399) | N/A |

DUNS 21-728-9842

## Rogerstone Woodworkers Ltd

8 Clifton Street, Newport, Gwent NP10 9GF
**Tel:** 01633893248
**Reg No:** 0709987 **Estd:** 1961 Private Limited Company
**Line of Business:** Building services
**Issued Capital:** £6,750
**Director:** T J Howell
**Co. Secretary:** Martin Howell
**US SIC:** 6552, 5072, 5039, 6531
**UK SIC:** 85000, 61500, 61300, 83400
**Auditors:** Ellis Lloyd Jones
**Bankers:** Lloyds TSB Bank plc (30-92-49)

| | 31-10-13 | 31-10-12 | 31-10-11 |
|---|---|---|---|
| TA | 5,694,147 | 6,567,806 | 4,738,834 |
| NW | 3,759,959 | 4,724,043 | 4,673,874 |
| WC | 2,136,084 | 3,824,854 | 3,018,449 |

DUNS 29-535-7685

## Rogge Global Partners Plc

(**Subsidiary of:** Old Mutual Plc)
Sion Hall, 56 Victoria Embankment, London EC4Y 0DZ
**Tel:** 020-7842-8420 **Fax:** 020-7842-8421
**Web:** www.rogge.co.uk
**Reg No:** 1902901 **Estd:** 1985 Public Limited Company
**Line of Business:** Underwriting
**Issued Capital:** £74,719
**Principals:** O Rogge *(Managing)*, I Gladman, P L Bain, J C Graham, D J Jacob, Ms M Conway, D R Gillard
**Co. Secretary:** David Witzer
**US SIC:** 6411 **UK SIC:** 83200
**Auditors:** KPMG Audit PLC
**Bankers:** Barclays Bank Plc (20-19-90)

| | 31-12-13 | 31-12-12 | 31-12-11 |
|---|---|---|---|
| TO | 46,888,768 | 47,326,423 | 41,864,818 |
| P/L | 11,428,257 | 12,360,609 | 10,715,404 |
| NW | 19,850,364 | 19,765,373 | 18,115,575 |
| WC | 15,717,737 | 16,371,034 | 15,298,992 |
| Emp. | 113 | 101 | 88 |

DUNS 23-213-0489

## Rohais Health Centre

Rohais, St Peter Port, Guernsey, Channel Islands GY1 1FF
**Tel:** 01481-723322
**Web:** www.healthcare.gg
**Partnership**
**Line of Business:** Medical practice activities
**Partners:** Dr D S Brand, Dr T R Gill, Dr S C Sweet, Dr B D Parkin, Dr M P Downing
**Responsibilities**
**Senior:** Lynne Mclagan *(Practice Manager)*
**Branches:** Rohais Health Centre, Route De Carteret, Guernsey, Channel Islands GY5 7HA
**US SIC:** 8011 **UK SIC:** 95300
**Employees:** 60

DUNS 22-813-6792 Imp

## Rohan Designs Ltd

(**Subsidiary of:** Rohan Group Ltd)
30 Maryland Road, Milton Keynes, Buckinghamshire MK15 8HN
**Tel:** 01394610840
**Web:** www.rohan.co.uk
**Reg No:** 1567549 **VAT No:** 679064301
**Estd:** 2012 Private Limited Company
**Line of Business:** Design consultants
**Issued Capital:** £50,000
**Directors:** R J Cann, M C Willison, B J Berryman, I D Palmer
**Responsibilities**
**Senior:** Karen Siddall *(Proprietor)*
**Marketing:** Luis Melendez *(Online Marketing Manager)*
**Operations:** Brendon Marczan *(Sourcing Director)*
**Branches:** Rohan Designs Ltd, 86B George Street, Edinburgh, Midlothian EH2 3BU
**US SIC:** 5699, 5961
**UK SIC:** 64500, 65600

**Auditors:** Mercer & Hole
**Bankers:** Bank Of Scotland (12-08-81)

| | 01-02-14 | 31-01-13 | 31-02-12 |
|---|---|---|---|
| TO | 27,252,000 | 25,979,000 | 23,882,000 |
| P/L | 1,295,000 | 68,000 | (2,723,000) |
| NW | 1,461,000 | (132,000) | (200,000) |
| WC | 4,890,000 | 3,066,000 | 3,094,000 |
| Emp. | 318 | 337 | 350 |

DUNS 21-689-1499 Exp

## Rohm & Haas (U K) Ltd

Herald Way, Coventry, West Midlands CV3 2RQ
**Tel:** 02476654400
**Web:** www.rohmhaas.com
**Reg No:** 0312415 **VAT No:** 217819156
**Estd:** 1936 Private Limited Company
**Line of Business:** Manufacturers of chemicals
**Export Markets:** Rest of Europe; USA;
**Trading Style:** Rohm & Haas European Operations, Rohm & Haas Powder Coatings
**Issued Capital:** £14,941,102
**Directors:** Miss N J Ephgrave, Mrs J West
**Co. Secretary:** Mrs Kim Fox
**Responsibilities**
**Senior:** P Barthelmes *(Proprietor)*
**Branches:** Rohm & Haas (U K) Ltd, Wholeflats Road, Grangemouth, Stirlingshire FK3 9UY
**US SIC:** 2899, 2821
**UK SIC:** 25670, 25140
**Auditors:** Deloitte LLP
**Bankers:** Lloyds TSB Bank plc (30-92-45)

| | 31-12-13 | 31-12-12 | 31-12-11 |
|---|---|---|---|
| TO | 14,501,000 | 27,956,000 | 35,914,000 |
| P/L | 1,474,000 | 271,000 | (976,000) |
| NW | 147,098,000 | 147,020,000 | 145,774,000 |
| WC | 99,715,000 | 98,954,000 | 95,924,000 |

DUNS 45-882-1915 Imp

## Rohr Aero Services Ltd

(**Subsidiary of:** United Technologies Corporation)
Technology House Maylands Avenue, Hemel Hempstead, Hertfordshire HP2 7DF
**Tel:** 01292670208 **Fax:** 01292-672854
**Web:** www.goodrich.com
**Reg No:** 0166785SC **VAT No:** 671761519
**Estd:** 1996 Private Limited Company
**Line of Business:** Manufacture of aircraft and spacecraft
**Export Sales:** £34,626,928
**Trading Style:** Bf Goodrich Corporation
**Issued Capital:** £6,049,463
**Directors:** A M Hodge, B Craig, S P Callan, D Harrison
**Co. Secretary:**
Edwin Coe Secretaries Limited
**Responsibilities**
**Senior:** Eugene Gallenagh *(CEO, Managing Director)*
**US SIC:** 3721 **UK SIC:** 36400
**Auditors:** Ernst & Young LLP
**Bankers:** The Royal Bank Of Scotland Plc (83-15-26)

| | 31-12-13 | 31-12-12 | 31-12-11 |
|---|---|---|---|
| TO | 48,086,282 | 43,472,106 | 37,521,326 |
| P/L | 7,217,007 | 4,642,584 | 4,376,554 |
| NW | 22,775,226 | 26,379,325 | 21,509,742 |
| WC | 9,065,265 | 11,411,151 | 5,955,837 |
| Emp. | 270 | 267 | 256 |

DUNS 34-588-5362

## Rojay Services Ltd

Blackhorse Street, Bolton, Lancashire BL1 1SY
**Tel:** 01204388125
**Web:** www.arriva.co.uk
**Reg No:** 2732657 **VAT No:** 597801985
**Estd:** 1990 Private Limited Company
**Line of Business:** Rail transport services
**Trading Style:** Blue Bus Lancashire
**Issued Capital:** £195
**Managing Director:** R C Jarvis
**Co. Secretary:** Ms Victoria Jarvis
**Responsibilities**
**Senior:** Henry Hughes *(General Manager)*
**US SIC:** 4011, 7513
**UK SIC:** 71000, 84802
**Bankers:** National Westminster Bank Plc (60-24-04)

| | 31-12-13 | 31-12-12 | 31-12-11 |
|---|---|---|---|
| TA | 104,736 | 140,401 | 177,946 |
| NW | 29,966 | 2,163 | (36,629) |
| WC | (10,096) | (31,692) | (77,919) |

DUNS 39-908-0761 Imp

## Rok Associates Ltd

Unit 1 Peckfield Business Park, Phoenix Avenue, Leeds, West Yorkshire LS25 4DY
**Tel:** 01133850200
**Reg No:** 2221377 **Estd:** 1988 Private Limited Company
**Line of Business:** Management activities of holding companies
**Issued Capital:** £120
**Principals:** M King *(Managing)*, S G Reeve
**Co. Secretary:** Michael King
**US SIC:** 6711, 3585
**UK SIC:** 83962, 32841

**Auditors:** Garbutt & Elliott Ltd
**Bankers:** Lloyds TSB Bank plc (30-00-05)

|     | 31-12-13 | 31-12-12 | 31-12-11 |
|-----|----------|----------|----------|
| TO  | 5,785,698 | 4,666,950 | 4,696,425 |
| P/L | 883,706 | 157,353 | 493,994 |
| NW  | 2,545,450 | 1,858,841 | 1,733,776 |
| WC  | (547,042) | (986,461) | (833,001) |
| Emp. | 67 | 64 | 64 |

DUNS 22-967-4700

## Rokeby Educational Trust Ltd
George Road, Kingston-Upon-Thames, Surrey KT2 7PB
**Tel:** 020-8942-2247
**Web:** www.rokebyschool.co.uk
**Reg No:** 0872414 **Estd:** 1980 Private Company Limited By Guarantee
**Line of Business:** General secondary education
**Trading Style:** Rokeby School
**Directors:** Dr A J Mayfield, Mrs A H Evans-Tovey, Ms K H Abbott, C W Carter, D P Viles, R M Webster, S B Allen
**Co. Secretary:** Mrs Maureen Adams
**Responsibilities**
**Senior:** Maureen Mclaughlin (Bursar), Christopher Merry (Manager), Jason Peck (Principal)
**Finance:** Maureen Mclaughlin (Bursar)
**IT:** Roger Lakhani (Head of IT)
**HR:** Maureen Mclaughlin (Bursar)
**Facilities:** Maureen Mclaughlin (Bursar)
**Purchasing:** Maureen Mclaughlin (Bursar)
**US SIC:** 8211 **UK SIC:** 93200
**Auditors:** Haysmacintyre
**Bankers:** Barclays Bank Plc (20-00-00)

|     | 31-08-13 | 31-08-12 | 31-08-11 |
|-----|----------|----------|----------|
| TO  | 5,039,100 | 4,757,790 | 4,550,434 |
| P/L | 233,269 | 174,794 | (66,644) |
| NW  | 5,929,593 | 5,682,253 | 5,498,167 |
| WC  | 414,582 | 1,244,835 | 2,620,412 |
| Emp. | 76 | 71 | 70 |

DUNS 42-424-4098

## Roko Health Clubs Ltd
(Subsidiary of: Civil Services Sports Council Ltd)
Wilford Lane, Nottingham, Nottinghamshire NG2 7RN
**Tel:** 01159827799
**Web:** www.roko.co.uk
**Reg No:** 4411979 **Estd:** 2002 Private Limited Company
**Line of Business:** Pre school education
**Issued Capital:** £10,000
**Directors:** R J Haskell, B Hunter
**Co. Secretary:** Nigel Maglione
**Responsibilities**
**Senior:** Sarah Bond (Proprietor)
**US SIC:** 8211 **UK SIC:** 93200

|     | 31-12-13 | 31-12-12 | 31-12-11 |
|-----|----------|----------|----------|
| TO  | 7,801,612 | 7,791,080 | 7,826,448 |
| P/L | 405,617 | 618,813 | 375,646 |
| NW  | (3,090,364) | (3,324,605) | (3,696,218) |
| WC  | (1,257,914) | (1,390,399) | (1,618,559) |
| Emp. | 162 | 155 | 162 |

DUNS 23-507-8011

## Rol-Lite Blinds Ltd
Copley Mill, Demesne Drive, St Pauls Trading Estate, Stalybridge, Cheshire SK15 2QF
**Tel:** 0161-338-2681
**Web:** www.blindsbyrol-lite.co.uk
**Reg No:** 2186004 **Estd:** 1973 Private Limited Company
**Line of Business:** Manufacturers and retailers of curtains
**Issued Capital:** £9,600
**Principals:** T M Hollis (Managing), A Stirrup, G G Millican
**Co. Secretary:** Ms Jacqueline Tierney
**Responsibilities**
**Senior:** D Hollis (Proprietor)
**US SIC:** 2392 **UK SIC:** 45550
**Auditors:** Gatley, Read & Co
**Bankers:** National Westminster Bank Plc (01-06-39)

|     | 30-11-13 | 30-11-12 | 30-11-11 |
|-----|----------|----------|----------|
| TA  | 1,359,323 | 1,214,395 | 1,113,105 |
| NW  | 1,012,949 | 916,464 | 841,660 |
| WC  | 760,961 | 637,771 | 553,151 |

DUNS 50-480-3339

## Roland Berger Strategy Consultants Ltd
(Subsidiary of: Roland Berger Strategy Consultants Holding Gmbh)
6th Floor, London W1U 8EW
**Tel:** 02030751100 **Fax:** 02072244110
**Web:** www.rolandberger.co.uk
**Reg No:** 2454242 **Estd:** 1989 Private Limited Company
**Line of Business:** Management and business consultants
**Issued Capital:** £750,000
**Directors:** Baron T J Collot D'Escury, Dr P M Jowett
**Co. Secretary:** Arifur Ali

**Responsibilities**
**Senior:** Chris Cardinal (Principal), Friedrich Demmer (Partner)
**US SIC:** 7392, 6111
**UK SIC:** 83951, 81501
**Auditors:** Moore Stephens LLP

|     | 31-12-13 | 31-12-12 | 31-12-11 |
|-----|----------|----------|----------|
| TA  | 4,347,522 | 5,126,430 | 6,461,494 |
| P/L | 166,240 | 673,455 | 410,179 |
| NW  | 916,240 | 1,395,872 | 722,417 |
| WC  | 952,394 | 1,323,426 | 600,210 |
| Emp. | 68 | 55 | 43 |

DUNS 21-720-3900    Imp

## Roland (U.K.) Ltd
(Subsidiary of: Roland Corporation)
Atlantic Close, Swansea Enterprise Park, Swansea, West Glamorgan SA7 9FJ
**Fax:** 01792 515048
**Web:** www.roland.co.uk
**Reg No:** 1216941 **Estd:** 1975 Private Limited Company
**Line of Business:** Activities of other transport agencies
**Export Sales:** £789,692
**Issued Capital:** £5,019,245
**Directors:** J Miki, T J Walter, G L Raison
**Responsibilities**
**Senior:** Dean Lawrence (Area Manager)
**Finance:** Tracy Richards (Management Accountant)
**Marketing:** Martyn Hopkins (Brand Manager)
**Admin:** Gail Dothae (Human Resources Manager), Janine Newton-Howes (PA to Managing Director)
**HR:** Gail Dothae (Human Resources Manager)
**Operations:** Sean Montgomery (Senior Product Manager)
**Branches:** Roland (U.k.) Ltd, 2 Bridge Road, Leeds, West Yorkshire LS5 3BL
**US SIC:** 4712 **UK SIC:** 77002
**Auditors:** Deloitte LLP
**Bankers:** National Westminster Bank Plc (60-08-46)

|     | 31-12-13 | 31-12-12 | 31-12-11 |
|-----|----------|----------|----------|
| TO  | 17,759,599 | 19,119,523 | 19,267,485 |
| P/L | 251,693 | 151,741 | 174,924 |
| NW  | 7,395,361 | 7,252,511 | 7,138,260 |
| WC  | 6,354,867 | 6,166,456 | 6,029,293 |
| Emp. | 70 | 79 | 82 |

DUNS 22-850-0112

## Roland Whatmore Ltd
Brook Street, Oswaldtwistle, Accrington, Lancashire BB5 3JH
**Tel:** 01254-233214 **Fax:** 01254-385747
**Reg No:** 0641002 **VAT No:** 174893714
**Estd:** 2002 Private Limited Company
**Line of Business:** Builders
**Issued Capital:** £61,200
**Principals:** B Thornton (Managing), M Hartley, Ms B A Thornton, J A Ormerod
**Co. Secretary:** Mrs Andrea Jones
**US SIC:** 1522, 1796, 1751
**UK SIC:** 50100, 50400
**Auditors:** Egan Roberts Ltd
**Bankers:** Yorkshire Bank Plc (05-03-53)

|     | 31-10-13 | 31-10-12 | 31-10-11 |
|-----|----------|----------|----------|
| TA  | 835,758 | 895,808 | 866,541 |
| NW  | 8,721 | 140,082 | 149,469 |
| WC  | 138,539 | 284,178 | 297,279 |

DUNS 42-385-4897

## Rolawn Ltd
York Road, Elvington, York, North Yorkshire YO41 4XR
**Tel:** 08456046075
**Web:** www.rolawn.co.uk
**Reg No:** 4373077 **Estd:** 2002 Private Limited Company
**Line of Business:** Growing of cereals and other crops not elsewhere classified
**Issued Capital:** £243,193
**Directors:** K E Dawson, G A Barrett, P A Dawson, J M Hill
**Co. Secretary:** Mrs Davina Turner
**Responsibilities**
**Senior:** Lorraine Willis (Marketing Executive)
**Marketing:** Lorraine Willis (Marketing Executive)
**Branches:** Rolawn Ltd, Tyttenhanger House, Coursers Road, Colney Heath, St Albans, St. Albans, Hertfordshire AL4 0PG
**US SIC:** 0119 **UK SIC:** 01001
**Bankers:** Lloyds TSB Bank plc (30-00-05)

|     | 28-02-14 | 28-02-13 | 29-02-12 |
|-----|----------|----------|----------|
| TO  | 10,092,954 | 10,394,537 | 12,709,392 |
| P/L | 529,332 | 173,539 | 15,676 |
| NW  | 2,738,041 | 2,566,455 | 2,415,768 |
| WC  | 1,865,645 | 1,955,401 | 1,853,414 |
| Emp. | 55 | 62 | 86 |

DUNS 23-827-1795    Exp

## Rolawn (Turf Growers) Ltd
York Road, Elvington, York, North Yorkshire YO41 4XR
**Tel:** 01904608661 **Fax:** 01904-608272
**Web:** www.rolawn.co.uk
**Reg No:** 0057391SC **Estd:** 1975 Private Limited Company

**Line of Business:** Growing of cereals and other crops not elsewhere classified
**Issued Capital:** £58,700
**Chairmen:** K E Dawson, P A Dawson
**Co. Secretary:** Mrs Davina Turner
**Responsibilities**
**Finance:** David Mumby (Financial Director)
**IT:** Alan Featherstone (IT Manager)
**Branches:** Rolawn (Turf Growers) Ltd, 102 Crowhill Road, Glasgow, Lanarkshire G64 1RP
**US SIC:** 0119 **UK SIC:** 01001
**Auditors:** Ernst & Young
**Bankers:** Lloyds TSB Bank plc (30-99-99)

|     | 28-02-14 | 28-02-13 | 29-02-12 |
|-----|----------|----------|----------|
| TA  | 58,700 | 58,700 | 58,700 |
| NW  | 58,700 | 58,700 | 58,700 |

DUNS 73-967-8295    Imp

## Roldvale Trading Ltd
Ramillies House, Ramillies Street, London W1F 7LN
**Tel:** 01992815151
**Reg No:** 5218684 **Estd:** 1975 Private Limited Company
**Line of Business:** Other letting of own property
**Issued Capital:** £100
**Director:** D Sullivan
**Co. Secretary:** Conegate Limited
**US SIC:** 6519, 6711
**UK SIC:** 85000, 83962

|     | 29-09-13 | 29-09-12 | 29-09-11 |
|-----|----------|----------|----------|
| TO  | 10,274,279 | 11,608,934 | 11,834,490 |
| P/L | 609,437 | 1,429,889 | 249,416 |
| NW  | 10,044,539 | 9,598,726 | 8,176,194 |
| WC  | 6,134,390 | 5,284,705 | 3,241,911 |
| Emp. | 206 | 214 | 208 |

DUNS 50-004-1454    Imp-Exp

## Rolec Services Ltd
Ralphs Lane, Boston, Lincolnshire PE20 1QU
**Tel:** 01205724754 **Fax:** 01205-724-876
**Web:** www.rolecserv.com
**Reg No:** 2294468 **VAT No:** 571624245
**Estd:** 2011 Private Limited Company
**Line of Business:** Other artistic and literary creation and interpretation
**Export Markets:** E U, Middle East
**Issued Capital:** £100,000
**Directors:** K J Alsop, Miss H T Brown, M Georgeson
**US SIC:** 8999, 7999
**UK SIC:** 83954, 97913
**Auditors:** Streets Audit LLP
**Bankers:** Barclays Bank Plc (20-97-34)

|     | 31-07-13 | 31-07-12 | 30-07-11 |
|-----|----------|----------|----------|
| TO  | 6,251,484 | 4,734,530 | N/A |
| P/L | 1,490,481 | 665,087 | N/A |
| NW  | 9,014,442 | 7,989,585 | 7,494,468 |
| WC  | 7,171,249 | 6,407,824 | 5,700,984 |
| Emp. | 91 | 63 | N/A |

DUNS 21-602-6690

## The Rolex Watch Company Ltd
(Subsidiary of: Fondation Hans Wilsdorf)
19 St James' Square, London SW1Y 4JE
**Tel:** 02070247300
**Web:** www.rolex.com
**Reg No:** 0142138 **Estd:** 1905 Private Limited Company
**Line of Business:** Wholesale of jewellery
**Export Sales:** £4,251,735
**Trading Style:** Rolex U K
**Issued Capital:** £120,000
**Directors:** R De Leyser, B Gros, Ms C M Thomson
**Co. Secretary:** Graham Richards
**Branches:** The Rolex Watch Company Ltd, 19 St. James's Square, London SW1Y 4JE
**US SIC:** 5094, 7631
**UK SIC:** 61900, 67302
**Auditors:** Deloitte LLP
**Bankers:** Lloyds TSB Bank plc (30-94-31)

|     | 31-12-13 | 31-12-12 | 31-12-11 |
|-----|----------|----------|----------|
| TO  | 156,647,787 | 142,588,045 | 133,026,553 |
| P/L | 15,703,061 | 15,481,255 | 5,135,258 |
| NW  | 90,589,446 | 82,802,636 | 69,938,703 |
| WC  | 56,176,797 | 47,939,011 | 36,612,352 |
| Emp. | 161 | 160 | 161 |

DUNS 22-805-6933    Imp-Exp

## Rolf C. Hagen (U.K.) Ltd
(Subsidiary of: Investissements Hagensons Inc)
Distribution Centre, California Drive, Castleford, West Yorkshire WF10 5QH
**Tel:** 01977-556622 **Fax:** 01977-513465
**Web:** www.hagen.com
**Reg No:** 1670484 **Estd:** 1982 Private Limited Company
**Line of Business:** Distribution service providers
**Export Markets:** North America, Asia, West Indies and Europe.
**Export Sales:** £405,855
**Issued Capital:** £100,000
**Principals:** L Milburn (Financial), R H Hagen, A N Burgess
**Co. Secretary:** Tom Hagen

**Responsibilities**
**Senior:** Andrew Bartyla (Manager)
**US SIC:** 4712, 5399
**UK SIC:** 77002, 65600
**Auditors:** Morgan Brown & Spofforth
**Bankers:** Barclays Bank Plc (20-48-46)

|     | 31-12-13 | 31-12-12 | 31-12-11 |
|-----|----------|----------|----------|
| TO  | 19,580,500 | 19,565,738 | 19,808,079 |
| P/L | 884,510 | 823,013 | 1,228,594 |
| NW  | 9,033,568 | 9,340,528 | 10,733,238 |
| WC  | 6,663,115 | 7,143,985 | 8,690,277 |
| Emp. | 76 | 75 | 74 |

DUNS 28-914-7761    Exp

## Rolfe Judd Architecture Ltd
(Subsidiary of: Rolfe Judd Holdings Ltd)
Old Church Court, Claylands Road, London SW8 1NZ
**Tel:** 020-7556-1500
**Web:** www.rolfe-judd.co.uk
**Reg No:** 1439773 **VAT No:** 730696229
**Estd:** 1979 Private Limited Company
**Line of Business:** Architectural activities
**Export Markets:** Italy & Eastern Europe
**Issued Capital:** £100
**Directors:** I Greves, C A Graham, S Harvey, J C Carter, S Drummond
**Co. Secretary:** Nathan Dhevarajah
**Responsibilities**
**Senior:** Daryl Mylroie (Manager)
**US SIC:** 8911, 7399
**UK SIC:** 83701, 83954
**Auditors:** Kingston Smith LLP
**Bankers:** HSBC Bank plc (40-02-02)

|     | 30-09-13 | 30-09-12 | 30-09-11 |
|-----|----------|----------|----------|
| TO  | 5,301,092 | N/A | 6,281,408 |
| P/L | 697,313 | N/A | 793,184 |
| NW  | 1,466,804 | 1,328,567 | 1,269,115 |
| WC  | 1,345,905 | 1,206,743 | 1,153,061 |

DUNS 23-699-6919    Imp

## Roll-A-Ramp (Europe) Ltd.
Unit 4 Bittacy Business Centre, Bittacy Hill, London NW7 1BA
**Tel:** 020-8346-4477 **Fax:** 02083466002
**Web:** www.rollaramp.co.uk
**Reg No:** 3694430 **Estd:** 2002 Private Limited Company
**Line of Business:** Agents specialising in the sale of particular products or ranges of products not elsewhere classified
**Issued Capital:** £2
**Director:** J S Salmon
**Co. Secretary:** Stuart Lake
**US SIC:** 5199 **UK SIC:** 61900
**Auditors:** Goodmakers

|     | 31-12-13 | 31-12-12 | 31-12-11 |
|-----|----------|----------|----------|
| TA  | 160,882 | 147,203 | 164,309 |
| NW  | 150,166 | 133,256 | 150,438 |
| WC  | 150,166 | 133,256 | 150,438 |

DUNS 23-696-6763

## Roll-Tec Safety Ltd
Middleton Business Park, Morecambe, Lancashire LA3 3FH
**Tel:** 01524-850686 **Fax:** 01534859681
**Web:** www.rolltecsafety.co.uk
**Reg No:** 3691401 **VAT No:** 746399387
**Estd:** 1999 Private Limited Company
**Line of Business:** Manufacture of other general purpose machinery not elsewhere classified
**Trading Style:** Fuelproof
**Issued Capital:** £12
**Directors:** Mrs R A Pilkington, Mrs F E Hargreaves, A R Hargreaves
**Co. Secretary:** Roger Pilkington
**Responsibilities**
**Finance:** Tamar Hodgeson (Senior Finance Administrator)
**Admin:** Tamar Hodgeson (Senior Finance Administrator)
**US SIC:** 3549, 3499
**UK SIC:** 32212, 31694
**Auditors:** Phil Dodgson & Partners Ltd

|     | 31-12-13 | 31-12-12 | 31-12-11 |
|-----|----------|----------|----------|
| TA  | 1,666,061 | 1,657,369 | 1,702,613 |
| NW  | 281,979 | 212,195 | 193,252 |
| WC  | (974,306) | (1,037,470) | (935,862) |

DUNS 23-688-0469

## Rollalong Ltd
(Subsidiary of: Newship Ltd)
Woolsbridge Industrial Estate, Three Legged Cross, Wimborne, Dorset BH21 6SF
**Tel:** 01202-824541
**Web:** www.rollalong.co.uk
**Reg No:** 3683003 **Estd:** 1935 Private Limited Company
**Line of Business:** Construction of commercial buildings
**Issued Capital:** £5,525,000
**Principals:** J D Clarkson (Managing), R J Newman, J W Newman, T J Woodley, M P Sayers, S E Compson
**Co. Secretary:** Andrew Bale
**US SIC:** 1541, 1522
**UK SIC:** 50100
**Auditors:** BDO LLP

**Bankers:** National Westminster Bank Plc (60-13-08)

| | 31-12-13 | 31-12-12 | 31-12-11 |
|---|---|---|---|
| TO | 19,150,000 | 17,086,000 | 30,120,000 |
| P/L | 525,000 | 2,795,000 | 3,029,000 |
| NW | 6,381,000 | 6,474,000 | 6,340,000 |
| WC | 5,945,000 | 5,947,000 | 6,087,000 |
| Emp. | 72 | 83 | 118 |

DUNS 23-352-6693

### Rolled Alloys International Ltd
(**Subsidiary of:** Rolled Alloys Inc.)
Unit 16 Walker Industrial Estate Walker, Road, Blackburn, Lancashire BB1 2QE
**Tel:** 01254-582999 **Fax:** 01254582666
**Web:** www.rolledalloys.co.uk
**Reg No:** 0024157FC **Estd:** 2002 Foreign Company
**Line of Business:** Treatment and coating of metals
**Director:** K Friedman
**Co. Secretary:** Shaun Hussey
**Responsibilities**
**Senior:** ian russell (general manager)
**US SIC:** 3398, 5051
**UK SIC:** 31380, 61200

DUNS 21-025-1609     Imp-Exp

### Rollins & Sons (London) Ltd
Rollins House, 1 Parkway, Harlow Business Park, Green Way, Harlow, Essex CM19 5QF
**Tel:** 01279401570 **Fax:** 01279-401581
**Web:** www.rollins.co.uk
**Reg No:** 0198889 **Estd:** 1866 Private Limited Company
**Line of Business:** Wholesale of hardware, plumbing and heating equipment and supplies
**Export Markets:** Worldwide
**Export Sales:** £1,387,569
**Issued Capital:** £10,000
**Principals:** A J White (Managing), D R Woolard, M G Tompsett, S C Elsom, R R Partridge
**Co. Secretary:** David Woollard
**US SIC:** 5074 **UK SIC:** 61300
**Auditors:** Price Bailey
**Bankers:** HSBC Bank plc (40-04-12)

| | 31-12-13 | 31-12-12 | 31-12-11 |
|---|---|---|---|
| TO | 14,597,771 | 13,804,359 | 12,414,878 |
| P/L | 142,993 | (108,759) | 169,529 |
| NW | 9,086,074 | 8,791,812 | 9,356,294 |
| WC | 7,956,442 | 8,011,135 | 7,767,984 |
| Emp. | 108 | 107 | 106 |

DUNS 28-883-8634

### Rollinson Safeway Ltd
65 Hall Lane, Armley, Leeds, West Yorkshire LS12 1PQ
**Tel:** 01132311355
**Web:** www.airlineconnections.co.uk
**Reg No:** 1210156 **Estd:** 1966 Private Limited Company
**Line of Business:** Taxi operation
**Trading Style:** Airline Connections, Moorside Private Hire
**Issued Capital:** £100
**Managing Director:** P Rollinson
**Co. Secretary:** Michael Joyce
**Responsibilities**
**Senior:** Peter Rollinson (Manager)
**Health & Safety:** Peter Battensby (Facilities Manager)
**Facilities:** Peter Battensby (Facilities Manager)
**US SIC:** 4121, 4142
**UK SIC:** 72200, 72102
**Auditors:** Thorntons
**Bankers:** Yorkshire Bank Plc (05-00-30)

| | 31-05-14 | 31-05-13 | 31-05-12 |
|---|---|---|---|
| TA | 2,626,025 | 2,235,340 | 1,993,318 |
| NW | 1,418,779 | 1,266,637 | 1,178,253 |
| WC | 44,887 | 164,610 | 243,548 |

DUNS 63-458-7299

### Rollit Solicitors
Rowntree Wharf, Navigation Road, York, North Yorkshire YO1 9WE
**Tel:** 01904652233
**Web:** www.rollits.com
**Estd:** 1984 Partnership
**Line of Business:** Solicitors
**Partners:** J Downing, S Trynka
**Responsibilities**
**Senior:** Caroline Hardcastle (Partner), Donna Ingleby (Partner), Tom Morrison (Partner)
**Finance:** Donald Robertson (Finance Director)
**Admin:** Wilf Fowler (Director of Administration)
**US SIC:** 8111 **UK SIC:** 83500
**Employees:** 100

DUNS 23-216-0465

### Rollits
Wilberforce Court, High Street, Hull, North Humberside HU1 1YJ
**Web:** www.rollits.co.uk
**VAT No:** 167886110 **Estd:** 1841 Partnership

**Line of Business:** Solicitors
**Partners:** C Platts, G Coyle, K Benton, Ms C Hedges, T Farrington, G Craft, D Oliver, N Sharf
**Responsibilities**
**Senior:** Sheridan Ball (Partner ? Lawyer/ Mediator), Ralph Coyle (Partner), Fiona Draper (Partner), Caroline Hardcastle (Partner), David Hextall (Partner), Donna Ingleby (Partner), Tom Morrison (Partner), Gerry Morrison (Head of Charities)
**Finance:** Donald Robertson (Financial Director), Donald Robertson (Director of Finance)
**Marketing:** Pat Coyle (Marketing Manager)
**Admin:** Wilf Fowler (Manager)
**IT:** Mike Wasling (IT Systems Manager), Mike Wasling (IT Director)
**HR:** Wilf Fowler (Manager)
**Facilities:** Wilf Fowler (Manager)
**Operations:** Wilf Fowler (Manager)
**Purchasing:** Wilf Fowler (Manager)
**Branches:** Rollits, 4 Bondgate, York, North Yorkshire YO62 5BS
**US SIC:** 8111 **UK SIC:** 83500
**Bankers:** Barclays Bank Plc (20-43-47)
**Employees:** 70

DUNS 21-135-7466

### Rolls-Royce Controls and Data Services Ltd
(**Subsidiary of:** Rolls-Royce Holdings Plc)
Po Box 31, Moor Lane, Derby, Derbyshire DE24 8BJ
**Tel:** 01332 242424 **Fax:** 01332 249936
**Web:** www.aeroenginecontrols.com
**Reg No:** 6686268 **VAT No:** 939396075
**Estd:** 1977 Private Limited Company
**Line of Business:** Other manufacturing not elsewhere classified
**Trading Style:** Aero Engine Controls
**Issued Capital:** £3,000
**Directors:** S A Ricketts, L J Haynes, M A Cowdry, C P Smith, A Wood, M J Mosley
**Co. Secretary:** Mrs Karen Waldron
**Responsibilities**
**Senior:** Stephen Churchhouse (Manager)
**Branches:** Rolls-Royce Controls and Data Services L, 4 Bruce Street, Belfast, Belfast BT2 7LA
**US SIC:** 3999, 3721
**UK SIC:** 49590, 36400
**Auditors:** KPMG LLP

| | 31-12-13 | 31-12-12 | 31-12-11 |
|---|---|---|---|
| TO | 233,400,000 | 211,600,000 | 208,200,000 |
| P/L | 5,100,000 | (3,900,000) | 200,000 |
| NW | 10,800,000 | 5,800,000 | 5,900,000 |
| WC | (40,100,000) | 44,100,000 | (20,900,000) |
| Emp. | 1,444 | 1,355 | 1,359 |

DUNS 36-801-1094

### Rolls Royce Leisure Associates
The Pavilion Moor Lane, Allenton, Allenton, Derby, Derbyshire DE24 9HY
**Tel:** 01332349048
**Web:** www.rolls-royce.com
**Proprietorship**
**Line of Business:** Sports clubs
**US SIC:** 7999 **UK SIC:** 97913
**Employees:** 50

DUNS 21-035-1668

### Rolls-Royce Leisure Association
Moor Lane, Allenton, Derby, Derbyshire DE24 9HY
**Tel:** 01332248027
**Web:** www.rolls-royce.com
**Estd:** 2009 Proprietorship
**Line of Business:** Sports clubs
**Proprietor:** C Bancroft
**US SIC:** 7999 **UK SIC:** 97913
**Employees:** 60

DUNS 34-636-6131     Imp

### Rolls-Royce Marine Electrical Systems Ltd
(**Subsidiary of:** Rolls-Royce Holdings Plc)
Northarbour Road, Portsmouth, Hampshire PO6 3TL
**Tel:** 023-9231-0000 **Fax:** 023-9231-0001
**Web:** www.rolls-royce.com
**Reg No:** 2766255 **Estd:** 1992 Private Limited Company
**Line of Business:** Marine electrical services
**Export Sales:** £1,320,000
**Trading Style:** Rolls-Royce Marine Electrical Systems Limited
**Issued Capital:** £2,500,000
**Directors:** M Toutant, S Slifkin
**Co. Secretary:** Mrs Delrose Goma
**Responsibilities**
**Marketing:** Robin Thuillier (Marketing Director)
**Branches:** Rolls-Royce Marine Electrical Systems Ltd, 10-12 Shield Drive, Manchester M28 2QB

**US SIC:** 3811, 3661
**UK SIC:** 37100, 34410
**Auditors:** KPMG Audit PLC

| | 31-12-13 | 31-12-12 | 31-12-11 |
|---|---|---|---|
| TO | 13,409,000 | 10,978,000 | 14,460,000 |
| P/L | 2,299,000 | 1,317,000 | 505,000 |
| NW | 4,539,000 | 8,671,000 | 7,684,000 |
| WC | 5,712,000 | 9,464,000 | 8,151,000 |
| Emp. | 77 | 76 | 93 |

DUNS 57-021-9634

### Rolls-Royce Military Aero Engines Ltd
(**Subsidiary of:** Rolls-Royce Holdings Plc)
Po Box 3, Bristol, Avon BS34 7QE
**Tel:** 01179791234 **Fax:** 01179797575
**Web:** www.rolls-royce.com
**Reg No:** 2868832 **Estd:** 2009 Private Limited Company
**Line of Business:** Engineers (general)
**Trading Style:** Rolls-Royce
**Issued Capital:** £1
**Directors:** W S Mansfield, Rolls-Royce Directorate Limited
**Co. Secretary:** Rolls-Royce Secretariat Limited
**Responsibilities**
**Senior:** Karen Doble (Marketing Communications)
**Marketing:** Karen Doble (Marketing Communications)
**Sales:** Adam Morton (Head of Business)
**US SIC:** 8911 **UK SIC:** 83701
**Bankers:** National Westminster Bank Plc (50-00-00)

| | 31-12-13 | 31-12-12 | 31-12-11 |
|---|---|---|---|
| TA | 1 | 1 | 1 |
| NW | 1 | 1 | 1 |

DUNS 23-523-6192     Imp

### Rolls-Royce Motor Cars Ltd
(**Subsidiary of:** Bayerische Motoren Werke Ag)
The Drive, Westhampnett, Chichester, West Sussex PO18 0SH
**Tel:** 01243-384000
**Web:** www.rolls-roycemotorcars.com
**Reg No:** 3522604 **Estd:** 1904 Private Limited Company
**Line of Business:** Manufacture of motor vehicles
**Issued Capital:** £41,500,003
**Directors:** T G Mueller-Oetvoes, N Wagner, Sir R Robins, C H March, P Schwarzenbauer
**Co. Secretary:** Ms Gillian Woolley
**Responsibilities**
**Engineering:** John McWilliam (Interior Trim Planner)
**Branches:** Rolls-Royce Motor Cars Ltd, New Era Estate, Oldlands Way, Southern Cross Trading Estate, Bognor Regis, West Sussex PO22 9SE
**US SIC:** 3711, 5511
**UK SIC:** 35101, 65100
**Auditors:** KPMG LLP

| | 31-12-13 | 31-12-12 | 31-12-11 |
|---|---|---|---|
| TO | 376,603,000 | 333,215,000 | 368,674,000 |
| P/L | 17,778,000 | 8,817,000 | 15,049,000 |
| NW | 102,568,000 | 89,562,000 | 84,635,000 |
| WC | 31,376,000 | 23,013,000 | 20,413,000 |
| Emp. | 899 | 826 | 807 |

DUNS 21-090-8687     Exp

### Rolls-Royce Plc
(**Subsidiary of:** Rolls-Royce Holdings Plc)
65 Buckingham Gate, London SW1E 6AT
**Tel:** 020 7222 9020
**Web:** www.rolls-royce.com
**Reg No:** 1003142 **VAT No:** 345886022
**Estd:** 1927 Public Limited Company
**Line of Business:** Manufacture of steam generators, except central heating hot water boilers
**Export Sales:** £1.371E+10
**Issued Capital:** £311,732,471
**Directors:** Mrs L R Cairnie, J F Rishton, L W Booth, C P Smith, H Y Lee, Ms J Staiblin, J M Neill, D W East
**Co. Secretary:** Ms Pamela Coles
**Responsibilities**
**Senior:** Helen Alexander (Business Manager), James Guyette (Director), Ian Strachan (Manager)
**HR:** Tom Brown (Human Resources Director)
**Health & Safety:** John Bullock (Site Manager)
**Facilities:** John Bullock (Site Manager)
**Operations:** John Bullock (Site Manager)
**Branches:** Rolls-Royce Plc, Loaninghill, Broxburn, West Lothian EH52 5DG
**US SIC:** 3443, 8911, 3519
**UK SIC:** 32051, 83701, 32811
**Auditors:** KPMG Audit PLC

**Bankers:** National Westminster Bank Plc (50-00-00)
Following financial data are in thousands

| | 31-12-13 | 31-12-12 | 31-12-11 |
|---|---|---|---|
| TO | 15,513,000 | 12,161,000 | 11,124,000 |
| P/L | 2,019,000 | 2,705,000 | 1,106,000 |
| NW | 2,449,000 | 3,861,000 | 1,795,000 |
| WC | 4,869,000 | 3,119,000 | 1,558,000 |
| Emp. | 55,200 | 42,800 | 40,400 |

DUNS 50-542-2964     Imp-Exp

### Rollstud Ltd
(**Subsidiary of:** Rollstud Holdings Ltd)
Units 5-7, Denmore Industrial Estate, Bridge Of Don, Aberdeen, Aberdeenshire AB23 8JW
**Tel:** 01224425300 **Fax:** 01224-425333
**Web:** www.rollstud.com
**Reg No:** 0124655SC **Estd:** 1990 Private Limited Company
**Line of Business:** Manufacture of fasteners, screw machine products, chains and springs
**Export Markets:** worldwide
**Issued Capital:** £140,133
**Principals:** A W Sinclair (Chairman), A Cadger (Managing)
**Co. Secretary:** Allan Johnston
**Responsibilities**
**Health & Safety:** Brian Gilkes-Imeson (Quality Manager)
**Operations:** Brian Gilkes-Imeson (Quality Manager)
**Branches:** Rollstud Ltd, Unit 25A, Parkview East Industrial Estat, Parkview Road East, Hartlepool, Cleveland TS25 1PG
**US SIC:** 3452 **UK SIC:** 31371
**Auditors:** Deloitte & Touche LLP
**Bankers:** Bank Of Scotland (80-05-14)

| | 31-05-14 | 31-05-13 | 31-05-12 |
|---|---|---|---|
| TO | 16,764,199 | 19,141,404 | 19,438,390 |
| P/L | 1,663,257 | 2,613,897 | 2,232,367 |
| NW | 8,586,617 | 7,390,843 | 5,448,558 |
| WC | 8,120,330 | 6,856,139 | 5,192,434 |
| Emp. | 112 | 116 | 118 |

DUNS 23-285-3296

### Roltech Engineering Ltd
The Acorn Works, Newcastle, Staffordshire ST5 9JA
**Tel:** 01782566523 **Fax:** 01782566274
**Web:** www.roltechengineering.com
**Reg No:** 4366413 **Estd:** 2002 Private Limited Company
**Line of Business:** Other building completion
**Issued Capital:** £100
**Principals:** H F Austin (Managing), S Baldwin, W A Durber
**Co. Secretary:** Anthony Beardmore
**US SIC:** 1799 **UK SIC:** 50000
**Auditors:** Bruce Marshall & Co

| | 31-03-13 | 31-03-12 | 31-03-11 |
|---|---|---|---|
| TO | 11,674,772 | N/A | N/A |
| P/L | 338,177 | N/A | N/A |
| NW | 93,201 | 38,543 | 20,404 |
| WC | 8,675 | (61,337) | (58,686) |
| Emp. | 80 | N/A | N/A |

DUNS 29-278-3610

### Rolton Group Ltd
(**Subsidiary of:** Rolton Holdings Ltd)
Charles Parker Buildings, Midland Road, Higham Ferrers, Rushden, Northamptonshire NN10 8DN
**Tel:** 01933410909 **Fax:** 08707-260222
**Web:** www.rolton.com
**Reg No:** 1547400 **VAT No:** 336255460
**Estd:** 1981 Private Limited Company
**Line of Business:** Engineers (consulting)
**Trading Style:** The Rolton Group, Delrig
**Issued Capital:** £15,147
**Principals:** P E Rolton (Chairman), C A Rose (Managing), G M Waring, C M Evans, D J Rolton, A Chisem
**Co. Secretary:** Cedric Rose
**Branches:** Rolton Group Ltd, Cumberland House, 35 Park Row, Nottingham, Nottinghamshire NG1 6EE
**US SIC:** 8911 **UK SIC:** 83701
**Auditors:** Grant Thornton UK LLP
**Bankers:** Barclays Bank Plc (20-61-51)

| | 30-09-13 | 30-09-12 | 30-09-11 |
|---|---|---|---|
| TA | 1,833,026 | 1,981,394 | 1,512,592 |
| NW | 949,042 | 872,626 | 816,634 |
| WC | 638,532 | 636,632 | 686,286 |

DUNS 36-535-1576     Imp-Exp

### Rom Group Ltd
(**Subsidiary of:** Ipo Wire Holdings Sa)
Eastern Avenue, Lichfield, Staffordshire WS13 6RS
**Tel:** 01543414111 **Fax:** 01543-421605
**Web:** www.romgroup.co.uk
**Reg No:** 3291151 **Estd:** 1996 Private Limited Company
**Line of Business:** Steel fabricators
**Export Markets:** Worldwide
**Export Sales:** £2,259,000
**Issued Capital:** £13,402,795
**Directors:** M L Mckillop, A J Fort, F Mesegue, L S Villares
**Co. Secretary:** Xavier Puig

**Responsibilities**
**Senior:** Raimon Fita (Manager), Robert Holton (Manager), Juan Puiggali (Manager), Francesc Rubio (Manager), Franciso Rubiralta (Manager)
**Health & Safety:** Rick Allwood (Health & Safety Officer)
**Facilities:** Jez Taylor (maintenance Manager)
**Branches:** Rom Group Ltd, Belgrave Street, Bellshill, Lanarkshire ML4 3NP
**US SIC:** 1622, 3441
**UK SIC:** 50200, 32042
**Auditors:** Ernst & Young LLP
**Bankers:** Barclays Bank Plc (20-07-71)

|     | 31-12-13 | 31-12-12 | 31-12-11 |
|-----|----------|----------|----------|
| TO  | 115,859,000 | 117,864,000 | 133,745,000 |
| P/L | 579,000 | 948,000 | 1,224,000 |
| NW  | 10,347,000 | 10,338,000 | 9,935,000 |
| WC  | 19,164,000 | 17,511,000 | 19,002,000 |
| Emp.| 253 | 279 | 288 |

DUNS 21-025-1732     **Imp-Exp**
## Rom Ltd
(**Subsidiary of:** Ipo Wire Holdings Sa)
Eastern Avenue, Lichfield, Staffordshire WS13 6RN
**Tel:** 01543414111 **Fax:** 01543421657
**Web:** www.rom.co.uk
**Reg No:** 0213629 **VAT No:** 792453504
**Estd:** 1926 Private Limited Company
**Line of Business:** Manufacture of other fabricated metal products not elsewhere classified
**Export Markets:** Europe
**Export Sales:** £79,000
**Trading Style:** Rom Group
**Issued Capital:** £20,501
**Directors:** A J Fort, L S Villares, F Mesegue, M L Mckillop
**Co. Secretary:** Xavier Puig
**Responsibilities**
**Sales:** Darren Royce (Area Sales Manager)
**IT:** Brian Livens (Network Manager)
**Health & Safety:** Rick Allwood (Health & Safety Officer)
**Facilities:** Jez Taylor (Head of Maintenance)
**Operations:** Rick Allwood (Health & Safety Officer)
**Branches:** Rom Ltd, Lund Point, Flat 118, London E15 2JP
**US SIC:** 3499, 1611
**UK SIC:** 31694, 50200
**Auditors:** PricewaterhouseCoopers
**Bankers:** Barclays Bank Plc (20-07-71)

|     | 31-12-13 | 31-12-12 | 31-12-11 |
|-----|----------|----------|----------|
| TO  | 77,145,000 | 77,823,000 | 85,151,000 |
| P/L | 1,134,000 | 845,000 | 1,043,000 |
| NW  | 9,924,000 | 9,415,000 | 9,028,000 |
| WC  | 13,689,000 | 11,769,000 | 12,377,000 |
| Emp.| 142 | 157 | 171 |

DUNS 22-168-2185
## Roman Glass Ltd
65 Lower Bristol Road, Green Park, Bath, Avon BA2 3BE
**Tel:** 01225-337433
**Web:** www.romanglass.co.uk
**Reg No:** 4186679 **VAT No:** 771274523
**Estd:** 1974 Private Limited Company
**Line of Business:** Painting and glazing
**Issued Capital:** £11,450
**Directors:** M Cains, W Dagger, C V Williams
**Co. Secretary:** Roger Hudd
**Branches:** Roman Glass Ltd, 2 Buckland Road, Yeovil, Somerset BA21 5EA
**US SIC:** 1721 **UK SIC:** 50400
**Auditors:** Baker Tilly UK Audit LLP
**Bankers:** Lloyds TSB Bank plc (30-00-01)

|     | 30-11-13 | 30-11-12 | 30-11-11 |
|-----|----------|----------|----------|
| TO  | 8,070,871 | 7,919,041 | 7,736,748 |
| P/L | 539,720 | 242,919 | (46,524) |
| NW  | 1,237,204 | 818,438 | 615,004 |
| WC  | 691,759 | 214,305 | (76,903) |
| Emp.| 137 | 142 | 141 |

DUNS 39-743-7740     **Imp**
## Roman Ltd
Whitworth Avenue, Aycliffe Business Park, Newton Aycliffe, County Durham DL5 6YN
**Tel:** 07748702095 **Fax:** 01325328027
**Web:** www.roman-showers.com
**Reg No:** 2184168 **VAT No:** 873307517
**Estd:** 1985 Private Limited Company
**Line of Business:** Manufacture of other fabricated metal products not elsewhere classified
**Export Sales:** £162,797
**Issued Capital:** £235,294
**Principals:** G C Osborne (Managing), J Wright, M G Spink, J M Franks, D C Osborne, Ms P Osborne, S M Teasdale, J Pearson
**Co. Secretary:** Ms Deborah Green
**Responsibilities**
**Senior:** Loraine Henderson (Sales & Marketing Director), Tim Mcnally (Proprietor)
**Marketing:** Loraine Henderson (Sales & Marketing Director)
**Sales:** Loraine Henderson (Sales & Marketing Director)

**IT:** Lawrence English (IT Manager)
**US SIC:** 3499 **UK SIC:** 31694
**Auditors:** KPMG LLP
**Bankers:** The Royal Bank Of Scotland Plc (16-17-31)

|     | 31-03-14 | 31-03-13 | 31-03-12 |
|-----|----------|----------|----------|
| TO  | 11,379,449 | 9,463,615 | 9,075,854 |
| P/L | 80,126 | (320,168) | (536,014) |
| NW  | 2,847,560 | 2,791,983 | 2,959,644 |
| WC  | 2,157,650 | 1,210,725 | 1,263,956 |
| Emp.| 153 | 140 | 142 |

DUNS 29-373-4984     **Imp**
## Roman Originals Plc
5 Wingfoot Close, Erdington, Birmingham, West Midlands B24 9JH
**Tel:** 01213801900
**Web:** www.romanoriginals.co.uk
**Reg No:** 0980843 **VAT No:** 111360723
**Estd:** 1970 Public Limited Company
**Line of Business:** Manufacturers of clothing and fabrics
**Issued Capital:** £190,010
**Managing Director:** E Christodoulou
**Co. Secretary:** Peter Christodoulou
**Responsibilities**
**Senior:** Rick Christo (Manager)
**HR:** Caroline Kisby (Human Resources Manager)
**Purchasing:** Michele Bastock (Senior Merchandiser)
**Engineering:** Pete Christo (Production Manager)
**Branches:** Roman Originals Plc, Unit 7, Festival Park Factory Outlet Shopping Centre, Ebbw Vale, Gwent NP23 8FP
**US SIC:** 2389, 5699
**UK SIC:** 45393, 64500
**Auditors:** Watergates
**Bankers:** Barclays Bank Plc (20-07-71)

|     | 31-12-13 | 31-12-12 | 31-12-11 |
|-----|----------|----------|----------|
| TO  | 35,151,044 | 28,429,335 | 22,838,534 |
| P/L | 3,161,279 | 1,450,884 | (396,024) |
| NW  | 7,275,087 | 5,148,524 | 4,542,546 |
| WC  | 3,894,101 | 2,874,300 | 2,644,296 |
| Emp.| 626 | 433 | 374 |

DUNS 50-571-7264
## Romanes & Paterson Ltd
(**Subsidiary of:** The Edinburgh Woollen Mill (Group) Ltd)
62 Princes Street, Edinburgh, Midlothian EH2 2DF
**Tel:** 01312254966
**Web:** www.ewm.co.uk
**Reg No:** 0126056SC **Estd:** 1990 Private Limited Company
**Line of Business:** Manufacture of other wearing apparel and accessories not elsewhere classified
**Issued Capital:** £2
**Director:** K B Lee
**Co. Secretary:** Ms June Carruthers
**US SIC:** 2389 **UK SIC:** 45393
**Bankers:** The Royal Bank Of Scotland Plc (83-24-13)

|     | 01-03-14 | 02-03-13 | 25-03-12 |
|-----|----------|----------|----------|
| NW  | (102,510) | (102,510) | (102,510) |

DUNS 21-824-7428
## Romanes Media Group Ltd
Carus House 201 Dumbarton Road, Clydebank, Dunbartonshire G81 4XJ
**Tel:** 01189553333
**Web:** www.romanesmediagroup.co.uk
**Reg No:** 0417529SC **Estd:** 2012 Private Limited Company
**Line of Business:** Other business activities not elsewhere classified
**Issued Capital:** £1,585
**Directors:** G T Morrison, G J Faulds, C J Allwood
**Co. Secretary:** Graham Faulds
**US SIC:** 7399 **UK SIC:** 83954

|     | 28-09-13 | 29-09-12 |
|-----|----------|----------|
| TO  | 18,105,575 | 9,184,665 |
| P/L | 1,640,351 | 266,167 |
| NW  | (15,379,159) | (16,553,963) |
| WC  | 462,719 | (289,965) |
| Emp.| 295 | 293 |

DUNS 21-554-5372
## Romans Group
33-34 Market Place, Reading, Berkshire RG1 2DE
**Tel:** 01189538710
**Web:** www.romans.co.uk
**Estd:** 2001 Proprietorship
**Line of Business:** Estate agents
**Proprietor:** J Roberts
**Branches:** Romans Group, Hnleazes Ho, 13 Harbury Rd, Bristol, Avon BS9 4PN
**US SIC:** 6531 **UK SIC:** 83400
**Employees:** 50

DUNS 39-711-8290
## The Romans Group (Uk) Ltd
(**Subsidiary of:** Romans 1 Ltd)
23 Market Place, Wokingham, Berkshire RG40 1AP
**Tel:** 01189743500 **Fax:** 01189-743528
**Web:** www.romans.co.uk
**Reg No:** 2161874 **Estd:** 1987 Private Limited Company
**Line of Business:** Real estate agencies
**Trading Style:** Romans Management
**Issued Capital:** £11,951
**Directors:** P Fuller, P Loverdos, T Shelford, V Courtney, P A Coles, M Salter, M E Palmer
**Co. Secretary:** Michael Palmer
**Responsibilities**
**Senior:** Matthew Witney (Manager)
**Branches:** The Romans Group (Uk) Ltd, 246 High Street, Crowthorne, Berkshire RG45 7AP
**US SIC:** 6531 **UK SIC:** 83400
**Auditors:** Deloitte & Touche
**Bankers:** National Westminster Bank Plc (60-03-23)

|     | 31-12-13 | 31-12-12 | 31-12-11 |
|-----|----------|----------|----------|
| TO  | 32,067,027 | 27,055,581 | 23,562,724 |
| P/L | 1,597,344 | 1,244,053 | 2,865,578 |
| NW  | 10,815,191 | 8,883,792 | 9,521,402 |
| WC  | 7,594,169 | 5,909,392 | 7,067,278 |
| Emp.| 472 | 442 | 338 |

DUNS 22-609-7939
## Romans of Farnborough Ltd
105 Farnborough Road, Farnborough, Hampshire GU14 6TL
**Tel:** 01252518185
**Web:** www.baronsbmw.co.uk
**Reg No:** 0456992 **Estd:** 1984 Private Limited Company
**Line of Business:** Business services
**Director:** R Leach
**US SIC:** 5511 **UK SIC:** 65100
**Employees:** 112

DUNS 23-715-7169
## Roma's
4-6 Regent Street, Newtownards, Co Down BT23 4LH
**Tel:** 028-9181-2841
**Web:** www.romas.co.uk
**Estd:** 1993 Proprietorship
**Line of Business:** Managed public houses and bars
**Proprietor:** J Mcerlean
**Responsibilities**
**Senior:** John Mccerlean (Partner)
**US SIC:** 5812 **UK SIC:** 66110
**Employees:** 49

DUNS 50-320-8084     **Imp-Exp**
## Romax Technology Limited.
Romax Technology Centre University Of, Nottingham Innovation Park, Triumph Road, Nottingham, Nottinghamshire NG7 2TU
**Tel:** 01159-518800
**Web:** www.romaxtech.com
**Reg No:** 2345696 **Estd:** 1989 Private Limited Company
**Line of Business:** Power transmission equipment
**Export Markets:** Worldwide
**Export Sales:** £12,575,000
**Issued Capital:** £101,577
**Principals:** P ( Poon (Managing), Ms N J Mccabe, R Irons, A Poon, P J Magowan, M B Wells
**Co. Secretary:** Fil Administration Limited
**Responsibilities**
**Senior:** Xiaobing Hu (Country Director (China)), Younsu Park (Manager), Michael Platten (Manager)
**Marketing:** Rohini Syal (Marketing Campaign Manager)
**Sales:** Grace Liu (Business Development Executive), Nigel Parlor (European Sales Manager - Fleet)
**IT:** Sean Akers (It Manager), Xiaoqin Ma (Head of Technology Development)
**Fleet:** Nigel Parlor (European Sales Manager - Fleet)
**Engineering:** Michael Platten (Manager), Dave Scott (Lead Design Engineer)
**US SIC:** 8911, 8922, 7379
**UK SIC:** 83701, 94000, 83940
**Auditors:** Deloitte LLP
**Bankers:** National Westminster Bank Plc (54-10-23)

|     | 31-03-14 | 31-03-13 | 31-03-12 |
|-----|----------|----------|----------|
| TO  | 15,724,000 | 12,515,000 | 12,154,000 |
| P/L | (1,491,000) | (3,518,000) | (1,566,000) |
| NW  | 4,513,000 | 6,082,000 | 9,343,000 |
| WC  | 3,293,000 | 5,085,000 | 8,707,000 |
| Emp.| 218 | 212 | 190 |

DUNS 21-768-2452
## Romec
Po Box 87, Warrington, Cheshire WA3 6YZ
**Tel:** 01925847600
**Web:** www.romec.co.uk
**Estd:** 2011
**Line of Business:** Facilities management services
**US SIC:** 7399 **UK SIC:** 83954
**Employees:** 50

DUNS 22-217-5981     **Imp**
## Romec Ltd
(**Subsidiary of:** Royal Mail Plc)
Applicon House, Exchange Street, Stockport, Cheshire SK3 0EE
**Tel:** 0161-475-3800
**Web:** www.romec.com
**Reg No:** 4235613 **Estd:** 1989 Private Limited Company
**Line of Business:** National post activities
**Issued Capital:** £102
**Directors:** M O Devanny, R L Dargue, M J Prince, G M Simpson, Mrs L Williamson, W J Petrie
**Co. Secretary:** Miss Claudine O'Connor
**Responsibilities**
**Senior:** Wendy Pollit (Organisation Development Manag)
**Finance:** John Marlor (Financial Director)
**IT:** Stuart Keating (Senior IS Manager)
**Branches:** Romec Ltd, North House, St. Edwards Way, Romford, Essex RM1 3PP
**US SIC:** 7399, 7393, 6531, 7349
**UK SIC:** 83954, 83400, 92300
**Auditors:** Deloitte & Touche LLP
**Bankers:** National Westminster Bank Plc (01-00-61)

|     | 31-03-14 | 31-03-13 | 31-03-12 |
|-----|----------|----------|----------|
| TO  | 193,335,000 | 159,497,000 | 139,193,000 |
| P/L | 7,015,000 | 1,381,000 | (14,549,000) |
| NW  | 8,309,000 | 3,004,000 | 2,879,000 |
| WC  | 10,555,000 | 5,430,000 | 3,544,000 |
| Emp.| 3,965 | 3,910 | 4,087 |

DUNS 21-729-2143
## Romford Stadium Ltd
(**Subsidiary of:** Gcg Manager S.A. Luxco Sca)
Ryan Court, 152-162 London Road, Romford, Essex RM7 9QP
**Tel:** 01708740296
**Web:** www.coral.co.uk
**Reg No:** 0307446 **Estd:** 1935 Private Limited Company
**Line of Business:** Stadiums and sports grounds
**Issued Capital:** £54,353
**Directors:** Gala Coral Nominees Limited, P Bowtell, R W Templeman, C A Leaver, Gala Coral Properties Limited
**Co. Secretary:** Gala Coral Secretaries Limited
**Responsibilities**
**Senior:** Carol Chown-Smith (General Manager)
**US SIC:** 7999 **UK SIC:** 97913
**Auditors:** Ernst & Young
**Bankers:** Barclays Bank Plc (20-12-75)

|     | 28-09-13 | 29-09-12 | 24-09-11 |
|-----|----------|----------|----------|
| TO  | 6,202,000 | 6,298,000 | 6,256,000 |
| P/L | (791,000) | (1,123,000) | 169,000 |
| NW  | 5,694,000 | 6,370,000 | 7,325,000 |
| WC  | 11,178,000 | 10,064,000 | 8,605,000 |
| Emp.| 182 | 216 | 211 |

DUNS 21-914-0329
## Romford Ymca
29 Rush Green Road, Romford, Essex RM7 0PH
**Tel:** 01708766211
**Web:** www.romfordymca.org
**Reg No:** 6102037 **Estd:** 2007 Private Company Limited By Guarantee
**Line of Business:** Hostels
**Directors:** A M Dyckhoff, P W Johnson, D L Potter, M D Howse, A Khan, Mrs V Clark, Mrs S Unsworth-Tomlinson, E J Galgano
**Co. Secretary:** Paul Setterfield
**Responsibilities**
**Senior:** Dave Ball (Chief Executive Officer), Faye Hoque (Director), Gaggandip Sandhu (Director)
**US SIC:** 7021 **UK SIC:** 66500
**Bankers:** National Westminster Bank Plc (60-06-08)

|     | 31-03-14 | 31-03-13 | 31-03-12 |
|-----|----------|----------|----------|
| TO  | 3,227,534 | 3,097,637 | 2,978,131 |
| P/L | 34,792 | 189,960 | (39,804) |
| NW  | 4,299,625 | 4,215,326 | 3,909,868 |
| WC  | 577,132 | 620,860 | 489,022 |
| Emp.| 71 | 70 | 70 |

DUNS 73-447-0409
## Romica Engineering Ltd
Suite 1 Minster House, 23 Flemming Gate, Beverley, North Humberside HU17 0NT
**Tel:** 01482853884 **Fax:** 01482853884
**Web:** www.romica.co.uk
**Reg No:** 4711361 **VAT No:** 830023190

**Estd:** 2005 Private Limited Company
**Line of Business:** Manufacture of lifting and handling equipment
**Issued Capital:** £100
**Director:** M Turner
**Co. Secretary:** Robert Turner
**US SIC:** 3534 **UK SIC:** 32553
**Auditors:** Sadofskys Chartered Accountants

|  | 31-03-14 | 31-03-13 | 31-03-12 |
|---|---|---|---|
| TA | 1,401,258 | 1,147,177 | 892,541 |
| NW | 1,016,647 | 900,199 | 672,712 |
| WC | 754,985 | 627,980 | 407,346 |

DUNS 22-294-7140
## Romie Care Services Ltd
50 High Street, Erdington, Birmingham, West Midlands B23 6RH
**Tel:** 01213734300
**Reg No:** 4312670 **Estd:** 2001 Private Limited Company
**Line of Business:** Other human health activities
**Issued Capital:** £20,000
**Director:** Dr H O Adenekan
**Co. Secretary:** Benjamin Awunor
**US SIC:** 8091 **UK SIC:** 95200

|  | 31-03-14 | 31-03-13 | 31-03-12 |
|---|---|---|---|
| TA | 438,739 | 306,960 | 378,403 |
| NW | 177,632 | 195,098 | 193,120 |
| WC | 154,645 | 196,478 | 183,587 |

DUNS 21-319-1237
## The Romilly
9-15 Romilly Road, Cardiff, South Glamorgan CF5 1FH
**Tel:** 029-2023-1903
**Web:** www.romillynursinghome.co.uk
**Estd:** 1979 Proprietorship
**Line of Business:** Nursing homes
**Partners:** J Duffield, Mrs P Duffield
**US SIC:** 8051 **UK SIC:** 95100
**Employees:** 75

DUNS 22-629-2605
## Romney Hythe & Dymchurch Railway Plc
New Romney Station, 2 Littlestone Road, Littlestone, New Romney, Kent TN28 8PL
**Tel:** 01797362353
**Web:** www.rhdr.org.uk
**Reg No:** 1031179 **Estd:** 1927 Public Limited Company
**Line of Business:** Train stations
**Trading Style:** R H D R
**Issued Capital:** £504,958
**Principals:** Sir W H Mcalpine (Chairman), K L Richardson, J G Butt, D W Martin, M G Boatman, F L Walton
**Co. Secretary:** Daniel Martin
**Responsibilities**
**Senior:** John Snell (Manager)
**Branches:** Romney Hythe & Dymchurch Railway Plc, New Romney Station, 2 Littlestone Road, New Romney, Kent TN28 8PL
**US SIC:** 4011 **UK SIC:** 71000
**Auditors:** Finn-Kelcey & Chapman
**Bankers:** Lloyds TSB Bank plc (30-90-28)

|  | 31-12-13 | 31-12-12 | 31-12-11 |
|---|---|---|---|
| TO | 2,043,268 | 1,944,564 | 1,954,066 |
| P/L | 125,823 | 129,079 | 74,123 |
| NW | 3,659,723 | 3,572,424 | 3,481,314 |
| WC | 1,076,867 | 860,613 | 729,706 |
| Emp. | 59 | 66 | 69 |

DUNS 23-441-0525
## Romney Tavern
The Parade, Greatstone, New Romney, Kent TN28 8RN
**Tel:** 01797363877
**Web:** www.park-resorts.com
**Estd:** 1964 Proprietorship
**Line of Business:** Other tourist or short-stay accommodation
**Proprietor:** Mrs K Cooper
**Responsibilities**
**Senior:** Samuel Gosden (General Manager)
**US SIC:** 7021 **UK SIC:** 66500
**Employees:** 92

DUNS 76-638-1065                          Imp-Exp
## Romo (Holdings) Ltd
Lowmoor Road, Kirkby-In-Ashfield, Sutton-In-Ashfield, Nottinghamshire NG17 7DE
**Tel:** 01623750005 **Fax:** 08451297071
**Web:** www.romo.com
**Reg No:** 2583111 **Estd:** 1991 Private Limited Company
**Line of Business:** Textile merchants
**Export Sales:** £48,714,000
**Trading Style:** Romo Fabrics
**Issued Capital:** £3,266,404
**Principals:** R A Mould (Managing), J F Mould, L P Biddulph, Ms E D Mould, Ms F M Mould
**Co. Secretary:** Neil Sexton

**Responsibilities**
**Senior:** Victor Fairbanks (Manager), Cicely Mould (Chairman of the Board and Dire), Lynn Stone (Manager)
**Finance:** Lynn Stone (Manager)
**Sales:** David Canovan (Sales Director)
**HR:** Lynn Stone (Manager)
**Purchasing:** David Canovan (Sales Director)
**US SIC:** 5133, 6519
**UK SIC:** 61600, 85000
**Auditors:** PricewaterhouseCoopers
**Bankers:** Barclays Bank Plc (20-55-62)

|  | 31-12-13 | 31-12-12 | 31-12-11 |
|---|---|---|---|
| TO | 70,635,000 | 64,355,000 | 61,612,000 |
| P/L | 10,013,000 | 7,614,000 | 8,651,000 |
| NW | 48,571,000 | 43,633,000 | 40,213,000 |
| WC | 39,114,000 | 36,437,000 | 34,968,000 |
| Emp. | 312 | 311 | 289 |

DUNS 22-008-2874
## Rompa Ltd
(Subsidiary of: Flaghouse Inc.)
Goyt Side Road, Chesterfield, Derbyshire S40 2PH
**Tel:** 01246-211777
**Web:** www.rompa.com
**Reg No:** 4011415 **VAT No:** 814513257
**Estd:** 2000 Private Limited Company
**Line of Business:** Retail sale via mail order house
**Trading Style:** Rompa, Snoezelen, Everysense
**Issued Capital:** £223,529
**Directors:** G A Carmel, D K Carmel, G A Corps, Mrs E M Kettlewood, Ms D C Hartley
**US SIC:** 5961, 5399
**UK SIC:** 65600
**Auditors:** Grant Thornton UK LLP
**Bankers:** National Westminster Bank Plc (54-41-34)

|  | 31-12-13 | 31-12-12 | 31-12-11 |
|---|---|---|---|
| TO | 6,290,000 | 6,100,000 | 6,560,000 |
| P/L | 272,000 | 49,000 | 277,000 |
| NW | 927,000 | 677,000 | 902,000 |
| WC | 710,000 | 561,000 | 973,000 |
| Emp. | 52 | 50 | 46 |

DUNS 29-165-1362
## Ron & Jill Pladdys Ltd
Brandon Road, Coventry, West Midlands CV3 2AN
**Tel:** 02476440444 **Fax:** 024-7665-2696
**Reg No:** 1805144 **Estd:** 1954 Private Limited Company
**Line of Business:** Management activities of holding companies
**Issued Capital:** £84,144
**Managing Director:** R F Pladdys
**Co. Secretary:** Scott Pladdys
**US SIC:** 6711 **UK SIC:** 83962
**Auditors:** Fox Evans
**Bankers:** Barclays Bank Plc (20-23-55)

|  | 31-12-13 | 31-12-12 | 31-12-11 |
|---|---|---|---|
| TA | 932,743 | 1,026,480 | 1,051,039 |
| NW | 904,493 | 998,983 | 1,025,163 |
| WC | 186,607 | 260,585 | 234,985 |

DUNS 21-815-1900
## Ron Brooks Ltd
The Gateway, Derby Road, Ilkeston, Derbyshire DE7 5FH
**Tel:** 01159302885 **Fax:** 01159-898519
**Web:** www.toyota.co.uk
**Reg No:** 0730852 **VAT No:** 116282291
**Estd:** 1962 Private Limited Company
**Line of Business:** New & used motor vehicle dealers
**Issued Capital:** £20,000
**Principals:** K C Slack (Managing), P Stephenson, Mrs E M Brooks
**Co. Secretary:** Jonathan Hagues
**Responsibilities**
**Sales:** Andrew Hoult (Sales Manager)
**Admin:** Angela Leatherland (Office Manager)
**HR:** Angela Leatherland (Office Manager), Adam Lyons (Group HR Manager)
**Purchasing:** Andrew Hoult (Sales Manager)
**US SIC:** 5511, 5521, 7539, 5531
**UK SIC:** 65100, 67100
**Auditors:** Blythens
**Bankers:** HSBC Bank plc (40-25-29)

|  | 30-06-14 | 30-06-13 | 30-06-12 |
|---|---|---|---|
| TO | 25,823,724 | 26,220,928 | 22,651,967 |
| P/L | 459,457 | 807,923 | 409,542 |
| NW | 4,277,590 | 4,022,164 | 3,464,671 |
| WC | 1,601,997 | 1,852,722 | 1,544,172 |
| Emp. | 93 | 90 | 93 |

DUNS 21-259-5730                          Imp
## Ron Chalker ( the Potato Man ) Ltd
Mellor Street, Rochdale, Lancashire OL11 1PF
**Tel:** 01706-644384 **Fax:** 01706-639926
**Web:** www.ronchalker.co.uk
**Reg No:** 1069111 **VAT No:** 145442576
**Estd:** 1972 Private Limited Company

**Line of Business:** Wholesale of fruit and vegetables
**Issued Capital:** £1,200
**Managing Director:** C J Chalker
**Responsibilities**
**Senior:** Kevin Ramsden (General Manager)
**Finance:** Kevin Ramsden (General Manager)
**IT:** Kevin Ramsden (General Manager)
**HR:** Lauren Chalker (Human Resources Manager), Beverley Chalker (Human Resources Manager)
**Health & Safety:** Kevin Ramsden (General Manager)
**Facilities:** Kevin Ramsden (General Manager)
**Operations:** Kevin Ramsden (General Manager)
**US SIC:** 5148 **UK SIC:** 61700
**Auditors:** Wyatt Morris Golland & Co
**Bankers:** National Westminster Bank Plc (01-07-44)

|  | 31-10-13 | 31-10-12 | 31-10-11 |
|---|---|---|---|
| TA | 1,064,477 | 993,440 | 2,806,942 |
| NW | 415,396 | 277,808 | 1,287,103 |
| WC | 205,251 | 52,460 | 1,003,849 |

DUNS 22-613-4054
## Ron Darch & Sons Ltd
35 Oxford Road, Pen Mill Trading Estate, Yeovil, Somerset BA21 5HR
**Tel:** 01935473302
**Web:** www.darchoil.co.uk
**Reg No:** 1702395 **VAT No:** 186031667
**Estd:** 1983 Private Limited Company
**Line of Business:** Other treatment of petroleum products (excluding petrochemicals manufacture)
**Issued Capital:** £160
**Directors:** J Darch, A T Darch, Mrs Y W Darch, N Darch, A R Darch, B R Darch, J P Darch, S L Darch
**Co. Secretary:** Simon Darch
**Responsibilities**
**Finance:** Rosemary Hopkins (Finance Director)
**Branches:** Ron Darch & Sons Ltd, 13A Buckland Road, Yeovil, Somerset BA21 5HA
**US SIC:** 2999 **UK SIC:** 11150
**Auditors:** Ivan Rendall & Co
**Bankers:** Barclays Bank Plc (20-99-40)

|  | 31-07-13 | 31-07-12 | 31-07-11 |
|---|---|---|---|
| TO | 26,953,129 | 22,431,227 | 20,768,473 |
| P/L | 1,017,719 | (235,060) | 733,574 |
| NW | 4,418,987 | 3,696,323 | 3,923,195 |
| WC | 2,951,917 | 2,195,115 | 2,480,829 |
| Emp. | 53 | 54 | 53 |

DUNS 22-195-9088
## Ron Smith (Recycling) Ltd
St Albans Farm, Staines Road, North Feltham, Feltham, Middlesex TW14 0HH
**Tel:** 02085703424 **Fax:** 02088140320
**Web:** www.ronsmithrecycling.co.uk
**Reg No:** 4213892 **VAT No:** 776271306
**Estd:** 2001 Private Limited Company
**Line of Business:** Collection and treatment of other waste
**Issued Capital:** £100
**Director:** I Hutchins
**Co. Secretary:** Miss Katie Hutchins
**Responsibilities**
**Senior:** Linda Hutchins (Manager)
**US SIC:** 4953, 4959
**UK SIC:** 92110
**Auditors:** Stiles & Co

|  | 31-05-13 | 31-05-12 | 31-05-11 |
|---|---|---|---|
| TO | 7,288,453 | 7,130,304 | 9,635,354 |
| P/L | 441,812 | 215,059 | 211,322 |
| NW | 1,549,868 | 1,474,001 | 1,588,922 |
| WC | (553,067) | (798,604) | (221,308) |
| Emp. | 82 | 82 | 82 |

DUNS 21-736-8737                          Exp
## Ronacrete Ltd
Ronac House, Flex Meadow, Harlow, Essex CM19 5TD
**Tel:** 01279-638700
**Web:** www.ronacrete.co.uk
**Reg No:** 0947913 **VAT No:** 918581007
**Estd:** 1969 Private Limited Company
**Line of Business:** Manufacturers and distributiors of concrete and mortar
**Export Markets:** Hong Kong, China, Singapore, Malaysia
**Export Sales:** £7,119,234
**Issued Capital:** £100,000
**Directors:** D N Osen, Mrs R D Freedman
**Co. Secretary:** Gary Sharman
**Responsibilities**
**Senior:** Maurice Osen (Chairman)
**Sales:** Daren Chambers (Sales Manager), Mike Rhodes (Sales Manager)
**Branches:** Ronacrete Ltd, 13 Lamson Rd Off Ferry La, Rainham, Essex RM13 9YY
**US SIC:** 3273 **UK SIC:** 24360
**Auditors:** Harris Lipman LLP

**Bankers:** National Westminster Bank Plc (60-01-38)

|  | 31-03-14 | 31-03-13 | 31-03-12 |
|---|---|---|---|
| TO | 9,435,972 | 11,457,316 | 9,198,954 |
| P/L | 264,138 | 516,576 | (89,461) |
| NW | 2,688,028 | 2,673,538 | 2,157,538 |
| WC | 2,203,143 | 2,420,018 | 1,912,553 |
| Emp. | 116 | 116 | 113 |

DUNS 21-773-2552
## Ronald Gibson House
Ronald Gibson House, 236 Burntwood Lane, London SW17 0AN
**Tel:** 02088779998
**Web:** www.brendoncare.org.uk
**Estd:** 2011 Proprietorship
**Line of Business:** Nursing homes
**Proprietor:** Mrs E Day
**Responsibilities**
**Senior:** Ann Hinds (Care Centre Manager), Victor Njoku (Care Home Manager)
**US SIC:** 8051 **UK SIC:** 95100
**Employees:** 90

DUNS 28-890-8668
## Ronald Hull Jnr. Ltd
Mangham Road, Parkgate, Rotherham, South Yorkshire S62 6EF
**Tel:** 01709524115 **Fax:** 01709-710110
**Web:** www.ronhull.co.uk
**Reg No:** 1278500 **Estd:** 1976 Private Limited Company
**Line of Business:** Waste disposal
**Export Sales:** £2,954,901
**Trading Style:** Ron Hull Group
**Issued Capital:** £50,000
**Principals:** R Hull (Managing), D J Hull, N P Hull, M R Hull
**Co. Secretary:** Ms Vivien Hull
**Responsibilities**
**Purchasing:** Paul Furney (Purchasing Manager)
**US SIC:** 4953, 3031
**UK SIC:** 92110, 48123
**Auditors:** Grant Thornton U K LLP
**Bankers:** National Westminster Bank Plc (56-00-66)

|  | 31-01-14 | 31-01-13 | 31-01-12 |
|---|---|---|---|
| TO | 33,994,093 | 40,848,102 | 52,591,478 |
| P/L | 1,517,932 | 1,006,105 | 1,619,805 |
| NW | 15,178,500 | 13,835,164 | 12,983,347 |
| WC | 6,802,811 | 5,018,998 | 5,223,664 |
| Emp. | 143 | 144 | 126 |

DUNS 21-715-7593
## Ronald Martin (Butchers) Ltd
Pennygillam Way, Pennygillam Industrial Estate, Launceston, Cornwall PL15 7ED
**Tel:** 01566-773526
**Reg No:** 0391405 **Estd:** 1944 Private Limited Company
**Line of Business:** Cash and carry wholesalers
**Trading Style:** Martins Cash & Carry, Bidders W A & Sons
**Issued Capital:** £12,948
**Principals:** C R Martin (Managing), Ms M Martin
**Co. Secretary:** Richard Martin
**US SIC:** 5199 **UK SIC:** 61900
**Auditors:** Northcott Trumfield
**Bankers:** HSBC Bank plc (40-27-04)

|  | 31-12-13 | 31-12-12 | 31-12-11 |
|---|---|---|---|
| TO | 7,835,017 | 8,217,719 | 7,755,240 |
| P/L | 31,372 | 131,697 | 115,567 |
| NW | 2,463,934 | 2,498,815 | 2,452,887 |
| WC | 1,328,967 | 1,355,523 | 1,317,969 |
| Emp. | 49 | 45 | 43 |

DUNS 39-945-9072
## Ronald McDonald House Charities (U K)
11-59 High Road, East Finchley, London N2 8AW
**Tel:** 08448400844
**Web:** www.rmhc.org.uk
**Reg No:** 2252337 **VAT No:** 371057172
**Estd:** 1988 Private Company Limited By Guarantee
**Line of Business:** Other tourist or short-stay accommodation
**Trading Style:** Rmhc
**Directors:** Ms P Hurst, S R Kirk, R P Forte, W D Anderson, Dr A A Ohrling, S Tomlin, Mrs A Sirkhot, Ms S K Hunsdale
**Co. Secretary:** Mrs Anne Ward
**Responsibilities**
**Senior:** Jeffrey Fergus (Director), Henry Trickey (Director)
**Finance:** Bhavna Rana (Fundraising Assistant)
**Branches:** Ronald Mcdonald House Charities (U K), 11 Caldecot Road, London SE5 9RL
**US SIC:** 7021, 6732
**UK SIC:** 66500, 83100
**Auditors:** Ernst & Young LLP

**Bankers:** Barclays Bank Plc (20-00-00)

| | 31-12-13 | 31-12-12 | 31-12-11 |
|---|---|---|---|
| TO | 9,088,021 | 7,448,664 | 6,657,232 |
| P/L | 4,258,383 | 2,890,531 | 3,272,654 |
| NW | 29,647,028 | 25,388,645 | 22,498,114 |
| WC | 6,785,885 | 5,818,275 | 8,552,807 |
| Emp. | 48 | 44 | 35 |

**DUNS 23-282-5679**

## Ronaldsway Aircraft (Holdings) Ltd

(Subsidiary of: Rlc Engineering Group Ltd)
Ballasalla, Douglas, Isle of Man IM9 2RY
**Tel:** 01624-820555
**Web:** www.rlc-ronaldsway.com
**Reg No:** 0054135M **Estd:** 1991 Private
Limited Company
**Line of Business:** Management activities of
holding companies
**Issued Capital:** £49,750
**Director:** Ms J P Holt
**Co. Secretary:** George Moore
**US SIC:** 6711, 3721
**UK SIC:** 83962, 36400
**Employees:** 300

**DUNS 50-472-3024**    Imp

## Rondanini U K Ltd

22 Bessemer Park, London SE24 0HG
**Tel:** 02077386669 **Fax:** 020-7738-5917
**Web:** www.rondanini.co.uk
**Reg No:** 2451201 **VAT No:** 548059521
**Estd:** 1989 Private Limited Company
**Line of Business:** Canteens and catering
**Export Sales:** £2,376,962
**Issued Capital:** £100,001
**Director:** A De Vito
**Co. Secretary:** Jason De Vito
**Responsibilities**
**Marketing:** Tereza Breckova (Customer
Insight Manager)
**US SIC:** 5812, 5149
**UK SIC:** 66110, 61700
**Auditors:** Proto & Co

| | 31-03-14 | 31-03-13 | 31-03-12 |
|---|---|---|---|
| TO | 64,761,782 | 60,398,205 | 60,378,706 |
| P/L | 2,324,871 | 2,296,835 | 2,190,187 |
| NW | 8,606,279 | 7,504,558 | 6,959,683 |
| WC | 4,693,159 | 4,172,487 | 3,278,700 |
| Emp. | 90 | 89 | 114 |

**DUNS 21-717-7559**

## Ronez Ltd

(Subsidiary of: Holcim U K Holdings Ltd)
Lane Route Du Nord, St John, Jersey,
Channel Islands JE3 4AR
**Tel:** 01534867200 **Fax:** 01534-864450
**Web:** www.ronez.com
**Reg No:** 0000041J **Estd:** 1921 Private
Limited Company
**Line of Business:** Manufacture of ready-
mixed concrete
**Issued Capital:** £2,500,000
**Principals:** A L Shearer (Chairman),
D F Gray (Managing), A Ayres, G R Shove,
V J Hansford
**Co. Secretary:** John Tanguy
**Responsibilities**
**Senior:** Mike Osbourne (Manager)
**Sales:** Carlton Moody (Sales Manager)
**HR:** Mike Osbourne (Manager)
**Health & Safety:** Mike Osbourne (Manager)
**Facilities:** Mike Osbourne (Manager)
**Operations:** Mike Osbourne (Manager)
**Branches:** Ronez Ltd, Les Vardes Quarry,
Guernsey, Channel Islands GY1 1BG
**US SIC:** 3273 **UK SIC:** 24360
**Employees:** 327

**DUNS 21-017-6195**

## Roodlane Medical Ltd

(Subsidiary of: Hca Holdings Inc.)
242 Marylebone Road, London NW1 6JL
**Tel:** 02077097171 **Fax:** 020-7377-4647
**Web:** www.roodlane.co.uk
**Reg No:** 6395903 **Estd:** 2007 Private
Limited Company
**Line of Business:** Doctors
**Issued Capital:** £50,036
**Directors:** J R Bugos, M T Neeb, J Reay,
Dr H Trakoshis, Dr G A Macleod
**Co. Secretary:** Mrs Jasy Loyal
**Branches:** Roodlane Medical Ltd, 2 More
London Riverside, London SE1 2AP
**US SIC:** 8011 **UK SIC:** 95300
**Bankers:** Barclays Bank Plc (20-03-80)

| | 31-12-13 | 31-12-12 | 31-12-11 |
|---|---|---|---|
| TO | 16,909,000 | 12,381,000 | 11,450,000 |
| P/L | 586,000 | (80,000) | (485,000) |
| NW | 2,227,000 | 1,585,000 | 1,379,000 |
| WC | 1,464,000 | 809,000 | 264,000 |
| Emp. | 183 | 158 | 136 |

**DUNS 39-974-4085**

## Roof Edge Fabrications Ltd

144-146 Dalsetter Avenue, Glasgow,
Lanarkshire G15 8TE
**Web:** www.roofedge.co.uk
**Reg No:** 0111926SC **Estd:** 1988 Private
Limited Company
**Line of Business:** Manufacture of other
fabricated metal products not elsewhere
classified
**Issued Capital:** £100
**Directors:** N Russ, C Milburn
**Responsibilities**
**Senior:** Peter Allan (Manager)
**Finance:** Angela Allan (Manager)
**Health & Safety:** Peter Allan (Manager)
**Facilities:** Peter Allan (Manager)
**US SIC:** 3499, 8911
**UK SIC:** 31694, 83701
**Auditors:** Murray & Co
**Bankers:** Bank Of Scotland (80-07-65)

| | 31-07-13 | 31-07-12 | 31-07-11 |
|---|---|---|---|
| TA | 397,646 | 460,034 | 408,771 |
| NW | 310,803 | 337,863 | 310,071 |
| WC | 283,424 | 318,445 | 281,968 |

**DUNS 21-304-1916**

## Roof Shop Ltd

(Subsidiary of: Sig Plc)
Grimshaw Street, Spring Vale, Darwen,
Lancashire BB3 2E3
**Tel:** 08456124304
**Reg No:** 1048980 **Estd:** 1977 Private
Limited Company
**Line of Business:** Agents involved in the
sale of timber and building materials
**Issued Capital:** £20,000
**Director:** I Jackson
**Co. Secretary:** Richard Monro
**Branches:** Roof Shop Ltd, Wretham
Rd,Soho Hill,Handsworth, Birmingham, West
Midlands B19 1ED
**US SIC:** 5072 **UK SIC:** 61500
**Bankers:** Lloyds TSB Bank plc (30-90-87)

| | 31-12-13 | 31-12-12 | 31-12-11 |
|---|---|---|---|
| TA | 20,000 | 20,000 | 20,000 |
| NW | 20,000 | 20,000 | 20,000 |

**DUNS 23-682-0937**

## Rooff Holdings Ltd

Rooff House, Cooks Road, London E15 2PN
**Reg No:** 3677170 **Estd:** 1929 Private
Limited Company
**Line of Business:** Management activities of
holding companies
**Issued Capital:** £37,154
**Directors:** M P Horn, A A Horn
**Co. Secretary:** John Pearson
**US SIC:** 6711 **UK SIC:** 83962
**Bankers:** The Bank Of Ireland (30-14-43)

| | 30-06-14 | 30-06-13 | 31-06-11 |
|---|---|---|---|
| TO | 22,823,579 | 17,603,715 | 17,297,639 |
| P/L | 1,118,218 | 61,684 | 1,484,187 |
| NW | 13,046,951 | 12,222,431 | 12,176,568 |
| WC | 1,998,299 | 1,023,971 | 1,269,284 |
| Emp. | 65 | 56 | 55 |

**DUNS 23-767-1610**

## Roofline Group Ltd

(Subsidiary of: Roofline Group (Holdings)
Ltd)
Euro House, Waterlooville, Hampshire PO7
7XE
**Web:** www.roofline.co.uk
**Reg No:** 3760657 **VAT No:** 755067126
**Estd:** 1997 Private Limited Company
**Line of Business:** Roofing contracting
services
**Issued Capital:** £240
**Directors:** Ms A J Van Der Heijdt, S A Jones,
T Dunaway
**Co. Secretary:** Mark Jones
**US SIC:** 1761 **UK SIC:** 50400
**Auditors:** Lowndes & Co
**Bankers:** National Westminster Bank Plc
(52-41-32)

| | 30-06-14 | 30-06-13 | 30-06-12 |
|---|---|---|---|
| TO | 9,703,106 | 9,713,805 | 13,120,934 |
| P/L | 723,805 | 303,394 | 763,547 |
| NW | 1,041,052 | 1,004,628 | 1,002,239 |
| WC | 994,188 | 947,804 | 927,405 |
| Emp. | 76 | 81 | 83 |

**DUNS 21-916-0117**

## Rooftechcare Ltd

Church Lane, Thornton, Kirkcaldy, Fife KY1
4BH
**Tel:** 01383647315
**Web:** www.rooftechcare.com
**Reg No:** 0435324SC **Estd:** 2012 Private
Limited Company
**Line of Business:** Erection of roof covering
and frames
**Issued Capital:** £1
**Director:** C T Gray
**US SIC:** 1761 **UK SIC:** 50400

| | 30-09-13 |
|---|---|
| TA | 30,221 |
| NW | 15,114 |
| WC | 5,940 |

**DUNS 21-587-1537**

## Rookery Radstock Care Home

The Rookery, Wells Road, Bath, Avon BA3
3RS
**Tel:** 01761438610
**Web:** www.priorygroup.com
**Estd:** 2010 Proprietorship
**Line of Business:** Residential care
establishments
**Proprietor:** Mrs D Pasley
**Responsibilities**
**Senior:** Jenny Abrahams (Home Manager)
**US SIC:** 8321 **UK SIC:** 96111
**Employees:** 50

**DUNS 28-853-2856**

## Rookwood School Trust Ltd

35-39 Weyhill Road, Andover, Hampshire
SP10 3AL
**Tel:** 01264-325900
**Web:** www.rookwood.hants.sch.uk
**Reg No:** 0758856 **Estd:** 1934 Private
Company Limited By Guarantee
**Line of Business:** General secondary
education
**Trading Style:** Rookwood School
**Directors:** K J Knight, Ms C Machin,
S Jenkinson, Mrs G S Cotton, D N Drew,
Mrs C Hardiman
**Co. Secretary:** Mrs Lisa Barton
**Responsibilities**
**Senior:** Jonathan Frost (Manager), Margaret
Langley (Headmistress), Patricia West
(Manager), Louise Whetstone
(Headmistress)
**IT:** Stephen Ungi (Head of IT)
**Purchasing:** Kakai Haig (Purchasing
Manager)
**US SIC:** 8211 **UK SIC:** 93200
**Auditors:** Beck Randall & Carpenter
**Bankers:** HSBC Bank plc (40-08-28)

| | 31-08-13 | 31-08-12 | 31-08-11 |
|---|---|---|---|
| TO | 3,453,303 | 3,443,880 | 3,320,407 |
| P/L | 266,690 | 186,599 | 147,155 |
| NW | 2,701,157 | 2,434,467 | 2,247,868 |
| WC | 360,809 | 288,462 | 270,967 |
| Emp. | 72 | 73 | 73 |

**DUNS 21-034-1356**

## Room Restaurant

Pro Manchester, 81 King Street, Manchester
M2 4AH
**Tel:** 01618392005
**Web:** www.roomrestaurants.com
**Estd:** 2006 Proprietorship
**Line of Business:** Licensed restaurants
**Proprietor:** I Murghwaite
**Responsibilities**
**Senior:** Unda Ozola (Manager)
**US SIC:** 5812, 5813
**UK SIC:** 66110, 66200
**Employees:** 60

**DUNS 21-616-4864**

## Room Three Shop

Trafalgar Square, London WC2N 5DN
**Web:** www.nationalgallery.co.uk
**Estd:** 2011
**Line of Business:** Gift shops
**US SIC:** 5399 **UK SIC:** 65600
**Employees:** 60

**DUNS 28-831-2366**    Imp

## Roomes Stores Ltd

22-24 Station Road, Upminster, Essex RM14
2UB
**Tel:** 01708250080 **Fax:** 01708-228108
**Web:** www.roomes.co.uk
**Reg No:** 0222504 **VAT No:** 246073175
**Estd:** 1927 Private Limited Company
**Line of Business:** Departmental stores
**Issued Capital:** £268,180
**Principals:** S J Roome (Managing),
M D Roome (Managing), Ms M G Roome
**Responsibilities**
**Senior:** Laura Davies (Manager)
**Branches:** Roomes Stores Ltd, 21-22 High
Chelmer, Chelmsford, Essex CM1 1XL
**US SIC:** 5399 **UK SIC:** 65600
**Auditors:** Bland Baker
**Bankers:** Barclays Bank Plc (20-72-89)

| | 01-02-14 | 26-01-13 | 28-02-12 |
|---|---|---|---|
| TO | 5,948,267 | 6,311,441 | 5,876,868 |
| P/L | (34,415) | (1,585) | 16,184 |
| NW | 5,247,106 | 5,281,546 | 5,283,250 |
| WC | 236,848 | 44,519 | (89,860) |
| Emp. | 55 | 55 | 52 |

**DUNS 21-558-2268**

## Roop Cottage Nursing Home

Wakefield Road, Fitzwilliam, Pontefract,
West Yorkshire WF9 5AN
**Tel:** 01977-610918
**Estd:** 1987 Partnership
**Line of Business:** Medical nursing home
activities
**Partners:** Dr R Kanani, Mrs M R Kanani

**Responsibilities**
**Senior:** Ann Egley (Manager)
**US SIC:** 8051 **UK SIC:** 95100
**Employees:** 50

**DUNS 50-647-3230**

## Roo's Leap

2 Traill Drive, Montrose, Angus DD10 8SW
**Tel:** 01674-672157
**Web:** www.roosleap.com
**Estd:** 1985 Partnership
**Line of Business:** American and Australian
style restaurant
**Partners:** M Johnson, Mrs H Johnson
**US SIC:** 5812 **UK SIC:** 66110
**Bankers:** Bank Of Scotland (80-17-59)
**Employees:** 70

**DUNS 21-411-9518**

## Roosters & Travelling

Bobbing Village School, Sheppey Way,
Bobbing, Sittingbourne, Kent ME9 8PL
**Tel:** 01795431890
**Web:** www.brewersfayre.co.uk
**Estd:** 2003 Proprietorship
**Line of Business:** Public house
**Proprietor:** J Charles
**Responsibilities**
**Senior:** Louise Ainsworth (Manager)
**US SIC:** 5813, 5812
**UK SIC:** 66200, 66110
**Employees:** 77

**DUNS 22-257-3888**

## RoOT3 Lighting Ltd

Beacon Innovation Centre, Camelot Road,
Beacon Park, Great Yarmouth, Norfolk NR31
7RA
**Tel:** 01493446525
**Web:** www.root3automation.com
**Reg No:** 4275443 **Estd:** 2013 Private
Limited Company
**Line of Business:** Electrical contractors and
electricians
**Issued Capital:** £200
**Director:** C Mccormick
**Co. Secretary:** Ms Lynne Mccormick
**US SIC:** 1731, 1796
**UK SIC:** 50300, 50400
**Auditors:** D R Carter

| | 28-02-14 | 28-02-13 | 29-02-12 |
|---|---|---|---|
| TA | 251,663 | 165,196 | 189,809 |
| NW | 48,068 | 21,111 | 22,078 |
| WC | (6,625) | (28,736) | (28,903) |

**DUNS 22-953-9598**    Exp

## The Rootstein Hopkins Group Ltd

(Subsidiary of: Yoshichu Mannequin Co.
Ltd.)
9 Beaumont Avenue, London W14 9LP
**Tel:** 020-7381-1447 **Fax:** 02073869594
**Web:** www.rhfoundation.org
**Reg No:** 1601375 **Estd:** 1981 Private
Limited Company
**Line of Business:** Other manufacturing not
elsewhere classified
**Export Markets:** Worldwide
**Export Sales:** £3,111,172
**Trading Style:** The Rootstein Hopkins Group
Ltd
**Issued Capital:** £842
**Principals:** T Yoshida (Chairman),
K Takemoto, J Morita
**Co. Secretary:** Ms Rita Conde
**US SIC:** 3999 **UK SIC:** 49590
**Auditors:** Ernst & Young
**Bankers:** Barclays Bank Plc (20-67-59)

| | 31-03-14 | 31-03-13 | 31-03-12 |
|---|---|---|---|
| TO | 3,704,809 | 5,318,057 | 6,362,673 |
| P/L | (2,615,286) | (736,105) | (172,919) |
| NW | 10,790,362 | 7,064,337 | 7,347,822 |
| WC | 5,718,306 | 2,797,024 | 3,401,801 |
| Emp. | 52 | 52 | 55 |

**DUNS 50-558-7162**    Imp-Exp

## Roper Industries Ltd

(Subsidiary of: Roper Industries Inc.)
Western Way, Bury St Edmunds, Suffolk
IP33 3SZ
**Tel:** 01284-762222 **Fax:** 01284-760256
**Web:** www.amot.com
**Reg No:** 2509935 **Estd:** 1990 Private
Limited Company
**Line of Business:** Control system equipment
**Export Sales:** £25,722,000
**Trading Style:** Amot, Media Cybernetics Uk
**Issued Capital:** £536,481
**Directors:** D B Liner, M S Firth,
J R Humphrey, P J Soni, E Schellenberger
**Co. Secretary:** John Bignall
**Responsibilities**
**Senior:** Michael Parks (Operations Director),
Nigel Whitmore (Operations Manager)
**IT:** Jason Turrell (IT Manager)
**HR:** H Caine (Personnel Manager), Julie
Chmiel (Human Resources Manager)

**Health & Safety:** Kelvin O'Brien *(Health & Safety Officer)*
**Facilities:** Michael Parks *(Operations Director)*
**Purchasing:** P Arthur *(Purchasing Manager)*
**Engineering:** Greg Astland *(Electronic Engineer)*
**Branches:** Roper Industries Ltd, Western Way, Bury St. Edmunds, Suffolk IP33 3SZ
**US SIC:** 3643, 3494
**UK SIC:** 34203, 32880
**Auditors:** PricewaterhouseCoopers LLP
**Bankers:** Barclays Bank Plc (20-16-12)

| | 31-12-13 | 31-12-12 | 31-12-11 |
|---|---|---|---|
| TO | 37,340,000 | 39,191,000 | 37,670,000 |
| P/L | 18,071,000 | 13,419,000 | 10,210,000 |
| NW | 40,386,000 | 22,315,000 | 37,680,000 |
| WC | 34,754,000 | 16,992,000 | 32,286,000 |
| Emp. | 157 | 161 | 156 |

DUNS 22-555-4666 Imp-Exp

## Roper Rhodes Ltd

Unit 1 Brassmill Lane Trading Estate, Bath, Avon BA1 3JF
**Tel:** 01225334148
**Web:** www.roperrhodes.co.uk
**Reg No:** 1568433 **Estd:** 1979 Private Limited Company
**Line of Business:** Manufacture of other fabricated metal products not elsewhere classified
**Export Markets:** Republic of Ireland
**Export Sales:** £442,834
**Issued Capital:** £141,853
**Principals:** P Roper *(Managing)*, M Roper, S P Taylor, L E Leather
**Co. Secretary:** Ms Helen Morgan
**Responsibilities**
**Senior:** Brian Roper *(Manager)*
**Marketing:** Alexis Leyland *(Graphic Design / Digital Marke)*
**Admin:** Kate Brown *(Office Manager)*
**IT:** Dean Taylor *(IT Director)*
**Operations:** Kate Brown *(Office Manager)*
**Branches:** Roper Rhodes Ltd, Unit 1 Chase Road Trad Est, 51 Chase Rd, London NW10 6LG
**US SIC:** 3499 **UK SIC:** 31694
**Auditors:** Richardson Groves
**Bankers:** National Westminster Bank Plc (56-00-34)

| | 31-07-13 | 31-07-12 | 31-07-11 |
|---|---|---|---|
| TO | 36,192,573 | 33,328,934 | 35,629,129 |
| P/L | 3,529,412 | 2,455,571 | 2,592,831 |
| NW | 21,757,178 | 19,545,241 | 18,034,673 |
| WC | 17,700,366 | 15,446,254 | 13,947,735 |
| Emp. | 113 | 101 | 99 |

DUNS 77-947-7249

## Ropner Insurance Holdings Ltd

Boundary House, 7-17 Jewry Street, London EC3N 2HP
**Tel:** 02074884533
**Web:** www.ropnerins.co.uk
**Reg No:** 3054049 **Estd:** 1995 Private Limited Company
**Line of Business:** Activities auxiliary to insurance and pension funding
**Issued Capital:** £691,963
**Director:** S A Ross
**Co. Secretary:** Andrew Hunter
**Responsibilities**
**Senior:** Vinodrai Desai *(Director)*, Frank Hindle *(Director)*, Alan Rixon *(Director)*, Richard Steel *(Director)*, Cosmo Whiteley *(Director)*
**US SIC:** 8999 **UK SIC:** 83954
**Auditors:** Hope Agar

| | 31-12-13 | 31-12-12 | 31-12-11 |
|---|---|---|---|
| TO | 6,658,204 | 6,770,455 | 6,905,892 |
| P/L | 35,533 | 535,579 | 622,738 |
| NW | 3,556,154 | 3,499,294 | 3,229,525 |
| WC | 3,393,427 | 3,335,319 | 3,057,255 |
| Emp. | 58 | 55 | 53 |

DUNS 22-621-7354 Imp

## Roquette Uk Ltd

**(Subsidiary of:** Roquette Freres)
Unit E-H, Cavendish Courtyard, Sallow Road, Corby, Northamptonshire NN17 5JX
**Tel:** 01536-273000
**Web:** www.roquette.com
**Reg No:** 1486339 **VAT No:** 339986000
**Estd:** 1980 Private Limited Company
**Line of Business:** Non-specialised wholesale of food, beverages and tobacco
**Issued Capital:** £98,550,000
**Directors:** S Baseden, C D Scarrott, T Magnien, G Patrucco, D Delloye, Ms S Price
**Co. Secretary:** Ms Susan Price
**Responsibilities**
**Senior:** Melvin Clarke *(Warehouse Manager)*, Marc Roquette *(Manager)*, Jean Willefert *(Manager)*
**Purchasing:** Nigel Streatfield *(Purchasing Manager)*
**US SIC:** 5149, 5084
**UK SIC:** 61700, 61490
**Auditors:** Deloitte & Touche LLP
**Bankers:** HSBC Bank plc (40-35-04)

| | 31-12-13 | 31-12-12 | 31-12-11 |
|---|---|---|---|
| TO | 174,069,000 | 157,272,000 | 169,973,000 |
| P/L | (810,000) | 1,261,000 | 9,647,000 |
| NW | 45,915,000 | 49,205,000 | 50,542,000 |
| WC | 7,146,000 | 7,779,000 | 12,312,000 |
| Emp. | 152 | 153 | 152 |

DUNS 64-090-9789

## Rory J Holbrook Ltd

Roudham Road, Harling Road, Norwich, Norfolk NR16 2QN
**Tel:** 01953718306
**Web:** www.roryjholbrook.com
**Reg No:** 4494452 **Estd:** 2004 Private Limited Company
**Line of Business:** Road haulage and transport services
**Issued Capital:** £100
**Director:** R J Holbrook
**Responsibilities**
**Finance:** Brian Brooker *(Finance Director)*
**US SIC:** 4789 **UK SIC:** 77002

| | 31-12-13 | 31-12-12 | 31-12-11 |
|---|---|---|---|
| TA | 3,404,527 | 2,631,368 | 2,705,864 |
| NW | 238,593 | 311,412 | 372,472 |
| WC | (164,231) | (268,630) | (399,035) |

DUNS 21-162-5025 Imp-Exp

## Roscolab Ltd

**(Subsidiary of:** Rosco Holdings Inc.)
Blanchard Works, Kangley Bridge Road, Sydenham, London SE26 5AQ
**Tel:** 02086592300
**Web:** www.rosco.com
**Reg No:** 1136899 **VAT No:** 219096651
**Estd:** 1973 Private Limited Company
**Line of Business:** Wholesale of other machinery for use in industry, trade and navigation
**Export Markets:** E U, S Africa & the 'Eastern Block'
**Export Sales:** £5,153,118
**Issued Capital:** £1,054
**Principals:** M Najur *(Financial)*, S Miller, K Frijters
**Co. Secretary:** Mark Engel
**Responsibilities**
**Senior:** Nina Harrup *(General Manager)*, Gordon Tomkins *(Manager)*
**IT:** Nina Harrup *(General Manager)*
**HR:** Nina Harrup *(General Manager)*
**Health & Safety:** Nina Harrup *(General Manager)*
**Facilities:** Nina Harrup *(General Manager)*
**US SIC:** 5084 **UK SIC:** 61490
**Auditors:** Sobell Rhodes
**Bankers:** Barclays Bank Plc (20-03-53)

| | 30-06-13 | 30-06-12 | 30-06-11 |
|---|---|---|---|
| TO | 8,311,481 | 7,670,926 | 7,787,240 |
| P/L | (35,557) | (29,887) | 20,595 |
| NW | 156,485 | 153,756 | 135,169 |
| WC | 1,090,366 | 1,055,248 | 1,130,573 |
| Emp. | 53 | 54 | 52 |

DUNS 22-069-1062 Imp

## Roscom Ltd

Bateman Street, Derby, Derbyshire DE23 8JQ
**Tel:** 01332344990 **Fax:** 01332-206424
**Web:** www.roscom.co.uk
**Reg No:** 4070645 **Estd:** 1978 Private Limited Company
**Line of Business:** Telecom services
**Export Sales:** £1,761,626
**Trading Style:** Roscom Ltd
**Issued Capital:** £289,282
**Director:** Mrs M J Blackburn
**Co. Secretary:** Simon Taylor
**Responsibilities**
**Finance:** Louise Green *(Senior Finance Administrator)*, Judith Howe *(Assistant Financial Controller)*
**Marketing:** Julia Ayling *(Marketing Director)*
**Sales:** Andy Harper *(Head of Commercial Operations)*
**Admin:** Louise Green *(Senior Finance Administrator)*
**Operations:** Andy Harper *(Head of Commercial Operations)*
**US SIC:** 4899, 4832
**UK SIC:** 79020, 97411
**Bankers:** The Royal Bank Of Scotland Plc (16-18-18)

| | 30-04-14 | 30-04-13 | 30-04-12 |
|---|---|---|---|
| TO | 2,726,193 | 3,027,425 | 3,464,265 |
| P/L | (208,945) | (5,818) | 244,629 |
| NW | 2,741,739 | 2,882,329 | 2,930,781 |
| WC | 1,080,250 | 1,291,429 | 1,488,145 |
| Emp. | 79 | 82 | 79 |

DUNS 22-519-0479 Imp-Exp

## Roscomac Ltd

Dominion Way, Worthing, West Sussex BN14 8NW
**Tel:** 01903-201701 **Fax:** 01903-201702
**Web:** www.roscomac.co.uk
**Reg No:** 1254467 **VAT No:** 192195349
**Estd:** 1976 Private Limited Company
**Line of Business:** Precision engineers
**Export Sales:** £10,745,304
**Issued Capital:** £10,000
**Principals:** F Martello *(Chairman and Managing)*, J G Martello *(Managing)*, N A Rolfe
**Co. Secretary:** Joseph Martello
**Responsibilities**
**Senior:** Dean Clayton *(Stores Manager)*
**Finance:** Jana Forshaw *(Financial Controller)*
**Sales:** Colin Alexander *(Operations Director)*
**HR:** Leanne Cumberland *(Human Resources Manager)*
**Operations:** Colin Alexander *(Operations Director)*
**Engineering:** Colin Alexander *(Operations Director)*
**US SIC:** 8911, 5199
**UK SIC:** 83701, 61900
**Auditors:** PFK (UK) LLP
**Bankers:** Barclays Bank Plc (20-49-76)

| | 28-02-14 | 28-02-13 | 29-02-12 |
|---|---|---|---|
| TO | 12,722,841 | 11,843,964 | 15,309,977 |
| P/L | 35,085 | (1,237,885) | 390,006 |
| NW | 2,732,972 | 2,373,976 | 3,532,451 |
| WC | 1,194,295 | 528,298 | 1,342,209 |
| Emp. | 175 | 150 | 200 |

DUNS 22-643-7820

## Rose Bruford College

Burnt Oak Lane Lamorbey Park, Sidcup, Kent DA15 9DF
**Tel:** 02083082600 **Fax:** 02083080542
**Web:** www.bruford.ac.uk
**Reg No:** 0508616 **Estd:** 1952 Private Company Limited By Guarantee
**Line of Business:** First-degree level higher education
**Directors:** Dr K Southworth, Professor M Earley, M J Mccart, Ms J M Sims, Miss E J Lang, D Massey, C E Campbell, Professor D M Willcocks
**Co. Secretary:** Ms Ruth Bourne
**Responsibilities**
**Senior:** David Ames *(Director)*, Philip Broadhead *(Director)*, Mike Dormer *(Manager)*, Rodney Gent *(Director)*, Kirsty Macdonald *(Manager)*, Steffani Nash *(Director)*, Cara Turtington *(Director)*
**Operations:** Rachel Candler *(Production Manager)*, Jayne Richards *(Programme Director)*
**US SIC:** 8221 **UK SIC:** 93100
**Auditors:** Buzzacott
**Bankers:** HSBC Bank plc (40-05-20)

| | 31-07-14 | 31-07-13 | 31-07-12 |
|---|---|---|---|
| TO | 7,609,000 | 7,444,000 | 7,083,000 |
| P/L | 192,000 | 241,000 | 150,000 |
| NW | 8,489,000 | 8,418,000 | 7,962,000 |
| WC | 251,000 | 357,000 | 267,000 |
| Emp. | 89 | 84 | 84 |

DUNS 29-660-8680 Imp-Exp

## Rose Cottage Care Ltd

Rose Cottage School Road, Broughton, Huntingdon, Cambridgeshire PE28 3AT
**Tel:** 01487822550 **Fax:** 020-8205-1192
**Web:** www.rosecottagecare.com
**Reg No:** 1987141 **VAT No:** 226355764
**Estd:** 1983 Private Limited Company
**Line of Business:** Other human health activities
**Export Markets:** France
**Issued Capital:** £100
**Managing Director:** J F Tillisch
**Co. Secretary:** Ms Christine Friend
**US SIC:** 8091, 8321
**UK SIC:** 95200, 96111
**Bankers:** Barclays Bank Plc (20-43-63)

| | 31-12-13 | 31-12-12 | 31-12-11 |
|---|---|---|---|
| TO | 1,537,742 | 1,983,344 | 1,955,061 |
| P/L | 115,835 | 65,822 | 167,649 |
| NW | 151,859 | (118,739) | (77,593) |
| WC | 74,318 | 21,772 | 59,516 |
| Emp. | 90 | 118 | 114 |

DUNS 73-282-7618

## Rose Group Ltd

Riverside House, Riverside Avenue East, Lawford, Manningtree, Essex CO11 1US
**Tel:** 01206-392613 **Fax:** 01206392680
**Web:** www.rosebuilders.co.uk
**Reg No:** 4556499 **Estd:** 2002 Private Limited Company
**Line of Business:** Management activities of construction holding companies
**Trading Style:** Rose Builders
**Issued Capital:** £50,000
**Directors:** S W Rose, W C Rose, Ms J M Rose
**Co. Secretary:** Andrew Bowles
**US SIC:** 6711 **UK SIC:** 83962

| | 31-03-14 | 31-03-13 | 31-03-12 |
|---|---|---|---|
| TO | 30,143,527 | 20,878,802 | 20,924,886 |
| P/L | 1,438,764 | 557,845 | 640,365 |
| NW | 5,337,365 | 4,432,501 | 4,003,597 |
| WC | 5,572,341 | 4,272,212 | 3,909,050 |
| Emp. | 123 | 110 | 111 |

DUNS 23-010-4549

## Rose Hill School

Coniston Avenue, Tunbridge Wells, Kent TN4 9SY
**Tel:** 01892-525591
**Web:** www.rosehillschool.co.uk
**Estd:** 1832
**Line of Business:** General secondary education
**Director:** D Westcombe
**Responsibilities**
**Senior:** Charles Broadie *(Manager)*, Susan Gates *(Manager)*
**US SIC:** 8211 **UK SIC:** 93200
**Employees:** 70

DUNS 38-764-9825

## The Rose Homes

Roseland, Garratts Lane, Banstead, Surrey SM7 2EQ
**Tel:** 01737-358796
**Web:** www.rosehomes.org.uk
**Estd:** 2002
**Line of Business:** Non-charitable social work activities with accommodation
**US SIC:** 8321 **UK SIC:** 96111
**Employees:** 80

DUNS 21-600-8236

## Rose House

Rose Grove, Armthorpe, Doncaster, South Yorkshire DN3 3AJ
**Tel:** 01302831450
**Estd:** 1953 Proprietorship
**Line of Business:** Non-charitable social work activities with accommodation
**Proprietor:** Mrs P Castle
**US SIC:** 8321 **UK SIC:** 96111
**Employees:** 48

DUNS 21-595-5462

## Rose Lodge Care Home

Carers Way, Newton Aycliffe, County Durham DL5 4SE
**Tel:** 01325271301
**Web:** www.countrywidecarehomes.co.uk
**Estd:** 2003
**Line of Business:** Residential care establishments
**Proprietor:** Mrs E Henman
**Responsibilities**
**Senior:** Karen Frew-Mcgill *(Home Manager)*
**US SIC:** 8321 **UK SIC:** 96111
**Employees:** 50

DUNS 21-581-0830

## Rose Lodge Nursing Home

185 Belsize Road, Lisburn, Co Antrim BT27 4LA
**Web:** www.roselodge.co.uk
**Estd:** 2011 Proprietorship
**Line of Business:** Nursing homes
**Proprietor:** M Warnock
**US SIC:** 8051 **UK SIC:** 95100
**Employees:** 100

DUNS 21-609-5828

## Rose of Colchester Ltd

Clough Road Severalls Industrial Estate, Colchester, Essex CO4 9QT
**Tel:** 01206-844500 **Fax:** 01206-845872
**Web:** www.cantsroses.co.uk
**Reg No:** 0575231 **VAT No:** 102584204
**Estd:** 1910 Private Limited Company
**Line of Business:** Publishing of books
**Issued Capital:** £253,061
**Principals:** C G Rose *(Managing)*, M Rose
**Co. Secretary:** Andrew Clement
**Responsibilities**
**Senior:** Elizabeth Rose *(Marketing Manager)*, Ralph White-Robinson *(Manager)*
**US SIC:** 3999 **UK SIC:** 49590
**Auditors:** Butt Cozens
**Bankers:** Lloyds TSB Bank plc (30-92-16)

| | 30-09-13 | 30-09-12 | 30-09-11 |
|---|---|---|---|
| TO | 5,599,791 | 5,384,531 | 5,657,696 |
| P/L | 253,398 | 207,861 | 447,646 |
| NW | 4,872,490 | 4,729,344 | 4,605,931 |
| WC | 3,155,602 | 2,912,544 | 2,854,939 |
| Emp. | 64 | 61 | 61 |

DUNS 73-299-8096

## Rose Petroleum Plc

4th Floor, 3 Shepherd Street, London W1J 7HL
**Tel:** 02072-254-590
**Web:** www.rosepetroleum.com
**Reg No:** 4573663 **Estd:** 2002 Public Limited Company
**Line of Business:** Holding companies management activities
**Export Sales:** £5,710,172
**Issued Capital:** £19,263,626
**Directors:** C J Eadie, K Hefton, K Scott, R F Kilmorey, M C Idiens, P E Jeffcock, J M Blair

**Co. Secretary:** Ian Mcneill
**Responsibilities**
**Senior:** Leavitt Arnold *(Manager)*, David Ingmire *(Manager)*
**US SIC:** 6711 **UK SIC:** 83962
**Auditors:** Baker Tilly UK Audit LLP
**Bankers:** Barclays Bank Plc (20-65-82)

| | 31-12-13 | 31-12-12 | 31-12-11 |
|---|---|---|---|
| TO | 5,710,172 | 5,759,225 | 3,678,126 |
| P/L | (2,981,301) | 54,304 | (1,528,732) |
| NW | 2,056,681 | 1,020,802 | 1,648,406 |
| WC | 2,357,601 | 1,232,910 | 2,253,895 |
| Emp. | 52 | 52 | 50 |

DUNS 28-903-7715
## The Rose Road Association
Bradbury Centre, Southampton, Hampshire SO16 5NA
**Tel:** 02380721234
**Web:** www.roseroad.org.uk
**Reg No:** 1366534 **Estd:** 1952 Private Limited Company
**Line of Business:** Organised childrens play schemes
**Directors:** C J Cundy, C J Attridge, D Miller, Dr R M Magdalena, Mrs S Parker, Mrs S James, Mrs P Porter, Mrs D G Heatly
**Responsibilities**
**Senior:** Heather Aspinall *(Chief Executive)*, Timothy Burbidge *(Director)*, Carol Cheesman *(Director)*, Jane Houghton *(Manager)*, Sandra Jay *(Director)*, Jane Lyon Maris *(Director)*, Susan Morse *(Manager)*, Christine Smalley *(Manager)*
**Sales:** Timothy Burbidge *(Director)*
**HR:** Emily Burke *(Personnel Manager)*, Emma Russo *(Human Resources Manager)*
**Branches:** The Rose Road Association, Rose Road, Southampton, Hampshire SO14 6TE
**US SIC:** 8211, 8321, 6732
**UK SIC:** 93200, 96111, 83100
**Auditors:** Nexi Audit Ltd
**Bankers:** National Westminster Bank Plc (55-50-21)

| | 31-03-14 | 31-03-13 | 31-03-12 |
|---|---|---|---|
| TO | 2,779,709 | 2,991,026 | 3,152,278 |
| P/L | 65,930 | 89,195 | 120,475 |
| NW | 3,204,019 | 3,138,089 | 5,018,062 |
| WC | 905,521 | 850,528 | 827,461 |
| Emp. | 195 | 224 | 211 |

DUNS 22-808-1675 Imp
## Rose Roofing Ltd
(**Subsidiary of:** B.R.T. Supplies Ltd)
1 Flass Lane, Castleford, West Yorkshire WF10 5JW
**Web:** www.rose-roofing.co.uk
**Reg No:** 1579418 **VAT No:** 591098319
**Estd:** 1982 Private Limited Company
**Line of Business:** Manufacture of other non-metallic mineral products not elsewhere classified
**Export Sales:** £351,544
**Issued Capital:** £30,000
**Principals:** M Abraham *(Managing)*, L Sykes *(Managing)*, N J Sykes
**Co. Secretary:** Mrs Ann Sykes
**Responsibilities**
**Senior:** John Tomney *(Production Manager)*
**Finance:** Les Pagett *(Financial Director)*
**IT:** Les Pagett *(Financial Director)*
**Purchasing:** John Tomney *(Production Manager)*
**Engineering:** John Tomney *(Production Manager)*
**US SIC:** 3299 **UK SIC:** 24504
**Auditors:** Horwath Clark Whitehill
**Bankers:** National Westminster Bank Plc (01-10-01)

| | 31-03-14 | 31-03-13 | 31-03-12 |
|---|---|---|---|
| TO | 16,079,835 | 13,682,017 | 14,690,459 |
| P/L | 1,320,674 | 945,339 | (249,121) |
| NW | 3,563,908 | 2,547,453 | 1,828,941 |
| WC | 3,891,273 | 2,852,543 | 2,103,427 |
| Emp. | 65 | 63 | 66 |

DUNS 50-690-6288
## Rose Tissues
Sefton Street, Hollingwood, Oldham, Lancashire OL9 7LT
**Web:** www.rosetissues.co.uk
**VAT No:** 457428033 **Estd:** 1985 Partnership
**Line of Business:** Toilet rolls & kitchen towels manufacturer
**Partners:** Mrs T Iqbal, Z Iqbal
**US SIC:** 2621 **UK SIC:** 47013
**Employees:** 52

DUNS 21-774-3487
## Rose Tree
Victoria Street, Bourton-On-The-Water, Cheltenham, Gloucestershire GL54 2BX
**Tel:** 01451820635
**Estd:** 1998 Proprietorship
**Line of Business:** Licensed restaurants
**Proprietor:** Mrs J Sands
**Responsibilities**
**Senior:** Jill Sands *(Proprietor)*
**US SIC:** 5812 **UK SIC:** 66110
**Employees:** 51

DUNS 21-333-2351
## Rose Villa
148-150 Eccleshall Road, Stafford, Staffordshire ST16 1JA
**Tel:** 01785-254760
**Web:** www.rosevillanursinghome.co.uk
**Estd:** 1997 Proprietorship
**Line of Business:** Nursing homes
**Proprietor:** P Patel
**US SIC:** 8051 **UK SIC:** 95100
**Employees:** 50

DUNS 42-446-6618
## Rose Villa Care Home Ltd
Rose Villa Nursing Home, Hull, North Humberside HU5 2ST
**Tel:** 01482472038 **Fax:** 01482-472038
**Reg No:** 4434303 **Estd:** 2002 Private Limited Company
**Line of Business:** Other human health activities
**Issued Capital:** £1,052
**Directors:** Dr J G Shores, Dr D N Kieran, Dr P Thackray, Dr G S Chauhan
**Responsibilities**
**Senior:** Jill Plater *(Business Manager)*
**Finance:** Jill Plater *(Business Manager)*
**Sales:** Jill Plater *(Business Manager)*
**IT:** Jill Plater *(Business Manager)*
**HR:** Alec Bauld *(Matron)*, Jill Plater *(Business Manager)*
**Health & Safety:** Alec Bauld *(Matron)*
**Facilities:** Jill Plater *(Business Manager)*
**US SIC:** 8091, 8321
**UK SIC:** 95200, 96111

| | 30-06-13 | 30-06-12 | 30-06-11 |
|---|---|---|---|
| TA | 307,230 | 319,946 | 324,602 |
| NW | 211,371 | 210,134 | 199,643 |
| WC | (30,689) | (37,388) | (56,359) |

DUNS 64-259-3263
## Rose Villa Nursing Home
269 Beverley Road, Hull, North Humberside HU5 2ST
**Tel:** 01482-472151
**Estd:** 1990 Partnership
**Line of Business:** Medical nursing home activities
**Partners:** C Chauhan, Dr J Shores, Mrs S Jordan, Dr P Thackeray
**Responsibilities**
**Senior:** J Plater *(Manager)*
**US SIC:** 8051 **UK SIC:** 95100
**Employees:** 50

DUNS 51-605-5563
## Rose Walter & Sons
21-22 Sidmouth Street, Devizes, Wiltshire SN10 1LD
**Web:** www.walterroseandson.co.uk
**Estd:** 1903 Proprietorship
**Line of Business:** Butchers
**Proprietor:** S Cook
**US SIC:** 5423 **UK SIC:** 64100
**Employees:** 60

DUNS 21-002-9068
## Roseberry Care Centres Gb Ltd
2 Defender Court, Sunderland, Tyne and Wear SR5 3PE
**Fax:** 0191 549 0508
**Web:** www.roseberrycarecentres.co.uk
**Reg No:** 6281674 **Estd:** 2011 Private Limited Company
**Line of Business:** Representative office
**Trading Style:** Roseberry Care Centres
**Issued Capital:** £2
**Directors:** R M Mcnamara, Mrs E Mcnamara, Miss L Mcnamara, Miss L Mcnamara
**Co. Secretary:** Ms Marie Royal
**Responsibilities**
**Senior:** Mark Dumble *(Financial Director)*, Maurine Henderson *(Director of Human Resources)*, Elaine McNamara *(Director)*
**Finance:** Mark Dumble *(Financial Director)*
**HR:** Maurine Henderson *(Director of Human Resources)*
**Branches:** Roseberry Care Centres Gb Ltd, Po Box 1229, Sunderland, Tyne and Wear SR5 9EB
**US SIC:** 8051, 6711
**UK SIC:** 95100, 83962
**Auditors:** Tait Walker LLP

| | 31-12-13 | 31-12-12 | 31-12-11 |
|---|---|---|---|
| TO | 11,135,455 | N/A | N/A |
| P/L | 154,150 | N/A | N/A |
| NW | 24,341 | (13,675) | (46,070) |
| WC | (136,574) | (107,299) | (18,647) |
| Emp. | 534 | N/A | N/A |

DUNS 21-585-4780
## Roseberry Park Hospital
Marton Road, Middlesbrough, Cleveland TS4 3AF
**Tel:** 01642837300
**Web:** www.tewv.nhs.uk
**Estd:** 2011 Proprietorship
**Line of Business:** Mental health centres
**Proprietor:** R Lamb
**Responsibilities**
**Senior:** Simon Lancashire *(Site Manager)*
**US SIC:** 8062 **UK SIC:** 95100
**Employees:** 1,000

DUNS 39-672-3348 Imp
## The Rosebery Group Ltd
Hastings House, 79-83 Station Road, Ellesmere Port, Cheshire CH65 4BN
**Tel:** 0151-357-1066
**Web:** www.rosebery.co.uk
**Reg No:** 2138483 **VAT No:** 477141537
**Estd:** 1987 Private Limited Company
**Line of Business:** Electrical contractors and electricians
**Issued Capital:** £1,000
**Principals:** T J Topping *(Chairman and Managing)*, C C Woodward *(Managing)*
**Co. Secretary:** Leslie Cooke
**Responsibilities**
**HR:** John Maher *(Human Resources Manager)*
**Purchasing:** Jeanette Nolan *(Purchasing Manager)*
**Engineering:** Ian Suckley *(Estimating Manager)*
**US SIC:** 1731 **UK SIC:** 50300
**Auditors:** McEwan Wallace
**Bankers:** National Westminster Bank Plc (60-07-35)

| | 30-09-13 | 30-09-12 | 30-09-11 |
|---|---|---|---|
| TO | 14,339,377 | 14,769,006 | 12,327,037 |
| P/L | 1,364,600 | 2,045,883 | 978,068 |
| NW | 4,131,700 | 3,126,351 | 1,633,752 |
| WC | 4,025,196 | 2,997,658 | 1,574,322 |
| Emp. | 124 | 116 | 109 |

DUNS 21-222-6874
## Rosebridge Court
190 Darby Lane, Wigan, Lancashire WN2 3DU
**Web:** www.hc-one.co.uk
**Estd:** 2004
**Line of Business:** Children's homes
**Proprietor:** P Mays
**Responsibilities**
**Finance:** Kerry Thomason *(Senior Finance Administrator)*
**US SIC:** 8321 **UK SIC:** 96111
**Employees:** 50

DUNS 21-568-1118
## Rosecroft
Westfield Drive, Workington, Cumbria CA14 5AR
**Tel:** 01900-604814
**Estd:** 1998 Proprietorship
**Line of Business:** Non-charitable social work activities with accommodation
**Proprietor:** Mrs B Hoban
**Responsibilities**
**Senior:** Elizabeth Bedford *(Manager)*
**US SIC:** 8321 **UK SIC:** 96111
**Employees:** 46

DUNS 21-205-5623
## Rosedale Nursing Home
Old Vicarage, Catterick Road, Catterick Garrison, North Yorkshire DL9 4DD
**Tel:** 01748834948
**Web:** www.maria-mallaband.co.uk
**Estd:** 1988 Proprietorship
**Line of Business:** Non-charitable social work activities with accommodation
**Proprietor:** K Davis
**Responsibilities**
**Senior:** Sylvia Greenhalgh *(Chief Clerk)*
**US SIC:** 8321 **UK SIC:** 96111
**Employees:** 80

DUNS 21-205-5631
## Rosedene Nursing Home
141-147 Trinity Road, London SW17 7HJ
**Web:** www.rosedenenursinghome.co.uk
**Estd:** 1954 Proprietorship
**Line of Business:** Nursing homes
**Proprietor:** T Lewis
**Responsibilities**
**Senior:** Pat Bareer *(Home Manager)*
**US SIC:** 8051 **UK SIC:** 95100
**Employees:** 50

DUNS 52-011-8175
## Roseguard Properties Ltd
(**Subsidiary of:** Fife Health Care Ltd)
Norcliffe House Station Road, Wilmslow, Cheshire SK9 1BU
**Reg No:** 3378572 **Estd:** 1997 Private Limited Company
**Line of Business:** Other human health activities
**Issued Capital:** £2
**Directors:** I R Smith, Ms M C Royston, B R Taberner
**Co. Secretary:** Mrs Abigail Mattison
**US SIC:** 8091 **UK SIC:** 95200
**Bankers:** Bank Of Scotland (80-16-84)

| | 31-12-13 | 31-12-12 | 31-12-11 |
|---|---|---|---|
| TO | 4,413,000 | 4,751,000 | 4,357,000 |
| P/L | (512,000) | (236,000) | (32,000) |
| NW | (678,000) | (166,000) | 70,000 |
| WC | (1,409,000) | (873,000) | (688,000) |
| Emp. | 196 | 203 | 197 |

DUNS 21-782-1865
## Rosehill Conference & Training Centre
Rose Hill, Cheltenham, Gloucestershire GL52 3LZ
**Tel:** 01242222444
**Web:** www.ucas.com
**Estd:** 2011
**Line of Business:** Conference centres and facilities
**Responsibilities**
**Senior:** Mary Curknock-Cook *(Chief Executive)*
**US SIC:** 7011 **UK SIC:** 66500
**Employees:** 400

DUNS 50-136-0150 Imp-Exp
## Rosehill Polymers Ltd
(**Subsidiary of:** Rosehill Polymers Group Ltd)
Spring Bank Mills, Watson Mill Lane, Sowerby Bridge, West Yorkshire HX6 3BW
**Tel:** 01422839456 **Fax:** 01422839610
**Web:** www.rosehillpolymers.com
**Reg No:** 2283308 **VAT No:** 516206181
**Estd:** 1989 Private Limited Company
**Line of Business:** Manufacture of other rubber products
**Export Markets:** Far East, U S A, E U, Canada, Australasia, Middle East
**Export Sales:** £9,678,198
**Trading Style:** Rosehill Polymers Ltd
**Issued Capital:** £27,004
**Principals:** J M Hopkinson *(Chairman)*, Dr W Stevens, Dr A Celik
**Co. Secretary:** David Beech
**Responsibilities**
**Senior:** Bran Whiteman *(Transport Manager)*
**Finance:** Jeanne Garside *(Financial Manager)*
**IT:** Carlos Matos *(Computer Coordinator)*
**Fleet:** Bran Whiteman *(Transport Manager)*
**US SIC:** 3069, 3079, 3559
**UK SIC:** 48123, 48360, 32863
**Auditors:** B.M. Howarth Ltd
**Bankers:** Barclays Bank Plc (20-35-84)

| | 31-03-14 | 31-03-13 | 31-03-12 |
|---|---|---|---|
| TO | 22,549,619 | 21,013,021 | 20,603,389 |
| P/L | 834,736 | 714,912 | 343,617 |
| NW | 4,241,701 | 3,782,115 | 4,028,060 |
| WC | (607,589) | (637,390) | (322,691) |
| Emp. | 80 | 77 | 87 |

DUNS 21-788-0918
## Rosehill School Association
St Matthias Road, Nottingham, Nottinghamshire NG3 2FE
**Tel:** 01159502038
**Web:** www.therosehillschool.co.uk
**Estd:** 1993
**Line of Business:** Education services
**US SIC:** 8299 **UK SIC:** 93300
**Employees:** 60

DUNS 22-173-1750
## Roseland Care Ltd
(**Subsidiary of:** Romac Investments Ltd)
1st Floor, Brunswick House, Regent Park, Leatherhead, Surrey KT22 7LU
**Tel:** 01872530972
**Web:** www.retirementvillages.co.uk
**Reg No:** 4191487 **Estd:** 2001 Private Limited Company
**Line of Business:** Rest and retirement homes
**Issued Capital:** £2
**Directors:** N Donaldson, N F Welby, P M Walsh
**Co. Secretary:** David Miller
**Responsibilities**
**Senior:** Clive Hayton *(Manager)*, Derek Pashley *(Manager)*

**US SIC:** 8321 **UK SIC:** 96111

| | 31-03-14 | 31-03-13 | 31-03-12 |
|---|---|---|---|
| TO | 1,897,354 | 2,046,419 | 1,884,529 |
| P/L | 349,295 | 534,669 | 508,245 |
| NW | 1,703,222 | 1,383,756 | 840,568 |
| WC | 1,611,343 | 1,251,178 | 684,825 |
| Emp. | 66 | 59 | 53 |

DUNS 21-717-0415

## The Roseland Community College

Tregony, Truro, Cornwall TR2 5SE
**Tel:** 01872530583
**Web:** www.theroseland.co.uk
**Reg No:** 7557817 **Estd:** 1994 Private Company Limited By Guarantee
**Line of Business:** Schools (local authority)
**Directors:** Ms D A Morse, S T Bundy, N A Hyde, A P Stephens, G Henderson, M J Wardle, Miss A L Yeo, Mrs P Appleyard
**Co. Secretary:** Mrs Laura Keam
**Responsibilities**
**Senior:** Kay Chapman *(Director)*, Kristy Gouldsmith *(Director)*, Jacqueline Vincent *(Director)*, Neil Wilkinson-Mckie *(Director)*, Jodie Winter *(PA to Head Teacher)*
**Finance:** Jackie Parker *(Business Manager)*
**Marketing:** Jackie Parker *(Business Manager)*
**IT:** John Mcdermott *(Network, Security Manager)*
**US SIC:** 8211 **UK SIC:** 93200
**Bankers:** Lloyds TSB Bank plc (30-12-21)

| | 31-08-14 | 31-08-13 | 31-08-12 |
|---|---|---|---|
| TO | 3,950,384 | 4,153,823 | 11,776,103 |
| P/L | 490,329 | 748,204 | 6,689,180 |
| NW | 7,385,713 | 7,271,384 | 6,512,180 |
| WC | 1,020,606 | 619,144 | 242,867 |
| Emp. | 71 | 78 | 74 |

DUNS 21-798-1187

## The Roseland Youth Community Group

Tregony, Truro, Cornwall TR2 5SE
**Tel:** 01872-530675
**Estd:** 1997 Proprietorship
**Line of Business:** Schools (local authority)
**Proprietor:** D Parker
**US SIC:** 8211 **UK SIC:** 93200
**Employees:** 120

DUNS 23-154-4318

## Roselodge Care Homes Ltd

185 Belsize Road, Lisburn, Co Antrim BT27 4LA
**Web:** www.roselodge.co.uk
**Reg No:** 0035541NI **Estd:** 2010 Private Limited Company
**Line of Business:** Au pair agencies
**Trading Style:** Rose Lodge Community Care Services
**Issued Capital:** £648,540
**Directors:** R D Dowling, E Warnock, Ms J Thompson, Ms D M Kidd
**Co. Secretary:** David Warnock
**Responsibilities**
**Senior:** Judith Warnock *(Director)*
**US SIC:** 8811 **UK SIC:** 99000
**Auditors:** Blythe Grace
**Bankers:** The Bank Of Ireland (90-22-23)

| | 28-02-14 | 28-02-13 | 29-02-12 |
|---|---|---|---|
| TA | 2,410,449 | 2,390,627 | 2,422,598 |
| NW | 2,152,553 | 2,139,024 | 2,160,393 |
| WC | 573,138 | 536,376 | 438,649 |

DUNS 45-868-5104 **Imp-Exp**

## Rosemary & Thyme Ltd

Progress Way, Mid Suffolk Business Park, Eye, Suffolk IP23 7HU
**Tel:** 01379-871007 **Fax:** 01379-871005
**Web:** www.rosemaryandthyme.co.uk
**Reg No:** 3211003 **Estd:** 1996 Private Limited Company
**Line of Business:** Herbs and spices suppliers and retailers
**Export Sales:** £2,036,790
**Trading Style:** Rosemary & Thyme Ltd
**Issued Capital:** £20,000
**Director:** P Farrow
**Co. Secretary:** Rik Jacob
**Responsibilities**
**Senior:** Dirk Decoster *(Manager)*
**Branches:** Rosemary & Thyme Ltd, Magdala Road, Nottingham, Nottinghamshire NG3 5DE
**US SIC:** 5499, 2099
**UK SIC:** 64100, 42399
**Auditors:** Haines Watts

| | 30-06-14 | 30-06-13 | 30-06-12 |
|---|---|---|---|
| TO | 22,594,359 | 21,345,446 | 20,578,991 |
| P/L | 975,189 | 1,212,011 | 1,606,577 |
| NW | 4,745,126 | 4,752,846 | 4,595,196 |
| WC | 7,567,602 | 5,858,774 | 4,408,697 |
| Emp. | 56 | 53 | 50 |

DUNS 51-566-6100

## Rosemont Holdings Ltd

**(Subsidiary of:** Perrigo Uk Finco Limited Partnership)
Yorkdale Industrial Park, Braithwaite Street, Leeds, West Yorkshire LS11 9XE
**Tel:** 01132977800
**Web:** www.rosemont-holdings.com
**Reg No:** 5848073 **Estd:** 2006 Private Limited Company
**Line of Business:** Manufacturers of pharmaceutical products
**Issued Capital:** £394,976
**Directors:** R P Howard, P Thompson, P M O'Sullivan, M A Tucker
**Co. Secretary:** Niall Kavanagh
**Responsibilities**
**Senior:** Neil Salvin *(Manager)*
**US SIC:** 2834 **UK SIC:** 25700
**Auditors:** PricewaterhouseCoopers LLP
**Bankers:** HSBC Bank plc (40-00-00)

| | 29-06-13 | 31-12-12 | 31-06-11 |
|---|---|---|---|
| TO | N/A | 38,066,000 | 35,818,000 |
| P/L | (506,000) | (197,000) | (3,032,000) |
| NW | 102,692,000 | (91,017,000) | (92,363,000) |
| WC | 102,692,000 | 11,945,000 | 9,135,000 |
| Emp. | N/A | 198 | 198 |

DUNS 21-299-7852 **Imp-Exp**

## Rosemont Pharmaceuticals Ltd

**(Subsidiary of:** Perrigo Company Public Limited Company)
Yorkdale Industrial Park, Braithwaite Street, Leeds, West Yorkshire LS11 9XE
**Tel:** 01132-441400 **Fax:** 01132-453567
**Web:** www.rosemontpharma.com
**Reg No:** 0924648 **VAT No:** 170604683
**Estd:** 1967 Private Limited Company
**Line of Business:** Pharmaceutical suppliers and wholesalers
**Export Markets:** Worldwide countries
**Export Sales:** £1,382,000
**Issued Capital:** £1,762,400
**Directors:** P M O'Sullivan, R P Howard, P Thompson, M A Tucker
**Co. Secretary:** Niall Kavanagh
**Responsibilities**
**Senior:** John Blythe *(Manager)*
**Marketing:** John Blythe *(Manager)*, Jan Flynn *(Marketing Manager)*
**Sales:** John Blythe *(Manager)*
**HR:** Claudette Rushworth *(Human Resources Officer)*
**US SIC:** 2834 **UK SIC:** 25700
**Auditors:** PricewaterhouseCoopers LLP
**Bankers:** National Westminster Bank Plc (60-60-05)

| | 29-06-13 | 31-12-12 | 31-06-11 |
|---|---|---|---|
| TO | 18,406,000 | 38,066,000 | 35,818,000 |
| P/L | 6,683,000 | 17,048,000 | 14,651,000 |
| NW | 94,338,000 | 88,967,000 | 74,741,000 |
| WC | 91,227,000 | 85,352,000 | 70,337,000 |
| Emp. | 198 | 198 | 198 |

DUNS 21-609-9374 **Imp-Exp**

## Rosemount Measurement Ltd

**(Subsidiary of:** Emerson Electric Co.)
158 Edinburgh Avenue, Slough, Berkshire SL1 4UE
**Tel:** 01753-756600 **Fax:** 01753-823589
**Web:** www.mobrey.com
**Reg No:** 0293743 **VAT No:** 425141094
**Estd:** 1934 Private Limited Company
**Line of Business:** Burglar alarm systems
**Export Sales:** £31,605,000
**Trading Style:** Emerson Process Management
**Issued Capital:** £18,114,512
**Directors:** A J Prain, C C Rooke, J Rowley
**Co. Secretary:** Ms Teresa Field
**Responsibilities**
**Senior:** William Lyall *(Manager)*, Thomas Moser *(Manager)*, Beverly Watson *(Senior Finance Manager)*, Joe Wilson *(Manager)*
**Finance:** Beverly Watson *(Senior Finance Manager)*
**Marketing:** Peta Glenister *(Group Marketing Manager)*
**Sales:** Stuart Rattlidge *(Sales Manager)*
**HR:** Denise Good *(Human Resources Manager)*
**Operations:** Richard Canham *(Project Manager)*
**Purchasing:** T Akar *(Purchasing Manager)*
**Branches:** Rosemount Measurement Ltd, Taywood Enterprise Centre, Unit P, Glasgow, Lanarkshire G73 1DR
**US SIC:** 3643, 8911
**UK SIC:** 34203, 83701
**Auditors:** KPMG LLP

| | 30-09-13 | 30-09-12 | 30-09-11 |
|---|---|---|---|
| TO | 35,059,000 | 35,551,000 | 34,823,000 |
| P/L | 6,071,000 | 6,441,000 | 7,716,000 |
| NW | 24,840,000 | 28,642,000 | 22,916,000 |
| WC | 22,244,000 | 26,550,000 | 21,866,000 |
| Emp. | 189 | 184 | 180 |

DUNS 23-223-9319

## Rosenblatt Solicitors

9-13 St Andrew Street, London EC4A 3AF
**Tel:** 020-7955-0880
**Web:** www.rosenblatt-law.co.uk
**VAT No:** 523071385 **Estd:** 1990 Partnership
**Line of Business:** Solicitors
**Trading Style:** Rosenblatt Solicitors
**Partners:** I Rosenblatt, H Salter
**Responsibilities**
**Admin:** Theresa John *(Office Manager)*
**IT:** James Bolger *(IT Manager)*
**US SIC:** 8111 **UK SIC:** 83500
**Employees:** 51

DUNS 21-228-9496

## Rosetrees Residential Care Homes

Asher Loftus Way, London N11 3ND
**Tel:** 020-89204150
**Web:** www.jcare.org
**Estd:** 1997
**Line of Business:** Residential care establishments
**Partner:** Ms A Prior
**US SIC:** 8321 **UK SIC:** 96111
**Employees:** 100

DUNS 21-215-3779

## Rosettes Direct Ltd

The Old Chappelle, Accrington, Lancashire BB5 1DN
**Tel:** 01254393711 **Fax:** 01254-394839
**Web:** www.rosettesdirect.com
**Reg No:** 1521420 **VAT No:** 343165864
**Estd:** 1980 Private Limited Company
**Line of Business:** Suppliers of trophies and medals
**Issued Capital:** £50,000
**Principals:** S R Freegard *(Managing)*, Ms L V Wilkinson
**Co. Secretary:** Stephen Freegard
**Responsibilities**
**Engineering:** Gail Grimmer *(Production Manager)*
**US SIC:** 3911 **UK SIC:** 49101

| | 31-12-13 | 31-12-12 | 31-12-11 |
|---|---|---|---|
| TA | 1 | 1 | 1 |

DUNS 34-622-7361

## Rosevale Holdings Ltd

Pitfold House, Woolmer Hill Road, Haslemere, Surrey GU27 1QA
**Tel:** 01428-661960
**Web:** www.rosevaleholdings.com
**Reg No:** 5429215 **Estd:** 2005 Private Limited Company
**Line of Business:** Holding companies management activities
**Issued Capital:** £105
**Directors:** S A Irons, Ms M Randles, J B Woodward
**Responsibilities**
**Senior:** Christine Churchley *(Manager)*
**Sales:** Mike Hughes *(Business Services Manager)*
**US SIC:** 6711 **UK SIC:** 83962
**Auditors:** Roffe Swayne

| | 31-01-14 | 31-01-13 | 31-01-12 |
|---|---|---|---|
| TO | 9,028,560 | 8,330,765 | 7,028,228 |
| P/L | 964,343 | 781,745 | 603,615 |
| NW | 6,595,718 | 6,024,380 | 3,146,301 |
| WC | (954,494) | (1,363,054) | (1,301,901) |
| Emp. | 296 | 295 | 259 |

DUNS 21-775-7154

## Rosewood

28-30 Norwood Avenue, Southport, Merseyside PR9 7EG
**Tel:** 01704509582
**Estd:** 2002 Proprietorship
**Line of Business:** Residential care establishments
**Proprietor:** J Little
**Responsibilities**
**Senior:** Mark Mussell *(Manager)*
**US SIC:** 8321 **UK SIC:** 96111
**Employees:** 700

DUNS 21-227-9684

## Rosewood Court Care Home

1 Shakespeare Close, Bradford, West Yorkshire BD3 9ES
**Tel:** 01274-308308
**Web:** www.handsale.co.uk
**Estd:** 2001 Proprietorship
**Line of Business:** Nursing homes
**Proprietor:** Mrs V Taylor
**US SIC:** 8051 **UK SIC:** 95100
**Employees:** 75

DUNS 21-210-9649

## Rosewood Manufacturing Co (Gateshead) Ltd

Unit 14, North Shields, Tyne and Wear NE29 8SD
**Tel:** 01912-936363 **Fax:** 01912936393
**Web:** www.rosewoodpackaging.co.uk
**Reg No:** 0526758 **VAT No:** 176581433
**Estd:** 2010 Private Limited Company
**Line of Business:** Manufacture of cartons, boxes and cases of non-corrugated paper and paperboard
**Trading Style:** Rosewood Packaging
**Issued Capital:** £100
**Principals:** S Lord *(Managing)*, M E Preston, P Evans, J G Lord
**Co. Secretary:** Stephen Lord
**Responsibilities**
**Senior:** Ged Wright *(Production Coordinator)*
**Engineering:** Ged Wright *(Production Coordinator)*
**Branches:** Rosewood Manufacturing Co (Gateshead) Ltd, Unit L92, Kingsway, Gateshead, Tyne and Wear NE11 0LB
**US SIC:** 2651, 2645
**UK SIC:** 47253, 47280
**Auditors:** Tenon Audit Ltd
**Bankers:** Barclays Bank Plc (20-62-09)

| | 31-12-13 | 31-12-12 | 31-12-11 |
|---|---|---|---|
| TO | 8,546,696 | 7,738,170 | 7,715,492 |
| P/L | 592,083 | 450,141 | 257,223 |
| NW | 1,427,445 | 1,269,074 | 1,143,513 |
| WC | (230,286) | (199,102) | (217,071) |
| Emp. | 88 | 90 | 94 |

DUNS 21-833-3102 **Imp-Exp**

## Rosewood Pet Products Ltd

45 Coalport Road, Broseley, Shropshire TF12 5AN
**Tel:** 01952-883408 **Fax:** 01952-884359
**Web:** www.rosewoodpet.com
**Reg No:** 0662785 **Estd:** 1960 Private Limited Company
**Line of Business:** Wholesale of live animals
**Export Markets:** E U, Hong Kong.
**Export Sales:** £2,127,834
**Issued Capital:** £3,000
**Principals:** N Panter *(Managing)*, N Cruickshank, M D Bollands, Mrs B Panter
**Responsibilities**
**Senior:** Harry Irving *(Manager)*, Stephen Switonski *(Warehouse Manager)*
**HR:** Stephen Switonski *(Warehouse Manager)*
**Health & Safety:** Stephen Switonski *(Warehouse Manager)*
**Facilities:** Stephen Switonski *(Warehouse Manager)*
**US SIC:** 5154 **UK SIC:** 61100
**Auditors:** Johnson Barton & Co
**Bankers:** Barclays Bank Plc (20-85-46)

| | 31-05-14 | 31-05-13 | 31-05-12 |
|---|---|---|---|
| TO | 19,672,469 | 16,844,230 | 17,667,026 |
| P/L | 902,032 | 643,623 | 630,752 |
| NW | 3,508,078 | 3,096,081 | 2,960,736 |
| WC | 3,259,345 | 2,806,724 | 2,717,391 |
| Emp. | 59 | 60 | 62 |

DUNS 21-825-9278

## Rosewood Primary School Ptfa

Rosewood Avenue, Burnley, Lancashire BB11 2PH
**Tel:** 01282463790
**Web:** www.rosewood.lancs.sch.uk
**Estd:** 2005
**Line of Business:** Schools (local authority)
**Proprietor:** I Mccann
**Responsibilities**
**Senior:** Ian McCann *(Proprietor)*
**US SIC:** 8211 **UK SIC:** 93200
**Employees:** 61

DUNS 23-736-8548

## Rosgal Ltd

Rosgal House, 15 Pollard Street East, Manchester M40 7FS
**Tel:** 01612257836 **Fax:** 01612736945
**Web:** www.rosgal.co.uk
**Reg No:** 3731189 **VAT No:** 733086539
**Estd:** 1999 Private Limited Company
**Line of Business:** Civil engineers
**Issued Capital:** £50
**Principals:** J G Breheny *(Managing)*, K A Breheny, S C Breheny
**Co. Secretary:** Ms Angela Breheny
**Responsibilities**
**Senior:** Kim Eagle *(Office Manager)*
**Admin:** Kim Eagle *(Office Manager)*
**US SIC:** 8911 **UK SIC:** 83701
**Auditors:** Moffatt & Co

| | 31-03-14 | 31-03-13 | 31-03-12 |
|---|---|---|---|
| TA | 620,100 | 425,335 | 762,600 |
| NW | 272,795 | 182,329 | 288,052 |
| WC | 195,882 | 81,649 | 158,320 |

DUNS 42-333-8958 **Imp**
## Roshan Frozen Foods Ltd
56-60 Wharf Road, Tyseley, Birmingham, West Midlands B11 2EB
**Tel:** 0121-706-8188
**Web:** www.humzafoods.co.uk
**Reg No:** 4321633 **Estd:** 2001 Private Limited Company
**Line of Business:** Non-specialised wholesale of food, beverages and tobacco
**Issued Capital:** £160
**Director:** W Liaqat
**Responsibilities**
**Senior:** Waqas Ali *(Manager)*, Jawad Ali *(Manager)*, Liaqat Ali *(Manager)*
**US SIC:** 5149, 5147
**UK SIC:** 61700

| | 30-11-13 | 30-11-12 | 30-11-11 |
|---|---|---|---|
| TA | 1,582,040 | 1,650,565 | 1,404,058 |
| NW | 499,973 | 476,263 | 433,043 |
| WC | (172,270) | (155,444) | (174,947) |

DUNS 21-039-8022 **Imp**
## The Roslin Institute
Marshall Building, Roslin, Midlothian EH25 9PS
**Tel:** 01316519100
**Web:** www.roslin.ac.uk
**Estd:** 1995 Partnership
**Line of Business:** Research institutions and organisations
**Partners:** Dr D Parnell, D Hume, Dr H Marriage, Professor J Tait, C Warkup, Dr J Brown
**Responsibilities**
**IT:** Matt Blair *(Network Manager)*
**HR:** Catherine Eastwood *(Personnel Manager)*, Susan McNeill *(Personnel Manager)*
**US SIC:** 7391 **UK SIC:** 94000
**Employees:** 300

DUNS 38-584-4022
## Roslin Nutrition Ltd
Gosford, Longniddry, East Lothian EH32 0PX
**Tel:** 01875-871270 **Fax:** 01875871268
**Web:** www.roslinnutrition.co.uk
**Reg No:** 0173850SC **Estd:** 1997 Private Limited Company
**Line of Business:** Animal husbandry service activities, except veterinary activities, not elsewhere classified
**Trading Style:** Roslin Nutrition Ltd
**Issued Capital:** £1
**Directors:** M Andrews, D J Currie, The Honourable J D Lord Douglas Of Neidpath, Ms A I Knox
**US SIC:** 0751, 2048
**UK SIC:** 01003, 42210
**Auditors:** Scott Moncrieff
**Bankers:** Bank Of Scotland (80-20-00)

| | 31-03-14 | 31-03-13 | 31-03-12 |
|---|---|---|---|
| TO | 1,000,153 | 1,432,974 | 1,753,006 |
| P/L | (137,476) | 38,953 | 48,187 |
| NW | 266,313 | 384,466 | 354,851 |
| WC | (81,452) | 43,966 | 27,574 |

DUNS 21-106-7783
## Rosling King Llp
10 Old Bailey, London EC4M 7NG
**Tel:** 02072468000 **Fax:** 02072468100
**Web:** www.rkllp.co.uk
**Reg No:** 0334495OC **Estd:** 1978 Private Limited Company
**Line of Business:** Solicitors
**Responsibilities**
**Senior:** Ann Ebberson *(Human Resources Manager)*, Jonathan Hyndman *(Partner)*, Amy Lacey *(Partner)*, Melissa Padoa *(Partner)*, Juliet Schalker *(Partner)*, Rebecca Sharpe *(Partner)*, Helen Thurkettle *(Partner)*
**HR:** Ann Ebberson *(Human Resources Manager)*
**US SIC:** 8111 **UK SIC:** 83500

| | 30-04-14 | 30-04-13 | 30-04-12 |
|---|---|---|---|
| TO | 12,202,136 | 9,926,683 | 12,190,295 |
| P/L | 5,910,420 | 4,010,651 | 6,534,911 |
| NW | 5,910,420 | 3,846,063 | 6,534,911 |
| WC | 10,917,578 | 10,294,697 | 10,164,494 |
| Emp. | 82 | 84 | 81 |

DUNS 22-266-4307
## Rosoft Training Ltd
14 Birchen Lee, Emerson Valley, Milton Keynes, Buckinghamshire MK4 2JX
**Tel:** 01908-330400
**Web:** www.rosoft.co.uk
**Reg No:** 4284389 **Estd:** 1901 Private Limited Company
**Line of Business:** Computer training
**Issued Capital:** £1,000
**Director:** M Gurner
**Co. Secretary:** Ms Joanne Gurner
**US SIC:** 8299, 8249
**UK SIC:** 93300

| | 30-09-13 | 30-09-12 | 30-09-11 |
|---|---|---|---|
| TO | N/A | N/A | 66,614 |
| P/L | N/A | N/A | 47,863 |
| NW | 2,847 | 5,496 | 1,865 |
| WC | 1,488 | 3,218 | 308 |

DUNS 21-148-7176
## Ross Aldridge Llp
Fifth Floor Eagle Tower, Montpellier Drive, Cheltenham, Gloucestershire GL50 1TA
**Tel:** 01242707400
**Web:** www.rossaldridge.co.uk
**Reg No:** 0342430OC **Estd:** 2009
**Line of Business:** Solicitors
**US SIC:** 8111 **UK SIC:** 83500

| | 31-03-14 | 31-03-13 | 31-03-12 |
|---|---|---|---|
| TO | 4,735,240 | 7,885,970 | 6,819,098 |
| NW | 5,686 | N/A | N/A |
| WC | (42,045) | 947,177 | 999,705 |
| Emp. | 84 | 149 | 129 |

DUNS 64-110-6182 **Imp**
## Ross & Catherall Ltd
**(Subsidiary of:** Government of Dubai)
Forge Lane, Sheffield, South Yorkshire S21 1BW
**Tel:** 01142-486404
**Web:** www.doncasters.com
**Reg No:** 4110786 **VAT No:** 125826076
**Estd:** 2000 Private Limited Company
**Line of Business:** Production of alloys
**Export Sales:** £33,980,000
**Issued Capital:** £1,000,002
**Directors:** M J Schurch, D Hinks
**Co. Secretary:** Ian Molyneux
**Responsibilities**
**Senior:** Bob Hunt *(Sales Manager)*
**US SIC:** 3325, 3999
**UK SIC:** 31110, 49590
**Auditors:** PricewaterhouseCoopers LLP

| | 31-12-13 | 31-12-12 | 31-12-11 |
|---|---|---|---|
| TO | 77,469,000 | 80,466,000 | 90,525,000 |
| P/L | 13,344,000 | 11,265,000 | 12,499,000 |
| NW | 118,042,000 | 104,577,000 | 93,137,000 |
| WC | 108,896,000 | 95,739,000 | 83,714,000 |
| Emp. | 158 | 143 | 140 |

DUNS 29-671-3654
## Ross & Liddell Ltd
60 St Enoch Square, Glasgow, Lanarkshire G1 4AW
**Tel:** 0141-221-9266
**Web:** www.ross-liddell.com
**Reg No:** 0097770SC **VAT No:** 481723146
**Estd:** 1854 Private Limited Company
**Line of Business:** Management of real estate on a fee or contract basis
**Trading Style:** Ross & Liddell Incorporating Winnings & Fulton
**Issued Capital:** £1,790
**Directors:** A Cunningham, Ms I C Devenny, B W Fulton, G Gilroy
**Co. Secretary:** Alexander Cassidy
**Responsibilities**
**Senior:** Keith Bagnall *(Information technology Executi)*, John Brolly *(Manager)*
**IT:** Keith Bagnall *(Information technology Executi)*
**Health & Safety:** Alan Beaver *(Facilities Manager)*
**Facilities:** Alan Beaver *(Facilities Manager)*
**Purchasing:** Alan Beaver *(Facilities Manager)*
**Branches:** Ross & Liddell Ltd, 6 Clifton Terrace, Edinburgh, Midlothian EH12 5DR
**US SIC:** 6531 **UK SIC:** 83400
**Auditors:** Ernst & Young LLP
**Bankers:** The Royal Bank Of Scotland Plc (83-41-00)

| | 31-03-14 | 31-03-13 | 31-03-12 |
|---|---|---|---|
| TO | 4,165,239 | 4,110,522 | 4,185,949 |
| P/L | 459,249 | 150,716 | 732,221 |
| NW | 2,585,982 | 2,842,278 | 2,851,519 |
| WC | 1,702,405 | 1,972,999 | 2,004,262 |
| Emp. | 78 | 88 | 82 |

DUNS 21-241-1029 **Exp**
## Ross Auto Engineering Ltd
**(Subsidiary of:** Ross Care Holdings Ltd)
2-3 Westfield Road, Wallasey, Merseyside CH44 7HX
**Tel:** 01516536000 **Fax:** 01516 538543
**Web:** www.rosselectricvehicles.co.uk
**Reg No:** 0469301 **VAT No:** 164356753
**Estd:** 1949 Private Limited Company
**Line of Business:** Car and commercial vehicle repairs
**Trading Style:** Ross Care Centres
**Issued Capital:** £14,625
**Principals:** J M Turner *(Managing)*, Mrs E M Turner, J F Parramore
**Co. Secretary:** Peter Smith
**Responsibilities**
**Senior:** Shirley Dempsey *(Operations Manager)*, Dave Munt *(Warehouse Manager)*
**IT:** Stephen Dean *(Operations Manager)*
**HR:** Shirley Dempsey *(Operations Manager)*
**Health & Safety:** Stephen Dean *(Operations Manager)*
**Operations:** Shirley Dempsey *(Operations Manager)*
**Purchasing:** David Clay *(Contract Coordinator)*
**Branches:** Ross Auto Engineering Ltd, Chester Road, Ellesmere Port, Cheshire CH65 6RX
**US SIC:** 3799 **UK SIC:** 36502
**Auditors:** Hollows Davies Crane
**Bankers:** National Westminster Bank Plc (60-20-11)

| | 30-06-13 | 30-06-12 | 30-06-11 |
|---|---|---|---|
| TO | 7,455,891 | 7,176,348 | 6,472,696 |
| P/L | 655,489 | 525,308 | 589,974 |
| NW | 2,647,755 | 2,165,141 | 1,799,171 |
| WC | 1,661,873 | 1,125,728 | 851,709 |
| Emp. | 147 | 149 | 139 |

DUNS 39-821-9568 **Imp-Exp**
## Ross Ceramics Ltd
**(Subsidiary of:** Rolls-Royce Holdings Plc)
Derby Road, Ripley, Derbyshire DE5 8NX
**Tel:** 01773-570800 **Fax:** 01773-570152
**Web:** www.rossceramics.co.uk
**Reg No:** 2220030 **Estd:** 1969 Private Limited Company
**Line of Business:** Manufacturers and suppliers of ceramics
**Export Markets:** U S A, W Europe, Australia, Japan
**Issued Capital:** £150,000
**Directors:** G A Ridgley, M A Hulands
**Co. Secretary:** Andrew Harvey-Wrate
**Responsibilities**
**Senior:** Anthony Cox *(Manager)*, Hedley Hazell *(Manager)*, Alex Hoolop *(Manager)*
**IT:** Paul Bain *(IT Manager)*
**US SIC:** 3269 **UK SIC:** 24894
**Auditors:** KPMG Audit Plc
**Bankers:** Lloyds TSB Bank plc (30-00-02)

| | 31-12-13 | 31-12-12 | 31-12-11 |
|---|---|---|---|
| TO | 12,766,000 | 12,343,000 | 13,284,000 |
| P/L | 101,000 | (239,000) | 471,000 |
| NW | 4,908,000 | 4,668,000 | 4,696,000 |
| WC | 2,735,000 | 2,610,000 | 3,224,000 |
| Emp. | 245 | 238 | 234 |

DUNS 21-808-9759
## Ross Coates Solicitors
15 High Street, City Centre, Ipswich, Suffolk IP1 3JZ
**Tel:** 01473222303
**Web:** www.rosscoates-conveyancing.co.uk
**Estd:** 2012
**Line of Business:** Solicitors
**US SIC:** 8111 **UK SIC:** 83500
**Employees:** 50

DUNS 28-822-0221
## Ross County Football Club Ltd
Jubilee Park Road, Dingwall, Ross-Shire IV15 9QZ
**Tel:** 01349860860 **Fax:** 01349-866277
**Web:** www.rosscountyfootballclub.co.uk
**Reg No:** 0033275SC **Estd:** 1958 Private Limited Company
**Line of Business:** Sports clubs
**Issued Capital:** £4,821,110
**Principals:** R J Macgregor *(Managing)*, G Ryder, G M Macrae, D W Mackenzie, A I Kennedy, J D Macdonald, L F Daly, J W Macgregor
**Co. Secretary:** Michael Kydd
**Responsibilities**
**Senior:** Ronald Fraser *(Director)*, Ronald Gilbert *(Head Of Administration)*, David Siegel *(Chairman)*
**Marketing:** Grant Wallace *(Marketing Manager)*
**US SIC:** 7999 **UK SIC:** 97913
**Auditors:** Ernst & Young LLP
**Bankers:** Bank Of Scotland (80-05-14)

| | 30-06-13 | 30-06-12 | 30-06-11 |
|---|---|---|---|
| TA | 2,960,181 | 2,803,907 | 742,408 |
| NW | 2,494,449 | 780,772 | 739,672 |
| WC | 1,870,077 | 156,400 | N/A |

DUNS 29-249-7138 **Imp-Exp**
## Ross Farm Machinery Ltd
Unit 8/9, Ross-On-Wye, Herefordshire HR9 5NB
**Tel:** 01989-768811 **Fax:** 01989-768465
**Web:** www.rossfarm.co.uk
**Reg No:** 1348974 **VAT No:** 549762594
**Estd:** 1978 Private Limited Company
**Line of Business:** Wholesale of agricultural machinery and accessories and implements, including tractors
**Export Markets:** W Europe; European Union (E U)
**Export Sales:** £1,339,515
**Trading Style:** Ross Trailer Centre, Raglan Trailer Centre
**Issued Capital:** £45,000
**Principals:** R A Brett *(Marketing)*, P C Kennedy, M S Stuffins
**Co. Secretary:** Paul Stuffins
**Responsibilities**
**Senior:** Anthony Dudfield *(Joint Managing Director)*, Francis Evans *(Workshop Manager)*
**HR:** Francis Evans *(Workshop Manager)*
**Health & Safety:** Francis Evans *(Workshop Manager)*
**Facilities:** Francis Evans *(Workshop Manager)*
**Purchasing:** Tony Farr *(Purchasing Manager)*
**Engineering:** Francis Evans *(Workshop Manager)*
**Branches:** Ross Farm Machinery Ltd, Unit 3 Maylite Trading Estate, Berrow Green Road, Martley, Worcester, Worcestershire WR6 6PQ
**US SIC:** 5083 **UK SIC:** 61490
**Auditors:** Grant Thornton
**Bankers:** HSBC Bank plc (40-22-09)

| | 31-05-14 | 31-05-13 | 31-05-12 |
|---|---|---|---|
| TO | 24,617,003 | 25,466,425 | 26,949,915 |
| P/L | 139,102 | 189,689 | 261,548 |
| NW | 2,330,525 | 2,268,406 | 2,168,218 |
| WC | 2,329,636 | 2,042,570 | 1,945,371 |
| Emp. | 49 | 51 | 50 |

DUNS 23-823-4194
## Ross Healthcare Ltd
**(Subsidiary of:** Majesticare Holdings 1 Ltd)
Holly Villa 27 Crewe Road, Alsager, Stoke-On-Trent, Staffordshire ST7 2EY
**Tel:** 01270878883
**Web:** www.majesticare.co.uk
**Reg No:** 3815444 **Estd:** 1999 Private Limited Company
**Line of Business:** Medical nursing home activities
**Issued Capital:** £100
**Directors:** Ms E J Hart, R W Pratap, M B Pratap
**Co. Secretary:** Steven Oakes
**Responsibilities**
**Senior:** Steven Barley *(Accountant)*
**Finance:** Steven Barley *(Accountant)*
**US SIC:** 7399 **UK SIC:** 83954

| | 30-09-13 | 30-09-12 | 30-09-11 |
|---|---|---|---|
| TO | 11,481,461 | 17,129,865 | 15,424,405 |
| P/L | 9,295,943 | 1,503,179 | 910,861 |
| NW | 8,654,104 | 3,455,196 | 1,972,495 |
| WC | 27,406,191 | 9,917,473 | 8,927,659 |
| Emp. | 436 | 637 | 581 |

DUNS 21-774-7860
## Ross High School
Well Wynd, Tranent, East Lothian EH33 2EQ
**Tel:** 01875610433
**Web:** www.ross.e-lothian.sch.uk
**Estd:** 1963 Proprietorship
**Line of Business:** Schools (local authority)
**Proprietor:** Mrs D Bartholomew
**US SIC:** 8211 **UK SIC:** 93200
**Employees:** 90

DUNS 58-495-5025 **Imp**
## Ross Holdings Ltd
1 Ross Street, Sheffield, South Yorkshire S9 4PU
**Tel:** 01142-447720
**Web:** www.allroofing.co.uk
**Reg No:** 2909651 **Estd:** 1984 Private Limited Company
**Line of Business:** Management activities of holding companies
**Issued Capital:** £157,002
**Principals:** J H Martin *(Managing)*, J B Elmore, G Brooks
**Co. Secretary:** Richard Christian
**US SIC:** 6711, 1761
**UK SIC:** 83962, 50400
**Auditors:** Wingfield Slater

| | 30-09-13 | 30-09-12 | 30-09-11 |
|---|---|---|---|
| TA | 625,474 | 579,760 | 626,058 |
| NW | 484,204 | 481,069 | 479,188 |
| WC | 301,871 | 312,889 | 305,653 |

DUNS 54-374-7893
## Ross Human Directions Ltd
**(Subsidiary of:** Ross Human Directions Limited)
Religare House, London EC4N 6EU
**Tel:** 020-7929-1199 **Fax:** 020-7929-7196
**Web:** www.rossjuliaross.com
**Reg No:** 3262728 **VAT No:** 697448078
**Estd:** 1996 Private Limited Company
**Line of Business:** Employment and recruitment companies and consultants
**Trading Style:** Rossjuliaross
**Issued Capital:** £100
**Directors:** G D Brooks, C J Judson
**Co. Secretary:** Jd Secretariat Limited
**Responsibilities**
**Senior:** Maria Jones *(Managing Director)*, Esther Marsden *(Manager)*
**US SIC:** 7361 **UK SIC:** 83954
**Auditors:** Slaven Jeffcote LLP
**Bankers:** Coutts & Co (18-00-02)

| | 30-06-14 | 30-06-13 | 30-06-12 |
|---|---|---|---|
| TO | 3,319,065 | 3,101,394 | 3,551,273 |
| P/L | 32,576 | 81,204 | 151,182 |
| NW | 562,673 | 537,722 | 616,234 |
| WC | 560,700 | 535,337 | 606,532 |
| Emp. | 131 | 157 | 158 |

DUNS 53-613-3697
## Ross-Shire Engineering Ltd
(**Subsidiary of:** Geg (Holdings) Ltd)
Muir Of Ord Industrial Estate Great, North Road, Muir of Ord, Ross-Shire IV6 7UA
**Tel:** 01463-870-049 **Fax:** 01463-871-020
**Web:** www.ross-eng.com
**Reg No:** 0177939SC **VAT No:** 694020737
**Estd:** 1997 Private Limited Company
**Line of Business:** Engineering services
**Export Sales:** £287,473
**Issued Capital:** £18,000
**Directors:** J D Macdonald, R J Macgregor, I R Macgregor, J I Macgregor, G G Grant
**Co. Secretary:** Allan Dallas
**Responsibilities**
**Health & Safety:** Tina Rawcliffe *(Health & Safety Officer)*
**Engineering:** Gordon Kellow *(Design Engineer)*
**US SIC:** 1711, 3559, 8911, 1799
**UK SIC:** 50300, 32863, 83701, 50000
**Auditors:** Ernst & Young LLP
**Bankers:** Bank Of Scotland (80-91-26)

| | 31-03-14 | 31-03-13 | 30-03-11 |
|---|---|---|---|
| TO | 37,059,355 | 57,707,884 | 16,970,056 |
| P/L | 2,583,660 | 2,905,695 | 711,363 |
| NW | 7,004,562 | 5,085,182 | 2,913,819 |
| WC | 3,566,179 | 2,134,606 | 784,706 |
| Emp. | 210 | 261 | 120 |

DUNS 64-266-4940 **Imp**
## Rossdale & Partners
Beaufort Cottage Stables, 140 High Street, Newmarket, Suffolk CB8 8JS
**Tel:** 01638-663150
**Web:** www.rossdales.com
**Estd:** 1978 Partnership
**Line of Business:** Veterinary activities
**Partners:** N Wingfield-Digby, Dr P Rossdale, Dr S Ricketts
**Responsibilities**
**Senior:** Tim Greet *(Managing Partner)*
**Health & Safety:** Robert Cash *(Health & Safety Officer)*
**Branches:** Rossdale & Partners, Cotton End Road, Exning, Newmarket, Suffolk CB8 7NN
**US SIC:** 0741 **UK SIC:** 95601
**Employees:** 50

DUNS 29-496-2899
## Rossefield Nursing Homes Ltd
(**Subsidiary of:** Rossefield Management Services Ltd)
122 Leylands Lane, Bradford, West Yorkshire BD9 5QU
**Tel:** 01274-488855 **Fax:** 01274-544801
**Web:** www.wellspringsnursinghome.co.uk
**Reg No:** 1859586 **Estd:** 1984 Private Limited Company
**Line of Business:** Nursing homes
**Trading Style:** Well Springs Nursing Home
**Issued Capital:** £100
**Managing Director:** J Redhead
**Co. Secretary:** Mrs Karen Redhead
**Responsibilities**
**Senior:** Susan Seal *(CEO, Managing Director)*
**HR:** Sue Walsh *(Human Resources Manager)*
**US SIC:** 8051 **UK SIC:** 95100

| | 31-10-14 | 31-10-13 | 31-10-12 |
|---|---|---|---|
| TA | 2,011,536 | 3,090,371 | 3,037,260 |
| NW | 11,201 | 1,174,244 | 1,005,721 |
| WC | (40,247) | 1,035,736 | 987,257 |

DUNS 21-212-5736
## Rossendale Group Ltd
Grange Road, Livingston, West Lothian EH54 5DE
**Tel:** 01506444455
**Web:** www.eurohiredrive.com
**Reg No:** 0463320 **Estd:** 2012 Private Limited Company
**Line of Business:** Manufacture of lifting and handling equipment
**Trading Style:** Rossendale Chain & Block Co, Abel Foxall Lifting Gear, Cymru Lifting Gear, Stockport Lifting Gear
**Issued Capital:** £80,000
**Principals:** S J Bamford *(Managing)*, J A Bamford
**Co. Secretary:** Ms Cynthia Bamford
**Responsibilities**
**Senior:** Adam Aziz *(Proprietor)*
**Branches:** Rossendale Group Ltd, Roman Way, Lincoln, Lincolnshire LN6 9UH
**US SIC:** 3534, 7394
**UK SIC:** 32553, 84000
**Auditors:** Waterworths
**Bankers:** HSBC Bank plc (40-20-20)

| | 31-03-14 | 31-03-13 | 31-03-12 |
|---|---|---|---|
| TA | 1,594,773 | 1,892,381 | 1,859,953 |
| NW | 1,018,176 | 1,012,176 | 877,091 |
| WC | 686,933 | 705,637 | 685,961 |

DUNS 23-161-4256
## Rossendale Holdings
Po Box 324, Rossendale, Lancashire BB4 0GE
**Tel:** 01706833770
**Web:** www.rossendales.com
**Estd:** 1980 Partnership
**Line of Business:** Other legal activities not elsewhere classified
**Partners:** Mrs J Green Jones, D Chapman, M Shang, A Clifton
**US SIC:** 8999 **UK SIC:** 83954
**Employees:** 124

DUNS 29-683-5762
## Rossendale Transport Ltd
(**Subsidiary of:** Rossendale Borough Council)
Knowsley Park Way, Knowsley Road Industrial Estate, Hasling, Rossendale, Lancashire BB4 4RS
**Web:** www.rossendalebus.co.uk
**Reg No:** 2004970 **Estd:** 1986 Private Limited Company
**Line of Business:** Bus operators and stations
**Issued Capital:** £645,000
**Directors:** M R Parkes, Miss C C Kelly, R Knowles, Dr C E Crawforth, R Wilkinson, B W Essex, M P Marriott, A C Cheetham
**Co. Secretary:** Matthew Parkes
**Responsibilities**
**Senior:** Brian Juffs *(Manager)*, Alastair Nuttall *(Manager)*, Edgar Oldham *(Manager)*, Trevor Unsworth *(Manager)*
**Branches:** Rossendale Transport Ltd, Mandale Park, Corporation Road, Rochdale, Lancashire OL11 4HJ
**US SIC:** 4119 **UK SIC:** 72200
**Auditors:** KPMG LLP
**Bankers:** National Westminster Bank Plc (01-07-29)

| | 31-03-14 | 31-03-13 | 31-03-12 |
|---|---|---|---|
| TO | 9,920,926 | 9,207,690 | 9,447,477 |
| P/L | 180,294 | (440,921) | (920,400) |
| NW | 1,050,908 | 1,134,149 | 1,721,578 |
| WC | (532,020) | (573,708) | (518,167) |
| Emp. | 253 | 253 | 268 |

DUNS 55-075-6258
## The Rossendale Trust
Rossendale Hall, Hollin Lane, Sutton, Macclesfield, Cheshire SK11 0HR
**Tel:** 01260252216
**Web:** www.rossendaletrust.org
**Estd:** 1973
**Line of Business:** Residential care establishments
**Chairman:** Mrs S Ferness
**Responsibilities**
**Senior:** Steve Nichols *(Chief Executive Officer)*
**Branches:** The Rossendale Trust, 3 Leefield Rd, High Peak, Derbyshire SK23 0LF
**US SIC:** 8091 **UK SIC:** 95200
**Employees:** 100

DUNS 21-153-9018
## Rossetts (Uk) Ltd
Meadow Road Industrial Estate, Worthing, West Sussex BN11 2RU
**Tel:** 01903-223400 **Fax:** 01903-223422
**Web:** www.rossetts.co.uk
**Reg No:** 6689316 **VAT No:** 938962173
**Estd:** 2009 Private Limited Company
**Line of Business:** Car dealers (used)
**Trading Style:** Rossetts Commercials
**Issued Capital:** £2,500,000
**Directors:** Mrs P M Mckeating, R G Maxwell, L N Mckibbin, P Reeves, E G Zoratti
**Co. Secretary:** Mrs Pauline Mckeating
**Responsibilities**
**Senior:** Brian Phippen *(Manager)*
**Finance:** Wayne Solomon *(Finance Director)*
**Sales:** Brian Phippen *(Manager)*
**IT:** John Logan *(IT Manager)*
**Branches:** Rossetts (Uk) Ltd, 1 Eastern Road, Aldershot, Hampshire GU12 4TB
**US SIC:** 5521, 7539
**UK SIC:** 65100, 67100
**Auditors:** PricewaterhouseCoopers LLP
**Bankers:** The Bank Of Ireland (90-21-27)

| | 31-12-13 | 31-12-12 | 31-12-11 |
|---|---|---|---|
| TO | 42,195,866 | 36,549,371 | 29,083,823 |
| P/L | 651,728 | 47,485 | 203,388 |
| NW | 3,358,521 | 2,870,085 | 2,783,707 |
| WC | 1,655,970 | 1,673,903 | 1,584,082 |
| Emp. | 146 | 150 | 158 |

DUNS 77-936-6137
## Rossie Young People's Trust
Rossie, Montrose, Angus DD10 9TN
**Tel:** 01674-820204
**Web:** www.rossie.org.uk
**Reg No:** 0157602SC **Estd:** 1995 Private Limited Company
**Line of Business:** Business services
**Directors:** J A Sutcliffe, Ms F Mackenzie, Dr M J Morphy, E O Russell, E J Foulis, Dr C J Urquhart, Ms C Richardson, A Y Chalmers
**Co. Secretary:** Thorntons Law Llp
**Responsibilities**
**IT:** Bob Condie *(Network Administrator)*
**US SIC:** 8999 **UK SIC:** 83954
**Auditors:** Murray Taylor (Scotland) Ltd
**Employees:** 135

DUNS 21-017-9195
## Rosskeen Scaffolding Ltd
Roskeen Old Manse, Rosskeen Bridge, Invergordon, Ross-Shire IV18 0PR
**Tel:** 01349853222
**Web:** www.mcdonaldscaffolding.com
**Reg No:** 0332393SC **Estd:** 2007 Private Limited Company
**Line of Business:** Building services
**Trading Style:** McDonald Scaffolding
**Issued Capital:** £35,002
**Director:** M M Mcdonald
**Co. Secretary:** James Cameron
**US SIC:** 1799 **UK SIC:** 50000

| | 30-11-13 | 30-11-12 | 30-11-11 |
|---|---|---|---|
| TO | 20,305,220 | 10,134,242 | 7,367,387 |
| P/L | 3,130,676 | 922,804 | 447,281 |
| NW | 5,638,967 | 3,380,832 | 2,766,554 |
| WC | 3,605,107 | 1,900,356 | 1,623,226 |
| Emp. | 225 | 119 | 90 |

DUNS 23-996-3494 **Imp**
## Rosti McKechnie Ltd
(**Subsidiary of:** Nordstjernan Ab)
Bridge Works, Stamford Bridge, York, North Yorkshire YO41 1AL
**Tel:** 01751472139 **Fax:** 01759-371517
**Web:** www.rosti.com
**Reg No:** 3984537 **VAT No:** 184473343
**Estd:** 2002 Private Limited Company
**Line of Business:** Plastic injection moulding
**Export Sales:** £5,577,000
**Trading Style:** McKechnie Plastic Components
**Issued Capital:** £10,000
**Directors:** M Dittmann, B Vernet, B Coughlan
**Responsibilities**
**Senior:** Barry Cuoghlin *(Manager)*, Michael Sturgess *(Financial Director)*
**Finance:** Michael Sturgess *(Financial Director)*
**Branches:** Rosti Mckechnie Ltd, Bridge Works, York, North Yorkshire YO41 1AL
**US SIC:** 3079, 3714
**UK SIC:** 48360, 35300
**Auditors:** PricewaterhouseCoopers LLP
**Bankers:** Lloyds TSB Bank plc (30-00-03)

| | 31-12-13 | 31-12-12 | 31-12-11 |
|---|---|---|---|
| TO | 95,621,000 | 79,429,000 | 70,770,000 |
| P/L | 6,594,000 | 4,216,000 | 2,051,000 |
| NW | 35,834,000 | 29,225,000 | 25,116,000 |
| WC | 17,460,000 | 14,391,000 | 12,374,000 |
| Emp. | 541 | 440 | 402 |

DUNS 50-546-7993 **Imp-Exp**
## Rosti Uk Ltd
(**Subsidiary of:** Nordstjernan Ab)
Baird Avenue, Larkhall, Lanarkshire ML9 2PJ
**Tel:** 01698552200 **Fax:** 01698 888389
**Web:** www.rosti.com
**Reg No:** 2501256 **Estd:** 1990 Private Limited Company
**Line of Business:** Manufacture of other plastic products
**Export Markets:** U S A
**Export Sales:** £982,567
**Issued Capital:** £250,000
**Managing Director:** B Coughlan
**Responsibilities**
**Senior:** Lillian He *(Financial Manager)*
**Finance:** Lillian He *(Financial Manager)*
**Facilities:** Jillian McNeil *(Plant Manager)*
**US SIC:** 3079 **UK SIC:** 48360
**Auditors:** PricewaterhouseCoopers LLP
**Bankers:** HSBC Bank plc (40-45-27)

| | 31-12-13 | 31-12-12 | 31-12-11 |
|---|---|---|---|
| TO | 22,270,772 | 19,294,354 | 15,743,454 |
| P/L | 1,218,390 | 723,388 | 224,409 |
| NW | 6,901,182 | 3,528,675 | 2,854,413 |
| WC | (117,706) | 1,836,017 | (1,291,353) |
| Emp. | 247 | 215 | 210 |

DUNS 21-580-3173
## Rosturk House
Carslogie Road, Cupar, Fife KY15 4HY
**Web:** www.rosturk.co.uk
**Estd:** 2003 Proprietorship
**Line of Business:** Residential care establishments
**Proprietor:** Mrs P Laidlaw
**Responsibilities**
**Senior:** Ashley Deacon *(Manager)*, Ashley Ferguson *(Senior Finance Administrator)*, Sandra Hackathorn *(Manager)*
**Finance:** Ashley Ferguson *(Senior Finance Administrator)*
**Admin:** Maureen White *(Administration Assistant)*
**US SIC:** 8321 **UK SIC:** 96111
**Employees:** 60

DUNS 23-729-7630
## Rosturk House Ltd
111 Loughborough Road, Kirkcaldy, Fife KY1 3DD
**Tel:** 01592652172
**Web:** www.rosturk.co.uk
**Reg No:** 0193979SC **Estd:** 1999 Private Limited Company
**Line of Business:** Residential care establishments
**Trading Style:** Wilby House
**Issued Capital:** £100
**Directors:** J Gaughan, Mrs W Mccarroll, G D Mccarroll
**Co. Secretary:** Mrs Susan Gaughan
**Responsibilities**
**Senior:** Ashley Deacon *(Manager)*, Ashley Ferguson *(Manager)*, Sandra Hackathorn *(Manager)*
**US SIC:** 8321 **UK SIC:** 96111
**Bankers:** Allied Irish Bank (gb) (83-91-06)

| | 31-03-14 | 31-03-13 | 31-03-12 |
|---|---|---|---|
| TO | 4,720,422 | 4,274,960 | 4,353,399 |
| P/L | 521,825 | 293,322 | 674,883 |
| NW | 625,043 | 371,584 | 290,408 |
| WC | 677,387 | 446,139 | 523,893 |
| Emp. | 160 | 175 | 175 |

DUNS 21-206-9413 **Imp-Exp**
## Rota Engineering Ltd
(**Subsidiary of:** Wharton Holdings Ltd)
Wellington Street, Bury, Lancashire BL8 2BD
**Tel:** 0161-764-0424 **Fax:** 0161-762-9729
**Web:** www.rota-eng.com
**Reg No:** 0415416 **VAT No:** 146214782
**Estd:** 1964 Private Limited Company
**Line of Business:** Manufacture of electronic instruments and appliances for measuring, checking, testing, navigating and other purposes, except industrial process control equipment
**Issued Capital:** £5,000
**Principals:** R Gething *(Managing)*, D J Sumner, M J Fawcett
**Co. Secretary:** Alan Hill
**Responsibilities**
**IT:** Brad Blower *(IT Manager)*, Brad French *(IT Manager)*
**US SIC:** 3829 **UK SIC:** 37100
**Auditors:** Edwards Veeder (Oldham) LLP
**Bankers:** HSBC Bank plc (40-15-21)

| | 31-08-13 | 31-08-12 | 31-08-11 |
|---|---|---|---|
| TO | 8,768,250 | N/A | N/A |
| P/L | 2,322,244 | N/A | N/A |
| NW | 4,264,420 | 2,553,258 | 1,435,821 |
| WC | 3,495,755 | 1,845,985 | 803,288 |
| Emp. | 59 | N/A | N/A |

DUNS 21-805-3932 **Imp-Exp**
## Rotadex Systems Ltd
(**Subsidiary of:** Redacell Ltd)
Systems House, Central Business Park, Birmingham, West Midlands B33 0JL
**Tel:** 0121-783-7411
**Web:** www.rotadex.co.uk
**Reg No:** 0527785 **Estd:** 1984 Private Limited Company
**Line of Business:** Printers general
**Export Markets:** Worldwide
**Issued Capital:** £71,300
**Principals:** W J White *(Managing)*, M J White *(Sales)*, M Bailey
**Co. Secretary:** Peter Talbot
**Responsibilities**
**HR:** Michael Guest *(Print Manager)*
**Purchasing:** June Gough *(Purchasing Manager)*
**US SIC:** 2599, 3499
**UK SIC:** 46720, 31694
**Auditors:** Cotterell & Co
**Bankers:** Barclays Bank Plc (20-77-62)

| | 31-12-13 | 31-12-12 | 31-12-11 |
|---|---|---|---|
| TA | 3,027,648 | 2,889,821 | 3,070,460 |
| NW | 731,378 | 550,471 | 562,507 |
| WC | 379,767 | 368,834 | 373,270 |

DUNS 34-528-3449
## Rotala Plc
Beacon House, Long Acre, Birmingham, West Midlands B7 5JJ
**Tel:** 01213222222 **Fax:** 01213222718
**Web:** www.rotalaplc.co.uk
**Reg No:** 5338907 **Estd:** 2005 Public Limited Company
**Line of Business:** Other scheduled passenger land transport not elsewhere classified
**Issued Capital:** £8,817,722
**Directors:** F G Flight, R A Dunn, J H Gunn, S L Dunn
**Co. Secretary:** Kim Taylor
**Responsibilities**
**Senior:** Antony Goozee *(Strategy/Business Development)*

**Sales:** Antony Goozee *(Strategy/Business Development)*, Stephen Haselden *(Group Business Development and)*
**US SIC:** 4119 **UK SIC:** 72200
**Auditors:** Grant Thornton UK LLP
**Bankers:** Barclays Bank Plc (20-00-00)

| | 30-11-13 | 30-11-12 | 30-11-11 |
|---|---|---|---|
| TO | 53,303,000 | 54,813,000 | 56,077,000 |
| P/L | 2,058,000 | 2,076,000 | 1,878,000 |
| NW | 14,102,000 | 12,394,000 | 11,576,000 |
| WC | (5,075,000) | (3,012,000) | (4,931,000) |
| Emp. | 1,073 | 1,089 | 1,200 |

DUNS 21-610-1386 **Imp-Exp**

## Rotalink Ltd

(**Subsidiary of:** Oval (259) Ltd)
Unit 4 Cropmead, Crewkerne, Somerset TA18 7HQ
**Tel:** 0146 072 000 **Fax:** 0146 074 278
**Web:** www.rotalink.com
**Reg No:** 0313872 **Estd:** 1936 Private Limited Company
**Line of Business:** Representative office
**Export Markets:** Worldwide
**Export Sales:** £5,670,037
**Issued Capital:** £72,500
**Principals:** M E Hazell *(Managing)*, Ms O S Hazell
**Co. Secretary:** Ms Rose Hazell
**Responsibilities**
**Senior:** David Auton *(Buyer)*
**Health & Safety:** David Auton *(Buyer)*
**Operations:** David Auton *(Buyer)*
**Purchasing:** David Auton *(Buyer)*
**Engineering:** Brendan Gale *(Production Manager)*
**US SIC:** 3621 **UK SIC:** 34201
**Auditors:** B.J. Dixon Walsh Ltd
**Bankers:** National Westminster Bank Plc (56-00-05)

| | 30-09-13 | 30-09-12 | 30-09-11 |
|---|---|---|---|
| TO | 7,587,947 | 7,433,482 | 7,976,745 |
| P/L | 1,520,939 | 1,557,973 | 1,705,066 |
| NW | 9,608,151 | 8,414,931 | 7,173,995 |
| WC | 8,796,496 | 7,547,390 | 6,337,641 |
| Emp. | 64 | 63 | 61 |

DUNS 57-040-1216 **Imp**

## Rotamat Ltd

(**Subsidiary of:** Hans Huber Gmbh & Co. Kg)
Unit C-D, Chippenham, Wiltshire SN14 6NQ
**Web:** www.huber.co.uk
**Reg No:** 2874696 **VAT No:** 639396393
**Estd:** 1993 Private Limited Company
**Line of Business:** Agents involved in the sale of machinery, industrial equipment, ships and aircraft
**Trading Style:** Huber Technology Uk
**Issued Capital:** £200,000
**Directors:** Huber Se, S Morris, N H Hunt, P D Thompson
**Responsibilities**
**Senior:** Adrian Gouldstone *(Manager)*
**HR:** Virginia Pollock-Siebert *(Personnel Manager)*
**Facilities:** Dave Thompson *(Operations Director)*
**US SIC:** 5084 **UK SIC:** 61490
**Auditors:** Chappell Associates
**Bankers:** Bayerische Vereinsbank Ag (30-10-61)

| | 31-12-13 | 31-12-12 | 31-12-11 |
|---|---|---|---|
| TO | 14,024,421 | 12,593,699 | N/A |
| P/L | 1,798,873 | 1,117,277 | 2,105,792 |
| NW | 2,701,329 | 2,164,645 | 2,315,243 |
| WC | 2,512,448 | 1,963,521 | 2,170,665 |
| Emp. | 73 | 72 | 73 |

DUNS 21-788-2351

## Rotary Club of Gillingham (Dorset) Trust Fund

Fern Brook Lane, Gillingham, Dorset SP8 4FL
**Tel:** 01747834020
**Web:** www.embracegroup.co.uk
**Estd:** 2012
**Line of Business:** Rest and retirement homes
**Responsibilities**
**Senior:** Karen Mandle *(Home Manager)*, Caroline Orrell *(Home Manager)*
**US SIC:** 8321 **UK SIC:** 96111
**Employees:** 50

DUNS 64-109-4024 **Imp**

## Rotary Watches Ltd

(**Subsidiary of:** The Dreyfuss Group Ltd)
84-86 Regent Street, London W1B 5RR
**Tel:** 020-7434-5500 **Fax:** 02074345548
**Web:** www.rotarywatches.com
**Reg No:** 4109554 **Estd:** 2000 Private Limited Company
**Line of Business:** Manufacture of watches and clocks
**Trading Style:** Dreyfuss Group
**Issued Capital:** £1,000,000
**Directors:** K L Hon, Ms M Lam, C W Fong, Ms L Lam, T Halim, R M Dreyfuss, A J Quinn, Ms V L Campbell
**Co. Secretary:** Gary Williams
**Responsibilities**
**Senior:** Li Tao *(Director)*, Thomas Tope *(Director)*
**Marketing:** Liz Sowden *(Head of Brand)*
**HR:** Chris Abey *(Human Resources Manager)*
**Purchasing:** Chris Timmins *(Purchasing Manager)*
**US SIC:** 3873, 5094
**UK SIC:** 37400, 61900
**Auditors:** BDO LLP

| | 31-12-13 | 31-12-12 | 31-12-11 |
|---|---|---|---|
| TO | 21,167,854 | 20,383,918 | 18,415,227 |
| P/L | 1,380,037 | 2,275,171 | 1,642,223 |
| NW | 3,917,501 | 1,969,607 | 207,862 |
| WC | 8,467,809 | 7,148,524 | 5,912,715 |
| Emp. | 99 | 91 | 86 |

DUNS 21-218-3933

## Rotary Yorkshire Ltd

(**Subsidiary of:** Pearl Holdings (Bermuda) Ltd)
4-5 Buslingthorpe Green, Leeds, West Yorkshire LS7 2HG
**Tel:** 01132-620911 **Fax:** 02890831201
**Web:** www.rotarygroup.com
**Reg No:** 0480195 **VAT No:** 169744811
**Estd:** 1927 Private Limited Company
**Line of Business:** Building services
**Issued Capital:** £10,400
**Directors:** D Salter, P J Hughes
**Co. Secretary:** Inbaraj Rajakumar
**Responsibilities**
**Senior:** John Balderstone *(Manager)*, Gary Bearsley *(Warehouse Manager)*, Jon Dunwell *(Manager)*
**Finance:** B Trafford *(Accounts Assistant)*
**IT:** T Bradder *(IT Manager)*
**US SIC:** 1622, 1731
**UK SIC:** 50200, 50300
**Auditors:** PricewaterhouseCoopers LLP
**Bankers:** HSBC Bank plc (40-27-15)

| | 31-12-13 | 31-12-12 | 30-12-12 |
|---|---|---|---|
| TO | 16,861,000 | 16,930,000 | 25,230,578 |
| P/L | (2,615,000) | 9,160,000 | (5,931,658) |
| NW | 10,000 | 7,438,000 | (2,339,232) |
| WC | N/A | 7,231,000 | (2,555,641) |
| Emp. | 95 | 130 | 155 |

DUNS 21-137-9754

## Rotational Moulding Group Ltd

Knowles Industrial Estate, Buxton Road, Furness Vale, High Peak, Derbyshire SK23 7PH
**Web:** www.rotationalmouldings.co.uk
**Reg No:** 6705878 **Estd:** 2008 Private Limited Company
**Line of Business:** Management activities of holding companies
**Issued Capital:** £1,960
**Directors:** J Rowbotham, V Olivier, P G Knowles
**Co. Secretary:** Ms Suzanne Rowbotham
**US SIC:** 6711 **UK SIC:** 83962
**Bankers:** The Royal Bank Of Scotland Plc (16-10-80)

| | 30-11-13 | 24-11-12 | 26-11-11 |
|---|---|---|---|
| TO | 9,256,770 | 9,309,218 | 8,951,650 |
| P/L | 344,208 | 562,160 | 237,855 |
| NW | 696,113 | 513,914 | 283,902 |
| WC | 609,606 | 557,048 | 427,968 |
| Emp. | 94 | 100 | 98 |

DUNS 57-841-5853 **Imp**

## Rotech Holdings Ltd

Rotech House, Whitemyres Avenue, Aberdeen, Aberdeenshire AB16 6HQ
**Tel:** 01224-698698
**Web:** www.rotech.co.uk
**Reg No:** 0148822SC **Estd:** 1994 Private Limited Company
**Line of Business:** Management activities of holding companies
**Trading Style:** Rotech Holdings Ltd
**Issued Capital:** £106,716
**Principals:** K R Stewart *(Managing)*, G S Bell, Dr D Stewart, Ms R S Stewart
**Co. Secretary:** George Bell
**US SIC:** 6711 **UK SIC:** 83962
**Auditors:** Ritson Smith

| | 30-06-13 | 30-06-12 | 30-06-11 |
|---|---|---|---|
| TO | 8,929,453 | 12,286,736 | 19,262,779 |
| P/L | 928,494 | 10,182,258 | 2,038,011 |
| NW | 13,671,039 | 12,953,928 | 6,452,816 |
| WC | 11,560,246 | 11,213,970 | 190,301 |
| Emp. | 59 | 78 | 125 |

DUNS 22-289-9176 **Imp-Exp**

## Rotex Europe Ltd

(**Subsidiary of:** Hillenbrand Switzerland Gmbh)
Whitehouse Vale, Aston Lane North, Runcorn, Cheshire WA7 3FA
**Tel:** 01928707800 **Fax:** 08707-529920
**Web:** www.tevapharm.com
**Reg No:** 4307924 **Estd:** 2001 Private Limited Company
**Line of Business:** Engineers (general)
**Export Sales:** £13,632,046
**Issued Capital:** £1,000
**Directors:** K A Cerniglia, R W Dieckman Jr
**Co. Secretary:** John Hill
**Responsibilities**
**Senior:** Anthony Casablanca *(Director)*, Robert Dieckman *(Director)*, Steve Forrester-Coles *(Manager)*
**US SIC:** 2834 **UK SIC:** 25700
**Auditors:** Hurst & Co Accountants LLP
**Bankers:** Lloyds TSB Bank plc (77-67-06)

| | 30-09-13 | 30-09-12 | 30-09-11 |
|---|---|---|---|
| TO | 15,206,880 | 15,218,558 | 10,357,164 |
| P/L | 1,491,434 | 1,441,688 | 1,294,724 |
| NW | 6,738,058 | 5,702,696 | 5,265,554 |
| WC | 5,502,276 | 4,354,336 | 4,003,054 |
| Emp. | 77 | 71 | 65 |

DUNS 22-638-9443 **Imp-Exp**

## Rothamsted Research Ltd

West Common, Harpenden, Hertfordshire AL5 2JQ
**Web:** www.rothamsted.ac.uk
**Reg No:** 2393175 **VAT No:** 197420151
**Estd:** 1989 Private Company Limited By Guarantee
**Line of Business:** Research institutions and organisations
**Export Markets:** worldwide
**Export Sales:** £1,638,000
**Trading Style:** Institute of Arable Crops Research Rothamsted
**Directors:** Ms C J Drummond, Professor M J Bailey, J R Beddington, Professor D M Winter, R L Brooks, D C Baulcombe, Dr G J Birch, Dr D K Lawrence
**Co. Secretary:** Miss Louise Warren
**Responsibilities**
**Senior:** Richard Bardgett *(Director)*, David Brightman *(Manager)*, Edward Cocking *(Manager)*, Sam Cook *(Executive)*, Michael Elves *(Manager)*, Hugh Godfray *(Director)*, Paul Leonard *(Director)*, Maurice Moloney *(Manager)*, Nicholas Talbot *(Manager)*
**Marketing:** Susannah Bolton *(Science Communication)*, Ian Pettitt *(Web Coordinator)*
**Admin:** Sheila Bishop *(Administrator)*
**Health & Safety:** Cliff Brookes *(Health & Safety Officer)*
**Facilities:** Keith Law *(Facilities Manager)*, Leona Pollock *(Accommodation Manager)*
**Operations:** Steve Mcgrath *(Head of Department)*
**Branches:** Rothamsted Research Limited, Higham, Bury St Edmunds, Bury St. Edmunds, Suffolk IP28 6NP
**US SIC:** 7391 **UK SIC:** 94000
**Auditors:** Baker Tilly UK Audit LLP
**Bankers:** Barclays Bank Plc (20-74-09)

| | 31-03-14 | 31-03-13 | 31-03-12 |
|---|---|---|---|
| TO | 38,053,000 | 43,279,000 | 36,814,000 |
| P/L | 3,787,000 | 7,235,000 | 1,400,000 |
| NW | 67,867,000 | 64,080,000 | 56,845,000 |
| WC | 21,962,000 | 16,531,000 | 6,499,000 |
| Emp. | 409 | 390 | 439 |

DUNS 21-912-5606 **Imp-Exp**

## Rothenberger (U.K.) Ltd

Unit 2, Kingsthorne Park, Henson Way, Kettering, Northamptonshire NN16 8PX
**Tel:** 01536-310300 **Fax:** 01536-310600
**Web:** www.rothenberger.com
**Reg No:** 1023214 **VAT No:** 119604867
**Estd:** 1971 Private Limited Company
**Line of Business:** Industrial services
**Export Markets:** Ireland; Iceland & Malta
**Export Sales:** £760,741
**Issued Capital:** £850,000
**Directors:** R Weber, J N Potter
**Co. Secretary:** Mark Phillips
**Responsibilities**
**Senior:** Helmut Rothenberger *(President)*, Alan Sparrow *(Chief Executive)*
**US SIC:** 5074 **UK SIC:** 61300
**Auditors:** Deloitte & Touche LLP
**Bankers:** Barclays Bank Plc (20-29-90)

| | 31-12-13 | 31-12-12 | 31-12-11 |
|---|---|---|---|
| TO | 15,158,799 | 15,007,825 | 15,646,379 |
| P/L | 1,771,098 | 1,911,157 | 2,361,150 |
| NW | 3,095,900 | 3,737,605 | 3,296,443 |
| WC | 2,943,923 | 3,587,194 | 3,252,758 |
| Emp. | 52 | 49 | 48 |

DUNS 23-617-7358

## Rother District Council

Town Hall, London Road, Bexhill-On-Sea, East Sussex TN39 3JX
**Tel:** 01424787878
**Web:** www.rother.gov.uk
**Estd:** 1974
**Line of Business:** Local government
**Directors:** D F Powell, D Turner, L Robinson, D Stevens
**Co. Secretary:** T Elliott
**Responsibilities**
**Finance:** Robin Vennard *(Head of Finance)*
**Sales:** S Grisbrook *(Head of Corporate Services)*
**Operations:** Anthony Leonard *(Community Services Director)*
**Branches:** Rother District Council, Battle Library, Market Square, Battle, East Sussex TN33 0XB
**US SIC:** 9121 **UK SIC:** 91110
**Bankers:** National Westminster Bank Plc (51-70-12)
**Employees:** 270

DUNS 21-779-9037

## Rother Valley College

Doe Quarry Lane, Sheffield, South Yorkshire S25 2NF
**Tel:** 01909559100
**Web:** www.rotherham.ac.uk
**Estd:** 2002 Proprietorship
**Line of Business:** Further education schools and colleges
**Proprietor:** Miss G Alton
**Responsibilities**
**IT:** Chris Muffitt *(IT Manager)*
**US SIC:** 8221 **UK SIC:** 93100
**Employees:** 1,200

DUNS 23-208-0903

## Rotherham Community Transport Ltd

Erskine Road, Rotherham, South Yorkshire S65 1RF
**Tel:** 01709516092 **Fax:** 01709517200
**Web:** www.rotherhamct.org.uk
**Reg No:** 0026853IP **VAT No:** 533902750
**Estd:** 1989 Friendly Society
**Line of Business:** Charities and charitable organisations
**Directors:** Mrs V Beckett, V Thornes, S May, D Martin, Miss K Bradshaw, Ms J Vollons, G Brittain, Ms P Qureshi
**Co. Secretary:** S Hewitson
**Responsibilities**
**Senior:** Stephen Hewitson *(General Manager)*
**Finance:** Debbie Pearson *(Finance Manager)*
**US SIC:** 8699 **UK SIC:** 96902
**Bankers:** The Co-Operative Bank Plc (08-90-87)
**Employees:** 52

DUNS 52-003-6674

## Rotherham Crossroads-Caring for Carers

Unit H, The Point, Rotherham, South Yorkshire S60 1BP
**Web:** www.crossroadsrotherham.co.uk
**Reg No:** 3370678 **Estd:** 1997 Private Limited Company
**Line of Business:** Home care service providers
**Directors:** D Lisgo, Mrs M Hudson, Dr M E Holt, T M Ensor, J Dearden, E Bennett, J Hacon, Ms L S Wainwright
**Co. Secretary:** Ms Elizabeth Bent
**Responsibilities**
**Senior:** Efra Bennett *(Chairman)*, Mary Doran *(Director)*
**US SIC:** 8091, 6732
**UK SIC:** 95200, 83100
**Auditors:** O'Brien & Co
**Bankers:** Barclays Bank Plc (20-76-89)

| | 31-03-14 | 31-03-13 | 31-03-12 |
|---|---|---|---|
| TO | 1,871,797 | 1,791,328 | 1,691,009 |
| P/L | 58,143 | 61,733 | 87,366 |
| NW | 449,796 | 391,653 | 329,920 |
| WC | 328,365 | 257,673 | 309,961 |
| Emp. | 115 | 112 | 106 |

DUNS 23-261-9085

## Rotherham Doncaster and South Humber Nhs Foundation Trust

Tickhill Road Hospital, Doncaster, South Yorkshire DN4 8QN
**Web:** www.rdash.nhs.uk
**Estd:** 1999
**Line of Business:** Public sector hospital activities, including nhs trusts
**Trading Style:** St Catherine's Hospital
**Issued Capital:** £1
**Director:** L Hayes
**Responsibilities**
**Senior:** Christine Bain *(Chief Executive)*, Helen Dabbs *(Deputy CEO / Executive Directo)*, Lawson Pater *(Trust Chairman)*
**IT:** Dave Coney *(IT Manager)*
**Health & Safety:** Allan Irwin *(Health & Safety Officer)*
**Purchasing:** Allan Makeman *(Purchasing Manager)*
**Branches:** Rotherham Doncaster and South Humber Nhs Foundation Trust, Wardens Flat, Ancholme Gardens, Brigg, South Humberside DN20 8LA
**US SIC:** 8062 **UK SIC:** 95100

**Auditors:** PricewaterhouseCoopers

| | 31-03-14 | 31-03-13 | 31-03-12 |
|---|---|---|---|
| TO | 156,790,000 | 160,796,000 | 161,358,000 |
| P/L | (1,191,000) | 760,000 | (102,000) |
| NW | 74,396,000 | 71,437,000 | 71,572,000 |
| WC | 3,856,000 | 3,211,000 | 3,775,000 |
| Emp. | 3,482 | 3,711 | 3,546 |

DUNS 34-747-9602

## Rotherham Healthcare Ltd

(**Subsidiary of:** Rotherham Healthcare Holdings Ltd)
Nightingale Close, Moorgate, Rotherham, South Yorkshire S60 2AB
**Tel:** 01709370763 **Fax:** 01709-835692
**Reg No:** 2783407 **Estd:** 1993 Private Limited Company
**Line of Business:** Social work activities with accommodation
**Issued Capital:** £150,000
**Managing Director:** G J Oliver
**Co. Secretary:** Trevor Payne
**US SIC:** 8321, 8999
**UK SIC:** 96111, 83954
**Auditors:** GBAC Ltd
**Bankers:** National Westminster Bank Plc (60-14-03)

| | 31-12-13 | 31-12-12 | 31-12-11 |
|---|---|---|---|
| TO | 4,328,216 | 3,806,380 | 2,705,885 |
| P/L | 1,158,778 | 651,907 | 296,060 |
| NW | 1,217,817 | 661,907 | 610,000 |
| WC | 1,269,426 | 825,737 | 868,166 |
| Emp. | 174 | 156 | 122 |

DUNS 39-909-4556

## The Rotherham Hospice Trust

Broom Road, Rotherham, South Yorkshire S60 2SW
**Web:** www.rotherhamhospice.org.uk
**Reg No:** 2234222 **Estd:** 1996 Private Limited Company
**Line of Business:** Hospices
**Directors:** Mrs J Flanagan, Professor B W Hancock, D W Wheater, Mrs E J Thompson, Mrs L W Shelton, J P Neal, Mrs B J Watson, Mrs P Hancock
**Co. Secretary:** Ms Deborah Barker
**Responsibilities**
**Senior:** Meredydd Hughes (Director), Ronald Johnson (Director)
**US SIC:** 8091, 8051, 8321
**UK SIC:** 95200, 95100, 96111
**Auditors:** Allotts

| | 31-03-14 | 31-03-13 | 31-03-12 |
|---|---|---|---|
| TO | 5,110,557 | 4,669,850 | 4,032,532 |
| P/L | (29,971) | (181,023) | (71,257) |
| NW | 4,995,296 | 5,046,806 | 5,193,243 |
| WC | 721,743 | 767,251 | 1,268,274 |
| Emp. | 136 | 136 | 121 |

DUNS 21-395-6132

## Rotherham Leisure Complex

Rotherham Eye Centre, 34 Wellgate, Rotherham, South Yorkshire S60 2LR
**Tel:** 01709722555
**Web:** www.rotherham.gov.uk
**Proprietorship**
**Line of Business:** Leisure centres
**Proprietor:** Miss C Pearce
**US SIC:** 5812 **UK SIC:** 66110
**Employees:** 50

DUNS 21-126-6937

## Rotherham Metropolitan Borough Council

Riverside House, Rotherham, South Yorkshire S60 1QY
**Tel:** 01709 382 121 **Fax:** 01709 366 837
**Web:** www.rotherham.gov.uk
**Estd:** 2002 Incorporate By Act Of Parliament
**Line of Business:** Local government
**Trading Style:** Rotherham Mbc Asylum
**Directors:** A G Carruthers, P Nolan, J Parkes, J Everitt, E P Jones, B H Yemm, H Bower
**Responsibilities**
**Senior:** Mike Cuff (Chief Executive), Martin Kimber (Chief Executive), Allan Lewis (Chairman)
**HR:** Tracey Priestley (Human Resources Officer), Odette Stringwell (Human Resources Manager)
**Operations:** Jasmine Swallow (Production and Operations Mana)
**Branches:** Rotherham Metropolitan Borough Council, Sycamore Avenue, Sheffield, South Yorkshire S26 5QU
**US SIC:** 9121 **UK SIC:** 91110
**Bankers:** The Co-Operative Bank Plc (08-90-87)
**Employees:** 2,000

DUNS 22-400-3744      Imp

## Rotherham Nhs Foundation Trust

Moorgate Road, Rotherham, South Yorkshire S60 2UD
**Web:** www.rothgen.nhs.uk
**Estd:** 2012
**Line of Business:** Hospitals

**Trading Style:** The Rotherham Nhs Foundation Trust
**Principals:** Ms M Oldfield (Chairman), M Lowry (Financial), B James, Ms J Wilson, Ms J Bird, G Bloomer, N Ruff, Ms J Hickton
**Responsibilities**
**Senior:** Louise Barnett (Chef Executive)
**Health & Safety:** Danielle Davis (Health & Safety Officer)
**Branches:** Rotherham Nhs Foundation Trust, Badsley Moor Lane, Rotherham, South Yorkshire S60 2UD
**US SIC:** 8062, 9121
**UK SIC:** 95100, 91110
**Auditors:** KPMG LLP

| | 31-03-14 | 31-03-13 | 31-03-11 |
|---|---|---|---|
| TO | 235,112,000 | 234,209,000 | 167,391,000 |
| P/L | (3,184,000) | (6,500,000) | (1,474,000) |
| NW | 56,729,000 | 55,002,000 | 67,684,000 |
| WC | (3,461,000) | (5,281,000) | (3,133,000) |
| Emp. | 3,688 | 3,769 | 3,003 |

DUNS 23-310-8112

## Rotherham Primary Care Trust

Oak House, Moorhead Way, Bramley, Rotherham, South Yorkshire S66 1YY
**Web:** www.rotherham.nhs.uk
**Estd:** 2002
**Line of Business:** Primary Care Trust.
**Issued Capital:** £1
**Principals:** A Spring (Financial), J Mciver
**Responsibilities**
**Senior:** Louise Barnett (Chief Executive Officer), John McIver (Chief Executive Officer)
**Finance:** Keely Firth (Financial Director)
**Branches:** Rotherham Primary Care Trust, Medical Centre Chapel Wy, Kiveton Pk, Sheffield, South Yorkshire S26 6QU
**US SIC:** 8062, 8091
**UK SIC:** 95100, 95200
**Auditors:** D Murray
**Employees:** 1,500

DUNS 21-810-3715

## Rothesay Joint Campus

High Street, Rothesay, Rothesay, Bute PA20 9JJ
**Tel:** 01700503227
**Web:** www.rothesayprimary.org
**Estd:** 1977
**Line of Business:** Pre school education
**Responsibilities**
**Senior:** Wendy Brownline (Schools - Principal)
**US SIC:** 8211 **UK SIC:** 93200
**Employees:** 70

DUNS 21-684-3156

## Rothiemurchus Estate by Abbeymoore

Inverdruie, Aviemore, Inverness-Shire PH22 1QH
**Web:** www.rothiemurchus.net
**Estd:** 1999 Proprietorship
**Line of Business:** Farming (mixed)
**Trading Style:** Clay Pidgeon Shoot
**Proprietor:** J P Grant
**US SIC:** 0291 **UK SIC:** 01001
**Employees:** 50

DUNS 21-128-3916

## Rothman Pantall & Co

232-233 Temple Chambers, 3-7 Temple Avenue, London EC4Y 0HP
**Tel:** 02078719711
**Web:** www.rothmansllp.com
**Estd:** 1955 Partnership
**Line of Business:** Chartered accountants.
**Principals:** Twenty-One, M Wells (Partner), J Poulter (Partner), D L Morgan (Partner), G J Hindley (Partner), B Lynch (Partner), G Pantall (Partner)
**Branches:** Rothman Pantall & Co, 229 West Street, Fareham, Hampshire PO16 0HZ
**US SIC:** 8931 **UK SIC:** 83600
**Employees:** 200

DUNS 21-149-4824

## Rothman Pantall Llp

Avebury House, 6 St Peter Street, Winchester, Hampshire SO23 8BN
**Tel:** 01962842345
**Web:** www.rothmansllp.com
**Reg No:** 0342585OC **Estd:** 1989 Private Limited Company
**Line of Business:** Accounting and auditing activities
**Responsibilities**
**Senior:** Brian Corlett (Non-designated Limited Liabili), Julian Sims (Non-designated Limited Liabili)
**Admin:** Debbie Dawson (Office Manager Manager)
**HR:** Debbie Dawson (Office Manager Manager)
**Health & Safety:** Debbie Dawson (Office Manager Manager)
**Facilities:** Ken Giles (Buildings Officer)

**Branches:** Rothman Pantall Llp, 24 Park Road South, Havant, Hampshire PO9 1HB
**US SIC:** 8931 **UK SIC:** 83600
**Auditors:** Mazars LLP

| | 31-03-14 | 31-03-13 | 31-03-12 |
|---|---|---|---|
| TO | 10,383,715 | 9,599,737 | 9,664,775 |
| P/L | 171,665 | 2,677,832 | 98,091 |
| NW | 951,000 | N/A | 1,000,000 |
| WC | 6,049,643 | 5,509,943 | 5,402,291 |
| Emp. | 154 | 144 | 147 |

DUNS 21-737-7100      Exp

## Rothschild Bank International Ltd

(**Subsidiary of:** Paris Orleans)
St Julians Court, Julians Avenue, Guernsey, Guernsey, Channel Islands GY1 3BP
**Tel:** 01481713713
**Web:** www.rothschild.com
**Reg No:** 0001088G **Estd:** 1967 Private Limited Company
**Line of Business:** Banks and financial institutions
**Issued Capital:** £5,000,000
**Principals:** D D Sullivan (Chairman), C P Tracy (Managing), D Oxburgh (Financial), J Cowley, D O Moon, W Lane, J B Soames, Ms C Banszky
**Co. Secretary:** Peter Rose
**Responsibilities**
**Senior:** Graham Curds (Director), Sinead Ferguson (Manager), Sinead Granville (Bank Manager), David Hoxburgh (Financial Director), Charles Keay (Director)
**Finance:** David Hoxburgh (Financial Director)
**Admin:** Bruce Spittal (Office Manager)
**IT:** Andrew Dimelow (Computer Manager)
**Facilities:** Ivan Fossey (Facilities Manager)
**Purchasing:** Andrew Dimelow (Computer Manager)
**US SIC:** 6012 **UK SIC:** 81402
**Auditors:** KMPG
**Employees:** 60

DUNS 23-174-2503

## Rothschild Trust (Guernsey) Ltd

(**Subsidiary of:** Paris Orleans)
Po Box 472 St Peter Port, Guernsey, Channel Islands GY1 6AX
**Tel:** 01481-707800 **Fax:** 01481-712686
**Web:** www.rothchild.de
**Reg No:** 0002154G **Estd:** 1970 Private Limited Company
**Line of Business:** Banks
**Issued Capital:** £6,000
**Directors:** Ms C Dickinson, W Lane, P Harwood, D Harris, N Moss, D Allison, C Ward
**US SIC:** 6012 **UK SIC:** 81402
**Employees:** 50

DUNS 39-712-6509

## Rothwell & Robertson Ltd

Castle Street, Beaumaris, Gwynedd LL58 8AP
**Tel:** 01248-810329 **Fax:** 01248-811294
**Web:** www.bullsheadinn.co.uk
**Reg No:** 1291866 **Estd:** 1976 Private Limited Company
**Line of Business:** Hotels and motels without restaurant
**Trading Style:** (The) Olde Bulls Head
**Issued Capital:** £2,000
**Director:** K W Rothwell
**Co. Secretary:** David Robertson
**US SIC:** 7011, 5813
**UK SIC:** 66500, 66200
**Auditors:** Haslam Tunstall

| | 31-03-14 | 31-03-13 | 31-03-12 |
|---|---|---|---|
| TA | 3,108,742 | 3,081,313 | 3,108,739 |
| NW | 1,325,426 | 1,209,976 | 1,166,061 |
| WC | (252,184) | (706,463) | (638,809) |

DUNS 52-015-8379

## Rothwell Plumbing Services Ltd

Stephens Way, Warrington Road Industrial Estate, Wigan, Lancashire WN3 6PH
**Tel:** 01942615840 **Fax:** 01695633249
**Web:** www.rothwellplumbing.co.uk
**Reg No:** 3382494 **Estd:** 1997 Private Limited Company
**Line of Business:** Plumbing
**Issued Capital:** £750
**Directors:** G W Rothwell, W H Rothwell, N Hanmer, J F Pearson, Mrs B Rothwell
**Co. Secretary:** Ms Diane Kirk
**Branches:** Rothwell Plumbing Services Ltd, Phoenix Park Industrial Estate, Phoenix Close, Heywood, Lancashire OL10 2JG
**US SIC:** 1711 **UK SIC:** 50300
**Auditors:** Livesey Spottiswood

**Bankers:** HSBC Bank plc (40-46-32)

| | 30-06-13 | 30-06-12 | 30-06-11 |
|---|---|---|---|
| TO | 17,678,213 | 26,377,294 | 22,063,599 |
| P/L | 110,964 | 635,105 | 986,705 |
| NW | 2,789,908 | 2,715,231 | 2,250,647 |
| WC | 2,602,772 | 2,515,957 | 2,072,863 |
| Emp. | 135 | 182 | 182 |

DUNS 21-735-1675      Exp

## Rotolok (Holdings) Ltd

1 Millennium Place, Tiverton Business Park, Tiverton, Tiverton, Devon EX16 6SB
**Tel:** 01884-232232
**Web:** www.rotolok.co.uk
**Reg No:** 1178138 **VAT No:** 453756036
**Estd:** 1974 Private Limited Company
**Line of Business:** Manufacture of other special purpose machinery not elsewhere classified
**Export Markets:** Worldwide
**Export Sales:** £20,424,590
**Issued Capital:** £106,885
**Principals:** D Mccauley (Managing), S J Swales
**Co. Secretary:** Mrs Ann Mccauley
**Responsibilities**
**Senior:** Daniel McCauley (Managing Director)
**IT:** Simon Bates (IT Manager)
**US SIC:** 3559, 6711
**UK SIC:** 32863, 83962
**Auditors:** Peplows
**Bankers:** Barclays Bank Plc (20-30-47)

| | 31-05-13 | 31-05-12 | 31-05-11 |
|---|---|---|---|
| TO | 23,758,432 | 22,336,456 | 16,924,584 |
| P/L | 5,037,209 | 4,181,894 | 3,103,689 |
| NW | 29,796,489 | 33,940,773 | 31,385,641 |
| WC | 12,181,834 | 12,226,185 | 12,041,738 |
| Emp. | 232 | 222 | 219 |

DUNS 76-948-2555      Exp

## Rotometrics International Ltd

(**Subsidiary of:** Roto-Die Company Inc.)
Walsall Road Walsall Business Park, Walsall, West Midlands WS9 0SW
**Tel:** 01922-610000 **Fax:** 01922-610100
**Web:** www.rotometrics.com
**Reg No:** 2368722 **VAT No:** 547207249
**Estd:** 1989 Private Limited Company
**Line of Business:** Manufacturers of machine tools
**Export Sales:** £8,152,031
**Issued Capital:** £1,775,000
**Directors:** P Emerson, M E Niemiec
**Co. Secretary:** Mark Walters
**Responsibilities**
**Finance:** Edward Salter (Financial Director), Andrew Speed (Finance Director)
**Sales:** Neil Lilly (Sales Manager)
**Admin:** Val Ball (Human Resources Administrator)
**HR:** Val Ball (Human Resources Administrator)
**Health & Safety:** Ian Davenport (Health & Safety Officer)
**Engineering:** James Wellsbury (Technical Manager)
**US SIC:** 3542 **UK SIC:** 32212
**Auditors:** BDO Stoy Hayward
**Bankers:** Lloyds TSB Bank plc (30-99-36)

| | 30-09-13 | 30-09-12 | 30-09-11 |
|---|---|---|---|
| TO | 15,477,388 | 14,261,328 | 15,646,050 |
| P/L | (1,050,205) | (620,074) | 984,577 |
| NW | (7,241,688) | (6,191,483) | (5,571,409) |
| WC | 2,181,588 | 2,912,293 | 3,396,630 |
| Emp. | 189 | 187 | 158 |

DUNS 21-601-9661

## Rotork P.L.C.

Rotork House, Brassmill Lane, Bath, Avon BA1 3JQ
**Tel:** 01225-733-200 **Fax:** 01225-733-381
**Web:** www.rotork.com
**Reg No:** 0578327 **VAT No:** 137485546
**Estd:** 1957 Public Limited Company
**Line of Business:** Management activities of holding companies
**Export Sales:** £546,675,000
**Issued Capital:** £4,378,369
**Directors:** P I France, G B Bullard, Ms S A James, R Arnold, Mrs L M Bell, R C Lockwood, M J Lamb, J E Nicholas
**Co. Secretary:** Stephen Jones
**Responsibilities**
**Senior:** Alex Busby (Managing Director, Rotork Flui), Dave Littlejohns (Managing Director, Rotork Gear), Graham Ogden (Director), Grant Wood (Manager)
**Finance:** Gary Waylen (CFO)
**Marketing:** Carlos Elvira (Group Sales and Marketing Dire), Tony Scott (Sales and Marketing Manager), Nigel Willis (Sales And Marketing Director)
**Sales:** Pamela Bingham (Group Business Development Dir), Ivan Burnell (Business Development Manager ()), Carlos Elvira (Group Sales and Marketing Dire), Jon Fowkes (Business Development Manager), Mike Howard (Sales Executive), Laurence Kettle (Sales Manager), Tony Scott (Sales and Marketing Manager), Nigel Willis (Sales And Marketing Director)

**Admin:** Sandro Necchi *(Sales Office Manager)*
**IT:** James Blannin *(Global IT Manager)*
**Facilities:** Mike Summerill *(Facilities Manager)*
**Operations:** Ralph Hibbert *(Service Coordinator)*, Alastair Spurr *(Group Operations Director)*
**US SIC:** 6711, 3829, 7399
**UK SIC:** 83962, 37100, 83954
**Auditors:** KPMG Audit PLC
**Bankers:** Barclays Bank Plc (20-13-42)

| | 31-12-13 | 31-12-12 | 31-12-11 |
|---|---|---|---|
| TO | 578,440,000 | 511,747,000 | 447,833,000 |
| P/L | 137,997,000 | 124,194,000 | 112,550,000 |
| NW | 173,448,000 | 147,851,000 | 117,385,000 |
| WC | 157,394,000 | 143,113,000 | 113,687,000 |
| Emp. | 2,892 | 2,581 | 2,192 |

DUNS 21-308-7851 **Imp-Exp**
### Rotork Uk Ltd
**(Subsidiary of:** Rotork P.L.C.)
Regina House, Ring Road, Bramley, Leeds, West Yorkshire LS13 4ET
**Tel:** 0113-256-7922 **Fax:** 01132057274
**Web:** www.exeeco.co.uk
**Reg No:** 1090344 **VAT No:** 180394459
**Estd:** 1973 Private Limited Company
**Line of Business:** Actuaries
**Export Markets:** Worldwide
**Export Sales:** £20,572,000
**Trading Style:** T/A Rotork, Fluid Power Division, Exeeco
**Issued Capital:** £6,250
**Directors:** P I France, D A Littlejohns
**Co. Secretary:** Stephen Jones
**Responsibilities**
**Senior:** Paul Root *(Production Director)*
**Finance:** William Rachmann *(Financial Director)*, William Rochemenn *(Finance Director)*
**HR:** Karen Black *(Training Manager)*, Lindsay Esdhus *(Human Resources Manager)*
**Purchasing:** Kath Sayer *(Buyer)*, Sara Veneillon *(Purchasing Manager)*
**Engineering:** Paul Root *(Production Director)*
**Branches:** Rotork Uk Ltd, Brookside Way, Nunn Pk, Sutton-In-Ashfield, Nottinghamshire NG17 2NL
**US SIC:** 8911 **UK SIC:** 83701
**Auditors:** KPMG Audit PLC
**Bankers:** Barclays Bank Plc (20-13-42)

| | 31-12-13 | 31-12-12 | 31-12-11 |
|---|---|---|---|
| TO | 49,153,000 | 34,362,000 | 34,431,000 |
| P/L | 7,100,000 | 3,872,000 | 5,183,000 |
| NW | 16,763,000 | 11,720,000 | 8,602,000 |
| WC | 9,756,000 | 7,166,000 | 6,662,000 |
| Emp. | 265 | 202 | 186 |

DUNS 21-919-4859 **Exp**
### Rotrex Group Ltd
Gryphon Works, Alfreton Industrial Estate, Wimsey Way, Alfreton, Derbyshire DE55 4LS
**Tel:** 01773603997 **Fax:** 01773-540566
**Web:** www.rotrexwinches.co.uk
**Reg No:** 1095234 **VAT No:** 344061287
**Estd:** 1973 Private Limited Company
**Line of Business:** Renting of other machinery and equipment not elsewhere classified
**Export Sales:** £1,369,000
**Trading Style:** Rotrex Winches, Rotrex Onsite
**Issued Capital:** £200,000
**Principals:** W B Parkinson *(Chairman and Managing)*, S H Butterworth *(Managing)*, I W Parkinson
**Co. Secretary:** Simon Butterworth
**Responsibilities**
**Senior:** Ian Bunting *(Commercial Manager)*, Louise Cail *(Manager)*
**Finance:** Alan Coxon *(Financial Director)*
**Sales:** Ian Bunting *(Commercial Manager)*
**Facilities:** Paul Land *(Facilities Manager)*
**Branches:** Rotrex Group Ltd, Gryphon Wks, Wimsey Way, Alfreterton Ind Est, Alfreton, Derbyshire DE55 4LS
**US SIC:** 7394, 6531
**UK SIC:** 84000, 83400
**Auditors:** PKF (UK) LLP
**Bankers:** National Westminster Bank Plc (60-01-28)

| | 30-04-14 | 30-04-13 | 30-04-12 |
|---|---|---|---|
| TO | 6,655,000 | 6,212,000 | 6,662,000 |
| P/L | 859,000 | 632,000 | 535,000 |
| NW | 840,000 | 404,000 | 688,000 |
| WC | 2,708,000 | 2,396,000 | 1,883,000 |
| Emp. | 57 | 59 | 56 |

DUNS 42-325-6437
### Rottingdean Nursing Home
30-32 Newlands Road, Rottingdean, Brighton, East Sussex BN2 7GD
**Estd:** 1987 Partnership
**Line of Business:** Nursing Homes
**Partners:** J Breeds, J Breeds, Mrs C Breeds, Mrs C Breeds
**Responsibilities**
**Senior:** John Breeds *(Proprietor)*
**US SIC:** 8051 **UK SIC:** 95100
**Employees:** 55

DUNS 21-290-2715
### Rou Bill
Senator House, Stadium Way, Harlow, Essex CM19 5GY
**Tel:** 01279630800
**Line of Business:** Retail sale of books, newspapers and stationery
**Proprietor:** Miss M Chevin
**US SIC:** 5942 **UK SIC:** 65300
**Employees:** 50

DUNS 21-604-8185
### Rouge Bouillon School & Nursery
Brighton Road, St Helier, Jersey, Channel Islands JE2 3YN
**Tel:** 01534705705
**Web:** http://vle.jeron.je
**Estd:** 1984 Proprietorship
**Line of Business:** Schools (local authority)
**Proprietor:** J Speight
**US SIC:** 8211 **UK SIC:** 93200
**Employees:** 50

DUNS 28-881-1458
### Rougemont School Trust Ltd
Llantarnam Hall, Malpas Road, Newport, Gwent NP20 6QB
**Tel:** 01633820800 **Fax:** 01633-855598
**Web:** www.rsch.co.uk
**Reg No:** 1178886 **Estd:** 1974 Private Company Limited By Guarantee
**Line of Business:** Schools (independent)
**Directors:** R S Green, I G Short, Ms C Thomas, M K Tebbutt, R C Pugsley, Dr J N Tribbick, H Clark, Ms J A Sollis
**Co. Secretary:** Ms Heidi Perry
**Responsibilities**
**Senior:** David Blayney *(Manager)*, Robert Carnecal *(Head Teacher)*, Jayne Clark *(Director)*, David Fone *(Director)*, Terence Rose *(Manager)*
**Branches:** Rougemont School Trust Ltd, Nant Coch House, Risca Rd, Newport, Gwent NP20 3FB
**US SIC:** 8211 **UK SIC:** 93200
**Auditors:** Bkr Hanies Watts
**Bankers:** Barclays Bank Plc (20-60-58)

| | 31-08-14 | 31-08-13 | 31-08-12 |
|---|---|---|---|
| TO | 5,809,752 | 5,781,703 | 5,682,167 |
| P/L | 285,368 | 156,091 | 210,142 |
| NW | 13,493,020 | 11,176,940 | 11,020,849 |
| WC | (832,076) | (1,039,695) | (892,741) |
| Emp. | 125 | 124 | 123 |

DUNS 21-228-4465
### Rougemont Thistle Hotel
Queen Street, Exeter, Devon EX4 3SP
**Tel:** 01392254982
**Web:** www.thistle.com
**Estd:** 1980 Proprietorship
**Line of Business:** Hotels
**Proprietor:** R Heale
**Responsibilities**
**Senior:** Mark Beedell *(Manager)*, Craig Findleton *(General Manager)*, Joe Hibberd *(General Manager)*, Georgia Suttie *(Sales)*
**Sales:** Georgia Suttie *(Sales)*
**US SIC:** 7011 **UK SIC:** 66500
**Employees:** 50

DUNS 77-514-4876 **Exp**
### Roughton (Holdings) Ltd
Unit A2 Omega Park, Electron Way, Chandler's Ford, Eastleigh, Hampshire SO53 4SE
**Web:** www.roughton.com
**Reg No:** 2985638 **Estd:** 1983 Private Limited Company
**Line of Business:** Engineers (consulting)
**Export Sales:** £12,623,664
**Trading Style:** Roughton International
**Issued Capital:** £163,477
**Directors:** B N Obika, S F Kimmett, R C Wotton
**Responsibilities**
**Marketing:** Simon Bratt *(IT Manager)*
**IT:** Simon Bratt *(IT Manager)*
**HR:** Alan Mulroney *(Human Resources Manager)*
**Operations:** Simon Bratt *(IT Manager)*
**US SIC:** 8911 **UK SIC:** 83701
**Auditors:** HLB A V Audit PLC
**Bankers:** Barclays Bank Plc (20-79-25)

| | 31-12-12 | 31-12-11 | 31-12-10 |
|---|---|---|---|
| TO | 14,158,939 | 15,062,676 | 12,793,676 |
| P/L | 617,546 | 725,573 | 331,910 |
| NW | 1,021,070 | 981,744 | 661,190 |
| WC | 1,896,640 | 1,891,704 | 1,942,687 |
| Emp. | 177 | 89 | 92 |

DUNS 21-223-0048
### Round & About Excursions
Heritage House, 7 Star Road, Horsham, West Sussex RH13 8RD
**Web:** www.heritage-coaches.com
**Estd:** 1999 Proprietorship
**Line of Business:** Coach and bus hire
**Proprietor:** C Rice
**US SIC:** 4119 **UK SIC:** 72200
**Employees:** 80

DUNS 21-783-1546
### Round Hill Primary School
Foster Avenue, Beeston, Nottingham, Nottinghamshire NG9 1AE
**Tel:** 01159179262
**Web:** www.roundhill.web6.devwebsite.co.uk
**Estd:** 1981 Proprietorship
**Line of Business:** Primary education
**Proprietor:** A Nash
**US SIC:** 8211 **UK SIC:** 93200
**Employees:** 55

DUNS 21-810-7648
### The Roundabout Childrens Centre
Whitehawk Road, Brighton, East Sussex BN2 5FL
**Tel:** 01273290300
**Web:** www.brighton-hove.gov.uk
**Estd:** 2012
**Line of Business:** Childcare services
**Responsibilities**
**Senior:** Marian Gerrett *(Manager)*, Sue Moore *(Manager)*
**US SIC:** 8321 **UK SIC:** 96111
**Employees:** 50

DUNS 22-802-4048 **Imp**
### Roundel Manufacturing Ltd
Harton Centre, South Shields, Tyne and Wear NE34 0EE
**Tel:** 0191-427-1222 **Fax:** 0191-427-0902
**Web:** www.roundelkitchens.co.uk
**Reg No:** 1586822 **Estd:** 1982 Private Limited Company
**Line of Business:** Manufacture of other kitchen furniture
**Trading Style:** Roundel Kitchens & Bedrooms, Nixons Kitchens
**Issued Capital:** £1,100
**Principals:** G K Oman *(Chairman)*, L Oman *(Managing)*, Ms M E Oman, J T Bebbington
**Co. Secretary:** Ms Elizabeth Oman
**Responsibilities**
**Senior:** Tom Middleton *(Warehouse Manager)*
**Marketing:** Doug Gordon *(Sales & Marketing Manager)*
**Sales:** Doug Gordon *(Sales & Marketing Manager)*
**Health & Safety:** Colin Grout *(Facilities Manager)*
**Facilities:** Colin Grout *(Facilities Manager)*
**Branches:** Roundel Manufacturing Ltd, Great North Road, Newcastle Upon Tyne, Tyne and Wear NE13 6BH
**US SIC:** 2599 **UK SIC:** 46720
**Auditors:** Torgersens
**Bankers:** HSBC Bank plc (40-43-24)

| | 31-01-14 | 31-01-13 | 31-01-12 |
|---|---|---|---|
| TO | 12,072,716 | 9,026,309 | 9,957,291 |
| P/L | 882,223 | 109,498 | 1,352 |
| NW | 3,624,970 | 2,951,491 | 2,822,229 |
| WC | 1,673,087 | 1,042,044 | 883,560 |
| Emp. | 132 | 120 | 136 |

DUNS 23-584-3864
### Roundhouse Holdings Ltd
11 Wigmore Street, London W1U 1PE
**Tel:** 02072976220
**Web:** www.roundhousedesign.com
**Reg No:** 3582057 **Estd:** 1998 Private Limited Company
**Line of Business:** Manufacture of other kitchen furniture
**Trading Style:** Roundhouse Design
**Issued Capital:** £1,000
**Directors:** W J Telford, C J Matson, C J Wilson
**Co. Secretary:** Christopher Wilson
**Responsibilities**
**Senior:** Mary Marriott *(Manager)*
**US SIC:** 2599 **UK SIC:** 46720

| | 30-06-13 | 30-06-12 | 30-06-11 |
|---|---|---|---|
| TO | 7,665,847 | 7,557,733 | N/A |
| P/L | 242,606 | 443,050 | N/A |
| NW | (193,824) | (178,192) | 12,047 |
| WC | (921,230) | (646,391) | (238,054) |
| Emp. | 78 | 73 | N/A |

DUNS 39-802-1840 **Imp**
### Roundstone Nurseries Ltd
Pagham Road, Lagness, Chichester, West Sussex PO20 1LL
**Tel:** 01243-755940
**Web:** www.roundstone.co.uk
**Reg No:** 2207753 **Estd:** 1987 Private Limited Company
**Line of Business:** Florists wholesale
**Export Sales:** £1,102
**Trading Style:** Roundstone Nurseries Ltd
**Issued Capital:** £2,917,500
**Directors:** R I Cahn, C C Need, M R Cahn, P Cook, Ms M L Rijks
**Co. Secretary:** Gavin Miskelly
**US SIC:** 5199 **UK SIC:** 61900
**Auditors:** Spofforths

| | 31-12-13 | 31-12-12 | 31-12-11 |
|---|---|---|---|
| TO | 18,763,286 | 21,235,685 | 21,378,869 |
| P/L | (86,465) | (702,987) | 1,744,354 |
| NW | 11,365,936 | 11,496,928 | 11,903,507 |
| WC | 6,256,984 | 5,668,006 | 6,267,176 |
| Emp. | 125 | 92 | 83 |

DUNS 21-030-3512
### Roundstone Surgery
Roundstone Surgery, Polebarn Circus, Trowbridge, Wiltshire BA14 7EH
**Tel:** 08444778952
**Estd:** 1991 Partnership
**Line of Business:** Doctors practice
**Trading Style:** Lovemead Group Practice
**Partners:** Dr S Smales, Dr D Lodge, Dr D Hales, Dr G Newcomb, Dr C Slack, Dr E Bryant, Dr T Duckworth
**US SIC:** 8011 **UK SIC:** 95300
**Employees:** 55

DUNS 21-853-6427
### Rouse & Co International Llp
11th Floor Exchange Tower, 1 Harbour Exchange Square, London E14 9GE
**Tel:** 02075364100
**Web:** www.rouse.com
**Reg No:** 0377595OC **Estd:** 2012 Private Limited Company
**Line of Business:** Other legal activities not elsewhere classified
**Responsibilities**
**Senior:** Yanli Chang *(Non-designated Limited Liabili)*, Karen Fong *(Non-designated Limited Liabili)*, Mark Foreman *(Non-designated Limited Liabili)*, Edward Hardcastle *(Non-designated Limited Liabili)*, Fang He *(Non-designated Limited Liabili)*, Ling Jing *(Non-designated Limited Liabili)*, Luke Minford *(Non-designated Limited Liabili)*, Rongde Qiao *(Non-designated Limited Liabili)*, Arathi Rajendra *(Non-designated Limited Liabili)*, Jason Rutt *(Non-designated Limited Liabili)*, Diana Sternfeld *(Non-designated Limited Liabili)*, Christopher Vale *(Non-designated Limited Liabili)*
**US SIC:** 8999 **UK SIC:** 83954

| | 30-04-13 |
|---|---|
| TO | 23,252,404 |
| P/L | 292,527 |
| NW | 7,540,686 |
| WC | 7,597,570 |
| Emp. | 329 |

DUNS 21-677-9639
### Rouse Partners Llp
55 Station Road, Beaconsfield, Buckinghamshire HP9 1QL
**Tel:** 01494675321
**Web:** www.rousepartners.co.uk
**Reg No:** 0355817OC **Estd:** 2010
**Line of Business:** Accounting activities
**US SIC:** 8931 **UK SIC:** 83600

| | 31-03-14 | 31-03-13 | 31-03-12 |
|---|---|---|---|
| TO | 4,529,909 | 4,672,689 | 4,530,972 |
| NW | (210,660) | (900,737) | (1,044,725) |
| WC | 1,765,621 | 1,937,351 | 1,664,545 |
| Emp. | 50 | 51 | 54 |

DUNS 21-416-5241
### Route 66
37-39 Guildhall Walk, Portsmouth, Hampshire PO1 2RY
**Tel:** 023-92863741
**Web:** www.route66portsmouth.co.uk
**Estd:** 1982
**Line of Business:** Bars
**Proprietor:** D Woods
**US SIC:** 5813 **UK SIC:** 66200
**Employees:** 49

DUNS 73-822-7318
### Route One Retail Ltd
**(Subsidiary of:** Route One (Holdings) Ltd)
The Rear Buffer Depot, Badminton Road, Badminton, Avon GL9 1HE
**Tel:** 01225338641
**Web:** www.routeone.co.uk
**Reg No:** 5078588 **Estd:** 2004 Private Limited Company
**Line of Business:** Retail sale of sports goods, games and toys, stamps and coins
**Export Sales:** £270,000

**Issued Capital:** £1,000
**Directors:** Ms J A Dixon, R X Boissevain
**Responsibilities**
**Senior:** Paul Wearmouth *(Director)*
**US SIC:** 5699, 5661
**UK SIC:** 64500, 64600
**Bankers:** Lloyds TSB Bank plc (30-00-01)

| | 31-01-14 | 31-01-13 | 31-01-12 |
|---|---|---|---|
| TO | 9,177,408 | 10,569,161 | 9,967,233 |
| P/L | 204,274 | 657,590 | 905,772 |
| NW | 2,264,005 | 2,111,270 | 1,621,832 |
| WC | 1,941,415 | 1,647,174 | 1,394,369 |
| Emp. | 97 | 108 | 103 |

DUNS 21-674-5205
## Routeco Group Holdings Ltd
Davy Avenue, Knowlhill, Milton Keynes, Buckinghamshire MK5 8HJ
**Tel:** 01908666777
**Web:** www.routeco.com
**Reg No:** 7264575 **Estd:** 2010 Private Limited Company
**Line of Business:** Wholesale of other electronic parts and equipment
**Export Sales:** £15,711,000
**Issued Capital:** £150,000
**Directors:** J J Verbeek, I Stewart, A Neocleous
**Co. Secretary:** Sean Evans
**Responsibilities**
**Senior:** Franck Bruel *(Director)*, Fran?s Poncet *(Director)*
**US SIC:** 5065 **UK SIC:** 61500
**Auditors:** Mazars LLP

| | 31-05-14 | 31-05-13 | 31-05-12 |
|---|---|---|---|
| TO | 109,894,000 | 100,076,000 | 97,074,000 |
| P/L | 5,816,000 | 5,498,000 | 5,352,000 |
| NW | 6,499,000 | 1,670,000 | (2,808,000) |
| WC | 6,791,000 | 3,962,000 | 936,000 |
| Emp. | 286 | 275 | 268 |

DUNS 73-286-0866
## Routes to Work Ltd
168-170 Main Street, Bellshill, Lanarkshire ML4 1AE
**Tel:** 01698346834
**Web:** www.routestowork.co.uk
**Reg No:** 0238030SC **Estd:** 2002 Private Company Limited By Guarantee
**Line of Business:** Training providers
**Directors:** J Mcdougall, H Curran, C Mcauley, K Nicholson, K Moffat, T Mcardle, M Mcguire, R King
**Co. Secretary:** Peter Lewis
**Responsibilities**
**Senior:** Robert Biggar *(Manager)*, Kenneth Newton *(Director)*
**US SIC:** 7361 **UK SIC:** 83954
**Bankers:** The Royal Bank Of Scotland Plc (83-25-45)

| | 31-03-14 | 31-03-13 | 31-03-12 |
|---|---|---|---|
| TO | 2,807,732 | 2,608,973 | 2,084,565 |
| P/L | 35,144 | 36,940 | 5,681 |
| NW | 640,894 | 605,750 | 568,810 |
| WC | 623,146 | 589,572 | 558,232 |
| Emp. | 77 | 72 | 54 |

DUNS 28-992-1009
## Roux Waterside Inn Ltd
Ferry Road Bray, Maidenhead, Berkshire SL6 2AT
**Tel:** 01628620691
**Web:** www.waterside-inn.co.uk
**Reg No:** 1826709 **Estd:** 1984 Private Limited Company
**Line of Business:** Hotels
**Issued Capital:** £1,000
**Directors:** A Roux, D C Brown, Mrs C Grant, M A Broadbent, D Masciaga
**Co. Secretary:** David Glaser
**US SIC:** 7011, 5812
**UK SIC:** 66500, 66110
**Auditors:** Roffe Swayne

| | 31-12-13 | 31-12-12 | 31-12-11 |
|---|---|---|---|
| TO | 5,934,036 | 5,466,756 | 6,100,972 |
| P/L | 801,500 | 264,653 | 508,439 |
| NW | 5,789,035 | 5,454,739 | 5,469,589 |
| WC | 1,003,799 | 535,684 | 753,104 |
| Emp. | 66 | 70 | 69 |

DUNS 22-770-1315
## Rover Finance Ltd
**(Subsidiary of:** Hm Treasury)
435 Stratford Road, Shirley, Solihull, West Midlands B90 4AA
**Tel:** 01217463000
**Reg No:** 1241118 **Estd:** 1976 Private Limited Company
**Line of Business:** Financial intermediation not elsewhere classified
**Issued Capital:** £1
**Directors:** N T Clibbens, A P Gadsby
**Co. Secretary:** Rbs Secretarial Services Limited
**Branches:** Rover Finance Ltd, 51 Field House, West Way, Oxford, Oxfordshire OX2 9JN
**US SIC:** 6111 **UK SIC:** 81501
**Auditors:** Deloitte & Touche

**Bankers:** National Westminster Bank Plc (54-30-36)

| | 30-09-14 | 30-09-13 | 30-09-12 |
|---|---|---|---|
| TA | 1 | 1 | 1 |
| NW | 1 | 1 | 1 |

DUNS 29-893-8697 Imp
## Rovi Europe Ltd
14-18 Bell Street, Maidenhead, Berkshire SL6 1BR
**Fax:** 01628677392
**Web:** www.rovicorp.co.uk
**Reg No:** 2096781 **Estd:** 1987 Private Limited Company
**Line of Business:** Other business activities not elsewhere classified
**Export Sales:** £10,119,000
**Issued Capital:** £15,000
**Directors:** Ms P A Sergeef, P Rojas
**Co. Secretary:** John Patterson
**Responsibilities**
**Sales:** Graham Byrne *(Major Account Manager)*, Charles Dawes *(Global Strategic Account Direc)*, David Scutt *(Senior Sales Director)*, Scott Winchester *(Sales Director)*
**Branches:** Rovi Europe Ltd, 52 Bermondsey Street, London SE1 3UD
**US SIC:** 7379 **UK SIC:** 83940
**Auditors:** Ernst & Young LLP
**Bankers:** Barclays Bank Plc (20-89-16)

| | 31-12-13 | 31-12-12 | 31-12-11 |
|---|---|---|---|
| TO | 10,119,000 | 9,332,000 | 9,019,000 |
| P/L | 732,000 | 725,000 | 6,567,000 |
| NW | 15,398,000 | 14,054,000 | 12,842,000 |
| WC | 15,326,000 | 13,970,000 | 12,716,000 |
| Emp. | 64 | 71 | 74 |

DUNS 39-804-7456
## Rowan & Co Capital Management Ltd
**(Subsidiary of:** Mattioli Woods Plc)
2 Queen Square, Bath, Avon BA1 2HQ
**Tel:** 01225-469424 **Fax:** 01225-428760
**Web:** www.rowanplc.com
**Reg No:** 2201679 **VAT No:** 806651335
**Estd:** 1987 Private Limited Company
**Line of Business:** Financial intermediation not elsewhere classified
**Trading Style:** Ashcourt Rowan
**Issued Capital:** £800,000
**Director:** A Tagliabue
**Co. Secretary:** Ms Rehana Hasan
**Responsibilities**
**Senior:** Jonathan Poland *(CEO)*
**IT:** Roger Rumble *(IT Manager)*
**Branches:** Rowan & Co Capital Management Ltd, St. Georges Square, Harding House, Taunton, Somerset TA1 3RX
**US SIC:** 6111 **UK SIC:** 81501
**Auditors:** KPMG Audit PLC
**Bankers:** The Royal Bank Of Scotland Plc (16-14-25)

| | 31-03-14 | 31-03-13 | 31-03-12 |
|---|---|---|---|
| TA | 1,237,196 | 1,237,196 | 1,237,196 |
| NW | 1,237,196 | 1,237,196 | 1,237,196 |

DUNS 23-080-9337
## Rowan Dartington & Co. Ltd
**(Subsidiary of:** Rowan Dartington Holdings Ltd)
Colston Tower, Colston Street, Bristol, Avon BS1 4RD
**Tel:** 01179-330000
**Web:** www.rowan-dartington.co.uk
**Reg No:** 2752304 **VAT No:** 609477023
**Estd:** 1992 Private Limited Company
**Line of Business:** Financial intermediation not elsewhere classified
**Issued Capital:** £2,084,333
**Directors:** G J Stephens, J N Cooper, Miss S E Evans, D W Snow, B D Cooper, G P Coxell, D Burrows
**Co. Secretary:** David Burrows
**Responsibilities**
**Senior:** Nigel Pavey *(Senior Broker)*
**Finance:** Nick Hodgkinson *(Financial Controller)*, Matt Shakeshaft *(Financial Controller)*
**Marketing:** Kirsty Abel *(Marketing Manager)*
**IT:** Alex Dredge *(IT Manager)*
**HR:** David Money *(Human Resources Manager)*
**Health & Safety:** Alison Crotch-Harvey *(Compliance Officer)*
**Facilities:** Rebecca Boulton *(Facilities Coordinator)*, Lydia Grant *(Facilities Coordinator)*
**Branches:** Rowan Dartington & Co. Ltd, Lloyds Bank Chambers, 115 High Street, Weston-Super-Mare, Avon BS23 1HQ
**US SIC:** 6111 **UK SIC:** 81501
**Auditors:** Deloitte LLP
**Bankers:** The Royal Bank Of Scotland Plc (15-10-00)

| | 31-12-13 | 31-12-12 | 31-12-11 |
|---|---|---|---|
| TA | 7,850,571 | 5,585,328 | 5,085,353 |
| P/L | 751,573 | 215,563 | 46,879 |
| NW | 2,852,744 | 2,040,404 | 1,776,838 |
| WC | 2,158,543 | 1,300,759 | 1,005,925 |
| Emp. | 71 | 67 | 66 |

DUNS 21-775-2007
## Rowan Gate Primary School
Finedon Road, Wellingborough, Northamptonshire NN8 4NS
**Tel:** 01933304970
**Web:** www.rowangate.ik.org
**Estd:** 1997 Proprietorship
**Line of Business:** Primary education
**Proprietor:** Mrs L Clarke
**US SIC:** 8211 **UK SIC:** 93200
**Employees:** 77

DUNS 76-934-7121
## Rowan International Ltd
**(Subsidiary of:** Vsl Group Holdings Ltd)
Endeavour Drive, Basildon, Essex SS14 3WF
**Tel:** 01268592000 **Fax:** 01268767808
**Web:** www.rowan.eu.com
**Reg No:** 2477215 **Estd:** 1945 Private Limited Company
**Line of Business:** Trade and business organisations
**Trading Style:** Rowan International
**Issued Capital:** £520,000
**Directors:** A J Saywell, P R Tissiman, A T Littmoden
**Co. Secretary:** Matthew Piears
**Responsibilities**
**HR:** Lindsay Edwards *(Head of Human Resources)*
**US SIC:** 5999 **UK SIC:** 65600
**Auditors:** Leigh Carr
**Bankers:** Lloyds TSB Bank plc (30-00-09)

| | 31-12-13 | 31-12-12 | 31-12-11 |
|---|---|---|---|
| TO | 66,707,904 | 56,561,132 | 52,715,167 |
| P/L | 3,661,343 | 3,621,732 | 3,222,432 |
| NW | 9,652,291 | 7,701,547 | 5,669,521 |
| WC | 5,234,223 | 3,422,213 | 1,938,005 |
| Emp. | 76 | 71 | 65 |

DUNS 23-448-1562
## The Rowan Organisation
Elliot Park Innovation Centre, Nuneaton, Warwickshire CV10 7RH
**Tel:** 02476322860 **Fax:** 02476374948
**Web:** www.therowan.org
**Reg No:** 2783681 **Estd:** 2008 Private Company Limited By Guarantee
**Line of Business:** Social work activities without accommodation
**Directors:** A Forwood, J N Deacon, Dr B A Lucas, Ms J Taylor, Mrs W P Betts, Miss D E Cambray, Ms J C Prout, Ms L Crawford
**Responsibilities**
**Senior:** Ian Keenan *(Director)*
**Finance:** Glyn Davies *(Director and Company Secretary)*
**Branches:** The Rowan Organisation, 330 Saxon Gate West, Milton Keynes, Buckinghamshire MK9 2ES
**US SIC:** 8321 **UK SIC:** 96111
**Auditors:** Bishop Simmons Ltd
**Bankers:** Barclays Bank Plc (20-85-13)

| | 31-03-14 | 31-03-13 | 31-03-12 |
|---|---|---|---|
| TO | 1,861,021 | 1,936,455 | 2,264,058 |
| P/L | 5,338 | (44,394) | (287,196) |
| NW | 118,377 | 113,039 | 264,217 |
| WC | 92,752 | 84,797 | 212,289 |
| Emp. | 79 | 72 | 70 |

DUNS 77-979-4374
## Rowan Telmac Holdings Ltd
Rowan House, Hortonwood 33, Telford, Shropshire TF1 7EX
**Tel:** 01952-677705 **Fax:** 01952605600
**Web:** www.rowantelmac.co.uk
**Reg No:** 5947786 **Estd:** 2006 Private Limited Company
**Line of Business:** Engineers (general)
**Issued Capital:** £10,000
**Director:** R J Mallard
**Co. Secretary:** Mrs Margaret Mallard
**US SIC:** 6711 **UK SIC:** 83962

| | 30-09-13 | 30-09-12 | 30-09-11 |
|---|---|---|---|
| TA | 1,614,591 | 1,616,692 | 1,620,092 |
| NW | 10,000 | 10,000 | 10,000 |
| WC | N/A | (57,899) | (54,499) |

DUNS 34-997-2864
## Rowanmoor Group Plc
Rowanmoor House, 46-50 Castle Street, Salisbury, Wiltshire SP1 3TS
**Tel:** 08445-440440 **Fax:** 08445440500
**Web:** www.rowanmoor.co.uk
**Reg No:** 5792242 **Estd:** 2006 Public Limited Company
**Line of Business:** Financial intermediation not elsewhere classified
**Trading Style:** Rowanmoor Pensions
**Issued Capital:** £242,001
**Directors:** C M Terrey, S C Whitmore, I D Hammond, D Saer, D O Downie, Ms L V Matthews
**Co. Secretary:** Ms Shirley Hylands
**Responsibilities**
**Marketing:** Emily Chuang-Neesham *(Online Marketing Coordinator)*
**Health & Safety:** June Jach *(Head of Property Services)*
**Facilities:** June Jach *(Head of Property Services)*
**US SIC:** 6111, 8999
**UK SIC:** 81501, 83954
**Auditors:** Nexia Smith & Williamson

| | 30-09-14 | 30-09-13 | 30-09-12 |
|---|---|---|---|
| TA | 6,619,000 | 6,606,000 | 6,407,000 |
| P/L | 126,000 | 1,553,000 | 418,000 |
| NW | 662,000 | 556,000 | (656,000) |
| WC | 214,000 | 206,000 | (895,000) |
| Emp. | 258 | 245 | 234 |

DUNS 39-978-7944
## The Rowans Hospice
Purbrook Heath Road, Purbrook, Waterlooville, Hampshire PO7 5RU
**Tel:** 023-9225-0001
**Web:** www.rowanshospice.co.uk
**Reg No:** 2275068 **VAT No:** 615153467
**Estd:** 1988 Private Company Limited By Guarantee
**Line of Business:** Medical practice activities
**Directors:** Ms C Hewitt, I J Young, Mrs L Dickens, The Very Reverend D C Brindley, Mrs E Emms, R C Tonge, I A Dillow, M Smith
**Co. Secretary:** Miss Anne Yendell
**Responsibilities**
**Senior:** Oliver Howard *(Director)*, Anne Powell *(Director)*, Ruth White *(CEO, Managing Director)*
**Operations:** Vanessa Gilding *(Operations Manager)*
**Branches:** The Rowans Hospice, 146 Fratton Road, Portsmouth, Hampshire PO1 5DD
**US SIC:** 8011 **UK SIC:** 95300
**Auditors:** Morris Crocker
**Bankers:** National Westminster Bank Plc (56-00-64)

| | 31-03-14 | 31-03-13 | 31-03-12 |
|---|---|---|---|
| TO | 6,934,438 | 5,514,655 | 3,810,508 |
| P/L | 676,811 | (156,260) | 79,229 |
| NW | 8,732,692 | 7,888,998 | 7,808,104 |
| WC | 1,382,694 | 764,482 | 876,783 |
| Emp. | 144 | 139 | 117 |

DUNS 21-607-3990
## Rowantree
10 Railway View Road, Clitheroe, Lancashire BB7 2HE
**Tel:** 01200427115
**Web:** www.the-rowan-tree.org.uk
**Estd:** 2003 Partnership
**Line of Business:** Guest houses
**Partners:** Miss L Murray, Mrs E Mckeegan
**Responsibilities**
**Senior:** Elizabeth McKeegan *(Partner)*, Peter Ritchie *(Proprietor)*
**US SIC:** 7011 **UK SIC:** 66500
**Employees:** 300

DUNS 52-560-3510
## Rowcliffe Holdings Ltd
78-88 East Reach, Taunton, Somerset TA1 3HF
**Web:** www.rowcliffes.co.uk
**Reg No:** 3246171 **Estd:** 1996 Private Limited Company
**Line of Business:** Other letting of own property
**Trading Style:** Rowcliffe Holdings Ltd
**Issued Capital:** £209,100
**Directors:** Mrs N C Rattray, T D Rowcliffe, Mrs L Darby, N T Rowcliffe
**Responsibilities**
**Senior:** Karen Bater *(General Manager)*
**US SIC:** 6519, 5521
**UK SIC:** 85000, 65100
**Auditors:** Albert Goodman
**Bankers:** Lloyds TSB Bank plc (30-98-45)

| | 30-06-14 | 30-06-13 | 30-06-12 |
|---|---|---|---|
| TA | 6,161,317 | 6,076,931 | 5,749,148 |
| NW | 5,354,284 | 5,257,903 | 4,980,446 |
| WC | (422,032) | (79,249) | (356,878) |

DUNS 28-937-5123
## The Rowcroft House Foundation Ltd
Avenue Road, Torquay, Devon TQ2 5LS
**Tel:** 01803210800
**Web:** www.rowcrofthospice.org.uk
**Reg No:** 1561601 **Estd:** 1982 Private Company Limited By Guarantee
**Line of Business:** Other human health activities
**Trading Style:** Rowcroft Hospice
**Directors:** C M Pincombe, Dr R W Ward, C L Hicks, R A Smith, W Grahamslaw, R J Brinsley
**Co. Secretary:** Giles Charnaud
**Responsibilities**
**Senior:** Susan Newman *(Director)*, Michael Pavey *(Director)*, Caroline Wannell *(Pa To The Chief Executive And)*
**Finance:** Jayne Owen *(Finance Manager)*
**HR:** Tracey Cole *(Director of Human Resources)*
**Facilities:** Simon Weal *(Estate Manager)*

**Purchasing:** Jayne Owen *(Finance Manager)*
**Branches:** The Rowcroft House Foundation Ltd, 1-3 Victoria Sq, Paignton, Devon TQ4 6PE
**US SIC:** 8011 **UK SIC:** 95300
**Auditors:** Hawes Richards & Co
**Bankers:** National Westminster Bank Plc (55-70-01)

| | 31-03-14 | 31-03-13 | 31-03-12 |
|---|---|---|---|
| TO | 7,203,511 | 6,869,812 | 6,599,891 |
| P/L | (1,114,219) | (700,822) | (112,866) |
| NW | 7,626,122 | 8,603,092 | 8,333,022 |
| WC | 1,421,761 | 2,347,062 | 1,514,990 |
| Emp. | 189 | 272 | 259 |

DUNS 29-629-5041
## Rowden House School Ltd
(**Subsidiary of:** Senad Group Limited)
Rowden House, Bromyard, Herefordshire HR7 4LS
**Fax:** 01885483361
**Web:** www.senadgroup.com
**Reg No:** 1955565 **Estd:** 1985 Private Limited Company
**Line of Business:** Schools (independent)
**Issued Capital:** £80,000
**Director:** B J Jones
**Co. Secretary:** James Atkinson
**Responsibilities**
**Senior:** Martin Carter *(Head Teacher)*
**US SIC:** 8211 **UK SIC:** 93200
**Auditors:** Ford Campbell
**Bankers:** HSBC Bank plc (40-31-24)

| | 31-08-13 | 31-08-12 | 31-08-11 |
|---|---|---|---|
| TO | 3,677,000 | 4,604,000 | 7,320,000 |
| P/L | (72,000) | (227,000) | 236,000 |
| NW | 481,000 | 513,000 | 637,000 |
| WC | 8,889,000 | (2,571,000) | (2,379,000) |
| Emp. | 123 | 133 | 185 |

DUNS 63-468-9848
## Rowe Veterinary Group
Veterinary Hospital, Wotton-Under-Edge, Gloucestershire GL12 7PP
**Tel:** 01453844337
**Web:** www.local-vets.net
**Partnership**
**Line of Business:** Veterinary activities
**Partner:** R Rowe
**Branches:** Rowe Veterinary Group, 3 Pullins Green, Bristol, Avon BS35 2AX
**US SIC:** 0741 **UK SIC:** 95601
**Employees:** 60

DUNS 21-282-3476
## Rowland Road Wmc
38 Rowland Road, Leeds, West Yorkshire LS11 6ED
**Tel:** 0113-2289333
**Line of Business:** Licensed clubs
**US SIC:** 5813 **UK SIC:** 66200
**Employees:** 47

DUNS 23-224-1661
## Rowlands Field Cunningham
Phoenix House, Manchester M2 4JF
**Tel:** 08449846000
**Web:** www.lindermyers.co.uk
**Estd:** 1996 Partnership
**Line of Business:** Solicitors
**Trading Style:** Linder Myers Solicitors
**Responsibilities**
**Senior:** Jon Andrews *(Partner)*, Suzanne Lurie *(Business Relationship Partner)*
**Finance:** Chris Hawley *(Finance Director)*
**Marketing:** Dougie Watt *(Marketing Director)*
**IT:** Michael McGuire *(Head of IT)*
**HR:** Mark Booth *(Compliance and Training Manage)*, Pauline Taylor *(HR Manager)*
**Branches:** Rowlands Field Cunningham, 16 Crofts Bank Road, Arrandale Court, Manchester M41 0UZ
**US SIC:** 8111 **UK SIC:** 83500
**Employees:** 80

DUNS 21-234-1124
## Rowlands Gill & District Live At Home Scheme
Strathmore Road, Rowlands Gill, Tyne and Wear NE39 1JB
**Tel:** 01207-549200
**Estd:** 2001
**Line of Business:** Community centres
**Proprietor:** Mrs T Dixon
**US SIC:** 8699 **UK SIC:** 96902
**Employees:** 70

DUNS 21-781-4626
## Rowlatt's Hill Primary School
Balderstone Close, Leicester, Leicestershire LE5 4ES
**Tel:** 01162768812
**Web:** www.rowlattshill.leicester.sch.uk
**Estd:** 1992 Proprietorship
**Line of Business:** Schools (local authority)
**Proprietor:** Ms J Virk
**US SIC:** 8211 **UK SIC:** 93200
**Employees:** 48

DUNS 49-725-6107
## Rowledge Conservative Club
Fullers Road, Rowledge, Farnham, Surrey GU10 4DE
**Tel:** 01252-793679
**Estd:** 2002
**Line of Business:** Clubs social and associations
**Chairman:** T Hill
**US SIC:** 8699 **UK SIC:** 96902
**Employees:** 200

DUNS 23-635-8115
## Rowley Ashworth
Kennedy Tower, Birmingham, West Midlands B4 6JG
**Tel:** 01212126800
**Web:** www.rowley-ashworth.co.uk
**Partnership**
**Line of Business:** Solicitors
**Partners:** T Sterling, Ms M O'Connor, K Roberts, R Ellis, Ms A Isaacson, J Parkhouse, J Mullen, Mrs S Hemsley
**Responsibilities**
**Senior:** Peter Carson *(Partner)*, Jan Dadd *(Partner)*, Karl De Loyde *(Partner)*, Steve Fitzwalter *(Partner)*, Alison Hunphry *(Partner)*, Mary O'Connor *(Partner)*, Martin Singh *(Partner)*, Edmund Young *(Partner)*
**Branches:** Rowley Ashworth, Brittany House, New North Road, Exeter, Devon EX4 4EP
**US SIC:** 8111 **UK SIC:** 83500
**Employees:** 200

DUNS 34-988-9258
## Rowley House Ltd
26 Rowley Avenue, Stafford, Staffordshire ST17 9AA
**Tel:** 01785-255279 **Fax:** 01785-259861
**Reg No:** 5784082 **Estd:** 1983 Private Limited Company
**Line of Business:** Medical nursing home activities
**Issued Capital:** £100
**Director:** M J O'Connell
**Co. Secretary:** Mrs Jillian O'Connell
**US SIC:** 8051 **UK SIC:** 95100

| | 31-08-14 | 31-08-13 | 31-08-12 |
|---|---|---|---|
| TA | 434,562 | 372,999 | 450,605 |
| NW | 315,683 | 252,377 | 162,546 |
| WC | 248,220 | 180,567 | 85,937 |

DUNS 76-722-4199
## Rowlinson Constructions Ltd
(**Subsidiary of:** Rowlinson Holdings Ltd)
London House, London Road South, Poynton, Stockport, Cheshire SK12 1YP
**Tel:** 01625-877177
**Web:** www.rowlinsonconstruction.co.uk
**Reg No:** 2596893 **Estd:** 1953 Private Limited Company
**Line of Business:** Development and selling of real estate
**Issued Capital:** £1,000
**Directors:** D S Chilton, S J Weir, D J Roberts
**Co. Secretary:** Adrian Simpson
**US SIC:** 6552, 1541
**UK SIC:** 85000, 50100
**Auditors:** Hurst & Co Accountants LLP
**Bankers:** The Royal Bank Of Scotland Plc (16-00-01)

| | 31-12-13 | 31-12-12 | 31-12-11 |
|---|---|---|---|
| TO | 15,007,044 | 12,426,480 | 17,511,361 |
| P/L | 441,201 | 396,331 | 619,082 |
| NW | 7,354,456 | 7,023,161 | 6,733,798 |
| WC | 6,650,767 | 6,714,919 | 6,401,485 |
| Emp. | 60 | 63 | 92 |

DUNS 21-882-9885 **Imp-Exp**
## Rowlinson Group Ltd
(**Subsidiary of:** Rowlinson Group Holdings Ltd)
Unit 2 Green Lane, Nantwich, Cheshire CW5 6BN
**Tel:** 01829260571 **Fax:** 01207065479
**Web:** www.rowlinson.co.uk
**Reg No:** 0682070 **Estd:** 1961 Private Limited Company
**Line of Business:** Other letting of own property
**Export Markets:** Europe; Far East
**Trading Style:** Rowlinson Garden Products
**Issued Capital:** £82
**Principals:** R J Rowlinson *(Managing)*, K P Douglas *(Financial)*, J M Brodie, J D Williams
**Co. Secretary:** William Kiernan
**Responsibilities**
**Health & Safety:** Peter Penlington *(Health & Safety Officer)*
**Branches:** Rowlinson Group Ltd, Unit 2, Green Lane, Nantwich, Cheshire CW5 6BN
**US SIC:** 6519, 6711
**UK SIC:** 85000, 83962
**Auditors:** Arthur Andersen
**Bankers:** The Royal Bank Of Scotland Plc (16-26-14)

| | 30-04-14 | 30-04-13 | 30-04-12 |
|---|---|---|---|
| TO | 46,933,495 | 31,246,029 | 47,891,801 |
| P/L | 363,255 | (38,060) | 432,442 |
| NW | 17,358,133 | 17,507,373 | 17,638,710 |
| WC | 9,321,918 | 9,970,466 | 9,954,084 |
| Emp. | 324 | 299 | 317 |

DUNS 21-607-3955
## Rownhams St Johns Primary School
Bakers Drove, Rownhams, Southampton, Hampshire SO16 8AD
**Tel:** 02380736417
**Web:** www.rownhams.hants.sch.uk
**Estd:** 1999
**Line of Business:** Schools (local authority)
**Proprietor:** Mrs M Knight
**Responsibilities**
**Senior:** Bernadette Fleet *(Acting Head Teacher)*
**US SIC:** 8211 **UK SIC:** 93200
**Employees:** 60

DUNS 21-919-6623
## Rowntrees (Market Street) Manchester Ltd
(**Subsidiary of:** Qmh Ltd)
Altrincham Road, Wilmslow, Cheshire SK9 4LR
**Tel:** 01625-889988
**Web:** www.manchester2002-uk.com
**Reg No:** 0948579 **Estd:** 1969 Private Limited Company
**Line of Business:** Hotels
**Trading Style:** Wilmslow Moat House
**Issued Capital:** £100
**Directors:** J Braidley, D Arzi
**US SIC:** 7011 **UK SIC:** 66500
**Auditors:** PricewaterhouseCoopers LLP
**Bankers:** Lloyds TSB Bank plc (30-95-42)

| | 31-12-13 | 31-12-12 | 31-12-11 |
|---|---|---|---|
| TO | N/A | 5,435,000 | 6,446,000 |
| P/L | 10,000 | 7,356,000 | (3,976,000) |
| NW | 10,000 | N/A | (8,303,000) |
| WC | N/A | N/A | (16,803,000) |
| Emp. | N/A | 121 | 129 |

DUNS 21-691-0448 **Imp-Exp**
## Rowse Honey Ltd
(**Subsidiary of:** Lydian Capital Partners L.P.)
Moreton Avenue, Wallingford, Oxfordshire OX10 9DE
**Tel:** 01491827400
**Web:** www.rowsehoney.co.uk
**Reg No:** 1024018 **VAT No:** 537596893
**Estd:** 1971 Private Limited Company
**Line of Business:** Manufacturers of food products
**Export Markets:** European Union (E U)
**Export Sales:** £362,000
**Issued Capital:** £18,934
**Directors:** J S Rodrigues, Mrs P K Briant
**Co. Secretary:**
Ogier Corporate Services (Uk) Li
**Responsibilities**
**Senior:** James Gidmore *(Manager)*, Jon Hather *(Manager)*, Patrick Robinson *(Operations Director)*, John Toomey *(Manager)*
**Finance:** Michael Lysaght *(Financial Controller)*
**Sales:** Jeff Hammond *(Sales Manager)*
**Health & Safety:** Richard Winfield *(Health & Safety Officer)*
**Purchasing:** John Feast *(Purchasing Manager)*
**US SIC:** 2099, 5149
**UK SIC:** 42399, 61700
**Auditors:** PricewaterhouseCoopers LLP
**Bankers:** Barclays Bank Plc (20-01-09)

| | 31-12-13 | 31-12-12 | 31-12-11 |
|---|---|---|---|
| TO | 85,096,000 | 73,553,000 | 73,044,000 |
| P/L | 7,313,000 | 6,116,000 | 23,889,000 |
| NW | 49,110,000 | 65,360,000 | 60,715,000 |
| WC | 42,357,000 | 59,275,000 | 54,792,000 |
| Emp. | 203 | 187 | 192 |

DUNS 52-566-1260
## Rowton Hall Hotel Ltd
Whitchurch Road., Chester, Cheshire CH3 6AD
**Tel:** 01244335262
**Web:** www.rowtonhallhotel.co.uk
**Reg No:** 3252288 **Estd:** 1996 Private Limited Company
**Line of Business:** Hotels
**Trading Style:** Rowton Hall Hotel and Spa
**Issued Capital:** £8,079
**Director:** G R Wigginton
**Co. Secretary:** Ms Hazel O'Hare
**US SIC:** 7011 **UK SIC:** 66500
**Auditors:** Qed Partnership
**Bankers:** National Westminster Bank Plc (60-40-08)

| | 31-03-14 | 31-03-13 | 31-03-12 |
|---|---|---|---|
| TO | 2,259,586 | 2,195,826 | 1,985,242 |
| P/L | 42,449 | 154,603 | 69,280 |
| NW | 876,599 | 851,608 | 576,513 |
| WC | (415,631) | (334,327) | (421,876) |
| Emp. | 64 | 62 | 60 |

DUNS 21-582-5503
## Rox Interiors
Palmerston Centre, Oxford Road, Wealdstone, Harrow, Middlesex HA3 7RG
**Web:** www.roxinteriors.com
**Estd:** 2011 Proprietorship
**Line of Business:** Speciality design activities
**Proprietor:** Mrs F Lanchhani
**US SIC:** 7399 **UK SIC:** 83954
**Employees:** 50

DUNS 22-149-6131 **Imp**
## Rox (U.K.) Ltd
(**Subsidiary of:** Rosebank Holdings Ltd.)
Argyll Arcade, Glasgow, Lanarkshire G2 8BG
**Tel:** 0141-221-0550 **Fax:** 0141-221-9877
**Web:** www.rox.co.uk
**Reg No:** 0216217SC **Estd:** 2002 Private Limited Company
**Line of Business:** Other business activities not elsewhere classified
**Export Sales:** £39,273
**Issued Capital:** £1,400,000
**Directors:** H S Mitchell, G L Mitchell
**Co. Secretary:** Kyron Keogh
**Responsibilities**
**Finance:** David boyle *(Finance director)*
**US SIC:** 7399 **UK SIC:** 83954
**Bankers:** The Royal Bank Of Scotland Plc (83-16-25)

| | 31-03-14 | 31-03-13 | 31-03-12 |
|---|---|---|---|
| TO | 11,351,699 | 10,221,742 | 9,922,763 |
| P/L | 251,702 | 196,759 | 279,971 |
| NW | 1,295,995 | 1,056,957 | 836,637 |
| WC | 1,128,898 | 838,462 | 891,963 |
| Emp. | 90 | 88 | 81 |

DUNS 21-777-9658
## Roxburghe Golf Course
The Roxburghe Hotel & Golf Course, Kelso, Roxburghshire TD5 8JZ
**Tel:** 01573450333
**Web:** www.roxburghe.net
**Estd:** 2011 Proprietorship
**Line of Business:** Other sporting activities not elsewhere classified
**Proprietor:** G Mack
**Responsibilities**
**Senior:** Duncan Evans *(General Manager)*
**US SIC:** 7999 **UK SIC:** 97913
**Employees:** 60

DUNS 23-041-2905
## The Roxburghe Hotel & Golf Course
Heiton By Kelso, Kelso, Kelso, Roxburghshire TD5 8JZ
**Tel:** 01573 450331
**Web:** www.roxburghe.net
**VAT No:** 356229838 **Estd:** 1996 Partnership
**Line of Business:** Hotels
**Partners:** D Roxburghe, D Roxburghe
**Responsibilities**
**Senior:** Duncan Evans *(General Manager)*
**US SIC:** 7011 **UK SIC:** 66500
**Employees:** 50

DUNS 73-269-5932 **Imp-Exp**
## Roxel (Uk Rocket Motors) Ltd
(**Subsidiary of:** Roxel)
Summerfield Lane, Summerfield, Kidderminster, Worcestershire DY11 7RZ
**Tel:** 01562-824061
**Web:** www.roxelgroup.com
**Reg No:** 4543318 **VAT No:** 799928923
**Estd:** 2002 Private Limited Company
**Line of Business:** Manufacture of weapons and ammunition
**Export Sales:** £10,622,000
**Issued Capital:** £50,001
**Directors:** J Desclaux, M Hardman, S A Liggitt
**Responsibilities**
**Senior:** David Quancard *(CEO)*
**IT:** John Ayris *(Engineering Manager)*, Phil Mock *(Computer Manager)*
**Facilities:** John Ayris *(Engineering Manager)*, Andy McIntyre *(Facilities Manager)*
**Operations:** John Ayris *(Engineering Manager)*
**Purchasing:** Graham Irving *(Purchasing Manager)*
**Engineering:** John Ayris *(Engineering Manager)*
**US SIC:** 3489, 3721
**UK SIC:** 32901, 36400
**Auditors:** KPMG Audit PLC

**Bankers:** HSBC Bank plc (40-02-50)

| | 31-12-13 | 31-12-12 | 31-12-11 |
|---|---|---|---|
| TO | 17,595,000 | 32,026,000 | 27,201,000 |
| P/L | 2,479,000 | 2,582,000 | 7,740,000 |
| NW | 5,610,000 | 4,214,000 | 2,198,000 |
| WC | 2,629,000 | 5,495,000 | 2,705,000 |
| Emp. | 150 | 150 | 144 |

DUNS 51-649-6481

## Roxi Petroleum Plc

5 New Street Square, London EC3A 3TW
**Web:** www.roxipetroleum.com
**Reg No:** 5966431 **Estd:** 2006 Public Limited Company
**Line of Business:** Oil and gas extraction
**Directors:** K R Oraziman, H S Jang, Lord E C Earl Of Limerick, C N Carver, K A Satylganov
**Co. Secretary:** Clive Carver
**US SIC:** 1311 **UK SIC:** 13000
**Auditors:** BDO LLP
**Employees:** 112
**Turnover:** £3,908,000

DUNS 23-895-7984

## Roxton Nursing Home Ltd

154 Birmingham Road, Sutton Coldfield, West Midlands B72 1LY
**Fax:** 0121-355-2135
**Web:** www.roxton.biz
**Reg No:** 3886617 **Estd:** 1936 Private Limited Company
**Line of Business:** Nursing homes
**Issued Capital:** £2
**Director:** K L Milligan
**Co. Secretary:** Phillip Milligan
**US SIC:** 8051 **UK SIC:** 95100

| | 31-12-13 | 31-12-12 | 31-12-11 |
|---|---|---|---|
| TA | 189,839 | 172,816 | 146,408 |
| NW | 65,619 | 51,465 | 49,732 |
| WC | 48,731 | 50,659 | 27,476 |

DUNS 73-297-6241

## Roy Beech (Surfacing) Ltd

60 Castleton Road, Lightwood, Stoke-On-Trent, Staffordshire ST3 7TD
**Tel:** 01782847925
**Web:** www.roybeech.co.uk
**Reg No:** 4571507 **Estd:** 2002 Private Limited Company
**Line of Business:** Civil Engineers
**Issued Capital:** £1
**Directors:** N G Bennett, I D Jennings
**Co. Secretary:** Adrian Williams
**US SIC:** 8911 **UK SIC:** 83701

| | 31-10-14 | 31-10-13 | 31-10-12 |
|---|---|---|---|
| TA | 1 | 1 | 1 |
| NW | 1 | 1 | 1 |

DUNS 21-718-2419

## Roy Bowles Transport Ltd

(**Subsidiary of:** Roy Bowles Services Ltd)
Hornblower House, Galleymead Road, Colnbrook, Slough, Berkshire SL3 0EN
**Tel:** 08438164752
**Web:** www.roybowles.net
**Reg No:** 1075529 **VAT No:** 208086864
**Estd:** 1972 Private Limited Company
**Line of Business:** Road haulage and transport services
**Issued Capital:** £99
**Directors:** Ms M Bowles, S N Bowles, Ms J L Bowles
**Co. Secretary:** Ms Sheila Nye
**Responsibilities**
**Senior:** Royston Bowles *(Health & Safety Director)*
**Finance:** Vic Gilliard *(Financial Director)*
**Health & Safety:** Royston Bowles *(Health & Safety Director)*
**Fleet:** Royston Bowles *(Health & Safety Director)*
**Engineering:** Royston Bowles *(Health & Safety Director)*
**Branches:** White Hart Ho, Silwood Rd, Sunninghill, Ascot Berks SL5 0DD.
**US SIC:** 4789 **UK SIC:** 77002
**Auditors:** S W Frankson & Co
**Bankers:** Barclays Bank Plc (20-78-58)

| | 31-12-13 | 31-12-12 | 31-12-11 |
|---|---|---|---|
| TA | 834,941 | 925,116 | 952,629 |
| NW | 407,961 | 403,559 | 508,485 |
| WC | 221,255 | 162,141 | 91,079 |

DUNS 77-956-0010

## Roy Castle Lung Cancer Foundation

4-6 Enterprise Way, Liverpool, Merseyside L13 1FB
**Tel:** 01512547200 **Fax:** 0151-254-7273
**Web:** www.roycastle.org
**Reg No:** 3059425 **Estd:** 1995 Private Company Limited By Guarantee
**Line of Business:** Clinics private
**Directors:** D S Maples, R J Donnelly, P J Rainey, G Gottig, Dr A J Coombs, Dr D Gilligan, Sir P D Carter, E Imrie
**Co. Secretary:** Mrs Paula Chadwick
**Responsibilities**
**Senior:** Sarah Burbridge *(Administration)*, James Couton *(Director)*
**Finance:** Mike Grundy *(Financial Controller)*
**IT:** Simon Critchley *(IT Officer)*
**Branches:** Roy Castle Lung Cancer Foundation, 98 Holm Street, Glasgow, Lanarkshire G2 6SY
**US SIC:** 8699 **UK SIC:** 96902
**Auditors:** HLB Kidsons
**Bankers:** Barclays Bank Plc (20-51-01)

| | 31-12-13 | 31-12-12 | 31-12-11 |
|---|---|---|---|
| TO | 4,679,833 | 4,953,840 | 5,227,741 |
| P/L | (750,985) | (43,487) | 354,140 |
| NW | 1,511,857 | 2,157,790 | 2,168,329 |
| WC | 293,805 | 1,046,147 | 1,094,482 |
| Emp. | 125 | 121 | 124 |

DUNS 73-350-3416

## Roy Fox Transport Ltd

(**Subsidiary of:** Kenneth Howley Transport Ltd)
Green Lane, Castleford, West Yorkshire WF10 2RY
**Tel:** 01977559539
**Web:** www.royfoxtransport.co.uk
**Reg No:** 4623957 **Estd:** 2002 Private Limited Company
**Line of Business:** Road haulage and transport services
**Issued Capital:** £100
**Director:** K T Howley
**Co. Secretary:** Gary Howley
**Responsibilities**
**Senior:** Liz Howley *(Manager)*
**US SIC:** 4789 **UK SIC:** 77002

| | 30-06-14 | 30-06-13 | 30-06-12 |
|---|---|---|---|
| TA | 294,125 | 299,572 | 381,847 |
| NW | 146 | 22,788 | 28,862 |
| WC | (178,220) | (150,015) | (233,667) |

DUNS 21-316-6887

## Roy Hankinson (Holdings) Ltd

Cotton Place, Birkenhead, Merseyside CH41 5EF
**Tel:** 08702953530 **Fax:** 0870-789-2021
**Web:** www.hankinson.co.uk
**Reg No:** 1230965 **VAT No:** 166243073
**Estd:** 1975 Private Limited Company
**Line of Business:** Painters and decorators
**Export Sales:** £359,831
**Trading Style:** Hankinson
**Issued Capital:** £92,500
**Directors:** W R Crocker, I A Thomas, A Westhead
**Co. Secretary:** Stephen Hankinson
**US SIC:** 1721 **UK SIC:** 50400
**Auditors:** Baker Tilly
**Bankers:** Lloyds TSB Bank plc (30-12-96)

| | 31-10-13 | 31-10-12 | 31-10-11 |
|---|---|---|---|
| TO | 19,751,961 | 16,619,437 | 15,571,972 |
| P/L | 451,573 | 477,996 | 511,081 |
| NW | 3,021,861 | 2,611,192 | 2,133,196 |
| WC | 3,762,550 | 4,715,914 | 5,521,192 |
| Emp. | 307 | 277 | 245 |

DUNS 21-761-9509

## Roy McConnachie

Unit 4 Ardyle Industrial Park, Dundee, Angus DD2 2RD
**Tel:** 07960-748333
**Estd:** 2011 Proprietorship
**Line of Business:** Joinery and carpentry
**Responsibilities**
**Senior:** Roy Mcconnachie *(Owner)*
**US SIC:** 2431 **UK SIC:** 46300
**Employees:** 50

DUNS 55-040-9825

## Roy Wilkinson

Canalside, St Michaels Road, Bilsborrow, Preston, Lancashire PR3 0RS
**Tel:** 01995-640020
**Estd:** 2004 Proprietorship
**Line of Business:** Public house
**Proprietor:** R Wilkinson
**US SIC:** 5813 **UK SIC:** 66200
**Employees:** 51

DUNS 21-005-1605 **Imp**

## The Royal Academy of Arts

Burlington House, London W1J 0BD
**Tel:** 02073008000
**Web:** www.royalacademy.org.uk
**Reg No:** 6298947 **Estd:** 2007 Private Company Limited By Guarantee
**Line of Business:** Art gallery
**Directors:** W R Woodrow, Ms A Christopher, P W Gough, Ms A Desmet, Dr B D Rae, Professor I Mckeever, B G Finucane, J Mcfadyen
**Co. Secretary:** Jonathon Cornaby
**Responsibilities**
**Senior:** Sarah Cranmer *(Curaotor)*, Mariella Frostrup *(Director)*, Julian Heslop *(Director)*, Timothy Hyman *(Director)*, Christopher Le Brun *(Director)*, Adrian Locke *(Director of Exhibitions)*, Cornelia Parker *(Director)*, Grayson Perry *(Director)*, Charles Saumarez-Smith *(Chief Executive)*, Emma Stibbon *(Director)*
**Marketing:** Daisy Bell *(Development Marketing Manager)*, Johanna Bennett *(Senior Press Officer)*, Alexandra Bradley *(Press Officer)*, Susie Gault *(Head of Press)*, Nina Sandhaus *(Press Assistant)*
**Sales:** Will Dallimore *(Commercial Director)*, Su Hsiao *(?Senior New Business Manager)*, Angharad Lloyd-Jones *(Deputy Director of Development)*, Aysen Yilmaz *(Senior Business Development Ma)*
**IT:** Brenda Hillary *(IT Systems Manager)*
**HR:** Laura Denton *(HR Business Partner)*, Sarah Myers *(Human Resources Manager)*
**US SIC:** 7911 **UK SIC:** 97913
**Bankers:** The Royal Bank Of Scotland Plc (16-00-38)

| | 31-08-14 | 31-08-13 | 31-08-12 |
|---|---|---|---|
| TO | 33,146,825 | 36,281,856 | 39,437,409 |
| P/L | 4,446,638 | 7,670,588 | 12,244,985 |
| NW | 37,500,637 | 33,420,167 | 25,699,579 |
| WC | 4,225,029 | 6,687,562 | 8,918,141 |
| Emp. | 282 | 256 | 261 |

DUNS 22-720-1175

## Royal Academy of Dance

36 Battersea Square, London SW11 3RA
**Tel:** 020-7326-8000
**Web:** www.rad.org.uk
**Reg No:** 0000436RC **Estd:** 1974
**Line of Business:** Dancing schools
**Trading Style:** Royal Academy of Dance
**Director:** D Watchman
**Responsibilities**
**Senior:** Sandra Elphinston *(Manager)*
**Finance:** Richard Slatford *(Financial Controller)*, Richard Thom *(Finance & Administration Direc)*
**Marketing:** Flavia Cerrone *(Press & Communications Manager)*, Penny Cotton *(Head of Membership)*, Penny Kearns *(Head of Membership)*, Melanie Murphy *(Director of Marketing Communic)*, Lorraine Nicholson *(Marketing Manager)*
**Admin:** Zofie Fraser *(Assistant to the Director of E)*, Louise Linford *(Programmes Administration Mana)*, Richard Thom *(Finance & Administration Direc)*
**IT:** Hitan Patel *(IT Manager)*
**HR:** Debbie Bolton *(Human Resources Manager)*
**Operations:** Paulette McKoy *(Professional Development & Qua)*
**US SIC:** 8299, 7911
**UK SIC:** 93300, 97913
**Bankers:** National Westminster Bank Plc (60-15-33)
**Employees:** 130

DUNS 64-254-8499

## Royal Academy of Dramatic Art

62-64 Gower Street, London WC1E 6ED
**Tel:** 02076367076
**Web:** www.rada.ac.uk
**Reg No:** 0000437RC **Estd:** 1902
**Line of Business:** Schools (local authority)
**Directors:** Lord R Attenborough, Ms A Russell
**Responsibilities**
**Senior:** Edward Kemp *(Manager)*
**Finance:** Linda Garforth *(Bursar)*
**Sales:** Marcelle Lorenzo *(Purchasing Manager)*
**Health & Safety:** Jim Keegan *(Facilities Manager)*
**Facilities:** Jim Keegan *(Facilities Manager)*
**Purchasing:** Marcelle Lorenzo *(Purchasing Manager)*
**US SIC:** 8299 **UK SIC:** 93300
**Auditors:** Saffery Champness

| | 31-07-14 | 31-07-13 | 31-07-12 |
|---|---|---|---|
| TO | 8,697,000 | 7,910,000 | 7,574,000 |
| P/L | 225,000 | 170,000 | 609,000 |
| NW | 37,059,000 | 36,650,000 | 35,034,000 |
| WC | 1,403,000 | 1,059,000 | 922,000 |
| Emp. | 96 | 94 | 92 |

DUNS 42-435-4447 **Imp**

## Royal Academy of Music

Marylebone Road, London NW1 5HT
**Tel:** 020-7873-7373
**Web:** www.ram.ac.uk
**Reg No:** 0000438RC **Estd:** 1990
**Line of Business:** University
**Principals:** G Whalley *(Chairman)*, C Price
**Responsibilities**
**Senior:** Jonathan Freeman-Attwood *(Principal)*, Chris Loake *(Senior Manager)*
**Finance:** Sandra Green *(Financial Director)*
**Marketing:** Peter Craik *(Marketing and Communications M)*, Carol McCormack *(Development Director)*
**Admin:** Catherine Jury *(Academic Secretary)*, Kate McKiernan *(PA to the Principal)*, Hannah Melville-Smith *(Administrator)*
**HR:** Gemma Davies *(HR Advisor)*, Isobel Palmer *(Human Resources)*, Paul Riddell *(Human Resources Manager)*
**US SIC:** 6732, 8299
**UK SIC:** 83100, 93300
**Auditors:** Kingston Smith
**Bankers:** National Westminster Bank Plc (50-30-25)
**Employees:** 500
**Turnover:** £18,223,000

DUNS 54-863-0896

## Royal Agricultural Society of England

Stoneleigh Park Mews, Stoneleigh Abbey, Kenilworth, Warwickshire CV8 2LF
**Tel:** 02476696969
**Web:** www.rase.org.uk
**Reg No:** 0000442RC **Estd:** 1981 Incorporate By Act Of Parliament
**Line of Business:** Activities of private training providers
**Trading Style:** N A C Stoneleigh Park, Stoneleigh Park
**Principals:** H R Oliver-Bellasis *(Chairman)*, N F Harris *(Financial)*, B Warren, G Hurst, G Vickers, H Cator, M Mcallister, R A Wood
**Responsibilities**
**Senior:** Ian Pegler *(Chief Executive)*, Emily Stlllwell *(Personal Assistant)*
**HR:** Heather Timms *(Human Resources Manager)*
**US SIC:** 8299, 6531
**UK SIC:** 93300, 83400
**Auditors:** Baker Tilly UK Audit LLP
**Bankers:** Coutts & Co (18-00-02)
**Turnover:** £8,682,000

DUNS 28-829-4374 **Imp**

## Royal Agricultural University

Stroud Road, Cirencester, Gloucestershire GL7 6JS
**Tel:** 01285889885
**Web:** www.rau.ac.uk
**Reg No:** 0099168 **Estd:** 2002 Private Company Limited By Guarantee
**Line of Business:** First-degree level higher education
**Trading Style:** The Rac
**Issued Capital:** £1,200
**Directors:** A O Colburn, C Musgrave, Mrs A H Bernays, M Amersi, Professor C Dennis, M D Osbaldeston, D J Slack, Professor J G Kydd
**Co. Secretary:** Ms Theresa Chapman
**Responsibilities**
**Senior:** Patricia Broadfoot *(Director)*, Susan Jebb *(Director)*, Philip Moody *(Director)*, Christopher Mullard *(Director)*, Christopher Musgrave *(Director)*, Thomas Overbury *(Farms Director)*, Colin Pett *(Director)*, Jean Roberts *(Director)*
**Admin:** Caroline Jenkins *(Secretary to the Principal)*
**IT:** William Amsden *(PC Manager)*
**HR:** Sue Norton *(Human Resources Manager)*
**Branches:** Royal Agricultural University, Eysey Manor, Eysey, Swindon, Wiltshire SN6 6LP
**US SIC:** 8221 **UK SIC:** 93100
**Auditors:** BDO LLP
**Bankers:** Lloyds TSB Bank plc (30-92-06)

| | 31-07-14 | 31-07-13 | 31-07-12 |
|---|---|---|---|
| TO | 17,267,000 | 16,347,000 | 16,118,000 |
| P/L | 250,000 | 1,270,000 | 309,000 |
| NW | 9,756,000 | 10,910,000 | 10,035,000 |
| WC | 935,000 | 1,324,000 | 1,089,000 |
| Emp. | 211 | 205 | 197 |

DUNS 23-685-6845

## The Royal Air Force Benevolent Fund

67 Portland Place, London W1B 1AR
**Tel:** 02075808343
**Web:** www.rafbf.org
**Reg No:** 0000201ZC **Estd:** 1919
**Line of Business:** Representative office
**Principals:** Sir A Swire *(Chairman)*, D W Cheyne, A Lea, A C Irvine, Air Commodore A Opie, Dr S R Critchley, S Dougherty, Ms A Hastie
**Co. Secretary:** Group Captain Michael Neville
**Responsibilities**
**Senior:** Pamela Bagnall *(Manager)*, Rob Bedford *(Facilities Manager)*, Nigel Beet *(Manager)*, Frances Brindle *(Director)*, David Cousins *(Chief Executive Officer)*, Mike Neville *(Director of Strategy and Fundr)*, Marie Orzel *(Director)*, Victoria Raffe *(Manager)*, David Rainford *(Manager)*, Hugh Trenchard *(Manager)*, Allan Vaughan *(Trustee)*
**Finance:** Lesley Baliga *(Finance Director)*, Mike Neville *(Director of Strategy and Fundr)*

**Marketing:** Samantha Budde (*Public Relations Officer*), Fiona Ferguson (*Communications Manager*)
**Sales:** Mike Neville (*Director of Strategy and Fundr*)
**IT:** Gary Ross (*Computer Manager*)
**Purchasing:** Rob Bedford (*Facilities Manager*)
**Branches:** The Royal Air Force Benevolent Fund, 299 Altrincham Rd, Manchester M22 4NY
**US SIC:** 7399   **UK SIC:** 83954
**Auditors:** Kingston Smith LLP
**Bankers:** Lloyds TSB Bank plc (30-00-08)

|     | 31-12-12 | 31-12-11 | 31-12-10 |
|-----|----------|----------|----------|
| TO | 17,301,000 | 17,910,000 | 18,372,000 |
| P/L | (8,128,000) | (11,664,000) | 3,256,000 |
| NW | 124,576,000 | 127,114,000 | 144,733,000 |
| WC | 5,659,000 | 16,143,000 | 7,715,000 |
| Emp. | 184 | 175 | 170 |

DUNS 71-940-6444

## The Royal Air Force Club
128 Piccadilly, London W1J 7PY
**Tel:** 020-7399-1000

**Web:** www.rafclub.org.uk
**Reg No:** 5321353   **Estd:** 2004 Private Company Limited By Guarantee
**Line of Business:** Clubs social and associations
**Directors:** Sir R Birch, K Warner, J Pelling, A Banks, J D Fisher, R S Peacock Ed, Mrs C A Lewis, Group Captain M Heffron
**Co. Secretary:** Peter Owen
**Responsibilities**
**Senior:** Ian Bruton (*Director*), Wendy Rothery (*Director*)
**US SIC:** 5813   **UK SIC:** 66200
**Bankers:** Coutts & Co (18-00-02)

|     | 31-12-13 | 31-12-12 | 31-12-11 |
|-----|----------|----------|----------|
| TO | 7,063,073 | 6,169,153 | 5,885,890 |
| P/L | 966,747 | 478,466 | 209,202 |
| NW | 4,904,967 | 3,938,220 | 3,459,754 |
| WC | 1,088,409 | 113,333 | (570,538) |
| Emp. | 118 | 97 | 112 |

DUNS 21-607-3963

## Royal Air Force St Mawgan
St Mawgan, Newquay, Cornwall TR8 4HP
**Tel:** 01637872201
**Estd:** 2011 Proprietorship
**Line of Business:** Defence activities
**Proprietor:** K Charlton
**US SIC:** 8999   **UK SIC:** 83954
**Employees:** 939

DUNS 50-646-4481

## Royal Air Forces Association Dunstable Branch
18 Montague Avenue, Luton, Bedfordshire LU4 9JG
**Web:** www.rafadunstable.co.uk
**Estd:** 2002
**Line of Business:** Charities and charitable organisations
**US SIC:** 6732   **UK SIC:** 83100
**Employees:** 190

DUNS 21-034-3721

## Royal Airforce Cosford
Cosford, Albrighton, Wolverhampton, West Midlands WV7 3EX
**Tel:** 01902-372393
**Web:** www.raf.mod.uk
**Estd:** 2002
**Line of Business:** Armed forces
**Responsibilities**
**Finance:** Diana Castree (*Financial Officer*)
**Health & Safety:** Pete Fitzsimmons (*Health & Safety Officer*)
**US SIC:** 9711   **UK SIC:** 83100
**Employees:** 3,000

DUNS 36-489-7418

## The Royal Alexandra & Albert School
The Royal Alexandra & Albert School, Gatton Park, Reigate, Surrey RH2 0TD
**Tel:** 01737649000
**Web:** www.raa-school.co.uk
**Estd:** 1949
**Line of Business:** Schools (local authority)
**US SIC:** 8211   **UK SIC:** 93200
**Auditors:** PricewaterhouseCoopers
**Employees:** 100
**Turnover:** £4,473,000

DUNS 21-614-8839

## Royal Alexandra Hospital
Royal Alexandra Hospital, Marine Drive, Rhyl, Clwyd LL18 3AS
**Tel:** 01745443000
**Web:** www.wales.nhs.uk
**Estd:** 2011 Proprietorship
**Line of Business:** Hospitals
**Proprietor:** Ms Y Drysdale

**Responsibilities**
**Senior:** Liz Morgan (*Community General Manager*)
**US SIC:** 8091   **UK SIC:** 95200
**Employees:** 500

DUNS 54-818-8796

## Royal Alfred Seafarers' Society
Weston Acres, Woodmansterne Lane, Banstead, Surrey SM7 3HB
**Web:** www.royalalfredseafarers.com
**Estd:** 1962
**Line of Business:** Nursing homes
**Trading Style:** Belvedere House
**Responsibilities**
**Senior:** Brian Boxall-Hunt (*Chief Executive officer*), Anne Kasey (*Home Manager*), A Sowamber (*Manager*)
**US SIC:** 8051   **UK SIC:** 95100
**Auditors:** haysmacintyre

|     | 31-12-12 | 31-12-11 | 31-12-10 |
|-----|----------|----------|----------|
| TO | 3,013,742 | 2,642,931 | 2,634,696 |
| P/L | (77,653) | (147,984) | 150,383 |
| NW | 12,821,167 | 12,287,304 | 12,783,701 |
| WC | 334,122 | 398,684 | 1,141,765 |
| Emp. | 78 | 67 | 59 |

DUNS 21-221-7756         Exp

## Royal & Sun Alliance Insurance Plc
(*Subsidiary of:* Rsa Insurance Group Plc)
St Marks Court, Chart Way, Horsham, West Sussex RH12 1XL
**Tel:** 01403-232-323 **Fax:** 01403-232-111
**Web:** www.rsagroup.com
**Reg No:** 0093792   **Estd:** 1920 Public Limited Company
**Line of Business:** Life insurance
**Trading Style:** Rsa
**Issued Capital:** £1,127,772,833
**Directors:** P Whittaker, W R Mcdonnell, D Coughlan, S Lewis, R D Houghton
**Co. Secretary:** Roysun Limited
**Responsibilities**
**Marketing:** Mike Holiday-Williams (*Marketing Manager*)
**Health & Safety:** Alex Rochford (*Health & Safety Officer*)
**Branches:** Royal & Sun Alliance Insurance Plc, Woollerton House, 7 High Street, Aylesbury, Buckinghamshire HP22 6DU
**US SIC:** 6311, 6399
**UK SIC:** 82002, 82001
**Auditors:** KPMG LLP
**Bankers:** Barclays Bank Plc (20-51-01)
**Following financial data are in thousands**

|     | 31-12-13 | 31-12-12 | 31-12-11 |
|-----|----------|----------|----------|
| TO | 3,527,000 | 3,461,000 | 3,065,000 |
| P/L | 128,000 | 406,000 | 425,000 |
| NW | 3,531,000 | 4,549,000 | 4,295,000 |
| WC | (3,706,000) | (3,376,000) | (4,122,000) |
| Emp. | 8,483 | 8,841 | 8,790 |

DUNS 57-021-1573

## Royal Armouries (International) P L C
1 Waterloo Street, Leeds, West Yorkshire LS10 1JL
**Tel:** 01132201916
**Web:** www.royalarmouries.org
**Reg No:** 2868025   **VAT No:** 613388540
**Estd:** 1993 Public Limited Company
**Line of Business:** Catering
**Issued Capital:** £948,642
**Directors:** J V Vincent, C G O'Boyle
**Co. Secretary:** Mark Burrows
**Responsibilities**
**Senior:** Jonathon Riley (*Manager*)
**Branches:** Royal Armouries (International) P L C, Fort Nelson, Portsdown Hill Road, Fareham, Hampshire PO17 6AN
**US SIC:** 5812, 6519
**UK SIC:** 66110, 85000
**Auditors:** Ernst & Young LLP
**Bankers:** Bank Of Scotland (12-08-83)

|     | 31-12-13 | 31-12-12 | 31-12-11 |
|-----|----------|----------|----------|
| TO | 3,532,000 | 4,018,000 | 3,796,000 |
| P/L | 288,000 | 481,000 | 123,000 |
| NW | 5,776,000 | 6,095,000 | 6,289,000 |
| WC | 134,000 | 36,000 | (53,000) |
| Emp. | 65 | 70 | 67 |

DUNS 21-690-0270

## Royal Armouries Trading & Enterprises Ltd
Armouries Drive, Leeds, West Yorkshire LS10 1LT
**Tel:** 01132201873
**Web:** www.royalarmouriesshop.org
**Reg No:** 7374477   **Estd:** 2010 Private Limited Company
**Line of Business:** Other retail sale in specialised stores not elsewhere classified
**Issued Capital:** £150,000
**Directors:** W I Paul, A P Ulster, H K Patel, Dr E A Impey, C J Case
**Responsibilities**
**Senior:** Jonathan Riley (*Director General*)
**US SIC:** 5999   **UK SIC:** 65600

**Bankers:** National Westminster Bank Plc (01-03-87)

|     | 31-03-14 | 31-03-13 | 31-03-12 |
|-----|----------|----------|----------|
| TO | 898,193 | 936,143 | 845,373 |
| P/L | 15,441 | (88,141) | N/A |
| NW | 77,300 | 61,859 | 150,000 |
| WC | 60,915 | 61,859 | 150,000 |

DUNS 21-581-7422

## The Royal Army School Music
Kneller Hall, Kneller Road, Twickenham, Middlesex TW2 7DU
**Tel:** 02087448684
**Estd:** 2011
**Line of Business:** Schools (local authority)
**US SIC:** 9711   **UK SIC:** 65600
**Employees:** 200

DUNS 23-596-8351

## The Royal Association for Deaf People
Century House South, Colchester, Essex C01 1RE
**Tel:** 0845-688-2525
**Web:** www.royaldeaf.org.uk
**Estd:** 2000
**Line of Business:** Charities and charitable organisations
**Trading Style:** All Saints Centre for Deaf People, Beverley Hall Centre for Deaf People, St Bede's Centre for Deaf People
**Principals:** J Wenger (*Chairman*), T Fenton, Rev D Paton, M Redshaw, G C Burgess, B Edmond
**Responsibilities**
**Senior:** Roger Beeson (*Manager*), Stephanie Bull (*Manager*), Toby Burton (*Board Member*), Julie Cartey (*Senior Manager*), David Cloake (*Manager*), Andrew Eadie (*Head of Children, Youth and Fa*), Abdi Gas (*Manager*), Sarah Gilson (*Senior Manager*), Nnaemeka Glover (*Manager*), Ann Goldfinch (*Board Member*), Eoin Heffernan (*Manager*), Margaret Joachim (*Board Member*), Thomas Lichy (*Manager*), David Moller (*Manager*), Mark Napier (*Manager*), Sarah Reed (*Manager*), Tony Sheill (*Board Member*), Shana Weinbaum (*Manager*), Tyron Woolfe (*Manager*)
**Finance:** Angela Galley (*Finance Assistant*), Susan Gudgeon (*Finance Assistant*)
**Marketing:** Amanda Casson-Webb (*Director of Communications Ser*), Linda Parkin (*Development Manager*)
**Admin:** Helen Barrett (*Administrator*), Natalie Creevy (*Project Administrator*), Emma Hampson (*Administrator*), Laura Herbert (*Interpreting Office Supervisor*), Bob Proctor (*Administration Assistant*), Emma Shallcross (*Administrative Assistant*), Heather Wadey (*Administrator*)
**HR:** Daniela Miller (*Human Resources Administrator*), Louise Mudie (*HR Executive*), Susie Slater (*HR Executive*)
**Operations:** Natalie Creevy (*Project Administrator*)
**Branches:** The Royal Association For Deaf People, 412 Clapham Rd, London SW9 9DA
**US SIC:** 8321   **UK SIC:** 96111
**Auditors:** Binder Hamlyn
**Bankers:** National Westminster Bank Plc (50-41-10)
**Employees:** 66

DUNS 21-039-8651

## Royal Automobile Club
Woodcote Park, Epsom, Surrey KT18 7EW
**Tel:** 01372-276311
**Web:** www.royalautomobileclub.co.uk
**Estd:** 1915
**Line of Business:** Clubs social and associations
**Partners:** D Renton, M Bovaird
**Responsibilities**
**Senior:** Tom Purves (*Chairman*), David Ranton (*CEO, Managing Director*), Simon Witt (*General Manager*)
**Admin:** Genevieve Mahoney (*PA to The Chairman & The Secre*)
**IT:** Gavin Duhaney (*Network, Security Manager*)
**US SIC:** 7999   **UK SIC:** 97913
**Employees:** 200

DUNS 23-572-3355

## The Royal Automobile Club Ltd
Pall Mall Clubhouse, London SW1Y 5HS
**Tel:** 020-7930-2345 **Fax:** 020-7976-1086
**Web:** www.royalautomobileclub.co.uk
**Reg No:** 3570702   **Estd:** 1991 Private Company Limited By Guarantee
**Line of Business:** Clubs social and associations
**Issued Capital:** £2
**Directors:** T F Purves, M J Turner, Sir S M Lamport, P G Read, C E Moyle, P Tyrie, A J Gow, Viscountess C J Mackintosh Of Halifax
**Co. Secretary:** Miles Wade

**Responsibilities**
**Senior:** Benjamin Cussons (*Director*), Ronald Fox (*Director*), Nick Joce (*Financial Director*), Simon Machell (*Manager*)
**Finance:** Nick Joce (*Financial Director*)
**Marketing:** Genevieve Mahoney (*Head of Membership and Board G*)
**Admin:** Lucy McCarthy (*PA to Club Secretary*)
**HR:** Helen Brodie (*Human Resources Manager*)
**Facilities:** Tony White (*Head of Maintenance*)
**Operations:** Daniel Pereira (*Head of Club Operations*)
**US SIC:** 8699, 7011
**UK SIC:** 96902, 66500
**Auditors:** Saffery Champness
**Bankers:** National Westminster Bank Plc (60-18-18)

|     | 31-12-13 | 31-12-12 | 31-12-11 |
|-----|----------|----------|----------|
| TO | 41,723,000 | 39,197,000 | 37,733,000 |
| P/L | 2,967,000 | 1,221,000 | 1,770,000 |
| NW | 79,195,000 | 74,069,000 | 68,802,000 |
| WC | 1,504,000 | (945,000) | (1,291,000) |
| Emp. | 530 | 528 | 510 |

DUNS 28-841-4212

## Royal Ballet School
46 Floral Street, London WC2E 9DA
**Tel:** 020-7836-8899
**Web:** www.royalballetschool.org.uk
**Reg No:** 0547018   **Estd:** 1955 Private Company Limited By Guarantee
**Line of Business:** Ballet schools
**Directors:** R F Wallace, D J Fletcher, K P O'Hare, J C Chenevix-Trench, Ms C M Hurst Brown, J C Cope, E A Wallis, R G Conway
**Co. Secretary:** Alan Winter
**Responsibilities**
**Senior:** Sarah Dorfman (*Director*), Antonia Douro (*Director*), Clarissa Farr (*Director*), Janet Lambert (*Director*), Margaret Maden (*Director*), Madeleine Plaut (*Director*), Kenneth Steele (*Director*), Gailene Stock (*Manager*)
**US SIC:** 8299, 8249
**UK SIC:** 93300
**Auditors:** Baker Tilly
**Bankers:** Coutts & Co (18-00-02)

|     | 31-08-13 | 31-08-12 | 31-08-11 |
|-----|----------|----------|----------|
| TO | 10,641,000 | 9,558,000 | 9,864,000 |
| P/L | 586,000 | (33,000) | 31,000 |
| NW | 33,325,000 | 32,803,000 | 33,314,000 |
| WC | 4,387,000 | 3,088,000 | 2,483,000 |
| Emp. | 114 | 136 | 138 |

DUNS 28-823-7878

## Royal Bank Leasing Ltd
(*Subsidiary of:* Hm Treasury)
24/25 St Andrew Square, Edinburgh, Midlothian EH2 1AF
**Tel:** 01242226200 **Fax:** 01242-262133
**Reg No:** 0058013SC   **VAT No:** 402809867
**Estd:** 1975 Private Limited Company
**Line of Business:** Financial intermediation not elsewhere classified
**Issued Capital:** £17,000,001
**Directors:** Mrs S J Caterer, T D Crome, A P Gadsby, N T Clibbens
**Co. Secretary:**
Rbs Secretarial Services Limited
**Branches:** Royal Bank Leasing Ltd, Exchange Court, 3 Bedford Pk, Croydon, Surrey CR0 2AQ
**US SIC:** 6111   **UK SIC:** 81501
**Auditors:** Deloitte & Touche LLP
**Bankers:** The Royal Bank Of Scotland Plc (16-16-13)
**Following financial data are in thousands**

|     | 30-09-13 | 30-09-12 | 30-09-11 |
|-----|----------|----------|----------|
| TA | 6,578,567 | 6,784,018 | 7,372,451 |
| P/L | 133,683 | 169,993 | 90,190 |
| NW | 256,081 | 138,513 | 39,363 |
| WC | 527,485 | 306,474 | 94,952 |

DUNS 21-737-7118

## Royal Bank of Canada (Channel Islands) Ltd
(*Subsidiary of:* Royal Bank of Canada)
Canada Court, Guernsey, Channel Islands GY1 3BQ
**Tel:** 0148 174 4000 **Fax:** 01481-744001
**Web:** www.rbcprivatebanking.com
**Reg No:** 0003295G   **Estd:** 1973 Private Limited Company
**Line of Business:** Banks
**Issued Capital:** £5,000,000
**Principals:** A A Webb (*Chairman*), A Holder (*Managing*), M J Lagopoulos, R Stanley, T J Betley
**Co. Secretary:** Peter Hanna
**Responsibilities**
**Senior:** Paul Patterson (*CEO, Managing Director*)
**Marketing:** Angela Le Bailly (*Marketing Manager*)
**IT:** Ellen Chalmers (*Computer Manager*)
**HR:** Petra Clayton (*Training Manager*)

**Operations:** Dave Thomas *(Chief Operating Officer)*
**US SIC:** 7399 **UK SIC:** 83954
**Employees:** 350

DUNS 38-544-5044
## Royal Bank of Canada Investment Management (Usa) Ltd
**(Subsidiary of:** Royal Bank of Canada)
71 Queen Victoria Street, London EC4V 4DE
**Tel:** 02072480800
**Web:** www.rbc.com
**Reg No:** 3327984 **Estd:** 1997 Private Limited Company
**Line of Business:** Fund management activities
**Issued Capital:** £2,150,000
**Directors:** M R Clatworthy, D L Ellis, S R Krag
**Co. Secretary:** Temitope Adejumo
**US SIC:** 6371 **UK SIC:** 82002
**Auditors:** PricewaterhouseCoopers

| | 31-10-14 | 31-10-13 | 31-10-12 |
|---|---|---|---|
| TO | 1,356,000 | 1,296,000 | 985,000 |
| P/L | (359,000) | (802,000) | (294,000) |
| NW | 575,000 | 790,000 | 1,468,000 |
| WC | 575,000 | 790,000 | 1,468,000 |

DUNS 22-950-0418
## Royal Bank of Canada Trust Co (Jersey) Ltd
**(Subsidiary of:** Royal Bank of Canada)
19-21 Broad Street, Jersey, Channel Islands JE2 3RR
**Tel:** 01534283000
**Web:** www.rbcwminternational.com
**Reg No:** 0001223J **Estd:** 1962 Private Limited Company
**Line of Business:** Banks and financial institutions
**Issued Capital:** £500,000
**Principals:** G Stick *(Financial)*, D J Clothier, K E Rayner, H M Macdougall, G H Jurat, T J Wacker, H L Dubras, L Joly
**Co. Secretary:** George Stick
**Responsibilities**
**Senior:** Chris Blampied *(Branch Manager)*, M Cornelissen *(Director)*, R Jeune *(Director)*, Robert Le Masurier Bse *(Director)*, H MacDougall *(Director)*, P Patterson *(Manager)*
**Marketing:** Gail McCourt *(Marketing Manager)*
**IT:** Derek Luxon *(IT Manager)*
**US SIC:** 6732 **UK SIC:** 83100
**Bankers:** Royal Bank Of Canada (jersey) Ltd (23-73-17)
**Employees:** 300

DUNS 21-036-1280
## The Royal Bank of Scotland
7-10 Brindley Place, Birmingham, West Midlands B1 2TZ
**Tel:** 01215661000
**Web:** www.rbs.com
**Estd:** 2012
**Line of Business:** Banks
**US SIC:** 8999 **UK SIC:** 83954
**Employees:** 2,000

DUNS 21-737-8488
## The Royal Bank of Scotland International Ltd
**(Subsidiary of:** Hm Treasury)
Royal Bank House, Jersey, Channel Islands JE4 8PJ
**Tel:** 01534-285200 **Fax:** 01534285588
**Web:** www.rbsinternational.com
**Reg No:** 0002304J **Estd:** 1966 Private Limited Company
**Line of Business:** Banks
**Issued Capital:** £86,539,817
**Director:** M R Mclean
**Responsibilities**
**Senior:** Stephen Camm *(Manager)*, M McLean *(Director)*, Christopher Nicol *(Manager)*
**Finance:** Lynn Cleary *(Finance Director)*
**Marketing:** Jerry Whitsey *(Head of Products and Marketing)*
**HR:** Ken Gunning *(Training Officer)*
**Health & Safety:** Richard Surcouf *(Buildings Manager)*
**Facilities:** Richard Surcouf *(Buildings Manager)*
**Operations:** Sue Horgan *(Risk Operations Manager)*
**Branches:** The Royal Bank Of Scotland International Ltd, Bank Of Scotland House, Prospect Hill, Douglas, Douglas, Isle Of Man IM1 1EJ
**US SIC:** 6012 **UK SIC:** 81402
**Employees:** 1,000

DUNS 22-912-3146
## The Royal Bank of Scotland Plc
**(Subsidiary of:** Hm Treasury)
36 St Andrew Square, Edinburgh, Midlothian EH2 2AD
**Tel:** 01315233636
**Web:** www.rbs.co.uk
**Reg No:** 0090312SC **Estd:** 1984 Public Limited Company
**Line of Business:** Banks
**Trading Style:** Rbs
**Issued Capital:** £6,609,113,809
**Directors:** B R Nelson, A Davis, E J Stevenson, Sir A M Crombie, R M Mcewan, M N Friis, Ms P L Hughes, Sir P R Hampton
**Co. Secretary:** Ms Aileen Taylor
**Branches:** The Royal Bank Of Scotland Plc, 19-21 Islington High Street, London N1 9LQ
**US SIC:** 6012, 6311, 8111
**UK SIC:** 81402, 82002, 83500
**Auditors:** Deloitte LLP
**Bankers:** The Royal Bank Of Scotland Plc (83-00-01)
**Following financial data are in thousands**

| | 31-12-13 | 31-12-12 | 31-12-11 |
|---|---|---|---|
| TA | 1,019,934,000 | 1,284,274,000 | 1,432,781,000 |
| P/L | (6,761,000) | (3,412,000) | (864,000) |
| NW | 36,434,000 | 46,885,000 | 49,361,000 |
| WC | 64,143,000 | 38,905,000 | 38,263,000 |
| Emp. | 107,100 | 108,600 | 110,900 |

DUNS 23-860-6045
## Royal Bay Care Homes Ltd
86 Barrack Lane, Bognor Regis, West Sussex PO21 4DG
**Tel:** 01243267755
**Web:** www.royalbay.co.uk
**Reg No:** 3852183 **Estd:** 2006 Private Limited Company
**Line of Business:** Medical nursing home activities
**Trading Style:** Royal Bay Retirement Residential Care Home, Aldwick Lodge
**Issued Capital:** £10,000
**Principals:** R L Wilson *(Managing)*, A F Wilson
**Co. Secretary:** Anthony Wilson
**Responsibilities**
**Admin:** Jenny Laatz *(Administrator)*
**Branches:** Royal Bay Care Homes Ltd, 86 Aldwick Road, Bognor Regis, West Sussex PO21 2PE
**US SIC:** 8051, 6519, 6732, 8321
**UK SIC:** 95100, 85000, 83100, 96111
**Auditors:** Watling & Hirst

| | 31-10-13 | 31-10-12 | 31-10-11 |
|---|---|---|---|
| TO | 8,539,384 | 8,656,509 | 8,054,660 |
| P/L | 483,182 | 597,230 | 484,364 |
| NW | 8,537,649 | 8,276,745 | 7,913,727 |
| WC | (119,326) | 81,708 | 1,042,662 |
| Emp. | 370 | 390 | 343 |

DUNS 55-045-5448
## Royal Bayswater Hotel
121-122 Bayswater Road, London W2 3JH
**Web:** www.royalbayswater.com
**Estd:** 1995 Proprietorship
**Line of Business:** Hotels
**Proprietor:** A Fyad
**US SIC:** 7011 **UK SIC:** 66500
**Employees:** 78

DUNS 23-599-8036
## Royal Belfast Academical Inst
College Square East, Belfast BT1 6DL
**Tel:** 02890240461
**Web:** www.rbai.org.uk
**Estd:** 2011
**Line of Business:** Schools (independent)
**Trading Style:** Inst
**Director:** J D Marshall
**Responsibilities**
**IT:** Rodger Wilson *(Senior IT Executive)*
**Operations:** Eamon Foster *(Dean)*, Eamon Foster *(Dean)*
**Branches:** Cranmore Rd, Belfast
**US SIC:** 8211 **UK SIC:** 93200
**Bankers:** Ulster Bank Ltd (98-00-00)
**Employees:** 100

DUNS 42-487-2653
## Royal Berkshire Fire & Rescue Service
Brigade Headquarters Newsham Court, Pincents Kiln, Calcot, Reading, Berkshire RG31 7SD
**Tel:** 01189-452888
**Web:** www.rbfrs.co.uk
**Estd:** 1974 Incorporate By Act Of Parliament
**Line of Business:** Fire stations
**Director:** D J Harper
**Responsibilities**
**Senior:** Andy Fry *(Chief Officer)*, Sylvia Simmonds *(P A To The Chief Officer)*
**Marketing:** Nicole Targett *(Corporate Communications Manag)*
**IT:** Alan Newcombe *(Technical Leader)*
**Health & Safety:** Tracey Mitchell *(Health & Safety Manager)*
**Branches:** Royal Berkshire Fire & Rescue Service, Fire Station, Denton Rd, Wokingham, Berkshire RG40 2DX
**US SIC:** 9224 **UK SIC:** 91400
**Employees:** 170

DUNS 23-088-6715
## The Royal Berkshire Hotel
London Road, Sunninghill, Ascot, Berkshire SL5 0PP
**Tel:** 01344623322
**Web:** www.ramadajarvis.co.uk
**Estd:** 1985 Proprietorship
**Line of Business:** Hotels
**Proprietor:** D Mcghee
**Responsibilities**
**Senior:** Jonathan Oldrowyd *(General Manager)*
**Finance:** Madhu Murtala *(Finance Manager)*, Barbara Royal *(Financial Manager)*
**Facilities:** Alan Bergin *(Maintenance Manager)*
**US SIC:** 7011 **UK SIC:** 66500
**Employees:** 50

DUNS 54-864-0036 **Imp**
## Royal Berkshire N H S Foundation Trust
London Road, Reading, Berkshire RG1 5AN
**Tel:** 01183225111
**Web:** www.royalberkshire.nhs.uk
**Estd:** 1993
**Line of Business:** Hospitals
**Issued Capital:** £1
**Principals:** C Maclean *(Chairman)*, M Sheldon *(Financial)*, B Raven *(Commercial)*, C Walsh, P Sheen, Ms I Inskip, K Hydon, R Sohpa
**Responsibilities**
**Senior:** Jean Callaghan *(Chief Executive)*, Edward Donald *(Chief Executive)*, Alistair Flowerdew *(Acting CEO)*
**Finance:** Graham Butler *(Senior Finance Administrator)*
**Marketing:** Nicola Wesson *(Press Officer)*, Joe Wise *(PR Manager)*
**Health & Safety:** Imogen Gray *(Risk Manager)*
**Facilities:** Philip Holmes *(Director of Facilities and Est)*
**Purchasing:** Neil Dowdell *(Contract Manager)*, Maria Yates *(Head of Procurement)*
**Engineering:** Malcolm Sperrin *(Director, Engineering)*
**Branches:** Royal Berkshire N H S Foundation Trust, 21 Craven Road, Reading, Berkshire RG1 5LE
**US SIC:** 8062 **UK SIC:** 95100
**Auditors:** KPMG LLP

| | 31-03-14 | 31-03-13 | 31-03-12 |
|---|---|---|---|
| TO | 343,755,000 | 333,417,000 | 294,947,000 |
| P/L | (6,593,000) | 539,000 | 1,016,000 |
| NW | 159,777,000 | 160,178,000 | 194,799,000 |
| WC | 2,173,000 | 4,437,000 | 2,130,000 |
| Emp. | 4,788 | 4,569 | 4,309 |

DUNS 21-778-7888
## Royal Black Country & Kings Cars
3 Lower High Street, Cradley Heath, West Midlands B64 5AB
**Tel:** 01384411007
**Estd:** 2011 Proprietorship
**Line of Business:** Taxi operation
**Proprietor:** A Jahangir
**US SIC:** 4121 **UK SIC:** 72200
**Employees:** 50

DUNS 23-698-3854
## Royal Blind Asylum & School
50 Gillespie Crescent, Edinburgh, Midlothian EH10 4HZ
**Tel:** 01312-291456
**Web:** www.royalblind.org
**Reg No:** 0000449RC **VAT No:** 270038093
**Estd:** 1793
**Line of Business:** Charities and charitable organisations
**Trading Style:** Royal Blind
**Principals:** D A Osler *(Chairman)*, Hon Lord Clyde (The), I Lumsden, D C Dunn, A Scott, K D Reid, G Waddell, D Fleck
**Responsibilities**
**Senior:** Gordon Banks *(Principal)*, Cllr Conor Snowden *(Principal)*, Robert Hodge *(Principal)*, Margery M Browning *(Board Member)*, James M Finlay *(Principal)*, Margaret M Sibbald *(Principal)*, Julie Sardell *(Principal)*, Janis Sugden *(Principal)*
**Marketing:** Davina Shiell *(Marketing & Fundraising Manage)*
**Branches:** Royal Blind Asylum & School, Royal Blind School, 2B Craigmillar Park, Edinburgh, Midlothian EH16 5NA
**US SIC:** 8211 **UK SIC:** 93200

**Auditors:** PKF (UK) LLP
**Bankers:** The Royal Bank Of Scotland Plc (83-20-03)

| | 31-03-13 | 31-03-12 | 31-03-11 |
|---|---|---|---|
| TO | 14,185,000 | 14,539,000 | 13,323,857 |
| P/L | 1,087,000 | 555,000 | (837,213) |
| NW | 53,042,000 | 48,717,000 | 48,800,425 |
| WC | 3,007,000 | 2,664,000 | 2,142,911 |
| Emp. | N/A | N/A | 370 |

DUNS 22-831-4522
## Royal Borough of Greenwich
The Woolwich Centre, 35 Wellington Street, London SE18 6HQ
**Tel:** 020 8854 8888
**Web:** www.greenwich.gov.uk
**Estd:** 1963
**Line of Business:** General (overall) public service activities
**Trading Style:** Crown Woods College
**Principals:** C Perry *(Financial)*, Ms M Ney
**Responsibilities**
**Finance:** Debbie Warren *(Financial Director)*
**Marketing:** Katrina Delaney *(Head of Communications)*
**HR:** Jean Heel *(Workforce Development Coordina)*
**Facilities:** Sue Butterfill *(Principal Community Manager)*
**Branches:** Royal Borough Of Greenwich, Foundation House, 2 Cutty Sark Gardens, London SE10 9LW
**US SIC:** 9121 **UK SIC:** 91110
**Auditors:** The Borough Treasurer, London Borough of Greenwich
**Employees:** 8,500

DUNS 21-112-4466 **Imp**
## Royal Borough of Kensington & Chelsea
Town Hall, Hornton Street, London W8 7NX
**Tel:** 02079375464 **Fax:** 020-7938-1445
**Web:** www.rbkc.gov.uk
**Estd:** 1974 Incorporate By Act Of Parliament
**Line of Business:** General (overall) public service activities
**Directors:** A Taylor, D Reeve
**Responsibilities**
**Senior:** Debbie Morris *(Manager)*
**Sales:** Raymond Brown *(Head of Business Management an)*
**IT:** Barry Goodall *(Support Unit Manager)*, Marion Sinclair *(IS Strategy and Change Manager)*
**Branches:** Royal Borough Of Kensington & Chelsea, Clareville Street, London SW7 5AQ
**US SIC:** 9121 **UK SIC:** 91110
**Bankers:** Lloyds TSB Bank plc (30-94-65)
**Employees:** 35,000

DUNS 77-936-0221
## The Royal Borough of Kensington & Chelsea Tenant Management Organisation Ltd
Town Hall, Hornton Street, London W8 7NX
**Tel:** 02073613000 **Fax:** 02073613000
**Web:** www.rbkc.gov.uk
**Reg No:** 3048135 **Estd:** 1995 Private Company Limited By Guarantee
**Line of Business:** Management of real estate on a fee or contract basis
**Trading Style:** Kensington & Chelsea T M O
**Directors:** K Kanodia, J M Blakeman, Miss A Duru, M Condon-Simmonds, Ms F M Edwards, Ms D L Price, P S Chapman, A A Preiskel
**Co. Secretary:** Miss Fola Kafidiya
**Responsibilities**
**Senior:** Anthony Annis *(Director)*, Meredith Benjamin *(Director)*, Simon Brissenden *(Director)*, Jeffrey Zitron *(Director)*
**US SIC:** 6531 **UK SIC:** 83400
**Auditors:** Baker Tilly UK Audit LLP

| | 31-03-14 | 31-03-13 | 31-03-12 |
|---|---|---|---|
| TO | 14,565,812 | 10,948,699 | 11,151,577 |
| P/L | (47,568) | (443,651) | (25,093) |
| NW | (3,773,904) | (4,204,637) | (9,719,731) |
| WC | 414,141 | 418,559 | 577,725 |
| Emp. | 210 | 165 | 165 |

DUNS 22-847-0233
## Royal Borough of Kingston-upon-Thames
Guildhall Complex, High Street, Kingston-Upon-Thames, Surrey KT1 1EU
**Tel:** 02085475000
**Web:** www.kingston.gov.uk
**Estd:** 2005
**Line of Business:** Local government
**Directors:** T Hornsby, S Chamberlain, T Knights, B Dickenson, P Taunton, M Gilks, R Taylor, B Mcdonald
**Responsibilities**
**Senior:** Bruce Macdonald *(Chief Executive)*
**HR:** Emma Stracy *(Human Resources Manager)*
**Facilities:** Steve Ladbroke *(Facilities Officer)*, Steve Manners *(Facilities Manager)*

**Branches:** Royal Borough Of Kingston-Upon-Thames, Surbiton Hill Road, Surbiton, Surrey KT6 4TU
**US SIC:** 9121 **UK SIC:** 91110
**Employees:** 4,000

DUNS 22-741-1998    Imp
## Royal Borough Windsor & Maidenhead
Town Hall, St Ives Road, Maidenhead, Berkshire SL6 1RF
**Tel:** 01628683800
**Web:** www.rbwm.gov.uk
**Estd:** 1974
**Line of Business:** Local government
**Trading Style:** Windsor & Maidenhead Social Services, Furze Platt Comprehensive School, Cookham Dean Primary School
**Director:** D Lunn
**Responsibilities**
**Senior:** Mike McGaughrin (CEO), Christabel Shawcross (Deputy Managing Director and S)
**Marketing:** Anne Dackcombe (Chief Public Relations Officer)
**Sales:** Don Pitts (Business Development Manager)
**IT:** Daniel Brookman (Head of IT)
**Operations:** Cathryn James (Strategic Director of Operatio)
**Branches:** Royal Borough Windsor & Maidenhead, Furze Platt Road, Maidenhead, Berkshire SL6 7NQ
**US SIC:** 9121 **UK SIC:** 91110
**Bankers:** Lloyds TSB Bank plc (30-95-36)
**Employees:** 7,000

DUNS 21-031-0364    Imp
## Royal Botanic Garden Edinburgh
20 Inverleith Row, Edinburgh, Midlothian EH3 5LR
**Tel:** 0131-552-7171
**Web:** www.rbge.org.uk
**Estd:** 2002 Partnership
**Line of Business:** Preservation of historical sites and buildings
**Partners:** E Bain, Mrs J Neville, Mrs N Stuart, I Laurie, G Love, Ms S Elliott
**Branches:** Royal Botanic Garden Edinburgh, Stobo, Peebles, Peeblesshire EH45 9JU
**US SIC:** 8411, 8421
**UK SIC:** 97700
**Employees:** 338

DUNS 22-822-2402    Imp-Exp
## Royal Botanic Gardens
Kew Green, Richmond, Surrey TW9 3AB
**Tel:** 02083325000
**Web:** www.kew.org
**Estd:** 1759 Incorporate By Act Of Parliament
**Line of Business:** Departmental stores
**Trading Style:** Kew Publications
**Principals:** The Viscount M Blakenham (Chairman), Professor G Prance (Managing), Sir J Bowman, S De Grey, Ms M Black, Ms Lennox-Boyd, E O Selborne, Professor H Dickinson
**Responsibilities**
**Senior:** Richard Deverell (Manager)
**Health & Safety:** Julie Bowers (Head of Corporate Services)
**Operations:** Julie Bowers (Head of Corporate Services)
**Branches:** Royal Botanic Gardens, Wakehurst Place, Haywards Heath, West Sussex RH17 6TN
**US SIC:** 8411, 7391
**UK SIC:** 97700, 94000
**Auditors:** John Bourn (Comptroller & Auditor General)
**Employees:** 800

DUNS 54-864-5043    Imp
## Royal Bournemouth Hospital & Christchurch Hospitals Nhs Foundation Trusts
Castle Lane East, Bournemouth, Dorset BH7 7DW
**Web:** www.rbch.nhs.uk
**Estd:** 1990
**Line of Business:** Hospitals
**Issued Capital:** £1
**Director:** T Spotswood
**Responsibilities**
**Senior:** Lesley Angus (Secretary)
**Marketing:** Tracey Hall (Head of Communications)
**Admin:** Debbie Detheridge (Administrator), Lorraine Hammond-Evans (Secretary), Janet Long (Secretary)
**IT:** Gary Desborough (Senior IT Executive)
**HR:** Jenny Dempsey (Human Resources Manager), Victoria Douglas (Human Resources Manager)
**Purchasing:** Eddie Rathbone (Purchasing Manager)

**Branches:** Royal Bournemouth Hospital & Christchurch Hospitals Nhs Foundation Tru, West Howe Clinic, Cunningham Crescent, Bournemouth, Dorset BH11 8DN
**US SIC:** 8062 **UK SIC:** 95100
**Auditors:** Deloitte LLP

| | 31-03-14 | 31-03-13 | 31-03-12 |
|---|---|---|---|
| TO | 260,323,000 | 249,180,000 | 220,409,000 |
| P/L | 463,000 | 3,634,000 | 4,516,000 |
| NW | 199,638,000 | 182,933,000 | 180,989,000 |
| WC | 41,211,000 | 41,337,000 | 36,036,000 |
| Emp. | 3,861 | 3,700 | 3,633 |

DUNS 23-992-6629
## The Royal British Legion
199 Borough High Street, London SE1 1AA
**Tel:** 020-3207-2100
**Web:** www.britishlegion.org.uk
**Reg No:** 0219279RC **Estd:** 1990
**Line of Business:** Clubs social and associations
**Principals:** J Farmer (Chairman), J Fisher Mbe, J Crisford, C Harper, I P Canell, R M Williams, Ms J Rowe, C Carson
**Responsibilities**
**Senior:** Peter Fiet (Manager), John Fisher MBE (Director), Eddie Hefferman MBE (Trustee)
**Finance:** Charles Byrne (Fundraising Director), Helen Downie (Chief Financial Officer)
**Marketing:** Louise Garrahan (PR Officer), Bethan Herbert (PR Officer), Rebecca Warren (Public Relations Manager)
**HR:** Helena Hamlyn (PR Officer), Sharron Lewis-James (Human Resources Director)
**Operations:** Sue Freeth (Director of Operations)
**Branches:** The Royal British Legion, Halsey House, 31 Norwich Road, Cromer, Norfolk NR27 0BA
**US SIC:** 6732 **UK SIC:** 83100
**Auditors:** PricewaterhouseCoopers LLP
**Bankers:** Barclays Bank Plc (20-06-05)
**Employees:** 1,089
**Turnover:** £136,185,000

DUNS 22-610-7266
## Royal British Legion Industries Ltd.
Ysbyty George Thomas, Cwmparc Road, Treorchy, Mid Glamorgan CF42 6YG
**Tel:** 01443430022
**Web:** www.rbli.co.uk
**Reg No:** 0158479 **VAT No:** 240800405
**Estd:** 1919 Private Company Limited By Guarantee
**Line of Business:** Charities and charitable organisations
**Directors:** R J Corben, F Martin, Mrs K A Bosley, J B Smithers, Brigadier H H Kerr, S W Kingsman, A B Gulland, C Abergavenny
**Co. Secretary:** Philip Defraine
**Responsibilities**
**Senior:** Peter Edgley (Trustee), Bruce Sorrell (Manager), Kerry Stapleford (Manager)
**Marketing:** Liz Rickaby (business dev director)
**Sales:** Geoff Streetley (Head of Commercial)
**Branches:** Royal British Legion Industries Ltd., Ste 6 Kingfisher Ct, Brambleside, Uckfield, East Sussex TN22 1QQ
**US SIC:** 8699, 3999, 8321
**UK SIC:** 96902, 49590, 96111
**Auditors:** PricewaterhouseCoopers
**Bankers:** Barclays Bank Plc (20-54-11)

| | 31-03-14 | 31-03-13 | 31-03-12 |
|---|---|---|---|
| TO | 15,479,000 | 12,762,000 | 12,386,000 |
| P/L | 230,000 | (418,000) | (1,107,000) |
| NW | 17,794,000 | 17,440,000 | 17,460,000 |
| WC | 2,078,000 | 1,924,000 | 472,000 |
| Emp. | 375 | 323 | 322 |

DUNS 21-293-3779
## The Royal British Legion Lister House
Lister House, Southgate, Ripon, North Yorkshire HG4 1PG
**Tel:** 01765694740
**Web:** www.britishlegion.org.uk
**Estd:** 1988
**Line of Business:** Residential care establishments
**Responsibilities**
**Senior:** Sue Bayran (Manager), P Fowlerwatts (Manager), Tracey Fullagar (Home Manager)
**US SIC:** 8321 **UK SIC:** 96111
**Employees:** 110

DUNS 21-722-2363
## The Royal British Legion Poppy Factory Ltd
20 Petersham Road, Richmond, Surrey TW10 6UR
**Tel:** 02089403305
**Web:** www.poppyfactory.org
**Reg No:** 0204405 **Estd:** 1925 Private Company Limited By Guarantee
**Line of Business:** Other manufacturing not elsewhere classified
**Directors:** Lt Col M A Overton, A J Truscott, S C Monger-Godfrey, P R Gill, C S Cook, H H Player, Dr G Strathdee, A R Sharpe
**Co. Secretary:** William Kay
**Responsibilities**
**Senior:** Bernard Cook (Manager), Thomas Longland (Manager), John Tedder (Manager), Melanie Waters (Ceo)
**US SIC:** 3999, 6519, 7361
**UK SIC:** 49590, 85000, 83954
**Auditors:** Nabarro
**Bankers:** Barclays Bank Plc (20-72-17)

| | 30-09-14 | 30-09-13 | 30-09-12 |
|---|---|---|---|
| TO | 3,801,461 | 3,799,138 | 3,547,635 |
| P/L | 179,911 | (339,285) | (336,373) |
| NW | 20,645,563 | 18,067,848 | 15,659,426 |
| WC | 996,047 | 683,985 | 1,148,947 |
| Emp. | 49 | 46 | 42 |

DUNS 22-741-1808
## The Royal British Legion Scotland
New Haig House, 66 Logie Green Road, Edinburgh, Midlothian EH7 4HR
**Tel:** 01315572782
**Web:** www.rblscotland.org.uk
**Estd:** 1921
**Line of Business:** Clubs social and associations
**Principals:** Sir M Gow (President), G R Miller (Chairman)
**Co. Secretary:** Brigadier Robert Riddle
**Responsibilities**
**Senior:** Kevin Grey (Head Of Administration)
**Branches:** The Royal British Legion Scotland, 26 Market Square, Stonehaven, Kincardineshire AB39 2BA
**US SIC:** 6732, 8111
**UK SIC:** 83100, 83500
**Employees:** 62

DUNS 23-929-0802
## Royal Brompton & Harefield Nhs Foundation Trust
Sydney Street, London SW3 6NP
**Tel:** 020-7352-8121
**Web:** www.rbht.nhs.uk
**VAT No:** 654968091 **Estd:** 1844
**Line of Business:** Hospitals
**Trading Style:** Royal Brompton Hospital, Harefield Hospital
**Issued Capital:** £1
**Principals:** Sir P Otton (Chairman), M Taylor, Prof P Poole-Wilson, B Mallion, J Chapman, Ms C Shuldhman, Prof A Newman-Taylor, D Vaughan
**Responsibilities**
**Senior:** Tom Carter (Manager), Gerrie Coertzen (Manager), Susanna Hammond (Principal), Nick Hunt (Board Member), Clothilde Kapufi-Morrison (Manager)
**Finance:** Alexandra Weller (Clinical Audit and Effectivene)
**Marketing:** Martin Carter (Interim Director of Communicat), Sian Carter (Interim Director of Communicat), Christine Denmark (?Marketing Communications Mana), Katherine Denney (Head of Marketing, Communicati), Alex Malloy (Communications Assistant)
**Sales:** Joanna Axon (Director of Capital Projects a)
**Admin:** Daisy Hayden (Infection Control Surveillance)
**IT:** Katherine Denney (Head of Marketing, Communicati), Ricardo Wage (Executive)
**Health & Safety:** Daisy Hayden (Infection Control Surveillance)
**Operations:** Kelly Goulding (Production and Operations Mana), Takis Kotis (Director, Production and Opera)
**Branches:** Royal Brompton & Harefield Nhs Foundation Trust, Hill End Road, Uxbridge, Middlesex UB9 6JH
**US SIC:** 8062 **UK SIC:** 95100
**Auditors:** Deloitte LLP
**Bankers:** Lloyds TSB Bank plc (30-91-86)

| | 31-03-14 | 31-03-13 | 31-03-12 |
|---|---|---|---|
| TO | 308,753,000 | 282,495,000 | 267,165,000 |
| P/L | 10,896,000 | 10,283,000 | 8,194,000 |
| NW | 216,622,000 | 189,498,000 | 215,631,000 |
| WC | 7,920,000 | 8,479,000 | 3,708,000 |
| Emp. | 3,274 | 2,877 | 3,008 |

DUNS 22-853-5316    Imp
## Royal Caribbean Cruise Line A/S
(**Subsidiary of:** Royal Caribbean Cruises Ltd.)
Aviator Park, Station Road, Addlestone, Surrey KT15 2PG
**Tel:** 01932-834200
**Web:** www.royalcaribbean.co.uk
**Reg No:** 0007848FC **VAT No:** 792400337
**Estd:** 1990 Foreign Company
**Line of Business:** Activities of travel agencies
**Trading Style:** Royal Caribbean Cruise Line A/S
**Director:** O M Osnes
**Responsibilities**
**Senior:** Michael Bayley (Manager)
**Finance:** Diane Allen (Financial Manager), Ian McIlrath (Financial Director)
**Marketing:** Jo Briody (Head of Marketing)
**IT:** Sally Briggs (IT Manager)
**HR:** S Gravestock (Training Manager), Jackie Wybrow (Human Resources Manager)
**Health & Safety:** Laura Duncan (Facilities Manager), Katherine Neilson (Facilities Manager)
**Facilities:** Laura Duncan (Facilities Manager), Katherine Neilson (Facilities Manager)
**Purchasing:** Laura Duncan (Facilities Manager), Katherine Neilson (Facilities Manager)
**US SIC:** 4722 **UK SIC:** 77001
**Bankers:** HSBC Bank plc (40-26-12)

DUNS 21-708-3463
## Royal Cars
2a Stephenson Street, Stockton-On-Tees, Cleveland TS17 6AL
**Tel:** 01642666666
**Web:** www.royalcarsne.co.uk
**Estd:** 1999 Proprietorship
**Line of Business:** Taxis and private hire vehicles
**Proprietor:** A Khan
**US SIC:** 4121 **UK SIC:** 72200
**Employees:** 50

DUNS 29-342-9015
## The Royal Central School of Speech & Drama
Eton Avenue, London NW3 3HY
**Tel:** 020-7722-8183 **Fax:** 020-7722-4132
**Web:** www.cssd.ac.uk
**Reg No:** 0203645 **Estd:** 1925 Private Company Limited By Guarantee
**Line of Business:** Drama schools
**Trading Style:** Embassy Theatre
**Directors:** Ms J L Webb, M Scott, P G Taiano, C J Perrin, Mrs V T Dickie, Professor S W Mcveigh, Mrs M L Mcgregor, Miss L M Twynam
**Co. Secretary:** Ms Deborah Scully
**Responsibilities**
**Senior:** Ross Brown (Dean of Studies and Professor), Gavin Henderson (Principal), Anne Mensah (Director), Lee Menzies (Manager), Jodi Myers (Director), Natalie Poernig (Director), Dominic Tulett (Director)
**Admin:** Becky Gooby (Research Administrator), Gail Hunt (Office Administrator), James Prince (Academic Registrar)
**IT:** Brian Harry (Computer Manager)
**HR:** Dominic Tulett (Director)
**Branches:** The Royal Central School of Speech & Drama, 1 Brixton Road, London SW9 6DE
**US SIC:** 8299, 8221, 7999
**UK SIC:** 93300, 93100, 97913
**Auditors:** PricewaterhouseCoopers

| | 31-07-14 | 31-07-13 | 31-07-12 |
|---|---|---|---|
| TO | 14,387,000 | 14,118,000 | 13,271,000 |
| P/L | (13,000) | 1,057,000 | 860,000 |
| NW | 20,597,000 | 21,580,000 | 19,744,000 |
| WC | 8,374,000 | 8,546,000 | 7,277,000 |
| Emp. | 249 | 188 | 186 |

DUNS 21-615-8328
## The Royal Centre
Theatre Square, Nottingham, Nottinghamshire NG1 5ND
**Tel:** 01159895500
**Web:** www.trch.co.uk
**Estd:** 2007 Partnership
**Line of Business:** Theatres & concert halls
**Partners:** J Ashworth, P Burgess
**Responsibilities**
**Marketing:** Sarah Newnes (Corporate Relations Manager), Magnus Pooole (Marketing Manager), Lucy Thomas (Press & PR Manager), Imogen Ward (Communications Officer)
**IT:** Dave Guy (Technical Director)
**US SIC:** 7911 **UK SIC:** 97913
**Employees:** 100

## DUNS 21-224-0880
### Royal China
24-26 Baker Street, Mayfair, London W1U 3BZ
**Tel:** 020-74874688
**Web:** www.rcguk.hk
**Estd:** 1997 Proprietorship
**Line of Business:** Restaurant - american
**Proprietor:** K Lok
**US SIC:** 5812   **UK SIC:** 66110
**Employees:** 50

## DUNS 21-525-2979
### Royal China Restaurant
13 Queensway, Bayswater, London W2 4QJ
**Tel:** 020-7221-2535
**Web:** www.royalchinagroup.co.uk
**Estd:** 1990
**Line of Business:** Restaurant - chinese
**Proprietor:** P Keung
**Responsibilities**
**Senior:** Peter Keung (Manager)
**US SIC:** 5812   **UK SIC:** 66110
**Employees:** 100

## DUNS 23-799-8518
### The Royal Clarence Hotel Ltd
(**Subsidiary of:** Andrew Brownsword Hotels Limited)
Cathedral Yard, Exeter, Devon EX1 1HD
**Tel:** 01392319955 **Fax:** 01392439423
**Web:** www.royalclarencehotel.co.uk
**Reg No:** 3792478   **VAT No:** 821211485
**Estd:** 1999 Private Limited Company
**Line of Business:** Hotels
**Trading Style:** Abode Exeter
**Issued Capital:** £24
**Directors:** J Carruthers, J D Hancock, A D Brownsword, Mrs A J Skedd
**Co. Secretary:** Mrs Alison Skedd
**Responsibilities**
**Senior:** Nicholas Halliday (Manager), Ewan Steele (General Manager), Julian Wilkinson (General Manager), Tom William-Hawkes (Head Chef)
**Finance:** Mhairi Innes (Financial Controller)
**IT:** Julian Wilkinson (General Manager)
**HR:** Julian Wilkinson (General Manager)
**Health & Safety:** Sara Lakin (Head Housekeeper)
**US SIC:** 7011, 5812, 5813
**UK SIC:** 66500, 66110, 66200
**Auditors:** O"Hara Wood
**Bankers:** National Westminster Bank Plc (56-00-49)

|     | 31-12-13 | 31-12-12 | 31-12-11 |
|-----|----------|----------|----------|
| TO  | 3,692,728 | 3,870,130 | 4,124,120 |
| P/L | 32,811 | 234,175 | 84,758 |
| NW  | 5,008,775 | 4,975,964 | 4,741,789 |
| WC  | (324,114) | (531,109) | (937,195) |
| Emp.| 115 | 114 | 117 |

## DUNS 23-679-5688   Imp
### Royal College of Anaesthetists
Churchill House, 35 Red Lion Square, London WC1R 4SG
**Tel:** 020-7092-1500
**Web:** www.rcoa.ac.uk
**Estd:** 2011
**Line of Business:** Charities and charitable organisations
**Principals:** Dr P Nightingle (President), Dr A A Tomlinson, P J Snyed, P J Snyed, Dr O R Dearlove, Dr D M Nolan, P J Bion, Dr J A Hulf
**US SIC:** 8221   **UK SIC:** 93100
**Auditors:** Crowe Clark Whitehill LLP
**Bankers:** The Royal Bank Of Scotland Plc (15-10-00)
**Employees:** 70
**Turnover:** £9,114,000

## DUNS 22-716-1213   Imp
### Royal College of Art
Cab Shelter, Kensington Road, London SW7 5EE
**Fax:** 020-7590-4500
**Web:** www.rca.ac.uk
**Reg No:** 0000456RC   **VAT No:** 240189968
**Estd:** 1986 Incorporate By Act Of Parliament
**Line of Business:** Colleges (higher education)
**Directors:** Prof C Frayling, A Selby
**Responsibilities**
**Marketing:** Aine Duffy (Marketing Manager)
**US SIC:** 8221   **UK SIC:** 93100
**Bankers:** National Westminster Bank Plc (56-00-17)
**Employees:** 400
**Turnover:** £28,826,000

## DUNS 21-236-4108
### The Royal College of General Practitioners
30 Euston Square, London NW1 2FB
**Tel:** 02031-887-400
**Web:** www.rcgp.org.uk
**VAT No:** 240751288   **Estd:** 1984
**Line of Business:** Training services
**Principals:** Dr I Heath (President), Dr C Gerada (Chairman), N Hunt
**Responsibilities**
**Senior:** Stuart Blake (Chairman), Steve Brinksman (Manager), Professor Carter (Manager), Antony Chuter (Chairman), Laurence Dorman (Executive), Nicola Edmunds (Manager), Boyd Gilmore (Executive), Philip Hannaford (Manager), Colin Hunter (Manager), Laura Kelleher (Senior Manager), Nigel Mathers (Vice Chair), Anthony Mathie (Manager), Mike Pringle (President), Rachel Vial (Manager), Valerie Wass (Chair), Josie Westley (Senior Manager), Jill Wilton (Area Manager - Northern Irelan)
**Finance:** Mark Gabbay (Treasurer), Jenny Stock (International Officer)
**Marketing:** Erika Niesner (Editor)
**Admin:** Tom Anstey (Administrator), Rebecca Black (Administrator), Birgitta Bowman (Executive Assistant), Liz Brown (Administrator), Heidi Cook (Administrator, Professional St), Dorothy Lewis (Administrator), Mona Lindsay (Administrator), Norman Maclean (Administrator), Angela Mclaughlin (Administrator), Bronagh Monaghan (Administrator), Mayuri Patel (Executive Assistant), Fiona Paterson (Administrator), Julianne Reddin (Policy Administrator), Christina Smith (Personal Assistant), Lindsay Wallace (Administrator), Lindsay Wilson (Administrative Assistant, Exec)
**IT:** Andy Smith (IT Manager)
**Operations:** Leanne Brown (Production and Operations Mana), Carol Edgar (Production and Operations Mana), Shelley Ell (Production and Operations Mana), Claire Godley (Production and Operations Mana), Bally Pabla (Production and Operations Mana), Diane Rich (Production and Operations Mana)
**Branches:** Royal College Of General Practitioners, David Anderson Bldg, Foresterhill Rd, Aberdeen, Aberdeenshire AB25 2ZP
**US SIC:** 8299   **UK SIC:** 93300
**Auditors:** Chantrey Vellacott DFK LLP
**Bankers:** Barclays Bank Plc (20-06-05)

|     | 31-03-12 | 31-03-11 | 31-03-10 |
|-----|----------|----------|----------|
| TO  | 33,017,181 | 33,111,406 | 29,984,998 |
| P/L | (445,953) | 1,548,356 | 2,305,097 |
| NW  | 46,578,084 | 49,838,931 | 12,809,795 |
| WC  | 6,415,930 | 3,844,810 | 6,402,289 |
| Emp.| 270 | 267 | 254 |

## DUNS 28-828-7535
### The Royal College of Midwives
15 Mansfield Street, London W1G 9NH
**Tel:** 020-7312-3535 **Fax:** 02073123536
**Web:** www.rcmawards.com
**Reg No:** 0030157   **Estd:** 1902 Private Company Limited By Guarantee
**Line of Business:** Activities of business and employers organisations
**Directors:** Ms H A Marshall, Dr P A Gillen, Ms V G Shand, Mrs L C Pacanowski, Ms A N Shasha, Professor J Sandall, Dr S Way, Ms M Mcdonald
**Responsibilities**
**Senior:** Melissa Cutlan (Manager), Amanda Hutcherson (Manager), Kathleen Jones (Manager), Barbara Kuypers (Director), Marlene Sinclair (Manager), Dale Spence (Manager), Cathy Warrick (Chief Executive Officer)
**Finance:** Harry Watkins (Financial Director)
**IT:** Carol Tiernan (IT Coordinator)
**HR:** John Skewes (Human Resources Director)
**Health & Safety:** Terry Mulford (Facilities Manager)
**Facilities:** Terry Mulford (Facilities Manager)
**Purchasing:** Terry Mulford (Facilities Manager)
**Branches:** The Royal College Of Midwives, 58 Howard Street, Belfast, Belfast BT1 6PJ
**US SIC:** 8611, 8631
**UK SIC:** 96312, 96313
**Auditors:** Horwath Clark Whitehill
**Bankers:** Lloyds TSB Bank plc (30-94-87)

|     | 31-12-13 | 31-12-12 | 31-12-11 |
|-----|----------|----------|----------|
| TO  | 8,672,181 | 8,433,037 | 7,896,199 |
| P/L | 411,534 | 359,970 | 814,085 |
| NW  | 4,091,393 | 2,227,491 | 2,645,707 |
| WC  | 2,541,344 | 2,231,653 | 2,035,103 |
| Emp.| 69 | 71 | 74 |

## DUNS 23-294-4082   Imp
### Royal College of Music
Prince Consort Road, London SW7 2BS
**Tel:** 02075893643 **Fax:** 020-7589-7740
**Web:** www.rcm.ac.uk
**Reg No:** 0000458RC   **Estd:** 1883
Incorporate By Act Of Parliament
**Line of Business:** Other adult and other education not elsewhere classified
**Principals:** M Mcdonald (Financial), S Savant, Ms T Hull, S Johns, R Wistreich, Professor C Lawson, K Porter
**Responsibilities**
**Senior:** David Burnand (Chairman), Amanda Glauert (Director of Programmes and Res), Frankie Hutchinson (Executive), Sophie Lockett (Vice President), Matt Nicholl (House Manager), Susan Sturrock (Director), Lance Whitehead (Executive), Rupert Whitehead (Executive)
**Finance:** Marcus McDonald (Director of Finance and Estate)
**Marketing:** John Fosbrook (Press Officer)
**Admin:** Sarah Hanratty (Personal Assistant), Alice Hughes (PA), Emma McCormack (Executive Assistant to the Dir), Sarah Thurlow (Administrator)
**IT:** Amanda Glauert (Director of Programmes and Res)
**HR:** Sophie Reef (Personnel Manager)
**Health & Safety:** Lynette Easterbrook (Welfare Officer), Andrew Mccarley (Safety and Maintenance Manager)
**Facilities:** Angela Escott (Orchestral and Choral Libraria)
**Operations:** Simon Channing (Head of Performance), Charlotte Martin (Projects Manager)
**Purchasing:** Matt Nicholl (House Manager)
**US SIC:** 8299, 8221
**UK SIC:** 93300, 93100
**Auditors:** BDO LLP UK

|     | 31-07-14 | 31-07-10 | 31-07-08 |
|-----|----------|----------|----------|
| TO  | 21,628,267 | 17,662,663 | 16,261,386 |
| P/L | 1,139,854 | 661,250 | 502,982 |
| NW  | 73,823,560 | 53,575,412 | 50,075,480 |
| WC  | 23,365,204 | (79,023) | 714,615 |
| Emp.| 187 | 179 | 186 |

## DUNS 22-710-6796
### The Royal College of Nursing of the United Kingdom
20 Cavendish Square, London W1G 0RN
**Tel:** 020-7409-3333 **Fax:** 020746473436
**Web:** www.rcn.org.uk
**Reg No:** 0000459RC   **Estd:** 2002
Incorporate By Act Of Parliament
**Line of Business:** Activities of trade unions
**Directors:** Ms M Hinds, Ms T Donnelly, T Golbourn, T Sandford, Ms J Davies, Prof A Kitson, Dr P Carter, Ms J Cox
**Responsibilities**
**IT:** Peter Rutland (IT Manager)
**Facilities:** E Arram (Facilities Manager)
**Branches:** The Royal College Of Nursing Of The United Kingdom, Church Street, Henfield, West Sussex BN5 9NP
**US SIC:** 7399   **UK SIC:** 83954
**Auditors:** PricewaterhouseCoopers LLP
**Bankers:** National Westminster Bank Plc (60-40-02)
**Employees:** 450
**Turnover:** £87,554,000

## DUNS 21-813-2346
### The Royal College of Obstetricians and Gynaecologists
27 Sussex Place, Regent's Park, London NW1 4RG
**Tel:** 020-7772-6200
**Web:** www.rcog.org.uk
**Reg No:** 0000792RC   **Estd:** 1929
**Line of Business:** Activities of professional organisations
**Principals:** S Simmons (President), Dr N Patel (President), P A Barnett, J Malvern
**US SIC:** 8621, 8091
**UK SIC:** 96311, 95200

|     | 31-12-12 |
|-----|----------|
| TO  | 13,171,896 |
| P/L | 578,317 |
| NW  | 27,704,171 |
| WC  | 5,516,723 |
| Emp.| 136 |

## DUNS 21-142-1628   Imp
### The Royal College of Paediatrics & Child Health
5-11 Theobalds Road, London WC1X 8SH
**Tel:** 02070926000
**Web:** www.rcpch.ac.uk
**Estd:** 1928
**Line of Business:** Colleges (higher education)
**Principals:** Professor R Cooke (President), Professor J Osbourne, Doctor K Dodd

## Responsibilities
**Senior:** Hiliary Caff (President), Chris Hanvey (Chief Executive), David Howely (Corporate Services Director), Len Tyler (Chief Executive)
**Marketing:** Debbie Sayers (Buildings Manager)
**Health & Safety:** Debbie Sayers (Buildings Manager)
**Facilities:** Debbie Sayers (Buildings Manager)
**US SIC:** 8699, 6732
**UK SIC:** 96902, 83100
**Bankers:** The Royal Bank Of Scotland Plc (16-00-37)
**Employees:** 100

## DUNS 23-635-9667   Imp
### The Royal College of Physicians
11 St Andrews Place, Camden Town, London NW1 4LE
**Tel:** 02079351174
**Web:** www.rcplondon.ac.uk
**Estd:** 2005
**Line of Business:** Activities of professional organisations
**Directors:** Sir R Thompson, C Clarke, A Burroughs, Prof I Gilmore, S Bennett, Dr M Chestire, L Cotter, Ms D Bax
**Responsibilities**
**Senior:** Elizabeth Berkin (Director), Susan Bews (Director), Nicholas Boon (Director), Rodney Burnham (Director), Michael Clements (Director), David Coggon (Director), Tim Felton (Director), Edward Glucksman (Director), Humphreys Hodgson (Director), Louise Sadler (Executive Assistant)
**Marketing:** Clive Constable (Professional and Regional Affa), Lisa Cunningham (Senior Public Affairs & PR Off), Orla Fee (Head of Publications), Tom Grinyer (Communications and External Af), Andrew McCracken (Communications Officer)
**Admin:** Louise Sadler (Executive Assistant)
**HR:** Linda Asamoah (Personnel Manager)
**Branches:** The Royal College Of Physicians, 4 St. Andrews Place, London NW1 4LB
**US SIC:** 8621   **UK SIC:** 96311
**Auditors:** Crowe Clarke Whitehill LLP

|     | 31-12-12 | 31-12-11 | 31-12-10 |
|-----|----------|----------|----------|
| TO  | 35,133,000 | 32,944,000 | 31,679,000 |
| P/L | 1,337,000 | 1,330,000 | 1,987,000 |
| NW  | 43,065,000 | 39,416,000 | 40,041,000 |
| WC  | 318,000 | (1,105,000) | 5,083,000 |
| Emp.| 334 | N/A | 320 |

## DUNS 21-580-1421
### Royal College of Psychiatrists
21 Mansell Street, London E1 8AA
**Tel:** 02079776655
**Web:** www.rcpsych.ac.uk
**Estd:** 1995 Proprietorship
**Line of Business:** Research institutions and organisations
**Proprietor:** Miss S Holder
**US SIC:** 7391   **UK SIC:** 94000
**Employees:** 79

## DUNS 23-696-8244
### The Royal College of Psychiatrists
21 Prescot Street, London E1 8BB
**Tel:** 020-7235-2351
**Web:** www.rcpsych.ac.uk
**Reg No:** 0228636RC   **VAT No:** 233868639
**Estd:** 1841 Incorporate By Act Of Parliament
**Line of Business:** Colleges (higher education)
**Principals:** Prof A C Sims (President), Dr W D Boyd
**Co. Secretary:** V Cameron
**Responsibilities**
**Senior:** Sue Bailey (President), Susan Halliwell-Bass (Manager), Dave Jago (Head Of Publications And Websi), Janet Parrott (Chairman)
**Marketing:** Liz Fox (Media and Communications Manag), Deborah Hart (Director of Communications & P), Dave Jago (Head Of Publications And Websi), Kathy Oxtoby (Media and Communications Manag), Veena Verdi (Website Officer)
**IT:** Gordon Malcolm (Computer Manager)
**HR:** E Donohoe (Personnel Coordinator)
**US SIC:** 8621, 7391
**UK SIC:** 96311, 94000
**Employees:** 100

## DUNS 23-620-2123   Imp
### Royal College of Surgeons of Edinburgh
Nicolson Street, Edinburgh, Midlothian EH8 9DW
**Tel:** 0131-527-1600
**Web:** www.rcsed.ac.uk
**Reg No:** 0000466RC   **Estd:** 1981

**Line of Business:** Further education schools and colleges
**Principals:** Professor G D Chisholm *(President)*, Professor A G Moran, Ms M Bean, A C Watson
**Responsibilities**
**Marketing:** Mark Baillie *(Communications & Marketing Dir)*, Mariel Roy *(Regional Manager)*
**Admin:** Emma Black *(Museum Administrator)*, Alice Brown *(Sab Administrator)*, Cathy McCartney *(Awards & Grants Secretary)*
**IT:** Alice Brown *(Sab Administrator)*, Kenneth Ryan *(IT Network Manager)*
**HR:** Yvonne Gallagher *(HR Officer)*, Helen MacDonald *(Personnel Officer)*, Siobhan Watts *(HR Advisor)*
**Health & Safety:** Bobby Ross *(Health & Safety Officer)*
**Facilities:** Jennifer McBurnie *(Facilities Manager)*
**Purchasing:** Helen MacDonald *(Personnel Officer)*
**Branches:** Royal College Of Surgeons Of Edinburgh, 61-63 Nicolson Street, Edinburgh, Midlothian EH8 9BZ
**US SIC:** 8221 **UK SIC:** 93100
**Employees:** 130

DUNS 22-845-3874 **Imp**
## Royal College of Surgeons of England
35-43 Lincoln's Inn Fields, London WC2A 3PE
**Web:** www.rcseng.ac.uk
**Estd:** 1800
**Line of Business:** Further education schools and colleges
**Trading Style:** Nuffield College of Surgical Sciences
**President:** N Profesor Browse
**Co. Secretary:** Roger Duffett
**Responsibilities**
**Senior:** Sam Alberti *(General Manager)*, Tom Bishop *(Chairman)*, Louise Walker *(Senior Manager)*
**Marketing:** Adam Brownsell *(Head of Publications & Marketi)*, Matthew Whittaker *(Editorial Manager)*
**HR:** Francine Alexander *(Training Director)*, Mervyn Milton *(Human Resources Manager)*
**Branches:** Royal College Of Surgeons Of England, 35-43 Lincoln's Inn Fields, London WC2A 3PE
**US SIC:** 8221 **UK SIC:** 93100
**Auditors:** Deloitte & Touche LLP
**Employees:** 309
**Turnover:** £25,145,000

DUNS 42-440-1800
## Royal College of Veterinary Surgeons
Belgravia House, London SW1P 2AF
**Tel:** 02072222001 **Fax:** 020-7222-2004
**Web:** www.rcvs.org.uk
**Reg No:** 0000467RC **Estd:** 1800
Incorporate By Act Of Parliament
**Line of Business:** Libraries
**Responsibilities**
**Senior:** Annette Amato *(Secretary)*, Sheila Crispin *(Board Member)*, Jerry Davies *(Vice President)*, Sandy Trees *(President)*, Bradley Viner *(Board Member)*
**Finance:** Corrie McCann *(Head of Finance)*
**HR:** Lesley Evans *(Recruitment Officer)*
**Health & Safety:** Martin Webster *(Facilities Manager)*
**Facilities:** Martin Webster *(Facilities Manager)*
**Operations:** Corrie McCann *(Head of Finance)*
**US SIC:** 8231 **UK SIC:** 97700
**Employees:** 65

DUNS 22-945-2826
## Royal Colleges of Physicians & Surgeons
232-242 St Vincent Street, Glasgow, Lanarkshire G2 5RJ
**Tel:** 0141-221-6072 **Fax:** 01412211804
**Web:** www.rcpsg.ac.uk
**Reg No:** 0000468RC **Estd:** 1881
Incorporate By Act Of Parliament
**Line of Business:** Colleges (higher education)
**Director:** R K Littlejohn
**Responsibilities**
**Senior:** Linda Irvine *(Manager)*, Roger Sturrock *(Chairman)*
**Finance:** Michelle Wylie *(head of Finance & support)*
**HR:** Susan McMahon *(Head of Education, Training &)*, Kay Rennie *(Deputy Head of Education, Trai)*
**US SIC:** 8221 **UK SIC:** 93100
**Bankers:** The Royal Bank Of Scotland Plc (83-54-60)
**Employees:** 75

DUNS 23-677-8098
## Royal Commission on the Ancient
John Sinclair House, 16 Bernard Terrace, Edinburgh, Midlothian EH8 9NX
**Web:** www.rcahms.gov.uk
**Estd:** 1992
**Line of Business:** Library and archive activities
**Trading Style:** R C A H M S
**Directors:** R J Mercer, Prof T C Snout, R Paxton, Prof R J Cramp, Prof J Dunbar-Naismith, Miss A Richards, Prof J M Coles, Cullen
**Responsibilities**
**Senior:** Deborah Howard *(Principal)*, Barbara Richards *(Principal)*
**Finance:** Elaine Fitzsimmons *(Financial Officer)*
**Marketing:** Rebecca Bailey *(Marketing Manager)*
**IT:** Jo McCoy *(IT Manager)*
**HR:** Sean Gallen *(Human Resources Officer)*
**US SIC:** 8999 **UK SIC:** 83954
**Bankers:** Clydesdale Bank Plc (82-62-34)
**Employees:** 100

DUNS 22-702-4320
## The Royal Commonwealth Society
22-25 Northumberland Avenue, London WC2N 5AP
**Tel:** 02079306733 **Fax:** 02077669222
**Web:** www.thercs.org
**Reg No:** 0000469RC **Estd:** 1868
Incorporate By Act Of Parliament
**Line of Business:** Caterers
**Director:** Sir D Thorn
**Responsibilities**
**Senior:** Andrew Goddhard *(General Manager)*, Micheal Lake *(Manager)*
**Operations:** Hans Schrader *(Operations Manager)*
**US SIC:** 6732, 7399
**UK SIC:** 83100, 83954
**Employees:** 50

DUNS 23-285-1287 **Imp-Exp**
## The Royal Commonwealth Society for the Blind
2a Halifax Road, Melksham, Wiltshire SN12 6YY
**Tel:** 01444446600
**Web:** www.sightsavers.org
**Reg No:** 0000706RC **VAT No:** 654340056
**Estd:** 1950 Incorporate By Act Of Parliament
**Line of Business:** Children's homes
**Export Markets:** Africa, Asia, Caribean
**Trading Style:** Sightsavers International
**Principals:** D Thompson *(Chairman)*, A Poffley *(Financial)*, Her Royal Highness Princess Alex, M Queen, Hon Lady Ogilvy (The), J Kerslake, J Hickman, R Porter
**Responsibilities**
**Marketing:** Andy Long *(Global Brand & Strategy Manage)*
**US SIC:** 8321, 7399, 8249, 8299
**UK SIC:** 96111, 83954, 93300
**Auditors:** Deloitte & Touche LLP
**Bankers:** HSBC Bank plc (40-23-27)
**Employees:** 120
**Turnover:** £31,778,000

DUNS 23-261-3302
## Royal Cornwall Hospitals Nhs Trust
Treliske Lane, Truro, Cornwall TR1 3QN
**Tel:** 01872255044
**Web:** www.cht.nhs.uk
**Estd:** 2002
**Line of Business:** Hospitals
**Issued Capital:** £1
**Principals:** M Watts *(Chairman)*, J Teape *(Financial)*, G Shaw, L Boswell, Ms S Hall, D Webb, Ms S Healy, R Evans
**Responsibilities**
**Senior:** Peter Colclough *(Acting Chief Executive)*, Roger Gazzard *(Non-Executive Director)*, Helen Ross-Mcgill *(Manager)*
**Marketing:** Laura Mason *(Communications Manager)*
**Facilities:** Mike Pearson *(Head of Hotel Services)*, Garth Weaver *(Acting Director of Estates)*
**Branches:** Royal Cornwall Hospitals Nhs Trust, St. Clare Street, Penzance, Cornwall TR18 2PF
**US SIC:** 9121, 8062
**UK SIC:** 91110, 95100
**Employees:** 10,000

DUNS 36-797-6834
## Royal County Down Golf Club
36 Golf Links Road, Newcastle, Co Down BT33 0AN
**Tel:** 02843723314
**Web:** www.royalcountydown.org
**Estd:** 1903
**Line of Business:** Golf clubs
**Co. Secretary:** James Laidler
**Responsibilities**
**Senior:** David' Wilson *(General Manager)*
**Finance:** David' Wilson *(General Manager)*
**Marketing:** David' Wilson *(General Manager)*
**IT:** David' Wilson *(General Manager)*
**HR:** David' Wilson *(General Manager)*
**Health & Safety:** David' Wilson *(General Manager)*
**Facilities:** David' Wilson *(General Manager)*
**Purchasing:** David' Wilson *(General Manager)*
**US SIC:** 7999 **UK SIC:** 97913
**Employees:** 50

DUNS 76-950-0299
## The Royal County of Berkshire Health & Racquets Club Ltd
**(Subsidiary of:** Virgin Group Holdings Limited)
Nine Mile Ride, Bracknell, Berkshire RG12 7PB
**Tel:** 01344382380
**Web:** www.esporta.com
**Reg No:** 2500623 **Estd:** 1990 Private Limited Company
**Line of Business:** Physical well-being activities
**Trading Style:** Virgin Active
**Issued Capital:** £50,000
**Directors:** M P Burrows, M W Bucknall, M G Merrick, P A Woolf
**Co. Secretary:** James Archibald
**US SIC:** 7299 **UK SIC:** 98902
**Auditors:** KPMG LLP

| | 31-12-13 | 31-12-12 | 31-12-11 |
|---|---|---|---|
| TO | N/A | N/A | 5,453,000 |
| P/L | 917,000 | N/A | 3,111,000 |
| NW | N/A | 3,155,000 | 3,095,000 |
| WC | N/A | N/A | 3,095,000 |
| Emp. | N/A | N/A | 73 |

DUNS 28-976-6818
## Royal Court Theatre Productions Ltd
Sloane Square, London SW1W 8AS
**Tel:** 02075655000
**Web:** www.royalcourttheatre.com
**Reg No:** 1759772 **Estd:** 1983 Private Limited Company
**Line of Business:** Theatres & concert halls
**Trading Style:** English Stage Company
**Issued Capital:** £100
**Directors:** S Daldry, M R Stafford-Clark, R M Fox, Ms J E Daish, A C Burton, Sir J C Mortimer, J L Tanner, Ms H Cruickshank
**Co. Secretary:** Mrs Lucy Glynn
**Responsibilities**
**Senior:** Dominic Cook *(Manager)*, Rachel Dudley *(Manager)*, Sonia Melchett *(Manager)*
**Branches:** Royal Court Theatre Productions Ltd, 309 Portobello Rd, London W10 5TD
**US SIC:** 7911, 8999
**UK SIC:** 97913, 83954
**Auditors:** haysmacintyre

| | 31-03-14 | 31-03-13 | 31-03-12 |
|---|---|---|---|
| TO | 3,020 | 42,999 | 911,540 |
| P/L | 2,130 | 26,364 | 111,194 |
| NW | 100 | 100 | 100 |
| WC | 100 | 100 | 100 |

DUNS 21-100-5731
## Royal Danish Embassy
55 Sloane Street, London SW1X 9SR
**Tel:** 020-7333-0200
**Web:** www.cfp-e.com
**Estd:** 1700
**Line of Business:** Embassies
**Branches:** Royal Danish Embassy, Powell Duffryn Herbert Walker Ave, 101 West End Dock, Southampton, Hampshire SO15 1HJ
**US SIC:** 9121 **UK SIC:** 91110
**Bankers:** National Westminster Bank Plc (60-19-27)
**Employees:** 46

DUNS 23-220-8629
## Royal Devon & Exeter N H S Foundation Trust
Royal Devon & Exeter Hospital, Barrack Road, Exeter, Devon EX2 5DW
**Tel:** 01392-411611
**Web:** www.rdehospital.nhs.uk
**VAT No:** 654938887 **Estd:** 1759 Incorporate By Act Of Parliament
**Line of Business:** Public sector hospital activities, including nhs trusts
**Trading Style:** Royal Devon & Exeter N H S Foundation Trust
**Issued Capital:** £1
**Principals:** Ms A Ballatti *(Chairman)*, Ms S Tracey *(Financial)*, Ms L Lane *(Personnel)*, Ms S Sutherland, Ms E Hobson, Ms A Pedder Obe, D Bishop, J Rackstraw
**Responsibilities**
**Senior:** Bob Baty OBE *(Non-Executive Director)*, Julian Bennet *(Head Of Community States)*, James Brent *(Chairperson)*, Gerald Sturtridge *(Non-Executive Director)*
**Branches:** Royal Devon & Exeter N H S Foundation Trust, Gladstone Road, Exeter, Devon EX1 2ED
**US SIC:** 8062 **UK SIC:** 95100
**Auditors:** PricewaterhouseCoopers LLP
**Bankers:** National Westminster Bank Plc (56-00-49)

| | 31-03-14 | 31-03-13 | 31-03-12 |
|---|---|---|---|
| TO | 316,374,000 | 300,852,000 | 287,244,000 |
| P/L | (8,427,000) | (21,580,000) | 3,030,000 |
| NW | 221,770,000 | 215,504,000 | 260,424,000 |
| WC | 28,685,000 | 32,377,000 | 38,699,000 |
| Emp. | 5,722 | 5,440 | 5,179 |

DUNS 21-330-4165
## Royal Exchange Theatre Co Ltd
St Anns Square, Manchester M2 7DH
**Tel:** 0161-833-9833 **Fax:** 0161-932-6696
**Web:** www.royalexchange.co.uk
**Reg No:** 0927203 **Estd:** 1968 Private Company Limited By Guarantee
**Line of Business:** Operation of arts facilities
**Directors:** G A Shindler, P A Lee, Ms S Greenaway, Ms J M Raffle, J King, M J Hutchins, Mrs T Black, Ms C Roberts Cherry
**Co. Secretary:** Ms Fiona Gasper
**Responsibilities**
**Senior:** Carol Arditti *(Manager)*, Peter Folkman *(Director)*, Anthony Gordon *(Director)*, Ann-Marie Humphreys *(Director)*, Jean Oglesby *(Director)*, Martyn Torevell *(Director)*, Keith Whitmore *(Director)*
**Marketing:** John Goodfellow *(Press & Communications Manager)*, Claire Will *(Marketing & Communications Dir)*, Val Young *(Development Director)*
**Admin:** Holli Leah *(Administrative Assistant)*
**IT:** Ean Burgon *(IT Manager)*
**HR:** Yvonne Cox *(HR Manager)*
**Branches:** Royal Exchange Theatre Co Ltd, Sterling House, 692 Bolton Rd, Manchester M27 6EL
**US SIC:** 7911 **UK SIC:** 97913
**Auditors:** Grant Thornton UK LLP
**Bankers:** National Westminster Bank Plc (01-10-01)

| | 31-08-13 | 31-08-12 | 31-08-11 |
|---|---|---|---|
| TO | 7,413,000 | 7,822,000 | 7,175,000 |
| P/L | (960,000) | (924,000) | (958,000) |
| NW | 11,978,000 | 12,938,000 | 13,862,000 |
| WC | 310,000 | 360,000 | 385,000 |
| Emp. | 154 | 158 | 159 |

DUNS 42-440-0315
## Royal Free Hospital
Pond Street, London NW3 2QG
**Tel:** 02037582000
**Web:** www.royalfree.org.uk
**Reg No:** 0000475RC **Estd:** 1975
**Line of Business:** Hospitals
**Director:** M Else
**US SIC:** 8062 **UK SIC:** 95100
**Employees:** 6,000

DUNS 23-989-2987 **Imp**
## Royal Free London Nhs Foundation Trust
Royal Free Hospital, Pond Street, London NW3 2QG
**Tel:** 02077-940-500
**Web:** www.royalfree.nhs.uk
**Estd:** 1991
**Line of Business:** Local government authority overseeing the provision of healthcare and acute hospital services.
**Trading Style:** The Royal Free Hospital / Barnet General Hospital, Mount Vernon Hospital / St Pancras Hospital, Edgware Community Hospital, Edgware Community Hospital
**Issued Capital:** £1
**Principals:** D Dodd *(Chairman)*, J Buggle *(Financial)*, C Bruce, D Sloman, A Schapira, R Chada, D Bernstein, D Pascall
**Responsibilities**
**Admin:** Tracey Clifford *(Administration Manager)*
**Operations:** Martin Hogarth *(Project Manager)*
**Branches:** Royal Free London Nhs Foundation Trust, Wells House Clinic, Well Walk, London NW3 1LE
**US SIC:** 9121, 8091, 8062
**UK SIC:** 91110, 95200, 95100
**Auditors:** PricewaterhouseCoopers LLP

**Bankers:** Lloyds TSB Bank plc (30-93-80)

| | 31-03-14 | 31-03-13 | 31-03-12 |
|---|---|---|---|
| TO | 593,741,000 | 577,061,000 | 486,809,000 |
| P/L | (21,973,000) | (8,995,000) | 11,822,000 |
| NW | 238,023,000 | 281,082,000 | 290,869,000 |
| WC | 21,624,000 | 7,256,000 | 12,467,000 |
| Emp. | 5,731 | 1,191 | 5,219 |

DUNS 21-811-9317
## Royal Free Neurological Rehabilitation Centre
Edgware Community Hospital, Burnt Oak Broadway, Edgware, Middlesex HA8 0AD
**Tel:** 02089512165
**Web:** www.royalfree.nhs.uk
**Estd:** 2012
**Line of Business:** Rehabilitation centres
**Responsibilities**
**Senior:** Fiona Kelly *(Clinical Lead)*
**US SIC:** 8062 **UK SIC:** 95100
**Employees:** 50

DUNS 77-932-5638
## Royal Garden Hotel Ltd
(**Subsidiary of:** Royal Garden Hotel (Jersey) Ltd)
2-24 Kensington High Street, London W8 4PT
**Tel:** 02073610602
**Web:** www.royalgardenhotel.co.uk
**Reg No:** 3045114 **Estd:** 1995 Private Limited Company
**Line of Business:** Restaurants
**Trading Style:** The Tenth Restaurant, Park Terrace Restaurant
**Issued Capital:** £40,000,000
**Directors:** Mrs M B Khoo, Mrs J Carmichael, K H Khoo, Ms E Khoo
**Co. Secretary:** Ms Jacqueline Khoo
**Responsibilities**
**Senior:** Massimo Devenuto *(Manager)*, Mavis Khoo Oei *(Manager)*, Joan Lau *(Company Representative)*, Jonathan Lowrey *(General Manager)*
**Marketing:** Matthew Burbidge-Airs *(E-Commerce Marketing Executive)*, Natalia Makarevich *(Sales & Marketing Coordinator)*, Marilyn Watkinson *(Assistant Director of Sales &)*
**Sales:** Natalia Makarevich *(Sales & Marketing Coordinator)*, Marilyn Watkinson *(Assistant Director of Sales &)*
**US SIC:** 5812 **UK SIC:** 66110
**Auditors:** PricewaterhouseCoopers

| | 30-09-13 | 30-09-12 | 30-09-11 |
|---|---|---|---|
| TO | 31,238,677 | 31,843,218 | 26,616,749 |
| P/L | 2,092,249 | 2,957,588 | 473,548 |
| NW | 69,069,644 | 67,962,597 | 66,353,224 |
| WC | (11,612,511) | (15,819,569) | (19,749,370) |
| Emp. | 364 | 358 | 343 |

DUNS 36-490-3869
## Royal Geographical Society (With the Institute of British Geographers)
1 Kensington Gore, London SW7 2AR
**Tel:** 020-7591-3000
**Web:** www.rgs.org
**Estd:** 1977
**Line of Business:** Adult education locations
**Trading Style:** Royal Geographical Society
**Principals:** Sir N Cosson *(President)*, D Lyon
**Responsibilities**
**Senior:** Rita Gardener *(Manager)*
**Finance:** David Riviere *(Head of Finance)*
**HR:** Steve Brace *(Development Officer)*
**Health & Safety:** Denise Prior *(Health & Safety Officer)*
**US SIC:** 8299 **UK SIC:** 93300
**Auditors:** Baker Tilly UK Audit LLP
**Employees:** 50
**Turnover:** £6,513,000

DUNS 21-606-7383
## Royal Glamorgan Hospital
Ynysmaerdy, Pontyclun, Mid Glamorgan CF72 8XR
**Tel:** 01443744800
**Estd:** 2011 Proprietorship
**Line of Business:** Hospitals
**Proprietor:** Mrs M Davies
**US SIC:** 8062 **UK SIC:** 95100
**Employees:** 1,500

DUNS 23-082-8126
## The Royal Grammar School
Amersham Road, High Wycombe, Buckinghamshire HP13 6QT
**Tel:** 01494524955
**Web:** www.rgshw.com
**Estd:** 2004
**Line of Business:** Schools (foundation)
**Directors:** T Tingle, D Leven
**Responsibilities**
**Senior:** Roger Pantridge *(Deputy Head Teacher)*
**IT:** Varsha Kirkby *(ICT Manager)*, Richard Shreeve *(IT Security)*
**US SIC:** 8211 **UK SIC:** 93200
**Employees:** 120

DUNS 85-614-5862
## The Royal Grammar School Worcester
R G S Worcester, Worcester, Worcestershire WR1 1HN
**Tel:** 01905-613391
**Web:** www.rgsao.org
**Reg No:** 6251081 **Estd:** 1991 Private Company Limited By Guarantee
**Line of Business:** Primary education
**Directors:** Dr E L Robinson, Miss K Meredith, Ms J Preedy, J Q Poole, B W Radford, Ms R F Ham, Mrs L M Cook, N C Fairlie
**Co. Secretary:** Ian Roberts
**Responsibilities**
**Senior:** Robert Ingles *(Manager)*
**US SIC:** 8211 **UK SIC:** 93200
**Auditors:** Baker Tilly Audit LLP

| | 31-08-14 | 31-08-13 | 31-08-12 |
|---|---|---|---|
| TO | 11,263,000 | 11,755,000 | 10,937,000 |
| P/L | 93,000 | 718,000 | 663,000 |
| NW | 19,058,000 | 18,937,000 | 18,215,000 |
| WC | 1,581,000 | 1,469,000 | 1,369,000 |
| Emp. | 204 | 199 | 187 |

DUNS 21-783-1475
## Royal Highland Hotel
Station Square, Academy Street, Inverness, Inverness-Shire IV1 1LG
**Web:** www.royalhighlandhotel.co.uk
**Estd:** 2011 Proprietorship
**Line of Business:** Other tourist assistance activities not elsewhere classified
**Proprietor:** I Banargee
**US SIC:** 7999 **UK SIC:** 97913
**Employees:** 50

DUNS 23-210-7532 Imp
## Royal Holloway University of London
Egham Hill, Egham, Surrey TW20 0EX
**Tel:** 01784443131
**Web:** www.rhul.ac.uk
**VAT No:** 212327410 **Estd:** 1991
**Line of Business:** Doctors
**Trading Style:** Royal Holloway and Bedford New College
**Director:** P Layzell
**Responsibilities**
**Senior:** Shawana Araf *(Doctor)*, Sheryl Simon *(Manager)*, Jean Strudley *(Manager)*, Adam Tickell *(Manager)*
**Finance:** Emma McMahon *(Finance and Facilities Coordin)*
**Marketing:** Sophia Haque *(Head of Press and PR)*, Paul Teed *(Head of Press and PR)*
**Sales:** Lauren Parker *(?Major Gifts Manager)*
**Admin:** Sandra Beaty *(Recruitment Administrator)*, Doreen Bravery *(Faculty Administrator)*, Gaenor Burchett-Vass *(Administrator)*, Marie Gallagher *(Deputy Head of School, Adminis)*, Tracey Jeffries *(Faculty Administrator)*, Pam Kaur *(Personal Assistant to the Depu)*, Sarah Moffat *(Senior Faculty Administrator)*, Nicola Moss *(Faculty Administrator)*, Finuala Shearman *(Executive Assistant to the Pri)*, Simon Suggate *(Administrator, Academic Staff)*, Anne Varty *(Admissions Tutor)*
**IT:** Judith Crocker *(Head of IT Development)*, Tristan Findley *(System Administrator)*, Claire Hudson *(Administrator, Information Sec)*, Liz Jenkins *(Systems Administrator)*
**HR:** Helen Angel *(Recruitment Officer)*, Cheryl Newsome *(HR Director)*, Karin Okuefuna-Budd *(Placement Tutor)*
**Facilities:** Emma McMahon *(Finance and Facilities Coordin)*
**Engineering:** Laura Perez *(Technical Engineer)*
**Branches:** Royal Holloway University Of London, Egham Hill, Egham, Surrey TW20 0EX
**US SIC:** 8221 **UK SIC:** 93100
**Auditors:** BDO LLP
**Bankers:** National Westminster Bank Plc (60-07-33)

| | 31-07-14 | 31-07-13 | 31-07-12 |
|---|---|---|---|
| TO | 148,263,000 | 141,980,000 | 136,759,000 |
| P/L | 7,765,000 | 5,964,000 | 7,586,000 |
| NW | 126,709,000 | 194,703,000 | 186,917,000 |
| WC | 37,401,000 | 33,613,000 | 33,026,000 |
| Emp. | 1,373 | 1,335 | 1,294 |

DUNS 23-553-5960
## Royal Horseguards Hotel
2 Whitehall Court, Westminster, London SW1A 2EJ
**Tel:** 08713769033
**Web:** www.guoman.com
**Estd:** 2012 Partnership
**Line of Business:** Hotels
**Trading Style:** Band of the Blues & Royals (Royak Horse Guards and 1st Dragoon
**Partners:** Mrs N Forsell, Ms L Lewis, J Beecroft, B Messaoud
**Responsibilities**
**Senior:** Neil Sherry *(General Manager)*
**Branches:** Royal Horseguards Hotel, Knightsbridge, London SW7 1SE
**US SIC:** 7011 **UK SIC:** 66500
**Employees:** 117

DUNS 22-546-5160 Imp-Exp
## The Royal Horticultural Society
80 Vincent Square, London SW1P 2PE
**Tel:** 08452605000 **Fax:** 020-7630-6060
**Web:** www.rhs.org.uk
**Reg No:** 0000480RC **Estd:** 2012 Incorporate By Act Of Parliament
**Line of Business:** Preservation of historical sites and buildings
**Trading Style:** R H S Gardens
**Responsibilities**
**Senior:** Jim Arbury *(Executive)*, Sue Biggs *(Manager)*, Louise Bowering *(Manager)*, Katie Draper *(Senior Manager)*, Andrew Halstead *(Chairman)*, Rachael Horsley *(Manager)*, Lucie Rudnicka *(Executive)*, Louise Tee *(Manager)*
**Marketing:** Jon Ardle *(technical editor)*, Kylie Balmain *(Head of Horticultural Trials a)*, Hayley Monckton *(Head of Communications)*, Elysa Rule *(Membership Marketing Executive)*, Natalie Searle *(Advertising Manager)*, Louisa Smith *(Membership Marketing Executive)*
**Sales:** Claire Custance *(Strategic Development Manager)*, William Havercroft *(Head of Retail)*
**Admin:** Mary Howard *(Personal Assistant)*, Carol Johns *(Personal Assistant)*
**IT:** Robert Reilly *(Head of IT)*
**HR:** Sarah Cathcart *(Training Director)*
**Operations:** Claire Hollis *(Manager)*, Diana Levy *(Print and Production Services)*
**Branches:** The Royal Horticultural Society, Rosemoor Garden, Torrington, Devon EX38 8PH
**US SIC:** 8411, 0729
**UK SIC:** 97700, 01003
**Auditors:** PKF (UK) LLP
**Turnover:** £64,552,000

DUNS 73-296-7240
## Royal Hospital for Neuro-Disability Services Ltd
(**Subsidiary of:** Royal Hospital for Neuro-Disability)
West Hill, London SW15 3SW
**Tel:** 020-8780-4500
**Web:** www.rhn.org.uk
**Reg No:** 4570542 **Estd:** 2002 Private Limited Company
**Line of Business:** Hospitals
**Issued Capital:** £1
**Directors:** L Kalkun, A J Somerville
**Co. Secretary:** Len Kalkun
**Responsibilities**
**Senior:** William Chidgey *(Director of Finance)*
**Finance:** William Chidgey *(Director of Financo)*
**US SIC:** 8011 **UK SIC:** 95300

| | 30-09-13 | 30-09-12 | 30-09-11 |
|---|---|---|---|
| TO | 66,689 | 61,469 | N/A |
| P/L | 44,438 | N/A | N/A |
| NW | 1 | 1 | 1 |
| WC | 1 | 1 | 1 |

DUNS 23-183-8033
## Royal Hospital for Sick Children
(**Subsidiary of:** Scottish Government)
Dalnair Street, Glasgow, Lanarkshire G3 8SJ
**Tel:** 0141 201 0000
**Web:** www.nhsgg.org.uk
**Estd:** 1883
**Line of Business:** Public sector hospital activities, including nhs trusts
**Issued Capital:** £1
**Principals:** Ms S Kuenssberg *(Chairman)*, J Bryden *(Financial)*
**Responsibilities**
**Health & Safety:** Frazer Holmes *(Health & Safety Officer)*
**Facilities:** Frank McGuire *(Facilities Manager)*
**US SIC:** 8062 **UK SIC:** 95100
**Employees:** 1,000

DUNS 42-319-5114
## Royal Hospital for Sick Children
Royal Hospital For Sick Children, 9 Sciennes Road, Edinburgh, Midlothian EH9 1LF
**Tel:** 0131-536-0000
**Web:** www.edinburghsickkids.org
**Estd:** 2002
**Line of Business:** Hospitals
**Trading Style:** Royal Hospital for Sick Children
**Principals:** G Miller *(Chairman)*, Ms S Goldsmith *(Financial)*, Dr M Godman, Ms W Miller, M Wright
**Responsibilities**
**Senior:** Dorothy Hanley *(Chief Nurse)*, Janice MacKenzie *(Principal Nurse)*, Sandra Mair *(General Manager)*
**Health & Safety:** Janice MacKenzie *(Principal Nurse)*
**Operations:** Janice MacKenzie *(Principal Nurse)*
**US SIC:** 8062 **UK SIC:** 95100
**Bankers:** Bank Of Scotland (80-02-83)
**Employees:** 1,100

DUNS 21-499-4621
## The Royal Hospital School
Park Cottage, Holbrook Gardens, Ipswich, Suffolk IP9 2QU
**Web:** www.royalhospitalschool.org
**Estd:** 2011
**Line of Business:** Schools (independent)
**Responsibilities**
**Senior:** James Lockwood *(Head Teacher)*
**IT:** Andy Wollard *(IT Director)*
**HR:** Maggie Cross *(Human Resources Manager)*
**Health & Safety:** Tony Nicoll *(Property Services Manager)*
**Facilities:** Tony Nicoll *(Property Services Manager)*
**Purchasing:** Tony Nicoll *(Property Services Manager)*
**US SIC:** 8211 **UK SIC:** 93200
**Employees:** 300

DUNS 21-071-7018
## Royal Hotel
Belgrave Road, Ventnor, Isle of Wight PO38 1JJ
**Tel:** 01983-852186
**Web:** www.royalhoteliow.co.uk
**Estd:** 1995 Proprietorship
**Line of Business:** Hotels
**Proprietor:** W Bailey
**Responsibilities**
**Finance:** Jennie McKee *(General Manager)*
**HR:** Jennie McKee *(General Manager)*
**Health & Safety:** Jennie McKee *(General Manager)*
**US SIC:** 7011 **UK SIC:** 66500
**Employees:** 50

DUNS 23-711-2701
## The Royal Hotel
64-72 Coagh Street, Cookstown, Co Tyrone BT80 8NG
**Tel:** 028-8676-2224
**Web:** www.theroyal-hotel.com
**Estd:** 1973 Proprietorship
**Line of Business:** Hotels and motels without restaurant
**Proprietor:** S Thom
**Responsibilities**
**Senior:** Stephen Thom *(Proprietor)*
**HR:** Tanya Thom *(Human Resources Manager)*
**US SIC:** 7011 **UK SIC:** 66500
**Bankers:** The Bank Of Ireland (90-48-19)
**Employees:** 47

DUNS 37-756-1527
## Royal Hotel Cromarty
Marine Terrace, Cromarty, Ross-Shire IV11 8YN
**Tel:** 01381-600217
**Web:** www.royalhotel-cromarty.co.uk
**Estd:** 1995 Proprietorship
**Line of Business:** Hotels
**Proprietor:** J Shearer
**Responsibilities**
**Senior:** Jenny Henderson *(Proprietor)*
**US SIC:** 7011 **UK SIC:** 66500
**Employees:** 49

DUNS 21-557-5230
## The Royal Household
1 Burnt Ash Hill, London SE12 0AA
**Tel:** 02088515234
**Web:** www.royal.gov.uk
**Estd:** 2012 Incorporate By Act Of Parliament
**Line of Business:** Restaurant - chinese
**Directors:** Sir M C Gerrard Peat, D A Walker, Lt Col A C Ford, The Rt Hon C E Wollaston Mackenzie Geidt, Sir A Reid, M Hunt-Davis, The Rt Hon W J Robert Peel, Sir H A Roberts
**Responsibilities**
**Senior:** Shi Han *(Proprietor)*, Sung Lai *(Proprietor)*, Christopher Wollaston MacKenzie Geidt *(Principal)*
**Marketing:** Susannah Mann *(Marketing Director)*
**US SIC:** 9121 **UK SIC:** 91110

**Auditors:** KPMG LLP

| | 31-03-12 | 31-03-11 | 31-03-09 |
|---|---|---|---|
| TO | 14,600,000 | 14,600,000 | 16,100,000 |
| P/L | 2,400,000 | 2,700,000 | 600,000 |
| NW | 12,500,000 | 11,300,000 | 7,300,000 |
| WC | 2,800,000 | 1,200,000 | (1,900,000) |
| Emp. | 100 | 106 | 109 |

DUNS 42-396-8379

## Royal Infirmary

51 Little France Crescent, Edinburgh, Midlothian EH16 4SA
**Web:** www.nhslothian.scot.nhs.uk
**Estd:** 2010
**Line of Business:** Hospitals
**Principals:** Ms M Duffy *(Financial)*, C Swainson
**Responsibilities**
**Finance:** Helen Amos *(Financial Manager)*
**US SIC:** 8062 **UK SIC:** 95100
**Employees:** 2,000

DUNS 23-271-4055 **Exp**

## Royal Institute of International Affairs

Chatham House, 10 St James's Square, London SW1Y 4LE
**Tel:** 020-7957-5700 **Fax:** 020-7957-5710
**Web:** www.chathamhouse.org
**Reg No:** 0000485RC **VAT No:** 653218153
**Estd:** 1994 Incorporate By Act Of Parliament
**Line of Business:** Research institutions and organisations
**Financial Director:** Ms L Allison
**Responsibilities**
**Senior:** Robin Niblett *(Manager)*
**Finance:** Paul Curtin *(Financial Director)*
**Marketing:** Esther Stoffels *(Marketing Manager)*
**HR:** Dawn Margrett *(Human Resources Manager)*
**Health & Safety:** Dawn Margrett *(Human Resources Manager)*
**Facilities:** Charag Ali *(Facilities Manager)*, Danny Allen *(Facilities Manager)*
**US SIC:** 7391, 8699, 6732
**UK SIC:** 94000, 96902, 83100
**Bankers:** Lloyds TSB Bank plc (30-00-08)
**Employees:** 75

DUNS 22-956-0545

## The Royal Institution of Chartered Surveyors

12 Great George St Parliament Square, London SW1P 3AD
**Tel:** 02072227000
**Web:** www.rics.org
**Reg No:** 0000487RC **VAT No:** 584940013
**Estd:** 2002 Incorporate By Act Of Parliament
**Line of Business:** Engineering related scientific and technical consulting activities
**Trading Style:** R I C S
**Principals:** C Lewis *(President)*, J L Armstrong *(Managing)*, M Clark, J Offen, R Swanston, S Pott, M Pattison
**Responsibilities**
**Marketing:** Joanne Lindon *(Head of Marketing)*
**Branches:** The Royal Institution Of Chartered Surveyors, 50 New Rd, High Wycombe, Buckinghamshire HP10 8DL
**US SIC:** 7399, 4511
**UK SIC:** 83954, 75000
**Auditors:** Deloitte & Touche LLP
**Bankers:** National Westminster Bank Plc (56-00-45)
**Employees:** 499
**Turnover:** £46,207,000

DUNS 21-205-5698

## Royal Leamington Spa Nursing Home

14-16 Adelaide Road, Leamington Spa, Warwickshire CV31 3PW
**Tel:** 01926426820
**Web:** www.careuk.com
**Estd:** 1992 Proprietorship
**Line of Business:** Nursing homes
**Proprietor:** M Mendelson
**Responsibilities**
**Senior:** Sue Chillars *(General Manager)*, Stephanie Webley *(Manager)*
**US SIC:** 8051 **UK SIC:** 95100
**Employees:** 60

DUNS 28-830-2961

## The Royal Leicestershire Rutland and Wycliffe Society for the Blind

Station Street, Birmingham, West Midlands B5 4DS
**Tel:** 08457404404
**Web:** www.wycliffebeds.co.uk
**Reg No:** 0163099 **Estd:** 1920 Private Company Limited By Guarantee
**Line of Business:** Social work activities with accommodation
**Directors:** H M Pearson, Ms V A Parsons, J J Godber, Mrs U D Dattani, Ms S V Disley, A J Harrop, Dr R Hill, Ms P G Cyhan
**Co. Secretary:** John Lewis
**Responsibilities**
**Senior:** Abdullah Ghanchi *(Manager)*
**Branches:** The Royal Leicestershire, Rutland and Wycliffe Society For The Blind, The New Wycliffe Home For The Blind, 111 Gleneagles Avenue, LE4 7YJ Leicester
**US SIC:** 8321 **UK SIC:** 96111
**Auditors:** KPMG
**Bankers:** National Westminster Bank Plc (60-15-31)

| | 31-03-14 | 31-03-13 | 31-03-12 |
|---|---|---|---|
| TO | 6,016,000 | 5,731,000 | 5,573,000 |
| P/L | 361,000 | (92,000) | (192,000) |
| NW | 5,524,000 | 5,417,000 | 5,582,000 |
| WC | 283,000 | 238,000 | 413,000 |
| Emp. | 198 | 201 | 206 |

DUNS 77-855-8858

## The Royal Life Saving Society U K

River House, High Street, Broom, Alcester, Warwickshire B50 4HN
**Tel:** 01789773994
**Web:** www.rlss.org.uk
**Reg No:** 3033781 **Estd:** 1995 Private Company Limited By Guarantee
**Line of Business:** Other adult and other education not elsewhere classified
**Trading Style:** The Royal Life Saving Society U K
**Directors:** M A Smith, C P Harper, Ms S J Andrews, I M Hutchings, Mrs D Hunt, W J Stainer, C P Burchell, P D Moyes
**Co. Secretary:** Ms Diane Steer
**Responsibilities**
**Senior:** Bryan Finlay *(Manager)*, Fredric Lang *(Director)*, Diane Standley *(Chief Executive)*
**Branches:** The Royal Life Saving Society U K, 9 Bentfield Cottages, Bradford, West Yorkshire BD14 6DJ
**US SIC:** 8299, 8091
**UK SIC:** 93300, 95200
**Auditors:** Eden Currie Ltd
**Bankers:** Coutts & Co (18-00-02)

| | 31-12-13 | 31-12-12 | 31-12-11 |
|---|---|---|---|
| TO | 4,489,327 | 4,735,702 | 4,282,852 |
| P/L | (400,311) | (110,451) | (154,117) |
| NW | 2,436,702 | 2,773,540 | 2,802,450 |
| WC | 944,554 | 1,340,617 | 1,530,517 |
| Emp. | 46 | 43 | 39 |

DUNS 21-034-8727

## Royal Liverpool Golf Club

30 Meols Drive, Wirral, Merseyside CH47 4AL
**Tel:** 01516323101
**Web:** www.royal-liverpool-golf.com
**Estd:** 2002 Proprietorship
**Line of Business:** Golf clubs
**Proprietor:** D Cromie
**Responsibilities**
**Senior:** Shaun Herbert *(House Manager)*
**US SIC:** 7999 **UK SIC:** 97913
**Employees:** 50

DUNS 22-851-6696 **Exp**

## The Royal Liverpool Philharmonic Society

Liverpool Masonic Hall, 22 Hope Street, Liverpool, Merseyside L1 9BY
**Tel:** 01512102895 **Fax:** 0151-210-2902
**Web:** www.liverpoolphil.com
**Reg No:** 0088235 **VAT No:** 849774462
**Estd:** 1906 Private Company Limited By Guarantee
**Line of Business:** Stadiums and sports grounds
**Trading Style:** Philharmonic Hall
**Directors:** M Eakin, J A Stone, Dr T Harvey, J A Corner, Ms W A Simon, Ms C Coker, D W Nicholls, A J Holladay
**Co. Secretary:** Dr Tony Harvey
**Responsibilities**
**Senior:** Timothy Johnston *(Board Of Directors)*, Lorraine Rogers *(Director)*
**Finance:** Deborah Dunning *(Group Accountant)*, Stephan Heaton *(Financial Director)*
**Marketing:** Jayne Garrity *(Head of Communications & Corpo)*, James Hanks *(Marketing Manager)*, Millicent Jones *(Executive Director Marketing,)*
**Sales:** Charlie Taylor *(Development Manager)*, Dawn Williams *(Senior Sales Executive)*
**Admin:** Rosemary Barton *(Administrator)*, Moira Hall *(Events Administrator)*, Jane Robins *(Executive assistant)*
**HR:** Judith Agnew *(Training Director)*, Andrew Choyce *(Head of Human Resources)*
**Health & Safety:** Steve Bragger *(Maintenance Manager)*
**Facilities:** Steve Bragger *(Maintenance Manager)*, Patricia Peter *(Facilities Manager)*
**Fleet:** Emma King *(Capital Development Director)*
**Engineering:** Steve Bragger *(Maintenance Manager)*
**US SIC:** 7911 **UK SIC:** 97913
**Auditors:** PricewaterhouseCoopers LLP
**Bankers:** Barclays Bank Plc (20-51-01)

| | 31-03-14 | 31-03-13 | 31-03-12 |
|---|---|---|---|
| TO | 12,790,000 | 10,488,000 | 9,738,000 |
| P/L | (3,713,000) | (371,000) | (541,000) |
| NW | 2,168,000 | 5,307,000 | 7,831,000 |
| WC | (243,000) | (1,979,000) | (1,812,000) |
| Emp. | 227 | 220 | 221 |

DUNS 21-025-4371 **Imp**

## The Royal London Mutual Insurance Society Ltd

55 Gracechurch Street, London EC3V 0RL
**Tel:** 02077870770 **Fax:** 01625-605400
**Web:** www.royallondon.com
**Reg No:** 0099064 **VAT No:** 368524427
**Estd:** 1908 Private Company Limited By Guarantee
**Line of Business:** Activities auxiliary to insurance and pension funding
**Directors:** A W Palmer, P D Loney, T W Harris, Mrs T Graham, Mrs S Bridgeland, J M Macdonald, I E Dilks, D A Weymouth
**Co. Secretary:** Royal London Management Services
**Responsibilities**
**Senior:** Tim Melville-Ross *(Non-Executive Chairman)*, Stephen Shone *(Group Finance Director)*
**Branches:** The Royal London Mutual Insurance Society,Limited, Morline Ho, London Rd, Barking, Essex IG11 8BB
**US SIC:** 6411 **UK SIC:** 83200
**Auditors:** PricewaterhouseCoopers LLP
**Bankers:** National Westminster Bank Plc (60-06-06)

**Following financial data are in thousands**

| | 31-12-13 | 31-12-12 | 31-12-11 |
|---|---|---|---|
| TO | 726,000 | 682,000 | 732,000 |
| P/L | 449,000 | 233,000 | 64,000 |
| NW | 1,964,000 | 1,565,000 | 1,279,000 |
| WC | (50,802,000) | 2,881,000 | 1,067,000 |
| Emp. | 3,050 | 2,787 | 2,692 |

DUNS 22-720-6901

## The Royal London Society for Blind People

Norton House, Exeter, Devon EX5 5AL
**Tel:** 01732-592500 **Fax:** 01732-592506
**Web:** www.rlsb.org.uk
**Reg No:** 0139928 **VAT No:** 227080874
**Estd:** 1915 Private Company Limited By Guarantee
**Line of Business:** Other adult and other education not elsewhere classified
**Directors:** I F Stephenson, P A Obey, M S Brignall, Mrs S Sood, R J Hart, Mrs V M May
**Co. Secretary:** Ms Alison Futtit
**Responsibilities**
**Senior:** Victoria Cleland *(Director)*, Ronald Edghill *(Trustee)*, Ian Godwin *(Director)*, Vivian Lawrence *(Director)*, Tom Pey *(Chief Executive)*
**Branches:** The Royal London Society For Blind People, Seal Drive, Sevenoaks, Kent TN15 0AH
**US SIC:** 8299, 8249
**UK SIC:** 93300
**Auditors:** haysmacintyre
**Bankers:** Barclays Bank Plc (20-00-50)

| | 31-12-13 | 31-12-12 | 31-12-11 |
|---|---|---|---|
| TO | 8,507,000 | 5,532,000 | 9,421,000 |
| P/L | 2,143,000 | (1,889,000) | (2,654,000) |
| NW | 4,005,000 | 5,939,000 | 7,871,000 |
| WC | 1,307,000 | 159,000 | (126,000) |
| Emp. | 111 | 136 | 175 |

DUNS 22-916-2276

## The Royal Lyceum Theatre Co Ltd

30b Grindlay Street, Edinburgh, Midlothian EH3 9AX
**Tel:** 01312484800
**Web:** www.lyceum.org.uk
**Reg No:** 0062065SC **VAT No:** 300377303
**Estd:** 1977 Private Company Limited By Guarantee
**Line of Business:** Theatrical presentation companies
**Directors:** Ms R A Silbert, A Mcgowan, Ms A L Macpherson, P D Watts, D M Thomson, R Lewis, S W Dunn, Ms J E Hepburn
**Co. Secretary:** Ms Jennifer Stewart
**Responsibilities**
**Senior:** Donald Emslie *(Chief Executive)*, L Godini *(Theatre Manager)*, Paul Godzik *(Manager)*, Kathleen Mackenzie *(Manager)*, Neil Menzies *(Manager)*
**Marketing:** Ben Jeffries *(Director of Communications & C)*, Michelle Mangan *(Press and PR Manager)*, Emma Robertson Werner *(Communications Manager)*
**Admin:** Ruth Butterworth *(Administration Manager)*
**IT:** Ruth Butterworth *(Administration Manager)*
**HR:** Ruth Butterworth *(Administration Manager)*
**Operations:** David Butterworth *(Head of Production)*, L Godini *(Theatre Manager)*
**Purchasing:** Ruth Butterworth *(Administration Manager)*
**Engineering:** David Butterworth *(Head of Production)*
**Branches:** The Royal Lyceum Theatre Co Ltd, 29 Roseburn St, Edinburgh, Midlothian EH12 5PE
**US SIC:** 8999 **UK SIC:** 83954
**Auditors:** Chiene & Tait CA
**Bankers:** Bank Of Scotland (80-11-94)

| | 05-04-14 | 06-04-13 | 31-04-12 |
|---|---|---|---|
| TO | 3,376,804 | 3,357,203 | 3,242,795 |
| P/L | (22,631) | (206,832) | (14,491) |
| NW | 477,384 | 500,015 | 706,847 |
| WC | 115,818 | 38,501 | 145,994 |
| Emp. | 82 | 90 | 86 |

DUNS 23-697-4366

## Royal Lymington Yacht Club

Bath Road, Lymington, Hampshire SO41 3SE
**Tel:** 01590-672677
**Web:** www.rlymyc.org.uk
**Estd:** 1922
**Line of Business:** Clubs social and associations
**Directors:** P R Major, M Raisen
**Co. Secretary:** Ian Gawn
**Responsibilities**
**Senior:** Duncan Macalister *(Board Member)*, Kevin Podger *(Secretary)*
**Finance:** Kerry Priday *(Accounts Manager)*
**Sales:** Kerry Priday *(Accounts Manager)*
**Operations:** Jon Chittock *(Operations Manager)*
**US SIC:** 5813 **UK SIC:** 66200
**Bankers:** HSBC Bank plc (40-30-36)
**Employees:** 40

DUNS 22-704-5366

## Royal Mail Group Ltd

**(Subsidiary of:** Royal Mail Plc)
100 Victoria Embankment, London EC4Y 0HQ
**Tel:** 03457740740 **Fax:** 02072-502-632
**Web:** www.royalmail.com
**Reg No:** 4138203 **VAT No:** 243170002
**Estd:** 2013 Private Limited Company
**Line of Business:** National post activities
**Trading Style:** Royal Mail Post Office Counters, Parcelforce, Royal Mail Relay
**Issued Capital:** £50,001
**Directors:** Ms M M Greene, D H Brydon, M J Lester
**Co. Secretary:** Ms Emily Pang
**Responsibilities**
**Senior:** Mark Higson *(Manager)*, Jonathan Millidge *(Manager)*
**Branches:** Royal Mail Group Ltd, 112-118 Barker Street, Norwich, Norfolk NR2 4HJ
**US SIC:** 4311 **UK SIC:** 79010
**Auditors:** Ernst & Young LLP
**Bankers:** Girobank Plc (72-00-00)

**Following financial data are in thousands**

| | 30-03-14 | 31-03-13 | 25-03-12 |
|---|---|---|---|
| TO | 7,782,000 | 7,758,000 | 7,167,000 |
| P/L | 1,519,000 | 520,000 | 239,000 |
| NW | 1,958,000 | 1,114,000 | (3,053,000) |
| WC | (766,000) | (385,000) | (572,000) |
| Emp. | 149,172 | 149,940 | 160,248 |

DUNS 23-168-2337 **Imp**

## The Royal Marsden Hospital Nhs Foundation Trust

369 Fulham Road, London SW10 9NH
**Tel:** 02087-468-000
**Web:** www.chelwest.nhs.uk
**VAT No:** 654915415 **Estd:** 1983
**Line of Business:** Hospitals
**Issued Capital:** £1
**Principals:** P Edwards *(Chairman)*, Ms L Bewes *(Financial)*, Ms H Lawrence, C Glass, C Wilson, A Havery, P Kitney Obe, Ms K Norman
**Responsibilities**
**Senior:** Saji Alexander *(Manager)*, Gubby Ayida *(Manager)*, Vivien Bell *(Head of Midwifery and General)*, Tony Bell *(CEO)*, Kidge Burns *(Executive)*, Leigh Chislett *(Manager)*, Alison Delamare *(Executive)*, Csilla Kanyaro *(Manager)*, Martin Lupton *(Manager)*, Kausikh Nandi *(Manager)*, Dimitrios Nikolaou *(Executive)*, Juling Ong *(Executive)*, Anton Pozniak *(Manager)*, Amanda Pritchard *(Deputy Chief Executive)*, James Smellie *(Doctor)*, Fiona Walkinshaw *(Manager)*, Marie Warner *(Manager)*, Angela Yates *(Chairman)*
**Admin:** Maureen Fortier *(Medical Secretary)*, Caroline Pooley *(Personal Assistant)*, Sue Stephens *(Personal Assistant)*, Tracy Stevenson *(Administrator)*
**IT:** Jason Devarajah *(Network, Security Manager)*

**HR:** Matt Guilfoyle *(Workforce and ESR Manager)*
**Operations:** Priti Bhatt *(Production and Operations Mana)*, Robert Hodgkiss *(Acting COO)*
**Purchasing:** Marie Courtney *(Transport Manager)*
**Fleet:** Marie Courtney *(Transport Manager)*
**Branches:** The Royal Marsden Hospital Nhs Foundation Trust, North West London Medical Centre, 56 Maida Vale, London W9 1PP
**US SIC:** 8062, 9121
**UK SIC:** 95100, 91110
**Auditors:** Deloitte LLP
**Bankers:** The Royal Bank Of Scotland Plc (16-00-84)

| | 31-03-14 | 31-03-13 | 31-03-12 |
|---|---|---|---|
| TO | 365,972,000 | 345,918,000 | 301,555,000 |
| P/L | 6,230,000 | 13,043,000 | 13,638,000 |
| NW | 341,822,000 | 332,872,000 | 320,621,000 |
| WC | 13,713,000 | 18,949,000 | 13,395,000 |
| Emp. | 3,494 | 3,417 | 3,301 |

DUNS 22-576-7276 **Imp**

## The Royal Marsden Junior League of Friends

Fulham Road, London SW3 6JJ
**Tel:** 02073523875
**Web:** www.royalmarsden.nhs.uk
**Estd:** 2002
**Line of Business:** Hospitals
**Principals:** Mrs T Green Cbe *(Chairman)*, A Goldsman *(Financial)*, Miss C Palmer Cbe, R Mullally, R Turnor, Sir J Craven, C Clark, G Andrews
**Responsibilities**
**Senior:** Tessa Green CBE *(Chairman)*, Jacquie Gulbenkian *(Chairperson)*, David Probert *(Executive Director)*, Professor Rigby *(Non Executive Member)*
**Branches:** The Royal Marsden Junior League Of Friends, Royal Marsden Hospital, Downs Road, Sutton, Surrey SM2 5PT
**US SIC:** 7999 **UK SIC:** 97913
**Auditors:** Deloitte LLP
**Bankers:** HSBC Bank plc (40-06-15)

| | 31-03-14 | 31-03-13 | 31-03-12 |
|---|---|---|---|
| TO | 266,887,000 | 247,026,000 | 226,056,000 |
| P/L | 1,656,000 | (3,841,000) | 6,902,000 |
| NW | 228,046,000 | 217,234,000 | 221,646,000 |
| WC | 6,421,000 | (1,159,000) | 5,184,000 |
| Emp. | 3,882 | 3,771 | 3,720 |

DUNS 23-931-8728

## Royal Masonic Benevolent Institution

Freemasons Hall, 60 Great Queen Street, London WC2B 5AZ
**Tel:** 02075962400
**Web:** www.rmbi.org.uk
**Estd:** 1842
**Line of Business:** Committee managed organisations
**Principals:** C J Caine, Dr J Reuther, D R Innes, J Newman, W Shackell, D V Frics, M Ward, R Marks
**Responsibilities**
**Senior:** Edna Darko'sarkwa *(Proprietor)*
**Branches:** Royal Masonic Benevolent Institution, 106-128 Alumhurst Road, Bournemouth, Dorset BH4 8HU
**US SIC:** 8621 **UK SIC:** 96311
**Auditors:** Knox Cropper

| | 31-03-14 | 31-03-13 | 31-03-11 |
|---|---|---|---|
| TO | 40,250,000 | 37,849,000 | 38,087,000 |
| P/L | (17,000) | (1,949,000) | 22,000 |
| NW | 115,703,000 | 112,556,000 | 116,716,000 |
| WC | 8,702,000 | 7,788,000 | 12,017,000 |
| Emp. | 1,506 | 1,495 | 1,349 |

DUNS 28-899-7786

## The Royal Masonic School for Girls

Rickmansworth Park, Rickmansworth, Hertfordshire WD3 4HF
**Tel:** 01923-773168 **Fax:** 0192896729
**Web:** www.royalmasonic.herts.sch.uk
**Reg No:** 1339867 **Estd:** 1788 Private Company Limited By Guarantee
**Line of Business:** General secondary education
**Directors:** K R Surry, Dr M Woodcock, H K Emmerson, R J Smith, J E Gould, D R Ellis, J Clappison, D R Yeaman
**Co. Secretary:** Mrs Diana Robinson
**Responsibilities**
**Senior:** Charles Cadogan *(Manager)*, Keith Carmichael *(Manager)*, James Flecker *(Director)*, Abigail Gray *(Director)*, Bryan Jones *(Manager)*, Hilary Porter *(Director)*, Diana Rose *(Headmistress)*
**Marketing:** Gail Braiden *(Admissions Secretary)*
**Sales:** Gail Braiden *(Admissions Secretary)*
**IT:** Joy Heaven *(Bursar)*
**HR:** Joy Heaven *(Bursar)*, Diana Rose *(Headmistress)*
**Health & Safety:** Joy Heaven *(Bursar)*
**Facilities:** Joy Heaven *(Bursar)*
**Purchasing:** Joy Heaven *(Bursar)*
**US SIC:** 8211 **UK SIC:** 93200

**Auditors:** Thorne Lancaster Parker
**Bankers:** National Westminster Bank Plc (60-17-32)

| | 31-08-14 | 31-08-13 | 31-08-12 |
|---|---|---|---|
| TO | 13,803,815 | 12,952,447 | 12,317,017 |
| P/L | 393,212 | 311,046 | 386,559 |
| NW | 1,699,514 | 1,285,320 | 958,943 |
| WC | 2,556,519 | 2,109,462 | 1,557,616 |
| Emp. | 231 | 226 | 238 |

DUNS 28-841-6035

## Royal Mencap Society

Carr House, Lysander Close, York, North Yorkshire YO30 4XB
**Tel:** 01904690187
**Web:** www.mencap.org.uk
**Reg No:** 0550457 **Estd:** 1955 Private Company Limited By Guarantee
**Line of Business:** Charities and charitable organisations
**Trading Style:** Hale Lodge Residential Home, Adcare, Golden Lane Housing, Lufton Manor College
**Directors:** Ms L R Redford, Professor R P Hastings, G T Williams, Ms K S Hollier, Ms J K Brown, S A Jack, J Phillips, G A Venus
**Co. Secretary:** Ms Oonagh Smyth
**Responsibilities**
**Senior:** Geoffrey Alltimes *(Director)*, Pete Bickers *(Manager)*, Mark Goldring *(CEO)*
**Branches:** Royal Mencap Society, Halgabron, Long Meadow, Wirral, Merseyside CH60 8QQ
**US SIC:** 8321, 6732
**UK SIC:** 96111, 83100
**Auditors:** Deloitte & Touche LLP
**Bankers:** Barclays Bank Plc (20-36-47)

| | 31-03-14 | 31-03-13 | 31-03-12 |
|---|---|---|---|
| TO | 201,195,000 | 196,584,000 | 200,597,000 |
| P/L | 8,683,000 | (2,257,000) | 10,566,000 |
| NW | 49,761,000 | 42,196,000 | 52,092,000 |
| WC | 17,008,000 | 11,022,000 | (3,305,000) |
| Emp. | 8,287 | 30 | 5,762 |

DUNS 36-794-7520

## Royal Mid-Surrey Golf Club

Twickenham Road Old Deer Park, Richmond, Surrey TW9 2SB
**Tel:** 020-8940-1894
**Web:** www.rmsgc.co.uk
**Estd:** 1900
**Line of Business:** Golf clubs
**Responsibilities**
**Senior:** Graham Dorward *(Finance Director)*
**Finance:** Graham Dorward *(Finance Director)*
**US SIC:** 7999 **UK SIC:** 97913
**Employees:** 49

DUNS 23-224-8794

## Royal Midland Home for the Physically Disabled

Castel Froma, 93 Lillington Road, Leamington Spa, Warwickshire CV32 6LL
**Tel:** 01926-427216
**Web:** www.castelfroma.co.uk
**Estd:** 1900
**Line of Business:** Charity involved in running a nursing home
**Trading Style:** Castelfroma
**US SIC:** 7231, 8091
**UK SIC:** 98200, 95200
**Employees:** 104

DUNS 21-812-0478

## Royal Military Police Ta

T A Centre, Norton Road, Stockton-On-Tees, Cleveland TS20 2QW
**Tel:** 01642366695
**Web:** www.armynet.com
**Estd:** 1946
**Line of Business:** Defence activities
**Responsibilities**
**Senior:** Alan Cavanagh *(Manager)*
**US SIC:** 8999 **UK SIC:** 83954
**Employees:** 108

DUNS 22-777-7463 **Imp-Exp**

## The Royal Mint

Llantrisant, Pontyclun, Mid Glamorgan CF72 8YT
**Tel:** 01443222111
**Web:** www.royalmint.com
**Estd:** 1811 Incorporate By Act Of Parliament
**Line of Business:** Collectors items
**Export Markets:** Worldwide
**Trading Style:** The British Royal Mint
**Directors:** C Boyle, R R Burchill, K Cottrell, R L De Holmes, Ms G Burg, L Haddon, S Taylor
**Co. Secretary:** Miss L Viner
**Responsibilities**
**Senior:** Gemma Archibald *(Client Services Manager)*, Anthony Sealey *(Stores Manager)*, Roger de Holmes *(Chief Executive)*
**IT:** Tina Oakes *(Head of IT)*
**Facilities:** Trevor Graham *(Facilities Manager)*
**Operations:** Shane Bissett *(Director of Commemorative Coin)*
**Fleet:** Anthony Sealey *(Stores Manager)*
**Branches:** The Royal Mint, 7 Grosvenor Gardens, London SW1W 0BD
**US SIC:** 3499, 3469, 5094
**UK SIC:** 31694, 31200, 61900
**Bankers:** Bank Of England (10-00-00)
**Employees:** 892

DUNS 21-172-2976

## The Royal Mint Ltd

Po Box 500, Pontyclun, Mid Glamorgan CF72 8WP
**Tel:** 08456088300 **Fax:** 01443-623-326
**Web:** www.royalmint.com
**Reg No:** 6964873 **VAT No:** 980738876
**Estd:** 2009 Private Limited Company
**Line of Business:** Striking of coins
**Export Sales:** £188,573,000
**Issued Capital:** £6,000,001
**Directors:** T C Martin, Mrs X M Fletcher, V S Wijeratne, P T Warry, D W Morgan, A T Lawrence
**Co. Secretary:** Ms Anne Jessopp
**Responsibilities**
**Senior:** Colin Balmer *(Manager)*, Mary Pears *(Manager)*
**US SIC:** 3911 **UK SIC:** 49101
**Auditors:** PricewaterhouseCoopers LLP

| | 31-03-14 | 31-03-13 | 31-03-12 |
|---|---|---|---|
| TO | 314,872,000 | 254,123,000 | 313,878,000 |
| P/L | 5,669,000 | (2,243,000) | 8,064,000 |
| NW | 53,379,000 | 54,661,000 | 64,472,000 |
| WC | 8,996,000 | 8,009,000 | 17,503,000 |
| Emp. | 801 | 861 | 915 |

DUNS 76-931-9583

## The Royal National College for the Blind

College Road, Hereford, Herefordshire HR1 1EB
**Tel:** 01432265725 **Fax:** 01432-376628
**Web:** www.rnc.ac.uk
**Reg No:** 2367626 **VAT No:** 337851534
**Estd:** 1989 Private Limited Company
**Line of Business:** Further education schools and colleges
**Trading Style:** R N C B
**Issued Capital:** £2
**Directors:** P Hatfield, C Vince, J H Bretherton, P Dean, Professor T J Thompson, C West, R P Mclellan, M J Edwards
**Co. Secretary:** Peter O'Keefe
**Responsibilities**
**Senior:** Albert Cooper *(Manager)*, Gillian Curtis *(Manager)*, Judith Harris *(Manager)*, Tracey Lancaster *(Director)*, Sheila Tallon *(Principal)*
**US SIC:** 8211, 8249, 7999
**UK SIC:** 93200, 93300, 97913
**Auditors:** Whittingham Riddell
**Bankers:** Barclays Bank Plc (20-39-64)

| | 31-07-13 | 31-07-12 | 31-07-11 |
|---|---|---|---|
| TO | 7,027,000 | 7,122,000 | 8,014,000 |
| P/L | (184,000) | (1,488,000) | (716,000) |
| NW | 13,120,000 | 12,750,000 | 16,489,000 |
| WC | (6,513,000) | (6,478,000) | (1,897,000) |
| Emp. | 160 | 197 | 198 |

DUNS 23-215-4435

## The Royal National Hospital for Rheumatoid Arthritis

Upper Borough Walls, Bath, Avon BA1 1RL
**Tel:** 01225-465941
**Web:** www.rnhrd.nhs.uk
**Estd:** 1993 Incorporate By Act Of Parliament
**Line of Business:** Other human health activities
**Principals:** J Thring *(Chairman)*, C Quinnell
**Responsibilities**
**Senior:** Kirsty Matthews *(Chief Executive)*
**Marketing:** Emma Mooney *(Marketing Manager)*
**IT:** Jackie Vincent *(Computer Manager)*
**HR:** Karen Kerley *(Personnel Manager)*, Marianne Spaans *(Personnel Manager)*
**Health & Safety:** Simon Evanson *(Health & Safety Officer)*
**US SIC:** 8091, 6732
**UK SIC:** 95200, 83100
**Employees:** 400

DUNS 22-716-6212 **Imp**

## The Royal National Institute for Deaf People

19-23 Featherstone Street, London EC1Y 8SL
**Tel:** 08088080123
**Web:** www.theloop.com
**Reg No:** 0454169 **Estd:** 1911 Private Company Limited By Guarantee
**Line of Business:** Retail sale via mail order house
**Trading Style:** Action of Hearing Loss
**Directors:** R J Jones, Professor A Q Summerfield, E Roux, S G Hill, R G Turner, W J Griffiths, P Clarke, C P Boland
**Co. Secretary:** Peter Robson
**Responsibilities**
**Senior:** Caroline Ashley *(Director)*, Jackie Ballard *(CEO)*, Harry Mcquillan *(Director)*, Janine Roebuck *(Director)*, Elizabeth Tait *(Director)*
**Branches:** The Royal National Institute For Deaf People, Crowngate Business Centre, 115-127 Brook St, Glasgow, Lanarkshire G40 3AP
**US SIC:** 5961, 7399, 8321
**UK SIC:** 65600, 83954, 96111
**Auditors:** Horwath Clark Whitehill LLP
**Bankers:** National Westminster Bank Plc (56-00-31)

| | 31-03-14 | 31-03-13 | 31-03-12 |
|---|---|---|---|
| TO | 47,090,000 | 37,426,000 | 37,533,000 |
| P/L | 8,265,000 | (853,000) | (2,073,000) |
| NW | 12,020,000 | 5,164,000 | 7,281,000 |
| WC | 15,933,000 | 3,913,000 | 5,073,000 |
| Emp. | 802 | 890 | 862 |

DUNS 22-723-0166

## Royal National Institute of Blind People

105 Judd Street, London WC1H 9NE
**Tel:** 02073881266
**Web:** www.rnib.org.uk
**Reg No:** 0000500RC **Estd:** 2012 Incorporate By Act Of Parliament
**Line of Business:** Social work activities
**Trading Style:** Rnib
**Principals:** K Carey *(Chairman)*, M Nussbaum *(Chairman)*, K Reid *(Chairman)*, T Rucinski *(Chairman)*, D Child, Ms E Southwood, T Moody, V Hjardeng
**Responsibilities**
**Senior:** Steven Alra *(Executive)*, Alice Armitage *(Member)*, Paul Barrowman *(Executive)*, Tony Bebbington *(Executive)*, Carol Borowski *(Owner)*, Rita Carden *(Executive)*, Simon Cavendish *(Member)*, Rory Cobb *(National Development Officer)*, John Dickinson-Lilley *(Executive)*, Katherin Ekstrom *(Manager)*, Eleanor Ellison *(Executive)*, Rosemary Frazer *(Senior Manager)*, Neil Heslop *(Group Director-RNIB Solutions)*, Lauren Kelly *(Executive)*, Donna Ledwidge *(Senior Manager)*, Tom Lewis-Reynier *(Manager)*, Shane Logan *(Board Member)*, Alison Long *(Senior Manager)*, Sarah Lupson *(Office Manager)*, Miriam Martin *(Group Director- Chief Executiv)*, Mark Masons *(Executive)*, Jonathan Mcinerny *(Manager)*, Richard Mckay *(Owner)*, Anne Mclean *(Board Member)*, Claire Milton *(Executive)*, Rachel Murphy *(Manager)*, Regina Reagan *(Executive)*, Sarah Rebus *(Member)*, Michele Richardson *(Senior Manager)*, James Risdon *(Executive)*, Catrin Roberts *(Executive)*, Jeannie Robertson *(Executive)*, Sarah Rochira *(Board Member)*, Archie Roy *(Executive)*, Dan Scorer *(Executive)*, Rachel Setchell *(Executive)*, Donna Smillie *(Executive)*, Anne Spinali *(Executive)*, Robin Spinks *(Manager)*, Andy Stowe *(Member)*, Alan Suttie *(Manager)*, Chris Tattersall *(Member)*, Mike Townsend *(Manager)*, Iris Vision *(Partner)*, Tony Warren *(Principal)*, Andy White *(Senior Manager)*
**Finance:** Wanda Hamilton *(Group Director - Fundraising)*, Keith Hickey *(Financial Director)*, Nigel Matt *(?Systems Accountant)*, Beth Picton *(Finance Manager)*, Neil Surridge *(Fundraising Insight Analyst)*
**Marketing:** Bill Alker *(Press Officer)*, Fiona Blakemore *(Head of Publishing and Interna)*, Louise Brown *(Relations Manager)*, Fiona Burles *(Director, Marketing and Commun)*, Rory Cobb *(National Development Officer)*, Sharon Cobley *(Telemarketing Manager)*, Mary Cox *(Librarian & Information Office)*, Angela Fuggle *(Marketing Director)*, Liz Gutteridge *(Marketing Director)*, Wanda Hamilton *(Group Director - Fundraising)*, Ann Henson *(Senior Manager)*, Leigh Iliffe *(Marketing Director)*, Julie Jennings *(Early Years Development Office)*, Gordon Matheson *(Press Manager)*, Leen Petre *(Principal Manager Media and Cu)*, Verity Pillenger Cork *(Senior Digital Manager)*, Thomas Quigley *(Comunications/PR Officer)*, Mikey Robinson *(Digital Marketing Manager)*, Ciara Smyth *(Spokesperson)*, Natalie Westwood *(Editor)*, John Whytock *(Product Manager)*, Sharon Wilding *(Marketing Manager)*
**Sales:** Nicky Fleming *(Business Development Officer)*, Tony Lee *(Business Development Manager)*, Tracy Riddell *(Business Development Manager)*
**Admin:** Lorena Carrasco *(Administrator)*, Karen Edwards *(Administrator)*, Hannah Evans *(Personal Assistant)*, Louise Hallsworth *(Personal Assistant)*, Sarah Lupson *(Office Manager)*, Gillian Mcgregor *(Administrator)*, Fran Mcsweeney *(Head of Information)*, Louise Neeson *(Administrator - Resource)*

**IT:** Barry Goold *(Manager, Information Systems a)*, Fran Mcsweeney *(Head of Information)*
**HR:** Maureen Biss *(Head of Personnel)*, David Carrington-Porter *(Training Director)*, Jacqui Hemming *(Executive)*, Shane McEwan *(Training Manager)*, Maureen Mcmahon *(Human Resources Manager)*, Sean Owen *(Employment Services Manager)*, Jonathan Rgibbin *(HR Executive)*, John Sole *(HR Executive)*, Madeleine Spears *(HR Executive)*
**Health & Safety:** Joe Rodriguez *(Health & Safety Advisor)*
**Facilities:** Sarah-Jane Casey *(Facilities Manager)*, Jeff Cochrane *(Facilities Manager)*
**Operations:** Helen Dearman *(Campaigns Officer)*, Deborah Hamlin *(Manager)*, Keith Hickey *(Financial Director)*, Joe Rodriguez *(Health & Safety Advisor)*, Steve Winyard *(Head of Campaigns)*
**Purchasing:** Sarah Lupson *(Office Manager)*, Jim Roberts *(Procurement Officer)*
**Engineering:** Colin Garnham *(Executive)*
**Branches:** Royal National Institute Of Blind People, 22 Park Road, Solihull, West Midlands B91 3SU
**US SIC:** 7399, 8299
**UK SIC:** 83954, 93300
**Auditors:** PricewaterhouseCoopers LLP
**Bankers:** The Royal Bank Of Scotland Plc (16-00-63)

| | 31-03-14 | 31-03-13 | 31-03-11 |
|---|---|---|---|
| TO | 118,647,000 | 117,023,000 | 116,311,000 |
| P/L | (1,957,000) | 590,000 | (3,470,000) |
| NW | 106,334,000 | 107,163,000 | 104,771,000 |
| WC | 12,271,000 | 9,901,000 | 11,370,000 |
| Emp. | 2,490 | 2,406 | 2,804 |

DUNS 22-550-4687

## Royal National Lifeboat Institution

1 West Quay Road, Poole, Dorset BH15 1JD
**Web:** www.rnli.org.uk
**Reg No:** 0000503RC **Estd:** 1984 Incorporate By Act Of Parliament
**Line of Business:** Lifeboat stations
**Trading Style:** R N L I
**Principals:** M Vernon *(Chairman)*, T Of Kent, K Lord, G Hale, Sir A Hezlet, Ms P C Denham, P Colville, Sir J Grandy
**Responsibilities**
**Senior:** F Baskerville *(Vice President)*, Paul Boissier *(Chief Executive)*, Peter Compston *(Vice President)*, Her Elizabeth The Queen Mother *(Principal)*, Matt Horton *(Executive)*, Charles Hunter-Pease *(Chairman)*, Rebecca Mccarthy *(Manager)*, Her Queen Elizabeth II *(Principal)*, Linda Rodgers *(Board Member)*, Roy Teggarty *(Manager)*, The of Kent *(Principal)*
**Finance:** Anna Classon *(Fundraising and Communications)*, Mark Hallam *(Finance and Information System)*, Dave Nicoll *(Area Fundraising Manager)*, Alan Pardon *(Finance Director)*
**Marketing:** Tim Ash *(Public Relations Manager)*, Anna Classon *(Fundraising and Communications)*, John Lerossignol *(Learning Resources Director)*, Alison Levett *(PR Manager)*, James Oxley *(Press Officer)*, Joanna Quinn *(Public Relations Officer)*, Hannah Randall *(Marketing Assistant)*, Pamela Saunders *(PR Manager)*, Dan Sumner *(Website Developer)*, James Vaughan *(Fundraising and Communications)*, Katie Wilton *(Internal Communications Office)*
**Sales:** Angela Rook *(Business Support & Development)*
**HR:** Heidi Allen *(Director of People)*, John Lerossignol *(Learning Resources Director)*
**Health & Safety:** Frankie Horne *(Senior Health and Safety Manag)*, Tony Wafer *(Coastal Safety Manager)*, Steve Wills *(Health and Safety Manager)*
**Operations:** James Ellerton *(Production Manager)*, George Rawlinson *(Operations Director)*, Michael Vlasto *(Operations Director)*
**Fleet:** David Tidman *(Transport Manager)*
**Engineering:** Neil Chaplin *(Principal Naval Architect)*, John Deas *(Senior Engineer)*, Holly Phillips *(Senior Naval Architect)*, Angus Watson *(Head of Construction & Mainten)*
**Branches:** Royal National Lifeboat Institution, 6 Strand, Teignmouth, Devon TQ14 8BW
**US SIC:** 6732 **UK SIC:** 83100
**Auditors:** Horwath Clark Whitehill LLP
**Bankers:** Coutts & Co (18-00-02)
**Employees:** 2,000
**Turnover:** £167,400,000

DUNS 23-505-4848

## The Royal National Mission to Deep Sea Fishermen

4400 Parkway, Fareham, Hampshire PO15 7FJ
**Tel:** 01489-566910
**Web:** www.fishermensmission.org
**Reg No:** 0024477 **VAT No:** 232640589
**Estd:** 1881 Private Company Limited By Guarantee
**Line of Business:** Charities and charitable organisations
**Trading Style:** Fishermen's Mission
**Directors:** Rear Admiral J S Lang, D W Lacy, I Gatt, J M De Halpert, D Young, Professor G M Tonge, J F Parker, Ms L Woodhatch
**Co. Secretary:** David Dickens
**Responsibilities**
**Senior:** Dan Conley *(Chief Executive)*, Simon Golding *(Director)*, Jill Henderson *(Director)*, James Portus *(Director)*, Kenneth Vlasto *(Director)*
**Branches:** The Royal National Mission To Deep Sea Fishermen, 196 Market Street, Aberdeen, Aberdeenshire AB11 5PQ
**US SIC:** 8321 **UK SIC:** 96111
**Auditors:** Mazars LLP
**Bankers:** Lloyds TSB Bank plc (30-95-74)

| | 31-10-13 | 31-10-12 | 31-10-11 |
|---|---|---|---|
| TO | 2,901,613 | 2,723,354 | 3,040,986 |
| P/L | 427,910 | 221,063 | 241,552 |
| NW | 9,091,848 | 7,586,492 | 8,196,180 |
| WC | 1,194,218 | 974,686 | 338,487 |
| Emp. | 53 | 64 | 64 |

DUNS 23-302-6603 **Imp**

## Royal National Orthopaedic Hospital

Brockley Hill, Stanmore, Middlesex HA7 4LP
**Tel:** 020-8954-2300
**Web:** www.rnoh.nhs.uk
**Reg No:** 0000504RC **Estd:** 1900
**Line of Business:** Hospitals
**Trading Style:** R N O H
**Principals:** A Koray *(Financial)*, M Vaughan *(Personnel)*, M Masters, Ms S Puckett, S Patel, C Sheldon, R Hurd, P Briggs
**Responsibilities**
**Senior:** Guy Billington *(Non-Executive Director)*, Helen Farrow *(Non-Executive Director)*, Rob Heard *(Manager)*, Suzy Hudson *(Executive)*, Benjamin Jacobs *(Board Member)*, Rachel Mandel *(Executive)*, Caroline Mckenna *(General Manager)*, Laurence Milsted *(Non Executive Member)*, Helen Nafis *(Executive)*, Edwina Neumann *(Executive)*, Prof Shorvon *(Non-Executive Director)*, Nikki Thorpe *(Executive)*, Laurent Wong *(Supplies Manager)*
**Marketing:** Anna Fox *(Communications Manager)*
**Admin:** Jane Batts *(Administrator)*, Siobhan Christian *(Secretary/Personal Assistant)*, Liane Levens *(Events Administrator)*, Kirti Popat *(Administrator)*
**IT:** Gemma Cannon *(IT Manager)*, Iva Hauptmannova *(Research and Development Manag)*, Karen Holmes *(IT Manager)*, Sabu Nair *(Network Manager)*, Colin Waller *(IT Manager)*
**HR:** John Masterson *(Human Resources Manager)*
**Health & Safety:** Sejel Sukhar *(Health & Safety Officer)*
**Operations:** Robin Maisey *(Capital Projects Manager)*
**Purchasing:** Laurent Wong *(Supplies Manager)*
**Branches:** Royal National Orthopaedic Hospital, 45 Bolsover Street, London W1W 5AQ
**US SIC:** 8062, 9121
**UK SIC:** 95100, 91110
**Employees:** 1,000

DUNS 23-505-6512 **Imp**

## The Royal National Theatre

Upper Ground, London SE1 9PX
**Tel:** 02074523333
**Web:** www.nationaltheatre.org.uk
**Reg No:** 0749504 **Estd:** 1963 Private Company Limited By Guarantee
**Line of Business:** Operation of arts facilities
**Trading Style:** National Theatre
**Directors:** Rt Hon J M Purnell, J C Makinson, D J Casserley, T N Clark, H J Davies, R N Macgregor, Mrs R M Haigh, Ms F Ramzan Golant
**Responsibilities**
**Senior:** Ursula Brennan *(Director)*, Susan Chinn *(Director)*, Glenn Earle *(Director)*, Aminatta Forna *(Director)*, Katharine Mosse *(Director)*, Clive Sherling *(Director)*
**Marketing:** Alex Bayley *(Director of Marketing)*, Michelle Kettner *(Marketing Officer)*, Lena Zimmer *(Digital Marketing Officer)*
**Sales:** Martin Prendergast *(Deputy Director of Development)*
**IT:** Lena Zimmer *(Digital Marketing Officer)*
**Branches:** The Royal National Theatre, 83-101 The Cut, London SE1 8LL
**US SIC:** 7911, 7922
**UK SIC:** 97913, 97412
**Auditors:** PricewaterhouseCoopers LLP
**Bankers:** Clydesdale Bank Plc (82-04-03)

| | 30-03-14 | 31-03-13 | 01-03-12 |
|---|---|---|---|
| TO | 124,100,000 | 97,600,000 | 86,500,000 |
| P/L | 20,700,000 | 6,000,000 | 9,700,000 |
| NW | 68,200,000 | 47,500,000 | 41,500,000 |
| WC | 14,600,000 | 14,400,000 | 19,900,000 |
| Emp. | 1,134 | 1,056 | 1,014 |

DUNS 50-706-3410

## Royal Naval Benevolent Trust

Castaway House, 311 Twyford Avenue, Portsmouth, Hampshire PO2 8RN
**Tel:** 02392690112
**Web:** www.rnbt.org.uk
**Estd:** 1942
**Line of Business:** Charities and charitable organisations
**Principals:** P H Swan *(President)*, J B Musters, J W Thompson
**Responsibilities**
**Senior:** Linda Frost *(Employment Consultant)*, Lyn Gannon *(Office Manager)*, Fabian Malbon *(president)*
**Admin:** Lyn Gannon *(Office Manager)*
**Branches:** Royal Naval Benevolent Trust, Pembroke House, 11 Oxford Road, Gillingham, Kent ME7 4BS
**US SIC:** 6732 **UK SIC:** 83100
**Auditors:** Horwath Clark Whitehill LLP
**Employees:** 10
**Turnover:** £4,629,534

DUNS 42-436-1145

## Royal Netherlands Embassy

38 Hyde Park Gate, London SW7 5DP
**Web:** www.unitedkingdom.nlembassy.org
**Estd:** 1957
**Line of Business:** Embassies
**Responsibilities**
**Senior:** Laetitia Assum *(Ambassador)*
**Branches:** Royal Netherlands Embassy, 3 Annandale Terr, Glasgow, Lanarkshire G60 5DJ
**US SIC:** 9121 **UK SIC:** 91110
**Employees:** 60

DUNS 21-360-8705

## Royal Northern Box Office

124 Oxford Road, Manchester M13 9RD
**Tel:** 01619075555
**Web:** www.rncm.ac.uk
**Estd:** 2004 Proprietorship
**Line of Business:** Schools of music
**Proprietor:** J Stockdale
**US SIC:** 8299 **UK SIC:** 93300
**Employees:** 500

DUNS 64-259-3362

## Royal Northern College of Music

124 Oxford Road, Manchester M13 9RD
**Tel:** 01619075300
**Web:** www.rncm.ac.uk
**VAT No:** 519615240 **Estd:** 2004
**Line of Business:** Further education schools and colleges
**Principals:** D Kent *(Financial)*, Professor E Gregson
**Responsibilities**
**Senior:** Geoffrey Reed *(Manager)*
**Finance:** Kerry Fairclough *(Student Finance Administrator)*, Julie Hardy *(Management Accountant)*, Jean Makins *(Finance Assistant)*
**Marketing:** Jennifer Hawkswell *(Marketing Assistant)*, Christine Henstock *(Development Manager)*, Roger Hildreth *(Marketing Officer)*, Rachael Howarth *(Digital Marketing & Communicat)*, Simon Oldknow *(Head of Marketing and Communic)*, Lisa Pring *(Marketing Manager)*, Liz Rowley *(PR and Media Relations Officer)*
**Admin:** Melissa Ellis *(Receptionist)*, Esther Wakeman *(Administrator)*, Lewis Woolcock *(Programmes Administrator)*
**Health & Safety:** Valerie Donovan *(Health & Safety Manager)*
**Facilities:** Neil Bohanna *(Maintenance Manager)*
**Operations:** Terence Ayebare *(Board Member)*, Matt Whitham *(Performance & Programming Admi)*
**Branches:** Royal Northern College Of Music, Alexandra Rd South, Manchester M16 8NH
**US SIC:** 8221 **UK SIC:** 93100
**Bankers:** The Royal Bank Of Scotland Plc (16-25-14)
**Employees:** 500

DUNS 21-570-4771

## Royal Oak Hotel

123 High Street, Great Ayton, Middlesbrough, Cleveland TS9 6BW
**Web:** www.royaloak-hotel.co.uk
**Estd:** 1980 Partnership
**Line of Business:** Public house
**Partner:** D Monaghan
**Responsibilities**
**Senior:** Simon Monaghan *(Proprietor)*
**US SIC:** 5813 **UK SIC:** 66200
**Employees:** 60

DUNS 28-871-5600

## Royal Oak Hotel (Betws-y-Coed) Ltd

Holyhead Road, Betws-Y-Coed, Gwynedd LL24 0AY
**Tel:** 01690710219
**Web:** www.royaloakhotel.net
**Reg No:** 1049407 **Estd:** 1968 Private Limited Company
**Line of Business:** Hotels
**Issued Capital:** £115
**Directors:** G H Evans, Miss S J Evans-Ward, J E Evans
**Co. Secretary:** Mrs Anna Evans
**Responsibilities**
**Senior:** Sian Hurmpherson *(Marketing Manager)*
**Marketing:** Sian Hurmpherson *(Marketing Manager)*, Katie Valentine *(Marketing Manager)*
**US SIC:** 7011 **UK SIC:** 66500
**Auditors:** Parker O'Regan Tann & Co
**Bankers:** HSBC Bank plc (40-10-11)

| | 31-01-14 | 31-01-13 | 31-01-12 |
|---|---|---|---|
| TO | 4,812,534 | 4,749,271 | 4,872,813 |
| P/L | 326,907 | 439,691 | 644,950 |
| NW | 4,319,657 | 4,187,976 | 3,951,653 |
| WC | (881,395) | (996,140) | (761,487) |
| Emp. | 140 | 124 | 120 |

DUNS 22-900-7406

## The Royal Observatory (Edinburgh) Trust

Royal Observatory, Blackford Hill, Edinburgh, Midlothian EH9 3HJ
**Tel:** 01316688100 **Fax:** 0131-668-8264
**Web:** www.roe.ac.uk
**Reg No:** 0069720SC **Estd:** 1979 Private Company Limited By Guarantee
**Line of Business:** Research and experimental development on natural sciences and engineering
**Principals:** E I Robson *(Managing)*, Professor G S Wright, T E O'Connor, Professor A Lawrence, I Murray, Professor J S Dunlop
**Co. Secretary:** Clive Davenhall
**Responsibilities**
**Senior:** Colin Cunningham *(Manager)*, Dan Hillier *(Manager)*, Adrian Townsend *(Manager)*
**IT:** Bryan Little *(Project Manager)*
**Operations:** Andy Longmore *(Production and Operations Mana)*
**Engineering:** Brian Stobie *(Engineer)*
**US SIC:** 7391, 8211
**UK SIC:** 94000, 93200
**Auditors:** KPMG
**Bankers:** Bank Of Scotland (80-02-77)

| | 05-10-13 | 05-10-12 | 05-10-11 |
|---|---|---|---|
| TO | N/A | N/A | 16 |
| P/L | (1,088) | (1,058) | (1,002) |
| NW | 27,184 | 28,272 | 29,320 |
| WC | 16,784 | 17,872 | 18,920 |

DUNS 22-950-1937 **Imp**

## Royal Opera House Covent Garden Foundation

Covent Garden, London WC2E 9DD
**Tel:** 02072129331 **Fax:** 02072129502
**Web:** www.roh.org.uk
**Reg No:** 0480523 **VAT No:** 769377565
**Estd:** 1974 Private Company Limited By Guarantee
**Line of Business:** Gift shops
**Directors:** L M Dorfman, Ms H V Rabbatts, Ms S Heywood, S C Robey, I R Taylor, M D Wyler, J Metherell, J Kingman
**Co. Secretary:** Ms Fiona Le Roy
**Responsibilities**
**Senior:** Genevieve Davies *(Director)*, Nicholas Hytner *(Director)*, Dr Mirza *(Director)*, Roland Rudd *(Director)*, Susan Street *(Director)*, Laura Wade-Gery *(Director)*
**Finance:** John Bernasko *(Financial Controller)*, Lindsey Glen *(Head of Strategic Funding)*, Mindy Kilby *(Director of Finance)*, Nicola Pirson *(Finance Administrator)*, Natalie Whyte *(Financial Controller)*
**Marketing:** Elizabeth Bell *(Head of Press and Communicatio)*, Jeff Coventry *(Head of Marketing (Enterprises)*, Dean Drury *(Commercial Manager)*, Kate Shaw *(Publications Manager)*, Ashley Woodfield *(Head of Ballet Press)*

**Sales:** Dean Drury *(Commercial Manager)*, Moya Maxwell *(Head of Commercial Programming)*, Amanda Saunders *(Director, Development)*
**IT:** Rob Greig *(Chief Technology Officer)*, Jason Oliver *(Head of Technology Operations)*, Jamie Tetlow *(Head of Digital Developmet)*
**HR:** Elizabeth Bridges *(Director of Personnel)*, Steven Foulston *(Human Resources Manager)*, Greg Jauncey *(Human Resources Manager)*
**Health & Safety:** Melanie Boucher *(Health and Safety Manager)*
**Engineering:** Stefano Pace *(Technical Director)*
**Branches:** Royal Opera House Covent Garden Foundation, Royal Opera House, Covent Garden, London WC2E 9DD
**US SIC:** 5399, 7911
**UK SIC:** 65600, 97913
**Auditors:** Grant Thornton UK LLP
**Bankers:** Coutts & Co (18-00-02)

| | 25-08-13 | 26-08-12 | 28-08-11 |
|---|---|---|---|
| TO | 111,933,000 | 109,793,000 | 112,074,000 |
| P/L | (2,414,000) | (1,536,000) | (2,478,000) |
| NW | 205,842,000 | 202,580,000 | 210,298,000 |
| WC | 17,704,000 | 16,204,000 | 7,806,000 |
| Emp. | 993 | 981 | 966 |

DUNS 28-995-4968
## Royal Ordnance (Crown Service) Pension Scheme Trustees Ltd
**(Subsidiary of:** Bae Systems Plc)
Central Avenue, Chorley, Lancashire PR7 6AD
**Tel:** 01772677200 **Fax:** 01257-260614
**Reg No:** 1842254 **Estd:** 1984 Private Limited Company
**Line of Business:** Compulsory social security activities
**Issued Capital:** £2
**Directors:** C C Mackenzie, M S Westcott, C J Kelly, M Copeland, C N Sparkes, B Halliwell, T F Eardley, M S Fullerton
**Co. Secretary:** Ms Marian Miller
**US SIC:** 6732 **UK SIC:** 83100

| | 31-12-13 | 31-12-12 | 31-12-11 |
|---|---|---|---|
| TA | 2 | 2 | 2 |
| NW | 2 | 2 | 2 |

DUNS 38-784-2974
## The Royal Orthopaedic Hospital Nhs Foundation Trust
Bristol Road South, Northfield, Birmingham, West Midlands B31 2AP
**Tel:** 0121-685-4000
**Web:** www.roh.nhs.uk
**Estd:** 2006
**Line of Business:** Hospitals
**Issued Capital:** £1
**Principals:** L James *(Chairman)*, S Bloomer *(Financial)*, Ms P Venables, P J Stevens, R Otto, L Jones, Ms E Hensel, C Monk
**Responsibilities**
**Senior:** Asterios Dramis *(Executive)*, Donal O'donoghue *(Chief Executive)*
**US SIC:** 8062 **UK SIC:** 95100
**Auditors:** Deloitte LLP

| | 31-03-14 | 31-03-13 | 31-03-12 |
|---|---|---|---|
| TO | 75,966,000 | 71,008,000 | 66,967,000 |
| P/L | (402,000) | 2,230,000 | 1,245,000 |
| NW | 57,520,000 | 57,673,000 | 55,326,000 |
| WC | 17,443,000 | 17,753,000 | 17,335,000 |
| Emp. | 923 | 894 | 872 |

DUNS 21-575-9101
## Royal Over-Seas League
Overseas House, London SW1A 1LR
**Tel:** 02074080214
**Web:** www.rosl.org.uk
**Reg No:** 0000511RC **VAT No:** 238827236
**Estd:** 1923
**Line of Business:** Clubs social and associations
**Trading Style:** Royal Overseas League
**Principals:** S Tayub *(Financial)*, R F Newell, R Lakin, Ms M Adrian-Vallance
**Responsibilities**
**Senior:** General Porter *(Director General)*, Roderick Porter *(Manager)*
**Marketing:** Eoghan O' Neill *(Marketing Director)*
**HR:** Tony Hanman *(Banqueting Manager)*
**Health & Safety:** Tony Hanman *(Banqueting Manager)*
**Branches:** Royal Over-Seas League, Overseas House, 100 Princes Street, Edinburgh, Midlothian EH2 3AB
**US SIC:** 8699 **UK SIC:** 96902
**Auditors:** Deloitte & Touche LLP
**Bankers:** Coutts & Co (18-00-02)
**Employees:** 130
**Turnover:** £3,319,988

DUNS 23-637-4922
## Royal Parks Agency
The Old Police House, Hyde Park, London W2 2UH
**Web:** www.royalparks.org.uk
**Estd:** 1993
**Line of Business:** Parks & gardens
**Trading Style:** Royal Parks Constabulary, Richmond Park, Brompton Emetary
**Director:** D Walsh
**Responsibilities**
**Senior:** Mark Camley *(Chief Executive)*, Linda Lenon *(Chief Executive)*, L Trenga *(Catering Manager)*
**Finance:** John Swainson *(Financial Manager)*
**Marketing:** Jason Dudley *(Sales & Marketing Manager)*
**Sales:** Jason Dudley *(Sales & Marketing Manager)*
**IT:** Angela Snowden *(IT Manager)*
**HR:** Teresa Marsh *(Personnel Manager)*
**Health & Safety:** Colin Buttery *(Parks Director)*
**Facilities:** Colin Buttery *(Parks Director)*
**Purchasing:** Mike Page *(Procurement Manager)*
**Branches:** Royal Parks Agency, Holly Lodge, Richmond Park, Richmond, Surrey TW10 5HS
**US SIC:** 8411, 7999
**UK SIC:** 97700, 97913
**Auditors:** T J Burr
**Employees:** 150

DUNS 22-706-6305 **Imp**
## Royal Pharmaceutical Society of Great Britain
1 Lambeth High Street, London SE1 7JN
**Tel:** 02077359141
**Web:** www.rpsgb.org
**Reg No:** 0000799RC **Estd:** 2002 Incorporate By Act Of Parliament
**Line of Business:** Trade assoc & regulatory bodies
**Trading Style:** Rpsgb
**Principals:** H R Patel *(President)*, P Green, L Braddick, D Pruce, Ms C O'Brien, Ms M Lavin, B Kelly, C Fry
**Responsibilities**
**Senior:** Seema Agha *(Designated Limited Liability P)*, Martin Ashbury *(President)*, Steve Churton *(President)*, Rob Darracott *(Manager Director)*, Howard Duff *(Director for England)*, John Jolley *(Manager)*, Alina Lourie *(Managing Director - Pharmaceut)*, Cath O'brien *(Director)*, Beverley Parkin *(Manager)*
**Finance:** Andrew Gush *(Treasurer)*
**Marketing:** Melissa Dear *(Campaigns and Corporate Commun)*, Elizabeth Gorrie *(Corporate Communications and D)*, Michelle Hyland *(PR Officer)*, Viola Lewis *(New Media and Corporate Commun)*, Sera Onofrei *(New Media and Corporate Commun)*, Neal Patel *(Head of Corporate Communicatio)*, Patrick Stubbs *(Director of Marketing and Memb)*
**Sales:** Catherine Duggan *(Director of Professional Devel)*, H Rai *(Sales Manager)*
**Admin:** Rebecca Braybrook *(Directorate Administrator)*, Yvonne Dennington *(Personal Assistant)*
**IT:** J Malinowski *(Computer Operations Manager)*
**HR:** Jenny Deere *(Senior HR Business Partner)*, Rebecca Mcdougall *(Human Resources Manager)*
**Purchasing:** Joyce Gibson *(Procurement Manager)*
**Branches:** Royal Pharmaceutical Society Of Great Britain, Customer Services, Wallingford, Oxfordshire OX10 8DG
**US SIC:** 8611, 2721
**UK SIC:** 96312, 47522
**Auditors:** Horwath Clark Whitehill LLP
**Bankers:** National Westminster Bank Plc (60-60-04)
**Employees:** 160
**Turnover:** £47,013,000

DUNS 22-430-4399
## Royal Pharmacy
57 High Town Road, Luton, Bedfordshire LU2 0BW
**Tel:** 01582-732312
**Estd:** 1947 Proprietorship
**Line of Business:** Dispensing chemists
**Proprietor:** N Shah
**Responsibilities**
**Finance:** Mina Shah *(Finance Director)*
**US SIC:** 5912 **UK SIC:** 64300
**Employees:** 96

DUNS 36-818-1350
## Royal Portrush Golf Club
Dunluce Road, Portrush, Co Antrim BT56 8JQ
**Tel:** 02870822311
**Web:** www.royalportrushgolfclub.com
**Estd:** 1888
**Line of Business:** Golf clubs
**US SIC:** 3949 **UK SIC:** 49420
**Employees:** 65

DUNS 21-590-2369
## Royal Robbins
16a Mill Street, Oakham, Leicestershire LE15 6EA
**Tel:** 01572771133
**Web:** www.royalrobbins.co.uk
**Estd:** 2011
**Line of Business:** Outdoor clothing and equipment
**US SIC:** 7999 **UK SIC:** 97913
**Employees:** 65

DUNS 21-137-6163 **Imp-Exp**
## Royal Sanders (Uk) Ltd
Red Scar Business Park, Preston, Lancashire PR2 5NA
**Tel:** 01772-662-400 **Fax:** 01772-662-402
**Web:** www.royalsanders.com
**Reg No:** 6703227 **Estd:** 1990 Private Limited Company
**Line of Business:** Beauty products
**Export Sales:** £2,500,000
**Issued Capital:** £16,885
**Directors:** D A Duggan, B O Hullegie, B C Barnes
**Responsibilities**
**Senior:** David Bannister *(Warehouse Manager)*, Paul Sellars *(Manager)*
**IT:** Stuart Lord *(IT Support Manager)*
**Facilities:** David Bannister *(Warehouse Manager)*
**Operations:** David Bannister *(Warehouse Manager)*
**US SIC:** 2844 **UK SIC:** 25820
**Auditors:** KPMG LLP
**Bankers:** Barclays Bank Plc (20-12-75)

| | 31-03-14 | 31-03-13 | 31-03-12 |
|---|---|---|---|
| TO | 13,411,000 | 21,307,000 | 16,164,000 |
| P/L | 210,000 | 1,056,000 | (932,000) |
| NW | 2,671,000 | 2,614,000 | 313,000 |
| WC | 1,383,000 | 2,208,000 | 159,000 |
| Emp. | 105 | 133 | 154 |

DUNS 42-345-8256
## The Royal School
Farnham Lane, Haslemere, Surrey GU27 1HQ
**Tel:** 01428605805
**Web:** www.royal-school.org
**Estd:** 2007
**Line of Business:** General secondary education
**Principals:** Mrs A Haddon-Cave *(Chairman)*, Sir J Dunt, A Day, Mrs L Taylor, Mrs S Stephenson, P F Allchurch, J Manley, C Chapman
**Responsibilities**
**Senior:** Lynne Taylor-Gooby *(Headmistress)*
**Marketing:** Kit Bithrey-George *(Marketing Manager)*
**Admin:** Sheila Sheehan *(Administrator)*
**IT:** Dean Hucklesby *(IT Manager)*
**Health & Safety:** Jackie Travis *(Domestic Bursar)*
**Branches:** The Royal School, Portsmouth Road, Hindhead, Surrey GU26 6BW
**US SIC:** 8211 **UK SIC:** 93200
**Auditors:** Menzies LLP
**Employees:** 3
**Turnover:** £5,789,237

DUNS 54-891-3359
## Royal School Armagh Ltd
College Hill, Armagh, Co Armagh BT61 9DH
**Tel:** 028-3752-2807 **Fax:** 028-3752-5014
**Web:** www.royalschoolarmagh.co.uk
**Reg No:** 0033458NI **Estd:** 1998 Private Limited Company
**Line of Business:** Schools (local authority)
**Issued Capital:** £2
**Co. Secretary:** Stephen Mcconnell
**Responsibilities**
**Senior:** Paul Crute *(principal)*
**US SIC:** 8211 **UK SIC:** 93200
**Bankers:** First Trust Bank (aib Group (uk) Plc) (93-81-65)

| | 31-03-14 | 31-03-13 | 31-03-12 |
|---|---|---|---|
| TA | 81,284 | 87,259 | 84,120 |
| NW | 1,561 | 1,718 | 1,947 |
| WC | 934 | 934 | 933 |

DUNS 23-251-4963
## Royal School Dungannon
2 Ranfurly Road, Dungannon, Co Tyrone BT71 6EG
**Tel:** 02887722710
**Web:** www.royaldungannon.com
**Line of Business:** Schools (independent)
**Responsibilities**
**IT:** Keith McGuinness *(Head of IT)*
**US SIC:** 8211 **UK SIC:** 93200
**Bankers:** Northern Bank Ltd (95-03-02)
**Employees:** 73

DUNS 23-082-8985
## The Royal School for the Blind
Church Road North, Liverpool, Merseyside L15 6TQ
**Tel:** 0151-733-1012
**Web:** www.rsblind.com
**Estd:** 1800
**Line of Business:** Schools (special)
**Trading Style:** Wavertree School for the Blind
**Director:** J Byrne
**Responsibilities**
**Senior:** Joseph Byrnes *(Head Teacher)*
**HR:** Clare Geraghty *(Deputy Head)*
**Health & Safety:** Clare Geraghty *(Deputy Head)*
**US SIC:** 8299 **UK SIC:** 93300
**Employees:** 97

DUNS 21-362-7349
## Royal School of Veterinary Studies
The University Of Edinburgh, Roslin, Midlothian EH25 9RG
**Tel:** 01316517300
**Web:** www.ed.ac.uk
**Estd:** 2006 Proprietorship
**Line of Business:** Veterinary activities
**Proprietor:** R Soutar
**US SIC:** 0741 **UK SIC:** 95601
**Employees:** 47

DUNS 28-821-7235
## Royal Scottish National Orchestra Society Ltd
73 Claremont Street, Glasgow, Lanarkshire G41 3LY
**Tel:** 0141 226 3868
**Web:** www.rsno.org.uk
**Reg No:** 0027809SC **VAT No:** 316344770
**Estd:** 1950 Private Company Limited By Guarantee
**Line of Business:** Musicians and orchestras
**Trading Style:** Royal Scottish National Orchestra
**Directors:** B A Lang, K J Leitch, Ms L J Rourke, M T Batho, J Clark, C R Van Der Kuyl, Ms N M Austin Hart, Ms A S Newton
**Co. Secretary:** Gordon Murray
**Responsibilities**
**Senior:** William Chandler *(Director)*, Keith Cochrane *(Director)*, Aileen Colleran *(Manager)*, Andrew Cornall *(Director)*, Ursula Heidecker Allen *(Director)*, David Hubbard *(Manager)*, Harriet Wilson *(Board Member)*, Katherine Wren *(Manager)*
**Finance:** Lynne Blevins *(Accounts and Office Manager)*, Keneth Osbourne *(Director of Finance and Corpor)*, Susan Rennie *(Finance Manager)*
**Marketing:** Manus Carey *(Executive Producer)*, Jane Donald *(Director of External Relations)*, Carol Fleming *(Head of Marketing)*, Daniel Pollitt *(Communications Manager)*
**Sales:** Mairi Foster *(Development Manager)*
**Operations:** Nick Lander *(Operations Director)*
**US SIC:** 7922 **UK SIC:** 97412
**Auditors:** Scott-Moncrieff
**Bankers:** The Royal Bank Of Scotland Plc (83-52-00)

| | 31-03-14 | 31-03-13 | 31-03-12 |
|---|---|---|---|
| TO | 7,056,690 | 7,474,840 | 7,620,928 |
| P/L | (396,735) | (44,758) | 711,977 |
| NW | 9,497,442 | 719,754 | 990,649 |
| WC | 2,294,976 | 1,199,792 | 881,210 |
| Emp. | 110 | 111 | 109 |

DUNS 22-702-6481
## The Royal Shakespeare Company
13 Waterside, Stratford Upon Avon, Stratford-Upon-Avon, Warwickshire CV37 6BA
**Tel:** 08448-001-110
**Web:** www.rsc.org.uk
**VAT No:** 272705851 **Estd:** 1991
**Line of Business:** Book retailers
**Principals:** H The Prince Of Wales *(President)*, Sir C Bland *(Chairman)*, G Harris, M Boyd, Ms N Dumezweni, M Foster, P Bate, D Burbidge

**Responsibilities**
**Senior:** Damon Buffini *(Director)*, Geoffrey Cass *(Vice President)*, Jane Drabble *(Director)*, Vikki Heywood *(Managing Director)*, McIntosh Hudnall *(Director)*, Paul Morrell *(Director)*, Louise Morris *(Manager)*, Tim Pigott-Smith *(Director)*, His The Prince of Wales *(President)*, Sainsbury Turville *(Vice Chairperson)*
**HR:** Adele Cope *(Head of Director)*
**Health & Safety:** Gail Miller *(Health & Safety Coordinator)*
**Purchasing:** Sarah Lovsey *(Retail Development Manager)*
**US SIC:** 7922 **UK SIC:** 97412
**Auditors:** Baker Tilly UK Audit LLP
**Bankers:** Barclays Bank Plc (20-59-42)
**Employees:** 500
**Turnover:** £46,716,000

DUNS 21-229-1951
## Royal Signals
Bolton Road, Windsor, Berkshire SL4 3JG
**Tel:** 01753-860600
**Web:** www.army.mod.uk
**Partnership**
**Line of Business:** Armed forces
**Partners:** J Knowles, P Samways, P Samway
**Responsibilities**
**Senior:** Justine Harris *(Manager)*
**US SIC:** 9711 **UK SIC:** 97412
**Employees:** 120

DUNS 28-845-3590
## The Royal Signals Trustee Ltd
Regimental H Q, The Royal School Of Signals, Blandford Camp, Blandford Forum, Dorset DT11 8RH
**Tel:** 01258459989
**Reg No:** 0622786 **Estd:** 1981 Private Limited Company
**Line of Business:** Ministry of defence site & training school
**Issued Capital:** £3
**Directors:** K J Bruce-Smith, G Norton, Ms S Nesmith, M G Taylor, R J Luke, T G Inshaw, J Cole, N F Wood
**Co. Secretary:** Colonel Terrance Canham
**Responsibilities**
**Senior:** Adam Forty *(General Manager)*
**Finance:** Colin Lee *(Budget Manager)*
**US SIC:** 8321 **UK SIC:** 96111

| | 31-12-13 | 31-12-12 | 31-12-11 |
|---|---|---|---|
| TA | 3 | 3 | 3 |
| NW | 3 | 3 | 3 |

DUNS 42-454-4526
## Royal Society
6-9 Carlton House Terrace, London SW1Y 5AG
**Tel:** 02074512500
**Web:** www.royalsociety.org
**Reg No:** 0000519RC **Estd:** 1981
**Line of Business:** Representative office
**Principals:** Lord R Of Ludlow *(President)*, D Dbe
**Responsibilities**
**Senior:** Dame DBE *(Vice President)*, Rachel Francis *(Executive)*, Paul MacDonald *(Manager)*, Julie Maxton *(Executive Director)*, Paul Nurse *(President)*, Sofia Pascu *(Executive)*, Carmel Toomes *(Senior Manager)*, Rees of Ludlow *(President)*
**Finance:** Anthony Cheetham *(Treasurer)*, Andy Hibbert *(Director of Finance and IT)*
**Marketing:** Peter Cotgreave *(Director, Fellowship and Scien)*, Catherine De Lange *(Press Officer)*, Helen Duriez *(ePublishing Manager)*, Bill Hartnett *(Head of Media and Public Relat)*, Katherine Jarrett *(Head of Science Communication)*, Nicola Kane *(Senior Press Officer)*, Charlotte Marling *(Corporate Communications Manag)*, Andrew Swailes *(Press Officer)*
**Admin:** John Pethica *(Physical Secretary)*, Martyn Poliakoff *(Foreign Secretary)*, Emma Tate *(Administrator)*
**Engineering:** Tony McBride *(Director, Science Policy Centr)*
**US SIC:** 8699, 8922
**UK SIC:** 96902, 94000
**Bankers:** Barclays Bank Plc (20-00-50)

| | 31-03-12 | 31-03-11 | 31-03-09 |
|---|---|---|---|
| TO | 70,838,000 | 72,863,000 | 80,374,000 |
| P/L | 2,620,000 | 1,471,000 | 17,155,000 |
| NW | 229,091,000 | 236,202,000 | 185,699,000 |
| WC | 356,000 | (5,766,000) | (626,000) |
| Emp. | 138 | 140 | 135 |

DUNS 21-795-5658
## Royal Society for Public Health
John Snow House, 59 Mansell Street, London E1 8AN
**Tel:** 02072657300
**Web:** www.rsph.org.uk
**Estd:** 2011 Proprietorship
**Line of Business:** Activities of other membership organisations not elsewhere classified
**Proprietor:** Professor R Parish
**Responsibilities**
**Senior:** Parthy Parthipan *(Manager)*
**US SIC:** 8699 **UK SIC:** 96902
**Employees:** 47

DUNS 23-592-5856
## The Royal Society for the Prevention of Accidents
353 Bristol Road, Birmingham, West Midlands B5 7SW
**Tel:** 01212-482-000
**Web:** www.rospa.com
**Reg No:** 0231435 **Estd:** 1928 Private Company Limited By Guarantee
**Line of Business:** Adult and other education not elsewhere classified
**Trading Style:** R O S P A, The Royal Society for the Prevention of Accidents
**Directors:** Dr D J Lloyd, Mrs J E Mcnulty, M D Hampson, P R Brown, Y Doyle, M D Parker, Mrs H Kondel, Dr M O'Mahony
**Co. Secretary:** Mark Penny
**Responsibilities**
**Senior:** Robert Bucknell *(Director)*, Thomas Mullarkey *(Chief Executive)*, Julian Redhead *(Director)*
**Marketing:** Frances Richardson *(Sales Manager)*
**Sales:** Frances Richardson *(Sales Manager)*
**HR:** Tracey Mansell *(Human Resources Manager)*, Denise Sandall *(Training Manager)*
**Health & Safety:** Anita Gouth *(Facilities Manager)*
**Facilities:** Anita Gouth *(Facilities Manager)*
**Purchasing:** Deborah Parslow *(Purchasing Manager)*
**Branches:** The Royal Society For The Prevention Of Accidents, 3 Abbey Rd, Durham, County Durham DH1 5DQ
**US SIC:** 8249, 8299
**UK SIC:** 93300
**Auditors:** BDO LLP

| | 31-03-14 | 31-03-13 | 31-03-12 |
|---|---|---|---|
| TO | 8,787,124 | 8,241,418 | 7,704,456 |
| P/L | 785 | 189,944 | 121,376 |
| NW | 165,541 | 44,935 | 701,831 |
| WC | 705,687 | 770,354 | 360,726 |
| Emp. | 104 | 102 | 103 |

DUNS 22-522-2447
## Royal Society for the Prevention of Cruelty to Animals
Wilberforce Way, Southwater, Horsham, West Sussex RH13 9RS
**Fax:** 03031230100
**Web:** www.rspca.org.uk
**VAT No:** 210702425 **Estd:** 1972 Incorporate By Act Of Parliament
**Line of Business:** Animal welfare and care organisations
**Trading Style:** Rspca
**Principals:** Mrs D Harris *(Chairman)*, M Tomlinson, Mrs M Baker, W Stubbs, T Bray
**Responsibilities**
**HR:** Brian Dalton *(Training Manager)*
**Facilities:** Ray Boxall *(Facilities Manager)*
**Branches:** Royal Society For The Prevention Of Cruelty To Animals, 16 St. Georges, Castle Douglas, Kirkcudbrightshire DG7 1LN
**US SIC:** 8699 **UK SIC:** 96902
**Auditors:** BDO Stoy Hayward LLP
**Bankers:** Coutts & Co (18-00-93)
**Employees:** 286
**Turnover:** £110,669,000

DUNS 22-639-1035 **Imp**
## Royal Society for the Protection of Birds
The Lodge, Potton Road, Sandy, Bedfordshire SG19 2DL
**Tel:** 01408634404
**Web:** www.rspb.org.uk
**Reg No:** 0000521RC **Estd:** 2002
**Line of Business:** Conservation organisations
**Trading Style:** Rspb
**Principals:** G Wynne *(Managing)*, A Sharpe *(Financial)*, Dr M Avery, S Housden, Mrs K Rothwell, A Gammell, Dr M Clarke, Ms A Harley
**Responsibilities**
**Senior:** Kevin Cox *(Manager)*, Kenny Graham *(Manager)*, Richard Thaxton *(Site Manager)*, Graeme Wallace *(Manager)*
**Marketing:** Gemma Butlin *(Consumer PR manager)*, Gemma Hogg *(Senior Media Officer)*, Henry Leyland *(Advertising Team Manager)*, Louise Savin *(Advertising Executive)*
**Admin:** Greatrex Lucy *(Personal Assistant)*
**IT:** Roger Summers *(Head of IT)*
**Branches:** Royal Society For The Protection Of Birds, Keble House, Southernhay Gardens, Exeter, Devon EX1 1NT
**US SIC:** 8321, 7391
**UK SIC:** 96111, 94000
**Auditors:** Crowe Clark Whitehill LLP
**Bankers:** The Co-Operative Bank Plc (08-90-28)

| | 31-03-14 | 31-03-13 | 31-03-12 |
|---|---|---|---|
| TO | 127,045,000 | 122,114,000 | 119,677,000 |
| P/L | 266,000 | 7,027,000 | 7,696,000 |
| NW | 117,829,000 | 113,093,000 | 126,182,000 |
| WC | 14,806,000 | 19,166,000 | 16,502,000 |
| Emp. | 2,217 | 2,151 | 2,110 |

DUNS 22-707-2329
## Royal Society of Chemistry
Burlington House, London W1J 0BA
**Tel:** 02074378656 **Fax:** 02074403393
**Web:** www.rsc.org
**Reg No:** 0000524RC **VAT No:** 342176471
**Estd:** 1841 Incorporate By Act Of Parliament
**Line of Business:** Information services
**Trading Style:** R S C Publishing
**Principals:** Dr R Parker *(Managing)*, W Beaumont *(Financial)*, Ms J Mitchell, Dr R Pike, Dr N Reed
**Responsibilities**
**Senior:** Colin Batchelor *(Senior Manager)*, Darren Holling *(Member)*, Dominic Tildesley *(President)*, Lesley Yellowlees *(President)*
**Marketing:** Brian Emsley *(Press Officer)*, Leanne Marle *(Commissioning Editor)*, Richard Porte *(Marketing Manager)*, Rebecca Quine *(Conference Development and Pro)*
**Admin:** Fiona Nalden *(Administrator)*
**IT:** Matthew Stiles *(Computer Manager)*
**Facilities:** Bob Shimmens *(Facilities Manager)*
**Branches:** Royal Society Of Chemistry, Blackhorse Rd, Letchworth, Hertfordshire SG6 1HN
**US SIC:** 8621, 2731
**UK SIC:** 96311, 47532
**Auditors:** Baker Tilly UK Audit LLP
**Bankers:** Coutts & Co (18-00-02)

| | 31-12-13 | 31-12-12 | 31-12-11 |
|---|---|---|---|
| TO | 51,602,000 | 49,126,000 | 45,102,000 |
| P/L | 10,127,000 | 6,696,000 | 5,003,000 |
| NW | 96,372,000 | 86,034,000 | 73,078,000 |
| WC | 5,752,000 | 3,719,000 | 5,400,000 |
| Emp. | 491 | 422 | 417 |

DUNS 34-876-7658
## Royal Society of Medicine Support Services Ltd
**(Subsidiary of:** Royal Society of Medicine)
1 Wimpole Street, London W1G 0AE
**Tel:** 02072902900
**Web:** www.1wimpolestreet.co.uk
**Reg No:** 2820374 **Estd:** 1993 Private Limited Company
**Line of Business:** Catering
**Issued Capital:** £1,000
**Directors:** I A Balmer, Professor D J Russell, M A Johnstone, Miss R Hargest, N Collett
**Co. Secretary:** Ms Felicity Nash
**Responsibilities**
**Senior:** Janice Liverseidge *(Director)*
**US SIC:** 5812 **UK SIC:** 66110
**Auditors:** Horwath Clark Whitehill
**Bankers:** Bank Of Scotland (12-11-03)

| | 30-09-13 | 30-09-12 | 30-09-11 |
|---|---|---|---|
| TO | 6,773,000 | 6,731,000 | 6,730,000 |
| P/L | 17,000 | 385,000 | 497,000 |
| NW | 278,000 | 351,000 | (34,000) |
| WC | 278,000 | 351,000 | (34,000) |
| Emp. | 227 | 230 | 223 |

DUNS 21-537-9665
## Royal St Georges Golf Club
Sandwich, Sandwich Bay, Sandwich, Kent CT13 9PB
**Tel:** 01304-613090
**Web:** www.royalstgeorges.com
**Estd:** 2002
**Line of Business:** Golf clubs
**Co. Secretary:** Christopher Cabbie
**Responsibilities**
**Senior:** Tim Checketts *(Manager)*
**IT:** Peter Fawcus *(Computer Manager)*
**US SIC:** 7999 **UK SIC:** 97913
**Employees:** 50

DUNS 21-225-5833
## Royal Standard
Leyfield Road, Liverpool, Merseyside L12 9EY
**Tel:** 0151-2209675
**Web:** www.thespiritgroup.com
**Estd:** 2005 Proprietorship
**Line of Business:** Managed public houses and bars
**Proprietor:** E Riley
**US SIC:** 5813 **UK SIC:** 66200
**Employees:** 50

DUNS 21-583-2383
## The Royal Star & Garter Home Solihull
Tudor Coppice, Solihull, West Midlands B91 3DE
**Tel:** 01217116330
**Web:** www.starandgarter.org
**Estd:** 2011 Proprietorship
**Line of Business:** Convalescent homes
**Proprietor:** Mrs S Tompkins
**US SIC:** 8321 **UK SIC:** 96111
**Employees:** 100

DUNS 22-504-6853
## The Royal Star & Garter Homes
Richmond Hill, Richmond, Surrey TW10 6RR
**Web:** www.starandgarter.org
**Reg No:** 0000713RC **Estd:** 1916
**Line of Business:** Other human health activities
**Trading Style:** Royal Star & Garter Home
**Presidents:** S Weston, D L Jacobs, Sir D Dobson, R U Thames, The Lord C O Radley, Princess H Alexandra, M O Solihull, Sir D Parry-Evans
**Responsibilities**
**Senior:** Princess Alexandra *(President)*, Mike Barter *(Chief Executive)*, John Stibbon *(Governor)*
**HR:** Siobhan Creighton *(Human Resources Manager)*
**US SIC:** 8091 **UK SIC:** 95200
**Auditors:** Horwath Clark Whitehill LLP
**Bankers:** National Westminster Bank Plc (60-17-31)

| | 31-12-12 | 31-12-11 | 31-12-10 |
|---|---|---|---|
| TO | 17,764,000 | 17,191,000 | 13,056,000 |
| P/L | 5,837,000 | 5,754,000 | 1,900,000 |
| NW | 67,123,000 | 60,436,000 | 55,823,000 |
| WC | 2,609,000 | 4,892,000 | (440,000) |
| Emp. | 231 | 230 | 224 |

DUNS 64-262-9968
## The Royal Station Hotel
Neville Street, Newcastle-Upon-Tyne, Tyne and Wear NE1 5DH
**Web:** www.royalstationhotel.com
**Estd:** 1991 Proprietorship
**Line of Business:** Hotels
**Proprietor:** A Hande
**Responsibilities**
**Senior:** Arran Hande *(Director)*, Michelle Harle *(General Manager)*
**Sales:** Michelle Harle *(General Manager)*
**HR:** Michelle Harle *(General Manager)*
**Health & Safety:** Michelle Harle *(General Manager)*, Chris Hunn *(Facilities Manager)*
**Facilities:** Chris Hunn *(Facilities Manager)*
**Branches:** The Royal Station Hotel, 10-18 Windsor Street, Edinburgh, Midlothian EH7 5JR
**US SIC:** 7011, 6531, 6519
**UK SIC:** 66500, 83400, 85000
**Employees:** 80

DUNS 28-839-8613
## Royal Surgical Aid Society
High Broom, Crowborough, East Sussex TN6 3SL
**Tel:** 01892611542
**Web:** www.agecare.org.uk
**Reg No:** 0515174 **Estd:** 1862 Private Company Limited By Guarantee
**Line of Business:** Social work activities with accommodation
**Trading Style:** Rsas Agecare
**Directors:** Ms M Spater, L R Marple, Mrs L E Bracken, Miss D A Woda, Dr A Burch, A M Lomax, Mrs E A Houlihan, Mrs C D Stevens
**Co. Secretary:** Mark Rogers
**Responsibilities**
**Senior:** Julie Fuller *(CEO)*, Hugh Risebrow *(Director)*
**Branches:** Royal Surgical Aid Society, Alice Bright La, Crowborough, East Sussex TN6 3SQ
**US SIC:** 8321 **UK SIC:** 96111
**Auditors:** Horwath Clark Whitehill LLP
**Bankers:** Barclays Bank Plc (20-32-29)

| | 30-09-13 | 30-09-12 | 30-09-11 |
|---|---|---|---|
| TO | 6,468,000 | 6,909,000 | 6,918,000 |
| P/L | (762,000) | (86,000) | 67,000 |
| NW | 7,833,000 | 8,464,000 | 8,450,000 |
| WC | 1,565,000 | 1,926,000 | 1,827,000 |
| Emp. | 290 | 315 | 306 |

DUNS 23-219-3532
## Royal Surrey County Hospital Nhs Foundation Trust
Royal Surrey County Hospital, Egerton Road, Guildford, Surrey GU2 7XX
**Tel:** 01483-571-122
**Web:** www.royalsurrey.nhs.uk
**Estd:** 1990
**Line of Business:** Foundation hospital
**Issued Capital:** £1

**Principals:** M Poole (Chairman), P Biddle (Financial), M Pantlin (Personnel), N Moberly, G Crouch, S Caswell, J Denning, Ms D Mckenzie
**Responsibilities**
**Senior:** Tony Harris (Non-Executive Director), Deborah McKenzie (Non-Executive Director)
**Health & Safety:** Nina Goodwin (Health & Safety Officer)
**Branches:** Royal Surrey County Hospital Nhs Foundation Trust, The Wheatsheaf, Chobham Road, Woking, Surrey GU21 4AL
**US SIC:** 8062, 8221
**UK SIC:** 95100, 93100
**Auditors:** KPMG LLP
**Bankers:** The Royal Bank Of Scotland Plc (16-20-30)

|  | 31-03-14 | 31-03-13 | 31-03-12 |
|---|---|---|---|
| TO | 245,865,000 | 257,441,000 | 218,359,000 |
| P/L | 2,758,000 | 2,659,000 | 3,582,000 |
| NW | 142,819,000 | 153,770,000 | 150,420,000 |
| WC | 11,527,000 | 10,409,000 | 8,141,000 |
| Emp. | 3,603 | 3,497 | 3,368 |

DUNS 23-055-9309
### Royal Terrace Hotel Leisure Club
18 Royal Terrace, Edinburgh, Midlothian EH7 5AQ
**Tel:** 0131-557-3222
**Web:** www.royalterracehotel.co.uk
**Estd:** 1988 Proprietorship
**Line of Business:** Hotels and motels without restaurant
**Proprietor:** Mrs C Quinn-Waugh
**US SIC:** 7011 **UK SIC:** 66500
**Employees:** 70

DUNS 21-663-4855
### The Royal Toby Hotel (Castleton) Ltd
(**Subsidiary of:** Deckers Hospitality Group Ltd)
The Royal Toby Hotel, Rochdale, Lancashire OL11 3HF
**Tel:** 01706861861
**Web:** www.thedeckergroup.com
**Reg No:** 7180111 **Estd:** 2010 Private Limited Company
**Line of Business:** Hotels
**Issued Capital:** £1
**Directors:** C Brierley, M J Brierley
**Co. Secretary:** Mrs Victoria Cosgrove
**Responsibilities**
**Senior:** Victoria Brierley (Manager)
**US SIC:** 7011, 5812
**UK SIC:** 66500, 66110
**Bankers:** Lloyds TSB Bank plc (30-95-42)

|  | 31-03-13 | 02-04-12 | 31-03-11 |
|---|---|---|---|
| TO | 2,683,442 | 2,698,165 | 2,663,131 |
| P/L | 204,025 | 259,564 | 134,682 |
| NW | 2,066,973 | 349,565 | 113,088 |
| WC | (3,616,324) | (3,863,328) | (4,206,188) |

DUNS 22-723-1818
### The Royal Town Planning Institute
41-42 Botolph Lane, London EC3R 8DL
**Tel:** 020-7929-9494
**Web:** www.rtpi.org.uk
**Reg No:** 0262865RC **VAT No:** 524318171
**Estd:** 1914
**Line of Business:** Town and city planning
**Trading Style:** Rtpi
**Principals:** M Wellbank (President), B Abbott, D Fryer
**Responsibilities**
**Senior:** Derek Bytheway (Manager), Neale Hall (Member), George Mcdonic (Manager)
**Marketing:** Suzanne Slack (Publisher)
**US SIC:** 8699, 8221
**UK SIC:** 96902, 93100
**Auditors:** Chantrey Vellacott DFK LLP
**Bankers:** HSBC Bank plc (40-03-15)
**Employees:** 50
**Turnover:** £6,671,000

DUNS 22-535-4976
### Royal United Kingdom Beneficent Association
6 Avonmore Road, London W14 8RL
**Tel:** 02076054200
**Web:** www.independentage.co.uk
**Reg No:** 0000530RC **Estd:** 1863
**Line of Business:** Charity organisation assisting the elderly and needy in the U K and Republic of Ireland.
**Principals:** of Abercorn (President), M Kench (Chairman), W S Wolft, W Rathbone, G A Whateley, N H Bibby, J R Ducker, Ms M E Martineau
**Responsibilities**
**Senior:** Archibald Birkmyre (Principal), Queen Elizabeth II (Principal), F Hervey Bathurst (Principal), T Jackson-Stops (Principal), Yehudi Menuhin (Vice President), N Whately (Vice President), Dean of Westminster (Vice President)

**IT:** Richard Ella (Training Manager)
**HR:** Richard Ella (Training Manager)
**Branches:** Royal United Kingdom Beneficent Association, Fernhill Road, Camberley, Surrey GU17 9HR
**US SIC:** 6732, 8361
**UK SIC:** 83100, 96112
**Auditors:** PricewaterhouseCoopers LLP
**Bankers:** National Westminster Bank Plc (60-80-08)

|  | 31-12-13 | 31-12-12 | 31-12-11 |
|---|---|---|---|
| TO | 8,168,000 | 9,443,000 | 14,669,000 |
| P/L | 2,215,000 | 1,543,000 | 5,321,000 |
| NW | 151,263,000 | 130,137,000 | 121,896,000 |
| WC | 10,084,000 | 12,070,000 | 5,617,000 |
| Emp. | 85 | 92 | 273 |

DUNS 42-440-0844      Imp
### The Royal Veterinary College
Royal College Street, London NW1 0TU
**Tel:** 02074-685-000
**Web:** www.rvc.ac.uk
**Reg No:** 0000532RC **VAT No:** 766414220
**Estd:** 2002
**Line of Business:** Schools (local authority)
**Trading Style:** Equine Referral Hospital, Rvc
**Directors:** L E Lanyon, A Smith
**Responsibilities**
**Senior:** Chris Lamb (Manager), C McKellar (Principal), Jane Tomlin (Assistant Director)
**Finance:** R Blennerhassett (Finance Manager), Jennifer Hydarl (Assistant Director of Finance), Sanjay Raikundalia (Senior Banking & Treasury Offi), Dimple Shah (Finance Officer)
**Marketing:** Paula Burton (Marketing Manager), Bevan McWilliam (Business Relationship Manager), Hannah Murray (Press Officer), Jackie Sharp (Marketing Assistant), Jack Sisterson (Web Editor / Designer)
**Sales:** Patricia Latter (Head of Business Development)
**Admin:** Kerry Adams (Receptionist), Pauline Ashley-Spike (PA to Director of HR), Debbie Avenell (PA to Chief Operating Officer), Izzy Hamer (Purchasing Administrator), Lisa Harber (Personal Assistant), Carol Lawson (Deputy Head of Research Admini)
**IT:** Rees Gates (Infrastructure Engineer), Arif Gulma (IT & Audio-Visual Support Anal), Sue Harrison (Project Manager (Data Manageme), David Maruta (IT Systems Engineer), Lakshyam Nanayakkara (IT & AV Technician), Nick Short (Head of eMedia Unit)
**HR:** Dominic Barfield (Senior Clinical Training Schol), Vikki Cannon (Head of Admissions and Recruit), Kerstin Erles (Senior Clinical Training Schol), Rosanne Jepson (Senior Clinical Training Schol), Hilary Orpet (Course Director), Matt Parkin (HR Adviser)
**Health & Safety:** Ian Constantine (Corporate Health and Safety Of)
**Operations:** Livia Benigni (Diagnostic Imaging Manager), Efstathios Giotis (Postdoctoral Fellow), Wenming Ji (Manager)
**Purchasing:** Penny Ireland (Business Contracts Manager), Minesh Shah (Head of Procurement)
**Branches:** The Royal Veterinary College, Royal Veterinary College, Hawkshead House, Hatfield, Hertfordshire AL9 7TA
**US SIC:** 8221, 0741
**UK SIC:** 93100, 95601
**Auditors:** Deloitte LLP
**Bankers:** The Royal Bank Of Scotland Plc (16-08-05)
**Employees:** 400
**Turnover:** £65,832,000

DUNS 23-291-1099
### Royal Victoria Hospital
274 Grosvenor Road, Belfast BT12 6BA
**Tel:** 02890240503
**Web:** www.royalhospitals.org
**Estd:** 1798
**Line of Business:** Hospitals
**Trading Style:** The Royal Hospital, Royal Maternity Hospital, Royal School of Dentristry
**Directors:** G Carson, Prof G Love, Mrs D O'Brien, H Mccaughey, Dr P Mcwilliams, Ms C Burns, Miss M Mallon, N Bennett
**Responsibilities**
**Senior:** Evan Bates (Director), William McKee (Chief Executive), Deirdre O' Brien (Director)
**Finance:** Martin Dillon (Financial Director), Wendy Gailbraith (Financial Manager)
**IT:** Paul Duffy (IT Manager)
**Branches:** Royal Victoria Hospital, 704 Shore Road, Belfast, Belfast BT15 4HU
**US SIC:** 8021 **UK SIC:** 95400
**Bankers:** Northern Bank Ltd (95-00-05)
**Employees:** 6,000

DUNS 23-035-8850
### Royal Victoria Hotel
Marina St Leonards On Sea, St Leonards-On-Sea, East Sussex TN38 0BD
**Tel:** 01424-445544
**Web:** www.bestwestern.co.uk
**Estd:** 2002 Proprietorship
**Line of Business:** Hotels
**Proprietor:** W Shin
**Responsibilities**
**Senior:** Ian Crow (General Manager), Wooseung Shin (Proprietor)
**Finance:** Wooseung Shin (Proprietor)
**Marketing:** Lucie Hide (Sales Manager)
**Sales:** Lucie Hide (Sales Manager)
**IT:** Wooseung Shin (Proprietor)
**HR:** Wooseung Shin (Proprietor)
**Health & Safety:** Wooseung Shin (Proprietor)
**Facilities:** Wooseung Shin (Proprietor)
**Purchasing:** Aaron Bryan (Operations Manager)
**US SIC:** 7011 **UK SIC:** 66500
**Employees:** 50

DUNS 50-638-2832
### The Royal Victoria Hotel
Llanberis, Caernarfon, Gwynedd LL55 4TY
**Tel:** 01286-870253
**Web:** www.theroyalvictoria.co.uk
**Estd:** 2002 Proprietorship
**Line of Business:** Hotels
**Proprietor:** R Ibbott
**Responsibilities**
**Senior:** Pete Hazlehurst (Head Chef), Tracey Salisbury (General Manager)
**Facilities:** Dennis Hughes (Maintenance Manager)
**Operations:** Tracey Salisbury (General Manager)
**Purchasing:** Pete Hazlehurst (Head Chef)
**US SIC:** 7011 **UK SIC:** 66500
**Employees:** 60

DUNS 50-572-4690
### Royal Voluntary Service
Beck Court, Pontprennau, Cardiff, South Glamorgan CF23 8RP
**Tel:** 02920739000 **Fax:** 01235-861166
**Web:** www.royalvoluntaryservice.org.uk
**Reg No:** 2520413 **Estd:** 2011 Private Company Limited By Guarantee
**Line of Business:** Activities of other membership organisations not elsewhere classified
**Directors:** W M Shannon, Ms S A Fox, M F Smith, R C Greenhalgh, Mrs E Burnley, Sir P M Williams, Miss R H Brook, T Jones
**Co. Secretary:** Ms Catherine Nightingale
**Responsibilities**
**Senior:** Alexis Jay (Director), Fiona Joyce (Director), David Mccullough (Chief Executive)
**Branches:** Royal Voluntary Service, 3 Edison Village, Nottingham Science & Technology Park, Nottingham, Nottinghamshire NG7 2RF
**US SIC:** 7399 **UK SIC:** 83954
**Auditors:** Baker Tilly UK Audit LLP
**Bankers:** The Royal Bank Of Scotland Plc (83-06-08)

|  | 30-03-14 | 31-03-13 | 31-03-12 |
|---|---|---|---|
| TO | 71,028,000 | 73,217,000 | 74,706,000 |
| P/L | (8,905,000) | (3,966,000) | (3,973,000) |
| NW | 35,620,000 | 44,427,000 | 47,127,000 |
| WC | 10,981,000 | 23,183,000 | 28,318,000 |
| Emp. | 1,592 | 1,723 | 1,974 |

DUNS 21-030-9401
### Royal West Sussex Trust
3 William Booker Yard, The Street, Walberton, Arundel, West Sussex BN18 0PF
**Tel:** 01243572433
**Web:** www.wsx-pct.nhs.uk
**Estd:** 2002 Partnership
**Line of Business:** Charities and charitable organisations
**Partners:** Mrs C Holloway, J Wilderspin
**Responsibilities**
**Senior:** Miranda Emmet (Manager), Geraldine Hamilton (Manager), Rita Hope (Manager), Diane Levantine (Manager), Valerie Seddon (Manager), Catherine Shaw (Manager)
**US SIC:** 8062 **UK SIC:** 95100
**Employees:** 125

DUNS 23-708-4629
### The Royal Wolverhampton Nhs Trust
Leachkin Road, Inverness, Inverness-Shire IV3 8NP
**Tel:** 01463704000
**Web:** www.royalwolverhamptonhospitals.nhs.uk
**Estd:** 1994
**Line of Business:** Nhs trust & acute hospital.
**Issued Capital:** £1

**Principals:** A Edwards (Chairman), K Stringer (Financial), Ms C Etches, G Penn, Ms D Harnin, D Loughton, B Millar
**Responsibilities**
**Senior:** Maxine Espley (Director of Planning and Contr), Sultan Mahmud (Interim Programme Integration)
**Marketing:** Vivien Hall (Marketing Manager)
**HR:** Diane Pugh (Director of Human Resources)
**Facilities:** Brian Midgelow-Marston (Estates Director)
**Branches:** The Royal Wolverhampton Nhs Trust, New Cross Hospital, Wolverhampton Road, Wolverhampton, West Midlands WV10 0QP
**US SIC:** 9121, 8062
**UK SIC:** 91110, 95100
**Employees:** 6,000

DUNS 28-837-3871
### The Royal Wolverhampton School
Penn Road, Wolverhampton, West Midlands WV3 0EG
**Tel:** 01902349101 **Fax:** 01902-344496
**Web:** www.theroyalschool.co.uk
**Reg No:** 0454793 **Estd:** 2000 Private Company Limited By Guarantee
**Line of Business:** Schools (independent)
**Trading Style:** The Young Royal's Nursery
**Directors:** Ms B J Dixon, R Hart, Ms J D Lawson, M R White, Mrs S L Seivewright, A K Rashid, M D Masters, P Hill
**Responsibilities**
**Senior:** Samson Chung (Director), Mark Heywood (Head Teacher), Harold Hilton (Director), Devis Penn (Bursar), Subashini Suresh (Director), David Swift (Director)
**Finance:** Devis Penn (Bursar)
**Marketing:** Meg Orton (Registrar)
**HR:** Devis Penn (Bursar)
**US SIC:** 8211 **UK SIC:** 93200
**Auditors:** Crowe Clark Whitehill LLP
**Bankers:** Barclays Bank Plc (20-97-78)

|  | 31-08-13 | 31-08-12 | 31-08-11 |
|---|---|---|---|
| TO | 5,842,106 | 5,562,549 | 4,857,574 |
| P/L | (366,893) | (586,206) | (489,106) |
| NW | 5,297,485 | 5,664,378 | 6,250,584 |
| WC | (2,835,745) | (2,509,271) | (1,967,528) |
| Emp. | 150 | 136 | 119 |

DUNS 21-031-9503
### The Royal Yacht Britannia
Ocean Drive, Edinburgh, Midlothian EH6 6JJ
**Tel:** 01315555566
**Web:** www.royalyachtbritannia.co.uk
**Estd:** 1998
**Line of Business:** Preservation of historical sites and buildings
**Partners:** E Milligan, B Downie, C Hammond, Rear Admiral N Rankin, T Smith, Sir T Clifford
**Responsibilities**
**Marketing:** Casey Rust (Marketing Manager)
**HR:** Vicki Bygrave (Human Resources Manager)
**US SIC:** 8411 **UK SIC:** 97700
**Employees:** 150

DUNS 23-558-0631
### The Royal Yacht Britannia Trust
100 Ocean Drive, Edinburgh, Midlothian EH6 6JJ
**Tel:** 0131-555-8800
**Web:** www.royalyachtbritannia.co.uk
**Reg No:** 0185443SC **Estd:** 1998 Private Unlimited Company
**Line of Business:** Social work activities
**Directors:** T P Smith, E Milligan, C G Hammond, J M Marsden, S R Paterson, Rear Admiral N E Rankin, Ms E P Denzler
**Co. Secretary:** Turcan Connell
**Responsibilities**
**Sales:** Sonia Lee (Head of Retail)
**Health & Safety:** Andrea Bradbury (Health & Safety Officer)
**Facilities:** Derek Miller (Maintenance Manager)
**Operations:** Andrea Bradbury (Health & Safety Officer)
**US SIC:** 7399 **UK SIC:** 83954
**Auditors:** McCabe Partnership
**Bankers:** Bank Of Scotland (80-11-00)

|  | 31-12-13 | 31-12-12 | 31-12-11 |
|---|---|---|---|
| TO | 5,460,366 | 5,454,475 | 5,013,452 |
| P/L | 177,055 | 186,925 | 259,747 |
| NW | 3,795,955 | 3,618,142 | 3,431,362 |
| WC | 1,101,031 | 1,005,643 | 1,076,922 |
| Emp. | 114 | 117 | 128 |

DUNS 28-860-3012      Imp
### Royal Yachting Association
Rya House, Southampton, Hampshire SO31 4YA
**Tel:** 02380604100
**Web:** www.rya.org.uk
**Reg No:** 0878357 **VAT No:** 239281352

**Estd:** 1875 Private Company Limited By Guarantee
**Line of Business:** Activities of professional organisations
**Export Sales:** £1,831,491
**Directors:** S Clark, J M Scott, Ms S L Treseder, Ms J Poulton, D Strain, M J Moore, O P Franks, P M Bryans
**Co. Secretary:** Angus Lewis
**Responsibilities**
**Senior:** John Friend *(Manager)*, Sarah Hanratty *(Director)*, Victoria Lenz *(General Manager)*, Denville Reed *(Manager)*
**Finance:** Kenneth Pollicott *(Treasurer)*
**Marketing:** Lindsey Bell *(Communications Manager)*, Emma Slater *(Press Officer)*
**Sales:** Guy Malpas *(Business Development Manager)*
**Admin:** Nicola Drummond *(Administrator)*, Jackie Reid *(Human Resources Manager)*
**IT:** Bas Edmonds *(Technical Manager)*, Andy Galvin *(IS Manager)*, Darrell Sears *(Senior Network Technician)*
**HR:** Richard Falk *(Training Manager)*, Jackie Reid *(Human Resources Manager)*
**Health & Safety:** Rod Annetts *(Facilities Manager)*
**Facilities:** Rod Annetts *(Facilities Manager)*
**Operations:** Chris Atherton *(High Performance Manager)*, Stuart Carruthers *(Cruising Manager)*, Graham Manchester *(Regional Development Officer)*, Amanda Van Santen *(?Chief Instructor, Dinghy and)*
**Purchasing:** Rod Annetts *(Facilities Manager)*
**Engineering:** Andy Galvin *(IS Manager)*
**Branches:** Royal Yachting Association, Rya Northern Ireland House Of Sport 2A Upper Malo, Belfast, Co Antrim BT9 5LA
**US SIC:** 8621, 7999, 8699
**UK SIC:** 96311, 97913, 96902
**Auditors:** haysmacintyre
**Bankers:** National Westminster Bank Plc (60-24-20)

| | 31-03-14 | 31-03-13 | 31-03-12 |
|---|---|---|---|
| TO | 19,341,326 | 20,927,759 | 20,309,426 |
| P/L | (124,402) | 1,135,549 | 1,310,437 |
| NW | 7,671,707 | 7,461,899 | 6,618,209 |
| WC | 277,855 | (235,204) | (809,996) |
| Emp. | 160 | 155 | 154 |

DUNS 22-916-3720 **Imp**

## The Royal Zoological Society of Scotland

134 Corstorphine Road, Edinburgh, Midlothian EH12 6TS
**Tel:** 01313 349171
**Web:** www.edinburghzoo.org.uk
**VAT No:** 270337179 **Estd:** 1909
**Line of Business:** Parks & gardens
**Principals:** J Spence *(President)*, Dr T Mitchell *(Chairman)*, J Peat *(Chairman)*, Ms K Carlton *(Chairman)*, P Galbraith, P Budd, G Brechin, Ms T Mcgregor
**Responsibilities**
**Senior:** George Corr *(Warehouse Manager)*, Daniella Gardner *(Marketing Executive)*
**Marketing:** Daniella Gardner *(Marketing Executive)*, Anthony Mcreavy *(Director of Development)*
**HR:** Stuart Jenkinson *(Health & Safety Manager)*
**Health & Safety:** Stuart Jenkinson *(Health & Safety Manager)*
**Facilities:** Stuart Jenkinson *(Health & Safety Manager)*
**US SIC:** 8411 **UK SIC:** 97700
**Employees:** 187

DUNS 23-518-4160

## Royale Research Ltd

**(Subsidiary of:** Cms Graphics Inc)
235 Record Street, London SE15 1TL
**Tel:** 02077322000 **Fax:** 020-7732-2233
**Web:** www.cmsnetwork.com
**Reg No:** 3517482 **Estd:** 1998 Private Limited Company
**Line of Business:** Courier activities other than national post activities
**Export Sales:** £1,158,975
**Trading Style:** Cms
**Issued Capital:** £250,000
**Directors:** S L Stokes, L Santorelli, Ms F A Santorelli
**Co. Secretary:** Stephen Libroia
**Responsibilities**
**Marketing:** Matthew Enion *(Marketing Manager)*
**HR:** Brett Harding *(Head of Human Resources)*
**Health & Safety:** Brett Harding *(Head of Human Resources)*
**US SIC:** 4311 **UK SIC:** 79010
**Auditors:** BDO LLP

| | 31-12-13 | 31-12-12 | 31-12-11 |
|---|---|---|---|
| TO | 10,942,611 | 9,178,196 | 11,519,088 |
| P/L | 1,870,196 | 881,852 | 2,349,427 |
| NW | 2,179,698 | 1,665,787 | 2,010,430 |
| WC | 2,136,854 | 1,601,452 | 1,943,622 |
| Emp. | 75 | 76 | 80 |

DUNS 73-554-2974

## Royce Peeling Green Ltd

**(Subsidiary of:** Rpg Holdings Ltd)
The Copper Room, Trinity Way Deva Centre, Manchester M3 7BG
**Tel:** 01616080000 **Fax:** 0161-608-0001
**Web:** www.rpg.co.uk
**Reg No:** 4816267 **Estd:** 1910 Private Limited Company
**Line of Business:** Accounting activities
**Issued Capital:** £1
**Directors:** J S Brownson, C M Slater, A R Burnett, P Randall, M A Chatten, C M Poston, I E Paramor, P J Buckley
**Co. Secretary:** John Redmond
**Responsibilities**
**Senior:** Norman Milligan *(Partner)*, S Murrills *(Partner)*, G Wardle *(Partner)*, Roderick Withinshaw *(License And Insolvency Practit)*
**Branches:** Royce Peeling Green Ltd, 15 Buckingham Gate, London SW1E 6LB
**US SIC:** 8931, 7392
**UK SIC:** 83600, 83951
**Bankers:** Barclays Bank Plc (20-54-58)

| | 31-12-13 | 31-12-12 | 31-12-11 |
|---|---|---|---|
| TO | 3,308,490 | 3,669,875 | 3,450,111 |
| P/L | 351,366 | 943,680 | 456,429 |
| NW | (317,510) | (332,154) | (622,177) |
| WC | 132,788 | (349,313) | (571,326) |
| Emp. | 49 | 50 | 48 |

DUNS 21-025-4454 **Imp**

## Royde & Tucker Ltd

**(Subsidiary of:** Royde & Tucker Holdings Ltd)
Bilton Road, Hitchin, Hertfordshire SG4 0SB
**Tel:** 01462-444444 **Fax:** 01462444433
**Web:** www.ratman.co.uk
**Reg No:** 0531276 **VAT No:** 220857377
**Estd:** 1924 Private Limited Company
**Line of Business:** Manufacture of locks and hinges
**Issued Capital:** £100,000
**Principals:** S W Jenkins *(Managing)*, J M Simms, S C Gardiner, N J Gadsby
**Co. Secretary:** Stephen Jenkins
**Responsibilities**
**Engineering:** Dennis Lambley *(Engineering Manager)*
**US SIC:** 3429 **UK SIC:** 31694
**Auditors:** Brindley Goldstein Ltd
**Bankers:** Lloyds TSB Bank plc (30-97-41)

| | 31-03-14 | 31-03-13 | 31-03-12 |
|---|---|---|---|
| TO | 6,266,247 | 5,580,953 | 5,355,741 |
| P/L | 241,578 | 115,894 | 179,513 |
| NW | 3,079,149 | 2,912,487 | 2,904,570 |
| WC | 2,217,766 | 2,051,915 | 2,029,033 |
| Emp. | 73 | 70 | 63 |

DUNS 21-162-6011

## Roydon Group Plc

Unit 16 Chichester Business Centre, Chichester Street, Rochdale, Lancashire OL16 2AU
**Tel:** 01706647643
**Web:** www.roydon.com
**Reg No:** 6890221 **Estd:** 2005 Public Limited Company
**Line of Business:** Recycling
**Export Sales:** £7,945,727
**Issued Capital:** £54,492
**Directors:** W Sumner, G R Wallwork
**Co. Secretary:** Mrs Sarah Sumner
**US SIC:** 3031 **UK SIC:** 48123
**Bankers:** Barclays Bank Plc (20-72-67)

| | 31-10-13 | 31-10-12 | 31-10-11 |
|---|---|---|---|
| TO | 20,578,942 | 15,611,859 | 16,748,756 |
| P/L | 1,695,674 | 103,221 | 586,760 |
| NW | 3,096,114 | 1,596,804 | 1,272,448 |
| WC | (70,406) | (1,261,886) | (224,366) |
| Emp. | 83 | 78 | 65 |

DUNS 21-010-2949

## Royds Llp

65 Carter Lane, London EC4V 5HF
**Tel:** 020-7583-2222
**Web:** www.roydsrdw.com
**Reg No:** 0330413OC **Estd:** 2007 Private Limited Company
**Line of Business:** Solicitors
**Responsibilities**
**Senior:** Gemma Ospedale *(Non-designated Limited Liabili)*
**Finance:** David Albans *(Office Manager)*
**Admin:** David Albans *(Office Manager)*
**HR:** Cheryl Sturdy *(Human Resources Manager)*
**Health & Safety:** Cheryl Sturdy *(Human Resources Manager)*
**Facilities:** David Albans *(Office Manager)*
**US SIC:** 8111 **UK SIC:** 83500
**Bankers:** Barclays Bank Plc (20-06-05)

| | 31-03-14 | 31-03-13 | 31-03-12 |
|---|---|---|---|
| TO | 7,100,928 | 6,483,634 | 5,478,068 |
| P/L | 1,559,195 | 1,757,053 | 1,220,396 |
| NW | N/A | N/A | 948,982 |
| WC | 1,845,110 | 1,892,787 | 1,169,468 |
| Emp. | 80 | 75 | 68 |

DUNS 23-055-7985

## Royland Contractors Ltd

Fairline House, George Summers Close Future Court, Rochester, Kent ME2 4EL
**Tel:** 01634715300
**Web:** www.royland.co.uk
**Reg No:** 2856742 **Estd:** 1993 Private Limited Company
**Line of Business:** Groundwork contractors
**Issued Capital:** £100
**Director:** R G Prior
**Co. Secretary:** Ms Susan Prior
**Responsibilities**
**Senior:** Jenny Bolton *(Manager)*
**Branches:** Homeward Bound, Gas House Rd, Rochester Kent ME1 1PN Tel 01634-404174
**US SIC:** 1622, 1795
**UK SIC:** 50200, 50000
**Auditors:** Beak Kemmenoe

| | 31-12-13 | 31-12-12 | 31-12-11 |
|---|---|---|---|
| TA | 4,959,680 | 4,489,597 | 4,048,152 |
| NW | 2,544,467 | 2,525,378 | 2,486,091 |
| WC | 1,649,633 | 1,675,811 | 1,646,349 |

DUNS 39-963-4021

## Royle Recruitment Ltd

5 Skeldergate, York, North Yorkshire YO1 6DG
**Tel:** 01904-610560 **Fax:** 01904-626631
**Web:** www.royle.co.uk
**Reg No:** 2263563 **Estd:** 1988 Private Limited Company
**Line of Business:** Employment and recruitment companies and consultants
**Issued Capital:** £21,957
**Directors:** Ms A N Craven, Ms L G Aston, J R Craven
**Co. Secretary:** Robert Craven
**US SIC:** 7361 **UK SIC:** 83954

| | 30-04-13 | 30-04-12 | 30-04-11 |
|---|---|---|---|
| TO | 17,965,937 | 15,286,368 | 12,803,049 |
| P/L | 95,504 | 107,085 | 40,619 |
| NW | 290,001 | 275,721 | 330,408 |
| WC | 232,460 | 215,411 | 275,508 |
| Emp. | 232 | 182 | 187 |

DUNS 23-528-0992 **Exp**

## Roy's Quality Foods Ltd

**(Subsidiary of:** Peter's Holdings Ltd)
Bedwas House Industrial Estate, Bedwas, Caerphilly, Mid Glamorgan CF83 8XP
**Tel:** 029-2085-3200
**Web:** www.petersfood.com
**Reg No:** 3526992 **Estd:** 1998 Private Limited Company
**Line of Business:** Other meat and poultry meat processing
**Trading Style:** Peter's Food Svc
**Issued Capital:** £2
**Director:** M J Grimwood
**Co. Secretary:** David Peek
**Responsibilities**
**Senior:** Wayne Richards *(Stores Controller)*
**HR:** Judith Caddy *(Personnel Manager)*
**Engineering:** Wayne Morgan *(Production Manager)*
**US SIC:** 2013 **UK SIC:** 41223
**Auditors:** PricewaterhouseCoopers

| | 31-05-14 | 31-05-13 | 31-05-12 |
|---|---|---|---|
| TA | 2 | 2 | 2 |
| NW | 2 | 2 | 2 |

DUNS 21-835-8604 **Imp**

## Roys (Wroxham) Ltd

Wroxham, Norwich, Norfolk NR12 8DB
**Tel:** 01603-782-131
**Web:** www.roys.co.uk
**Reg No:** 0256574 **Estd:** 1931 Private Limited Company
**Line of Business:** General retailers
**Trading Style:** Roys of Wroxham
**Issued Capital:** £1,000,000
**Directors:** T How, Ms M D Roy, J Wheeler, P A Roy
**Co. Secretary:** Edward Roy
**Responsibilities**
**Senior:** Roger Ridley-Thomas *(Director)*
**IT:** Brett Martin *(PC Manager)*
**Branches:** Roys (Wroxham) Ltd, Great Eastern Road, Sudbury, Suffolk CO10 2TJ
**US SIC:** 5399, 5411
**UK SIC:** 65600, 64100
**Auditors:** PricewaterhouseCoopers LLP
**Bankers:** Barclays Bank Plc (20-62-53)

| | 25-01-14 | 26-01-13 | 28-01-12 |
|---|---|---|---|
| TO | 51,054,802 | 48,355,219 | 45,392,362 |
| P/L | 661,432 | 1,141,130 | 1,415,444 |
| NW | 30,933,530 | 30,614,214 | 29,900,568 |
| WC | 5,035,167 | 7,737,525 | 9,071,182 |
| Emp. | 842 | 767 | 747 |

DUNS 21-532-8340

## Royston Bowling Club

47 Green Drift, Royston, Hertfordshire SG8 5BX
**Estd:** 2002
**Line of Business:** Sports clubs
**Director:** G Lewis
**Responsibilities**
**Senior:** Stanley Whitehouse *(Club Secretary)*
**US SIC:** 7999 **UK SIC:** 97913
**Employees:** 90

DUNS 77-796-3877

## Royston Labels Ltd

Unit 18 Orchard Road, Royston, Hertfordshire SG8 5HD
**Tel:** 01763-212020
**Web:** www.roystonlabels.co.uk
**Reg No:** 3027229 **VAT No:** 215880657
**Estd:** 1995 Private Limited Company
**Line of Business:** Labels finishing and supply
**Export Sales:** £495,248
**Issued Capital:** £1,000
**Managing Director:** P M Clayton
**Co. Secretary:** Ms Sharon Clayton
**US SIC:** 2752 **UK SIC:** 47544
**Auditors:** Peters Elworthy & Moore
**Bankers:** HSBC Bank plc (40-25-22)

| | 30-04-14 | 30-04-13 | 30-04-12 |
|---|---|---|---|
| TO | 8,189,758 | 7,517,847 | 6,547,339 |
| P/L | 564,470 | 528,702 | 336,831 |
| NW | 4,383,748 | 4,059,352 | 3,635,088 |
| WC | 2,810,050 | 2,521,829 | 1,789,176 |
| Emp. | 58 | 57 | 57 |

DUNS 21-325-9195 **Exp**

## Royston Ltd

**(Subsidiary of:** Royston Power Generation Ltd)
Unit 3 Walker Riverside, Newcastle-Upon-Tyne, Tyne and Wear NE6 3PF
**Tel:** 01912958000
**Web:** www.royston.co.uk
**Reg No:** 1384241 **VAT No:** 621360381
**Estd:** 1978 Private Limited Company
**Line of Business:** Marine engines and engineering
**Export Markets:** E U, Africa, Australasia, Eastern Europe
**Export Sales:** £3,156,647
**Trading Style:** Royston Engineering
**Issued Capital:** £50,000
**Principals:** L J Brown *(Managing)*, G R Denholm, Ms S Wade
**Co. Secretary:** Graham Denholm
**Responsibilities**
**Marketing:** Damian Mccann *(Product Manager)*
**US SIC:** 8911, 5999
**UK SIC:** 83701, 65600
**Auditors:** Ernst & Young LLP
**Bankers:** National Westminster Bank Plc (60-15-08)

| | 28-02-14 | 28-02-13 | 29-02-12 |
|---|---|---|---|
| TO | 12,033,674 | 11,141,198 | 9,335,601 |
| P/L | 471,743 | 432,774 | 1,860 |
| NW | 1,878,141 | 1,492,637 | 1,130,765 |
| WC | 1,427,717 | 1,110,726 | 759,848 |
| Emp. | 63 | 66 | 64 |

DUNS 21-783-6536

## Royston Social Work Area Office

15 Glenbarr Street, Glasgow, Lanarkshire G21 2NW
**Tel:** 01412767010
**Estd:** 2011
**Line of Business:** The dss
**US SIC:** 8321 **UK SIC:** 96111
**Employees:** 150

DUNS 23-697-3756

## Roythorne & Co

Enterprise Way, Pinchbeck, Spalding, Lincolnshire PE11 3YR
**Web:** www.roythorne.co.uk
**VAT No:** 119939139 **Estd:** 1920 Partnership
**Line of Business:** Solicitors
**Partners:** R C Tongue, G C Smith, J F Danks, D R Proctor, G M Orton, L P Fidler, Ms J M Ratcliffe, M E Fielding
**Responsibilities**
**Senior:** D Bambridge *(Partner)*, Caroline Gumbrell *(Partner)*, G Harrod *(Partner)*, Nick Ingrey *(Partner)*, Paul Osbourne *(Managing Partner)*, Alan Plummer *(Partner)*, Jeanette Sharpe *(Partner)*
**HR:** Jackie Kirkland *(Human Resources Manager)*, Rachel Wood *(HR Manager)*
**Facilities:** Jackie Sterling *(Facilities Manager)*
**Purchasing:** Jackie Sterling *(Facilities Manager)*
**Branches:** Roythorne & Co, 27 Wide Bargate, Boston, Lincolnshire PE21 6SR
**US SIC:** 8111 **UK SIC:** 83500
**Bankers:** HSBC Bank plc (40-43-01)
**Employees:** 150

**DUNS 21-125-9711**

## Roythornes Ltd
Roythornes Limited, Enterprise Way, Spalding, Lincolnshire PE11 3YR
Tel: 01775-842500 Fax: 01775-725736
Web: www.roythornes.co.uk
Reg No: 6611251 Estd: 2008 Private Limited Company
Line of Business: Solicitors
Issued Capital: £648,000
Directors: A M Czajka, T J Russ, V Mortlock, Ms J J Ladds, N G Ingrey, J T Wright, T G Foottit, P R Osborne
Co. Secretary: Samuel Elkin
Responsibilities
Senior: Phillip Cookson (Director)
US SIC: 7399 UK SIC: 83954

| | 30-06-14 | 30-06-13 | 30-06-12 |
|---|---|---|---|
| TO | 7,008,638 | N/A | N/A |
| P/L | 1,619,501 | N/A | N/A |
| NW | (907,096) | 2,436,905 | 1,757,188 |
| WC | 1,579,790 | 1,521,562 | 919,411 |

**DUNS 21-596-7137**

## Royton Health & Wellbeing Centre
Park Street, Royton, Oldham, Lancashire OL2 6QW
Tel: 01613624002
Web: www.hoperomania.org.uk
Estd: 2011 Proprietorship
Line of Business: Hospitals
Proprietor: Ms S Langley
US SIC: 8062 UK SIC: 95100
Employees: 250

**DUNS 21-327-8125**

## Rozelle Home Farm
4-8 Home Farm Road, Ayr, Ayrshire KA7 4XH
Tel: 01292445400
Estd: 1989 Proprietorship
Line of Business: Nursing homes
Proprietor: F Robertson
Responsibilities
Senior: Patricia Morgan (General Manager)
IT: Heather Thorburn (Computer Manager)
HR: Patricia Morgan (General Manager)
Health & Safety: Patricia Morgan (General Manager)
US SIC: 8051 UK SIC: 95100
Employees: 70

**DUNS 21-323-9270**    Imp

## R.P. Tyson Construction Ltd
1 Mitcham Road, Blackpool, Lancashire FY4 4QN
Tel: 01253-696800 Fax: 01253-696801
Web: www.tysonconstruction.co.uk
Reg No: 0877069 VAT No: 153767641
Estd: 1966 Private Limited Company
Line of Business: Building of complete constructions or parts thereof; civil engineering
Issued Capital: £12,000
Principals: D J Whittle (Chairman and Managing), P Whelan, A Brumwell, N G Bell, J P Whittle, T F Wright
Co. Secretary: Ms Irene Jones
Responsibilities
Senior: Roy Bingham (Manager)
US SIC: 1541 UK SIC: 50100
Auditors: Sheards
Bankers: National Westminster Bank Plc (60-03-04)

| | 30-06-14 | 30-06-13 | 30-06-12 |
|---|---|---|---|
| TO | 10,337,773 | 9,515,202 | 12,873,548 |
| P/L | (56,842) | 42,050 | 381,111 |
| NW | 1,790,921 | 1,836,774 | 1,840,983 |
| WC | 2,086,658 | 1,563,422 | 1,557,373 |
| Emp. | 101 | 99 | 111 |

**DUNS 76-622-5106**

## Rpc Group Plc
Sapphire House, Crown Way, Rushden, Northamptonshire NN10 6FB
Tel: 01933416523
Web: www.rpc-group.com
Reg No: 2578443 VAT No: 684319216
Estd: 1991 Public Limited Company
Line of Business: Management activities of holding companies
Export Sales: £777,100,000
Issued Capital: £8,300,129
Directors: Ms I Haaijer, M G Towers, G S Wong, J R Pike, P R Vervaat, Dr L Drummond, S J Kesterton, S Rojahn
Co. Secretary: Ms Rebecca Joyce
Responsibilities
Senior: Joanne Pack (Marketing Manager), Neil Skeats (Factory Manager), David Wilbraham (Manager)
Finance: Helen Craik (Group Tax Manager)
Marketing: Joanne Pack (Marketing Manager)
HR: Shaheen Sheikh (Personnel Manager)
Branches: Rpc Group Plc, The Crown Business Park, Station Road, Old Dalby, Melton Mowbray, Leicestershire LE14 3NQ

US SIC: 6711, 3079, 2654
UK SIC: 83962, 48360, 47280
Auditors: KPMG Audit PLC
Bankers: National Westminster Bank Plc (56-00-55)
Following financial data are in thousands

| | 31-03-14 | 31-03-13 | 31-03-12 |
|---|---|---|---|
| TO | 1,046,900 | 1,051,300 | 1,129,900 |
| P/L | 59,000 | 40,300 | 59,600 |
| NW | 91,400 | 170,300 | 167,200 |
| WC | 28,100 | 46,700 | 44,700 |
| Emp. | 7,493 | 7,188 | 7,326 |

**DUNS 23-734-9548**

## Rpc Land & New Homes Ltd
89 King Street, Maidstone, Kent ME14 1BG
Tel: 01622691911
Web: www.rpcland.co.uk
Reg No: 3729331 Estd: 1999 Private Limited Company
Line of Business: Estate agents
Issued Capital: £6,209
Directors: M J Linington, P T Randall
Co. Secretary: Mark Linington
Branches: Rpc Land & New Homes Ltd, 158 High Street, Tonbridge, Kent TN9 1BB
US SIC: 6531 UK SIC: 83400
Auditors: John D Coleman

| | 31-12-13 | 31-12-12 | 31-12-11 |
|---|---|---|---|
| TO | 1,436,802 | 1,294,994 | 955,410 |
| P/L | 161,959 | 291,379 | 9,639 |
| NW | 791,865 | 765,742 | 584,287 |
| WC | 768,094 | 749,916 | 564,447 |

**DUNS 36-529-8801**

## Rpc Tedeco-Gizeh (Uk) Ltd
Kenfig Ind. Estate, Water Street, Port Talbot, West Glamorgan SA13 2PG
Tel: 01656749183 Fax: 01656-743074
Web: www.rpc-tedeco-gizeh.com
Reg No: 3289951 VAT No: 684319216
Estd: 1992 Private Limited Company
Line of Business: Manufacture of plastics in primary forms
Issued Capital: £2
Directors: P R Vervaat, S J Kesterton
Co. Secretary: Ms Rebecca Joyce
Responsibilities
HR: Lewis King (Human Resources Manager), Sara Powell (Human Resources Manager)
Health & Safety: Lewis King (Human Resources Manager), Sara Powell (Human Resources Manager)
US SIC: 2821, 7399
UK SIC: 25140, 83954
Auditors: KPMG LLP
Bankers: National Westminster Bank Plc (60-60-06)

| | 31-03-14 | 31-03-13 | 31-03-12 |
|---|---|---|---|
| TO | N/A | 22,591,000 | 18,292,000 |
| P/L | N/A | 3,591,000 | 2,198,000 |
| NW | 10,545,000 | 10,545,000 | 7,776,000 |
| WC | N/A | N/A | (868,000) |
| Emp. | N/A | 81 | 74 |

**DUNS 21-822-5985**

## R.P.Colman & Co; Ltd
Colman House, Avian Way, Salhouse Road, Norwich, Norfolk NR7 9AR
Tel: 01603486900
Web: www.colmangroup.com
Reg No: 0624771 VAT No: 104600525
Estd: 1880 Private Limited Company
Line of Business: Commercial lithographic printers
Trading Style: Colman Wholesale, Colman Print, Stationary Stop, Owl Brand Stationary
Issued Capital: £8,000
Principals: A J Colman (Managing), Mrs J P Colman, W R Colman
Co. Secretary: Robert Colman
Branches: R.p.colman & Co; Ltd, Prestige House, Avian Way, Salhouse Road, Norwich, Norfolk NR7 9AR
US SIC: 2752, 5199, 5999
UK SIC: 47544, 61900, 65600
Auditors: Lovewell Blake
Bankers: Barclays Bank Plc (20-62-53)

| | 31-12-13 | 31-12-12 | 31-12-11 |
|---|---|---|---|
| TA | 2,291,661 | 2,261,193 | 1,695,363 |
| NW | 876,682 | 915,197 | 931,210 |
| WC | 655,751 | 801,406 | 757,094 |

**DUNS 73-974-0228**

## Rpm London Holdings Ltd
The Old Treacle Factory, London W12 9JW
Tel: 02087355144
Web: www.rpmltd.com
Reg No: 5224866 Estd: 2004 Private Limited Company
Line of Business: Management and business consultants
Trading Style: Rpm London Holdings Ltd
Issued Capital: £1,121
Directors: L Farrant, H S Robertson, D J Robertson
Co. Secretary: Robin Burman
Responsibilities
Marketing: James Poletti (Head Of Digital Strategy)

Sales: Rebecca Collins (New Business Manager), Jamie Green (Senior Account Director)
IT: Dermot Mc Quaid (Technical Director)
US SIC: 7392 UK SIC: 83951

| | 31-03-14 | 31-03-13 | 31-03-12 |
|---|---|---|---|
| TO | 19,366,124 | 22,256,296 | 25,070,772 |
| P/L | 396,839 | 938,541 | 1,630,649 |
| NW | 3,470,113 | 3,618,090 | 3,129,655 |
| WC | 2,653,683 | 2,549,162 | 1,913,172 |
| Emp. | 250 | 333 | 337 |

**DUNS 50-054-8367**

## Rpmi Ltd
Stooperdale Offices, Brinkburn Road, Darlington, County Durham DL3 6EH
Tel: 01325342829
Web: www.rpmi.co.uk
Reg No: 2315380 Estd: 1988 Private Limited Company
Line of Business: Pension companies
Trading Style: Pensions Management
Issued Capital: £102
Directors: C J Hitchen, J C Hamilton, G T Towse, D Maddison, C F Johnson, D Tyson, C B Ramamurthy, C R Goldson
Co. Secretary: Ms Lisa Sunner
Responsibilities
Senior: David Teasdale (Director)
Finance: David Teasdale (Director)
Marketing: Peter Ennis (Business Assurance Manager)
HR: Paul Sheldrick (Human Resources Manager)
US SIC: 6371 UK SIC: 82002
Auditors: KPMG LLP
Bankers: The Royal Bank Of Scotland Plc (16-04-00)

| | 31-12-13 | 31-12-12 | 31-12-11 |
|---|---|---|---|
| TO | 47,397,000 | 42,406,000 | 45,055,000 |
| P/L | 263,000 | (1,188,000) | 3,519,000 |
| NW | 4,639,000 | (5,240,000) | (4,492,000) |
| WC | 5,513,000 | 6,445,000 | 423,000 |
| Emp. | 337 | 337 | 284 |

**DUNS 21-659-9970**

## Rpp Ltd
(Subsidiary of: Rpp Group Holdings Ltd)
Blenwood Court, 451 Cleckheaton Road, Low Moor, Bradford, West Yorkshire BD12 0NY
Tel: 01274693622
Web: www.rpp-constructionconsultants.co.uk
Reg No: 7159352 VAT No: 169518331
Estd: 2010 Private Limited Company
Line of Business: Building construction management
Trading Style: Rex Procter & Partners
Issued Capital: £852,460
Directors: G Mcgeough, A Blenard, P H Mackie, J Deegan, M Cooper, A Cooper, J G Crowther, I W Tomlinson
Responsibilities
Senior: Daren Chessun (Director), Ronald Linton (Manager)
Branches: Rpp Ltd - 3 Blenheim Court, LS2 9AE Leeds
US SIC: 8911 UK SIC: 83701
Auditors: Mazars LLP

| | 31-03-14 | 31-03-13 | 31-03-12 |
|---|---|---|---|
| TO | 5,967,139 | 5,863,291 | 5,670,870 |
| P/L | 761,200 | 381,888 | 500,774 |
| NW | (1,164,830) | (2,091,976) | (3,397,039) |
| WC | 992,865 | 666,013 | 631,679 |
| Emp. | 78 | 83 | 82 |

**DUNS 50-502-9165**

## Rps Us Holdings Ltd
(Subsidiary of: R P S Group Plc)
Centurion Court, 85 Milton Park, Abingdon, Oxfordshire OX14 4RY
Tel: 01235-863206
Reg No: 2470604 Estd: 1971 Private Limited Company
Line of Business: Engineering services
Directors: P C Fearn, G R Young, Dr J P Williams, Dr A S Hearne, K Cruthirds
Co. Secretary: Nicholas Rowe
US SIC: 8911 UK SIC: 83701

| | 31-12-12 | 31- -11 | |
|---|---|---|---|
| TA | 2 | 2 | |
| NW | 2 | 2 | |

**DUNS 21-138-7991**    Imp

## Rr Donnelley Global Document Solutions Group Ltd
(Subsidiary of: R.R. Donnelley & Sons Company)
Tower Close, Huntingdon, Cambridgeshire PE29 7YD
Tel: 02030475500 Fax: 01480 426201
Web: www.rrd.com
Reg No: 6711794 Estd: 2008 Private Limited Company
Line of Business: Other business activities not elsewhere classified
Export Sales: £47,601,000
Trading Style: Rr Donnelley
Issued Capital: £100,001

Directors: M S Gordon, K T Woor, J S Farmer
Co. Secretary: Jonathan Dally
Branches: Rr Donnelley Global Document Solutions Group Ltd, 85 Gracechurch Street, London EC3V 0AA
US SIC: 7399 UK SIC: 83954
Auditors: Deloitte LLP
Bankers: National Westminster Bank Plc (60-11-30)

| | 31-12-13 | 31-12-12 | 31-12-11 |
|---|---|---|---|
| TO | 236,863,000 | 286,786,000 | 266,945,000 |
| P/L | 1,708,000 | 7,678,000 | 3,542,000 |
| NW | (11,175,000) | (13,767,000) | (17,273,000) |
| WC | 32,503,000 | 34,396,000 | 38,557,000 |
| Emp. | 2,153 | 2,254 | 2,062 |

**DUNS 29-401-6134**

## R.R. Donnelley Pension Trustee Company Ltd
(Subsidiary of: R.R. Donnelley & Sons Company)
Flaxby Moor, Knaresborough, North Yorkshire HG5 0XJ
Tel: 01423796100
Web: www.rrdonnelley.com
Reg No: 1337495 Estd: 1977 Private Limited Company
Line of Business: Other business activities not elsewhere classified
Trading Style: R.R. Donnelley, R.R. Donnelley Global Print Management
Issued Capital: £2
Directors: M Reynolds, D P Stobbs, J W Ward, Mrs E K Harvey, S Rayner, S Karim
Co. Secretary: Mrs Terry Gordon
US SIC: 7399 UK SIC: 83954
Auditors: Deloitte LLP
Bankers: HSBC Bank plc (40-47-31)

| | 31-03-14 | 31-03-13 | 31-03-12 |
|---|---|---|---|
| TA | 2 | 2 | 2 |
| NW | 2 | 2 | 2 |

**DUNS 50-391-3121**    Exp

## R.R. Spink & Sons (Arbroath) Ltd
(Subsidiary of: Dawnfresh Holdings Ltd)
Sir William Smith Road, Kirkton Industrial Estate, Arbroath, Angus DD11 3RD
Tel: 01241-872023
Web: www.dawnfresh.co.uk
Reg No: 0118747SC VAT No: 270126980
Estd: 1920 Private Limited Company
Line of Business: Processing and preserving of fish and fish products
Issued Capital: £592,857
Directors: A E Salvesen, A T Cooksey
Co. Secretary: Mrs Helen Muir
Responsibilities
Senior: Ronald Dacre (Manager), Stephen Flack (Manager), James Gourley (Manager), Muir Hunter (Manager), L Kucerova (Despatch Manager), Joseph McManus (Manager), Kirsteen Stewart (Site Manager)
US SIC: 2092 UK SIC: 41501
Auditors: Grant Thornton UK LLP
Bankers: The Royal Bank Of Scotland Plc (83-15-22)

| | 31-03-14 | 31-03-13 | 31-03-12 |
|---|---|---|---|
| TO | 15,705,709 | 10,481,026 | 9,882,216 |
| P/L | 206,318 | 199,343 | 19,857 |
| NW | (2,072,976) | (2,279,294) | (2,478,637) |
| WC | (936,768) | (450,314) | (647,291) |
| Emp. | 91 | 68 | 89 |

**DUNS 76-647-7392**

## R.R. Transport Ltd
Stanley Way, Cardrew, Redruth, Cornwall TR15 1SP
Tel: 01209-310816
Web: www.rrtransport.com
Reg No: 2584166 Estd: 1991 Private Limited Company
Line of Business: Road haulage and transport services
Export Sales: £3,900
Issued Capital: £600,000
Director: M G Bailey
Co. Secretary: Ms Kathryn Bailey
US SIC: 4789, 4226
UK SIC: 77002, 77003
Auditors: Walker Moyle
Bankers: Barclays Bank Plc (20-87-94)

| | 31-01-14 | 31-01-13 | 31-01-12 |
|---|---|---|---|
| TO | 8,352,648 | 7,543,545 | N/A |
| P/L | 485,226 | 245,695 | N/A |
| NW | 555,582 | 183,410 | 5,715 |
| WC | (404,562) | (168,173) | (41,003) |
| Emp. | 75 | 69 | N/A |

DUNS 21-822-9045

## R.Robinson & Co.(Motor Services) Ltd

Heigham Causeway, Heigham Street, Norwich, Norfolk NR2 4LX
**Tel:** 01603-612111
**Web:** www.robinsonsvolkswagen.co.uk
**Reg No:** 0561428 **Estd:** 1928 Private Limited Company
**Line of Business:** Management activities of holding companies
**Trading Style:** The Robinsons Group
**Issued Capital:** £158,334
**Directors:** R Robinson, Mrs C E Kenvyn, T E Robinson, M B Wallace
**Co. Secretary:** David Bonfield
**Responsibilities**
**Senior:** Andrew Bracking *(General Manager)*
**US SIC:** 6711, 7539
**UK SIC:** 83962, 67100
**Auditors:** Sexty & Co
**Bankers:** HSBC Bank plc (40-35-10)

| | 31-12-13 | 31-12-12 | 31-12-11 |
|---|---|---|---|
| TO | 283,333,841 | 197,911,467 | 176,429,207 |
| P/L | 5,225,903 | 4,300,440 | 3,305,098 |
| NW | 22,213,504 | 19,083,374 | 16,659,111 |
| WC | 6,314,542 | 6,455,585 | 4,304,764 |
| Emp. | 580 | 473 | 450 |

DUNS 21-244-7858

## R.S. Cockerill (York) Ltd

**(Subsidiary of:** Providence Holdings Ltd)
Stamford Bridge Road, Dunnington, York, North Yorkshire YO19 5AE
**Tel:** 01904-481111 **Fax:** 01904 486100
**Web:** www.cockerill.co.uk
**Reg No:** 0598050 **Estd:** 1935 Private Limited Company
**Line of Business:** Agents specialising in the sale of particular products or ranges of products not elsewhere classified
**Issued Capital:** £9,001
**Principals:** M R Cockerill *(Managing)*, C J Ingle, R J Pilgrim, M J Dangerfield
**Co. Secretary:** Ms Pamela Cockerill
**Responsibilities**
**Marketing:** Joanne Forster *(Marketing)*
**Branches:** R.s. Cockerill (York) Ltd, Stamford Bridge Road, York, North Yorkshire YO19 5AE
**US SIC:** 5199 **UK SIC:** 61900
**Auditors:** Hunter Gee Holroyd
**Bankers:** Barclays Bank Plc (20-99-56)

| | 30-06-14 | 30-06-13 | 30-06-12 |
|---|---|---|---|
| TO | 44,281,065 | 46,455,175 | 34,455,842 |
| P/L | 2,105,882 | 378,130 | 1,504,946 |
| NW | 6,083,729 | 5,448,051 | 5,118,158 |
| WC | 3,054,328 | 2,569,365 | 1,623,240 |
| Emp. | 91 | 93 | 81 |

DUNS 21-090-8414

## Rs Components Ltd

**(Subsidiary of:** Electrocomponents Public Limited Company)
Po Box 99, Corby, Northamptonshire NN17 9RS
**Tel:** 01132311211 **Fax:** 01536 405678
**Web:** www.rs.com
**Reg No:** 1002091 **VAT No:** 243164091
**Estd:** 2011 Private Limited Company
**Line of Business:** Distribution service providers
**Trading Style:** Verospeed, R S, Electromail, Electrospeed
**Issued Capital:** £50,000
**Directors:** I Mason, S Boddie
**Co. Secretary:** Ian Haslegrave
**Branches:** Rs Components Ltd, 1 Maverton Road, London E3 2JE
**US SIC:** 4712, 5065
**UK SIC:** 77002, 61500
**Auditors:** KPMG Audit PLC
**Bankers:** HSBC Bank plc (40-18-12)

| | 31-03-14 | 31-03-13 | 31-03-12 |
|---|---|---|---|
| TO | 626,700,000 | 624,600,000 | 624,900,000 |
| P/L | 58,700,000 | 55,400,000 | 58,400,000 |
| NW | 111,200,000 | 115,900,000 | 113,200,000 |
| WC | 46,400,000 | 47,400,000 | 33,700,000 |
| Emp. | 2,913 | 3,005 | 3,038 |

DUNS 34-636-6370

## Rs Consulting Ltd

**(Subsidiary of:** Cello Group Plc)
Studio 2, Priory House, Battersea Park Road Cloisters Business, Centre, London SW8 4BG
**Tel:** 02076277810
**Web:** www.rsconsulting.com
**Reg No:** 2766279 **VAT No:** 608032668
**Estd:** 1984 Private Limited Company
**Line of Business:** Market research organisations
**Export Sales:** £5,277,066
**Trading Style:** Mruk
**Issued Capital:** £175,000
**Directors:** Ms J E Shirley, C Smith, M Scott, M Bentley, P G Stubington, Ms C E Anderson
**Co. Secretary:** Chris Stead
**Responsibilities**
**Senior:** Kate Anderson *(Manager)*, Bryan Atkin *(Manager)*
**Branches:** RS CONSULTING LTD: MRUK, 40 Princess Street, M1 6DE, MANCHESTER.
**US SIC:** 7392, 7399
**UK SIC:** 83951, 83954
**Auditors:** PricewaterhouseCoopers LLP
**Bankers:** Bank Of Scotland (12-11-03)

| | 31-12-13 | 31-12-12 | 31-12-11 |
|---|---|---|---|
| TO | 9,139,337 | 8,380,083 | 8,403,330 |
| P/L | 527,448 | 382,199 | 480,643 |
| NW | 1,481,093 | 1,023,300 | 983,609 |
| WC | 1,380,295 | 960,476 | 946,676 |
| Emp. | 60 | 54 | 57 |

DUNS 23-834-5201

## Rsa Insurance Group Plc

20 Fenchurch Street, London EC3M 3AU
**Tel:** 02071117000 **Fax:** 02076363451
**Web:** www.rsagroup.com
**Reg No:** 2339826 **Estd:** 1989 Public Limited Company
**Line of Business:** Management activities of holding companies
**Issued Capital:** £1,101,943,893
**Directors:** R D Houghton, A W Barbour, Ms K M Shailer, H S Mitchell, M A Scicluna, Mrs J E Waterous, S A Hester, J B Streppel
**Co. Secretary:** Derek Walsh
**Responsibilities**
**Senior:** Enrico Cucchiani *(Director)*
**Marketing:** Anna Campbell *(Marketing Capabilities Manager)*, Dominic Grounsell *(Sales & Marketing Director)*, Louise Shield *(External Communications Direct)*, David Shortland *(Head of Global Marketing)*
**Sales:** Dominic Grounsell *(Sales & Marketing Director)*
**Engineering:** John Ahern *(Engineering Portfolio Manager)*
**Branches:** Rsa Insurance Group Plc, 109 New Kings Rd, London SW6 4SJ
**US SIC:** 6711, 6411
**UK SIC:** 83962, 83200
**Auditors:** KPMG LLP
**Bankers:** Lloyds TSB Bank plc (30-00-02)
**Following financial data are in thousands**

| | 31-12-13 | 31-12-12 | 31-12-11 |
|---|---|---|---|
| TO | 8,594,000 | 8,167,000 | 7,856,000 |
| P/L | (244,000) | 479,000 | 613,000 |
| NW | 1,790,000 | 2,261,000 | 2,442,000 |
| WC | (10,475,000) | (9,093,000) | (10,675,000) |
| Emp. | 23,872 | 23,824 | 23,240 |

DUNS 23-242-7547

## Rsa Northern Ireland Insurance Ltd

**(Subsidiary of:** Rsa Insurance Group Plc)
Law Society House, 106 Victoria Street, Belfast BT1 3GN
**Tel:** 028-9032-0190
**Web:** www.europageneral.com
**Reg No:** 0039814NI **Estd:** 2000 Private Limited Company
**Line of Business:** Activities auxiliary to insurance and pension funding
**Trading Style:** Europa General Underwriters (N.I.) Limited
**Issued Capital:** £10,000
**Directors:** J Mcilduff, R ( Keenan
**Co. Secretary:** Mrs Pamela Cree
**Responsibilities**
**Senior:** Paul Kierans *(Manager)*
**Finance:** Des Doherty *(Accounts Manager)*
**HR:** Des Doherty *(Accounts Manager)*
**Facilities:** Des Doherty *(Accounts Manager)*
**US SIC:** 6411 **UK SIC:** 83200
**Auditors:** Deloitte & Touche
**Bankers:** The Bank Of Ireland (90-21-78)

| | 31-12-13 | 31-12-12 | 31-12-11 |
|---|---|---|---|
| TO | 8,425,464 | 5,214,321 | 2,537,638 |
| P/L | 981,543 | 987,799 | 354,217 |
| NW | 2,982,195 | 2,255,707 | 1,532,583 |
| WC | 2,401,759 | 2,040,771 | 1,352,898 |
| Emp. | 54 | 46 | 44 |

DUNS 21-590-1137

## Rsa Security Division

R S A House, Western Road, Bracknell, Berkshire RG12 1RT
**Tel:** 01344781000
**Web:** www.rsa.com
**Estd:** 2011
**Line of Business:** Internet security
**US SIC:** 7379 **UK SIC:** 83940
**Employees:** 200

DUNS 23-767-8342 **Imp**

## Rsk Group Plc

Spring Lodge, 172 Chester Road, Frodsham, Cheshire WA6 0AR
**Tel:** 01928726006
**Web:** www.rsk.co.uk
**Reg No:** 3761340 **VAT No:** 918476001
**Estd:** 2012 Public Limited Company
**Line of Business:** Environmental consultants
**Export Sales:** £22,751,000
**Issued Capital:** £1,314,826
**Directors:** Ms S Sljivic, N P Board, Dr M A Smyth, M W Mason, P J Witherington, G Charnock, J R Jones, I H Strudwick
**Co. Secretary:** Steven Mills
**Responsibilities**
**Senior:** Stefan Bangels *(Director)*, Abigail Draper *(Director)*, Gareth Moorhead *(Associate Director)*, Alasdair Ryder *(Director)*, Paul Upton *(International Operations Direc)*
**Finance:** Edward Halliwell *(UK Finance Director)*
**Operations:** Paul Upton *(International Operations Direc)*
**US SIC:** 8911 **UK SIC:** 83701
**Auditors:** Ross Brooke Ltd
**Bankers:** HSBC Bank plc (40-31-24)

| | 31-03-14 | 31-03-13 | 31-03-12 |
|---|---|---|---|
| TO | 73,531,000 | 63,578,000 | 60,677,000 |
| P/L | 1,294,000 | 1,162,000 | (985,000) |
| NW | (23,788,000) | (20,342,000) | (20,831,000) |
| WC | 4,297,000 | 180,000 | 1,337,000 |
| Emp. | 824 | 806 | 800 |

DUNS 23-290-8272

## Rsl Enterprises Ltd

9 Decimus Park, Kingstanding Way, Tunbridge Wells, Kent TN2 3GP
**Tel:** 08432080610
**Web:** www.rsl-group.co.uk
**Reg No:** 4119470 **Estd:** 2002 Private Limited Company
**Line of Business:** Management activities of holding companies
**Issued Capital:** £100
**Director:** S Debeger
**Co. Secretary:** Richard Stevens
**US SIC:** 6711 **UK SIC:** 83962

| | 31-12-13 | 31-12-12 | 31-12-11 |
|---|---|---|---|
| TO | 7,014,953 | 1,011,771 | 6,433,140 |
| P/L | 1,225,763 | 922,271 | 835,269 |
| NW | 3,608,800 | 3,235,609 | 3,573,063 |
| WC | 791,233 | 92,646 | 607,364 |
| Emp. | 97 | 11 | 93 |

DUNS 34-770-5613

## Rsl Steeper Holdings Ltd

Artificial Limb Unit, Sykes Street, Hull, North Humberside HU2 8BB
**Tel:** 01482325645
**Web:** www.rslsteeper.co.uk
**Reg No:** 5571486 **Estd:** 2004 Private Limited Company
**Line of Business:** Management activities of holding companies
**Issued Capital:** £10,348,259
**Directors:** N P Winks, N D Hoare
**Co. Secretary:** John Midgley
**Responsibilities**
**Senior:** Paul Laverick *(General Manager)*
**US SIC:** 6711 **UK SIC:** 83962
**Auditors:** BDO LLP

| | 28-02-14 | 28-02-13 | 29-02-12 |
|---|---|---|---|
| TO | 31,783,258 | 29,980,757 | 28,492,893 |
| P/L | 7,864 | (2,795) | (1,776) |
| NW | (5,938,511) | (6,406,688) | (6,516,315) |
| WC | 595,785 | 796,000 | 1,469,419 |
| Emp. | 421 | 400 | 365 |

DUNS 23-631-9500

## Rsm Leisure Ltd

Haunch Lane, Lea Marston, Sutton Coldfield, West Midlands B76 0BY
**Tel:** 01675-470468 **Fax:** 01675470871
**Web:** www.leamarstonhotel.co.uk
**Reg No:** 3628906 **Estd:** 2000 Private Limited Company
**Line of Business:** Management activities of holding companies
**Trading Style:** Lea Marston Hotel
**Issued Capital:** £1,250,002
**Principals:** M I Blake *(Managing)*, R J Blake, J R Blake, S D Blake
**Co. Secretary:** Mark Blake
**Responsibilities**
**Senior:** Tom Kirkham *(Manager)*
**Finance:** Adam Small *(Accountant)*
**US SIC:** 6711, 7011
**UK SIC:** 83962, 66500
**Auditors:** HLB Kidsons

| | 31-03-14 | 31-03-13 | 31-03-12 |
|---|---|---|---|
| TO | 8,823,070 | 8,414,347 | 8,436,629 |
| P/L | 371,757 | 202,338 | 180,652 |
| NW | 5,502,659 | 5,188,902 | 5,042,564 |
| WC | (1,175,632) | (1,133,971) | (965,625) |
| Emp. | 292 | 299 | 297 |

DUNS 21-667-0282

## Rsm McClure Watters Ltd

1 Lanyon Quay, Belfast BT1 3LG
**Tel:** 02890234343
**Web:** www.rsmmcclurewatters.com
**Reg No:** 0602692NI **Estd:** 2005 Private Limited Company
**Line of Business:** Tax consultancy
**Issued Capital:** £200
**Directors:** M Blair, R W Gardiner, D W Gray, D S Watters
**Co. Secretary:** David Gray
**US SIC:** 8931 **UK SIC:** 83600

| | 31-03-14 | 31-03-13 | 31-03-12 |
|---|---|---|---|
| TA | 200 | 200 | 1 |
| NW | 200 | 200 | 1 |

DUNS 21-300-1266 **Imp**

## Rss Jet Centre Ltd

**(Subsidiary of:** Landmark Aviation (Uk) Ltd)
Britannia House, Frank Lester Way, London Luton Airport, Luton, Bedfordshire LU2 9NQ
**Tel:** 01582798400 **Fax:** 0161-436-3450
**Web:** www.oceansky.com
**Reg No:** 0711628 **Estd:** 1961 Private Limited Company
**Line of Business:** Scheduled passenger air transport
**Export Sales:** £447,481
**Issued Capital:** £355,646
**Directors:** R A Ashcraft, D E Barnes
**Responsibilities**
**Senior:** Edward Allison *(Manager)*
**Branches:** Rss Jet Centre Ltd, 111 Easy Way, Luton, Bedfordshire LU2 9DH
**US SIC:** 4511 **UK SIC:** 75000
**Auditors:** Deloitte LLP
**Bankers:** Lloyds TSB Bank plc (30-95-42)

| | 31-12-13 | 31-12-12 | 31-12-11 |
|---|---|---|---|
| TO | 17,755,737 | 18,285,398 | 18,894,446 |
| P/L | (4,971,063) | (2,674,318) | (3,157,396) |
| NW | (13,870,095) | (8,979,585) | (6,197,239) |
| WC | (18,804,136) | 157,882 | (3,020,525) |
| Emp. | 90 | 79 | 138 |

DUNS 22-378-3411

## R.S.S.B

Unit 10 Lyng Lane, West Bromwich, West Midlands B70 7RW
**Tel:** 01215253166
**Web:** www.rssb.co.uk
**Estd:** 2010 Proprietorship
**Line of Business:** Religious organisations and places of worship
**Proprietor:** D Paul
**Responsibilities**
**Senior:** Vipal Kumar *(Manager)*
**US SIC:** 8661 **UK SIC:** 96600
**Employees:** 280

DUNS 21-626-5066 **Exp**

## R.Swain & Sons Ltd

Priory Road, Rochester, Kent ME2 2BD
**Tel:** 01634733333 **Fax:** 01634-739589
**Web:** www.rswain.com
**Reg No:** 0371501 **VAT No:** 303869943
**Estd:** 1941 Private Limited Company
**Line of Business:** Road haulage and transport services
**Issued Capital:** £8,550
**Principals:** R J Swain *(Managing)*, A W Swain, C Dyke, P M Burridge, M G Swain, S Baker
**Co. Secretary:** Andrew Swain
**Responsibilities**
**Senior:** Graham Lord *(Transport Manager)*
**Finance:** Terry Birley *(Finance Director)*
**IT:** Stuart Wake *(Computer Manager)*
**HR:** Amanda Rootes *(Personnel Director)*
**Health & Safety:** Amanda Rootes *(Personnel Director)*
**Facilities:** Peter Standen *(Facilities Manager)*
**Fleet:** Graham Lord *(Transport Manager)*
**Branches:** R.swain & Sons Ltd, Potters La, Wednesbury, West Midlands WS10 0AT
**US SIC:** 4789 **UK SIC:** 77002
**Auditors:** Beak Kemmenoe
**Bankers:** Barclays Bank Plc (20-54-11)

| | 31-12-13 | 31-12-12 | 31-12-11 |
|---|---|---|---|
| TO | 34,876,539 | 31,810,865 | 29,123,910 |
| P/L | 1,342,553 | 1,087,314 | 705,210 |
| NW | 5,193,098 | 4,180,741 | 4,177,153 |
| WC | (408,146) | (597,928) | (1,001,201) |
| Emp. | 441 | 376 | 349 |

DUNS 21-164-3195

## Rt Infrastructure Solutions Ltd

91 Dales Road, Ipswich, Suffolk IP1 4JR
**Tel:** 01473242330
**Web:** www.rt-is.co.uk
**Reg No:** 6903399 **Estd:** 2009 Private Limited Company
**Line of Business:** Employment and recruitment companies and consultants
**Issued Capital:** £50,001
**Directors:** S E Jamieson, A R Thomas
**Co. Secretary:** Andrew Thomas
**Responsibilities**
**Senior:** Mary Wood *(Operations Manager)*
**US SIC:** 7361 **UK SIC:** 83954

| | 31-08-14 | 31-08-13 | 31-08-12 |
|---|---|---|---|
| TA | 1,040,644 | 891,800 | 1 |
| NW | 56,321 | 118,777 | 1 |
| WC | 37,056 | 111,277 | N/A |

DUNS 28-956-5855

## R.T. Keedwell Ltd

(**Subsidiary of:** R. T. Keedwell Holdings Ltd)
Commerce Way, Highbridge, Somerset TA9 4AG
**Tel:** 01278-788731 **Fax:** 01278-795241
**Web:** www.rtkeedwellgroup.co.uk
**Reg No:** 1658126 **VAT No:** 130309320
**Estd:** 2009 Private Limited Company
**Line of Business:** Road haulage and transport services
**Trading Style:** R.T. Keedwell Ltd
**Issued Capital:** £100
**Principals:** R T Keedwell *(Managing)*, S R Keedwell, J D White
**Co. Secretary:** Mrs Pauline Keedwell
**US SIC:** 4789 **UK SIC:** 77002
**Auditors:** T.P. Lewis & Partners (BOS) Ltd
**Bankers:** Barclays Bank Plc (20-94-74)

| | 31-10-13 | 31-10-12 | 31-10-11 |
|---|---|---|---|
| TO | 13,482,499 | 12,148,886 | 12,574,836 |
| P/L | 879,134 | 475,394 | 761,171 |
| NW | 9,867,255 | 9,156,050 | 8,701,992 |
| WC | 4,829,885 | 4,653,461 | 4,247,741 |
| Emp. | 122 | 106 | 115 |

DUNS 21-402-4010

## R.T. Stuart Ltd

Number 3, Newbridge, Midlothian EH28 8NB
**Tel:** 01313350940 **Fax:** 01333-420020
**Web:** www.scotlandfoodanddrink.org
**Reg No:** 0021805SC **VAT No:** 268337726
**Estd:** 1857 Private Limited Company
**Line of Business:** Manufacture of bread; manufacture of fresh pastry goods and cakes
**Trading Style:** Scotland Food & Drink
**Issued Capital:** £24,350
**Principals:** A J Stuart *(Managing)*, K Stuart, Ms J M Stuart, D Mcmahon
**Co. Secretary:** Stephen Haig
**Responsibilities**
**Senior:** James Withers *(Chief Executive Officer)*
**Finance:** Gillian Cullen *(Finance Administrator)*
**IT:** Heath Booth *(IT Manager)*
**Branches:** R.t. Stuart Ltd, 37 High Street, Leven, Fife KY8 4NE
**US SIC:** 2051, 5423
**UK SIC:** 41960, 64100
**Auditors:** Carters
**Bankers:** The Royal Bank Of Scotland Plc (83-24-24)

| | 31-03-14 | 31-03-13 | 31-03-12 |
|---|---|---|---|
| TA | 2,586,854 | 2,265,420 | 2,376,616 |
| NW | 1,082,567 | 977,066 | 947,575 |
| WC | (355,070) | (312,142) | (352,686) |

DUNS 21-000-1780 Imp

## Rta Trading Ltd

Asher House, Blackburn Road, London NW6 1AW
**Tel:** 020-7447-3900
**Web:** www.accurist.co.uk
**Reg No:** 0419400 **Estd:** 1946 Private Limited Company
**Line of Business:** Manufacture of watches and clocks
**Issued Capital:** £200,000
**Principals:** A D Loftus *(Managing)*, R I Loftus, A L Loftus
**Co. Secretary:** Horace Hickson
**Responsibilities**
**Marketing:** Mark Gwinnett *(Sales Manager)*
**Sales:** Mark Gwinnett *(Sales Manager)*
**US SIC:** 3873 **UK SIC:** 37400
**Auditors:** Silver Altman

| | 30-04-14 | 31-03-13 | 31-04-12 |
|---|---|---|---|
| TO | 10,525,896 | 10,329,745 | 10,324,339 |
| P/L | 3,903,189 | 346,895 | 90,108 |
| NW | 6,759,553 | 3,312,330 | 3,489,276 |
| WC | 7,240,788 | 4,026,315 | 3,999,513 |
| Emp. | 52 | 52 | 55 |

DUNS 39-029-0229 Imp

## Rtc Europe Ltd

(**Subsidiary of:** Rtc Industries Inc)
Eurolink Industrial Centre, Castle Road, Sittingbourne, Kent ME10 3RN
**Tel:** 01795-412795
**Web:** www.retailactivation.com
**Reg No:** 2108779 **VAT No:** 662200082
**Estd:** 1987 Private Limited Company
**Line of Business:** Display equipment and fixtures
**Export Sales:** £3,076,504
**Issued Capital:** £2,675,000
**Directors:** R L Nathan, W Nathan
**Co. Secretary:** Mark Jerram
**US SIC:** 7319, 2794
**UK SIC:** 83800, 47545
**Auditors:** Perrys
**Bankers:** Barclays Bank Plc (20-36-16)

| | 31-12-13 | 31-12-12 | 31-12-11 |
|---|---|---|---|
| TO | 23,102,031 | 12,745,669 | 10,654,022 |
| P/L | 933,678 | 647,596 | 131,819 |
| NW | 3,797,253 | 3,153,317 | 2,578,222 |
| WC | 5,307,353 | 1,789,979 | 1,057,386 |
| Emp. | 71 | 59 | 57 |

DUNS 76-414-6841

## Rtc Group Plc

The Derby Conference Centre, Derby, Derbyshire DE24 8UX
**Tel:** 01332861345 **Fax:** 08708901880
**Web:** www.rtcgroupplc.co.uk
**Reg No:** 2558971 **VAT No:** 567785673
**Estd:** 1990 Public Limited Company
**Line of Business:** Employment and recruitment companies and consultants
**Trading Style:** A T A Selection
**Issued Capital:** £135,116
**Directors:** W J Douie, A M Pendlebury, Mrs S L Dye, T D Jackson
**Co. Secretary:** Mrs Sarah Dye
**Responsibilities**
**Senior:** Scott Bulloch *(Manager)*
**Branches:** Rtc Group Plc, York House, 38 Great Charles St Queensway, Birmingham, West Midlands B3 3JY
**US SIC:** 7361 **UK SIC:** 83954
**Auditors:** PKF (UK) LLP
**Bankers:** Barclays Bank Plc (20-05-06)

| | 31-12-13 | 31-12-12 | 31-12-11 |
|---|---|---|---|
| TO | 48,817,000 | 42,963,000 | 29,519,000 |
| P/L | 736,000 | 474,000 | (561,000) |
| NW | 1,701,000 | 1,171,000 | 637,000 |
| WC | 1,182,000 | 529,000 | 213,000 |
| Emp. | 219 | 200 | 173 |

DUNS 21-692-3961

## R.T.H. Holdings Ltd

Shotover Kilns Shotover Hill, Oxford, Oxfordshire OX3 8ST
**Tel:** 01865-742300 **Fax:** 01865-741405
**Web:** www.rtharris.co.uk
**Reg No:** 0651550 **Estd:** 1947 Private Limited Company
**Line of Business:** Apartment buildings
**Issued Capital:** £2,750
**Principals:** I R Harris *(Chairman)*, M R Harris
**Co. Secretary:** Frances Harris
**US SIC:** 6519, 6711
**UK SIC:** 85000, 83962
**Auditors:** Wenn Townsend
**Bankers:** Lloyds TSB Bank plc (30-94-04)

| | 30-04-14 | 30-04-13 | 30-04-12 |
|---|---|---|---|
| TO | 5,002,262 | 8,066,725 | 4,428,255 |
| P/L | 993,347 | 734,103 | 288,124 |
| NW | 4,314,672 | 3,606,991 | 3,044,314 |
| WC | 224,773 | 356,890 | (119,510) |
| Emp. | 53 | 54 | 54 |

DUNS 50-497-1995 Imp-Exp

## Rtkl-Uk Ltd.

(**Subsidiary of:** Arcadis N.V.)
25 Farringdon St 10th Floor, London EC4A 4AB
**Tel:** 02073060404 **Fax:** 020-7306-0405
**Web:** www.rtkl.com
**Reg No:** 2465376 **VAT No:** 497645093
**Estd:** 1990 Private Limited Company
**Line of Business:** Architects
**Issued Capital:** £18,000
**Directors:** B Barker, T Lundgren, J G Beroiz, L Josal, J E Badman, Ms M M Sobik, K J Christian, M Faruqi
**Co. Secretary:** Randall Pace
**Responsibilities**
**Senior:** Harold Thompson *(Director)*
**US SIC:** 8911 **UK SIC:** 83701
**Auditors:** KPMG LLP
**Bankers:** Barclays Bank Plc (20-65-82)

| | 31-12-13 | 31-12-12 | 31-12-11 |
|---|---|---|---|
| TO | 12,784,429 | 8,812,130 | 9,836,146 |
| P/L | (466,503) | (969,392) | 62,789 |
| NW | 1,546,158 | 1,699,961 | 3,041,207 |
| WC | 71,647 | (220,686) | 2,671,890 |
| Emp. | 72 | 63 | 64 |

DUNS 21-614-9617

## R.T.Rate Ltd

Hogg Lane, Grays, Essex RM17 5QL
**Tel:** 01375-391234
**Web:** www.rates.co.uk
**Reg No:** 0553972 **Estd:** 1945 Private Limited Company
**Line of Business:** New & used motor vehicle dealers
**Trading Style:** Rates of Grays, Rapidfit
**Issued Capital:** £6,666
**Principals:** C J Rate *(Chairman and Managing)*, M Day, Mrs C A Rate, A W Brigden
**Co. Secretary:** Anthony Cade
**US SIC:** 5511, 5521, 7539, 5531
**UK SIC:** 65100, 67100
**Auditors:** Elliott Mortlock Busby & Co
**Bankers:** National Westminster Bank Plc (60-09-11)

| | 31-12-13 | 31-12-12 | 31-12-11 |
|---|---|---|---|
| TO | 42,137,285 | 34,328,020 | 31,084,262 |
| P/L | 615,194 | 444,472 | 261,060 |
| NW | 3,911,010 | 3,567,045 | 3,299,748 |
| WC | 2,397,055 | 2,175,492 | 1,980,496 |
| Emp. | 59 | 60 | 63 |

DUNS 21-625-2969

## Rts Consultants (International) Ltd

(**Subsidiary of:** Rts Consultants (Uk) Ltd.)
1 Langley Road, Chippenham, Wiltshire SN15 1BP
**Web:** www.rtsgroup.com
**Reg No:** 7051657 **Estd:** 2009 Private Limited Company
**Line of Business:** Business and management consultancy activities not elsewhere classified
**Issued Capital:** £100
**Directors:** M J Miller, R S Wells
**Co. Secretary:** Alison Noble
**US SIC:** 7392 **UK SIC:** 83951

| | 30-06-13 | 30-06-12 | 30-06-11 |
|---|---|---|---|
| TA | 273,614 | 218,726 | 407,261 |
| NW | (52,985) | (88,053) | (40,270) |
| WC | (53,635) | (89,735) | (42,275) |

DUNS 21-600-4630 Imp-Exp

## R.Twining & Company Ltd

(**Subsidiary of:** Wittington Investments Ltd)
South Way, Walworth Industril Estate, Andover, Hampshire SP10 5AQ
**Tel:** 01264334477
**Web:** www.jacksonsofpiccadilly.co.uk
**Reg No:** 0525071 **VAT No:** 730168554
**Estd:** 1953 Private Limited Company
**Line of Business:** Road haulage and transport services
**Export Markets:** Worldwide
**Export Sales:** £160,574,000
**Trading Style:** Twining, Jacksons of Piccadilly
**Issued Capital:** £40,940
**Directors:** G T Mccallum, R E Tavener, N S Revett
**Co. Secretary:** Mrs Rosalyn Schofield
**Responsibilities**
**Senior:** Ben Matley *(Manager)*
**Purchasing:** Mike Wright *(New Product Development Manage)*
**Branches:** R.twining & Company Ltd, 110 Cambuslang Road, Glasgow, Lanarkshire G73 1BQ
**US SIC:** 4789, 5199
**UK SIC:** 77002, 61900
**Auditors:** KPMG Audit PLC
**Bankers:** Lloyds TSB Bank plc (30-00-02)

| | 31-08-14 | 31-08-13 | 15-08-12 |
|---|---|---|---|
| TO | 280,543,000 | 273,240,000 | 265,242,000 |
| P/L | 43,147,000 | 23,969,000 | 17,114,000 |
| NW | 18,123,000 | 7,607,000 | 8,908,000 |
| WC | (1,226,000) | (15,319,000) | (12,034,000) |
| Emp. | 478 | 512 | 514 |

DUNS 22-851-1879

## Rubax Lifts Ltd

(**Subsidiary of:** Frostall Ltd)
Wilson House, Warrington, Cheshire WA2 0XP
**Tel:** 01925849200
**Web:** www.rubax.co.uk
**Reg No:** 1509899 **VAT No:** 343906649
**Estd:** 1979 Private Limited Company
**Line of Business:** Lifts (maintenance and repair)
**Issued Capital:** £5,000
**Principals:** P Verey *(Managing)*, D P Verey
**Co. Secretary:** Mrs Maureen Verey
**Branches:** Rubax Lifts Ltd, Wilson House, Unit 6, Warrington, Cheshire WA2 0XP
**US SIC:** 3534, 7341
**UK SIC:** 32553, 92300
**Auditors:** Allens Accountants Ltd
**Bankers:** National Westminster Bank Plc (01-06-88)

| | 31-12-13 | 31-12-12 | 31-12-11 |
|---|---|---|---|
| TO | 9,798,062 | 9,507,283 | 8,425,380 |
| P/L | 1,076,981 | 1,249,980 | 1,240,686 |
| NW | 3,735,032 | 2,906,651 | 1,968,085 |
| WC | 3,023,821 | 2,309,224 | 1,261,590 |
| Emp. | 75 | 70 | 66 |

DUNS 21-318-6687 Imp-Exp

## Rubb Buildings Ltd

(**Subsidiary of:** Rubb Group As)
Team Valley Trading Estate, Gateshead, Tyne and Wear NE11 0QE
**Tel:** 0191-482-2211 **Fax:** 0191-482-2516
**Web:** www.rubb.com
**Reg No:** 1309845 **VAT No:** 301034337
**Estd:** 1977 Private Limited Company
**Line of Business:** Portable buildings
**Export Markets:** Germany, Turkey, Italy, Middle East, France
**Export Sales:** £69,070
**Issued Capital:** £30,000
**Principals:** W F Wood *(Managing)*, I Hindmoor, T Torgersen, J E Torgersen
**Co. Secretary:** Finn Haldorsen
**Responsibilities**
**Senior:** Michael Halpin *(Warehouse Manager)*
**Admin:** Lynn Hindson *(office Manager)*, Liz Spurr *(Office Manager)*
**HR:** Liz Spurr *(Office Manager)*
**Health & Safety:** Mike Mote *(Quality Manager)*
**Operations:** Mike Mote *(Quality Manager)*, Liz Spurr *(Office Manager)*
**US SIC:** 3499 **UK SIC:** 31694
**Auditors:** PricewaterhouseCoopers
**Bankers:** Barclays Bank Plc (20-33-51)

| | 31-12-13 | 31-12-12 | 31-12-11 |
|---|---|---|---|
| TO | 3,768,964 | 8,244,749 | 6,653,357 |
| P/L | (248,841) | 1,075,618 | 340,349 |
| NW | 2,029,019 | 2,814,488 | 2,210,265 |
| WC | 1,791,078 | 2,543,550 | 1,895,645 |
| Emp. | 51 | 59 | 55 |

DUNS 21-627-0237

## Rubber Astic Ltd

(**Subsidiary of:** The Wilkes Partnership Llp)
Vulcan Road, Bilston, West Midlands WV14 7HT
**Tel:** 01902407150
**Web:** www.rubberastic.com
**Reg No:** 7064963 **Estd:** 2005 Private Limited Company
**Line of Business:** Manufacturers of rubber products
**Trading Style:** Ramsay Rubber
**Issued Capital:** £1
**Director:** M H Dell
**Co. Secretary:** Mrs Lisa Botfield
**Responsibilities**
**Senior:** Paul Killeen *(Manager)*
**US SIC:** 3069 **UK SIC:** 48123

| | 30-11-13 | 30-11-12 | 30-11-11 |
|---|---|---|---|
| TA | 1 | 1 | 1 |
| NW | 1 | 1 | 1 |

DUNS 76-910-2922 Exp

## Rubberatkins Ltd

Hydro House, Claymore Avenue, Aberdeen, Aberdeenshire AB23 8GW
**Tel:** 01224246777 **Fax:** 01224-248342
**Web:** www.rubberatkins.co.uk
**Reg No:** 0109744SC **VAT No:** 498174691
**Estd:** 1988 Private Limited Company
**Line of Business:** Manufacture of other rubber products
**Export Sales:** £6,193,175
**Issued Capital:** £30,242
**Managing Director:** N Atkins
**Co. Secretary:** Ms Jill Webster
**Responsibilities**
**Senior:** Andy More *(Factory Manager)*
**Finance:** June Chisholm *(Office Manager)*
**Admin:** Susan Caroline *(IT Administrator)*, June Chisholm *(Office Manager)*
**HR:** Jacqueline Rennison *(Human Resources Advisor)*
**Health & Safety:** Andy More *(Factory Manager)*
**Facilities:** Ronnie Milne *(Maintenance Manager)*, Stan Walker *(Maintenance Manager)*
**US SIC:** 3069 **UK SIC:** 48123
**Auditors:** Williamson & Dunn
**Bankers:** Lloyds TSB Bank plc (30-10-01)

| | 30-09-13 | 30-09-12 | 30-09-11 |
|---|---|---|---|
| TO | 9,352,841 | N/A | N/A |
| P/L | 2,353,088 | N/A | N/A |
| NW | 4,783,208 | 3,056,958 | 1,704,685 |
| WC | 3,016,379 | 1,757,530 | 1,017,401 |
| Emp. | 90 | N/A | N/A |

DUNS 21-810-8991 Imp-Exp

## Rubery Owen Holdings Ltd

Po Box 10, Wednesbury, West Midlands WS10 8JD
**Tel:** 01215263131 **Fax:** 0121-526-2869
**Web:** www.ruberyowen.com
**Reg No:** 0166447 **Estd:** 2012 Private Limited Company
**Line of Business:** Investment companies and vehicles
**Export Markets:** W Europe
**Export Sales:** £1,728,614
**Trading Style:** Rubery Owen Group Services, Rozonne, Roteck Laboratories, Burrows Grass Machinery
**Issued Capital:** £1,029,408
**Principals:** J E Owen *(Managing)*, C W Owen, D F Allison, R M Jenkins, J P Owen
**Co. Secretary:** Ms Elaine Eaton
**US SIC:** 6711 **UK SIC:** 83962
**Auditors:** Mazars LLP

| | 31-12-13 | 31-12-12 | 30-12-11 |
|---|---|---|---|
| TO | 52,066,731 | 53,319,033 | 38,791,105 |
| P/L | 877,319 | (352,520) | (233,522) |
| NW | 10,758,398 | 9,335,389 | 10,549,389 |
| WC | 4,092,061 | 3,280,263 | 3,416,097 |
| Emp. | 170 | 153 | 168 |

DUNS 28-942-4731

## Rubicon Drinks Ltd

(**Subsidiary of:** A.G. Barr P.L.C.)
Unit 5, Rubicon House, Second Way, Wembley, Middlesex HA9 0YJ
**Tel:** 02089009944 **Fax:** 02089009955
**Web:** www.rubiconexotic.com
**Reg No:** 1585600 **VAT No:** 346676814
**Estd:** 1981 Private Limited Company

**Line of Business:** Manufacture of mineral waters and soft drinks
**Trading Style:** Rubicon Foods, Rubicon Beverages
**Issued Capital:** £15,000
**Directors:** R A White, S W Lorimer
**Co. Secretary:** Miss Julie Barr
**Branches:** Rubicon Drinks Ltd, Unit 25, Tafarnaubach Industrial Estate, Tredegar, Gwent NP22 3AA
**US SIC:** 2086 **UK SIC:** 42831
**Auditors:** Sterling
**Bankers:** Lloyds TSB Bank plc (30-96-29)

| | 26-01-14 | 26-01-13 | 28-01-12 |
|---|---|---|---|
| TO | 49,747,000 | 48,716,000 | 47,864,000 |
| P/L | 12,304,000 | 9,567,000 | 8,125,000 |
| NW | 40,943,000 | 31,500,000 | 24,260,000 |
| WC | 39,902,000 | 30,312,000 | 22,786,000 |
| Emp. | N/A | N/A | 2 |

DUNS 45-805-3022
## Rubicon Pastimes Ltd
12-14 The Front, Hartlepool, Cleveland TS25 1BS
**Tel:** 01429266371
**Reg No:** 3163234 **Estd:** 1998 Private Limited Company
**Line of Business:** Other entertainment activities not elsewhere classified
**Issued Capital:** £716,400
**Director:** S L Nichols
**Co. Secretary:** Ms Helen Nichola
**US SIC:** 7999 **UK SIC:** 97913
**Auditors:** Baines Goldston
**Bankers:** Yorkshire Bank Plc (05-06-01)

| | 31-10-13 | 31-10-12 | 31-10-11 |
|---|---|---|---|
| TO | 3,658,097 | 3,601,700 | N/A |
| P/L | 33,987 | (36,588) | N/A |
| NW | 1,312,456 | 1,330,357 | 1,375,533 |
| WC | 70,614 | (112,994) | (231,725) |
| Emp. | 84 | 82 | N/A |

DUNS 23-509-6745 Imp
## Rubie's Masquerade Co (U K) Ltd
3-4 Moses Winter Way, Wallingford, Oxfordshire OX10 9FE
**Tel:** 01491-826500
**Web:** www.rubiesuk.com
**Reg No:** 3508897 **VAT No:** 628760417
**Estd:** 1998 Private Limited Company
**Line of Business:** Other wholesale
**Export Sales:** £38,800,000
**Issued Capital:** £6,549,246
**Directors:** C J Isitt, H Beige
**Co. Secretary:** Marc Beige
**Responsibilities**
**Finance:** Linda Bassett *(Financial Controller)*
**US SIC:** 5199 **UK SIC:** 61900
**Auditors:** Richardson Jones

| | 30-06-13 | 30-06-12 | 30-06-11 |
|---|---|---|---|
| TO | 67,722,000 | 21,336,155 | 20,587,887 |
| P/L | 3,315,000 | 826,701 | 486,904 |
| NW | 10,142,000 | 7,255,690 | 6,596,243 |
| WC | 8,883,000 | 3,204,415 | 2,645,484 |
| Emp. | 202 | 86 | 84 |

DUNS 21-231-9070
## Ruckland Court
Ruckland Avenue, Lincoln, Lincolnshire LN1 3TP
**Tel:** 01522-530217
**Web:** www.lacehousing.org
**Estd:** 1990
**Line of Business:** Rest and retirement homes
**Partners:** Miss F Naylor, Mrs F Naylor
**Responsibilities**
**Senior:** Angie Smith *(Home Manager)*
**Finance:** Dee Chapman *(Senior Finance Administrator)*
**US SIC:** 8321 **UK SIC:** 96111
**Employees:** 53

DUNS 21-552-7974
## Rudding Park Golf Club
Follifoot Road, Harrogate, North Yorkshire HG3 1ES
**Tel:** 01423-872100
**Web:** www.ruddingpark.co.uk
**Estd:** 1987 Proprietorship
**Line of Business:** Golf clubs
**Proprietor:** G Molyneux
**Responsibilities**
**Senior:** Judith Mackaness *(Manager)*
**US SIC:** 7999 **UK SIC:** 97913
**Employees:** 195

DUNS 29-536-8781
## Ruddington Homes Ltd
**(Subsidiary of:** Moriah House Ltd)
46 Easthorpe Street, Nottingham, Nottinghamshire NG11 6LA
**Tel:** 01159-217610
**Web:** www.ruddingtonhomes.co.uk
**Reg No:** 1903864 **Estd:** 1985 Private Limited Company
**Line of Business:** Social work activities with accommodation
**Trading Style:** Orchard House Residential Home, St Peters Rest Home, Balmore Nursing Home
**Issued Capital:** £25,000
**Director:** P Hearn
**Branches:** Ruddington Homes Ltd, 15 Vicarage Lane, Nottingham, Nottinghamshire NG11 6HB
**US SIC:** 8321 **UK SIC:** 96111
**Auditors:** Hobsons
**Bankers:** National Westminster Bank Plc (60-13-23)

| | 31-12-13 | 31-12-12 | 30-12-11 |
|---|---|---|---|
| TO | 2,592,350 | N/A | N/A |
| P/L | 26,250 | N/A | N/A |
| NW | 2,733,124 | 2,667,461 | 2,236,612 |
| WC | 1,119,767 | 945,787 | 864,809 |
| Emp. | 107 | N/A | N/A |

DUNS 22-525-7609 Imp
## Ruddy Joinery Ltd
Unit 10 Enterprise Way, Flitwick, Bedford, Bedfordshire MK45 5BS
**Tel:** 01525-716603 **Fax:** 01525-718595
**Web:** www.ruddy.co.uk
**Reg No:** 1352763 **VAT No:** 706323266
**Estd:** 1978 Private Limited Company
**Line of Business:** Manufacturers of joinery
**Issued Capital:** £9,000
**Principals:** P J Ruddy *(Chairman)*, A J Ruddy, L M Ruddy, Mrs E C Ruddy, B J Drane, M Mc Gilloway
**Responsibilities**
**Marketing:** John Doody *(Joint Managing Director)*
**Branches:** Ruddy Joinery Ltd, Ealing Studios Ealing Gn, London W5 5EP
**US SIC:** 2431 **UK SIC:** 46300
**Auditors:** Riordan O' Sullivan & Co
**Bankers:** Allied Irish Bank (gb) (23-83-95)

| | 31-12-13 | 31-12-12 | 31-12-11 |
|---|---|---|---|
| TO | 58,697,794 | 47,413,607 | 35,864,281 |
| P/L | 3,885,125 | 2,955,837 | 2,270,224 |
| NW | 13,757,545 | 10,855,809 | 9,123,897 |
| WC | 14,687,654 | 11,326,197 | 9,289,214 |
| Emp. | 145 | 130 | 135 |

DUNS 76-398-9175 Imp
## Ruder Finn U K Ltd
**(Subsidiary of:** Ruder Finn Group Inc.)
2nd Floor, London WC2E 9HG
**Tel:** 02074383050 **Fax:** 020-7462-8999
**Web:** www.ruderfinn.com
**Reg No:** 2556531 **Estd:** 1990 Private Limited Company
**Line of Business:** Public relations activities
**Export Sales:** £2,008,881
**Issued Capital:** £100
**Principals:** Ms K Bloomgarden *(President)*, N J Leonard
**Co. Secretary:** Alison Denham
**Responsibilities**
**Senior:** Peter Finn *(Vice Chairman)*
**US SIC:** 7392 **UK SIC:** 83951
**Auditors:** Grant Thornton
**Bankers:** Lloyds TSB Bank plc (30-97-71)

| | 31-12-13 | 31-12-12 | 31-12-11 |
|---|---|---|---|
| TO | 4,783,050 | 3,895,017 | 3,265,383 |
| P/L | 393,223 | 250,909 | 15,250 |
| NW | 1,447,702 | 1,145,841 | 942,572 |
| WC | 1,330,617 | 992,833 | 801,195 |

DUNS 21-774-5684
## Rudheath High School
Shipbrook Road, Rudheath, Northwich, Cheshire CW9 7DT
**Tel:** 0160642515
**Web:** www.rudheathhs.cheshire.co.uk
**Estd:** 2011 Partnership
**Line of Business:** Schools (local authority)
**Partners:** M Wood, M Hayhurst
**US SIC:** 8211 **UK SIC:** 93200
**Employees:** 100

DUNS 29-012-6846
## Rudolf Steiner School Kings Langley Ltd
Langley Hill, King's Langley, Hertfordshire WD4 9HG
**Tel:** 01923-262505
**Reg No:** 0395056 **Estd:** 1945 Private Limited Company
**Line of Business:** Adult and other education not elsewhere classified
**Directors:** Mrs J Etchell, Mrs K Goode, T Hart-Shea, G J Dalrymple, Mrs S Alkema, P Murray, Dr S Peat
**Co. Secretary:** Mrs Carol Langley
**US SIC:** 8249 **UK SIC:** 93300
**Bankers:** National Westminster Bank Plc (60-00-08)

| | 31-07-14 | 31-07-13 | 31-07-12 |
|---|---|---|---|
| TO | 3,094,688 | 2,834,445 | 2,785,414 |
| P/L | 348,082 | 137,155 | 33,838 |
| NW | 2,249,624 | 1,902,055 | 1,764,104 |
| WC | 1,107,194 | 625,035 | 584,725 |
| Emp. | 59 | 67 | 65 |

DUNS 23-890-9613
## Rudolph & Hellmann Automotive Ltd
Charter House, Sandford Street, Lichfield, Staffordshire WS13 6QA
**Tel:** 01543-441670
**Web:** www.rh-automotive.co.uk
**Reg No:** 3881895 **Estd:** 1999 Private Limited Company
**Line of Business:** Operation of storage facilities
**Issued Capital:** £50,000
**Directors:** P Weide, J R Hyde, M J Rollings, T Rudolph, A Connor, B W Oevermann, M F Cranidge
**Co. Secretary:** Jeffrey Hyde
**US SIC:** 4226 **UK SIC:** 77003
**Auditors:** Mazars LLP
**Bankers:** Yorkshire Bank Plc (05-03-03)

| | 31-12-13 | 31-12-12 | 31-12-11 |
|---|---|---|---|
| TO | 14,616,994 | 12,632,991 | 10,483,269 |
| P/L | 146,824 | 670,047 | 582,752 |
| NW | 2,066,153 | 2,344,665 | 2,794,890 |
| WC | 1,921,009 | 2,238,511 | 2,659,942 |
| Emp. | 303 | 261 | 234 |

DUNS 23-934-2210
## Rudridge Ltd
2 Coxbridge Business Park, Alton Road, Farnham, Surrey GU10 5EH
**Tel:** 01252-711911 **Fax:** 01252-718623
**Web:** www.rudridge.co.uk
**Reg No:** 3923995 **VAT No:** 733675516
**Estd:** 2000 Private Limited Company
**Line of Business:** Activities of other transport agencies
**Issued Capital:** £51,613
**Managing Director:** A Betteridge
**Co. Secretary:** Robert Rudd
**Branches:** Rudridge Ltd, Mark Lane, Gravesend, Kent DA12 2QB
**US SIC:** 4712 **UK SIC:** 77002

| | 30-06-14 | 30-06-13 | 30-06-12 |
|---|---|---|---|
| TO | 41,397,474 | 31,592,574 | 27,412,566 |
| P/L | 2,026,063 | 997,734 | 1,121,326 |
| NW | 2,578,720 | 1,557,804 | 2,220,080 |
| WC | 2,361,388 | 1,333,776 | 2,120,945 |
| Emp. | 69 | 50 | 43 |

DUNS 21-773-6194
## Rudyard Kipling Primary School
Chalkland Rise, Brighton, East Sussex BN2 6RH
**Tel:** 01273303328
**Web:** www.kiplink.co.uk
**Estd:** 2000 Proprietorship
**Line of Business:** Primary education
**Proprietor:** Mrs J Aldridge
**US SIC:** 8211 **UK SIC:** 93200
**Employees:** 65

DUNS 73-797-7835
## Ruffer Management Ltd
80 Victoria Street, London SW1E 5JL
**Tel:** 020-7963-8100 **Fax:** 02072080096
**Web:** www.ruffer.co.uk
**Reg No:** 2929040 **Estd:** 1994 Private Limited Company
**Line of Business:** Investment companies and vehicles
**Issued Capital:** £100
**Directors:** M C Marmion, Ms R J Tufnell, R C Odey, The Right Honourable R W 14th Earl Ferrers, J G Ruffer
**Co. Secretary:** Ms Edwina Blackford
**Responsibilities**
**Senior:** Derek Berry *(Manager)*, Henry Maxey *(Chief Executive)*, Russell Whitefoord *(Manager)*, Robert th Earl Ferrers *(Director)*
**Sales:** Guy Shirley *(Business Projects Manager)*
**HR:** William Jutsum *(HR Director)*, Vanessa Webster *(Head of HR)*
**Operations:** Dave Francis *(Chief Operating Officer)*, Nick Horder *(Operations Director)*, Russell Vickers *(Operations Processing Manager)*
**US SIC:** 6111 **UK SIC:** 81501
**Auditors:** Dixon Wilson
**Bankers:** Bank Of Scotland (12-21-37)

| | 31-03-14 | 31-03-13 | 31-03-12 |
|---|---|---|---|
| TA | 124,398,850 | 117,839,254 | 108,822,988 |
| P/L | 124,564,053 | 115,302,761 | 108,079,823 |
| NW | 8,827,697 | 8,191,252 | 6,656,570 |
| WC | 82,606,950 | 98,159,229 | 92,217,027 |
| Emp. | 145 | 123 | 116 |

DUNS 23-727-2133
## Rufflets Country House Hotel
Strathkinness Low Road, St Andrews, Fife KY16 9TX
**Tel:** 01334-472594
**Web:** www.rufflets.co.uk
**Estd:** 1952 Proprietorship
**Line of Business:** Hotels and motels without restaurant
**Proprietor:** Mrs A Murray-Smith
**Responsibilities**
**Senior:** Gavin Aitken *(Food & Beverage Manager)*, Ann Murray-smith *(Proprietor)*
**Marketing:** Ann Murray-smith *(Proprietor)*
**Facilities:** Ann Murray-smith *(Proprietor)*
**US SIC:** 7011 **UK SIC:** 66500
**Employees:** 50

DUNS 76-944-7988
## Rufford Stud Ltd
**(Subsidiary of:** Eastwood Anglo-European Investments Ltd)
Rufford Abbey, Rufford, Newark, Nottinghamshire NG22 9DF
**Tel:** 01623822944
**Web:** www.nottinghamshire.gov.uk
**Reg No:** 1515848 **Estd:** 1980 Private Limited Company
**Line of Business:** Farming (livestock)
**Issued Capital:** £57,000
**Director:** W H Eastwood
**Co. Secretary:** Thomas Eastwood
**US SIC:** 0279, 7999
**UK SIC:** 01001, 97913
**Bankers:** National Westminster Bank Plc (60-14-03)

| | 31-03-14 | 31-03-13 | 31-03-12 |
|---|---|---|---|
| TA | 445 | 445 | 445 |
| NW | (296,725) | (296,725) | (296,725) |
| WC | (296,725) | (296,725) | (296,725) |

DUNS 42-416-2704
## Rufford Veterinary Group Ltd
9 Holly Lane, Rufford, Ormskirk, Lancashire L40 1SH
**Tel:** 01704821204 **Fax:** 01704-822902
**Web:** www.ruffordvets.com
**Reg No:** 4403963 **Estd:** 1902 Private Limited Company
**Line of Business:** Veterinary activities
**Issued Capital:** £10,000
**Directors:** I J Fraser, S Miller, J Greenwood
**Co. Secretary:** Seamus Miller
**US SIC:** 0741 **UK SIC:** 95601

| | 30-09-13 | 30-09-12 | 30-09-11 |
|---|---|---|---|
| TA | 1,221,035 | 1,085,177 | 1,101,257 |
| NW | 661,452 | 623,632 | 637,774 |
| WC | 274,705 | 206,774 | 322,143 |

DUNS 39-751-4209
## Rufforth Park Equestrian
Rufforth Park Equestrian, Wether, York, North Yorkshire YO23 3QH
**Tel:** 01617922152
**Web:** www.rufforthcarboot.com
**Reg No:** 2190821 **Estd:** 1987 Private Limited Company
**Line of Business:** Arts the
**Issued Capital:** £100
**Managing Director:** R M Ginley
**Co. Secretary:** Ms Angela Ginley
**US SIC:** 8999 **UK SIC:** 83954
**Auditors:** Garbutt & Elliot, York.
**Bankers:** Barclays Bank Plc (20-99-56)

| | 30-09-13 | 30-09-12 | 30-09-11 |
|---|---|---|---|
| TO | 2,808,594 | 2,901,874 | 2,964,028 |
| P/L | 146,314 | 308,445 | 145,017 |
| NW | 2,848,415 | 2,593,880 | 3,455,173 |
| WC | (599,775) | (901,247) | (744,356) |
| Emp. | 53 | 54 | 81 |

DUNS 51-981-0790
## Rufus Leonard Ltd
Drill Hall, Pretoria Road, London E4 7HA
**Web:** www.rufusleonard.com
**Reg No:** 3348509 **Estd:** 1997 Private Limited Company
**Line of Business:** Engineering design activities for industrial process and production
**Export Sales:** £42,683
**Issued Capital:** £1,500
**Principals:** N V Svensen *(Managing)*, P Barker, D C Worthington, L Wall
**Responsibilities**
**Senior:** Freddie Baveystock *(Consultant)*, Ali Wiser *(Production and Operations Mana)*
**Marketing:** Anastasia Innes *(Marketing Manager)*, James Ramsden *(Communications Director)*
**Sales:** Charlotte Anderson *(Business Development Director)*, Charly Dove *(New Business Director)*
**Admin:** Lucy Barker *(Head of Human Resources & Faci)*
**HR:** Lucy Barker *(Head of Human Resources & Faci)*
**Health & Safety:** Lucy Barker *(Head of Human Resources & Faci)*
**Facilities:** Lucy Barker *(Head of Human Resources & Faci)*
**Operations:** Ali Wiser *(Production and Operations Mana)*
**Purchasing:** Lucy Barker *(Head of Human Resources & Faci)*
**US SIC:** 7399, 7379
**UK SIC:** 83954, 83940
**Auditors:** Silver Altman

**Bankers:** Coutts & Co (18-00-98)

| | 30-04-13 | 30-04-12 | 30-04-11 |
|---|---|---|---|
| TO | 11,367,810 | 9,988,264 | 11,832,971 |
| P/L | 452,117 | 15,185 | 123,742 |
| NW | 1,687,541 | 1,351,147 | 1,313,962 |
| WC | 1,442,997 | 1,652,279 | 1,395,501 |
| Emp. | 87 | 81 | 86 |

DUNS 21-113-3867
## The Rug Co (Holdings) Ltd
119b Portland Road, London W11 4LN
**Tel:** 020-7229-5148
**Web:** www.therugcompany.com
**Reg No:** 6541563 **Estd:** 2008 Private Limited Company
**Line of Business:** Retail sale of floor coverings
**Export Sales:** £12,087,405
**Issued Capital:** £231,646
**Directors:** Ms S M Sharp, C R Sharp, C J Curry, Mrs L A Kitchener, R Harding
**Co. Secretary:** Robin Harding
**US SIC:** 5713 **UK SIC:** 64700

| | 30-03-14 | 31-03-13 | 01-03-12 |
|---|---|---|---|
| TO | 22,422,346 | 20,046,622 | 17,727,759 |
| P/L | 3,496,536 | 3,213,008 | 3,200,555 |
| NW | 6,621,815 | 5,789,220 | 4,927,139 |
| WC | 5,158,086 | 3,727,835 | 3,436,747 |
| Emp. | 100 | 95 | 74 |

DUNS 22-518-8515 Imp-Exp
## Rug Doctor Ltd
Unit 29 Decoy Road, Worthing, West Sussex BN14 8ND
**Tel:** 01903-235558 **Fax:** 01903-209671
**Web:** www.rugdoctor.co.uk
**Reg No:** 1544366 **VAT No:** 322059293
**Estd:** 1981 Private Limited Company
**Line of Business:** Washing and dry cleaning of textile and fur products
**Export Markets:** European Union (E U); Africa; Middle East
**Export Sales:** £413,522
**Issued Capital:** £276,000
**Directors:** K S Dosanjh, J P Shields, T J Wall
**Co. Secretary:** Paul Lynch
**Responsibilities**
**Senior:** Mike Holden *(Manager)*, Kimberly Whitehead *(Manager)*
**Finance:** Paul Hansford *(Financial Manager)*
**Branches:** Darlington, Wolverhampton, Mildenhall, Glasgow and Worthing.
**US SIC:** 7219 **UK SIC:** 98110
**Auditors:** Deloitte & Touche LLP
**Bankers:** Bank Of Scotland (12-12-68)

| | 31-12-13 | 31-12-12 | 31-12-11 |
|---|---|---|---|
| TO | 8,270,447 | 8,210,938 | 8,355,299 |
| P/L | 481,872 | 371,144 | 908,247 |
| NW | 6,765,665 | 6,370,225 | 6,394,076 |
| WC | 4,967,112 | 3,641,215 | 3,633,033 |
| Emp. | 73 | 82 | 66 |

DUNS 34-622-6009
## Rugby Football Development Ltd
**(Subsidiary of:** Rugby Football Union)
198 Whitton Road, Twickenham, Middlesex TW2 7BA
**Tel:** 02088922000
**Web:** www.rfu.com
**Reg No:** 5429073 **Estd:** 2005 Private Limited Company
**Line of Business:** Operation of other sports arenas and stadiums not elsewhere classified
**Issued Capital:** £1,000
**Directors:** R W Daniel, S P Brown
**Co. Secretary:** Karena Vleck
**US SIC:** 7999 **UK SIC:** 97913
**Auditors:** Mazars LLP

| | 30-06-14 | 30-06-13 | 30-06-12 |
|---|---|---|---|
| TO | 27,247,000 | 25,423,000 | 21,585,000 |
| P/L | 417,000 | 964,000 | 1,149,000 |
| NW | 4,613,000 | 4,308,000 | 3,594,000 |
| WC | 4,478,000 | 4,268,000 | 3,492,000 |
| Emp. | 252 | 252 | N/A |

DUNS 23-207-7479
## Rugby Football Union
15-19 York Street, Twickenham, Middlesex TW1 3JZ
**Tel:** 08712222120
**Web:** www.rfu.com
**Reg No:** 0027981IP **Estd:** 1994 Friendly Society
**Line of Business:** Membership sports and recreation clubs
**Principals:** B E Baister *(Chairman)*, F Cotton, G Cattermole, W B Beaumont, F S Baron, M S Phillips, D P Rogers, E Blackman
**Responsibilities**
**Senior:** Jonathan Dance *(Designated Limited Liability P)*, Keith Kent *(Head Groundsman)*
**Sales:** Neil Armit *(Business Development Manager)*, Sophie Goldschmidt *(Chief Commercial Officer)*
**Admin:** Alisha Bird *(Office Manager)*
**Facilities:** Keith Kent *(Head Groundsman)*
**Branches:** Rugby Football Union, Castlecroft Stadium, Castlecroft Road, Wolverhampton, West Midlands WV3 8NA
**US SIC:** 7999 **UK SIC:** 97913
**Auditors:** Mazars Neville Russell
**Employees:** 120

DUNS 23-604-3493
## Rugby School
10 Little Church Street, Rugby, Warwickshire CV21 3AW
**Tel:** 01788556261
**Web:** www.rugbyschool.net
**Proprietorship**
**Line of Business:** Museum activities
**Principals:** W M Fowle *(Chairman)*, Mrs P A Williams *(Chairman)*, R W Swannell *(Chairman)*, M Dunne, Ms D F Caldicott, C H Imray, M J Mansell, P Cattell
**Responsibilities**
**Senior:** P Berners-Price *(Principal)*, Michael Mavor *(Director)*, Lady McFarlane *(Governor)*, Gerry Randall *(Principal)*
**Branches:** Rugby School, Horton Crescent, Rugby, Warwickshire CV22 5DJ
**US SIC:** 8411, 8211
**UK SIC:** 97700, 93200
**Auditors:** Crowe Clark Whitehill LLP
**Bankers:** National Westminster Bank Plc (54-41-00)

| | 31-07-13 | 31-07-12 | 31-07-11 |
|---|---|---|---|
| TO | 30,369,000 | 28,579,000 | 28,065,000 |
| P/L | 2,748,000 | 2,161,000 | 3,134,000 |
| NW | 99,765,000 | 90,639,000 | 88,789,000 |
| WC | 1,808,000 | 2,316,000 | 5,064,000 |
| Emp. | 234 | 220 | 227 |

DUNS 21-910-0484 Exp
## Rugeley Aluminium Products Ltd
**(Subsidiary of:** Rugeley Metals Ltd)
5a Knighton Road, Sutton Coldfield, West Midlands B74 4NY
**Tel:** 01213530006 **Fax:** 01213535586
**Reg No:** 1084115 **VAT No:** 100607430
**Estd:** 1972 Private Limited Company
**Line of Business:** Casting of light metals
**Export Markets:** E U, U.S.A, Canada and Far East.
**Trading Style:** Westland Castings
**Issued Capital:** £500,000
**Director:** P S Borland
**Co. Secretary:** Ms Karen Borland
**US SIC:** 3361, 5051
**UK SIC:** 31120, 61200
**Auditors:** Price Pearson
**Bankers:** Lloyds TSB Bank plc (30-99-83)

| | 30-09-13 | 30-09-12 | 30-09-11 |
|---|---|---|---|
| TA | 654,752 | 776,465 | 682,635 |
| NW | 648,030 | 766,843 | 677,155 |
| WC | 50,387 | 423,847 | 334,159 |

DUNS 37-849-7879
## Rugeley Power Generation Ltd
**(Subsidiary of:** Gdf Suez)
Rugeley Power Station, Rugeley, Staffordshire WS15 1PR
**Tel:** 01889572171
**Reg No:** 3300792 **Estd:** 1997 Private Limited Company
**Line of Business:** Generation Of Electricity
**Issued Capital:** £2
**Directors:** S D Pinnell, I Kajimura, A W Garner, K A Dibble
**Co. Secretary:** Ms Hillary Berger
**US SIC:** 4911 **UK SIC:** 16101
**Auditors:** KPMG Audit Plc

| | 31-12-13 | 31-12-12 | 31-12-11 |
|---|---|---|---|
| TA | 2 | 2 | 2 |
| NW | 2 | 2 | 2 |

DUNS 22-194-3892 Imp
## Rugeley Power Ltd
**(Subsidiary of:** Gdf Suez)
Rugeley Power Station, Rugeley, Staffordshire WS15 1PR
**Tel:** 01889572100
**Web:** www.rugeleypower.com
**Reg No:** 4212554 **Estd:** 2001 Private Limited Company
**Line of Business:** Electricity companies
**Trading Style:** Rugeley Power Station
**Issued Capital:** £1,003
**Directors:** R Okaniwa, P W Evans, D G Alcock, S D Pinnell
**Co. Secretary:** Ms Hillary Berger
**Responsibilities**
**Senior:** David Leich *(Station Manager)*, Toru Takahashi *(Manager)*
**Finance:** Doug Alston *(Financial Manager)*, Jacqui Ashforth *(Finance Director)*
**IT:** Donna McCourt *(Computer Manager)*
**HR:** Kim Hensby *(Human Resources Manager)*
**Purchasing:** Jenny Ludlow *(Purchasing Manager)*
**Branches:** Rugeley Power Ltd, Rugeley Power Station, Rugeley, Staffordshire WS15 1PR
**US SIC:** 4911 **UK SIC:** 16101
**Auditors:** KPMG Audit PLC

| | 31-12-13 | 31-12-12 | 31-12-11 |
|---|---|---|---|
| TO | 379,456,000 | 291,771,000 | 271,934,000 |
| P/L | 9,314,000 | 8,062,000 | (157,609,000) |
| NW | 52,035,000 | 47,772,000 | (76,065,000) |
| WC | 77,627,000 | 47,347,000 | 105,768,000 |
| Emp. | 168 | 169 | N/A |

DUNS 77-086-8487
## Ruggles & Jeffery Ltd
**(Subsidiary of:** Ruggles & Jeffery Holdings Ltd)
Britaney House, Hodgson Way, Wickford, Essex SS11 8YG
**Tel:** 01268572332 **Fax:** 01268-572337
**Web:** www.rugglesandjeffery.co.uk
**Reg No:** 2672506 **Estd:** 1992 Private Limited Company
**Line of Business:** Construction of commercial buildings
**Issued Capital:** £11,000
**Principals:** I H Jeffery *(Managing)*, B W Ruggles *(Managing)*, H A Hannon, G C Flanagan
**Co. Secretary:** Ian Jeffery
**US SIC:** 1541, 2599
**UK SIC:** 50100, 46720
**Auditors:** Venthams
**Bankers:** Lloyds TSB Bank plc (30-10-52)

| | 31-03-14 | 31-03-13 | 31-03-12 |
|---|---|---|---|
| TA | 1,663,017 | 1,160,247 | 859,138 |
| NW | 274,371 | 72,875 | 30,567 |
| WC | 224,462 | 30,304 | (26,353) |

DUNS 56-990-9930 Imp-Exp
## Ruia Group Ltd
Kearsley Mill, Stoneclough Radcliffe, Manchester M26 1RH
**Tel:** 01204702300
**Web:** www.ruia.co.uk
**Reg No:** 2858400 **Estd:** 1966 Private Limited Company
**Line of Business:** Management activities of holding companies
**Trading Style:** Richard Howorth, Osam, Drew Brady, Kearsley Manufacturing
**Issued Capital:** £160,000
**Principals:** S Ruia *(Managing)*, A Ruia *(Managing)*, R Ruia *(Managing)*, V Ruia *(Financial)*, A Ruia
**Co. Secretary:** Philip Campbell
**US SIC:** 6711, 5133
**UK SIC:** 83962, 61600
**Auditors:** Grant Thornton UK LLP
**Bankers:** HSBC Bank plc (40-05-15)

| | 30-04-14 | 30-04-13 | 30-04-12 |
|---|---|---|---|
| TO | 50,495,626 | 49,088,553 | 49,843,102 |
| P/L | 5,625,913 | 6,796,302 | 8,089,284 |
| NW | 17,262,043 | 17,486,755 | 17,375,612 |
| WC | 14,411,816 | 15,726,831 | 16,089,931 |
| Emp. | 317 | 307 | 286 |

DUNS 53-623-3364
## Rules Restaurant Ltd
**(Subsidiary of:** Lartington Estates Ltd)
35 Maiden Lane, Covent Garden, London WC2E 7LB
**Tel:** 020-7836-5314 **Fax:** 020-7497-1081
**Web:** www.rules.co.uk
**Reg No:** 3428308 **Estd:** 1798 Private Limited Company
**Line of Business:** Licensed restaurants
**Issued Capital:** £1
**Directors:** R M Mcmenemy, Lartington Estates Limited
**Co. Secretary:** Michael White
**Responsibilities**
**Senior:** Terence Bowler *(Manager)*, John Mayhew *(Owner)*, Demis Rossi *(Restaurant Manager)*
**Finance:** Terence Bowler *(Manager)*, Colin Moseley *(Senior Finance Manager)*
**Facilities:** Mike Stockham *(Facilities Manager)*
**US SIC:** 5812 **UK SIC:** 66110
**Auditors:** Allen Sykes
**Bankers:** Lloyds TSB Bank plc (30-92-32)

| | 31-08-14 | 31-08-13 | 31-08-12 |
|---|---|---|---|
| TA | 3,130,822 | 2,936,756 | 2,735,801 |
| NW | 2,355,054 | 2,249,989 | 2,093,814 |
| WC | 1,920,006 | 1,709,712 | 1,581,701 |

DUNS 34-806-1037
## Rullion Ltd
Trafalgar House, 110 Manchester Road, Altrincham, Cheshire WA14 1NU
**Tel:** 01616022380 **Fax:** 01616022381
**Web:** www.rullion.co.uk
**Reg No:** 2790818 **Estd:** 1993 Private Limited Company
**Line of Business:** Management activities of holding companies
**Trading Style:** Rullionbuild Ltd
**Issued Capital:** £225,000
**Principals:** R Scott *(Managing)*, T M Saoulli, Ms R M Saoulli, J B Saoulli
**Co. Secretary:** Matthew Hart
**Responsibilities**
**Senior:** William O' Donnell *(Manager)*
**Branches:** Rullion Ltd, Cotton Exchange Building, Old Hall Street, Liverpool, Merseyside L3 9LQ
**US SIC:** 6711, 7361
**UK SIC:** 83962, 83954
**Auditors:** Beever & Struthers
**Bankers:** National Westminster Bank Plc (01-10-01)

| | 31-12-13 | 31-12-12 | 31-12-11 |
|---|---|---|---|
| TO | 326,243,392 | 278,271,616 | 262,119,617 |
| P/L | 2,764,054 | 2,361,915 | 3,537,859 |
| NW | 7,401,991 | 6,292,427 | 5,497,641 |
| WC | 8,712,503 | 7,131,145 | 6,257,912 |
| Emp. | 1,478 | 1,310 | 1,327 |

DUNS 29-848-0591 Imp
## Rulmeca Uk Ltd
Brunel Road, Corby, Northamptonshire NN17 4UX
**Tel:** 01536-748525
**Web:** www.rulmeca.com
**Reg No:** 2051312 **Estd:** 1986 Private Limited Company
**Line of Business:** Material handling equipment
**Export Sales:** £849,428
**Trading Style:** Rulmeca Uk Limited
**Issued Capital:** £775,000
**Principals:** R Ball *(Managing)*, S Cortese, C Spanggaard, M A Ghisalberti
**Co. Secretary:** Fabio Ghisalberti
**US SIC:** 3534, 3532
**UK SIC:** 32553, 32510
**Auditors:** Grant Thornton UK LLP
**Bankers:** National Westminster Bank Plc (60-06-11)

| | 31-12-13 | 31-12-12 | 31-12-11 |
|---|---|---|---|
| TO | 6,967,506 | 5,771,021 | 6,628,646 |
| P/L | 206,792 | 112,958 | 155,208 |
| NW | 2,689,895 | 2,535,657 | 2,454,343 |
| WC | 1,281,533 | 1,970,820 | 2,234,649 |
| Emp. | 55 | 43 | 42 |

DUNS 34-548-2447
## Rumara Ltd
**(Subsidiary of:** Arg Holdings (Jersey) Limited)
25 Quarry Park Close, Moulton Park, Northampton, Northamptonshire NN3 6QB
**Tel:** 01604670056
**Reg No:** 5358259 **Estd:** 2005 Private Limited Company
**Line of Business:** Holding companies management activities
**Issued Capital:** £1
**Director:** Mrs L O'Shea
**Responsibilities**
**Senior:** Mark Coetzee *(Manager)*
**US SIC:** 6711, 7361
**UK SIC:** 83962, 83954
**Auditors:** Grant Thornton
**Bankers:** National Westminster Bank Plc (60-15-55)
**Employees:** 10
**Turnover:** £3,591,019

DUNS 22-013-3115 Exp
## Rumenco Ltd
Stretton House, Derby Road, Burton-On-Trent, Staffordshire DE13 0DW
**Tel:** 01283511211
**Web:** www.rumenco.co.uk
**Reg No:** 4016333 **Estd:** 2000 Private Limited Company
**Line of Business:** Manufacture of prepared pet foods
**Export Sales:** £11,459,835
**Issued Capital:** £2,130,000
**Principals:** F C Heap *(Managing)*, Dr R Knight, N J Duncalf, N R Lyon
**Co. Secretary:** Nicholas Duncalf
**Responsibilities**
**Admin:** Sheila Grover *(Administrator)*
**HR:** Sheila Grover *(Administrator)*
**US SIC:** 2048, 2099
**UK SIC:** 42210, 42399
**Auditors:** BDO LLP
**Bankers:** Bank Of Scotland (12-09-26)

| | 30-06-13 | 30-06-12 | 30-06-11 |
|---|---|---|---|
| TO | 43,594,880 | 34,659,603 | 29,076,512 |
| P/L | 2,570,521 | 2,010,366 | 1,601,881 |
| NW | 7,275,236 | 5,023,013 | 6,965,772 |
| WC | 4,763,344 | 4,369,342 | 5,202,371 |
| Emp. | 144 | 110 | 89 |

DUNS 21-773-6541
## Rumney High School
Newport Road, Cardiff, South Glamorgan CF3 3XG
**Tel:** 02920792751
**Web:** www.rumney.cardiff.sch.uk
**Estd:** 1964 Proprietorship
**Line of Business:** Schools (foundation)
**Proprietor:** G Cooke
**Responsibilities**
**Senior:** Wendy Rees *(Head Teacher)*
**US SIC:** 8211 **UK SIC:** 93200
**Employees:** 60

DUNS 21-005-2854

## Runnett & Co Ltd

Elm Court Cowbridge Road, Bridgend, Mid Glamorgan CF31 3SR
**Tel:** 01656665850
**Web:** www.runnettlaw.co.uk
**Reg No:** 6299873 **Estd:** 2007 Private Limited Company
**Line of Business:** Solicitors
**Trading Style:** Runnett & Co Property Lawyers
**Issued Capital:** £100
**Directors:** B D Lewis, M T Lewis
**Responsibilities**
**Senior:** Jena Dight *(Partner)*
**US SIC:** 8111 **UK SIC:** 83500
**Auditors:** KTS Owens Thomas Ltd

| | 31-03-13 | 30-09-11 | 30-03-10 |
|---|---|---|---|
| TO | 6,162,845 | N/A | N/A |
| P/L | 410,888 | N/A | N/A |
| NW | 54,628 | (349,341) | (10,287) |
| WC | 16,502 | (379,284) | (11,281) |
| Emp. | 54 | N/A | N/A |

DUNS 23-609-4673

## Running Deep Ltd

(**Subsidiary of:** Emih Ltd)
The Deep Business Ctr, Tower Street, Hull, North Humberside HU1 4DP
**Tel:** 01482381000
**Web:** www.thedeep.co.uk
**Reg No:** 3606689 **Estd:** 1998 Private Limited Company
**Line of Business:** Other letting of own property
**Issued Capital:** £2
**Directors:** Ms J Reuben, A J Hunt, D W Gemmell, C C Brown, J A Parkes, Professor G Chesters, Professor C W Pistorius
**Co. Secretary:** Neil Porteus
**US SIC:** 6519, 8249, 8421
**UK SIC:** 85000, 93300, 97700
**Auditors:** Ernst & Young LLP
**Bankers:** National Westminster Bank Plc (56-00-06)

| | 31-01-14 | 31-01-13 | 31-01-12 |
|---|---|---|---|
| TO | 6,114,307 | 6,963,381 | 6,675,716 |
| P/L | 399,800 | 163,715 | 232,402 |
| NW | 1,159,886 | 777,884 | 138,032 |
| WC | 486,569 | 195,850 | 86,136 |
| Emp. | 137 | 127 | 116 |

DUNS 21-122-1741

## Runnymede Borough Council

Civic Offices, Addlestone, Surrey KT15 2AH
**Tel:** 01932-838383
**Web:** www.runnymede.gov.uk
**Estd:** 1974 Partnership
**Line of Business:** Health authorities
**Partners:** A Pearson, P Turrell, D Thomas, S Cawthorne
**Responsibilities**
**Senior:** Sonia Druce *(Executive Assistant)*, Bernard Fleckney *(Board Member)*, John Gurmin *(Board Member)*, Carol Holehouse *(Board Member)*
**Admin:** Sonia Druce *(Executive Assistant)*, Julie Kitchenside *(Administration Manager)*
**IT:** Helen Dunn *(Head of ICT)*
**Engineering:** Penny Shields *(Officer)*, Peter Sims *(Director, Technical Services)*
**Branches:** Runnymede Borough Council, The Old Library, Church Road, Addlestone, Surrey KT15 1RW
**US SIC:** 9121 **UK SIC:** 91110
**Employees:** 350

DUNS 21-602-1937

## Runshaw Business Centre

Euxton Lane, Euxton, Chorley, Lancashire PR7 6AQ
**Tel:** 01772643008
**Estd:** 2001 Proprietorship
**Line of Business:** Training centres
**Proprietor:** Mrs C Foreman
**US SIC:** 8299 **UK SIC:** 93300
**Employees:** 60

DUNS 23-996-1485

## Runshaw College

Langdale Road, Preston, Lancashire PR25 3DQ
**Tel:** 01772-622677
**Web:** www.runshaw.ac.uk
**Estd:** 1983
**Line of Business:** Further education schools and colleges
**Trading Style:** Runshaw Business Centre
**Principals:** M Smith *(Financial)*, B O'Connell, Ms M Parsons
**Responsibilities**
**Senior:** Bernard O'connell *(Director)*, Janet Wales *(Manager)*
**Sales:** Colin Burrow *(Commercial Manager)*
**HR:** Tracey Croft *(Personnel Officer)*
**Branches:** Runshaw College, Euxton Lane, Euxton, Chorley, Lancashire PR7 6AQ
**US SIC:** 8221 **UK SIC:** 93100
**Bankers:** Barclays Bank Plc (20-69-85)
**Employees:** 800

DUNS 22-228-4486

## Runswick Ltd

Westfield Road, Slyfield Industrial Estate, Guildford, Surrey GU1 1RR
**Tel:** 01483-506678
**Web:** www.runswickmotorcompany.co.uk
**Reg No:** 4246433 **Estd:** 2001 Private Limited Company
**Line of Business:** Holding companies management activities
**Export Sales:** £601,048
**Trading Style:** John Dennis Coach Builders
**Issued Capital:** £200,000
**Directors:** A Mcclafferty, J B Leathers, G S Pitt
**Co. Secretary:** Ms Gwen Mcclafferty
**US SIC:** 6711, 3711
**UK SIC:** 83962, 35101

| | 30-09-13 | 30-09-12 | 30-09-11 |
|---|---|---|---|
| TO | 14,923,998 | 14,947,581 | 16,144,469 |
| P/L | 144,523 | 309,734 | 638,181 |
| NW | 3,153,899 | 3,043,966 | 2,803,365 |
| WC | 1,998,932 | 1,854,295 | 1,454,141 |
| Emp. | 90 | 85 | 117 |

DUNS 45-853-1803

## Runtech Ltd

Unit 5, Llewellyns Quay, Port Talbot, West Glamorgan SA13 1RF
**Tel:** 01639890800
**Web:** www.runtech.ltd.uk
**Reg No:** 3199248 **VAT No:** 681731034
**Estd:** 1996 Private Limited Company
**Line of Business:** Road haulage and transport services
**Issued Capital:** £200,000
**Directors:** I Gorvett, M J Hazell
**Co. Secretary:** Ms Samantha Gorvett
**US SIC:** 7513, 4213, 7394
**UK SIC:** 84802, 72300, 84000
**Auditors:** Morgan Hemp & Co Ltd
**Bankers:** Barclays Bank Plc (20-58-72)

| | 31-07-13 | 31-07-12 | 31-07-11 |
|---|---|---|---|
| TO | 7,794,492 | N/A | N/A |
| P/L | 44,409 | N/A | N/A |
| NW | 973,707 | 986,312 | 1,164,448 |
| WC | 576,269 | (610,799) | (127,293) |
| Emp. | 64 | N/A | N/A |

DUNS 23-907-4581

## Runtime Collective Ltd

Sovereign House, Church Street, 2nd Floor, Brighton, East Sussex BN1 1UJ
**Tel:** 01273234290 **Fax:** 01273325459
**Web:** www.brandwatch.com
**Reg No:** 3898053 **VAT No:** 754750710
**Estd:** 2000 Private Limited Company
**Line of Business:** Hardware consultancy
**Export Sales:** £5,559,823
**Trading Style:** Brand Watch, Brandwatch
**Issued Capital:** £313
**Directors:** M A Heeley, B Tookey, S W Brooks, J G Moore, C Ferrer Roqueta, Dr F Retkowsky
**Co. Secretary:** Giles Palmer
**Responsibilities**
**Senior:** Marshall King *(Manager)*
**US SIC:** 7379 **UK SIC:** 83940
**Auditors:** Armstrong & Co

| | 31-12-13 | 31-12-12 | 31-12-11 |
|---|---|---|---|
| TO | 8,804,153 | N/A | N/A |
| P/L | (1,898,388) | N/A | N/A |
| NW | 849,693 | 2,394,564 | 1,236,635 |
| WC | 525,505 | 1,519,776 | 662,180 |
| Emp. | 127 | N/A | N/A |

DUNS 21-789-6300

## Runwood Homes

Tallis House, Neal Court, Waltham Abbey, Essex EN9 3EH
**Tel:** 01992713336
**Web:** www.runwoodhomes.co.uk
**Estd:** 2011 Proprietorship
**Line of Business:** Rest and retirement homes
**Proprietor:** Miss E Weeks
**Responsibilities**
**Senior:** Lennie Terrado *(Home Manager)*
**US SIC:** 8321 **UK SIC:** 96111
**Employees:** 108

DUNS 28-851-6594

## Runwood Homes Ltd

Runwood House, 107 London Road, Hadleigh, Benfleet, Essex SS7 2QL
**Tel:** 01702-559797 **Fax:** 01702-558984
**Web:** www.runwoodhomes.co.uk
**Reg No:** 0731250 **Estd:** 1962 Private Limited Company
**Line of Business:** Residential care establishments
**Issued Capital:** £50,000,000
**Principals:** G G Sanders *(Managing)*, M Robinson, T Sanders, Mrs J Fitzgerald, D J Spencer, E Kupfuwa, Mrs S J Sanders, N Logeswaren
**Co. Secretary:** Jamie Davidson
**Responsibilities**
**Senior:** Joanne Cauchi *(Manager)*, Kathryn Davidson *(Facilities Director)*, Laura Glyde *(Manager)*, Rona Johnson *(Manager)*, Pauline Kelly *(Manager)*, Stephen Larkin *(Financial Director)*, Sue Loftus *(Manager)*, Logan Logeswaran *(Manager)*, Mercy Mahupete *(Manager)*, Janet Moffat *(Manager)*, Janice Sanders *(Manager)*, Evelyn Sanders *(Manager)*, Peter Skeats *(Manager)*, Donna Winterborne *(Manager)*
**Finance:** Stephen Larkin *(Financial Director)*
**Branches:** Runwood Homes Ltd, Frank Foster House, Loughton Lane, Epping, Essex CM16 7LD
**US SIC:** 7399 **UK SIC:** 83954
**Auditors:** Crowe Clark Whitehill LLP
**Bankers:** Barclays Bank Plc (20-79-73)

| | 30-09-13 | 30-09-12 | 30-09-11 |
|---|---|---|---|
| TO | 93,707,931 | 73,849,671 | 63,323,892 |
| P/L | 12,226,388 | 10,878,411 | 9,312,452 |
| NW | 159,607,472 | 138,018,472 | 114,349,922 |
| WC | (7,176,638) | (227,904) | 175,419 |
| Emp. | 3,571 | 2,986 | 2,567 |

DUNS 23-552-2646

## Rupert House School

90-92 Bell Street, Henley-On-Thames, Oxfordshire RG9 2BN
**Tel:** 01491-574263
**Web:** www.ruperthouse.org
**Reg No:** 0569365 **Estd:** 1933 Private Company Limited By Guarantee
**Line of Business:** Schools (independent)
**Directors:** S Boddie, A G Davies, Mrs R M Murison, J J Hamilton-Smith, E Hellings, M B Denehy, M A Antingham, Mrs K A Macaulay
**Co. Secretary:** Kim Rawlingson
**Responsibilities**
**Senior:** Caroline Barker *(Manager)*, Neil Boddington *(Director)*, Elizabeth Collinson *(Director)*, Niki Gan *(Principal)*, Gillian Little *(Director)*, Clare Lynas *(Head Teacher)*, Helen Mackman *(Bursar)*, Michelle Martin *(Director)*, Clair Overend *(Manager)*, Paul Stott *(Manager)*
**Finance:** Helen Mackman *(Bursar)*, A Shawcross *(BURSAR)*
**IT:** Sarah Mowberly *(IT Coordinator)*
**HR:** Helen Mackman *(Bursar)*
**Health & Safety:** Helen Mackman *(Bursar)*
**Facilities:** Helen Mackman *(Bursar)*
**Purchasing:** Helen Mackman *(Bursar)*
**US SIC:** 8211 **UK SIC:** 93200
**Auditors:** Cave Harper & Co
**Bankers:** Unity Trust Bank Plc (08-60-01)

| | 31-08-13 | 31-08-12 | 31-08-11 |
|---|---|---|---|
| TO | 1,908,156 | 1,850,305 | 1,972,322 |
| P/L | 81,886 | 72,866 | 186,166 |
| NW | 2,133,530 | 2,051,644 | 1,978,778 |
| WC | 471,943 | 343,633 | 694,819 |
| Emp. | 46 | 44 | 44 |

DUNS 42-363-3296

## Rural Community Network (Ni)

38a Oldtown Street, Cookstown, Co Tyrone BT80 8EF
**Tel:** 028-8676-6670 **Fax:** 028-8676-6006
**Web:** www.ruralcommunitynetwork.org
**Reg No:** 0031418NI **Estd:** 1991 Private Company Limited By Guarantee
**Line of Business:** Community networks
**Directors:** H G Francis, R M Craig, G A Hatch, N J Moore, R O'Brien, J K Rankin, J M Mccartney, Ms K M Armstrong
**Responsibilities**
**Senior:** Kate Clifford *(Development Manager)*, Paul Dinsmore *(Trustee)*, Siobhan Kearney *(Director)*, Sharon Loane *(Director)*, Declan Mc Ateer *(Director)*, Patrick O'Hanlon *(Director)*, Frances Spence *(Director)*
**US SIC:** 7399 **UK SIC:** 83954
**Auditors:** PricewaterhouseCoopers LLP
**Bankers:** The Bank Of Ireland (90-48-19)

| | 31-03-14 | 31-03-13 | 31-03-12 |
|---|---|---|---|
| TO | 326,902 | 1,153,993 | 2,152,211 |
| P/L | 51,827 | (235,459) | (72,629) |
| NW | 631,810 | 579,983 | 815,442 |
| WC | 270,428 | 208,601 | 427,594 |
| Emp. | 21 | 47 | 43 |

DUNS 39-802-0529

## Rural Insurance Group Ltd

(**Subsidiary of:** Uk General Insurance Holdings Limited)
Unit J2 Hornbeam Park Park Drive, Harrogate, North Yorkshire HG2 8RE
**Tel:** 01423-876000
**Web:** www.ruralinsurance.co.uk
**Reg No:** 2207611 **Estd:** 1995 Private Limited Company
**Line of Business:** Non-life insurance
**Issued Capital:** £1,000
**Directors:** L D Harvey, R M Gill, P J Hubbard, I J Barclay, M P Smith
**Co. Secretary:** Jeffrey Orton
**Responsibilities**
**Senior:** Stacey Zaczkiewicz *(Manager)*
**Branches:** Rural Insurance Group Ltd, 11 Carcraig Place, Dunfermline, Fife KY11 9ST
**US SIC:** 6399 **UK SIC:** 82001
**Auditors:** Price Waterhouse
**Bankers:** Barclays Bank Plc (20-00-00)

| | 31-03-14 | 31-03-13 | 31-03-12 |
|---|---|---|---|
| TO | 4,023,256 | 3,973,458 | 2,995,125 |
| P/L | 223,882 | 28,653 | 160,995 |
| NW | 713,660 | 198,838 | 184,110 |
| WC | 1,448,562 | 1,176,875 | 1,770,991 |
| Emp. | 55 | 47 | 40 |

DUNS 21-627-4998

## Rural Payments Agency

Northgate House, 21-23 Valpy Street, Reading, Berkshire RG1 1AF
**Tel:** 0118-958-3626
**Web:** www.rpa.gov.uk
**Estd:** 2001
**Line of Business:** Environmental consultants
**Directors:** J Marshall, S Pearce, R Moulson, D Healsey, T Cooper
**Responsibilities**
**Senior:** Mark Grimshaw *(Chief Executive)*
**HR:** Kathleen Evans *(Training Manager)*
**Facilities:** Richard Workman *(Facilities Manager)*
**Branches:** Rural Payments Agency, Eden Bridge House, Lowther Street, Carlisle, Cumbria CA3 8DX
**US SIC:** 8911 **UK SIC:** 83701
**Employees:** 3,000

DUNS 77-222-9100

## Rural Retreats Holidays Ltd

(**Subsidiary of:** Hpb Holdings Ltd)
Station Road, Blockley, Gloucester, Gloucestershire GL56 9JY
**Tel:** 01386701177 **Fax:** 01386-701178
**Web:** www.ruralretreats.co.uk
**Reg No:** 2711772 **Estd:** 1992 Private Limited Company
**Line of Business:** Other provision of lodgings not elsewhere classified
**Issued Capital:** £2
**Directors:** G D Baber, R Seager, J C Boyce, R G Boyce
**Co. Secretary:** Ms Maxine Bambury
**Responsibilities**
**Senior:** Caroline Beddington *(Manager)*, Charles Millward *(Manager)*
**US SIC:** 7011 **UK SIC:** 66500

| | 30-09-13 | 30-09-12 | 30-09-11 |
|---|---|---|---|
| TA | 2,846,517 | 2,928,529 | 3,086,024 |
| NW | (2,367,467) | (2,201,448) | (2,055,183) |
| WC | (1,277,524) | (74,021) | (45,772) |

DUNS 73-550-7241

## Rurelec P L C

Prince Consort House, London SE1 7TJ
**Tel:** 02077935610
**Web:** www.rurelec.com
**Reg No:** 4812855 **Estd:** 2003 Public Limited Company
**Line of Business:** Electricity companies
**Export Sales:** £9,651,000
**Issued Capital:** £1,090,310,752
**Directors:** Ms E R Shaw, C P Blanco Quintanilla, A J Morris, C J Emson, P R Earl, B Rowbotham
**Co. Secretary:** Ms Susan Laker
**Responsibilities**
**Senior:** Robin Christopher *(Non-Executive Director)*
**US SIC:** 4911 **UK SIC:** 16101
**Auditors:** Grant Thornton UK LLP
**Bankers:** HSBC Bank plc (40-06-15)

| | 31-12-13 | 31-12-12 | 31-12-11 |
|---|---|---|---|
| TO | 15,093,000 | 13,373,000 | 13,522,000 |
| P/L | (39,384,000) | (2,546,000) | 1,897,000 |
| NW | 53,231,000 | 78,144,000 | 82,460,000 |
| WC | (998,000) | 46,195,000 | 51,006,000 |
| Emp. | 60 | 45 | 42 |

DUNS 29-822-1318

## Rusdene Services Ltd

(**Subsidiary of:** Rusdene Holdings Ltd)
1 South Lane, Waterlooville, Hampshire PO8 0RB
**Tel:** 02392570080
**Web:** www.rusdene.co.uk
**Reg No:** 2040250 **VAT No:** 448843903
**Estd:** 1986 Private Limited Company
**Line of Business:** Petrol service stations
**Issued Capital:** £100
**Principals:** D R Lodge *(Managing)*, O R Lodge, Mrs E Lodge, P S Lodge
**Co. Secretary:** Mrs Emma Lodge
**Branches:** Rusdene Services Ltd, Station Hill, Southampton, Hampshire SO30 2DN
**US SIC:** 5541 **UK SIC:** 65200
**Auditors:** BDO Stoy Hayward
**Bankers:** National Westminster Bank Plc (56-00-64)

| | 30-09-13 | 30-09-12 | 30-09-11 |
|---|---|---|---|
| TO | 21,467,229 | 34,459,787 | 40,220,483 |
| P/L | 595,770 | 719,646 | 155,741 |
| NW | 1,141,030 | 1,166,669 | 764,325 |
| WC | (1,096,349) | (890,391) | (1,049,842) |
| Emp. | N/A | 74 | 83 |

DUNS 21-318-7961
## Rush Croft School
Rushcroft Road, London E4 8SG
**Tel:** 020-8531-9231
**Web:** www.rushcroft.waltham.sch.uk
**Estd:** 2002 Proprietorship
**Line of Business:** Schools (local authority)
**Proprietor:** Ms P Cutler
**Responsibilities**
**Senior:** Jurek Jacyna (Senior Deputy Head Teacher), Mark Morrall (Head Teacher)
**Marketing:** Carol Carroll (Business Manager)
**IT:** Colin Golding (ICT Systems Manager)
**US SIC:** 8221 **UK SIC:** 93100
**Employees:** 120

DUNS 21-776-3871
## Rush Hair
3rd Floor, Century House, 57 Frith Road, Croydon, Surrey CR0 1TB
**Tel:** 02082412086
**Web:** www.rush.co.uk
**Estd:** 2011 Proprietorship
**Line of Business:** Hairdressing and other beauty treatment
**Proprietor:** A Phouli
**US SIC:** 7399 **UK SIC:** 83954
**Employees:** 200

DUNS 22-747-3808
## Rushcliffe Borough Council
Civic Centre, Pavilion Road, Nottingham, Nottinghamshire NG2 5FE
**Web:** www.rushcliffe.gov.uk
**Estd:** 1974
**Line of Business:** Local government
**Directors:** A Graham, C Bullett
**Responsibilities**
**Finance:** Peter Steed (Executive Manager Finance and)
**Marketing:** Kath Marriott (Executive Manager Transformati), Dave Mitchell (Executive Manager Communities)
**Admin:** Karen Shepperson (Executive support worker)
**Health & Safety:** Joanne Wilkinson (Health & Safety Advisor)
**Facilities:** Joanne Wilkinson (Health & Safety Advisor)
**Operations:** Daniel Swaine (Executive Manager Operations a)
**Fleet:** Darryl Burch (Waste & Fleet Operations Manag)
**Branches:** Rushcliffe Borough Council, Mere Way, Ruddington Fields Business Park, Ruddington, Nottingham, Nottinghamshire NG11 6JS
**US SIC:** 9121 **UK SIC:** 91110
**Bankers:** Lloyds TSB Bank plc (30-96-18)
**Employees:** 350

DUNS 34-616-1979
## Rushcliffe Care Ltd
Epinal Way Care Centre, Epinal Way, Loughborough, Leicestershire LE11 3GD
**Tel:** 01509219605 **Fax:** 01509-262710
**Web:** www.rushcliffecare.co.uk
**Reg No:** 2753596 **Estd:** 1989 Private Limited Company
**Line of Business:** Medical nursing home activities
**Issued Capital:** £167,600
**Managing Director:** S S Rai
**Co. Secretary:** David Kaplan
**Responsibilities**
**Senior:** Sue Wilkinson (Financial Director)
**Finance:** Sue Wilkinson (Financial Director)
**Health & Safety:** Darren Carmwell (Health & Safety Manager)
**Branches:** Rushcliffe Care Ltd, 41 Cartwright Street, Loughborough, Leicestershire LE11 1JW
**US SIC:** 8051 **UK SIC:** 95100
**Auditors:** Greenhalgh & Co
**Bankers:** Lloyds TSB Bank plc (30-95-21)

|     | 30-11-13 | 30-11-12 | 30-11-11 |
|-----|----------|----------|----------|
| TO  | 36,231,341 | 33,616,979 | 31,744,239 |
| P/L | 1,561,817 | (4,891,367) | 816,505 |
| NW  | 156,027 | (1,634,077) | (3,139,875) |
| WC  | (3,718,142) | (5,324,724) | (5,026,684) |
| Emp. | 1,348 | 1,325 | 1,182 |

DUNS 76-958-9391
## Rushes Postproduction Ltd
(**Subsidiary of:** Macandrews & Forbes Holdings Inc.)
Film House, 142 Wardour Street, London W1F 8DD
**Tel:** 02074378676 **Fax:** 020-7734-2519
**Web:** www.rushes.co.uk
**Reg No:** 2623334 **VAT No:** 539105549
**Estd:** 1977 Private Limited Company
**Line of Business:** Other motion picture and video production activities
**Issued Capital:** £250,000
**Directors:** K S Sonnenfeld, Miss J R Capper
**Co. Secretary:** James Watson

**Responsibilities**
**Senior:** Christopher Catterall (Manager), Sharon Hill (Head of Dispatch)
**Finance:** Harry Ash (Accounts Department)
**Marketing:** Thom Trigger (PR & Marketing Manager)
**Health & Safety:** Robin Durham (Facilities Manager)
**Facilities:** Robin Durham (Facilities Manager)
**Operations:** Carl Grinter (Production Manager), Anthony McCaffery (Head of Production)
**Engineering:** Carl Grinter (Production Manager)
**US SIC:** 7819 **UK SIC:** 97111
**Auditors:** KPMG
**Bankers:** Barclays Bank Plc (20-78-98)

|     | 31-12-13 | 31-12-12 | 31-12-11 |
|-----|----------|----------|----------|
| TO  | 12,550,000 | 10,069,000 | 10,517,520 |
| P/L | 1,360,000 | 1,002,000 | 1,680,223 |
| NW  | 13,076,000 | 11,716,000 | 10,713,591 |
| WC  | 12,371,000 | 10,807,000 | 9,476,834 |
| Emp. | 141 | 111 | 98 |

DUNS 23-635-6945
## Rushey Mead Secondary School
Melton Road, Leicester, Leicestershire LE4 7AN
**Tel:** 01162-663730
**Web:** www.rusheymead-sec.leicester.sch.uk
**Estd:** 1960
**Line of Business:** Schools (local authority)
**Directors:** Ms N Patel, S J White
**Responsibilities**
**Senior:** Caroline Robson (CEO, Managing Director)
**IT:** David Wiffen (Senior IT Executive)
**US SIC:** 8211 **UK SIC:** 93200
**Bankers:** National Westminster Bank Plc (60-60-06)
**Employees:** 100

DUNS 73-791-0419
## Rushlift (Uk) Ltd
(**Subsidiary of:** The Specialist Hire Group Ltd)
Longfield Road, Bishop Auckland, County Durham DL14 6XB
**Tel:** 01753501910 **Fax:** 01388770725
**Web:** www.rushliftuk.co.uk
**Reg No:** 5047628 **Estd:** 2004 Private Limited Company
**Line of Business:** Material handling equipment
**Trading Style:** Rushlift Ltd
**Issued Capital:** £1,145,000
**Directors:** G Holyland, J Chappell, P Cosgrove
**Co. Secretary:** Ms Lynn Cosgrove
**Responsibilities**
**Finance:** Malcolm Beadle (Finance Manager)
**US SIC:** 3534, 7394
**UK SIC:** 32553, 84000

|     | 31-08-13 | 31-08-12 | 31-08-11 |
|-----|----------|----------|----------|
| TA  | 1,070,000 | 1,070,000 | 1,070,000 |
| NW  | 1,070,000 | 1,070,000 | 1,070,000 |

DUNS 23-260-7606
## Rushmoor Borough Council
Council Offices, Farnborough Road, Farnborough, Hampshire GU14 7JU
**Tel:** 01252398399
**Web:** www.rushmoor.gov.uk
**Estd:** 1986 Incorporate By Act Of Parliament
**Line of Business:** Local government
**Directors:** D Hartley, A P Richards, W D Cooke, P Merriman, R Sharpe, S P Taylor Head of Legal Servic, W D Cooke, R W Fisher
**Responsibilities**
**Senior:** Diane Bedford (Chairman), I Betts (Principal), Annie Denton (Partner), Richard Greaney (Executive), Ian May (Executive), Sally Ravenhill (Manager), V Richardson (Director), F Woodhall (Principal)
**Finance:** Amanda Fahey (Head of Finance)
**Marketing:** Karen Edwards (Head of Strategy and Communica), Rachael Goodchild (Communications Officer), Kathy O'Rourke (Marketing Officer)
**Admin:** Sharon Sullivan (Administrative Assistant)
**HR:** Nikki Astill (Principal Personnel Officers)
**Health & Safety:** Colin Alborough (Health & Safety Officer), Roger Sanders (Health and Safety Officer)
**Branches:** Rushmoor Borough Council, Cove Manor County Junior & Infant School, Fernhill Road, Farnborough, Hampshire GU14 9DX
**US SIC:** 9121 **UK SIC:** 91110
**Employees:** 350

DUNS 28-859-0615
## Rushmoor School Ltd
58-60 Shakespeare Road, Bedford, Bedfordshire MK40 2DL
**Tel:** 01234-352031
**Web:** www.rushmoorschool.co.uk
**Reg No:** 0856842 **Estd:** 1965 Private Company Limited By Guarantee
**Line of Business:** General secondary education
**Principals:** G M Bates (Chairman), J Wilkinson, J J Leydon, D Eyton-Williams, M J Neal, R O Gaskell, B H Thompson, M J Grafton
**Co. Secretary:** Ivan Flack
**Responsibilities**
**Senior:** Mary Burt (Director), Clive Simmonds (Director), Jean Skelton (Manager)
**Finance:** H Hawkes (Bursar)
**Marketing:** H Hawkes (Bursar)
**HR:** H Hawkes (Bursar)
**Health & Safety:** H Hawkes (Bursar)
**US SIC:** 8249 **UK SIC:** 93300
**Auditors:** MacIntyre Hudson
**Bankers:** HSBC Bank plc (40-10-02)

|     | 31-08-13 | 31-08-12 | 31-08-11 |
|-----|----------|----------|----------|
| TO  | 2,736,751 | 2,401,201 | 2,091,483 |
| P/L | 360,984 | 297,820 | 211,549 |
| NW  | 4,179,521 | 3,818,537 | 3,520,717 |
| WC  | 1,431,623 | 1,003,172 | 760,266 |
| Emp. | 50 | 48 | 46 |

DUNS 21-123-5412
## Rushton Hinchy Solicitors Ltd
(**Subsidiary of:** Rushton Hinchy Holdings Ltd)
1 Mill Lane Mill Brook Business Park, St Helens, Merseyside WA11 8LZ
**Tel:** 01744887800
**Web:** www.rushtonhinchy.co.uk
**Reg No:** 6674924 **Estd:** 2008 Private Limited Company
**Line of Business:** Solicitors
**Issued Capital:** £100,000
**Directors:** Miss H S Cliffe, S Rushton, C S Hinchy
**US SIC:** 8111 **UK SIC:** 83500

|     | 30-09-13 | 30-09-12 | 30-09-11 |
|-----|----------|----------|----------|
| TO  | 4,071,241 | 5,824,764 | N/A |
| P/L | (1,142,786) | 2,325,704 | N/A |
| NW  | 3,718,611 | 1,664,772 | (276,501) |
| WC  | N/A | 1,641,911 | (308,470) |
| Emp. | 62 | 63 | N/A |

DUNS 21-331-8863
## Rushy Meadow Primary School
Rushy Meadow Lane, Carshalton, Surrey SM5 2SG
**Tel:** 020-8669-7588
**Web:** www.rushymeadow.sutton.sch.uk
**Estd:** 1992
**Line of Business:** Schools (local authority)
**Proprietor:** Ms K Rhodes
**US SIC:** 8211 **UK SIC:** 93200
**Employees:** 60

DUNS 49-455-1112
## Rusi Trading Ltd
(**Subsidiary of:** The Royal United Services Institute for Defence St)
Whitehall, London SW1A 2ET
**Tel:** 02079305854
**Web:** www.rusi.org
**Reg No:** 3147032 **Estd:** 1903 Private Limited Company
**Line of Business:** Letting of conference and exhibition centres
**Trading Style:** Rusi
**Issued Capital:** £100
**Directors:** Mrs D Pourkarimi, Professor M Clarke, Mrs K Vagneur
**Co. Secretary:** Philip Matfield
**Responsibilities**
**Senior:** Michael Maiden (vice chairman)
**US SIC:** 6519 **UK SIC:** 85000
**Auditors:** PKF

|     | 31-03-14 | 31-03-13 | 31-03-12 |
|-----|----------|----------|----------|
| TO  | 779,667 | 780,065 | 957,887 |
| P/L | N/A | N/A | 446,538 |
| NW  | 100 | 100 | 100 |
| WC  | 100 | 100 | 100 |

DUNS 22-859-1376 **Imp-Exp**
## Ruskim Seafoods Ltd
Marine House, Stafford Park 15, Telford, Shropshire TF3 3BB
**Tel:** 01952-293344 **Fax:** 01952-293345
**Web:** www.ruskim.co.uk
**Reg No:** 1634987 **VAT No:** 320248009
**Estd:** 1982 Private Limited Company
**Line of Business:** Wholesale of other food including fish, crustaceans and molluscs
**Export Markets:** Worldwide
**Export Sales:** £5,083,748
**Trading Style:** Ruskim Seafoods Limited
**Issued Capital:** £50,000

**Principals:** W S Mooney (Managing), A I Russell, R Mooney, K Williamson, I D Harley
**Co. Secretary:** Lesley Mooney
**Responsibilities**
**Senior:** Jack Makin (Manager)
**Branches:** Ruskin Seafoods Ltd, Unit 99, Whitley Road, Newcastle Upon Tyne, Tyne and Wear NE12 9SZ
**US SIC:** 5146 **UK SIC:** 61700
**Auditors:** RSM Tenon Audit Ltd
**Bankers:** HSBC Bank plc (40-29-26)

|     | 30-06-14 | 30-06-13 | 30-06-12 |
|-----|----------|----------|----------|
| TO  | 90,388,942 | 81,714,002 | 79,730,256 |
| P/L | 1,193,231 | 555,467 | 535,139 |
| NW  | 7,479,499 | 7,044,962 | 6,997,243 |
| WC  | 4,930,695 | 4,382,204 | 4,272,501 |
| Emp. | 231 | 206 | 189 |

DUNS 21-807-1736 **Imp-Exp**
## Ruskin Air Management Ltd
(**Subsidiary of:** Qs0004 Sa)
Stourbridge Road, Bridgnorth, Shropshire WV15 5BB
**Tel:** 01746-761921
**Web:** www.ruskinuk.co.uk
**Reg No:** 0738495 **VAT No:** 274123279
**Estd:** 1962 Private Limited Company
**Line of Business:** Fabricated metal products
**Export Markets:** Europe, Africa, Middle East and other countries
**Export Sales:** £5,473,000
**Issued Capital:** £5,322,088
**Directors:** A Mckay, R B Mcdonald, B J Stief, F Voltolina, B Cadwallader, T R Edwards
**Responsibilities**
**Senior:** Richard Goulds (Manager), Elizabeth Lewzey (Manager), Andrew McKay (Finance Director), Manoj Shah (Manager)
**Finance:** Andrew McKay (Finance Director)
**Branches:** Ruskin Air Management Ltd, South Street, Whitstable, Kent CT5 3DU
**US SIC:** 3441 **UK SIC:** 32042
**Auditors:** Deloitte LLP
**Bankers:** HSBC Bank plc (40-02-50)

|     | 31-12-13 | 31-12-12 | 31-12-11 |
|-----|----------|----------|----------|
| TO  | 22,833,000 | 20,774,000 | 20,072,000 |
| P/L | 2,181,000 | 1,467,000 | 1,276,000 |
| NW  | 7,364,000 | 6,763,000 | 13,034,000 |
| WC  | 5,908,000 | 5,331,000 | 17,969,000 |
| Emp. | 210 | 204 | 217 |

DUNS 33-963-1483
## Ruskin Mill College
Ruskin Mill, Millbottom, Nailsworth, Stroud, Gloucestershire GL6 0LA
**Web:** www.rmt.org
**Line of Business:** Other adult and other education not elsewhere classified
**Trading Style:** Living Earth Produce, Ruskin Mill College
**Co. Secretary:** John Gush
**Responsibilities**
**IT:** Richard MacBeth (Computer Manager)
**US SIC:** 8299, 8221
**UK SIC:** 93300, 93100
**Employees:** 250

DUNS 42-394-8447
## Ruskin Mill Further Education College
Millbottom, Nailsworth, Stroud, Gloucestershire GL6 0LA
**Web:** www.ruskin-mill.org.uk
**Estd:** 1986
**Line of Business:** Further education schools and colleges
**Trading Style:** Ruskin Mill Fisheries
**Director:** A Gordon
**Responsibilities**
**Senior:** Laura Cammish (Manager)
**Branches:** Ruskin Mill Further Education College, Wollaston Road, Stourbridge, West Midlands DY8 4HF
**US SIC:** 8221 **UK SIC:** 93100
**Employees:** 130

DUNS 21-672-9978
## Ruskin Mill Trust Ltd
65 Carter Lane, London EC4V 5HF
**Tel:** 01142525993
**Web:** www.rmt.org
**Reg No:** 7252866 **Estd:** 2010 Private Company Limited By Guarantee
**Line of Business:** Adult and other education not elsewhere classified
**Directors:** R Ballard, Dr P Gruenewald, A C Gordon, B Martin-Simpson, Mrs P Eblett, Mrs C Tennyson, Mrs H M Kippax
**Co. Secretary:** Ms Katherine Harrington
**US SIC:** 8249 **UK SIC:** 93300
**Bankers:** Lloyds TSB Bank plc (30-98-29)

|     | 31-08-13 | 31-08-12 | 31-08-11 |
|-----|----------|----------|----------|
| TO  | 20,485,512 | 20,479,552 | 12,592,708 |
| P/L | 615,879 | 148,217 | 157,948 |
| NW  | 697,192 | 98,479 | (60,669) |
| WC  | (655,632) | (972,877) | (939,715) |
| Emp. | 308 | 351 | 296 |

DUNS 21-038-0042

## Ruskin Private Hire

6 Camberwell Road, London SE5 0EN
**Tel:** 02072526805
**Web:** www.ruskin-privatehire.com
**Estd:** 2002 Proprietorship
**Line of Business:** Taxi operation
**Proprietor:** R Lynch
**US SIC:** 4121 **UK SIC:** 72200
**Employees:** 120

DUNS 21-751-3099

## Ruspetro Plc

First Floor, Berkeley Square House, Berkeley Square, London W1J 6BD
**Tel:** 02078-877-624
**Web:** www.ruspetro.com
**Reg No:** 7817695 **Estd:** 2011 Public Limited Company
**Line of Business:** Extraction of crude petroleum and natural gas
**Directors:** K G Androsov, M G Dijols, S Gordeev, A N Chistyakov, R J Jenkins, J M Conlin, F J Monstrey, C M Pearson
**Co. Secretary:** Prism Cosec Limited
**US SIC:** 1311 **UK SIC:** 13000
**Auditors:** PricewaterhouseCoopers LLP
**Employees:** 211
**Turnover:** £79,849,000

DUNS 21-606-4816 **Imp**

## Russell & Bromley Ltd

24-34 Farwig Lane, Bromley, Kent BR1 3RB
**Fax:** 020 8460 4424
**Web:** www.russellandbromley.co.uk
**Reg No:** 0512958 **VAT No:** 205469959
**Estd:** 1952 Private Limited Company
**Line of Business:** Retail sale of footwear
**Issued Capital:** £1,020,000
**Principals:** R J Bromley *(Managing)*, S P Bromley, A M Bromley
**Co. Secretary:** Philip Wright
**Responsibilities**
**Senior:** Avril Copeland *(Manager)*
**Finance:** Avril Copeland *(Manager)*
**IT:** Stuart Parkes *(IT Manager)*
**Branches:** Russell & Bromley Ltd, 100 Promenade, Cheltenham, Gloucestershire GL50 1NB
**US SIC:** 5661, 5621
**UK SIC:** 64600, 64500
**Auditors:** Ernst & Young LLP
**Bankers:** National Westminster Bank Plc (60-04-02)

| | 31-12-13 | 31-12-12 | 31-12-11 |
|---|---|---|---|
| TO | 117,568,732 | 107,383,634 | 101,007,906 |
| P/L | 21,955,814 | 19,514,980 | 20,865,365 |
| NW | 64,611,212 | 58,595,183 | 52,548,044 |
| WC | 36,660,030 | 32,041,429 | 25,640,513 |
| Emp. | 1,096 | 1,082 | 1,038 |

DUNS 42-353-3038

## Russell & Russell Business Advisers Ltd

4 Royal Crescent, Glasgow, Lanarkshire G3 7SL
**Tel:** 01413326331 **Fax:** 01204-389223
**Web:** www.growyourbusiness.co.uk
**Reg No:** 0226378SC **Estd:** 2001 Private Limited Company
**Line of Business:** Accounting activities
**Issued Capital:** £330
**Directors:** A W Russell, Mrs R Mcmaster, I Mcmonagle
**Co. Secretary:** Kenneth Russell
**Branches:** Russell & Russell Business Advisers Ltd, Russell & Russell Solicitors, Churchill House, Bolton, Lancashire BL1 1EE
**US SIC:** 8931, 7392
**UK SIC:** 83600, 83951

| | 31-01-14 | 31-01-13 | 31-01-12 |
|---|---|---|---|
| TA | 909,650 | 884,365 | 829,855 |
| NW | 514,504 | 416,216 | 340,571 |
| WC | 345,761 | 250,786 | 328,108 |

DUNS 64-254-8655

## Russell & Russell Solicitors

Churchill House, 7-13 Wood Street, Bolton, Lancashire BL1 1EE
**Tel:** 01204399299
**Web:** www.russellrussell.co.uk
**Estd:** 2002 Partnership
**Line of Business:** Solicitors
**Partners:** A Walsh, J Matthews
**Responsibilities**
**Senior:** Judith Bromley *(Senior Partner)*, Andrew Costello *(Partner / Solicitor)*, Nick Ross *(Partner / Solicitor)*, Adam Whittaker *(Partner / Solicitor)*
**Finance:** Jill Chan *(Finance Administrator)*
**IT:** Nigel Greensitt *(IT Manager)*, Steve Sarab *(IT Manager)*
**HR:** Emma Hughes *(Human Resources Manager)*, Sharon Matthews *(Human Resources Manager)*
**Health & Safety:** Sharon Matthews *(Human Resources Manager)*
**Facilities:** Sharon Matthews *(Human Resources Manager)*
**Branches:** Russell & Russell Solicitors, 43 Market Street, Manchester M46 0GQ
**US SIC:** 8111 **UK SIC:** 83500
**Employees:** 120

DUNS 38-549-4182

## Russell Bedford International

65 St Paul's Churchyard, London EC4M 8AB
**Fax:** 02075492337
**Web:** www.russellbedford.com
**Reg No:** 3331251 **Estd:** 1983 Private Limited Company
**Line of Business:** Activities of professional organisations
**Directors:** H Kligman, W Rucci, D L Ryba, J Ngai, J Jimenez Lizardi, Dr K Hillebrand, A P Bezzant, L D Newman
**Co. Secretary:** Mrs Vanessa Clark
**Responsibilities**
**Senior:** Thomas Donovan *(Director)*, Geoffrey Goodyear *(Manager)*, Ken Harper *(Marketing Manager)*, Katharine Lebihan *(Manager)*, Abir Raveh *(Director)*, Carlos Tortelli *(Partner)*
**Marketing:** Kempton Bedell-Harper *(Marketing Director)*
**US SIC:** 8621 **UK SIC:** 96311
**Bankers:** HSBC Bank plc (40-05-01)

| | 30-06-13 | 30-06-12 | 30-06-11 |
|---|---|---|---|
| TA | 381,982 | 312,125 | 383,101 |
| NW | 292,763 | 242,968 | 254,250 |
| WC | 291,493 | 242,102 | 253,593 |

DUNS 21-825-2088 **Imp-Exp**

## Russell Burgess Ltd

1 Commerce Road, Lynch Wood, Peterborough, Cambridgeshire PE2 6LR
**Tel:** 01733-240491 **Fax:** 01733244572
**Web:** www.produceworld.co.uk
**Reg No:** 0557434 **VAT No:** 119403978
**Estd:** 1943 Private Limited Company
**Line of Business:** Convenience stores
**Export Markets:** European Union (E U)
**Export Sales:** £154,000
**Trading Style:** Produce World
**Issued Capital:** £18,320
**Principals:** H Z Brown *(Managing)*, J C Burgess, D S Burgess, A S Burgess
**Co. Secretary:** David Burgess
**US SIC:** 6711 **UK SIC:** 83962
**Auditors:** Bulley Davey
**Bankers:** Barclays Bank Plc (20-67-37)

| | 28-06-13 | 29-06-12 | 01-06-11 |
|---|---|---|---|
| TO | 186,003,000 | 178,680,000 | 206,240,000 |
| P/L | 3,151,000 | (5,087,000) | (11,636,000) |
| NW | 2,453,000 | 1,236,000 | 4,367,000 |
| WC | (6,049,000) | (14,615,000) | (11,445,000) |
| Emp. | 772 | 1,113 | 1,306 |

DUNS 29-768-2437

## Russell Cawberry Ltd

(**Subsidiary of:** Minter International Ltd)
31 The Broadway, Sutton, Surrey SM3 8BL
**Tel:** 020-8643-9521
**Web:** www.russellcawberry.com
**Reg No:** 2031233 **Estd:** 1986 Private Limited Company
**Line of Business:** Construction of commercial buildings
**Issued Capital:** £14,705
**Directors:** A F Dillon, P F Ryan, F J Minter
**Co. Secretary:** Frederick Minter
**US SIC:** 1541 **UK SIC:** 50100
**Auditors:** Stewart & Co
**Bankers:** The Royal Bank Of Scotland Plc (16-32-45)

| | 31-03-14 | 31-03-13 | 31-03-12 |
|---|---|---|---|
| TO | 30,039,814 | 18,810,354 | 21,310,635 |
| P/L | 116,048 | 80,934 | 147,272 |
| NW | 534,738 | 568,178 | 666,789 |
| WC | 534,579 | 564,807 | 652,532 |
| Emp. | 61 | 66 | 71 |

DUNS 85-614-3086

## Russell-Cooke Llp

2 Putney Hill, London SW15 6AB
**Tel:** 02085466111 **Fax:** 02087801194
**Web:** www.russell-cooke.co.uk
**Reg No:** 0327450OC **Estd:** 1982 Private Limited Company
**Line of Business:** Solicitors
**Responsibilities**
**Senior:** Lesley Alderson *(Designated Limited Liability P)*, Jessica Asher *(Partner)*, Alex Bearman *(Partner)*, Rita Bhargava *(Partner)*, Deborah Blythe *(Designated Limited Liability P)*, Jae Carwardine *(Partner)*, Judith Carwardine *(Designated Limited Liability P)*, Nigel Coates *(Managing Partner)*, Dominic Fairclough *(Partner)*, Rebecca Fisher *(Partner)*, Richard Frimston *(Designated Limited Liability P)*, Arnold Isaacson *(Designated Limited Liability P)*, Francesca Kaye *(Designated Limited Liability P)*, Samantha Little *(Designated Limited Liability P)*, Lee Ranford *(Designated Limited Liability P)*, James Sinclair-taylor *(Proprietor)*
**Marketing:** Janev Djemil *(Marketing Assistant)*, Stephanie Efah *(Marketing Assistant)*, Kate Wreford-Glanvill *(Marketing Assistant)*
**Branches:** Russell-Cooke Llp, 8 Bedford Row, London WC1R 4BX
**US SIC:** 8111 **UK SIC:** 83500
**Bankers:** National Westminster Bank Plc (60-00-01)

| | 30-06-14 | 30-06-13 | 30-06-12 |
|---|---|---|---|
| TO | 28,152,924 | 25,959,284 | 24,724,533 |
| NW | N/A | 4,756,193 | 4,401,559 |
| WC | 18,037,337 | 15,606,370 | 15,230,311 |
| Emp. | 227 | 228 | 213 |

DUNS 50-028-1761

## Russell Court Ltd

Russell Square, Longfield, Kent DA3 7RY
**Tel:** 01474-708151
**Web:** www.russellcourt.co.uk
**Reg No:** 2287130 **VAT No:** 586464789
**Estd:** 2012 Private Limited Company
**Line of Business:** Nursing homes
**Trading Style:** Russel Court Nursing Home
**Issued Capital:** £10,000
**Director:** A E West
**Co. Secretary:** Ms Astrid West
**Responsibilities**
**Senior:** Rachel Caveney *(Manager)*
**Admin:** Ann Glanville *(Administrator)*
**Purchasing:** Ann Glanville *(Administrator)*
**US SIC:** 8051 **UK SIC:** 95100
**Bankers:** Barclays Bank Plc (20-25-42)

| | 30-04-14 | 30-04-13 | 30-04-12 |
|---|---|---|---|
| TA | 3,051,514 | 3,006,917 | 2,972,371 |
| NW | 1,044,972 | 956,828 | 826,087 |
| WC | 127,949 | 129,185 | 89,850 |

DUNS 21-097-6494 **Imp-Exp**

## Russell Finex Ltd

Browells Lane, Feltham, Middlesex TW13 7EW
**Tel:** 02088182000
**Web:** www.russellfinex.com
**Reg No:** 0294532 **Estd:** 1934 Private Limited Company
**Line of Business:** Manufacture of machinery for food, beverage and tobacco processing
**Issued Capital:** £181,443
**Directors:** S J Keyworth, M W Chipperfield, Dr N J Mainwaring, R Singh, R J O'Connell, K J Armour
**Co. Secretary:** Ms Carolyn Mcdermott
**Responsibilities**
**Senior:** Timothy Corn *(Manager)*, Michael Henson *(Manager)*, Radhika Singh *(Sales Director)*, Ray Singh *(Manager)*
**Marketing:** Radhika Singh *(Sales Director)*
**Sales:** Radhika Singh *(Sales Director)*
**US SIC:** 3551, 3559
**UK SIC:** 32441, 32863
**Auditors:** Michael Letch & Partners LLP
**Bankers:** HSBC Bank plc (40-21-22)

| | 31-01-14 | 31-01-13 | 31-01-12 |
|---|---|---|---|
| TO | 23,919,373 | 23,008,129 | 22,140,998 |
| P/L | 1,930,936 | 1,939,778 | 2,552,628 |
| NW | 11,685,771 | 11,743,132 | 13,074,330 |
| WC | 9,271,088 | 8,938,439 | 7,693,814 |
| Emp. | 299 | 297 | 261 |

DUNS 22-121-9459

## Russell House School Ltd

Station Road, Otford, Otford, Sevenoaks, Kent TN14 5QU
**Tel:** 01959-522352
**Web:** www.russellhouse.kent.sch.uk
**Reg No:** 4140981 **Estd:** 1901 Private Limited Company
**Line of Business:** Primary education
**Issued Capital:** £100
**Directors:** Ms J Imas, Ms E Lindsay, R A Lindsay
**Co. Secretary:** Dr Yvonne Lindsay
**Responsibilities**
**Senior:** Alison Cooke *(Head Teacher)*, Keith Lindsay *(Manager)*, Craig Mccarthy *(Head Teacher)*
**Finance:** Patricia Reeve *(Bursar)*
**US SIC:** 8211 **UK SIC:** 93200

| | 31-08-13 | 31-08-12 | 31-08-11 |
|---|---|---|---|
| TA | 1,138,550 | 1,008,494 | 894,856 |
| NW | 949,558 | 859,250 | 804,390 |
| WC | 711,674 | 645,246 | 541,865 |

DUNS 49-380-9149

## Russell Hume Ltd

3 Pinnacle Way, Derby, Derbyshire
**Tel:** 08000850801 **Fax:** 01332-332862
**Web:** www.russellhume.com
**Reg No:** 3127969 **VAT No:** 354304476
**Estd:** 1996 Private Limited Company
**Line of Business:** Production of meat and poultry meat products
**Issued Capital:** £1,047,165
**Directors:** P Herlihy, I Gould, D A Holding, Mrs P K Purewal
**Co. Secretary:** Richard Kay
**Responsibilities**
**IT:** Martin Basford *(Computer Manager)*
**Branches:** Russell Hume Ltd, 47 Shady Lane, Birmingham, West Midlands B44 9ER
**US SIC:** 5149 **UK SIC:** 61700
**Auditors:** RSM Tenon Audit Ltd
**Bankers:** National Westminster Bank Plc (60-12-01)

| | 31-03-14 | 31-03-13 | 31-03-12 |
|---|---|---|---|
| TO | 126,087,000 | 115,665,000 | 101,665,000 |
| P/L | 3,698,000 | 3,726,000 | 3,013,000 |
| NW | 27,630,000 | 24,712,000 | 21,828,000 |
| WC | 24,164,000 | 21,091,000 | 18,420,000 |
| Emp. | 395 | 379 | 351 |

DUNS 29-883-2692 **Imp**

## Russell Investments Ltd

(**Subsidiary of:** Russell Systems Ltd)
Rex House, 4-12 Regent Street, London SW1Y 4PE
**Tel:** 02070246000 **Fax:** 020-7024-6001
**Web:** www.russell.com
**Reg No:** 2086230 **Estd:** 1986 Private Limited Company
**Line of Business:** Investment consultants
**Issued Capital:** £10,341,000
**Directors:** P Duval, P D Gonella, C Caspar, J J Beveridge, R Bishop, K Willman, B C Tipple
**Co. Secretary:** Tmf Corporate Administration Ser
**Responsibilities**
**Senior:** Ian Battye *(Manager)*, Johan Cras *(Manager)*, James Firn *(Manager)*, Alexandra Haggard *(Managing Director, Product & M)*, Martijn Kuipers *(Managing Director, Benelux & N)*, Shamindra Perera *(Managing Director, Head of Pen)*
**Marketing:** Alexandra Haggard *(Managing Director, Product & M)*
**Sales:** Ronan O'Riordan *(Business Development Manager)*, Guy Wickramanayake *(Head of Product & Business Man)*
**US SIC:** 6111 **UK SIC:** 81501
**Auditors:** PricewaterhouseCoopers LLP

| | 31-12-13 | 31-12-12 | 31-12-11 |
|---|---|---|---|
| TA | 35,387,066 | 28,148,986 | 27,104,398 |
| P/L | 4,471,291 | (3,519,094) | (7,247,273) |
| NW | 16,816,853 | 13,115,922 | 11,468,404 |
| WC | 17,505,590 | 13,753,085 | 11,808,380 |
| Emp. | 149 | 142 | 146 |

DUNS 54-313-5206 **Imp**

## Russell Reynolds Associates Ltd

(**Subsidiary of:** Russell Reynolds Associates Inc.)
Almack House, 26-28 King Street, London SW1Y 6QW
**Tel:** 02078397788 **Fax:** 02078399295
**Web:** www.russellreynolds.com
**Reg No:** 3258089 **Estd:** 1969 Private Limited Company
**Line of Business:** Management and business consultants
**Issued Capital:** £50
**Director:** E Allen
**Co. Secretary:** James Bichener
**Responsibilities**
**Senior:** Jim Hinds *(Manager)*, Patrick Johnson *(Manager)*, Suzzane Wood *(MD of Financial Officers)*
**Finance:** Albert Morris *(Chief Financial Officer)*, Suzzane Wood *(MD of Financial Officers)*
**Admin:** Stacey Parsons *(Health & Safety Officer)*
**IT:** Tristan Jervis *(Associate in Technology & Corp)*
**HR:** Fiona Griffiths *(Human Resources Manager)*
**Health & Safety:** Stacey Parsons *(Health & Safety Officer)*
**Branches:** Russell Reynolds Associates Ltd, 24 Melville St, Edinburgh, Midlothian EH3 7NS
**US SIC:** 7392 **UK SIC:** 83951
**Auditors:** PricewaterhouseCoopers LLP
**Bankers:** Barclays Bank Plc (20-65-82)

| | 31-12-13 | 31-12-12 | 31-12-11 |
|---|---|---|---|
| TO | 39,914,000 | 38,280,000 | 38,747,000 |
| P/L | 1,283,000 | 3,201,000 | (61,000) |
| NW | 3,436,000 | 2,569,000 | 4,299,000 |
| WC | 845,000 | (470,000) | 784,000 |
| Emp. | 146 | 147 | 148 |

DUNS 21-440-5615

## Russell Roof Tiles Ltd

(**Subsidiary of:** Cemex S.A.B. De C.V.)
Nicolson Way, Burton-On-Trent, Staffordshire DE14 2AW
**Tel:** 01283-517070
**Web:** www.russell-rooftiles.co.uk
**Reg No:** 0028252SC **Estd:** 1951 Private Limited Company
**Line of Business:** Manufacture of other non-metallic mineral products not elsewhere classified
**Trading Style:** Russell Roof Tiles Ltd
**Issued Capital:** £10,000
**Principals:** P G Rosie *(Managing)*, M L Collins
**Co. Secretary:** Ms Daphne Murray
**Responsibilities**
**Senior:** Andrew haywood *(Director sales)*

**US SIC:** 3272 **UK SIC:** 24370
**Bankers:** Barclays Bank Plc (20-13-42)

| | 31-12-13 | 31-12-12 | 31-12-11 |
|---|---|---|---|
| TA | 10,000 | 10,000 | 10,000 |
| NW | 10,000 | 10,000 | 10,000 |

DUNS 21-216-3208
## Russell's (Kirbymoorside) Ltd
Eden Works, Edenhouse Road, Old Malton, Malton, North Yorkshire YO17 6RD
**Web:** http://russells.uk.com
**Reg No:** 0178738 **VAT No:** 167140473
**Estd:** 1922 Private Limited Company
**Line of Business:** Agricultural machinery sales service and repair
**Trading Style:** Russell Farm Machinery
**Issued Capital:** £110,000
**Directors:** W G Shaw, H E Shaw, T P Russell, Major J Shaw, J R Archer
**Co. Secretary:** Robert Whitehead
**Branches:** Russell's (Kirbymoorside) Ltd, Milby, Boroughbridge, York, North Yorkshire YO51 9BL
**US SIC:** 3523 **UK SIC:** 32113
**Auditors:** Winn & Co
**Bankers:** Barclays Bank Plc (20-99-56)

| | 31-10-13 | 31-10-12 | 31-10-11 |
|---|---|---|---|
| TO | 29,972,918 | 33,642,957 | 31,588,514 |
| P/L | 388,631 | 782,145 | 674,339 |
| NW | 6,256,013 | 5,655,257 | 5,299,549 |
| WC | 4,048,413 | 3,778,488 | 3,752,061 |
| Emp. | 91 | 90 | 88 |

DUNS 23-230-3313
## Russet Homes Ltd
Basted House, Harrison Road, Borough Green, Sevenoaks, Kent TN15 8PB
**Tel:** 01732-780999
**Web:** www.russethomes.org
**Reg No:** 0027076IP **VAT No:** 573555517
**Estd:** 1991 Friendly Society
**Line of Business:** Housing associations societies trusts & co-operatives
**Principals:** M Webber *(Chairman)*, Mrs S Farmer, R Mackay, H Simmons, P West, C Ainsworth, F Groves, R Barden
**Co. Secretary:** John Ridley
**Responsibilities**
**Senior:** Marion Cole *(Designated Limited Liability P)*, John Figgett *(Designated Limited Liability P)*, Charles Gadd *(Designated Limited Liability P)*, Georgina Gradwell *(Designated Limited Liability P)*, Joy Johnson *(Designated Limited Liability P)*, Arnold Jones *(Designated Limited Liability P)*, Nan Lynch *(Designated Limited Liability P)*, Peter Reed *(Designated Limited Liability P)*, Constance Ward *(Designated Limited Liability P)*, Steven Woodcock *(Manager)*
**Admin:** Carol Whitfield *(Office Manager)*
**Facilities:** Carol Whitfield *(Office Manager)*
**Operations:** Carol Whitfield *(Office Manager)*
**Purchasing:** Carol Whitfield *(Office Manager)*
**US SIC:** 8321 **UK SIC:** 96111
**Bankers:** National Westminster Bank Plc (55-81-07)

| | 31-03-12 | 31-03-11 | 31-03-10 |
|---|---|---|---|
| TO | 37,090,000 | 35,597,000 | 34,628,000 |
| P/L | 8,286,000 | 11,441,000 | 10,347,000 |
| NW | 25,190,000 | 19,672,000 | 4,362,000 |
| WC | (148,598,000) | (151,759,000) | (3,922,000) |
| Emp. | 69 | 64 | 61 |

DUNS 21-117-5617 **Imp-Exp**
## Rustins Ltd
51 Waterloo Road, London E10 7HR
**Tel:** 020-8450-4666
**Web:** www.rustins.co.uk
**Reg No:** 0162273 **VAT No:** 226532967
**Estd:** 1924 Private Limited Company
**Line of Business:** Manufacturers of paints
**Export Markets:** Eire; Cyprus; Russia; Australia; Greece; Norway; Sweden; Finland; New Zealand
**Export Sales:** £1,117,496
**Trading Style:** Rustin Clark
**Issued Capital:** £15,961
**Directors:** E P Krawitt, Mrs B Berman, A Rustin, M G Rustin
**Co. Secretary:** Pankaj Shah
**Responsibilities**
**Senior:** Paresh Soni *(Works Manager)*
**Marketing:** Vince McDonagh *(Design Marketing Manager)*
**Facilities:** Paresh Soni *(Works Manager)*
**Operations:** Paresh Soni *(Works Manager)*
**Purchasing:** Paresh Soni *(Works Manager)*
**Engineering:** Paresh Soni *(Works Manager)*
**US SIC:** 2891 **UK SIC:** 25620
**Auditors:** PKF
**Bankers:** Barclays Bank Plc (20-92-60)

| | 31-12-13 | 31-12-12 | 31-12-11 |
|---|---|---|---|
| TO | 7,224,781 | 5,990,984 | 5,238,350 |
| P/L | 861,139 | 588,770 | 286,916 |
| NW | 4,808,012 | 5,160,047 | 4,758,692 |
| WC | 1,832,515 | 2,106,933 | 1,696,394 |
| Emp. | 56 | 52 | N/A |

DUNS 21-585-5846
## Rutherglen High School
Langlea Road, Cambuslang, Glasgow, Lanarkshire G72 8ES
**Tel:** 01416433480
**Web:** www.rutherglen.s-lanark.sch.uk
**Estd:** 2010 Proprietorship
**Line of Business:** Schools (special)
**Proprietor:** Mrs J Allan
**Responsibilities**
**Senior:** Janet Allan *(Head Teacher)*
**US SIC:** 8299 **UK SIC:** 93300
**Employees:** 50

DUNS 50-544-4885
## Ruthin School Charity
Mold Road, Ruthin, Clwyd LL15 1EG
**Tel:** 01824-702543 **Fax:** 01824-707141
**Web:** www.ruthinschool.co.uk
**Reg No:** 2498499 **Estd:** 1990 Private Limited Company
**Line of Business:** Schools (independent)
**Directors:** C W Conway, Dr G H Roberts, I Trigger, J E Sharples, Rev J S Evans, Ms J C Oldbury, Ms T O Kerrigan, A R Bale
**Co. Secretary:** Toby Belfield
**Responsibilities**
**Admin:** Judy Salt *(Office Coordinator)*
**Health & Safety:** Catherine Bland *(Matron)*
**Purchasing:** Judy Salt *(Office Coordinator)*
**US SIC:** 8211 **UK SIC:** 93200
**Employees:** 40

DUNS 23-993-5216
## Rutland County Council
Catmose House, Catmos Street, Oakham, Leicestershire LE15 6HP
**Tel:** 01572-722577
**Web:** www.rutland.gov.uk
**Estd:** 1997
**Line of Business:** Local government
**Trading Style:** Rutland Housing Services
**Directors:** Dr J Morphet, B Phillips, R Adams
**Responsibilities**
**Senior:** Roger Begy *(Chairman)*, Helen Briggs *(Chief Executive)*
**Finance:** Debbie Mogg *(Director of Resources)*
**Sales:** Libby Kingsley *(Senior Economic Development Ma)*
**IT:** Matt Callan *(IT Manager)*
**HR:** Tish Barnwell *(Road Safety Officer)*, Carol Chambers *(Training Director)*
**Health & Safety:** Ian Watt *(Health & Safety Officer)*
**Facilities:** Birinder Rakhra *(Facilities Manager)*
**Operations:** Dave Brown *(Director of Places Environment)*, Stephen Tee *(Team Leader)*
**Branches:** Rutland County Council, 69 High Street, Southwold, Suffolk IP18 6DS
**US SIC:** 9121 **UK SIC:** 91110
**Bankers:** Barclays Bank Plc (20-63-66)
**Employees:** 450

DUNS 42-368-0896
## The Rutland Hotel (Sheffield) Ltd
(**Subsidiary of:** Claypenny Hotels Ltd)
452 Glossop Road, Sheffield, South Yorkshire S10 2PY
**Tel:** 01142-664411
**Web:** www.rutlandhotel-sheffield.com
**Reg No:** 4355709 **Estd:** 1986 Private Limited Company
**Line of Business:** Hotels
**Issued Capital:** £1
**Directors:** G P Ludlam, C J Dowie
**Co. Secretary:** Fraser Ludlam
**Responsibilities**
**Senior:** Sarah Bakewell *(Manager)*, Frederick Pickworth *(Manager)*, Jacqueline Pickworth *(Manager)*
**Finance:** Simone Pickworth *(Finance Director)*, Anne Roper *(Financial Manager)*
**Marketing:** Katey Dent *(Sales & Marketing Manager)*
**Sales:** Katey Dent *(Sales & Marketing Manager)*
**IT:** Kirsty Butterfield *(General Manager)*
**HR:** Gail Plant *(Human Resources Manager)*
**Facilities:** Rod Dixon *(Facilities Manager)*
**Operations:** Katey Dent *(Sales & Marketing Manager)*
**Purchasing:** Kirsty Butterfield *(General Manager)*
**US SIC:** 7011 **UK SIC:** 66500
**Auditors:** HLB AV Audit PLC

| | 29-06-14 | 30-06-13 | 01-06-12 |
|---|---|---|---|
| TA | 2,752,781 | 2,697,978 | 2,908,253 |
| NW | 407,497 | 293,655 | 118,052 |
| WC | (330,833) | (480,547) | (674,707) |

DUNS 49-743-8473
## Rutland House
67 All Saints Road, Sutton, Surrey SM1 3DQ
**Tel:** 020-8644-5699
**Estd:** 1988 Proprietorship
**Line of Business:** Residential care establishments
**Proprietor:** R Parouty
**Responsibilities**
**Senior:** Donna Konthasindhe *(Manager)*
**US SIC:** 8321 **UK SIC:** 96111

DUNS 21-779-0126
## Rutland Manor
99-109 Heanor Road, Ilkeston, Derbyshire DE7 8TA
**Tel:** 01159440322
**Web:** www.monarchhealthcare.co.uk
**Estd:** 1989 Partnership
**Line of Business:** Nursing homes
**Partners:** Mrs A Martin, Mrs E Mellard
**US SIC:** 8051 **UK SIC:** 95100
**Employees:** 55

DUNS 21-824-7666 **Imp-Exp**
## Rutland Plastics Ltd
Cold Overton Road, Oakham, Leicestershire LE15 6NU
**Tel:** 01572723476
**Web:** www.rutlandplastics.co.uk
**Reg No:** 0560131 **VAT No:** 330356390
**Estd:** 1956 Private Limited Company
**Line of Business:** Manufacture of other plastic products
**Export Markets:** W Europe
**Issued Capital:** £23,900
**Principals:** M E Ayre *(Managing)*, S R Ayre, Mrs S E Ayre, Mrs C R Johnston, S A Johnston
**Co. Secretary:** Mark Dolby
**Responsibilities**
**Senior:** Darren Wiggins *(Warehouse Manager)*
**HR:** Alistair Forbes *(Operations Manager)*
**Health & Safety:** Alistair Forbes *(Operations Manager)*
**Operations:** Alistair Forbes *(Operations Manager)*
**US SIC:** 3079 **UK SIC:** 48360
**Auditors:** Rowleys
**Bankers:** HSBC Bank plc (40-28-08)

| | 31-12-13 | 31-12-12 | 31-12-11 |
|---|---|---|---|
| TO | 8,999,309 | 8,848,361 | 9,273,061 |
| P/L | 248,317 | 258,808 | 321,989 |
| NW | 9,540,738 | 9,523,548 | 9,536,863 |
| WC | 3,871,958 | 3,915,012 | 3,927,571 |
| Emp. | 102 | 103 | 102 |

DUNS 73-783-6387
## Rutland Water Cycling Ltd
(**Subsidiary of:** Rutland Cycling 2013 Ltd)
Whitwell Leisure Park, Oakham, Leicestershire LE15 8BL
**Tel:** 01780460705
**Web:** www.rutlandcycling.com
**Reg No:** 2926548 **VAT No:** 974976545
**Estd:** 1994 Private Limited Company
**Line of Business:** Cycle shops
**Export Sales:** £61,365
**Issued Capital:** £80
**Directors:** P M Archer, Ms S M Middlemiss, D Middlemiss
**Co. Secretary:** Ms Karen Archer
**Responsibilities**
**Senior:** Dan Murtaugh *(Manager)*
**Marketing:** Kerry Rough *(Marketing Manager)*
**US SIC:** 5941, 7999
**UK SIC:** 65400, 97913
**Auditors:** Cheney & Co

| | 31-01-14 | 31-01-13 | 31-01-12 |
|---|---|---|---|
| TO | 9,202,795 | 10,872,259 | 10,456,198 |
| P/L | (303,624) | (1,765) | 169,810 |
| NW | 505,815 | 903,052 | 900,849 |
| WC | 174,662 | 808,509 | 281,407 |
| Emp. | 81 | 77 | 90 |

DUNS 23-232-3691
## Rutledge Recruitment & Training Ltd
(**Subsidiary of:** Rutledge Training & Recruitment Ltd)
25-27 New Row, Coleraine, Co Londonderry BT52 1AD
**Tel:** 02870356710 **Fax:** 028-3834-7885
**Web:** www.rutledgegroup.co.uk
**Reg No:** 0028890NI **Estd:** 1994 Private Limited Company
**Line of Business:** Labour recruitment and provision of personnel
**Issued Capital:** £100
**Director:** J N Doherty
**Co. Secretary:** Jonathan Doherty
**Responsibilities**
**Senior:** Edward Lane *(Finance Director)*
**Finance:** Edward Lane *(Finance Director)*
**Health & Safety:** Philip Rankin *(Quality Coordinator)*
**US SIC:** 8999, 7361
**UK SIC:** 83954

| | 31-03-14 | 31-03-13 | 31-03-12 |
|---|---|---|---|
| TA | 4,934,367 | 5,471,894 | 5,727,909 |
| P/L | 460,259 | 71,761 | 685,363 |
| NW | 1,903,143 | 1,571,322 | 1,628,706 |
| WC | (710,940) | (1,113,191) | (967,355) |
| Emp. | 270 | 325 | 421 |

DUNS 34-712-4104
## Rutronik Uk Ltd
Dunscar House, Deakins Business Park, Blackburn Road, Egerton, Bolton, Lancashire BL7 9RP
**Tel:** 01204-602200 **Fax:** 01204602210
**Web:** www.rutronik.com
**Reg No:** 5516352 **Estd:** 1996 Private Limited Company
**Line of Business:** Manufacturers and distributors of electronic components
**Issued Capital:** £1
**Directors:** H L Rudel, T M Rudel
**Co. Secretary:** Alexander Schroer
**Responsibilities**
**Senior:** Giselle Hardern *(CEO, Managing Director)*, Jezel Hardern *(Manager)*
**US SIC:** 3679, 5199
**UK SIC:** 34542, 61900
**Auditors:** Cowgill Holloway LLP
**Bankers:** The Royal Bank Of Scotland Plc (16-00-01)

| | 31-12-13 | 31-12-12 | 31-12-11 |
|---|---|---|---|
| TO | 19,225,249 | 18,037,577 | N/A |
| P/L | 997,076 | 1,541,573 | N/A |
| NW | 3,118,931 | 2,370,595 | 1,237,046 |
| WC | 3,118,931 | 2,370,595 | 2,087,479 |
| Emp. | 46 | 44 | N/A |

DUNS 21-879-5133
## Rutson Hospital
The Rutson Rehabilitation Unit, Northallerton, North Yorkshire DL6 1JG
**Tel:** 01609764818
**Estd:** 2002
**Line of Business:** General Medical And Surgical Hospitals
**US SIC:** 8062 **UK SIC:** 95100
**Employees:** 1,000

DUNS 22-850-7828 **Exp**
## Ruttle Plant Holdings Ltd
Lancaster House, Chorley, Lancashire PR7 1NH
**Web:** www.ruttle.co.uk
**Reg No:** 1333237 **Estd:** 1977 Private Limited Company
**Line of Business:** Plant hire and leasing
**Export Markets:** U S A & Canada
**Issued Capital:** £2,000
**Principals:** G H Ruttle *(Managing)*, T K Ruttle
**Co. Secretary:** Arthur Ruttle
**Branches:** Ruttle Plant Holdings Ltd, Killean, Cara, Tarbert, Argyll PA29 6XF
**US SIC:** 6711, 6552
**UK SIC:** 83962, 85000
**Auditors:** James Todd & Co
**Bankers:** Barclays Bank Plc (20-69-85)

| | 30-09-13 | 30-09-12 | 30-09-11 |
|---|---|---|---|
| TO | N/A | N/A | 6,190,377 |
| P/L | N/A | N/A | (602,356) |
| NW | 17,866,477 | 17,614,244 | 17,406,800 |
| WC | 2,857,291 | 715,733 | 4,545,343 |
| Emp. | N/A | N/A | 4 |

DUNS 21-747-5987 **Imp**
## Ruxley Manor Garden Centre Ltd
(**Subsidiary of:** H.Evans & Sons Ltd)
Maidstone Road, Sidcup, Kent DA14 5BQ
**Tel:** 020-8300-0084 **Fax:** 02083023879
**Web:** www.ruxley-manor.co.uk
**Reg No:** 1170687 **VAT No:** 299327311
**Estd:** 1974 Private Limited Company
**Line of Business:** Erection of roof covering and frames
**Issued Capital:** £100
**Principals:** R T Evans *(Managing)*, A R Evans, J S Evans, K Baker
**Co. Secretary:** Richard Evans
**Responsibilities**
**Marketing:** Lisa Bottomley *(Marketing Manager)*
**HR:** Allyson Barnard *(Human Resources Manager)*
**Facilities:** Roger Juby *(Facilities Manager)*
**US SIC:** 1761, 5999
**UK SIC:** 50400, 65600
**Auditors:** McBrides
**Bankers:** HSBC Bank plc (40-42-01)

| | 31-12-13 | 31-12-12 | 31-12-11 |
|---|---|---|---|
| TO | 8,446,460 | 7,339,585 | 7,521,732 |
| P/L | (103,744) | (32,686) | 404,340 |
| NW | 2,923,098 | 3,026,842 | 3,086,015 |
| WC | 1,576,125 | 1,686,661 | 2,528,806 |
| Emp. | 111 | 101 | 89 |

DUNS 29-517-7224 Exp

## Rvl Aviation Ltd

(**Subsidiary of:** Reconnaissance Ventures Ltd)
Hanger 6 Coventry Airport, Kenilworth, Warwickshire CV8 3AZ
**Tel:** 02476305731 **Fax:** 02476305170
**Web:** www.rvl-group.com
**Reg No:** 1880927 **VAT No:** 911374348
**Estd:** 1985 Private Limited Company
**Line of Business:** Airlines
**Trading Style:** Rvl Group
**Issued Capital:** £4,250,000
**Director:** C H Dennis
**Co. Secretary:** Stephen Guynan
**US SIC:** 4511, 7399
**UK SIC:** 75000, 83954
**Auditors:** Jerroms LLP
**Bankers:** National Westminster Bank Plc (60-12-03)

| | 31-12-13 | 31-12-12 | 31-12-11 |
|---|---|---|---|
| TA | 865,399 | 1,061,913 | 727,789 |
| NW | 790,296 | 900,211 | 727,789 |
| WC | 790,295 | 900,210 | N/A |

DUNS 29-525-9519 Imp-Exp

## Rvl Holdings Plc

Estate Way, 210 Church Road, London E10 7JN
**Tel:** 02085581234 **Fax:** 02089888149
**Web:** www.gbnservices.co.uk
**Reg No:** 1893445 **Estd:** 1985 Public Limited Company
**Line of Business:** Management activities of holding companies
**Export Markets:** E U
**Export Sales:** £4,319,219
**Trading Style:** Rvl Holdings Public Limited Company
**Issued Capital:** £103,060
**Principals:** D W Thompson *(Chairman)*, G D Thompson, G M Hobson
**Co. Secretary:** Frederick Black
**Responsibilities**
**Senior:** Angela Roe *(Manager)*
**Sales:** Bobby Patel *(Senior Sales Executive)*
**IT:** David Totty *(Senior IT Executive)*
**US SIC:** 6711 **UK SIC:** 83962
**Auditors:** Brindley Goldstein Ltd
**Bankers:** Barclays Bank Plc (20-00-30)

| | 31-03-14 | 31-03-13 | 31-03-12 |
|---|---|---|---|
| TO | 35,636,879 | 29,712,949 | 26,655,822 |
| P/L | 2,976,530 | 3,580,192 | 1,544,338 |
| NW | 22,455,158 | 19,651,480 | 16,620,485 |
| WC | 160,682 | (2,154,056) | (2,050,452) |
| Emp. | 251 | 202 | 240 |

DUNS 21-139-8056

## Rvs Engineering (2008) Ltd

Ynys Bridge, Tongwynlais, Cardiff, South Glamorgan CF15 7NT
**Tel:** 02920811663 **Fax:** 0292081359
**Web:** www.rvsengineering.co.uk
**Reg No:** 6719531 **Estd:** 2008 Private Limited Company
**Line of Business:** General mechanical engineering
**Issued Capital:** £1
**Director:** D M Mathias
**Responsibilities**
**HR:** Mike Duffy *(Human Resources Manager)*
**US SIC:** 8911, 7699
**UK SIC:** 83701, 67303

| | 30-09-13 | 30-09-12 | 30-09-11 |
|---|---|---|---|
| TA | 400,226 | 346,722 | 442,263 |
| NW | (315,062) | (316,296) | (201,912) |
| WC | 155,945 | 97,866 | 121,716 |

DUNS 23-538-9892

## R.V.W. Pugh Ltd.

Mellington, Church Stoke, Montgomery, Powys SY15 6TQ
**Tel:** 01588-620545 **Fax:** 01588-620515
**Web:** www.rvwpugh.co.uk
**Reg No:** 3537677 **VAT No:** 326522963
**Estd:** 1978 Private Limited Company
**Line of Business:** Manufacture of other agricultural and forestry machinery
**Export Sales:** £324,452
**Issued Capital:** £2
**Director:** R V Pugh
**Co. Secretary:** Ms Caroline Pugh
**US SIC:** 3523 **UK SIC:** 32113
**Auditors:** Davies Edwards & Co

| | 28-02-14 | 28-02-13 | 29-02-12 |
|---|---|---|---|
| TO | 15,993,759 | 18,962,927 | 18,621,772 |
| P/L | 767,642 | 671,156 | 441,462 |
| NW | 5,437,317 | 4,720,420 | 4,198,408 |
| WC | 4,557,347 | 3,908,414 | 3,287,257 |
| Emp. | 54 | 48 | 49 |

DUNS 29-573-5682

## R.W. Hill (Piling) Ltd

(**Subsidiary of:** The Hill Group (1985) Ltd)
Unit 1 Springfield Industrial Estate, Springfield Road, Southminster, Essex CM0 8UA
**Tel:** 01621 785954 **Fax:** 01621786135
**Web:** www.hillpiling.co.uk
**Reg No:** 1935383 **VAT No:** 675138222
**Estd:** 1995 Private Limited Company
**Line of Business:** Other construction work involving special trades
**Issued Capital:** £750
**Directors:** Ms D J Richardson, H Sidebottom
**Co. Secretary:** Ms Joanne Hallel
**Responsibilities**
**Senior:** Joanne Whiteside *(Manager)*
**Branches:** R.w. Hill (Piling) Ltd, Unit 1, Springfield Road, Burnham-On-Crouch, Essex CM0 8UA
**US SIC:** 1799 **UK SIC:** 50000
**Auditors:** Bland Baker
**Bankers:** National Westminster Bank Plc (60-22-06)

| | 31-12-13 | 31-12-12 | 31-12-11 |
|---|---|---|---|
| TA | 2,934,232 | 2,174,980 | 1,984,231 |
| NW | 170,492 | 87,791 | 165,091 |
| WC | (343,560) | (283,438) | (112,213) |

DUNS 23-957-6163

## R.W. McConnell & Son (Pharmacy) Ltd

27 Mauchline Road, Hurlford, Kilmarnock, Ayrshire KA1 5AB
**Tel:** 01563-525393
**Reg No:** 0205011SC **Estd:** 1962 Private Limited Company
**Line of Business:** Dispensing chemists
**Issued Capital:** £100
**Director:** Mrs U M Balls
**Co. Secretary:** Walter Mcconnell
**Responsibilities**
**Senior:** Morag Mcconnell *(Manager)*, Alison Tait *(Practice Manager)*
**US SIC:** 5912 **UK SIC:** 64300

| | 30-04-14 | 30-04-13 | 30-04-12 |
|---|---|---|---|
| TA | 1,455,503 | 1,379,252 | 1,514,794 |
| NW | 717,144 | 698,524 | 828,699 |
| WC | 532,072 | 489,305 | 590,654 |

DUNS 21-455-5674 Exp

## R.W. Pierce (Ni) Ltd

(**Subsidiary of:** Sentry Enterprises Ltd)
17 Dargan Crescent, Belfast BT3 9RP
**Tel:** 02890371010
**Web:** www.thepiercepartnership.com
**Reg No:** 0029923NI **VAT No:** 286584605
**Estd:** 1929 Private Limited Company
**Line of Business:** Digital services
**Export Markets:** Republic of Ireland
**Trading Style:** The Pierce Partnership
**Issued Capital:** £200,002
**Director:** R L Pierce
**Co. Secretary:** John Pierce
**Responsibilities**
**HR:** Jennifer Eccles *(Human Resources Assistant)*
**US SIC:** 7399, 7311
**UK SIC:** 83954, 83800
**Auditors:** Grant Thornton
**Bankers:** Northern Bank Ltd (95-01-41)

| | 31-08-13 | 31-08-12 | 31-08-11 |
|---|---|---|---|
| TA | 839,402 | 982,865 | 683,958 |
| NW | 548,619 | 531,890 | 550,918 |
| WC | 91,220 | 51,756 | 302,489 |

DUNS 21-711-7829

## R.W.Armstrong & Sons Ltd

Armstrong House, Aldermaston Road, Basingstoke, Hampshire RG24 9JZ
**Tel:** 01256-850177
**Web:** www.rwarmstrong.co.uk
**Reg No:** 0719464 **VAT No:** 199151237
**Estd:** 1962 Private Limited Company
**Line of Business:** Property refurbishment contractors
**Trading Style:** R.W.Armstrong & Sons Ltd
**Issued Capital:** £42
**Principals:** N J Armstrong *(Managing)*, S L Pearson, Mrs G Hall, S D Lewis
**Co. Secretary:** Ms Ashley Tirri
**Responsibilities**
**Finance:** Hannah Townson *(Accounts Administrator)*
**US SIC:** 1799, 1541
**UK SIC:** 50000, 50100
**Auditors:** Grant Thornton UK LLP
**Bankers:** Barclays Bank Plc (20-05-00)

| | 31-03-14 | 31-03-13 | 31-03-12 |
|---|---|---|---|
| TO | 32,185,774 | 26,733,045 | 25,260,201 |
| P/L | 360,918 | 423,531 | 475,437 |
| NW | 869,831 | 744,722 | 550,673 |
| WC | 491,066 | 372,293 | 218,639 |
| Emp. | 178 | 162 | 153 |

DUNS 23-518-5456

## Rwc Partners Ltd

60 Petty France, London SW1H 9EU
**Tel:** 02072276000 **Fax:** 02072276003
**Web:** www.rwcpartners.com
**Reg No:** 3517613 **Estd:** 1998 Private Limited Company
**Line of Business:** Investment companies and vehicles
**Export Sales:** £33,584,916
**Trading Style:** Rwc Partners Ltd
**Issued Capital:** £144,000
**Directors:** R D Goodchild, P Harrison, J H Innes, D C Mannix, P Larche, Ms G M Bainbridge
**Co. Secretary:** James Kaufmann
**Responsibilities**
**Senior:** Tina Banks *(Office Manager)*, Kenneth Lambden *(Non Executive Director)*
**US SIC:** 6111 **UK SIC:** 81501
**Auditors:** Rees Pollock
**Bankers:** HSBC Bank plc (40-38-10)

| | 31-12-13 | 31-12-12 | 31-12-11 |
|---|---|---|---|
| TA | 24,662,720 | 14,629,956 | 13,788,915 |
| P/L | 14,256,597 | 7,604,783 | 12,298,861 |
| NW | 13,810,438 | 9,275,921 | 8,759,308 |
| WC | 14,182,156 | 7,727,685 | 7,615,456 |
| Emp. | 68 | 63 | 59 |

DUNS 23-859-0215

## Rwe Dea Uk Holdings Ltd

(**Subsidiary of:** Rwe Ag)
4th Floor, London WC1V 6LJ
**Tel:** 02031160200 **Fax:** 02031160205
**Web:** www.rwe.com
**Reg No:** 0200459SC **Estd:** 2001 Private Limited Company
**Line of Business:** Extraction of crude petroleum and natural gas
**Issued Capital:** £74,327,239
**Directors:** Ms A Lippold, Dr P T Jeffs, Dr T Kremski, D Schoene
**Co. Secretary:** Ms Gemma Byrne
**Responsibilities**
**Senior:** Manfred Boeckmann *(General Manager, New Ventures)*, Sandra Redding *(Manager)*
**Sales:** Anjela Maharajah *(Commercial Manager)*
**HR:** Veronica Judge *(Human Resources Manager)*
**Engineering:** Dirk Kowalczyk *(Waste Management Engineer)*
**US SIC:** 1311 **UK SIC:** 13000
**Auditors:** PricewaterhouseCoopers LLP

| | 31-12-13 | 31-12-12 | 31-12-11 |
|---|---|---|---|
| TA | 360,694,000 | 270,587,000 | 246,404,000 |
| P/L | 1,796,000 | 719,000 | 445,000 |
| NW | 231,444,000 | 229,674,000 | 239,119,000 |
| WC | 74,686,000 | 72,689,000 | 81,998,000 |
| Emp. | 72 | 53 | 57 |

DUNS 67-223-3181

## Rwe Gbs Uk Ltd

(**Subsidiary of:** Rwe Ag)
Mistral, Swindon, Wiltshire SN5 7EZ
**Tel:** 01793893985
**Web:** www.rwe.com
**Reg No:** 6052966 **Estd:** 1991 Private Limited Company
**Line of Business:** Computer services
**Issued Capital:** £74,000,000
**Directors:** Mrs B M Lichtenstein, M M Neff, C J Pilgrim
**Responsibilities**
**Senior:** Jane Kilmartin *(Director)*
**US SIC:** 7379 **UK SIC:** 83940
**Auditors:** PricewaterhouseCoopers LLP

| | 31-12-13 | 31-12-12 | 31-12-11 |
|---|---|---|---|
| TO | 138,457,000 | 157,384,000 | 161,419,000 |
| P/L | (54,159,000) | (6,577,000) | (11,531,000) |
| NW | 22,927,000 | 12,499,000 | 18,702,000 |
| WC | 20,757,000 | (331,000) | 3,880,000 |
| Emp. | 536 | 683 | 713 |

DUNS 23-902-1210 Imp

## Rwe Generation Uk Plc

(**Subsidiary of:** Rwe Ag)
Windmill Hill Business Park, Whitehill Way, Swindon, Wiltshire SN5 6PB
**Tel:** 01793877777
**Web:** www.npower.com
**Reg No:** 3892782 **VAT No:** 524921354
**Estd:** 1958 Public Limited Company
**Line of Business:** Distribution and trade in electricity
**Trading Style:** Rwe Npower, Rwe Power International, Tsg Ferrybridge, Generation Aggregates
**Issued Capital:** £5,960,847
**Directors:** Dr F T Weigand, Mrs R C Wall, A K Robinson, R H Miesen, Dr K J Nix, T C Glover, Rwe Generation Se
**Co. Secretary:** Jason Keene
**Branches:** Rwe Generation Uk Plc, R W E Npower, Little Barford Power Station, St. Neots, Cambridgeshire PE19 6YT
**US SIC:** 4911, 4932
**UK SIC:** 16101, 16200
**Auditors:** PricewaterhouseCoopers LLP

Following financial data are in thousands

| | 31-12-13 | 31-12-12 | 31-12-11 |
|---|---|---|---|
| TO | 566,000 | 665,000 | 687,000 |
| P/L | (146,000) | 440,000 | (38,000) |
| NW | 1,576,000 | 1,684,000 | 1,214,000 |
| WC | 415,000 | 881,000 | (2,404,000) |
| Emp. | 1,992 | 2,352 | 2,409 |

DUNS 21-102-5772

## Rwe Supply & Trading Participations Ltd

(**Subsidiary of:** Rwe Ag)
60 Fred Needle Street, London EC2R 8HP
**Tel:** 020 7898 1930 **Fax:** 020 7898 1940
**Web:** www.rwe.com
**Reg No:** 6457522 **Estd:** 2007 Private Limited Company
**Line of Business:** Distribution and trade of gaseous fuels through mains
**Trading Style:** Rwe Supply & Trading
**Directors:** R Khosla, Dr R Becker, M W Rees, S K Judisch
**Co. Secretary:** Michael Rees
**Responsibilities**
**Senior:** Helmut Hammerschmid *(LNG Commercial Director)*, Gunnar Janson *(Manager)*, Jurgen Juttermann *(Manager)*, Alexander Thistlethwayte *(Manager)*
**Sales:** Helmut Hammerschmid *(LNG Commercial Director)*
**US SIC:** 4932 **UK SIC:** 16200
**Auditors:** PricewaterhouseCoopers LLP
**Employees:** 160

DUNS 50-442-2833 Imp-Exp

## Rwg (Repair & Overhauls) Ltd

Rolls Wood House, Aberdeen, Aberdeenshire AB21 7GA
**Tel:** 01224797000
**Web:** www.rwgroup.com
**Reg No:** 0120673SC **VAT No:** 552882715
**Estd:** 1989 Private Limited Company
**Line of Business:** Manufacturers of turbines and parts thereof
**Export Markets:** Worldwide
**Export Sales:** £91,210,000
**Issued Capital:** £1,000,000
**Directors:** W Meixner, N C Gilman, M P Gray, B D Byrne, G A Brown, N J Blaskoski
**Co. Secretary:** Nicholas Gilman
**Responsibilities**
**Purchasing:** Jackie Sim *(Purchasing Assistant)*
**Fleet:** Jackie Sim *(Purchasing Assistant)*
**US SIC:** 3519 **UK SIC:** 32811
**Auditors:** PricewaterhouseCoopers LLP
**Bankers:** Clydesdale Bank Plc (82-40-00)

| | 31-12-13 | 31-12-12 | 31-12-11 |
|---|---|---|---|
| TO | 164,167,000 | 174,858,000 | 180,874,000 |
| P/L | 23,870,000 | 28,537,000 | 22,619,000 |
| NW | 74,530,000 | 66,009,000 | 54,443,000 |
| WC | 65,203,000 | 57,944,000 | 49,216,000 |
| Emp. | 489 | 496 | 487 |

DUNS 53-649-4636

## Rwm Dorset Ltd

(**Subsidiary of:** Rwm Food Group Holdings Ltd)
Chetnole Road, Sherborne, Dorset DT9 6HQ
**Tel:** 01935874129
**Web:** www.abplamb.com
**Reg No:** 3454792 **Estd:** 1997 Private Limited Company
**Line of Business:** Frozen food processors and distributors
**Trading Style:** Abp Yetminster
**Issued Capital:** £1,000
**Directors:** J M Burton, T J Kirwan, P J Finnerty
**Co. Secretary:** John Mclaughlin
**Responsibilities**
**Senior:** Mark Eastwood *(Production Director)*, Robert Heffer *(Manager)*
**Health & Safety:** Mark Eastwood *(Production Director)*
**Facilities:** Mark Eastwood *(Production Director)*
**Engineering:** Mark Eastwood *(Production Director)*
**US SIC:** 5149, 5147
**UK SIC:** 61700
**Auditors:** Milsted Langdon

| | 31-03-14 | 31-03-13 | 01-03-12 |
|---|---|---|---|
| TO | N/A | 60,782,000 | 133,563,000 |
| P/L | N/A | 3,362,000 | 379,000 |
| NW | 27,000 | 33,000 | 6,893,000 |
| WC | 27,000 | N/A | 2,099,000 |
| Emp. | N/A | 242 | 221 |

DUNS 77-612-8431

## Rws Holdings Plc

Europa House, Gerrards Cross, Buckinghamshire SL9 9FG
**Fax:** 01753-480280
**Web:** www.rws.com
**Reg No:** 3002645 **Estd:** 1994 Public Limited Company

**Line of Business:** Management activities of other non-financial holding companies not elsewhere classified
**Export Sales:** £29,160,000
**Issued Capital:** £2,115,629
**Directors:** D E Shrimpton, R K Ottway, A S Brode, R J Thompson, P Mountford, Mrs E A Lucas
**Co. Secretary:** Richard Thompson
**Responsibilities**
**Senior:** Mike Mccarthy *(Finance Director)*, Neil Simpkin *(General Manager)*
**Finance:** Mike Mccarthy *(Finance Director)*
**IT:** Roberto Aletto *(IT Manager)*
**US SIC:** 6711 **UK SIC:** 83962
**Auditors:** BDO LLP

| | 30-09-14 | 30-09-13 | 30-09-12 |
|---|---|---|---|
| TO | 93,556,000 | 77,404,000 | 68,825,000 |
| P/L | 19,629,000 | 20,510,000 | 16,598,000 |
| NW | 39,694,000 | 31,492,000 | 44,902,000 |
| WC | 24,463,000 | 21,093,000 | 28,841,000 |
| Emp. | 593 | 532 | 488 |

DUNS 21-197-6899 Imp-Exp
## R.W.Simon Ltd
System Works, Hatchmoor Industrial Estate, Torrington, Devon EX38 7HP
**Tel:** 01805-623721 **Fax:** 01805-624578
**Web:** www.rwsimon.co.uk
**Reg No:** 0615240 **VAT No:** 231416110
**Estd:** 1958 Private Limited Company
**Line of Business:** Manufacture of other plastic products
**Export Markets:** Holland, New Zealand, Canada
**Export Sales:** £169,629
**Issued Capital:** £60,004
**Principals:** R A Simon *(Managing)*, J G Simon, Mrs H J Woolley
**Co. Secretary:** Terence Hitchins
**Responsibilities**
**Senior:** Jackie Coggins *(Accounts Administrator)*
**Finance:** Jackie Coggins *(Accounts Administrator)*
**IT:** Martyn Griffiths *(Quality Manager)*
**Engineering:** David Edwick *(Production Manager)*
**US SIC:** 3079 **UK SIC:** 48360
**Auditors:** Sully & Co
**Bankers:** Lloyds TSB Bank plc (30-90-78)

| | 31-03-14 | 31-03-13 | 31-03-12 |
|---|---|---|---|
| TO | 6,870,206 | 6,268,732 | 5,859,931 |
| P/L | 87,152 | (527,788) | (42,481) |
| NW | 2,327,763 | 2,059,864 | 2,608,680 |
| WC | 1,609,480 | 1,645,257 | 1,746,040 |
| Emp. | 96 | 87 | 85 |

DUNS 22-543-8472
## R.W.T. Edworthy & Sons Ltd
Johnsland, Bow, Crediton, Devon EX17 6HG
**Tel:** 0136382283
**Reg No:** 1977072 **Estd:** 1986 Private Limited Company
**Line of Business:** Road haulage and transport services
**Issued Capital:** £2
**Director:** P T Edworthy
**Co. Secretary:** Reginald Edworthy
**US SIC:** 4789, 4213
**UK SIC:** 77002, 72300
**Auditors:** Simpkins Edwards

| | 31-12-13 | 31-12-12 | 31-12-11 |
|---|---|---|---|
| TA | 948,791 | 924,526 | 718,967 |
| NW | 647,714 | 542,125 | 402,447 |
| WC | 501,824 | 393,923 | 225,995 |

DUNS 29-389-2006
## Ryan Insurance Group Ltd
Crane Hall, London Road, Ipswich, Suffolk IP2 0AL
**Fax:** 08704444302
**Web:** www.ryan-group.co.uk
**Reg No:** 1217489 **Estd:** 1975 Private Limited Company
**Line of Business:** Insurance brokers
**Issued Capital:** £2,000
**Directors:** R S Belsom, T J Larke, T M Ryan
**Co. Secretary:** Trevor Ward
**Responsibilities**
**Senior:** John Girling *(Associate Director)*, Gemma Handy *(General Manager)*, Colin Ryan *(Manager)*
**Branches:** Ryan Insurance Group Ltd, 3 St. Benedicts Street, Woolgate Court, Norwich, Norfolk NR2 4AP
**US SIC:** 6411 **UK SIC:** 83200
**Auditors:** Ensors
**Bankers:** Lloyds TSB Bank plc (30-94-55)

| | 31-12-13 | 31-12-12 | 31-12-11 |
|---|---|---|---|
| TA | 2,653,538 | 2,655,132 | 2,724,117 |
| NW | 1,410,814 | 1,403,625 | 1,347,926 |
| WC | 444,463 | 415,085 | 378,279 |

DUNS 29-649-2598 Imp
## Ryan-Jayberg Ltd
(**Subsidiary of:** Ryjabe Ltd)
Delta House, Riverside Road, London SW17 0BA
**Tel:** 020-8944-6288
**Web:** www.ryan-jayberg.co.uk
**Reg No:** 1975488 **VAT No:** 440327090
**Estd:** 1987 Private Limited Company
**Line of Business:** Plumbing
**Issued Capital:** £1,100,000
**Directors:** N C Jamieson, C M Green
**Co. Secretary:** Rakesh Patel
**Responsibilities**
**Senior:** Steve Borg *(Stores Manager)*, Fred Jamieson *(Chairman)*
**Marketing:** Raman Patel *(Senior Marketing Executive)*
**HR:** Mary Steel *(Human Resources Manager)*
**Facilities:** Steve Borg *(Stores Manager)*
**Branches:** Ryan-Jayberg Ltd, Mitchell Point, Unit 5, Southampton, Hampshire SO31 4RF
**US SIC:** 1711 **UK SIC:** 50300
**Auditors:** Deloitte & Touche LLP
**Bankers:** Barclays Bank Plc (20-90-69)

| | 31-12-13 | 31-12-12 | 31-12-11 |
|---|---|---|---|
| TO | 23,525,393 | 22,890,591 | 23,918,909 |
| P/L | 1,991,997 | 1,824,641 | 1,976,995 |
| NW | 8,993,241 | 7,466,814 | 6,084,174 |
| WC | 9,349,935 | 7,141,968 | 5,789,665 |
| Emp. | 127 | 111 | 91 |

DUNS 28-984-9499
## Ryan Poultry Services Ltd
Heath Road, Norwich, Norfolk NR16 2DG
**Tel:** 01953681475
**Reg No:** 1796298 **Estd:** 1983 Private Limited Company
**Line of Business:** Cleaning contracting commercial
**Issued Capital:** £19,000
**Principals:** B J Gooderham *(Chairman)*, R J Gooderham *(Managing)*
**Co. Secretary:** Robert Gooderham
**US SIC:** 7349 **UK SIC:** 92300
**Auditors:** Martin & Acock
**Bankers:** National Westminster Bank Plc (60-15-31)

| | 31-03-14 | 31-03-13 | 31-03-12 |
|---|---|---|---|
| TO | 5,849,722 | 7,184,675 | 6,548,320 |
| P/L | 399,075 | 182,687 | 514,467 |
| NW | 2,880,606 | 2,573,684 | 2,532,216 |
| WC | 1,963,939 | 1,447,856 | 1,527,738 |
| Emp. | 134 | 136 | 132 |

DUNS 34-587-8136 Imp
## Ryan Turner Hope Plc
Pegasus Woodward Avenue Westerleigh, Business Park, Bristol, Avon BS37 5YS
**Web:** www.rthgroup.co.uk
**Reg No:** 2731954 **VAT No:** 581976392
**Estd:** 1992 Public Limited Company
**Line of Business:** Activities of exhibition and fair organisers
**Export Sales:** £6,368,549
**Trading Style:** Rth Group
**Issued Capital:** £50,001
**Directors:** N J Ryan, J M Turner, D A Deacon, M Fletcher, J B Hope, J M Ryan
**Co. Secretary:** Ms Margaret Young
**Responsibilities**
**Senior:** Barry Hope *(Manager)*
**US SIC:** 7399, 2421
**UK SIC:** 83954, 46101
**Auditors:** Leigh Saxton Green
**Bankers:** Barclays Bank Plc (20-13-08)

| | 31-12-13 | 31-12-12 | 31-12-11 |
|---|---|---|---|
| TO | 12,958,273 | 12,828,036 | 13,209,086 |
| P/L | 95,984 | 570,790 | 458,777 |
| NW | 1,283,059 | 1,326,380 | 1,088,044 |
| WC | 1,131,128 | 1,228,906 | 972,458 |
| Emp. | 51 | 47 | 48 |

DUNS 21-788-5228
## Ryan's Cleaning Event Specialists
Unit 37 Elmdon Trading Estate, Bickenhill Lane, Birmingham, West Midlands B37 7HE
**Tel:** 01217829750
**Web:** www.ryanscleaning.com
**Estd:** 2011 Proprietorship
**Line of Business:** Cleaning contracting commercial
**Proprietor:** Mrs S Cavanagh
**Responsibilities**
**Senior:** Elaine Ryan *(Manager)*
**US SIC:** 7349 **UK SIC:** 92300
**Employees:** 50

DUNS 77-915-7481
## Rybrook Holdings Ltd
Unit 6, Athena Court, Athena Drive, Warwick, Warwickshire CV34 6RT
**Tel:** 01926359966
**Web:** www.rybrook.co.uk
**Reg No:** 5818940 **Estd:** 1991 Private Limited Company
**Line of Business:** Representative office

**Issued Capital:** £22,400,000
**Directors:** H W Whale, K D Simpson, P W Whale, R S Kirby, K D Simpson
**Co. Secretary:** Keith Hampson
**Responsibilities**
**Operations:** Geoff Tew *(Project Manager)*
**US SIC:** 6711 **UK SIC:** 83962

| | 31-12-13 | 31-12-12 | 31-12-11 |
|---|---|---|---|
| TO | 377,089,000 | 356,156,000 | 331,868,000 |
| P/L | 2,019,000 | 2,857,000 | 1,504,000 |
| NW | 10,843,000 | 9,068,000 | 9,156,000 |
| WC | 6,428,000 | 5,546,000 | 5,444,000 |
| Emp. | 757 | 744 | 745 |

DUNS 21-156-8626
## Ryburn Valley High School
St Peters Avenue, Sowerby Bridge, West Yorkshire HX6 1DF
**Tel:** 01422-832070
**Web:** www.rvhs.co.uk
**Estd:** 2012
**Line of Business:** Schools (foundation)
**Responsibilities**
**Finance:** Julie Kendall *(Business Manager)*, Mark Thoroughly *(Finance)*
**Marketing:** Julie Kendall *(Business Manager)*
**Health & Safety:** Julie Kendall *(Business Manager)*
**Facilities:** Julie Kendall *(Business Manager)*
**US SIC:** 8211 **UK SIC:** 93200
**Employees:** 130

DUNS 21-235-8212
## Rycroft Vehicles Ltd
(**Subsidiary of:** Penske Automotive Group Inc.)
Montgomery Way, Rosehill Industrial Estate, Carlisle, Cumbria CA1 2RW
**Tel:** 01228541111
**Web:** www.stockton.rycroft.co.uk
**Reg No:** 0248481 **Estd:** 1942 Private Limited Company
**Line of Business:** Sale of new motor vehicles
**Trading Style:** Mercedes-Benz of Carlisle
**Issued Capital:** £240,000
**Directors:** G E Nieuwenhuys, A Collinson
**Co. Secretary:** Adam Collinson
**Responsibilities**
**Finance:** Steven Jeff *(Senior Financial Executive)*
**Branches:** Rycroft Vehicles Ltd, Hylton Grange, Sunderland, Tyne and Wear SR5 3HR
**US SIC:** 5511, 7539, 5531
**UK SIC:** 65100, 67100
**Auditors:** PricewaterhouseCoopers
**Bankers:** Barclays Bank Plc (20-07-71)

| | 31-12-13 | 31-12-12 | 31-12-11 |
|---|---|---|---|
| TO | N/A | 118,533,000 | 112,115,000 |
| P/L | N/A | 2,157,000 | 1,354,000 |
| NW | 240,000 | 13,394,000 | 11,843,000 |
| WC | N/A | N/A | 3,940,000 |
| Emp. | N/A | 223 | 220 |

DUNS 23-592-5315
## Rydal Penrhos (Sports & Leisure) Ltd
Pwllycrochan Avenue, Colwyn Bay, Clwyd LL29 7BT
**Tel:** 01492-530155
**Web:** www.rydalpenrhos.com
**Reg No:** 3590034 **Estd:** 1998 Private Limited Company
**Line of Business:** Schools (independent)
**Issued Capital:** £3
**Directors:** A D Johnson, J I Morris
**Co. Secretary:** Ms Kathryn Baines
**Responsibilities**
**Senior:** Patrick Lee-Browne *(Head Teacher)*
**US SIC:** 8211 **UK SIC:** 93200
**Auditors:** Mitchell Charlesworth

| | 31-08-13 | 31-08-12 | 31-08-11 |
|---|---|---|---|
| TO | 2,640 | 2,640 | 2,640 |
| P/L | 763 | (976) | (2,300) |
| NW | 5,881 | 5,118 | 6,094 |
| WC | 5,881 | 5,118 | 5,675 |

DUNS 76-962-4958
## Rydale Windows (Manufacturing) Ltd
(**Subsidiary of:** Rydale Group Ltd)
Rydale House, 33 Long Lane, Halesowen, West Midlands B62 9LS
**Tel:** 01215594211
**Web:** www.rydalewindows.co.uk
**Reg No:** 2627171 **VAT No:** 632120101
**Estd:** 1991 Private Limited Company
**Line of Business:** Manufacturers of window frames
**Issued Capital:** £2
**Director:** F Large
**Co. Secretary:** Stuart Humpherson
**Responsibilities**
**Senior:** Malcolm Caldicott *(Manager)*
**IT:** Mike Homer *(IT Manager)*
**Branches:** Rydale Windows (Manufacturing) Ltd, Rydale House, 32-33 Long Lane, Halesowen, West Midlands B62 9LS

**US SIC:** 3442, 3999
**UK SIC:** 31420, 49590
**Auditors:** F E Sidaway Son & Co
**Bankers:** Lloyds TSB Bank plc (30-90-88)

| | 30-04-14 | 30-04-13 | 30-04-12 |
|---|---|---|---|
| TA | 755,912 | 726,238 | 697,501 |
| NW | 291,036 | 262,958 | 301,579 |
| WC | 291,036 | 262,958 | 301,579 |

DUNS 73-958-3701
## Ryde House Llp
Binstead Road, Ryde, Ryde, Isle of Wight PO33 3NF
**Web:** www.rydehouse.com
**Reg No:** 0309044OC **Estd:** 2004
**Line of Business:** Representative office
**US SIC:** 7399 **UK SIC:** 83954

| | 31-08-13 | 31-08-12 | 31-08-11 |
|---|---|---|---|
| TO | 4,461,104 | 4,184,643 | 3,791,801 |
| P/L | N/A | N/A | 270,136 |
| NW | (72,600) | (79,200) | (85,800) |
| WC | (677,942) | (450,521) | (523,259) |
| Emp. | 183 | 153 | 143 |

DUNS 73-571-0761
## Ryde Marina Bowls Club Ltd
Esplanade, Ryde, Isle of Wight PO33 1JA
**Tel:** 01983-564477
**Web:** www.rydemarinabowlsclub.co.uk
**Reg No:** 4832760 **Estd:** 2003 Private Company Limited By Guarantee
**Line of Business:** Sports clubs
**Directors:** B Rodwell, Mrs J Lee, J E Baker-Deam, D W Mulhern, M J Mccreanor, Ms D Wallace, A D Cawdell, Mrs P Evans
**Co. Secretary:** Alan Cawdell
**US SIC:** 7999 **UK SIC:** 97913

| | 30-09-14 | 30-09-13 | 30-09-12 |
|---|---|---|---|
| TA | 748,088 | 750,280 | 750,418 |
| NW | 746,122 | 748,265 | 748,644 |
| WC | 69,950 | 66,504 | 61,635 |

DUNS 28-836-6156
## Ryde School
7 Queens Road, Ryde, Isle of Wight PO33 3BE
**Tel:** 01983-562229
**Web:** www.rydeschool.org.uk
**Reg No:** 0432077 **Estd:** 1921 Private Company Limited By Guarantee
**Line of Business:** Schools (local authority)
**Directors:** Ms L M Dennis, Dr A Mcisaac, Ms E E Bladon, G E Morris, Ms E C Millett, P I Weeks, J H Fisher, Ms J E Bland
**Co. Secretary:** Peter Taylor
**Responsibilities**
**Senior:** Raymond Bradbury *(Manager)*, Cassandra Clark *(Director)*, Chantal Doerries *(Director)*, Nicholas England *(Headmaster)*, Annabelle Harvey *(Director)*, Michelle Legg *(Director)*, Joanna Minchin *(Director)*, Caroline Pepys *(Manager)*, Nisha Pillah *(Director)*, Nicholas Wakefield *(Director)*
**Marketing:** Sarah Noyes *(Office Manager)*
**Admin:** Sarah Noyes *(Office Manager)*
**IT:** Tony Johnson *(IT Manager)*
**Facilities:** Adrian Davies *(Maintenance Manager)*
**Branches:** Ryde School, Hillway Road, Bembridge, Isle Of Wight PO35 5PH
**US SIC:** 8211 **UK SIC:** 93200
**Auditors:** Morris Crocker
**Bankers:** Barclays Bank Plc (20-60-55)

| | 31-08-13 | 31-08-12 | 31-08-11 |
|---|---|---|---|
| TO | 8,230,295 | 7,984,435 | 7,673,190 |
| P/L | 450,107 | 359,693 | 444,031 |
| NW | 12,576,818 | 11,974,198 | 11,573,660 |
| WC | (315,548) | (239,859) | (778,691) |
| Emp. | 176 | 171 | 173 |

DUNS 73-917-8791
## Ryden L L P
46 North Castle Street, Edinburgh, Midlothian EH2 3BN
**Tel:** 01312256612
**Web:** www.ryden.co.uk
**Reg No:** 0300405SO **VAT No:** 270061788
**Estd:** 1959
**Line of Business:** Commercial property agents
**Responsibilities**
**Senior:** Timothy Bunker *(Designated Limited Liability P)*, Ewan Cameron *(Designated Limited Liability P)*, Marc Giles *(Designated Limited Liability P)*, Roy Ritchie *(Designated Limited Liability P)*, Brian Ronnie *(Designated Limited Liability P)*, Kenneth Shaw *(Designated Limited Liability P)*, Gerard Smith *(Designated Limited Liability P)*, James Swanson *(Designated Limited Liability P)*, Derek Tillery *(Designated Limited Liability P)*
**Branches:** Ryden L L P, 130 St Vincent Street, Glasgow, Lanarkshire G2 5HF
**US SIC:** 7397 **UK SIC:** 83702
**Auditors:** Baker Tilly UK Audit LLP

**Bankers:** The Royal Bank Of Scotland Plc (83-18-44)

| | 30-04-14 | 30-04-13 | 30-04-12 |
|---|---|---|---|
| TO | 13,192,957 | 11,281,976 | 10,590,172 |
| P/L | 6,002,823 | 4,057,534 | 2,203,096 |
| NW | N/A | N/A | 2,162,109 |
| WC | 5,559,937 | 3,654,110 | 3,549,192 |
| Emp. | 140 | 139 | 140 |

DUNS 67-146-4829

## Ryder & Dutton Ltd

(**Subsidiary of:** Edge View Holdings Ltd)
St James"s Court, Brown Street, Manchester M2 1DH
**Tel:** 0161-925-3232
**Web:** www.ryder-dutton.co.uk
**Reg No:** 6005064 **Estd:** 2006 Private Limited Company
**Line of Business:** Real estate agencies
**Issued Capital:** £50
**Directors:** D J Ebden, J D Roberts, I Hill, J White
**Co. Secretary:** Richard Powell
**US SIC:** 6531 **UK SIC:** 83400

| | 31-12-13 | 31-12-12 | 31-12-11 |
|---|---|---|---|
| TA | 2,394,607 | 2,379,338 | 2,479,772 |
| NW | (751,972) | (993,440) | (1,093,313) |
| WC | 325,864 | 199,391 | 69,395 |

DUNS 29-489-5388

## Ryder Architecture Ltd

Coppers Studios, 14 Westgate Road, Newcastle-Upon-Tyne, Tyne and Wear NE1 3NN
**Tel:** 01912-695454 **Fax:** 0191-269-5455
**Web:** www.ryderarchitecture.com
**Reg No:** 1852938 **Estd:** 1950 Private Limited Company
**Line of Business:** Architects
**Issued Capital:** £625
**Directors:** P Buchan, M R Thompson
**Co. Secretary:** Graeme Hurworth
**Responsibilities**
**Facilities:** Norma Vinton *(Facilities Manager)*
**Branches:** Ryder Architecture Ltd, 33 Gresse Street, London W1T 1QU
**US SIC:** 8911 **UK SIC:** 83701
**Auditors:** Brennan Neil & Leonard
**Bankers:** HSBC Bank plc (40-34-18)

| | 30-04-14 | 30-04-13 | 30-04-12 |
|---|---|---|---|
| TO | 8,111,507 | 7,118,155 | 5,818,420 |
| P/L | 655,923 | 729,145 | 142,855 |
| NW | 334,849 | 427,240 | 629,602 |
| WC | 103,993 | 310,717 | 366,728 |
| Emp. | 119 | 101 | 81 |

DUNS 21-093-6845

## Ryder Ltd

(**Subsidiary of:** Ryder Capital U K Holdings Llp)
1 Herald Way, Coventry, West Midlands CV3 2NY
**Tel:** 02476654800 **Fax:** 01380720785
**Web:** www.ryder.com
**Reg No:** 1019474 **Estd:** 1971 Private Limited Company
**Line of Business:** Freight transport by road not elsewhere classified
**Trading Style:** Rds Transport
**Issued Capital:** £3,063,168
**Directors:** Mrs C F Candela, D R Hunt, S J Hodes, B K Moll
**Co. Secretary:** Ms Anya Calcott
**Responsibilities**
**Senior:** David Pointon *(Health & Safety Officer)*
**Marketing:** Robin White *(Marketing Director)*
**Health & Safety:** David Pointon *(Health & Safety Officer)*
**Operations:** Robin White *(Marketing Director)*
**Branches:** Ryder Ltd, Eldon Way, Northampton, Northamptonshire NN6 7SL
**US SIC:** 4213 **UK SIC:** 72300
**Auditors:** PricewaterhouseCoopers LLP
**Bankers:** National Westminster Bank Plc (60-19-28)

| | 31-12-13 | 31-12-12 | 31-12-11 |
|---|---|---|---|
| TO | 237,376,000 | 241,364,000 | 204,643,000 |
| P/L | 10,181,000 | 17,438,000 | 19,373,000 |
| NW | 137,681,000 | 85,650,000 | 113,507,000 |
| WC | 43,193,000 | 10,543,000 | 56,570,000 |
| Emp. | 1,268 | 1,251 | 1,150 |

DUNS 39-996-6514 Exp

## Ryder System Holdings (Uk) Ltd

(**Subsidiary of:** Ryder Capital U K Holdings Llp)
Unit 2-3 Prince Maurice Court, Hambleton Avenue, Devizes, Wiltshire SN10 2RT
**Tel:** 01380731500 **Fax:** 01380720785
**Web:** www.ryder.com
**Reg No:** 2284754 **Estd:** 1988 Private Limited Company
**Line of Business:** Van hire
**Export Markets:** E U
**Issued Capital:** £12,005,922
**Directors:** D M Beilin, D R Hunt, Ms C F Candela
**Responsibilities**
**Senior:** Terry Dilon *(Manager)*
**Branches:** Ryder System Holdings (Uk) Ltd, Bucklers Lane, St Austell, St. Austell, Cornwall PL25 3JL
**US SIC:** 6711 **UK SIC:** 83962
**Auditors:** PricewaterhouseCoopers LLP
**Bankers:** Barclays Bank Plc (20-65-82)

| | 31-12-13 | 31-12-12 | 31-12-11 |
|---|---|---|---|
| TA | 143,068,000 | 142,438,000 | 90,914,741 |
| P/L | (6,735,000) | 40,595,000 | N/A |
| NW | 10,517,000 | 14,854,000 | 88,943,038 |
| WC | 2,742,000 | 42,997,000 | N/A |

DUNS 22-952-2511

## Rydon Group Ltd

(**Subsidiary of:** Rydon Holdings Ltd)
Rydon House, Forest Row, East Sussex RH18 5DW
**Tel:** 01342-825151 **Fax:** 01342-824676
**Web:** www.rydon.co.uk
**Reg No:** 1583757 **Estd:** 1976 Private Limited Company
**Line of Business:** Management activities of holding companies
**Issued Capital:** £1,331,954
**Directors:** W J Barnes, N G Panes, Mrs A A Ivanec, J D Henton, R Bond, A D Wilkinson, S M Collinson, M Mitchener
**Co. Secretary:** Antony Wilkinson
**Responsibilities**
**Senior:** Dave Gardner *(Manager)*, David Hay *(Managing Director, Ryhurst)*
**Sales:** Malcolm Pollard *(Commercial Director)*, Tom Rigby *(Development Director)*, Laurence Rudman *(Development Director)*
**HR:** Maggie Greaves *(Training Director)*
**Facilities:** Paul Holder *(Maintenance Manager)*
**Operations:** Richard Pickup *(Service Manager)*
**Purchasing:** Ian Watkinson *(Contracts Director)*
**Engineering:** Clifford Yeend *(Technical Manager)*
**Branches:** Rydon Group Ltd, 226 Holtye Rd, East Grinstead, West Sussex RH19 3EY
**US SIC:** 6711, 1522
**UK SIC:** 83962, 50100
**Auditors:** Mazars LLP
**Bankers:** Barclays Bank Plc (20-23-97)

| | 30-09-13 | 30-09-12 | 30-09-11 |
|---|---|---|---|
| TO | 128,486,000 | 145,635,000 | 115,831,000 |
| P/L | 4,210,000 | 5,502,000 | 6,414,000 |
| NW | 27,680,000 | 24,510,000 | 20,839,000 |
| WC | 32,747,000 | 29,649,000 | 27,619,000 |
| Emp. | 573 | 584 | 502 |

DUNS 21-880-5223

## Rydon Property Maintainence - Dartford

Unit 14 Quadrant Court, Charles Park Crossways Business Park, Greenhithe, Kent DA9 9AY
**Tel:** 08452692982
**Web:** www.rydon.co.uk
**Estd:** 2012
**Line of Business:** Estate management services
**Responsibilities**
**Senior:** Barrie Beckett *(Manager)*
**US SIC:** 6531 **UK SIC:** 83400
**Employees:** 52

DUNS 21-775-9320

## Rydon Ward Somerset Partnership Nhs Foundation Trust

Cheddon Road, Taunton, Somerset TA2 7AZ
**Tel:** 01823333437
**Web:** www.sompar.nhs.uk
**Estd:** 2011 Proprietorship
**Line of Business:** Hospitals
**Proprietor:** T Young
**US SIC:** 8091 **UK SIC:** 95200
**Employees:** 101

DUNS 50-469-1411

## Rye Cutters Ltd

36-38 Cinque Ports Street, Rye, East Sussex TN31 7AN
**Tel:** 01797-222211
**Web:** www.theryeretreat.co.uk
**Reg No:** 2448067 **Estd:** 1989 Private Limited Company
**Line of Business:** Hairdressers (unisex)
**Issued Capital:** £41,667
**Director:** Ms J J Sperring
**Co. Secretary:** Ralph Sperring
**Responsibilities**
**Senior:** Carole Beecroft *(Manager)*, Felicity Parsons *(Manager)*
**US SIC:** 7231 **UK SIC:** 98200
**Auditors:** Gibbons And Mannington
**Bankers:** Barclays Bank Plc (20-88-13)

| | 31-12-13 | 31-12-12 | 31-12-11 |
|---|---|---|---|
| TA | 116,918 | 116,931 | 116,931 |
| NW | 2,748 | 2,761 | 2,761 |
| WC | 2,648 | 2,661 | 2,661 |

DUNS 21-781-3606

## Rye Hills School

Redcar Lane, Redcar, Cleveland TS10 2HN
**Tel:** 01642484269
**Web:** www.ryehills.com
**Estd:** 2008 Proprietorship
**Line of Business:** Schools (foundation)
**Proprietor:** N Appleby
**Responsibilities**
**IT:** Ben Stonehouse *(IT Manager)*
**US SIC:** 8211 **UK SIC:** 93200
**Employees:** 100

DUNS 28-844-7782

## Rye St. Antony School Ltd

Pullens Lane, Headington, Oxford, Oxfordshire OX3 0BY
**Tel:** 01865-762802 **Fax:** 01865-763611
**Web:** www.ryestantony.co.uk
**Reg No:** 0612426 **Estd:** 1958 Private Limited Company
**Line of Business:** Primary education
**Trading Style:** Beechtree Nursery School
**Issued Capital:** £1,000
**Directors:** Dr J C Byren, Dr T M Czepiel, R D Potts, Ms H J Stafford Northcote, Mrs S H Mcgregor, D J Parke, S K Calnan, J Jackson
**Co. Secretary:** Ms Teresa Hudson
**Responsibilities**
**Senior:** Ian Callaghan *(Director)*, Susan Hampshire *(Director)*, Patricia Kennett *(Manager)*, Eleanor Lowe *(Director)*, Timothy Morton *(Director)*
**Finance:** Nimmy Sanhotra *(Finance Officer)*
**Admin:** Elizabeth Cheeseman *(PA)*
**IT:** Drew Pocock *(Senior IT Executive)*
**HR:** Ellen Phelips *(Human Resources Manager)*
**US SIC:** 8211 **UK SIC:** 93200
**Auditors:** Bronsens
**Bankers:** Barclays Bank Plc (20-65-21)

| | 31-08-13 | 31-08-12 | 31-08-11 |
|---|---|---|---|
| TO | 5,218,020 | 4,974,599 | 4,600,602 |
| P/L | 425,832 | 553,968 | 457,170 |
| NW | 6,668,375 | 6,242,543 | 5,688,575 |
| WC | 764,773 | 431,914 | 439,604 |
| Emp. | 135 | 152 | 138 |

DUNS 23-344-6137

## Rye Street Coachworks Ltd

Rye Street, Bishops Stortford, Hertfordshire CM23 2HA
**Tel:** 01279505405 **Fax:** 01279506787
**Web:** www.ryestreetgroup.com
**Reg No:** 2712853 **Estd:** 1992 Private Limited Company
**Line of Business:** Maintenance and repair of motor vehicles
**Issued Capital:** £2,856
**Principals:** T A Mcnaughton *(Managing)*, L Mcnaughton, S S Duffy
**Co. Secretary:** Thomas Mcnaughton
**Responsibilities**
**Finance:** Colin Gill *(Head of Finance)*
**Health & Safety:** Janine Mcnaughton *(Administrator)*
**Facilities:** Janine Mcnaughton *(Administrator)*
**Branches:** Rye Street Coachworks Ltd, The Fairways, New River Trading Est, Waltham Cross, Hertfordshire EN8 0NL
**US SIC:** 7539 **UK SIC:** 67100
**Auditors:** Philip T Chave & Co
**Bankers:** National Westminster Bank Plc (60-18-01)

| | 31-05-14 | 31-05-13 | 31-05-12 |
|---|---|---|---|
| TO | 13,438,514 | 12,146,813 | 11,889,753 |
| P/L | 1,042,773 | 756,697 | 646,265 |
| NW | 608,772 | 414,186 | 386,202 |
| WC | 116,664 | 14,724 | 16,827 |
| Emp. | 140 | 125 | 131 |

DUNS 23-708-7569

## Ryecroft Glenton Audit Services Ltd

32 Portland Terrace, Newcastle-Upon-Tyne, Tyne and Wear NE2 1QP
**Tel:** 0191-281-1292
**Web:** www.ryecroftglenton.com
**Reg No:** 3703877 **Estd:** 1999 Private Limited Company
**Line of Business:** Accounting activities
**Issued Capital:** £1
**Director:** D R Anderson
**Responsibilities**
**Senior:** Geoff Cawthorn *(Partner)*, Claire Charlton *(Partner)*, Tony Glenton *(Senior Partner)*, Deborah Graham *(Partner)*, David Milligan *(Partner)*, Charles Pearson *(Partner)*, Alan Woolhead *(Partner)*, Nigel Wyrley-Birch *(Partner)*
**Finance:** Carl Swansbury *(Director, Corporate Finance)*
**IT:** Linda Adams *(IT Services Consultant)*, Sean Stambridge *(IT Manager)*
**US SIC:** 8621 **UK SIC:** 96311

| | 30-04-14 | 30-04-13 | 30-04-12 |
|---|---|---|---|
| TA | 1 | 1 | 1 |
| NW | 1 | 1 | 1 |

DUNS 21-782-1197

## Ryecroft Primary School

Stonebridge Grove, Leeds, West Yorkshire LS12 5AW
**Tel:** 01132632433
**Web:** www.ryecroftprimaryschool.co.uk
**Estd:** 2011
**Line of Business:** Schools (foundation)
**Proprietor:** Mrs J Tootill
**Responsibilities**
**Senior:** Soheila Mathison *(Acting Head Teacher)*, Jan Tothill *(Head Teacher)*
**US SIC:** 8211 **UK SIC:** 93200
**Employees:** 50

DUNS 73-874-1847

## Ryedale Group Ltd

2 Hall Garth, Pickering, North Yorkshire YO18 7AW
**Tel:** 01751-432505
**Reg No:** 5128618 **Estd:** 2004 Private Limited Company
**Line of Business:** Holding companies management activities
**Export Sales:** £192,030
**Issued Capital:** £24,000
**Director:** J P Buffoni
**Co. Secretary:** Stephen Buffoni
**US SIC:** 6711 **UK SIC:** 83962

| | 30-06-13 | 30-06-12 | 30-06-11 |
|---|---|---|---|
| TO | 6,965,172 | 7,156,019 | 8,233,166 |
| P/L | (156,263) | 207,192 | 573,093 |
| NW | 2,483,775 | 2,708,121 | 2,544,754 |
| WC | 903,798 | 1,207,486 | 1,267,122 |
| Emp. | 78 | 76 | 77 |

DUNS 23-692-1818

## Ryemarc Ltd

Ashworth Road, Bridgemead, Swindon, Wiltshire SN5 7XW
**Tel:** 01793-520581
**Reg No:** 3687080 **Estd:** 1996 Private Limited Company
**Line of Business:** Management activities of holding companies
**Issued Capital:** £100,459
**Director:** R C Tutt
**US SIC:** 6711 **UK SIC:** 83962
**Auditors:** Grant Thornton
**Bankers:** National Westminster Bank Plc (01-00-04)

| | 31-12-13 | 31-12-12 | 31-12-11 |
|---|---|---|---|
| TO | 13,038,743 | 10,751,251 | 9,760,825 |
| P/L | 485,414 | 117,909 | 204,255 |
| NW | 1,027,795 | 712,401 | 732,293 |
| WC | (273,911) | (211,944) | 139,088 |
| Emp. | 127 | 116 | 110 |

DUNS 21-773-8729

## Ryeoak Primary School & Childrens Centre

Whorlton Road, London SE15 3PD
**Tel:** 02076393914
**Web:** www.ryeoak.southwark.sch.uk
**Estd:** 2001 Proprietorship
**Line of Business:** Schools (local authority)
**Proprietor:** Ms V Bridge
**Responsibilities**
**Senior:** Manda George *(Head Teacher)*
**US SIC:** 8211 **UK SIC:** 93200
**Employees:** 85

DUNS 21-880-4022

## Ryes College & Community

New Road, Aldham, Colchester, Essex CO6 3PN
**Tel:** 01206243473
**Web:** www.theryescollege.org.uk
**Estd:** 2012
**Line of Business:** Schools (special)
**Responsibilities**
**Senior:** Maria Marques-Nevis *(Manager)*, Kate Yarbo *(Principal)*
**US SIC:** 8299 **UK SIC:** 93300
**Employees:** 100

DUNS 21-770-5515

## Ryfields Retirement Village

Ryfields Village, Arena Gardens, Warrington, Cheshire WA2 7GB
**Web:** www.extracare.org.uk
**Estd:** 2005 Proprietorship
**Line of Business:** Non-charitable social work activities with accommodation
**Proprietor:** J Hammond
**Responsibilities**
**Senior:** Judith Lathey *(Manager)*, Carl Walmsley *(Manager)*
**US SIC:** 8321 **UK SIC:** 96111
**Employees:** 80

DUNS 21-714-2561

## Rygor Group Ltd

**(Subsidiary of:** Rygor Holdings Ltd)
The Broadway, West Wilts Trading Estate, Westbury, Wiltshire BA13 4JX
**Tel:** 01373-855555 **Fax:** 01373855525
**Web:** www.rygor.co.uk
**Reg No:** 0936467 **VAT No:** 423007208
**Estd:** 1961 Private Limited Company
**Line of Business:** Other business activities not elsewhere classified
**Issued Capital:** £250,000
**Principals:** B W Whitfield *(Managing)*, T B Stacey *(Financial)*, P Reed
**Co. Secretary:** Graham Drake
**Responsibilities**
**Health & Safety:** Jim Pascoe *(operations manager)*
**Branches:** Rygor Group Ltd, Hambridge Business Centre, Unit 13, Newbury, Berkshire RG14 5TU
**US SIC:** 7399, 5511
**UK SIC:** 83954, 65100
**Auditors:** BDO Stoy Hayward LLP
**Bankers:** Barclays Bank Plc (20-05-06)

| | 30-04-14 | 30-04-13 | 30-04-12 |
|---|---|---|---|
| TO | 154,588,000 | 124,430,834 | 106,128,405 |
| P/L | 778,000 | 1,567,458 | 963,179 |
| NW | 8,226,000 | 7,873,577 | 7,774,899 |
| WC | 155,000 | (1,055,099) | 749,935 |
| Emp. | 556 | 536 | 436 |

DUNS 23-848-5705

## Rykneld Tean (Holdings) Ltd

Hansard Gate, West Meadows Industrial Estate, Derby, Derbyshire DE21 6RR
**Web:** www.rykneldtean.co.uk
**Reg No:** 3840551 **Estd:** 1999 Private Limited Company
**Line of Business:** Management activities of holding companies
**Issued Capital:** £300
**Directors:** A Oppermann, G Specht, R J Wilkinson
**Responsibilities**
**Senior:** Claire Jones *(Manager)*, William Rollason *(Manager)*
**US SIC:** 6711, 5133
**UK SIC:** 83962, 61600

| | 31-03-14 | 31-03-13 | 31-03-12 |
|---|---|---|---|
| TA | 670,025 | 670,025 | 670,025 |
| NW | (437,445) | (437,445) | (437,445) |
| WC | (1,106,602) | (1,106,602) | (1,106,602) |

DUNS 21-255-0944

## Ryland Honda

230 Penarth Road, Cardiff Do, Cardiff, South Glamorgan CF11 8TU
**Tel:** 029-2037-6000
**Web:** www.rylandhonda.co.uk
**Estd:** 1991 Partnership
**Line of Business:** Car dealers (new & used)
**Partners:** M Evans, K Hampson, R Dixon, A Page, Mrs M Simmons, Ms N Haberfield
**Responsibilities**
**Senior:** Karl Harris *(Service Manager)*
**Finance:** Robert Pitt *(Finance Manager)*
**Health & Safety:** Karl Harris *(Service Manager)*
**Facilities:** Karl Harris *(Service Manager)*
**Operations:** Karl Harris *(Service Manager)*
**US SIC:** 5511 **UK SIC:** 65100
**Employees:** 50

DUNS 21-860-4783

## Ryland Investments Ltd

**(Subsidiary of:** Penske Automotive Group Inc.)
70a St Philips Court, Church Hill, Birmingham, West Midlands B46 3AD
**Tel:** 01675-466566
**Web:** www.ryland.com
**Reg No:** 0491856 **Estd:** 1951 Private Limited Company
**Line of Business:** Holding companies management activities
**Trading Style:** Ryland Ryfield, Rydale Ryland Ford, Rycroft, Rybrook
**Issued Capital:** £3,032,384
**Directors:** G E Nieuwenhuys, A Collinson
**Co. Secretary:** Adam Collinson
**Responsibilities**
**Finance:** Stephen Jeff *(Management Accountant)*
**IT:** Stephen Jeff *(Management Accountant)*
**Branches:** Ryland Investments Ltd, Sytner, Usk Way, Newport, Gwent NP20 2DS
**US SIC:** 6711, 5511
**UK SIC:** 83962, 65100
**Auditors:** PricewaterhouseCoopers LLP
**Bankers:** Barclays Bank Plc (20-07-71)

| | 31-12-13 | 31-12-12 | 31-12-11 |
|---|---|---|---|
| TA | 10,516,000 | 18,710,000 | 18,711,000 |
| P/L | 60,531,000 | N/A | N/A |
| NW | 10,505,000 | 16,695,000 | 16,684,000 |
| WC | 9,948,000 | (2,010,000) | (2,021,000) |

DUNS 23-548-9978

## The Ryleys School Ltd

Ryleys Lane, Wilmslow, Cheshire SK9 7UY
**Tel:** 01625-583241
**Web:** www.theryleys.com
**Reg No:** 0895208 **Estd:** 1904 Private Limited Company
**Line of Business:** Schools (independent)
**Issued Capital:** £12
**Directors:** Mrs J M Lort-Limond, Mrs A Hudson, B L Staples, O J Robinson, C J Williams, M S Bird, D Slack, J Parker
**Co. Secretary:** Mrs Amanda Webb
**Responsibilities**
**Senior:** Vikki Ashton *(Director)*, Jeremy Banks *(Director)*, Martin Cropper *(Director)*, Andrew Lowcock *(Manager)*, Jane Nichols *(Manager)*, Samantha Raper *(Bursar)*
**Finance:** Samantha Raper *(Bursar)*
**Sales:** Samantha Raper *(Bursar)*
**HR:** Barbara Barrett *(Human Resources Manager)*
**Health & Safety:** Samantha Raper *(Bursar)*
**Facilities:** Samantha Raper *(Bursar)*
**US SIC:** 8211 **UK SIC:** 93200
**Auditors:** R Sutton & Co
**Bankers:** Bank Of Scotland (80-02-52)

| | 31-08-13 | 31-08-12 | 31-08-11 |
|---|---|---|---|
| TO | 2,016,369 | 1,891,790 | 1,848,673 |
| P/L | 59,178 | (81,005) | (144,777) |
| NW | 394,563 | 335,385 | 416,390 |
| WC | (222,634) | (326,381) | (299,628) |
| Emp. | 49 | 48 | 50 |

DUNS 77-706-5673

## Ryman Ltd

**(Subsidiary of:** Sixfathers Ltd)
Ryman House, Savoy Road, Crewe, Cheshire CW1 6NA
**Tel:** 01270-505888
**Web:** www.ryman.co.uk
**Reg No:** 3007166 **Estd:** 1995 Private Limited Company
**Line of Business:** Retail sale of books, newspapers and stationery
**Issued Capital:** £1,500,000
**Directors:** R E Towner, S J Lakin, K Kyprianou, M S Cooke, T Paphitis, T Paphitis, I M Childs
**Co. Secretary:** Ms Ann Mantz
**Responsibilities**
**Health & Safety:** Debbie Price *(Health & Safety Manager)*
**Branches:** Ryman Ltd, Ryman The Stationer, 3 Middle Street, Yeovil, Somerset BA20 1LE
**US SIC:** 7399, 5021
**UK SIC:** 83954, 61500
**Auditors:** BDO LLP
**Bankers:** National Westminster Bank Plc (60-04-04)

| | 29-03-14 | 30-03-13 | 31-03-12 |
|---|---|---|---|
| TO | 130,622,000 | 125,384,000 | 124,368,000 |
| P/L | 7,673,000 | 7,263,000 | 14,449,000 |
| NW | 41,439,000 | 37,644,000 | 34,493,000 |
| WC | 28,084,000 | 24,665,000 | 21,448,000 |
| Emp. | 2,170 | 3,711 | 2,224 |

DUNS 64-076-0612

## Ryness 1 Ltd

**(Subsidiary of:** Ryness Holdings Ltd)
The Point Building, London N1 9HP
**Tel:** 02073530575
**Reg No:** 4479395 **Estd:** 2002 Private Limited Company
**Line of Business:** Holding companies management activities
**Issued Capital:** £100
**Directors:** N J Palmer, S Westbrook
**Co. Secretary:** Steven Westbrook
**Responsibilities**
**Senior:** Sean Mcevoy *(Manager)*, Bill Smith *(Manager)*
**US SIC:** 6711 **UK SIC:** 83962
**Bankers:** HSBC Bank plc (40-02-38)

| | 31-12-13 | 31-12-12 | 26-12-11 |
|---|---|---|---|
| TA | 100 | 100 | 100 |
| NW | 100 | 100 | 100 |

DUNS 21-025-5956 **Imp**

## Ryness Ltd

**(Subsidiary of:** Ryness Holdings Ltd)
191 Clapham Road, London SW9 0QE
**Tel:** 02072787469 **Fax:** 020-7239-8332
**Web:** www.ryness.co.uk
**Reg No:** 0693658 **VAT No:** 799168163
**Estd:** 1955 Private Limited Company
**Line of Business:** Electrical products (sales)
**Issued Capital:** £100
**Directors:** S Westbrook, N J Palmer
**Co. Secretary:** Steven Westbrook
**Responsibilities**
**Senior:** James Shortridge *(Manager)*
**HR:** Beatrix O'Conner *(Human Resources Manager)*
**Health & Safety:** Alan Woodhouse *(Health & Safety Officer)*
**Branches:** Ryness Ltd, 306 High Holborn, London WC1V 7JS
**US SIC:** 5065, 5064

**UK SIC:** 61500
**Auditors:** Hazlewoods LLP
**Bankers:** Bank Of Scotland (80-20-00)

| | 31-12-13 | 31-12-12 | 26-12-11 |
|---|---|---|---|
| TA | 100 | 100 | 100 |
| NW | 100 | 100 | 100 |

DUNS 23-841-9790 **Imp-Exp**

## Ryobi Aluminium Casting (U.K.) Ltd

**(Subsidiary of:** Ryobi Limited)
5 Meadowbank Road, Carrickfergus, Co Antrim BT38 8YF
**Tel:** 028-9335-1043
**Web:** www.ryobi.co.uk
**Reg No:** 0024284NI **Estd:** 1990 Private Limited Company
**Line of Business:** Manufacturers of aluminium
**Export Markets:** Germany
**Issued Capital:** £8,000,000
**Directors:** T Yokoyama, J M Hughes
**Co. Secretary:** Hiroyuki Kawaguchi
**Responsibilities**
**Senior:** Gwyneth Evans *(Training Manager)*
**Marketing:** Sam Bell *(Sales & Marketing Manager)*
**Sales:** Sam Bell *(Sales & Marketing Manager)*
**HR:** Chris McCullough *(Training Manager)*
**Health & Safety:** Chris McCullough *(Training Manager)*
**Facilities:** Jim Logan *(Facilities Engineer)*
**Purchasing:** Stephen McCullough *(Purchasing Manager)*
**US SIC:** 3334 **UK SIC:** 22451
**Auditors:** Deloitte LLP

| | 31-12-13 | 31-12-12 | 31-12-11 |
|---|---|---|---|
| TO | 54,912,659 | 38,189,742 | 40,869,271 |
| P/L | 2,090,804 | (3,569,714) | 119,986 |
| NW | 23,620,594 | 19,550,440 | 22,173,788 |
| WC | 5,996,681 | (4,902,941) | 2,121,665 |
| Emp. | 277 | 231 | 221 |

DUNS 22-952-1778

## Rysaffe Trustees (C I) Co Ltd

P O Box 141, Tunnel House, Guernsey, Channel Islands GY1 3HS
**Tel:** 01481721374 **Fax:** 01481-722046
**Web:** www.fery.gg
**Reg No:** 0005643G **Estd:** 1976 Private Limited Company
**Line of Business:** Trustee holding company
**Issued Capital:** £7
**Directors:** P Murrin, I C Domaille, R Sinclair, Ms R Hancock, J Gardner, Ms M Guilbert, Ms L M Gervaise-Brazier
**US SIC:** 6733 **UK SIC:** 83100
**Employees:** 80

# S

DUNS 37-973-0773 **Imp-Exp**

## S + B Uk Ltd

**(Subsidiary of:** Snb 06 Ltd)
Labtec Street, Pendlebury, Swinton, Manchester M27 8SE
**Tel:** 0161 793 9333
**Web:** www.splusb.co.uk
**Reg No:** 3280435 **VAT No:** 880990286
**Estd:** 2007 Private Limited Company
**Line of Business:** Wholesale of other machinery for use in industry, trade and navigation
**Trading Style:** S + B Uk Ltd
**Issued Capital:** £1,000,000
**Principals:** M T Serridge *(Managing)*, C Norris, P J Bentham
**Responsibilities**
**Senior:** Jim Burtess *(Purchasing Manager)*, Angela Yorke *(Financial Controller)*
**Finance:** Angela Yorke *(Financial Controller)*
**HR:** Angela Yorke *(Financial Controller)*
**Operations:** Angela Yorke *(Financial Controller)*
**Purchasing:** Jim Burtess *(Purchasing Manager)*
**US SIC:** 5199 **UK SIC:** 61900
**Bankers:** The Co-Operative Bank Plc (08-90-00)

| | 31-12-13 | 31-12-12 | 31-12-11 |
|---|---|---|---|
| TA | 2,914,556 | 3,050,139 | 3,074,141 |
| NW | 1,915,999 | 1,811,507 | 1,613,856 |
| WC | 1,499,435 | 1,486,305 | 1,364,413 |

DUNS 21-833-0173 **Imp-Exp**

## S + C Bowers & Jones Ltd

**(Subsidiary of:** Schmidt + Clemens Gmbh + Co. Kg)
Unit 4 Hilton Cross Business Park, Featherstone, Wolverhampton, West Midlands WV10 7QZ
**Tel:** 01902-732110
**Web:** www.bowersjones.com
**Reg No:** 0546897 **VAT No:** 897395840
**Estd:** 1955 Private Limited Company
**Line of Business:** Manufacturers general
**Export Markets:** European Union
**Export Sales:** £2,904,741
**Issued Capital:** £96,960
**Directors:** M J Sommerville, R Klausmeier, D Otte
**Responsibilities**
**Senior:** Henning Kreisel *(Manager)*, James Willmott *(Manager)*
**Finance:** Martyn Thompson *(Financial Director)*
**US SIC:** 3999, 3423
**UK SIC:** 49590, 31612
**Auditors:** Muras Baker Jones
**Bankers:** HSBC Bank plc (40-22-26)

| | 31-12-13 | 31-12-12 | 31-12-11 |
|---|---|---|---|
| TO | 5,330,033 | 5,081,907 | N/A |
| P/L | (291,085) | (635,054) | N/A |
| NW | 749,134 | 1,040,219 | 1,675,273 |
| WC | (855,044) | (497,866) | 419,665 |
| Emp. | 47 | 56 | N/A |

DUNS 21-636-8605

## S A Brain & Company Ltd

The Cardiff Brewery, Crawshay Street, Cardiff, South Glamorgan CF10 5DS
**Tel:** 029-2040-2060
**Web:** www.brainstenancies.com
**Reg No:** 0052099 **VAT No:** 700806962
**Estd:** 1882 Private Limited Company
**Line of Business:** Manufacture of beer
**Trading Style:** Brains, The Pilot
**Issued Capital:** £2,574,746
**Directors:** J F Rhys, M S Reed, D P Bonney, A G Arkley, J S Waddington
**Co. Secretary:** Charles Brain
**Responsibilities**
**Senior:** Philip Lay *(Manager)*
**Branches:** S.a.brain & Company,Limited, Jolly Sailor, 1 Church Street, Porthcawl, Mid Glamorgan CF36 5PD
**US SIC:** 2082, 5182, 5813
**UK SIC:** 42702, 61700, 66200
**Auditors:** Deloitte LLP
**Bankers:** HSBC Bank plc (40-16-15)

| | 28-09-13 | 29-09-12 | 01-09-11 |
|---|---|---|---|
| TO | 122,181,000 | 120,745,000 | 113,643,000 |
| P/L | 109,000 | (2,077,000) | 1,840,000 |
| NW | 49,769,000 | 59,281,000 | 67,093,000 |
| WC | (7,658,000) | (6,544,000) | 1,695,000 |
| Emp. | 2,224 | 2,216 | 1,994 |

DUNS 23-989-6942

## S A L Group Ltd

376 London Road, Hadleigh, Benfleet, Essex SS7 2DA
**Tel:** 01268694447
**Web:** www.thesalgroup.com
**Reg No:** 3977940 **Estd:** 2000 Private Limited Company
**Line of Business:** Management activities of holding companies
**Export Sales:** £54,551,022
**Issued Capital:** £10
**Directors:** A J Elliott, D M Champ, P J Dare, S Y Kim, N S Goldstone, V J Pais, S Bhattacharji
**Co. Secretary:** Ms Jennifer Elliott
**Branches:** S A L Group Ltd, Chadwick House, Warrington Road, Warrington, Cheshire WA3 6AE
**US SIC:** 6711 **UK SIC:** 83962
**Bankers:** HSBC Bank plc (40-23-33)

| | 31-03-14 | 31-12-12 | 31-03-11 |
|---|---|---|---|
| TO | 72,859,379 | 57,946,869 | 52,134,838 |
| P/L | (2,115,836) | 784,090 | 1,339,735 |
| NW | 842,330 | 2,205,383 | 1,298,145 |
| WC | 1,056,686 | 2,205,610 | 1,801,532 |
| Emp. | 103 | 90 | 79 |

DUNS 21-880-1227

## S A S M I Gateshead College

Washington Road, Sunderland, Tyne and Wear SR5 3HE
**Tel:** 01914902499
**Web:** www.gateshead.ac.uk
**Estd:** 2012
**Line of Business:** Further education schools and colleges
**US SIC:** 8221 **UK SIC:** 93100
**Employees:** 50

**DUNS 73-737-7148**

## S & A Foods Group Ltd
37 Shaftesbury St South, Derby, Derbyshire DE23 8YH
**Tel:** 01332270670
**Web:** www.sa-foods.co.uk
**Reg No:** 4995676 **Estd:** 2000 Private Limited Company
**Line of Business:** Manufacture of other food products not elsewhere classified
**Export Sales:** £1,056,000
**Issued Capital:** £778
**Directors:** Ms P Warsi, C R Sharpe
**US SIC:** 2099, 2013
**UK SIC:** 42399, 41223
**Auditors:** KPMG LLP
**Bankers:** Barclays Bank Plc (20-07-71)

| | 31-03-14 | 31-03-13 | 31-03-12 |
|---|---|---|---|
| TO | 44,245,000 | 51,541,000 | 57,600,000 |
| P/L | 313,000 | 692,000 | 551,000 |
| NW | 7,429,000 | 7,366,000 | 7,825,000 |
| WC | (509,000) | (888,000) | (844,000) |
| Emp. | 388 | 471 | 563 |

**DUNS 50-512-1475**     Imp

## S & A Produce (Uk) Ltd
(Subsidiary of: S & A Group Holdings Ltd)
Brook Farm, Hereford, Herefordshire HR1 3ET
**Tel:** 01432880235 **Fax:** 01432-880044
**Web:** www.sagroup.co.uk
**Reg No:** 2480021 **Estd:** 1990 Private Limited Company
**Line of Business:** Fruit and vegetable (producers)
**Issued Capital:** £1,000,472
**Directors:** F M Green, D H Martin, J W Naerebout
**Co. Secretary:** Trevor Gregory
**Branches:** S & A Produce (Uk) Ltd, Highstreet Road, Faversham, Kent ME13 9EJ
**US SIC:** 0179 **UK SIC:** 01002
**Auditors:** Deloitte LLP

| | 31-12-13 | 31-12-12 | 31-12-11 |
|---|---|---|---|
| TO | 57,124,887 | 53,985,926 | 56,023,685 |
| P/L | 863,574 | 1,086,863 | 428,327 |
| NW | 6,236,066 | 5,283,408 | 4,177,886 |
| WC | 5,277,534 | 3,620,837 | 2,601,631 |
| Emp. | 184 | 175 | 228 |

**DUNS 22-625-4332**

## S & B Commercials Plc
Travellers Lane, Welham Green, North Mymms, Hatfield, Hertfordshire AL9 7HN
**Tel:** 01707-261111 **Fax:** 01707274546
**Web:** www.sbcommercials.co.uk
**Reg No:** 1635078 **VAT No:** 370799807
**Estd:** 1982 Public Limited Company
**Line of Business:** Van and truck dealers
**Issued Capital:** £50,000
**Directors:** D J Holmes, I T Oakes, A B Welch
**Co. Secretary:** Andrew Welch
**Responsibilities**
**Senior:** Ronald Holmes (Dealer Principal)
**Finance:** Frank Warren (Financial Controller)
**IT:** Frank Warren (Financial Controller)
**HR:** Judy Gosnell (Human Resources Manager)
**Branches:** S & B Commercials Plc, Unit 2A, Start Hill, Bishop's Stortford, Hertfordshire CM22 7DG
**US SIC:** 5511, 5521
**UK SIC:** 65100
**Auditors:** Landau Morley LLP
**Bankers:** Barclays Bank Plc (20-92-54)

| | 31-12-13 | 31-12-12 | 31-12-11 |
|---|---|---|---|
| TO | 110,098,058 | 95,096,055 | 78,159,216 |
| P/L | 2,001,323 | 1,519,690 | 765,203 |
| NW | 10,287,542 | 9,010,461 | 8,003,692 |
| WC | 4,623,554 | 3,384,630 | 2,632,885 |
| Emp. | 268 | 271 | 282 |

**DUNS 21-329-6312**     Imp

## S & B Eps Ltd
Grieves Row, Cramlington, Northumberland NE23 7PX
**Tel:** 01912500818 **Fax:** 0191-250-0548
**Web:** www.sandbeps.com
**Reg No:** 1646418 **VAT No:** 376432145
**Estd:** 1982 Private Limited Company
**Line of Business:** Packaging equipment
**Issued Capital:** £20,000
**Principals:** H C Smith (Managing), D C Smith (Financial), D Davison, Ms D L Davison, P Banks, J Smith
**Co. Secretary:** Henry Smith
**US SIC:** 3079, 1541
**UK SIC:** 48360, 50100
**Auditors:** Gilchrist Tash
**Bankers:** Barclays Bank Plc (20-62-09)

| | 30-04-14 | 30-04-13 | 30-04-12 |
|---|---|---|---|
| TO | 12,937,323 | N/A | N/A |
| P/L | 1,270,450 | N/A | N/A |
| NW | 1,933,332 | 1,373,933 | 1,081,275 |
| WC | 430,716 | 74,684 | 179,284 |
| Emp. | 46 | N/A | N/A |

**DUNS 21-581-2479**

## S & B Productions
3 Enterprise Way, Newtownabbey, Co Antrim BT36 4EW
**Tel:** 02890343000
**Web:** www.diageo.com
**Estd:** 2011 Proprietorship
**Line of Business:** Distilleries
**Proprietor:** M Hails
**Responsibilities**
**Senior:** Manus Rogan (Manager)
**US SIC:** 2085 **UK SIC:** 42402
**Employees:** 50

**DUNS 23-698-4451**

## S & B Property Ltd
Unit A, Bristol, Avon BS3 4AG
**Tel:** 01179-533001
**Web:** www.sandbaa.com
**Reg No:** 3693182 **Estd:** 1998 Private Company Limited By Guarantee
**Line of Business:** Training services
**Export Sales:** £22,601
**Directors:** A D Jolliffe, M Read, S J Curtis
**Co. Secretary:** Justin Patterson
**Responsibilities**
**Senior:** Tom May (Business Development Manager)
**US SIC:** 8299, 8221
**UK SIC:** 93300, 93100
**Auditors:** Blackmore & Co

| | 31-07-14 | 31-07-13 | 31-07-12 |
|---|---|---|---|
| TO | 3,404,295 | 3,477,700 | 3,501,923 |
| P/L | 145,397 | 1,530 | 40,267 |
| NW | 2,869,161 | 2,753,402 | 2,772,222 |
| WC | 552,689 | 411,613 | 498,640 |
| Emp. | 56 | 55 | 51 |

**DUNS 23-448-0242**     Imp

## S & B Waste Management & Recycling Ltd
(Subsidiary of: S & B Industrial Investments Ltd)
Purbrook Road Unit 26, Stowheath Industrial Esta, Wolverhampton, West Midlands WV1 2EJ
**Tel:** 01902459900
**Web:** www.sbwastemanagementrecycling.co.uk
**Reg No:** 2780778 **VAT No:** 559373405
**Estd:** 2002 Private Limited Company
**Line of Business:** Skip hire
**Issued Capital:** £100
**Director:** S Broadley
**Co. Secretary:** Ms Karen Broadley
**US SIC:** 7394, 4953
**UK SIC:** 84000, 92110
**Auditors:** Crowther Jordan Ltd

| | 31-03-14 | 31-03-13 | 31-03-12 |
|---|---|---|---|
| TO | 7,796,054 | 6,744,395 | 7,058,833 |
| P/L | 97,056 | 47,456 | 814,862 |
| NW | 2,990,345 | 2,932,184 | 2,898,060 |
| WC | 2,990,345 | 2,932,184 | 2,898,060 |
| Emp. | 52 | 54 | 59 |

**DUNS 21-584-3636**

## S & H Kickboxing
Wye Road Community Centre, Wye Road, Newcastle, Staffordshire ST5 4AZ
**Tel:** 07834875420
**Web:** www.shkickboxing.co.uk
**Estd:** 2011 Proprietorship
**Line of Business:** Martial art instruction
**Proprietor:** S Hallan
**US SIC:** 7999 **UK SIC:** 97913
**Employees:** 300

**DUNS 28-823-2788**

## S & J D Robertson North Air Ltd
Building 10, Derby, Derbyshire DE74 2SA
**Tel:** 01332810459
**Reg No:** 0051614SC **Estd:** 1972 Private Limited Company
**Line of Business:** Wholesale of petroleum and petroleum products
**Issued Capital:** £4,225,100
**Directors:** P Van Espen, P Workman, Dr. I C Harrison, P Westerman
**Co. Secretary:** Paul Workman
**Branches:** S & J D Robertson North Air Ltd, Viscount Road, Building 10, Derby, Derbyshire DE74 2SA
**US SIC:** 5171 **UK SIC:** 61200
**Auditors:** Ernst & Young LLP
**Bankers:** The Royal Bank Of Scotland Plc (83-24-07)

| | 31-12-13 | 31-12-12 | 31-12-11 |
|---|---|---|---|
| TO | 18,031,527 | 15,282,600 | 13,814,748 |
| P/L | 733,428 | 701,457 | 483,712 |
| NW | 2,427,115 | 1,727,506 | 977,484 |
| WC | 1,392,225 | (144,616) | 1,443,984 |
| Emp. | 203 | 187 | 179 |

**DUNS 39-802-4562**

## S & J European Haulage Ltd
Unit C Ashfordby Business Park, Melton Mowbray, Leicestershire LE14 0EJ
**Tel:** 01664-810060 **Fax:** 01664-810061
**Web:** www.sj-haulage.co.uk
**Reg No:** 2208036 **Estd:** 1980 Private Limited Company
**Line of Business:** Road haulage and transport services
**Issued Capital:** £100
**Principals:** S Haines (Managing), P Pugsley, M Haines
**Co. Secretary:** Mrs Jane Haines
**Responsibilities**
**IT:** Carl Musson (IT Manager)
**Health & Safety:** Carl Musson (IT Manager)
**Branches:** S & J European Haulage Ltd, 64 Snow Hill Industrial Estate, Melton Mowbray, Leicestershire LE13 1PD
**US SIC:** 4789 **UK SIC:** 77002
**Auditors:** Mulligan Williams
**Bankers:** Lloyds TSB Bank plc (30-95-52)

| | 30-11-13 | 30-11-12 | 30-11-11 |
|---|---|---|---|
| TO | 6,927,992 | 6,531,161 | N/A |
| P/L | 54,097 | (31,358) | N/A |
| NW | 306,412 | 284,341 | 312,056 |
| WC | (1,003,737) | (916,524) | (833,580) |
| Emp. | 72 | 75 | N/A |

**DUNS 64-715-8781**

## S & J Pierce Transport
Firbank Way, Leighton Buzzard, Bedfordshire LU7 4YP
**Estd:** 1986 Partnership
**Line of Business:** Local Trucking Without Storage
**Partners:** Mrs J Pierce, S Pierce
**US SIC:** 4212 **UK SIC:** 72300
**Employees:** 50

**DUNS 73-586-7710**

## S & L Catering Ltd
(Subsidiary of: Hopton Brow Ltd)
Shaw & Lisle Catering, Unit N-P, Shaw Park, Silver Street, Huddersfield, West Yorkshire HD5 9AF
**Tel:** 01484-304401 **Fax:** 01484-304402
**Web:** www.slcatering.co.uk
**Reg No:** 4848218 **Estd:** 2003 Private Limited Company
**Line of Business:** Manufacturers of food products
**Issued Capital:** £100
**Directors:** S Tidball, Ms J E Dedman
**Co. Secretary:** Simon Shaw
**Responsibilities**
**Senior:** Richard Lisle (Manager)
**US SIC:** 2099 **UK SIC:** 42399
**Auditors:** Armitages Chartered Accountants

| | 31-12-13 | 31-12-12 | 31-12-11 |
|---|---|---|---|
| TA | 2,212,742 | 1,748,935 | 1,624,843 |
| NW | (465,230) | (400,371) | (379,395) |
| WC | (690,120) | (659,664) | (662,745) |

**DUNS 21-751-6681**     Imp-Exp

## S. & L. United Storage Systems Ltd
United House, The Street Takeley, Bishops Stortford, Hertfordshire CM22 6QR
**Tel:** 01279871633 **Fax:** 01992-524198
**Web:** www.unitedstorage.co.uk
**Reg No:** 1313816 **VAT No:** 291616253
**Estd:** 1977 Private Limited Company
**Line of Business:** Railway attractions
**Export Markets:** Europe
**Trading Style:** United Storage Systems
**Issued Capital:** £100
**Principals:** V J Smith (Chairman), P A Beszant, M H Smith, S V Miller
**Co. Secretary:** Philip Mullens
**Branches:** S. & L. United Storage Systems Ltd, Unit 5, North Weald Airfield, Epping, Essex CM16 6AA
**US SIC:** 2599, 5084
**UK SIC:** 46720, 61490
**Auditors:** Knight Wheeler Ltd
**Bankers:** HSBC Bank plc (40-25-27)

| | 30-06-13 | 30-06-12 | 30-06-11 |
|---|---|---|---|
| TO | 4,802,977 | 9,957,211 | 10,666,075 |
| P/L | (810,660) | 12,936 | 32,339 |
| NW | 1,801,557 | 2,758,946 | 2,771,386 |
| WC | 649,951 | 1,619,903 | 1,586,687 |
| Emp. | 50 | 57 | 51 |

**DUNS 21-174-0933**     Imp

## S & M Tyres Holdings Ltd
Elite Garages Brighton Road, Mannings Heath, Horsham, West Sussex RH13 6HY
**Tel:** 01403 213380
**Web:** www.elitegarages.co.uk
**Reg No:** 6978507 **VAT No:** 991249489
**Estd:** 2009 Private Limited Company
**Line of Business:** Management activities of holding companies
**Trading Style:** Eg Wholesale
**Issued Capital:** £100
**Directors:** M P Whittemore, Mrs S D Whittemore

**Co. Secretary:** Richard Whittemore
**US SIC:** 6711 **UK SIC:** 83962
**Auditors:** RSM Tenon Audit Ltd
**Bankers:** National Westminster Bank Plc (60-11-17)

| | 31-01-14 | 31-01-13 | 31-01-12 |
|---|---|---|---|
| TO | 42,138,213 | 44,003,786 | 41,839,293 |
| P/L | 1,031,273 | 958,127 | 433,763 |
| NW | 4,605,435 | 4,287,478 | 3,946,688 |
| WC | (2,008,676) | (1,499,947) | (1,419,892) |
| Emp. | 196 | 193 | 201 |

**DUNS 73-757-9776**     Exp

## S & P Coil Products Ltd
S P C House, Evington Valley Road, Leicester, Leicestershire LE5 5LU
**Tel:** 01162-490044
**Web:** www.spcoils.co.uk
**Reg No:** 5015411 **Estd:** 2004 Private Limited Company
**Line of Business:** Manufacture of non-domestic cooling and ventilation equipment
**Export Sales:** £3,141,517
**Issued Capital:** £5,000
**Principals:** A J Westbury (Managing), K Davinson, K N Cockwill, P I Pritchett, P J Teasdale, W Taylor
**Responsibilities**
**Senior:** Terry Johnson (Manufacturing Coordinator)
**Sales:** David Birtles (National Key Account Manager), Charles Hart (Regional Sales Manager)
**Purchasing:** Terry Johnson (Manufacturing Coordinator)
**US SIC:** 3585 **UK SIC:** 32841

| | 29-03-14 | 30-03-13 | 31-03-12 |
|---|---|---|---|
| TO | 8,843,423 | 9,310,532 | 10,246,820 |
| P/L | 112,361 | 358,761 | 627,536 |
| NW | 2,532,195 | 2,389,658 | 2,181,887 |
| WC | 760,613 | 549,407 | 308,741 |
| Emp. | 83 | 83 | 84 |

**DUNS 22-926-2647**

## S. & R. Electric Ltd
56 Holywood Road, Belfast BT4 1NT
**Tel:** 02890655929 **Fax:** 02890658846
**Web:** www.sr-electric.com
**Reg No:** 0017617NI **Estd:** 1972 Private Limited Company
**Line of Business:** Retail sale of electrical household appliances and radio and television goods
**Issued Capital:** £4,899
**Directors:** S G Duff, Ms J M Duff, R H Duff
**Co. Secretary:** Ms Pauline Sergeant
**Responsibilities**
**Senior:** Tom Harper (Service Manager)
**US SIC:** 5732, 5719
**UK SIC:** 64800, 64700
**Auditors:** Flannigan Edmonds Bannon
**Bankers:** Ulster Bank Ltd (98-00-30)

| | 30-06-13 | 30-06-12 | 30-06-11 |
|---|---|---|---|
| TO | 2,923,535 | 3,202,450 | 4,130,849 |
| NW | 1,165,697 | 1,063,423 | 1,403,879 |
| WC | (670,443) | (548,520) | (933,492) |

**DUNS 21-880-4434**

## S & R Nelson Ltd Nelson Parks
Sheriff Hutton Road, York, North Yorkshire YO32 5TL
**Tel:** 01904492912
**Web:** www.nelsonparks.co.uk
**Estd:** 2012
**Line of Business:** Holidays (self catering)
**Responsibilities**
**Senior:** Kelli Barrett (Manager), Shadrack Nelson (Proprietor)
**US SIC:** 7021 **UK SIC:** 66500
**Employees:** 150

**DUNS 21-025-3033**

## S & R Smith & Sons
Hedley Avenue, Grays, Essex RM20 4EL
**Tel:** 01708892490
**Web:** www.sr-smith.com
**Estd:** 2012
**Line of Business:** Freight transport by road not elsewhere classified
**US SIC:** 4213 **UK SIC:** 72300
**Employees:** 60

**DUNS 34-721-5126**

## S & S Care (Uk) Ltd
88 Clayhall Avenue, Clayhall, Ilford, Essex IG5 0LF
**Tel:** 01978769385
**Reg No:** 5525079 **Estd:** 2005 Private Limited Company
**Line of Business:** Home care service providers
**Issued Capital:** £2
**Director:** S S Sunnar
**Co. Secretary:** Sukhbir Sahota
**US SIC:** 8091 **UK SIC:** 95200

| | 31-08-13 | 31-08-12 | 31-08-11 |
|---|---|---|---|
| TO | 2,269,533 | 2,250,974 | 2,289,410 |
| P/L | (47,561) | (105,257) | (205,814) |
| NW | (873,267) | (883,132) | (859,481) |
| WC | (894,659) | (860,795) | (915,058) |
| Emp. | 127 | 139 | 138 |

DUNS 28-934-6280
## S & S Contract Cleaning Services Ltd
Nexus House, 2 Cray Road, Sidcup, Kent DA14 5DA
**Tel:** 01959534257
**Reg No:** 1547189 **Estd:** 1981 Private Limited Company
**Line of Business:** Traditional cleaning activities
**Issued Capital:** £100
**Managing Director:** M F Snell
**Co. Secretary:** Ms Linda Fogarty
**US SIC:** 7349 **UK SIC:** 92300
**Bankers:** Barclays Bank Plc (20-06-72)

| | 28-02-14 | 28-02-13 | 28-02-12 |
|---|---|---|---|
| TA | 23,940 | 23,847 | 32,566 |
| NW | 5,452 | 10,530 | 23,383 |
| WC | 4,138 | 8,973 | 21,535 |

DUNS 22-611-2423
## S & S Services
Postern Industrial Estate, 400 Vale Road, Tonbridge, Kent TN9 1SW
**Tel:** 01732-358800
**Web:** www.ssdistribution.co.uk
**VAT No:** 210259311 **Estd:** 1969 Partnership
**Line of Business:** Haulage contractors and warehousemen.
**Partners:** J Sanderson, K Sanderson, D Sanderson, Ms D Sanderson
**US SIC:** 4311, 4213
**UK SIC:** 79010, 72300
**Bankers:** National Westminster Bank Plc (60-21-28)
**Employees:** 75

DUNS 23-741-3005 **Imp**
## S & T Audio Ltd
48-50 Queens Road, Southend-On-Sea, Essex SS1 1NL
**Tel:** 01702-436501
**Web:** www.pmtonline.co.uk
**Reg No:** 3735541 **Estd:** 1999 Private Limited Company
**Line of Business:** Musical instruments and sheet music retailers
**Trading Style:** Pmt Professional Music Technologies
**Issued Capital:** £100
**Director:** T A Hope
**Co. Secretary:** Simon Gilson
**Branches:** S & T Audio Ltd, Tyndale House, Cowley Road, Oxford, Oxfordshire OX4 1JQ
**US SIC:** 5732, 2741
**UK SIC:** 64800, 47541
**Auditors:** Mudd & Co

| | 30-04-13 | 30-04-12 | 30-04-11 |
|---|---|---|---|
| TO | 21,099,174 | 19,199,057 | 14,509,183 |
| P/L | 843,718 | 562,906 | 413,343 |
| NW | 3,439,505 | 2,790,178 | 2,572,121 |
| WC | 3,523,377 | 2,930,232 | 2,757,931 |
| Emp. | 139 | 131 | 123 |

DUNS 21-805-4468 **Exp**
## S & U Plc
Royal House, Solihull, West Midlands B91 3QQ
**Tel:** 0121-705-7777
**Web:** www.suplc.co.uk
**Reg No:** 0342025 **Estd:** 1938 Public Limited Company
**Line of Business:** Finance brokers
**Trading Style:** S & U
**Issued Capital:** £2,120,591
**Principals:** F Coombs *(Managing)*, D Markou, K R Smith, M J Thompson, G D Coombs, J G Thompson, C H Redford, M Mullins
**Co. Secretary:** Mrs Manjeet Bhogal
**Responsibilities**
**HR:** Emma Helliwell *(Group Human Resources Manager)*
**Branches:** S & U Plc, Beech Business Park, Unit 9, Hereford, Herefordshire HR4 9QJ
**US SIC:** 6111 **UK SIC:** 81501
**Auditors:** Deloitte LLP
**Bankers:** HSBC Bank plc (40-11-18)

| | 31-01-14 | 31-01-13 | 31-01-12 |
|---|---|---|---|
| TA | 109,951,000 | 88,714,000 | 79,749,000 |
| P/L | 17,287,000 | 14,230,000 | 12,216,000 |
| NW | 69,410,000 | 61,066,000 | 54,862,000 |
| WC | 47,648,000 | 42,775,000 | 43,877,000 |
| Emp. | 386 | 372 | 375 |

DUNS 21-735-6815
## S B A (Manufacturing) Ltd
**(Subsidiary of:** S B A Ltd.)
Freemans Common, Leicester, Leicestershire LE2 7SQ
**Tel:** 01162-576595
**Web:** www.sba.co.uk
**Reg No:** 1173209 **Estd:** 1974 Private Limited Company
**Line of Business:** Other wholesale
**Issued Capital:** £10,000
**Principals:** R Smith *(Managing)*, Ms K L Webber
**US SIC:** 5199 **UK SIC:** 61900
**Auditors:** Tenon Ltd
**Bankers:** HSBC Bank plc (40-28-06)

| | 31-12-13 | 31-12-12 | 31-12-11 |
|---|---|---|---|
| TA | 1 | 10,000 | 10,000 |
| NW | 1 | 10,000 | 10,000 |

DUNS 23-868-3457 **Imp**
## S B Components (International) Ltd
Millennium Works, Wisbech, Cambridgeshire PE14 0SB
**Tel:** 01945-475234
**Web:** www.sb-components.com
**Reg No:** 3859796 **Estd:** 1999 Private Limited Company
**Line of Business:** Manufacture of tanks, reservoirs and containers of metal
**Issued Capital:** £1,000
**Directors:** Mrs C A Oldfield, J Warren, J Bushell
**Co. Secretary:** Steven Bushell
**Responsibilities**
**Marketing:** Matthew Warren *(Sales & Marketing Manager)*
**Sales:** Paul Boyce *(Sales Support)*, Matthew Warren *(Sales & Marketing Manager)*
**Operations:** Daniel Burrowes *(Operations Manager)*, Matthew Warren *(Sales & Marketing Manager)*
**Purchasing:** Andy Withers *(Purchasing Manager)*
**US SIC:** 3443 **UK SIC:** 32051
**Auditors:** Buting & Co

| | 31-03-14 | 31-03-13 | 31-03-12 |
|---|---|---|---|
| TA | 5,684,777 | 3,786,060 | 3,786,157 |
| P/L | 1,067,851 | 453,813 | N/A |
| NW | 2,686,573 | 2,082,266 | 1,912,348 |
| WC | 1,846,659 | 1,601,026 | 1,411,535 |
| Emp. | 95 | 83 | N/A |

DUNS 21-580-3330 **Imp**
## S B F I
Unit 1a-1d Hawthorne Industrial Estate, Avis Way, Newhaven, East Sussex BN9 0DJ
**Web:** www.sbfi.com
**Estd:** 1985 Proprietorship
**Line of Business:** Manufacturers of household furnishings
**Proprietor:** M Banwell
**US SIC:** 2517 **UK SIC:** 46714
**Employees:** 59

DUNS 21-771-6215
## S C A
Riverbank Works, 166 Riverford Road, Glasgow, Lanarkshire G43 1PT
**Tel:** 01416320999
**Web:** www.dssmith.com
**Estd:** 2005 Partnership
**Line of Business:** Printers general
**Trading Style:** Ds Smith Packaging Ltd
**Partners:** B Miller, G Lethan
**Responsibilities**
**Senior:** Jim Jackson *(Plant Manager)*
**US SIC:** 2752 **UK SIC:** 47544
**Employees:** 200

DUNS 23-208-8179
## S C A Community Care Services Ltd
Lower Brownhill Road, Southampton, Hampshire SO16 9LA
**Tel:** 02380771808
**Reg No:** 0027461IP **Estd:** 1984 Friendly Society
**Line of Business:** Residential care establishments
**Trading Style:** Brownhill House Information Services
**Principals:** Dame S Quinn *(Chairman)*, J J Farrow, D R Palmer, J J Coffey, Miss M A Goodman, R Hallett, F Davis, P M Fenner
**Responsibilities**
**Senior:** s Quinn *(Chairperson)*
**Admin:** B Strevens *(Secretary)*
**US SIC:** 8321 **UK SIC:** 96111
**Auditors:** Abraham & Dobell
**Employees:** 340

DUNS 42-395-1508
## S C B Vehicle Dismantlers & Salvage Dealers
Newbridge Industrial Estate, Newbridge, Midlothian EH28 8LZ
**Tel:** 01313331098
**Web:** www.scbvehicledismantlers.co.uk
**Estd:** 1961 Proprietorship
**Line of Business:** Vehicle salvage dealers
**Proprietor:** H Irvine
**Branches:** S C B Vehicle Dismantlers & Salvage Dealers, Unit 3, Newbridge Industrial Estate, Newbridge, Midlothian EH28 8PJ
**US SIC:** 5093 **UK SIC:** 62200
**Bankers:** Bank Of Scotland (80-20-00)
**Employees:** 55

DUNS 28-986-8325
## S. C. Motor Factors Ltd
**(Subsidiary of:** Genghis Topco Ltd)
Units 4-6 Ruxley Corner Industrial, Estate, Edgington Way, Sidcup, Kent DA14 5BL
**Tel:** 020-8302-7624
**Web:** www.scmf.co.uk
**Reg No:** 1804705 **VAT No:** 412902092
**Estd:** 1984 Private Limited Company
**Line of Business:** Sale of motor vehicle parts and accessories
**Issued Capital:** £7,500
**Directors:** M E Murray, P C Sephton
**Responsibilities**
**Senior:** Richard Cserjen *(Financial Manager)*, Andy Rogers *(Regional Manager)*, Jeremy Stopher *(Managing Director)*
**Finance:** Richard Cserjen *(Financial Manager)*
**Admin:** Richard Cserjen *(Financial Manager)*
**US SIC:** 5531 **UK SIC:** 65100
**Auditors:** BDO LLP

| | 30-04-14 | 30-04-13 | 31-04-12 |
|---|---|---|---|
| TO | 18,261,425 | 16,135,504 | 18,134,960 |
| P/L | (89,874) | (716,387) | 690,663 |
| NW | 1,516,148 | 1,606,022 | 2,324,479 |
| WC | 773,821 | 951,431 | 1,982,036 |
| Emp. | 206 | 200 | 196 |

DUNS 21-388-3397
## S C R A
The Exchange, 62-104 Market Street, Aberdeen, Aberdeenshire AB11 5PJ
**Tel:** 03002002166
**Web:** www.scra.gov.uk
**Estd:** 2007
**Line of Business:** Childcare services
**Proprietor:** M Cooke
**Responsibilities**
**Senior:** Elizabeth Templeton *(Authority Reporter)*
**US SIC:** 8321 **UK SIC:** 96111
**Employees:** 400

DUNS 21-807-3799 **Exp**
## S. Cartwright & Sons (Coachbuilders) Ltd
Atlantic Street, Altrincham, Cheshire WA14 5DH
**Tel:** 01619-280966
**Web:** www.cartwright-group.co.uk
**Reg No:** 0687816 **Estd:** 1961 Private Limited Company
**Line of Business:** Manufacture of motor vehicles
**Trading Style:** Cartwright Group
**Issued Capital:** £966,666
**Principals:** P S Cartwright *(Managing)*, W L Cartwright, Ms L C Lee, Mrs C Cartwright, Ms N M Cartwright, M R Cartwright
**Co. Secretary:** Peter Cartwright
**Responsibilities**
**Senior:** B Potts *(Production Manager)*
**Finance:** I McEwan *(Accountant)*
**Facilities:** B Potts *(Production Manager)*
**Engineering:** B Potts *(Production Manager)*
**Branches:** S. Cartwright & Sons (Coachbuilders) Ltd, Atlantic St, Altrincham, Cheshire WA14 5DH
**US SIC:** 3713 **UK SIC:** 35201
**Auditors:** Kay Johnson Gee
**Bankers:** National Westminster Bank Plc (01-10-01)

| | 31-03-14 | 06-04-13 | 31-03-12 |
|---|---|---|---|
| TO | 89,099,710 | 77,946,387 | 79,254,183 |
| P/L | 1,525,504 | 2,702,052 | 2,358,558 |
| NW | 12,452,908 | 12,774,211 | 12,124,436 |
| WC | (1,636,943) | (5,463,467) | (3,998,446) |
| Emp. | 525 | 442 | 484 |

DUNS 21-911-5086 **Imp**
## S. Collins & Co. Ltd
Unit 2-3, Collins Court, Ascot Road, Nottingham, Nottinghamshire NG8 5HD
**Tel:** 01159425522
**Web:** www.collinscashandcarry.co.uk
**Reg No:** 0484469 **VAT No:** 116492669
**Estd:** 1950 Private Limited Company
**Line of Business:** Cash and carry wholesalers
**Trading Style:** Super C's, Collins Cash & Carry
**Issued Capital:** £51,500
**Principals:** F J Collins *(Managing)*, Mrs S A Collins
**Co. Secretary:** Frank Collins
**US SIC:** 5199, 5136
**UK SIC:** 61900, 61600
**Auditors:** J H Trease & Co
**Bankers:** Barclays Bank Plc (20-63-25)

| | 31-01-14 | 31-01-13 | 31-01-12 |
|---|---|---|---|
| TO | N/A | 5,300,782 | 5,436,352 |
| P/L | N/A | 163,793 | 140,995 |
| NW | 3,064,314 | 3,301,050 | 3,283,808 |
| WC | 1,945,989 | 2,216,165 | 2,166,483 |
| Emp. | N/A | 50 | 57 |

DUNS 21-809-6188
## S. Cooper Holdings Ltd
Unit 8-9 Nat Lane Business Park, Nat Lane, Winsford, Cheshire CW7 3BS
**Tel:** 01606863888
**Web:** www.minsteronline.co.uk
**Reg No:** 0344767 **VAT No:** 158231176
**Estd:** 1938 Private Limited Company
**Line of Business:** Cladding and insulation materials
**Issued Capital:** £11,000
**Principals:** J R Howarth *(Chairman and Managing)*, R J Howarth, K Howarth
**Co. Secretary:** Kate Buckwell
**Responsibilities**
**Senior:** Judith Evans *(Manager)*
**Branches:** S. Cooper Holdings Ltd, Unit G1, Talbot Rd, Hyde, Cheshire SK14 4UQ
**US SIC:** 6519, 4213
**UK SIC:** 85000, 72300
**Auditors:** BDO Stoy Hayward
**Bankers:** National Westminster Bank Plc (51-61-11)

| | 31-03-14 | 31-03-13 | 31-03-12 |
|---|---|---|---|
| TO | 11,511,803 | 10,746,501 | 10,708,842 |
| P/L | 333,702 | 201,654 | 238,366 |
| NW | 1,727,663 | 1,692,121 | 1,878,882 |
| WC | 254,933 | (6,299) | 54,891 |
| Emp. | 137 | 138 | 131 |

DUNS 29-687-5099 **Imp-Exp**
## S D A Protec Ltd
**(Subsidiary of:** Synectics Plc)
Axis 7, Rhodes Way, Watford, Hertfordshire WD24 4YW
**Tel:** 01923211550 **Fax:** 01923-211590
**Web:** www.sda-protec.co.uk
**Reg No:** 2011062 **Estd:** 1986 Private Limited Company
**Line of Business:** Electrical contractors and electricians
**Export Markets:** countries worldwide
**Issued Capital:** £50,000
**Director:** M J Stilwell
**Co. Secretary:** Nigel Poultney
**Branches:** S D A Protec Ltd, 3rd Floor, The Triangle, Exchange Sq, Manchester M4 3TR
**US SIC:** 1731, 7393
**UK SIC:** 50300, 83954
**Auditors:** PKF
**Bankers:** Barclays Bank Plc (20-74-09)

| | 30-11-13 | 30-11-12 | 30-11-11 |
|---|---|---|---|
| TA | 1,154,204 | 1,154,204 | 1,154,204 |
| NW | 1,154,204 | 1,154,204 | 1,154,204 |

DUNS 29-154-5226
## S D C (Holdings) Ltd
**(Subsidiary of:** The Sdc Ebt Ltd)
Limegrove House, Caxton Road, Elm Farm Industrial Estate, Bedford, Bedfordshire MK41 0QQ
**Tel:** 01234363155
**Web:** www.sdc.co.uk
**Reg No:** 1756144 **Estd:** 1983 Private Limited Company
**Line of Business:** Management activities of construction holding companies
**Issued Capital:** £65,001
**Directors:** C W Millar, G L Wykes, F P Shiner
**Co. Secretary:** Martin Lowndes
**US SIC:** 6711, 1522, 1761
**UK SIC:** 83962, 50100, 50400
**Auditors:** Haysom Silverton & Partners Ltd
**Bankers:** Barclays Bank Plc (20-05-74)

| | 30-09-14 | 30-09-13 | 30-09-12 |
|---|---|---|---|
| TO | 126,997,689 | 103,932,654 | 93,818,310 |
| P/L | 818,914 | 876,310 | (104,871) |
| NW | 5,335,068 | 4,722,620 | 4,105,782 |
| WC | (1,928,592) | (463,727) | (760,048) |
| Emp. | 248 | 213 | 221 |

DUNS 21-241-1896 **Imp-Exp**
## S Dugdale Son & Co Ltd
**(Subsidiary of:** Vinpol Ltd)
Valley Mill, Holmes Road, Sowerby Bridge, West Yorkshire HX6 2AA
**Tel:** 01422-832501
**Web:** www.dugdaleplc.com
**Reg No:** 0652435 **Estd:** 1896 Private Limited Company
**Line of Business:** Manufacture of plastics in primary forms
**Export Markets:** E U
**Issued Capital:** £36,000
**Directors:** T F Durkin, R H Bickerton
**Co. Secretary:** Darren Rowell
**US SIC:** 2821 **UK SIC:** 25140
**Bankers:** Lloyds TSB Bank plc (30-93-76)

| | 31-12-13 | 31-12-12 | 31-12-11 |
|---|---|---|---|
| TA | 4,289,223 | 4,289,223 | 4,289,223 |
| NW | 4,289,223 | 4,289,223 | 4,289,223 |

DUNS 22-116-3301

## S E A Transport Ltd

25 Bluestem Road, Ipswich, Suffolk IP3 9RR
**Tel:** 01473276400 **Fax:** 01473717533
**Web:** www.seatrans.co.uk
**Reg No:** 4135441 **Estd:** 2001 Private Limited Company
**Line of Business:** Road haulage and transport services
**Issued Capital:** £100
**Directors:** Mrs S Smith, F R Smith, Mrs J Smith, C M Smith
**Co. Secretary:** Frazer Smith
**Branches:** S E A Transport Ltd, Unit 25, Bluestem Road, Ipswich, Suffolk IP3 9RR
**US SIC:** 4789 **UK SIC:** 77002

| | 31-12-13 | 31-12-12 | 31-12-11 |
|---|---|---|---|
| TO | 6,656,899 | 6,581,049 | 5,942,324 |
| P/L | 144,322 | 35,417 | 154,448 |
| NW | 144,679 | 138,127 | 224,595 |
| WC | (447,625) | (448,652) | (240,906) |
| Emp. | 58 | 59 | 61 |

DUNS 77-903-5588

## S E C Recruitment Ltd

**(Subsidiary of:** Rdl Corporation Ltd)
R D L House, 1 Chertsey Road, Woking, Surrey GU21 5AD
**Tel:** 01483228190
**Web:** www.secrecruitment.com
**Reg No:** 5808613 **Estd:** 2006 Private Limited Company
**Line of Business:** Labour recruitment and provision of personnel
**Export Sales:** £9,673,443
**Issued Capital:** £1
**Director:** S G Britton
**Co. Secretary:** James Gardner
**US SIC:** 7361 **UK SIC:** 83954
**Bankers:** Barclays Bank Plc (20-72-17)

| | 31-12-13 | 31-12-12 | 31-12-11 |
|---|---|---|---|
| TO | 15,758,943 | 14,610,176 | 13,562,248 |
| P/L | 930,062 | 850,405 | 886,991 |
| NW | 1,923,839 | 1,827,746 | 1,780,780 |
| WC | 1,888,294 | 1,763,129 | 1,739,312 |
| Emp. | 52 | 61 | 44 |

DUNS 21-899-8946

## S E Davis & Son Ltd

Edgioake Lane, Astwood Bank, Redditch, Worcestershire B96 6BG
**Tel:** 01527892716 **Fax:** 01527-893356
**Web:** www.sedavis.co.uk
**Reg No:** 0943697 **VAT No:** 110285025
**Estd:** 1960 Private Limited Company
**Line of Business:** Road haulage and transport services
**Issued Capital:** £100
**Principals:** R H Davis *(Managing)*, A W Jenkins, A M Davis, P A Davis, Ms L A Davis, Mrs S T Davis, Miss S E Davis
**Co. Secretary:** Mrs Christine Davis
**US SIC:** 4789, 4213
**UK SIC:** 77002, 72300
**Auditors:** Rigbey Harrison
**Bankers:** HSBC Bank plc (40-38-07)

| | 30-11-13 | 30-11-12 | 30-11-11 |
|---|---|---|---|
| TA | 7,242,167 | 5,885,429 | 5,307,815 |
| NW | 5,106,871 | 4,369,807 | 4,015,245 |
| WC | 1,529,982 | 1,501,137 | 1,342,517 |

DUNS 21-820-7954

## S E Dykes Bower Will Trust

6 High Street, Bishops Stortford, Hertfordshire CM23 2LU
**Tel:** 01223702435
**Web:** www.stanleytee.co.uk
**Estd:** 1995
**Line of Business:** Solicitors
**US SIC:** 8111 **UK SIC:** 83500
**Employees:** 160

DUNS 23-350-4211 **Imp**

## S. E. Marshall & Co. Ltd

Alconbury Hill, Huntingdon, Cambridgeshire PE28 4HY
**Tel:** 08445576700
**Web:** www.marshalls-seeds.co.uk
**Reg No:** 0048629NI **Estd:** 2012 Private Limited Company
**Line of Business:** Growing of cereals and other crops not elsewhere classified
**Issued Capital:** £85
**Directors:** J B Mcveigh, E J Conroy, R H Lavery, F Keenan
**Co. Secretary:** John Mcveigh
**Branches:** S E Marshall & Co Alconbury hill,Huntingdon Cambridgeshire PE28 4HY
**US SIC:** 0119 **UK SIC:** 01001
**Auditors:** McKeague Morgan & Co
**Bankers:** The Bank Of Ireland (90-23-97)

| | 31-08-13 | 31-08-12 | 31-08-11 |
|---|---|---|---|
| TA | 1,381,191 | 1,449,192 | 1,089,983 |
| NW | 433,488 | 264,289 | 68,667 |
| WC | 462,723 | 206,435 | 58,750 |

DUNS 21-779-7282

## S E V Group

Unit 3 Park Square, Thorncliffe Park Estate, Newton Chambers Road, Chapeltown, Sheffield, South Yorkshire S35 2PH
**Tel:** 01142965737
**Web:** www.sev.co.uk
**Estd:** 2011 Partnership
**Line of Business:** Electrical engineers
**Partner:** T Fisher
**US SIC:** 8911 **UK SIC:** 83701
**Employees:** 200

DUNS 73-604-0101 **Exp**

## S F Ltd

Riverside Road, Barnstaple, Devon EX31 1LZ
**Tel:** 01271326633
**Web:** www.sflchimneys.com
**Reg No:** 4865090 **VAT No:** 811395247
**Estd:** 2003 Private Limited Company
**Line of Business:** Chimney builders
**Export Sales:** £2,517,718
**Trading Style:** Sfl
**Issued Capital:** £2,561,990
**Directors:** J Lee, Ms M S Stamm
**Co. Secretary:** Arthur Stamm
**Responsibilities**
**Senior:** Ben Gibbs *(Marketing Coordinator)*
**Marketing:** Ben Gibbs *(Marketing Coordinator)*
**Sales:** john dyson *(Sales Manager)*
**Health & Safety:** Steve Whitten *(Health & Safety Officer)*
**Facilities:** Steve Slade *(Facilities Manager)*
**Branches:** S F Ltd, Unit 7, Mullacott Cross Industrial Estate, Ilfracombe, Devon EX34 8PL
**US SIC:** 1799, 8911
**UK SIC:** 50000, 83701
**Auditors:** BDO Stoy Hayward LLP
**Bankers:** Fortis Bank London Bch (formerly Generale Bk) (40-52-62)

| | 30-06-14 | 30-06-13 | 30-06-12 |
|---|---|---|---|
| TO | 9,322,949 | 9,127,810 | 8,208,128 |
| P/L | 610,281 | 683,382 | 318,807 |
| NW | 4,207,870 | 3,719,920 | 3,202,219 |
| WC | 3,212,098 | 2,895,746 | 2,342,738 |
| Emp. | 86 | 80 | 76 |

DUNS 21-043-8023

## S F T Dental Laboratory

120 Turves Green, Birmingham, West Midlands B31 4BL
**Tel:** 01214-751001
**Web:** www.sftdentallab.co.uk
**Estd:** 2000 Partnership
**Line of Business:** Dental practice activities
**Proprietor:** K Fields
**US SIC:** 8021 **UK SIC:** 95400
**Employees:** 93

DUNS 21-741-0836 **Imp**

## S G A Technologies Ltd

**(Subsidiary of:** Cbpg Innovations Ltd)
Shire Hill, Saffron Walden, Essex CB11 3AQ
**Tel:** 01799-527264 **Fax:** 01799-528066
**Web:** www.sgatech.co.uk
**Reg No:** 0968536 **VAT No:** 214149687
**Estd:** 1969 Private Limited Company
**Line of Business:** Manufacturers and suppliers of seals
**Export Sales:** £363,380
**Issued Capital:** £3,000
**Director:** P J Game
**Co. Secretary:** Christopher Brown
**Responsibilities**
**Senior:** Melvin Patient *(Production Manager)*
**Health & Safety:** Melvin Patient *(Production Manager)*
**Facilities:** Steven Desilva *(Operations Coordinator)*
**Engineering:** Melvin Patient *(Production Manager)*
**US SIC:** 3494, 3999
**UK SIC:** 32880, 49590
**Auditors:** Deloitte & Touche
**Bankers:** National Westminster Bank Plc (60-18-10)

| | 30-06-13 | 30-06-12 | 30-06-11 |
|---|---|---|---|
| TO | 4,880,075 | N/A | N/A |
| P/L | 161,162 | N/A | N/A |
| NW | 3,257,017 | 3,083,747 | 3,011,006 |
| WC | 2,871,239 | 2,697,543 | 2,532,817 |
| Emp. | 84 | N/A | N/A |

DUNS 73-996-4976

## S G Court Ltd

Warren House Warren Road, Kingston-Upon-Thames, Surrey KT2 7HY
**Tel:** 01892542275
**Web:** www.sgcourt.co.uk
**Reg No:** 5246907 **Estd:** 1982 Private Limited Company
**Line of Business:** Chemists dispensing
**Issued Capital:** £14,000,000
**Directors:** Dr P J Brown, Mrs V K Good, O L O'Callaghan-Brown
**Co. Secretary:** Mrs Patricia Brown
**US SIC:** 5912 **UK SIC:** 64300
**Auditors:** Alan Cooper Saunders Angel

| | 31-03-14 | 31-03-13 | 31-03-12 |
|---|---|---|---|
| TO | 15,233,026 | 14,090,715 | 15,137,591 |
| P/L | (633,952) | (809,342) | (500,760) |
| NW | 4,226,931 | 3,934,364 | 3,792,824 |
| WC | 2,847,384 | 2,472,511 | 2,580,514 |
| Emp. | 177 | 174 | 169 |

DUNS 21-701-0050

## S G H Properties Llp

Tonge Bridge Industrial Estate, Bolton, Lancashire BL2 6AA
**Tel:** 01204529374
**Web:** www.sghmoulds.co.uk
**Reg No:** 0360041OC **Estd:** 1977
**Line of Business:** Precision engineers
**Responsibilities**
**Finance:** Lyn Farrow *(Senior Finance Administrator)*
**HR:** Kevin Mclarty *(Human Resources Manager)*
**US SIC:** 8911 **UK SIC:** 83701

| | 31-03-14 | 31-03-13 | 31-03-12 |
|---|---|---|---|
| TA | 4,355,327 | 3,112,722 | 3,144,893 |
| NW | 640,000 | 720,000 | 700,632 |
| WC | 1,961,495 | 1,478,261 | 1,411,843 |

DUNS 21-737-7001

## S G Hambros Trust Company (Guernsey) Ltd

**(Subsidiary of:** Societe Generale)
Hambro House Po Box 6, St Julians Avenue Street Peter Port, Guernsey, Channel Islands GY1 3AE
**Tel:** 01481726521 **Fax:** 01481710742
**Web:** www.sghambros.com
**Reg No:** 0001093G **Estd:** 1967 Private Limited Company
**Line of Business:** Banks and financial institutions
**Issued Capital:** £2,500,000
**Principals:** C E Hambro *(Chairman)*, B A Taylor *(Managing)*, P J Morgan, J F Tuke, J M Beaumont, T P O'Leary, E E Barnett, Mrs S M Cross
**Co. Secretary:** A Boss
**Responsibilities**
**Senior:** Alan Boss *(Human Resources Manager)*, R Olliver *(Chief Executive Officer)*
**IT:** David Blondel *(IT Manager)*
**HR:** Alan Boss *(Human Resources Manager)*, Camilla Le-Maitre *(Personnel Manager)*
**Health & Safety:** Camilla Le-Maitre *(Personnel Manager)*
**Facilities:** Camilla Le-Maitre *(Personnel Manager)*
**Purchasing:** Colin Penny *(Purchasing Manager)*
**US SIC:** 6012 **UK SIC:** 81402
**Employees:** 100

DUNS 50-511-1930

## S G Petch Ltd

Mcmullen Road, Darlington, County Durham DL1 1XZ
**Tel:** 08009804532 **Fax:** 01325362637
**Web:** www.imgroup.co.uk
**Reg No:** 2479069 **Estd:** 1995 Private Limited Company
**Line of Business:** Sale of new motor vehicles
**Trading Style:** S G Petch Ltd
**Issued Capital:** £56,897
**Principals:** S G Petch *(Managing)*, A Hodgson, Ms S M Petch
**Co. Secretary:** Simon Rees
**Branches:** S G Petch Ltd, 20 Green Howards Road, Richmond, North Yorkshire DL10 4SY
**US SIC:** 5511, 5521, 5531
**UK SIC:** 65100
**Auditors:** Kenneth Easby & Co
**Bankers:** Barclays Bank Plc (20-25-29)

| | 30-04-14 | 30-04-13 | 30-04-12 |
|---|---|---|---|
| TO | 127,273,833 | 110,654,763 | 111,440,515 |
| P/L | 858,340 | 108,314 | 697,913 |
| NW | 5,637,398 | 5,183,239 | 5,154,870 |
| WC | (948,882) | (843,946) | (1,239,332) |
| Emp. | 269 | 246 | 236 |

DUNS 73-748-0467

## S G S Ltd

Unit 39 Stoneferry Park, Foster Street, Hull, North Humberside HU8 8BT
**Tel:** 01482-610488
**Web:** www.sg-scaffolding.com
**Reg No:** 2923721 **Estd:** 1994 Private Limited Company
**Line of Business:** Scaffolds and work platform erectors
**Issued Capital:** £5,000
**Principals:** S J Gainey *(Managing)*, J Balmer
**Branches:** S G S Ltd, Airport Road West, Belfast, Belfast BT3 9ED
**US SIC:** 1799 **UK SIC:** 50000
**Auditors:** Dutton Moore

| | 31-03-14 | 31-03-13 | 31-03-12 |
|---|---|---|---|
| TA | 2,045,532 | 1,151,616 | 1,141,670 |
| NW | 178,909 | (190,407) | (370,559) |
| WC | 616,202 | 300,100 | 37,023 |

DUNS 21-588-0882

## S G S Studios

Unit 3 Priory Park East, Hull, North Humberside HU1 3HA
**Tel:** 01482973000
**Estd:** 2011 Proprietorship
**Line of Business:** Copying services
**Proprietor:** Miss J Holmes
**US SIC:** 2753 **UK SIC:** 47545
**Employees:** 70

DUNS 39-713-6961 **Imp**

## S G Technologies Ltd

**(Subsidiary of:** S G Technologies Group Ltd)
Ferry Lane, Rainham, Essex RM13 9YH
**Tel:** 01708558411 **Fax:** 01708554021
**Web:** www.sgmagnets.com
**Reg No:** 2163295 **VAT No:** 798622962
**Estd:** 1987 Private Limited Company
**Line of Business:** Manufacture of electronic instruments and appliances for measuring, checking, testing, navigating and other purposes, except industrial process control equipment
**Export Sales:** £12,797,000
**Trading Style:** Sg Technologies Group
**Issued Capital:** £2,960,002
**Directors:** J Swift, S T Williams, T G Robinson, J S Taylor, S A Hutcheon
**Co. Secretary:** Brian Mabbott
**Responsibilities**
**Senior:** Lee Dudack *(Manager)*
**US SIC:** 3999, 3079
**UK SIC:** 49590, 48360
**Auditors:** Arram Berlyn Gardner
**Bankers:** Barclays Bank Plc (20-95-61)

| | 31-03-14 | 31-03-13 | 31-03-12 |
|---|---|---|---|
| TO | 13,197,000 | 11,007,000 | 11,387,000 |
| P/L | 1,144,000 | 457,000 | 733,000 |
| NW | 3,219,000 | 1,778,000 | 2,037,000 |
| WC | 5,614,000 | 4,792,000 | 3,913,000 |
| Emp. | 152 | 145 | 138 |

DUNS 42-471-1075

## S H A C Ltd

29 Bedford Street, Belfast BT2 7EJ
**Tel:** 02890246811
**Web:** www.shac.freeserve.co.uk
**Reg No:** 0000187IP **Estd:** 1977 Friendly Society
**Line of Business:** Individual & Family Social Services
**Principals:** Miss J Fullerton *(Chairman)*, Miss U Leahy, Miss E Fitzgerald, Miss E Himpey, B Corrigan, Miss E Trainor, Miss S Mccoy, D Carson
**Responsibilities**
**Senior:** Gtainne Leppard *(Director)*
**Admin:** Alison Ahern *(Secretary)*
**Branches:** S H A C Ltd, Unit 3, 126 Strand Rd, Londonderry, Co Londonderry BT48 7PB
**US SIC:** 8321 **UK SIC:** 96111
**Auditors:** BDO Stoy Hayward
**Employees:** 52

DUNS 22-505-9559 **Imp-Exp**

## S H L Group Ltd

**(Subsidiary of:** The Corporate Executive Board Company)
The Pavilion, 1 Atwell Place, Thames Ditton, Surrey KT7 0NE
**Tel:** 02083358000
**Web:** www.shl.com
**Reg No:** 1328744 **Estd:** 1977 Private Limited Company
**Line of Business:** Management and business consultants
**Export Markets:** Worldwide
**Trading Style:** Ceb
**Issued Capital:** £677,273,069
**Directors:** D E Ryell, M D Franks
**Responsibilities**
**Senior:** Diane Hove *(Vice President)*, Caroline Paxman *(President, Americas)*, Jason Pilbrow *(Manager)*, Emanual Rhilac *(Manager)*, Helen Shipp *(Distribution Controller)*, Scott Troeller *(Non-Executive Director)*
**Marketing:** Monika Baran *(Senior E-Marketing Manager)*, Paul Levett *(Chief Product Officer)*, Edina Racz *(Marketing Manager)*, Julian Wenban *(Marketing Director)*
**Sales:** Mohamed Farid *(Regional Manager - Middle East)*, Catherine Harms *(Manager, Sales)*, Hayley Moorhouse *(Account Manager)*
**IT:** Claire Little *(Head of Training)*, Andy McCallum *(IT Manager)*
**HR:** Claire Little *(Head of Training)*, Paul Wesley *(Human Resources Director)*
**Health & Safety:** Mark Eates *(Facilities Manager)*

**Facilities:** Mark Eates *(Facilities Manager)*
**Purchasing:** Mark Eates *(Facilities Manager)*
**Branches:** S H L Group Ltd, Woodstock House, Woodstock Lane North, Surbiton, Surrey KT6 5HN
**US SIC:** 7392 **UK SIC:** 83951
**Auditors:** KPMG LLP
**Bankers:** HSBC Bank plc (40-44-11)

| | 31-12-13 | 31-12-12 | 31-12-11 |
|---|---|---|---|
| TO | 27,625,000 | 26,884,000 | 26,534,000 |
| P/L | 15,886,000 | 81,134,000 | 13,624,000 |
| NW | 210,582,000 | 193,979,000 | 110,345,000 |
| WC | 193,154,000 | 176,551,000 | 17,261,000 |
| Emp. | 455 | 391 | 352 |

DUNS 21-626-5439 **Imp-Exp**

## S H Racing Ltd

90 Main Road, Hawkwell, Hockley, Essex SS5 4JH
**Web:** www.auto-plas.co.uk
**Reg No:** 0665717 **VAT No:** 250569361
**Estd:** 1960 Private Limited Company
**Line of Business:** Other service activities not elsewhere classified
**Export Markets:** Germany; Italy; U S A
**Issued Capital:** £1,250
**Director:** S Harris
**Responsibilities**
**Senior:** Gwendoline Harris *(Manager)*
**US SIC:** 8999 **UK SIC:** 83954
**Auditors:** MWS
**Bankers:** National Westminster Bank Plc (60-17-38)

| | 31-12-13 | 31-12-12 | 31-12-11 |
|---|---|---|---|
| TA | 3,226,598 | 4,028,502 | 3,999,631 |
| NW | 2,761,971 | 3,690,460 | 3,719,411 |
| WC | 429,084 | 959,626 | 1,138,408 |

DUNS 21-585-7996

## S H S Group Ltd

S H S House, Airport Road West, Belfast BT3 9ED
**Tel:** 028-9045-4647 **Fax:** 028-9073-4834
**Web:** www.shs-group.co.uk
**Reg No:** 0011256NI **Estd:** 1975 Private Limited Company
**Line of Business:** Agents involved in the sale of food, beverages and tobacco
**Export Sales:** £27,546,429
**Trading Style:** S H S Sales & Marketing
**Issued Capital:** £250,000
**Directors:** Mrs B A Salters, Ms E Birchall, Ms E Sloan, J Sloan, Ms K Salters, R M Howard, A W Richmond
**Co. Secretary:** Arthur Richmond
**Responsibilities**
**Senior:** Barry Vance *(Despatch Manager)*
**HR:** Barry Vance *(Despatch Manager)*
**Health & Safety:** Barry Vance *(Despatch Manager)*
**Facilities:** Barry Vance *(Despatch Manager)*
**Fleet:** Barry Vance *(Despatch Manager)*
**Branches:** S H S Group Ltd, 2-3 Oriel Villas, Oriel Road, Cheltenham, Gloucestershire GL50 1XN
**US SIC:** 5149 **UK SIC:** 61700
**Auditors:** Grant Thornton UK LLP
**Bankers:** Northern Bank Ltd (95-00-01)

| | 03-01-14 | 28-12-12 | 30-01-11 |
|---|---|---|---|
| TO | 393,273,381 | 391,229,330 | 430,230,993 |
| P/L | 19,415,403 | 18,363,543 | 25,752,259 |
| NW | 45,914,326 | 41,724,566 | 35,964,183 |
| WC | 56,189,773 | 50,886,770 | 45,868,999 |
| Emp. | 737 | 688 | 710 |

DUNS 23-907-0204

## S Harris Ophthalmic Optician

65 High Street, West Wickham, Kent BR4 0LS
**Tel:** 020-8777-1337
**Web:** www.stevenharris-opticians.com
**VAT No:** 523518755 **Estd:** 1974 Partnership
**Line of Business:** Retail of optical goods
**Partners:** S Harris, Mrs S Harris
**Branches:** S Harris Ophthalmic Optician, 88 High Street, London SE20 7HB
**US SIC:** 5999 **UK SIC:** 65600
**Employees:** 60

DUNS 22-335-4494

## S Hill

Unit 3 Caddick Road, Knowsley Business Park, Prescot, Merseyside L34 9HP
**Tel:** 01515494000
**Web:** www.barringtonscleaning.co.uk
**Proprietorship**
**Line of Business:** Traditional cleaning activities
**Proprietor:** S Hill
**US SIC:** 7349 **UK SIC:** 92300
**Employees:** 400

DUNS 23-589-6172 **Imp**

## S I A S Ltd

37 Manor Place, Edinburgh, Midlothian EH3 7EB
**Web:** www.sias.com
**Reg No:** 0112949SC **Estd:** 1988 Private Limited Company
**Line of Business:** Transportation consultants
**Issued Capital:** £63,738
**Principals:** S Druitt *(Managing)*, Ms S Muirhead, B Mathieson
**Co. Secretary:** Hbjg Secretarial Limited
**Responsibilities**
**Marketing:** Pete Sykes *(Sales & Marketing Manager)*
**Sales:** Pete Sykes *(Sales & Marketing Manager)*
**Branches:** S I A S Ltd, Sias Ltd, 13 Rose Terrace, Perth, Perthshire PH1 5HA
**US SIC:** 4712, 8911
**UK SIC:** 77002, 83701
**Auditors:** Lyon Windram Crolla
**Bankers:** Clydesdale Bank Plc (82-45-05)

| | 31-12-13 | 31-12-12 | 31-12-11 |
|---|---|---|---|
| TA | 1,365,527 | 1,461,593 | 1,222,016 |
| NW | 961,605 | 983,479 | 882,929 |
| WC | 890,211 | 943,226 | 843,252 |

DUNS 21-824-8763 **Imp-Exp**

## S I Group - Uk Ltd

(**Subsidiary of:** Si Group Inc.)
Four Ashes, Wolverhampton, West Midlands WV10 7BT
**Tel:** 01902-790555
**Web:** www.siigroup.com
**Reg No:** 0667049 **VAT No:** 278810429
**Estd:** 1960 Private Limited Company
**Line of Business:** Manufacture of mastics and sealants
**Export Markets:** Europe; Middle East; S Africa; Ghana; Nigeria; Sri Lanka
**Export Sales:** £44,209,000
**Issued Capital:** £53,039,820
**Directors:** Z G Steele, A H Missy, R Barlow, P J Ingham, S T Haller
**Co. Secretary:** Mrs Barbara Dias
**Responsibilities**
**Senior:** Frank A Bozich *(President and Chief Executive)*, William A Scheffer *(Vice President, Operational Ex)*, Christopher T Roberts *(Vice President, Sourcing and C)*
**Marketing:** Neil Greeff *(Senior Marketing Executive)*
**Sales:** Jackie Holmes *(Senior Sales Executive)*, Christopher T Roberts *(Vice President, Sourcing and C)*
**US SIC:** 2891 **UK SIC:** 25620
**Auditors:** KPMG LLP
**Bankers:** Barclays Bank Plc (20-93-15)

| | 31-12-13 | 31-12-12 | 31-12-11 |
|---|---|---|---|
| TO | 49,449,000 | 48,374,000 | 56,718,000 |
| P/L | 1,708,000 | 1,147,000 | 5,916,000 |
| NW | 18,140,000 | 13,747,000 | 16,134,000 |
| WC | 14,230,000 | 14,120,000 | 15,081,000 |
| Emp. | 79 | 75 | 71 |

DUNS 23-112-8653 **Imp**

## S I S (Science in Sport) Ltd

(**Subsidiary of:** Science in Sport Plc)
Ashwood, Blackburn, Lancashire BB6 8BB
**Tel:** 01254246060
**Web:** www.scienceinsport.com
**Reg No:** 2742833 **VAT No:** 604598037
**Estd:** 1993 Private Limited Company
**Line of Business:** Manufacture of homogenised food preparations and dietetic food
**Trading Style:** Science in Sport
**Issued Capital:** £599,383
**Directors:** Mrs V Sparks, S N Moon
**Co. Secretary:** Mrs Vivienne Sparks
**US SIC:** 2023, 5122
**UK SIC:** 41303, 61800
**Auditors:** Bishops
**Bankers:** HSBC Bank plc (40-13-15)

| | 31-03-14 | 31-03-13 | 31-03-12 |
|---|---|---|---|
| TO | 6,846,809 | 5,522,240 | 6,113,880 |
| P/L | (948,901) | (185,855) | (282,635) |
| NW | 391,721 | 674,144 | 764,085 |
| WC | (452,837) | 54,675 | 244,943 |
| Emp. | 55 | 48 | 48 |

DUNS 51-649-8755

## S J K Taxis

Coney Park Industrial Estate, Coney Park Harrogate Road, Yeadon, Leeds, West Yorkshire LS19 7XS
**Tel:** 01132588600
**Web:** www.sjktaxis.co.uk
**Estd:** 1978 Proprietorship
**Line of Business:** Taxis
**Proprietor:** J Kotchie
**Responsibilities**
**Senior:** Simon Murphey *(Manager)*
**US SIC:** 4121 **UK SIC:** 72200
**Employees:** 100

DUNS 51-566-0723

## S J R Holdings Ltd

Lowfield, Marton, Welshpool, Powys SY21 8JX
**Tel:** 01743-891858
**Web:** www.sjroberts.com
**Reg No:** 5847509 **VAT No:** 870176814
**Estd:** 2006 Private Limited Company
**Line of Business:** Management activities of holding companies
**Issued Capital:** £103
**Directors:** S J Roberts, M Phillips
**Co. Secretary:** Ms Linda Evans
**US SIC:** 6711 **UK SIC:** 83962

| | 30-06-13 | 30-06-12 | 30-06-11 |
|---|---|---|---|
| TO | 16,193,691 | 13,272,349 | 10,764,572 |
| P/L | 316,088 | 408,400 | (221,466) |
| NW | 2,116,726 | 1,934,434 | 1,690,884 |
| WC | 612,672 | 522,809 | 311,123 |
| Emp. | 92 | 75 | 78 |

DUNS 50-583-1313

## S J S Cleaning Services Ltd

1 Lakeside, Oxen Lease, Ashford, Kent TN23 4GU
**Tel:** 01233666026
**Web:** www.sjscleaning.net
**Reg No:** 2525814 **Estd:** 1990 Private Limited Company
**Line of Business:** Traditional cleaning activities
**Issued Capital:** £8,500
**Principals:** M G Sutherland *(Managing)*, G West, B Hemsworth
**Co. Secretary:** Ms Beryl Sutherland
**US SIC:** 7399 **UK SIC:** 83954
**Auditors:** Magee Gammon
**Bankers:** HSBC Bank plc (40-08-32)

| | 31-03-14 | 31-03-13 | 31-03-12 |
|---|---|---|---|
| TA | 289,231 | 320,757 | 418,052 |
| NW | 145,284 | 156,692 | 233,953 |
| WC | 104,558 | 103,740 | 190,641 |

DUNS 28-871-0742 **Imp**

## S K S Ltd

Unit 2, Berkhamsted, Hertfordshire HP4 1EG
**Tel:** 01442-291400 **Fax:** 01442-863683
**Web:** www.skskeys.co.uk
**Reg No:** 1042581 **VAT No:** 424122889
**Estd:** 1972 Private Limited Company
**Line of Business:** Wholesale of hardware, plumbing and heating equipment and supplies
**Issued Capital:** £200
**Principals:** T W Brett *(Managing)*, Mrs R Brett, R Hawkins
**Co. Secretary:** Ms Lorna Betts
**Branches:** S K S Ltd, 25 Belmont Circlekenton Lane Kenton, Harrow, Middlesex HA3 8RF
**US SIC:** 5074 **UK SIC:** 61300
**Auditors:** Gowers
**Bankers:** The Royal Bank Of Scotland Plc (16-20-38)

| | 31-12-13 | 31-12-12 | 31-12-11 |
|---|---|---|---|
| TO | 7,392,703 | 7,250,576 | N/A |
| P/L | 932,993 | 934,956 | N/A |
| NW | 3,593,745 | 3,090,756 | 2,579,308 |
| WC | 2,764,815 | 2,272,679 | 1,803,792 |
| Emp. | 47 | 42 | N/A |

DUNS 21-929-3537

## S L Engineering Ltd.

Manor Farm, Sleaford, Lincolnshire NG34 0HJ
**Tel:** 01778-440228
**Web:** www.sl-engineering.co.uk
**Reg No:** 1147082 **VAT No:** 129496436
**Estd:** 1973 Private Limited Company
**Line of Business:** Precision engineers
**Issued Capital:** £10,000
**Principals:** J L Pickard *(Financial)*, Ms G Stevenson, S Fox, Mrs C S Pickard, S Eggleton, S C Stevenson
**US SIC:** 3499 **UK SIC:** 31694
**Bankers:** Barclays Bank Plc (20-34-60)

| | 28-02-14 | 28-02-13 | 29-02-12 |
|---|---|---|---|
| TA | 2,195,983 | 1,643,670 | 1,766,784 |
| NW | 1,053,181 | 773,362 | 869,348 |
| WC | 651,916 | 351,191 | 410,671 |

DUNS 23-301-7982

## S L P Decorations

16 Grindstone Crescent, Knaphill, Woking, Surrey GU21 2RY
**Tel:** 01483-475447
**VAT No:** 641365156 **Estd:** 2004 Proprietorship
**Line of Business:** Painters and decorators
**Proprietor:** Ms S Fox
**US SIC:** 1721 **UK SIC:** 50400
**Employees:** 50

DUNS 34-905-8490

## S Luca Ltd

32-38 High Street, Musselburgh, Midlothian EH21 7AG
**Web:** www.lucasicecream.co.uk
**Reg No:** 0296884SC **Estd:** 2008 Private Limited Company
**Line of Business:** Manufacture of rusks and biscuits; manufacture of preserved pastry goods and cakes
**Issued Capital:** £2
**Directors:** Ms Y Luca, M Luca
**US SIC:** 2052, 5462
**UK SIC:** 41970, 64100

| | 31-03-14 | 31-03-13 | 31-03-12 |
|---|---|---|---|
| TA | 2 | 2 | 2 |
| NW | 2 | 2 | 2 |

DUNS 77-517-3255

## S M C Design & Draughting Services Ltd

No 6 Colwick Road, Nottingham, Nottinghamshire NG2 4BU
**Tel:** 0115-940-0002 **Fax:** 0115-961-4491
**Web:** www.smcdesign.com
**Reg No:** 2986708 **Estd:** 1994 Private Limited Company
**Line of Business:** Other engineering activities
**Issued Capital:** £2
**Director:** S Mcballantine
**Co. Secretary:** Ms Diane Mcballantine
**Responsibilities**
**Senior:** Steven McBallantine *(Director)*
**US SIC:** 8911 **UK SIC:** 83701
**Bankers:** National Westminster Bank Plc (60-80-09)

| | 30-11-13 | 30-11-12 | 30-11-11 |
|---|---|---|---|
| TA | 5,749,795 | 4,873,446 | 3,246,895 |
| NW | 3,763,217 | 3,255,862 | 2,446,474 |
| WC | 3,544,503 | 3,021,329 | 2,394,735 |

DUNS 42-353-2816

## S M C Ltd

4 Canterbury Road, Sittingbourne, Kent ME10 4SB
**Tel:** 01795592100 **Fax:** 07789006473
**Web:** www.smc-cars.com
**Reg No:** 0226356SC **Estd:** 1964 Private Limited Company
**Line of Business:** Car dealers (new & used)
**Issued Capital:** £450
**Director:** M Stenhouse
**Co. Secretary:** Alison Stenhouse
**Branches:** S M C Ltd, 325-327 Long Lane, Uxbridge, Middlesex UB10 9JU
**US SIC:** 5511 **UK SIC:** 65100

| | 31-03-14 | 31-03-13 | 31-03-12 |
|---|---|---|---|
| TA | 17,699 | 11,079 | 20,283 |
| NW | 931 | 597 | 1,284 |
| WC | 507 | 33 | 860 |

DUNS 21-381-9233 **Imp**

## S M E

Mill Road, Steyning, West Sussex BN44 3GY
**Tel:** 01903814321
**Web:** www.sme.ltd.uk
**Estd:** 1946 Proprietorship
**Line of Business:** Precision engineers
**Proprietor:** A Standard
**Responsibilities**
**Senior:** Ray Byrne *(Warehouse Manager)*
**Purchasing:** Ray Byrne *(Warehouse Manager)*
**US SIC:** 8911 **UK SIC:** 83701
**Bankers:** Woolwich Plc (10-80-02)
**Employees:** 56

DUNS 77-471-5403

## S M H Products Ltd

29-35 Maxwell Street, South Shields, Tyne and Wear NE33 4PU
**Tel:** 01914566000 **Fax:** 01914-567777
**Web:** www.smhproducts.com
**Reg No:** 2968133 **Estd:** 1994 Private Limited Company
**Line of Business:** Asbestos products & removal
**Export Sales:** £2,921,080
**Issued Capital:** £750
**Directors:** O S Smith, D T Rowe, D Meehan
**Responsibilities**
**Finance:** Sarah Bezuidenhout *(Financial Director)*
**Branches:** S M H Products Ltd, 186 Drews Lane, Birmingham, West Midlands B8 2SL
**US SIC:** 1799, 3549, 7394
**UK SIC:** 50000, 32212, 84000
**Auditors:** Robson Laidler LLP
**Bankers:** Barclays Bank Plc (20-80-47)

| | 28-02-14 | 28-02-13 | 29-02-12 |
|---|---|---|---|
| TO | 15,277,293 | 13,776,969 | 13,095,290 |
| P/L | 895,222 | 398,187 | 249,330 |
| NW | 2,694,343 | 1,906,582 | 1,585,268 |
| WC | 1,550,145 | 626,915 | 290,488 |
| Emp. | 115 | 113 | 119 |

DUNS 21-398-3922

## S M K Building Contractors

Unit 15 Palmerston Road Palmers Vale, Business Centre, Barry, South Glamorgan CF63 2XA
**Tel:** 01446-741888
**Web:** www.smkbuilding.com
**Estd:** 1999 Proprietorship
**Line of Business:** Building construction contractors
**Proprietor:** M Perry
**US SIC:** 1522 **UK SIC:** 50100
**Employees:** 100

DUNS 73-716-1380
### S M P Group Holdings Ltd
2 Swan Road, London SE18 5TT
**Tel:** 020-8855-5535 **Fax:** 02083177414
**Web:** www.smpgroup.co.uk
**Reg No:** 2918389 **Estd:** 1993 Private Limited Company
**Line of Business:** Printing not elsewhere classified
**Trading Style:** S M P Group Holdings Ltd
**Issued Capital:** £2,061
**Principals:** P J Mitchell *(Managing)*, D R Jarvis, Dr J W Oppenheimer, B Slade
**Co. Secretary:** Paul Chapman
**US SIC:** 2752, 7399
**UK SIC:** 47544, 83954
**Auditors:** Baker Tilly
**Bankers:** Barclays Bank Plc (20-24-61)

| | 31-12-13 | 31-12-12 | 31-12-11 |
|---|---|---|---|
| TO | 32,268,405 | 30,471,022 | 30,124,837 |
| P/L | 2,537,933 | 2,180,434 | 1,989,871 |
| NW | 8,572,151 | 7,538,186 | 6,475,545 |
| WC | 5,940,125 | 4,920,412 | 2,645,271 |
| Emp. | 170 | 162 | 159 |

DUNS 51-998-7085
### S M R S Ltd
Express Networks 2, Manchester M4 6BD
**Tel:** 0161-200-1444 **Fax:** 0161-200-1455
**Web:** www.smrs.co.uk
**Reg No:** 3365804 **Estd:** 1997 Private Limited Company
**Line of Business:** Advertising agency services
**Issued Capital:** £20,000
**Directors:** R N Lewis, A D Jeal, Ms S Sturgess, T C Windsor
**Co. Secretary:** Anthony Blease
**Responsibilities**
**Purchasing:** Cathy Young *(Office Products Buyer)*
**US SIC:** 7319, 7311
**UK SIC:** 83800
**Auditors:** Finlay Robertson
**Bankers:** HSBC Bank plc (40-31-28)

| | 31-10-13 | 31-10-12 | 31-10-11 |
|---|---|---|---|
| TO | 17,751,428 | 17,158,850 | 14,721,461 |
| P/L | 1,022,960 | 1,031,396 | 721,547 |
| NW | 734,875 | 714,920 | 408,578 |
| WC | (764,929) | (780,436) | (881,824) |
| Emp. | 56 | 46 | 41 |

DUNS 23-312-0455 **Imp**
### S McConnell & Sons Ltd
184 Carrigenagh Road, Kilkeel, Newry, Co Down BT34 4QA
**Tel:** 028-4176-3717
**Web:** www.smcconnellandsons.com
**Reg No:** 0046012NI **Estd:** 1963 Private Limited Company
**Line of Business:** Stone and exterior cleaning
**Issued Capital:** £30,000
**Directors:** H Mcconnell, R Mcconnell, W Mcconnell, K S Mcconnell, D I Mcconnell, S S Mcconnell, A W Mcconnell, S L Mcconnell
**Co. Secretary:** Alan Mcconnell
**Branches:** S Mcconnell & Sons Ltd, 2 Ascham Rd, Bournemouth, Dorset BH8 8LX
**US SIC:** 1799, 3281
**UK SIC:** 50000, 24503
**Bankers:** First Trust Bank (aib Group (uk) Plc) (93-83-27)

| | 31-03-14 | 31-03-13 | 31-03-12 |
|---|---|---|---|
| TO | N/A | 4,166,251 | 6,820,438 |
| P/L | N/A | 138,962 | 242,847 |
| NW | 663,240 | 726,953 | 683,721 |
| WC | 418,204 | 356,918 | 345,768 |
| Emp. | N/A | 64 | 100 |

DUNS 21-636-7045 **Imp**
### S Morris Ltd
Tout Quarry, Tout Road, Somerton, Somerset TA11 7AN
**Tel:** 01458-223991 **Fax:** 01458-223181
**Web:** www.smorris.co.uk
**Reg No:** 0781444 **VAT No:** 185555922
**Estd:** 1963 Private Limited Company
**Line of Business:** Manufacture of concrete products for construction purposes
**Issued Capital:** £5,000
**Principals:** B S Perry *(Managing)*, Mrs R J Perry
**Co. Secretary:** Brian Perry
**Responsibilities**
**Senior:** Dave Hanney *(General Manager)*
**Branches:** S Morris Ltd, 20 Gazelle Road, Lynx Trading Estate, Yeovil, Somerset BA20 2PJ
**US SIC:** 3271, 3273
**UK SIC:** 24370, 24360
**Auditors:** Milsted Langdon
**Bankers:** National Westminster Bank Plc (60-24-37)

| | 30-04-14 | 30-04-13 | 30-04-12 |
|---|---|---|---|
| TO | 19,603,248 | 13,963,800 | 13,356,238 |
| P/L | 2,467,069 | 542,937 | 82,481 |
| NW | 12,324,852 | 10,386,856 | 9,867,977 |
| WC | 2,340,267 | 304,637 | (113,649) |
| Emp. | 56 | 54 | 53 |

DUNS 23-362-8671
### S N C B C
Winchester House, Baxter Road, Sunderland, Tyne and Wear SR5 4LW
**Tel:** 01915373231
**Web:** www.sunderlandcommunitynetwork.org.uk
**Estd:** 1987 Proprietorship
**Line of Business:** Business and commerce centres
**Principals:** R Symonds *(Chairman)*, Miss N Vokes *(Proprietor)*
**Branches:** Sunderland North Community Business Centre, 283 Southwick Road, Sunderland, Tyne and Wear SR5 2AB
**US SIC:** 7361, 7392
**UK SIC:** 83954, 83951
**Employees:** 170

DUNS 21-318-7453 **Imp**
### S. Norton & Co Ltd
Bankfield House, Regent Road, Bootle, Merseyside L20 8RQ
**Tel:** 01519 553300 **Fax:** 01519 553399
**Web:** www.snorton.com
**Reg No:** 1859428 **VAT No:** 164589624
**Estd:** 1964 Private Limited Company
**Line of Business:** Recycling
**Issued Capital:** £100,000
**Principals:** J A Harry *(Managing)*, M P Harry
**Co. Secretary:** Charles Harry
**Branches:** S. Norton & Co Ltd, Regent Rd, Liverpool, Merseyside L20 1DQ
**US SIC:** 3031, 3341
**UK SIC:** 48123, 22470
**Auditors:** PricewaterhouseCoopers LLP

| | 31-12-13 | 31-12-12 | 31-12-11 |
|---|---|---|---|
| TO | 208,637,000 | 276,856,000 | 352,250,000 |
| P/L | (2,545,000) | 1,965,000 | 15,888,000 |
| NW | 89,494,000 | 96,468,000 | 94,887,000 |
| WC | 67,620,000 | 74,636,000 | 74,030,000 |
| Emp. | 135 | 136 | 122 |

DUNS 73-458-0447 **Imp-Exp**
### S P C International Ltd
Unit 5 The Grand Union Office Park, Packet Boat Lane, Uxbridge, Middlesex UB8 2GH
**Tel:** 01895430900
**Web:** www.spcint.com
**Reg No:** 4722278 **Estd:** 2001 Private Limited Company
**Line of Business:** Cash machines
**Export Sales:** £8,108,893
**Issued Capital:** £5,000
**Directors:** J R Hemphill, T M Hope, D C Clarke
**Co. Secretary:** Brian Orr
**Responsibilities**
**IT:** Terry Spall *(Systems Manager)*
**Operations:** Wendy Deamer *(Operations Manager)*
**Branches:** S P C International Ltd, Unit 6-7, Bennetts Field Trading Estate, Wincanton, Somerset BA9 9DT
**US SIC:** 3579, 6711
**UK SIC:** 33010, 83962
**Auditors:** MHA MacIntyre Hudson
**Bankers:** National Westminster Bank Plc (60-17-21)

| | 30-09-13 | 30-09-12 | 30-09-11 |
|---|---|---|---|
| TO | 18,003,089 | 17,494,287 | 16,108,896 |
| P/L | 613,281 | 196,914 | 392,572 |
| NW | 939,351 | 222,535 | (84,487) |
| WC | 372,975 | 402,563 | 873,157 |
| Emp. | 210 | 190 | 190 |

DUNS 22-952-6876
### S P G Media Group Ltd
**(Subsidiary of:** Progressive Digital Media Group Plc)
Brunel House, London W2 1LA
**Tel:** 02079159660
**Web:** www.spgmedia.com
**Reg No:** 1309004 **VAT No:** 242281093
**Estd:** 1996 Private Limited Company
**Line of Business:** Book publishers
**Issued Capital:** £4,556,056
**Directors:** M T Danson, S J Pyer
**Co. Secretary:** Stephen Bradley
**US SIC:** 7311 **UK SIC:** 83800
**Auditors:** Grant Thornton UK LLP
**Bankers:** Barclays Bank Plc (20-71-64)

| | 31-12-13 | 31-12-12 | 31-12-11 |
|---|---|---|---|
| TA | 11,564,000 | 11,914,000 | 15,861,000 |
| P/L | (47,000) | (3,770,000) | (256,000) |
| NW | 11,214,000 | 11,261,000 | 15,031,000 |
| WC | 6,407,000 | 6,465,000 | 6,454,000 |

DUNS 23-719-1127
### S P Graham Ltd
Ground Floor, Belfast BT1 6GE
**Tel:** 02890963963 **Fax:** 028-9096-3988
**Web:** www.seangraham.com
**Reg No:** 0009702NI **Estd:** 1970 Private Limited Company
**Line of Business:** Gambling and betting activities
**Issued Capital:** £1
**Directors:** B Hayes, Mrs B E Graham, G D Graham
**Co. Secretary:** Ms Brenda Graham
**Branches:** S P Graham Ltd, 49 Church Place, Craigavon, Co Armagh BT66 6HD
**US SIC:** 7999 **UK SIC:** 97913
**Auditors:** B P Tanney & Co

| | 31-03-13 | 31-03-12 | 31-03-11 |
|---|---|---|---|
| TO | 5,835,978 | 5,575,062 | 5,759,375 |
| P/L | (1,299,668) | (114,281) | 736,835 |
| NW | 1,374,599 | 2,382,209 | 2,213,680 |
| WC | 515,234 | 882,243 | (676,457) |
| Emp. | 144 | 138 | 134 |

DUNS 21-811-2107
### S P I Associates
Arishi House, 20-22 Curtain Road, London EC2A 3NF
**Tel:** 02076554449
**Web:** www.spiassociates.com
**Estd:** 2012
**Line of Business:** Security activities
**US SIC:** 7393 **UK SIC:** 83954
**Employees:** 50

DUNS 73-578-0624 **Imp-Exp**
### S P P Pumps Ltd
**(Subsidiary of:** Kirloskar Brothers Limited)
1420 Lakeview, Arlington Business Park, Theale, Reading, Berkshire RG7 4SA
**Tel:** 01189-323-123
**Web:** www.spppumps.com
**Reg No:** 4839607 **VAT No:** 823268334
**Estd:** 2003 Private Limited Company
**Line of Business:** Manufacture of pumps
**Export Sales:** £64,441,590
**Issued Capital:** £1,950,000
**Directors:** O Shevlin, A S Kirloskar, S C Kirloskar, P B Shirke, A S Kirloskar
**Co. Secretary:** Jonathan Powell
**Responsibilities**
**Senior:** Mark Fussey *(Field Service Sales Manager)*
**IT:** Damian Hudson *(Information Systems Manager)*
**Purchasing:** Graham Brain *(Buyer)*
**Branches:** S P P Pumps Ltd, Unit 1, Stanstead Road, Eastleigh, Hampshire SO50 4RZ
**US SIC:** 3561, 5084
**UK SIC:** 32870, 61490
**Auditors:** Deloitte LLP
**Bankers:** Barclays Bank Plc (20-00-00)

| | 31-12-13 | 31-12-12 | 31-12-11 |
|---|---|---|---|
| TO | 87,141,845 | 67,997,448 | 69,204,842 |
| P/L | 5,864,716 | 5,543,291 | 5,037,819 |
| NW | 18,398,698 | 15,983,640 | 13,204,905 |
| WC | 12,702,907 | 10,835,568 | 9,262,127 |
| Emp. | 437 | 422 | 382 |

DUNS 21-810-4693 **Imp-Exp**
### S P S Technologies Ltd
Troon Industrial Area, 191 Barkby Road, Leicester, Leicestershire LE4 9HX
**Web:** www.spstech.com
**Reg No:** 0303951 **VAT No:** 566146331
**Estd:** 1935 Private Limited Company
**Line of Business:** Fasteners and fixings
**Export Markets:** E C, North America, South America and Worldwide
**Export Sales:** £47,925,000
**Trading Style:** T J Brooks Division, S P S Unbrako
**Issued Capital:** £6,208,779
**Directors:** Mrs S R Hagel, R S Pattee, Ms R A Beyer, J Randeria, A V Masterman, R P Becker, M J Quinn, S C Blackmore
**Co. Secretary:** Paul Edelstyn
**Responsibilities**
**Senior:** Sean Barrett *(Manager)*
**IT:** Matt Willey *(IT Manager)*
**Branches:** S P S Technologies Ltd, Po Box 76, Smethwick, West Midlands B66 2WE
**US SIC:** 3452, 3714
**UK SIC:** 31371, 35300
**Auditors:** Deloitte LLP

| | 30-03-14 | 31-03-13 | 31-03-12 |
|---|---|---|---|
| TO | 88,854,000 | 80,507,000 | 68,604,000 |
| P/L | 21,811,000 | 16,059,000 | 14,176,000 |
| NW | 78,428,000 | 66,267,000 | 50,728,000 |
| WC | 51,039,000 | 36,581,000 | 24,789,000 |
| Emp. | 654 | 597 | 523 |

DUNS 29-509-7240
### S Pugh & Son (Garden Centre) Ltd
Ty Nant Road, Morganstown, Cardiff, South Glamorgan CF15 8LB
**Tel:** 08445731007 **Fax:** 029-2084-3277
**Web:** www.robinsonsequestrian.com
**Reg No:** 1872960 **Estd:** 1955 Private Limited Company
**Line of Business:** Riding wear and equestrian supplies
**Trading Style:** Pugh's Garden Centre
**Issued Capital:** £5,000
**Principals:** C W Pugh *(Managing)*, I M Pugh, G N Pugh
**Co. Secretary:** Ms Winifred Pugh
**Responsibilities**
**Senior:** Jim Bentham *(Manager)*, Laura O'brien *(Store Manager)*
**Branches:** S Pugh & Son (Garden Centre) Ltd, Treerbert Rd, Cwmbran, Gwent NP44 2BZ
**US SIC:** 3161, 5431
**UK SIC:** 44201, 64100
**Auditors:** Hodge Bakshi
**Bankers:** National Westminster Bank Plc (56-00-41)

| | 31-01-14 | 31-01-13 | 31-01-12 |
|---|---|---|---|
| TA | 1,996,401 | 1,787,364 | 1,773,904 |
| NW | 991,308 | 940,269 | 938,225 |
| WC | 336,160 | 128,394 | 148,707 |

DUNS 21-778-4999
### S R A
50 Woodside, Thornwood, Epping, Essex CM16 6LJ
**Estd:** 2011
**Line of Business:** Traditional cleaning activities
**US SIC:** 7399 **UK SIC:** 83954
**Employees:** 48

DUNS 23-410-2445
### S R B Care Ltd
29a Castlegore Road, Castlederg, Co Tyrone BT81 7RU
**Tel:** 028 8167 9574 **Fax:** 028 8167 9494
**Web:** www.silverdalecare.co.uk
**Reg No:** 0055838NI **Estd:** 1991 Private Limited Company
**Line of Business:** Medical nursing home activities
**Trading Style:** Silverdale Care Home
**Issued Capital:** £1
**Director:** Mrs S R Brownlee
**Co. Secretary:** Ms Victoria Carroll
**Responsibilities**
**Senior:** Geraldine Browne *(Manageress)*
**US SIC:** 8051 **UK SIC:** 95100
**Auditors:** Brian McDaid & Co
**Bankers:** Northern Bank Ltd (95-02-64)

| | 31-03-14 | 31-03-13 | 31-03-12 |
|---|---|---|---|
| TA | 1,002,701 | 1,045,461 | 1,089,010 |
| NW | 211,295 | 187,626 | 164,669 |
| WC | (189,120) | (181,261) | (166,528) |

DUNS 34-837-6609
### S R Bailey Ltd
9 Station Road, Crynant, Neath, West Glamorgan SA10 8NW
**Tel:** 01639-750238 **Fax:** 01639751060
**Web:** www.srbaileypharmacies.com
**Reg No:** 2803757 **Estd:** 2002 Private Limited Company
**Line of Business:** Dispensing chemists
**Issued Capital:** £2
**Directors:** R A Street, K Rajja
**Responsibilities**
**Senior:** William Plenty *(Manager)*
**Branches:** S R Bailey Ltd, Dulais Road, Nant Y Cafn, Neath, West Glamorgan SA10 9EY
**US SIC:** 5912 **UK SIC:** 64300
**Auditors:** W R King & Co
**Bankers:** Barclays Bank Plc (20-58-72)

| | 31-08-13 | 31-08-12 | 31-08-11 |
|---|---|---|---|
| TO | 6,924,000 | 7,310,053 | 7,221,251 |
| P/L | 260,000 | 294,051 | 221,201 |
| NW | 1,318,000 | 910,720 | 496,028 |
| WC | 397,000 | 115,430 | (347,444) |
| Emp. | 62 | N/A | N/A |

DUNS 21-592-3776
### S R C Bede Sixth Form
Marsh House Avenue, Billingham, Cleveland TS23 3HB
**Web:** www.stockton.ac.uk
**Estd:** 2011 Proprietorship
**Line of Business:** Sixth form colleges
**Proprietor:** Mrs M Stanton
**US SIC:** 8221 **UK SIC:** 93100
**Employees:** 70

DUNS 21-123-7217 **Imp**
### S R M Industries Ltd
**(Subsidiary of:** Stanford Directors Ltd)
Station Road, Hatton, Derby, Derbyshire DE65 5EL
**Tel:** 01283814411
**Web:** www.srm-industries.com
**Reg No:** 6699670 **VAT No:** 939763174
**Estd:** 1988 Private Limited Company
**Line of Business:** Manufacture of other rubber products
**Issued Capital:** £160
**Directors:** M J Spare, P R Barton, J N Rodgers
**Co. Secretary:** Martin Spare
**Responsibilities**
**Senior:** Yvonne Spare *(Manager)*, Michael Spare *(CEO, Managing Director)*
**Finance:** Yvonne Spare *(Manager)*
**US SIC:** 3069 **UK SIC:** 48123
**Auditors:** McGregors Business Services
**Bankers:** HSBC Bank plc (40-33-30)

| | 31-10-13 | 31-10-12 | 31-10-11 |
|---|---|---|---|
| TA | 1,307,198 | 1,336,729 | 1,324,976 |
| NW | 87,818 | 141,872 | 145,918 |
| WC | 17,882 | 40,616 | (2,571) |

DUNS 29-880-8973

## S R S Rail System Ltd

(Subsidiary of: Srs Rail System (Holdings) Ltd)
Unit 3 Riverside Way, Bolsover, Chesterfield, Derbyshire S44 6GA
Tel: 01246241312 Fax: 01246825076
Web: www.srsrailuk.co.uk
Reg No: 2083871 Estd: 1986 Private Limited Company
Line of Business: Plant hire and leasing
Issued Capital: £20,000
Directors: S J Whatley, N J Whatley, J D Rooke, R M Whatley
Responsibilities
Senior: Karen Clark (Administrator)
Sales: Gethin Thomas (Business Development Manager)
US SIC: 7394 UK SIC: 84000
Auditors: Pesters

|  | 30-04-14 | 30-04-13 | 30-04-12 |
|---|---|---|---|
| TO | 8,047,692 | 5,407,537 | 5,383,522 |
| P/L | 1,064,505 | 491,165 | 626,837 |
| NW | 5,069,791 | 4,249,703 | 3,844,906 |
| WC | 2,300,032 | 1,668,079 | 1,780,110 |
| Emp. | 66 | 61 | 68 |

DUNS 29-858-1992     Imp

## S. Riddler Ltd

(Subsidiary of: Vistgate Ltd)
Saber Close, Newton Abbot, Devon TQ12 6TW
Tel: 01626835100
Web: www.riddlers.net
Reg No: 2060546 Estd: 1926 Private Limited Company
Line of Business: Fish merchants (wholesale)
Trading Style: Riddlers Quality Fish
Issued Capital: £1,000
Director: J A Lakeman
Co. Secretary: Edward Lakeman
US SIC: 5146 UK SIC: 61700
Bankers: Lloyds TSB Bank plc (30-96-06)

|  | 30-11-13 | 30-11-12 | 30-11-11 |
|---|---|---|---|
| TO | 14,433,715 | 13,745,589 | 9,867,877 |
| P/L | 603,808 | 541,994 | 90,515 |
| NW | 737,286 | 287,399 | (129,069) |
| WC | 634,854 | 217,650 | (327,331) |
| Emp. | 88 | 96 | 73 |

DUNS 23-763-9146

## S S E Energy Supply Ltd

(Subsidiary of: Sse Plc)
55 Vastern Road, Reading, Berkshire RG1 8BU
Tel: 08009808831
Web: www.sserugby.com
Reg No: 3757502 VAT No: 553769603
Estd: 1998 Private Limited Company
Line of Business: Distribution and trade in electricity
Trading Style: Southern Electric
Issued Capital: £147,500,001
Directors: A E Keeling, W K Morris
Co. Secretary: Peter Lawns
Branches: S S E Energy Supply Ltd, 18 Holton Rd, Barry, South Glamorgan CF63 4HD
US SIC: 7399 UK SIC: 83954
Auditors: KPMG Audit PLC
Following financial data are in thousands

|  | 31-03-14 | 31-03-13 | 31-03-12 |
|---|---|---|---|
| TO | 29,953,300 | 27,835,700 | 32,007,900 |
| P/L | 141,300 | (5,200) | (6,900) |
| NW | 169,300 | 146,600 | 310,700 |
| WC | 397,100 | 400,200 | 619,800 |
| Emp. | 1,190 | 1,385 | 1,937 |

DUNS 21-600-6322

## S S Osmund & Andrews R C P School

Falkirk Drive, Bolton, Lancashire BL2 6NW
Tel: 01204333070
Web: www.ss-osands.bolton.sch.uk
Estd: 1989
Line of Business: Schools (local authority)
Proprietor: J Thorpe
US SIC: 8211 UK SIC: 93200
Employees: 50

DUNS 34-939-7195

## S S P Group Plc

169 Euston Road, London NW1 2AE
Tel: 02075433300
Web: www.foodtravelexperts.com
Reg No: 5735966 Estd: 2006 Public Limited Company
Line of Business: Holding companies management activities
Export Sales: £1,106,600,000
Issued Capital: £5,376,837
Directors: Ms K E Swann, R J Barton, D Hennequin, J O Davies, I Dyson, P Franzen, V O Soerensen
Co. Secretary: Mrs Helen Byrne

Responsibilities
Senior: Leslie Cappetta (Chief Executive, America), Nick Inkster (Chief Executive, Northern and)
Sales: Sukh Tiwana (Group Commercial Director)
Admin: Helen Rylands (Personal Assistant)
HR: Chris Rayner (Human Resources Director)
US SIC: 6711, 5813, 5812
UK SIC: 83962, 66200, 66110
Auditors: KPMG LLP
Following financial data are in thousands

|  | 30-09-14 | 30-09-13 | 30-09-12 |
|---|---|---|---|
| TO | 1,827,100 | 1,827,200 | 1,737,500 |
| P/L | (13,500) | 16,200 | 14,400 |
| NW | (427,700) | (909,700) | (909,100) |
| WC | (132,500) | (41,600) | (40,900) |
| Emp. | 29,457 | 29,529 | 29,796 |

DUNS 23-569-7620     Imp-Exp

## S. Sacker (Claydon) Ltd

Gipping Road, Great Blakenham, Ipswich, Suffolk IP6 0JB
Tel: 01473830373
Web: www.sackers.co.uk
Reg No: 1526052 VAT No: 344544751
Estd: 1981 Private Limited Company
Line of Business: Rubber reclaimers
Export Markets: Worldwide
Export Sales: £17,631,538
Trading Style: Sackers Recycling
Issued Capital: £100
Principals: D G Dodds (Managing), A A Dodds (Managing), Mrs B I Dodds, C A Dodds
Co. Secretary: Ewan Dodds
Responsibilities
Senior: Agen Dodds (Manager)
Sales: Nigel Slinn (Commercial Manager)
Operations: Nigel Slinn (Commercial Manager)
Fleet: Stuart Spreadbridge (Transport Manager)
US SIC: 3031, 4953, 3341, 4959
UK SIC: 48123, 92110, 22470
Auditors: Ensors
Bankers: HSBC Bank plc (40-43-37)

|  | 30-04-14 | 30-04-13 | 30-04-12 |
|---|---|---|---|
| TO | 23,360,434 | 24,599,737 | 26,485,804 |
| P/L | (480,796) | 476,206 | 594,131 |
| NW | 3,324,858 | 3,534,962 | 3,188,220 |
| WC | (371,359) | (142,563) | 433,157 |
| Emp. | 61 | 57 | 58 |

DUNS 23-210-6497

## S T A Promotions

Second Floor, 3 Portwall Lane, Bristol, Avon BS1 6NB
Tel: 01179065905
Partnership
Line of Business: Marketing consultants
Partners: Mrs C Edwards, Mrs E Davige
US SIC: 7392 UK SIC: 83951
Employees: 50

DUNS 21-160-0861

## S T L Group P L C

St Johns Road, Woking, Surrey GU21 7SE
Tel: 01483715355 Fax: 01483-221854
Web: www.stlgroup.co.uk
Reg No: 1171409 Estd: 1974 Public Limited Company
Line of Business: Other business activities not elsewhere classified
Issued Capital: £50,000
Directors: A B Thorogood, M J Killeen
Branches: S T L Group P L C, 77 Maid Marian Way, Nottingham, Nottinghamshire NG1 6AJ
US SIC: 7399 UK SIC: 83954
Auditors: Grant Thornton UK LLP
Bankers: National Westminster Bank Plc (60-24-20)

|  | 31-03-14 | 31-03-13 | 31-03-12 |
|---|---|---|---|
| TO | 9,487,465 | 7,333,813 | 6,910,465 |
| P/L | 548,164 | 163,224 | 137,931 |
| NW | 1,003,478 | 1,076,155 | 1,104,378 |
| WC | 842,080 | 905,829 | 889,391 |
| Emp. | 85 | 72 | 62 |

DUNS 21-584-6227

## S T L Logistics

52 Mallusk Road, Newtownabbey, Co Antrim BT36 4PX
Tel: 02890831130
Web: www.stllogistics.ie
Estd: 2011
Line of Business: Driver hire agencies
Responsibilities
Senior: Terence Dougan (Manager)
US SIC: 4789 UK SIC: 77002
Employees: 80

DUNS 21-590-9464

## S T R C Coleg Sir Gar

Jobs Well Campus, Job's Well Road, Carmarthen, Dyfed SA31 3HY
Web: www.colegsirgar.ac.uk
Estd: 2011

Line of Business: Manufacture of workwear
Responsibilities
Senior: Gill Cole (Manager)
US SIC: 7399 UK SIC: 83954
Employees: 200

DUNS 52-623-3085

## S T R Enterprises Ltd

Waverley House, 30 The Oval, Benton, Benton, Newcastle-Upon-Tyne, Tyne and Wear NE12 9PP
Tel: 01912662800
Web: www.strenterprises.co.uk
Reg No: 3256878 VAT No: 686524401
Estd: 1996 Private Limited Company
Line of Business: Hotels, motels, and tourist resorts
Trading Style: Victoria Hotel, The Manor House Hotel & Country Club, The Honest Lawer Hotel
Issued Capital: £210,000
Directors: R A Sanderson, J T Sanderson, C S Sanderson, J J Sanderson
Co. Secretary: Ms Elizabeth Sanderson
Branches: S T R Enterprises Ltd, Croxdale Bridge, Croxdale, Durham, County Durham DH1 3SP
US SIC: 7011, 5812, 7999
UK SIC: 66500, 66110, 97913
Auditors: Glen C Rodger Ltd
Bankers: Bank Of Scotland (80-20-00)

|  | 31-01-14 | 31-01-13 | 31-01-12 |
|---|---|---|---|
| TO | 6,102,112 | 6,223,329 | 5,254,026 |
| P/L | 335,249 | 263,704 | 192,821 |
| NW | 4,332,580 | 4,175,590 | 4,040,583 |
| WC | (1,832,574) | (1,664,677) | (3,106,048) |
| Emp. | 193 | 193 | 185 |

DUNS 21-900-8286

## S T Services Electrical Ltd

Brulimar House Jubilee Road, Middleton, Manchester M24 2LX
Tel: 01618724755
Web: www.pfjones.co.uk
Reg No: 6086384 Estd: 2003 Private Limited Company
Line of Business: Electrical contractors and electricians
Issued Capital: £4
Director: A J Boardman
Co. Secretary: Ms Michelle Hooker
Responsibilities
Senior: Les Bailey (Sales Director)
Sales: Les Bailey (Sales Director)
US SIC: 1731 UK SIC: 50300

|  | 28-02-13 | 29-02-12 | 28-02-11 |
|---|---|---|---|
| TA | 38,412 | 57,700 | 61,006 |
| NW | 2,390 | 3,994 | 1,332 |
| WC | (6,707) | 13,997 | 10,547 |

DUNS 21-931-7880     Imp

## S. Teasdale (Hospital Equipment) Ltd

Haigh Avenue, Whitehill Industrial Estate, Stockport, Cheshire SK4 1NU
Tel: 01614805779
Web: www.teasdalehealthcare.com
Reg No: 1242976 Estd: 1976 Private Limited Company
Line of Business: Hospital equipment
Export Sales: £80,529
Issued Capital: £55,554
Principals: B C Teasdale (Managing), E Stott (Financial), Ms E L Palmer
Co. Secretary: Barry Teasdale
Responsibilities
Senior: Anne Teasdale (Manager)
US SIC: 5199, 3841
UK SIC: 61900, 37201
Auditors: Hurst & Co Accountants LLP
Bankers: National Westminster Bank Plc (01-08-38)

|  | 31-03-14 | 31-03-13 | 31-03-12 |
|---|---|---|---|
| TO | 8,041,674 | 7,335,213 | 6,862,110 |
| P/L | 875,302 | 241,136 | 310,447 |
| NW | 2,133,904 | 2,255,424 | 2,082,982 |
| WC | 1,307,182 | 1,063,811 | 920,318 |
| Emp. | 140 | 141 | 136 |

DUNS 50-112-1917

## S. Thorogood & Sons (Covent Garden) Ltd

Hammonds Farm, Hammonds Road, Little Baddow, Chelmsford, Essex CM3 4BJ
Tel: 01245-473362
Reg No: 2318779 Estd: 1994 Private Limited Company
Line of Business: Wholesalers of fruit and vegetable
Issued Capital: £810
Principals: G H Thorogood (Chairman), T J Thorogood, S J Thorogood
Co. Secretary: Andrew Thorogood
Responsibilities
Senior: Anthony Shamash (Manager)
Branches: S. Thorogood & Sons (Covent Garden) Ltd, Stand 87-88A New Spitalfields Market, 23 Sherrin Road, London E10 5SQ
US SIC: 5148 UK SIC: 61700
Auditors: Clemence Hoar Cummings

Bankers: National Westminster Bank Plc (60-18-01)

|  | 31-10-14 | 31-10-13 | 31-10-12 |
|---|---|---|---|
| TO | 17,696,560 | 20,128,260 | 17,151,810 |
| P/L | (43,265) | (154,250) | (180,842) |
| NW | 551,005 | 595,680 | 764,562 |
| WC | 200,374 | 326,617 | 533,802 |
| Emp. | 58 | 60 | 56 |

DUNS 23-530-5211

## S W Bruce & Company Ltd

(Subsidiary of: S W B Holdings Ltd)
Unit 1a, Goodwin Road Dominion Business Park, London N9 0BG
Tel: 020-8807-1089
Web: www.swbruce.co.uk
Reg No: 3529448 Estd: 1950 Private Limited Company
Line of Business: Other construction work involving special trades
Trading Style: S W Bruce & Company Ltd
Issued Capital: £90,001
Principals: R Messling (Managing), Ms P Messling
Co. Secretary: Lee Messling
Responsibilities
Senior: David Messling (Manager)
US SIC: 1799, 1751
UK SIC: 50000, 50400
Auditors: Barnes Roffe

|  | 30-06-13 | 30-06-12 | 30-06-11 |
|---|---|---|---|
| TO | 15,109,177 | 18,898,872 | 16,413,868 |
| P/L | 654,660 | 1,516,084 | 1,281,788 |
| NW | 1,624,473 | 2,139,090 | 2,318,807 |
| WC | 1,421,397 | 1,928,553 | 2,176,426 |
| Emp. | 50 | 50 | 51 |

DUNS 42-367-1143

## S W C Composite Products Ltd

Unit 1 The Gateway, Dunslow Road Eastfield, Scarborough, North Yorkshire YO11 3UT
Tel: 01723-582666 Fax: 01723582667
Web: www.swctradeframes.co.uk
Reg No: 4354732 Estd: 1989 Private Limited Company
Line of Business: Management activities of production holding companies
Trading Style: Swc Trade Frames
Issued Capital: £253,101
Director: P Richings
Co. Secretary: Mrs Susan Richings
Responsibilities
Sales: Mark Catchpole (Sales Director)
IT: Mike Moore (IT Manager)
US SIC: 6711 UK SIC: 83962
Bankers: Barclays Bank Plc (20-00-00)

|  | 31-03-13 | 31-03-12 | 31-03-10 |
|---|---|---|---|
| TO | 8,407,793 | 9,510,366 | 8,136,686 |
| P/L | (87,885) | (126,333) | (124,571) |
| NW | 429,803 | 357,621 | 304,381 |
| WC | (90,275) | (156,360) | (113,668) |
| Emp. | 93 | 89 | 85 |

DUNS 21-724-6248     Exp

## S W Group Logistics Ltd

Unit 6, Swindon, Wiltshire SN2 2QJ
Tel: 01793-523750 Fax: 01793-542304
Web: www.swgrouplogistics.com
Reg No: 1439705 Estd: 1967 Private Limited Company
Line of Business: Road haulage and transport services
Trading Style: Car & Truck Services
Issued Capital: £9,097
Directors: R Knox, K G Knox
Co. Secretary: Mrs Pauline Knox
Responsibilities
Finance: Tony Nash (Financial Director)
Marketing: Tony Nash (Financial Director)
Branches: S W Group Logistics Ltd, Chelworth Industrial Estate, Unit A, Swindon, Wiltshire SN6 6HE
US SIC: 4789 UK SIC: 77002
Auditors: Bentley Jennison
Bankers: National Westminster Bank Plc (60-21-40)

|  | 31-12-13 | 31-12-12 | 31-12-11 |
|---|---|---|---|
| TO | 11,119,677 | 9,857,966 | 8,591,199 |
| P/L | 244,797 | 173,185 | 142,733 |
| NW | 1,830,457 | 1,649,683 | 1,532,723 |
| WC | 453,316 | 324,390 | 315,542 |
| Emp. | 135 | 119 | 105 |

DUNS 21-602-1595

## S W N Y Mor Holiday Park

Aberlerry, Ynyslas, Borth, Dyfed SY24 5JU
Tel: 01970871233
Web: www.sunbourne.com
Estd: 1996 Proprietorship
Line of Business: Camping site operators
Proprietor: A Crutchley
Responsibilities
Senior: William Lloyd-Jones (General Manager)
US SIC: 7033 UK SIC: 66701
Employees: 50

DUNS 22-247-1067
## S Walker Transport Ltd
Bransons Cross Farm, Beoley Lane, Redditch, Worcestershire B98 9DP
**Tel:** 01564-742426 **Fax:** 01564-742455
**Reg No:** 4265074 **Estd:** 1990 Private Limited Company
**Line of Business:** Road haulage and transport services
**Issued Capital:** £467,200
**Director:** S Walker
**Co. Secretary:** Ms Rosemarie Walker
**US SIC:** 4789 **UK SIC:** 77002

| | 30-09-13 | 30-09-12 | 30-09-11 |
|---|---|---|---|
| TA | 2,180,543 | 2,623,183 | 3,225,187 |
| NW | 640,782 | 377,166 | 243,790 |
| WC | (267,341) | (685,338) | (898,288) |

DUNS 29-691-9053
## S Y S (Scaffolding Contractors) Ltd
Old North Ropery Works, Carr Hill, Doncaster, South Yorkshire DN4 8DE
**Tel:** 01302340132 **Fax:** 01302-730275
**Web:** www.sysscaffolding.com
**Reg No:** 2015440 **VAT No:** 436588710
**Estd:** 1986 Private Limited Company
**Line of Business:** Scaffolds and work platform erectors
**Trading Style:** S Y S (Scaffolding Contractors) Ltd
**Issued Capital:** £38,000
**Managing Director:** J T Pearce
**Co. Secretary:** Joseph Pearce
**Responsibilities**
**Finance:** Janet Pearce *(Operations Director)*
**HR:** Janet Pearce *(Operations Director)*
**US SIC:** 7394, 5082
**UK SIC:** 84000, 61490
**Auditors:** Johnson Walker
**Bankers:** HSBC Bank plc (40-45-29)

| | 31-03-14 | 31-03-13 | 31-03-12 |
|---|---|---|---|
| TA | 1,895,912 | 2,021,006 | 2,314,883 |
| NW | 423,899 | 594,664 | 671,144 |
| WC | (497,203) | (252,314) | 183,792 |

DUNS 21-143-8243
## S1 Taxis Ltd
Globe 2 Business Centre, 128 Maltravers Road, Sheffield, South Yorkshire S2 5AZ
**Tel:** 01142-555111
**Web:** www.s1taxis.com
**Reg No:** 6746788 **Estd:** 2008 Private Limited Company
**Line of Business:** Taxis and private hire vehicles
**Issued Capital:** £3
**Directors:** H Rehman, R G Khan
**Co. Secretary:** Arshad Ali
**Responsibilities**
**Senior:** Mohammed Faryad *(Manager)*
**US SIC:** 4121 **UK SIC:** 72200

| | 31-03-14 | 31-03-13 | 31-03-12 |
|---|---|---|---|
| TO | 350,294 | 78,354 | 83,996 |
| P/L | 30,606 | (17,605) | (418) |
| NW | (28,345) | (58,951) | (41,346) |
| WC | 34,325 | 2,718 | (1,254) |

DUNS 23-711-9529
## S2 Partnership Ltd
23 Station Road, Sheringham, Norfolk NR26 8RF
**Tel:** 01412783108
**Reg No:** 3706897 **Estd:** 1999 Private Limited Company
**Line of Business:** Technical testing and analysis
**Issued Capital:** £2,200
**Directors:** S R Smith, R C Mead, R J Bagley, Ms L Harrison
**Co. Secretary:** Ms Susan Smith
**Branches:** S2 Partnership Ltd, Avenue Business Park, Unit 14-16, Cambridge, Cambridgeshire CB23 4EY
**US SIC:** 7397 **UK SIC:** 83702

| | 31-01-14 | 31-01-13 | 31-01-12 |
|---|---|---|---|
| TA | 1,771,146 | 1,849,603 | 1,719,755 |
| NW | 1,058,491 | 1,200,428 | 1,033,754 |
| WC | 1,016,978 | 1,175,737 | 996,723 |

DUNS 21-970-1377 **Imp**
## S247 Plc
**(Subsidiary of:** S247 Group Ltd)
Units 3 And 4 Lower Park Farm, Birmingham, West Midlands B48 7ER
**Tel:** 01527-598388
**Web:** www.sports2000-srcc.com
**Reg No:** 6151896 **VAT No:** 916598189
**Estd:** 2007 Public Limited Company
**Line of Business:** Retail sale via mail order house
**Export Sales:** £4,515,112
**Issued Capital:** £50,000
**Directors:** S J Millington, J C Lawrance, O G Nation, Mrs S J Millington
**Co. Secretary:** David Rice
**Responsibilities**
**Senior:** Roger Eden *(Manager)*
**US SIC:** 5961 **UK SIC:** 65600
**Auditors:** Deloitte LLP

| | 30-09-13 | 30-09-12 | 30-09-11 |
|---|---|---|---|
| TO | 18,055,522 | 16,414,840 | 13,652,729 |
| P/L | 109,204 | 1,029,894 | 1,018,455 |
| NW | 3,648,536 | 3,753,069 | 2,839,970 |
| WC | 3,105,929 | 3,339,820 | 2,477,475 |
| Emp. | 46 | 44 | 38 |

DUNS 23-544-4432
## S4C Rhyngwladol Cyf
**(Subsidiary of:** Welsh Fourth Channel Authority)
Parc Ty Glas, Llanishen, Cardiff, South Glamorgan CF14 5DU
**Fax:** 029-2075-4444
**Web:** www.s4c.co.uk
**Reg No:** 3542938 **Estd:** 1997 Private Limited Company
**Line of Business:** Motion picture and video distribution
**Trading Style:** S4c
**Issued Capital:** £1
**Directors:** D T Bryant, E G Morris, I H Jones, Dr C Bell, G M Roberts, H H Evans, D J Sanders
**Co. Secretary:** Elin Morris
**Responsibilities**
**Senior:** Kathryn Morris *(Financial Director)*
**Finance:** Kathryn Morris *(Financial Director)*
**IT:** Huw Edmunds *(Head of IT)*
**US SIC:** 7829, 4833
**UK SIC:** 97112, 07411
**Auditors:** Grant Thornton
**Bankers:** Bank Of Wales Plc (12-23-00)

| | 31-03-14 | 31-12-12 | 31-03-11 |
|---|---|---|---|
| TO | 2,696,395 | 2,791,466 | 2,465,076 |
| P/L | 1,078,771 | 1,279,659 | 829,789 |
| NW | 103,702 | 354,931 | 325,272 |
| WC | 103,702 | 354,931 | 325,272 |

DUNS 73-933-5961
## S5 Agency World Ltd
Vintage Yard, 61 Bermondsey Street, London SE1 3XF
**Tel:** 0207939953
**Web:** www.s-5.org
**Reg No:** 5186549 **VAT No:** 898702957
**Estd:** 2004 Private Limited Company
**Line of Business:** Shipping companies
**Issued Capital:** £116,650
**Directors:** Ms A Y Lam, K H Peters, F F Kanoo, A Campoy Garcia, J Tapias Herrero, E P Lim, R Moss
**Co. Secretary:** Graham Bog
**US SIC:** 4712 **UK SIC:** 77002
**Auditors:** Montpelier Audit Ltd

| | 31-12-13 | 31-12-12 | 31-12-11 |
|---|---|---|---|
| TA | 692,904 | 1,581,742 | 5,023,243 |
| NW | (333,795) | (468,075) | (1,075,933) |
| WC | (391,514) | (479,641) | (1,075,933) |

DUNS 21-925-9348
## S.A. & Partners (Cardiff) Ltd
Hadfield Road, Cardiff, South Glamorgan CF11 8AQ
**Tel:** 029 2022 9962 **Fax:** 029 2023 8581
**Web:** www.ba-cc.co.uk
**Reg No:** 1429865 **Estd:** 1979 Private Limited Company
**Line of Business:** Non-specialised wholesale of food, beverages and tobacco
**Trading Style:** B.A. Cash & Carry
**Issued Capital:** £51,484
**Principals:** S Ahmed *(Managing)*, Z Ahmed, T Ahmed
**Co. Secretary:** Sabri Ahmed
**US SIC:** 5149, 5182
**UK SIC:** 61700
**Auditors:** Hayvenhursts Ltd
**Bankers:** Barclays Bank Plc (20-18-15)

| | 28-02-14 | 28-02-13 | 29-02-12 |
|---|---|---|---|
| TO | 93,519,264 | 95,153,151 | 96,376,605 |
| P/L | 3,140,909 | 825,852 | 871,154 |
| NW | 8,709,725 | 6,565,095 | 6,331,592 |
| WC | (548,199) | (2,796,904) | (3,077,225) |
| Emp. | 177 | 171 | 177 |

DUNS 28-980-6333
## S.A. Labels Ltd
**(Subsidiary of:** S.A. Labels Group Ltd)
Station Road, Oakworth, Keighley, West Yorkshire BD22 0ED
**Tel:** 01535646177 **Fax:** 01535-646739
**Web:** www.salabels.co.uk
**Reg No:** 1777502 **VAT No:** 405939342
**Estd:** 1983 Private Limited Company
**Line of Business:** Labelling stamping and imprinting equipment
**Issued Capital:** £250,000
**Principals:** J Hutton *(Managing)*, Mrs J M Hutton
**Co. Secretary:** Jonathan Hutton
**Responsibilities**
**Marketing:** Mike Reynolds *(Sales & Marketing Director)*
**Sales:** Mike Reynolds *(Sales & Marketing Director)*
**Admin:** Liz Carter *(Administration Manager)*
**HR:** Liz Carter *(Administration Manager)*, Mike Reynolds *(Sales & Marketing Director)*
**Operations:** Mike Reynolds *(Sales & Marketing Director)*
**Engineering:** Anthony Coulthard *(Production Manager)*
**Branches:** S.a. Labels Ltd, 1 Malin Close, Haverhill, Suffolk CB9 0LY
**US SIC:** 3551 **UK SIC:** 32441
**Auditors:** Baker Tilly
**Bankers:** Yorkshire Bank Plc (05-05-35)

| | 28-02-14 | 28-02-13 | 28-02-12 |
|---|---|---|---|
| TO | N/A | N/A | 6,298,758 |
| P/L | N/A | N/A | 149,508 |
| NW | 1,789,568 | 1,729,042 | 1,561,141 |
| WC | 927,321 | 890,734 | 568,549 |
| Emp. | N/A | N/A | 45 |

DUNS 39-951-2250
## Saab G B Pension Plan Trustee Co Ltd
Griffin House, Osborne Road, Luton, Bedfordshire LU1 3YT
**Tel:** 08453009395 **Fax:** 01582426693
**Web:** www.saab.co.uk
**Reg No:** 2257413 **Estd:** 1988 Private Limited Company
**Line of Business:** Other business activities not elsewhere classified
**Issued Capital:** £12
**Directors:** C Gentleman, R B Hulme
**Co. Secretary:** Eversecretary Limited
**US SIC:** 7399 **UK SIC:** 83954

| | 31-03-14 | 31-03-13 | 31-03-12 |
|---|---|---|---|
| TA | 12 | 12 | 12 |
| NW | 12 | 12 | 12 |

DUNS 39-702-0801 **Imp-Exp**
## Saab Seaeye Ltd
**(Subsidiary of:** Saab Ab)
20 Brunel Way, Segensworth East, Fareham, Hampshire PO15 5SD
**Fax:** 01489898001
**Web:** www.saabgroup.com
**Reg No:** 2022671 **Estd:** 1986 Private Limited Company
**Line of Business:** Manufacturers of photographic equipment and supplies
**Export Sales:** £26,630,574
**Issued Capital:** £14,084
**Directors:** M R Exeter, J M Robertson, Ms A M Kammeby, B A Johansson, B S Svensson
**Co. Secretary:** Matthew Bates
**Responsibilities**
**Finance:** Simon Warne *(Financial Controller)*
**IT:** Colin Leigh *(IT Manager)*, Ash Ridley *(IT Manager)*
**HR:** Pete Vallender *(Production Manager)*
**Facilities:** Simon Warne *(Financial Controller)*
**Engineering:** Pete Vallender *(Production Manager)*
**US SIC:** 3861, 3559
**UK SIC:** 37330, 32863
**Auditors:** Hopper Williams & Bell Ltd

| | 31-12-13 | 31-12-12 | 31-12-11 |
|---|---|---|---|
| TO | 32,780,706 | 25,831,922 | 24,048,208 |
| P/L | 4,689,802 | 3,771,258 | 3,218,759 |
| NW | 18,272,780 | 14,703,651 | 11,847,021 |
| WC | 14,310,463 | 13,833,203 | 10,510,602 |
| Emp. | 154 | 126 | 101 |

DUNS 28-969-7088 **Imp-Exp**
## Saab Technologies Uk Ltd
**(Subsidiary of:** Saab Ab)
16 Harcourt Street, London W1H 4AD
**Tel:** 02075353430
**Web:** www.saabgroup.com
**Reg No:** 1724399 **Estd:** 1983 Private Limited Company
**Line of Business:** Activities of private training providers
**Export Markets:** Worldwide
**Trading Style:** Saab Training Systems, Saab Training Systems Uk
**Issued Capital:** £100,000
**Directors:** J F Ohlson, J M Robertson, M Franklin, G T Samuelsson
**Co. Secretary:**
Norose Company Secretarial Servi
**Responsibilities**
**Senior:** Nils Hultin *(Manager)*, Mikael Nord *(Manager)*
**US SIC:** 8999 **UK SIC:** 83954
**Auditors:** Fawcetts
**Bankers:** Skandinaviska Enskilda Banken Ab (publ) (40-48-65)

| | 31-12-13 | 31-12-12 | 31-12-11 |
|---|---|---|---|
| TO | 7,308,953 | 6,008,433 | 5,379,723 |
| P/L | 607,688 | 391,141 | 323,446 |
| NW | 1,660,859 | 1,210,293 | 938,177 |
| WC | 1,466,583 | 972,208 | 661,444 |
| Emp. | 46 | 41 | 33 |

DUNS 21-664-0739 **Imp**
## Saacke Combustion Services Ltd
Level 3 Room 2 Empress Business Centre, Chester Road, Manchester M16 9EA
**Tel:** 01618775113
**Web:** www.saacke.com
**Reg No:** 7184556 **Estd:** 2010 Private Limited Company
**Line of Business:** Engineers (general)
**Trading Style:** Saacke Combustion Services Limited
**Issued Capital:** £350,000
**Director:** M J Cook
**Co. Secretary:** Stephen Donald
**US SIC:** 8911 **UK SIC:** 83701
**Auditors:** Jones Avens
**Bankers:** Lloyds TSB Bank plc (30-96-11)

| | 31-12-13 | 31-12-12 | 31-12-11 |
|---|---|---|---|
| TO | 9,202,244 | 8,842,320 | 8,150,038 |
| P/L | 1,068,537 | 1,114,279 | 1,372,119 |
| NW | 1,558,073 | 1,459,425 | 1,337,194 |
| WC | 1,403,978 | 1,241,106 | 1,131,393 |
| Emp. | 72 | 77 | 68 |

DUNS 21-011-4914
## Saatchi & Saatchi Group Ltd
**(Subsidiary of:** Publicis Groupe S.A.)
80 Charlotte Street, London W1A 1AQ
**Tel:** 020-7636-5060 **Fax:** 02074361998
**Web:** www.saatchimasius.co.uk
**Reg No:** 0231824 **Estd:** 1928 Private Limited Company
**Line of Business:** Planning, creation and placement of advertising activities
**Export Sales:** £32,237,000
**Issued Capital:** £286,448
**Directors:** A Harker, M Djaba
**Co. Secretary:** Mrs Sarah Bailey
**Branches:** Saatchi & Saatchi Group Ltd, 15 Lower Regent St, London SW1Y 4LR
**US SIC:** 7311 **UK SIC:** 83800
**Auditors:** Ernst & Young LLP
**Bankers:** Bank Of Scotland (12-11-03)

| | 31-12-13 | 31-12-12 | 31-12-11 |
|---|---|---|---|
| TO | 57,497,000 | 99,377,000 | 99,585,000 |
| P/L | 27,046,000 | 14,499,000 | 12,819,000 |
| NW | 72,419,000 | 56,294,000 | 44,330,000 |
| WC | 71,640,000 | 58,454,000 | 49,185,000 |
| Emp. | 369 | 318 | 341 |

DUNS 29-891-6628 **Imp**
## Sabeti Wain Aerospace Ltd
Diamond House, Lane End Road, High Wycombe, Buckinghamshire HP12 4HX
**Tel:** 01494512664
**Web:** www.sabetiwainaerospace.com
**Reg No:** 2094671 **Estd:** 1987 Private Limited Company
**Line of Business:** Other software consultancy and supply
**Issued Capital:** £99,996
**Directors:** Mrs M S Wain, N Wain, P Sabeti, Mrs M Sabeti, P Sabeti
**Co. Secretary:** Parviz Sabeti
**US SIC:** 7399 **UK SIC:** 83954
**Auditors:** O"Sullivan & Co
**Bankers:** Lloyds TSB Bank plc (30-94-28)

| | 31-07-13 | 29-02-12 | 28-07-11 |
|---|---|---|---|
| TA | 2,484,932 | 3,434,372 | 1,830,977 |
| NW | 1,361,932 | 1,309,119 | 1,129,605 |
| WC | 502,301 | 503,058 | 708,450 |

DUNS 77-126-1237
## Sabhal Mor Ostaig (Developments) Ltd
Sleat, Isle of Skye IV44 8RQ
**Tel:** 01471888000 **Fax:** 01471888000
**Web:** www.smo.uhi.ac.uk
**Reg No:** 0137223SC **VAT No:** 624008182
**Estd:** 1973 Private Limited Company
**Line of Business:** Other letting of own property
**Issued Capital:** £2
**Directors:** D ( Munro, M Campbell
**Responsibilities**
**Senior:** Boyd Robertson *(Principal)*
**Marketing:** Angela MacGillivray *(Marketing Manager)*, Ange McKay *(Marketing Officer)*
**Facilities:** Carlotta Graham *(Facilities Manager)*
**Branches:** Sabhal Mor Ostaig (Developments) Ltd, 2 Wentworth Street, Portree, Isle Of Skye IV51 9EJ
**US SIC:** 6519, 8221
**UK SIC:** 85000, 93100
**Auditors:** Mann Judd Gordon
**Bankers:** Bank Of Scotland (12-01-22)

| | 31-07-13 | 31-07-12 | 31-07-11 |
|---|---|---|---|
| TO | 260,574 | 260,573 | N/A |
| P/L | 35 | 13 | N/A |
| NW | 2,783,631 | 2,866,155 | 6,213 |
| WC | 6,263 | 6,227 | 6,214 |

DUNS 23-773-7338

### Sabic Uk Petrochemicals Ltd

(**Subsidiary of:** Saudi Basic Indutries Corporation (Sabic))
Po Box 99 Wilton Centre, Redcar, Cleveland TS10 4YA
**Fax:** 01642-834622
**Web:** www.sabic-europe.com
**Reg No:** 3767075 **VAT No:** 895164093
**Estd:** 2009 Private Limited Company
**Line of Business:** Manufacturers of chemicals
**Export Sales:** £315,200,000
**Issued Capital:** £445,000,002
**Directors:** R N Grant, M L Williams, A Wasson, P Booth, Ms C L Watson, M E Ducker, J Middleton, J Den Holder
**Co. Secretary:** John Middleton
**Responsibilities**
**Senior:** J Prowes *(Vice President)*, Daren Smith *(Director)*
**Branches:** Sabic Uk Petrochemicals Ltd, North Tees Works, Seaton Road, Port Clarence, Middlesbrough, Cleveland TS2 1TT
**US SIC:** 2899, 2879
**UK SIC:** 25670, 25680
**Auditors:** Ernst & Young LLP

| | 31-12-13 | 31-12-12 | 31-12-11 |
|---|---|---|---|
| TO | 330,500,000 | 317,500,000 | 319,800,000 |
| P/L | (400,000) | (5,800,000) | 28,900,000 |
| NW | 525,700,000 | 618,800,000 | 632,800,000 |
| WC | 90,900,000 | 64,400,000 | 69,100,000 |
| Emp | 699 | 728 | 700 |

DUNS 23-138-2995 Imp

### Sabichi Homewares Ltd

Sabichi House 5 Wadsworth Road, Greenford, Middlesex UB6 7JD
**Tel:** 02087997474 **Fax:** 02087997478
**Web:** www.sabichi.co.uk
**Reg No:** 2947642 **VAT No:** 225798137
**Estd:** 1984 Private Limited Company
**Line of Business:** Serviced office facilities
**Issued Capital:** £25,000
**Principals:** T Bagga *(Managing)*, S Bagga, Ms S Bagga
**Co. Secretary:** Mrs Mukesh Bagga
**US SIC:** 5021, 5199
**UK SIC:** 61500, 61900
**Auditors:** Jacob Cavenagh & Skeet
**Bankers:** Barclays Bank Plc (20-06-05)

| | 31-10-13 | 31-10-12 | 31-10-11 |
|---|---|---|---|
| TA | 8,205,969 | 8,352,515 | 7,974,210 |
| P/L | 175,530 | 300,045 | 340,956 |
| NW | 6,117,282 | 5,941,483 | 5,656,997 |
| WC | 6,075,326 | 5,877,588 | 5,566,605 |
| Emp. | 46 | 46 | 48 |

DUNS 23-649-2265

### Sabio Ltd

Enterprise House, London SE1 9PG
**Tel:** 02076333900 **Fax:** 02076333901
**Web:** www.sabio.co.uk
**Reg No:** 3644452 **VAT No:** 723073755
**Estd:** 1998 Private Limited Company
**Line of Business:** Telecom services
**Export Sales:** £5,323,000
**Issued Capital:** £72,000
**Directors:** K Hitchen, A C Roberts, P Began, L D Shorten, S Henkes, A Faulkner
**Co. Secretary:** Robert Prosser
**Responsibilities**
**Senior:** Stuart Dorman *(Chairman)*
**Finance:** Chris Dumpleton *(Account Manager)*
**Sales:** Chris Dumpleton *(Account Manager)*
**Admin:** Alice Flook *(Office Manager)*
**IT:** Rob Scutchings *(Chief Technology Officer and F)*
**HR:** Danielle Godsell *(Human Resources Manager)*
**Health & Safety:** Alice Flook *(Office Manager)*
**Branches:** Sabio Ltd, 1 Tontine House, 8 Gordon Street, Glasgow, Lanarkshire G1 3PL
**US SIC:** 4899, 7379
**UK SIC:** 79020, 83940
**Auditors:** PricewaterhouseCoopers LLP
**Bankers:** Lloyds TSB Bank plc (30-94-77)

| | 30-09-14 | 30-09-13 | 30-09-12 |
|---|---|---|---|
| TO | 34,436,000 | 28,074,000 | 24,904,000 |
| P/L | 1,634,000 | 42,000 | 211,000 |
| NW | 1,748,000 | 685,000 | 784,000 |
| WC | 705,000 | (626,000) | (328,000) |
| Emp. | 184 | 167 | 156 |

DUNS 21-948-2212

### Sabmiller Corporate Services Ltd

(**Subsidiary of:** Sabmiller Plc)
S A B Miller House, Church Street West, Woking, Surrey GU21 6HS
**Tel:** 01483264000
**Reg No:** 8575040 **Estd:** 2013 Private Limited Company
**Line of Business:** Management activities of holding companies
**Trading Style:** S A B Miller Plc
**Directors:** T M Boucher, Ms V J Balchin, D P Mallac, S V Shapiro, J K Gay, P H Learoyd
**Co. Secretary:** William Warner
**US SIC:** 6711 **UK SIC:** 83962
**Employees:** 450
**Turnover:** £424,000

DUNS 23-529-5586 Imp

### Sabmiller Plc

Sabmiller House, Church Street West, Woking, Surrey GU21 6HS
**Tel:** 02076590100 **Fax:** 01483-264-117
**Web:** www.sabmiller.com
**Reg No:** 3528416 **Estd:** 1895 Public Limited Company
**Line of Business:** Manufacture of beer
**Trading Style:** Sabmiller
**Directors:** J A Manzoni, A J Clark, P J Manser, J P Du Plessis, H A Willard, G R Elliott, M H Armour, L M Knox
**Co. Secretary:** Stephen Shapiro
**Responsibilities**
**Senior:** Geoffrey Bible *(Director)*, Dinyar Devitre *(Director)*, Graham Mckay *(Chairman)*, Dambisa Moyo *(Director)*, Carlos Perez Davila *(Director)*, Alejandro Santo Domingo Davila *(Director)*
**Branches:** Sabmiller Plc, S A B Miller House, Church Street West, Woking, Surrey GU21 6HS
**US SIC:** 2082, 2086, 5182
**UK SIC:** 42702, 42831, 61700
**Auditors:** PricewaterhouseCoopers LLP
**Employees:** 69,947
**Turnover:** £2.231E+10

DUNS 22-644-6375

### S.A.Brazier Ltd

(**Subsidiary of:** B.& M. Dairies Ltd)
Oxhey Lane, Watford, Hertfordshire WD19 5RJ
**Tel:** 02084287334
**Web:** www.pensworth.co.uk
**Reg No:** 0563085 **Estd:** 2002 Private Limited Company
**Line of Business:** Dairies
**Trading Style:** Carpenters Park Dairy, Braziers Dairy
**Issued Capital:** £5,000
**Director:** Ms S A Alban
**Co. Secretary:** Ms Susan Alban
**Responsibilities**
**Senior:** Roy Brazier *(Manager)*, Arthur Dunn *(Manager)*
**Branches:** S.a.brazier Ltd, Bellingdon Road, Chesham, Buckinghamshire HP5 2NN
**US SIC:** 0241 **UK SIC:** 01001
**Auditors:** Oury Clark Chartered Accountants
**Bankers:** Barclays Bank Plc (20-91-79)

| | 31-03-14 | 31-03-13 | 31-03-12 |
|---|---|---|---|
| TA | 1,624,324 | 1,753,603 | 1,737,243 |
| NW | 491,591 | 455,715 | 415,191 |
| WC | (1,067,409) | (1,103,285) | (1,143,809) |

DUNS 89-635-9460

### Sabre Controls Ltd

(**Subsidiary of:** Bancroft Holdings (Sussex) Ltd)
8-10 Chandler Road, Bexhill-On-Sea, East Sussex TN39 3QN
**Tel:** 01424732424
**Web:** www.sabrecontrols.co.uk
**Reg No:** 3317153 **VAT No:** 583654018
**Estd:** 1991 Private Limited Company
**Line of Business:** Manufacture of electronic valves and tubes and other electronic components
**Issued Capital:** £100,000
**Managing Director:** R A Bancroft
**Co. Secretary:** Alison Bancroft
**Responsibilities**
**Senior:** Robert Bamber *(Print Manager)*
**Finance:** John Higginbottom *(Financial Director)*
**IT:** Tim Waddell *(Technical Director)*
**Facilities:** Tim Waddell *(Technical Director)*
**Operations:** Tim Waddell *(Technical Director)*
**Engineering:** Bob Heatley *(Engineering Manager)*
**US SIC:** 3679 **UK SIC:** 34542
**Auditors:** David Watson & Co
**Bankers:** Barclays Bank Plc (20-27-91)

| | 30-04-14 | 30-04-13 | 30-04-12 |
|---|---|---|---|
| TA | 769,672 | 629,347 | 696,571 |
| NW | 445,988 | 427,022 | 404,403 |
| WC | 400,348 | 384,724 | 361,915 |

DUNS 39-672-9147 Exp

### Sabre Instrument Valves Ltd

(**Subsidiary of:** Sabre Holdings (U K) Ltd)
Golf Road, Hale, Altrincham, Cheshire WA15 8AH
**Tel:** 01619254020
**Web:** www.sabre-valves.com
**Reg No:** 2139085 **Estd:** 1987 Private Limited Company
**Line of Business:** Manufacturers of valves
**Export Markets:** Europe, South East Asia
**Issued Capital:** £800,100
**Principals:** S R Buckley *(Chairman)*, P F Veitch *(Managing)*, R H Clegg *(Technical)*, E F Buckley
**Co. Secretary:** Peter Veitch
**Responsibilities**
**Senior:** Nigel Pegram *(Manager)*
**US SIC:** 3494 **UK SIC:** 32880
**Auditors:** Hale Financial Ltd
**Bankers:** National Westminster Bank Plc (60-70-08)

| | 31-12-13 | 31-12-12 | 31-12-11 |
|---|---|---|---|
| TA | 3,754,408 | 3,411,056 | 3,118,942 |
| NW | 2,082,368 | 1,717,455 | 1,507,970 |
| WC | 1,965,038 | 1,679,178 | 1,387,105 |

DUNS 50-378-0066 Exp

### Sabre Insurance Co Ltd

(**Subsidiary of:** Binomial Group Ltd)
Sabre House, 150 South Street, Dorking, Surrey RH4 2YY
**Fax:** 08443876996
**Web:** www.sabre-ins.co.uk
**Reg No:** 2387080 **Estd:** 1989 Private Limited Company
**Line of Business:** Insurance - car and automotive
**Issued Capital:** £20,000,000
**Directors:** P Swords, T N Webb, S P Curzio, J H Cronly, D J Hindley, A Ball, J P Hosgood, I E Clark
**Co. Secretary:** Keith Morris
**Responsibilities**
**Senior:** John Kavanaugh *(Manager)*
**Finance:** Allan Brett *(Senior Finance Administrator)*
**Marketing:** Wendy Bamping *(Human Resources Manager)*
**IT:** Paul Notte *(Senior IT Executive)*
**HR:** Wendy Bamping *(Human Resources Manager)*
**Health & Safety:** Wendy Bamping *(Human Resources Manager)*
**Branches:** Sabre Insurance Co Ltd, Bradney Fm Ho, Bradney, Bridgnorth, Shropshire WV15 5NT
**US SIC:** 6411 **UK SIC:** 83200
**Auditors:** PricewaterhouseCoopers
**Bankers:** HSBC Bank plc (40-00-00)

| | 31-12-13 | 31-12-12 | 31-12-11 |
|---|---|---|---|
| TO | 138,317,000 | 153,626,000 | 157,918,000 |
| P/L | 56,576,000 | 39,249,000 | 24,761,000 |
| NW | 68,192,000 | 47,263,000 | 45,921,000 |
| WC | 3,644,000 | 11,879,000 | 15,536,000 |
| Emp. | 131 | 129 | 124 |

DUNS 76-901-6932

### Sabre Rail Services Ltd

Grindon Way, Aycliffe Business Park, Newton Aycliffe, County Durham DL5 6SH
**Tel:** 01325300505
**Web:** www.sabre-rail.co.uk
**Reg No:** 2140843 **VAT No:** 459884576
**Estd:** 1987 Private Limited Company
**Line of Business:** Manufacture of railway and tramway locomotives and rolling stock
**Issued Capital:** £20,000
**Principals:** D A Thompson *(Managing)*, S M Thompson
**Co. Secretary:** Ms Glenys Thompson
**Responsibilities**
**Marketing:** Adrian Handley *(Marketing Manager)*
**IT:** James Skidd *(IT Administrator)*
**Health & Safety:** Brian Capeling *(Operations Manager)*
**Facilities:** Brian Capeling *(Operations Manager)*
**Operations:** Brian Capeling *(Operations Manager)*
**Purchasing:** James Skidd *(IT Administrator)*
**US SIC:** 3743 **UK SIC:** 36201
**Bankers:** Barclays Bank Plc (20-25-29)

| | 30-09-13 | 30-09-12 | 30-09-11 |
|---|---|---|---|
| TA | 2,155,288 | 2,043,511 | 2,170,244 |
| NW | 1,457,353 | 1,389,772 | 1,308,446 |
| WC | 934,776 | 884,040 | 780,239 |

DUNS 21-169-0598 Imp

### Sabre Retail Llp

Prospect House, Crendon Street, High Wycombe, Buckinghamshire HP13 6LA
**Tel:** 01494-435123
**Web:** www.mintvelvet.co.uk
**Reg No:** 0346577OC **Estd:** 2009 Private Limited Company
**Line of Business:** Retail sale of other women's clothing
**Trading Style:** Mint Velvet
**US SIC:** 5621 **UK SIC:** 64500
**Auditors:** Deloitte LLP
**Bankers:** Lloyds TSB Bank plc (30-16-85)

| | 30-04-14 | 30-04-13 | 30-04-12 |
|---|---|---|---|
| TO | N/A | N/A | 20,553,000 |
| P/L | N/A | 6,091,000 | 464,000 |
| NW | N/A | N/A | (128,000) |
| WC | N/A | N/A | 1,511,000 |
| Emp. | N/A | 4 | 309 |

DUNS 34-710-8362

### Sabre Safety Holdings Ltd

Cupar Trading Estate, Cupar, Fife KY15 4SX
**Tel:** 01334-656645 **Fax:** 01334-656646
**Web:** www.sabreh2s.com
**Reg No:** 0287793SC **Estd:** 2005 Private Limited Company
**Line of Business:** Engineering related scientific and technical consulting activities
**Export Sales:** £3,089,884
**Issued Capital:** £349
**Directors:** Ms J A Cameron, D J Smith
**Responsibilities**
**Admin:** Pauline Hackett *(Office Administrator)*
**Health & Safety:** Marion Peat *(IMS Director)*
**US SIC:** 8911 **UK SIC:** 83701

| | 31-12-13 | 31-12-12 | 31-12-11 |
|---|---|---|---|
| TO | 11,183,153 | 8,846,194 | N/A |
| P/L | 203,970 | 1,139,981 | (1,652) |
| NW | 2,437,322 | 2,248,007 | 246,218 |
| WC | (1,203,230) | (599,951) | 233,536 |
| Emp. | 122 | 76 | N/A |

DUNS 21-013-7983

### Sabrina Health Care Ltd

77 Cardigan Road, Bridlington, North Humberside YO15 3JU
**Tel:** 01262673566 **Fax:** 01262602679
**Web:** www.sabrinahealthcare.co.uk
**Reg No:** 6366199 **Estd:** 2007 Private Limited Company
**Line of Business:** Social work activities with accommodation
**Issued Capital:** £100
**Director:** T Seeneevassen
**Responsibilities**
**Senior:** Sue Tyler *(General Manager)*
**US SIC:** 7399 **UK SIC:** 83954

| | 28-02-14 | 28-02-13 | 29-02-12 |
|---|---|---|---|
| TO | 2,635,781 | 2,580,365 | 2,484,897 |
| P/L | 71,629 | (129,185) | (103,152) |
| NW | 161,320 | 62,907 | 139,745 |
| WC | (665,433) | (1,014,092) | (605,453) |
| Emp. | 110 | 102 | 101 |

DUNS 64-092-4143

### Saccs Care Ltd

(**Subsidiary of:** Advanced Childcare Services Ltd)
4th Floor, Waterfront Building, Hammersmith Embankment, London W6 9RU
**Tel:** 01743-850015
**Web:** www.saccs.co.uk
**Reg No:** 4495879 **Estd:** 2002 Private Limited Company
**Line of Business:** Social work activities with accommodation
**Issued Capital:** £1
**Directors:** M S Asaria, A P Griffith
**Co. Secretary:** Paul Wright
**Responsibilities**
**Senior:** Rizwan Khan *(Manager)*, Forbes Stuart *(Manager)*
**Branches:** Saccs Care Ltd, Relay Point, Tamworth, Staffordshire B77 5PA
**US SIC:** 8321, 6732
**UK SIC:** 96111, 83100
**Auditors:** PKF (UK) LLP
**Bankers:** Clydesdale Bank Plc (82-04-03)

| | 31-12-13 | 31-12-12 | 31-12-11 |
|---|---|---|---|
| TO | 12,785,432 | 13,933,495 | 10,058,954 |
| P/L | 3,084,593 | (158,772) | 292,624 |
| NW | 4,970,812 | 1,760,863 | 1,856,485 |
| WC | N/A | 1,546,328 | 1,679,565 |
| Emp. | 171 | 195 | 175 |

DUNS 63-454-1007

### Sacker & Partners

20 Gresham Street, London EC2V 7JE
**Tel:** 02079159505
**Web:** www.sacker-partners.co.uk
**Estd:** 1970 Partnership
**Line of Business:** Solicitors
**Partner:** J Seres
**US SIC:** 8111 **UK SIC:** 83500
**Employees:** 90

DUNS 73-880-9578

### Sacker & Partners Llp

20 Gresham Street, London EC2V 7JE
**Tel:** 02073296699
**Web:** www.sacker-partners.co.uk
**Reg No:** 0308089OC **Estd:** 1970 Partnership
**Line of Business:** Solicitors
**Trading Style:** Sacker & Partners Llp
**Responsibilities**
**Senior:** Jonathan Berman *(Partner)*, Michaela Berry *(Partner)*, Claire Carey *(Designated Limited Liability P)*, Christopher Close *(Designated Limited Liability P)*, Nick Couldrey *(Partner)*, Alison Cribbs *(Partner)*, Eleanor Daplyn *(Partner)*, Katharine Dickson *(Designated Limited Liability P)*, Peter Docking *(Partner)*, Emily Forrest *(Partner)*, Edward Hayes *(Designated Limited Liability P)*, Caroline Legg *(Non-designated Limited*

Liabili), Zoe Lynch (Partner), Stuart O' Brien (Partner), Ian Pittaway (Managing Director), Fuat Sami (Non-designated Limited Liabili), Pauline Sibbit (Designated Limited Liability P), Robin Simmons (Partner), Claire Van Rees (Non-designated Limited Liabili)
**Finance:** David Leather (Finance Director)
**Marketing:** Mark Wileman (Business Development Manager)
**Sales:** Mark Wileman (Business Development Manager)
**Admin:** Amanda Kemp (Secretary), Verity Miller (Personal Assistant)
**HR:** Julia Perrin (Human Resources Manager)
**Health & Safety:** David Leather (Finance Director)
**Facilities:** David Leather (Finance Director)
**US SIC:** 8111  **UK SIC:** 83500
**Auditors:** BDO LLP

|      | 31-12-13   | 31-12-12   | 31-12-11   |
|------|------------|------------|------------|
| TO   | 24,236,855 | 24,679,665 | 24,478,144 |
| NW   | 10,825,661 | 10,994,461 | N/A        |
| WC   | 11,027,523 | 10,880,274 | 10,160,726 |
| Emp. | 104        | 107        | 104        |

DUNS 21-727-5848
### Saco the Serviced Apartment Co Ltd
(Subsidiary of: Saco Group Holdings Ltd)
6th Floor Embassy House, Queens Avenue, Bristol, Avon BS8 1SB
**Tel:** 01179706999
**Web:** www.sacoapartments.com
**Reg No:** 7638220  **Estd:** 2011 Private Limited Company
**Line of Business:** Representative office
**Export Sales:** £1,012,919
**Issued Capital:** £100
**Directors:** S A Hanton, D M Freed, P A Deeley, Mrs L A Freed
**Co. Secretary:** Philip Briggs
**US SIC:** 7399  **UK SIC:** 83954
**Auditors:** BDO LLP

|      | 30-04-14   | 30-04-13   | 29-04-12 |
|------|------------|------------|----------|
| TO   | 25,131,727 | 22,088,111 | N/A      |
| P/L  | 797,294    | 863,653    | N/A      |
| NW   | 839,803    | (9,142)    | 1        |
| WC   | 981,629    | 71,151     | N/A      |
| Emp. | 168        | 152        | N/A      |

DUNS 21-754-4104
### Sacred Heart Catholic High School
Fenham Hall Drive, Newcastle-Upon-Tyne, Tyne and Wear NE4 9YH
**Tel:** 01912747373
**Web:** www.sacredheart-high.newcastle.sch.uk
**Reg No:** 7841435  **Estd:** 2011 Private Company Limited By Guarantee
**Line of Business:** General secondary education
**Directors:** T Braun, L G Clarke, C O'Connor, Ms D M Kendall, Ms M T Choat, J Dunne, B J Fitzgerald, B Fitzpatrick
**Responsibilities**
**Senior:** Mary Awcock (Director), Anita Bath (Director), Julia Freer (Director), Patricia Gilbert (Director), Veronica Goatman (Director), Florence Kirkby (Director), Elizabeth Payne (Director)
**US SIC:** 8211  **UK SIC:** 93200
**Bankers:** National Westminster Bank Plc (54-10-31)

|      | 31-08-14   | 31-08-13   | 31-08-12   |
|------|------------|------------|------------|
| TO   | 9,016,000  | 8,818,000  | 22,752,000 |
| P/L  | 758,000    | 756,000    | 16,770,000 |
| NW   | 18,176,000 | 17,383,000 | 16,560,000 |
| WC   | 2,725,000  | 3,403,000  | 3,114,000  |
| Emp. | 140        | 137        | 142        |

DUNS 64-255-2426
### Sacred Heart College
Kevlin Road, Omagh, Co Tyrone BT78 1LG
**Tel:** 028-8224-2717
**Web:** www.shcomagh.co.uk
**Estd:** 2002 Proprietorship
**Line of Business:** Schools (local authority)
**Proprietor:** D Clarke
**US SIC:** 8211  **UK SIC:** 93200
**Employees:** 177

DUNS 23-083-2391
### Sacred Heart of Mary Girls School
70 St Marys Lane, Upminster, Essex RM14 2QR
**Tel:** 01708-222660
**Web:** www.mary.havering.sch.uk
**Estd:** 1927
**Line of Business:** Schools (local authority)
**Director:** Mrs B Williams
**US SIC:** 8211  **UK SIC:** 93200
**Employees:** 130

DUNS 21-167-4747
### Sacred Heart R C Primary School
2 Oakleigh Park South, London N20 9JU
**Tel:** 020-8445-3854
**Web:** www.sacredheartprimary.co.uk
**Estd:** 1929 Proprietorship
**Line of Business:** Schools (local authority)
**Proprietor:** Mrs M Ruane
**Responsibilities**
**Senior:** Catheline Mcmahon (Head Teacher), Maureen Ruane (Head Teacher)
**US SIC:** 8211  **UK SIC:** 93200
**Employees:** 50

DUNS 21-156-8741
### Sacred Heart R C Secondary School
Camberwell New Road, London SE5 0RP
**Tel:** 020-7274-6844
**Web:** www.sacredheart.southwark.sch.uk
**Estd:** 1965 Proprietorship
**Line of Business:** Schools (local authority)
**Proprietor:** Ms S Coates
**Responsibilities**
**Senior:** Serge Cefai (Head Teacher)
**Sales:** Savita Pindoria (Executive Business Manager)
**IT:** Jason Goodrich (Network, Security Manager)
**US SIC:** 8211  **UK SIC:** 93200
**Employees:** 70

DUNS 28-827-8997
### Sacro
29 Albany Street, Edinburgh, Midlothian EH1 3QN
**Tel:** 01316247270
**Web:** www.sacro.org.uk
**Reg No:** 0086651SC  **Estd:** 1971 Private Company Limited By Guarantee
**Line of Business:** Rehabilitation centres
**Directors:** Mrs J Knox, Mrs E Carmichael, G Paterson, A Cameron, D E Gunn, Dr S Siddique, Ms E Dalgleish, G H Palmer
**Co. Secretary:** Thomas Halpin
**Responsibilities**
**Senior:** David Croft (Manager), Linda Mcdowall (Director), Paul Morron (Chairman), Lindsay Thomson (Manager), andrew philip (Director of corporate service)
**Finance:** andrew philip (Director of corporate service)
**Branches:** Sacro, S A C R O, 110 Crown Street, Aberdeen, Aberdeenshire AB11 6HJ
**US SIC:** 8321  **UK SIC:** 96111
**Auditors:** Scott-Moncreiff
**Bankers:** The Royal Bank Of Scotland Plc (83-19-04)

|      | 31-03-14  | 31-03-13  | 31-03-12  |
|------|-----------|-----------|-----------|
| TO   | 8,205,234 | 7,661,796 | 7,418,531 |
| P/L  | 525,625   | 365,243   | 401,391   |
| NW   | 8,697,709 | 7,911,084 | 3,797,841 |
| WC   | 4,635,309 | 4,570,684 | 4,162,841 |
| Emp. | 295       | 310       | 330       |

DUNS 23-933-7025
### Sadler Tankers Ltd
(Subsidiary of: Vision Capital Partners V-A L.P.)
Wilson Street, Stockton-On-Tees, Cleveland TS17 7AR
**Tel:** 01642607777
**Reg No:** 2341288  **VAT No:** 499496166
**Estd:** 1989 Private Limited Company
**Line of Business:** Haulage contractors of bulk liquid chemical and petroleum products.
**Issued Capital:** £211,268
**Directors:** D Wake, T W Minett
**Co. Secretary:** Ms Sharon Armitage
**Branches:** Sadler Tankers Ltd, Bell Street, Oldham, Lancashire OL1 3PY
**US SIC:** 4213, 4212
**UK SIC:** 72300
**Bankers:** National Westminster Bank Plc (54-10-04)

|    | 31-03-14  | 31-03-13  | 31-03-12  |
|----|-----------|-----------|-----------|
| TA | 1,613,481 | 1,613,481 | 1,613,481 |
| NW | 1,613,481 | 1,613,481 | 1,613,481 |

DUNS 22-519-9199
### Sadler's Wells Trust Ltd
Rosebery Avenue, London EC1R 4TN
**Tel:** 02072783330
**Web:** www.sadlerswells.com
**Reg No:** 1488786  **VAT No:** 649178496
**Estd:** 2012 Private Company Limited By Guarantee
**Line of Business:** Newsagents
**Trading Style:** Sadler's Wells Trust Ltd
**Directors:** T Marlow, Ms C A Lake, Sir D C Bell, M Compagnoni, R A Glick, Ms S Butcher, R A Bennetts, Mrs S W Ulrich
**Co. Secretary:** Alistair Spalding

**Responsibilities**
**Senior:** Julian Burns (Director), Joachim Fleury (Manager), Hannah Kirkpatrick (NYDC Company Manager), Britannia Morton (Director, Visitor Services and), Robin Pauley (Manager), Arlene Phillips (Manager), Emma Ponsford (General Manager), Robin Saunders (Director), Sanoke Viswanathan (Director)
**Finance:** Miranda Schnitger (Capital Fundraising Manager)
**Marketing:** Caroline Ansdell (Press Officer), Maxwell Baker (Marketing Publications Officer), Dave Barros (Digital Communications Officer), Sebastian Cheswright (Director of Marketing and Sale), Sally Daniels (Marketing Officer), Abigail Desch (Head of Press), Mark Doerfel (Web Manager), Terrie McCann (Development Manager, Trusts &), Georgie Shields (Director of Brand, Communicati), Sammie Squire (Senior Marketing Manager)
**Sales:** Sebastian Cheswright (Director of Marketing and Sale)
**IT:** Alec Cuffy (Information Technology Manager), Peter Maniam (Projects Manager), Kieron Mohindra (Head of IT), Raymond Neequaye (IT Systems & Network Manager)
**Facilities:** Marguerite Bullard (Senior House ManagerMarguerite), Chris Harmer (House Manager), Zahir Jaffer (House Manager), Hannah Sless (House Manager)
**Operations:** Russell Lynch (Building Services Manager), Britannia Morton (Director, Visitor Services and)
**Engineering:** Roman Bezdyk (Technical Manager), Adam CarrUe (Technical Production Manager), Christian Wallace (Technical Manager)
**Branches:** Sadler's Wells Trust Ltd, Rosebery Avenue, London EC1R 4TN
**US SIC:** 7999  **UK SIC:** 97913
**Auditors:** Moore Stephens
**Bankers:** National Westminster Bank Plc (56-00-20)

|      | 31-03-14   | 31-03-13   | 31-03-12   |
|------|------------|------------|------------|
| TO   | 26,836,000 | 25,659,000 | 22,771,000 |
| P/L  | 334,000    | 938,000    | (153,000)  |
| NW   | 3,361,000  | 3,036,000  | 2,089,000  |
| WC   | 2,230,000  | 1,630,000  | 619,000    |
| Emp. | 206        | 205        | 199        |

DUNS 21-779-0271
### Safari Restaurant
Crawley Road, Woburn, Milton Keynes, Buckinghamshire MK17 9QN
**Tel:** 01525290406
**Web:** www.woburn.co.uk
**Estd:** 1993 Proprietorship
**Line of Business:** Caterers
**Proprietor:** D Mullin
**Responsibilities**
**Senior:** Kaja Hutson (Head Of Catering)
**US SIC:** 5812  **UK SIC:** 66110
**Employees:** 50

DUNS 21-740-8863
### Safari Service Station Ltd
79 Morland Road, Croydon, Surrey CR0 6HA
**Fax:** 020-8656-0054
**Web:** www.classicautomobiles.co.uk
**Reg No:** 1100346  **VAT No:** 218558838
**Estd:** 1973 Private Limited Company
**Line of Business:** Garage related services
**Issued Capital:** £4
**Managing Director:** I Beaton
**Co. Secretary:** Michael Anderson
**Branches:** Safari Service Station Ltd, 79 Morland Road, Croydon, Surrey CR0 6HA
**US SIC:** 7539  **UK SIC:** 67100
**Auditors:** F Winter & Co
**Bankers:** National Westminster Bank Plc (60-01-04)

|    | 05-04-14 | 05-04-13 | 05-04-12 |
|----|----------|----------|----------|
| TA | 908,778  | 547,093  | 548,153  |
| NW | 541,448  | 327,153  | 295,765  |
| WC | 532,463  | 317,525  | 283,658  |

DUNS 22-860-9327                                   Imp-Exp
### Safc Hitech Ltd
(Subsidiary of: Sigma-Aldrich Corporation)
Power Road, Bromborough, Wirral, Merseyside CH62 3QF
**Tel:** 01513342774  **Fax:** 0151-334-6422
**Web:** www.safchitech.com
**Reg No:** 1670306  **VAT No:** 368132743
**Estd:** 1982 Private Limited Company
**Line of Business:** Representative office
**Export Markets:** U S A; Belgium; Germany; France; Japan
**Issued Capital:** £20,673
**Director:** D Goss
**Co. Secretary:** Geoffrey Wynne
**Responsibilities**
**Senior:** Vicky Arundale (Shipping Manager), Martin Skitt (Production Manager)
**Marketing:** Sarah Leese (Sales & Marketing Manager)
**Sales:** Sarah Leese (Sales & Marketing Manager)

**HR:** Hilary Parker (Human Resources Manager)
**Health & Safety:** Anthony Pickford (Health & Safety Manager)
**Operations:** Sarah Leese (Sales & Marketing Manager)
**Engineering:** Martin Skitt (Production Manager)
**Branches:** Safc Hitech Ltd, 26 James Carter Rd, Mildenhall, Bury St Edmunds, Suffolk IP28 7DE
**US SIC:** 2899, 2819
**UK SIC:** 25670, 25110
**Auditors:** KPMG LLP
**Bankers:** Barclays Bank Plc (20-50-36)

|      | 31-12-13    | 31-12-12   | 31-12-11   |
|------|-------------|------------|------------|
| TO   | 17,706,000  | 30,939,000 | 32,668,000 |
| P/L  | (4,040,000) | 1,887,000  | 5,211,000  |
| NW   | 11,242,000  | 14,791,000 | 13,316,000 |
| WC   | 7,912,000   | 14,171,000 | 13,150,000 |
| Emp. | 96          | 101        | 99         |

DUNS 76-511-9789
### Safe Cellars Ltd
(Subsidiary of: International Bonded Warehouses Ltd)
Malta Mill, Mills Hill Road, Manchester M24 2FD
**Tel:** 01613454848
**Web:** www.safecellars.co.uk
**Reg No:** 2568851  **VAT No:** 562621941
**Estd:** 1990 Private Limited Company
**Line of Business:** Storage and warehousing
**Issued Capital:** £10
**Director:** A J Taylor
**Responsibilities**
**Senior:** Gordon Haynes (Manager)
**Branches:** Safe Cellars Ltd, Majestic Mill, Dunham St, Waterhead, Oldham, Lancashire OL4 3NT
**US SIC:** 4226  **UK SIC:** 77003
**Auditors:** Topping Partnership
**Bankers:** National Westminster Bank Plc (01-06-39)

|    | 31-03-14 | 31-03-13  | 31-03-12  |
|----|----------|-----------|-----------|
| TA | 383,684  | 1,223,931 | 1,532,645 |
| NW | 57,131   | 173,591   | 178,668   |
| WC | (8,952)  | 433,221   | 502,123   |

DUNS 34-739-4590
### Safe Computing Holdings Ltd
20 Freeschool Lane, Leicester, Leicestershire LE1 4FY
**Tel:** 01162629321
**Web:** www.safecomputing.co.uk
**Reg No:** 5541359  **Estd:** 2005 Private Limited Company
**Line of Business:** Hardware consultancy
**Export Sales:** £743,745
**Issued Capital:** £1,054
**Directors:** J C Brooks, J G Griffiths, P E Presland, Mrs P E Rule, A W Scott
**Co. Secretary:** Mark James
**US SIC:** 7379  **UK SIC:** 83940

|      | 31-12-13   | 31-12-12   | 31-12-11   |
|------|------------|------------|------------|
| TO   | 15,918,884 | 14,019,249 | 12,022,390 |
| P/L  | 1,593,022  | 1,240,148  | 1,531,583  |
| NW   | 2,451,396  | 579,878    | 458,073    |
| WC   | 1,328,585  | 372,022    | 121,304    |
| Emp. | 188        | 183        | 158        |

DUNS 21-164-2974
### Safe Events Security Co Ltd
42 Minford Gardens, London W14 0AN
**Tel:** 07786375728
**Web:** www.safe-events-security.co.uk
**Reg No:** 6903215  **Estd:** 2009 Private Limited Company
**Line of Business:** Security activities
**Issued Capital:** £1
**Director:** A P Hayes
**Co. Secretary:** Anthony Hayes
**US SIC:** 7393  **UK SIC:** 83954

|    | 31-05-14 | 31-05-13 | 31-05-12 |
|----|----------|----------|----------|
| TA | 74       | 2,386    | 4        |
| NW | (301)    | (211)    | (1,818)  |
| WC | (301)    | (211)    | (1,818)  |

DUNS 21-708-9114
### Safe Harbour
254 Hagley Road, Stourbridge, West Midlands DY9 0RW
**Web:** www.safeharbour.co.uk
**Estd:** 2004 Partnership
**Line of Business:** Non-charitable social work activities with accommodation
**Partners:** Dr A Kumar, L Copeland
**Responsibilities**
**Senior:** Lorna Priest (Home Manager)
**US SIC:** 8321  **UK SIC:** 96111
**Employees:** 50

DUNS 45-835-8058
### Safe in Tees Valley Ltd
Safe in Tees Valley, Richard House, Stockton-On-Tees, Cleveland TS17 6DA
**Tel:** 01642664440
**Web:** www.safeinteesvalley.org
**Reg No:** 3186535  **Estd:** 1990 Private Limited Company

**Line of Business:** Public security, law and order activities
**Directors:** Ms A Skelton, Mrs J D Bruce, Dr A J Gillham, H Ian, Ms J A Cheer, M F Home, Ms W Balmain
**US SIC:** 9221 **UK SIC:** 91300
**Auditors:** Baines Goldston

| | 31-03-14 | 31-03-13 | 31-03-12 |
|---|---|---|---|
| TO | 1,369,865 | 2,674,028 | 3,163,613 |
| P/L | (30,627) | (158,134) | 154,500 |
| NW | 497,166 | 527,793 | 685,927 |
| WC | 485,787 | 502,419 | 645,588 |
| Emp. | 46 | 55 | 162 |

DUNS 21-584-7549
### Safe Style Uk
Unit 2 Legrams Terrace Fieldhead, Business Centre, Fieldhead Business Centre, Bradford, West Yorkshire BD7 1LN
**Tel:** 01274354864
**Web:** www.safestyle-windows.co.uk
**Estd:** 2011 Proprietorship
**Line of Business:** Double glazing installers
**Proprietor:** A Clarke
**Responsibilities**
**Senior:** Leon Binns *(Manager)*
**US SIC:** 1721 **UK SIC:** 50400
**Employees:** 200

DUNS 29-682-1184
### Safechem Ltd
Drum House, Chester-Le-Street, County Durham DH2 1SR
**Tel:** 0191-410-8668
**Web:** www.safechem.co.uk
**Reg No:** 2005633 **VAT No:** 459728887
**Estd:** 1987 Private Limited Company
**Line of Business:** Cleaning materials and equipment
**Issued Capital:** £1,000
**Principals:** N L Bruce *(Managing)*, Ms E Lumley, J Bruce, Ms C Bruce
**Responsibilities**
**Senior:** Emma Bruce *(Manager)*, Colin Silvester *(Sales & Marketing Manager)*
**Marketing:** Colin Silvester *(Sales & Marketing Manager)*
**Sales:** Colin Silvester *(Sales & Marketing Manager)*
**Purchasing:** Neil Frost *(Buyer)*
**US SIC:** 5199 **UK SIC:** 61900
**Auditors:** T W Tasker FCA
**Bankers:** Barclays Bank Plc (20-27-41)

| | 31-01-14 | 31-01-13 | 31-01-12 |
|---|---|---|---|
| TA | 2,646,938 | 2,432,767 | 2,446,872 |
| NW | 1,672,422 | 1,672,312 | 1,590,237 |
| WC | 1,238,079 | 1,275,694 | 1,237,730 |

DUNS 34-882-3402
### Safecourt Ltd
89 High St South, Dunstable, Bedfordshire LU6 3SF
**Web:** www.dunstablelock.co.uk
**Reg No:** 2821172 **Estd:** 1987 Private Limited Company
**Line of Business:** Locksmiths
**Trading Style:** Dunstable Lock & Safe Co
**Issued Capital:** £1,000
**Director:** Mrs M L Freeman
**Co. Secretary:** Steven Freeman
**Responsibilities**
**Admin:** Cathy Mayfield *(Office Manager)*
**US SIC:** 3429 **UK SIC:** 31694
**Auditors:** F M C B

| | 31-07-13 | 31-07-12 | 31-07-11 |
|---|---|---|---|
| TA | 79,110 | 74,397 | 45,069 |
| NW | 44,021 | 37,091 | 19,976 |
| WC | 31,262 | 25,896 | 10,045 |

DUNS 76-996-5963
### Safedale Ltd
Unit 6c, Dominion Business Park, Goodwin Road, London N9 0BG
**Tel:** 020-8803-6222
**Web:** www.safedale-ltd.co.uk
**Reg No:** 2651047 **Estd:** 1991 Private Limited Company
**Line of Business:** Chemists dispensing
**Issued Capital:** £137,500
**Principals:** B K Patel *(Managing)*, A Patel, P K Patel
**Co. Secretary:** Mrs Kumud Patel
**Responsibilities**
**Senior:** Bk Patel *(Manager)*
**Branches:** Safedale Ltd, Safedale Pharmacy, 2-3 Albion Road, London N16 0TA
**US SIC:** 5912 **UK SIC:** 64300
**Auditors:** Ashfords Goyal Partnership

| | 31-10-13 | 31-10-12 | 31-10-11 |
|---|---|---|---|
| TO | 11,866,117 | 12,001,115 | 16,818,141 |
| P/L | 371,031 | 595,404 | 395,957 |
| NW | 1,464,426 | 1,318,771 | 1,058,870 |
| WC | 509,696 | 303,873 | 1,071,603 |
| Emp. | 98 | 96 | 92 |

DUNS 22-906-2195
### Safedem Ltd
Arthurstone House, Liff Road, Dundee, Angus DD2 4TD
**Tel:** 01382811444 **Fax:** 01382-828244
**Web:** www.safedem.co.uk
**Reg No:** 0057536SC **Estd:** 1975 Private Limited Company
**Line of Business:** Demolition and wrecking of buildings; earth moving
**Trading Style:** Safedem Ltd
**Issued Capital:** £1,000
**Principals:** W Sinclair *(Managing)*, Ms M P Smith
**Co. Secretary:** Ms Tracey Sinclair
**US SIC:** 1795 **UK SIC:** 50000
**Auditors:** French Duncan LLP
**Bankers:** Bank Of Scotland (80-73-31)

| | 31-05-14 | 31-05-13 | 31-05-12 |
|---|---|---|---|
| TO | 12,972,019 | 10,828,524 | 10,319,182 |
| P/L | 1,019,515 | 743,559 | 1,131,956 |
| NW | 2,409,168 | 1,966,996 | 1,774,157 |
| WC | (226,517) | (628,454) | (803,889) |
| Emp. | 59 | 66 | 70 |

DUNS 21-615-3403
### Safeguard Coaches Ltd
Ridgemount, Guildford, Surrey GU2 7TH
**Tel:** 01483-561103
**Web:** www.safeguardcoaches.co.uk
**Reg No:** 0273953 **VAT No:** 211884767
**Estd:** 1933 Private Limited Company
**Line of Business:** Coach and bus hire
**Issued Capital:** £4,000
**Directors:** M G Newman, D K Newman, Mrs J C Newman, Ms T Hunter
**Co. Secretary:** Andrew Halliday
**Responsibilities**
**Health & Safety:** Brett Lambley *(Health & Safety Officer)*
**Branches:** Farnham Coaches, Odiham Rd, Ewshot, Farnham Surrey GU10 5AG.
**US SIC:** 4119, 4141, 4789
**UK SIC:** 72200, 72102, 77002
**Auditors:** Garner Bleasdale Chandler
**Bankers:** National Westminster Bank Plc (60-09-21)

| | 31-12-13 | 31-12-12 | 31-12-11 |
|---|---|---|---|
| TO | 3,427,522 | 3,289,930 | 3,094,480 |
| P/L | 358,962 | 195,348 | 226,705 |
| NW | 4,529,001 | 4,388,795 | 4,364,961 |
| WC | 1,128,469 | 941,558 | 694,165 |
| Emp. | N/A | N/A | 63 |

DUNS 76-739-9355
### Safeguard Pest Control & Environmental Services Ltd
6 Churchill Business Park, The Flyers Way, Westerham, Kent TN16 1BT
**Tel:** 01959565777 **Fax:** 01959-565888
**Web:** www.safeguardpestcontrol.co.uk
**Reg No:** 2597625 **VAT No:** 425253667
**Estd:** 1987 Private Limited Company
**Line of Business:** Pest control
**Trading Style:** Safeguard Pest Control
**Issued Capital:** £200
**Directors:** P C Butterick, T C Sheehan
**Co. Secretary:** Ms Penelope Gadd
**US SIC:** 4959 **UK SIC:** 92110
**Auditors:** Tryhorn & Hall
**Bankers:** National Westminster Bank Plc (60-02-48)

| | 30-04-14 | 30-04-13 | 30-04-12 |
|---|---|---|---|
| TO | N/A | N/A | 3,137,240 |
| P/L | N/A | N/A | 310,571 |
| NW | 1,439,616 | 1,415,680 | 1,474,601 |
| WC | 1,199,475 | 1,224,667 | 1,286,629 |

DUNS 22-138-1564
### Safeguard Security Group Ltd
Safeguard House, Leeds, West Yorkshire LS27 7QZ
**Tel:** 01132539710 **Fax:** 0845-072-9998
**Web:** www.safeguardgroup.co.uk
**Reg No:** 4157058 **VAT No:** 915825022
**Estd:** 2001 Private Limited Company
**Line of Business:** Security activities
**Issued Capital:** £100
**Directors:** S P Richardson, Mrs D S Mitchell, M N Green
**US SIC:** 7393 **UK SIC:** 83954

| | 30-06-13 | 30-06-12 | 30-06-11 |
|---|---|---|---|
| TA | 2,547,835 | 2,398,319 | 1,984,765 |
| NW | 262,110 | 18,825 | (34,544) |
| WC | 236,292 | (5,799) | (60,813) |

DUNS 21-100-2406
### Safeguard World International Ltd
Suite 3 -5 Edwin Foden Business Centre, Sandbach, Cheshire CW11 3AE
**Tel:** 01270 758 020
**Web:** www.safeguardworld.com
**Reg No:** 6439329 **Estd:** 2007 Private Limited Company
**Line of Business:** Financial intermediation not elsewhere classified
**Export Sales:** £7,485,853
**Issued Capital:** £6,803
**Directors:** R Martin, J Coker, B J Thew
**Co. Secretary:** John Giles
**Responsibilities**
**Senior:** Bjorn Reynolds *(Chief Executive Officer)*
**US SIC:** 8931, 7374
**UK SIC:** 83600, 83940
**Auditors:** Grant Thornton UK LLP
**Bankers:** HSBC Bank plc (40-49-19)

| | 31-12-13 | 31-12-12 | 31-12-11 |
|---|---|---|---|
| TO | 16,924,416 | 12,378,141 | 8,466,614 |
| P/L | (1,625,224) | (385,126) | 116,889 |
| NW | (276,180) | 6,168 | 361,287 |
| WC | 31,941 | (145,168) | 684,875 |
| Emp. | 190 | 122 | N/A |

DUNS 21-661-1603
### Safehands Cleaning Services
3 Riverside Terrace, Clarkston, Glasgow, Lanarkshire G76 8EA
**Tel:** 01416440965
**Web:** http://safehandscleaning.com
**Estd:** 1994 Partnership
**Line of Business:** Cleaning contracting commercial
**Partners:** Mrs K O'Leary, P O'Leary
**Responsibilities**
**Senior:** P O' Leary *(Partner)*, Kerry O'Leary *(Partner)*
**US SIC:** 7349 **UK SIC:** 92300
**Employees:** 100

DUNS 21-686-4291
### Safehands Corporation Ltd
3 Neptune Court, Whitehills Business Park, Blackpool, Lancashire FY4 5LZ
**Tel:** 08448482810
**Web:** www.safehandscare.com
**Reg No:** 7354779 **Estd:** 2010 Private Limited Company
**Line of Business:** Management activities of other non-financial holding companies not elsewhere classified
**Issued Capital:** £100
**Directors:** P D Manning, W S Rigby, M J Darch
**US SIC:** 6711 **UK SIC:** 83962
**Auditors:** Moore & Smalley LLP

| | 31-12-13 | 31-12-12 | 31-12-11 |
|---|---|---|---|
| TO | 5,958,039 | 4,630,563 | N/A |
| P/L | 232,993 | 127,370 | N/A |
| NW | 632,904 | 408,751 | 100 |
| WC | (1,210,130) | (1,390,007) | N/A |
| Emp. | 358 | N/A | N/A |

DUNS 73-743-0210 Imp
### Safehouse Habitats (Scotland) Ltd
**(Subsidiary of:** Saffron Lux Holdco Sarl)
Unit 2, Bowbridge Works, Thistle Street, Dundee, Angus DD3 7RF
**Tel:** 01382-814122 **Fax:** 01382-489952
**Web:** www.safehouseltd.com
**Reg No:** 0261216SC **Estd:** 2004 Private Limited Company
**Line of Business:** Service activities incidental to oil and gas extraction excluding surveying
**Issued Capital:** £100
**Directors:** M T Garty, G A Mackay, A Poddar, R P Clark, P G Watters, J A Smith, A V Gronlund
**Co. Secretary:** Burness Paull Llp
**Responsibilities**
**Senior:** Mark Garty *(Manager)*, Dave Hanlon *(Health and Safety Executive)*
**Admin:** Suzanne Garty *(Office Manager)*
**IT:** Stephanie Paton *(Chief Technology Officer)*
**Health & Safety:** Dave Hanlon *(Health and Safety Executive)*
**Engineering:** Gordon Priestley *(Development Engineer)*
**US SIC:** 1389 **UK SIC:** 13000
**Auditors:** Walker Dunnett & Co

| | 31-05-14 | 31-05-13 | 31-05-12 |
|---|---|---|---|
| TO | 19,194,319 | 17,127,253 | 15,568,098 |
| P/L | 5,149,724 | 6,126,086 | 6,680,429 |
| NW | 9,527,012 | 8,664,327 | 7,529,775 |
| WC | 7,118,907 | 5,639,747 | 6,192,825 |
| Emp. | 101 | 107 | 80 |

DUNS 39-952-9767 Imp-Exp
### Safenet Uk Ltd
**(Subsidiary of:** Sfnt Netherlands Coöperatief B.A.)
3 Meadows Drive, Camberley, Surrey GU15 1GA
**Tel:** 01276-608000 **Fax:** 01276-608080
**Web:** www.safenet-inc.com
**Reg No:** 2258824 **VAT No:** 494014647
**Estd:** 1988 Private Limited Company
**Line of Business:** Other computer related activities
**Export Markets:** countries worldwide
**Issued Capital:** £50,000
**Directors:** P Panjwani, G A Clark
**Co. Secretary:** Kevin Hicks
**Responsibilities**
**Senior:** Roozbeh Barkhordari *(Manager)*, Chris Fedde *(Manager)*, Nick Glass *(Networks Administrator)*
**Finance:** Richard Dodridge *(Financial Director)*
**Marketing:** Nicki Wallace *(Marketing Manager)*
**HR:** Susie Andrew *(Human Resources Director)*
**Health & Safety:** Susie Andrew *(Human Resources Director)*
**Branches:** Safenet Uk Ltd, 55 High Street, Bromsgrove, Worcestershire B61 8AJ
**US SIC:** 7379 **UK SIC:** 83940
**Auditors:** Ernst & Young LLP
**Bankers:** Barclays Bank Plc (20-65-18)

| | 31-12-13 | 31-12-12 | 31-12-11 |
|---|---|---|---|
| TO | 11,002,533 | 10,750,630 | 6,058,811 |
| P/L | 363,965 | 322,931 | 376,503 |
| NW | (1,140,040) | 682,533 | 569,085 |
| WC | (1,393,747) | 444,839 | 284,214 |
| Emp. | 104 | 102 | 93 |

DUNS 34-804-8489
### Safer Places
9 Bush House, Bush Fair, Harlow, Essex CM18 6NS
**Tel:** 01279899253
**Web:** www.labellezzawithin.co.uk
**Reg No:** 2789572 **Estd:** 1980 Private Limited Company
**Line of Business:** Hairdressing and other beauty treatment
**Directors:** P Nosa Samuel, Ms J Mcrae, J Chapman, D Wildey, Ms S L Rodie, Miss R M Parmenter, Ms S M Johnson
**Co. Secretary:** Ms Allison Mann
**Responsibilities**
**Senior:** Bianca Preston *(Manager)*
**US SIC:** 7231, 8321
**UK SIC:** 98200, 96111
**Auditors:** Price Bailey LLP
**Bankers:** HSBC Bank plc (40-23-10)

| | 31-03-14 | 31-03-13 | 31-03-12 |
|---|---|---|---|
| TO | 2,955,578 | 2,924,965 | 2,076,466 |
| P/L | 23,774 | 333,912 | (79,807) |
| NW | 481,001 | 593,226 | (862,686) |
| WC | 898,225 | 957,595 | 512,113 |
| Emp. | 72 | 75 | 60 |

DUNS 34-900-0732
### Saferoad Uk Ltd
**(Subsidiary of:** Cidron Triangle Sarl)
Dragonby Vale Enterprise Park, Mannaberg Way, Scunthorpe, South Humberside DN15 8XF
**Tel:** 01724-289119
**Web:** www.balmer-group.co.uk
**Reg No:** 5697518 **Estd:** 2006 Private Limited Company
**Line of Business:** Construction of motorways, roads, railways, airfields and sports facilities
**Trading Style:** Saferoad Blg Limited
**Issued Capital:** £10
**Directors:** S F Cummings, T Boe
**Co. Secretary:** Michael Sheffield
**US SIC:** 1611 **UK SIC:** 50200
**Auditors:** Ernst & Young LLP
**Bankers:** Unibank A/s (40-48-78)

| | 31-12-13 | 31-12-12 | 31-12-11 |
|---|---|---|---|
| TO | 3,257,599 | 3,639,173 | N/A |
| P/L | 4,221,015 | (253,251) | N/A |
| NW | 2,218,754 | (2,003,248) | (1,749,997) |
| WC | (1,433,523) | (2,180,950) | (1,750,000) |

DUNS 77-751-4357
### Saferworld
The Grayston Centre, 28 Charles Square, London N1 6HT
**Web:** www.saferworld.co.uk
**Reg No:** 3015948 **Estd:** 1995 Private Limited Company
**Line of Business:** Other publishing
**Directors:** Dr O Greene, M G Chalmers, J P Lester, C H Marshall, F A Judd, D C Norman, Professor A E Hills, Ms S Joss
**Co. Secretary:** Ms Susan Maskell
**Responsibilities**
**Senior:** Godfrey Allen *(Director)*, Roy Isbister *(Senior Manager)*, Richard Nabudere *(Team Leader)*
**Finance:** Helen Macfoy *(Finance Officer, UK)*, Enzo Martinelli *(Head of Funding)*, Esther Waweru *(Finance Manager)*
**Marketing:** Elizabeth Bourne *(PR Manager)*
**HR:** Marie Aziz *(Operations/HR Manager)*
**Operations:** Marie Aziz *(Operations/HR Manager)*, Evelyn Vancollie *(Project Officer)*
**Purchasing:** Richard Callaghan *(Director of Finance and Procur)*
**US SIC:** 2741, 8299
**UK SIC:** 47541, 93300
**Bankers:** The Co-Operative Bank Plc (08-92-40)

| | 31-03-14 | 31-03-13 | 31-03-12 |
|---|---|---|---|
| TO | 11,069,000 | 9,061,000 | 6,664,000 |
| P/L | 2,060,000 | 1,053,000 | (787,000) |
| NW | 4,818,000 | 2,758,000 | 1,705,000 |
| WC | 4,747,000 | 2,757,000 | 1,705,000 |
| Emp. | 119 | 93 | 74 |

DUNS 34-911-1310

## Safeskys Ltd

Abbey House, 84b Easton Street, High Wycombe, Buckinghamshire HP11 1LT
**Web:** www.safeskys.co.uk
**Reg No:** 2833067 **Estd:** 1993 Private Limited Company
**Line of Business:** Other supporting air transport activities
**Issued Capital:** £2,000
**Principals:** R H Barber *(Managing)*, Mrs E A Smith, Ms S A Benn
**Co. Secretary:** Mrs Shirley Benn
**Branches:** Safeskys Ltd, Bird Control Unit, Exeter Airport, Exeter, Devon EX5 2BD
**US SIC:** 4582, 7342, 8249
**UK SIC:** 76400, 92110, 93300
**Bankers:** Lloyds TSB Bank plc (30-93-74)

| | 31-07-13 | 31-07-12 | 31-07-11 |
|---|---|---|---|
| TA | 818,111 | 845,075 | 865,446 |
| NW | 664,817 | 745,790 | 633,300 |
| WC | 330,802 | 413,010 | 322,301 |

DUNS 73-462-3429

## Safestore Holdings Plc

Brittanic House, Stirling Way, Borehamwood, Hertfordshire WD6 2BT
**Tel:** 020-8732-1500 **Fax:** 02087321510
**Web:** www.safestore.co.uk
**Reg No:** 4726380 **Estd:** 2003 Public Limited Company
**Line of Business:** Management activities of holding companies
**Export Sales:** £25,900,000
**Issued Capital:** £1,881,351
**Directors:** F Vecchioli, K G Edelman, A S Lewis, A H Martin, I S Krieger, A B Jones, Ms J L Kenrick
**Co. Secretary:** Sam Ahmed
**Responsibilities**
**Senior:** Peter Gowers *(ceo)*, Richard Hodsden *(Manager)*, Frederic Vecchioli *(Chief Executive Officer)*
**Finance:** Richard Hodsden *(Manager)*
**Sales:** Stuart Beavers *(Head of Retail Services)*
**Purchasing:** Nigel Welling *(Buyer)*
**Branches:** Safestore Holdings Plc, 50 York Road, Leeds, West Yorkshire LS9 8SY
**US SIC:** 6711 **UK SIC:** 83962
**Auditors:** PricewaterhouseCoopers LLP

| | 31-10-13 | 31-10-12 | 31-10-11 |
|---|---|---|---|
| TO | 96,100,000 | 98,836,000 | 95,060,000 |
| P/L | 48,600,000 | (19,463,000) | 8,547,000 |
| NW | 345,900,000 | 243,385,000 | 275,159,000 |
| WC | (16,600,000) | (16,760,000) | (23,383,000) |
| Emp. | 575 | 569 | 521 |

DUNS 22-217-1782

## Safestyle Security Services Ltd

Executive Suit 1, Cardiff, South Glamorgan CF10 2EQ
**Tel:** 02920221711 **Fax:** 02920234592
**Web:** www.safestylesecurity.co.uk
**Reg No:** 4235179 **VAT No:** 779382863
**Estd:** 2001 Private Limited Company
**Line of Business:** Security activities
**Issued Capital:** £1
**Director:** D A Edwards
**US SIC:** 7393 **UK SIC:** 83954

| | 30-06-14 | 30-06-13 | 30-06-12 |
|---|---|---|---|
| TA | 1,256,421 | 1,222,613 | 1,147,721 |
| NW | 1,074,720 | 1,033,310 | 1,017,410 |
| WC | 896,602 | 899,311 | 1,015,924 |

DUNS 21-779-1405

## Safestyle Uk

Unit 1 Clayfield Industrial Estate Tick, Hill Road, Doncaster, South Yorkshire DN4 8QG
**Tel:** 01302515956
**Web:** www.safestyle-windows.co.uk
**Estd:** 1992 Proprietorship
**Line of Business:** Painting and glazing
**Proprietor:** N Holmes
**Responsibilities**
**Senior:** Gary Brooker *(Manager)*
**US SIC:** 1721 **UK SIC:** 50400
**Employees:** 50

DUNS 42-416-9204

## Safety Engineering Systems Ltd

10 Seaforth Park, Hecklegirth, Annan, Dumfriesshire DG12 6HX
**Tel:** 01461202583
**Web:** www.dewsburyrams.co.uk
**Reg No:** 0229669SC **Estd:** 2002 Private Limited Company
**Line of Business:** Business and management consultancy activities not elsewhere classified
**Issued Capital:** £1
**Managing Director:** E W Foster
**Co. Secretary:** Ms Anne Foster
**US SIC:** 8911 **UK SIC:** 83701

**Bankers:** The Royal Bank Of Scotland Plc (83-15-19)

| | 31-03-14 | 31-03-13 | 31-03-12 |
|---|---|---|---|
| TA | 145,683 | 183,047 | 191,055 |
| NW | 104,542 | 141,625 | 148,026 |
| WC | 53,497 | 91,476 | 99,312 |

DUNS 28-845-3558 **Imp**

## Safety First Aid Group Ltd

Unit 15-17, Irving Way Garrick Industrial Centre, London NW9 6AQ
**Tel:** 02082027447
**Web:** www.safetyfirstaid.co.uk
**Reg No:** 0622741 **VAT No:** 229664142
**Estd:** 1914 Private Limited Company
**Line of Business:** Other adult and other education not elsewhere classified
**Issued Capital:** £100
**Managing Directors:** R J Froomberg, Ms B H Froomberg
**Co. Secretary:** Robert Froomberg
**Responsibilities**
**Senior:** Derek Froomberg *(Manager)*
**Marketing:** Daniela Iurascu *(Marketing Assistant)*
**HR:** Lesley Grazeley *(Human Resources Manager)*, Lisa Rose *(Human Resources Manager)*
**Health & Safety:** Lesley Grazeley *(Human Resources Manager)*, Lisa Rose *(Human Resources Manager)*
**Operations:** Lesley Grazeley *(Human Resources Manager)*, Lisa Rose *(Human Resources Manager)*
**US SIC:** 5199 **UK SIC:** 61900
**Auditors:** Leslie Michael Lipowicz & Co
**Bankers:** National Westminster Bank Plc (50-30-20)

| | 31-12-13 | 31-12-12 | 31-12-11 |
|---|---|---|---|
| TA | 2,788,029 | 2,166,420 | 2,080,031 |
| NW | 208,149 | 71,243 | 47,196 |
| WC | 80,989 | (15,752) | (46,692) |

DUNS 21-723-9391 **Imp-Exp**

## Safety-Kleen U.K. Ltd

(**Subsidiary of:** Wp Safety-Kleen (Cayman) Limited)
Profile West, 950 Great West Road, Brentford, Middlesex TW8 9ES
**Tel:** 02082327510
**Web:** www.kirbygroup.co.uk
**Reg No:** 1190039 **VAT No:** 720544561
**Estd:** 2011 Private Limited Company
**Line of Business:** Engineering, architectural, & surveying
**Export Markets:** W Europe, U S A, Canada, Australasia, Puerto Rico
**Issued Capital:** £10,000
**Directors:** G M Baldock, K Buchborn-Klos, Ms S L Cramer, P R Mauguy
**Co. Secretary:** Geoffrey Baldock
**Responsibilities**
**Senior:** Stephen Brain *(Chief Executive Officer)*, Mark Flanagan *(Manager)*, Chris Handley *(Manager)*, Lee Hosier *(Operations Director)*
**Finance:** Richard Goodley *(Financial Manager)*, Gregory Peacock *(Finance Director)*
**Marketing:** Matt Trace *(Press Enquirers)*
**HR:** Josephine Binder *(Human Resources Manager)*, Cathy Burrell *(Human Resources Manager)*
**Health & Safety:** Cathy Burrell *(Human Resources Manager)*
**Facilities:** Lee Hosier *(Operations Director)*
**Operations:** Lee Hosier *(Operations Director)*
**Purchasing:** Lee Hosier *(Operations Director)*
**Branches:** Safety-Kleen U.k. Ltd, Christy Way, Basildon, Essex SS15 6TR
**US SIC:** 8911, 4953
**UK SIC:** 83701, 92110
**Auditors:** PricewaterhouseCoopers LLP
**Bankers:** Barclays Bank Plc (20-42-73)

| | 28-12-13 | 29-12-12 | 31-12-11 |
|---|---|---|---|
| TO | 56,036,000 | 57,420,000 | 58,449,000 |
| P/L | 8,501,000 | 11,383,000 | 13,137,000 |
| NW | 101,319,000 | 92,152,000 | 80,102,000 |
| WC | 89,686,000 | 80,414,000 | 69,093,000 |
| Emp. | 475 | 468 | 489 |

DUNS 21-315-6839 **Imp-Exp**

## Safety Systems Uk Ltd

(**Subsidiary of:** Pentair Flow Control Holdings Limited)
Sharp Street, Worsley, Manchester M28 3NA
**Tel:** 01617907741 **Fax:** 016-1799-4335
**Web:** www.safetysystemsuk.com
**Reg No:** 0030037 **VAT No:** 144998715
**Estd:** 1832 Private Limited Company
**Line of Business:** Manufacturers of valves
**Export Markets:** Worldwide
**Export Sales:** £21,759,000
**Issued Capital:** £100,000
**Directors:** M D Lawrence, K W Ford, Ms S A Greenway, M S Boardman, T Toffolo, N G Petty, P Cox
**Co. Secretary:** Ms Sophie Grundy
**Responsibilities**
**Senior:** Alison Boldison *(Manager)*, James Wainwright *(General Manager)*
**HR:** Louise Keeley *(Human Resources)*
**Branches:** Safety Systems Uk Ltd, Wobaston Road, Wolverhampton, West Midlands WV10 6QJ
**US SIC:** 3494 **UK SIC:** 32880
**Auditors:** Deloitte LLP
**Bankers:** National Westminster Bank Plc (60-22-46)

| | 31-12-13 | 31-12-12 | 30-12-11 |
|---|---|---|---|
| TO | 29,660,000 | 35,736,000 | 30,106,000 |
| P/L | 1,479,000 | 1,790,000 | 1,194,000 |
| NW | 29,852,000 | 28,384,000 | 26,966,000 |
| WC | 27,824,000 | 27,231,000 | 25,002,000 |
| Emp. | 226 | 227 | 230 |

DUNS 29-488-2592

## Saffery Champness

Lion House 72 75, Red Lion Street, London WC1R 4GB
**Tel:** 020-7841-4000
**Web:** www.saffery.com
**Reg No:** 1851581 **Estd:** 1984 Private Unlimited Company
**Line of Business:** Accounting and auditing activities
**Trading Style:** Saffery Champness
**Issued Capital:** £4
**Directors:** R T Elliott, C A Nicholson
**Responsibilities**
**Senior:** Jonathan Fox *(Managing Partner)*
**Admin:** Jonathan Fox *(Managing Partner)*
**Branches:** Saffery Champness, Saffery Champness, Fox House, High Wycombe, Buckinghamshire HP13 5DR
**US SIC:** 8931 **UK SIC:** 83600
**Auditors:** Coombs Wales Quinnell
**Bankers:** Barclays Bank Plc (20-19-90)
**Employees:** 281

DUNS 23-650-9043 **Imp**

## Saffil Ltd

(**Subsidiary of:** Unifrax Ltd)
Pilkington Sullivan Site, Widnes, Cheshire WA8 0US
**Tel:** 01514-226-700 **Fax:** 01514-226-701
**Web:** www.saffil.com
**Reg No:** 3646114 **Estd:** 1998 Private Limited Company
**Line of Business:** Cladding and insulation materials
**Export Sales:** £19,245,889
**Issued Capital:** £2
**Directors:** S ' Martins, J C Dandolph Iv, F B Von Arx, Dr M W Briscoe
**Responsibilities**
**Senior:** Lee Attwood *(Finance Director)*, Christopher Honeyborne *(Manager)*
**Finance:** Lee Attwood *(Finance Director)*
**HR:** Pauline Lightfoot *(Human Resources Manager)*
**Health & Safety:** Pauline Lightfoot *(Human Resources Manager)*
**US SIC:** 3079, 2821
**UK SIC:** 48360, 25140
**Auditors:** Ernst & Young LLP

| | 31-12-13 | 31-12-12 | 31-12-11 |
|---|---|---|---|
| TO | 27,387,227 | 25,815,671 | 6,705,537 |
| P/L | (3,048,020) | 1,544,918 | 1,072,124 |
| NW | 2,209,591 | 6,321,693 | 4,390,767 |
| WC | (37,082,341) | (33,328,146) | (10,147,882) |
| Emp. | 76 | 67 | 64 |

DUNS 21-879-8828

## Saffron & Eyres Monsell Neighbourhood Housing

499 Saffron Lane, Leicester, Leicestershire LE2 6UQ
**Tel:** 01162527007
**Estd:** 2012
**Line of Business:** Housing advice
**US SIC:** 8321 **UK SIC:** 96111
**Employees:** 50

DUNS 22-647-3411

## Saffron Building Society

Saffron House, 1a Market Place, Saffron Walden, Essex CB10 1HX
**Tel:** 01799522211
**Web:** www.swhebs.co.uk
**Estd:** 1847
**Line of Business:** Building societies
**Principals:** P Harrison *(Chairman)*, C Plumbrige *(Financial)*, J Hall, T Bayley, Ms J Smith, G Dunn, C Wilson
**Responsibilities**
**Senior:** Andy Golding *(Chief Executive)*, Alan Goodman *(Non-Executive Director)*
**Marketing:** Michelle Monk *(Marketing Manager)*, Zoe Neville-Smith *(Marketing Manager)*
**Admin:** Tracy Gumus *(Office Manager)*
**HR:** Sue Philby *(Training Manager)*
**Health & Safety:** Tracy Gumus *(Office Manager)*
**Facilities:** Richard Pellatt *(Facilities Manager)*
**Branches:** Saffron Building Society, 32 Connaught Avenue, Frinton-On-Sea, Essex CO13 9PR
**US SIC:** 6111 **UK SIC:** 81501
**Auditors:** Deloitte LLP
**Bankers:** Barclays Bank Plc (20-74-05)
**Employees:** 139

DUNS 42-383-5508

## Saffron Digital Ltd

(**Subsidiary of:** Cdmg Holdings Uk Ltd)
25 Farringdon Street, London EC4A 4AB
**Tel:** 02074046333 **Fax:** 020-7421-2555
**Web:** www.saffrondigital.com
**Reg No:** 4371159 **Estd:** 2002 Private Limited Company
**Line of Business:** Audio/visual production services
**Export Sales:** £10,343,724
**Issued Capital:** £2,966,387
**Directors:** J J Keane, S G Brown
**Co. Secretary:** Davin Mcdermott
**Responsibilities**
**Admin:** Harriet Lee *(Office Manager)*
**Branches:** Saffron Digital Ltd, 2 Brunel Road, Reading, Berkshire RG30 3JH
**US SIC:** 7819 **UK SIC:** 97111

| | 31-12-12 | 31-12-11 | 31-12-10 |
|---|---|---|---|
| TO | 12,516,562 | 8,215,822 | 5,274,005 |
| P/L | 47,823 | 1,056,694 | 656,518 |
| NW | 3,039,380 | 2,991,557 | (1,147,025) |
| WC | 1,995,075 | 2,680,842 | (1,310,853) |
| Emp. | 107 | 90 | N/A |

DUNS 89-636-0187

## Saffron Homes Ltd

(**Subsidiary of:** Jason Tonge Ltd)
Devon Road, Bristol, Avon BS5 9AD
**Tel:** 01179396681
**Web:** www.brunelcare.org.uk
**Reg No:** 3317226 **Estd:** 2003 Private Limited Company
**Line of Business:** Other letting of own property
**Issued Capital:** £20,000
**Director:** J A Tonge
**Co. Secretary:** Ms Helen Tonge
**US SIC:** 6519 **UK SIC:** 85000

| | 05-04-14 | 05-04-13 | 05-04-12 |
|---|---|---|---|
| TA | 558,785 | 553,663 | 433,477 |
| NW | 187,779 | 175,399 | 162,248 |
| WC | (305,119) | (183,929) | (189,632) |

DUNS 21-173-2224

## Saffron Insurance Holdings Ltd

67 High Street, Saffron Walden, Essex CB10 1AA
**Tel:** 01799522293
**Web:** www.saffroninsurance.co.uk
**Reg No:** 6971834 **Estd:** 2009 Private Limited Company
**Line of Business:** Management activities of holding companies
**Trading Style:** Saffron Insurance Services Limited
**Issued Capital:** £1,017
**Directors:** D C Beswick, D C Wardley, C J Fellows
**US SIC:** 6711, 6399
**UK SIC:** 83962, 82001

| | 31-12-13 | 31-12-12 | 31-12-11 |
|---|---|---|---|
| TO | 6,557,340 | 7,110,897 | 7,319,621 |
| P/L | 184,770 | 795,587 | 1,092,038 |
| NW | (1,309,664) | (1,246,344) | (1,831,148) |
| WC | (50,481) | 442,308 | (96,688) |
| Emp. | 120 | 123 | 122 |

DUNS 50-481-7495

## Saffron Walden Property Developments Ltd

(**Subsidiary of:** Saffron Building Society)
Saffron House, Market Place, Saffron Walden, Essex CB10 1HX
**Tel:** 01799516517
**Web:** www.saffronbs.co.uk
**Reg No:** 2455568 **Estd:** 1989 Private Limited Company
**Line of Business:** Banks and financial institutions
**Issued Capital:** £2
**Director:** G R Dunn
**Co. Secretary:** Richard Barrett
**US SIC:** 6012 **UK SIC:** 81402

| | 31-12-13 | 31-12-12 | 31-12-11 |
|---|---|---|---|
| TA | 2 | 2 | 2 |
| NW | 2 | 2 | 2 |

DUNS 21-627-2039

## Saffron Walden Steam Laundry Company Ltd

(**Subsidiary of:** Swsl Holdings Ltd)
13-17 Gold Street, Saffron Walden, Essex CB10 1EN
**Tel:** 01799-522588
**Web:** www.saffronlaundry.co.uk
**Reg No:** 0054073 **VAT No:** 213466189
**Estd:** 1897 Private Limited Company

**Line of Business:** Dry cleaners
**Issued Capital:** £750
**Financial Director:** S Griffiths
**Co. Secretary:** Ms Helen Larsen
**Branches:** Saffron Walden Steam Laundry Company Ltd, 15 The Traverse, Bury St. Edmunds, Suffolk IP33 1BJ
**US SIC:** 7219 **UK SIC:** 98110
**Auditors:** David Verney & Co
**Bankers:** Lloyds TSB Bank plc (30-97-24)

| | 31-12-13 | 31-12-12 | 31-12-11 |
|---|---|---|---|
| TA | 1,232,135 | 1,253,735 | 1,231,481 |
| NW | 486,125 | 480,889 | 453,331 |
| WC | 121,086 | 122,464 | 191,213 |

DUNS 34-648-0882

## Safilo U K Ltd

**(Subsidiary of:** Safilo International B.V.)
Savoy Hill House, 7-10 Savoy Hill, London WC2R 0BU
**Tel:** 02078415990 **Fax:** 02078415991
**Web:** www.safilo.com
**Reg No:** 2773194 **Estd:** 1992 Private Limited Company
**Line of Business:** Wholesalers of optical goods
**Trading Style:** Safilo U K Limited
**Issued Capital:** £250
**Directors:** E Frixa, H M Blomqvist, E Stefanutto
**Co. Secretary:** Luca Beatrice
**Responsibilities**
**Senior:** Andrea Busato *(Director)*, Keith Gardner *(Financial Manager)*
**Finance:** Keith Gardner *(Financial Manager)*
**Marketing:** Kerri Campbell *(Trade Marketing Manager)*
**Branches:** Safilo U K Limited, Savoy Hill House, 7-10 Savoy Hill, London WC2R 0BU
**US SIC:** 3861 **UK SIC:** 37330
**Auditors:** PricewaterhouseCoopers LLP
**Bankers:** Lloyds TSB Bank plc (30-93-91)

| | 31-12-13 | 31-12-12 | 31-12-11 |
|---|---|---|---|
| TO | 28,528,866 | 23,156,432 | 16,313,258 |
| P/L | 757,683 | 102,050 | (2,101,662) |
| NW | 2,464,396 | 1,944,435 | 1,844,816 |
| WC | 2,317,949 | 1,844,211 | 1,816,174 |
| Emp. | 52 | 67 | 69 |

DUNS 23-523-7310 **Imp-Exp**

## Saft Ltd

**(Subsidiary of:** Saft Finance Sarl)
River Drive, South Shields, Tyne and Wear NE33 2TR
**Tel:** 0191-456-1451 **Fax:** 0191-456-6383
**Web:** www.saftbatteries.com
**Reg No:** 0328857 **Estd:** 1937 Private Limited Company
**Line of Business:** Battery suppliers
**Export Sales:** £2,251,000
**Issued Capital:** £5,839,754
**Directors:** B J Dathis, Mrs T Collinson, J N Taylor
**Co. Secretary:** Christopher Land
**Responsibilities**
**Senior:** Alan Averre *(Engineering Services Manager)*
**HR:** Amanda rutherford *(HR Manager)*
**Engineering:** Alan Averre *(Engineering Services Manager)*
**Branches:** Saft Ltd, 5 Astra Centre, Edinburgh Way, Harlow, Essex CM20 2BN
**US SIC:** 3692 **UK SIC:** 34321
**Auditors:** PricewaterhouseCoopers LLP
**Bankers:** HSBC Bank plc (40-02-50)

| | 31-12-13 | 31-12-12 | 31-12-11 |
|---|---|---|---|
| TO | 6,824,000 | 10,530,000 | 8,812,000 |
| P/L | 541,000 | 1,379,000 | 1,048,000 |
| NW | 5,852,000 | 6,351,000 | 5,936,000 |
| WC | 3,933,000 | 4,347,000 | 3,937,000 |
| Emp. | 87 | 99 | 100 |

DUNS 22-602-6177

## Saftdwin Ltd

London Road, Old Basing, Basingstoke, Hampshire RG24 7NZ
**Tel:** 01256-867000
**Web:** www.martins.uk.com
**Reg No:** 1426887 **VAT No:** 314354386
**Estd:** 1979 Private Limited Company
**Line of Business:** Sale of new motor vehicles
**Trading Style:** Martins of Basingstoke
**Issued Capital:** £325,210
**Principals:** B M Martin *(Managing)*, T J Handley, Ms S L Graham, Ms J R Lock
**Co. Secretary:** John Miles
**Branches:** Saftdwin Ltd, London Road, Basingstoke, Hampshire RG24 7NZ
**US SIC:** 5511 **UK SIC:** 65100
**Auditors:** Moore Stephens
**Bankers:** HSBC Bank plc (40-46-39)

| | 31-12-13 | 31-12-12 | 31-12-11 |
|---|---|---|---|
| TO | 91,022,266 | 75,925,076 | 73,700,326 |
| P/L | 1,022,686 | 1,040,543 | 849,598 |
| NW | 7,334,639 | 6,651,532 | 6,380,578 |
| WC | 401,978 | 52,481 | 428,091 |
| Emp. | 294 | 269 | 271 |

DUNS 29-573-9361 **Imp-Exp**

## Saftronics Ltd

**(Subsidiary of:** Saftronics Group Ltd)
Pearson Street, Leeds, West Yorkshire LS10 1BQ
**Tel:** 01132-457170
**Web:** www.saftronics.co.uk
**Reg No:** 1935773 **VAT No:** 427773818
**Estd:** 1979 Private Limited Company
**Line of Business:** Manufacture of other electrical equipment not elsewhere classified
**Issued Capital:** £6,922
**Directors:** J P Robinson, A H Rayner, M C Godfrey
**Co. Secretary:** Richard Kinder
**Responsibilities**
**HR:** Sian Andrews *(Human Resources Manager)*
**Health & Safety:** Sian Andrews *(Human Resources Manager)*
**Operations:** Sian Andrews *(Human Resources Manager)*
**Purchasing:** Val Cuthbertson *(Purchasing Manager)*
**US SIC:** 3629, 3829
**UK SIC:** 34350, 37100
**Auditors:** Bentley Jennison
**Bankers:** Bank Of Scotland (12-08-83)

| | 31-12-13 | 31-12-12 | 31-12-11 |
|---|---|---|---|
| TA | 3,138,489 | 3,533,109 | 3,182,923 |
| NW | 1,617,682 | 1,840,461 | 1,774,538 |
| WC | 1,612,137 | 1,831,384 | 1,767,199 |

DUNS 21-878-9737

## Saga Home Care

Oak Cottage, 13 The Square, Liphook, Hampshire GU30 7AB
**Tel:** 01428722848
**Web:** www.saga.co.uk
**Estd:** 1992
**Line of Business:** Nursing agencies
**Responsibilities**
**Senior:** Roshell Rowland *(Branch Manager)*
**US SIC:** 8091 **UK SIC:** 95200
**Employees:** 178

DUNS 73-992-4525

## Saga Independent Living (Hove) Ltd

**(Subsidiary of:** Acromas Holdings Ltd)
78 A Goldstone Villas, Hove, East Sussex BN3 3RU
**Tel:** 01273770202 **Fax:** 01273-771787
**Web:** www.sussexhomecareagency.co.uk
**Reg No:** 5242898 **Estd:** 1999 Private Limited Company
**Line of Business:** Other human health activities
**Issued Capital:** £4
**Directors:** D S Gibson, J H Whitehead
**Co. Secretary:** Ms Victoria Haynes
**Responsibilities**
**Senior:** Kerry Stone *(Branch Manager)*
**US SIC:** 8091 **UK SIC:** 95200
**Auditors:** Ernst & Young LLP

| | 31-01-14 | 31-01-13 | 31-01-12 |
|---|---|---|---|
| TA | 511,000 | 511,000 | 511,000 |
| NW | 511,000 | 511,000 | 511,000 |

DUNS 50-429-7672 **Exp**

## Saga Leisure Ltd

**(Subsidiary of:** Acromas Holdings Ltd)
Enbrook Park, Sandgate High Street, Sandgate, Folkestone, Kent CT20 3SE
**Tel:** 01303771111 **Fax:** 01303256676
**Web:** www.saga.co.uk
**Reg No:** 2421829 **Estd:** 1989 Private Limited Company
**Line of Business:** Management activities of holding companies
**Export Markets:** U S A, Australia
**Trading Style:** Saga Service, Saga Group, Saga Holidays
**Issued Capital:** £2,027,331
**Directors:** L H Batchelor, S M Howard, J A Goodsell
**Co. Secretary:** Ms Victoria Haynes
**US SIC:** 6711, 4722
**UK SIC:** 83962, 77001
**Bankers:** National Westminster Bank Plc (52-41-42)

| | 31-01-14 | 31-01-13 | 31-01-12 |
|---|---|---|---|
| TA | 49,661,000 | 49,661,000 | 49,661,000 |
| NW | 4,059,000 | 4,059,000 | 4,059,000 |

DUNS 21-171-2322 **Imp**

## Sage Automotive Interiors Ltd

Wellington Street, Bury, Lancashire BL8 2AL
**Tel:** 01617-623-686
**Web:** www.sageautomotiveinteriors.co.uk
**Reg No:** 6956549 **Estd:** 2009 Private Limited Company
**Line of Business:** Manufacture of other textiles not elsewhere classified
**Export Sales:** £6,209,919
**Issued Capital:** £100
**Directors:** D R Pieper, D F Russian, D N Campbell
**US SIC:** 2299, 3714
**UK SIC:** 43992, 35300
**Auditors:** RSM Tenon Audit Ltd

| | 31-12-13 | 31-12-12 | 31-12-11 |
|---|---|---|---|
| TO | 6,959,780 | N/A | N/A |
| P/L | (676,023) | N/A | N/A |
| NW | 2,129,600 | 2,728,215 | 2,162,329 |
| WC | (1,398,650) | 1,800,228 | 1,840,511 |
| Emp. | 84 | N/A | N/A |

DUNS 39-906-1407 **Imp**

## The Sage Group Plc.

North Park Avenue, Newcastle-Upon-Tyne, Tyne and Wear NE13 9AA
**Tel:** 01912943000
**Web:** www.sage.com
**Reg No:** 2231246 **Estd:** 1988 Public Limited Company
**Line of Business:** Management activities of holding companies
**Issued Capital:** £12,063,834
**Directors:** J W Hall, S Hare, N A Berkett, Ms I A Kuznetsova, Ms R Markland, J A Howell, D H Brydon, S P Kelly
**Co. Secretary:** Michael Robinson
**Responsibilities**
**Senior:** Jayne Archbold *(Manager)*, Steve Attwell *(General Manager, Business Part)*, Greg Hammermaster *(President)*, Stuart Lynn *(Chief Technical Officer)*, Paul Say *(Marketing Director)*
**Finance:** Jayne Archbold *(Manager)*, Barry Cochrane *(Accountants' Division)*, Natalie Coulthard *(Board Member)*
**Marketing:** Connie Davison *(Marketing Director)*, Matthew Forrest *(European Strategy Director Acc)*, Lisa Graveling *(Media and Public Relations)*, Amanda Jobbins *(CMO)*, Jenny Masters *(?Mid-Market Europe Marketing C)*, Jennie Whitell *(Group PR Manager)*
**Sales:** James Beard *(Head of Business Development &)*, Tony Callaghan *(Commercial Manager)*, June Horne *(Regional Account Manager)*, Cath Sheldon *(Social Business Manager)*, Piers Thom *(Sales Executive)*
**Admin:** Angela Burgon *(UK Travel and Reception Manage)*, Joanna Reilly *(Personal Assistant)*
**IT:** David Beard *(CRM Principal)*, Stuart Lynn *(Chief Technical Officer)*, Kerry Sinclair *(Head of Information Systems)*
**HR:** Leisa Docherty *(People Services Director)*, Richard Drury *(Group HR Director)*, Adrienne Mcfarland *(Human Resources Director)*, Tina Welch *(Human Resources Consultant)*
**Facilities:** Tony Dodds *(Facilities Manager)*
**Operations:** Andy Harrison *(Production and Operations Mana)*, Ken Rose *(Head of Business Services)*
**Engineering:** Stuart Lynn *(Chief Technical Officer)*
**US SIC:** 6711, 7372
**UK SIC:** 83962, 83940
**Auditors:** PricewaterhouseCoopers LLP
**Bankers:** Lloyds TSB Bank plc (30-90-50)
**Following financial data are in thousands**

| | 30-09-14 | 30-09-13 | 30-09-12 |
|---|---|---|---|
| TO | 1,306,800 | 1,376,100 | 1,340,200 |
| P/L | 277,500 | 164,100 | 334,300 |
| NW | (747,200) | (757,400) | (579,100) |
| WC | (444,600) | (375,100) | (420,500) |
| Emp. | 12,594 | 13,242 | 13,193 |

DUNS 29-888-5906

## Sage Number 3 Ltd

**(Subsidiary of:** Starwood Capital Group Global L.P.)
Wilderspool House, Greenalls Avenue, Warrington, Cheshire WA4 6RH
**Tel:** 01253290979 **Fax:** 01925-413137
**Reg No:** 2091581 **Estd:** 1987 Private Limited Company
**Line of Business:** Misc grocery wholesalers
**Trading Style:** G & J Drinks, Greenalls Pubs & Restaurants, The Griffin Inn
**Issued Capital:** £1,000
**Directors:** A M Coppel, C Elliot
**Branches:** Sage Number 3 Ltd, Ironbridge Road, Telford, Shropshire TF7 5HX
**US SIC:** 5149, 5921, 5813
**UK SIC:** 61700, 64200, 66200
**Auditors:** Ernst & Young LLP
**Employees:** 19,795

DUNS 21-112-7036 **Imp-Exp**

## Sagentia Group Plc

Harston Mill, Harston, Cambridge, Cambridgeshire CB22 7GG
**Web:** www.sagentia.com
**Reg No:** 6536543 **Estd:** 2008 Public Limited Company
**Line of Business:** Design consultants
**Export Sales:** £23,166,000
**Issued Capital:** £420,420
**Directors:** M R Ratcliffe, M J Lacey-Solymar, Professor K Glover, D J Courtley, Ms R A Hemsted
**Co. Secretary:** Ms Sarah Cole
**Responsibilities**
**Senior:** Dan Edwards *(Manager)*, Paul Wilkins *(SVP, Head of Medical)*
**Finance:** Guy McCarthy *(Financial Director)*
**Marketing:** Iain Ansell *(Head of Product Development)*, Charlotte Gynane *(Marketing Manager)*
**Sales:** Alun James *(Commercial Director)*, Tamara Kahn *(SVP Corporate Development & St)*
**Admin:** Marian Green *(Personal Assistant)*
**IT:** Gregory Berman *(Head Innovation and Technology)*, Peter Norton *(IT Manager)*
**HR:** Alison Grant *(Human Resources Manager)*, Anna Jackson *(HR Manager)*, Rebecca Lawrence *(Human Resources)*
**Operations:** Euan Morrison *(Intelliguage Project Manager)*
**US SIC:** 8911, 7391, 7399
**UK SIC:** 83701, 94000, 83954
**Auditors:** Grant Thornton UK LLP

| | 31-12-13 | 31-12-12 | 31-12-11 |
|---|---|---|---|
| TO | 30,596,000 | 22,268,000 | 23,568,000 |
| P/L | 4,939,000 | 2,998,000 | 3,346,000 |
| NW | 25,433,000 | 25,251,000 | 26,420,000 |
| WC | 19,420,000 | 15,257,000 | 17,732,000 |
| Emp. | 190 | 156 | 154 |

DUNS 76-386-5284 **Imp**

## Sagittarius Ltd

Lower Victoria Street, Oldham, Lancashire OL9 9TU
**Tel:** 0161-620-2029 **Fax:** 01616287102
**Web:** www.sagittarius.demon.co.uk
**Reg No:** 2554830 **VAT No:** 562550055
**Estd:** 1990 Private Limited Company
**Line of Business:** Wholesale of hardware, plumbing and heating equipment and supplies
**Issued Capital:** £111
**Directors:** D Watkinson, D Parkinson
**Co. Secretary:** Mrs Kathleen Casey
**Branches:** Sagittarius Ltd, Willan Enterprise Centre Watts Street, Oldham, Lancashire OL9 9LT
**US SIC:** 5074 **UK SIC:** 61300
**Auditors:** Royce Peeling Green

| | 31-12-13 | 31-12-12 | 31-12-11 |
|---|---|---|---|
| TA | 1,740,923 | 1,564,801 | 1,692,192 |
| NW | 1,027,456 | 1,062,703 | 1,061,389 |
| WC | 915,428 | 956,983 | 949,270 |

DUNS 23-834-4639

## S.A.H Nursing Homes Ltd

**(Subsidiary of:** A.G.E. Nursing Homes Ltd)
Roslyn House, King Street, Dunstable, Bedfordshire LU5 5TT
**Tel:** 01582-896600
**Web:** www.roslynhouse.co.uk
**Reg No:** 3826287 **Estd:** 1999 Private Limited Company
**Line of Business:** Nursing homes
**Issued Capital:** £2,100
**Director:** S A Hainsworth
**Co. Secretary:** Ms Julia Hainsworth-Adams
**Responsibilities**
**Senior:** Marge Feltcher *(Manager)*
**Operations:** Sarah Betts *(Manager)*
**US SIC:** 8051 **UK SIC:** 95100

| | 31-12-13 | 31-12-12 | 31-12-11 |
|---|---|---|---|
| TA | 2,081,472 | 2,054,106 | 1,899,082 |
| NW | 1,649,981 | 1,508,296 | 1,387,907 |
| WC | (201,809) | (334,289) | (214,411) |

DUNS 23-958-6550

## Sahara Holdings Ltd

Williams House 61 Hailey Road, Erith, Kent DA18 4AA
**Tel:** 020-8319-7700
**Reg No:** 3947832 **Estd:** 2000 Private Limited Company
**Line of Business:** Wholesale of other electronic parts and equipment
**Export Sales:** £5,180,996
**Issued Capital:** £50,000
**Directors:** N Batley, K Batley
**Co. Secretary:** Nigel Batley
**US SIC:** 5065 **UK SIC:** 61500
**Bankers:** Barclays Bank Plc (20-00-30)

| | 31-12-13 | 31-12-12 | 31-12-11 |
|---|---|---|---|
| TO | 28,111,318 | 20,930,550 | 17,061,811 |
| P/L | 1,743,837 | 518,739 | 737,241 |
| NW | 4,461,311 | 3,835,125 | 3,629,937 |
| WC | 4,645,879 | 3,606,895 | 3,209,934 |
| Emp. | 68 | 63 | 62 |

DUNS 21-690-9365 **Imp**

## Sahaviriya Steel Industries Uk Ltd

**(Subsidiary of:** Sahaviriya Steel Industries Public Company Limited)
Steel House, Redcar, Cleveland TS10 5QW
**Tel:** 01642-408000
**Web:** www.ssi-steel.co.uk
**Reg No:** 7381674 **Estd:** 2010 Private Limited Company
**Line of Business:** Manufacture of basic iron and steel and of ferro-alloys
**Trading Style:** Ssi Uk
**Directors:** K Mapanao, S Sivapaiboon, V R Conti, R H Mathis, W Viriyaprapaikit

**Co. Secretary:** Simon Melhuish-Hancock
**US SIC:** 3325 **UK SIC:** 31110
**Auditors:** KPMG LLP
**Employees:** 1,741
**Turnover:** £1,514,721,000

DUNS 21-210-8893
### Sahbourne Health Carc
Sodbury Road, Wotton-Under-Edge, Gloucestershire GL12 8NR
**Tel:** 01454-294426
**Web:** www.bettercaring.co.uk
**Estd:** 1987 Proprietorship
**Line of Business:** Nursing homes
**Proprietor:** Ms A Waldron
**Responsibilities**
**Senior:** Christina Arriola (Manager), Tess Breen (Manager)
**US SIC:** 8051 **UK SIC:** 95100
**Employees:** 64

DUNS 50-445-5916 **Imp**
### Sai Automotive Fradley Ltd
(**Subsidiary of:** Peugeot Sa)
Common Lane, Fradley, Lichfield, Staffordshire WS13 8NQ
**Tel:** 01543445218
**Web:** www.faurecia.com
**Reg No:** 2433456 **VAT No:** 652204665
**Estd:** 1810 Private Limited Company
**Line of Business:** Manufacturers of vehicle components
**Trading Style:** Faurecia
**Issued Capital:** £121,700,000
**Directors:** Faurecia Automotive Holdings, Y Cantieni
**Co. Secretary:**
Jordan Company Secretaries Limit
**Responsibilities**
**Senior:** Nick Hayton (Plant Manager)
**HR:** Emma Muller (Human Resources Manager), Faye Norris (Manager)
**Engineering:** Lee Matthews (Maintenance Manager)
**US SIC:** 3714 **UK SIC:** 35300
**Auditors:** Ernst & Young LLP
**Bankers:** HSBC Bank plc (40-02-50)

| | 31-12-12 | 31-12-11 | 31-12-10 |
|---|---|---|---|
| TO | 80,143,000 | 62,411,000 | 55,143,000 |
| P/L | 11,717,000 | 4,617,000 | 1,787,000 |
| NW | 15,768,000 | 7,461,000 | 1,898,000 |
| WC | 7,037,000 | 7,274,000 | 204,000 |
| Emp. | 292 | 249 | 253 |

DUNS 50-444-2245 **Imp-Exp**
### Sai Automotive Washington Ltd
(**Subsidiary of:** Peugeot Sa)
Staithes Road, Washington, Tyne and Wear NE38 8NW
**Tel:** 01914192156
**Web:** www.egger.co.uk
**Reg No:** 2432086 **VAT No:** 551216277
**Estd:** 2011 Private Limited Company
**Line of Business:** Recycling
**Export Markets:** Sweden
**Trading Style:** Faurecia
**Issued Capital:** £7,222,000
**Directors:** J M Membrillera, Sai Automotive Fradley Ltd
**Co. Secretary:**
Jordan Company Secretaries Limit
**Responsibilities**
**Senior:** Mark Hayton (Manager), Julie Head (Logistics Coordinator)
**HR:** Karen Almond (Human Resources Manager)
**Operations:** Julie Head (Logistics Coordinator)
**Fleet:** Julie Head (Logistics Coordinator)
**Branches:** Sai Automotive Washington Ltd, Centurion Pk, Watling St, Tamworth, Staffordshire B77 5PN
**US SIC:** 3031, 2211
**UK SIC:** 48123, 43220
**Auditors:** Ernst & Young LLP
**Bankers:** Barclays Bank Plc (20-98-61)

| | 31-12-13 | 31-12-12 | 31-12-11 |
|---|---|---|---|
| TO | 27,631,000 | 27,877,000 | 30,059,000 |
| P/L | (1,037,000) | (128,000) | 3,627,000 |
| NW | 1,154,000 | 2,106,000 | 5,112,000 |
| WC | 2,848,000 | 3,985,000 | 4,268,000 |
| Emp. | 161 | 155 | 142 |

DUNS 23-695-8067
### Sai Global Assurance Services Ltd
(**Subsidiary of:** Sai Global Limited)
Partis House, Milton Keynes, Buckinghamshire MK5 8HJ
**Tel:** 02921510190
**Reg No:** 3690660 **VAT No:** 716584026
**Estd:** 1998 Private Limited Company
**Line of Business:** Business and management consultancy activities not elsewhere classified
**Trading Style:** Sai Global Assurance Services Ltd
**Issued Capital:** £80,000

**Directors:** P J Mullins, P R Butcher, G P Richardson
**Co. Secretary:** Ms Hanna Myllyoja
**Responsibilities**
**Senior:** Christopher Bloon (Manager), Duncan Lilley (Manager), Anthony Scotton (CEO)
**US SIC:** 7399 **UK SIC:** 83954
**Auditors:** Ashbys

| | 30-06-13 | 30-06-12 | 30-06-11 |
|---|---|---|---|
| TO | 13,329,231 | 12,131,909 | 11,062,795 |
| P/L | (379,531) | 708,748 | 422,782 |
| NW | 1,915 | 675,553 | 2,318,628 |
| WC | (4,795,241) | (4,181,666) | 1,745,929 |
| Emp. | 180 | 203 | 213 |

DUNS 21-632-8253
### Sai Global Ltd
Partis House Davy Avenue, Knowlhill, Milton Keynes, Buckinghamshire MK5 8HJ
**Tel:** 01908249974
**Web:** www.saiglobal.com
**Reg No:** 7109048 **Estd:** 2009 Private Limited Company
**Line of Business:** Legal activities
**Issued Capital:** £1
**Directors:** G P Richardson, P R Butcher, P J Mullins
**Co. Secretary:** Ms Hanna Myllyoja
**Responsibilities**
**Senior:** Mario Balotelli (Manager)
**US SIC:** 8111 **UK SIC:** 83500

| | 30-06-13 | 30-06-12 | 30-06-11 |
|---|---|---|---|
| TA | 1 | 1 | 1 |
| NW | 1 | 1 | 1 |

DUNS 23-779-2952
### Sai School of Harrow
10 Wrenwood Way, Pinner, Middlesex HA5 2HS
**Tel:** 020-8868-1693
**Web:** www.saischool.com
**Reg No:** 3772546 **Estd:** 1999 Private Company Limited By Guarantee
**Line of Business:** Schools (foundation)
**Directors:** R Mehta Radia, N Badiani
**Co. Secretary:** Anil Gadhia
**US SIC:** 8211 **UK SIC:** 93200

| | 31-05-13 | 31-05-12 | 31-05-11 |
|---|---|---|---|
| TO | 20,367 | 19,433 | 18,096 |
| P/L | (67) | 4,130 | 3,202 |
| NW | 27,713 | 27,780 | 23,650 |
| WC | 27,245 | 27,156 | 22,818 |

DUNS 34-631-1538 **Imp**
### Saic Motor Uk Technical Centre Ltd
(**Subsidiary of:** Shanghai Automotive Industry Corporation (Group))
Lowhill Lane, Birmingham, West Midlands B31 2BQ
**Tel:** 01212-513700 **Fax:** 01212-513600
**Web:** www.saicmotor.co.uk
**Reg No:** 5437330 **Estd:** 2005 Private Limited Company
**Line of Business:** Design consultants
**Export Sales:** £38,149,000
**Issued Capital:** £2
**Directors:** J Zhang, D M Lindley, X Wang, P M Mcnamara, M Wu
**Co. Secretary:** Lian Su
**Responsibilities**
**Engineering:** Julian Harper-Cuss (Engineering Manager)
**US SIC:** 8911, 7397
**UK SIC:** 83701, 83702
**Auditors:** Deloitte & Touche LLP
**Bankers:** HSBC Bank plc (40-05-30)

| | 31-12-13 | 31-12-12 | 31-12-11 |
|---|---|---|---|
| TO | 38,149,000 | 30,730,000 | 30,777,000 |
| WC | (4,000,000) | (4,105,000) | (2,948,000) |
| Emp. | 155 | 141 | 131 |

DUNS 21-782-8597
### Saica Pack Uk
Cloberfield Factory, Milngavie, Glasgow, Lanarkshire G62 7LN
**Tel:** 01419562323
**Web:** www.seica.com
**Estd:** 1986 Partnership
**Line of Business:** Manufacturers of boxes and cartons
**Partners:** J Williams, R Hogg, R Sharp, D Kesson, W Mckelvie
**Responsibilities**
**Senior:** William McKelvie (Partner)
**US SIC:** 2651 **UK SIC:** 47253
**Employees:** 130

DUNS 29-235-5351 **Imp-Exp**
### Saica Pack Uk Ltd
(**Subsidiary of:** Aragocias Sociedad Anonima)
144 Manchester Road, Carrington, Trafford, Manchester M31 4QN
**Tel:** 01617767000
**Web:** www.saica.com
**Reg No:** 1218445 **VAT No:** 974812586
**Estd:** 1975 Private Limited Company

**Line of Business:** Manufacture of other containers
**Export Markets:** European Union (E U)
**Export Sales:** £18,096,000
**Issued Capital:** £84,730,625
**Directors:** A R Alejandro Balet, P Giraud, B Lister, T A Rice, Ms S Alejandro Balet
**Co. Secretary:** Steven Petty
**Responsibilities**
**Senior:** Vince Alcock (Warehouse Manager), Pedro Gutierrez Rodriguez (Manager)
**Branches:** Saica Pack Uk Ltd, Warrington Road, Wigan, Lancashire WN3 6XD
**US SIC:** 2654, 2653
**UK SIC:** 47280, 47251
**Auditors:** Ernst & Young LLP
**Bankers:** National Westminster Bank Plc (60-15-29)

| | 31-12-13 | 31-12-12 | 31-12-11 |
|---|---|---|---|
| TO | 287,695,000 | 288,128,000 | 284,178,000 |
| P/L | 6,848,000 | 11,119,000 | (613,000) |
| NW | 213,705,000 | 209,462,000 | 199,390,000 |
| WC | 102,026,000 | 91,828,000 | 75,666,000 |
| Emp. | 1,484 | 1,517 | 1,508 |

DUNS 34-864-4217
### Saif Charter Ltd
3a Bullfields, Sawbridgeworth, Hertfordshire CM21 9DB
**Tel:** 0845-230-6777
**Web:** www.saif.org.uk
**Reg No:** 5663828 **Estd:** 2005 Private Limited Company
**Line of Business:** Management activities of holding companies
**Issued Capital:** £1
**Directors:** G A Neill, E J West
**Co. Secretary:** Richard Edwards
**US SIC:** 6711, 8631
**UK SIC:** 83962, 96313
**Bankers:** Lloyds TSB Bank plc (30-10-01)

| | 31-03-14 | 31-03-13 | 31-03-12 |
|---|---|---|---|
| TO | 32,603,610 | 21,313,861 | 12,678,650 |
| P/L | 1,007,771 | (5,216) | 85,332 |
| NW | 1,320,503 | 540,090 | 567,450 |
| WC | 840,623 | (11,938) | 438,381 |
| Emp. | 355 | 246 | 136 |

DUNS 29-935-9307 **Imp-Exp**
### Sailing Holidays Ltd
105 Mount Pleasant Road, Harlesden, London NW10 3EH
**Tel:** 020-8459-8787
**Web:** www.sailingholidays.com
**Reg No:** 2104689 **VAT No:** 539246329
**Estd:** 1989 Private Limited Company
**Line of Business:** Tour operators
**Export Markets:** Greece
**Issued Capital:** £30,000
**Principals:** B E Neilson (Managing), F M Burdett-Coutts
**Co. Secretary:** Mrs Heidi Neilson
**US SIC:** 4722 **UK SIC:** 77001
**Auditors:** Trotman & Co
**Bankers:** Barclays Bank Plc (20-96-55)

| | 31-10-14 | 31-10-13 | 31-10-12 |
|---|---|---|---|
| TO | 8,863,281 | 9,156,194 | 9,086,599 |
| P/L | 146,109 | 147,912 | 125,286 |
| NW | 3,691,880 | 3,643,568 | 3,604,447 |
| WC | 49,304 | (150,696) | (27,332) |
| Emp. | 93 | 89 | 81 |

DUNS 22-630-3923 **Imp**
### Sailors' Society
350 Shirley Road, Southampton, Hampshire SO15 3HY
**Fax:** 02380981386
**Web:** www.bifs.org.uk
**Reg No:** 0086942 **VAT No:** 248821835
**Estd:** 1905 Private Company Limited By Guarantee
**Line of Business:** Activities of other membership organisations not elsewhere classified
**Trading Style:** B I S S Trading, British & International Sailors Society
**Directors:** Captain J R Stoneley, A Fischbacher, Mrs N C Shaw, C A Mcmurray, M J Burridge, S K Sharma, Dr P M Swift, J Holloway
**Co. Secretary:** Stuart Rivers
**Responsibilities**
**Senior:** Michael Drayton (Director), Peter Goldberg (Director)
**Finance:** Andrew Pitcher (Director of Finance)
**Branches:** Sailors' Society, 2-3 Orchard Place, Southampton, Hampshire SO14 3BR
**US SIC:** 8699, 8321, 8999
**UK SIC:** 96902, 96111, 83954
**Auditors:** Saffery Champness
**Bankers:** National Westminster Bank Plc (56-00-68)

| | 31-12-13 | 31-12-12 | 31-12-11 |
|---|---|---|---|
| TO | 4,332,000 | 3,359,000 | 3,460,000 |
| P/L | 572,000 | (382,000) | (44,000) |
| NW | 18,007,000 | 15,689,000 | 15,242,000 |
| WC | 1,713,000 | 1,097,000 | 1,291,000 |
| Emp. | 112 | 117 | 126 |

DUNS 23-675-0352
### Sailors the Soldiers Airmen and Families Association - Forces Help
4 St Dunstan's Hill, London EC3R 8AD
**Tel:** 02074 038 783
**Web:** https://www.ssafa.org.uk
**Reg No:** 0000571RC **Estd:** 1990 Incorporate By Act Of Parliament
**Line of Business:** Counselling & advice services
**Trading Style:** Ssafa - Forces Help
**Principals:** P M Of Kent (President), K Wood (Financial), Major General C R Grey, Lt Col H B Singer, B Best
**Responsibilities**
**Senior:** Kevin O'donoghue (Chairman), Prince of Kent (President)
**Marketing:** Ann-Mari Freebairn (?Director of Marketing and Com)
**HR:** Susie Worley (Training Director)
**Branches:** Sailors The Soldiers Airmen and Families Association - Forces Help, Saatchi Gallery, Duke Of Yorks Headquarters, London SW3 4RY
**US SIC:** 8321, 8699
**UK SIC:** 96111, 96902
**Bankers:** Coutts & Co (18-00-02)
**Employees:** 732

DUNS 21-326-4008
### Sainsbury's
915-921 Fulham Road, London SW6 5HU
**Tel:** 02072008710
**Web:** www.sainsburys.co.uk
**Estd:** 2012 Proprietorship
**Line of Business:** Retail sale in non-specialised stores (excluding ctns) holding an alcohol licence with food, beverages or tobacco predominating
**Proprietor:** I Charles
**Responsibilities**
**Senior:** Richard Coppin (Manager), Levon Gumbs (Manager)
**US SIC:** 5199 **UK SIC:** 61900
**Employees:** 500

DUNS 21-879-0739
### Sainsbury's Distribution Centre
Fleming Road, Waltham Abbey, Essex EN9 3BZ
**Tel:** 01992766000
**Web:** www.sainsburys.co.uk
**Estd:** 2012
**Line of Business:** Distribution service providers
**US SIC:** 4712 **UK SIC:** 77002
**Employees:** 1,600

DUNS 21-155-2547
### St. Aidans Day Nursery
Lismore Place, Carlisle, Cumbria CA1 1LY
**Tel:** 01228631266
**Web:** www.st-aidans.cumbria.sch.uk
**Estd:** 1970
**Line of Business:** Social work activities without accommodation
**Principals:** Ms J Watson (Financial), M Murphy
**US SIC:** 8321 **UK SIC:** 96111
**Employees:** 116

DUNS 21-043-4553
### Saint & Co
Lakeland Business Park, Lamplugh Road, Cockermouth, Cumbria CA13 0QT
**Tel:** 01900824118
**Web:** www.saint.co.uk
**Estd:** 1978
**Line of Business:** Accounting activities
**Proprietor:** W Moore
**US SIC:** 8931 **UK SIC:** 83600
**Employees:** 57

DUNS 23-562-8596 **Imp**
### St.Andrews Bay Development Ltd
Fairmont St Andrews, St Andrews, Fife KY16 8PN
**Tel:** 01334-837000
**Web:** www.fairmontstandrews.com
**Reg No:** 0185639SC **VAT No:** 889069458
**Estd:** 2003 Private Limited Company
**Line of Business:** Hotels
**Trading Style:** Fairmont St Andrews
**Issued Capital:** £10,101,010
**Directors:** P R Hewetson, G Doshi, Ms P Singla
**Responsibilities**
**Senior:** Robert Glashan (General Manager), Luke Hamill (Manager), Michael Pashley (overall Director), Garrett Turta (General Manager)
**Sales:** Jane Frazer (Sales Director)

**HR:** Jackie Cannon *(Human Resources Manager)*
**US SIC:** 7011, 7999
**UK SIC:** 66500, 97913
**Auditors:** Deloitte LLP
**Bankers:** Bank Of Scotland (80-05-10)

| | 31-12-13 | 31-12-12 | 31-12-11 |
|---|---|---|---|
| TO | 13,808,631 | 13,159,400 | 12,721,986 |
| P/L | (464,821) | (12,836,033) | (3,866,230) |
| NW | (30,462,323) | (30,715,939) | (19,419,314) |
| WC | (63,243,904) | (65,737,882) | (57,502,696) |
| Emp. | 207 | 221 | 225 |

DUNS 21-179-0250
## Saint Andrews Ltd
10 Lakesmere Close, North Oxford Business Park, Kidlington, Oxfordshire OX5 1LG
**Tel:** 01865841362
**Web:** www.homeinstead.co.uk
**Reg No:** 7016634 **Estd:** 2009 Private Limited Company
**Line of Business:** Home care and help services
**Issued Capital:** £2
**Directors:** Mrs S Dunster, M A Owen
**Co. Secretary:** Mrs Alison Simpson
**US SIC:** 8811 **UK SIC:** 99000

| | 30-09-13 | 30-09-12 | 30-09-11 |
|---|---|---|---|
| TA | 78,606 | 101,938 | 57,702 |
| NW | (577) | 22,294 | (15,047) |
| WC | (16,730) | 8,133 | (16,245) |

DUNS 76-914-8685
## St. Andrew's School (Rochester) Ltd
28 Watts Avenue, Rochester, Kent ME1 1SA
**Tel:** 01634-843479
**Web:** www.st-andrews.rochester.sch.uk
**Reg No:** 0733743 **Estd:** 1945 Private Limited Company
**Line of Business:** Schools (independent)
**Issued Capital:** £100
**Director:** J C Tweedale
**Responsibilities**
**Senior:** Clive Adderley *(Manager)*, Timothy Emmett *(Manager)*, Joan Jabbour *(Principal)*
**US SIC:** 8211 **UK SIC:** 93200
**Auditors:** JAD Audit Ltd
**Bankers:** National Westminster Bank Plc (60-17-36)

| | 31-03-13 | 31-03-12 | 31-03-11 |
|---|---|---|---|
| TA | 100 | 1 | 1 |
| NW | 100 | 1 | 1 |

DUNS 77-009-1957
## St. Andrews University Services Ltd
North Street, St Andrews, Fife KY16 9AL
**Web:** www.st-andrews.ac.uk
**Reg No:** 0134798SC **Estd:** 1991 Private Limited Company
**Line of Business:** Hotels
**Issued Capital:** £2
**Directors:** B Stuart, D A Watson
**Co. Secretary:** Roy Drummond
**US SIC:** 7011 **UK SIC:** 66500
**Auditors:** Ernst & Young LLP

| | 31-07-14 | 31-07-13 | 31-07-12 |
|---|---|---|---|
| TO | 2,148,684 | 2,723,857 | 2,369,656 |
| NW | 2 | 2 | 2 |
| WC | 2 | 2 | 2 |

DUNS 29-580-4355
## St. Andrew's (Woking) School Trust
Church Hill House, Wilson Way, Woking, Surrey GU21 4QW
**Web:** www.st-andrews.woking.sch.uk
**Reg No:** 1942216 **Estd:** 1985 Private Limited Company
**Line of Business:** General secondary education
**Directors:** N A Moden, Mrs E S Mcquater, Ms J J Way, Mrs T C Gill Parker, J E Tufts, A O Wingfield Digby, J H Gibson, D S Knapp
**Co. Secretary:** Miss Karen Windegaard
**Responsibilities**
**Senior:** David Jarrett *(Manager)*, Julian Jeffrey *(Manager)*, Jane Lunnon *(Manager)*
**Marketing:** Tracey Cole *(Marketing Manager)*
**Health & Safety:** Juliette McKenzie *(Health & Safety Coordinator)*
**US SIC:** 8211 **UK SIC:** 93200
**Auditors:** Fraser Russell
**Bankers:** Barclays Bank Plc (20-97-58)

| | 31-08-13 | 31-08-12 | 31-08-11 |
|---|---|---|---|
| TO | 3,021,641 | 3,001,904 | 2,997,956 |
| P/L | 140,915 | 11,657 | 31,858 |
| NW | 1,649,159 | 1,508,244 | 1,496,587 |
| WC | 942,337 | 794,905 | 1,139,665 |
| Emp. | 60 | 62 | 63 |

DUNS 76-913-0253
## St. Anne's Nursing Home Ltd
**(Subsidiary of:** Cedarwood Residential Care Ltd)
Crossway Grn, Chepstow, Gwent NP16 5LX
**Tel:** 01291622050
**Reg No:** 0393186 **Estd:** 1945 Private Limited Company
**Line of Business:** Social work activities with accommodation
**Issued Capital:** £1,170
**Director:** B P Hadley
**US SIC:** 8321 **UK SIC:** 96111
**Auditors:** KPMG

| | 31-05-14 | 31-05-13 | 31-05-12 |
|---|---|---|---|
| TA | 1,051,980 | 1,016,788 | 939,221 |
| NW | 680,786 | 733,365 | 820,167 |
| WC | 28,311 | (177,654) | 41,510 |

DUNS 28-864-4297
## St. Ann's Hospice
St Anns Road North, Cheadle, Cheshire SK8 3SZ
**Tel:** 0161-437-8136
**Web:** www.sah.org.uk
**Reg No:** 0947220 **Estd:** 1990 Private Company Limited By Guarantee
**Line of Business:** Hospital activities
**Directors:** A Hillier, Ms S J Merchant, Ms M K Bashir, E O'Neal, Mrs C Gibbons, A J Bond, Ms H E Chilton, L Dillon
**Co. Secretary:** Miss Victoria Yates
**Responsibilities**
**Senior:** Christopher Bracegirdle *(Manager)*, Julie Foley *(Support Services Manager)*, Anne Mack *(Director)*
**Finance:** Katrina Bury *(Fundraising Manager)*
**Marketing:** Margaret Beck *(Fundraising Officer)*, Carrie Bradshaw *(Fundraising and Communications)*, Katrina Bury *(Fundraising Manager)*, Danielle Carney *(Fundraising and Communications)*, Anna Ross *(Marketing and Communications O)*, John Soonaye *(Marketing & Communications Man)*
**HR:** Gill Turnpenney *(HR Director)*, Mary Veevers *(Human Resources Manager)*
**Health & Safety:** Jane Close *(Health & Safety Officer)*
**Facilities:** Julie Foley *(Support Services Manager)*
**Operations:** Sian Burgess *(Clinical Operations Manager)*, Bernadette Quinn *(Clinical Operations Manager)*
**Purchasing:** Julie Foley *(Support Services Manager)*
**Branches:** St. Ann's Hospice, 82 School Road, Sale, Cheshire M33 7XB
**US SIC:** 8062 **UK SIC:** 95100
**Auditors:** Deloitte & Touche
**Bankers:** The Royal Bank Of Scotland Plc (16-00-01)

| | 31-03-14 | 31-03-13 | 31-03-12 |
|---|---|---|---|
| TO | 11,869,495 | 9,708,015 | 9,883,995 |
| P/L | 1,118,150 | (877,204) | 107,289 |
| NW | 11,973,772 | 10,266,568 | 11,061,878 |
| WC | 3,064,205 | 1,946,769 | 2,851,157 |
| Emp. | 242 | 243 | 246 |

DUNS 23-666-3308
## Saint Anselm's College
Nazareth House, Manor Hill, Prenton, Merseyside CH43 1UG
**Tel:** 0151-652-1408
**Web:** www.st-anselms.com
**Estd:** 1933
**Line of Business:** Schools (local authority)
**Directors:** C Cleugh, Mrs S Mcgraffney
**Responsibilities**
**Senior:** Simon Duggin *(Headmaster)*
**IT:** Colin Hawksworth *(Senior ICT Services Manager)*
**US SIC:** 8211 **UK SIC:** 93200
**Employees:** 60

DUNS 21-727-6089
## St. Anselm's College Edmund Rice Academy Trust
St Anselm's College Manor Hill, Birkenhead, Merseyside CH43 1UQ
**Tel:** 01516521957
**Web:** www.st-anselms.com
**Reg No:** 7638417 **Estd:** 2011 Private Company Limited By Guarantee
**Line of Business:** Schools (local authority)
**Directors:** J M Greaves, Mrs M Martin, G J Davies, W B Iveson, J S Brown, Mrs P Young, A R Wood, P J Wyness
**Co. Secretary:** Brian Morgan
**Responsibilities**
**Senior:** Brian Cummings *(Director)*, Kenneth Diaz *(Director)*, Richard Duggan *(Director)*, Pamela Green *(Director)*, John Oates *(Director)*, Jean Rawsthorne *(Director)*, Michael Redfearn *(Director)*
**US SIC:** 8211 **UK SIC:** 93200

**Bankers:** Lloyds TSB Bank plc (30-00-00)

| | 31-08-13 | 31-08-12 |
|---|---|---|
| TO | 6,659,000 | 6,132,510 |
| P/L | 1,797,000 | (569,145) |
| NW | 1,200,000 | (610,145) |
| WC | 388,000 | 172,114 |
| Emp. | 97 | 86 |

DUNS 21-042-1485
## St. Antony's Catholic College
St Antony's Catholic College Bradfield, Road, Manchester M41 9PD
**Tel:** 01619118001
**Web:** www.st-antonys.com
**Estd:** 2012
**Line of Business:** General secondary education
**Responsibilities**
**Senior:** Bill Byford *(Principal)*, Keith Turmeau *(Principal)*, Fiona Wright *(Head Teacher)*
**US SIC:** 8211 **UK SIC:** 93200
**Employees:** 70

DUNS 23-541-6674
## St. Aubyn's (Woodford Green) School Trust
Bunces Lane, Woodford Green, Essex IG8 9DU
**Tel:** 02085041577
**Web:** www.staubyns.com
**Reg No:** 1218766 **Estd:** 1890 Private Company Limited By Guarantee
**Line of Business:** Schools (independent)
**Directors:** Mrs J E Ruff, A J Botha, Ms S Evans, D I Davies, Mrs M Lalude, D Shah, Mrs E Blewett, M R Foster
**Co. Secretary:** Mrs Maureen Foakes
**Responsibilities**
**Senior:** Kenneth Farmer *(Director)*, Gordon James *(Headmaster)*, Patricia Russell *(Director)*
**Marketing:** Georgina Hogwood *(Marketing Manager)*
**IT:** Neil Colton *(Network Manager)*
**HR:** Gordon James *(Headmaster)*
**US SIC:** 8211 **UK SIC:** 93200
**Auditors:** Haslers
**Bankers:** HSBC Bank plc (40-06-23)

| | 31-07-14 | 31-07-13 | 31-07-12 |
|---|---|---|---|
| TO | 4,782,301 | 4,572,315 | 4,662,997 |
| P/L | 612,677 | 566,441 | 835,937 |
| NW | 6,061,779 | 5,449,102 | 4,882,661 |
| WC | 713,783 | 2,007,125 | 1,840,559 |
| Emp. | 80 | 81 | 83 |

DUNS 64-079-5956
## St. Augustine's Priory School Ltd
Hillcrest Road, London W5 2JL
**Tel:** 020-8997-2022
**Web:** www.saintaugustinespriory.org.uk
**Reg No:** 4482913 **Estd:** 2002 Private Company Limited By Guarantee
**Line of Business:** General secondary education
**Directors:** D P Murphy, Ms C Mcintyre, Ms D A Neilson, Rt Rev K T Conry, C N Bennett, Ms C M Murphy, Ms A M Fitzgerald
**Co. Secretary:** Sriranjan Waas
**US SIC:** 8211 **UK SIC:** 93200
**Bankers:** HSBC Bank plc (40-02-26)

| | 31-07-13 | 31-07-12 | 31-07-11 |
|---|---|---|---|
| TO | 4,977,853 | 5,222,696 | 5,335,319 |
| P/L | (999,003) | 216,367 | (53,832) |
| NW | 1,442,687 | 2,385,381 | 2,166,352 |
| WC | 1,143,279 | 2,258,977 | 2,151,637 |
| Emp. | 90 | 76 | 81 |

DUNS 64-729-4594
## St. Augustines R C Primary School
St Wilfrids Circus, Leeds, West Yorkshire LS8 3PF
**Tel:** 01132-930350
**Web:** www.staugustinesleeds.org.uk
**Estd:** 1996
**Line of Business:** Schools (local authority)
**Proprietor:** M Teggart
**Responsibilities**
**Senior:** Susan O'brien *(Head Teacher)*
**US SIC:** 8211 **UK SIC:** 93200
**Employees:** 50

DUNS 21-627-5024 Imp
## St.Austell Brewery Company Ltd
63 Trevarthian Road, St Austell, Cornwall PL25 4BY
**Web:** www.staustellbrewery.co.uk
**Reg No:** 0107021 **VAT No:** 131603807
**Estd:** 1910 Private Limited Company
**Line of Business:** Manufacture of beer
**Export Sales:** £394,000
**Issued Capital:** £1,792,384

**Principals:** C J Stratton *(Financial)*, K R Georgel, G H Barnes, T A Luck, W F Michelmore, J B Neame, P M Thompson, S J Staughton
**Responsibilities**
**Sales:** Ian Blunt *(Sales Director)*, Pete Wilkie *(Sales Development Manager)*
**Facilities:** Graham Sandercock *(Property Maintenance Manager)*
**Operations:** Will Aldrez *(Laboratory Manager)*, Roger Ryman *(Head Brewer)*
**Purchasing:** Vivian May *(Purchasing Manager)*
**Fleet:** Ian Blunt *(Sales Director)*
**Branches:** St.austell Brewery Company Ltd, St. Clare Street, Penzance, Cornwall TR18 2PD
**US SIC:** 2082, 5182, 5813
**UK SIC:** 42702, 61700, 66200
**Auditors:** Deloitte LLP
**Bankers:** Barclays Bank Plc (20-74-20)

| | 28-12-13 | 29-12-12 | 31-12-11 |
|---|---|---|---|
| TO | 116,562,000 | 106,069,000 | 99,081,000 |
| P/L | 10,433,000 | 10,350,000 | 10,304,000 |
| NW | 78,791,000 | 70,557,000 | 66,572,000 |
| WC | 735,000 | 2,162,000 | 1,985,000 |
| Emp. | 1,043 | 1,010 | 935 |

DUNS 39-980-9623
## St. Bede's College Ltd
Alexandra Road South, Manchester M16 8HX
**Tel:** 01612263323 **Fax:** 0161-226-3813
**Web:** www.stbedescollege.co.uk
**Reg No:** 2277006 **Estd:** 1896 Private Limited Company
**Line of Business:** Schools (independent)
**Directors:** Rev P Daly, J Moynihan, Mrs R M Kennedy, G J Macmillan, J B Ainscough, S Parkinson, D T Coffey, T A Richards
**Co. Secretary:** John Fletcher
**Responsibilities**
**Senior:** Clare Finnigan *(Manager)*, Michael Gillespie *(Governor)*, Timothy Hopkins *(Governor)*, Daniel Kearny *(Head Teacher)*, Gerard Lanigan *(Manager)*, Patrick McMahon *(Director)*, Sandra Pike *(Head Teacher)*, Terence Walsh *(Director)*, Helen West *(Director)*
**IT:** C Earles *(Computer Coordinator)*, Paul Mcdaid *(Senior IT Executive)*
**US SIC:** 8211 **UK SIC:** 93200
**Auditors:** Baker Tilly
**Bankers:** The Royal Bank Of Scotland Plc (16-00-02)

| | 31-08-13 | 31-08-12 | 31-08-11 |
|---|---|---|---|
| TO | 6,303,503 | 6,530,884 | 6,682,455 |
| P/L | (96,830) | 27,517 | (263,294) |
| NW | 8,775,454 | 9,715,409 | 9,687,892 |
| WC | (1,225,731) | (1,208,570) | (1,196,049) |
| Emp. | 147 | 145 | 119 |

DUNS 45-815-2097
## St. Benedict's College Foundation Ltd
Norman Way, Colchester, Essex CO3 3US
**Tel:** 01206549222
**Web:** www.stbenedicts.essex.sch.uk
**Reg No:** 3172895 **Estd:** 1963 Private Company Limited By Guarantee
**Line of Business:** Schools (foundation)
**Trading Style:** St. Benedict's College
**Directors:** M W O Connor, A W Livesley
**Co. Secretary:** Timothy Moriarty
**Responsibilities**
**Senior:** Joanne Santinelli *(Principal)*
**US SIC:** 8211, 8999
**UK SIC:** 93200, 83954
**Auditors:** A R Tilsley
**Bankers:** HSBC Bank plc (40-18-51)

| | 31-12-13 | 31-12-12 | 31-12-11 |
|---|---|---|---|
| TO | 25,655 | 31,978 | 80,159 |
| P/L | 22,484 | 28,048 | 71,758 |
| NW | 371,321 | 334,590 | 276,000 |
| WC | 371,321 | 334,590 | 275,998 |

DUNS 23-910-1434
## St. Bride's Spa Hotel Ltd
Tradewinds, Sandy Hill Road, Saundersfoot, Dyfed SA69 9PL
**Fax:** 01834-811766
**Web:** www.stpridesspahotel.com
**Reg No:** 3900656 **Estd:** 1999 Private Limited Company
**Line of Business:** Hotels
**Trading Style:** St Prides Spa Hotel
**Issued Capital:** £1,000,002
**Director:** A M Evans
**Co. Secretary:** Lindsey Evans
**US SIC:** 7011, 5812
**UK SIC:** 66500, 66110

| | 31-03-13 | 31-03-12 | 31-03-11 |
|---|---|---|---|
| TO | 2,756,962 | 2,591,156 | 3,242,243 |
| P/L | 538,466 | (297,911) | 276,950 |
| NW | 2,823,463 | 1,402,034 | 1,732,660 |
| WC | (42,879) | (1,580,102) | (1,148,968) |
| Emp. | 55 | 55 | 86 |

DUNS 23-777-0052
## St. Catherine's Hospice (Lancashire) Ltd
Lostock Lane, Lostock Hall, Preston, Lancashire PR5 5XU
**Tel:** 01772-629171 **Fax:** 01772696339
**Web:** www.stcatherines.co.uk
**Reg No:** 1602467 **Estd:** 1981 Private Limited Company
**Line of Business:** Adult and other education not elsewhere classified
**Trading Style:** St. Catherine's Hospice
**Issued Capital:** £2
**Directors:** P R Jones, A E Harrisson, J G Chesworth, Dr F M Duncan, J Holden, J C Hughes, M J Lough, J A Bonser
**Co. Secretary:** Stephen Greenhalgh
**Responsibilities**
**Senior:** Russell Atkinson *(Trustee)*, Mary Elliker *(Senior Manager)*, Lesley Fraser *(Director)*, Stephen Greenhouse *(Chief Executive)*
**US SIC:** 8249, 8091
**UK SIC:** 93300, 95200
**Auditors:** Moore & Smalley
**Bankers:** Lloyds TSB Bank plc (30-16-79)

| | 31-03-14 | 31-03-13 | 31-03-12 |
|---|---|---|---|
| TO | 6,013,000 | 6,140,745 | 5,622,117 |
| P/L | 162,000 | 442,450 | (84,676) |
| NW | 9,845,000 | 9,681,767 | 9,230,075 |
| WC | 4,009,000 | 4,201,527 | 3,774,251 |
| Emp. | 116 | 116 | 113 |

DUNS 28-930-5914
## St. Catherine's Hospice Ltd
Malthouse Road, Crawley, West Sussex RH10 6BH
**Tel:** 01293-447333 **Fax:** 01293447390
**Web:** www.stch.org.uk
**Reg No:** 1525404 **Estd:** 1980 Private Company Limited By Guarantee
**Line of Business:** Retail sale of other second-hand goods in stores
**Trading Style:** St. Catherine"s Hospice Ltd
**Directors:** Ms Y Rajani, D G Jones, R A Richman, D H Rudkin, Mrs B Williams, R W Leason, D S Yates, S R Turpitt
**Responsibilities**
**Senior:** Eileen Cowley *(Manager)*, Alexander Cuppage *(Manager)*, John Mansfield *(Director)*, Shaun O' Leary *(Chief Executive)*, Marion Sheahan *(Development Manager)*, Michael Waldron *(Trustee)*
**Finance:** Eric Norman *(Head of Finance)*
**Marketing:** Rebecca Day *(Marketing Director)*, Samantha Rider *(Marketing Director)*
**Admin:** Zena Cairns *(Services Director)*
**IT:** Richard Tullett *(IT Manager)*, Alison Tulley *(IT Manager)*
**HR:** Gina Starnes *(Head of Nursing Practice)*, Anne Truett *(Education and Training Manager)*
**Health & Safety:** Tom Botting *(Facilities Manager)*, Bob Harman *(Facilities Manager)*
**Facilities:** Tom Botting *(Facilities Manager)*, Bob Harman *(Facilities Manager)*
**Operations:** Rebecca Day *(Marketing Director)*
**Purchasing:** Tom Botting *(Facilities Manager)*, Bob Harman *(Facilities Manager)*
**Engineering:** Shaun O' Leary *(Chief Executive)*
**Branches:** St. Catherine's Hospice Ltd, Spring Cottage Stenners Yard, Hartcliffe Way, Bristol, Avon BS3 5RN
**US SIC:** 7399 **UK SIC:** 83954
**Auditors:** Baker Tilly
**Bankers:** Barclays Bank Plc (20-23-97)

| | 31-03-14 | 31-03-13 | 31-03-12 |
|---|---|---|---|
| TO | 13,372,452 | 8,765,246 | 8,156,202 |
| P/L | 4,389,070 | 360,752 | (54,761) |
| NW | 16,148,344 | 11,173,439 | 9,886,320 |
| WC | 12,166,643 | 7,227,407 | 6,077,915 |
| Emp. | 187 | 181 | 177 |

DUNS 28-855-4975
## St.Cedd's School Educational Trust Ltd
178 New London Road, Chelmsford, Essex CM2 0AR
**Tel:** 01245392810
**Web:** www.stcedds.org.uk
**Reg No:** 0795895 **Estd:** 2012 Private Company Limited By Guarantee
**Line of Business:** General secondary education
**Directors:** B J Read, P Copeland, J L Dagg, M K Bryant, D K Thompson, F M Hargreaves, Mrs L Hall
**Co. Secretary:** Mrs Susan Sutcliffe
**Responsibilities**
**Senior:** B Windley *(Headmistress)*
**IT:** A Lowe-Wheeler *(Computer Manager)*
**Health & Safety:** B Windley *(Headmistress)*
**Facilities:** B Windley *(Headmistress)*
**US SIC:** 8211 **UK SIC:** 93200
**Auditors:** HLB Kidsons
**Bankers:** National Westminster Bank Plc (60-05-13)

| | 31-08-13 | 31-08-12 | 31-08-11 |
|---|---|---|---|
| TO | 3,435,049 | 3,452,993 | 4,422,690 |
| P/L | 316,330 | 159,007 | (494,819) |
| NW | 2,487,077 | 2,170,747 | 2,011,740 |
| WC | (32,208) | (333,846) | (423,992) |
| Emp. | 57 | 61 | 63 |

DUNS 21-500-0371
## St. Charles Catholic Sixth Form College
St Charles Square, London W10 6EY
**Tel:** 02089687755
**Web:** www.stcharles.ac.uk
**Estd:** 2011 Partnership
**Line of Business:** Further education schools and colleges
**Partners:** P O'Shea, P O"Shea
**Responsibilities**
**Senior:** Paul O"shea *(Partner)*
**Admin:** Debbie O'Sullivan *(PA to Principal)*
**IT:** Robin Dearing *(MIS Manager)*
**US SIC:** 8221 **UK SIC:** 93100
**Employees:** 100

DUNS 50-708-9696
## St. Christopher Fellowship
1 Putney High Street, London SW15 1SZ
**Tel:** 020-8780-7800
**Web:** www.stchris.org.uk
**Estd:** 1936
**Line of Business:** Housing associations societies trusts & co-operatives
**Principals:** E Whyms, J Farrow
**Responsibilities**
**Senior:** Janelle Howell *(Manager)*, Susan Kent *(Financial Director)*, Donna Kerr *(Area Manager)*, Paul Kissack *(Manager)*, Jeremy Lamb *(Manager)*, Annette Richards *(Regional Manager)*, Harry Wilkinson *(Executive)*
**Finance:** Susan Kent *(Financial Director)*
**Marketing:** Tony Bridger *(Communications Manager)*
**Sales:** Sam Olsen *(Director of Strategy and Devel)*
**Admin:** Michelle Jones *(Office Manager)*, Michelle Rabbitte *(Office Manager)*
**Facilities:** Michelle Jones *(Office Manager)*, Michelle Rabbitte *(Office Manager)*
**Operations:** Ron Giddens *(Director of Operations)*, Michelle Jones *(Office Manager)*, Michelle Rabbitte *(Office Manager)*
**Branches:** St. Christopher Fellowship, West Point First Floor, 39-40 Warple Way, London W3 0RG
**US SIC:** 8321, 7399
**UK SIC:** 96111, 83954
**Auditors:** Beever & Struthers

| | 31-03-12 | 31-03-11 | 31-03-10 |
|---|---|---|---|
| TO | 16,396,000 | 18,578,000 | 20,662,000 |
| P/L | (209,000) | 206,000 | 298,000 |
| NW | 4,935,000 | 5,182,000 | 4,581,000 |
| WC | 3,667,000 | 3,339,000 | 3,313,000 |
| Emp. | 276 | 299 | 331 |

DUNS 28-833-3982
## St.Christophers Fellowship
9 Fairlawns, Twickenham, Middlesex TW1 2JY
**Tel:** 02089792220 **Fax:** 020-8544-1633
**Web:** www.stchris.org.uk
**Reg No:** 0321509 **Estd:** 1936 Private Company Limited By Guarantee
**Line of Business:** Social work activities with accommodation
**Directors:** Ms H M Barker, D C Visavadia, Ms S T O'Neill, Mrs A M Lennon, D Hobbs, H Barma, Dr D J Brown, A K Alexander
**Co. Secretary:** Jonathan Farrow
**Responsibilities**
**Senior:** Christopher Borkowski *(Director)*, Bert O'Donoghue *(Director)*
**Branches:** St.christophers Fellowship, 338 Lewisham High Street, London SE13 6LE
**US SIC:** 8321 **UK SIC:** 96111
**Auditors:** Beever & Struthers
**Bankers:** National Westminster Bank Plc (60-24-06)

| | 31-03-14 | 31-03-13 | 31-03-12 |
|---|---|---|---|
| TO | 15,670,000 | 14,882,000 | 16,396,000 |
| P/L | 231,000 | 210,000 | 98,000 |
| NW | 5,505,000 | 4,937,000 | 4,935,000 |
| WC | 3,880,000 | 3,729,000 | 3,667,000 |
| Emp. | 251 | 238 | 276 |

DUNS 22-714-0993
## St. Christophers Hospice
51-59 Lawrie Park Road, London SE26 6DZ
**Tel:** 020-8768-4500 **Fax:** 02087684513
**Web:** www.stchristophers.org.uk
**Reg No:** 0681880 **Estd:** 1961 Private Company Limited By Guarantee
**Line of Business:** Hospices
**Trading Style:** St. Christophers Hospice
**Directors:** J C Houlton, R J Raeburn, M K Davis, R B Saunders, T I Collis, Mrs B Noble, Mrs G E Baker, Mrs J E Walters
**Co. Secretary:** Martin Belham
**Responsibilities**
**Senior:** Phyllis Cunningham *(Manager)*, Joanna Donaldson *(Director)*, Tyrrell Evans *(Director)*, Jonathan Hosie *(Manager)*, Barry Kidson *(Manager)*, Shaun O'leary *(Chief Executive Officer)*
**IT:** Reg van Selm *(IT Manager)*
**HR:** Arthur Tanner *(Personnel Director)*
**Branches:** St. Christophers Hospice, 171 High Street, London SE20 7DS
**US SIC:** 8091 **UK SIC:** 95200
**Auditors:** Haysmacintyre
**Bankers:** HSBC Bank plc (40-02-07)

| | 31-03-14 | 31-03-13 | 31-03-12 |
|---|---|---|---|
| TO | 19,170,000 | 17,644,000 | 18,241,000 |
| P/L | (4,111,000) | 137,000 | 1,199,000 |
| NW | 27,954,000 | 32,185,000 | 31,061,000 |
| WC | 3,706,000 | 4,765,000 | 2,845,000 |
| Emp. | 311 | 293 | 279 |

DUNS 28-844-1488
## St.Christophers(Glossop) Ltd
Redcourt, Hollincross Lane, Glossop, Derbyshire SK13 8JH
**Tel:** 01457899250
**Web:** www.stchristopherstrust.org
**Reg No:** 0600800 **Estd:** 1958 Private Company Limited By Guarantee
**Line of Business:** Social work activities with accommodation
**Directors:** Mrs C Madge, Mrs J Roebuck, A Hargreaves, Ms T Owen, A D Wilkinson, Mrs C Lobley
**Co. Secretary:** Mrs Emma Oakes
**US SIC:** 8321 **UK SIC:** 96111
**Auditors:** Kidsons Impey
**Bankers:** National Westminster Bank Plc (01-03-38)

| | 31-03-14 | 31-03-13 | 31-03-12 |
|---|---|---|---|
| TO | 1,909,426 | 1,916,188 | 1,923,225 |
| P/L | 200,782 | 328,098 | 391,138 |
| NW | 1,759,989 | 1,559,207 | 1,231,109 |
| WC | 420,636 | 193,443 | 325,375 |
| Emp. | 99 | 94 | 98 |

DUNS 29-660-6031 **Exp**
## St. Clare's Oxford.
18 Bardwell Road, Oxford, Oxfordshire OX2 6SP
**Tel:** 01865-552031
**Web:** www.stclares.ac.uk
**Reg No:** 1986868 **VAT No:** 448623333
**Estd:** 1953 Private Company Limited By Guarantee
**Line of Business:** Language schools
**Export Markets:** Europe, Japan, Korean Democratic Peoples Republic, Taiwan, U S A
**Directors:** Ms A W Lewis, P M Oppenheimer, P L Mason, J F Offen, J E Church, Mrs M E Darlington, C R Dick, L A Whitehead
**Co. Secretary:** Nicholas Paladina
**Responsibilities**
**Senior:** Paula Holloway *(Principal)*, Yao Hu *(Director)*, Irina Kirillova *(Director)*
**Marketing:** Patricia Alvarez *(Sales And Marketing Manager)*
**Sales:** Patricia Alvarez *(Sales And Marketing Manager)*
**IT:** John Boschen *(Computer Manager)*
**Health & Safety:** Anne Jeffs *(Health & Safety Officer)*
**US SIC:** 8249, 8221
**UK SIC:** 93300, 93100
**Auditors:** Grant Thornton
**Bankers:** Brown, Shipley & Co Ltd (60-01-68)

| | 31-08-14 | 31-08-13 | 31-08-12 |
|---|---|---|---|
| TO | 13,967,000 | 14,120,000 | 13,021,000 |
| P/L | 313,000 | 562,000 | 404,000 |
| NW | 17,361,000 | 17,048,000 | 16,465,000 |
| WC | (3,870,000) | (962,000) | (1,087,000) |
| Emp. | 235 | 236 | 236 |

DUNS 21-526-6565
## St. Clares Senior School
Newton, Porthcawl, Mid Glamorgan CF36 5NR
**Tel:** 01656-782509
**Web:** www.stclares-school.co.uk
**Estd:** 1999 Proprietorship
**Line of Business:** Schools (independent)
**Proprietor:** Mrs C Barnard
**Responsibilities**
**Senior:** Simon Antwis *(Headmaster)*
**US SIC:** 8211 **UK SIC:** 93200
**Employees:** 50

DUNS 21-760-1060
## St. Clement Danes School
Chenies Road, Chorleywood, Rickmansworth, Hertfordshire WD3 6EW
**Tel:** 01923284169
**Web:** www.stclementdanes.org.uk
**Reg No:** 7671949 **Estd:** 2011 Private Limited Company
**Line of Business:** General secondary education
**Directors:** Mrs G R Collison, D M Swain, Ms R A Hatfield, M G Jordan, A G Hatfield, M J Austen, I J Birkett, R Campanini
**Responsibilities**
**Senior:** Michael Brasier *(Director)*, Mohan Gharial *(Director)*, Rosemary Hadfield *(Director)*, David Heward *(Director)*
**IT:** Tom Phillips *(Head of IT)*
**US SIC:** 8211 **UK SIC:** 93200
**Bankers:** Lloyds TSB Bank plc (77-95-26)

| | 31-08-13 | 31-08-12 |
|---|---|---|
| TO | 7,790,223 | 24,353,365 |
| P/L | 34,934 | 15,387,689 |
| NW | 15,331,623 | 15,272,689 |
| WC | 1,050,851 | 665,531 |
| Emp. | 128 | 125 |

DUNS 39-905-7272
## St. Cloud Care Ltd
The Boynes, Upper Hook Road, Upton-Upon-Severn, Worcester, Worcestershire WR8 0SB
**Tel:** 01428652622
**Web:** www.stcloudcare.co.uk
**Reg No:** 2230827 **Estd:** 1993 Private Limited Company
**Line of Business:** Other human health activities
**Issued Capital:** £50,000
**Directors:** A N Rubinstein, E P Robson
**Responsibilities**
**Senior:** Linton Connell *(Manager)*, Philip Connoll *(Managor)*
**Branches:** St. Cloud Care Ltd, Old Hills, Worcester, Worcestershire WR2 4TQ
**US SIC:** 8091 **UK SIC:** 95200
**Auditors:** Elman Wall Ltd
**Bankers:** National Westminster Bank Plc (55-81-57)

| | 31-03-14 | 31-03-13 | 31-03-12 |
|---|---|---|---|
| TO | 11,328,418 | 10,241,336 | 8,843,936 |
| P/L | 2,062,950 | 1,337,788 | 610,698 |
| NW | 1,950,995 | 1,250,452 | 1,703,014 |
| WC | 946,570 | 843,931 | 1,326,648 |
| Emp. | 399 | 399 | 320 |

DUNS 21-472-6064
## St. Columbanus College
Ballymaconnell Road, Bangor, Co Down BT20 5PU
**Tel:** 028-9127-0927
**Web:** www.stcolumbanus.org.uk
**Estd:** 1963
**Line of Business:** Schools (local authority)
**Principals:** Mrs B Bordan, Mrs B Bordan
**Responsibilities**
**Senior:** Liam Perry *(Head Teacher)*
**Finance:** Brian Jamison *(Bursar)*
**HR:** Brian Jamison *(Bursar)*
**US SIC:** 8211 **UK SIC:** 93200
**Employees:** 60

DUNS 28-823-0683
## St. Columba's Hospice Ltd
15 Boswall Road, Edinburgh, Midlothian EH5 3RW
**Tel:** 01315511381 **Fax:** 01315512771
**Web:** www.stcolumbashospice.org.uk
**Reg No:** 0048700SC **Estd:** 1971 Private Company Limited By Guarantee
**Line of Business:** Hospices
**Directors:** Dr F M Skinner, M F Johnston, Ms L E Sydie, N M Bryson, I A Mclaren, Ms E M Moir Obe, Professor R H Macdougall, J A Hammond-Chambers
**Co. Secretary:** Tm Company Services Limited
**Responsibilities**
**Senior:** Ian Adam *(Director)*, Graham Burnside *(Director)*, Patricia Cantley *(Director)*, David Coltman *(Manager)*, Margaret Dunbar *(Chief Executive Officer)*, David Dunsire *(Director)*, Brian Hilsley *(Director)*
**Finance:** Lesley Christie *(Director, Fundraising)*
**Sales:** Kim Donaldson *(Development Officer)*
**Admin:** Alison George *(Administrator)*, Susan Thorburn *(Administrator)*
**HR:** Nick Dey *(Human Resources Manager)*, Bill Kerr *(Human Resources Manager)*
**Health & Safety:** Margaret Dunbar *(Chief Executive Officer)*
**Operations:** Margaret Dunbar *(Chief Executive Officer)*
**Purchasing:** Margaret Dunbar *(Chief Executive Officer)*
**US SIC:** 8062 **UK SIC:** 95100
**Auditors:** Chiene & Tait CA
**Bankers:** The Royal Bank Of Scotland Plc (83-00-80)

| | 31-03-14 | 31-03-13 | 31-03-12 |
|---|---|---|---|
| TO | 8,743,905 | 9,811,186 | 8,840,134 |
| P/L | 723,753 | 2,417,797 | 1,313,973 |
| NW | 54,950,716 | 53,392,105 | 47,577,405 |
| WC | 1,051,348 | 1,271,768 | 952,646 |
| Emp. | 170 | 167 | 159 |

DUNS 21-033-1688

## St. Comgall's Primary School

1 Ballymena Road, Antrim, Co Antrim BT41 4JG
**Tel:** 028-9442-8837
**Web:** www.stcomgalls.com
**Estd:** 1955 Proprietorship
**Line of Business:** Schools (local authority)
**Proprietor:** H Cush
**Responsibilities**
**Senior:** Haliry Cush *(Head Teacher)*, Jim Matthews *(Principal)*
**US SIC:** 8211 **UK SIC:** 93200
**Employees:** 60

DUNS 76-902-6485

## St. Cuthbert's Hospice Durham

Park House Road, Durham, County Durham DH1 3QF
**Tel:** 01913861170
**Web:** www.stcuthbertshospice.com
**Reg No:** 2208426 **Estd:** 1987 Private Limited Company
**Line of Business:** Hospices
**Directors:** I R Dewhirst, Dr J L Mcmichael, J W Griffiths, J Graydon, Mrs J A Brown, Ms S M Chapman, Dr A Galloway, Dr A Macintyre
**Co. Secretary:** Richard Langdon
**Responsibilities**
**Senior:** Ronald Dickie *(Director)*, Sandra Ruskin *(Director)*, Eunice Sneddon *(Director)*, Kevin Whitfield *(Director)*
**US SIC:** 8091, 8011
**UK SIC:** 95200, 95300
**Bankers:** National Westminster Bank Plc (52-30-44)

| | 31-03-14 | 31-03-13 | 31-03-12 |
|---|---|---|---|
| TO | 2,866,093 | 2,412,954 | 2,194,063 |
| P/L | 265,541 | 253,472 | 168,372 |
| NW | 5,114,127 | 4,847,488 | 4,594,317 |
| WC | 1,768,319 | 1,482,752 | 1,205,198 |
| Emp. | 76 | 69 | 63 |

DUNS 77-127-9098

## St. David's Foundation Hospice Care

Blackett Avenue, Newport, Gwent NP20 6NH
**Tel:** 01633851051 **Fax:** 01633851052
**Web:** www.stdavidsfoundation.co.uk
**Reg No:** 2700097 **Estd:** 1979 Private Limited Company
**Line of Business:** Charities and charitable organisations
**Directors:** Dr R Lurvey, J O Thompson, Mrs P A White, I S Burge, Lieutenant Colonel D Evans, M Davies, Mrs J E Child, Mrs P J Davies
**Co. Secretary:** Mrs Katherine Saysell
**Responsibilities**
**Senior:** Kris Broome *(Director, Fundraising and Lott)*, Michael Hine *(Director)*, Denis Jessopp *(Director)*, Gill Tanner *(Senior Manager)*, Margaret Van De Weyer *(Director)*
**Finance:** Kris Broome *(Director, Fundraising and Lott)*
**Branches:** St. David's Foundation Hospice Care, 35 Bridge Street, Usk, Gwent NP15 1BQ
**US SIC:** 8091 **UK SIC:** 95200
**Auditors:** Arthur Gait & Co
**Bankers:** National Westminster Bank Plc (56-00-59)

| | 31-03-14 | 31-03-13 | 31-03-12 |
|---|---|---|---|
| TO | 7,376,000 | 6,058,708 | 7,278,202 |
| P/L | 267,000 | (133,453) | 1,480,581 |
| NW | 5,609,000 | 5,341,253 | 5,476,418 |
| WC | 1,660,000 | 1,327,291 | 1,744,064 |
| Emp. | 277 | 256 | 244 |

DUNS 22-773-4548

## St. Dominic's Brewood Trust

32 Bargate Street, Brewood, Stafford, Staffordshire ST19 9BA
**Tel:** 01902-850248
**Web:** www.stdominicsschool.co.uk
**Reg No:** 1226758 **Estd:** 1975 Private Company Limited By Guarantee
**Line of Business:** Schools (independent)
**Directors:** Mrs S K Gidda, Mrs M E Peakman, R P Turton, Ms B S Jones, K A Paulins, Mrs J Thomas, A J Clare-Hay
**Responsibilities**
**Senior:** Nicholas Berriman *(Manager)*, Pieter Hazenberg *(Manager)*, Dennis Marrison *(Manager)*, Raymond Wallis *(Bursar)*
**Finance:** Raymond Wallis *(Bursar)*
**HR:** Raymond Wallis *(Bursar)*
**Health & Safety:** Raymond Wallis *(Bursar)*
**Facilities:** Raymond Wallis *(Bursar)*
**Purchasing:** Raymond Wallis *(Bursar)*
**US SIC:** 8211 **UK SIC:** 93200
**Auditors:** Garratt & Co
**Bankers:** Lloyds TSB Bank plc (30-98-00)

| | 31-08-13 | 31-08-12 | 31-08-11 |
|---|---|---|---|
| TO | 2,190,612 | 2,204,024 | 2,592,166 |
| P/L | 7,431 | 11,883 | 93,412 |
| NW | 2,052,729 | 2,045,298 | 2,033,415 |
| WC | (587,056) | (596,259) | (606,818) |
| Emp. | 67 | 71 | 76 |

DUNS 45-855-1421

## St. Edmund's School Canterbury

St Thomas Hill, Canterbury, Kent CT2 8HU
**Tel:** 01227-475600 **Fax:** 01227-471083
**Web:** www.stedmunds.org.uk
**Reg No:** 3201223 **Estd:** 1996 Private Company Limited By Guarantee
**Line of Business:** Primary education
**Directors:** Colonel P R Whittington, Dr L Naylor, Mrs M L Lacamp, Dr P D Eichorn, C P Irvine, J P Coleman, P A Todd, Mrs S J Winning
**Co. Secretary:** Nicholas Lewis
**Responsibilities**
**Senior:** Peter Atkins *(Governor)*, Christopher Harbridge *(Director)*, Nichola Leatherbarrow *(Director)*, Louise Moelwyn-Hughes *(Head Teacher)*, Michael Punt *(Director)*
**Admin:** Carol Hawkins *(Administrator)*
**US SIC:** 8211 **UK SIC:** 93200
**Auditors:** Saffery Champness
**Bankers:** National Westminster Bank Plc (60-04-27)

| | 31-08-14 | 31-08-13 | 31-08-12 |
|---|---|---|---|
| TO | 9,119,340 | 8,537,640 | 8,162,032 |
| P/L | 318,172 | 6,955 | 13,098 |
| NW | 2,895,431 | 2,535,947 | 2,466,949 |
| WC | (2,046,911) | (2,358,485) | (2,013,311) |
| Emp. | 126 | 128 | 130 |

DUNS 28-829-6403

## St.Edward's School

Woodstock Road, Oxford, Oxfordshire OX2 7NN
**Tel:** 01865319204 **Fax:** 01865319286
**Web:** www.stedwardsoxford.org
**Reg No:** 0116784 **VAT No:** 195115657
**Estd:** 1911 Private Company Limited By Guarantee
**Line of Business:** Schools (independent)
**Directors:** C I Jones, P M Oppenheimer, M P Stanfield, Sir R P Reid, Dr L L Fawcett Posada, G R Howe, D J Jackson, Mrs J M Peach
**Co. Secretary:** Stephen Withers Green
**Responsibilities**
**Senior:** Caroline Baggs *(Director)*, Georgina Dennis *(Director)*, Alexandra Holloway *(Director)*, Katherine Ross *(Manager)*, Andrew Trotman *(Headmaster)*
**Marketing:** Rebecca Ting *(Marketing Manager)*, Tracy Van Der Heiden *(Marketing Manager)*
**Branches:** St.edward's School, Woodstock Rd, Oxford, Oxfordshire OX2 7NN
**US SIC:** 8211 **UK SIC:** 93200
**Auditors:** Critchleys
**Bankers:** Barclays Bank Plc (20-65-18)

| | 31-07-14 | 31-07-13 | 31-07-12 |
|---|---|---|---|
| TO | 19,459,000 | 18,131,000 | 17,531,000 |
| P/L | 679,000 | 638,000 | 371,000 |
| NW | 32,342,000 | 31,542,000 | 30,388,000 |
| WC | 761,000 | (1,521,000) | (392,000) |
| Emp. | 317 | 322 | 312 |

DUNS 28-984-6354 **Imp**

## St. Elizabeth Hospice (Suffolk)

565 Foxhall Road, Ipswich, Suffolk IP3 8LX
**Tel:** 01473727776
**Web:** www.stelizabethhospice.org.uk
**Reg No:** 1794927 **Estd:** 1984 Private Company Limited By Guarantee
**Line of Business:** Charities and charitable organisations
**Directors:** Mrs S J Shrubshall, W D Barnes, Mrs G C Drummond, D R Wilkes, Mrs A N Hogarth, M W Nicholls, Mrs E L Wellesley Wesley, I J Turner
**Co. Secretary:** Brian Bolt
**Responsibilities**
**Senior:** Cynthia Conquest *(Director)*, Nigel Gibbons *(Director)*, Srah Hewetson *(Manager)*, Linda Laisure *(General Manager)*, Eliot Morgan *(Manager)*, Jane Petit *(Chief Executive)*, Suzy Powling *(Manager)*, Bridget Wiseman *(Manager)*
**Finance:** Ray Chaplin *(Financial Manager)*
**Marketing:** Carl Brooks *(Business Income Generation Man)*, Patrica Johnson *(Fundraising Manager)*, Alison Lanchester *(Director of Income Generation)*
**Sales:** Jason Rudderham *(Retail Sales Manager)*
**IT:** Bill Weston *(Computer Manager)*
**Purchasing:** Susan Bryant *(Purchasing Manager)*
**Branches:** St. Elizabeth Hospice (Suffolk), 12B Bury Street, Stowmarket, Suffolk IP14 1HA
**US SIC:** 8091, 8321
**UK SIC:** 95200, 96111
**Auditors:** BDO Stoy Hayward
**Bankers:** The Royal Bank Of Scotland Plc (16-22-17)

| | 31-03-14 | 31-03-13 | 31-03-12 |
|---|---|---|---|
| TO | 9,104,525 | 7,191,544 | 7,664,160 |
| P/L | 4,667 | (1,168,752) | 290,465 |
| NW | 15,711,909 | 15,420,370 | 15,639,357 |
| WC | 565,666 | 232,624 | 291,568 |
| Emp. | 173 | 159 | 145 |

DUNS 21-616-3821

## St. Enoch Centre

Unit 55 St Enoch Centre, 55 St Enoch Square, Glasgow, Lanarkshire G1 4BW
**Tel:** 01412043900
**Web:** www.stenoch.co.uk
**Estd:** 2011
**Line of Business:** Shopping centres
**Responsibilities**
**Senior:** Anne Ledgerwood *(General Manager)*
**US SIC:** 5399 **UK SIC:** 65600
**Employees:** 100

DUNS 22-010-2722 **Imp**

## St. Ermin's Operating (Uk) Ltd

**(Subsidiary of:** St. Ermin's Coöperatieve U.A.)
2 Caxton Street, London SW1H 0QW
**Tel:** 02072227888 **Fax:** 020-7222-6914
**Web:** www.sterminshotel.co.uk
**Reg No:** 4013347 **VAT No:** 766415217
**Estd:** 2000 Private Limited Company
**Line of Business:** Hotels
**Trading Style:** St Ermin's Operating (Uk) Limited
**Issued Capital:** £1,000
**Directors:** J Kuan- Wen Chen, R Kuan- Chun Chen, Ms W Chun- Yu Teng, E Kuan- Jai Chen, T F Chen, S Chun- Hwa Chen Beutler, O L Chen
**Co. Secretary:** Mitre Secretaries Limited
**Responsibilities**
**Senior:** Michael Chang *(Director)*, Douglas Mchugh *(General manager)*, Daniel Pound *(Director)*, Joseph Wekselblatt *(Director)*, Kirk Wickman *(Director)*
**Marketing:** Stuart Leckie *(Sales and Marketing Director)*
**Sales:** Stuart Leckie *(Sales and Marketing Director)*, Gemma Wren *(Catering Sales Manager)*
**Admin:** Frederick Christoph *(Front Office Manager)*
**Operations:** Nishma Patel *(Reservations Manager)*
**US SIC:** 7011 **UK SIC:** 66500
**Auditors:** Deloitte LLP
**Bankers:** Barclays Bank Plc (20-06-05)

| | 31-12-13 | 31-12-12 | 31-12-11 |
|---|---|---|---|
| TO | 20,136,731 | 17,442,571 | 7,060,592 |
| P/L | 1,244,605 | 804,288 | (2,742,526) |
| NW | 397,766 | (1,515,657) | (2,010,923) |
| WC | (4,992,482) | (7,006,287) | (7,629,798) |
| Emp. | N/A | N/A | 137 |

DUNS 28-833-2927

## Saint Felix Schools

Halesworth Road, Reydon, Southwold, Suffolk IP18 6SD
**Tel:** 01502722175
**Web:** www.stfelix.co.uk
**Reg No:** 0316883 **Estd:** 1936 Private Company Limited By Guarantee
**Line of Business:** Schools (independent)
**Directors:** L W Dawson, K Dobson, N Johnson, Dr J Hunt, Mrs L Rous, R Stephens, J W Whyte, Dr J F Kelly
**Co. Secretary:** Mrs Helen Watkins
**Responsibilities**
**Senior:** Hazel Anthony *(Director)*, Raewyn Hope Cobbold *(Director)*, Barrie Slatter *(Director)*
**Branches:** Saint Felix Schools, Halesworth Road, Southwold, Suffolk IP18 6SD
**US SIC:** 8211 **UK SIC:** 93200
**Auditors:** Larking Gowen
**Bankers:** The Royal Bank Of Scotland Plc (16-00-30)

| | 31-08-13 | 31-08-12 | 31-08-11 |
|---|---|---|---|
| TO | 4,082,626 | 4,321,870 | 4,368,949 |
| P/L | (152,018) | 113,539 | 51,911 |
| NW | 1,489,191 | 1,641,209 | 1,527,670 |
| WC | (680,576) | (585,345) | (891,072) |
| Emp. | 148 | 137 | 135 |

DUNS 28-903-9430

## Saint Francis Hospice

The Hall, Broxhill Road, Havering-Atte-Bower, Romford, Essex RM4 1QH
**Tel:** 01708753319
**Web:** www.stfrancishospice.co.uk
**Reg No:** 1367828 **Estd:** 1978 Private Company Limited By Guarantee
**Line of Business:** Hospital activities
**Directors:** D G Burton, P D Crutchett, Dr R M Weatherstone, P Adams, C L Ghiotti, S J Roome, N A Brown, Mrs S Holland
**Responsibilities**
**Senior:** Gurdev Saini *(Director)*
**Finance:** Martin Barkwitch *(Finance Manager)*, Donald May *(Treasurer)*
**Admin:** Michael Pointer *(Secretary)*
**HR:** Caroline Scates *(Education Coordinator)*
**Facilities:** Valerie Harding *(Facilities Manager)*
**Branches:** Saint Francis Hospice, 20 Station Lane, Hornchurch, Essex RM12 6NJ
**US SIC:** 8062, 8321
**UK SIC:** 95100, 96111
**Auditors:** Mazars Neville Russell
**Bankers:** Barclays Bank Plc (20-00-00)

| | 31-03-14 | 31-03-13 | 31-03-12 |
|---|---|---|---|
| TO | 10,845,000 | 9,028,000 | 9,559,000 |
| P/L | 1,152,000 | 192,000 | 839,000 |
| NW | 10,852,000 | 9,527,000 | 9,073,000 |
| WC | 3,854,000 | 3,104,000 | 2,985,000 |
| Emp. | 248 | 289 | 478 |

DUNS 76-689-5742

## The St. Gabriel Schools Foundation

Sandleford Priory, Newtown Road, Newtown, Newbury, Berkshire RG20 9BD
**Tel:** 01635555680
**Web:** www.stgabriels.co.uk
**Reg No:** 2590761 **Estd:** 1991 Private Limited Company
**Line of Business:** Schools (independent)
**Directors:** M W Scholl, N C Garland, Mrs S A Bowen, D I Mcallan, Mrs J Whitehead, S R Barrett, S M Ryan, Reverend J Toogood
**Co. Secretary:** Mrs Julia Bond
**Responsibilities**
**Senior:** Lucy Hobby *(governor)*, Amanda Rowse *(Director)*
**Finance:** Noel Erskine *(Bursar)*
**Marketing:** Jane Benney *(Marketing Manager)*
**IT:** John Mannion *(Head of IT)*
**HR:** Noel Erskine *(Bursar)*
**Health & Safety:** Noel Erskine *(Bursar)*
**US SIC:** 8211 **UK SIC:** 93200
**Auditors:** Brading Cryer
**Bankers:** National Westminster Bank Plc (60-15-07)

| | 31-07-13 | 31-07-12 | 31-07-11 |
|---|---|---|---|
| TO | 5,789,709 | 5,800,676 | 5,835,779 |
| P/L | 339,016 | 234,812 | 439,852 |
| NW | 3,068,401 | 3,786,805 | 3,561,588 |
| WC | 25,684 | 361,567 | 246,157 |
| Emp. | 90 | 94 | 97 |

DUNS 34-648-7499

## St. Gemma's Hospice

329 Harrogate Road, Moortown, Leeds, West Yorkshire LS17 6QD
**Web:** www.st-gemma.co.uk
**Reg No:** 2773867 **Estd:** 1999 Private Company Limited By Guarantee
**Line of Business:** Hospital activities
**Directors:** A C Alderson, A Martin, M Traynor, Mrs R D Weinberg, C S Millar, Mrs J A Toovey, Professor P M Hopkins, E Fucito
**Co. Secretary:** Jason Kirk
**Responsibilities**
**Senior:** Arif Ahmad *(Director)*, Susan Ansbro *(Director)*, Peter Belfield *(Director)*, Elizabeth Carmody *(Director)*, Kerry Jackson *(Chief Executive)*, Helen Kemp *(Financial Director)*, Marie O'Sullivan *(Director)*
**Finance:** Helen Kemp *(Financial Director)*
**Marketing:** Tracy Dick *(Business Development Manager)*
**IT:** Paul Williment *(Computer Manager)*
**HR:** Cath Miller *(Director of Nursing)*
**Purchasing:** Tracy Dick *(Business Development Manager)*
**Branches:** St. Gemma's Hospice, 49 Street Lane, Leeds, West Yorkshire LS8 1AP
**US SIC:** 8062 **UK SIC:** 95100
**Auditors:** Sagars
**Bankers:** HSBC Bank plc (40-27-14)

| | 31-03-14 | 31-03-13 | 31-03-12 |
|---|---|---|---|
| TO | 9,682,073 | 9,273,132 | 9,044,886 |
| P/L | 287,072 | (26,821) | (56,222) |
| NW | 12,403,409 | 11,884,082 | 11,456,511 |
| WC | 3,040,165 | 3,247,043 | 2,940,492 |
| Emp. | 241 | 257 | 245 |

DUNS 28-860-8391

## St. George Hotel (Chatham) Ltd

**(Subsidiary of:** Sylenta Properties Ltd)
7-8 New Road Avenue, Chatham, Kent ME4 6BB
**Tel:** 01634835989 **Fax:** 01634-812109
**Web:** www.george-hotel.co.uk
**Reg No:** 0887540 **Estd:** 1966 Private Limited Company
**Line of Business:** Hotels
**Issued Capital:** £27,812
**Principals:** A E Stanley *(Managing)*, Ms C L Amos, R A Stanley
**Co. Secretary:** Jonathan Hadlow
**US SIC:** 7011 **UK SIC:** 66500
**Auditors:** Woolmer & Kennedy

| | 31-10-13 | 31-10-12 | 31-10-11 |
|---|---|---|---|
| TA | 360,283 | 403,247 | 374,317 |
| NW | 139,677 | 146,361 | 112,519 |
| WC | 16,479 | 14,522 | (3,751) |

DUNS 36-812-6439

## St. George's Coachworks (Camberley)

20 Doman Road, Camberley, Surrey GU15 3DF
**Estd:** 1997 Proprietorship
**Line of Business:** Car body repairers
**Proprietor:** T Chantrey
**US SIC:** 7539 **UK SIC:** 67100
**Employees:** 46

DUNS 28-928-3228

## St. George's Hospital Ltd

(**Subsidiary of:** Law 873 Ltd)
De Lane Warr Road, Milford On Sea, Lymington, Hampshire SO41 0PS
**Tel:** 01590648000
**Web:** www.stgeorgescare.co.uk
**Reg No:** 1513903 **VAT No:** 619783009
**Estd:** 1980 Private Limited Company
**Line of Business:** Medical nursing home activities
**Trading Style:** St George's Hospital & Nursing Home
**Issued Capital:** £2
**Director:** T M Russell
**Responsibilities**
**Senior:** Petrina Russell *(Manager)*
**US SIC:** 8051, 8091
**UK SIC:** 95100, 95200
**Auditors:** Compass Accountants Ltd
**Bankers:** Barclays Bank Plc (20-53-53)

| | 31-01-14 | 31-01-13 | 31-01-12 |
|---|---|---|---|
| TA | 412,909 | 404,237 | 325,961 |
| NW | 97,674 | 89,038 | 39,438 |
| WC | 7,029 | 32,400 | (21,405) |

DUNS 50-342-9664

## St. George's Hotel (Llandudno) Ltd

(**Subsidiary of:** St. George's Group of Hotels (Marketing) Ltd)
The Promenade, Penmaenmawr, Gwynedd LL34 6NJ
**Tel:** 01492-877544
**Web:** www.stgeorgeswales.co.uk
**Reg No:** 2363157 **Estd:** 1989 Private Limited Company
**Line of Business:** Hotels
**Trading Style:** The St George's Hotel
**Issued Capital:** £3,099,902
**Directors:** S M Fish, M J Chapelow
**Co. Secretary:** Pall Mall Registrars Limited
**Responsibilities**
**Senior:** Paul Brodrick *(Food & Beverage Manager)*, Tony Byrnes *(General Manager)*
**Finance:** Joe Bills *(Financial Controller)*
**Marketing:** Nicky Fare *(Conference Manager)*
**Sales:** June Thomas *(Office Manager)*
**Admin:** June Thomas *(Office Manager)*
**IT:** Joe Bills *(Financial Controller)*
**HR:** Tony Byrnes *(General Manager)*
**Health & Safety:** Tony Byrnes *(General Manager)*
**Operations:** Tony Byrnes *(General Manager)*
**Purchasing:** Tony Byrnes *(General Manager)*
**US SIC:** 7011 **UK SIC:** 66500
**Auditors:** Howard Kennedy
**Bankers:** Barclays Bank Plc (20-51-23)

| | 30-09-13 | 30-09-12 | 30-09-11 |
|---|---|---|---|
| TA | 1,128,000 | 1,128,000 | 1,128,000 |
| NW | 1,128,000 | 1,128,000 | 1,128,000 |

DUNS 39-925-6874

## St. George's Investment Company

(**Subsidiary of:** Hammerson Plc)
Lanesborough Place, London SW1X 7TA
**Tel:** 02072595599
**Web:** www.lanesborough.com
**Reg No:** 2239800 **Estd:** 1988 Private Unlimited Company
**Line of Business:** Hotels
**Trading Style:** The Lanesborough
**Issued Capital:** £100
**Directors:** C J Kingham, A K Alqubaisi, M A Alqubaisi
**Co. Secretary:** Manacor (Jersey) Limited
**Responsibilities**
**Senior:** Khaled Alkhajeh *(Director)*, Majed Alromaithi *(Director)*, Khalil Foulathi *(Manager)*, Abdulla Kindi *(Manager)*, Khalifa Mansoori *(Manager)*, J Mulla *(Manager)*, Charles Scragg *(Director)*
**Finance:** Fardan Al Fardan *(Director and Company Secretary)*
**Branches:** St. George's Investment Company, Lanesborough Place, London SW1X 7TA
**US SIC:** 7011 **UK SIC:** 66500
**Auditors:** PricewaterhouseCoopers
**Bankers:** National Bank Of Abu Dhabi (60-93-60)

| | 31-12-13 | 31-12-12 | 31-12-10 |
|---|---|---|---|
| TA | 1,000 | 1,000 | 1,000 |
| P/L | (76,666) | N/A | N/A |
| NW | (75,666) | 1,000 | 1,000 |
| WC | (75,666) | N/A | N/A |

DUNS 21-530-7104

## St. Giles School

Babworth Road, Retford, Nottinghamshire DN22 7NJ
**Tel:** 01777-703683
**Web:** www.st-giles.notts.sch.uk
**Estd:** 1992 Proprietorship
**Line of Business:** Schools (special)
**Proprietor:** Mrs C Kirk
**Responsibilities**
**Senior:** Hilary Short *(Head Teacher)*
**US SIC:** 8299 **UK SIC:** 93300
**Employees:** 50

DUNS 22-950-5771 **Imp-Exp**

## Saint-Gobain Building Distribution Ltd

(**Subsidiary of:** Compagnie De Saint Gobain Les Miroirs La Defense 3)
Saint-Gobain House, Binley Business Park, Coventry, West Midlands CV3 2TT
**Web:** www.saint-gobain.com
**Reg No:** 1647362 **VAT No:** 394121263
**Estd:** 1982 Private Limited Company
**Line of Business:** Kitchenware
**Trading Style:** International Timber / Jewson / Greenworks / Normans, Calders&Grandidge / Ideal Bathrooms / George Boyd, International Decorative Surfaces / British Gypsum, Ashworth / Gibbs&Dandy / Jp Corry / Ctd Group / Frazer
**Issued Capital:** £51,023,401
**Directors:** E Du Moulin, Dr P Hindle Mbe, B Bazin, M A Rayfield, T G Dufour
**Co. Secretary:** Alun Oxenham
**Responsibilities**
**Senior:** Raja Hussain *(Branch Manager)*
**Branches:** Saint-Gobain Building Distribution Ltd, Ditton Rd, Widnes, Cheshire WA8 0QG
**US SIC:** 5199, 5039
**UK SIC:** 61900, 61300
**Auditors:** KPMG Audit PLC
**Bankers:** National Westminster Bank Plc (56-00-13)

| | 31-12-13 | 31-12-12 | 31-12-11 |
|---|---|---|---|
| TO | 623,912,000 | 593,725,000 | 534,833,000 |
| P/L | (39,426,000) | 28,555,000 | 4,280,000 |
| NW | 138,071,000 | 153,037,000 | 154,470,000 |
| WC | (71,590,000) | (72,563,000) | (95,864,000) |
| Emp. | 2,760 | 2,837 | 2,449 |

DUNS 21-705-0327 **Imp-Exp**

## Saint-Gobain Industrial Ceramics Ltd

(**Subsidiary of:** Compagnie De Saint Gobain Les Miroirs La Defense 3)
St Gobain Industrial Ceramics, St Helens, Merseyside WA11 8LP
**Tel:** 01744-882941 **Fax:** 01744-883514
**Web:** www.saint-gobain.co.uk
**Reg No:** 0909697 **VAT No:** 374137647
**Estd:** 1910 Private Limited Company
**Line of Business:** Paving supplies
**Export Markets:** Worldwide
**Export Sales:** £5,476,000
**Issued Capital:** £11,450,000
**Directors:** R Granger, P Hindle Mbe
**Co. Secretary:** Alun Oxenham
**Responsibilities**
**Finance:** Nigel Hales *(Financial Manager)*
**Health & Safety:** David Anderton *(Purchasing Manager)*
**Facilities:** Mark Hayton *(Engineering Manager)*
**Operations:** David Anderton *(Purchasing Manager)*
**Purchasing:** David Anderton *(Purchasing Manager)*
**Engineering:** Mark Hayton *(Engineering Manager)*
**US SIC:** 5072 **UK SIC:** 61500
**Auditors:** KPMG Audit PLC

| | 31-12-13 | 31-12-12 | 31-12-11 |
|---|---|---|---|
| TO | 6,734,000 | 8,346,000 | 8,328,000 |
| P/L | 358,000 | 1,114,000 | 541,000 |
| NW | 9,535,000 | 9,121,000 | 8,772,000 |
| WC | 7,355,000 | 7,085,000 | 7,106,000 |
| Emp. | 54 | 61 | 53 |

DUNS 76-312-6844 **Exp**

## Saint-Gobain Weber Ltd

(**Subsidiary of:** Compagnie De Saint Gobain Les Miroirs La Defense 3)
Dickens House, Bedford, Bedfordshire MK45 5BY
**Tel:** 08703330070 **Fax:** 01525-718988
**Web:** www.saint-gobain.co.uk
**Reg No:** 2544294 **Estd:** 1990 Private Limited Company
**Line of Business:** Manufacture of insulated wire and cable
**Trading Style:** Weber Building
**Issued Capital:** £6,500,002
**Directors:** M S Chaldecott, P Hindle Mbe, E Du Moulin, P J Barry
**Co. Secretary:** Alun Oxenham
**Responsibilities**
**Facilities:** Alan Tysom *(Facilities Manager)*
**Branches:** Saint-Gobain Weber Ltd, Unit 1 Spiersbridge Business Park, Spiersbridge Avenue, Thornliebank, Glasgow, Lanarkshire G46 8NL
**US SIC:** 3357, 3299
**UK SIC:** 22470, 24504
**Auditors:** KPMG Audit PLC

| | 31-12-13 | 31-12-12 | 31-12-11 |
|---|---|---|---|
| TO | 47,578,000 | 41,697,000 | 37,705,000 |
| P/L | 904,000 | (189,000) | 1,053,000 |
| NW | 2,536,000 | 1,401,000 | 1,944,000 |
| WC | (2,747,000) | (3,303,000) | (2,687,000) |
| Emp. | 199 | 208 | 198 |

DUNS 21-600-6561

## St. Helena Hospice

62 Rosemary Road, Clacton-On-Sea, Essex CO15 1TE
**Tel:** 01255475055
**Web:** www.sthelenahospice.org.uk
**Estd:** 1991 Proprietorship
**Line of Business:** Charity shops
**Proprietor:** Mrs K Moore
**US SIC:** 8321 **UK SIC:** 96111
**Employees:** 93

DUNS 22-630-8278

## St. Helena Hospice Ltd

Myland Hall, Barncroft Close, Highwoods, Colchester, Essex CO4 9JU
**Tel:** 01206845566
**Web:** www.sthelenahospice.org.uk
**Reg No:** 1511841 **Estd:** 1985 Private Company Limited By Guarantee
**Line of Business:** Hospices
**Trading Style:** St. Helena Hospice
**Directors:** Ms I Martin, Ms M M Sparke, D Cresswell, R E Sirman, C Bull, Dr S I Mackenzie, A Wassell, K J Aldred
**Co. Secretary:** Duncan Turner
**Responsibilities**
**Senior:** Tracey Dickens *(Director)*, Andrew Dickerson *(Director)*, Mark Jarman-Howe *(CEO)*, Carol Munn-giddings *(Director)*, Stephen Razzell *(Director)*, Mary Sample *(Director)*, Peter Vergo *(Director)*
**Finance:** Sarah Green *(Director of Income and Communi)*
**Sales:** Stella Fletcher *(Director of Business Transform)*
**HR:** Tracey Salisbury *(Human Resources Manager)*
**Branches:** St. Helena Hospice Ltd, 4A Arthur St, Colchester, Essex CO2 7DT
**US SIC:** 8091 **UK SIC:** 95200
**Auditors:** Baker Chapman & Bussey
**Bankers:** National Westminster Bank Plc (60-06-06)

| | 31-03-14 | 31-03-13 | 31-03-12 |
|---|---|---|---|
| TO | 9,092,127 | 7,062,222 | 6,695,470 |
| P/L | 364,655 | 228,063 | 606,916 |
| NW | 13,051,993 | 12,355,367 | 11,477,762 |
| WC | 1,123,545 | 678,079 | 686,624 |
| Emp. | 178 | 149 | 139 |

DUNS 50-053-4029

## St. Helens & Knowsley Caring Association

St Bartholomews Court, Woodfield Road, Liverpool, Merseyside L36 4PJ
**Tel:** 0151-480-9997 **Fax:** 01514805505
**Web:** www.bettercaring.com
**Reg No:** 2313902 **Estd:** 1989 Private Limited Company
**Line of Business:** Nursing homes
**Trading Style:** St Bartholomew's Court Nursing Home
**Directors:** Doctor A Arain, Doctor A Arain, Ms M H Henley, Dr M A Sadiq, J D Green, A J Tallon, F C Johnson, Ms P A Gentry
**Co. Secretary:** Mrs Yvonne Houghton
**Responsibilities**
**Senior:** Elaine Allison *(Matron Manager)*, Allastair Davey *(Director)*
**US SIC:** 8051, 8091
**UK SIC:** 95100, 95200
**Auditors:** C A Hunter & Partners
**Bankers:** National Westminster Bank Plc (60-70-08)

| | 31-03-14 | 31-03-13 | 31-03-12 |
|---|---|---|---|
| TO | 1,787,261 | 1,764,371 | 1,786,415 |
| P/L | 23,069 | 21,473 | (3,000) |
| NW | 262,916 | 239,847 | 208,307 |
| WC | 479,113 | 448,178 | 394,316 |
| Emp. | 88 | N/A | N/A |

DUNS 23-554-3261

## St.Helens Y.M.C.A.

Central Court, 2 North Road, St Helens, Merseyside WA10 2TJ
**Tel:** 01744455030
**Web:** www.sthelensymca.org.uk
**Reg No:** 1947323 **Estd:** 1998 Private Company Limited By Guarantee
**Line of Business:** Non-charitable social work activities without accommodation
**Trading Style:** St.Helens Y.M.C.A
**Directors:** J Frodsham, D L Hickman, F Grayson, L F Rigby, K Jackson, R I Tully
**Co. Secretary:** Justin Hill
**Responsibilities**
**Senior:** Catherine Groves *(Manager)*, William Lawrenson *(Manager)*, Andrew Leakey *(Manager)*, Pat Lockhart *(Executive)*, Christine Mcgovern *(Executive)*
**HR:** Sarah Parsonage *(Human Resources Manager)*
**Purchasing:** Joe O' Reilly *(Purchasing Manager)*
**Branches:** St.helens Y.m.c.a., Central Court, 2 North Rd, St. Helens, Merseyside WA10 2TJ
**US SIC:** 8321, 7299
**UK SIC:** 96111, 98902
**Auditors:** Beever & Struthers
**Bankers:** National Westminster Bank Plc (60-70-08)

| | 31-03-14 | 31-03-13 | 31-03-12 |
|---|---|---|---|
| TO | 1,940,613 | 1,935,978 | 1,963,901 |
| P/L | 202,791 | (1,981,434) | (77,375) |
| NW | 2,501,742 | 2,298,952 | 4,280,386 |
| WC | 852,893 | 743,749 | 918,974 |
| Emp. | 58 | 60 | 62 |

DUNS 28-828-9333

## St. Hilda's East

18 Club Row, London E2 7EY
**Tel:** 020-7739-8066
**Web:** www.sthildas.org.uk
**Reg No:** 0052880 **Estd:** 1867 Private Company Limited By Guarantee
**Line of Business:** Community centres
**Directors:** N F Khan, Ms N Basuthakur, A Miah, Miss H E Edwards, Ms J G Locker, A Klarfeld, Ms S J Barry, Mrs S M Jaigirdar
**Co. Secretary:** Rupert Williams
**Responsibilities**
**Senior:** Jill Pittaway *(treasuers)*, Dennis Twomey *(treasurers)*
**Finance:** Fatima Begum *(Financial Director)*
**Marketing:** Ashras Hoque *(Administrator)*
**Admin:** Victoria Bamber *(Administration Manager)*, Ashras Hoque *(Administrator)*
**IT:** Ashras Hoque *(Administrator)*
**HR:** Ashras Hoque *(Administrator)*
**Facilities:** Uster Ullah *(Facilities Manager)*
**Purchasing:** Ashras Hoque *(Administrator)*
**US SIC:** 8321 **UK SIC:** 96111
**Auditors:** Ramon Lee & Partners
**Bankers:** Cafcash Ltd (40-52-40)

| | 31-03-14 | 31-03-13 | 31-03-12 |
|---|---|---|---|
| TO | 1,903,247 | 1,941,848 | 1,925,969 |
| P/L | (121,750) | 19,060 | 15,202 |
| NW | 2,455,923 | 2,573,904 | 2,555,799 |
| WC | 658,274 | 755,186 | 680,455 |
| Emp. | 53 | 51 | 51 |

DUNS 21-335-8596

## Saint Ignatius College

Turkey Street, Enfield, Middlesex EN1 4NP
**Tel:** 01992-717835
**Web:** www.st-ignatius.enfield.sch.uk
**Estd:** 1920
**Line of Business:** Schools (local authority)
**Director:** M Blundell
**Responsibilities**
**Senior:** Jp Morrison *(Head Teacher)*
**IT:** Martin Stevens *(IT Manager)*
**US SIC:** 8211 **UK SIC:** 93200
**Employees:** 151

DUNS 34-898-2661

## St. Ives Hotel Ltd

7-9 South Promenade, Lytham St Annes, Lancashire FY8 1LS
**Fax:** 01253-722873
**Web:** www.thestiveshotel.co.uk
**Reg No:** 2829187 **Estd:** 1993 Private Limited Company
**Line of Business:** Hotels
**Issued Capital:** £1,000
**Directors:** M Hothersall, M D Webb
**Co. Secretary:** Ms Sharon Webb
**Responsibilities**
**Senior:** Caroline Patterson *(General Manager)*
**Finance:** Louise Mathieson *(Accountant)*
**US SIC:** 7011 **UK SIC:** 66500
**Auditors:** J Morris & Co

| | 30-09-13 | 30-09-12 | 30-09-11 |
|---|---|---|---|
| TA | 1,296,119 | 1,358,442 | 1,197,769 |
| NW | 188,132 | 127,633 | 17,080 |
| WC | (50,814) | (190,816) | (625,319) |

DUNS 22-146-7462 **Imp**

## St. James Hotel Ltd

(**Subsidiary of:** Soc Hoteliere De Paris Les Halles)
6 Waterloo Place, London SW1Y 4AN
**Tel:** 020-7747-2280 **Fax:** 020-7747-2281
**Web:** www.sophidale.com
**Reg No:** 4165524 **Estd:** 2001 Private Limited Company

**Line of Business:** Hotels and motels, with restaurant (licensed)
**Issued Capital:** £15,000,000
**Directors:** T A Dubsere, R C Nottage, N Y Nasib, L R Cross, C Karaoglanian
**Co. Secretary:** Robert Bush
**Responsibilities**
**Senior:** Robert Gaymer-Jones *(Manager)*
**US SIC:** 7011 **UK SIC:** 66500
**Auditors:** Ernst & Young LLP

| | 31-12-13 | 31-12-12 | 31-12-11 |
|---|---|---|---|
| TO | 21,977,000 | 22,035,000 | 20,637,000 |
| P/L | 1,824,000 | 1,817,000 | 1,534,000 |
| NW | 16,516,000 | 14,561,000 | 13,162,000 |
| WC | 7,828,000 | 5,935,000 | 2,820,000 |
| Emp. | 191 | 192 | 178 |

DUNS 21-822-1868
## St. James the Great R.C. Primary & Nursery School
Windsor Road, Thornton Heath, Surrey CR7 8HJ
**Tel:** 02087713424
**Web:** www.stjamesthegreat.org
**Reg No:** 7937939 **Estd:** 2012 Private Company Limited By Guarantee
**Line of Business:** Schools (local authority)
**Directors:** S Beck, D A Byrne, A C Willis
**Co. Secretary:** Mrs Patricia Spinks
**US SIC:** 8211 **UK SIC:** 93200
**Bankers:** Allied Irish Bank (gb) (23-83-95)

| | 31-08-13 | 31-08-12 |
|---|---|---|
| TO | 9,505,464 | 898,920 |
| P/L | 7,472,277 | 67,341 |
| NW | 6,527,618 | 67,341 |
| WC | 22,156 | 12,029 |
| Emp. | 81 | 86 |

DUNS 77-479-4333
## The St. James's Club Ltd
**(Subsidiary of:** Residentia Holdings Pte. Ltd.)
7 Park Place, London SW1A 1LS
**Tel:** 02073161619 **Fax:** 020-7491-0987
**Web:** www.stjameshotelandclub.com
**Reg No:** 2968645 **VAT No:** 649539489
**Estd:** 1975 Private Limited Company
**Line of Business:** Hotels
**Issued Capital:** £3,750,000
**Directors:** I H Mansha, H Mansha
**Responsibilities**
**Senior:** Henrik Muehler *(General Manager)*, Christophe Thuilot *(Food & Beverage Manager)*
**Admin:** blanche Devon *(Secretary)*
**US SIC:** 7011 **UK SIC:** 66500
**Auditors:** BDO LLP
**Bankers:** National Westminster Bank Plc (56-00-27)

| | 31-12-13 | 31-12-12 | 31-12-11 |
|---|---|---|---|
| TO | 6,494,041 | 6,663,110 | 6,256,904 |
| P/L | 962,292 | 1,146,878 | 991,584 |
| NW | 2,939,087 | 2,285,865 | 1,640,500 |
| WC | 1,320,546 | 1,736,805 | 2,308,860 |
| Emp. | 86 | 86 | 80 |

DUNS 76-963-2159
## St. James's Place Uk Plc
**(Subsidiary of:** St. James's Place Plc)
Tetbury Road 1, Thomas Street, Cirencester, Gloucestershire GL7 1FP
**Tel:** 01285640302
**Reg No:** 2628062 **Estd:** 1992 Public Limited Company
**Line of Business:** Life insurance
**Trading Style:** J Rothschild Partnership, St James Place Partnership
**Issued Capital:** £110,000,001
**Directors:** D C Bellamy, D J Lamb, A M Croft, I S Gascoigne
**Co. Secretary:**
St. James'S Place Corporate Secr
**Responsibilities**
**Senior:** Hugh Gladman *(Manager)*
**Branches:** St. James's Place Uk Plc, Concorde House Concorde Way, Preston Farm Indstl Est, Stockton-On-Tees, Cleveland TS18 3RB
**US SIC:** 6311, 6371
**UK SIC:** 82002
**Auditors:** KPMG Audit Plc
**Bankers:** National Westminster Bank Plc (60-05-41)

**Following financial data are in thousands**

| | 31-12-13 | 31-12-12 | 31-12-11 |
|---|---|---|---|
| TO | 4,655,019 | 22,319 | 24,571 |
| P/L | 261,276 | 158,785 | 145,108 |
| NW | 639,616 | 652,402 | 549,189 |
| WC | 161,556 | (11,647) | (107,491) |

DUNS 76-962-8488
## St. James's Place Wealth Management Group Plc
**(Subsidiary of:** St. James's Place Plc)
St James's Place House, 1 Tetbury Road, Cirencester, Gloucestershire GL7 1FP
**Tel:** 08000138137
**Web:** www.heraldwealth.co.uk
**Reg No:** 2627518 **VAT No:** 243455077
**Estd:** 1991 Public Limited Company
**Line of Business:** Management activities of holding companies
**Issued Capital:** £95,465,135
**Directors:** I S Gascoigne, D J Lamb, D C Bellamy, A M Croft
**Co. Secretary:**
St. James'S Place Corporate Secr
**US SIC:** 6711, 6311
**UK SIC:** 83962, 82002
**Auditors:** KPMG Audit Plc
**Bankers:** National Westminster Bank Plc (60-05-41)

| | 31-12-13 | 31-12-12 | 31-12-11 |
|---|---|---|---|
| TO | 8,762,000 | N/A | N/A |
| P/L | 90,453,000 | 63,497,000 | 43,057,000 |
| NW | 104,895,000 | 103,242,000 | 102,955,000 |
| WC | (71,187,000) | (57,840,000) | (58,127,000) |

DUNS 22-166-9976
## The St. John & Red Cross Defence Medical Welfare Service
The Old Stables, Redenham Park, Andover, Hampshire SP11 9AQ
**Tel:** 01264774000 **Fax:** 01264773677
**Web:** www.dmws.org.uk
**Reg No:** 4185635 **Estd:** 2001 Private Company Limited By Guarantee
**Line of Business:** Other human health activities
**Directors:** Dr J G Paterson, L H March, S J Cowden, T Shepherd, Mrs M Burton, A Buckham, Mrs S P Rouse, Ms B Young
**Co. Secretary:** Miss Ruth Martindale
**Responsibilities**
**Senior:** David Keenan *(Director)*, Simon Patten *(Director)*, James Plastow *(Director)*, Fiona Walters *(Marketing Manager)*
**US SIC:** 8091 **UK SIC:** 95200
**Bankers:** National Westminster Bank Plc (60-19-27)

| | 31-03-14 | 31-03-13 | 31-03-12 |
|---|---|---|---|
| TO | 3,562,686 | 2,526,840 | 2,338,176 |
| P/L | 976,010 | 97,167 | 73,424 |
| NW | 1,758,542 | 782,532 | 685,365 |
| WC | 1,758,542 | 782,532 | 685,365 |
| Emp. | 55 | 51 | 44 |

DUNS 29-847-6110
## St. John Cooper Associates Ltd
Atlantic Business Centre, Altrincham, Cheshire WA14 5NQ
**Tel:** 01666511300
**Web:** www.stjohnassociates.com
**Reg No:** 2050450 **VAT No:** 560948517
**Estd:** 1986 Private Limited Company
**Line of Business:** Business and management consultancy activities not elsewhere classified
**Issued Capital:** £120
**Principals:** K J Cooper *(Managing)*, B C Cooper
**Co. Secretary:** Ms Claire Brewerton
**US SIC:** 7392, 3679
**UK SIC:** 83951, 34542
**Bankers:** Barclays Bank Plc (20-01-96)

| | 31-10-13 | 31-10-12 | 31-10-11 |
|---|---|---|---|
| TA | 16,697 | 11,973 | 11,829 |
| NW | (60,502) | (63,846) | (67,121) |
| WC | (65,396) | (68,791) | (72,127) |

DUNS 76-976-3517
## St. John of God (Community Developments) Ltd
Morton Park Way, Darlington, County Durham DL1 4XZ
**Tel:** 01325373705 **Fax:** 01325-373708
**Web:** www.sjog.org
**Reg No:** 2637928 **Estd:** 1991 Private Limited Company
**Line of Business:** Other letting of own property
**Issued Capital:** £2
**Directors:** W M Forkan, R Moore, M J Neild
**Co. Secretary:** Michael Neild
**Branches:** St. John Of God (Community Developments) Ltd, 99 Old Oscott Hill, Birmingham, West Midlands B44 9SR
**US SIC:** 6519 **UK SIC:** 85000
**Auditors:** PKF
**Bankers:** Barclays Bank Plc (20-25-29)

| | 31-12-13 | 31-12-12 | 31-12-12 |
|---|---|---|---|
| TO | 60,000 | 45,000 | 60,000 |
| NW | (264,222) | (264,222) | (264,222) |
| WC | 103,724 | 63,549 | 38,848 |

DUNS 34-513-3297
## Saint John of God Hospitaller Services
Morton Park Way, Darlington, County Durham DL1 4XZ
**Tel:** 01325373700 **Fax:** 01325-373708
**Web:** www.saintjohnofgod.org
**Reg No:** 5324279 **Estd:** 2005 Private Company Limited By Guarantee
**Line of Business:** Other human health activities
**Trading Style:** Balmachel
**Directors:** E Francis, W Brennan-Whitmore, R Moore, W M Forkan, J G Pepper, M J Neild
**Responsibilities**
**Senior:** Douglas Ball *(Trustee)*, Bridget Doogan *(Chief Executive)*, Anna Mccann *(Trustee)*
**Marketing:** Karen Gilroy *(Marketing Manager)*
**HR:** Kay Taylor *(Human Resources Manager)*
**Branches:** Saint John Of God Hospitaller Services, 1 Leeming Lane, Richmond, North Yorkshire DL10 7NG
**US SIC:** 8091, 8321
**UK SIC:** 95200, 96111
**Bankers:** Barclays Bank Plc (20-25-29)

| | 31-12-13 | 31-12-12 | 31-12-12 |
|---|---|---|---|
| TO | 23,595,000 | 17,726,000 | 24,604,000 |
| P/L | (882,000) | (241,000) | 435,000 |
| NW | 1,315,000 | 2,035,000 | 2,273,000 |
| WC | (426,000) | (423,000) | (80,000) |
| Emp. | 852 | 882 | 872 |

DUNS 21-479-7834
## St. John Payne Roman Catholic Comprehensive School
Patching Hall Lane, Chelmsford, Essex CM1 4BS
**Tel:** 01245256030
**Web:** www.sjp.essex.sch.uk
**Estd:** 1976
**Line of Business:** General secondary education
**US SIC:** 8211 **UK SIC:** 93200
**Employees:** 120

DUNS 77-952-4594
## St. Johns Buildings Ltd
24a-28 St John Street, Manchester M3 4DJ
**Tel:** 0161-214-1500
**Web:** www.stjohnsbuildings.com
**Reg No:** 3058225 **Estd:** 1995 Private Limited Company
**Line of Business:** Barristers at law
**Issued Capital:** £510,638
**Directors:** A J O'Byrne, Ms S Harrison, J P Hedgecoe, R Norton, D C Taylor, J P O'Brien, D Berkley, Miss L Harrison
**Co. Secretary:** David Anderson
**Responsibilities**
**Senior:** Guy Matthieson *(Director)*, Michael Redfern QC *(Head of Chambers)*, Karl Rowley *(Director)*
**US SIC:** 7399 **UK SIC:** 83954
**Auditors:** Moore & Smalley
**Bankers:** National Westminster Bank Plc (01-67-14)

| | 30-09-13 | 30-09-12 | 29-09-11 |
|---|---|---|---|
| TO | 4,241,723 | N/A | N/A |
| P/L | 68,657 | N/A | N/A |
| NW | 4,667,452 | 4,499,165 | 3,074,276 |
| WC | 1,075,199 | 243,723 | (28,334) |
| Emp. | 70 | N/A | N/A |

DUNS 39-229-8691
## St. John's College Ltd
Newport Road, Cardiff, South Glamorgan CF3 5YX
**Tel:** 029-2077-8936
**Web:** www.stjohnscollegecardiff.com
**Reg No:** 2114449 **Estd:** 1987 Private Company Limited By Guarantee
**Line of Business:** Schools (independent)
**Directors:** Ms P J Smerald, M J Prior
**Co. Secretary:** Simon James
**US SIC:** 8211 **UK SIC:** 93200
**Auditors:** Deloitte & Touche
**Bankers:** Bank Of Wales Plc (12-01-36)

| | 31-08-13 | 31-08-12 | 31-08-11 |
|---|---|---|---|
| TO | 4,486,973 | 3,955,725 | 3,944,404 |
| P/L | 599,304 | 412,165 | 642,866 |
| NW | 6,681,194 | 6,081,890 | 5,669,725 |
| WC | 2,414,305 | 2,034,585 | 2,923,217 |
| Emp. | 80 | 80 | 80 |

DUNS 64-255-1568
## St.John's Hospice
Slyne Road, Lancaster, Lancashire LA2 6ST
**Tel:** 01524-382538
**Web:** www.sjhospice.org.uk
**Estd:** 2010
**Line of Business:** Hospices
**Director:** R Ward
**Responsibilities**
**Senior:** Susan Mcgraw *(Chief Executive)*, Julie Reid *(General Clerk)*
**HR:** Fiona Lewis *(Human Resources Manager)*
**US SIC:** 8699 **UK SIC:** 96902
**Employees:** 100

DUNS 22-605-2017 **Imp**
## St.John's Nurseries (North Devon) Ltd
St Johns Lane, Newport, Barnstaple, Devon EX32 9DD
**Tel:** 01271-343884
**Web:** www.stjohnsgardencentre.co.uk
**Reg No:** 0612259 **VAT No:** 144153982
**Estd:** 1958 Private Limited Company
**Line of Business:** Other retail sale in specialised stores not elsewhere classified
**Trading Style:** St Johns Garden Centre
**Issued Capital:** £4,301
**Directors:** N Oliver, S C Oliver
**Co. Secretary:** Thomas Oliver
**Branches:** St.john's Nurseries (North Devon) Ltd, Priory Way, Taunton, Somerset TA1 2BB
**US SIC:** 5999 **UK SIC:** 65600
**Auditors:** Simpkins Edwards
**Bankers:** Barclays Bank Plc (20-13-42)

| | 30-09-13 | 30-09-12 | 30-09-11 |
|---|---|---|---|
| TO | 3,099,589 | 3,132,030 | 3,277,978 |
| P/L | 162,595 | 106,409 | (55,301) |
| NW | 2,678,515 | 2,584,245 | 2,469,493 |
| WC | 787,079 | 752,113 | 707,742 |
| Emp. | 77 | 70 | 68 |

DUNS 21-705-0703
## St. Joseph's College Edmund Rice Academy Trust
London Road, Stoke-On-Trent, Staffordshire ST4 5NT
**Tel:** 01782 848008
**Web:** www.stjosephstrentvale.com
**Reg No:** 7490390 **Estd:** 2011 Private Company Limited By Guarantee
**Line of Business:** General secondary education
**Directors:** D D O'Neill, A Franks, Ms R Maguire
**Co. Secretary:** Ms Karen Cleverley
**US SIC:** 8211 **UK SIC:** 93200
**Bankers:** Lloyds TSB Bank plc (30-93-83)

| | 31-08-14 | 31-08-13 | 31-08-12 |
|---|---|---|---|
| TO | 7,035,781 | 9,317,567 | 6,748,230 |
| P/L | (253,993) | 2,755,619 | 461,362 |
| NW | 8,436,412 | 3,113,298 | 335,679 |
| WC | 413,514 | 410,615 | 332,777 |
| Emp. | 142 | 128 | 120 |

DUNS 28-908-4683
## St. Joseph's College Reading Trust
Upper Redlands Road, Reading, Berkshire RG1 5JT
**Tel:** 01189-661000
**Web:** www.st-josephs.reading.sch.uk
**Reg No:** 1400984 **Estd:** 1978 Private Limited Company
**Line of Business:** General secondary education
**Directors:** Ms M A Banning, C J Murray, Dr M E Cross, Ms D M Mason, J M Hennah, D I Halle, M J Reynolds, Mrs J Feeney
**Co. Secretary:** Anthony Leggett
**Responsibilities**
**Senior:** Ndong Bonaventure *(Director)*, Susan Buckle *(Director)*, Katie Gripton *(Director)*
**US SIC:** 8211 **UK SIC:** 93200
**Bankers:** Lloyds TSB Bank plc (30-91-31)

| | 31-08-13 | 31-08-12 | 31-08-11 |
|---|---|---|---|
| TO | 3,735,521 | 3,624,360 | 8,409,867 |
| P/L | (259,184) | (192,298) | 4,872,239 |
| NW | 4,834,873 | 5,094,057 | 5,286,354 |
| WC | (421,737) | (216,352) | 86,168 |
| Emp. | 69 | 74 | 69 |

DUNS 50-435-8730 **Imp**
## St. Jude Medical U.K. Ltd
**(Subsidiary of:** St. Jude Medical Inc.)
Capulet House, Stratford Business & Technology Park, Banbury Road, Stratford-Upon-Avon, Warwickshire CV37 7GX
**Tel:** 01789207600 **Fax:** 01789207601
**Web:** www.sjm.com
**Reg No:** 2423907 **VAT No:** 536433154
**Estd:** 1978 Private Limited Company
**Line of Business:** Other human health activities
**Trading Style:** St. Jude Medical U.K. Ltd
**Issued Capital:** £2
**Directors:** J C Heinmiller, J A Zellers
**Co. Secretary:** Dodd Gray
**Responsibilities**
**Senior:** Pamela Krop *(Manager)*
**HR:** Susan Martin *(Human Resources Manager)*
**US SIC:** 8091 **UK SIC:** 95200
**Auditors:** Ernst & Young LLP
**Bankers:** Bank Of America, Na (16-50-50)

| | 31-12-13 | 31-12-12 | 31-12-11 |
|---|---|---|---|
| TO | 21,019,667 | 23,603,773 | 24,402,028 |
| P/L | 6,219,426 | 3,170,795 | 6,959,388 |
| NW | 20,721,467 | 16,303,154 | 14,363,743 |
| WC | 20,642,220 | 16,113,390 | 12,806,368 |
| Emp. | 141 | 135 | 134 |

DUNS 39-817-8566
## St. Kentigern Hospice
Upper Denbigh Road, St Asaph, Clwyd LL17 0RS
**Tel:** 01745585221
**Web:** www.stkentigernhospice.org.uk
**Reg No:** 2216886 **Estd:** 1988 Private Limited Company
**Line of Business:** Hospices
**Directors:** S D Cheshire, Mrs S J Last, G R Thompson, Ms S B England, Dr D Gozzard, Professor M Lloyd Williams, R Bartley, T G Jones
**Co. Secretary:** David Thomas
**Responsibilities**
**Senior:** Lady Langford *(Manager)*
**US SIC:** 8091 **UK SIC:** 95200
**Auditors:** J V Banks & Co
**Bankers:** The Royal Bank Of Scotland Plc (16-28-29)

| | 31-03-14 | 31-03-13 | 31-03-12 |
|---|---|---|---|
| TO | 2,612,392 | 2,253,817 | 2,068,115 |
| P/L | 848,453 | 510,338 | 723,161 |
| NW | 3,159,575 | 2,294,871 | 1,782,913 |
| WC | 2,600,757 | 1,709,657 | 1,174,994 |
| Emp. | 51 | 51 | N/A |

DUNS 49-120-6827
## St. Lawrence College Enterprises Ltd
College Road, Ramsgate, Kent CT11 7AE
**Tel.** 01843-587666
**Web:** www.slcuk.com
**Reg No:** 3100304 **Estd:** 1996 Private Limited Company
**Line of Business:** General secondary education
**Issued Capital:** £100
**Director:** M Iliff
**Co. Secretary:** James Connelly
**US SIC:** 8211 **UK SIC:** 93200
**Auditors:** Reeves & Neylan

| | 31-08-13 | 31-08-12 | 31-08-11 |
|---|---|---|---|
| TO | N/A | 15,656 | 19,556 |
| NW | 456 | 456 | 456 |
| WC | (59,091) | (71,001) | 456 |

DUNS 21-036-8100
## Saint Lazarus Hospice Association
53 Thurlby Road, London SE27 0RN
**Web:** www.saintlazarus.co.uk
**Line of Business:** Charitable organisation engaged as a fund raising organisation
**Responsibilities**
**Senior:** John Hoff *(Clubs - President)*
**US SIC:** 6732, 7399
**UK SIC:** 83100, 83954
**Employees:** 70

DUNS 28-916-8221
## St. Leonard's Hospice York
Tadcaster Road, York, North Yorkshire YO24 1GL
**Web:** www.stleonardshospice.org.uk
**Reg No:** 1451533 **Estd:** 1985 Private Limited Company
**Line of Business:** Other human health activities
**Directors:** M W Sturge, D J Miller, Dr D S Kemp, Mrs H Smith, A M Shepherd, Dr C A Kirk, A M Duncan, D J Alexander
**Co. Secretary:** Ms Karen Johnson
**Responsibilities**
**Senior:** Michael Bainbridge *(Director)*, David Mazza *(Director)*, Graham Millar *(Director)*
**Branches:** St. Leonard's Hospice York, 72 The Village, York, North Yorkshire YO32 2HY
**US SIC:** 8091 **UK SIC:** 95200
**Auditors:** Garbutt & Elliott Ltd
**Bankers:** National Westminster Bank Plc (56-00-70)

| | 31-03-14 | 31-03-13 | 31-03-12 |
|---|---|---|---|
| TO | 5,117,058 | 5,406,134 | 4,080,791 |
| P/L | 366,166 | 1,076,855 | 68,140 |
| NW | 12,760,490 | 12,133,516 | 10,440,507 |
| WC | 728,777 | 180,464 | 330,121 |
| Emp. | 114 | 104 | 153 |

DUNS 23-037-6881
## St. Leonards-Mayfield School
The Old Palace, Mayfield, East Sussex TN20 6PH
**Tel:** 01435874600
**Web:** www.mayfieldgirls.org
**Reg No:** 3068144 **Estd:** 1995 Private Company Limited By Guarantee
**Line of Business:** Schools (independent)
**Directors:** M Dinnendahl, P S Thomas, E T Walshe, C J Buxton, Mrs K Douglas, J Lancaster, Mrs E Byrne Hill, Miss J L Bowden
**Co. Secretary:** Lt Col Anthony Bayliss
**Responsibilities**
**Senior:** Anthonya Beary *(CEO, Managing Director)*, Chantal Davies *(Director)*, Sara Hullbert-Powell *(Governor)*, Maureen Martin *(Director)*, Clotilde Moody *(Director)*, Marie Quayle *(Director)*
**IT:** Caroline Barry *(Computer Operations Manager)*
**US SIC:** 8211 **UK SIC:** 93200
**Auditors:** Macintyre & Co
**Bankers:** National Westminster Bank Plc (60-10-30)

| | 31-08-14 | 31-08-13 | 31-08-12 |
|---|---|---|---|
| TO | 8,326,110 | 8,474,981 | 8,104,383 |
| P/L | 298,118 | 309,325 | 407,894 |
| NW | 9,518,846 | 9,177,289 | 8,828,851 |
| WC | (198,893) | (105,521) | 972,949 |
| Emp. | 149 | 138 | 150 |

DUNS 21-735-5189
## St.Leonards Motors Ltd
3 John Macadam Way, St Leonards-On-Sea, East Sussex TN37 7SQ
**Tel:** 01424852233 **Fax:** 01424853915
**Web:** www.slm.co.uk
**Reg No:** 0672274 **VAT No:** 201831706
**Estd:** 1960 Private Limited Company
**Line of Business:** Car dealers (new & used)
**Trading Style:** St Leonards Motors Vauxhall, St Leonards Motors Toyota, S L M Body Repair Centre, St Leonards Motors Nissan
**Issued Capital:** £265,600
**Principals:** I C Wakeford *(Sales)*, M Phillips, B Cunningham
**Co. Secretary:** Raymond Billenness
**Responsibilities**
**Senior:** Kevin Maynard *(Parts Manager)*
**Marketing:** Mel Ball *(Marketing Manager)*, Lee Oliver *(Showroom Controller & Motab Sp)*, Julia Tutt *(Marketing Manager)*
**Sales:** Laura Bloe *(Sales Executive)*, Jack Craddock *(Sales Executive)*, Neal Hood *(Sales Manager)*, Daniel Killick *(Sales Executive)*, Brett King *(Sales Executive & Motability S)*, Jonathan Tatlock *(Retail Operator)*, Paul Tree *(After Sales Manager)*, Gus Wakeford *(Dealer Principal and After Sal)*
**Admin:** Lynn Billenness *(Administration manager)*
**IT:** Mike Flenley *(IT Manager)*
**HR:** Julia Tutt *(Marketing Manager)*
**Operations:** Steve Batchelor *(Parts Manager)*, Louise Evans *(Motability Specialist)*, Jay Lorton *(Parts Manager)*, Julie Parsons *(Motability Specialist)*, Tony Ray *(Parts Manager)*, Glyn Sharman *(Workshop Controller)*
**Branches:** St.leonards Motors Ltd, Junction Road, Eastbourne, East Sussex BN21 3QR
**US SIC:** 5511, 5521, 7539, 5531
**UK SIC:** 65100, 67100
**Auditors:** Ogilvie Booth & Associates
**Bankers:** HSBC Bank plc (40-40-09)

| | 31-12-13 | 31-12-12 | 31-12-11 |
|---|---|---|---|
| TO | 45,037,280 | 43,077,553 | 34,250,432 |
| P/L | 124,994 | (172,649) | 74,166 |
| NW | 5,475,670 | 5,384,039 | 5,550,272 |
| WC | 49,988 | 186,887 | 147,252 |
| Emp. | 170 | 174 | 164 |

DUNS 28-862-8449
## St. Luke's Hospice
Little Common Lane, Sheffield, South Yorkshire S11 9NE
**Web:** www.stlukeshospice.org.uk
**Reg No:** 0922448 **Estd:** 1967 Private Company Limited By Guarantee
**Line of Business:** Other human health activities
**Directors:** Mrs S Inglis, Professor B W Hancock, L M Gavin, N A Macdonald, A W Pettifer, Professor R E Coleman, Dr D F Da Costa, M N Pestereff
**Co. Secretary:** Peter Hartland
**Responsibilities**
**Senior:** Petra Billing *(Director)*, Andrew Coombe *(Manager)*, Tracy Fletcher *(Director)*, Alan Spier *(Manager)*, Hazel Wills *(Director)*
**Marketing:** Una Moran *(Director of Funding)*
**Health & Safety:** Steve Hogg *(Health & Safety Manager)*
**Facilities:** Steve Hogg *(Health & Safety Manager)*
**Purchasing:** Amanda Lowe *(Buyer)*
**Branches:** St. Luke's Hospice, 17 Cornwall Street, Plymouth, Devon PL1 1NL
**US SIC:** 8091 **UK SIC:** 95200
**Auditors:** KPMG
**Bankers:** National Westminster Bank Plc (54-41-48)

| | 31-03-14 | 31-03-13 | 31-03-12 |
|---|---|---|---|
| TO | 9,682,292 | 10,602,058 | 6,871,927 |
| P/L | 2,252,837 | 3,055,634 | 508,246 |
| NW | 12,503,059 | 10,187,414 | 7,131,780 |
| WC | 1,697,541 | 3,374,470 | 3,339,419 |
| Emp. | 226 | 220 | 212 |

DUNS 28-988-7549
## St. Luke's Hospice (Basildon & District) Ltd
Fobbing Farm, Nethermayne, Basildon, Essex SS16 5NJ
**Tel:** 01268524973 **Fax:** 01268272292
**Web:** www.stlukeshospice.com
**Reg No:** 1812104 **Estd:** 1980 Private Limited Company
**Line of Business:** Medical practice activities
**Directors:** Dr R Maunder, Mrs R M Booth, R M Smith, Dr J M D'Mello, Ms M P Bartlett, G W Peaty, Ms M Moura, K Potticary
**Co. Secretary:** Ms Eileen Marshall
**Responsibilities**
**Senior:** Ilene Marshall *(Chief Executive)*
**Marketing:** Sharon Quinn *(Community Services & Developme)*
**HR:** Sally Bingham *(Head of HR)*
**US SIC:** 8011 **UK SIC:** 95300
**Auditors:** Connah Goldsworthy

| | 31-03-14 | 31-03-13 | 31-03-12 |
|---|---|---|---|
| TO | 4,848,006 | 4,280,861 | 4,115,592 |
| P/L | 6,233 | (173,140) | 701 |
| NW | 4,782,408 | 4,776,175 | 4,949,315 |
| WC | 2,639,717 | 2,954,750 | 3,119,998 |
| Emp. | 96 | 90 | 87 |

DUNS 39-780-4428
## St. Luke's Hospice (Harrow & Brent) Ltd.
The Kenton Grange, Kenton Road, Kenton, Harrow, Middlesex HA3 0YG
**Tel:** 020-8382-8000
**Web:** www.stlukeshospice.org
**Reg No:** 2141770 **Estd:** 1987 Private Company Limited By Guarantee
**Line of Business:** Miscellaneous health & allied services
**Directors:** P R O'Neill, S C Radia, Mrs A D Vekaria, Ms J Newland, J Mcdonald, Dr G I Schiller, M S Redhouse, Mrs F Rahman
**Responsibilities**
**Senior:** Sharon Aldridge-Bent *(Director)*, Rameshchandra Bhanderi *(Director)*, Rajesh Bhatia *(Director)*, Claire Buckland *(Director)*, John Carling *(Manager)*, Julie Fewtrell *(Director)*, Jean Gaffin *(Manager)*, Dee Holden *(Manager)*, Aeneas Mee *(Manager)*, Ashok Parmar *(Manager)*, Robin Webb *(Chief Executive)*
**Branches:** St. Luke's Hospice (Harrow & Brent) Ltd., St. Lukes Kenton Grange Hospice Shop, 349 Rayners Lane, Pinner, Middlesex HA5 5EN
**US SIC:** 8091, 8321
**UK SIC:** 95200, 96111
**Auditors:** Sproull & Co
**Bankers:** National Westminster Bank Plc (60-12-17)

| | 31-12-13 | 31-12-12 | 31-12-11 |
|---|---|---|---|
| TO | 6,299,000 | 5,716,000 | 5,356,000 |
| P/L | 487,000 | (102,000) | (117,000) |
| NW | 7,405,000 | 6,782,000 | 6,789,000 |
| WC | 1,081,000 | 702,000 | 690,000 |
| Emp. | 116 | 123 | 115 |

DUNS 28-926-7551
## St. Luke's Hospice Plymouth
Stamford Road, Plymouth, Devon PL9 9XA
**Web:** www.stlukes-hospice.org.uk
**Reg No:** 1505753 **Estd:** 1982 Private Company Limited By Guarantee
**Line of Business:** Hospices
**Directors:** S Elford, Dr J Grose, Mrs C M Postle-Hacon, C J Cavanagh, Dr. S Hobbs, Dr C E Davies, Mrs J A Wills, Mrs L Thomas
**Co. Secretary:** Ms Sally Taylor
**Responsibilities**
**Senior:** Tracey Holeman *(Manager)*, Guy Northcott *(Director)*, David Shepperd *(Director)*, Eugene Van Jaarsveldt *(Director)*, Marianne Williams *(Director)*
**Admin:** Carol Dodridge *(Office Manager)*
**HR:** Steve Statham *(Human Resources Manager)*
**Branches:** St. Luke's Hospice Plymouth, 11 Victoria Rd, Plymouth, Devon PL5 1RW
**US SIC:** 8091 **UK SIC:** 95200
**Auditors:** PricewaterhouseCoopers
**Bankers:** HSBC Bank plc (40-36-22)

| | 31-03-14 | 31-03-13 | 31-03-12 |
|---|---|---|---|
| TO | 9,988,531 | 8,729,386 | 7,837,085 |
| P/L | 1,063,877 | 67,717 | (514,040) |
| NW | 6,864,323 | 5,770,177 | 5,578,160 |
| WC | 2,437,784 | 1,313,010 | 962,592 |
| Emp. | 256 | 203 | 239 |

DUNS 29-663-1252
## St. Luke's Oxford
Mcmaster House, Oxford, Oxfordshire OX3 7PX
**Tel:** 01865228800
**Web:** www.stlukeshosp.co.uk
**Reg No:** 1989868 **Estd:** 1957 Private Company Limited By Guarantee
**Line of Business:** Hospital activities
**Trading Style:** St Luke's Radiology, St Lukes Home
**Directors:** G M Wareing, S J Dare, N Talbot Rice, Mrs C C Williams, L A Ponsonby, Mrs S Cellan-Jones, P A Mclean, R J Hawes
**Co. Secretary:** Gary Hunt
**Responsibilities**
**Senior:** Christopher Cash *(Director)*
**US SIC:** 8062, 8091
**UK SIC:** 95100, 95200
**Auditors:** Nick Westbury & Co Ltd
**Bankers:** Lloyds TSB Bank plc (77-23-09)

| | 31-03-14 | 31-03-13 | 31-03-12 |
|---|---|---|---|
| TO | 2,153,109 | 2,091,560 | 2,124,728 |
| P/L | 239,625 | (69,135) | 222,345 |
| NW | 6,693,079 | 6,389,107 | 6,458,242 |
| WC | 2,909,077 | 2,497,105 | 2,458,240 |
| Emp. | 70 | 68 | 70 |

DUNS 21-181-2297
## St. Lukes Surgery
St Luke's Road, Beckington, Frome, Somerset BA11 6SE
**Estd:** 2011 Partnership
**Line of Business:** Cosmetic surgery
**Trading Style:** Beckington Family Practice
**Partners:** D Gibbs, Dr J Bevan, Dr D Archer, Dr J D Brookes, Dr B Mansfield
**US SIC:** 8011 **UK SIC:** 95300
**Employees:** 50

DUNS 42-359-8044
## St. Margaret's School Bushey
St Margaret?s School Gym, Mer, Watford, Bushey, Hertfordshire WD23 1DT
**Tel:** 02089010870
**Web:** www.stmargaretsbushey.co.uk
**Reg No:** 3201182 **Estd:** 1996 Private Company Limited By Guarantee
**Line of Business:** Primary education
**Directors:** Mrs A S Lovett, Rev W J Gibbs, P Walton, Ms M F Rudland, Mrs S L Shepherd, Mrs R F Hodgson, J Hill, Ms J E Fenn
**Co. Secretary:** Dr Kenneth Young
**Responsibilities**
**Senior:** David Clout *(Director)*, Brian Coulshed *(Director)*, Diella Singarayer *(Director)*
**US SIC:** 8211, 7999, 7941
**UK SIC:** 93200, 97913, 97911
**Auditors:** Macintyre & Co
**Bankers:** Barclays Bank Plc (20-91-79)

| | 31-07-14 | 31-07-13 | 31-07-12 |
|---|---|---|---|
| TO | 7,147,995 | 6,495,585 | 6,516,782 |
| P/L | 515,955 | 138,369 | 430,528 |
| NW | 10,914,055 | 10,398,100 | 10,259,731 |
| WC | (980,907) | 961,425 | 888,688 |
| Emp. | 94 | 91 | 90 |

DUNS 28-821-1576
## St. Margaret's School for Girls (Incorporated).
15-17 Albyn Place, Aberdeen, Aberdeenshire AB10 1RU
**Tel:** 01224584466
**Web:** www.st-margaret.aberdeen.sch.uk
**Reg No:** 0012585SC **Estd:** 1846 Private Company Limited By Guarantee
**Line of Business:** General secondary education
**Trading Style:** St Margarets School
**Directors:** J M Baillie, A J Bannister, Professor J Harper, M A Ruddiman, J N Gifford, Mrs A C Everest, D B Wood, Mrs J A Craik
**Co. Secretary:** Anthony Mountain
**Responsibilities**
**Senior:** Michael Grattidge *(Director)*, L McKie *(Head Teacher)*, Anna Tomlinson *(Head Teacher)*
**HR:** Wendy Main *(Training Manager)*
**US SIC:** 8211 **UK SIC:** 93200
**Auditors:** Ritson Smith
**Bankers:** The Royal Bank Of Scotland Plc (83-15-31)

| | 31-07-13 | 31-07-12 | 31-07-11 |
|---|---|---|---|
| TO | 3,880,317 | 3,771,041 | 3,789,441 |
| P/L | 52,172 | 122,940 | 141,041 |
| NW | 2,349,374 | 2,279,382 | 2,150,740 |
| WC | 922,327 | 876,491 | 738,094 |
| Emp. | 83 | 82 | 82 |

DUNS 28-920-4448
## St. Margaret's Somerset Hospice
Heron Drive, Bishops Hull, Taunton, Somerset TA1 5HA
**Tel:** 01823-259394 **Fax:** 01823354021
**Web:** www.somerset-hospice.org.uk
**Reg No:** 1471345 **VAT No:** 666479678
**Estd:** 1987 Private Company Limited By Guarantee
**Line of Business:** Other human health activities
**Trading Style:** St. Margaret's Somerset Hospice
**Directors:** A J Snell, T G Samuel, Mrs R S Davies, J C Langdon, Dr D J Stalker, D L Jenkins, J H Buckley, Dr J H Yoxall
**Co. Secretary:** Kevin Jones
**Responsibilities**
**Senior:** Ann Andrewes *(Manager)*, Jennifer Board *(Director)*, Nicholas Chapman *(Manager)*, Bernard Newmarch *(Manager)*, Robin Ray *(Manager)*
**IT:** Tim Netto *(Computer Assistant)*
**Branches:** St. Margaret's Somerset Hospice, 71 High Street, Wells, Somerset BA5 2AQ
**US SIC:** 8091 **UK SIC:** 95200
**Auditors:** Francis Clark

**Bankers:** Barclays Bank Plc (20-85-26)

| | 31-03-14 | 31-03-13 | 31-03-12 |
|---|---|---|---|
| TO | 10,924,084 | 8,872,512 | 8,522,638 |
| P/L | 1,264,126 | (753,273) | (1,270,556) |
| NW | 16,019,115 | 14,679,609 | 15,124,302 |
| WC | 317,899 | 162,083 | (236,398) |
| Emp. | 232 | 231 | 242 |

DUNS 21-476-8256

## St. Mark S C of E Primary School

Danebury Road, Basingstoke, Hampshire RG22 4US
**Tel:** 01256346111
**Web:** www.st-markscofe.hants.sch.uk
**Estd:** 2002
**Line of Business:** Schools (local authority)
**Principals:** Mrs E Jones, Mrs E Jones
**Responsibilities**
**Senior:** Sally Jenkins *(Head Teacher)*
**Admin:** Annette Donnelly *(Clerk to Governors)*, Natalie Greer *(Administrative Assistant)*, Claire Howes *(Office Manager)*, Sandra Sim *(Administrative Assistant)*
**Health & Safety:** Tracey Dobell *(Health And Safety)*
**US SIC:** 8211 **UK SIC:** 93200
**Employees:** 70

DUNS 21-549-3029

## St. Mark's Nursing Home

145 Hylton Road, Millfield, Sunderland, Tyne and Wear SR4 7YQ
**Tel:** 01915-674-321
**Web:** www.stmarksnursinghome.co.uk
**Estd:** 1995 Proprietorship
**Line of Business:** Clinics private
**Proprietor:** Dr L Wind
**US SIC:** 8051 **UK SIC:** 95100
**Employees:** 47

DUNS 21-734-9805

## St. Mark's West Essex Catholic School

Tripton Road, Harlow, Essex CM18 6AA
**Tel:** 01279421267
**Web:** www.st-marks.essex.sch.uk
**Reg No:** 7694563 **Estd:** 2011 Private Company Limited By Guarantee
**Line of Business:** General secondary education
**Directors:** Ms R C Harding, Ms K M Hay, T T Austin, J Baker, Reverend B Soley, N J Ehigie-Obano, Ms M Roberts, Mrs J A Delves
**Co. Secretary:** Peter Walsh
**Responsibilities**
**Senior:** Nicole Balloqui *(Director)*, David Brunwin *(Head Teacher)*, Patrick Hay *(Director)*, Ellen Heaphy *(Director)*, Pamela Plowman *(Director)*
**Admin:** Ethel Riley *(Secretary)*
**US SIC:** 8211 **UK SIC:** 93200
**Bankers:** Lloyds TSB Bank plc (30-00-00)

| | 31-08-14 | 31-08-13 | 31-08-12 |
|---|---|---|---|
| TO | 6,445,281 | 6,967,386 | 7,558,779 |
| P/L | (70,522) | 295,466 | 908,573 |
| NW | 603,517 | 991,039 | 758,573 |
| WC | 1,575,543 | 1,537,418 | 1,162,915 |
| Emp. | 116 | 116 | 178 |

DUNS 23-666-8617

## St. Martha's Ltd

16-17 Thornhill Park, Sunderland, Tyne and Wear SR2 7LA
**Tel:** 0191-565-6443 **Fax:** 01915108810
**Web:** www.stmarthasltd.com
**Reg No:** 3661733 **Estd:** 1990 Private Limited Company
**Line of Business:** Rest and retirement homes
**Issued Capital:** £6
**Director:** Ms G Swalwell
**Co. Secretary:** Ms Donna Mccann
**Responsibilities**
**Senior:** Michele Harrison *(Manager)*
**US SIC:** 8321 **UK SIC:** 96111
**Auditors:** Ainleys Accountants

| | 30-11-13 | 30-11-12 | 30-11-11 |
|---|---|---|---|
| TO | 1,284,430 | N/A | N/A |
| P/L | 25,116 | N/A | N/A |
| NW | 965,292 | 935,826 | 919,809 |
| WC | 456,321 | 436,883 | 445,553 |

DUNS 29-893-7830

## St. Martin-in-the Fields Ltd

St Martin's Place, London WC2N 4JH
**Tel:** 02077661122 **Fax:** 020-7839-5163
**Web:** www.stmartin-in-the-fields.org
**Reg No:** 2096693 **VAT No:** 446273639
**Estd:** 1987 Private Limited Company
**Line of Business:** Other retail sale in non-specialised stores
**Trading Style:** St. Martin-In-The-Fields Ltd
**Issued Capital:** £3
**Principals:** Ms J A Hargreaves *(Managing)*, C S Cowls, Ms A M Lyon, M D Whalley, Dame D Brittan, J J O'Brien, S M Wells, K J Hedderly
**Co. Secretary:** Mrs Joanne Hargreaves
**Branches:** St. Martin-In-The Fields Ltd, 6-7 Little Russell Street, London WC1A 2HR
**US SIC:** 5399, 5812
**UK SIC:** 65600, 66110
**Auditors:** Kingston Smith
**Bankers:** National Westminster Bank Plc (60-40-05)

| | 31-12-13 | 31-12-12 | 31-12-11 |
|---|---|---|---|
| TO | 4,260,147 | 3,918,787 | 3,847,615 |
| P/L | (3,915) | 10,375 | (3,371) |
| NW | 60,541 | 64,456 | 54,081 |
| WC | (58,030) | (50,533) | (44,016) |

DUNS 56-976-3402

## St. Martin's Care Ltd

(**Subsidiary of:** Darnley Bidco Ltd)
Vestry Building, 23 Fawcett Street, Sunderland, Tyne and Wear SR1 1RH
**Tel:** 0191-565-2294
**Web:** www.stmartinscare.co.uk
**Reg No:** 2853138 **Estd:** 1993 Private Limited Company
**Line of Business:** Residential care establishments
**Issued Capital:** £100
**Director:** K Pattison
**Responsibilities**
**Senior:** Margaret Garner *(Manager)*, Barry Garner *(Manager)*
**US SIC:** 8321 **UK SIC:** 96111
**Auditors:** Rowlands
**Bankers:** The Co-Operative Bank Plc (08-90-06)

| | 31-03-13 | 31-03-12 | 31-03-11 |
|---|---|---|---|
| TO | 9,323,293 | 8,667,186 | N/A |
| P/L | 1,317,040 | 810,924 | N/A |
| NW | 568,871 | 190,476 | (620,448) |
| WC | 38,635 | (494,299) | (1,402,255) |
| Emp. | 365 | 361 | N/A |

DUNS 28-850-2768

## St.Martins' (Northwood) Preparatory School Trust Ltd

40 Moor Park Road, Northwood, Middlesex HA6 2DJ
**Tel:** 01923828837
**Web:** www.stmartins.org.uk
**Reg No:** 0709159 **Estd:** 1961 Private Limited Company
**Line of Business:** Schools (local authority)
**Directors:** V W Hales, Mrs B Vaughan, Dr I S Gould, Mrs R Uppal, R E Jakes, M R Jordan, Mrs C A Marks, S J Everson
**Co. Secretary:** Stephen Gower
**US SIC:** 8211 **UK SIC:** 93200
**Auditors:** Hardcastle Burton
**Bankers:** National Westminster Bank Plc (60-15-30)

| | 31-08-13 | 31-08-12 | 31-08-11 |
|---|---|---|---|
| TO | 4,744,765 | 4,581,456 | 4,224,496 |
| P/L | 400,511 | 312,278 | 198,427 |
| NW | 9,429,322 | 9,028,811 | 8,716,534 |
| WC | 1,319,200 | 1,162,592 | 1,032,160 |
| Emp. | 72 | 72 | 72 |

DUNS 23-565-0447

## Saint Martin's (Solihull) Ltd

St Martins, Solihull, West Midlands B91 3EN
**Tel:** 01217112557
**Web:** www.saintmartins-school.com
**Reg No:** 0772557 **Estd:** 1944 Private Company Limited By Guarantee
**Line of Business:** Nursery schools
**Trading Style:** Saint Martin"s (Solihull) Ltd
**Directors:** N G Manley, J Shepherd, V K Hallan, Mrs F E De Minckwitz, I P Ralph, Reverend D C Ballard, Mrs G E Tillman, Mrs P M Harbour
**Co. Secretary:** Simon Brown
**Responsibilities**
**Senior:** Kelly Kemp *(Manager)*, Carol Mcnidder *(Director)*
**Finance:** Mike Llewellyn *(Bursar)*
**IT:** Carolyn Dance *(Head of IT)*
**HR:** Mike Llewellyn *(Bursar)*
**Health & Safety:** Mike Llewellyn *(Bursar)*
**Facilities:** Mike Llewellyn *(Bursar)*
**Purchasing:** Mike Llewellyn *(Bursar)*
**US SIC:** 8211 **UK SIC:** 93200
**Auditors:** Michael Kay & Co
**Bankers:** Lloyds TSB Bank plc (30-97-78)

| | 31-08-14 | 31-08-13 | 31-08-12 |
|---|---|---|---|
| TO | 3,811,270 | 3,863,119 | 3,744,708 |
| P/L | (88,971) | 94,983 | 148,572 |
| NW | 5,411,077 | 5,481,135 | 5,346,875 |
| WC | 379,828 | 433,435 | 332,604 |
| Emp. | 112 | 110 | 111 |

DUNS 21-042-1705

## St. Marylebone C of E Secondary School

64 Marylebone High Street, London W1U 5BA
**Tel:** 02079-354704
**Web:** www.stmaryleboneschool.com
**Estd:** 2002 Partnership
**Line of Business:** Schools (local authority)
**Partner:** Mrs E Phillips
**Responsibilities**
**Senior:** Kathryn Pugh *(Head Teacher)*
**US SIC:** 8211 **UK SIC:** 93200
**Employees:** 140

DUNS 28-879-7152

## St. Mary's Hospice Ltd

176 Raddlebarn Road, Birmingham, West Midlands B29 7DA
**Web:** www.birminghamhospice.org.uk
**Reg No:** 1161308 **Estd:** 1979 Private Company Limited By Guarantee
**Line of Business:** Hospices
**Trading Style:** St Mary''s Hospice (Trading)
**Directors:** S W Leyland, M J Russell, V Randeniya, Ms G M Stanley, J K Crawford, Professor A D Walmsley, G S Mandla, C L Graham
**Co. Secretary:** Ms Tina Swani
**Responsibilities**
**Senior:** Collette Clifford *(Manager)*, Judith Millward *(Manager)*
**Finance:** Judith Millward *(Manager)*
**Branches:** St. Mary's Hospice Ltd, 31 Raddlebarn Road, Birmingham, West Midlands B29 6HH
**US SIC:** 8091, 6531
**UK SIC:** 95200, 83400
**Auditors:** BDO Stoy Hayward
**Bankers:** National Westminster Bank Plc (60-22-22)

| | 31-03-14 | 31-03-13 | 31-03-12 |
|---|---|---|---|
| TO | 7,468,378 | 6,815,299 | 6,405,658 |
| P/L | 64,218 | 92,215 | (149,903) |
| NW | 7,123,439 | 6,907,595 | 6,636,472 |
| WC | 3,551,623 | 3,450,944 | 3,084,924 |
| Emp. | 150 | 185 | 182 |

DUNS 55-054-6337

## Saint Marys Hospital

West Wing, Milton Road, Portsmouth, Hampshire PO3 6AD
**Tel:** 02392680000
**Web:** www.solent.nhs.uk
**Estd:** 2012
**Line of Business:** Health centres
**Responsibilities**
**Senior:** Sue Robson *(Manager)*
**Finance:** Malcolm Dennett *(Financial Director)*
**IT:** Philip Kenney *(Head of ICT)*
**Health & Safety:** Peter Fisk *(Health & Safety Coordinator)*
**US SIC:** 8062 **UK SIC:** 95100
**Employees:** 2,000

DUNS 64-741-7351

## St. Mary's Kenmure School

St Marys Road, Glasgow, Lanarkshire G64 2EH
**Tel:** 0141-586-1200
**Web:** www.stmaryskenmure.org.uk
**Line of Business:** General secondary education
**Director:** W Duffy
**Responsibilities**
**Senior:** Jim Crawford *(Principal)*
**IT:** Gerry Sullivan *(Head of Service Education)*
**US SIC:** 8211 **UK SIC:** 93200
**Employees:** 135

DUNS 23-592-5930 **Imp**

## St. Mary's School (Calne)

63 Curzon Street, Calne, Wiltshire SN11 0DF
**Tel:** 01249-857200
**Web:** www.stmaryscalne.org
**Reg No:** 0235572 **Estd:** 1873 Private Company Limited By Guarantee
**Line of Business:** Schools (independent)
**Trading Style:** St Mary's Calne
**Directors:** P V Allen, S F Knight, J S Smith, Dr T R Hands, Ms C M Lough, H S Ringrose, Mrs V J Wilson, Mrs V J Nye
**Co. Secretary:** Richard Gordon
**Responsibilities**
**Senior:** Julia Buckingham *(Director)*, Brian Fall *(Manager)*, Anne Ferguson *(Governor)*, Felicia Kirk *(Principal)*, Patrick Macdougall *(Manager)*, Michael Pipes *(Director)*, Richard Southwell *(Manager)*
**Marketing:** Stephanie Bryan *(Marketing and Communications M)*, Kelly Crockett *(Publication and Events Manager)*, Cari Depla *(Marketing Manager)*
**IT:** Matt Rus *(Head of IT)*, Anne Thornton *(Computer Operations Manager)*
**US SIC:** 8211 **UK SIC:** 93200
**Auditors:** J & A W Sully & Co
**Bankers:** Lloyds TSB Bank plc (30-91-99)

| | 31-08-13 | 31-08-12 | 31-08-11 |
|---|---|---|---|
| TO | 12,560,047 | 11,813,295 | 11,243,792 |
| P/L | 1,272,899 | 981,206 | 894,359 |
| NW | 10,329,224 | 9,039,215 | 8,244,188 |
| WC | 205,931 | 528,279 | (114,102) |
| Emp. | 175 | 169 | 166 |

DUNS 23-530-0399

## St. Mary's School Cambridge

Bateman Street, Cambridge, Cambridgeshire CB2 1LY
**Tel:** 01223-353253
**Web:** www.stmaryscambridge.co.uk
**Reg No:** 1840431 **Estd:** 1898 Private Limited Company
**Line of Business:** Schools
**Directors:** W F Orchard, Ms J L Driscoll, A S Milne, G S Minto, A R Grant, F V Morgan, M D Ledzion, Dr B N Ward
**Co. Secretary:** Duncan Askew
**Responsibilities**
**Senior:** Charlotte Avery *(Headmistress)*, Judith Bates *(Director)*, Peter Chamberlain *(Governor)*, Linda Fairbrother *(Governor)*, Andrew Freeman *(Director)*, Peter Leeming *(Director)*
**Marketing:** Laura Morris *(Marketing Manager)*
**HR:** Charlotte Avery *(Headmistress)*, Kate Ross *(Human Resources Manager)*
**US SIC:** 8211, 8249
**UK SIC:** 93200, 93300
**Auditors:** Peters Elworthy & Moore
**Bankers:** Lloyds TSB Bank plc (30-13-55)

| | 31-08-13 | 31-08-12 | 31-08-11 |
|---|---|---|---|
| TO | 9,228,289 | 9,274,233 | 9,491,972 |
| P/L | 1,000,933 | 848,176 | 1,606,872 |
| NW | 9,879,289 | 8,857,626 | 8,003,247 |
| WC | 4,377,197 | 3,659,570 | 2,618,074 |
| Emp. | 139 | 136 | 138 |

DUNS 76-916-1894

## St. Mary's School (Colchester) Ltd

91 Lexden Road, Colchester, Essex CO3 3RB
**Tel:** 01206-572544 **Fax:** 01206-576437
**Web:** www.stmaryscolchester.org.uk
**Reg No:** 0988976 **Estd:** 1970 Private Company Limited By Guarantee
**Line of Business:** Primary education
**Directors:** Mrs E C Waters, Ms M Livingstone, J R Pendle, Mrs A C Woods, Ms S Foakes, Ms H Borgartz, Ms K Burns, Mrs M K Loxley
**Co. Secretary:** Ms Anne Walker
**Responsibilities**
**Senior:** Robert Lambert *(Director)*
**US SIC:** 8211 **UK SIC:** 93200
**Auditors:** Horwath Clark Whitehill LLP
**Bankers:** The Royal Bank Of Scotland Plc (16-16-31)

| | 31-08-13 | 31-08-12 | 31-08-11 |
|---|---|---|---|
| TO | 3,910,658 | 3,794,241 | 3,937,414 |
| P/L | 31,416 | (77,516) | (76,181) |
| NW | 3,228,528 | 3,197,112 | 3,274,628 |
| WC | 905,969 | 810,192 | 775,922 |
| Emp. | 60 | 61 | 61 |

DUNS 76-985-6279

## St. Mary's School Hampstead

47 Fitzjohns Avenue, Hampstead, London NW3 6PG
**Tel:** 020-7435-1868 **Fax:** 020-7794-7922
**Web:** www.stmh.co.uk
**Reg No:** 2643515 **Estd:** 1992 Private Company Limited By Guarantee
**Line of Business:** General secondary education
**Directors:** K Wilkins, Ms S A Mccarron, P Minns, Mrs M B Jeffrey, K A Murphy, Miss D E Rowe, D H Rands
**Co. Secretary:** Jonathan Davies
**Responsibilities**
**Senior:** Angela Rawlinson *(Principal)*, Owen Wynne *(Manager)*
**Finance:** Charlotte Hall *(Bursar)*
**Sales:** Charlotte Hall *(Bursar)*
**IT:** Madeleine Campbell *(Computer Manager)*
**HR:** Angela Rawlinson *(Principal)*
**Health & Safety:** Charlotte Hall *(Bursar)*
**Facilities:** Charlotte Hall *(Bursar)*
**US SIC:** 8211 **UK SIC:** 93200
**Auditors:** MacIntyre & Co
**Bankers:** National Westminster Bank Plc (60-00-01)

| | 31-08-14 | 31-08-13 | 31-08-12 |
|---|---|---|---|
| TO | 3,737,560 | 3,532,121 | 3,355,468 |
| P/L | 164,969 | 235,260 | 354,477 |
| NW | 4,454,059 | 4,289,090 | 4,053,830 |
| WC | 992,273 | 1,018,069 | 868,564 |
| Emp. | 49 | 51 | 51 |

DUNS 29-622-5238

## St. Mary's School Shaftesbury Trust

Donhead St Mary, Shaftesbury, Dorset SP7 9LP
**Web:** www.st-marys-shaftesbury.co.uk
**Reg No:** 1949068 **Estd:** 1985 Private Limited Company
**Line of Business:** General secondary education
**Directors:** S J Roberts, Miss V M Younghusband, Dr K Mounde, C Mcveigh, R T Moulding, M B Catchpole, Ms J M Taylor, Mrs B E Quest-Ritson

**Co. Secretary:** Louis Tuson
**Responsibilities**
**Senior:** Clare Asquith *(Governor)*, Robert Carson *(Manager)*, David Ceiriog-Hughes *(Director)*, Lucretia Eeles *(Manager)*, Anne May *(Governor)*
**US SIC:** 8211 **UK SIC:** 93200
**Auditors:** Mazars LLP
**Bankers:** Lloyds TSB Bank plc (30-99-72)

| | 31-08-13 | 31-08-12 | 31-08-11 |
|---|---|---|---|
| TO | 6,765,117 | 6,451,003 | 6,234,422 |
| P/L | 188,651 | 70,974 | (120,737) |
| NW | 5,394,365 | 5,141,639 | 5,027,401 |
| WC | (1,645,228) | (1,123,252) | (1,266,847) |
| Emp. | 213 | 214 | 70 |

DUNS 28-838-3946
## St.Marys School(Lincoln) Ltd
5 Pottergate, Lincoln, Lincolnshire LN2 1PH
**Tel:** 01522-524622
**Web:** www.lincolnminsterschool.co.uk
**Reg No:** 0482093 **Estd:** 1950 Private Company Limited By Guarantee
**Line of Business:** Schools (independent)
**Directors:** Mrs S L Johnston, T Overton, Mrs A Crowe
**Responsibilities**
**Senior:** Hazel Belcher *(Manager)*, Rebecca Blackwood *(Manager)*, Russell Eke *(Manager)*, Derek James *(Manager)*, Rachel Pareezer *(Manager)*, Fiona Thomas *(Head Mistress)*, clive rickart *(Principal)*
**US SIC:** 8211 **UK SIC:** 93200
**Auditors:** Streets & Co
**Bankers:** National Westminster Bank Plc (60-13-15)

| | 31-08-11 |
|---|---|
| TO | 1,080,097 |
| P/L | (131,089) |
| Emp. | 58 |

DUNS 21-558-2062
## St. Matthew Housing Ltd
Elseys Yard, Risbygate Street, Bury St Edmunds, Suffolk IP33 3AA
**Web:** www.genefiahomes.co.uk
**Estd:** 2007
**Line of Business:** Social work activities
**Trading Style:** Genesis Housing Association
**Directors:** Ms N A Lucking, M G Swiney, Ms V S Connolly, J Norman, Ms J A Manser, C D Gale, Ms H Shellens
**Responsibilities**
**Senior:** Susie Mills *(Business Manager)*
**Finance:** Susie Mills *(Business Manager)*
**US SIC:** 6732 **UK SIC:** 83100
**Auditors:** KPMG LLP
**Employees:** 19
**Turnover:** £7,455,641

DUNS 21-040-0382
## St. Matthews C of E Primary School
New Hall Lane, Preston, Lancashire PR1 5XB
**Tel:** 01772-794482
**Web:** www.stmatthews.kingston.sch.uk
**Estd:** 2002 Proprietorship
**Line of Business:** Schools (local authority)
**Proprietor:** R Small
**Responsibilities**
**Senior:** Roger Small *(Head Teacher)*
**US SIC:** 8211 **UK SIC:** 93200
**Employees:** 80

DUNS 21-660-7049
## St. Michael S Hospice
Bartestree, Hereford, Herefordshire HR1 4HA
**Tel:** 01432272364
**Web:** www.st-michaels-hospice.org.uk
**Estd:** 2011
**Line of Business:** Charity shops
**Responsibilities**
**Senior:** Claire Carr *(Manager)*
**US SIC:** 8321 **UK SIC:** 96111
**Employees:** 150

DUNS 21-491-8562
## St.Michaels College
Chanterhill Road, Enniskillen, Co Fermanagh BT74 6DG
**Tel:** 028-6632-2935
**Web:** www.saintmichaels.org.uk
**Estd:** 1890 Proprietorship
**Line of Business:** Schools (foundation)
**Proprietor:** E Mccullough
**Responsibilities**
**IT:** Aidan Power *(IT Manager)*
**US SIC:** 8211 **UK SIC:** 93200
**Employees:** 50

DUNS 76-853-1121
## Saint Michael's College (Tenbury) Ltd
**(Subsidiary of:** Chopping Hart & Biddlecomb Limited)
Oldwood Road, St Michaels, Tenbury Wells, Worcestershire WR15 8PH
**Web:** www.st-michaels.uk.com
**Reg No:** 2608682 **Estd:** 1994 Private Limited Company
**Line of Business:** General secondary education
**Export Sales:** £4,934,082
**Issued Capital:** £2
**Directors:** S M Higgins, Dr R G Fry
**Co. Secretary:** Miss Tasha Hunt
**Branches:** Saint Michael's College (Tenbury) Ltd, Oldwood Road, St. Michaels, Tenbury Wells, Worcestershire WR15 8PH
**US SIC:** 8211 **UK SIC:** 93200

| | 31-08-13 | 31-08-12 | 31-08-11 |
|---|---|---|---|
| TO | 4,934,082 | N/A | N/A |
| P/L | 241,714 | N/A | N/A |
| NW | 505,233 | 279,416 | 353,444 |
| WC | (1,472,057) | (890,281) | (692,714) |
| Emp. | 125 | N/A | N/A |

DUNS 21-101-8051
## Saint Michael's Grammar School
12 Cornakinnegar Road, Lurgan, Craigavon, Co Armagh BT67 9JW
**Tel:** 028-3832-3192
**Web:** www.stmichaelslurgan.org.uk
**Estd:** 2004
**Line of Business:** Schools (independent)
**Responsibilities**
**Senior:** Gerard Adams *(Head Teacher)*
**Finance:** Maria Hoy *(Senior Finance Administrator)*
**IT:** Kate Mccann *(Senior IT Executive)*
**US SIC:** 8211 **UK SIC:** 93200
**Employees:** 85

DUNS 22-282-4364
## St. Michael's Hotel Ltd
Stracey Road, Falmouth, Cornwall TR11 4NB
**Tel:** 01326312707 **Fax:** 01326211772
**Web:** www.stmichaelshotel.co.uk
**Reg No:** 4300398 **Estd:** 2001 Private Limited Company
**Line of Business:** Hotels
**Issued Capital:** £1,000
**Directors:** Ms J Carpenter, N J Carpenter
**Co. Secretary:** Ms Julie Carpenter
**Responsibilities**
**Senior:** Nick Hodges *(Executive Head Chef)*
**US SIC:** 7011, 5813
**UK SIC:** 66500, 66200

| | 31-03-14 | 31-03-13 | 31-03-12 |
|---|---|---|---|
| TA | 3,472,544 | 997,488 | 429,099 |
| NW | (103,229) | (391,465) | (594,948) |
| WC | 892,136 | (304,532) | (839,422) |

DUNS 28-858-7470
## St.Michael's Manor Ltd
Fishpool Street, St Albans, Hertfordshire AL3 4RY
**Tel:** 01727-864444 **Fax:** 01727-848909
**Web:** www.stmichaelsmanor.com
**Reg No:** 0850748 **Estd:** 1985 Private Limited Company
**Line of Business:** Hotels
**Trading Style:** St.Michael's Manor Hotel
**Issued Capital:** £100
**Directors:** E G Gibson, Ms S B Newling Ward, Mrs P Sale
**Co. Secretary:** Geoffrey Goddard
**Responsibilities**
**Senior:** Oliviier Deluanoy *(Manager)*, Leslie Furnell *(Manager)*, Richard Marrett *(Manager)*, Richard Newling Ward *(Manager)*, David Newling-Ward *(Proprietor)*
**Marketing:** Emma Cook *(Sales & Marketing Manager)*
**Sales:** Emma Cook *(Sales & Marketing Manager)*
**US SIC:** 7011, 5812
**UK SIC:** 66500, 66110
**Auditors:** Churchmill Partnership

| | 30-06-13 | 30-06-12 | 30-06-11 |
|---|---|---|---|
| TO | 2,609,266 | 2,540,552 | 2,116,693 |
| P/L | 188,517 | 234,124 | 121,726 |
| NW | 7,136,864 | 6,974,410 | 6,879,772 |
| WC | (398,903) | (448,871) | (384,133) |
| Emp. | 51 | 37 | 38 |

DUNS 28-912-0040
## St. Michael's School (Bryn) Ltd
**(Subsidiary of:** Broadway Education Ltd)
Bryn, Bryn, Llanelli, Dyfed SA14 9TU
**Tel:** 01554-820325
**Web:** www.stmikes.co.uk
**Reg No:** 1424406 **Estd:** 1979 Private Limited Company
**Line of Business:** Schools (independent)
**Issued Capital:** £82,800
**Director:** M Broadway
**Co. Secretary:** Paul Broadway
**Responsibilities**
**Senior:** Emma Lewis *(Head Teacher)*, Taiwo Okeneye *(It Manager)*, Daniel Sheeham *(Headmaster)*
**Marketing:** Daniel Sheeham *(Headmaster)*
**Sales:** Daniel Sheeham *(Headmaster)*
**IT:** Alan Jeffery *(IT Manager)*, Taiwo Okeneye *(It Manager)*
**Purchasing:** Philippa Chapel *(Purchasing Manager)*
**US SIC:** 8211 **UK SIC:** 93200
**Auditors:** PricewaterhouseCoopers

| | 31-08-13 | 31-08-12 | 31-08-11 |
|---|---|---|---|
| TO | 4,023,811 | 4,014,513 | 3,979,588 |
| P/L | 714,863 | 861,459 | 3,451,184 |
| NW | 5,635,918 | 5,546,575 | 5,340,149 |
| WC | 3,885,744 | 4,793,656 | 5,224,012 |
| Emp. | 100 | 100 | 96 |

DUNS 28-821-0412
## The St. Mirren Football Club Ltd.
**(Subsidiary of:** Douglas Street Ltd)
St Mirren Park, 75 Greenhill Road, Paisley, Renfrewshire PA3 1RU
**Tel:** 0141-889-2558
**Web:** www.saintmirren.net
**Reg No:** 0005773SC **Estd:** 1970 Private Limited Company
**Line of Business:** Sports clubs
**Issued Capital:** £95,250
**Directors:** G Campbell, A W Marshall, C W Stewart, S G Gilmour, B A Mcausland
**Co. Secretary:** Christopher Stewart
**Responsibilities**
**Senior:** Brian Caldwell *(General Manager)*, Kenneth Mcgeoch *(Manager)*
**Marketing:** Campbell Kennedy *(Marketing Manager)*
**Health & Safety:** Finley Macauly *(Safety Officer)*
**US SIC:** 7999 **UK SIC:** 97913
**Auditors:** JRD LLP
**Bankers:** Clydesdale Bank Plc (82-69-20)

| | 31-05-14 | 31-05-13 | 31-05-12 |
|---|---|---|---|
| TO | 3,183,296 | 3,459,679 | 3,263,795 |
| P/L | (408,100) | (251,255) | (290,455) |
| NW | 9,777,406 | 10,177,906 | 10,304,161 |
| WC | (543,465) | (400,694) | (380,824) |
| Emp. | 65 | 74 | 65 |

DUNS 28-827-9466
## St. Modans Care Home Ltd
**(Subsidiary of:** Meallmore Ltd)
17 Wyvis Road, Nairn, Nairnshire IV12 5NR
**Tel:** 01667453902
**Reg No:** 0086885SC **Estd:** 1984 Private Limited Company
**Line of Business:** Nursing homes
**Issued Capital:** £20,100
**Directors:** G J Hennessey, A P Hennessey
**Co. Secretary:** Gavin Mackenzie
**US SIC:** 8051, 1541
**UK SIC:** 95100, 50100
**Auditors:** Saffery Champness
**Bankers:** Bank Of Scotland (80-09-17)

| | 31-03-14 | 31-03-13 | 31-03-12 |
|---|---|---|---|
| TO | N/A | N/A | 1,668,812 |
| P/L | 449,015 | 206,291 | 95,937 |
| NW | 3,786,673 | 3,147,361 | 4,332,071 |
| WC | (1,411,184) | (2,174,652) | (910,022) |
| Emp. | 78 | 78 | 73 |

DUNS 21-880-3377
## St. Modwen Properties Plc
Sir Stanley Clarke House, Birmingham, West Midlands B32 1AF
**Tel:** 01212-229-400 **Fax:** 01212-229-401
**Web:** www.stmodwen.co.uk
**Reg No:** 0349201 **VAT No:** 299056611
**Estd:** 1939 Public Limited Company
**Line of Business:** Development and selling of real estate
**Issued Capital:** £22,037,699
**Directors:** W A Oliver, S J Burke, J H Salmon, L James, S W Clarke, W M Shannon, I A Bull, R S Mully
**Co. Secretary:** Ms Tanya Stote
**Responsibilities**
**Marketing:** Bev Hall *(Residential Director of Sales)*, Charlotte McCarthy *(Marketing Manager)*
**Sales:** Bev Hall *(Residential Director of Sales)*, Stephen Prosser *(Regional Manager, Yorkshire)*
**Health & Safety:** Desmond Kemp *(Property Administrator)*
**Facilities:** Desmond Kemp *(Property Administrator)*
**Branches:** St. Modwen Properties Plc, Trentham Estate, Stone Road, Stoke-On-Trent, Staffordshire ST4 8AX
**US SIC:** 6552 **UK SIC:** 85000
**Auditors:** Deloitte LLP
**Bankers:** National Westminster Bank Plc (52-10-35)

| | 30-11-13 | 30-11-12 | 30-11-11 |
|---|---|---|---|
| TO | 161,100,000 | 219,100,000 | 109,600,000 |
| P/L | 80,500,000 | 47,400,000 | 50,400,000 |
| NW | 614,200,000 | 502,600,000 | 464,400,000 |
| WC | 36,900,000 | 68,400,000 | 115,100,000 |
| Emp. | 255 | 240 | 234 |

DUNS 21-094-9504
## Saint Nicholas Health Centre
The Surgery, Canterbury Way, Stevenage, Hertfordshire SG1 4LH
**Tel:** 01438-747064
**Estd:** 1978 Partnership
**Line of Business:** Public sector hospital activities, including nhs trusts
**Partners:** Dr M Delayni, Dr S Zaidi, Dr A J Wilson, Dr C Saunders
**Responsibilities**
**Senior:** Susan Shanbrook *(Practice Manager)*
**US SIC:** 8062 **UK SIC:** 95100
**Employees:** 60

DUNS 28-974-3130
## St. Nicholas Hospice (Suffolk)
Hardwick Lane Macmillan Way, Bury St Edmunds, Suffolk IP33 2QY
**Web:** www.stnicholashospice.org.uk
**Reg No:** 1748046 **Estd:** 1983 Private Company Limited By Guarantee
**Line of Business:** Hospices
**Directors:** R H Norburn, D W Barclay, M J Vernon, Mrs M C Miles, M A Leith, A S Williams, Mrs S M Hayter, I C Morgan
**Co. Secretary:** Ms Julie Roy
**Responsibilities**
**Senior:** Loreen Macklin *(Director)*, Brigid Martineau *(Director)*, Elisabeth Wallace *(Director)*
**US SIC:** 8091, 8321
**UK SIC:** 95200, 96111
**Auditors:** BDO Stoy Hayward
**Bankers:** Barclays Bank Plc (20-16-12)

| | 31-03-14 | 31-03-13 | 31-03-12 |
|---|---|---|---|
| TO | 5,856,381 | 5,788,410 | 5,298,521 |
| P/L | 321,495 | 876,774 | 537,574 |
| NW | 11,613,794 | 11,186,848 | 9,797,833 |
| WC | 1,313,451 | 2,091,767 | 1,138,734 |
| Emp. | 115 | 106 | 102 |

DUNS 28-859-9780
## St. Nicholas' School (Fleet) Educational Trust Ltd
Redfields Lane, Fleet, Hampshire GU52 0RF
**Tel:** 01252-850121
**Web:** www.st-nicholas.hants.sch.uk
**Reg No:** 0872200 **Estd:** 1935 Private Limited Company
**Line of Business:** General secondary education
**Trading Style:** St. Nicholas' School
**Directors:** Ms S L Raynsford, N W Gradidge, Mrs N S Eastwood, S H Sturge, G R Cockayne, Ms J Ash
**Co. Secretary:** Ms Caroline Taylor
**Responsibilities**
**Senior:** Margaret Cairns *(Manager)*, Peter Keep *(Manager)*
**IT:** Laura Johnson *(IT Manager)*
**Health & Safety:** Michele Axton *(Health & Safety Officer)*
**Facilities:** Peter Sleet *(Facilities Manager)*
**US SIC:** 8211 **UK SIC:** 93200
**Auditors:** Haysmacintyre
**Bankers:** Lloyds TSB Bank plc (30-93-32)

| | 31-07-13 | 31-07-12 | 31-07-11 |
|---|---|---|---|
| TO | 4,243,835 | 3,992,754 | 3,937,266 |
| P/L | 314,602 | 277,990 | 218,187 |
| NW | 4,803,235 | 4,488,633 | 4,210,643 |
| WC | 887,745 | 721,207 | 468,279 |
| Emp. | 52 | 58 | 56 |

DUNS 28-851-0555
## St.Nicholas School(Harlow) Ltd
Hillingdon House, Harlow, Essex CM17 0NJ
**Tel:** 01279-429910
**Web:** www.saintnicholasschool.net
**Reg No:** 0721476 **Estd:** 1962 Private Limited Company
**Line of Business:** Schools (independent)
**Directors:** R G Ellice, Mrs D J Spellman, Mrs J M Templeton-Knight, A E Johnson, S K Penney
**Co. Secretary:** Mrs Lucy Maunder
**Responsibilities**
**Senior:** Pauline Jones *(Bursar)*, Keith Knight *(Headmaster)*
**Finance:** Lorna Baufrere *(Accounts Administrator)*, Pauline Jones *(Bursar)*
**Marketing:** Caroline Furneaux *(Deputy Head of Lower School)*
**Admin:** Lorna Baufrere *(Accounts Administrator)*, Beverly Brooks *(Recptionist)*, Yvette Mardel *(Office Manager)*
**IT:** Kate Foxwell *(Network Manager)*
**Health & Safety:** Pauline Jones *(Bursar)*
**Facilities:** Pauline Jones *(Bursar)*

**Operations:** Martin Glen *(Operations Manager)*, Pauline Jones *(Bursar)*
**Purchasing:** Pauline Jones *(Bursar)*
**Engineering:** Vera Dawkins *(Resources Technician)*
**US SIC:** 8211 **UK SIC:** 93200
**Auditors:** Willis Burnell
**Bankers:** Barclays Bank Plc (20-05-06)

| | 31-07-14 | 31-07-13 | 31-07-12 |
|---|---|---|---|
| TO | 3,345,729 | 3,464,054 | 3,366,867 |
| P/L | (63,665) | 110,961 | 132,596 |
| NW | 3,970,145 | 4,033,810 | 3,922,849 |
| WC | 961,069 | 1,001,152 | 843,640 |
| Emp. | 79 | N/A | 75 |

DUNS 23-562-9656
## St. Oswald's Hospice Ltd
Regent Avenue, Newcastle-Upon-Tyne, Tyne and Wear NE3 1EE
**Tel:** 0191-285-0063
**Web:** www.stoswaldsuk.org
**Reg No:** 1166239 **Estd:** 1974 Private Limited Company
**Line of Business:** Hospices
**Trading Style:** St. Oswalds Hospice
**Directors:** Dr H H Lucraft, Mrs K G Jobson, Mrs D Clasper, Dr S M Blades, Mrs M Liston, K Fanibunda, Mrs J Clarke, I G Kelsall
**Co. Secretary:** Ms Helen Eadington
**Responsibilities**
**Senior:** James Ellam *(Chief Executive)*, Julie Harrison *(Director)*, Kathryn Mannix *(Trustee)*, Anthony Mooney *(Director)*, Sheralyn Pinner *(Manager)*, Mike Robson *(Director)*, Susan Stirling *(Manager)*
**Finance:** Gill Gregory *(Financial Director)*
**Marketing:** Debra Daglish *(Marketing Manager)*
**Admin:** Jenny Ranson *(Personal Assistant)*
**HR:** Pat Bolland *(Human Resources Manager)*, Deborah Heron *(Human Resources Manager)*
**Health & Safety:** Jane Hamblin *(Facilities Manager)*
**Facilities:** Jane Hamblin *(Facilities Manager)*
**US SIC:** 8091 **UK SIC:** 95200
**Auditors:** RMT
**Bankers:** Barclays Bank Plc (20-59-61)

| | 31-03-14 | 31-03-13 | 31-03-12 |
|---|---|---|---|
| TO | 11,268,812 | 10,482,377 | 9,518,491 |
| P/L | 238,306 | 278,994 | 12,771 |
| NW | 16,078,977 | 15,806,887 | 15,425,353 |
| WC | 3,066,046 | 3,062,615 | 2,660,712 |
| Emp. | 230 | 220 | 214 |

DUNS 23-703-7663
## St. Patrick's International College Ltd
24 Great Chapel Street, London W1F 8FS
**Tel:** 02035351155 **Fax:** 02072876665
**Web:** www.st-patricks.ac.uk
**Reg No:** 3698965 **Estd:** 1998 Private Limited Company
**Line of Business:** General secondary education
**Issued Capital:** £2
**Directors:** Mrs M Ludhor, D Y Khan
**Co. Secretary:**
Thomas Eggar Secretaries Limited
**Responsibilities**
**Senior:** Girish Chandra *(Manager)*, Sunita Chandra *(Manager)*, Trevor Cocking *(Facilities Director)*
**Finance:** Dinsesh Bist *(Financial Manager)*
**IT:** Shashi Bhushan *(IT Manager)*
**Health & Safety:** Esther Hardy *(Health & Safety Officer)*
**US SIC:** 8211, 8299
**UK SIC:** 93200, 93300
**Auditors:** Jefferys Henry LLP
**Bankers:** HSBC Bank plc (40-05-20)

| | 30-11-12 | 29-04-12 | 31-11-10 |
|---|---|---|---|
| TA | 7,786,193 | 2,510,306 | 1,022,921 |
| NW | 1,241,819 | 235,267 | 217,622 |
| WC | 2,990,358 | 113,867 | 564,773 |

DUNS 37-895-5249 **Imp**
## St. Paul's Cathedral Enterprises Ltd
The Chapterhouse, St Paul's Churchyard, London EC4M 8AD
**Web:** www.stpauls.co.uk
**Reg No:** 3313320 **Estd:** 2000 Private Limited Company
**Line of Business:** Places of worship
**Issued Capital:** £150,000
**Directors:** Major General N J Cottam, M O Pennington, P D Hillas, A W Bird, Ms S Fellows, M R Mcvay
**Co. Secretary:** Mrs Ruth Moore
**Responsibilities**
**Senior:** Lee Amaitis *(Manager)*, Barry Bateman *(Vice Chairman)*, Michael Gifford *(Manager)*, Roger Walkinton *(CEO, Managing Director)*
**Marketing:** Ed Holmes *(Press & Communications Manager)*
**US SIC:** 5399 **UK SIC:** 65600
**Auditors:** PricewaterhouseCoopers
**Bankers:** Lloyds TSB Bank plc (30-91-83)

| | 31-12-13 | 31-12-12 | 31-12-11 |
|---|---|---|---|
| TO | 2,527,946 | 2,222,553 | 2,068,880 |
| P/L | 1,132,400 | 926,385 | 790,316 |
| NW | 150,000 | 150,000 | 150,000 |
| WC | 150,000 | 149,352 | 148,550 |

DUNS 28-912-9314
## St. Paul's Community Development Trust
73 Hertford Street, Birmingham, West Midlands B12 8NJ
**Web:** www.stpaulstrust.org.uk
**Reg No:** 1429707 **Estd:** 1979 Private Company Limited By Guarantee
**Line of Business:** Primary education
**Directors:** R Sadikot, M P Riley, J Mcfarlane, M Jaspal, R Buckman, Ms J C Webster, Mrs S P Fry, Ms G Coffin
**Co. Secretary:** Mrs Marion Ridsdill
**Responsibilities**
**Senior:** Shashi Bhana *(Manager)*, Shazim Husayn *(Manager)*, Tony Kennedy *(Director)*, David Lane *(Director)*, Judith Millington *(Director)*, Constance Perris *(Director)*, Jacqui Ure *(Director)*, Patrick Wing *(Director)*
**Branches:** St. Paul's Community Development Trust, 10 Malvern Street, Birmingham, West Midlands B12 8NN
**US SIC:** 8211, 8091
**UK SIC:** 93200, 95200
**Auditors:** Burman & Co
**Bankers:** Unity Trust Bank Plc (08-60-01)

| | 31-03-14 | 31-03-13 | 31-03-12 |
|---|---|---|---|
| TO | 3,572,105 | 2,969,819 | 3,095,196 |
| P/L | 310,740 | (23,169) | 112,219 |
| NW | 2,739,085 | 2,428,345 | 2,451,514 |
| WC | 1,362,756 | 1,431,008 | 1,368,476 |
| Emp. | 155 | 141 | 122 |

DUNS 21-719-7433 **Imp**
## St. Peters Garden Centre Ltd
Avenue De Lane Reine, Elizabeth, Jersey, Channel Islands JE3 7BP
**Tel:** 01534-745903 **Fax:** 01534-746774
**Web:** www.stpetersgardencentre.co.uk
**Reg No:** 0002001J **Estd:** 1997 Private Limited Company
**Line of Business:** Garden centre proprietors
**Principals:** M Vaudin *(Managing)*, G R Dorey, P J Le Sueur, M H Berresford
**Responsibilities**
**Senior:** Mark Mabbett *(General Manager)*, Pepin le Sueur *(Director)*
**US SIC:** 0181, 5261
**UK SIC:** 01002, 65400
**Employees:** 57

DUNS 29-873-2926
## St. Peter's School Commercial Company
Clifton, York, North Yorkshire YO30 6AB
**Tel:** 01904527300 **Fax:** 01904521301
**Web:** www.stpetersyork.org.uk
**Reg No:** 2076568 **Estd:** 1986 Private Unlimited Company
**Line of Business:** General management consultancy activities
**Issued Capital:** £3
**Directors:** N L Winkley, Ms K V Hodges, R M Schofield
**Co. Secretary:** Richard Schofield
**Responsibilities**
**Senior:** Nick Sheppard *(Manager)*
**Finance:** P Lacy *(Bursar)*
**Marketing:** Hannah Hamilton *(Marketing Officer)*
**HR:** P Lacy *(Bursar)*
**Health & Safety:** P Lacy *(Bursar)*
**Facilities:** Graham Fennell *(Estates Manager)*
**Branches:** St. Peter's School Commercial Company, 13 The Avenue, York, North Yorkshire YO30 6AS
**US SIC:** 7392, 8211
**UK SIC:** 83951, 93200

| | 31-08-13 | 31-08-12 |
|---|---|---|
| TO | 125,223 | 184,426 |
| NW | 3 | 3 |
| WC | 3 | 3 |

DUNS 21-318-4042
## St. Philomenas Catholic High School for Girls
Pound Street, Carshalton, Surrey SM5 3PS
**Tel:** 020-8642-2025
**Web:** www.stphils.org.uk
**Estd:** 2002 Proprietorship
**Line of Business:** Post-graduate level higher education
**Proprietor:** Mrs J Johnson
**Responsibilities**
**Finance:** Christine Eadie *(Senior Finance Administrator)*
**US SIC:** 8221 **UK SIC:** 93100
**Employees:** 100

DUNS 28-871-4090
## St.Piran's School Ltd
Gringer Hill, Maidenhead, Berkshire SL6 7LZ
**Tel:** 01628-594300
**Web:** www.stpirans.co.uk
**Reg No:** 1047287 **Estd:** 1972 Private Company Limited By Guarantee
**Line of Business:** Schools (independent)
**Directors:** Mrs H Ness-Gifford, S A Nokes, E J Parrott, Mrs K J Snowden Taylor, C B Mcarthur, Mrs E Marriner, Ms S Ayre, C Lambert
**Co. Secretary:** Ms Christine Murray
**Responsibilities**
**Senior:** Alexandra Acton *(Manager)*, Jonathon Carroll *(Head Teacher)*, Johnatan Carroll *(Head Teacher)*, Keith Spicer *(Director)*, William Stileman *(Director)*, Robert Vaux *(Manager)*
**IT:** Jackie Quinn *(Computer Manager)*
**US SIC:** 8211 **UK SIC:** 93200
**Bankers:** Barclays Bank Plc (20-71-03)

| | 31-08-13 | 31-08-12 | 31-08-11 |
|---|---|---|---|
| TO | 4,266,640 | 4,189,972 | 4,047,028 |
| P/L | 90,812 | 28,353 | (19,301) |
| NW | 1,580,740 | 1,489,928 | 1,461,575 |
| WC | (1,300,238) | (1,104,480) | (1,044,802) |
| Emp. | 64 | 65 | 63 |

DUNS 29-487-2486
## St. Richard's Hospice Foundation
Wildwood Drive, Worcester, Worcestershire WR5 2QT
**Fax:** 01905760938
**Web:** www.strichards.org.uk
**Reg No:** 1850502 **Estd:** 1984 Private Company Limited By Guarantee
**Line of Business:** Hospices
**Directors:** Dr V Wilkie, Prof R A Lewis, Mrs A L Palmer, Mrs H E Edwards, Ms B Sheridan, A C Roberts, J G Bartholomew, Ms J P Cowpe
**Co. Secretary:** Lt Col Mark Jackson
**Responsibilities**
**Senior:** John Bawden *(Director)*, Peter Flagg *(Director)*, Helen Griffee *(Communications Manager)*, Simon Hyslop *(Director)*, Janet Quallington *(Director)*, Margaret Sullivan *(Director)*
**Marketing:** Helen Griffee *(Communications Manager)*
**Branches:** St. Richard's Hospice Foundation, 19 Mealcheapen St, Reindeer Court, Worcester, Worcestershire WR1 2DS
**US SIC:** 8091, 6732, 8321
**UK SIC:** 95200, 83100, 96111
**Auditors:** John Yelland & Co
**Bankers:** National Westminster Bank Plc (55-81-36)

| | 31-03-14 | 31-03-13 | 31-03-12 |
|---|---|---|---|
| TO | 7,704,543 | 7,220,716 | 5,642,799 |
| P/L | 1,274,421 | 1,330,893 | 316,977 |
| NW | 12,192,248 | 10,918,062 | 9,350,470 |
| WC | 2,590,787 | 2,373,336 | 954,669 |
| Emp. | 197 | 182 | 162 |

DUNS 21-491-3761
## St. Richards R.C Secondary School
Ashdown Road, Bexhill-On-Sea, East Sussex TN40 1SE
**Tel:** 01424-731070
**Web:** www.st-richards.e-sussex.sch.uk
**Line of Business:** General secondary education
**Responsibilities**
**Senior:** D Cronin *(Head Teacher)*
**US SIC:** 8211 **UK SIC:** 93200
**Employees:** 100

DUNS 28-938-2707
## St. Rocco's Hospice
Lockton Lane, Warrington, Cheshire WA5 0BW
**Tel:** 01925-575780
**Web:** www.stroccos.org.uk
**Reg No:** 1565543 **Estd:** 1981 Private Company Limited By Guarantee
**Line of Business:** Hospices
**Directors:** M Coates, A D Tilston, Dr C E Walshe, Z Clements, Rev J Bellfield, M F Rashid, Mrs D W Webb, N L Banner
**Co. Secretary:** John Farquharson
**Responsibilities**
**Senior:** Zak Clements *(Director)*, Edwin Holland *(Director)*, David Kendrick *(Director)*, Pam Massey *(Chief Executive Officer)*, Geoffrey Player *(Director)*, Mary Rudkin *(Director)*, Margaret Wright *(Director)*
**Branches:** St. Rocco's Hospice, 99 London Road, Warrington, Cheshire WA4 6LG
**US SIC:** 8091 **UK SIC:** 95200
**Auditors:** Haslam Tunstall
**Bankers:** HSBC Bank plc (40-45-24)

| | 05-04-14 | 05-04-13 | 05-04-12 |
|---|---|---|---|
| TO | 4,118,063 | 3,660,128 | 3,945,082 |
| P/L | 415,409 | (19,346) | 518,175 |
| NW | 9,389,031 | 8,927,667 | 8,853,973 |
| WC | 2,347,354 | 3,700,885 | 3,632,600 |
| Emp. | 116 | 116 | 107 |

DUNS 73-293-9678
## St. Roch's Childcare Service
Unit W/14, 141 Charles Street, Glasgow, Lanarkshire G21 2QA
**Tel:** 01415643020
**Reg No:** 0238421SC **Estd:** 2002 Private Company Limited By Guarantee
**Line of Business:** Primary education
**Directors:** Ms C O'Hara, Ms A F Umeh, Ms J Mundy, Ms H Hunter, Ms M J Jones, Ms C Gallacher, Ms D Black, Ms D Mundy
**Responsibilities**
**Senior:** Anne Sweeney *(Manager)*
**Branches:** St. Roch's Childcare Service, Forge St, Glasgow, Lanarkshire G21 2AH
**US SIC:** 8211 **UK SIC:** 93200
**Bankers:** Clydesdale Bank Plc (82-64-26)

| | 31-03-14 | 31-03-13 | 31-03-12 |
|---|---|---|---|
| TO | 710,282 | 689,419 | 646,925 |
| P/L | 17,635 | (33,406) | (48,345) |
| NW | 8,232 | (9,403) | 24,003 |
| WC | 3,249 | (12,763) | (24,364) |
| Emp. | 46 | 47 | 43 |

DUNS 21-494-6803
## St. Roses Special School
Stratford Lawn, Stroud, Gloucestershire GL5 4AP
**Tel:** 01453-763793
**Web:** www.stroses.org.uk
**Estd:** 2002 Proprietorship
**Line of Business:** Schools (special)
**Proprietor:** Mrs F Billington
**Responsibilities**
**Senior:** Jan Daines *(Head Teacher)*
**US SIC:** 8299 **UK SIC:** 93300
**Employees:** 95

DUNS 22-606-0705
## St.Swithuns School(Winchester)
Alresford Road, Winchester, Hampshire SO21 1HA
**Tel:** 01962835700 **Fax:** 01962-835779
**Web:** www.stswithuns.com
**Reg No:** 0110692 **VAT No:** 631653844
**Estd:** 1870 Private Company Limited By Guarantee
**Line of Business:** Primary education
**Directors:** Miss R L Rothman, E M Berry, J B Russell, J E Atwell, L H Meynell, Dr H M Mycock, A M Reid, T J Bremridge
**Responsibilities**
**Senior:** Natalie Lee *(Director)*, Sarah Parrish *(Director)*, Julian Whitehouse *(Director)*
**Marketing:** Simon Mayes *(Marketing Manager)*
**IT:** Adam King *(IT Manager)*
**Health & Safety:** Jim Ewing *(Estate Manager)*
**Facilities:** Jim Ewing *(Estate Manager)*
**US SIC:** 8211 **UK SIC:** 93200
**Auditors:** Baker Tilly UK Audit LLP
**Bankers:** National Westminster Bank Plc (55-81-26)

| | 31-07-13 | 31-07-12 | 31-07-11 |
|---|---|---|---|
| TO | 11,478,660 | 10,738,886 | 10,899,494 |
| P/L | 1,251,926 | 621,446 | 1,181,723 |
| NW | 25,646,036 | 24,591,951 | 24,199,219 |
| WC | 4,922,483 | 4,889,108 | 4,379,988 |
| Emp. | 164 | 159 | 161 |

DUNS 21-557-6955
## St.Teresa's Catholic Church
Haig Road, Biggin Hill, Westerham, Kent TN16 3LJ
**Tel:** 01959-571404
**Web:** www.st-theresas-bigginhill.weebly.com
**Estd:** 1988
**Line of Business:** Places of worship
**Proprietor:** Reverend G Flood
**US SIC:** 8661 **UK SIC:** 96600
**Employees:** 170

DUNS 21-735-3042
## St. Thomas More High School
Kenilworth Gardens, Westcliff-On-Sea, Essex SS0 0BW
**Tel:** 01702344933
**Web:** www.st-thomasmore.southend.sch.uk
**Reg No:** 7696989 **Estd:** 2011 Private Company Limited By Guarantee
**Line of Business:** Schools (foundation)
**Directors:** Mrs G A Ackred, V S Copeland, J C Foster, J F O'Brien, M K Lambert, F Keenan, Mrs M M Lewis, M E Barry
**Co. Secretary:** Geoffrey Prior
**Responsibilities**
**Senior:** David Micklewright *(Director)*, Joseph Parsad *(Director)*, Susan Turrell *(Director)*, Jeffrey Woolnough *(Director)*

**US SIC:** 8211 **UK SIC:** 93200

| | 31-08-14 | 31-08-13 | 31-08-12 |
|---|---|---|---|
| TO | 5,817,649 | 5,940,113 | 6,109,655 |
| P/L | (167,587) | (150,114) | (98,368) |
| NW | (494,069) | (583,482) | (374,368) |
| WC | 755,893 | 784,176 | 849,003 |
| Emp. | 116 | 108 | 144 |

DUNS 23-990-4787

## St. Vincent Care Homes Ltd

Forton Road, Gosport, Hampshire PO12 4TH
**Tel:** 02392358062
**Web:** www.stvincentcare.co.uk
**Reg No:** 3978762 **Estd:** 1986 Private Limited Company
**Line of Business:** Residential care establishments
**Trading Style:** St. Vincent House Residential Home
**Issued Capital:** £363,000
**Directors:** Mrs C L Shann, C F Downs, Ms C F Downs, R A Shann
**Co. Secretary:** Ms Nicola Canbek
**Responsibilities**
**Senior:** Vivian Coombs *(Manager)*
**US SIC:** 8321 **UK SIC:** 96111
**Bankers:** National Westminster Bank Plc (56-00-64)

| | 31-03-14 | 31-03-13 | 31-03-12 |
|---|---|---|---|
| TO | 3,173,869 | 3,098,215 | 2,928,153 |
| P/L | 138,140 | 147,749 | 270,825 |
| NW | 1,505,579 | 1,361,618 | 1,214,471 |
| WC | (001,041) | (010,017) | (590,209) |
| Emp. | 180 | 172 | 151 |

DUNS 22-196-4435

## St. Vincent's & St. George's Association

Well Close, Lansdown Parade, Cheltenham, Gloucestershire GL50 2LH
**Tel:** 01242511237 **Fax:** 01242242627
**Web:** www.stvsandstgs.org.uk
**Reg No:** 4214557 **Estd:** 2001 Private Company Limited By Guarantee
**Line of Business:** Individual & family social services
**Directors:** A W Brookes, L Bonney, P Ireland, P Sayers, Ms P Tudhope, Ms J Gregory, D G Draper, A Winwood
**Co. Secretary:** Mrs Lisa Gettins
**Responsibilities**
**Senior:** Jane Cussons *(Director)*
**Branches:** St. Vincent's & St. George's Association, 127 Promenade, Cheltenham, Gloucestershire GL50 1NW
**US SIC:** 8321, 8091, 7299
**UK SIC:** 96111, 95200, 98902
**Auditors:** Accounting For The Future Ltd
**Bankers:** National Westminster Bank Plc (60-05-16)

| | 31-01-14 | 31-01-13 | 31-01-12 |
|---|---|---|---|
| TO | 1,351,015 | 1,658,426 | 1,182,512 |
| P/L | (73,902) | 305,854 | (924) |
| NW | 1,912,475 | 1,986,340 | 1,667,076 |
| WC | 507,553 | 382,367 | 558,549 |
| Emp. | 71 | N/A | 66 |

DUNS 28-937-6204

## St. Wilfrid's Hospice (South Coast) Ltd

Grosvenor Road, Chichester, West Sussex PO19 8FP
**Tel:** 01243775302
**Web:** www.stwh.co.uk
**Reg No:** 1562110 **Estd:** 1981 Private Limited Company
**Line of Business:** Hospices
**Directors:** C R Cameron, A J Lewis, P N Stoakley, C J Dicks, Mrs A P Wormald, M G Bevis, Ms A S Sharp, Dr A Copsey
**Responsibilities**
**Senior:** Alec Dewhurst *(Director)*, Alison Moorey *(Ceo)*, Elisabeth Spence *(Director)*, Martin Troy *(Director)*, Malcolm Williams *(Director)*
**Finance:** Alison Moorey *(Ceo)*
**US SIC:** 8091, 6732
**UK SIC:** 95200, 83100
**Auditors:** Sheen Stickland
**Bankers:** National Westminster Bank Plc (60-05-24)

| | 31-03-14 | 31-03-13 | 31-03-12 |
|---|---|---|---|
| TO | 5,250,934 | 7,476,656 | 6,519,677 |
| P/L | (948,632) | 1,564,472 | 821,045 |
| NW | 15,255,421 | 16,256,457 | 13,553,497 |
| WC | 2,018,815 | 4,046,026 | 2,661,854 |
| Emp. | 126 | 126 | 122 |

DUNS 51-636-2592

## Saints Solicitors Llp

45 Villa Road, Birmingham, West Midlands B19 1BH
**Tel:** 01215237865
**Reg No:** 0322891OC **Estd:** 2006 Private Limited Company
**Line of Business:** Solicitors
**US SIC:** 8111 **UK SIC:** 83500
**Bankers:** Lloyds TSB Bank plc (30-00-01)

| | 31-03-14 | 31-03-13 | 31-03-12 |
|---|---|---|---|
| TA | 146,884 | 111,767 | 75,392 |
| NW | (70,545) | (70,545) | (70,545) |
| WC | (82,904) | (83,977) | (84,249) |

DUNS 21-099-7964

## Saints Transport Grp Ltd

Unit 14, Halo House, Galleymead Road, Slough, Berkshire SL3 0EN
**Tel:** 01753682999
**Web:** www.saints.co.uk
**Reg No:** 6435925 **Estd:** 2007 Private Limited Company
**Line of Business:** Road haulage and transport services
**Issued Capital:** £100
**Directors:** M Carroll, S L Beeches, P Carroll
**Co. Secretary:** Kevin Beeches
**US SIC:** 4213 **UK SIC:** 72300

| | 31-12-13 | 31-12-12 | 31-12-11 |
|---|---|---|---|
| TO | 24,873,087 | 24,288,012 | 23,198,282 |
| P/L | 574,995 | 343,447 | 1,484,078 |
| NW | 1,274,847 | 814,368 | 885,113 |
| WC | (2,650,970) | (2,651,924) | (3,189,994) |
| Emp. | 363 | 335 | 330 |

DUNS 21-665-4443

## Saipem Ltd

**(Subsidiary of:** Saipem Spa)
Conquest House, Wood Street, Kingston-Upon-Thames, Surrey KT1 1AB
**Tel:** 02086125000 **Fax:** 02082 965100
**Web:** www.saipem.com
**Reg No:** 7195109 **Estd:** 2013 Private Limited Company
**Line of Business:** Oil and gas exploration services
**Issued Capital:** £7,500,000
**Directors:** N Swinnerton, G Di Pietro, P Formica, J J Chassagne
**Co. Secretary:** Edgar Van Stijn
**Responsibilities**
**Senior:** Elizabeth Turkson *(Manager)*, Marco Villa *(Manager)*
**Marketing:** Massimo Fontolan *(Business Development Director)*, Ray Hutton *(Commercial Manager)*
**Branches:** Saipem Ltd, Tern Place, Aberdeen, Aberdeenshire AB23 8JX
**US SIC:** 1389 **UK SIC:** 13000
**Auditors:** Ernst & Young LLP

| | 31-12-13 | 31-12-12 | 31-12-11 |
|---|---|---|---|
| TO | 497,060,000 | 853,656,000 | 753,260,000 |
| P/L | 98,797,000 | 153,061,000 | 126,389,000 |
| NW | 154,540,000 | 155,683,000 | 52,712,000 |
| WC | 98,652,000 | 93,201,000 | (19,727,000) |
| Emp. | 833 | 961 | 758 |

DUNS 50-055-0702

## Saks Hair (Holdings) Ltd

55-59 Duke Street, Darlington, County Durham DL3 7SD
**Tel:** 08456780290
**Web:** www.saks.co.uk
**Reg No:** 2315625 **VAT No:** 441500006
**Estd:** 1988 Private Limited Company
**Line of Business:** Hairdressers (unisex)
**Issued Capital:** £50,200
**Directors:** S Kee, D Cheesebrough
**Co. Secretary:** Dennis Cheesebrough
**Branches:** Saks Hair (Holdings) Ltd, 2 Peel Court, 24 St. Cuthberts Way, Darlington, County Durham DL1 1GB
**US SIC:** 7231, 8999
**UK SIC:** 98200, 83954
**Auditors:** CP Waites
**Bankers:** Barclays Bank Plc (20-25-29)

| | 31-12-13 | 31-12-12 | 31-12-11 |
|---|---|---|---|
| TA | 1,221,115 | 1,020,059 | 561,548 |
| NW | 389,107 | 260,225 | 205,365 |
| WC | 277,268 | 260,119 | 205,264 |

DUNS 39-346-5257 **Exp**

## Saladin Holdings Ltd

7 Abingdon Road, London W8 6AH
**Tel:** 02073762655
**Web:** www.saladin-security.com
**Reg No:** 2120198 **Estd:** 1987 Private Limited Company
**Line of Business:** Wheel clamping
**Export Markets:** Europe & worldwide
**Export Sales:** £7,376,520
**Trading Style:** Saladin Security
**Issued Capital:** £700
**Directors:** D J Walker, D H Walker
**Co. Secretary:** Ms Susan Merrick
**US SIC:** 7393, 6711
**UK SIC:** 83954, 83962
**Bankers:** HSBC Bank plc (40-04-01)

| | 30-06-13 | 30-06-12 | 30-06-11 |
|---|---|---|---|
| TO | 9,784,207 | 10,840,209 | 11,208,354 |
| P/L | 631,172 | 1,762,890 | (2,608,295) |
| NW | 1,105,327 | 1,323,539 | 363,058 |
| WC | 1,627,055 | 2,254,764 | 1,378,113 |
| Emp. | 636 | 610 | 1,272 |

DUNS 22-012-1185

## Salads to Go Ltd

**(Subsidiary of:** Soc Coop Agric Agro Alimentaire)
1 Penketh Place, Skelmersdale, Lancashire WN8 9QX
**Tel:** 01695-550088 **Fax:** 01695550099
**Web:** www.saladstogo.co.uk
**Reg No:** 4015138 **Estd:** 2000 Private Limited Company
**Line of Business:** Non-specialised wholesale of food, beverages and tobacco
**Issued Capital:** £1,000
**Directors:** B R Totel, D Hayat, T S Proudlove, Mrs M Le Meur Tiphaigne, N P Sanderson
**Co. Secretary:** Dan Hayat
**Responsibilities**
**Senior:** Helen Semmens *(Manager)*
**US SIC:** 5149 **UK SIC:** 61700
**Auditors:** PricewaterhouseCoopers LLP
**Bankers:** Bank Of Scotland (12-17-40)

| | 31-12-13 | 31-12-12 | 31-12-11 |
|---|---|---|---|
| TO | 23,903,000 | 25,461,000 | 32,711,000 |
| P/L | 550,000 | (1,416,000) | (2,241,000) |
| NW | 292,000 | (84,000) | 1,014,000 |
| WC | (2,128,000) | (2,653,000) | (1,746,000) |
| Emp. | 287 | 328 | 158 |

DUNS 42-345-9320

## Salamanca Group Trust (Jersey) Ltd

**(Subsidiary of:** Investec Plc)
5 Castle Street, Jersey, Channel Islands JE2 3RT
**Tel:** 01534512512
**Reg No:** 0058347J **Estd:** 1994 Private Limited Company
**Line of Business:** Trust management services
**Issued Capital:** £100
**Principals:** T Grimes *(Financial)*, C E Lloyd, P J Burton, R A Clifford
**Co. Secretary:** Onband Secretaries Ltd
**US SIC:** 6733, 7392
**UK SIC:** 83100, 83951
**Bankers:** National Westminster Bank Plc (60-12-03)
**Employees:** 50

DUNS 77-965-4180

## Salamander Energy Plc

4th Floor, 25 Great Pulteney Street, London W1F 9LT
**Tel:** 020 7432 2680
**Web:** www.salamander-energy.com
**Reg No:** 5934263 **Estd:** 2006 Public Limited Company
**Line of Business:** Oil and gas exploration services
**Directors:** C J Jamieson, M J Pavia, R M Cathery, M J Buck, K J Crowle, Dr J M Copus, Dr C Bell, J G Menzies
**Co. Secretary:** Charles Morgan
**Responsibilities**
**Senior:** Dave Robertson *(Director)*
**Sales:** Nick Ingrassia *(Corporate Business Development)*
**US SIC:** 1389, 1311
**UK SIC:** 13000
**Auditors:** Deloitte LLP
**Bankers:** HSBC Bank plc (40-00-00)
**Employees:** 195
**Turnover:** £482,220,000

DUNS 34-692-2131 **Imp-Exp**

## Salamander Pumped Shower Systems Ltd

**(Subsidiary of:** Davidson Holdings Ltd)
Unit 2c Colima Avenue, Enterprise Park West, Sunderland, Tyne and Wear SR5 3XE
**Tel:** 01915162002 **Fax:** 01234355939
**Web:** www.salamanderpumps.co.uk
**Reg No:** 2778382 **VAT No:** 694558969
**Estd:** 1993 Private Limited Company
**Line of Business:** Manufacture of pumps
**Export Markets:** Eire, Cyprus
**Trading Style:** Salamander Pumps
**Issued Capital:** £1,222
**Directors:** K G Boiston, G Richards, A L Graves, C P Vallance, G S Gestetner
**Co. Secretary:** Stuart Johnson
**Branches:** Salamander Pumped Shower Systems Ltd, Unit 89, Alexandra Ave, Sunderland Indstl Est, Sunderland, Tyne and Wear SR5 2TB
**US SIC:** 3561 **UK SIC:** 32870
**Auditors:** Mazars Neville Russell

| | 30-04-14 | 30-04-13 | 30-04-12 |
|---|---|---|---|
| TO | 9,260,069 | 9,160,488 | 7,986,088 |
| P/L | 964,551 | 1,040,092 | 938,762 |
| NW | 5,385,549 | 4,687,092 | 3,950,127 |
| WC | 5,246,037 | 4,578,510 | 3,866,969 |
| Emp. | 54 | 54 | 56 |

DUNS 34-859-6854

## Salans Fmc Snr Denton Europe Llp

One Fleet Place, London EC4P 4GD
**Tel:** 02072 421 212
**Web:** www.salans.co.uk
**Reg No:** 0316822OC **VAT No:** 888651364
**Estd:** 2008
**Line of Business:** Solicitors
**Trading Style:** Salans
**Responsibilities**
**Senior:** Sahin Ardiyok *(Non-designated Limited Liabili)*, Aurlien Chardeau *(Non-designated Limited Liabili)*, Markus Diepold *(Non-designated Limited Liabili)*, Doran Doeh *(Non-designated Limited Liabili)*, Ramin Hariri *(Non-designated Limited Liabili)*, Smeetesh Kakkad *(Managing Partner)*, Vincent Lacombe *(Non-designated Limited Liabili)*, Raul Mihu *(Non-designated Limited Liabili)*, Dominic Pellew *(Non-designated Limited Liabili)*, Alexandre Poupard *(Non-designated Limited Liabili)*, Maxime Simonnet *(Non-designated Limited Liabili)*, Victoria Simonova *(Non-designated Limited Liabili)*, Philipp Windemuth *(Non-designated Limited Liabili)*, Roman Zaitsev *(Non-designated Limited Liabili)*, Almas Zhaiylgan *(Non-designated Limited Liabili)*, Birzhan Zharasbayev *(Non-designated Limited Liabili)*
**Finance:** Michael Kallenberg *(Head of Accounts)*
**Marketing:** J Naqvi *(Marketing Manager)*
**Purchasing:** Tanya Martin *(Purchasing Manager)*
**US SIC:** 8111 **UK SIC:** 83500
**Auditors:** BDO LLP

| | 31-12-13 | 31-12-12 | 31-12-11 |
|---|---|---|---|
| TO | 175,400,000 | 180,115,000 | 181,325,000 |
| P/L | 1,750,000 | 159,000 | 421,000 |
| NW | 36,174,000 | 41,879,000 | 42,547,000 |
| WC | 43,777,000 | 61,252,000 | 51,880,000 |
| Emp. | 1,317 | 1,396 | 1,604 |

DUNS 28-838-9505 **Imp**

## Saldon Products Ltd

**(Subsidiary of:** Saldon Ltd)
Park Farm Industrial Estate, Redditch, Worcestershire B98 0HU
**Tel:** 01527517777
**Web:** www.tamlite.co.uk
**Reg No:** 0494829 **VAT No:** 272745345
**Estd:** 1951 Private Limited Company
**Line of Business:** Manufacturers of lighting equipment
**Trading Style:** Tamlite Lighting, Tamlite Hid, Tamtec Electronics
**Issued Capital:** £5,000,000
**Director:** J R Allden
**Co. Secretary:** Andrew Swift
**Responsibilities**
**Sales:** Graham Marshall *(Senior Sales Executive)*
**IT:** Aaron Vowles *(IT Manager)*
**Branches:** Saldon Products Ltd, Unit 48A, Pipers Road, Park Farm Industrial Estate, Redditch, Worcestershire B98 0HU
**US SIC:** 3648 **UK SIC:** 34702
**Auditors:** Crowe Clark Whitehill LLP
**Bankers:** HSBC Bank plc (40-26-04)

| | 30-04-14 | 30-04-13 | 30-04-12 |
|---|---|---|---|
| TO | 46,927,085 | 40,245,882 | 40,658,090 |
| P/L | 6,426,888 | 2,875,298 | 4,982,863 |
| NW | 15,028,944 | 9,648,318 | 11,739,677 |
| WC | 14,008,157 | 8,598,120 | 10,770,549 |
| Emp. | 341 | 336 | 356 |

DUNS 21-617-3468

## Sales Support Group Ltd

**(Subsidiary of:** Akzo Nobel N.V.)
Manchester Road West, West Timperley, Altrincham, Cheshire WA14 5PG
**Tel:** 01753550000
**Web:** www.salessupportgroup.com
**Reg No:** 0891336 **Estd:** 1993 Private Limited Company
**Line of Business:** Other business activities not elsewhere classified
**Issued Capital:** £2,050
**Directors:** M K Roberts, M Pullen
**Co. Secretary:** O.H. Secretariat Limited
**US SIC:** 7399 **UK SIC:** 83954
**Auditors:** KPMG Audit PLC
**Bankers:** HSBC Bank plc (40-24-38)

| | 31-12-13 | 31-12-12 | 31-12-11 |
|---|---|---|---|
| TA | 1,393,209 | 1,592,760 | 1,530,396 |
| P/L | 120,000 | 120,000 | 120,000 |
| NW | 639,760 | 639,760 | 639,760 |
| WC | 639,760 | 639,760 | 639,760 |
| Emp. | 222 | 225 | 241 |

DUNS 73-838-7492 **Imp**

## Salesforce.Com Emea Ltd

**(Subsidiary of:** Salesforce.Com Inc.)
Block Two, Lotus Park, The Causeway, Staines, Middlesex TW18 3AG
**Tel:** 01784607000
**Web:** www.salesforce.com
**Reg No:** 5094083 **Estd:** 2004 Private Limited Company

**Line of Business:** Other computer related activities
**Trading Style:** Salesforce.Com
**Issued Capital:** £1
**Directors:** H J Wettermark, J L Moura Neto
**Co. Secretary:** Abogado Nominees Limited
**Branches:** SFDC UK Ltd. - Village 9, Floor 26 Heron Tower, 110 Bishopsgate, London, EC2N 4AY.
**US SIC:** 7379 **UK SIC:** 83940
**Auditors:** Ernst & Young

|      | 31-01-14 | 31-01-13 | 31-01-12 |
|------|----------|----------|----------|
| TO   | 102,521,844 | 80,394,169 | 56,622,800 |
| P/L  | 5,440,672 | 4,475,287 | 2,825,913 |
| NW   | 31,180,093 | 25,052,099 | 20,047,780 |
| WC   | 27,485,840 | 24,059,623 | 18,962,047 |
| Emp. | 409 | N/A | 234 |

DUNS 54-905-0979
**Salesian College**
Surrey Lane, London SW11 3PB
**Tel:** 02072282857
**Web:** www.salesiancollege.co.uk
**Estd:** 1897
**Line of Business:** Schools (local authority)
**Chairman:** A Richins
**Responsibilities**
**Senior:** Steve McAnn (Head Teacher)
**US SIC:** 8211 **UK SIC:** 93200
**Employees:** 65

DUNS 21-144-6494
**Salesian College Farnborough Ltd**
Reading Road, Farnborough, Hampshire GU14 6PA
**Tel:** 01252893000
**Web:** www.salesiancollege.com
**Reg No:** 6753037 **Estd:** 1997 Private Company Limited By Guarantee
**Line of Business:** Schools (independent)
**Directors:** M I Chatterton, Rev J Gallagher, P A Turrell, A P Gribbon, Mrs A C Leforte, Mrs A C Nash, A K Lion, Reverend D O'Riordan
**Co. Secretary:** Robert Lougee
**Responsibilities**
**Senior:** Clayton Almeida (Director), Bob Colgate (Site Manager), Kevin Mcgill (Director), Gerard Owens (Director), Paul Page-Tickell (Director)
**Facilities:** Bob Colgate (Site Manager)
**US SIC:** 8211 **UK SIC:** 93200

|      | 31-08-14 | 31-08-13 | 31-08-12 |
|------|----------|----------|----------|
| TO   | 6,395,650 | 5,946,382 | 5,763,345 |
| P/L  | 567,465 | 461,789 | 327,968 |
| NW   | 2,495,619 | 1,928,154 | 1,466,365 |
| WC   | 366,386 | (211,529) | (593,892) |
| Emp. | 89 | 95 | 88 |

DUNS 21-845-6144
**Salford Academy Trust**
Frontier House Merchants Quay, Salford, Lancashire M50 3SR
**Tel:** 01618488873
**Reg No:** 8115121 **Estd:** 2012 Private Company Limited By Guarantee
**Line of Business:** General secondary education
**Directors:** Miss G Lagan, Mrs C A Starbuck, A Fidler, Mrs B Rogers, D A Cowpe, Professor M A Pearson, H P Wilson, D Wootton
**Co. Secretary:** Paul Leigh
**Responsibilities**
**Senior:** Kimberley Cash (Director), Leon Dowd (Director), Colleen Taylor (Director)
**US SIC:** 8211 **UK SIC:** 93200
**Bankers:** Lloyds TSB Bank plc (30-95-42)

|      | 31-08-14 | 31-08-13 |
|------|----------|----------|
| TO   | 11,467,000 | 26,243,000 |
| P/L  | 1,459,000 | 16,946,000 |
| NW   | 18,140,000 | 17,084,000 |
| WC   | 1,173,000 | 1,296,000 |
| Emp. | 187 | 198 |

DUNS 64-254-8911
**Salford City College**
Worsley Campus, Walkden Road, Manchester M28 7QD
**Tel:** 01616315000
**Web:** www.salfordcc.ac.uk
**Estd:** 1900
**Line of Business:** Colleges (higher education)
**Principals:** C Brooks (Financial), Mrs A Bowes
**Responsibilities**
**Senior:** A McMann (Manager), Jackie Moores (Vice Chancellor), Martin Sim (Principal), Greg Skarratt (Manager), John Walls (Estates Manager), Rebeckah Wilkins (Marketing Manager)
**Finance:** Louise Donaldson (Financial Director)
**Marketing:** Rebeckah Wilkins (Marketing Manager)
**Admin:** Barbara Weilding (Administration Coordinator)
**IT:** James Mortlock (Computer Manager)

**HR:** Una Gillham (Training Director), Warren O'Donovan (Human Resources Manager)
**Health & Safety:** John Walls (Estates Manager)
**Facilities:** John Walls (Estates Manager)
**Operations:** Barbara Weilding (Administration Coordinator)
**Purchasing:** John Walls (Estates Manager)
**US SIC:** 8221, 8249
**UK SIC:** 93100, 93300
**Employees:** 1,000

DUNS 23-260-5519
**Salford City Council**
Civic Centre, Chorley Road, Manchester M27 5FJ
**Tel:** 0161-794-4711 **Fax:** 0161-794-6595
**Web:** www.salford.gov.uk
**Estd:** 1974 Incorporate By Act Of Parliament
**Line of Business:** Employment and recruitment companies and consultants
**Principals:** J Spink (Financial), M Sykes, J Willis, G Bannister
**Co. Secretary:** Alan Westwood
**Responsibilities**
**Senior:** Peter Kidd (Manager), Jim Taylor (CEO)
**Sales:** Michaela Haines (Strategic Manager)
**IT:** Noel Baxendale (IT Manager)
**HR:** Debbie Brown (Head of Human Resources)
**Operations:** Deborah Keelan (Project Manager)
**Engineering:** Alan Fitzsimons (Technical Engineer)
**Branches:** Salford City Council, Civic Centre, Chorley Road, Manchester M27 5DA
**US SIC:** 9121 **UK SIC:** 91110
**Bankers:** The Co-Operative Bank Plc (08-90-00)
**Employees:** 9,987

DUNS 21-749-0478
**Salford Community Leisure Ltd**
Civic Centre, Chorley Road, Swinton, Manchester M27 5DA
**Tel:** 01617780372
**Reg No:** 00029627IP **Estd:** 2003
**Line of Business:** Local government
**US SIC:** 7999 **UK SIC:** 97913
**Auditors:** Beever & Struthers

|      | 31-03-13 |
|------|----------|
| TO   | 12,939,431 |
| P/L  | 36,660 |
| NW   | (2,814,859) |
| WC   | 532,227 |
| Emp. | 359 |

DUNS 21-580-1474
**Salford Family Information Service**
Minerva House, Pendlebury Road, Swinton, Manchester M27 4EQ
**Tel:** 08001955565
**Estd:** 2011
**Line of Business:** Misc Schools & Educational Services
**US SIC:** 8299 **UK SIC:** 93300
**Employees:** 360

DUNS 54-864-0333
**Salford Primary Care Trust**
St James House, Pendleton Way, Salford, Lancashire M6 5FW
**Tel:** 0161-212-4800
**Web:** www.gmcsu.co.uk
**Estd:** 2011
**Line of Business:** Healthcare companies
**Issued Capital:** £1
**Principals:** M Gibbs (Managing), Ms C Yarwood (Financial), M Clough, M Burrows, Ms J Higgins, A Campbell
**Responsibilities**
**Senior:** Lee Griffin (Manager)
**Branches:** Salford Primary Care Trust, St. James House, Pendleton Way, Salford, Lancashire M6 5FW
**US SIC:** 9121 **UK SIC:** 91110
**Employees:** 200

DUNS 54-864-0515
**Salford Royal Nhs Foundation Trust**
Stott Lane, Salford, Lancashire M6 8HD
**Tel:** 0161-789 7373
**Web:** www.srht.nhs.uk
**Estd:** 1995
**Line of Business:** Hospitals
**Issued Capital:** £1
**Principals:** J J Potter (Chairman), T Whitfield (Financial), D Wood, D N Dalton, J Willis, Ms A Williams, D Thompson, M Halsall

**Responsibilities**
**Senior:** Stewart Almond (Manager), Anthony Bannister (Manager), Diane Brown (Non-Executive Director), Sally Cockshaw (Manager), Carol Crossley (Purchasing Manager), Michael Dulhanty (Manager), Howard Forster (Non-Executive Director), Stephanie Gibson (Divisional Managing Director o), Elaine Inglesby-Burke (Executive Nurse Director and D), Kenneth Palmer (Manager)
**Finance:** Joanne Entwistle (Financial Manager)
**Sales:** Jack Sharp (Executive Director of Service)
**Admin:** Emma Butler (Administrator), Karen Wynn (Secretary)
**HR:** Carole Swindells (Training Manager)
**Health & Safety:** John Crosby (Health & Safety Advisor)
**Facilities:** Harry Evans (Estates Manager)
**Purchasing:** Carol Crossley (Purchasing Manager)
**Branches:** Salford Royal Nhs Foundation Trust, Hope Hospital, Summerfield House, Salford, Lancashire M6 8HD
**US SIC:** 8062 **UK SIC:** 95100
**Auditors:** Grant Thornton UK LLP

|      | 31-03-14 | 31-03-13 | 31-03-12 |
|------|----------|----------|----------|
| TO   | 382,972,000 | 363,469,000 | 340,363,000 |
| P/L  | 13,912,000 | (3,090,000) | (14,064,000) |
| NW   | 122,304,000 | 102,698,000 | 106,928,000 |
| WC   | 20,773,000 | 13,469,000 | 7,977,000 |
| Emp. | 6,224 | 5,745 | 5,432 |

DUNS 21-788-9471
**Salford Royal Nhs Foundation Trust General Charitable Fund**
Hope Hospital, Stott Lane, Salford, Lancashire M6 8HD
**Web:** www.srht.nhs.uk
**Estd:** 1995
**Line of Business:** Hospitals
**Trading Style:** Hope Hospital
**US SIC:** 6732 **UK SIC:** 83100
**Employees:** 6,000

DUNS 52-004-1385
**The Salford Valve Co Ltd**
Sherburn, Malton, North Yorkshire YO17 1SW
**Tel:** 01944-710000 **Fax:** 01944710907
**Reg No:** 3371104 **Estd:** 1997 Private Limited Company
**Line of Business:** Oil and gas extraction
**Issued Capital:** £1
**Directors:** Professor G G Nasr, G Hawthorne, G G Tulloch, M Waters
**Co. Secretary:** Thomas Goldberg
**US SIC:** 4925, 8911
**UK SIC:** 25670, 83701

|    | 30-06-13 | 30-06-12 | 30-06-11 |
|----|----------|----------|----------|
| TA | 1 | 1 | 1 |
| NW | 1 | 1 | 1 |

DUNS 21-293-9599     **Exp**
**Salford Van Hire Ltd**
43 Sherborne Street, Manchester M3 1EJ
**Tel:** 0161-833-0771
**Web:** www.salfordvanhire.com
**Reg No:** 0864602 **VAT No:** 147275749
**Estd:** 1965 Private Limited Company
**Line of Business:** Renting of other land transport equipment
**Export Markets:** E U
**Export Sales:** £12,660,747
**Issued Capital:** £2,148,250
**Principals:** R Bacci (Managing), A Bacci, N M Evers, Ms P Bacci
**Co. Secretary:** Ms Eda Bacci
**Responsibilities**
**Senior:** Roberto Bacci (Chairman), Graziella Bacci-Evers (Manager)
**Engineering:** Stephen McNally (Fleet Engineering Manager)
**Branches:** Salford Van Hire Ltd, 82 Great Ducie Street, Manchester M3 1LT
**US SIC:** 7513, 7512
**UK SIC:** 84802, 84801
**Auditors:** PKF
**Bankers:** HSBC Bank plc (40-31-23)

|      | 31-12-13 | 31-12-12 | 31-12-11 |
|------|----------|----------|----------|
| TO   | 55,258,694 | 57,168,614 | 58,670,969 |
| P/L  | 794,134 | 1,628,174 | 2,928,412 |
| NW   | 51,855,168 | 51,091,948 | 50,319,182 |
| WC   | (29,151,640) | (37,063,020) | (32,626,090) |
| Emp. | 195 | 193 | 194 |

DUNS 21-035-6139     **Imp**
**Salinity**
Po Box 390, Hoddesdon, Hertfordshire EN11 1GR
**Tel:** 01992447095
**Web:** www.salinity.co.uk
**Estd:** 2012 Proprietorship
**Line of Business:** Wholesale suppliers of salt
**Responsibilities**
**Senior:** Luke Hodgson (Manager)
**US SIC:** 1476 **UK SIC:** 23300
**Employees:** 50

DUNS 28-839-1261
**The Salisbury Arts Theatre Ltd**
Malthouse Lane, Salisbury, Wiltshire SP2 7RA
**Tel:** 01722320333
**Web:** www.salisburyplayhouse.com
**Reg No:** 0499076 **Estd:** 1951 Private Company Limited By Guarantee
**Line of Business:** Theatres & concert halls
**Trading Style:** Salisbury Playhouse
**Directors:** A J Bridewell, D A Bossom, N H Frankfort, Mrs R E Macdoanld, Miss S J Butcher, T F Clay, Mrs S E Shaw, T J Crarer
**Co. Secretary:** Richard Warrack
**Responsibilities**
**Senior:** Michelle Carwardine-palmer (Executive Director), Gareth Machin (Artistic Director), Victoria Maycock (Manager), Simon Trewin (Director)
**Finance:** Vivienne Franklin (Financial Director)
**Marketing:** Tim Croall (Head of Marketing)
**IT:** Michelle Carwardine-palmer (Executive Director)
**HR:** Michelle Carwardine-palmer (Executive Director)
**Health & Safety:** John Titcombe (Health & Safety Officer)
**Purchasing:** Michelle Carwardine-palmer (Executive Director)
**Branches:** The Salisbury Arts Theatre Ltd, 2 Malthouse Lane, Salisbury, Wiltshire SP2 7RA
**US SIC:** 7911, 5812
**UK SIC:** 97913, 66110
**Auditors:** Smith & Williamson
**Bankers:** National Westminster Bank Plc (54-41-19)

|      | 31-03-14 | 31-03-13 | 31-03-12 |
|------|----------|----------|----------|
| TO   | 3,140,805 | 3,020,816 | 3,108,387 |
| P/L  | (128,902) | (118,769) | (42,056) |
| NW   | 2,574,241 | 2,703,143 | 2,821,912 |
| WC   | (67,296) | 14,284 | 39,813 |
| Emp. | 73 | 75 | 77 |

DUNS 21-035-9828
**Salisbury Cathedral**
33 The Close, Salisbury, Wiltshire SP1 2EJ
**Tel:** 01722555120
**Web:** www.salisburycathedral.org.uk
**Proprietorship**
**Line of Business:** Places of worship
**Proprietor:** Miss M Water
**Responsibilities**
**Senior:** June Osbourne (Dean Of Salisbury)
**US SIC:** 8661 **UK SIC:** 96600
**Employees:** 70

DUNS 29-352-0789
**Salisbury Cathedral Enterprises Ltd**
6 The Close, Salisbury, Wiltshire SP1 2EN
**Tel:** 01722555144
**Web:** www.salisburycathedralstainedglass.co.uk
**Reg No:** 0556116 **Estd:** 1955 Private Limited Company
**Line of Business:** Painting and glazing
**Issued Capital:** £10
**Directors:** Mrs K E Sporle, S A Radford, S E Mullally, C Hurford-Jones, R P Gurd, E C Probert, Mrs K F Beckett, D Coulthard
**Branches:** Salisbury Cathedral Enterprises Ltd, The Kings House, 65 The Close, Salisbury, Wiltshire SP1 2EN
**US SIC:** 1721, 5942, 5812
**UK SIC:** 50400, 65300, 66110
**Auditors:** Fletcher & Partners

|      | 31-03-14 | 31-03-13 | 31-03-12 |
|------|----------|----------|----------|
| TO   | 1,047,535 | 1,053,800 | 1,055,973 |
| P/L  | 346,597 | 369,438 | 360,209 |
| NW   | (726) | (726) | (726) |
| WC   | 31,306 | 30,655 | 29,861 |

DUNS 42-474-2455
**Salisbury Cathedral School Ltd**
1 The Close, Salisbury, Wiltshire SP1 2EQ
**Tel:** 01722555300
**Web:** www.salisburycathedralschool.com
**Reg No:** 4461932 **Estd:** 2002 Private Company Limited By Guarantee
**Line of Business:** General secondary education
**Directors:** Mrs J E Lee, T E Clammer, Dr L A Brown, F L Wain, Ms C Leslie, T E Foster, J Fletcher, J Osborne
**Co. Secretary:** Mrs Andrea Clarke
**Responsibilities**
**Senior:** Clive Barnett (Director), Yury Beylin (Director), Richard Folkes (Director), Clive Marriott (Head Teacher), Laura Philips (Director)
**Admin:** Jane Mundy (Administration Manager)

**US SIC:** 8211 **UK SIC:** 93200

| | 31-08-14 | 31-08-13 | 31-08-12 |
|---|---|---|---|
| TO | 2,117,720 | 2,257,322 | 2,074,018 |
| P/L | (124,853) | 99,007 | 184,519 |
| NW | 1,082,558 | 1,196,831 | 1,085,531 |
| WC | 818,132 | 869,588 | 813,410 |
| Emp. | 53 | 48 | 51 |

DUNS 28-828-6776
## The Salisbury Diocesan Board of Finance
Church House, 99 Crane Street, Salisbury, Wiltshire SP1 2QB
**Web:** www.salisbury.anglican.org
**Reg No:** 0017442 **Estd:** 2002 Private Limited Company
**Line of Business:** Religious organisations and places of worship
**Directors:** M P Armstrong, P S Taylor, The Reverend G R Kings, Ms B M Trump, D W Harris, W H Wilks, Ms C Corteen, Dr J Matthews
**Co. Secretary:** Ms Lucinda Herklots
**Responsibilities**
**Senior:** Maureen Allchin *(Director)*, Margaret Chinchen *(Director)*, Alan Ely *(Director)*, Peter Hime *(Director)*, Alan Jeans *(Director)*, Simon Key *(Director)*, Debrah Mcisaac *(Director)*, Robert Thorn *(Director)*, John Walmsley *(Director)*, Gilbert Williams *(Director)*
**Branches:** The Salisbury Diocesan Board Of Finance, Church Office St. Marys Street, Weymouth, Dorset DT4 8PB
**US SIC:** 8661 **UK SIC:** 96600
**Auditors:** Messrs Fletcher & Partners

| | 31-12-13 | 31-12-12 | 31-12-11 |
|---|---|---|---|
| TO | 12,626,000 | 12,324,000 | 12,174,000 |
| P/L | (798,000) | (566,000) | (2,771,000) |
| NW | 122,900,000 | 122,030,000 | 120,175,000 |
| WC | 5,120,000 | 3,983,000 | 2,320,000 |
| Emp. | 50 | 46 | 46 |

DUNS 21-731-4541
## Salisbury Glass Centre Ltd
(**Subsidiary of:** Salisbury Glass Holdings Ltd)
Newton Road, Churchfields Industrial Estate, Salisbury, Wiltshire SP2 7QA
**Tel:** 01722-328985 **Fax:** 01722-338784
**Web:** www.salisbury-glass.com
**Reg No:** 1256872 **VAT No:** 189940896
**Estd:** 1952 Private Limited Company
**Line of Business:** Painting and glazing
**Issued Capital:** £100
**Directors:** I Paton, M S Gower, D W Naish, C Grigg
**Co. Secretary:** Ms Julie Gower
**Responsibilities**
**Finance:** Anne Heather *(Commercial Finance Administrat)*
**Sales:** Tony Horton *(Domestic Sales Manager)*, Paul Thomlinson *(Commercial Manager)*
**Admin:** Anne Heather *(Commercial Finance Administrat)*
**Purchasing:** Mark Lenihan *(Purchase Manager)*
**Branches:** 87-89 Gigant St, Salisbury
**US SIC:** 1721, 1751
**UK SIC:** 50400
**Auditors:** Thwaites Blackwell Bailey & Co
**Bankers:** HSBC Bank plc (40-40-14)

| | 31-05-14 | 31-05-13 | 31-05-12 |
|---|---|---|---|
| TO | 16,092,460 | 19,964,780 | 10,676,919 |
| P/L | 905,069 | 1,134,121 | 368,446 |
| NW | 6,327,617 | 5,620,946 | 4,979,388 |
| WC | 5,937,247 | 5,299,162 | 4,810,595 |
| Emp. | 158 | 154 | 142 |

DUNS 23-181-1758 **Imp**
## Salisbury Nhs Foundation Trust
Public Health Laboratory, Odstock Hospital, Salisbury, Wiltshire SP2 8BJ
**Tel:** 01722-336262
**Web:** www.salisbury.nhs.uk
**VAT No:** 654939884 **Estd:** 1948 Incorporate By Act Of Parliament
**Line of Business:** Public sector hospital activities, including nhs trusts
**Trading Style:** Salisbury District Hospital
**Issued Capital:** £1
**Director:** F Harsent
**Branches:** Salisbury Nhs Foundation Trust, 3 Ashfield Road Trading Estate, Salisbury, Wiltshire SP2 7HL
**US SIC:** 8062 **UK SIC:** 95100
**Auditors:** KPMG LLP

| | 31-03-14 | 31-03-13 | 31-03-12 |
|---|---|---|---|
| TO | 178,954,000 | 166,734,000 | 168,330,000 |
| P/L | 2,925,000 | 1,632,000 | 1,139,000 |
| NW | 138,287,000 | 113,336,000 | 114,117,000 |
| WC | 14,573,000 | 9,744,000 | 8,025,000 |
| Emp. | 2,972 | 2,789 | 2,817 |

DUNS 49-014-5166 **Exp**
## Salisbury Poultry (Midlands) Ltd
(**Subsidiary of:** Mehta Holdings Ltd)
Salisbury Court, 19 Hare Street, Bilston, West Midlands WV14 7DX
**Tel:** 01902-490222
**Web:** www.salisburypoultry.co.uk
**Reg No:** 3073979 **VAT No:** 431384664
**Estd:** 1995 Private Limited Company
**Line of Business:** Wholesale of meat and meat products
**Export Markets:** Republic of Ireland
**Issued Capital:** £10,000
**Managing Director:** T R Mehta
**Co. Secretary:** Mrs Kaljinder Mehta
**Responsibilities**
**Senior:** Telford Mehta *(Managing Director)*
**HR:** Claire Logan *(Human Resources Manager)*
**US SIC:** 5147, 2013
**UK SIC:** 61700, 41223
**Auditors:** Garratts
**Bankers:** Barclays Bank Plc (20-97-78)

| | 30-06-13 | 30-06-12 | 30-06-11 |
|---|---|---|---|
| TO | 46,963,512 | 47,078,586 | 45,195,966 |
| P/L | 1,325,671 | 430,000 | 587,591 |
| NW | 2,416,628 | 1,411,184 | 1,104,941 |
| WC | 2,336,573 | 1,327,179 | 1,451,462 |
| Emp. | 347 | 327 | 314 |

DUNS 50-132-1947
## Saliwawadon Ltd
(**Subsidiary of:** Starwood Capital Group L.L.C.)
Bawtry Road, Doncaster, South Yorkshire DN4 7PD
**Tel:** 01302370770
**Web:** www.campanile.com
**Reg No:** 2320204 **VAT No:** 518194438
**Estd:** 2001 Private Limited Company
**Line of Business:** Hotels
**Trading Style:** Campanile Hotel
**Issued Capital:** £15,000
**Directors:** X P Douchy, M A Aldridge
**Co. Secretary:** Mark Aldridge
**Responsibilities**
**Senior:** Olivier Derycke *(Manager)*, Victoria Fletcher *(General Manager)*, Didier Laporte *(Manager)*
**Finance:** Aline Durieu *(Finance Director)*
**Branches:** Saliwawadon Ltd, Evans Business Centre, Monckton Road, Wakefield, West Yorkshire WF2 7AS
**US SIC:** 7011 **UK SIC:** 66500
**Auditors:** Deloitte & Touche LLP
**Bankers:** Barclays Bank Plc (20-82-94)

| | 31-12-13 | 31-12-12 | 31-12-11 |
|---|---|---|---|
| TO | 5,557,541 | 5,112,536 | 4,877,577 |
| P/L | 1,223,668 | (257,638) | 460,918 |
| NW | (1,352,786) | (2,416,362) | (2,190,147) |
| WC | (8,192,716) | (8,734,709) | (9,147,404) |
| Emp. | 107 | 110 | 109 |

DUNS 21-580-1448
## Sally Beauty Holdings Group
Evanton Drive, Thornliebank, Glasgow, Lanarkshire G46 8HZ
**Tel:** 01416213600
**Estd:** 1971 Proprietorship
**Line of Business:** Hairdressers supplies
**Proprietor:** Ms K Mitchell
**Responsibilities**
**Senior:** David Boyle *(General Manager)*
**US SIC:** 7231 **UK SIC:** 98200
**Employees:** 80

DUNS 21-583-4458 **Imp**
## Sally Salon Services Ltd
(**Subsidiary of:** Sally Beauty International Holdings C.V.)
210 Wharfedale Road, Winnersh, Wokingham, Berkshire RG41 5TP
**Tel:** 01189447000
**Web:** www.sallyexpress.com
**Reg No:** 1060763 **VAT No:** 260924169
**Estd:** 1972 Private Limited Company
**Line of Business:** Representative office
**Trading Style:** Sally Salon Services Ltd
**Issued Capital:** £8,326,375
**Directors:** S Peckham, R G Hull, M Faulkner
**Co. Secretary:** Ms Nina Azemoudeh
**Branches:** Sally Salon Services Ltd, Shop 3, Loddon Vale Centre, Reading, Berkshire RG5 4UL
**US SIC:** 2844, 5999
**UK SIC:** 25820, 65600
**Auditors:** KPMG LLP
**Bankers:** National Westminster Bank Plc (60-02-49)

| | 30-09-13 | 30-09-12 | 30-09-11 |
|---|---|---|---|
| TO | 133,270,000 | 130,995,000 | 127,699,000 |
| P/L | 1,400,000 | 760,000 | 3,488,000 |
| NW | 23,421,000 | 22,490,000 | 20,794,000 |
| WC | 2,113,000 | 8,527,000 | 10,274,000 |
| Emp. | 1,620 | 1,552 | 1,638 |

DUNS 50-336-7914
## Salmon Ltd
(**Subsidiary of:** Wpp Plc)
64 Clarendon Road, Watford, Hertfordshire WD17 1DA
**Tel:** 01923320000
**Web:** www.salmon.com
**Reg No:** 2360867 **VAT No:** 489306607
**Estd:** 1989 Private Limited Company
**Line of Business:** It consultants
**Export Sales:** £610,000
**Issued Capital:** £5,520
**Directors:** J N Eggar, N Stewart, D A Roth, M R Pring, M J Read
**Co. Secretary:** Wpp Group (Nominees) Limited
**Responsibilities**
**Senior:** Christopher Hoskin *(Chief Marketing Officer)*
**Marketing:** Christopher Hoskin *(Chief Marketing Officer)*, Susan Pratt *(Head Of Marketing)*
**HR:** Sam Cottenden *(Human Resources Manager)*
**Health & Safety:** Lorraine Kennelay *(Facilities Manager)*
**Facilities:** Lorraine Kennelay *(Facilities Manager)*
**Engineering:** Glen Burson *(Head of Architecture & Technic)*
**Branches:** Salmon Ltd, The Gate Ho, Fretherne Rd, Welwyn Garden City, Hertfordshire AL8 6NS
**US SIC:** 7379 **UK SIC:** 83940
**Auditors:** Charterhouse

| | 31-12-13 | 31-10-12 | 31-12-11 |
|---|---|---|---|
| TO | 42,367,042 | 34,207,925 | 26,380,642 |
| P/L | 3,080,554 | 3,790,202 | 2,863,019 |
| NW | 7,072,562 | 4,489,389 | 1,831,537 |
| WC | 6,634,773 | 3,933,405 | 1,621,220 |
| Emp. | 197 | 175 | 136 |

DUNS 22-878-0714
## Salmons Caterers Ltd
Rivington Lane, Rivington, Bolton, Lancashire BL6 7SB
**Tel:** 01204697180
**Web:** www.rivingtonhallbarn.co.uk
**Reg No:** 0583046 **VAT No:** 145231006
**Estd:** 1953 Private Limited Company
**Line of Business:** Caterers
**Issued Capital:** £3,000
**Principals:** K W Salmon *(Financial)*, Ms P M Hayes
**US SIC:** 5812 **UK SIC:** 66110
**Auditors:** Abrams Ashton
**Bankers:** The Royal Bank Of Scotland Plc (16-16-22)

| | 30-04-14 | 30-04-13 | 30-04-12 |
|---|---|---|---|
| TA | 1,164,260 | 1,061,096 | 975,490 |
| NW | 666,205 | 629,930 | 607,391 |
| WC | 156,237 | 134,264 | 165,602 |

DUNS 23-965-9097 **Imp-Exp**
## Salmor Industries Ltd
(**Subsidiary of:** Crh Plc)
4 Silverwood Road Silverwood Industrial, Area, Craigavon, Co Armagh BT66 6LN
**Tel:** 028-3831-3100 **Fax:** 028-3831-7770
**Web:** www.salmor.co.uk
**Reg No:** 0025807NI **VAT No:** 697102030
**Estd:** 1982 Private Limited Company
**Line of Business:** Casting of iron
**Export Markets:** Europe
**Trading Style:** Cubas Industries Ltd
**Issued Capital:** £100,000
**Directors:** E Sweeney, M Wightman, B H Scott
**Co. Secretary:** Ms Denise Geddis
**US SIC:** 3321 **UK SIC:** 31110
**Auditors:** Moore Stephens
**Bankers:** The Bank Of Ireland (90-07-70)

| | 31-12-13 | 31-12-12 | 31-12-11 |
|---|---|---|---|
| TA | 7,084,046 | 7,084,046 | 7,084,046 |
| NW | 7,084,046 | 7,084,046 | 7,084,046 |

DUNS 29-637-2212 **Imp**
## Salon Success Ltd
Millennium Point, Broadfields, Aylesbury, Buckinghamshire HP19 8YH
**Tel:** 01296390500
**Web:** www.salonsuccess.co.uk
**Reg No:** 1963398 **VAT No:** 490881318
**Estd:** 1982 Private Limited Company
**Line of Business:** Wholesale of perfume and cosmetics
**Export Sales:** £5,652,772
**Trading Style:** Paul Mitchell, 3.6.5
**Issued Capital:** £1,000
**Directors:** M Faulkner, S A Tickler
**Co. Secretary:** Ms Nina Azemoudeh
**Branches:** Salon Success Ltd, Fast Track House, Station Approach, Aylesbury, Buckinghamshire HP22 6BN
**US SIC:** 5122, 7399
**UK SIC:** 61800, 83954
**Auditors:** Ashby's

**Bankers:** National Westminster Bank Plc (60-02-13)

| | 30-09-13 | 30-09-12 | 30-09-11 |
|---|---|---|---|
| TO | 15,999,368 | 15,761,978 | 17,107,085 |
| P/L | 1,775,600 | 1,869,552 | 1,706,363 |
| NW | 14,865,361 | 13,712,765 | 10,949,797 |
| WC | 14,914,229 | 13,736,519 | 10,840,188 |
| Emp. | 94 | 96 | 92 |

DUNS 77-756-5797
## Salons Direct Ltd
Valley Road Business Park, Birkenhead, Merseyside CH41 7EL
**Tel:** 0844-875-7775 **Fax:** 01516709233
**Web:** www.salonsdirect.com
**Reg No:** 3018632 **Estd:** 1995 Private Limited Company
**Line of Business:** Hairdressers supplies
**Issued Capital:** £5,150
**Principals:** S Hill *(Financial)*, Ms D Roberts, D G Roberts, Mrs G Langman, G M Jones
**Co. Secretary:** Ms Valerie Roberts
**US SIC:** 5961 **UK SIC:** 65600
**Auditors:** Priory Practice Ltd

| | 31-03-14 | 31-03-13 | 31-03-12 |
|---|---|---|---|
| TO | 10,463,099 | 9,454,599 | 7,737,360 |
| P/L | 361,811 | 332,382 | 268,477 |
| NW | 540,296 | 499,073 | 477,180 |
| WC | 183,538 | 68,941 | 17,634 |
| Emp. | 78 | 69 | 64 |

DUNS 21-964-4502
## Salop Leisure Holdings Ltd
Salop Leisure Emstrey, Shrewsbury, Shropshire SY5 6QS
**Tel:** 08442471840 **Fax:** 01743282404
**Web:** www.salopleisure.co.uk
**Reg No:** 6146154 **Estd:** 2007 Private Limited Company
**Line of Business:** Other entertainment activities not elsewhere classified
**Issued Capital:** £990
**Directors:** M E Bebb, A T Bywater
**Co. Secretary:** Dylan Roberts
**US SIC:** 7999 **UK SIC:** 97913

| | 30-09-13 | 30-09-12 | 30-09-11 |
|---|---|---|---|
| TO | 21,853,170 | 23,256,326 | 24,652,270 |
| P/L | 1,040,454 | 1,117,775 | 862,457 |
| NW | 3,518,309 | 3,043,474 | 2,610,393 |
| WC | 1,435,702 | 1,957,554 | 1,757,907 |
| Emp. | 142 | 115 | 129 |

DUNS 50-460-0453
## Salram Ltd
(**Subsidiary of:** Sedale Investments Limited)
Claremount, 5 Station Road, Preston, Lancashire PR4 6SN
**Tel:** 01772814098
**Web:** www.numarkpharmacists.com
**Reg No:** 0121294SC **VAT No:** 732399125
**Estd:** 1982 Private Limited Company
**Line of Business:** Dispensing chemists
**Trading Style:** Hesketh Bank Pharmacy
**Issued Capital:** £225,000
**Director:** D K Jones
**Co. Secretary:** Raymond Roberts
**Branches:** Salram Ltd, 7 Lido Buildings, Lytham Road, Blackpool, Lancashire FY4 1EW
**US SIC:** 5912 **UK SIC:** 64300
**Auditors:** Finlay Robertson

| | 30-09-13 | 30-09-12 | 30-09-11 |
|---|---|---|---|
| TO | 6,420,936 | 6,605,571 | 7,163,424 |
| P/L | (61,534) | 100,836 | (24,554) |
| NW | 856,751 | 861,171 | 749,076 |
| WC | (408,245) | (397,369) | (52,981) |
| Emp. | 60 | 60 | 62 |

DUNS 29-650-9615
## Saltash Enterprises Ltd
(**Subsidiary of:** Saltash Enterprises Holdings Ltd)
110-116 Ormside Street, Peckham, London SE15 1TF
**Tel:** 020-7277-5661 **Fax:** 020-7277-5662
**Web:** www.saltashconstruction.co.uk
**Reg No:** 1977118 **Estd:** 1986 Private Limited Company
**Line of Business:** Development and selling of real estate
**Issued Capital:** £50,000
**Principals:** R J Raymond *(Managing)*, Ms D V Raymond
**Co. Secretary:** Mrs Dawn Raymond
**Responsibilities**
**Senior:** Wesley Flaherty *(Procurement & Supply Chain Man)*, Joanna Gibbons *(Manager)*
**Finance:** Peter Gibons *(Joint Managing Director)*, Jacky Herger *(Accounts Manager)*
**Sales:** Lee Stevens *(Business Development Manager)*
**Purchasing:** Wesley Flaherty *(Procurement & Supply Chain Man)*
**US SIC:** 6552, 1541, 1522
**UK SIC:** 85000, 50100

**Auditors:** Walker, Sutcliffe & Cooper

| | 30-09-13 | 30-09-12 | 30-09-11 |
|---|---|---|---|
| TO | 13,621,745 | 13,331,165 | 12,785,310 |
| P/L | 951,393 | 834,550 | 708,341 |
| NW | 2,384,656 | 2,212,238 | 1,721,569 |
| WC | 2,352,924 | 2,446,789 | 2,012,221 |
| Emp. | 50 | 49 | 52 |

DUNS 21-602-1732
## Saltash Leisure Centre
Callington Road, Saltash, Cornwall PL12 6DJ
**Tel:** 01752840940
**Web:** www.cornwall.gov.uk
**Estd:** 1996 Proprietorship
**Line of Business:** Leisure centres
**Proprietor:** B Price
**US SIC:** 7999 **UK SIC:** 97913
**Employees:** 48

DUNS 54-428-7428
## Saltend Cogeneration Co Ltd
**(Subsidiary of:** Gdf Suez)
Senator House, London EC4V 4DP
**Tel:** 01482895500
**Web:** www.internationalpowerplc.com
**Reg No:** 3274929 **VAT No:** 991260803
**Estd:** 1989 Private Limited Company
**Line of Business:** Electrical distribution companies
**Trading Style:** International Power
**Issued Capital:** £23,786,000
**Directors:** D Alcock, S D Pinnell, P W Evans, R Okaniwa
**Co. Secretary:** Ms Hillary Berger
**Responsibilities**
**Senior:** Mick Farr *(Station Manager)*, Jan Flachet *(Chief Executive and President,)*, Isabelle Kocher *(Non-Executive Director)*, Shankar Krishnamoorthy *(Chief Executive and President,)*, Gerard Lamarche *(Non-Executive Director)*, Zin Smati *(Chief Executive and President,)*, Serdar Tusekcr *(Station Manager)*, Michael Zaoui *(Non-Executive Director)*
**Admin:** Francois Graux *(General Counsel and Company So)*, Emma Mallia *(PA to IT Manager)*
**IT:** Martin Proudlove *(IT Managerm)*
**HR:** Gavin Firth *(Human Resources Manager)*
**Facilities:** Denise Phillips *(Facilities Manager)*, Barry Winter *(Engineering Manager)*
**Operations:** Craig Jenkinson *(Chemist)*
**Engineering:** Matthias Sander *(Renewable Engineer)*
**Branches:** Saltend Cogeneration Co Ltd, P O Box 1063, Hull, North Humberside HU12 8YG
**US SIC:** 4911 **UK SIC:** 16101
**Auditors:** KPMG Audit PLC

| | 31-12-13 | 31-12-12 | 31-12-11 |
|---|---|---|---|
| TO | 408,306,000 | 447,303,000 | 434,084,000 |
| P/L | (151,340,000) | 20,370,000 | 25,246,000 |
| NW | 23,150,000 | 139,876,000 | 121,905,000 |
| WC | 28,722,000 | (118,243,000) | 73,160,000 |

DUNS 23-596-3647
## Salter Baxter Communications Ltd
202 Kensington Church Street, London W8 4DP
**Web:** www.salterbaxter.com
**Reg No:** 3593800 **Estd:** 1998 Private Limited Company
**Line of Business:** Speciality design activities
**Issued Capital:** £9,000
**Directors:** Ms P L Baxter, R Johansson, A L Kempe, N J Salter, P J Miller
**Co. Secretary:** Mrs Raj Basran
**US SIC:** 7399 **UK SIC:** 83954
**Auditors:** Haines Watts
**Bankers:** HSBC Bank plc (40-07-14)

| | 31-12-13 | 31-12-12 | 31-12-11 |
|---|---|---|---|
| TA | 3,204,616 | 2,465,830 | 2,514,243 |
| NW | 1,010,409 | 953,457 | 726,243 |
| WC | 793,496 | 642,372 | 381,863 |

DUNS 21-774-4016
## Saltergate School
3 Cousland Road, Dalkeith, Midlothian EH22 2PS
**Tel:** 01316544703
**Estd:** 2011 Proprietorship
**Line of Business:** Schools (special)
**Proprietor:** J Loughlin
**Responsibilities**
**Senior:** Fiona Hume *(Head Teacher)*
**US SIC:** 8299 **UK SIC:** 93300
**Employees:** 76

DUNS 22-557-6222 Imp
## Salterns Marina Ltd
40 Salterns Way, Poole, Dorset BH14 8JR
**Web:** www.salterns.co.uk
**Reg No:** 0957868 **Estd:** 1969 Private Limited Company
**Line of Business:** Other supporting water transport activities
**Trading Style:** Salterns Marina
**Issued Capital:** £305,752
**Principals:** J N Smith *(Managing)*, J Eads, N J Smith, M Mandy, M R Bizzell
**Co. Secretary:** Mark Mandy
**Responsibilities**
**Senior:** Louisa Barber *(Food & Beverage Manager)*, James Sydenatm *(Manager)*
**HR:** Tina Young *(Human Resources Manager)*
**Health & Safety:** Mike Wilcock *(Health & Safety Officer)*
**Branches:** Salterns Marina Ltd, Salterns Harbourside Hotel, 38 Salterns Way, Poole, Dorset BH14 8JR
**US SIC:** 4469 **UK SIC:** 76300
**Auditors:** Saffery Champness
**Bankers:** Barclays Bank Plc (20-68-79)

| | 31-03-14 | 31-03-13 | 31-03-12 |
|---|---|---|---|
| TO | 14,542,386 | 12,890,637 | 14,487,808 |
| P/L | 29,616 | 30,134 | 115,800 |
| NW | 4,406,798 | 4,369,783 | 4,330,265 |
| WC | 1,749,906 | 1,856,956 | 1,790,635 |
| Emp. | 88 | 84 | 94 |

DUNS 45-847-4160 Imp-Exp
## Saltire Energy Ltd
Badentoy Road, Aberdeen, Aberdeenshire AB12 4YA
**Tel:** 01224872228 **Fax:** 01224897541
**Web:** www.saltire-energy.com
**Reg No:** 0165384SC **VAT No:** 671112664
**Estd:** 1996 Private Limited Company
**Line of Business:** Drilling and boring equipment
**Export Sales:** £21,615,366
**Issued Capital:** £1,240
**Directors:** P T Gray, G D Leslie, M D Loggie
**Co. Secretary:** Bryan Keenan
**Responsibilities**
**Finance:** Pauline Perfect *(Accountant)*
**US SIC:** 3531, 5084
**UK SIC:** 32541, 61490
**Auditors:** Bower & Smith
**Bankers:** Bank Of Scotland (80-29-01)

| | 30-06-14 | 30-06-13 | 30-06-12 |
|---|---|---|---|
| TO | 36,314,194 | 32,993,127 | 21,678,505 |
| P/L | 17,693,867 | 17,192,003 | 13,198,456 |
| NW | 41,153,804 | 26,510,913 | 12,816,195 |
| WC | (7,327,332) | (3,474,544) | (12,421,365) |
| Emp. | 65 | 52 | 42 |

DUNS 22-079-0179
## Saltire Facilities Management Ltd
**(Subsidiary of:** Alhco Group Ltd)
10 James Street, Glasgow, Lanarkshire
**Tel:** 01698312033 **Fax:** 01236754507
**Web:** www.saltire.co.uk
**Reg No:** 0211524SC **Estd:** 2000 Private Limited Company
**Line of Business:** Plumbing
**Trading Style:** Saltire
**Issued Capital:** £1,000
**Directors:** Mrs K M Hassell, J Reynolds, D L Weston, Mrs L J Keohane, J Brooks
**Co. Secretary:** Mrs Lynda Keohane
**Responsibilities**
**Senior:** Andrew Stirling *(Manager)*
**US SIC:** 1711 **UK SIC:** 50300
**Auditors:** Wylie & Bisset LLP
**Bankers:** Barclays Bank Plc (20-13-42)

| | 31-12-13 | 31-12-12 | 31-12-11 |
|---|---|---|---|
| TO | 19,678,717 | 18,296,858 | 19,620,534 |
| P/L | 2,431 | 681,386 | 276,998 |
| NW | 593,885 | 1,098,137 | 882,170 |
| WC | 292,329 | 783,834 | 642,829 |
| Emp. | 291 | 281 | 293 |

DUNS 73-918-3341
## Saltire Press Ltd
**(Subsidiary of:** Trinity Mirror Plc)
110 Fifty Pitches Place, Glasgow, Lanarkshire G51 4EA
**Tel:** 0141-309-3733
**Web:** www.saltirepress.co.uk
**Reg No:** 0151303SC **Estd:** 1900 Private Limited Company
**Line of Business:** Publishing of newspapers
**Issued Capital:** £18,000,000
**Directors:** S R Fox, T M Directors Limited, V L Vaghela
**Co. Secretary:** T M Secretaries Limited
**Responsibilities**
**HR:** Laura Fitzsimmons *(Human Resources Manager)*
**Health & Safety:** Peter Hutchison *(Health & Safety Officer)*
**Facilities:** David Beagan *(Chief Engineer)*
**Engineering:** David Beagan *(Chief Engineer)*
**US SIC:** 2711 **UK SIC:** 47512
**Auditors:** McGrigor Donald

| | 29-12-13 | 30-12-12 | 01-12-12 |
|---|---|---|---|
| TA | 19,215,000 | 19,215,000 | 20,354,000 |
| NW | 19,215,000 | 19,215,000 | 19,215,000 |
| WC | N/A | N/A | 19,215,000 |

DUNS 54-429-2675
## Saltire Taverns Ltd
25 George Iv Bridge, Edinburgh, Midlothian EH1 1EN
**Tel:** 01316221820 **Fax:** 0131-220-0106
**Web:** www.lemondehotel.co.uk
**Reg No:** 0169679SC **Estd:** 1996 Private Limited Company
**Line of Business:** Copper production
**Issued Capital:** £3,699,997
**Principals:** T Mcgrath *(Managing)*, W Lowe *(Managing)*, Ms K A Lowe, Ms M L Parker-Burnell, A G Manson
**Co. Secretary:** Hbjg Secretarial Limited
**Branches:** Saltire Taverns Ltd, 22 Netherkirkgate, Aberdeen, Aberdeenshire AB10 1AU
**US SIC:** 7399 **UK SIC:** 83954
**Auditors:** Deloitte & Touche
**Bankers:** Clydesdale Bank Plc (82-63-01)

| | 31-01-14 | 31-01-13 | 31-01-12 |
|---|---|---|---|
| TO | 7,436,112 | 6,914,520 | 5,827,970 |
| P/L | 6,307 | 25,168 | (32,720) |
| NW | 10,249,129 | 10,163,232 | 9,988,905 |
| WC | (711,563) | (1,090,552) | (908,812) |
| Emp. | 169 | 172 | 129 |

DUNS 22-753-2058
## Saltmarine
Tamnamore Road, Dungannon, Co Tyrone BT71 6HW
**Tel:** 028-8772-3376
**Web:** www.saltmarine-mazda.co.uk
**VAT No:** 255435164 **Estd:** 1969 Proprietorship
**Line of Business:** Car dealers (new & used)
**Proprietor:** N Salt
**US SIC:** 5511 **UK SIC:** 65100
**Bankers:** Northern Bank Ltd (95-03-02)
**Employees:** 50

DUNS 39-465-3190
## Salts Estates Ltd
Salts Mill, Victoria Road, Shipley, West Yorkshire BD18 3LA
**Tel:** 01274531163 **Fax:** 01274-531184
**Web:** www.saltsmill.org.uk
**Reg No:** 2123490 **VAT No:** 447784796
**Estd:** 1986 Private Limited Company
**Line of Business:** Retail sale of books, newspapers and stationery
**Trading Style:** Hockney 1853 Gallery
**Issued Capital:** £100
**Principals:** R J Silver *(Managing)*, M Miller *(Financial)*, Ms Z Silver, Mrs M Silver, Ms D Silver, Ms Z Silver
**Co. Secretary:** Ms Linda Wilkinson
**Responsibilities**
**Senior:** P Breeze *(Reverend)*
**US SIC:** 8661, 5812
**UK SIC:** 96600, 66110
**Auditors:** Leslie Bray & Co
**Bankers:** Barclays Bank Plc (20-11-81)

| | 31-12-13 | 31-12-12 | 31-12-11 |
|---|---|---|---|
| TO | 2,316,837 | 2,406,445 | 2,283,086 |
| P/L | (29,414) | (73,855) | 273,777 |
| NW | 8,195,007 | 8,338,317 | 8,363,933 |
| WC | 1,356,070 | 1,341,962 | 1,638,873 |
| Emp. | 95 | 100 | 90 |

DUNS 23-702-4740
## Salts Gallery
Victoria Road, Shipley, West Yorkshire BD18 3LA
**Tel:** 01274530533
**Web:** www.saltsmill.org.uk
**Estd:** 1992 Proprietorship
**Line of Business:** Restaurant - american
**Proprietor:** Mrs M Silver
**Responsibilities**
**Senior:** Nigel Kay *(Manager)*
**US SIC:** 5812, 8411
**UK SIC:** 66110, 97700
**Employees:** 50

DUNS 21-805-4690 Imp-Exp
## Salts Healthcare Ltd
Unit 1, Richard Street, Birmingham, West Midlands B7 4AA
**Tel:** 0121 333 2000
**Web:** www.salts.co.uk
**Reg No:** 0074096 **VAT No:** 110399004
**Estd:** 1793 Private Limited Company
**Line of Business:** First aid supplies
**Export Markets:** Netherlands, Sweden, Switzerland, Denmark, Republic of Ireland, S Afric, Australia, S America, Middle East, Eastern Europe
**Export Sales:** £14,022,711
**Trading Style:** Salts Techstep
**Issued Capital:** £49,975
**Principals:** P W Salt *(Managing)*, P E Salt, R J Salt
**Co. Secretary:** Ian Taylor
**Branches:** Salts Healthcare Ltd, 53 Valley Road, Plymouth, Devon PL7 1RF
**US SIC:** 5122, 2834
**UK SIC:** 61800, 25700
**Auditors:** Grant Thornton UK LLP
**Bankers:** Lloyds TSB Bank plc (30-00-03)

| | 31-12-13 | 31-12-12 | 31-12-11 |
|---|---|---|---|
| TO | 63,931,916 | 58,746,018 | 52,546,577 |
| P/L | 3,494,992 | 4,266,836 | 3,589,162 |
| NW | 12,610,782 | 14,970,498 | 11,464,760 |
| WC | 7,136,436 | 7,004,329 | 4,927,351 |
| Emp. | 538 | 495 | 419 |

DUNS 21-066-1760
## Salutation Hotel
30-34 South Street, Perth, Perthshire PH2 8PH
**Tel:** 01738-630066
**Web:** www.strathmorehotel.co.uk
**Estd:** 1988 Proprietorship
**Line of Business:** Hotels and motels without restaurant
**Proprietor:** G Paterson
**US SIC:** 7011 **UK SIC:** 66500
**Employees:** 50

DUNS 22-710-6473 Exp
## The Salvation Army
99-101 Newington Causeway, London SE1 6BN
**Tel:** 02073320101
**Web:** www.salvationarmy.org
**VAT No:** 577712802 **Estd:** 1990
**Line of Business:** Religious organisations and places of worship
**Directors:** G A Birkett, Ms W R Chalmers, J M Barr, K M Graham, G A Pilkington, D H Paul, Ms B R Dickens, Ms M E Drew
**Responsibilities**
**Senior:** Clifford Bradbury *(Trustee)*, John Metear *(Commander)*
**Marketing:** Julius Woolfe-Ingham *(Sales & Marketing Director)*
**Sales:** Julius Woolfe-Ingham *(Sales & Marketing Director)*
**IT:** Martin Croft *(Computer Manager)*
**Branches:** The Salvation Army, 99-101 Newington Causeway, London SE1 6BN
**US SIC:** 8661 **UK SIC:** 96600
**Auditors:** Knox Cropper
**Bankers:** Reliance Bank Ltd (60-01-73)

| | 31-03-13 | 31-03-12 | 31-03-09 |
|---|---|---|---|
| TO | 181,516,000 | 162,208,000 | 152,140,000 |
| P/L | 5,241,000 | 2,523,000 | 20,377,000 |
| NW | 491,158,000 | 486,028,000 | 466,290,000 |
| WC | 101,736,000 | 106,684,000 | 126,785,000 |
| Emp. | 2,778 | 2,671 | 3,689 |

DUNS 76-906-3546
## Salvation Army Housing Association
Barber Surgeon's Hall, 1a Monkwell Square, London EC2Y 5BL
**Tel:** 08009706363
**Web:** www.saha.org.uk
**Reg No:** 0152109IP **Estd:** 1959 Friendly Society
**Line of Business:** Residential care establishments
**Principals:** D Pender *(Chairman)*, A Vince, Ms S Johnston-Wood, M Tiplady, P Smith, L Spencer, R Jones, J Peddley
**Co. Secretary:** Ms Margery Mansfield-Cooke
**Responsibilities**
**Senior:** Margaret Bassingthwaite *(Director)*, John Bayliss *(Director)*, Jill Coller *(Director)*, Iris Medlicott *(Director)*, Bryan Stobart *(Director)*
**Branches:** Salvation Army Housing Association, Tyneside Foyer, 114 Westgate Rd, Newcastle Upon Tyne, Tyne and Wear NE1 4AQ
**US SIC:** 8321 **UK SIC:** 96111
**Bankers:** Barclays Bank Plc (20-74-09)

| | 31-03-12 | 31-03-11 | 31-03-10 |
|---|---|---|---|
| TO | 43,344,564 | 43,561,912 | 42,791,565 |
| P/L | 2,079,946 | 15,882,837 | 2,183,292 |
| NW | 28,680,546 | 33,583,143 | 17,700,342 |
| WC | 3,792,548 | 3,979,806 | 3,714,269 |
| Emp. | 143 | 140 | 126 |

DUNS 21-391-8848
## The Salvation Army Limavady
72-76 Main Street, Limavady, Co Londonderry BT49 0EX
**Tel:** 028-77722613
**Web:** www.salvationarmy.org.uk
**Estd:** 2009 Proprietorship
**Line of Business:** Places of worship
**Proprietor:** Captain J Archibald
**Responsibilities**
**Senior:** Edmund Archibald *(Manager)*
**US SIC:** 8661 **UK SIC:** 96600
**Employees:** 250

DUNS 21-558-3319
## The Salvation Army Social Work Trust
99-101 Newington Causeway, London SE1 6BN
**Tel:** 02073674890
**Web:** www.salvationarmy.org.uk
**Estd:** 1891

**Line of Business:** Charities and charitable organisations
**Directors:** A Read, B D Peddle, K G Manners, J Matear, G A Pilkington, W R Chalmers, Ms M E Drew, J M Barr
**Responsibilities**
**Senior:** John Mateur *(Chief of The Staff)*
**US SIC:** 6732 **UK SIC:** 83100
**Auditors:** Knox Cropper

| | 31-03-12 | 31-03-10 | 31-03-09 |
|---|---|---|---|
| TO | 107,809,000 | 95,554,000 | 93,213,000 |
| P/L | 5,799,000 | 6,824,000 | 84,727,000 |
| NW | 288,873,000 | 168,349,000 | 149,036,000 |
| WC | 49,994,000 | 37,957,000 | 34,712,000 |
| Emp. | 3,063 | 3,113 | 3,055 |

DUNS 76-846-2186
### Salvation Army Trading Co Ltd
66-78 Dennington Road, Wellingborough, Northamptonshire NN8 2QH
**Tel:** 01933441086
**Web:** www.satradingco.org
**Reg No:** 2605817 **VAT No:** 577816686
**Estd:** 1991 Private Limited Company
**Line of Business:** Retail sale of other second-hand goods in stores
**Export Sales:** £27,660,736
**Issued Capital:** £3,076,920
**Directors:** Major M Ord, Major R M Welch, T P Caffull, Mrs M Adams, J B Stubbings, Captain H M Mcclintock, A Read, Major D Lees
**Co. Secretary:** Mrs Beverley Phillips
**Responsibilities**
**Senior:** Stephen Cobb *(Director)*, Martyn Croft *(Director)*, Melvyn Jones *(Manager)*, Elizabeth Matear *(Manager)*
**Branches:** Salvation Army Trading Co Ltd, 5 Penn Street, Bristol, Avon BS1 3AW
**US SIC:** 5931, 6732
**UK SIC:** 65400, 83100
**Auditors:** Knox Cropper

| | 31-03-14 | 31-03-13 | 31-03-12 |
|---|---|---|---|
| TO | 46,309,125 | 44,699,093 | 26,159,836 |
| P/L | 3,958,629 | 4,784,648 | 2,512,789 |
| NW | 6,707,888 | 2,701,755 | 9,240,198 |
| WC | 342,552 | 1,873,731 | 4,104,170 |
| Emp. | 600 | 467 | 416 |

DUNS 22-720-3403 **Imp**
### The Salvation Army Trustee Company
99-101 Newington Causeway, London SE1 6BN
**Tel:** 020-7367-4500 **Fax:** 02073674501
**Web:** www.salvationarmy.org.uk
**Reg No:** 0259322 **Estd:** 1891 Private Company Limited By Guarantee
**Line of Business:** Individual & family social services
**Directors:** M C Caffull, M Adams, Major A L Sawyer, G A Pilkington, Major R M Welch, Ms B R Dickens, P Gale, Lieut Colonel M C Fincham
**Co. Secretary:** Elliot Thomas
**Responsibilities**
**Senior:** Clive Adams *(Director)*, Clifford Bradbury *(Trustee)*, Walter Chalmers *(Director)*, Suzanne Fincham *(Member)*, Sylvia Hinton *(Director)*, John Metear *(Commander)*, Yvonne Roufett *(Member)*
**Marketing:** Joanna Inskip *(Head of Media)*, Julius Woolfe-Ingham *(Sales & Marketing Director)*
**Sales:** Julius Woolfe-Ingham *(Sales & Marketing Director)*
**IT:** Martyn Croft *(IT director)*, Neil Edmonds *(IT Operations Manager)*
**Branches:** The Salvation Army Trustee Company, 190 Seabourne Rd, Bournemouth, Dorset BH5 2JB
**US SIC:** 8321, 8661
**UK SIC:** 96111, 96600
**Auditors:** Knox Cropper
**Bankers:** National Westminster Bank Plc (70-09-12)
**Employees:** 3,040

DUNS 21-848-2244
### Salvatorian College
High Road, Harroweld, Harrow, Middlesex HA3 5DY
**Tel:** 02088632706
**Web:** www.salvatoriancollege.co.uk
**Reg No:** 8134861 **Estd:** 2012 Private Company Limited By Guarantee
**Line of Business:** Schools (local authority)
**Directors:** P Kassapian, B J Morahan, Ms B Osayi, Ms L Elliott, Ms L M Mckenna, Ms R C Caiado, A Mcallister, K S Daly
**Responsibilities**
**Senior:** Debbie Carroll *(Director)*, Richard Mway Zeng *(Director)*, Margaret Newton *(Director)*, Bernadette O'Reilly *(Director)*, Theresa O'Sullivan *(Director)*, Gary Prazer *(Director)*, Margaret Reynolds *(Director)*
**Finance:** Patricia Garside *(Treasurer)*
**US SIC:** 8211 **UK SIC:** 93200
**Bankers:** Lloyds TSB Bank plc (30-15-93)

| | 31-08-14 | 31-08-13 |
|---|---|---|
| TO | 4,306,425 | 11,939,993 |
| P/L | (164,374) | 6,704,177 |
| NW | 5,320,803 | 5,696,177 |
| WC | 282,178 | 191,838 |
| Emp. | 93 | 93 |

DUNS 21-827-3910
### Salvesen Logistics Ltd
(**Subsidiary of:** Dentressangle Intitiatives)
Righead Industrial Estate, Bellshill, Lanarkshire ML4 3LA
**Tel:** 01698844050
**Web:** www.norbert-dentressangle.co.uk
**Reg No:** 0346268 **Estd:** 1928 Private Limited Company
**Line of Business:** Distribution service providers
**Issued Capital:** £77,010,000
**Directors:** Ms L G Navid Lane, M Wilson, P J Shaw, H F Montjotin, D S Myers, G De La Rochebrochard, P Bataillard, N P Sargeant
**Co. Secretary:** Ms Lyndsay Navid Lane
**Branches:** Salvesen Logistics Ltd, Amble Ind Est, Amble, Morpeth, Northumberland NE65 0PE
**US SIC:** 6711, 4213
**UK SIC:** 83962, 72300
**Auditors:** Grant Thornton UK LLP
**Bankers:** HSBC Bank plc (40-35-04)

| | 31-12-13 | 31-12-12 | 31-12-11 |
|---|---|---|---|
| TA | 194,294,000 | 192,162,000 | 197,399,000 |
| P/L | 12,992,000 | 3,996,000 | 707,000 |
| NW | 141,374,000 | 139,707,000 | 133,310,000 |
| WC | 192,801,000 | 190,787,000 | 195,310,000 |
| Emp. | N/A | N/A | 11,814 |

DUNS 37-784-7421
### Salvo's Barber Shop
4 Queen Victoria Street, Reading, Berkshire RG1 1TG
**Tel:** 01189-507772
**Web:** www.salvoandalex.co.uk
**Estd:** 2010 Proprietorship
**Line of Business:** Hairdressers (unisex)
**Proprietor:** S Ballairno
**Responsibilities**
**Senior:** Salvo Ballarino *(Manager)*
**US SIC:** 7231 **UK SIC:** 98200
**Bankers:** Barclays Bank Plc (20-71-02)
**Employees:** 305

DUNS 23-526-3936
### Salvo's Restaurant Ltd
Salvos, 107 Otley Road, Leeds, West Yorkshire LS6 3PX
**Tel:** 01132755017
**Web:** www.salvos.co.uk
**Reg No:** 1264823 **Estd:** 1976 Private Limited Company
**Line of Business:** Restaurant - italian
**Trading Style:** Salvos
**Issued Capital:** £5,000
**Principals:** G Dammone *(Managing)*, G Dammone *(Financial)*, Mrs G Dammone, Ms J Dammone
**Co. Secretary:** Gianfranco Dammone
**Responsibilities**
**Senior:** John Dammone *(Owner)*
**US SIC:** 5812 **UK SIC:** 66110
**Auditors:** Sochall & Smith
**Bankers:** Yorkshire Bank Plc (05-01-61)

| | 31-08-13 | 31-08-12 | 31-08-11 |
|---|---|---|---|
| TA | 595,948 | 688,774 | 529,339 |
| NW | 150,651 | 83,912 | 161,719 |
| WC | (265,784) | (396,291) | (94,394) |

DUNS 21-583-6245
### Sam Beare Hospice Book Shop
7 High Street, Weybridge, Surrey KT13 8AX
**Tel:** 01932878439
**Web:** www.wsbhospices.co.uk
**Estd:** 2011 Proprietorship
**Line of Business:** Dress agencies
**Proprietor:** Ms C Wrag
**US SIC:** 8321 **UK SIC:** 96111
**Employees:** 50

DUNS 49-389-3994
### Sam Dowden Ltd
33 Mount Road, Sunderland, Tyne and Wear SR4 7PX
**Tel:** 0191-528-3712
**Web:** www.samdowdenltd.com
**Reg No:** 3136429 **Estd:** 1995 Private Limited Company
**Line of Business:** Manufacture of electric domestic appliances
**Trading Style:** After Hours Cleaning Services
**Issued Capital:** £100
**Director:** S Dowden
**Co. Secretary:** Ms Hazel Dowden
**US SIC:** 3639, 5084
**UK SIC:** 34600, 61490
**Auditors:** A W S
**Bankers:** The Royal Bank Of Scotland Plc (16-32-36)

| | 28-02-14 | 28-02-13 | 29-02-12 |
|---|---|---|---|
| TA | 83,542 | 79,800 | 79,837 |
| NW | 25,756 | 23,139 | 17,039 |
| WC | 4,776 | (618) | (9,238) |

DUNS 77-109-2202
### Sam Hagan Leisure (Uk) Ltd
Skinburness Drive, Silloth, Wigton, Cumbria CA7 4QQ
**Fax:** 01697332553
**Web:** www.hagansleisure.co.uk
**Reg No:** 2686607 **Estd:** 1992 Private Limited Company
**Line of Business:** Holiday parks and camps
**Trading Style:** Solway Holiday Village, Lido Residential Park
**Issued Capital:** £100,000
**Principals:** S J Hagan *(Managing)*, Mrs D J Hagan
**Responsibilities**
**Senior:** John Finlinson *(Manager)*, Geraldine Hagan *(Manager)*, Terry Rodger *(Manager)*
**Branches:** Sam Hagan Leisure (Uk) Ltd, Skinburness Drive, Wigton, Cumbria CA7 4QQ
**US SIC:** 7021 **UK SIC:** 66500
**Auditors:** RWCA Ltd
**Bankers:** HSBC Bank plc (40-10-50)

| | 31-10-13 | 31-10-12 | 31-10-11 |
|---|---|---|---|
| TO | N/A | N/A | 3,816,437 |
| P/L | N/A | N/A | 31,439 |
| NW | 3,937,046 | 3,805,202 | 3,788,457 |
| WC | (50,911) | 141,203 | 42,422 |
| Emp. | N/A | N/A | 63 |

DUNS 21-589-5445
### Sam Jacks
The Gate, Newgate Street, Newcastle-Upon-Tyne, Tyne and Wear NE1 5TG
**Tel:** 01912618982
**Web:** www.samjacks.com
**Estd:** 2011 Proprietorship
**Line of Business:** Bars
**Proprietor:** Mrs L Harrison
**US SIC:** 5813 **UK SIC:** 66200
**Employees:** 60

DUNS 21-233-2720
### Sam Turner & Sons Ltd
Northallerton Road, Northallerton, North Yorkshire DL6 2QR
**Tel:** 01609772422
**Web:** www.sam-turner.co.uk
**Reg No:** 0402201 **VAT No:** 257505159
**Estd:** 1945 Private Limited Company
**Line of Business:** Agricultural merchants
**Issued Capital:** £34,854
**Directors:** C M Turner, B M Turner, C E Turner, M S Turner
**Co. Secretary:** John Turner
**Responsibilities**
**Admin:** Diane Nixon *(Administrator)*
**IT:** Ian Place *(IT Manager)*
**Purchasing:** Diane Nixon *(Administrator)*
**Branches:** Sam Turner & Sons Ltd, 17 Ellerbeck Court, Middlesbrough, Cleveland TS9 5PT
**US SIC:** 5159 **UK SIC:** 61100
**Auditors:** Anderson Barroweliff
**Bankers:** Barclays Bank Plc (20-61-46)

| | 30-09-13 | 30-09-12 | 30-09-11 |
|---|---|---|---|
| TO | 12,079,453 | 11,899,263 | 11,184,131 |
| P/L | 270,103 | 276,927 | 368,645 |
| NW | 6,216,737 | 6,016,830 | 5,848,048 |
| WC | 2,001,737 | 2,328,346 | 2,296,330 |
| Emp. | 134 | 125 | 87 |

DUNS 22-632-5546
### Samaritans
The Upper Mill, Kingston Road, Epsom, Surrey KT17 2AF
**Tel:** 02083948300
**Web:** www.samaritans.org
**Reg No:** 0757372 **Estd:** 1963 Private Company Limited By Guarantee
**Line of Business:** Activities of other membership organisations not elsewhere classified
**Directors:** M A Rogerson, Dr J Craissati, Mrs C J Pearce, Ms J M Mccartney, Ms G Leo, K Walker, Ms R Howell, C J Mill
**Co. Secretary:** Ms Catherine Johnstone
**Responsibilities**
**Senior:** Kevin Corrigan *(Director)*, Terry Holland *(Director)*, Kathleen Jones *(Manager)*, Michael Kirkman *(Director)*, Anita Lawlor *(Director)*, Amanda Perrin *(Director)*
**Branches:** Samaritans, 18 Clarendon Street, Nottingham, Nottinghamshire NG1 5HQ
**US SIC:** 8699 **UK SIC:** 96902
**Auditors:** Smith & Williamson
**Bankers:** Lloyds TSB Bank plc (30-97-73)

| | 31-03-14 | 31-03-13 | 31-03-12 |
|---|---|---|---|
| TO | 12,507,000 | 12,943,000 | 11,557,000 |
| P/L | 717,000 | (433,000) | 12,000 |
| NW | 7,229,000 | 6,525,000 | 6,797,000 |
| WC | 2,453,000 | 1,719,000 | 2,063,000 |
| Emp. | 108 | 108 | 101 |

DUNS 50-444-2179
### Sambro International Ltd
Dumers Lane, Bury, Manchester
**Tel:** 0845-873-9380 **Fax:** 0845-873-9381
**Web:** www.sambro.co.uk
**Reg No:** 2432079 **VAT No:** 519486415
**Estd:** 1989 Private Limited Company
**Line of Business:** Wholesale of other household goods not elsewhere classified
**Export Sales:** £13,418,804
**Trading Style:** New World Toys, Stocklot
**Issued Capital:** £50,000
**Directors:** N M Samuels, T J Duffy, J P Clynes, B Samuels
**Co. Secretary:** Brian Robinson
**Responsibilities**
**Senior:** Nikki Samules *(Manager)*
**Branches:** Sambro International Ltd, Hardys Gate, Dumers Lane, Bury, Lancashire BL9 9UE
**US SIC:** 5199, 3944
**UK SIC:** 61900, 49410
**Auditors:** Royce Peeling Green Ltd
**Bankers:** HSBC Bank plc (40-31-24)

| | 31-12-13 | 31-12-12 | 31-12-11 |
|---|---|---|---|
| TO | 35,012,573 | 29,839,033 | 26,058,150 |
| P/L | 1,329,097 | (884,729) | 695,122 |
| NW | 4,184,629 | 3,121,706 | 3,848,769 |
| WC | 4,073,307 | 2,595,729 | 3,371,531 |
| Emp. | 77 | 69 | 74 |

DUNS 21-032-3398
### Same Day Solutions
8 Honeywood Road, London NW10 4UU
**Tel:** 07968637281
**Estd:** 2005 Proprietorship
**Line of Business:** Computer repair and maintenance services
**Proprietor:** R Patel
**US SIC:** 7379 **UK SIC:** 83940
**Employees:** 700

DUNS 21-176-7469
### Sammon Contracting Uk Ltd
(**Subsidiary of:** Sammon Contracting Group Limited)
Suite 4, London EC1M 5UT
**Tel:** 020-7374-2135
**Web:** www.sammongroup.com
**Reg No:** 6999019 **Estd:** 2009 Private Limited Company
**Line of Business:** Construction of commercial buildings
**Issued Capital:** £100
**Director:** M Sammon
**Co. Secretary:** Miceal Sammon
**Responsibilities**
**Senior:** Mukund Patel *(Development Director)*
**US SIC:** 1541 **UK SIC:** 50100

| | 31-12-13 | 31-12-12 | 31-12-11 |
|---|---|---|---|
| TA | 9,309 | 9,309 | 11,751 |
| NW | 9,309 | 9,309 | 9,309 |
| WC | N/A | N/A | 9,309 |

DUNS 21-780-5836
### Sampford Care Home
27 Shurnhold, Melksham, Wiltshire SN12 8DD
**Tel:** 01225896200
**Web:** www.majesticare.co.uk
**Estd:** 2011 Proprietorship
**Line of Business:** Residential care establishments
**Proprietor:** Mrs A Cole
**Responsibilities**
**Senior:** Vicky Higginson *(Home Manager)*, Nickola Pritchard *(Home Manager)*, Amanda Ring *(Home Manager)*
**US SIC:** 8321 **UK SIC:** 96111
**Employees:** 50

DUNS 21-249-2203
### Sams Sales and Marketing Services
Furness House, 5 Furness Road, Urmston, Manchester M41 0UQ
**Tel:** 0161-7468757
**Web:** www.sams.uk.net
**Estd:** 2005 Proprietorship
**Line of Business:** Business and management consultancy activities not elsewhere classified
**Responsibilities**
**Senior:** Tracy Chapman *(Manager)*
**US SIC:** 7399 **UK SIC:** 83954
**Employees:** 55

DUNS 28-972-3512
### Sam's Transport (Heathrow) Ltd
West Side Mill Road, Rugby, Warwickshire CV21 1BZ
**Tel:** 01788571102 **Fax:** 01895-436228
**Web:** www.samstransport.co.uk
**Reg No:** 1738215 **Estd:** 1983 Private Limited Company

**Line of Business:** Freight transport by road not elsewhere classified
**Issued Capital:** £100
**Principals:** B S Samra *(Managing)*, Ms S Samra
**Co. Secretary:** Balwant Samra
**Branches:** Sam's Transport (Heathrow) Ltd, Tavistock Road, West Drayton, Middlesex UB7 7QT
**US SIC:** 4213, 4226
**UK SIC:** 72300, 77003
**Bankers:** National Westminster Bank Plc (53-61-58)

| | 30-06-14 | 30-06-13 | 30-06-12 |
|---|---|---|---|
| TA | 1,205,098 | 996,269 | 706,964 |
| NW | 630,173 | 448,366 | 376,003 |
| WC | 251,294 | 141,137 | 138,060 |

DUNS 76-622-3028 Imp
## Samsara Ltd
Millennium Way, Vale Park, Evesham, Worcestershire WR11 1GR
**Tel:** 01386422922
**Web:** www.samsara.ltd
**Reg No:** 2578225 **VAT No:** 577288192
**Estd:** 1991 Private Limited Company
**Line of Business:** Food packers
**Issued Capital:** £5,000
**Principals:** R M Suarez *(Managing)*, A Zarei *(Financial)*, Ms C K Hall, Ms R L Quiney
**Responsibilities**
**Senior:** Sylvia Bamford *(Manager)*
**Finance:** Jo Limrick *(Accountant)*
**US SIC:** 7399 **UK SIC:** 83954
**Auditors:** Hazlewoods
**Bankers:** Bank Of Scotland (12-12-82)

| | 01-08-14 | 26-07-13 | 27-08-12 |
|---|---|---|---|
| TO | 21,344,380 | 26,992,857 | 30,252,636 |
| P/L | 10,282 | 196,091 | 1,375,140 |
| NW | 2,499,591 | 2,523,329 | 2,503,453 |
| WC | 1,048,071 | 296,001 | 1,932,165 |
| Emp. | 51 | 51 | 49 |

DUNS 21-860-2924
## Samsung Cambridge Solution Centre Ltd
St Johns Innovation Park, Cowley Road, Cambridge, Cambridgeshire CB4 0DS
**Web:** www.samsung.com
**Reg No:** 8226456 **Estd:** 2012 Private Limited Company
**Line of Business:** Telecom consultants
**Directors:** Y J Kim, R S Gawera, H K Lee, M G Kim
**Responsibilities**
**Senior:** Young Doo *(Director)*, Roger Fince *(Manager)*, Suk Kim *(Director)*, Youngho Lee *(Manager)*, Byunghoon Suh *(Manager)*
**US SIC:** 4899 **UK SIC:** 79020

| | 31-12-13 |
|---|---|
| TO | 64,910,279 |
| P/L | 4,030,016 |
| NW | 27,809,536 |
| WC | 24,810,974 |
| Emp. | 176 |

DUNS 49-080-6437 Imp-Exp
## Samsung Electronics (Uk) Ltd
**(Subsidiary of:** Samsung Electronics Co. Ltd.)
Samsung House, 1000 Hillswood Drive, Chertsey, Surrey KT16 0PS
**Tel:** 01932 455 000 **Fax:** 01932 875 030
**Web:** www.samsungelectronics.co.uk
**Reg No:** 3086621 **VAT No:** 689376366
**Estd:** 1995 Private Limited Company
**Line of Business:** Manufacture of other electrical equipment not elsewhere classified
**Export Markets:** Europe; Worldwide
**Issued Capital:** £109,546,000
**Directors:** G Song, S H Jo, A R Griffiths, S W Kang
**Co. Secretary:** Sung Kang
**Responsibilities**
**Senior:** David Song *(Manager)*
**Finance:** Bill Shon *(Financial Director)*
**Marketing:** Jessica Arnould *(Marketing Administrator)*
**IT:** Richard Sterry *(IT Manager)*
**HR:** David Diamond *(Human Resources Manager)*
**Health & Safety:** Carl Glassar *(Facilities Manager)*
**Facilities:** Carl Glassar *(Facilities Manager)*
**Purchasing:** Carl Glassar *(Facilities Manager)*
**US SIC:** 3629, 6711
**UK SIC:** 34350, 83962
**Auditors:** PricewaterhouseCoopers LLP
**Bankers:** HSBC Bank plc (40-13-21)
**Following financial data are in thousands**

| | 31-12-13 | 31-12-12 | 31-12-11 |
|---|---|---|---|
| TO | 3,423,500 | 3,208,259 | 2,142,251 |
| P/L | 59,412 | 56,936 | 39,940 |
| NW | 384,640 | 338,834 | 303,239 |
| WC | 408,282 | 371,854 | 322,736 |
| Emp. | 1,244 | 1,005 | 917 |

DUNS 21-674-3214
## Samsung Hospitality U.K. Ltd
**(Subsidiary of:** Hotel Shilla Co. Ltd.)
Samsung House, 1000 Hillswood Drive, Chertsey, Surrey KT16 0PS
**Tel:** 01932455018
**Web:** www.samsung.com
**Reg No:** 7263011 **Estd:** 2010 Private Limited Company
**Line of Business:** Transportation consultants
**Issued Capital:** £25,000
**Directors:** H Jae-Ho, L Myung-Jin, L Yoo-Seog
**US SIC:** 4712 **UK SIC:** 77002

| | 31-12-13 | 31-12-12 | 31-12-11 |
|---|---|---|---|
| TO | N/A | 194,249 | N/A |
| P/L | N/A | 51,799 | N/A |
| NW | 171,472 | 137,577 | 96,304 |
| WC | 170,085 | 135,518 | 93,576 |

DUNS 23-975-6617 Imp
## Samsung Sds Europe Ltd
**(Subsidiary of:** Samsung Sds Co. Ltd.)
No 5, First Floor, The Heights, Brooklands, Weybridge, Surrey KT13 0NY
**Tel:** 01932834000
**Web:** www.sdsesamsung.com
**Reg No:** 3964307 **Estd:** 2000 Private Limited Company
**Line of Business:** Computer software (development)
**Export Sales:** £115,326,000
**Issued Capital:** £1,000,000
**Directors:** J Lee, J Kim
**Co. Secretary:** Jinbok Kim
**Responsibilities**
**Senior:** Jeong Moon *(Manager)*
**HR:** Natalie Law *(Hr Advisor)*
**Branches:** Samsung Sds Europe Limited, Samsung House, 1000 Hillswood Drive, Chertsey, Surrey KT16 0PS
**US SIC:** 7379, 7372
**UK SIC:** 83940
**Auditors:** PricewaterhouseCoopers LLP

| | 31-12-13 | 31-12-12 | 31-12-11 |
|---|---|---|---|
| TO | 129,266,000 | 83,892,000 | 54,253,000 |
| P/L | 13,347,000 | 9,686,000 | 7,691,000 |
| NW | 32,759,000 | 22,128,000 | 16,888,000 |
| WC | 16,133,000 | 15,203,000 | 13,016,000 |
| Emp. | 272 | 253 | 171 |

DUNS 42-355-8068
## Samsung Techwin Europe Ltd
**(Subsidiary of:** Samsung Techwin Co. Ltd.)
2nd Floor, No 5 The Heights, Weybridge, Surrey KT13 0NY
**Web:** www.samsungsecurity.co.uk
**Reg No:** 4343432 **Estd:** 2001 Private Limited Company
**Line of Business:** Wholesale of other electronic parts and equipment
**Export Sales:** £66,419,000
**Issued Capital:** £6,500,000
**Directors:** J W Lim, B H Lee
**Co. Secretary:** Beom Lee
**Responsibilities**
**Senior:** Tae In *(Manager)*, Dong Lee *(Manager)*
**US SIC:** 5065 **UK SIC:** 61500
**Auditors:** PricewaterhouseCoopers LLP

| | 31-12-13 | 31-12-12 | 31-12-11 |
|---|---|---|---|
| TO | 79,223,000 | 86,487,000 | 84,750,000 |
| P/L | 445,000 | 2,761,000 | 1,605,000 |
| NW | 11,311,000 | 11,102,000 | 9,039,000 |
| WC | 10,885,000 | 10,779,000 | 8,679,000 |
| Emp. | 101 | 79 | 70 |

DUNS 76-970-3885 Exp
## Samuel Banner & Co. Ltd
**(Subsidiary of:** 2m Group Ltd)
Hampton Court Tudor Road, Runcorn, Cheshire WA7 1TU
**Tel:** 01928-597000 **Fax:** 01642231780
**Web:** www.bannerchemicals.com
**Reg No:** 2631366 **Estd:** 1991 Private Limited Company
**Line of Business:** Manufacture of other chemical products not elsewhere classified
**Export Markets:** Worldwide
**Export Sales:** £4,639,762
**Issued Capital:** £2,301,180
**Directors:** C R Boyle, M Kessler, D R Dalton
**Co. Secretary:** Brian Perry
**Responsibilities**
**Marketing:** Jim Bell *(Marketing Manager)*
**US SIC:** 2899, 5161
**UK SIC:** 25670, 61200
**Auditors:** UHY Hacker Young
**Bankers:** Yorkshire Bank Plc (05-05-73)

| | 30-04-14 | 30-04-13 | 30-04-12 |
|---|---|---|---|
| TO | 48,813,055 | 44,388,374 | 46,108,912 |
| P/L | 304,839 | 190,142 | 1,016,714 |
| NW | 9,960,331 | 9,566,995 | 14,311,570 |
| WC | 11,011,661 | 6,913,856 | 12,720,196 |
| Emp. | 81 | 76 | 79 |

DUNS 21-879-6665
## Samuel Cody Specialist Sports College
School House, Ballantyne Road, Farnborough, Hampshire GU14 8SN
**Tel:** 01252514194
**Web:** www.samuelcody.hants.sch.uk
**Estd:** 2012
**Line of Business:** Other adult and other education not elsewhere classified
**Responsibilities**
**Senior:** Anna Dawson *(Head Teacher)*
**US SIC:** 8299 **UK SIC:** 93300
**Employees:** 50

DUNS 22-788-1943 Imp-Exp
## Samuel Grant Group Ltd
146-148 Garnet Road, Leeds, West Yorkshire LS11 5LA
**Tel:** 01132-707221
**Web:** www.samuelgrant.co.uk
**Reg No:** 0174855 **VAT No:** 168835225
**Estd:** 1891 Private Limited Company
**Line of Business:** Packaging equipment
**Export Markets:** E U
**Issued Capital:** £9,381
**Directors:** Ms S M Grant, A D Grant, M P Grant
**Co. Secretary:** Ashley Dean
**Responsibilities**
**Senior:** Malcolm Dudley *(Facilities Manager)*, Ivan Ficenec *(Manager)*
**Admin:** Lorraine Lapping *(Office Manager)*
**Health & Safety:** Malcolm Dudley *(Facilities Manager)*
**Facilities:** Malcolm Dudley *(Facilities Manager)*
**Fleet:** Malcolm Dudley *(Facilities Manager)*
**Branches:** Samuel Grant Group Ltd, Unit 15, Tanfield Lea Industrial Estate North, Tanfield Lea, Stanley, County Durham DH9 9NX
**US SIC:** 6711 **UK SIC:** 83962
**Auditors:** Horwath Clark Whitehill (Yorkshire) LLP
**Bankers:** National Westminster Bank Plc (60-60-05)

| | 31-12-13 | 31-12-12 | 31-12-11 |
|---|---|---|---|
| TO | 22,302,434 | 20,196,772 | 19,264,612 |
| P/L | 1,057,833 | 873,136 | 539,739 |
| NW | 8,900,210 | 8,359,781 | 7,794,816 |
| WC | 4,052,335 | 3,719,062 | 3,409,379 |
| Emp. | 105 | 112 | 86 |

DUNS 21-803-6754 Imp-Exp
## Samuel Heath and Sons Plc
Leopold Street, Birmingham, West Midlands B12 0UP
**Tel:** 01217722303 **Fax:** 0121-772-3334
**Web:** www.samuel-heath.co.uk
**Reg No:** 0031942 **VAT No:** 109524969
**Estd:** 1929 Public Limited Company
**Line of Business:** Manufacture of other fabricated metal products not elsewhere classified
**Export Markets:** W Europe, U S A, Africa, S & S E Asia, Australasia
**Export Sales:** £4,246,000
**Trading Style:** Perkins & Powell, Adams W & Sons
**Issued Capital:** £253,432
**Principals:** S B Heath *(Chairman)*, D J Pick *(Managing)*, M J Legge, P B Turner, M P Whieldon, N Bosworth, M P Green, A R Buttanshaw
**Co. Secretary:** John Park
**Responsibilities**
**Marketing:** Vanessa Allan *(Senior Marketing Executive)*
**IT:** James Grinnell *(Computer Operations Manager)*, Nigel Titley *(Senior IT Executive)*
**Engineering:** Mark Stonelake *(Development Engineer)*
**US SIC:** 3499, 3261
**UK SIC:** 31694, 24892
**Auditors:** RSM Tenon Audit Ltd
**Bankers:** Barclays Bank Plc (20-07-71)

| | 31-03-14 | 31-03-13 | 31-03-12 |
|---|---|---|---|
| TO | 10,979,000 | 10,083,000 | 9,782,000 |
| P/L | 610,000 | 633,000 | 632,000 |
| NW | 3,924,000 | 3,742,000 | 4,986,000 |
| WC | 5,462,000 | 5,292,000 | 5,351,000 |
| Emp. | 132 | 131 | 131 |

DUNS 21-582-7582
## Samuel Hobson House
Knutton Road, Newcastle, Staffordshire ST5 0HU
**Tel:** 01782620011
**Web:** www.samuelhobsonhouse.co.uk
**Estd:** 2011 Proprietorship
**Line of Business:** Medical nursing home activities
**Proprietor:** Mrs B Turner
**US SIC:** 8051 **UK SIC:** 95100
**Employees:** 48

DUNS 21-229-7474
## Samuel Johnson Community Hospital
Windsor Court, Trent Valley Road, Lichfield, Staffordshire WS13 6EU
**Tel:** 01543-412900
**Estd:** 2008 Proprietorship
**Line of Business:** Hospitals
**Proprietor:** Miss J Docksey
**US SIC:** 8062 **UK SIC:** 95100
**Employees:** 1,000

DUNS 21-242-1523 Imp-Exp
## Samuel Smith Old Brewery (Tadcaster)
Old Brewery, High Street, Tadcaster, North Yorkshire LS24 9SB
**Tel:** 01937-832225 **Fax:** 01937-834673
**Web:** www.samuelsmithsbrewery.co.uk
**Reg No:** 0188027 **VAT No:** 169514441
**Estd:** 1758 Private Unlimited Company
**Line of Business:** Brewers
**Issued Capital:** £1,885,972
**Principals:** H R Smith *(Chairman and Managing)*, O G Smith *(Managing)*, S G Smith
**Co. Secretary:** Mark Butler
**Responsibilities**
**Marketing:** Simon Poynton *(Marketing Manager)*
**HR:** Laurie Capon *(Training Manager)*
**Health & Safety:** Colin Carbert *(Chief Engineer)*
**Facilities:** Colin Carbert *(Chief Engineer)*
**Operations:** Colin Carbert *(Chief Engineer)*, Simon Poynton *(Marketing Manager)*
**Branches:** Samuel Smith Old Brewery (Tadcaster), 37 Redcar Road, Guisborough, Cleveland TS14 6HR
**US SIC:** 2082, 5182
**UK SIC:** 42702, 61700
**Bankers:** National Westminster Bank Plc (60-60-05)
**Employees:** 1,164

DUNS 28-823-0642
## Samuel Solley (Hotels) Ltd
100 Milton Road East, Edinburgh, Midlothian EH15 2NP
**Tel:** 0131-669-0444
**Web:** www.bestwestern.co.uk
**Reg No:** 0048634SC **Estd:** 1971 Private Limited Company
**Line of Business:** Hotels
**Trading Style:** Pitbauchlie House Hotel, Kings Manor Hotel
**Issued Capital:** £58,534
**Directors:** S H Solley, L A Solley
**Co. Secretary:** Ian Solley
**Responsibilities**
**Marketing:** Alistair Paul *(Marketing Manager)*
**HR:** Garry Burness *(Human Resources Manager)*
**Operations:** Alistair Paul *(Marketing Manager)*
**Branches:** Samuel Solley (Hotels) Ltd, 100 Milton Road East, Edinburgh, Midlothian EH15 2NP
**US SIC:** 7011 **UK SIC:** 66500
**Auditors:** Bannerman Johnstone Maclay

| | 30-04-14 | 30-04-13 | 30-04-12 |
|---|---|---|---|
| TO | 6,135,505 | 5,875,314 | 5,757,660 |
| P/L | 162,095 | 325,543 | 102,566 |
| NW | 5,421,280 | 5,296,992 | 5,017,298 |
| WC | (248,786) | (185,703) | (606,156) |
| Emp. | 217 | 214 | 210 |

DUNS 21-805-9509 Imp-Exp
## Samuel Taylor Ltd
**(Subsidiary of:** Samuel Taylor Group Ltd)
Unit 91 Arthur Street, Redditch, Worcestershire B98 8JY
**Tel:** 01527 504 910 **Fax:** 01527 500 869
**Web:** www.samueltaylor.co.uk
**Reg No:** 0063351 **VAT No:** 109679929
**Estd:** 1899 Private Limited Company
**Line of Business:** Manufacturers and wholesalers of electrical products
**Export Markets:** E U, Africa, S & S E Asia, Australasia
**Export Sales:** £12,467,998
**Issued Capital:** £7,999
**Principals:** J A Gordon *(Managing)*, R A Gordon *(Commercial)*, Ms J K Gordon
**Co. Secretary:** Richard Pick
**Responsibilities**
**Senior:** Alastair Gordon *(Manager)*, Carl Siviter *(Sales Director)*
**Marketing:** Alastair Gordon *(Manager)*
**Sales:** Alastair Gordon *(Manager)*, Carl Siviter *(Sales Director)*
**HR:** Alastair Gordon *(Manager)*
**US SIC:** 3629 **UK SIC:** 34350
**Auditors:** Nicklin LLP

**Bankers:** Lloyds TSB Bank plc (30-93-66)

| | 31-05-13 | 31-05-12 | 31-05-11 |
|---|---|---|---|
| TO | 16,271,473 | 25,362,317 | 19,240,864 |
| P/L | 105,560 | 1,145,609 | 886,541 |
| NW | 3,753,882 | 3,620,865 | 3,198,362 |
| WC | 1,524,329 | 1,903,171 | 1,048,945 |
| Emp. | 81 | 77 | 76 |

DUNS 42-462-3556

## Samways Fish Merchants & International Transporters Ltd

Gore Cross Business Park, Corbin Way, Bradpole, Bridport, Dorset DT6 3UX
**Tel:** 01308-422201
**Web:** www.samwaysfish.com
**Reg No:** 4449949 **Estd:** 2002 Private Limited Company
**Line of Business:** Fish merchants (wholesale)
**Export Sales:** £5,248,956
**Issued Capital:** £22,660
**Directors:** C A Samways, Ms S J Samways
**Co. Secretary:** Ms Sarah Samways
**Responsibilities**
**Sales:** Catherine Robinson (Accounts Manager)
**US SIC:** 5146 **UK SIC:** 61700

| | 31-08-14 | 31-08-13 | 31-08-12 |
|---|---|---|---|
| TO | 9,060,785 | 10,890,438 | N/A |
| P/L | 124,833 | 55,001 | N/A |
| NW | 685,040 | 681,644 | 654,855 |
| WC | 935,389 | 902,601 | 841,628 |
| Emp. | 71 | 72 | N/A |

DUNS 34-557-2700

## The Samworth Academy

Trenant Road, Leicester, Leicestershire LE2 6UA
**Tel:** 01162780232
**Web:** www.samworthenterpriseacademy.org
**Reg No:** 5367105 **Estd:** 2005 Private Company Limited By Guarantee
**Line of Business:** Schools
**Directors:** T R Stratford, P Drabble
**Co. Secretary:** James Cook
**Responsibilities**
**Senior:** Jo Brodrick (Director), Ann Chandler (Director), Cheryl Crewe (Director), Pat Dubass (Principal), Benjamin Long (Director), Alison Roche (Director), Robert Stretton (Director), Caroline Whitty (Director)
**US SIC:** 8211, 8249
**UK SIC:** 93200, 93300
**Bankers:** HSBC Bank plc (40-35-18)

| | 31-08-13 | 31-08-12 | 31-08-11 |
|---|---|---|---|
| TO | 7,778,188 | 7,644,073 | 6,985,265 |
| P/L | (218,088) | 19,078 | (219,706) |
| NW | 17,850,142 | 18,020,230 | 18,559,152 |
| WC | 483,186 | 282,398 | 242,036 |
| Emp. | 227 | 235 | 232 |

DUNS 49-196-3880

## Samworth Brothers Ltd

(**Subsidiary of:** Samworth Brothers (Holdings) Ltd)
Chetwode House, 1 Samworth Way, Melton Mowbray, Leicestershire LE13 1GA
**Web:** www.samworthbrothers.co.uk
**Reg No:** 3116767 **VAT No:** 728127826
**Estd:** 1896 Private Limited Company
**Line of Business:** Bakers shops
**Trading Style:** Walkers Midshire Foods Walkers & Son, Kettleby Foods Bradgate Bakery, Westward Laboratories, Salad Works Walkers Charnwood Bakery
**Issued Capital:** £5,535
**Directors:** I A Fletcher, M C Samworth, G R Lewis, M F Duddridge, L J Pownall, S M Draisey, Ms A M Barker, Mrs M Lake
**Co. Secretary:** Timothy Barker
**Responsibilities**
**Senior:** Alan Barton (Manager)
**Branches:** Samworth Brothers Ltd, Ratby Road, Leicester, Leicestershire LE3 3JZ
**US SIC:** 6711 **UK SIC:** 83962
**Auditors:** KPMG LLP
**Bankers:** National Westminster Bank Plc (60-08-28)

| | 28-12-13 | 29-12-12 | 31-12-11 |
|---|---|---|---|
| TO | 791,363,000 | 767,205,000 | 744,527,000 |
| P/L | 33,459,000 | 41,443,000 | 43,611,000 |
| NW | 163,102,000 | 161,911,000 | 154,759,000 |
| WC | 110,105,000 | 96,939,000 | 71,663,000 |
| Emp. | 7,482 | 7,372 | 7,320 |

DUNS 21-905-0981

## The Samworth Church Academy

Sherwood Hall Road, Mansfield, Nottinghamshire NG18 2DY
**Tel:** 01623663450
**Web:** www.samworthchurchacademy.co.uk
**Reg No:** 6091123 **Estd:** 2005 Private Company Limited By Guarantee
**Line of Business:** Schools (local authority)
**Directors:** E M Astley-Arlington, S N Garner, Mrs V J Leivers, N Smith, N S Linney, Mrs B Nita, B L Found, M Longdon
**Co. Secretary:** Robert Munro

**Responsibilities**
**Senior:** Tony Eggington (Director), Anthony Gabb (Director), Andrew Longdon (Director), Gwendoline Mountain (Director), Nigel Spraggins (Director), Caroline Whitty (Director)
**Finance:** Marks Robert (Finance Director)
**US SIC:** 8211 **UK SIC:** 93200

| | 31-08-14 | 31-08-13 | 31-08-12 |
|---|---|---|---|
| TO | 6,659,517 | 6,283,781 | 5,866,004 |
| P/L | (130,149) | (418,262) | (414,485) |
| NW | 608,630 | 1,765,150 | 2,030,984 |
| WC | 719,519 | 700,623 | 660,449 |
| Emp. | 149 | 143 | 130 |

DUNS 21-595-6419

## San Carlo

38-40 Granby Street, Leicester, Leicestershire LE1 1DE
**Tel:** 01162519332
**Web:** www.sancarlo.co.uk
**Estd:** 2000
**Line of Business:** Restaurant - italian
**Partners:** G Balduini, F Vassallo
**Responsibilities**
**Senior:** Vito Farro (Branch Manager)
**US SIC:** 5812 **UK SIC:** 66110
**Employees:** 50

DUNS 21-612-5793

## San Lorenzo

22 Beauchamp Place, London SW3 1NH
**Tel:** 02075841074
**Web:** www.sanlorenzolondon.com
**Estd:** 1969 Proprietorship
**Line of Business:** Licensed restaurants
**Proprietor:** L Berni
**Responsibilities**
**Senior:** Mara Berni (Partner)
**US SIC:** 5812 **UK SIC:** 66110
**Employees:** 50

DUNS 54-822-0326

## San Lorenzo Restaurant

22 Beauchamp Place, London SW3 1NH
**Tel:** 02075841074
**Web:** www.sanlorenzo.com
**Estd:** 1964 Partnership
**Line of Business:** Restaurants
**Partners:** Ms M T Berni, L Berni
**Responsibilities**
**Senior:** Domenico Loi (CEO)
**US SIC:** 5812 **UK SIC:** 66110
**Employees:** 50

DUNS 21-121-2116

## Sancta Maria Hospital

Ffynone Road, Swansea, West Glamorgan SA1 6DF
**Tel:** 01792-479040
**Web:** www.sanctamaria.co.uk
**Estd:** 1988
**Line of Business:** Hospitals
**Partners:** M Davies, S Hammond
**Responsibilities**
**Senior:** Ann Palmer (Site Director)
**Marketing:** Ann Palmer (Site Director)
**HR:** Ann Palmer (Site Director)
**Health & Safety:** Ann Palmer (Site Director)
**Purchasing:** Ann Palmer (Site Director)
**US SIC:** 8062 **UK SIC:** 95100
**Employees:** 108

DUNS 23-526-7577

## Sancton Wood School Ltd

(**Subsidiary of:** August Equity Partners Iii A Lp)
1-2 St Pauls Road, Cambridge, Cambridgeshire CB1 2EZ
**Tel:** 01223471703
**Web:** www.sanctonwood.co.uk
**Reg No:** 3525719 **Estd:** 1998 Private Limited Company
**Line of Business:** Primary education
**Issued Capital:** £410
**Directors:** Mrs C A Robertson, T M Milner, Mrs E V Simpson
**Responsibilities**
**Senior:** Richard Settle (Headmaster)
**US SIC:** 8211 **UK SIC:** 93200
**Auditors:** Wilson Sandford (Hove) Ltd

| | 31-08-13 | 31-08-12 | 31-08-11 |
|---|---|---|---|
| TA | 967,965 | 798,820 | 596,389 |
| NW | 683,916 | 493,043 | 300,206 |
| WC | 634,069 | 519,540 | 371,296 |

DUNS 21-322-5886

## Sancton Wood Senior & Infant School

2 St Pauls Road, Cambridge, Cambridgeshire CB1 2EZ
**Tel:** 01223-359488
**Web:** www.sanctonwood.co.uk
**Estd:** 1975 Partnership
**Line of Business:** General secondary education

**Partners:** Miss H Sturdy, D Sturdy, Miss R Atkins
**Responsibilities**
**Senior:** Richard Settle (Head Teacher)
**US SIC:** 8211, 6732
**UK SIC:** 93200, 83100
**Employees:** 50

DUNS 55-057-9395

## Sanctuary Care Property (1) Ltd

Sanctuary House, Chamber Court, Castle Street, Worcester, Worcestershire WR1 3ZQ
**Tel:** 03458 500500
**Reg No:** 0028885IP **Estd:** 1999 Friendly Society
**Line of Business:** Residential care home
**Branches:** Sanctuary Care Property (1) Limited, Heart Of England Housing & Care, Breme House, Bromsgrove, Worcestershire B61 8EF
**US SIC:** 6733 **UK SIC:** 83100
**Bankers:** Barclays Bank Plc (20-00-00)

| | 31-03-14 | 31-03-13 | 31-03-12 |
|---|---|---|---|
| TO | 13,073,000 | 12,316,000 | 11,799,000 |
| P/L | 1,303,000 | 1,013,000 | 617,000 |
| NW | 3,743,000 | 1,884,000 | 1,326,000 |
| WC | 1,368,000 | 534,000 | (59,000) |
| Emp. | 403 | 396 | 377 |

DUNS 21-595-6436

## Sanctuary Housing

Camping Close, Haddenham, Ely, Cambridgeshire CB6 3UA
**Web:** www.sanctuary-housing.co.uk
**Estd:** 2011 Proprietorship
**Line of Business:** Non-charitable social work activities with accommodation
**Proprietor:** E Dillon
**US SIC:** 8321 **UK SIC:** 96111
**Employees:** 91

DUNS 22-610-4024      Exp

## Sanctuary Housing Association

Sanctuary House, Chamber Court, Castle Street, Worcester, Worcestershire WR1 3ZQ
**Fax:** 01905 334958
**Web:** www.sanctuary-housing.co.uk
**Reg No:** 0019059IP **Estd:** 1969 Friendly Society
**Line of Business:** Housing associations societies trusts & co-operatives
**Principals:** N Baldwin (Chairman), C Moule (Financial), D Bennett, J Lander, I Mcdermott, J Doughty, R Mccomb, Ms T Stober
**Co. Secretary:** Ms Sophie Atkinson
**Responsibilities**
**Senior:** Rosemary Crawley (Manager), Victoria Elvidge (Vice Chairman), Debbie Hay (Manager), Rober McComb (Board Member), Nikki Mcdivitt (Manager), Liz Meek (Board Member), Elwyn Roberts (Board Member), Barry Stanford (Manager)
**Marketing:** Lindsay Evans (Group Public Relations Manager), Gareth Holmes (PR Manager), Meghan Zinkewich-Peotti (Neighbourhood Partnerships Man)
**IT:** Martyn Lucking (PC Manager)
**Operations:** Joanne Bain (Business Information Manager), Ian McDermott (Chartered Surveyor)
**Branches:** Sanctuary Housing Association, Avro House, 49 Lancaster Way Business Park, Ely, Cambridgeshire CB6 3NW
**US SIC:** 6531, 6732
**UK SIC:** 83400, 83100
**Auditors:** PricewaterhouseCoopers
**Bankers:** Barclays Bank Plc (20-00-00)

| | 31-03-14 | 31-03-13 | 31-03-12 |
|---|---|---|---|
| TO | 592,300,000 | 474,000,000 | 431,500,000 |
| P/L | 42,300,000 | 72,000,000 | 23,700,000 |
| NW | 752,800,000 | 723,800,000 | 669,000,000 |
| WC | 104,700,000 | 107,500,000 | 1,300,000 |
| Emp. | 8,004 | 6,622 | 5,731 |

DUNS 56-977-3849

## The Sanctuary Ltd

(**Subsidiary of:** The Sanctuary Spa Group Ltd)
12 Floral Street, London WC2E 9DH
**Tel:** 08455214567 **Fax:** 08700630303
**Web:** www.thesanctuary.co.uk
**Reg No:** 2853755 **Estd:** 1993 Private Limited Company
**Line of Business:** Other retail sale in specialised stores not elsewhere classified
**Issued Capital:** £2
**Directors:** J Lang, B H Leigh
**Co. Secretary:** Martyn Campbell
**Responsibilities**
**Senior:** Isabel Blinder (Food & Beverage Manager)
**Marketing:** Emma Keyworth (Marketing Manager)
**US SIC:** 5999 **UK SIC:** 65600

| | 31-05-13 | 31-05-12 | 31-05-11 |
|---|---|---|---|
| TA | 2 | 2 | 2 |
| NW | 2 | 2 | 2 |

DUNS 21-153-7285

## Sanctuary Maintenance Contractors Ltd

(**Subsidiary of:** Sanctuary Housing Association)
Chamber Court, Castle Street, Worcester, Worcestershire WR1 3ZQ
**Reg No:** 6822831 **Estd:** 2009 Private Limited Company
**Line of Business:** Property maintenance services
**Issued Capital:** £1
**Directors:** I J Mcdermott, R D Barclay, D J Bennett, S J Wood, C J Moule
**Co. Secretary:** Ms Sophie Atkinson
**Responsibilities**
**Senior:** Dennis Evans (Manager)
**US SIC:** 6519 **UK SIC:** 85000
**Bankers:** Barclays Bank Plc (20-00-00)

| | 31-03-14 | 31-03-13 | 31-03-12 |
|---|---|---|---|
| TO | 112,924,000 | 84,392,640 | 2,815,222 |
| P/L | 698,000 | 265,000 | 276,557 |
| NW | 514,000 | 231,702 | 1 |
| WC | 514,000 | 231,702 | (4,206) |
| Emp. | 1,260 | 1,035 | N/A |

DUNS 21-782-6454

## Sanctuary Midlands

Knight House 2 4, Woodhouse Street, Stoke-On-Trent, Staffordshire ST4 1EJ
**Tel:** 08000234503
**Web:** www.housing.org.uk
**Estd:** 1987 Partnership
**Line of Business:** Housing associations societies trusts & co-operatives
**Partners:** D Bennet, L Bradshaw
**US SIC:** 8321 **UK SIC:** 96111
**Employees:** 100

DUNS 21-132-7978

## Sanctuary (North West) Housing Association Ltd

Marybone House, 2 Marybone, Liverpool, Merseyside L3 2BY
**Tel:** 08001313348 **Fax:** 01512274991
**Web:** www.sanctuary-housingnorthwest.co.uk
**Reg No:** 0019012IP **Estd:** 1969 Friendly Society
**Line of Business:** Housing associations societies trusts & co-operatives
**Trading Style:** Sanctuary Housing
**Principals:** Ms H Gardner (Chairman), I Mcdermott, M M Morris, Ms J Riley, N Warren, Ms S Anderson
**Responsibilities**
**Senior:** Ian McDermott (Director), Julie Mcnally (Executive), Andrea Murray (Executive), Geoffrey Redhead (Chief Executive)
**Finance:** Lynda Beck (Income Officer), Karen Cheung (Senior Manager Income)
**IT:** Kelly Harris (Allocations and Support Assist)
**Facilities:** Sasha Buckley (Resident Involvement Assistant), Ria Burns (Housing Officer), Vicky Jemson (Allocations Officer)
**Branches:** SANCTUARY (NORTH WEST) 36 Bentinck Street, Runcorn WA7 1ES
**US SIC:** 6531 **UK SIC:** 83400
**Auditors:** PKF (UK) LLP
**Bankers:** Barclays Bank Plc (20-67-59)

| | 31-03-14 | 31-03-13 | 31-03-11 |
|---|---|---|---|
| TO | 17,021,000 | 17,844,000 | 12,792,809 |
| P/L | (1,371,000) | (5,432,000) | 545,494 |
| NW | 5,239,000 | (996,000) | 20,927,517 |
| WC | 12,012,000 | 2,790,000 | 4,107,186 |
| Emp. | 93 | 140 | N/A |

DUNS 51-656-6374

## Sanctuary Personnel Ltd

Sanctuary Social Care, Ipswich, Suffolk IP4 1AX
**Tel:** 01473280844 **Fax:** 08000468103
**Web:** www.sanctuarypersonnel.com
**Reg No:** 5972910 **VAT No:** 900452370
**Estd:** 2006 Private Limited Company
**Line of Business:** Labour recruitment and provision of personnel
**Issued Capital:** £1,122
**Directors:** D A Hill, J Rook, Mrs P A Mcpherson
**US SIC:** 7361 **UK SIC:** 83954
**Auditors:** Scrutton Bland

| | 31-10-13 | 31-10-12 | 31-10-11 |
|---|---|---|---|
| TO | 61,018,021 | 41,364,866 | 36,390,757 |
| P/L | 4,019,863 | 3,247,205 | 2,019,806 |
| NW | 8,953,824 | 6,795,147 | 4,437,240 |
| WC | 8,745,780 | 6,781,625 | 5,382,695 |
| Emp. | 112 | 86 | 73 |

DUNS 21-410-4680

## Sanctuary Shaftesbury

Estuary House, Peninsula Park, Rydon Lane, Exeter, Devon EX2 7XE
**Tel:** 08456021214
**Web:** www.sanctuary-housing.co.uk
**Estd:** 1990
**Line of Business:** Housing associations societies trusts & co-operatives

**Responsibilities**
**Senior:** Richard Heeley *(General Manager)*
**US SIC:** 8321 **UK SIC:** 96111
**Employees:** 70

DUNS 21-583-2414
## Sanctum Soho Hotel London
20 Warwick Street, London W1B 5NF
**Tel:** 02072926100
**Web:** www.sanctumsoho.com
**Estd:** 2011 Proprietorship
**Line of Business:** Hotels
**Proprietor:** S Carrodus
**US SIC:** 7011 **UK SIC:** 66500
**Employees:** 70

DUNS 29-543-8287
## Sand Le Mere Caravan Park Ltd
(**Subsidiary of:** Kings Park Capital (Jersey) Limited)
Southfield Lane, Main Street, Tunstall, Hull, North Humberside HU12 0JF
**Tel:** 01964670403
**Web:** www.sand-le-mere.co.uk
**Reg No:** 1910554 **Estd:** 1985 Private Limited Company
**Line of Business:** Camping site operators
**Issued Capital:** £300,000
**Directors:** S J Williams, S J Elliott, A S Howe
**Co. Secretary:** Simon Elliott
**US SIC:** 7033, 7399
**UK SIC:** 66701, 83954
**Auditors:** Rushtons
**Bankers:** National Westminster Bank Plc (01-01-35)

| | 31-12-13 | 31-12-12 | 31-12-11 |
|---|---|---|---|
| TO | 4,905,071 | 4,615,748 | 3,578,772 |
| P/L | 965,631 | 785,189 | 563,268 |
| NW | 5,581,440 | 4,805,475 | 3,926,948 |
| WC | (369,409) | (287,858) | (699,879) |

DUNS 28-905-6707
## Sandal Motors (Bayern) Ltd
(**Subsidiary of:** Findpath Ltd)
Jewsbury Road, Wakefield, West Yorkshire WF1 1RE
**Tel:** 01924433533 **Fax:** 01924384064
**Web:** www.sandalbmw.co.uk
**Reg No:** 1381018 **VAT No:** 518290151
**Estd:** 1978 Private Limited Company
**Line of Business:** Car dealers (new & used)
**Trading Style:** Sandal B M W
**Issued Capital:** £50,000
**Principals:** D Bosomworth *(Managing)*, J T Carter
**Co. Secretary:** Timothy Simons
**Responsibilities**
**Senior:** Lee Ogden *(Parts Manager)*
**Marketing:** Greg Stainton *(Marketing Manager)*
**Sales:** Matthew Crowhirst *(Sales Manager)*
**Branches:** Sandal Motors (Bayern) Ltd, Dewsbury Road, Wakefield, West Yorkshire WF2 9BE
**US SIC:** 5511, 5521, 5531
**UK SIC:** 65100
**Auditors:** Ernst & Young LLP
**Bankers:** The Royal Bank Of Scotland Plc (16-23-37)

| | 31-12-13 | 31-12-12 | 31-12-11 |
|---|---|---|---|
| TO | 53,326,442 | 47,738,051 | 42,294,914 |
| P/L | 624,672 | 540,083 | 33,744 |
| NW | 4,941,087 | 4,626,919 | 4,304,512 |
| WC | 2,470,347 | 2,236,463 | 2,092,844 |
| Emp. | 105 | 103 | 106 |

DUNS 21-028-1572 **Imp**
## S&B Herba Foods Ltd
(**Subsidiary of:** Ebro Foods Sa)
Berwick House, Orpington, Kent BR6 0EL
**Tel:** 01689878700
**Web:** www.sbhf.com
**Reg No:** 0156737 **VAT No:** 863963089
**Estd:** 1919 Private Limited Company
**Line of Business:** Import and export agents
**Export Sales:** £2,316,000
**Trading Style:** S B Herba Foods
**Issued Capital:** £408
**Directors:** R L Holben, A H Callejas, R A Lopez Relimpio, F H Callejas
**Co. Secretary:** Peter Cattaneo
**Responsibilities**
**Senior:** Amanda Haynes *(General Manager)*, Mark Malone *(General Manager, Liverpool Fac)*
**HR:** Clare Syers *(Human Resources Manager)*
**Operations:** Piers Stevens *(Product Manager)*
**Branches:** S&b Herba Foods Ltd, 7 West Pallant, Chichester, West Sussex PO19 1TD
**US SIC:** 4712, 0729
**UK SIC:** 77002, 01003
**Auditors:** Deloitte LLP

**Bankers:** Barclays Bank Plc (20-00-00)

| | 31-12-13 | 31-12-12 | 31-12-11 |
|---|---|---|---|
| TO | 76,661,000 | 79,429,000 | 80,593,000 |
| P/L | 4,082,000 | 5,166,000 | 6,403,000 |
| NW | 41,364,000 | 37,267,000 | 33,518,000 |
| WC | 38,450,000 | 34,663,000 | 29,960,000 |
| Emp. | 95 | 95 | 96 |

DUNS 21-693-9412
## Sandbach High School & Sixth Form College
Middlewich Road, Sandbach, Cheshire CW11 3NT
**Tel:** 01270765031
**Web:** www.sandhigh.cheshire.sch.uk
**Reg No:** 7404747 **Estd:** 2010 Private Company Limited By Guarantee
**Line of Business:** General secondary education
**Directors:** Mrs J Bailey, G W Heath, Mrs S Joyce, Mrs M A Hoole, T P Jones, Ms J Astins, Mrs K Butler, Mrs J Flaherty
**Responsibilities**
**Senior:** Alan Bell *(Director)*, Alan Bradley *(Director)*, Ella Brett *(Director)*, Deborah Broad *(Director)*, Maxwell Leese *(Director)*, Brian Mcgivern *(Director)*, Stephanie Owen *(Director)*, Joanne Wilkins *(Director)*, Dig Woodvine *(Director)*
**Marketing:** Jane Street *(Business Manager)*
**US SIC:** 8211 **UK SIC:** 93200
**Bankers:** Lloyds TSB Bank plc (30-99-65)

| | 31-08-13 | 31-08-12 | 31-08-11 |
|---|---|---|---|
| TO | 7,163,000 | 6,789,000 | 21,297,000 |
| P/L | (279,000) | (255,000) | 14,001,000 |
| NW | 14,155,000 | 14,362,000 | 14,897,000 |
| WC | 381,000 | 342,000 | 390,000 |
| Emp. | 204 | 139 | 140 |

DUNS 21-106-2394
## Sandbach School
Crewe Road, Sandbach, Cheshire CW11 3NS
**Tel:** 01270758870
**Web:** www.sandbachschool.cheshire.sch.uk
**Reg No:** 6486255 **Estd:** 2008 Private Company Limited By Guarantee
**Line of Business:** Schools (local authority)
**Directors:** J D Cargill, Ms P G Kelly, Ms S A Kennerley, C J Tyler, S J Robertson, M F Roberts, B Gribbin, P J Sherrat
**Co. Secretary:** Ms Deborah Torjussen
**Responsibilities**
**Senior:** Sarah Burns *(Head Teacher)*, Emily Hankey *(Director)*, Stephen Hodgkinson *(Director)*, Shena Lewington *(Director)*, Clare Longden *(Director)*, Gillian Merry *(Director)*, Philip Michell *(Director)*, Chris Sheardown *(Director)*, Dominic Surry *(Director)*
**Marketing:** Sarah Burns *(Head Teacher)*
**US SIC:** 8211, 8249
**UK SIC:** 93200, 93300
**Bankers:** Lloyds TSB Bank plc (30-12-59)

| | 31-08-14 | 31-08-13 | 31-08-12 |
|---|---|---|---|
| TO | 6,814,768 | 6,864,197 | 7,036,430 |
| P/L | (98,489) | 91,185 | 530,535 |
| NW | 5,931,042 | 6,116,348 | 5,907,511 |
| WC | (137,122) | (148,986) | (251,029) |
| Emp. | 138 | 162 | 158 |

DUNS 21-724-6164
## Sandbanks Hotel Ltd
15 Banks Road, Poole, Dorset BH13 7PS
**Tel:** 01202708283
**Web:** www.thewatersportsacademy.com
**Reg No:** 0556842 **VAT No:** 619671514
**Estd:** 2003 Private Limited Company
**Line of Business:** Watersport activities
**Trading Style:** Haven Sports & Leisure Club
**Issued Capital:** £200
**Principals:** J G Butterworth *(Managing)*, Ms E J Adlem
**Co. Secretary:** Joy Barcellos
**Responsibilities**
**Senior:** John Belk *(General Manager)*, Dave Hartswell *(Manager)*, Philippa Thompson *(General Manager)*
**US SIC:** 7999 **UK SIC:** 97913
**Auditors:** Schofields
**Bankers:** Lloyds TSB Bank plc (30-12-05)

| | 31-03-14 | 31-03-13 | 31-03-11 |
|---|---|---|---|
| TO | 7,505,207 | 8,276,068 | 6,296,604 |
| P/L | 391,651 | 3,834,007 | 485,983 |
| NW | 14,179,698 | 13,264,725 | 10,130,586 |
| WC | 4,715,401 | 3,662,233 | 271,771 |
| Emp. | 176 | 167 | 155 |

DUNS 73-434-7979
## Sandberg Llp
40 Grosvenor Gardens, London SW1W 0EB
**Tel:** 020-7565-7000
**Web:** www.sandberg.co.uk
**Reg No:** 0304229OC **VAT No:** 239135757
**Estd:** 2003
**Line of Business:** Engineering consultative and design activities
**Branches:** Sandberg Llp, Station Road, Chepstow, Gwent NP16 5YL
**US SIC:** 7399 **UK SIC:** 83954

**Bankers:** National Westminster Bank Plc (50-41-01)

| | 30-04-14 | 30-04-13 | 30-04-12 |
|---|---|---|---|
| TO | 6,313,522 | 5,644,220 | 5,293,562 |
| P/L | 576,939 | 335,403 | 336,026 |
| NW | 721,939 | 524,403 | 306,026 |
| WC | 1,173,310 | 911,207 | 1,113,076 |
| Emp. | 91 | 85 | 78 |

DUNS 23-890-1933
## Sandco F.P.S. Ltd
South Tyne Mill, Fourstones, Hexham, Northumberland NE46 3SD
**Tel:** 01434-602444 **Fax:** 01434607046
**Web:** www.fourstonespapermill.co.uk
**Reg No:** 3881192 **Estd:** 1999 Private Limited Company
**Line of Business:** Other business activities not elsewhere classified
**Issued Capital:** £2
**Director:** Mrs P Duxbury
**Co. Secretary:** Peter Duxbury
**US SIC:** 7399, 6711
**UK SIC:** 83954, 83962
**Bankers:** National Westminster Bank Plc (53-50-46)

| | 31-03-14 | 31-03-13 | 31-03-12 |
|---|---|---|---|
| TO | 20,173,815 | 18,330,892 | 16,010,345 |
| P/L | 1,263,214 | 718,592 | 163,100 |
| NW | 4,871,932 | 4,282,703 | 3,885,883 |
| WC | (765,616) | (1,542,002) | (459,393) |
| Emp. | 117 | 109 | 105 |

DUNS 22-627-2839 **Imp-Exp**
## Sanden International (Europe) Ltd
(**Subsidiary of:** Sanden Corporation)
Hampshire International Business Park, Crockford Lane, Chineham, Basingstoke, Hampshire RG24 8WH
**Tel:** 01256-708888
**Web:** www.sanden-europe.com
**Reg No:** 1432637 **VAT No:** 314595455
**Estd:** 1979 Private Limited Company
**Line of Business:** Air/heating/refrigeration equipment mfrs
**Export Markets:** Other EU Member states, Other
**Export Sales:** £380,456,000
**Issued Capital:** £17,685,142
**Directors:** R Ushikubo, O Campy, E Koller, T Shimizu, Y Takeuchi, S Ichikawa
**Co. Secretary:** Douglas Black
**Responsibilities**
**Senior:** Maria W ensch-Guaraldi *(Director)*
**US SIC:** 3585, 5084
**UK SIC:** 32841, 61490
**Auditors:** KPMG LLP

| | 31-03-14 | 31-03-13 | 31-03-12 |
|---|---|---|---|
| TO | 426,160,000 | 421,171,000 | 449,894,000 |
| P/L | 2,721,000 | 17,488,000 | 14,571,000 |
| NW | 76,953,000 | 77,778,000 | 76,207,000 |
| WC | 65,317,000 | 42,484,000 | 16,156,000 |
| Emp. | 117 | 117 | 38 |

DUNS 21-584-1618
## The Sanderling
Glasgow Airport Airside, Abbotsinch, Paisley, Renfrewshire PA3 2ST
**Tel:** 01418484877
**Web:** www.jdwetherspoon.co.uk
**Estd:** 2011
**Line of Business:** Public house
**Proprietor:** B Martin
**US SIC:** 5813 **UK SIC:** 66200
**Employees:** 50

DUNS 21-826-4042 **Imp-Exp**
## Sanders & Sanders Ltd
Spencer Road, Rushden, Northamptonshire NN10 6AE
**Tel:** 01933-353066
**Web:** www.sanders-uk.com
**Reg No:** 0343139 **VAT No:** 120038823
**Estd:** 1873 Private Limited Company
**Line of Business:** Manufacturers of footwear
**Export Markets:** Middle East, Far East, E U, Africa
**Export Sales:** £4,372,771
**Issued Capital:** £20,800
**Principals:** G E Sanders *(Chairman and Managing)*, H B Sanders *(Managing)*, L R Whitmore
**Co. Secretary:** Mrs Susan Whatton
**Responsibilities**
**Senior:** David Overton *(Manager)*
**Finance:** David Overton *(Manager)*
**IT:** David Overton *(Manager)*
**Branches:** Sanders & Sanders Ltd, Unit 3 Wilford Bridge Road, Woodbridge, Suffolk IP12 1RB
**US SIC:** 3149 **UK SIC:** 45100
**Auditors:** Grant Thornton UK LLP
**Bankers:** National Westminster Bank Plc (54-41-05)

| | 28-02-14 | 28-02-13 | 29-02-12 |
|---|---|---|---|
| TO | 5,973,731 | 5,364,079 | 4,566,715 |
| P/L | 535,286 | 449,434 | 288,928 |
| NW | 1,632,235 | 1,337,119 | 1,057,991 |
| WC | 1,419,595 | 1,153,166 | 889,503 |

DUNS 73-319-1592
## Sanders Coaches Ltd
Heath Drive, Holt, Norfolk NR25 6ER
**Tel:** 01263-712800 **Fax:** 01263-710920
**Web:** www.sanderscoaches.com
**Reg No:** 4592984 **Estd:** 2002 Private Limited Company
**Line of Business:** Other scheduled passenger land transport not elsewhere classified
**Issued Capital:** £400
**Director:** P F Sanders
**Co. Secretary:** Charles Sanders
**Responsibilities**
**Senior:** Gladys Sanders *(Partner)*
**Finance:** Carole Willimott *(Administration Manager)*
**Marketing:** Carole Willimott *(Administration Manager)*
**Admin:** Carole Willimott *(Administration Manager)*
**HR:** Carole Willimott *(Administration Manager)*
**Operations:** Carole Willimott *(Administration Manager)*
**Fleet:** Nigel Trowman *(Transport Manager)*
**US SIC:** 4119 **UK SIC:** 72200

| | 30-04-14 | 30-04-13 | 30-04-12 |
|---|---|---|---|
| TA | 3,015,351 | 2,921,805 | 3,109,075 |
| NW | 1,150,656 | 1,249,427 | 1,297,538 |
| WC | (243,891) | (128,175) | 74,610 |

DUNS 21-754-2559
## Sanders Gardenworld
Bristol Road, Brent Knoll, Highbridge, Somerset TA9 4HJ
**Tel:** 08442885188
**Web:** www.thegardencentregroup.co.uk
**Estd:** 2000 Partnership
**Line of Business:** Other retail sale in specialised stores not elsewhere classified
**Partners:** A Jenkinson, N Marshall, R Kozlowski, D Pierpoint
**Responsibilities**
**Senior:** Hedley Triggs *(Manager)*
**Facilities:** Mervyn Rawlings *(Facilities Manager)*
**US SIC:** 5999 **UK SIC:** 65600
**Employees:** 100

DUNS 29-874-6694 **Imp-Exp**
## Sanders Polyfilms Ltd
Westfields Trading Estate, Hereford, Herefordshire HR4 9NS
**Fax:** 01432-357409
**Web:** www.theshrinkfilmcompany.com
**Reg No:** 2077853 **VAT No:** 549677874
**Estd:** 1986 Private Limited Company
**Line of Business:** Packaging equipment
**Export Markets:** E U
**Export Sales:** £6,951,851
**Issued Capital:** £1,625,000
**Principals:** B G Davies *(Chairman)*, A R Aftalion *(Managing)*, A G Struthers *(Sales)*, Ms S Mohan
**Co. Secretary:** Ms Elizabeth Fairclough
**US SIC:** 3551 **UK SIC:** 32441
**Auditors:** Baker Tilly
**Bankers:** National Westminster Bank Plc (53-50-41)

| | 31-12-13 | 31-12-12 | 31-12-11 |
|---|---|---|---|
| TO | 24,764,271 | 26,508,186 | 29,082,468 |
| P/L | 330,310 | 478,123 | 228,722 |
| NW | 2,762,738 | 2,360,963 | 2,022,297 |
| WC | 1,109,783 | 944,002 | 696,699 |
| Emp. | 94 | 97 | 101 |

DUNS 73-709-7563
## Sanderson Group Plc
Sanderson House, Manor Road, Coventry, West Midlands CV1 2GF
**Tel:** 03331231400
**Web:** www.sanderson.com
**Reg No:** 4968444 **Estd:** 1999 Public Limited Company
**Line of Business:** Computer software (development)
**Issued Capital:** £4,367,595
**Directors:** C Winn, P E Kelly, J C Paterson, I Newcombe
**Co. Secretary:** Adrian Frost
**Responsibilities**
**Senior:** Paul Bywater *(Managing Director, Manufacturi)*, David O'Byrne *(Group Projects Director)*
**Operations:** David O'Byrne *(Group Projects Director)*
**US SIC:** 7379, 7372
**UK SIC:** 83940
**Auditors:** Grant Thornton UK LLP

| | 30-09-14 | 30-09-13 | 30-09-12 |
|---|---|---|---|
| TO | 16,411,000 | 13,828,000 | 13,374,000 |
| P/L | 1,916,000 | 1,943,000 | 1,481,000 |
| NW | (2,697,000) | (2,295,000) | (2,374,000) |
| WC | 2,462,000 | 456,000 | 320,000 |
| Emp. | 193 | 154 | 146 |

DUNS 21-612-5662
## Sanderson Hotel
50 Berners Street, London W1T 3NG
**Tel:** 02073001400
**Web:** www.sandersonlondon.com
**Estd:** 2003 Partnership
**Line of Business:** Hotels
**Partners:** D Bowd, Miss A Golden
**Responsibilities**
**Senior:** Fakirahmed Kaldane *(Manager)*
**Marketing:** Fiona Morgan *(Senior Marketing Executive)*
**IT:** Darrell Spencer *(Regional IT Director)*
**US SIC:** 7299 **UK SIC:** 98902
**Employees:** 105

DUNS 77-479-7393
## Sanderson Logistics Ltd
Poplar Way, Catcliffe, Rotherham, South Yorkshire S60 5TR
**Tel:** 01709373715
**Web:** www.whitbysrestaurant.co.uk
**Reg No:** 2968972 **Estd:** 1994 Private Limited Company
**Line of Business:** Restaurant - american
**Issued Capital:** £1
**Directors:** C Winn, A D Frost
**Co. Secretary:** Mark Adamson
**Responsibilities**
**Senior:** James Foers *(Proprietor)*
**Branches:** Sanderson Logistics Ltd, 3A Heron Wharf, Heron Road, Belfast, Belfast BT3 9LE
**US SIC:** 5812 **UK SIC:** 66110
**Auditors:** Grant Thornton UK LLP

| | 30-09-13 | 30-09-12 | 30-09-11 |
|---|---|---|---|
| TA | 1 | 1 | 1 |
| NW | 1 | 1 | 1 |

DUNS 23-749-5358 Exp
## Sanderson Ltd
(**Subsidiary of:** Sanderson Group Plc)
720 Aztec West, Bristol, Avon BS32 4UD
**Tel:** 01454892500
**Web:** www.sanderson.com
**Reg No:** 3743507 **Estd:** 1973 Private Limited Company
**Line of Business:** Other computer related activities
**Issued Capital:** £2,100,002
**Director:** C P Bywater
**Co. Secretary:** Adrian Frost
**Responsibilities**
**Senior:** Brian Dewis *(Manager)*, P Oldershaw *(Manager)*
**US SIC:** 7379 **UK SIC:** 83940
**Auditors:** Grant Thornton UK LLP
**Bankers:** The Royal Bank Of Scotland Plc (16-12-21)

| | 30-09-13 | 30-09-12 | 30-09-11 |
|---|---|---|---|
| TO | 6,123,000 | 5,854,000 | 5,899,000 |
| P/L | 1,187,000 | 127,000 | (39,000) |
| NW | (1,444,000) | (2,899,000) | (3,027,000) |
| WC | 11,092,000 | 9,017,000 | 7,932,000 |
| Emp. | 63 | 60 | 58 |

DUNS 73-721-9618
## Sanderson Recruitment Plc
(**Subsidiary of:** Resource Solutions Group P L C)
First Floor Clifton Down House, Bristol, Avon BS8 2NH
**Tel:** 01179-706666
**Web:** www.sandersonplc.com
**Reg No:** 2919156 **Estd:** 1975 Public Limited Company
**Line of Business:** Labour recruitment and provision of personnel
**Trading Style:** The Resource Solution Group
**Issued Capital:** £50,000
**Principals:** K W Dawe *(Managing)*, N Walrond
**Co. Secretary:** Neil Pollinger
**Responsibilities**
**Senior:** Sarah Pitkin *(Business Director)*
**Finance:** Sarah Pitkin *(Business Director)*
**IT:** Lawrence Harris *(Computer Manager)*
**HR:** Denise Gywther *(Head of HR)*, Sarah Pitkin *(Business Director)*
**Health & Safety:** Sarah Pitkin *(Business Director)*
**Facilities:** Sarah Pitkin *(Business Director)*
**US SIC:** 7361 **UK SIC:** 83954
**Auditors:** Robson Taylor LLP
**Bankers:** National Westminster Bank Plc (56-00-05)

| | 30-06-14 | 30-06-13 | 30-06-12 |
|---|---|---|---|
| TO | 86,690,000 | 87,388,000 | 71,215,940 |
| P/L | 16,000 | 16,000 | 26,002 |
| NW | 842,000 | 834,000 | 814,264 |
| WC | 842,000 | 834,000 | 814,264 |
| Emp. | 65 | 89 | 85 |

DUNS 57-892-0316
## Sanderson Townend Ltd
18-24 Grey Street, Newcastle-Upon-Tyne, Tyne and Wear NE1 6AD
**Tel:** 0191-261-2681
**Web:** www.sw.co.uk
**Reg No:** 2903380 **Estd:** 1994 Private Limited Company
**Line of Business:** Architectural woodwork
**Trading Style:** Sanderson Weatherall Llt
**Issued Capital:** £2
**Director:** C H Noble
**Co. Secretary:** Martin Archer
**Branches:** Sanderson Townend Ltd, Bede House, All Saints Business Centre, Newcastle Upon Tyne, Tyne and Wear NE1 2ES
**US SIC:** 8911 **UK SIC:** 83701

| | 31-03-14 | 31-03-13 | 31-03-12 |
|---|---|---|---|
| TA | 2 | 2 | 2 |
| NW | 2 | 2 | 2 |

DUNS 64-107-3200
## Sanderson Watts Associates Ltd
(**Subsidiary of:** Swa Consultants Ltd)
100 Chapel Lane, Wigan, Lancashire WN3 4HG
**Tel:** 01942491777
**Web:** www.sandersonwatts.com
**Reg No:** 4107494 **Estd:** 2000 Private Limited Company
**Line of Business:** Structural consultants
**Issued Capital:** £47,922
**Directors:** E C Webb, B A Adeyefa
**Co. Secretary:** Edward Webb
**Responsibilities**
**Senior:** John Bousfield *(Manager)*, Christine Bousfield *(Manager)*, Christine Harris *(Manager)*
**Admin:** Alicia Bennett *(Office Manager)*
**Health & Safety:** Alicia Bennett *(Office Manager)*
**US SIC:** 6711 **UK SIC:** 83962
**Auditors:** Fairhurst

| | 30-06-14 | 30-06-13 | 30-06-12 |
|---|---|---|---|
| TO | N/A | N/A | 4,736,067 |
| P/L | N/A | N/A | 653,606 |
| NW | 2,718,102 | 2,302,200 | 2,063,275 |
| WC | 2,658,721 | 2,291,912 | 2,104,375 |
| Emp. | N/A | N/A | 24 |

DUNS 73-609-4447
## Sanderson Weatherall Group Ltd
25 Wellington Street, Leeds, West Yorkshire LS1 4WG
**Fax:** 01132216200
**Web:** www.sandersonweatherall.co.uk
**Reg No:** 4870380 **Estd:** 2003 Private Limited Company
**Line of Business:** Real estate agencies
**Issued Capital:** £1,071,005
**Directors:** S P Heather, C M Tucker, P B Kenny, I R Naylor, T A Kelly, R M Farr, W R Tubman, M D Hardy
**Co. Secretary:** Martin Archer
**Responsibilities**
**Senior:** Neil Bss *(Partner - Asset Advisory & Rec)*, Adam Burkinshaw *(Partner)*, Lesley Charlton *(Manager)*, Robert Dagwell *(Partner)*, Bob Fletcher *(Partner)*, Peter Heron *(Partner)*, Graham Isle *(Partner)*, Stephen Jefferies *(Partner)*, Matthew Lawrence *(Partner)*, Matthew Midwinter *(Director)*, David Rastrick *(Director)*, Mark Swiers *(Partner)*, Diana Warr *(Partner)*
**Finance:** Yvonne Gilmore *(Accounts Manager)*, Janet Wallis *(Accounts Manager)*
**Marketing:** Timothy Catterall *(Sales & Marketing Manager)*, Hayley McMillan *(Marketing Manager)*
**Sales:** Timothy Catterall *(Sales & Marketing Manager)*
**Admin:** Tim Carter *(Office Executive)*
**HR:** Marnie Smith *(Personnel Manager)*, Kay Vaughan-Payne *(HR Manager)*
**Health & Safety:** John Peckett *(Health & Safety Officer)*
**Operations:** Liz Mcloughlin *(Senior Surveyor)*
**Engineering:** Neil Bss *(Partner - Asset Advisory & Rec)*
**Branches:** Sanderson Weatherall Group Ltd, Caxton House, London Road, Derby, Derbyshire DE24 8UP
**US SIC:** 6531 **UK SIC:** 83400
**Auditors:** Baker Tilly U K Audit LLP

| | 31-03-14 | 31-03-13 | 31-03-12 |
|---|---|---|---|
| TO | 14,581,477 | 13,288,559 | 13,148,186 |
| P/L | 263,753 | (872,073) | 209,524 |
| NW | (151,812) | (764,225) | 854,190 |
| WC | 1,656,695 | 1,393,397 | 2,241,711 |
| Emp. | 215 | 220 | 222 |

DUNS 21-160-1462
## Sanderson Weatherall Llp
25 Wellington Street, Leeds, West Yorkshire LS1 4WG
**Tel:** 01133696000
**Web:** www.sandersonweatherall.com
**Reg No:** 0344770OC **VAT No:** 945674483
**Estd:** 2009
**Line of Business:** Surveyors and valuers
**Responsibilities**
**Senior:** Timothy Catterall *(Designated Limited Liability P)*, Robert Dagwell *(Non-designated Limited Liabili)*, Chris Deacon *(Non-designated Limited Liabili)*, David Downing *(Non-designated Limited Liabili)*, David Fairley *(Non-designated Limited Liabili)*, David Fawcett *(Non-designated Limited Liabili)*, Peter Heron *(Non-designated Limited Liabili)*, Stephen Jefferies *(Non-designated Limited Liabili)*, David Rastrick *(Designated Limited Liability P)*, Adrian Rich *(Non-designated Limited Liabili)*, Mark Swiers *(Designated Limited Liability P)*
**US SIC:** 8911 **UK SIC:** 83701
**Auditors:** Baker Tilly UK Audit LLP
**Bankers:** National Westminster Bank Plc (60-60-05)

| | 31-03-14 | 31-03-13 | 31-03-12 |
|---|---|---|---|
| TO | 14,581,477 | 13,288,559 | 13,148,186 |
| NW | (1,002,313) | (1,109,136) | (525,139) |
| WC | 1,919,445 | 1,875,232 | 3,161,663 |
| Emp. | 215 | 220 | 171 |

DUNS 21-779-5407
## Sandgate Primary School
Coolinge Lane, Folkestone, Kent CT20 3QU
**Tel:** 01303257280
**Web:** www.sandgateprimary.co.uk
**Estd:** 2011 Proprietorship
**Line of Business:** Schools (local authority)
**Proprietor:** Mrs H Tait
**US SIC:** 8211 **UK SIC:** 93200
**Employees:** 65

DUNS 21-490-3838
## Sandhall Residential Nursing Home
Sandhall Drive, Goole, North Humberside DN14 5HY
**Tel:** 01405-765132
**Web:** www.mimosahealthcare.com
**Estd:** 1996 Partnership
**Line of Business:** Rest and retirement homes
**Partners:** A Musurri, Mrs J Musurri
**Responsibilities**
**Senior:** Joanne Coolledge *(Manager)*, Yan Huang *(Manager)*, Pauline Mountford *(Manager)*
**US SIC:** 8321 **UK SIC:** 96111
**Employees:** 53

DUNS 34-799-1247
## Sandhata Technologies Ltd
Synegis House, 21 Crockhamwell Road, Woodley, Reading, Berkshire RG5 3LE
**Tel:** 02071291190
**Web:** www.sandhata.com
**Reg No:** 5599334 **Estd:** 2005 Private Limited Company
**Line of Business:** Computer software (development)
**Issued Capital:** £470
**Directors:** S B Vundavilli, S C Alluri, K Narayanan, K C Kalakudiah Chelladurai, G Thornhill
**Co. Secretary:** Satyanarayana Vundavilli
**US SIC:** 7379, 7372, 7374
**UK SIC:** 83940

| | 31-03-14 | 31-03-13 | 31-03-12 |
|---|---|---|---|
| TA | 264,628 | 597,267 | 548,550 |
| NW | 119,947 | 222,444 | 183,758 |
| WC | 111,083 | 220,332 | 178,022 |

DUNS 77-022-5159
## Sandhill Park Ltd
10a Middle Street, Taunton, Somerset TA1 1SH
**Tel:** 01823-257192
**Web:** www.sandhillpark.com
**Reg No:** 2664610 **Estd:** 1991 Private Limited Company
**Line of Business:** Other letting of own property
**Issued Capital:** £506,875
**Directors:** S V Fineberg, P F Fineberg, D Fineberg
**Co. Secretary:** Ms Sylvia Fineberg
**US SIC:** 6519 **UK SIC:** 85000

| | 30-06-14 | 30-06-13 | 30-06-12 |
|---|---|---|---|
| TA | 8,476,942 | 8,224,218 | 8,238,005 |
| NW | 8,022,754 | 7,734,791 | 7,794,374 |
| WC | 8,021,570 | 7,733,212 | 7,792,005 |

DUNS 21-744-6712
## Sandhills East Ltd.
3rd Floor, 1 Ashley Road, Altrincham, Cheshire WA14 2DT
**Tel:** 08456475555
**Web:** www.sandhillseast.co.uk
**Reg No:** 7768642 **Estd:** 2011 Private Limited Company
**Line of Business:** Newspapers publishing
**Issued Capital:** £10,000
**Director:** S T Peed
**Co. Secretary:** Oakwood Corporate Secretary Limi
**US SIC:** 2711 **UK SIC:** 47512

| | 28-12-13 | 31-12-12 |
|---|---|---|
| TO | 2,736,028 | 1,250,588 |
| P/L | (9,979,060) | (6,509,118) |
| NW | (16,483,302) | (6,505,672) |
| WC | 348,949 | 247,357 |
| Emp. | 54 | 26 |

DUNS 53-638-2344 Imp
## Sandhurst Autoprint Ltd
Unit 1 Vulcan Way, Sandhurst, Berkshire GU47 9DB
**Tel:** 01252-749808 **Fax:** 01252-879564
**Web:** www.sandhurstautoprint.co.uk
**Reg No:** 3443003 **Estd:** 1997 Private Limited Company
**Line of Business:** Number plate suppliers
**Issued Capital:** £50,000
**Director:** T M Sanders
**Co. Secretary:** Ms Judith Sanders
**US SIC:** 3714 **UK SIC:** 35300
**Auditors:** Stewart & Co
**Bankers:** National Westminster Bank Plc (60-11-01)

| | 31-07-13 | 31-07-12 | 31-07-11 |
|---|---|---|---|
| TO | 9,987,219 | 8,296,019 | 7,581,592 |
| P/L | 831,107 | 651,961 | 601,958 |
| NW | 2,617,455 | 2,044,586 | 1,669,270 |
| WC | 1,690,008 | 1,496,308 | 1,047,648 |
| Emp. | 58 | 47 | 45 |

DUNS 21-143-8305
## Sandhurst Plant Ltd
Medway City Estate, Whitewall Road, Rochester, Kent ME2 4DZ
**Tel:** 08451206633 **Fax:** 0845-120-6644
**Web:** www.sandhurst.co.uk
**Reg No:** 6746840 **Estd:** 2008 Private Limited Company
**Line of Business:** Agents involved in the sale of machinery, industrial equipment, ships and aircraft
**Issued Capital:** £1,000
**Directors:** P L Dean, T W Dean
**Co. Secretary:** Jeffrey Young
**Responsibilities**
**Sales:** Harry Backhouse *(Dealer Principal)*
**Health & Safety:** Hugh Boorman *(Service Manager)*
**Operations:** Hugh Boorman *(Service Manager)*
**US SIC:** 5084 **UK SIC:** 61490
**Auditors:** Barnes Roffe LLP

| | 31-05-14 | 31-05-13 | 31-05-12 |
|---|---|---|---|
| TA | 2,398 | 2,398 | 2,398 |
| NW | 2,398 | 2,398 | 2,398 |

DUNS 45-847-1133
## Sandicliffe Ltd
(**Subsidiary of:** Sandicliffe Motor Holdings Ltd)
154 Welford Road, Leicester, Leicestershire LE2 6BW
**Tel:** 01162332332
**Web:** www.sandicliffe.co.uk
**Reg No:** 3193805 **Estd:** 1960 Private Limited Company
**Line of Business:** Sale of new motor vehicles
**Issued Capital:** £7,274,415
**Principals:** T H Barton *(Managing)*, T H Barton, J R Woodhouse, R Tutt, R A Woodhouse
**Co. Secretary:** Nicholas Woodhouse
**Responsibilities**
**Senior:** Nigel Falkiner *(Group Marketing Manager)*
**Finance:** John Storer *(Financial Director)*
**HR:** Ivor Birkin *(Human Resources Manager)*
**US SIC:** 5511, 5521, 5531
**UK SIC:** 65100
**Auditors:** KPMG LLP
**Bankers:** The Royal Bank Of Scotland Plc (16-26-32)

| | 31-12-13 | 31-12-12 | 31-12-11 |
|---|---|---|---|
| TO | 220,224,000 | 183,434,000 | 176,526,000 |
| P/L | 731,000 | 357,000 | 93,000 |
| NW | 15,238,000 | 15,308,000 | 15,119,000 |
| WC | 1,162,000 | 2,504,000 | 3,495,000 |
| Emp. | 574 | 537 | 563 |

DUNS 49-389-8316
## Sandicliffe Motor Group Ltd
(**Subsidiary of:** Sandicliffe Motor Holdings Ltd)
280 Nottingham Road, Nottingham, Nottinghamshire NG7 7DG
**Tel:** 01159422100 **Fax:** 01159423453
**Web:** www.sandicliffe.co.uk
**Reg No:** 3136847 **Estd:** 1995 Private Limited Company
**Line of Business:** New & used motor vehicle dealers
**Issued Capital:** £293,000
**Directors:** T H Barton, T H Barton, R A Woodhouse, J R Woodhouse
**Co. Secretary:** Nicholas Woodhouse
**Branches:** Sandicliffe Motor Group Ltd, West Bridgford House, Loughborough Road, Nottingham, Nottinghamshire NG2 7UN
**US SIC:** 5511, 5521, 7539, 5531
**UK SIC:** 65100, 67100
**Auditors:** KPMG
**Bankers:** The Royal Bank Of Scotland Plc (16-26-32)

|  | 31-12-13 | 31-12-12 | 31-12-11 |
|---|---|---|---|
| TA | 4,761,000 | 4,761,000 | 4,761,000 |
| NW | 102,000 | 102,000 | 102,000 |
| WC | 22,000 | 22,000 | 22,000 |

DUNS 73-335-4505
## Sandicliffe Motor Holdings Ltd
152 Nottingham Road, Nottingham, Nottinghamshire NG9 3PP
**Tel:** 01159395000
**Web:** www.sandicliffe.co.uk
**Reg No:** 4609153 **Estd:** 2002 Private Limited Company
**Line of Business:** Sale of new motor vehicles
**Trading Style:** Sandicliffe Motor Group
**Issued Capital:** £293,000
**Directors:** R A Woodhouse, Ms P E Hills, Ms E A Murfitt, J R Woodhouse, T H Barton, T H Barton
**Co. Secretary:** Nicholas Woodhouse
**Responsibilities**
**Senior:** Brien Probert (Manager)
**US SIC:** 5511, 5521, 7539, 5531
**UK SIC:** 65100, 67100
**Bankers:** The Royal Bank Of Scotland Plc (16-26-32)

|  | 31-12-13 | 31-12-12 | 31-12-11 |
|---|---|---|---|
| TO | 221,491,000 | 186,188,000 | 177,220,000 |
| P/L | 1,501,000 | 754,000 | 328,000 |
| NW | 15,130,000 | 15,167,000 | 14,774,000 |
| WC | (2,739,000) | (918,000) | (230,000) |
| Emp. | 611 | 573 | 598 |

DUNS 21-735-3639
## The Sandon School Academy Trust
Molrams Lane, Chelmsford, Essex CM2 7AQ
**Tel:** 01245473611
**Reg No:** 7697483 **Estd:** 2011 Private Company Limited By Guarantee
**Line of Business:** General secondary education
**Directors:** D Owen, P Athey, T Brown, Dr J Lawrence, Ms C F Greenwood, Mrs C J Amos, Ms A S Whelpdale, Ms C Fitzsimmons
**Co. Secretary:** Ms Karen Bayley
**Responsibilities**
**Senior:** Maxine Dodd (Director), Clive Hodges (Director), Daryle Mountford (Director), Duncan Robertson (Director), Jonathon Wincott (Director)
**US SIC:** 8211 **UK SIC:** 93200

|  | 31-08-13 | 31-08-12 |
|---|---|---|
| TO | 8,016,276 | 12,050,625 |
| P/L | (191,604) | 4,972,394 |
| NW | 4,466,790 | 4,739,394 |
| WC | 903,616 | 969,880 |
| Emp. | 159 | 129 |

DUNS 23-254-3335
## Sandown Nursing Home
28 Grove Road, Sandown, Isle of Wight PO36 9BE
**Tel:** 01983408574
**Web:** www.sandownnursinghome.co.uk
**Estd:** 2012 Proprietorship
**Line of Business:** Nursing homes
**Proprietor:** R Davies
**Responsibilities**
**Senior:** Ann-Marie Jordan (Home Manager)
**Finance:** Ann-Marie Jordan (Home Manager)
**Marketing:** Ann-Marie Jordan (Home Manager)
**Admin:** Donna Cafferky (Administrator)
**HR:** Ann-Marie Jordan (Home Manager)
**Health & Safety:** Jingle Santos (Matron)
**Facilities:** Ann-Marie Jordan (Home Manager)
**Purchasing:** Ann-Marie Jordan (Home Manager)
**US SIC:** 8051 **UK SIC:** 95100
**Employees:** 48

DUNS 77-756-6142
## Sandown Surrey & Hampshire Ltd
(**Subsidiary of:** Selanac Holdings Limited)
1-3 Edison Road, Basingstoke, Hampshire RG21 6YH
**Tel:** 01256464050 **Fax:** 01483 654500
**Web:** www.mercedes-benzofbasingstoke.co.uk
**Reg No:** 3018671 **VAT No:** 642230574
**Estd:** 1995 Private Limited Company
**Line of Business:** Sale of new motor vehicles
**Trading Style:** Mercedes-Benz of Guildford
**Issued Capital:** £500,000
**Directors:** G R Copling, G A Mcallister, P Todd
**Co. Secretary:** Gareth Copling
**Responsibilities**
**Senior:** Anthony Purslow (Manager)
**IT:** Andy Walker (IT Manager)
**Branches:** Sandown Surrey & Hampshire Ltd, Seven Thorns Lane, Hindhead, Surrey GU26 6DF
**US SIC:** 5511, 5521, 7539, 5531
**UK SIC:** 65100, 67100
**Auditors:** BDO LLP
**Bankers:** National Westminster Bank Plc (54-30-03)

|  | 31-12-13 | 31-12-12 | 31-12-11 |
|---|---|---|---|
| TO | 72,258,000 | 58,826,000 | 49,798,000 |
| P/L | 1,145,000 | 1,458,000 | 656,000 |
| NW | 4,364,000 | 3,498,000 | 2,314,000 |
| WC | 3,700,000 | 3,000,000 | 1,887,000 |
| Emp. | 152 | 151 | 141 |

DUNS 22-521-8163  Exp
## Sandoz Ltd
(**Subsidiary of:** Novartis Ag)
Unit 37 Woolmer Way, Bordon, Hampshire GU35 9QE
**Tel:** 01276 698020
**Web:** www.sandoz.com
**Reg No:** 1547204 **VAT No:** 615030685
**Estd:** 1981 Private Limited Company
**Line of Business:** Manufacture of basic pharmaceutical products
**Export Markets:** Worldwide
**Export Sales:** £229,000
**Issued Capital:** £2,000,000
**Directors:** S Eder, N R Haggar, E H Arrocha, Ms S A Webb
**Co. Secretary:** Roy Henry
**US SIC:** 2834 **UK SIC:** 25700
**Auditors:** PricewaterhouseCoopers LLP
**Bankers:** Barclays Bank Plc (20-91-79)

|  | 31-12-13 | 31-12-12 | 31-12-11 |
|---|---|---|---|
| TO | 88,571,000 | 69,352,000 | 61,682,000 |
| P/L | 17,351,000 | 4,180,000 | 8,668,000 |
| NW | 22,322,000 | 10,658,000 | 5,892,000 |
| WC | 20,610,000 | 7,867,000 | 5,356,000 |
| Emp. | 82 | 82 | 73 |

DUNS 23-157-7198
## Sandpiper Ci
1-3 L"Abenue Le Bas, Lonquebille, Jersey, Channel Islands JE4 8NB
**Tel:** 01534508508
**Web:** www.sandpiperci.com
**Proprietorship**
**Line of Business:** Retail sale in non-specialised stores (excluding ctns) holding an alcohol licence with food, beverages or tobacco predominating
**Proprietor:** P Vernon
**Responsibilities**
**Senior:** Nick Henderson (Buying Director), Tony O'Neill (Manager)
**IT:** Alistair Wild (IT Manager)
**Purchasing:** Nick Henderson (Buying Director)
**US SIC:** 5411 **UK SIC:** 64100
**Employees:** 100

DUNS 21-070-6477
## Sandpiperci Ltd
123 L"Avenue Le Bas, Longville, St Helier, Jersey, Channel Islands JE4 8NB
**Tel:** 01534508200
**Web:** www.sandpiperci.com
**Reg No:** 0097653J **Estd:** 2007 Private Limited Company
**Line of Business:** Convenience stores
**Responsibilities**
**Senior:** Tony O'Neill (Manager)
**Marketing:** Barbara Holyhead (Marketing Director), Brain Le Ion (Marketing Director)
**US SIC:** 5411 **UK SIC:** 64100
**Employees:** 3,000

DUNS 23-337-4284
## Sandpiperci Retail Ltd
1-3 L'Avenue Le Bas Longueville, Jersey, Channel Islands JE4 8NB
**Tel:** 01534508620
**Web:** www.sandpiperci.com
**Reg No:** 0083291J **Estd:** 2002 Private Limited Company
**Line of Business:** Other retail sale in specialised stores not elsewhere classified

**Branches:** Sandpiperci Retail Limited, Admiral Park, Elizabeth Avenue, Guernsey, Channel Islands GY1 2AL
**US SIC:** 7399, 5399, 6531, 6111
**UK SIC:** 83954, 65600, 83400, 81501
**Auditors:** Deloitte & Touche
**Bankers:** HSBC Bank plc (40-25-33)
**Turnover:** £326,100,000

DUNS 21-228-0679
## Sandringham Care Home
24 Sandringham, Craigavon, Co Armagh BT63 5BW
**Tel:** 028-38394194
**Web:** www.fshc.co.uk
**Proprietorship**
**Line of Business:** Nursing homes
**Proprietor:** A Moriarty
**Responsibilities**
**Senior:** Niamh Murray (General Manager)
**Finance:** Elaine Gilchrist (Senior Finance Administrator)
**US SIC:** 8051 **UK SIC:** 95100
**Employees:** 70

DUNS 23-709-7050
## Sandringham Estate
233 Regents Park Road, London N3 3PQ
**Web:** www.sandringhamestate.co.uk
**Estd:** 2010
**Line of Business:** Estate management services
**Trading Style:** Sandringham Estate Shop, Sandringham House Museum & Grounds, Sandringham Estate Saw Mills
**Manager:** Mrs G Pattinson
**Responsibilities**
**Senior:** Marcus O'Lone (Land Agent), Malcolm Ziff (Manager)
**Finance:** Marcus O'Lone (Land Agent)
**Marketing:** Helen Walch (Public Enterprise Manager)
**IT:** Marcus O'Lone (Land Agent)
**HR:** Marcus O'Lone (Land Agent)
**Health & Safety:** Alexander George (Health & Safety Officer)
**Branches:** Sandringham Estate, Appleton Farm, King's Lynn, Norfolk PE31 6AY
**US SIC:** 2421 **UK SIC:** 46101
**Bankers:** Coutts & Co (18-50-01)
**Employees:** 100

DUNS 28-893-8186
## Sandringham Hotels (Isle of Wight) Ltd
High Street, Sandown, Isle of Wight PO36 8AH
**Tel:** 01983-406655
**Web:** www.sandringhamhotel.co.uk
**Reg No:** 1303729 **VAT No:** 108891451
**Estd:** 1977 Private Limited Company
**Line of Business:** Hotels
**Issued Capital:** £33,629
**Directors:** M Moorman, N J Spyker
**Co. Secretary:** Ms Josephine Moorman
**US SIC:** 7011 **UK SIC:** 66500
**Auditors:** HLB AV Audit PLC
**Bankers:** Lloyds TSB Bank plc (77-95-35)

|  | 31-03-14 | 31-03-13 | 31-03-12 |
|---|---|---|---|
| TA | 1,961,464 | 2,091,687 | 1,891,119 |
| NW | 1,007,853 | 936,534 | 959,370 |
| WC | 703,741 | 637,776 | 642,859 |

DUNS 28-841-7439
## Sandroyd School Trust Ltd
Rushmore Park, Tollard Royal, Salisbury, Wiltshire SP5 5QD
**Web:** www.sandroyd.org
**Reg No:** 0552767 **Estd:** 1955 Private Limited Company
**Line of Business:** General secondary education
**Trading Style:** Sandroyd School
**Directors:** Mrs H Bell, P J Bourke, K Fuller, Mrs E Brierley, D M Gregg, O H Stanley, T C Hextall, S W Barber
**Co. Secretary:** Christopher Stewart
**Responsibilities**
**Senior:** Paul Bowen (Manager), Penelope Brewer (Manager), William Hillary (Manager), Emma Mckendrick (Director), Simon O'Malley (Director), Rhodri Thomas (Director), Felicity Wilson (Director)
**Branches:** Rushmore Pk, Tollard Royal, Salisbury, Wiltshire SP5 5QD
**US SIC:** 8211 **UK SIC:** 93200
**Auditors:** Fawcetts
**Bankers:** Barclays Bank Plc (20-75-01)

|  | 31-08-14 | 31-08-13 | 31-08-12 |
|---|---|---|---|
| TO | 3,764,779 | 3,794,949 | 3,666,369 |
| P/L | 21,345 | 212,355 | 225,879 |
| NW | 3,754,186 | 3,732,841 | 3,520,486 |
| WC | (925,439) | (1,029,574) | (926,168) |
| Emp. | 84 | 86 | 84 |

DUNS 34-625-0533
## Sands Leisure (Portland) Ltd
Portland Heights Hotel, Portland, Dorset DT5 2EN
**Tel:** 01305-821361
**Web:** www.heightshotel.com
**Reg No:** 2758887 **Estd:** 1992 Private Limited Company
**Line of Business:** Hotels
**Trading Style:** Portland Heights Hotel
**Issued Capital:** £901
**Director:** P Wogman
**Co. Secretary:** Ms Tracy Wogman
**Responsibilities**
**Operations:** Angie Mustill (Operations Director)
**US SIC:** 7011, 5812
**UK SIC:** 66500, 66110
**Auditors:** Gerald Edelman

|  | 31-10-13 | 31-10-12 | 31-10-11 |
|---|---|---|---|
| TA | 6,542,229 | 6,710,537 | 6,718,043 |
| NW | 4,030,738 | 4,016,584 | 3,917,869 |
| WC | (351,918) | (251,900) | (232,091) |

DUNS 50-558-5026
## Sandtoft Roof Tiles Ltd
(**Subsidiary of:** Wienerberger Ag)
Belton Road, Sandtoft, Doncaster, South Yorkshire DN8 5SY
**Tel:** 01427-871200
**Web:** www.sandtoft.com
**Reg No:** 2509718 **Estd:** 1990 Private Limited Company
**Line of Business:** Other building completion
**Trading Style:** Sandtoft
**Issued Capital:** £11,029
**Directors:** K S Barker, C Domenig, H A Schwarzmayr, P Stevenson
**Co. Secretary:** Michael Grace
**Responsibilities**
**Senior:** S Aldridge (Manager), Anthony Carter (Sales Director), Simon Oldridge (Director), Nicholas Oldridge (Director)
**Sales:** Anthony Carter (Sales Director)
**Branches:** Sandtoft Roof Tiles Ltd, Brooks Dr, Cheadle Roayl Bp, Cheadle, Cheshire SK8 3SA
**US SIC:** 1799, 3271, 3251
**UK SIC:** 50000, 24370, 24100
**Bankers:** National Westminster Bank Plc (51-81-34)

|  | 31-12-13 | 31-12-12 | 31-12-11 |
|---|---|---|---|
| TO | 48,327,000 | 42,776,000 | 43,125,000 |
| P/L | 3,104,000 | 3,010,000 | 3,160,000 |
| NW | 48,493,000 | 46,142,000 | 43,945,000 |
| WC | 14,320,000 | 11,365,000 | 13,398,000 |
| Emp. | 348 | 327 | 353 |

DUNS 21-904-0193  Exp
## Sandtoft Trading Ltd
(**Subsidiary of:** Wienerberger Ag)
Sandtoft Roof Tiles Ltd, Barrow-Upon-Humber, South Humberside DN19 7EN
**Tel:** 01469535600
**Web:** www.sandtoft.com
**Reg No:** 1094518 **VAT No:** 555428527
**Estd:** 1904 Private Limited Company
**Line of Business:** Manufacture of bricks, tiles and construction products, in baked clay
**Export Markets:** U S A, E U
**Issued Capital:** £1,000
**Director:** P Stevenson
**Co. Secretary:** Michael Grace
**Responsibilities**
**Senior:** Kaye Few (Manager), Nicholas Oldridge (Director), Martin Oldridge (Director), Simon Oldridge (Director), Paul Staves (Works Engineer)
**Facilities:** Paul Staves (Works Engineer)
**Engineering:** Paul Staves (Works Engineer)
**Branches:** Sandtoft Trading Ltd, Broomfleet, Brough, North Humberside HU15 1RS
**US SIC:** 3251, 3271
**UK SIC:** 24100, 24370
**Auditors:** PricewaterhouseCoopers LLP
**Bankers:** National Westminster Bank Plc (51-81-34)

|  | 31-12-13 | 31-12-12 | 31-12-11 |
|---|---|---|---|
| TA | 14,414,000 | 14,150,000 | 13,915,000 |
| P/L | 357,000 | 389,000 | 397,000 |
| NW | 14,378,000 | 14,104,000 | 13,810,000 |
| WC | 14,378,000 | 14,104,000 | 13,810,000 |

DUNS 28-974-2108
## Sandtoft Transport Centre Ltd
Belton Road, Sandtoft, Doncaster, South Yorkshire DN8 5SY
**Tel:** 01427872696
**Web:** www.sandtoft.com
**Reg No:** 1747475 **Estd:** 1983 Private Limited Company
**Line of Business:** Museum activities
**Directors:** A G Ferris, I H Wilson, F R Whitehead, S J Harrison, C N Proctor, N Broxholme, G P Bilbe
**Co. Secretary:** Christopher Lake
**US SIC:** 8411 **UK SIC:** 97700

**Auditors:** David Watson

| | 31-01-14 | 31-01-13 | 31-01-12 |
|---|---|---|---|
| TO | 127,158 | 130,087 | 132,652 |
| P/L | 40,955 | 39,319 | 34,654 |
| NW | 494,564 | 453,609 | 414,291 |
| WC | 182,111 | 136,022 | 105,753 |

DUNS 42-473-0062

## Sandtrend Ltd

Grove Road, Newbury, Berkshire RG14 2LA
**Tel:** 01635581000 **Fax:** 01635-552259
**Web:** www.macdonaldhotels.co.uk
**Reg No:** 4460633 **Estd:** 1993 Private Limited Company
**Line of Business:** Other sporting activities not elsewhere classified
**Trading Style:** Donnington Grove Golf and Country Club
**Issued Capital:** £2
**Directors:** R M Davies, T Gwyn Jones
**Co. Secretary:** Malcolm Hezel
**Responsibilities**
**Senior:** Kathleen Bainbridge *(Manager)*, Rosemary Davies *(Manager)*, Nigel Green *(General Manager)*
**US SIC:** 7999, 7941
**UK SIC:** 97913, 97911
**Auditors:** Mazars LLP
**Bankers:** National Westminster Bank Plc (60-15-07)

| | 26-09-13 | 27-09-12 | 30-09-11 |
|---|---|---|---|
| TO | 1,583,571 | 1,574,826 | 1,695,069 |
| P/L | (864,982) | (706,392) | (319,995) |
| NW | (5,912,902) | (5,047,920) | (4,341,528) |
| WC | (4,158,862) | (2,694,911) | (247,000) |
| Emp. | 51 | 50 | 59 |

DUNS 21-443-5505 **Imp-Exp**

## Sandusky Ltd

**(Subsidiary of:** Metaltek International Inc.)
Viewfield, Glenrothes, Fife KY6 2RQ
**Web:** www.metaltek.com
**Reg No:** 0737075 **VAT No:** 268318927
**Estd:** 1962 Private Limited Company
**Line of Business:** Mechanical engineering general
**Export Markets:** Worldwide
**Export Sales:** £6,949,711
**Trading Style:** Metaltek International
**Issued Capital:** £350,000
**Directors:** A G Cope, R M Danning, R J Smickley, T G Gibb
**Co. Secretary:** Martin Handyside
**Responsibilities**
**Senior:** Angela Forster-Rainey *(Buyer)*, Richard Hargrave *(Vice President)*, Edward Ryan *(Manager)*
**Sales:** Graeme Duncan *(Sales Manager)*
**HR:** Nicola Howe *(Human Resources Manager)*
**Purchasing:** Angela Forster-Rainey *(Buyer)*
**US SIC:** 3325, 3369
**UK SIC:** 31110, 31120
**Auditors:** BSN Associates Ltd
**Bankers:** Clydesdale Bank Plc (82-45-05)

| | 30-06-13 | 30-06-12 | 30-06-11 |
|---|---|---|---|
| TO | 7,061,397 | 7,566,603 | 10,412,939 |
| P/L | (585,365) | (316,172) | 696,493 |
| NW | (1,338,896) | (521,749) | 926,432 |
| WC | (110,361) | 174,865 | 595,405 |
| Emp. | 64 | 64 | 56 |

DUNS 73-363-2264 **Imp**

## Sandvik Construction Mobile Crushers & Screens Ltd

**(Subsidiary of:** Sandvik Ab)
Hearthcote Road, Swadlincote, Derbyshire DE11 9DU
**Tel:** 01283-818-400 **Fax:** 01283-818-360
**Web:** www.miningandconstruction.sandvik.com
**Reg No:** 4636796 **VAT No:** 806399995
**Estd:** 2003 Private Limited Company
**Line of Business:** Manufacture of other general purpose machinery not elsewhere classified
**Export Sales:** £124,129,000
**Issued Capital:** £15,512,050
**Directors:** A Kjellberg, T Allison, J A Boulton, Ms J K Cooke
**Co. Secretary:** Gregory Cooper
**Responsibilities**
**Senior:** Andrew McManus *(Manager)*, Duncan Mcgregor *(President Product Area Breaker)*
**Finance:** Thomas Warringer *(Executive Vice President Finan)*
**US SIC:** 3549, 3542
**UK SIC:** 32212
**Auditors:** KPMG LLP
**Bankers:** HSBC Bank plc (40-41-08)

| | 31-12-13 | 31-12-12 | 31-12-11 |
|---|---|---|---|
| TO | 153,792,000 | 161,225,000 | 155,676,000 |
| P/L | (2,420,000) | (2,965,000) | 3,241,000 |
| NW | 9,772,000 | 11,325,000 | 14,630,000 |
| WC | 34,652,000 | 10,615,000 | 13,075,000 |
| Emp. | 566 | 552 | 543 |

DUNS 21-814-0317 **Imp**

## Sandvik Ltd

**(Subsidiary of:** Sandvik Ab)
Manor Way, Halesowen, West Midlands B62 8QZ
**Tel:** 01215045000 **Fax:** 01215045554
**Web:** www.sandvik.com
**Reg No:** 0136547 **VAT No:** 281452560
**Estd:** 1914 Private Limited Company
**Line of Business:** Retail sale of hardware, paints and glass
**Export Sales:** £91,853,000
**Trading Style:** Sandvik Coromant Uk / Sandvik Hard Materials, Sandvik Steel Uk / Sandvik Hyperion, Sandvik Information Systems Uk
**Issued Capital:** £15,000,000
**Directors:** J A Boulton, M H Walker, P L Lehnbom
**Co. Secretary:** Stephen Brabham
**Responsibilities**
**Senior:** Magnus Ekback *(Manager)*
**Finance:** Alison Ronnie *(Financial Controller)*
**Marketing:** David Harbon *(Sales and Marketing Manager)*
**Sales:** David Harbon *(Sales and Marketing Manager)*
**HR:** Elaine Buckley *(Human Resources Manager)*, Magnus Ekback *(Manager)*
**Purchasing:** James Doughty *(Purchasing Manager)*
**Branches:** Sandvik Ltd, 150 Helen Street, Glasgow, Lanarkshire G51 3JS
**US SIC:** 5251, 3423, 3499
**UK SIC:** 64800, 31612, 31694
**Auditors:** KPMG LLP
**Bankers:** Barclays Bank Plc (20-76-89)

| | 31-12-13 | 31-12-12 | 31-12-11 |
|---|---|---|---|
| TO | 149,865,000 | 163,971,000 | 161,862,000 |
| P/L | 2,051,000 | 6,367,000 | 9,890,000 |
| NW | 51,914,000 | 49,639,000 | 44,669,000 |
| WC | 24,812,000 | 23,417,000 | 17,392,000 |
| Emp. | 512 | 524 | 491 |

DUNS 22-762-9664 **Imp-Exp**

## Sandvik Osprey Ltd

Milland Road, Neath, West Glamorgan SA11 1NJ
**Tel:** 01639-634121
**Web:** www.sandvik.com
**Reg No:** 1189998 **VAT No:** 124668756
**Estd:** 1974 Private Limited Company
**Line of Business:** Manufacture of other fabricated metal products not elsewhere classified
**Export Markets:** E U, U S A, Worldwide
**Export Sales:** £22,520,000
**Issued Capital:** £1
**Directors:** S Brabham, P Yu, Miss A M Genschou, R J Park
**Co. Secretary:** Paul Williams
**Responsibilities**
**Senior:** Reginald Brooks *(Manager)*, Mats Gunnarsson *(CEO)*, Olof Wijk *(Manager)*
**IT:** Derek Jackson *(Computer Manager)*
**Engineering:** Ian Bath *(Production Manager)*, Ian Stimpson *(Production Manager)*
**US SIC:** 3999 **UK SIC:** 49590
**Auditors:** KPMG LLP

| | 31-12-13 | 31-12-12 | 31-12-11 |
|---|---|---|---|
| TO | 22,863,000 | 22,332,000 | 20,818,000 |
| P/L | 5,310,000 | 5,283,000 | 5,020,000 |
| NW | 16,072,000 | 11,993,000 | 8,006,000 |
| WC | 9,589,000 | 6,034,000 | 4,133,000 |
| Emp. | 111 | 108 | 98 |

DUNS 21-783-1035

## Sandwell Academy School

Sandwell Academy, Halfords Lane, West Bromwich, West Midlands B71 4LG
**Tel:** 01215251700
**Web:** www.sandwellacademy.com
**Estd:** 2007 Partnership
**Line of Business:** Schools (foundation)
**Partners:** S Topper, S Topper
**US SIC:** 8211 **UK SIC:** 93200
**Employees:** 250

DUNS 23-440-5751

## Sandwell College

High Street, West Bromwich, West Midlands B70 8ND
**Tel:** 01215566000
**Web:** www.sandwell.ac.uk
**Estd:** 2003 Proprietorship
**Line of Business:** Further education schools and colleges
**Proprietor:** Ms V Bailey
**Responsibilities**
**Senior:** Graham Pennington *(Principal)*
**US SIC:** 8221 **UK SIC:** 93100
**Employees:** 300

DUNS 36-516-7857

## The Sandwell Community Caring Trust

9th Floor West Palza, 144 High Street, West Bromwich, West Midlands B70 6JJ
**Tel:** 01215532722
**Web:** www.sandwellcct.org.uk
**Reg No:** 3286106 **Estd:** 1996 Private Limited Company
**Line of Business:** Charities and charitable organisations
**Directors:** Mrs S A Rogers, J Haynes, Ms J H Jones, F A Betteridge, R L Alsop
**Co. Secretary:** Mrs Tracy Graham
**Responsibilities**
**Senior:** Christine D'Amore *(Finance Director)*, Amy Macwatt *(Volunteer Manager)*
**Finance:** Christine D'Amore *(Finance Director)*
**Branches:** The Sandwell Community Caring Trust, 51 Lodge Rd, West Bromwich, West Midlands B70 8NZ
**US SIC:** 8321 **UK SIC:** 96111
**Auditors:** Clement Keys
**Bankers:** Barclays Bank Plc (20-93-15)

| | 31-03-14 | 31-03-13 | 31-03-12 |
|---|---|---|---|
| TO | 15,283,186 | 14,546,228 | 11,090,377 |
| P/L | 342,956 | (433,821) | 422,158 |
| NW | 666,490 | (1,408,466) | 908,355 |
| WC | 439,259 | 365,090 | 583,061 |
| Emp. | 634 | 600 | 450 |

DUNS 73-777-7479

## Sandwell Homes Ltd

Dartmouth House, Sandwell Road, West Bromwich, West Midlands B70 8TQ
**Tel:** 01215696000
**Web:** www.sandwell.gov.uk
**Reg No:** 5034622 **Estd:** 2004 Private Company Limited By Guarantee
**Line of Business:** General (overall) public service activities
**Trading Style:** Sandwell Metropolitan Council
**Director:** G J Lewis
**Co. Secretary:** Ms Kaye Coulthard
**Responsibilities**
**Senior:** Norman Fletcher *(General Manager - Housing Serv)*
**Finance:** Judy Guest *(Finance Officer)*
**Marketing:** Janette Coughlan *(Head of Business Transformatio)*
**US SIC:** 9121 **UK SIC:** 91110
**Auditors:** Baker Tilly UK Audit LLP
**Bankers:** The Co-Operative Bank Plc (08-90-01)

| | 01-01-13 | 31-03-12 |
|---|---|---|
| TO | 67,243,000 | 96,103,000 |
| P/L | 37,037,000 | (4,369,000) |
| NW | N/A | (19,368,000) |
| WC | N/A | 16,238,000 |
| Emp. | 987 | 1,077 |

DUNS 21-604-5201

## Sandwell Leisure Trust

Wednesbury Oak Road, Tipton, West Midlands DY4 0BS
**Tel:** 08456594815
**Web:** www.slt-leisure.co.uk
**Estd:** 2008 Proprietorship
**Line of Business:** Leisure centres
**Partners:** D Cosgrove, Mrs R Clayton
**US SIC:** 7999 **UK SIC:** 97913
**Employees:** 167

DUNS 21-590-5671

## Sandwell Metropolitan Borough Council

Sandwell Council House, Oldbury, West Midlands B69 3DE
**Tel:** 01215692200
**Web:** www.sandwell.gov.uk
**Estd:** 2011
**Line of Business:** Central Government
**Responsibilities**
**Marketing:** Mark Waldman *(Senior Marketing Executive)*
**Purchasing:** Neil Whitehouse *(Purchasing Manager)*
**US SIC:** 9121 **UK SIC:** 91110
**Employees:** 14,000

DUNS 23-891-3024 **Imp**

## Sandwell Metropolitan Borough Council

Freeth Street, Oldbury, West Midlands B69 3DE
**Tel:** 08453582200
**Web:** www.sandwell.gov.uk
**Estd:** 2011
**Line of Business:** Local government
**Trading Style:** Sandwell Metropolitan Borough Council
**Directors:** F N Summers, Ms L Bateman, E J Gamble
**Responsibilities**
**Senior:** Jan Britton *(Chief Executive Officer)*, Carrol Rowe *(Manager)*
**IT:** Matthew Howe *(PC Manager)*
**HR:** Melanie Dudley *(Human Resources Manager)*
**Branches:** Sandwell Metropolitan Borough Council, Hydes Road, Wodensborough Community Technology Colle, West Bromwich, West Midlands WS10 0DR
**US SIC:** 8211 **UK SIC:** 93200
**Bankers:** The Co-Operative Bank Plc (08-90-01)
**Employees:** 14,000

DUNS 36-517-7042

## Sandwell Primary Care Trust

Kingston House, 438-450 High Street, West Bromwich, West Midlands B70 9LD
**Tel:** 01216121500
**Web:** www.blackcountry.nhs.uk
**Estd:** 2006
**Line of Business:** Primary care trusts
**Principals:** R Nugent *(Chairman)*, R Bacon
**US SIC:** 8062 **UK SIC:** 95100
**Employees:** 1,800

DUNS 34-843-1438

## Sandwich & District Growers Ltd

Grove Road, Canterbury, Kent CT3 1EF
**Tel:** 01227722247
**Web:** www.salvatori.com
**Reg No:** 2806417 **Estd:** 1993 Private Limited Company
**Line of Business:** Storage and warehousing
**Trading Style:** A Salvatori & Son
**Issued Capital:** £1,000
**Chairman:** D A Salvatori
**Co. Secretary:** David Tobin
**Responsibilities**
**Senior:** R Laslett *(Vice Chairman)*
**Branches:** Sandwich & District Growers Ltd, Lwr Santon Lane, Canterbury, Kent CT3 1JF
**US SIC:** 4226, 5511
**UK SIC:** 77003, 65100
**Auditors:** McCabe Ford Williams
**Bankers:** National Westminster Bank Plc (60-04-27)

| | 31-12-13 | 30-09-12 | 30-12-11 |
|---|---|---|---|
| TO | 6,493,636 | N/A | N/A |
| P/L | 201,857 | N/A | N/A |
| NW | 1,004,990 | 394,653 | 328,057 |
| WC | (864,812) | (150,751) | (183,861) |
| Emp. | 99 | N/A | N/A |

DUNS 45-847-8146

## The Sandwich Factory Holdings Ltd

**(Subsidiary of:** Cranswick Plc)
Atherstone Signs, Carlyon Road, Carlyon Road Industrial Estate, Atherstone, Warwickshire CV9 1LQ
**Tel:** 01827-719100 **Fax:** 01827719101
**Web:** www.tsfl.co.uk
**Reg No:** 3194496 **Estd:** 1996 Private Limited Company
**Line of Business:** Manufacture of other food products not elsewhere classified
**Issued Capital:** £2,252,000
**Directors:** M T Davey, N Anderson, A H Couch, G Landsborough, J M Bottomley
**Co. Secretary:** Malcolm Windeatt
**Responsibilities**
**Finance:** Phil Reader *(Head of Finance)*
**IT:** Kyle Mckay *(IT Manager)*
**US SIC:** 2099 **UK SIC:** 42399
**Auditors:** PricewaterhouseCoopers
**Bankers:** Bank Of Scotland (12-05-65)

| | 31-03-14 | 31-03-13 | 31-03-12 |
|---|---|---|---|
| TO | 44,918,000 | 50,810,000 | 47,642,000 |
| P/L | 1,706,000 | (262,000) | (240,000) |
| NW | 7,365,000 | 5,819,000 | 5,628,000 |
| WC | 6,739,000 | 4,913,000 | 5,863,000 |
| Emp. | 638 | 777 | 726 |

DUNS 21-693-5103

## Sandwich Technology School

Deal Road, Sandwich, Kent CT13 0BU
**Tel:** 01304610000 **Fax:** 01304610100
**Web:** www.sandwich-tech.kent.sch.uk
**Reg No:** 7401373 **Estd:** 2010 Private Company Limited By Guarantee
**Line of Business:** Schools (foundation)
**Directors:** Mrs D S Hogben, J Kirtley, J E Flannery, A J Chapman, G E Rorke, Mrs S Summers, L B Ridings, S R Pinfold
**Co. Secretary:** Mrs Lynn Walters
**Responsibilities**
**Senior:** Kimberley Anderson *(Director)*, Adem Azira *(Governor)*, Laura Campbell *(Director)*, Bruce Eccles *(Director)*, Veronica Gomez *(Director)*, David Hampson-Ghani *(Director)*, Charles James *(Director)*, David Larkins *(Director)*, Mark Mucklow *(Manager)*, Sam O'Hara *(Manager)*, Donna Purvis *(General Manager)*, Gillian Rowland *(Director)*, Gaynor Smissen *(Director)*
**Finance:** Julie Platts *(Senior Finance Administrator)*

**IT:** Liz Williamson *(Director of IT)*
**US SIC:** 8211, 8249, 8221
**UK SIC:** 93200, 93300, 93100

| | 31-08-13 | 31-08-12 | 31-08-11 |
|---|---|---|---|
| TO | 7,871,958 | 8,374,466 | 23,917,597 |
| P/L | (108,684) | 607,647 | 17,586,626 |
| NW | 16,517,589 | 16,688,273 | 16,510,626 |
| WC | 1,420,856 | 1,604,994 | 935,074 |
| Emp. | 130 | 195 | 201 |

DUNS 21-319-9487
## Sandwich Techology School
Dover Road, Sandwich, Kent CT13 0FA
**Tel:** 01304613071
**Web:** www.sandwich-tech.kent.sch.uk
**Estd:** 2010
**Line of Business:** Schools (foundation)
**Chairman:** Lady J Pender
**Responsibilities**
**Senior:** Veronica Gomez *(Head Teacher)*
**US SIC:** 8211 **UK SIC:** 93200
**Employees:** 200

DUNS 52-024-0169
## Sandwood Design & Build Ltd
155 Tottenham Lane, London N8 9BT
**Tel:** 020-8348-8180
**Web:** www.sandwood.co.uk
**Reg No:** 3390506 **Estd:** 1991 Private Limited Company
**Line of Business:** Builders
**Issued Capital:** £55,009
**Directors:** J Millen, T J Barlow
**Co. Secretary:** Richard Garland
**Branches:** Sandwood Design & Build Ltd, Carlton Drive, London SW15 2BZ
**US SIC:** 1522 **UK SIC:** 50100
**Auditors:** Brian D Hogg

| | 31-12-13 | 31-12-12 | 31-12-11 |
|---|---|---|---|
| TO | 6,430,289 | 7,892,822 | 7,004,668 |
| P/L | 4,337 | (396,841) | 110,921 |
| NW | 1,791,190 | 1,851,275 | 2,252,475 |
| WC | 1,791,839 | 1,858,606 | 2,253,227 |
| Emp. | 46 | 45 | 53 |

DUNS 22-550-8340
## Sandy Balls Estate Ltd
Godshill, Fordingbridge, Fordingbridge, Hampshire SP6 2JZ
**Tel:** 08446931050
**Web:** www.sandy-balls.co.uk
**Reg No:** 0631600 **VAT No:** 186539128
**Estd:** 1920 Private Limited Company
**Line of Business:** Other sporting activities not elsewhere classified
**Trading Style:** Sandy Balls Holiday Centre
**Issued Capital:** £100
**Directors:** Mrs H R Quinn, I B Brown, R P Westlake, M Stone
**Responsibilities**
**Senior:** Micheen Stone *(Guest Services Manager)*
**Finance:** Del Granger *(Finance Director)*
**IT:** Neil Long *(Head of IT)*, Dan Rook *(Head of IT)*
**HR:** Lynne Bennett *(Human Resources Manager)*
**Branches:** Sandy Balls Estate Ltd, Sandy Balls Estate, Fordingbridge, Hampshire SP6 2JZ
**US SIC:** 7999, 7021
**UK SIC:** 97913, 66500
**Auditors:** Lanham & Francis
**Bankers:** Lloyds TSB Bank plc (30-97-08)

| | 31-12-13 | 31-12-12 | 31-12-11 |
|---|---|---|---|
| TO | 8,752,937 | 9,097,874 | 8,570,951 |
| P/L | 627,151 | 258,517 | 313,272 |
| NW | 8,014,338 | 7,558,145 | 7,550,017 |
| WC | (601,254) | (762,227) | (836,821) |
| Emp. | 201 | 214 | 197 |

DUNS 21-580-5840
## Sandy Bay Caravan Park
North Seaton Road, Ashington, Northumberland NE63 8ST
**Tel:** 01670815055
**Web:** www.park-resorts.com
**Estd:** 2011 Proprietorship
**Line of Business:** Caravan parks
**Proprietor:** T Chelton
**Responsibilities**
**Senior:** Dominic Devine *(CEO, Managing Director)*
**US SIC:** 7033 **UK SIC:** 66701
**Employees:** 50

DUNS 21-717-7367
## Sandye Place Academy
Park Road, Sandy, Bedfordshire SG19 1JD
**Tel:** 01767680420 **Fax:** 01767691141
**Web:** www.sandyeplaceacademy.org.uk
**Reg No:** 7563116 **Estd:** 2011 Private Company Limited By Guarantee
**Line of Business:** Schools (foundation)
**Directors:** M J Sale, S R Watson, D W Jaeger, M T Greener
**Co. Secretary:** Ms Sharon Kane
**Responsibilities**
**Senior:** Kim Mccamley *(Principal)*
**US SIC:** 8211 **UK SIC:** 93200

**Bankers:** National Westminster Bank Plc (60-02-29)

| | 31-08-14 | 31-08-13 | 31-08-12 |
|---|---|---|---|
| TO | 2,823,366 | 3,277,535 | 3,203,085 |
| P/L | 120,176 | 819,792 | 965,451 |
| NW | 1,744,370 | 1,768,194 | 946,402 |
| WC | 532,939 | 560,002 | 1,100,344 |
| Emp. | 55 | 55 | 47 |

DUNS 21-772-5707
## Sandygate
57 Sandygate, Wath-Upon-Dearne, Rotherham, South Yorkshire S63 7LU
**Tel:** 01709877463
**Web:** www.mha.org.uk
**Estd:** 1999 Proprietorship
**Line of Business:** Rest and retirement homes
**Proprietor:** Mrs A Martin
**Responsibilities**
**Senior:** Tracey Marsden *(Manager)*
**US SIC:** 8321 **UK SIC:** 96111
**Employees:** 50

DUNS 22-930-9943
## Sandyholm Garden Centre
Crossford, Crossford, Carluke, Lanarkshire ML8 5QF
**Web:** www.sandyholmgardencentre.co.uk
**VAT No:** 261420690 **Estd:** 1978 Partnership
**Line of Business:** Garden centres
**Partners:** Ms A Warnock, D Warnock, W Warnock
**US SIC:** 5999 **UK SIC:** 65600
**Bankers:** Bank Of Scotland (80-17-02)
**Employees:** 120

DUNS 21-777-6552
## Sandylands Community Primary School
Hampton Road, Morecambe, Lancashire LA3 1EJ
**Tel:** 01524410286
**Web:** www.sandylands.lancs.sch.uk
**Estd:** 1907 Proprietorship
**Line of Business:** Schools (local authority)
**Proprietor:** Miss A Hickson
**Responsibilities**
**Finance:** Karen Garsorth *(Bursar)*
**US SIC:** 8211 **UK SIC:** 93200
**Employees:** 80

DUNS 36-487-7659
## Saneux
4 Imperial Way, Croydon, Surrey CR0 4RR
**Web:** www.saneux.com
**Reg No:** 0011536LP **Estd:** 2010 Limited Partnership
**Line of Business:** Manufacture of taps and valves
**Partners:** K Cooper, Mrs R Cooper, I Cooper, Mrs D Cooper
**Responsibilities**
**Senior:** Iain Cooper *(Sales Manager)*
**US SIC:** 3494 **UK SIC:** 32880
**Employees:** 60

DUNS 23-766-7428
## Sanford C. Bernstein Ltd
(**Subsidiary of:** Axa Direction Juridique Centrale)
Barclays Street, London W1J 8SB
**Tel:** 02071705000 **Fax:** 020-7170-5001
**Web:** https://www.alliancebernstein.com
**Reg No:** 3760267 **Estd:** 1999 Private Limited Company
**Line of Business:** Security broking and related activities
**Issued Capital:** £22
**Directors:** S Chellappah, T M Bayliss, J P Hagemeier, C E Hogbin, Ms R Singer, J N Doyle, D Gordon, Ms A P Perricone
**Co. Secretary:** Hackwood Secretaries Limited
**Responsibilities**
**Senior:** Peter Kraus *(Chief Executive Officer)*, Robert Van Brugge *(Director)*
**Finance:** John Weisenseel *(Chief Financial Officer)*
**Marketing:** Claire Olsen *(Office Manager)*
**Admin:** Claire Olsen *(Office Manager)*
**Purchasing:** Claire Olsen *(Office Manager)*
**US SIC:** 6211 **UK SIC:** 83100
**Auditors:** PricewaterhouseCoopers LLP
**Bankers:** HSBC Bank plc (40-05-26)

| | 31-12-13 | 31-12-12 | 31-12-11 |
|---|---|---|---|
| TA | 329,235,643 | 250,384,462 | 357,856,549 |
| P/L | (536,058) | (7,555,792) | (27,344,743) |
| NW | 21,367,917 | 17,530,822 | 23,996,886 |
| WC | 27,867,917 | 24,030,822 | 30,496,886 |
| Emp. | 132 | 124 | 126 |

DUNS 22-932-3050
## Sangers (Northern Ireland) Ltd
(**Subsidiary of:** Udg Healthcare Public Limited Company)
2 Marshalls Road, Belfast BT5 6SR
**Tel:** 02890401111 **Fax:** 02890-401240
**Web:** www.sangerspharmacynews.com
**Reg No:** 0018941NI **VAT No:** 574903027
**Estd:** 1830 Private Limited Company
**Line of Business:** Pharmaceutical suppliers and wholesalers
**Trading Style:** Pemberton Marketing, Sangers Distribution, Primacare Services
**Issued Capital:** £100
**Directors:** P G Lemon, Mrs J Dougan, L M Fitzgerald, S Coyle, E Bleakley, P R Surgenor, D Jackson, Mrs N Meier
**Co. Secretary:** Peter Surgenor
**Responsibilities**
**Senior:** Alison Mcbride *(Personal Assistant)*
**Branches:** Sangers (Northern Ireland) Ltd, 286 Maryland Industrial Estate, Newtownards, Co Down BT23 6BL
**US SIC:** 5122 **UK SIC:** 61800
**Auditors:** KPMG
**Bankers:** First Trust Bank (aib Group (uk) Plc) (93-83-43)

| | 30-09-13 | 30-09-12 | 30-09-11 |
|---|---|---|---|
| TO | 225,611,650 | 223,284,365 | 215,393,280 |
| P/L | 6,926,888 | 8,579,990 | 5,737,211 |
| NW | 13,334,508 | 10,043,083 | 9,550,747 |
| WC | 852,815 | 619,882 | 3,144,235 |
| Emp. | 227 | 235 | 284 |

DUNS 21-135-8925 **Imp**
## Sangwin Holdings Ltd
Dansom Lane, Hull, North Humberside HU8 7LN
**Tel:** 01482-329921 **Fax:** 01482-215353
**Web:** www.sangwin.co.uk
**Reg No:** 6687485 **Estd:** 1922 Private Limited Company
**Line of Business:** Manufacture of concrete products for construction purposes
**Issued Capital:** £31,463
**Directors:** I D Sangwin, N J Sangwin
**Co. Secretary:** David Spurgeon
**Responsibilities**
**Health & Safety:** Dave Richardson *(Health & Safety Manager)*
**Facilities:** Dave Richardson *(Health & Safety Manager)*
**US SIC:** 7399 **UK SIC:** 83954
**Auditors:** Smailes Goldie

| | 28-02-14 | 28-02-13 | 29-02-12 |
|---|---|---|---|
| TO | 19,705,117 | 22,206,017 | 19,428,260 |
| P/L | 909,980 | 1,237,060 | 590,653 |
| NW | 3,406,964 | 3,147,544 | 2,660,070 |
| WC | 1,059,803 | 1,158,717 | 275,212 |
| Emp. | 136 | 147 | 152 |

DUNS 45-859-6533 **Imp**
## Sanjeev 1979 Ltd
1st Floor Concept, 6 Magnickle Drive, London NW10 7AW
**Tel:** 020 8961 0187
**Web:** www.influencefashion.co.uk
**Reg No:** 3205716 **Estd:** 1996 Private Limited Company
**Line of Business:** Wholesale of clothing and footwear
**Export Sales:** £7,804,016
**Trading Style:** Influence
**Issued Capital:** £2
**Directors:** S Kumar, B Kumar, Ms S Kumar, R Kumar
**Co. Secretary:** Sanjeev Kumar
**Responsibilities**
**Health & Safety:** Gaura Deb *(general manager)*
**Branches:** Sanjeev 1979 Ltd, 140 Cheetham Hill Road, Manchester M8 8PZ
**US SIC:** 5199, 7399
**UK SIC:** 61900, 83954
**Auditors:** Mitchell Charlesworth
**Bankers:** Barclays Bank Plc (20-12-05)

| | 30-06-13 | 30-06-12 | 30-06-11 |
|---|---|---|---|
| TO | 28,679,338 | 30,529,051 | 31,549,123 |
| P/L | 21,521 | 456,536 | 249,135 |
| NW | 2,289,455 | 2,477,557 | 2,224,729 |
| WC | 439,886 | 693,505 | 532,676 |
| Emp. | 118 | 138 | 142 |

DUNS 28-837-9977 **Imp-Exp**
## Sankey Laminations Ltd
(**Subsidiary of:** Sumitomo Corporation)
Anchor Lane, Bilston, West Midlands WV14 9NE
**Tel:** 01902-693000 **Fax:** 01902 661100
**Web:** www.cogent-power.com
**Reg No:** 0472505 **VAT No:** 410076306
**Estd:** 1949 Private Limited Company
**Line of Business:** Manufacturers and distributors of press tools and jigs
**Export Markets:** Scandinavia, Germany, U S A
**Export Sales:** £11,213,000
**Trading Style:** Kienle + Spiess Uk
**Issued Capital:** £25,000
**Directors:** A Gohring, W Werheid
**Co. Secretary:** Ms Hazel Gilhooly
**Responsibilities**
**Senior:** Matteo Fassio *(Manager)*
**HR:** Jennifer Gibson *(Human Resources Manager)*
**Health & Safety:** Jennifer Gibson *(Human Resources Manager)*
**Facilities:** Martin Pitt *(Maintenance Manager)*
**Purchasing:** Sylvester Phillips *(Purchasing Manager)*
**Branches:** Sankey Laminations Ltd, Anchor Lane, Bilston, West Midlands WV14 9NE
**US SIC:** 3542, 3999
**UK SIC:** 32212, 49590
**Auditors:** PricewaterhouseCoopers LLP
**Bankers:** Lloyds TSB Bank plc (30-00-02)

| | 31-12-13 | 31-12-12 | 31-12-11 |
|---|---|---|---|
| TO | 16,082,000 | 19,917,000 | 15,453,000 |
| P/L | 433,000 | 1,706,000 | 1,089,000 |
| NW | 6,849,000 | 6,600,000 | 7,600,000 |
| WC | 2,935,000 | 3,924,000 | 5,062,000 |
| Emp. | 141 | 141 | 139 |

DUNS 39-706-7612 **Imp-Exp**
## Sanko Gosei Uk Ltd
(**Subsidiary of:** Sanko Gosei Ltd.)
15-17 Seddon Place, Skelmersdale, Lancashire WN8 8EB
**Tel:** 08707503400
**Web:** www.sankogosei.com
**Reg No:** 2159382 **VAT No:** 480196537
**Estd:** 1986 Private Limited Company
**Line of Business:** Plastic injection moulding
**Export Sales:** £7,596,013
**Issued Capital:** £4,170,000
**Directors:** L P Tabner, T Shibata, A Kusumi, K Kajiya, H Aoki, W Ash, Y Shibata
**Co. Secretary:** Mrs Jane Harris
**Responsibilities**
**IT:** Phil Gault *(IT Manager)*
**HR:** Karen Houghton *(Human Resources Manager)*
**Health & Safety:** Karen Houghton *(Human Resources Manager)*
**US SIC:** 3079, 2834
**UK SIC:** 48360, 25700
**Auditors:** KPMG LLP
**Bankers:** National Westminster Bank Plc (60-19-49)

| | 31-05-14 | 31-05-13 | 31-05-12 |
|---|---|---|---|
| TO | 26,596,174 | 20,464,673 | 18,638,374 |
| P/L | 1,379,699 | 2,439 | (393,347) |
| NW | 2,743,443 | 1,279,165 | 1,170,795 |
| WC | 362,123 | 331,313 | (551,686) |
| Emp. | 164 | 188 | 119 |

DUNS 21-729-0034
## Sankofa Group Ltd
New Broad Street House, 35 New Broad Street, London EC2M 1NH
**Tel:** 020-7096-0250
**Web:** www.sankofa-group.com
**Reg No:** 7649043 **Estd:** 2011 Private Limited Company
**Line of Business:** Management activities of holding companies
**Issued Capital:** £17,400
**Director:** Dr B I Horsford
**Co. Secretary:** Fanon Healthcare
**US SIC:** 6711 **UK SIC:** 83962

| | 31-05-14 | 31-05-13 | 31-05-12 |
|---|---|---|---|
| TA | 104,479 | 52,463 | 14,117 |
| NW | 100,264 | 48,247 | 11,951 |
| WC | 96,328 | 42,625 | 4,743 |

DUNS 22-505-2984
## Sanlam Life & Pensions Uk Ltd
(**Subsidiary of:** Sanlam Ltd)
St Bartholomews House, Lewins Mead, Bristol, Avon BS1 2NH
**Tel:** 0117-926-6366 **Fax:** 0117-975-2144
**Web:** www.merchant-investors.co.uk
**Reg No:** 0980142 **Estd:** 1970 Private Limited Company
**Line of Business:** Life insurance
**Trading Style:** Sanlam Investor
**Issued Capital:** £25,000,000
**Directors:** A J Morley, L Lambrechts, I Plenderleith, J P Gibson, A Gildenhuys, J A Samuels, P R Bradshaw, R Roux
**Co. Secretary:** Mrs Rehana Loram
**Responsibilities**
**Senior:** Nicholas Parry *(Director)*
**Marketing:** Herman Sandrock *(Sales & Marketing Manager)*
**Sales:** Herman Sandrock *(Sales & Marketing Manager)*
**Admin:** Mitch Williamson *(Office Manager)*
**IT:** Shaun Glass *(IT Manager)*
**HR:** Joanne Beech *(Human Resources Coordinator)*
**Health & Safety:** Mitch Williamson *(Office Manager)*
**Purchasing:** Mitch Williamson *(Office Manager)*
**Branches:** Sanlam Life & Pensions Uk Ltd, 32 Cornhill, London EC3V 3LJ
**US SIC:** 6311, 6371
**UK SIC:** 82002
**Auditors:** Ernst & Young LLP

**Bankers:** Barclays Bank Plc (20-13-42)

| | 31-12-13 | 31-12-12 | 31-12-11 |
|---|---|---|---|
| TO | 225,368,000 | 124,804,000 | 118,412,000 |
| P/L | 12,055,000 | 7,121,000 | 6,862,000 |
| NW | 33,464,000 | 34,292,000 | 32,461,000 |
| WC | 26,935,000 | 23,483,000 | 17,310,000 |
| Emp. | 108 | 105 | 101 |

DUNS 29-823-7769

## Sanlam Private Investments (Uk) Ltd

(**Subsidiary of:** Sanlam Ltd)
16 South Park, Sevenoaks, Kent TN13 1AN
**Tel:** 01732-740700 **Fax:** 01732-740287
**Web:** www.spi.sanlam.co.uk
**Reg No:** 2041819 **VAT No:** 644353148
**Estd:** 1987 Private Limited Company
**Line of Business:** Fund management activities
**Trading Style:** Sanlam Private Investments (Uk) Ltd.
**Issued Capital:** £100,000
**Directors:** Mrs A L Barwell, D J Gager, F Bruwer, J L Amor, C A Massey, D E Kriel, B Smith, H H Titcomb
**Co. Secretary:** Duncan Gager
**Responsibilities**
**Senior:** Charles Brand *(Director)*, Chris Brocklehurst *(Head of Risk)*, Johannes Petrus *(Manager)*, Christopher Tolkien *(IT Manager)*
**Sales:** Chris Beecroft *(Sales Support)*, Adrian Jewitt *(Head of Intermediary Sales)*, Phil Valentine *(Sales Support)*
**Admin:** Rachael Aldous *(Senior Administrator)*, Mandy Stell *(Office Manager)*
**IT:** Christopher Tolkien *(IT Manager)*
**Facilities:** Mandy Stell *(Office Manager)*
**Operations:** Christopher Tolkien *(IT Manager)*
**Purchasing:** Mandy Stell *(Office Manager)*
**Branches:** Sanlam Private Investments (Uk) Ltd, 5 Miles's Buildings, Bath, Avon BA1 2QS
**US SIC:** 6371 **UK SIC:** 82002
**Auditors:** Ernst & Young LLP
**Bankers:** Barclays Bank Plc (20-76-55)

| | 31-12-13 | 31-12-12 | 31-12-11 |
|---|---|---|---|
| TO | 23,030,000 | 18,078,000 | 14,058,000 |
| P/L | 4,803,000 | 2,120,000 | 1,317,000 |
| NW | 9,942,000 | 6,325,000 | 4,759,000 |
| WC | 10,115,000 | 6,462,000 | 5,024,000 |
| Emp. | 122 | 123 | 102 |

DUNS 23-888-9294

## Sanlam Wealth Planning Uk Ltd

(**Subsidiary of:** Sanlam Ltd)
Derwen House, Ffordd Derwen, Rhyl, Clwyd LL18 2LS
**Tel:** 01745-345131
**Web:** www.sanlamprivatewealth.co.uk
**Reg No:** 3879955 **Estd:** 1999 Private Limited Company
**Line of Business:** Miscellaneous financial institutions
**Issued Capital:** £2,750,010
**Directors:** A J Morley, J P Gibson, P R Bradshaw, R Briesies, N Speirs, L Van Der Walt, J A Samuels
**Responsibilities**
**Senior:** Andy Davies *(Head Of Group Development)*
**US SIC:** 6111 **UK SIC:** 81501

| | 31-12-13 | 31-12-12 | 31-12-11 |
|---|---|---|---|
| TA | 3,776,439 | 3,034,545 | 1,992,255 |
| P/L | 749,733 | 258,001 | (668,432) |
| NW | 1,522,551 | 762,107 | (155,674) |
| WC | 2,135,151 | 1,103,205 | 244,851 |
| Emp. | 49 | 54 | 54 |

DUNS 22-901-4584 **Imp-Exp**

## Sanmex International Ltd

(**Subsidiary of:** Sanmex Holdings Ltd)
5-9 Dalmarnock Road, Glasgow, Lanarkshire G73 1NY
**Tel:** 01416472244 **Fax:** 01416-131228
**Web:** www.sanmex.com
**Reg No:** 0079216SC **Estd:** 1982 Private Limited Company
**Line of Business:** Manufacture of cleaning and polishing preparations
**Export Markets:** Middle East, Africa, China, Western Europe, South America
**Export Sales:** £3,018,243
**Issued Capital:** £10,000
**Directors:** J T Agnew, W Macmillan, E K Woolfson
**Co. Secretary:** Steven Groden
**Responsibilities**
**Senior:** Allan Groden *(Manager)*, Bernard Groden *(Manager)*
**US SIC:** 2842, 2844
**UK SIC:** 25990, 25820
**Auditors:** Grant Thornton UK LLP

**Bankers:** The Royal Bank Of Scotland Plc (83-07-06)

| | 30-01-14 | 30-01-13 | 30-01-12 |
|---|---|---|---|
| TO | 14,819,062 | 16,977,511 | 16,088,947 |
| P/L | 206,308 | 491,815 | 615,084 |
| NW | 2,953,874 | 2,710,944 | 2,168,250 |
| WC | 1,268,217 | 1,375,662 | 1,152,796 |
| Emp. | 71 | 69 | 69 |

DUNS 42-382-8115

## Sanmina-Sci U.K. Ltd

(**Subsidiary of:** Sanmina Corporation)
7 West Nile Street, Glasgow, Lanarkshire G1 2PR
**Tel:** 01475746811
**Web:** www.sanmina-sci.com
**Reg No:** 4370464 **Estd:** 1988 Private Limited Company
**Line of Business:** Manufacture of electronic valves and tubes and other electronic components
**Directors:** C K Sadeghian, L F Clothier
**Co. Secretary:** Broughton Secretaries Limited
**Responsibilities**
**Senior:** Todd Schull *(Manager)*
**Branches:** Sanmina-Sci U.k. Ltd, Kingston Business Park, Unit 2, Port Glasgow, Renfrewshire PA14 5DG
**US SIC:** 3679 **UK SIC:** 34542
**Auditors:** KPMG LLP
**Bankers:** Citibank Na (18-50-08)
**Employees:** 215
**Turnover:** £17,805,000

DUNS 76-852-2369 **Imp-Exp**

## Sanoh Uk Manufacturing Ltd

(**Subsidiary of:** Sanoh Industrial Co. Ltd.)
Grandeur Point, Fourth Way, Bristol, Avon BS11 8DL
**Tel:** 01179-828260
**Web:** www.sanoh.com
**Reg No:** 2607806 **Estd:** 1991 Private Limited Company
**Line of Business:** Manufacturers of vehicle components
**Export Markets:** Czech Republic; Germany; France
**Export Sales:** £4,110,000
**Issued Capital:** £390,000
**Directors:** Y Takeda, J Hayashi, R Harada, N Tanaka, P K Davis, S Tanaka
**Co. Secretary:** Wilfrid Burke
**Responsibilities**
**IT:** Mike Boote *(IT Manager)*
**US SIC:** 3714 **UK SIC:** 35300
**Auditors:** PricewaterhouseCoopers LLP
**Bankers:** Lloyds TSB Bank plc (30-99-38)

| | 31-03-14 | 31-03-13 | 31-03-12 |
|---|---|---|---|
| TO | 26,571,000 | 26,385,000 | 21,049,000 |
| P/L | 3,728,000 | 2,304,000 | 215,000 |
| NW | 7,230,000 | 4,364,000 | 2,620,000 |
| WC | 3,849,000 | 759,000 | 200,000 |
| Emp. | 313 | 311 | 275 |

DUNS 22-900-5327 **Imp**

## Sanquhar Tile Services Ltd

(**Subsidiary of:** Styletuft Ltd)
Blackaddie Road Industrial Estate, Sanquhar, Dumfriesshire DG4 6DB
**Tel:** 01659-50497 **Fax:** 01659-58384
**Web:** www.sanquhartilesltd.co.uk
**Reg No:** 0009331SC **VAT No:** 428102677
**Estd:** 1971 Private Limited Company
**Line of Business:** Manufacturers of carpets and rugs
**Export Sales:** £1,417,887
**Issued Capital:** £67,720
**Principals:** D Watters *(Financial)*, D Lind, F C Williamson
**Co. Secretary:** Wjm Secretaries Limited
**US SIC:** 2279 **UK SIC:** 43852
**Auditors:** BDO LLP
**Bankers:** Bank Of Scotland (80-18-62)

| | 31-12-13 | 31-12-12 | 31-12-11 |
|---|---|---|---|
| TO | 14,038,606 | 14,426,763 | 13,448,437 |
| P/L | 291,639 | 362,129 | 257,839 |
| NW | 4,601,796 | 4,067,912 | 3,966,601 |
| WC | 2,741,632 | 2,542,570 | 2,385,333 |
| Emp. | 110 | 113 | 113 |

DUNS 42-416-3582

## Sant Tysilio Nursing Home

Llanfairpwllgwyngyll, Llanfairpwllgwyngyll, Llanfairpwllgwyngyll, Gwynedd LL61 5YR
**Tel:** 01248-716400
**Web:** www.santtysilio.org.uk
**Estd:** 1990 Partnership
**Line of Business:** Nursing homes
**Trading Style:** Rhys Williams
**Partners:** H K Mehta, Mrs M H Mehta
**Responsibilities**
**Senior:** Liji Joby *(Manager)*
**US SIC:** 8051 **UK SIC:** 95100
**Employees:** 70

DUNS 50-327-0886 **Imp**

## Santa Maria Uk Ltd

(**Subsidiary of:** Discovery Ltd)
Nimbus House, Maidstone Road, Kingston, Milton Keynes, Buckinghamshire MK10 0BD
**Tel:** 01908-933000
**Web:** www.santamariafoodservice.co.uk
**Reg No:** 2351789 **VAT No:** 545896393
**Estd:** 1989 Private Limited Company
**Line of Business:** Manufacture of bread; manufacture of fresh pastry goods and cakes
**Issued Capital:** £200,000
**Directors:** J A Sundelin, H P Samuelson, J Tanayama, J O Malmus, Mrs D Mckenna
**Co. Secretary:** Nicholas Hayman
**Responsibilities**
**Senior:** Diane McKenna *(Human Resources Manager)*
**Sales:** Martin Purdy *(Country Sales Manager)*
**HR:** Diane McKenna *(Human Resources Manager)*
**Health & Safety:** Roy Laurie *(Health & Safety Officer)*
**US SIC:** 2051 **UK SIC:** 41960
**Auditors:** King Loose & Co
**Bankers:** National Westminster Bank Plc (60-50-50)

| | 31-12-13 | 31-12-12 | 31-12-11 |
|---|---|---|---|
| TO | 46,298,000 | 47,717,000 | 48,754,000 |
| P/L | 1,048,000 | (1,087,000) | (4,798,000) |
| NW | 91,000 | (957,000) | (47,000) |
| WC | 4,959,000 | 4,041,000 | 6,204,000 |
| Emp. | 157 | 156 | 215 |

DUNS 22-278-8908

## Santana Ltd

61 Church Street, London NW8 8EU
**Tel:** 02074027873
**Reg No:** 4296860 **Estd:** 2001 Private Limited Company
**Line of Business:** Hardware and ironmongers merchants
**Issued Capital:** £2
**Director:** J D Wittich
**Co. Secretary:** Mrs Mary Wittich
**US SIC:** 6711 **UK SIC:** 83962
**Bankers:** Barclays Bank Plc (20-00-00)

| | 29-12-13 | 30-12-12 | 01-12-12 |
|---|---|---|---|
| TA | 5,173 | 649 | 286,230 |
| NW | N/A | (167,634) | (15,221) |
| WC | N/A | (167,724) | (298,647) |

DUNS 21-028-3759

## Santander

Po Box 545 1921 Commercial Street, St Helier, Jersey, Channel Islands JE4 8XG
**Tel:** 01534885000
**Web:** www.santanderpb.je
**Proprietorship**
**Line of Business:** Banks
**Proprietor:** N Crolla
**Responsibilities**
**Senior:** Jeone Advocate *(Manager)*, Colin Huelin *(Manager)*, D Robbie *(Manager)*, Roger Wiseman *(Head of Systems)*
**Finance:** Paul Nayar *(Head of Finance)*
**Admin:** Janette Doidge *(Administration Manager)*
**IT:** Stephen France *(Head of Systems)*
**US SIC:** 6012 **UK SIC:** 81402
**Employees:** 120

DUNS 29-434-0922 **Imp**

## Santander Asset Finance (December) Ltd

(**Subsidiary of:** Banco Santander Sa)
Carlton Park, Narborough, Leicester, Leicestershire LE19 0AL
**Tel:** 01162011000
**Reg No:** 1562865 **Estd:** 1981 Private Limited Company
**Line of Business:** Financial leasing
**Issued Capital:** £100
**Directors:** M W Evans, C R Morley, A N Mussert
**Co. Secretary:** Santander Secretariat Services L
**US SIC:** 6111 **UK SIC:** 81501
**Auditors:** Deloitte & Touche LLP
**Bankers:** Girobank Plc (72-16-00)

| | 31-12-13 | 31-12-12 | 31-12-11 |
|---|---|---|---|
| TA | 262,542,180 | 306,497,096 | 350,275,311 |
| P/L | 10,659,665 | 18,826,459 | 11,844,158 |
| NW | 31,322,379 | 23,641,824 | 8,608,814 |
| WC | (171,658,715) | (235,175,834) | (239,455,894) |

DUNS 39-712-6004

## Santander Asset Management Uk Ltd

(**Subsidiary of:** Banco Santander Sa)
301 St Vincent Street, Glasgow, Lanarkshire G2 5HN
**Tel:** 08456000181
**Web:** www.santanderam.co.uk
**Reg No:** 0106669SC **Estd:** 1987 Private Limited Company
**Line of Business:** Financial intermediation not elsewhere classified
**Issued Capital:** £24,196,000
**Directors:** J I Gella Rodero, S J Pateman, J C Scott, A Ceschia, R L Noach, D Lessner, Ms G E Glen
**Co. Secretary:** Jagjit Nazran
**US SIC:** 6111 **UK SIC:** 81501
**Auditors:** Deloitte LLP

| | 31-12-13 | 31-12-12 | 31-12-11 |
|---|---|---|---|
| TA | 45,639,613 | 55,277,737 | 24,307,868 |
| P/L | (4,149,778) | 4,971,942 | 2,582,660 |
| NW | 17,341,344 | 29,546,938 | 10,805,147 |
| WC | 17,143,912 | 29,257,837 | 10,805,147 |

DUNS 23-943-1914

## Santander Cards Ltd

(**Subsidiary of:** Banco Santander Sa)
2-3 Triton Square, London NW1 3AN
**Tel:** 08715225151
**Web:** www.santandercards.com
**Reg No:** 3932752 **Estd:** 1979 Private Limited Company
**Line of Business:** Credit granting by non-deposit taking finance houses and other specialist consumer credit grantors
**Issued Capital:** £179,999,901
**Directors:** R Attar-Zadeh, J R Aboukhair-Hurtado, J D De La Vega, N D Wren, C H Gibson
**Co. Secretary:** Santander Secretariat Services L
**US SIC:** 6111 **UK SIC:** 81501
**Auditors:** Deloitte LLP
**Following financial data are in thousands**

| | 31-12-13 | 31-12-12 | 31-12-11 |
|---|---|---|---|
| TA | 1,608,600 | 1,355,400 | 1,277,100 |
| P/L | 60,200 | 300 | (9,600) |
| NW | 64,900 | 16,500 | 13,900 |
| WC | 64,900 | 16,500 | 13,900 |
| Emp. | 78 | 43 | 49 |

DUNS 39-935-4273

## Santander Consumer (Uk) Plc

(**Subsidiary of:** Banco Santander Sa)
3 Princess Way, Redhill, Surrey RH1 1SR
**Tel:** 08712004150
**Web:** www.santanderconsumer.co.uk
**Reg No:** 2248870 **Estd:** 1988 Public Limited Company
**Line of Business:** Banks and financial institutions
**Trading Style:** Santander Consumer Finance
**Issued Capital:** £150,000,000
**Directors:** B Montalvo Wilmot, J Anton San Pablo, V T Hill, S J Pateman, A R Goldhagen, Ms M Cueva Diaz, Ms D E Roberts
**Co. Secretary:** Santander Secretariat Services L
**Responsibilities**
**Senior:** Vik Hill *(Manager)*
**US SIC:** 6111 **UK SIC:** 81501
**Auditors:** Deloitte LLP
**Following financial data are in thousands**

| | 31-12-13 | 31-12-12 | 31-12-11 |
|---|---|---|---|
| TA | 4,264,535 | 4,036,863 | 3,641,563 |
| P/L | 120,937 | 111,372 | 85,544 |
| NW | 380,978 | 298,794 | 214,737 |
| WC | (196,114) | (1,221,597) | (1,162,027) |
| Emp. | 472 | 476 | 502 |

DUNS 29-422-8796

## Santander Insurance Services Uk Ltd

(**Subsidiary of:** Banco Santander Sa)
Abbey National House, 2 Triton Square Regents Place, London NW1 3AN
**Tel:** 08009175090
**Reg No:** 1492302 **Estd:** 1980 Private Limited Company
**Line of Business:** Financial intermediation not elsewhere classified
**Issued Capital:** £2
**Directors:** J R Aboukhair Hurtado, D J Hickman, F D Ayuso, J Olaizola, A L Rodriguez, J De La Vega
**Co. Secretary:** Santander Secretariat Services L
**US SIC:** 6111 **UK SIC:** 81501
**Auditors:** Deloitte LLP

| | 31-12-13 | 31-12-12 | 31-12-11 |
|---|---|---|---|
| TA | 57,321,000 | 53,160,000 | 47,223,000 |
| P/L | 1,144,000 | 4,913,000 | 4,163,000 |
| NW | 32,932,000 | 32,076,000 | 28,402,000 |
| WC | 32,932,000 | 32,076,000 | 28,402,000 |
| Emp. | 52 | 52 | 51 |

DUNS 73-935-6830

## Santander Isa Managers Ltd

(**Subsidiary of:** Banco Santander Sa)
287 St Vincent Street, Glasgow, Lanarkshire G2 5NB
**Fax:** 01412-759230
**Web:** www.isamarkets.com
**Reg No:** 0151605SC **Estd:** 1999 Private Limited Company
**Line of Business:** Financial intermediation not elsewhere classified
**Issued Capital:** £37,000,000
**Directors:** Ms A Wakelin, J Alzamora, S J Pateman, Ms P C Ickinger, J De La Vega
**Co. Secretary:** Santander Secretariat Services L

**US SIC:** 6111 **UK SIC:** 81501
**Auditors:** Deloitte & Touche LLP

| | 31-12-13 | 31-12-12 | 31-12-11 |
|---|---|---|---|
| TA | 8,929,850 | 29,496,786 | 35,047,728 |
| P/L | (1,116,714) | 1,689,019 | 2,105,037 |
| NW | 5,143,324 | 20,738,845 | 19,450,501 |
| WC | 5,143,324 | 23,721,299 | 26,077,820 |

DUNS 50-005-2220
## Santander Uk Plc
(**Subsidiary of:** Banco Santander Sa)
2-3 Triton Square, Regents Place, London NW1 3AN
**Tel:** 08706076000
**Web:** www.santander.co.uk
**Reg No:** 2294747 **Estd:** 2001 Public Limited Company
**Line of Business:** Banks and financial institutions
**Issued Capital:** £3,430,476,889
**Directors:** R D Brown, S J Pateman, J M Carballo Cotanda, Ms R P Thorne, Ms A P Botin-Sanz De Sautuola Y O'She, J S Wheway, A H Dromer, M L Amato
**Co. Secretary:** Shaun Coles
**Responsibilities**
**Senior:** Nathan Bostock *(Director)*, Terence Burns *(Chairman)*, Antonio Escamez Torres *(Director)*, Jose Fuster Van Bendegem *(Director)*, Juan Inciarte *(Director)*, Manuel Soto Serrano *(Director)*, Richard Truelove *(General Manager)*
**Finance:** Rachel Baynes *(Head of Brand and Communicatio)*, Rachel Morrison *(Director of Financial Control)*, Umesh Ramji *(Fraud Mitigation Manager)*
**Marketing:** Rachel Baynes *(Head of Brand and Communicatio)*, James Cairns *(Head of Customer Insight & Pro)*, Charlotte Cleeton *(Corporate Communication and Ev)*, Sara Garcia Moran *(Marketing Manager)*, Keith Moor *(Chief Marketing Officer)*, Dan Sherwood *(Head of Marketing Strategy, Ev)*, Kirsty Wilson *(Multi Channel Marketing Manage)*
**Sales:** Ben Barbanel *(Business Development Director)*, John Hennessy *(Chief Risk Officer, Wholesale)*, Allison Moulton *(Head of Specialist Products)*, Graham Sellar *(?Head of Business Development)*
**IT:** John Dempsey *(Head of IT)*, Manuel Porcel *(Software Development Manager)*
**HR:** Wendy Carr *(People & Talent - Resourcing B)*
**Purchasing:** Suzanne Batten *(Head of Retail Management)*
**Branches:** Santander Uk Plc, Santander Uk Plc, 161-163 High Street, Birmingham, West Midlands B14 7DJ
**US SIC:** 6012, 7399
**UK SIC:** 81402, 83954
**Auditors:** Deloitte LLP
**Bankers:** Bank Of England (10-00-00)
**Following financial data are in thousands**

| | 31-12-13 | 31-12-12 | 31-12-11 |
|---|---|---|---|
| TA | 270,305,000 | 293,044,000 | 297,574,000 |
| P/L | 1,139,000 | 1,231,000 | 1,261,000 |
| NW | 10,185,000 | 10,624,000 | 10,524,000 |
| WC | 8,940,000 | 9,988,000 | 34,251,000 |
| Emp. | 20,064 | 21,090 | 21,371 |

DUNS 73-667-2895 **Imp**
## Sante Verte Ltd
(**Subsidiary of:** Ndg Group Sa)
Unit E, Ashford, Kent TN24 0SH
**Tel:** 01233504444
**Web:** www.sante-verte.com
**Reg No:** 4926782 **Estd:** 2003 Private Limited Company
**Line of Business:** Non-specialised wholesale of food, beverages and tobacco
**Export Sales:** £26,575,563
**Issued Capital:** £1
**Director:** D Le Normand
**US SIC:** 5149, 5122
**UK SIC:** 61700, 61800
**Auditors:** Magee Gammon Corporate Ltd

| | 31-12-13 | 31-12-12 | 31-12-11 |
|---|---|---|---|
| TO | 26,881,763 | 24,611,286 | 20,516,759 |
| P/L | 4,420,047 | 4,742,766 | 4,098,882 |
| NW | 8,530,842 | 5,385,180 | 3,497,209 |
| WC | 8,209,612 | 5,064,621 | 3,278,397 |
| Emp. | 124 | 111 | 102 |

DUNS 21-710-9923
## Santia Consulting Ltd
(**Subsidiary of:** Becap Santia Limited)
Santia House, Parc, Nantgarw, Cardiff, South Glamorgan CF15 7QX
**Tel:** 02920852852
**Web:** www.santiaconsulting.com
**Reg No:** 7511553 **Estd:** 2011 Private Limited Company
**Line of Business:** Safety advisers and technicians
**Export Sales:** £656,831
**Trading Style:** Safecontractor
**Issued Capital:** £1
**Directors:** Ms J H Hext, A Franklin

**Responsibilities**
**Senior:** Lawrence Rawlinson *(Company SOLITCOR)*
**US SIC:** 7392 **UK SIC:** 83951
**Auditors:** Grant Thornton UK LLP
**Bankers:** National Westminster Bank Plc (50-00-00)

| | 31-01-14 | 31-01-13 | 31-01-12 |
|---|---|---|---|
| TO | 15,106,984 | 15,903,041 | 22,415,089 |
| P/L | (3,471,717) | (4,306,604) | (4,707,436) |
| NW | (14,932,236) | (11,910,388) | (8,330,122) |
| WC | (3,552,234) | (896,578) | 1,514,218 |
| Emp. | 328 | 399 | 438 |

DUNS 21-710-9919
## Santia Holdco Ltd
(**Subsidiary of:** Becap Santia Limited)
Santia House Parc Nantgarw, Nantgarw, Cardiff, South Glamorgan CF15 7QX
**Tel:** 08455040402
**Reg No:** 7511550 **Estd:** 2011 Private Limited Company
**Line of Business:** Management activities of holding companies
**Export Sales:** £1,249,000
**Issued Capital:** £1,000
**Directors:** A Franklin, Mrs K Halford, R M Leighton, Ms J Hext, T G Bouzac, P Ollerton
**US SIC:** 6711 **UK SIC:** 83962
**Bankers:** National Westminster Bank Plc (50-00-00)

| | 31-01-14 | 31-01-13 | 31-01-12 |
|---|---|---|---|
| TO | 28,885,000 | 29,237,000 | 32,385,000 |
| P/L | (2,362,000) | (3,151,000) | (5,226,000) |
| NW | (14,321,000) | (10,914,000) | (8,459,000) |
| WC | (3,702,000) | (150,000) | 1,129,000 |
| Emp. | 500 | 511 | 642 |

DUNS 29-560-3419
## Santoro Ltd
Rotunda Point, 11 Hartfield Crescent, London SW19 3RL
**Tel:** 02087811106
**Web:** www.santoro-london.com
**Reg No:** 1924562 **Estd:** 1985 Private Limited Company
**Line of Business:** E-commerce
**Issued Capital:** £100,000
**Principals:** L A Santoro *(Managing)*, J C Freeman, Ms M Santoro
**Co. Secretary:** Godlove Quaye
**Responsibilities**
**Senior:** Yvette Wilmot *(Assistant to Director)*
**Branches:** Santoro Ltd, Unit 11 Atlas North Indstl Est, Atlas Way, Sheffield, South Yorkshire S4 7QQ
**US SIC:** 2731 **UK SIC:** 47532
**Auditors:** H W Fisher & Co

| | 31-12-13 | 31-12-12 | 31-12-11 |
|---|---|---|---|
| TA | 7,825,768 | 7,177,096 | 5,419,241 |
| NW | 6,396,275 | 5,839,506 | 4,722,255 |
| WC | 5,734,917 | 5,204,192 | 4,083,786 |

DUNS 39-695-1675 **Imp-Exp**
## Sap (Uk) Ltd
(**Subsidiary of:** Sap Se)
Clockhouse Place, Feltham, Middlesex TW14 8HD
**Tel:** 0870-608-4000
**Web:** www.sap.com
**Reg No:** 2152073 **VAT No:** 494703129
**Estd:** 1987 Private Limited Company
**Line of Business:** Computer software (development)
**Issued Capital:** £10,000,000
**Directors:** L Mucic, Mrs E Shishkina, D Roos
**Co. Secretary:** Howard Bennett
**Responsibilities**
**Senior:** Frederic Arrouays *(Chief Financial Officer)*, Jonathan Trew *(Manager)*, Sarah Woodman *(Facilities Manager)*
**Finance:** Frederic Arrouays *(Chief Financial Officer)*
**Marketing:** Valentina Pettenati *(Senior Marketing Specialist)*, Sian Smith *(Marketing Director)*
**Sales:** Peter Heffner *(Sales Director)*
**Admin:** Corrin Cole *(?Executive Assistant - SVP Mar)*
**IT:** Thomas Mocek *(IT Manager)*
**HR:** Laura Burton *(Human Resources Director)*
**Facilities:** Sarah Woodman *(Facilities Manager)*
**Operations:** Guy Armstrong *(Chief Operations Officer)*
**Purchasing:** Frederic Arrouays *(Chief Financial Officer)*
**Branches:** Sap (Uk) Ltd, 1 Noble Drive, Bath Road, Hayes, Middlesex UB3 5EY
**US SIC:** 7379 **UK SIC:** 83940
**Auditors:** KPMG LLP
**Bankers:** Lloyds TSB Bank plc (30-93-08)

| | 31-12-13 | 31-12-12 | 31-12-11 |
|---|---|---|---|
| TO | 693,164,000 | 613,348,000 | 583,019,000 |
| P/L | 20,872,000 | 5,679,000 | 28,075,000 |
| NW | (6,681,000) | (21,061,000) | 1,352,000 |
| WC | (12,890,000) | 60,917,000 | 105,098,000 |
| Emp. | 1,397 | 1,185 | 1,066 |

DUNS 85-613-3694
## Sapa Aluminium Extrusion Ltd
Sawpit Lane Industrial Estate Mansfield, Road, Alfreton, Derbyshire DE55 5NH
**Tel:** 01773872761
**Web:** www.sapagroup.com
**Reg No:** 6249949 **Estd:** 1968 Private Limited Company
**Line of Business:** Aluminium products
**Export Sales:** £4,813,000
**Issued Capital:** £1,000
**Directors:** J F Tate, A Couturier
**Co. Secretary:** James Tate
**Responsibilities**
**Marketing:** Jude Howson *(Marketing Manager)*
**IT:** Richard Tuck *(IT Manager)*
**US SIC:** 3334 **UK SIC:** 22451
**Bankers:** Barclays Bank Plc (20-20-15)

| | 31-12-13 | 31-12-12 | 31-12-11 |
|---|---|---|---|
| TO | 98,554,000 | 93,208,000 | 98,592,000 |
| P/L | 4,498,000 | 2,444,000 | 3,266,000 |
| NW | 36,952,000 | 32,969,000 | 31,048,000 |
| WC | 17,475,000 | 17,867,000 | 16,651,000 |
| Emp. | 326 | 337 | 331 |

DUNS 21-726-3284 **Exp**
## Sapa Building Systems Ltd
(**Subsidiary of:** Orkla Asa)
Alexandra Way, Ashchurch, Tewkesbury, Gloucestershire GL20 8NB
**Tel:** 01684853500
**Web:** www.sapagroup.com
**Reg No.** 1029071 **Estd.** 1971 Private Limited Company
**Line of Business:** Wholesale of metals and ores
**Export Sales:** £526,000
**Trading Style:** Glostal Monach
**Issued Capital:** £1,420,320
**Principals:** N K Sissons *(Financial)*, P C Strong, J P Vos, S N Viner, M P Robinson, N A Eley, J P Palethorpe, Ms K Cookson
**Co. Secretary:** Simon Viner
**Responsibilities**
**Senior:** Hans Johansson *(Manager)*
**Health & Safety:** Paul Perrott *(Health & Safety Officer)*
**Facilities:** Steve Stack *(Logistics Manager)*
**Purchasing:** Ray Simmonds *(Purchasing Manager)*
**Fleet:** Steve Stack *(Logistics Manager)*
**US SIC:** 5051, 3999
**UK SIC:** 61200, 49590
**Auditors:** Ernst & Young LLP
**Bankers:** Barclays Bank Plc (20-20-15)

| | 31-12-13 | 31-12-12 | 31-12-11 |
|---|---|---|---|
| TO | 33,933,000 | 32,368,000 | 31,024,000 |
| P/L | 605,000 | 747,000 | 692,000 |
| NW | 8,097,000 | 9,746,000 | 11,160,000 |
| WC | 6,009,000 | 7,528,000 | 8,765,000 |
| Emp. | 146 | 151 | 164 |

DUNS 22-778-1788 **Imp**
## Sapa Building Systems (Wakefield) Ltd
(**Subsidiary of:** Sapa As)
Hbs Centre, Silkwood Park, Wakefield, West Yorkshire WF5 9TG
**Tel:** 08456028799
**Web:** www.hydro.com
**Reg No:** 1420752 **VAT No:** 675388093
**Estd:** 1963 Private Limited Company
**Line of Business:** Wholesale of wood, construction materials and sanitary equipment
**Export Sales:** £1,377,000
**Trading Style:** Technal Uk, Wicona Uk
**Issued Capital:** £1,200,000
**Director:** N K Sissons
**Co. Secretary:** Simon Viner
**Responsibilities**
**Senior:** Lars Ringvold *(Manager)*, Christine Simms *(Marketing Manager)*
**Branches:** Sapa Building Systems (Wakefield) Ltd, The Lodden Centre, Unit J, Basingstoke, Hampshire RG24 8FL
**US SIC:** 5039 **UK SIC:** 61300
**Auditors:** KPMG LLP
**Bankers:** National Westminster Bank Plc (60-01-35)

| | 31-12-13 | 31-12-12 | 31-12-11 |
|---|---|---|---|
| TO | 15,015,000 | 15,083,000 | 16,860,000 |
| P/L | (647,000) | (827,000) | (944,000) |
| NW | 2,464,000 | 3,235,000 | 4,060,000 |
| WC | 2,125,000 | 2,828,000 | 3,602,000 |
| Emp. | 54 | 61 | 70 |

DUNS 85-613-3512
## Sapa Components Uk Ltd
(**Subsidiary of:** Sapa As)
Barbot Hall Industrial Estate, Rotherham, South Yorkshire S62 6EF
**Tel:** 0 1709 833 959 **Fax:** 01709 829 251
**Web:** www.sapagroup.com
**Reg No:** 6249930 **Estd:** 1954 Private Limited Company
**Line of Business:** Manufacture of builders carpentry and joinery
**Export Sales:** £9,576,000
**Trading Style:** Sapa Group
**Issued Capital:** £1,000
**Directors:** A Couturier, C Carpenter, Mrs C L Butler
**Co. Secretary:** Mrs Claire Butler
**Branches:** Sapa Components Uk Limited, Unit 5, Kingsditch Lane, Cheltenham, Gloucestershire GL51 9PX
**US SIC:** 2431, 3334
**UK SIC:** 46300, 22451
**Auditors:** Ernst & Young LLP
**Bankers:** Barclays Bank Plc (20-20-15)

| | 31-12-13 | 31-12-12 | 31-12-11 |
|---|---|---|---|
| TO | 38,127,000 | 30,189,000 | 35,161,000 |
| P/L | 2,062,000 | (248,000) | (3,250,000) |
| NW | 718,000 | (1,520,000) | (1,482,000) |
| WC | 11,782,000 | 9,854,000 | 9,995,000 |
| Emp. | 246 | 226 | 275 |

DUNS 21-711-6953 **Imp**
## Sapa Profiles Uk Ltd
(**Subsidiary of:** Sapa As)
Pantglas Industrial Estate, Caerphilly, Mid Glamorgan CF83 8DR
**Tel:** 01452634070 **Fax:** 02920865229
**Web:** www.sapagroup.cpm
**Reg No:** 0961843 **VAT No:** 134635770
**Estd:** 2000 Private Limited Company
**Line of Business:** Aluminium production
**Export Sales:** £1,465,000
**Trading Style:** Bedwas Plant
**Issued Capital:** £53,376,000
**Directors:** A R Couturier, J F Tate, S M Meeuwissen-True
**Co. Secretary:** David Williams
**Responsibilities**
**Senior:** Gwyn Powell *(Manager)*, Paul Randle *(Director)*, Derrick Webb *(Manager)*
**Branches:** Sapa Profiles Uk Limited, Pantglas Industrial Estate, Bedwas, Bedwas, Caerphilly, Mid Glamorgan CF83 8DR
**US SIC:** 3334 **UK SIC:** 22451
**Auditors:** KPMG LLP
**Bankers:** Commerzbank Ag (30-12-42)

| | 31-12-13 | 31-12-12 | 31-12-11 |
|---|---|---|---|
| TO | 59,818,000 | 63,142,000 | 72,776,000 |
| P/L | (11,500,000) | (2,999,000) | (1,226,000) |
| NW | 3,733,000 | 14,762,000 | 17,436,000 |
| WC | 7,873,000 | 9,544,000 | 11,072,000 |
| Emp. | 283 | 290 | 302 |

DUNS 23-597-9312
## Sapiens (Uk) Insurance Software Solutions Ltd
Building 1 Caspian Point, Pier Head Street, Cardiff, South Glamorgan CF10 4DQ
**Tel:** 02920-448-600 **Fax:** 02920-504-286
**Web:** www.sapiens.com
**Reg No:** 3595317 **Estd:** 1998 Private Limited Company
**Line of Business:** Other business activities not elsewhere classified
**Export Sales:** £1,937,262
**Issued Capital:** £1
**Directors:** R Al-Dor, P Slattery, R Giladi
**Co. Secretary:** Roni Giladi
**US SIC:** 7399 **UK SIC:** 83954
**Auditors:** Levy Cohen & Co

| | 31-12-13 | 31-12-12 | 31-12-11 |
|---|---|---|---|
| TO | 14,032,544 | 12,406,263 | 7,887,347 |
| P/L | 483,059 | 151,133 | 167,561 |
| NW | 3,250,774 | 2,872,088 | 2,721,577 |
| WC | 2,946,695 | 2,686,042 | 2,600,030 |
| Emp. | 128 | 93 | 72 |

DUNS 49-433-0988 **Imp**
## Sapient Ltd
(**Subsidiary of:** Sapient Corporation)
Eden House, London E1 6DX
**Tel:** 01670812772 **Fax:** 020-7786-4600
**Web:** www.sapient.com
**Reg No:** 3144067 **Estd:** 1990 Private Limited Company
**Line of Business:** Internet services
**Issued Capital:** £7,950,457
**Directors:** J M Reid, N G Vaz, J S Tibbetts Jr
**Co. Secretary:** Clyde Secretaries Limited
**Responsibilities**
**Senior:** Joseph Tibbetts *(Director)*, Valerie Vena *(Manager)*
**Sales:** Shailesh Joshi *(Director of Business Consultin)*, Anant Saxena *(Senior Account Director)*, Mihir Vaidya *(Business Consulting Manager)*
**US SIC:** 7379 **UK SIC:** 83940
**Auditors:** PricewaterhouseCoopers LLP
**Bankers:** National Westminster Bank Plc (50-00-00)

| | 31-12-13 | 31-12-12 | 31-12-11 |
|---|---|---|---|
| TO | 108,224,000 | 103,127,000 | 97,792,000 |
| P/L | 573,000 | 2,452,000 | 2,539,000 |
| NW | 18,235,000 | 23,031,000 | 18,968,000 |
| WC | 25,374,000 | 34,710,000 | 34,277,000 |
| Emp. | 788 | 795 | 754 |

DUNS 77-515-3604

## Sapienza Consulting Ltd

5 Birtley Courtyard, Guildford, Surrey GU5 0LA
**Tel:** 01483-890298
**Web:** www.sapienzaconsulting.com
**Reg No:** 2986023 **Estd:** 1994 Private Limited Company
**Line of Business:** Building construction contractors
**Issued Capital:** £250
**Director:** T Larfaoui
**Co. Secretary:** Michael Bearman
**Responsibilities**
**Senior:** Frederique Berenbach *(Manager)*
**Sales:** Frederique Berenbach *(Manager)*
**Engineering:** Andrea Bennetti *(Commercial Director of Space P)*
**Branches:** Sapienza Consulting Ltd, 38 Parkway, Welwyn Garden City, Hertfordshire AL8 6HQ
**US SIC:** 7379 **UK SIC:** 83940
**Auditors:** Alexander Mayerson & Co

| | 31-12-13 | 31-12-12 | 31-12-11 |
|---|---|---|---|
| TO | 7,678,428 | N/A | N/A |
| P/L | (24,584) | N/A | N/A |
| NW | 219,788 | 403,445 | 514,037 |
| WC | 138,318 | 306,232 | 395,314 |
| Emp. | 98 | N/A | N/A |

DUNS 22-214-2775

## Sapphire Cards Ltd

(**Subsidiary of:** Bank of America Corporation)
28 St Andrew Square, Edinburgh, Midlothian EH2 1AF
**Tel:** 07712848300 **Fax:** 01603-215700
**Web:** www.virginmoney.com
**Reg No:** 4232392 **Estd:** 2001 Private Limited Company
**Line of Business:** Activities auxiliary to financial intermediation not elsewhere classified
**Issued Capital:** £100
**Directors:** C W Bradley, J P Metcalfe, J B West
**Co. Secretary:** Mrs Alyson Mulholland
**Responsibilities**
**Senior:** Marian Watson *(Manager)*
**HR:** Simon Leeming *(Human Resources Director)*
**Health & Safety:** David Wadham *(Facilities Manager)*
**Facilities:** David Wadham *(Facilities Manager)*
**US SIC:** 7399 **UK SIC:** 83954
**Auditors:** KPMG LLP
**Bankers:** HSBC Bank plc (40-00-00)

| | 31-12-13 | 31-12-12 | 31-12-11 |
|---|---|---|---|
| TO | N/A | 79,732,000 | 117,601,000 |
| P/L | (4,491,591) | 27,936,000 | 79,572,000 |
| NW | (13,018,350) | 113,617,000 | 92,628,000 |
| WC | (13,018,350) | 113,617,000 | 92,628,000 |

DUNS 22-025-0828

## Sapphire Energy Recovery Ltd

(**Subsidiary of:** Lafarge Tarmac Holdings Ltd)
Yelsway Lane, Stoke-On-Trent, Staffordshire ST10 3AZ
**Tel:** 01538-309400
**Web:** www.sapphirerecovery.co.uk
**Reg No:** 4027738 **Estd:** 2001 Private Limited Company
**Line of Business:** Agents involved in the sale of fuels, ores, metals and industrial chemicals
**Issued Capital:** £3,500,000
**Directors:** Lafarge Tarmac Directors (Uk) Li, R Hodder, C Law, J Janse Van Rensburg
**Co. Secretary:** Lafarge Tarmac Secretaries (Uk)
**US SIC:** 5199 **UK SIC:** 61900
**Auditors:** Deloitte LLP

| | 31-12-13 | 31-12-12 | 31-12-11 |
|---|---|---|---|
| TO | 8,752,396 | 9,352,880 | 7,877,501 |
| P/L | 94,842 | (42,403) | 245,589 |
| NW | 1,519,656 | 1,218,127 | 1,218,875 |
| WC | 455,619 | (194,086) | (164,685) |
| Emp. | 46 | 53 | 51 |

DUNS 42-451-2015

## Sapphire Garage Ltd

Quantum Business Park, Monsall Road, Manchester M40 8FY
**Tel:** 0161-202-8680 **Fax:** 01612028697
**Web:** www.sapphiregarage.co.uk
**Reg No:** 4438851 **Estd:** 2002 Private Limited Company
**Line of Business:** Car body repairers
**Issued Capital:** £112
**Director:** A Arnone
**Co. Secretary:** Ms Paula Arnone
**US SIC:** 7539 **UK SIC:** 67100

| | 31-12-13 | 31-12-12 | 30-12-11 |
|---|---|---|---|
| TO | 6,809,886 | 9,812,024 | 6,563,745 |
| P/L | 289,656 | 623,676 | 516,746 |
| NW | 1,713,344 | 1,432,528 | 1,008,862 |
| WC | (762,881) | (423,249) | (654,409) |
| Emp. | 75 | 59 | 67 |

DUNS 22-704-4963

## Sapphire Laundry Ltd

Sultra House, London SE1 4SB
**Tel:** 020-7232-2904 **Fax:** 020-7231-8332
**Reg No:** 1589271 **VAT No:** 243037785
**Estd:** 1981 Private Limited Company
**Line of Business:** Linen hire
**Issued Capital:** £100
**Director:** Ms T Chung
**Co. Secretary:** Ms Kerstin Lydon
**Responsibilities**
**Senior:** Kristine Lydan *(CEO, Managing Director)*, Christine Lydon *(Manager)*
**Health & Safety:** Lincoln Honer *(Health & Safety Officer)*
**Purchasing:** Christine Lydon *(Manager)*
**US SIC:** 7219 **UK SIC:** 98110
**Auditors:** Lustigman & Co

| | 30-11-13 | 30-11-12 | 30-11-11 |
|---|---|---|---|
| TA | 519,960 | 524,631 | 501,697 |
| NW | 273,616 | 266,786 | 268,278 |
| WC | (55,431) | (69,605) | (61,998) |

DUNS 21-715-7701

## Sapphire Power Management Ltd

Sapphire House, Roundtree Way, Norwich, Norfolk NR7 8SQ
**Tel:** 01603480560
**Reg No:** 7540060 **Estd:** 2011 Private Limited Company
**Line of Business:** Manufacture of telegraph and telephone apparatus and equipment
**Issued Capital:** £999
**Directors:** N J Carter, A J Rackham, B J Kreyling
**US SIC:** 3661 **UK SIC:** 34410

| | 31-07-14 | 31-07-13 | 31-07-12 |
|---|---|---|---|
| TA | 1,328,061 | 1,280,215 | 1,200,698 |
| NW | 819,836 | 597,846 | 366,316 |
| WC | 49,308 | (12,682) | (84,212) |

DUNS 34-691-4849 **Exp**

## Sapphire Systems Plc

The Northern & Shell Building, 10 Lower Thames Street, London EC3R 6AD
**Tel:** 02076482000
**Web:** www.sapphiresystems.co.uk
**Reg No:** 2777799 **VAT No:** 597442007
**Estd:** 1993 Public Limited Company
**Line of Business:** Hardware consultancy
**Export Markets:** Ireland, Malasia & Singapore.
**Export Sales:** £4,330,888
**Issued Capital:** £50,000
**Principals:** I E Caswell *(Managing)*, D Healy, M Royle
**Co. Secretary:** Ralph Bolton
**Responsibilities**
**Marketing:** Kathryn Boast *(Online Marketing Executive)*, Victoria Park *(Sales & Marketing Manager)*, Pavlina Wrzecka *(Online Marketing)*
**Sales:** Clare Howard *(Business Development Manager)*, Victoria Park *(Sales & Marketing Manager)*
**Admin:** Melanie Barnes *(Health & Safety Officer)*
**HR:** Sharon Stevenson *(Training Manager)*
**Health & Safety:** Melanie Barnes *(Health & Safety Officer)*
**Facilities:** Melanie Barnes *(Health & Safety Officer)*
**Engineering:** Peter Brett *(Support Manager)*
**Branches:** Sapphire Systems Plc, The Northern & Shell Building, 10 Lower Thames Street, London EC3R 6AD
**US SIC:** 7379 **UK SIC:** 83940
**Auditors:** Glazers
**Bankers:** Barclays Bank Plc (20-44-22)

| | 31-03-14 | 31-03-13 | 31-03-12 |
|---|---|---|---|
| TO | 20,408,521 | 18,635,056 | 16,902,820 |
| P/L | 2,829,066 | 2,932,618 | 2,959,865 |
| NW | 192,074 | 103,254 | (36,578) |
| WC | (64,480) | (178,280) | (274,775) |
| Emp. | 146 | 128 | 121 |

DUNS 21-668-3009

## Sapphire Vehicle Services Ltd

(**Subsidiary of:** Ballyvesey Holdings Limited)
Little Wigston Tamworth Road, Appleby Magna, Swadlincote, Derbyshire DE12 7BJ
**Tel:** 01933232600
**Web:** www.intercounty-contracts.com
**Reg No:** 7216859 **Estd:** 2010 Private Limited Company
**Line of Business:** Sale of motor vehicles
**Trading Style:** Intercounty Truck and Van
**Issued Capital:** £100
**Directors:** H H Montgomery, S Hunt, D Birkmyre, D N Birkmyre
**Co. Secretary:** Harold Montgomery
**Responsibilities**
**Senior:** Stephen Kidney *(Finance Director)*
**Finance:** Stephen Kidney *(Finance Director)*
**US SIC:** 5511, 5531
**UK SIC:** 65100

**Bankers:** The Royal Bank Of Scotland Plc (83-27-14)

| | 30-09-13 | 30-09-12 | 30-09-11 |
|---|---|---|---|
| TA | 9,551,873 | 7,336,193 | 5,447,320 |
| P/L | 471,968 | 518,501 | 507,279 |
| NW | 1,116,411 | 756,534 | 369,621 |
| WC | 811,980 | 601,381 | 140,976 |
| Emp. | 124 | 83 | 78 |

DUNS 23-953-4428

## Sara-Int Ltd

King Street, London W6 9JT
**Tel:** 02088463600
**Web:** www.saraint.co.uk
**Reg No:** 3942716 **Estd:** 2000 Private Limited Company
**Line of Business:** Accounting activities
**Issued Capital:** £100
**Director:** W Witkowski
**Co. Secretary:** Radoslaw Staszewski
**Responsibilities**
**Senior:** Kris Gondek *(Manager)*
**IT:** Marcin Podlasinski *(IT Manager)*
**US SIC:** 8931, 1751
**UK SIC:** 83600, 50400

| | 31-03-14 | 31-03-13 | 31-03-12 |
|---|---|---|---|
| TO | 3,661,498 | 3,755,965 | 3,434,576 |
| P/L | 90,914 | 122,180 | 101,678 |
| NW | 412,606 | 365,481 | 251,267 |
| WC | 265,495 | (214,947) | (148,829) |

DUNS 22-109-2062

## Sarah's Snacks Cymru Ltd

1 James Street, Brithdir, New Tredegar, Gwent NP24 6JN
**Tel:** 01443832342
**Web:** www.sarahs-snacks.com
**Reg No:** 4128467 **Estd:** 2000 Private Limited Company
**Line of Business:** Canteens and catering
**Issued Capital:** £2
**Director:** P W Morris
**Co. Secretary:** John Morris
**US SIC:** 5812 **UK SIC:** 66110
**Bankers:** National Westminster Bank Plc (55-81-47)

| | 30-11-13 | 30-11-12 | 30-11-11 |
|---|---|---|---|
| TA | 52,088 | 63,799 | 38,040 |
| NW | 32,570 | 40,707 | 28,565 |
| WC | 28,987 | 31,672 | 17,932 |

DUNS 28-974-4344 **Imp**

## Sarasin (U.K.) Ltd

(**Subsidiary of:** J. Safra Sarasin Holding Ag)
Juxon House, 100 St Paul's Churchyard, London EC4M 8BU
**Tel:** 02070387000
**Web:** www.sarasin.co.uk
**Reg No:** 1748643 **Estd:** 1983 Private Limited Company
**Line of Business:** Investment consultants
**Trading Style:** Sarasin International
**Issued Capital:** £17,900,000
**Principals:** T N Service *(Financial)*, O A Cartade, R M Clinton, J G Monson, S A Penchas
**Co. Secretary:** Mrs Sarah Larkins
**Responsibilities**
**Senior:** Fidelis Goetz *(Manager)*, Burkhard Varnholt *(Manager)*
**US SIC:** 6111, 6211
**UK SIC:** 81501, 83100
**Auditors:** Nexia Audit Ltd

| | 31-12-13 | 31-12-12 | 31-12-11 |
|---|---|---|---|
| TA | 85,802,000 | 85,601,000 | 91,053,000 |
| P/L | 26,574,000 | 16,751,000 | 18,356,000 |
| NW | 21,695,000 | 26,252,000 | 20,058,000 |
| WC | 35,393,000 | 40,626,000 | 30,360,000 |
| Emp. | 182 | 177 | 176 |

DUNS 23-923-0290 **Imp-Exp**

## Sarclad Ltd

(**Subsidiary of:** The Heico Companies L L C)
Unit 3 Whittle Way, Catcliffe, Rotherham, South Yorkshire S60 5BL
**Tel:** 0114 293 9300 **Fax:** 0114 293 9301
**Web:** www.sarclad.com
**Reg No:** 3913109 **VAT No:** 738304336
**Estd:** 2000 Private Limited Company
**Line of Business:** Sheet metal fabrication equipment
**Export Sales:** £16,197,560
**Issued Capital:** £1
**Directors:** E A Roskovensky, R S Cowlishaw, Ms E H Stoeckel
**Co. Secretary:** Stanley Meadows
**Responsibilities**
**Senior:** Emily Roskovensky *(Chairman)*, Keith Shillam *(Manager)*
**Finance:** Julie Dawtry *(Accountant)*
**IT:** Steve Shillito *(Technical Manager)*, Mark Wybrow *(IT Manager)*
**Health & Safety:** Nicola Gregory *(Purchasing Manager)*
**Purchasing:** Nicola Gregory *(Purchasing Manager)*
**Branches:** Sarclad Ltd, Advanced Manufacturing Park,, Rotherham, South Yorkshire S60 5WG
**US SIC:** 3542 **UK SIC:** 32212
**Auditors:** Grant Thornton UK LLP
**Bankers:** HSBC Bank plc (40-17-15)

| | 31-12-13 | 31-12-12 | 31-12-11 |
|---|---|---|---|
| TO | 16,644,026 | 13,618,468 | 9,510,107 |
| P/L | 1,935,708 | (864,190) | 714,267 |
| NW | 3,853,125 | 3,766,019 | 4,418,442 |
| WC | 4,052,090 | 4,228,835 | 4,440,431 |
| Emp. | 59 | 52 | 44 |

DUNS 28-865-9956

## Sarco Ltd

Runnings Road, Kings Ditch Trading Estate, Cheltenham, Gloucestershire GL51 9NQ
**Tel:** 01242583100
**Web:** www.spiraxsarco.com
**Reg No:** 0969972 **Estd:** 1970 Private Limited Company
**Line of Business:** Manufacture of electricity distribution and control apparatus
**Issued Capital:** £2
**Directors:** D J Meredith, A J Robson
**Co. Secretary:** Andrew Robson
**Responsibilities**
**IT:** Tim Ingman *(IT Manager)*
**US SIC:** 3643 **UK SIC:** 34203

| | 31-12-13 | 31-12-12 | 31-12-11 |
|---|---|---|---|
| NW | (21,457) | (21,457) | (21,457) |

DUNS 23-257-0168

## Sarens (Uk) Ltd

(**Subsidiary of:** Sarens Bestuur Nv)
Booth House, Middlesbrough, Cleveland TS2 1UT
**Web:** www.sarens.com
**Reg No:** 2322823 **Estd:** 1997 Private Limited Company
**Line of Business:** Asbestos products & removal
**Export Sales:** £3,244,000
**Issued Capital:** £90,660
**Directors:** B A Sarens, L Sarens, B M Bentley
**Co. Secretary:** Mrs Michelle O'Brien
**US SIC:** 1799 **UK SIC:** 50000
**Auditors:** Nicholsons
**Bankers:** National Westminster Bank Plc (54-41-26)

| | 31-12-13 | 31-12-12 | 31-12-11 |
|---|---|---|---|
| TO | 42,696,000 | 41,629,000 | 21,910,271 |
| P/L | 1,297,000 | 4,988,000 | 788,648 |
| NW | 9,993,000 | 8,886,000 | 4,956,161 |
| WC | 3,171,000 | 1,382,000 | (1,388,007) |
| Emp. | 171 | 160 | 88 |

DUNS 21-819-8588

## Sargeant Turner & Sons Ltd

Sargeant Turner Trading Estate, Stourbridge, West Midlands DY9 8HZ
**Tel:** 01384-422532
**Reg No:** 0077256 **Estd:** 1903 Private Limited Company
**Line of Business:** Other letting of own property
**Issued Capital:** £27,071
**Director:** R L Davies
**Co. Secretary:** Ms Kay Davies
**US SIC:** 6519 **UK SIC:** 85000
**Bankers:** HSBC Bank plc (40-43-17)

| | 31-12-13 | 31-12-12 | 31-12-11 |
|---|---|---|---|
| TA | 565,035 | 563,081 | 578,786 |
| NW | 532,468 | 532,763 | 542,364 |
| WC | 49,657 | 48,992 | 60,643 |

DUNS 89-635-6300

## Sargent Electrical Services Ltd

Unit 39 Tokenspire Business Park, Hull Road, Woodmansey, Beverley, North Humberside HU17 0TB
**Tel:** 01482-881655
**Web:** www.sargentshop.co.uk
**Reg No:** 3316790 **Estd:** 1997 Private Limited Company
**Line of Business:** Manufacture of insulated wire and cable
**Issued Capital:** £1,000
**Managing Director:** I L Sargent
**Co. Secretary:** Neil Sargent
**US SIC:** 3357 **UK SIC:** 22470
**Auditors:** Baker Tilly UK Audit LLP

| | 30-11-13 | 30-11-12 | 30-11-11 |
|---|---|---|---|
| TO | 9,349,477 | 8,891,304 | 9,365,485 |
| P/L | 1,507,748 | 1,525,512 | 1,313,275 |
| NW | 4,758,808 | 4,018,188 | 3,221,160 |
| WC | 4,595,029 | 3,853,062 | 3,087,435 |
| Emp. | 105 | 96 | 102 |

DUNS 21-005-4758

## Sargents Bakeries Ltd

Shaw Lane Industrial Estate, Ogden Road, Doncaster, South Yorkshire DN2 4SE
**Tel:** 01302-363336
**Web:** www.sargentsbakeries.co.uk
**Reg No:** 6301340 **Estd:** 2007 Private Limited Company
**Line of Business:** Retail sale of bread, cakes, flour confectionery and sugar confectionery
**Export Sales:** £806,650
**Issued Capital:** £1
**Director:** I D Allen

**Responsibilities**
**Senior:** Peter Maycock *(General Manager)*, Mandy Yates *(General Manager)*
**IT:** Sarah Whitrod *(IT Manager)*
**US SIC:** 3999 **UK SIC:** 49590

| | 31-12-13 | 30-06-13 | 30-12-12 |
|---|---|---|---|
| TO | 8,962,182 | N/A | N/A |
| P/L | 372,612 | N/A | N/A |
| NW | 651,804 | 361,655 | (277,721) |
| WC | (2,339,129) | (2,575,669) | (533,717) |
| Emp. | 85 | N/A | N/A |

DUNS 21-209-5889 Imp-Exp

## Saria Ltd

(**Subsidiary of:** Rethmann Se & Co. Kg)
Ings Road, Doncaster, South Yorkshire DN5 9TL
**Fax:** 01302390743
**Web:** www.saria.co.uk
**Reg No:** 0547564 **Estd:** 1955 Private Limited Company
**Line of Business:** Animal feed and pet foods
**Export Markets:** E U, Middle Ezst, Far East
**Export Sales:** £27,677,509
**Issued Capital:** £211,188
**Directors:** P A Morris, A J De Mulder, P N De Mulder, R V Ratcliffe, P A Simpson, A R Smith, R A De Mulder, F B Thier
**Co. Secretary:** Jonathan Braide
**Responsibilities**
**Senior:** William Braide *(Manager)*, Keith Jennison *(HR Director)*, Richard Mulder *(Manager)*
**IT:** Neil Shukla *(IT Manager)*
**Branches:** Saria Ltd, Sheffield Rd, Doncaster, South Yorkshire DN12 2BT
**US SIC:** 2047, 6711
**UK SIC:** 42221, 83962
**Auditors:** Paylings
**Bankers:** Barclays Bank Plc (20-26-55)

| | 31-12-13 | 31-12-12 | 31-12-12 |
|---|---|---|---|
| TO | 65,594,663 | 167,787,463 | 222,407,119 |
| P/L | (300,129) | (1,985,319) | (14,816,385) |
| NW | 115,059,607 | 120,679,925 | 127,342,123 |
| WC | 97,169,846 | 18,483,366 | 25,927,854 |
| Emp. | 88 | 881 | 873 |

DUNS 64-728-6327

## Saris Automotive & Industrial Coatings

Unit 1, Burton-On-Trent, Staffordshire DE14 1PT
**Tel:** 01283532006
**Web:** www.sariscoatings.com
**Estd:** 1975 Proprietorship
**Line of Business:** Wholesalers of automotive supplies and parts
**Proprietor:** P Simpson
**US SIC:** 5013 **UK SIC:** 61480
**Employees:** 50

DUNS 23-193-3524

## Sarsen Housing Association Ltd

1 Campbell Place, Stoke-On-Trent, Staffordshire ST4 1ND
**Tel:** 08456051605 **Fax:** 01380-735400
**Web:** www.astercommunities.co.uk
**Reg No:** 0028077IP **Estd:** 1995 Friendly Society
**Line of Business:** Other letting of own property
**Trading Style:** Aster Communities
**Directors:** A Edwards, H Begley, Dr B Jamieson, Ms S Haigh, H Mitchell, C Martin, A Light, J Heffer
**Responsibilities**
**Senior:** Louise Angell *(Board Member)*, Jacqueline Archer *(Executive)*, Carole Blake *(Executive)*, Gill Boden *(Manager)*, Tim Bridger *(Board Member)*, Fiona Buchan *(Board Member)*, Natasha Burke *(Executive)*, Nicola Churches *(Board Member)*, Gail Deimert *(Senior Manager)*, Helen Dodds *(Executive)*, Hannah Enderby *(Executive)*, Julia Frost *(Executive)*, Annette Gilbert *(Executive)*, Linda Gillam *(General Manager)*, Shirley Gray *(Executive)*, Zoi Hayes *(Board Member)*, Antony Higgins *(Manager)*, Sue Hiscock *(Executive)*, Annette Holdsworth *(Senior Manager)*, Bjorn Howard *(Chief Executive)*, Susie Ingram *(Executive)*, Beth Ireson *(Board Member)*, Debbie James *(Board Member)*, Gary Kearley *(Executive)*, Mark Lake *(Board Member)*, Ian Lister *(Board Member)*, Yvette Lloyd *(Senior Manager)*, Katy Mascall *(Executive)*, Joy Merrett *(Executive)*, Donna Mosses *(Board Member)*, Kerry Muir *(Executive)*, Sarah Paget *(Executive)*, Jodie Pitcher *(Executive)*, Carol Sainsbury *(Executive)*, Scott Simmons *(Board Member)*, Ruth Simmons *(Executive)*, Hayley Steffens *(Board Member)*, Leanne Stone *(Board Member)*, Kathryn Unsworth *(Manager)*, Leanna Waters *(Board Member)*
**Marketing:** Andrew Buley *(Relations Manager)*
**Admin:** Ged Hopgood *(Administrator)*, Teresa Morgan *(Personal Assistant)*, Steve Phillip *(Executive Assistant)*, Debbie Varney *(Administrator)*, Chris Welford *(Administrator)*
**Operations:** Justin Messenger *(Operations Manager)*
**US SIC:** 7399 **UK SIC:** 83954
**Auditors:** Deloitte & Touche
**Bankers:** Barclays Bank Plc (20-04-50)
**Employees:** 116
**Turnover:** £30,235,000

DUNS 77-271-0968 Exp

## Sartex Quilts & Textiles Ltd

Castle Mill, Rochdale, Lancashire OL11 2NY
**Tel:** 01706-357490 **Fax:** 01706-657642
**Web:** www.sartexquilts.co.uk
**Reg No:** 2715284 **Estd:** 1992 Private Limited Company
**Line of Business:** Manufacturers of textiles
**Export Sales:** £57,168
**Issued Capital:** £2,000
**Directors:** Z Ali, S Khalid, I A Randhawa, M Ahmed, S Gauhar
**Co. Secretary:** Maqbool Ahmed
**Branches:** Sartex Quilts & Textiles Ltd, Castle Mill, Queensway, Rochdale, Lancashire OL11 2NY
**US SIC:** 2392, 5133
**UK SIC:** 45550, 61600
**Auditors:** Tenon Audit Ltd
**Bankers:** Barclays Bank Plc (20-72-67)

| | 31-07-13 | 31-07-12 | 31-07-11 |
|---|---|---|---|
| TO | 10,564,489 | 14,312,152 | 10,664,970 |
| P/L | 277,681 | 2,006,428 | (529,129) |
| NW | 539,678 | 558,962 | (439,875) |
| WC | 838,128 | 1,137,051 | 95,738 |
| Emp. | 98 | 107 | 81 |

DUNS 34-588-1551 Imp

## Sartorius Stedim Lab Ltd

(**Subsidiary of:** Sartorius Ag)
Unit 6 Oldends Lane, Stonedale Road, Stonehouse, Gloucestershire GL10 3RQ
**Tel:** 01453821972
**Web:** www.sartorius.co.uk
**Reg No:** 2732279 **Estd:** 1992 Private Limited Company
**Line of Business:** Manufacture of other plastic products
**Issued Capital:** £695,900
**Directors:** Dr J Kreuzburg, Dr R Lausch, C R Biddell, V Niebel
**Co. Secretary:** Anthony Sweetman
**Responsibilities**
**Senior:** Uwe Becker *(Director)*, Charles Nickerson *(Director)*
**Branches:** Sartorius Stedim Lab Ltd, Unit 6, Oldends Industrial Estate, Stonehouse, Gloucestershire GL10 3RQ
**US SIC:** 3079 **UK SIC:** 48360
**Auditors:** Wilkinson Latham
**Bankers:** Barclays Bank Plc (20-10-53)

| | 31-12-13 | 31-12-12 | 31-12-11 |
|---|---|---|---|
| TO | 6,262,023 | 5,573,525 | 4,270,627 |
| P/L | 1,519,182 | 1,423,190 | 883,189 |
| NW | 1,680,986 | 1,591,520 | 1,589,206 |
| WC | 298,176 | 566,718 | 606,943 |
| Emp. | 84 | 73 | 59 |

DUNS 21-731-5589 Imp

## Sartorius Uk Ltd

(**Subsidiary of:** Sartorius Ag)
Longmead Business Centre, Bleinheim Road, Epsom, Surrey KT19 9QQ
**Tel:** 01372737102 **Fax:** 01372729927
**Web:** www.sartorius.co.uk
**Reg No:** 1126814 **VAT No:** 217028979
**Estd:** 1973 Private Limited Company
**Line of Business:** Wholesale of other electronic parts and equipment
**Issued Capital:** £1,150,000
**Directors:** Ms D Winzker-Demes, D A Newble, D Campbell
**Co. Secretary:** David Campbell
**Responsibilities**
**Senior:** J?rg Pfirrmann *(Director)*, Jens Reichel *(Manager)*
**Finance:** Donna Pearce *(Finance Manager)*, Jens Reichel *(Manager)*
**Admin:** Jens Reichel *(Manager)*
**HR:** John Courtney *(Human Resources Coordinator)*
**Health & Safety:** John Courtney *(Human Resources Coordinator)*
**US SIC:** 5065, 5084
**UK SIC:** 61500, 61490
**Auditors:** Wilkinson Latham
**Bankers:** National Westminster Bank Plc (60-21-08)

| | 31-12-13 | 31-12-12 | 31-12-11 |
|---|---|---|---|
| TO | 9,968,808 | 8,056,554 | 7,771,177 |
| P/L | (1,525,522) | (1,492,522) | (128,450) |
| NW | (597,907) | 120,116 | 1,737,495 |
| WC | (496,092) | (201,959) | 278,373 |
| Emp. | 86 | 77 | 62 |

DUNS 21-623-2115

## Sarum Academy

Westwood Road, Salisbury, Wiltshire SP2 9HS
**Tel:** 01722323431
**Web:** www.sarumacademy.org
**Reg No:** 7035327 **Estd:** 2009 Private Company Limited By Guarantee
**Line of Business:** Other sporting activities not elsewhere classified
**Directors:** Reverend J M Guillebaud, E C Probert, A C Hartley, Mrs R A Stiven, R T Rogers, N Boulton, Mrs C A Simon, Mrs A Siggs
**Co. Secretary:** Mrs Jean Campbell
**Responsibilities**
**Senior:** Mark Deketelaere *(Director)*, Ruth Johnson *(Director)*, Mark Manterfield *(Director)*
**US SIC:** 7999 **UK SIC:** 97913

| | 31-08-14 | 31-08-13 | 31-08-12 |
|---|---|---|---|
| TO | 19,624,354 | 4,016,242 | 4,520,296 |
| P/L | 14,528,326 | (764,529) | (703,550) |
| NW | 18,366,863 | 3,973,537 | 4,680,066 |
| WC | 263,934 | 372,781 | 429,568 |
| Emp. | 75 | 91 | 103 |

DUNS 42-479-2518

## The Sas Business Group Ltd

Blackhouse Farm, Blackhouse Road, Colgate, Horsham, West Sussex RH13 6HS
**Tel:** 08455-194-190
**Web:** www.sas.co.uk
**Reg No:** 4466865 **Estd:** 2002 Private Limited Company
**Line of Business:** Computer services
**Issued Capital:** £100
**Directors:** C D Davis, N Cothill
**Co. Secretary:** David Biggins
**Responsibilities**
**Senior:** Simon Cranford *(Manager)*
**US SIC:** 4899, 1731
**UK SIC:** 79020, 50300

| | 31-12-13 | 31-08-12 | 31-12-11 |
|---|---|---|---|
| TA | 100 | 100 | 100 |
| NW | 100 | 100 | 100 |

DUNS 21-100-0227

## Sas Daniels Llp

30 Greek Street, Stockport, Cheshire SK3 8AD
**Tel:** 01614757676
**Web:** www.sasdaniels.co.uk
**Reg No:** 0333138OC **Estd:** 1976
**Line of Business:** Solicitors
**Responsibilities**
**Senior:** Shelley Chesworth *(Non-designated Limited Liabili)*, Timothy Lomas *(Non-designated Limited Liabili)*, Christopher Maccafferty *(Non-designated Limited Liabili)*, Helen Thompson *(Non-designated Limited Liabili)*
**US SIC:** 8111 **UK SIC:** 83500
**Auditors:** DTE Business Advisory Ltd
**Bankers:** The Royal Bank Of Scotland Plc (16-19-20)

| | 30-04-14 | 30-04-13 | 30-04-12 |
|---|---|---|---|
| TA | 2,519,927 | 2,986,491 | 3,067,333 |
| P/L | (78,000) | (84,000) | (90,000) |
| NW | 1,043,748 | 964,899 | 1,278,610 |

DUNS 42-330-9983

## The Sas Group of Companies Ltd.

S A S House Blackhouse Farm, Blackhouse Road, Colgate, Horsham, West Sussex RH13 6HS
**Tel:** 0845-643-1431
**Web:** www.sas.co.uk
**Reg No:** 4318754 **Estd:** 2001 Private Limited Company
**Line of Business:** Management activities of holding companies
**Export Sales:** £563,900
**Issued Capital:** £112,000
**Directors:** N Cothill, C D Davis
**Co. Secretary:** David Biggins
**US SIC:** 6711 **UK SIC:** 83962

| | 31-12-13 | 31-08-12 | 31-12-11 |
|---|---|---|---|
| TO | 17,038,259 | 12,495,187 | 10,463,653 |
| P/L | 1,542,291 | 1,982,667 | 1,702,751 |
| NW | 1,587,228 | 2,417,328 | 1,019,205 |
| WC | 924,477 | 1,671,459 | 513,202 |
| Emp. | 118 | 87 | 73 |

DUNS 28-964-2852 Imp

## Sas Holdings Ltd

31 Suttons Business Park, Reading, Berkshire RG6 1AZ
**Tel:** 01189385900
**Web:** www.sasint.co.uk
**Reg No:** 1697448 **Estd:** 2011 Private Limited Company
**Line of Business:** Property refurbishment contractors
**Export Sales:** £17,433,000
**Trading Style:** S A S International
**Issued Capital:** £228,484
**Principals:** E A Mcelhinney *(Chairman)*, J M King, A H Gammon, R C Altman, H E Balfour, A J Williams, M E Mcelhinney, Ms S Mcelhinney
**Co. Secretary:** Mrs Brigid Matthews
**Responsibilities**
**Senior:** Neil Adams *(Contracts Manager)*
**IT:** Sarah De-Bank *(IT Manager)*
**Operations:** Stephen Burlton *(Project Manager)*
**Branches:** Sas Holdings Ltd, Guinness Circle, Manchester M17 1EB
**US SIC:** 1799, 5039
**UK SIC:** 50000, 61300
**Auditors:** PKF (UK) LLP
**Bankers:** Barclays Bank Plc (20-71-03)

| | 31-12-13 | 31-12-12 | 31-12-11 |
|---|---|---|---|
| TO | 72,344,000 | 80,691,000 | 83,582,000 |
| P/L | (616,000) | 4,978,000 | 6,793,000 |
| NW | 51,008,000 | 51,409,000 | 47,747,000 |
| WC | 21,967,000 | 20,885,000 | 19,442,000 |
| Emp. | 699 | 718 | 708 |

DUNS 22-529-3703 Imp-Exp

## Sas Software Ltd

(**Subsidiary of:** Sas Institute Inc.)
Wittington House, Henley Road, Medmenham, Marlow, Buckinghamshire SL7 2EB
**Tel:** 01628-486933 **Fax:** 01628-483203
**Web:** www.sas.com
**Reg No:** 1316437 **Estd:** 1977 Private Limited Company
**Line of Business:** Computer software (development)
**Export Sales:** £665,514
**Trading Style:** Sas Institute
**Issued Capital:** £1,000
**Director:** A M Hagstrom
**Co. Secretary:** Keith Valder
**Responsibilities**
**Senior:** Cheryl Remsbury *(Distribution Manager)*
**Finance:** Sue Reynolds *(Head of Financial Services Mar)*
**Marketing:** Sally Hanson *(Marketing Communications Direc)*, Richard Kellett *(Marketing Manager)*, Amanda Koenig *(Marketing Manager)*, Mui Luc *(Corporate Communications Manag)*
**IT:** Wensley Tristram *(IT Manager)*
**HR:** Mandy Devonal-Batt *(Personnel Manager)*
**Facilities:** Peter Dorrington *(Business Solutions Manager)*
**Operations:** Peter Dorrington *(Business Solutions Manager)*
**Branches:** Sas Software Ltd, Quay Plaza, The Quays, Salford, Lancashire M50 3BA
**US SIC:** 7379 **UK SIC:** 83940
**Auditors:** BDO LLP

| | 31-12-13 | 31-12-12 | 31-12-11 |
|---|---|---|---|
| TO | 122,584,503 | 113,778,497 | 115,267,613 |
| P/L | (6,631,189) | 1,211,353 | 4,502,299 |
| NW | 282,406 | 5,849,444 | 5,346,542 |
| WC | (11,476,230) | (7,248,009) | (10,506,855) |
| Emp. | 492 | 442 | 404 |

DUNS 22-813-7592 Imp-Exp

## Sash U K Ltd

Ferrymoor Way, Grimethorpe, Barnsley, South Yorkshire S72 7BN
**Tel:** 01226715619
**Web:** www.sashuk.com
**Reg No:** 1548780 **VAT No:** 364104381
**Estd:** 1965 Private Limited Company
**Line of Business:** Double glazing installers
**Export Markets:** Worldwide; U S A; Faroe Islands
**Issued Capital:** £1,000
**Directors:** T Morrell, Mrs J Bean, S T Morrell, Mrs M J Morrell, R F Bean
**Co. Secretary:** Mrs Julie Bell
**Responsibilities**
**Senior:** Glenn Trevelyan *(IT Systems Manager)*
**Finance:** Robert Heatherington *(Financial Director)*
**Branches:** Sash U K Ltd, Badsley Moor La, Rotherham, South Yorkshire S65 2QN
**US SIC:** 3079 **UK SIC:** 48360
**Auditors:** Kubinski
**Bankers:** HSBC Bank plc (40-09-12)

| | 30-09-13 | 30-09-12 | 30-09-11 |
|---|---|---|---|
| TO | 12,358,710 | 10,937,808 | 10,831,356 |
| P/L | 812,108 | 327,557 | 390,524 |
| NW | 3,535,076 | 2,916,218 | 2,656,390 |
| WC | (267,641) | (362,951) | (372,365) |
| Emp. | 137 | 130 | 120 |

DUNS 57-844-1982

## The Sash Window Workshop Trading Ltd

(**Subsidiary of:** The Sash Window Workshop Ltd)
Kiln Lane, Bracknell, Berkshire RG12 1NA
**Tel:** 01344-868668
**Web:** www.sashwindow.com
**Reg No:** 2897134 **Estd:** 1994 Private Limited Company
**Line of Business:** Windows specialised

**Trading Style:** The Sash Window Workshop
**Issued Capital:** £200
**Directors:** D G Dollar, Mrs S Kainth
**Co. Secretary:** Richard Dollar
**Responsibilities**
**Senior:** Debbie Van Den Brink *(Manager)*
**HR:** Wayne Bailey *(Human Resources Manager)*
**Health & Safety:** Debbie McAll *(Health & Safety Officer)*
**Engineering:** David Davitt *(Production Manager)*
**US SIC:** 3231, 5199
**UK SIC:** 24791, 61900
**Auditors:** Hare Wilson & Co
**Bankers:** HSBC Bank plc (40-13-10)

| | 31-12-13 | 31-12-12 | 31-12-11 |
|---|---|---|---|
| TA | 2,549,064 | 1,947,859 | 2,169,811 |
| NW | 145,811 | 190,951 | 278,538 |
| WC | 316,653 | 381,243 | 448,176 |

DUNS 21-699-4626

## Sasse Ltd

**(Subsidiary of:** Dr. Sasse Ag)
1000 Great West Road, Brentford, Middlesex TW8 9HH
**Tel:** 01332 362 425 **Fax:** 01332 208 456
**Web:** www.sasse.de
**Reg No:** 7447234 **Estd:** 2010 Private Limited Company
**Line of Business:** Sanitation, remediation and similar activities
**Export Sales:** £37,174
**Issued Capital:** £1
**Director:** B Wunderlich
**Co. Secretary:** Christopher Sayer
**Branches:** Sasse Ltd, Wyvern House, Railway Terrace, Derby, Derbyshire DE1 2RU
**US SIC:** 4959, 7349
**UK SIC:** 92110, 92300
**Auditors:** Andrew Hamilton & Co Ltd
**Bankers:** The Royal Bank Of Scotland Plc (83-00-80)

| | 31-12-13 | 31-12-12 | 31-12-11 |
|---|---|---|---|
| TO | 4,797,139 | 5,035,340 | 5,168,026 |
| P/L | 195,482 | 238,171 | 70,421 |
| NW | 421,442 | 242,811 | 56,598 |
| WC | 348,043 | 105,799 | (100,616) |
| Emp. | 222 | 240 | 271 |

DUNS 73-956-2267 Imp

## Satcom Global Ltd

**(Subsidiary of:** Broadband Satellite Services Ltd)
Tanners' Bank, North Shields, Tyne and Wear NE30 1JH
**Fax:** 01722410777
**Web:** www.satcomgroup.com
**Reg No:** 5208041 **Estd:** 2004 Private Limited Company
**Line of Business:** Telecommunications
**Directors:** I A Robinson, C Leydon, R A Howes
**Co. Secretary:** Robert Howes
**Responsibilities**
**Senior:** Theresa Griffiths *(Manager)*, Alexandra Johnson *(Manager)*, Richard Vos *(Chairman)*
**US SIC:** 4899 **UK SIC:** 79020
**Bankers:** National Westminster Bank Plc (54-41-19)
**Employees:** 50
**Turnover:** £32,022,017

DUNS 21-825-7559

## Satellite Applications Catapult Ltd

Electron Building Fermi Avenue, Harwell, Didcot, Oxfordshire OX11 0QR
**Web:** www.inventorthon.com
**Reg No:** 7964746 **Estd:** 2012 Private Company Limited By Guarantee
**Line of Business:** Other business activities not elsewhere classified
**Directors:** S D Martin, Ms L M Patmore, T E Just, T R Sherwood, W N Hutton, Ms S M Hunt, Mrs C E Mealing-Jones, R J Pinto
**US SIC:** 7399 **UK SIC:** 83954

| | 31-03-14 | 28-03-13 |
|---|---|---|
| TO | 16,830,637 | 4,122,937 |
| P/L | 9,480,374 | 2,783,822 |
| NW | 12,263,241 | 2,782,867 |
| WC | 218,776 | (955) |
| Emp. | 58 | 7 |

DUNS 29-578-0787 Imp-Exp

## Satellite Information Services (Holdings) Ltd

2 Whitehall Avenue, Milton Keynes, Buckinghamshire MK10 0AX
**Tel:** 01908865252 **Fax:** 020-7251-3737
**Web:** www.sis.tv
**Reg No:** 1939932 **Estd:** 1985 Private Limited Company
**Line of Business:** Television activities
**Export Markets:** W Europe
**Issued Capital:** £19,953
**Directors:** A R Lyman, M D Stewart, C D Evans, C H Mills, S R Reid, R W Devlin, Ms S D Flanagan, F Done
**Co. Secretary:** Sis Cosec Limited
**Responsibilities**
**Marketing:** Donna Palumbo *(Marketing Manager)*
**Sales:** Nigel Boardman *(Head of Retail)*, Katie Steele *(Sales Executive)*
**HR:** Nicky Clark *(Human Resources Manager)*
**US SIC:** 4833 **UK SIC:** 97411
**Auditors:** PricewaterhouseCoopers
**Bankers:** The Royal Bank Of Scotland Plc (16-01-29)

| | 31-03-14 | 31-03-13 | 31-03-12 |
|---|---|---|---|
| TO | 253,764,000 | 260,758,000 | 239,583,000 |
| P/L | 12,349,000 | 27,720,000 | 25,328,000 |
| NW | 5,145,000 | (11,776,000) | (27,045,000) |
| WC | (20,160,000) | (18,726,000) | (27,612,000) |
| Emp. | 821 | 813 | 839 |

DUNS 22-225-3168 Exp

## Satellite Information Services Ltd

**(Subsidiary of:** Satellite Information Services (Holdings) Ltd)
Satellite House 17 Corsham Stree, London N1 6DR
**Fax:** 020-7251-3737
**Web:** www.sis.tv
**Reg No:** 4243307 **Estd:** 1987 Private Limited Company
**Line of Business:** Television activities
**Trading Style:** Sis Link, Sis Live
**Issued Capital:** £1
**Directors:** G G Irvine, Mrs N C Clark, G J Smith, D Meynell
**Co. Secretary:** Sis Cosec Limited
**Responsibilities**
**Senior:** Warwick Bartlett *(Manager)*, David Holdgate *(Chief Executive Officer)*, Mathew Masters *(Manager)*
**Branches:** Satellite Information Services Ltd, Denbigh Hall Industrial Estate, Denbigh Hall, Bletchley, Milton Keynes, Buckinghamshire MK3 7QT
**US SIC:** 4833 **UK SIC:** 97411
**Auditors:** Ernst & Young LLP

| | 31-03-14 | 31-03-13 | 31-03-12 |
|---|---|---|---|
| TO | 218,717,000 | 208,281,000 | 189,152,000 |
| P/L | 20,599,000 | 1,570,000 | 28,541,000 |
| NW | (12,241,000) | (36,731,000) | (20,220,000) |
| WC | (37,456,000) | (31,362,000) | (24,695,000) |
| Emp. | 605 | 574 | 502 |

DUNS 23-824-3757

## Satellite Solutions (Uk) Ltd

**(Subsidiary of:** Gl & Jk Investments Ltd)
Unit 5 Redbourne Park, Liliput Road Brackmills In, Northampton, Northamptonshire NN4 7DT
**Tel:** 08456444000
**Reg No:** 3816399 **Estd:** 1990 Private Limited Company
**Line of Business:** Television and satellite retailer
**Trading Style:** Solutions Group U K
**Issued Capital:** £2
**Director:** G M Lester
**Co. Secretary:** Jeremy Kennedy
**Branches:** Satellite Solutions (Uk) Ltd, Unit 9, Upton Road, Poole, Dorset BH17 7AF
**US SIC:** 4712 **UK SIC:** 77002
**Auditors:** PKF

| | 31-07-13 | 31-07-12 | 31-07-11 |
|---|---|---|---|
| TA | 2 | 2 | 2 |
| NW | 2 | 2 | 2 |

DUNS 21-860-6051 Imp-Exp

## Sato U K Ltd

**(Subsidiary of:** Sato Holdings Corporation)
Valley Road, Harwich, Essex CO12 4RR
**Tel:** 01255240000 **Fax:** 01255-240111
**Web:** www.satoeurope.com
**Reg No:** 0604144 **VAT No:** 666000068
**Estd:** 1958 Private Limited Company
**Line of Business:** Manufacture of machinery for food, beverage and tobacco processing
**Export Markets:** E U
**Export Sales:** £1,599,000
**Issued Capital:** £10,801,501
**Directors:** M Hayama, N J Batchelor
**Responsibilities**
**Senior:** Lee Garnham *(Distribution Manager)*, Paula Wilkinson *(Human Resources Manager)*, Jason Wise *(Operations Director)*
**Finance:** Lorraine Heath *(Financial Manager)*
**Marketing:** Jason Wise *(Operations Director)*
**Sales:** Jason Wise *(Operations Director)*
**HR:** Paula Wilkinson *(Human Resources Manager)*
**Health & Safety:** Trevor Clifford *(Quality Assurance Manager)*
**Facilities:** Jim Mann *(Maintenance Manager)*
**Operations:** Trevor Clifford *(Quality Assurance Manager)*, Jason Wise *(Operations Director)*
**Branches:** Sato U K Ltd, Horncastle Road, Barrow Upon Soar, Boston, Lincolnshire PE21 9HZ
**US SIC:** 3551 **UK SIC:** 32441
**Auditors:** Deloitte LLP
**Bankers:** Lloyds TSB Bank plc (30-92-72)

| | 31-03-14 | 31-03-13 | 31-03-12 |
|---|---|---|---|
| TO | 13,310,000 | 12,558,000 | 12,321,000 |
| P/L | (208,000) | (699,000) | (189,000) |
| NW | (3,213,000) | (8,534,000) | (9,158,000) |
| WC | (1,547,000) | (1,721,000) | (818,000) |
| Emp. | 104 | 106 | 109 |

DUNS 21-114-0934 Exp

## Satra

Wyndham Way, Kettering, Northamptonshire NN16 8SD
**Tel:** 01536410000
**Web:** www.satra.co.uk
**Reg No:** 0153475 **VAT No:** 119923455
**Estd:** 2000 Private Company Limited By Guarantee
**Line of Business:** Research and experimental development on natural sciences and engineering
**Export Markets:** Worldwide
**Trading Style:** Satra Technology Centre
**Directors:** Dr R E Whittaker, T J Blades, A C Simmons, R J Denton, S Etheridge, S D Botterill, A J Perillo
**Responsibilities**
**Senior:** Liz Mawby *(General Manager)*
**US SIC:** 7391 **UK SIC:** 94000
**Auditors:** Grant Thornton UK LLP
**Bankers:** National Westminster Bank Plc (53-61-33)

| | 31-12-13 | 31-12-12 | 31-12-11 |
|---|---|---|---|
| TO | 11,380,000 | 10,444,000 | 9,462,000 |
| P/L | 583,000 | 482,000 | 466,000 |
| NW | 4,507,000 | 5,549,000 | 4,952,000 |
| WC | 3,419,000 | 3,511,000 | 3,492,000 |
| Emp. | 194 | 181 | 170 |

DUNS 21-595-7011

## Saturn Taxis

Autoreps Clive Road, Gravesend, Kent DA11 0RS
**Tel:** 01474247011
**Estd:** 2011
**Line of Business:** Taxicab Operators
**Proprietor:** N Thandi
**US SIC:** 4121 **UK SIC:** 72200
**Employees:** 49

DUNS 29-630-0148 Imp-Exp

## Sauflon Pharmaceuticals Ltd

**(Subsidiary of:** The Cooper Companies Inc)
49-53 York Street, Twickenham, Middlesex TW1 3LP
**Tel:** 02083-224200 **Fax:** 08450518702
**Web:** www.sauflon.co.uk
**Reg No:** 1071033 **VAT No:** 563044066
**Estd:** 1985 Private Limited Company
**Line of Business:** Manufacturers of optical products
**Export Markets:** Middle East; Australia; W Europe; Africa; Caribbean; Hong Kong; Taiwan; Egypt
**Issued Capital:** £292,815
**Directors:** K P Barrett, G W Matz, S Mathieson, G T Markham, N A Penfold, M F Wilkinson, M S Harty, Ms C R Kaufman
**Responsibilities**
**Senior:** Francis Erard *(Company Director)*, Howard Griffiths *(Technical Director)*, Bradley Wells *(Joint Managing Director)*
**Finance:** Andres Gaviria *(?Group Financial Controller)*, P Hawdio *(Financial Controller)*
**Marketing:** Angela Bossert *(Marketing Services Manager)*, Myles Hustler *(?International Marketing Manag)*
**Sales:** Pardeep Kalia *(Business Development Manager)*, Peter Manford *(Commercial Director)*
**IT:** Howard Griffiths *(Technical Director)*, Ben Surendranath *(IT Manager)*
**HR:** Susan Ings *(Human Resources Manager)*, John McManus *(International Technical Produc)*
**Health & Safety:** M Botting *(Health & Safety Officer)*
**Engineering:** Howard Griffiths *(Technical Director)*, James Lonnen *(Technical Projects Manager)*
**Branches:** Sauflon Pharmaceuticals Ltd, Unit 3-11, Mace Industrial Estate, Ashford, Kent TN24 8PE
**US SIC:** 3861 **UK SIC:** 37330
**Auditors:** Ward Williams
**Bankers:** Barclays Bank Plc (20-91-79)

| | 31-10-13 | 31-10-12 | 31-10-11 |
|---|---|---|---|
| TO | 101,588,000 | 84,176,000 | 68,245,000 |
| P/L | 11,602,000 | 9,098,000 | 5,908,000 |
| NW | 23,168,000 | 20,654,000 | 13,019,000 |
| WC | 32,004,000 | 12,030,000 | 8,712,000 |
| Emp. | 1,012 | 823 | 713 |

DUNS 73-286-4934

## Saul Pension Services Ltd

1 King's Arms Yard, London EC2R 7AF
**Tel:** 08458720339
**Web:** www.stcpm.co.uk
**Reg No:** 4560260 **Estd:** 2002 Private Limited Company
**Line of Business:** Business services
**Issued Capital:** £50,000
**Directors:** W Causon, Mrs S Applegarth, C Gosling
**Co. Secretary:** Mrs Jadranka Maros
**US SIC:** 7399 **UK SIC:** 83954

| | 31-03-14 | 31-03-13 | 31-03-12 |
|---|---|---|---|
| TO | 283,921 | 283,235 | 252,362 |
| P/L | 126,231 | 3,306 | 7,928 |
| NW | 129,464 | 30,133 | 27,834 |
| WC | 169,464 | 70,133 | 67,834 |
| Emp. | 76 | N/A | 50 |

DUNS 57-022-0053

## Saul Trustee Company

1 Kings Arms Yard, London EC2R 7AF
**Tel:** 020 7776 4340 **Fax:** 020 7776 4341
**Web:** www.saul.org.uk
**Reg No:** 2868875 **Estd:** 1993 Private Limited Company
**Line of Business:** Pension funding
**Directors:** P G Fraser, J W Foster, J G Tregoning, Lawdeb Pension Trustees, S Large, C A Robinson, Mrs L Lindsey, W Causon
**Co. Secretary:** Mrs Jadranka Maros
**Responsibilities**
**Senior:** Dennis Buckley *(Director)*, Partha Dasgupta *(Manager)*, Penny Green *(Manager)*, Peter Leishman *(Director)*
**US SIC:** 6371 **UK SIC:** 82002
**Auditors:** PricewaterhouseCoopers LLP

| | 31-03-14 | 31-03-13 | 31-03-12 |
|---|---|---|---|
| TO | 13,525,000 | 12,404,000 | 10,629,000 |
| WC | (3,828,000) | (2,105,000) | (360,000) |
| Emp. | 76 | 71 | 50 |

DUNS 21-114-2681

## Saunders Gotch & Surridge Llp

35 Headlands, Kettering, Northamptonshire NN15 7ES
**Tel:** 01536-513165 **Fax:** 01536-410226
**Web:** www.gotch.co.uk
**Reg No:** 0336029OC **Estd:** 1900 Private Limited Company
**Line of Business:** Architects
**Branches:** Gotch, Saunders & Surridge Llp, Hornbean Park Developments, The Tower, Harrogate, North Yorkshire HG2 8QT
**US SIC:** 8911 **UK SIC:** 83701
**Auditors:** Grant Thornton UK LLP

| | 30-06-14 | 30-06-13 | 30-06-12 |
|---|---|---|---|
| TA | 1,271,274 | 1,206,643 | 1,705,010 |
| NW | 336,483 | N/A | 1,162,826 |
| WC | 367,270 | 753,865 | 1,075,804 |

DUNS 34-846-7148

## Saunders Partnership Design Ltd

Studio Four, 37 Broad Water Road, Welwyn Garden City, Hertfordshire AL7 3AX
**Tel:** 01707385300 **Fax:** 01707385333
**Web:** www.saundersarchitect.com
**Reg No:** 5645709 **Estd:** 2005 Private Limited Company
**Line of Business:** Architectural activities
**Issued Capital:** £406
**Directors:** K M Seggery, M R Williams, S J Hutchinson, R M Weedon, C Saunders
**Co. Secretary:** Kevin Seggery
**US SIC:** 8911 **UK SIC:** 83701

| | 31-07-13 | 31-07-12 | 31-07-11 |
|---|---|---|---|
| TA | 6,289,358 | 6,282,441 | 6,282,455 |
| NW | 2,959,900 | 2,952,983 | 3,242,997 |
| WC | (892,498) | N/A | (44,245) |

DUNS 29-371-2048

## Saunderson House Ltd

**(Subsidiary of:** I F G Group Plc)
1 Long Lane, London EC1A 9HF
**Tel:** 02073 156 500 **Fax:** 02073 156 550
**Web:** www.saundersonhouse.co.uk
**Reg No:** 0940473 **VAT No:** 514035880
**Estd:** 2011 Private Limited Company
**Line of Business:** Life insurance
**Issued Capital:** £86,000
**Directors:** J O Hagger, R A Phipps, C O'Reilly, C V Sexton, A R Overy, J A Watson, A W Wellby, I R Mcnally
**Co. Secretary:** Conleth O'Reilly
**Responsibilities**
**Senior:** Tony Clarke *(Director)*
**Finance:** Tony Clarke *(Director)*
**Marketing:** Beverly Landais *(Marketing and Business Develop)*
**Operations:** Duncan Ross *(COO)*
**Branches:** Prospect Ho, 32 Sovereign St, Leeds, Lees
**US SIC:** 6311, 7399
**UK SIC:** 82002, 83954
**Auditors:** PricewaterhouseCoopers

**Bankers:** Barclays Bank Plc (20-17-19)

| | 31-12-13 | 31-12-12 | 31-12-11 |
|---|---|---|---|
| TO | 20,700,118 | 18,484,407 | 19,212,529 |
| P/L | 4,046,857 | 3,811,975 | 3,744,632 |
| NW | 3,453,272 | 2,666,991 | 2,375,807 |
| WC | 2,913,410 | 2,259,409 | 1,885,725 |
| Emp. | 109 | 107 | 103 |

DUNS 21-742-3631 **Imp-Exp**

## Sauter Automation Ltd

(**Subsidiary of:** Fr. Sauter Holding Ag)
Inova House, Crockford Lane, Hampshire Int Business Park, Chineh, Basingstoke, Hampshire RG24 8WH
**Tel:** 01256-374400 **Fax:** 01256-374455
**Web:** www.sauterautomation.co.uk
**Reg No:** 1292827 **Estd:** 1976 Private Limited Company
**Line of Business:** Building services
**Export Markets:** Switzerland, Germany, Eire, France, Belgium, Spain, Hong Kong, Austria, Sweden, U S A, Czech Republic
**Issued Capital:** £250,000
**Directors:** W Karlen, C R Church, J Schwartzentruber, M J Clinch
**Co. Secretary:** John Buckley
**Responsibilities**
**Senior:** Bertram Schmitz *(Manager)*, Harald Ziegler *(Manager)*
**Sales:** Geoff Woodhouse *(Sales Coordinator)*
**Health & Safety:** Amanda Mitchell *(Health & Safety Officer)*
**Branches:** Sauter Automation Ltd, Court La, Newent, Gloucestershire GL18 1AR
**US SIC:** 1622 **UK SIC:** 50200
**Auditors:** PricewaterhouseCoopers
**Bankers:** Barclays Bank Plc (20-78-58)

| | 31-12-13 | 31-12-12 | 31-12-11 |
|---|---|---|---|
| TO | 8,136,000 | 8,184,000 | 8,722,000 |
| P/L | 458,000 | 321,000 | 629,000 |
| NW | 3,551,000 | 3,183,000 | 3,001,000 |
| WC | 2,662,000 | 2,391,000 | 2,507,000 |
| Emp. | 66 | 70 | 74 |

DUNS 23-196-0050

## Savage & Whitten Wholesale Ltd

(**Subsidiary of:** Savage Whitten Holdings Limited)
Carnbane Business Park, Newry, Co Down BT35 6QH
**Tel:** 02830257700 **Fax:** 028-3026-3143
**Web:** www.savageandwhitten.co.uk
**Reg No:** 0038618NI **Estd:** 2000 Private Limited Company
**Line of Business:** Cash and carry wholesalers
**Issued Capital:** £10,000
**Directors:** J T Whitten, R L Whitten, B Duffy, A C Dorman, M Windebank, N Savage, M Skelton
**Co. Secretary:** Barry Duffy
**US SIC:** 5199 **UK SIC:** 61900
**Bankers:** The Bank Of Ireland (90-23-38)

| | 31-12-13 | 31-12-12 | 31-12-11 |
|---|---|---|---|
| TO | 58,564,827 | 47,839,429 | 38,988,843 |
| P/L | 1,017,416 | 424,007 | 568,815 |
| NW | 4,273,678 | 3,521,894 | 3,230,070 |
| WC | 3,702,896 | 2,850,427 | 2,524,629 |
| Emp. | 174 | 129 | 98 |

DUNS 21-118-7152

## Save & Claim Ltd

Anchor Building, Westgate, Morecambe, Lancashire LA3 3DD
**Tel:** 08009903215
**Web:** www.saveandclaim.com
**Reg No:** 6582527 **Estd:** 2012 Private Limited Company
**Line of Business:** Legal services
**Issued Capital:** £50
**Director:** D J Furey
**Responsibilities**
**Senior:** Julian Mash *(Manager)*
**US SIC:** 8111 **UK SIC:** 83500

| | 31-05-13 | 31-05-12 | 31-05-11 |
|---|---|---|---|
| TA | 609,705 | 630,659 | 123,305 |
| NW | 508,329 | 444,768 | 61,426 |
| WC | 408,092 | 363,904 | 26,862 |

DUNS 28-830-5220 **Imp**

## Save the Children Fund

1 St John's Lane, London EC1M 4AR
**Fax:** 020-7012-6963
**Web:** www.savethechildren.org.uk
**Reg No:** 0178159 **Estd:** 1919 Private Company Limited By Guarantee
**Line of Business:** Activities of other membership organisations not elsewhere classified
**Directors:** Ms J A Cooper-Hohn, A Parker, Ms F C Mcbain, G T Davies, Mrs A H Anderson, M Esiri, Honourable S R James, R C Hingley
**Co. Secretary:** Andrew Willis
**Responsibilities**
**Senior:** Diana Carney *(Director)*, Naomi Eisenstadt *(Director)*, Nyaradzayi Gumbonzvanda *(Manager)*, Devi Sridhar *(Director)*, Kevin Watkins *(Director)*
**Branches:** Save The Children Fund, Fore Street, Castle Cary, Somerset BA7 7BG
**US SIC:** 8699 **UK SIC:** 96902
**Auditors:** Deloitte LLP
**Bankers:** National Westminster Bank Plc (60-80-07)

| | 31-12-13 | 31-12-12 | 31-12-11 |
|---|---|---|---|
| TO | 342,594,000 | 283,748,000 | 332,881,000 |
| P/L | 33,682,000 | (33,285,000) | 10,302,000 |
| NW | 93,748,000 | 54,843,000 | 85,083,000 |
| WC | 109,588,000 | 80,676,000 | 104,785,000 |
| Emp. | 3,551 | 4,025 | 4,947 |

DUNS 23-737-9362

## Save the Children International

St Vincent House, 30 Orange Street, London WC2H 7HH
**Tel:** 02032720300
**Web:** www.savethechildren.net
**Reg No:** 3732267 **Estd:** 1999 Private Company Limited By Guarantee
**Line of Business:** Non-charitable social work activities without accommodation
**Directors:** P Lopez, C Perrin, Dr I Khan, H Singh, Dr M Romisch, C F Maccormack, J N Powell, Ms A H Anderson
**Co. Secretary:** Ms Lauren Ellery
**Responsibilities**
**Senior:** Inger Ashing *(Director)*, Vivien Bridgwater *(Director)*, Mimi Jakobsen *(Director)*, Bradley Palmer *(Director)*, Nils Øveraas *(Director)*
**US SIC:** 8321 **UK SIC:** 96111
**Bankers:** Cafcash Ltd (40-52-40)
**Employees:** 11,061
**Turnover:** £874,497,000

DUNS 39-779-1336

## Savers Health & Beauty Ltd

(**Subsidiary of:** A.S. Watson (Europe) Holdings B.V.)
118 Beddington Lane, Croydon, Surrey CR0 4TB
**Web:** www.savers.co.uk
**Reg No:** 2202838 **VAT No:** 777947160
**Estd:** 1988 Private Limited Company
**Line of Business:** Holding companies management activities
**Trading Style:** Superdrug
**Issued Capital:** £1,400,000
**Directors:** Ms G G Smith, P W Macnab, Dr A J Heaton, D K Lai
**Co. Secretary:** Ms Edith Shih
**Responsibilities**
**Senior:** Joey Wat *(Manager)*
**Branches:** Savers Health & Beauty Ltd, Unit 2, Walsall Road, Birmingham, West Midlands B42 1AA
**US SIC:** 6711 **UK SIC:** 83962
**Auditors:** PricewaterhouseCoopers LLP
**Bankers:** National Westminster Bank Plc (60-00-01)

| | 28-12-13 | 29-12-12 | 31-12-11 |
|---|---|---|---|
| TO | 246,593,000 | 214,499,000 | 189,149,000 |
| P/L | 9,026,000 | 6,952,000 | (368,000) |
| NW | (36,853,000) | (43,509,000) | (48,935,000) |
| WC | (48,307,000) | (64,709,000) | (58,001,000) |
| Emp. | 2,573 | 2,498 | 2,491 |

DUNS 28-829-5454

## Savile Club Ltd

69 Brook Street, London W1K 4ER
**Tel:** 020-7629-5462
**Web:** www.savileclub.co.uk
**Reg No:** 0108260 **Estd:** 1910 Private Limited Company
**Line of Business:** Clubs social and associations
**Issued Capital:** £7
**Directors:** J G Davis, C Hayward-Hughes, D J Bradbury, Dr S M Ginn, A W Hilton, A J Stranger-Jones, A J Miller, B John
**Co. Secretary:** Julian Malone Lee
**Responsibilities**
**Senior:** Peter Allinson *(Director)*, Clifford Beal *(Director)*, Andrew Blakesley *(Manager)*, Alan Cameron *(Manager)*, Cuffe Jonathan *(Director)*, Julian Malone-Lee *(Club Secretary)*, Michael Senior *(Manager)*, Phillip Sober *(Director)*, William Stockbridge *(Director)*, Martin Vander Weyer *(Director)*, Geoffrey Vevers *(Director)*, Nick Wilkinson *(Chairman)*, Edward Willmott *(Director)*, Max Wiltshire *(Director)*
**Admin:** Julian Malone-Lee *(Club Secretary)*
**US SIC:** 5813 **UK SIC:** 66200
**Auditors:** Shipleys
**Bankers:** Lloyds TSB Bank plc (30-91-37)

| | 31-12-13 | 31-12-12 | 31-12-11 |
|---|---|---|---|
| TO | 1,310,828 | 1,267,814 | 1,171,568 |
| P/L | 170,293 | 149,985 | 499,981 |
| NW | 2,569,830 | 2,407,351 | 2,259,386 |
| WC | (683,856) | (592,963) | (440,068) |
| Emp. | 46 | 45 | 40 |

DUNS 49-138-8245

## Saville & Holdsworth Ltd

(**Subsidiary of:** The Corporate Executive Board Company)
The Pavilion, 1 Atwell Place, Thames Ditton, Surrey KT7 0NE
**Tel:** 02083358010
**Web:** www.shlsolutionpartner.com
**Reg No:** 3109058 **Estd:** 1995 Private Limited Company
**Line of Business:** Management activities of other non-financial holding companies not elsewhere classified
**Trading Style:** S H L
**Issued Capital:** £100
**Directors:** D E Ryell, M D Franks
**US SIC:** 6711, 1099
**UK SIC:** 83962, 21000
**Auditors:** KPMG LLP

| | 31-12-13 | 31-12-12 | 31-12-11 |
|---|---|---|---|
| TA | 33,144,000 | 32,466,000 | 31,913,000 |
| P/L | 678,000 | 553,000 | 392,000 |
| NW | 33,144,000 | 32,466,000 | 31,913,000 |

DUNS 73-850-7859

## Saville Consulting Uk Ltd

(**Subsidiary of:** Saville Consulting Group Limited)
Claygate House, Littleworth Road, Esher, Surrey KT10 9PN
**Tel:** 02086199000 **Fax:** 02086199001
**Web:** www.savilleconsulting.com
**Reg No:** 5105906 **Estd:** 2004 Private Limited Company
**Line of Business:** Business and management consultancy activities not elsewhere classified
**Issued Capital:** £1
**Directors:** K J O'Connor, C Small, I R Maciver, Ms G A Parry, Professor P F Saville
**Co. Secretary:** Graham Seager
**US SIC:** 7392, 7361
**UK SIC:** 83951, 83954

| | 31-12-13 | 31-12-12 | 31-12-11 |
|---|---|---|---|
| TA | 2,496,309 | 1,841,061 | 1,152,888 |
| NW | 1,101,910 | (1,023,691) | (1,221,263) |
| WC | 911,789 | 622,794 | 421,983 |

DUNS 77-527-9011

## Saville Estates Ltd

Innovation Court, 121 Edmund Street, Birmingham, West Midlands B3 2HJ
**Tel:** 01216333733
**Web:** www.savills.co.uk
**Reg No:** 2991311 **Estd:** 1994 Private Limited Company
**Line of Business:** Development and selling of real estate
**Trading Style:** Savilles
**Issued Capital:** £500,000
**Directors:** G J Vale, N T Harber, Mrs A E Wilkinson, J S Lucas
**Co. Secretary:** Mrs Pauline Vale
**US SIC:** 6552, 1522, 6519
**UK SIC:** 85000, 50100
**Auditors:** Farmiloes

| | 30-04-14 | 30-04-13 | 30-04-12 |
|---|---|---|---|
| TA | 4,867,087 | 4,434,121 | 4,439,070 |
| NW | 2,638,811 | 2,769,386 | 2,820,139 |
| WC | 1,689,035 | 1,819,610 | 1,868,653 |

DUNS 29-494-5423

## Saville's Freights Ltd

Aldermoor Way, Longwell Green, Bristol, Avon BS30 7DA
**Tel:** 01179600778 **Fax:** 01179-352172
**Web:** www.savillesfreights.co.uk
**Reg No:** 1857882 **VAT No:** 399056505
**Estd:** 1984 Private Limited Company
**Line of Business:** Representative office
**Issued Capital:** £6,000
**Principals:** A M Saville *(Managing)*, Ms J Saville, G M Dunford, D P Saville
**Co. Secretary:** Mrs Carol Saville
**Branches:** Saville's Freights Ltd, Saville House, 12-13 Bonville Road, Bristol, Avon BS4 5QG
**US SIC:** 7399, 4226
**UK SIC:** 83954, 77003
**Auditors:** Grant Thornton
**Bankers:** The Royal Bank Of Scotland Plc (16-14-25)

| | 31-12-13 | 31-12-12 | 31-12-11 |
|---|---|---|---|
| TO | 4,796,054 | 5,144,937 | 5,919,506 |
| P/L | 75,346 | 179,997 | 275,413 |
| NW | 4,161,220 | 3,958,198 | 4,073,774 |
| WC | 897 | 33,823 | (116,512) |
| Emp. | 49 | 53 | 46 |

DUNS 76-840-2596

## Savills Commercial Ltd

(**Subsidiary of:** Savills Plc)
Belvedere, 12 Booth Street, Manchester M2 4AW
**Tel:** 01612368644 **Fax:** 020 749 53773
**Web:** www.savills.com
**Reg No:** 2605125 **Estd:** 2011 Private Limited Company
**Line of Business:** Surveyors and valuers
**Issued Capital:** £2,000,000
**Directors:** J J Ridley, T S Maynard, N P Herward
**Co. Secretary:** Christopher Lee
**Responsibilities**
**Senior:** Patrick Joynson *(Head Of Office)*
**Branches:** Savills Commercial Ltd, Wessex House, Priors Walk, Wimborne, Dorset BH21 1PB
**US SIC:** 6531 **UK SIC:** 83400
**Auditors:** PricewaterhouseCoopers LLP

| | 31-12-13 | 31-12-12 | 31-12-11 |
|---|---|---|---|
| TO | N/A | 152,337,000 | 106,284,000 |
| P/L | 61,000 | 18,295,000 | 11,758,000 |
| NW | 10,375,000 | 5,454,000 | 12,726,000 |
| WC | 10,375,000 | 14,794,000 | 22,772,000 |
| Emp. | N/A | 845 | 672 |

DUNS 39-415-3332

## Savills Plc

33 Margaret Street, London W1G 0JD
**Tel:** 020-7499-8644 **Fax:** 020-7495-3773
**Web:** www.savills.co.uk
**Reg No:** 2122174 **Estd:** 1987 Public Limited Company
**Line of Business:** Management activities of holding companies
**Export Sales:** £442,500,000
**Trading Style:** Savills Uk
**Issued Capital:** £3,337,667
**Directors:** M D Angle, P A Smith, C S Mcveigh Iii, Ms E A Hewitt, T G Freshwater, S J Shaw, J C Helsby
**Co. Secretary:** Christopher Lee
**Responsibilities**
**Senior:** Richard Addington *(Head of Office - Exeter)*, Billy Chau *(Manager)*, Paul Cheung *(Manager)*, Neal Hudson *(Associate Director - Residenti)*, Alexander Joslin *(Associate Director UK Investme)*, Kendrew Leung *(Manager)*, Katrina Mackay *(Associate Director)*, Philip Mahler *(Manager)*, Tom Mellows *(Associate Director, Regional O)*, Duncan Miller *(Associate Director Investment)*, Christopher Nicolle *(Senior Advisor)*, Alex Palfreyman *(Associate Director)*, Jonathan Phelps *(Associate Director - Developme)*, Sam Pilgrim *(Associate Director)*, Colin Rees-Smith *(Director - Healthcare)*, Borja Sierra *(Chief Executive Officer)*, Paul Tostevin *(Associate Director - Research)*, Matt Willcock *(Director - National Developmen)*
**Finance:** David Cunnington *(Head of Corporate Finance)*, Claire Fahey *(Associate Director - Finance)*, Alex Heaton *(Assistant Finance Manager)*, Nicola Hordern *(Head of Fund Finance)*, James Howard *(Finance Manager)*, Danny O'Donnell *(Director Corporate Finance)*, Matt Probert *(Head of Tax)*
**Marketing:** Steve Carrick *(Sales & Marketing Manager)*, Alison Dean *(Head of Marketing)*, Chioma Ibe *(Marketing Manager)*, Amy Ng *(Marketing Manager)*, Neville Page *(International Marketing and Bu)*
**Sales:** Simon Aldous *(Sales Executive)*, Sam Arrowsmith *(Retail Research Analyst)*, Clare Bailey *(Commercial Research Analyst)*, Christopher Blair *(Director Retail)*, Nicola Bradley *(Residential Development Sale M)*, Steve Carrick *(Sales & Marketing Manager)*, Jon Crossfield *(Director Central London Market)*, Gill Daniels *(Sales Manager)*, Maria Eivers *(Associate - Residential Develo)*, Jennifer Goldie *(Sales Manager)*, Eri Mitsostergiou *(Director - Commercial Research)*, Karen Mole *(Director Residential Developme)*, Mat Oakley *(Director Commercial Research)*, Abbie Pearson *(Residential Development Sales)*, Lee Pickles *(Director Commercial Management)*, Dominic Rodbourne *(Director Out of Town Retail)*, Miles Rowe *(Sales Director)*, Peter Tyson *(Sales Director)*, Tim Whittington *(Retail Research Director)*, Peter Yuen *(Sales Director)*
**Admin:** Nina Burley *(PA - World Research)*, Chloe Fowler *(Personal Assistant)*, Jayne Glenn *(Reception Manager)*, Alison Mennecier *(Secretary)*, Alice Wigram *(Personal Assistant)*
**IT:** Emma Self *(Systems Manager)*
**HR:** Sarah Allan *(Head of Human Resources)*
**Facilities:** Ned Baring *(Director of Residential Develo)*, Clive Beer *(Head of Professional Services)*, Richard Gayner *(Head of Country Houses)*, Jonathan Ottewell *(Associate)*, William Peppitt *(Estate Agent Director)*, Stefan Saul *(Associate)*, Rupert Sebag-Montefiore *(Head of Global Residential)*
**Operations:** Richard Aldous *(Head of New Homes)*, Steve Carrick *(Sales & Marketing Manager)*, Belinda Nowland *(Project Manager)*, Daniel Parker *(Operations Manager)*
**Fleet:** Toby Green *(Director Industrial & Logistic)*
**Branches:** Savills Plc, Savills (L & P) Ltd, 12 Clerk Street, Brechin, Angus DD9 6AE
**US SIC:** 6711, 6531
**UK SIC:** 83962, 83400
**Auditors:** PricewaterhouseCoopers LLP

**Bankers:** Barclays Bank Plc (20-00-00)

|  | 31-12-13 | 31-12-12 | 31-12-11 |
|---|---|---|---|
| TO | 904,800,000 | 806,400,000 | 721,500,000 |
| P/L | 70,100,000 | 54,200,000 | 40,000,000 |
| NW | 118,900,000 | 78,700,000 | 53,100,000 |
| WC | 67,600,000 | 55,500,000 | 36,700,000 |
| Emp. | 26,287 | 25,016 | 23,555 |

DUNS 21-005-1550    Imp

## Saving Energy Ltd
Unit 19 Oban Court, Hurricane Way, Wickford, Essex SS11 8YB
**Tel:** 08009549689
**Web:** www.savingenergyuk.co.uk
**Reg No:** 6298898 **Estd:** 2007 Private Limited Company
**Line of Business:** Insulation installers
**Issued Capital:** £1,000,100
**Directors:** Miss S J Fulker, G Coulson, Mrs A L Coulson, C K Langley
**Co. Secretary:** Miss Danielle Fulker
**US SIC:** 1742 **UK SIC:** 50400

|  | 31-12-13 | 31-12-12 | 31-12-11 |
|---|---|---|---|
| TA | 2,447,938 | 2,049,998 | 1,803,112 |
| NW | 1,211,213 | 1,168,237 | 877,723 |
| WC | 929,532 | 918,820 | 636,212 |

DUNS 73-501-4396

## Savona Provisions Ltd
Oxonian Park, Langford Locks, Kidlington, Oxfordshire OX5 1FP
**Tel:** 01865-852010 **Fax:** 01865-841345
**Web:** www.savona.co.uk
**Reg No:** 4764681 **Estd:** 2013 Private Limited Company
**Line of Business:** Catering food and drink suppliers
**Issued Capital:** £9,500
**Directors:** K J Holloway, J N Vokes, K J Knowland
**Co. Secretary:** Trude Knowland
**US SIC:** 5149 **UK SIC:** 61700
**Auditors:** Baker Tilly Audit Ltd
**Bankers:** National Westminster Bank Plc (60-10-28)

|  | 28-06-14 | 29-06-13 | 30-06-12 |
|---|---|---|---|
| TO | 14,185,762 | 13,270,914 | 12,587,474 |
| P/L | 220,207 | 152,982 | 290,000 |
| NW | 1,704,123 | 1,526,863 | 1,400,232 |
| WC | 1,337,392 | 1,219,483 | 1,007,099 |
| Emp. | 78 | 74 | 71 |

DUNS 53-652-3731

## Savoy Asset Management Plc
**(Subsidiary of:** Mattioli Woods Plc)
60 Queen Victoria Street, London EC4N 4TR
**Tel:** 02078717300 **Fax:** 02078717339
**Web:** www.savoyim.com
**Reg No:** 3457951 **Estd:** 1997 Private Limited Company
**Line of Business:** Financial intermediation not elsewhere classified
**Trading Style:** Ashcourt Rowan, Savoy Investment Manager
**Issued Capital:** £1,081,188
**Directors:** J C Polin, A Tagliabue
**Co. Secretary:** Ms Rehana Hasan
**Responsibilities**
**Senior:** Christopher Jeffreys (Chief Executive Officer)
**HR:** Sharon Cunningham (Head of Human Resources)
**US SIC:** 6111 **UK SIC:** 81501
**Auditors:** Saffery Champness
**Bankers:** HSBC Bank plc (40-31-24)

|  | 31-03-14 | 31-03-13 | 31-03-12 |
|---|---|---|---|
| TA | 6,304,300 | 6,282,112 | 6,113,809 |
| P/L | 5,695 | 21,455 | (8,641) |
| NW | 4,635,999 | 4,630,304 | 4,608,849 |
| WC | (1,457,555) | (1,434,637) | (1,256,092) |

DUNS 23-674-5449

## The Savoy Hotel Ltd
**(Subsidiary of:** D.W. Director 1 Ltd)
The Strand, London WC2R 0EU
**Tel:** 020-7836-4343 **Fax:** 020-7240-6040
**Web:** www.fairmont.com
**Reg No:** 3669255 **Estd:** 1998 Private Limited Company
**Line of Business:** Hotels
**Trading Style:** Savoy
**Issued Capital:** £150,000
**Directors:** G A Drake, A Fernandes, C K Broderick, M Kandrac
**Co. Secretary:**
D.W. Company Services Limited
**Responsibilities**
**Senior:** Shawn Halloran (Director Housekeeping)
**Facilities:** Jack Harding (Director of Engineering)
**Purchasing:** Shawn Halloran (Director Housekeeping)
**Branches:** The Savoy Hotel Ltd, 100 Strand, London WC2R 0EW
**US SIC:** 7011 **UK SIC:** 66500
**Auditors:** Deloitte LLP

**Bankers:** Bank Of Scotland (12-01-03)

|  | 31-12-13 | 31-12-12 | 31-12-11 |
|---|---|---|---|
| TO | 56,748,000 | 58,455,000 | 56,517,000 |
| P/L | (32,092,000) | (21,494,000) | (25,388,000) |
| NW | 59,719,000 | 92,235,000 | 114,416,000 |
| WC | 2,817,000 | (10,189,000) | (12,525,000) |
| Emp. | 531 | 489 | 497 |

DUNS 34-724-1593

## Savoy Theatre Group Ltd
**(Subsidiary of:** Atg Luxco Sarl)
7 Church Path, Woking, Surrey GU21 6EJ
**Tel:** 01483776610
**Web:** http://maiawoking.com
**Reg No:** 5527723 **Estd:** 2008 Private Limited Company
**Line of Business:** Other entertainment activities not elsewhere classified
**Issued Capital:** £100
**Directors:** P R Kavanagh, D Blyth, M C Lynas, Mrs H J Enright, H H Panter, N G Potter, Ms R A Squire
**US SIC:** 7999 **UK SIC:** 97913
**Bankers:** National Westminster Bank Plc (50-42-28)

|  | 29-03-14 | 30-03-13 | 31-03-12 |
|---|---|---|---|
| TO | N/A | 3,471,192 | 3,072,516 |
| P/L | (80,552) | 1,293,800 | 547,072 |
| NW | 452,390 | 3,305,639 | 2,319,358 |
| WC | (7,409,926) | (2,920,407) | (5,324,452) |
| Emp. | N/A | 53 | 61 |

DUNS 28-828-9424

## Savoy Theatre Ltd
**(Subsidiary of:** Atg Luxco Sarl)
Savoy Court, Strand, London WC2R 0ET
**Tel:** 08448717644
**Web:** www.savoytheatre.org
**Reg No:** 0053830 **Estd:** 1897 Private Limited Company
**Line of Business:** Theatres & concert halls
**Issued Capital:** £41,250
**Directors:** Ms R A Squire, Mrs H J Enright, H H Panter, D Blyth, M C Lynas, N G Potter, P R Kavanagh
**Responsibilities**
**Senior:** Glenn Cottenden (Theatre Manager)
**US SIC:** 8999 **UK SIC:** 83954
**Auditors:** Deloitte & Touche
**Bankers:** Coutts & Co (18-00-93)

|  | 29-03-14 | 30-03-13 | 31-03-12 |
|---|---|---|---|
| TO | 3,238,104 | 3,471,192 | 3,072,516 |
| P/L | 901,536 | 1,403,712 | 666,082 |
| NW | 8,079,400 | 7,368,933 | 6,372,740 |
| WC | 5,766,819 | (556,135) | (1,502,773) |
| Emp. | 59 | 53 | 61 |

DUNS 50-424-0920    Imp

## Savoy Timber Ltd
**(Subsidiary of:** Savoy Holdings Ltd)
Old Cinema Building (By The Bridge), Ashton Street, Ashton-On-Ri, Preston, Lancashire PR2 2PP
**Tel:** 01772729165
**Web:** www.savoytimber.com
**Reg No:** 2416333 **VAT No:** 534544154
**Estd:** 1946 Private Limited Company
**Line of Business:** Retail sale of hardware, paints and glass
**Issued Capital:** £8,350
**Principals:** G L Cornwell (Managing), P J Cornwell, Mrs L Royle, P H Cornwell
**Co. Secretary:** Ms Sara Braithwaite
**Responsibilities**
**Senior:** Ian Cornwall (Manager), Bill Woods (Branch Manager)
**Branches:** Savoy Timber Ltd, 95-97 Talbot Road, Blackpool, Lancashire FY1 3QX
**US SIC:** 5251, 5074
**UK SIC:** 64800, 61300
**Auditors:** Moore & Smalley LLP
**Bankers:** Barclays Bank Plc (20-12-75)

|  | 30-11-13 | 30-11-12 | 30-11-11 |
|---|---|---|---|
| TO | 6,147,182 | N/A | N/A |
| P/L | 203,050 | N/A | N/A |
| NW | 1,982,224 | 1,968,569 | 1,987,937 |
| WC | 1,887,445 | 1,927,402 | 1,928,649 |
| Emp. | 53 | N/A | N/A |

DUNS 67-220-8936

## Savoy Ventures Ltd
Stone Castle Drive, Greenhithe, Kent DA9 9XL
**Tel:** 01322 389393 **Fax:** 01322 388818
**Web:** www.savoyventures.com
**Reg No:** 6050564 **Estd:** 2007 Private Limited Company
**Line of Business:** Hospital activities
**Issued Capital:** £100
**Directors:** R L Adams, M R Clayton
**Responsibilities**
**Senior:** Brian Wren (Manager)
**US SIC:** 8062, 8091
**UK SIC:** 95100, 95200
**Auditors:** Jennifer M. Richardson Ltd

|  | 30-04-13 | 30-04-12 | 30-04-11 |
|---|---|---|---|
| TO | 13,259,385 | 12,017,734 | 9,542,736 |
| P/L | 210,941 | 350,172 | (443,333) |
| NW | 431,189 | 255,766 | (17,534) |
| WC | (1,036,583) | (1,343,249) | (1,835,680) |
| Emp. | 135 | 307 | N/A |

DUNS 21-098-4637

## Savvy Marketing Ltd
**(Subsidiary of:** Get Savvy Group Ltd)
15-17 High Court Lane The Call, Leeds, West Yorkshire LS2 7EU
**Tel:** 01132376500
**Web:** www.getsavvy.com
**Reg No:** 6425646 **Estd:** 2011 Private Limited Company
**Line of Business:** Other business activities not elsewhere classified
**Issued Capital:** £100
**Director:** Ms C Shuttleworth
**Responsibilities**
**Senior:** Bev D''Ambrisio (Manager)
**Finance:** Bev D''Ambrisio (Manager)
**Marketing:** James Lunn (Innovations Director)
**Sales:** Lauren Pickering (?Senior Account Director)
**Health & Safety:** Jonathon Brockett (Facilities Manager)
**Facilities:** Jonathon Brockett (Facilities Manager)
**US SIC:** 7399 **UK SIC:** 83954

|  | 31-12-13 | 31-12-12 | 31-12-11 |
|---|---|---|---|
| TA | 100 | 100 | 100 |
| NW | 100 | 100 | 100 |

DUNS 21-759-8052

## Sawston Village College
New Road, Sawston, Cambridge, Cambridgeshire CB22 3BP
**Tel:** 01223712777
**Web:** www.sawstonvc.org
**Reg No:** 7627138 **Estd:** 2011 Private Limited Company
**Line of Business:** Schools (local authority)
**Directors:** Ms S Hickling, J M Culpin, Dr C G Kenney, V T Kitay, Ms J Bennett, M K Postle, D R Lamkin, Miss S Gelder
**Co. Secretary:** Brian Croft
**Responsibilities**
**Senior:** John Ashurst (Director), Victoria Benedikz (Director), June Cannie (Head Teacher), Mark Dawe (Director), Shaun Fitzgerald (Director), Sarah Franklin (Director), Michelle Murray (Proprietor), Polly Stanton (Director), Edward Westrip (Director), Jacqueline Worster (Director)
**US SIC:** 8211 **UK SIC:** 93200
**Bankers:** Barclays Bank Plc (20-74-05)

|  | 31-08-14 | 31-08-13 | 31-08-12 |
|---|---|---|---|
| TO | 6,131,631 | 5,961,394 | 24,178,233 |
| P/L | (440,026) | (459,084) | 15,928,800 |
| NW | 14,469,690 | 15,298,716 | 15,659,800 |
| WC | 703,957 | 705,220 | 772,857 |
| Emp. | 124 | 121 | 116 |

DUNS 21-736-1734

## Sawtry Community College
Fen Lane, Huntingdon, Cambridgeshire PE28 5TQ
**Tel:** 01487830701
**Web:** www.sawtrycc.com
**Reg No:** 7703775 **Estd:** 1993 Private Company Limited By Guarantee
**Line of Business:** Nursery schools
**Directors:** R Tuplin, P Leaton, Professor J M Weeks
**Co. Secretary:** Mrs Lisa Killner
**Responsibilities**
**Senior:** Christine Laxton (Manager), Dawn Quince (Manager)
**US SIC:** 8211 **UK SIC:** 93200
**Bankers:** Lloyds TSB Bank plc (30-00-00)

|  | 31-08-13 | 31-08-12 |
|---|---|---|
| TO | 7,317,194 | 17,277,540 |
| P/L | (311,088) | 8,572,912 |
| NW | 8,256,824 | 8,481,912 |
| WC | 45,668 | 218,837 |
| Emp. | 162 | 157 |

DUNS 23-280-9376

## Sawyers Transport Ltd
Armagh Road, Dungannon, Co Tyrone BT71 7SD
**Tel:** 02887 789 522 **Fax:** 02887 789 525
**Web:** www.sawyerstransport.com
**Reg No:** 0026029NI **Estd:** 1984 Private Limited Company
**Line of Business:** Freight transport by road not elsewhere classified
**Export Sales:** £3,495,769
**Issued Capital:** £2
**Directors:** L Sawyers, D R Sawyers, A Sawyers, Ms Y Sawyers
**Co. Secretary:** Ms Sonya Mckelvey
**US SIC:** 4213 **UK SIC:** 72300
**Auditors:** McElhom & Co
**Bankers:** Ulster Bank Ltd (98-04-50)

|  | 31-01-14 | 31-01-13 | 31-01-12 |
|---|---|---|---|
| TO | 64,647,505 | 54,422,845 | 45,107,005 |
| P/L | 938,140 | 766,733 | 607,783 |
| NW | 4,221,547 | 3,598,267 | 3,388,050 |
| WC | 852,282 | 621,059 | 1,105,327 |
| Emp. | 93 | 79 | 59 |

DUNS 21-324-0745

## Saxlingham Hall Nursing Home
The Green, Saxlingham Nethergate, Norwich, Norfolk NR15 1TH
**Tel:** 01508-499225
**Web:** www.saxlinghamhallnursinghome.com
**Estd:** 1953 Proprietorship
**Line of Business:** Clinics private
**Proprietor:** A Bird
**US SIC:** 8051 **UK SIC:** 95100
**Employees:** 63

DUNS 22-634-4158    Imp-Exp

## Saxon Industries Ltd
Everland Road, Hungerford, Berkshire RG17 0DX
**Tel:** 01488-689400
**Web:** www.saxon-brands.com
**Reg No:** 1751487 **Estd:** 1979 Private Limited Company
**Line of Business:** Distribution service providers
**Issued Capital:** £60,000
**Director:** Dr R Samann
**Co. Secretary:** Alan Mcivor
**Responsibilities**
**Senior:** Neil Haines (Operations Director), Len Hillier (Operations Director), Jody Lalone (Manager), Rhona Shirewood (Purchasing Manager)
**Finance:** Thomas Redfern (Finance Director)
**Marketing:** Danielle Kay (Product Manager), Romeo de Lima Pereira (Marketing Director)
**HR:** Len Hillier (Operations Director)
**Health & Safety:** Len Hillier (Operations Director)
**Facilities:** Neil Haines (Operations Director), Jim Hale (Facilities Manager)
**Operations:** Romeo de Lima Pereira (Marketing Director)
**Purchasing:** Richard Amor (Purchasing Manager)
**US SIC:** 4712 **UK SIC:** 77002

|  | 30-09-13 | 30-09-12 | 30-09-11 |
|---|---|---|---|
| TA | 271,985 | 271,985 | 271,985 |
| NW | 271,985 | 271,985 | 271,985 |

DUNS 29-654-8639    Imp

## Saxon Packaging Ltd
28-32 Harvest Drive South Lowestoft, Industrial Estate, Lowestoft, Suffolk NR33 7NJ
**Tel:** 01502509711 **Fax:** 01502583627
**Web:** www.saxonpackaging.co.uk
**Reg No:** 1981173 **VAT No:** 428091453
**Estd:** 1986 Private Limited Company
**Line of Business:** Packaging equipment
**Issued Capital:** £22,000
**Managing Director:** P W King
**Co. Secretary:** Ms Joanne King
**Responsibilities**
**Senior:** Steve Hindes (Factory Manager), Rory King (Executive), Andy Smith (Health & Safety Officer & Gene)
**Finance:** Trevor Hook (Financial Director), Andrew Reeder (Credit Control)
**Sales:** Carly Blowers (Sales Office), John Stembridge (Sales Executive)
**IT:** Andy Smith (Health & Safety Officer & Gene)
**Health & Safety:** Andy Smith (Health & Safety Officer & Gene)
**Purchasing:** Andy Smith (Health & Safety Officer & Gene)
**Fleet:** Sandra Jenkins (Planning & Transport Controlle)
**US SIC:** 2651 **UK SIC:** 47253
**Auditors:** Sexty & Co
**Bankers:** Lloyds TSB Bank plc (30-94-55)

|  | 28-02-14 | 28-02-13 | 29-02-12 |
|---|---|---|---|
| TA | 2,199,702 | 2,175,779 | 2,443,164 |
| NW | 384,388 | 383,452 | 373,421 |
| WC | (459,235) | (429,520) | (324,724) |

DUNS 21-690-0721

## Saxon Quality Foods Ltd
**(Subsidiary of:** Abbeydale Food Group Ltd)
Unit 5 Atkinsons Way, Foxhills Industrial Estate, Scunthorpe, South Humberside DN15 8QJ
**Tel:** 01724280664
**Web:** www.saxonqualityfoods.co.uk
**Reg No:** 7374852 **Estd:** 2010 Private Limited Company
**Line of Business:** Manufacturers of food products
**Issued Capital:** £1
**Directors:** C V Wright, J S Beach, R M Firth, D W Figg, A P Hayes
**Co. Secretary:** David Figg
**US SIC:** 2099 **UK SIC:** 42399

|  | 28-02-14 | 28-02-13 | 28-02-12 |
|---|---|---|---|
| TA | 2,040,640 | 966,012 | 626,415 |
| NW | 176,685 | 122,004 | 29,052 |
| WC | (401,008) | (6,461) | 10,135 |

DUNS 23-855-9368
## Saxon Weald Homes Ltd
Saxon Weald House, 38-42 Worthing Road, Horsham, West Sussex RH12 1DT
**Web:** www.saxonweald.com
**Reg No:** 3847737 **Estd:** 1999 Private Limited Company
**Line of Business:** Representative office
**Directors:** Ms S C Sjuve, M Loates, Ms S J White, Ms C F Moore, R Perry, R H Venables Kyrke, Ms D J Joseph, D J Standfast
**Co. Secretary:** Norman Hill
**Responsibilities**
**Senior:** Anthony Bevis *(Manager)*, Mary Short *(Chairman)*, Vanessa Williams *(Director)*
**Finance:** Peter Lansberry *(Finance Director)*
**Admin:** Jim Dean *(Head of Service Improvement)*, Helen Neeve *(Human Resource Administrator)*, Ruth Skipper *(Human Resource Administrator)*
**IT:** Alex Gunter *(IT Manager)*
**HR:** Kath Hicks *(Older People?s Services Direct)*, Linda Kawycz *(Human Resources Manager)*, Helen Neeve *(Human Resource Administrator)*, Ruth Skipper *(Human Resource Administrator)*
**Health & Safety:** Linda Kawycz *(Human Resources Manager)*
**Branches:** Saxon Weald Homes Ltd, Adur View, Dawn Cres, Upper Beeding, Steyning, West Sussex BN44 3WY
**US SIC:** 6519, 7399
**UK SIC:** 85000, 83954
**Auditors:** Baker Tilly
**Bankers:** National Westminster Bank Plc (60-11-17)

| | 31-03-14 | 31-03-13 | 31-03-12 |
|---|---|---|---|
| TO | 36,574,000 | 38,392,000 | 33,354,000 |
| P/L | 960,000 | (27,916,000) | 4,496,000 |
| NW | 24,780,000 | 20,267,000 | 49,206,000 |
| WC | 48,236,000 | 62,935,000 | 10,744,000 |
| Emp. | 164 | 189 | 171 |

DUNS 29-755-0360
## Saxton Bampfylde Hever Ltd
**(Subsidiary of:** Chatel 08 Ltd)
35 Old Queen Street, London SW1H 9JA
**Tel:** 020-7227-0800
**Web:** www.saxbam.com
**Reg No:** 2018211 **VAT No:** 444011789
**Estd:** 1986 Public Limited Company
**Line of Business:** Employment and recruitment companies and consultants
**Export Sales:** £434,934
**Issued Capital:** £50,000
**Principals:** S J Bampfylde *(Managing)*, Mrs D Loudon, J Morgan, P D Stevenson, Ms R Hubbard, Ms I B Napier
**Co. Secretary:** James Kempton
**Responsibilities**
**Senior:** Ann Bourne *(Executive Search Consultant)*, Sarah Orwin *(General Manager)*, James Spearpoint *(Executive)*
**Admin:** Belinda Beck *(Administration)*, Anneliese Boz *(Personal Assistant)*, Tessa Dain *(Assistant)*
**Branches:** Saxton Bampfylde Hever Ltd, 38-42 Chertsey Street, Guildford, Surrey GU1 4HD
**US SIC:** 7361 **UK SIC:** 83954
**Auditors:** Nexia Audit Ltd
**Bankers:** Coutts & Co (18-00-02)

| | 30-09-13 | 30-09-12 | 30-09-11 |
|---|---|---|---|
| TO | 8,478,239 | N/A | N/A |
| P/L | 1,112,331 | N/A | N/A |
| NW | 1,630,010 | 821,962 | 493,955 |
| WC | 1,485,642 | 807,406 | 627,053 |
| Emp. | 61 | N/A | N/A |

DUNS 21-716-2387
## Saxton Drilling Ltd
**(Subsidiary of:** Saxton Holdings Ltd)
Cardrew Industrial Estate, Redruth, Cornwall TR15 1SS
**Tel:** 01209315100
**Reg No:** 0925272 **VAT No:** 591460531
**Estd:** 1967 Private Limited Company
**Line of Business:** Drilling and boring equipment
**Issued Capital:** £150,000
**Principals:** A C Thomas *(Managing)*, Mrs L M Thomas
**Co. Secretary:** Mrs Lynda Thomas
**Responsibilities**
**Finance:** Carole Pengilly *(Accounts Manager)*
**IT:** Carole Pengilly *(Accounts Manager)*
**HR:** Stella Fuller *(Human Resources Administrator)*
**Branches:** Saxton Drilling Ltd, Old Pound, St. Austell, Cornwall PL26 7XS
**US SIC:** 3531, 1799
**UK SIC:** 32541, 50000
**Auditors:** Lang Bennetts
**Bankers:** Lloyds TSB Bank plc (30-98-76)

| | 31-12-13 | 31-12-12 | 31-12-11 |
|---|---|---|---|
| TA | 2,925,813 | 2,783,519 | 2,840,714 |
| NW | 1,829,003 | 1,696,210 | 1,571,095 |
| WC | 1,137,906 | 1,062,745 | 1,013,944 |

DUNS 71-933-1121
## Say Scaffolding Ltd
Say House Rudgate Business Centre, Wighill Lane, Thorp Arch, Wetherby, West Yorkshire LS23 7AT
**Tel:** 01937-848480 **Fax:** 01904737702
**Web:** www.sayltd.co.uk
**Reg No:** 5314071 **VAT No:** 852549603
**Estd:** 2006 Private Limited Company
**Line of Business:** Other construction work involving special trades
**Trading Style:** Say Scaffolding Ltd
**Issued Capital:** £2
**Director:** P J Wetten
**Co. Secretary:** Ms Amanda Wetten
**US SIC:** 1799 **UK SIC:** 50000
**Auditors:** HPH

| | 31-05-14 | 31-05-13 | 31-05-12 |
|---|---|---|---|
| TA | 2,772,288 | 2,251,965 | 2,038,156 |
| NW | 1,106,551 | 902,411 | 900,469 |
| WC | (50,961) | (477,675) | (55,937) |

DUNS 37-798-4133
## Sayer Vincent
Unit 8, Angel Gate, 326 City Road, London EC1V 2SJ
**Web:** www.sayervincent.co.uk
**Estd:** 1992 Partnership
**Line of Business:** Accounting and auditing activities
**Partners:** Ms H Elliot, Mrs P Craig, I Pritchyard, Ms K Sayer
**Branches:** Sayer Vincent, Kings House, 14 Orchard Street, Bristol, Avon BS1 5EH
**US SIC:** 8931 **UK SIC:** 83600
**Employees:** 51

DUNS 21-118-6871
## Sayers the Bakers Ltd
**(Subsidiary of:** Stb Holdings Ltd)
Sidney Street, Bolton, Lancashire BL3 6BG
**Tel:** 01253393660 **Fax:** 01204-380140
**Web:** www.sayersthebakers.co.uk
**Reg No:** 6582290 **Estd:** 2004 Private Limited Company
**Line of Business:** Bakers shops
**Trading Style:** Sayers the Bakers Ltd
**Issued Capital:** £1
**Directors:** D Silvester, M S James, A P Birnie
**Responsibilities**
**Senior:** Kim Oke *(Manager)*, Michael Quinlan *(Manager)*
**Finance:** Anne-Marie Goodchild *(Financial controller)*
**Health & Safety:** Karen Marsay *(Health & Safety Officer)*
**US SIC:** 5462, 5499
**UK SIC:** 64100

| | 30-09-14 | 30-09-13 | 30-09-12 |
|---|---|---|---|
| TO | 45,357,000 | 42,371,000 | 42,520,000 |
| P/L | 469,000 | (82,000) | 229,000 |
| NW | (177,000) | (515,000) | (430,000) |
| WC | (2,509,000) | (2,462,000) | (2,269,000) |
| Emp. | 1,519 | 1,470 | 1,463 |

DUNS 21-235-3254
## Sayes & Co Ltd
**(Subsidiary of:** Sayes Holdings Ltd)
Grangefield, Richardshaw Road, Pudsey, West Yorkshire LS28 6BR
**Tel:** 01132-578411 **Fax:** 0112569275
**Web:** www.sayesandcoltd.co.uk
**Reg No:** 0257299 **VAT No:** 179860411
**Estd:** 1931 Private Limited Company
**Line of Business:** Heating contractors
**Issued Capital:** £2,500
**Directors:** G M Walton, N W Jackson, A C Barker, Ms J E Jackson, P A Jackson, Ms D M Barker
**Co. Secretary:** Ms Jane Jackson
**US SIC:** 1711 **UK SIC:** 50300
**Auditors:** David Lacey & Co
**Bankers:** Lloyds TSB Bank plc (30-91-12)

| | 30-06-13 | 30-06-12 | 30-06-11 |
|---|---|---|---|
| TO | 5,285,331 | N/A | N/A |
| P/L | 320,534 | N/A | N/A |
| NW | 963,852 | 924,184 | 916,404 |
| WC | 861,632 | 826,468 | 802,788 |

DUNS 21-690-7923 Imp-Exp
## Saywell International Ltd
Downland Business Park, Lyons Way, Worthing, West Sussex BN14 9LA
**Tel:** 01903704900 **Fax:** 01903-705701
**Web:** www.saywell.co.uk
**Reg No:** 0579488 **VAT No:** 210393406
**Estd:** 1946 Private Limited Company
**Line of Business:** Other supporting air transport activities
**Export Markets:** Worldwide
**Export Sales:** £34,236,034
**Issued Capital:** £150
**Principals:** P L Saywell *(Managing)*, R Tudor, Mrs M E Saywell, S Sutaria
**Co. Secretary:** Mrs Heather Edmonds
**Responsibilities**
**Senior:** Heather Saywell *(Manager)*
**Finance:** Yvette Grout *(Accounts Manager)*
**US SIC:** 4582 **UK SIC:** 76400
**Auditors:** Deloitte LLP
**Bankers:** National Westminster Bank Plc (54-41-54)

| | 31-08-13 | 31-08-12 | 31-08-11 |
|---|---|---|---|
| TO | 45,957,724 | 38,680,825 | 34,643,593 |
| P/L | 3,462,303 | 2,615,176 | 3,013,261 |
| NW | 11,588,757 | 9,789,133 | 8,737,432 |
| WC | 17,686,025 | 13,786,139 | 11,544,834 |
| Emp. | 74 | 73 | 71 |

DUNS 73-281-9615
## Sb Drug Discovery Ltd
Telford Pavilion, Block H, Todd Campus, West Of Scotland, Glasgow, Lanarkshire G33 6HZ
**Tel:** 01415-876100 **Fax:** 01415876110
**Web:** www.scottish-biomedical.com
**Reg No:** 0237873SC **Estd:** 2002 Private Limited Company
**Line of Business:** Research and experimental development on natural sciences and engineering
**Issued Capital:** £5,380
**Directors:** Dr. I Mcphee, Dr. D Dalrymple
**Co. Secretary:** Eric Smith
**Responsibilities**
**Senior:** Ian McPhee *(Director)*
**US SIC:** 7391 **UK SIC:** 94000

| | 31-03-14 | 31-03-13 | 31-03-12 |
|---|---|---|---|
| TA | 532,760 | 356,677 | 522,993 |
| NW | 117,504 | 90,106 | 161,961 |
| WC | 22,265 | 45,845 | 113,877 |

DUNS 21-787-5992
## Sbe
Unit 11 Carousel Way, Riverside Business Park, Northampton, Northamptonshire NN3 9HG
**Tel:** 01604412919
**Estd:** 2011
**Line of Business:** Telecom consultants
**Responsibilities**
**Senior:** Olivier Maldeghem *(General Manager)*
**US SIC:** 4899 **UK SIC:** 79020
**Employees:** 100

DUNS 45-857-0876
## S.B.E. Ltd.
**(Subsidiary of:** Societe Boulonnaise Electronique)
Beaver Industrial Estate, Beaver Road, Ashford, Kent TN23 7SH
**Tel:** 01233-619-320 **Fax:** 01233-638-547
**Web:** www.sbe-online.com
**Reg No:** 3203217 **Estd:** 1996 Private Limited Company
**Line of Business:** Management activities of other non-financial holding companies not elsewhere classified
**Issued Capital:** £10,000
**Directors:** P Beseme, M Rattu, S Lambert, X Lalouet, H Beseme, M K Schroder
**Co. Secretary:** Herve Beseme
**Responsibilities**
**Senior:** David Rosenberg *(Manager)*
**US SIC:** 7399, 7699, 7379
**UK SIC:** 83954, 67303, 83940
**Auditors:** Wilkins Kennedy FKC
**Bankers:** National Westminster Bank Plc (54-21-07)

| | 31-12-13 | 31-12-12 | 31-12-11 |
|---|---|---|---|
| TO | 84,607,143 | 99,391,813 | 74,109,876 |
| P/L | 161,591 | 1,829,796 | 2,862,153 |
| NW | 6,488,319 | 6,379,746 | 5,501,890 |
| WC | 5,462,859 | 5,221,891 | 4,330,660 |
| Emp. | 431 | 427 | 458 |

DUNS 71-917-6617
## Sbfi Ltd
**(Subsidiary of:** Five Fingers (Holdings) Ltd)
1h, First Floor, International House, St Katherines Way, London E1W 1TW
**Tel:** 02074-801-320
**Web:** www.sbfi.com
**Reg No:** 5299222 **Estd:** 2004 Private Limited Company
**Line of Business:** Manufacturers of furniture fittings
**Export Sales:** £4,187,000
**Issued Capital:** £114,944
**Directors:** A F Hynd, S M Finch, T L Finger
**Co. Secretary:** Stephen Finch
**US SIC:** 2599 **UK SIC:** 46720
**Auditors:** Baker Tilly UK Audit LLP

| | 30-11-13 | 30-11-12 | 30-11-11 |
|---|---|---|---|
| TO | 5,851,000 | 8,278,000 | 11,923,000 |
| P/L | (896,000) | 539,000 | 1,568,000 |
| NW | 4,087,000 | 4,778,000 | 4,323,000 |
| WC | 4,079,000 | 4,538,000 | 4,244,000 |
| Emp. | 49 | 61 | 70 |

DUNS 23-633-8591 Exp
## Sbj Group Ltd
**(Subsidiary of:** Axa Direction Juridique Centrale)
Matrix House, 9 Aldgate High Street, London EC3N 1AH
**Tel:** 02072043600
**Web:** www.sbjgroupinc.com
**Reg No:** 3630730 **Estd:** 1998 Private Limited Company
**Line of Business:** Holding companies management activities
**Trading Style:** Lonmar Global Risks Limited
**Issued Capital:** £28,256
**Directors:** C G Bobby, B M Poupart-Lafarge
**Co. Secretary:** Jeremy Small
**Responsibilities**
**Senior:** Graham Harvey *(Manager)*, Simon Rice *(Chief Executive Officer)*
**Marketing:** Marc Petherick *(Head of Communications)*
**Facilities:** Carol Lamborn *(Purchasing Coordinator)*
**Purchasing:** Carol Lamborn *(Purchasing Coordinator)*
**US SIC:** 6711 **UK SIC:** 83962
**Auditors:** PricewaterhouseCoopers LLP

| | 31-12-13 | 31-12-12 | 31-12-11 |
|---|---|---|---|
| TO | 7,393,000 | 23,462,000 | 268,110 |
| P/L | (6,672,000) | (28,374,000) | (97,759,759) |
| NW | 62,182,000 | 65,253,000 | 68,487,094 |
| WC | 79,381,000 | 85,478,000 | 25,580,682 |
| Emp. | 89 | 639 | N/A |

DUNS 23-998-2262
## Sbs Insurance Services Ltd
Block East, Beecroft Court, Beecroft Road, Cannock, Staffordshire WS11 1JP
**Tel:** 01543-505011 **Fax:** 01543-505550
**Web:** www.sbs-claims.co.uk
**Reg No:** 3986368 **VAT No:** 754031750
**Estd:** 2000 Private Limited Company
**Line of Business:** Other software consultancy and supply
**Issued Capital:** £25,000
**Directors:** Mrs T J Rees, S Crowley, A J Parkes, P Fairbrass
**Co. Secretary:**
Clever Management Solutions Limi
**Responsibilities**
**Senior:** Olga Bibikoff *(Director)*, Alan Cable *(Manager)*, Sue Comlay *(H R & Communications Director)*
**Marketing:** Sue Comlay *(H R & Communications Director)*
**US SIC:** 7379, 6399
**UK SIC:** 83940, 82001
**Auditors:** HKM Ltd
**Bankers:** Yorkshire Bank Plc (05-03-57)

| | 30-04-14 | 30-04-13 | 30-04-12 |
|---|---|---|---|
| TO | 14,087,813 | 18,422,671 | 18,443,809 |
| P/L | 193,394 | 794,156 | 754,772 |
| NW | 597,913 | 723,831 | 570,547 |
| WC | 582,963 | 669,156 | 474,334 |
| Emp. | 62 | 65 | 67 |

DUNS 50-525-6206
## S.B.T. Engineering Services Ltd
**(Subsidiary of:** Sbt Holdings Ltd)
Atlantic Works, Empress Street, Old Trafford, Manchester M16 9EN
**Tel:** 0161-877-7755
**Web:** www.sbtengineering.co.uk
**Reg No:** 2483687 **VAT No:** 560805645
**Estd:** 1990 Private Limited Company
**Line of Business:** Industrial engineers
**Issued Capital:** £5,000
**Principals:** W J Coplin *(Managing)*, P Laidlaw
**Co. Secretary:** Ms Samantha Mills
**US SIC:** 8911, 3568
**UK SIC:** 83701, 32613
**Auditors:** Gowgill Holloway
**Bankers:** Barclays Bank Plc (20-02-77)

| | 28-02-14 | 28-02-13 | 29-02-12 |
|---|---|---|---|
| TA | 6,101,124 | 4,470,350 | 3,058,677 |
| NW | 4,984,770 | 3,121,280 | 1,627,803 |
| WC | 4,913,297 | 3,052,845 | 1,538,134 |

DUNS 34-939-1503
## Sbu Ltd
Kestia House, Market Flat Lane, Knaresborough, North Yorkshire HG5 9JA
**Tel:** 01423-866180 **Fax:** 01423865679
**Web:** www.sb-utilities.com
**Reg No:** 5735517 **Estd:** 2006 Private Limited Company
**Line of Business:** Civil engineers
**Trading Style:** S & B Utilities
**Issued Capital:** £3,220
**Directors:** D P Swales, R K Swales
**Co. Secretary:** Mrs Karen Cocker
**Responsibilities**
**Senior:** Karen Blackwood *(Manager)*
**US SIC:** 1522, 1541, 1622
**UK SIC:** 50100, 50200
**Auditors:** Unknown Auditor

**Bankers:** Yorkshire Bank Plc (05-04-54)

|      | 30-04-14 | 30-04-13 | 30-04-12 |
|------|----------|----------|----------|
| TO   | 6,694,457 | 7,406,250 | N/A |
| P/L  | 931,928 | 498,046 | N/A |
| NW   | 364,092 | 2,090 | 582,599 |
| WC   | (400,658) | (679,880) | (1,563,695) |
| Emp. | 51 | 57 | N/A |

DUNS 23-906-3451

## Sca Group Ltd

Unit 7, Woolsbridge Small Business Centr, Crane Way, Three Legge, Wimborne, Dorset BH21 6FA

**Tel:** 01202-820-820 **Fax:** 0870-241-7124

**Web:** www.sca-group.com

**Reg No:** 3896934 **Estd:** 1999 Private Limited Company

**Line of Business:** Renting of scaffold

**Export Sales:** £14,033

**Issued Capital:** £1,982

**Directors:** S A King, L R Bennett, S J Bicknell

**US SIC:** 1799 **UK SIC:** 50000

**Auditors:** Nexia Smith & Williamson

**Bankers:** National Westminster Bank Plc (60-24-43)

|      | 30-06-14 | 30-06-13 | 30-06-12 |
|------|----------|----------|----------|
| TO   | 8,852,029 | 7,157,133 | 3,439,234 |
| P/L  | 124,893 | 373,541 | 292,049 |
| NW   | 1,229,912 | 1,192,072 | 1,000,276 |
| WC   | (380,935) | (283,110) | (431,193) |
| Emp. | 103 | 114 | N/A |

DUNS 21-834-8601

## Sca Hygiene Products Tissue Ltd

(**Subsidiary of:** Sca Uk Holdings Ltd)

Llangynwyd, Bridgend, Mid Glamorgan CF34 9RS

**Tel:** 01656-684-500

**Web:** www.sca.com

**Reg No:** 8033620 **Estd:** 2012 Private Limited Company

**Line of Business:** Manufacture of household and sanitary goods and of toilet requisites

**Export Sales:** £3,395,000

**Issued Capital:** £1

**Directors:** P A Bailey, Mrs S A Barker, A Richards

**Co. Secretary:** Paul Bailey

**Responsibilities**

**Senior:** Mike Docker (Manager), Rob Mcgraw (Manager), Carys Williams (Manager)

**US SIC:** 2647 **UK SIC:** 47220

**Auditors:** PricewaterhouseCoopers LLP

**Bankers:** The Royal Bank Of Scotland Plc (16-14-29)

|      | 31-12-13 | 31-12-12 |
|------|----------|----------|
| TO   | 127,547,000 | 108,472,000 |
| P/L  | (40,339,000) | 9,662,000 |
| NW   | 8,711,000 | 7,060,000 |
| WC   | (8,439,000) | (27,015,000) |
| Emp. | 473 | 868 |

DUNS 45-889-0126                                   Imp-Exp

## Sca Hygiene Products Uk Ltd

(**Subsidiary of:** Sca Uk Holdings Ltd)

Southfields Road, Dunstable, Bedfordshire LU6 3EJ

**Tel:** 01582677400 **Fax:** 01582 677502

**Web:** www.sca-hygiene.co.uk

**Reg No:** 3226403 **VAT No:** 600433106

**Estd:** 1996 Private Limited Company

**Line of Business:** Manufacture of household and sanitary goods and of toilet requisites

**Export Sales:** £19,931,000

**Trading Style:** Tork, Cushelle, Tena, Velvet

**Issued Capital:** £288,325,190

**Directors:** Mrs C M Rydebrink, Mrs S A Barker, A Richards

**Co. Secretary:** Paul Bailey

**Responsibilities**

**Marketing:** Bill Dawson (it director)

**IT:** Bill Dawson (it director)

**Operations:** Bill Dawson (it director)

**Branches:** Sca Hygiene Products Uk Ltd, Oakenholt Papermill, Chester Road, Flint, Clwyd CH6 5PU

**US SIC:** 2647 **UK SIC:** 47220

**Auditors:** PricewaterhouseCoopers LLP

**Bankers:** National Westminster Bank Plc (60-00-01)

|      | 31-12-13 | 31-12-12 | 31-12-11 |
|------|----------|----------|----------|
| TO   | 638,169,000 | 549,668,000 | 534,858,000 |
| P/L  | 69,502,000 | 40,941,000 | 26,293,000 |
| NW   | 327,199,000 | 281,346,000 | 240,994,000 |
| WC   | 190,125,000 | 176,049,000 | 165,311,000 |
| Emp. | 1,056 | 1,017 | 1,030 |

DUNS 76-258-9323                                          Imp

## Sca Timber Supply Ltd

(**Subsidiary of:** Svenska Cellulosa Ab Sca)

Etruscan Street, Stoke-On-Trent, Staffordshire ST1 5PG

**Tel:** 01782202122 **Fax:** 01782 224 200

**Web:** www.sca.com

**Reg No:** 2541468 **Estd:** 2003 Private Limited Company

**Line of Business:** Timber merchants

**Export Sales:** £237,000

---

**Issued Capital:** £2,000,000

**Directors:** A I Ek, M A Kenny, S King, E J Griffiths

**Co. Secretary:** Raymond Mills

**Responsibilities**

**Health & Safety:** Bob Bastow (Health & Safety Officer)

**US SIC:** 2421 **UK SIC:** 46101

**Auditors:** PricewaterhouseCoopers LLP

**Bankers:** HSBC Bank plc (40-35-18)

|      | 31-12-13 | 31-12-12 | 31-12-11 |
|------|----------|----------|----------|
| TO   | 75,507,000 | 56,118,000 | 61,907,000 |
| P/L  | (5,832,000) | 2,613,000 | 323,000 |
| NW   | 1,321,000 | 5,889,000 | 2,954,000 |
| WC   | (5,918,000) | 1,784,000 | (10,989,000) |
| Emp. | 154 | 131 | 129 |

DUNS 21-580-1488

## Scaffold Access Yorkshire

S A Y House, Unit 2-3 Rudgate Business Centre, Thorp Arch, Wetherby, West Yorkshire LS23 7AU

**Tel:** 01904737701

**Web:** www.sayltd.co.uk

**Estd:** 2011 Proprietorship

**Line of Business:** Scaffolds and work platform erectors

**Proprietor:** P Wetton

**US SIC:** 1799 **UK SIC:** 50000

**Employees:** 48

DUNS 21-907-8920

## Scaffold Erection Services Ltd

221-225 Tyburn Road, Birmingham, West Midlands B24 8NB

**Tel:** 01213-222088 **Fax:** 01213-272592

**Web:** www.scaffolder.com

**Reg No:** 1189840 **VAT No:** 112491109

**Estd:** 1974 Private Limited Company

**Line of Business:** Scaffolds and work platform erectors

**Issued Capital:** £39

**Directors:** P Heffernan, P T Sprason, Mrs J Ward

**Co. Secretary:** Ms Joanne Ward

**US SIC:** 7394 **UK SIC:** 84000

**Auditors:** HW Chartered Accountants

**Bankers:** Lloyds TSB Bank plc (30-98-37)

|      | 30-04-14 | 30-04-13 | 30-04-12 |
|------|----------|----------|----------|
| TA   | 2,998,996 | 2,578,699 | 1,820,150 |
| NW   | 2,049,555 | 1,257,071 | 1,007,746 |
| WC   | 1,076,596 | 582,781 | 407,091 |

DUNS 73-392-2087

## Scaffolding Group Ltd

Unit 10 Tongue Lane Industrial Estate, Dew Pond Lane, Buxton, Derbyshire SK17 7LF

**Tel:** 01298-214214 **Fax:** 01298-22255

**Web:** www.scaffolding-group.co.uk

**Reg No:** 4665911 **VAT No:** 809008150

**Estd:** 2004 Private Limited Company

**Line of Business:** Renting of scaffold

**Issued Capital:** £2

**Director:** J S Rowland

**Co. Secretary:** Ms Charlotte Needham

**Responsibilities**

**Admin:** Joanne Beesley (Office Manager)

**Branches:** Scaffolding Group Ltd, Brierley Park Close, Sutton-In-Ashfield, Nottinghamshire NG17 3FW

**US SIC:** 1799, 5072, 7394

**UK SIC:** 50000, 61500, 84000

**Bankers:** National Westminster Bank Plc (60-40-09)

|      | 28-02-14 | 28-02-13 | 29-02-12 |
|------|----------|----------|----------|
| TA   | 1,293,011 | 1,643,294 | 1,275,076 |
| NW   | 213,310 | 166,448 | 147,902 |
| WC   | (551,604) | (608,542) | (371,181) |

DUNS 21-211-7852

## Scalford Court Care Home

Melton Road, Scalford, Melton Mowbray, Leicestershire LE14 4UB

**Tel:** 01664-444696

**Web:** www.scalfordcourt.co.uk

**Estd:** 1987 Partnership

**Line of Business:** Residential care establishments

**Partners:** Mrs R M Fricker, Mrs M Nussey, D M Nussey

**Responsibilities**

**Senior:** Jeremy Lord (Manager)

**US SIC:** 8321 **UK SIC:** 96111

**Employees:** 48

DUNS 21-564-1922

## Scalini Restaurant

85 Botanic Avenue, Belfast BT7 1JL

**Tel:** 028-9032-0303

**Web:** www.scalinirestaurant.co.uk

**Estd:** 2002 Proprietorship

**Line of Business:** Restaurant - italian

**Proprietor:** P Gordano

**Responsibilities**

**Senior:** Dario Giordano (Manager), Tony Gordano (Proprietor)

**US SIC:** 5812 **UK SIC:** 66110

**Employees:** 160

---

DUNS 29-663-9271

## Scamp Security Ltd

(**Subsidiary of:** Scamp Security Services Ltd)

Wassand Street, Hull, North Humberside HU3 4AL

**Tel:** 01482-329271 **Fax:** 01482219350

**Web:** www.scampsecurity.co.uk

**Reg No:** 1990041 **VAT No:** 433635458

**Estd:** 1986 Private Limited Company

**Line of Business:** Security activities

**Trading Style:** Scamp Security Services

**Issued Capital:** £1,000

**Managing Director:** R Pallier

**Co. Secretary:** Mrs Deborah Pallier

**Responsibilities**

**Finance:** Sarah Pallier (Senior Finance Administrator)

**Marketing:** Tracy Sadler (Senior Marketing Executive)

**Sales:** Gavin Moulds (Sales Manager)

**Admin:** Lynne Aherne (Office Manager), Sarah Pallier (Senior Finance Administrator), Tracy Sadler (Senior Marketing Executive)

**HR:** Lynne Aherne (Office Manager)

**Operations:** Tracey Cowling (Technical, Production Manager), Gavin Moulds (Sales Manager)

**Purchasing:** Lynne Aherne (Office Manager)

**US SIC:** 7393, 8999

**UK SIC:** 83954

**Auditors:** Sadofskys

**Bankers:** Barclays Bank Plc (20-99-56)

|      | 31-05-14 | 31-05-13 | 31-05-12 |
|------|----------|----------|----------|
| TA   | 1,487,942 | 1,518,256 | 1,681,560 |
| NW   | 936,710 | 925,304 | 918,603 |
| WC   | 739,075 | 670,994 | 618,731 |

DUNS 22-753-0540

## Scan Alarms & Security Systems (U.K.) Ltd

(**Subsidiary of:** Scan Alarms Ltd)

52 Trench Road, Newtownabbey, Co Antrim BT36 4TY

**Tel:** 028-9034-2233

**Web:** www.scanalarms.co.uk

**Reg No:** 0015649NI **Estd:** 1982 Private Limited Company

**Line of Business:** Security and related activities

**Issued Capital:** £100

**Directors:** D M Allen, D Allen

**Co. Secretary:** Ms Leanne Allen

**Responsibilities**

**IT:** Darren Lamont (IT and Quality Manager)

**Facilities:** Hilton McGregor (Facilities Manager)

**Purchasing:** Stuart McQuiston (Purchasing Manager)

**US SIC:** 8999, 3629

**UK SIC:** 83954, 34350

**Auditors:** Grant Thornton

**Bankers:** Ulster Bank Ltd (98-00-90)

|      | 31-03-14 | 31-03-13 | 31-03-12 |
|------|----------|----------|----------|
| TA   | 1,148,458 | 1,077,231 | 1,068,169 |
| NW   | 535,357 | 493,446 | 429,528 |
| WC   | 489,510 | 451,695 | 380,592 |

DUNS 21-588-5187

## Scan Building Services Ltd

35 Byron Street, Dundee, Angus DD3 6QT

**Web:** www.scanbs.co.uk

**Reg No:** 0072076SC **VAT No:** 345323766

**Estd:** 1980 Private Limited Company

**Line of Business:** Building services

**Issued Capital:** £10,000

**Principals:** D W Anderson (Managing), F Mclaren (Financial), C Lees, G Prophet

**Co. Secretary:** Thorntons Law Llp

**US SIC:** 1711, 1541

**UK SIC:** 50300, 50100

**Auditors:** Henderson Loggie

**Bankers:** Clydesdale Bank Plc (82-44-04)

|      | 31-10-13 | 31-10-12 | 31-10-11 |
|------|----------|----------|----------|
| TO   | N/A | N/A | 5,257,317 |
| P/L  | N/A | N/A | (8,568) |
| NW   | 643,190 | 683,301 | 789,646 |
| WC   | 382,736 | 426,632 | 518,962 |

DUNS 21-279-1768                                       Imp-Exp

## Scan Coin Ltd.

(**Subsidiary of:** Scan Coin Holding Ab)

Dutch House, 110 Broadway, Salford Quays, Salford, Lancashire M50 2UW

**Tel:** 01618730500

**Web:** www.scancoin.co.uk

**Reg No:** 0518608 **VAT No:** 519594608

**Estd:** 1953 Private Limited Company

**Line of Business:** Cash register and epos equipment

**Export Markets:** Worldwide

**Export Sales:** £136,628

**Issued Capital:** £9,500

**Principals:** J G Carr (Managing), P Wessner, B K Renulf, S Fitton

**Co. Secretary:** John-Paul Yates

**Responsibilities**

**IT:** David Thornber (IT Officer)

---

**US SIC:** 3579 **UK SIC:** 33010

**Auditors:** PricewaterhouseCoopers LLP

**Bankers:** HSBC Bank plc (40-31-24)

|      | 31-12-13 | 31-12-12 | 31-12-11 |
|------|----------|----------|----------|
| TO   | 6,014,079 | 6,834,133 | 7,961,519 |
| P/L  | 209,722 | (690,016) | 458,030 |
| NW   | 452,790 | 212,818 | 1,587,818 |
| WC   | (93,988) | (390,430) | 1,200,561 |
| Emp. | 57 | 61 | 64 |

DUNS 76-940-4138

## Scan Computers International Ltd

25-28 Enterprise Park, Horwich, Bolton, Lancashire BL6 6PE

**Tel:** 01204474747 **Fax:** 01204474748

**Web:** www.scan.co.uk

**Reg No:** 2620081 **Estd:** 1991 Private Limited Company

**Line of Business:** Computer systems and software (sales)

**Export Sales:** £291,896

**Trading Style:** Scan International, Scan Computers

**Issued Capital:** £31,000

**Director:** S Raja

**Co. Secretary:** Nilendra Raja

**US SIC:** 5946, 5081

**UK SIC:** 65400, 61490

**Auditors:** Warings Business Advisers LLP

**Bankers:** Barclays Bank Plc (20-10-71)

|      | 30-06-13 | 30-06-12 | 30-06-11 |
|------|----------|----------|----------|
| TO   | 63,771,764 | 58,867,742 | 55,611,912 |
| P/L  | 573,409 | 755,633 | 1,019,691 |
| NW   | 7,021,319 | 6,831,772 | 6,503,595 |
| WC   | 3,370,956 | 3,147,324 | 3,337,097 |
| Emp. | 148 | 138 | 145 |

DUNS 28-837-5504

## Scandinavian Airlines System (Investments) Ltd

1 World Business Centre Heathrow, Newall Road, London Heathrow Airport, Hounslow, Middlesex TW6 2RE

**Tel:** 02089907000 **Fax:** 020-8990-7127

**Web:** www.flysas.co.uk

**Reg No:** 0459408 **VAT No:** 606050482

**Estd:** 1948 Private Limited Company

**Line of Business:** Buying and selling of own real estate

**Trading Style:** Scandinavian Airlines Travel Agent Support, Sas

**Issued Capital:** £700

**Directors:** Ms J Utter, H W Dyhrfort

**Co. Secretary:** Hans Dyhrfort

**Branches:** Scandinavian Airlines System (Investments) Ltd, World Business Centre 2, Newall Rd, Hounslow, Middlesex TW6 2RQ

**US SIC:** 6531 **UK SIC:** 83400

**Auditors:** Auren & Co Ltd

**Bankers:** HSBC Bank plc (40-06-02)

|      | 31-10-13 | 31-12-12 | 31-10-11 |
|------|----------|----------|----------|
| TA   | 1,704,657 | 1,701,186 | 1,683,452 |
| P/L  | 3,471 | 10,288 | (18,509) |
| NW   | 1,696,566 | 1,693,447 | 1,683,398 |
| WC   | 1,696,566 | 1,693,447 | 1,683,398 |

DUNS 28-829-7989                                          Imp

## Scandinavian Tobacco Group United Kingdom Ltd

(**Subsidiary of:** Augustinus Fonden)

Unit 250 Centennial Park, Centennial Avenue, Elstree, Borehamwood, Hertfordshire WD6 3TH

**Tel:** 020-8731-3400 **Fax:** 020-8207-7977

**Web:** www.st-group.com

**Reg No:** 0130335 **Estd:** 2005 Private Limited Company

**Line of Business:** Wholesale of tobacco products

**Issued Capital:** £7

**Directors:** H Williams, C H Sorensen

**Responsibilities**

**Finance:** Neil Lambert (Financial Manager)

**Marketing:** Regis Broersma (Marketing Manager)

**IT:** Nikki Rayner (Computer Manager)

**US SIC:** 5194 **UK SIC:** 61700

**Auditors:** PricewaterhouseCoopers LLP

**Bankers:** Den Danske Bank Aktieselskab (30-12-81)

|      | 31-12-13 | 31-12-12 | 31-12-11 |
|------|----------|----------|----------|
| TO   | 80,381,334 | 81,985,138 | 71,093,223 |
| P/L  | 5,635,474 | 6,579,626 | 5,854,887 |
| NW   | 19,304,046 | 14,985,922 | 14,026,355 |
| WC   | 19,105,988 | 14,728,876 | 13,769,402 |
| Emp. | 50 | 49 | 51 |

DUNS 28-825-2232

## Scandinavian Village Ltd

Aviemore Centre Mountain Resort, Aviemore, Inverness-Shire PH22 1PF

**Tel:** 01479810500 **Fax:** 01479-811604

**Web:** www.scandinavian-village.co.uk

**Reg No:** 0070383SC **Estd:** 1977 Private Limited Company

**Line of Business:** Timeshare operations

**Issued Capital:** £1,000

**Directors:** J Mckie, Mrs M Pollock, E Monks, J D Doyle, J Falconer, T B Moar

**Co. Secretary:** Edward Monks
**Responsibilities**
**Senior:** Miriam Grant *(General Manager)*
**US SIC:** 6531, 7011
**UK SIC:** 83400, 66500
**Bankers:** Bank Of Scotland (80-05-40)

| | 31-12-13 | 31-12-12 | 31-12-11 |
|---|---|---|---|
| TA | 774,801 | 706,453 | 576,641 |
| NW | 384,823 | 369,861 | 338,993 |
| WC | 69,921 | 76,899 | 63,304 |

DUNS 21-618-2113 **Imp**
## Scania (Great Britain) Ltd
(**Subsidiary of:** Volkswagen Ag)
Delaware Drive, Tongwell, Milton Keynes, Buckinghamshire MK15 8HB
**Tel:** 01908210210
**Web:** www.scania.com
**Reg No:** 0831017 **Estd:** 1964 Private Limited Company
**Line of Business:** Agents involved in the sale of a variety of goods
**Export Sales:** £18,319,000
**Trading Style:** Scania
**Issued Capital:** £8,000,000
**Directors:** B A Thorsson, C I Podgorski, P C Jacobsson, U B Erdtman
**Co. Secretary:** Richard Gray
**Responsibilities**
**Senior:** Mark Begley *(Warehouse Maanager)*, Sven Grundstromer *(Manager)*, Claes Jacobsson *(Manager)*, Arne Karlsson *(Manager)*
**Finance:** Steven Wager *(Finance Director)*
**Sales:** Martin Hay *(Sales Manager)*
**Operations:** Mark Begley *(Warehouse Maanager)*
**Purchasing:** Astrid Lagerberg *(Head of Purchasing)*
**Branches:** Scania (Great Britain) Ltd, Heathhall Industrial Estate, Dumfries, Dumfriesshire DG1 3PH
**US SIC:** 5199 **UK SIC:** 61900
**Auditors:** Ernst & Young LLP
**Bankers:** Barclays Bank Plc (20-57-40)

| | 31-12-13 | 31-12-12 | 31-12-11 |
|---|---|---|---|
| TO | 733,054,000 | 602,835,000 | 598,216,000 |
| P/L | 46,595,000 | 33,941,000 | 39,866,000 |
| NW | 47,126,000 | 38,429,000 | 46,555,000 |
| WC | (44,651,000) | (52,067,000) | (11,139,000) |
| Emp. | 1,414 | 1,373 | 1,364 |

DUNS 21-911-1705
## Scanlink Ltd
(**Subsidiary of:** Volkswagen Ag)
Ripley Drive, Normanton, West Yorkshire WF6 1QT
**Tel:** 01924891254 **Fax:** 01924-897536
**Web:** http://scan-link.com
**Reg No:** 1147878 **VAT No:** 129466056
**Estd:** 1969 Private Limited Company
**Line of Business:** Van hire
**Issued Capital:** £1,871,875
**Directors:** R K Gray, P C Jacobsson
**Co. Secretary:** Ms Kareen Cranston
**Responsibilities**
**Senior:** Neal Walker *(Manager)*
**Sales:** John Mortimor *(Sales Manager)*
**Branches:** Scanlink Ltd, Grange Lane North, Scunthorpe, South Humberside DN16 1BT
**US SIC:** 5511, 7539
**UK SIC:** 65100, 67100
**Auditors:** PKF
**Bankers:** Skandinaviska Enskilda Banken Ab (publ) (40-48-65)

| | 31-12-13 | 31-12-12 | 31-12-11 |
|---|---|---|---|
| TA | 1,956,000 | 1,956,000 | 1,956,000 |
| NW | 1,956,000 | 1,956,000 | 1,956,000 |

DUNS 50-471-6044
## Scantec Personnel Ltd
Morpeth Wharf, Birkenhead, Merseyside CH41 1LF
**Tel:** 01516668999 **Fax:** 01516668998
**Web:** www.scantec.co.uk
**Reg No:** 2450519 **VAT No:** 534763237
**Estd:** 1989 Private Limited Company
**Line of Business:** Labour recruitment and provision of personnel
**Trading Style:** Weider Publishing Limited
**Issued Capital:** £100
**Directors:** Miss V A Lawton, P J Bates, A Spelman, Mrs K Bates, J E Robinson
**Co. Secretary:** Mrs Penelope Robinson
**Branches:** Scantec Personnel Ltd, 26 Hamilton Square, Birkenhead, Merseyside CH41 6AY
**US SIC:** 7361 **UK SIC:** 83954
**Auditors:** Lerman Quaile Ltd

| | 31-12-13 | 31-12-12 | 31-12-11 |
|---|---|---|---|
| TO | 65,681,110 | 53,922,800 | 49,506,344 |
| P/L | 982,269 | 1,011,959 | 699,498 |
| NW | 661,387 | 1,213,576 | 1,056,655 |
| WC | 609,261 | 1,146,713 | 969,318 |
| Emp. | 57 | 48 | 47 |

DUNS 21-202-5803
## Scapa Group Plc
997 Manchester Road, Ashton-Under-Lyne, Lancashire OL7 0ED
**Tel:** 01613017400 **Fax:** 01613017591
**Web:** www.scapa.com
**Reg No:** 0826179 **VAT No:** 326018484
**Estd:** 1964 Public Limited Company
**Line of Business:** Management activities of holding companies
**Export Sales:** £195,900,000
**Trading Style:** Scapa Group Plc
**Issued Capital:** £7,320,440
**Directors:** R J Perry, M C Buzzacott, H R Chae, J A Wallace, P Edwards, M T Sawkins
**Co. Secretary:** Ms Rebecca Smith
**Responsibilities**
**Senior:** Joe Davin *(Group President Healthcare)*
**HR:** Clare Douglas *(Group HR Director)*
**US SIC:** 6711, 2891
**UK SIC:** 83962, 25620
**Auditors:** PricewaterhouseCoopers LLP

| | 31-03-14 | 31-03-13 | 31-03-12 |
|---|---|---|---|
| TO | 226,100,000 | 208,800,000 | 195,600,000 |
| P/L | 11,200,000 | 12,300,000 | 10,500,000 |
| NW | 20,200,000 | 30,100,000 | 34,400,000 |
| WC | 33,900,000 | 31,400,000 | 31,300,000 |
| Emp. | 1,223 | 1,209 | 1,167 |

DUNS 29-883-7014 **Imp**
## Scarab Holdings Ltd
(**Subsidiary of:** Fayat)
Pattenden Lane, Marden, Marden, Tonbridge, Kent TN12 9QD
**Tel:** 01622-831006 **Fax:** 01622-831417
**Web:** www.scarab
**Reg No:** 2086673 **VAT No:** 374500268
**Estd:** 1987 Private Limited Company
**Line of Business:** Management activities of holding companies
**Export Sales:** £18,954,256
**Trading Style:** Scarab Sweepers
**Issued Capital:** £13,600
**Directors:** D J Cassingham, L N Galdeano, J C Fayat, A Farley
**Responsibilities**
**Senior:** John Affleck *(Manager)*, Stephen Hoadley *(Manager)*
**Finance:** John Affleck *(Manager)*
**US SIC:** 6711, 3711
**UK SIC:** 83962, 35101
**Auditors:** Reeves & Co LLP
**Bankers:** HSBC Bank plc (40-44-20)

| | 30-09-13 | 30-09-12 | 31-09-11 |
|---|---|---|---|
| TO | 33,294,455 | 34,514,413 | 25,327,952 |
| P/L | 2,197,049 | 1,362,203 | 1,748,839 |
| NW | 10,228,278 | 8,542,546 | 7,546,208 |
| WC | 9,530,408 | 7,836,909 | 6,832,037 |
| Emp. | 216 | 206 | 191 |

DUNS 23-644-1325
## Scarborough Borough Council
Town Hall, St Nicholas Street, Scarborough, North Yorkshire YO11 2HG
**Tel:** 01723-232323
**Web:** www.scarborough.gov.uk
**VAT No:** 168444244
**Line of Business:** Borough council headquarters
**Trading Style:** Harbour Master Office
**Principals:** J M Trebble *(Managing)*, M J Barratt *(Financial)*
**Co. Secretary:** Michael Barratt
**Responsibilities**
**Senior:** Jim Dillon *(Chief Executive)*
**IT:** Greg Harper *(IT Director)*
**Branches:** Scarborough Borough Council, Beckhole Road, Whitby, North Yorkshire YO22 5ND
**US SIC:** 9121 **UK SIC:** 91110
**Employees:** 300

DUNS 22-818-2499
## Scarborough Building Society
16-17 Westborough, Scarborough, North Yorkshire YO11 1UH
**Tel:** 01723360461
**Web:** www.scarborough.co.uk
**Reg No:** 0000500D **Estd:** 1846 Friendly Society
**Line of Business:** Other credit granting not elsewhere classified
**Trading Style:** Skipton Building Society
**Principals:** W R Worsley *(Chairman)*, R S Litten *(Financial)*, N H Wrigley, Mrs K Priestley, Mrs D N Jagger, R L Grunwell, Mrs B M Richmond, J J Carrier
**Branches:** Scarborough Building Society, Prospect Ho, Po Box 6, Scarborough, North Yorkshire YO11 3WZ
**US SIC:** 6111 **UK SIC:** 81501
**Auditors:** KPMG Audit PLC
**Bankers:** HSBC Bank plc (40-40-22)
**Employees:** 325

DUNS 28-828-9077
## Scarborough College Ltd
Filey Road, Scarborough, North Yorkshire YO11 3BA
**Tel:** 01723360620 **Fax:** 01723380607
**Web:** www.scarboroughcoll.co.uk
**Reg No:** 0050404 **Estd:** 1896 Private Limited Company
**Line of Business:** General secondary education
**Trading Style:** Scarborough College Ltd
**Issued Capital:** £5,507
**Directors:** S N Fairbank, Reverend T L Jones, J J Cook, Mrs G A Braithwaite, M J Baines, Dr I G Renwick, Dr J Renshaw, Dr C A Rhodes
**Co. Secretary:** Timothy Fenton
**Responsibilities**
**Senior:** Lindsey Griffin *(Manager)*, Fay Humphries *(Director)*, Isobel Nixon *(Headmistress)*, Mark Precious *(Director)*
**US SIC:** 8211 **UK SIC:** 93200
**Auditors:** Moore Stephens
**Bankers:** The Royal Bank Of Scotland Plc (16-31-14)

| | 31-08-13 | 31-08-12 | 31-08-11 |
|---|---|---|---|
| TO | 3,359,625 | 2,981,134 | 3,439,258 |
| P/L | (313,495) | (778,445) | (301,134) |
| NW | 2,707,032 | 3,005,287 | 3,783,732 |
| WC | (1,384,209) | (904,963) | (406,625) |
| Emp. | 72 | 72 | 82 |

DUNS 21-227-3071
## Scarborough Court
Alexandra Way, Cramlington, Northumberland NE23 6ED
**Tel:** 01670-712215
**Web:** www.rmbi.org.uk
**Estd:** 1967
**Line of Business:** Residential care establishments
**Partners:** Mrs C Edden, Mrs C Edden
**Responsibilities**
**Senior:** Lesley Dawson *(Home Manager)*
**US SIC:** 8321 **UK SIC:** 96111
**Employees:** 47

DUNS 67-250-6995
## Scarborough Group International Ltd
93 George Street, Stirling, Stirlingshire
**Tel:** 01132840800
**Web:** www.scarboroughgroup.com
**Reg No:** 0319817SC **Estd:** 2007 Private Limited Company
**Line of Business:** Management activities of other non-financial holding companies not elsewhere classified
**Export Sales:** £234,000
**Issued Capital:** £137,391,360
**Directors:** J J Tutton, S R Mccabe, S A Marshall, S C Mccabe, K C Mccabe
**Co. Secretary:**
Esplanade Secretarial Services L
**US SIC:** 6711 **UK SIC:** 83962

| | 28-02-14 | 28-02-13 | 29-02-12 |
|---|---|---|---|
| TO | 49,126,000 | 71,488,000 | 80,031,000 |
| P/L | (498,000) | (4,790,000) | (29,061,000) |
| NW | 15,775,000 | 15,763,000 | 16,570,000 |
| WC | 97,242,000 | 9,715,000 | 45,479,000 |
| Emp. | 168 | 247 | 264 |

DUNS 21-770-6958
## Scarborough Talking News
181 Dean Road, Scarborough, North Yorkshire YO12 7JH
**Tel:** 01723363344
**Estd:** 1982 Proprietorship
**Line of Business:** Social work activities without accommodation
**Proprietor:** H Dolan
**US SIC:** 8321 **UK SIC:** 96111
**Employees:** 50

DUNS 28-856-6540
## Scarborough Theatre Trust Ltd
48 Westborough, Scarborough, North Yorkshire YO11 1UN
**Tel:** 01723-370540
**Web:** www.sjt.uk.com
**Reg No:** 0815227 **Estd:** 1964 Private Company Limited By Guarantee
**Line of Business:** Artistic and literary creation and interpretation
**Trading Style:** The Stephen Joseph Theatre
**Directors:** Ms H Boaden, P F Worsley, T E Watton, M J Wilkinson, A J Smith, Mrs H S Truefitt, J G Armistead, Ms K A Carmichael
**Co. Secretary:** Ian Wyatt
**Responsibilities**
**Senior:** Christine Fitzpatrick *(Director)*, Helen Swiers *(Director)*, Patricia Weller *(Director)*
**Branches:** Scarborough Theatre Trust Ltd, Westborough, Scarborough, North Yorkshire YO11 1JW
**US SIC:** 7999, 7922
**UK SIC:** 97913, 97412

**Auditors:** Winn & Co
**Bankers:** Barclays Bank Plc (20-75-92)

| | 31-03-14 | 31-03-13 | 31-03-12 |
|---|---|---|---|
| TO | 2,393,560 | 2,330,108 | 2,624,979 |
| P/L | (129,662) | (13,361) | 70,811 |
| NW | 30,906 | 160,568 | 173,929 |
| WC | (49,255) | 91,882 | 109,059 |
| Emp. | 88 | 73 | 78 |

DUNS 29-578-3260
## S.C.A.R.F.
1 Cotton Street, Aberdeen, Aberdeenshire AB11 5EE
**Tel:** 01224-213005 **Fax:** 01224-213650
**Web:** www.scarf.org.uk
**Reg No:** 0094819SC **Estd:** 1985 Private Company Limited By Guarantee
**Line of Business:** Business and management consultancy activities not elsewhere classified
**Directors:** Ms J S Morrison, J D Gordon, E C Rennie, Ms J L Nicol, R G Milne, J A Tomlinson, R R Webster, D A Bodie
**Co. Secretary:**
Stronachs Secretaries Limited
**Responsibilities**
**Senior:** Alister Leitch *(Manager)*, Billy Sloen *(CEO)*
**IT:** Louis McRobbie *(IT Manager)*
**Branches:** S.c.a.r.f., Balgray Pl, Dundee, Angus DD3 8SH
**US SIC:** 7392 **UK SIC:** 83951
**Auditors:** Anderson Anderson & Brown

| | 31-03-14 | 31-03-13 | 31-03-12 |
|---|---|---|---|
| TO | 1,593,358 | 2,272,379 | 1,967,743 |
| P/L | (244,749) | 257,790 | (11,272) |
| NW | 1,492,933 | 1,598,682 | 2,116,893 |
| WC | 1,676,178 | 1,838,246 | 1,520,427 |
| Emp. | 63 | 74 | 77 |

DUNS 52-022-7117
## Scarlets Regional Ltd
6 Parc Pemberton Retail Park, Llanelli, Dyfed SA14 9UZ
**Tel:** 01554784050
**Web:** www.scarlets.co.uk
**Reg No:** 3389199 **Estd:** 1995 Private Limited Company
**Line of Business:** Other sporting activities not elsewhere classified
**Issued Capital:** £9,088,681
**Principals:** H D Evans *(Chairman)*, O G Jones, P J Morgan, W M Morgan, E W Evans, J D Daniels, R A Cammish, G H Wise
**Co. Secretary:** Phillip Morgan
**Responsibilities**
**Senior:** Hefin Jenkins *(Manager)*, Nigel Short *(Director)*
**HR:** Gene Parker *(Human Resources Manager)*
**Health & Safety:** Dave Healey *(Facilities Manager)*
**Facilities:** Dave Healey *(Facilities Manager)*
**Branches:** Scarlets Regional Ltd, New Clubhouse, Stradey Park, Llanelli, Dyfed SA15 4BT
**US SIC:** 7999 **UK SIC:** 97913
**Auditors:** Grant Thornton
**Bankers:** Bank Of Scotland (12-05-77)

| | 30-06-13 | 30-06-12 | 30-06-11 |
|---|---|---|---|
| TO | 7,992,436 | 7,980,249 | 7,591,035 |
| P/L | (690,701) | (1,297,186) | (1,819,158) |
| NW | (3,545,236) | (3,344,324) | (2,069,686) |
| WC | (4,541,865) | (4,598,550) | (3,380,882) |
| Emp. | 162 | 137 | 125 |

DUNS 21-774-9858
## Scarletts Residential Care Home
Recreation Road, Colchester, Essex CO1 2HJ
**Tel:** 01206792429
**Web:** www.scarlettscottage.co.uk
**Estd:** 2002 Proprietorship
**Line of Business:** Residential care establishments
**Proprietor:** Ms M Faires
**Responsibilities**
**Senior:** Paula Johnston *(Manager)*
**US SIC:** 8321 **UK SIC:** 96111
**Employees:** 48

DUNS 21-236-4587
## Scarman & Radcliffe House Management Training Centres
Scarman Road, Coventry, West Midlands CV4 7AL
**Tel:** 024-7622-1111
**Web:** www.warwickconferences.com
**Estd:** 1999 Proprietorship
**Line of Business:** Other adult and other education not elsewhere classified
**Proprietor:** B Healey
**US SIC:** 8299 **UK SIC:** 93300
**Employees:** 100

DUNS 23-111-5924
## Scartop Country Pine
Moor Lodge, Oldfield, Keighley, West Yorkshire BD22 0JL
**Tel:** 01535642585
**Web:** www.scartop.com
**VAT No:** 363745534 **Estd:** 1974 Partnership
**Line of Business:** Pine furniture
**Partners:** T Johnson, S Johnson
**Branches:** Scartop Country Pine, Bury Old Road, Heywood, Lancashire OL10 3HU
**US SIC:** 5719 **UK SIC:** 64700
**Bankers:** Barclays Bank Plc (20-11-81)
**Employees:** 62

DUNS 21-218-3982     **Imp**
## Scattergood & Johnson Ltd
**(Subsidiary of:** S & J Industries Ltd)
Lowfields Road, Leeds, West Yorkshire LS12 6ET
**Fax:** 01132-420-959
**Web:** www.scatts.co.uk
**Reg No:** 0199809 **VAT No:** 613190570
**Estd:** 1899 Private Limited Company
**Line of Business:** Wholesale of other machinery for use in industry, trade and navigation
**Trading Style:** Scatts
**Issued Capital:** £28,600
**Principals:** R C Hargreaves (Chairman and Managing), I R Manson (Financial), R P Lumley
**Co. Secretary:** Richard Lumley
**Responsibilities**
**Senior:** Jean Hargreaves (Manager)
**Branches:** Scattergood & Johnson Limited, 80 Fifty Pitches Road, Glasgow, Lanarkshire G51 4EB
**US SIC:** 5084, 5064
**UK SIC:** 61490, 61500
**Auditors:** Sagars Accountants Ltd
**Bankers:** Lloyds TSB Bank plc (30-00-05)

| | 30-04-14 | 30-04-13 | 30-04-12 |
|---|---|---|---|
| TO | 27,602,616 | 27,136,209 | 27,162,898 |
| P/L | 1,013,560 | 910,979 | 860,153 |
| NW | 3,784,329 | 3,711,792 | 3,693,146 |
| WC | 3,469,883 | 3,305,309 | 3,343,003 |
| Emp. | 118 | 105 | 100 |

DUNS 22-548-3593
## S.C.C. Ltd
Kenwood Road, Stockport, Cheshire SK5 6PH
**Tel:** 0161-432-7700
**Web:** www.sccltd.co.uk
**Reg No:** 1434172 **VAT No:** 306675551
**Estd:** 1979 Private Limited Company
**Line of Business:** Construction of domestic buildings
**Trading Style:** Structural Concrete Contractors
**Issued Capital:** £100,000
**Principals:** M J O'Donnell (Chairman), M O'Donnell (Chairman and Managing), P A Mcdaid (Managing), E O'Donnell
**Co. Secretary:** Michael O'Donnell
**Responsibilities**
**Senior:** Eamonn O' Donnell (Director), Manus O' Donnell (Director)
**Branches:** S.c.c. Ltd, Park Square, Unit 1A, Sheffield, South Yorkshire S35 2PH
**US SIC:** 1522, 1799
**UK SIC:** 50100, 50000
**Auditors:** Edwards Veeder
**Bankers:** National Westminster Bank Plc (01-08-52)

| | 31-08-14 | 31-08-13 | 31-08-12 |
|---|---|---|---|
| TO | 24,868,548 | 13,656,086 | 15,973,540 |
| P/L | 186,407 | (310,984) | (122,680) |
| NW | 4,223,947 | 4,048,037 | 4,359,037 |
| WC | 818,058 | 575,650 | 803,780 |
| Emp. | 145 | 91 | 107 |

DUNS 34-626-9145
## Scci Alphatrack Ltd
**(Subsidiary of:** Suissefonds Sa)
Unit 14 West Place, West Road, Harlow, Essex CM20 2GY
**Tel:** 01279630400 **Fax:** 01992-641655
**Web:** www.sccialphatrack.co.uk
**Reg No:** 2760731 **VAT No:** 590059142
**Estd:** 1992 Private Limited Company
**Line of Business:** Cctv & video equipment
**Issued Capital:** £102,831
**Directors:** R C Wickings, H D Mackenzie Smith, A M Kearns, D J Fogelman, P W Dellow
**Co. Secretary:** Trethowans Services Limited
**Responsibilities**
**Senior:** Hugo Smith (Manager)
**Marketing:** Marina Vrahimi (Sales & Marketing Manager)
**Sales:** Marina Vrahimi (Sales & Marketing Manager)
**Branches:** Scci Alphatrack Ltd, Unit 6, Fieldings Rd, Waltham Cross, Hertfordshire EN8 9TJ
**US SIC:** 7394, 1799
**UK SIC:** 84000, 50000
**Auditors:** Fiander Tovell LLP

**Bankers:** Barclays Bank Plc (20-20-37)

| | 31-05-14 | 31-05-13 | 31-05-12 |
|---|---|---|---|
| TO | 26,160,886 | 20,788,697 | 25,187,139 |
| P/L | 1,614,392 | 1,533,720 | 2,279,666 |
| NW | 8,056,613 | 7,296,791 | 6,935,673 |
| WC | 6,893,443 | 6,080,790 | 6,005,889 |
| Emp. | 234 | 186 | 173 |

DUNS 21-903-8903
## Scci Group Ltd
**(Subsidiary of:** Suissefonds Sa)
The Pavilion, Botleigh Grange Business Park, Southampton, Hampshire SO30 2AF
**Tel:** 01603425400
**Web:** www.sccialphatrack.co.uk
**Reg No:** 6089974 **Estd:** 2007 Private Limited Company
**Line of Business:** Other business activities not elsewhere classified
**Issued Capital:** £1,000
**Directors:** R C Wickings, Ms L J Hutchings, H D Mackenzie Smith, P W Dellow, D J Fogelman
**Co. Secretary:** Trethowans Services Limited
**US SIC:** 7399 **UK SIC:** 83954

| | 31-05-14 | 31-05-13 | 31-05-12 |
|---|---|---|---|
| TO | 43,574,122 | 34,253,727 | 46,974,953 |
| P/L | (1,835,830) | 1,149,275 | 3,519,266 |
| NW | (3,330,378) | (4,500,312) | (5,227,541) |
| WC | 16,133,258 | 15,998,898 | 16,918,860 |
| Emp. | 394 | 399 | 411 |

DUNS 37 874 0675
## Scd Group Ltd
Radial Park, Manston Lane, Leeds, West Yorkshire LS15 8ST
**Tel:** 03707506416 **Fax:** 03707506417
**Web:** www.scd-ltd.com
**Reg No:** 3307132 **Estd:** 1997 Private Limited Company
**Line of Business:** Building of complete constructions or parts thereof; civil engineering
**Issued Capital:** £200
**Director:** C Durkan
**Co. Secretary:** Ms Ann Durkan
**US SIC:** 1541 **UK SIC:** 50100
**Auditors:** Burrow & Crowe

| | 31-03-13 | 31-03-12 | 31-03-11 |
|---|---|---|---|
| TA | 6,675,588 | 3,354,925 | 3,239,242 |
| NW | 2,071,233 | 1,935,217 | 1,769,694 |
| WC | 976,089 | 1,236,462 | 1,444,872 |

DUNS 76-925-1257     **Exp**
## Scena Works Ltd
**(Subsidiary of:** Scena Holdings Ltd)
240 Camberwell Road, London SE5 0DP
**Tel:** 020-7358-5800
**Web:** www.scenapro.com
**Reg No:** 2295424 **VAT No:** 626349234
**Estd:** 1994 Private Limited Company
**Line of Business:** Other construction work involving special trades
**Issued Capital:** £2
**Principals:** D J Thompson (Managing), M D Hubbard, P Winder
**Co. Secretary:** Paul Norman
**Responsibilities**
**IT:** Gary Winder (IT Manager)
**US SIC:** 1799 **UK SIC:** 50000
**Auditors:** Audit Assure
**Bankers:** National Westminster Bank Plc (50-41-10)

| | 30-11-13 | 30-11-12 | 30-11-11 |
|---|---|---|---|
| TA | 2 | 2 | 2 |
| NW | 2 | 2 | 2 |

DUNS 38-568-3305
## Sceptre-Europe Ltd
**(Subsidiary of:** Avis Budget Group Inc.)
Victoria House, 150-182 The Quays, Salford, Lancashire M50 3SP
**Tel:** 01618762000
**Reg No:** 3337481 **Estd:** 1997 Private Limited Company
**Line of Business:** Other service activities not elsewhere classified
**Issued Capital:** £100
**Directors:** Ms J E Spiers, J C Turner
**Co. Secretary:** Broughton Secretaries Limited
**US SIC:** 8999 **UK SIC:** 83954
**Auditors:** PricewaterhouseCoopers
**Bankers:** The Royal Bank Of Scotland Plc (16-00-02)
**Employees:** 180

DUNS 45-839-5332
## Sceptre Leisure Plc
Bamber Bridge, Preston, Lancashire PR5 8BF
**Fax:** 01772-694-243
**Web:** www.sceptreleisureplc.co.uk
**Reg No:** 3189747 **Estd:** 1996 Public Limited Company
**Line of Business:** Other business activities not elsewhere classified
**Issued Capital:** £2,849,479
**Directors:** K B Turner, M A White
**Co. Secretary:** Mark White

**US SIC:** 7399 **UK SIC:** 83954
**Auditors:** Grant Thornton UK LLP
**Bankers:** Barclays Bank Plc (20-44-22)

| | 30-04-13 | 30-04-12 | 30-04-11 |
|---|---|---|---|
| TO | 32,845,000 | 35,834,000 | 38,627,000 |
| P/L | (5,471,000) | (1,499,000) | 1,640,000 |
| NW | 7,553,000 | 10,495,000 | 8,685,000 |
| WC | (13,636,000) | (9,233,000) | (8,209,000) |
| Emp. | 369 | 372 | 418 |

DUNS 23-681-0375
## Sceptre Leisure Solutions Ltd.
**(Subsidiary of:** Sceptre Leisure Plc)
Emmanuel Trading Estate, Springwell Road, Leeds, West Yorkshire LS12 1AT
**Tel:** 01132428106
**Web:** www.sceptreleisure.co.uk
**Reg No:** 3675579 **Estd:** 1998 Private Limited Company
**Line of Business:** Gambling and betting activities
**Issued Capital:** £51,020
**Directors:** P R Robinson, A L Yates, M A White, K B Turner
**Co. Secretary:** Mark White
**Responsibilities**
**Senior:** Bola Messenger (Manager)
**Branches:** Sceptre Leisure Solutions Ltd., 9 Dunlin Court, Bellshill, Lanarkshire ML4 3NH
**US SIC:** 7999 **UK SIC:** 97913
**Auditors:** Baker Tilly
**Bankers:** National Westminster Bank Plc (60-19-38)

| | 30-04-13 | 30-04-12 | 30-04-11 |
|---|---|---|---|
| TO | 30,505,452 | 33,137,162 | 35,382,944 |
| P/L | (3,323,326) | 937,096 | 1,439,970 |
| NW | 4,741,566 | 6,931,490 | 6,106,298 |
| WC | (16,001,705) | (15,470,091) | (15,539,449) |
| Emp. | 343 | 336 | 375 |

DUNS 39-809-3229     **Imp**
## Schades Ltd
**(Subsidiary of:** Schades Holding A/S)
Brittain Drive, Ripley, Derbyshire DE5 3RZ
**Tel:** 01773-748721 **Fax:** 01773-745061
**Web:** www.schades.com
**Reg No:** 2213725 **VAT No:** 509106175
**Estd:** 1988 Private Limited Company
**Line of Business:** Paper and paperboard suppliers
**Export Sales:** £3,259,998
**Issued Capital:** £1,333,000
**Directors:** S J Kim, J A Osborne, P Moller
**Co. Secretary:** Erling Sorenson
**Responsibilities**
**Senior:** Ren?edholt Andersen (Director), Emma Haynes (Manager), Jack Hugill (Manager), Erling Sorensen (Director)
**Finance:** Emma Haynes (Manager)
**Health & Safety:** Steve Grainger (factory Manager)
**US SIC:** 2631 **UK SIC:** 47017
**Auditors:** Grant Thornton
**Bankers:** HSBC Bank plc (40-38-22)

| | 31-12-13 | 31-12-12 | 31-12-11 |
|---|---|---|---|
| TO | 22,213,899 | 21,926,791 | 20,466,003 |
| P/L | (468,610) | 637,871 | 971,524 |
| NW | 2,876,146 | 3,991,974 | 5,620,165 |
| WC | 2,234,125 | 2,497,782 | 4,706,983 |
| Emp. | 49 | 53 | 45 |

DUNS 34-645-7237
## Schaeffler Automotive Aftermarket (Uk) Ltd
**(Subsidiary of:** Ina-Holding Schaeffler Gmbh & Co. Kg)
Holme Lacy Road, Fir Tree Lane, Rotherwas Industrial Estate, Hereford, Herefordshire HR2 6LA
**Tel:** 01432 264264 **Fax:** 01432275146
**Web:** www.schaeffler-aftermarket.de
**Reg No:** 2770881 **Estd:** 1980 Private Limited Company
**Line of Business:** Sale of motor vehicle parts and accessories
**Issued Capital:** £1,000
**Directors:** M W Soeding, N Morgan
**Co. Secretary:** Peter Evans
**Responsibilities**
**Senior:** Warren Barnett (General Manager), Werner Schultz (Manager)
**Finance:** M Brisland (Financial Controller), Juergen Maedge (Finance Director)
**Branches:** Schaeffler Automotive Aftermarket (Uk) Ltd, Holme Lacy Road, Hereford, Herefordshire HR2 6LA
**US SIC:** 5531 **UK SIC:** 65100
**Auditors:** KPMG LLP
**Bankers:** Barclays Bank Plc (20-76-89)

| | 31-12-13 | 31-12-12 | 31-12-11 |
|---|---|---|---|
| TO | 105,666,764 | 97,009,658 | 90,182,018 |
| P/L | 10,919,103 | 8,787,132 | 8,361,946 |
| NW | 49,582,869 | 41,588,684 | 34,544,091 |
| WC | 49,683,508 | 41,304,211 | 34,765,449 |
| Emp. | 103 | 106 | 109 |

DUNS 34-810-6241
## Schaeffler (U K) Pension Trustee Ltd
Forge Lane Minworth Industrial Park, Sutton Coldfield, West Midlands B76 1AP
**Tel:** 01554772288
**Web:** www.schaeffler.com
**Reg No:** 5610565 **Estd:** 2005 Private Company Limited By Guarantee
**Line of Business:** Pension funding
**Directors:** P J Evans, P R Tarry, W A Boersig, D R Gaskell, N Akers, R Gingell, A R Roberts
**Co. Secretary:** Aaron Brock
**US SIC:** 6371 **UK SIC:** 82002
**Employees:** 400

DUNS 21-640-0069     **Imp-Exp**
## Schaeffler (Uk) Ltd
**(Subsidiary of:** Ina-Holding Schaeffler Gmbh & Co. Kg)
Forge Lane, Minworth, Sutton Coldfield, West Midlands B76 1AP
**Tel:** 01213513833
**Web:** www.schaeffler.com
**Reg No:** 0556493 **VAT No:** 122075412
**Estd:** 1955 Private Limited Company
**Line of Business:** Manufacturers of bearings
**Export Markets:** U S A: Germany: Europe
**Issued Capital:** £1,000,000
**Directors:** R J Hall, J R Evans, Prof. P Pleus
**Co. Secretary:** Aaron Brock
**Responsibilities**
**Senior:** Mike Barbar (Facilities Manager), Karen Preston (Sales & Marketing Manager)
**Marketing:** Kay Chapman (Marketing Officer), Karen Preston (Sales & Marketing Manager)
**Sales:** Karen Preston (Sales & Marketing Manager)
**Admin:** Andrew Parkhouse (IT Manager)
**IT:** Andrew Parkhouse (IT Manager)
**Facilities:** Mike Barbar (Facilities Manager)
**Engineering:** Richard Granger (Power Generation Sector Manage), Des Pattinson (Vice President - Industrial), Alena Useinovic (Vice President - Automotive), Dave Wall (Senior Application Engineer)
**Branches:** Schaeffler (Uk) Ltd, Bynea, Llanelli, Dyfed SA14 9TG
**US SIC:** 3568, 3714
**UK SIC:** 32613, 35300
**Auditors:** MacIntyre Hudson LLP
**Bankers:** Barclays Bank Plc (20-51-32)

| | 31-12-13 | 31-12-12 | 31-12-11 |
|---|---|---|---|
| TO | 73,225,665 | 66,769,360 | 62,480,775 |
| P/L | 7,631,846 | 5,115,787 | 4,617,303 |
| NW | 28,695,033 | 26,237,923 | 20,438,004 |
| WC | 11,768,265 | 5,149,991 | 4,070,510 |
| Emp. | 308 | 317 | 324 |

DUNS 53-657-3421     **Imp-Exp**
## Schawk Uk Ltd
**(Subsidiary of:** Schawk Wace Group)
St Marks House, Shepherdess Walk, Islington, London N1 7LH
**Tel:** 020-7861-7777 **Fax:** 02078717701
**Web:** www.schawk.com
**Reg No:** 3462552 **Estd:** 1923 Private Limited Company
**Line of Business:** Marketing consultants
**Export Markets:** U S A; Australia
**Export Sales:** £21,600,000
**Issued Capital:** £100,000
**Directors:** A A Sarkisian, D A Schawk
**Co. Secretary:** Ronald Vittorini
**Responsibilities**
**Senior:** Ray Keiser (Manager)
**Branches:** Schawk Uk Ltd, Unit A, Kingsway North, Gateshead, Tyne and Wear NE11 0JH
**US SIC:** 7392 **UK SIC:** 83951
**Auditors:** Ernst & Young LLP
**Bankers:** National Westminster Bank Plc (60-30-03)

| | 31-12-13 | 31-12-12 | 31-12-11 |
|---|---|---|---|
| TO | 39,427,000 | 38,632,000 | 36,244,000 |
| P/L | 952,000 | 566,000 | 1,394,000 |
| NW | 2,108,000 | 897,000 | (224,000) |
| WC | 187,000 | (633,000) | (1,855,000) |
| Emp. | 467 | 473 | 458 |

DUNS 29-843-8656
## Scheff Foods Ltd
Unit 2 Hawthorns Business Park, Halfords Lane, Smethwick, West Midlands B66 1EL
**Tel:** 01215652280
**Web:** www.scheff-foods.com
**Reg No:** 2011961 **VAT No:** 443679227
**Estd:** 1986 Private Limited Company
**Line of Business:** Manufacturers of food products
**Export Sales:** £11,951
**Issued Capital:** £20,100
**Principals:** M K Chauhan (Managing), S Chauhan, R Chauhan
**Co. Secretary:** Mohan Chauhan
**US SIC:** 2099 **UK SIC:** 42399
**Auditors:** J W Hinks

**Bankers:** Lloyds TSB Bank plc (30-93-82)

| | 31-12-13 | 31-12-12 | 31-12-11 |
|---|---|---|---|
| TO | 8,221,454 | 8,643,846 | 9,923,417 |
| P/L | 107,865 | 703,206 | 605,774 |
| NW | 2,777,971 | 2,709,200 | 2,233,870 |
| WC | (144,998) | (9,867) | (246,853) |
| Emp. | 134 | 120 | 117 |

DUNS 23-813-2687 Imp

## Scheidt & Bachmann (U K) Ltd

**(Subsidiary of:** Scheidt & Bachmann Gmbh)
Unit 7-8, Leatherhead Road Silverglade Business, Park, Chessington, Surrey KT9 2QL
**Tel:** 01732763322
**Web:** www.scheidt-bachmann.de
**Reg No:** 3805576 **VAT No:** 725020968
**Estd:** 1999 Private Limited Company
**Line of Business:** Manufacture of tools
**Issued Capital:** £10,000
**Principals:** M Hughes *(Managing)*, M Augustynik, M Kammler, G J Straetener, J Heilingbrunner, D Ambrose, I R Jacques
**Co. Secretary:** Johannes Peschen
**US SIC:** 3423, 7699
**UK SIC:** 31612, 67303
**Auditors:** Perrys

| | 31-12-13 | 31-12-12 | 31-12-11 |
|---|---|---|---|
| TO | 12,345,549 | 9,963,376 | 9,433,139 |
| P/L | 1,098,277 | 873,133 | 868,592 |
| NW | 1,683,844 | 1,360,103 | 1,502,102 |
| WC | 1,330,959 | 1,149,696 | 1,287,244 |
| Emp. | 100 | 90 | 86 |

DUNS 34-733-3283

## Schenck Process Uk Ltd

**(Subsidiary of:** S-Process Equipment International Sarl)
Carolina Court Lakeside, Doncaster, South Yorkshire DN4 5RA
**Tel:** 01302 321313
**Web:** www.schenckprocess.com
**Reg No:** 5535492 **VAT No:** 868574464
**Estd:** 2012 Private Limited Company
**Line of Business:** Manufacture of other general purpose machinery not elsewhere classified
**Export Sales:** £9,120,372
**Issued Capital:** £272,001
**Directors:** N P Jones, R G Ellis
**Co. Secretary:** Nicholas Jones
**Responsibilities**
**Senior:** Steve Nixon *(Manager)*, Ian Woolf *(Manager)*
**US SIC:** 3549 **UK SIC:** 32212
**Auditors:** Deloitte LLP

| | 31-12-13 | 31-12-12 | 31-12-11 |
|---|---|---|---|
| TO | 24,989,720 | 25,440,178 | 13,790,701 |
| P/L | (3,560,426) | (1,649,376) | (2,488,495) |
| NW | (7,972,235) | (4,510,839) | (2,798,171) |
| WC | (8,829,081) | (5,096,634) | (41,414,283) |
| Emp. | 110 | 108 | 86 |

DUNS 22-650-0825

## Schenker-B T L Ltd

**(Subsidiary of:** Bundesrepublik Deutschland)
Eastfield Road, South Killingholme, Immingham, South Humberside DN40 3DQ
**Tel:** 01469-571755
**Web:** www.shenker.com
**Reg No:** 1060439 **VAT No:** 168191640
**Estd:** 1972 Private Limited Company
**Line of Business:** Freight forwarders
**Trading Style:** Schenker Ltd.
**Issued Capital:** £1,050,000
**Director:** Ms P Kuester
**Co. Secretary:** Pekka Hale
**Responsibilities**
**Senior:** Andrew Amis *(Depot Manager)*, Per Holst-Nielsen *(Manager)*
**Finance:** Malcolm Webster *(Finance Director)*
**Branches:** Schenker-B T L Ltd, Kelsey Close, Nuneaton, Warwickshire CV11 6XN
**US SIC:** 4712 **UK SIC:** 77002
**Bankers:** Skandinaviska Enskilda Banken Ab (publ) (40-48-65)

| | 31-12-13 | 31-12-12 | 31-12-11 |
|---|---|---|---|
| TA | 261,000 | 261,000 | 261,000 |
| NW | 261,000 | 261,000 | 261,000 |

DUNS 21-026-0212 Imp-Exp

## Schenker Ltd

**(Subsidiary of:** Bundesrepublik Deutschland)
Schenker House, Unit 3 Lhr Portal, Scylla Road, Hounslow, Middlesex TW6 3FE
**Tel:** 02088314511 **Fax:** 02088314697
**Web:** www.schenker.co.uk
**Reg No:** 0383914 **VAT No:** 656921313
**Estd:** 1943 Private Limited Company
**Line of Business:** Other scheduled air transport
**Export Sales:** £75,463,000
**Issued Capital:** £700,095
**Directors:** M A Sims, Ms P Kuester, S W Bruce, Ms H O Ingolfsson, R M Anderson, F Fabbroni, M Kraus
**Co. Secretary:** Ms Petra Kuester
**Responsibilities**
**Senior:** Jochen Mueller *(Chief Executive Officer)*
**Branches:** Schenker Ltd, International House, Ledson Road, Roundthorn Industrial Estate, Manchester M23 9LP
**US SIC:** 4511, 4411, 4712
**UK SIC:** 75000, 74001, 77002
**Auditors:** Ernst & Young LLP
**Bankers:** Barclays Bank Plc (20-19-90)

| | 31-12-13 | 31-12-12 | 31-12-11 |
|---|---|---|---|
| TO | 280,718,000 | 341,162,000 | 307,479,000 |
| P/L | (3,328,000) | 429,000 | 1,378,000 |
| NW | 8,275,000 | 12,772,000 | 16,795,000 |
| WC | 9,958,000 | 16,846,000 | 20,575,000 |
| Emp. | 813 | 891 | 850 |

DUNS 50-007-6070 Exp

## Schering-Plough Holdings Ltd

**(Subsidiary of:** Msd International Finance Coöperatief U.A.)
Schering-Plough House, Welwyn Garden City, Hertfordshire AL7 1TW
**Tel:** 01707-363636
**Reg No:** 2297208 **Estd:** 1989 Private Limited Company
**Line of Business:** Management activities of holding companies
**Export Markets:** Worldwide
**Issued Capital:** £500,002
**Directors:** Ms M S Leonard, S Nicholson, Mrs K E White, M T Nally
**Co. Secretary:** Richard Robinski
**US SIC:** 6711, 2834
**UK SIC:** 83962, 25700
**Auditors:** PricewaterhouseCoopers LLP
**Bankers:** National Westminster Bank Plc (60-04-16)

| | 31-12-13 | 31-12-12 | 31-12-11 |
|---|---|---|---|
| TA | 464,026,000 | 473,846,000 | 483,134,000 |
| P/L | 120,047,000 | 80,000 | 60,121,000 |
| NW | 402,236,000 | 412,208,000 | 412,028,000 |
| WC | (50,218,000) | (40,246,000) | (40,341,000) |

DUNS 73-798-6682

## Schiedel Chimney Systems Ltd

**(Subsidiary of:** Monier Holdings Sca)
Crowther Road Industrial Estate, Washington, Tyne and Wear NE38 0AQ
**Tel:** 01914-161150 **Fax:** 01914-151263
**Web:** www.ritevent.co.uk
**Reg No:** 5055083 **VAT No:** 675311731
**Estd:** 1968 Private Limited Company
**Line of Business:** Other construction work involving special trades
**Issued Capital:** £2,550,000
**Directors:** T Muehl, M C Ball
**Co. Secretary:** Geoffrey Shepheard
**Responsibilities**
**Senior:** Alessandro Cappellini *(Manager)*, Wendy Pearson *(Personal Assistant)*
**IT:** Steve Lovett *(IT Manager)*
**Purchasing:** Karen Fulton *(Procurement Manager)*
**Branches:** Schiedel Chimney Systems Ltd, 1 Washingbay Road, Dungannon, Co Tyrone BT71 4ND
**US SIC:** 5074, 8299
**UK SIC:** 61300, 93300
**Auditors:** KPMG LLP
**Bankers:** The Bank Of Ireland (90-48-51)

| | 31-12-13 | 31-12-12 | 31-12-11 |
|---|---|---|---|
| TO | 18,633,000 | 16,543,000 | 17,844,000 |
| P/L | (890,000) | (81,000) | (445,000) |
| NW | (18,379,000) | (17,503,000) | (17,436,000) |
| WC | (21,109,000) | (21,345,000) | (21,589,000) |
| Emp. | 103 | 104 | 112 |

DUNS 34-888-7709

## Schlegel Uk (2006) Ltd

**(Subsidiary of:** Tyman Plc)
29 Queen Anne's Gate, London SW1H 9BU
**Web:** www.schlegel.com
**Reg No:** 5686601 **Estd:** 2006 Private Limited Company
**Line of Business:** Management activities of holding companies
**Export Sales:** £3,164,000
**Issued Capital:** £5,201,100
**Directors:** P R Santo, J R Swan
**Co. Secretary:** Kevin O'Connell
**US SIC:** 6711 **UK SIC:** 83962

| | 31-12-13 | 31-12-12 | 31-12-11 |
|---|---|---|---|
| TO | 8,756,000 | 10,181,000 | 10,766,000 |
| P/L | 132,000 | 480,000 | 1,205,000 |
| NW | (1,692,000) | (2,946,000) | (657,000) |
| WC | 983,000 | 1,107,000 | 4,003,000 |
| Emp. | 58 | 62 | 65 |

DUNS 22-639-9731 Imp-Exp

## Schleifring Systems Ltd

**(Subsidiary of:** Wegmann Unternehmens-Holding Gmbh & Co. Kg)
Abex Road, Newbury, Berkshire RG14 5EY
**Tel:** 0163536363 **Fax:** 0163538334
**Web:** www.schleifring.co.uk
**Reg No:** 1800218 **Estd:** 1984 Private Limited Company
**Line of Business:** Manufacturers and wholesalers of electrical products
**Export Markets:** Scandinavia, France, Germany, U.S.A., Middle East
**Issued Capital:** £1,480,400
**Directors:** D P Finnegan, R G Simpson
**Co. Secretary:** Ms Linda Parsons
**Responsibilities**
**Senior:** Gregory Knapp *(Manager)*
**Finance:** Debbie Niven *(Financial controller)*
**Marketing:** Alan Meredith *(International Sales Manager)*
**Sales:** Alan Meredith *(International Sales Manager)*
**Health & Safety:** Debbie Niven *(Financial controller)*
**US SIC:** 3629, 3621
**UK SIC:** 34350, 34201
**Auditors:** Martin & Co
**Bankers:** Barclays Bank Plc (20-59-14)

| | 31-12-13 | 31-12-12 | 31-12-11 |
|---|---|---|---|
| TO | 5,432,419 | 6,174,299 | 6,082,946 |
| P/L | 329,190 | 250,870 | 287,170 |
| NW | 3,381,658 | 2,886,510 | 2,701,024 |
| WC | 1,946,053 | 1,385,070 | 1,331,960 |
| Emp. | 59 | 58 | 70 |

DUNS 22-138-8460

## Schlumberger Oilfield Uk Plc

**(Subsidiary of:** Schlumberger N.V.)
Schlumberger House, Horley, Surrey RH6 0NZ
**Tel:** 01293556655 **Fax:** 01293556080
**Web:** www.slb.com
**Reg No:** 4157867 **VAT No:** 743869490
**Estd:** 1955 Public Limited Company
**Line of Business:** Oil and gas exploration services
**Export Sales:** £488,062,000
**Trading Style:** Western Geco
**Issued Capital:** £200,000,000
**Directors:** R A Kidd, S Smoker, S M White, K K Chong, Ms C Mccandless, Mrs K A Hoeing-Cosentino, M E Mannering, D Marsh
**Co. Secretary:** Ms Pauline Droy Moore
**Responsibilities**
**Senior:** Dalton Boutte *(CEO, Managing Director)*, Carel Hooijkaas *(Manager)*, Olayinka Ilori *(Manager)*, Vladimir Tertychny *(Director)*
**Marketing:** Rhonda Boon *(Senior Marketing Executive)*
**Branches:** Schlumberger Oilfield Uk Plc, Lambourn Court, Abingdon Technology Centre, Abingdon, Oxfordshire OX14 1UJ
**US SIC:** 1389, 7391
**UK SIC:** 13000, 94000
**Auditors:** PricewaterhouseCoopers LLP

| | 31-12-13 | 31-12-12 | 31-12-11 |
|---|---|---|---|
| TO | 715,693,000 | 690,638,000 | 614,905,000 |
| P/L | 29,570,000 | 35,476,000 | 132,565,000 |
| NW | 285,312,000 | 311,850,000 | 345,200,000 |
| WC | 395,932,000 | 413,753,000 | 465,570,000 |
| Emp. | 2,530 | 2,366 | 2,465 |

DUNS 39-689-1350 Imp-Exp

## Schneider Electric Ltd

**(Subsidiary of:** Schneider Electric Sa)
Stafford Park 5, Telford, Shropshire TF3 3BL
**Tel:** 08706-088-608 **Fax:** 02031-071-611
**Web:** www.clipsal.com
**Reg No:** 1407228 **VAT No:** 301428505
**Estd:** 1978 Private Limited Company
**Line of Business:** Manufacture of electricity distribution and control apparatus
**Export Sales:** £57,659,000
**Issued Capital:** £60,000,000
**Directors:** S J Thorogood, T Lambeth, A W Taylor, E Coxon
**Responsibilities**
**Sales:** Paul Markham *(Customer Care Manager)*
**Operations:** Paul Markham *(Customer Care Manager)*, Paul Trattles *(Quality Manager)*
**Branches:** Schneider Electric Limited, 112 Cornwall Street South, Glasgow, Lanarkshire G41 1AA
**US SIC:** 3643, 7399
**UK SIC:** 34203, 83954
**Auditors:** Mazars LLP
**Bankers:** Barclays Bank Plc (20-48-46)

| | 31-12-13 | 31-12-12 | 31-12-11 |
|---|---|---|---|
| TO | 639,925,000 | 587,243,000 | 444,113,000 |
| P/L | 23,108,000 | 50,495,000 | 28,387,000 |
| NW | (10,792,000) | (21,165,000) | 82,213,000 |
| WC | 230,127,000 | 233,275,000 | 188,004,000 |
| Emp. | 2,907 | 2,774 | 1,882 |

DUNS 39-736-2641

## Schneider Industry (U K) Ltd

**(Subsidiary of:** Gli International)
Schneider Industry, Occupation Road, Stoney Stanton, Leicester, Leicestershire LE9 4JJ
**Web:** www.schneider-industry.co.uk
**Reg No:** 0107153SC **VAT No:** 624098440
**Estd:** 1987 Private Limited Company
**Line of Business:** Agents involved in the sale of machinery, industrial equipment, ships and aircraft
**Issued Capital:** £699,182
**Directors:** R Cato, C Vallat
**Co. Secretary:** Francis Frene
**Branches:** Schneider Industry (U K) Ltd, Alveley Indstl Est, Alverley, Bridgnorth, Shropshire WV15 6HG
**US SIC:** 5084, 8999
**UK SIC:** 61490, 83954
**Auditors:** Cooper Parry LLP
**Bankers:** The Royal Bank Of Scotland Plc (83-15-11)

| | 31-12-13 | 31-12-12 | 31-12-11 |
|---|---|---|---|
| TA | 153,749 | 166,766 | 150,233 |
| NW | (896,297) | (919,530) | (980,506) |
| WC | 35,725 | 10,947 | 9,120 |

DUNS 21-726-8449

## Schoeller Allibert Ltd

**(Subsidiary of:** La Holding Ltd)
17 Quinton Business Park Ridgeway, Birmingham, West Midlands B32 1AF
**Tel:** 0121 506 0100 **Fax:** 0121 422 1771
**Web:** www.linpacallibert.com
**Reg No:** 7632708 **Estd:** 2011 Private Limited Company
**Line of Business:** Business services
**Export Sales:** £19,789,000
**Issued Capital:** £2
**Directors:** D Oliynik, J Blakiston
**Co. Secretary:** John Blakiston
**US SIC:** 3999, 2654, 2651
**UK SIC:** 49590, 47280, 47253
**Auditors:** KPMG LLP

| | 31-12-13 | 31-12-12 | 31-12-11 |
|---|---|---|---|
| TO | 62,231,000 | 48,082,000 | N/A |
| P/L | 6,318,000 | 10,754,000 | N/A |
| NW | 15,388,000 | 15,615,000 | 1 |
| WC | 3,747,000 | 3,058,000 | N/A |
| Emp. | 218 | 233 | N/A |

DUNS 56-950-1117 Imp-Exp

## Schoeller-Bleckmann Darron Ltd

Howe Moss Terrace, Aberdeen, Aberdeenshire AB21 0GR
**Tel:** 01224-799600
**Web:** www.sbdl.co.uk
**Reg No:** 0145802SC **VAT No:** 605105096
**Estd:** 1993 Private Limited Company
**Line of Business:** Oil and gas exploration services
**Export Markets:** Africa; European Union (E U); Libya; Norway; Venezuela; Tunisia
**Export Sales:** £11,504,372
**Trading Style:** Darron-Sb0
**Issued Capital:** £4,365,000
**Directors:** Miss K Limer, M Fosleitner, G Grohmann, F Gritsch, W H Bailey
**Co. Secretary:** Raeburn Christie Clark & Wallace
**Responsibilities**
**Senior:** Donna Findlay *(Manager)*, Jamie Frazer *(Quality Manager)*
**Admin:** Donna Findlay *(Manager)*
**Operations:** Donna Findlay *(Manager)*
**Engineering:** Jamie Frazer *(Quality Manager)*, Sandy Stephen *(Workshop Manager)*
**Branches:** Schoeller-Bleckmann Darron Ltd, Unit 47 Howe Moss Terrace, Aberdeen, Aberdeenshire AB21 0GR
**US SIC:** 1389, 7394
**UK SIC:** 13000, 84000
**Auditors:** Ritson Smith
**Bankers:** Clydesdale Bank Plc (82-62-22)

| | 31-12-13 | 31-12-12 | 31-12-11 |
|---|---|---|---|
| TO | 11,504,372 | 11,190,400 | 18,990,323 |
| P/L | 2,555,688 | 2,135,915 | 4,633,416 |
| NW | 7,582,247 | 6,275,225 | 12,804,952 |
| WC | 2,617,136 | 2,120,170 | 8,524,321 |
| Emp. | 62 | 55 | 97 |

DUNS 21-213-9661 Exp

## Schofield & Smith (Huddersfield) Ltd

**(Subsidiary of:** Schofield & Smith (Holdings) Ltd)
Unit 26, Huddersfield, West Yorkshire HD7 5HA
**Tel:** 01484-842471
**Web:** www.schofieldandsmith.co.uk
**Reg No:** 0482361 **Estd:** 1904 Private Limited Company
**Line of Business:** Manufacture of household textiles
**Export Markets:** Worldwide
**Trading Style:** Oswald Supertex
**Issued Capital:** £55,000
**Director:** O Franco
**US SIC:** 2392, 5133
**UK SIC:** 45550, 61600
**Auditors:** Mazars
**Bankers:** HSBC Bank plc (40-25-10)

| | 31-12-13 | 31-12-12 | 31-12-11 |
|---|---|---|---|
| TA | 824,553 | 1,059,348 | 1,124,462 |
| NW | 485,046 | 750,714 | 785,114 |
| WC | 767,679 | 1,003,318 | 1,036,598 |

**DUNS 50-427-7849**

## Schofield Construction Ltd

Unit 41 Trinity Enterprise Centre, Furness Business Park, Barrow-In-Furness, Cumbria LA14 2PN
**Web:** www.plumber-blackburn.com
**Reg No:** 2419938 **VAT No:** 531487838
**Estd:** 1989 Private Limited Company
**Line of Business:** Building construction contractors
**Issued Capital:** £3,000
**Managing Director:** P Schofield
**Co. Secretary:** Ms Michelle Schofield
**Responsibilities**
**Health & Safety:** Steve Anderton (contracts manager)
**Facilities:** Steve Anderton (contracts manager)
**US SIC:** 1522, 7349
**UK SIC:** 50100, 92300
**Bankers:** The Royal Bank Of Scotland Plc (16-12-27)

|  | 31-12-13 | 31-12-12 | 31-12-11 |
|---|---|---|---|
| TA | 958,967 | 824,532 | 658,098 |
| NW | 528,112 | 535,780 | 451,072 |
| WC | 485,548 | 493,676 | 423,373 |

**DUNS 21-602-1962**

## Schofield Dyers & Finishers

Gala Mill, Huddersfield Street, Galashiels, Selkirkshire TD1 3AY
**Web:** www.schofield-df.co.uk
**Estd:** 1983 Proprietorship
**Line of Business:** Dyers
**Proprietor:** D Ormiston
**US SIC:** 2269 **UK SIC:** 43702
**Employees:** 53

**DUNS 21-139-5390**

## Schofield Lothian Ltd

Temple Chambers 3 7, Temple Avenue, London EC4Y 0DT
**Tel:** 02078420920
**Web:** www.schofieldlothian.com
**Reg No:** 6717705 **Estd:** 2008 Private Limited Company
**Line of Business:** Business and management consultancy activities not elsewhere classified
**Issued Capital:** £1,001
**Directors:** B W Impey, T L Mcauliffe, K F Corcoran, R M Palphramand, M J Upton
**US SIC:** 7392 **UK SIC:** 83951

|  | 31-12-13 | 31-12-12 | 31-12-11 |
|---|---|---|---|
| TO | N/A | N/A | 5,839,753 |
| P/L | N/A | N/A | (69,273) |
| NW | 709,811 | 546,858 | (992,177) |
| WC | 705,763 | 531,212 | 739,667 |
| Emp. | N/A | N/A | 62 |

**DUNS 23-762-7307**

## Schofield Publishing Ltd

10 Cringleford Business Centre, Norwich, Norfolk NR4 6AU
**Tel:** 01603274130 **Fax:** 01603-274131
**Web:** www.schofieldpublishing.co.uk
**Reg No:** 3756336 **Estd:** 2000 Private Limited Company
**Line of Business:** Publishing of books
**Issued Capital:** £80,771
**Directors:** M M Tulloch, A J Schofield
**Co. Secretary:** Andrew Schofield
**Responsibilities**
**Senior:** Robert Dickson (Finance Director), Brian Reshefsky (Manager)
**Finance:** Robert Dickson (Finance Director)
**Admin:** Tracy Chynoweth (Purchasing Manager)
**Facilities:** Tracy Chynoweth (Purchasing Manager)
**Purchasing:** Tracy Chynoweth (Purchasing Manager)
**US SIC:** 2731 **UK SIC:** 47532
**Auditors:** Banham Graham
**Bankers:** National Westminster Bank Plc (60-15-31)

|  | 30-06-13 | 30-06-12 | 30-06-11 |
|---|---|---|---|
| TO | N/A | N/A | 2,993,797 |
| P/L | N/A | N/A | 68,423 |
| NW | 48,030 | 369,501 | 642,707 |
| WC | 41,279 | 361,785 | 632,447 |

**DUNS 73-321-2398**

## Schofield Sweeney Llp

Church Bank House, Church Bank, Bradford, West Yorkshire BD1 4DY
**Web:** www.schofieldsweeney.co.uk
**Reg No:** 0303400OC **Estd:** 1995
**Line of Business:** Solicitors
**Responsibilities**
**Senior:** Alexandra Clements (Non-designated Limited Liabili), Laurence Dale (Designated Limited Liability P), Robert Hayes (Designated Limited Liability P), Dean Jowett (Non-designated Limited Liabili), Nigel Middlemass (Non-designated Limited Liabili), Amar Rashid (Non-designated Limited Liabili), Richard Stockdale (Non-designated Limited Liabili), Graham Sweeney (Non-designated Limited Liabili)

**US SIC:** 8111 **UK SIC:** 83500

|  | 31-12-13 | 31-12-12 | 31-12-11 |
|---|---|---|---|
| TO | 6,542,313 | 6,894,550 | N/A |
| WC | 2,273,064 | 2,382,065 | 1,806,445 |
| Emp. | 95 | 93 | N/A |

**DUNS 21-233-4251**

## Scholars Catering

Foster Building, Preston, Lancashire PR1 2HE
**Tel:** 01772-892080
**Web:** www.uclan.ac.uk
**Partnership**
**Line of Business:** Caterers
**Partners:** Miss D Lishman, Miss L Holding
**Responsibilities**
**Senior:** Jackie Cunningham (Manager)
**US SIC:** 5812 **UK SIC:** 66110
**Employees:** 70

**DUNS 21-198-6815**     **Imp**

## Scholastic Ltd

(**Subsidiary of:** Scholastic Corporation)
Unit 6, Southam, Warwickshire CV47 0RA
**Tel:** 01926813910
**Web:** www.scholastic.com
**Reg No:** 0701339 **VAT No:** 241359376
**Estd:** 2002 Private Limited Company
**Line of Business:** Book publishers
**Export Sales:** £9,315,719
**Trading Style:** Scholastic Childrens Books, Scholastic Online Resources, Scholastic Book Fairs
**Issued Capital:** £45,019,500
**Principals:** M R Robinson (Chairman), Mrs C Moreton, S K Thompson
**Co. Secretary:** Mrs Nicola Dixon
**Responsibilities**
**Senior:** Julie Goodchild (Manager), Alan Hurchombe (Manager)
**Branches:** Scholastic Ltd, Touchet Hall Road, Steakhill Industrial Estate, Manchester M24 2FL
**US SIC:** 2731, 2741, 5963
**UK SIC:** 47532, 47541, 65600
**Auditors:** Ernst & Young LLP
**Bankers:** HSBC Bank plc (40-42-15)

|  | 31-05-13 | 31-05-12 | 31-05-11 |
|---|---|---|---|
| TO | 33,584,382 | 35,892,761 | 26,020,288 |
| P/L | 1,962,259 | 2,205,466 | 7,042,369 |
| NW | 16,662,289 | 16,138,600 | 16,143,113 |
| WC | 24,504,978 | 22,985,337 | 22,065,112 |
| Emp. | 222 | 227 | 280 |

**DUNS 64-072-2633**     **Imp**

## Scholle Europe Ltd

(**Subsidiary of:** Scholle Corporation)
Unit 12a Follingsby Close, Gateshead, Tyne and Wear NE10 8YG
**Tel:** 01914193900 **Fax:** 01914196311
**Web:** www.scholle.com
**Reg No:** 3467709 **Estd:** 1998 Private Limited Company
**Line of Business:** Manufacture of plastic packing goods
**Issued Capital:** £2,630,154
**Directors:** S J Waller, T J Bickford, L P Gianneschi
**Co. Secretary:** Jack Moore
**Branches:** Scholle Europe Ltd, Hempstead Road Industrial Estate, Fakenham, Norfolk NR21 8SN
**US SIC:** 3079 **UK SIC:** 48360
**Auditors:** BDO LLP
**Bankers:** Lloyds TSB Bank plc (30-93-71)

|  | 30-09-13 | 30-09-12 | 30-09-11 |
|---|---|---|---|
| TO | 19,765,398 | 17,053,439 | 15,936,473 |
| P/L | 1,289,497 | 1,198,405 | 958,339 |
| NW | 4,106,849 | 3,634,872 | 6,276,987 |
| WC | 3,319,937 | 2,852,000 | 5,431,589 |
| Emp. | 77 | 83 | 91 |

**DUNS 21-556-0156**

## School Bargain Bookshop Ltd

Rollesby Road, Hardwick Industrial Estate, King's Lynn, Norfolk PE30 4LS
**Tel:** 01553816083
**Web:** www.schoolbargainbookshop.co.uk
**Reg No:** 6828890 **Estd:** 1989 Private Limited Company
**Line of Business:** Adult and other education not elsewhere classified
**Issued Capital:** £1
**Co. Secretary:** David Clark
**US SIC:** 8249 **UK SIC:** 93300

|  | 28-02-14 | 28-02-13 | 28-02-12 |
|---|---|---|---|
| TA | 2 | 2 | 2 |
| NW | 2 | 2 | 2 |

**DUNS 21-100-7770**

## School Business Services Ltd.

26a Parkstone Road, Poole, Dorset BH15 2PG
**Tel:** 08453008179
**Web:** www.schoolbusinessservices.co.uk
**Reg No:** 6443524 **Estd:** 2007 Private Limited Company
**Line of Business:** Secretarial and translation activities
**Issued Capital:** £3

**Directors:** M Tadman, Mrs T L Brown
**US SIC:** 7399 **UK SIC:** 83954

|  | 31-12-13 | 31-12-12 | 31-12-11 |
|---|---|---|---|
| TA | 1,045,889 | 923,171 | 756,780 |
| NW | 211,830 | 172,239 | 98,013 |
| WC | (330,507) | 48,255 | 3,566 |

**DUNS 21-579-7102**

## The School for Policy Studies

6-8 Priory Road, Bristol, Avon BS8 1TZ
**Tel:** 01179546755
**Web:** www.bristol.ac.uk
**Estd:** 2002 Proprietorship
**Line of Business:** University
**Proprietor:** R Forrest
**Responsibilities**
**Senior:** Alex Marsh (Head Of School)
**US SIC:** 8221 **UK SIC:** 93100
**Employees:** 70

**DUNS 21-779-5695**

## The School for Profound Education

Tadworth Court, Tadworth, Surrey KT20 5RU
**Web:** www.thechildrenstrust.org.uk
**Estd:** 2011 Proprietorship
**Line of Business:** Schools (special)
**Proprietor:** Mrs J Cunningham
**Responsibilities**
**Senior:** Silvia Kerambrum (Head Teacher)
**US SIC:** 8299 **UK SIC:** 93300
**Employees:** 100

**DUNS 51-984-5569**

## School-Home Support Service (U K)

Cityside House, London E1 1EE
**Tel:** 02074265001
**Web:** www.schoolhomesupport.org.uk
**Reg No:** 3991440 **Estd:** 2000 Private Unlimited Company
**Line of Business:** Charities and charitable organisations
**Directors:** B W Olson, R L Phillips, A J Scott-Barrett, Ms S Scheiber, I R Woolf, R S Evans, Ms E Wolverson, A J Dowell
**Co. Secretary:** Ms Alexine Horsup
**Responsibilities**
**Senior:** David Marriage (Director), Ian Stickley (Manager), Jan Tallis (Chief Executive)
**US SIC:** 8211, 8299
**UK SIC:** 93200, 93300
**Bankers:** Barclays Bank Plc (20-51-01)

|  | 31-08-13 | 31-08-12 | 31-08-11 |
|---|---|---|---|
| TO | 3,686,019 | 4,119,885 | 7,252,919 |
| P/L | 244,842 | (111,707) | (429,224) |
| NW | 546,440 | 270,767 | 374,676 |
| WC | 411,648 | 211,936 | 291,191 |
| Emp. | 129 | 105 | 158 |

**DUNS 23-116-3630**

## School House Leisure Ltd

Moddershall, Moddershall, Stone, Staffordshire ST15 8TG
**Tel:** 01782399000 **Fax:** 01782399662
**Web:** www.moddershalloaks.com
**Reg No:** 3679011 **Estd:** 2000 Private Limited Company
**Line of Business:** Hairdressing and other beauty treatment
**Trading Style:** Moddershall Oaks Health Spa
**Issued Capital:** £970,000
**Directors:** P G Holland, Ms P E Holland
**Co. Secretary:** Ms Delia Holland
**US SIC:** 7231 **UK SIC:** 98200
**Auditors:** Hammond McNulty

|  | 31-03-14 | 31-03-13 | 31-03-12 |
|---|---|---|---|
| TO | 2,273,626 | 2,347,411 | 2,019,284 |
| P/L | 353,489 | 248,930 | 182,194 |
| NW | 2,343,193 | 1,996,257 | 1,747,327 |
| WC | (470,702) | (470,189) | (449,951) |
| Emp. | 65 | 56 | 59 |

**DUNS 64-718-2617**

## The School House Nursery

Pannal Green, Pannal, Harrogate, North Yorkshire HG3 1LH
**Web:** www.kidsatheart.co.uk
**Estd:** 1995 Proprietorship
**Line of Business:** Nursery schools
**Proprietor:** Mrs J Shaw
**US SIC:** 8211 **UK SIC:** 93200
**Employees:** 60

**DUNS 21-041-7140**

## School of Biological Sciences

Biological Sciences Building, Bristol, Avon BS8 1UG
**Tel:** 01179287475
**Web:** www.bristol.ac.uk
**Estd:** 2005
**Line of Business:** University
**Responsibilities**
**IT:** Keir Mobbf (Senior IT Executive)
**US SIC:** 8221 **UK SIC:** 93100
**Employees:** 150

**DUNS 21-880-0358**

## School of Computer Science

University Of Nottingham, Wollaton Road, Nottingham, Nottinghamshire NG8 1BB
**Web:** www.nottingham.ac.uk
**Estd:** 2012
**Line of Business:** University
**Responsibilities**
**Senior:** Uwe Aickelin (Head Teacher)
**US SIC:** 8221 **UK SIC:** 93100
**Employees:** 50

**DUNS 21-580-1476**

## School of Computing

Borough Road, Middlesbrough, Cleveland TS1 3BA
**Tel:** 01642342631
**Estd:** 2005 Proprietorship
**Line of Business:** Computer training
**Proprietor:** Miss K Alexander
**US SIC:** 8221 **UK SIC:** 93100
**Employees:** 500

**DUNS 21-035-5507**

## School of Computing Communications & Electronics

Drake Circus, Plymouth, Devon PL4 8AA
**Tel:** 01752586200
**Web:** www.plymouth.ac.uk
**Estd:** 1990
**Line of Business:** University
**Proprietor:** S Furnell
**US SIC:** 8221 **UK SIC:** 93100
**Employees:** 100

**DUNS 21-880-1734**

## School of Construction Management

2 Nd Floor Whiteknights, Reading, Berkshire RG6 6AW
**Estd:** 2012
**Line of Business:** Colleges (higher education)
**US SIC:** 8221 **UK SIC:** 93100
**Employees:** 5,000

**DUNS 21-601-0042**

## School of Engineering

Singleton Park, Swansea, West Glamorgan SA2 8PP
**Estd:** 2011 Proprietorship
**Line of Business:** Colleges (higher education)
**Proprietor:** J Bomet
**US SIC:** 8221 **UK SIC:** 93100
**Employees:** 150

**DUNS 21-581-4662**

## The School of Engineering

Drake Circus, Plymouth, Devon PL4 8AA
**Tel:** 01752233664
**Web:** www.plymouth.ac.uk
**Estd:** 2011
**Line of Business:** University
**Responsibilities**
**Senior:** Barabara Fuller (Personal Assistant)
**US SIC:** 8221 **UK SIC:** 93100
**Employees:** 300

**DUNS 21-391-3373**

## School of Health

Walsall Campus, Gorway Road, Walsall, West Midlands WS1 3BD
**Tel:** 01902-518800
**Web:** www.wlv.ac.uk
**Estd:** 1993
**Line of Business:** University
**Partners:** Professor L Lang, Mrs M Chevannes
**US SIC:** 8221 **UK SIC:** 93100
**Employees:** 60

**DUNS 21-773-0676**

## School of Law

Wills Memorial Building, Queens Road, Clifton, Bristol, Avon BS8 1RJ
**Tel:** 01179545356
**Web:** www.bristol.ac.uk
**Estd:** 1932 Proprietorship
**Line of Business:** University
**Proprietor:** Ms C Andrews
**Responsibilities**
**Senior:** Caroline Andrews (School Manager)
**US SIC:** 8221 **UK SIC:** 93100
**Employees:** 54

DUNS 21-590-6166

## The School of Life Sciences

Riverside East, Garthdee Road, Aberdeen, Aberdeenshire AB10 7GJ
**Tel:** 01224262800
**Web:** www.rgu.ac.uk
**Estd:** 2011
**Line of Business:** Post-graduate level higher education
**Responsibilities**
**Senior:** Donald Cairns *(Head Of School)*
**US SIC:** 8221 **UK SIC:** 93100
**Employees:** 100

DUNS 21-039-8077

## The School of Management University of Surrey

University Of Surrey, Guildford, Surrey GU2 7XH
**Web:** www.surrey.ac.uk
**Line of Business:** First-degree level higher education
**Trading Style:** The School of Management University of Surrey
**US SIC:** 8221 **UK SIC:** 93100
**Employees:** 100

DUNS 21-591-7516

## School of Mechanical Engineering

Woodhouse Lane, Leeds, West Yorkshire LS2 9JT
**Tel:** 01133432186
**Web:** www.leeds.ac.uk
**Estd:** 2011
**Line of Business:** University
**US SIC:** 8221 **UK SIC:** 93100
**Employees:** 350

DUNS 22-576-6021 **Imp**

## School of Oriental & African Studies

Thornhaugh Street, London WC1H 0XG
**Tel:** 020-7637-2388
**Web:** www.soas.ac.uk
**Reg No:** 0000541RC **Estd:** 2011 Incorporate By Act Of Parliament
**Line of Business:** University
**Trading Style:** School of Advanced Study
**Principals:** T Lancaster, J Faulkner
**Co. Secretary:** Frank Dabell
**Responsibilities**
**Senior:** Emmon Bach *(External Member)*, Cedric Barnes *(External Member)*, Maxine Brown *(Senior Manager)*, Tom Castle *(Manager)*, Carlos Chirinos *(Manager)*, Wayne Dooling *(Manager)*, Alicia Fernandez *(Executive)*, Almut Hintze *(Doctor)*, John Hollingworth *(Executive)*, Stephen Hopgood *(Executive)*, Bernard Howard *(Manager)*, Chris Ince *(Deputy Secretary)*, Machiko Nissanke *(Executive)*, Martin Orwin *(Chairman)*, Katerina Pavlakis *(Senior Manager)*, Richard Poulson *(Facilities Manager)*, Paul Webley *(Manager)*
**Finance:** Graeme Appleby *(Financial Director)*, Norbert Chan *(Financial Accountant)*, Barry Douglas *(Assistant Director of Finance)*, Julie Hammond *(Credit Controller)*, Richard Lucus *(Senior Financial Accountant)*, Pamela McLeary *(Credit Controller)*, Mariam Noor *(Management Accounting Assistan)*, Anne Perkins *(Research & Enterprise Finance)*, Kemi Rockson *(Financial Controller)*, Carol Roycroft *(Accounts Assistants)*, Hannah Sharpe *(Management Accountant)*, Jane Wood *(Accounting Officer)*
**Marketing:** Kobir Ahmed *(Web Content Assistant)*, Henty Bulley *(Marketing Officer - Advertisin)*, Catriona Finlayson *(Head of Communications)*, Duncan Franklin *(Marketing Manager)*, Payal Gaglani-Bhatt *(Senior Marketing and Events Of)*, Fiona McWilliams *(Director of External Relations)*, Andrew Osmond *(Marketing Officer - Advertisin)*, Katie Price *(Interim Head of Communications)*, Clare Rhodes *(External Relations Officer)*, Louise Roberts *(Enterprise Manager)*, Sophie Salffner *(Web Development Executive)*, Michael Sherry *(Head of Marketing Publications)*, Vesna Siljanovska *(Communications Officer)*, Becky Unitt *(Marketing Officer (Campaigns))*, Jamie Wells *(Marketing Manager)*, Kerry Whitston *(Publications Manager)*
**Sales:** Valerie De Ruyter *(Business Development Manager)*, Sophie Dilley *(Business Development Officer)*
**Admin:** Alexander Andreou *(Librarian)*, Simon Buller *(Administrator)*, Nina Chang *(Administrative Assistant)*, Alan Cummings *(Admissions Tutor)*, Ayo Duyile *(Clerical Officer)*, Jo Fung *(Clerical Officer)*, Carolyn Heath *(Administrator)*, Fujiko Kobayashi *(Legal Executive)*, Celine Noguera *(Clerical Officer)*, Roger Nuthall *(Administrator)*, Gary Somers *(Clerical Officer, Admissions)*, Sarah Tucker *(Administrator, Academic Develo)*, Natasha Williams *(Administrator)*
**IT:** Denson Abrahams *(IT & Media Services Support An)*, Beth Clark *(Head of Electronic Services)*, Mike Humphrey *(IS Project Manager)*, Andrew Leedham *(Corporate Systems Manager)*, Liz Mags *(IS Project Manager)*, Robert Mertling-Blake *(Network Officer)*, Ed Spick *(ICT Manager)*, Martin Whiteside *(Assistant Director, Informatio)*, Lindsay Whittome *(Senior Networks Officer)*, Joseph Yau *(Telecom Manager)*
**HR:** Maxine Brown *(Senior Manager)*, Fon Browndy *(Staff Development Officer)*, Chris Byrne *(Human Resources Manager)*, Emily Crofts *(Human Resources Manager)*, Marva De La Coudray *(Head of Widening Participation)*, Norman Flynn *(Director, Studies)*, Simon Gwynne *(Human Resources Projects Coord)*, Carol John *(Training Director)*, Jakob Klein *(Lecturer)*, Clive Lawton *(Training Director)*, Brenda Lett *(HR Manager)*, Trevor Marchand *(Senior Lecturer, Social Anthro)*, David Mosse *(Senior Lecturer, Social Anthro)*, Caroline Nield *(Human Resources Officer)*, Hellen Onaba *(Human Resources Assistant)*, Carol Rifkin *(Training Director)*, Seema Sanyal *(HR Manager)*, Rebecca Tyler *(Human Resources Assistant)*, Serena Yeo *(Human Resources Manager)*
**Health & Safety:** Heidi Alderton *(Safety Officer)*
**Facilities:** Mike Haddon *(Head of Facilities Management)*, Richard Poulson *(Facilities Manager)*
**Operations:** Renata Albuquerque *(Project Manager)*, Lucy Allan *(Project Executive)*, Nic Crotch *(Programme Manager)*, Regina Everitt *(Assistant Director, Operations)*
**Purchasing:** Katie Price *(Interim Head of Communications)*, Mark Sellick *(Purchasing Assistant)*, Adeola Talabi *(Purchase Ledger Supervisor)*
**Engineering:** Barbara Spina *(Head of Technical Services)*
**Branches:** School Of Oriental & African Studies, Dinwiddy House, 189-205 Pentonville Rd, London N1 9NF
**US SIC:** 8221 **UK SIC:** 93100
**Employees:** 2,600
**Turnover:** £47,596,000

DUNS 21-591-7454

## School of Psychology

Woodhouse Lane, Leeds, West Yorkshire LS2 9JT
**Tel:** 01133435724
**Web:** www.leeds.ac.uk
**Estd:** 2011
**Line of Business:** Post-graduate level higher education
**Responsibilities**
**Senior:** Mark Mon-Williams *(Head Of Institute)*
**US SIC:** 8221 **UK SIC:** 93100
**Employees:** 60

DUNS 21-691-5120

## School Partnership Trust Academies

Education House Fusion Court, Aberford Road Garforth, Leeds, West Yorkshire LS25 2GH
**Tel:** 01133368615
**Reg No:** 7386086 **Estd:** 2010 Private Company Limited By Guarantee
**Line of Business:** Primary education
**Directors:** S P Hodsman, Sir R P Edwards, Mrs S L Bailey, I Garforth, P Forbes, S P Cavan, Mrs N P Cox, P Hirst
**US SIC:** 8211, 8249
**UK SIC:** 93200, 93300
**Bankers:** The Royal Bank Of Scotland Plc (16-00-08)

| | 31-08-14 | 31-08-13 | 31-08-12 |
|---|---|---|---|
| TO | 145,776,000 | 136,262,000 | 151,839,000 |
| P/L | 29,703,000 | 21,035,000 | 72,118,000 |
| NW | 149,760,000 | 121,663,000 | 100,560,000 |
| WC | 26,075,000 | 16,017,000 | 10,529,000 |
| Emp. | 2,404 | 2,128 | 1,925 |

DUNS 34-840-5098

## The School Photography Co Ltd

(**Subsidiary of:** Tsgp Group Ltd)
Unit B Beaumont Close, Banbury, Oxfordshire OX16 1TG
**Tel:** 01295-250812
**Web:** www.schoolphotographs.co.uk
**Reg No:** 5639678 **Estd:** 2005 Private Limited Company
**Line of Business:** Photographic activities not elsewhere classified
**Issued Capital:** £3,000
**Directors:** N R Owen, D V Wallbank, S Solomons
**Co. Secretary:** David Fonge
**US SIC:** 7333 **UK SIC:** 83953

| | 31-03-14 | 31-03-13 | 31-03-12 |
|---|---|---|---|
| TA | 1,322,021 | 1,063,710 | 1,203,931 |
| NW | 53,928 | 147,998 | 45,978 |
| WC | (340,746) | (139,023) | (280,405) |

DUNS 64-150-1689

## School Trend

Carley Drive, Westfield, Sheffield, South Yorkshire S20 8NQ
**Tel:** 08701650161
**Web:** www.schooltrends.co.uk
**Line of Business:** School outfitters
**Proprietor:** P Beal
**Responsibilities**
**Finance:** Wendy Laycock *(Financial Director)*
**US SIC:** 5611, 2392
**UK SIC:** 64500, 45550
**Employees:** 120

DUNS 50-593-5270

## School Trends Ltd

(**Subsidiary of:** New School Trends Ltd)
10 Carley Drive, Sheffield, South Yorkshire S20 8NQ
**Tel:** 08701650161 **Fax:** 08001970161
**Web:** www.schooltrends.co.uk
**Reg No:** 2532511 **Estd:** 2011 Private Limited Company
**Line of Business:** Retail sale of children's and infants' clothing
**Issued Capital:** £9,961
**Directors:** Mrs L Wills, Mrs K Peat, D Brown, P J Westerman, M W Newell
**Co. Secretary:** Derry Mather
**US SIC:** 5641 **UK SIC:** 64500
**Auditors:** Barber Harrison & Platt

| | 31-12-13 | 31-12-12 | 31-12-11 |
|---|---|---|---|
| TO | 9,359,310 | 10,158,704 | 9,814,115 |
| P/L | 397,810 | 448,128 | 255,921 |
| NW | 3,713,527 | 3,357,137 | 3,012,251 |
| WC | 3,620,288 | 3,363,175 | 3,022,841 |
| Emp. | 138 | 143 | 142 |

DUNS 29-523-2144

## Schoolbus Ltd

(**Subsidiary of:** Stagecoach Group Plc)
Business Station, Sandgate, Ayr, Ayrshire KA7 1DD
**Fax:** 01292-613501
**Web:** www.stagecoachbus.com
**Reg No:** 0091904SC **Estd:** 1913 Private Limited Company
**Line of Business:** Bus operators and stations
**Trading Style:** Stagecoach
**Issued Capital:** £2
**Director:** C Brown
**Co. Secretary:** Michael Vaux
**Responsibilities**
**Senior:** Alan Henry *(Marketing Manager)*, Alan Whitnall *(Manager)*
**US SIC:** 4119 **UK SIC:** 72200
**Bankers:** The Royal Bank Of Scotland Plc (83-46-00)

| | 30-04-14 | 30-04-13 | 30-04-12 |
|---|---|---|---|
| TA | 2 | 2 | 2 |
| NW | 2 | 2 | 2 |

DUNS 21-400-5928 **Exp**

## Schoolhill Hydraulic Engineering Company Ltd

4 Greenbank Place, East Tullos Industrial Estate, Aberdeen, Aberdeenshire AB12 3RJ
**Tel:** 01224-871086
**Web:** www.schoolhillengineering.com
**Reg No:** 0077775SC **VAT No:** 268063741
**Estd:** 1982 Private Limited Company
**Line of Business:** Engineering consultative and design activities
**Export Markets:** France, Spain and Trinidad
**Issued Capital:** £50,000
**Principals:** R N Whyte *(Managing)*, Mrs J Whyte
**US SIC:** 3999, 3559
**UK SIC:** 49590, 32863
**Bankers:** Clydesdale Bank Plc (82-69-27)

| | 31-10-13 | 31-10-12 | 31-10-11 |
|---|---|---|---|
| TA | 1,900,366 | 1,529,407 | 1,172,764 |
| NW | 654,385 | 620,837 | 661,079 |
| WC | 428,901 | 349,014 | 395,081 |

DUNS 73-262-5632

## Schoolhouse Daycare Ltd

45 De Lane Beche Road, Sketty, Swansea, West Glamorgan SA2 9EA
**Tel:** 01792202900
**Web:** www.schoolhouse-daycare.co.uk
**Reg No:** 4536396 **Estd:** 1996 Private Limited Company
**Line of Business:** Pre school education
**Issued Capital:** £100
**Director:** Ms A J Bennett
**Responsibilities**
**Senior:** Annie Kettley *(Manager)*
**US SIC:** 8211 **UK SIC:** 93200

| | 31-12-13 | 31-12-12 | 31-12-11 |
|---|---|---|---|
| TA | 350,817 | 345,141 | 394,573 |
| NW | (35,574) | (115,799) | (135,840) |
| WC | (75,456) | (155,251) | (179,805) |

DUNS 21-778-8290

## Schools Academy for Health

D B H House, 105 Boundary Street, Liverpool, Merseyside L5 9YJ
**Tel:** 01514825678
**Web:** www.skillsacademyforhealth.org.uk
**Estd:** 2011 Proprietorship
**Line of Business:** Training providers
**Proprietor:** Mrs J Mcgregor
**Responsibilities**
**Senior:** Judith McGregor *(Proprietor)*
**US SIC:** 8299 **UK SIC:** 93300
**Employees:** 50

DUNS 22-676-3035

## The Schools of King Edward the Sixth in Birmingham

Edgbaston Park Road, Birmingham, Birmingham, West Midlands B15 2UD
**Tel:** 01215544036
**Web:** www.kingedwardthesixth.org
**Estd:** 1650
**Line of Business:** Schools (local authority)
**Principals:** M J Price *(Chairman)*, P Burns, S G Campbell, G P Thomas, Mrs A Tonks, C W Hughes, M B Squires, Dr L K Harding
**US SIC:** 8211 **UK SIC:** 93200
**Auditors:** Baker Tilly UK Audit LLP
**Employees:** 306
**Turnover:** £19,275,919

DUNS 21-716-2906

## Schools With Schools (Kingfisher) Ltd

Foxdenton Lane, Chadderton, Oldham, Lancashire OL9 9QR
**Tel:** 01617705910
**Web:** www.schoolswithschools.co.uk
**Reg No:** 7552072 **Estd:** 2011 Private Company Limited By Guarantee
**Line of Business:** General secondary education
**Trading Style:** The Kingfisher Comunity Special School
**Directors:** Ms S Caine, K Fennelley, Ms A S Redmond, Ms D J Lucas, M Unsworth, Ms S V Pass
**Responsibilities**
**Admin:** Kath Cooper *(Office Administrator)*
**US SIC:** 8299 **UK SIC:** 93300

| | 31-03-14 | 31-03-13 | 31-03-12 |
|---|---|---|---|
| TA | 184,727 | 228,054 | 1 |
| NW | (5,385) | (1,065) | 1 |
| WC | (5,385) | (1,065) | N/A |

DUNS 76-972-0814

## Schottlander Ltd

Fifth Avenue, Letchworth, Hertfordshire SG6 2WD
**Web:** www.schottlander.com
**Reg No:** 2633400 **Estd:** 1991 Private Limited Company
**Line of Business:** Management activities of holding companies
**Issued Capital:** £11,802
**Directors:** B D Schottlander, I J Schottlander, Mrs S A Schottlander
**Co. Secretary:** Paul Peacock
**US SIC:** 6711 **UK SIC:** 83962

| | 31-12-13 | 31-12-12 | 31-12-11 |
|---|---|---|---|
| TO | 16,082,521 | 16,667,922 | N/A |
| P/L | 1,249,010 | 1,342,573 | N/A |
| NW | 8,467,107 | 7,390,994 | 2 |
| WC | 8,357,600 | 7,306,845 | N/A |
| Emp. | 54 | 54 | N/A |

DUNS 23-339-5938 **Imp-Exp**

## Schrader Electronics Ltd

(**Subsidiary of:** Sensata Technologies Holding N.V.)
11 Belfast Road Technology Park, Antrim, Co Antrim BT41 1QS
**Tel:** 028 9446 1300 **Fax:** 028 9446 8440
**Web:** www.schraderelectronics.com
**Reg No:** 0025720NI **Estd:** 1991 Private Limited Company
**Line of Business:** Manufacturers of automotive components
**Export Markets:** European Union (E U); U S A
**Issued Capital:** £2,550,000
**Director:** G M Thompson
**Co. Secretary:** Graeme Thompson
**Responsibilities**
**Marketing:** Carl Wacker *(Sales & Marketing Manager)*
**Sales:** David Caskey *(Senior Sales Executive)*, Carl Wacker *(Sales & Marketing Manager)*
**Admin:** Meg McClelland *(Receptionist)*
**IT:** Emma Proctor *(IT Manager)*
**Operations:** Paul Ritchie *(Production Manager)*, Carl Wacker *(Sales & Marketing Manager)*
**Engineering:** Elsa Degabbey *(Engineer)*
**Branches:** Schrader Electronics Ltd, 2 Meadowbank Rd, Carrickfergus, Co Antrim BT38 8YF
**US SIC:** 3714, 7399

**UK SIC:** 35300, 83954
**Auditors:** Deloitte LLP
**Bankers:** The Bank Of Ireland (90-21-27)

| | 31-12-13 | 31-12-12 | 31-12-11 |
|---|---|---|---|
| TO | 193,322,000 | 172,629,000 | 169,808,000 |
| P/L | 22,189,000 | 16,617,000 | 15,331,000 |
| NW | 46,118,000 | 35,618,000 | 28,070,000 |
| WC | 23,350,000 | 23,808,000 | 15,769,000 |
| Emp. | 1,045 | 964 | 936 |

DUNS 23-919-6673

## Schroders Plc

Garrard House, 31-45 Gresham Street, London EC2V 7QA
**Tel:** 020-7658-6000 **Fax:** 02076586965
**Web:** www.schroders.com
**Reg No:** 3909886 **Estd:** 2000 Public Limited Company
**Line of Business:** Investment companies and vehicles
**Issued Capital:** £282,528,000
**Directors:** B L Schroder, A M Almanza, Lord P E Howard, A N Beeson, R J Keers, M Tosato, P S Mallinckrodt, M W Dobson
**Co. Secretary:** Graham Staples
**Responsibilities**
**Senior:** Tom Cha *(Vice President)*, Murray Coble *(Manager)*, Lieven Debruyne *(Chief Executive Officer)*, Roger Doig *(Executive)*, Noel Fessey *(Manager)*, Shaun Levesque *(Sales Director)*, Merlyn Lowther *(Non-Executive Director and Cha)*, Tim Main *(General Manager)*, George Mallinckrodt *(President)*, Sue Noffke *(General Manager)*, Nichola Pease *(Director)*, Ross Pritchard *(Manager)*, Christopher Smiley *(Client Director)*, Maha Soueissy *(Executive)*, Massismo Tosato *(Executive Vice-Chairman and Gl)*, Matthew Whyte *(Deputy Company Secretary)*, Lucette Yvernault *(Manager)*, Azad Zangana *(Executive)*
**Finance:** Justin Bisseker *(European Banks Analyst)*, Clive Dennis *(Head of Currency)*, John Ibbotson *(Head of Finance)*, Merlyn Lowther *(Non-Executive Director and Cha)*, Nicholas Morse *(Latin America Fund Manager)*, Keith Wade *(Chief Economist)*
**Marketing:** Emma Anderson *(Global Marketing Liaison Execu)*, Charlotte Banks *(Intermediary PR)*, James Cardew *(Global Head Of Marketing)*, Grace Ho *(Marketing Director)*, Sasha Miller *(Market Analysis & Strategy Man)*, Giles Neville *(Head of Charities)*, Beth Saint *(International PR)*, Kathryn Sutton *(International PR)*
**Sales:** Claire Glennon *(UK Institutional Business Deve)*, Shaun Levesque *(Sales Director)*, Jacqueline Loh *(Head of Trading)*, Miles O' Connor *(Head of UK Institutional Busin)*, John Troiano *(Deputy Head of Distribution &)*, Hilary Vince *(Contribution Strategy Manager)*
**Admin:** Christopher Biggs *(Administrator)*, Sophie Djura *(Personal Assistant)*, Donna Douglas *(Administrator)*, Helen Fitzgerald *(Administrator)*, Mary Wang *(Secretary)*, Diana Weyden *(Personal Assistant)*, Lara Zunino *(Personal Assistant for CEO / M)*
**Facilities:** Christopher Biggs *(Administrator)*
**Operations:** Tom Dorey *(Product Manager)*, Manu George *(Product Manager)*, Matthew Michael *(Product Manager)*, Rupert Rucker *(Head of Product Asia)*, Lilian Tham *(Chief Operating Officer)*, Massismo Tosato *(Executive Vice-Chairman and Gl)*, Paul Truscott *(Product Development Director)*, Stephanie Whitford *(Head of Derivative Operations)*, Christopher Wyke *(Product Manager)*
**US SIC:** 6711 **UK SIC:** 83962
**Auditors:** PricewaterhouseCoopers LLP
**Following financial data are in thousands**

| | 31-12-13 | 31-12-12 | 31-12-11 |
|---|---|---|---|
| TO | 1,838,700 | 1,464,600 | 1,501,900 |
| P/L | 447,500 | 360,000 | 407,300 |
| NW | 1,779,600 | 1,927,800 | 1,757,500 |
| WC | 1,513,100 | 956,700 | (84,200) |
| Emp. | 3,304 | 2,969 | 2,848 |

DUNS 21-624-9181 Imp

## Schueco Uk Ltd

**(Subsidiary of:** Otto Fuchs - Kg -)
Whitehall Avenue, Kingston, Milton Keynes, Buckinghamshire MK10 0AL
**Tel:** 01908282111 **Fax:** 01908282124
**Web:** www.schueco.co.uk
**Reg No:** 7048715 **Estd:** 2009 Private Limited Company
**Line of Business:** Manufacturers of window frames
**Issued Capital:** £10,000,000
**Directors:** M J Lane, T S Humpf, A Engelhardt
**Co. Secretary:** David Dees
**Responsibilities**
**Senior:** Dirk Hindrichs *(Manager)*, Nico Reiner *(Manager)*, Marc Von Briel *(Manager)*
**Finance:** Stuart Gosling *(Financial Controller)*
**HR:** Dawn Kneasfey *(Human Resources Director)*
**US SIC:** 3442, 5051
**UK SIC:** 31420, 61200
**Auditors:** PricewaterhouseCoopers LLP
**Bankers:** Deutsche Bank Ag (40-48-28)

| | 31-12-13 | 31-12-12 | 31-12-11 |
|---|---|---|---|
| TO | 50,470,000 | 56,856,000 | 105,051,000 |
| P/L | 8,955,000 | 3,483,000 | 12,251,000 |
| NW | 22,305,000 | 19,093,000 | 24,875,000 |
| WC | 17,171,000 | 14,454,000 | 18,861,000 |
| Emp. | 127 | 147 | 151 |

DUNS 50-555-5912 Imp

## Schuh Ltd

**(Subsidiary of:** Genesco Inc.)
1 Neilson Square, Livingston, West Lothian EH54 8RQ
**Tel:** 01506460250 **Fax:** 01506460251
**Web:** www.schuhstore.co.uk
**Reg No:** 0125327SC **VAT No:** 553611358
**Estd:** 1981 Private Limited Company
**Line of Business:** Representative office
**Export Sales:** £18,644,000
**Issued Capital:** £206,492
**Directors:** R Dennis, J Estepa, J S Gulmi, C Temple, D Spencer, K Ball
**Co. Secretary:** Mark Crutchley
**Responsibilities**
**IT:** Scott Curran *(Internet Development Team Lead)*
**Branches:** Schuh Ltd, Schuh, 113 Queen Street, Cardiff, South Glamorgan CF10 2BH
**US SIC:** 5661 **UK SIC:** 64600
**Auditors:** KPMG LLP
**Bankers:** Lloyds Tsb Scotland Plc (87-70-01)

| | 01-02-14 | 02-02-13 | 28-02-12 |
|---|---|---|---|
| TO | 229,969,000 | 232,986,000 | 168,665,000 |
| P/L | 12,089,000 | 25,634,000 | (140,000) |
| NW | 77,757,000 | 77,358,000 | 57,015,000 |
| WC | 73,457,000 | 58,891,000 | 41,947,000 |
| Emp. | 1,816 | 1,721 | 1,461 |

DUNS 21-731-2297 Imp

## Schunk U.K. Ltd

**(Subsidiary of:** Ludwig Schunk-Stiftung E.V.)
Europa Works, Richardshaw Drive, Pudsey, West Yorkshire LS28 6QR
**Tel:** 01132-567238
**Web:** www.schunk-carbon.co.uk
**Reg No:** 0737825 **VAT No:** 239527049
**Estd:** 1962 Private Limited Company
**Line of Business:** Manufacture of tools
**Issued Capital:** £250,000
**Director:** N A Harvey
**Responsibilities**
**Senior:** Steven Benn *(Storeman)*, Heinz Maeurer *(Manager)*, Robert Rack *(Manager)*, Wilfried Seidt *(Manager)*
**Operations:** Bob Milne *(Product Manager)*
**US SIC:** 3999, 5199
**UK SIC:** 49590, 61900
**Auditors:** Clough & Co LLP
**Bankers:** Lloyds TSB Bank plc (30-91-12)

| | 31-12-13 | 31-12-12 | 31-12-11 |
|---|---|---|---|
| TA | 1,993,083 | 1,887,929 | 1,689,311 |
| NW | 1,399,208 | 1,383,173 | 1,302,728 |
| WC | 982,439 | 1,039,504 | 939,780 |

DUNS 50-322-8827 Imp

## Schutz (U.K.) Ltd

**(Subsidiary of:** Schütz Verwaltungs Gmbh)
Claylands Avenue, Worksop, Nottinghamshire S81 7BE
**Tel:** 01909478863
**Web:** www.schuetz.net
**Reg No:** 2347670 **VAT No:** 646306049
**Estd:** 2011 Private Limited Company
**Line of Business:** Plastic injection moulding
**Export Sales:** £1,489,000
**Issued Capital:** £1,000,000
**Directors:** V Enders, R Strassburger, Dr J C Meier
**Co. Secretary:** Martin Colley
**US SIC:** 3079 **UK SIC:** 48360
**Auditors:** Deloitte & Touche LLP
**Bankers:** Barclays Bank Plc (20-55-62)

| | 31-12-13 | 31-12-12 | 31-12-11 |
|---|---|---|---|
| TO | 51,835,000 | 50,564,000 | 48,654,000 |
| P/L | 5,817,000 | 2,618,000 | 3,486,000 |
| NW | 28,684,000 | 25,972,000 | 26,043,000 |
| WC | 17,725,000 | 13,413,000 | 12,237,000 |
| Emp. | 118 | 122 | 120 |

DUNS 42-435-1203

## Sci-Fi Channel Europe L.L.C.

**(Subsidiary of:** Comcast Corporation)
Universal Networks International, 1 Central Saint Giles, St Giles High Street, London WC2H 8NU
**Tel:** 02036188000
**Web:** www.syfy.co.uk
**Reg No:** 0019016FC **VAT No:** 662537916
**Estd:** 1996 Foreign Company
**Line of Business:** Television activities
**Trading Style:** Syfy
**Directors:** O Canning, J D Burnett, Ms D E Klein, G Matson, M G Heaton Cooper, S S Brainch, Ms R R Khanna, C R Mcleod
**Co. Secretary:** Ms Gabriela Kornzweig
**Responsibilities**
**Senior:** Nicola Douglas *(Director)*
**US SIC:** 4833 **UK SIC:** 97411

DUNS 21-330-1377

## Sciama Family Trustees Ltd

Moss Rose Mill, Springfield Road, Kearsley, Bolton, Lancashire BL4 8JW
**Tel:** 01204-571686 **Fax:** 01204861447
**Web:** www.john-holden.com
**Reg No:** 0874207 **Estd:** 1966 Private Limited Company
**Line of Business:** Lamination services
**Trading Style:** John Holden & Son (Kearsley), John Holden
**Issued Capital:** £20,000
**Principals:** A M Sciama *(Managing)*, M E Sciama *(Financial)*, R N Sciama, F Simons
**Co. Secretary:** Andrew Sciama
**US SIC:** 3079 **UK SIC:** 48360
**Auditors:** Waterworths

| | 31-03-14 | 31-03-13 | 31-03-12 |
|---|---|---|---|
| TA | 85 | 85 | 85 |
| NW | 85 | 85 | 85 |

DUNS 21-746-2063

## Science and Technology Facilities Council

Rutherford Appleton Laboratory, Didcot, Oxfordshire OX11 0QX
**Web:** www.scitech.ac.uk
**VAT No:** 618367325 **Estd:** 2010
**Line of Business:** Research and laboratory based activities
**Trading Style:** Stfc
**Principals:** Ms P Foster *(Financial)*, J Womersley, Dr A Taylor, Dr S Cosgrove, Dr T Bestwick, G Blair, G Stewart, Mrs S Bonfield
**Responsibilities**
**Senior:** Colin Whitehouse *(Assistant Chief Executive Offi)*
**Sales:** Linda Baines *(Head of Commercial Development)*
**US SIC:** 7391 **UK SIC:** 94000
**Employees:** 1,800

DUNS 50-146-7781

## Science Engineering & Manufacturing Technologies Alliance

Unit 2 Greycaine Road, Watford, Hertfordshire WD24 7GP
**Tel:** 01923-238441 **Fax:** 01923-652401
**Web:** www.semta.org.uk
**Reg No:** 2324869 **VAT No:** 579154406
**Estd:** 1991 Private Company Limited By Guarantee
**Line of Business:** Production engineers
**Trading Style:** S E M T A
**Directors:** A J Connelly, J M Hillier, T C Scuoler, I Gray, I M Mukerjee, S Ball, I Waddell, J Greenwell
**Co. Secretary:** Stephen Ball
**Responsibilities**
**Senior:** Graham Althorpe *(Manager)*, Dolores Byrne *(Manager)*, Margaret Gildea *(Manager)*, Lynn Minella *(Director)*
**Finance:** Barry Finnan *(Financial Director)*
**Branches:** Science Engineering & Manufacturing Technologies Alliance, 22 Old Queen St, London SW1H 9HP
**US SIC:** 8911 **UK SIC:** 83701
**Auditors:** Haysmacintyre
**Bankers:** Barclays Bank Plc (20-91-79)

| | 31-03-14 | 31-03-13 | 31-03-12 |
|---|---|---|---|
| TO | 16,854,000 | 18,056,000 | 14,763,000 |
| P/L | 1,875,000 | 1,611,000 | (227,000) |
| NW | 30,488,000 | 28,731,000 | 26,455,000 |
| WC | (907,000) | (1,490,000) | (1,737,000) |
| Emp. | 170 | 172 | 161 |

DUNS 22-985-0722 Imp

## The Science Museum

Exhibition Road, South Kensington, London SW7 2DD
**Tel:** 02079424000
**Web:** www.sciencemuseum.org.uk
**VAT No:** 503511496 **Estd:** 1883 Incorporate By Act Of Parliament
**Line of Business:** Museum activities
**Trading Style:** The National Media Museum, The National Railway Museum, Locomotion: the National Railway Museum At Shildon, The Science Museum At Wroughton
**Principals:** Dr D Gurr *(Chairman)*, Lord . Grade Of Yarmouth, J Smith, Ms L Jordanova, Lady . Chisholm, Sir H Newby, C Swinson, Ms A Macdonald
**Responsibilities**
**Senior:** Ian Blatchford *(Manager)*, Adele Mcallister *(Personnel Manager)*
**Marketing:** Andrea Dearden *(Senior Marketing Executive)*, Julia Murray *(Senior Press Officer)*, Laura Singleton *(Press Officer)*, William Stanley *(Press Officer)*
**Admin:** Mary Witton *(PA to Managing Director)*
**HR:** Adele Mcallister *(Personnel Manager)*
**Health & Safety:** Alex McClerie *(Health & Safety Officer)*
**Facilities:** John Bevin *(Head of Estates)*
**Operations:** Jonathan Newby *(Chief Operating Officer)*
**Branches:** National Museum Of Science & Industry, Science Museum, Exhibition Road, London SW7 2DD
**US SIC:** 8411, 5961
**UK SIC:** 97700, 65600
**Auditors:** Amyas C E Morse
**Bankers:** Barclays Bank Plc (20-80-14)

| | 31-03-14 | 31-03-11 |
|---|---|---|
| TO | 79,285,000 | 63,354,000 |
| P/L | (1,191,000) | (5,265,000) |
| NW | 387,254,000 | 278,854,000 |
| WC | 7,201,000 | 15,757,000 |
| Emp. | 795 | 899 |

DUNS 39-745-6369 Imp

## Science Projects

14 Colville Road, London W3 8BL
**Tel:** 020-8741-2305
**Web:** www.science-projects.org
**Reg No:** 2186073 **Estd:** 1987 Private Company Limited By Guarantee
**Line of Business:** Other adult and other education not elsewhere classified
**Trading Style:** Science Projects
**Principals:** S Pizzey *(Managing)*, Ms J C Allen, Ms A E Derbyshire, R B Scholefield
**Co. Secretary:** Richard Allsop
**Responsibilities**
**Senior:** Tim Holdsworth *(Production Manager)*
**Finance:** Sue Farrer *(Accountant)*
**Branches:** Science Projects, St Michael's Church, Coslany St, Norwich, Norfolk NR3 3DT
**US SIC:** 3999, 8299
**UK SIC:** 49590, 93300
**Auditors:** Grant Thornton
**Bankers:** Barclays Bank Plc (20-35-90)

| | 31-12-13 | 31-12-12 | 31-12-11 |
|---|---|---|---|
| TO | 1,666,986 | 1,753,938 | 2,006,669 |
| P/L | 78,268 | 72,142 | 277,890 |
| NW | 1,393,178 | 1,314,910 | 1,242,768 |
| WC | 1,191,318 | 1,233,890 | 1,133,465 |
| Emp. | 50 | 48 | 44 |

DUNS 77-104-3775

## Science Recruitment Group Ltd

**(Subsidiary of:** Impellam Group Plc)
800 Capability Green, Luton, Bedfordshire LU1 3BA
**Tel:** 01582692699
**Web:** www.srg.co.uk
**Reg No:** 2681320 **Estd:** 1992 Private Limited Company
**Line of Business:** Employment and recruitment companies and consultants
**Export Sales:** £2,529,000
**Trading Style:** S R G
**Issued Capital:** £100
**Directors:** Ms J Robertson, Ms R J Watson
**Co. Secretary:** Ms Rebecca Watson
**Responsibilities**
**Senior:** Andrew Burchall *(Manager)*, Danni Cassar *(Manager)*
**Branches:** Science Recruitment Group Ltd, Regents Park House, Regent Street, Leeds, West Yorkshire LS2 7QN
**US SIC:** 7361 **UK SIC:** 83954
**Auditors:** PricewaterhouseCoopers LLP
**Bankers:** Barclays Bank Plc (20-78-58)

| | 27-12-13 | 28-12-12 | 30-12-11 |
|---|---|---|---|
| TO | 66,854,000 | 15,592,000 | N/A |
| P/L | 4,687,000 | 662,000 | N/A |
| NW | 5,638,000 | 2,040,000 | 1,552,363 |
| WC | 5,534,000 | 1,882,000 | N/A |
| Emp. | 113 | 29 | N/A |

DUNS 21-117-8712

## Scientia Resource Management Ltd

C P C 1, Capital Park, Fulbourn, Cambridge, Cambridgeshire CB21 5XE
**Tel:** 01223884949
**Web:** www.scientia.com
**Reg No:** 6576048 **Estd:** 1989 Private Limited Company
**Line of Business:** Computer software (development)
**Export Sales:** £8,588,521
**Issued Capital:** £102,092
**Directors:** Ms Y Laird, Baron S C Bentinck, Dr G A Forster
**Co. Secretary:** Peter Loomes
**US SIC:** 7379 **UK SIC:** 83940
**Bankers:** Barclays Bank Plc (20-17-19)

| | 31-12-13 | 31-12-12 | 31-12-11 |
|---|---|---|---|
| TO | 12,770,424 | 12,123,681 | 11,222,038 |
| P/L | 2,087,726 | 2,417,270 | 1,501,944 |
| NW | (1,383,096) | (2,231,249) | (2,219,085) |
| WC | (1,567,206) | (2,435,425) | (2,365,638) |
| Emp. | 95 | 87 | 91 |

**DUNS 57-829-5834**    Imp
## Scientific Analysis Instruments Ltd
**(Subsidiary of:** Hallco 479 Ltd)
Hadfield House, 9 Hadfield Street, Manchester M16 9FE
**Tel:** 0161 874 2460 **Fax:** 0161 874 2461
**Web:** www.saiman.co.uk
**Reg No:** 2887821 **Estd:** 1994 Private Limited Company
**Line of Business:** Manufacture of other electrical equipment not elsewhere classified
**Trading Style:** S A I, S A L
**Issued Capital:** £2
**Directors:** D Blyth, V C Parr
**Co. Secretary:** Karl Moss
**US SIC:** 3629 **UK SIC:** 34350
**Auditors:** RSM Tenon Ltd

| | 31-12-13 | 31-12-12 | 31-12-11 |
|---|---|---|---|
| TA | 2,610,148 | 1,553,411 | 1,405,838 |
| NW | (181,404) | (289,291) | (635,992) |
| WC | (278,751) | 733,452 | 868,860 |

**DUNS 23-273-4830**    Imp
## Scientific Analysis Laboratories Ltd
**(Subsidiary of:** Concept Life Sciences Ltd)
Hadfield House, Manchester M16 9FE
**Tel:** 0161-874-2400 **Fax:** 01618271414
**Web:** www.salltd.co.uk
**Reg No:** 2514788 **VAT No:** 560870632
**Estd:** 1990 Private Limited Company
**Line of Business:** Other engineering activities
**Export Sales:** £754,297
**Trading Style:** S A L
**Issued Capital:** £42,837
**Directors:** K A Moss, D Wood, A S Morgan, P Mccluskey
**Co. Secretary:** Paul Mccluskey
**Responsibilities**
**Senior:** Jayne Blyth (Manager), Christina Wood (Manager)
**Finance:** Ruth Cowley (Financial Manager)
**Sales:** Ruth Cowley (Financial Manager), Chris Roper (Sales Manager)
**Fleet:** Ruth Cowley (Financial Manager), Rick Shaw (Transport Manager)
**Branches:** Scientific Analysis Laboratories Ltd, 25-27 Langlands Place, Kelvin South Business Park, Glasgow, Lanarkshire G75 0YF
**US SIC:** 8911, 7399
**UK SIC:** 83701, 83954
**Auditors:** RSM Tenon Audit Ltd
**Bankers:** National Westminster Bank Plc (01-09-17)

| | 31-12-13 | 31-12-12 | 31-12-11 |
|---|---|---|---|
| TO | 11,187,008 | 10,292,450 | 10,082,282 |
| P/L | 1,047,148 | 597,872 | 1,630,746 |
| NW | 1,781,143 | 1,824,859 | 1,415,394 |
| WC | (524,509) | (658,151) | (1,221,987) |
| Emp. | 208 | 203 | 184 |

**DUNS 22-680-2312**    Imp
## Scientific & Chemical Supplies Ltd
**(Subsidiary of:** Scichem Uk Ltd)
Carlton House, Livingstone Road, Bilston, West Midlands WV14 0QZ
**Tel:** 01902-402402
**Web:** www.scichem.co.uk
**Reg No:** 0588778 **VAT No:** 277053156
**Estd:** 1957 Private Limited Company
**Line of Business:** Wholesale of pharmaceutical goods
**Export Sales:** £3,079,891
**Issued Capital:** £31,318
**Principals:** J R Turton (Chairman), B K Cartland (Managing), P Palser, T W Avery, G R Owen
**Co. Secretary:** Gary Owen
**Responsibilities**
**Senior:** Andy Ellett (Warehouse Manager), Bethany Harding (Manager), Phillip Palser (Operations Manager), Elaine Parkin (Purchasing Manager)
**Marketing:** Liz Allen (Marketing Manager), Sarah Bullivont (Marketing Manager)
**Sales:** S D'arcy (Sales Director)
**IT:** Phillip Palser (Operations Manager)
**HR:** R Spurrier (Purchasing Director)
**Facilities:** Andy Ellett (Warehouse Manager)
**Operations:** Phillip Palser (Operations Manager)
**Purchasing:** Elaine Parkin (Purchasing Manager)
**Branches:** Scientific & Chemical Supplies Ltd, 39 Back Sneddon Street, Paisley, Renfrewshire PA3 2DE
**US SIC:** 5199 **UK SIC:** 61900
**Auditors:** Bloomer Heaven Ltd

| | 31-12-13 | 31-12-12 | 31-12-11 |
|---|---|---|---|
| TO | 15,515,823 | 16,654,981 | 16,756,542 |
| P/L | 141,170 | 167,428 | 302,409 |
| NW | 727,410 | 698,911 | 660,717 |
| WC | (136,797) | 32,634 | (272,948) |
| Emp. | 100 | 103 | 112 |

**DUNS 29-621-7367**    Imp
## Scientific Drilling Controls Ltd
**(Subsidiary of:** Scientific Drilling International Inc.)
Dyce Industrial Park, Aberdeen, Aberdeenshire AB21 7GA
**Tel:** 01224724535
**Web:** www.scientificdrilling.com
**Reg No:** 1948245 **VAT No:** 268209835
**Estd:** 1985 Private Limited Company
**Line of Business:** Drilling and boring equipment
**Director:** G W Thomson
**Co. Secretary:** Michael Leahy
**Responsibilities**
**Senior:** Brett Steenwyk (Manager), Donald Steenwyk (Manager), Kedrin Steenwyk (Manager), Scott Watson (Manager)
**Branches:** Scientific Drilling Controls Limited, Unit 1, Bessemer Wayharfreys Ind Est, Great Yarmouth, Norfolk NR31 0LX
**US SIC:** 3531, 3532
**UK SIC:** 32541, 32510
**Auditors:** Anderson Anderson & Brown LLP
**Bankers:** Clydesdale Bank Plc (82-62-22)
**Employees:** 183
**Turnover:** £59,271,272

**DUNS 42-372-2953**
## Scientific Games International Holdings Ltd
**(Subsidiary of:** Scientific Games Corporation)
3 George Mann Road, Leeds, West Yorkshire LS10 1DJ
**Tel:** 01133-855000
**Reg No:** 4359953 **Estd:** 2002 Private Limited Company
**Line of Business:** Gambling and betting activities
**Trading Style:** Ets London
**Issued Capital:** £36,755,683
**Directors:** J B Sarno, J Walsh, C Kometer, M W Scholey, J E Bunitsky
**Co. Secretary:** Terence Mcqueen
**Responsibilities**
**Senior:** Ira Raphaelson (Manager), James Trask (Manager)
**US SIC:** 7999 **UK SIC:** 97913
**Auditors:** Deloitte LLP
**Bankers:** HSBC Bank plc (40-27-15)

| | 31-12-13 | 31-12-12 | 31-12-11 |
|---|---|---|---|
| TA | 404,840,000 | 350,228,000 | 327,001,000 |
| P/L | (17,541,000) | (17,634,000) | (4,581,000) |
| NW | 46,707,000 | 64,248,000 | 81,882,000 |
| WC | (250,609,000) | (92,306,000) | (83,757,000) |

**DUNS 22-814-4184**    Imp-Exp
## Scientific Games International Ltd
**(Subsidiary of:** Scientific Games Corporation)
3 George Mann Road, Leeds, West Yorkshire LS10 1DJ
**Tel:** 01133855000 **Fax:** 01132045200
**Web:** www.scigames.co.uk
**Reg No:** 1754767 **Estd:** 1923 Private Limited Company
**Line of Business:** Printers general
**Export Markets:** Worldwide
**Export Sales:** £46,110,000
**Trading Style:** Norton & Wright, Knightway Promotions, Scientific Connections, Scientific Games
**Issued Capital:** £1,100
**Directors:** C Kometer, J E Bunitsky, J B Sarno, M W Scholey
**Co. Secretary:** Terence Mcqueen
**Responsibilities**
**Senior:** Paul Bosworth (Logistics Manager), Jeffrey Lipkin (Manager), Ira Raphaelson (Manager)
**Marketing:** Phil McGeever (IT Manager)
**IT:** Phil McGeever (IT Manager)
**HR:** Katherine Clark (HR Manager)
**Operations:** Phil McGeever (IT Manager)
**Purchasing:** Paul Bosworth (Logistics Manager)
**Fleet:** Paul Bosworth (Logistics Manager)
**Branches:** Scientific Games International Ltd, Unit 2, Phoenix Way, Bradford, West Yorkshire BD4 8JP
**US SIC:** 2752 **UK SIC:** 47544
**Auditors:** Deloitte LLP
**Bankers:** First Union National Bank (40-51-33)

| | 31-12-13 | 31-12-12 | 31-12-11 |
|---|---|---|---|
| TO | 63,813,000 | 58,550,000 | 51,271,000 |
| P/L | 26,450,000 | 23,045,000 | 17,412,000 |
| NW | 139,819,000 | 113,641,000 | 89,480,000 |
| WC | 33,103,000 | 63,531,000 | 53,044,000 |
| Emp. | 252 | 266 | 266 |

**DUNS 76-905-2788**    Exp
## Scientific Laboratory Supplies Ltd
**(Subsidiary of:** Sls Group Ltd)
Unit 14, Orchard House, The Square, Hessle, North Humberside HU13 0AE
**Tel:** 01482-649665 **Fax:** 01482-649667
**Web:** www.scientificlabs.co.uk
**Reg No:** 2577009 **VAT No:** 572692021
**Estd:** 1992 Private Limited Company
**Line of Business:** Manufacturers of scientific machinery and instrument
**Export Markets:** Middle East, Far East, Africa
**Trading Style:** A R Horwell, S L S
**Issued Capital:** £400,000
**Principals:** R P Chapman (Chairman and Managing), J J Chapman, P R Dunning, P J Lister, I A Roulstone, A W Monkman
**Co. Secretary:** Anthony Cherry
**Branches:** Scientific Laboratory Supplies Ltd, 28 Greenheys Business Centre, Pencroft Way, Manchester M15 6JJ
**US SIC:** 3829 **UK SIC:** 37100
**Auditors:** Sadofskys
**Bankers:** Barclays Bank Plc (20-43-47)

| | 30-04-14 | 30-04-13 | 30-04-12 |
|---|---|---|---|
| TO | 36,044,575 | 31,327,934 | 26,446,913 |
| P/L | 1,336,444 | 666,942 | 377,754 |
| NW | 2,823,557 | 1,916,253 | 1,521,675 |
| WC | 2,161,695 | 1,350,840 | 1,113,131 |
| Emp. | 147 | 130 | 114 |

**DUNS 36-517-0810**    Imp
## Scientifica Ltd
**(Subsidiary of:** Judges Scientific Plc)
Kingfisher Court, Uckfield, East Sussex TN22 1QQ
**Tel:** 01825-749933 **Fax:** 01825-749934
**Web:** www.scientifica.uk.com
**Reg No:** 3286415 **Estd:** 2010 Private Limited Company
**Line of Business:** Manufacturers of scientific machinery and instrument
**Export Sales:** £3,084,117
**Issued Capital:** £1,000
**Directors:** M Kemp, M Johnson, D Barnbrook, D E Cicurel, R L Cohen
**Co. Secretary:** Ralph Cohen
**Responsibilities**
**Senior:** Marck Johnson (Joint Managing Director), David Rogerson (Joint Managing Director)
**Finance:** Marck Johnson (Joint Managing Director)
**Branches:** Scientifica Ltd, Unit 8, Woodlands Park Avenue, Maidenhead, Berkshire SL6 3UA
**US SIC:** 3829 **UK SIC:** 37100
**Bankers:** National Westminster Bank Plc (60-22-05)

| | 31-12-13 | 25-06-13 | 31-12-12 |
|---|---|---|---|
| TO | 5,055,929 | 11,286,305 | N/A |
| P/L | 777,862 | 2,522,015 | N/A |
| NW | 4,244,525 | 3,634,379 | 1,450,047 |
| WC | 4,084,397 | 3,465,595 | 1,300,266 |
| Emp. | 66 | 51 | N/A |

**DUNS 28-906-0931**
## Scimitar Care Hotels Plc
The Lodge, Coopers Lane Road, Potters Bar, Hertfordshire EN6 4AD
**Tel:** 01707665515
**Web:** www.scimitarcare.co.uk
**Reg No:** 1383875 **Estd:** 1978 Public Limited Company
**Line of Business:** Other tourist or short-stay accommodation
**Issued Capital:** £729,019
**Principals:** M P Gerrard (Chairman and Managing), P D Sargeant, L M Sargeant
**Co. Secretary:** Mrs Valerie Gerrard
**Responsibilities**
**Senior:** Julie Ball (Manager), Valerie Sargeant (Manager)
**Branches:** Scimitar Care Hotels Plc, 35-49 Bullsmoor Lane, Enfield, Middlesex EN3 6TE
**US SIC:** 7399 **UK SIC:** 83954
**Auditors:** Bennett Nash Woolf
**Bankers:** National Westminster Bank Plc (51-61-34)

| | 31-10-14 | 31-10-13 | 31-10-12 |
|---|---|---|---|
| TO | 9,539,968 | 8,319,630 | 7,919,432 |
| P/L | 1,736,389 | 1,431,161 | 1,661,867 |
| NW | 28,852,918 | 27,423,948 | 22,635,724 |
| WC | 249,773 | 172,825 | (1,967,970) |
| Emp. | 319 | 286 | 269 |

**DUNS 22-878-8642**
## Scintilla Links Ltd
Coopers Building, Church Street, Liverpool, Merseyside L1 3AA
**Tel:** 01517093173
**Web:** www.linktranslation.co.uk
**Reg No:** 1887742 **Estd:** 1985 Private Limited Company
**Line of Business:** Other business activities not elsewhere classified
**Issued Capital:** £1,300

**Directors:** D A Gill, R Bartle, Ms G H Smaggasgale, Dr J M Potter, Ms J C Freeman, Dr T L Brand
**Co. Secretary:** Nicholas Manley
**Responsibilities**
**Senior:** Robert Ackroyd (Director)
**US SIC:** 7399 **UK SIC:** 83954

| | 31-07-13 | 31-07-12 | 31-07-11 |
|---|---|---|---|
| TA | 36,155 | 38,422 | 10,957 |
| NW | 31,545 | 2,924 | 2,952 |
| WC | 31,542 | 2,921 | 2,949 |

**DUNS 73-705-4168**
## Scio Healthcare Ltd
26 Arthurs Hill, Shanklin, Isle of Wight PO37 6EX
**Tel:** 01983-862934
**Web:** www.sciohealthcare.co.uk
**Reg No:** 4964072 **Estd:** 2003 Private Limited Company
**Line of Business:** Healthcare companies
**Trading Style:** Scio Healthcare Ltd
**Issued Capital:** £50,002
**Directors:** Ms S Dannatt, Ms P Flux, T J Flux, M J Flux
**Co. Secretary:** Kevin Dannatt
**US SIC:** 8091 **UK SIC:** 95200
**Auditors:** Bayliss Ware Ltd

| | 31-03-14 | 31-03-13 | 31-03-12 |
|---|---|---|---|
| TO | 5,181,808 | 4,784,803 | 4,502,071 |
| P/L | 708,735 | 191,708 | (46,260) |
| NW | (674,329) | (1,238,185) | (1,411,863) |
| WC | (305,832) | (9,580,026) | (9,811,980) |
| Emp. | 229 | 228 | 231 |

**DUNS 21-779-9672**
## Scissett Middle School
Wakefield Road, Scissett, Huddersfield, West Yorkshire HD8 9JX
**Tel:** 01484222930
**Web:** www.scissettmiddleschool.org.uk
**Estd:** 1954 Proprietorship
**Line of Business:** Schools (local authority)
**Proprietor:** Mrs H Baxter
**Responsibilities**
**IT:** James Ambler (IT Manager)
**US SIC:** 8211 **UK SIC:** 93200
**Employees:** 50

**DUNS 42-353-3764**
## Scitech Engineering Ltd
Connaught House, Portsmouth Road, Send, Woking, Surrey GU23 7JY
**Web:** www.scitecheng.com
**Reg No:** 4341006 **VAT No:** 786877054
**Estd:** 2001 Private Limited Company
**Line of Business:** Design consultants
**Export Sales:** £3,912,780
**Issued Capital:** £241,758
**Directors:** R A Frankland, D F Jackson, C K Parks, D I Grant, N A Thompson
**Co. Secretary:** Neil Thompson
**Responsibilities**
**Sales:** Andy Twyford (Commercial director)
**US SIC:** 8911, 7399
**UK SIC:** 83701, 83954
**Auditors:** Alliotts

| | 31-12-13 | 31-12-12 | 31-12-11 |
|---|---|---|---|
| TO | 21,042,002 | 20,184,698 | 9,130,468 |
| P/L | 337,741 | 637,762 | 385,616 |
| NW | 1,472,078 | 1,518,291 | 1,606,694 |
| WC | 1,430,169 | 1,492,273 | 1,587,570 |
| Emp. | 50 | 48 | 45 |

**DUNS 22-147-3627**
## Scj Eurafne Ltd
**(Subsidiary of:** S. C. Johnson & Son Inc.)
Frimley Green Road, Frimley Green, Camberley, Surrey GU16 7AJ
**Tel:** 01276852000 **Fax:** 01276852660
**Web:** www.scjohnson.co.uk
**Reg No:** 4166158 **Estd:** 2001 Private Limited Company
**Line of Business:** Manufacture of cleaning and polishing preparations
**Export Sales:** £14,647,000
**Trading Style:** Sc Johnson
**Issued Capital:** £25,369,332
**Directors:** M J Worden, T P Howard
**Co. Secretary:** John Hayes
**Responsibilities**
**Senior:** Bradley Goodwin (Manager)
**Branches:** Scj Eurafne Ltd, Milton Park, Stroude Road, Egham, Surrey TW20 9UH
**US SIC:** 2842 **UK SIC:** 25990
**Auditors:** Ernst & Young LLP

| | 28-06-13 | 29-06-12 | 01-06-11 |
|---|---|---|---|
| TO | 15,479,000 | 31,431,000 | 21,071,000 |
| P/L | (415,000) | 1,236,000 | (8,741,000) |
| NW | 37,561,000 | 36,984,000 | 35,621,000 |
| WC | 36,466,000 | 35,343,000 | 34,224,000 |
| Emp. | 128 | 321 | 362 |

**DUNS 21-585-0818**
## Scm Canterbury Press
3rd Floor Invicta House, London EC1Y 0TG
**Tel:** 02077767540
**Web:** www.churchtimes.co.uk
**Estd:** 2011 Proprietorship

**Line of Business:** Advertising publications & publishers
**Proprietor:** D Vaughan
**Responsibilities**
**Senior:** Sue Stapleford *(Group Finance Director)*
**Finance:** Sue Stapleford *(Group Finance Director)*
**Marketing:** Michael Addison *(Sales and Marketing Director)*, Josie Gunn *(Sales and Marketing Controller)*, Mary Matthews *(Editorial Manager)*
**Sales:** Michael Addison *(Sales and Marketing Director)*, Josie Gunn *(Sales and Marketing Controller)*, Aude Pasquier *(Key Account Manager)*
**US SIC:** 7319 **UK SIC:** 83800
**Employees:** 75

DUNS 21-408-1374
## ScO13284 Ltd
**(Subsidiary of:** Cie Gen Des Ets Michelin)
Vantage Point, 20 Upper Portland Street, Birmingham, West Midlands B6 5TW
**Web:** www.atseuromaster.co.uk
**Reg No:** 0013284SC **VAT No:** 259690611
**Estd:** 1961 Private Limited Company
**Line of Business:** Car accessories and parts
**Trading Style:** A T S Euromaster
**Issued Capital:** £1
**Directors:** Mrs R Mcmullen, M Tomlinson
**Co. Secretary:** Mark Tomlinson
**Responsibilities**
**Senior:** Peter Allan *(Manager)*
**Branches:** SCO13284 Ltd, Bonnington Rd, Edinburgh, Midlothian EH6 5JD
**US SIC:** 5531 **UK SIC:** 65100
**Auditors:** Deloitte LLP
**Bankers:** The Royal Bank Of Scotland Plc (83-07-06)

| | 31-12-11 |
|---|---|
| TO | 118,000 |
| P/L | 180,000 |
| NW | 3,689,000 |

DUNS 21-562-1459 Imp-Exp
## Scobie & Junor (Holdings) Ltd
1 Singer Road, East Kilbride, Glasgow, Lanarkshire G75 0XS
**Tel:** 01355576308 **Fax:** 01355-263585
**Web:** www.scobie-junor.co.uk
**Reg No:** 0047779SC **Estd:** 1970 Private Limited Company
**Line of Business:** Holding companies management activities
**Export Sales:** £6,114,359
**Issued Capital:** £28,000
**Principals:** W T Wicklow *(Managing)*, G T Wicklow, A J Wicklow
**Co. Secretary:** Maclay Murray & Spens Llp
**Responsibilities**
**Senior:** Vicky Mc Clain *(Human Resources Manager)*
**US SIC:** 6711, 5084
**UK SIC:** 83962, 61490
**Auditors:** Henderson Loggie Sinclair Wood
**Bankers:** The Royal Bank Of Scotland Plc (83-28-13)

| | 30-06-13 | 30-06-12 | 30-06-11 |
|---|---|---|---|
| TO | 27,304,676 | 25,036,514 | 20,854,409 |
| P/L | 795,133 | 1,731,128 | 354,391 |
| NW | 2,877,765 | 2,315,007 | 1,429,466 |
| WC | 3,726,370 | 3,512,406 | 3,252,128 |
| Emp. | 127 | 118 | 94 |

DUNS 21-406-1285 Imp-Exp
## Scobie & McIntosh Ltd
1 Broomhills, Steading, 45 Frogston Road East, Edinburgh, Midlothian EH17 8RT
**Tel:** 02086147770
**Web:** www.scobie-equipment.com
**Reg No:** 0012259SC **VAT No:** 380094752
**Estd:** 2012 Private Limited Company
**Line of Business:** Confectioners (retail)
**Export Markets:** Belarus
**Export Sales:** £20,000
**Issued Capital:** £18,060
**Principals:** G P Alderson *(Chairman and Managing)*, A B Alderson, Ms P A Alderson
**Co. Secretary:** Christopher Barlow
**Responsibilities**
**Senior:** Timothy Alderson *(Manager)*, Duncan Macfarlane *(Manager)*
**Branches:** Scobie & Mcintosh Ltd, 46-50 Elswick Road, Newcastle Upon Tyne, Tyne and Wear NE4 6JH
**US SIC:** 5462 **UK SIC:** 64100
**Auditors:** Geoghegan & Co
**Bankers:** Bank Of Scotland (80-02-85)

| | 31-12-13 | 31-12-12 | 31-12-11 |
|---|---|---|---|
| TO | 12,680,000 | 11,214,947 | 11,945,562 |
| P/L | 457,000 | 604,482 | 970,679 |
| NW | 2,465,000 | 2,143,170 | 1,546,611 |
| WC | 2,654,000 | 2,320,125 | 1,866,616 |
| Emp. | 93 | 82 | 81 |

DUNS 50-565-2529 Imp-Exp
## Scolmore (International) Ltd
Scolmore Park, 1 Landsberg, Tamworth, Staffordshire B79 7XB
**Fax:** 0182763362
**Web:** www.scolmore.com
**Reg No:** 2513009 **VAT No:** 555096427
**Estd:** 1990 Private Limited Company
**Line of Business:** Electrical wholesalers
**Export Markets:** Worldwide
**Export Sales:** £3,944,615
**Trading Style:** Scolmore (International) Ltd
**Issued Capital:** £50,000
**Principals:** B Mordue *(Managing)*, S Taylor, I Hunter, P R Dawson, P A Bridgwater, G C Mordue
**Co. Secretary:** Jonathan Rogers
**Branches:** Scolmore (International) Ltd, 24 Erleigh Drive, Chippenham, Wiltshire SN15 2NQ
**US SIC:** 5074, 3643, 5084
**UK SIC:** 61300, 34203, 61490
**Auditors:** Harbach Tibbetts
**Bankers:** Barclays Bank Plc (20-85-13)

| | 30-04-14 | 30-04-13 | 30-04-12 |
|---|---|---|---|
| TO | 37,046,537 | 29,429,473 | 31,876,622 |
| P/L | 4,523,724 | 3,936,028 | 4,857,328 |
| NW | 15,860,181 | 14,081,254 | 12,635,039 |
| WC | 8,426,808 | 7,569,905 | 7,154,435 |
| Emp. | 105 | 100 | 89 |

DUNS 53 638 6057
## Scoonie House Ltd
Windygates Road, Leven, Fife KY8 4DP
**Tel:** 01333426735
**Web:** www.caringhomes.co.uk
**Reg No:** 0179355SC **Estd:** 1997 Private Limited Company
**Line of Business:** Non-charitable social work activities with accommodation
**Issued Capital:** £1
**Director:** J D Farkas
**Co. Secretary:** Sanne Group Secretaries (Uk) Lim
**Responsibilities**
**Senior:** Andrew Fairchild *(Manager)*, Melanie Macdonald *(Home Manager)*, Mathieu Streiff *(Director)*
**HR:** Melanie Macdonald *(Home Manager)*
**Health & Safety:** Melanie Macdonald *(Home Manager)*
**US SIC:** 8321 **UK SIC:** 96111

| | 31-03-13 | 31-12-12 |
|---|---|---|
| TO | N/A | 414,843 |
| P/L | N/A | 140,916 |
| NW | 1 | 1 |

DUNS 49-426-8360
## Scooter Store Ltd
Unit 11 Italstyle Buildings, Cambridge Road, Harlow, Essex CM20 2HE
**Tel:** 01279-453565
**Web:** www.scooterstore.co.uk
**Reg No:** 3141502 **Estd:** 1995 Private Limited Company
**Line of Business:** Manufacture of cutlery
**Issued Capital:** £100
**Principals:** S M Wass *(Managing)*, A M Wass, Ms A J Wass, Mrs D Wass
**Co. Secretary:** Ms Angela Wass
**Responsibilities**
**Facilities:** Matt Chandler *(operations manager)*
**Operations:** Matt Chandler *(operations manager)*
**Branches:** Scooter Store Ltd, 71-75 Beaconsfield Road, Brighton, East Sussex BN1 4QJ
**US SIC:** 3421 **UK SIC:** 31621
**Auditors:** Giess Wallis Crisp

| | 31-12-13 | 31-12-12 | 31-12-11 |
|---|---|---|---|
| TA | 100,085 | 85,621 | 70,054 |
| NW | 659 | 8,160 | 13,162 |
| WC | (19,951) | (9,737) | (6,645) |

DUNS 22-714-5695
## Scope
Market Road, London N7 9PW
**Tel:** 020-7619-7100
**Web:** www.scope.org.uk
**Reg No:** 0520866 **VAT No:** 805156939
**Estd:** 1952 Private Company Limited By Guarantee
**Line of Business:** Social work activities
**Trading Style:** Options With Scope (Birmingham), Plymouth Skills Development Centre
**Directors:** Ms C Atherton, Dr A J Mcdonald, Miss V E Mcdermott, Ms A M Fletcher, J M Gilbert, Ms H A Samson-Barry, Ms R T Wallach, Ms C M Thomas
**Co. Secretary:** Ms Jacqueline Penalver
**Responsibilities**
**Senior:** Rosemary Bolinger *(Trustee)*, John Corneille *(Trustee)*, Jaspal Dhani *(Trustee)*, Robert Eames *(Trustee)*, Richard Hawkes *(Chief Executive)*, Jagroop Kaur *(Director)*, Alice Maynard *(Manager)*, Gavin Poole *(Director)*, John Yeats *(Manager)*
**Marketing:** Reyna Desai *(Marketing Officer)*, Claire Whitney *(Creative Resources Manager)*
**Sales:** Andrew Adair *(Retail Director)*
**Branches:** Scope, 22 Mansfield St, Glasgow, Lanarkshire G11 5QP
**US SIC:** 7399, 8091
**UK SIC:** 83954, 95200
**Auditors:** KPMG LLP
**Bankers:** National Westminster Bank Plc (60-00-01)

| | 31-03-14 | 31-03-13 | 31-03-12 |
|---|---|---|---|
| TO | 102,635,000 | 102,961,000 | 104,288,000 |
| P/L | (660,000) | (349,000) | 1,359,000 |
| NW | 30,480,000 | 31,722,000 | 32,286,000 |
| WC | 3,964,000 | 3,622,000 | 4,080,000 |
| Emp. | 2,700 | 2,710 | 2,753 |

DUNS 21-811-9959
## Scope Sharon Colins Resource Centre
13 Albion Street, Brighton, East Sussex BN2 9NE
**Tel:** 01273695675
**Estd:** 2012
**Line of Business:** Disability services
**US SIC:** 8321 **UK SIC:** 96111
**Employees:** 60

DUNS 76-625-6549 Imp
## Scopus Engineering Ltd
**(Subsidiary of:** Amec Foster Wheeler Plc)
Howe Moss Drive, Kirkhill Industrial Estate, Dyce, Aberdeen, Aberdeenshire AB21 0GL
**Tel:** 01224-214400 **Fax:** 01224-729585
**Web:** www.scopuseng.com
**Reg No:** 0129734SC **Estd:** 1991 Private Limited Company
**Line of Business:** Engineers (general)
**Issued Capital:** £100
**Directors:** A J Johnstone, G B Sleigh, C R Fleming
**Co. Secretary:** Christopher Fidler
**Responsibilities**
**Senior:** Mike Elrick *(Manager)*, Mark Fraser *(Manager)*
**Branches:** Scopus Engineering Ltd, Baker House, Admiralty Rd, Great Yarmouth, Norfolk NR30 3PU
**US SIC:** 4469, 8911
**UK SIC:** 76300, 83701
**Auditors:** PricewaterhouseCoopers LLP
**Bankers:** Bank Of Scotland (80-05-14)

| | 30-04-14 | 30-04-13 | 30-04-12 |
|---|---|---|---|
| TO | 25,127,230 | 17,214,424 | 13,126,552 |
| P/L | 4,762,910 | 3,988,616 | 2,408,921 |
| NW | 8,052,053 | 5,365,206 | 3,397,503 |
| WC | 6,461,621 | 4,470,717 | 2,621,091 |
| Emp. | 133 | 129 | 50 |

DUNS 22-532-8202
## Scor (U.K.) Group Ltd
**(Subsidiary of:** Scor)
10 Lime Street, London EC3M 7AA
**Tel:** 02072837485 **Fax:** 020-7256-3092
**Web:** www.cheaney.co.uk
**Reg No:** 1356873 **VAT No:** 447270250
**Estd:** 1978 Private Limited Company
**Line of Business:** Insurance - other
**Issued Capital:** £32,700,000
**Directors:** V Y Peignet, B Gentsch, M C Newman, C Delannes, J A Bayfield
**Co. Secretary:** Adrian Hacking
**US SIC:** 6399 **UK SIC:** 82001
**Auditors:** Mazars LLP

| | 31-12-13 | 31-12-12 | 31-12-11 |
|---|---|---|---|
| TA | 32,851,000 | 32,851,000 | 32,876,000 |
| P/L | N/A | (3,000) | (3,000) |
| NW | 32,851,000 | 32,851,000 | 32,828,000 |
| WC | N/A | N/A | 328,000 |

DUNS 29-563-0628 Imp-Exp
## Score (Europe) Ltd
**(Subsidiary of:** Score Group Plc)
33-36 Southgates Road, Great Yarmouth, Norfolk NR30 3LL
**Tel:** 01493845760
**Web:** www.score-group.com
**Reg No:** 0094003SC **Estd:** 2011 Private Limited Company
**Line of Business:** Manufacturers of valves
**Export Markets:** Worldwide
**Export Sales:** £15,680,000
**Issued Capital:** £2,500,000
**Principals:** C B Ritchie *(Chairman and Managing)*, A Marshall, M J Billington, S B Will, J Geddes, L A Willox, C S Ritchie
**Co. Secretary:** Ms Anita Mcrobbie
**Responsibilities**
**Senior:** Kevin Macfarlane *(CEO, Managing Director)*, Ally Marshall *(Manager)*
**Finance:** Kevin Macfarlane *(CEO, Managing Director)*
**Health & Safety:** Neil Porter *(Health & Safety Officer)*
**Branches:** Score (Europe) Ltd, The Paragon Works, Woodend Place, Cowdenbeath, Fife KY4 8EE
**US SIC:** 3494, 8911
**UK SIC:** 32880, 83701
**Auditors:** KPMG LLP
**Bankers:** Clydesdale Bank Plc (82-67-12)

| | 26-09-13 | 27-09-12 | 29-09-11 |
|---|---|---|---|
| TO | 88,237,000 | 72,810,000 | 61,372,000 |
| P/L | 12,665,000 | 6,666,000 | 2,865,000 |
| NW | 16,036,000 | 15,144,000 | 10,310,000 |
| WC | 11,477,000 | 13,446,000 | 8,502,000 |
| Emp. | 876 | 796 | 746 |

DUNS 37-876-9012 Imp
## Scorpio Worldwide Ltd
**(Subsidiary of:** Heinemann Scorpio International Holdings Ltd)
International House, Unit D2, Crawley, West Sussex RH11 0PR
**Tel:** 01293-411733 **Fax:** 01293-414544
**Web:** www.scorpdis.com
**Reg No:** 3308665 **Estd:** 1997 Private Limited Company
**Line of Business:** Distribution service providers
**Issued Capital:** £1,345
**Principals:** S Mcguire *(Managing)*, R C Kennedy, Ms N K Heubel, I S Cowie
**Co. Secretary:** Ian Cowie
**Responsibilities**
**Senior:** Gunnar Heinemann *(Manager)*, Thorsten Repenning *(Manager)*, Kay Spanger *(Manager)*
**Branches:** Scorpio Worldwide Ltd, Kelvin House, Suite 3, Crawley, West Sussex RH10 9WE
**US SIC:** 4712, 5999
**UK SIC:** 77002, 65600
**Auditors:** LB Group
**Bankers:** The Royal Bank Of Scotland Plc (16-08-05)

| | 31-12-13 | 31-12-12 | 31-12-11 |
|---|---|---|---|
| TO | 34,867,402 | 31,767,337 | 29,640,222 |
| P/L | (217,747) | 703,482 | 1,543,822 |
| NW | 2,227,208 | 2,940,255 | 3,448,796 |
| WC | 2,014,551 | 2,714,385 | 3,373,989 |
| Emp. | 58 | 57 | 51 |

DUNS 34-840-4807 Imp-Exp
## Scorpion Exhausts Ltd
Unit 3 High Holborn Road, Codnor Gate Business Park, Ripley, Derbyshire DE5 3NW
**Tel:** 01773-744123 **Fax:** 01773513731
**Web:** www.scorpion-exhausts.com
**Reg No:** 2803997 **VAT No:** 593308622
**Estd:** 1993 Private Limited Company
**Line of Business:** Manufacture of parts and accessories for motor vehicles and their engines
**Export Markets:** Albania,France (including French Guyane,Switzerland ,United States of America (including Virgin Islands of the United States
**Issued Capital:** £100
**Director:** S Leonard
**Co. Secretary:** Ms Kathleen Holmes
**US SIC:** 3714 **UK SIC:** 35300
**Auditors:** Cooper Parry LLP
**Bankers:** National Westminster Bank Plc (60-10-29)

| | 31-12-13 | 31-12-12 | 31-12-11 |
|---|---|---|---|
| TA | 1,804,758 | 1,467,435 | 1,405,509 |
| NW | 547,085 | 396,998 | 261,184 |
| WC | 129,162 | 99,423 | (32,652) |

DUNS 45-824-8671
## Scorpion Ribs Ltd
Haven Quay, Mill Lane, Lymington, Hampshire SO41 9AZ
**Tel:** 01590677080
**Web:** www.scorpionribs.com
**Reg No:** 3177988 **Estd:** 2002 Private Limited Company
**Line of Business:** Building and repairing of pleasure and sporting boats
**Issued Capital:** £1,975,002
**Director:** V P Byrne
**Co. Secretary:** Ms Tina Price
**US SIC:** 3732 **UK SIC:** 36102
**Auditors:** The Crest Partnership Ltd

| | 30-09-13 | 30-09-12 | 30-09-11 |
|---|---|---|---|
| TA | 696,937 | 570,081 | 591,920 |
| NW | 305,006 | 215,042 | 149,415 |
| WC | 287,581 | 194,007 | 92,523 |

DUNS 50-380-9659
## Scot Frame Timber Engineering Ltd
**(Subsidiary of:** Scotframe Ltd)
Souterford Avenue, Inverurie Business Park, Inverurie, Aberdeenshire AB51 0ZJ
**Web:** www.scotframe.co.uk
**Reg No:** 0118213SC **VAT No:** 498492968
**Estd:** 1989 Private Limited Company
**Line of Business:** Other manufacturing not elsewhere classified
**Issued Capital:** £20,000
**Principals:** R T Edwards *(Managing)*, C J Irwin, A Cruickshank, M R Simpson, D B Barron, M G Cruickshank, A K Milne
**Co. Secretary:** Ian Mcdougall
**Responsibilities**
**Senior:** Terry Rait *(Production Controller)*
**Purchasing:** Ally Duguid *(Buyer)*

**Engineering:** Terry Rait (*Production Controller*)
**Branches:** Scot Frame Timber Engineering Ltd, 4 Grayshill Road, Glasgow, Lanarkshire G68 9HQ
**US SIC:** 3999　**UK SIC:** 49590
**Auditors:** MacPherson & Co
**Bankers:** Bank Of Scotland (80-09-38)

|  | 30-04-14 | 30-04-13 | 30-04-12 |
|---|---|---|---|
| TO | 27,899,024 | 25,129,509 | 28,441,798 |
| P/L | 1,006,529 | 347,119 | 617,331 |
| NW | 7,967,893 | 7,533,778 | 7,354,951 |
| WC | 6,029,345 | 5,495,864 | 5,307,667 |
| Emp. | 143 | 142 | 142 |

DUNS 38-546-8806
### Scot Home Care Ltd
(**Subsidiary of:** Acromas Holdings Ltd)
Scotnursing Crosslet House Argyll Avenue, Dumbarton, Dunbartonshire G82 3NS
**Tel:** 01389762162 **Fax:** 01389768555
**Web:** www.scotnursing.com
**Reg No:** 0173276SC **Estd:** 2008 Private Limited Company
**Line of Business:** Nursing agencies
**Trading Style:** Scot Nursing
**Issued Capital:** £2
**Directors:** J H Whitehead, D S Gibson
**Co. Secretary:** Ms Victoria Haynes
**Responsibilities**
**Senior:** Ann Sinclaire (*Manager*)
**Finance:** Ann Sinclaire (*Manager*)
**Marketing:** Ann Sinclaire (*Manager*)
**HR:** Margaret Mason (*Human Resources Manager*)
**Branches:** Scot Home Care Ltd, 9 Gateside Street, Hamilton, Lanarkshire ML3 7HT
**US SIC:** 7361, 8091
**UK SIC:** 83954, 95200
**Auditors:** Anne Sinclair

|  | 31-01-14 | 31-01-13 | 30-01-11 |
|---|---|---|---|
| TA | 2 | 2 | 2 |
| NW | 2 | 2 | 2 |

DUNS 53-654-5858
### Scot Jcb (Holdings) Ltd
398 Townmill Road, Glasgow, Lanarkshire G31 3AR
**Tel:** 0141-556-6521
**Web:** www.scot-jcb.co.uk
**Reg No:** 0180256SC **Estd:** 1972 Private Limited Company
**Line of Business:** Agents involved in the sale of machinery, industrial equipment, ships and aircraft
**Issued Capital:** £72,222
**Directors:** R J Bryant, S I Bryant, D Park, S C Bryant, D M Donoghue
**Co. Secretary:** Stephen Barker
**Responsibilities**
**Sales:** Colin Buchanan (*Sales Office Manager*), Jim Foley (*Sales Engineer*), Billy Thomas (*Sales Manager*)
**Branches:** Scot Jcb (Holdings) Ltd, Unit 2, Wellheads Crescent, Wellheads Industrial Estate, Aberdeen, Aberdeenshire AB21 7GA
**US SIC:** 5084, 5082
**UK SIC:** 61490
**Auditors:** PricewaterhouseCoopers LLP

|  | 31-12-13 | 31-12-12 | 31-12-11 |
|---|---|---|---|
| TO | 102,964,000 | 91,356,000 | 86,732,000 |
| P/L | 3,761,000 | 2,434,000 | 3,101,000 |
| NW | 18,530,000 | 16,173,000 | 14,702,000 |
| WC | 17,029,000 | 14,807,000 | 13,293,000 |
| Emp. | 188 | 186 | 178 |

DUNS 22-102-4842　　　　　　　Imp
### Scot Seat Direct Ltd.
Gainford Business Centre, Fenwick, Kilmarnock, Ayrshire KA3 6AR
**Tel:** 01560600100
**Web:** www.scotseats.co.uk
**Reg No:** 0213634SC **Estd:** 2000 Private Limited Company
**Line of Business:** Car trimmers and upholsterers
**Issued Capital:** £250,000
**Directors:** J A Young, A A Young
**Co. Secretary:** Ms Carol Young
**Responsibilities**
**Finance:** Ruby Goldie (*Financial Director*)
**Marketing:** Sharon Hollis (*Marketing Manager*)
**Sales:** Alan Rilley (*Senior IT Executive*)
**IT:** Alan Rilley (*Senior IT Executive*)
**US SIC:** 2599　**UK SIC:** 46720
**Auditors:** Illegible Auditor Name

|  | 31-12-13 | 31-12-12 | 31-12-11 |
|---|---|---|---|
| TA | 1,183,963 | 1,219,854 | 1,198,812 |
| NW | 117,237 | (57,479) | (128,660) |
| WC | 291,581 | 154,724 | 93,953 |

DUNS 42-390-8297
### Scot Truck (Holdings) Ltd
Units 8 & 9, M8 Interlink Estate Kirkshaws Ro, Coatbridge, Lanarkshire ML5 4RP
**Tel:** 08452411300 **Fax:** 08452411301
**Web:** www.scottruck.co.uk
**Reg No:** 0228367SC **Estd:** 2002 Private Limited Company

**Line of Business:** Management activities of other non-financial holding companies not elsewhere classified
**Issued Capital:** £115,000
**Co. Secretary:** Ian Nish
**Branches:** Scot Truck (Holdings) Ltd, Penilee Road, Hillington Industrial Estate, Glasgow, Lanarkshire G52 4UU
**US SIC:** 6711　**UK SIC:** 83962
**Bankers:** The Royal Bank Of Scotland Plc (83-26-22)

|  | 31-03-14 | 31-03-13 | 31-03-12 |
|---|---|---|---|
| TA | 65,015 | 65,015 | 102,189 |
| NW | (229,227) | (229,227) | (214,227) |
| WC | (229,227) | (229,227) | (229,227) |

DUNS 21-912-8477　　　　　Imp-Exp
### Scot Young Research Ltd
Lye By Pass, Stourbridge, West Midlands DY9 8HG
**Tel:** 01384-892021 **Fax:** 01384-422675
**Web:** www.syrclean.com
**Reg No:** 0481830 **VAT No:** 277229728
**Estd:** 1955 Private Limited Company
**Line of Business:** Manufacture of other plastic products
**Export Markets:** Worldwide
**Export Sales:** £1,161,238
**Trading Style:** Scot Young Research
**Issued Capital:** £55,100
**Directors:** L Staves, A M Jones
**Co. Secretary:** Surjinder Dhillon
**Responsibilities**
**IT:** David Matty (*Senior IT Executive*)
**HR:** Brian Shuard (*Human Resources Manager*)
**Branches:** Scot Young Research Ltd, 10 Harts Farm Way, Broadmarsh Business & Innovation Centre, Havant, Hampshire PO9 1HS
**US SIC:** 3079, 7539
**UK SIC:** 48360, 67100
**Auditors:** dhjh Ltd
**Bankers:** National Westminster Bank Plc (60-09-39)

|  | 31-08-13 | 31-08-12 | 31-08-11 |
|---|---|---|---|
| TO | 13,824,114 | 14,086,144 | 14,185,407 |
| P/L | 513,152 | 256,332 | 1,001,859 |
| NW | 5,921,616 | 5,557,425 | 5,378,734 |
| WC | 3,222,070 | 2,723,995 | 2,806,259 |
| Emp. | 125 | 145 | 144 |

DUNS 23-078-6972
### Scotbake Ltd
(**Subsidiary of:** Marixin Ltd)
38 Seafield Road, Inverness, Inverness-Shire IV1 1SG
**Tel:** 01463711357 **Fax:** 01463-242244
**Web:** www.scotlandfoodanddrink.org
**Reg No:** 0142086SC **VAT No:** 624398523
**Estd:** 1993 Private Limited Company
**Line of Business:** Retail sale of bread, cakes, flour confectionery and sugar confectionery
**Issued Capital:** £150,000
**Principals:** D J Skeoch (*Managing*), D C Smith, C E Smith
**Co. Secretary:** David Skeoch
**Responsibilities**
**Finance:** Sheila Dalgetty (*Office Manager*), Graeme Moffat (*Finance Director*)
**Admin:** Sheila Dalgetty (*Office Manager*)
**IT:** Sheila Dalgetty (*Office Manager*)
**HR:** Sheila Dalgetty (*Office Manager*)
**Health & Safety:** Sheila Dalgetty (*Office Manager*)
**Facilities:** Jim Slaven (*Engineering Manager*)
**Branches:** Scotbake Ltd, 6 Queensgate, Inverness, Inverness-Shire IV1 1PQ
**US SIC:** 5462　**UK SIC:** 64100
**Bankers:** Clydesdale Bank Plc (82-63-07)

|  | 30-04-14 | 30-04-13 | 30-04-12 |
|---|---|---|---|
| TO | 2,944,584 | 3,205,426 | 3,191,733 |
| P/L | 216,647 | 450,159 | 205,724 |
| NW | 913,818 | 735,830 | 339,475 |
| WC | (282,773) | 1,074,672 | (525,427) |
| Emp. | 73 | 70 | 70 |

DUNS 76-236-0030
### Scotcall Ltd
Spectrum House, Glasgow, Lanarkshire G2 7AT
**Tel:** 01412488098 **Fax:** 01412486616
**Web:** www.scotcall.co.uk
**Reg No:** 0127277SC **Estd:** 2001 Private Limited Company
**Line of Business:** Debt collection agencies
**Trading Style:** Scotcall
**Issued Capital:** £8,000
**Directors:** E A Turner, Mrs A G Mcvicker, D Stevenson, Ms B Stevenson
**Co. Secretary:** Alistair Smith
**Responsibilities**
**Sales:** Stephen Tyacke (*Director, Group Business Devel*)
**US SIC:** 7321　**UK SIC:** 83954
**Auditors:** KPMG

**Bankers:** Bank Of Scotland (80-07-73)

|  | 30-09-13 | 30-09-12 | 30-09-11 |
|---|---|---|---|
| TO | 10,257,712 | 10,841,166 | 9,134,117 |
| P/L | 606,600 | 957,640 | 502,496 |
| NW | 1,023,801 | 1,236,236 | 992,308 |
| WC | 495,381 | 867,945 | 588,467 |
| Emp. | 177 | 84 | 154 |

DUNS 21-559-8350　　　　　　Imp
### Scotch Frost of Glasgow Ltd
(**Subsidiary of:** S F G Holdings Ltd)
Block 3, Bothwell Park Industrial Estate, Glasgow, Lanarkshire G71 6NZ
**Tel:** 01698-810099
**Web:** www.scotchfrost.com
**Reg No:** 0045152SC **VAT No:** 260160010
**Estd:** 1967 Private Limited Company
**Line of Business:** Non-specialised wholesale of food, beverages and tobacco
**Issued Capital:** £1,000,000
**Principals:** D G Louden (*Sales*), J P Mc Shane, J R Speirs, G Kelly, Ms P J Harvey, Miss A M Doherty
**Co. Secretary:** Adrian Louden
**Responsibilities**
**Senior:** Pamela Cochran (*Manager*)
**Branches:** Scotch Frost Of Glasgow Ltd, Unit 14 Earlsfield Close, Lincoln, Lincolnshire LN6 3RT
**US SIC:** 5149, 5148, 5147
**UK SIC:** 61700
**Auditors:** Wylie & Bisset LLP
**Bankers:** The Royal Bank Of Scotland Plc (83-00-40)

|  | 31-05-14 | 31-05-13 | 31-05-12 |
|---|---|---|---|
| TO | 53,813,720 | 50,785,340 | 48,317,716 |
| P/L | 391,171 | 221,348 | 123,559 |
| NW | 4,601,478 | 4,295,651 | 3,954,763 |
| WC | 2,581,121 | 2,462,540 | 2,423,408 |
| Emp. | 152 | 148 | 128 |

DUNS 29-818-4508
### The Scotch Whisky Heritage Centre Ltd
Scotch Whisky Heritage Centre, Edinburgh, Midlothian EH1 2NE
**Fax:** 0131-220-6288
**Web:** www.whisky-heritage.co.uk
**Reg No:** 0100141SC **Estd:** 1986 Private Limited Company
**Line of Business:** Heritage centre
**Issued Capital:** £258,000
**Principals:** A S Mcintosh (*Managing*), M Leask, H D Fetter, K W Grier, P F Smith, Ms S Morrison, K R Robertson, R Paterson
**Co. Secretary:** Anthony Dick
**Responsibilities**
**Senior:** Angela Keir (*Deputy General Manager*), Kenneth Mckinlay (*Director*), Patrick Millet (*Manager*)
**Finance:** Anthony Schofield (*Finance Director*)
**IT:** Ross Morris (*IT Manager*)
**Purchasing:** Ross Morris (*IT Manager*)
**US SIC:** 8411　**UK SIC:** 97700
**Auditors:** PricewaterhouseCoopers
**Bankers:** Bank Of Scotland (80-02-38)

|  | 30-11-13 | 30-11-12 | 30-11-11 |
|---|---|---|---|
| TO | 5,519,478 | 4,741,143 | 4,376,497 |
| P/L | 703,676 | 504,357 | 457,855 |
| NW | 4,055,026 | 3,486,877 | 3,142,374 |
| WC | 439,321 | (66,514) | 65,765 |
| Emp. | 65 | 62 | 61 |

DUNS 49-136-6209
### Scotco Restaurants Ltd
(**Subsidiary of:** Scotco (Eastern) Ltd)
1 Chargers Paddock Harleyford, Henley Road, Marlow, Buckinghamshire SL7 2DX
**Tel:** 01628487804
**Web:** www.scotcorestaurants.co.uk
**Reg No:** 3107170 **Estd:** 1995 Private Limited Company
**Line of Business:** Unlicensed restaurants and cafes
**Trading Style:** Kentucky Fried Chicken
**Issued Capital:** £42,839
**Directors:** L E Herbert, A G Purnell
**Co. Secretary:** Andrew Purnell
**Responsibilities**
**Senior:** Hilary Ford (*Personal Assistant*)
**Branches:** Scotco Restaurants Ltd, Select, Unit 215, Tunbridge Wells, Kent TN1 2SS
**US SIC:** 7399　**UK SIC:** 83954
**Auditors:** Grant Thornton
**Bankers:** The Royal Bank Of Scotland Plc (15-10-00)

|  | 01-12-13 | 02-12-12 | 04-12-11 |
|---|---|---|---|
| TO | 30,187,357 | 23,751,995 | 23,141,367 |
| P/L | 2,365,116 | 712,210 | 1,893,379 |
| NW | 6,212,365 | 6,685,208 | 6,476,141 |
| WC | 2,326,671 | 2,983,264 | 3,377,985 |
| Emp. | 732 | 469 | 458 |

DUNS 42-394-9317
### Scotco Restaurants Southern Ltd
46 High Street, Hassocks, West Sussex BN6 9RG
**Tel:** 01273-834566
**Reg No:** 4382569 **Estd:** 2002 Private Limited Company
**Line of Business:** Restaurants
**Issued Capital:** £50,000
**Director:** A G Purnell
**Co. Secretary:** Andrew Purnell
**Responsibilities**
**Senior:** Belinda Coates (*Manager*), Jonathan Coates (*Manager*), Simon Coates (*Manager*)
**Branches:** Scotco Restaurants Southern Ltd, 1 Lottbridge Drove, Eastbourne, East Sussex BN22 7SG
**US SIC:** 7399　**UK SIC:** 83954
**Auditors:** Baker Tilly UK Audit LLP

|  | 30-09-13 | 30-09-12 | 30-09-11 |
|---|---|---|---|
| TO | 7,360,442 | 7,569,741 | 7,291,944 |
| P/L | 510,124 | 654,126 | 691,602 |
| NW | (169,889) | (135,877) | (296,488) |
| WC | (1,281,245) | (971,348) | (1,400,866) |
| Emp. | 148 | 144 | 153 |

DUNS 76-676-9954
### Scotgrip (U.K.) Ltd
Units 8-9, Banchory, Kincardineshire AB31 5YR
**Tel:** 01330825335 **Fax:** 01330-825260
**Web:** www.scotgrip.com
**Reg No:** 0130388SC **Estd:** 1991 Private Limited Company
**Line of Business:** Safety equipment suppliers
**Issued Capital:** £142
**Principals:** C Prise (*Managing*), Ms M D Prise, O R Prise, C M Prise
**Co. Secretary:** Lc Secretaries Limited
**US SIC:** 5999　**UK SIC:** 65600
**Auditors:** MacPherson & Co
**Bankers:** The Royal Bank Of Scotland Plc (83-15-31)

|  | 31-03-14 | 31-03-13 | 31-03-12 |
|---|---|---|---|
| TA | 1,404,234 | 1,106,434 | 748,428 |
| NW | 1,031,453 | 795,059 | 519,273 |
| WC | 888,238 | 688,219 | 430,402 |

DUNS 21-124-0444　　　　　　Imp
### Scotia Binding Supplies Ltd
Unit 22 Optima Park, Thames Road, Crayford, Dartford, Kent DA1 4QX
**Fax:** 08712000909
**Web:** www.bindingsupplies.co.uk
**Reg No:** 6740138 **Estd:** 2008 Private Limited Company
**Line of Business:** Commercial stationery supplies
**Issued Capital:** £250
**Directors:** P Aldred, C Buckingham
**Responsibilities**
**Senior:** Martin Ball (*Manager*)
**US SIC:** 5942　**UK SIC:** 65300

|  | 31-03-14 | 31-03-13 | 31-03-12 |
|---|---|---|---|
| TA | 864,970 | 1,001,291 | 913,350 |
| NW | 53,306 | 35,821 | (7,559) |
| WC | 68,121 | 43,847 | 87,157 |

DUNS 50-569-5130
### Scotia Clean Teck Ltd
1 West Gorgie Parks, Edinburgh, Midlothian EH14 1UT
**Tel:** 01314434455 **Fax:** 0131-444-1909
**Web:** www.scotiacleanteck.co.uk
**Reg No:** 0125938SC **VAT No:** 553592916
**Estd:** 1990 Private Limited Company
**Line of Business:** Cleaning contracting commercial
**Issued Capital:** £58,984
**Principals:** Mrs E J Aitken (*Managing*), Ms A Hume
**Responsibilities**
**Senior:** Elaine Morris (*Manager*)
**Finance:** Brian Corrigan (*Finance Director*)
**US SIC:** 7349　**UK SIC:** 92300
**Auditors:** Neil Nisbet & Co
**Bankers:** Bank Of Scotland (80-02-71)

|  | 31-03-14 | 31-03-13 | 31-03-12 |
|---|---|---|---|
| TA | 359,860 | 332,565 | 324,621 |
| NW | 95,565 | 79,722 | 77,591 |
| WC | 80,616 | 66,204 | 59,608 |

DUNS 22-904-9788
### Scotia Double Glazing Ltd
(**Subsidiary of:** Ayrshire Aluminium Co. Ltd)
Bonnyton Industrial Estate, Munro Place, Kilmarnock, Ayrshire KA1 2NP
**Tel:** 01563541111
**Web:** www.scotiadg.co.uk
**Reg No:** 0084590SC **Estd:** 1983 Private Limited Company
**Line of Business:** Double glazing installers
**Issued Capital:** £6,000
**Directors:** M A Smith, G F Smith, J D Glen
**Co. Secretary:** Robert Mcknight
**Responsibilities**
**Senior:** Ricky Campbell (*Works Manager*)

**Finance:** Robert McKnight *(Financial Director)*
**Sales:** George Dunn *(General Sales Manager)*
**IT:** Robert McKnight *(Financial Director)*
**Health & Safety:** Ricky Campbell *(Works Manager)*
**Facilities:** Ricky Campbell *(Works Manager)*
**Engineering:** Ricky Campbell *(Works Manager)*
**Branches:** Scotia Double Glazing Ltd, Block 2, Unit 7, Burnbank Road, Hamilton, Lanarkshire ML3 9AZ
**US SIC:** 1721 **UK SIC:** 50400
**Auditors:** BDO Stoy Hayward
**Bankers:** Bank Of Scotland (80-08-53)

| | 30-06-14 | 30-06-13 | 30-06-12 |
|---|---|---|---|
| TO | 9,975,072 | 9,915,237 | 9,300,658 |
| P/L | 594,985 | 306,849 | 178,116 |
| NW | 1,830,039 | 1,263,917 | 1,032,911 |
| WC | 1,179,302 | 933,438 | 669,082 |
| Emp. | 100 | 96 | 84 |

DUNS 73-699-3762

## Scotia Gas Networks Ltd

St Lawrence House, Station Approach, Horley, Surrey RH6 9HJ
**Tel:** 08450701432
**Web:** https://www.sgn.co.uk
**Reg No:** 4958135 **VAT No:** 864416218
**Estd:** 2003 Private Limited Company
**Line of Business:** Management activities of holding companies
**Issued Capital:** £200,006,277
**Directors:** R Mcdonald, Ms O P Steedman, J J Mcmanus, Ms N M Flageul, J Mcphillimy, S B Sherman, F M Alexander
**Co. Secretary:** Ms Nicola Shand
**Responsibilities**
**Marketing:** Victoria Richardson *(Digital Development Manager)*
**Branches:** Scotia Gas Networks Ltd, 95 Kilbirnie Street, Glasgow, Lanarkshire G5 8JD
**US SIC:** 6711, 4932
**UK SIC:** 83962, 16200
**Auditors:** Deloitte LLP
**Following financial data are in thousands**

| | 31-03-14 | 31-03-13 | 31-03-12 |
|---|---|---|---|
| TO | 1,096,800 | 965,300 | 928,700 |
| P/L | 110,900 | (11,800) | (20,000) |
| NW | (1,262,800) | (1,225,400) | (1,159,200) |
| WC | (144,300) | (220,400) | (151,200) |
| Emp. | 9 | 3,740 | 3,854 |

DUNS 73-771-6626

## Scotia Health Care Ltd

(**Subsidiary of:** Falcon Capital Investments Ltd)
Scotia Road, Stoke-On-Trent, Staffordshire ST6 4HA
**Tel:** 01782829100
**Web:** www.scotiahealth.com
**Reg No:** 5028745 **Estd:** 2004 Private Limited Company
**Line of Business:** Other human health activities
**Trading Style:** Scotia Heights
**Issued Capital:** £1
**Directors:** D Rowe-Bewick, Ms T Duke, E D Craig, Mrs T J Clarkson, D Collinge, Mrs L Thomas
**Co. Secretary:** Mrs Tracy Clarkson
**US SIC:** 8091, 8321
**UK SIC:** 95200, 96111
**Auditors:** KPMG LLP

| | 31-03-14 | 31-03-13 | 25-03-12 |
|---|---|---|---|
| TO | 4,592,855 | 4,880,035 | 4,354,845 |
| P/L | 416,379 | 713,731 | 408,138 |
| NW | (3,146,253) | 953,513 | 1,649,156 |
| WC | 1,158,444 | 798,387 | 1,504,691 |
| Emp. | 158 | 181 | 165 |

DUNS 34-627-8880

## Scotia Homes Ltd

21 Bridge Street, Ellon, Aberdeenshire AB41 9AA
**Tel:** 01224318792 **Fax:** 01738448561
**Web:** www.scotia-homes.co.uk
**Reg No:** 0141011SC **Estd:** 1999 Private Limited Company
**Line of Business:** Buying and selling of own real estate
**Issued Capital:** £3,976,547
**Directors:** R S Dryburgh, R G Begbie, D R Thomson, D W Watt, W H Bruce, W L Macleod, S Burnett, P J Boyle
**Co. Secretary:** Michael Zanre
**Responsibilities**
**Senior:** Carol Beaton *(Director)*, Francis Fairlie *(Director)*, Debbie Johnston *(Sales Advisor)*, Andrew Lonie *(Director)*
**Sales:** Debbie Johnston *(Sales Advisor)*
**Branches:** Scotia Homes Ltd, 9 Redwood Ave, Inverness, Inverness-Shire IV2 6HA
**US SIC:** 6531 **UK SIC:** 83400
**Auditors:** Bain Henry Reid
**Bankers:** Bank Of Scotland (80-06-71)

| | 30-04-14 | 30-04-13 | 30-04-12 |
|---|---|---|---|
| TO | 42,012,903 | 32,914,112 | 21,164,876 |
| P/L | 3,023,356 | 3,603,083 | 2,339,463 |
| NW | 32,241,683 | 30,270,865 | 29,544,739 |
| WC | 55,208,135 | 58,822,279 | 48,084,053 |
| Emp. | 181 | 176 | 141 |

DUNS 22-900-5046 **Imp**

## Scotia Instrumentation Ltd

Campus 1 Aberdeen Science & Technology, Park, Balgownie Road, Bridge Of Don, Aberdeen, Aberdeenshire AB22 8GT
**Tel:** 01224222888 **Fax:** 01224-826299
**Web:** www.scotia-instrumentation.com
**Reg No:** 0074997SC **Estd:** 1982 Private Limited Company
**Line of Business:** Calibration equipment services
**Issued Capital:** £30,000
**Principals:** J W Thom *(Chairman and Managing)*, A J Smith *(Financial)*
**Co. Secretary:** John Davie
**Responsibilities**
**Marketing:** Brian Mclaren *(Technical Director)*
**IT:** Brian Mclaren *(Technical Director)*
**HR:** Brian Mclaren *(Technical Director)*, Theresa Munro *(Human Resources Manager)*
**Health & Safety:** George Weir *(Health & Safety Officer)*
**Branches:** Scotia Instrumentation Ltd, Unit 5C, New York Way, Newcastle Upon Tyne, Tyne and Wear NE27 0QF
**US SIC:** 3811 **UK SIC:** 37100
**Auditors:** Anderson Anderson & Brown
**Bankers:** Bank Of Scotland (80-05-17)

| | 31-12-13 | 31-12-12 | 31-12-11 |
|---|---|---|---|
| TO | 11,461,589 | 10,087,848 | 9,433,445 |
| P/L | 1,732,617 | 999,411 | 1,140,257 |
| NW | 5,240,968 | 4,114,228 | 3,189,806 |
| WC | 2,403,041 | 1,464,298 | 629,010 |
| Emp. | 91 | 88 | 83 |

DUNS 29-364-9653 **Exp**

## Scotiabank Europe Plc

(**Subsidiary of:** Bank of Nova Scotia The)
201 Bishopsgate, London EC2M 3NS
**Tel:** 020-7638-5644 **Fax:** 020-7638-8488
**Web:** www.gbm.scotiabank.com
**Reg No:** 0817692 **VAT No:** 238772824
**Estd:** 1964 Public Limited Company
**Line of Business:** Banks and financial institutions
**Export Markets:** W Europe
**Directors:** C E Leaver, P S Smith, R Wild, Mrs J M Lloyd, P M Cutts, M E Caplan, S M Lowe
**Co. Secretary:** Julian Rhys
**Branches:** Scotiabank Europe Plc, 48 Berkeley Square, London W1J 5AX
**US SIC:** 6012, 6111
**UK SIC:** 81402, 81501
**Auditors:** KPMG Audit PLC
**Employees:** 59
**Turnover:** £291,633,000

DUNS 21-558-0652

## Scotland Excel

Renfrewshire House, Cotton Street, Paisley, Renfrewshire PA1 1AR
**Tel:** 03003001200
**Web:** www.scotland-excel.com
**Estd:** 1996 Partnership
**Line of Business:** Other business activities not elsewhere classified
**Directors:** Ms D Cowie, M Mcdonald, J Robb, J Stewart, C Mcmaster, N Baker, G Douglas, P Argyle
**Responsibilities**
**Senior:** J Beare *(Principal)*, N Elliott-Cannon *(Principal)*, B Howatson *(Principal)*, M McDonald *(Principal)*, C McMaster *(Principal)*, L Rosin *(Principal)*, M Salmond *(Principal)*
**Admin:** Jim McLaggan *(Business Services Manager)*
**US SIC:** 7399 **UK SIC:** 83954
**Employees:** 65

DUNS 21-773-1638

## Scotland Gas Network

95 Kilbirnie Street, Glasgow, Lanarkshire G5 8JD
**Tel:** 01414184121
**Web:** www.sgn.co.uk
**Estd:** 2011 Proprietorship
**Line of Business:** Gas companies
**Proprietor:** J Deveney
**US SIC:** 4925 **UK SIC:** 25670
**Employees:** 190

DUNS 73-799-8448

## Scotland Gas Networks Plc

(**Subsidiary of:** Scotia Gas Networks Ltd)
Inveralmond House, Perth, Perthshire PH1 3AQ
**Tel:** 08450701432
**Web:** www.sgn.co.uk
**Reg No:** 0264065SC **Estd:** 2004 Public Limited Company
**Line of Business:** Distribution and trade of gaseous fuels through mains
**Issued Capital:** £49,392,787
**Directors:** J Mcphillimy, P R Jeffrey, Ms N M Flageul, Ms O P Steedman, J J Mcmanus, R Mcdonald, F M Alexander, G G Juggins
**Co. Secretary:** Ms Nicola Shand
**Responsibilities**
**Senior:** John Morea *(Chief Executive Officer)*
**Branches:** Scotland Gas Networks Plc, Perrie Street, Lochee, DD2 2rd Dundee
**US SIC:** 4932 **UK SIC:** 16200
**Auditors:** Deloitte LLP

| | 31-03-14 | 31-03-13 | 31-03-12 |
|---|---|---|---|
| TO | 319,100,000 | 297,600,000 | 283,500,000 |
| P/L | 44,300,000 | 38,500,000 | 28,900,000 |
| NW | 34,600,000 | (18,000,000) | (50,800,000) |
| WC | 202,500,000 | 118,200,000 | 101,600,000 |
| Emp. | 589 | 628 | 655 |

DUNS 21-581-7451

## Scotland Televisons

George Street, Edinburgh, Midlothian EH2 2DU
**Tel:** 01312008200
**Web:** www.stv.tv
**Estd:** 2011
**Line of Business:** Radio broadcasting services
**Proprietor:** M Sichi
**US SIC:** 4833 **UK SIC:** 97411
**Employees:** 500

DUNS 21-589-1722 **Imp-Exp**

## Scotlog Sales Ltd

41 Culduthel Road, Inverness, Inverness-Shire IV2 4AT
**Tel:** 01463223821 **Fax:** 01463220901
**Web:** www.scotbarkuk.com
**Reg No:** 0066812SC **VAT No:** 415744258
**Estd:** 1993 Private Limited Company
**Line of Business:** Horticultural plant and equipment servicing
**Export Markets:** Sweden
**Trading Style:** Scotbark
**Issued Capital:** £12,546
**Principals:** A G Catto *(Managing)*, G J Catto, S A Catto
**Responsibilities**
**Senior:** Michael Boyle *(Proprietor)*, John Ligertwood *(Manager)*
**Branches:** Scotlog Sales Ltd, 313 Blochairn Rd, Glasgow, Lanarkshire G21 2RX
**US SIC:** 5083 **UK SIC:** 61490
**Auditors:** Frame Kennedy
**Bankers:** Clydesdale Bank Plc (82-70-13)

| | 31-03-14 | 31-03-13 | 31-03-12 |
|---|---|---|---|
| TO | 14,279,857 | 12,002,648 | 12,764,990 |
| P/L | 1,163,080 | (5,309) | 1,139,461 |
| NW | 7,395,148 | 6,337,458 | 6,449,786 |
| WC | (2,023,476) | (2,019,818) | (1,575,826) |
| Emp. | 77 | 74 | 78 |

DUNS 23-879-8057

## Scotmore Investments Ltd

Thistle House, 3 Scholars Gate, Glasgow, Lanarkshire G75 9JL
**Tel:** 01412218251
**Reg No:** 0201301SC **Estd:** 1947 Private Limited Company
**Line of Business:** Other business activities not elsewhere classified
**Issued Capital:** £200
**Directors:** Ms W L Crozier, Ms I A Philp, I Philp
**Co. Secretary:** Brodies Secretarial Services Lim
**US SIC:** 7399 **UK SIC:** 83954
**Auditors:** PricewaterhouseCoopers

| | 31-12-13 | 31-12-12 | 31-12-11 |
|---|---|---|---|
| TO | 171,652 | 171,700 | 146,805 |
| P/L | 123,548 | 121,547 | 113,507 |
| NW | 454,867 | 357,285 | 267,547 |
| WC | (31,789) | (35,872) | (29,100) |

DUNS 22-906-8960 **Imp-Exp**

## Scotoil Services Ltd

(**Subsidiary of:** Grupo Tradebe Medio Ambiente Sociedad Limitada)
Miller Street, Aberdeen, Aberdeenshire AB11 5AN
**Tel:** 01224-571491 **Fax:** 01224-580861
**Web:** www.scotoil.co.uk
**Reg No:** 0077501SC **VAT No:** 456493026
**Estd:** 1984 Private Limited Company
**Line of Business:** Oil and gas exploration services
**Export Markets:** Europe; Africa
**Issued Capital:** £500,000
**Directors:** Tradebe Management Sl, V Creixell De Villalonga, S J Mcgown
**Responsibilities**
**Senior:** Alastair Lindsay *(Manager)*
**Finance:** Lesley Milne *(Senior Finance Administrator)*
**US SIC:** 1389 **UK SIC:** 13000
**Auditors:** Johnston Carmichael
**Bankers:** Bank Of Scotland (80-73-30)

| | 31-12-13 | 31-12-12 | 31-12-11 |
|---|---|---|---|
| TO | 8,358,015 | 6,622,789 | 6,331,518 |
| P/L | 2,083,390 | 1,424,271 | 1,808,007 |
| NW | 8,112,764 | 7,264,769 | 6,439,729 |
| WC | 6,299,239 | 5,321,340 | 4,310,133 |
| Emp. | 56 | 52 | 47 |

DUNS 23-628-8150 **Imp**

## Scotprime Seafoods Ltd

11 Whitfield Drive, Heathfield Industrial Estate, Ayr, Ayrshire KA8 9RX
**Tel:** 01292611942 **Fax:** 01292280475
**Web:** www.scotprime.com
**Reg No:** 3625848 **Estd:** 1998 Private Limited Company
**Line of Business:** Fish merchants (wholesale)
**Export Sales:** £4,968,669
**Issued Capital:** £8,333
**Directors:** J Boada, E Salsas Boada, Ms M Boada Descalzo, M Boada Rovira, Ms C Boada Rovira
**Co. Secretary:** Robert Crano
**Responsibilities**
**Senior:** Kenny Hastie *(Factory Manager)*
**Facilities:** Kenny Hastie *(Factory Manager)*
**Branches:** Scotprime Seafoods Ltd, 66 Sinclair Rd, Aberdeen, Aberdeenshire AB11 9PP
**US SIC:** 5146 **UK SIC:** 61700
**Auditors:** Baker Tilly

| | 31-12-13 | 31-12-12 | 31-12-11 |
|---|---|---|---|
| TO | 10,406,004 | 11,233,763 | 11,753,620 |
| P/L | 58,970 | 128,626 | 246,062 |
| NW | 1,802,991 | 1,758,326 | 1,644,272 |
| WC | 1,300,085 | 1,229,448 | 1,147,599 |
| Emp. | 56 | 56 | 64 |

DUNS 73-927-7564

## Scotrail Railways Ltd

(**Subsidiary of:** National Express Group Plc)
P O Box 7030, Fort William, Inverness-Shire PH33 6WX
**Tel:** 03303030112 **Fax:** 0141-335-4592
**Web:** www.scotrail.co.uk
**Reg No:** 2938994 **Estd:** 1994 Private Limited Company
**Line of Business:** Train stations
**Issued Capital:** £1,000,001
**Directors:** A N Chivers, R J Bowley
**Co. Secretary:** Ms Dianne Robinson
**Responsibilities**
**Senior:** Peter Cotton *(Manager)*, Barbara Lees *(Manager)*
**Finance:** Billy Connelly *(Acting Finance Director)*
**Engineering:** Ken Docherty *(Engineering Director)*
**Branches:** Scotrail Railways Ltd, Scotland Electronics International Ltd, 28 West Road, Forres, Morayshire IV36 2GW
**US SIC:** 4011 **UK SIC:** 71000
**Auditors:** Ernst & Young
**Bankers:** HSBC Bank plc (40-02-50)

| | 31-12-13 | 31-12-12 | 31-12-11 |
|---|---|---|---|
| TA | N/A | 1,028,000 | 251,000 |
| P/L | 66,861,000 | (4,154,000) | (937,000) |
| NW | N/A | (66,861,000) | (63,724,000) |
| WC | N/A | (66,861,000) | (63,724,000) |

DUNS 34-960-9169

## Scots Bearings Ltd

5916 Robert Leonard, Kirkhill Industial Estate, Dice, Aberdeen, Aberdeenshire AB21 0GG
**Tel:** 01224-770346
**Web:** www.scots-bearings.co.uk
**Reg No:** 0299694SC **Estd:** 2006 Private Limited Company
**Line of Business:** Wholesale of other machinery for use in industry, trade and navigation
**Issued Capital:** £67,751
**Director:** D J Jackson
**Co. Secretary:** Ms Ann Jackson
**US SIC:** 8999 **UK SIC:** 83954
**Bankers:** Bank Of Scotland (80-06-60)

| | 31-03-14 | 31-12-12 | 31-03-11 |
|---|---|---|---|
| TO | 13,338,415 | 10,304,827 | 9,244,629 |
| P/L | 287,652 | 480,121 | 534,410 |
| NW | 829,931 | 704,996 | 477,657 |
| WC | 59,541 | (2,667) | 436,611 |
| Emp. | 61 | 62 | 51 |

DUNS 21-808-4036 **Imp**

## Scotsdale Nursery & Garden Centre Ltd

120 Cambridge Road, Cambridge, Cambridgeshire CB2 2JT
**Tel:** 01223-842777
**Web:** www.scotsdalegardencentre.co.uk
**Reg No:** 0820387 **VAT No:** 213415996

**Estd:** 1964 Private Limited Company
**Line of Business:** Garden centres
**Trading Style:** Scotsdale Nursery & Garden Centre Ltd
**Issued Capital:** £100,000
**Principals:** D A Rayner *(Chairman)*, Mrs C Owen *(Managing)*, B T Rayner
**Co. Secretary:** Mrs June Cullum
**Responsibilities**
**HR:** Sam Carlton *(Training Manager)*
**Health & Safety:** Sam Carlton *(Training Manager)*
**US SIC:** 5999 **UK SIC:** 65600
**Auditors:** Bradshaw Johnson
**Bankers:** Lloyds TSB Bank plc (30-91-56)

|  | 31-07-13 | 31-07-12 | 31-07-11 |
|---|---|---|---|
| TO | 14,920,489 | 14,527,990 | 14,878,375 |
| P/L | 612,572 | 938,809 | 1,019,405 |
| NW | 10,037,859 | 9,855,145 | 9,120,849 |
| WC | 6,035,552 | 5,469,515 | 4,687,427 |
| Emp. | 196 | 164 | 152 |

DUNS 22-715-0216

## Scotstoun Property Ltd
**(Subsidiary of:** Ove Arup Partnership Trust Corporation Ltd)
13 Fitzroy Street, London W1T 4BQ
**Tel:** 01904652373 **Fax:** 02074653669
**Web:** www.arup.com
**Reg No:** 0894934 **Estd:** 2012 Private Limited Company
**Line of Business:** Architectural services
**Trading Style:** Ove Arup Partnership
**Issued Capital:** £100
**Director:** D A Whittleton
**Co. Secretary:** Matthew Tweedie
**Responsibilities**
**Senior:** Geoff Davidson *(Manager)*
**US SIC:** 8911 **UK SIC:** 83701
**Auditors:** PricewaterhouseCoopers LLP

|  | 31-03-14 | 31-03-13 | 31-03-12 |
|---|---|---|---|
| TA | 2,039,157 | 2,886,602 | 3,733,057 |
| P/L | (847,525) | (847,866) | (874,582) |
| NW | 2,039,157 | (2,259,674) | (1,411,808) |

DUNS 57-837-8374

## Scott Aerospace Ltd
**(Subsidiary of:** Scott Aerospace Holdings Ltd)
Woodward Avenue, Yate, Bristol, Avon BS37 5YS
**Web:** www.scottaero.co.uk
**Reg No:** 2890968 **VAT No:** 902773822
**Estd:** 2003 Private Limited Company
**Line of Business:** Engineers (general)
**Trading Style:** Scott Aerospace Ltd
**Issued Capital:** £100
**Principals:** M Trigg *(Managing)*, M J Scott
**Co. Secretary:** William Anstee
**Responsibilities**
**Marketing:** Tony Davies *(Marketing Manager)*
**Sales:** Sandra Molton *(Sales Manager)*
**Admin:** Lisa Stephens *(Quality & Administration Manag)*
**Health & Safety:** Lisa Stephens *(Quality & Administration Manag)*, Tony Veale *(Health & Safety Officer)*
**Operations:** Lisa Stephens *(Quality & Administration Manag)*, Tony Veale *(Health & Safety Officer)*
**US SIC:** 8911, 3542
**UK SIC:** 83701, 32212
**Auditors:** R S Porter & Co
**Bankers:** National Westminster Bank Plc (52-10-03)

|  | 31-12-13 | 31-12-12 | 31-12-11 |
|---|---|---|---|
| TO | 7,977,969 | 4,167,228 | 4,815,277 |
| P/L | 191,149 | 440,518 | 103,316 |
| NW | 1,634,052 | 1,474,542 | 972,571 |
| WC | 1,291,132 | 1,326,223 | 795,246 |
| Emp. | 54 | 61 | 61 |

DUNS 21-449-1540 **Imp-Exp**

## Scott & Fyfe Ltd
Tayport Works, Newport-On-Tay, Fife DD6 9EE
**Tel:** 01382 554000 **Fax:** 01382554005
**Web:** www.scott-fyfe.com
**Reg No:** 0017244SC **VAT No:** 269314247
**Estd:** 1933 Private Limited Company
**Line of Business:** Manufacturers of textiles
**Export Markets:** E U; Middle East; Canada; Africa; Australasia; U.S.A.
**Export Sales:** £2,815,000
**Issued Capital:** £634,900
**Directors:** D P Tough, Professor N C Kuenssberg, J C Lupton, J G Palmer
**Co. Secretary:** Colin Cameron
**Responsibilities**
**Senior:** Richard Tough *(Operations Director)*
**Marketing:** Michelle Quadrelli *(Business Manager)*
**Sales:** Paul McMullan *(Business Manager)*, Michaela Millar *(Business Development Officer)*, Duncan Wilcox *(Sales Executive)*
**Health & Safety:** Richard Tough *(Operations Director)*
**Operations:** Richard Tough *(Operations Director)*

**Purchasing:** Roland Pap *(Purchasing Manager)*
**US SIC:** 2392 **UK SIC:** 45550
**Auditors:** EQ Accountants LLP
**Bankers:** Clydesdale Bank Plc (82-67-01)

|  | 31-12-13 | 31-12-12 | 31-12-11 |
|---|---|---|---|
| TO | 9,318,000 | 10,500,000 | 13,166,000 |
| P/L | (678,000) | 353,000 | (71,000) |
| NW | 8,536,000 | 4,290,000 | 10,136,000 |
| WC | 6,263,000 | 2,640,000 | 9,917,000 |
| Emp. | 87 | 104 | 186 |

DUNS 50-574-1314 **Imp**

## Scott & Sons Ltd
81-83 Old Watford Road, St Albans, Hertfordshire AL2 3UN
**Tel:** 01923682856 **Fax:** 01923-682857
**Web:** www.scott-sons.co.uk
**Reg No:** 2522429 **VAT No:** 991238203
**Estd:** 1990 Private Limited Company
**Line of Business:** Commercial premises cleaning
**Issued Capital:** £5,000
**Principals:** M D Scott *(Managing)*, G D Scott, Ms J Scott
**Responsibilities**
**Senior:** June Scott *(Manager)*
**US SIC:** 7349, 1796
**UK SIC:** 92300, 50400
**Auditors:** Rayner Essex LLP
**Bankers:** The Bank Of Ireland (30-11-70)

|  | 30-09-13 | 30-09-12 | 30-09-11 |
|---|---|---|---|
| TA | 483,652 | 463,127 | 481,111 |
| NW | 102,031 | 120,574 | 159,081 |
| WC | 144,517 | 157,055 | 139,069 |

DUNS 22-955-0470

## Scott Bader Commonwealth Ltd
Wollaston Hall, Wollaston, Wollaston, Wellingborough, Northamptonshire NN29 7RL
**Tel:** 01933663100
**Web:** www.scottbader.com
**Reg No:** 0496082 **Estd:** 1951 Private Company Limited By Guarantee
**Line of Business:** Management activities of holding companies
**Directors:** J Pike, Ms J O Findlay, K H Funke, Dr L S Norwood, Ms J Rogers, Dr S O Hayat, Ms A Atkinson-Clark, C Caulier
**Co. Secretary:** Ms Susan Carter
**Responsibilities**
**Senior:** Richard Hirst *(Director)*, Andrew Radford *(Director)*
**Branches:** Scott Bader Commonwealth Ltd, 9-13 Lenton Drive, Leeds, West Yorkshire LS11 5JW
**US SIC:** 6711, 2821
**UK SIC:** 83962, 25140
**Auditors:** PricewaterhouseCoopers LLP
**Bankers:** National Westminster Bank Plc (55-70-37)

|  | 31-12-13 | 31-12-12 | 31-12-11 |
|---|---|---|---|
| TO | 199,033,000 | 188,622,000 | 200,545,000 |
| P/L | 1,049,000 | 3,074,000 | 1,109,000 |
| NW | 40,612,000 | 42,078,000 | 45,324,000 |
| WC | 25,323,000 | 28,033,000 | 27,373,000 |
| Emp. | 640 | 615 | 612 |

DUNS 21-588-2457

## Scott Bros
206 Strathmartine Road, Dundee, Angus DD3 8DE
**Web:** www.scottbrothers.net
**VAT No:** 270107006 **Estd:** 1935 Partnership
**Line of Business:** Retail sale of meat and meat products
**Trading Style:** Scott Brothers Butchers
**Partners:** D Jarron, G Jarron, S Jarron
**Branches:** Wellgate, Markethill, Dundee
**US SIC:** 5423, 5499, 5149
**UK SIC:** 64100, 61700
**Bankers:** The Royal Bank Of Scotland Plc (83-50-00)
**Employees:** 50

DUNS 54-900-9736

## Scott Bros Ltd
Haverton Hill Road, Billingham, Cleveland TS23 1PY
**Web:** www.scottbros.com
**VAT No:** 921442648 **Estd:** 2006 Proprietorship
**Line of Business:** Road haulage and transport services
**Proprietor:** D Scott
**US SIC:** 7394, 5999, 1611, 3031
**UK SIC:** 84000, 65600, 50200, 48123
**Employees:** 60

DUNS 21-009-1378

## Scott Bros. Ltd
**(Subsidiary of:** Scott Bros. Holdings Ltd)
Haverton Hill Road, Billingham, Cleveland TS23 1PY
**Tel:** 01642750444
**Web:** www.scottbros.com
**Reg No:** 6329873 **Estd:** 2006 Private Limited Company
**Line of Business:** Road haulage and transport services
**Issued Capital:** £1
**Directors:** F Cooke, R J Borthwick
**Co. Secretary:**
 Endeavour Secretary Limited
**Responsibilities**
**Senior:** John Dee *(General Manager)*
**US SIC:** 4789 **UK SIC:** 77002

|  | 30-06-13 | 30-06-12 | 30-06-11 |
|---|---|---|---|
| TO | 4,715,777 | 4,668,166 | 5,473,897 |
| P/L | 5,761 | (149,521) | 95,361 |
| NW | 42,408 | 19,647 | (79,803) |
| WC | 29,985 | (142,761) | 33,180 |
| Emp. | 90 | 89 | 80 |

DUNS 73-616-7433

## Scott Brownrigg Group Ltd
77 Endell Street, London WC2H 9DZ
**Tel:** 01483568686
**Web:** www.scottbrownrigg.com
**Reg No:** 4877539 **Estd:** 1993 Private Limited Company
**Line of Business:** Architects
**Export Sales:** £1,093,632
**Issued Capital:** £2,961,401
**Directors:** R Mccarthy, N L Macomish, J G Hill, D E Comber, A M Olliff
**Responsibilities**
**Senior:** Caroline Holden *(Manager)*, Panayiotis Panayiotou *(Manager)*, Martyn Stutchbury *(Manager)*
**Finance:** Caroline More *(Finance Director)*
**Marketing:** Claire Donald *(Senior Marketing Executive)*
**US SIC:** 8911, 7399
**UK SIC:** 83701, 83954

|  | 31-07-14 | 31-07-13 | 31-07-12 |
|---|---|---|---|
| TO | 14,896,628 | 11,913,611 | 11,504,270 |
| P/L | 1,092,102 | 864,181 | 512,558 |
| NW | 5,897,052 | 3,065,542 | 3,027,351 |
| WC | 2,828,957 | 2,499,483 | 2,699,644 |
| Emp. | 168 | 142 | 137 |

DUNS 34-826-7774 **Exp**

## Scott Brownrigg Ltd
**(Subsidiary of:** Scott Brownrigg Group Ltd)
77 Endell Street, London WC2H 9DZ
**Tel:** 020 7240 7766
**Web:** www.scottbrownrigg.com
**Reg No:** 2800215 **VAT No:** 591954693
**Estd:** 1910 Private Limited Company
**Line of Business:** Architectural activities
**Export Markets:** Europe, Africa, Middle East, Far East
**Export Sales:** £431,672
**Issued Capital:** £8,698
**Principals:** J G Hill *(Managing)*, R Mccarthy, A M Olliff, N L Macomish, D E Comber
**Responsibilities**
**Senior:** Amanda Lopez *(Manager)*, Caroline More *(Manager)*
**Admin:** Duncan Greenaway *(Office Manager)*
**HR:** Kim Balchin *(Human Resources Director)*, Aleksandra Paduch *(Human Resources Officer)*
**Operations:** Duncan Greenaway *(Office Manager)*
**Branches:** Scott Brownrigg Ltd, 1 St. Augustines Yard, Gaunts Lane, Bristol, Avon BS1 5DE
**US SIC:** 8911 **UK SIC:** 83701
**Auditors:** Baker Tilly UK Audit LLP
**Bankers:** National Westminster Bank Plc (60-09-21)

|  | 31-07-14 | 31-07-13 | 31-07-12 |
|---|---|---|---|
| TO | 14,144,668 | 11,549,957 | 10,549,595 |
| P/L | 1,328,236 | 1,204,292 | 661,869 |
| NW | 8,721,391 | 10,182,666 | 10,832,473 |
| WC | 5,695,323 | 5,479,265 | 5,785,190 |
| Emp. | 161 | 131 | 122 |

DUNS 21-109-8258

## Scott Dunn Holdings Ltd
Scott Dunn Madgwick Lane, Westhampnett, Chichester, West Sussex PO18 0FB
**Tel:** 01243792900
**Reg No:** 6514320 **Estd:** 2008 Private Limited Company
**Line of Business:** Management activities of holding companies
**Issued Capital:** £64,047
**Directors:** S J Russell, G R Trotter, O Evans, G Horner, J Ghinn, B P Rose
**Co. Secretary:** Julian Ghinn
**US SIC:** 6711 **UK SIC:** 83962

**Bankers:** National Westminster Bank Plc (51-81-41)

|  | 30-06-13 | 30-06-12 | 30-06-11 |
|---|---|---|---|
| TO | 34,510,028 | 27,396,486 | 25,033,195 |
| P/L | 990,156 | (887,553) | 959,994 |
| NW | 3,184,839 | 2,592,638 | 3,427,994 |
| WC | 2,926,075 | 2,185,619 | 3,232,275 |
| Emp. | 192 | 170 | 154 |

DUNS 21-172-3222

## Scott Ferguson Building Co. Ltd
Unit 17-18, Kilwee Business Park, Upper Dunmurry Lane, Dunmurry, Belfast BT17 0HD
**Tel:** 02890302900
**Reg No:** 0073098NI **Estd:** 2002 Private Limited Company
**Line of Business:** Builders
**Issued Capital:** £2
**Directors:** Ms O M Scott, G M Scott
**Responsibilities**
**Senior:** Jerry Scott *(Manager)*
**US SIC:** 1522, 1751, 1721
**UK SIC:** 50100, 50400

|  | 31-07-13 | 31-07-12 | 31-07-11 |
|---|---|---|---|
| TA | 539,490 | 299,974 | 2 |
| NW | 479,588 | 299,974 | 2 |
| WC | 479,588 | N/A | N/A |

DUNS 73-762-5306

## Scott Group Investments Ltd
75-76 Whitecraigs Road, Glenrothes, Fife KY6 2RX
**Fax:** 01383 627 101
**Web:** www.scottgroupltd.com
**Reg No:** 0262153SC **Estd:** 2004 Private Limited Company
**Line of Business:** Management activities of holding companies
**Trading Style:** Scott Group, Scott Pallets, Scott Packaging, Scott Direct
**Issued Capital:** £5,200
**Directors:** R W Maclean, Mrs T J Trotter, A Gibson
**Co. Secretary:** Norman Scott
**US SIC:** 6711, 2449
**UK SIC:** 83962, 46402
**Auditors:** Campbell Dallas LLP

|  | 31-12-13 | 31-12-12 | 31-12-11 |
|---|---|---|---|
| TO | 106,550,000 | 102,361,000 | 95,988,000 |
| P/L | 2,309,000 | 2,637,000 | 3,573,000 |
| NW | 4,016,000 | 1,640,000 | 1,356,000 |
| WC | 7,150,000 | 1,014,000 | 3,159,000 |
| Emp. | 854 | 867 | 833 |

DUNS 21-318-3932 **Imp-Exp**

## Scott Health & Safety Ltd
**(Subsidiary of:** Tyco International Finance Sa)
Pimbo Road, Skelmersdale, Lancashire WN8 9RA
**Tel:** 01695727171 **Fax:** 01695711772
**Web:** www.scottsafety.com
**Reg No:** 0413886 **VAT No:** 864426018
**Estd:** 1946 Private Limited Company
**Line of Business:** Health & safety products
**Export Markets:** E U, U S A, Far East
**Export Sales:** £66,059,000
**Trading Style:** Protector, Sabre, Scott Safety
**Issued Capital:** £6,300,000
**Directors:** A E Chrostowski, R W Waters, B Lerner, P A Benny
**Co. Secretary:** Paul Benny
**Responsibilities**
**Senior:** Steve Burne *(Manager)*
**Marketing:** Nicola Whitehead *(Marketing Manager)*
**HR:** Frank Angear *(Product Manager)*
**Branches:** Scott Health & Safety Ltd, Matteson House, 225 Ash Rd, Aldershot, Hampshire GU12 4DD
**US SIC:** 5999 **UK SIC:** 65600
**Auditors:** Deloitte LLP
**Bankers:** Barclays Bank Plc (20-96-37)

|  | 26-09-14 | 27-09-13 | 30-09-12 |
|---|---|---|---|
| TO | 85,941,000 | 71,557,000 | 62,099,000 |
| P/L | 6,426,000 | 6,527,000 | 5,009,000 |
| NW | 35,855,000 | 29,650,000 | 22,902,000 |
| WC | 23,778,000 | 24,181,000 | 17,418,000 |
| Emp. | 359 | 300 | 273 |

DUNS 34-569-2490 **Imp**

## Scott Logic Ltd
6 Charlotte Square, Newcastle-Upon-Tyne, Tyne and Wear NE1 4XF
**Tel:** 08452241930
**Web:** www.scottlogic.co.uk
**Reg No:** 5377430 **Estd:** 2005 Private Limited Company
**Line of Business:** Computer software (development)
**Export Sales:** £2,871,525
**Issued Capital:** £20,000
**Director:** G Scott
**Co. Secretary:** Dr Helen Estyn-Jones
**Responsibilities**
**Sales:** Phil Pounder *(Senior Business Development Ma)*
**US SIC:** 7379 **UK SIC:** 83940

**Auditors:** Robson Laidler LLP

| | 31-12-13 | 31-12-12 | 31-12-11 |
|---|---|---|---|
| TO | 7,003,720 | N/A | N/A |
| P/L | 1,031,072 | N/A | N/A |
| NW | 3,466,555 | 2,572,312 | 1,829,274 |
| WC | 3,382,967 | 2,473,305 | 1,789,543 |
| Emp. | 100 | N/A | N/A |

DUNS 21-003-7115 **Imp-Exp**

### Scott Ltd

(**Subsidiary of:** Kimberly-Clark Corporation)
Beech House, 35 London Road, Reigate, Surrey RH2 9HZ
**Tel:** 0800626008
**Web:** www.stuartscottltd.com
**Reg No:** 0563798 **Estd:** 1932 Private Limited Company
**Line of Business:** Paper products
**Export Markets:** Middle East, Africa, S & S E Asia
**Issued Capital:** £35,000,002
**Directors:** L A Quaranto, G W Childers
**Co. Secretary:** Issy Aydiner
**Branches:** Barrow-In-Furness
**US SIC:** 2654, 2647
**UK SIC:** 47280, 47220
**Auditors:** Coopers & Lybrand
**Bankers:** National Westminster Bank Plc (60-09-10)
**Employees:** 847

DUNS 22-988-0885

### Scott-Moncrieff

Exchange Place, 3 Semple Street, Edinburgh, Midlothian EH3 8BL
**Tel:** 01314733500
**Web:** www.scott-moncrieff.com
**Estd:** 1993 Partnership
**Line of Business:** Accounting and auditing activities
**Principals:** N B Bennett *(Partner)*, I Patterson *(Partner)*, R G Thom *(Partner)*, M Hawthorne
**Responsibilities**
**Senior:** Helen Berry *(Senior Manager)*, David Eardley *(Senior Manager)*, Andrew Fay *(Manager)*, Donald Forsythe *(Manager)*, Alan Glen *(Manager)*, Barry Truswell *(Senior Manager)*
**Finance:** Dianne King *(CFO)*
**Marketing:** Suzanne Chaudhry *(Marketing Director)*
**Sales:** Jennifer Hansen *(Business Development Manager)*, Fiona Watson *(Account Manager)*
**IT:** Ryan Knowles *(IT Manager)*
**HR:** Joanne Brooks *(Training Manager)*
**Health & Safety:** Claire McKean *(Facilities Manager)*
**Facilities:** Claire McKean *(Facilities Manager)*, Kathleen Revel *(Facilities Manager)*
**Purchasing:** Claire McKean *(Facilities Manager)*
**Branches:** Scott-Moncrieff, Graham Street, Airdrie, Lanarkshire ML6 6DD
**US SIC:** 8931 **UK SIC:** 83600
**Employees:** 100

DUNS 64-226-0954

### Scott Rees and Co

Centaur House, Gardiners Place, Skelmersdale, Lancashire WN8 9SP
**Tel:** 01695722222
**Web:** www.scottrees.co.uk
**Estd:** 1990 Partnership
**Line of Business:** Solicitors
**Partners:** J Fenney, R Smith, D Rees, P Scott
**Responsibilities**
**Senior:** S McKinnon *(Practice Manager)*
**Finance:** Stuart Mackinnon *(Finance Director)*
**Marketing:** H Blythe *(Marketing Manager)*
**Admin:** Sharon King *(Office Manager)*, Michelle Mcmahon *(Personal Assistant)*
**IT:** Andrew Gavin *(IT Manager)*
**Health & Safety:** Sharon King *(Office Manager)*
**Operations:** Sharon King *(Office Manager)*
**Purchasing:** Sharon King *(Office Manager)*
**Branches:** Scott Rees and Co, Cassiobury House 11-19, Station Road, Watford, Hertfordshire WD17 1AP
**US SIC:** 8111 **UK SIC:** 83500
**Employees:** 253

DUNS 21-138-0446

### The Scott Trust Ltd

Kings Place, 90 York Way, London N1 9GU
**Tel:** 02033532000
**Web:** www.gmgplc.co.uk
**Reg No:** 6706464 **Estd:** 2008 Private Limited Company
**Line of Business:** Management activities of holding companies
**Issued Capital:** £250,000
**Directors:** A Graham, W N Hutton, Ms E J Bell, Ms H Stewart, A A Miller, A M Salz, A C Rusbridger, A W Graham
**Co. Secretary:** Philip Tranter
**Responsibilities**
**Senior:** Elizabeth Forgan *(Director)*
**US SIC:** 6711, 2711
**UK SIC:** 83962, 47512
**Auditors:** PricewaterhouseCoopers LLP

**Following financial data are in thousands**

| | 30-03-14 | 31-03-13 | 01-03-12 |
|---|---|---|---|
| TO | 210,200 | 206,800 | 254,400 |
| P/L | (26,300) | 22,500 | (75,800) |
| NW | 1,082,300 | 532,700 | 428,800 |
| WC | 659,500 | 84,300 | 61,300 |

DUNS 21-776-5477

### Scotthall Bmw

Sheepscar Way, Gemini Business P, Leeds, West Yorkshire LS7 3JB
**Tel:** 01132620641
**Estd:** 2011 Proprietorship
**Line of Business:** New & Used Motor Vehicle Dealers
**Proprietor:** B Fielding
**US SIC:** 5511 **UK SIC:** 65100
**Employees:** 130

DUNS 21-038-8514

### Scotthall Hampshire

1 Stoneycroft Rise, Chandler's Ford, Eastleigh, Hampshire SO53 3YU
**Tel:** 023-8068-9800
**Web:** www.partridgebmw.co.uk
**Estd:** 2000 Proprietorship
**Line of Business:** Car dealers (new & used)
**Proprietor:** D Starse
**US SIC:** 5511 **UK SIC:** 65100
**Employees:** 74

DUNS 22-902-4062 **Imp**

### Scottish African Safari Park Ltd

Blair Drummond, Stirling, Stirlingshire FK9 4UR
**Tel:** 01786-841456
**Web:** www.blairdrummond.com
**Reg No:** 0977880 **Estd:** 1970 Private Limited Company
**Line of Business:** A zoo
**Trading Style:** Blair Drummond Safari & Adventure Park
**Issued Capital:** £73,817
**Directors:** J A Muir, W A Muir
**Co. Secretary:** James Muir
**US SIC:** 8421 **UK SIC:** 97700
**Auditors:** Dickson Middleton & Co

| | 31-12-13 | 31-12-12 | 31-12-11 |
|---|---|---|---|
| TA | 2,398,697 | 1,955,408 | 1,720,849 |
| NW | 1,609,677 | 1,256,081 | 1,032,621 |
| WC | 202,288 | 20,153 | 164,913 |

DUNS 23-033-4914

### Scottish Agricultural College

Riverside Campus, University Avenue, Ayr, Ayrshire KA8 0SX
**Tel:** 0800269453
**Web:** www.sac.ac.uk
**Estd:** 2011
**Line of Business:** Further education schools and colleges
**Proprietor:** A Leggape
**US SIC:** 8221 **UK SIC:** 93100
**Auditors:** Ernst & Young LLP
**Employees:** 52
**Turnover:** £47,424,000

DUNS 21-038-9218

### Scottish Agricultural Science Agency

1 Roddinglaw Road, Edinburgh, Midlothian EH12 9FJ
**Fax:** 0131-244-8940
**Web:** www.sasa.gov.uk
**Estd:** 1913 Incorporate By Act Of Parliament
**Line of Business:** Research and experimental development on natural sciences and engineering
**Trading Style:** Science and Advice for Scottich Agricultural, Sasa
**US SIC:** 7391 **UK SIC:** 94000
**Employees:** 130

DUNS 21-406-1681

### Scottish & Newcastle Ltd

(**Subsidiary of:** L'Arche Green N.V.)
2-4 Broadway Park, South Gyle Broadway, Edinburgh, Midlothian EH12 9JZ
**Tel:** 08459009074
**Web:** www.starpubs.co.uk
**Reg No:** 0016288SC **Estd:** 1978 Private Limited Company
**Line of Business:** Management activities of holding companies
**Trading Style:** Heineken Uk
**Issued Capital:** £188,988,883
**Directors:** D M Forde, Mrs K Taylor-Welsh, Miss L J Nicoll, Miss R C Hunter, J P Van Der Burg
**Co. Secretary:** Graeme Colquhoun
**Responsibilities**
**Senior:** Jeremy Blood *(Manager)*, John Botia *(Manager)*, Willie Crawshay *(Manager)*, Mark Gerken *(Manager)*, Paul Hoffman *(Manager)*
**Branches:** Scottish & Newcastle Ltd, 68 George Street, Altrincham, Cheshire WA14 1RF
**US SIC:** 6711 **UK SIC:** 83962
**Auditors:** KPMG LLP
**Bankers:** Bank Of Scotland (80-11-00)

**Following financial data are in thousands**

| | 31-12-13 | 31-12-12 | 31-12-11 |
|---|---|---|---|
| TA | 7,392,600 | 7,011,800 | 6,536,400 |
| P/L | 59,000 | 65,100 | 57,300 |
| NW | 3,125,200 | 3,061,700 | 3,005,500 |
| WC | (256,100) | (230,200) | (232,600) |
| Emp. | 130 | 126 | 118 |

DUNS 42-454-4450

### The Scottish Arts Council

Waverley Gate, Edinburgh, Midlothian EH3 7DD
**Tel:** 01312266051
**Web:** www.creativescotland.com
**Reg No:** 0000743RC **Estd:** 1969 Incorporate By Act Of Parliament
**Line of Business:** Institutes
**Principals:** M Linklater *(Chairman)*, Ms T Jackson
**Responsibilities**
**Senior:** Janet Archer *(Chief Executive Officer)*, Morag Arnot *(Chief Executive)*, Jim Tough *(Chief Executive)*
**Marketing:** Sophie Bamborough *(PR & Media Officer)*, Wendy Grannon *(Media and PR Manager)*, Katherine Green *(Marketing Manager)*, Oliver Kass *(Web Officer)*, Maggie Page *(Communications Officer)*, Morgan Petrie *(Portfolio Manager)*, Charonne Ruth *(IT Manager)*, Helen Sim *(Media & PR Assistant)*
**Sales:** Amanda Catto *(Portfolio Manager Internationa)*, Clare Hewitt *(Development Officer)*, Janice Kelly *(Head of Audience Development)*
**IT:** Charonne Ruth *(IT Manager)*
**Branches:** The Scottish Arts Council, Unit 6 Stenhouse Mill Wynd, Edinburgh, Midlothian EH11 3XX
**US SIC:** 8699 **UK SIC:** 96902
**Auditors:** Scott-Moncrieff
**Turnover:** £66,146,000

DUNS 22-907-0107 **Imp**

### The Scottish Association for Marine Science

Dunstaffnage Marine Laboratory, Dunbeg, Oban, Argyll PA37 1QA
**Tel:** 01631-559-000 **Fax:** 01631-559-001
**Web:** www.smi.ac.uk
**Reg No:** 0009292SC **Estd:** 1914 Private Company Limited By Guarantee
**Line of Business:** Miscellaneous membership organisations
**Directors:** Professor J E Francis, Mrs M A Jeffcoat, Dr R C Ferrier, Dr M Chierici, Professor I G Priede, A A Ross, K A Rundle, S G Cannon
**Co. Secretary:** Ms Elaine Walton
**Responsibilities**
**Senior:** Geoffrey Boulton *(Director)*, Keith Duff *(Manager)*, Leaurnece Mee *(Manager)*, Roger Scrutton *(Manager)*, Tracy Shimmield *(Manager)*, Ian Townend *(Manager)*, Alexander Tudhope *(Director)*
**IT:** Steve Gontarek *(Senior IT Executive)*
**US SIC:** 7399, 7391, 8221
**UK SIC:** 83954, 94000, 93100
**Auditors:** Ernst & Young LLP
**Bankers:** Bank Of Scotland (80-17-99)

| | 31-03-14 | 31-03-13 | 31-03-12 |
|---|---|---|---|
| TO | 11,275,000 | 11,633,000 | 10,398,000 |
| P/L | 26,000 | (400,000) | (337,000) |
| NW | 17,259,000 | 17,233,000 | 17,743,000 |
| WC | 463,000 | 801,000 | 1,061,000 |
| Emp. | 185 | 147 | 131 |

DUNS 22-911-9888

### Scottish Association for Mental Health

Brunswick House, Glasgow, Lanarkshire G1 1UZ
**Web:** www.samh.org.uk
**Reg No:** 0082340SC **VAT No:** 429303658
**Estd:** 1950 Private Company Limited By Guarantee
**Line of Business:** Social work activities with accommodation
**Principals:** Ms P A Aniello *(Financial)*, Ms L Russell, A R Dick, W G Gallagher, Dr L E Burley, Mrs J E Maclennan, Mrs J H Ferguson, J Law
**Responsibilities**
**Senior:** Christopher Creegan *(Director)*, Kay Hampton *(Executive Director)*, Keir Hardie *(Executive Director)*, Douglas Hutchens *(Manager)*, Pamela Mitchell *(Manager)*, Billy Watson *(Chief Executive Officer)*, Peter Woolfson *(Manager)*
**Marketing:** Pamela Graham *(Communications Officer)*
**Admin:** Una McLean *(Senior Service Support Officer)*
**IT:** John Stoner *(IT Manager)*
**Branches:** Scottish Association For Mental Health, Ailsa Hospital, Dalmellington Road, Ayr, Ayrshire KA6 6AB
**US SIC:** 8321 **UK SIC:** 96111
**Auditors:** Ernst & Young LLP
**Bankers:** Bank Of Scotland (80-11-20)

| | 31-03-14 | 31-03-13 | 31-03-12 |
|---|---|---|---|
| TO | 21,882,878 | 20,977,644 | 21,199,805 |
| P/L | 61,819 | 119,235 | 381,434 |
| NW | 5,031,998 | 4,950,208 | 4,812,663 |
| WC | 3,000,664 | 3,437,746 | 3,543,101 |
| Emp. | 694 | 639 | 730 |

DUNS 29-486-2610

### The Scottish Association of Citizens Advice Bureaux

Spectrum House, 2 Powderhall Road, Edinburgh, Midlothian EH7 4GB
**Tel:** 01315-501000
**Web:** www.citizensadvice.org.uk
**Reg No:** 0089892SC **Estd:** 2002 Private Limited Company
**Line of Business:** Activities of other membership organisations not elsewhere classified
**Trading Style:** Citizens Advice Scotland
**Directors:** D M Dennett, W Mitchell, Mrs S A Peart, Mrs S F Beer, J S Miller, M J Mcginley, C Keegan, Mrs A Robson
**Co. Secretary:** Ms Margaret Lynch
**Responsibilities**
**Senior:** Kate Hinder *(Marketing Manager)*, Mary Kinninmonth *(Director)*, Flora Martin *(Director)*, Dominic Notarangelo *(Director)*
**Branches:** The Scottish Association Of Citizens Advice Bureaux, 34 Alexander Street, Clydebank, Dunbartonshire G81 1RZ
**US SIC:** 8699 **UK SIC:** 96902
**Auditors:** BDO LLP
**Bankers:** Bank Of Scotland (80-02-73)

| | 31-03-14 | 31-03-13 | 31-03-12 |
|---|---|---|---|
| TO | 10,153,844 | 10,197,663 | 6,689,967 |
| P/L | 44,593 | 1,468,227 | 394,955 |
| NW | 3,273,102 | 3,228,509 | 1,760,282 |
| WC | 2,850,276 | 2,927,474 | 1,276,643 |
| Emp. | 79 | 70 | 71 |

DUNS 28-826-8964

### Scottish Autism

Alloa Business Centre, The Whins, Alloa, Clackmannanshire FK10 3SA
**Web:** www.scottishautism.org
**Reg No:** 0081123SC **Estd:** 1982 Private Company Limited By Guarantee
**Line of Business:** Disability services
**Directors:** Mrs S Clark, K M Wardrop, Mrs C M Scott, L G Ebner, I Mcphail, A J Lester, Dr P G Prescott, Mrs C Robertson
**Co. Secretary:** Mrs Sharon Stewart
**Responsibilities**
**Senior:** Susan Fletcher-Watson *(Director)*, Alison Leask *(Director)*, Alan Somerville *(Chief Executive)*
**IT:** Colin Sharp *(IT Manager)*
**Branches:** Scottish Autism, 100 Smithfield Loan, Alloa, Clackmannanshire FK10 1NP
**US SIC:** 8321, 8091
**UK SIC:** 96111, 95200
**Auditors:** Cheetham & Co
**Bankers:** The Royal Bank Of Scotland Plc (83-15-15)

| | 31-03-14 | 31-03-13 | 31-03-12 |
|---|---|---|---|
| TO | 21,360,439 | 20,786,702 | 19,670,037 |
| P/L | 375,605 | 664,115 | 933,817 |
| NW | 4,946,371 | 6,611,381 | 7,793,372 |
| WC | 6,343,803 | 5,752,278 | 4,919,465 |
| Emp. | 958 | 892 | 860 |

DUNS 22-902-8667

### Scottish Ballet

Tramway, 25 Albert Drive, Glasgow, Lanarkshire G41 2PE
**Tel:** 01413312931 **Fax:** 01414240757
**Web:** www.scottishballet.co.uk
**Reg No:** 0065497SC **Estd:** 1970 Private Company Limited By Guarantee
**Line of Business:** Entertainers
**Directors:** C A Meikle, Dr C M Sughrue, N Scott, J P Curran, Ms J F Craw, Ms C A Roxburgh, A Giri, M P Berry
**Co. Secretary:** Mrs Julie Merrilees
**Responsibilities**
**Senior:** Catherine Cassidy *(Associate Director, Education)*, Mike Ewart *(Board Member)*, Anne Gallacher *(Director)*, Rachel Gwyon *(Director)*, Steven Spier *(Board Member)*, Cindy Sughrue *(Chief Executive)*, Zoe Van Zwanenberg *(Chair of Board of Directors)*

**Finance:** Fiona Donaldson *(Financial Controller)*, Paul Hacket *(Director of Resources)*, Kae Sakurai *(Finance Assistant)*
**Marketing:** Clare Campbell *(Marketing Officer)*, Kirsten Cockburn *(Head of Marketing)*, Charlotte Gross *(Sales & Marketing Manager)*, Ann Nugent *(Communications Manager)*, Christina Riley *(Marketing & Communications Edi)*
**Sales:** Charlotte Gross *(Sales & Marketing Manager)*
**Admin:** Yvonne Halliday *(Receptionist/ Administrator)*, Laura Keceyapan *(Administration Officer)*, Joanna Millard *(Human Resources Manager)*
**HR:** Joanna Millard *(Human Resources Manager)*
**Operations:** Sheelagh Mccabe *(Stage Manager)*, Joanna Mclean *(Wardrobe Assistant)*
**Engineering:** Matthew Strachan *(Chief Electrician)*
**US SIC:** 7911, 8999
**UK SIC:** 97913, 83954
**Auditors:** Grant Thornton
**Bankers:** Clydesdale Bank Plc (82-20-00)

| | 31-03-14 | 31-03-13 | 31-03-12 |
|---|---|---|---|
| TO | 7,144,816 | 6,821,840 | 7,702,374 |
| P/L | 605,922 | 302,114 | 1,055,923 |
| NW | 12,396,191 | 11,790,269 | 11,488,155 |
| WC | 1,744,515 | 1,029,310 | 443,545 |
| Emp. | 83 | 88 | 89 |

DUNS 21-119-6886
## Scottish Borders Council
Council Headquarters, Melrose, Roxburghshire TD6 0SA
**Tel:** 01835-824000 **Fax:** 01835-825001
**Web:** www.scotborders.gov.uk
**Estd:** 2010 Incorporate By Act Of Parliament
**Line of Business:** Central government
**Directors:** K Clarke, P Jeary, A Croall, A Bowman
**Responsibilities**
**Admin:** Linda Young *(Office Supervisor)*
**Health & Safety:** Graham Cresswell *(Health & Safety Officer)*
**Facilities:** David Romanis *(Buildings Maintenance Manager)*
**Operations:** Graham Cresswell *(Health & Safety Officer)*
**Branches:** Scottish Borders Council, 3 St. John Street, Galashiels, Selkirkshire TD1 3JX
**US SIC:** 9121 **UK SIC:** 91110
**Bankers:** The Royal Bank Of Scotland Plc (83-26-34)
**Employees:** 590

DUNS 21-122-1617
## Scottish Borders Housing Associationltd.
South Bridge House, Whinfield Road, Selkirk, Selkirkshire TD7 5DT
**Tel:** 01750-724444
**Web:** www.sbha.org.uk
**Reg No:** 0002573IP **Estd:** 2002
**Line of Business:** Housing associations societies trusts & co-operatives
**Trading Style:** Scottish Borders Housing Association
**Proprietor:** Mrs J Cambridge
**Responsibilities**
**Senior:** Janice Cambridge *(Chief Executive)*
**Finance:** Carly Stewart *(Director of Finance)*
**HR:** David McCracken *(Human Resource Manager)*
**Facilities:** Maria Lyle *(Director of Housing Services)*
**US SIC:** 8321 **UK SIC:** 96111
**Auditors:** Chiene & Tait
**Bankers:** Lloyds TSB Bank plc (30-13-01)
**Employees:** 70
**Turnover:** £15,968,736

DUNS 22-912-7030
## Scottish Building Society
193 Dalry Road, Edinburgh, Midlothian EH11 2EF
**Tel:** 0131-313-7700
**Web:** www.scottishbs.co.uk
**Reg No:** 0000032T **Estd:** 1848 Friendly Society
**Line of Business:** Building societies
**Principals:** P C Brown *(Chairman)*, D D Carmichael, R Matteson, W A Johnston, F C Barron, E I Cuthbertson, W A Munro, R M Sherriff
**Co. Secretary:** Scott Oswald & Co
**Responsibilities**
**Senior:** Janet Gillespie *(Executive Assistant)*, Gerry Kaye *(Chief Executive)*, Mark Thomson *(Chief Executive Officer)*
**US SIC:** 6111 **UK SIC:** 81501
**Bankers:** The Royal Bank Of Scotland Plc (83-06-08)
**Employees:** 40

DUNS 63-454-1221
## The Scottish Childrens Reporter Administration
Ochil House, Springkerse Business Park, Stirling, Stirlingshire FK7 7XE
**Tel:** 03002001555
**Web:** www.scra.gov.uk
**Estd:** 2012
**Line of Business:** Central government
**Chairman:** Ms S Kuenssberg
**Responsibilities**
**Senior:** Michelle Rice *(Administration Manager)*
**Branches:** The Scottish Childrens Reporter Administration, Campfield House, Wellside Place, Falkirk, Stirlingshire FK1 5RL
**US SIC:** 6732 **UK SIC:** 83100
**Employees:** 60

DUNS 28-821-9868
## The Scottish Council of Law Reporting
26-27 Drumsheugh Gardens, Edinburgh, Midlothian EH3 7YR
**Tel:** 01314779000 **Fax:** 0131-225-2934
**Web:** www.scottishlawreports.org.uk
**Reg No:** 0032729SC **Estd:** 1949 Private Company Limited By Guarantee
**Line of Business:** Other publishing
**Directors:** J A Millar, Mrs J Cherry Qc, K J Campbell, R J Waldhelm, Ms J Mcrae
**Co Secretary:** Anthony Kinahan
**US SIC:** 2741 **UK SIC:** 47541
**Auditors:** KPMG
**Bankers:** Clydesdale Bank Plc (82-45-05)

| | 31-12-13 | 31-12-12 | 31-12-11 |
|---|---|---|---|
| TO | 233,083 | 163,378 | 194,775 |
| P/L | 25,588 | 18,605 | (63,110) |
| NW | 355,960 | 311,567 | 281,414 |
| WC | 167,598 | 142,010 | 173,405 |

DUNS 54-897-2298
## Scottish Council Y W C A Housing Association Ltd
188 Bawtry Road, Bramley, Rotherham, South Yorkshire S66 2TR
**Tel:** 01709702411 **Fax:** 0131-229-8236
**Reg No:** 0001477IP **Estd:** 2012 Friendly Society
**Line of Business:** Residential care establishments
**Trading Style:** Haven Housing Association
**Responsibilities**
**Senior:** Maureen Spencer *(Manager)*
**Branches:** Scottish Council Y W C A Housing Association Ltd, Craigellachie Crescent, Aviemore, Inverness-Shire PH22 1PA
**US SIC:** 6531 **UK SIC:** 83400
**Employees:** 60

DUNS 23-310-9920
## Scottish Court Service
Saughton House, Broomhouse Drive, Edinburgh, Midlothian EH11 3XD
**Tel:** 01314443300
**Web:** www.scotcourts.gov.uk
**Estd:** 1995
**Line of Business:** Justice and judicial activities
**Director:** Ms E Emberson
**Responsibilities**
**Senior:** Janet Blackstock *(Sheriff Clerk)*, Graeme Marwick *(Member)*, Eric McQueen *(Chief Executive)*, Gillian Prentice *(Member)*
**US SIC:** 9211 **UK SIC:** 91200
**Employees:** 100

DUNS 21-453-5523
## Scottish Crime and Drug Enforcement
Osprey House, Inchinnan Road, Paisley, Renfrewshire PA3 2RE
**Tel:** 01413021000 **Fax:** 01413-021090
**Estd:** 2000 Incorporate By Act Of Parliament
**Line of Business:** Drug enforcement agency. MISSION STATEMENT: To drive and co-ordinate a substantially enhanced multi agency response to combat the threat from drug trafficking and other serious and organised crime in Scotland.
**Trading Style:** Scde
**Director:** G Pearson
**US SIC:** 9221 **UK SIC:** 91300
**Employees:** 203

DUNS 28-821-8027 **Imp-Exp**
## The Scottish Crop Research Institute
Errol Road, Invergowrie, Invergowrie, Dundee, Angus DD2 5DA
**Tel:** 01382562731 **Fax:** 01382-562426
**Web:** www.scri.ac.uk
**Reg No:** 0029367SC **Estd:** 1953 Private Company Limited By Guarantee
**Line of Business:** Research institutions and organisations
**Trading Style:** James Hutton Institute
**Directors:** A M Stevenson, Professor D Boxer
**Co. Secretary:** Elizabeth Corcoran
**Responsibilities**
**Senior:** Steve Petrie *(Head of Maintenance)*
**Finance:** Neil Hattersley *(Financial Director)*
**Marketing:** Jonathan Snape *(Sales & Marketing Manager)*
**Sales:** Jonathan Snape *(Sales & Marketing Manager)*
**Admin:** Alison Cartwright *(Office Manager)*
**IT:** Scott Clark *(IS Manager)*
**HR:** Alison Cartwright *(Office Manager)*
**Health & Safety:** Frances Rowe *(Health & Safety Officer)*
**Facilities:** Steve Petrie *(Head of Maintenance)*
**Engineering:** Steve Petrie *(Head of Maintenance)*
**Branches:** The Scottish Crop Research Institute, University Of Edinburgh, James Clerk Maxwell Building, Edinburgh, Midlothian EH9 3JZ
**US SIC:** 7391 **UK SIC:** 94000
**Auditors:** PricewaterhouseCoopers
**Bankers:** Bank Of Scotland (80-73-31)
**Employees:** 300

DUNS 21-442-6348
## Scottish Daily Record & Sunday Mail Ltd
(**Subsidiary of:** Trinity Mirror Plc)
Daily Record Building, 40 Anderston Quay, Glasgow, Lanarkshire G3 8DA
**Tel:** 0141-309-3000
**Web:** www.dailyrecord.co.uk
**Reg No:** 0012921SC **Estd:** 1923 Private Limited Company
**Line of Business:** Printing of newspapers
**Issued Capital:** £1,022,084
**Directors:** V L Vaghela, S R Fox
**Co. Secretary:** T M Secretaries Limited
**Responsibilities**
**Senior:** Mark Hollinshead *(General Manager)*
**Finance:** Maria Henry *(Senior Finance Administrator)*, Mark Mountford *(Financial Director)*
**Marketing:** Mark Hollinshead *(General Manager)*, Mark Mountford *(Financial Director)*
**Admin:** Alec MacDonald *(Facilities Manager)*
**Health & Safety:** Alec MacDonald *(Facilities Manager)*
**Facilities:** Alec MacDonald *(Facilities Manager)*
**Operations:** Alec MacDonald *(Facilities Manager)*
**Purchasing:** Alec MacDonald *(Facilities Manager)*
**Fleet:** Alec MacDonald *(Facilities Manager)*
**Branches:** Scottish Daily Record & Sunday Mail Ltd, 1 Canada Square, London E14 5AR
**US SIC:** 2711 **UK SIC:** 47512
**Auditors:** Deloitte & Touche LLP
**Bankers:** The Royal Bank Of Scotland Plc (83-44-00)

| | 29-12-13 | 30-12-12 | 01-12-12 |
|---|---|---|---|
| TO | 73,607,000 | 78,851,000 | 85,310,000 |
| P/L | 11,896,000 | 13,151,000 | 8,888,000 |
| NW | 102,966,000 | 93,774,000 | 83,837,000 |
| WC | 83,135,000 | 72,798,000 | 61,658,000 |
| Emp. | 338 | 303 | 342 |

DUNS 42-319-6625
## Scottish Development International
5 Atlantic Quay, Glasgow, Lanarkshire G2 8LU
**Tel:** 01412282828
**Web:** www.sdi.co.uk
**Line of Business:** Development agencies
**Principals:** Scottish Enterprise, Scottish Enterprise, Business Gateway Scotland, TalentScotland, Highlands and Islands Enterprise
**Responsibilities**
**Senior:** Anne MacColl *(chief executive)*, Linda Mcdowall *(Manager)*, Alex Mcguire *(international senior manager)*
**Finance:** Gerry Boyce *(International Finance Manager)*, Kenneth Clark *(Trade and Investment Manager)*
**Marketing:** Sarah Cross *(PR Executive)*, Joanne Murphy *(International Business Executi)*
**Sales:** Graeme White *(Business Developer)*
**Admin:** Caroline Greig *(renewable energy senior admini)*
**IT:** Mike Shiel *(Head Of Technology)*
**Operations:** John Carmichael *(Project Manager)*, John McGinnes *(Senior International Trade Exe)*
**Engineering:** Laura Campbell *(Technology & Creative Industri)*
**US SIC:** 9121 **UK SIC:** 91110
**Employees:** 65

DUNS 21-588-8611 **Imp**
## Scottish Enterprise
150 Broomielaw, Glasgow, Lanarkshire G2 8LU
**Tel:** 01412041111
**Web:** www.scottish-enterprise.com
**Estd:** 1990 Incorporate By Act Of Parliament
**Line of Business:** Management and business consultants
**Trading Style:** Careers Scotland
**Directors:** T Farmer, C Beveridge, Ms G Hogarth-Coull, C Gray, Sir G Hills, C Mclatchie, Professor A Bain, Professor J S Calman
**Responsibilities**
**Senior:** Adrian Gillespie *(Managing Director Operations)*, Anne MacColl *(Managing Director Operations)*, Cameron McLatchie *(Director)*, Yvonne Strachan *(Director)*
**Marketing:** Jamie Crawford *(International Marketing Senior)*
**Sales:** Amanda Dutton *(Assistance Development Executi)*, Gerry Love *(Senior International Business)*, Lorna MacMillan *(International Business Executi)*, Catriona Wilson *(International Business Executi)*
**Operations:** Shaqil Gastasab *(International Executive)*, Anne MacColl *(Managing Director Operations)*, Mark McMullen *(International Senior Manager)*, Andy Vaughan *(Senior International Executive)*
**Purchasing:** Murray Bainbridge *(Senior International Trade Exe)*
**Branches:** Scottish Enterprise, 14 St. Vincent Place, Glasgow, Lanarkshire G1 2EU
**US SIC:** 9121 **UK SIC:** 91110
**Auditors:** KPMG LLP
**Employees:** 200
**Turnover:** £48,668,000

DUNS 50-574-4342 **Exp**
## Scottish Enterprise Glasgow
50 Waterloo Street, Glasgow, Lanarkshire G2 6HQ
**Tel:** 01412041111
**Web:** www.scottish-enterprise.com
**Reg No:** 0126249SC **Estd:** 1990 Private Limited Company
**Line of Business:** General (overall) public service activities
**Export Markets:** E U, Worldwide
**Trading Style:** Scottish Enterprise
**Issued Capital:** £2
**Directors:** I Scott, D L Colquhoun
**Co. Secretary:** Ms Jacqueline Edwards
**Responsibilities**
**Senior:** Euan Dobson *(Manager)*, Linda Hanna *(Managing Director, Strategy &)*, Anne MacColl *(Chief Executive, Scottish Deve)*
**Sales:** Lindsay Branston *(Business Development Manager)*, Gavin Hanna *(Account Manager)*, Linda McDowall *(Executive Director, Business N)*, Colin Morris *(Commercial Director)*, laura birch *(commercial manager)*
**Admin:** Geraldine Shanahan *(Office Manager)*
**HR:** Carolyn Stewart *(Human Resources Director)*
**Health & Safety:** Geraldine Shanahan *(Office Manager)*
**Operations:** David Garry *(Project Manager)*, Adrian Gillespie *(Managing Director Operations -)*, Terry Hogg *(Project Manager)*, John MacLennan *(Project Manager)*
**Branches:** Scottish Enterprise Glasgow, Unit 9, Maryhill Road, Glasgow, Lanarkshire G20 0SP
**US SIC:** 9121 **UK SIC:** 91110
**Auditors:** KPMG LLP
**Bankers:** Bank Of Scotland (80-11-80)

| | 31-03-12 |
|---|---|
| P/L | (894,000) |

DUNS 50-379-3150
## Scottish Enterprise Grampian
27 Albyn Place, Aberdeen, Aberdeenshire AB10 1DB
**Tel:** 01224252000 **Fax:** 01224-213417
**Web:** www.scottish-enterprise.com
**Reg No:** 0118134SC **VAT No:** 552946812
**Estd:** 1989 Private Company Limited By Guarantee
**Line of Business:** Financial intermediation not elsewhere classified
**Directors:** I Scott, D L Colquhoun
**Co. Secretary:** Stuart Clarke
**Responsibilities**
**Senior:** Maggie McGuinlay *(Chief Executive)*
**Sales:** Lynn Davie *(Account Manager)*
**Facilities:** Angela McLean *(Facilities Manager)*
**Branches:** Scottish Enterprise Grampian, Seagate, Peterhead, Aberdeenshire AB42 1JP
**US SIC:** 6111 **UK SIC:** 81501
**Auditors:** KPMG LLP

**Bankers:** Clydesdale Bank Plc (82-60-11)

| | 31-03-12 |
|---|---|
| P/L | (366,000) |

DUNS 50-541-7972

## Scottish Enterprise Lanarkshire

New Lanarkshire House, Dove Wynd, Strathclyde Business Park, Bellshill, Lanarkshire ML4 3AD
**Tel:** 01698745454
**Web:** www.scottish-enterprise.com
**Reg No:** 0124620SC **Estd:** 2002 Private Company Limited By Guarantee
**Line of Business:** Activities of business and employers organisations
**Directors:** I Scott, D Colquhoun
**Co. Secretary:** Stuart Clarke
**Responsibilities**
**Senior:** Micheal Mchugh (Manager)
**Marketing:** Karen Eadie (Office Manager), Geraldine Shanahan (Office Manager)
**Sales:** Karen Eadie (Office Manager), Geraldine Shanahan (Office Manager)
**Admin:** Karen Eadie (Office Manager), Geraldine Shanahan (Office Manager)
**HR:** Lynne Shearer (Human Resources Manager)
**Health & Safety:** Geraldine Shanahan (Office Manager)
**Operations:** Geraldine Shanahan (Office Manager)
**Purchasing:** Karen Eadie (Office Manager), Geraldine Shanahan (Office Manager)
**Branches:** Scottish Enterprise Lanarkshire, 4 Platthorn Rd, Glasgow, Lanarkshire G74 1NW
**US SIC:** 8611 **UK SIC:** 96312
**Auditors:** KPMG LLP
**Bankers:** The Royal Bank Of Scotland Plc (83-22-26)

| | 31-03-12 |
|---|---|
| P/L | (957,000) |

DUNS 23-599-4449

## Scottish Environment Protection Agency

Strathallan House, The Castle Business Park, Stirling, Stirlingshire FK9 4TZ
**Tel:** 01786-457700 **Fax:** 01786-446885
**Web:** www.sepa.org.uk
**Estd:** 1996 Incorporate By Act Of Parliament
**Line of Business:** Other engineering activities
**Trading Style:** S E P A
**Directors:** Ms T Henton, J Ford
**Responsibilities**
**Senior:** Jacqueline Macmillan (Senior Manager)
**Finance:** Bill Lyons (Head of Resilience), Stuart McGregor (Chief Financial Officer), Fiona Wright (Finance Manager)
**Admin:** Fiona Weatherly (National Waste Strategy Techni)
**HR:** Jennifer Russell (Human Resources Manager)
**Facilities:** Stephen Field (Land Unit Manager)
**Operations:** Neil Archibald (Head of Business Support), Janice Milne (Head of National Operations)
**Purchasing:** Myles O' Reilly (Contract Manager), Clare Scanlan (Contract Manager)
**Branches:** Scottish Environment Protection Agency, 2 Alloway Pl, Ayr, Ayrshire KA7 2AA
**US SIC:** 8911 **UK SIC:** 83701
**Bankers:** The Royal Bank Of Scotland Plc (83-34-00)
**Employees:** 300

DUNS 34-873-4930

## Scottish Equitable Plc

(**Subsidiary of:** Aegon N.V.)
Edinburgh Park 1-3, Lochside Crescent, Edinburgh, Midlothian EH12 9SE
**Tel:** 08702-426789
**Web:** www.aegon.co.uk
**Reg No:** 0144517SC **VAT No:** 502229195
**Estd:** 1993 Public Limited Company
**Line of Business:** Life insurance
**Trading Style:** Aegonse Scottish Equitable
**Issued Capital:** £625,000,000
**Directors:** J Ewing, A M Eastwood, S J Gulliford, P C Easter, Mrs C F Ramsay, M R Tuohy, Ms C Bousfield, D D Button
**Co. Secretary:** Ms Marian Glen
**Responsibilities**
**Senior:** Maurice Brunet (Head of Customer Services), Feilim Mackle (Manager), Michael Merrick (Director)
**HR:** Sandy Begbie (Human Resources Director)
**Operations:** Maurice Brunet (Head of Customer Services)
**Branches:** Scottish Equitable Plc, 7th Floor, Southgate Ho, Wood St, Cardiff, South Glamorgan CF10 1EW
**US SIC:** 6311, 6371

---

**UK SIC:** 82002
**Auditors:** Ernst & Young LLP
**Bankers:** The Royal Bank Of Scotland Plc (83-06-08)
Following financial data are in thousands

| | 31-12-13 | 31-12-12 | 31-12-11 |
|---|---|---|---|
| TO | 5,547,000 | 4,899,600 | 5,516,100 |
| P/L | 96,200 | 198,500 | (51,000) |
| NW | 3,861,600 | 4,013,900 | 3,431,100 |
| WC | (52,336,000) | (54,647,600) | 46,658,200 |
| Emp. | 3,500 | N/A | N/A |

DUNS 22-907-0289

## Scottish Exhibition Centre Ltd

Exhibition Way, Glasgow, Lanarkshire G3 8YW
**Tel:** 08700404000
**Web:** www.secc.co.uk
**Reg No:** 0082081SC **VAT No:** 382955512
**Estd:** 1983 Private Limited Company
**Line of Business:** Exhibition and trade centres
**Issued Capital:** £21,900,000
**Directors:** W P Mcfadyen, W E Whitehorn, Ms M Mcneill, T F Turley, G Hendry, Ms C Forrest, Ms P A Lafferty, P G Duthie
**Co. Secretary:** William Mcfadyen
**Responsibilities**
**Senior:** Malcolm Close (Manager), Bernard Goedegebuure (Manager), Morag Johnston (Director)
**Finance:** Billy McFadyen (Financial Director)
**Marketing:** Sean Murray (Head of Marketing)
**HR:** Lilias Bennie (Human Resources Manager)
**Health & Safety:** Alan Cuggy (Health & Safety Officer)
**US SIC:** 6519, 8999
**UK SIC:** 85000, 83954
**Auditors:** Ernst & Young LLP
**Bankers:** Bank Of Scotland (80-54-01)

| | 31-03-14 | 31-03-13 | 31-03-12 |
|---|---|---|---|
| TO | 23,321,828 | 29,508,149 | 27,087,709 |
| P/L | 61,409 | 1,432,293 | (29,838,047) |
| NW | 42,050,642 | 42,417,341 | 40,456,052 |
| WC | (15,300,149) | 19,790,460 | 9,429,493 |
| Emp. | 217 | 211 | 222 |

DUNS 42-487-3024

## Scottish Fire and Rescue Service

99 Bothwell Road, Hamilton, Lanarkshire ML3 0EA
**Fax:** 01698-338444
**Web:** www.firescotland.gov.uk
**VAT No:** 680443927 **Estd:** 1974 Incorporate By Act Of Parliament
**Line of Business:** Fire service activities
**Trading Style:** Strathclyde Fire
**Director:** J Jameson
**Responsibilities**
**Senior:** John Cairns (Executive), Martin Gordon (Group Manager)
**Finance:** Eileen Beard (Financial director)
**HR:** Mary Corry (Training Manager), Pauline Docherty (Personnel Officer)
**Health & Safety:** Mick Hydes (Senior Health and Safety Manag)
**Operations:** Grace Quigley (Project Executive)
**Engineering:** Grace Quigley (Project Executive)
**Branches:** Scottish Fire and Rescue Service, West Command Headquarters, 4 Barr Street, Ardrossan, Ayrshire KA22 8HD
**US SIC:** 7399 **UK SIC:** 83954
**Employees:** 350

DUNS 22-902-4427

## Scottish Fishermen's Organisation Ltd

601 Queensferry Road, Edinburgh, Midlothian EH4 6EA
**Web:** www.scottishfishermen.co.uk
**Reg No:** 0053475SC **Estd:** 1973 Private Company Limited By Guarantee
**Line of Business:** Fish processing
**Trading Style:** S F O, Brarhead (S F O Enterprises)
**Directors:** J R Clark, G R West, A M Kenning, R Skinner, A West, J A Macdougall, I Murray, J Macalister
**Co. Secretary:** Iain Macsween
**Responsibilities**
**Senior:** Bruce Buchan (Director), James Buchan (Director), Tommy Finn (Director), Peter Lovie (Director), Ian Mac Sween (CEO), Alexander Mcleman (Director), Adam Tait (Director), James Thores (Manager), William Wiseman (Manager)
**Branches:** Scottish Fishermen's Organisation Ltd, 8 Bridge Street, Peterhead, Aberdeenshire AB42 1DH
**US SIC:** 0921 **UK SIC:** 03002
**Auditors:** Blueprint Scotland

---

**Bankers:** Bank Of Scotland (80-20-00)

| | 31-12-13 | 31-12-12 | 31-12-11 |
|---|---|---|---|
| TO | 14,420,870 | 15,887,383 | 15,792,587 |
| P/L | 1,084,137 | 711,942 | 934,254 |
| NW | 13,158,845 | 12,178,235 | 11,162,401 |
| WC | 11,079,012 | 9,667,989 | 9,674,018 |
| Emp. | 68 | 61 | 61 |

DUNS 28-821-0370                                    **Imp**

## The Scottish Football Association Ltd

Hampden Park, Letherby Drive, Glasgow, Lanarkshire G42 9BA
**Tel:** 01416204550 **Fax:** 01416166001
**Web:** www.scottishfa.co.uk
**Reg No:** 0005453SC **Estd:** 1873 Private Company Limited By Guarantee
**Line of Business:** Sports clubs
**Trading Style:** Scottish Schools Football Association
**Directors:** R M Petrie, A Mcrae, S M Regan, T A Johnston, B M Jackson, P T Lawwell, R C Ogilvie, R J Topping
**Co. Secretary:** Heather-Anne Barton
**Responsibilities**
**Senior:** John Gold (Manager), Thomas Mckeown (National Secretary), Alexander Stables (board member)
**Marketing:** Kenny MacLeod (Commercial Director)
**Sales:** Kenny MacLeod (Commercial Director)
**Admin:** Thomas Mckeown (National Secretary)
**IT:** Scott MacIntosh (IT Manager)
**HR:** Vivien Coady (Human Resources Manager)
**US SIC:** 7999, 3652, 7941
**UK SIC:** 97913, 34520, 97911
**Auditors:** Grant Thornton
**Bankers:** Bank Of Scotland (80-83-33)

| | 31-12-13 | 31-12-12 | 31-12-11 |
|---|---|---|---|
| TO | 32,915,264 | 33,268,611 | 32,385,675 |
| P/L | 554,673 | 698,614 | 278,003 |
| NW | 11,045,358 | 7,925,015 | 6,543,550 |
| WC | 1,918,127 | 1,987,708 | 1,626,878 |
| Emp. | 183 | 178 | 148 |

DUNS 23-703-5928

## Scottish Friendly Assurance

Scottish Friendly House, 16 Blythswood Square, Glasgow, Lanarkshire G2 4HJ
**Tel:** 01412755000 **Fax:** 0141-221-4864
**Web:** www.scottishfriendly.co.uk
**Reg No:** 0000034SP **Estd:** 1890 Friendly Society
**Line of Business:** Activities of open-ended investment companies
**Directors:** A J Agnew, A D Forbes, G H Webster, A Gilchrist, W E Aiton, I B Smail, S M Smith, R G Thomson
**Co. Secretary:** A Bramley
**Responsibilities**
**Senior:** J Bairdwatson (Director), Fiona Mcbaine (Chief Executive Officer)
**Finance:** Colin Saxby (Financial Director)
**Marketing:** Callum Bennie (Marketing Manager)
**Sales:** Callum Bennie (Marketing Manager)
**IT:** Jeffrey Wilson (IT Manager)
**Facilities:** Jeffrey Wilson (IT Manager)
**Operations:** Jeffrey Wilson (IT Manager)
**Purchasing:** Callum Bennie (Marketing Manager)
**US SIC:** 6724, 6111, 6732
**UK SIC:** 81502, 81501, 83100
**Auditors:** KPMG Audit PLC

| | 31-12-12 | 31-12-09 | 31-12-08 |
|---|---|---|---|
| TA | 822,764,000 | 755,102,000 | 704,583,000 |
| P/L | N/A | 24,271,000 | N/A |
| NW | N/A | N/A | 71,218,000 |
| WC | 248,373,000 | 78,036,000 | 108,313,000 |
| Emp. | 136 | 143 | 93 |

DUNS 23-183-9726                                    **Imp**

## Scottish Funding Council

Apex 2, Edinburgh, Midlothian EH12 5HD
**Tel:** 0131-313-6500
**Web:** www.sfc.ac.uk
**Estd:** 1999
**Line of Business:** Education agencies and authorities
**Principals:** J Mcclelland (Chairman), R Mcclure
**Responsibilities**
**Senior:** Duncan Condie (Executive), Paul Hagan (Director, Research and Innovat), Judith Henderson (Director, Strategic Developmen), Laurence Howells (Senior Director, Research & Kn), John Mcclelland (Chairperson), Roger McClure (Chief Executive Officer), Keith McDonald (General Manager), Ann Millar (Director, Research Policy and), Ian Murning (Board Member), Esther Roberton (Chairman)
**Finance:** Riona Bell (Finance Director), Dorothy Carson (Financial Analyst), Jennifer Mcgregor (Head of HEI Funding), Mark Naylor (Funding Officer)
**Marketing:** Judith Henderson (Director, Strategic Developmen)
**Admin:** Derek Horsburgh (Clerk)

---

**IT:** Laurence McDonald (Computer Manager)
**US SIC:** 8299 **UK SIC:** 93300
**Employees:** 120

DUNS 52-006-4478

## Scottish Gas Ltd

(**Subsidiary of:** Centrica Plc)
1 Waterfront Avenue, Edinburgh, Midlothian EH5 1SG
**Tel:** 08003161651 **Fax:** 01313446943
**Web:** www.scotland.gov.uk
**Reg No:** 0175628SC **Estd:** 1997 Private Limited Company
**Line of Business:** Central heating supplies
**Trading Style:** British Gas
**Issued Capital:** £2
**Directors:** Ms N M Carroll, Centrica Directors Limited
**Co. Secretary:** Centrica Secretaries Limited
**Responsibilities**
**Senior:** David Ramsay (Programme Manager)
**HR:** Gillian Stephenson (Training Manager)
**Facilities:** Neil Hollis (Facilities Manager)
**US SIC:** 7399, 4932
**UK SIC:** 83954, 16200

| | 31-12-13 | 31-12-12 | 31-12-11 |
|---|---|---|---|
| TA | 2 | 2 | 2 |
| NW | 2 | 2 | 2 |

DUNS 23-222-6415

## Scottish Government

St Andrews House, 2 Regent Road, Edinburgh, Midlothian EH1 3DG
**Tel:** 01315568400 **Fax:** 0139795001
**Web:** www.scotland.gov.uk
**Estd:** 1999 Incorporate By Act Of Parliament
**Line of Business:** Central Government
**Trading Style:** Scottish Procurement
**Responsibilities**
**Finance:** Alyson Stafford (Director General Finance)
**Branches:** Scottish Government, New Abbey Corn Mill, Dumfries, Dumfriesshire DG2 8BU
**US SIC:** 9111 **UK SIC:** 91110
**Bankers:** Bank Of England (10-14-99)
**Employees:** 2,500

DUNS 23-557-2398

## The Scottish Institute of Sport

Fairview, Airthrey Road, Stirling, Stirlingshire FK9 5PH
**Tel:** 01786-460100 **Fax:** 01786-460101
**Web:** www.sisport.com
**Reg No:** 0185362SC **Estd:** 1998 Private Unlimited Company
**Line of Business:** Other sporting activities not elsewhere classified
**Director:** S G Harris
**Responsibilities**
**Senior:** Alistair Call (Manager)
**Finance:** Tracy Austin (Financial Manager)
**Marketing:** Matt Lock (Communications Manager)
**Admin:** Tracy Austin (Financial Manager)
**IT:** Laura Carey (Network Performance Psychologi), Mark Ritchie (Network Manager)
**Health & Safety:** Kristine Dun (Sport Psychologist)
**Operations:** Cate Brewster (Head Performance Coach), Karen Mccall (Production and Operations Mana), Fiona Simpson (Production and Operations Mana)
**US SIC:** 7999 **UK SIC:** 97913
**Employees:** 70

DUNS 21-402-3038

## Scottish Leather Group Ltd

1 Seedhill, Paisley, Renfrewshire PA1 1JL
**Tel:** 01418-474-520
**Web:** www.scottishleathergroup.com
**Reg No:** 0042020SC **VAT No:** 264644348
**Estd:** 1965 Private Limited Company
**Line of Business:** Tanning and dressing of leather
**Issued Capital:** £1,025,936
**Directors:** I F Mcfadyen, R M Brown, I A Lundie, J Davidson, J A Muirhead, I D Duffin, Mrs M K Marshall, W J Lang
**Co. Secretary:** Ronald Brown
**Responsibilities**
**IT:** Vincent Morris (IT Director)
**US SIC:** 3111 **UK SIC:** 44101
**Auditors:** KPMG LLP
**Bankers:** Clydesdale Bank Plc (82-20-00)

| | 31-03-14 | 31-03-13 | 31-03-12 |
|---|---|---|---|
| TO | 136,227,000 | 115,522,000 | 119,304,000 |
| P/L | 4,537,000 | 4,484,000 | 8,683,000 |
| NW | 52,824,000 | 50,932,000 | 49,978,000 |
| WC | 32,294,000 | 29,492,000 | 30,955,000 |
| Emp. | 561 | 564 | 505 |

DUNS 23-187-9586

## Scottish Legal Aid Board

44 Drumsheugh Gardens, Edinburgh, Midlothian EH3 7SW
**Tel:** 0131-226-7061
**Web:** www.slab.org.uk
**Estd:** 1987
**Line of Business:** Information services
**Principals:** J Edgar *(Financial)*, R Scott, P O'Connell
**Responsibilities**
**Senior:** Lindsay Montgomery *(Chief Executive)*
**Finance:** Vince Simmons *(Financial Controller)*
**Admin:** Julie Garvey *(Executive Assistant)*, Yvonne Stuart *(Legal Secretary)*
**IT:** John McLeod *(Head of IT)*
**HR:** Linda Laughland *(Personnel Manager)*
**Operations:** Steven Carrie *(Technical, Production Manager)*
**US SIC:** 8111 **UK SIC:** 83500
**Bankers:** The Royal Bank Of Scotland Plc (83-06-08)
**Employees:** 300

DUNS 28-823-2127

## The Scottish Life Guarantee Company Ltd.

**(Subsidiary of:** The Royal London Mutual Insurance Society Limited)
Royal London House, Alderley Road, Wilmslow, Cheshire SK9 1PF
**Tel:** 08456050050 **Fax:** 01314567880
**Web:** www.royal-london.co.uk
**Reg No:** 0050741SC **Estd:** 1996 Private Limited Company
**Line of Business:** Activities auxiliary to insurance and pension funding
**Trading Style:** Royal London
**Issued Capital:** £1
**Director:** Ms J M Murray
**Co. Secretary:**
Royal London Management Services
**Responsibilities**
**Senior:** Christopher Aujard *(Manager)*, Stephen Shone *(Finance Director)*
**Finance:** Stephen Shone *(Finance Director)*
**US SIC:** 6411 **UK SIC:** 83200
**Auditors:** KPMG Audit Plc
**Bankers:** Bank Of Scotland (80-11-00)

| | 31-12-13 | 31-12-12 | 31-12-11 |
|---|---|---|---|
| TA | 1 | 1 | 1 |
| NW | 1 | 1 | 1 |

DUNS 21-829-9785

## Scottish Masonic Homes Ltd

Freemasons Hall, 96 George Street, Edinburgh, Midlothian EH2 3DH
**Tel:** 01312266665
**Reg No:** 0419899SC **Estd:** 2012 Private Company Limited By Guarantee
**Line of Business:** Social work activities with accommodation
**Directors:** J Bell, D M Begg, T C Smith
**US SIC:** 8321 **UK SIC:** 96111
**Bankers:** Bank Of Scotland (80-11-00)

| | 31-03-13 |
|---|---|
| TO | 1,432,220 |
| P/L | 911,655 |
| NW | 911,655 |
| WC | (132,292) |
| Emp. | 64 |

DUNS 21-587-6566 Imp

## Scottish Midland Co-Operative Society Ltd

Unit 61 Longwood Road, Newtownabbey, Co Antrim BT37 9UL
**Tel:** 01313 354400 **Fax:** 01313356500
**Web:** www.scotmid.com
**Reg No:** 0002059T **VAT No:** 269727214
**Estd:** 1859 Friendly Society
**Line of Business:** Supermarkets
**Trading Style:** Scotmid, Semichem
**Directors:** J Hill, G Manderson, C Kerr, Ms A Williamson, R Smith, Mrs M Hume, D Moon, G A Hill
**Co. Secretary:** Colin Bird
**Responsibilities**
**Senior:** J Gillhurst *(Director)*, John Roady *(Chief Executive)*, H Smallman *(President)*
**Branches:** Scottish Midland Co-Operative Society Limited, 46-50 Drysdale St, Alloa, Clackmannanshire FK10 1JL
**US SIC:** 5411, 5999
**UK SIC:** 64100, 65600
**Auditors:** Deloitte LLP
**Employees:** 4,211
**Turnover:** £322,338,000

DUNS 22-901-2588

## Scottish Motor Auctions Ltd

**(Subsidiary of:** Sma Vehicle Remarketing Ltd)
1 Dunlop Square, Deans Industrial Estate Deans, Livingston, West Lothian EH54 8SB
**Tel:** 01506418309 **Fax:** 01577-864474
**Web:** www.smag.co.uk
**Reg No:** 0067431SC **VAT No:** 356088827
**Estd:** 1980 Private Limited Company
**Line of Business:** Other non-store retail sale
**Trading Style:** Scottish Motor Option Group
**Issued Capital:** £129,020
**Principals:** R J Anderson *(Managing)*, N M Richards, D J Seabridge, M V Rijkse, M A Stewart
**Branches:** Scottish Motor Auctions Ltd, Portobello Industrial Estate, Shadon Way, Birtley, Chester Le Street, County Durham DH3 2SW
**US SIC:** 5963 **UK SIC:** 65600
**Auditors:** Grant Thornton UK LLP
**Bankers:** The Royal Bank Of Scotland Plc (83-23-47)

| | 31-10-13 | 30-04-13 | 31-10-11 |
|---|---|---|---|
| TO | 11,879,800 | 29,727,974 | 16,816,859 |
| P/L | (20,942) | 1,403,934 | (229,345) |
| NW | 15,424,376 | 15,455,749 | 14,056,246 |
| WC | 14,936,601 | 15,299,803 | 13,313,809 |
| Emp. | 335 | 310 | 273 |

DUNS 21-811-2574

## Scottish Motor Auctions Technical Services

2 Arrol Square Deans Industrial Estate, Livingston, West Lothian EH54 8QZ
**Tel:** 01506466000
**Web:** www.icvd.co.uk
**Estd:** 1990
**Line of Business:** Road haulage and transport services
**Responsibilities**
**Senior:** Ronnie Stewart *(Branch Manager)*
**US SIC:** 4789 **UK SIC:** 77002
**Employees:** 150

DUNS 76-984-9274

## Scottish Mutual Assurance Ltd

**(Subsidiary of:** Phoenix Life Holdings Ltd)
301 St Vincent Street, Glasgow, Lanarkshire G2 5HN
**Tel:** 08452710900
**Web:** www.scotprov.co.uk
**Reg No:** 0133846SC **Estd:** 1996 Private Limited Company
**Line of Business:** Activities auxiliary to insurance and pension funding
**Trading Style:** Scottish Mutual
**Issued Capital:** £10
**Directors:** R K Thakrar, S J Perowne, J Mcconville
**Co. Secretary:**
Pearl Group Secretariat Services
**Branches:** Scottish Mutual Assurance Ltd, 31 Great George Street, Bristol, Avon BS1 5QD
**US SIC:** 7399 **UK SIC:** 83954
**Auditors:** Ernst & Young LLP
**Bankers:** The Royal Bank Of Scotland Plc (16-04-00)

**Following financial data are in thousands**

| | 31-12-13 | 31-12-12 | 31-12-11 |
|---|---|---|---|
| TO | 31,000 | 47,300 | 43,400 |
| P/L | 31,000 | 47,300 | 43,400 |
| NW | 1,485,100 | 1,454,700 | 1,708,300 |

DUNS 21-442-6561

## The Scottish Mutual Assurance Society

301 St Vincent Street, Glasgow, Lanarkshire G2 5NB
**Tel:** 01732427112 **Fax:** 0141-221-1230
**Web:** www.phoenixlifegroup.co.uk
**Reg No:** 0000015SZ **Estd:** 1883 Incorporate By Act Of Parliament
**Line of Business:** Insurance companies and agents
**Trading Style:** Scottish Providence
**Directors:** Ms S D Mcinnes, A Kassimiotis, K J Arnott, A Moss, S Mohammed, S Fawcett, L A Nuttall
**Co. Secretary:**
Pearl Group Secretariat Services
**Branches:** Subject has branches throughout country.
**US SIC:** 6411 **UK SIC:** 83200
**Bankers:** The Royal Bank Of Scotland Plc (83-07-06)
**Employees:** 1,012

DUNS 23-677-9807 Imp

## Scottish Natural Heritage

Great Glenn House, Inverness, Inverness-Shire IV3 8NW
**Tel:** 01463725000
**Web:** www.snh.org.uk
**Estd:** 1958
**Line of Business:** Non-charitable social work activities without accommodation
**Directors:** M Forsythe, R Crofts, M Magnusson
**Responsibilities**
**Senior:** David Bale *(Area Manager)*, Richard Kilpatrick *(Manager)*, Cassandra Macdougall *(Office Manager)*, Craig Nisbet *(Manager)*, David Pickett *(Reserve manager)*, Andrew Rayburn *(Chairman)*, Stuart Shaw *(General Manager)*, Iain Sime *(General Manager)*, Rob Threadgould *(Manager)*, Carole Wells *(Senior Manager)*
**Finance:** Hayley Lewis *(Finance Manager)*, Jane Macdonald *(Business Support Services Mana)*
**Marketing:** Eleanor Macdonald *(Campaign Manager)*, Christine Moodie *(Events & Marketing Officer)*, Dougie Pollok *(Communications Officer)*, Kristin Scott *(Communications Manager)*, Tony Wemyss *(Media Support Officer)*
**Admin:** Nicola Dando *(Personal Assistant)*, Rhoda Davidson *(Administrator)*, Helena McIntyre *(Office Manager)*
**IT:** Kenneth MacLean *(Information Security Manager)*
**Operations:** Andrew Bachell *(Director of Operations)*
**Engineering:** Robert Youngson *(Technical Director)*
**Branches:** Scottish Natural Heritage, 46 Crossgate, Cupar, Fife KY15 5HS
**US SIC:** 8321 **UK SIC:** 96111
**Bankers:** The Royal Bank Of Scotland Plc (83-06-08)
**Employees:** 50

DUNS 22-900-9139 Imp

## Scottish Opera

39 Elmbank Crescent, Glasgow, Lanarkshire G2 4PT
**Tel:** 0141-248-4567 **Fax:** 0141-221-8812
**Web:** www.scottishopera.org.uk
**Reg No:** 0037531SC **Estd:** 1962 Private Company Limited By Guarantee
**Line of Business:** Representative office
**Directors:** Sir J W Elvidge, S L Patrick, A W Burton, C Mccallum, T M Hatton, J Mccormick, W S Henderson, A Reedijk
**Co. Secretary:** Miss Judith Patrickson
**Responsibilities**
**Senior:** Gloria Del Monte *(Executive)*, Mark Harrod *(Workshop Manager)*, Anne Higgins *(Manager)*, Ben Howell *(Executive)*, Andrew Lockyer *(Director)*, Colin Mcclatchie *(Manager)*, Carole Mcwilliam *(Manager)*, Dorothy Miell *(Director)*, Stephen Powles *(Executive)*
**Finance:** Pauline Hodgert *(Finance Officer)*, Lorraine Kelly *(Finance Officer)*
**Marketing:** Gemma Couper *(Press Officer)*, Catorina Downie *(Marketing Manager)*, Catriona Hutchinson *(Marketing Manager)*, Helen Ireland *(Sales Manager)*, Marissa McTeague *(Senior Marketing Officer)*, Emma York *(Press Officer)*, Kenny Young *(Press Manager)*
**Sales:** Helen Ireland *(Sales Manager)*
**Admin:** Karen Gilchrist *(Personal Assistant)*, Iona Jack *(Personal Assistant)*
**HR:** Hazel Kirkpatrick *(Human Resource Advisor)*, Hazel Mcintyre *(Human Resources)*, Catherine Shaw *(Human Resources Manager)*
**Operations:** Amy Burkitt Harrington *(Assistant Production Manager)*
**Fleet:** Audrey Blake *(Logistics Manager)*
**Engineering:** Steven Mcbride *(Maintenance Technician)*, Katie Poulter *(Technical Engineer)*
**Branches:** Scottish Opera, 54 High Street, Biggar, Lanarkshire ML12 6BJ
**US SIC:** 7399 **UK SIC:** 83954
**Auditors:** Ernst & Young
**Bankers:** Clydesdale Bank Plc (82-50-00)

| | 31-03-14 | 31-03-13 | 31-03-12 |
|---|---|---|---|
| TO | 16,777,345 | 16,682,482 | 11,809,245 |
| P/L | 4,672,691 | 5,458,399 | 520,372 |
| NW | 13,716,915 | 9,044,226 | 3,585,827 |
| WC | 2,299,323 | 4,210,697 | 470,335 |
| Emp. | 151 | 141 | 140 |

DUNS 21-748-6930

## Scottish Police Authority

65 West Regent Street, Glasgow, Lanarkshire G2 2AF
**Tel:** 01415-858300
**Web:** www.spa.police.uk
**Estd:** 2003
**Line of Business:** Public security, law and order activities
**Trading Style:** S P A, Scottish Police College
**Directors:** J Geates, Mrs M Barr, T Ward
**Branches:** Scottish Police Authority, Queen Street, Aberdeen, Aberdeenshire AB10 1ZA
**US SIC:** 9221 **UK SIC:** 91300
**Employees:** 150

DUNS 21-700-0832

## Scottish Power Energy Networks Holdings Ltd

**(Subsidiary of:** Iberdrola Sociedad Anonima)
10 Technology Avenue, Hamilton International Technology Park, Glasgow, Lanarkshire G72 0HT
**Tel:** 01416140008
**Web:** www.spenergynetworks.com
**Reg No:** 0389555SC **Estd:** 2010 Private Limited Company
**Line of Business:** Management activities of holding companies
**Issued Capital:** £819,257,993
**Directors:** J R Mcdonald, A Espinosa De Los Monteros Herrera, J Izaguirre Nazar, J Villalba Sanchez, Dr E Z Haywood, Ms N M Connelly, Ms W J Barnes, S H Mathieson
**Co. Secretary:** Seumus O'Gorman
**Responsibilities**
**Senior:** Vicky Kelsall *(Customer Service Director)*
**HR:** Sarah Brannan *(Head of Human Resources)*
**Health & Safety:** Andy Bird *(Head of Health & safety)*
**US SIC:** 6711 **UK SIC:** 83962
**Auditors:** Ernst & Young LLP

**Following financial data are in thousands**

| | 31-12-13 | 31-12-12 | 31-12-11 |
|---|---|---|---|
| TO | 1,042,700 | 969,200 | N/A |
| P/L | 486,000 | 535,400 | 194,500 |
| NW | 1,040,000 | 943,200 | 825,300 |
| WC | (1,196,200) | (919,800) | (813,200) |
| Emp. | 2,838 | 2,723 | N/A |

DUNS 21-781-5878

## Scottish Power Network Connections

55 Fullarton Drive, Glasgow East Investment Park, Glasgow, Lanarkshire G32 8FA
**Tel:** 01416140010
**Web:** www.scottishpower.com
**Estd:** 2011
**Line of Business:** Distribution and trade in electricity
**Responsibilities**
**Senior:** Iain Steele *(Site Manager)*
**US SIC:** 4911 **UK SIC:** 16101
**Employees:** 200

DUNS 23-617-0593

## Scottish Power Uk Plc

**(Subsidiary of:** Iberdrola Sociedad Anonima)
1 Atlantic Quay, Robertson Street, Glasgow, Lanarkshire G2 8SP
**Tel:** 01415-682000 **Fax:** 0141-568-2017
**Web:** www.scottishpower.com
**Reg No:** 0117120SC **VAT No:** 259547811
**Estd:** 1989 Public Limited Company
**Line of Business:** Management activities of holding companies
**Trading Style:** Scottish Power, Scottish Power Ash Sales
**Issued Capital:** £871,991,551
**Directors:** Ms M Venman, D J Wright, D Alcain
**Co. Secretary:** Ms Marion Venman
**Responsibilities**
**HR:** Paul McKelvie *(Learning Director)*
**Branches:** Scottish Power Uk Plc, 23 High Street, Paisley, Renfrewshire PA1 2AF
**US SIC:** 6711, 4911
**UK SIC:** 83962, 16101
**Auditors:** Ernst & Young LLP
**Bankers:** The Royal Bank Of Scotland Plc (83-06-08)

**Following financial data are in thousands**

| | 31-12-13 | 31-12-12 | 31-12-11 |
|---|---|---|---|
| TO | 8,230,700 | 7,803,100 | 6,440,900 |
| P/L | 553,500 | 741,700 | 294,800 |
| NW | 2,863,700 | 2,588,900 | 2,506,900 |
| WC | (2,472,200) | (1,928,700) | (1,333,100) |
| Emp. | 7,112 | 7,190 | 7,721 |

DUNS 23-225-0365

## Scottish Prison Service

Communications Branch, Room 338, Calton House, 5 Redheughs Rigg, Edinburgh, Midlothian EH12 9HW
**Web:** www.sps.gov.uk
**Estd:** 1885
**Line of Business:** Central government
**Trading Style:** S P S
**Financial Director:** W Pretswell
**Responsibilities**
**Senior:** Rachel Gwyon *(Principal)*, Sharon Ritchie *(Executive)*, Eric Sept *(Board Member)*, Stewart Tweedlie *(Executive)*
**HR:** George Kerr *(Training Standards Team)*
**Branches:** Scottish Prison Service, Peterhead, Aberdeenshire AB42 2YY
**US SIC:** 9121 **UK SIC:** 91110
**Employees:** 300

DUNS 50-572-3577

### Scottish Provincial Press Ltd

(**Subsidiary of:** Peter Press Ltd)
Stadium Road, Inverness, Inverness-Shire IV1 1SP
**Tel:** 01463-246575 **Fax:** 01463-221251
**Web:** www.spp-group.com
**Reg No:** 0126102SC **Estd:** 1990 Private Limited Company
**Line of Business:** Newspapers publishing
**Issued Capital:** £4,500,000
**Principals:** P G Fowler *(Chairman and Managing)*, R P Iliffe, N P Hillyard, R J Fowler, D S Fordham, Mrs T Henderson
**Co. Secretary:** Dr Richard Dudley
**Responsibilities**
**Senior:** Calum Mcleod *(General Manager)*
**Finance:** Kim Macgillvray *(Senior Finance Administrator)*
**Branches:** Scottish Provincial Press Ltd, Monzie Square, Fort William, Inverness-Shire PH33 6AG
**US SIC:** 2711, 2721
**UK SIC:** 47512, 47522
**Auditors:** Rothman Pantall LLP
**Bankers:** The Royal Bank Of Scotland Plc (83-23-10)

| | 30-09-13 | 30-09-12 | 30-09-11 |
|---|---|---|---|
| TO | 12,741,000 | 12,674,000 | 12,765,000 |
| P/L | 1,715,000 | 1,877,000 | 1,526,000 |
| NW | 1,259,000 | 444,000 | (493,000) |
| WC | 1,726,000 | 1,547,000 | 1,418,000 |
| Emp. | 239 | 243 | 264 |

DUNS 21-422-4407

### Scottish Public Services Ombudsman

4-6 Melville Street, Edinburgh, Midlothian EH3 7NS
**Tel:** 0800-3777330
**Web:** www.spso.org.uk
**Estd:** 2010 Proprietorship
**Line of Business:** Ombudsman
**Proprietor:** J Martin
**US SIC:** 8111 **UK SIC:** 83500
**Employees:** 50

DUNS 21-225-7682

### Scottish Qualifications Authority

22 Wester Shawfair, Danderhall, Dalkeith, Midlothian EH22 1FD
**Tel:** 03452791000
**Web:** www.sqa.org.uk
**Estd:** 2011
**Line of Business:** Education agencies and authorities
**Proprietor:** Ms J Brown
**Responsibilities**
**Admin:** Paula Petersen *(Administrator)*
**Branches:** Scottish Qualifications Authority, 5OPtima Building, Glasgow, Lanarkshire G2 5DQ
**US SIC:** 8299 **UK SIC:** 93300
**Bankers:** The Royal Bank Of Scotland Plc (83-17-26)
**Employees:** 500

DUNS 76-890-2843

### Scottish Rugby Union Plc

Murrayfield, Edinburgh, Midlothian EH12 5PJ
**Tel:** 01313465000 **Fax:** 01313 465001
**Web:** www.scottishrugby.org
**Reg No:** 0132061SC **VAT No:** 592882686
**Estd:** 1991 Public Limited Company
**Line of Business:** Sports clubs
**Trading Style:** Caithness Rugby Football Club
**Issued Capital:** £50,000
**Directors:** I R Barr, D C Mckay, Ms L E Thomson, C S Grassie, I Mclauchlan, F J Neil, A P Healy, I T Rankin
**Co. Secretary:** Robert Howat
**Responsibilities**
**Senior:** Edward Crozier *(Manager)*, Nicole Kelly *(Human Resources Manager)*, Jock Millican *(Council Member)*, Michael Monro *(Director)*
**HR:** Nicole Kelly *(Human Resources Manager)*
**Branches:** Scottish Rugby Union Plc, 27 Stewarton Road, Kilmarnock, Ayrshire KA3 4AD
**US SIC:** 7999 **UK SIC:** 97913
**Auditors:** PricewaterhouseCoopers LLP
**Bankers:** The Royal Bank Of Scotland Plc (83-06-08)

| | 31-05-14 | 30-04-13 | 30-05-12 |
|---|---|---|---|
| TO | 43,728,000 | 39,273,000 | 38,224,000 |
| P/L | 860,000 | 858,000 | 1,580,000 |
| NW | (8,933,000) | (9,793,000) | (10,651,000) |
| WC | (6,304,000) | (5,514,000) | (16,633,000) |
| Emp. | 317 | 303 | 295 |

DUNS 39-740-3080 **Imp-Exp**

### The Scottish Salmon Co Ltd

(**Subsidiary of:** The Scottish Salmon Company Plc)
8 Melville Cresent, Edinburgh, Midlothian EH3 7JE
**Tel:** 01317188500 **Fax:** 01499-600232
**Web:** www.scottishsalmon.com
**Reg No:** 0107275SC **VAT No:** 498711694
**Estd:** 1988 Private Limited Company
**Line of Business:** Fish processing
**Export Markets:** E U
**Export Sales:** £30,039,000
**Trading Style:** The Scottish Salmon Co Ltd
**Issued Capital:** £20,000,000
**Directors:** Mrs S M Cox, C Anderson, Mrs F M Larkin
**Co. Secretary:** Morisons Secretaries Limited
**Responsibilities**
**Senior:** Stewart Mclelland *(Manager)*
**Branches:** The Scottish Salmon Co Ltd, Quarry Point, The Cabin, Inveraray, Argyll PA32 8YA
**US SIC:** 0921 **UK SIC:** 03002
**Auditors:** Campbell Dallas LLP
**Bankers:** Clydesdale Bank Plc (82-60-19)

| | 31-12-13 | 31-12-12 | 31-12-11 |
|---|---|---|---|
| TO | 85,338,000 | 82,436,000 | 90,306,000 |
| P/L | (3,156,000) | (7,607,000) | 10,766,000 |
| NW | 4,762,000 | 7,745,000 | 13,649,000 |
| WC | 34,801,000 | 27,826,000 | 34,691,000 |
| Emp. | 393 | 400 | 374 |

DUNS 21-122-2658 **Exp**

### Scottish Sea Farms Ltd

(**Subsidiary of:** Norskott Havbruk As)
South Shian, Oban, Argyll PA37 1SB
**Tel:** 01786445521 **Fax:** 01786451563
**Web:** www.scottishseafarms.com
**Reg No:** 0958001 **VAT No:** 699607859
**Estd:** 2003 Private Limited Company
**Line of Business:** Fish farms
**Export Markets:** Europe, U S A, Japan, Hong Kong and South America
**Issued Capital:** £21,400,000
**Directors:** H K Beltestad, J Rea, J F Gallagher, L I Nordhammer, G Witzoe, H Singelstad
**Co. Secretary:** Dermot Anderson
**Responsibilities**
**Marketing:** Rory Conn *(Marketing Manager)*, Ewan Mackintosh *(Marketing Manager)*
**HR:** Jane McCusker *(Personnel Manager)*
**Branches:** Scottish Sea Farms Ltd, Sand, Shetland, Shetland ZE2 9NQ
**US SIC:** 0921 **UK SIC:** 03002
**Auditors:** Ernst & Young LLP
**Bankers:** National Westminster Bank Plc (60-08-46)

| | 31-12-13 | 31-12-12 | 31-12-11 |
|---|---|---|---|
| TO | 130,865,000 | 102,296,000 | 88,721,000 |
| P/L | 22,198,000 | 4,696,000 | 12,645,000 |
| NW | 44,351,000 | 26,998,000 | 23,396,000 |
| WC | 49,040,000 | 21,259,000 | 23,154,000 |
| Emp. | 375 | 376 | 358 |

DUNS 23-514-9387

### Scottish Seabird Centre Trading Ltd

(**Subsidiary of:** Scottish Seabird Centre)
The Harbour, North Berwick, East Lothian EH39 4SS
**Tel:** 01620-890202
**Web:** www.seabird.org
**Reg No:** 0183214SC **Estd:** 2000 Private Limited Company
**Line of Business:** Aquarium and pond suppliers
**Trading Style:** Scottish Seabird Centre
**Issued Capital:** £1
**Directors:** T Brock, Mrs D M Murray, D M Windmill, Ms L Presslie
**Co. Secretary:** David Reith
**US SIC:** 5999, 8411
**UK SIC:** 65600, 97700
**Auditors:** Chiene & Tait CA

| | 31-01-14 | 31-01-13 | 31-01-12 |
|---|---|---|---|
| TO | 705,687 | 670,743 | 675,373 |
| P/L | 760 | 229 | (991) |
| NW | 38,592 | 37,869 | 37,640 |
| WC | 17,397 | 34,813 | 31,863 |

DUNS 50-395-3002 **Exp**

### Scottish Seafoods Ltd

(**Subsidiary of:** Liongem Sweden 1 Ab)
Port Street, Annan, Dumfriesshire DG12 6BN
**Tel:** 01461207460 **Fax:** 01461205641
**Web:** www.youngsseafood.co.uk
**Reg No:** 0118977SC **Estd:** 2010 Private Limited Company
**Line of Business:** Fish processing
**Export Markets:** E U
**Issued Capital:** £1,000,000
**Directors:** M H Lofts, Mrs J N Loncaster
**Co. Secretary:** Wilkin Chapman Company Secretari
**Responsibilities**
**Senior:** Rory Furgusson *(Operations Manager)*
**Branches:** Scottish Seafoods Ltd, Import Dock, Blyth, Northumberland NE24 3DZ
**US SIC:** 2092, 5146
**UK SIC:** 41501, 61700
**Auditors:** PricewaterhouseCoopers
**Bankers:** National Westminster Bank Plc (56-00-52)

| | 30-09-13 | 30-09-12 | 31-09-11 |
|---|---|---|---|
| TA | 1,007,211 | 1,007,211 | 1,007,211 |
| NW | 1,007,211 | 1,007,211 | 1,007,211 |

DUNS 21-755-0172

### Scottish Social Services Council

Compass House, 11 Riverside Drive, Dundee, Angus DD1 4NY
**Tel:** 08456030891
**Web:** www.sssc.uk.com
**Estd:** 2010
**Line of Business:** The dss
**Responsibilities**
**Finance:** Nicky Anderson *(Senior Accountant)*, Gordon Weir *(Director of Resources)*
**Marketing:** Nicola Gilray *(Communications and Public Affa)*, Vanessa Glenday *(Communications Manager)*, Sandra Wilson *(Communications Officer)*
**Sales:** Lorriane Gray *(Head of Strategic Performance)*
**Admin:** Shirley Gibson *(Administrative Support Assista)*, Anne Reid *(PA to Registrar)*, Melanie Taylor *(Administrative Assistant)*, Audrey Wallace *(Administrator)*
**IT:** Keith Quinn *(?Learning Technologies Manager)*
**HR:** Jess Alexander *(Workforce Development and Plan)*, Bryan Healy *(Workforce Intelligence Manager)*, Susan Sneddon *(HR Manager)*
**Operations:** Mike Docherty *(Development Officer)*
**US SIC:** 9121 **UK SIC:** 91110
**Employees:** 200

DUNS 23-881-3567

### Scottish Society for the Prevention of Cruelty to Animals

6 U Halbeath Interchange Business Park, Kingseat Road, Halbeath, Inverkeithing, Fife KY11 8RY
**Tel:** 03000-999999
**Web:** www.scottishspca.org
**Reg No:** 0201401SC **Estd:** 1999 Private Company Limited By Guarantee
**Line of Business:** Activities of other membership organisations not elsewhere classified
**Directors:** N W Alexander, R H Soutar, S Earley, Ms K E Peebles, H Haworth, I D Turnbull, K J Chandler, Dr S Rusbridge
**Co. Secretary:** David Webster
**Responsibilities**
**Senior:** Fiona Davis *(Director)*, Harry Smith *(Director)*
**Branches:** Scottish Society For The Prevention Of Cruelty To Animals, 10 The Glebe, Oban, Argyll PA34 4XF
**US SIC:** 8699 **UK SIC:** 96902
**Auditors:** Baker Tilly UK Audit LLP
**Bankers:** Clydesdale Bank Plc (82-48-08)

| | 31-12-13 | 31-12-12 | 31-12-11 |
|---|---|---|---|
| TO | 13,824,000 | 15,190,000 | 14,829,000 |
| P/L | 30,000 | 2,785,000 | 3,886,000 |
| NW | 39,644,000 | 38,140,000 | 34,445,000 |
| WC | 5,332,000 | 5,501,000 | 4,679,000 |
| Emp. | 328 | 310 | 298 |

DUNS 23-276-3107

### Scottish Water

Castle House, Dunfermline, Fife KY11 8GG
**Tel:** 01383848200
**Web:** www.scottishwater.co.uk
**Estd:** 2002 Incorporate By Act Of Parliament
**Line of Business:** Water authorities
**Principals:** J D Millician *(Financial)*, Dr J Hargreaves
**Responsibilities**
**Senior:** Thomas Axford *(Manager)*, Peter Farrer *(Chief Operating Officer)*, Rob Mustard *(General Manager)*, Kenny Naylor *(Chief Executive Officer)*, Chris Wallace *(Director of Communications)*, Steven Webster *(Manager)*
**Marketing:** Colleen Knight *(Public Affairs Officer)*, Jim Savage *(Public Affairs Officer)*, Chris Wallace *(Director of Communications)*
**Sales:** Jody Campbell *(Senior Business Analyst)*, Stephen Griffen *(Regional Manager)*, Malcolm Hunter *(Commercial Programme Manager)*, David Weber *(Sales and Contracts Manager)*
**IT:** Katie Phizacklea *(IT Manager)*
**Facilities:** Barbara Hendry *(Facilities Service Coordinator)*
**Operations:** Peter Farrer *(Chief Operating Officer)*, Derek Ogilvie *(Operations Manager)*, Janice Reilly *(Product Manager)*, Lynsey Tweedlie *(Project Manager)*
**Purchasing:** Lorna Mcgregor *(Purchasing Director)*
**Branches:** Scottish Water, Child & Family Centre, Gowans Terrace, Perth, Perthshire PH1 5AX
**US SIC:** 4941 **UK SIC:** 17000
**Auditors:** KPMG LLP
**Employees:** 250
**Turnover:** £895,300,000

DUNS 34-864-1288

### Scottish Water Business Stream Ltd

(**Subsidiary of:** Scottish Water)
7 Lochside View, Edinburgh, Midlothian EH12 9DH
**Tel:** 0845-602-8855 **Fax:** 08456-046431
**Web:** www.business-stream.co.uk
**Reg No:** 0294924SC **VAT No:** 945850885
**Estd:** 2006 Private Limited Company
**Line of Business:** Collection, purification and distribution of water
**Issued Capital:** £11,500,000
**Directors:** Mrs J Dow, Ms A E Mcmillan, R E Mercer, D W Macdiarmid
**Co. Secretary:** Charles Smith
**US SIC:** 4941, 5052
**UK SIC:** 17000, 61200
**Auditors:** PricewaterhouseCoopers LLP
**Bankers:** Bank Of Scotland (12-22-91)

| | 31-03-14 | 31-03-13 | 31-03-12 |
|---|---|---|---|
| TO | 364,200,000 | 361,500,000 | 357,400,000 |
| P/L | 38,300,000 | 35,300,000 | 32,800,000 |
| NW | 91,700,000 | 72,200,000 | 55,100,000 |
| WC | 98,100,000 | 80,000,000 | 74,900,000 |
| Emp. | 289 | 267 | 218 |

DUNS 54-916-0869

### Scottish Widows Bank Plc

(**Subsidiary of:** Lloyds Banking Group Plc)
67 Morrison Street, Edinburgh, Midlothian EH3 8HH
**Tel:** 01316555000 **Fax:** 0131-220-3074
**Web:** www.scottishwidows.co.uk
**Reg No:** 0154554SC **Estd:** 1994 Public Limited Company
**Line of Business:** Banks and financial institutions
**Issued Capital:** £120,000,000
**Directors:** S J Noakes, G Mcgregor, M J Jones, G F Bowden
**Co. Secretary:** Mrs Margaret Watson
**Responsibilities**
**Marketing:** Ross Keany *(Head of Media Relations)*
**Branches:** Scottish Widows Bank Plc, 37 Melville St, Edinburgh, Midlothian EH3 7JF
**US SIC:** 6012 **UK SIC:** 81402
**Auditors:** PricewaterhouseCoopers LLP

**Following financial data are in thousands**

| | 31-12-13 | 31-12-12 | 31-12-11 |
|---|---|---|---|
| TA | 8,473,109 | 10,562,491 | 9,565,125 |
| P/L | 17,268 | 24,947 | 11,857 |
| NW | 154,109 | 200,295 | 230,902 |
| WC | 153,855 | 1,496,166 | (5,061,709) |
| Emp. | 162 | 182 | 223 |

DUNS 23-844-0338

### Scottish Widows Plc

(**Subsidiary of:** Lloyds Banking Group Plc)
69 Morrison Street, Edinburgh, Midlothian EH3 8YD
**Tel:** 08457678910
**Web:** www.scottishwidows.co.uk
**Reg No:** 0199549SC **VAT No:** 244155576
**Estd:** 1999 Public Limited Company
**Line of Business:** Life insurance
**Trading Style:** Lloyds Banking
**Issued Capital:** £1,470,092,770
**Directors:** C J Thornton, Mrs J E Curtis, D J Oldfield, R L Wohanka, A M Parsons, M G Culmer, V Maru, N E Prettejohn
**Co. Secretary:** Mrs Joanne Jolly
**Responsibilities**
**Senior:** Robin Bulloch *(CEO / Managing Director)*, Jeremy Goford *(Non-Executive Director)*, Camilla Grove *(Manager)*, Lindsey Montgomery *(Marketing Manager)*
**Marketing:** Kirsty Chalmers *(Marketing Manager New Business)*, Lindsey Montgomery *(Marketing Manager)*
**Sales:** John Farrelly *(Head of Advised Distribution)*
**US SIC:** 6311 **UK SIC:** 82002
**Auditors:** PricewaterhouseCoopers LLP

**Following financial data are in thousands**

| | 31-12-13 | 31-12-12 | 31-12-11 |
|---|---|---|---|
| TO | 6,848,000 | 6,553,000 | 5,189,000 |
| P/L | 667,000 | 205,000 | 391,000 |
| NW | 4,831,000 | 3,616,000 | 3,656,000 |
| WC | (98,932,000) | (839,000) | 47,943,000 |
| Emp. | 2,497 | 6,333 | 3,832 |

DUNS 28-822-4801

### The Scottish Wildlife Trust

Cramond House, 3 Kirk Cramond, Edinburgh, Midlothian EH4 6HZ
**Web:** www.scottishwildlifetrust.org.uk
**Reg No:** 0040247SC **VAT No:** 402875263
**Estd:** 1964 Private Company Limited By Guarantee

**Line of Business:** Activities of other membership organisations not elsewhere classified
**Directors:** D I Lindgren, Dr K Taylor, T W Hailey, A J Grier, R A Mann, Dr J Barnes, Ms K Chambers, Colonel P D Baird
**Co. Secretary:** Ms Susan Mckenzie
**Responsibilities**
**Senior:** David Ashford *(Council Member)*, Allan Bantick *(Chairman)*, Jean Barr *(Council Member)*, Christopher Spray *(Director)*
**Branches:** The Scottish Wildlife Trust, Dyeworks, New Lanark Mills, Lanark, Lanarkshire ML11 9DB
**US SIC:** 7399 **UK SIC:** 83954
**Auditors:** Scott-Moncrieff
**Bankers:** The Royal Bank Of Scotland Plc (83-06-08)

| | 31-03-14 | 31-03-13 | 31-03-12 |
|---|---|---|---|
| TO | 5,148,570 | 4,271,746 | 5,166,582 |
| P/L | 218,878 | (363,754) | (34,773) |
| NW | 7,275,624 | 6,962,656 | 6,831,501 |
| WC | 1,331,656 | 677,594 | 865,286 |
| Emp. | 106 | 96 | 141 |

DUNS 29-868-8557

## Scottish Woodlands Ltd

**(Subsidiary of:** Swl Ltd)
Research Park, Edinburgh, Midlothian EH14 4AP
**Tel:** 01314-515154
**Web:** www.scottishwoodlands.co.uk
**Reg No:** 0101787SC **VAT No:** 269354133
**Estd:** 1980 Private Limited Company
**Line of Business:** Forestry advisers
**Trading Style:** Scottish Woodlands
**Issued Capital:** £364,625
**Directors:** C Mann, S A Johnston, A R Browne, S A Stanley, S T Oldham
**Co. Secretary:** Geoffrey Craythorne
**Responsibilities**
**Senior:** Douglas Hyslop *(General Manager of Timber)*, Craig Nimmo *(General Manager of Railways)*
**Sales:** James Adamson *(Investment and Business Develo)*
**Facilities:** Duncan Gilchrist *(Senior Estates Manager)*
**Branches:** Scottish Woodlands Ltd, Brynkinalt Business Centre, Sawmill, Wrexham, Clwyd LL14 5NS
**US SIC:** 0851 **UK SIC:** 02000
**Auditors:** Johnston Carmichael LLP
**Bankers:** Bank Of Scotland (80-20-00)

| | 30-09-14 | 30-09-13 | 30-09-12 |
|---|---|---|---|
| TO | 73,875,000 | 63,908,000 | 63,901,000 |
| P/L | 1,134,000 | 627,000 | 842,000 |
| NW | 6,192,000 | 5,907,000 | 5,642,000 |
| WC | 6,458,000 | 5,750,000 | 5,347,000 |
| Emp. | 141 | 143 | 142 |

DUNS 51-657-9435

## Scottish Youth Hostels Association

7 Glebe Crescent, Stirling, Stirlingshire FK8 2JA
**Tel:** 01786-891400
**Web:** www.syha.org.uk
**Reg No:** 0310841SC **Estd:** 2006 Private Company Limited By Guarantee
**Line of Business:** Activities of other membership organisations not elsewhere classified
**Directors:** Dr A C Pia, Ms J H Overton, M J Ambrose, D Calder, Mrs S Mayer, M T Anderson, G B Fisher, D M Craig
**Co. Secretary:** Ms Margo Paterson
**Responsibilities**
**Senior:** Andrew Waugh *(Director)*
**Finance:** Vic Bourne *(Treasurer)*
**Branches:** Scottish Youth Hostels Association, 7-8 Park Terrace, Glasgow, Lanarkshire G3 6BY
**US SIC:** 8699 **UK SIC:** 96902
**Bankers:** The Royal Bank Of Scotland Plc (83-27-09)

| | 31-01-14 | 31-01-13 | 31-01-12 |
|---|---|---|---|
| TO | 9,539,732 | 8,146,939 | 7,947,377 |
| P/L | (593,602) | (937,512) | (475,245) |
| NW | 8,654,983 | 9,248,402 | 10,177,628 |
| WC | 1,609,722 | (781,470) | (328,336) |
| Emp. | 244 | 441 | 457 |

DUNS 23-654-0386

## Scottishpower Energy Retail Ltd

**(Subsidiary of:** Iberdrola Sociedad Anonima)
1 Atlantic Quay, Robertson Street, Glasgow, Lanarkshire G2 8SP
**Tel:** 01416143449
**Web:** www.scottishpower.co.uk
**Reg No:** 0190287SC **Estd:** 1998 Private Limited Company
**Line of Business:** Transmission of electricity
**Trading Style:** Scottish Power
**Issued Capital:** £55,407,000
**Directors:** M Rossi, N D Clitheroe, A M Raigoso
**Co. Secretary:** Alistair Orr
**Branches:** Scottishpower Energy Retail Ltd, Unit 4, Watling Street, Cannock, Staffordshire WS11 1TD
**US SIC:** 4911, 4932
**UK SIC:** 16101, 16200
**Auditors:** Ernst & Young LLP
**Following financial data are in thousands**

| | 31-12-13 | 31-12-12 | 31-12-11 |
|---|---|---|---|
| TO | 4,133,300 | 3,818,200 | 3,377,900 |
| P/L | 167,500 | 174,500 | (14,200) |
| NW | (45,500) | 30,300 | 79,500 |
| WC | (104,900) | (34,400) | 38,700 |
| Emp. | 2,172 | 2,368 | 2,686 |

DUNS 22-925-9890 **Exp**

## Scotts Bakery Co

169 Ballagh Road, Fivemiletown, Co Tyrone BT75 0QP
**Tel:** 028-8952-1295
**Estd:** 1986 Partnership
**Line of Business:** Retail sale of bread, cakes, flour confectionery and sugar confectionery
**Export Markets:** Republic Of Ireland
**Partners:** R Elliott, G Elliott
**Responsibilities**
**Senior:** Robert Coulter *(Manager)*
**US SIC:** 3999, 5145
**UK SIC:** 49590, 61700
**Bankers:** First Trust Bank (aib Group (uk) Plc) (93-80-76)
**Employees:** 58

DUNS 76-491-4271

## The Scotts Co (Manufacturing) Ltd

**(Subsidiary of:** The Scotts Miracle-Gro Company)
Howden Dyke, Goole, North Humberside DN14 7UF
**Tel:** 01430434301 **Fax:** 01430-431658
**Web:** www.scotts.com
**Reg No:** 2566745 **Estd:** 2010 Private Limited Company
**Line of Business:** Manufacture of fertilisers and nitrogen compounds
**Issued Capital:** £1,760,100
**Directors:** D Larson, Ms A Deluca
**Co. Secretary:** Tmf Corporate Administration Ser
**Responsibilities**
**Senior:** Paul Bend *(Production Manager)*, Martin Breddy *(Managing Director)*, Mark Filer *(Logistics Manager)*
**Finance:** Debbie Wetherill *(Management Accountant)*
**Facilities:** Shirley Mortimer *(Facilities Manager)*
**Fleet:** Mark Filer *(Logistics Manager)*
**Engineering:** Paul Bend *(Production Manager)*
**US SIC:** 2873, 2899
**UK SIC:** 25130, 25670
**Auditors:** PricewaterhouseCoopers
**Bankers:** Bank Of Scotland (80-20-00)

| | 30-09-13 | 30-09-12 | 30-09-11 |
|---|---|---|---|
| TO | 3,804,000 | 3,622,000 | 3,574,000 |
| P/L | 178,000 | 170,000 | 131,000 |
| NW | 5,195,000 | 5,069,000 | 4,944,000 |
| WC | 776,000 | 134,000 | 1,261,000 |
| Emp. | 60 | 69 | 61 |

DUNS 73-752-7895 **Imp-Exp**

## The Scotts Co (Uk) Ltd

**(Subsidiary of:** The Scotts Miracle-Gro Company)
Salisbury House, Weyside Park, Catteshall Lane, Godalming, Surrey GU7 1XE
**Tel:** 01483-410210
**Web:** www.lovethegarden.com
**Reg No:** 2924130 **VAT No:** 637919007
**Estd:** 1994 Private Limited Company
**Line of Business:** Extraction and agglomeration of peat
**Export Sales:** £14,564,000
**Issued Capital:** £70,999,999
**Directors:** D Larson, Ms A Deluca
**Co. Secretary:** Tmf Corporate Administration Ser
**Responsibilities**
**Senior:** Martin Breddy *(Managing Director)*, Edward Claggett *(Manager)*, A Winden *(Manager)*
**Finance:** Matthew Dunsmore *(Financial Director)*
**Marketing:** Paula Parker *(Marketing Director)*
**HR:** Julie Friend *(Human Resources Manager)*, Sophie Shillinglaw *(Human resources Manager)*
**Facilities:** Martin Breddy *(Managing Director)*
**Branches:** The Scotts Co (Uk) Ltd, Paper Mill Lane, Ipswich, Suffolk IP8 4BZ
**US SIC:** 1499, 2873
**UK SIC:** 23960, 25130
**Auditors:** Deloitte LLP
**Bankers:** National Westminster Bank Plc (53-61-24)

| | 30-09-13 | 30-09-12 | 30-09-11 |
|---|---|---|---|
| TO | 81,284,000 | 84,171,000 | 95,924,000 |
| P/L | 59,000 | (4,427,000) | (26,899,000) |
| NW | 9,528,000 | (59,431,000) | (51,616,000) |
| WC | 4,704,000 | (62,230,000) | (52,058,000) |
| Emp. | 177 | 198 | 195 |

DUNS 49-737-3332

## Scott's Hospital

Gladstone Road, Huntly, Aberdeenshire AB54 8BD
**Estd:** 1901
**Line of Business:** Children's homes
**Proprietor:** Miss E Alexander
**US SIC:** 8321 **UK SIC:** 96111
**Employees:** 54

DUNS 76-347-9524 **Imp**

## Scotts Ltd

**(Subsidiary of:** Horton United Co Inc)
1 Crompton Road, Groundwell, Swindon, Wiltshire SN25 5AW
**Tel:** 01793 707 700 **Fax:** 08444821103
**Web:** www.scottsofstow.co.uk
**Reg No:** 2548299 **Estd:** 1991 Private Limited Company
**Line of Business:** Mail order houses
**Trading Style:** Scotts & Co, Spirito Di Artigiano, Artigiano, Scotts of Stow
**Issued Capital:** £400,000
**Directors:** Ms V Laws, A S Walsham, N V Swaboy, A J Oldham
**Co. Secretary:** Andrew Walsham
**Branches:** Scotts Ltd, The Square, Stow-On-The-Wold, Cheltenham, Gloucestershire GL54 1AF
**US SIC:** 5961, 5021
**UK SIC:** 65600, 61500
**Auditors:** KPMG LLP
**Bankers:** Barclays Bank Plc (20-20-15)

| | 30-06-13 | 30-06-12 | 26-06-11 |
|---|---|---|---|
| TO | 51,591,000 | 64,138,000 | 63,802,000 |
| P/L | 404,000 | (785,000) | 1,581,000 |
| NW | 1,946,000 | 1,617,000 | 2,124,000 |
| WC | 1,440,000 | 327,000 | 1,522,000 |
| Emp. | 282 | 338 | 298 |

DUNS 23-332-6453

## Scotts Nightclub

Brook Street, Wrexham, Clwyd LL13 7LH
**Tel:** 01978310580
**Web:** www.liquidclubs.com
**Estd:** 1989 Proprietorship
**Line of Business:** Nightclub
**Proprietor:** R W Scott
**Responsibilities**
**Senior:** David McCarroll *(Manager)*
**US SIC:** 5813 **UK SIC:** 66200
**Employees:** 50

DUNS 22-160-4049

## Scotts of Thrapston Ltd

**(Subsidiary of:** Scottco Holdings Ltd)
Bridge Street, Thrapston, Kettering, Northamptonshire NN14 4LR
**Tel:** 01832732366 **Fax:** 01832733703
**Web:** www.scottsofthrapston.co.uk
**Reg No:** 4178948 **Estd:** 2001 Private Limited Company
**Line of Business:** Timber merchants
**Export Sales:** £10,088
**Trading Style:** Scotts of Thrapston Ltd
**Issued Capital:** £10,000
**Directors:** J A Scott, D J Scott
**Co. Secretary:** Peter Waddup
**Responsibilities**
**Marketing:** Julia Berrie *(Marketing Manager)*
**US SIC:** 5072 **UK SIC:** 61500
**Bankers:** National Westminster Bank Plc (55-70-37)

| | 31-12-13 | 31-12-12 | 31-12-11 |
|---|---|---|---|
| TO | 7,949,219 | 7,764,137 | 10,266,728 |
| P/L | 235,734 | 227,510 | 950,360 |
| NW | 857,990 | 834,476 | 1,153,250 |
| WC | 580,201 | 616,549 | 924,167 |
| Emp. | 82 | 87 | 89 |

DUNS 29-576-0615 **Imp**

## Scotvalve Services Ltd

**(Subsidiary of:** Petrofac Ltd)
Howemoss Cresent, Kirkhill Industrial Estate, Aberdeen, Aberdeenshire AB21 0GN
**Tel:** 01467631400
**Web:** www.scotvalves.co.uk
**Reg No:** 0094733SC **VAT No:** 430029596
**Estd:** 1985 Private Limited Company
**Line of Business:** Welding services
**Issued Capital:** £15,000
**Principals:** R Burnett *(Managing)*, G Smith, Mrs E Bentley
**Responsibilities**
**Senior:** Frederick Hearle *(Manager)*
**Health & Safety:** Darren Still *(QHSE Manager)*
**Facilities:** Darren Still *(QHSE Manager)*
**Operations:** Darren Still *(QHSE Manager)*
**US SIC:** 3494, 8911
**UK SIC:** 32880, 83701
**Auditors:** Ernst & Young LLP
**Bankers:** Bank Of Scotland (80-73-30)

| | 31-12-13 | 31-12-12 | 31-12-11 |
|---|---|---|---|
| TO | 4,715,000 | 5,564,000 | 5,323,000 |
| P/L | (836,000) | 833,000 | 1,309,000 |
| NW | 3,492,000 | 4,263,000 | 3,676,000 |
| WC | 489,000 | 3,647,000 | 2,970,000 |
| Emp. | 51 | 47 | 44 |

DUNS 22-504-9816 **Imp**

## The Scout Association

Baden-Powell House, Queen's Gate, London SW7 5JS
**Tel:** 08453001818
**Web:** www.scout.org.uk
**Reg No:** 0000547RC **VAT No:** 240314904
**Estd:** 1907 Incorporate By Act Of Parliament
**Line of Business:** Youth centres and associations
**Principals:** J Bevan *(Chairman)*, G H Mitchell, W G Purdy, J R Emly, D Capper, J C Bailey, W Mcdonald, D M Twine
**Responsibilities**
**Senior:** B Clay *(Vice President)*, Sima Fenton *(Manager)*, William Gladstone *(Vice President)*, W McDonald *(Director)*, Sharon Smithen *(Office Services Manager)*, Queen The Second *(Principal)*
**Branches:** The Scout Association, Edward St, Newcastle-Upon-Tyne, Newcastle Upon Tyne, Tyne and Wear NE3 1EA
**US SIC:** 8699 **UK SIC:** 96902
**Auditors:** Mazars LLP
**Bankers:** Barclays Bank Plc (20-06-05)
**Turnover:** £49,688,000

DUNS 21-585-5927

## Scouting 26TH Dundee

St Johns Cross Church, Blackness Avenue, Dundee, Angus DD2 1ER
**Web:** www.26thscoutgroup.org.uk
**Estd:** 2011 Proprietorship
**Line of Business:** Scout, guides, cubs and brownie groups
**Proprietor:** D Cox
**US SIC:** 8699 **UK SIC:** 96902
**Employees:** 200

DUNS 21-675-1801

## Scp Admin Solutions Ltd

80-83 Long Lane, London EC1A 9ET
**Tel:** 01278782505
**Reg No:** 7269558 **Estd:** 2010 Private Limited Company
**Line of Business:** Word processing service
**Issued Capital:** £100
**Director:** Ms S C Boyce
**US SIC:** 7379 **UK SIC:** 83940

| | 30-06-12 | 30-06-11 |
|---|---|---|
| TA | 15,377 | 13,243 |
| NW | (33,749) | (42,216) |
| WC | (34,749) | (43,716) |

DUNS 23-112-8125

## Screen Solutions Ltd

Unit A1-2, Beaufort House, Greenwich Way, Peacehaven, East Sussex BN10 8HS
**Tel:** 01273-589922
**Web:** www.screensolutions.co.uk
**Reg No:** 2795048 **Estd:** 1993 Private Limited Company
**Line of Business:** Office furniture and equipment suppliers
**Issued Capital:** £27,210
**Principals:** J G Grindall *(Managing)*, D Valovin, M E Stevens, S Woods, R D Mackenzie, P Saunders
**Co. Secretary:** Ms Sally Evans
**Responsibilities**
**Senior:** Geoff Bagshaw *(Purchasing Manager)*
**Purchasing:** Geoff Bagshaw *(Purchasing Manager)*
**Branches:** Screen Solutions Ltd, 9 Springfield Close, Windsor, Berkshire SL4 3PT
**US SIC:** 2599 **UK SIC:** 46720
**Auditors:** Baker Tilly
**Bankers:** HSBC Bank plc (40-25-06)

| | 31-12-13 | 31-12-12 | 31-12-11 |
|---|---|---|---|
| TO | 6,778,882 | 5,740,983 | 6,426,947 |
| P/L | 647,461 | 363,000 | 404,100 |
| NW | 817,530 | 707,758 | 682,296 |
| WC | (252,722) | (345,749) | (336,670) |
| Emp. | 66 | 62 | 67 |

DUNS 28-969-3343

## Screenprint Productions Ltd

Calderbank, River Street, Brighouse, West Yorkshire HD6 1LU
**Tel:** 01484726272 **Fax:** 01484726273
**Web:** www.screenprintproductions.com
**Reg No:** 1722391 **Estd:** 1983 Private Limited Company
**Line of Business:** Manufacturers of albums
**Issued Capital:** £100
**Managing Director:** C B White
**Co. Secretary:** Mrs Janine White

**Responsibilities**
**Senior:** Martyn Hicks *(Sales Director)*
**Sales:** Martyn Hicks *(Sales Director)*
**Health & Safety:** Susan Earl *(Quality & Health & Safety Mana)*
**Engineering:** Paul Chaplin *(Production Manager)*
**US SIC:** 2752 **UK SIC:** 47544
**Auditors:** Peel, Walker & Co
**Bankers:** Yorkshire Bank Plc (05-04-69)

| | 31-05-14 | 31-05-13 | 31-05-12 |
|---|---|---|---|
| TO | 7,880,804 | N/A | N/A |
| P/L | 485,585 | N/A | N/A |
| NW | 1,069,980 | 1,177,764 | 1,026,276 |
| WC | 455,099 | 531,127 | 254,791 |
| Emp. | 56 | N/A | N/A |

DUNS 77-696-7606
## Screwfix Direct Ltd
(**Subsidiary of:** Kingfisher Plc)
Trade House, Mead Avenue, Houndstone Business Park, Yeovil, Somerset BA22 8RT
**Tel:** 01935414100 **Fax:** 01935-414-100
**Web:** www.screwfix.com
**Reg No:** 3006378 **VAT No:** 232555575
**Estd:** 2012 Private Limited Company
**Line of Business:** Hardware
**Issued Capital:** £50,459
**Directors:** J S Mackenzie, J M Mewett, W A Livingston, G R Bell, R I Bell, S B Willett, Mrs L J Haselhurst
**Co. Secretary:** Matthew Smith
**Responsibilities**
**Senior:** Nick Emms *(Hedge End Branch Manager)*, Janet Maggs *(Director)*, Sam Sturgess *(Manager)*, Rachel Vincent *(Senior Manager)*
**Finance:** Richard Shoteh *(Finance Manager)*
**Marketing:** Colin McMahon *(Head of Marketing)*, John Mewett *(Marketing Director)*
**IT:** Phil Slawson *(IT Manager)*
**Branches:** Screwfix Direct Ltd, Unit 5, Worcester Road, Kidderminster, Worcestershire DY11 7AR
**US SIC:** 3499, 5251, 5961
**UK SIC:** 31694, 64800, 65600
**Auditors:** Deloitte LLP
**Bankers:** Barclays Bank Plc (20-99-40)

| | 01-02-14 | 02-02-13 | 28-02-12 |
|---|---|---|---|
| TO | 665,263,000 | 577,247,000 | 515,128,000 |
| P/L | 45,328,000 | 34,223,000 | 30,697,000 |
| NW | 223,625,000 | 191,332,000 | 163,672,000 |
| WC | 140,399,000 | 110,707,000 | 84,518,000 |
| Emp. | 5,442 | 4,727 | 3,945 |

DUNS 29-500-2414
## Scribbler Holdings Ltd
9 Harmsworth Street, London SE17 3TJ
**Tel:** 02070912640 **Fax:** 020-7287-5473
**Web:** www.scribbler.com
**Reg No:** 1863486 **VAT No:** 672405736
**Estd:** 2010 Private Limited Company
**Line of Business:** Retail sale of books, newspapers and stationery
**Trading Style:** Scribbler
**Issued Capital:** £112,000
**Director:** Mrs J L Procter
**Co. Secretary:** John Procter
**Responsibilities**
**Senior:** Gemma Rochester *(Personal Assistant)*
**Marketing:** Emily Ridgwell *(e-Commerce Executive)*
**Branches:** Scribbler Holdings Ltd, Unit 1B, Hammersmith Broadway, London W6 9YD
**US SIC:** 7399, 6711
**UK SIC:** 83954, 83962
**Auditors:** Smethers & Co
**Bankers:** National Westminster Bank Plc (56-00-27)

| | 31-08-13 | 31-08-12 | 31-08-11 |
|---|---|---|---|
| TO | 9,065,120 | 8,070,947 | N/A |
| P/L | 558,740 | 471,311 | N/A |
| NW | 1,697,634 | 1,235,285 | 1,064,252 |
| WC | (116,589) | (353,029) | (505,573) |
| Emp. | 140 | 140 | N/A |

DUNS 73-812-8300 **Exp**
## Scripps Networks International (Uk) Ltd
(**Subsidiary of:** Southbank Media Ltd)
100 Buchingham Place Road, London SW1W 0SR
**Tel:** 02075789520 **Fax:** 020-7636-6424
**Web:** www.travelchannel.co.uk
**Reg No:** 5068968 **VAT No:** 835543323
**Estd:** 2004 Private Limited Company
**Line of Business:** Radio and television production services
**Export Sales:** £19,685,000
**Trading Style:** Travel Channel
**Issued Capital:** £312,640
**Directors:** Ms C L Gibson, J R Sichel-Outcalt, J G Necastro, J Samples, S Nardi
**Co. Secretary:** Dentons Secretaries Limited
**US SIC:** 4833 **UK SIC:** 97411
**Auditors:** Deloitte LLP
**Bankers:** HSBC Bank plc (40-01-13)

| | 31-12-13 | 31-12-12 | 31-12-11 |
|---|---|---|---|
| TO | 27,319,000 | 16,588,000 | 15,973,000 |
| P/L | (10,735,000) | 4,409,000 | 4,307,000 |
| NW | 2,912,000 | 7,652,000 | 5,627,000 |
| WC | 5,119,000 | 7,328,000 | 5,281,000 |
| Emp. | 92 | 46 | 47 |

DUNS 22-800-7803
## Scriptide Ltd
4 Mill St East, Dewsbury, West Yorkshire WF12 9AQ
**Tel:** 01924-455804 **Fax:** 01924-465925
**Reg No:** 1641996 **Estd:** 1982 Private Limited Company
**Line of Business:** Packaging activities
**Issued Capital:** £100
**Director:** R E Yates
**Co. Secretary:** Mrs Penelope Yates
**US SIC:** 7399 **UK SIC:** 83954
**Auditors:** Walter Dawson & Son

| | 30-06-13 | 30-06-12 | 30-06-11 |
|---|---|---|---|
| TA | 286,246 | 292,640 | 323,256 |
| NW | (45,072) | (43,368) | (37,532) |
| WC | (57,078) | (53,664) | (47,205) |

DUNS 21-152-6884 **Imp-Exp**
## Scripture Union
207-209 Queensway, Bletchley, Milton Keynes, Buckinghamshire MK2 2EB
**Web:** www.scriptureunion.org.uk
**Reg No:** 0039828 **VAT No:** 233473180
**Estd:** 1867 Private Company Limited By Guarantee
**Line of Business:** Publishing of books
**Export Markets:** Worldwide
**Directors:** R Barnes, D W Adams, K B Civval, C Beard, E F Scrase-Field, Mrs C A Walker
**Co. Secretary:** Mrs Susan Winning
**Responsibilities**
**Senior:** Penny Boshoff *(Manager)*
**Branches:** Scripture Union, St Johns Church Hall, The Green, Havering-Atte-Bower, Romford, Essex RM4 1PL
**US SIC:** 2731, 2741
**UK SIC:** 47532, 47541
**Auditors:** Binder Hamlyn
**Bankers:** HSBC Bank plc (40-14-13)

| | 31-03-14 | 31-03-13 | 31-03-12 |
|---|---|---|---|
| TO | 5,840,000 | 6,369,000 | 6,736,000 |
| P/L | 49,000 | 111,000 | 93,000 |
| NW | 6,928,000 | 6,785,000 | 6,468,000 |
| WC | 4,398,000 | 4,298,000 | 4,417,000 |
| Emp. | 68 | 72 | 78 |

DUNS 22-756-4416
## Scripture Union Scotland
70 Milton Street, Glasgow, Lanarkshire G4 0HR
**Web:** www.suscotland.org.uk
**Reg No:** 0054297SC **Estd:** 1973 Private Company Limited By Guarantee
**Line of Business:** Activities of religious organisations
**Directors:** Mrs S M Sydserff, J S Gladstone, N Maclennan, J L Gray, S M Mackay, Miss K Carmichael, A Jones, Mrs L M Scott
**Co. Secretary:** Robin Maclellan
**Responsibilities**
**Senior:** Andy Bathgate *(Chief Executive)*, James Dewar *(Director)*, Beth Dickson *(Trustee)*, Robin Easton *(Manager)*, Barry Elder *(Manager)*, Alistair Macleod *(Manager)*, Alasdair Morrison *(Manager)*, Hugh O'Brien *(Director)*
**Finance:** Sarah Lynch *(Accountant)*
**Branches:** Scripture Union Scotland, 2 Oxgangs Path, Edinburgh, Midlothian EH13 9LX
**US SIC:** 7399 **UK SIC:** 83954
**Auditors:** Mazars LLP

| | 31-03-14 | 31-03-13 | 31-03-12 |
|---|---|---|---|
| TO | 3,763,753 | 3,227,727 | 3,060,959 |
| P/L | 606,243 | (44,701) | (30,220) |
| NW | 6,248,024 | 5,641,781 | 5,686,482 |
| WC | 1,929,814 | 884,392 | 1,136,779 |
| Emp. | 102 | 107 | 103 |

DUNS 21-805-5192 **Imp**
## Scrivens Ltd
(**Subsidiary of:** Seamap Ltd)
Scrivens House, 60 Islington Row Middleway, Edgbaston, Birmingham, West Midlands B15 1PH
**Tel:** 0121-456-8700
**Web:** www.scrivens.com
**Reg No:** 0377588 **Estd:** 2012 Private Limited Company
**Line of Business:** Representative office
**Trading Style:** Scrivens Opticians & Hearing Care
**Issued Capital:** £203,487
**Directors:** M A Georgevic, Mrs A M Georgevic, N J Georgevic, D B Harris, M A Georgevic, Mrs K R Georgevic
**Co. Secretary:** Nicholas Georgevic
**Responsibilities**
**Senior:** Darren Haylings *(Stock Controller)*
**Marketing:** Richard Cobb *(Marketing Manager)*
**Branches:** Scrivens Limited, 47 Howardsgate, Welwyn Garden City, Hertfordshire AL8 6AP
**US SIC:** 5999 **UK SIC:** 65600
**Auditors:** Nyman Libson Paul
**Bankers:** HSBC Bank plc (40-11-18)

| | 27-10-13 | 28-10-12 | 30-10-11 |
|---|---|---|---|
| TO | 29,051,074 | 24,503,261 | 24,453,435 |
| P/L | 1,950,194 | 1,560,190 | 1,512,887 |
| NW | (2,728,678) | (3,314,244) | (3,644,665) |
| WC | (6,076,562) | (6,559,228) | (7,167,108) |
| Emp. | 811 | 707 | 740 |

DUNS 22-661-3370
## Scrutton Bland
Fitzroy House, Ipswich, Suffolk IP1 3LG
**Tel:** 01473267000
**Web:** www.scruttonbland.co.uk
**Estd:** 1929 Partnership
**Line of Business:** Accounting and auditing activities
**Partners:** J C Pickering, M A Farrow, Mrs S Gull, Ms S Gravner, C J Dolton
**Responsibilities**
**Senior:** Emma Clifton *(Manager)*, Emma Emerson *(Account Executive)*, Jason Fayers *(Partner)*, Sharon Gravener *(Partner)*, Julia Norman *(Assistant Manager)*, Tim O' Connor *(Partner)*
**Finance:** Robert Brigg *(Tax Manager)*, Grant Buchanan *(Finance Manager)*, Debbie Heron *(Financal Advisor)*
**Sales:** Emma Emerson *(Account Executive)*, Shirley Greer *(Commercial Account Executive)*, Emma Hood *(Private Client Account Handler)*
**Admin:** Jackie Mitchell *(Personal Assistant)*
**HR:** Debbie Sawyer *(Personnel Officer)*
**Health & Safety:** Jason Fayers *(Partner)*
**Branches:** Scrutton Bland, 62 Connaught Ave, Frinton-On-Sea, Essex CO13 9PT
**US SIC:** 8931, 6311
**UK SIC:** 83600, 82002
**Employees:** 75

DUNS 29-395-8005
## Scrutton Bland Ltd
820 The Crescent, Colchester Business Park, Colchester, Essex CO4 9YQ
**Tel:** 01206-838400 **Fax:** 01206838401
**Web:** www.scruttonbland.co.uk
**Reg No:** 1288848 **Estd:** 1976 Private Limited Company
**Line of Business:** Accounting activities
**Issued Capital:** £15,000
**Principals:** T J Mulley *(Managing)*, D J Bligh, G L Riches, J G Buchanan, S Mills, N Hewitt, N L Banks, A P Strickland
**Co. Secretary:** Truan Death
**Responsibilities**
**Senior:** Nigel Hutchinson *(Manager)*, Simon McKay *(Manager)*, E Twinn *(Senior Partner)*
**IT:** Ian Doe *(Computer Manager)*
**Health & Safety:** Penny Pearce *(Administrator)*
**Facilities:** Penny Pearce *(Administrator)*
**US SIC:** 8931, 6399
**UK SIC:** 83600, 82001
**Auditors:** Bird Luckin
**Bankers:** The Royal Bank Of Scotland Plc (16-16-31)

| | 31-03-14 | 31-03-13 | 31-03-12 |
|---|---|---|---|
| TO | N/A | 3,442,413 | 3,448,309 |
| P/L | N/A | 695,277 | 708,273 |
| NW | 1,269,879 | 585,372 | 289,999 |
| WC | 578,432 | 519,217 | 240,010 |
| Emp. | N/A | 62 | 63 |

DUNS 23-013-2107
## Scruttons (Ni) Ltd
(**Subsidiary of:** J. & J. Denholm Ltd)
2-10 Duncrue Road, Belfast BT3 9BP
**Tel:** 02890740777 **Fax:** 028-9074-2211
**Web:** www.hamiltonshipping.com
**Reg No:** 0036855NI **Estd:** 1999 Private Limited Company
**Line of Business:** Shipping companies
**Export Sales:** £2,060,916
**Issued Capital:** £2
**Directors:** S B Hughes, J N Denholm, G F Hamilton, S R Allen, M J Beveridge, D G Boyle
**Co. Secretary:** Gregory Hanson
**Responsibilities**
**Senior:** Gareth Jess *(Director of Operations)*
**Finance:** Martina Kenny *(Credit Controller)*
**Sales:** Joe Peoples *(Accounts Manager)*
**Admin:** Tara Johnston *(Administrator)*
**Operations:** Gareth Jess *(Director of Operations)*
**US SIC:** 4712 **UK SIC:** 77002
**Auditors:** Grant Thornton
**Bankers:** The Bank Of Ireland (90-21-27)

| | 31-12-13 | 31-12-12 | 31-12-11 |
|---|---|---|---|
| TO | 9,046,934 | 8,551,763 | 7,853,723 |
| P/L | 1,427,780 | 926,749 | 795,569 |
| NW | 721,688 | 625,212 | 1,329,413 |
| WC | 504,242 | 501,813 | 1,206,182 |
| Emp. | 102 | 98 | 95 |

DUNS 50-428-3524
## Sct Pension Trustees Ltd
(**Subsidiary of:** Dubai World Corporation)
204-206 Berth, Southampton, Hampshire SO15 1DA
**Tel:** 02380701701
**Web:** www.dpworldsouthampton.com
**Reg No:** 2420498 **Estd:** 1989 Private Limited Company
**Line of Business:** Business services
**Trading Style:** Southampton Container Terminals Ltd
**Issued Capital:** £100
**Directors:** Ms J G Berry, M J Mills, D E Walker, N P Loader, M R Swann, C G Beeson, P A Walker, M A Gibson
**Co. Secretary:** Ms Jane Healy
**Responsibilities**
**Senior:** Philip Kenley *(Manager)*, Valerie Milne *(Director)*
**US SIC:** 7399 **UK SIC:** 83954

| | 31-12-13 | 31-12-12 | 31-12-11 |
|---|---|---|---|
| TA | 100 | 100 | 100 |
| NW | 100 | 100 | 100 |

DUNS 28-829-7211
## Scunthorpe United Football Club Ltd
Glanford Park, Doncaster Road, Scunthorpe, South Humberside DN15 8TD
**Tel:** 08712211899
**Web:** www.scunthorpe-united.co.uk
**Reg No:** 0123622 **VAT No:** 128523474
**Estd:** 1912 Private Limited Company
**Line of Business:** Sports clubs
**Trading Style:** Glanford Park Restaurant
**Issued Capital:** £985,080
**Directors:** P D Swann, C Swann, J Oxenforth, K Wagstaff, Mrs K L Swann
**Co. Secretary:** David Beeby
**Responsibilities**
**Senior:** Jane Laws *(Centre Manager)*
**Finance:** Louise Whittaker *(Accountant)*
**Marketing:** Michelle Harness *(Commercial Manager)*
**Sales:** Michelle Harness *(Commercial Manager)*
**Purchasing:** Michelle Harness *(Commercial Manager)*
**US SIC:** 7999 **UK SIC:** 97913
**Auditors:** Forrester Boyd
**Bankers:** Barclays Bank Plc (20-76-14)

| | 30-06-14 | 30-06-13 | 30-06-12 |
|---|---|---|---|
| TO | 2,350,582 | 2,451,752 | 3,289,377 |
| P/L | (1,120,862) | (1,505,395) | (1,990,762) |
| NW | 2,178,621 | 3,022,455 | 4,240,162 |
| WC | (778,400) | (672,889) | (463,918) |
| Emp. | 191 | 178 | 227 |

DUNS 21-255-3176
## Scurrah-Nassau Ltd
Haverigg Industrial Estate, Millom, Cumbria LA18 4NG
**Tel:** 01229772685
**Web:** www.scurrahnassau.com
**Reg No:** 1112216 **VAT No:** 257110778
**Estd:** 1935 Private Limited Company
**Line of Business:** Steel fabricators
**Issued Capital:** £100
**Principals:** J B Keen *(Managing)*, Mrs Y Keen, A B Keen
**Co. Secretary:** John Keen
**Responsibilities**
**Senior:** Dave Brewer *(General Manager)*
**IT:** Dave Brewer *(General Manager)*, Edna Milligan *(Computer Manager)*
**Facilities:** Dave Brewer *(General Manager)*
**Engineering:** Dave Brewer *(General Manager)*
**Branches:** Scurrah-Nassau Ltd, Cavendish Dock Road, Barrow-In-Furness, Cumbria LA14 2LA
**US SIC:** 1622 **UK SIC:** 50200
**Auditors:** J L Winder & Co
**Bankers:** Barclays Bank Plc (20-04-68)

| | 31-12-13 | 31-12-12 | 31-12-11 |
|---|---|---|---|
| TA | 530,056 | 325,401 | 253,175 |
| NW | 45,798 | 59,795 | 91,605 |
| WC | 1,633 | 9,481 | 48,685 |

DUNS 22-668-4314
## S.C.W.S. Ltd
(**Subsidiary of:** S.C.W.S. (Holdings) Ltd)
Rear Of 59, Clifton Street, Cardiff, South Glamorgan CF24 1LT
**Tel:** 08457404404
**Web:** www.scws.co.uk
**Reg No:** 1794582 **Estd:** 1966 Private Limited Company
**Line of Business:** Construction of commercial buildings
**Issued Capital:** £3,000
**Principals:** A W Scales *(Managing)*, B G Watson, D E Green, Mrs L M Scales
**Co. Secretary:** Andrew Scales
**Responsibilities**
**Senior:** Christopher Coulson *(Manager)*, Sean Middleton *(Works Manager)*
**Finance:** Eddie Howard *(Financial Director)*

**Admin:** Kirsty Hill (Office Manager)
**IT:** Kirsty Hill (Office Manager)
**HR:** Kirsty Hill (Office Manager), Nicky Scales (Training Coordinator)
**Health & Safety:** Sean Middleton (Works Manager)
**Facilities:** Sean Middleton (Works Manager)
**US SIC:** 1541, 5051
**UK SIC:** 50100, 61200
**Auditors:** Baker Tilly UK Audit LLP
**Bankers:** National Westminster Bank Plc (60-07-47)

|  | 31-03-14 | 31-03-13 | 31-03-12 |
|---|---|---|---|
| TO | 11,543,007 | 15,426,701 | 12,176,941 |
| P/L | 140,150 | 148,929 | 176,027 |
| NW | 854,606 | 734,550 | 621,126 |
| WC | 447,477 | 482,845 | 258,230 |
| Emp. | 79 | 78 | 65 |

DUNS 73-477-5724     **Imp**

## Scx Ltd
Roman Ridge Road, Sheffield, South Yorkshire S9 1GA
**Tel:** 01142-431142
**Web:** www.scx.co.uk
**Reg No:** 4741414 **Estd:** 2003 Private Limited Company
**Line of Business:** Management activities of other non-financial holding companies not elsewhere classified
**Issued Capital:** £18,002
**Directors:** Mrs S A Vickers, M Street, S J Eastwood
**Co. Secretary:** Ms Sophie Stead
**Responsibilities**
**Operations:** Andy Whitworth (Projects Director)
**US SIC:** 6711, 3534
**UK SIC:** 83962, 32553
**Bankers:** Barclays Bank Plc (20-76-89)

|  | 31-03-14 | 31-03-13 | 31-03-12 |
|---|---|---|---|
| TO | 19,818,535 | 17,300,767 | 15,556,901 |
| P/L | 2,191,514 | 1,844,257 | 1,613,661 |
| NW | 7,368,605 | 6,172,401 | 4,704,506 |
| WC | 3,380,869 | 2,610,900 | 1,396,670 |
| Emp. | 134 | 113 | 112 |

DUNS 21-580-6712     **Imp**

## S.D. Kells Ltd
Lackaghboy Industrial Estate, Enniskillen, Co Fermanagh BT74 4RL
**Tel:** 028-6632-0600 **Fax:** 028-6772-1078
**Web:** www.sdkells.co.uk
**Reg No:** 0020251NI **VAT No:** 254504082
**Estd:** 1928 Private Limited Company
**Line of Business:** Departmental stores
**Issued Capital:** £400,000
**Directors:** A J Kells, S Mcelwaine, A D Kells, I A Kells, R A Kells, Mrs S Kells
**Co. Secretary:** Howard Mcmorris
**Responsibilities**
**Senior:** Ain Kelly (Proprietor)
**Branches:** S.d. Kells Ltd, 3-5 Scarffes Entry, Omagh, Co Tyrone BT78 1JH
**US SIC:** 5399 **UK SIC:** 65600
**Auditors:** Roger Morrison & Co Ltd
**Bankers:** Ulster Bank Ltd (98-09-70)

|  | 19-01-14 | 19-01-13 | 19-01-12 |
|---|---|---|---|
| TO | 9,780,691 | 9,246,860 | 8,836,451 |
| P/L | 828,502 | 739,669 | 438,494 |
| NW | 6,447,336 | 5,869,190 | 5,342,816 |
| WC | 1,486,099 | 1,098,886 | 297,885 |
| Emp. | 151 | 147 | 140 |

DUNS 73-907-6722

## Sdi Media Ltd
**(Subsidiary of:** Bnp Paribas)
Cambridge House, 100 Cambridge Grove, London W6 0LE
**Tel:** 020-8237-7900 **Fax:** 02082377950
**Web:** www.sdimedia.com
**Reg No:** 5161289 **Estd:** 2004 Private Limited Company
**Line of Business:** Other motion picture and video production activities
**Issued Capital:** £100
**Directors:** R J Peckham, A Abisso, R P Flynn
**Co. Secretary:** Alistair Agnew
**Responsibilities**
**Senior:** Joe Sage (Manager)
**US SIC:** 7819 **UK SIC:** 97111
**Auditors:** Deloitte LLP
**Bankers:** Barclays Bank Plc (20-00-00)

|  | 31-12-13 | 31-12-12 | 31-12-11 |
|---|---|---|---|
| TA | 13,170,688 | 13,170,688 | 13,170,688 |
| P/L | (370,680) | (170,538) | (572,085) |
| NW | 4,409,253 | 4,779,933 | 4,950,471 |
| WC | (5,828,710) | (5,458,030) | (5,287,492) |

DUNS 28-984-0803     **Imp-Exp**

## Sdl Group Ltd
Britannia Centre, Bentley Wood Way, Network 65 Business Park, Burnley, Lancashire BB11 5ST
**Tel:** 01282-418418 **Fax:** 01282-418419
**Web:** www.sdlgroupltd.com
**Reg No:** 1792430 **VAT No:** 151234014
**Estd:** 1977 Private Limited Company
**Line of Business:** Suppliers of trophies and medals

---

**Export Markets:** Europe; Australia; Middle East; S Africa
**Export Sales:** £942,004
**Trading Style:** Sdl Trophies
**Issued Capital:** £87,691
**Principals:** G E Lord (Managing), Y C Tam, P J Lord, Ms N J Lord, K L Lam, C G Lord
**Co. Secretary:** Geoffrey Lord
**Responsibilities**
**Senior:** Karen Hartley (Business Development Manager)
**Branches:** Sdl Group Ltd, 26 Castle Hill, Dudley, West Midlands DY1 4QQ
**US SIC:** 3911 **UK SIC:** 49101
**Auditors:** Moss & Williamson
**Bankers:** National Westminster Bank Plc (01-07-29)

|  | 31-12-13 | 31-12-12 | 31-12-11 |
|---|---|---|---|
| TO | 6,364,895 | 5,928,251 | 6,283,273 |
| P/L | 252,691 | 235,905 | 138,958 |
| NW | 1,447,414 | 1,353,661 | 1,243,603 |
| WC | 1,557,226 | 1,547,443 | 1,242,163 |
| Emp. | 59 | 60 | 65 |

DUNS 77-087-9856     **Exp**

## Sdl Plc
Globe House, Clivemont Road, Maidenhead, Berkshire SL6 7DY
**Tel:** 01628-410-100 **Fax:** 01628-410-150
**Web:** www.sdl.com
**Reg No:** 2675207 **VAT No:** 578231228
**Estd:** 1993 Public Limited Company
**Line of Business:** Other software consultancy and supply
**Export Markets:** worldwide
**Export Sales:** £202,200,000
**Issued Capital:** £802,112
**Principals:** M J Lancaster (Managing), C M Batterham, A J Gradden, Ms A J Gradden, G Collinson, A J Mcwalter, D H Clayton, D Lavelle
**Co. Secretary:** Ms Pamela Pickering
**Responsibilities**
**Senior:** Rachael Allan (General Manager), Joseph Campbell (Manager), Jaz Sehmi (General Manager), Michelle Wilson (Program Manager), Debbie Young (Operations Director), Silke Zschweigert (Manager)
**Finance:** Bernadette Nixon (Chief Revenue Officer)
**Marketing:** Paul Filkin (Relations Director), Massimo Ghislandi (Marketing Director), Elliott Harley (Online Website Assistant), Argyro Kyriakidou (Marketing Manager), Garry Levitt (Business Unit Director), Paige O'Neill (Chief Marketing Officer)
**Sales:** Tomas Ezpeleta (Business Development Manager), Frances Fenn (Sales Manager), Allan Hall (VP Sales & Operations), Fluer Schut (Sales Manager), Vincenta Soriano (Sales Manager)
**IT:** Craig Somers (Global IT Manager), Dennis van der Veeke (Chief Technology Officer)
**HR:** Roddy Temperley (Global Head of Human Resources)
**Facilities:** Clara Von Horn (Office And Facilities Manager)
**Operations:** Jean-Pierre Dekker (Chief Operating Officer), John Fennell (Chief Operating Officer), Sarah Joslin (Commercial Operations Manager), Dominic Kinnon (CEO SDL Global Solutions Divis), Cristina Lancaster (Global Operations Consultant), Melanie Priest (Project Manager), Debbie Young (Operations Director)
**Branches:** Sdl Plc, Aspect Court, Pond Hill, Sheffield, South Yorkshire S1 2BG
**US SIC:** 7379, 7339
**UK SIC:** 83940, 83954
**Auditors:** KPMG Audit PLC
**Bankers:** Barclays Bank Plc (20-78-58)

|  | 31-12-13 | 31-12-12 | 31-12-11 |
|---|---|---|---|
| TO | 266,100,000 | 269,323,000 | 229,001,000 |
| P/L | (24,400,000) | 27,397,000 | 33,761,000 |
| NW | (12,500,000) | (6,740,000) | 62,688,000 |
| WC | (17,900,000) | (10,289,000) | 58,854,000 |
| Emp. | 3,177 | 2,750 | 2,278 |

DUNS 21-002-9948     **Imp**

## Sdv Ltd
**(Subsidiary of:** Bollore Participations)
Bernard House, 52-54 Peregrine Road, Ilford, Essex IG6 3SZ
**Tel:** 02085 599911 **Fax:** 02085599922
**Web:** www.sdv.com
**Reg No:** 0232744 **Estd:** 1928 Private Limited Company
**Line of Business:** Freight forwarders
**Trading Style:** Sdv Limited
**Issued Capital:** £200,000
**Directors:** T Ehrenbogen, H A Le Gouis, D Smith
**Co. Secretary:** John Love
**Responsibilities**
**Senior:** Herbert De St Simon (Chief Executive Officer), Andrea Eusebi (Industrial Project General Man), Bertrand Jannin (Manager), Moira Walsh (Human Resources Director)

---

**Marketing:** Lisa Brewster (Director Marketing & Communica)
**Sales:** Natalie Hart (Business Development Manager)
**IT:** Michael Rumsey (Senior IT Executive)
**HR:** Moira Walsh (Human Resources Director)
**Engineering:** Andrea Eusebi (Industrial Project General Man)
**Branches:** Sdv Limited, Ninian Park, Ninian Way, Tamworth, Staffordshire B77 5ES
**US SIC:** 4712 **UK SIC:** 77002
**Auditors:** Constantin
**Bankers:** National Westminster Bank Plc (60-05-01)

|  | 31-12-13 | 31-12-12 | 31-12-11 |
|---|---|---|---|
| TO | 124,102,941 | 128,507,481 | 127,710,900 |
| P/L | 4,958,471 | 4,139,040 | 3,308,987 |
| NW | 8,004,960 | 5,703,199 | 4,486,842 |
| WC | 3,638,561 | 1,088,383 | 511,267 |
| Emp. | 424 | 427 | 425 |

DUNS 22-440-8083

## Sea Cadet Corps (Crawley)
Longmere Road, Crawley, West Sussex RH10 8ND
**Tel:** 01293-529585
**Estd:** 1997 Proprietorship
**Line of Business:** Associations
**Proprietor:** Ms G Cruise
**Responsibilities**
**Senior:** Darren Erb (Commanding Officer)
**US SIC:** 8699 **UK SIC:** 96902
**Employees:** 99

DUNS 22-900-5574

## Sea Fish Industry Authority
18 Logie Mill, Edinburgh, Midlothian EH7 4HS
**Tel:** 0131-558-3331
**Web:** www.seafish.org
**Estd:** 1952
**Line of Business:** Trade assoc & regulatory bodies
**Trading Style:** Seafish
**Principals:** A Dewer-Burie (Chairman), J E Tumilty (Technical), K D Waind, J Rutherford
**Co. Secretary:** D Robertson
**Responsibilities**
**Senior:** Ivan Bartolo (Board Member)
**Finance:** Declan Byrne (Finance Manager), Hazel Curtis (Chief Economist), Angus Garrett (Senior Economist), Stuart Jeffery (Finance Officer), Carol Lynch (Project Finance Officer)
**Marketing:** Joanna Dunlop (Marketing Executive), Karen McGalloway (Market Planning & Strategy Man), Heather Middleton (Marketing Manager), Dani Sewell (Industry Communications), Dawn Sneddon (Office Manager)
**Sales:** Malcolm Large (Partnerships Manager)
**Admin:** Dawn Sneddon (Office Manager)
**IT:** Michaela Archer (Project Manager), Richard Caslake (Project Manager), Marcus Jacklin (Project Manager)
**HR:** Richard Wardell (Standards Supply)
**Facilities:** Dawn Sneddon (Office Manager)
**Operations:** Janice Anderson (Business Services Director), Mick Bacon (Project Officer)
**Engineering:** Mike Montgomerie (Gear Technologist)
**Branches:** Sea Fish Industry Authority, Glenugie Business Centre, Unit 12A, Peterhead, Aberdeenshire AB42 1UH
**US SIC:** 8621 **UK SIC:** 96311
**Bankers:** Clydesdale Bank Plc (82-45-05)
**Employees:** 50

DUNS 45-885-1318

## Sea Holdings Ltd
Millfield Lane, Nether Poppleton, York, North Yorkshire YO26 6PQ
**Tel:** 01904-782782 **Fax:** 01904-782700
**Web:** www.saville-av.com
**Reg No:** 3222660 **Estd:** 1996 Private Limited Company
**Line of Business:** Management activities of other non-financial holding companies not elsewhere classified
**Export Sales:** £1,478,539
**Trading Style:** Saville Audiovisual, The Saville Group
**Issued Capital:** £648,446
**Principals:** J P Sills (Managing), M N Nisbet, E J Everard, A J Dyson
**Co. Secretary:** Colin Nixey
**US SIC:** 3999 **UK SIC:** 49590
**Auditors:** HPH
**Bankers:** HSBC Bank plc (40-47-31)

|  | 31-12-13 | 31-12-12 | 31-12-11 |
|---|---|---|---|
| TO | 36,773,414 | 34,635,061 | 30,752,742 |
| P/L | 205,659 | 503,693 | 179,864 |
| NW | 2,815,198 | 2,549,570 | 2,114,881 |
| WC | 1,152,349 | 1,072,866 | 1,511,495 |
| Emp. | 255 | 244 | 241 |

---

DUNS 21-391-6690

## Sea Hotel
Sea Road, South Shields, Tyne and Wear NE33 2LD
**Tel:** 0191-427-0999
**Web:** www.bestwestern.co.uk
**VAT No:** 177399115 **Estd:** 1986 Partnership
**Line of Business:** Hotels
**Partners:** Mrs D James, F Bassett
**Responsibilities**
**Finance:** Jill Halliday (Head of Accounts)
**US SIC:** 7011 **UK SIC:** 66500
**Employees:** 70

DUNS 22-198-5687

## Sea Shell Trust
160-166 Stanley Road, Cheadle, Cheshire SK8 6RQ
**Tel:** 0161-610-0100
**Web:** www.seashelltrust.org.uk
**Reg No:** 4216714 **Estd:** 2001 Private Company Limited By Guarantee
**Line of Business:** Schools (special)
**Directors:** B T Exell, P J Walker, Ms G Carr, Ms D Whalley, D C Shipley, N J Gower, E Baines, Doctor D Sanders
**Co. Secretary:** Mark Ascroft
**Responsibilities**
**Senior:** Stephen Gillingham (Director), Afshan Khawaja (Director), Anthony Snape (Director)
**Admin:** Bev Mars (Head of Access, Admissions & A), Hayley Rose (PA to the Chief Executive)
**HR:** Nikola Giles (Director of HR)
**Engineering:** Geoff Grasse (Maintenance Manager)
**Branches:** Sea Shell Trust, Griffin Lane Lodge 4-5, Heald Green, Cheadle, Cheshire SK8 3PZ
**US SIC:** 8299, 8091, 8321, 7999
**UK SIC:** 93300, 95200, 96111, 97913
**Bankers:** The Royal Bank Of Scotland Plc (16-10-80)

|  | 31-08-13 | 31-08-12 | 31-08-11 |
|---|---|---|---|
| TO | 12,544,000 | 11,986,000 | 12,160,000 |
| P/L | 336,000 | (46,000) | 145,000 |
| NW | 11,096,000 | 10,409,000 | 10,290,000 |
| WC | 4,402,000 | 2,251,000 | 3,387,000 |
| Emp. | 413 | 396 | 372 |

DUNS 21-712-1219     **Imp-Exp**

## Sea Sure Ltd
The Clocktower, 2 Shore Road, Southampton, Hampshire SO31 9GQ
**Tel:** 01489-885401
**Web:** www.sea-sure.co.uk
**Reg No:** 0887907 **VAT No:** 107757950
**Estd:** 1966 Private Limited Company
**Line of Business:** Building and repairing of pleasure and sporting boats
**Export Markets:** Europe, U S A, Canada, Australasia, Far East
**Issued Capital:** £19,002
**Directors:** G E Brown, Ms M A Mugridge
**Co. Secretary:** Edward Brown
**Responsibilities**
**Senior:** Mark Acaster (Manager)
**US SIC:** 3732, 3999
**UK SIC:** 36102, 49590

|  | 30-09-13 | 30-09-12 | 30-09-11 |
|---|---|---|---|
| TA | 1,341,074 | 1,340,911 | 1,380,149 |
| NW | 759,544 | 732,056 | 718,514 |
| WC | 429,855 | 440,937 | 461,165 |

DUNS 76-691-6241

## Seabank Power Ltd
Severn Road, Hallen, Bristol, Avon BS10 7SP
**Tel:** 01179387800 **Fax:** 0117-938-7821
**Web:** www.seabank.co.uk
**Reg No:** 2591188 **Estd:** 1991 Private Limited Company
**Line of Business:** Production of electricity
**Trading Style:** Uk Coal Mining Ltd
**Issued Capital:** £5,280
**Directors:** D N Macrae, J A Sutherland, A J Hunter, P R Smith, Ms W Tong Barnes, M J Pibworth, N D Mcgee, C Tsai
**Co. Secretary:** Ms Laura Pittam
**Responsibilities**
**Senior:** Stuart Mayer (General manager), Laura Mcvean (Manager)
**Admin:** Glynis Walker (Administrator)
**HR:** Glynis Walker (Administrator)
**US SIC:** 4911 **UK SIC:** 16101
**Auditors:** PricewaterhouseCoopers LLP
**Bankers:** The Royal Bank Of Scotland Plc (15-20-25)

|  | 31-12-13 | 31-12-12 | 31-12-11 |
|---|---|---|---|
| TO | 124,135,000 | 130,665,000 | 122,308,000 |
| P/L | 51,745,000 | 46,177,000 | 13,284,000 |
| NW | 122,080,000 | 102,450,000 | 85,933,000 |
| WC | 1,600,000 | (5,873,000) | (328,000) |
| Emp. | 54 | 55 | 63 |

**DUNS 77-443-8642**
## Seaborne Plastics Ltd
2-3 Manfield Park, Cranleigh, Surrey GU6 8PT
**Tel:** 01483-272-282 **Fax:** 01483-272-283
**Web:** www.seaborne.co.uk
**Reg No:** 2953469 **Estd:** 1994 Private Limited Company
**Line of Business:** Vacuum formed plastics
**Issued Capital:** £212,000
**Principals:** M A Bollands (Managing), Ms A M Wettern, J I Hawkins
**Responsibilities**
**Senior:** Jennifer Fish (Manager)
**Purchasing:** Kevin Winn (Purchasing Manager)
**US SIC:** 3079 **UK SIC:** 48360
**Auditors:** Menzies LLP

|     | 31-12-13 | 31-12-12 | 31-12-11 |
|-----|----------|----------|----------|
| TA | 2,654,352 | 2,434,593 | 2,611,501 |
| NW | 969,318 | 891,767 | 805,156 |
| WC | 359,019 | 387,055 | 352,154 |

**DUNS 21-585-1169**
## Seabourn Cruise Line
Carnival House, 100 Harbour Parade, Southampton, Hampshire SO15 1ST
**Tel:** 08450700500
**Web:** www.seabourn.com
**Estd:** 2011 Partnership
**Line of Business:** Cruiselines
**Partners:** P Beale, Ms L Havis
**US SIC:** 4452 **UK SIC:** 74002
**Employees:** 50

**DUNS 21-152-2826**    Imp-Exp
## Seabourne Group Ltd
(**Subsidiary of:** C J Bourne (Asset Management) Ltd)
U C H House, Suite 102 Old Bath Road, Colnbrook, Slough, Berkshire SL3 0NW
**Tel:** 01753680376
**Web:** www.seabourne-group.com
**Reg No:** 1060736 **VAT No:** 239848219
**Estd:** 1972 Private Limited Company
**Line of Business:** Import and export agents
**Export Markets:** Worldwide
**Issued Capital:** £400,000
**Principals:** N C Hudson (Financial), Lady J H Bourne, D J Flitterman
**Co. Secretary:** Donald Hayes
**Responsibilities**
**Senior:** Grant Marshall (Manager)
**Health & Safety:** Jess Wise (personal assistant)
**Facilities:** Jess Wise (personal assistant)
**Branches:** Seabourne Group Ltd, Forward House, Birmingham, West Midlands B26 3QT
**US SIC:** 4712, 4311
**UK SIC:** 77002, 79010
**Auditors:** Bright Grahame Murray
**Bankers:** Barclays Bank Plc (20-36-47)

|     | 30-06-13 | 30-06-12 | 30-06-11 |
|-----|----------|----------|----------|
| TO | 30,990,162 | 31,780,180 | 33,458,047 |
| P/L | 194,103 | (8,127) | (29,810) |
| NW | 340,723 | 955,920 | 1,014,540 |
| WC | 1,175,782 | 95,973 | 457,744 |
| Emp. | 343 | 334 | 292 |

**DUNS 54-906-5811**
## Seabourne Residential Home
1 Clifton Road, Bournemouth, Dorset BH6 3NZ
**Web:** www.luxurycare.co.uk
**Estd:** 2000 Proprietorship
**Line of Business:** Residential care establishments
**Proprietor:** Miss S Johnson
**US SIC:** 8321, 6732
**UK SIC:** 96111, 83100
**Employees:** 49

**DUNS 21-781-2230**
## Seabridge Primary School
Roe Lane, Newcastle, Staffordshire ST5 3PJ
**Tel:** 01782297361
**Web:** www.seabridge-primary.staffs.sch.uk
**Estd:** 1999 Proprietorship
**Line of Business:** Primary education
**Proprietor:** Mrs S Mitchell
**US SIC:** 8211 **UK SIC:** 93200
**Employees:** 50

**DUNS 34-907-0628**
## Seabrook Group Ltd
Seabrook House, Duncombe Street, Bradford, West Yorkshire BD8 9AJ
**Tel:** 01274-546405
**Web:** www.seabrookcrists.com
**Reg No:** 5704256 **Estd:** 2006 Private Limited Company
**Line of Business:** Management activities of holding companies
**Trading Style:** Seabrook Group Limited
**Issued Capital:** £120

**Directors:** Ms S C Brook-Chrispin, Mrs J C Brook-Chrispin, D R Woodwards, K Brook-Chrispin, Miss C M Brook-Chrispin, J Bye
**Co. Secretary:** Daniel Woodwards
**US SIC:** 6711, 2099
**UK SIC:** 83962, 42399
**Auditors:** Grant Thornton UK LLP
**Bankers:** HSBC Bank plc (40-27-15)

|     | 30-03-14 | 31-03-13 | 01-03-12 |
|-----|----------|----------|----------|
| TO | 24,535,000 | 22,817,000 | 12,370,123 |
| P/L | 1,148,000 | (366,000) | (219,413) |
| NW | 272,000 | (652,000) | (376,034) |
| WC | 47,000 | (615,000) | 363,171 |
| Emp. | 157 | 168 | 184 |

**DUNS 77-934-8317**
## Seabrook Warehousing Ltd
(**Subsidiary of:** Seabrook Holdings Ltd)
90 New Road, Rainham, Essex RM13 8DB
**Tel:** 020-859-67500 **Fax:** 02085967501
**Web:** www.seabrookwarehousing.com
**Reg No:** 3046974 **Estd:** 2002 Private Limited Company
**Line of Business:** Warehouses
**Issued Capital:** £100
**Directors:** M R Seabrook, Mrs P Seabrook
**Co. Secretary:** Michael Seabrook
**Responsibilities**
**HR:** David Tanner (Manager)
**US SIC:** 4226 **UK SIC:** 77003
**Auditors:** Taylor Viney & Marlow

|     | 31-07-13 | 31-07-12 | 31-07-11 |
|-----|----------|----------|----------|
| TO | 13,717,221 | 11,987,646 | 12,658,743 |
| P/L | 810,778 | 378,214 | 2,036,009 |
| NW | 3,387,538 | 2,714,206 | 2,459,291 |
| WC | 2,730,974 | 2,164,253 | 2,264,122 |
| Emp. | 83 | 76 | 78 |

**DUNS 23-811-4867**    Imp
## Seacatch (U K) Ltd
Estate Road 7, South Humberside Industrial Estate, Grimsby, South Humberside DN31 2TP
**Tel:** 01472-360370 **Fax:** 01472-361371
**Web:** www.seacatch.co.uk
**Reg No:** 3803850 **Estd:** 1999 Private Limited Company
**Line of Business:** Fish processing
**Issued Capital:** £110
**Directors:** Ms B A Chapman, Ajr Developments Limited, Ms N Eddowes, J A Jenkinson, R A Masterson
**Co. Secretary:** Simon Chapman
**Responsibilities**
**Finance:** David De Freitas (Financial Director)
**Sales:** April Dows (Sales)
**IT:** Claire Smalley (technical manager)
**Health & Safety:** Claire Smalley (technical manager)
**Facilities:** Barry Washington (Facilities Manager)
**Operations:** Elaine Smalley (Technical Manager)
**US SIC:** 2092, 5146
**UK SIC:** 41501, 61700
**Bankers:** HSBC Bank plc (40-22-24)

|     | 31-03-13 | 31-03-12 | 31-03-11 |
|-----|----------|----------|----------|
| TO | N/A | 7,202,440 | N/A |
| P/L | N/A | 153,213 | N/A |
| NW | 58,376 | 399,136 | 397,993 |
| WC | (591,802) | (64,042) | 47,137 |

**DUNS 21-017-1908**
## Seacole Ltd
2007 12 Norwich Road, Great Yarmouth, Norfolk NR30 5JT
**Tel:** 08447361458 **Fax:** 08447-36281
**Web:** www.seacole.org
**Reg No:** 6392530 **Estd:** 2007 Private Limited Company
**Line of Business:** Activities of other transport agencies
**Issued Capital:** £100
**Director:** B Mukuya
**Co. Secretary:** Miss Nicole Anderson
**US SIC:** 4712, 7361
**UK SIC:** 77002, 83954

|     | 31-10-13 | 31-10-12 | 31-10-11 |
|-----|----------|----------|----------|
| TA | 30,550 | 14,393 | 12,437 |
| NW | 10,367 | 354 | 12,437 |
| WC | 2,151 | (6,583) | N/A |

**DUNS 29-932-7882**    Imp
## Seacon (Europe) Ltd
(**Subsidiary of:** Brantner and Associates Inc.)
Seacon House Hewett Road, Gapton Hall Industrial Estate, Great Yarmouth, Norfolk NR31 0RB
**Tel:** 01493652733 **Fax:** 01493-652840
**Web:** www.seaconeurope.com
**Reg No:** 2101490 **VAT No:** 460340971
**Estd:** 1987 Private Limited Company
**Line of Business:** Manufacture of insulated wire and cable
**Export Sales:** £9,249,792
**Issued Capital:** £1,000
**Directors:** D W Sites, H G Barksdale, C A Newell, S C Cooper

**Responsibilities**
**Marketing:** Melanie Harrison (Marketing Manager)
**Operations:** Melanie Harrison (Marketing Manager)
**Engineering:** Lee Stevenson (Engineering Manager)
**US SIC:** 3357 **UK SIC:** 22470
**Auditors:** Cunninghams
**Bankers:** National Westminster Bank Plc (53-81-16)

|     | 31-12-13 | 31-12-12 | 31-12-11 |
|-----|----------|----------|----------|
| TO | 17,761,287 | 12,677,474 | 10,030,523 |
| P/L | 4,139,785 | 2,551,059 | 1,858,972 |
| NW | 7,104,749 | 5,389,906 | 4,353,516 |
| WC | 6,486,663 | 5,064,818 | 4,019,726 |
| Emp. | 128 | 110 | 97 |

**DUNS 22-203-0731**
## Seacon Group Ltd
Tower Warf, North Fleet, Northfleet, Northfleet, Gravesend, Kent DA11 9BD
**Tel:** 01474-320000 **Fax:** 01474329945
**Web:** www.seacon.co.uk
**Reg No:** 4221248 **Estd:** 2001 Private Limited Company
**Line of Business:** Shipping companies
**Issued Capital:** £250,017
**Directors:** M Dale, J A Roth
**Co. Secretary:** Kevin Jeeves
**Branches:** Seacon Group Ltd, Trelawny House, Room 115, Felixstowe, Suffolk IP11 3GB
**US SIC:** 6711, 4712
**UK SIC:** 83962, 77002
**Auditors:** Barnes Roffe LLP
**Bankers:** National Westminster Bank Plc (57-00-00)

|     | 30-09-13 | 30-09-12 | 30-09-11 |
|-----|----------|----------|----------|
| TO | 23,120,919 | 30,461,103 | 31,796,543 |
| P/L | (1,987,775) | (461,740) | (136,427) |
| NW | 8,578,449 | 4,709,113 | 5,663,932 |
| WC | (2,581,797) | (2,113,591) | (1,082,725) |
| Emp. | 144 | 186 | 172 |

**DUNS 23-112-4710**
## Seacore Trustees Ltd
(**Subsidiary of:** Fugro N.V.)
Lower Quay, Gweek, Helston, Cornwall TR12 6UD
**Tel:** 01326-221771
**Web:** www.seacore.com
**Reg No:** 2909001 **Estd:** 1978 Private Limited Company
**Line of Business:** Financial intermediation not elsewhere classified
**Issued Capital:** £2
**Director:** W S Rainey
**Co. Secretary:** Gordon Duncan
**Responsibilities**
**Senior:** Douglas Simpson (Manager)
**US SIC:** 6111 **UK SIC:** 81501
**Auditors:** Kitchen & Brown

|     | 31-03-14 | 31-03-13 | 31-03-12 |
|-----|----------|----------|----------|
| TA | 74,073 | 74,073 | 74,073 |
| NW | (1) | (1) | (1) |
| WC | (1) | (1) | (1) |

**DUNS 21-222-8041**
## Seacroft Holiday Village
Beach Road, Hemsby, Great Yarmouth, Norfolk NR29 4HR
**Tel:** 01493733610
**Web:** www.richardsonsholidayvillages.co.uk
**Estd:** 2002 Proprietorship
**Line of Business:** Other tourist or short-stay accommodation
**Proprietor:** J Ettridge
**Responsibilities**
**Health & Safety:** John Foreman (Health & Safety Officer)
**Facilities:** Paul Tidman (Maintenance Manager)
**US SIC:** 7021 **UK SIC:** 66500
**Employees:** 120

**DUNS 21-866-8741**
## Seadrill Management Ltd.
(**Subsidiary of:** Seadrill Limited)
Building 11, Chiswick Park, 566 Chiswick High Road, London W4 5YS
**Fax:** 02088114701
**Web:** www.seadrill.com
**Reg No:** 8276358 **Estd:** 2012 Private Limited Company
**Line of Business:** Oil and gas extraction
**Directors:** R M Lundetrae, D S Sneddon, P Wulff, Ms G Sousa
**Responsibilities**
**Senior:** Robert Hingley Wilson (Manager)
**US SIC:** 1311 **UK SIC:** 13000
**Employees:** 80
**Turnover:** £83,394,010

**DUNS 39-698-2514**
## Seafab Consultants Ltd
(**Subsidiary of:** Kerrow Ltd)
Wellheads Terrace, Wellheads Industrial Estate, Aberdeen, Aberdeenshire AB21 7GF
**Tel:** 01224797940 **Fax:** 01224-723400
**Web:** www.seafab.co.uk
**Reg No:** 0106030SC **VAT No:** 268268422
**Estd:** 1987 Private Limited Company
**Line of Business:** Steel fabricators
**Issued Capital:** £100
**Principals:** N Green (Managing), N N Green
**Co. Secretary:** Ms June Palin
**Responsibilities**
**Senior:** Stewart Cardno (Procurement Manager)
**Finance:** Florence Mckay (Accounts Manager)
**IT:** Florence Mckay (Accounts Manager)
**Health & Safety:** Alex Keith (Quality Assurance Manager)
**Purchasing:** Stewart Cardno (Procurement Manager)
**US SIC:** 1622, 3499
**UK SIC:** 50200, 31694
**Auditors:** Anderson Anderson & Brown
**Bankers:** Bank Of Scotland (80-05-14)

|     | 31-03-14 | 31-03-13 | 31-03-12 |
|-----|----------|----------|----------|
| TA | 1,753,723 | 2,466,629 | 2,526,860 |
| NW | 853,446 | 1,165,002 | 1,074,504 |
| WC | (478,460) | (108,701) | (236,776) |

**DUNS 23-576-4524**    Exp
## Seafield Pedigrees Ltd
Seafield Farm, Seafield Lane, Redditch, Worcestershire B98 9DB
**Tel:** 01527-66191 **Fax:** 01527-62975
**Web:** www.attwellfarm.com
**Reg No:** 3574319 **Estd:** 1968 Private Limited Company
**Line of Business:** Production of meat products
**Trading Style:** Seafield Pedigrees Ltd
**Issued Capital:** £2
**Directors:** M W Attwell, C M Attwell
**Co. Secretary:** Ms Susan Attwell
**Responsibilities**
**Engineering:** Simon Maddocks (Production Manager)
**US SIC:** 2013, 0259
**UK SIC:** 41223, 01001
**Auditors:** Mitchell Meredith Ltd

|     | 31-12-13 | 31-12-12 | 31-12-11 |
|-----|----------|----------|----------|
| TA | 2,228,503 | 2,145,593 | 2,278,476 |
| NW | (255,794) | 108,765 | 242,445 |
| WC | (751,167) | (367,213) | (136,402) |

**DUNS 21-561-3282**    Imp-Exp
## Seafish U.K. Ltd
45-55 Wassand Street, Hull, North Humberside HU3 4AN
**Tel:** 01482-223648 **Fax:** 01482-216230
**Web:** www.seafishuk.co.uk
**Reg No:** 0058333SC **Estd:** 1922 Private Limited Company
**Line of Business:** Processing and preserving of fish and fish products
**Export Markets:** U S A, Australia, France, Germany
**Issued Capital:** £2,229,998
**Managing Director:** R A Carter
**Co. Secretary:** Ms Cheryl Carter
**Responsibilities**
**Finance:** Una O'Donovan (Accounts Assistant), nick smith (Financial Director)
**Sales:** Laura Dibnah (Sales Administrator), Michelle Elland (Sales Administrator)
**Admin:** Linda Cawthra (Receptionist), Carly Deery (Office Administrator), Laura Dibnah (Sales Administrator), Melissa Dunhill (Office Administrator), Michelle Elland (Sales Administrator), Sarah Rimmington (Office Manager)
**IT:** Edward Fleming (Technical Manager)
**Health & Safety:** Paul Rimmington (Safety Officer)
**Operations:** Edward Fleming (Technical Manager)
**Purchasing:** Paul Rimmington (Safety Officer)
**Engineering:** Edward Fleming (Technical Manager)
**Branches:** Seafish U.k. Ltd, Easterdale, Hamnavoe Burra, Lerwick, Shetland, Shetland ZE2 9LB
**US SIC:** 2092 **UK SIC:** 41501
**Auditors:** Gillani & Co
**Bankers:** The Royal Bank Of Scotland Plc (83-24-22)

|     | 31-12-13 | 31-12-12 | 31-12-11 |
|-----|----------|----------|----------|
| TO | 15,655,095 | 12,023,709 | 12,192,562 |
| P/L | 823,042 | 434,389 | 489,650 |
| NW | 3,822,896 | 3,187,547 | 2,767,230 |
| WC | 2,717,646 | 2,121,487 | 1,737,562 |
| Emp. | 92 | 82 | 77 |

DUNS 50-415-5425 **Imp-Exp**

## Seafood Ecosse Ltd

**(Subsidiary of:** Sco-Bere Seafoods (Holdings) Ltd)
Dales Industrial Estate, Peterhead, Aberdeenshire AB42 3JF
**Tel:** 01779475718 **Fax:** 01779475846
**Web:** www.sco-bere.freeserve.co.uk
**Reg No:** 0119437SC **VAT No:** 553294141
**Estd:** 1992 Private Limited Company
**Line of Business:** Shell fish suppliers and processors
**Export Markets:** E U
**Export Sales:** £20,310,112
**Issued Capital:** £182,000
**Principals:** F Gault *(Managing)*, J M Stephen *(Financial)*, D Leiper, C J Gault, D West, W Leiper
**Co. Secretary:** Peterkins
**US SIC:** 0912, 5423
**UK SIC:** 03001, 64100
**Auditors:** Murray, Taylor (Scotland) Ltd
**Bankers:** The Royal Bank Of Scotland Plc (83-26-16)

| | 31-12-13 | 31-12-12 | 31-12-11 |
|---|---|---|---|
| TO | 21,770,199 | 19,649,520 | 18,871,315 |
| P/L | 1,628,786 | 859,754 | 1,169,631 |
| NW | 5,825,499 | 5,147,826 | 5,092,042 |
| WC | 4,976,932 | 4,331,669 | 4,245,499 |
| Emp. | 57 | 56 | 56 |

DUNS 22-208-9190 **Imp**

## Seafood Holdings Ltd

**(Subsidiary of:** The Bidvest Group Ltd)
Unit 14-15, Bermondsey Trading Estate, Rotherhithe New Road, London SE16 3LL
**Tel:** 02073-581617
**Web:** www.directseafoodslondon.co.uk
**Reg No:** 4227047 **VAT No:** 778259081
**Estd:** 1991 Private Limited Company
**Line of Business:** Wholesale of other food including fish, crustaceans and molluscs
**Trading Style:** Direct Seafoods, Direct Seafoods
**Issued Capital:** £125
**Directors:** B P Hall, P M Gower, Miss I Nicholson, Ms J C Roberts, S A Oswald, S D Bender
**Co. Secretary:** Miss Ingrid Nicholson
**Responsibilities**
**Senior:** Debbie Baughan *(Office Manager)*, Darren North *(Manager)*
**US SIC:** 5146 **UK SIC:** 61700
**Auditors:** KPMG LLP
**Bankers:** National Westminster Bank Plc (01-10-01)

| | 30-06-13 | 30-06-12 | 30-06-11 |
|---|---|---|---|
| TO | 90,554,915 | 82,442,542 | 111,944,867 |
| P/L | 3,908,803 | 2,625,918 | (3,113,687) |
| NW | (13,248,288) | (16,281,871) | (18,148,847) |
| WC | 3,738,149 | 4,233,662 | 3,816,226 |
| Emp. | 542 | 512 | 491 |

DUNS 21-630-2221

## The Seafood Restaurant (Padstow) Ltd

Riverside, Padstow, Cornwall PL28 8BY
**Tel:** 01841532700
**Web:** www.rickstein.com
**Reg No:** 7089657 **Estd:** 2009 Private Limited Company
**Line of Business:** Management activities of holding companies
**Issued Capital:** £135,000
**Directors:** Ms J Stein, C R Stein, N J Mcleod
**Co. Secretary:** Neil Mcleod
**US SIC:** 6711 **UK SIC:** 83962
**Bankers:** Barclays Bank Plc (20-87-94)

| | 29-12-13 | 30-12-12 | 31-12-11 |
|---|---|---|---|
| TO | 15,067,000 | 14,603,000 | 15,239,000 |
| P/L | 986,000 | 148,000 | 626,000 |
| NW | 8,380,000 | 7,926,000 | 7,822,000 |
| WC | (949,000) | (1,495,000) | (1,314,000) |
| Emp. | 289 | 321 | 327 |

DUNS 22-520-4171

## Seaford College

Lavington Park, Petworth, West Sussex GU28 0LE
**Web:** www.seaford.org
**Estd:** 1884
**Line of Business:** Schools (independent)
**Director:** T J Mullins
**US SIC:** 8211 **UK SIC:** 93200
**Bankers:** National Westminster Bank Plc (56-00-64)
**Employees:** 150

DUNS 21-588-1640

## Seaforth Hotel (Stornoway) Ltd

**(Subsidiary of:** Seaforth Hotel (Stornoway) Holdings Ltd)
James Street, Stornoway, Isle of Lewis HS1 2QN
**Tel:** 01851-702740
**Web:** www.calahotels.com
**Reg No:** 0064817SC **Estd:** 1971 Private Limited Company
**Line of Business:** Hotels
**Issued Capital:** £105,364
**Principals:** K A Mackenzie *(Managing)*, Ms L A Murray, N Mackenzie, R Mackenzie
**Co. Secretary:** Kenneth Mackenzie
**Responsibilities**
**Senior:** Christina Maciver *(Hotel Manager)*, Isobel Mackenzie *(Director)*
**Branches:** Seaforth Hotel (Stornoway) Ltd, Manor Park, Perceval Road South, Stornoway, Isle Of Lewis HS1 2EU
**US SIC:** 7011 **UK SIC:** 66500
**Auditors:** Scott-Morncrieff
**Bankers:** Bank Of Scotland (80-09-73)

| | 31-12-13 | 31-12-12 | 31-12-11 |
|---|---|---|---|
| TA | 1,545,069 | 1,415,344 | 1,683,561 |
| NW | 676,440 | 585,864 | 487,831 |
| WC | 16,143 | (149,290) | 50,922 |

DUNS 21-042-9211

## Seafresh Wholesale

27a Thorncliffe Road, Bradford, West Yorkshire BD8 7DD
**Tel:** 01274-492044
**Web:** www.adam-braches.com
**Estd:** 1984
**Line of Business:** Non-specialised wholesale of food, beverages and tobacco
**Proprietor:** A Perviz
**US SIC:** 5149 **UK SIC:** 61700
**Employees:** 100

DUNS 49-387-8573 **Imp**

## Seagate Systems (Uk) Ltd

**(Subsidiary of:** Xyratex Ltd)
Langstone Technology Park, Langstone Road, Havant, Hampshire PO9 1SA
**Tel:** 02392-496000
**Web:** www.xyratex.com
**Reg No:** 3134912 **VAT No:** 643353154
**Estd:** 1994 Private Limited Company
**Line of Business:** Manufacturers of pcs
**Trading Style:** Seagate
**Directors:** P O'Malley, J J Lerner
**Co. Secretary:** Kenneth Massaroni
**Responsibilities**
**Senior:** Malcolm Rule *(Manager)*
**Marketing:** Judy Redgrove *(Marketing Manager)*
**HR:** Jeremy Dyer *(Human Resources Manager)*
**US SIC:** 3573, 7397
**UK SIC:** 33020, 83702
**Auditors:** PricewaterhouseCoopers LLP
**Employees:** 641
**Turnover:** £809,846,000

DUNS 23-219-3995 **Imp**

## Seagate Technology (Ireland)

**(Subsidiary of:** Seagate Technology Public Limited)
1 Disc Drive, Springtown Industrial Estate, Londonderry, Co Londonderry BT48 0BF
**Tel:** 028 7127 4000 **Fax:** 028 7127 4202
**Web:** www.seagate.com
**Reg No:** 0003090NF **Estd:** 1994 Foreign Company
**Line of Business:** Manufacturers of pcs
**Directors:** P O'Malley, K M Massaroni
**Co. Secretary:** Stephen Sedler
**Responsibilities**
**Senior:** Ryan Burns *(Manager)*, Brian Burns *(Manager)*, E McIvor *(Stores Manager)*
**Finance:** David McHugh *(Financial Manager)*
**IT:** Bob Hunter *(Senior IT Executive)*, Ben McLaughlin *(IT Manager)*
**HR:** Kevin Calldwell *(Human Resources Manager)*, Michael Harper *(Human Resources Manager)*
**Health & Safety:** Bernadette McDermott *(Health & Safety Officer)*
**Facilities:** Mark Moroney *(Facilities Director)*
**Operations:** Bernadette McDermott *(Health & Safety Officer)*
**Purchasing:** Billy Doherty *(Purchasing Coordinator)*
**Engineering:** Paul O"Neill *(Production Manager)*
**US SIC:** 3573, 3679
**UK SIC:** 33020, 34542
**Bankers:** The Bank Of Ireland (90-49-74)

DUNS 42-441-5206

## Seager Heating Ltd

1 Seager Court, Crockatt Road, Hadleigh, Ipswich, Suffolk IP7 6RL
**Tel:** 01473-824884
**Web:** www.seagerhomesolutions.com
**Reg No:** 3395937 **Estd:** 1996 Private Limited Company
**Line of Business:** Plumbers
**Trading Style:** Seager Homes Solutions
**Issued Capital:** £31,000
**Directors:** Ms M Ramplin, G Seager, A C Seager, K M Greaves
**Responsibilities**
**Senior:** Julie Seager *(Manager)*, Kelly Seager *(Manager)*
**Finance:** Rebecca Martin *(Finance Manager)*
**Branches:** Seager Heating Ltd, Vendas Farm, Bury St. Edmunds, Suffolk IP29 4UR
**US SIC:** 1711 **UK SIC:** 50300
**Auditors:** Wilkins McLeese

| | 31-10-13 | 31-10-12 | 31-10-11 |
|---|---|---|---|
| TO | N/A | N/A | 5,777,013 |
| P/L | N/A | N/A | 221,539 |
| NW | 950,169 | 761,070 | 598,378 |
| WC | 380,616 | 246,634 | 135,465 |

DUNS 21-706-9965

## Seagoe Hotel 2007 Llp

Upper Church Lane, Portadown, Craigavon, Co Armagh BT63 5JE
**Tel:** 02838333076
**Web:** www.seagoe.com
**Reg No:** 0000266NC **Estd:** 2007
**Line of Business:** Hotels
**Responsibilities**
**Senior:** Brian Scullion *(Joint Managing Director)*
**Finance:** Miles Scullion *(Joint Managing Director)*
**US SIC:** 7011 **UK SIC:** 66500

| | 30-06-13 | 30-06-12 | 30-06-11 |
|---|---|---|---|
| TA | 7,713,843 | 8,118,472 | 7,786,131 |
| NW | (404,629) | N/A | (245,994) |
| WC | (7,531,219) | (7,531,219) | (7,527,990) |

DUNS 45-816-6208 **Imp**

## Seagold Ltd

**(Subsidiary of:** Samherji Hf)
Hesslewood Hall, Hessle, North Humberside HU13 0LH
**Tel:** 01482645500 **Fax:** 01482643580
**Web:** www.samherji.is
**Reg No:** 3193323 **Estd:** 1996 Private Limited Company
**Line of Business:** Import and export agents
**Export Sales:** £18,719,927
**Issued Capital:** £100,000
**Director:** P M Baldvinsson
**Co. Secretary:** Gustaf Baldvinsson
**Responsibilities**
**Senior:** Victoria Evins *(Personal Assistant)*
**US SIC:** 4712 **UK SIC:** 77002
**Auditors:** Streets & Co
**Bankers:** HSBC Bank plc (40-25-14)

| | 31-12-13 | 31-12-12 | 31-12-11 |
|---|---|---|---|
| TO | 82,232,790 | 71,466,121 | 72,320,859 |
| P/L | 714,785 | 392,044 | 335,874 |
| NW | 3,832,780 | 3,290,796 | 3,011,113 |
| WC | 3,692,878 | 3,130,193 | 2,797,332 |
| Emp. | 49 | 46 | 45 |

DUNS 21-782-8577

## Seagulls Sure Start Childrens Centre

Magdalen Way, Gorleston, Great Yarmouth, Norfolk NR31 7BP
**Tel:** 01493660090
**Web:** www.priorycentre.co.uk
**Estd:** 2002 Proprietorship
**Line of Business:** Community networks
**Proprietor:** R Mills
**US SIC:** 8211 **UK SIC:** 93200
**Employees:** 50

DUNS 21-825-7563

## Seajacks International Ltd

**(Subsidiary of:** Atlantis Investorco Ltd)
South Denes Business Park, South Beach Parade, Great Yarmouth, Norfolk NR30 3QR
**Tel:** 01493841400
**Web:** www.seajacks.com
**Reg No:** 7964749 **Estd:** 2012 Private Limited Company
**Line of Business:** Management activities of other non-financial holding companies not elsewhere classified
**Directors:** T Toyoda, T Furuta, T Mamiya, T Nishiwaki, W B Ainslie, S Nakagawa, S Inoue
**Co. Secretary:** Burness Paull Llp
**US SIC:** 6711 **UK SIC:** 83962
**Employees:** 7
**Turnover:** £219,193,000

DUNS 22-186-0666 **Imp**

## Seaking Electrical Ltd

70 Old Bidston Road, Birkenhead, Merseyside CH41 8BL
**Tel:** 0151-652-4821 **Fax:** 0151-653-8076
**Web:** www.seakinggroup.co.uk
**Reg No:** 4204287 **Estd:** 2002 Private Limited Company
**Line of Business:** Marine engines and engineering
**Issued Capital:** £2,500
**Directors:** D L Gillam, M K Sealeaf, C G Dahill
**Co. Secretary:** Eric King
**US SIC:** 8911, 3629, 3519
**UK SIC:** 83701, 34350, 32811
**Auditors:** Cowgill Holloway
**Bankers:** Bank Of Scotland (12-17-40)

| | 31-07-13 | 31-07-12 | 31-07-11 |
|---|---|---|---|
| TO | 12,899,412 | 10,847,552 | 6,283,436 |
| P/L | 1,115,715 | 446,157 | (243,466) |
| NW | 970,646 | 403,579 | 179,035 |
| WC | 620,633 | 186,205 | 8,153 |
| Emp. | 128 | 127 | 85 |

DUNS 21-158-7154

## Seal County Primary School

East Street, Selsey, Chichester, West Sussex PO20 0BN
**Tel:** 01243-602746
**Web:** www.seal.w-sussex.sch.uk
**Estd:** 1986
**Line of Business:** Schools (foundation)
**Proprietor:** Miss L Reynolds
**Responsibilities**
**Senior:** Matthew Batchelor *(Head Teacher)*
**US SIC:** 8211 **UK SIC:** 93200
**Employees:** 60

DUNS 64-083-7873 **Imp**

## Seal It Services Ltd

Unit G16, River Bank Way, Lowfields Business Park, Elland, West Yorkshire HX5 9DN
**Tel:** 01422-315300
**Web:** www.bond-it.co.uk
**Reg No:** 4487206 **Estd:** 2002 Private Limited Company
**Line of Business:** Manufacture of glues and gelatine
**Trading Style:** Bond It
**Issued Capital:** £100
**Directors:** D A Moore, S P Engineer, Mrs J S Engineer, G M Helm
**Responsibilities**
**Finance:** Sarah Sharkey *(Financial Controller)*, Rachel Skelly *(Accounts Associate)*
**Sales:** Christine Bray *(Sales Manager)*
**IT:** Sarah Sharkey *(Financial Controller)*
**Health & Safety:** Mark Kemp *(Production Manager)*
**Engineering:** Mark Kemp *(Production Manager)*
**US SIC:** 2891 **UK SIC:** 25620
**Auditors:** BDO Northern Ireland

| | 31-03-14 | 31-03-13 | 31-03-12 |
|---|---|---|---|
| TO | 13,286,021 | 11,704,523 | 11,429,470 |
| P/L | 592,608 | 627,060 | 559,321 |
| NW | 1,730,195 | 1,371,951 | 995,980 |
| WC | 1,752,319 | 1,550,569 | 1,485,763 |
| Emp. | 66 | 57 | 55 |

DUNS 21-090-9032

## Seal Sands Storage Ltd

**(Subsidiary of:** Inter Pipeline Europe Ltd)
Seal Sands, Middlesbrough, Cleveland TS2 1UB
**Tel:** 01642-546775 **Fax:** 01642-546076
**Web:** www.simonstorage.com
**Reg No:** 0465548 **Estd:** 1940 Private Limited Company
**Line of Business:** Storage and warehousing
**Issued Capital:** £5,004
**Directors:** M J Lyons, K L Jackson, P B Channing
**Co. Secretary:** Nicholas Coldrey
**Responsibilities**
**Senior:** Richard Sammons *(Manager)*
**Branches:** Seal Sands Storage Ltd, Seal Sands, Middlesbrough, Cleveland TS2 1UB
**US SIC:** 4226 **UK SIC:** 77003
**Auditors:** KPMG Audit Plc
**Bankers:** Barclays Bank Plc (20-00-00)

| | 31-12-13 | 31-12-12 | 31-12-11 |
|---|---|---|---|
| TO | 14,024,000 | 13,564,000 | 13,005,000 |
| P/L | 5,282,000 | 5,016,000 | 4,737,000 |
| NW | 11,591,000 | 16,330,000 | 15,922,000 |
| WC | (5,580,000) | (331,000) | (716,000) |
| Emp. | 67 | 69 | 68 |

DUNS 53-635-3014

## Sealant & Construction Services Ltd

Boundary Farm, Stowmarket, Suffolk IP14 6LH
**Tel:** 01728-860198
**Web:** www.sealantconstruction.co.uk
**Reg No:** 3440074 **VAT No:** 571332458
**Estd:** 1997 Private Limited Company
**Line of Business:** Building construction contractors
**Trading Style:** Scs
**Issued Capital:** £1,000
**Director:** D Rogers
**Co. Secretary:** Alison Rogers
**Responsibilities**
**Senior:** Philip Alden *(Manager)*, Pip Holden *(Manager)*
**Branches:** Sealant & Construction Services Ltd, Unit 2 620-636 South Street, Glasgow, Lanarkshire G14 0TR
**US SIC:** 1622 **UK SIC:** 50200

**Auditors:** Knights Lowe

| | 30-10-14 | 30-10-13 | 30-10-12 |
|---|---|---|---|
| TA | 1,170,710 | 1,248,150 | 1,269,689 |
| NW | 687,784 | 922,493 | 946,757 |
| WC | 627,436 | 634,468 | 630,767 |

DUNS 53-659-0953 Imp

## Sealants International Ltd

Farndon Business Centre, Farndon Road, Market Harborough, Leicestershire LE16 9NP
**Web:** www.sealants-int.com
**Reg No:** 3464200 **Estd:** 1997 Private Limited Company
**Line of Business:** Manufacturers and distribution of adhesive
**Issued Capital:** £100
**Directors:** P B Cooper, H W Parlour, D P Parr, G R Trahearn, K H Parlour
**Co. Secretary:** Fenton Parlour
**US SIC:** 2891, 2899
**UK SIC:** 25620, 25670

| | 31-03-14 | 31-03-13 | 31-03-12 |
|---|---|---|---|
| TA | 1,556,648 | 1,314,583 | 1,131,975 |
| NW | 1,259,493 | 1,038,785 | 873,069 |
| WC | 1,213,920 | 1,003,015 | 837,671 |

DUNS 73-637-2124

## Seale Enterprises Ltd

Eastern Avenue, Burton-On-Trent, Staffordshire DE13 0BB
**Tel:** 01283-530930
**Web:** www.mcdonalds.co.uk
**Reg No:** 4897443 **Estd:** 2003 Private Limited Company
**Line of Business:** Restaurants
**Trading Style:** McDonalds
**Issued Capital:** £100
**Directors:** Ms L Nash, A Nash
**Co. Secretary:** Ms Lorraine Nash
**Responsibilities**
**Senior:** Nigel Seale *(CEO, Managing Director)*
**US SIC:** 5812 **UK SIC:** 66110

| | 31-12-13 | 31-12-12 | 31-12-11 |
|---|---|---|---|
| NW | (36,991) | (36,991) | (36,991) |

DUNS 51-980-9920 Imp-Exp

## Sealed Air Ltd

(**Subsidiary of:** Sealed Air Corporation)
Clifton House, 1 Marston Road, St Neots, Cambridgeshire PE19 2HN
**Tel:** 01480224000 **Fax:** 01480224066
**Web:** www.sealedair-emea.com
**Reg No:** 3443946 **Estd:** 1997 Private Limited Company
**Line of Business:** Manufacturers of packaging materials
**Export Sales:** £43,064,000
**Trading Style:** Cryovac
**Issued Capital:** £59,087,957
**Directors:** W G Stiehl, Ms D A Macdonald, M A Oxford, M P Thurland, N D Finch Junior, Ms A F Assis, M J Chapman
**Co. Secretary:** Michael Chapman
**Responsibilities**
**Senior:** Tod Christie *(Director)*, Norman Finch *(Director)*, William Hickey *(President)*, David Kelsey *(Manager)*, Fabrice Leric *(Finance Director)*, Ranjan Tirimanne *(Supply Chain Manager)*, Chris Woodbridge *(Vice President)*
**Finance:** Fabrice Leric *(Finance Director)*
**Marketing:** Linsey Crowhurst *(Human Resources Director)*
**Sales:** Sandra Schneider *(Sales Manager)*
**IT:** Neil Parker *(IT Technician)*
**HR:** Linsey Crowhurst *(Human Resources Director)*, Rebecca Hutchinson *(Training Officer)*
**Health & Safety:** Michelle Wilson *(Health & Safety Officer)*
**Facilities:** Tony Batten *(Facilities Manager)*
**Operations:** Linsey Crowhurst *(Human Resources Director)*
**Branches:** Sealed Air Ltd, Stafford Park 9, Telford, Shropshire TF3 3BZ
**US SIC:** 2654 **UK SIC:** 47280
**Auditors:** KPMG LLP
**Bankers:** Barclays Bank Plc (20-65-63)

| | 31-12-13 | 31-12-12 | 31-12-11 |
|---|---|---|---|
| TO | 180,120,000 | 195,840,000 | 176,211,000 |
| P/L | 5,543,000 | 42,350,000 | 14,802,000 |
| NW | 62,821,000 | 53,375,000 | 3,792,000 |
| WC | 45,743,000 | 40,515,000 | 35,867,000 |
| Emp. | 632 | 714 | 748 |

DUNS 21-113-9183 Exp

## Sealed Air Packaging Ltd

(**Subsidiary of:** Sealed Air Corporation)
Telford Way, Telford Way Industrial Estate, Kettering, Northamptonshire NN16 8UN
**Tel:** 01536-315-700
**Web:** www.sealedaircorp.com
**Reg No:** 1560613 **Estd:** 1972 Private Limited Company
**Line of Business:** Manufacture of other containers
**Issued Capital:** £100
**Directors:** M J Chapman, M P Thurland
**Co. Secretary:** Michael Chapman
**Responsibilities**
**Senior:** Jason King *(Production Director)*, Matt Tartaglia *(Vp Finance)*
**US SIC:** 2654 **UK SIC:** 47280
**Bankers:** Barclays Bank Plc (20-45-77)

| | 31-12-13 | 31-12-12 | 31-12-11 |
|---|---|---|---|
| TA | 2,990,000 | 2,990,000 | 2,990,000 |
| NW | 1,334,000 | 1,334,000 | 1,334,000 |
| WC | N/A | (11,000) | (11,000) |

DUNS 22-755-1371 Imp

## Sealex Ltd

(**Subsidiary of:** Newseal Finance Ltd)
Poole Hall Industrial Estate, Ellesmere Port, Cheshire CH66 1ST
**Tel:** 0151-357-1551
**Web:** www.sealexltd.co.uk
**Reg No:** 1657257 **VAT No:** 373943621
**Estd:** 1982 Private Limited Company
**Line of Business:** Manufacturers of gaskets
**Issued Capital:** £523
**Directors:** M N Horton, G C Maters
**Co. Secretary:** Mark Crossley
**Responsibilities**
**Senior:** Steven Clarkson *(Manager)*, Stanley Harper *(Manager)*, Ian Marray *(Manager)*, Terry Marray *(Manager)*
**Finance:** Julie Griffin *(Accounts Manager)*
**Purchasing:** Tony Darcy *(Purchasing Director)*
**US SIC:** 5531, 3499
**UK SIC:** 65100, 31694
**Auditors:** John Graham & Co
**Bankers:** Barclays Bank Plc (20-29-50)

| | 31-12-13 | 31-12-12 | 31-12-11 |
|---|---|---|---|
| TO | 5,953,195 | 3,284,308 | 3,311,119 |
| P/L | 786 | (22,805) | 304,959 |
| NW | (849,619) | 700,138 | 714,256 |
| WC | 381,955 | 589,199 | 645,061 |
| Emp. | 46 | 34 | 32 |

DUNS 50-523-4617

## Sealey (U K) Ltd

Kempson Way, Suffolk Business Park, Bury St Edmunds, Suffolk IP32 7AR
**Tel:** 01284-757500
**Web:** www.sealey.co.uk
**Reg No:** 2481552 **Estd:** 1981 Private Limited Company
**Line of Business:** Management activities of holding companies
**Export Sales:** £6,239,000
**Issued Capital:** £11,500
**Managing Director:** J L Sealey
**Co. Secretary:** Ms Patricia Sealey
**Responsibilities**
**Senior:** Mark Sweetman *(Manager)*
**Finance:** Mark Sweetman *(Manager)*
**US SIC:** 6711, 5531
**UK SIC:** 83962, 65100
**Auditors:** Scrutton Bland
**Bankers:** Barclays Bank Plc (20-83-50)

| | 30-04-14 | 30-04-13 | 30-04-12 |
|---|---|---|---|
| TO | 54,994,000 | 51,023,000 | 51,681,000 |
| P/L | 5,339,000 | 4,990,000 | 5,180,000 |
| NW | 46,890,000 | 42,916,000 | 39,258,000 |
| WC | 32,775,000 | 28,148,000 | 28,211,000 |
| Emp. | 333 | 320 | 309 |

DUNS 21-199-2953 Imp-Exp

## Sealion Shipping Ltd

(**Subsidiary of:** Toisa Limited)
Gostrey House, Union Road, Farnham, Surrey GU9 7PT
**Tel:** 01252-737773
**Web:** www.sealionshipping.co.uk
**Reg No:** 1154180 **VAT No:** 241160312
**Estd:** 1974 Private Limited Company
**Line of Business:** Ships agents
**Export Markets:** Europe and Far East
**Issued Capital:** £5,000
**Directors:** A Varvaros, P J Wood, R W Baldwin, J C Golding, S R Marshall
**Co. Secretary:** Kenneth Thomas
**Responsibilities**
**Senior:** John Golding *(Catering Director)*
**HR:** Ann Falls *(Human Resources Manager)*
**US SIC:** 4712 **UK SIC:** 77002
**Auditors:** Moore Stephens
**Bankers:** HSBC Bank plc (40-22-26)

| | 31-12-13 | 31-12-12 | 31-12-11 |
|---|---|---|---|
| TO | 88,740,000 | 82,513,000 | 76,400,000 |
| P/L | 265,000 | 208,000 | 335,000 |
| NW | 2,423,000 | 2,199,000 | 2,019,000 |
| WC | 2,094,000 | 1,774,000 | 1,547,000 |
| Emp. | 69 | 68 | 69 |

DUNS 23-994-7281 Imp

## Sealord Caistor Ltd

(**Subsidiary of:** Kura Limited)
Unit 6/7, North Kelsey Road, Caistor, Market Rasen, Lincolnshire LN7 6PX
**Web:** www.sealord.com
**Reg No:** 3982958 **Estd:** 1992 Private Limited Company
**Line of Business:** Wholesale of other food including fish, crustaceans and molluscs
**Export Sales:** £697,978
**Issued Capital:** £1,000
**Directors:** A Crookes, S A Yung
**Co. Secretary:** Ms Susan Prowse
**Responsibilities**
**Senior:** Andrian Crookes *(Ceo)*, Micheal Gleissner *(General Manager, Corporate Str)*, Simon Paul *(It Manager)*
**Finance:** Andrian Crookes *(Ceo)*
**Marketing:** Michelle Rowell *(Marketing Manager)*
**IT:** Simon Paul *(It Manager)*
**US SIC:** 5146, 7399
**UK SIC:** 61700, 83954
**Auditors:** Ernst & Young LLP
**Bankers:** HSBC Bank plc (40-22-24)

| | 28-09-13 | 28-09-12 | 28-09-11 |
|---|---|---|---|
| TO | 53,684,574 | 51,540,342 | 61,928,420 |
| P/L | 1,758,367 | 1,370,815 | 3,714,582 |
| NW | 18,067,877 | 16,710,291 | 15,688,268 |
| WC | 18,886,125 | 17,706,725 | 14,684,128 |
| Emp. | 208 | 223 | 225 |

DUNS 73-666-0791

## Sealskinz Ltd

(**Subsidiary of:** Sealskinz Holdings Ltd)
36 Oldmedow Road, Hardwick Industrial Estate, King's Lynn, Norfolk PE30 4PP
**Tel:** 01553-817990 **Fax:** 01553772662
**Web:** www.sealskinz.com
**Reg No:** 4925632 **Estd:** 2007 Private Limited Company
**Line of Business:** Clothing wholesale and suppliers
**Export Sales:** £1,447,080
**Trading Style:** Sealskinz Ltd
**Issued Capital:** £1,200,000
**Directors:** S N Riley, I N Blackman, A J Tait, A J Tillen, J P Adams, H C Farrer, T Ives
**Co. Secretary:** Hadleigh Farrer
**Responsibilities**
**Senior:** Andrew Dahl *(Manager)*, David Jesson *(Manager)*
**US SIC:** 5136 **UK SIC:** 61600

| | 30-06-13 | 30-06-12 | 30-06-11 |
|---|---|---|---|
| TO | 7,535,189 | 6,923,536 | 5,883,839 |
| P/L | (1,369,247) | 635,480 | 205,750 |
| NW | 734,814 | 1,977,085 | 1,450,853 |
| WC | 542,655 | 1,812,828 | 1,275,300 |
| Emp. | 56 | 56 | 55 |

DUNS 21-774-6311

## Seamab Schhol

Rumbling Bridge, Kinross, Kinross-Shire KY13 0PT
**Tel:** 01577840307
**Web:** www.seamab.org.uk
**Estd:** 2011 Proprietorship
**Line of Business:** Schools (foundation)
**Proprietor:** Ms A Anderson
**Responsibilities**
**Senior:** Joanna Mccreadie *(Chief Executive)*
**US SIC:** 8211 **UK SIC:** 93200
**Employees:** 50

DUNS 76-595-3369 Imp-Exp

## Seamark Plc

Hulme Hall Lane, Manchester M40 8AD
**Tel:** 01612055000
**Web:** www.seamark.co.uk
**Reg No:** 2575875 **VAT No:** 606300291
**Estd:** 1991 Public Limited Company
**Line of Business:** Production and preserving of poultry meat
**Export Markets:** Worldwide
**Export Sales:** £50,195,884
**Trading Style:** Seamark, Vermilion & Cinnabar, Restaurant Wholesale
**Issued Capital:** £60,000
**Principals:** I Ahmed *(Managing)*, K Ahmed
**Co. Secretary:** Bilal Ahmed
**Responsibilities**
**Marketing:** Graeme Kerr *(Sales Director)*
**Sales:** Graeme Kerr *(Sales Director)*
**HR:** Sue Stockley *(Human Resources Manager)*
**Branches:** Seamark Plc, Seamark Ho Edge La, Manchester M43 6BB
**US SIC:** 5146, 2092
**UK SIC:** 61700, 41501
**Auditors:** BDO LLP
**Bankers:** HSBC Bank plc (40-37-27)

| | 31-12-13 | 31-12-12 | 31-12-11 |
|---|---|---|---|
| TO | 67,551,331 | 59,845,598 | 69,316,997 |
| P/L | 1,718,853 | (663,038) | 1,478,438 |
| NW | 17,006,607 | 15,673,564 | 15,506,321 |
| WC | 8,907,555 | 7,713,005 | 8,942,936 |
| Emp. | 168 | 174 | 187 |

DUNS 49-001-5104

## Seamill Hydro Services Ltd

(**Subsidiary of:** Seamill Glenfoot Ltd)
Ardrossan Road, Seamill, West Kilbride, Ayrshire KA23 9ND
**Tel:** 01294-822217
**Web:** www.seamillhydro.co.uk
**Reg No:** 0158722SC **Estd:** 1995 Private Limited Company
**Line of Business:** Hotels and motels without restaurant
**Issued Capital:** £2
**Directors:** Ms L Mccomb, Ms M T Sweeney, S Sweeney
**Co. Secretary:** Sylvester Sweeney
**US SIC:** 7011 **UK SIC:** 66500

| | 30-04-14 | 30-04-13 | 30-04-12 |
|---|---|---|---|
| TA | 920,481 | 1,214,330 | 1,248,566 |
| NW | 338,096 | 1,014,497 | 1,072,360 |
| WC | 288,096 | (10,703) | 23,860 |

DUNS 23-222-0350

## Sean Graham Ltd

Oyster House, 12 Wellington Place, Belfast BT1 6GE
**Tel:** 02890963963
**Web:** www.seangraham.com
**Reg No:** 0028674NI **Estd:** 1994 Private Limited Company
**Line of Business:** Bookmakers and turf accountants
**Issued Capital:** £2
**Director:** Mrs B E Graham
**Co. Secretary:** Brendan Hayes
**Responsibilities**
**Senior:** Chris Deery *(Manager)*
**Branches:** Sean Graham Ltd, 66 Victoria Road, Aberdeen, Aberdeenshire AB11 9DS
**US SIC:** 7999 **UK SIC:** 97913

| | 31-08-13 | 31-08-12 | 31-08-11 |
|---|---|---|---|
| TA | 2 | 2 | 2 |
| NW | 2 | 2 | 2 |
| WC | 2 | N/A | N/A |
| Emp. | 100 | N/A | N/A |

DUNS 22-161-0103

## Sean Hanna Ltd

26 Jubilee Place, London E14 5NY
**Tel:** 02075132660
**Web:** www.seanhanna.com
**Reg No:** 4179577 **Estd:** 1998 Private Limited Company
**Line of Business:** Hairdressers (unisex)
**Issued Capital:** £100
**Directors:** Y Obrien, S Hanna
**Co. Secretary:** Mrs Lynn Hickey
**Branches:** Sean Hanna Ltd, 4 The Quadrant, Epsom, Surrey KT17 4RH
**US SIC:** 7231 **UK SIC:** 98200

| | 31-05-13 | 31-05-12 | 31-05-11 |
|---|---|---|---|
| TA | 457,572 | 561,881 | 479,705 |
| NW | 16,143 | 81,339 | (57,474) |
| WC | (38,073) | 74,362 | (76,853) |

DUNS 23-014-8376 Exp

## Sean Timoney & Sons Ltd

Mullenanaskea, Enniskillen, Co Fermanagh BT74 4JQ
**Tel:** 02866329252 **Fax:** 02866324262
**Web:** www.timoneywindows.com
**Reg No:** 0037381NI **Estd:** 2010 Private Limited Company
**Line of Business:** Wholesale of wood, construction materials and sanitary equipment
**Export Markets:** Republic Of Ireland
**Issued Capital:** £300
**Directors:** S Timoney, R Timoney
**Co. Secretary:** Ms Marie Timoney
**Responsibilities**
**IT:** Darren Timoney *(Senior IT Executive)*
**US SIC:** 5039 **UK SIC:** 61300

| | 31-01-14 | 31-01-13 | 31-01-12 |
|---|---|---|---|
| TA | 1,572,419 | 1,878,340 | 2,290,686 |
| NW | 1,293,543 | 1,419,200 | 1,843,537 |
| WC | 478,593 | 241,237 | 784,747 |

DUNS 23-974-7400

## Seap

Aquila House Breeds Place, Hastings, East Sussex TN34 3UY
**Tel:** 03304409000
**Web:** www.seap.org.uk
**Reg No:** 3963421 **Estd:** 2000 Private Company Limited By Guarantee
**Line of Business:** Other service activities not elsewhere classified
**Directors:** Ms V S Briant, G J Parker, Ms S Holmes Smith, Ms E H Sherwood, Ms A L Heslop
**Co. Secretary:** Ms Veronique Briant
**Branches:** Seap, 42 Robertson Street, Hastings, East Sussex TN34 1HL
**US SIC:** 8999 **UK SIC:** 83954
**Bankers:** The Co-Operative Bank Plc (08-90-00)

| | 31-03-14 | 31-03-13 | 31-03-12 |
|---|---|---|---|
| TO | 3,147,633 | 5,086,728 | 5,087,224 |
| P/L | (82,054) | 300,649 | 41,016 |
| NW | 1,679,812 | 1,761,866 | 1,461,217 |
| WC | 1,603,151 | 1,666,717 | 1,304,591 |
| Emp. | 90 | 126 | 132 |

DUNS 23-943-6629

## Seapet Centres

1 Tollgate Road, Stanway, Colchester, Essex CO3 8RF
**Tel:** 01206-764777
**Web:** www.seapets.co.uk
**Estd:** 1977 Proprietorship
**Line of Business:** Retailer of pet supplies
**Proprietor:** J F Arnold
**Responsibilities**
**Senior:** Jim Lloyd *(General Manager)*

**Branches:** Unit 21 Beardmore Park, Ipswich, Suffolk IP5 3RX
**US SIC:** 5999 **UK SIC:** 65600
**Employees:** 48

DUNS 23-919-6806
## Search Consultancy Group Ltd
(**Subsidiary of:** Saints Management Llc)
117-119 High Street, Crawley, West Sussex RH10 1DD
**Tel:** 01293-848100 **Fax:** 0129-384-8190
**Web:** www.searchconsultancy.co.uk
**Reg No:** 3909899 **Estd:** 2008 Private Limited Company
**Line of Business:** Employment and recruitment companies and consultants
**Trading Style:** Search Consultancy
**Issued Capital:** £139,838
**Directors:** S J Dick, G R Sharpe, G C Caswell, Ms J L Crawford, D J Smith
**Co. Secretary:** Graham Sharpe
**US SIC:** 7361 **UK SIC:** 83954
**Auditors:** Deloitte LLP
**Bankers:** Barclays Bank Plc (20-00-62)

| | 05-01-14 | 30-12-12 | 31-01-11 |
|---|---|---|---|
| TO | 135,442,000 | 124,885,000 | 115,683,000 |
| P/L | (606,000) | 94,000 | (1,457,000) |
| NW | (14,969,000) | (14,294,000) | (14,862,000) |
| WC | (2,718,000) | (1,785,000) | (1,034,000) |
| Emp. | 520 | 476 | 483 |

DUNS 39-686-7335
## Search Consultancy Ltd
(**Subsidiary of:** Saints Management Llc)
198 West George Street, Glasgow, Lanarkshire G2 2NR
**Fax:** 01412727788
**Web:** www.searchconsultancy.co.uk
**Reg No:** 0105640SC **VAT No:** 751115367
**Estd:** 2000 Private Limited Company
**Line of Business:** Labour recruitment and provision of personnel
**Trading Style:** Search Recruitment & Selection
**Issued Capital:** £1,000
**Directors:** G R Sharpe, G C Caswell, S J Dick
**Responsibilities**
**Senior:** Simone Lockhart *(Manager)*, Gerald McGrath *(Manager)*
**HR:** Kathryn Boyd *(Human Resources Director)*
**Health & Safety:** Kathryn Boyd *(Human Resources Director)*
**Branches:** Search Consultancy Ltd, 9 St. Colme Street, Edinburgh, Midlothian EH3 6AA
**US SIC:** 7361 **UK SIC:** 83954
**Auditors:** Deloitte LLP
**Bankers:** Barclays Bank Plc (20-33-70)

| | 05-01-14 | 30-12-12 | 31-01-11 |
|---|---|---|---|
| TO | 135,442,000 | 124,883,000 | 115,676,000 |
| P/L | 2,821,000 | 2,781,000 | 1,080,000 |
| NW | 8,825,000 | 12,887,000 | 10,652,000 |
| WC | 7,573,000 | 11,370,000 | 8,923,000 |
| Emp. | 517 | 473 | 480 |

DUNS 21-136-9070
## Search Group Holdings Ltd
Market Works, Leeds, West Yorkshire LS12 6EP
**Tel:** 01132639081
**Web:** www.wgsearch.co.uk
**Reg No:** 6697872 **Estd:** 2008 Private Limited Company
**Line of Business:** Builders
**Trading Style:** Wg Search
**Issued Capital:** £1,300,000
**Director:** J C Search
**Co. Secretary:** Richard Search
**Responsibilities**
**IT:** Linda Gaunt *(IT Manager)*
**US SIC:** 6711 **UK SIC:** 83962
**Bankers:** HSBC Bank plc (40-46-78)

| | 31-12-13 | 31-12-12 | 31-12-11 |
|---|---|---|---|
| TO | 10,959,578 | 11,714,635 | 10,830,036 |
| P/L | 350,092 | 449,974 | 224,022 |
| NW | 6,394,898 | 6,557,319 | 6,475,207 |
| WC | 34,868 | (228,129) | (407,454) |
| Emp. | 121 | 121 | 119 |

DUNS 34-808-4992
## Search Laboratory Ltd
Blok Haus, Ring Road, West Park, Leeds, West Yorkshire LS16 6QG
**Tel:** 01132-121211 **Fax:** 01133930697
**Web:** www.searchlaboratory.com
**Reg No:** 5608449 **Estd:** 2005 Private Limited Company
**Line of Business:** Internet services
**Export Sales:** £795,867
**Issued Capital:** £71
**Directors:** I M Harris, Mrs L P Byrne, T Carr
**Co. Secretary:** Ronald Harris
**US SIC:** 7379 **UK SIC:** 83940

| | 31-10-13 | 31-10-12 | 31-10-11 |
|---|---|---|---|
| TO | 7,663,671 | N/A | N/A |
| P/L | 1,192,942 | N/A | N/A |
| NW | 944,085 | 557,149 | 259,975 |
| WC | 759,217 | 382,502 | 194,980 |
| Emp. | 142 | N/A | N/A |

DUNS 21-278-4052
## Search (Sheffield) Ltd
(**Subsidiary of:** Search Group Holdings Ltd)
191 Woodbourn Road, Sheffield, South Yorkshire S9 3LQ
**Tel:** 01142-446521 **Fax:** 01142-562093
**Web:** www.sheffieldhaworth.com
**Reg No:** 0828066 **Estd:** 1964 Private Limited Company
**Line of Business:** Plant hire and leasing
**Issued Capital:** £53,000
**Director:** J C Search
**Co. Secretary:** Richard Search
**Responsibilities**
**Senior:** Andrew Collings *(Group Hire Operations Manager)*
**US SIC:** 7394 **UK SIC:** 84000
**Auditors:** Sagars
**Bankers:** HSBC Bank plc (40-27-15)

| | 31-12-14 | 31-12-13 | 31-12-12 |
|---|---|---|---|
| TA | 53,050 | 53,050 | 53,050 |
| NW | 53,050 | 53,050 | 53,050 |

DUNS 22-083-3722
## Searchflow Ltd
(**Subsidiary of:** Property Data Holdings Lp)
42 Kingshill Avenue, Kingshill, West Malling, Kent ME19 4AJ
**Tel:** 08707877625 **Fax:** 08709909949
**Web:** https://www.searchflow.co.uk
**Reg No:** 4084804 **Estd:** 2000 Private Limited Company
**Line of Business:** Data processing
**Issued Capital:** £1,000,000
**Directors:** M F Milner, D W Callcott, Ms S A Richards
**Co. Secretary:** David Callcott
**Responsibilities**
**Senior:** Marshall King *(Chief Executive Officer)*, Terrence Piche *(Manager)*
**Marketing:** Perran Moon *(Marketing Director)*
**Sales:** Lianne Goddard *(Sales Director)*, Ben Hobbs *(Sales Manager)*
**HR:** Catherine Carr *(HR Director)*
**Purchasing:** Adam Ralph *(Purchasing Manager)*
**US SIC:** 7374 **UK SIC:** 83940
**Auditors:** KPMG Audit PLC

| | 31-12-13 | 31-12-12 | 31-12-11 |
|---|---|---|---|
| TO | 65,951,211 | 57,683,810 | 60,143,187 |
| P/L | 3,747,104 | 3,619,457 | 8,368,594 |
| NW | 1,192,478 | (2,024,570) | (833,647) |
| WC | 380,811 | (3,325,305) | (1,670,936) |
| Emp. | 75 | 65 | 97 |

DUNS 21-229-3716 **Imp**
## Searchlight Electric Ltd
900 Oldham Road, Manchester M40 2BS
**Tel:** 0161-203-3300
**Web:** www.searchlightelectric.com
**Reg No:** 1169504 **VAT No:** 149697311
**Estd:** 1974 Private Limited Company
**Line of Business:** Lighting wholesale and supply
**Export Sales:** £7,644,600
**Trading Style:** Illuma Lighting
**Issued Capital:** £1,063,980
**Principals:** D S Joyce *(Managing)*, H E Hamburger *(Managing)*, M E Hamburger, D S Hamburger, Ms G J Lenham
**Co. Secretary:** David Hamburger
**Responsibilities**
**Finance:** Janice Garrett *(Senior Finance Administrator)*
**Sales:** Maurice Hamburger *(Senior Sales Executive)*
**IT:** Lorraine Fletcher *(Computer Operations Manager)*, Chris Pearce *(IT Manager)*
**HR:** Wendy Egerton *(Human Resources Manager)*
**Health & Safety:** Mick Byrne *(Facilities Manager)*
**Facilities:** Mick Byrne *(Facilities Manager)*
**Purchasing:** Dov Hamburger *(Purchasing Manager)*
**US SIC:** 3648 **UK SIC:** 34702
**Auditors:** Jack Ross
**Bankers:** Barclays Bank Plc (20-54-58)

| | 30-06-13 | 30-06-12 | 30-06-11 |
|---|---|---|---|
| TO | 27,496,301 | 29,696,310 | 30,731,559 |
| P/L | 1,686,896 | 1,984,335 | 2,034,682 |
| NW | 15,663,275 | 15,435,072 | 13,959,683 |
| WC | 11,347,560 | 11,347,732 | 9,590,927 |
| Emp. | 161 | 159 | 166 |

DUNS 55-080-7085
## Searchlight Workshops
Claremont Road, Newhaven, East Sussex BN9 0NQ
**Tel:** 01273-514007
**Web:** www.fitzroy.org
**Estd:** 1935
**Line of Business:** Residential care establishments
**Chairman:** D Bray
**Responsibilities**
**Senior:** Denise Wareing *(Service Manager)*
**US SIC:** 8321 **UK SIC:** 96111
**Employees:** 53

DUNS 21-026-1988
## Searcy Tansley & Co Ltd
(**Subsidiary of:** Hp Investco (Catering) Ltd)
1 Bridges Court, London SW11 3BB
**Tel:** 02075850505 **Fax:** 02073-501748
**Web:** www.searcys.co.uk
**Reg No:** 0331909 **VAT No:** 603176273
**Estd:** 1990 Private Limited Company
**Line of Business:** Catering
**Trading Style:** Searcy's Brasserie, Searcys, Paddington Champagne Bar
**Issued Capital:** £7,500
**Directors:** C J Maddison, A D Storey, M Bradley, G R Sutherland
**Co. Secretary:** Marc Bradley
**Responsibilities**
**Senior:** Richard Goodhew *(Manager)*, Nigel Goodhew *(Manager)*, Doug Tetleys *(Chief Executive)*
**Facilities:** Jim Coles *(Maintenance Officer)*
**Branches:** Searcy Tansley & Co Ltd, 41 Covent Garden Piazza, The Market, London WC2E 8RF
**US SIC:** 7399, 5813
**UK SIC:** 83954, 66200
**Auditors:** BSG Valentine
**Bankers:** Barclays Bank Plc (20-36-47)

| | 30-06-13 | 30-06-12 | 30-06-11 |
|---|---|---|---|
| TO | 34,198,446 | 33,700,712 | 47,190,845 |
| P/L | (63,506) | 17,323 | 270,510 |
| NW | 397,301 | 462,145 | 681,942 |
| WC | 1,894,882 | (999,121) | 525,287 |
| Emp. | 1,037 | 1,068 | 1,037 |

DUNS 28-840-4395
## Searles (Camping Ground) Ltd
South Beach Road, Hunstanton, Norfolk PE36 5BB
**Tel:** 01485-534211 **Fax:** 01485-533815
**Web:** www.searles.co.uk
**Reg No:** 0528033 **VAT No:** 105903201
**Estd:** 1954 Private Limited Company
**Line of Business:** Caravan parks
**Trading Style:** Searles Leisure Resort
**Issued Capital:** £600
**Directors:** P R Searle, Mrs J A Searle, W J Searle, A J Searle
**Co. Secretary:** Ms Victoria Searle
**Responsibilities**
**Senior:** Gene Detton *(Accommodation Services Manager)*, Richard Gowen *(General Manager)*
**HR:** Bev Playford *(Human Resources Manager)*
**Health & Safety:** Gene Detton *(Accommodation Services Manager)*, Richard Gowen *(General Manager)*
**Purchasing:** Gene Detton *(Accommodation Services Manager)*, Richard Gowen *(General Manager)*
**US SIC:** 7033, 7032
**UK SIC:** 66701, 66702
**Auditors:** Stephenson Smart
**Bankers:** Barclays Bank Plc (20-46-65)

| | 31-12-13 | 31-12-12 | 31-12-11 |
|---|---|---|---|
| TO | 10,553,333 | 9,490,465 | 9,526,218 |
| P/L | 369,633 | 81,837 | 237,873 |
| NW | 3,747,922 | 3,598,403 | 3,730,878 |
| WC | (10,878,662) | (8,923,031) | (10,846,355) |
| Emp. | 178 | 183 | 165 |

DUNS 64-226-1093
## Searles of Hunstanton
South Beach Road, Hunstanton, Norfolk PE36 5BB
**Tel:** 01485534444
**Web:** www.seatours.co.uk
**Estd:** 1952 Proprietorship
**Line of Business:** Excursions and sightseeing activities
**Proprietor:** R Searle
**US SIC:** 7999 **UK SIC:** 97913
**Employees:** 129

DUNS 23-908-9027
## Searoute Group Ltd
Suite 15 Dunnswood House, Dunnswood Road, Glasgow, Lanarkshire G67 3EN
**Tel:** 01236-861230
**Web:** www.searoute.co.uk
**Reg No:** 0202649SC **VAT No:** 762110761
**Estd:** 2000 Private Limited Company
**Line of Business:** Secretarial and translation activities
**Trading Style:** Searoute Group Ltd
**Issued Capital:** £1,000
**Principals:** A Porter *(Managing)*, M P Breingan
**Co. Secretary:** John Sloss
**US SIC:** 7339, 4712
**UK SIC:** 83954, 77002
**Auditors:** William Duncan & Co
**Bankers:** The Royal Bank Of Scotland Plc (83-17-31)

| | 31-03-14 | 31-03-13 | 31-03-12 |
|---|---|---|---|
| TO | 10,489,506 | 13,652,342 | 13,114,171 |
| P/L | 255,372 | 370,364 | 228,883 |
| NW | 1,557,926 | 1,502,114 | 1,386,540 |
| WC | 1,703,532 | 1,632,410 | 1,446,197 |
| Emp. | 59 | 63 | 93 |

DUNS 21-923-8474 **Imp-Exp**
## Sears Manufacturing Co. (Europe) Ltd
(**Subsidiary of:** Sears Manufacturing Co.)
Unit 42 Rassau Industrial Estate, Ebbw Vale, Gwent NP23 5SD
**Fax:** 01495-304452
**Web:** www.searsseating.com
**Reg No:** 1275439 **VAT No:** 273903253
**Estd:** 1976 Private Limited Company
**Line of Business:** Manufacturers of seats
**Export Markets:** Netherlands, Scandinavia
**Export Sales:** £14,007,393
**Issued Capital:** £732,000
**Managing Directors:** K Wichelt, J Sears
**Co. Secretary:** Philip Jones
**Responsibilities**
**IT:** Carl Davies *(IT Director)*, Tyrone Sandercock *(Engineering Manager)*
**Operations:** Tyrone Sandercock *(Engineering Manager)*
**Engineering:** Tyrone Sandercock *(Engineering Manager)*
**US SIC:** 2599 **UK SIC:** 46720
**Auditors:** PricewaterhouseCoopers LLP
**Bankers:** National Westminster Bank Plc (52-21-06)

| | 31-12-13 | 31-12-12 | 31-12-11 |
|---|---|---|---|
| TO | 20,957,503 | 18,305,266 | 17,820,271 |
| P/L | 265,611 | 61,584 | 131,832 |
| NW | 494,150 | (38,557) | (100,141) |
| WC | 1,759,239 | 1,167,719 | 1,237,194 |
| Emp. | 102 | 96 | 82 |

DUNS 23-895-9980
## Seascope Shipping Investments Ltd
(**Subsidiary of:** Braemar Shipping Services Plc)
35 Cosway Street, London NW1 5BT
**Tel:** 02079032600 **Fax:** 020-8953-4718
**Web:** www.seascope.co.uk
**Reg No:** 3886820 **Estd:** 1999 Private Limited Company
**Line of Business:** Freight sea and coastal water transport
**Issued Capital:** £100
**Director:** R Harwood
**Co. Secretary:** James Kidwell
**US SIC:** 4411 **UK SIC:** 74001

| | 28-02-14 | 28-02-13 | 29-02-12 |
|---|---|---|---|
| TA | 100 | 100 | 100 |
| NW | 100 | 100 | 100 |

DUNS 28-838-4423
## Seashore Enterprises (Porthcawl) Ltd
Mackworth Road, Porthcawl, Mid Glamorgan CF36 5BT
**Tel:** 01656782432
**Web:** www.hi-tide.co.uk
**Reg No:** 0483382 **Estd:** 1950 Private Limited Company
**Line of Business:** Public house
**Issued Capital:** £500
**Directors:** G Dower, Ms F R Dower
**Co. Secretary:** Ms Melanie Quantock Shuldham
**Responsibilities**
**Senior:** Christine Malvisi *(Manager)*, Melanie Shuldham *(Manager)*
**US SIC:** 5813, 6519
**UK SIC:** 66200, 85000
**Auditors:** Clay Shaw Thomas

| | 31-03-14 | 31-03-13 | 31-03-12 |
|---|---|---|---|
| TA | 2,497,189 | 2,641,502 | 2,607,656 |
| NW | 1,416,064 | 1,412,356 | 1,459,967 |
| WC | (440,559) | (387,675) | (371,784) |

DUNS 21-417-3423
## Seasons Events
The Gibson Hall, 13 Bishopsgate, London EC2N 3BA
**Tel:** 020-72362149
**Web:** www.seasonedevents.co.uk
**Estd:** 2005 Proprietorship
**Line of Business:** Caterers
**Proprietor:** C Beer

**Responsibilities**
**Senior:** Colin Sayers *(Manager)*, Chantelle Scullion *(Sales Manager)*, Piers Zangana *(Head of Communications)*
**US SIC:** 5812 **UK SIC:** 66110
**Employees:** 50

DUNS 36-480-0458
## Seasons Holidays Plc
Wynchgate House, Woodlands Lane, Bradley Stoke, Bristol, Avon BS32 4JT
**Tel:** 01454613366 **Fax:** 01454618325
**Web:** www.seasonsholidays.com
**Reg No:** 3283015 **Estd:** 1996 Public Limited Company
**Line of Business:** Holiday centres and holiday villages
**Issued Capital:** £50,000
**Directors:** B T Hurley, Ms S A Kinsella
**Co. Secretary:** Barry Hurley
**Branches:** Seasons Holidays Plc, Lanugh Park, Lanugh, Carmarthen, Dyfed SA33 4PD
**US SIC:** 7399 **UK SIC:** 83954
**Auditors:** The Mudd Partnership
**Bankers:** National Westminster Bank Plc (60-10-20)

| | 31-12-13 | 31-12-12 | 31-12-11 |
|---|---|---|---|
| TO | 11,931,861 | 28,579,547 | 11,903,241 |
| P/L | 934,555 | 3,622,219 | (4,948,906) |
| NW | (3,291,999) | (4,615,873) | (2,337,214) |
| WC | 17,221,656 | (1,878,696) | 912,268 |
| Emp. | 351 | 343 | 282 |

DUNS 21-613-5601
## Seat Hobin of Manchester
266 Bury New Road, Salford, Lancashire M7 2YJ
**Tel:** 01617089000
**Web:** www.lookers.co.uk
**Estd:** 2011 Proprietorship
**Line of Business:** Car dealers (new & used)
**Proprietor:** D Hobin
**Responsibilities**
**Senior:** Scott Kershaw *(Dealer Principal)*, Duncan Mafee *(Dealer Principal)*
**US SIC:** 5511 **UK SIC:** 65100
**Employees:** 50

DUNS 39-698-2472
## Seatec Uk Ltd
(**Subsidiary of:** Royal Bank of Canada)
The Skypark, 8 Elliot Place, Glasgow, Lanarkshire G3 8EP
**Tel:** 01413051370
**Web:** www.marlins.co.uk
**Reg No:** 0106026SC **Estd:** 1991 Private Limited Company
**Line of Business:** Other business activities not elsewhere classified
**Issued Capital:** £51
**Directors:** A G Trevarthen, J Muir, M T Stafford
**Co. Secretary:** James Muir
**Responsibilities**
**Senior:** Catherine Logie *(Manager)*
**US SIC:** 7399 **UK SIC:** 83954
**Auditors:** Ernst & Young

| | 31-12-13 | 31-12-12 | 31-12-11 |
|---|---|---|---|
| TO | 31,376,916 | 27,817,295 | 11,165,265 |
| P/L | 7,384,986 | 4,251,720 | 3,171,780 |
| NW | 6,479,331 | 1,145,584 | 5,215,184 |
| WC | 5,804,826 | 551,801 | 4,532,205 |
| Emp. | 96 | 137 | N/A |

DUNS 50-705-0862
## Seaton Lane Inn
Seaton Lane, Seaton, Seaham, County Durham SR7 0LP
**Tel:** 01915812038
**Web:** www.seatonlaneinn.com
**Estd:** 1996 Proprietorship
**Line of Business:** Hotels
**Proprietor:** N Bergen
**US SIC:** 7011 **UK SIC:** 66500
**Employees:** 50

DUNS 21-240-6318
## Seaton Valley Co-Operative Society Ltd
Delaval House, Avenue Road, Seaton Delaval, Whitley Bay, Tyne and Wear NE25 0DS
**Tel:** 0191-237-1010
**Web:** www.seatonvalleyco-op.co.uk
**Reg No:** 0016818IP **VAT No:** 177261646
**Estd:** 1910 Friendly Society
**Line of Business:** Supermarkets
**Principals:** J Moody *(Chairman)*, A Covell, T Waugh, C Brown, W Midgley, G Winter
**Co. Secretary:** Malcolm Rutherford
**US SIC:** 5411 **UK SIC:** 64100
**Auditors:** Robinson & Co
**Bankers:** The Co-Operative Bank Plc (08-90-06)
**Employees:** 70

DUNS 77-524-2555
## Seatrax (U.K.) Ltd
Southtown Road, Great Yarmouth, Norfolk NR31 0JJ
**Tel:** 01493651311 **Fax:** 01493443666
**Web:** www.seatrax.co.uk
**Reg No:** 2989264 **VAT No:** 651065066
**Estd:** 1994 Private Limited Company
**Line of Business:** Manufacturers of cranes
**Issued Capital:** £300
**Director:** J P Emrick
**Co. Secretary:** Michael Cleghorn
**Responsibilities**
**HR:** Dean Barlow *(Operations Manager)*
**Facilities:** Dean Barlow *(Operations Manager)*
**Operations:** Dean Barlow *(Operations Manager)*
**Fleet:** Dean Barlow *(Operations Manager)*
**US SIC:** 3534, 5084
**UK SIC:** 32553, 61490
**Auditors:** Lovewell Blake

| | 31-03-13 | 31-03-12 | 31-03-11 |
|---|---|---|---|
| TO | 19,781,594 | 13,322,378 | 9,617,048 |
| P/L | 2,144,042 | 633,408 | 2,387,859 |
| NW | 7,759,417 | 6,138,022 | 5,665,846 |
| WC | 8,982,672 | 5,167,019 | 7,105,112 |
| Emp. | 95 | 80 | 63 |

DUNS 50-542-2998 **Imp-Exp**
## Seatronics Ltd
4 Denmore Industrial Estate, Denmore Road, Bridge Of Don, Aberdeen, Aberdeenshire AB23 8JW
**Tel:** 01224853100 **Fax:** 01224-853101
**Web:** www.seatronics-group.com
**Reg No:** 0124658SC **VAT No:** 552937911
**Estd:** 1990 Private Limited Company
**Line of Business:** Marine services
**Export Markets:** U S A; Norway; Australasia; Middle East
**Issued Capital:** £100,000
**Directors:** D R Currie, Dr B Bruggaier
**Co. Secretary:** Burness Paull Llp
**Responsibilities**
**Finance:** John Cope *(Financial Director)*
**IT:** James Gomez *(It Director)*
**Branches:** Seatronics Ltd, Unit 1 Block 2 Blackhouse Circle, Peterhead, Aberdeenshire AB42 1BN
**US SIC:** 3811, 7394
**UK SIC:** 37100, 84000
**Auditors:** KPMG LLP
**Bankers:** Bank Of Scotland (80-06-71)

| | 31-12-13 | 31-12-12 | 31-12-11 |
|---|---|---|---|
| TO | 34,513,000 | 27,874,000 | 23,031,000 |
| P/L | 9,636,000 | 8,164,000 | 7,231,000 |
| NW | 42,094,000 | 34,848,000 | 28,976,000 |
| WC | 26,398,000 | 20,946,000 | 18,259,000 |
| Emp. | 81 | 73 | 67 |

DUNS 34-763-4995
## Seatruck Ferries Holding Ltd
(**Subsidiary of:** Clipper Group Ltd)
North Quay, Heysham, Morecambe, Lancashire LA3 2XF
**Tel:** 01524853512
**Web:** www.merchantferries.co.uk
**Reg No:** 5564629 **Estd:** 2005 Private Limited Company
**Line of Business:** Ferry operators
**Issued Capital:** £23,626,667
**Directors:** H L Dal, A J Eagles, O Frie, K Morch
**Co. Secretary:** Ms Karen Donaldson
**US SIC:** 4712 **UK SIC:** 77002
**Auditors:** Deloitte LLP
**Bankers:** Ulster Bank Ltd (98-14-90)

| | 31-12-13 | 31-12-12 | 31-12-11 |
|---|---|---|---|
| TO | 74,095,958 | 68,157,309 | 64,345,443 |
| P/L | 5,288,777 | (4,468,032) | (14,619,907) |
| NW | 38,125,837 | 32,628,143 | 15,861,006 |
| WC | 9,072,840 | (65,822,603) | (5,971,097) |
| Emp. | 90 | 98 | 98 |

DUNS 34-852-3577
## Seatruck Ferries Ltd
(**Subsidiary of:** Clipper Group Ltd)
Sea Truck House, The Docks, Newry, Co Down BT34 3JR
**Tel:** 02841754411 **Fax:** 02841773737
**Web:** www.seatruckferries.com
**Reg No:** 5651131 **Estd:** 1996 Private Limited Company
**Line of Business:** Freight forwarders
**Issued Capital:** £1
**Directors:** K Morch, H L Dal, A J Eagles, O Frie
**Co. Secretary:** Mrs Karen Donaldson
**Responsibilities**
**Senior:** Eoin McShane *(Operations Manager)*
**HR:** Jim Daly *(Human Resources Manager)*
**Health & Safety:** Eoin McShane *(Operations Manager)*
**Facilities:** Eoin McShane *(Operations Manager)*
**Operations:** Eoin McShane *(Operations Manager)*
**US SIC:** 4712 **UK SIC:** 77002

**Bankers:** Northern Bank Ltd (95-04-40)

| | 31-12-13 | 31-12-12 | 31-12-11 |
|---|---|---|---|
| TO | 74,455,958 | 68,154,901 | 64,705,443 |
| P/L | 7,592,031 | (4,635,969) | (2,217,722) |
| NW | 8,354,296 | 2,711,871 | (32,633,247) |
| WC | 11,854,119 | 2,995,340 | (1,544,328) |
| Emp. | 75 | 83 | 84 |

DUNS 21-613-4001
## Seattle Restaurant
Waterfrontbrighton Marina Villag, Brighton, East Sussex BN2 5WA
**Tel:** 01273679799
**Web:** www.hotelseattlebrighton.com
**Estd:** 2011
**Line of Business:** Hotels and motels without restaurant
**Responsibilities**
**Senior:** Matt Linkin *(General Manager)*
**US SIC:** 7011 **UK SIC:** 66500
**Employees:** 60

DUNS 73-943-6926
## Seattle Software Ltd.
(**Subsidiary of:** Seattle Holdings Ltd)
111 Buckingham Palace Road, London SW1W 0SR
**Tel:** 0870-991-1851
**Web:** www.orbussoftware.com
**Reg No:** 5190435 **Estd.** 2004 Private Limited Company
**Line of Business:** Other software consultancy and supply
**Trading Style:** Orbus Software
**Issued Capital:** £100
**Directors:** S K Lawrence, A P Donoguue
**US SIC:** 7379 **UK SIC:** 83940
**Auditors:** Menzies LLP

| | 31-12-13 | 31-12-12 | 31-12-11 |
|---|---|---|---|
| TO | N/A | N/A | 2,843,690 |
| P/L | N/A | N/A | 113,883 |
| NW | 1,207,145 | 1,115,627 | 775,233 |
| WC | 1,441,612 | 1,250,210 | 978,633 |

DUNS 51-562-3622
## Seatwave Ltd
6 Moorgate, London EC2M 6UR
**Tel:** 02070-828-282
**Web:** www.seatwave.com
**Reg No:** 5843832 **Estd:** 2006 Private Limited Company
**Line of Business:** Operation of tickets agencies.
**Issued Capital:** £1
**Directors:** D N Hamilton, M J Yovich, C A Homann
**Responsibilities**
**Senior:** Ajay Chowdhury *(Chief Executive Officer)*, Joseph Cohen *(Chairman)*, Eleanor Krivicic *(Manager)*
**IT:** Ged Waring *(IT Director)*
**US SIC:** 8999, 7911, 7399
**UK SIC:** 83954, 97913
**Auditors:** PricewaterhouseCoopers LLP

| | 31-12-13 | 31-12-12 | 31-12-11 |
|---|---|---|---|
| TO | 7,858,000 | 7,944,000 | 7,080,000 |
| P/L | (1,191,000) | (1,596,000) | (2,415,000) |
| NW | 753,000 | (2,621,000) | (2,481,000) |
| WC | 653,000 | (2,763,000) | (2,613,000) |
| Emp. | 59 | 60 | 54 |

DUNS 28-959-8898 **Imp-Exp**
## Seaward Electronic Ltd
(**Subsidiary of:** Seaward Holding Co Ltd)
15-18 Bracken Hill, South West Industrial Estate, Peterlee, County Durham SR8 2SW
**Tel:** 0191-586-3511
**Web:** www.seaward.co.uk
**Reg No:** 1674384 **Estd:** 1982 Private Limited Company
**Line of Business:** Manufacture of electronic instruments and appliances for measuring, checking, testing, navigating and other purposes, except industrial process control equipment
**Export Markets:** Australia, Africa, West Europe
**Trading Style:** The Seaward Group
**Issued Capital:** £200,000
**Principals:** R G Taylor *(Managing)*, I West, M Marsh, J Grant, Dr M T Ying, A R Upton, Miss L V Armstrong, D J Clarke
**Co. Secretary:** Ms Rosemary Taylor
**Responsibilities**
**Senior:** Eric Blakie *(Manager)*
**HR:** Wendy Chaplian *(Human Resources Manager)*
**Health & Safety:** Steven Mugridge
**Operations:** Steven Mugridge
**US SIC:** 3829 **UK SIC:** 37100
**Auditors:** Baker Tilly
**Bankers:** Lloyds TSB Bank plc (30-95-96)

| | 31-03-14 | 31-03-13 | 31-03-12 |
|---|---|---|---|
| TO | 13,349,576 | 12,143,389 | 12,257,015 |
| P/L | 1,154,028 | 701,350 | 923,336 |
| NW | 6,181,515 | 5,400,298 | 4,842,118 |
| WC | 4,951,088 | 4,211,690 | 3,639,764 |
| Emp. | 149 | 151 | 151 |

DUNS 45-845-6431 **Exp**
## The Sebden Group Ltd
Craven House Craven Road, Altrincham, Cheshire WA14 5DY
**Tel:** 0161-928-8548 **Fax:** 01619417061
**Web:** www.sebden.com
**Reg No:** 3192327 **Estd:** 1996 Private Limited Company
**Line of Business:** Steel stockholders
**Issued Capital:** £24,112
**Directors:** B J Sanders, M C Weisselberg, M P Whitby, R E Hill, K Scholes
**Responsibilities**
**Senior:** Rob Hatton *(Business Director)*, Craig Hodson *(Sales Director)*
**Sales:** Craig Hodson *(Sales Director)*
**US SIC:** 5051 **UK SIC:** 61200
**Auditors:** Lathams Blueprint
**Bankers:** National Westminster Bank Plc (01-05-31)

| | 30-04-14 | 30-04-13 | 30-04-12 |
|---|---|---|---|
| TO | 90,838,000 | 87,099,000 | 98,356,000 |
| P/L | 639,000 | 283,000 | 543,000 |
| NW | 10,790,000 | 10,155,000 | 11,410,000 |
| WC | 330,000 | (628,000) | 4,868,000 |
| Emp. | 188 | 205 | 203 |

DUNS 23-223-4398
## Sebright House Nursing Home
10-12 Leam Terrace, Leamington Spa, Warwickshire CV31 1BB
**Estd:** 1992 Proprietorship
**Line of Business:** Non-charitable social work activities with accommodation
**Proprietor:** Mrs J Shuker
**Responsibilities**
**Senior:** Belinda Hughes *(Home Manager)*, Marie Woodcock *(Home Manager)*
**US SIC:** 8321 **UK SIC:** 96111
**Employees:** 49

DUNS 54-382-6408
## Sec Lighting Services Trading Ltd
(**Subsidiary of:** Sse Plc)
Southdown View Road, Worthing, West Sussex BN14 8NL
**Tel:** 01293509100
**Web:** www.ssecontracting.co.uk
**Reg No:** 3267621 **Estd:** 1996 Private Limited Company
**Line of Business:** Electrical contractors and electricians
**Trading Style:** Edf Energy
**Issued Capital:** £10,000,002
**Directors:** A Peters, G W Mackinlay
**Co. Secretary:** Gavin Mackinlay
**Branches:** Sec Lighting Services Trading Ltd, 58 Arndale Centre, Eastbourne, East Sussex BN21 3NW
**US SIC:** 1731 **UK SIC:** 50300
**Auditors:** Deloitte LLP

| | 31-03-14 | 31-03-13 | 31-03-12 |
|---|---|---|---|
| TA | 47,360,000 | 9,932,000 | 9,932,000 |
| NW | 9,907,000 | 9,907,000 | 9,907,000 |
| WC | 46,365,000 | 9,785,000 | 9,785,000 |

DUNS 23-716-2594
## Secal Laser Ltd
(**Subsidiary of:** R.J.T. Enterprises Ltd)
Unit C1-C4, Halesfield 5, Telford, Shropshire TF7 4QJ
**Tel:** 01952-588231
**Web:** www.secal-laser.co.uk
**Reg No:** 3711104 **Estd:** 1999 Private Limited Company
**Line of Business:** Sheet metal fabricators
**Export Sales:** £97,525
**Issued Capital:** £100
**Principals:** R L Lavender *(Managing)*, D J Shimmons, J L Collins
**Co. Secretary:** Ms Angela Griffiths
**Responsibilities**
**Health & Safety:** Stefan Parkes *(Health & Safety Officer)*
**US SIC:** 3469, 7399
**UK SIC:** 31200, 83954
**Auditors:** Phillips Ltd
**Bankers:** National Westminster Bank Plc (60-21-57)

| | 31-12-13 | 31-12-12 | 31-12-11 |
|---|---|---|---|
| TO | 6,543,654 | 7,157,094 | 6,830,570 |
| P/L | 552,908 | 315,130 | 252,834 |
| NW | 704,565 | 582,962 | 397,078 |
| WC | 272,860 | 161,102 | (149,846) |
| Emp. | 67 | 80 | 78 |

DUNS 34-804-0114
## Secal Sheet Metal (Midlands) Ltd
(**Subsidiary of:** P & B Holdings Ltd)
Unit J3, Telford, Shropshire TF7 4QJ
**Tel:** 01952684140
**Web:** www.secal.co.uk
**Reg No:** 2789163 **Estd:** 1993 Private Limited Company
**Line of Business:** Manufacture of other fabricated metal products not elsewhere classified

Issued Capital: £1,000
Director: S M Mills
Co. Secretary: Ms Angela Griffiths
Responsibilities
HR: Bev Neville *(Personnel Manager)*
Purchasing: Sharon Maloney *(Contract / Purchasing Manager)*
US SIC: 3499, 3398
UK SIC: 31694, 31380
Auditors: Rochesters
Bankers: Lloyds TSB Bank plc (30-18-55)

| | 31-05-14 | 30-11-12 | 30-05-11 |
|---|---|---|---|
| TA | 2,129,306 | 1,732,868 | 2,713,372 |
| NW | 130,582 | 129,197 | 119,003 |
| WC | 4,144 | (75,217) | (33,868) |

DUNS 36-533-8313
## The Seckford Foundation
Marryott Jouse, Burkitt Road, Woodbridge, Suffolk IP12 4JJ
Tel: 01394-615100
Web: www.seckford-foundation.org.uk
Reg No: 5522615 Estd: 2005 Private Limited Company
Line of Business: Schools
Directors: Ms M A King, M T Sylvester, J D Wellesley Wesley, D P Grant, Ms I M Grimsey, Mrs W S Evans Hendrick, K S Mccormack, R J Finbow
Co. Secretary: Graham Watson
Responsibilities
Senior: John Carrington *(Manager)*, Jonathan Ripman *(Director)*
US SIC: 8211, 8321
UK SIC: 93200, 96111
Bankers: Barclays Bank Plc (20-03-80)

| | 31-08-13 | 31-08-12 | 31-08-11 |
|---|---|---|---|
| TO | 18,937,000 | 18,968,000 | 12,698,062 |
| P/L | 2,692,000 | 5,592,000 | 79,420 |
| NW | 28,155,000 | 24,591,000 | 19,147,291 |
| WC | (2,396,000) | (2,113,000) | (2,267,630) |
| Emp. | 380 | 333 | 320 |

DUNS 28-836-6834
## Seckford Hall Hotel Ltd
(Subsidiary of: Ravenscroft Investments Ltd)
Seckford Hall Road, Woodbridge, Suffolk IP13 6NU
Tel: 01394-385678
Web: www.seckford.co.uk
Reg No: 0434025 VAT No: 103247024
Estd: 1947 Private Limited Company
Line of Business: Hotels
Issued Capital: £10,000
Directors: S Pankhurst, Ms J K Pankhurst
Responsibilities
Senior: Christine Bunn *(Manager)*, Denis Frucot *(Manager)*
Finance: Ken Burr *(Financial Director)*
Admin: Julie Waters *(Office Manager)*
Facilities: Jim Wyard *(Maintenance Coordinator)*
Operations: Mark Suddes *(Operations Director)*
Purchasing: Julie Waters *(Office Manager)*
US SIC: 7011 UK SIC: 66500
Auditors: Bird Luckin

| | 31-03-14 | 31-03-13 | 31-03-12 |
|---|---|---|---|
| TA | 2,337,864 | 1,512,765 | 1,488,276 |
| NW | 43,310 | 157,741 | 71,080 |
| WC | (74,206) | (125,636) | (458,838) |

DUNS 21-906-9606 Imp-Exp
## Seco Tools (U.K.) Ltd
(Subsidiary of: Sandvik Ab)
Adams Way, Springfield Business Park, Alcester, Warwickshire B49 6PU
Tel: 01789764220 Fax: 01789-761170
Web: www.secotools.com
Reg No: 1151087 VAT No: 276207160
Estd: 1973 Private Limited Company
Line of Business: Distribution service providers
Export Markets: E U, North America
Issued Capital: £750,000
Directors: J Boyer, A Eller, H Hellgren, R L Jelfs
Co. Secretary: Christopher Gillespie
Responsibilities
Senior: Patrik Johnson *(Manager)*, Paul Laferen *(Manager)*
HR: Sara Robeson *(Human Resource Manager)*
Health & Safety: Philip Madkins *(Quality Manager)*
Operations: Philip Madkins *(Quality Manager)*
Engineering: Peter Wiseman *(Technical Manager)*
US SIC: 4712 UK SIC: 77002
Auditors: PricewaterhouseCoopers LLP
Bankers: Svenska Handelsbanken Ab (publ) (40-51-62)

| | 31-12-13 | 31-12-12 | 31-12-11 |
|---|---|---|---|
| TO | 26,806,000 | 27,669,000 | 25,412,000 |
| P/L | 872,000 | 1,527,000 | 2,800,000 |
| NW | 3,781,000 | 4,417,000 | 5,409,000 |
| WC | 2,345,000 | 2,493,000 | 6,735,000 |
| Emp. | 98 | 104 | 103 |

DUNS 76-667-6092
## Secom Plc
(Subsidiary of: Secom Co. Ltd.)
Secom House, 52 Godstone Road, Purley, Surrey CR8 5JF
Tel: 02086455400 Fax: 02086455500
Web: www.secom.plc.uk
Reg No: 2585807 Estd: 1991 Public Limited Company
Line of Business: Security and related activities
Issued Capital: £44,126,304
Directors: A Blake, A D Gover, M Takezawa, H Ishikawa
Co. Secretary: Paul Simpson
Responsibilities
Marketing: Dionne Fenech-Soler *(Marketing Manager)*, David Whitley *(Head of Marketing)*
IT: Brian Webster *(IT Manager)*
Facilities: Mick Smith *(Facilities Manager)*
Branches: Secom Plc, Gee House, Holborn Hill, Birmingham, West Midlands B7 5PA
US SIC: 7393 UK SIC: 83954
Auditors: KPMG LLP
Bankers: HSBC Bank plc (40-18-41)

| | 31-12-13 | 31-12-12 | 31-12-11 |
|---|---|---|---|
| TO | 51,051,000 | 49,758,000 | 45,750,000 |
| P/L | 2,566,000 | 1,925,000 | 2,436,000 |
| NW | 22,260,000 | 20,462,000 | 17,521,000 |
| WC | 16,012,000 | 14,210,000 | 13,696,000 |
| Emp. | 668 | 685 | 671 |

DUNS 22-705-5852 Imp-Exp
## Second Nature Ltd
(Subsidiary of: Second Nature (Holdings) Ltd)
10 Malton Road, London W10 5UP
Tel: 020-8960-0212
Web: www.secondnature.co.uk
Reg No: 1594736 VAT No: 340278276
Estd: 1981 Private Limited Company
Line of Business: Publishing of books
Export Markets: Canada, U S A, Europe, Africa
Issued Capital: £171,470
Director: T Schragger
Co. Secretary: Rodney Schragger
Responsibilities
Senior: Martin Skelcey *(Head Of Production)*
Finance: Harry Devlia *(Financial Controller)*
Branches: Second Nature Ltd, Second Nature Ltd, Unit 2-4, Cowes, Isle Of Wight PO31 8AP
US SIC: 2731, 7311
UK SIC: 47532, 83800
Auditors: Morley & Scott

| | 31-12-13 | 31-12-12 | 31-12-11 |
|---|---|---|---|
| TO | N/A | N/A | 5,535,609 |
| P/L | N/A | N/A | 7,843 |
| NW | 940,266 | 923,606 | 858,931 |
| WC | 853,993 | 966,927 | 734,225 |
| Emp. | N/A | N/A | 50 |

DUNS 23-679-2479
## Second Step Housing Association
9 Brunswick Square, Bristol, Avon BS2 8PE
Tel: 0117-909-6630 Fax: 0117-909-8807
Web: www.second-step.co.uk
Reg No: 0025597IP Estd: 1995 Friendly Society
Line of Business: Housing associations societies trusts & co-operatives
Principals: C Trowell *(Chairman)*, M Forrest, P Siddall, A Howarth, Ms A Edwards, G Monaghan, G Scott, P Cooney
Branches: Second Step Housing Association, The Office Jasmine Ct, Hopkins Street, Weston-Super-Mare, Avon BS23 1RS
US SIC: 8321 UK SIC: 96111
Auditors: RSM Tenon Audit Ltd

| | 31-03-13 |
|---|---|
| TO | 5,581,000 |
| P/L | 37,000 |
| NW | 2,180,000 |
| WC | 2,064,000 |
| Emp. | 166 |

DUNS 22-156-9333
## Seconique Holdings Ltd
Meashill House, Shifnal, Shropshire TF11 8QB
Tel: 0121-506-4888
Web: www.seconique.co.uk
Reg No: 4175603 Estd: 2001 Private Limited Company
Line of Business: Furniture wholesale
Export Sales: £130,459
Issued Capital: £500,005
Director: Ms H Barker
Co. Secretary: Ms Leah Ellington
Responsibilities
Senior: Roger Evans-Southall *(Manager)*, Heather Shepherd *(Manager)*
US SIC: 6711 UK SIC: 83962

Bankers: Allied Irish Bank (gb) (23-85-85)

| | 30-06-13 | 30-06-12 | 30-06-11 |
|---|---|---|---|
| TO | 26,718,234 | 27,028,667 | 35,430,525 |
| P/L | 1,177,904 | 1,611,285 | (428,808) |
| NW | 4,044,577 | 3,662,945 | 2,389,337 |
| WC | 12,482,874 | 6,922,565 | 5,625,354 |
| Emp. | 129 | 134 | 165 |

DUNS 21-180-2790
## Secret Escapes Ltd
29-35 Farringdon Road, London EC1M 3JB
Tel: 08432277777
Web: www.secretescapes.com
Reg No: 7026107 Estd: 2009 Private Limited Company
Line of Business: Airline ticket suppliers and agencies
Issued Capital: £1,332
Directors: A S Saint, T J Valentine, L P Laffy, T D Collins, B J Holmes, A D Cole
Co. Secretary: Ohs Secretaries Limited
Responsibilities
Senior: Shane Simpson *(Head Of Customer Services)*
US SIC: 7999 UK SIC: 97913

| | 31-12-13 | 31-12-12 | 31-12-11 |
|---|---|---|---|
| TO | 11,596,876 | N/A | N/A |
| P/L | (3,523,646) | N/A | N/A |
| NW | (625,653) | 2,725,025 | 2,126,845 |
| WC | (712,885) | 2,652,483 | 2,101,144 |
| Emp. | 56 | N/A | N/A |

DUNS 67-137-9704 Imp
## Secret Sales Ltd
Newcombe House, 45 Notting Hill Gate, London W11 3LQ
Tel: 08458-739-522
Web: www.secretsales.com
Reg No: 5996763 VAT No: 906580029
Estd: 2007 Private Limited Company
Line of Business: Retail sale via mail order house
Trading Style: Secret Sales.Com, Secretsales
Issued Capital: £3,669,063
Directors: S A Dias, N P Grierson, F Halley, N Kukadia, C B Anderson
Co. Secretary: Michael Cody
US SIC: 5961, 5699
UK SIC: 65600, 64500
Auditors: Baker Tilly UK Audit LLP
Bankers: Barclays Bank Plc (20-73-53)

| | 31-12-13 | 31-12-12 | 31-12-11 |
|---|---|---|---|
| TO | 18,163,382 | 10,820,112 | 8,876,485 |
| P/L | (3,960,226) | (3,979,667) | (3,248,482) |
| NW | (3,558,025) | 316,686 | (1,714,476) |
| WC | (2,300,418) | 13,687 | (1,804,797) |
| Emp. | 74 | 59 | 48 |

DUNS 21-130-4451
## Secrets
62 Glenthorne Road, London W6 0LR
Tel: 020-8563-7974
Web: www.secrets-clubs.co.uk
Estd: 1993 Proprietorship
Line of Business: Nightclub
Proprietor: Ms N Girardot
Responsibilities
Senior: Jane Hurlow *(Manager)*, Atif Manzoor *(Manager)*
Finance: Michelle Woollen *(Financial Director)*
US SIC: 5813 UK SIC: 66200
Employees: 50

DUNS 77-774-8500
## Sector Security Services Ltd
27-29 Blackpool Road, Preston, Lancashire PR2 6BT
Tel: 01772794728
Web: www.sectorsecurity.com
Reg No: 3022368 Estd: 1995 Private Limited Company
Line of Business: Security activities
Issued Capital: £3,780
Principals: Ms M F Wilson *(Managing)*, N Karia, D Wilson
Responsibilities
Senior: Ian Garrett *(Manager)*
Branches: Sector Security Services Ltd, 1 Castle Street, Manchester M29 8FP
US SIC: 7393 UK SIC: 83954
Auditors: THR
Bankers: Barclays Bank Plc (20-69-85)

| | 31-05-13 | 31-05-12 | 31-05-11 |
|---|---|---|---|
| TA | 2,073,732 | 1,899,893 | 1,789,695 |
| NW | 770,464 | 665,988 | 566,877 |
| WC | 336,408 | 182,975 | 117,406 |

DUNS 23-116-3908
## Securahome P V C U Ltd
Unit C1-C2, Kestrel Way, Garngoch Industrial Estate, Gorseinon, Swansea, West Glamorgan SA4 9WN
Tel: 01792-224090 Fax: 01792-224099
Web: www.securahome.co.uk
Reg No: 2929292 Estd: 1994 Private Limited Company
Line of Business: Manufacture of other builders ware of plastic

Trading Style: Conservatory Roofing Direct
Issued Capital: £200,100
Director: J M Jenkins
Co. Secretary: Nigel Williams
US SIC: 3079 UK SIC: 48360
Auditors: K B Ferguson
Bankers: HSBC Bank plc (40-22-15)

| | 31-05-13 | 31-05-12 | 31-05-11 |
|---|---|---|---|
| TA | 1,024,976 | 1,080,633 | 1,035,232 |
| NW | 581,209 | 626,484 | 591,568 |
| WC | 259,834 | 295,939 | 256,525 |

DUNS 21-693-3605
## Secure Direct Ltd
14 Factory Street, Darlaston, Wednesbury, West Midlands WS10 8QX
Tel: 07826848714
Web: www.securedirectltd.com
Reg No: 7400241 Estd: 2010 Private Limited Company
Line of Business: Security activities
Issued Capital: £100
Directors: Ms E J Turner, S Wilkes, C D Hartland
US SIC: 7393 UK SIC: 83954

| | 31-10-12 | 31-10-11 |
|---|---|---|
| TA | 1,000 | 5,000 |
| NW | 1,000 | 4,000 |
| WC | N/A | 4,000 |

DUNS 45-880-8482 Exp
## Secure Holdings Ltd
Pyronix House, Braithwell Way, Hellaby, Rotherham, South Yorkshire S66 8QY
Tel: 01709-700100 Fax: 01709-701042
Web: www.secureholdings.co.uk
Reg No: 3218507 Estd: 1996 Private Limited Company
Line of Business: Management activities of wholesale holding companies
Issued Capital: £36,336
Directors: J S Herrera, Mrs J A Kenny, C M Beresford
US SIC: 6711, 3629
UK SIC: 83962, 34350
Auditors: PKF
Bankers: Barclays Bank Plc (20-76-89)

| | 31-12-13 | 31-12-12 | 31-12-11 |
|---|---|---|---|
| TO | 18,503,000 | 16,345,000 | 14,146,000 |
| P/L | 686,000 | 441,000 | 286,000 |
| NW | 3,118,000 | 2,696,000 | 2,247,000 |
| WC | 1,313,000 | 1,057,000 | 822,000 |
| Emp. | 145 | 142 | 132 |

DUNS 73-492-8463
## Secure I T Disposals Ltd
Unit 53 Kettles Wood Drive, Birmingham, West Midlands B32 3DB
Web: www.sitd.co.uk
Reg No: 4756286 Estd: 2010 Private Limited Company
Line of Business: Security and related activities
Issued Capital: £600
Directors: M G Burgoyne, L R Speedie, M J Burke, D W Miller
Co. Secretary: Andrew Speedie
US SIC: 7399, 7379
UK SIC: 83954, 83940
Bankers: Lloyds TSB Bank plc (77-85-20)

| | 31-05-14 | 31-05-13 | 31-05-12 |
|---|---|---|---|
| TA | 825,297 | 919,387 | 919,682 |
| NW | 367,797 | 520,847 | 554,385 |
| WC | 64,488 | 150,663 | 156,979 |

DUNS 39-762-5799 Imp-Exp
## Secure Meters (Uk) Ltd
(Subsidiary of: Secure Meters Limited)
Secure House, Moorside Road, Winchester, Hampshire SO23 7RX
Tel: 01962-840048
Web: www.securetogether.com
Reg No: 2199653 Estd: 1988 Private Limited Company
Line of Business: Manufacturers of meters
Export Markets: Europe, Asia, Africa, Australasia
Export Sales: £13,411,626
Trading Style: Polymeters International, Polymeters, P R I
Issued Capital: £8,086,430
Directors: S Singhal, K Patel, K Ghosh
Co. Secretary: Hemender Pandwal
Responsibilities
Senior: Vineet Agrawal *(Manager)*, Leslie Woolner *(Manager)*
IT: Dave Nessling *(Computer Manager)*
HR: Sara Chubb *(Human Resources Manager)*
US SIC: 3811 UK SIC: 37100
Auditors: James Cowper LLP
Bankers: HSBC Bank plc (40-46-39)

| | 31-03-14 | 31-03-13 | 31-03-12 |
|---|---|---|---|
| TO | 102,569,795 | 61,415,215 | 40,947,165 |
| P/L | 2,722,773 | (1,031,798) | 350,491 |
| NW | 11,427,455 | 11,065,790 | 10,958,984 |
| WC | 4,133,126 | 4,181,855 | 6,045,509 |
| Emp. | 181 | 132 | 128 |

DUNS 34-596-3334 **Imp-Exp**

## Secure Microsystems Ltd

(**Subsidiary of:** 21st Century Technology Plc)
Drake Road, Mitcham, Surrey CR4 4HQ
**Tel:** 02089084708 **Fax:** 020-8710-7771
**Web:** www.maverick-telemarketing.co.uk
**Reg No:** 2740409 **VAT No:** 603497051
**Estd:** 1993 Private Limited Company
**Line of Business:** Telephone marketing services
**Export Markets:** Eire
**Trading Style:** Sigma
**Issued Capital:** £9,992
**Directors:** R C Singleton, G Robinson
**Co. Secretary:** Glenn Robinson
**Responsibilities**
**Senior:** Christopher Massey *(Sales Director)*
**Sales:** Christopher Massey *(Sales Director)*
**Branches:** Secure Microsystems Ltd, 1 Seymour Court, Runcorn, Cheshire WA7 1SY
**US SIC:** 3629 **UK SIC:** 34350
**Auditors:** Ernst & Young
**Bankers:** Barclays Bank Plc (20-01-96)

| | 31-12-13 | 31-12-12 | 31-12-11 |
|---|---|---|---|
| TA | 9,992 | 9,992 | 9,992 |
| NW | 9,992 | 9,992 | 9,992 |

DUNS 22 780 4317

## Secure Trust Bank Plc

1 Arleston Way, Shirley, Solihull, West Midlands B90 4LH
**Tel:** 08451117117
**Web:** www.securetrustbank.com
**Reg No:** 0541132 **Estd:** 2012 Public Limited Company
**Line of Business:** Financial intermediation not elsewhere classified
**Issued Capital:** £6,259,260
**Principals:** H Angest *(Chairman)*, N Kapur, Lord M B Forsyth, P A Lynam, P Marrow, Mrs C F Sergeant, A A Salmon
**Co. Secretary:** Alan Karter
**Responsibilities**
**Senior:** Paul Lineham *(Chief Executive Officer)*
**IT:** Steve Bevan *(IT Director)*
**HR:** Frances Lees *(Human Resources Manager)*
**Branches:** Secure Trust Bank Plc, 43 High Street, Walsall, West Midlands WS3 4LT
**US SIC:** 6111 **UK SIC:** 81501
**Auditors:** KPMG Audit PLC
**Bankers:** Barclays Bank Plc (20-07-82)

| | 31-12-13 | 31-12-12 | 31-12-11 |
|---|---|---|---|
| TA | 525,900,000 | 474,599,000 | 307,840,000 |
| P/L | 17,100,000 | 17,165,000 | 7,280,000 |
| NW | 51,700,000 | 50,690,000 | 23,129,000 |
| WC | 45,200,000 | 41,390,000 | 18,300,000 |
| Emp. | 530 | 399 | 229 |

DUNS 23-077-1359

## Secure Valeting Ltd

(**Subsidiary of:** Secure Group Limited)
8 Marlborough Road, Colmworth Business Park, Eaton Socon, St Neots, Cambridgeshire PE19 8YP
**Tel:** 01480216700
**Web:** www.secureplc.com
**Reg No:** 3609741 **VAT No:** 806640342
**Estd:** 1998 Private Limited Company
**Line of Business:** Maintenance and repair of motor vehicles
**Issued Capital:** £50,000
**Directors:** F Beccles, D Johnston, C Reynolds, G T Gray
**Co. Secretary:** Jonathan Evens
**US SIC:** 7539 **UK SIC:** 67100
**Auditors:** French Duncan LLP
**Bankers:** The Royal Bank Of Scotland Plc (16-13-18)

| | 31-03-14 | 31-12-12 | 31-03-11 |
|---|---|---|---|
| TO | 28,405,064 | 18,261,779 | 15,412,910 |
| P/L | 378,169 | 123,916 | 183,940 |
| NW | 665,485 | 727,554 | 696,436 |
| WC | 68,872 | 926,884 | 547,592 |
| Emp. | 148 | 147 | 81 |

DUNS 85-611-7986

## Securecare (Uk) Ltd

First Floor 557 Cranbrook Road, Ilford, Essex IG2 6HE
**Tel:** 08456769247
**Web:** www.impactcareservices.co.uk
**Reg No:** 6248454 **Estd:** 2007 Private Limited Company
**Line of Business:** Labour recruitment and provision of personnel
**Issued Capital:** £100
**Director:** Z A Choudhry
**US SIC:** 7361 **UK SIC:** 83954

| | 31-05-13 | 31-05-12 | 31-05-11 |
|---|---|---|---|
| TA | 280,766 | 160,582 | 40,984 |
| NW | 122,154 | 68,693 | (6,951) |
| WC | 104,735 | 46,919 | 20,376 |

DUNS 52-036-6147

## Secured by Design Ltd

12 Davy Avenue, Knowlhill, Milton Keynes, Buckinghamshire MK5 8NL
**Tel:** 01908-305101
**Web:** www.sbd.co.uk
**Reg No:** 3403037 **Estd:** 1997 Private Limited Company
**Line of Business:** Other software consultancy and supply
**Trading Style:** S B D
**Issued Capital:** £30,003
**Principals:** D A Bell *(Managing)*, D E Mcclure
**Co. Secretary:** Gareth Jones
**Responsibilities**
**Senior:** Dawn Maycock *(Office Manager)*
**US SIC:** 7399 **UK SIC:** 83954
**Auditors:** Cottons Accountants LLP
**Bankers:** The Royal Bank Of Scotland Plc (16-23-15)

| | 31-03-14 | 31-03-13 | 31-03-12 |
|---|---|---|---|
| TA | 1,279,824 | 1,336,468 | 1,364,413 |
| NW | 896,019 | 954,774 | 678,386 |
| WC | 844,438 | 903,582 | 631,860 |

DUNS 73-573-3243

## Secured Express Ltd

(**Subsidiary of:** Next Wave Partners Llp)
Calver Road, Win Wick Quay, Warrington, Cheshire WA2 8UD
**Tel:** 01925657564 **Fax:** 08704-141700
**Web:** www.securedmail.co.uk
**Reg No:** 4834987 **Estd:** 2003 Private Limited Company
**Line of Business:** Courier activities other than national post activities
**Trading Style:** Secured Mail
**Issued Capital:** £40
**Directors:** J H Wilkins, T G Kilroy, M Owen
**Co. Secretary:** Mark Bigley
**US SIC:** 4311 **UK SIC:** 79010
**Auditors:** Saffery Champness

| | 31-07-13 | 31-07-12 | 31-07-11 |
|---|---|---|---|
| TO | 78,495,803 | 66,795,901 | 47,929,102 |
| P/L | (2,860,687) | (1,715,273) | 480,015 |
| NW | (4,108,747) | (1,248,060) | 144,630 |
| WC | (6,600,601) | (3,258,297) | (689,234) |
| Emp. | 154 | 136 | 87 |

DUNS 21-127-8458

## Secured Group Ltd

(**Subsidiary of:** Next Wave Partners Llp)
Calver Road, Winwick Quay, Warrington, Cheshire WA2 8UD
**Tel:** 01925406577
**Web:** www.securedmail.co.uk
**Reg No:** 6625531 **Estd:** 2008 Private Limited Company
**Line of Business:** Courier activities other than national post activities
**Trading Style:** Secured Mail
**Issued Capital:** £1,053
**Directors:** T G Kilroy, J H Wilkins, M Owen, M S Bigley
**Co. Secretary:** Mark Bigley
**Responsibilities**
**Senior:** Sandra Lennox *(Health & Safety Officer)*
**Health & Safety:** Sandra Lennox *(Health & Safety Officer)*
**Facilities:** Paul Bowers *(Maintenance Manager)*
**US SIC:** 4311 **UK SIC:** 79010

| | 31-07-13 | 31-07-12 | 31-07-11 |
|---|---|---|---|
| TA | 560,278 | 560,278 | 1,878,884 |
| P/L | N/A | N/A | 26,621 |
| NW | 560,278 | 560,278 | 560,278 |
| WC | N/A | N/A | 144,715 |
| Emp. | N/A | N/A | 4 |

DUNS 42-378-3005 **Imp**

## Securedata Europe Ltd

(**Subsidiary of:** August Equity Partners Ii A)
Hermitage Court, Hermitage Lane, Maidstone, Kent ME16 9NT
**Tel:** 01622 723400
**Web:** www.secdata.com
**Reg No:** 4365896 **Estd:** 2002 Private Limited Company
**Line of Business:** Other computer related activities
**Issued Capital:** £13,581
**Directors:** G M Legg, M C Tomlinson, E Greeff, R P Nagevadia
**US SIC:** 7379, 5081
**UK SIC:** 83940, 61490
**Auditors:** Grant Thornton UK LLP
**Bankers:** Lloyds TSB Bank plc (30-16-87)

| | 31-07-14 | 31-07-13 | 31-07-12 |
|---|---|---|---|
| TO | 27,230,070 | 19,704,028 | 19,447,216 |
| P/L | 1,922,154 | 1,265,715 | 1,353,605 |
| NW | 5,345,187 | 3,558,353 | 2,516,417 |
| WC | 7,794,677 | 6,240,383 | 4,614,757 |
| Emp. | 101 | 99 | 82 |

DUNS 21-142-9652

## Secureforce Uk Ltd

Unit 22 Cavalier Road Samara Business, Park, Newton Abbot, Devon TQ12 6TR
**Tel:** 01626362424
**Web:** www.secureforceuk.com
**Reg No:** 6741338 **Estd:** 2008 Private Limited Company
**Line of Business:** Security and related activities
**Issued Capital:** £300
**Director:** M Wain
**Co. Secretary:** Kevin Schmidt
**Branches:** Secureforce Uk Ltd, Fronds Park, Frouds Lane, Aldermaston, Reading, Berkshire RG7 4LH
**US SIC:** 7393 **UK SIC:** 83954

| | 31-12-13 | 31-12-12 | 31-12-11 |
|---|---|---|---|
| TA | 229,361 | 173,473 | 140,311 |
| NW | 39,340 | 24,555 | 18,982 |
| WC | 35,003 | 16,076 | 7,665 |

DUNS 73-312-4270

## Securetrading Group Ltd

(**Subsidiary of:** Uc Group Ltd)
Willoughby Lane, Bromley, Kent BR1 3FZ
**Tel:** 02082909890
**Web:** www.securetrading.com
**Reg No:** 4586150 **Estd:** 2002 Private Limited Company
**Line of Business:** Hardware consultancy
**Trading Style:** Secure Trading
**Issued Capital:** £9,501
**Directors:** D I Holden, J A Paulsen
**Co. Secretary:** Daniel Holden
**US SIC:** 7379, 6711
**UK SIC:** 83940, 83962
**Auditors:** The Gallagher Partnership LLP
**Bankers:** The Hongkong And Shanghai Banking Corporation Ltd (40-48-01)

| | 31-12-13 | 31-12-12 | 31-12-11 |
|---|---|---|---|
| TO | 6,557,955 | 7,322,229 | 10,451,526 |
| P/L | (7,705,673) | (3,149,008) | (1,373,921) |
| NW | (11,192,013) | (4,025,905) | (1,242,117) |
| WC | (3,427,317) | (4,190,792) | (1,384,326) |
| Emp. | 56 | 43 | 48 |

DUNS 23-693-4316

## Securex Ltd

First Floor, 962 Old Lode Lane, Solihull, West Midlands B92 8LN
**Tel:** 01217424333
**Web:** www.securexsecurity.com
**Reg No:** 3688240 **Estd:** 1998 Private Limited Company
**Line of Business:** Security and related activities
**Issued Capital:** £100
**Director:** G P Wardell
**Co. Secretary:** Ms Dawn Wardell
**US SIC:** 7393 **UK SIC:** 83954

| | 31-01-14 | 31-01-13 | 31-01-12 |
|---|---|---|---|
| TA | 74,355 | 67,000 | 63,861 |
| NW | 45,721 | 38,955 | 30,342 |
| WC | 40,116 | 33,915 | 26,332 |

DUNS 21-741-2454

## Securi-Guard (Holdings) Ltd

Darklake View Estover, Plymouth, Devon PL6 7TL
**Tel:** 01752512120
**Reg No:** 7742735 **Estd:** 2011 Private Limited Company
**Line of Business:** Security and related activities
**Issued Capital:** £2,777,492
**Directors:** T S Boyd, T P Boyd, Mrs K M Precious
**Responsibilities**
**Senior:** Margaret Boyd *(Director)*, Bill Boyd *(Manager)*
**US SIC:** 7393 **UK SIC:** 83954

| | 30-04-14 | 30-04-13 | 30-04-12 |
|---|---|---|---|
| TO | 7,460,641 | 7,169,013 | 3,810,254 |
| P/L | 243,762 | 250,889 | 111,175 |
| NW | (18,592) | (239,773) | (449,808) |
| WC | 265,650 | 107,168 | 139,191 |
| Emp. | 175 | 175 | 196 |

DUNS 76-636-1968

## Securi-Guard South West Ltd

(**Subsidiary of:** Securi-Guard (Holdings) Ltd)
Darklake View, Estover, Plymouth, Devon PL6 7TL
**Tel:** 01752512134 **Fax:** 01752-204912
**Reg No:** 2582835 **VAT No:** 557508028
**Estd:** 1982 Private Limited Company
**Line of Business:** Security and related activities
**Issued Capital:** £10,000
**Principals:** T S Boyd *(Managing)*, Ms K M Precious *(Managing)*, T P Boyd
**Co. Secretary:** Ms Kimberley Precious
**Responsibilities**
**Senior:** Margaret Boyd *(Director)*
**US SIC:** 7393 **UK SIC:** 83954
**Auditors:** Mark Holt & Co Ltd

**Bankers:** Lloyds TSB Bank plc (30-96-68)

| | 30-04-14 | 30-04-13 | 30-04-12 |
|---|---|---|---|
| TA | 10,000 | 10,000 | 10,000 |
| NW | 10,000 | 10,000 | 10,000 |

DUNS 39-935-8191 **Imp**

## Securi-Plex Ltd

Aviation House, 11 Swordfish Way, Leeds, West Yorkshire LS25 6NG
**Tel:** 01977680700 **Fax:** 01977-680701
**Web:** www.securi-plex.co.uk
**Reg No:** 2249277 **VAT No:** 482065251
**Estd:** 1988 Private Limited Company
**Line of Business:** Burglar alarm systems
**Issued Capital:** £20,000
**Directors:** S Wilson, D F Cavell, M Shann, S R Lawson
**Co. Secretary:** Jean Lawson
**US SIC:** 7393 **UK SIC:** 83954
**Auditors:** Birdsall & Bennett
**Bankers:** Barclays Bank Plc (20-33-42)

| | 31-05-14 | 31-05-13 | 31-05-12 |
|---|---|---|---|
| TO | 5,991,607 | 6,937,591 | 6,829,245 |
| P/L | 68,576 | 198,362 | 317,962 |
| NW | 3,241,621 | 3,197,683 | 3,046,695 |
| WC | 2,566,877 | 2,446,683 | 2,300,582 |
| Emp. | 57 | 58 | 56 |

DUNS 21-778-5717

## Securicor Cash Services

Stonebridge Trading Estate, Rowley Drive, Coventry, West Midlands CV3 4FG
**Tel:** 02476305507
**Web:** www.g4s.com
**Estd:** 2011 Proprietorship
**Line of Business:** Security activities
**Proprietor:** R Flint
**US SIC:** 7393 **UK SIC:** 83954
**Employees:** 100

DUNS 21-131-6608

## Securigroup Ltd

349 Bath Street, Glasgow, Lanarkshire G2 4AA
**Tel:** 08448080999
**Web:** www.securigroup.co.uk
**Reg No:** 0346167SC **Estd:** 2009 Private Limited Company
**Line of Business:** Management activities of other non-financial holding companies not elsewhere classified
**Issued Capital:** £100
**Directors:** A Morton, R Kerr
**Responsibilities**
**Senior:** Scott Weatherby *(Manager)*
**IT:** Lisa Lilley *(Office Manager)*
**US SIC:** 6711 **UK SIC:** 83962

| | 30-03-14 | 31-03-13 | 31-03-12 |
|---|---|---|---|
| TO | 21,341,537 | 18,111,066 | 13,630,160 |
| P/L | 587,832 | 357,921 | 496,021 |
| NW | 397,943 | 394,289 | 211,122 |
| WC | (382,349) | (229,003) | (131,904) |
| Emp. | 1,395 | 1,208 | 934 |

DUNS 73-390-2394

## Securigroup Services Ltd

(**Subsidiary of:** Securigroup Ltd)
Venlaw Building, 349 Bath Street, Glasgow, Lanarkshire G2 4AA
**Tel:** 01412 215448
**Web:** www.securigroup.co.uk
**Reg No:** 0243826SC **Estd:** 2003 Private Limited Company
**Line of Business:** Security activities
**Issued Capital:** £2
**Directors:** R Kerr, A Morton, V Garvie
**Responsibilities**
**Senior:** Peter Nokes *(Manager)*
**US SIC:** 7393 **UK SIC:** 83954
**Auditors:** Gilliland & Co

| | 30-03-14 | 31-03-13 | 31-03-12 |
|---|---|---|---|
| TO | 20,935,841 | 17,749,213 | 13,383,086 |
| P/L | 547,624 | 321,475 | 533,128 |
| NW | 381,532 | 251,075 | 188,072 |
| WC | 265,340 | (75,678) | (38,048) |

DUNS 21-179-1161

## Securist Ltd

7 Kennard Road, Bristol, Avon BS15 8AA
**Tel:** 01179600471
**Web:** www.securist.co.uk
**Reg No:** 7017273 **Estd:** 2009 Private Limited Company
**Line of Business:** Security activities
**Issued Capital:** £1
**Director:** K Davis
**Co. Secretary:** Evans & Partners Ltd
**Responsibilities**
**Senior:** Sophia Rowe *(Office Manager)*
**US SIC:** 7393 **UK SIC:** 83954

| | 30-09-13 | 30-09-12 | 30-09-11 |
|---|---|---|---|
| TA | 44,543 | 74,623 | 9,945 |
| NW | 10,222 | 9,058 | 537 |
| WC | 4,692 | 6,486 | (1,096) |

DUNS 21-739-1622 **Imp-Exp**

## Securistyle Ltd

(**Subsidiary of:** Assa Abloy Ab)
Unit A-F, Kingsmead Industrial Estate, Cheltenham, Gloucestershire GL51 7RE
**Tel:** 01242-221200 **Fax:** 01242-520828
**Web:** www.securistyle.co.uk
**Reg No:** 1381767 **Estd:** 1975 Private Limited Company
**Line of Business:** Manufacture of locks and hinges
**Export Markets:** countries worldwide.
**Export Sales:** £5,336,000
**Issued Capital:** £667,954
**Directors:** C D Browning, N A Vann, A D Talbot-Cooper
**Co. Secretary:** Graham Penter
**Responsibilities**
**Senior:** Keith Agnew *(Warehouse Manager)*, Andrew Large *(Manager)*
**Marketing:** Rosemary Hartland *(Personnel Administrator)*
**IT:** Malcolm Hill *(Computer Network Supervisor)*, Grant Stratford *(Technical Manager)*
**HR:** Rosemary Hartland *(Personnel Administrator)*
**Health & Safety:** Richard Kitley *(Manufacturing Manager)*
**Operations:** Grant Stratford *(Technical Manager)*
**Engineering:** Richard Kitley *(Manufacturing Manager)*
**US SIC:** 3429 **UK SIC:** 31694
**Auditors:** Ernst & Young LLP
**Bankers:** Lloyds TSB Bank plc (30-96-18)

| | 31-12-13 | 31-12-12 | 31-12-11 |
|---|---|---|---|
| TO | 19,088,000 | 20,254,000 | 20,273,000 |
| P/L | 2,034,000 | (747,000) | 1,652,000 |
| NW | 28,602,000 | 27,051,000 | 27,638,000 |
| WC | 29,226,000 | 28,131,000 | 25,755,000 |
| Emp. | 199 | 220 | 228 |

DUNS 76-870-5659

## Securit Midlands Ltd

(**Subsidiary of:** Securit (East Midlands) Ltd)
25 Wellington Road, Bilston, West Midlands WV14 6AH
**Tel:** 01902492415
**Web:** www.secur-it.co.uk
**Reg No:** 2614109 **Estd:** 1991 Private Limited Company
**Line of Business:** Security activities
**Issued Capital:** £2
**Directors:** R Cooke, S Hands, M P Fisher
**Responsibilities**
**Senior:** Fraser Tranter *(Manager)*
**US SIC:** 7393 **UK SIC:** 83954
**Auditors:** Madeley Jones

| | 30-06-13 | 30-06-12 | 30-06-11 |
|---|---|---|---|
| TA | 1,760,273 | 1,560,520 | 1,292,403 |
| NW | 1,498,307 | 1,241,429 | 919,361 |
| WC | 1,489,600 | 1,230,046 | 903,630 |

DUNS 21-198-0032 **Exp**

## Securitas Security Personnel Ltd

(**Subsidiary of:** Securitas Ab)
1 Regent Business Park, 37 Booth Drive, Park Farm Industrial Estate, Wellingborough, Northamptonshire NN8 6GR
**Tel:** 01933671000 **Fax:** 01933671001
**Web:** www.securitas.com
**Reg No:** 1062876 **Estd:** 1968 Private Limited Company
**Line of Business:** Security and related activities
**Issued Capital:** £100
**Directors:** S W Kennedy, J J Collins
**Co. Secretary:** Goodwille Limited
**Responsibilities**
**Senior:** Jackie Gregory *(Marketing Manager)*, John Savill *(Chief Operator Officer)*, Geoffrey Zeidler *(Manager)*
**Branches:** Securitas Security Personnel Ltd, Prospect Ho, 9-11 Commonside East, Mitcham, Surrey CR4 2QA
**US SIC:** 7393, 7399
**UK SIC:** 83954
**Auditors:** PKF (UK) LLP
**Bankers:** National Westminster Bank Plc (50-00-00)

| | 31-12-12 | 31-12-11 |
|---|---|---|
| TO | N/A | 115,502,000 |
| P/L | N/A | (5,235,000) |
| NW | 7,780,000 | 7,780,000 |
| WC | N/A | 8,397,000 |
| Emp. | N/A | 5,033 |

DUNS 76-981-3288

## Securitas Security Services Ltd

(**Subsidiary of:** Securitas Ab)
271 High Street, Uxbridge, London
**Tel:** 01895-276-300 **Fax:** 0845-409-9437
**Web:** www.securitas.com
**Reg No:** 2630124 **Estd:** 1991 Private Limited Company
**Line of Business:** Security and related activities
**Issued Capital:** £1
**Directors:** J J Collins, S W Kennedy
**Co. Secretary:** Goodwille Limited
**Responsibilities**
**Senior:** Ashley Bailey *(Manager)*, Lars Blecko *(Manager)*, Amanda Dempsey *(Personal Assistant)*
**Branches:** Securitas Security Services Ltd, Cuckoo Wharf, Unit 2, Birmingham, West Midlands B6 7SS
**US SIC:** 8999 **UK SIC:** 83954
**Auditors:** PricewaterhouseCoopers LLP
**Bankers:** National Westminster Bank Plc (50-00-00)

| | 31-12-13 | 31-12-12 | 31-12-11 |
|---|---|---|---|
| TO | N/A | N/A | 60,721,140 |
| P/L | (4,238) | (2,487,436) | (8,606,316) |
| NW | 2,553,964 | 474,115 | (3,427,359) |
| WC | N/A | N/A | 188,567 |
| Emp. | N/A | N/A | 3,029 |

DUNS 21-159-3546

## Securitas Security Services (Uk) Ltd

(**Subsidiary of:** Securitas Ab)
Main Avenue, Treforest Industrial Estate, Pontypridd, Mid Glamorgan CF37 5UR
**Tel:** 01443841118 **Fax:** 0118-930-5397
**Web:** www.securitas.com
**Reg No:** 1146486 **Estd:** 2011 Private Limited Company
**Line of Business:** Business services
**Issued Capital:** £7,070
**Directors:** B R Nielsen, J J Collins, S W Kennedy
**Co. Secretary:** Goodwille Limited
**Responsibilities**
**Senior:** Adam Griffiths *(Operations Manager)*
**Branches:** Securitas Security Services (Uk) Ltd, Unit 4, Gatwick Road, Crawley, West Sussex RH10 9RF
**US SIC:** 7393, 9221, 9224
**UK SIC:** 83954, 91300, 91400
**Auditors:** PricewaterhouseCoopers LLP
**Bankers:** National Westminster Bank Plc (56-00-46)

| | 31-12-13 | 31-12-12 | 31-12-11 |
|---|---|---|---|
| TO | 338,401,375 | 350,679,715 | 205,199,131 |
| P/L | 86,117 | (2,261,529) | (5,401,835) |
| NW | 806,910 | (11,377,436) | (4,984,908) |
| WC | 45,743,403 | (1,996,924) | (3,338,492) |
| Emp. | 14,707 | 15,025 | 7,383 |

DUNS 49-495-0140

## Securitay Ltd

31 Church Street, Broughty Ferry, Dundee, Angus DD5 1HB
**Tel:** 01382732090
**Web:** www.securitay.co.uk
**Reg No:** 0163291SC **Estd:** 1985 Private Limited Company
**Line of Business:** Security activities
**Issued Capital:** £2
**Managing Director:** N M Cameron
**Co. Secretary:** Ms Catriona Mcwilliam
**Responsibilities**
**Senior:** Tricia Jennings *(Manager)*
**Branches:** Securitay Ltd, 72 Carden Pl, Aberdeen, Aberdeenshire AB10 1UL
**US SIC:** 7393 **UK SIC:** 83954
**Auditors:** Richard Han & Co
**Bankers:** Bank Of Scotland (80-05-80)

| | 28-02-14 | 28-02-13 | 29-02-12 |
|---|---|---|---|
| TA | 850,099 | 1,121,341 | 1,125,738 |
| NW | 502,226 | 533,732 | 554,780 |
| WC | 438,399 | 475,450 | 513,616 |

DUNS 77-110-5004

## Securities & Investment Institute

S I I, London EC3M 1AE
**Tel:** 020-7645-0600 **Fax:** 020-7645-0601
**Web:** www.cisi.org
**Reg No:** 2687534 **VAT No:** 644856995
**Estd:** 1992 Private Company Limited By Guarantee
**Line of Business:** Activities of professional organisations
**Trading Style:** Chartered Institute for Securites & Investment
**Directors:** S H Culhane, Chartered Institute For Securiti, E S Brunel-Cohen
**Co. Secretary:** Broadway Secretaries Limited
**Responsibilities**
**Senior:** David Brewer *(Manager)*, Linda Raven *(Manager)*
**US SIC:** 8621 **UK SIC:** 96311
**Auditors:** Deloitte & Touche
**Bankers:** National Westminster Bank Plc (60-00-01)
**Employees:** 280

DUNS 21-686-0243

## The Security Group (National) Ltd

1b St Georges House, St Georges Road, Aldershot, Hampshire GU12 4LD
**Tel:** 01252345100
**Web:** www.tsg-uk.com
**Reg No:** 7353891 **Estd:** 2010 Private Limited Company
**Line of Business:** Security activities
**Issued Capital:** £1,000
**Directors:** B F Mein, J L Liddle
**US SIC:** 7393 **UK SIC:** 83954

| | 30-04-14 | 30-04-13 | 24-04-12 |
|---|---|---|---|
| TO | 9,053,661 | 9,204,171 | 9,811,136 |
| P/L | 49,882 | (25,018) | (30,497) |
| NW | (169,698) | (332,750) | (309,655) |
| WC | (297,982) | (457,521) | (455,483) |
| Emp. | 320 | 317 | 376 |

DUNS 21-867-7412

## Security Industry Authority

Po Box 1293, Liverpool, Merseyside L69 1AX
**Tel:** 0844-892-1025 **Fax:** 0844-892-0975
**Web:** www.sia.homeoffice.gov.uk
**Estd:** 2003 Incorporate By Act Of Parliament
**Line of Business:** Licencing & regulatory body for the private security industry. Reports to the Home Secretary, under the terms of the Private Security Industry Act 2001.
**Principals:** Baroness R Henig Cbe *(Chairman)*, B Butler, R Dahlberg, E Weiss, Ms L Sharpe, B Matthews
**Responsibilities**
**Senior:** Ruth Henig CBE *(Chairperson)*
**Branches:** SECURITY INDUSTRY AUTHORITY: Approved Contractor Scheme, PO Box 49768, WC1V 6WY, LONDON.
**US SIC:** 9111, 7393, 8999
**UK SIC:** 91110, 83954
**Employees:** 234

DUNS 34-513-6779

## Security Management South West Ltd

237 Union Street, Plymouth, Devon PL1 3HQ
**Tel:** 01752-227731
**Web:** www.smsw.co.uk
**Reg No:** 5324647 **Estd:** 2005 Private Limited Company
**Line of Business:** Security and related activities
**Issued Capital:** £100
**Director:** J Morrish
**Co. Secretary:** Ken York
**US SIC:** 7393 **UK SIC:** 83954
**Auditors:** David Mayer Accounting Services

| | 28-02-14 | 28-02-13 | 28-02-12 |
|---|---|---|---|
| TA | 201,012 | 183,038 | 172,696 |
| NW | 1,295 | 1,789 | 236 |
| WC | (23,153) | (15,320) | (18,470) |

DUNS 22-801-3348 **Imp**

## Security Print Solutions Ltd

Northumbria House, Unit 38 Number One Industrial Estate, Consett, County Durham DH8 6TW
**Tel:** 01207590185
**Web:** www.securityps.co.uk
**Reg No:** 1642326 **Estd:** 1982 Private Limited Company
**Line of Business:** Printers general
**Export Sales:** £530,332
**Issued Capital:** £14,432
**Principals:** J Crowther *(Managing)*, G C Mcguire, S Wilson, M Crowther
**Co. Secretary:** James Crowther
**US SIC:** 2752 **UK SIC:** 47544
**Auditors:** Ernst & Young
**Bankers:** Barclays Bank Plc (20-58-17)

| | 30-04-14 | 30-04-13 | 30-04-12 |
|---|---|---|---|
| TO | 6,063,549 | 5,028,566 | 5,138,649 |
| P/L | 538,952 | 84,023 | 130,781 |
| NW | 2,568,854 | 2,052,804 | 1,888,954 |
| WC | 829,498 | 481,620 | 385,185 |
| Emp. | 59 | 56 | 60 |

DUNS 21-918-9099

## Security Products Uk Ltd

(**Subsidiary of:** Assa Abloy Ab)
Portebello Works, School Street, Willenhall, West Midlands WV13 3PW
**Tel:** 01902-366911 **Fax:** 01902364666
**Web:** www.assaabloy.co.uk
**Reg No:** 1403050 **Estd:** 2000 Private Limited Company
**Line of Business:** Suppliers of locks
**Trading Style:** Assa Abbloy
**Issued Capital:** £51,070,715
**Directors:** N A Vann, J A Sasse, C D Browning
**Co. Secretary:** Graham Penter
**Responsibilities**
**Senior:** Sara Fisher *(Executive Assistant)*
**Branches:** Security Products Uk Ltd, 1 Factory, Charlotte Rd, Birmingham, West Midlands B30 2BP

**US SIC:** 7393 **UK SIC:** 83954

| | 31-12-13 | 31-12-12 | 31-12-11 |
|---|---|---|---|
| TA | 48,514,000 | 50,887,000 | 50,887,000 |
| P/L | (2,373,000) | N/A | N/A |
| NW | 48,514,000 | 50,887,000 | 50,887,000 |

DUNS 45-813-1323 **Exp**

## Security Research Group Plc

133 Ebury Street, London SW1W 9QU
**Tel:** 020-7881-0800
**Web:** www.srgroupplc.com
**Reg No:** 3170812 **Estd:** 1996 Public Limited Company
**Line of Business:** Manufacturers of security equipment suppliers and
**Export Sales:** £780,932
**Trading Style:** Psg Solutions
**Issued Capital:** £3,885,265
**Directors:** T M Brown, J D Holme, B C Connor, J P Mervis
**Co. Secretary:** John Warwick
**Branches:** Security Research Group Plc, 27 Riverbank Drive, Bury, Lancashire BL8 1UR
**US SIC:** 6711 **UK SIC:** 83962
**Auditors:** Milsted Langdon LLP

| | 31-03-14 | 31-03-13 | 31-03-12 |
|---|---|---|---|
| TO | 9,061,054 | 29,363,893 | 37,272,645 |
| P/L | 1,739,315 | 4,978,290 | 7,933,254 |
| NW | 5,646,218 | 3,947,780 | 13,501,488 |
| WC | 4,985,581 | 3,224,165 | 11,795,421 |
| Emp. | 98 | 193 | 158 |

DUNS 23-261-7084

## Security Services

2 Berry Street, Stoke-On-Trent, Staffordshire ST4 1AY
**Tel:** 01332369668
**Web:** www.uksecurityservices.com
**VAT No:** 368124251 **Estd:** 1982 Partnership
**Line of Business:** Security activities
**Trading Style:** Bryan Enterprises
**Partners:** A Mcglaughlin, Ms J Mcglaughlin
**Responsibilities**
**Senior:** Jean McGlaughlin *(Partner)*, Adrian Mclaughlin *(Manager)*
**Branches:** Security Services, 31 Firs St, Dudley, West Midlands DY2 7DW
**US SIC:** 1731 **UK SIC:** 50300
**Employees:** 66

DUNS 21-772-9077

## Security Vetting Appeals Panel

70 Whitehall, London SW1A 2AS
**Tel:** 02072765645
**Estd:** 2011 Partnership
**Line of Business:** Central Government
**Partner:** Sir G Newman
**US SIC:** 9121 **UK SIC:** 91110
**Employees:** 1,500

DUNS 23-523-2936

## The Security Watchdog Ltd

Cross & Pillory House, Cross & Pillory Lane, Alton, Hampshire GU34 1HL
**Tel:** 01420593830 **Fax:** 01428725716
**Web:** www.securitywatchdog.org.uk
**Reg No:** 3522258 **Estd:** 1998 Private Limited Company
**Line of Business:** Security and related activities
**Issued Capital:** £6,000
**Directors:** J Parkhouse, T C Richards, P J Bluck, Capita Corporate Director Limite
**Co. Secretary:** Capita Group Secretary Limited
**US SIC:** 7393 **UK SIC:** 83954
**Auditors:** Harvey Montgomery

| | 31-12-13 | 31-12-12 | 30-12-11 |
|---|---|---|---|
| TO | 1,816,612 | 7,733,261 | N/A |
| P/L | 375,186 | 852,224 | N/A |
| NW | 381,120 | 607,816 | 94,361 |
| WC | 381,120 | 436,975 | 171,531 |
| Emp. | 112 | 104 | N/A |

DUNS 21-690-7253 **Imp-Exp**

## Securon Manufacturing Ltd

Winchmore Hill, Amersham, Buckinghamshire HP7 0NZ
**Tel:** 01494434455
**Web:** www.securon.co.uk
**Reg No:** 0432663 **VAT No:** 207824468
**Estd:** 1947 Private Limited Company
**Line of Business:** Manufacture of parts and accessories for motor vehicles and their engines
**Export Markets:** European Union (E U)
**Export Sales:** £4,990,546
**Issued Capital:** £3,300
**Principals:** R A Proctor *(Managing)*, Ms A A Proctor, W D John
**Co. Secretary:** William John
**Responsibilities**
**Senior:** Timothy Proctor *(Manager)*
**US SIC:** 3714, 6711
**UK SIC:** 35300, 83962
**Auditors:** Caldwell & Braham

**Bankers:** Barclays Bank Plc (20-19-90)

| | 31-12-13 | 31-12-12 | 31-12-11 |
|---|---|---|---|
| TO | 7,339,696 | 6,369,361 | 6,830,826 |
| P/L | 1,141,418 | 580,367 | 956,752 |
| NW | 6,824,051 | 6,401,779 | 5,968,308 |
| WC | 6,478,915 | 6,074,096 | 5,614,487 |
| Emp. | 87 | 82 | 85 |

DUNS 21-624-9888 **Imp-Exp**
## Seda Uk Ltd
(**Subsidiary of:** Seda International Packaging Group Spa)
Hawtin Park, Gellihaf, Blackwood, Gwent NP12 2EU
**Tel:** 01443-811888
**Web:** www.sedagroup.org
**Reg No:** 0297265 **VAT No:** 532531375
**Estd:** 1935 Private Limited Company
**Line of Business:** Manufacturers of boxes and cartons
**Export Markets:** Export
**Export Sales:** £12,441,954
**Issued Capital:** £11,000
**Principals:** Dr A D'Amato *(Chairman)*, G D'Amato
**Co. Secretary:** Giulio Grandoni
**Responsibilities**
**Senior:** Gianfranco D' Amato *(Director)*, Tony Picciano *(Factory Manager)*
**IT:** Alberto Desantis *(Computer Manager)*, Gary Mulvihill *(Senior IT Executive)*
**HR:** Christina Calver *(Human Resources Manager)*, Rhian Williams *(Hr Assistant)*
**Operations:** Jim Statts *(Quality Manager)*
**Engineering:** Tony Henderson *(Engineering Manager)*
**Branches:** Bicester Rd, Aylesbury
**US SIC:** 2651, 6711
**UK SIC:** 47253, 83962
**Auditors:** Ernst & Young LLP
**Bankers:** Barclays Bank Plc (20-40-71)

| | 31-12-13 | 31-12-12 | 31-12-11 |
|---|---|---|---|
| TO | 77,069,195 | 76,478,161 | 75,326,121 |
| P/L | 13,855,297 | 14,466,904 | 11,566,291 |
| NW | 33,643,510 | 32,749,876 | 33,935,965 |
| WC | 14,179,187 | 16,577,973 | 16,842,766 |
| Emp. | 310 | 277 | 240 |

DUNS 28-995-6880
## Sedac Ltd
Triple House, Whitehill Road, Crowborough, East Sussex TN6 1JP
**Tel:** 01892669944 **Fax:** 01892-669955
**Web:** www.sedac.co.uk
**Reg No:** 1843231 **VAT No:** 412371489
**Estd:** 1984 Private Limited Company
**Line of Business:** Development and selling of real estate
**Issued Capital:** £20,000
**Principals:** G L Paddy *(Managing)*, G I Heath, J I Hunt
**Co. Secretary:** Ms Margaret Wakeling
**US SIC:** 6552 **UK SIC:** 85000
**Auditors:** Creaseys
**Bankers:** National Westminster Bank Plc (60-10-25)

| | 31-08-13 | 31-08-12 | 31-08-11 |
|---|---|---|---|
| TA | 1,385,397 | 826,140 | 1,028,356 |
| NW | 160,199 | 144,105 | 167,994 |
| WC | 121,676 | 100,475 | 120,404 |

DUNS 23-690-3415
## Sedbergh School
The Bursary, Sedbergh School, Sedbergh, Cumbria LA10 5RY
**Web:** www.sedberghschool.org
**Estd:** 1996 Partnership
**Line of Business:** Schools (foundation)
**Partners:** R Napier, C Hirst, P Marshall
**Responsibilities**
**Senior:** Andrew Fleck *(Headmaster)*
**Branches:** Sedbergh School, Huddersfield Road, Bradford, West Yorkshire BD6 1DJ
**US SIC:** 8211 **UK SIC:** 93200
**Employees:** 400

DUNS 23-580-3645
## Seddon Construction Ltd
(**Subsidiary of:** Seddon Solutions Ltd)
Plodder Lane, Edge Fold, Farnworth, Bolton, Lancashire BL4 0NN
**Tel:** 01204570400 **Fax:** 01204570401
**Web:** www.gjseddon.com
**Reg No:** 3578140 **Estd:** 1998 Private Limited Company
**Line of Business:** Development and selling of real estate
**Issued Capital:** £1,155
**Directors:** P J Jackson, C G Wilde, John Howard Shaw, C J Seddon, L Wilkinson, E J Burns, J F Seddon, Mrs N J Hodkinson
**Co. Secretary:** Christopher Wilcox
**Responsibilities**
**Senior:** Keith Waddington *(Director)*
**US SIC:** 6552, 8911
**UK SIC:** 85000, 83701
**Auditors:** Grant Thornton UK LLP
**Bankers:** Barclays Bank Plc (20-55-34)

| | 31-12-13 | 31-12-12 | 31-12-11 |
|---|---|---|---|
| TO | 149,135,000 | 161,631,000 | 153,077,000 |
| P/L | 4,122,000 | 1,997,000 | 1,866,000 |
| NW | 43,554,000 | 40,276,000 | 39,416,000 |
| WC | 40,886,000 | 37,025,000 | 38,495,000 |
| Emp. | 623 | 671 | 699 |

DUNS 52-563-5900 **Exp**
## Seddon Group Ltd
Manor House, Holmes Chapel Business Centre, Manor Lane, Holmes Chapel, Crewe, Cheshire CW4 8AF
**Web:** www.seddongroup.co.uk
**Reg No:** 3249290 **Estd:** 2003 Private Limited Company
**Line of Business:** Estate management services
**Issued Capital:** £225,847
**Directors:** G Seddon, J Seddon, C J Seddon
**Co. Secretary:** David Handley
**Responsibilities**
**Senior:** Rodney Sellers *(Manager)*
**Fleet:** Steve Paget *(Transport Manager)*
**Branches:** Seddon Group Limited, Unit 34A, Brownsburn Industrial Estate, Airdrie, Lanarkshire ML6 9SE
**US SIC:** 6531, 1721
**UK SIC:** 83400, 50400
**Auditors:** Grant Thornton UK LLP
**Bankers:** Barclays Bank Plc (20-55-34)

| | 31-12-12 | 31-12-11 | 31-12-10 |
|---|---|---|---|
| TO | 306,580,000 | 281,279,000 | 200,900,000 |
| P/L | 4,532,000 | 5,430,000 | 8,792,000 |
| NW | 93,182,000 | 93,006,000 | 90,155,000 |
| WC | 88,448,000 | 90,310,000 | 91,628,000 |
| Emp. | 1,737 | 1,774 | 1,843 |

DUNS 77-932-7493
## Seddon Homes Ltd
(**Subsidiary of:** Seddon Solutions Ltd)
3 Crab Lane Cinnamon Park, Warrington, Cheshire WA2 0XP
**Tel:** 01925839500
**Web:** www.seddonhomes.co.uk
**Reg No:** 3045309 **Estd:** 1995 Private Limited Company
**Line of Business:** Property developers
**Issued Capital:** £2
**Directors:** S J Seddon, D A Maddock, A Thompson, M R Jefferson, J F Seddon, C W Graham
**Co. Secretary:** Stuart Mclaughlin
**Responsibilities**
**Senior:** Kenton Whitaker *(Manager)*
**US SIC:** 1799, 1541
**UK SIC:** 50000, 50100
**Auditors:** Grant Thornton UK LLP
**Bankers:** Barclays Bank Plc (20-55-34)

| | 31-12-13 | 31-12-12 | 31-12-11 |
|---|---|---|---|
| TO | 31,851,000 | 25,564,795 | 22,200,243 |
| P/L | (1,190,000) | 594,400 | 1,510,293 |
| NW | 9,261,000 | 20,883,527 | 20,824,758 |
| WC | 12,307,000 | 41,430,560 | 41,214,837 |
| Emp. | 47 | 39 | 36 |

DUNS 21-934-5646
## Seddon Property Services Ltd
(**Subsidiary of:** Seddon Solutions Ltd)
Seddon Building Plodder Lane, Edge Fold, Bolton, Lancashire BL4 0NN
**Tel:** 08435073092
**Web:** www.gjseddon.co.uk
**Reg No:** 8471367 **Estd:** 2013 Private Limited Company
**Line of Business:** Building services
**Issued Capital:** £2
**Directors:** C J Seddon, J F Seddon
**Co. Secretary:** Christopher Wilcox
**US SIC:** 7399 **UK SIC:** 83954

| | 31-12-13 |
|---|---|
| TA | 2 |
| NW | 2 |

DUNS 21-203-8319 **Exp**
## Seddons (Plant & Engineers) Ltd
(**Subsidiary of:** Krmco Holdings Ltd)
P O Box 41, Bolton, Lancashire BL4 0LS
**Tel:** 01204854600
**Web:** www.seddonplant.co.uk
**Reg No:** 0499299 **VAT No:** 147627743
**Estd:** 1951 Private Limited Company
**Line of Business:** Plant dealers
**Export Sales:** £30,267
**Issued Capital:** £8,954
**Principals:** S J Seddon *(Managing)*, P A Goulbourne, S C Brown, N Beswick
**Co. Secretary:** Mrs Sarah Cook
**Responsibilities**
**Marketing:** Justin Smith *(Sales & Marketing Director)*
**Sales:** Justin Smith *(Sales & Marketing Director)*
**Branches:** Seddons (Plant & Engineers) Ltd, Unit 8 Hadrians Ct,Seventh Ave, Team Valley Trad Est, Gateshead, Tyne and Wear NE11 0XW
**US SIC:** 5084 **UK SIC:** 61490
**Auditors:** Grant Thornton UK LLP
**Bankers:** Barclays Bank Plc (20-55-34)

| | 31-12-13 | 31-12-12 | 31-12-11 |
|---|---|---|---|
| TO | 15,783,209 | 14,264,123 | 13,668,025 |
| P/L | 233,910 | 61,409 | 181,524 |
| NW | 5,068,913 | 4,877,729 | 4,879,865 |
| WC | 4,891,899 | 4,399,753 | 4,318,635 |
| Emp. | 66 | 66 | 65 |

DUNS 23-211-9508
## Seddons Solicitors
5 Portman Square, London W1H 6NT
**Web:** www.seddons.co.uk
**Estd:** 1990 Partnership
**Line of Business:** Solicitors
**Partners:** C Evans, A Seddon, H Imgram
**Responsibilities**
**Senior:** Robin Austin *(Managing Partner)*, Lili Davarzani *(Partner)*, Leon Golstein *(Partner)*, Graham Honey *(Partner)*, Kyle Irvine *(Partner)*, Deborah Jeff *(Partner)*, James Liffen *(Partner)*, Charles Maxwell *(Partner - Commercial Property)*, Marvin Simons *(Partner)*
**Sales:** Lois Davidson *(Account Manager)*
**HR:** Louise Pye *(HR Manager)*
**US SIC:** 8111 **UK SIC:** 83500
**Employees:** 65

DUNS 22-756-9712
## Sedgefield Borough Council
Council Offices, Spennymoor, County Durham DL16 6JQ
**Tel:** 08455055500
**Web:** www.sedgefield.gov.uk
**Estd:** 1974
**Line of Business:** General (overall) public service activities
**Principals:** B Stephens *(Chairman)*, B Allen *(Financial)*, INC By Charter/Special Act of Pa
**Branches:** Sedgefield Borough Council, Hackworth Clo, Shildon, County Durham DL4 1PL
**US SIC:** 9121 **UK SIC:** 91110
**Bankers:** The Co-Operative Bank Plc (08-90-70)
**Employees:** 500

DUNS 21-120-4011
## Sedgemoor District Council
Bridgwater House, King Square, Bridgwater, Somerset TA6 3AR
**Tel:** 08454082540
**Web:** www.sedgemoor.gov.uk
**Estd:** 1974
**Line of Business:** Local government
**Principals:** C A Buchanan *(Chairman)*, K Rickards
**Responsibilities**
**Senior:** Doug Bamsey *(Manager)*, Bob Brown *(Partner)*, Allison Parsons *(Manager)*
**Finance:** Allison Griffin *(Corporate Director)*
**Marketing:** Claire Faun *(Marketing Manager)*
**HR:** Melanie Wellman *(Legal Service & Procurement)*
**Health & Safety:** Mary Fray *(Health & Safety Manager)*
**Fleet:** Bob Kondys *(Transport Manager)*
**Branches:** Sedgemoor District Council, South Esplanade, Burnham-On-Sea, Somerset TA8 1BU
**US SIC:** 9121 **UK SIC:** 91110
**Bankers:** Barclays Bank Plc (20-85-26)
**Employees:** 730

DUNS 21-811-6175
## Sedgley Lodge
10 Woodcross Street, Bilston, West Midlands WV14 9RT
**Web:** www.cambiangroup.com
**Estd:** 2012
**Line of Business:** Mental health centres
**US SIC:** 8062 **UK SIC:** 95100
**Employees:** 1,000

DUNS 21-011-5260
## See Group Ltd
(**Subsidiary of:** Uk Ticketing Ltd)
Norfolk House, 47 Upper Parliament Street, Nottingham, Nottinghamshire NG1 2AB
**Tel:** 08702643333
**Web:** www.seethreesixty.co.uk
**Reg No:** 6348619 **Estd:** 2007 Private Limited Company
**Line of Business:** Other entertainment activities not elsewhere classified
**Issued Capital:** £443,549
**Directors:** C Sere-Annichini, S Gillham, R I Wilmshurst, J C Bonamy
**Co. Secretary:** Mrs Leanne Lipscombe
**US SIC:** 7999 **UK SIC:** 97913

| | 31-12-13 | 31-12-12 | 31-12-11 |
|---|---|---|---|
| TO | 7,998,000 | 7,733,000 | 12,215,000 |
| P/L | 1,652,000 | 2,192,000 | 8,434,000 |
| NW | 48,923,000 | 46,990,000 | 44,847,000 |
| WC | (10,728,000) | (12,397,000) | (13,713,000) |
| Emp. | 106 | 116 | 147 |

DUNS 21-420-7980
## See Tickets
Manor House, 21 Soho Square, London W1D 3QP
**Tel:** 01159129200
**Web:** www.seetickets.com
**Estd:** 2011 Proprietorship
**Line of Business:** Other entertainment activities
**Proprietor:** A Peaches
**US SIC:** 8999 **UK SIC:** 83954
**Employees:** 50

DUNS 33-974-4419
## See Woo Cash & Carry
108 Horn Lane, London SE10 0RT
**Tel:** 020-8293-9393
**Web:** www.seewoo.com
**Estd:** 2010 Partnership
**Line of Business:** Cash and carry wholesalers
**Partners:** S Chi, L Low
**Responsibilities**
**Senior:** San Kong *(General Manager)*
**US SIC:** 5199 **UK SIC:** 61900
**Employees:** 70

DUNS 36-521-8457
## See Woo Foods
Saracen Street, Glasgow, Lanarkshire G22 5HT
**Tel:** 08450788818
**Web:** www.seewoo.com
**Estd:** 2009 Proprietorship
**Line of Business:** Supermarkets
**Proprietor:** P Lam
**US SIC:** 5411 **UK SIC:** 64100
**Employees:** 50

DUNS 23-615-5669
## Seeability
Newplan House, Epsom, Surrey KT17 1BL
**Tel:** 01372-755-000
**Web:** www.seeability.org
**VAT No:** 235566158 **Estd:** 1993
**Line of Business:** Representative office
**Principals:** Mrs E Wagstaff *(Chairman)*, J R Deeley, M Buckingham, D A Hopkins, Mrs S Yarwood, G V Malachowski, Mrs E Wagstaff, Mrs C M Rollinson
**Responsibilities**
**Senior:** Lady Colman *(Vice President)*, Jane Hunnable *(Executive)*, Roger Mattingly *(Vice President)*, Sue Ogden *(Health & Safety Officer)*, David Scott-Ralphs *(Chief Executive)*
**Finance:** Brian Newcombe *(Finance & Resources Director)*
**Marketing:** Jane McGann *(Public Relations Manager)*, Paula Spinks- Chamberlain *(Director of Advisory)*
**Sales:** Heather Salisbury *(New Business Manager)*
**HR:** Sheila Tuck *(Human Resources Manager)*
**Health & Safety:** Sue Ogden *(Health & Safety Officer)*
**Facilities:** Justin Roxburgh *(Housing & Developments Directo)*
**Branches:** Seeability, 35 Fore Street, Wellington, Somerset TA21 8AG
**US SIC:** 7399 **UK SIC:** 83954
**Auditors:** haysmacintyre
**Bankers:** Lloyds TSB Bank plc (30-92-70)
**Employees:** 650
**Turnover:** £12,440,422

DUNS 23-730-5128 **Imp**
## Seebyte Ltd
Level 7 Orchard Brae House, 30 Queensferry Road, Edinburgh, Midlothian EH4 2HS
**Tel:** 0131-447-4200
**Web:** www.seebyte.com
**Reg No:** 0194014SC **Estd:** 2001 Private Limited Company
**Line of Business:** Computer software (development)
**Export Sales:** £3,071,263
**Issued Capital:** £981
**Directors:** B W Miller, S A Genet, Dr R K Black, F Byus
**Responsibilities**
**Senior:** Andrew Byatt *(Manager)*, Caroline Kellock *(office manager)*, Ralph Taylor-Smith *(Director)*
**Sales:** Ioseba Tena *(Sales Manager)*
**Admin:** Barbara Johnston *(Office Manager)*, Caroline Kellock *(office manager)*
**Engineering:** Alastair Cormack *(Engineer Manager)*, Matt Fitchett *(Engineer)*, Scott Reed *(Engineering Manager)*, Chris Tierney *(Engineer)*
**US SIC:** 7379 **UK SIC:** 83940

**Auditors:** BDO LLP

| | 31-12-13 | 31-12-12 | 31-12-11 |
|---|---|---|---|
| TO | 5,484,398 | 4,423,488 | N/A |
| P/L | 2,127,582 | 1,429,230 | N/A |
| NW | 3,042,246 | 3,485,272 | 2,302,449 |
| WC | 2,959,459 | 3,411,616 | 2,227,966 |

DUNS 21-930-2767 **Imp-Exp**

## Seetall Furniture Ltd

Swansea Road, Swansea, West Glamorgan SA4 9DZ
**Tel:** 01792-897464 **Fax:** 01792-893180
**Web:** www.seetall.com
**Reg No:** 1323135 **Estd:** 1977 Private Limited Company
**Line of Business:** Manufacture of other furniture
**Export Markets:** European Union (E U); U S A
**Issued Capital:** £310,000
**Directors:** M W Fury, Ms A C Riseborough, P C Fury
**Co. Secretary:** Ms Anna Riseborogh
**US SIC:** 2517 **UK SIC:** 46714
**Auditors:** P.W. Lang & Co
**Bankers:** Barclays Bank Plc (20-12-25)

| | 28-02-14 | 28-02-13 | 29-02-12 |
|---|---|---|---|
| TA | 2,682,933 | 2,627,028 | 2,391,464 |
| NW | 1,614,521 | 1,556,403 | 1,508,809 |
| WC | 1,283,739 | 1,225,158 | 1,166,425 |

DUNS 50-000-6234

## Seetec Business Technology Centre Ltd

Frogmoor, Main Road, Hockley, Essex SS5 4RG
**Tel:** 01702201070
**Web:** www.seetec.co.uk
**Reg No:** 2291188 **VAT No:** 507510475
**Estd:** 1988 Private Limited Company
**Line of Business:** Computer software (development)
**Issued Capital:** £100
**Principals:** P A Cooper *(Managing)*, Miss A J Bunney, L Barry, J P Nutter, G B Martin
**Co. Secretary:** John Baumback
**Responsibilities**
**Admin:** Kate Fee *(Office Manager)*
**HR:** Elaine Cole *(Personnel Assistant)*, Vanessa Storey *(Training Manager)*
**Facilities:** Sharon Adams *(Commercial Property Manager)*
**Purchasing:** Michelle Hall *(Purchasing Manager)*
**Branches:** Seetec Business Technology Centre Ltd, 56 Brushfield St, London E1 6AG
**US SIC:** 8299, 7361
**UK SIC:** 93300, 83954
**Auditors:** Goldwyns Ltd
**Bankers:** Barclays Bank Plc (20-79-73)

| | 31-03-14 | 31-03-13 | 31-03-12 |
|---|---|---|---|
| TO | 70,537,607 | 54,834,570 | 57,683,493 |
| P/L | 7,604,694 | 8,320,796 | 8,217,543 |
| NW | 24,274,486 | 23,332,376 | 19,997,649 |
| WC | 27,481,911 | 20,876,552 | 18,102,626 |
| Emp. | 974 | 809 | 577 |

DUNS 39-414-6047 **Imp-Exp**

## Seevent Plastics Ltd

Unit 2-5, Lancing, West Sussex BN15 8TH
**Web:** www.seevent.co.uk
**Reg No:** 2121368 **VAT No:** 461845533
**Estd:** 1987 Private Limited Company
**Line of Business:** Sppliers of bags various types
**Export Markets:** Worldwide
**Export Sales:** £229,429
**Issued Capital:** £30,000
**Director:** N J Gates
**Co. Secretary:** Neil Gates
**Responsibilities**
**Facilities:** Frank Tarjanyi *(Maintenance Manager)*
**US SIC:** 2645, 2752
**UK SIC:** 47280, 47544
**Auditors:** Sharnock Skinner & Co
**Bankers:** National Westminster Bank Plc (53-61-43)

| | 28-02-14 | 28-02-13 | 29-02-12 |
|---|---|---|---|
| TO | 8,375,394 | 7,311,165 | 7,470,460 |
| P/L | 633,877 | 476,823 | 460,680 |
| NW | 1,632,308 | 1,435,477 | 1,369,501 |
| WC | 899,006 | 743,673 | 663,517 |
| Emp. | 49 | 49 | 51 |

DUNS 23-703-1554

## Seevic College

Runnymeade Chase, Benfleet, Essex SS7 1TW
**Tel:** 01268-756111 **Fax:** 01268-565515
**Web:** www.seevic-college.ac.uk
**Estd:** 1975 Incorporate By Act Of Parliament
**Line of Business:** Further education schools and colleges
**Director:** G Arnott
**Responsibilities**
**Senior:** Murray Higgs *(Facilities Manager)*, Nick Spenceley *(Principal & CEO)*
**Finance:** Bruce Balicki *(Financial Manager)*
**Marketing:** Andrew Westerby *(Marketing Manager)*
**Sales:** Eileen O Gara *(Commercial Development Directo)*
**Admin:** Sally Hamilton *(Administration Officer)*
**IT:** John Revill *(Director of Information Servic)*
**HR:** Janet McGready *(Development Manager)*, Kim Morton *(Human Resources Manager)*
**Health & Safety:** Murray Higgs *(Facilities Manager)*
**Facilities:** Murray Higgs *(Facilities Manager)*
**Purchasing:** Murray Higgs *(Facilities Manager)*
**Branches:** Seevic College, Rocheway, Rochford, Essex SS4 1DQ
**US SIC:** 8221, 8249
**UK SIC:** 93100, 93300
**Bankers:** Barclays Bank Plc (20-70-93)
**Employees:** 300

DUNS 21-161-0464 **Imp-Exp**

## Seewoo Foods Ltd

**(Subsidiary of:** Seewoo Group Ltd)
Seewoo House, London NW10 7NU
**Tel:** 0845-076-8888 **Fax:** 08458768899
**Web:** www.seewoo.com
**Reg No:** 1295299 **Estd:** 2005 Private Limited Company
**Line of Business:** Import and export agents
**Export Sales:** £372,227
**Trading Style:** See Woo Supermarket, See Woo Cash & Carry
**Issued Capital:** £45,500
**Principals:** H W Tse *(Managing)*, N H Tse, S Tse, K S Chan
**Co. Secretary:** Hon Tse
**Responsibilities**
**Sales:** Henry Piri *(Senior Sales Executive)*
**IT:** Ben Brettenny *(Computer Operations Manager)*, Ian Shepard *(Senior IT Executive)*
**HR:** Marion Jiang *(Human Resources Manager)*
**Health & Safety:** Steve Claridge *(Health & Safety Officer)*
**Facilities:** C Tse *(Operations Director)*
**Purchasing:** A Lew *(Buyer)*
**Branches:** Seewoo Foods Ltd, 19 Lisle Street, London WC2H 7BE
**US SIC:** 4712, 5411
**UK SIC:** 77002, 64100
**Auditors:** Rayner Essex
**Bankers:** HSBC Bank plc (40-39-13)

| | 31-03-14 | 31-03-13 | 31-03-12 |
|---|---|---|---|
| TO | 61,599,643 | 62,555,133 | 63,698,322 |
| P/L | 396,045 | 439,987 | 1,272,179 |
| NW | 8,754,795 | 8,632,815 | 8,484,926 |
| WC | 7,114,681 | 6,854,310 | 6,631,047 |
| Emp. | 283 | 288 | 282 |

DUNS 23-107-6373

## Sefton Council

Town Hall, Oriel Road, Bootle, Merseyside L20 7AE
**Tel:** 01519224040
**Web:** www.sefton.gov.uk
**VAT No:** 165662152 **Estd:** 2002
**Line of Business:** Local government
**Financial Director:** P Corthorn
**Responsibilities**
**Senior:** Graham Haywood *(Chief Executive)*
**Branches:** Sefton Council, Albion Works, Silver St, Oldham, Lancashire OL1 1HU
**US SIC:** 9121 **UK SIC:** 91110
**Employees:** 11,000

DUNS 34-910-9876

## Sefton Council for Voluntary Service

16 Crosby Road North, Waterloo, Liverpool, Merseyside L22 0NY
**Tel:** 0151-920-0726
**Web:** www.seftoncvs.co.uk
**Reg No:** 2832920 **Estd:** 1999 Private Limited Company
**Line of Business:** Charities and charitable organisations
**Directors:** D Mcgregor, Ms P Lappin, M Sonne, Dr M J Homfray, Ms E A Barnett, S J Sharman, U D Russell, D W Roscoe
**Co. Secretary:** Ms Angela White
**Responsibilities**
**Senior:** Paul Cummins *(Director)*, Margaret Hardman *(Manager)*, Vaughan Smart *(Manager)*
**Branches:** Sefton Council For Voluntary Service, 40-48 Carr Meadow Hey, Bootle, Merseyside L30 2NZ
**US SIC:** 8699 **UK SIC:** 96902
**Auditors:** Gasking Lace & Co
**Bankers:** HSBC Bank plc (40-12-26)

| | 31-03-14 | 31-03-13 | 31-03-12 |
|---|---|---|---|
| TO | 2,741,555 | 3,168,699 | 2,997,156 |
| P/L | (77,621) | (45,321) | (46,867) |
| NW | 1,702,384 | 1,780,005 | 1,825,326 |
| WC | 1,602,728 | 1,705,576 | 1,827,499 |
| Emp. | 62 | 86 | 82 |

DUNS 22-871-3525

## Sefton Group Plc

The Sefton, Douglas, Isle of Man IM1 2RW
**Tel:** 01624645500
**Web:** www.seftonhotel.co.im
**Reg No:** 0000439M **Estd:** 1923 Public Limited Company
**Line of Business:** Hotels
**Principals:** W J Cowell *(Chairman)*, C R Robertshaw *(Managing)*, M J Proffitt, R T Dursley-Stott
**Co. Secretary:** Christopher Robertshaw
**Responsibilities**
**Senior:** Brett Martin *(Chief Executive Officer)*, David Woodiwiss *(Manager)*
**Marketing:** Elanna Swindon *(Business Development Manager)*
**Sales:** David Woodiwiss *(Manager)*
**Health & Safety:** Amanda Fairburn *(Health & Safety Officer)*, Jilly Joyce *(Health & Safety Officer)*
**Operations:** Mark Lewin *(Chief Operating Officer)*
**Purchasing:** David Woodiwiss *(Manager)*
**US SIC:** 7011, 5812, 5813, 7399
**UK SIC:** 66500, 66110, 66200, 83954
**Auditors:** Pannell Kerr Forster,
**Bankers:** Isle Of Man Bank (55-91-00)
**Employees:** 60

DUNS 21-029-4673

## Sefton Mbc

1st Floor, Bootle, Merseyside L20 3NJ
**Tel:** 0151-934-3452
**Web:** www.investsefton.com
**Proprietorship**
**Line of Business:** Central Government
**Responsibilities**
**Sales:** Mike Mullin *(Business Support Manager)*, Gavin Quinn *(Business Development Manager)*, Kristina Swift *(Business Partnerships Manager)*
**Admin:** Angela Baruch *(Business Systems Administrator)*
**IT:** Angela Baruch *(Business Systems Administrator)*
**US SIC:** 9121 **UK SIC:** 91110
**Employees:** 10,000

DUNS 21-776-3839

## Sefton Metropolitan Borough Council

Town Hall, Oriel Road, Bootle, Merseyside L20 7AE
**Web:** www.sefton.gov.uk
**Estd:** 2011 Proprietorship
**Line of Business:** Local government
**Proprietor:** Mrs M Carney
**US SIC:** 9121 **UK SIC:** 91110
**Employees:** 7,000

DUNS 67-223-1144

## Sefton New Directions Ltd

**(Subsidiary of:** Sefton Council)
375 Stanley Road, Bootle, Merseyside L20 3EF
**Tel:** 01519343726
**Web:** www.ndirections.co.uk
**Reg No:** 6052757 **Estd:** 2007 Private Limited Company
**Line of Business:** Home care service providers
**Issued Capital:** £1,000
**Directors:** Ms M Carney, R J Brennan, D P Rimmer
**Co. Secretary:** Mrs Penelope Fell
**US SIC:** 8091 **UK SIC:** 95200
**Bankers:** National Westminster Bank Plc (60-20-23)

| | 31-03-14 | 31-03-13 | 31-03-12 |
|---|---|---|---|
| TO | 9,264,209 | 9,390,843 | 10,311,660 |
| P/L | 985,288 | 879,005 | (764,576) |
| NW | (417,604) | (6,149,903) | (5,352,455) |
| WC | 1,708,355 | 1,412,067 | 32,688 |
| Emp. | 339 | 403 | 474 |

DUNS 21-580-8600

## Sefton Park

St Bartholomews Road, Bristol, Avon BS7 9BJ
**Web:** www.seftonparkschools.bristol.sch.uk
**Estd:** 2011 Proprietorship
**Line of Business:** Schools (local authority)
**Proprietor:** Ms J Lonsdale
**US SIC:** 8211 **UK SIC:** 93200
**Employees:** 60

DUNS 22-737-7454 **Imp-Exp**

## Sega Amusements Europe Ltd

42 Barwell Business Park, Leatherhead Road, Chessington, Surrey KT9 2NY
**Tel:** 02083918090 **Fax:** 020-8391-8099
**Web:** www.sega-amusements.co.uk
**Reg No:** 1711515 **VAT No:** 391624247
**Estd:** 1984 Private Limited Company
**Line of Business:** Manufacturers of games, toys and sporting products
**Export Markets:** Europe
**Export Sales:** £16,455,000
**Issued Capital:** £25,972,823
**Directors:** P Williams, S Yamashita, J Yamada, S Yamakata
**Co. Secretary:** Roger Pennington
**Responsibilities**
**Senior:** Justin Burke *(General Manager)*, Steve D' Arcy *(Sales Director)*, Aaron Gilbey *(Sales Director)*
**Sales:** Steve D' Arcy *(Sales Director)*, Aaron Gilbey *(Sales Director)*
**Engineering:** Gamini Bandara *(Technical Service Manager)*
**Branches:** Sega Amusements Europe Limited, 27 Brain Wwest Rd, Brentford, Middlesex TW8 9BW
**US SIC:** 3949, 5944
**UK SIC:** 49420, 65400
**Auditors:** KPMG LLP
**Bankers:** Barclays Bank Plc (20-00-00)

| | 31-03-14 | 31-03-13 | 31-03-12 |
|---|---|---|---|
| TO | 24,166,000 | 30,041,000 | 25,106,000 |
| P/L | 943,000 | 2,684,000 | 2,310,000 |
| NW | 12,292,000 | 9,792,000 | 7,855,000 |
| WC | 11,704,000 | 7,884,000 | 5,700,000 |
| Emp. | 51 | 51 | 52 |

DUNS 28-958-8386 **Imp-Exp**

## Sega Europe Ltd

27 Great West Road, Brentford, Middlesex TW8 9BW
**Tel:** 02089-953399
**Web:** www.sega.co.uk
**Reg No:** 1669057 **Estd:** 1982 Private Limited Company
**Line of Business:** Publishing of software
**Export Markets:** Worldwide
**Export Sales:** £38,549,000
**Issued Capital:** £10,000,000
**Directors:** Y Sugino, H Satomi, T Miyazaki, J Post
**Co. Secretary:** Ms Nicola Ormrod
**Responsibilities**
**Senior:** Nicola Boxall *(Manager)*
**Branches:** Sega Europe Limited, 70-74 Harvey Centre, Harlow, Essex CM20 1XS
**US SIC:** 7372 **UK SIC:** 83940
**Auditors:** KPMG LLP
**Bankers:** Lloyds TSB Bank plc (30-12-18)

| | 31-03-14 | 31-03-13 | 31-03-12 |
|---|---|---|---|
| TO | 51,710,000 | 75,683,000 | 81,515,000 |
| P/L | 2,228,000 | 17,653,000 | (34,384,000) |
| NW | 41,600,000 | 40,413,000 | 23,007,000 |
| WC | 40,506,000 | 38,325,000 | 20,780,000 |
| Emp. | 154 | 171 | 278 |

DUNS 71-928-0104

## Segen Ltd

Havelock House, Barrack Road, Aldershot, Hampshire GU11 3NP
**Tel:** 01252310033
**Web:** www.segen.co.uk
**Reg No:** 5309114 **VAT No:** 855284207
**Estd:** 2005 Private Limited Company
**Line of Business:** Manufacture of electronic valves and tubes and other electronic components
**Export Sales:** £526,897
**Issued Capital:** £223
**Directors:** Ms M Roberts, Ms E A Macfarlane, J Hawkey, A J Pegg
**Responsibilities**
**Sales:** Nick Hudson *(Sales Representative)*
**HR:** Michelle Gough *(Hr Director)*
**Branches:** Segen Limited, Wimberley Mills, Stroud, Gloucestershire GL5 2TH
**US SIC:** 8999, 1799
**UK SIC:** 83954, 50000
**Auditors:** Menzies LLP

| | 30-11-13 | 30-11-12 | 30-11-11 |
|---|---|---|---|
| TO | 53,643,056 | 83,610,639 | 129,876,030 |
| P/L | 1,970,415 | (302,126) | 8,384,238 |
| NW | 8,388,595 | 7,959,706 | 8,130,985 |
| WC | 8,201,787 | 7,732,903 | 7,954,927 |
| Emp. | 54 | 73 | 53 |

DUNS 29-644-3351

## Segesta Ltd

Bloomfield Road, Blackpool, Lancashire FY1 6JJ
**Tel:** 08704431953 **Fax:** 01253-405011
**Web:** www.segesta.com
**Reg No:** 1970661 **Estd:** 1985 Private Limited Company
**Line of Business:** Stadiums and sports grounds
**Trading Style:** Blackpool Football Club
**Issued Capital:** £1,650,618
**Directors:** O J Oyston, K S Oyston
**Co. Secretary:** Roderick Dyer
**US SIC:** 7999 **UK SIC:** 97913
**Auditors:** A I Cherry
**Bankers:** National Westminster Bank Plc (01-09-51)

| | 31-05-13 | 31-05-12 | 31-05-11 |
|---|---|---|---|
| TO | 23,340,919 | 29,118,660 | 51,785,327 |
| P/L | 5,518,406 | 15,510,488 | 20,451,017 |
| NW | 20,984,217 | 14,562,949 | 7,458,533 |
| WC | 8,642,415 | 5,777,097 | (2,783,774) |
| Emp. | 161 | 150 | 127 |

**DUNS 21-629-0031**   Imp-Exp
## Segro Plc
234 Bath Road, Slough, Berkshire SL1 4EE
**Tel:** 01753-537171
**Web:** www.segro.com
**Reg No:** 0167591 **Estd:** 1920 Public Limited Company
**Line of Business:** Management activities of holding companies
**Export Markets:** Canada, USA, Europe, Australia
**Export Sales:** £200,400,000
**Issued Capital:** £74,219,143
**Directors:** P A Redding, Baroness M A Ford, N M Rich, D J Sleath, D R Webb, M R Moore, A S Gulliford, J R Read
**Co. Secretary:** Ms Elizabeth Blease
**Responsibilities**
**Senior:** Simon Hollins (Investment Director), Mark Robertshaw (Non-Executive Director), Thom Wernink (Independent Non-Executive Dire)
**Finance:** Simon Carlyon (Group Financial Controller)
**Marketing:** Neil Impiazzi (Partnership Development Manage)
**Admin:** Joanne Kirby (Property Administrator), Helen Murray (Secretary), Colette Sharp (Property Administrator)
**IT:** David Drummond (Head of Data Centres)
**Facilities:** Barry Thomas (Property Services Manager)
**Operations:** Allan Davey (Project Manager), Deborah George (Operations Manager), Rowan Harper (Operations Manager), Roger Heywood (Operations Manager), Natalie Price (Operations Manager), Graham Wilder (Project Manager)
**Fleet:** Ken Butcher (Asset Manager - Logistics)
**Branches:** Segro Plc, Unit 15-17, Kings Norton Business Centre, Birmingham, West Midlands B30 3HG
**US SIC:** 6711 **UK SIC:** 83962
**Auditors:** Deloitte LLP
**Bankers:** Barclays Bank Plc (20-78-58)
Following financial data are in thousands

| | 31-12-13 | 31-12-12 | 31-12-11 |
|---|---|---|---|
| TO | 273,800 | 305,400 | 326,100 |
| P/L | 212,100 | (202,200) | (53,600) |
| NW | 2,341,200 | 2,231,000 | 2,554,000 |
| WC | 435,300 | 49,600 | 149,800 |
| Emp. | 238 | 252 | 276 |

**DUNS 50-380-9402**
## S.E.H. (Ipswich) Ltd
(Subsidiary of: One Group Construction Ltd)
Crowcroft Road Industrial Estate, Crowcroft Road, Nedging Tye, Ipswich, Suffolk IP7 7HR
**Tel:** 01449-740971
**Web:** www.sehipswich.co.uk
**Reg No:** 2389994 **Estd:** 1989 Private Limited Company
**Line of Business:** Construction of motorways, roads, railways, airfields and sports facilities
**Issued Capital:** £6,000
**Directors:** R W Neall, R P Garrard, P A Firman, C D Driver
**Co. Secretary:** Trevor Dixon
**Responsibilities**
**Senior:** Graham Emmerson (Manager), Simon Girling (Manager)
**US SIC:** 1611, 1541, 1795
**UK SIC:** 50200, 50100, 50000
**Auditors:** BDO LLP
**Bankers:** Lloyds TSB Bank plc (30-94-55)

| | 31-12-13 | 31-12-12 | 31-12-11 |
|---|---|---|---|
| TO | 7,463,336 | 8,013,229 | 7,388,263 |
| P/L | 472,522 | 302,735 | 525,722 |
| NW | 838,437 | 553,818 | 360,000 |
| WC | 431,960 | 123,646 | (106,736) |
| Emp. | 65 | 67 | 66 |

**DUNS 73-643-9865**
## S.E.H. Jackson Ltd
(Subsidiary of: One Group Construction Ltd)
30 White House Road, Ipswich, Suffolk IP1 5LT
**Tel:** 01473238570 **Fax:** 01473238301
**Web:** www.sehfrench.co.uk
**Reg No:** 4904038 **Estd:** 2012 Private Limited Company
**Line of Business:** Building construction contractors
**Trading Style:** Jackson Engineering
**Issued Capital:** £2,900,000
**Directors:** R W Neall, J D Chaplin, T M Dixon, A J Tuke
**Co. Secretary:** Trevor Dixon
**Responsibilities**
**Senior:** Graham Emmerson (Chief Executive Officer), Simon Girling (Manager)
**US SIC:** 1522, 1611
**UK SIC:** 50100, 50200
**Auditors:** PKF (UK) LLP

| | 31-12-13 | 31-12-12 | 31-12-11 |
|---|---|---|---|
| TA | 1 | 1 | 237,334 |
| NW | (914,044) | (914,044) | (914,044) |
| WC | (914,044) | (914,044) | (914,045) |

**DUNS 22-278-7447**
## Seh Windows & Doors Ltd
6 Wyncolls Road Crown Gate, Colchester, Essex CO4 9HZ
**Tel:** 01206-841811 **Fax:** 01206-841818
**Web:** www.sehbac.co.uk
**Reg No:** 4296709 **Estd:** 1985 Private Limited Company
**Line of Business:** Architectural guilding and decorating
**Issued Capital:** £10
**Director:** R W Neall
**Co. Secretary:** Trevor Dixon
**Responsibilities**
**Senior:** Graham Emmerson (Proprietor)
**Branches:** Seh Windows & Doors Ltd, 30 White House Road, Ipswich, Suffolk IP1 5LT
**US SIC:** 1721 **UK SIC:** 50400
**Auditors:** PKF (UK) LLP

| | 31-12-13 | 31-12-12 | 31-12-11 |
|---|---|---|---|
| TA | 10 | 1 | 10 |
| NW | 10 | 1 | 10 |

**DUNS 29-621-3192**
## Sehbac Ltd
(Subsidiary of: One Group Construction Ltd)
Unit 1, Ipswich, Suffolk IP1 5LN
**Tel:** 01473461171 **Fax:** 01473-462-240
**Web:** www.sehbac.com
**Reg No:** 1047808 **Estd:** 1986 Private Limited Company
**Line of Business:** Other building installation
**Trading Style:** Sehbac Retail
**Issued Capital:** £102
**Directors:** J C Savage, N P Hornigold, R W Neall
**Co. Secretary:** Trevor Dixon
**Responsibilities**
**Senior:** Graham Emmerson (Manager)
**Branches:** Sehbac Ltd, 6 Wyncolls Road, Crown Gate, Colchester, Essex CO4 9HZ
**US SIC:** 1796, 1721
**UK SIC:** 50400
**Auditors:** BDO LLP
**Bankers:** Lloyds TSB Bank plc (30-94-55)

| | 31-12-13 | 31-12-12 | 31-12-11 |
|---|---|---|---|
| TO | 14,919,758 | 12,473,706 | 12,637,146 |
| P/L | 274,472 | (453,784) | (835,077) |
| NW | (2,119,310) | (2,336,564) | (1,976,136) |
| WC | (2,612,982) | (2,339,225) | (1,920,188) |
| Emp. | 74 | 70 | 87 |

**DUNS 21-620-9031**   Imp-Exp
## Sehlbach & Whiting Ltd
(Subsidiary of: Sehlbach & Whiting Holdings Ltd)
Exclusive House, Oldfield Road, Maidenhead, Berkshire SL6 1TA
**Tel:** 01628-591600
**Web:** www.sehlbach.co.uk
**Reg No:** 0180727 **VAT No:** 207958243
**Estd:** 1922 Private Limited Company
**Line of Business:** Haberdashers
**Export Markets:** France; European Union (EU); New Zealand; W Indies
**Trading Style:** Exclusive
**Issued Capital:** £18,251
**Directors:** M Holman, J Hope, P Pandya
**Co. Secretary:** Parimal Pandya
**Responsibilities**
**Senior:** Bruce Ripley (Manager), Phillip Ripley (Manager)
**Sales:** Phillip Ripley (Manager)
**US SIC:** 5136, 5199
**UK SIC:** 61600, 61900
**Auditors:** Harper Broom
**Bankers:** National Westminster Bank Plc (60-00-01)

| | 31-12-13 | 31-12-12 | 31-12-11 |
|---|---|---|---|
| TO | 4,882,816 | 5,669,198 | N/A |
| P/L | 10,050 | 10,639 | N/A |
| NW | 3,496,044 | 3,524,594 | 3,555,462 |
| WC | 3,354,327 | 3,368,008 | 3,409,059 |
| Emp. | 48 | 51 | N/A |

**DUNS 51-995-3111**
## Sehmi Builders Merchants Ltd
8a Hayes Road Canal Yard, Southall, Middlesex UB2 5NA
**Tel:** 02088439955 **Fax:** 02088430950
**Web:** www.sehmis.co.uk
**Reg No:** 3362456 **Estd:** 1982 Private Limited Company
**Line of Business:** Builders merchants
**Issued Capital:** £1,000
**Director:** M S Sehmi
**Responsibilities**
**Senior:** Narinder Sehmi (Manager), Kalwinder Sehmi (Manager)
**Branches:** Sehmi Builders Merchants Ltd, Marsh Road, Wembley, Middlesex HA0 1ES
**US SIC:** 5072 **UK SIC:** 61500
**Auditors:** D.S. Ahluwalia

| | 30-06-13 | 30-06-12 | 30-06-11 |
|---|---|---|---|
| TO | N/A | 7,890,547 | 7,453,077 |
| P/L | N/A | 51,351 | 137,407 |
| NW | 39,766 | 452,769 | 388,481 |
| WC | 1,078,208 | 2,555,508 | 1,850,116 |
| Emp. | N/A | 46 | 46 |

**DUNS 23-644-4985**   Imp
## Sei Interconnect Products (Europe) Ltd
Axis Court, Riverside Business Park Mallard Way, Swansea, West Glamorgan SA7 0AJ
**Tel:** 01792-487290
**Web:** www.sumi-electric.com
**Reg No:** 3639819 **VAT No:** 713023292
**Estd:** 1998 Private Limited Company
**Line of Business:** Cable and wire supply and distribution
**Directors:** Y Miyata, A Hiroto
**Co. Secretary:** Dean Gillett
**Responsibilities**
**Marketing:** Neil Perkins (Sales & Marketing Manager)
**Sales:** Neil Perkins (Sales & Marketing Manager)
**US SIC:** 3357 **UK SIC:** 22470
**Auditors:** KPMG LLP

| | 31-03-14 | 31-03-13 | 31-03-12 |
|---|---|---|---|
| TO | 42,056,446 | 39,204,005 | 30,610,013 |
| P/L | 120,473 | 367,589 | 960,947 |
| NW | (983,087) | (1,191,232) | 3,873,310 |
| WC | (1,613,266) | (1,968,187) | 3,177,060 |
| Emp. | 82 | 75 | 33 |

**DUNS 23-771-9336**   Imp
## Sei Investments (Europe) Ltd
Time And Life Building, London W1J 6TL
**Tel:** 02075188950 **Fax:** 02075188951
**Web:** www.seic.com
**Reg No:** 3765319 **Estd:** 1999 Private Limited Company
**Line of Business:** Investment companies and vehicles
**Issued Capital:** £77,060,410
**Directors:** R A Goldspink, P W Disney, R A Nesher, B S Williams, J P Ujobai, A Mallick, W M Doran
**Co. Secretary:**
Jordan Company Secretaries Limit
**Responsibilities**
**Senior:** Hannah Clarke (Front Of House Manager)
**Finance:** Kevin Barr (Executive Vice President, Inve), Dennis McGonigle (Chief Financial Officer), Stephen Meyer (Executive Vice President, Head)
**Marketing:** Sarah Griffin (Marketing Manager), Mark Samuels (Chief Marketing Officer)
**HR:** Anita Juneja (Relationship Director - Global)
**US SIC:** 6111 **UK SIC:** 81501
**Auditors:** PricewaterhouseCoopers LLP

| | 31-12-13 | 31-12-12 | 31-12-11 |
|---|---|---|---|
| TA | 50,114,000 | 46,468,000 | 32,301,000 |
| P/L | (5,899,000) | (9,224,000) | (10,876,000) |
| NW | 31,821,000 | 32,731,000 | 22,241,000 |
| WC | 31,273,000 | 32,202,000 | 22,164,000 |
| Emp. | 240 | 198 | 173 |

**DUNS 21-197-2211**   Imp-Exp
## Seiko U.K. Ltd
(Subsidiary of: Seiko Holdings Corporation)
S C House, Vanwall Road, Maidenhead, Berkshire SL6 4UW
**Tel:** 01628770988
**Web:** www.seiko.co.uk
**Reg No:** 1032911 **Estd:** 1971 Private Limited Company
**Line of Business:** Watch and clock sales & repairs
**Export Markets:** Gibraltar; Turkey; Africa
**Issued Capital:** £5,500,000
**Directors:** S Tanaka, M Shoyama, R Wilson, H Umemoto, N Hirooka, S Kawanishi, D A Hamby
**Co. Secretary:** Ms Julie Powell
**Responsibilities**
**Senior:** Atsushi Kakizaki (Manager), Hiroyuki Ouchi (Manager), Matthew Sloane (Warehouse Manager), Toyoji Todaka (Manager), Richard Whitbread (General Manager)
**Finance:** Richard Whitbread (General Manager)
**Marketing:** Kirsten Crisford (Marketing Manager), Paul Simmonds (Sales & Marketing Executive -)
**Sales:** Paul Simmonds (Sales & Marketing Executive -)
**IT:** Richard Whitbread (General Manager)
**Health & Safety:** Mara Thorne (Personnel Senior Officer)
**Branches:** Seiko U.k. Ltd, Berkeley Sq House, Berkeley Sq, London W1J 6BR
**US SIC:** 3873 **UK SIC:** 37400
**Auditors:** Deloitte & Touche LLP
**Bankers:** National Westminster Bank Plc (60-13-35)

| | 31-03-14 | 31-03-13 | 31-03-12 |
|---|---|---|---|
| TO | 68,528,000 | 65,002,000 | 64,647,000 |
| P/L | 1,714,000 | 1,866,000 | 2,601,000 |
| NW | 34,837,000 | 32,471,000 | 30,248,000 |
| WC | 18,283,000 | 17,297,000 | 16,754,000 |
| Emp. | 297 | 296 | 296 |

**DUNS 21-700-7536**   Imp
## Sekisui Diagnostics (Uk) Ltd
(Subsidiary of: Sekisui Chemical Co. Ltd.)
50 Gibson Drive, Kings Hill, West Malling, Kent ME19 4AF
**Tel:** 01732220022
**Web:** www.sekisuidiagnostics.com
**Reg No:** 7457131 **Estd:** 2010 Private Limited Company
**Line of Business:** Manufacture of medical and surgical equipment and orthopaedic appliances
**Export Sales:** £28,400,515
**Issued Capital:** £36,000,000
**Directors:** H Tagashira, E Takahashi, T Kon
**Responsibilities**
**Senior:** Mutsumi Fukuda (Manager), Mitsuhisa Manabe (Manager), Will Stockburn (Senior Operations Director)
**IT:** David Roff (System Administrator)
**HR:** Maxine Goodearl (Associate HR Business Partner)
**US SIC:** 3841 **UK SIC:** 37201
**Bankers:** The Bank Of Tokyo-Mitsubishi, Ltd (60-01-09)

| | 31-03-14 | 31-03-13 | 31-03-11 |
|---|---|---|---|
| TO | 30,684,586 | 32,693,496 | 25,410,685 |
| P/L | 5,203,414 | 2,620,261 | 1,267,340 |
| NW | 16,757,383 | 10,818,356 | 9,363,820 |
| WC | 6,719,729 | 176,721 | 9,200,426 |
| Emp. | 117 | 117 | 124 |

**DUNS 73-317-0422**   Imp
## Seko Logistics (London) Ltd
(Subsidiary of: Seko Logistics Group Ltd)
Birch House, Fairfield Avenue, Staines, Middlesex TW18 4AB
**Tel:** 01784417120 **Fax:** 01753 588700
**Web:** www.sekologistics.com
**Reg No:** 4590887 **VAT No:** 804760145
**Estd:** 2004 Private Limited Company
**Line of Business:** Import and export agents
**Export Sales:** £3,519,487
**Issued Capital:** £17
**Directors:** D J Emerson, K Gaskin, D Perry, M L White, M R Claydon
**Co. Secretary:** Keith O'Brien
**Responsibilities**
**Senior:** Patrick Daye (Manager)
**US SIC:** 4712 **UK SIC:** 77002
**Auditors:** LBCA Ltd

| | 31-12-13 | 31-12-12 | 30-12-12 |
|---|---|---|---|
| TO | 38,391,692 | 15,144,503 | 29,040,574 |
| P/L | 1,845,450 | 539,521 | 1,453,594 |
| NW | 2,695,916 | 1,403,452 | 1,450,041 |
| WC | 1,753,028 | 726,212 | 804,304 |
| Emp. | 100 | 68 | 69 |

**DUNS 45-816-0256**
## Sekura Trade Frames Ltd
12 Walton Road, Pattinson North, Washington, Tyne and Wear NE38 8QE
**Tel:** 01914179620 **Fax:** 01914187293
**Web:** www.sekuragroup.co.uk
**Reg No:** 3173704 **VAT No:** 675223040
**Estd:** 1996 Private Limited Company
**Line of Business:** Other manufacturing not elsewhere classified
**Trading Style:** Sekura Trade Frames Ltd
**Issued Capital:** £270
**Directors:** Mrs S Curtis, C Hill
**Co. Secretary:** Ms Michelle Ayre
**Branches:** Sunderland
**US SIC:** 3999, 3442
**UK SIC:** 49590, 31420
**Auditors:** TTR Barnes
**Bankers:** Barclays Bank Plc (20-27-41)

| | 31-05-13 | 31-05-12 | 31-05-11 |
|---|---|---|---|
| TO | 8,464,686 | 10,138,847 | 10,581,932 |
| P/L | 1,103,828 | 503,393 | 1,218,842 |
| NW | 6,776,123 | 5,771,321 | 5,623,495 |
| WC | 6,706,972 | 5,623,649 | 5,296,079 |
| Emp. | 99 | 96 | 100 |

**DUNS 21-145-6420**
## Sel World Ltd
No 19 1-13 Adler Street, London E1 1EG
**Tel:** 02088844054
**Reg No:** 6760692 **Estd:** 2001 Private Limited Company
**Line of Business:** Manufacturers of clothing accessories
**Issued Capital:** £1
**Director:** H Altunatmaz
**Responsibilities**
**Senior:** Kenan Kasha (Manager)
**US SIC:** 2389 **UK SIC:** 45393

| | 30-11-12 | 30-11-11 | 30-11-10 |
|---|---|---|---|
| TA | 173,477 | 179,549 | 94,790 |
| NW | 30,263 | 11,784 | 10,833 |
| WC | 19,742 | (1,367) | N/A |

**DUNS 34-709-0073**
## Selborne Care Ltd
97 Friar Street, Droitwich, Worcestershire WR9 8EG
**Web:** www.selbornecare.com
**Reg No:** 5513162 **Estd:** 2005 Private Limited Company
**Line of Business:** Representative office

**Issued Capital:** £4
**Directors:** M A Stratford, J Mcallister
**Co. Secretary:** Simon Bishop
**Responsibilities**
**Senior:** John McAllister (Director)
**Branches:** Selborne Care Ltd, 36-37 South Road, Smethwick, West Midlands B67 7BU
**US SIC:** 7399 **UK SIC:** 83954
**Bankers:** The Royal Bank Of Scotland Plc (16-16-13)

| | 31-12-13 | 31-12-12 | 31-12-11 |
|---|---|---|---|
| TO | 11,043,838 | 10,422,520 | 9,435,210 |
| P/L | 1,179,858 | 1,246,616 | 1,089,491 |
| NW | 7,394,623 | 92,509 | (399,498) |
| WC | 347,858 | (201,457) | (305,130) |
| Emp. | 495 | 476 | 404 |

DUNS 42-466-5404
## Selby College
Abbots Road, Selby, North Yorkshire YO8 8AT
**Tel:** 0175721097
**Web:** www.selby.ac.uk
**Estd:** 1984 Proprietorship
**Line of Business:** Colleges (higher education)
**Director:** A Stewart
**Responsibilities**
**Senior:** Liz Ridley (Manager), Allan Stuart (Head Teacher)
**Finance:** Pamela Olbison (Finance Administrator)
**Admin:** Pamela Olbison (Finance Administrator)
**IT:** Mike Pilling (IT Manager)
**Branches:** Selby College, 10-12A North St, Wetherby, West Yorkshire LS22 6NN
**US SIC:** 8221 **UK SIC:** 93100
**Employees:** 200

DUNS 23-981-6721
## Selby District Council
Civic Centre, Doncaster Road, Selby, North Yorkshire YO8 9FT
**Tel:** 01757-705101
**Web:** www.selby.gov.uk
**Estd:** 1974
**Line of Business:** Local government
**Directors:** M Connor, A Wilson
**Responsibilities**
**Senior:** Gillian Ivey (Chairman), Denise Richardson (Business Support Lead Officer), Mary Weastel (CEO)
**Finance:** Karen Iveson (Head of Finance), Dean Richardson (Business Manager), Eileen Scothern (Business Manager)
**Marketing:** Mike James (Communications Manager)
**HR:** Janette Barlow (Human Resources Manager)
**Health & Safety:** Ben Hymers (Health & Safety Officer), Andy Rouse (Utilities Manager)
**Branches:** Selby District Council, Civic Centre, Portholme Road, Selby, North Yorkshire YO8 4SB
**US SIC:** 9121 **UK SIC:** 91110
**Employees:** 450

DUNS 22-186-0393
## Selby Salads Ltd
C/O Hedon Salads Ltd, Brough, North Humberside HU15 2PR
**Tel:** 01757-611000
**Web:** www.selbysaladsltd.com
**Reg No:** 4204258 **Estd:** 2001 Private Limited Company
**Line of Business:** Growing of vegetables, horticultural specialities and nursery products
**Issued Capital:** £100
**Directors:** G Colletti, S Cannatella, A Magistro-Contenta
**Co. Secretary:** Salvatore Cannatella
**US SIC:** 0161 **UK SIC:** 01001
**Bankers:** Barclays Bank Plc (20-20-37)

| | 30-11-13 | 30-11-12 | 30-11-11 |
|---|---|---|---|
| TA | 1,590,828 | 1,809,885 | 1,985,366 |
| NW | (166,454) | 742,121 | 857,189 |
| WC | (1,449,710) | (438,959) | (269,642) |

DUNS 22-153-9856 **Imp**
## Selcia Ltd
**(Subsidiary of:** Selcia Holdings Ltd)
Fyfield Business & Research Park, Ongar, Essex CM5 0GS
**Tel:** 01277-367000 **Fax:** 01277-367099
**Web:** www.selcia.com
**Reg No:** 4172701 **Estd:** 1901 Private Limited Company
**Line of Business:** Research institutions and organisations
**Export Sales:** £5,735,390
**Trading Style:** Selcia Ltd
**Issued Capital:** £160,500
**Principals:** H G Fliri (Managing), P L Hurley, C Cornell, Dr A Rummelt
**Co. Secretary:** Kerry Williams

**Responsibilities**
**Senior:** Carol Austin (Senior Manager), Dave Roberts (Business Development Director)
**Marketing:** Dave Roberts (Business Development Director)
**Sales:** Dave Roberts (Business Development Director)
**HR:** Liz King (Human Resources Manager)
**US SIC:** 7391 **UK SIC:** 94000
**Auditors:** Deloitte & Touche LLP
**Bankers:** HSBC Bank plc (40-06-15)

| | 31-12-13 | 31-12-12 | 31-12-11 |
|---|---|---|---|
| TO | 8,178,686 | 8,243,371 | 8,031,153 |
| P/L | 84,806 | (54,053) | 393,632 |
| NW | 3,741,596 | 3,619,638 | 3,690,691 |
| WC | 2,951,267 | 2,645,146 | 2,529,675 |
| Emp. | 73 | 79 | 77 |

DUNS 64-118-5400
## Selclene (Docklands) Ltd
14-18 Forest Road, Loughton, Essex IG10 1DX
**Tel:** 020-8262-5878
**Web:** www.eastlondoncleaning.co.uk
**Reg No:** 4118630 **Estd:** 2000 Private Limited Company
**Line of Business:** Cleaning activities not elsewhere classified
**Issued Capital:** £100
**Director:** F W Donnellan
**Co. Secretary:** Majella Donnellan
**US SIC:** 7349, 8999
**UK SIC:** 92300, 83954

| | 30-11-13 | 30-11-12 | 30-11-11 |
|---|---|---|---|
| TA | 8,592 | 10,159 | 12,180 |
| NW | 1,877 | 1,010 | 780 |
| WC | 1,737 | 823 | 532 |

DUNS 39-741-6751
## Selco Trade Centres Ltd
**(Subsidiary of:** Grafton Group (Uk) Plc)
Boundary House, Birmingham, West Midlands B47 6LW
**Tel:** 01564821000 **Fax:** 0121-415-7294
**Web:** www.selcobw.com
**Reg No:** 2182671 **VAT No:** 110412150
**Estd:** 1987 Private Limited Company
**Line of Business:** Other wholesale
**Trading Style:** Selco Builders Merchants
**Issued Capital:** £160,000
**Directors:** G Slark, C A Rinn, R D Brewill, D L Arnold, C S Cunliffe
**Co. Secretary:**
Grafton Group Secretarial Servic
**Responsibilities**
**Senior:** Malcolm Aldridge (Manager), Matthew Keith (Manager)
**Marketing:** Simon Humpage (Sales & Marketing Manager)
**Sales:** Simon Humpage (Sales & Marketing Manager)
**Branches:** Selco Trade Centres Ltd, 292 Wharfdale Road, Birmingham, West Midlands B11 2DT
**US SIC:** 5199 **UK SIC:** 61900
**Auditors:** KPMG LLP
**Bankers:** National Westminster Bank Plc (52-21-10)

| | 31-12-13 | 31-12-12 | 31-12-11 |
|---|---|---|---|
| TO | 261,622,000 | 230,299,000 | 207,434,000 |
| P/L | 25,051,000 | 21,142,000 | 17,886,000 |
| NW | 50,605,000 | 46,801,000 | 44,089,000 |
| WC | 20,589,000 | 16,306,000 | 13,840,000 |
| Emp. | 1,595 | 1,514 | 1,432 |

DUNS 21-720-5699 **Imp-Exp**
## Selden Masts Ltd
**(Subsidiary of:** Furlex International Ab)
Lederle Lane, Lee-On-The-Solent, Hampshire PO13 0FZ
**Tel:** 01329504000 **Fax:** 01329-504049
**Web:** www.seldenmast.co.uk
**Reg No:** 0952439 **VAT No:** 188268220
**Estd:** 1969 Private Limited Company
**Line of Business:** Yacht masts and spars
**Trading Style:** Selden Masts
**Issued Capital:** £42,000
**Principals:** P Ronnback (Chairman), A Mccormack
**Co. Secretary:** Stephen Norbury
**Responsibilities**
**Purchasing:** Sofia Reis (Purchasing Manager)
**US SIC:** 3799 **UK SIC:** 36502
**Auditors:** BDO Stoy Hayward
**Bankers:** Barclays Bank Plc (20-79-25)

| | 31-12-13 | 31-12-12 | 31-12-11 |
|---|---|---|---|
| TA | 6,406,247 | 6,033,407 | 6,402,798 |
| NW | 3,124,935 | 3,024,302 | 2,898,042 |
| WC | (703,782) | 675,446 | 605,093 |

DUNS 21-910-4841 **Imp-Exp**
## Selden Research Ltd
Staden Business Park, Buxton, Derbyshire SK17 9RZ
**Tel:** 0129826226 **Fax:** 01298-26540
**Web:** www.selden.co.uk
**Reg No:** 0984285 **VAT No:** 157511665
**Estd:** 1967 Private Limited Company

**Line of Business:** Manufacturers of chemicals
**Export Markets:** Meddle East; Far East; Europe
**Issued Capital:** £12,000
**Principals:** D E Woodhead (Managing), M A Woodhead, D A Woodhead, P P Woodhead
**Co. Secretary:** Ms Sandra Woodhead
**Responsibilities**
**IT:** Graeme Overton (Computer Manager)
**HR:** Yvonne Watson (Human Resources Manager)
**Health & Safety:** Mike Cartwright (Works Chemist)
**Operations:** Mike Cartwright (Works Chemist)
**Purchasing:** Mike Cartwright (Works Chemist), Toni Cox (Purchasing Administrator)
**Engineering:** Andy Pleavin (Engineering Manager)
**US SIC:** 2899 **UK SIC:** 25670
**Auditors:** Hallidays
**Bankers:** The Royal Bank Of Scotland Plc (16-00-01)

| | 31-03-14 | 31-03-13 | 31-03-12 |
|---|---|---|---|
| TO | 24,647,824 | 20,771,841 | 17,440,292 |
| P/L | 1,056,496 | (672,119) | 331,281 |
| NW | 4,647,129 | 2,469,813 | 7,339,728 |
| WC | 2,194,374 | 1,300,753 | 1,887,471 |
| Emp. | 158 | 144 | 118 |

DUNS 21-412-0224
## Seldons
15 The Quay, Bideford, Devon EX39 2EZ
**Tel:** 01237477997
**Web:** www.seldons-solicitors.co.uk
**Estd:** 2010 Proprietorship
**Line of Business:** Estate agents
**Proprietor:** Ms C Marsh
**Responsibilities**
**Senior:** David Dark (Manager)
**US SIC:** 8111 **UK SIC:** 83500
**Employees:** 50

DUNS 21-772-5374
## Sele Medical Practice
Hexham General Hospital, Hexham, Northumberland NE46 1QJ
**Tel:** 01434602237
**Web:** www.selemedicalpractice.co.uk
**Estd:** 2012 Proprietorship
**Line of Business:** Cosmetic surgery
**Proprietor:** Mrs A Brooks
**US SIC:** 8011 **UK SIC:** 95300
**Employees:** 50

DUNS 21-846-8751
## The Sele School
Welwyn Road, Hertford, Hertfordshire SG14 2DG
**Tel:** 01992581455
**Web:** www.sele.herts.sch.uk
**Reg No:** 8124615 **Estd:** 2012 Private Company Limited By Guarantee
**Line of Business:** General secondary education
**Directors:** Ms S A Bruton, Mrs S L Beytell, Mrs P A Moore, Miss M A Cooke, D J Futter, P J Pickard, Mrs S A Blore, N J Binder
**Responsibilities**
**Senior:** Peter Beattie (Director), Alan Cohen (Director), Julia Hays-Bateson (Director), Hilary Warne (Director), Bruce White (Director)
**US SIC:** 8211 **UK SIC:** 93200

| | 31-08-14 | 31-08-13 |
|---|---|---|
| TO | 3,754,969 | 13,548,413 |
| P/L | (150,211) | 9,197,042 |
| NW | 8,943,831 | 9,208,042 |
| WC | 947,673 | 852,919 |
| Emp. | 67 | 62 |

DUNS 21-678-8970
## Select Calls Ltd
Lakeview West, Galleon Boulevard, Dartford, Kent DA2 6QE
**Tel:** 08447792251
**Web:** www.true-telecom.com
**Reg No:** 7298032 **Estd:** 2010 Private Limited Company
**Line of Business:** Telecom services
**Issued Capital:** £1
**Director:** M A Baines
**US SIC:** 7399 **UK SIC:** 83954
**Employees:** 50

DUNS 34-582-6796
## Select Engineering Ltd
**(Subsidiary of:** Drivefields Ltd)
1st Floor, Broadway House, 1-7 The Broadway, Wickford, Essex SS11 7AD
**Tel:** 01245403560 **Fax:** 01268-573111
**Web:** www.select-engineering.net
**Reg No:** 2729801 **Estd:** 2005 Private Limited Company
**Line of Business:** Employment and recruitment companies and consultants

**Trading Style:** Select Employment
**Issued Capital:** £100
**Managing Director:** Mrs D L Foster
**Co. Secretary:** Clive Foster
**Responsibilities**
**Senior:** Laura Hobson (Manager)
**US SIC:** 7361 **UK SIC:** 83954
**Auditors:** Kenneth Tointon Associates Ltd
**Bankers:** HSBC Bank plc (40-13-22)

| | 31-12-13 | 31-12-12 | 31-12-11 |
|---|---|---|---|
| TA | 3,382,109 | 1,762,357 | 1,453,146 |
| NW | 1,687,155 | 756,411 | 417,954 |
| WC | 1,655,067 | 748,962 | 389,577 |

DUNS 77-522-1609
## Select Enterprises (South East) Ltd
**(Subsidiary of:** Select Enterprises (Holdings) Ltd)
28 Lewis Grove, London SE13 6BG
**Fax:** 02089838099
**Web:** www.seenterprise.co.uk
**Reg No:** 2988507 **Estd:** 1994 Private Limited Company
**Line of Business:** Primary education
**Trading Style:** See
**Issued Capital:** £25,000
**Directors:** S S Kalsi, S S Kalsi
**Co. Secretary:** Balvinder Kalsi
**US SIC:** 8211 **UK SIC:** 93200
**Auditors:** Bennett & Co

| | 31-01-14 | 31-01-13 | 31-01-12 |
|---|---|---|---|
| TO | 6,398,128 | 5,898,255 | 5,306,765 |
| P/L | 488,448 | 531,392 | 458,464 |
| NW | 2,804,506 | 2,658,169 | 2,506,383 |
| WC | 2,035,506 | 2,732,640 | 2,716,513 |
| Emp. | 245 | 230 | 205 |

DUNS 21-028-4417
## Select Facilities Management
Unit 12-13, Newton Road The Brunel Centre, Crawley, West Sussex RH10 9TU
**Tel:** 02077388444
**Web:** www.select-fs.com
**Estd:** 1991
**Line of Business:** Business and management consultancy activities not elsewhere classified
**US SIC:** 7392 **UK SIC:** 83951
**Employees:** 123

DUNS 50-559-6080
## Select Gaming Ltd
Unit 5-6 Motorway Industrial Estate, Forstal Road, Aylesford, Kent ME20 7AF
**Tel:** 08456426464
**Web:** www.selectgaming.com
**Reg No:** 2510846 **VAT No:** 573547809
**Estd:** 1990 Private Limited Company
**Line of Business:** Amusement and gaming machines
**Issued Capital:** £68,453
**Principals:** J S Oversby-Powell (Managing), P R Gordon, A G Oversby Powell, J Oversby Powell
**Co. Secretary:** Ms Sally Oversby-Powell
**US SIC:** 3944 **UK SIC:** 49410
**Auditors:** Dendy Neville
**Bankers:** National Westminster Bank Plc (60-50-06)

| | 30-11-13 | 30-11-12 | 30-11-11 |
|---|---|---|---|
| TO | 7,880,195 | 8,385,825 | N/A |
| P/L | 172,975 | 264,219 | N/A |
| NW | 483,140 | 544,058 | 699,802 |
| WC | (1,912,443) | (1,451,032) | (1,055,464) |
| Emp. | 137 | 136 | N/A |

DUNS 29-088-9377 **Imp-Exp**
## Select Hardware Ltd
Station Road, Rowley Regis, West Midlands B65 0LJ
**Tel:** 0121-561-6070 **Fax:** 0121-561-6080
**Web:** www.selecthardware.com
**Reg No:** 1418418 **Estd:** 1979 Private Limited Company
**Line of Business:** Builders merchants
**Export Markets:** E U
**Export Sales:** £1,044,483
**Trading Style:** Map Hardware
**Issued Capital:** £2,303,388
**Directors:** T W Blashill, N S Mcwalter, B E Hanaway
**Co. Secretary:** Raymond Birkin
**US SIC:** 5072 **UK SIC:** 61500
**Auditors:** RSM Tenon Audit Ltd
**Bankers:** National Westminster Bank Plc (60-04-30)

| | 31-12-13 | 31-12-12 | 31-12-11 |
|---|---|---|---|
| TO | 7,472,388 | 7,991,993 | 6,620,146 |
| P/L | 589,963 | 377,982 | 146,264 |
| NW | 6,123,642 | 6,480,956 | 6,140,414 |
| WC | 4,189,819 | 4,515,553 | 4,115,733 |
| Emp. | 47 | 46 | 66 |

DUNS 34-926-6440
## Select Health Care (2006) Ltd
(**Subsidiary of:** Select Healthcare (South) Ltd)
32 Victoria Street, Brierley Hill, West Midlands DY5 1RD
**Tel:** 01843831667 **Fax:** 01843-836152
**Web:** www.selecthealthcare.co.uk
**Reg No:** 5723335 **Estd:** 2006 Private Limited Company
**Line of Business:** Other human health activities
**Issued Capital:** £1
**Directors:** B R Bernard, P M Cooke
**Responsibilities**
**Senior:** Pauline Jones *(Manager)*
**US SIC:** 8091, 6732
**UK SIC:** 95200, 83100

| | 31-03-14 | 31-03-13 | 31-03-12 |
|---|---|---|---|
| TO | 9,384,600 | 9,788,292 | 9,204,381 |
| P/L | 1,037,181 | 970,806 | (281,113) |
| NW | (257,583) | (1,134,639) | (1,864,824) |
| WC | (362,386) | (859,648) | 1,435,166 |
| Emp. | 416 | 584 | 582 |

DUNS 29-647-1444 Imp
## Select Plant Hire Co Ltd
(**Subsidiary of:** Suffolk Partners Corporation)
Bridge Place 1-2, Anchor Boulevard, Crossways Business Park, Dartford, Kent DA2 6SN
**Tel:** 01322-296990 **Fax:** 01375-392087
**Web:** www.laingorourke.com
**Reg No:** 1973463 **VAT No:** 549347706
**Estd:** 1985 Private Limited Company
**Line of Business:** Plant and tool hire
**Issued Capital:** £100
**Directors:** P Mcnerney, H D O'Rourke, C M Tuckett
**Co. Secretary:** Mrs Teresa Styant
**Responsibilities**
**Senior:** Stephen Hollingshead *(Chief Executive Officer)*, Philip Wainwright *(Manager)*
**Branches:** Select Plant Hire Co Ltd, Salcey Forest Depot, Quinton Rd, Northampton, Northamptonshire NN7 2HX
**US SIC:** 7394 **UK SIC:** 84000
**Auditors:** PricewaterhouseCoopers LLP
**Bankers:** Barclays Bank Plc (20-65-82)

| | 31-03-14 | 31-03-13 | 31-03-12 |
|---|---|---|---|
| TO | 194,835,000 | 184,219,000 | 180,070,000 |
| P/L | 11,152,000 | 12,847,000 | 5,379,000 |
| NW | 113,607,000 | 104,252,000 | 94,889,000 |
| WC | 44,904,000 | 30,931,000 | 26,766,000 |

DUNS 21-630-7272
## Select Service Partner Retail Catering Ltd
(**Subsidiary of:** S S P Group Plc)
The Heights, Brooklands, Weybridge, Surrey KT13 0NY
**Fax:** 01932-792480
**Web:** www.monart.ie
**Reg No:** 0623378 **Estd:** 1959 Private Limited Company
**Line of Business:** Eating places
**Issued Capital:** £1,000
**Directors:** M E Collins, L L Tait, J O Davies, J D Brook, M Rainbow
**Co. Secretary:** Mrs Helen Byrne
**Branches:** Select Service Partner Retail Catering Ltd, Fantasy Island, Sea La, Ingoldmells, Skegness, Lincolnshire PE25 1RH
**US SIC:** 5812 **UK SIC:** 66110

| | 25-09-13 | 26-09-12 | 28-09-11 |
|---|---|---|---|
| TA | 158,332 | 158,332 | 158,332 |
| NW | 158,332 | 158,332 | 158,332 |

DUNS 21-583-4051
## Select Services Partners
Diamond House, Birmingham Airport, Birmingham, West Midlands B26 3QJ
**Tel:** 01217677942
**Estd:** 2011 Proprietorship
**Line of Business:** Advertising activities not elsewhere classified
**Proprietor:** Miss S Price
**US SIC:** 7319 **UK SIC:** 83800
**Employees:** 150

DUNS 76-897-7449
## Select Windows (Home Improvements) Ltd
(**Subsidiary of:** Select Group Holdings Ltd)
Select House, Walsall Road, Walsall Wood, Walsall, West Midlands WS9 9AQ
**Tel:** 01543-370666
**Web:** www.selectwindows.co.uk
**Reg No:** 2616087 **VAT No:** 346812252
**Estd:** 1980 Private Limited Company
**Line of Business:** Manufacture of other plastic products
**Issued Capital:** £1,000
**Principals:** J S Wood *(Managing)*, G R Wylde, A V Wood
**Responsibilities**
**Senior:** Nigel Court *(General Manager)*
**Health & Safety:** Nigel Court *(General Manager)*
**Facilities:** Nigel Court *(General Manager)*
**Branches:** Select Windows (Home Improvements) Ltd, 28 Goosemoor La, Birmingham, West Midlands B23 5PN
**US SIC:** 3079, 1796
**UK SIC:** 48360, 50400
**Auditors:** Nicklin LLP
**Bankers:** Barclays Bank Plc (20-90-08)

| | 31-12-13 | 30-11-12 | 30-12-11 |
|---|---|---|---|
| TA | 1,408,575 | 1,635,225 | 1,310,467 |
| NW | 222,365 | 174,194 | 166,719 |
| WC | 121,892 | 68,949 | 37,859 |

DUNS 28-952-9430 Imp-Exp
## Selecta Systems Ltd
(**Subsidiary of:** Select Profiles Ltd)
Selecta House, Winster Grove Industrial Estate, Birmingham, West Midlands B44 9EG
**Tel:** 01213-252100 **Fax:** 01213666360
**Web:** www.selectasystems.com
**Reg No:** 1638655 **VAT No:** 370095266
**Estd:** 1982 Private Limited Company
**Line of Business:** Manufacturers and suppliers of pvc based products
**Export Markets:** Eire, Germany & France
**Export Sales:** £239,378
**Trading Style:** Selecta Extruders, Selecta Profiles
**Issued Capital:** £5,000
**Director:** M Weihe
**Responsibilities**
**Finance:** Maria Lawrence *(Accounts Manager)*
**HR:** Jane Bushell *(Personnel Manager)*
**Operations:** Dean Taylor *(Operations Director)*
**US SIC:** 3079 **UK SIC:** 48360
**Auditors:** Burrows Scarborough Silk Ltd
**Bankers:** National Westminster Bank Plc (60-22-22)

| | 31-12-13 | 31-12-12 | 31-12-11 |
|---|---|---|---|
| TO | 12,892,184 | 12,217,363 | 12,836,953 |
| P/L | 149,367 | 8,869 | (297,970) |
| NW | 3,697,831 | 3,615,362 | 3,602,896 |
| WC | 3,420,125 | 3,261,153 | 3,196,955 |
| Emp. | 114 | 112 | 105 |

DUNS 21-913-7023
## Selecta Tyre Ltd
117 Montagu Street, Kettering, Northamptonshire NN16 8XJ
**Tel:** 01536520450 **Fax:** 01536511830
**Web:** www.selectatyre.co.uk
**Reg No:** 1093373 **Estd:** 1973 Private Limited Company
**Line of Business:** Tyre dealers
**Issued Capital:** £3,600
**Principals:** Captain S J Pashley *(Managing)*, R Knight, N D Henshall, Ms F J Pashley, D P Rees
**Co. Secretary:** Ms Fiona Pashley
**Responsibilities**
**Senior:** Richard Aridegbe *(Site Manager)*, Ellis Barnett *(Site Manager)*, Philip Tyrer *(Manager)*
**Branches:** Selecta Tyre Ltd, New Row, Grantham, Lincolnshire NG31 8HJ
**US SIC:** 5531 **UK SIC:** 65100
**Auditors:** J R Antoine & Partners
**Bankers:** Lloyds TSB Bank plc (30-94-68)

| | 31-12-13 | 31-12-12 | 31-12-11 |
|---|---|---|---|
| TO | 8,285,692 | 8,588,917 | 8,235,638 |
| P/L | 479,212 | 450,933 | 405,894 |
| NW | 4,184,377 | 3,908,361 | 4,061,209 |
| WC | 933,071 | 828,838 | 598,253 |
| Emp. | 89 | 91 | 86 |

DUNS 22-700-0601 Imp
## Selecta Uk Ltd
(**Subsidiary of:** Acp Vermögensverwaltung Gmbh & Co. Kg Nr. 4 D)
1st Floor, Spinnaker House, Basingstoke, Hampshire RG24 8GG
**Tel:** 01256340600
**Web:** www.selecta.com
**Reg No:** 0157122 **VAT No:** 244522871
**Estd:** 1919 Private Limited Company
**Line of Business:** Other non-store retail sale
**Issued Capital:** £31,180,000
**Directors:** D G Jones, C A Stevenson, G Hughes
**Responsibilities**
**Senior:** Andrew Mee *(Manager)*, Martin Schwab *(Manager)*
**Marketing:** Dina Soliman *(Sales & Marketing Manager)*
**Sales:** Dina Soliman *(Sales & Marketing Manager)*
**Operations:** David Birtwistle *(Business Services UK Operation)*
**Branches:** Selecta Uk Ltd, 28 Duncrue Road, Belfast, Belfast BT3 9BP
**US SIC:** 5963, 7394
**UK SIC:** 65600, 84000
**Auditors:** KPMG LLP
**Bankers:** National Westminster Bank Plc (56-00-27)

| | 30-09-13 | 30-09-12 | 30-09-11 |
|---|---|---|---|
| TO | 63,823,000 | 75,868,000 | 81,836,000 |
| P/L | (13,414,000) | (6,985,000) | (6,731,000) |
| NW | 18,029,000 | (9,107,000) | (2,172,000) |
| WC | 4,055,000 | (28,837,000) | (25,904,000) |
| Emp. | 816 | 1,016 | 1,078 |

DUNS 21-735-5171 Imp-Exp
## Selectaglaze Ltd
(**Subsidiary of:** Albansky Holdings Ltd)
Alban Park, Hatfield Road, St Albans, Hertfordshire AL4 0JJ
**Tel:** 01727837271 **Fax:** 01727-844053
**Web:** www.selectaglaze.co.uk
**Reg No:** 0879879 **VAT No:** 197447416
**Estd:** 1966 Private Limited Company
**Line of Business:** Double glazing installers
**Export Markets:** Republic of Ireland
**Issued Capital:** £1,000
**Principals:** M M Childerstone *(Managing)*, Ms K Childerstone, C M Bignell, K A Mercer
**Co. Secretary:** Patrick Donovan
**Responsibilities**
**Senior:** Brian Steventon *(Sales Director)*
**Sales:** Brian Steventon *(Sales Director)*
**HR:** Michelle Bolino *(Human Resources Manager)*
**Health & Safety:** Gail Newman *(PA to Managing Director)*
**US SIC:** 1721, 1751
**UK SIC:** 50400
**Auditors:** The KBSP Partnership
**Bankers:** Barclays Bank Plc (20-53-30)

| | 31-12-13 | 31-12-12 | 31-12-11 |
|---|---|---|---|
| TO | 7,139,507 | 7,819,805 | 6,838,465 |
| P/L | (1,509,630) | 900,252 | 801,643 |
| NW | 2,412,023 | 4,211,065 | 3,681,943 |
| WC | 1,947,786 | 1,519,526 | 952,513 |
| Emp. | 92 | 86 | 77 |

DUNS 34-624-8859
## Selection Services Ltd
(**Subsidiary of:** Selection Services Investments Ltd)
Provident House, 122 High Street, Bromley, Kent BR1 1EZ
**Tel:** 08448-741-000 **Fax:** 08448-741-001
**Web:** www.selection.co.uk
**Reg No:** 2758710 **VAT No:** 608048548
**Estd:** 1988 Private Limited Company
**Line of Business:** Other software consultancy and supply
**Issued Capital:** £5
**Principals:** G Harrington *(Managing)*, P Clark, P A Offord, J M Rowbotham, M J Woodall
**Co. Secretary:** Mark Woodall
**Branches:** Selection Services Ltd, Provident House, 122 High Street, Bromley, Kent BR1 1EZ
**US SIC:** 7374, 7379, 7399
**UK SIC:** 83940, 83954
**Auditors:** BDO LLP
**Bankers:** Barclays Bank Plc (20-32-29)

| | 30-06-13 | 30-06-12 | 30-06-11 |
|---|---|---|---|
| TO | 31,376,107 | 27,559,555 | 23,561,589 |
| P/L | 229,491 | 2,058,418 | 1,613,735 |
| NW | 685,668 | 3,565,498 | 1,228,794 |
| WC | 462,858 | 2,673,229 | 638,388 |
| Emp. | 379 | 364 | 325 |

DUNS 53-638-8853
## Selection Services Supportnet Ltd
(**Subsidiary of:** Selection Services Investments Ltd)
Forester House, 2 Cromwell Avenue, Keston, Kent BR2 9BF
**Tel:** 0870-163-9000 **Fax:** 0870-163-9001
**Web:** www.selection.co.uk
**Reg No:** 3444455 **Estd:** 1997 Private Limited Company
**Line of Business:** Data processing
**Issued Capital:** £2
**Directors:** G Harrington, M J Woodall
**Co. Secretary:** Mark Woodall
**US SIC:** 7374 **UK SIC:** 83940
**Auditors:** BDO Stoy Hayward

| | 30-06-14 | 30-06-13 | 30-06-12 |
|---|---|---|---|
| TA | 2 | 2 | 2 |
| NW | 2 | 2 | 2 |

DUNS 21-932-4902 Imp-Exp
## Selective Marketplace Ltd
Belton Road West, Loughborough, Leicestershire LE11 5XL
**Tel:** 01509638600
**Web:** www.selective.co.uk
**Reg No:** 1566688 **VAT No:** 355300482
**Estd:** 1958 Private Limited Company
**Line of Business:** Mail order houses
**Export Markets:** Australia, New Zealand
**Export Sales:** £15,092,443
**Issued Capital:** £800,000
**Principals:** J C Dashper *(Managing)*, L Dashper, Ms J E Dashper
**Co. Secretary:** John Dashper
**Responsibilities**
**Senior:** Hannah Dashper *(General Manager)*
**IT:** Anita Clarke *(It Manager)*
**Branches:** Selective Marketplace Ltd, 126-128 New Kings Road, London SW6 4LZ
**US SIC:** 5961 **UK SIC:** 65600
**Auditors:** T.J. Killick & Co
**Bankers:** Lloyds TSB Bank plc (30-95-21)

| | 31-12-13 | 31-12-12 | 31-12-11 |
|---|---|---|---|
| TO | 30,706,021 | 31,489,086 | 33,851,193 |
| P/L | (566,673) | 2,249,262 | 780,128 |
| NW | 4,554,966 | 4,948,495 | 3,249,599 |
| WC | 4,324,622 | 4,739,721 | 3,057,606 |
| Emp. | 111 | 141 | 143 |

DUNS 50-571-5425
## Selex Es Infrared Ltd
(**Subsidiary of:** Finmeccanica Spa)
Millbrook Industrial Estate, Southampton, Hampshire SO15 0LG
**Tel:** 02380702300
**Web:** www.selexgalileo.com
**Reg No:** 2519499 **Estd:** 1993 Private Limited Company
**Line of Business:** Military equipment dealers
**Issued Capital:** £2
**Directors:** D Mackinnon, G F Munday
**Responsibilities**
**Senior:** Jeremy Crouch *(Manager)*, Stewart Miller *(Vice President)*
**Marketing:** David Bishton *(Marketing Manager)*
**Sales:** David Bishton *(Marketing Manager)*
**HR:** Pippa McMurray *(Human Resources Manager)*
**US SIC:** 5999, 3629
**UK SIC:** 65600, 34350

| | 31-12-13 | 31-12-12 | 31-12-11 |
|---|---|---|---|
| TA | 2 | 2 | 2 |
| NW | 2 | 2 | 2 |

DUNS 50-438-1468 Exp
## Selex Es Ltd
(**Subsidiary of:** Finmeccanica Spa)
Sigma House, Christopher Martin Road, Basildon, Essex SS14 3EL
**Tel:** 01268522822
**Web:** www.selex-es.com
**Reg No:** 2426132 **VAT No:** 849774658
**Estd:** 1950 Private Limited Company
**Line of Business:** Defence activities
**Export Sales:** £398,381,000
**Issued Capital:** £270,000,100
**Directors:** N J Bone, F Giulianini, G F Munday
**Co. Secretary:** Federico Bonaiuto
**Responsibilities**
**Senior:** Colin Musgrave *(Manager)*, Remo Pertica *(Chairman)*
**Finance:** David MacKinnon *(Accountant)*
**Marketing:** Penny McPherson *(?Head of Marketing Communicati)*
**Health & Safety:** Steve Wilcox *(Health & Safety Executive)*
**Operations:** Mike McPartlin *(Project Manager)*, A Poynter *(Purchasing Manager)*
**Purchasing:** A Poynter *(Purchasing Manager)*
**Branches:** Selex Es Ltd, First Avenue, Southampton, Hampshire SO15 0LG
**US SIC:** 9711, 5065
**UK SIC:** 65600, 34350
**Auditors:** KPMG LLP
**Following financial data are in thousands**

| | 31-12-13 | 31-12-12 | 31-12-11 |
|---|---|---|---|
| TO | 910,572 | 910,277 | 1,001,292 |
| P/L | 61,169 | 100,193 | 90,598 |
| NW | 259,287 | 301,169 | 282,354 |
| WC | (85,958) | 144,105 | 124,117 |
| Emp. | 4,521 | 3,801 | 3,909 |

DUNS 67-206-0022
## Self Help Services Ltd
339 Stretford Road, Manchester M15 4ZY
**Tel:** 01612263871 **Fax:** 01612261096
**Web:** www.selfhelpservices.org.uk
**Reg No:** 6036050 **Estd:** 2008 Private Company Limited By Guarantee
**Line of Business:** Social work activities without accommodation
**Directors:** Mrs E J Robinson, P Ferry, Ms F L Selvan, Ms A Young
**Co. Secretary:** Mark Fitzgibbon
**Responsibilities**
**Senior:** Nicky Alidbetter *(Chief Officer)*
**US SIC:** 8321 **UK SIC:** 96111
**Bankers:** The Royal Bank Of Scotland Plc (16-10-80)

| | 31-03-14 | 31-03-13 | 31-03-12 |
|---|---|---|---|
| TO | 2,834,950 | 2,337,968 | 1,740,280 |
| P/L | 145,548 | 168,804 | 122,188 |
| NW | 826,334 | 680,786 | 511,982 |
| WC | 824,712 | 678,623 | 509,098 |
| Emp. | 95 | 78 | 54 |

DUNS 21-605-5613
## Self Unlimited
Furlong Close, Rowde, Devizes, Wiltshire SN10 2TQ
**Tel:** 01380725455
**Web:** www.care-ltd.co.uk
**Estd:** 1994
**Line of Business:** Charities and charitable organisations
**Proprietor:** Mrs S Peskett
**US SIC:** 8321 **UK SIC:** 96111
**Employees:** 50

DUNS 73-459-5759
## Selfridges Holdings Ltd
(**Subsidiary of:** Roundwood Holdings Limited)
400 Oxford Street, London W1A 1AB
**Tel:** 01133698040 **Fax:** 02073182331
**Web:** www.selfridges.com
**Reg No:** 4723822 **Estd:** 2003 Private Limited Company
**Line of Business:** Departmental stores
**Issued Capital:** £225,000,001
**Directors:** P G Kelly, A Batty, J A Skelton, Ms K L Nurse
**Co. Secretary:** Ms Sarah Hemsley
**Responsibilities**
**Senior:** Alec Latimer *(Manager)*, Meave Wall *(Store Manager)*
**US SIC:** 6711, 5399
**UK SIC:** 83062, 65600
**Auditors:** PricewaterhouseCoopers LLP

| | 01-02-14 | 02-02-13 | 28-02-12 |
|---|---|---|---|
| TO | 530,000,000 | 487,500,000 | 464,800,000 |
| P/L | 89,200,000 | 73,500,000 | 80,500,000 |
| NW | 270,100,000 | 248,500,000 | 264,000,000 |
| WC | 130,200,000 | 135,700,000 | 143,700,000 |
| Emp. | 2,392 | 2,285 | 2,304 |

DUNS 21-128-2727 Imp-Exp
## Selig Uk Ltd
635-639 Ajax Avenue, Slough, Berkshire SL1 4BH
**Tel:** 01753773154 **Fax:** 01753 773111
**Web:** www.seligsealing.com
**Reg No:** 6628891 **VAT No:** 936120444
**Estd:** 1889 Private Limited Company
**Line of Business:** Manufacture of other plastic products
**Export Sales:** £11,629,000
**Issued Capital:** £37,602,001
**Directors:** G R Lu, P Schellinger, S D Goffin, S Cassidy
**Co. Secretary:** Simon Goffin
**Responsibilities**
**Senior:** Andrew McLean *(Executive Vice President)*, Alex Meeuwissen *(Warehouse Manager)*
**Engineering:** Warren Thornhill *(Operations Director)*
**US SIC:** 3559 **UK SIC:** 32863
**Auditors:** Grant Thornton UK LLP
**Bankers:** The Chase Manhattan Bank (60-92-42)

| | 31-10-13 | 31-10-12 | 31-10-11 |
|---|---|---|---|
| TO | 21,889,000 | 20,533,000 | 24,321,000 |
| P/L | (12,079,000) | (5,470,000) | (7,504,000) |
| NW | 14,797,000 | 7,764,000 | 5,544,000 |
| WC | 13,393,000 | 4,221,000 | 4,539,000 |
| Emp. | 108 | 103 | 98 |

DUNS 28-981-2141 Exp
## Selima Ltd
(**Subsidiary of:** Selima Holding Co Ltd)
Unit 7, Signet House, Europa View, Sheffield, South Yorkshire S9 1XH
**Tel:** 01618208240
**Web:** www.selima.co.uk
**Reg No:** 1780317 **VAT No:** 390976408
**Estd:** 1983 Private Limited Company
**Line of Business:** Computer software (development)
**Issued Capital:** £100
**Directors:** Ms J Mercer, M Parry, W J Blakemore
**Co. Secretary:** Wayne Blakemore
**US SIC:** 7379 **UK SIC:** 83940
**Bankers:** National Westminster Bank Plc (56-00-09)

| | 31-12-13 | 31-12-12 | 31-12-11 |
|---|---|---|---|
| TA | 2,248,624 | 2,061,091 | 1,912,049 |
| NW | 1,132,204 | 955,134 | 599,598 |
| WC | 1,104,216 | 915,555 | 552,638 |

DUNS 77-972-1104
## Sella Ltd
Unit 3, Ashby-De-La-Zouch, Leicestershire LE65 2AB
**Tel:** 01614-294500
**Web:** www.hima-sella.co.uk
**Reg No:** 5940692 **Estd:** 2006 Private Limited Company
**Line of Business:** Other manufacturing not elsewhere classified
**Export Sales:** £801,406
**Trading Style:** Hema Sella Ltd
**Issued Capital:** £480,000

**Directors:** I F Wright, E A Turnock, P T Garland
**Co. Secretary:** John Blackwell
**Responsibilities**
**Senior:** Nigel Banner *(Manager)*, Emma Warburton *(Manager)*
**Sales:** Iain Wilkinson *(Business Development Manager)*
**Admin:** Julie Cheadle *(Office Manager)*
**Health & Safety:** Steve Ashton *(Safety Engineer)*, Stuart Blackhall *(Safety, Quality and Environmen)*
**Engineering:** Steve Ashton *(Safety Engineer)*, Tim Marsden *(Principal Engineer)*, Carl Toft *(Principal Engineer)*, Andrew Yard *(Automation Engineer)*
**US SIC:** 3999, 3643
**UK SIC:** 49590, 34203
**Bankers:** The Co-Operative Bank Plc (08-90-96)

| | 31-03-14 | 31-03-13 | 31-03-12 |
|---|---|---|---|
| TO | 9,665,192 | 9,450,670 | 10,567,077 |
| P/L | 81,937 | 321,129 | 320,469 |
| NW | (2,244,482) | (2,839,473) | (3,501,156) |
| WC | (1,217,261) | (764,809) | (481,140) |
| Emp. | 100 | 99 | 96 |

DUNS 73-846-9274
## Sellars Agriculture Ltd
Meadows Industrial Estate, Station Road, Oldmeldrum, Inverurie, Aberdeenshire AB51 0EZ
**Tel:** 01651872891 **Fax:** 01651-872750
**Web:** www.sellar.co.uk
**Reg No:** 0266513SC **Estd:** 2004 Private Limited Company
**Line of Business:** Agricultural machinery sales service and repair
**Issued Capital:** £237,500
**Directors:** C E Last, N A Wattie
**Branches:** Sellars Agriculture Ltd, Sellar Agriculture, 6 West Road, Forres, Morayshire IV36 2GW
**US SIC:** 3523, 5999
**UK SIC:** 32113, 65600

| | 30-09-13 | 30-09-12 | 30-09-11 |
|---|---|---|---|
| TO | 31,884,202 | 36,235,969 | 29,322,253 |
| P/L | 396,671 | 662,956 | 692,869 |
| NW | 3,469,978 | 3,308,747 | 2,934,905 |
| WC | 3,263,317 | 3,134,420 | 2,797,239 |
| Emp. | 80 | 81 | 81 |

DUNS 73-850-2421
## Selleck Nicholls Holdings Ltd
Polhilsa, Stoke Climsland, Callington, Cornwall PL17 8PP
**Tel:** 01579-370740 **Fax:** 01579-370920
**Web:** www.sellecknicholls.com
**Reg No:** 5105338 **Estd:** 2004 Private Limited Company
**Line of Business:** Management activities of holding companies
**Issued Capital:** £2,010
**Director:** A D Selleck
**Co. Secretary:** Ms Sharon Selleck
**Responsibilities**
**Finance:** Sharon Gorman *(Financial Director)*, Rachel Mather *(Financial Director)*
**Marketing:** Sarah Parsley *(Office Manager)*
**HR:** Sarah Parsley *(Office Manager)*
**US SIC:** 6711 **UK SIC:** 83962

| | 30-09-13 | 30-09-12 | 30-09-11 |
|---|---|---|---|
| TA | 12,140 | 12,030 | 12,030 |
| NW | 12,140 | 12,030 | 12,030 |

DUNS 45-883-6525
## Sellerdeck Ltd
(**Subsidiary of:** Private Software Ltd)
Globe House, Lavender Park Road, West Byfleet, Surrey KT14 6ND
**Tel:** 08451294888 **Fax:** 01932358341
**Web:** www.actinic.co.uk
**Reg No:** 3221222 **Estd:** 1996 Private Limited Company
**Line of Business:** Miscellaneous computer services
**Trading Style:** Sellerdeck
**Issued Capital:** £330
**Directors:** P H Rothwell, C L Bray
**Co. Secretary:** Paul Lawrence
**Responsibilities**
**Senior:** Chris Barley *(Manager)*, Kevin Grumball *(Manager)*
**US SIC:** 7379, 7374
**UK SIC:** 83940
**Auditors:** BDO Stoy Hayward
**Bankers:** Barclays Bank Plc (20-65-18)

| | 30-09-13 | 30-09-12 | 30-09-11 |
|---|---|---|---|
| TO | N/A | N/A | 1,887,000 |
| P/L | N/A | N/A | 801,000 |
| NW | 93,000 | 183,000 | 232,000 |
| WC | 71,000 | 159,000 | 214,000 |
| Emp. | N/A | N/A | 30 |

DUNS 22-894-1936
## Sellers Containers
Sellers Way, Oldham, Lancashire OL9 8EY
**Tel:** 0161-681-5846
**Web:** www.sellersengineering.co.uk
**Estd:** 1977 Proprietorship

**Line of Business:** Waste disposers installation and repair
**Proprietor:** B Sellers
**Responsibilities**
**Senior:** John Beech *(Finance Director)*, Gary Birney *(Manager)*, Kathleen Sellers *(Manager)*, Alexander Sellers *(Manager)*
**Finance:** John Beech *(Finance Director)*
**IT:** Alan Kennedy *(IT Director)*
**US SIC:** 7513, 3441
**UK SIC:** 84802, 32042
**Employees:** 150

DUNS 22-137-0856
## Sellick Partnership Ltd
Queens Court, 24 Queen Street, Manchester M2 5HX
**Tel:** 0161 834 1642
**Web:** www.sellickpartnership.co.uk
**Reg No:** 4156002 **VAT No:** 864288095
**Estd:** 2001 Private Limited Company
**Line of Business:** Other business activities not elsewhere classified
**Issued Capital:** £100
**Directors:** T J Sellick, Mrs M J Sellick, Ms H Cottam, R Wareing
**Responsibilities**
**Senior:** Peter Tootell *(Manager)*
**Branches:** Sellick Partnership Ltd, 17 Park Place, Leeds, West Yorkshire LS1 2SJ
**US SIC:** 7399 **UK SIC:** 83954
**Auditors:** Mitten Clarke Ltd
**Bankers:** Lloyds TSB Bank plc (30-95-42)

| | 28-02-14 | 28-02-13 | 29-02-12 |
|---|---|---|---|
| TO | 25,697,589 | 20,998,440 | 17,733,961 |
| P/L | 241,854 | (148,163) | (91,261) |
| NW | (242,656) | (399,479) | (287,059) |
| WC | (292,109) | (417,564) | (289,872) |
| Emp. | 544 | 470 | 385 |

DUNS 21-812-2173
## Selly Oak Local Authority
St Marys C Of E Junior & Infant School, Lodge Hill Road, Birmingham, West Midlands B29 6NU
**Tel:** 01216751729
**Web:** www.stmryb29.bham.sch.uk
**Estd:** 2012
**Line of Business:** Schools (local authority)
**Responsibilities**
**Senior:** Alisa Hathaway *(Head Teacher)*
**US SIC:** 8211 **UK SIC:** 93200
**Employees:** 50

DUNS 22-513-1085
## Selsdon Park Hotel & Golf Course
126 Addington Road, South Croydon, Surrey CR2 8YA
**Tel:** 02086578811
**Web:** www.principal-hayley.com
**VAT No:** 523665543 **Estd:** 1996 Proprietorship
**Line of Business:** Other tourist assistance activities not elsewhere classified
**Proprietor:** M Churchill
**Responsibilities**
**Senior:** Lisa Mackenzie *(Manager)*, Caroline Morrone *(General Manager)*
**HR:** Megan Darroch *(Human Resources Manager)*
**Health & Safety:** Megan Darroch *(Human Resources Manager)*
**Facilities:** Clifford South *(Maintenance Manager)*
**US SIC:** 7999 **UK SIC:** 97913
**Bankers:** Barclays Bank Plc (20-24-61)
**Employees:** 200

DUNS 21-750-8422
## Selwood Academy
Selwood Academy Berkley Road, Frome, Somerset BA11 2EF
**Web:** www.selwood.somerset.sch.uk
**Reg No:** 7814065 **Estd:** 2011 Private Company Limited By Guarantee
**Line of Business:** General secondary education
**Directors:** Mrs K A Kirkwood, N A Maxted, R Phillips, Mrs J D Hopegood, C J Bailey-Green, R O Sage, Mrs R L Clarke, Mrs M Bailey
**Co. Secretary:** Mrs Rosalind Clark
**Responsibilities**
**Senior:** Clare Cardnell *(Director)*
**US SIC:** 8211 **UK SIC:** 93200
**Bankers:** Lloyds TSB bank plc (30-93-40)

| | 31-08-14 | 31-08-13 | 31-08-12 |
|---|---|---|---|
| TO | 3,297,313 | 3,366,786 | 7,970,426 |
| P/L | (221,761) | 134,396 | 5,792,342 |
| NW | 5,391,977 | 5,662,738 | 5,578,342 |
| WC | 548,578 | 618,126 | 367,921 |
| Emp. | 67 | 66 | 66 |

DUNS 21-097-1803
## Selwood Holdings Ltd
Bournemouth Road, Chandler's Ford, Eastleigh, Hampshire SO53 3ZL
**Tel:** 02380266311
**Web:** www.selwood.co.uk
**Reg No:** 6415716 **Estd:** 2007 Private Limited Company
**Line of Business:** Plant and tool hire
**Export Sales:** £9,171,000
**Issued Capital:** £4,900,000
**Directors:** B Watson, R J Conway, C M Garrett, M Page, R J Dudman, R A Brown
**Co. Secretary:** Ian Carter
**US SIC:** 7394 **UK SIC:** 84000
**Bankers:** National Westminster Bank Plc (51-81-41)

| | 31-12-13 | 31-12-12 | 31-12-11 |
|---|---|---|---|
| TO | 56,231,000 | 55,477,000 | 45,607,000 |
| P/L | 9,858,000 | 6,901,000 | 4,142,000 |
| NW | 15,974,000 | 8,562,000 | 4,163,000 |
| WC | (3,654,000) | 3,310,000 | 3,243,000 |
| Emp. | 416 | 420 | 410 |

DUNS 22-149-5554
## Selwood Housing Society Ltd
Bradford Road Bryer Ash Business Park, Trowbridge, Wiltshire BA14 8RT
**Tel:** 01225-715715
**Web:** www.selwoodhousing.com
**Reg No:** 4168336 **Estd:** 2001 Private Limited Company
**Line of Business:** Housing associations societies trusts & co-operatives
**Directors:** J C Noeken, L S O'Bryan, R Britton, B A Cosstick, S Darvell, Mrs M A Haylock, M I Macdonald, Mrs B A Wayman
**Co. Secretary:** Ms Diane Hall
**Responsibilities**
**Senior:** Alison Christy *(Director)*, Una Davis *(Manager)*, Rod Eaton *(Manager)*, Barry Hughes *(Chief Executive)*, Scott Kinnaird *(Manager)*, James McGee *(Manager)*, Amanda Meanwell *(Director)*, Pip Ridout *(Manager)*, Anthony Roddis *(Manager)*
**Marketing:** Rebecca O'Neil *(Sales & Marketing Manager)*
**Sales:** Rebecca O'Neil *(Sales & Marketing Manager)*
**US SIC:** 8321 **UK SIC:** 96111
**Auditors:** Beever & Struthers
**Bankers:** Lloyds TSB Bank plc (30-98-75)

| | 31-03-14 | 31-03-13 | 31-03-12 |
|---|---|---|---|
| TO | 29,695,000 | 28,309,000 | 26,909,000 |
| P/L | 9,019,000 | 8,381,000 | 5,922,000 |
| NW | 49,203,000 | 39,284,000 | 32,592,000 |
| WC | (905,000) | (755,000) | (3,255,000) |
| Emp. | 127 | 120 | 144 |

DUNS 21-607-4494
## Selworthy School
Selworthy Road, Taunton, Somerset TA2 8HD
**Tel:** 01823284970
**Web:** www.selworthy.somerset.sch.uk
**Estd:** 1993
**Line of Business:** Schools (special)
**Proprietor:** Ms K Milton
**US SIC:** 8299 **UK SIC:** 93300
**Employees:** 80

DUNS 23-314-0958
## Selwyn Building Services Ltd
Tarran Road, Tarran Industrial Estate, Wirral, Merseyside CH46 4TU
**Tel:** 01516782919 **Fax:** 0151-488-5387
**Web:** www.selwyngroup.co.uk
**Reg No:** 4576697 **Estd:** 2003 Private Limited Company
**Line of Business:** Miscellaneous business services
**Issued Capital:** £200
**Principals:** B M Evans *(Managing)*, Mrs H C Davis, J G Doherty, M Roberts
**Responsibilities**
**Senior:** Nathan Daniels *(Manager)*
**US SIC:** 7399, 1711, 1799, 8911
**UK SIC:** 83954, 50300, 50000, 83701

| | 31-10-13 | 31-10-12 | 31-10-11 |
|---|---|---|---|
| TO | 8,318,915 | N/A | N/A |
| P/L | 348,492 | N/A | N/A |
| NW | 368,674 | 350,959 | 418,351 |
| WC | 278,319 | 327,522 | 410,782 |
| Emp. | 89 | N/A | N/A |

DUNS 42-454-4658
## Selwyn College Cambridge
Grange Road, Cambridge, Cambridgeshire CB3 9DQ
**Web:** www.sel.cam.ac.uk
**Estd:** 1882
**Line of Business:** Education services.
**Directors:** Professor R Bowring, N Downer
**US SIC:** 8299 **UK SIC:** 93300

**Auditors:** Peters Elworthy & Moore

| | 30-06-13 | 30-06-12 | 30-06-11 |
|---|---|---|---|
| TO | 7,426,153 | 7,382,286 | 7,239,011 |
| P/L | (127,029) | 342,556 | 318,282 |
| NW | 77,068,493 | 82,800,556 | 81,180,231 |
| WC | (1,457,239) | (676,270) | 300,607 |
| Emp. | 147 | 147 | 147 |

DUNS 21-602-1907 **Imp-Exp**

## Sem Ltd

(**Subsidiary of:** Dr. Johannes Heidenhain-Stiftung Gmbh)
Faraday House, Faraday Way, Orpington, Kent BR5 3QT
**Tel:** 01689-884700
**Web:** www.sem.co.uk
**Reg No:** 0138006 **VAT No:** 205878546
**Estd:** 1914 Private Limited Company
**Line of Business:** Manufacture of electric motors, generators and transformers
**Export Markets:** Worldwide
**Issued Capital:** £8,900,000
**Director:** T P Walther
**Co. Secretary:** Michael Laming
**US SIC:** 3621 **UK SIC:** 34201
**Auditors:** Friend-james
**Bankers:** National Westminster Bank Plc (60-02-12)

| | 31-12-13 | 31-12-12 | 31-12-11 |
|---|---|---|---|
| TO | 16,644,947 | 17,724,519 | 17,734,888 |
| P/L | (200,385) | (1,134,998) | 1,018,564 |
| NW | 10,494,693 | 3,695,078 | 4,830,076 |
| WC | 7,661,504 | 2,154,050 | 3,091,653 |
| Emp. | 182 | 206 | 201 |

DUNS 39-793-1296 **Imp-Exp**

## Sematic U.K. Ltd

(**Subsidiary of:** Sapa Spa)
Meadow Gate, Valley Park Industrial Estate, Wombwell, Wombwell, Barnsley, South Yorkshire S73 0UN
**Web:** www.sematic.com
**Reg No:** 2205395 **VAT No:** 500260807
**Estd:** 1988 Private Limited Company
**Line of Business:** Manufacture of other fabricated metal products not elsewhere classified
**Export Markets:** European Union (E U); Europe; Scandinavia
**Export Sales:** £8,613,018
**Issued Capital:** £3,000,000
**Managing Director:** S K Brunton
**Co. Secretary:** Dr Ing Zappa
**Responsibilities**
**Health & Safety:** Alan Tonks *(Health & Safety Advisor)*
**US SIC:** 3499 **UK SIC:** 31694
**Auditors:** Pannell Kerr Forster
**Bankers:** National Westminster Bank Plc (60-06-39)

| | 31-12-13 | 31-12-12 | 31-12-11 |
|---|---|---|---|
| TO | 9,638,643 | 9,696,301 | 10,244,686 |
| P/L | 690,150 | 1,620,112 | 2,164,424 |
| NW | 4,528,284 | 5,245,173 | 6,242,951 |
| WC | 2,839,308 | 3,525,380 | 4,296,391 |
| Emp. | 71 | 65 | 62 |

DUNS 73-362-7538 **Imp**

## Sembcorp Utilities (Uk) Ltd

(**Subsidiary of:** Sembcorp Industries Ltd)
Po Box 1985, Wilton International, Middlesbrough, Cleveland TS90 8WS
**Tel:** 01642212000
**Web:** www.sembutilities.co.uk
**Reg No:** 4636301 **VAT No:** 809090530
**Estd:** 1998 Private Limited Company
**Line of Business:** Other manufacturing not elsewhere classified
**Trading Style:** Sembcorp
**Issued Capital:** £31,900,000
**Directors:** M P Ng, D S Annan, A S Wong, K F Tang
**Co. Secretary:** Stephen Hands
**Responsibilities**
**Senior:** Paul Gavens *(Manager)*
**Finance:** David Guy *(Financial Director)*
**HR:** Joanne Potter *(Human Resources Manager)*
**US SIC:** 3999, 4911
**UK SIC:** 49590, 16101
**Auditors:** KPMG LLP
**Bankers:** National Westminster Bank Plc (54-10-04)

| | 31-12-13 | 31-12-12 | 31-12-11 |
|---|---|---|---|
| TO | 174,100,000 | 168,633,000 | 145,797,000 |
| P/L | (39,929,000) | (3,601,000) | 8,373,000 |
| NW | 107,243,000 | 153,655,000 | 155,303,000 |
| WC | 23,328,000 | 26,365,000 | 21,949,000 |
| Emp. | 390 | 391 | 398 |

DUNS 21-680-6899

## Sembmarine Slp Ltd

(**Subsidiary of:** Sembcorp Marine Ltd)
Hamilton Dock, Hamilton Road, Lowestoft, Suffolk NR32 1XF
**Tel:** 01502548000 **Fax:** 01502-512589
**Web:** www.slp-eng.com
**Reg No:** 7311944 **Estd:** 2010 Private Limited Company
**Line of Business:** Building and repairing of ships
**Trading Style:** Slp Engineering Ltd
**Issued Capital:** £1,000,000
**Directors:** N S Ho, C T Tan, J T Lawrence, P D Thomson, L Chiang Theng, W S Wong
**Co. Secretary:** Colin Yaxley
**Responsibilities**
**Sales:** Chris Boswell *(Commercial Manager)*
**Operations:** Gavin Crisp *(Production Services Manager)*, Brett Hurrell *(Offshore Manager)*, Michael Morely *(Fabrication Manager)*, Matthew Wooltorten *(Project Manager)*
**Purchasing:** Stephen Powley *(Procurement Manager)*
**Engineering:** Mervyn Dalley *(Piping Mechanical Manager)*
**US SIC:** 1799, 1796
**UK SIC:** 50000, 50400
**Auditors:** PricewaterhouseCoopers LLP

| | 31-12-13 | 31-12-12 | 31-12-11 |
|---|---|---|---|
| TO | 36,140,869 | 23,689,692 | 14,300,573 |
| P/L | 63,870 | 184,463 | (1,499,784) |
| NW | 1,832,151 | 1,768,281 | (2,861,378) |
| WC | 285,531 | 828,324 | (3,200,810) |
| Emp. | 251 | 99 | 85 |

DUNS 21-950-7659

## Semcon Product Information Uk Ltd

(**Subsidiary of:** Semcon Ab)
8 Brook Business Park, Brookhampton Lane, Kineton, Warwick, Warwickshire CV35 0JA
**Tel:** 01926 642935
**Web:** www.semcon.com
**Reg No:** 6132347 **Estd:** 2007 Private Limited Company
**Line of Business:** Other engineering activities
**Issued Capital:** £10
**Directors:** J M Granlund, J Ekener, T Sundin
**Responsibilities**
**Senior:** Semcon Informatic *(Partner)*
**US SIC:** 7399 **UK SIC:** 83954
**Auditors:** Wright Vigar Ltd

| | 31-12-13 | 31-12-12 | 31-12-11 |
|---|---|---|---|
| TO | 14,314,509 | 12,593,378 | 9,760,332 |
| P/L | 2,987,777 | 2,755,076 | 1,307,915 |
| NW | 3,639,353 | 3,366,101 | 2,792,950 |
| WC | 3,453,432 | 3,062,834 | 2,685,275 |
| Emp. | 90 | 79 | 55 |

DUNS 22-913-9985 **Imp-Exp**

## Semefab Ltd

(**Subsidiary of:** Hicks (1) Ltd)
Newark Road South, Glenrothes, Fife KY7 4NS
**Tel:** 01592-630630 **Fax:** 01592-775265
**Web:** www.semefab.com
**Reg No:** 0100193SC **Estd:** 1987 Private Limited Company
**Line of Business:** Manufacturers of semiconductors
**Export Markets:** Switzerland, Hong Kong
**Export Sales:** £6,046,325
**Trading Style:** Semefab Ltd
**Issued Capital:** £1,001,000
**Principals:** A D James *(Managing)*, Doctor J M Bruce
**Co. Secretary:** Ccw Secretaries Limited
**Responsibilities**
**Senior:** Lorraine Carr *(Hr Assistant)*
**Marketing:** Shona Ray *(Development Manager)*
**IT:** Paul Gorniak *(IT Manager)*
**HR:** J Cushnie *(Personnel Officer)*
**US SIC:** 3999, 3629
**UK SIC:** 49590, 34350
**Auditors:** Tenon Audit Ltd
**Bankers:** Barclays Bank Plc (20-57-40)

| | 31-10-13 | 31-10-12 | 31-10-11 |
|---|---|---|---|
| TO | 7,949,378 | 7,347,349 | 8,650,044 |
| P/L | 127,065 | (847,743) | 253,985 |
| NW | 4,417,331 | 4,185,217 | 5,141,834 |
| WC | 152,443 | 1,366,065 | 1,974,936 |
| Emp. | 81 | 91 | 94 |

DUNS 28-825-9237

## Semi-Chem (Toiletries) Ltd

Hillwood House, 2 Harvest Drive, Newbridge, Midlothian EH28 8QJ
**Tel:** 02890236177
**Web:** www.semichem.co.uk
**Reg No:** 0075371SC **Estd:** 1901 Private Limited Company
**Line of Business:** Beauty products
**Issued Capital:** £5,000
**Directors:** J Watson, H P Cairney
**Co. Secretary:** John Dalley
**Responsibilities**
**Senior:** Hollis Smallman *(Manager)*
**Branches:** Semi-Chem (Toiletries) Ltd, 37 Park Centre, Donegall Road, Belfast, Belfast BT12 6HN
**US SIC:** 2844 **UK SIC:** 25820
**Auditors:** Deloitte & Touche

| | 25-01-14 | 26-01-13 | 28-01-12 |
|---|---|---|---|
| TA | 5,000 | 5,000 | 5,000 |
| NW | 5,000 | 5,000 | 5,000 |

DUNS 21-918-5709 **Imp-Exp**

## Seminar Components (U.K.) Ltd

(**Subsidiary of:** Seminar Components Holdings Ltd)
Unit 4-6, Carmarthen Road Cwmdu Industrial Estate, Swansea, West Glamorgan SA5 8JF
**Tel:** 01792588553
**Web:** www.seminar-components.co.uk
**Reg No:** 1191770 **VAT No:** 124455093
**Estd:** 1974 Private Limited Company
**Line of Business:** Manufacture of other fabricated metal products not elsewhere classified
**Export Markets:** Spain, Belgium, Germany
**Issued Capital:** £57,100
**Principals:** N M Hale *(Managing)*, R J Hale *(Managing)*, J Phillpart, S R Hale
**Co. Secretary:** Nicholas Hale
**US SIC:** 3499, 8999
**UK SIC:** 31694, 83954
**Auditors:** Bevan & Buckland
**Bankers:** Lloyds TSB Bank plc (30-95-46)

| | 31-03-14 | 31-03-13 | 31-03-12 |
|---|---|---|---|
| TA | 3,138,923 | 2,490,002 | 2,046,794 |
| NW | 2,158,982 | 1,740,799 | 1,479,217 |
| WC | 1,844,754 | 1,541,030 | 1,225,351 |

DUNS 23-604-5972

## Semlogistics Milford Haven Ltd

(**Subsidiary of:** Semeuro Ltd)
Main Road, Milford Haven, Dyfed SA73 1DP
**Tel:** 01646691201
**Web:** www.semgrouplp.com
**Reg No:** 3601913 **Estd:** 1998 Private Limited Company
**Line of Business:** Other storage and warehousing not elsewhere classified
**Export Sales:** £3,469,000
**Issued Capital:** £2
**Directors:** N R Passmore, R Fitztgerald, C H Thomas, C Conner
**Co. Secretary:** Mrs Candice Cheeseman
**US SIC:** 4226 **UK SIC:** 77003
**Auditors:** PricewaterhouseCoopers LLP

| | 31-12-13 | 31-12-12 | 31-12-11 |
|---|---|---|---|
| TO | 7,505,000 | 7,769,000 | 14,526,000 |
| P/L | (12,243,000) | (4,498,000) | 2,049,000 |
| NW | 25,817,000 | 35,702,000 | 39,052,000 |
| WC | 266,000 | 3,630,000 | 10,559,000 |
| Emp. | 52 | 49 | 61 |

DUNS 23-726-6908 **Imp**

## Semper Holdings Ltd

Unit 5a, East Way, Rivergreen Industrial Estate, Sunderland, Tyne and Wear SR4 6AD
**Tel:** 0191-564-0898
**Web:** www.icwpower.com
**Reg No:** 3721334 **VAT No:** 735843806
**Estd:** 1999 Private Limited Company
**Line of Business:** Manufacture of other electrical equipment not elsewhere classified
**Issued Capital:** £100,000
**Directors:** D A Sharpe, R G Melgaard, R J Mills
**Responsibilities**
**Senior:** Nicholas Melgaard *(Manager)*
**US SIC:** 3629 **UK SIC:** 34350
**Auditors:** Baker Tilly UK Audit LLP
**Bankers:** Barclays Bank Plc (20-74-09)

| | 31-03-13 | 31-03-12 | 31-03-11 |
|---|---|---|---|
| TO | 11,361,409 | 8,170,813 | 7,667,676 |
| P/L | 97,305 | 202,342 | 125,163 |
| NW | 1,472,131 | (1,016,938) | (1,153,970) |
| WC | 1,170,475 | 1,252,204 | 1,386,933 |
| Emp. | 53 | 55 | 54 |

DUNS 67-153-0202

## Semperian Capital Management Ltd

(**Subsidiary of:** Semperian Ppp Investment Partners Lp)
Third Floor Broad Quay House, Prince Street, Bristol, Avon BS1 4DJ
**Reg No:** 5991860 **Estd:** 2006 Private Limited Company
**Line of Business:** Financial intermediation not elsewhere classified
**Issued Capital:** £300,000
**Directors:** A E Birch, J M Simpson
**Co. Secretary:** Michael Saunders
**Responsibilities**
**Health & Safety:** Emry Pritchard *(health & safety manager)*
**US SIC:** 6111, 6211
**UK SIC:** 81501, 83100
**Auditors:** PricewaterhouseCoopers LLP

| | 31-03-14 | 31-03-13 | 31-03-12 |
|---|---|---|---|
| TA | 15,309,913 | 11,003,130 | 13,741,211 |
| P/L | 213,100 | 160,215 | 363,294 |
| NW | 3,029,227 | 2,954,118 | 2,866,493 |
| WC | 2,145,696 | 2,276,570 | 2,098,304 |
| Emp. | 145 | 144 | 137 |

DUNS 21-148-9374

## Semperian Ltd

(**Subsidiary of:** Semperian Ppp Investment Partners Lp)
Third Floor Broad Quay House, Prince Street, Bristol, Avon BS1 4DJ
**Tel:** 020 3405 1300 **Fax:** 020 7184 9288
**Web:** www.semperian.co.uk
**Reg No:** 6786026 **Estd:** 2009 Private Limited Company
**Line of Business:** Business services
**Issued Capital:** £1
**Directors:** C Burlton, A E Birch
**Co. Secretary:** Semperian Secretariat Services L
**US SIC:** 7399, 6211
**UK SIC:** 83954, 83100

| | 31-03-14 | 31-03-13 | 31-03-12 |
|---|---|---|---|
| TA | 1 | 1 | 1 |
| NW | 1 | 1 | 1 |

DUNS 42-395-7369 **Imp**

## Sen Medicine Co Ltd

Hutchison House 5 Hester Road, London SW11 4AN
**Tel:** 02073940745 **Fax:** 020-7231-9215
**Web:** www.senhealth.com
**Reg No:** 4383420 **Estd:** 2002 Private Limited Company
**Line of Business:** Medical practice activities
**Issued Capital:** £1
**Directors:** J C Cheng, S C To, C L Hogg, Mrs S M Chow
**Co. Secretary:** Ms Edith Shih
**US SIC:** 8011 **UK SIC:** 95300

| | 31-12-13 | 31-12-12 | 31-12-11 |
|---|---|---|---|
| TO | N/A | 477,136 | 1,720,933 |
| P/L | (81,690) | (1,843,160) | (837,633) |
| NW | (11,756,381) | (11,674,691) | (9,856,230) |
| WC | 221,522 | 351,777 | 2,150,312 |
| Emp. | N/A | 20 | 38 |

DUNS 29-386-0664

## Senad Ltd

(**Subsidiary of:** Senad Group Limited)
St Georges Vernon Gate, Derby, Derbyshire DE1 1UQ
**Tel:** 01332378840
**Web:** www.senadgroup.com
**Reg No:** 1176549 **Estd:** 1974 Private Limited Company
**Line of Business:** Adult and other education not elsewhere classified
**Issued Capital:** £300,000
**Managing Director:** B J Jones
**Co. Secretary:** James Atkinson
**Responsibilities**
**Senior:** Victoria Finn *(Hr Manager)*
**HR:** Victoria Finn *(Hr Manager)*
**Branches:** Senad Ltd, Blithbury House, Blithbury Rd, Rugeley, Staffordshire WS15 3HR
**US SIC:** 8249 **UK SIC:** 93300
**Auditors:** Smith Cooper
**Bankers:** Barclays Bank Plc (20-25-85)

| | 31-08-13 | 31-08-12 | 31-08-11 |
|---|---|---|---|
| TO | 16,487,000 | 17,151,000 | 17,943,000 |
| P/L | 1,792,000 | 2,770,000 | 2,698,000 |
| NW | 7,918,000 | 6,497,000 | 4,424,000 |
| WC | 14,686,000 | (4,512,000) | (6,487,000) |
| Emp. | 495 | 465 | 488 |

DUNS 21-323-9189 **Imp-Exp**

## Senator International Ltd

Syke Side Drive, Altham Business Park, Altham, Accrington, Lancashire BB5 5YE
**Web:** www.senator.co.uk
**Reg No:** 1323955 **Estd:** 1977 Private Limited Company
**Line of Business:** Manufacturers of office equipments
**Export Markets:** U S A; European Union (E U)
**Export Sales:** £22,367,000
**Issued Capital:** £10,000
**Principals:** C G Mustoe *(Managing)*, P Clarke, J Simpson, B Martin, Mrs J E Davies, Ms J Mustoe
**Co. Secretary:** Robert Mustoe
**Responsibilities**
**Senior:** Julia Mustoe *(Manager)*
**Finance:** Claire Johnson *(Financial Manager)*, P Truehurst *(Financial Controller)*
**Sales:** Pauline Hancock *(Senior Sales Executive)*
**IT:** Justin Fairley *(PC Manager)*
**Facilities:** Dominic Gorrell *(Engineering Manager)*
**Engineering:** Dominic Gorrell *(Engineering Manager)*
**Branches:** Senator International Ltd, Huncoat Business Pk, Accrington, Lancashire BB5 5JW
**US SIC:** 3579, 2599
**UK SIC:** 33010, 46720
**Auditors:** Egan Roberts Ltd

**Bankers:** Barclays Bank Plc (20-09-72)

| | 31-12-13 | 31-12-12 | 31-12-11 |
|---|---|---|---|
| TO | 107,683,000 | 98,108,000 | 100,951,000 |
| P/L | 7,820,000 | 6,118,000 | 3,336,000 |
| NW | 38,437,000 | 32,860,000 | 28,396,000 |
| WC | 14,526,000 | 12,180,000 | 11,858,000 |
| Emp. | 1,017 | 1,017 | 978 |

DUNS 67-241-1055
## Senator Security South Ltd
Solent Business Centre, Southampton, Hampshire SO15 0HW
**Tel:** 02380780614
**Web:** www.senatorsecuritysouth.co.uk
**Reg No:** 6124650 **Estd:** 2007 Private Limited Company
**Line of Business:** Security and related activities
**Issued Capital:** £100
**Director:** Ms M Lethbridge
**Co. Secretary:** Mellony Lethbridge
**Responsibilities**
**Senior:** Mellony Brown (Manager), Andrew Glass (Manager), Derek Winn (Manager)
**Health & Safety:** Malcolm Broomfield (Health & Safety Officer)
**US SIC:** 7393 **UK SIC:** 83954

| | 31-03-14 | 31-03-13 | 31-03-12 |
|---|---|---|---|
| TA | 308,134 | 276,693 | 181,990 |
| NW | 490 | 3,925 | 307 |
| WC | (4,957) | (2,963) | (8,379) |

DUNS 39-028-5781 **Imp-Exp**
## Sencon (U K) Ltd
Stonebridge Cross Business Park, Droitwich, Worcestershire WR9 0LW
**Web:** www.sencon.net
**Reg No:** 2108329 **VAT No:** 454893312
**Estd:** 1987 Private Limited Company
**Line of Business:** Manufacturers and suppliers of bakery equipment
**Export Markets:** European Union (E U)
**Trading Style:** Sencon
**Issued Capital:** £1,000
**Principals:** P Craddock (Managing), W Shields, R Churchill, N H Tipping
**Co. Secretary:** Mrs Elizabeth Craddock
**US SIC:** 3551, 5065
**UK SIC:** 32441, 61500
**Auditors:** Kendall Wadley
**Bankers:** National Westminster Bank Plc (55-81-36)

| | 31-12-13 | 31-12-12 | 31-12-11 |
|---|---|---|---|
| TO | 6,665,515 | 8,230,367 | N/A |
| P/L | 557,674 | 1,375,479 | N/A |
| NW | 2,033,903 | 2,967,865 | 2,360,777 |
| WC | 1,806,178 | 2,681,740 | 1,966,947 |
| Emp. | 47 | 47 | N/A |

DUNS 50-558-4565 **Imp**
## Senergy (Gb) Ltd
(Subsidiary of: Senergy Group Ltd)
Ternan House, North Deeside Road, Banchory, Kincardineshire AB31 5YR
**Tel:** 01330825188
**Web:** www.senergyworld.com
**Reg No:** 0125513SC **Estd:** 1994 Private Limited Company
**Line of Business:** Oil and gas exploration services
**Issued Capital:** £19,469
**Directors:** J G Mccallum, A Buchanan
**Co. Secretary:** Neil Campbell
**Responsibilities**
**Senior:** Terry Carr (Location Manager)
**Finance:** Mike McEwan (VP of Finance and Information)
**HR:** Vivien Broughton (VP - Human Resources)
**Branches:** Senergy (Gb) Ltd, 2-3 Queens Terrace, Aberdeen, Aberdeenshire AB10 1XL
**US SIC:** 1389 **UK SIC:** 13000
**Auditors:** Anderson Anderson & Brown LLP

| | 31-05-13 | 31-05-12 | 31-05-11 |
|---|---|---|---|
| TO | 41,659,877 | 44,422,961 | 42,461,437 |
| P/L | (1,189,308) | 3,645,557 | 7,588,986 |
| NW | 25,253,511 | 26,179,762 | 22,582,672 |
| WC | 23,811,730 | 24,757,294 | 21,256,170 |
| Emp. | 140 | 172 | 192 |

DUNS 23-918-8944
## Senior Architectural Systems Ltd
(Subsidiary of: Clytha Holdings Ltd)
Eland Road, Doncaster, South Yorkshire DN12 4HA
**Tel:** 01709-772600
**Web:** www.seniorarchitectural.co.uk
**Reg No:** 3909137 **Estd:** 2000 Private Limited Company
**Line of Business:** Manufacturers of window frames
**Issued Capital:** £50,000
**Principals:** S O Jonsson (Managing), J R Keeling-Heane, M V Wadsworth, D Fletcher, J S Hopkins, S J Wightman
**Co. Secretary:** James Hopkins
**US SIC:** 3442 **UK SIC:** 31420
**Auditors:** KPMG LLP

**Bankers:** HSBC Bank plc (40-41-07)

| | 30-06-14 | 30-06-13 | 30-06-12 |
|---|---|---|---|
| TO | 20,807,371 | 20,473,444 | 21,802,033 |
| P/L | 820,896 | 970,326 | 902,638 |
| NW | 3,288,672 | 2,653,458 | 1,884,645 |
| WC | 1,633,009 | 960,688 | 132,197 |
| Emp. | 122 | 115 | 114 |

DUNS 21-051-4501 **Imp-Exp**
## Senior Plc
59-61 High Street, Rickmansworth, Hertfordshire WD3 1RH
**Web:** www.seniorplc.com
**Reg No:** 0282772 **Estd:** 1933 Public Limited Company
**Line of Business:** Management activities of holding companies
**Export Markets:** Rest of Europe; North America & Worldwide
**Export Sales:** £646,000,000
**Trading Style:** Senior
**Issued Capital:** £41,593,384
**Directors:** D J Harding, A N Hamment, G F Kerr, Dr C F Baxter, M E Vernon, M Rollins, C A Berry
**Co. Secretary:** Andrew Bodenham
**Branches:** Senior Plc, Gt Bridge St, West Bromwich, West Midlands B70 0DA
**US SIC:** 6711, 8911
**UK SIC:** 83962, 83701
**Auditors:** Deloitte LLP
**Bankers:** National Westminster Bank Plc (60-00-01)

| | 31-12-13 | 31-12-12 | 31-12-11 |
|---|---|---|---|
| TO | 775,100,000 | 712,000,000 | 640,700,000 |
| P/L | 83,800,000 | 83,400,000 | 72,700,000 |
| NW | 119,000,000 | 74,100,000 | 49,500,000 |
| WC | 101,100,000 | 94,800,000 | 75,000,000 |
| Emp. | 6,362 | 6,081 | 5,374 |

DUNS 23-691-9994
## Senior Response Ltd
Unit 15-17 Blythe Valley Innovation, Centre, Central Boulevard, Shirley, Solihull, West Midlands B90 8AJ
**Tel:** 01215069200
**Web:** www.seniorresponse.co.uk
**Reg No:** 3686881 **Estd:** 1998 Private Limited Company
**Line of Business:** Call centre activities
**Issued Capital:** £20,100
**Director:** M J Bingham
**Co. Secretary:** Christopher Aldcroft
**Responsibilities**
**HR:** Alison Bates (Director of Operations)
**Health & Safety:** Alison Bates (Director of Operations)
**Operations:** Alison Bates (Director of Operations)
**US SIC:** 7399 **UK SIC:** 83954

| | 31-12-13 | 31-12-12 | 31-12-11 |
|---|---|---|---|
| TA | 557,408 | 471,800 | 373,764 |
| NW | 343,858 | 334,172 | 321,919 |
| WC | 332,182 | 324,905 | 314,892 |

DUNS 29-566-1110 **Imp-Exp**
## Senior Uk Ltd
(Subsidiary of: Senior Plc)
Adlington Business Park, Adlington, Macclesfield, Cheshire SK10 4NL
**Tel:** 01625872261
**Web:** www.seniorplc.com
**Reg No:** 1928053 **Estd:** 1992 Private Limited Company
**Line of Business:** Manufacture of non-domestic cooling and ventilation equipment
**Export Markets:** worldwide
**Trading Style:** Senior Aerospace B W T, Senior Aerospace Bird Bellows
**Issued Capital:** £2,000,000
**Directors:** M Rollins, M Sheppard, D J Harding
**Co. Secretary:** Andrew Bodenham
**Responsibilities**
**Senior:** Simon Ashley (Works Manager), Dean Ballenger (Chief Executive Officer)
**Finance:** Darren Butterworth (Financial Director)
**Marketing:** Carl Baskerville (Head of Marketing), Mark Jenkings (Sales & Marketing Director)
**Sales:** Mark Jenkings (Sales & Marketing Director)
**IT:** Bev Hardman (Network Manager)
**HR:** Sally Kennedy (Human Resources Manager)
**Operations:** Mark Jenkings (Sales & Marketing Director)
**Engineering:** Simon Ashley (Works Manager)
**Branches:** Senior Uk Ltd, Cleton Street Business Park, Unit 1, Tipton, West Midlands DY4 7TR
**US SIC:** 3585 **UK SIC:** 32841
**Auditors:** Deloitte LLP
**Bankers:** HSBC Bank plc (40-03-27)

| | 31-12-13 | 31-12-12 | 31-12-11 |
|---|---|---|---|
| TO | 80,033,000 | 71,538,000 | 70,632,000 |
| P/L | 17,751,000 | 16,636,000 | 13,757,000 |
| NW | 47,486,000 | 30,021,000 | 12,590,000 |
| WC | 11,854,000 | 22,717,000 | 5,865,000 |
| Emp. | 761 | 656 | 609 |

DUNS 50-472-7678
## Senior Wright Holdings Ltd
Boundary House 7-17, Jewry Street, London EC3N 2EX
**Fax:** 020-7680-5777
**Web:** www.seniorwright.co.uk
**Reg No:** 2451678 **Estd:** 1989 Private Limited Company
**Line of Business:** Non-life insurance
**Issued Capital:** £2
**Managing Director:** M Griffin
**Co. Secretary:** Mrs Janet Griffin
**Branches:** Senior Wright Holdings Ltd, 2 Hagley Court South, Level Street, Brierley Hill, West Midlands DY5 1XE
**US SIC:** 6399, 6411
**UK SIC:** 82001, 83200
**Auditors:** Saffery Champness
**Bankers:** HSBC Bank plc (40-35-34)

| | 31-12-13 | 31-12-12 | 31-12-11 |
|---|---|---|---|
| TO | 5,137,812 | 5,436,194 | 5,793,671 |
| P/L | (290,079) | (1,169,010) | (896,500) |
| NW | 2,974,784 | 3,311,835 | 4,447,818 |
| WC | 2,743,800 | 3,821,232 | 4,890,405 |
| Emp. | 70 | 74 | 78 |

DUNS 51-610-4770
## Seniorlink Eldercare Llp
847 Burnley Road, Loveclough, Rossendale, Lancashire BB4 8QL
**Tel:** 08456015844
**Web:** www.seniorlinkeldercare.co.uk
**Reg No:** 0321280OC **VAT No:** 890243424
**Estd:** 2006 Private Limited Company
**Line of Business:** Social alarm monitoring and mobile response
**US SIC:** 7399 **UK SIC:** 83954
**Auditors:** Tenon Ltd
**Bankers:** Barclays Bank Plc (20-00-00)

| | 31-08-13 | 31-08-12 | 31-08-11 |
|---|---|---|---|
| TA | 2,027,528 | 1,921,835 | 1,829,766 |
| NW | 200 | 200 | 100 |
| WC | 915,307 | 694,109 | 560,199 |

DUNS 50-575-8383 **Imp-Exp**
## Sennheiser U K Ltd
(Subsidiary of: Sennheiser Electronic Gmbh & Co. Kg)
Pacific House, Third Avenue, Globe Park, Marlow, Buckinghamshire SL7 1EY
**Tel:** 03332408185 **Fax:** 01494-551550
**Web:** www.sennheiser.co.uk
**Reg No:** 2523629 **VAT No:** 538045250
**Estd:** 1990 Private Limited Company
**Line of Business:** Manufacturers of sound systems
**Export Markets:** E U, Eire, Middle East
**Export Sales:** £7,017,296
**Issued Capital:** £210,000
**Principals:** P E Whiting (Managing), D Sennheiser
**Co. Secretary:** Philip Massey
**Responsibilities**
**Senior:** Stefan Junker (Manager), Steyson Patterson (Warehouse Manager), Susanne Seidel (Manager)
**Marketing:** Victoria Cheriah (Corporate Communications Manag)
**Purchasing:** Steyson Patterson (Warehouse Manager)
**Fleet:** Steyson Patterson (Warehouse Manager)
**US SIC:** 3651 **UK SIC:** 34541
**Auditors:** Barnes Roffe
**Bankers:** HSBC Bank plc (40-24-17)

| | 31-12-13 | 31-12-12 | 31-12-11 |
|---|---|---|---|
| TO | 42,447,773 | 41,811,447 | 41,840,492 |
| P/L | 123,290 | (104,935) | 131,500 |
| NW | 7,916,255 | 7,835,657 | 8,364,141 |
| WC | 6,946,333 | 7,341,748 | 7,994,337 |
| Emp. | 73 | 70 | 64 |

DUNS 23-732-2347
## Senoble Uk Holdings Ltd
(Subsidiary of: Senoble Groupe Services)
4 Berrington Road, Leamington Spa, Warwickshire CV31 1NB
**Tel:** 01926-311531
**Web:** www.senoble.com
**Reg No:** 3726718 **Estd:** 1999 Private Limited Company
**Line of Business:** Manufacture of other food products not elsewhere classified
**Export Sales:** £3,008,000
**Issued Capital:** £22,135,362
**Directors:** O Besset, S International, A Peck
**US SIC:** 2099 **UK SIC:** 42399
**Auditors:** KPMG LLP

| | 31-12-13 | 31-12-12 | 31-12-11 |
|---|---|---|---|
| TO | 65,359,000 | 69,958,000 | 73,377,000 |
| P/L | (1,540,000) | (4,294,000) | (11,402,000) |
| NW | 1,146,000 | (954,000) | 2,521,000 |
| WC | (24,985,000) | (28,992,000) | (26,883,000) |
| Emp. | 665 | 718 | 835 |

DUNS 21-040-0810
## Sense
12 Hyde Close, Barnet, Hertfordshire EN5 5TJ
**Tel:** 02084490964
**Web:** www.sense.org.uk
**Estd:** 2010 Proprietorship
**Line of Business:** Activities of other membership organisations not elsewhere classified
**Responsibilities**
**Senior:** A Adegbuyi (Manager), Jackie Landsbury (Manager)
**US SIC:** 8699, 6732
**UK SIC:** 96902, 83100
**Employees:** 60

DUNS 22-832-3440
## Sense (East)
11-13 Clifton Terrace, London N4 3JP
**Tel:** 084 5127 0060
**Web:** www.sense.org.uk
**VAT No:** 524704461 **Estd:** 1956
**Line of Business:** Charitable social work activities without accommodation
**Principals:** Ms J Hills (Chairman), D Harker (Managing), M Matthews, J Swindells, R Clark
**Branches:** Sense (East), Sense Charity Shop, 53A Southgate, Sleaford, Lincolnshire NG34 7SY
**US SIC:** 6732 **UK SIC:** 83100
**Bankers:** National Westminster Bank Plc (60-12-14)
**Employees:** 500

DUNS 57-031-7768
## Sense Scotland
43 Middlesex Street, Glasgow, Lanarkshire G41 1EE
**Tel:** 0141-429-0294
**Web:** www.sensescotland.org.uk
**Reg No:** 0147570SC **Estd:** 1993 Private Company Limited By Guarantee
**Line of Business:** Social work activities
**Directors:** T D Tannahil, Mrs A A Clements, Dr U Rehman, R F Cox, G M Simpson, N Farquharson, G J Seenan, D B Newton
**Co. Secretary:** John O'Connor
**Responsibilities**
**Senior:** Isobel Allan (Director), Carol Bradly (Office manager), Joe Gibson (Senior Manager), Eileen Henighen (Director), John O' Connor (Financial Director), Norman Richie (Director), Kim Watt (Vocational Qualifications Mana)
**Finance:** John O' Connor (Financial Director)
**Marketing:** Graham Thompson (Senior Marketing Executive), Graeme Thomson (Marketing Manager)
**Admin:** Anne McLaughlan (Manager), John O' Connor (Financial Director), Anne Sutherland (Administrator)
**Health & Safety:** John O' Connor (Financial Director)
**Branches:** Sense Scotland, Debra, 19-27 Bridge Street, Dunfermline, Fife KY12 8AQ
**US SIC:** 7399, 8321
**UK SIC:** 83954, 96111
**Auditors:** PricewaterhouseCoopers LLP
**Bankers:** Bank Of Scotland (80-07-65)

| | 31-03-14 | 31-03-13 | 31-03-12 |
|---|---|---|---|
| TO | 21,650,161 | 20,978,231 | 19,761,524 |
| P/L | (115,701) | 1,406,585 | 1,870,916 |
| NW | 13,233,967 | 13,349,666 | 11,943,080 |
| WC | 7,341,068 | 7,381,552 | 6,480,577 |
| Emp. | 726 | 694 | 648 |

DUNS 29-169-7209
## Sense the National Deafblind & Rubella Association
101 Pentonville Road, London N1 9LG
**Tel:** 01924298000 **Fax:** 020-7520-0958
**Web:** www.sense.org.uk
**Reg No:** 1825301 **Estd:** 1984 Private Company Limited By Guarantee
**Line of Business:** Other human health activities
**Trading Style:** Sense Trading
**Directors:** Mrs S G Turner, R Staines, J R Crabtree, I Harley, Dr D A Reeves, T D Tannahill, S Armstrong, Ms N Assad
**Co. Secretary:** Mrs Gillian Morbey
**Responsibilities**
**Senior:** Virginia Bartlett (Director), Nicholas Keegan (Director), Richard Kramer (Deputy CEO), Desmond Lucy (Director), James Mcmanus (Director), Justin Molloy (Director)
**Finance:** Alana Tubasei (Director of Fundraising)
**Marketing:** James Thornberry (Director, International)
**Admin:** Fiona Markey (Director, Corporate Secretaria)
**HR:** Toni Dumolo (HR Director)
**Facilities:** Marc Kimpton (Head of Estates)
**Operations:** Peter Cheer (Operations Director)

**Branches:** Sense The National Deafblind & Rubella Association, 428-430 Gillott Rd, Birmingham, West Midlands B16 9LP
**US SIC:** 8091 **UK SIC:** 95200
**Auditors:** PricewaterhouseCoopers LLP
**Bankers:** National Westminster Bank Plc (60-12-14)

|      | 31-03-14 | 31-03-13 | 31-03-12 |
|------|----------|----------|----------|
| TO   | 81,807,742 | 79,477,801 | 78,354,387 |
| P/L  | (810,062) | 1,900,232 | 2,748,781 |
| NW   | 40,426,111 | 46,016,986 | 41,864,788 |
| WC   | 17,366,556 | 20,492,141 | 20,089,230 |
| Emp. | 3,287 | 3,223 | 3,130 |

DUNS 21-040-6978
## Sense West
9a Birkdale Avenue, Selly Oak, Birmingham, West Midlands B29 6UB
**Tel:** 01214-152720
**Web:** www.sense.org.uk
**Estd:** 2003
**Line of Business:** Home care and help services
**Trading Style:** Sense
**Principals:** Mrs C Cieslik, Mrs C Cieslik
**Responsibilities**
**Senior:** Peter Cheer (Group Director)
**Admin:** Laura Davies (Receptionist)
**HR:** Baljinder Kang (Human Resources Manager)
**Health & Safety:** Allan Powers (Health & Safety Officer)
**Facilities:** Bob Fisher (Facilities Manager)
**US SIC:** 8699, 6732
**UK SIC:** 96902, 83100
**Employees:** 50

DUNS 22-625-6733    **Imp-Exp**
## Sensient Flavors Ltd
(**Subsidiary of:** Sensient Technologies Corporation)
Bilton Road, Bletchley, Milton Keynes, Buckinghamshire MK1 1HP
**Tel:** 01908-270-270
**Web:** www.sensient-tech.com
**Reg No:** 1514781 **VAT No:** 335959321
**Estd:** 1932 Private Limited Company
**Line of Business:** Manufacturers and distribution of food colouring, flavouring & additives
**Export Markets:** Far East; Europe; Denmark; Israel
**Export Sales:** £17,604,420
**Issued Capital:** £609,000
**Directors:** J T Makal, M F De Meyer
**Responsibilities**
**Senior:** Paul Heesterman (Manager), Steffen Sonnenberg (Director)
**HR:** Dilwen Henson (Personnel Manager), Olive Williams (Human Resources Manager)
**Operations:** Ian Norris (Laboratory Manager)
**US SIC:** 2099 **UK SIC:** 42399
**Auditors:** Ernst & Young LLP

|      | 31-12-13 | 31-12-12 | 31-12-11 |
|------|----------|----------|----------|
| TO   | 34,082,968 | 32,363,656 | 33,339,214 |
| P/L  | 1,451,516 | 906,168 | 423,914 |
| NW   | 6,863,094 | 5,779,692 | 5,092,521 |
| WC   | 7,844,982 | (4,914,180) | (3,543,571) |
| Emp. | 181 | 169 | 169 |

DUNS 21-322-3274    **Imp-Exp**
## Sensing Devices Ltd
97 Tithebarn Road, Southport, Merseyside PR8 6AG
**Tel:** 01704546161 **Fax:** 01704546231
**Web:** www.sensing-devices.co.uk
**Reg No:** 1018313 **VAT No:** 163684738
**Estd:** 1971 Private Limited Company
**Line of Business:** Electronic equipment (assembly)
**Trading Style:** Sdl
**Issued Capital:** £14,000
**Managing Director:** J C Halstead
**Co. Secretary:** Ms Susan Halstead
**Responsibilities**
**Senior:** Lyn Arnold (Sales & Marketing Director), Bernard Cox (Production Manager)
**Marketing:** Lyn Arnold (Sales & Marketing Director)
**Sales:** Lyn Arnold (Sales & Marketing Director)
**HR:** Karen Stuart (Personnel Manager)
**Health & Safety:** Bernard Cox (Production Manager)
**Operations:** Lyn Arnold (Sales & Marketing Director), Bernard Cox (Production Manager)
**Engineering:** Bernard Cox (Production Manager)
**US SIC:** 3643 **UK SIC:** 34203
**Auditors:** J & D Pennington
**Bankers:** Barclays Bank Plc (20-51-01)

|      | 31-08-14 | 31-08-13 | 31-08-12 |
|------|----------|----------|----------|
| TA   | 1,165,948 | 1,141,238 | 1,149,776 |
| NW   | 938,535 | 880,046 | 828,526 |
| WC   | 686,689 | 625,207 | 559,610 |

DUNS 23-514-6110
## Sensitisers Group Ltd.
Kernick Road, Penryn, Cornwall TR10 9DQ
**Tel:** 01326-373147 **Fax:** 01326376614
**Web:** www.sensitisers.com
**Reg No:** 3513777 **Estd:** 1998 Private Limited Company
**Line of Business:** Holding company
**Export Sales:** £10,994,940
**Issued Capital:** £520
**Directors:** K C Boyes, P M Bartlett, B Colak, P A Newell
**Co. Secretary:** Kevin Boyes
**Branches:** Sensitisers Group Ltd., 6 The Hatches, Camberley, Surrey GU16 6HE
**US SIC:** 2752, 6111
**UK SIC:** 47544, 81501
**Auditors:** Robinson Reed Layton

|      | 31-03-14 | 31-03-13 | 31-03-12 |
|------|----------|----------|----------|
| TA   | 11,396,206 | 11,040,422 | 10,376,439 |
| P/L  | 1,412,917 | 1,093,149 | 1,135,532 |
| NW   | 9,434,878 | 9,331,731 | 8,419,048 |
| WC   | 7,345,729 | 7,238,776 | 6,296,596 |
| Emp. | 106 | 104 | 101 |

DUNS 73-886-4201    **Imp**
## Sensortech Uk Ltd
9 Southgate Industrial Park, Heywood, Lancashire OL10 1ND
**Tel:** 01706625060 **Fax:** 01706625961
**Web:** http://sensortech.weebly.com
**Reg No:** 5140570 **Estd:** 1989 Private Limited Company
**Line of Business:** Other manufacturing not elsewhere classified
**Issued Capital:** £100
**Director:** G Wild
**Co. Secretary:** Richard Wild
**US SIC:** 3999 **UK SIC:** 49590

|      | 31-03-14 | 31-03-13 | 31-03-12 |
|------|----------|----------|----------|
| TA   | 100 | 100 | 100 |
| NW   | 100 | 100 | 100 |

DUNS 21-228-9761
## Sensory Impaired Childrens Service
Elmfield House, Greystoke Avenue, Bristol, Avon BS10 6AY
**Tel:** 01179038441
**Web:** www.sensorysupportservice.org.uk
**Estd:** 2005 Proprietorship
**Line of Business:** Education services
**Proprietor:** Mrs J Roe
**US SIC:** 8299 **UK SIC:** 93300
**Employees:** 89

DUNS 21-362-1414
## Sensory Inclusion Service
2nd Floor Darby House, Lawn Central, Town Centre, Telford, Shropshire TF3 4JA
**Tel:** 01952-385269
**Web:** www.inclusion.taw.org.uk
**Estd:** 2007 Proprietorship
**Line of Business:** Education services
**Proprietor:** A Broughton
**Responsibilities**
**Senior:** Lindsay Bout (Team Leader)
**US SIC:** 8299 **UK SIC:** 93300
**Employees:** 47

DUNS 23-504-9421    **Imp**
## Senstronics Ltd
(**Subsidiary of:** Senstronics Holdings Ltd)
Unit 2/3, Newton Aycliffe, County Durham DL5 6BG
**Tel:** 01325-328500
**Web:** www.senstronics.com
**Reg No:** 3504198 **Estd:** 1998 Private Limited Company
**Line of Business:** Manufacture of electronic instruments and appliances for measuring, checking, testing, navigating and other purposes, except industrial process control equipment
**Export Sales:** £8,794,000
**Trading Style:** Senstronics
**Issued Capital:** £768,749,897
**Directors:** A Junker, S P Lovass, M F Donahue, T Koniordos
**Co. Secretary:**
  Bird & Bird Company Secretaries
**Responsibilities**
**Senior:** John Hague (Manager), Kjeld Kuckelhahn (Manager), Jona Ulrich Vase (Manager)
**US SIC:** 3829, 3714, 7399
**UK SIC:** 37100, 35300, 83954
**Auditors:** KPMG LLP
**Bankers:** HSBC Bank plc (40-14-12)

|      | 31-12-13 | 31-12-12 | 31-12-11 |
|------|----------|----------|----------|
| TO   | 9,460,000 | 8,672,000 | 7,762,000 |
| P/L  | 549,000 | 415,000 | 163,000 |
| NW   | 3,214,000 | 2,665,000 | 2,250,000 |
| WC   | 2,650,000 | 2,048,000 | 1,436,000 |
| Emp. | 79 | 73 | 76 |

DUNS 73-668-8230
## Sentimental Care Ltd
Hamilton Road, Taunton, Somerset TA1 2EH
**Fax:** 01823254212
**Reg No:** 4928318 **Estd:** 1990 Private Limited Company
**Line of Business:** Nursing homes
**Issued Capital:** £2
**Directors:** Mrs V M Saunders, Mrs T Kasmani, J B Ellis
**Co. Secretary:** David Aukett
**Responsibilities**
**Senior:** Sharron Williams (Manager)
**US SIC:** 8051 **UK SIC:** 95100
**Bankers:** The Royal Bank Of Scotland Plc (16-18-18)

|      | 31-10-13 | 31-10-12 | 31-10-11 |
|------|----------|----------|----------|
| TO   | 3,001,587 | 2,919,956 | 2,824,870 |
| P/L  | 345,085 | 250,794 | 196,264 |
| NW   | 821,577 | 740,122 | 628,850 |
| WC   | 391,201 | 448,172 | 484,956 |
| Emp. | 133 | 133 | 133 |

DUNS 21-712-5594
## Sentinel Enterprises Ltd
Water Lane, Lowestoft, Suffolk NR32 2NH
**Tel:** 01502588444
**Web:** www.waveney.gov.uk
**Reg No:** 7523567 **Estd:** 2011 Private Limited Company
**Line of Business:** Leisure centres
**Issued Capital:** £1
**Directors:** J Godbold, A Wilson-Sutter, J A Annis, J M Starling
**US SIC:** 8321 **UK SIC:** 96111

|      | 31-03-14 | 31-03-13 | 31-03-12 |
|------|----------|----------|----------|
| TO   | N/A | N/A | 450,951 |
| NW   | 1 | 1 | 1 |
| WC   | (19,645) | (22,097) | (2,245) |

DUNS 34-627-7205
## Sentinel Health Care Ltd
Fritham House, Lyndhurst, Hampshire SO43 7HH
**Web:** www.sentinel-healthcare.co.uk
**Reg No:** 2761889 **Estd:** 1992 Private Limited Company
**Line of Business:** Hotels
**Trading Style:** Sentinel Health Care Limited
**Issued Capital:** £8,065
**Directors:** C M Brumpton, A L Donnelly, C M Brumpton
**Co. Secretary:** Russell Donnelly
**Responsibilities**
**Senior:** Alison Bruce (Manager of health care), Michelle Fog (Centre Manager), Sharon Palser (Manager)
**Finance:** Tina Follins (Accounts Administrator), Lyn Hargett (Senior Finance Administrator)
**US SIC:** 7011, 8051
**UK SIC:** 66500, 95100
**Auditors:** Freeman & Partners
**Bankers:** Barclays Bank Plc (20-72-37)

|      | 31-01-14 | 31-01-13 | 31-01-12 |
|------|----------|----------|----------|
| TO   | 8,956,920 | 8,944,107 | 8,774,312 |
| P/L  | 200,258 | 678,846 | 762,421 |
| NW   | 14,692,825 | 14,599,532 | 13,977,207 |
| WC   | 1,734,962 | 1,437,137 | 978,327 |
| Emp. | 214 | 181 | 169 |

DUNS 23-209-6503
## Sentinel Housing Association Ltd
56 Kingsclere Road, Basingstoke, Hampshire RG21 6XG
**Tel:** 01256338800
**Web:** https://www.sentinelha.org.uk
**Reg No:** 0027940IP **VAT No:** 641751642
**Estd:** 1994 Friendly Society
**Line of Business:** Housing associations societies trusts & co-operatives
**Directors:** Mrs P Phipps, A D Thacker, R Smith, Mrs B Huckle, P Keaney, J J Macro, I Butell, C E Hall
**Co. Secretary:** W Okoya
**Responsibilities**
**Senior:** Andrew Cobb (Manager), P Durrans (Director), Warick Lovegrove (Director)
**Finance:** Lionel Haynes (Finance Director)
**Facilities:** Bob Grover (Executive)
**Operations:** Julian Chun (Operations Director)
**US SIC:** 8699 **UK SIC:** 96902
**Auditors:** Nexia Smith & Williamson
**Bankers:** The Royal Bank Of Scotland Plc (16-12-35)

|      | 31-03-12 | 31-03-11 | 31-03-10 |
|------|----------|----------|----------|
| TO   | 53,540,000 | 44,454,000 | 42,266,000 |
| P/L  | 12,558,000 | 14,046,000 | 8,372,000 |
| NW   | 88,767,000 | 70,953,000 | 59,770,000 |
| WC   | 9,229,000 | 972,000 | 1,189,000 |
| Emp. | 200 | 188 | 421 |

DUNS 34-627-1773
## Sentinel Performance Solutions Ltd
(**Subsidiary of:** Sentinel Performance Solutions Group Ltd)
7650 Daresbury Park, Warrington, Cheshire WA4 4BS
**Tel:** 08003 894670 **Fax:** 01928562070
**Web:** www.sentinel-solutions.net
**Reg No:** 5433529 **Estd:** 1988 Private Limited Company
**Line of Business:** Manufacturers of chemicals
**Issued Capital:** £116,013
**Directors:** G J Roebuck, A K Lumley, S M Goodwin
**Co. Secretary:** Adam Lumley
**US SIC:** 2899 **UK SIC:** 25670
**Auditors:** Deloitte LLP

|      | 31-03-14 | 31-03-13 | 31-03-12 |
|------|----------|----------|----------|
| TO   | 17,203,000 | 15,801,000 | 18,166,000 |
| P/L  | 1,946,000 | 1,667,000 | 858,000 |
| NW   | 12,955,000 | 10,390,000 | 8,102,000 |
| WC   | 9,183,000 | 6,498,000 | 4,496,000 |
| Emp. | 67 | 59 | 53 |

DUNS 23-838-8123
## Sentry Ltd
The Hall, Willisham, Ipswich, Suffolk IP8 4SL
**Tel:** 08453458058 **Fax:** 01473-658059
**Web:** www.sentryfarms.co.uk
**Reg No:** 3830499 **Estd:** 1999 Private Limited Company
**Line of Business:** Farming (arable)
**Issued Capital:** £251,250
**Principals:** A B Mason (Managing), C E Last, J C Fuller, T J Atkinson
**Co. Secretary:** Steven Farrar
**Responsibilities**
**Senior:** Linda Lanton (Personnel Manager)
**Finance:** Rebecca Arkley (Head of Advisory / Accountant)
**Admin:** Hanna Coyne (Office Assistant), Linda Lanton (Personnel Manager)
**IT:** Debbie Brannick (IT Coordinator)
**HR:** Linda Lanton (Personnel Manager)
**Health & Safety:** Roger Connah (Health & Safety Officer)
**Branches:** Sentry Ltd, Lansdowne, Dorchester, Dorset DT2 7BN
**US SIC:** 0119, 0729, 7392
**UK SIC:** 01001, 01003, 83951
**Auditors:** Larking Gowen
**Bankers:** Barclays Bank Plc (20-44-51)

|      | 30-04-14 | 30-04-13 | 30-04-12 |
|------|----------|----------|----------|
| TO   | 9,762,950 | 9,914,604 | 10,969,822 |
| P/L  | 932,775 | 650,253 | 671,767 |
| NW   | 2,091,203 | 2,671,453 | 2,501,571 |
| WC   | 1,168,540 | 2,207,328 | 1,875,544 |
| Emp. | 76 | 74 | 94 |

DUNS 73-597-4060    **Imp**
## Senvion Uk Ltd
10 Waterloo Place, Edinburgh, Midlothian EH1 3EG
**Tel:** 01316239286 **Fax:** 01316239284
**Web:** www.senvion.com
**Reg No:** 0253885SC **Estd:** 2003 Private Limited Company
**Line of Business:** Manufacturers of turbines and parts thereof
**Trading Style:** Repower Uk Ltd
**Issued Capital:** £100,000
**Directors:** K M Sharma, R A Gilfedder
**Co. Secretary:** Paul Richards
**Responsibilities**
**Senior:** Richard Eggleston (Manager), Anurag Rai (Business Development Manager)
**Marketing:** Stephanie Oxley (Marketing & Communications Man)
**Sales:** Gordon Christison (Business Development Manager), Ranjit Mene (Head of UK Offshore Sales), Anurag Rai (Business Development Manager), Carys Thomas (Offshore Commercial Sales Supp), Shona Watson (Contracts Manager)
**Admin:** Christina Duffle (Administrator), Ruth Mileham (Office Manager)
**Fleet:** Murray Gardiner (Logistics Manager)
**Engineering:** Sigrid Bolik (Principal Electrical Engineer)
**US SIC:** 3519 **UK SIC:** 32811
**Auditors:** Ernst & Young LLP
**Bankers:** Barclays Bank Plc (20-00-50)

|      | 31-03-14 | 31-03-13 | 31-03-12 |
|------|----------|----------|----------|
| TO   | 14,017,962 | 13,614,019 | 11,419,994 |
| P/L  | 735,500 | 677,344 | 1,337,091 |
| NW   | 3,339,617 | 2,799,551 | 2,288,896 |
| WC   | 2,872,254 | 2,281,698 | 2,010,629 |
| Emp. | 154 | 139 | 118 |

DUNS 21-412-5985
## Sepa
Inverdee House, Baxter Street, Aberdeen, Aberdeenshire AB11 9QA
**Tel:** 01224-266600
**Web:** www.sepa.org.uk
**Estd:** 1988

**Line of Business:** Activities of other membership organisations not elsewhere classified
**Proprietor:** C Dermmell
**Responsibilities**
**Senior:** James Curran (Chief Executive)
**US SIC:** 8699 **UK SIC:** 96902
**Employees:** 150

DUNS 23-275-0513
## Sepa Enterprises Ltd
31 Ballsmill Road, Newry, Co Down BT35 9ED
**Fax:** 028-3088-8082
**Reg No:** 0023258NI **Estd:** 1989 Private Limited Company
**Line of Business:** Joinery installation
**Issued Capital:** £34,000
**Director:** S Murphy
**Co. Secretary:** Aislinn Murphy
**US SIC:** 1751, 1799
**UK SIC:** 50400, 50000
**Auditors:** John Mac Mahon & Co
**Bankers:** The Bank Of Ireland (90-22-82)

|     | 28-02-14 | 28-02-13 | 28-02-12 |
|-----|----------|----------|----------|
| TA  | 26,297   | 38,727   | 156,838  |
| NW  | (142,356)| (98,838) | (2,406)  |
| WC  | (155,941)| (116,948)| (40,814) |

DUNS 42-366-1615     **Imp-Exp**
## Sepura Plc
Radio House, St Andrews Road, Cambridge, Cambridgeshire CB4 1GR
**Tel:** 01223876000
**Web:** www.sepura.co.uk
**Reg No:** 4353801 **Estd:** 2002 Public Limited Company
**Line of Business:** Research and experimental development on natural sciences and engineering
**Export Sales:** £84,816,000
**Issued Capital:** £68,659
**Directors:** S K Chamberlain, S P Kearsey, R J King, G M Stuart, N W Smith, G J Watling, J L Hughes
**Co. Secretary:** Anthony Hunter
**Responsibilities**
**Senior:** David Tilston (Manager)
**Finance:** Jane Farebrother (Financial Controller)
**Marketing:** Steve Barber (Head of Product Strategy), Karl Forbes (Head of Product Realisation), Rebecca Greenall (Sales Support Team Manager), Vitor Rodrigues (Regional Director - Latin Amer), Barbara Sankl (Product Manager)
**Sales:** Emanuele Algieri (Sales Director), David Armitstead (Business Development Manager), Doug Bowden (Senior Business Development Ma), Chris D'Aguiar (VP Commercial), Rebecca Greenall (Sales Support Team Manager)
**HR:** Trevor Boulding (Human Resources Manager)
**Operations:** Mark Barnby (Product Manager)
**Engineering:** Daniel Sherwood (Software Engineer), Mike Slade (Director of Engineering)
**US SIC:** 7391, 3559
**UK SIC:** 94000, 32863
**Auditors:** PricewaterhouseCoopers LLP
**Bankers:** Barclays Bank Plc (20-57-40)

|     | 28-03-14    | 29-03-13    | 30-03-12    |
|-----|-------------|-------------|-------------|
| TO  | 101,679,000 | 88,490,000  | 69,408,000  |
| P/L | 12,363,000  | 6,656,000   | 3,829,000   |
| NW  | 19,640,000  | 18,468,000  | 25,226,000  |
| WC  | 16,605,000  | 15,318,000  | 24,478,000  |
| Emp.| 345         | 311         | 266         |

DUNS 22-752-3750     **Imp**
## Sequani Ltd
Bromyard Road, Ledbury, Herefordshire HR8 1LH
**Tel:** 01531-634121
**Web:** www.sequani.com
**Reg No:** 1008026 **VAT No:** 243486356
**Estd:** 1971 Private Limited Company
**Line of Business:** Research and experimental development on natural sciences and engineering
**Export Sales:** £3,997,631
**Issued Capital:** £16,783
**Directors:** Supersummer Services Limited, S Eckley
**Responsibilities**
**Senior:** Nigel Edmondson (Executive)
**Branches:** Sequani Ltd, New Street, Ledbury, Herefordshire HR8 2DX
**US SIC:** 7399 **UK SIC:** 83954
**Auditors:** Baker Tilly UK Audit LLP

|     | 31-07-13  | 31-07-12  | 31-07-11   |
|-----|-----------|-----------|------------|
| TO  | 8,964,859 | 9,564,918 | 12,373,405 |
| P/L | 418,659   | 981,919   | 3,117,944  |
| NW  | 10,522,008| 9,918,850 | 8,863,106  |
| WC  | 8,677,916 | 8,308,435 | 7,501,465  |
| Emp.| 153       | 164       | 161        |

DUNS 85-623-2256
## Sequence Care Ltd
(Subsidiary of: Corinthian Healthcare Ltd)
Highbury Crescent Rooms, 70 Ronalds Road, London N5 1XA
**Tel:** 01992-785460
**Web:** www.curocare.co.uk
**Reg No:** 6259354 **Estd:** 2007 Private Limited Company
**Line of Business:** Hospital activities
**Issued Capital:** £1
**Directors:** Ms K F Ford, C F Doleman, R R Perry
**Responsibilities**
**Senior:** Raoul Federman (Financial Director), Renos Sideras (Manager), Elaine Sideras (Project Director)
**US SIC:** 8062, 8091
**UK SIC:** 95100, 95200

|     | 31-03-13  | 31-03-12  | 31-03-11  |
|-----|-----------|-----------|-----------|
| TO  | 8,625,211 | 6,118,078 | 4,112,125 |
| P/L | 447,732   | (18,320)  | 164,239   |
| NW  | 417,362   | 107,133   | 127,220   |
| WC  | 496,190   | 494,516   | 674,654   |
| Emp.| 228       | 159       | 110       |

DUNS 49-000-0882
## Sequence Collective Ltd
Gloworks, Heol Porth Teigr, Cardiff, South Glamorgan CF10 4GA
**Tel:** 02920935200 **Fax:** 029-2025-2444
**Web:** www.sequence.co.uk
**Reg No:** 3068061 **Estd:** 1995 Private Limited Company
**Line of Business:** Web site design and development
**Issued Capital:** £100
**Principals:** R L Baker (Managing), J Stoneman, P A Thomas, P L Schmidt
**Responsibilities**
**Senior:** Paul Osbaldeston (Manager)
**Finance:** Allie Symonds (operations Director)
**Operations:** Allie Symonds (operations Director)
**US SIC:** 7379 **UK SIC:** 83940
**Auditors:** HWCA Ltd
**Bankers:** Barclays Bank Plc (20-12-25)

|     | 31-07-14  | 31-07-13  | 31-07-12 |
|-----|-----------|-----------|----------|
| TA  | 786,096   | 425,356   | 657,635  |
| NW  | (281,185) | (435,264) | 10,269   |
| WC  | (26,454)  | (125,929) | (72,471) |

DUNS 28-889-4033
## Serais Investments Ltd
(Subsidiary of: Steinhoff International Holdings Ltd)
Unit A9a Dovers Corner Industria, New Road, Rainham, Essex RM13 8QT
**Tel:** 08000323864 **Fax:** 01708-521514
**Web:** www.waste-man.co.uk
**Reg No:** 1264703 **Estd:** 1976 Private Limited Company
**Line of Business:** Management activities of holding companies
**Trading Style:** Harveys Furnishing Group
**Issued Capital:** £101
**Directors:** J H Robins, P J Dieperink
**Co. Secretary:** John Robins
**Responsibilities**
**Senior:** Terry Grant (Manager)
**US SIC:** 6711 **UK SIC:** 83962
**Auditors:** Deloitte & Touche LLP

|     | 29-06-13  | 30-06-12  | 25-06-11  |
|-----|-----------|-----------|-----------|
| TO  | 32,000    | 34,000    | 34,000    |
| P/L | 5,187,000 | 1,000     | 1,000     |
| NW  | 4,779,000 | (408,000) | (409,000) |
| WC  | 4,779,000 | N/A       | N/A       |

DUNS 21-582-4386
## Seramams Metal Technologies
Fudan Way, Thornaby, Stockton-On-Tees, Cleveland TS17 6EN
**Tel:** 01642662100
**Web:** www.siemens.co.uk
**Estd:** 2011 Proprietorship
**Line of Business:** Forging, pressing, stamping and roll forming of metal; powder metallurgy
**Proprietor:** G Wingrove
**Responsibilities**
**Senior:** David Haughe (Facilities Manager)
**US SIC:** 3469 **UK SIC:** 31200
**Employees:** 100

DUNS 21-623-5847
## Seraphina Translations Ltd
37 Sudbury Avenue, North Wembley, Wembley, Middlesex HA0 3AN
**Tel:** 02087950891 **Fax:** 02087950700
**Web:** www.seraphinatranslations.com
**Reg No:** 7038095 **Estd:** 2011 Private Limited Company
**Line of Business:** Translation activities
**Issued Capital:** £100
**Director:** M Whig
**Co. Secretary:** Manohar Whig

**US SIC:** 7339 **UK SIC:** 83954

|     | 31-12-13 | 31-12-12 | 31-12-11 |
|-----|----------|----------|----------|
| TA  | 5,634    | 4,990    | 9,007    |
| NW  | 358      | 1,413    | 978      |
| WC  | (2,564)  | 799      | 5,365    |

DUNS 42-419-1588
## Seraphine Ltd
29 Kimberley Court, Kimberley Road, London NW6 7SL
**Tel:** 020-7794-0805
**Web:** www.seraphine.com
**Reg No:** 4406761 **Estd:** 2002 Private Limited Company
**Line of Business:** Retail sale of clothing
**Issued Capital:** £9,528
**Director:** Ms C H Reinaud
**Co. Secretary:** John Bailey
**US SIC:** 5699 **UK SIC:** 64500
**Bankers:** HSBC Bank plc (40-03-36)

|     | 31-03-14  | 31-03-13  | 31-03-12 |
|-----|-----------|-----------|----------|
| TO  | 8,280,371 | N/A       | N/A      |
| P/L | 1,083,240 | N/A       | N/A      |
| NW  | 1,947,407 | 1,122,605 | 862,875  |
| WC  | 1,821,380 | 1,049,150 | 766,066  |
| Emp.| 53        | N/A       | N/A      |

DUNS 21-775-0461
## Serc
25 Castle Street, Lisburn, Co Antrim BT27 4SU
**Tel:** 02892677225
**Web:** www.serc.ac.uk
**Estd:** 2011 Proprietorship
**Line of Business:** Further education schools and colleges
**Proprietor:** K Webb
**Branches:** Downpatrick Campus, County Down BT30 6LZ Market Street
**US SIC:** 8221 **UK SIC:** 93100
**Employees:** 1,000

DUNS 39-969-5105     **Imp-Exp**
## Sercel England Ltd
(Subsidiary of: Cgg)
Birchwood Way, Somercotes, Alfreton, Derbyshire DE55 4QQ
**Tel:** 01773-605078 **Fax:** 01773-541778
**Web:** www.sercel.com
**Reg No:** 0111791SC **VAT No:** 509256150
**Estd:** 1988 Private Limited Company
**Line of Business:** Marine services
**Export Markets:** E U
**Export Sales:** £8,617,000
**Issued Capital:** £240,100
**Principals:** D K Mcconnachie (Managing), R G Basset, A C Surpas
**Co. Secretary:** Davidson Chalmers (Secretarial S
**Responsibilities**
**Senior:** Jean Dalongeville (Manager)
**Finance:** Jeanette Butler (Financial Manager)
**Marketing:** Philip Hauton (Purchasing Manager)
**Sales:** Philip Hauton (Purchasing Manager)
**HR:** Elaine England (Human Resources Manager)
**Facilities:** Trevor Benson (Senior Engineer)
**Operations:** Philip Hauton (Purchasing Manager)
**Purchasing:** Philip Hauton (Purchasing Manager)
**US SIC:** 4469, 3829, 3357, 8911
**UK SIC:** 76300, 37100, 22470, 83701
**Auditors:** Mazars LLP
**Bankers:** National Westminster Bank Plc (60-01-10)

|     | 31-12-13  | 31-12-12   | 31-12-11   |
|-----|-----------|------------|------------|
| TO  | 9,023,000 | 14,756,000 | 41,197,000 |
| P/L | 3,805,000 | 1,921,000  | 4,662,000  |
| NW  | 10,224,000| 8,712,000  | 10,344,000 |
| WC  | 9,100,000 | 7,621,000  | 9,652,000  |
| Emp.| 69        | 85         | 89         |

DUNS 21-811-8121
## Serco Co British Airways
Hangar 6, Perimeter Road South, London Gatwick Airport, Horley, Surrey RH6 0PQ
**Web:** www.serco.com
**Estd:** 2012
**Line of Business:** Property maintenance services
**Responsibilities**
**Senior:** Michael Jays (Contract Manager)
**US SIC:** 1799 **UK SIC:** 50000
**Employees:** 53

DUNS 21-553-5050
## Serco Defence Science & Nuclear
Hms Seahawk, Helston, Cornwall TR12 7RH
**Web:** www.serco.com
**Line of Business:** Manufacture of aircraft and spacecraft

**Responsibilities**
**Senior:** Rachel Stevenson (Contract Manager)
**US SIC:** 7999 **UK SIC:** 97913
**Employees:** 350

DUNS 34-847-2577
## Serco Global Services (Uk) Ltd
(Subsidiary of: Serco Bpo Private Limited)
Serco House, 16 Bartley Wood Business Park, Hook, Hampshire RG27 9UY
**Tel:** 01415684000
**Web:** www.serco.com
**Reg No:** 5646273 **Estd:** 2005 Private Limited Company
**Line of Business:** Call centre activities
**Issued Capital:** £4,652,000
**Directors:** R Judge, A Telang
**Co. Secretary:** Serco Corporate Services Limited
**Branches:** Serco Global Services (Uk) Ltd, Intercity House, Plymouth Railway Station, Plymouth, Devon PL4 6AB
**US SIC:** 7399 **UK SIC:** 83954
**Auditors:** Grant Thornton UK LLP

|     | 31-03-13  | 31-03-12    | 31-03-11    |
|-----|-----------|-------------|-------------|
| TO  | 255,000   | 8,840,000   | 6,861,000   |
| P/L | (6,000)   | (1,373,000) | (2,129,000) |
| NW  | 5,044,000 | (2,340,000) | (1,301,000) |
| WC  | (560,000) | 1,133,000   | 1,430,000   |
| Emp.| N/A       | 352         | 204         |

DUNS 29-845-2707     **Exp**
## Serco Group Plc
Serco House, 16 Bartley Wood Business Park, Bartley W, Hook, Hampshire RG27 9UY
**Tel:** 01256-745900
**Web:** www.serco.com
**Reg No:** 2048608 **Estd:** 1986 Public Limited Company
**Line of Business:** Management activities of holding companies
**Export Sales:** £2,216,600,000
**Trading Style:** Serco Shared Service Centre
**Issued Capital:** £9,971,400
**Directors:** M Clasper, A D Lyons, M I Wyman, Mrs A S Risley, A G Cockburn, Ms J R Lomax, E J Casey Jr, Ms T Ingram
**Co. Secretary:** David Eveleigh
**Responsibilities**
**Senior:** Edward Casey (Director), Ralph Crosby (Director)
**Branches:** Serco Group Plc, Building 11 Duke Of Yorks Royal Military School, Guston, Dover, Kent CT15 5EQ
**US SIC:** 6711, 7379
**UK SIC:** 83962, 83940
**Auditors:** Deloitte LLP
Following financial data are in thousands

|     | 31-12-13  | 31-12-12  | 31-12-11  |
|-----|-----------|-----------|-----------|
| TO  | 4,288,100 | 4,913,000 | 4,646,400 |
| P/L | 106,600   | 302,000   | 238,300   |
| NW  | (361,300) | (411,600) | (440,100) |
| WC  | 199,100   | 145,900   | 67,400    |
| Emp.| 94,980    | 96,113    | 76,670    |

DUNS 23-656-6795
## Serco Listening Co Ltd
(Subsidiary of: Serco Group Plc)
Auriol House, Richmond, Surrey TW9 1DL
**Tel:** 020-8484-1000 **Fax:** 020-8484-1001
**Web:** www.serco.com
**Reg No:** 3651678 **Estd:** 1998 Private Limited Company
**Line of Business:** Call centres
**Issued Capital:** £959,861
**Directors:** R F Holland, M A Morley, N J Cossey, Ms M A Mcphail
**Co. Secretary:** Serco Corporate Services Limited
**Responsibilities**
**Marketing:** Laura New (Marketing Manager)
**HR:** Reena Parshar (Training Manager)
**US SIC:** 7399, 7319
**UK SIC:** 83954, 83800
**Auditors:** Deloitte LLP
**Bankers:** National Westminster Bank Plc (60-40-02)

|     | 31-12-13    | 31-12-12    | 31-12-11    |
|-----|-------------|-------------|-------------|
| TO  | 118,719,000 | 120,856,000 | 87,323,000  |
| P/L | 12,141,000  | 45,482,000  | (9,513,000) |
| NW  | 35,267,000  | 43,049,000  | (3,537,000) |
| WC  | 58,679,000  | 35,623,000  | 7,851,000   |
| Emp.| 3,065       | 2,121       | 3,589       |

DUNS 21-811-2318
## Serco Marine Services
Great Harbour, Greenock, Renfrewshire PA15 2AR
**Tel:** 01475731540
**Web:** www.serco.com
**Estd:** 2012
**Line of Business:** Other supporting water transport activities
**Responsibilities**
**Senior:** Phil Ireland (Manager)
**US SIC:** 4469 **UK SIC:** 76300
**Employees:** 300

**DUNS 21-036-4531**

## Serco Uk and Europe Defence

Raf Tcs, Oakhanger, Bordon, Hampshire GU35 9JE
**Web:** www.sstd.rl.ac.uk
**Proprietorship**
**Line of Business:** Engineers (consulting)
**Responsibilities**
**Senior:** Roy Bolinger (Contract Manager)
**IT:** Anthony Nowak (Computer Manager)
**HR:** Liz Hammond (Human Resources Manager)
**Health & Safety:** Dave Wyatt (Health & Safety Officer)
**Facilities:** Roy Bolinger (Contract Manager)
**Operations:** Dave Wyatt (Health & Safety Officer)
**US SIC:** 8911   **UK SIC:** 83701
**Employees:** 90

**DUNS 51-652-1403**

## Sercon Support Services Ltd

Kent House, 21 Whittle Place, South Newmoor Industrial Estat, Irvine, Ayrshire KA11 4HR
**Tel:** 01294-217600 **Fax:** 01294217633
**Web:** www.serconltd.co.uk
**Reg No:** 0310397SC **Estd:** 2001 Private Limited Company
**Line of Business:** Security activities
**Issued Capital:** £302
**Directors:** I J Murray, Ms L Stevely
**Co. Secretary:** Paul Gratton
**US SIC:** 7361, 6531, 7349
**UK SIC:** 83954, 83400, 92300

|      | 31-03-14 | 31-03-13 | 31-03-12 |
|------|----------|----------|----------|
| TA   | 1,545,879 | 1,303,970 | 1,109,533 |
| NW   | 409,692 | 219,464 | 231,782 |
| WC   | 88,485 | 73,687 | 67,315 |

**DUNS 42-454-1951**

## Sere Ltd

(**Subsidiary of:** S.E.R.E. Holdings Ltd)
7-13 Boucher Road, Belfast BT12 6HR
**Tel:** 028-9020-5100 **Fax:** 02890205120
**Web:** www.seremotors.com
**Reg No:** 0032529NI **Estd:** 2001 Private Limited Company
**Line of Business:** Car and commercial vehicle repairs
**Issued Capital:** £1,250,002
**Directors:** P Kearney, S Edgar, T J Megarry, W Mcnally, T B Thompson
**Responsibilities**
**HR:** Claire Grady (Human Resources Manager)
**Health & Safety:** Claire Grady (Human Resources Manager)
**US SIC:** 5511   **UK SIC:** 65100
**Auditors:** Trevor Jones & Co
**Bankers:** HSBC Bank plc (40-10-50)

|      | 31-12-13 | 31-12-12 | 31-12-11 |
|------|----------|----------|----------|
| TO   | 28,991,712 | 28,808,458 | 30,887,804 |
| P/L  | 527,325 | 147,513 | (189,996) |
| NW   | 1,534,624 | 1,088,489 | 1,567,189 |
| WC   | 390,847 | 252,937 | 155,314 |
| Emp. | 91 | 98 | 106 |

**DUNS 23-599-1820**

## Seren Ffestiniog Cyf.

Unit 1-2, Llwyn Gell Industrial Estate, Blaenau Ffestiniog, Gwynedd LL41 3NE
**Tel:** 01766832378
**Web:** www.serencys.org.com
**Reg No:** 3596581 **Estd:** 2006 Private Limited Company
**Line of Business:** General (overall) public service activities
**Trading Style:** Cwmni Seren
**Directors:** G C Price, E J Lewis, J E Ellis, A L Ellis, E M Jones, Mrs A Ellis, W A Evans, Ms L A Jones
**Co. Secretary:** Mrs Krystle Madoc-Jones
**Responsibilities**
**Senior:** Krystle Murphy (Manager)
**US SIC:** 9121   **UK SIC:** 91110
**Auditors:** Dunn & Ellis

|      | 31-03-14 | 31-03-13 | 31-03-12 |
|------|----------|----------|----------|
| TO   | 2,018,107 | 1,135,791 | 1,136,622 |
| P/L  | 687,846 | 5,761 | 56,621 |
| NW   | 1,468,132 | 776,731 | 761,170 |
| WC   | 91,378 | 206,590 | 216,882 |
| Emp. | 55 | 58 | N/A |

**DUNS 36-484-4196**

## Seren Group Ltd

The Old Post Office, High Street, Newport, Gwent NP20 1AA
**Tel:** 01633679911
**Web:** www.seren-group.co.uk
**Reg No:** 0029682IP **Estd:** 2004
**Line of Business:** Housing associations societies trusts & co-operatives
**Trading Style:** Charter Housing
**Principals:** B Hutchings (Chairman), M Williams, G Rawlings, Ms B Morris, M Davies, S Murton, M Lawson-Jones, Ms L Moseley

**Responsibilities**
**Senior:** Darrell Bolton (Manager), Graham Graham (Manager), Adrianne Jones (Designated Limited Liability P)
**IT:** Chris Cherryman (IT Operations Manager)
**US SIC:** 8321   **UK SIC:** 96111
**Auditors:** KPMG LLP
**Bankers:** Lloyds TSB Bank plc (77-62-02)
**Employees:** 692
**Turnover:** £40,333,000

**DUNS 21-154-2097**      Exp

## Serena Software Europe Ltd

(**Subsidiary of:** Merant Holdings)
Abbey View, Everard Close, St Albans, Hertfordshire AL1 2PS
**Tel:** 01727-812812
**Web:** www.serena.com
**Reg No:** 1272886 **Estd:** 1976 Private Limited Company
**Line of Business:** Other computer related activities
**Export Markets:** Worldwide
**Export Sales:** £3,929,000
**Issued Capital:** £17,101
**Director:** K R Jukes
**Co. Secretary:** Edward Malysz
**Responsibilities**
**Senior:** Michael Lindner (Vice President)
**Branches:** Serena Software Europe Ltd, 7 Oxford Rd, Link View, Newbury, Berkshire RG14 3AD
**US SIC:** 7379   **UK SIC:** 83940
**Auditors:** KPMG Audit PLC

|      | 31-01-14 | 31-01-13 | 31-01-12 |
|------|----------|----------|----------|
| TO   | 13,672,000 | 13,893,000 | 15,154,000 |
| P/L  | (254,000) | 3,341,000 | 5,744,000 |
| NW   | 2,132,000 | 27,003,000 | 23,928,000 |
| WC   | 3,015,000 | 27,108,000 | 24,216,000 |
| Emp. | 75 | 103 | 104 |

**DUNS 21-017-8686**

## Serendipity Healthcare Ltd

(**Subsidiary of:** Seren Holdings (Uk) Ltd)
Seren House, Unit 26 Vanguard Trading Estate, Chesterfield, Derbyshire S40 2TZ
**Tel:** 01246260843
**Web:** www.serendipityhealthcare.co.uk
**Reg No:** 6397807 **Estd:** 2007 Private Limited Company
**Line of Business:** Activities of households as employers of domestic staff
**Issued Capital:** £12
**Director:** C J Pickles
**Co. Secretary:** Mrs Sarah Pickles
**US SIC:** 8811   **UK SIC:** 99000

|      | 31-12-13 | 31-12-12 | 31-12-11 |
|------|----------|----------|----------|
| TA   | 552,853 | 432,957 | 322,520 |
| NW   | 413,069 | 348,960 | 234,769 |
| WC   | 403,529 | 337,333 | N/A |

**DUNS 22-641-2013**

## Serenity Holidays Ltd.

Atlantic House, Fareham, Hampshire PO15 7AN
**Tel:** 01489866901 **Fax:** 01489866917
**Web:** www.serenity.co.uk
**Reg No:** 1744872 **VAT No:** 386066134
**Estd:** 1983 Private Limited Company
**Line of Business:** Activities of travel organisers
**Trading Style:** The Gambia Experience, Serenity Golf, Kololi Flight Cub
**Issued Capital:** £100,470
**Principals:** S F Wilde (Managing), C P Ayling, C J Rowles, Ms S M Wilde
**Co. Secretary:** Robert Lane
**Responsibilities**
**Marketing:** Jenny Adams (PR Manager)
**Sales:** Jason Dicks (Sales Manager)
**US SIC:** 4722   **UK SIC:** 77001
**Auditors:** Rossell Hicks
**Bankers:** National Westminster Bank Plc (60-18-46)

|      | 31-10-13 | 31-10-12 | 31-10-11 |
|------|----------|----------|----------|
| TO   | 26,981,579 | 24,788,694 | 24,744,458 |
| P/L  | 312,535 | 844,094 | 838,576 |
| NW   | 3,826,029 | 3,937,473 | 3,255,836 |
| WC   | 2,858,053 | 1,726,416 | 1,179,830 |
| Emp. | 243 | 246 | 243 |

**DUNS 73-784-3834**

## Serif Group Ltd

The Software Centre, 12 Nottingham South & Wilford In, Nottingham, Nottinghamshire NG11 7EP
**Tel:** 01159142000
**Reg No:** 5041038 **Estd:** 2004 Private Limited Company
**Line of Business:** Other software consultancy and supply
**Export Sales:** £3,012,805
**Issued Capital:** £48,750
**Directors:** J D Bryce, A T Hewson
**Co. Secretary:** Gary Bates
**US SIC:** 7379   **UK SIC:** 83940

**Bankers:** Bank Of Scotland (12-09-26)

|      | 31-12-13 | 31-12-12 | 31-12-11 |
|------|----------|----------|----------|
| TO   | 11,569,848 | 15,749,469 | 17,214,787 |
| P/L  | 923,431 | 619,834 | 922,090 |
| NW   | 2,627,084 | 2,089,607 | 2,056,736 |
| WC   | 2,495,485 | 2,002,756 | 1,936,608 |
| Emp. | 182 | 249 | 249 |

**DUNS 28-825-6811**

## Serimax Ltd

16 Airfield Road, Dingwall, Ross-Shire IV16 9XJ
**Tel:** 01349-831-122 **Fax:** 01349-831-133
**Web:** www.serimax.com
**Reg No:** 0073616SC **Estd:** 1981 Private Limited Company
**Line of Business:** Pipework contractors
**Export Sales:** £9,946,667
**Issued Capital:** £12,100,000
**Director:** F Castrec
**Co. Secretary:** Burness Paull Llp
**Responsibilities**
**Senior:** Les Dickson (Vice President), Helen Dornan (Manager), Elodie Penet (Executive), Malcolm Watt (Manager)
**Sales:** Kenny Coutts (Vice President, Group Business)
**IT:** Kelly O Connor (Head of IT)
**Operations:** Dave Mackay (Vice President of Operations)
**Branches:** Serimax Ltd, 35 Henderson Drive, Inverness, Inverness-Shire IV1 1TR
**US SIC:** 4619, 7699
**UK SIC:** 72601, 67303
**Auditors:** Deloitte LLP
**Bankers:** The Royal Bank Of Scotland Plc (83-15-31)

|      | 31-12-13 | 31-12-12 | 31-12-11 |
|------|----------|----------|----------|
| TO   | 35,184,534 | 24,920,300 | 27,460,738 |
| P/L  | (2,192,324) | (224,351) | (5,611,416) |
| NW   | (828,553) | 1,541,843 | (10,300,716) |
| WC   | (3,815,023) | (700,819) | (12,606,369) |
| Emp. | 249 | 197 | 226 |

**DUNS 73-364-6223**

## Serious Crews Ltd

(**Subsidiary of:** Serious Ventures Ltd)
Tor Hill Works, Tor Hill, Wells, Somerset BA5 3NT
**Tel:** 01749-899188
**Web:** www.stages.co.uk
**Reg No:** 4637657 **Estd:** 2003 Private Limited Company
**Line of Business:** Other artistic and literary creation and interpretation
**Issued Capital:** £1
**Directors:** S Allen, Mrs H C Corfield Moore
**Co. Secretary:** Steven Corfield Moore
**US SIC:** 8999   **UK SIC:** 83954
**Bankers:** Barclays Bank Plc (20-99-40)

|      | 31-12-13 | 31-12-12 | 31-12-11 |
|------|----------|----------|----------|
| TA   | 854 | 81,923 | 81,923 |
| NW   | 854 | 854 | 854 |
| WC   | N/A | 854 | 854 |

**DUNS 23-995-0249**

## Serious Fraud Office

2-4 Cockspur Street, London SW1Y 5BS
**Tel:** 020-7239-7272
**Web:** www.sfo.gov.uk
**Estd:** 2002
**Line of Business:** Central government
**Principals:** Mrs R Wright, R Wardell
**Responsibilities**
**IT:** Abdul Abdi (IT Manager)
**Facilities:** Mina Sharma (Head of Facilities)
**Purchasing:** Mina Sharma (Head of Facilities)
**Branches:** various depts country wide
**US SIC:** 9121   **UK SIC:** 91110
**Employees:** 300

**DUNS 23-807-7288**

## Serjeant Security Ltd.

10 Kent House, Bourne Road, Old Bexley Business Park, Bexley, Kent DA5 1LR
**Tel:** 01322-315501
**Web:** www.serjeantsecurityltd.co.uk
**Reg No:** 3800134 **Estd:** 1999 Private Limited Company
**Line of Business:** Security and related activities
**Issued Capital:** £100
**Director:** D C Scrivens
**Co. Secretary:** Ms Christine Scrivens
**US SIC:** 7393   **UK SIC:** 83954
**Auditors:** Hedley Dunk Ltd

|      | 31-07-14 | 31-07-13 | 31-07-12 |
|------|----------|----------|----------|
| TA   | 600,820 | 511,102 | 600,229 |
| NW   | 208,805 | 287,325 | 290,916 |
| WC   | 202,948 | 279,228 | 281,003 |

**DUNS 73-927-7085**

## Serlo Enterprises Ltd

Bishopscourt, Pitt Street, Gloucester, Gloucestershire GL1 2BQ
**Tel:** 01452-337337 **Fax:** 01452-337314
**Web:** www.thekingsschool.co.uk
**Reg No:** 2938904 **Estd:** 1997 Private Limited Company

**Line of Business:** Catering
**Trading Style:** King's School
**Issued Capital:** £3
**Directors:** C M Collier, P F Markey, A K Macnaughton
**Co. Secretary:** Ms Jacqueline Millar
**Responsibilities**
**Senior:** A Mcnaughton (Head Teacher)
**Marketing:** Sharon Bird (Registrar)
**Sales:** Sharon Bird (Registrar)
**HR:** Adrienne McMeeken (Human Resources Manager), Vivienne Scholes (Deputy Head)
**US SIC:** 5812   **UK SIC:** 66110
**Auditors:** Horwath Clark Whitehill LLP
**Bankers:** Lloyds TSB Bank plc (30-93-48)

|      | 31-08-14 | 31-08-13 | 31-08-12 |
|------|----------|----------|----------|
| TO   | 52,459 | 92,496 | 65,217 |
| P/L  | (1,135) | N/A | N/A |
| NW   | (353) | 782 | 782 |
| WC   | (353) | 782 | 782 |

**DUNS 34-539-2356**

## Sermatech International Uk Ltd

Sermatech (Uk) Lincoln, Lincoln, Lincolnshire LN6 3DL
**Tel:** 01522878207 **Fax:** 01773-512344
**Reg No:** 5349513 **Estd:** 2005 Private Limited Company
**Line of Business:** Treatment and coating of metals
**Issued Capital:** £100
**Directors:** J Winterburn, S Cast
**Co. Secretary:** Julian Winterburn
**US SIC:** 3398   **UK SIC:** 31380
**Auditors:** PricewaterhouseCoopers LLP
**Bankers:** National Westminster Bank Plc (51-81-41)

|      | 31-12-13 | 31-12-12 | 31-12-11 |
|------|----------|----------|----------|
| TA   | 3,574,000 | 3,567,000 | 3,557,000 |
| P/L  | 6,000 | 10,000 | 11,000 |
| NW   | 3,554,000 | 3,551,000 | 3,547,000 |
| WC   | 3,554,000 | 3,551,000 | 3,547,000 |

**DUNS 21-175-0157**

## Sermo Telecom Ltd

16 Phillips Hatch, Wonersh, Guildford, Surrey GU5 0PX
**Tel:** 08454507950
**Web:** www.sermotelecom.co.uk
**Reg No:** 6985713 **Estd:** 2009 Private Limited Company
**Line of Business:** Telecom services
**Issued Capital:** £100
**Director:** A J Silver
**Co. Secretary:** Ms Samantha Silver
**US SIC:** 4899   **UK SIC:** 79020

|      | 31-08-13 | 31-08-12 | 31-08-11 |
|------|----------|----------|----------|
| TA   | 95,111 | 48,062 | 12,448 |
| NW   | (19,750) | (21,992) | (28,996) |
| WC   | (30,373) | (23,716) | (31,294) |

**DUNS 85-617-7451**

## Serocor Holdings Ltd

Langstone Road, Havant, Hampshire PO9 1SA
**Tel:** 02392458080
**Web:** www.serocor.com
**Reg No:** 6254182 **Estd:** 2007 Private Limited Company
**Line of Business:** Employment and recruitment companies and consultants
**Issued Capital:** £173,200
**Directors:** S J Church, M J Gawthorne, S M Lawton, M W Hunt, P A Huntingdon
**Co. Secretary:** Mark Gawthorne
**US SIC:** 6711   **UK SIC:** 83962

|      | 28-02-14 | 28-02-13 | 31-02-11 |
|------|----------|----------|----------|
| TO   | 109,369,000 | 168,746,000 | 98,840,000 |
| P/L  | (1,650,000) | 2,578,000 | 3,707,000 |
| NW   | 4,102,000 | 5,352,000 | 3,131,000 |
| WC   | 5,933,000 | 7,128,000 | 5,234,000 |
| Emp. | 204 | 196 | 157 |

**DUNS 39-692-9200**      Imp

## The Serpentine Trust

Kensington Gardens, London W2 3XA
**Tel:** 02077064907 **Fax:** 020-7402-4103
**Web:** www.serpentinegalleries.org
**Reg No:** 2150221 **Estd:** 2010 Private Company Limited By Guarantee
**Line of Business:** Art gallery
**Trading Style:** Serpentine Gallery
**Directors:** R J Bramble, B Townsley, C D Tweedy, The Lord P G Palumbo, M J Boyle, M Bloomberg, M Compagnoni, D J Fletcher
**Co. Secretary:** Weil Secretaries Limited
**Responsibilities**
**Senior:** Mark Booth (Manager), Robert Hersov (Director), Julia Patent- Jones (Manager), Julia Peyton-Jones (Operations Director), Felicity Waley-Cohen (Director)
**Marketing:** Rose Dempsey (Head of Press)
**HR:** Elizabeth Clayton (Human Resources Manager), Julia Peyton-Jones (Operations Director)
**Facilities:** Julie Burnell (Head of Operations)
**Branches:** The Serpentine Trust, 54 Warren St, London W1T 5NN

**US SIC:** 7911, 8249
**UK SIC:** 97913, 93300
**Auditors:** Horwath Clark Whitehill
**Bankers:** Coutts & Co (18-00-02)

| | 31-03-14 | 31-03-13 | 31-03-12 |
|---|---|---|---|
| TO | 9,167,841 | 6,704,852 | 9,962,400 |
| P/L | 2,350,857 | 614,900 | 4,892,456 |
| NW | 13,157,999 | 10,807,142 | 10,192,242 |
| WC | (898,213) | 433,836 | 5,451,402 |
| Emp. | 64 | 57 | 48 |

DUNS 73-687-4764

## Sers Energy Solutions Group Ltd

**(Subsidiary of:** Sers Energy Solutions Holdings Ltd)
Unit 3a, Parc Pontypandy, Caerphilly, Mid Glamorgan CF83 3GX
**Tel:** 01387811222
**Web:** www.sersltd.co.uk
**Reg No:** 4946501 **Estd:** 2003 Private Limited Company
**Line of Business:** Management activities of holding companies
**Issued Capital:** £250,002
**Directors:** L M Jones, M J Barker, M J Roberts, A B Robb
**Co. Secretary:** Miss Gaynor Howells
**US SIC:** 6711 **UK SIC:** 83962

| | 31-12-13 | 31-12-12 | 31-12-11 |
|---|---|---|---|
| TO | 28,124,690 | 26,660,334 | 14,431,599 |
| P/L | 522,617 | 3,262,329 | 348,757 |
| NW | 3,083,408 | 2,978,573 | 919,732 |
| WC | 2,781,439 | 2,903,966 | 943,567 |
| Emp. | 147 | 120 | 64 |

DUNS 76-934-1090

## Sers Energy Solutions Ltd

**(Subsidiary of:** Sers Energy Solutions Holdings Ltd)
Cefn Nyddfa, Commercial Street, Blackwood, Gwent NP12 3TX
**Tel:** 01443-821349 **Fax:** 01443836549
**Web:** www.sersltd.co.uk
**Reg No:** 2473034 **VAT No:** 540837151
**Estd:** 1990 Private Limited Company
**Line of Business:** Building services
**Trading Style:** S E R S
**Issued Capital:** £2
**Principals:** L M Jones *(Managing)*, M J Barker, M J Roberts, A B Robb
**Co. Secretary:** Miss Gaynor Howells
**Responsibilities**
**Purchasing:** Gloria Browning *(Purchasing Manager)*
**US SIC:** 1742 **UK SIC:** 50400
**Auditors:** Neil Hodge & Co Ltd
**Bankers:** Barclays Bank Plc (20-10-26)

| | 31-12-13 | 31-12-12 | 31-12-11 |
|---|---|---|---|
| TO | 27,956,540 | 26,200,941 | 12,690,667 |
| P/L | 603,161 | 2,731,492 | 594,395 |
| NW | 3,297,215 | 3,240,498 | 1,436,682 |
| WC | 2,862,673 | 2,939,566 | 1,210,517 |
| Emp. | 116 | 92 | 56 |

DUNS 42-408-1482 **Imp**

## Sert-Mst Plc

**(Subsidiary of:** Artrade Holdings Ltd)
Tetron Point, William Nadin Way, Swadlincote, Derbyshire DE11 0BB
**Tel:** 01159425577 **Fax:** 01159425588
**Web:** www.sert-mst.com
**Reg No:** 4395793 **VAT No:** 784412910
**Estd:** 2002 Public Limited Company
**Line of Business:** Non-specialised wholesale of food, beverages and tobacco
**Export Sales:** £7,621,304
**Trading Style:** Crown Cress
**Issued Capital:** £4,499,105
**Directors:** S R Tayub, Mrs S Tayub
**Co. Secretary:** Abdul Tayub
**US SIC:** 5149 **UK SIC:** 61700
**Auditors:** PKF (UK) LLP
**Bankers:** Lloyds TSB Bank plc (30-92-59)

| | 31-03-14 | 31-03-13 | 31-03-12 |
|---|---|---|---|
| TO | 89,961,540 | 114,800,253 | 120,111,288 |
| P/L | 717,111 | 3,835,522 | 2,076,700 |
| NW | 23,108,423 | 24,912,639 | 21,844,508 |
| WC | 14,957,332 | 20,303,438 | 15,765,197 |
| Emp. | 115 | 128 | 123 |

DUNS 21-880-6487 **Imp-Exp**

## Sertec (Birmingham) Ltd

**(Subsidiary of:** Sertec Group Holdings Ltd)
Gorsey Lane, Coleshill, Birmingham, West Midlands B46 1JU
**Tel:** 01675-463361 **Fax:** 01675-465539
**Web:** www.sertec.co.uk
**Reg No:** 0719490 **VAT No:** 661546431
**Estd:** 1962 Private Limited Company
**Line of Business:** Engineers (general)
**Export Markets:** Europe
**Export Sales:** £1,813,238
**Issued Capital:** £1,500
**Principals:** G R Mosedale *(Managing)*, M A Hughes *(Financial)*, G W Adams, S J Morley, Ms R A Jessop, D G Steggles, J A O'Shea
**Co. Secretary:** Graham Mosedale
**Branches:** Sertec (Birmingham) Ltd, Essex Works, Holborn Hill, Birmingham, West Midlands B6 7QT
**US SIC:** 3714, 8911
**UK SIC:** 35300, 83701
**Auditors:** Harrison Beale
**Bankers:** Lloyds TSB Bank plc (30-00-06)

| | 31-03-14 | 31-03-13 | 31-03-12 |
|---|---|---|---|
| TO | 76,341,950 | 66,159,742 | 61,009,060 |
| P/L | 5,713,399 | 3,862,814 | 3,774,905 |
| NW | 19,862,281 | 15,182,576 | 12,989,467 |
| WC | 11,555,223 | 7,195,303 | 6,111,806 |
| Emp. | 343 | 295 | 232 |

DUNS 38-547-6007

## Servaccomm Redhall Ltd

Patrington Road, Ottringham, Hull, North Humberside HU12 0AD
**Tel:** 01964-624444
**Web:** www.servaccomm.co.uk
**Reg No:** 3329199 **VAT No:** 686656867
**Estd:** 1997 Private Limited Company
**Line of Business:** Erection of roof covering and frames
**Trading Style:** Servaccomm Redhall Ltd
**Issued Capital:** £151,650
**Directors:** M J Hardy, J Gilfoyle, D B Winn, T Hebb, S N Dennis, M R Marriott, D S Anderson
**Responsibilities**
**Senior:** Edward Delaney *(Chairman)*, Mary Fairweather *(Manager)*
**US SIC:** 1761, 3441
**UK SIC:** 50400, 32042
**Auditors:** Smailes Goldie

| | 31-03-14 | 31-03-13 | 31-03-12 |
|---|---|---|---|
| TO | 14,735,086 | 15,328,069 | 12,751,035 |
| P/L | 125,429 | (281,585) | 196,392 |
| NW | 1,518,412 | 1,954,442 | 2,171,128 |
| WC | 851,908 | 878,543 | 1,103,385 |
| Emp. | 80 | 78 | 71 |

DUNS 77-442-2000

## Serve

19 Church Street, Rushden, Northamptonshire NN10 9YU
**Tel:** 01933-315555
**Web:** www.serve.org.uk
**Reg No:** 2951827 **Estd:** 1981 Private Limited Company
**Line of Business:** Charities and charitable organisations
**Directors:** L H Meakings, C O Parker, A Armson, Ms P L Hooton, M B Neville, B Coker
**Co. Secretary:** James Kearns
**Responsibilities**
**Senior:** Cate Carmichael *(Chief Executive Officer)*, Barry Graves *(Chief Executive)*, Betty Harris *(Manager)*, Gopalan Pillai *(Manager)*
**Branches:** Serve, 20 Ockley Road, London SW16 1UB
**US SIC:** 8699 **UK SIC:** 96902
**Auditors:** Phipps Henson McAllister
**Bankers:** HSBC Bank plc (40-39-15)

| | 31-03-14 | 31-03-13 | 31-03-12 |
|---|---|---|---|
| TO | 2,349,645 | 1,668,865 | 1,350,612 |
| P/L | 27,451 | 22,910 | 187,053 |
| NW | 376,927 | 349,476 | 326,566 |
| WC | 267,613 | 251,479 | 229,695 |
| Emp. | 135 | 99 | 81 |

DUNS 21-118-4958

## Servebase Group Ltd

63 Braemar Avenue Wimbledon Park, London SW19 8AY
**Tel:** 07775-766565
**Web:** www.abacuspartners.co.uk
**Reg No:** 6580786 **Estd:** 2008 Private Limited Company
**Line of Business:** Business services
**Issued Capital:** £1,511,458
**Directors:** K Hedjri, J G Leigh, R R Steytler, M J Weigold, J Bennett, E W Chandler
**Co. Secretary:** Robert Hoskin
**US SIC:** 7399 **UK SIC:** 83954

| | 31-03-14 | 31-03-13 | 31-03-12 |
|---|---|---|---|
| TO | 3,872,121 | 4,091,631 | 3,806,073 |
| P/L | (1,818,854) | (2,191,819) | (1,885,689) |
| NW | (5,753,621) | (5,649,875) | (4,703,663) |
| WC | 179,242 | (2,844) | 79,871 |
| Emp. | 55 | 65 | 69 |

DUNS 77-534-8089

## Servecorp Ltd

76 Victoria Road, Burgess Hill, West Sussex RH15 9LH
**Tel:** 01444871574
**Web:** http://servecorpsvs.com
**Reg No:** 2992782 **Estd:** 1994 Private Limited Company
**Line of Business:** Airline related services
**Issued Capital:** £2
**Director:** N G White
**Co. Secretary:** Ms Amanda White
**Responsibilities**
**HR:** Lorna Leggett *(Human Resources Manager)*
**Health & Safety:** Lorna Leggett *(Human Resources Manager)*
**Facilities:** Brendan Digges *(Maintenance Engineer)*
**Branches:** Servecorp Ltd, Unit B, 1 Woolborough Lane, Crawley, West Sussex RH10 9AQ
**US SIC:** 4582 **UK SIC:** 76400
**Auditors:** Wood Branson Dickinson
**Bankers:** HSBC Bank plc (40-18-22)

| | 30-04-14 | 30-04-13 | 30-04-12 |
|---|---|---|---|
| TA | 1,619,760 | 2,207,893 | 2,159,054 |
| NW | 1,311,204 | 894,050 | 539,815 |
| WC | 328,472 | (1,691) | (277,869) |

DUNS 49-115-8143 **Imp**

## Servelec Group Plc

Rotherside Road, Eckington, Sheffield, South Yorkshire S21 4HL
**Tel:** 01246-437500 **Fax:** 01246-437401
**Web:** www.cse-healthcare.com
**Reg No:** 3098411 **VAT No:** 648280518
**Estd:** 1995 Public Limited Company
**Line of Business:** Management activities of holding companies
**Export Sales:** £5,337,000
**Trading Style:** C S E Healthcare Systems
**Issued Capital:** £4,578,500
**Directors:** R S Mcdowell, R Last, B J Waldron, A Stubbs, M G Cane
**Co. Secretary:** Michael Cane
**US SIC:** 6711 **UK SIC:** 83962
**Auditors:** Ernst & Young LLP
**Bankers:** HSBC Bank plc (40-27-15)

| | 31-12-13 | 31-12-12 | 31-12-11 |
|---|---|---|---|
| TO | 41,995,000 | 40,814,000 | 43,117,000 |
| P/L | 10,908,000 | 10,386,000 | 8,797,000 |
| NW | 23,929,000 | 22,421,000 | 15,714,000 |
| WC | 23,700,000 | 21,159,000 | 14,612,000 |
| Emp. | 436 | 397 | 404 |

DUNS 21-155-1742 **Imp**

## Servequip Ltd

Suite 8, Croydon, Surrey CR0 4XG
**Tel:** 02086-868855 **Fax:** 02086-817509
**Web:** www.servequip.co.uk
**Reg No:** 1065251 **VAT No:** 218482457
**Estd:** 1970 Private Limited Company
**Line of Business:** Catering equipment
**Issued Capital:** £43,522
**Principals:** R J Cumbo *(Chairman and Managing)*, N T Pearson
**Responsibilities**
**Senior:** Shawn Drury *(Northern Area Manager)*, Costas Skrvis *(Warehouse Manager)*, Ahsam Zameer *(Marketing Manager)*
**Marketing:** Ahsam Zameer *(Marketing Manager)*
**Admin:** Lisa Bagheri *(Service Administration Manager)*
**Purchasing:** Paula Bedingfield *(Purchasing Manager)*
**Branches:** Servequip Ltd, Rear Of 1 Cromwell Rd, Walton-On-Thames, Surrey KT12 3NL
**US SIC:** 3551 **UK SIC:** 32441
**Auditors:** Mazars LLP
**Bankers:** National Westminster Bank Plc (60-06-20)

| | 31-12-13 | 31-12-12 | 31-12-11 |
|---|---|---|---|
| TO | 64,484 | N/A | N/A |
| P/L | (6,285) | 65,464 | N/A |
| NW | (124,513) | (118,201) | (142,838) |
| WC | 280,854 | 302,203 | 332,360 |

DUNS 76-512-2866

## Servest Catering Ltd

**(Subsidiary of:** Servest (Pty) Ltd)
Drayton Manor Business Park, Coleshill Road, Tamworth, Staffordshire B78 3TL
**Tel:** 01827-259600 **Fax:** 01827-259506
**Web:** www.servest.com
**Reg No:** 2569158 **Estd:** 1994 Private Limited Company
**Line of Business:** Canteens and catering
**Issued Capital:** £100
**Directors:** D C Griffiths, M Johnson, P Morris, P H Watts, R Legge
**Co. Secretary:** Daniel Dickson
**Responsibilities**
**Senior:** Nicola Boothright *(Manager)*, Mark Boothwright *(Proprietor)*, Colette Reeves *(Finance Director)*
**Finance:** Colette Reeves *(Finance Director)*
**HR:** Paul Chetwynd *(Personnel Manager)*
**Branches:** Servest Catering Ltd, Rockingham Way, Redhouse Interchange, Adwick-Le-Street, Doncaster, South Yorkshire DN6 7FB
**US SIC:** 5812 **UK SIC:** 66110
**Auditors:** H W
**Bankers:** Barclays Bank Plc (20-07-71)

| | 30-09-14 | 30-09-13 | 31-09-12 |
|---|---|---|---|
| TO | 58,619,520 | 81,927,468 | 61,611,396 |
| P/L | 3,786,809 | 3,722,035 | 2,172,265 |
| NW | 8,059,965 | 5,026,644 | 5,263,751 |
| WC | 7,639,408 | 4,953,993 | 5,213,876 |
| Emp. | 2,099 | 2,278 | 2,301 |

DUNS 21-012-3801

## Servest Group Ltd

**(Subsidiary of:** Servest (Pty) Ltd)
Servest House, Heath Farm Business Centre, Fornham All Saints, Bury St Edmunds, Suffolk IP28 6LG
**Tel:** 01284703535
**Web:** www.servest.co.uk
**Reg No:** 6355228 **Estd:** 2007 Private Limited Company
**Line of Business:** Management of real estate on a fee or contract basis
**Issued Capital:** £1,665,003
**Directors:** K J Fine, D C Zietsman, J A Venter, R Legge, Miss C Green, A Sugars, P Morris
**Co. Secretary:** Daniel Dickson
**Responsibilities**
**Senior:** Sara Gage *(Operations Administrator)*, Paul Middleton *(Manager)*
**US SIC:** 6531 **UK SIC:** 83400
**Auditors:** PKF (UK) LLP

| | 30-09-14 | 30-09-13 | 30-09-12 |
|---|---|---|---|
| TO | 215,269,838 | 169,409,726 | 82,831,017 |
| P/L | 2,334,894 | 4,184,213 | 2,461,994 |
| NW | (33,881,041) | (35,941,516) | (14,124,698) |
| WC | 15,448,052 | (12,916,844) | (7,886,625) |
| Emp. | 16,576 | 13,672 | 9,235 |

DUNS 21-918-3274

## Service Ceilings Ltd

Trafalgar Industrial Estate, Sovereign Way, Downham Market, Norfolk PE38 9SW
**Tel:** 01366388783 **Fax:** 01366-388511
**Web:** www.serviceceilings.co.uk
**Reg No:** 1452966 **VAT No:** 324578055
**Estd:** 1979 Private Limited Company
**Line of Business:** Other building completion
**Trading Style:** S C L Interiors
**Issued Capital:** £5,000
**Principals:** A J Nurse *(Managing)*, T J Nurse *(Managing)*, N F Roper, Mrs M C Nurse
**Co. Secretary:** Stephen Nixon
**Branches:** Service Ceilings Ltd, Unit E, 29 Olympus Close, Ipswich, Suffolk IP1 5LJ
**US SIC:** 1799 **UK SIC:** 50000
**Auditors:** Wheeler & Co

| | 31-03-14 | 31-03-13 | 31-03-12 |
|---|---|---|---|
| TO | 12,146,831 | 12,159,300 | 15,605,548 |
| P/L | 47,991 | (29,185) | 181,518 |
| NW | 1,011,076 | 985,104 | 1,020,070 |
| WC | 678,234 | 509,000 | 585,172 |
| Emp. | 100 | 105 | 96 |

DUNS 21-600-4675

## Service Force

Cornwall House, 55-57 High Street, Slough, Berkshire SL1 1DZ
**Tel:** 08705929929
**Estd:** 2011
**Line of Business:** Washing machines service and repair
**US SIC:** 7629 **UK SIC:** 67301
**Employees:** 754

DUNS 21-106-0808

## Service Glasgow Llp

220 High Street, Glasgow, Lanarkshire G4 0QW
**Tel:** 01412-878104
**Web:** www.access.uk.com
**Reg No:** 0301705SO **Estd:** 2008
**Line of Business:** Business services
**Trading Style:** Access
**US SIC:** 7399 **UK SIC:** 83954
**Auditors:** Deloitte LLP

| | 31-12-13 | 31-12-12 | 31-12-11 |
|---|---|---|---|
| TO | 55,720,000 | 52,870,000 | 47,608,000 |
| P/L | (139,000) | (167,000) | 50,000 |
| NW | (1,049,000) | (167,000) | N/A |
| WC | (1,049,000) | (167,000) | N/A |
| Emp. | 410 | 374 | 339 |

DUNS 22-720-2439 **Imp-Exp**

## Service Innovation Group-Uk Ltd

**(Subsidiary of:** Hopp Beteiligungsges. Mbh & Co. Kg)
51 Clarendon Road, Watford, Hertfordshire WD17 1HP
**Tel:** 02084576400 **Fax:** 020-8203-7722
**Web:** www.innovation-group.com
**Reg No:** 1443016 **Estd:** 1979 Private Limited Company
**Line of Business:** Conference centres and facilities
**Trading Style:** Brann Ellert
**Issued Capital:** £2
**Directors:** T Lark, J Mueller
**Co. Secretary:** Mrs Melanie Moodley
**Responsibilities**
**Senior:** Kate Hendry *(Business Development Manager)*, Annette Lacey *(Manager)*, Nico van Santvoort *(Manager)*
**Marketing:** George Seal *(Office Manager)*
**Admin:** Jose Rampini *(IT Administrator)*
**IT:** Jose Rampini *(IT Administrator)*
**Facilities:** George Seal *(Office Manager)*
**US SIC:** 7399 **UK SIC:** 83954

**Auditors:** BDO LLP
**Bankers:** Barclays Bank Plc (20-71-74)

| | 30-09-13 | 30-09-12 | 30-09-11 |
|---|---|---|---|
| TO | 6,603,000 | 9,327,000 | 8,628,000 |
| P/L | (719,000) | 349,000 | 953,000 |
| NW | 135,000 | 763,000 | 506,000 |
| WC | 217,000 | 722,000 | 456,000 |
| Emp. | 459 | 527 | 504 |

DUNS 22-831-5644    **Imp-Exp**
## Service Metals (Midlands) Ltd
Unit 2, Jamage Industrial Estate, Stoke-On-Trent, Staffordshire ST7 1XW
**Tel:** 0844-848-7020 **Fax:** 0844-848-7021
**Web:** www.servicemetals.co.uk
**Reg No:** 2107614 **Estd:** 1987 Private Limited Company
**Line of Business:** Manufacture of other fabricated metal products not elsewhere classified
**Export Markets:** Worldwide
**Issued Capital:** £10,000
**Directors:** J M Winn, A P Walley
**Co. Secretary:** Graham Wilson
**US SIC:** 3499 **UK SIC:** 31694
**Auditors:** Frank W. Dobby & Co Ltd
**Bankers:** National Westminster Bank Plc (55-70-23)

| | 31-12-13 | 31-12-12 | 31-12-11 |
|---|---|---|---|
| TO | 12,798,180 | 12,374,156 | 12,280,479 |
| P/L | 168,524 | 167,793 | 118,783 |
| NW | 1,091,083 | 962,342 | 837,953 |
| WC | 852,522 | 739,897 | 642,568 |
| Emp. | 49 | 49 | 49 |

DUNS 21-005-2125
## Service-Now.Com Uk Ltd
Ambassador House, Paradise Road, Richmond, Surrey TW9 1SQ
**Web:** www.servicenow.com
**Reg No:** 6299383 **Estd:** 2007 Private Limited Company
**Line of Business:** Telecom consultants
**Issued Capital:** £1
**Directors:** M P Scarpelli, R Van Der Meij, M Aardema
**Responsibilities**
**Senior:** Frank Slootman (Chief Executive)
**US SIC:** 7379 **UK SIC:** 83940

| | 31-12-13 | 31-12-12 | 30-12-11 |
|---|---|---|---|
| TO | 30,085,178 | 28,338,301 | N/A |
| P/L | 1,045,901 | 2,056,911 | N/A |
| NW | 6,407,323 | 5,093,627 | 455,606 |
| WC | 1,669,161 | 1,975,657 | 167,952 |
| Emp. | 180 | N/A | N/A |

DUNS 39-962-8890    **Imp**
## Service Timber Ltd
Breighton The Airfield, Breighton, Selby, North Yorkshire YO8 6DJ
**Tel:** 01757289109
**Web:** www.servicetimber.co.uk
**Reg No:** 2241351 **VAT No:** 457515923
**Estd:** 1986 Private Limited Company
**Line of Business:** Agents involved in the sale of timber and building materials
**Issued Capital:** £40,000
**Principals:** M J Eveson (Managing), P G Eveson
**Co. Secretary:** Miss Claire Eveson
**Branches:** Service Timber Ltd, 69F Market Pl, York, North Yorkshire YO43 3AN
**US SIC:** 5072, 5039
**UK SIC:** 61500, 61300
**Auditors:** Haines Flowers
**Bankers:** National Westminster Bank Plc (56-00-06)

| | 31-01-14 | 31-01-13 | 31-01-12 |
|---|---|---|---|
| TO | 13,690,929 | 12,779,281 | 13,286,686 |
| P/L | 173,893 | 222,608 | 94,686 |
| NW | 1,938,841 | 1,826,022 | 1,660,224 |
| WC | (195,335) | 192,383 | 400,781 |
| Emp. | 55 | 50 | 50 |

DUNS 73-787-6875
## Service Underwriting Agency Ltd
1 Eridge Road Linden Close, Tunbridge Wells, Kent TN4 8HH
**Tel:** 01892532677 **Fax:** 01892532477
**Web:** www.service-policies.com
**Reg No:** 5044350 **Estd:** 1996 Private Limited Company
**Line of Business:** Activities auxiliary to insurance and pension funding
**Trading Style:** Service Policies
**Issued Capital:** £20,000
**Directors:** S R Tidd, S A Salter
**Co. Secretary:** Mrs Adele Mcgeechan
**Responsibilities**
**Senior:** Neil Fanthome-Hodgson (Manager), Mike Lewis (Manager), Christopher Messer (Director), Beverley Shreeve (Manager)
**Finance:** Neil Fanthome-Hodgson (Manager)
**Health & Safety:** Ann Law (PA)
**US SIC:** 6411 **UK SIC:** 83200
**Auditors:** Baker Tilly UK Audit LLP

**Bankers:** Svenska Handelsbanken Ab (publ) (40-51-62)

| | 31-12-13 | 31-12-12 | 31-12-11 |
|---|---|---|---|
| TO | 7,923,504 | 7,146,842 | 7,117,373 |
| P/L | (121,417) | 483,106 | 404,698 |
| NW | 1,866,634 | 1,969,250 | 1,614,161 |
| WC | 2,603,959 | 2,081,523 | 2,029,482 |
| Emp. | 105 | 91 | 81 |

DUNS 73-655-4200
## Service Works International Ltd
(**Subsidiary of:** Service Works Group Ltd)
S W G House, 4 Keswick Road, London SW15 2JN
**Tel:** 08707360000
**Web:** www.serviceworks.co.uk
**Reg No:** 4915227 **Estd:** 2003 Private Limited Company
**Line of Business:** Computer systems and software (sales)
**Issued Capital:** £1
**Director:** G Watkins
**Co. Secretary:** Mrs Anne Gales
**US SIC:** 7374 **UK SIC:** 83940

| | 31-10-13 | 31-10-12 | 31-10-11 |
|---|---|---|---|
| TA | 265,074 | 210,100 | 12,258 |
| NW | 82,190 | 34,717 | 2,304 |
| WC | 82,190 | 34,717 | 2,304 |

DUNS 77-781-7156    **Exp**
## Servicecare Support Services Ltd
(**Subsidiary of:** Knaresborough Investments Ltd)
Hollinwood Works, Manchester Road, Oldham, Lancashire OL9 7AA
**Tel:** 0161-688-1999 **Fax:** 01616881998
**Web:** www.servicecare.co.uk
**Reg No:** 3024924 **VAT No:** 732419054
**Estd:** 1995 Private Limited Company
**Line of Business:** Electrical appliance repairs
**Issued Capital:** £12,638
**Directors:** D A Hodkin, S E Fahey, M A Mcmanus, A G Mannix, D A Aspin, S N Parkin
**Co. Secretary:** David Hodkin
**Responsibilities**
**Senior:** Hayley May (Manager), John Zwiggelaar (Financial Director)
**Finance:** John Zwiggelaar (Financial Director)
**IT:** Paul Giesberts (IT and QA Manager), Steve Peers (Operations Manager)
**HR:** Hayley May (Manager)
**Health & Safety:** Dennis Wardlow (Health & Safety Officer)
**US SIC:** 7629, 7397
**UK SIC:** 67301, 83702
**Auditors:** Kay Johnson Gee
**Bankers:** HSBC Bank plc (40-20-14)

| | 30-09-13 | 30-09-12 | 30-09-11 |
|---|---|---|---|
| TO | 10,380,364 | 9,597,130 | 8,282,797 |
| P/L | 980,162 | 1,022,239 | 738,860 |
| NW | 2,277,286 | 1,288,745 | 958,702 |
| WC | 2,128,889 | 1,138,158 | 800,270 |
| Emp. | 138 | 119 | 116 |

DUNS 21-590-6580
## Serviced Office Company
Davenport House 16 Pepper Street, London E14 9RP
**Tel:** 08003196600
**Web:** www.servicedofficecompany.co.uk
**Estd:** 2011 Proprietorship
**Line of Business:** Office rental
**Proprietor:** S Eastlake
**US SIC:** 7339 **UK SIC:** 83954
**Employees:** 100

DUNS 21-787-7035
## Serviced Office Group
Westside, London Road, Hemel Hempstead, Hertfordshire HP3 9TD
**Tel:** 01442840300
**Web:** www.sogplc.com
**Estd:** 2011 Proprietorship
**Line of Business:** Secretarial and translation activities
**Proprietor:** Miss L Stodart
**Responsibilities**
**Senior:** Shukla Sachin (Manager), Sachin Shukla (Business Centre Manager)
**US SIC:** 7339 **UK SIC:** 83954
**Employees:** 60

DUNS 23-251-0532
## Servicemaster
Excalibur Industrial Estate, Fields Road, Alsager, Stoke-On-Trent, Staffordshire ST7 2LX
**Web:** www.smcleaningcontractors.co.uk
**Estd:** 2002 Proprietorship
**Line of Business:** Hygiene and cleaning services
**Proprietor:** T Quinn
**US SIC:** 7349 **UK SIC:** 92300
**Employees:** 150

DUNS 49-715-6083
## Servicemaster (Lincs)
Fulbeck Low Fields, Fulbeck, Grantham, Lincolnshire NG32 3JD
**Web:** www.lrs-online.co.uk
**Estd:** 2007 Partnership
**Line of Business:** Cleaning contracting commercial
**Partners:** Mrs W Hinton, K R Hinton
**Responsibilities**
**Senior:** Kennith Hinton (Manager)
**US SIC:** 7349 **UK SIC:** 92300
**Bankers:** Lloyds TSB Bank plc (30-95-05)
**Employees:** 90

DUNS 21-926-0999    **Imp-Exp**
## Servicemaster Ltd
(**Subsidiary of:** Svm Finance Luxembourg 2 Sarl)
Tigers Road, Wigston, Leicestershire LE18 4WS
**Tel:** 01162-759000
**Web:** www.servicemaster.co.uk
**Reg No:** 1250088 **VAT No:** 241642974
**Estd:** 1959 Private Limited Company
**Line of Business:** Cleaning/maintenance svcs to buildings
**Export Sales:** £28,206
**Trading Style:** Merrymaids, Furniture Medic
**Issued Capital:** £550,000
**Directors:** D T Ford, A P Lewin
**Co. Secretary:** Damien Ford
**Responsibilities**
**Senior:** Stephen Emmerson (Manager), Ashley Green (Stores Manager), Hugh Walwyn (Manager)
**IT:** Darshan Patel (Senior IT Executive)
**HR:** Don Pringle (Director of Supply & Communica)
**Health & Safety:** Don Pringle (Director of Supply & Communica)
**Facilities:** Don Pringle (Director of Supply & Communica)
**Branches:** Servicemaster Ltd, Laurieston Industrial Estate, Unit 2C, Falkirk, Stirlingshire FK2 9JU
**US SIC:** 7349, 2517, 8999
**UK SIC:** 92300, 46714, 83954
**Auditors:** Deloitte LLP
**Bankers:** HSBC Bank plc (40-28-03)

| | 31-12-13 | 31-12-12 | 31-12-11 |
|---|---|---|---|
| TO | 17,889,479 | 19,252,000 | 21,731,000 |
| P/L | 45,386 | 80,000 | 267,000 |
| NW | 2,898,181 | 2,400,000 | 2,344,000 |
| WC | 2,561,274 | 2,111,000 | 2,212,000 |
| Emp. | 60 | 63 | 65 |

DUNS 23-951-6268
## Servicepower Technologies Plc
Petersgate House, 64 Street Petersgate, Stockport, Cheshire SK1 1HE
**Tel:** 0161-476-2277
**Web:** www.servicepower.com
**Reg No:** 3941006 **Estd:** 2000 Public Limited Company
**Line of Business:** Other software consultancy and supply
**Export Sales:** £8,448,000
**Issued Capital:** £2,000,303
**Directors:** R E Mace, H Fitzwilliam - Lay, L C Bury, T S Sandhu, M E Martin
**Co. Secretary:** Tajinder Sandhu
**Responsibilities**
**Senior:** Mark Duffin (Chief Executive), Waqar Hussain (Accountant)
**Finance:** Sally Gillings (Group Accountant)
**Marketing:** Mark Homer (Sales & Marketing Manager)
**Sales:** Mark Homer (Sales & Marketing Manager)
**HR:** Sally Gillings (Group Accountant)
**US SIC:** 7379 **UK SIC:** 83940
**Auditors:** Deloitte LLP
**Bankers:** HSBC Bank plc (40-47-37)

| | 31-12-13 | 31-12-12 | 31-12-11 |
|---|---|---|---|
| TO | 14,002,000 | 11,142,000 | 13,284,000 |
| P/L | 45,000 | (1,796,000) | 1,108,000 |
| NW | 1,570,000 | 1,389,000 | 2,937,000 |
| WC | 1,441,000 | 1,335,000 | 2,792,000 |
| Emp. | 98 | 71 | 67 |

DUNS 73-351-3589
## Services for Independent Living
Services For Independent Living, Unit 1-, The Business Plaza, Ow, Leominster, Herefordshire HR6 0LA
**Tel:** 01568616653
**Web:** www.s4il.co.uk
**Reg No:** 4624968 **Estd:** 2002 Private Company Limited By Guarantee
**Line of Business:** Non-charitable social work activities with accommodation
**Directors:** Ms M O'Neill, J Rogers, G C Hopper, Ms D Crook, T R Misselbrook, Mrs C Warner, Mrs S Nicholls, C N Javens
**Co. Secretary:** Miss Kate Thomas

**Responsibilities**
**Senior:** Marion Tweed-Ryecroft (Chief Executive)
**US SIC:** 8321 **UK SIC:** 96111
**Auditors:** Kendall Wadley LLP
**Bankers:** National Westminster Bank Plc (53-70-12)

| | 31-03-14 | 31-03-13 | 31-03-12 |
|---|---|---|---|
| TO | 1,996,743 | 1,859,376 | 1,660,482 |
| P/L | 27,895 | 47,334 | 97,076 |
| NW | 884,310 | 856,415 | 809,081 |
| WC | 544,136 | 507,067 | 458,340 |
| Emp. | 131 | 105 | 100 |

DUNS 22-620-0475    **Imp-Exp**
## Services Sound & Vision Corporation
Chalfont Grove, Narcot Lane, Gerrards Cross, Buckinghamshire SL9 8TN
**Tel:** 01494874461
**Web:** www.ssvc.com
**Reg No:** 0407270 **VAT No:** 349127936
**Estd:** 1946 Private Company Limited By Guarantee
**Line of Business:** Retail sale of electrical household appliances and radio and television goods
**Export Markets:** Far East, E U
**Trading Style:** S S V C, B S B S
**Directors:** H S Perlin, Mrs M A Carver, A G Vallance, A J Hales, Major General C C Wilson, Mrs C E Colacicchi, S P Purvis, Captain G D Robinson
**Co. Secretary:** David Hamilton
**Responsibilities**
**Senior:** Robert Dungate (Manager), Joanne Holt (General Manager), Andrew Parfitt (Director), Jenny Rye (Head of Personnel)
**Finance:** Nicky Ness (Controller)
**Admin:** Kelly Alford (Events Administrator)
**IT:** Simon Shute (Technical Director)
**HR:** Jenny Rye (Head of Personnel)
**Health & Safety:** Jenny Rye (Head of Personnel)
**Operations:** Jennifer Holdford (Cinema Operations Manager), Sakina Kajee (Project Coordinator), Janice Lorimer (Cinema Projects Manager)
**Engineering:** Simon Shute (Technical Director)
**Branches:** Services Sound & Vision Corporation, Raf Marham, King's Lynn, Norfolk PE33 9NP
**US SIC:** 5732, 4832, 4833, 8231
**UK SIC:** 64800, 97411, 97700
**Auditors:** Grant Thornton UK LLP
**Bankers:** HSBC Bank plc (40-22-05)

| | 31-03-14 | 31-03-13 | 31-03-12 |
|---|---|---|---|
| TO | 30,283,000 | 33,818,000 | 34,549,000 |
| P/L | 1,390,000 | 4,983,000 | 4,490,000 |
| NW | 37,701,000 | 36,311,000 | 28,831,000 |
| WC | 7,076,000 | 11,994,000 | 7,630,000 |
| Emp. | 248 | 241 | 247 |

DUNS 77-155-5265
## Servicescale Ltd
(**Subsidiary of:** Servicescale Personnel Ltd)
117 High Street, Barnet, Hertfordshire EN5 5UZ
**Tel:** 02084416868
**Web:** www.personnel-bank.co.uk
**Reg No:** 2707580 **Estd:** 1992 Private Limited Company
**Line of Business:** Labour recruitment and provision of personnel
**Issued Capital:** £100
**Managing Director:** Ms R L Payne
**Co. Secretary:** James Ainscow
**Branches:** Servicescale Ltd, 8A Church Rd, Welwyn Garden City, Hertfordshire AL8 6PS
**US SIC:** 7361 **UK SIC:** 83954
**Auditors:** Kevan R Kynaston & Co
**Bankers:** National Westminster Bank Plc (51-61-34)

| | 31-05-13 | 31-05-12 | 31-05-11 |
|---|---|---|---|
| TO | 8,164,103 | 8,429,465 | 17,463,060 |
| P/L | 97,322 | 65,182 | (349,248) |
| NW | 1,100,020 | 1,023,551 | 1,024,450 |
| WC | 1,040,287 | 967,987 | 948,280 |
| Emp. | 407 | 439 | 619 |

DUNS 73-677-2513    **Imp**
## Servicetec Global Services Ltd
Spirella Buildings, Bridge Road, Letchworth, Hertfordshire SG6 4ET
**Web:** www.servicetec.com
**Reg No:** 4936619 **Estd:** 2003 Private Limited Company
**Line of Business:** Other computer related activities
**Export Sales:** £5,036,738
**Issued Capital:** £749
**Directors:** D J Ison, B E Mills, A Anderson
**Co. Secretary:** Ms Lynne Harrison
**US SIC:** 7379, 7399
**UK SIC:** 83940, 83954

**Bankers:** HSBC Bank plc (40-05-20)

| | 30-06-14 | 30-06-13 | 30-06-12 |
|---|---|---|---|
| TO | 7,489,821 | 7,567,627 | 7,095,801 |
| P/L | (86,241) | (194,637) | (550,959) |
| NW | 1,158,981 | 1,298,219 | 1,320,011 |
| WC | 1,847,353 | 1,849,044 | 1,826,682 |
| Emp. | 133 | 128 | 129 |

DUNS 21-616-0655

## Servier Laboratories Ltd

(**Subsidiary of:** Servier Sas)
Wexham Springs, Framewood Road, Wexham, Slough, Berkshire SL3 6PJ
**Tel:** 01753-662744 **Fax:** 01753-663456
**Web:** www.servier.co.uk
**Reg No:** 0783023 **Estd:** 1963 Private Limited Company
**Line of Business:** Manufacturers of pharmaceutical products
**Trading Style:** Servier
**Issued Capital:** £1,219,000
**Directors:** P J Andriot, E M Bodineau, H C Renaut
**Co. Secretary:** Charles Brooks
**Responsibilities**
**Marketing:** Jill Jackling *(Digital Marketing Projects Man)*
**Sales:** Tom Ellis *(National Healthcare Developmen)*
**IT:** Iain Steedmen *(IT Manager)*
**US SIC:** 5122, 2834
**UK SIC:** 61800, 25700
**Auditors:** Ernst & Young LLP
**Bankers:** Societe Generale (23-63-91)

| | 30-09-13 | 30-09-12 | 30-09-11 |
|---|---|---|---|
| TO | 27,918,000 | 26,079,000 | 22,706,000 |
| P/L | 774,000 | 6,314,000 | 155,000 |
| NW | 6,804,000 | 6,034,000 | 33,000 |
| WC | 5,799,000 | 5,217,000 | (578,000) |
| Emp. | 118 | 124 | 130 |

DUNS 21-109-8438

## Servio Technology Ltd

Eagle House 69 The Street, Basingstoke, Hampshire RG24 7BY
**Tel:** 01256376930
**Web:** www.serviotechnology.com
**Reg No:** 6514473 **Estd:** 2008 Private Limited Company
**Line of Business:** Wholesale of computers, computer peripheral equipment and software
**Issued Capital:** £100
**Director:** M C Charlton
**Co. Secretary:** Matthew Haystaff
**US SIC:** 5081, 1711
**UK SIC:** 61490, 50300

| | 31-03-14 | 31-03-13 | 31-03-12 |
|---|---|---|---|
| TA | 427,317 | 1,938,131 | 762,938 |
| NW | 69,041 | 372,605 | 260,061 |
| WC | 65,351 | 366,346 | 256,996 |

DUNS 52-528-1671

## Servisair (Contract Handling) Ltd

(**Subsidiary of:** Pai Partners)
19-21 Ack Lane East, Stockport, Cheshire SK7 2BE
**Tel:** 01614893238 **Fax:** 0161-439-9316
**Web:** www.servisair.com
**Reg No:** 3234040 **Estd:** 1959 Private Limited Company
**Line of Business:** Other supporting air transport activities
**Trading Style:** Servisair U K
**Issued Capital:** £1
**Director:** T Watt
**Co. Secretary:** Eversecretary Limited
**US SIC:** 4582 **UK SIC:** 76400
**Auditors:** KPMG LLP

| | 31-12-13 | 30-09-13 | 30-12-12 |
|---|---|---|---|
| TA | 1 | 1 | 1 |
| NW | 1 | 1 | 1 |

DUNS 22-754-8633

## Servisair Uk Ltd

(**Subsidiary of:** Pai Partners)
Business Development, Runcorn, Cheshire WA7 1TT
**Tel:** 01928570120 **Fax:** 01614905700
**Web:** www.servisaircargo.com
**Reg No:** 0509585 **Estd:** 1952 Private Limited Company
**Line of Business:** Other supporting air transport activities
**Trading Style:** Swissport
**Issued Capital:** £10,100
**Directors:** D Harding, J Gaskell, T Watt, A Gomez-Reino
**Co. Secretary:** Eversecretary Limited
**Responsibilities**
**Senior:** Abderrahmane Aoufir *(Ceo)*, Daniel Derichebourg *(Manager)*, Abderaman Lelaoufir *(Chief Executive Officer)*, Bernard Regis *(Manager)*
**Branches:** Servisair Uk Ltd, The Transit Shed, Leeds, West Yorkshire LS19 7TZ
**US SIC:** 4582, 4712
**UK SIC:** 76400, 77002
**Auditors:** PricewaterhouseCoopers LLP

**Bankers:** Societe Generale (23-63-91)

| | 31-12-13 | 30-09-13 | 30-12-12 |
|---|---|---|---|
| TO | 50,122,000 | 201,517,000 | 205,113,000 |
| P/L | 1,109,000 | 16,281,000 | 15,109,000 |
| NW | 15,654,000 | 16,543,000 | 15,116,000 |
| WC | 23,952,000 | 20,589,000 | 9,278,000 |
| Emp. | 4,537 | 4,051 | 4,760 |

DUNS 76-970-1111

## Servlite U.K. Ltd

(**Subsidiary of:** Aidenhall Ltd)
Priestley Road, Manchester M28 2LX
**Tel:** 0161-727-0110 **Fax:** 01617270127
**Web:** www.servlite.co.uk
**Reg No:** 2631082 **Estd:** 1991 Private Limited Company
**Line of Business:** Lighting wholesale and supply
**Export Sales:** £41,449
**Issued Capital:** £5,000
**Principals:** P A Abrahams *(Managing)*, P Isaacs *(Financial)*, D B Miller
**Co. Secretary:** Paul Abrahams
**Branches:** Servlite U.k. Ltd, Unit 39C, Irish Tapestry Bldg, South St, Newtownards, Co Down BT23 4JU
**US SIC:** 5199 **UK SIC:** 61900
**Auditors:** PM & M Solutions For Business LLP
**Bankers:** National Westminster Bank Plc (01-05-31)

| | 31-07-13 | 31-07-12 | 31-07-11 |
|---|---|---|---|
| TO | 8,980,032 | 9,320,649 | N/A |
| P/L | 353,201 | 552,378 | N/A |
| NW | 1,107,020 | [illegible] | 737,249 |
| WC | 1,032,775 | 854,070 | 611,134 |
| Emp. | 47 | 47 | N/A |

DUNS 76-982-6017

## Servoca Plc

41 Whitcomb Street, London WC2H 7DT
**Tel:** 02077473030 **Fax:** 020-7747-3031
**Web:** www.servoca.com
**Reg No:** 2641313 **VAT No:** 608839117
**Estd:** 1991 Public Limited Company
**Line of Business:** Management activities of holding companies
**Issued Capital:** £1,255,760
**Directors:** G Swaby, Ms E J Sugarman, A M Church, A L Morton, J R Foley
**Co. Secretary:** Glenn Swaby
**Responsibilities**
**Senior:** Stephen Shipley *(Manager)*, glenn swaby *(finance director)*
**Finance:** glenn swaby *(finance director)*
**IT:** Dean Gilbert *(IT Manager)*
**Branches:** Servoca Plc, Mill Lane Industrial Estate, Unit 2, Croydon, Surrey CR0 4AA
**US SIC:** 6711 **UK SIC:** 83962
**Auditors:** Baker Tilly UK Audit LLP
**Bankers:** Barclays Bank Plc (20-05-75)

| | 30-09-14 | 30-09-13 | 30-09-12 |
|---|---|---|---|
| TO | 48,989,000 | 43,058,000 | 42,485,000 |
| P/L | 1,569,000 | 672,000 | 46,000 |
| NW | 3,054,000 | 1,715,000 | 1,006,000 |
| WC | 2,335,000 | 892,000 | 322,000 |
| Emp. | 202 | 188 | 207 |

DUNS 29-576-9541

## Servomex Ltd

(**Subsidiary of:** Spectris Plc)
Millbrook Industrial Estate, Sybron Way, Crowborough, East Sussex TN6 3FB
**Tel:** 01892-652181
**Web:** www.servomex.com
**Reg No:** 1938746 **VAT No:** 522607763
**Estd:** 1985 Private Limited Company
**Line of Business:** Manufacturers of scientific machinery and instrument
**Trading Style:** Bicotest, Buhler Montec
**Issued Capital:** £516,953
**Directors:** R J Stephens, C G Watson
**Co. Secretary:** Robert Martin
**Responsibilities**
**Senior:** Chris Cottrell *(Manager)*
**US SIC:** 6711 **UK SIC:** 83962
**Auditors:** KPMG Audit Plc
**Bankers:** Barclays Bank Plc (20-88-13)

| | 31-12-13 | 31-12-12 | 31-12-11 |
|---|---|---|---|
| TA | 5,317,000 | 5,503,000 | 5,038,000 |
| P/L | 162,000 | 281,000 | 135,000 |
| NW | 5,317,000 | 5,206,000 | 4,963,000 |
| WC | N/A | 5,206,000 | 4,913,000 |

DUNS 21-117-8494

## Servotest Ltd

(**Subsidiary of:** Servotest Testing Systems Ltd)
Unit 1 Beta Way, Egham, Surrey TW20 8RE
**Tel:** 01784274410
**Web:** www.servotestsystems.com
**Reg No:** 6575864 **Estd:** 2008 Private Limited Company
**Line of Business:** Other business activities not elsewhere classified
**Issued Capital:** £2
**Director:** B D Ferris
**US SIC:** 7399 **UK SIC:** 83954

| | 30-04-14 | 30-04-13 | 30-04-12 |
|---|---|---|---|
| TA | 2 | 2 | 2 |
| NW | 2 | 2 | 2 |

DUNS 29-546-4200 **Imp**

## Servtech Ltd

2 Abbotswell Road, Aberdeen, Aberdeenshire AB12 3AB
**Tel:** 01224-878322 **Fax:** 01224-895080
**Web:** www.servtech.co.uk
**Reg No:** 0093422SC **Estd:** 1985 Private Limited Company
**Line of Business:** Oil and gas exploration services
**Export Sales:** £24,971,000
**Issued Capital:** £1,000
**Directors:** N A Johnson, S A Mitchell
**Co. Secretary:** Pinsent Masons Secretarial Limit
**US SIC:** 1389 **UK SIC:** 13000
**Auditors:** Ritson Smith
**Bankers:** The Royal Bank Of Scotland Plc (83-49-40)

| | 31-12-13 | 30-06-12 | 30-12-11 |
|---|---|---|---|
| TO | 34,545,000 | 16,166,883 | 11,524,381 |
| P/L | 2,929,000 | 2,532,700 | 1,703,504 |
| NW | 3,077,000 | 1,792,890 | 602,797 |
| WC | 2,974,000 | 1,673,259 | 511,918 |
| Emp. | 181 | 68 | 63 |

DUNS 73-462-1865

## Ses Autoparts Ltd

Alexandra House, Winchester Hill, Romsey, Hampshire SO51 7ND
**Fax:** 01794-529789
**Web:** www.sesautoparts.co.uk
**Reg No:** 2912863 **Estd:** 1994 Private Limited Company
**Line of Business:** Maintenance and repair of motor vehicles
**Trading Style:** Ses Autoparts Ltd
**Issued Capital:** £275
**Principals:** C C Wilson *(Managing)*, S C Wilson, M A Rigler, R A Wilson, T Coombes
**Co. Secretary:** Ms Patricia Wilson
**Branches:** Ses Autoparts Ltd, Unit 2 Station Approach, Fareham, Hampshire PO16 0UT
**US SIC:** 5531 **UK SIC:** 65100
**Auditors:** Graham Martin & Co

| | 30-04-14 | 30-04-13 | 30-04-12 |
|---|---|---|---|
| TO | 8,908,188 | 10,347,928 | 10,749,111 |
| P/L | 201,239 | 157,498 | 320,070 |
| NW | 630,770 | 624,382 | 701,899 |
| WC | 240,619 | 246,441 | 307,658 |
| Emp. | 111 | 126 | 128 |

DUNS 73-666-4611

## Ses Avocet Ltd

(**Subsidiary of:** Specialist Education Services (Holdings) Ltd)
The Old Vicarage, School Lane, Heckingham, Norwich, Norfolk NR14 6QP
**Tel:** 01508549320
**Web:** www.specialisteducation.co.uk
**Reg No:** 4926028 **Estd:** 2003 Private Limited Company
**Line of Business:** Miscellaneous business services
**Issued Capital:** £1,000
**Director:** J J Lees
**Co. Secretary:** Stephen Lord
**Responsibilities**
**Senior:** Neil Dawson *(Principal)*
**US SIC:** 7399, 8211, 8249, 8321
**UK SIC:** 83954, 93200, 93300, 96111

| | 31-08-13 | 31-08-12 | 31-08-11 |
|---|---|---|---|
| TA | 1,130,713 | 1,338,035 | 1,022,367 |
| NW | 557,685 | 415,015 | 364,739 |
| WC | 667,843 | 559,409 | 473,058 |

DUNS 73-888-1486

## S.E.S. Holdings (Uk) Ltd

S.E.S. House, Blyth Road Harworth Park, Doncaster, South Yorkshire DN11 8DB
**Tel:** 01302733681
**Web:** www.ses-holdings.com
**Reg No:** 5142324 **Estd:** 2004 Private Limited Company
**Line of Business:** Management activities of holding companies
**Trading Style:** Ses Holdings
**Issued Capital:** £6,000
**Directors:** D Hyland, W T Shinkins
**Responsibilities**
**Senior:** Pat Mchale *(director of rail services)*
**Health & Safety:** Chris Meggett *(health & safety manager)*
**US SIC:** 6711, 1622, 1611
**UK SIC:** 83962, 50200
**Auditors:** Smailes Goldie

| | 31-03-14 | 31-03-13 | 31-03-12 |
|---|---|---|---|
| TO | 48,126,331 | 46,864,228 | 40,888,907 |
| P/L | 468,196 | 287,870 | 640,373 |
| NW | 1,454,993 | 1,372,033 | 1,291,434 |
| WC | 1,513,655 | 1,449,863 | 1,380,102 |
| Emp. | 486 | 501 | 442 |

DUNS 77-952-0451

## S.E.S. Ltd.

Unit 2 Southport Business Park, Wight Moss Way, Southport, Merseyside PR8 4HQ
**Tel:** 01704552270 **Fax:** 0845-310-0044
**Web:** www.ses.ltd.uk
**Reg No:** 3057795 **Estd:** 1995 Private Limited Company
**Line of Business:** Security and related activities
**Issued Capital:** £4,000
**Directors:** Ms C Shuker, S Mawdsley, D C Quinn
**Co. Secretary:** Ms Sylvia Kent
**US SIC:** 7393 **UK SIC:** 83954
**Auditors:** Stubbs Parkin Taylor & Co
**Bankers:** National Westminster Bank Plc (60-20-11)

| | 31-05-14 | 31-05-13 | 31-05-12 |
|---|---|---|---|
| TO | 9,781,401 | 8,160,539 | 7,437,791 |
| P/L | 970,001 | 951,372 | 685,333 |
| NW | 969,823 | 867,217 | 540,649 |
| WC | (1,098,646) | (768,060) | (746,690) |
| Emp. | 173 | 169 | 167 |

DUNS 56-950-9946

## Sesame Ltd

(**Subsidiary of:** Friends Life Group Limited)
Independence House, Hollybank Road, Huddersfield, West Yorkshire HD3 3HN
**Tel:** 01484422224 **Fax:** 01484426152
**Web:** www.sesame.co.uk
**Reg No:** 2844161 **Estd:** 1993 Private Limited Company
**Line of Business:** Auditors
**Issued Capital:** £60,021,154
**Directors:** N Criticos, Mrs D S Miller, J Cowan, J A Newman
**Co. Secretary:** Friends Life Secretarial Service
**Responsibilities**
**Senior:** John Cupis *(Manager)*
**Finance:** Linda Todd *(Compliance Support Unit Manage)*
**Marketing:** Jared Aitken *(Head of Media Relations)*
**IT:** Peter Billington *(Head of IT)*
**HR:** Anna Masheter *(People Development Manager)*, Kate Sparkes *(Head of HR)*, Emma Townsend *(HR Consultant)*
**US SIC:** 8931 **UK SIC:** 83600
**Auditors:** Ernst & Young LLP
**Bankers:** National Westminster Bank Plc (60-11-17)

| | 31-12-12 | 31-12-11 | 31-12-10 |
|---|---|---|---|
| TO | 180,155,000 | 170,323,000 | 162,944,000 |
| P/L | (9,342,000) | (2,410,000) | 1,070,000 |
| NW | 59,374,000 | 68,425,000 | 70,285,000 |
| WC | 118,714,000 | 121,372,000 | 123,092,000 |

DUNS 76-929-7763

## Sesame Services Ltd

(**Subsidiary of:** Friends Life Group Limited)
1-5 Oasis Park, Stanton Harcourt Road, Witney, Oxfordshire OX29 4AE
**Tel:** 08451221515 **Fax:** 01865886001
**Web:** www.sesame.gov.uk
**Reg No:** 2338540 **Estd:** 1989 Private Limited Company
**Line of Business:** Other business activities not elsewhere classified
**Issued Capital:** £5,598,591
**Directors:** S C Gazard, J A Newman, Mrs L Winnard
**Co. Secretary:** Friends Life Secretarial Service
**Branches:** Sesame Services Ltd, Southmark Building, 3 Barrington Road, Altrincham, Cheshire WA14 1GY
**US SIC:** 7399 **UK SIC:** 83954
**Auditors:** KPMG Audit PLC
**Bankers:** Lloyds TSB Bank plc (30-00-06)

| | 31-12-12 | 31-12-11 | 31-12-10 |
|---|---|---|---|
| TO | 32,180,000 | 25,999,000 | 28,802,000 |
| P/L | (1,770,000) | 8,813,000 | 157,000 |
| NW | 74,608,000 | 73,843,000 | 63,112,000 |
| WC | 73,958,000 | 71,919,000 | 61,533,000 |
| Emp. | 402 | 369 | 355 |

DUNS 21-607-4498

## Sesnha Care

Aveley House, Arcany Road, South Ockendon, Essex RM15 5SX
**Tel:** 01708856444
**Estd:** 2002 Proprietorship
**Line of Business:** Home care service providers
**Proprietor:** C Bidmead
**Responsibilities**
**Senior:** Joyce Bristow *(Chief Executive)*, Jeff Grace *(Care Manager)*
**US SIC:** 8091 **UK SIC:** 95200
**Employees:** 250

DUNS 73-433-6816
### Sessions Spa Ltd
The Sessions House, New Walk, Beverley, North Humberside HU17 7AE
**Tel:** 01482873000
**Web:** www.sessionsspa.co.uk
**Reg No:** 4706592 **Estd:** 2003 Private Limited Company
**Line of Business:** Hairdressers (unisex)
**Issued Capital:** £100
**Director:** J W Parkinson
**Co. Secretary:** Georgina Parkinson
**US SIC:** 7231 **UK SIC:** 98200

| | 31-12-13 | 31-12-12 | 31-12-11 |
|---|---|---|---|
| TA | 246,960 | 325,872 | 361,290 |
| NW | (28,926) | (13,402) | 21,225 |
| WC | (145,139) | (136,694) | (107,116) |

DUNS 54-378-1322
### Set & Strike Ltd
Imperial House, 21 25 North Street, Bromley, Kent BR1 1SD
**Tel:** 020-8462-3059 **Fax:** 020-8462-3059
**Web:** www.setandstrike.com
**Reg No:** 3265929 **Estd:** 1997 Private Limited Company
**Line of Business:** Other construction work involving special trades
**Issued Capital:** £15
**Director:** S P Barker
**Responsibilities**
**Senior:** Margaret Barker *(Senior IT Executive)*
**IT:** Margaret Barker *(Senior IT Executive)*
**US SIC:** 1799 **UK SIC:** 50000
**Auditors:** Downs & Co

| | 30-06-14 | 31-12-12 | 31-06-11 |
|---|---|---|---|
| TA | 126,039 | 547,112 | 634,304 |
| NW | 104,425 | 344,632 | 406,115 |
| WC | 104,425 | 331,682 | 389,593 |

DUNS 28-847-1238 **Exp**
### Set Copyrights Ltd
Faber & Faber Ltd, London WC1N 3AU
**Tel:** 02074650045
**Web:** www.faber.co.uk
**Reg No:** 0654302 **Estd:** 1960 Private Limited Company
**Line of Business:** Book publishers
**Trading Style:** Faber & Faber
**Issued Capital:** £100
**Directors:** L P Longe, Ms J M Hooper, Ms C Reihill
**Responsibilities**
**Senior:** Clare Reinhill *(Director)*
**US SIC:** 2731, 8999
**UK SIC:** 47532, 83954
**Auditors:** Auditor Name Illegible
**Bankers:** Lloyds TSB Bank plc (30-97-81)

| | 31-03-14 | 31-03-13 | 31-03-12 |
|---|---|---|---|
| TA | 15,500,254 | 15,335,466 | 14,578,629 |
| NW | 15,455,172 | 15,180,249 | 14,518,121 |
| WC | 5,330,044 | 6,096,985 | 5,775,966 |

DUNS 29-497-9091
### Set in Hand Specialist Services Ltd
Unit 1-2, Combs Tannery, Tannery Road, Stowmarket, Suffolk IP14 2EN
**Web:** www.setinhand.com
**Reg No:** 1861191 **VAT No:** 410653782
**Estd:** 1985 Private Limited Company
**Line of Business:** Activities of other transport agencies
**Trading Style:** Set in Hand
**Issued Capital:** £100,000
**Principals:** J W Smithies *(Managing)*, Ms T L Davies
**Co. Secretary:** Ms Ivy Smithies
**Responsibilities**
**Senior:** Richard Stanton *(Manager)*, William Stanton *(Manager)*
**US SIC:** 7399, 4213
**UK SIC:** 83954, 72300
**Auditors:** Walter Wright
**Bankers:** The Royal Bank Of Scotland Plc (16-22-17)

| | 31-12-13 | 31-12-12 | 31-12-11 |
|---|---|---|---|
| TA | 915,800 | 962,582 | 840,326 |
| NW | 122,159 | 101,524 | 94,716 |
| WC | 17,671 | 24,268 | (27,104) |

DUNS 50-544-1394
### S.E.T. (Office Supplies) Ltd.
Llandough Trading Estate, Penarth Road, Cardiff, South Glamorgan CF11 8RR
**Tel:** 02920225555 **Fax:** 029-2022-1922
**Web:** www.setoffice.co.uk
**Reg No:** 2498167 **VAT No:** 535285242
**Estd:** 1975 Private Limited Company
**Line of Business:** Retail sale of books, newspapers and stationery
**Issued Capital:** £964
**Principals:** P G Amos *(Chairman)*, N Griffiths *(Managing)*
**Co. Secretary:** Ms Vivienne Amos
**Responsibilities**
**Finance:** Janice Hendon *(Financial Director)*
**IT:** Janice Hendon *(Financial Director)*
**Branches:** S.e.t. (Office Supplies) Ltd., S E T Stationery Supplies, 38 Bridge Street, Haverfordwest, Dyfed SA61 2AD
**US SIC:** 5942 **UK SIC:** 65300
**Auditors:** Hayvenhursts Ltd
**Bankers:** Lloyds TSB Bank plc (30-91-63)

| | 30-06-14 | 30-06-13 | 30-06-12 |
|---|---|---|---|
| TO | 15,721,052 | 14,473,892 | 14,333,255 |
| P/L | 1,500,273 | 1,080,996 | 1,754,034 |
| NW | 6,694,368 | 6,074,914 | 5,524,666 |
| WC | 5,742,923 | 5,203,327 | 4,667,142 |
| Emp. | 140 | 134 | 134 |

DUNS 49-394-3690
### Setml Transportation Ltd
**(Subsidiary of:** Bombardier Inc)
Friars Bridge Court, 41-45 Blackfriars Road, London SE1 8NZ
**Tel:** 02076205000
**Web:** www.southeasternrailway.co.uk
**Reg No:** 3138390 **Estd:** 1995 Private Limited Company
**Line of Business:** Manufacture of railway and tramway locomotives and rolling stock
**Trading Style:** South Eastern Railway
**Issued Capital:** £38,000,000
**Directors:** N J Travers, Mrs J D Stoney, Miss L S West
**Co. Secretary:** Mrs Sharmila Sylvester
**US SIC:** 3743, 4011
**UK SIC:** 36201, 71000
**Auditors:** Nelsons Solicitors
**Bankers:** Barclays Bank Plc (20-00-00)

| | 31-12-13 | 31-12-12 | 31-12-11 |
|---|---|---|---|
| TA | 4,987,000 | 4,987,000 | 4,987,000 |
| NW | 4,987,000 | 4,987,000 | 4,987,000 |

DUNS 21-771-1091
### Seton Hall
Seton Hall, Ord Road, Berwick-Upon-Tweed, Northumberland TD15 2UT
**Tel:** 01289306391
**Web:** www.setoncare.org.uk
**Estd:** 2011 Proprietorship
**Line of Business:** Residential care establishments
**Proprietor:** Mrs S Mcdougal
**Responsibilities**
**Senior:** Shirley Mcdougall *(Manager)*, Vanessa Nisbett *(Manager)*
**US SIC:** 8321 **UK SIC:** 96111
**Employees:** 60

DUNS 84-690-8189
### Setsquare Staging (Holdings) Ltd
3-9 Willow Lane, Mitcham, Surrey CR4 4NA
**Tel:** 02086877400
**Web:** www.setsquarestaging.com
**Reg No:** 6232118 **Estd:** 2007 Private Limited Company
**Line of Business:** Holding companies management activities
**Export Sales:** £1,169,884
**Issued Capital:** £400
**Directors:** M J Clemitson, J J O'Gorman, A M Tudor-Hart, Mrs I C O&Apos;Gorman
**Co. Secretary:** Ms Imogen O'Gorman
**Responsibilities**
**Senior:** Imogen O Apos Gorman *(Director)*
**US SIC:** 6711 **UK SIC:** 83962
**Bankers:** Barclays Bank Plc (20-21-78)

| | 31-05-13 | 31-05-12 | 31-05-11 |
|---|---|---|---|
| TO | 8,500,411 | N/A | N/A |
| P/L | 326,598 | N/A | N/A |
| NW | 994,239 | 259,485 | 234,990 |
| WC | 200,148 | (149,691) | (186,755) |
| Emp. | 49 | N/A | N/A |

DUNS 21-154-6902
### Sevacare Holdings Ltd
Unit 9 Sidestrand, Pendeford Business Park, Wolverhampton, West Midlands WV9 5HD
**Tel:** 01902625070
**Web:** www.sevacare.org.uk
**Reg No:** 6829537 **Estd:** 2009 Private Limited Company
**Line of Business:** Social work activities without accommodation
**Issued Capital:** £11,155,000
**Directors:** A S Bains, Mrs R K Bains, R S Bains, R S Bains
**Co. Secretary:** Philip Talbot
**Responsibilities**
**Senior:** Gillian Earnshaw *(Manageress)*
**US SIC:** 8091 **UK SIC:** 95200

| | 31-08-13 | 31-08-12 | 31-08-11 |
|---|---|---|---|
| TO | 54,949,532 | 42,901,695 | 32,059,032 |
| P/L | 1,821,768 | 1,508,499 | 1,478,446 |
| NW | (2,089,161) | (3,480,912) | (2,519,529) |
| WC | 2,306,746 | 794,544 | 688,306 |
| Emp. | 3,633 | 2,728 | 2,081 |

DUNS 51-997-8373
### Sevan Leisure Holdings Ltd
Market Towers, 1 Nine Elms Lane, London SW8 5NQ
**Tel:** 02077209200 **Fax:** 020-7627-1918
**Web:** www.clubcolosseum.com
**Reg No:** 3364956 **Estd:** 1997 Private Limited Company
**Line of Business:** Holding companies management activities
**Trading Style:** Club Colosseum
**Issued Capital:** £54,764
**Directors:** E Halil, Ms T A Bamford
**Co. Secretary:** Rezvan Halil
**Branches:** Sevan Leisure Holdings Ltd, 17-21 Tavistock St, London WC2E 7PS
**US SIC:** 6711, 5813
**UK SIC:** 83962, 66200

| | 30-06-14 | 30-06-13 | 30-06-12 |
|---|---|---|---|
| TO | 2,405,983 | 2,574,594 | 2,466,743 |
| P/L | 4,128,646 | 216,360 | (26,809) |
| NW | 2,044,906 | (1,488,833) | (1,660,469) |
| WC | 1,830,827 | (267,652) | (469,501) |

DUNS 21-317-7447 **Imp-Exp**
### Sevcon Ltd
**(Subsidiary of:** Sevcon Inc.)
Kingsway South, Team Valley Trading Estate, Gateshead, Tyne and Wear NE11 0QA
**Tel:** 0191-497-9000
**Web:** www.sevcon.com
**Reg No:** 0500106 **VAT No:** 178546912
**Estd:** 1951 Private Limited Company
**Line of Business:** Electric vehicles
**Issued Capital:** £140,353
**Directors:** B Start, M Boyle, F Wang, W Ketelhut, M Helmsley, D Steadman, P Stump, P Rosenberg
**Co. Secretary:** Paul Farquhar
**Responsibilities**
**Senior:** Richard Clennell *(Vice President of Quality)*, Marvin Schorr *(Director)*
**Finance:** Kevin Alderson *(Planning Manager)*, Chris Southward *(Financial Controller)*
**Sales:** Mark Durrant *(Vice President of Global Sales)*
**IT:** Darren Errington *(Vice President and Chief Infor)*
**Operations:** Steve Savage *(Projects Manager)*
**Engineering:** Peter G Barrass *(Engineering Manager)*, Dave Lamb *(Global Applications Engineerin)*
**US SIC:** 3799 **UK SIC:** 36502
**Auditors:** Baker Tilly UK Audit LLP
**Bankers:** Barclays Bank Plc (20-59-42)

| | 30-09-13 | 30-09-12 | 30-09-11 |
|---|---|---|---|
| TO | 14,872,760 | 16,771,476 | 14,638,817 |
| P/L | (866,716) | 1,160,623 | 606,770 |
| NW | 1,568,000 | 1,547,915 | 2,224,370 |
| WC | 3,550,303 | 3,973,122 | 3,323,800 |
| Emp. | 95 | 91 | 84 |

DUNS 53-601-9391
### Seven Asset Ltd
35-37 St Peters Street, Ipswich, Suffolk IP1 1XF
**Tel:** 01473-261777 **Fax:** 01473-261770
**Web:** www.sevenasset.co.uk
**Reg No:** 3407135 **Estd:** 1997 Private Limited Company
**Line of Business:** Leasing companies
**Issued Capital:** £10,000
**Directors:** T Forman *(Managing)*, M Forsdyke, S T Cole, Mrs J H Dunnett, R V Dunnett, W R Dunnett
**Co. Secretary:** Mark Harman
**Responsibilities**
**Senior:** Carley porter *(HR manager)*
**HR:** Carley porter *(HR manager)*
**US SIC:** 7512, 7394
**UK SIC:** 84801, 84000
**Auditors:** Grant Thornton

| | 30-09-13 | 30-09-12 | 30-09-11 |
|---|---|---|---|
| TO | 17,746,219 | 17,987,833 | 17,066,034 |
| P/L | 251,756 | 327,894 | 201,173 |
| NW | 2,529,985 | 2,267,304 | 1,970,301 |
| WC | (2,127,748) | (1,749,382) | (1,502,308) |
| Emp. | 57 | 54 | 57 |

DUNS 71-887-1176
### Seven Lincs Ltd
Fagbury Road, The Dock, Felixstowe, Suffolk IP11 4HQ
**Tel:** 01394673777 **Fax:** 01394 673138
**Web:** http://sevenlincs.com
**Reg No:** 5269482 **Estd:** 2004 Private Limited Company
**Line of Business:** Other supporting land transport activities
**Issued Capital:** £1,000
**Directors:** P Woodley, I D Mcallister, R V Dunnett, T Forman
**Co. Secretary:** Mark Harman
**Responsibilities**
**Senior:** Charles Garn *(Manager)*, Mike Thorsdyke *(Manager)*
**Fleet:** Mike Thorsdyke *(Manager)*
**Branches:** Seven Lincs Ltd, Armada House, Tilbury Freeport, Tilbury, Essex RM18 7ET
**US SIC:** 4789 **UK SIC:** 77002
**Auditors:** Ensors

| | 30-09-13 | 30-09-12 | 30-09-11 |
|---|---|---|---|
| TO | 9,005,615 | 8,852,350 | 7,619,598 |
| P/L | 3,337 | 2,381 | (166,901) |
| NW | (536,589) | (550,426) | (563,307) |
| WC | (308,915) | (321,086) | (334,327) |
| Emp. | 59 | 49 | 52 |

DUNS 21-392-7640
### Seven Locks Housing Association
1a Anson House, Market Harborough, Leicestershire LE16 9HW
**Tel:** 01858-414500
**Web:** www.sevenlockshousing.co.uk
**Estd:** 2005 Proprietorship
**Line of Business:** Housing associations societies trusts & co-operatives
**Proprietor:** Ms H Clarke
**US SIC:** 8321 **UK SIC:** 96111
**Employees:** 50

DUNS 73-428-2614
### Seven 'O' Six Cars Ltd
430 Marfleet Lane, Hull, North Humberside HU9 3NA
**Web:** www.706taxic.com
**Reg No:** 4701193 **Estd:** 2003 Private Limited Company
**Line of Business:** Taxis and private hire vehicles
**Issued Capital:** £3
**Director:** R G Murray
**Co. Secretary:** Magnus Murray
**US SIC:** 4121 **UK SIC:** 72200

| | 31-03-14 | 31-03-13 | 31-03-12 |
|---|---|---|---|
| TA | 31,357 | 19,596 | 27,017 |
| NW | 209 | 67 | 1,859 |
| WC | (9,945) | (11,439) | (12,648) |

DUNS 73-547-0200
### Seven Publishing Group Ltd
3-7 Herbal Hill, London EC1R 5EJ
**Tel:** 02077757775 **Fax:** 02077757705
**Web:** www.seven.co.uk
**Reg No:** 4809240 **Estd:** 2003 Private Limited Company
**Line of Business:** Publishing of journals and periodicals
**Issued Capital:** £43,199
**Directors:** A Hudson, N Mccarthy, T H Trotter, S S King, J Gibson, S M Bliss
**Co. Secretary:** Derringtons Limited
**Responsibilities**
**Senior:** Nic McCarthy *(Content Director)*
**Finance:** Dave Buck *(Finance Director Operations)*, Andrew Tkaczyk *(Senior Account Manager)*
**Admin:** Amy Barry *(Personal Assistant)*
**HR:** Sarah Wheeler *(HR Director)*
**Health & Safety:** Matthew Gisborne *(Facilities Manager)*
**Facilities:** Matthew Gisborne *(Facilities Manager)*
**Operations:** Robin Bonn *(Business Development Director)*
**US SIC:** 2721 **UK SIC:** 47522
**Auditors:** Brener Allen & Trapp

| | 31-12-13 | 31-12-12 | 31-12-11 |
|---|---|---|---|
| TO | 21,185,000 | 24,501,000 | 27,652,000 |
| P/L | 38,000 | 164,000 | 221,000 |
| NW | 1,290,000 | 1,035,000 | 342,000 |
| WC | 1,034,000 | 487,000 | (185,000) |
| Emp. | 161 | 163 | 169 |

DUNS 21-214-8746 **Imp-Exp**
### Seven Seas Ltd
**(Subsidiary of:** Merck Kg Auf Aktien)
Hedon Road, Hull, North Humberside HU9 5NJ
**Tel:** 01482-375234 **Fax:** 01482-374345
**Web:** www.seven-seas.com
**Reg No:** 0351663 **VAT No:** 167427151
**Estd:** 1935 Private Limited Company
**Line of Business:** Manufacturers of food products
**Issued Capital:** £50,001
**Directors:** S Kratzer, J D Binnington, K J White, A J Wines
**Co. Secretary:** A G Secretarial Limited
**Responsibilities**
**Senior:** Chris Kitchman *(Procurement Manager)*, Martin Sillitto *(Manager)*, Wendy Spivey *(Warehouse & Distributions Mana)*
**Marketing:** Catheryne Dymond *(Marketing Director)*, Neil Hepplewhite *(Marketing Director)*
**IT:** Steve Crook *(IT Manager)*
**Purchasing:** Malcolm Doubtfire *(Procurement Manager)*
**Branches:** Seven Seas Ltd, South Orbital Trading Park, Unit 1, Hull, North Humberside HU9 1NJ
**US SIC:** 2099, 2079
**UK SIC:** 42399, 41150
**Auditors:** KPMG LLP

**Bankers:** Barclays Bank Plc (20-92-54)

| | 31-12-13 | 31-12-12 | 31-12-11 |
|---|---|---|---|
| TO | 41,332,000 | 49,835,000 | 60,816,000 |
| P/L | (3,949,000) | (29,058,000) | 1,742,000 |
| NW | (29,263,000) | (26,193,000) | (5,572,000) |
| WC | 8,079,000 | 13,818,000 | 12,354,000 |
| Emp. | 216 | 254 | 273 |

DUNS 49-487-4530

## Seven Seas Worldwide Ltd

(**Subsidiary of:** Seven Seas Worldwide Group Ltd)
Paddock Cottage, Ashford, Kent TN25 6SP
**Tel:** 0800-216-698
**Web:** www.sevenseasworldwide.com
**Reg No:** 3152376 **Estd:** 1996 Private Limited Company
**Line of Business:** Cargo handling
**Issued Capital:** £10,100
**Directors:** J W Henderson, Ms G M Wilkinson
**Co. Secretary:** William Henderson
**Branches:** Seven Seas Worldwide Ltd, Bramble Road, Swindon, Wiltshire SN2 8HB
**US SIC:** 4712 **UK SIC:** 77002
**Auditors:** Spain Brothers & Co

| | 31-12-13 | 31-12-12 | 31-12-11 |
|---|---|---|---|
| TA | 1,821,098 | 2,096,224 | 2,271,338 |
| NW | 524,933 | 534,878 | 587,121 |
| WC | 91,006 | 21,671 | 21,473 |

DUNS 22-159-2293

## Seven Stories Trading Ltd

(**Subsidiary of:** The Centre for Children's Books)
The Centre For Childrens Books, 30 Lime St Ouseburn Valley, Newcastle-Upon-Tyne, Tyne and Wear NE1 2PQ
**Tel:** 01912612000
**Web:** www.sevenstories.org.uk
**Reg No:** 4177830 **Estd:** 2001 Private Limited Company
**Line of Business:** Book retailers
**Issued Capital:** £1
**Directors:** Ms K Chaplin, M T Mcwhinnie, J R Turner, Ms S Redpath, Ms M R Briggs, Ms A J Scott, C W Hoult
**Co. Secretary:** Jon Riley
**Responsibilities**
**Senior:** Kate Edwards *(Chief Executive)*, Lauren Regan-Ingram *(Marketing & Digital Coordinato)*
**Marketing:** Lauren Regan-Ingram *(Marketing & Digital Coordinato)*
**US SIC:** 7911 **UK SIC:** 97913

| | 31-03-14 | 31-03-13 | 31-03-12 |
|---|---|---|---|
| TA | 139,298 | 149,236 | 134,006 |
| NW | 1 | 1 | |
| WC | 1 | 1 | |

DUNS 23-610-0913

## Sevenoaks District Council

Council Offices, Argyle Road, Sevenoaks, Kent TN13 1HG
**Tel:** 01732-227000
**Web:** www.sevenoaks.gov.uk
**Estd:** 1974 Incorporate By Act Of Parliament
**Line of Business:** General (overall) public service activities
**Principals:** J H Sandeford *(Chairman)*, R Schulder, D Coates, D Williamson, P Godfrey
**Responsibilities**
**Senior:** Hayley Baldock *(Manager)*, Cllr Bosley *(Board Member)*, Cllr Bracken *(Board Member)*, Cllr Clark *(Board Member)*, Nicola Clinch *(Executive)*, Ray Froud *(Executive)*, Robin Hales *(Chief Executive)*, Avril Hunter *(Board Member)*, Cllr Hunter *(Board Member)*, Cllr Ramsay *(Board Member)*
**Marketing:** Merle Bigden *(Head of Community Development)*, Hayley Brooks *(Community Development Officer)*, Alison Bythway *(Performance & Communications S)*, Rebecca Perkins *(Community Officer)*
**IT:** Jim Carrington-West *(Senior IT Executive)*, Michael Laver-Smith *(Computer Manager)*
**HR:** Cathy Pitcher *(Head Personnel & Development)*
**Branches:** Sevenoaks District Council, London Road, Sevenoaks, Kent TN13 1ZZ
**US SIC:** 9121 **UK SIC:** 91110
**Bankers:** Barclays Bank Plc (20-76-55)
**Employees:** 300

DUNS 73-649-0140

## Sevenoaks School

High Street, Sevenoaks, Kent TN13 1HU
**Web:** www.sevenoaksschool.org
**Reg No:** 4908949 **Estd:** 2003 Private Company Limited By Guarantee
**Line of Business:** Schools (independent)
**Directors:** A R Little, Ms S J Dunnett, N G May, A B Boulton, Mrs E J Ecclestone, Lord A C Colgrain, Professor M J Waring, J F London
**Co. Secretary:** Andrew Burton
**Responsibilities**
**Senior:** Alison Beckett *(Director)*, Sian Carr *(Director)*, Belinda Giles *(Manager)*, Cyndi Goh *(Director)*, Katie Ricks *(Principal)*, Derick Walker *(Manager)*
**Marketing:** Katie Ricks *(Principal)*
**Admin:** Astria Nairn *(Assistant)*, Jo Nowicki *(Assistant)*
**Health & Safety:** Linda Kilgallon *(Health & Safety Officer)*
**Facilities:** Sebastien Coquelin *(Housemaster)*, Alan Pople *(Estates Bursar)*
**Engineering:** Graeme Lawrie *(Design & Technology Teacher)*
**US SIC:** 8211 **UK SIC:** 93200
**Bankers:** National Westminster Bank Plc (60-19-02)

| | 31-07-13 | 31-07-12 | 31-07-11 |
|---|---|---|---|
| TO | 24,575,718 | 24,061,517 | 23,152,412 |
| P/L | 2,389,650 | 2,573,917 | 2,444,169 |
| NW | 22,384,261 | 18,820,251 | 17,479,767 |
| WC | 18,731,359 | 17,276,258 | 14,708,017 |
| Emp. | 265 | 263 | 254 |

DUNS 77-720-0262

## Sevenoaks Sound & Vision Ltd

109-113 London Road, Sevenoaks, Kent TN13 1BH
**Fax:** 01732-743981
**Web:** www.ssav.com
**Reg No:** 3008095 **Estd:** 1995 Private Limited Company
**Line of Business:** Retail sale of electrical household appliances and radio and television goods
**Issued Capital:** £10,000
**Directors:** R J Lawley, J Roberts, P W Lee Kemp
**Co. Secretary:** Peter O'Brien
**Responsibilities**
**Senior:** R Burn *(Manager)*, Daniel Marchant *(Manager)*
**Branches:** Sevenoaks Sound & Vision Ltd, 597-599 Mansfield Road, Nottingham, Nottinghamshire NG5 2FW
**US SIC:** 5732 **UK SIC:** 64800
**Auditors:** Baker Tilly
**Bankers:** HSBC Bank plc (40-40-32)

| | 30-06-13 | 30-06-12 | 30-06-11 |
|---|---|---|---|
| TO | 15,046,231 | 12,685,567 | 14,243,226 |
| P/L | (187,495) | (121,866) | 308,849 |
| NW | 1,904,695 | 1,856,448 | 1,740,112 |
| WC | 1,507,830 | 1,413,435 | 1,352,951 |
| Emp. | 68 | 57 | 50 |

DUNS 64-107-3747 **Exp**

## Severfield (Design & Build) Ltd

(**Subsidiary of:** Atlas Ward Holdings Ltd)
St Hildas Street, Malton, North Yorkshire YO17 8PZ
**Tel:** 01944 710421 **Fax:** 01944710759
**Web:** www.severfield.com
**Reg No:** 4107553 **Estd:** 2000 Private Limited Company
**Line of Business:** Steel fabricators
**Issued Capital:** £1
**Directors:** G B Jones, J R Martindale, A D Dunsmore, I Lawson, D Ward, R H Pratt, S P Barnes
**Co. Secretary:** Darrell Ward
**Responsibilities**
**Senior:** Peter Davison *(Manager)*, Ian Rackham *(Manager)*
**HR:** Andrea Woodhead *(Human Resources Manager)*
**Purchasing:** Maurice Trousdale *(Head of Purchasing)*
**Branches:** Severfield (Design & Build) Ltd, St. Hildas Street Sherburn, Sherburn, Malton, North Yorkshire YO17 8PZ
**US SIC:** 1622 **UK SIC:** 50200
**Auditors:** Deloitte LLP
**Bankers:** National Australia Bank Ltd (16-55-90)

| | 31-03-14 | 31-03-13 | 31-03-11 |
|---|---|---|---|
| TO | 53,623,000 | 60,676,000 | 49,235,000 |
| P/L | 5,398,000 | 4,470,000 | 4,346,000 |
| NW | 32,402,000 | 28,238,000 | 24,182,000 |
| WC | 30,871,000 | 26,417,000 | 21,949,000 |
| Emp. | 217 | 209 | 207 |

DUNS 21-449-7240 **Imp-Exp**

## Severfield (Ni) Ltd

(**Subsidiary of:** Severfield Plc)
Main Street, Ballinamallard, Enniskillen, Co Fermanagh BT94 2FY
**Tel:** 028-6638-8521 **Fax:** 028-6638-8706
**Web:** www.severfield.com
**Reg No:** 0010328NI **Estd:** 1950 Private Limited Company
**Line of Business:** Engineers (structural)
**Export Markets:** Republic of Ireland
**Trading Style:** Severfield
**Issued Capital:** £37,000
**Directors:** B R Keys, A D Dunsmore, I R Cochrane, I Lawson
**Co. Secretary:** Wesley Knox
**Responsibilities**
**IT:** Carl Mcmally *(Computer Manager)*
**Health & Safety:** Barry Brunty *(Health & Safety Manager)*
**Purchasing:** Gary Culbert *(Purchasing Manager)*
**Branches:** Severfield (Ni) Ltd, Unit C3, 9 Ferguson Drive, Lisburn, Co Antrim BT28 2EX
**US SIC:** 8911, 1761
**UK SIC:** 83701, 50400
**Auditors:** Deloitte LLP
**Bankers:** Northern Bank Ltd (95-03-36)

| | 31-03-14 | 31-03-13 | 31-03-11 |
|---|---|---|---|
| TO | 50,741,559 | 59,603,562 | 59,922,580 |
| P/L | 1,142,479 | 973,788 | 6,101,444 |
| NW | 21,362,646 | 25,427,259 | 29,677,057 |
| WC | 16,266,117 | 21,148,721 | 25,597,993 |
| Emp. | 282 | 286 | 281 |

DUNS 22-808-0040 **Exp**

## Severfield Plc

Severs House, Thirsk, North Yorkshire YO7 3JN
**Tel:** 01845-577896 **Fax:** 01845-577411
**Web:** www.severfield.com
**Reg No:** 1721262 **Estd:** 1983 Public Limited Company
**Line of Business:** Manufacture of metal structures and parts of structures
**Export Markets:** Europe & other countries
**Export Sales:** £12,396,000
**Trading Style:** Severfield-Rowen
**Issued Capital:** £7,437,590
**Directors:** K I Whiteman, J Dodds, I R Cochrane, A D Dunsmore, Prof D Randall, I Lawson, A H Griffiths, N C Holt
**Co. Secretary:** Mark Sanderson
**Responsibilities**
**Senior:** John Osbaldiston *(Director)*, Nigel Pickard *(Managing Director Atlas Ward S)*
**Purchasing:** Sharon Fell *(Purchasing Manager)*
**Engineering:** Steve Raw *(Principal Engineering Manager)*
**US SIC:** 3441, 1799
**UK SIC:** 32042, 50000
**Auditors:** Deloitte LLP
**Bankers:** Yorkshire Bank Plc (05-00-20)

| | 31-03-14 | 31-03-13 | 31-03-11 |
|---|---|---|---|
| TO | 231,312,000 | 318,256,000 | 267,778,000 |
| P/L | (4,057,000) | (28,858,000) | 6,782,000 |
| NW | 78,841,000 | 32,589,000 | 59,359,000 |
| WC | 14,243,000 | (32,060,000) | (3,059,000) |
| Emp. | 1,203 | 1,265 | 1,207 |

DUNS 50-361-0081 **Imp-Exp**

## Severn & Wye Smokery Ltd

The Smoke House, Chaxhill, Newnham, Gloucestershire GL14 1QW
**Tel:** 01452760190
**Web:** www.severnandwye.co.uk
**Reg No:** 2377918 **VAT No:** 535600955
**Estd:** 1989 Private Limited Company
**Line of Business:** Fish smokers and curers
**Export Markets:** Greece; France
**Export Sales:** £5,415,709
**Issued Capital:** £90,100
**Managing Director:** R N Cook
**Co. Secretary:** Ms Shirley Cook
**Responsibilities**
**Health & Safety:** Malcolm Graves *(Quality Manager)*
**Facilities:** Malcolm Graves *(Quality Manager)*
**Branches:** Severn & Wye Smokery Ltd, Walmore Hill, Gloucester, Gloucestershire GL2 8LA
**US SIC:** 2092 **UK SIC:** 41501
**Auditors:** Upstone Blencowe
**Bankers:** Lloyds TSB Bank plc (30-93-48)

| | 31-03-14 | 31-03-13 | 31-03-12 |
|---|---|---|---|
| TO | 40,415,738 | 30,510,561 | 30,731,101 |
| P/L | 708,813 | 1,147,615 | 1,705,244 |
| NW | 5,742,984 | 5,245,778 | 4,399,358 |
| WC | 2,908,090 | 2,356,988 | 2,635,349 |
| Emp. | 121 | 136 | 129 |

DUNS 89-678-0103

## Severn Controls Ltd

Unit 3 The Perry Centre, Davy Way, Waterwells Business Park, Quedgeley, Gloucester, Gloucestershire GL2 2AD
**Tel:** 01452-727610 **Fax:** 01452-727611
**Web:** www.severncontrols.co.uk
**Reg No:** 3343337 **Estd:** 1997 Private Limited Company
**Line of Business:** Energy management control systems
**Issued Capital:** £200
**Directors:** C Rowston, R Bolton, A P Bolton
**Co. Secretary:** Ms Lynette Bolton
**Responsibilities**
**HR:** Jennifer Whitehead *(Facilities Officer)*
**Health & Safety:** Jennifer Whitehead *(Facilities Officer)*
**Facilities:** Jennifer Whitehead *(Facilities Officer)*
**Purchasing:** Stuart Wissett *(Purchasing Manager)*
**US SIC:** 3643, 3823, 3629
**UK SIC:** 34203, 37100, 34350

| | 31-05-14 | 31-05-13 | 31-05-12 |
|---|---|---|---|
| TA | 1,145,879 | 1,272,650 | 1,093,892 |
| NW | 384,497 | 325,340 | 416,638 |
| WC | 263,882 | 193,307 | 256,623 |

DUNS 23-249-2574 **Imp-Exp**

## Severn Delta Ltd

Showground Road, Bridgwater, Somerset TA6 6AJ
**Tel:** 01278-428200 **Fax:** 01278-458766
**Web:** www.sarah-smith.co.uk
**Reg No:** 4269451 **VAT No:** 793728185
**Estd:** 2003 Private Limited Company
**Line of Business:** Other manufacturing not elsewhere classified
**Export Markets:** France (including French Guyane,Spain (including Spanish territories in North Africa with Ceuta and Melilla)
**Trading Style:** Sarah Smith
**Issued Capital:** £50,030
**Principals:** C G Birnie *(Managing)*, Mrs P T Shiner, Ms K Birnie
**Co. Secretary:** Martyn Shiner
**Responsibilities**
**Health & Safety:** Simon Dawton *(quality manager)*
**Facilities:** Simon Dawton *(quality manager)*
**US SIC:** 3999, 5199
**UK SIC:** 49590, 61900
**Auditors:** Maxwells
**Bankers:** HSBC Bank plc (40-14-13)

| | 31-12-13 | 31-12-12 | 31-12-11 |
|---|---|---|---|
| TA | 2,535,327 | 2,783,258 | 2,886,429 |
| NW | 600,276 | 603,110 | 588,044 |
| WC | 155,615 | 160,180 | (26,318) |

DUNS 39-668-4748

## Severn Glocon Group Plc

The Olympus Centre, Gloucester, Gloucestershire GL2 4NF
**Fax:** 08452232041
**Web:** www.severnglocon.co.uk
**Reg No:** 2134858 **Estd:** 1988 Public Limited Company
**Line of Business:** Manufacture of pumps
**Export Sales:** £68,481,371
**Issued Capital:** £50,000
**Directors:** Mrs M J Critchley, C C Powell
**Co. Secretary:** Maurice Critchley
**Responsibilities**
**Finance:** Merrilyn Millington *(group financial director)*
**US SIC:** 3561 **UK SIC:** 32870
**Auditors:** Hazlewoods LLP
**Bankers:** Barclays Bank Plc (20-33-83)

| | 31-12-13 | 31-12-12 | 31-12-11 |
|---|---|---|---|
| TO | 94,442,399 | 79,833,850 | 53,350,334 |
| P/L | 13,213,047 | 9,483,206 | 5,980,277 |
| NW | 22,546,651 | 14,476,332 | 14,980,981 |
| WC | 13,923,103 | 9,539,649 | 11,087,186 |
| Emp. | 778 | 762 | 572 |

DUNS 28-947-0767

## Severn Hospice Ltd

Bicton Heath, Shrewsbury, Shropshire SY3 8HS
**Tel:** 01743-236565
**Web:** www.severnhospice.org.uk
**Reg No:** 1608025 **Estd:** 1982 Private Limited Company
**Line of Business:** Hospices
**Directors:** Mrs A H Tudor, M J Tudor, A J Cordery, Dr T D Ryan, B Tweedie, Ms G De Wet, P J Donohue, F A Yates
**Co. Secretary:** Paul Cronin
**Responsibilities**
**Senior:** Sarah Broomhead *(Director)*, John Fairclough *(Director)*, Zara Oliver *(Director)*, Marilyn Rydstrom *(Director)*, Susan Trevor *(Director)*, Barbara-ann Tweedie *(Trustee)*, Wendy Walton *(Director)*
**Branches:** Severn Hospice Ltd, 45 High St, Bridgnorth, Shropshire WV16 4DX
**US SIC:** 8091 **UK SIC:** 95200
**Auditors:** Whittingham Riddell
**Bankers:** National Westminster Bank Plc (55-50-05)

| | 31-03-14 | 31-03-13 | 31-03-12 |
|---|---|---|---|
| TO | 10,282,578 | 9,198,847 | 8,866,723 |
| P/L | 1,196,242 | 157,866 | 414,576 |
| NW | 17,479,832 | 16,250,279 | 15,954,774 |
| WC | 7,739,571 | 8,220,277 | 8,057,979 |
| Emp. | 209 | 201 | 200 |

DUNS 21-924-4670

## Severn Insulation Co Ltd

Unit L1, South Point, Clos Marion, Cardiff, South Glamorgan CF10 4LQ
**Tel:** 029-2047-1040 **Fax:** 029-2047-1044
**Web:** www.severninsulation.co.uk
**Reg No:** 1170999 **VAT No:** 137214587
**Estd:** 1974 Private Limited Company
**Line of Business:** Insulation installers
**Issued Capital:** £14,000
**Principals:** D Waters *(Managing)*, R Herdman, M E Morgan
**Co. Secretary:** Carl Waters
**Responsibilities**
**Senior:** Roger Sellick *(Operations Director)*

**Finance:** Karl Stephens *(Financial Controller)*, Dianne Tyley *(Payroll & Contracts Administra)*
**Health & Safety:** Nick Cox *(Health & Safety Officer)*
**Operations:** Guto Eames *(Project Manager)*, Roger Sellick *(Operations Director)*
**Purchasing:** Natalie Sellick *(Buyer & Logistics Manager)*, Dianne Tyley *(Payroll & Contracts Administra)*
**Fleet:** Natalie Sellick *(Buyer & Logistics Manager)*
**Branches:** Severn Insulation Co. Ltd, 4 Ardmore Rd, South Ockendon, Essex RM15 5TH
**US SIC:** 1742, 1799
**UK SIC:** 50400, 50000
**Auditors:** Arthur Gait & Co
**Bankers:** Barclays Bank Plc (20-60-58)

| | 31-03-14 | 31-03-13 | 31-03-12 |
|---|---|---|---|
| TA | 3,005,885 | 2,816,210 | 2,641,982 |
| NW | 1,595,553 | 1,543,698 | 1,460,593 |
| WC | 1,001,876 | 1,009,862 | 984,817 |

DUNS 54-864-0168

## Severn N H S Trust

Rikenel, Montpellier, Gloucester, Gloucestershire GL1 1LY
**Tel:** 01452894269
**Web:** www.swrecovery.org.uk
**Line of Business:** N H S Trust. Accountability:- Each Trust Board is directly accountable to the Secretary of State via the National Health Service Executive.
**Director:** R James
**Branches:** Severn N H S Trust, Bailey Hill, Lydney, Gloucestershire GL15 4RS
**US SIC:** 8062 **UK SIC:** 95100
**Employees:** 385

DUNS 50-364-7331

## Severn River Crossing Plc

Severn Bridge Maintenance Unit, Bristol, Avon BS35 4BD
**Tel:** 01454-635000
**Web:** www.severnbridge.co.uk
**Reg No:** 2379695 **VAT No:** 577050631
**Estd:** 1989 Public Limited Company
**Line of Business:** Property developers
**Issued Capital:** £50,000
**Directors:** M Vial, D Wells, A S Pearson, A H Moore, M Stringer, D J Rushton, J P Conway, A P Battersby
**Co. Secretary:** James Rawle
**Responsibilities**
**Senior:** James Clune *(General Manager)*, Pierre Delseny *(Director)*, Herve Le Caignec *(Director)*, Olivier Mathieu *(Manager)*, Paul Ramshaw *(Facilities Manager)*
**Sales:** Mike Gudgeon *(Commercial Manager)*
**IT:** Greg Cooke *(Technical & Systems Support Co)*, Jake Whity *(Computer Manager)*
**Facilities:** Peter Neale *(Facilities Manager)*
**Operations:** James Clune *(General Manager)*
**Engineering:** Scott Michell *(IT Systems Engineer)*
**US SIC:** 6552 **UK SIC:** 85000
**Auditors:** Unknown Auditor
**Bankers:** Lloyds TSB Bank plc (30-91-89)

| | 31-12-13 | 31-12-12 | 31-12-11 |
|---|---|---|---|
| TO | 85,435,000 | 81,222,000 | 77,623,000 |
| P/L | 10,059,000 | (2,679,000) | (13,690,000) |
| NW | (26,959,000) | (33,563,000) | (24,494,000) |
| WC | (8,853,000) | (54,435,000) | 127,292,000 |
| Emp. | 183 | 183 | 185 |

DUNS 23-776-0236 Imp-Exp

## Severn Trent Plc

Severn Trent Centre, 2 St John's Street, Coventry, West Midlands CV1 2LZ
**Tel:** 02477715000
**Web:** www.severntrentcostain.com
**Reg No:** 2366619 **Estd:** 1989 Public Limited Company
**Line of Business:** Management activities of holding companies
**Export Sales:** £239,800,000
**Issued Capital:** £233,347,420
**Responsibilities**
**Senior:** Anthony Ballance *(Director)*, Olivia Garfield *(Director)*, Martin Kane *(Director)*, Michael Mckeon *(Director)*, Ted Pearce *(Property Director)*, Antony Wray *(Chief Executive)*
**Health & Safety:** Christina Craddock *(Health & Safety Officer)*
**Facilities:** Christina Craddock *(Health & Safety Officer)*, Ted Pearce *(Property Director)*
**Branches:** Severn Trent Plc, Avon House, St. Martins Road, Coventry, West Midlands CV3 6PR
**US SIC:** 6711, 9121
**UK SIC:** 83962, 91110
**Auditors:** Deloitte LLP
**Bankers:** Lloyds TSB Bank plc (30-00-03)

**Following financial data are in thousands**

| | 31-03-14 | 31-03-13 | 31-03-12 |
|---|---|---|---|
| TO | 1,856,700 | 1,831,600 | 1,770,600 |
| P/L | 282,700 | 215,200 | 156,700 |
| NW | 982,600 | 692,200 | 812,600 |
| WC | 37,300 | 402,200 | 288,000 |
| Emp. | 7,992 | 8,221 | 8,051 |

DUNS 76-433-5154

## Severn Trent Retail & Utility Services Ltd

**(Subsidiary of:** Severn Trent Plc)
2297 Coventry Road, Birmingham, West Midlands B26 3PU
**Tel:** 01159713550
**Web:** www.stwater.co.uk
**Reg No:** 2562471 **Estd:** 1990 Private Limited Company
**Line of Business:** Other business activities not elsewhere classified
**Issued Capital:** £2
**Responsibilities**
**Senior:** Mark Dovey *(Director)*, Bronagh Kennedy *(Director)*, Robert Mcpheely *(Director)*
**US SIC:** 7399 **UK SIC:** 83954
**Auditors:** Deloitte LLP
**Bankers:** Lloyds TSB Bank plc (30-00-03)

| | 31-03-14 | 31-03-13 | 31-03-12 |
|---|---|---|---|
| TO | N/A | 10,111,000 | 10,110,000 |
| P/L | 43,000 | 3,864,000 | 4,116,000 |
| NW | 11,839,000 | 11,841,000 | 9,461,000 |
| WC | 11,641,000 | 13,063,000 | 9,070,000 |
| Emp. | 50 | 47 | 53 |

DUNS 22-050-3788

## Severn Trent Services Operations Uk Ltd

**(Subsidiary of:** Severn Trent Plc)
Unit 3900, Parkside, Birmingham Business Park, Birmingham, West Midlands B37 7YG
**Tel:** 08450340864
**Web:** www.severntrentcostain.com
**Reg No:** 4052522 **Estd:** 2000 Private Limited Company
**Line of Business:** Collection, purification and distribution of water
**Issued Capital:** £1,000
**Responsibilities**
**Senior:** Dave Godfrey *(Manager)*, Robert Mcpheely *(Director)*, Neil Miles *(Director)*
**US SIC:** 4941 **UK SIC:** 17000
**Auditors:** Deloitte LLP
**Bankers:** Lloyds TSB Bank plc (30-00-03)

| | 31-03-14 | 31-03-13 | 31-03-12 |
|---|---|---|---|
| TO | 18,119,000 | 19,401,000 | 18,492,000 |
| P/L | 4,407,000 | 4,711,000 | 2,238,000 |
| NW | 10,418,000 | 10,339,000 | 9,568,000 |
| WC | 18,159,000 | 17,101,000 | 16,242,000 |
| Emp. | N/A | 53 | 110 |

DUNS 54-901-5287

## Severn Vale Housing Society Ltd

Unit 18 Shannon Way, Ashchurch, Tewkesbury, Gloucestershire GL20 8ND
**Tel:** 01684272700
**Web:** www.svhs.org.uk
**Reg No:** 0028557IP **Estd:** 1998 Friendly Society
**Line of Business:** Housing associations societies trusts & co-operatives
**Responsibilities**
**Marketing:** Darren Knight *(Customer Services Manager)*
**HR:** Corry Ravenscroft *(Human Resources Manager)*
**Health & Safety:** Corry Ravenscroft *(Human Resources Manager)*
**Operations:** Corry Ravenscroft *(Human Resources Manager)*
**Branches:** Severn Vale Housing Society Ltd, 3 Parklands, Gloucester, Gloucestershire GL3 1JS
**US SIC:** 8699 **UK SIC:** 96902
**Auditors:** Grant Thornton UK LLP
**Bankers:** Bank Of Scotland (12-12-82)

| | 31-03-12 | 31-03-11 | 31-03-10 |
|---|---|---|---|
| TO | 16,952,000 | 15,200,000 | 16,034,000 |
| P/L | (213,000) | 28,000 | (497,000) |
| NW | (27,457,000) | (27,054,000) | (28,905,000) |
| WC | 1,643,000 | (486,000) | (1,266,000) |
| Emp. | 117 | 105 | 100 |

DUNS 21-926-3357

## Severn Valley Railway (Holdings) Plc

The Railway Station, Railway Station, Bewdley, Worcestershire DY12 1BG
**Tel:** 01299-403816
**Web:** www.svr.co.uk
**Reg No:** 1046274 **VAT No:** 275555431
**Estd:** 1972 Public Limited Company
**Line of Business:** Transport via railways
**Issued Capital:** £6,335,591
**Principals:** M R York *(Chairman)*, D C Williams, A G Bending, A D Owen, S C White, C W Walton, J A Dunster, N C Paul
**Co. Secretary:** Matthew Harris
**Responsibilities**
**Senior:** Alvin Barker *(Manager)*, Andy Barr *(Director)*, David Mee *(Marketing Manager)*, Peter Pearson *(Director)*, Nick Ralls *(general manager)*
**Marketing:** David Mee *(Marketing Manager)*
**Branches:** Severn Valley Railway (Holdings) Plc, Bridgnorth Railway Station, Bridgnorth, Shropshire WV16 5DT
**US SIC:** 4011 **UK SIC:** 71000
**Auditors:** Horwath Clark Whitehill
**Bankers:** HSBC Bank plc (40-26-08)

| | 05-01-14 | 06-01-13 | 31-01-11 |
|---|---|---|---|
| TO | 6,009,266 | 5,371,952 | 5,538,945 |
| P/L | 61,891 | 58,158 | 58,605 |
| NW | 7,261,114 | 6,225,035 | 5,110,401 |
| WC | 980,226 | 372,052 | (326,487) |
| Emp. | 135 | 127 | 141 |

DUNS 29-758-8048 Imp

## Severn Valley Woodworks Ltd

Calders Yard, Church Lane, Northwood Green, Newnham, Gloucestershire GL14 1ND
**Web:** www.svw2000.co.uk
**Reg No:** 2021938 **Estd:** 1970 Private Limited Company
**Line of Business:** Saw milling and planing of wood, impregnation of wood
**Export Sales:** £131,128
**Issued Capital:** £62,000
**Principals:** A F Jenkins *(Managing)*, A J Sterry, S J Brown, D R Twigg, R T Simpson
**Co. Secretary:** Terrence Jenkins
**Responsibilities**
**Senior:** Nicholas Jenkins *(Production Director)*
**Admin:** Judy Brown *(Office Manager)*
**IT:** Nicholas Jenkins *(Production Director)*
**HR:** Judy Brown *(Office Manager)*
**Engineering:** Nicholas Jenkins *(Production Director)*
**US SIC:** 2421 **UK SIC:** 46101
**Auditors:** Target Consulting Ltd
**Bankers:** National Westminster Bank Plc (60-05-16)

| | 31-10-14 | 31-10-13 | 31-10-12 |
|---|---|---|---|
| TO | 11,583,419 | 9,831,021 | 10,260,739 |
| P/L | 116,290 | 165,495 | 271,637 |
| NW | 1,680,028 | 1,633,581 | 1,546,663 |
| WC | 551,419 | 544,007 | 417,163 |
| Emp. | 76 | 67 | 67 |

DUNS 23-621-5690

## Severn Waste Services Ltd

Kings Road, Evesham, Worcestershire WR11 3XZ
**Tel:** 01386-443376
**Web:** www.severnwaste.com
**Reg No:** 3618688 **VAT No:** 715537435
**Estd:** 1998 Private Limited Company
**Line of Business:** Collection and treatment of other waste
**Issued Capital:** £250,000
**Directors:** Urbaser Limited, A Serrano Minchan, Fcc Environment Services (Uk) Li, J Peiro Balaguer
**Co. Secretary:** Tmf Corporate Administration Ser
**Responsibilities**
**HR:** Tony Perry *(Credit/Payroll)*
**Branches:** Severn Waste Services Ltd, Crossgate Depot, Crossgate Rd, Redditch, Worcestershire B98 7SN
**US SIC:** 7399, 4953, 3341
**UK SIC:** 83954, 92110, 22470
**Auditors:** Deloitte & Touche LLP
**Bankers:** HSBC Bank plc (40-47-17)

| | 31-12-13 | 28-12-12 | 31-12-11 |
|---|---|---|---|
| TO | 33,196,425 | 30,895,457 | 28,445,914 |
| P/L | 9,276 | 9,182 | 7,826 |
| NW | 343,847 | 307,057 | 328,887 |
| WC | 323,847 | 335,057 | 337,787 |
| Emp. | 262 | 251 | 236 |

DUNS 21-747-3594 Imp

## Severnprint Ltd

Ashville Trading Estate, Gloucester, Gloucestershire GL2 5EU
**Tel:** 01452416391
**Web:** www.severnprint.co.uk
**Reg No:** 1317797 **VAT No:** 302352902
**Estd:** 1977 Private Limited Company
**Line of Business:** Printers general
**Trading Style:** Sprinters
**Issued Capital:** £7,300
**Principals:** S R Pealing *(Managing)*, Mrs D Pealing, N J Pealing
**Co. Secretary:** David Pealing
**Responsibilities**
**Sales:** Anita Barry *(Account Manager)*, Andy Jordan *(Account Manager)*
**HR:** Caitriona Clucas *(Human Resources Manager)*
**Health & Safety:** Caitriona Clucas *(Human Resources Manager)*
**Operations:** Lyndon Murray *(Production Manager)*
**US SIC:** 2794, 2752
**UK SIC:** 47545, 47544
**Auditors:** Griffiths Marshall
**Bankers:** National Westminster Bank Plc (60-09-02)

| | 30-11-13 | 30-11-12 | 30-11-11 |
|---|---|---|---|
| TO | N/A | N/A | 3,454,813 |
| P/L | N/A | N/A | (8,216) |
| NW | 2,373,457 | 2,418,306 | 2,488,399 |
| WC | 1,033,359 | 978,015 | 998,366 |
| Emp. | N/A | N/A | 59 |

DUNS 22-023-1281

## Severnside Housing

Brassey Road, Shrewsbury, Shropshire SY3 7FA
**Tel:** 01743285000
**Web:** www.severnsidehousing.co.uk
**Reg No:** 4025816 **Estd:** 1900 Private Company Limited By Guarantee
**Line of Business:** Housing associations societies trusts & co-operatives
**Directors:** M T Price, Ms C K Robinson, P D Price, J A Lindsay, A J Parkes, G E Evans, P V Williams, Miss A C Lanning
**Co. Secretary:** Mrs Irene Molyneux
**Responsibilities**
**Senior:** Sarah Boden *(Chief Executive)*, Susan Ganderton *(Director)*, Rory O'Byrne *(Director)*, Benjamin Proltor *(Director)*
**Marketing:** Matt Critchley *(Marketing Manager)*, Helen Pugh *(Development Officer)*, Kerry Stanley *(Head of Marketing)*
**Purchasing:** Matt Akers *(Procurement Manager)*
**Branches:** Severnside Housing, Holland Clo, Shrewsbury, Shropshire SY3 0NY
**US SIC:** 6519 **UK SIC:** 85000
**Auditors:** KPMG LLP
**Bankers:** National Westminster Bank Plc (55-50-05)

| | 31-03-14 | 31-03-13 | 31-03-12 |
|---|---|---|---|
| TO | 25,895,000 | 23,734,000 | 22,644,000 |
| P/L | 1,631,000 | 829,000 | 1,307,000 |
| NW | 2,329,000 | (4,109,000) | (2,318,000) |
| WC | (2,763,000) | (2,732,000) | (601,000) |
| Emp. | 242 | 228 | 240 |

DUNS 55-080-7143

## Sevington Mill

Sevington Lane, Willesborough, Willesborough, Ashford, Kent TN24 0LB
**Tel:** 01233639800
**Estd:** 1986
**Line of Business:** Non-charitable social work activities with accommodation
**Proprietor:** M Crouickshanks
**Responsibilities**
**Senior:** Clare Battin *(Manager)*
**US SIC:** 8321 **UK SIC:** 96111
**Employees:** 50

DUNS 21-112-8525 Exp

## Sew-Eurodrive Ltd

**(Subsidiary of:** Bv Beteiligung Gmbh & Co Kg)
Beckbridge Road, Normanton, West Yorkshire WF6 1QR
**Tel:** 01924-893-855 **Fax:** 01924-893-702
**Web:** www.sew-eurodrive.co.uk
**Reg No:** 0947360 **VAT No:** 170908656
**Estd:** 1969 Private Limited Company
**Line of Business:** Renting of automobiles
**Export Markets:** E U
**Export Sales:** £1,482,802
**Trading Style:** Eurodrive, S E W
**Issued Capital:** £3,500,000
**Directors:** J D Blickle, M Holmes
**Co. Secretary:** John Pickup
**Responsibilities**
**Senior:** Rainer Blickle *(Director & Chairman)*
**Branches:** Sew-Eurodrive Ltd, S E W Eurodrive Ltd, Sugarbrook Court, Bromsgrove, Worcestershire B60 3EX
**US SIC:** 3999 **UK SIC:** 49590
**Auditors:** Jolliffe Cork LLP
**Bankers:** HSBC Bank plc (40-45-11)

| | 28-02-14 | 28-02-13 | 29-02-12 |
|---|---|---|---|
| TO | 38,265,280 | 34,287,944 | 32,419,081 |
| P/L | 7,115,422 | 6,954,239 | 6,626,514 |
| NW | 33,596,518 | 28,633,227 | 22,678,497 |
| WC | 15,700,109 | 11,632,717 | 15,167,365 |
| Emp. | 147 | 147 | 146 |

DUNS 21-810-8320

## Seward Accident Repair Centre

Langstone House, Southmoor Lane, Havant, Hampshire PO9 1JW
**Tel:** 08448460270
**Web:** www.sewardaccidentrepairs.co.uk
**Estd:** 2012
**Line of Business:** Car Body Repair
**Responsibilities**
**Senior:** Nigel Loughman *(Manager)*
**US SIC:** 7531 **UK SIC:** 67100
**Employees:** 60

DUNS 50-453-2938

## Sewell Retail Ltd

**(Subsidiary of:** Sewell Ventures Ltd)
Holme Church Lane, Beverley, North Humberside HU17 0QB
**Tel:** 01482-882302
**Web:** www.sewell-group.co.uk
**Reg No:** 2435966 **Estd:** 1989 Private Limited Company
**Line of Business:** Petrol service stations
**Issued Capital:** £70
**Directors:** Ms S A Sewell, P E Sewell, S J Davison, P A Sewell, D Craven-Jones
**Co. Secretary:** David Leedham
**Responsibilities**
**Senior:** Tom Massey *(Branch Manager)*, Mary Sewell *(Manager)*, Dennis Sewell *(Manager)*
**US SIC:** 5541 **UK SIC:** 65200
**Auditors:** PricewaterhouseCoopers

| | 31-12-13 | 31-12-12 | 31-12-11 |
|---|---|---|---|
| TO | 54,553,000 | 53,891,000 | 53,123,000 |
| P/L | 234,000 | 365,000 | 465,000 |
| NW | 1,625,000 | 1,425,000 | 1,121,000 |
| WC | (2,252,000) | (2,457,000) | (1,606,000) |
| Emp. | 177 | 177 | 174 |

DUNS 28-964-7299 **Imp-Exp**

## Sewtec Automation Ltd

**(Subsidiary of:** Sewtec Holdings Ltd)
1-3 Riverside Way, Dewsbury, West Yorkshire WF13 3LG
**Tel:** 01924-494047
**Web:** www.sewtec.co.uk
**Reg No:** 1699297 **VAT No:** 361694044
**Estd:** 1983 Private Limited Company
**Line of Business:** Packaging equipment
**Export Markets:** Worldwide
**Issued Capital:** £1,000
**Director:** B J Meehan
**Co. Secretary:** Ms Helen Meehan
**Responsibilities**
**Finance:** Paul Tansey *(Finance Director)*
**US SIC:** 3551 **UK SIC:** 32441
**Auditors:** Mazars LLP
**Bankers:** National Westminster Bank Plc (60-60-05)

| | 28-02-14 | 28-02-13 | 31-02-11 |
|---|---|---|---|
| TO | 20,522,155 | N/A | N/A |
| P/L | 6,253,654 | N/A | N/A |
| NW | 2,743,238 | 2,511,627 | 2,015,677 |
| WC | 2,044,923 | 1,821,749 | 1,710,937 |
| Emp. | 74 | N/A | N/A |

DUNS 21-522-7120

## Sexual Health Clinic

The Royal London Hospital, Po Box 59, Whitechapel, London E1 1BB
**Tel:** 020-7377-7307
**Proprietorship**
**Line of Business:** General Medical And Surgical Hospitals
**Proprietor:** Mrs E Snooks
**US SIC:** 8062 **UK SIC:** 95100
**Employees:** 50

DUNS 21-396-1708

## Sexual Health Promotion Service

Tennyson Medical Centre, 1 Tennyson Avenue, Chesterfield, Derbyshire S40 4SN
**Tel:** 01246559431
**Web:** www.dchs.nhs.uk
**Estd:** 2009 Proprietorship
**Line of Business:** Nhs clinics
**Proprietor:** R Marriott
**Responsibilities**
**Senior:** Paula Newbert *(Service Manager)*
**US SIC:** 8062 **UK SIC:** 95100
**Employees:** 50

DUNS 21-231-8032

## Sexual Health Services Pct

Owen Road, Lancaster, Lancashire LA1 2LN
**Tel:** 0845-059-0015
**Proprietorship**
**Line of Business:** Hospitals
**Proprietor:** Dr A Greenwood
**US SIC:** 8062 **UK SIC:** 95100
**Employees:** 60

DUNS 21-325-8353

## Seymour (Civil Engineering Contractors) Ltd.

**(Subsidiary of:** Renew Holdings Plc.)
30-34 Navigation Point, Middleton Road, Hartlepool, Cleveland TS24 0UQ
**Tel:** 01429-233521 **Fax:** 01429-862504
**Web:** www.seymourcec.co.uk
**Reg No:** 1374637 **VAT No:** 605789218
**Estd:** 1978 Private Limited Company
**Line of Business:** Construction of civil engineering constructions
**Issued Capital:** £2,100,000
**Directors:**
Renew Corporate Director Limited, K J Byrne, B W May
**Co. Secretary:** Reneew Nominees Limited
**Responsibilities**
**Senior:** Tammy Bennett *(Business Development)*, David Millwaid *(Buyer)*
**Facilities:** Stephen Seymour *(Fleet Manager)*
**US SIC:** 1622 **UK SIC:** 50200
**Auditors:** Tait Walker
**Bankers:** Yorkshire Bank Plc (05-09-75)

| | 30-09-13 | 30-09-12 | 30-09-11 |
|---|---|---|---|
| TO | 19,760,000 | 16,423,000 | 20,777,000 |
| P/L | 465,000 | (1,611,000) | (431,000) |
| NW | 2,220,000 | 1,783,000 | 1,497,000 |
| WC | 1,417,000 | 891,000 | (889,000) |
| Emp. | 170 | 153 | 194 |

DUNS 77-444-9748 **Imp**

## Seymour Distribution Ltd

2 East Poultry Avenue, London EC1A 9PT
**Tel:** 02074293600 **Fax:** 020-7429-4001
**Web:** www.seymour.co.uk
**Reg No:** 2954685 **Estd:** 1938 Private Limited Company
**Line of Business:** Distribution service providers
**Issued Capital:** £1,500
**Directors:** P L Hampel, J M Lambert, Ms T F O'Sullivan, F C Straetmans
**Co. Secretary:**
Bauer Group Secretariat Limited
**Responsibilities**
**Senior:** Karen Rooks *(Internationa and IS Director)*
**Admin:** Sharon Boyle *(Office Manager)*
**HR:** Fiona Winchester *(Human Resources Manager)*
**Health & Safety:** Sharon Boyle *(Office Manager)*
**Facilities:** Sharon Boyle *(Office Manager)*
**US SIC:** 4712 **UK SIC:** 77002
**Auditors:** PricewaterhouseCoopers LLP
**Bankers:** The Royal Bank Of Scotland Plc (16-71-67)

| | 31-12-13 | 31-12-12 | 31-12-11 |
|---|---|---|---|
| TO | 105,785,000 | 113,099,000 | 125,125,000 |
| P/L | 298,000 | 728,000 | 993,000 |
| NW | 204,000 | 344,000 | 426,000 |
| WC | (162,000) | (341,000) | (544,000) |
| Emp. | 86 | 91 | 93 |

DUNS 28-953-2525 **Exp**

## Seymour-Powell Ltd

**(Subsidiary of:** Writtle Holdings Ltd)
327 Lillie Road, London SW6 7NR
**Tel:** 020-7381-6433 **Fax:** 020-7381-9081
**Web:** www.seymourpowell.com
**Reg No:** 1640184 **VAT No:** 394607228
**Estd:** 1984 Private Limited Company
**Line of Business:** Design consultants
**Export Markets:** Japan; Korean Democratic Peoples Republic; Malaysia; India; European Union (E U); Scandinavia; U S A
**Export Sales:** £5,527,650
**Issued Capital:** £1,690
**Principals:** D H Powell *(Managing)*, R Lloyd *(Financial)*, G R Harris, A B Caroen, N Hirst, R W Seymour, R T Essex, E Hebblethwaite
**Co. Secretary:** Matthew Gilmore
**Responsibilities**
**Senior:** Dick Powell *(Joint Managing Director)*
**US SIC:** 8999 **UK SIC:** 83954
**Auditors:** Hextall Meakin
**Bankers:** Coutts & Co (18-00-14)

| | 31-12-13 | 31-12-12 | 31-12-11 |
|---|---|---|---|
| TO | 8,824,195 | 8,843,510 | 9,045,259 |
| P/L | 397,668 | 476,089 | 121,877 |
| NW | 1,344,861 | 1,395,190 | 713,197 |
| WC | 1,081,397 | 1,387,978 | 628,829 |
| Emp. | 94 | 94 | 92 |

DUNS 23-777-0789

## Seymour Valentine Ltd

4 Bermondsey Trading Estate, London SE16 3LL
**Tel:** 02072312131 **Fax:** 020-7231-7171
**Web:** www.seymourvalentine.co.uk
**Reg No:** 2368423 **VAT No:** 494564993
**Estd:** 1989 Private Limited Company
**Line of Business:** Vending machines sale, rental and supply
**Issued Capital:** £50,000
**Director:** C Riza
**Responsibilities**
**Operations:** Mohammed Hasib *(Fleet Operations Manager)*
**US SIC:** 5963, 5149
**UK SIC:** 65600, 61700
**Auditors:** Sylvester & Co
**Bankers:** The Royal Bank Of Scotland Plc (16-11-30)

| | 30-06-14 | 30-06-13 | 31-06-11 |
|---|---|---|---|
| TA | 1,551,869 | 1,411,425 | 2,166,535 |
| NW | (15,226) | (278,826) | 308,044 |
| WC | 8,922 | (189,017) | 91,599 |

DUNS 21-851-9636

## Sf Recruitment Ltd

**(Subsidiary of:** Sf Resourcing Ltd)
6 Millennium Way West, Phoenix Park, London
**Tel:** 01216841555
**Web:** www.sfrecruitment.co.uk
**Reg No:** 8163422 **Estd:** 2012 Private Limited Company
**Line of Business:** Labour recruitment and provision of personnel
**Issued Capital:** £1,356,452
**Directors:** T N Ramus, D Stuart-Smith, A I Minnis, A J Fletcher, D Jalan
**Co. Secretary:** Graham Dolan
**US SIC:** 7361 **UK SIC:** 83954
**Bankers:** The Co-Operative Bank Plc (08-90-74)

| | 29-12-13 |
|---|---|
| TO | 16,281,881 |
| P/L | 564,416 |
| NW | (2,185,518) |
| WC | (2,218,240) |
| Emp. | 100 |

DUNS 21-031-9745 **Exp**

## S.F. Williams (Foils) Ltd

**(Subsidiary of:** A M (Holdings) Ltd)
1 The Forum, Coopers Way, Temple Farm Industrial Estate, Southend-On-Sea, Essex SS2 5TE
**Tel:** 01702-445-851
**Web:** www.sfw.co.uk
**Reg No:** 0595486 **Estd:** 1957 Private Limited Company
**Line of Business:** Manufacturers of packaging materials.
**Export Markets:** Australia, New Zealand, Germany, Canada
**Trading Style:** Am Holdings Group, S F Williams
**Issued Capital:** £40,000
**Principals:** D J Watson *(Chairman)*, P S Watson
**Co. Secretary:** David Barnish
**Responsibilities**
**Engineering:** Frank Dixon *(Engineering Manager)*
**US SIC:** 2654, 5199
**UK SIC:** 47280, 61900
**Auditors:** Wilkins Kennedy LLP

| | 28-02-14 | 28-02-13 | 29-02-12 |
|---|---|---|---|
| TO | N/A | N/A | 3,469,315 |
| P/L | N/A | N/A | 82,362 |
| NW | 1,550,052 | 1,461,688 | 1,358,803 |
| WC | 1,247,769 | 1,288,008 | 1,200,280 |

DUNS 22-653-0004

## Sfc (Midlands) Ltd

**(Subsidiary of:** Syston Fencing Co Ltd)
Unit 75-78 The Burrows, East Goscote, Leicester, Leicestershire LE7 3XD
**Tel:** 01162602610 **Fax:** 01509816252
**Web:** www.sfcmidlands.co.uk
**Reg No:** 1420808 **VAT No:** 350202708
**Estd:** 1979 Private Limited Company
**Line of Business:** Steel fabricators
**Issued Capital:** £3,000
**Principals:** J R Stone *(Managing)*, D Sleeman
**Co. Secretary:** Jamie Mcloughlin
**US SIC:** 1622, 2421
**UK SIC:** 50200, 46101
**Auditors:** Stafford & Co
**Bankers:** National Westminster Bank Plc (60-13-39)

| | 31-03-14 | 31-03-13 | 31-03-12 |
|---|---|---|---|
| TA | 854,185 | 1,027,069 | 1,283,885 |
| NW | 101,711 | 100,796 | 88,874 |
| WC | 94,983 | 88,839 | 65,020 |

DUNS 73-960-3707 **Imp**

## Sfs Fire Services Ltd

**(Subsidiary of:** United Technologies Corporation)
Clapgate Lane, Birmingham, West Midlands B32 3BU
**Tel:** 01214-213311 **Fax:** 01214-217428
**Web:** www.hkfire.co.uk
**Reg No:** 5211559 **VAT No:** 864449980
**Estd:** 1970 Private Limited Company
**Line of Business:** Security and related activities
**Trading Style:** Hall & Kay Fire Engineering Limited
**Issued Capital:** £10,000
**Directors:** A E Kenny, P Salmons, B Glastonbury
**Co. Secretary:** Paul Salmons
**Responsibilities**
**Senior:** Simon Rooks *(Manager)*, peter adcock *(regional director)*
**Branches:** Sfs Fire Services Ltd, Sefton Lodge, Clewer Hill Road, Windsor, Berkshire SL4 4FT
**US SIC:** 7393, 3629
**UK SIC:** 83954, 34350
**Auditors:** PricewaterhouseCoopers LLP
**Bankers:** Barclays Bank Plc (20-07-71)

| | 31-12-13 | 31-12-12 | 31-12-11 |
|---|---|---|---|
| TO | 73,172,000 | 100,734,000 | 85,474,000 |
| P/L | (9,089,000) | 409,000 | 8,849,000 |
| NW | (8,705,000) | (5,680,000) | (5,488,000) |
| WC | (6,242,000) | (5,346,000) | (5,217,000) |
| Emp. | 366 | 441 | 401 |

DUNS 22-613-1332 **Imp-Exp**

## Sfs Intec Holdings Ltd

**(Subsidiary of:** Sfs Group Ag)
153 Kirkstall Road, Leeds, West Yorkshire LS4 2AT
**Tel:** 01132085500 **Fax:** 01132085573
**Web:** www.mangeard.eu
**Reg No:** 1737942 **Estd:** 1983 Private Limited Company
**Line of Business:** Haberdashers
**Export Markets:** U S A, Asia, E U, Australasia, Africa
**Export Sales:** £5,655,000
**Issued Capital:** £2,000,000
**Directors:** T Bamberger, M Jaeger, A Blank
**Co. Secretary:** Markus Jaeger
**US SIC:** 6711 **UK SIC:** 83962
**Auditors:** PricewaterhouseCoopers
**Bankers:** Ubs Ag (60-01-55)

| | 31-12-13 | 31-12-12 | 31-12-11 |
|---|---|---|---|
| TO | 20,162,000 | 20,147,000 | 21,529,000 |
| P/L | (307,000) | (204,000) | 548,000 |
| NW | 10,071,000 | 10,292,000 | 10,767,000 |
| WC | 7,880,000 | 7,651,000 | 6,040,000 |
| Emp. | 89 | 94 | 94 |

DUNS 34-596-2286

## Sfw Ltd

Southern House, Station Approach, Woking, Surrey GU22 7UY
**Web:** www.sfwltd.co.uk
**Reg No:** 2740301 **VAT No:** 591784202
**Estd:** 2002 Private Limited Company
**Line of Business:** Other software consultancy and supply
**Export Sales:** £292,797
**Issued Capital:** £15,465
**Principals:** P Hornsby *(Managing)*, S J Elliott
**Co. Secretary:** Ms Eileen Ryder
**Responsibilities**
**Senior:** Sharron Hornsby *(Manager)*
**US SIC:** 7379, 7374
**UK SIC:** 83940
**Auditors:** Menzies LLP
**Bankers:** National Westminster Bank Plc (60-24-20)

| | 31-03-14 | 31-03-13 | 31-03-12 |
|---|---|---|---|
| TO | 7,957,467 | 7,600,583 | 7,361,577 |
| P/L | 857,327 | 648,026 | 637,987 |
| NW | 2,056,245 | 1,718,401 | 1,552,332 |
| WC | 1,695,942 | 1,497,652 | 1,293,274 |
| Emp. | 144 | 82 | N/A |

DUNS 21-013-2080

## Sg Hambros Bank Ltd

**(Subsidiary of:** Societe Generale)
Norfolk House, 31 St James's Square, London SW1Y 4JR
**Tel:** 02075973000 **Fax:** 02075973056
**Web:** www.sghambros.com
**Reg No:** 0964058 **Estd:** 1790 Private Limited Company
**Line of Business:** Banks
**Issued Capital:** £143,800,000
**Principals:** W J Newbury *(Managing)*, O D Meredith, S Collins, Mrs D M Seiglie, Ms H I Thomas, S W Barnett, Mrs G A Branson, J Flais
**Co. Secretary:** Ms Talia Foa
**Responsibilities**
**Senior:** Ange Beretti *(Director)*, Jean Mazaud *(Director)*
**Branches:** Sg Hambros Bank Ltd, The Old Courthouse, 275 High Street, Dorking, Surrey RH4 1YB
**US SIC:** 6012 **UK SIC:** 81402
**Auditors:** Ernst & Young LLP
**Bankers:** Bank Of England (10-00-00)
**Following financial data are in thousands**

| | 31-12-13 | 31-12-12 | 31-12-11 |
|---|---|---|---|
| TA | 1,318,481 | 1,265,919 | 1,260,518 |
| P/L | 47,079 | 4,771 | 3,011 |
| NW | 242,679 | 250,045 | 243,531 |
| WC | (349,990) | 168,865 | (288,648) |
| Emp. | 198 | 194 | 209 |

DUNS 21-041-5442

## Sg Smith

Unit 2 Beddington Cross 136-138, Beddington Farm Road, Croydon, Surrey CR0 4XH
**Tel:** 02076391366
**Web:** www.sgsmith.co.uk
**Estd:** 2010 Proprietorship
**Line of Business:** Van and truck dealers
**Partners:** R Smith, M Wilson, Ms J Gibbs
**US SIC:** 5511 **UK SIC:** 65100
**Employees:** 51

DUNS 28-845-3236

## S.G. Smith Automotive Ltd
25 Dulwich Village, London SE21 7BW
**Tel:** 020-8693-0202
**Web:** www.sgsmith.com
**Reg No:** 0622112 **Estd:** 1959 Private Limited Company
**Line of Business:** Car dealers (new & used)
**Issued Capital:** £96,223
**Principals:** R C Smith (Chairman), P R Smith
**Co. Secretary:** Martin Wilson
**US SIC:** 5511 **UK SIC:** 65100
**Auditors:** Kingston Smith
**Bankers:** Barclays Bank Plc (20-66-51)

| | 31-12-13 | 31-12-12 | 31-12-11 |
|---|---|---|---|
| TO | 163,333,501 | 139,077,771 | 124,073,964 |
| P/L | 2,483,812 | 368,050 | (536,748) |
| NW | 10,070,267 | 8,972,532 | 9,372,382 |
| WC | (1,082,770) | (2,197,350) | (2,202,675) |
| Emp. | 397 | 410 | 400 |

DUNS 53-646-5164      Imp-Exp

## Sg World Ltd
Duchy Road, Crewe, Cheshire CW1 6ND
**Tel:** 01270-500921
**Web:** www.safeguard-europe.com
**Reg No:** 3451910 **Estd:** 1969 Private Limited Company
**Line of Business:** Payroll services
**Export Sales:** £986,812
**Issued Capital:** £121,147
**Principals:** A N Haase (Managing), M P Haase, S E Floodgate, D H Kinsman
**Co. Secretary:** Tom Mulvaney
**Responsibilities**
**Senior:** James Hilditch (Manager), Thomas Mulvaney (Financial Director)
**Finance:** Thomas Mulvaney (Financial Director)
**Marketing:** Lisa Robinson (Marketing Director)
**Health & Safety:** Russell Barnard (Health & Safety Officer)
**Purchasing:** Jason Basford (Purchasing Officer)
**Branches:** Sg World Ltd, Duchy Rd, Crewe, Cheshire CW1 6NB
**US SIC:** 2648, 2649
**UK SIC:** 47231, 47280
**Auditors:** Baker Tilly UK Audit LLP
**Bankers:** Barclays Bank Plc (20-00-00)

| | 31-03-14 | 31-03-13 | 31-03-12 |
|---|---|---|---|
| TO | 9,795,960 | 9,096,994 | 9,201,598 |
| P/L | 432,709 | 458,134 | 284,409 |
| NW | 1,486,679 | 1,522,872 | 1,197,222 |
| WC | 343,928 | 346,130 | 254,354 |
| Emp. | 152 | 149 | 143 |

DUNS 23-586-4258

## S.G.D. Security Ltd.
Unit 5 Melyn Mair Business Centre, Cardiff, South Glamorgan CF3 2EX
**Tel:** 029-2083-9940 **Fax:** 02920839941
**Web:** www.sgdsecurity.co.uk
**Reg No:** 3584065 **Estd:** 2006 Private Limited Company
**Line of Business:** Burglar alarm systems
**Trading Style:** Sgd Group
**Issued Capital:** £2,000
**Directors:** R N Riley, Mrs B J Witts, J J Witts, Mrs N J Alexander, D N Witts Price
**Co. Secretary:** Ms Lisa Duprey
**Responsibilities**
**Finance:** Nicola Price (Financial Director)
**US SIC:** 3643, 8999
**UK SIC:** 34203, 83954
**Auditors:** Huw J. Edmund Chartered Accountants

| | 31-07-13 | 31-07-12 | 31-07-11 |
|---|---|---|---|
| TA | 1,174,152 | 1,297,967 | 1,545,643 |
| NW | (267,522) | (375,074) | (478,381) |
| WC | (446,092) | (520,792) | (563,551) |

DUNS 22-212-6810

## Sgh Martineau Llp
One America Square, 17 Crosswall, London EC3N 2SG
**Tel:** 02072644444
**Web:** www.sghmartineau.com
**Reg No:** 0300228OC **Estd:** 2001 Private Limited Company
**Line of Business:** Solicitors
**Trading Style:** Sgh Martineau Llp
**Responsibilities**
**Senior:** Bhavesh Amlani (Non-designated Limited Liabili), Jane Byford (Non-designated Limited Liabili), Oliver Gutman (Non-designated Limited Liabili), Nikesh Haria (Non-designated Limited Liabili), Smita Jamdar (Non-designated Limited Liabili), Mary Kaye (Non-designated Limited Liabili), Adam Mcgiveron (Non-designated Limited Liabili), Samuel Payne (Non-designated Limited Liabili), Clive Read (Non-designated Limited Liabili), James Spreckley (Non-designated Limited Liabili), Naomi Tudor (Non-designated Limited Liabili)
**US SIC:** 8111 **UK SIC:** 83500

**Auditors:** Chantrey Vellacott DFK LLP

| | 30-04-14 | 30-04-13 | 30-04-12 |
|---|---|---|---|
| TO | 27,554,010 | 28,197,088 | 16,235,619 |
| WC | 5,858,920 | 5,186,129 | 6,322,441 |
| Emp. | 237 | 280 | 221 |

DUNS 21-737-5150

## Sgh (No. 2) Ltd
Christopher Grey Court Lakeside, Llantarnam Industrial Park, Cwmbran, Gwent NP44 3SE
**Tel:** 01633482509
**Web:** www.springfieldsguesthouse.com
**Reg No:** 7714168 **Estd:** 2011 Private Limited Company
**Line of Business:** Manufacture of plastic packing goods
**Directors:** R Spear, M J Henry, R F Spear
**Co. Secretary:** Michael Henry
**US SIC:** 3079 **UK SIC:** 48360
**Employees:** 651
**Turnover:** £186,374,000

DUNS 36-484-2729

## Sgh Trustees (Jersey) Ltd
S G Hambros House, P O Box 78, 18 Esplanade, Jersey, Channel Islands JE4 8PR
**Tel:** 01534815555
**Web:** www.sghambros.com
**Reg No:** 0077460J **Estd:** 1067 Private Limited Company
**Line of Business:** Security broking and related activities
**Responsibilities**
**Finance:** Ray Sutcliffe (MLRO)
**US SIC:** 7399 **UK SIC:** 83954
**Employees:** 121

DUNS 22-857-6286      Imp-Exp

## Sgl Carbon Fibers Ltd
(**Subsidiary of:** Sgl Carbon Se)
Great North Road, Muir of Ord, Ross-Shire IV6 7UA
**Tel:** 01463274100
**Web:** www.sglgroup.com
**Reg No:** 0078081SC **Estd:** 1982 Private Limited Company
**Line of Business:** Carbon products
**Export Markets:** Europe, U S A and other countries
**Trading Style:** Sgl Group
**Issued Capital:** £620,000
**Directors:** C W Hauswirth, J E Park, A G Fear, J K Becker
**Co. Secretary:** Ledingham Chalmers Llp
**Responsibilities**
**Senior:** Lance Hill (Manager), Juergen Koehler (Manager), Daniel Pichler (Manager), Jan Verdenhalven (Business Director)
**Operations:** Stephen Easton (Operations Manager)
**Branches:** Sgl Carbon Fibers Ltd, Brighton Rd, Heaton Norris, Cheshire Stockport
**US SIC:** 2873, 2824
**UK SIC:** 25130, 26000
**Auditors:** Ernst & Young LLP
**Bankers:** Bank Of Scotland (80-05-87)

| | 31-12-13 | 31-12-12 | 31-12-11 |
|---|---|---|---|
| TO | 56,705,000 | 41,468,000 | 58,281,000 |
| P/L | (12,304,000) | (4,699,000) | 184,000 |
| NW | 31,479,000 | 23,850,000 | 28,564,000 |
| WC | 4,624,000 | (4,027,000) | (430,000) |
| Emp. | 215 | 248 | 254 |

DUNS 21-911-2708

## Sgm Contracts Members Llp
Sgm House, Belleknowes Industrial Estate, Dunfermline, Fife KY11 1HZ
**Tel:** 01383 413333
**Web:** www.sgm-uk.com
**Reg No:** 0301206SO **VAT No:** 939951762
**Estd:** 2007
**Line of Business:** Foundry machinery and supplies
**US SIC:** 5999 **UK SIC:** 65600
**Auditors:** Condie & Co

| | 31-03-14 | 31-03-13 | 31-03-12 |
|---|---|---|---|
| TA | 2,265,005 | 2,663,084 | 3,751,918 |
| NW | N/A | 123,140 | 253,479 |
| WC | (513,492) | (762,203) | (1,052,136) |

DUNS 23-959-9298

## Sgp Property Services Ltd
(**Subsidiary of:** Bell Rock Bidco Ltd)
Sunningdale Road, Leicester, Leicestershire LE3 1UR
**Tel:** 01162016999 **Fax:** 01162016990
**Web:** www.sgp.co.uk
**Reg No:** 3948975 **Estd:** 1999 Private Limited Company
**Line of Business:** Building consultants and advisors
**Issued Capital:** £7
**Directors:** M J Holt, D C Wilton
**Co. Secretary:** David Wilton
**Responsibilities**
**Senior:** Kevin Elliott (Manager)

**Health & Safety:** Geoff Houghton (Health & Safety Officer)
**Purchasing:** Martyn Sherrington (Procurement Manager)
**US SIC:** 6531 **UK SIC:** 83400
**Auditors:** PricewaterhouseCoopers LLP
**Bankers:** Barclays Bank Plc (20-54-58)

| | 31-12-12 | 31-12-11 |
|---|---|---|
| TA | N/A | 28,000 |
| P/L | (28,000) | N/A |
| NW | N/A | 28,000 |
| WC | N/A | 28,000 |

DUNS 21-860-5325

## Sgs Hotels (Uk) Ltd
The Square, Town Centre, Solihull, West Midlands B91 3RF
**Tel:** 01217112121
**Reg No:** 8228301 **Estd:** 2012 Private Limited Company
**Line of Business:** Hotels
**Issued Capital:** £1,000,000
**Directors:** M Gulati, S Gulati, S Gulati
**Responsibilities**
**Senior:** Shareesh Singh (On Site Manager)
**US SIC:** 7011 **UK SIC:** 66500

| | 31-03-14 | 29-09-13 |
|---|---|---|
| TO | 1,627,534 | 2,491,146 |
| P/L | 22,329 | (258,061) |
| NW | 1,679,270 | 651,941 |
| WC | (113,141) | (941,855) |
| Emp. | 86 | 82 |

DUNS 29-088-4345      Exp

## Sgs M-Scan Ltd
(**Subsidiary of:** Sgs Sa)
3 Fishponds Close Millars Business, Centre, Wokingham, Berkshire RG41 2TZ
**Tel:** 01189896940
**Web:** www.m-scan.com
**Reg No:** 1414639 **VAT No:** 321317796
**Estd:** 2004 Private Limited Company
**Line of Business:** Chemists consulting
**Export Markets:** E U, Isrel, South Korea
**Export Sales:** £2,781,000
**Trading Style:** Sgs M-Scan Ltd
**Issued Capital:** £139
**Directors:** Mrs P Earl, Mrs C J Griffiths
**Co. Secretary:** Mrs Catherine Aldag
**Responsibilities**
**Marketing:** Dale Hirst (Marketing Executive)
**US SIC:** 5912 **UK SIC:** 64300
**Auditors:** Cooper Dawn Jerrom Ltd
**Bankers:** National Westminster Bank Plc (51-50-01)

| | 31-12-13 | 31-12-12 | 31-12-11 |
|---|---|---|---|
| TO | 7,234,000 | 5,948,000 | 4,382,000 |
| P/L | 852,000 | 1,912,000 | 1,360,000 |
| NW | 5,852,000 | 5,195,000 | 3,739,000 |
| WC | 3,699,000 | 4,171,000 | 2,771,000 |
| Emp. | 56 | 38 | 30 |

DUNS 28-845-8656      Imp-Exp

## Sgs Packaging Europe Ltd
(**Subsidiary of:** Logo Holdings I Corporation)
Citadel Trading Park, Hull, North Humberside HU9 1TQ
**Tel:** 01482-225835
**Web:** www.sgsintl.eu
**Reg No:** 0631503 **VAT No:** 433615466
**Estd:** 2005 Private Limited Company
**Line of Business:** Design consultants
**Export Markets:** Germany, Netherlands, France
**Export Sales:** £18,234,000
**Issued Capital:** £400,000
**Principals:** R R Jones (Financial), H R Baughman, B Mcgrath, L C Naccarato
**Co. Secretary:** Richard Jones
**Responsibilities**
**Senior:** Steve Babb (Manager)
**IT:** Mark Furniss (IT Director)
**US SIC:** 2794 **UK SIC:** 47545
**Auditors:** BDO LLP
**Bankers:** HSBC Bank plc (40-11-18)

| | 31-12-13 | 31-12-12 | 31-12-11 |
|---|---|---|---|
| TO | 31,390,000 | 26,377,000 | 24,664,000 |
| P/L | 2,142,000 | 1,355,000 | 2,115,000 |
| NW | 9,771,000 | 7,882,000 | 6,683,000 |
| WC | 5,436,000 | 4,541,000 | 4,322,000 |
| Emp. | 443 | 388 | 308 |

DUNS 28-882-4352      Imp

## Sgs United Kingdom Ltd
(**Subsidiary of:** Sgs Sa)
Inward Way, Rossmore Business Park, Ellesmere Port, Cheshire CH65 3EN
**Tel:** 0151-350-6666
**Web:** www.sgs.com
**Reg No:** 1193985 **VAT No:** 208660468
**Estd:** 2012 Private Limited Company
**Line of Business:** Gas safety testing & inspection
**Export Sales:** £39,834,000
**Issued Capital:** £8,000,000
**Directors:** Ms C J Griffiths, Ms P Earl
**Co. Secretary:** Ms Catherine Aldag
**Branches:** Sgs United Kingdom Ltd, Old Time Office, Avonmouth Dock, Bristol, Avon BS11 9DH
**US SIC:** 8911 **UK SIC:** 83701

**Auditors:** Deloitte LLP
**Bankers:** National Westminster Bank Plc (51-81-22)

| | 31-12-13 | 31-12-12 | 31-12-11 |
|---|---|---|---|
| TO | 121,945,000 | 115,216,000 | 102,095,000 |
| P/L | 12,735,000 | 10,109,000 | 18,877,000 |
| NW | 25,169,000 | 22,769,000 | 21,578,000 |
| WC | 42,000 | 4,108,000 | 7,864,000 |
| Emp. | 1,268 | 1,161 | 1,017 |

DUNS 28-833-6654

## S.H. Harrold Holdings Ltd
130-131 High Street, Uxbridge, Middlesex UB8 1JX
**Tel:** 01895237799
**Web:** www.harroldopticians.co.uk
**Reg No:** 0332247 **Estd:** 1939 Private Limited Company
**Line of Business:** Management activities of holding companies
**Trading Style:** Harrold S H (1937), Fairplay Optical Company
**Issued Capital:** £24,501
**Principals:** I R Harrold (Chairman and Managing), D Reeves (Managing), Mrs S E Harrold
**Co. Secretary:** David Reeves
**Branches:** S.h. Harrold Holdings Ltd, Crendon House, Drakes Drive, Long Crendon, Aylesbury, Buckinghamshire HP18 9BB
**US SIC:** 6711, 5999
**UK SIC:** 83962, 65600
**Auditors:** Godfrey Laws & Co Ltd
**Bankers:** National Westminster Bank Plc (60-08-34)

| | 30-09-13 | 30-09-12 | 30-09-11 |
|---|---|---|---|
| TA | 1,880,523 | 1,536,900 | 1,530,982 |
| NW | 1,376,436 | 1,386,507 | 1,379,421 |
| WC | 576,776 | 380,555 | 363,427 |

DUNS 21-608-6322      Imp

## S.H. Pratt & Co. (Bananas) Ltd
Laporte Way, Luton, Bedfordshire LU4 8WL
**Tel:** 01582436500
**Web:** www.shpratt.com
**Reg No:** 0637730 **VAT No:** 207666358
**Estd:** 1959 Private Limited Company
**Line of Business:** Processing and preserving of fruit and vegetables not elsewhere classified
**Trading Style:** Pratts Bananas
**Issued Capital:** £13,729
**Principals:** R F Wells (Chairman), R J Wells (Managing), Mrs M M Wells, Mrs F M Hallam, Mrs S Mohamed, D V Bateman
**Co. Secretary:** Mrs Shahida Mohamed
**Responsibilities**
**Senior:** David Lane (Manager)
**Finance:** Keith Goodlad (Financial Director)
**US SIC:** 2033 **UK SIC:** 41473
**Auditors:** Miller & Co
**Bankers:** Lloyds TSB Bank plc (77-95-11)

| | 26-10-13 | 27-10-12 | 29-10-11 |
|---|---|---|---|
| TO | 117,726,564 | 112,098,848 | 104,942,069 |
| P/L | 697,978 | 701,874 | 597,645 |
| NW | 8,842,102 | 8,114,055 | 7,562,226 |
| WC | (1,211,967) | (1,809,372) | (3,356,213) |
| Emp. | 271 | 304 | 263 |

DUNS 34-606-0874

## S.H. Structures Ltd
Moor Lane Trading Estate, Leeds, West Yorkshire LS25 6DX
**Tel:** 01977681931
**Web:** www.shstructures.com
**Reg No:** 2747449 **VAT No:** 598973548
**Estd:** 1992 Private Limited Company
**Line of Business:** Steel fabricators
**Issued Capital:** £22,000
**Principals:** S J Holden (Managing), M S Randerson, I D Smith
**Co. Secretary:** Simon Holden
**Responsibilities**
**Senior:** Wendy Holden (Manager)
**IT:** Gareth Rhodes (IT Manager)
**US SIC:** 1622, 3441
**UK SIC:** 50200, 32042
**Auditors:** Horwath Clark Whitehill
**Bankers:** National Westminster Bank Plc (60-13-38)

| | 30-11-13 | 30-11-12 | 30-11-11 |
|---|---|---|---|
| TO | 5,810,053 | 7,492,780 | 11,509,598 |
| P/L | (22,093) | 124,680 | 132,451 |
| NW | 651,410 | 669,790 | 570,936 |
| WC | 701,470 | 797,565 | 777,056 |
| Emp. | 60 | 60 | 63 |

DUNS 22-528-0643

## Shackleton & Wintle Ltd
(**Subsidiary of:** Rogers & Heffter Holdings Ltd)
3 Station Mews, Liddington Industrial Estate, Old Statio, Cheltenham, Gloucestershire GL53 0DL
**Tel:** 01242222641
**Web:** www.shackleton-wintle.co.uk
**Reg No:** 1736379 **VAT No:** 326370371
**Estd:** 1978 Private Limited Company
**Line of Business:** Plumbers
**Issued Capital:** £100

**Director:** R C Heffter
**Co. Secretary:** John Rogers
**Responsibilities**
**Senior:** Malcolm Faulkner *(Manager)*
**Finance:** Marina Green *(Accounts Manager)*
**Branches:** Shackleton & Wintle Ltd, 47 Cleeveland St, Cheltenham, Gloucestershire GL51 9HT
**US SIC:** 1711 **UK SIC:** 50300
**Auditors:** Berkeley Hamilton
**Bankers:** Lloyds TSB Bank plc (30-91-87)

|  | 31-07-13 | 31-07-12 | 31-07-11 |
|---|---|---|---|
| TO | 9,330,039 | 9,467,035 | 9,092,867 |
| P/L | 170,913 | 355,776 | 651,752 |
| NW | 1,692,108 | 1,619,520 | 1,398,800 |
| WC | 1,491,718 | 1,408,033 | 1,263,460 |
| Emp. | 67 | 77 | 67 |

---

DUNS 23-930-7627

## Shackletons Ltd

Lucas House, Weaving Lane, Dewsbury, West Yorkshire WF12 9QR
**Tel:** 01924868470 **Fax:** 01924-868490
**Web:** www.shackletonsltd.co.uk
**Reg No:** 3920668 **Estd:** 2000 Private Limited Company
**Line of Business:** Manufacture of other office and shop furniture
**Issued Capital:** £1,000
**Directors:** M K Higgins, M K Higgins
**Co. Secretary:** Ms Tracy Higgins
**Responsibilities**
**Senior:** Bill Marshall *(Branch Manager)*
**US SIC:** 2599 **UK SIC:** 46720
**Auditors:** Clough & Co

|  | 31-12-13 | 31-12-12 | 31-12-11 |
|---|---|---|---|
| TO | 7,761,337 | 8,637,164 | 6,350,448 |
| P/L | 212,873 | 552,805 | 357,469 |
| NW | 1,540,006 | 1,541,965 | 1,282,039 |
| WC | 377,524 | 578,855 | 407,935 |
| Emp. | 80 | 71 | 68 |

---

DUNS 21-626-8003

## Shadforth Pharmaceutical Company Ltd

Unit 11 Robjohns Road, Chelmsford, Essex CM1 3AG
**Tel:** 01708446462
**Reg No:** 0143500 **VAT No:** 246308173
**Estd:** 1916 Private Limited Company
**Line of Business:** Dispensing chemists
**Trading Style:** Burntwood Pharmacy, Shadworth W & Co
**Issued Capital:** £6,500
**Principals:** R M Shadforth *(Chairman and Managing)*, Ms D E Harrison, T W Shadforth
**Co. Secretary:** Ms Wendy Houghton
**Responsibilities**
**Senior:** Penelope Skellern *(Manager)*
**Branches:** Shadforth Pharmaceutical Company Ltd, 53 High Street, Wickford, Essex SS12 9AQ
**US SIC:** 7399 **UK SIC:** 83954
**Auditors:** Maurice J Bushell & Co
**Bankers:** Barclays Bank Plc (20-19-95)

|  | 31-01-14 | 31-01-13 | 31-01-12 |
|---|---|---|---|
| TO | 8,467,379 | 8,738,590 | 8,960,643 |
| P/L | 164,267 | 330,437 | 226,640 |
| NW | 3,586,545 | 3,632,288 | 3,522,353 |
| WC | 2,321,580 | 2,532,578 | 2,800,804 |
| Emp. | 113 | 111 | 104 |

---

DUNS 23-313-4832

## Shadow Cars

74 Cordwallis Road, Maidenhead, Berkshire SL6 7BR
**Estd:** 1990 Proprietorship
**Line of Business:** Taxi operation
**Proprietor:** A Zaman
**Responsibilities**
**Senior:** Alfred Zaman *(Manager)*
**US SIC:** 4121 **UK SIC:** 72200
**Employees:** 200

---

DUNS 52-006-0708

## Shadow Sales & Service Ltd

15 Turbary Avenue, Worcester, Worcestershire WR4 0PS
**Tel:** 01905384648 **Fax:** 01905798399
**Web:** www.shadowsalesandservice.co.uk
**Reg No:** 3372999 **Estd:** 2003 Private Limited Company
**Line of Business:** Cleaning activities not elsewhere classified
**Issued Capital:** £2
**Directors:** Mrs V C Williams, M B Williams, M B Williams
**Co. Secretary:** Michael Williams
**US SIC:** 7349 **UK SIC:** 92300

|  | 30-09-14 | 30-09-13 | 30-09-12 |
|---|---|---|---|
| TA | 23,247 | 19,233 | 14,209 |
| NW | 422 | (10,438) | (11,106) |
| WC | (1,229) | (11,712) | N/A |

---

DUNS 42-346-7880					Imp

## Shadowline Holdings Ltd

The Leeson Building, Canning Place, Leicester, Leicestershire LE1 3ER
**Tel:** 01162886551
**Web:** www.ftcgroup.co.uk
**Reg No:** 4334449 **Estd:** 2001 Private Limited Company
**Line of Business:** Wholesale of textiles
**Export Sales:** £2,191,642
**Issued Capital:** £7,500
**Directors:** C H Wei, D Wall, M J Holley
**Co. Secretary:** Michael Condon
**US SIC:** 5133 **UK SIC:** 61600
**Auditors:** PKF (UK) LLP
**Bankers:** HSBC Bank plc (40-28-03)

|  | 31-03-14 | 31-03-13 | 31-03-12 |
|---|---|---|---|
| TO | 14,278,519 | 15,220,648 | 20,903,291 |
| P/L | 286,524 | 615,636 | 1,104,602 |
| NW | 6,974,498 | 6,747,783 | 6,283,909 |
| WC | 6,236,354 | 6,043,399 | 5,496,967 |
| Emp. | 46 | 49 | 55 |

---

DUNS 39-760-4620					Imp

## Shadwell Estate Co Ltd

Nunnery Stud, Thetford, Norfolk IP24 2QE
**Web:** www.shadwellstud.co.uk
**Reg No:** 2197466 **Estd:** 1987 Private Limited Company
**Line of Business:** Horse breeders
**Issued Capital:** £2
**Principals:** R J Lancaster *(Managing)*, M Alsayegh
**Co. Secretary:** Christopher Kennard
**Responsibilities**
**Marketing:** Audrey Leyval *(Marketing Manager)*
**Admin:** Simon Beet *(Administration Manager)*
**IT:** Genene Constance *(Computer Manager)*, Janine Constance *(IT Manager)*
**HR:** Simon Beet *(Administration Manager)*, Harry Steed *(Health & Safety Officer)*
**Health & Safety:** Harry Steed *(Health & Safety Officer)*
**Purchasing:** Louise Brett *(Stores Assistant)*
**Branches:** Shadwell Estate Co Ltd, Newmarket Road, Newmarket, Suffolk CB8 9EH
**US SIC:** 0214 **UK SIC:** 01001
**Auditors:** PricewaterhouseCoopers LLP
**Bankers:** National Westminster Bank Plc (60-21-55)

|  | 31-12-13 | 31-03-12 | 31-12-09 |
|---|---|---|---|
| TA | 2 | 2 | 2 |
| NW | 2 | 2 | 2 |
| WC | 2 | 2 | N/A |
| Emp. | 50 | 50 | N/A |

---

DUNS 21-861-2680

## Shaftec Automotive Components Holdings Ltd

Soho Poolway Park Road, Hockley, Birmingham, West Midlands B18 5JA
**Tel:** 01213593232
**Web:** www.shaftec.co.uk
**Reg No:** 8233886 **Estd:** 2012 Private Limited Company
**Line of Business:** Management activities of other non-financial holding companies not elsewhere classified
**Export Sales:** £397,566
**Issued Capital:** £2
**Directors:** T R Curtis, R S Jones, S Marshall
**US SIC:** 6711 **UK SIC:** 83962

|  | 31-12-13 |
|---|---|
| TO | 7,048,181 |
| P/L | 591,713 |
| NW | 1,362,218 |
| WC | 772,408 |
| Emp. | 55 |

---

DUNS 22-574-9787

## Shaftesbury Homes & Arethusa

The Chapel, London SW18 3SX
**Tel:** 020-8875-1555 **Fax:** 02088752360
**Web:** www.shaftesbury.org.uk
**Reg No:** 0081186 **Estd:** 1843 Private Company Limited By Guarantee
**Line of Business:** Other adult and other education not elsewhere classified
**Trading Style:** Shaftesbury Homes
**Directors:** J G Minett, H E Salmon, M J Kaltz, Ms A M Brough
**Co. Secretary:** Dr Robert Goldfield
**Responsibilities**
**Senior:** Carol Elstub Leggatt *(Manager)*, Andy Haines *(Chief Executive Officer)*, Dave Neita *(Trustee)*, Colin Renwick *(Manager)*, Allistair Tulloch *(Manager)*
**US SIC:** 7011, 7392
**UK SIC:** 66500, 83951
**Auditors:** haysmacintyre

---

Bankers: The Royal Bank Of Scotland Plc (16-00-80)

|  | 31-03-14 | 31-03-13 | 31-03-12 |
|---|---|---|---|
| TO | 2,346,000 | 4,493,000 | 4,354,000 |
| P/L | (363,000) | 291,000 | (1,034,000) |
| NW | 4,476,000 | 4,819,000 | 4,462,000 |
| WC | 800,000 | 1,169,000 | 580,000 |
| Emp. | 56 | 84 | 125 |

---

DUNS 23-263-6860

## The Shakespeare Birthplace Trust

Shakespeare Centre, Henley Street, Stratford-Upon-Avon, Warwickshire CV37 6QW
**Tel:** 01789-204016
**Web:** www.shakespeare.org.uk
**Estd:** 1891
**Line of Business:** Museums
**Principals:** Prof S Wells *(Chairman)*, N Walsh, R Pringle
**Responsibilities**
**Sales:** Sue Croxford *(Senior Sales Executive)*
**Admin:** Julia Howells *(Secretary to Trustees)*
**IT:** Dan Moran *(Head of IT)*
**Branches:** The Shakespeare Birthplace Trust, Halls Croft, Mews Flat, Stratford-Upon-Avon, Warwickshire CV37 6BG
**US SIC:** 8411, 7999
**UK SIC:** 97700, 97913
**Auditors:** KPMG LLP
**Employees:** 250
**Turnover:** £5,757,000

---

DUNS 21-177-6650					Imp

## Shakespeare Engineering International (Asia) Ltd

91 Haltwhistle Road, South Woodham Ferrers, Chelmsford, Essex CM3 5ZA
**Tel:** 01245328118
**Web:** www.shakesp.demon.co.uk
**Reg No:** 7006110 **Estd:** 2009 Private Limited Company
**Line of Business:** Precision engineers
**Export Sales:** £177,727
**Trading Style:** Shakespear Enginerring Limited
**Issued Capital:** £101
**Director:** N B Shakespeare
**Co. Secretary:** Andrew Mair
**US SIC:** 8911 **UK SIC:** 83701

|  | 30-09-13 | 30-09-12 | 30-09-11 |
|---|---|---|---|
| TO | 9,329,248 | 10,570,512 | 7,181,317 |
| P/L | 569,679 | 1,053,005 | 955,418 |
| NW | 1,115,394 | 412,532 | (503,471) |
| WC | (377,655) | (664,276) | (284,097) |
| Emp. | 106 | 50 | 58 |

---

DUNS 23-563-2726

## The Shakespeare Globe Trust

21 New Globe Walk, London SE1 9DT
**Tel:** 02079025970
**Web:** www.shakespearesglobe.com
**Reg No:** 1152238 **Estd:** 1973 Private Company Limited By Guarantee
**Line of Business:** Non-charitable social work activities without accommodation
**Directors:** M I Ispahani, Lord C L Falconer, Dame M Richardson, D Witter, Dame R M De Souza, M A Clarke, Ms J M Topper, D R Butter
**Responsibilities**
**Senior:** Martin Ayres *(Manager)*, Ian Blair *(Director)*, Bruce Carnegie Brown *(Director)*, Neil Constable *(Chief Executive)*, Laurie Maguire *(Director)*, Emma Stenning *(Director)*
**Sales:** Laura Trigg *(Box Office Manager)*
**Health & Safety:** Andy Scorgie *(Facilities Manager)*
**Facilities:** Andy Scorgie *(Facilities Manager)*
**US SIC:** 7999, 7922, 8999, 7911
**UK SIC:** 97913, 97412, 83954
**Auditors:** Kpmg Llp
**Bankers:** Lloyds TSB Bank plc (30-91-59)

|  | 31-10-13 | 31-10-12 | 31-10-11 |
|---|---|---|---|
| TO | 21,662,000 | 20,423,000 | 16,170,000 |
| P/L | 3,699,000 | 3,166,000 | 1,633,000 |
| NW | 40,411,000 | 36,712,000 | 33,234,000 |
| WC | 8,627,000 | 10,395,000 | 8,394,000 |
| Emp. | 309 | 278 | 258 |

---

DUNS 21-580-9718

## Shakespeare Primary School

Shakespeare Avenue, Leeds, West Yorkshire LS9 7HP
**Tel:** 01133368340
**Web:** www.shakespeareleeds.org.uk
**Estd:** 2011 Proprietorship
**Line of Business:** Schools (local authority)
**Proprietor:** J Gorton
**US SIC:** 8211 **UK SIC:** 93200
**Employees:** 60

---

DUNS 64-139-7427

## Shakespeare's Globe Restaurant

21 New Globe Walk, London SE1 9DT
**Tel:** 02079021500
**Web:** www.shakespearesglobe.com
**Estd:** 2006 Proprietorship
**Line of Business:** Theatres & concert halls
**Proprietor:** Miss T Horienka
**US SIC:** 7911 **UK SIC:** 97913
**Employees:** 100

---

DUNS 34-981-2524

## Shakespeares Legal Llp

Somerset House, Temple Street, Birmingham, West Midlands B2 5DJ
**Tel:** 0121-237-3000
**Web:** www.shakespeares.co.uk
**Reg No:** 0319029OC **Estd:** 2006
**Line of Business:** Law firm with 40 partners
**Responsibilities**
**Senior:** Robert Adey *(Designated Limited Liability P)*, Simon Astill *(Partner)*, Keith Blizzard *(Partner)*, Andrew Breakwell *(Designated Limited Liability P)*, Nicholas Briggs *(Designated Limited Liability P)*, Paul Crutchley *(Partner)*, Alan Dark *(Associate, Employment Team)*, Mark Dunkley *(Designated Limited Liability P)*, Katherine Hall *(Designated Limited Liability P)*, Tony Hannington *(Partner)*, Richard Hartshorn *(Designated Limited Liability P)*, Michael Hibbs *(Designated Limited Liability P)*, Helen Holden *(Designated Limited Liability P)*, Sundeep Ladwa *(Designated Limited Liability P)*, Clare Laird *(Designated Limited Liability P)*, Phillip Lane *(Designated Limited Liability P)*, Janet Luckhurst *(Partner)*, Kevin Nagle *(Designated Limited Liability P)*, Mauro Paiano *(Partner)*, Lisa Rhodes *(Partner)*, Vicki Simpson *(Partner)*, Alan Sinnett *(Partner)*, Steven Warburton *(Partner)*, Pamela Whelan *(Designated Limited Liability P)*
**IT:** Marie Bridges *(Facilities Manager)*, Andrew Seaman *(IT Manager)*
**Operations:** Ian Smit *(Operations Director)*
**Purchasing:** Marie Bridges *(Facilities Manager)*
**US SIC:** 8111 **UK SIC:** 83500
**Auditors:** KPMG LLP

|  | 30-04-14 | 30-04-13 | 30-04-12 |
|---|---|---|---|
| TO | 48,010,000 | 39,926,000 | 28,494,000 |
| P/L | 2,165,000 | 2,507,000 | 2,192,000 |
| NW | 2,093,000 | 2,282,000 | 1,475,000 |
| WC | 14,351,000 | 14,190,000 | 8,252,000 |
| Emp. | 779 | 663 | 443 |

---

DUNS 50-348-9957

## Shakespeares Legal Secretaries Ltd

20 New Wk, Leicester, Leicestershire LE1 6TX
**Tel:** 01162-545454 **Fax:** 01162-554559
**Web:** www.harveyingram.com
**Reg No:** 2371054 **Estd:** 1989 Private Limited Company
**Line of Business:** Business and management consultancy activities not elsewhere classified
**Issued Capital:** £2
**Directors:** K H Spedding, R Botterill
**US SIC:** 7392 **UK SIC:** 83951

|  | 31-03-14 | 31-03-13 | 31-03-12 |
|---|---|---|---|
| TA | 2 | 2 | 2 |
| NW | 2 | 2 | 2 |

---

DUNS 21-057-5917

## Shalom Nursing & Caring Services

Unit 99 Hellidon Close Cariocca Business, Park, Manchester M12 4AH
**Web:** www.shalominternational.com
**Estd:** 2003 Proprietorship
**Line of Business:** Home care and help services
**Proprietor:** G Adunola
**Responsibilities**
**Senior:** Stella Adunola *(Proprietor)*
**US SIC:** 8811 **UK SIC:** 99000
**Employees:** 70

---

DUNS 21-908-0124					Imp-Exp

## Shand Engineering Ltd

*(Subsidiary of: Sturrock and Robson International B.V.)*
Kiln Lane, Stallingborough, Grimsby, South Humberside DN41 8DL
**Tel:** 01469-571586 **Fax:** 01469-571073
**Web:** www.shanduk.com
**Reg No:** 1083861 **VAT No:** 526104087
**Estd:** 1972 Private Limited Company
**Line of Business:** Manufacture of other fabricated metal products not elsewhere classified
**Export Markets:** Worldwide
**Export Sales:** £5,464,375
**Trading Style:** Shand U K
**Issued Capital:** £200,000

**Directors:** J M Little, I M Pillay, M J Currie
**Co. Secretary:** David Robinson
**Responsibilities**
**Senior:** Trevor Hayllar *(Factory Manager)*
**Health & Safety:** Trevor Hayllar *(Factory Manager)*
**Facilities:** Trevor Hayllar *(Factory Manager)*
**Engineering:** Trevor Hayllar *(Factory Manager)*
**US SIC:** 3499, 3317
**UK SIC:** 31694, 22200
**Auditors:** KPMG LLP
**Bankers:** Barclays Bank Plc (20-00-00)

| | 29-06-14 | 30-06-13 | 01-06-12 |
|---|---|---|---|
| TO | 9,564,127 | 16,953,150 | 12,417,741 |
| P/L | (211,188) | 1,872,908 | 1,892,501 |
| NW | 4,512,365 | 5,670,470 | 4,238,157 |
| WC | 2,637,286 | 4,393,810 | 2,978,200 |
| Emp. | 68 | 71 | 66 |

DUNS 39-729-5825 **Imp**
## Shaneel Enterprises Ltd
Amertrans Park, Bushey Mill Lane, Watford, Hertfordshire WD24 7JG
**Tel:** 01923204450
**Web:** www.shaneel.com
**Reg No:** 2171783 **VAT No:** 504973048
**Estd:** 1987 Private Limited Company
**Line of Business:** Import and export agents
**Export Sales:** £36,807,719
**Issued Capital:** £1,880,000
**Directors:** H B Mehta, D B Mehta
**Co. Secretary:** Mrs Chetna Mehta
**Responsibilities**
**Senior:** Joe Anthony *(Manager)*
**Admin:** Amrit Bajaj *(Administrator)*
**US SIC:** 4712, 5999
**UK SIC:** 77002, 65600
**Auditors:** R.R. Shah & Co
**Bankers:** Hamburgische Landesbank Girozentrale (40-52-41)

| | 31-03-14 | 31-03-13 | 31-03-12 |
|---|---|---|---|
| TO | 75,886,702 | 59,754,421 | 50,537,784 |
| P/L | 9,053,325 | 6,527,892 | 5,596,403 |
| NW | 23,741,885 | 16,700,700 | 1,869,865 |
| WC | 22,842,858 | 15,770,688 | 657,099 |
| Emp. | 278 | 261 | 240 |

DUNS 21-026-4347 **Imp-Exp**
## Shani Group Ltd
1st Floor 1 The Orient Centre, Watford, Hertfordshire WD24 7GT
**Tel:** 01923 210 111
**Web:** www.shanigroup.com
**Reg No:** 0490704 **Estd:** 1951 Private Limited Company
**Line of Business:** Business services
**Export Markets:** U K, Europe, Rest of World
**Export Sales:** £1,977,004
**Trading Style:** Shani Fashions
**Issued Capital:** £1,459,230
**Principals:** M Hollis *(Chairman and Managing)*, B S Hollis
**Co. Secretary:** Mark Hollis
**Branches:** Shani Group Ltd, Sandall Carr Rd, Doncaster, South Yorkshire DN3 1QL
**US SIC:** 7399 **UK SIC:** 83954
**Auditors:** Citroen Wells
**Bankers:** Barclays Bank Plc (20-65-82)

| | 31-12-13 | 31-12-12 | 31-12-11 |
|---|---|---|---|
| TO | 22,160,876 | 19,087,580 | 25,546,444 |
| P/L | (490,129) | 477,633 | 386,016 |
| NW | 3,688,740 | 4,386,758 | 4,266,087 |
| WC | 3,763,005 | 4,390,846 | 4,347,750 |
| Emp. | 84 | 73 | 84 |

DUNS 22-073-1512
## Shanks Argyll & Bute Ltd
**(Subsidiary of:** Shanks Group Plc)
Dunedin House, Auckland Park, Mount Farm, Milton Keynes, Buckinghamshire MK1 1BU
**Tel:** 01546-603795
**Web:** www.shanks.co.uk
**Reg No:** 0211187SC **Estd:** 2000 Private Limited Company
**Line of Business:** Collection and treatment of other waste
**Issued Capital:** £1
**Directors:** D K Mulligan, M A Turner, P D Eglinton
**Co. Secretary:** Philip Griffin-Smith
**Responsibilities**
**Senior:** Gail Orr *(Contracts Manager)*
**US SIC:** 4953 **UK SIC:** 92110
**Auditors:** PricewaterhouseCoopers LLP

| | 31-03-14 | 31-03-13 | 31-03-12 |
|---|---|---|---|
| TO | 7,962,000 | 7,934,000 | 8,016,000 |
| P/L | 1,392,000 | 1,465,000 | 1,289,000 |
| NW | 3,792,000 | 3,563,000 | 2,299,000 |
| WC | (76,000) | (277,000) | (1,720,000) |

DUNS 28-826-2819 **Imp-Exp**
## Shanks Group Plc
Dunedin House, Auckland Park, Mount Farm, Milton Keynes, Buckinghamshire MK1 1BU
**Tel:** 01908-650-650
**Web:** www.shanks.co.uk
**Reg No:** 0077438SC **VAT No:** 259547713
**Estd:** 1982 Public Limited Company
**Line of Business:** Collection and treatment of other waste
**Export Markets:** Europe, Rest of the World
**Export Sales:** £495,400,000
**Issued Capital:** £39,754,163
**Directors:** J F Petry, Dr S Riley, E A Van Amerongen, T R Woolrych, A R Auer, Ms M M Wyatt, P G Dilnot
**Co. Secretary:** Philip Griffin-Smith
**Responsibilities**
**Marketing:** Michelle Biscoe *(Marketing Executive)*
**HR:** Michelle Cummins, *(Group HR Director)*
**Branches:** Shanks Group Plc, Belasis Business Centre, Coxwold Way, Belasis Hall Technology Pk, Billingham, Cleveland TS23 4EA
**US SIC:** 8999 **UK SIC:** 83954
**Auditors:** PricewaterhouseCoopers LLP
**Bankers:** The Royal Bank Of Scotland Plc (16-04-00)

| | 31-03-14 | 31-03-13 | 31-03-12 |
|---|---|---|---|
| TO | 636,400,000 | 670,000,000 | 750,100,000 |
| P/L | 7,700,000 | (35,300,000) | 31,400,000 |
| NW | 61,300,000 | 62,300,000 | 99,600,000 |
| WC | 33,700,000 | (14,200,000) | (5,100,000) |
| Emp. | 3,741 | 4,086 | 4,094 |

DUNS 50-384-3765
## Shanks Waste Management Ltd
**(Subsidiary of:** Shanks Group Plc)
Dunedin House, Auckland Park, Bletchley, Milton Keynes, Buckinghamshire MK1 1BU
**Tel:** 01908650580
**Web:** www.shanks.co.uk
**Reg No:** 2393309 **Estd:** 1986 Private Limited Company
**Line of Business:** Waste disposal
**Issued Capital:** £54,023,000
**Directors:** M A Turner, D K Mulligan, P D Eglinton, T R Woolrych
**Co. Secretary:** Philip Griffin-Smith
**Responsibilities**
**Senior:** Ian Goodfellow *(Managing Director, UK)*, Jonny Kappen *(Managing Director, Hazardous W)*, Henk Kaskens *(Managing Director, Shanks Orga)*, Michael van Hulst *(Managing Director, Benelux)*
**Branches:** Shanks Waste Management Ltd, Greenbank Road, East Tullos Industrial Estate, Aberdeen, Aberdeenshire AB12 3BQ
**US SIC:** 4953, 3341
**UK SIC:** 92110, 22470
**Auditors:** PricewaterhouseCoopers LLP

| | 31-03-14 | 31-03-13 | 31-03-12 |
|---|---|---|---|
| TO | 142,013,000 | 136,558,000 | 145,489,000 |
| P/L | (27,377,000) | (22,536,000) | (3,188,000) |
| NW | 8,709,000 | (23,728,000) | 8,336,000 |
| WC | (20,247,000) | (58,416,000) | (38,749,000) |
| Emp. | 777 | 813 | 790 |

DUNS 21-119-0662
## Shanks Waste Operations Ltd
**(Subsidiary of:** Shanks Group Plc)
Dunedin House, Auckland Park, Bletchley, Milton Keynes, Buckinghamshire MK1 1BU
**Tel:** 08000282877
**Web:** www.shanks.co.uk
**Reg No:** 6585068 **Estd:** 1999 Private Limited Company
**Line of Business:** Recycling of non-metal waste and scrap
**Issued Capital:** £1
**Directors:** M A Turner, D K Mulligan, P D Eglinton
**Co. Secretary:** Philip Griffin-Smith
**Responsibilities**
**IT:** David Skett *(ICT Manager)*
**HR:** Samantha Lock *(Head of HR)*
**US SIC:** 7399 **UK SIC:** 83954

| | 31-03-14 | 31-03-13 | 31-03-12 |
|---|---|---|---|
| TO | 33,955,000 | 31,086,000 | 29,044,000 |
| P/L | 4,179,000 | 3,246,000 | 2,572,000 |
| NW | 1,351,000 | 5,133,000 | 2,666,000 |
| WC | 1,351,000 | 5,133,000 | 2,666,000 |

DUNS 49-725-7733
## Shannon Centre
14 Cameron Road, Ilford, Essex IG3 8LA
**Tel:** 020-8597-7014
**Web:** www.clubbersnetwork.co.uk
**Estd:** 1979 Partnership
**Line of Business:** Licensed clubs
**Partners:** T Watson, B Greenan, B O'Connor
**Responsibilities**
**Senior:** B O'connor *(Partner)*
**US SIC:** 5813, 5812
**UK SIC:** 66200, 66110
**Employees:** 60

DUNS 42-421-1845
## Shannon Court Nursing Home
112-114 Radcliffe Road, Bolton, Lancashire BL2 1NY
**Tel:** 01204-396641
**Web:** www.shannoncourt.eu
**Estd:** 1992 Partnership
**Line of Business:** Nursing homes
**Partners:** Ms C Flood, S Flood
**US SIC:** 8051 **UK SIC:** 95100
**Employees:** 60

DUNS 42-363-3887
## Shannon Rail Services Ltd
Watford Depot Orphanage Road, Watford, Hertfordshire WD17 1PG
**Tel:** 01923254567 **Fax:** 01923255678
**Web:** www.shannonrail.co.uk
**Reg No:** 4351029 **Estd:** 2006 Private Limited Company
**Line of Business:** Operators of railway
**Issued Capital:** £100
**Director:** M Mcanulty
**Co. Secretary:** N W Secretaries Limited
**US SIC:** 4011 **UK SIC:** 71000

| | 31-08-13 | 31-08-12 | 31-08-11 |
|---|---|---|---|
| TA | 1,155,870 | 959,695 | 825,098 |
| NW | 579,932 | 484,369 | 350,705 |
| WC | 278,249 | 338,910 | 254,390 |

DUNS 29-584-8006
## Shap Ltd
81 Ness Road, Shoeburyness, Southend-On-Sea, Essex SS3 9DB
**Tel:** 01744454056 **Fax:** 01744 617034
**Web:** www.shap.org.uk
**Reg No:** 1946544 **Estd:** 1985 Private Company Limited By Guarantee
**Line of Business:** Miscellaneous business services
**Directors:** Mrs C M Ingle, Ms M Milton, D Tighe
**Co. Secretary:** Mark Weights
**Branches:** Shap Ltd, 35 Queens Avenue, Widnes, Cheshire WA8 8HR
**US SIC:** 7399, 8091
**UK SIC:** 83954, 95200
**Auditors:** C.A. Hunter & Partners
**Bankers:** Yorkshire Bank Plc (05-07-44)

| | 31-03-14 | 31-03-13 | 31-03-12 |
|---|---|---|---|
| TO | 3,327,641 | 3,160,297 | 3,099,049 |
| P/L | 80,894 | 63,194 | 44,066 |
| NW | 871,170 | 789,276 | 729,082 |
| WC | 825,630 | 760,728 | 687,898 |
| Emp. | 84 | 85 | 78 |

DUNS 21-323-2226
## Shapwells Developments Ltd
Shap, Penrith, Cumbria CA10 3QU
**Tel:** 01931-716628
**Web:** www.shapwells.com
**Reg No:** 0511459 **VAT No:** 256790134
**Estd:** 1952 Private Limited Company
**Line of Business:** Building services
**Issued Capital:** £1,100
**Principals:** G Metcalfe *(Chairman and Managing)*, D N Metcalfe, Ms U G Doodson
**US SIC:** 6552 **UK SIC:** 85000
**Auditors:** Greaves Grindle
**Bankers:** Barclays Bank Plc (20-66-97)

| | 31-10-13 | 31-10-12 | 31-10-11 |
|---|---|---|---|
| TA | 2,705,011 | 2,813,401 | 2,925,772 |
| NW | 2,621,263 | 2,727,990 | 2,843,529 |
| WC | 2,327,155 | 2,424,343 | 2,528,948 |

DUNS 50-493-7533
## The Share Centre Ltd
**(Subsidiary of:** Share Plc)
Oxford House, Oxford Road, Aylesbury, Buckinghamshire HP21 8ZB
**Tel:** 01296414141 **Fax:** 01296-414140
**Web:** www.share.com
**Reg No:** 2461949 **VAT No:** 596391882
**Estd:** 1991 Private Limited Company
**Line of Business:** Stockbrokers
**Issued Capital:** £229,002
**Principals:** G D Oldham *(Managing)*, M D Birkett, R I Tolkien, R W Stone, G V Thomas, Ms F E Ecsery, J V Sargeant
**Co. Secretary:** Ms Barbara Pierssene
**Responsibilities**
**IT:** Des Barry *(IT Director)*
**US SIC:** 6211 **UK SIC:** 83100
**Auditors:** Deloitte LLP

| | 31-12-13 | 31-12-12 | 31-12-11 |
|---|---|---|---|
| TA | 30,255,000 | 23,492,000 | 20,298,000 |
| P/L | 2,271,000 | 2,023,000 | 2,043,000 |
| NW | 15,180,000 | 13,360,000 | 11,739,000 |
| WC | 12,919,000 | 12,016,000 | 10,828,000 |
| Emp. | 138 | 147 | 146 |

DUNS 42-409-7178
## Share Scotland
6b Moorpark Court, Glasgow, Lanarkshire G51 2JA
**Tel:** 01414458992
**Web:** www.sharescotland.org.uk
**Estd:** 1999 Proprietorship
**Line of Business:** Charities and charitable organisations
**Proprietor:** Mrs I Russell
**Responsibilities**
**Senior:** Robert Bogle *(Board Member)*, Eileen Gorrie *(Board Member)*, Gordon Hutcheson *(Board Member)*, Robin MacKenzie *(Board Member)*, Lorraine MacKenzie *(Board Member)*, Ronnie McPhee *(Board Member)*, Brian Venters *(Chairman)*, Joe Whyte *(CEO, Managing Director)*, Karen Wishart *(Board Member)*
**Finance:** Tom Gorrie *(Finance Director)*
**Marketing:** Dougie Reid *(Development Manager)*
**HR:** Lyn Todd *(Human Resources Manager)*
**Branches:** Share Scotland, 5 Wauchope Place, Edinburgh, Midlothian EH16 4NF
**US SIC:** 8699 **UK SIC:** 96902
**Employees:** 124

DUNS 21-880-1214
## Shared Life
Canon Pinnington Mews, Bingley, West Yorkshire BD16 1AQ
**Tel:** 01274432211
**Web:** www.bradford.gov.uk
**Estd:** 2012
**Line of Business:** Disability services
**Responsibilities**
**Senior:** Nancy Plowes *(Team Manager)*
**US SIC:** 8321 **UK SIC:** 96111
**Employees:** 70

DUNS 21-169-7574
## Shark Corporation Ltd
**(Subsidiary of:** Shark Management Ltd)
Office 16, Consett, County Durham DH8 5XP
**Tel:** 01916542070
**Web:** www.shark-ml.com
**Reg No:** 6945039 **VAT No:** 984720292
**Estd:** 2009 Private Limited Company
**Line of Business:** Labour recruitment and provision of personnel
**Issued Capital:** £2,053
**Directors:** J Maier, M Borlinghaus, S Greenwell
**Co. Secretary:** Mrs Marian Mcmanus
**US SIC:** 7361 **UK SIC:** 83954

| | 30-06-13 | 30-06-12 | 30-06-11 |
|---|---|---|---|
| TA | 90,469 | 136,301 | 153,897 |
| NW | (28,392) | 66,397 | 59,385 |
| WC | (38,290) | 34,215 | 53,524 |

DUNS 53-604-4613 **Exp**
## Sharksfin Holdings Ltd
6 Perry Way, Witham, Essex CM8 3SX
**Tel:** 01376500222
**Web:** www.dental-directory.co.uk
**Reg No:** 3409683 **Estd:** 1997 Private Limited Company
**Line of Business:** Dental equipment suppliers
**Issued Capital:** £50,500
**Director:** M A Mills
**Responsibilities**
**Senior:** Gordon Mills *(Manager)*, Paul O'leary *(Financial Controller)*
**Finance:** Paul O'leary *(Financial Controller)*
**Marketing:** Mike Volk *(Head of Marketing)*
**Admin:** Sally Slater *(Administration Manager)*
**Health & Safety:** Kevin Perry *(Operations Manager)*
**Facilities:** Kevin Perry *(Operations Manager)*
**Operations:** Sally Slater *(Administration Manager)*
**US SIC:** 3841 **UK SIC:** 37201

| | 31-12-13 | 31-12-12 | 31-12-11 |
|---|---|---|---|
| TO | 102,881,494 | 101,802,347 | 105,255,577 |
| P/L | 7,751,687 | 4,302,565 | 1,761,679 |
| NW | 38,587,760 | 32,815,445 | 29,709,204 |
| WC | 33,763,025 | 27,463,549 | 24,138,132 |
| Emp. | 228 | 230 | 227 |

DUNS 77-948-2074
## Sharman Shaw Exhibitions Ltd
Unit S Gildersome Spur, Morley, Morley, Leeds, West Yorkshire LS27 7JZ
**Tel:** 01132-897733
**Web:** www.sharmanshaw.co.uk
**Reg No:** 3054555 **VAT No:** 640674930
**Estd:** 1995 Private Limited Company
**Line of Business:** Activities of exhibition and fair organisers
**Issued Capital:** £125
**Directors:** T Longhurst, C M Sharman
**Responsibilities**
**Senior:** Graham Mortimer *(Manager)*, Joyce Sharman *(Manager)*
**US SIC:** 7399, 7999
**UK SIC:** 83954, 97913
**Auditors:** Kirk Newsholme

| | 31-12-13 | 31-12-12 | 31-12-11 |
|---|---|---|---|
| TO | N/A | 4,274,968 | 5,095,227 |
| P/L | N/A | 332,412 | 248,769 |
| NW | 140,157 | 148,490 | 93,458 |
| WC | 113,244 | 164,182 | 74,134 |

DUNS 21-821-0698
## Sharmans Agricultural Ltd
College Farm, Gonerby Moor, Grantham, Lincolnshire NG32 2AB
**Tel:** 01476-562561
**Web:** www.sharmans-agri.co.uk
**Reg No:** 0199317 **VAT No:** 114585475
**Estd:** 1924 Private Limited Company
**Line of Business:** Agricultural machinery sales service and repair
**Trading Style:** Sharmans Agricultural Ltd
**Issued Capital:** £1,775

**Directors:** F J Disney, S J Barclay, Mrs S Hazard
**Co. Secretary:** Mrs Elizabeth Marshall
**Responsibilities**
**Senior:** Elizabeth Harmsworth *(Manager)*, Duncan Hood *(Group Sales Manager)*, Andrew Woolerton *(Service Manager)*
**Marketing:** Martin Jarvis *(Marketing Manager)*
**Sales:** Duncan Hood *(Group Sales Manager)*
**Admin:** Bridget Tarry *(Office Manager)*
**HR:** Martin Jarvis *(Marketing Manager)*
**Health & Safety:** Andrew Woolerton *(Service Manager)*
**Facilities:** Andrew Woolerton *(Service Manager)*
**Branches:** Sharmans Agricultural Ltd, The Old Grain Store, Old Epperstone Road, Lowdham, Nottingham, Nottinghamshire NG14 7BS
**US SIC:** 3523, 5084, 5083
**UK SIC:** 32113, 61490
**Auditors:** Sinclair Wood & Co
**Bankers:** HSBC Bank plc (40-32-14)

| | 31-12-13 | 31-12-12 | 31-12-11 |
|---|---|---|---|
| TO | 27,479,714 | 30,323,118 | 31,468,116 |
| P/L | 2,360,396 | 2,214,564 | 3,064,309 |
| NW | 15,493,443 | 13,662,361 | 12,711,292 |
| WC | 10,707,343 | 8,135,899 | 8,358,452 |
| Emp. | 65 | 64 | 61 |

DUNS 21-709-4784
## Sharnbrook Academy Federation
Shambrook Upper School, Odell Road, Bedford, Bedfordshire MK44 1JL
**Tel:** 01234782191
**Web:** www.shambrook.beds.sch.uk
**Reg No:** 7500018 **Estd:** 2011 Private Company Limited By Guarantee
**Line of Business:** General secondary education
**Directors:** I G Denning, J Hepburn, Ms J Harrison, H A Carr-Archer, R J Paterson, K Williams, W Chalker, A Bahia
**Co. Secretary:** Mrs Julie Brasier
**Responsibilities**
**Senior:** Michael Lavelle *(Director)*, Stephen Mortimer *(Director)*
**US SIC:** 8211 **UK SIC:** 93200

| | 31-08-13 | 31-08-12 | 31-08-11 |
|---|---|---|---|
| TO | 20,753,411 | 21,845,835 | 54,198,010 |
| P/L | (1,001,041) | 1,915,509 | 43,150,313 |
| NW | 43,506,781 | 44,495,822 | 43,270,313 |
| WC | 1,848,632 | 2,072,244 | 2,289,988 |
| Emp. | 406 | 391 | 388 |

DUNS 21-783-8517
## Sharnbrook House
High Street, Sharnbrook, Bedford, Bedfordshire MK44 1PB
**Tel:** 01234781294
**Web:** www.greensleeves.org.uk
**Estd:** 1957 Proprietorship
**Line of Business:** Residential care establishments
**Proprietor:** Mrs S Whitehouse
**Responsibilities**
**Senior:** Elizabeth Turton *(Manager)*
**US SIC:** 8321 **UK SIC:** 96111
**Employees:** 50

DUNS 39-670-8117
## Sharp Business Systems Uk Plc
(**Subsidiary of:** Sharp Corporation)
Northern House, Moor Knoll Lane, East Ardsley, Wakefield, West Yorkshire WF3 2EE
**Tel:** 01924823455 **Fax:** 01924-820433
**Web:** www.iotplc.com
**Reg No:** 2136901 **Estd:** 1987 Private Limited Company
**Line of Business:** Renting of office machinery and equipment including computers
**Trading Style:** Sharp
**Issued Capital:** £50,000
**Directors:** R Hardiman, M Mccarney, S R Sykes, J Giles
**Co. Secretary:** Matthew Burton
**Responsibilities**
**Senior:** Stephen Nichols *(Manager)*
**Branches:** Sharp Business Systems Uk Plc, Unit 4, Antler Court, Wigan, Lancashire WN4 8DU
**US SIC:** 7379, 7699
**UK SIC:** 83940, 67303
**Auditors:** KPMG LLP
**Bankers:** Lloyds TSB Bank plc (30-98-93)

| | 31-03-14 | 31-03-13 | 31-03-12 |
|---|---|---|---|
| TO | 36,784,000 | 30,296,000 | 30,580,000 |
| P/L | 1,398,000 | (4,522,000) | 1,977,000 |
| NW | 10,077,000 | 10,825,000 | 15,797,000 |
| WC | 9,946,000 | 10,779,000 | 15,761,000 |
| Emp. | 231 | 206 | 167 |

DUNS 76-946-7788
## Sharp Clinical Services (Uk) Ltd
(**Subsidiary of:** Udg Healthcare Public Limited Company)
Unit 1 3 Waller House, Elvicta Estates, Crickhowell, Powys NP8 1DF
**Tel:** 01873812182 **Fax:** 01873810836
**Web:** www.sharpclinical.com
**Reg No:** 2234557 **VAT No:** 492081836
**Estd:** 1988 Private Limited Company
**Line of Business:** Manufacture of basic pharmaceutical products
**Issued Capital:** £24,500
**Directors:** I C Morgan, M Gannon, A Ralph
**Co. Secretary:** Ms Tara Grimley
**Responsibilities**
**Senior:** John Bath *(Manager)*, Edna Scott *(Manager)*
**Branches:** Sharp Clinical Services (Uk) Ltd, Unit 1-3 Elvicta Estates, Crickhowell, Powys NP8 1DF
**US SIC:** 2834 **UK SIC:** 25700
**Auditors:** Solomon Hare Audit LLP
**Bankers:** HSBC Bank plc (40-16-13)

| | 30-09-13 | 31-03-12 | 31-09-11 |
|---|---|---|---|
| TO | 8,239,374 | 5,829,484 | 3,227,361 |
| P/L | 934,331 | 978,493 | (172,752) |
| NW | (342,091) | 1,392,083 | 604,693 |
| WC | (1,125,299) | 907,335 | 132,446 |

DUNS 21-300-1571 **Imp-Exp**
## Sharp Electronics (U.K.) Ltd
(**Subsidiary of:** Sharp Corporation)
Sharp House, Llay Industrial Estate Davy Way, Wrexham, Clwyd LL12 0PG
**Tel:** 01978853939 **Fax:** 02087342400
**Web:** www.sharp.co.uk
**Reg No:** 0965877 **VAT No:** 144909062
**Estd:** 1969 Private Limited Company
**Line of Business:** Manufacture of other electrical equipment not elsewhere classified
**Export Sales:** £203,290,000
**Trading Style:** Sharp Manufacturing Company
**Issued Capital:** £48,115,800
**Directors:** H Sasaoka, H Ito, T Kawamura
**Co. Secretary:** Gosia Grant Lipinska
**Responsibilities**
**Senior:** Shingo Hato *(President)*, Paul Hide *(Manager)*, Noboru Igarashi *(Chief Executive Officer)*, Paul Molyneux *(Manager)*
**Marketing:** Philip Care *(Marketing Manager)*, Tom Linklater *(e-Commerce & Marketing Manager)*
**IT:** Tom Linklater *(e-Commerce & Marketing Manager)*
**Health & Safety:** Bob Neighbour *(Facilities Manager)*
**Facilities:** Mike Holmes *(Facilities Manager)*, Bob Neighbour *(Facilities Manager)*
**Branches:** Sharp Electronics (U.k.) Ltd, Sherbourne Ho, Croxley Business Park, Watford, Hertfordshire WD18 8YE
**US SIC:** 3629, 5081, 5064
**UK SIC:** 34350, 61490, 61500
**Auditors:** KPMG LLP
**Bankers:** HSBC Bank plc (40-31-24)

| | 31-03-13 | 31-03-12 | 31-03-11 |
|---|---|---|---|
| TO | 322,078,000 | 481,340,000 | 597,335,000 |
| P/L | (16,469,000) | 3,424,000 | 17,468,000 |
| NW | 69,348,000 | 91,012,000 | 96,708,000 |
| WC | 63,821,000 | 50,122,000 | 44,745,000 |
| Emp. | 537 | 565 | 575 |

DUNS 21-692-5597 **Imp**
## Sharpak Aylesham Ltd
(**Subsidiary of:** Groupe Guillin)
Aylesham Industrial Estate, Aylesham, Canterbury, Kent CT3 3EF
**Tel:** 01304-840-581 **Fax:** 01304-841-922
**Web:** en.sharpinterpack.com
**Reg No:** 7394042 **Estd:** 2010 Private Limited Company
**Line of Business:** Manufacturers of packaging materials
**Export Sales:** £5,533,000
**Issued Capital:** £12,091,345
**Director:** Mrs S Guillin-Frappier
**Co. Secretary:** Francois Guillin
**Responsibilities**
**Senior:** Charles Maignien *(Finance Director)*, Julie Parkin *(Pa To The Managing Director)*, Michelle Pentecost *(Buyer)*, Fiona Weatherley *(Human Resources Manager)*
**US SIC:** 2654, 3079
**UK SIC:** 47280, 48360
**Auditors:** KPMG LLP
**Bankers:** HSBC Bank plc (40-05-20)

| | 31-12-13 | 31-12-12 | 31-12-11 |
|---|---|---|---|
| TO | 28,643,000 | 28,173,000 | 31,401,000 |
| P/L | 1,055,000 | (406,000) | 261,000 |
| NW | 11,813,000 | 11,019,000 | 11,352,000 |
| WC | 5,669,000 | 4,404,000 | 4,585,000 |
| Emp. | 130 | 145 | 158 |

DUNS 21-692-5619 **Imp**
## Sharpak Bridgwater Ltd
(**Subsidiary of:** Groupe Guillin)
Colley Lane Estate, Bridgwater, Somerset TA6 5YS
**Fax:** 01278 423019
**Web:** www.sharpakbridgewater.co.uk
**Reg No:** 7394059 **Estd:** 2010 Private Limited Company
**Line of Business:** Manufacture of plastic packing goods
**Export Sales:** £7,710,000
**Issued Capital:** £17,789,860
**Director:** Mrs S Guillin-Frappier
**Co. Secretary:** Francois Guillin
**US SIC:** 3079 **UK SIC:** 48360
**Auditors:** KPMG LLP
**Bankers:** HSBC Bank plc (40-05-20)

| | 31-12-13 | 31-12-12 | 31-12-11 |
|---|---|---|---|
| TO | 34,470,000 | 37,366,000 | 40,439,000 |
| P/L | (3,541,000) | (2,040,000) | (1,645,000) |
| NW | 12,364,000 | 15,167,000 | 16,684,000 |
| WC | 2,361,000 | 5,578,000 | 8,328,000 |
| Emp. | 205 | 205 | 212 |

DUNS 21-692-5612 **Imp**
## Sharpak Yate Ltd
(**Subsidiary of:** Groupe Guillin)
Highway, Yate, Bristol, Avon BS37 7AA
**Tel:** 01454 874 100
**Web:** www.en.sharpinterpack.com
**Reg No:** 7394053 **Estd:** 2010 Private Limited Company
**Line of Business:** Manufacture of machinery for food, beverage and tobacco processing
**Export Sales:** £1,953,000
**Trading Style:** Sharpak Yate Ltd
**Issued Capital:** £6,746,338
**Director:** Mrs S Guillin-Frappier
**Co. Secretary:** Francois Guillin
**Responsibilities**
**IT:** Ian Roge *(IT Manager)*
**US SIC:** 3551 **UK SIC:** 32441
**Bankers:** HSBC Bank plc (40-05-20)

| | 31-12-13 | 31-12-12 | 31-12-11 |
|---|---|---|---|
| TO | 27,377,000 | 25,181,000 | 29,505,000 |
| P/L | (773,000) | (1,128,000) | 646,000 |
| NW | 5,160,000 | 5,737,000 | 6,814,000 |
| WC | 703,000 | 566,000 | 848,000 |
| Emp. | 153 | 160 | 174 |

DUNS 21-587-7648
## Sharpe Mechanical Services
57 Sydenham Road, Belfast BT3 9DJ
**Tel:** 028-9045-8185 **Fax:** 028-9073-1034
**Web:** www.sharpegroup.com
**Reg No:** 0011704NI **Estd:** 1976 Private Unlimited Company
**Line of Business:** Specialised building trade contractors
**Trading Style:** Sharpe Ventilation
**Issued Capital:** £10,001
**Directors:** Ms J Mcmaster, P Mcmaster, E Mcmaster
**Co. Secretary:** Ms Julie Mcmaster
**Responsibilities**
**Facilities:** Norman Burn *(Maintenance Officer)*
**US SIC:** 1799 **UK SIC:** 50000
**Auditors:** McDaid McCullough Moore
**Bankers:** First Trust Bank (aib Group (uk) Plc) (93-83-43)

| | 30-09-13 | 30-09-12 | 30-09-11 |
|---|---|---|---|
| TO | 11,862,239 | 9,252,994 | 8,028,758 |
| P/L | 430,931 | 85,171 | 140,170 |
| NW | 1,939,581 | 1,938,258 | 2,343,200 |
| WC | 395,013 | 473,533 | 826,604 |
| Emp. | 46 | 47 | 48 |

DUNS 21-803-0572
## Sharps Bedrooms
Unit 9 Pinchington Lane Newbury Retail, Park, Newbury, Berkshire RG14 7HU
**Tel:** 01635552875
**Web:** www.sharps.co.uk
**Estd:** 2011
**Line of Business:** Bedroom furnishers and planners
**Responsibilities**
**Senior:** Boorea Koshi *(Manager)*
**US SIC:** 2517 **UK SIC:** 46714
**Employees:** 200

DUNS 21-733-7905
## Sharps Bedrooms Ltd
(**Subsidiary of:** Hf Group Lux Sarl)
218 Bradford Road, Batley, West Yorkshire WF17 6JF
**Tel:** 01924467155 **Fax:** 01902 483 001
**Web:** www.sharps.co.uk
**Reg No:** 7685430 **Estd:** 2011 Private Limited Company
**Line of Business:** Manufacture of other furniture
**Issued Capital:** £710
**Director:** K J Smith
**Branches:** Sharps Bedrooms Ltd, Pines Way, Bath, Avon BA2 3ET
**US SIC:** 2517 **UK SIC:** 46714

**Bankers:** Barclays Bank Plc (20-35-81)

| | 30-06-13 | 01-07-12 |
|---|---|---|
| TO | 58,262,000 | 44,584,000 |
| P/L | 2,610,000 | (5,289,000) |
| NW | (6,510,000) | (10,819,000) |
| WC | (8,635,000) | (1,537,000) |
| Emp. | 608 | 595 |

DUNS 73-465-6809
## Sharp's Brewery Ltd
(**Subsidiary of:** Molson Coors Brewing Company)
Pityme Business Centre, Wadebridge, Cornwall PL27 6NU
**Tel:** 01208-862121
**Web:** www.sharpsbrewery.co.uk
**Reg No:** 4729760 **Estd:** 2003 Private Limited Company
**Line of Business:** Manufacture of beer
**Issued Capital:** £200
**Directors:** S Kerry, M Coyle, Ms E Bebbington, F Landtmeters
**Co. Secretary:** Stephen Shepherd
**Responsibilities**
**Senior:** Nick Baker *(Manager)*
**Finance:** Joe Keohane *(Finance Director)*, Andy Oakley *(Finance Director)*
**Sales:** Victoria Segebarth *(Head of Craft Businesses)*
**US SIC:** 2082 **UK SIC:** 42702
**Auditors:** PricewaterhouseCoopers LLP
**Bankers:** National Westminster Bank Plc (57-00-00)

| | 31-12-13 | 29-12-12 | 31-12-11 |
|---|---|---|---|
| TO | 36,924,477 | 31,876,901 | 28,710,980 |
| P/L | 2,335,425 | 1,692,873 | 2,159,236 |
| NW | 6,562,370 | 4,442,268 | 2,417,065 |
| WC | 2,805,797 | 1,858,855 | 3,341,932 |
| Emp. | 110 | 105 | 83 |

DUNS 33-983-9821
## Sharrow Bay Country House Hotel
Lake Ullswater, Howtown, Penrith, Cumbria CA10 2LZ
**Tel:** 01768-486301
**Web:** www.sharrowbay.co.uk
**Estd:** 1948 Proprietorship
**Line of Business:** Chocolate fountains
**Principals:** B Sack, N Lightburn *(Proprietor)*
**Responsibilities**
**Senior:** Alan Farkins *(Restaurant Manager)*
**Admin:** Christine Lightburn *(Office Manager)*
**US SIC:** 7011, 5812
**UK SIC:** 66500, 66110
**Employees:** 50

DUNS 34-714-0725 **Imp**
## Shasonic Ltd
22 Aintree Road, Perivale, Greenford, Middlesex UB6 7LA
**Tel:** 02088109982 **Fax:** 020 7636 5533
**Web:** www.shasonic.co.uk
**Reg No:** 2780417 **VAT No:** 626332847
**Estd:** 1993 Private Limited Company
**Line of Business:** Electrical products (sales)
**Export Sales:** £1,955,876
**Issued Capital:** £10,000
**Principals:** N D Shah *(Managing)*, P D Shah
**Responsibilities**
**Senior:** Prabagar Narayanasamy *(Manager)*, John Shah *(Manager)*
**Branches:** Shasonic Ltd, 28 Tottenham Court Road, London W1T 1BT
**US SIC:** 5732 **UK SIC:** 64800
**Auditors:** The JMO Practice
**Bankers:** Barclays Bank Plc (20-41-12)

| | 30-06-12 | 30-06-11 | 30-06-10 |
|---|---|---|---|
| TO | 16,206,745 | 20,163,029 | 18,167,372 |
| P/L | 41,896 | 312,260 | 230,950 |
| NW | 2,312,651 | 2,314,262 | 2,068,800 |
| WC | 1,668,084 | 1,490,763 | 1,550,627 |
| Emp. | 53 | 99 | 103 |

DUNS 34-915-7623 **Imp-Exp**
## Shasun Pharma Solutions Ltd
(**Subsidiary of:** Shasun Pharmaceuticals Limited)
Dudley Lane, Cramlington, Northumberland NE23 7QG
**Tel:** 01912500471
**Web:** www.shasun.com
**Reg No:** 5712796 **Estd:** 1976 Private Limited Company
**Line of Business:** Manufacture of basic pharmaceutical products
**Export Sales:** £26,018,000
**Issued Capital:** £4,965,706
**Directors:** S R Rangaswamy, V K Shankarlal, Dr D Shankarlal, A K Shankarlal, J Wiper, K P Cook
**Responsibilities**
**HR:** Colin Dunbar *(Training Manager)*, Janice Gibson *(Human Resources Manager)*
**US SIC:** 2834 **UK SIC:** 25700

**Auditors:** KPMG LLP

|      | 31-03-14 | 31-03-13 | 31-03-12 |
|------|----------|----------|----------|
| TO   | 28,776,000 | 34,505,000 | 42,171,000 |
| P/L  | (382,000) | 3,750,000 | 4,971,000 |
| NW   | 6,676,000 | 6,402,000 | 2,126,000 |
| WC   | (4,863,000) | (2,886,000) | (7,209,000) |
| Emp. | 279 | 296 | 304 |

DUNS 51-998-2388
### Shaun Stokoe Electrical Services Ltd
Unit 25 Derwentside Business Centre, Villa Real, Consett, County Durham DH8 6BP
**Reg No:** 4102802  **Estd:** 2000 Private Limited Company
**Line of Business:** Electrical contractors and electricians
**Issued Capital:** £320
**Directors:** S Bradley, S M Stokoe
**Co. Secretary:** Shaun Stokoe
**US SIC:** 1731  **UK SIC:** 50300
**Auditors:** Murray & Lamb Accountants

|    | 31-05-13 | 31-05-12 | 31-05-11 |
|----|----------|----------|----------|
| TA | 303,950 | 282,230 | 359,976 |
| NW | 124,873 | 124,631 | 74,765 |
| WC | 108,390 | 107,698 | 54,593 |

DUNS 22-522-3049
### Shaunaks Ltd
Shaunak House, Netham Road Netham Industrial Estate, Bristol, Avon BS5 9PJ
**Tel:** 01179550154
**Web:** www.pharmacynow.co.uk
**Reg No:** 1456399  **VAT No:** 302990861
**Estd:** 1979 Private Limited Company
**Line of Business:** Dispensing chemists
**Trading Style:** Shaunaks Pharmacy
**Issued Capital:** £20,100
**Principals:** D Shaunak (Managing), V D Shaunak, K D Shaunak, T D Shaunak
**Co. Secretary:** Kishen Shaunak
**Branches:** Shaunaks Ltd, 88 Ashcombe Rd, Weston-Super-Mare, Avon BS23 3DX
**US SIC:** 5912  **UK SIC:** 64300
**Auditors:** Wormald & Partners
**Bankers:** Barclays Bank Plc (20-13-42)

|      | 28-02-14 | 28-02-13 | 29-02-12 |
|------|----------|----------|----------|
| TO   | 14,693,393 | 14,732,068 | 13,478,952 |
| P/L  | 1,916,881 | 1,469,184 | 1,001,358 |
| NW   | 2,077,888 | 455,964 | (1,160,322) |
| WC   | 2,927,033 | 1,650,030 | 409,832 |
| Emp. | 102 | 110 | 98 |

DUNS 21-585-9154
### Shavington High School
Rope Lane, Shavington, Crewe, Cheshire CW2 5DH
**Tel:** 01270685111
**Web:** www.shavington.cheshire.sch.uk
**Estd:** 2011 Proprietorship
**Line of Business:** Schools (local authority)
**Proprietor:** Mrs C White
**US SIC:** 8211  **UK SIC:** 93200
**Employees:** 60

DUNS 56-948-4892
### Shaw & Sons (Holdings) Ltd
(Subsidiary of: Shaw & Sons Group Ltd)
Shaway House Unit 21, Bourne Industrial Park, Bourne Road, Dartford, Kent DA1 4BZ
**Tel:** 01322621100
**Web:** www.shaws.co.uk
**Reg No:** 2841590  **Estd:** 1993 Private Limited Company
**Line of Business:** Other publishing
**Trading Style:** Shaw & Sons, Shaws
**Issued Capital:** £12,150
**Directors:** C M Williams, R H Smith, Mrs K M Larwood
**Co. Secretary:** Crispin Williams
**US SIC:** 2741  **UK SIC:** 47541
**Auditors:** Grant Thornton

|    | 30-06-14 | 30-06-13 | 30-06-12 |
|----|----------|----------|----------|
| TA | 1,262,369 | 1,262,369 | 1,262,369 |
| NW | 1,230,000 | 1,230,000 | 1,230,000 |

DUNS 21-584-0134
### Shaw-Crete Concretes
Green Lane, Nantwich, Cheshire CW5 6DB
**Web:** www.nickbrookes.co.uk
**Estd:** 2011
**Line of Business:** Mortar ready mixed
**Responsibilities**
**Senior:** Nick Brookes (Manager)
**US SIC:** 3273  **UK SIC:** 24360
**Employees:** 70

DUNS 39-803-5188
### Shaw Gibbs Ltd
264 Banbury Road, Oxford, Oxfordshire OX2 7DY
**Tel:** 01865292200  **Fax:** 01865-310025
**Web:** www.shawgibbs.com
**Reg No:** 2209123  **Estd:** 2008 Private Limited Company
**Line of Business:** Accounting activities
**Issued Capital:** £2,000

**Directors:** Ms L Watson, S H Neal, L R Smith, Miss E Hall, Ms A G Caiger, D J Rickwood, S J Wetherall, E B Edgar-Gibson
**Co. Secretary:** Mrs Angela Caiger
**Responsibilities**
**Senior:** David Cadwallader (Manager), Clive Everitt (Director), Graham Henley (Director), Nicola Jaques (Manager), Donal Oconnell (Director)
**Sales:** Matt Wistow (Business Development Officer)
**US SIC:** 8931  **UK SIC:** 83600

|      | 31-03-14 | 31-03-13 | 30-03-12 |
|------|----------|----------|----------|
| TO   | 4,791,954 | 4,249,662 | 4,609,842 |
| P/L  | 725,485 | 1,295,700 | 1,224,352 |
| NW   | (2,877,733) | (2,427,471) | (3,004,285) |
| WC   | (1,848,731) | (648,733) | (268,623) |
| Emp. | 65 | 63 | 65 |

DUNS 64-070-1124                                      Exp
### Shaw Group (Uk) Ltd
(Subsidiary of: Chicago Bridge & Iron Company N.V.)
Stores Road, Derby, Derbyshire DE21 4BG
**Tel:** 01332291122
**Web:** www.cbi.com
**Reg No:** 3465952  **VAT No:** 706043861
**Estd:** 1997 Private Limited Company
**Line of Business:** Other construction work involving special trades
**Export Sales:** £132,000
**Issued Capital:** £5,350,002
**Director:** A R Latham
**Co. Secretary:** Mark Phillips
**Responsibilities**
**Senior:** Derek Hunter (Manager), Ronald Oakley (Manager)
**Purchasing:** Steve Lees (Purchasing Manager)
**Branches:** Shaw Group (Uk) Ltd, 335 High St, Rochester, Kent ME1 1DA
**US SIC:** 1799, 8911
**UK SIC:** 50000, 83701
**Auditors:** KPMG LLP
**Bankers:** Abn Amro Bank Nv (40-50-30)

|      | 31-12-13 | 31-08-12 | 31-12-11 |
|------|----------|----------|----------|
| TO   | 24,064,000 | 21,792,000 | 50,578,000 |
| P/L  | 953,000 | 732,000 | 1,612,000 |
| NW   | (3,008,000) | (18,796,000) | (18,401,000) |
| WC   | 4,099,000 | (13,039,000) | (13,212,000) |
| Emp. | 198 | 159 | 396 |

DUNS 21-781-3987
### Shaw Healthcare
Elizabeth House 83 Victoria Driv, Bognor Regis, West Sussex PO21 2TB
**Tel:** 01243880810
**Web:** www.beslimm.com
**Estd:** 2011 Proprietorship
**Line of Business:** Residential care establishments
**Proprietor:** Mrs D Denyer
**US SIC:** 8321  **UK SIC:** 96111
**Employees:** 85

DUNS 34-583-3565
### Shaw Healthcare (Group) Ltd
Unit 1, Links Court, Fortran Road, Cardiff, South Glamorgan CF3 0LT
**Tel:** 029-2036-4411
**Web:** www.shaw.co.uk
**Reg No:** 5391089  **Estd:** 1994 Private Limited Company
**Line of Business:** Medical nursing home activities
**Trading Style:** Shaw Healthcare (North Somerset), Shaw Healthcare Development, Shaw Healthcare Manage Services, Shaw Healthcare Specialict Services
**Issued Capital:** £50,000
**Directors:** P J Nixey, A C Savery, R S Brown, K Miller, Ms S D Hughes, M Heywood-Briggs, A Thomas
**Responsibilities**
**Senior:** Frances Cloud (Chairperson), Jonathan Pain (Manager)
**US SIC:** 7399  **UK SIC:** 83954
**Auditors:** Deloitte & Touche LLP
**Bankers:** Allied Irish Bank (gb) (23-85-86)

|      | 31-03-14 | 31-03-13 | 31-03-12 |
|------|----------|----------|----------|
| TO   | 87,516,000 | 84,644,000 | 85,034,000 |
| P/L  | 851,000 | 1,869,000 | 3,707,000 |
| NW   | 3,682,000 | 3,785,000 | 3,803,000 |
| WC   | 19,588,000 | 18,776,000 | 15,878,000 |
| Emp. | 3,675 | 3,543 | 3,265 |

DUNS 21-340-0257
### Shaw Hill Primary School
Anthony Road, Birmingham, West Midlands B8 3AN
**Tel:** 01214642131
**Web:** www.shawhill.bham.sch.uk
**Estd:** 2011 Proprietorship
**Line of Business:** Schools (local authority)
**Proprietor:** Mrs M Barnfield
**Responsibilities**
**Senior:** Nadeen Bhatti (Head Teacher)
**US SIC:** 8211  **UK SIC:** 93200
**Employees:** 70

DUNS 21-883-3978                                      Imp-Exp
### Shaw-Munster Ltd
Winster Grove, Birmingham, West Midlands B44 9EG
**Tel:** 0121-360-4279  **Fax:** 0121-360-4265
**Web:** www.shawmunstergroup.co.uk
**Reg No:** 0956969  **Estd:** 2009 Private Limited Company
**Line of Business:** Manufacture of jewellery and related articles not elsewhere classified
**Export Markets:** Norway, France and Germany.
**Issued Capital:** £10,000
**Managing Director:** M J Tyler
**Co. Secretary:** Mrs Wendy Tyler
**US SIC:** 3911  **UK SIC:** 49101
**Auditors:** Bentley Jennison
**Bankers:** HSBC Bank plc (40-11-36)

|    | 31-05-13 | 31-05-12 | 31-05-11 |
|----|----------|----------|----------|
| TA | 387,432 | 880,691 | 874,643 |
| NW | 136,117 | 123,615 | 118,255 |
| WC | 108,762 | 96,266 | 88,747 |

DUNS 21-315-0220
### Shaw Pallet Ltd
(Subsidiary of: Shaw Pallet (Holdings) Ltd)
Bridge Street, Slaithwaite, Huddersfield, West Yorkshire HD7 5JN
**Tel:** 01484-848400
**Web:** www.shawpallet.com
**Reg No:** 1150422  **Estd:** 1973 Private Limited Company
**Line of Business:** Manufacture of wooden containers
**Issued Capital:** £30,000
**Principals:** C J Hillaby (Managing), J M Coupland
**Co. Secretary:** Michael Dragicevic
**Responsibilities**
**Senior:** Christopher Hilloughby (Manager), Stuart Quarmby (Manager)
**Health & Safety:** Stuart Quarmby (Manager)
**US SIC:** 2449  **UK SIC:** 46402
**Auditors:** Grant Thornton
**Bankers:** National Westminster Bank Plc (53-61-07)

|      | 31-03-14 | 31-03-13 | 31-03-12 |
|------|----------|----------|----------|
| TO   | 4,965,126 | 5,357,029 | 6,017,857 |
| P/L  | 242,640 | 269,432 | 356,553 |
| NW   | 2,172,079 | 2,090,932 | 2,000,728 |
| WC   | 2,017,594 | 1,943,851 | 1,844,396 |
| Emp. | 50 | 53 | 55 |

DUNS 21-325-8445
### Shaw Timber Ltd
(Subsidiary of: Shaw Timber (Holdings) Ltd)
Bridge Street, Slaithwaite, Huddersfield, West Yorkshire HD7 5JN
**Tel:** 01484-848484
**Web:** www.shawtimber.com
**Reg No:** 1271632  **Estd:** 1976 Private Limited Company
**Line of Business:** Timber engineers
**Issued Capital:** £9,100
**Principals:** C Woodhead (Managing), S J Mullany
**Co. Secretary:** Michael Dragicevic
**Branches:** Shaw Timber Ltd, Bridge Street, Huddersfield, West Yorkshire HD7 5JN
**US SIC:** 1522, 5039
**UK SIC:** 50100, 61300
**Auditors:** Grant Thornton
**Bankers:** National Westminster Bank Plc (53-61-07)

|      | 30-09-13 | 30-09-12 | 30-09-11 |
|------|----------|----------|----------|
| TO   | 4,661,412 | 5,803,174 | N/A |
| P/L  | 117,679 | 455,725 | N/A |
| NW   | 2,256,090 | 2,291,807 | 2,138,663 |
| WC   | 1,918,927 | 1,937,434 | 1,817,347 |
| Emp. | 52 | 52 | N/A |

DUNS 28-973-5243
### The Shaw Trust Ltd
114 Lichfield Street, Walsall, West Midlands WS1 1SZ
**Tel:** 01922623535  **Fax:** 01225-716334
**Web:** www.shaw-trust.org.uk
**Reg No:** 1744121  **Estd:** 1982 Private Company Limited By Guarantee
**Line of Business:** Non-charitable social work activities with accommodation
**Trading Style:** Shaw Trust Employment, Shaw Trust Horticulture
**Directors:** Ms V H Miner, F J Mccrindle, P M Hollins, Ms J M Allen, J Norman, P D Holmes, Ms A J Lloyd, M Hawker
**Co. Secretary:** Nicholas Carey
**Responsibilities**
**Finance:** Jerome Walls (Chief Financial Officer)
**Sales:** Nick Mason (National Retail Director)
**Branches:** The Shaw Trust Ltd, 39 St. Peters Court, High Street, Gerrards Cross, Buckinghamshire SL9 9QQ
**US SIC:** 8321  **UK SIC:** 96111
**Auditors:** PricewaterhouseCoopers LLP

**Bankers:** Barclays Bank Plc (20-05-06)

|      | 31-03-14 | 31-03-13 | 31-03-12 |
|------|----------|----------|----------|
| TO   | 107,897,000 | 96,590,000 | 85,634,000 |
| P/L  | 2,294,000 | (3,821,000) | (392,000) |
| NW   | 42,576,000 | 40,826,000 | 42,204,000 |
| WC   | 22,196,000 | 18,967,000 | 25,749,000 |
| Emp. | 1,474 | 1,543 | 1,136 |

DUNS 21-122-5537
### Shawbrook Bank Ltd
(Subsidiary of: Laidlaw Acquisitions Ltd)
Lutea House, Warley Hill Business Park, The Drive, Great Warley, Brentwood, Essex CM13 3BE
**Tel:** 08452666611  **Fax:** 0161-833-5434
**Web:** www.swift.co.uk
**Reg No:** 0388466  **Estd:** 2012 Private Limited Company
**Line of Business:** Investment consultants
**Trading Style:** Shawbrook Asset Finance
**Issued Capital:** £111,989,866
**Directors:** T F Wood, Mrs L V Mcmurray, R J Ashton, R A Pyman, Sir G R Mathewson, Sir B G Ivory, G P Alcock, R V Lovering
**Co. Secretary:** Daniel Rushbrook
**US SIC:** 6012  **UK SIC:** 81402
**Auditors:** KPMG Audit PLC
**Bankers:** Whiteaway Laidlaw Bank Ltd (16-58-73)
Following financial data are in thousands

|      | 31-12-13 | 31-12-12 | 31-12-11 |
|------|----------|----------|----------|
| TA   | 1,661,601 | 1,044,106 | 217,132 |
| P/L  | 16,788 | (7,775) | (10,299) |
| NW   | 113,743 | 83,556 | 30,798 |
| WC   | 89,647 | (145,089) | (36,866) |
| Emp. | 281 | 179 | 71 |

DUNS 29-866-4822
### Shawfield Greyhound Stadium Ltd
Rutherglen Road, Rutherglen, Glasgow, Lanarkshire G73 1SZ
**Tel:** 01416475041
**Web:** www.shawfieldgreyhounds.com
**Reg No:** 0101716SC  **Estd:** 1986 Private Limited Company
**Line of Business:** Operation of sports arenas and stadiums
**Issued Capital:** £400,000
**Director:** Ms M Simpson
**Co. Secretary:** Ms Melanie King
**Responsibilities**
**Senior:** Patricia Henry (Manager), Robert Lithgow (Manager)
**US SIC:** 7941  **UK SIC:** 97911
**Auditors:** Wylie & Bisset
**Bankers:** Bank Of Scotland (80-07-12)

|      | 31-03-14 | 31-03-13 | 31-03-12 |
|------|----------|----------|----------|
| TO   | N/A | N/A | 637,012 |
| P/L  | N/A | N/A | 166,154 |
| NW   | 5,430,173 | 5,336,283 | 5,215,929 |
| WC   | 4,883,121 | 4,814,581 | 4,710,723 |
| Emp. | N/A | N/A | 47 |

DUNS 21-159-9909
### Shaws of Darwen Ltd
Waterside, Waterside, Darwen, Lancashire BB3 3NX
**Tel:** 01254775111
**Web:** www.shaws-of-darwen.co.uk
**Reg No:** 6870273  **Estd:** 1903 Private Limited Company
**Line of Business:** Manufacturers of kitchen furniture
**Issued Capital:** £10,000
**Directors:** M W Ashton, A Clarfield, D J Dare
**Co. Secretary:** Miss Katherine Hughes
**US SIC:** 2599  **UK SIC:** 46720
**Auditors:** Mazars LLP
**Bankers:** Barclays Bank Plc (20-00-30)

|      | 31-12-13 | 31-12-12 | 31-12-11 |
|------|----------|----------|----------|
| TO   | N/A | 6,823,339 | N/A |
| P/L  | N/A | 351,223 | N/A |
| NW   | 623,039 | 1,082,706 | 742,585 |
| WC   | 463,102 | 992,129 | 669,835 |
| Emp. | N/A | 97 | N/A |

DUNS 22-233-3267
### Shawston International Ltd
(Subsidiary of: Shawston Holdings Ltd)
Great Norbury Street, Hyde, Cheshire SK14 1BW
**Tel:** 0161-368-4545  **Fax:** 0161-367-8114
**Web:** www.shawston.co.uk
**Reg No:** 4251302  **VAT No:** 781535906
**Estd:** 2001 Private Limited Company
**Line of Business:** Pipework contractors
**Issued Capital:** £10,000
**Directors:** Ms M D Davenport, G Wilkins, R G Davenport
**Co. Secretary:** Mark Roberts
**Branches:** Shawston International Ltd, Heston Industl Mall, Church Rd, Hounslow, Middlesex TW5 0LD
**US SIC:** 1711, 8911
**UK SIC:** 50300, 83701

**Auditors:** Hurst & Co

| | 31-03-14 | 31-03-13 | 31-03-12 |
|---|---|---|---|
| TO | 12,243,040 | 10,747,776 | 9,813,706 |
| P/L | 1,107,454 | 1,087,176 | 99,200 |
| NW | 2,480,256 | 1,818,871 | 1,016,374 |
| WC | 3,852,551 | 1,820,025 | 1,061,808 |
| Emp. | 64 | 48 | 46 |

DUNS 64-109-8343
## Shaylor Group Plc
(**Subsidiary of:** Shaylor Holdings Ltd)
52 Wharf Approach, Walsall, West Midlands WS9 8BX
**Tel:** 01922-741570
**Web:** www.shaylorgroup.com
**Reg No:** 4513210 **Estd:** 1974 Public Limited Company
**Line of Business:** Construction of domestic buildings
**Issued Capital:** £105,263
**Directors:** Professor M W Chambers, S C Shaylor, R L Shaylor, C Madden
**Co. Secretary:** Gary Turley
**Responsibilities**
**Senior:** Philip Farnworth *(Manager)*, Frederick Shaylor *(Chairman)*
**US SIC:** 1522, 1799
**UK SIC:** 50100, 50000
**Auditors:** KPMG LLP

| | 30-09-14 | 30-09-13 | 30-09-12 |
|---|---|---|---|
| TO | 70,072,000 | 43,490,000 | 79,363,000 |
| P/L | 2,709,000 | 1,468,000 | (1,976,000) |
| NW | 10,356,000 | 8,439,000 | 8,169,000 |
| WC | 9,763,000 | 8,024,000 | 7,511,000 |
| Emp. | 157 | 132 | 149 |

DUNS 21-018-1220
## Shaylor Holdings Ltd
11a The Wharf, Bridge Street, Birmingham, West Midlands B1 2JS
**Tel:** 01216335800
**Web:** www.shaylorgroup.com
**Reg No:** 6399739 **Estd:** 2007 Private Limited Company
**Line of Business:** Holding companies management activities
**Issued Capital:** £53,113
**Directors:** R L Shaylor, S C Shaylor
**Co. Secretary:** Gary Turley
**Responsibilities**
**Senior:** Frederick Shaylor *(Chairman)*
**US SIC:** 6711 **UK SIC:** 83962
**Auditors:** KPMG LLP

| | 30-09-13 | 30-09-12 | 31-09-11 |
|---|---|---|---|
| TO | 43,490,000 | 79,363,000 | 44,680,000 |
| P/L | 885,000 | (2,930,000) | (151,000) |
| NW | (1,159,000) | (2,119,000) | (188,000) |
| WC | (1,124,000) | (2,163,000) | (1,067,000) |
| Emp. | 132 | 149 | 159 |

DUNS 51-992-0594 **Imp**
## Shazam Entertainment Ltd
26 Hammersmith Grove, London W6 7HA
**Tel:** 02087426820 **Fax:** 020 8742 6821
**Web:** www.shazam.com
**Reg No:** 3998831 **VAT No:** 766118223
**Estd:** 2001 Private Limited Company
**Line of Business:** Performing arts management and promotion
**Issued Capital:** £5,296,556
**Directors:** M J Murphy, K Lovell, N J Marovac, A Fisher, Ms L J Zalaznick, R J Riley, C A Smart, C J Barton
**Co. Secretary:** Bridget Kerle
**US SIC:** 4899 **UK SIC:** 79020
**Auditors:** PricewaterhouseCoopers LLP
**Bankers:** HSBC Bank plc (40-05-33)

| | 31-12-13 | 30-06-13 | 30-12-12 |
|---|---|---|---|
| TO | 16,889,630 | 31,017,466 | 21,806,832 |
| P/L | (5,302,243) | (1,277,962) | (2,977,928) |
| NW | 22,334,605 | 25,117,257 | 12,276,253 |
| WC | 21,638,692 | 25,456,254 | 12,432,145 |
| Emp. | 197 | 167 | 143 |

DUNS 22-557-3500
## S.H.B. Hire Ltd
18 Premier Way, Romsey, Hampshire SO51 9DQ
**Tel:** 01794511458
**Web:** www.shb.co.uk
**Reg No:** 1391731 **VAT No:** 320567282
**Estd:** 1968 Private Limited Company
**Line of Business:** Vehicle rental (car)
**Trading Style:** 4 X 4 Sales S H B Self Drive, Rangefinder, Country Car Hire Dormobile, Professional 4 X 4
**Issued Capital:** £25,000
**Principals:** M G Street *(Managing)*, P Street, Ms N J Simpson, R G Taylor
**Co. Secretary:** Ms Sharon Grantham-Davis
**Responsibilities**
**Purchasing:** Don Rae *(Purchasing Manager)*
**Branches:** S.h.b. Hire Ltd, Unit 8 Jardine Park, Bradman Way, Marsh Barton Trading Estate, Exeter, Devon EX2 8PE
**US SIC:** 7512, 7513
**UK SIC:** 84801, 84802
**Auditors:** Boler Wiseman

**Bankers:** Fortis Bank London Bch (formerly Generale Bk) (40-52-62)

| | 31-12-13 | 31-12-12 | 31-12-11 |
|---|---|---|---|
| TO | 69,041,856 | 62,912,570 | 53,577,887 |
| P/L | 6,440,603 | 6,317,558 | 4,434,725 |
| NW | 27,366,979 | 22,126,812 | 16,874,125 |
| WC | (28,316,882) | (22,281,678) | (21,023,969) |
| Emp. | 507 | 442 | 399 |

DUNS 45-835-2952
## Sheard Properties Ltd
Solar Works, Calder Street, Greetland, Halifax, West Yorkshire HX4 8AQ
**Tel:** 01422-373-649 **Fax:** 01422-310-090
**Web:** www.sheard.co.uk
**Reg No:** 3186042 **Estd:** 1996 Private Limited Company
**Line of Business:** Other letting of own property
**Export Sales:** £1,408,743
**Issued Capital:** £3,033,333
**Director:** J S Whittaker
**Co. Secretary:** Ms Barbara Whittaker
**Responsibilities**
**Senior:** Claire Greenwater *(Manager)*, Rodger Whittaker *(Manager)*
**US SIC:** 6519 **UK SIC:** 85000
**Auditors:** Baker Tilly Audit Ltd
**Bankers:** HSBC Bank plc (40-23-05)

| | 30-04-14 | 30-04-13 | 30-04-12 |
|---|---|---|---|
| TO | 33,571,413 | 27,578,585 | 30,899,007 |
| P/L | 4,751,278 | 4,157,373 | 4,261,250 |
| NW | 17,237,155 | 14,994,326 | 12,516,757 |
| WC | 8,529,832 | 8,807,476 | 6,552,447 |
| Emp. | 141 | 130 | 151 |

DUNS 71-890-1395
## Shearings Group Ltd
(**Subsidiary of:** Aghoco 1217 Ltd)
Victoria Mill, Miry Lane, Wigan, Lancashire WN3 4AG
**Web:** www.shearings.com
**Reg No:** 5272464 **Estd:** 2004 Private Limited Company
**Line of Business:** Management activities of holding companies
**Trading Style:** Shearings Holidays
**Issued Capital:** £1,094,670
**Directors:** G J Rogers, D Wormwell, Ms J Burke, G Speakman, V Flower
**Co. Secretary:** A G Secretarial Limited
**Branches:** Shearings Group Ltd, The Portpatrick, Stranraer, Wigtownshire DG9 8TQ
**US SIC:** 6711, 7011
**UK SIC:** 83962, 66500
**Auditors:** Deloitte LLP
**Bankers:** Lloyds TSB Bank plc (30-00-04)

| | 31-12-13 | 31-12-12 | 31-12-11 |
|---|---|---|---|
| TO | 195,013,000 | 195,570,000 | 193,657,000 |
| P/L | (2,196,000) | (2,742,000) | (3,581,000) |
| NW | (1,736,000) | (1,900,000) | (1,850,000) |
| WC | (27,232,000) | (28,286,000) | (29,603,000) |
| Emp. | 2,683 | 2,778 | 2,809 |

DUNS 21-590-4046
## Shearings Hotels Ltd
(**Subsidiary of:** Aghoco 1217 Ltd)
Mariners Way, Ashton-On-Ribble, Preston, Lancashire PR2 2YN
**Tel:** 01772333860 **Fax:** 01803-213989
**Web:** www.shearings.com
**Reg No:** 0024759SC **Estd:** 1946 Private Limited Company
**Line of Business:** Estate agents
**Trading Style:** Shearings Hotels, Post and Country Hotels
**Issued Capital:** £19,000,000
**Directors:** D Wormwell, S J Boricic, V Flower, G Speakman, Ms J Burke
**Co. Secretary:** A G Secretarial Limited
**Responsibilities**
**Senior:** Karl Emmott *(Hotel Director)*, David Newbold *(Finance director)*, Dennis Wormwell *(Managing Director)*
**Branches:** Shearings Hotels Ltd, Sands Road, Paignton, Devon TQ4 6EG
**US SIC:** 7011 **UK SIC:** 66500
**Auditors:** Deloitte LLP
**Bankers:** National Westminster Bank Plc (01-10-01)

| | 31-12-13 | 31-12-12 | 31-12-11 |
|---|---|---|---|
| TO | 71,696,000 | 71,346,000 | 70,793,000 |
| P/L | (2,310,000) | (1,964,000) | (2,670,000) |
| NW | 13,913,000 | 15,709,000 | 17,200,000 |
| WC | 133,000 | (294,000) | 1,180,000 |
| Emp. | 1,732 | 1,803 | 1,776 |

DUNS 39-978-8827
## Shearline Holdings Ltd
Precision House, St Thomas Place, Ely, Cambridgeshire CB7 4EX
**Tel:** 01353-668668
**Web:** www.shearline.co.uk
**Reg No:** 2275157 **Estd:** 1988 Private Limited Company
**Line of Business:** Precision engineers
**Export Sales:** £928,589
**Trading Style:** Shearline Holdings Ltd
**Issued Capital:** £2,500
**Directors:** D H Littlechild, I P Radford
**Co. Secretary:** Ian Radford

**Responsibilities**
**Senior:** Andrew Hayward *(Manager)*
**Finance:** Kevin Gouldthorp *(Finance Director)*
**HR:** Hilary Bacon *(Human Resources Manager)*
**US SIC:** 8911 **UK SIC:** 83701

| | 31-03-14 | 31-03-13 | 01-03-12 |
|---|---|---|---|
| TO | 6,592,903 | 6,423,622 | 6,065,389 |
| P/L | 544,257 | 490,330 | 234,414 |
| NW | 1,662,871 | 1,201,426 | 819,051 |
| WC | 481,728 | 347,631 | 475,572 |
| Emp. | 99 | 101 | 97 |

DUNS 28-900-4954
## Shears Brothers (Transport) Ltd.
Building 427 Aviation Business Park, Viscount Road, Hurn, Christchurch, Dorset BH23 6NW
**Tel:** 01202593555
**Web:** www.sbtl.co.uk
**Reg No:** 1344118 **Estd:** 2002 Private Limited Company
**Line of Business:** Road haulage and transport services
**Trading Style:** Lightfreight
**Issued Capital:** £247,540
**Directors:** Pall-Ex Group Limited, N Tancock, I J Shears, P F Shears
**Co. Secretary:** Anthony Rawlins
**Branches:** Shears Brothers (Transport) Ltd., Building 103, Aviation Business Park, Christchurch, Dorset BH23 6NW
**US SIC:** 4780 **UK SIC:** 77002
**Auditors:** Stephenson & Co
**Bankers:** HSBC Bank plc (40-46-37)

| | 30-11-13 | 30-11-12 | 30-11-11 |
|---|---|---|---|
| TA | 2,029,384 | 1,758,906 | 1,719,622 |
| NW | (81,262) | (36,324) | (45,601) |
| WC | (420,965) | (342,835) | (395,846) |

DUNS 21-604-8224
## Shearwater
18 Moorings Way, Southsea, Hampshire PO4 8QW
**Tel:** 02392776130
**Web:** www.portsmouth.gov.uk
**Estd:** 1988 Proprietorship
**Line of Business:** Residential care establishments
**Partner:** Mrs C Kirk
**Responsibilities**
**Senior:** Susan Mcmanus *(Unit Manager)*
**US SIC:** 8321 **UK SIC:** 96111
**Employees:** 50

DUNS 34-604-8341 **Imp**
## Shearwell Data Ltd
Putham Farm, Cutcombe, Wheddon Cross, Minehead, Somerset TA24 7AS
**Tel:** 01643841611
**Web:** www.sheeptags.co.uk
**Reg No:** 2746241 **Estd:** 1992 Private Limited Company
**Line of Business:** Manufacturers general
**Export Sales:** £912,827
**Trading Style:** Shearwell Data Ltd
**Issued Capital:** £53,350
**Principals:** R S Webber *(Managing)*, R S Webber
**Co. Secretary:** Mrs Carolyne Webber
**Branches:** Shearwell Data Ltd, East Shawtonhill Farm, Chapelton, Strathaven, Lanarkshire ML10 6SH
**US SIC:** 3357, 7399
**UK SIC:** 22470, 83954
**Auditors:** Albert Goodman

| | 30-09-13 | 30-09-12 | 30-09-11 |
|---|---|---|---|
| TO | 5,905,035 | 6,098,951 | N/A |
| P/L | 395,811 | 549,747 | N/A |
| NW | 1,047,966 | 674,954 | 445,893 |
| WC | 304,296 | 308,881 | 643,296 |
| Emp. | 57 | 58 | N/A |

DUNS 21-490-4828
## Shebbear College
Shebbear, Beaworthy, Devon EX21 5HJ
**Web:** www.mandgautos.com
**Estd:** 2002
**Line of Business:** Garage related services
**Principals:** L Clark, R Collings, B Horn, Mrs J Roe
**Responsibilities**
**Senior:** Martin Hedger *(Manager)*
**US SIC:** 7539 **UK SIC:** 67100
**Employees:** 50

DUNS 34-581-8496
## Shebbear College Enterprises Ltd
Shebbear College, Shebbear, Beaworthy, Devon EX21 5HJ
**Web:** www.shebbearcollege.co.uk
**Reg No:** 2728991 **Estd:** 1992 Private Limited Company
**Line of Business:** Primary education
**Issued Capital:** £2
**Directors:** M Saltmarsh, P A Sanders

**Co. Secretary:** Bradley Horn
**Responsibilities**
**Senior:** Annie Farrell *(Deputy Head)*, Simon Weale *(Head Master)*
**IT:** Pam Thomas *(Computer Manager)*
**US SIC:** 8211 **UK SIC:** 93200
**Auditors:** Haysmacintyre

| | 31-08-13 | 31-08-12 | 31-08-11 |
|---|---|---|---|
| TO | 111,203 | 74,585 | 49,338 |
| P/L | N/A | 17,721 | N/A |
| NW | (161) | (161) | (161) |
| WC | (407) | (489) | (599) |

DUNS 21-385-9710
## Shed
26 Langside Avenue, Glasgow, Lanarkshire G41 2QS
**Tel:** 01416495020
**Web:** www.shedglasgow.com
**Line of Business:** Nightclub
**Responsibilities**
**Senior:** Gemma Blair *(Manager)*
**US SIC:** 5813 **UK SIC:** 66200
**Employees:** 71

DUNS 21-601-9834
## The Shed
22 Dean Street, London W1D 3RX
**Tel:** 02031007800
**Web:** www.farmgroup.tv
**Estd:** 2011 Proprietorship
**Line of Business:** Film production services and studios
**Proprietor:** Ms C Barratt
**Responsibilities**
**Senior:** Jason Elliott *(Group Sales Director)*
**Sales:** Jason Elliott *(Group Sales Director)*
**US SIC:** 7319 **UK SIC:** 83800
**Employees:** 210

DUNS 54-866-2360
## Sheddon Macintosh
120 Dumbarton Road, Clydebank, Dunbartonshire G81 1UG
**Tel:** 0141-941-1087
**Web:** www.officestarsheddenmacintosh.co.uk
**Estd:** 1984 Proprietorship
**Line of Business:** Commercial stationery supplies
**Proprietor:** S Macintosh
**Responsibilities**
**Senior:** Scott MacIntosh *(Proprietor)*
**US SIC:** 5942 **UK SIC:** 65300
**Employees:** 75

DUNS 29-675-2744
## Sheehans Ltd
Knightsbridge Farm, Kidlington, Oxfordshire OX5 1PH
**Tel:** 01865-379931 **Fax:** 01865841216
**Web:** www.sheehancontractors.co.uk
**Reg No:** 2001591 **VAT No:** 448502153
**Estd:** 1986 Private Limited Company
**Line of Business:** Other letting of own property
**Issued Capital:** £100
**Principals:** C J Sheehan *(Managing)*, Miss T L Sheehan
**Co. Secretary:** Christopher Sheehan
**US SIC:** 6519, 1622
**UK SIC:** 85000, 50200
**Auditors:** Chapman Robinson & Moore
**Bankers:** Barclays Bank Plc (20-65-18)

| | 31-12-13 | 31-12-12 | 31-12-11 |
|---|---|---|---|
| TA | 2,557,307 | 2,640,165 | 2,437,660 |
| NW | 926,845 | 847,593 | 742,648 |
| WC | 288,210 | 457,545 | 387,459 |

DUNS 23-190-3498
## Sheepdrove Organic Farm
Warren Farm, Sheepdrove, Lambourn, Hungerford, Berkshire RG17 7UU
**Tel:** 0148871659
**Web:** www.sheepdrove.com
**Estd:** 1996 Partnership
**Line of Business:** Organic food production and supply
**Partners:** P J Kindersley, Mrs J Kindersley
**Branches:** Sheepdrove Organic Farm, Sheepdrove Organic Farm Family Butcher, 3 Lower Redland Road, Bristol, Avon BS6 6TB
**US SIC:** 5499 **UK SIC:** 64100
**Bankers:** Barclays Bank Plc (20-72-17)
**Employees:** 56

DUNS 22-134-0008
## Sheer Projects Ltd
(**Subsidiary of:** Sheer Corporation Ltd)
Prince Consort House Albert Embankment, London SE1 7TJ
**Tel:** 02030550850
**Web:** www.sheerprojects.com
**Reg No:** 4152945 **Estd:** 2001 Private Limited Company
**Line of Business:** Construction of commercial buildings
**Issued Capital:** £1,000

**Principals:** M G Pangherz *(Managing)*, M Steeds, M Poteratchi
**Co. Secretary:** Mark Steeds
**US SIC:** 1541 **UK SIC:** 50100

| | 31-03-14 | 31-03-13 | 31-03-12 |
|---|---|---|---|
| TA | 903,054 | 543,731 | 293,133 |
| NW | (69,705) | (180,339) | (236,968) |
| WC | (91,107) | (208,875) | (270,040) |

DUNS 34-865-7768

### Sheermans Ltd

(**Subsidiary of:** Sheermans Ss Ltd)
London House 243-253, Lower Mortlake Road, Richmond, Surrey TW9 2LL
**Tel:** 02089485166 **Fax:** 020-7836-4988
**Web:** www.dominos.co.uk
**Reg No:** 2817653 **Estd:** 1993 Private Limited Company
**Line of Business:** Take away meal outlets
**Trading Style:** Domino's Pizza
**Issued Capital:** £100
**Directors:** Mrs N Shakarchi, S Shakarchi
**Co. Secretary:** Tyrone Curtis
**Branches:** Sheermans Ltd, Central House, 1 Ballards Lane, Finchley, London N3 1UX
**US SIC:** 5812 **UK SIC:** 66110
**Auditors:** A V Audit Ltd
**Bankers:** National Westminster Bank Plc (60-17-31)

| | 31-07-13 | 31-07-12 | 31-07-11 |
|---|---|---|---|
| TO | 13,879,298 | 13,914,874 | 12,338,225 |
| P/l | 1,309,364 | 1,025,413 | 903,899 |
| NW | 4,998,278 | 3,975,969 | 3,242,450 |
| WC | 4,611,530 | 4,421,914 | 4,211,422 |
| Emp. | 407 | 418 | 409 |

DUNS 73-873-7381

### Sheermans Ss Ltd

68 Argyle Street, Birkenhead, Merseyside CH41 6AF
**Tel:** 02088319595
**Web:** www.shearman.com
**Reg No:** 5128157 **Estd:** 2004 Private Limited Company
**Line of Business:** Management activities of holding companies
**Issued Capital:** £1,000,000
**Director:** S Shakarchi
**Co. Secretary:** Tyrone Curtis
**US SIC:** 6711 **UK SIC:** 83962

| | 31-07-13 | 31-07-12 | 31-07-11 |
|---|---|---|---|
| TO | 13,879,298 | 13,914,874 | 12,338,225 |
| P/L | 1,066,684 | 782,735 | 661,219 |
| NW | (13,660) | (1,035,970) | (1,769,489) |
| WC | (400,408) | (590,025) | (800,517) |
| Emp. | 407 | 418 | 409 |

DUNS 21-880-4060 **Exp**

### Sheetfabs (Nottingham) Ltd

Nottingham Road, Attenborough, Beeston, Beeston, Nottingham, Nottinghamshire NG9 6DR
**Tel:** 01159-258101
**Web:** www.sheetfabs.co.uk
**Reg No:** 0426392 **VAT No:** 117138586
**Estd:** 1919 Private Limited Company
**Line of Business:** Fabricated metal products
**Export Markets:** European Union (E U); U S A
**Issued Capital:** £49,400
**Principals:** A Herrod *(Chairman and Managing)*, D C Mason
**Co. Secretary:** Mark Herrod
**Responsibilities**
**Purchasing:** Richard Sefton *(Purchasing Manager)*
**US SIC:** 3441, 3442
**UK SIC:** 32042, 31420
**Auditors:** Page Kirk
**Bankers:** Yorkshire Bank Plc (05-06-41)

| | 31-12-13 | 31-12-12 | 31-12-11 |
|---|---|---|---|
| TA | 3,637,813 | 3,321,632 | 3,757,572 |
| NW | 2,448,432 | 2,415,995 | 2,413,461 |
| WC | 2,195,278 | 2,053,571 | 2,214,915 |

DUNS 76-203-2860

### Sheffcare Ltd

192 Penrith Road, Sheffield, South Yorkshire S5 8UG
**Tel:** 01142213222
**Web:** www.sheffcare.co.uk
**Reg No:** 2538734 **Estd:** 1994 Private Limited Company
**Line of Business:** Social work activities with accommodation
**Issued Capital:** £100
**Directors:** R P Taylor, S M Huslter, Ms A Pittard, Mrs M J Surrell, Ms R A Dutton, I P Carey, Ms E M Bashforth, S W Sanderson
**Co. Secretary:** Mrs Elaine Parkinson
**Responsibilities**
**Senior:** Pamela Boulton *(Manager)*, Belinda Gibson *(Chief Executive)*, Adele Jagger *(Manager)*, Sally Pritchard *(Chief Executive)*, Mavis Sellars *(Manager)*, Anthony Warnes *(Manager)*, David Waxman *(Director)*
**Operations:** Tracey Payne *(Director of Care)*
**Branches:** Sheffcare Ltd, 11 Stanwood Road, Sheffield, South Yorkshire S6 5JE
**US SIC:** 7399 **UK SIC:** 83954
**Auditors:** KPMG LLP

**Bankers:** The Co-Operative Bank Plc (08-90-75)

| | 31-03-14 | 31-03-13 | 31-03-12 |
|---|---|---|---|
| TO | 9,271,182 | 9,056,027 | 8,901,517 |
| P/L | 613,341 | 471,562 | 328,148 |
| NW | 1,825,254 | 504,913 | 1,099,351 |
| WC | 1,542,132 | 1,519,694 | 1,290,062 |
| Emp. | 455 | 341 | 352 |

DUNS 54-868-2236

### Sheffield Assay Office

Hillsborough Leisure Centre, Beulah Road, Sheffield, South Yorkshire S6 2AN
**Tel:** 01142312121 **Fax:** 01142-756473
**Web:** www.assayoffice.co.uk
**VAT No:** 172572164 **Estd:** 1700 Incorporate By Act Of Parliament
**Line of Business:** Certification and accreditation bodies
**Principals:** J E Eardley *(Chairman)*, A M Carson *(Managing)*
**Responsibilities**
**HR:** Nicola Guest *(Human Resources Manager)*
**Health & Safety:** Andy Gaymond *(Facilities Manager)*
**Facilities:** Andy Gaymond *(Facilities Manager)*
**US SIC:** 8621 **UK SIC:** 96311
**Bankers:** The Royal Bank Of Scotland Plc (16-00-08)
**Employees:** 100

DUNS 76-907-8429

### Sheffield Children's Centre Ltd

101 Shoreham Street, Sheffield, South Yorkshire S1 4SR
**Tel:** 01142798236 **Fax:** 01142-768891
**Web:** www.sheffinfolink.org.uk
**Reg No:** 0265259IP **Estd:** 1985 Private Limited Company
**Line of Business:** Pre school education
**Responsibilities**
**Senior:** Annie Daquila *(Manager)*
**Branches:** Sheffield Children's Centre Ltd, 7 Paternoster Row, Sheffield, South Yorkshire S1 2BX
**US SIC:** 8211 **UK SIC:** 93200
**Employees:** 28

DUNS 23-265-7572 **Imp**

### Sheffield Childrens Nhs Foundation Trust

Western Bank, Sheffield, South Yorkshire S10 2TH
**Tel:** 01142717000
**Web:** www.sheffieldchildrens.nhs.uk
**Estd:** 1992
**Line of Business:** Hospitals
**Issued Capital:** £1
**Principals:** S Hunter *(Chairman)*, S Ned *(Personnel)*, Ms I Hemmings, P Lamberton, J Loeb, C Sharratt, D Williams, Ms S Jones
**Responsibilities**
**Senior:** Shona Ashworth *(Manager)*, Simon Murren *(Chief Executive)*
**Marketing:** Russell Banks *(it manager)*
**Admin:** Pamela Canham *(Medical Secretary)*
**IT:** Russell Banks *(it manager)*
**Operations:** Russell Banks *(it manager)*
**Branches:** Sheffield Childrens Nhs Foundation Trust, Western Bank, Sheffield, South Yorkshire S10 2TH
**US SIC:** 8062 **UK SIC:** 95100
**Auditors:** KPMG LLP

| | 31-03-14 | 31-03-13 | 31-03-12 |
|---|---|---|---|
| TO | 159,611,000 | 153,907,000 | 123,984,000 |
| P/L | 2,414,000 | 3,640,000 | 5,417,000 |
| NW | 81,413,000 | 78,811,000 | 75,715,000 |
| WC | 18,961,000 | 22,833,000 | 18,779,000 |
| Emp. | 2,485 | 2,346 | 2,269 |

DUNS 21-782-9957

### Sheffield City College

Granville Road, Sheffield, South Yorkshire S2 2RL
**Web:** www.sheffcol.ac.uk
**Estd:** 2011 Proprietorship
**Line of Business:** Further education schools and colleges
**Proprietor:** Mrs H Mcdonald
**US SIC:** 8221 **UK SIC:** 93100
**Employees:** 1,500

DUNS 22-815-3011

### Sheffield City Council

Town Hall, Pinstone Street, Sheffield, South Yorkshire S1 2HH
**Tel:** 01142734567 **Fax:** 01142 736844
**Web:** www.sheffield.gov.uk
**VAT No:** 173548838 **Estd:** 1976 Incorporate By Act Of Parliament
**Line of Business:** Local government
**Principals:** G Sherwin *(Financial)*, E Boylan, Ms P Thompson, J Crossley-Holland, J Mothersole, R W Kerslake
**Responsibilities**
**Senior:** Steve Danford *(Manager)*
**Sales:** Angela Cawkwell *(Head of Business Change and Pr)*
**Branches:** Sheffield City Council, The Sheffield Law Courts, 50 West Bar, Sheffield, South Yorkshire S3 8PH
**US SIC:** 9121 **UK SIC:** 91110
**Bankers:** The Co-Operative Bank Plc (08-90-75)
**Employees:** 20,000

DUNS 23-221-0500

### Sheffield College

Granville Road, Sheffield, South Yorkshire S2 2RL
**Web:** www.citycollegenursery.
**Estd:** 2012
**Line of Business:** Nursery schools
**Trading Style:** Norton College, Hillsborough College
**Director:** J Taylor
**Responsibilities**
**Senior:** Joanne Hardy *(Senior Nursery Manager)*, Heather MacDonald *(Principal)*
**IT:** Martin Plummer *(IT Manager)*
**Health & Safety:** Seamus Dooris *(Health & Safety Officer)*
**Facilities:** David Battell *(Estates Manager)*
**Branches:** Sheffield College, Arundel Gate Multistorey Car Park, Arundel Gate, Sheffield, South Yorkshire S1 2PN
**US SIC:** 8221 **UK SIC:** 93100
**Employees:** 2,500

DUNS 21-246-8768

### Sheffield Conservation Volunteers

P O Box 510, Sheffield, South Yorkshire S4 8YX
**Tel:** 01142-223701
**Line of Business:** Committee managed organisations
**Principals:** P Worthington, Ms C Ankerstein
**US SIC:** 8699, 7399
**UK SIC:** 96902, 83954
**Employees:** 50

DUNS 23-880-3352

### Sheffield Eagles 2000 Ltd

Unit 1b Enterprise Court, Farfield Park, Manvers, Rotherham, South Yorkshire S63 5DB
**Tel:** 01142610326
**Web:** www.sheffieldeagles.com
**Reg No:** 3871551 **Estd:** 1999 Private Limited Company
**Line of Business:** Sports clubs
**Issued Capital:** £189,000
**Directors:** M R Aston, D Johnston, I J Anniss, C Noble, P Clarke, J Whaling
**Co. Secretary:** Ian Swire
**Responsibilities**
**Senior:** Andy Giles *(General Manager)*, Simon Proctor *(General Manager)*
**US SIC:** 7999 **UK SIC:** 97913

| | 30-09-13 | 30-09-12 | 30-09-11 |
|---|---|---|---|
| TO | N/A | 810,544 | 801,960 |
| P/L | N/A | (4,896) | 9,852 |
| NW | (46,874) | (48,415) | (48,519) |
| WC | (46,874) | (48,415) | (48,519) |
| Emp. | N/A | 79 | 81 |

DUNS 21-170-4847

### Sheffield Foods (Uk) Ltd

Fairway Works, 75/129 Carlisle Street, Sheffield, South Yorkshire S4 7LJ
**Tel:** 01142-750408 **Fax:** 01142797110
**Web:** www.sheffieldfoods.co.uk
**Reg No:** 6950674 **Estd:** 2000 Private Limited Company
**Line of Business:** Manufacturers of food products
**Trading Style:** Sheffield Foods (Uk) Limited
**Issued Capital:** £100
**Director:** A Ahmed
**Responsibilities**
**IT:** Deborah Todd *(IT Manager)*
**US SIC:** 2099 **UK SIC:** 42399

| | 30-06-13 | 30-06-12 | 30-06-11 |
|---|---|---|---|
| TA | 1,185,288 | 1,399,307 | 1,086,590 |
| NW | 95,174 | 195,438 | 123,231 |
| WC | (8,159) | 115,698 | 85,394 |

DUNS 73-623-0728

### Sheffield Forgemasters International Ltd

P O Box 286, Sheffield, South Yorkshire S9 2RU
**Tel:** 01142-449071
**Web:** www.sheffieldforgemasters.com
**Reg No:** 4883675 **VAT No:** 865477674
**Estd:** 2005 Private Limited Company
**Line of Business:** Manufacture of basic iron and steel and of ferro-alloys
**Export Sales:** £60,970,000
**Trading Style:** Sheffield Forgemasters International Ltd
**Issued Capital:** £212,026
**Directors:** N A Maskrey, P Birtles, A P Pedder, Dr G A Honeyman
**Co. Secretary:** John Lovell
**US SIC:** 3325, 6711
**UK SIC:** 31110, 83962
**Auditors:** KPMG LLP
**Bankers:** Barclays Bank Plc (20-04-48)

| | 30-06-13 | 30-06-12 | 30-06-11 |
|---|---|---|---|
| TO | 100,092,000 | 106,815,000 | 107,544,000 |
| P/L | 1,556,000 | 4,429,000 | 1,269,000 |
| NW | 44,420,000 | 43,107,000 | 37,828,000 |
| WC | 8,197,000 | 10,698,000 | 7,290,000 |
| Emp. | 779 | 811 | 817 |

DUNS 77-462-0611

### Sheffield Futures

Star House, 43 Division Street, Sheffield, South Yorkshire S1 4GE
**Tel:** 01142012800 **Fax:** 01142-012757
**Web:** www.sheffieldfutures.org.uk
**Reg No:** 2963378 **Estd:** 1994 Private Limited Company
**Line of Business:** Business and management consultancy activities not elsewhere classified
**Directors:** J Doyle, Mrs D Fox, A Peaden, A Cropley, W Jones, S Green, L Clewes, M J Hemmingway
**Co. Secretary:** Liam Gilligan
**Responsibilities**
**Senior:** June Braithwait *(CEO's PA)*, Antony Hughes *(Manager)*, Christopher Humphries *(Director)*, Edward Ryder *(Director)*
**Branches:** Sheffield Futures, 36-42 Union Street, Sheffield, South Yorkshire S1 2JP
**US SIC:** 7392 **UK SIC:** 83951
**Auditors:** Grant Thornton UK LLP
**Bankers:** Allied Irish Bank (gb) (23-84-02)

| | 31-03-14 | 31-03-13 | 31-03-12 |
|---|---|---|---|
| TO | 6,398,262 | 5,919,084 | 6,354,490 |
| P/L | 1,022,257 | 602,172 | 119,078 |
| NW | (359,137) | (5,591,394) | (4,021,566) |
| WC | 1,864,101 | 1,207,612 | 593,894 |
| Emp. | 124 | 124 | 132 |

DUNS 77-117-5692

### Sheffield Haworth Ltd

60 Gresham Street, London EC2V 7BB
**Tel:** 020-7236-2400
**Web:** www.sheffieldhaworth.com
**Reg No:** 2690067 **VAT No:** 625571536
**Estd:** 1992 Private Limited Company
**Line of Business:** Employment and recruitment companies and consultants
**Export Sales:** £10,058,949
**Issued Capital:** £237,862
**Principals:** T J Sheffield *(Managing)*, C G Clothier, M P Hammond, S J Roberts, Ms M A Record, P D Morrissey, M A Spencer, M B Swann
**Co. Secretary:** Miss Erin Smith
**Responsibilities**
**Senior:** Charles Bruce-Smythe *(Managing Director, Global Weal)*, Mark Esposito *(Managing Director)*, Daniel Solo *(Executive Director)*
**Finance:** Monica Bedi *(Finance Manager)*, Michelle Henry *(Global Head of Business & Prof)*
**Admin:** Claire Dunt *(Office Manager)*, Claire Edmondson *(Office Manager)*
**IT:** Nilly Chaudhuri *(Head of Information Technology)*
**HR:** Claire Dunt *(Office Manager)*, Claire Edmondson *(Office Manager)*
**Health & Safety:** Claire Dunt *(Office Manager)*, Claire Edmondson *(Office Manager)*
**Facilities:** Claire Dunt *(Office Manager)*, Claire Edmondson *(Office Manager)*
**US SIC:** 7361 **UK SIC:** 83954
**Auditors:** Morley & Scott
**Bankers:** HSBC Bank plc (40-14-13)

| | 31-12-13 | 31-12-12 | 31-12-11 |
|---|---|---|---|
| TO | 16,666,848 | 12,241,407 | 16,971,138 |
| P/L | 1,742,781 | (688,686) | 2,045,180 |
| NW | 7,337,181 | 6,894,663 | 7,961,916 |
| WC | 6,601,835 | 6,357,465 | 7,135,274 |
| Emp. | 105 | 108 | 112 |

DUNS 54-864-1281

### Sheffield Health and Social Care Nhs Foundation Trust

Fulwood House, Old Fulwood Road, Sheffield, South Yorkshire S10 3TH
**Tel:** 01142718750
**Web:** www.shsc.nhs.uk
**Estd:** 1994
**Line of Business:** Public sector hospital activities, including nhs trusts
**Issued Capital:** £1
**Principals:** A Walker *(Chairman)*, C Kazoka, K Taylor, Ms S Rodgers, M Thomas, A Clayton, M Rosling, M Rooney
**Responsibilities**
**Senior:** Mick Rodgers *(Financial Director)*
**Finance:** Mick Rodgers *(Financial Director)*
**IT:** Tom Davidson *(Contracts Director)*
**HR:** Karen Dickinson *(Training Manager)*
**Branches:** Sheffield Health and Social Care Nhs Foundation Trust, Central Health Clinic, Mulberry Street, Sheffield, South Yorkshire S1 2PJ
**US SIC:** 8062 **UK SIC:** 95100

**Auditors:** Damian Murray

| | 31-03-14 | 31-03-13 | 31-03-12 |
|---|---|---|---|
| TO | 130,030,000 | 128,382,000 | 86,961,000 |
| P/L | 2,513,000 | 3,532,000 | 1,991,000 |
| NW | 77,205,000 | 71,223,000 | 69,018,000 |
| WC | 21,893,000 | 17,311,000 | 13,661,000 |
| Emp. | 2,716 | 2,661 | 2,746 |

DUNS 21-583-3822
## Sheffield Insulations
Hornhouse Lane, Knowsley Industrial Park, Liverpool, Merseyside L33 7YQ
**Tel:** 01515477680
**Web:** www.sheffins.co.uk
**Estd:** 2011 Proprietorship
**Line of Business:** Other construction work involving special trades
**Proprietor:** Mrs S Massey
**US SIC:** 1799 **UK SIC:** 50000
**Employees:** 50

DUNS 39-886-3779
## Sheffield International Venues Ltd
Don Valley Stadium, Sheffield, South Yorkshire S9 3TL
**Tel:** 01142233856
**Web:** www.sheffieldeagles.com
**Reg No:** 2226575 **VAT No:** 471029758
**Estd:** 1999 Private Limited Company
**Line of Business:** Stadiums and sports grounds
**Issued Capital:** £100
**Directors:** S Brailey, G G Sherwin, N G Gibson, Ms D L Hickman, L Clark, S G Britland
**Co. Secretary:** Andrew Snelling
**Responsibilities**
**Senior:** Andy Giles *(General Manager)*
**Marketing:** Liam Claffey *(Marketing Executive)*
**Facilities:** Martin Crookes *(Facilities Manager)*
**Purchasing:** Martin Crookes *(Facilities Manager)*
**Branches:** Sheffield International Venues Ltd, 95 Broughton La, Sheffield, South Yorkshire S9 2DE
**US SIC:** 7941, 7999
**UK SIC:** 97911, 97913
**Auditors:** KPMG LLP
**Bankers:** The Co-Operative Bank Plc (08-90-75)

| | 31-03-14 | 31-03-13 | 31-03-12 |
|---|---|---|---|
| TO | 11,696,000 | 14,077,000 | 13,940,000 |
| P/L | 137,000 | (1,023,000) | (209,000) |
| NW | (8,137,000) | (9,299,000) | (5,935,000) |
| WC | (8,879,000) | (6,611,000) | (4,077,000) |
| Emp. | 980 | 644 | 1,137 |

DUNS 21-773-8619
## Sheffield Job Lot Trading Co
939 Barnsley Road, Sheffield, South Yorkshire S5 0QJ
**Tel:** 01142576692
**Web:** www.joblotltd.co.uk
**Estd:** 2000 Proprietorship
**Line of Business:** Convenience stores
**Proprietor:** M Todd
**US SIC:** 5411 **UK SIC:** 64100
**Employees:** 50

DUNS 50-465-3619
## The Sheffield Media & Exhibition Centre Ltd
15 Paternoster Row, Sheffield, South Yorkshire S1 2BX
**Tel:** 01142765141
**Web:** www.sheffdocfest.com
**Reg No:** 2444438 **Estd:** 1993 Private Company Limited By Guarantee
**Line of Business:** Film distribution services
**Trading Style:** The Showroom Cinema
**Directors:** Ms S M Harvey, D B Gormley, Ms M Ellis, Mrs A Bouchier, Miss J P Dunn, Mrs S J Sanderson, P J Brooks, T L Rippon
**Co. Secretary:** Ms Julie Simpson
**Responsibilities**
**Senior:** Heather Croall *(Festival Director)*, Simon Gedye *(Director)*, Julie Muscroft *(Manager)*, Charlie Phillips *(Deputy Director)*, Colin Pons *(Director)*, Lisa Rowley *(Director)*
**Finance:** Julie Mitchell *(Management Accountant)*, Sylvia Wroblewska *(Business & Marketing Director)*, Sohil Zokari *(Assistant Management Accountan)*
**Marketing:** Kat Chirnside *(Marketing Coordinator)*, Nikki Cummins *(Press Consultant)*, Felicity Hoy *(Publications Coordinator)*, Karolina Lidin *(Marketplace Executive Producer)*, Anna Parker *(Marketplace Manager)*, Madelaine Russo *(Marketplace Sessions Coordinat)*, Becky Webb *(Marketplace Assistant)*, Sylvia Wroblewska *(Business & Marketing Director)*
**HR:** Elva Lynch-Bathgate *(Volunteers Coordinator)*, Maria Stoneman *(HR and Project Manager)*
**Branches:** The Sheffield Media & Exhibition Centre Ltd, The Workstation, 15 Paternoster Row, Sheffield, South Yorkshire S1 2BX
**US SIC:** 7829, 7832, 8299, 7911
**UK SIC:** 97112, 97113, 93300, 97913
**Auditors:** Barber Harrison & Platt
**Bankers:** National Westminster Bank Plc (56-00-09)

| | 31-03-14 | 31-03-13 | 31-03-12 |
|---|---|---|---|
| TO | 4,021,354 | 3,572,411 | 3,278,293 |
| P/L | (117,110) | (179,977) | (139,877) |
| NW | 4,207,715 | 3,879,669 | 4,544,995 |
| WC | (527,481) | (650,639) | (669,556) |
| Emp. | 93 | 99 | 99 |

DUNS 45-810-7968
## Sheffield Mencap
Norfolk Lodge, Park Grange Road, Sheffield, South Yorkshire S2 3QF
**Tel:** 01142-767757
**Web:** www.sheffieldmencap.org.uk
**Reg No:** 3168775 **Estd:** 1996 Private Limited Company
**Line of Business:** Education services
**Trading Style:** Sheffield Mencap
**Directors:** D Wand, Mrs L E Ward, R Kirkham, C Sterry, G Drabble, Mrs R Ardern, Mrs C Walker, Mrs C J Booth
**Co. Secretary:** Ms Janet Sullivan
**Responsibilities**
**Senior:** Geoffrey Birkett *(Director)*, Patricia Carey *(Director)*, Christine Gamble *(Director)*, Jean-Marc Michel *(Director)*, Norma Morgan *(Director)*, Stephen Newcombe *(Manager)*
**US SIC:** 8299 **UK SIC:** 93300
**Auditors:** Hawleys Ltd
**Bankers:** Lloyds TSB Bank plc (30-97-51)

| | 31-03-14 | 31-03-13 | 31-03-12 |
|---|---|---|---|
| TO | 849,030 | 902,233 | 931,693 |
| P/L | (76,591) | 30,557 | 71,856 |
| NW | 794,244 | 870,835 | 840,278 |
| WC | 574,149 | 651,403 | 653,424 |
| Emp. | 61 | 58 | 52 |

DUNS 21-328-0951 **Imp-Exp**
## Sheffield Refractories Ltd
**(Subsidiary of:** Tjs Holdings Ltd)
Jubilee House, 113 Laughton Road, Sheffield, South Yorkshire S25 2PP
**Tel:** 01909-568444
**Web:** www.sheffieldrefractories.com
**Reg No:** 1279115 **VAT No:** 646510151
**Estd:** 1976 Private Limited Company
**Line of Business:** Refractory materials
**Export Markets:** E U
**Export Sales:** £2,827,483
**Issued Capital:** £1,000
**Directors:** J Gray, T Staton
**Co. Secretary:** Trevor Staton
**US SIC:** 3269 **UK SIC:** 24894
**Auditors:** Deloitte & Touche
**Bankers:** HSBC Bank plc (40-41-08)

| | 30-09-13 | 30-09-12 | 30-09-11 |
|---|---|---|---|
| TO | 7,626,688 | 8,176,821 | 6,745,665 |
| P/L | 259,488 | 165,450 | 53,386 |
| NW | 2,628,713 | 2,377,260 | 2,358,249 |
| WC | 2,036,793 | 1,663,911 | 1,757,874 |
| Emp. | 47 | 50 | N/A |

DUNS 21-309-8908 **Imp**
## Sheffield Refrigeration Ltd
Leigh Street, Sheffield, South Yorkshire S9 2PR
**Tel:** 01142-560020
**Web:** www.srl-countertech.co.uk
**Reg No:** 2046069 **VAT No:** 173632463
**Estd:** 1987 Private Limited Company
**Line of Business:** Plumbing
**Issued Capital:** £123,596
**Managing Director:** J H Clarke
**Co. Secretary:** Paul Wells
**Branches:** Sheffield Refrigeration Ltd, 2 Progress Pk, Toddington Rd, Luton, Bedfordshire LU4 9UR
**US SIC:** 8999, 2517
**UK SIC:** 83954, 46714
**Auditors:** Hart Shaw LLP
**Bankers:** HSBC Bank plc (40-41-08)

| | 31-08-14 | 31-08-13 | 31-08-12 |
|---|---|---|---|
| TA | 731,611 | 676,312 | 925,325 |
| NW | 221,172 | 209,197 | 514,499 |
| WC | 134,537 | 90,201 | 383,179 |

DUNS 77-946-9923
## The Sheffield Royal Society for the Blind
5 Mappin Street, Sheffield, South Yorkshire S1 4DT
**Tel:** 01142722757
**Web:** www.srsb.org.uk
**Reg No:** 3053277 **Estd:** 1860 Private Limited Company
**Line of Business:** Activities of other membership organisations not elsewhere classified
**Directors:** Mrs C J Pattison, B S Campbell, N Wragg, S G Blacksell, Miss J Smethurst, E R Hill, A P Cooper, P W Lee
**Co. Secretary:** Steven Hambleton
**Responsibilities**
**Senior:** Katrina Hulse *(Director)*
**Finance:** Sue Coggin *(Fundraising and Marketing Mana)*
**Marketing:** Sue Coggin *(Fundraising and Marketing Mana)*
**HR:** Dyane Midgley *(Training Manager)*
**US SIC:** 8699, 8321
**UK SIC:** 96902, 96111
**Auditors:** Grant Thornton
**Bankers:** Barclays Bank Plc (20-76-89)

| | 30-06-14 | 30-06-13 | 30-06-12 |
|---|---|---|---|
| TO | 1,287,678 | 1,367,317 | 1,766,845 |
| P/L | (151,325) | (39,114) | 380,439 |
| NW | 6,795,824 | 6,636,963 | 6,212,913 |
| WC | 40,455 | 96,989 | 75,058 |
| Emp. | 71 | 68 | 68 |

DUNS 29-845-4513
## Sheffield Specsavers Ltd
**(Subsidiary of:** Specsavers International Healthcare Limited)
121-123 Pinstone Street, Sheffield, South Yorkshire S1 2HL
**Tel:** 01142755121 **Fax:** 01142-780111
**Web:** www.specsavers.co.uk
**Reg No:** 2048790 **Estd:** 1986 Private Limited Company
**Line of Business:** Opticians ophthalmic
**Issued Capital:** £100
**Directors:** G Bamford, Mrs M L Perkins, P Mcginty
**Co. Secretary:** Specsavers Optical Group Limited
**Responsibilities**
**Senior:** Paul McGinty *(Director)*
**US SIC:** 5999 **UK SIC:** 65600
**Auditors:** BDO LLP

| | 28-02-14 | 28-02-13 | 29-02-12 |
|---|---|---|---|
| TA | 175,736 | 184,392 | 150,094 |
| NW | (402,051) | (417,157) | (322,688) |
| WC | (505,676) | (526,616) | (423,246) |

DUNS 22-809-3340
## Sheffield Sports Stadium Ltd
**(Subsidiary of:** The A & S Leisure Group Ltd)
Owlerton Sports Stadium, Penistone Road, Sheffield, South Yorkshire S6 2DE
**Tel:** 01142-343074
**Web:** www.owlertonstadium.co.uk
**Reg No:** 0707406 **VAT No:** 172930558
**Estd:** 1961 Private Limited Company
**Line of Business:** Racecourses and racetracks
**Trading Style:** Owlerton Stadium
**Issued Capital:** £9,006
**Principals:** D E Allen *(Chairman)*, Ms L Clark, M Allen, J R Gilburn
**Co. Secretary:** Ashley Miles
**Responsibilities**
**Senior:** Godfrey Lakin *(Manager)*
**Admin:** Vicky Hearley *(Assistant Marketing Manager)*
**IT:** Louise Richards *(IT Manager)*
**Health & Safety:** Matt Hamilton *(Health & Safety Officer)*
**Branches:** Sheffield Sports Stadium Ltd, Owlerton Sports Stadium, Penistone Road, Sheffield, South Yorkshire S6 2DE
**US SIC:** 7999 **UK SIC:** 97913
**Auditors:** West & Foster
**Bankers:** Lloyds TSB Bank plc (30-97-51)

| | 30-09-13 | 30-09-12 | 30-09-11 |
|---|---|---|---|
| TO | 6,061,148 | 6,065,566 | 5,963,265 |
| P/L | 957,264 | 1,023,514 | 1,001,371 |
| NW | 5,400,281 | 5,302,713 | 5,173,418 |
| WC | 610,338 | 426,303 | 373,411 |
| Emp. | 188 | 195 | 187 |

DUNS 49-478-6163
## Sheffield Supplies Ltd
Guardian's Hall, Beulah Road, Sheffield, South Yorkshire S6 2AN
**Tel:** 01142318160 **Fax:** 01142-756473
**Web:** www.assayoffice.co.uk
**Reg No:** 3147906 **Estd:** 1996 Private Limited Company
**Line of Business:** Business services
**Trading Style:** Assay Office
**Issued Capital:** £2
**Managing Director:** A Carson
**US SIC:** 7399 **UK SIC:** 83954
**Auditors:** Pannell Kerr Forster
**Bankers:** The Royal Bank Of Scotland Plc (16-00-08)

| | 30-06-14 | 30-06-13 | 30-06-12 |
|---|---|---|---|
| TA | 2 | 2 | 2 |
| NW | 2 | 2 | 2 |

DUNS 21-778-5886 **Imp**
## Sheffield Teaching Hospitals
Herries Road, Sheffield, South Yorkshire S5 7AU
**Tel:** 01142434343
**Web:** www.sth.nhs.uk
**Estd:** 1999 Proprietorship
**Line of Business:** Hospitals
**Proprietor:** A Cash
**Responsibilities**
**Marketing:** James Coxon *(Communications Specialist)*, Laura Kirby *(Communication Specialist)*, Kirsten Major *(Director of Service Developmen)*, Julie Phelan *(Communications Director)*
**HR:** Mark Gwilliam *(Human Resources Director)*
**US SIC:** 8062 **UK SIC:** 95100
**Employees:** 3,000

DUNS 23-260-8476
## Sheffield Teaching Hospitals Nhs Foundation Trust
Royal Hallamshire Hospital, Glossop Road, Sheffield, South Yorkshire S10 2JF
**Tel:** 01142711900
**Web:** www.sth.nhs.uk
**Estd:** 2001
**Line of Business:** Public sector hospital activities, including nhs trusts
**Trading Style:** Royal Hallamshire Hospital, Genito-Urinary Medicine
**Issued Capital:** £1
**Principals:** D Stone Obe *(Chairman)*, N Priestly *(Financial)*, J Watts *(Personnel)*, C Welsh Obe, C Linacre, Sir A Cash Obe, C Suddes, J Donnelley
**Responsibilities**
**Senior:** Dotty Watkins *(Nurse Director)*
**Marketing:** Julie Phelan *(Communications and Marketing D)*
**Sales:** Kirsten Major *(Director of Strategy and Opera)*
**Branches:** Sheffield Teaching Hospitals Nhs Foundation Trust, Tree Route Work, Sheffield, South Yorkshire S10 3SF
**US SIC:** 8062 **UK SIC:** 95100
**Auditors:** KPMG LLP

| | 31-03-14 | 31-03-13 | 31-03-12 |
|---|---|---|---|
| TO | 932,870,000 | 909,487,000 | 716,978,000 |
| P/L | 7,264,000 | 2,416,000 | 7,979,000 |
| NW | 403,542,000 | 384,741,000 | 375,206,000 |
| WC | 20,156,000 | 14,200,000 | 16,056,000 |
| Emp. | 14,078 | 13,684 | 13,720 |

DUNS 21-888-1592
## Sheffield United (Hotel) Ltd
Europa House 20 Esplanade, Scarborough, North Yorkshire YO11 2AQ
**Tel:** 01142721100
**Web:** www.gymplus.co.uk
**Reg No:** 6072337 **Estd:** 2007 Private Limited Company
**Line of Business:** Hotels
**Issued Capital:** £5,640,286
**Directors:** Esplanade Director Limited, S R Mccabe
**Co. Secretary:** Esplanade Secretarial Services L
**US SIC:** 7011 **UK SIC:** 66500
**Bankers:** Bank Of Scotland (12-01-06)

| | 31-12-13 | 31-12-12 | 31-12-11 |
|---|---|---|---|
| TO | 2,979,357 | 2,776,184 | 4,374,436 |
| P/L | (954,320) | (360,316) | 191,037 |
| NW | (1,788,361) | (1,000,707) | (692,839) |
| WC | (11,668,175) | (11,234,259) | (11,330,523) |
| Emp. | 68 | 64 | 62 |

DUNS 21-279-1537 **Imp-Exp**
## Sheffield United Ltd
Bramall Lane, Cherry Street, Sheffield, South Yorkshire S2 4SU
**Tel:** 08719951899 **Fax:** 01142723030
**Web:** www.sufc.co.uk
**Reg No:** 0396956 **Estd:** 1944 Private Limited Company
**Line of Business:** Management activities of other non-financial holding companies not elsewhere classified
**Export Markets:** Worldwide
**Issued Capital:** £8,452,670
**Directors:** K C Mccabe, J J Tutton, S R Mccabe, S C Mccabe
**Co. Secretary:** Esplanade Secretarial Services L
**Branches:** Sheffield United Ltd, Unit 11 Farm Castle Duchess Pl, Glasgow, Lanarkshire G73 1DR
**US SIC:** 6711 **UK SIC:** 83962
**Auditors:** Grant Thornton UK LLP
**Bankers:** HSBC Bank plc (40-41-13)

| | 30-06-14 | 30-06-13 | 30-06-12 |
|---|---|---|---|
| TO | 128,865 | 8,928,000 | 10,263,000 |
| P/L | (3,448,324) | (4,634,000) | (12,978,000) |
| NW | 211,334 | (3,563,000) | 3,687,000 |
| WC | (22,955,692) | (21,587,000) | (14,696,000) |
| Emp. | 4 | 222 | 258 |

DUNS 50-558-7584
## Sheffield Wednesday Football Club Ltd
Hillsborough Stadium, Sheffield, South Yorkshire S6 1SW
**Tel:** 08719-951867
**Web:** www.swfc.co.uk
**Reg No:** 2509978 **Estd:** 2013 Private Limited Company
**Line of Business:** Sports clubs
**Issued Capital:** £1,000
**Directors:** M Mandaric, P Aldridge

**Responsibilities**
**Senior:** Allister Wilson *(Ticket Office Manager)*
**Sales:** Andy Daykin *(Commercial Director)*, Peter Pridmore *(Head of Retail)*
**Branches:** Sheffield Wednesday Football Club Ltd, Penistone Rd, Sheffield, South Yorkshire S6 1SW
**US SIC:** 7999 **UK SIC:** 97913
**Auditors:** Barber Harrison & Platt
**Bankers:** The Co-Operative Bank Plc (08-90-75)

| | 31-05-13 | 31-05-12 | 31-05-11 |
|---|---|---|---|
| TO | 14,916,000 | 10,944,000 | 9,401,000 |
| P/L | (3,737,000) | (5,191,000) | 15,784,000 |
| NW | 299,000 | 4,596,000 | 12,950,000 |
| WC | (16,543,000) | (13,230,000) | (9,142,000) |
| Emp. | 221 | 204 | 247 |

DUNS 23-590-0115
## Sheffield Wildlife Trust
Victoria Hall, 37 Stafford Road, Sheffield, South Yorkshire S2 2SF
**Tel:** 0114 263 4335
**Web:** www.wildsheffield.com
**Reg No:** 2287928 **Estd:** 1988 Private Company Limited By Guarantee
**Line of Business:** Technical and vocational secondary education
**Directors:** Mrs A P Clegg, P Quinn, A C Whiting, C H Pennell, Dr P H Warren, N Mcivor, Miss A Puritz, Mrs K Craik
**Co. Secretary:** Ms Elizabeth Ballard
**Responsibilities**
**Senior:** Anne Ashe *(Director)*, Laura Boyles *(Manager)*, Roderick Lees *(Partner)*, Richard Pethen *(Director)*, Frazer Snowdon *(Director)*, Margaret Spencer *(Partner)*, Greg Whitmore *(Director)*
**Sales:** Linda Baldwin *(Business Development Manager)*
**HR:** Andrew McNiven *(Human Resources and Payroll Ma)*
**Branches:** Sheffield Wildlife Trust, Elmfield House, Alma Road, Rotherham, South Yorkshire S60 2HZ
**US SIC:** 8249, 8421
**UK SIC:** 93300, 97700
**Auditors:** Hart Shaw LLP
**Bankers:** Unity Trust Bank Plc (08-60-01)

| | 31-03-14 | 31-03-13 | 31-03-12 |
|---|---|---|---|
| TO | 1,924,073 | 1,481,248 | 2,108,188 |
| P/L | 178,718 | 12,081 | 583,958 |
| NW | 1,668,455 | 1,530,940 | 1,471,278 |
| WC | 485,834 | 430,039 | 417,866 |
| Emp. | 65 | 57 | 57 |

DUNS 21-042-1446
## Sheffield Youth Offending Team
Star House, 43 Division Street, Sheffield, South Yorkshire S1 4GE
**Tel:** 01142288555
**Web:** www.sheffield-yos.org.uk
**Estd:** 2011
**Line of Business:** Probation services
**Responsibilities**
**Senior:** Joel Hanna *(Service Manager)*
**US SIC:** 9121 **UK SIC:** 91110
**Employees:** 100

DUNS 73-414-5662
## Shekinah Mission (Plymouth) Ltd
Bath Street, Plymouth, Devon PL1 3LT
**Tel:** 01752-203480 **Fax:** 01752-265916
**Web:** www.shekinahmission.co.uk
**Reg No:** 4687832 **Estd:** 2003 Private Company Limited By Guarantee
**Line of Business:** Community projects
**Directors:** A J Thomas, Dr J R Butler, R Morgan, Mrs M R Luckhurst, Mrs G Parker, A G Serpell, V Panandikar, W R Styring
**Co. Secretary:** Peter Woad
**US SIC:** 8321 **UK SIC:** 96111
**Bankers:** HSBC Bank plc (40-36-22)

| | 31-03-14 | 31-03-13 | 31-03-12 |
|---|---|---|---|
| TO | 1,192,242 | 1,438,020 | 1,851,878 |
| P/L | (31,025) | (110,399) | 42,088 |
| NW | 606,670 | 637,695 | 748,094 |
| WC | (29,463) | (25,192) | 53,257 |
| Emp. | 62 | 74 | 78 |

DUNS 21-752-4654
## Shel Holdings Europe Ltd
(**Subsidiary of:** Roundwood Holdings Limited)
400 Oxford Street, London W1A 1AB
**Tel:** 0800123400
**Reg No:** 7826605 **Estd:** 2011 Private Limited Company
**Line of Business:** Holding companies management activities
**Export Sales:** £469,200,000
**Issued Capital:** £5,002
**Directors:** J A Skelton, P G Kelly, A Batty, Mrs M J Stanford, A R Graham
**Co. Secretary:** Ms Sarah Hemsley
**US SIC:** 6711 **UK SIC:** 83962
**Auditors:** PricewaterhouseCoopers LLP

Following financial data are in thousands

| | 01-02-14 | 02-02-13 |
|---|---|---|
| TO | 999,200 | 1,122,000 |
| P/L | 25,700 | 39,400 |
| NW | (66,700) | (78,400) |
| WC | 169,000 | 95,900 |
| Emp. | 6,030 | 6,382 |

DUNS 22-935-2612
## Shelbourne Motors Ltd
334 Tandragee Road, Portadown, Craigavon, Co Armagh BT62 3RB
**Tel:** 02838396800 **Fax:** 02838395805
**Web:** www.shelbournemotors.com
**Reg No:** 0019993NI **VAT No:** 434202983
**Estd:** 1973 Private Limited Company
**Line of Business:** Car dealers (new & used)
**Issued Capital:** £30,000
**Directors:** F Ward, S P Ward, R F Ward, Mrs B Ward
**Co. Secretary:** Mrs Caroline Willis
**Responsibilities**
**Senior:** Darren Mcsherry *(Marketing Manager)*
**US SIC:** 5511, 7539
**UK SIC:** 65100, 67100
**Auditors:** Barry Thompson & Co
**Bankers:** Northern Bank Ltd (95-04-38)

| | 31-12-13 | 31-12-12 | 31-12-11 |
|---|---|---|---|
| TO | 28,281,326 | 23,601,013 | 26,808,668 |
| P/L | 362,191 | 117,292 | 192,099 |
| NW | 4,777,205 | 4,638,753 | 4,624,740 |
| WC | 240,480 | (598,745) | (164,310) |
| Emp. | 94 | 96 | 95 |

DUNS 21-908-7582 **Imp-Exp**
## Shelbourne Reynolds Engineering Ltd
(**Subsidiary of:** Russian Shelbourne Ltd)
Shepards Grove, Stanton, Bury St Edmunds, Suffolk IP31 2AR
**Web:** www.shelbourne.com
**Reg No:** 1055939 **VAT No:** 102008053
**Estd:** 1972 Private Limited Company
**Line of Business:** Agricultural machinery sales service and repair
**Export Markets:** Worldwide
**Issued Capital:** £298,278
**Directors:** N Gorbunov, N M Smith, Ms C J Bloomfield, Russian Shelbourne Limited, A E Budakov, A Kuznetsov
**Co. Secretary:** Mrs Claire Bloomfield
**US SIC:** 3559 **UK SIC:** 32863
**Auditors:** BDO Stoy Hayward
**Bankers:** National Westminster Bank Plc (60-04-23)

| | 30-09-13 | 30-09-12 | 30-09-11 |
|---|---|---|---|
| TO | 19,256,888 | 16,855,077 | 15,304,842 |
| P/L | 4,390,434 | 2,344,102 | 1,540,853 |
| NW | 8,364,430 | 5,172,289 | 4,482,490 |
| WC | 7,349,649 | 4,315,805 | 3,897,344 |
| Emp. | 114 | 112 | 99 |

DUNS 73-446-4600
## Shelbourne Senior Living Ltd
(**Subsidiary of:** Health Care Reit Inc.)
125 London Wall, London EC2Y 5AL
**Tel:** 01590684900
**Web:** www.shelbourneseniorliving.com
**Reg No:** 4699262 **Estd:** 2003 Private Limited Company
**Line of Business:** Representative office
**Issued Capital:** £1,805,562
**Directors:** Ms E C Ibele, K Crockett, J A Goodey, J Skiver
**US SIC:** 7399 **UK SIC:** 83954
**Auditors:** Myles C. Ronan & Associates
**Bankers:** National Westminster Bank Plc (56-00-27)

| | 31-12-13 | 31-12-12 | 31-12-11 |
|---|---|---|---|
| TO | 2,976,000 | 2,636,061 | 2,067,188 |
| P/L | 124,000 | (1,073,053) | (3,968,353) |
| NW | 9,803,000 | (9,155,892) | (8,082,839) |
| WC | 407,000 | (18,548,279) | (17,818,591) |
| Emp. | 93 | 99 | 75 |

DUNS 21-784-2589
## The Shelburne Hospital
Queen Alexandra Road, High Wycombe, Buckinghamshire HP11 2TR
**Tel:** 01494888700
**Web:** www.bmihealthcare.co.uk
**Estd:** 2008 Proprietorship
**Line of Business:** Hospitals
**Proprietor:** A Peake
**Responsibilities**
**Senior:** Rory Passmore *(Regional Director, South)*, john pullin *(manager)*
**IT:** Tracey McDermott *(Chief Information Officer)*
**Purchasing:** Garry Sitter *(Purchasing Manager)*
**US SIC:** 8062 **UK SIC:** 95100
**Employees:** 300

DUNS 21-156-5730
## Sheldon Clayton Holdings Ltd
Cygnus Point, Black Country New Road, West Bromwich, West Midlands B70 0BD
**Tel:** 0121 520 7070
**Web:** www.sheldonclaytongroup.co.uk
**Reg No:** 6844187 **VAT No:** 974962659
**Estd:** 2007 Private Limited Company
**Line of Business:** Management activities of holding companies
**Export Sales:** £3,721,913
**Trading Style:** Sheldon Clayton Logistics
**Issued Capital:** £14,211
**Directors:** Mrs K S Thomas, S Pollock, Ms P M Sheldon
**Responsibilities**
**Senior:** Lewis Griffiths *(Manager)*, Dave Kemp *(Manager)*
**US SIC:** 6711 **UK SIC:** 83962
**Auditors:** J.W. Hinks

| | 31-03-14 | 31-03-13 | 31-03-12 |
|---|---|---|---|
| TO | 16,389,753 | 15,322,754 | 15,680,050 |
| P/L | 797,913 | 607,267 | 593,559 |
| NW | 3,282,071 | 2,295,894 | 2,422,795 |
| WC | (1,561,703) | (1,661,729) | (1,636,192) |
| Emp. | 126 | 117 | 105 |

DUNS 21-716-8320
## Sheldon School
Hardenhuish Lane, Chippenham, Wiltshire SN14 6HJ
**Tel:** 01249651056
**Web:** www.sheldonschool.org
**Reg No:** 7556236 **Estd:** 1976 Private Company Limited By Guarantee
**Line of Business:** Schools (local authority)
**Directors:** P C Story, Ms V H Minors, Ms K P Sayers, J R Girvan, Mrs S M Brentnall, N C Spurdell, Mrs J M Needham, Ms K E Read
**Responsibilities**
**Senior:** Deborah Andrews *(Director)*, Nicholas Bartlett *(Director)*, Louise Carver *(Director)*, Dominic Corrywright *(Director)*, Caroline Fowke *(Director)*, Lynne Gill *(Sports Hall Supervsory Officer)*, Caroline Hiorns *(Director)*, Thomas Jacques *(Director)*, Robin Philip *(Director)*
**Finance:** Roger Hammett *(Finance Director)*
**Marketing:** Carl Orlans *(Marketing Director)*
**US SIC:** 7999 **UK SIC:** 97913
**Bankers:** Lloyds TSB Bank plc (30-92-16)

| | 31-08-14 | 31-08-13 | 31-08-12 |
|---|---|---|---|
| TO | 9,798,502 | 10,095,211 | 35,788,755 |
| P/L | 81,845 | 634,001 | 22,831,633 |
| NW | 23,113,479 | 23,266,634 | 22,570,633 |
| WC | 1,067,298 | 1,046,729 | 831,850 |
| Emp. | 176 | 177 | 173 |

DUNS 21-143-6273
## Shelfield Community Academy
Broad Way, Pelsall, Walsall, West Midlands WS4 1BW
**Tel:** 01922685777 **Fax:** 01922694267
**Web:** www.scacademy.co.uk
**Reg No:** 6745236 **Estd:** 2012 Private Company Limited By Guarantee
**Line of Business:** Schools (local authority)
**Directors:** Mrs J M Monckton, Mrs P Ward
**Responsibilities**
**Senior:** Bernard Dickenson *(Principal)*, Michael Riley *(Senior Vice Principle)*
**Finance:** Claire Pritchard *(Senior Finance Administrator)*
**Admin:** Claire Pritchard *(Senior Finance Administrator)*
**IT:** Amrick Taggar *(Senior IT Executive)*
**US SIC:** 8211 **UK SIC:** 93200

| | 31-08-14 | 31-08-13 | 31-08-12 |
|---|---|---|---|
| TO | 8,718,000 | 8,996,000 | 8,364,000 |
| P/L | (414,000) | (84,000) | (352,000) |
| NW | (939,000) | (706,000) | (693,000) |
| WC | 607,000 | 726,000 | 852,000 |
| Emp. | 173 | 169 | 165 |

DUNS 53-615-3992
## Shell Aviation Ltd
(**Subsidiary of:** Royal Dutch Shell Plc)
Site Office, London SE1 7NJ
**Tel:** 02079342000 **Fax:** 020-7546-2026
**Web:** www.shell.com
**Reg No:** 3420547 **Estd:** 1997 Private Limited Company
**Line of Business:** Agents involved in the sale of fuels, ores, metals and industrial chemicals
**Directors:** X Zhang, Ms V Guy, A R Harrison, A Pannall
**Co. Secretary:** Shell Corporate Secretary Limite
**Responsibilities**
**Senior:** John Lo *(General Manager, Strategy & Po)*
**Branches:** Shell Aviation Ltd, Aberdeen Airport Montrose Close, Aberdeen, Aberdeenshire AB21 0LL
**US SIC:** 5199 **UK SIC:** 61900
**Auditors:** PricewaterhouseCoopers LLP
**Employees:** 59

DUNS 21-026-5559 **Imp**
## Shell International Petroleum Co Ltd
(**Subsidiary of:** Royal Dutch Shell Plc)
Shell Ctr, 2 York Road, London SE1 7NA
**Tel:** 020 7934 4248
**Web:** www.shell.com
**Reg No:** 0621148 **VAT No:** 235763255
**Estd:** 1959 Private Limited Company
**Line of Business:** Wholesale of petroleum and petroleum products
**Issued Capital:** £196,400,000
**Directors:** H Von Der Linde, G R Van'T Hoff, B A Fermin
**Co. Secretary:** Shell Corporate Secretary Limite
**Branches:** Shell International Petroleum Co Ltd, 141 Bothwell Street, Glasgow, Lanarkshire G2 7EQ
**US SIC:** 7399, 5171
**UK SIC:** 83954, 61200
**Auditors:** PricewaterhouseCoopers LLP
**Bankers:** Lloyds TSB Bank plc (30-00-09)

Following financial data are in thousands

| | 31-12-13 | 31-12-12 | 31-12-11 |
|---|---|---|---|
| TO | 1,949,300 | 2,198,900 | 2,214,200 |
| P/L | (106,300) | (79,800) | 76,000 |
| NW | 105,300 | 207,600 | 281,700 |
| WC | 83,400 | 218,700 | 163,700 |
| Emp. | 975 | 955 | 1,084 |

DUNS 21-026-5542 **Imp**
## Shell International Trading & Shipping Co Ltd
(**Subsidiary of:** Royal Dutch Shell Plc)
Shell Mex House, London WC2R 0ZA
**Tel:** 02075465000
**Web:** www.shell.com
**Reg No:** 0525037 **VAT No:** 235763255
**Estd:** 1953 Private Limited Company
**Line of Business:** Activities of other transport agencies
**Trading Style:** Stasco
**Issued Capital:** £54,750,000
**Directors:** G Henderson, A J Lumens, S Preocanin, M Quartermain, M W Muller, M F Conway
**Co. Secretary:** Thomas Brandt
**Responsibilities**
**Senior:** Adam Ritchie *(General Manager - Global Tradi)*
**Sales:** Adam Ritchie *(General Manager - Global Tradi)*
**Branches:** Shell International Trading & Shipping Co Ltd, Shell Centre, York Road, London SE1 7NA
**US SIC:** 4712, 7399, 6211
**UK SIC:** 77002, 83954, 83100
**Auditors:** PricewaterhouseCoopers LLP
**Bankers:** Lloyds TSB Bank plc (30-00-09)

| | 31-12-13 | 31-12-12 | 31-12-11 |
|---|---|---|---|
| TA | 303,593,168 | 306,984,800 | 312,561,829 |
| P/L | 1,660,891 | (564,229) | (8,810,364) |
| NW | 105,045,160 | 107,987,040 | 104,627,550 |
| WC | 178,586,655 | 175,189,407 | 169,128,320 |
| Emp. | 907 | 800 | 803 |

DUNS 28-829-6114
## Shell Malaysia Ltd
(**Subsidiary of:** Royal Dutch Shell Plc)
Lloyds Tsb Bank Plc, London SE1 7LZ
**Tel:** 02079346244
**Reg No:** 0114428 **Estd:** 1911 Private Limited Company
**Line of Business:** Other business activities not elsewhere classified
**Directors:** H Z Wong, A B Ismail, I J Lo
**Co. Secretary:** Ms Yuen Tai
**Responsibilities**
**Senior:** Rodziah Zainudin *(Manager)*
**US SIC:** 7399, 7339
**UK SIC:** 83954
**Auditors:** PricewaterhouseCoopers LLP
**Employees:** 49
**Turnover:** £1,624,000

DUNS 23-220-4503
## Shell Marine Personnel (I O M) Ltd
(**Subsidiary of:** Royal Dutch Shell Plc)
Mannanan House, Market Square, Castletown, Douglas, Isle of Man IM9 1RB
**Tel:** 01624-825566
**Reg No:** 0031385M **Estd:** 1986 Private Limited Company
**Line of Business:** Employment service
**Issued Capital:** £100
**Principals:** G S Morton *(Managing)*, A G Chivers, Captain D Smith, H Mitchell, W J Mccallion, P B Games
**Co. Secretary:** Eddie Giddes
**Responsibilities**
**Senior:** William McCallion *(Director)*
**US SIC:** 7361 **UK SIC:** 83954
**Bankers:** Barclays Bank Plc (20-26-74)
**Employees:** 1,000

DUNS 21-778-2190
## Shell Uk
M5 Northbound Edingworth Weston Super, Mare, Bleadon, Weston-Super-Mare, Avon BS24 0LJ
**Tel:** 01934750659
**Web:** www.shell.co.uk
**Estd:** 2010
**Line of Business:** Petrol Service Stations
**Trading Style:** Welcome Break
**Responsibilities**
**Senior:** Kate Durban *(Unit Business Manager)*, David Hewish *(Manager)*
**US SIC:** 5541 **UK SIC:** 65200
**Employees:** 100

DUNS 22-955-3664
## Shelter the National Campaign for Homeless People Ltd
88 Old Street, London EC1V 9HU
**Tel:** 03445151199
**Web:** www.shelter.org.uk
**Reg No:** 1038133 **VAT No:** 626555624
**Estd:** 1972 Private Company Limited By Guarantee
**Line of Business:** Housing advice
**Trading Style:** Shelter Northwest Regional Office, Shelter Southwest Regional Office, Shelter Scottish Campaign for the Homeless
**Directors:** D J Myers, Ms J Simons, Ms J S Bentley, Ms R Hilary, S Somerville, Ms R Micklem, W A Rice, K A Macdonald
**Co. Secretary:** Daniel Oppenheimer
**Responsibilities**
**Senior:** Paola Barbarino *(Director)*, Anthony Crook *(Manager)*, Jonathan Kenworthy *(Director)*, Dominic McKenna *(Manager)*, Hugh Norton *(Manager)*, Campbell Robb *(Chief Executive)*, Gavin Sanderson *(Director)*, Daniel oppenheimer *(Financial director)*
**Finance:** Daniel oppenheimer *(Financial director)*
**IT:** Stuart McSkimming *(Head of IT)*
**HR:** Karen Simeon *(Human Resources Manager)*
**Health & Safety:** Paul Bassett *(Senior Health & Safety Officer)*
**Facilities:** Andy Christophi *(Facilities Manager)*
**Branches:** Shelter The National Campaign For Homeless People Ltd, 87 High Street, Stoke-On-Trent, Staffordshire ST6 5TA
**US SIC:** 8321, 2711
**UK SIC:** 96111, 47512
**Auditors:** Deloitte & Touche LLP
**Bankers:** Barclays Bank Plc (20-80-57)

| | 31-03-14 | 31-03-13 | 31-03-12 |
|---|---|---|---|
| TO | 57,540,000 | 53,537,000 | 52,859,000 |
| P/L | 35,200,000 | (5,249,000) | 1,437,000 |
| NW | 18,737,000 | 17,562,000 | 22,158,000 |
| WC | 3,148,000 | 3,157,000 | 3,481,000 |
| Emp. | 1,122 | 1,099 | 1,014 |

DUNS 76-558-0741
## Shelter Trading Ltd
**(Subsidiary of:** Shelter the National Campaign for Homeless People)
88 Old Street, London EC1V 9HU
**Tel:** 08445152000
**Web:** www.sheltercymru.org.uk
**Reg No:** 2573404 **Estd:** 1991 Private Limited Company
**Line of Business:** Other retail sale in non-specialised stores
**Issued Capital:** £80,000
**Director:** D A Oppenheimer
**Co. Secretary:** Mrs Joanna Quirk
**Responsibilities**
**Senior:** Paola Barbarino *(Board Member)*, Dominic McKenna *(Manager)*, Hugh Norton *(Manager)*, Denis Robertson Sullivan *(Chairman)*
**Finance:** Tracy Griffin *(Fundraising Director)*
**Marketing:** Tracy Griffin *(Fundraising Director)*
**IT:** Stuart McSkimming *(Head of IT)*
**HR:** Karen Simeon *(Human Resources Manager)*
**Health & Safety:** Paul Bassett *(Senior Health & Safety Officer)*
**Facilities:** Andy Christophi *(Facilities Manager)*
**Operations:** Diana Fawcett *(Operations Director)*
**Branches:** Shelter Trading Ltd, 7 Manor Rd, Gravesend, Kent DA12 1AA
**US SIC:** 5399, 5931
**UK SIC:** 65600, 65400
**Auditors:** Binder Hamlyn

| | 31-03-14 | 31-03-13 | 31-03-12 |
|---|---|---|---|
| TO | 3,386,070 | 1,978,256 | 1,870,011 |
| NW | 95,113 | 95,113 | 95,113 |
| WC | 95,113 | 95,113 | 95,113 |
| Emp. | 51 | 51 | 52 |

DUNS 77-963-6471
## Shelton Care Ltd
75-77 Shelton New Road, Stoke-On-Trent, Staffordshire ST4 7AA
**Tel:** 01782263104
**Web:** www.richmondcaregroup.com
**Reg No:** 3066903 **Estd:** 1995 Private Limited Company
**Line of Business:** Nursing homes
**Trading Style:** Richmond Care Group
**Issued Capital:** £200
**Directors:** Ms L B Vincent, J W Cullen, D Vincent
**Co. Secretary:** Ms Rebecca Bostock
**US SIC:** 8051, 8091
**UK SIC:** 95100, 95200
**Bankers:** The Royal Bank Of Scotland Plc (16-20-35)

| | 31-08-13 | 31-08-12 | 31-08-11 |
|---|---|---|---|
| TO | 7,035,976 | 6,463,898 | 6,085,884 |
| P/L | 67,100 | 173,280 | 263,776 |
| NW | 5,838,975 | 5,689,054 | 5,622,022 |
| WC | 713,117 | 738,937 | 830,506 |
| Emp. | 347 | 301 | 277 |

DUNS 22-171-2354
## Shenfield Taxis Ltd
4 Woodbrook Crescent, Billericay, Essex CM12 0EQ
**Tel:** 01277225544
**Web:** www.shenfieldtaxis-limited.co.uk
**Reg No:** 4189590 **Estd:** 2001 Private Limited Company
**Line of Business:** Taxi operation
**Issued Capital:** £120,000
**Director:** Ms K Schofield
**US SIC:** 4121 **UK SIC:** 72200
**Auditors:** The Mudd Partnership

| | 30-09-13 | 30-09-12 | 31-09-11 |
|---|---|---|---|
| TA | 29,073 | 29,778 | 25,770 |
| NW | 94 | (9,258) | (5,717) |
| WC | 29 | 1,155 | 4,644 |

DUNS 77-905-0108
## Shepherd & Wedderburn Llp
1 Exchange Crescent, Edinburgh, Midlothian EH3 8UL
**Tel:** 0131-228-9900
**Web:** www.shepwedd.co.uk
**Reg No:** 0300895SO **Estd:** 2013
**Line of Business:** Solicitors
**Responsibilities**
**Senior:** Colin Archibald *(Partner)*, Patrick Bell *(Non-designated Limited Liabili)*, Andrew Blain *(Designated Limited Liability P)*, Rodger Cairns *(Partner)*, Paul Carlyle *(Non-designated Limited Liabili)*, James Dobie *(Partner)*, Paul Donald *(Partner)*, Gordon Downie *(Partner)*, Guy Harvey *(Non-designated Limited Liabili)*, Lilian Hawthorn *(Non-designated Limited Liabili)*, Andrew Holehouse *(Partner)*, Andrew Kinnes *(Partner)*, Danny Lee *(Partner)*, Christopher McGill *(Partner)*, Euan Mcleod *(Partner - Construction)*, Edwin Mustard *(Partner)*, Fiona Paterson *(Partner)*, Neil Rainey *(Partner)*, Scott Ritchie *(Partner)*, Ian Rollo *(Non-designated Limited Liabili)*, Malcolm Rust *(Partner)*, Karen Shaw *(Non-designated Limited Liabili)*, Hugh Smith *(Partner)*, Stephen Trombala *(Partner)*, James Will *(Partner & Chairman)*, Robert Winter *(Non-designated Limited Liabili)*
**Finance:** Gillian Arthur *(Tax Manager)*, Patrick Bell *(Non-designated Limited Liabili)*, Andrew Blain *(Designated Limited Liability P)*
**Sales:** Cara Gorman *(Business Development Executive)*, Sarah McLean *(Business Development Director)*
**Admin:** Kristine Dudgeon *(Personal Assistant)*, Gail Dundas *(Personal Assistant)*, Hannah Quig *(Personal Assistant)*
**IT:** Paddy Toner *(IT Director)*
**HR:** Alison Sutherland *(HR Manager)*
**US SIC:** 8111 **UK SIC:** 83500
**Auditors:** Grant Thornton UK LLP
**Bankers:** Bank Of Scotland (80-11-30)

| | 30-04-14 | 30-04-13 | 30-04-12 |
|---|---|---|---|
| TO | 38,260,000 | 35,864,000 | 36,570,000 |
| P/L | 14,356,000 | 6,541,000 | 6,775,000 |
| NW | (466,000) | 7,521,000 | 10,379,000 |
| WC | 12,534,000 | 11,862,000 | 12,091,000 |
| Emp. | 357 | 369 | 375 |

DUNS 21-623-2579 **Imp**
## Shepherd & Woodward Ltd
109-113 High Street, Oxford, Oxfordshire OX1 4BT
**Web:** www.shepherdandwoodward.co.uk
**Reg No:** 0610771 **Estd:** 1958 Private Limited Company
**Line of Business:** Retail sale of clothing
**Issued Capital:** £31,000
**Principals:** J R Venables *(Chairman)*, P T Venables *(Financial)*, A J Palfreyman
**Co. Secretary:** Michael Crabtree
**Responsibilities**
**Senior:** Martin Neale *(Manager)*
**Branches:** Shepherd & Woodward Ltd, Walters & Co (Oxford) Ltd, 9-11 Turl Street, Oxford, Oxfordshire OX1 3DN
**US SIC:** 5611, 5661

**UK SIC:** 64500, 64600
**Auditors:** Wenn Townsend
**Bankers:** Barclays Bank Plc (20-65-18)

| | 31-01-14 | 31-01-13 | 31-01-12 |
|---|---|---|---|
| TO | 4,716,180 | 5,744,093 | 5,932,582 |
| P/L | 452,247 | 250,226 | 463,448 |
| NW | 6,040,363 | 5,945,272 | 6,009,621 |
| WC | 2,601,665 | 2,471,954 | 2,527,289 |
| Emp. | 67 | 81 | 84 |

DUNS 21-245-0225
## Shepherd Building Group Ltd
Huntington House, Jockey Lane, Huntington, York, North Yorkshire YO32 9XW
**Tel:** 01904650700 **Fax:** 01904650701
**Web:** www.shepherd-group.com
**Reg No:** 0653663 **VAT No:** 170779243
**Estd:** 1960 Private Limited Company
**Line of Business:** Management activities of holding companies
**Trading Style:** Shepherd Construction, Portakabin
**Issued Capital:** £860,219
**Directors:** A M Shepherd, P M Shepherd, M Perkins, K D Parker, D P Carter, S Price, D J Williams
**Co. Secretary:** Philip Clarke
**Responsibilities**
**Marketing:** Kurt Calder *(Corporate Relations Manager)*
**HR:** Liz Dean *(Personnel Director)*
**Health & Safety:** Liz Dean *(Personnel Director)*
**US SIC:** 6711 **UK SIC:** 83962
**Auditors:** KPMG LLP
**Bankers:** HSBC Bank plc (40-46-78)

| | 30-06-14 | 30-06-13 | 30-06-12 |
|---|---|---|---|
| TO | 686,000,000 | 748,000,000 | 671,600,000 |
| P/L | 11,400,000 | 13,000,000 | 27,600,000 |
| NW | 220,500,000 | 228,500,000 | 227,300,000 |
| WC | 102,500,000 | 122,900,000 | 124,300,000 |
| Emp. | 3,235 | 3,228 | 3,146 |

DUNS 21-245-0241
## Shepherd Construction Ltd
**(Subsidiary of:** Shepherd Building Group Ltd)
Frederick House, Fulford Road, York, North Yorkshire YO10 4EA
**Tel:** 01904634431 **Fax:** 01904610175
**Web:** www.shepherd-construction.co.uk
**Reg No:** 0201860 **VAT No:** 450761359
**Estd:** 1924 Private Limited Company
**Line of Business:** Building construction management
**Issued Capital:** £6,000,000
**Directors:** Mrs L G Stevenson, M Porter, M Perkins
**Co. Secretary:** Philip Clarke
**Responsibilities**
**Senior:** Kelly Atherton *(Human Business Parter)*, Jason Dimelow *(Senior Build Manager)*, Philip Greer *(Manager)*, Allan McDougall *(Chief Executive)*, Richard Vining *(Chief Executive)*
**Marketing:** Francesca Tomlimson *(Divisional Marketing Director)*
**Sales:** Gary Walton *(Commercial Director)*
**Admin:** Louise Gaze *(Personal Assistant)*
**IT:** Jon Mangham *(Project Manager)*, Steve Slater *(ICT Manager)*
**HR:** Kelly Atherton *(Human Business Parter)*
**Operations:** Mick Bodecott *(Project Director)*
**Engineering:** Graham Pycroft *(Chief Estimator of Infrastruct)*
**Branches:** Shepherd Construction Ltd, Woodgate Business Park, Birmingham, West Midlands B32 3DS
**US SIC:** 1622, 1522
**UK SIC:** 50200, 50100
**Auditors:** KPMG LLP
**Bankers:** HSBC Bank plc (40-47-31)

| | 30-06-14 | 30-06-13 | 30-06-12 |
|---|---|---|---|
| TO | 240,447,000 | 356,480,000 | 297,420,000 |
| P/L | (8,165,000) | 3,039,000 | 4,665,000 |
| NW | 20,143,000 | 25,777,000 | 22,978,000 |
| WC | 18,035,000 | 27,867,000 | 23,182,000 |
| Emp. | 415 | 435 | 443 |

DUNS 67-228-3561
## Shepherd Direct Ltd
3-4 Regan Way, Chilwell, Beeston, Nottingham, Nottinghamshire NG9 6RZ
**Tel:** 08702111399
**Web:** www.shepherddirect.co.uk
**Reg No:** 6055271 **Estd:** 2007 Private Limited Company
**Line of Business:** Management activities of holding companies
**Issued Capital:** £4,000,000
**Directors:** C C Hickling, I J Fergusson, P R Gratton, R M Clifford, J W Bloomer, N V Tamplin, G P Brewster
**Co. Secretary:** Ms Catherine Staley
**US SIC:** 6711 **UK SIC:** 83962
**Bankers:** HSBC Bank plc (40-35-18)

| | 31-03-14 | 31-03-13 | 31-03-12 |
|---|---|---|---|
| TO | 19,337,772 | 15,301,871 | 12,915,439 |
| P/L | (8,607,699) | 511,715 | (1,611,786) |
| NW | (10,874,023) | (4,779,303) | (5,819,843) |
| WC | (7,585,633) | (1,399,493) | (1,137,508) |
| Emp. | 205 | 174 | 178 |

DUNS 23-879-3785
## Shepherd Foods Holdings Ltd
2-5 Duke Of York Square, Chelsea, London SW3 4LY
**Tel:** 02077300651 **Fax:** 02072408633
**Web:** www.partridges.co.uk
**Reg No:** 3870621 **Estd:** 1999 Private Limited Company
**Line of Business:** Supermarkets
**Issued Capital:** £100,000
**Directors:** J A Shepherd, R C Shepherd
**Co. Secretary:** Sylvester Gomes
**US SIC:** 5411 **UK SIC:** 64100

| | 29-12-13 | 31-12-12 | 25-12-11 |
|---|---|---|---|
| TO | 4,129,703 | 4,143,151 | 4,078,061 |
| P/L | 221,156 | 237,331 | 254,720 |
| NW | 6,059,961 | 5,940,168 | 5,810,669 |
| WC | 832,597 | 790,424 | 800,602 |
| Emp. | 56 | 62 | 66 |

DUNS 21-613-6259 **Imp-Exp**
## Shepherd Neame Ltd
17 Court Street, Faversham, Kent ME13 7AX
**Tel:** 01795-532206 **Fax:** 01795-538907
**Web:** www.shepherdneame.co.uk
**Reg No:** 0138256 **VAT No:** 472781717
**Estd:** 1914 Private Limited Company
**Line of Business:** Brewers
**Export Markets:** France, Sweden, U S A
**Export Sales:** £2,730,000
**Trading Style:** Todd Vintners Vine Inn (The), King William Iv, The Wheelright Arms, Flying Horse Inn
**Issued Capital:** £12,817,500
**Principals:** J B Neame *(Managing)*, W J Brett, O W Barnes, G H Barnes, J H Leigh Pemberton, M H Templeman, M J Rider, N J Bunting
**Co. Secretary:** Robin Duncan
**Responsibilities**
**Senior:** Graeme Craig *(Sales & Marketing Director)*, Thomas Falcon *(Production Director)*
**Marketing:** Graeme Craig *(Sales & Marketing Director)*
**Sales:** Graeme Craig *(Sales & Marketing Director)*, Giles Hilton *(Head of Sales)*
**Health & Safety:** Robert Pooley *(Health & Safety Officer)*
**Facilities:** Martin Godden *(Property Officer)*
**Engineering:** Thomas Falcon *(Production Director)*
**Branches:** Shepherd Neame Ltd, 72 Margate Road, Ramsgate, Kent CT11 7SG
**US SIC:** 2082, 5182, 7011, 5813
**UK SIC:** 42702, 61700, 66500, 66200
**Auditors:** Deloitte LLP
**Bankers:** National Westminster Bank Plc (56-00-51)

| | 29-06-13 | 30-06-12 | 25-06-11 |
|---|---|---|---|
| TO | 134,906,000 | 133,025,000 | 121,346,000 |
| P/L | 7,107,000 | 9,061,000 | 6,485,000 |
| NW | 125,802,000 | 123,170,000 | 119,526,000 |
| WC | 4,844,000 | 4,657,000 | 7,913,000 |
| Emp. | 1,211 | 1,178 | 1,098 |

DUNS 21-101-7039
## Shepherd Offshore Group Ltd
Offshore Technology Park, 1 Rendle Road, Newcastle-Upon-Tyne, Tyne and Wear NE6 3NH
**Tel:** 01912629614 **Fax:** 01912639872
**Web:** www.shepherdoffshore.com
**Reg No:** 6450756 **Estd:** 2007 Private Limited Company
**Line of Business:** Other letting of own property
**Issued Capital:** £1,004
**Directors:** W F Shepherd, B S Shepherd
**Co. Secretary:** Shaun Ward
**Responsibilities**
**Senior:** Ted Lincoln *(General Manager)*
**Admin:** Tracy Hogg *(Office Manager)*
**Operations:** Robert Swalwell *(Operations Manager)*
**US SIC:** 6519, 4226
**UK SIC:** 85000, 77003
**Bankers:** Barclays Bank Plc (20-62-09)

| | 30-04-14 | 30-04-13 | 30-04-12 |
|---|---|---|---|
| TO | 27,732,874 | 19,212,551 | 15,375,060 |
| P/L | 4,685,964 | 4,978,283 | 3,910,366 |
| NW | 46,266,886 | 49,931,604 | 46,352,612 |
| WC | 40,304,180 | 37,354,625 | 33,956,109 |
| Emp. | 82 | 72 | 66 |

DUNS 23-294-4058 **Imp**
## Shepherd Widnes Ltd
**(Subsidiary of:** Shepherd Widnes Ltd.)
Moss Bank Road, Widnes, Cheshire WA8 0RU
**Tel:** 01514 249156 **Fax:** 0151-424-3539
**Web:** www.shepherdwidnes.com
**Reg No:** 0018633FC **VAT No:** 643776019
**Estd:** 1995 Foreign Company
**Line of Business:** Representative office
**Directors:** J Shepherd, T L Shepherd
**US SIC:** 2899 **UK SIC:** 25670

DUNS 23-212-9445

## Shepherds Bush Housing Association

1 Essex Place Square, Chiswick, London W4 5UJ
**Tel:** 020-8996-4200
**Web:** www.sbha.co.uk
**Reg No:** 0016442IP **VAT No:** 626822238
**Estd:** 1963 Friendly Society
**Line of Business:** Housing associations societies trusts & co-operatives
**Trading Style:** Shepherds Bush Housing Group
**Principals:** W Patrickson *(Chairman)*, P Warner, L Thomson, D Margetts, F Churamowicz, R Lawrence, M Mccarthy, G Pilkington
**Co. Secretary:** P Humberstone
**Responsibilities**
**Senior:** M Amucha *(Director)*, R Brunwin *(Director)*, Paul Doe *(Chief Executive)*, Patricia Humberstone *(Financial Director)*, M McCarthy *(Director)*, Amanda Morrison *(Director Of Housing Operations)*, J Navin *(Director)*, Dudley Savill *(Director)*
**Finance:** Patricia Humberstone *(Financial Director)*
**Sales:** Mary Caravan *(Director, Business Support)*
**Facilities:** Pam Sedgwick *(Director, Staying First)*
**Purchasing:** Anil Pandey *(?Building Services Procurement)*
**Engineering:** Patrick Ochola *(Maintenance Surveyor)*
**US SIC:** 8321 **UK SIC:** 96111
**Auditors:** BDO LLP

| | 31-03-12 | 31-03-11 | 31-03-10 |
|---|---|---|---|
| TO | 38,192,000 | 40,498,000 | 43,829,000 |
| P/L | 2,646,000 | 2,175,000 | 2,339,000 |
| NW | 27,841,000 | 27,337,000 | 32,527,000 |
| WC | 8,667,000 | 4,663,000 | 3,433,000 |
| Emp. | 219 | 237 | 179 |

DUNS 23-626-7977

## The Shepherds Friendly Society Ltd

Shepherds House, Stockport Road, Cheadle, Cheshire SK8 2AA
**Tel:** 01614281212
**Web:** www.shepherdsfriendly.co.uk
**Reg No:** 0000240IP **Estd:** 1826 Friendly Society
**Line of Business:** Life assurance services
**Principals:** I Turner *(Chairman)*, Ms E A Mason, P A Hill, A D Mckinnon, J L Semple, J Walker, M Symonds, E E Mills
**Responsibilities**
**Senior:** Alistair McKinnon *(Director)*, Robert Mewha *(Director)*
**Finance:** Diane Payne *(Financial Director)*
**Marketing:** Max Jarrold *(Marketing Executive)*, Libbi Martin *(Marketing Manager)*, Ann-Marie O'Dea *(Marketing Manager)*
**Admin:** Sam Chivers *(Information Systems Manager)*
**IT:** Sam Chivers *(Information Systems Manager)*
**US SIC:** 6411, 6111
**UK SIC:** 83200, 81501
**Bankers:** The Royal Bank Of Scotland Plc (16-00-01)
**Employees:** 90

DUNS 45-884-8272

## Shepley Spring Ltd

P O Box 645, Shepley, Huddersfield, West Yorkshire HD8 8EA
**Tel:** 01484-609330
**Web:** www.shepleyspring.co.uk
**Reg No:** 3222399 **VAT No:** 675449885
**Estd:** 1996 Private Limited Company
**Line of Business:** Manufacture of mineral waters and soft drinks
**Trading Style:** Shepley Spring Ltd
**Issued Capital:** £12,502
**Directors:** J Barlow, J S Smith, C A Smith, J M Smith
**Co. Secretary:** Alison Horn
**US SIC:** 2086 **UK SIC:** 42831
**Auditors:** Walker & Sutcliffe
**Bankers:** Barclays Bank Plc (20-43-04)

| | 31-01-14 | 31-01-13 | 31-01-12 |
|---|---|---|---|
| TO | 14,986,505 | 14,107,097 | 12,417,845 |
| P/L | 326,216 | 169,488 | 104,237 |
| NW | 918,576 | 791,995 | 643,786 |
| WC | 866,584 | 726,077 | 587,108 |
| Emp. | 52 | 49 | 54 |

DUNS 22-950-6274

## Shepperton Group Ltd

**(Subsidiary of:** Shepperton Ventures Limited)
28 Circus Mews, Bath, Avon BA1 2PW
**Tel:** 01225422569
**Web:** www.shepperton.com
**Reg No:** 1305567 **Estd:** 1977 Private Limited Company
**Line of Business:** Management activities of holding companies
**Issued Capital:** £2,020
**Principals:** G K Davis *(Chairman and Managing)*, G P Braddick, R Power
**Co. Secretary:** Graham Braddick
**US SIC:** 6711, 1522
**UK SIC:** 83962, 50100
**Auditors:** Nexia Smith & Williamson LLP
**Bankers:** The Co-Operative Bank Plc (08-90-08)

| | 30-04-14 | 30-04-13 | 30-04-12 |
|---|---|---|---|
| TO | 19,601,759 | 11,889,352 | 13,165,411 |
| P/L | 94,881 | (130,868) | (106,233) |
| NW | 7,931,519 | 7,858,381 | 7,989,249 |
| WC | 6,973,957 | 7,012,330 | 7,232,004 |
| Emp. | 54 | 47 | 56 |

DUNS 28-859-7073

## Shepperton Hotels Ltd

**(Subsidiary of:** Shepperton Hotels Holdings Ltd)
Church Square, Shepperton, Middlesex TW17 9JZ
**Tel:** 01932243377
**Web:** www.homecountiespubs.co.uk
**Reg No:** 0867971 **VAT No:** 208696144
**Estd:** 1966 Private Limited Company
**Line of Business:** Hotels
**Issued Capital:** £100,000
**Directors:** D G Gordon, A R Gordon, J D Gordon
**Co. Secretary:** Patrick Gordon
**Responsibilities**
**Senior:** Douglas Gordon *(Manager)*
**Branches:** Shepperton Hotels Ltd, Church Square, Shepperton, Middlesex TW17 9JZ
**US SIC:** 7011 **UK SIC:** 66500
**Auditors:** Coventry Nicholls
**Bankers:** National Westminster Bank Plc (56-00-03)

| | 30-09-13 | 30-09-12 | 30-09-11 |
|---|---|---|---|
| TO | N/A | N/A | 3,563,599 |
| P/L | N/A | N/A | 440,773 |
| NW | 4,033,998 | 3,485,186 | 3,061,639 |
| WC | (2,341,075) | (2,187,103) | (1,933,822) |

DUNS 77-490-6432

## Shepperton Studios Ltd

**(Subsidiary of:** Pinewood Shepperton Plc)
Studios Road, Shepperton, Middlesex TW17 0QD
**Tel:** 01932-562611 **Fax:** 01753656140
**Web:** www.pinewoodgroup.com
**Reg No:** 2974333 **Estd:** 1993 Private Limited Company
**Line of Business:** Film production services and studios
**Issued Capital:** £2
**Directors:** N Shulman, I P Dunleavy, D A Wight, A M Smith, C Naisby, N D Smith
**Co. Secretary:** Andrew Smith
**Responsibilities**
**Senior:** Peter Hicks *(Studio Manager)*, Ronald Stocks *(Manager)*
**Sales:** Peter Hicks *(Studio Manager)*
**IT:** Peter Hicks *(Studio Manager)*
**HR:** Emma Norman *(Training Manager)*
**Facilities:** Peter Hicks *(Studio Manager)*
**Branches:** Shepperton Studios Ltd, Shepperton Studios, Studios Road, Shepperton, Middlesex TW17 0QD
**US SIC:** 7819, 4833
**UK SIC:** 97111, 97411
**Auditors:** Ernst & Young
**Bankers:** Barclays Bank Plc (20-78-98)

| | 31-03-14 | 31-03-13 | 31-03-12 |
|---|---|---|---|
| TO | 12,624,000 | 12,258,000 | 14,559,000 |
| P/L | 2,525,000 | 2,616,000 | 2,994,000 |
| NW | 40,079,000 | 37,550,000 | 35,268,000 |
| WC | 35,218,000 | 32,880,000 | 31,048,000 |
| Emp. | 67 | 69 | 68 |

DUNS 57-844-4341

## Shepshed Carers Ltd

Field House, 19-23 Field Street, Loughborough, Leicestershire LE12 9AL
**Tel:** 01509-505243
**Web:** www.shepshedcarers.co.uk
**Reg No:** 2897384 **Estd:** 1994 Private Limited Company
**Line of Business:** Other human health activities
**Principals:** Mrs S C Pollard *(Financial)*, Mrs A A Johnson
**Co. Secretary:** Lee Sanders
**Responsibilities**
**Senior:** Christine Obahiagbon *(Manager)*
**US SIC:** 8091 **UK SIC:** 95200
**Auditors:** K Rimmer
**Bankers:** HSBC Bank plc (40-30-24)

| | 31-03-14 | 31-03-13 | 31-03-12 |
|---|---|---|---|
| TO | 1,488,928 | 1,343,429 | 1,227,070 |
| P/L | 9,144 | 3,603 | 5,702 |
| NW | 107,196 | 99,227 | 96,625 |
| WC | 93,392 | 87,852 | 82,677 |

DUNS 21-324-5140

## Shepton Mallet Community Hospital

Old Wells Road, Shepton Mallet, Somerset BA4 4PG
**Tel:** 01749333600
**Web:** www.somersetpct.nhs.uk
**Estd:** 2009 Proprietorship
**Line of Business:** Hospitals
**Proprietor:** Mrs K Thomas
**Responsibilities**
**Senior:** Chester Barnes *(Manager)*
**Admin:** Pauline Ashford *(Personal Assistant)*
**US SIC:** 8062 **UK SIC:** 95100
**Employees:** 100

DUNS 23-555-0878

## Shepway District Council

Castle Hill Avenue, Civic Centre, Folkestone, Kent CT20 2QY
**Tel:** 01303850388
**Web:** www.shepway.gov.uk
**VAT No:** 202376008
**Line of Business:** Local government
**Principals:** R A Pascoe *(Chairman)*, L Avory, I R Russell, S F Hagues, R Thompson
**Responsibilities**
**Senior:** Kathryn Beldon *(Deputy Chief Executive Officer)*, George Bunting *(Chairman)*, Ed Elcock *(Head of Technical Services)*, Tamasin Jarrett *(Executive)*, Mike Macdonald *(Executive)*, Bob Porter *(Housing Manager)*, Shelley Squance *(Manager)*
**Finance:** Gary Whittaker *(Financial Services Director)*
**Marketing:** Sandy Fleming *(Marketing Manager)*
**IT:** Ed Elcock *(Head of Technical Services)*, Steve Makin *(Computer Manager)*
**Health & Safety:** Arthur Atkins *(Health & Safety Officer)*
**Facilities:** Ed Elcock *(Head of Technical Services)*
**Operations:** Simon Burchell *(Contracts Manager)*
**Purchasing:** Dreda Van-Beer *(Procurement Manager)*
**Branches:** Shepway District Council, Chart Road, Folkestone, Kent CT19 4EW
**US SIC:** 9121 **UK SIC:** 91110
**Employees:** 450

DUNS 21-442-7288 **Imp-Exp**

## Sher Brothers (Glasgow) Ltd

39-45 Stromness Street, Glasgow, Lanarkshire G5 8HS
**Tel:** 0141-429-3671
**Web:** www.sherbros.demon.co.uk
**Reg No:** 0053476SC **VAT No:** 261951258
**Estd:** 1973 Private Limited Company
**Line of Business:** Clothing wholesale and suppliers
**Export Markets:** Europe
**Issued Capital:** £8,931,000
**Co. Secretary:** Munawar Hayat
**Responsibilities**
**Senior:** Tariq Ali *(Manager)*, Nazim Bashair *(IT Director)*
**IT:** Nazim Bashair *(IT Director)*
**Purchasing:** J Alley *(Buyer)*
**Branches:** Sher Brothers (Glasgow) Ltd, 39-45 Stromness Street, Glasgow, Lanarkshire G5 8HS
**US SIC:** 5133, 5199
**UK SIC:** 61600, 61900
**Auditors:** Ballantyne & Co
**Bankers:** Bank Of Scotland (80-07-67)

| | 31-12-12 | 31-12-11 | 31-12-10 |
|---|---|---|---|
| TO | 56,505,418 | 54,535,281 | 58,652,947 |
| P/L | (393,967) | (182,654) | 427,648 |
| NW | 19,623,821 | 19,735,926 | 20,278,876 |
| WC | 3,110,363 | 3,357,285 | 3,523,997 |
| Emp. | 184 | 194 | 183 |

DUNS 49-180-7335

## Sheraton Hotels (U.K.) P L C

Bath Road, Hayes, Middlesex UB3 5BP
**Tel:** 02087592535 **Fax:** 02087509150
**Web:** www.sherriton.com
**Reg No:** 3114981 **Estd:** 1969 Public Limited Company
**Line of Business:** Hotels
**Trading Style:** Starward Hotels & Resorts
**Issued Capital:** £33,461,672
**Directors:** C Bennett, M T Dojlidko
**Co. Secretary:** Stefaan Haegeman
**Responsibilities**
**Senior:** Jireiah Kececian *(CEO, Managing Director)*, Naval Patel *(Manager)*
**HR:** Jane Clements *(Human Resources Manager)*
**US SIC:** 7011 **UK SIC:** 66500
**Auditors:** Ernst & Young LLP

| | 31-12-13 | 31-12-12 | 31-12-11 |
|---|---|---|---|
| TA | 64,165,000 | 77,962,000 | 84,586,000 |
| P/L | (10,975,000) | 4,846,000 | 6,729,000 |
| NW | 42,972,000 | 55,235,000 | 51,486,000 |
| WC | 20,113,000 | 17,181,000 | 5,332,000 |

DUNS 21-006-2629

## Sherborne Holdings Ltd

45-47 Ashley Road, Bournemouth, Dorset BH1 4LG
**Tel:** 01202303585
**Reg No:** 6307541 **Estd:** 2007 Private Limited Company
**Line of Business:** Management activities of holding companies
**Issued Capital:** £1,946,992
**Directors:** C J Sherbone, J R Sherbone, M J Meyer
**Co. Secretary:** Raymond Pride
**US SIC:** 6711 **UK SIC:** 83962

| | 31-03-14 | 31-03-13 | 31-03-12 |
|---|---|---|---|
| TO | 50,658,053 | 44,083,540 | 45,827,211 |
| P/L | 3,531,547 | 2,003,701 | 3,521,200 |
| NW | 21,846,113 | 18,777,445 | 20,703,375 |
| WC | 6,566,375 | 4,574,952 | 7,385,772 |
| Emp. | 362 | 347 | 341 |

DUNS 50-472-9385

## Sherborne Leather Ltd.

Pasture Lane, Bradford, West Yorkshire BD14 6LT
**Web:** www.sherborneupholstery.co.uk
**Reg No:** 2451855 **Estd:** 1989 Private Limited Company
**Line of Business:** Furniture for home and office
**Issued Capital:** £2
**Director:** C D Fort
**Co. Secretary:** Andrew Sparkes
**Responsibilities**
**IT:** Heath Hague *(IT System Manager)*
**US SIC:** 2599 **UK SIC:** 46720

| | 30-06-14 | 30-06-13 | 30-06-12 |
|---|---|---|---|
| TA | 2 | 2 | 2 |
| NW | 2 | 2 | 2 |

DUNS 23-543-4078

## Sherborne Preparatory School

Acreman Street, Sherborne, Dorset DT9 3NY
**Tel:** 01935812097 **Fax:** 01935-813948
**Web:** www.sherborneprep.org
**Reg No:** 3541911 **Estd:** 1998 Private Limited Company
**Line of Business:** Schools (independent)
**Directors:** Ms J M Taylor, Mrs T Cosham, P H Lapping, C J Davis, D J Fowler Watt, T D Hague, Mrs J C Dwyer, C Banbury
**Co. Secretary:** Michael Burton Brown
**Responsibilities**
**Senior:** Fiona Ashley Miller *(Director)*, Richard Bromell *(Director)*, Emma Ramsay *(Director)*
**IT:** Daniel Fernley *(Computer Manager)*
**US SIC:** 8211 **UK SIC:** 93200
**Auditors:** Baker Tilly
**Bankers:** The Royal Bank Of Scotland Plc (15-10-00)

| | 31-08-14 | 31-08-13 | 31-08-12 |
|---|---|---|---|
| TO | 2,976,711 | 2,954,941 | 2,865,920 |
| P/L | 171,832 | 202,348 | 178,695 |
| NW | 3,134,410 | 2,962,432 | 2,760,406 |
| WC | 47,377 | (56,892) | (52,725) |
| Emp. | 70 | 69 | 69 |

DUNS 23-907-1843

## Sherborne Processing Co Ltd

**(Subsidiary of:** Pearce Seeds (Holdings) Ltd)
Rosedown Farm, Sherborne, Dorset DT9 4SX
**Tel:** 01935811400
**Web:** www.pearceseeds.co.uk
**Reg No:** 3897775 **Estd:** 1999 Private Limited Company
**Line of Business:** Wholesale suppliers of seeds
**Issued Capital:** £4
**Director:** K L Tuffin
**Co. Secretary:** Mrs Christine Tuffin
**US SIC:** 5153 **UK SIC:** 61100

| | 31-12-13 | 31-12-12 | 31-12-11 |
|---|---|---|---|
| TA | 4 | 4 | 20,942 |
| NW | 4 | 4 | 4 |
| WC | N/A | N/A | 4 |

DUNS 51-995-9014

## Sherborne School

Abbey Road, Sherborne, Dorset DT9 3AP
**Tel:** 01935810548
**Web:** www.sherborne.org.uk
**Reg No:** 4002575 **Estd:** 2000 Private Company Limited By Guarantee
**Line of Business:** Other sporting activities not elsewhere classified
**Trading Style:** Sherborne School Sailing Club
**Directors:** R A Leach, Major General P A Cordingley, Mrs I A Burke, M J Whittell, Professor R Hodder Williams, Mrs V Cotter, Dr S E Ball, A Charlton
**Co. Secretary:** Mrs Lucy Robins

**Responsibilities**
**Senior:** Michael Beaumont *(Manager)*, Nigel Bowles *(Manager)*, Simon Eliot *(Head Teacher)*, Roger Fidgen *(Director)*, Fiona Maddocks *(Manager)*, Gordon Parry *(Director)*, Eric Woods *(Director)*
**Branches:** Sherborne School, Newell, Sherborne, Dorset DT9 4EZ
**US SIC:** 7999 **UK SIC:** 97913
**Auditors:** Crowe Clark Whitehill LLP
**Bankers:** Lloyds TSB Bank plc (30-99-98)

| | 30-06-13 | 30-06-12 | 30-06-11 |
|---|---|---|---|
| TO | 24,877,000 | 24,157,000 | 23,636,000 |
| P/L | 1,285,000 | 1,190,000 | 2,013,000 |
| NW | 36,141,000 | 34,377,000 | 33,640,000 |
| WC | (1,215,000) | (1,895,000) | (1,112,000) |
| Emp. | 426 | 391 | 384 |

DUNS 21-606-7522
## Sherbrooke Lodge
41-43 Newark Drive, Glasgow, Lanarkshire G41 4QA
**Tel:** 01414238525
**Web:** www.lambhillcourt.ltd.uk
**Estd:** 2011 Proprietorship
**Line of Business:** Residential care establishments
**Proprietor:** Mrs J Duncan
**Responsibilities**
**Senior:** Laura Flanagan *(Manager)*, Alison Price *(Manager)*
**US SIC:** 8321 **UK SIC:** 96111
**Employees:** 65

DUNS 21-580-1521
## Sherburn Hospital
Durham, Durham, County Durham DH1 2SE
**Tel:** 01913722551
**Web:** www.sherburnhouse.org
**Estd:** 2003 Proprietorship
**Line of Business:** Residential care establishments
**Proprietor:** S Hallett
**US SIC:** 8321 **UK SIC:** 96111
**Employees:** 50

DUNS 21-534-9973
## Sherburn House Charity
Sherburn Hospital, Durham, County Durham DH1 2SE
**Tel:** 0191-372-0421
**Web:** www.sherburnhouse.org
**Estd:** 1949
**Line of Business:** Residential care establishments
**Trading Style:** Christs Hospital in Sherburn
**Principals:** S Gorton *(Financial)*, S Hallett, S Black *(Manager)*
**Responsibilities**
**Senior:** Joanne Carr *(Manager)*
**US SIC:** 8321 **UK SIC:** 96111
**Auditors:** RSM Tenon Audit Ltd

| | 31-03-12 | 31-03-11 | 31-03-10 |
|---|---|---|---|
| TO | 1,606,687 | 1,574,112 | 1,637,373 |
| P/L | 70,014 | 123,130 | 944,463 |
| NW | 27,863,790 | 27,502,751 | 26,404,720 |
| WC | (78,119) | (56,755) | (159,463) |
| Emp. | 55 | 55 | 51 |

DUNS 28-870-8449 **Exp**
## Sherburn Minerals Ltd
15 Front Street, Sherburn Hill, Durham, County Durham DH6 1PA
**Tel:** 01913720636 **Fax:** 0191-372-0312
**Reg No:** 1039631 **Estd:** 1972 Private Limited Company
**Line of Business:** Other mining and quarrying not elsewhere classified
**Export Markets:** Norway & Germany.
**Export Sales:** £757,491
**Trading Style:** Sherburn Stone, Tynedock Asphalt Plant
**Issued Capital:** £466,000
**Director:** J P Allison
**Co. Secretary:** James Connolly
**Branches:** Sherburn Minerals Ltd, Helbeck Low Farm Cottage, Kirkby Stephen, Cumbria CA17 4DD
**US SIC:** 1499 **UK SIC:** 23960
**Auditors:** Blueprint Audit Ltd
**Bankers:** HSBC Bank plc (40-43-24)

| | 31-03-14 | 31-03-13 | 31-03-12 |
|---|---|---|---|
| TO | 15,831,761 | 14,090,492 | 15,254,768 |
| P/L | (52,397) | 359,493 | 58,214 |
| NW | 4,204,013 | 4,197,869 | 3,826,526 |
| WC | 215,593 | (971,343) | (938,569) |
| Emp. | 107 | 120 | 117 |

DUNS 23-702-8969
## Shere Khan Restaurants Ltd
50-52 Wilmslow Road, Manchester M14 5TQ
**Tel:** 0161-256-2624 **Fax:** 01619279401
**Web:** www.sherekhan.com
**Reg No:** 3698110 **Estd:** 1999 Private Limited Company
**Line of Business:** Licensed restaurants
**Issued Capital:** £10,000
**Principals:** N B Awan *(Managing)*, R A Awan
**Co. Secretary:** Nighat Awan
**Branches:** Shere Khan Restaurants Ltd, 9-11 Old Market Place, Altrincham, Cheshire WA14 4NP
**US SIC:** 5812 **UK SIC:** 66110
**Auditors:** Madisons
**Bankers:** Lloyds TSB Bank plc (30-16-79)

| | 30-04-14 | 30-04-13 | 30-04-12 |
|---|---|---|---|
| TA | 601,011 | 610,758 | 581,631 |
| NW | (478,222) | (668,880) | (843,192) |
| WC | (290,334) | (486,504) | (673,123) |

DUNS 76-855-3208
## Sherico Care Services Ltd
2 Balmoral Road, London E10 5ND
**Tel:** 02085587569
**Web:** www.shericocareservices.com
**Reg No:** 2610830 **Estd:** 1991 Private Limited Company
**Line of Business:** Representative office
**Issued Capital:** £1,000
**Directors:** Ms B Walsh Andrews, S Hasmat-Ali
**Co. Secretary:** Ms Jasbir Panesar
**Responsibilities**
**Senior:** Reyaz Ali *(Manager)*, Noor Hasmat Ali *(Manager)*
**US SIC:** 7399 **UK SIC:** 83954
**Auditors:** Illegible

| | 30-11-13 | 30-11-12 | 30-11-11 |
|---|---|---|---|
| TA | 1,593,305 | 1,803,397 | 1,629,121 |
| NW | 1,038,876 | 1,093,869 | 926,408 |
| WC | 217,703 | 377,068 | 320,399 |

DUNS 49-387-0315 **Imp**
## Sheridan Fabrications Ltd
New Sheridan House, Don Pedro Avenue, Normanton, West Yorkshire WF6 1TD
**Tel:** 08456182800 **Fax:** 08456182824
**Web:** www.sheridan-uk.com
**Reg No:** 3134076 **Estd:** 2009 Private Limited Company
**Line of Business:** Wholesale of wood, construction materials and sanitary equipment
**Issued Capital:** £96
**Director:** J N Blackburn
**Co. Secretary:** Mrs Rachel Garner
**Responsibilities**
**Marketing:** Craig Probyn *(Sales & Marketing Director)*
**Sales:** Craig Probyn *(Sales & Marketing Director)*
**IT:** Steve Beardwood *(IT Manager)*
**US SIC:** 5039 **UK SIC:** 61300
**Auditors:** Auker Rhodes Ltd
**Bankers:** Barclays Bank Plc (20-11-81)

| | 31-12-13 | 31-12-12 | 31-12-11 |
|---|---|---|---|
| TO | 7,375,939 | 6,839,197 | 6,296,556 |
| P/L | 4,358 | 22,380 | 82,203 |
| NW | 923,043 | 920,607 | 915,658 |
| WC | 1,321,232 | 2,162,084 | 2,013,289 |
| Emp. | 101 | 91 | 98 |

DUNS 23-708-1179
## Sheridans
Whittington House, London WC1E 7EA
**Web:** www.sheridans.co.uk
**Estd:** 1963 Partnership
**Line of Business:** Solicitors
**Trading Style:** Sheridans Solicitors
**Partners:** R Roberts, J Soneji, M Thomas, S Luckman, I Watson, H Jones, G Stafford, R Gifford
**Responsibilities**
**Senior:** Zareen Ali *(Partner)*, Alan Daniel *(Partner)*, Cyril Glasser *(Partner)*, Stephen Kempner *(Partner)*, Rex Nwakodo *(Partner)*, Howard Rubin *(Partner)*, Bernard Sheridan *(Partner)*
**Admin:** Kaz Reilly *(Secretary)*
**US SIC:** 8111 **UK SIC:** 83500
**Employees:** 65

DUNS 21-584-1448
## Sheriff Court
1 Carlton Place, Glasgow, Lanarkshire G5 9DA
**Tel:** 01414298888
**Web:** www.scotcourts.gov.uk
**Estd:** 2011
**Line of Business:** Sheriffs officers
**US SIC:** 9221 **UK SIC:** 91300
**Employees:** 190

DUNS 76-551-5770
## Sherika Ltd
100 London Road, Hemel Hempstead, Hertfordshire HP3 9SD
**Tel:** 01442-268383
**Web:** www.pjdunphy.com
**Reg No:** 2571769 **Estd:** 1991 Private Limited Company
**Line of Business:** Technical testing and analysis
**Issued Capital:** £100
**Director:** P J Dunphy
**Co. Secretary:** Ms Wendy Dunphy
**US SIC:** 7397 **UK SIC:** 83702
**Auditors:** Ames & Co

| | 31-03-14 | 31-03-13 | 31-03-12 |
|---|---|---|---|
| TA | 2,054,110 | 1,750,580 | 1,833,122 |
| NW | 1,731,811 | 1,597,451 | 1,561,861 |
| WC | 1,531,910 | 1,396,238 | 1,363,806 |

DUNS 77-127-6557
## Sheriol Thirty - Two Ltd
10 Romsey Road, Eastleigh, Hampshire SO50 9AL
**Tel:** 02380-614555
**Web:** www.rothman-pantall.co.uk
**Reg No:** 2699826 **Estd:** 1992 Private Limited Company
**Line of Business:** Business services
**Issued Capital:** £1,010
**Directors:** E M Samuel Camps, R T Sperring
**Co. Secretary:**
Fryern Company Secretarial Servi
**US SIC:** 7399, 6711
**UK SIC:** 83954, 83962
**Auditors:** Rothman Pantall & Co

| | 31-10-13 | 31-10-12 | 31-10-11 |
|---|---|---|---|
| TA | 5,131,698 | 5,118,367 | 5,161,359 |
| NW | 2,989,179 | 3,055,686 | 3,011,204 |
| WC | 967,349 | 1,168,927 | 1,223,142 |

DUNS 23-819-7540 **Imp**
## Sherlock Holmes Park Plaza Ltd
(**Subsidiary of:** Park Plaza Coöperatief U.A.)
108 Baker Street, London W1U 6LJ
**Web:** www.parkplazasherlockholmes.com
**Reg No:** 3811881 **Estd:** 1999 Private Limited Company
**Line of Business:** Hotels
**Issued Capital:** £2
**Directors:** C C Moravsky, Euro Sea Hotels Nv
**Co. Secretary:** Mrs Inbar Zilberman
**Responsibilities**
**Senior:** Michelle World *(General Manager)*
**US SIC:** 7011 **UK SIC:** 66500
**Auditors:** Mazars LLP

| | 31-12-13 | 31-12-12 | 31-12-11 |
|---|---|---|---|
| TO | 6,515,000 | 6,518,000 | 6,783,000 |
| P/L | 295,000 | 301,000 | 480,000 |
| NW | (596,000) | (891,000) | (1,192,000) |
| WC | (596,000) | (891,000) | (1,192,000) |
| Emp. | 55 | 57 | 59 |

DUNS 77-270-1827
## Sherlock Interiors Contracting Ltd
20-22 Vestry Street, London N1 7RE
**Tel:** 020-7336-7337
**Web:** www.sherlockinteriors.com
**Reg No:** 2714699 **VAT No:** 673024647
**Estd:** 1992 Private Limited Company
**Line of Business:** Construction of domestic buildings
**Issued Capital:** £78
**Directors:** S C Pollard, M R Langdon, M J Pearson, R J Sherlock
**Co. Secretary:** Neal Harvey
**US SIC:** 1522 **UK SIC:** 50100
**Auditors:** Horwath Clark Whitehill
**Bankers:** Yorkshire Bank Plc (05-09-72)

| | 30-04-14 | 30-04-13 | 30-04-12 |
|---|---|---|---|
| TO | 14,083,405 | 10,436,591 | 8,842,069 |
| P/L | (66,174) | 149,959 | 148,402 |
| NW | 609,304 | 747,641 | 723,244 |
| WC | 594,902 | 722,453 | 696,040 |
| Emp. | 52 | 47 | 47 |

DUNS 21-077-9158
## Sherman & Sterling
9 Appold Street, London EC2A 2AP
**Web:** www.sherman.com
**Estd:** 1960 Partnership
**Line of Business:** Solicitors
**Partner:** Mrs P Gibson
**Responsibilities**
**Finance:** Ben Howard *(Financial Manager)*
**HR:** Lois Gordon *(Human Resources Manager)*
**Health & Safety:** Lois Gordon *(Human Resources Manager)*
**Facilities:** Kirsty Scott *(Facilities Manager)*
**US SIC:** 8111 **UK SIC:** 83500
**Employees:** 280

DUNS 28-834-7040
## Sherrardswood School
Sherrardswood School, Lockleys, Welwyn, Hertfordshire AL6 0BL
**Tel:** 01438-714282 **Fax:** 01438-840616
**Web:** www.sherrardswood.plus.com
**Reg No:** 0370409 **Estd:** 1930 Private Limited Company
**Line of Business:** Schools (independent)
**Directors:** B Kenyon, P M Buss, D Chapman, S Thompson, R Stattersfield, J M Phillips, Mrs T J Petri, A Khan
**Co. Secretary:** Neil Hounsom
**Responsibilities**
**Senior:** Lynda Corry *(Headmistress)*, Anthony Downs *(Manager)*, Patience Purchas *(Manager)*, James Swede *(Manager)*
**Marketing:** Michelle Gahan *(Registrar)*, Victoria Wells *(Marketing Executeve)*
**IT:** Christian Bernardo *(IT Manager)*
**Facilities:** Darryn Stewart *(Site Manager)*
**Purchasing:** Lynda Corry *(Headmistress)*
**US SIC:** 8211, 8221, 8249
**UK SIC:** 93200, 93100, 93300
**Auditors:** Kingston Smith LLP
**Bankers:** HSBC Bank plc (40-46-08)

| | 31-07-13 | 31-07-12 | 31-07-11 |
|---|---|---|---|
| TO | 3,438,743 | 3,364,867 | 3,636,714 |
| P/L | (70,912) | (188,686) | (279,366) |
| NW | 713,249 | 784,160 | 972,846 |
| WC | (2,872,968) | (2,663,026) | (2,551,813) |
| Emp. | 69 | 73 | 67 |

DUNS 63-458-7950
## Sherrington & Co
66 Chorley Street, Bolton, Lancashire BL1 4AL
**Tel:** 01204-391420
**Estd:** 1993 Proprietorship
**Line of Business:** Solicitors
**Proprietor:** J Sherrington
**US SIC:** 8111 **UK SIC:** 83500
**Employees:** 65

DUNS 51-999-1509
## Sherrington Law Ltd
Sherrington House, 66 Chorley Street Bolton, Lancashire BL1 4AL
**Tel:** 01204361799 **Fax:** 01204-362988
**Web:** www.seriousinjurylaw.co.uk
**Reg No:** 3366212 **Estd:** 1997 Private Limited Company
**Line of Business:** Solicitors
**Trading Style:** Serious Law Ltd
**Issued Capital:** £2
**Director:** J H Sherrington
**Co. Secretary:** Timothy Walters
**US SIC:** 8111 **UK SIC:** 83500

| | 30-04-14 | 30-04-13 | 30-04-12 |
|---|---|---|---|
| TA | 1 | 1 | 1 |
| NW | 1 | 1 | 1 |

DUNS 28-977-3772
## Sherrygreen Ltd
Teresa Gavin House, Southend Road, Woodford Green, Essex IG8 8FA
**Tel:** 020-8551-9999
**Web:** www.mulalley.co.uk
**Reg No:** 1762648 **Estd:** 1983 Private Limited Company
**Line of Business:** Holding companies management activities
**Trading Style:** Mulalley & Co
**Issued Capital:** £168,000
**Principals:** B O'Malley *(Managing)*, V O'Malley, S O'Malley, Ms T Taylor
**Co. Secretary:** Eamon O'Malley
**Responsibilities**
**Senior:** Vincent O' Malley *(Director)*, Shaun O' Malley *(Director)*, Eamon O' Malley *(Sales & Marketing Director)*
**Marketing:** Eamon O' Malley *(Sales & Marketing Director)*
**Sales:** Eamon O' Malley *(Sales & Marketing Director)*
**HR:** Angela Bowen *(Human Resources Manager)*
**Purchasing:** Richard Hatcher *(Purchasing Manager)*
**US SIC:** 6711, 6531
**UK SIC:** 83962, 83400
**Auditors:** Neiman Walters Niman

| | 31-03-14 | 31-03-13 | 31-03-12 |
|---|---|---|---|
| TO | 162,775,000 | 135,226,000 | 134,033,000 |
| P/L | 13,016,000 | 8,472,000 | 9,081,000 |
| NW | 61,989,000 | 53,043,000 | 47,660,000 |
| WC | 28,438,000 | 19,538,000 | 13,563,000 |
| Emp. | 589 | 597 | 609 |

DUNS 21-009-5211
## Shervey Ltd
First Floor Cef Building, Broomhill Way, Torquay, Devon TQ2 7QN
**Web:** www.bestcarehomes.co.uk
**Reg No:** 6333002 **Estd:** 2007 Private Limited Company
**Line of Business:** Management activities of other non-financial holding companies not elsewhere classified
**Issued Capital:** £50,000
**Director:** D G Henson
**Co. Secretary:** Nicholas Meyer
**US SIC:** 6711 **UK SIC:** 83962
**Auditors:** Mark Ward

| | 31-07-13 | 31-07-12 | 31-07-11 |
|---|---|---|---|
| TO | 3,234,884 | 3,074,198 | 2,666,652 |
| P/L | 454,979 | 497,009 | 220,985 |
| NW | (280,479) | (524,157) | (907,637) |
| WC | (600,169) | (463,840) | (411,913) |
| Emp. | 129 | 123 | 121 |

## DUNS 77-479-6080    Exp
### Sherwin-Williams Diversified Brands Ltd
(Subsidiary of: The Sherwin-Williams Company)
Thorncliffe Road, Thorncliffe Park Estate, Sheffield, South Yorkshire S35 2YP
Tel: 01142467171
Web: www.ronseal.co.uk
Reg No: 2968830 Estd: 1992 Private Limited Company
Line of Business: Adhesive & sealant manufacturers
Export Markets: Worldwide
Export Sales: £5,354,943
Issued Capital: £18,659,926
Principals: P Barrow (Managing), C M Connor, S Hennessy
Co. Secretary: Howard Hargreaves
Responsibilities
Senior: Jason Thorton (Warehouse Manager)
Marketing: Kate Hodge (Communications Manager)
Sales: Patrick Byrnes (Sales Director), Simon Garvey (National Account Manager)
IT: Lisa Brammer (MIS Manager), Ian Greaves (MIS Manager)
HR: Andrea Greensmith (Human Resources Manager)
Health & Safety: Keith Stephenson (Health & Safety Manager)
Facilities: Ian McCarthy (Facilities Manager)
Operations: Nicola Budge (Operations Director), Keith Stephenson (Health & Safety Manager)
Purchasing: Kevin Stafford (Purchasing Manager)
US SIC: 2891, 2899
UK SIC: 25620, 25670
Auditors: Deloitte LLP
Bankers: HSBC Bank plc (40-17-04)

|       | 31-12-13   | 31-12-12   | 31-12-11   |
|-------|-----------|-----------|-----------|
| TO    | 66,903,773 | 60,750,629 | 60,506,366 |
| P/L   | (243,475)  | 968,175    | 1,490,051  |
| NW    | 15,689,158 | 17,585,467 | 16,353,936 |
| WC    | 6,360,973  | 5,980,900  | 4,060,752  |
| Emp.  | 293        | 267        | 287        |

## DUNS 21-203-6735    Exp
### Sherwin-Williams Protective & Marine Coatings
(Subsidiary of: The Sherwin-Williams Company)
Tower Works, Bolton, Lancashire BL2 2AL
Tel: 01204-521771
Web: http://protectiveemea.sherwin-williams.com
Reg No: 0893081 VAT No: 146032692
Estd: 1929 Private Unlimited Company
Line of Business: Manufacture of paints, varnishes and similar coatings, printing ink and mastics
Trading Style: Leighs Paints
Issued Capital: £93,521
Directors: C M Connor, H S Hargreaves, V Miller, S P Hennessy
Responsibilities
Senior: Matt Hudson (Purchasing Manager)
Marketing: Lisa Usher (Communications Coordinator)
IT: Arthur Adams (IT Manager), Duncan Gettins (Non-PC Systems Manager), Alan Moon (IT Manager)
Health & Safety: Martin Aldred (Health & Safety Manager)
Operations: Martin Aldred (Health & Safety Manager)
Purchasing: Matt Hudson (Purchasing Manager)
Branches: Sherwin-Williams Protective & Marine Coatings, 4 Braeview Pl, Glasgow, Lanarkshire G74 3XH
US SIC: 2851, 3999
UK SIC: 25510, 49590
Auditors: Wheawill & Sudworth
Bankers: National Westminster Bank Plc (01-30-99)

|       | 31-12-13   | 31-12-12   | 31-12-11    |
|-------|-----------|-----------|------------|
| TO    | 44,843,655 | 44,300,669 | 38,525,635 |
| P/L   | 571,194    | 3,497,554  | (2,096,407) |
| NW    | 10,173,096 | 10,035,317 | 6,746,788  |
| WC    | 5,941,896  | 6,762,119  | 2,926,310  |
| Emp.  | 252        | 246        | 269        |

## DUNS 54-864-0366    Imp
### Sherwood Forest Hospitals N H S Foundation Trust
Mansfield Road, Sutton-In-Ashfield, Nottinghamshire NG17 4JL
Web: www.sfh-tr.nhs.uk
VAT No: 654927013 Estd: 2013 Incorporate By Act Of Parliament
Line of Business: Public sector hospital activities, including nhs trusts
Issued Capital: £1
Principals: Ms T Doucet (Chairman), L Bond (Financial), Ms K Fisher (Personnel), Ms C White, J Watkinson, D Heathcote, D Leah, S Pearson

Responsibilities
Senior: James Grasar (Non-Executive Director), Bonnie Jones (Non-Executive Director)
Marketing: Jack Adlam (Deputy Head of Communications), Yolanda Martin (Head of Communications), Jayne Morton (Communications Officer), Sophie Wragg (Primary Care Liaison Manager)
IT: Mike Press (Computer Director)
HR: Joe Forde (Human Resources Director)
Facilities: Alan Pritchett (Estates Manager)
Branches: Sherwood Forest Hospitals N H S Foundation Trust, Newark Hospital, Boundary Road, Newark, Nottinghamshire NG24 4DE
US SIC: 8062, 9121
UK SIC: 95100, 91110
Auditors: KPMG LLP

|       | 31-03-14     | 31-03-13     | 31-03-12     |
|-------|-------------|-------------|-------------|
| TO    | 266,158,000  | 255,784,000  | 208,246,000  |
| P/L   | (23,502,000) | (15,464,000) | (6,197,000)  |
| NW    | (139,204,000)| (143,761,000)| (128,722,000)|
| WC    | (22,125,000) | (19,108,000) | (5,594,000)  |
| Emp.  | 3,749        | 3,631        | 3,547        |

## DUNS 21-784-3110
### Sherwood House Independent Hospital
Rufford Colliery Lane, Rainworth, Mansfield, Nottinghamshire NG21 0HR
Tel: 01623499010
Web: www.cambiangroup.com
Estd: 2011 Proprietorship
Line of Business: Mental health centres
Proprietor: Miss N Roper
US SIC: 8091 UK SIC: 95200
Employees: 100

## DUNS 22-660-3918    Imp
### The Sherwood Press (Nottingham) Ltd
Haddon Court, Glaisdale Parkway, Nottingham, Nottinghamshire NG8 4GP
Tel: 01159-287766
Web: www.sherwood-press.co.uk
Reg No: 1881167 VAT No: 309402580
Estd: 1976 Private Limited Company
Line of Business: Printing not elsewhere classified
Issued Capital: £20,000
Principals: J T Bacon (Managing), R G Bacon, G R Garrod, S B King
Co. Secretary: Jeremy Bacon
US SIC: 2752 UK SIC: 47544
Auditors: UHY Hacker Young
Bankers: HSBC Bank plc (40-10-06)

|       | 30-04-14   | 30-04-13   | 30-04-12   |
|-------|-----------|-----------|-----------|
| TO    | 10,499,543 | 13,446,000 | 11,862,000 |
| P/L   | 227,287    | 216,000    | (20,000)   |
| NW    | 3,003,257  | 3,962,000  | 3,929,000  |
| WC    | 1,199,504  | 970,000    | 1,399,000  |
| Emp.  | 99         | 227        | 97         |

## DUNS 21-142-2059
### Sherwood Restaurants Ltd
Bawtry Road, Doncaster, South Yorkshire DN4 7PD
Tel: 01302535634
Reg No: 6739405 Estd: 2008 Private Limited Company
Line of Business: Restaurants
Issued Capital: £100
Director: M T Clapham
Co. Secretary: Ms Sally Clapham
US SIC: 5812 UK SIC: 66110
Bankers: The Royal Bank Of Scotland Plc (16-18-30)

|       | 31-12-13  | 31-12-12 | 31-12-11 |
|-------|----------|---------|---------|
| TO    | 9,227,747 | N/A     | N/A     |
| P/L   | 128,385   | N/A     | N/A     |
| NW    | (433,364) | 54,626  | 34,082  |
| WC    | (173,945) | (52,597)| (118,827)|
| Emp.  | 338       | N/A     | N/A     |

## DUNS 34-752-0223
### Sherwood Rise Ltd
Autumn Grange, Nottingham, Nottinghamshire NG5 1BS
Tel: 01158417470 Fax: 01159-620061
Web: www.autumngrange.com
Reg No: 2784528 Estd: 1979 Private Limited Company
Line of Business: Residential care establishments
Trading Style: Autumn Grange Nursing Home
Issued Capital: £9,375
Principals: M Khan (Chairman), Y Khan
Responsibilities
Senior: Paulette Gee (Manager), Azad Khan (Manager), Nasreem Kieni (Company Director)
Finance: Nasreem Kieni (Company Director)
US SIC: 8321 UK SIC: 96111
Auditors: McBoyle & Co

Bankers: National Westminster Bank Plc (60-11-33)

|       | 31-03-14   | 31-03-13   | 31-03-12   |
|-------|-----------|-----------|-----------|
| TA    | 600,183    | 1,119,626  | 2,423,821  |
| NW    | (196,117)  | 332,603    | 1,715,098  |
| WC    | (761,117)  | (732,397)  | (667,678)  |

## DUNS 50-415-4295    Imp-Exp
### Sherwood Stainless Steel (Service Centre) Ltd
The Science Park, Wolverhampton, West Midlands WV10 9TF
Tel: 01902-422215
Web: www.sherwoodstainless.co.uk
Reg No: 2412308 VAT No: 559331329
Estd: 1990 Private Limited Company
Line of Business: Stainless steel stockholders
Issued Capital: £37,500
Principals: T Franklin (Managing), P Thurston
Co. Secretary: Patrick Megarity
Responsibilities
Senior: Geoff Woodfield (Works Manager)
Finance: Sarah Dainty (Credit Control)
Sales: Paul Grimsley (Sales Manager)
Health & Safety: David Hollis (Health & Safety Officer)
Facilities: Geoff Woodfield (Works Manager)
Operations: David Hollis (Health & Safety Officer)
Engineering: Geoff Woodfield (Works Manager)
US SIC: 5051 UK SIC: 61200
Auditors: Jordan & Co
Bankers: National Westminster Bank Plc (60-02-35)

|       | 31-03-14   | 31-03-13   | 31-03-12   |
|-------|-----------|-----------|-----------|
| TO    | 13,983,548 | 12,225,816 | 10,116,793 |
| P/L   | 904,055    | 443,407    | 462,606    |
| NW    | 1,150,721  | 1,092,671  | 1,035,301  |
| WC    | (438,812)  | (262,710)  | (215,603)  |
| Emp.  | 60         | 56         | 49         |

## DUNS 21-595-8192
### Sherwoods
Concord Douglas Close, Preston Farm Industrial Estate, Stockton-On-Tees, Cleveland TS18 3SB
Tel: 01642633333
Web: www.sherwoods-stockton.co.uk
Estd: 2011 Partnership
Line of Business: Car dealers (new & used)
Partners: R Pratt, Ms L Pratt
US SIC: 5511 UK SIC: 65100
Employees: 50

## DUNS 57-043-0587
### Sherwoods (Darlington) Ltd
Chesnut Street, Darlington, County Durham DL1 1RJ
Tel: 01325466155 Fax: 01325376030
Web: www.sherwoodsgroup.co.uk
Reg No: 2876229 VAT No: 633238551
Estd: 1993 Private Limited Company
Line of Business: Car dealers (new & used)
Trading Style: Masterfit
Issued Capital: £1,900,000
Principals: A Macconachie (Managing), F D Lord, Motors Directors Limited
Co. Secretary: Motors Secretaries Limited
Responsibilities
Senior: Andrew Hodgeson (After Sales Manager), Simon MacConachie (General Manager)
Finance: Catherine Elgey (Finance Director), Rob Richards (Finance Business Manager)
Marketing: Angela Lleuellyn (Marketing)
Sales: Andrew Hodgeson (After Sales Manager)
Branches: Sherwoods (Darlington) Ltd, Standard Way Industrial Estate, Standard Way Business Park, Northallerton, North Yorkshire DL6 2XA
US SIC: 5511, 5521
UK SIC: 65100
Auditors: Grant Thornton UK LLP
Bankers: Barclays Bank Plc (20-25-29)

|       | 31-12-13   | 31-12-12   | 31-12-11   |
|-------|-----------|-----------|-----------|
| TO    | 61,127,772 | 54,897,932 | 51,450,456 |
| P/L   | 421,891    | 138,246    | 204,763    |
| NW    | 1,528,916  | 1,856,224  | 1,846,696  |
| WC    | (206,943)  | (43,076)   | 408,459    |
| Emp.  | 153        | 148        | 147        |

## DUNS 29-581-5849    Imp-Exp
### Shetland Catch Ltd
Gremista Industrial Estate, Gremista, Lerwick, Shetland ZE1 0PX
Tel: 01595-695740
Web: www.shetlandcatch.com
Reg No: 0094953SC VAT No: 430177773
Estd: 1989 Private Limited Company
Line of Business: Wholesale of other food including fish, crustaceans and molluscs
Export Markets: Europe and Worldwide
Issued Capital: £4,000,000

Directors: T Vikenes, J K Angus, E M Haugstad, B Anderson, C A Grains, Miss S M Laurenson, J H Goodlad, S N Leiper
Co. Secretary: Darren Leask
Responsibilities
Senior: Brian Isbister (Director)
Sales: Norma Williamson (Sales Executive)
US SIC: 5146 UK SIC: 61700
Auditors: Baker Tilly UK Audit LLP
Bankers: Bank Of Scotland (80-08-82)

|       | 31-03-14   | 31-03-13   | 31-03-12   |
|-------|-----------|-----------|-----------|
| TO    | 63,626,160 | 73,053,984 | 48,662,639 |
| P/L   | 3,112,127  | 1,420,087  | (6,038,478) |
| NW    | 21,656,133 | 19,261,477 | 15,053,000 |
| WC    | 11,461,920 | 11,133,770 | 7,662,288  |
| Emp.  | 87         | 86         | 89         |

## DUNS 77-946-2014
### Shetland Hotels Ltd
One America Square, 17 Crosswall, London EC3N 2SG
Tel: 01595692826
Web: www.shetlandhotels.co.uk
Reg No: 5915727 Estd: 2006 Private Limited Company
Line of Business: Hotels
Issued Capital: £1,000,000
Directors: C J Emson, H T Mackenzie-Smith
Co. Secretary: John Bottomley
US SIC: 7399 UK SIC: 83954

|       | 30-06-13    | 30-06-12    | 30-06-11   |
|-------|------------|------------|-----------|
| TO    | 4,078,361   | 3,111,324   | N/A       |
| P/L   | (3,114,351) | (3,643,189) | N/A       |
| NW    | (11,875,655)| (9,018,426) | (4,355,052)|
| WC    | 11,791      | (70,768)    | 1,595,871 |
| Emp.  | 167         | 120         | N/A       |

## DUNS 21-122-1189
### Shetland Islands Council
Town Hall, Hillhead, Shetland ZE1 0HB
Web: www.shetland.gov.uk
Line of Business: General (overall) public service activities
Director: N Reiter
Responsibilities
Senior: Mark Boden (Chief Executive Officer), Michael Craigie (Executive Manager for Transpor)
Fleet: Michael Craigie (Executive Manager for Transpor)
Branches: Shetland Islands Council, 96 Gilbertson Road, Shetland, Shetland ZE1 0QJ
US SIC: 9121 UK SIC: 91110
Employees: 2,100

## DUNS 50-383-5456
### Shetland Seafoods Ltd
(Subsidiary of: Scotprime Seafoods Ltd)
11 Whitfield Drive, Heathfield Industrial Estate, Ayr, Ayrshire KA8 9RX
Tel: 01292611161 Fax: 01292280475
Web: www.shetlandauction.com
Reg No: 2392476 Estd: 1990 Private Limited Company
Line of Business: Exporters of fresh fish
Trading Style: Scotprime Seafoods
Issued Capital: £2
Director: J Boada
Co. Secretary: Robert Crane
US SIC: 5146 UK SIC: 61700
Auditors: Baker Tilly

|       | 31-12-13 | 31-12-12 | 31-12-11 |
|-------|---------|---------|---------|
| TA    | 2       | 2       | 2       |
| NW    | 2       | 2       | 2       |

## DUNS 64-265-8850
### Shettleston Health Centre
420 Old Shettleston Road, Glasgow, Lanarkshire G32 7JZ
Tel: 01415316240
Web: www.themcglonepractice.co.uk
Estd: 2010 Partnership
Line of Business: Doctors
Partner: Dr M Mckenner
Responsibilities
Senior: Anne Coventry (Practice Manager), Margaret McKenner (Partner)
US SIC: 8011 UK SIC: 95300
Employees: 74

## DUNS 21-115-2977
### Shield Commercial Cleaning Ltd
Llan Coed Court, Darcy Business Park, Llandarcy, Neath, West Glamorgan SA10 6FG
Tel: 01792323238
Web: www.servicemasterofficecleaning.co.uk
Reg No: 6556122 Estd: 2007 Private Limited Company
Line of Business: Cleaning contracting commercial
Issued Capital: £1
Director: T C Vincent
Co. Secretary: Kenneth Williamson
Responsibilities
Senior: Jayne Gethin (Manager)

**US SIC:** 7349 **UK SIC:** 92300

| | 30-04-14 | 30-04-13 | 30-04-12 |
|---|---|---|---|
| TA | 1 | 1 | 1 |
| NW | 1 | 1 | 1 |

DUNS 21-660-5935

## Shield Contract Services (Uk) Ltd

Princess Mary House, 4 Bluecoats Avenue, Hertford, Hertfordshire SG14 1PB
**Tel:** 01992500236
**Web:** www.shieldcontractservices.co.uk
**Reg No:** 7163830 **Estd:** 2010 Private Limited Company
**Line of Business:** Building of complete constructions or parts thereof; civil engineering
**Issued Capital:** £100
**Directors:** G G Bough, S A Casha, C Belsey, L T Woods
**US SIC:** 1541, 1799
**UK SIC:** 50100, 50000
**Bankers:** HSBC Bank plc (40-23-10)

| | 31-03-14 | 31-03-13 | 31-03-12 |
|---|---|---|---|
| TO | 51,510,009 | 30,934,433 | 19,356,006 |
| P/L | 483,628 | 326,030 | 107,578 |
| NW | 96,193 | 119,288 | 21,076 |
| WC | 44,968 | 82,455 | (29,801) |
| Emp. | 1,820 | 1,142 | 585 |

DUNS 77-969-8922

## Shield Environmental Holdings Ltd

Shield House, Crown Way, Warmley, Bristol, Avon BS30 8XJ
**Tel:** 01179606366
**Web:** www.shieldenvironmental.co.uk
**Reg No:** 5938654 **Estd:** 2006 Private Limited Company
**Line of Business:** Asbestos products & removal
**Issued Capital:** £2,550,896
**Directors:** L P House, P A House, J House
**Co. Secretary:** Darren Sheppard
**Responsibilities**
**HR:** Tracey Redmond *(Human Resources Manager)*, Kevin Staniforth *(Training Manager)*
**US SIC:** 4959 **UK SIC:** 92110
**Bankers:** National Westminster Bank Plc (60-12-22)

| | 31-07-13 | 31-07-12 | 31-07-11 |
|---|---|---|---|
| TO | 20,932,290 | 18,208,468 | 15,249,194 |
| P/L | 2,252,138 | 397,210 | 1,097,608 |
| NW | (370,560) | (2,355,671) | (2,942,999) |
| WC | 1,959,061 | 1,309,576 | 1,372,431 |
| Emp. | 297 | 260 | 209 |

DUNS 29-859-4060

## The Shield Guarding Co Ltd

**(Subsidiary of:** Topsgrup Electronic Systems Limited)
250 Kennington Lane, London SE11 5RD
**Tel:** 08000930248
**Web:** www.theshieldgroup.com
**Reg No:** 2062725 **VAT No:** 437374828
**Estd:** 1986 Private Limited Company
**Line of Business:** Security and related activities
**Issued Capital:** £54,376
**Directors:** J A Roddy, Dr R R Nanda, A E Brundle, R R Iyer, A Chatrath
**Co. Secretary:** Andrew Brundle
**Responsibilities**
**Senior:** Peter Aaronson *(Managing Director Shield Group)*, Barry Baldwin *(Manager)*, James Firebrace *(Financial Director)*, David Kedward *(Manager)*, Richie Nanda *(Manager)*, Gerald Paxton *(Manager)*, Anthony Whitwam *(Manager)*
**Finance:** Robert Platais *(Financial Director)*
**Marketing:** Roger Sears *(Sales & Marketing Director)*
**Sales:** Stephen Hollings *(Commercial Director)*, Faye Pay *(Corporate Account Director)*, Roger Sears *(Sales & Marketing Director)*
**IT:** Stuart Kedward *(Operations Manager)*
**HR:** Nigel Jameson *(Head of HR)*, Stuart Kedward *(Operations Manager)*
**Health & Safety:** Greg North *(Health & Safety Officer)*
**Branches:** The Shield Guarding Co Ltd, 1 Vine La, London SE1 2JP
**US SIC:** 7399 **UK SIC:** 83954
**Auditors:** Grant Thornton UK LLP
**Bankers:** Lloyds TSB Bank plc (30-12-95)

| | 31-03-13 | 31-03-12 | 31-03-11 |
|---|---|---|---|
| TO | 54,558,483 | 55,364,708 | 53,316,951 |
| P/L | 19,923 | (425,432) | 502,133 |
| NW | 4,345,462 | 4,433,614 | 4,975,718 |
| WC | 3,942,546 | 3,175,802 | 4,109,850 |
| Emp. | 1,913 | 1,968 | 1,906 |

DUNS 50-346-0008 **Imp-Exp**

## Shield Medicare Ltd

**(Subsidiary of:** Shield Holdings Ltd)
Unit 1 Wernddu Court, Caerphilly, Mid Glamorgan CF83 3SG
**Tel:** 01252-717-616 **Fax:** 01252-717-942
**Web:** www.ecolabcc.com
**Reg No:** 2366120 **Estd:** 1989 Private Limited Company
**Line of Business:** Cleaning contracting commercial
**Export Markets:** Republic of Ireland
**Trading Style:** Ecolab
**Issued Capital:** £100
**Directors:** C R Lee, R E Gichtbrock
**Co. Secretary:** Miss Wendy Joyce
**Responsibilities**
**Senior:** Matt Cokely *(Manager)*, Axel Degremont *(Manager)*, Toni Lennox-Gentle *(Manager)*, Andy Newsome *(Vice President Global)*
**Finance:** Matt Cokely *(Manager)*
**Marketing:** Emily Buck *(Global Communications Manager)*, Don Cunningham *(Global Portfolio Manager - Equ)*, Axel Degremont *(Manager)*, Carolyn Longman *(Marketing Assistant)*
**Sales:** Sarah Anning *(Regional Sales Manager - UK, I)*, Lauren Clement *(National Sales Manager UK)*, Paul Frostick *(Territory Manager - UK Central)*, Dewi Lewis *(Global Corporate Account Manag)*, Michael Richter *(Global Corporate Account Direc)*, Eleanor Slevin *(Key Account Manager)*, Darren Webster *(Sales Manager)*
**Branches:** Shield Medicare Ltd, 123 Hunslet Road, Leeds, West Yorkshire LS10 1LD
**US SIC:** 7349, 7391
**UK SIC:** 92300, 94000
**Auditors:** PricewaterhouseCoopers LLP
**Bankers:** National Westminster Bank Plc (56-00-46)

| | 30-11-12 | 30-11-11 |
|---|---|---|
| TO | N/A | 23,207,000 |
| P/L | (51,000) | 6,685,000 |
| NW | N/A | 10,501,000 |
| WC | N/A | 6,975,000 |
| Emp. | N/A | 114 |

DUNS 21-997-3695

## Shield Security Service Ltd

Darcy Business Park Llandarcy, Neath, West Glamorgan SA10 6EJ
**Tel:** 01792-323000
**Web:** www.shieldsecurity.co.uk
**Reg No:** 6178619 **Estd:** 2007 Private Limited Company
**Line of Business:** Security and related activities
**Issued Capital:** £1,000
**Director:** T C Vincent
**Co. Secretary:** Kenneth Williamson
**US SIC:** 7393 **UK SIC:** 83954

| | 31-12-13 | 31-03-13 | 31-12-12 |
|---|---|---|---|
| TA | 596,549 | 1 | 1,000 |
| NW | (274,845) | 1 | 1,000 |
| WC | (308,456) | N/A | N/A |

DUNS 29-882-3386

## Shield Security Services Ltd

Shield House, 294 High Street, Aldershot, Hampshire GU12 4LT
**Tel:** 01252319899 **Fax:** 01252329354
**Web:** www.shieldsecurity.co.uk
**Reg No:** 2085388 **VAT No:** 413861462
**Estd:** 1986 Private Limited Company
**Line of Business:** Security and related activities
**Issued Capital:** £10,695
**Principals:** A Abdel-Hadi *(Managing)*, B Joshi, K B Thapa, Ms A J Durban
**Co. Secretary:** Adil Abdel-Hadi
**Responsibilities**
**Senior:** Abdul Abdel-Hadi *(Managing Director)*
**Finance:** Christine Harwood *(Financial Controller)*
**IT:** Bruce Waller *(IT Manager)*
**HR:** Amy Lock *(HR and Facilities Manager)*
**US SIC:** 7393 **UK SIC:** 83954
**Bankers:** Barclays Bank Plc (20-61-82)

| | 30-04-14 | 30-04-13 | 30-04-12 |
|---|---|---|---|
| TA | 1,129,746 | 1,369,376 | 1,069,771 |
| NW | 332,388 | 387,702 | 401,606 |
| WC | 179,455 | 137,599 | 276,983 |

DUNS 42-477-0688

## Shield Security Services (Yorkshire) Ltd

**(Subsidiary of:** Comack Limited)
7 Earls Court, Hull, North Humberside HU4 7DY
**Tel:** 01482-300833
**Web:** www.shield-security.co.uk
**Reg No:** 4464684 **VAT No:** 828189885
**Estd:** 2002 Private Limited Company
**Line of Business:** Security and related activities
**Issued Capital:** £100
**Director:** D Frank
**Co. Secretary:** Philip Mackay
**US SIC:** 7393 **UK SIC:** 83954

| | 31-03-14 | 31-03-13 | 31-03-12 |
|---|---|---|---|
| TA | 1,160,806 | 986,985 | 1,127,462 |
| NW | 217,247 | 164,974 | 130,995 |
| WC | 172,719 | 149,308 | 186,586 |

DUNS 23-575-0812

## Shield Service Group Plc

42 Westway, Caterham, Surrey CR3 5TP
**Tel:** 01883-345111 **Fax:** 01883-345200
**Web:** www.shieldgroup.co.uk
**Reg No:** 3573049 **Estd:** 1998 Public Limited Company
**Line of Business:** Cleaning contracting commercial
**Issued Capital:** £771,002
**Directors:** M J Rose, O W Weisflog, T R Pritchard, K J Macpherson
**Co. Secretary:** Martin Goddard
**US SIC:** 7349 **UK SIC:** 92300
**Auditors:** Jeffreys Henry LLP

| | 31-05-14 | 31-05-13 | 31-05-12 |
|---|---|---|---|
| TO | 6,158,817 | 6,258,678 | 6,364,441 |
| P/L | 206,348 | 190,725 | 193,770 |
| NW | (76,913) | (309,890) | (501,183) |
| WC | 390,178 | 305,681 | 113,500 |
| Emp. | 843 | 858 | 922 |

DUNS 73-858-6002

## Shields Environmental Group (Holdings) Ltd

Kerry Avenue, Purfleet Industrial Park, South Ockendon, Essex RM15 4YE
**Tel:** 01708684000
**Web:** www.shields-e.com
**Reg No:** 5113546 **Estd:** 2004 Private Limited Company
**Line of Business:** Telecommunications
**Export Sales:** £14,493,000
**Issued Capital:** £76,810
**Directors:** D Shields, S A Shields, G S Shields
**Co. Secretary:** Daniel Jones
**US SIC:** 4899 **UK SIC:** 79020

| | 30-06-14 | 30-06-13 | 30-06-12 |
|---|---|---|---|
| TO | 19,004,000 | 24,465,000 | 15,413,000 |
| P/L | (231,000) | 387,000 | 867,000 |
| NW | 3,950,000 | 4,345,000 | 4,460,000 |
| WC | 932,000 | 1,741,000 | 2,749,000 |
| Emp. | 138 | 100 | 79 |

DUNS 21-163-5735 **Imp**

## Shilcroft Ltd

32 High Road, London N2 9PJ
**Tel:** 020-8883-1559
**Web:** www.numarkpharmacists.com
**Reg No:** 1337007 **Estd:** 1980 Private Limited Company
**Line of Business:** Wholesale of perfume and cosmetics
**Trading Style:** C W Andrews, Maddox Health & Beauty
**Issued Capital:** £1,000
**Director:** J H Shah
**Co. Secretary:** Pradip Shah
**Branches:** Shilcroft Ltd, 45 Maddox Street, London W1S 2PE
**US SIC:** 5122, 5912
**UK SIC:** 61800, 64300
**Auditors:** Braham Noble Denholm & Co

| | 28-02-14 | 28-02-13 | 28-02-12 |
|---|---|---|---|
| TA | 719,459 | 755,216 | 808,255 |
| NW | 485,582 | 499,512 | 524,260 |
| WC | 371,489 | 369,045 | 376,924 |

DUNS 21-311-9134 **Exp**

## Shildon Controls Ltd

**(Subsidiary of:** Dialight Plc)
Hackworth Industrial Park, Shildon, County Durham DL4 1LH
**Tel:** 01388773065
**Web:** www.shildoncontrols.com
**Reg No:** 0977320 **VAT No:** 196909701
**Estd:** 1970 Private Limited Company
**Line of Business:** Process control engineers
**Export Markets:** Worldwide
**Issued Capital:** £4,080
**Director:** T R Burton
**Co. Secretary:** Nicholas Giles
**Branches:** Shildon Controls Ltd, Millbrook Business Centre, Floats Rd, Manchester M23 9YJ
**US SIC:** 3823, 3829
**UK SIC:** 37100
**Auditors:** KPMG Audit PLC
**Bankers:** Barclays Bank Plc (20-09-44)

| | 31-12-13 | 31-12-12 | 31-12-11 |
|---|---|---|---|
| TA | 2,011,000 | 2,011,000 | 2,011,000 |
| NW | 1,503,000 | 1,503,000 | 1,503,000 |
| WC | 1,503,000 | 1,503,000 | 1,503,000 |

DUNS 21-782-8609

## Shillington Lower School

Greenfields, Shillington, Hitchin, Hertfordshire SG5 3NX
**Tel:** 01462711637
**Estd:** 2011 Proprietorship
**Line of Business:** Schools (local authority)
**Proprietor:** Mrs T Callender
**Responsibilities**
**Senior:** Ingrid Alsop *(Head Teacher)*
**US SIC:** 8211 **UK SIC:** 93200
**Employees:** 75

DUNS 21-236-5928 **Imp-Exp**

## Shiloh Ltd

**(Subsidiary of:** Synergy Health Plc)
1 Western Avenue, Buckshaw Village, Chorley, Lancashire PR7 7NB
**Tel:** 01772299900 **Fax:** 01772-299901
**Web:** www.shiloh.com
**Reg No:** 0516671 **Estd:** 1953 Private Limited Company
**Line of Business:** Management activities of production holding companies
**Export Markets:** Europe
**Trading Style:** Synergy Health Plc
**Issued Capital:** £1,688,502
**Directors:** T S Fowler, Ms T A Miles, M Sutcliffe, J P Turner, Doctor R M Steeves, G Hill
**Co. Secretary:** Jonathan Turner
**Responsibilities**
**Senior:** David Stubbins *(Manager)*
**US SIC:** 8999, 2281
**UK SIC:** 83954, 43211
**Auditors:** Grant Thornton UK LLP
**Bankers:** Barclays Bank Plc (20-64-12)

| | 30-03-14 | 31-03-13 | 01-03-12 |
|---|---|---|---|
| TA | 36,299,475 | 36,204,157 | 36,199,302 |
| P/L | (5,816) | 644 | 190,030 |
| NW | 30,387,059 | 30,274,615 | 30,273,969 |
| WC | 29,387,059 | 29,274,615 | 29,782,326 |

DUNS 73-301-1691

## Shilton Sharpe Quarry Ltd

167 Fleet Street, London EC4A 2EA
**Tel:** 020-7187-7400
**Web:** www.ssq.com
**Reg No:** 4575013 **Estd:** 2002 Private Limited Company
**Line of Business:** Employment and recruitment companies and consultants
**Export Sales:** £4,253,785
**Issued Capital:** £11,883
**Directors:** N E Shilton, G D Quarry
**Co. Secretary:** Ms Jennifer Shilton
**Responsibilities**
**Senior:** Nishan Balasunderam *(Senior Manager)*, Matthew Bold *(Manager)*, Laura Field *(Senior Manager)*, Benji Field *(Manager)*, Matt Franklin *(Manager)*, Alana Gross *(Senior Manager)*, Becky Mackarel *(Manager)*, Laila Martin *(Senior Manager)*, June Mesrie *(Manager)*, Helmut Rogalla *(Manager)*, Rebecca Rogers *(Senior Manager)*, Jago Verna *(Manager)*
**US SIC:** 7361 **UK SIC:** 83954
**Auditors:** Simmons Gainsford LLP

| | 31-12-13 | 31-12-12 | 31-12-11 |
|---|---|---|---|
| TO | 13,896,061 | 13,160,537 | 12,173,192 |
| P/L | 4,030,737 | 3,955,866 | 3,640,883 |
| NW | 3,854,280 | 941,404 | 3,961,888 |
| WC | 3,717,625 | 741,299 | 3,746,414 |
| Emp. | 80 | 71 | 74 |

DUNS 53-604-0413

## Shimadzu Europe Ltd.

**(Subsidiary of:** Shimadzu Corporation)
Wharfside Trafford, Wharf Road, Trafford Park, Manchester M17 1GP
**Tel:** 01618884420 **Fax:** 01908552211
**Web:** www.srlab.co.uk
**Reg No:** 3409229 **Estd:** 1996 Private Limited Company
**Line of Business:** Management activities of other non-financial holding companies not elsewhere classified
**Issued Capital:** £13,380,117
**Directors:** Y Yamamoto, M Koyazaki, K Shimazu
**US SIC:** 6711 **UK SIC:** 83962
**Auditors:** Deloitte & Touche LLP
**Bankers:** The Bank Of Tokyo-Mitsubishi, Ltd (60-01-09)

| | 31-03-14 | 31-03-13 | 31-03-11 |
|---|---|---|---|
| TA | 13,328,790 | 13,339,589 | 13,355,182 |
| P/L | (10,547) | (13,230) | (10,129) |
| NW | 13,320,905 | 13,331,452 | 13,344,682 |
| WC | 190,788 | 201,335 | 214,565 |

DUNS 34-531-6785 **Imp**

## Shimadzu Uk Ltd

Unit 1a, Featherstone Road Mill Court, Milton Keynes, Buckinghamshire MK12 5RD
**Tel:** 01908552200 **Fax:** 08708375211
**Web:** www.shimadzu.co.uk
**Reg No:** 5342169 **Estd:** 2005 Private Limited Company
**Line of Business:** Wholesale of pharmaceutical goods
**Issued Capital:** £696,278
**Directors:** Y Yamamoto, P Yorke
**Co. Secretary:** Yasunori Yamamoto
**Responsibilities**
**Senior:** Colin Jump *(Manager)*
**Finance:** Yasuo Miura *(Director and Company Secretary)*
**US SIC:** 7399 **UK SIC:** 83954

**Auditors:** Deloitte LLP
**Bankers:** The Bank Of Tokyo-Mitsubishi, Ltd (60-01-09)

| | 31-03-14 | 31-03-13 | 31-03-12 |
|---|---|---|---|
| TO | 9,138,397 | 1,737,334 | 6,740,948 |
| P/L | 385,368 | (349,962) | (164,570) |
| NW | (1,630,169) | (2,015,537) | (1,665,575) |
| WC | (1,677,201) | (2,035,975) | (1,687,665) |
| Emp. | 50 | 50 | 50 |

DUNS 49-389-6476 **Imp**

## Shimizu Industry Uk Ltd

**(Subsidiary of:** Denso Corporation)
Unit 4, Welshpool, Powys SY21 8SL
**Tel:** 01938-556446
**Web:** www.shimiz-uk.com
**Reg No:** 3136742 **Estd:** 1995 Private Limited Company
**Line of Business:** Plastic injection moulding
**Export Sales:** £36,272
**Issued Capital:** £11,300,000
**Directors:** M Hayward, M Nicolelli
**Responsibilities**
**Senior:** Kenji Sakamaki *(Manager)*, Dean Thomas *(CEO, Managing Director)*
**Marketing:** Jason Whotton *(IT Manager)*
**IT:** Jason Watson *(Senior IT Executive)*, Jason Whotton *(IT Manager)*
**Operations:** Jason Whotton *(IT Manager)*
**US SIC:** 3079 **UK SIC:** 48360
**Auditors:** Dyke Yaxley Ltd
**Bankers:** Barclays Bank Plc (20-61-08)

| | 31-03-13 | 31-03-12 | 31-03-11 |
|---|---|---|---|
| TO | 11,848,451 | 11,640,828 | 15,887,820 |
| P/L | (989,639) | (1,932,048) | (3,107,492) |
| NW | (419,155) | 570,484 | 398,662 |
| WC | (2,510,627) | (874,195) | (1,830,755) |
| Emp. | 151 | 155 | 186 |

DUNS 23-219-0785

## Shimna Integrated College Ltd

King Street, Newcastle, Co Down BT33 0HD
**Tel:** 02843726107 **Fax:** 028-4372-6109
**Web:** www.shimnacollege.org.uk
**Reg No:** 0028059NI **Estd:** 1994 Private Limited Company
**Line of Business:** Schools (foundation)
**Directors:** Mrs D C Skillen, Mrs J M Boyle, J A Lovell, Ms J J Temple, D W O'Flaherty, Mrs A T Fitzpatrick, Mrs P A Quinn, T J Henderson
**Responsibilities**
**Senior:** Rachel Corrigan *(Director)*, Noreen Doran-Lahey *(Director)*, Geraldine Graham *(Director)*, Catherine Greene *(Director)*, Isobel Jones *(Director)*, Kevin Lambe *(Principal)*, Neil Mcgrady *(Director)*, Alasdair Spence *(Director)*
**US SIC:** 8211 **UK SIC:** 93200
**Auditors:** Cochrane & Co

| | 31-03-14 | 31-03-13 | 31-03-12 |
|---|---|---|---|
| TA | 288,646 | 116,907 | 38,083 |
| NW | 5,657 | 8,559 | 15,254 |
| WC | 5,657 | 8,559 | 15,254 |

DUNS 22-909-9635 **Imp-Exp**

## Shin-Etsu Handotai Europe Ltd

**(Subsidiary of:** Shin-Etsu Chemical Co. Ltd.)
Wilson Road, Livingston, West Lothian EH54 7DA
**Tel:** 01506-415555 **Fax:** 01506417171
**Web:** www.sehe.com
**Reg No:** 0087947SC **VAT No:** 402896644
**Estd:** 1984 Private Limited Company
**Line of Business:** Manufacture of electronic valves and tubes and other electronic components
**Export Markets:** Western Europe
**Export Sales:** £105,374,000
**Issued Capital:** £73,000,000
**Directors:** S Onishi, J S Wallace, T Ito
**Co. Secretary:** Burness Paull Llp
**Responsibilities**
**Senior:** H Hirooka *(Production Manager)*, Douglas Hughes *(Accounts Manager)*
**Finance:** Douglas Hughes *(Accounts Manager)*
**Health & Safety:** Stewart Cook *(Health & Safety Officer)*
**Operations:** Stewart Cook *(Health & Safety Officer)*
**Engineering:** H Hirooka *(Production Manager)*, John Wastle *(Engineering Manager)*
**US SIC:** 3679 **UK SIC:** 34542
**Auditors:** Ernst & Young LLP
**Bankers:** Bank Of Scotland (80-08-80)

| | 31-12-13 | 31-12-12 | 31-12-11 |
|---|---|---|---|
| TO | 116,544,000 | 135,214,000 | 185,024,000 |
| P/L | 2,679,000 | 7,608,000 | 16,568,000 |
| NW | 80,281,000 | 84,002,000 | 77,366,000 |
| WC | 26,134,000 | 14,594,000 | 23,901,000 |
| Emp. | 401 | 404 | 415 |

DUNS 22-751-9675 **Imp**

## Shine Food Machinery Ltd

New Quay Road, Felnex Industrial Estate, Newport, Gwent NP19 4PL
**Tel:** 01633-294800
**Web:** www.shine.co.uk
**Reg No:** 1443265 **VAT No:** 337650253
**Estd:** 1979 Private Limited Company
**Line of Business:** Catering equipment
**Issued Capital:** £10,000
**Principals:** J Shine *(Chairman and Managing)*, J J Shine *(Managing)*, J I Shine
**Co. Secretary:** Julian Shine
**Responsibilities**
**Senior:** Byron Parnell *(Manager)*
**Marketing:** Sharon Ryan *(Administration Coordinator)*
**Admin:** Sharon Ryan *(Administration Coordinator)*
**HR:** Sharon Ryan *(Administration Coordinator)*
**Branches:** Shine Food Machinery Ltd, New Quay Road, Stevenson Street Industrial Esta, Newport, Gwent NP19 4PL
**US SIC:** 3551, 8999, 5199
**UK SIC:** 32441, 83954, 61900
**Auditors:** Paul Phillis & Co Ltd
**Bankers:** Barclays Bank Plc (20-18-15)

| | 31-12-13 | 31-12-12 | 31-12-11 |
|---|---|---|---|
| TO | 7,820,724 | 8,286,641 | 10,887,843 |
| P/L | 13,086 | (526,880) | 281,444 |
| NW | 583,822 | 567,771 | 1,055,023 |
| WC | 54,792 | 58,684 | 655,295 |
| Emp. | 52 | 56 | 55 |

DUNS 51-995-2597 **Imp**

## Shine Ltd

**(Subsidiary of:** Nc Shine Acquisition Ltd.)
Primrose Studios, 109a Regents Park Road, London NW1 8UR
**Tel:** 02079857000 **Fax:** 020-7985-7001
**Web:** www.shinelimited.com
**Reg No:** 4001973 **Estd:** 2001 Private Limited Company
**Line of Business:** Film production services and studios
**Export Sales:** £291,000
**Issued Capital:** £4,204
**Directors:** T Hincks, C G Carey, Ms S Turner Laing, K R Murdoch
**US SIC:** 7819 **UK SIC:** 97111
**Auditors:** Deloitte LLP
**Bankers:** Barclays Bank Plc (20-71-74)

| | 30-06-14 | 30-06-13 | 01-06-12 |
|---|---|---|---|
| TO | 294,000 | 750,000 | 632,000 |
| P/L | (39,052,000) | (10,753,000) | 22,204,000 |
| NW | 80,097,000 | 109,300,000 | 119,207,000 |
| WC | (137,064,000) | (119,784,000) | (111,631,000) |
| Emp. | 76 | 73 | 70 |

DUNS 34-791-4454 **Imp**

## Shine-Mart Ltd

Unit 1 Spilsby Road, Harold Hill, Romford, Essex RM3 8SB
**Tel:** 01708374500
**Web:** www.shinemart.co.uk
**Reg No:** 5591927 **Estd:** 2005 Private Limited Company
**Line of Business:** Import and export agents
**Issued Capital:** £100
**Director:** M N Islam
**Co. Secretary:** Mohammed Manon
**US SIC:** 4712 **UK SIC:** 77002

| | 31-10-13 | 31-10-12 | 31-10-11 |
|---|---|---|---|
| TA | 1,485,869 | 1,158,601 | 921,193 |
| NW | 595,621 | 373,467 | 176,476 |
| WC | 296,296 | 177,519 | 52,880 |

DUNS 21-605-9741 **Imp-Exp**

## Shiner Ltd

1700 Park Avenue, Bristol, Avon BS5 9JB
**Tel:** 01179556035
**Web:** www.shiner.co.uk
**Reg No:** 0315108 **VAT No:** 137554850
**Estd:** 1936 Private Limited Company
**Line of Business:** Other wholesale
**Export Markets:** E U, Canada, U S A
**Export Sales:** £3,774,783
**Issued Capital:** £26,667
**Principals:** M J Allen *(Managing)*, L T Wilson, C J Allen, R N Allen, C N Allen, R A Staite, Ms V S Allen, Mrs V S Ruddlesdin
**Co. Secretary:** Christopher Allen
**Responsibilities**
**Marketing:** Vicki Ruddlesdin *(Marketing Director)*
**HR:** Marie Hodgson *(HR Manager)*
**US SIC:** 5199 **UK SIC:** 61900
**Auditors:** Whyatt Pakeman Partners
**Bankers:** Barclays Bank Plc (20-13-42)

| | 30-04-14 | 30-04-13 | 30-04-12 |
|---|---|---|---|
| TO | 13,024,021 | 8,725,213 | 9,563,936 |
| P/L | 117,425 | (423,378) | 1,061,815 |
| NW | 7,032,077 | 6,848,461 | 7,205,117 |
| WC | 4,737,442 | 4,525,796 | 5,538,220 |
| Emp. | 52 | 47 | 34 |

DUNS 21-484-6862

## Shinewater C P School

Milfoil Drive, Eastbourne, East Sussex BN23 8ED
**Tel:** 01323762129
**Web:** www.shinewater.e-sussex.sch.uk
**Estd:** 2012
**Line of Business:** Schools (local authority)
**Responsibilities**
**Senior:** Theresa Buttery *(Head Teacher)*
**US SIC:** 8699 **UK SIC:** 96902
**Employees:** 60

DUNS 28-844-7972

## Shiplake Court Ltd

Shiplake Court, Shiplake, Henley-On-Thames, Oxfordshire RG9 4BW
**Tel:** 01189402455
**Web:** www.shiplake.org.uk
**Reg No:** 0612809 **Estd:** 1959 Private Limited Company
**Line of Business:** Schools (independent)
**Trading Style:** Shiplake College
**Issued Capital:** £16
**Directors:** I G Howell, Ms S J Ryan, Mrs M M Elms, Sir W H Mcalpine, R C Dempster, J Dunston, M G Mackenzie-Charrington, J S Gordon
**Co. Secretary:** John Walne
**Responsibilities**
**Senior:** David Dalzell *(Manager)*, Jonathan Hobbs *(Director)*, Nathalie Phillimore *(Director)*, Stewart Roberts *(Manager)*, David Tanner Cbe *(Director)*
**Marketing:** Emily Hatch *(Manager)*, Sam Kilgour *(Marketing Manager)*, Charlotte Stow *(Manager)*
**US SIC:** 8211 **UK SIC:** 93200
**Auditors:** Ernest Francis
**Bankers:** Barclays Bank Plc (20-39-53)

| | 31-08-13 | 31-08-12 | 31-08-11 |
|---|---|---|---|
| TO | 8,730,071 | 8,358,201 | 7,521,317 |
| P/L | 591,979 | 298,671 | 297,233 |
| NW | 10,172,002 | 9,580,023 | 9,281,352 |
| WC | 2,470,403 | 2,047,690 | 3,576,652 |
| Emp. | 128 | 140 | 130 |

DUNS 34-826-2999

## Shipley Brothers Ltd

Scala House, Abbey Street, Nuneaton, Warwickshire CV11 5BZ
**Tel:** 02476385728
**Reg No:** 2799746 **VAT No:** 585264708
**Estd:** 1993 Private Limited Company
**Line of Business:** Gambling and betting activities
**Trading Style:** H J M Cateras, Shipley Amusement Centres
**Issued Capital:** £100
**Managing Director:** H J Shipley
**Co. Secretary:** Jonathan Shipley
**Branches:** Shipley Brothers Ltd, 4-5 Frederick St, Cardiff, South Glamorgan CF10 2DB
**US SIC:** 7999 **UK SIC:** 97913
**Auditors:** KPMG LLP
**Bankers:** National Westminster Bank Plc (56-00-45)

| | 31-03-14 | 31-03-13 | 31-03-12 |
|---|---|---|---|
| TO | 11,323,885 | 11,745,727 | 11,750,537 |
| P/L | 330,853 | 963,456 | 1,307,743 |
| NW | 6,771,507 | 6,447,920 | 5,842,001 |
| WC | 817,065 | 718,179 | (340,011) |
| Emp. | 135 | 141 | 152 |

DUNS 23-223-9376

## Shipley College

Salt Building, Victoria Road, Shipley, West Yorkshire BD18 3LQ
**Tel:** 01274-327222
**Web:** www.shipley.ac.uk
**Estd:** 2002
**Line of Business:** Colleges (higher education)
**Co. Secretary:** Jean Mcallister
**Responsibilities**
**Senior:** Nav Chohan *(Principal)*, Alison Coles *(Sales & Marketing Manager)*, Ian Durham *(Estates Manager)*, Jean McAllister *(Principal)*
**Finance:** Lorraine Swift *(Financial Officer)*
**Marketing:** Alison Coles *(Sales & Marketing Manager)*
**Sales:** Alison Coles *(Sales & Marketing Manager)*
**HR:** Jeremy Stott *(Head of Human Resources)*
**Facilities:** Ian Durham *(Estates Manager)*
**Operations:** Ian Durham *(Estates Manager)*
**US SIC:** 8221 **UK SIC:** 93100
**Employees:** 300

DUNS 57-840-9385 **Imp**

## Shipley Estates Ltd

Etcehell Road, Tamworth, Staffordshire B78 3HF
**Tel:** 01827-311441
**Web:** www.shipleyestates.co.uk
**Reg No:** 2893985 **Estd:** 1994 Private Limited Company

**Line of Business:** Amusement park activities
**Trading Style:** National Leisure
**Issued Capital:** £243,132
**Directors:** W Shipley, H J Shipley, H J Shipley
**Co. Secretary:** Ms Lavinia Shipley
**US SIC:** 7996 **UK SIC:** 97913
**Auditors:** KpmG

| | 30-03-14 | 31-03-13 | 25-03-12 |
|---|---|---|---|
| TO | 5,067,076 | 4,962,112 | 4,131,119 |
| P/L | 454,524 | 241,230 | 542,476 |
| NW | 6,346,081 | 6,022,894 | 5,882,429 |
| WC | (141,312) | (720,042) | (405,940) |
| Emp. | 71 | 73 | 66 |

DUNS 52-028-3334

## Shipleys Trustees Ltd

10 Orange Street, London WC2H 7DQ
**Tel:** 020-7312-0000 **Fax:** 020-7312-0022
**Web:** www.shipleys.com
**Reg No:** 3394826 **Estd:** 1997 Private Limited Company
**Line of Business:** Other business activities not elsewhere classified
**Trading Style:** Shipleys Llp
**Issued Capital:** £1
**Directors:** M D Luckett, K S Roberts
**Co. Secretary:** Kenneth Roberts
**Responsibilities**
**Senior:** J McCuin *(Manager)*
**Marketing:** Stuart Dey *(Marketing Manager)*
**IT:** Naresh Valji *(IT Manager)*
**Branches:** Shipleys Trustees Ltd, Market House, 10 Market Walk, Saffron Walden, Essex CB10 1JZ
**US SIC:** 7399 **UK SIC:** 83954

| | 30-04-14 | 30-04-13 | 30-04-12 |
|---|---|---|---|
| TA | 1 | 1 | 1 |
| NW | 1 | 1 | 1 |

DUNS 73-400-4901

## Shipman Security Systems Ltd

638 High Road, Benfleet, Essex SS7 5SU
**Tel:** 01268-757677 **Fax:** 01268795630
**Web:** www.shipmansecuritysystems.co.uk
**Reg No:** 4673800 **Estd:** 2003 Private Limited Company
**Line of Business:** Fire alarm systems
**Issued Capital:** £500
**Director:** J Shipman
**Co. Secretary:** Mrs Holly Hayhow
**US SIC:** 3643, 3629
**UK SIC:** 34203, 34350
**Bankers:** Barclays Bank Plc (20-12-21)

| | 31-03-14 | 31-03-13 | 31-03-12 |
|---|---|---|---|
| TA | 523,378 | 558,498 | 499,991 |
| NW | 404,515 | 412,078 | 342,249 |
| WC | 178,315 | 169,203 | 307,580 |

DUNS 29-864-1085

## The Shipowners Protection Ltd

St Clare House, 30-33 Minories, London EC3N 1BP
**Tel:** 020-7488-0911
**Web:** www.shipownersclub.com
**Reg No:** 2067444 **VAT No:** 447099617
**Estd:** 1986 Private Limited Company
**Line of Business:** Management activities of holding companies
**Issued Capital:** £20,000
**Principals:** L Aspinall *(Financial)*, S J Swallow *(Commercial)*, Ms B Pickering, S Curtis, D F Heaselden, I Edwards, C W Hume
**Co. Secretary:** Mrs Lauretta Dodsworth
**US SIC:** 6711 **UK SIC:** 83962
**Auditors:** Moore Stephens LLP
**Bankers:** Lloyds TSB Bank plc (30-93-23)

| | 20-02-14 | 20-02-13 | 20-02-12 |
|---|---|---|---|
| TA | 1,267,993 | 1,683,324 | 1,646,016 |
| NW | 20,764 | 20,764 | 20,764 |
| WC | (117,710) | (569,706) | (624,893) |

DUNS 21-853-4137

## Shipston High School

Darlingscote Road, Shipston-On-Stour, Warwickshire CV36 4DY
**Tel:** 01608661833
**Web:** www.shipstonhigh.co.uk
**Reg No:** 8174462 **Estd:** 2012 Private Company Limited By Guarantee
**Line of Business:** Schools (local authority)
**Directors:** R M Armstrong, B Punt, C J Saint, Ms C M Kovacs, G Feary, J Baker, Mrs K E Gaymond, P G Chapman
**Co. Secretary:** Ms Yuhong Meads
**Responsibilities**
**Senior:** David Beeton *(Director)*, Robert Macpherson *(Director)*, Mark Singleton *(Director)*
**US SIC:** 8211 **UK SIC:** 93200
**Bankers:** Lloyds TSB Bank plc (30-98-26)

| | 31-08-14 | 31-08-13 |
|---|---|---|
| TO | 2,820,000 | 10,756,000 |
| P/L | 184,000 | 7,790,000 |
| NW | 7,909,000 | 7,876,000 |
| WC | 954,000 | 718,000 |
| Emp. | 54 | 56 |

DUNS 21-805-5812

## Shipton & Co Ltd

(**Subsidiary of:** Shipton & Co. 1870 Ltd)
27 Spencer Street, Birmingham, West Midlands B18 6DL
**Tel:** 01212362427
**Web:** www.shiptonia.co.uk
**Reg No:** 0243143 **VAT No:** 109515578
**Estd:** 1929 Private Limited Company
**Line of Business:** Jewellery retailers
**Trading Style:** The Cornish Stone Co, Lakeland Jewellers, Derwent Jewellers
**Issued Capital:** £12,819
**Principals:** Lord J B May Of Weybridge *(Managing)*, Lady J May
**Co. Secretary:** John Daly
**Responsibilities**
**Senior:** Jasper May *(Manager)*
**Branches:** Shipton & Co.,Ltd, Corran Esplanade, Oban, Argyll PA34 5PT
**US SIC:** 5944 **UK SIC:** 65400
**Auditors:** James, Stanley & Co
**Bankers:** HSBC Bank plc (40-11-36)

| | 31-12-13 | 31-12-12 | 31-12-11 |
|---|---|---|---|
| TA | 2,376,454 | 2,174,706 | 2,258,648 |
| NW | 1,420,424 | 1,363,457 | 1,355,837 |
| WC | 1,295,791 | 1,185,004 | 1,027,331 |

DUNS 29-883-9382

## Shire Garden Buildings Ltd

Unit 1 Brigstock Road, Wisbech, Cambridgeshire PE13 3JJ
**Tel:** 01945465295 **Fax:** 01945-502070
**Web:** www.shiregb.co.uk
**Reg No:** 2086921 **Estd:** 1987 Private Limited Company
**Line of Business:** Portable buildings
**Issued Capital:** £2
**Managing Director:** S V Smeeth
**Co. Secretary:** Ms Carolyn Smeeth
**Responsibilities**
**Senior:** S Ablett *(Manager)*, M Bullen *(Works Manager)*, Dee Shore *(General Manager)*
**Finance:** K Clayton *(Head of Accounts)*
**Engineering:** Ray Stroud *(Production Manager)*
**US SIC:** 2499 **UK SIC:** 46500

| | 31-12-13 | 31-12-12 | 31-12-12 |
|---|---|---|---|
| TA | 2 | 2 | 2 |
| NW | 2 | 2 | 2 |

DUNS 21-584-7790

## Shire Hall Care Home

Overstone Court, Cardiff, South Glamorgan CF10 5NT
**Tel:** 02920537800
**Web:** www.hallmarkcarehomes.co.uk
**Estd:** 2011 Proprietorship
**Line of Business:** Other human health activities
**Proprietor:** K Walsh
**Responsibilities**
**Senior:** Karen Grapes *(Manager)*
**US SIC:** 8091 **UK SIC:** 95200
**Employees:** 150

DUNS 21-878-7276

## Shire Hall Study Centre

Market Avenue, Norwich, Norfolk NR1 3JU
**Tel:** 01603493625
**Web:** www.norfolk.gov.uk
**Estd:** 2012
**Line of Business:** Research institutions and organisations
**Responsibilities**
**Senior:** Rachel Kirk *(Manager)*
**US SIC:** 7391 **UK SIC:** 94000
**Employees:** 200

DUNS 50-508-6363

## Shire Leasing Plc

1 Calico Business Park, Sandy Way, Tamworth, Staffordshire B77 4BF
**Tel:** 01827689390 **Fax:** 01827-68672
**Web:** www.shireleasing.co.uk
**Reg No:** 2476571 **VAT No:** 558894080
**Estd:** 2004 Public Limited Company
**Line of Business:** Leasing companies
**Issued Capital:** £263,006
**Principals:** J Worton *(Managing)*, M E Smith, A H Rutherford, R C Hayes, M D Picken, Mrs S Price, J J Flounders, Ms H Lumb
**Co. Secretary:** Mrs Helen Lumb
**Responsibilities**
**Senior:** Ann Fortnam *(Manager)*
**Admin:** Deborah Amos *(Office Manager)*
**IT:** Graham Coe *(Computer Manager)*
**HR:** Deborah Amos *(Office Manager)*
**Health & Safety:** Deborah Amos *(Office Manager)*
**Facilities:** Lindsey Webster *(Facilities Manager)*
**US SIC:** 7394, 6111
**UK SIC:** 84000, 81501
**Auditors:** PricewaterhouseCoopers LLP
**Bankers:** Yorkshire Bank Plc (05-03-87)

| | 31-03-14 | 31-03-13 | 31-03-12 |
|---|---|---|---|
| TA | 53,679,000 | 49,558,000 | 46,154,000 |
| P/L | (295,000) | 2,509,000 | 3,507,000 |
| NW | 9,421,000 | 10,942,000 | 9,606,000 |
| WC | 31,311,000 | 26,017,000 | 22,134,000 |
| Emp. | 143 | 136 | 132 |

DUNS 21-122-2147

## Shire Plc

Unity Place, Hampshire International Business Park, Basingstoke, Hampshire RG24 8EP
**Tel:** 01256894000 **Fax:** 01256894708
**Web:** www.shire.com
**Reg No:** 0099854J **Estd:** 2008 Public Limited Company
**Line of Business:** Wholesale of perfume and cosmetics
**Responsibilities**
**Senior:** Roger Adsett *(?Senior Vice President)*, Sara Aswegan *(VP Product Strategy Team Lead)*, Tony Barber *(Associate Director Operational)*, Norman Barton *(Medical Director)*, Heidi Chandonnet *(Executive)*, Mike Christian *(Board Member)*, Jeannine Firestone *(Associate Director, Global Reg)*, David Ginsburg *(Non-Executive Director)*, Pierre Gosselin *(Senior Director, Business Deve)*, Tony Guthrie *(Deputy Company Secretary)*, Joe Homan *(Associate Director, Lean Sigma)*, Zohra Lomri *(Associate Director, Regulatory)*, Maureen Martini *(Manager)*, Anne Minto *(Non-Executive Director)*, Flemming Ornskov *(Chief Executive Officer)*, Kelly Rodeghiero *(HR Director)*, Harris Rotman *(Senior Manager)*, Michael Skoien *(Vice President)*, David Stout *(Non-Executive Director)*, Mort Sullivan *(Executive)*, Michael Sumner *(Vice President Clinical Develo)*, Leonhard Terp *(General Manager)*, Arthur Tzianabos *(Vice President, Program Manage)*, Steven Vaghefi *(Executive)*, Steven Valliere *(Manager)*, Phillip Wang *(Associate Director, Bioscience)*, Mike Ward *(Executive)*, Krystene Woodard *(Manager)*, Michael Yasick *(Vice President)*
**Finance:** Eduardo Gutierrez *(Financial Director)*
**Marketing:** Sara Aswegan *(VP Product Strategy Team Lead)*, Jessica Cotrone *(Senior Director, Corporate Com)*, Craig Dimblebee *(?Marketing and Events Innovati)*, Stephanie Fagan *(Senior Vice President Corporat)*, Gwen Fisher *(Senior Director Corporate Comm)*, Michelle Hickin *(e Marketing Operations Special)*, Xavier Petit *(Marketing Manager)*, Marc Weeks *(Digital Communications Manager)*
**Sales:** Carrie Burke *(Regional Business Development Manager)*, David Colpman *(Global Business Development Di)*, Richard Ferguson *(Director, Commercial Assessmen)*, Pierre Gosselin *(Senior Director, Business Deve)*, Cherise Kent *(Director, Business Development)*, Christy Richards *(Senior Sales Training)*, Mark Timko *(Sales Executive)*
**HR:** Ginger Gregory *(Chief Human Resources Officer)*, Ken Harris *(Human Resources Manager)*, Christy Richards *(Senior Sales Training)*, Kelly Rodeghiero *(HR Director)*
**Operations:** Jeffrey Dragan *(Senior Quality Engineer)*, Douglas Ducharme *(Manufacturing Supervisor)*, Rebekah Gorney *(Production and Operations Mana)*, Anthony Haskell *(Senior Project Manager)*, MaryAnn Livolsi *(Manager)*, Pat Sacco *(Engineer)*, David Stanmore *(Director, International Qualit)*, Stan Szpindor *(Quality Director)*
**Engineering:** Bill Hannula *(Engineer)*, Patricia Nugent *(Plant Engineer)*, Cheryl Stearns *(Senior Maintenance Planning Sp)*, Suzanne Stuhler *(Engineer)*
**US SIC:** 5122, 2834
**UK SIC:** 61800, 25700
**Employees:** 3,875
**Turnover:** £4,934,300,000

DUNS 49-388-6105

## Shire Timber & Truss Ltd

(**Subsidiary of:** Beautifulfuture Ltd)
Knowsthorpe Gate, Leeds, West Yorkshire LS9 0NP
**Web:** www.shiretimber.co.uk
**Reg No:** 3135648 **VAT No:** 664780013
**Estd:** 1995 Private Limited Company
**Line of Business:** Saw milling and planing of wood, impregnation of wood
**Issued Capital:** £120,000
**Principals:** M A Crowther *(Managing)*, M Onions
**Co. Secretary:** James Butler
**Responsibilities**
**Admin:** Nick Jagger *(Office Manager)*
**IT:** Matthew Crowther *(Sales Manager)*
**HR:** Pat Crowther *(Personnel Manager)*
**Health & Safety:** Pat Crowther *(Personnel Manager)*
**Facilities:** Martyn Britton *(Production Manager)*
**Engineering:** Martyn Britton *(Production Manager)*
**Branches:** Shire Timber & Truss Limited, Ample House, 76A South Park, Lincoln, Lincolnshire LN5 8ES
**US SIC:** 2421, 2499
**UK SIC:** 46101, 46500
**Auditors:** Kirk Newsholme
**Bankers:** The Royal Bank Of Scotland Plc (16-23-37)

| | 30-04-14 | 30-04-13 | 31-04-11 |
|---|---|---|---|
| TA | 1,847,165 | 1,602,183 | 1,668,515 |
| NW | 732,199 | 728,498 | 172,505 |
| WC | 814,979 | 704,393 | 227,105 |

DUNS 67-222-3976

## Shireland Learning Ltd

Waterloo Road, Smethwick, West Midlands B66 4ND
**Tel:** 01215658816
**Web:** www.collegiateacademy.org.uk
**Reg No:** 6052021 **Estd:** 1997 Private Company Limited By Guarantee
**Line of Business:** Schools (local authority)
**Trading Style:** Shireland Collegiate Academy
**Directors:** Sir M Grundy, A M Savell Boss, D M Irish
**Co. Secretary:** Ian Foyle
**Responsibilities**
**IT:** Harpreet Mudhar *(IT Manager)*
**US SIC:** 8211 **UK SIC:** 93200
**Auditors:** Gilbert & Co

| | 31-08-13 | 31-08-12 | 31-08-11 |
|---|---|---|---|
| TA | 3,187 | 30,904 | 112,923 |
| NW | 2,638 | 2,638 | 2,638 |
| WC | 2,638 | 2,638 | 2,638 |

DUNS 89-636-0922

## Shires Pharmacies Ltd

2 The Green, Clowne, Chesterfield, Derbyshire S43 4JJ
**Tel:** 01246810278
**Reg No:** 3317302 **Estd:** 2008 Private Limited Company
**Line of Business:** Dispensing chemists
**Issued Capital:** £430,004
**Director:** G Myers
**Co. Secretary:** Mrs Rosalyn Myers
**Branches:** Shires Pharmacies Ltd, 37-39 Jaunty Way, Sheffield, South Yorkshire S12 3DZ
**US SIC:** 5912 **UK SIC:** 64300
**Auditors:** Landin Wilcock & Co

| | 31-05-14 | 31-05-13 | 31-05-12 |
|---|---|---|---|
| TO | 4,982,623 | 4,978,027 | 5,148,290 |
| P/L | (61,318) | 564,631 | 613,525 |
| NW | (188,469) | 207,600 | 102,797 |
| WC | (137,304) | (581) | (169,408) |
| Emp. | 58 | 56 | 56 |

DUNS 21-606-9159

## Shirley Oaks Hospital

Poppy Lane, Croydon, Surrey CR9 8AB
**Web:** www.bmihealthcare.co.uk
**Estd:** 2011
**Line of Business:** Hospitals
**Proprietor:** J Hare
**US SIC:** 8062 **UK SIC:** 95100
**Employees:** 200

DUNS 21-675-4756

## Shirley Shelley Industrial Cleaners Ltd

725a Woodbridge Road, Ipswich, Suffolk IP4 4NB
**Tel:** 01473729208
**Web:** www.shirleyshelley.co.uk
**Reg No:** 7271924 **Estd:** 1984 Private Limited Company
**Line of Business:** Cleaning activities not elsewhere classified
**Trading Style:** Shirley Shelley Contract Cleaners
**Issued Capital:** £100
**Director:** M R Shelley
**Co. Secretary:** Mrs Shirley Shelley
**US SIC:** 7349 **UK SIC:** 92300

| | 30-04-14 | 30-04-13 | 30-04-12 |
|---|---|---|---|
| TA | 830,436 | 764,232 | 808,294 |
| NW | 161,697 | 23,200 | (128,367) |
| WC | 49,921 | (53,042) | (211,167) |

DUNS 21-932-6097

## Shirley's Transport Ltd

Mount Garage, Leek Road, Stoke-On-Trent, Staffordshire ST9 0DQ
**Web:** www.shirleystransport.co.uk
**Reg No:** 0817080 **VAT No:** 279027144
**Estd:** 1936 Private Limited Company
**Line of Business:** Other supporting land transport activities
**Issued Capital:** £1,775
**Director:** M J Shirley
**Co. Secretary:** Arthur Shirley
**Responsibilities**
**Facilities:** Alan Basnett *(Facilities Manager)*
**US SIC:** 4789 **UK SIC:** 77002
**Auditors:** Hardwicks
**Bankers:** Barclays Bank Plc (20-48-70)

| | 31-03-14 | 31-03-13 | 31-03-12 |
|---|---|---|---|
| TO | 9,126,108 | 10,066,229 | 9,552,673 |
| P/L | 561,068 | 785,624 | 666,944 |
| NW | 2,900,055 | 2,489,844 | 1,923,120 |
| WC | 949,415 | 906,436 | 522,688 |
| Emp. | 79 | 82 | 82 |

DUNS 29-822-0948 **Imp-Exp**

## Shiseido U K Co Ltd

(**Subsidiary of:** Shiseido Company Limited)
Gillingham House 38 44 Gillingha, London SW1V 1HU
**Tel:** 02073134774
**Web:** www.shiseido.co.uk
**Reg No:** 2040213 **VAT No:** 447183340
**Estd:** 1986 Private Limited Company
**Line of Business:** Wholesale of perfume and cosmetics
**Export Markets:** Japan
**Issued Capital:** £858,290
**Director:** E M Morizot
**Responsibilities**
**Senior:** Atsushi Sato *(Director)*
**US SIC:** 5122 **UK SIC:** 61800
**Auditors:** KPMG LLP
**Bankers:** The Dai-Ichi Kangyo Bank, Ltd. (40-50-69)

| | 31-12-13 | 31-12-12 | 31-12-11 |
|---|---|---|---|
| TO | 3,102,220 | 3,267,232 | 3,588,184 |
| P/L | (748,379) | (688,724) | (802,465) |
| NW | (7,857,660) | (7,109,281) | (5,744,853) |
| WC | (8,029,546) | (7,355,500) | (6,022,355) |
| Emp. | 70 | 81 | 78 |

DUNS 21-529-0151

## Shiskine Golf Club

Blackwaterfoot, Brodick, Isle of Arran KA27 8HA
**Tel:** 01770-860226
**Web:** www.shiskinegolf.com
**Estd:** 2002
**Line of Business:** Golf clubs
**Principals:** A Johnstone *(Chairman)*, Mrs F Crawford *(Manager)*
**Responsibilities**
**Senior:** Dougie Bell *(Professional)*
**Admin:** Pietra Johnston *(Club Secretary)*
**US SIC:** 7999 **UK SIC:** 97913
**Employees:** 700

DUNS 77-978-5166

## Shiva Excel Ltd

Regent House Allum Gate, Theobald Street Elstree, Borehamwood, Hertfordshire WD6 4RS
**Tel:** 02083271331
**Reg No:** 5946952 **Estd:** 2006 Private Limited Company
**Line of Business:** Hotels
**Issued Capital:** £1,000
**Directors:** R G Sachdev, R R Sachdev, U Vyas
**US SIC:** 7011 **UK SIC:** 66500
**Auditors:** KPMG LLP

| | 25-03-13 | 25-03-12 | 25-03-11 |
|---|---|---|---|
| TO | 6,785,614 | 7,230,850 | 6,470,755 |
| P/L | 41,137 | 262,157 | 85 |
| NW | 208,576 | 188,003 | 49,032 |
| WC | 49,051 | 303,011 | 138,830 |
| Emp. | 71 | 71 | 73 |

DUNS 76-988-7126

## Shoda Sauces Europe Co Ltd

(**Subsidiary of:** Shoda Shoyu Co. Ltd.)
Unit 19-20, Rising Sun Industrial Estate, Blaina, Abertillery, Gwent NP13 3JW
**Tel:** 01495-290393 **Fax:** 01495-291831
**Web:** www.shodasauceseu.com
**Reg No:** 2646875 **VAT No:** 626806430
**Estd:** 1991 Private Limited Company
**Line of Business:** Manufacturers of food products
**Issued Capital:** £5,349,034
**Directors:** M Kasahara, K Miyahara, T Shoda, M Hirata
**Co. Secretary:** Toshio Shoda
**Responsibilities**
**Senior:** Ken Watanabe *(Factory Manager)*
**Purchasing:** Tracey Briggs *(Purchasing Manager)*
**Branches:** Shoda Sauces Europe Co Ltd, Plateau, Unit 34, Ebbw Vale, Gwent NP23 5SD
**US SIC:** 2099, 2033
**UK SIC:** 42399, 41473
**Auditors:** G Foxwell & Co
**Bankers:** HSBC Bank plc (40-04-37)

| | 31-07-14 | 31-07-13 | 31-07-12 |
|---|---|---|---|
| TO | 10,464,281 | N/A | N/A |
| P/L | 744,947 | N/A | N/A |
| NW | 1,592,701 | 847,754 | 137,446 |
| WC | 1,310,058 | 545,384 | 61,662 |
| Emp. | 50 | N/A | N/A |

DUNS 21-565-4088
### Shoe Fair Sports
25-31 Newry Street, Banbridge, Co Down BT32 3EA
**Tel:** 028-4066-2750
**Web:** www.donaghys.co.uk
**VAT No:** 253217384 **Estd:** 1960 Partnership
**Line of Business:** Retail of sports goods
**Partners:** Ms A Mcreath, M Donaghy
**Responsibilities**
**Senior:** Anne McReath *(Partner)*
**Branches:** Shoe Fair Sports, 77 Bow Street, Lisburn, Co Antrim BT28 1BN
**US SIC:** 5941, 5699
**UK SIC:** 65400, 64500
**Bankers:** Ulster Bank Ltd (98-03-30)
**Employees:** 60

DUNS 21-817-1718 **Imp-Exp**
### Shoe Zone Retail Ltd
(**Subsidiary of:** Slawston Ltd)
Humberstone Road Haramead Business, Centre, Leicester, Leicestershire LE1 2LH
**Web:** www.shoezone.com
**Reg No:** 0148038 **Estd:** 1917 Private Limited Company
**Line of Business:** Retail sale of footwear
**Export Sales:** £6,320,000
**Issued Capital:** £10,050,000
**Principals:** A E Smith *(Managing)*, Ms N T Shefford, J C Smith, N J Davis, Ms C A Howes, C R Bloor
**Co. Secretary:** Keith Phillips
**Responsibilities**
**Senior:** John Markham *(Warehouse Manager)*
**Marketing:** Amy Johnson *(Marketing Officer)*, Aimee Johnson *(Marketing Administrator)*
**Sales:** Philip Doorly *(Retail Operations Manager)*
**IT:** Nigel Humphries *(IT Manager)*
**HR:** Lynne Brown *(Personnel Manager)*
**Health & Safety:** Lynne Brown *(Personnel Manager)*, Jamie Footitt *(Property Manager)*
**Facilities:** Jamie Footitt *(Property Manager)*
**Fleet:** Nigel Humphries *(IT Manager)*
**Branches:** Shoe Zone Retail Ltd, Park Centre Donegall Road, Belfast, Belfast BT12 6HN
**US SIC:** 5661 **UK SIC:** 64600
**Auditors:** PKF (UK) LLP
**Bankers:** HSBC Bank plc (40-28-04)

| | 05-10-13 | 29-09-12 | 01-10-11 |
|---|---|---|---|
| TO | 193,882,000 | 189,423,000 | 119,898,000 |
| P/L | 9,529,000 | 8,488,000 | (7,627,000) |
| NW | 45,666,000 | 36,609,000 | 33,600,000 |
| WC | 36,950,000 | 30,105,000 | 21,878,000 |
| Emp. | 4,560 | 4,591 | 4,409 |

DUNS 21-761-0608
### Shoeburyness High School
Caulfield Road, Shoeburyness, Shoeburyness, Southend-On-Sea, Essex SS3 9LL
**Web:** www.shoebury.energise.com
**Reg No:** 7825856 **Estd:** 2011 Private Limited Company
**Line of Business:** Schools (local authority)
**Directors:** P D Heron, E Lee, R Knight, Ms D Brazier, M Sweeting, S Goodall, Mrs L Rudd, S J Tollworthy
**Co. Secretary:** Ms Kathleen Hodgson
**Responsibilities**
**Senior:** Diane Burgess *(Director)*, Ruth Dalton *(Director)*, Jacqueline Holdsworth *(Director)*, Lisa Jarentowski *(Director)*, Lisa Johnson-Geach *(Director)*, Ronald Waelend *(Director)*
**US SIC:** 8211 **UK SIC:** 93200

| | 31-08-14 | 31-08-13 | 31-08-12 |
|---|---|---|---|
| TO | 10,983,465 | 10,934,046 | 23,515,465 |
| P/L | (615,881) | (597,308) | 15,471,723 |
| NW | 13,926,534 | 14,021,415 | 14,819,723 |
| WC | 1,477,715 | 1,253,667 | 1,242,169 |
| Emp. | 238 | 234 | 230 |

DUNS 23-583-4715 **Imp**
### Shoereuse Ltd
Unit 6-7 Omega Business Village, Thurston Road, Northallerton, North Yorkshire DL6 2NJ
**Tel:** 01609780555 **Fax:** 01609780452
**Web:** www.nextbestclothing.com
**Reg No:** 3581137 **Estd:** 1998 Private Limited Company
**Line of Business:** Wholesale of waste and scrap
**Issued Capital:** £100
**Directors:** M S Fitch-Peyton, C P Juniper
**Co. Secretary:** Ms Susan Drummond
**Responsibilities**
**Senior:** Marcus Peyton *(Manager)*
**US SIC:** 5093 **UK SIC:** 62200

| | 31-12-13 | 31-12-12 | 31-12-11 |
|---|---|---|---|
| TA | 1,100,408 | 705,283 | 769,282 |
| NW | (69,849) | 90,140 | 76,253 |
| WC | (131,413) | 26,703 | 22,701 |

DUNS 21-579-0724
### The Sholing Technology College
Middle Road, Southampton, Hampshire SO19 8PH
**Tel:** 02380448861
**Web:** www.sholingtc.org.uk
**Proprietorship**
**Line of Business:** Schools (foundation)
**Proprietor:** Ms J Dagwell
**US SIC:** 8211 **UK SIC:** 93200
**Employees:** 80

DUNS 28-987-6518 **Imp**
### Shone Building Ltd
Derby Road, Derby, Derbyshire DE73 7HL
**Tel:** 01283-702921 **Fax:** 01283-703241
**Web:** www.shone.uk.com
**Reg No:** 1807867 **Estd:** 1984 Private Limited Company
**Line of Business:** Building of complete constructions or parts thereof; civil engineering
**Issued Capital:** £100
**Principals:** T C Shone *(Managing)*, A Oldham, Mrs L Manning
**Co. Secretary:** Mrs Anne Shone
**Responsibilities**
**Senior:** Lorraine Mannings *(Accountant)*, Alan Urry *(Contracts Manager)*
**Finance:** Lorraine Mannings *(Accountant)*
**Marketing:** Alan Urry *(Contracts Manager)*
**Sales:** Alan Urry *(Contracts Manager)*
**Purchasing:** Sally Hurren *(Purchasing Manager)*
**US SIC:** 2599, 1751
**UK SIC:** 46720, 50400
**Auditors:** McGregors Accountancy Services Ltd
**Bankers:** National Westminster Bank Plc (60-14-19)

| | 31-07-13 | 31-07-12 | 31-07-11 |
|---|---|---|---|
| TA | 3,101,084 | 3,113,175 | 2,017,250 |
| NW | 805,377 | 655,388 | 331,694 |
| WC | 778,019 | 628,581 | 299,080 |

DUNS 21-837-0979
### Shoon (Trading) Ltd
(**Subsidiary of:** Shoon (Holdings) Ltd)
Southover, Wells, Somerset BA5 1UH
**Web:** www.shoon.com
**Reg No:** 8050525 **Estd:** 2012 Private Limited Company
**Line of Business:** Retail sale of footwear
**Issued Capital:** £90,000
**Directors:** S J Sanders, J Carroll, P J Phillips, K Bartle
**Co. Secretary:**
Shakespeares Legal Secretaries L
**US SIC:** 5661 **UK SIC:** 64600
**Bankers:** Barclays Bank Plc (20-13-34)

| | 01-02-14 | 26-01-13 |
|---|---|---|
| TO | 8,372,214 | 7,103,720 |
| P/L | (1,282,970) | 957,376 |
| NW | (235,594) | 842,120 |
| WC | 676,675 | 950,547 |
| Emp. | 149 | 123 |

DUNS 21-837-9656
### Shoosmiths Llp
Witan Gate House 500 600, Witan Gate West, Milton Keynes, Buckinghamshire MK9 1SH
**Tel:** 01908488300
**Web:** www.shoosmith.co.uk
**Reg No:** 0374987OC **VAT No:** 119570856
**Estd:** 2012
**Line of Business:** Solicitors
**Trading Style:** Shoosmiths Solicitors
**Responsibilities**
**Senior:** Simon Boss *(Non-designated Limited Liabili)*, Harold Brako *(Non-designated Limited Liabili)*, Sean Burke *(Non-designated Limited Liabili)*, Melanie Chell *(Non-designated Limited Liabili)*, Alan Corcoran *(Non-designated Limited Liabili)*, Paul De Vince *(Non-designated Limited Liabili)*, Christopher Garnett *(Non-designated Limited Liabili)*, Deborah Gordon Brown *(Non-designated Limited Liabili)*, Kirsten Hewson *(Non-designated Limited Liabili)*, Nicholas Shepherd *(Non-designated Limited Liabili)*, Sean Wright *(Non-designated Limited Liabili)*
**Branches:** Shoosmiths Llp, Premier Inn, The Lakes, Northampton, Northamptonshire NN4 7YD
**US SIC:** 8111 **UK SIC:** 83500

| | 30-04-14 | 30-04-13 |
|---|---|---|
| TO | 92,976,000 | 86,875,000 |
| P/L | 12,244,000 | 11,245,000 |
| NW | 20,227,000 | 20,752,000 |
| WC | 18,100,000 | 16,336,000 |
| Emp. | 1,276 | 1,175 |

DUNS 34-804-8807
### Shoosmiths Services Ltd
Witan Gate House 500-600, Witan Gate West, Milton Keynes, Buckinghamshire MK9 1SH
**Tel:** 08700868300
**Web:** www.shoosmiths.co.uk
**Reg No:** 5604947 **Estd:** 2005 Private Limited Company
**Line of Business:** Solicitors
**Trading Style:** Shoosmiths
**Issued Capital:** £2,000,001
**Directors:** Mrs C M Rowe, Mrs L Hadland, C P Stanton, A R Tubbs, Ms C J Light
**Co. Secretary:**
Shoosmiths Secretaries Limited
**Responsibilities**
**Senior:** Steve Wiltshire *(head of Office)*
**US SIC:** 7399, 8111
**UK SIC:** 83954, 83500
**Bankers:** The Royal Bank Of Scotland Plc (15-10-00)

| | 30-04-14 | 30-04-13 | 30-04-12 |
|---|---|---|---|
| TO | 74,651,000 | 66,037,000 | 59,657,000 |
| P/L | 1,979,000 | 66,000 | 59,000 |
| NW | 4,427,000 | 4,336,000 | 4,481,000 |
| WC | (5,000) | (2,551,000) | 426,000 |
| Emp. | 1,276 | 1,175 | 1,144 |

DUNS 23-733-3070
### Shoosmiths Shareholders Ltd
Witan Gate House, 500-600 Witan Gate West, Milton Keynes, Buckinghamshire MK9 1SH
**Tel:** 03700868300 **Fax:** 0870-086-8301
**Web:** www.shoosmiths.co.uk
**Reg No:** 3727751 **Estd:** 1999 Private Limited Company
**Line of Business:** Solicitors
**Trading Style:** Shoosmiths Solicitors
**Issued Capital:** £1
**Directors:** A R Tubbs, Shoosmiths Nominees Limited
**Co. Secretary:**
Shoosmiths Secretaries Limited
**Responsibilities**
**Senior:** Steve Wiltshire *(Head Of Office)*
**US SIC:** 8111 **UK SIC:** 83500

| | 30-04-14 | 30-04-13 | 30-04-12 |
|---|---|---|---|
| TA | 1 | 1 | 1 |
| NW | 1 | 1 | 1 |

DUNS 21-584-7535
### Shoosmiths Solicitors
38 Colmore Circus Queensway, Birmingham, West Midlands B4 6SH
**Tel:** 03700864000
**Web:** www.shoosmiths.co.uk
**Estd:** 2011 Proprietorship
**Line of Business:** Solicitors
**Proprietor:** M Anslow
**US SIC:** 8111 **UK SIC:** 83500
**Employees:** 1,500

DUNS 21-866-1286
### Shooters Hill Campus
Red Lion Lane, London SE18 4LD
**Tel:** 02083199700 **Fax:** 02088856542
**Web:** https://www.shootershill.ac.uk
**Reg No:** 8270802 **Estd:** 2012 Private Company Limited By Guarantee
**Line of Business:** General secondary education
**Directors:** Ms M C Donovan, Ms S Parker-Gore, M Hage, Ms J Warren, G Lamb
**Co. Secretary:** Stephen Greenman
**Responsibilities**
**Senior:** Susan Middlemiss *(Manager)*, Nick Morris *(CEO, Managing Director)*
**US SIC:** 8211, 8249
**UK SIC:** 93200, 93300
**Bankers:** Lloyds TSB Bank plc (30-93-60)

| | 31-08-14 | 31-08-13 |
|---|---|---|
| TO | 11,119,000 | 39,037,000 |
| P/L | (64,000) | 30,092,000 |
| NW | 29,819,000 | 29,478,000 |
| WC | 1,044,000 | 991,000 |
| Emp. | 191 | 175 |

DUNS 51-594-3319
### Shootfactory Ltd
7.25 Alaska Buildings, Grange Road, London SE1 3BD
**Tel:** 020-7252-3900 **Fax:** 0845-123-5418
**Web:** www.shootfactory.co.uk
**Reg No:** 5874983 **Estd:** 2006 Private Limited Company
**Line of Business:** Photographers (general)
**Issued Capital:** £2
**Director:** J King
**Co. Secretary:** Michael Minns
**US SIC:** 7333 **UK SIC:** 83953

| | 31-07-13 | 31-07-12 | 31-07-11 |
|---|---|---|---|
| TO | N/A | N/A | 826,611 |
| P/L | N/A | N/A | 83,634 |
| NW | 8,691 | 8,713 | 43,816 |
| WC | 32,103 | (3,698) | 37,158 |

DUNS 73-792-5966
### Shooting Star Chase
Bridge House, Addlestone Road, Addlestone, Surrey KT15 2UE
**Tel:** 01932823100 **Fax:** 01932858399
**Web:** www.shootingstarchase.org.uk
**Reg No:** 2927688 **Estd:** 1994 Private Limited Company
**Line of Business:** Hospices
**Directors:** Ms T Morris-Thompson, Mrs J Ader, B Peet, J Mayne, Ms K D Mcnamara Goodger, K Bell, K Doherty, K G Hanna
**Co. Secretary:** Piers Vimpany
**Responsibilities**
**Senior:** Paul Boughton *(Director)*, David Burland *(Chief Executive Officer)*, Kevin Dewey *(Director)*
**Marketing:** Adam Petrie *(Marketing Director)*
**IT:** Tom Bradley *(Head of IT)*
**HR:** Sandi Hillery *(HR Manager)*
**Branches:** Shooting Star Chase, Loseley Park, Guildford, Surrey GU3 1HS
**US SIC:** 8091 **UK SIC:** 95200
**Auditors:** KPMG
**Bankers:** Lloyds TSB Bank plc (30-94-77)

| | 31-03-14 | 31-03-13 | 31-03-12 |
|---|---|---|---|
| TO | 8,501,204 | 7,934,489 | 8,920,822 |
| P/L | (547,892) | (1,207,408) | (440,888) |
| NW | 14,455,178 | 14,792,981 | 15,588,246 |
| WC | 4,315,019 | 3,613,534 | 4,466,895 |
| Emp. | N/A | 166 | 168 |

DUNS 21-231-1525
### Shooting Star House
The Avenue, Hampton, Middlesex TW12 3RA
**Tel:** 020-87832000
**Web:** www.shootingstarchase.org.uk
**Estd:** 2005 Proprietorship
**Line of Business:** Hospices
**Proprietor:** Mrs V Mason
**Responsibilities**
**Senior:** Caroline Beazley *(Manager)*, Sandi Hillery *(Director Of Care)*
**US SIC:** 8091 **UK SIC:** 95200
**Employees:** 50

DUNS 73-387-4916
### Shop Direct Finance Company Ltd
(**Subsidiary of:** Transport International Holdings Limited)
Aintree Innovation Centre, Park, Lane, Netherton, Bootle, Merseyside L30 1SL
**Tel:** 08442-924-799
**Web:** www.shopdirect.com
**Reg No:** 4660974 **Estd:** 2003 Private Limited Company
**Line of Business:** Miscellaneous financial institutions
**Trading Style:** Littlewoods, Isme.Com, Very.Co.Uk, Woolworths.Co.Uk
**Issued Capital:** £170,000,000
**Directors:** C D Fletcher, R L Banks, Ms K J Machin, D W Kershaw, A D Baldock, N Chandler
**Co. Secretary:**
Shop Direct Secretarial Services
**US SIC:** 6111, 7339, 5961
**UK SIC:** 81501, 83954, 65600
**Auditors:** Deloitte LLP

| | 30-06-13 | 30-06-12 | 30-06-11 |
|---|---|---|---|
| TA | 446,379,000 | 560,066,000 | 509,044,000 |
| P/L | 2,024,000 | (8,224,000) | (22,533,000) |
| NW | 216,005,000 | 204,746,000 | 207,970,000 |
| WC | 221,709,000 | 187,872,000 | 105,115,000 |
| Emp. | 789 | 1,060 | 1,041 |

DUNS 73-947-5072
### Shop Direct Group Financial Services Ltd
(**Subsidiary of:** Transport International Holdings Limited)
Park Lane, Bootle, Merseyside L30 1SL
**Tel:** 08442925000
**Web:** www.shopdirect.com
**Reg No:** 5200103 **Estd:** 2004 Private Limited Company
**Line of Business:** Financial intermediation not elsewhere classified
**Issued Capital:** £100,000,000
**Directors:** H M Barclay, S A Winton, M Seal, P L Peters, A S Barclay
**Co. Secretary:**
Shop Direct Secretarial Services
**Responsibilities**
**Senior:** Marie Marsden *(Manager)*
**Branches:** Shop Direct Group Financial Services Ltd, 39 East Street, Chichester, West Sussex PO19 1HX
**US SIC:** 6111, 6711
**UK SIC:** 81501, 83962
**Auditors:** PricewaterhouseCoopers LLP

| | 30-06-13 | 30-06-12 | 30-06-11 |
|---|---|---|---|
| TA | 375,000,000 | 375,000,000 | 375,000,000 |
| NW | 375,000,000 | 375,000,000 | 375,000,000 |

DUNS 73-466-7145
## Shop Direct Ltd
**(Subsidiary of:** Transport International Holdings Limited)
Skyways House, Speke Road, Liverpool, Merseyside L70 1AB
**Tel:** 0844 292 1000
**Web:** www.shopdirect.com
**Reg No:** 4730752 **Estd:** 2003 Private Limited Company
**Line of Business:** Representative office
**Export Sales:** £46,300,000
**Issued Capital:** £264,400,000
**Directors:** S A Winton, A D Baldock, A S Barclay, M Seal, D W Kershaw, M Mcmenemy, P L Peters, H M Barclay
**Co. Secretary:**
  Shop Direct Secretarial Services
**Branches:** Shop Direct Ltd, Bardel Court, Unit 8, Yeovil, Somerset BA22 8RU
**US SIC:** 6111, 6711
**UK SIC:** 81501, 83962
**Auditors:** Deloitte LLP
Following financial data are in thousands

|      | 30-06-13 | 30-06-12 | 30-06-11 |
|------|----------|----------|----------|
| TA   | 1,266,200 | 1,223,100 | 1,218,000 |
| P/L  | 6,600 | (57,700) | (113,900) |
| NW   | 108,900 | 79,200 | 116,900 |
| WC   | 3,000 | (36,100) | (11,900) |
| Emp. | 5,146 | 7,068 | 7,509 |

DUNS 21-401-4529
## Shop Mobility At the Oracle
Management Suite, The Oracle Centre, Riverside Level, Reading, Berkshire RG1 2AG
**Tel:** 01189659008
**Web:** www.theoracle.com
**Proprietorship**
**Line of Business:** Renting of other machinery and equipment not elsewhere classified
**Responsibilities**
**Senior:** Steve Belam (Centre Manager), Sam French (Marketing Manager)
**Finance:** Elena Efamba (Financial Director)
**Marketing:** Sue Doddington (Marketing Coordinator)
**HR:** Sonia Gordon (Human Resources Coordinator)
**Health & Safety:** Bill Duke (Facilities Manager)
**Facilities:** Bill Duke (Facilities Manager)
**US SIC:** 7394 **UK SIC:** 84000
**Employees:** 50

DUNS 23-583-0770    **Imp**
## Shopfittings Direct Ltd
Sunningdale, The Belfry, Colonial Way, Watford, Hertfordshire WD24 4WH
**Tel:** 01923-232425
**Web:** www.sfd.co.uk
**Reg No:** 3580800 **VAT No:** 718820231
**Estd:** 1998 Private Limited Company
**Line of Business:** Manufacturers of shop fittings
**Export Sales:** £4,223,832
**Trading Style:** S F D
**Issued Capital:** £200
**Managing Director:** D N Brookstein
**Co. Secretary:** Paul Brooks
**US SIC:** 2599 **UK SIC:** 46720
**Auditors:** Shelley Stock Hutter LLP
**Bankers:** National Westminster Bank Plc (60-00-08)

|      | 30-09-13 | 30-09-12 | 30-09-11 |
|------|----------|----------|----------|
| TA   | 21,714,228 | 19,361,878 | 12,919,542 |
| P/L  | 1,061,779 | 2,129,900 | 1,049,137 |
| NW   | 3,002,450 | 2,658,352 | 1,348,754 |
| WC   | 2,664,096 | 2,445,865 | 1,268,268 |

DUNS 73-508-7996
## Shore Capital Markets Ltd
**(Subsidiary of:** Shore Capital Group Limited)
Bond Street House, 14 Clifford Street, London W1S 4JU
**Tel:** 02074084050
**Web:** www.shorecap.gg
**Reg No:** 4771893 **Estd:** 2003 Private Limited Company
**Line of Business:** Financial intermediation not elsewhere classified
**Issued Capital:** £945
**Directors:** D H Danford, R M Armitage, S P Fine, M L Van Messel, Dr C W Black, H P Shore, E Flanagan
**Co. Secretary:** David Kaye
**US SIC:** 6111 **UK SIC:** 81501
**Bankers:** The Royal Bank Of Scotland Plc (15-10-00)

|      | 31-12-13 | 31-12-12 | 31-12-11 |
|------|----------|----------|----------|
| TA   | 5,302,492 | 5,353,534 | 5,364,085 |
| P/L  | 2,299,888 | 1,899,869 | 2,499,902 |
| NW   | 3,813,193 | 3,814,235 | 3,714,471 |
| WC   | (1,186,806) | (1,185,764) | (1,285,528) |

DUNS 29-486-8641
## Shore Capital Stockbrokers Ltd
**(Subsidiary of:** Shore Capital Group Limited)
Bond St House, 14 Clifford Street, London W1S 4JU
**Tel:** 02070791670
**Web:** www.shorecap.co.uk
**Reg No:** 1850105 **Estd:** 1984 Private Limited Company
**Line of Business:** Security broking and related activities
**Issued Capital:** £1,639,899
**Principals:** H P Shore (Managing), S P Fine, Dr C W Black, R M Armitage, E Flanagan
**Co. Secretary:** Michael Van Messel
**Branches:** Shore Capital Stockbrokers Ltd, Corn Exchange Building, Fenwick Street, Liverpool, Merseyside L2 7RB
**US SIC:** 6211 **UK SIC:** 83100
**Auditors:** Deloitte & Touche
**Bankers:** The Royal Bank Of Scotland Plc (16-00-83)

|      | 31-12-13 | 31-12-12 | 31-12-11 |
|------|----------|----------|----------|
| TA   | 78,361,000 | 67,512,000 | 47,994,000 |
| P/L  | 5,505,000 | 3,497,000 | 4,030,000 |
| NW   | 27,863,000 | 24,620,000 | 23,583,000 |
| WC   | 27,280,000 | 23,933,000 | 23,250,000 |
| Emp. | 72 | 71 | 70 |

DUNS 76-851-5025
## Shore Laminates Ltd
**(Subsidiary of:** Strata Group Holdings (Scotland) Ltd)
Friarton Bridge Park, Friarton Road, Perth, Perthshire PH2 8DD
**Tel:** 01738-634455 **Fax:** 01738-441622
**Web:** www.shorelaminates.com
**Reg No:** 0131630SC **VAT No:** 561655531
**Estd:** 1991 Private Limited Company
**Line of Business:** Lamination services
**Issued Capital:** £20,100
**Principals:** S M Howie (Managing), M Elwine
**Co. Secretary:** David Cowper
**Responsibilities**
**Senior:** Andy Caldwell (General Manager), Alistair Pringle (Manager)
**Health & Safety:** Dennis Jackson (Production Manager)
**Facilities:** Dennis Jackson (Production Manager)
**Engineering:** Dennis Jackson (Production Manager)
**US SIC:** 5084 **UK SIC:** 61490
**Auditors:** Finlaysons
**Bankers:** The Royal Bank Of Scotland Plc (83-47-00)

|      | 31-12-13 | 31-12-12 | 31-12-11 |
|------|----------|----------|----------|
| TO   | 7,936,549 | 8,373,805 | 8,492,615 |
| P/L  | 1,205,093 | 1,224,232 | 717,856 |
| NW   | 7,567,238 | 5,935,734 | 4,653,795 |
| WC   | 6,132,636 | 4,830,973 | 3,849,896 |
| Emp. | 55 | 54 | 60 |

DUNS 22-904-0225    **Imp-Exp**
## The Shore Porters Society
1 Baltic Place, Aberdeen, Aberdeenshire AB11 5EW
**Tel:** 01224569569
**Web:** www.shoreporters.com
**Estd:** 1998 Partnership
**Line of Business:** Removals and storage activities (domestic)
**Export Markets:** Worldwide
**Trading Style:** Rumsey & Sons
**Partners:** G Winton, S Simpson, K L Brown, G L Burnett, A Davidson, M Chegwin
**Branches:** The Shore Porters Society, Power House, 27 Market Road, Richmond, Surrey TW9 4LZ
**US SIC:** 4214, 4226, 4213
**UK SIC:** 72300, 77003
**Bankers:** Clydesdale Bank Plc (82-60-11)
**Employees:** 100

DUNS 23-086-5169
## Shorefield Country Pk
Shorefield Road, Lymington, Hampshire SO41 0LH
**Tel:** 01590648300
**Web:** www.shorefield.co.uk
**Estd:** 1970
**Line of Business:** Caravan parks
**Proprietor:** S Pollock
**Responsibilities**
**Senior:** Simon Bransgrove (Marketing Manager)
**Sales:** David Goldsmith (Senior Sales Executive)
**IT:** Chris Jolly (Computer Operations Manager)
**US SIC:** 7033 **UK SIC:** 66701
**Employees:** 100

DUNS 22-550-9298
## Shorefield Holidays Ltd
Shorefield Road, Lymington, Hampshire SO41 0LH
**Tel:** 01590648331 **Fax:** 01590-645610
**Web:** www.shorefield.co.uk
**Reg No:** 0607997 **Estd:** 1958 Private Limited Company
**Line of Business:** Health clubs
**Issued Capital:** £31,800
**Principals:** S G Pollock (Managing), Mrs S Morley, Mrs P J Curtis, Mrs L Lawrence, Miss A Pollock, A J Bowden
**Co. Secretary:** Mrs Sara Bertin
**Responsibilities**
**Senior:** Justine Smart (General Manager), Richard Tricker (Manager)
**Branches:** Shorefield Holidays Ltd, Oakdene Holiday Park, St Leonards, Ringwood, Hampshire BH24 2RZ
**US SIC:** 7299 **UK SIC:** 98902
**Auditors:** Grant Thornton
**Bankers:** HSBC Bank plc (40-15-26)

|      | 31-10-13 | 31-10-12 | 31-10-11 |
|------|----------|----------|----------|
| TO   | 17,419,480 | 14,786,922 | 14,877,009 |
| P/L  | 1,500,115 | 1,291,563 | 1,306,010 |
| NW   | 27,201,152 | 25,697,111 | 24,684,079 |
| WC   | (5,171,508) | (5,503,888) | (5,388,539) |
| Emp. | 249 | 246 | 248 |

DUNS 21-772-3788
## Shoreham Academy
Kingston Lane, Shoreham-By-Sea, West Sussex BN43 6YT
**Tel:** 01273274100
**Web:** www.kingsmanor.w-sussex.sch.uk
**Estd:** 2002 Partnership
**Line of Business:** Schools (local authority)
**Partners:** Mrs R Bowker, Mrs H Brown, D Maclean, J Sale, Mrs T Steponitis
**US SIC:** 8211 **UK SIC:** 93200
**Employees:** 195

DUNS 49-385-4624
## Shoreham Ferry Services Ltd
Basin Road South, Portslade, Brighton, East Sussex BN41 1WF
**Tel:** 01273-417757
**Web:** www.shorehamferryservicesltd.com
**Reg No:** 3132479 **Estd:** 1995 Private Limited Company
**Line of Business:** Employment and recruitment companies and consultants
**Issued Capital:** £3,000
**Director:** V B Stupple
**Co. Secretary:** Ms Jacqueline Gawlik
**US SIC:** 7361 **UK SIC:** 83954
**Auditors:** The Sinden Thackeray Partnership

|      | 31-03-14 | 31-03-13 | 31-03-12 |
|------|----------|----------|----------|
| TA   | 124,387 | 73,324 | 61,617 |
| NW   | 45,366 | 30,465 | 22,204 |
| WC   | 44,999 | 29,939 | 22,204 |

DUNS 22-514-1555    **Exp**
## Shoreham Port Authority
90 Albion Street, Southwick, Brighton, East Sussex BN42 4DP
**Tel:** 01273598101
**Web:** www.shorehamportauthority.co.uk
**Estd:** 2013 Incorporate By Act Of Parliament
**Line of Business:** Operation of habours and ports
**Export Markets:** W Europe; Middle East; Africa
**Principals:** B Wheeler (Chairman), R Alete (Financial), C Robinson, I W Dodd, Capt J Robertson, B J Wilson, J Rosenfeld, A Vaughan
**Co. Secretary:** Roger Barrell
**Responsibilities**
**Senior:** Phillip Lacey (General Manager)
**Operations:** Alan Motterhan (Commercial And Operations Dire)
**Branches:** Shoreham Port Authority, 140 Albion St, Brighton, East Sussex BN42 4DP
**US SIC:** 4469 **UK SIC:** 76300
**Auditors:** Baker Tilly UK Audit LLP
**Employees:** 95
**Turnover:** £9,537,000

DUNS 22-656-3278
## Shoreheat Ltd
**(Subsidiary of:** Grafton Group (Uk) Plc)
Progress Group Plc, Cirencester, Gloucestershire GL7 4DS
**Tel:** 01285-713055
**Web:** www.progressgroup.co.uk
**Reg No:** 1566154 **VAT No:** 484608812
**Estd:** 1981 Private Limited Company
**Line of Business:** Other wholesale
**Issued Capital:** £48,422
**Directors:** B O'Hara, J P Sowton
**Co. Secretary:**
  Grafton Group Secretarial Servic
**Responsibilities**
**Senior:** Brian O' Hara (Director), Colm O' Nuallain (Manager)

**Branches:** Shoreheat Ltd, 2 Smyth Road, Bristol, Avon BS3 2BX
**US SIC:** 5199 **UK SIC:** 61900
**Auditors:** Grant Thornton
**Bankers:** Barclays Bank Plc (20-20-15)

|      | 31-12-13 | 31-12-12 | 31-12-11 |
|------|----------|----------|----------|
| TO   | N/A | 7,672,136 | 14,246,980 |
| P/L  | N/A | (185,168) | 28,006 |
| NW   | 2,709,756 | 2,703,756 | 2,894,924 |
| WC   | 2,691,139 | 2,685,139 | 2,334,878 |
| Emp. | N/A | 57 | 54 |

DUNS 51-032-6523
## Shoreland Projects Ltd
**(Subsidiary of:** Shoreland Holdings Ltd)
Woodhouse Lane, Botley, Southampton, Hampshire SO30 2EZ
**Web:** www.shoreland.co.uk
**Reg No:** 3296249 **VAT No:** 692630127
**Estd:** 1998 Private Limited Company
**Line of Business:** Other engineering activities
**Issued Capital:** £1,170
**Directors:** S A Allen, S G Bell
**Co. Secretary:** Richard Goodman
**Responsibilities**
**HR:** Maggi Potts (Administration Manager)
**Facilities:** Maggi Potts (Administration Manager)
**Operations:** Maggi Potts (Administration Manager)
**Purchasing:** Mark Bowley (Purchasing Manager)
**US SIC:** 8911 **UK SIC:** 83701
**Auditors:** Alliott Wingham Ltd
**Bankers:** The Bank Of Ireland (30-15-73)

|      | 31-12-13 | 31-12-12 | 31-12-11 |
|------|----------|----------|----------|
| TA   | 1,768,671 | 1,103,321 | 835,219 |
| NW   | 693,646 | 531,581 | 394,220 |
| WC   | 693,646 | 531,581 | 394,220 |

DUNS 73-740-0692
## Shoreline Housing Partnership Ltd
Shoreline House Westgate Park, Charlton Street, Grimsby, South Humberside DN31 1SQ
**Tel:** 08458492000
**Web:** www.shorelinehp.com
**Reg No:** 4997871 **Estd:** 2003 Private Company Limited By Guarantee
**Line of Business:** Other letting of own property
**Directors:** Mrs M Lalor, S Cousins, Mrs K A Rastall, A E Baxter, Ms M Edge, D M Howie
**Co. Secretary:** Michael Walters
**US SIC:** 6519 **UK SIC:** 85000
**Auditors:** Beever & Struthers
**Bankers:** National Westminster Bank Plc (60-13-20)

|      | 31-03-14 | 31-03-13 | 31-03-12 |
|------|----------|----------|----------|
| TO   | 31,801,000 | 30,910,000 | 30,171,000 |
| P/L  | 921,000 | 6,006,000 | 4,321,000 |
| NW   | 31,237,000 | 28,850,000 | 24,542,000 |
| WC   | 22,313,000 | 18,988,000 | 9,373,000 |
| Emp. | 212 | 218 | 206 |

DUNS 50-546-5401
## Shorewood Leisure Group Ltd
Seaside Road, Aldbrough, Hull, North Humberside HU11 4SA
**Tel:** 01964529292
**Web:** www.aldbroughleisurepark.co.uk
**Reg No:** 2501010 **VAT No:** 551796220
**Estd:** 1990 Private Limited Company
**Line of Business:** Holiday centres and holiday villages
**Issued Capital:** £10,000
**Managing Director:** D R Allison
**Co. Secretary:** Neil Willson
**Responsibilities**
**Marketing:** Karen Hague (Sales & Marketing Director)
**Sales:** Karen Hague (Sales & Marketing Director)
**US SIC:** 7032 **UK SIC:** 66702
**Auditors:** Lloyd Dowson & Co
**Bankers:** Yorkshire Bank Plc (05-05-10)

|      | 31-12-12 | 31-12-11 | 31-12-10 |
|------|----------|----------|----------|
| TO   | 16,089,451 | 16,017,134 | 17,687,006 |
| P/L  | 548,172 | 358,754 | 748,802 |
| NW   | 20,171,157 | 19,721,329 | 19,412,132 |
| WC   | (14,852,764) | (2,468,000) | (2,292,381) |
| Emp. | 97 | 91 | 101 |

DUNS 22-161-2281
## Shorrock Trichem Ltd
Unit 20 Tyldesley Old Road Chanters, Industrial Estate, Manchester M46 9SD
**Tel:** 01616525353 **Fax:** 01942870952
**Web:** www.shorrocktrichem.com
**Reg No:** 4179799 **VAT No:** 732829814
**Estd:** 2011 Private Limited Company
**Line of Business:** Manufacturers of chemicals
**Issued Capital:** £998
**Directors:** D P Allison, Mrs C M Darlington, D Fishwick, D L Oliver, M Denning, K E Shorrock, I J Eckersley
**Co. Secretary:** Joel Lewis

**Responsibilities**
**Health & Safety:** Lois Amos (PA to directors)
**Fleet:** Peter Cotton (Transport Manager)
**US SIC:** 2899, 4953
**UK SIC:** 25670, 92110
**Auditors:** Allen Mills Howard & Co

| | 31-12-13 | 31-12-12 | 31-12-11 |
|---|---|---|---|
| TO | 18,951,735 | 18,209,496 | 17,433,948 |
| P/L | 803,269 | 936,441 | 749,142 |
| NW | 5,390,340 | 4,557,472 | 3,755,399 |
| WC | 4,143,093 | 3,405,337 | 2,646,935 |
| Emp. | 200 | 194 | 193 |

**DUNS 21-455-7183**
### Short Brothers Plc
(**Subsidiary of:** Bombardier Inc)
Airport Road, Belfast BT3 9DZ
**Tel:** 02890-458-444
**Web:** www.bombardier.com
**Reg No:** 0001062NI **Estd:** 1908 Public
Limited Company
**Line of Business:** Manufacture of aircraft
and spacecraft
**Trading Style:** Short Brothers Plc, Shorts
**Directors:** Mrs M Mcgivern, D R Hendron,
G E Cox, M Ryan, R R Barnett, J Seguin,
S Dorgan, K S Brundle
**Co. Secretary:** Colin Thompson
**Responsibilities**
**Senior:** Andy Bann (Terminal Manager), Guy
Hutchey (CEO, Managing Director), Graham
Skinner (Director)
**Operations:** Mark Edgar (Senior
Manufacturing Engineer), Robert burke
(Director Manufacturing Enginee)
**Engineering:** Niall Bell (Composite
Manufacturing Engine), Michael Ernesti
(Manufacturing Engineering Sect), Stephen
McLaughlin (Materials and Processes
Engine), Justin Morrison (Senior
Manufacturing Engineer), Joe Nwaejike
(Research Composite Manufacturi)
**US SIC:** 3999, 3721, 8911
**UK SIC:** 49590, 36400, 83701
**Auditors:** Ernst & Young LLP
**Bankers:** HSBC Bank plc (40-00-00)
**Employees:** 4,954
**Turnover:** £904,551,000

**DUNS 21-777-5556**
### Short Term Assessment & Re-Ablement Service
1 Staff House, Ilkeston Avenue, Goole, North
Humberside DN14 6PZ
**Tel:** 01405768544
**Web:** www.eastriding.co.uk
**Estd:** 1997 Proprietorship
**Line of Business:** Home care service
providers
**Proprietor:** Mrs A Bulmer
**US SIC:** 8091 **UK SIC:** 95200
**Employees:** 60

**DUNS 23-638-6095**
### Shorterm Group Ltd
The Barn, Philpots Close, West Drayton,
Middlesex UB7 7RY
**Tel:** 08001223456 **Fax:** 01895-420041
**Web:** www.shorterm.co.uk
**Reg No:** 3635466 **Estd:** 1987 Private
Limited Company
**Line of Business:** Employment and
recruitment companies and consultants
**Issued Capital:** £6,246,330
**Directors:** Ms J L Crawford, S Gallucci,
P F Keenan
**Responsibilities**
**Health & Safety:** Julia Hudson-Morgan
(Health & Safety Officer)
**US SIC:** 7361 **UK SIC:** 83954
**Auditors:** BDO Stoy Hayward LLP
**Bankers:** National Westminster Bank Plc
(51-50-01)

| | 31-12-13 | 31-12-12 | 31-12-11 |
|---|---|---|---|
| TO | 71,074,000 | 56,943,000 | 64,762,000 |
| P/L | 244,000 | 103,000 | 16,000 |
| NW | (2,697,000) | (2,934,000) | (3,377,000) |
| WC | 317,000 | 576,000 | 439,000 |
| Emp. | 82 | 64 | 60 |

**DUNS 56-977-0738** Imp
### Shortridge Ltd
Joseph Noble Road, Lillyhall Industrial
Estate, Lillyhall, Workington, Cumbria CA14
4JX
**Tel:** 01900-606696
**Web:** www.shortridgelaundry.co.uk
**Reg No:** 2853436 **VAT No:** 621162189
**Estd:** 1993 Private Limited Company
**Line of Business:** Laundries
**Trading Style:** Short Ridge
**Issued Capital:** £39,200
**Principals:** P A Hinckley (Managing),
Ms C E Greenwell, D W Greenwell
**Co. Secretary:** Io Strong
**Branches:** Shortridge Ltd, Unit 5, Irongray
Road, Dumfries, Dumfriesshire DG2 0JE
**US SIC:** 7219 **UK SIC:** 98110
**Auditors:** Christian Douglass LLP

**Bankers:** HSBC Bank plc (40-26-06)

| | 30-09-13 | 30-09-12 | 30-09-11 |
|---|---|---|---|
| TA | 4,008,830 | 3,084,544 | 3,244,158 |
| NW | 1,698,238 | 1,543,446 | 1,507,336 |
| WC | 294,272 | 872,325 | 983,950 |

**DUNS 21-917-7912**
### Shorts Auto Electrical (Swansea) Ltd
43-51 Station Road, Landore, Swansea,
West Glamorgan SA1 2JE
**Tel:** 01792-469595
**Web:** www.shortsauto.co.uk
**Reg No:** 0983150 **Estd:** 2009 Private
Limited Company
**Line of Business:** Garage related services
**Issued Capital:** £100
**Directors:** Mrs C A Discombe,
Mrs J D Roberts, Mrs A J Bowman,
Mrs J Short, W R Short
**Co. Secretary:** David Roberts
**Responsibilities**
**Senior:** Eric Frost (Stores Coordinator)
**Branches:** Shorts Auto Electrical (Swansea)
Ltd, Lansdowne Road, Cardiff, South
Glamorgan CF5 1JU
**US SIC:** 7539, 5531
**UK SIC:** 67100, 65100
**Auditors:** Gerald Thomas & Co
**Bankers:** Lloyds TSB Bank plc (30-95-46)

| | 31-07-13 | 31-07-12 | 31-07-11 |
|---|---|---|---|
| TA | 738,166 | 708,623 | 604,045 |
| NW | 32,681 | 64,678 | 131,099 |
| WC | 61,135 | 66,968 | 44,618 |

**DUNS 21-720-2811**
### Shorts of Ascot Ltd
(**Subsidiary of:** Shorts Services Ltd)
Station Works, Lyndhurst Road, Ascot,
Berkshire SL5 9ED
**Tel:** 01344620316 **Fax:** 01344-624572
**Web:** www.shorts-group.co.uk
**Reg No:** 0614056 **Estd:** 1958 Private
Limited Company
**Line of Business:** Renting of construction
and civil engineering machinery and
equipment
**Issued Capital:** £5,000
**Director:** G D Short
**Co. Secretary:** Mrs Sylvia Short
**Responsibilities**
**Senior:** Mike Banham (General Manager)
**Finance:** Lindsey Pawlyszyn (Accounts
Manager)
**Marketing:** Alison Pike (Marketing Manager)
**Sales:** Tom Cobley (Commercial
Development Manager)
**Operations:** Jason Southam (Production
and Operations Mana), Lee Spicer
(Operations Manager)
**Purchasing:** Justin Lucas (Contracts
Manager)
**Fleet:** Steve Meade (Transport Manager)
**US SIC:** 7394, 9121
**UK SIC:** 84000, 91110
**Bankers:** Lloyds TSB Bank plc (30-90-24)

| | 31-05-14 | 31-05-13 | 31-05-12 |
|---|---|---|---|
| TA | 5,000 | 5,000 | 5,000 |
| NW | 5,000 | 5,000 | 5,000 |

**DUNS 77-101-8132**
### Shotley Holdings Ltd
64 Ladbroke Road, London W11 3NR
**Tel:** 02072212748
**Reg No:** 2678812 **VAT No:** 571447336
**Estd:** 1992 Private Limited Company
**Line of Business:** Renting of other
machinery and equipment not elsewhere
classified
**Trading Style:** Collin's Skip Hire
**Issued Capital:** £180
**Directors:** A W Fane, R Snelling
**Co. Secretary:** Timothy Richmond
**US SIC:** 7394, 8999
**UK SIC:** 84000, 83954
**Auditors:** Ballams
**Bankers:** The Royal Bank Of Scotland Plc
(15-80-00)

| | 31-12-13 | 31-12-12 | 31-12-11 |
|---|---|---|---|
| TO | 6,383,956 | 5,553,435 | N/A |
| P/L | 606,484 | 439,278 | N/A |
| NW | 4,650,833 | 4,248,463 | 3,681,343 |
| WC | 676,114 | 191,052 | (101,791) |
| Emp. | 59 | 56 | N/A |

**DUNS 39-695-5791**
### Shotley Park Homes for the Elderly Ltd
Shotley Park, Consett, County Durham DH8
0TJ
**Tel:** 01207-502052
**Reg No:** 2152496 **Estd:** 1987 Private
Limited Company
**Line of Business:** Residential care
establishments
**Issued Capital:** £1,000
**Directors:** Ms T Langdon, Dr I A Ansari,
B Swinburne, M Muthurangu
**Co. Secretary:** David James

**Responsibilities**
**Senior:** Vanessa Eccles (Manager)
**US SIC:** 8321 **UK SIC:** 96111
**Auditors:** David Coates & Co
**Bankers:** Allied Irish Bank (gb) (23-92-82)

| | 31-03-14 | 31-03-13 | 31-03-12 |
|---|---|---|---|
| TA | 932,893 | 881,989 | 894,296 |
| NW | 574,003 | 543,795 | 525,571 |
| WC | 69,205 | 53,641 | 47,668 |

**DUNS 21-581-2200**
### Show & Event Security
60-62 Papyrus Road, Peterborough,
Cambridgeshire PE4 5BH
**Tel:** 01733576222
**Web:** www.showandevent.com
**Estd:** 2011 Proprietorship
**Line of Business:** Security activities
**Proprietor:** R Bennett
**Responsibilities**
**Senior:** Adam Mowles (Office Manager)
**US SIC:** 7393 **UK SIC:** 83954
**Employees:** 60

**DUNS 22-123-1504**
### Show Attack Ltd
St James Business Park, Grantham Road,
Nottingham, Nottinghamshire NG12 2JP
**Tel:** 01159331666 **Fax:** 01159894924
**Reg No:** 4142180 **Estd:** 2001 Private
Limited Company
**Line of Business:** Other building installation
**Issued Capital:** £100
**Director:** M Sheppard
**Co. Secretary:** Ms Gillian Sheppard
**US SIC:** 1796 **UK SIC:** 50400
**Bankers:** Lloyds TSB Bank plc (30-93-72)

| | 31-03-14 | 31-03-13 | 31-03-12 |
|---|---|---|---|
| TA | 427,589 | 439,739 | 492,713 |
| NW | 65,704 | 94,552 | (18,478) |
| WC | 40,631 | 72,092 | (60,789) |

**DUNS 77-766-6652** Imp
### Showa Uk Ltd
(**Subsidiary of:** Showa K.K.)
Aberaman Industrial Estate, Aberaman,
Aberdare, Mid Glamorgan CF44 6DA
**Fax:** 01685-885806
**Web:** www.showa1.co.uk
**Reg No:** 3021272 **Estd:** 1996 Private
Limited Company
**Line of Business:** Manufacture of parts and
accessories for motor vehicles and their
engines
**Issued Capital:** £7,000,000
**Directors:** D P Enoch, T Nagao, K Iijima,
T Atkins
**Co. Secretary:** Ceri Connolly
**Responsibilities**
**Senior:** Masahiro Himura (Manager), Kenshi
Hirai (Manager), Masato Ishikawa
(Manager), Wayne Parry (Logistics
Manager), Kazuhito Umetsu (Manager)
**Marketing:** Robert Greenin (Sales &
Marketing Manager)
**Sales:** Robert Greenin (Sales & Marketing
Manager)
**IT:** Scott Edwards (IT Coordinator), Jonathan
Pollard (IT Engineer)
**Purchasing:** Wayne Parry (Logistics
Manager)
**Fleet:** Wayne Parry (Logistics Manager)
**Engineering:** Keri Allan (Maintenance
Engineer)
**US SIC:** 3714, 5531
**UK SIC:** 35300, 65100
**Auditors:** Ernst & Young LLP
**Bankers:** The Mitsubishi Trust & Banking
Corporation (62-21-11)

| | 31-12-13 | 31-12-12 | 31-12-11 |
|---|---|---|---|
| TO | 36,688,040 | 50,125,760 | 30,339,317 |
| P/L | 3,359,659 | 1,878,989 | (2,200,834) |
| NW | 14,534,986 | 12,230,209 | 9,644,463 |
| WC | 7,586,202 | 4,866,480 | 1,235,596 |
| Emp. | 122 | 141 | 133 |

**DUNS 21-746-4158**
### Showcard Print Ltd
(**Subsidiary of:** Ingleby (1884) Ltd)
Fontana House, Works Road, Letchworth,
Hertfordshire SG6 1LD
**Tel:** 01462 677148
**Web:** www.showcardprint.com
**Reg No:** 7781894 **Estd:** 2011 Private
Limited Company
**Line of Business:** Printers general
**Export Sales:** £1,547,000
**Issued Capital:** £1
**Directors:** M W Smith, M Hawkins,
J Fletcher
**Co. Secretary:** Mark Hawkins
**US SIC:** 2794 **UK SIC:** 47545
**Auditors:** Grant Thornton LLP

| | 31-12-13 | 31-12-12 |
|---|---|---|
| TO | 24,571,000 | 15,097,000 |
| P/L | 4,007,000 | 2,150,000 |
| NW | 5,209,000 | 1,985,000 |
| WC | 2,288,000 | (303,000) |
| Emp. | 129 | 117 |

**DUNS 77-777-2971**
### Showforce Services Ltd
Unit 1 Stratford Workshops, Burford Road,
London E15 2SP
**Tel:** 02085195252 **Fax:** 020-8519-9006
**Web:** www.showforce.com
**Reg No:** 3023380 **VAT No:** 549277209
**Estd:** 1995 Private Limited Company
**Line of Business:** Activities of exhibition and
fair organisers
**Trading Style:** Showforce Services Ltd
**Issued Capital:** £2
**Director:** C Martelly
**Co. Secretary:** Ms Kathleen Panzavechia
**Responsibilities**
**Senior:** Esteban Benedicto (Sales
Executive), Karyn Halifax (Operations
Director), Ian Spendlove (Manager)
**Finance:** Debbie Ricketts (Finance and
Operations Coordin)
**Sales:** Esteban Benedicto (Sales Executive),
Oliver Charldwood (Business Development
Manager)
**Operations:** Dave Bellamy (Key Client
Relationship Manage), Karyn Halifax
(Operations Director), Ashley Palser (Senior
Operations Coordinator), Sharelle Velinor
(Operations Coordinator)
**Fleet:** Aldo Bardetti (Transport Coordinator),
Barrie Spendlove (Transport Manager)
**Branches:** Showforce Services Ltd, 7
Caernarvon Close, Wirral, Merseyside CH49
4PL
**US SIC:** 7399 **UK SIC:** 83954
**Bankers:** HSBC Bank plc (40-25-27)

| | 30-04-14 | 30-04-13 | 30-04-12 |
|---|---|---|---|
| TA | 1,113,514 | 1,193,309 | 1,274,914 |
| NW | 557,249 | 726,422 | 247,764 |
| WC | 522,810 | 688,695 | 210,277 |

**DUNS 21-023-9455** Exp
### Showpla Plastics Ltd
(**Subsidiary of:** Synchemicals Ltd)
Landywood Lane, Cheslyn Hay, Walsall,
West Midlands WS6 7AL
**Tel:** 01922-419203
**Web:** www.showplaplastics.co.uk
**Reg No:** 0529119 **VAT No:** 238032581
**Estd:** 1954 Private Limited Company
**Line of Business:** Plastic injection moulding
**Issued Capital:** £3,000
**Directors:** I Rickuss, S Hutt, T R Sweet,
P A Gooding
**Co. Secretary:** Julian Plews
**Responsibilities**
**Health & Safety:** Maxine Davies (Health &
Safety Officer)
**Operations:** Dave Gibbons (Production
Manager), Edwin Heminsley (Quality Control
Manager)
**Fleet:** Roger Swinderman (Logistics
Controller)
**Branches:** Showpla Plastics Ltd, Landywood
Lane, Walsall, West Midlands WS6 7AL
**US SIC:** 3079 **UK SIC:** 48360
**Auditors:** RSM Tenon Audit Ltd

| | 31-08-13 | 31-08-12 | 31-08-11 |
|---|---|---|---|
| TO | 7,891,000 | 7,521,000 | 6,517,000 |
| P/L | 254,000 | 265,000 | 314,000 |
| NW | 2,086,000 | 1,889,000 | 1,698,000 |
| WC | 1,855,000 | 1,562,000 | 1,696,000 |
| Emp. | 56 | 55 | 57 |

**DUNS 39-747-4644**
### Showsec International Ltd
(**Subsidiary of:** Live Nation Entertainment
Inc.)
Regent House, 16 West Walk, Leicester,
Leicestershire LE1 7NA
**Tel:** 01162-043333 **Fax:** 01162-043300
**Web:** www.showsec.co.uk
**Reg No:** 2187286 **VAT No:** 350658453
**Estd:** 1987 Private Limited Company
**Line of Business:** Security and related
activities
**Export Sales:** £17,325
**Trading Style:** Showsec International
**Issued Capital:** £106
**Directors:** S Battersby, G P Van Duijkeren,
M Logan, M A Harding
**Co. Secretary:** Gerardus Van Duijkeren
**Responsibilities**
**Finance:** Wayne Latts (Head of finance)
**HR:** Debbie Atherton (Human Resources
Manager), Charlie Hannah (Training
Consultant)
**Branches:** Showsec International Ltd,
Connies Ho, Rhymney River Bridge Road,
Cardiff, South Glamorgan CF23 9AF
**US SIC:** 7393 **UK SIC:** 83954
**Auditors:** Ernst & Young LLP
**Bankers:** Barclays Bank Plc (20-95-61)

| | 31-12-13 | 31-12-12 | 31-12-11 |
|---|---|---|---|
| TO | 21,709,951 | 24,013,249 | 16,340,293 |
| P/L | 1,253,460 | 1,668,515 | 1,007,576 |
| NW | 1,396,560 | 1,477,068 | 997,415 |
| WC | 1,305,861 | 1,366,084 | 815,829 |
| Emp. | 2,318 | 2,246 | 1,986 |

DUNS 22-044-8810 **Imp**

## Shred-It Ltd

(**Subsidiary of:** Shred-It International Ulc)
Unit 1 Foresters Green, Trafford Park, Manchester M17 1EJ
**Tel:** 01617-721-700
**Web:** www.shredit.com
**Reg No:** 4047194 **VAT No:** 818302936
**Estd:** 2003 Private Limited Company
**Line of Business:** Business services
**Issued Capital:** £100
**Co. Secretary:** James Rudyk
**Responsibilities**
**Senior:** Colin Cassel *(Operations Manager)*
**Branches:** Shred-It Ltd, Chohan House, 177 Cross Street, Sale, Cheshire M33 7JQ
**US SIC:** 3031 **UK SIC:** 48123
**Auditors:** Ernst & Young LLP
**Bankers:** HSBC Bank plc (40-13-21)

| | 31-12-13 | 31-12-12 | 31-12-11 |
|---|---|---|---|
| TO | 36,341,886 | 29,604,818 | 29,797,625 |
| P/L | 4,582,723 | (1,137,120) | 1,702,894 |
| NW | (30,874,491) | (29,892,307) | (21,701,972) |
| WC | 20,836,574 | 14,006,131 | 9,947,864 |
| Emp. | 458 | 379 | 369 |

DUNS 42-402-9791

## Shrewsbury & Telford Hospitals N H S Trust

Mytton Oak Road, Shrewsbury, Shropshire SY3 8XQ
**Tel:** 01743-261-000 **Fax:** 01743-261-006
**Web:** www.sath.nhs.uk
**Estd:** 1993 Incorporate By Act Of Parliament
**Line of Business:** Hospitals
**Issued Capital:** £1
**Principals:** B Marsh *(Chairman)*, P Jones *(Financial)*, Dr A Fraser, Mrs V Howell, A Mckeever, Mrs B Price, H Scurfield, A V Nicholson
**Responsibilities**
**Senior:** Paul Corbett *(Telephone Engineer)*, Mike Hallworth *(Chairman)*, Anthony McKeever *(Chief Executive Officer)*
**Finance:** Neil Nisbet *(Director of Finance)*
**Marketing:** Andy Rogers *(Communications Manager)*
**Sales:** Debbie Vogler *(Director of Business and Enter)*
**Admin:** AnneMarie Brandon *(Personal Assistant to the chie)*, Rachel Hammer *(PA to Head of Midwifery)*
**HR:** Nia Kimm *(Human Resources Manager)*
**Operations:** Debbie Kadum *(Chief Operating Officer)*
**Branches:** Shrewsbury & Telford Hospitals N H S Trust, Lancaster Rd, Shrewsbury, Shropshire SY1 3ND
**US SIC:** 8091 **UK SIC:** 95200
**Bankers:** The Royal Bank Of Scotland Plc (16-31-23)
**Employees:** 2,500

DUNS 56-958-6969

## Shrewsbury Diocese Commercial Co Ltd

2 Park Road South, Prenton, Merseyside CH43 4UX
**Tel:** 0151-652-9855
**Web:** www.dioceseofshrewsbury.org
**Reg No:** 2848927 **Estd:** 1982 Private Limited Company
**Line of Business:** Licensed clubs
**Issued Capital:** £450,000
**Directors:** B J Hoban, Rev P J Moor, Mrs C Lawrence
**Co. Secretary:** Mrs Carol Lawrence
**Branches:** Shrewsbury Diocese Commercial Co Ltd, Flint Close, Hazel Grove, Stockport, Cheshire SK7 5PU
**US SIC:** 5813 **UK SIC:** 66200
**Auditors:** PKF
**Bankers:** The Royal Bank Of Scotland Plc (16-24-06)

| | 31-03-14 | 31-03-13 | 31-03-12 |
|---|---|---|---|
| TA | 887,631 | 882,680 | 809,348 |
| NW | 417,797 | 413,209 | 413,205 |
| WC | 80,922 | 92,371 | 121,270 |

DUNS 21-776-5366

## Shrewsbury High Prep School

Kingsland Grange School The New Teaching, Block Old Roman Roa, Shrewsbury, Shropshire SY3 9AH
**Tel:** 01743494200
**Web:** www.shrewsburyhigh.gdst.net
**Estd:** 1993
**Line of Business:** Primary education
**US SIC:** 8211 **UK SIC:** 93200
**Employees:** 50

DUNS 21-783-9868

## Shrewsbury High School

32 Town Walls, Shrewsbury, Shropshire SY1 1TN
**Tel:** 01743494000
**Web:** www.gdst.net
**Estd:** 2000 Proprietorship
**Line of Business:** General secondary education
**Proprietor:** Mrs M Cass
**Responsibilities**
**Senior:** Michael Getty *(Head Teacher)*
**US SIC:** 8211 **UK SIC:** 93200
**Employees:** 130

DUNS 28-909-8659

## Shrewsbury House School Trust Ltd

107 Ditton Road, 107 Ditton Road, Surbiton, Surrey KT6 6RL
**Tel:** 020-8399-3066 **Fax:** 020-8339-9529
**Web:** www.shrewsburyhouse.net
**Reg No:** 1411417 **Estd:** 1979 Private Company Limited By Guarantee
**Line of Business:** Schools (independent)
**Directors:** A L Lee, F G Corbett, A J Cornelius, Mrs C Linney, W H Davies, D M Johns, A J Sinfield, S J Harries
**Co. Secretary:** Mrs Monica Palmer
**Responsibilities**
**Senior:** Lesley Bell *(Manager)*, Michael Crow *(Governor)*, Hywel George *(Governor)*, Vivien Gillman *(Manager)*, Brian Howard *(Manager)*, Joanna Le Grice *(Director)*, Andrew Weiss *(Manager)*, kevin dobel *(Principal)*
**Marketing:** Jan Hand *(Head of Marketing)*
**US SIC:** 8211 **UK SIC:** 93200
**Auditors:** Haysmacintyre
**Bankers:** National Westminster Bank Plc (60-60-02)

| | 31-08-13 | 31-08-12 | 31-08-11 |
|---|---|---|---|
| TO | 6,103,424 | 5,963,396 | 5,598,494 |
| P/L | 367,019 | 304,312 | 332,340 |
| NW | 5,906,335 | 5,539,316 | 5,235,004 |
| WC | 214,158 | 407,869 | 237,103 |
| Emp. | 106 | 99 | 93 |

DUNS 23-680-6816

## Shrewsbury Sixth Form College

Priory Road, Shrewsbury, Shropshire SY1 1RX
**Tel:** 01743-235491
**Web:** www.ssfc.ac.uk
**Estd:** 1993
**Line of Business:** Further education schools and colleges
**Principals:** W Dowell, Ms G Bell *(Manager)*
**Responsibilities**
**IT:** Adrian Bayling *(Senior IT Executive)*
**US SIC:** 8221, 8211
**UK SIC:** 93100, 93200
**Bankers:** Lloyds TSB Bank plc (77-27-01)
**Employees:** 152

DUNS 28-833-2661

## Shrewsbury Town Football Club Ltd

Greenhous Meadow, Oteley Road, Shrewsbury, Shropshire SY2 6ST
**Tel:** 01743-289177
**Web:** www.shrewsburytown.com
**Reg No:** 0315587 **VAT No:** 160366087
**Estd:** 1936 Private Limited Company
**Line of Business:** Operation of other sports arenas and stadiums not elsewhere classified
**Issued Capital:** £1,945,703
**Directors:** R E Wycherley, J C Hughes
**Co. Secretary:** Michael Parry
**Responsibilities**
**Senior:** Sib Hayes *(Stores Manager)*
**Marketing:** Ian Whitfield *(Media Manager)*
**IT:** Ian Whitfield *(Media Manager)*
**US SIC:** 7999 **UK SIC:** 97913
**Auditors:** Whittingham Riddell LLP
**Bankers:** Lloyds TSB Bank plc (30-97-62)

| | 30-06-13 | 30-06-12 | 30-06-11 |
|---|---|---|---|
| TO | 3,823,518 | 3,877,911 | 4,415,058 |
| P/L | (383,497) | (275,047) | 20,046 |
| NW | 14,454,860 | 14,857,870 | 15,146,969 |
| WC | 373,135 | 793,972 | 911,936 |
| Emp. | 172 | 175 | 182 |

DUNS 21-198-6930 **Imp-Exp**

## Shrewville Ltd

Imperial House, Redlands, Coulsdon, Surrey CR5 2HT
**Tel:** 02086680931 **Fax:** 020-8668-2396
**Web:** www.simsonsfisheries.co.uk
**Reg No:** 1167195 **VAT No:** 244600880
**Estd:** 1974 Private Limited Company
**Line of Business:** Wholesale of other food including fish, crustaceans and molluscs
**Export Markets:** E U
**Trading Style:** Simson's Fisheries
**Issued Capital:** £300,000
**Directors:** S Boyd, T Lucas
**Branches:** Shrewville Ltd, Imperial House, Redlands, Coulsdon, Surrey CR5 2HT
**US SIC:** 5146 **UK SIC:** 61700
**Auditors:** CSL Partnership Ltd
**Bankers:** Barclays Bank Plc (20-38-83)

| | 30-04-14 | 30-04-13 | 30-04-12 |
|---|---|---|---|
| TO | N/A | 8,238,184 | 11,527,970 |
| P/L | N/A | (529,389) | (322,493) |
| NW | (620,532) | (682,409) | (153,020) |
| WC | (788,387) | (988,456) | (536,204) |
| Emp. | N/A | 49 | 59 |

DUNS 21-775-5477

## Shropshire Council County Training

Hollinswood House, Stafford Park 1, Telford, Shropshire TF3 3DD
**Tel:** 01952200677
**Web:** www.countytraining.com
**Estd:** 1997 Proprietorship
**Line of Business:** Training services
**Proprietor:** K Humphries
**US SIC:** 8249 **UK SIC:** 93300
**Employees:** 80

DUNS 23-275-1292

## Shropshire County Primary Care Trust

William Farr House, Mytton Oak Road, Shrewsbury, Shropshire SY3 8XL
**Tel:** 01743277500
**Web:** www.shropscommunityhealth.nhs.uk
**Estd:** 1983
**Line of Business:** Schools (local authority)
**Trading Style:** Shropshire County P C T
**Principals:** N Webb *(Financial)*, Mrs J Grant
**Responsibilities**
**Senior:** Mark Crisp *(Health & Safety Manager)*, Leigh Griffin *(Manager)*, Karen Moreton *(Chief Executive)*, Penny Pritchard *(General Manager)*
**IT:** Barry Patsalides *(IT Manager)*
**HR:** Paul Draycott *(Human Resources Director)*
**Health & Safety:** Mark Crisp *(Health & Safety Manager)*
**Branches:** Shropshire County Primary Care Trust, Station Drive, Ludlow, Shropshire SY8 2AB
**US SIC:** 8211 **UK SIC:** 93200
**Auditors:** Tony Corcoran
**Employees:** 100

DUNS 21-231-9178

## Shropshire Dairies

32 Vanguard Way, Shrewsbury, Shropshire SY1 3TG
**Tel:** 01743-344494
**Web:** www.cotteswold-dairy.co.uk
**Estd:** 1994 Proprietorship
**Line of Business:** Dairies
**Proprietor:** L Raymer
**US SIC:** 5199 **UK SIC:** 61900
**Employees:** 50

DUNS 22-780-8656

## Shropshire Homes Ltd

The Old Workhouse, The Chestnuts, Cross Houses, Shrewsbury, Shropshire SY5 6JH
**Tel:** 01743-761789
**Web:** www.shropshire-homes.com
**Reg No:** 1567991 **VAT No:** 351740078
**Estd:** 1981 Private Limited Company
**Line of Business:** Property developers
**Issued Capital:** £10,000
**Principals:** H T Thorne *(Managing)*, G S Rogers, R C Bowler
**Responsibilities**
**Senior:** Howard Trevor-Thorne *(Managing Director)*
**Finance:** Howard Trevor-Thorne *(Managing Director)*
**Admin:** Karen Trusselle *(Office Manager)*
**IT:** Ian Norris *(Purchasing Manager)*
**HR:** Karen Trusselle *(Office Manager)*
**Purchasing:** Ian Norris *(Purchasing Manager)*
**Branches:** Shropshire Homes Ltd, 50 Clock Tower View, Stourbridge, West Midlands DY8 5TJ
**US SIC:** 1522 **UK SIC:** 50100
**Auditors:** Caerwyn Jones & Co
**Bankers:** Barclays Bank Plc (20-53-22)

| | 31-12-13 | 31-12-12 | 31-12-11 |
|---|---|---|---|
| TO | 17,136,175 | 19,662,403 | 14,461,315 |
| P/L | 1,938,203 | 1,299,058 | 800,182 |
| NW | 4,646,678 | 4,113,736 | 3,130,530 |
| WC | 3,771,152 | 3,302,468 | 2,369,358 |
| Emp. | 80 | 82 | 80 |

DUNS 21-557-7533

## Shropshire Housing Ltd

The Gateway, The Auction Yard, Bucknell, Shropshire SY7 9BW
**Web:** www.sshropsha.co.uk
**Reg No:** 0030269IP **Estd:** 2012
**Line of Business:** Housing associations societies trusts & co-operatives
**Principals:** Ms S Latto *(Chairman)*, Ms I Overton, R Jaboor, M Buxey, G Hodgkiss, Ms L Hyde, J Thomas, S Mclaren
**Responsibilities**
**Senior:** Stuart McLaren *(Principal)*
**US SIC:** 8699 **UK SIC:** 96902
**Auditors:** Mazars LLP

| | 31-03-12 | 31-03-11 | 31-03-10 |
|---|---|---|---|
| TO | 21,472,418 | 20,768,760 | 21,153,583 |
| P/L | 3,030,226 | 2,992,555 | 3,309,875 |
| NW | 12,978,525 | 8,743,296 | 5,295,736 |
| WC | 23,221,619 | 23,102,639 | 34,223,429 |
| Emp. | 230 | 230 | 223 |

DUNS 21-911-5615

## Shropshire Leisure Group Ltd

(**Subsidiary of:** Rcapital Ltd)
Brook Buildings, Gobowen, Oswestry, Shropshire SY11 3JP
**Tel:** 01691684400
**Reg No:** 1181552 **Estd:** 1974 Private Limited Company
**Line of Business:** Building services
**Issued Capital:** £4,242
**Principals:** D W Dulson *(Managing)*, Obs Directors Llp, N A Dulson
**Co. Secretary:** Jamie Constable
**US SIC:** 6552, 5999, 5813
**UK SIC:** 85000, 65600, 66200
**Auditors:** Turner Peachey
**Bankers:** The Royal Bank Of Scotland Plc (16-31-23)

| | 31-12-13 | 31-12-12 | 31-12-11 |
|---|---|---|---|
| TO | 10,267,579 | 10,926,654 | 8,576,006 |
| P/L | (395,670) | (5,785,092) | 415,497 |
| NW | (6,253,172) | (5,857,502) | (2,777,299) |
| WC | (10,494,950) | (3,426,309) | (2,499,890) |
| Emp. | 322 | 330 | 325 |

DUNS 23-082-9769

## The Shrubbery School

Walmley Ash Road, Sutton Coldfield, West Midlands B76 1HY
**Tel:** 01213511582
**Web:** www.shrubberyschool.co.uk
**Estd:** 1930 Partnership
**Line of Business:** General secondary education
**Principals:** Mrs H Cooke, P Terry *(Partner)*, E Allen *(Partner)*
**Responsibilities**
**Senior:** Hillary Atkins *(Head Teacher)*
**US SIC:** 8211 **UK SIC:** 93200
**Employees:** 50

DUNS 23-519-4235

## Shs Integrated Services Ltd

Unit 15a Atlantic Trading Estate, Barry, South Glamorgan CF63 3RF
**Tel:** 01446-735364
**Web:** www.shs.uk.com
**Reg No:** 3518462 **Estd:** 1998 Private Limited Company
**Line of Business:** Scaffolds and work platform erectors
**Trading Style:** S H S Scaffolding
**Issued Capital:** £1,606
**Directors:** G Payne, J D Hawkes, P Smith, R Wint, P L Oldham, R A Kilner
**Responsibilities**
**Finance:** Sian Lewis *(financial manager)*
**US SIC:** 1799 **UK SIC:** 50000
**Bankers:** Barclays Bank Plc (20-18-15)

| | 31-12-13 | 31-07-12 | 31-12-11 |
|---|---|---|---|
| TO | 17,198,593 | 14,014,207 | 8,890,337 |
| P/L | (718,886) | 982,004 | 242,635 |
| NW | 899,794 | 1,363,530 | 728,381 |
| WC | 1,019,068 | (498,891) | (1,018,717) |
| Emp. | 192 | 182 | 139 |

DUNS 21-221-5628 **Imp-Exp**

## Shs International Ltd

(**Subsidiary of:** Danone Holdings (Uk))
100 Wavertree Boulevard, Liverpool, Merseyside L7 9PT
**Tel:** 01512288161 **Fax:** 01512-282650
**Web:** www.nutricia.com
**Reg No:** 0112075 **Estd:** 1879 Private Limited Company
**Line of Business:** Doctors
**Export Markets:** Australia; U S A; Europe; Middle East
**Trading Style:** Numico
**Issued Capital:** £552,017
**Directors:** Ms C Gravemaker, A W Wilkinson, P Cowley
**Responsibilities**
**IT:** Phil McCready *(IS Manager)*
**Branches:** Shs International Ltd, White Horse Business Pk, New Market Ave, Trowbridge, Wiltshire BA14 0XQ
**US SIC:** 8011, 2834
**UK SIC:** 95300, 25700
**Auditors:** Mazars LLP
**Bankers:** National Westminster Bank Plc (60-13-19)

| | 31-12-13 | 31-12-12 | 31-12-11 |
|---|---|---|---|
| TO | 80,659,000 | 76,788,000 | 87,824,000 |
| P/L | 17,820,000 | 12,959,000 | 18,943,000 |
| NW | 31,724,000 | 25,387,000 | 24,196,000 |
| WC | 15,173,000 | 7,007,000 | 3,558,000 |
| Emp. | 261 | 265 | 281 |

DUNS 21-026-7092 **Imp-Exp**

## Shubette of London Ltd

**(Subsidiary of:** Shubette Group of Companies Ltd)
Shubette House, 2 Apsley Way, London NW2 7HF
**Tel:** 020-8438-2000
**Web:** www.shubette.com
**Reg No:** 0622183 **Estd:** 1915 Private Limited Company
**Line of Business:** Ladies fashionwear (wholesale)
**Export Markets:** Worldwide
**Trading Style:** Shubette Group, Mister Ant, Shubette of London, Gina Battoni
**Issued Capital:** £1,000,000
**Principals:** G B Offenbach *(Managing)*, C D Offenbach, M J Offenbach
**Responsibilities**
**Marketing:** Carol McKeown *(Sales & Marketing Manager)*
**Sales:** Carol McKeown *(Sales & Marketing Manager)*
**IT:** William Colacicco *(IT Manager)*, Raj Kashyap *(Computer Operations Manager)*
**Operations:** Carol McKeown *(Sales & Marketing Manager)*
**Branches:** Shubette Of London Ltd, 32-34 Dale Street, Manchester M1 1FY
**US SIC:** 5136, 2341
**UK SIC:** 61600, 45362
**Auditors:** Nyman Libson Paul
**Bankers:** Barclays Bank Plc (20-36-47)

| | 30-09-13 | 30-09-12 | 30-09-11 |
|---|---|---|---|
| TO | 10,952,367 | 12,955,008 | 13,098,426 |
| P/L | 681,952 | 206,619 | 342,060 |
| NW | 797,987 | 308,551 | 2,386,315 |
| WC | 850,632 | 599,286 | 2,881,082 |
| Emp. | 60 | 59 | 60 |

DUNS 29-692-7403

## Shufflebottom Ltd

**(Subsidiary of:** Waa (Holdings) Ltd)
Heol Parc Mawr, Cross Hands Industrial Estate, Cross Hands, Llanelli, Dyfed SA14 6RE
**Tel:** 01269-831831 **Fax:** 01269-831031
**Web:** www.shufflebottom.co.uk
**Reg No:** 2016366 **VAT No:** 431861068
**Estd:** 1986 Private Limited Company
**Line of Business:** Steel constructed buildings
**Issued Capital:** £100
**Directors:** D A Davies, Mrs E A Shufflebottom, W W Shufflebottom
**Co. Secretary:** Mrs Emily Shufflebottom
**Responsibilities**
**Senior:** Emily Jones *(Manager)*
**US SIC:** 7399, 3499
**UK SIC:** 83954, 31694
**Auditors:** Deloitte & Touche
**Bankers:** National Westminster Bank Plc (51-81-27)

| | 30-09-13 | 30-09-12 | 30-09-11 |
|---|---|---|---|
| TO | 10,714,338 | 12,431,262 | 12,922,386 |
| P/L | 38,858 | 132,175 | 97,023 |
| NW | 4,008,887 | 3,950,172 | 3,863,138 |
| WC | 2,421,543 | 2,361,136 | 2,229,562 |
| Emp. | 69 | 67 | 76 |

DUNS 52-565-1766

## Shulmans Legal Services Ltd

10 Wellington Place, Leeds, West Yorkshire LS1 4AP
**Tel:** 01132-452833 **Fax:** 01132-467326
**Web:** www.shulmans.co.uk
**Reg No:** 3251455 **Estd:** 1977 Private Limited Company
**Line of Business:** Solicitors
**Trading Style:** Shulman Solicitors
**Issued Capital:** £1
**Director:** J I Shulman
**US SIC:** 8111 **UK SIC:** 83500

| | 31-03-14 | 31-03-13 | 31-03-12 |
|---|---|---|---|
| TA | 1 | 1 | 1 |
| NW | 1 | 1 | 1 |

DUNS 76-436-4808

## Shumei Eiko Ltd

Somerfield House, 59 London Road, Maidstone, Kent ME16 8JH
**Tel:** 01227787800
**Reg No:** 2562565 **Estd:** 1990 Private Company Limited By Guarantee
**Line of Business:** First-degree level higher education
**Directors:** Dr. M Horii, P A Todd, Professor M Sekiguchi, K Kawashima, P J Dalton, Professor K Yoshikawa
**Co. Secretary:** Gary Rigden
**Branches:** Shumei Eiko Ltd, Coolinge La, Folkestone, Kent CT20 3QS
**US SIC:** 8221 **UK SIC:** 93100
**Bankers:** HSBC Bank plc (40-16-11)

| | 31-03-14 | 31-03-13 | 29-03-12 |
|---|---|---|---|
| TO | 3,841,027 | 3,121,864 | 3,438,274 |
| P/L | (1,638) | (931,928) | (47,559) |
| NW | 11,685,024 | 11,686,662 | 12,618,590 |
| WC | (259,145) | (267,243) | (278,482) |
| Emp. | 74 | 77 | 78 |

DUNS 53-649-4495 **Imp**

## Shurgard Storage Centres U K Ltd

**(Subsidiary of:** Shurgard Holding Luxembourg Sarl)
2 A C Court, High Street, Thames Ditton, Surrey KT7 0SR
**Tel:** 020-8339-2700 **Fax:** 020-8339-2800
**Web:** www.shurgard.co.uk
**Reg No:** 3454778 **Estd:** 1997 Private Limited Company
**Line of Business:** Other storage and warehousing not elsewhere classified
**Issued Capital:** £100
**Director:** M P Oursin
**Co. Secretary:** Rjp Secretaries Limited
**Responsibilities**
**Senior:** Duncan Bells *(Marketing Manager)*
**Branches:** Shurgard Storage Centres U K Ltd, Shurguard Shelf Storage, Shurguard House, Hayes, Middlesex UB4 0HD
**US SIC:** 4226 **UK SIC:** 77003
**Auditors:** Deloitte & Touche LLP
**Bankers:** Allied Irish Bank (gb) (23-84-81)

| | 31-12-13 | 31-12-12 | 31-12-11 |
|---|---|---|---|
| TO | N/A | 7,979,665 | 10,317,960 |
| P/L | N/A | 59,626,032 | 4,370,237 |
| NW | 100 | 100 | 33,158,598 |
| WC | N/A | N/A | 24,937,995 |
| Emp. | N/A | 21 | 28 |

DUNS 21-012-4008 **Imp**

## Shuropody Ltd

Priory Gates, Priory Road, Wolston, Wolston, Kenilworth, Warwickshire CV8 3FX
**Tel:** 02476 545545 **Fax:** 02476 545969
**Web:** www.shuropody.com
**Reg No:** 6355404 **Estd:** 2007 Private Limited Company
**Line of Business:** Other business activities not elsewhere classified
**Issued Capital:** £15,714
**Directors:** G C Horsfield, Mrs J M Pilkington, I Downing, S P Bakewell, D Brown, F M Duffy
**Co. Secretary:** Dean Brown
**Responsibilities**
**Admin:** Shammy Hothi *(H R Administrator)*
**Branches:** Shuropody Ltd, Brent Cross Shopping Village, Tilling Road, London NW2 1LJ
**US SIC:** 7399, 8011
**UK SIC:** 83954, 95300
**Auditors:** BDO LLP

| | 31-12-13 | 31-12-12 | 31-12-11 |
|---|---|---|---|
| TO | 17,806,913 | 15,670,192 | 15,804,487 |
| P/L | (1,410,643) | (1,128,041) | 159,624 |
| NW | (2,095,529) | (675,634) | (1,039,914) |
| WC | 42,864 | 592,731 | (750,582) |
| Emp. | 489 | 444 | 432 |

DUNS 77-445-0050

## Sia Abrafoam Ltd

**(Subsidiary of:** R O B E R T B O S C H S T I F T U N G Gesellschaft)
Ellistones Lane, Halifax, West Yorkshire HX4 8NH
**Tel:** 01773832524
**Web:** www.sia-abrafoam.co.uk
**Reg No:** 2954615 **Estd:** 1994 Private Limited Company
**Line of Business:** Production of abrasive products
**Export Sales:** £9,855,000
**Issued Capital:** £100
**Directors:** A R Castle, Ms U T Lepple, I M Timmins
**Co. Secretary:** Jonathan Burton
**Responsibilities**
**Senior:** Graham Cobham *(Manager)*, John Cobham *(Manager)*, Keith Danby *(Warehouse Manager)*, Roland Eberle *(Manager)*, Roger Eleutheri *(Manager)*, Rachel Motteram *(Manager)*, Beat Staeheli *(Manager)*
**Finance:** Graham Cobham *(Manager)*
**US SIC:** 3291 **UK SIC:** 24600
**Auditors:** Mitchells
**Bankers:** Barclays Bank Plc (20-35-81)

| | 31-12-13 | 31-12-12 | 31-12-11 |
|---|---|---|---|
| TO | 10,353,000 | 7,710,000 | 7,584,000 |
| P/L | (31,000) | (842,000) | (676,000) |
| NW | 702,000 | 752,000 | 1,389,000 |
| WC | (426,000) | (108,000) | 610,000 |
| Emp. | 103 | 105 | 104 |

DUNS 39-741-7627 **Exp**

## Sia Anisa Ltd

**(Subsidiary of:** Anisa Group Holdings Ltd)
140 Buckingham Palace Road, London SW1W 9SA
**Tel:** 02078812500 **Fax:** 02078812501
**Web:** www.obs-logistics.com
**Reg No:** 2182758 **Estd:** 1989 Private Limited Company
**Line of Business:** Other business activities not elsewhere classified
**Trading Style:** Open Business Solutions
**Issued Capital:** £500,000
**Director:** R Telford
**Co. Secretary:** Lionel Moore
**Responsibilities**
**IT:** Phil Holloway *(IT Manager)*
**Branches:** Sia Anisa Ltd, Warwickgate House, 7 Warwick Road, Old Trafford, Manchester M16 0RZ
**US SIC:** 7399 **UK SIC:** 83954
**Bankers:** Coutts & Co (18-00-02)

| | 31-12-13 | 31-12-12 | 31-12-11 |
|---|---|---|---|
| TA | 500,000 | 500,000 | 500,000 |
| NW | 500,000 | 500,000 | 500,000 |

DUNS 21-802-8524

## Siam Thai Lounge

24 High Street, Lyndhurst, Hampshire SO43 7BG
**Tel:** 02380283061
**Web:** www.siamthailounge.com
**Estd:** 2011
**Line of Business:** Restaurant - thai
**Responsibilities**
**Senior:** A Chowdhury *(Manager)*
**US SIC:** 5812 **UK SIC:** 66110
**Employees:** 73

DUNS 73-496-0318

## Sian Formwork Ltd

Stonebridge Road, Gravesend, Kent DA11 9BA
**Tel:** 01474365300 **Fax:** 01474365329
**Web:** www.sianformwork.co.uk
**Reg No:** 4759389 **Estd:** 2008 Private Limited Company
**Line of Business:** Concrete reinforcements
**Issued Capital:** £100
**Directors:** J S Sian, A S Sian
**Co. Secretary:** Jugjit Sian
**US SIC:** 3271, 1799
**UK SIC:** 24370, 50000
**Auditors:** Nijjer & Co Accountants

| | 31-10-13 | 31-10-12 | 31-10-11 |
|---|---|---|---|
| TA | 2,396,819 | 2,021,871 | 2,267,574 |
| NW | 1,864,116 | 1,741,898 | 1,652,298 |
| WC | 1,545,948 | 1,475,115 | 1,505,981 |

DUNS 21-387-6563

## Sibbertoft Manor

Sibbertoft Manor, 3 Church Street, Market Harborough, Leicestershire LE16 9UA
**Tel:** 01858881304
**Web:** www.sibbertoftmanor.com
**Estd:** 1998
**Line of Business:** Nursing homes
**Proprietor:** Mrs P Bevin
**Responsibilities**
**Senior:** Patricia Bevin *(Matron)*
**US SIC:** 8321 **UK SIC:** 96111
**Employees:** 70

DUNS 21-584-3343

## Sibcas Ltd

**(Subsidiary of:** Sibcas (Holdings) Ltd)
Easton Road, Bathgate, West Lothian EH48 2SF
**Tel:** 01506-633122 **Fax:** 01506-634320
**Web:** www.sibcas.co.uk
**Reg No:** 0052604SC **VAT No:** 270980052
**Estd:** 1973 Private Limited Company
**Line of Business:** Portable buildings
**Issued Capital:** £100
**Principals:** A R Storrie *(Managing)*, W Lightbody, M A Smith, J Storrie, N D Robinson, E D Macleod
**Co. Secretary:** William Storrie
**Responsibilities**
**Senior:** Stuart Whitehead *(Manager)*
**HR:** Billy John *(Human Resources Manager)*
**Operations:** Billy Lightbuddy *(Production and Operations Mana)*
**Branches:** Sibcas Ltd, Salters Lane, Stockton-On-Tees, Cleveland TS21 3EE
**US SIC:** 1761, 6531
**UK SIC:** 50400, 83400
**Auditors:** Scott-Moncrieff
**Bankers:** The Royal Bank Of Scotland Plc (83-16-05)

| | 31-03-14 | 31-03-13 | 31-03-12 |
|---|---|---|---|
| TO | 20,641,958 | 20,407,526 | 22,371,274 |
| P/L | 171,962 | 169,089 | 162,366 |
| NW | 3,014,900 | 2,878,154 | 2,743,837 |
| WC | 3,014,900 | 2,878,154 | 2,743,837 |
| Emp. | 145 | 151 | 168 |

DUNS 21-809-2849 **Imp-Exp**

## Sibelco Uk Ltd

**(Subsidiary of:** Scr - Sibelco Nv)
Brookside Hall, Congleton Road, Sandbach, Cheshire CW11 4TF
**Tel:** 01270752752
**Web:** www.sibelco.co.uk
**Reg No:** 0578631 **VAT No:** 209571166
**Estd:** 1957 Private Limited Company
**Line of Business:** Quarrying of sand and clay
**Issued Capital:** £220,402
**Directors:** J A Deleersnyder, M C James, J L Herremans, J Emsens, J Pritchard, T C Cutbush, F Moreno Diaz
**Responsibilities**
**Marketing:** Robert Sproston *(Marketing Manager)*
**Sales:** Andy Brook *(Sales Manager)*, Alastair Kearton *(Sales Manager)*
**Admin:** Sarah Jenkins *(Office Coordinator)*
**IT:** David Rovira *(IS Manager)*
**HR:** Sarah Jenkins *(Office Coordinator)*
**Operations:** Robert Sproston *(Marketing Manager)*
**Branches:** Sibelco Uk Ltd, Moneystone Quarry, Oakamoor Road, Stoke-On-Trent, Staffordshire ST10 2DZ
**US SIC:** 1499, 3299
**UK SIC:** 23960, 24504
**Auditors:** KPMG LLP
**Bankers:** National Westminster Bank Plc (56-00-09)

| | 31-12-13 | 31-12-12 | 31-12-11 |
|---|---|---|---|
| TO | 112,379,169 | 108,247,398 | 122,948,627 |
| P/L | 400,153 | 6,313,445 | 3,860,121 |
| NW | 31,271,513 | 36,434,591 | 31,850,923 |
| WC | 35,289,859 | 16,622,264 | 22,349,437 |
| Emp. | 375 | 411 | 436 |

DUNS 64-092-6101

## Sibford School

Sibford Ferris, Banbury, Oxfordshire OX15 5QL
**Tel:** 01295781200
**Web:** www.sibford.oxon.sch.uk
**Reg No:** 3487651 **Estd:** 1876 Private Unlimited Company
**Line of Business:** Primary education
**Directors:** Ms C Merry, J A Brown, Ms H V Scott, Ms S C Lane, S P Fowler, P Jones, R J Hughes, Ms L Poulton
**Co. Secretary:** Peter Robinson
**Responsibilities**
**Senior:** Richard Bee *(Director)*, Sarah Bicheno *(Director)*, Katherine Davison *(Director)*, Alisrair Fuller *(Director)*, Peter Neighbour *(Manager)*, Simon Risley *(Director)*, Derry Sharman *(Director)*, Margaret Shelley *(Director)*, Diana Smith *(Manager)*, Seren Wildwood *(Director)*
**Finance:** Peter Neighbour *(Manager)*
**IT:** Martin Checkley *(Network Manager)*
**US SIC:** 8211 **UK SIC:** 93200
**Auditors:** haysmacintyre
**Bankers:** Allied Irish Bank (gb) (23-85-85)

| | 31-07-13 | 31-07-12 | 31-07-11 |
|---|---|---|---|
| TO | 5,988,042 | 6,130,120 | 6,076,975 |
| P/L | (293,713) | 102,004 | 41,656 |
| NW | 7,440,696 | 7,722,320 | 7,621,665 |
| WC | (439,063) | 169,239 | (15,237) |
| Emp. | 126 | 129 | 122 |

DUNS 21-028-5470

## Siblu Reservations

Bryanston Court, Selden Hill, Hemel Hempstead, Hertfordshire HP2 4TN
**Tel:** 08702427777
**Web:** www.siblu.com
**Estd:** 2004 Proprietorship
**Line of Business:** Holidays (self catering)
**Proprietor:** L Hurste
**Responsibilities**
**Senior:** Simon Crabbe *(Manager)*, Leslie Hurst *(Director)*, Katherine Locke *(Manager)*, Paul Popplestone *(Manager)*
**Finance:** Christopher Mutter *(Director and Company Secretary)*
**US SIC:** 7021 **UK SIC:** 66500
**Employees:** 58

DUNS 89-649-6437 **Imp-Exp**

## Sicame Uk Ltd

**(Subsidiary of:** Soc Indust Constr Apparei Materiel Ele)
Church Manorway, Erith, Kent DA8 1EX
**Tel:** 01322-444500 **Fax:** 01322-444502
**Web:** www.wt-henley.com
**Reg No:** 3319466 **Estd:** 1887 Private Limited Company
**Line of Business:** Design, develop and manufacture cable connectors
**Export Sales:** £3,281,000
**Issued Capital:** £2,250,000
**Principals:** Ms A P Giggins *(Financial)*, D P Marshman, G V Linsley, P G Brown, N Smith, P Francois
**Co. Secretary:** Mrs Anne Giggins
**Responsibilities**
**Senior:** Nick Jupp *(Manufacturing Manager)*
**IT:** Steve Thorley *(Computer Manager)*
**Facilities:** Nick Jupp *(Manufacturing Manager)*
**US SIC:** 5074 **UK SIC:** 61300
**Auditors:** KPMG Audit PLC
**Bankers:** National Westminster Bank Plc (60-13-08)

| | 31-12-13 | 31-12-12 | 31-12-11 |
|---|---|---|---|
| TO | 15,424,000 | 15,209,000 | 13,432,000 |
| P/L | 1,576,000 | 1,699,000 | 1,179,000 |
| NW | 6,338,000 | 5,606,000 | 5,193,000 |
| WC | 5,663,000 | 4,697,000 | 4,297,000 |
| Emp. | 60 | 57 | 53 |

DUNS 22-632-6171 **Imp**

## Sick (Uk) Ltd.

(**Subsidiary of:** Sick Holding Gmbh)
39 Hedley Road, Harpenden, Hertfordshire AL5 1BN
**Tel:** 01727-831121
**Web:** www.sick.co.uk
**Reg No:** 1147832 **VAT No:** 198362030
**Estd:** 1973 Private Limited Company
**Line of Business:** Safety equipment suppliers
**Export Sales:** £772,971
**Issued Capital:** £1,000
**Directors:** F R Hehl, M Goekstorp
**Co. Secretary:** Alan Reeves
**Responsibilities**
**Senior:** Rudolf Kast *(Vice President)*, Claus Melder *(Manager)*, Markus Paschmann *(Manager)*
**US SIC:** 5999, 3662, 3829
**UK SIC:** 65600, 34430, 37100
**Auditors:** Ernst & Young LLP
**Bankers:** Deutsche Bank Ag (30-00-55)

| | 31-12-13 | 31-12-12 | 31-12-11 |
|---|---|---|---|
| TO | 25,112,508 | 22,875,720 | 23,328,073 |
| P/L | 3,580,746 | 2,730,096 | 3,006,266 |
| NW | 5,264,158 | 5,025,800 | 4,973,377 |
| WC | 4,670,977 | 4,370,870 | 4,283,148 |
| Emp. | 69 | 70 | 69 |

DUNS 21-090-6749 **Imp-Exp**

## Sico Europe Ltd

(**Subsidiary of:** Sico Inc.)
The Link Park, Hythe, Kent CT21 4LR
**Tel:** 01303261218 **Fax:** 01303-234001
**Web:** www.sico-europe.com
**Reg No:** 0902613 **VAT No:** 218120111
**Estd:** 2012 Private Limited Company
**Line of Business:** Manufacture of other furniture
**Export Sales:** £4,202,378
**Issued Capital:** £38,940
**Principals:** H K Wilson *(Chairman)*, S B Mason, C E Wilson
**Co. Secretary:** Michael Bundock
**Responsibilities**
**Senior:** Steve Plant *(Proprietor)*, Andrew Shea *(Manager)*
**US SIC:** 2517, 5199
**UK SIC:** 46714, 61900
**Auditors:** Larkings Ltd
**Bankers:** Barclays Bank Plc (20-02-62)

| | 30-11-13 | 30-11-12 | 30-11-11 |
|---|---|---|---|
| TO | 10,536,412 | 10,761,453 | 10,579,168 |
| P/L | (110,313) | 70,970 | (36,498) |
| NW | 2,119,663 | 2,200,726 | 2,250,484 |
| WC | 1,129,919 | 1,138,049 | 1,123,044 |
| Emp. | 80 | 74 | 74 |

DUNS 29-890-4079

## Sidcot School

Oakridge Lane, Winscombe, Avon BS25 1PD
**Tel:** 01934843102
**Web:** www.sidcot.org.uk
**Reg No:** 2093340 **Estd:** 1808 Private Company Limited By Guarantee
**Line of Business:** Schools (independent)
**Directors:** Ms T Tyldesley, Mrs R E Carr, D S Whiting, C M Fincken, Ms S Harvey, Ms J Hicks, R L Starr, T C Niblock
**Co. Secretary:** Steve Harris
**Responsibilities**
**Senior:** Hilary Atkin *(Director Of Operations)*, Falcon Bell *(Manager)*, Desmond Harris *(Manager)*, Michael Len *(Manager)*, Duncan Pittaway *(Director)*, Andrew Putin *(Director)*, John Walmsley *(Headmaster)*
**Finance:** Michael Pentecost *(Bursar)*
**Marketing:** Alison Wilde *(Marketing Manager)*
**HR:** Michael Pentecost *(Bursar)*
**Health & Safety:** Michael Pentecost *(Bursar)*
**Facilities:** Michael Pentecost *(Bursar)*
**Purchasing:** John Walmsley *(Headmaster)*
**US SIC:** 8211 **UK SIC:** 93200
**Auditors:** Winters
**Bankers:** Lloyds TSB Bank plc (30-91-84)

| | 31-08-14 | 31-08-13 | 31-08-12 |
|---|---|---|---|
| TO | 9,346,820 | 8,734,000 | 8,488,000 |
| P/L | 192,542 | 188,000 | 279,000 |
| NW | 9,123,026 | 8,900,000 | 8,643,000 |
| WC | (520,075) | (500,000) | (736,000) |
| Emp. | 145 | 148 | 144 |

DUNS 21-211-5596

## Siddall & Hilton Fencing Products Ltd

(**Subsidiary of:** Siddall Investments Ltd)
Holmfield Industrial Estate, Holmfield, Halifax, West Yorkshire HX2 9TN
**Tel:** 01422415204
**Web:** www.halifaxskips.com
**Reg No:** 0228013 **Estd:** 1922 Private Limited Company
**Line of Business:** Manufacture of medical and surgical equipment and orthopaedic appliances
**Trading Style:** Preece Division, Siddall & Hilton Hospital Furniture, Redfearns Wire Products, Sidhil Limited
**Issued Capital:** £8,112
**Principals:** P R Siddall *(Chairman)*, A J Siddall
**Co. Secretary:** John Firth
**Responsibilities**
**Health & Safety:** Carl Haydock *(Health & Safety Officer)*
**Branches:** Siddall & Hilton Fencing Products Ltd, Caldervale Works, Brighouse, West Yorkshire HD6 1JS
**US SIC:** 3841 **UK SIC:** 37201
**Bankers:** National Westminster Bank Plc (60-09-27)

| | 31-12-13 | 31-12-12 | 31-12-11 |
|---|---|---|---|
| TA | 8,112 | 8,112 | 8,112 |
| NW | 8,112 | 8,112 | 8,112 |

DUNS 53-655-1310

## Siddall & Hilton Products Ltd

(**Subsidiary of:** Siddall Products Ltd)
Birds Royd Lane, Brighouse, West Yorkshire HD6 1LT
**Tel:** 01484-401-610
**Web:** www.sandhp.com
**Reg No:** 3460387 **Estd:** 1997 Private Limited Company
**Line of Business:** Manufacturers of wire products
**Export Sales:** £1,398,000
**Issued Capital:** £2
**Directors:** C P Siddall, A J Siddall, J C Siddall, P R Siddall, N A Stewardson, J E Mcgee, Mrs C M Siddall
**Co. Secretary:** John Firth
**US SIC:** 3357 **UK SIC:** 22470
**Auditors:** Saffery Champness
**Bankers:** National Westminster Bank Plc (60-09-27)

| | 31-12-13 | 31-12-12 | 31-12-11 |
|---|---|---|---|
| TO | 13,833,000 | 17,730,000 | 19,033,000 |
| P/L | 54,000 | 127,000 | 32,000 |
| NW | 1,902,000 | 1,988,000 | 2,448,000 |
| WC | (622,000) | 883,000 | 2,169,000 |
| Emp. | 65 | 77 | 84 |

DUNS 22-046-7166

## Siddall Group Ltd

(**Subsidiary of:** Siddall Medequip Ltd)
Sidhil Business Park, Holmfield, Halifax, West Yorkshire HX2 9TN
**Web:** www.siddallandhilton.com
**Reg No:** 4048974 **Estd:** 2000 Private Limited Company
**Line of Business:** Management activities of holding companies
**Issued Capital:** £22,840
**Directors:** P R Siddall, J E Mcgee, C P Siddall
**Co. Secretary:** Jeremy Siddall
**US SIC:** 6711 **UK SIC:** 83962
**Auditors:** KPMG
**Bankers:** National Westminster Bank Plc (60-09-27)

| | 31-12-13 | 31-12-12 | 31-12-11 |
|---|---|---|---|
| TA | 1,989,000 | 1,989,000 | 1,989,000 |
| P/L | N/A | N/A | 2,518,000 |
| NW | 24,000 | 24,000 | 24,000 |
| Emp. | N/A | N/A | 4 |

DUNS 22-627-5410 **Exp**

## Sidebell Ltd

(**Subsidiary of:** Sidebell Capital Partners Ltd)
The Coach House, Wokingham, Berkshire RG40 5QT
**Tel:** 01189776696
**Web:** www.sidebell.co.uk
**Reg No:** 0780147 **Estd:** 1963 Private Limited Company
**Line of Business:** Management activities of holding companies
**Export Markets:** W Europe, Far East
**Export Sales:** £1,413,727
**Issued Capital:** £3,310,000
**Principals:** S A Richards *(Chairman and Managing)*, K E Taplin, T J Richards, Mrs E W Richards, M A Richards
**Co. Secretary:** Mrs Alison Richards
**Responsibilities**
**Finance:** Conley Fairbrother *(Accountant)*
**US SIC:** 6711 **UK SIC:** 83962
**Auditors:** Haines Watts
**Bankers:** Lloyds TSB Bank plc (30-97-20)

| | 31-12-13 | 31-12-12 | 31-12-11 |
|---|---|---|---|
| TO | 5,615,277 | 6,484,925 | 7,110,129 |
| P/L | 1,299,980 | 476,690 | 484,533 |
| NW | 10,435,594 | 9,505,848 | 7,656,607 |
| WC | 6,195,288 | 2,844,059 | 2,823,295 |
| Emp. | 82 | 86 | 88 |

DUNS 21-775-0213

## Sidegate Primary School

Sidegate Lane, Ipswich, Suffolk IP4 4JD
**Tel:** 01473727319
**Web:** www.sidegate.net
**Estd:** 1942 Proprietorship
**Line of Business:** Primary education
**Proprietor:** Mrs W James
**US SIC:** 8211 **UK SIC:** 93200
**Employees:** 78

DUNS 50-386-1692

## Siderise (Holdings) Ltd

Unit 21 Lady Lane Industrial Estate, Ipswich, Suffolk IP7 6BQ
**Web:** www.siderise.com
**Reg No:** 2395079 **Estd:** 1989 Private Limited Company
**Line of Business:** Management activities of holding companies
**Export Sales:** £792,310
**Issued Capital:** £1,000
**Principals:** S W Bond *(Managing)*, A R James, S C Swales, L G Palmer
**Co. Secretary:** Leigh Palmer
**Responsibilities**
**Senior:** Andrew Dewhurst *(Manager)*
**US SIC:** 6711 **UK SIC:** 83962
**Auditors:** Keen Dicey Grover
**Bankers:** National Westminster Bank Plc (60-24-28)

| | 31-12-13 | 31-12-12 | 31-12-11 |
|---|---|---|---|
| TO | 7,545,807 | 6,965,370 | 6,962,857 |
| P/L | 839,964 | 494,737 | 344,007 |
| NW | 5,140,023 | 4,851,541 | 4,486,511 |
| WC | 3,697,499 | 3,378,637 | 3,027,859 |
| Emp. | 75 | 85 | 80 |

DUNS 76-855-2028

## Sidey Ltd

36 Cumberland Avenue Park Park Royal, London NW10 7RQ
**Tel:** 08444722222 **Fax:** 01738-631-335
**Web:** www.sidey.co.uk
**Reg No:** 0131851SC **VAT No:** 882837870
**Estd:** 1932 Private Limited Company
**Line of Business:** Freight transport by road not elsewhere classified
**Issued Capital:** £100,008
**Directors:** S Hardy, A J Litster, A D Ramsay, G Mckenna, R Hendry, P C Howe
**Co. Secretary:** Andrew Litster
**Branches:** Sidey Ltd, West Huntingtower, Crieff Rd, Perth, Perthshire PH1 2SJ
**US SIC:** 4213, 3629
**UK SIC:** 72300, 34350
**Auditors:** Bell & Company
**Bankers:** Bank Of Scotland (80-06-57)

| | 27-06-14 | 30-06-13 | 01-06-12 |
|---|---|---|---|
| TO | 24,969,808 | 20,832,893 | 24,763,594 |
| P/L | 327,457 | 146,799 | 444,212 |
| NW | 2,253,376 | 1,985,208 | 1,863,444 |
| WC | 671,077 | 451,925 | 179,559 |
| Emp. | 161 | 160 | 174 |

DUNS 22-702-7950 **Imp**

## Sidley Austin

Woolgate Exchange, 25 Basinghall Street, London EC2V 5HA
**Tel:** 020-7360-3600
**Web:** www.sidley.com
**Estd:** 2008 Proprietorship
**Line of Business:** Solicitors
**Proprietor:** D Scott
**Responsibilities**
**Marketing:** Katie Morgan *(Marketing Director)*
**IT:** James Searle *(Computer Manager)*
**HR:** Jerry Gallagher *(Human Resources Director)*
**Health & Safety:** David English *(Facilities Manager)*
**Facilities:** David English *(Facilities Manager)*
**Purchasing:** David English *(Facilities Manager)*
**US SIC:** 8111 **UK SIC:** 83500
**Bankers:** Bank One Na (40-50-20)
**Employees:** 240

DUNS 22-025-7070

## Sidmouth Hotels Ltd

The Esplanade, Sidmouth, Devon EX10 8AT
**Tel:** 01395513503
**Web:** www.hotels-sidmouth.co.uk
**Reg No:** 4028342 **Estd:** 2000 Private Limited Company
**Line of Business:** Hotels
**Issued Capital:** £100
**Director:** M Seward
**Co. Secretary:** Ms Joanna Seward
**US SIC:** 7011 **UK SIC:** 66500
**Bankers:** HSBC Bank plc (40-42-02)

| | 31-01-14 | 31-01-13 | 31-01-12 |
|---|---|---|---|
| TO | 2,099,096 | 2,038,214 | 3,008,301 |
| P/L | 347,709 | 258,087 | 353,860 |
| NW | 1,830,011 | 1,596,156 | 1,533,348 |
| WC | (344,108) | (428,618) | (1,068,418) |
| Emp. | 47 | 55 | 75 |

DUNS 21-242-8452

## Sidney Raines Ltd

Raines House, Denby Dale Road, Wakefield, West Yorkshire WF1 1HR
**Tel:** 01924886464
**Web:** www.rainesrecruitment.co.uk
**Reg No:** 0378791 **VAT No:** 419350556
**Estd:** 2010 Private Limited Company
**Line of Business:** Office rental
**Trading Style:** Raines Business Services, Raines Secretarial & Computer Training Centre
**Issued Capital:** £60,000
**Director:** J R Gill
**Co. Secretary:** Ms Dorothea Gill
**US SIC:** 6519, 7399
**UK SIC:** 85000, 83954
**Auditors:** Walter Dawson & Son

| | 30-06-13 | 30-06-12 | 30-06-11 |
|---|---|---|---|
| TA | 239,413 | 352,277 | 362,448 |
| NW | 16,190 | 50,742 | 65,359 |
| WC | (124,792) | (96,703) | (84,755) |

DUNS 36-487-7634

## Sidney Sussex College

Sidney Street, Cambridge, Cambridgeshire CB2 3HU
**Web:** www.sid.cam.ac.uk
**Estd:** 1904
**Line of Business:** University
**Directors:** N Allen, M M Beber, S Dawson, Dr A Al-Tabbaa, Dr I R Baxendale, Prof R V Penty, Prof. T C W. Blanning, Dr I Black
**Responsibilities**
**Senior:** Nick Allen *(Bursar)*, B Billups *(Principal)*, Richard Penty *(Acting Master)*, Keith Straughan *(Principal)*, T W Blanning *(Principal)*, Andrew Wallace-Hadrill *(Headmaster)*
**Finance:** C Larkham *(Bursar)*
**US SIC:** 8221 **UK SIC:** 93100
**Auditors:** Peters Elworthy & Moore

| | 30-06-13 | 30-06-12 | 30-06-11 |
|---|---|---|---|
| TO | 8,406,834 | 8,015,618 | 7,983,842 |
| P/L | 25,639 | 244,913 | 309,452 |
| NW | 105,423,906 | 101,310,147 | 87,374,629 |
| WC | (466,636) | 194,167 | 765,741 |
| Emp. | 154 | 152 | 151 |

DUNS 21-409-6280

## Sids Private Hire

Unit 1 Holditch Road, Newcastle, Staffordshire ST5 9JA
**Tel:** 01782713999
**Estd:** 2011 Proprietorship
**Line of Business:** Taxis and private hire vehicles
**Proprietor:** J Hamond
**Responsibilities**
**Senior:** Jeff Hammond *(Proprietor)*
**US SIC:** 4121 **UK SIC:** 72200
**Employees:** 150

DUNS 22-121-0144

## Siemens Financial Services Holdings Ltd

(**Subsidiary of:** Siemens Ag)
Sefton Park, Slough, Berkshire SL2 4JS
**Tel:** 01753434259 **Fax:** 01844-266512
**Web:** https://www.google.co.uk
**Reg No:** 4140043 **Estd:** 2001 Private Limited Company
**Line of Business:** Financial intermediation not elsewhere classified
**Issued Capital:** £118,006,579
**Directors:** B K Schneider, S J Mason, J Andrew, J T Gearey
**Co. Secretary:** Ralph Britton
**US SIC:** 6111 **UK SIC:** 81501

| | 30-09-13 | 30-09-12 | 30-09-11 |
|---|---|---|---|
| TA | 118,007,000 | 118,007,000 | 118,007,000 |
| P/L | N/A | 66,000,000 | N/A |
| NW | 118,007,000 | 118,007,000 | 118,007,000 |

DUNS 21-609-8459 **Imp**

## Siemens Hearing Instruments Ltd

(**Subsidiary of:** Siemens Ag)
Platinum House, Crawley, West Sussex RH10 9NH
**Tel:** 01293-423-700 **Fax:** 01293-403-080
**Web:** www.siemens.co.uk
**Reg No:** 0203774 **Estd:** 2010 Private Limited Company
**Line of Business:** Hearing aid suppliers
**Issued Capital:** £2,000,000
**Director:** T Andrews
**Co. Secretary:** David Smith
**Responsibilities**
**Marketing:** Mark Laben *(Marketing Manager)*, Stefan Schaller *(Vice President - Strategy - Si)*
**Sales:** Wendy Davies *(National Sales and Audiology M)*, James Goggin *(Regional Sales Manager)*, Mark Laben *(Marketing Manager)*, Robert Ryman *(Business Development Manager)*
**IT:** Gary Stenning *(Network Coordinator)*
**Facilities:** Lance Pelling *(Site Services Manager)*
**Purchasing:** Pat Drew *(Buyer)*, Mark Elmer *(Materials Manager)*
**US SIC:** 3841 **UK SIC:** 37201
**Auditors:** Ernst & Young LLP

**Bankers:** National Westminster Bank Plc (60-06-20)

| | 30-09-13 | 30-09-12 | 30-09-11 |
|---|---|---|---|
| TO | 25,065,000 | 20,691,000 | 22,324,000 |
| P/L | 1,237,000 | 1,808,000 | (1,672,000) |
| NW | 9,235,000 | 11,153,000 | 9,431,000 |
| WC | 8,064,000 | 9,437,000 | 7,172,000 |
| Emp. | 77 | 85 | 92 |

DUNS 73-465-6551 **Imp-Exp**

## Siemens Industrial Turbomachinery Ltd

(**Subsidiary of:** Siemens Ag)
Witham Park, 1 Waterside South, Lincoln, Lincolnshire LN5 7FB
**Web:** www.siemens.com
**Reg No:** 4729734 **VAT No:** 809499286
**Estd:** 1974 Private Limited Company
**Line of Business:** Manufacture of non-electronic instruments and appliances for measuring, checking, testing, navigating and other purposes, except industrial process control equipment
**Issued Capital:** £183,000,000
**Directors:** N Harris, J G Hunt, N A Corner
**Co. Secretary:** Ms Helen Carless
**Branches:** Siemens Industrial Turbomachinery Ltd, Kirkton Drive, Pitmedden Industrial Estate Dyce, Aberdeen, Aberdeenshire AB21 0BG
**US SIC:** 3811, 6711
**UK SIC:** 37100, 83962
**Auditors:** Ernst & Young LLP

| | 30-09-14 | 30-09-13 | 30-09-12 |
|---|---|---|---|
| TO | 334,955,000 | 353,592,000 | 345,298,000 |
| P/L | 64,182,000 | 59,289,000 | 36,602,000 |
| NW | 184,816,000 | 134,009,000 | 97,986,000 |
| WC | 160,287,000 | 107,457,000 | 73,710,000 |
| Emp. | 1,521 | 1,541 | 1,524 |

DUNS 64-081-2681 **Imp-Exp**

## Siemens Industry Software Ltd

(**Subsidiary of:** Siemens Ag)
Sir William Siemens Square, Camberley, Surrey GU16 8QD
**Tel:** 01276413200
**Web:** www.plm.automation.siemens.com
**Reg No:** 3476850 **VAT No:** 709342439
**Estd:** 1968 Private Limited Company
**Line of Business:** Hardware consultancy
**Issued Capital:** £8,393,105
**Directors:** R J Hancock, B A Holliday, D L Macaskill
**Co. Secretary:** Ms Sarah Brufal-De-Melgarejo
**Responsibilities**
**Senior:** Harry Volande *(Manager)*
**Marketing:** Neil Dunsmuir *(Marketing Manager)*
**HR:** Jo Bradfield *(Recruitment Lead - Entry Level)*
**Branches:** Siemens Industry Software Ltd, Parker House, 46 Regent Street, Cambridge, Cambridgeshire CB2 1DP
**US SIC:** 7379 **UK SIC:** 83940
**Auditors:** Ernst & Young LLP

| | 30-09-14 | 30-09-13 | 30-09-12 |
|---|---|---|---|
| TO | 55,618,000 | 56,677,000 | 57,487,000 |
| P/L | 5,665,000 | 9,496,000 | 6,691,000 |
| NW | 39,309,000 | 34,947,000 | 27,634,000 |
| WC | 38,414,000 | 33,812,000 | 26,685,000 |
| Emp. | 422 | 419 | 431 |

DUNS 21-604-1988 **Imp**

## Siemens Plc

(**Subsidiary of:** Siemens Ag)
Outrams Wharf, Little Eaton, Derby, Derbyshire DE21 5EL
**Tel:** 01332387300 **Fax:** 01344396761
**Web:** www.evoqua.com
**Reg No:** 0727817 **VAT No:** 479985260
**Estd:** 1989 Public Limited Company
**Line of Business:** Effluent treatment plant and equipment
**Trading Style:** Siemens Medical Solutions Siemens Measurement, Siemens Power Generation Siemens Water Technologies, Siemens Microelectronics Siemens Automation and Drive, Siemens It Services Siemens Traffic Control Siemens Healthcare
**Issued Capital:** £1,000,000
**Directors:** Ms H C Carless, A Hall, J W Maier
**Co. Secretary:** Ms Helen Carless
**Responsibilities**
**Senior:** Christiana Awofesobi *(Manager)*, Roland Jaksch *(Chief Financial Officer)*, Clark Macfarlane *(Managing Director, Offshore, W)*
**Finance:** Roland Jaksch *(Chief Financial Officer)*, Garry Knapper *(Financial Director)*
**Marketing:** Maurice Carter *(Head of Maintenance Strategy a)*, Dale Geach *(Innovation Manager - Strategy)*, Andy Kennington *(Marketing Director)*, Helen Moon *(Head of Marketing Communicatio)*, Geraldine Roy *(Proposals Manager)*, Michelle Thomson *(Communications Manager)*, Laurie Waugh *(Head of Communications)*
**Sales:** Gary Carroll *(Business Development Manager -)*, David Darlow *(Strategic Sales Manager)*, Mark Hoffman *(Head of Sales (UK & Ireland))*, Oliver Kuhn *(Senior Sales Manager)*, Bettina Peck *(Head of Business Development)*, Carla Remedios *(Sales Support Manager)*, Miriam Scheer *(Commercial Manager)*, Ray Thompson *(Business Development Manager)*, Jill Truman *(Sales Support and Administrati)*, Emily Wright *(Business Excellence Manager)*
**Facilities:** Laurence Knappert *(Manager Rolling Stock Maintena)*
**Operations:** Stuart Driver *(Research and Development Opera)*, Christine Longthorne *(Project Manager)*, Stephen Pead *(Project Manager)*, Anne Thornton *(Operations Manager - Grid Conn)*, Charles Wheaton *(Senior Projects Manager)*
**Fleet:** Mick Hill *(Fleet Manager)*, Paul Tate *(Head of Fleet)*
**Engineering:** Nick Anderson *(Manufacturing Engineering Team)*, Gareth Meehan *(Manufacturing Engineering Mana)*, James Oddie *(Instruments Manufacturing Mana)*, Nick Pegg *(Engineering Operations Manager)*, Steve Scrimshaw *(Head of Rolling Stock)*, Ralph Seidler *(Manufacturing Director)*
**Branches:** Siemens Plc, Nasmyth Building, Nasmyth Ave, Glasgow, Lanarkshire G75 0QU
**US SIC:** 4952, 3629
**UK SIC:** 92120, 34350
**Auditors:** Ernst & Young LLP
**Bankers:** Barclays Bank Plc (20-71-06)
**Following financial data are in thousands**

| | 30-09-14 | 30-09-13 | 30-09-12 |
|---|---|---|---|
| TO | 3,082,427 | 2,664,590 | 3,307,349 |
| P/L | 149,035 | 235,585 | 167,709 |
| NW | 456,953 | 59,380 | (23,136) |
| WC | 650,901 | 519,340 | 55,936 |
| Emp. | 8,287 | 8,339 | 8,227 |

DUNS 23-730-3636 **Imp**

## Siemens Protection Devices Ltd

(**Subsidiary of:** Siemens Ag)
Po Box 8, North Farm Road, Hebburn, Tyne and Wear NE31 1TZ
**Tel:** 01914017901 **Fax:** 0191-401-5575
**Web:** www.siemens.com
**Reg No:** 3724899 **Estd:** 1959 Private Limited Company
**Line of Business:** Manufacture of electronic valves and tubes and other electronic components
**Issued Capital:** £6,290,002
**Directors:** P Maher, M Bell, I Erkens, G S Weir
**Co. Secretary:** Ms Helen Carless
**Responsibilities**
**Senior:** Gerard Gent *(Manager)*, Andreas Heine *(Manager)*, Michael Jesberger *(Manager)*
**US SIC:** 3679 **UK SIC:** 34542
**Auditors:** KPMG Audit PLC

| | 30-09-14 | 30-09-13 | 30-09-12 |
|---|---|---|---|
| TO | 24,730,000 | 24,643,000 | 18,081,000 |
| P/L | 1,426,000 | 417,000 | 1,529,000 |
| NW | 2,799,000 | 1,763,000 | 1,718,000 |
| WC | 7,792,000 | 7,998,000 | 6,509,000 |
| Emp. | 145 | 154 | 156 |

DUNS 21-031-4878

## Siemens Rail Automation Holdings Ltd

(**Subsidiary of:** Siemens Ag)
Langley Park, Langely Road, Chippenham, Wiltshire SN15 1JD
**Tel:** 0124-944-1441
**Reg No:** 0016033 **Estd:** 1881 Private Limited Company
**Line of Business:** Railway sleepers
**Export Sales:** £59,988,000
**Issued Capital:** £10,664,136
**Directors:** P J Copeland, O Yilmaz
**Co. Secretary:** Ms Helen Carless
**Branches:** Siemens Rail Automation Holdings Ltd, Euston House, 7th Floor, London NW1 1AD
**US SIC:** 2421 **UK SIC:** 46101
**Auditors:** Ernst & Young LLP
**Bankers:** Barclays Bank Plc (20-53-30)

| | 02-05-13 | 31-03-12 | 31-05-11 |
|---|---|---|---|
| TO | 261,014,000 | 282,349,000 | 246,152,000 |
| P/L | (31,261,000) | (380,000) | 11,810,000 |
| NW | 231,417,000 | 274,193,000 | 279,451,000 |
| WC | 292,989,000 | 318,426,000 | 317,383,000 |
| Emp. | 1,657 | 1,735 | 1,788 |

DUNS 23-523-9258 **Imp**

## Siemens Transmission & Distribution Ltd

(**Subsidiary of:** Siemens Ag)
2 Koppers Way, Monkton Business Park, Hebburn, Tyne and Wear NE31 2EZ
**Tel:** 01914-952-244 **Fax:** 01315-610-801
**Web:** www.siemens.co.uk
**Reg No:** 0631825 **Estd:** 1961 Private Limited Company
**Line of Business:** Manufacture of electricity distribution and control apparatus
**Issued Capital:** £20,000,000
**Directors:** A J Gemmell, D R Wilson
**Co. Secretary:** Ms Helen Carless
**Responsibilities**
**Senior:** Dave Elliott *(Area Manager)*, Gerard Gent *(Manager)*, Neil Lane *(Senior Operational Excellence)*
**Branches:** Siemens Transmission & Distribution Ltd, Unit 5G, Birkdale Road, Scunthorpe, South Humberside DN17 2AU
**US SIC:** 3643, 3629, 4911
**UK SIC:** 34203, 34350, 16101
**Auditors:** Ernst & Young LLP
**Bankers:** National Westminster Bank Plc (50-00-00)

| | 30-09-13 | 30-09-12 | 30-09-11 |
|---|---|---|---|
| TO | 240,835,000 | 292,164,000 | 316,457,000 |
| P/L | 22,257,000 | 38,299,000 | 34,723,000 |
| NW | 119,950,000 | 104,981,000 | 87,729,000 |
| WC | 145,089,000 | 128,480,000 | 111,729,000 |
| Emp. | 789 | 792 | 788 |

DUNS 21-595-8346

## Siemens Water Technologies

Priory Works, Five Oak Green Road, Tonbridge, Kent TN11 0QN
**Tel:** 01732771777
**Web:** www.siemens.co.uk
**Estd:** 2012 Proprietorship
**Line of Business:** Water treatment services
**Proprietor:** C Dean
**US SIC:** 4941 **UK SIC:** 17000
**Employees:** 161

DUNS 76-798-3992 **Imp-Exp**

## The Siemon Co Ltd

Siemon House, 36-48 Windsor Street, Chertsey, Surrey KT16 8AS
**Tel:** 01932 571771
**Web:** www.callgps.com
**Reg No:** 2601151 **VAT No:** 584335228
**Estd:** 2003 Private Limited Company
**Line of Business:** Manufacturers general
**Export Markets:** Europe
**Issued Capital:** £165,675
**Directors:** C N Siemon, S Foster, K V Astin, N P Edwards
**Co. Secretary:** Neil Edwards
**Responsibilities**
**Senior:** Sue Corbin *(Human Resources Manager)*
**HR:** Sue Corbin *(Human Resources Manager)*
**Facilities:** Sue Corbin *(Human Resources Manager)*
**US SIC:** 3357 **UK SIC:** 22470
**Auditors:** Saffery Champness
**Bankers:** Barclays Bank Plc (20-11-74)

| | 31-12-13 | 31-12-12 | 31-12-11 |
|---|---|---|---|
| TO | 20,539,363 | 18,719,143 | 19,503,354 |
| P/L | 1,982,135 | 1,749,617 | 1,350,950 |
| NW | 3,264,540 | 1,711,918 | 347,596 |
| WC | 4,681,509 | 3,691,244 | 2,961,798 |
| Emp. | 66 | 60 | 59 |

DUNS 21-715-9493

## Sierra Support Services Ltd

(**Subsidiary of:** Millington Ltd)
Unit 14-15 Harbour Court, Sydenham Business Park Heron Road, Belfast BT3 9HB
**Tel:** 02890498310 **Fax:** 02890-498301
**Web:** www.sierra.ie
**Reg No:** 0606408NI **Estd:** 2011 Private Limited Company
**Line of Business:** Home care service providers
**Issued Capital:** £1,000
**Directors:** A Doherty, S Corkery, T J Malone, P Carolan
**Co. Secretary:** Patrick Carolan
**Responsibilities**
**Senior:** Thomas Jenkinson *(Operations Manager)*
**US SIC:** 8091 **UK SIC:** 95200
**Bankers:** Northern Bank Ltd (95-00-01)

| | 31-12-13 | 30-04-13 | 31-12-12 |
|---|---|---|---|
| TO | 3,059,696 | 6,695,158 | 2,550,446 |
| P/L | 237,427 | 372,860 | 74,232 |
| NW | 609,363 | 371,936 | 55,930 |
| WC | 470,031 | 196,055 | (128,165) |
| Emp. | 95 | 98 | 91 |

DUNS 21-414-5604

## Siesta

Unit D, Long Meadow Industrial Estate, Ringwood Road, Wimborne, Dorset BH21 6RD
**Web:** www.siestaframes.com
**Estd:** 1998 Partnership
**Line of Business:** Other retail sale in specialised stores not elsewhere classified
**Partners:** Mrs S Salvage, R Agar
**US SIC:** 5199 **UK SIC:** 61900
**Employees:** 49

DUNS 73-618-7498 **Imp**

## Siesta Frames Ltd

Unit D Long Meadow Industrial Estate, Ringwood Road, Three Legged Cross, Wimborne, Dorset BH21 6RD
**Web:** www.siestaframes.com
**Reg No:** 4879492 **Estd:** 2003 Private Limited Company
**Line of Business:** Other retail sale in specialised stores not elsewhere classified
**Issued Capital:** £130
**Directors:** Ms C L Agar, R J Agar
**Co. Secretary:** Colin Salvage
**US SIC:** 5199 **UK SIC:** 61900

| | 31-08-14 | 31-08-13 | 31-08-12 |
|---|---|---|---|
| TA | 410,545 | 381,513 | 367,115 |
| NW | 90,187 | 93,681 | 75,456 |
| WC | 80,422 | 80,040 | 58,738 |

DUNS 22-805-5455 **Imp-Exp**

## Siesta International Holidays Ltd

Siesta House, Lamport Street, Middlesbrough, Cleveland TS1 5QL
**Tel:** 08452712443
**Web:** www.siestaholidays.co.uk
**Reg No:** 1492986 **Estd:** 1980 Private Limited Company
**Line of Business:** Travel agency activities
**Export Markets:** Italy, Spain, France, Austria
**Trading Style:** Tragvel Europe
**Issued Capital:** £40,000
**Principals:** P R Herbert *(Managing)*, C P Herbert, Ms S E Herbert
**Co. Secretary:** Miss Julie Gofton
**Branches:** Siesta International Holidays Ltd, 103 High Street, Birmingham, West Midlands B23 6SA
**US SIC:** 4722 **UK SIC:** 77001
**Auditors:** King Hope & Co
**Bankers:** Barclays Bank Plc (20-56-74)

| | 30-09-13 | 30-09-12 | 30-09-11 |
|---|---|---|---|
| TO | 5,521,614 | 5,525,090 | 5,133,038 |
| P/L | (5,364) | 4,151 | (367,933) |
| NW | 4,267,314 | 3,715,041 | 3,317,899 |
| WC | 416,037 | 437,232 | 172,555 |
| Emp. | 59 | 60 | 64 |

DUNS 45-897-5562

## Sift Ltd

Bridge House 48-52, Baldwin Street, Bristol, Avon BS1 1QB
**Tel:** 01179150423 **Fax:** 01179-159630
**Web:** www.siftmedia.co.uk
**Reg No:** 3230061 **Estd:** 1995 Private Limited Company
**Line of Business:** Advertising publications & publishers
**Export Sales:** £651,672
**Trading Style:** Sift Software, Sift Media
**Issued Capital:** £796,157
**Directors:** B Heald, P S Phippen, W T Fraser-Allen
**Co. Secretary:** Steven Priscott
**Responsibilities**
**Marketing:** Ian Robins *(Marketing)*
**HR:** Georgina Dalby *(Human Resources)*
**US SIC:** 7379 **UK SIC:** 83940
**Auditors:** KPMG
**Bankers:** Lloyds TSB Bank plc (30-00-01)

| | 31-12-13 | 31-12-12 | 31-12-11 |
|---|---|---|---|
| TO | 8,063,862 | 8,038,414 | 8,062,190 |
| P/L | (31,970) | (441,577) | (20,076) |
| NW | (924,301) | (1,423,305) | (1,072,959) |
| WC | (187,125) | (673,893) | (359,877) |
| Emp. | 131 | 143 | 129 |

DUNS 21-300-6174

## Sig Plc

Hillsbrough Works, Langsett Road, Sheffield, South Yorkshire S6 2LW
**Tel:** 01142-856-300
**Web:** www.sigplc.co.uk
**Reg No:** 0998314 **VAT No:** 487017333
**Estd:** 1970 Public Limited Company
**Line of Business:** Management activities of holding companies
**Export Sales:** £1,404,900,000
**Trading Style:** Carpets & Flooring, A Steadman & Sons, Sig Insulation & Interiors
**Issued Capital:** £59,087,045
**Directors:** C V Geoghegan, D G Robertson, M Ewell, L V Walle, J C Nicholls, Ms J E Ashdown, S R Mitchell
**Co. Secretary:** Richard Monro
**Responsibilities**
**Senior:** Leslie Van De Walle *(Non-Executive Director)*
**HR:** Andrew Mander *(Personnel Director)*
**Facilities:** Scott Gary *(Logistics Manager)*
**Branches:** Sig Plc, 15 Apple Business Centre, Frobisher Way, Taunton, Somerset TA2 6BB
**US SIC:** 6711, 5039
**UK SIC:** 83962, 61300
**Auditors:** Deloitte LLP

**Bankers:** National Westminster Bank Plc (56-00-09)

Following financial data are in thousands

|  | 31-12-13 | 31-12-12 | 31-12-11 |
|---|---|---|---|
| TO | 2,719,800 | 2,635,500 | 2,808,400 |
| P/L | 2,100 | 43,700 | 7,500 |
| NW | 225,600 | 224,700 | 212,400 |
| WC | 369,100 | 292,400 | 363,800 |
| Emp. | 9,806 | 10,228 | 11,105 |

DUNS 50-544-6807
### Sig Trading (Ksa) Ltd
(**Subsidiary of:** Sig Plc)
Units 1/5, Crawley, West Sussex RH10 9RT
**Tel:** 01293592500
**Web:** www.sigblindsandgraphics.com
**Reg No:** 2498697 **Estd:** 1990 Private Limited Company
**Line of Business:** Agents involved in the sale of timber and building materials
**Issued Capital:** £2
**Director:** I Jackson
**Co. Secretary:** Richard Monro
**Responsibilities**
**Senior:** Mick O'callaghan (Manager)
**US SIC:** 5072 **UK SIC:** 61500

|  | 31-12-13 | 31-12-12 | 31-12-11 |
|---|---|---|---|
| TA | 2 | 2 | 2 |
| NW | 2 | 2 | 2 |

DUNS 21-724-4185 **Imp**
### Siga (Electronics) Ltd
(**Subsidiary of:** Siga Ltd)
3 Darlington Close Sunderland Road, Sandy, Bedfordshire SG19 1RW
**Tel:** 01767681266
**Web:** www.sigatransformers.co.uk
**Reg No:** 0683581 **VAT No:** 197097514
**Estd:** 1961 Private Limited Company
**Line of Business:** Manufacturers of electronic equipment and components
**Issued Capital:** £1,052
**Managing Director:** R J Thrussell
**Co. Secretary:** Mrs Christine Thrussell
**Responsibilities**
**Marketing:** Alex Diram (Marketing Manager)
**Facilities:** Stephen Blow (Purchasing Manager)
**Operations:** Dawn Walker (Purchasing Manager)
**Purchasing:** Stephen Blow (Purchasing Manager), Dawn Walker (Purchasing Manager)
**US SIC:** 3679 **UK SIC:** 34542
**Auditors:** Peters Elworthy & Moore
**Bankers:** Barclays Bank Plc (20-74-81)

|  | 31-03-14 | 31-03-13 | 31-03-12 |
|---|---|---|---|
| TA | 1,501,392 | 1,487,162 | 1,311,135 |
| NW | 923,293 | 1,006,274 | 806,179 |
| WC | 794,415 | 912,648 | 729,969 |

DUNS 21-784-5674
### Sight & Sound Security Solutions Ltd.
Airport House, Purley Way, Croydon, Surrey CR0 0XZ
**Tel:** 02086671560
**Estd:** 2011 Proprietorship
**Line of Business:** Misc Fabricated Metal Product Mfrs
**Proprietor:** P Purcase
**US SIC:** 3499 **UK SIC:** 31694
**Employees:** 50

DUNS 28-986-7129
### Sigma 3 (County) Ltd
(**Subsidiary of:** Sigma 3 (Holdings) Ltd)
Sigma House, Llantrisant Business Park, Llantrisant, Pontyclun, Mid Glamorgan CF72 8LF
**Tel:** 01443664000
**Web:** www.sigma3.co.uk
**Reg No:** 1804130 **Estd:** 1984 Private Limited Company
**Line of Business:** Joinery installation
**Issued Capital:** £100
**Director:** B C Lakin
**US SIC:** 1751, 5719
**UK SIC:** 50400, 64700
**Auditors:** Clay Shaw Thomas
**Bankers:** National Westminster Bank Plc (54-30-05)
**Employees:** 50

DUNS 22-003-1392
### Sigma 3 (Holdings) Ltd
Llantrisant Business Park, Llantrisant, Pontyclun, Mid Glamorgan CF72 8LF
**Tel:** 01443-237732
**Web:** www.sigma3.co.uk
**Reg No:** 4006412 **Estd:** 2000 Private Limited Company
**Line of Business:** Kitchen planners and installers
**Issued Capital:** £50,000
**Directors:** B C Lakin, P S Thomas, G Jones, Ms E M Lakin
**US SIC:** 1751 **UK SIC:** 50400

**Bankers:** Barclays Bank Plc (20-97-09)

|  | 10-11-13 | 11-11-12 | 13-11-11 |
|---|---|---|---|
| TO | 13,774,380 | 12,956,499 | 13,027,069 |
| P/L | 383,996 | 569,804 | (721,722) |
| NW | 3,806,707 | 3,503,874 | 3,608,595 |
| WC | 732,577 | 586,010 | 566,028 |
| Emp. | 130 | 128 | 153 |

DUNS 39-792-4143 **Imp-Exp**
### Sigma-Aldrich Co Ltd
(**Subsidiary of:** Sigma-Aldrich Corporation)
The Old Brickyard, New Road, Gillingham, Dorset SP8 4XF
**Fax:** 01747833313
**Web:** www.sigmaaldrich.com
**Reg No:** 2204655 **VAT No:** 501928855
**Estd:** 1987 Private Limited Company
**Line of Business:** Chemicals and allied products
**Export Markets:** Worldwide
**Export Sales:** £48,201,000
**Trading Style:** Sigma Aldrich, Supelca, Fluka Riedel-De Haen
**Issued Capital:** £1,000
**Directors:** Ms F Oldfield, L Schraishuhn, M J Hollenkamp, G J Van Den Dool
**Co. Secretary:** Graham Lucas
**Branches:** Sigma Aldrich, Second Avenue, Irvine, Ayrshire KA12 8NB
**US SIC:** 2899, 5161
**UK SIC:** 25670, 61200
**Auditors:** KPMG LLP
**Bankers:** HSBC Bank plc (40-45-02)

|  | 31-12-13 | 31-12-12 | 31-12-11 |
|---|---|---|---|
| TO | 137,184,000 | 134,811,000 | 131,437,000 |
| P/L | 12,363,000 | 14,158,000 | 18,124,000 |
| NW | 108,938,000 | 96,108,000 | 83,456,000 |
| WC | 48,033,000 | 45,326,000 | 36,593,000 |
| Emp. | 622 | 624 | 578 |

DUNS 37-972-9528
### Sigma-Genosys Ltd
(**Subsidiary of:** Sigma-Aldrich Corporation)
Sigma-Aldrich House, Haverhill, Suffolk CB9 8QP
**Fax:** 01440767099
**Web:** www.sigmaaldrich.com
**Reg No:** 3280305 **Estd:** 1992 Private Limited Company
**Line of Business:** Manufacture of other chemical products not elsewhere classified
**Issued Capital:** £2
**Director:** G Van Den Dool
**Co. Secretary:** Graham Lucas
**US SIC:** 2899 **UK SIC:** 25670
**Auditors:** KPMG LLP
**Bankers:** Barclays Bank Plc (20-17-35)

|  | 31-12-14 | 31-12-13 | 31-12-12 |
|---|---|---|---|
| TA | 4,691,172 | 4,691,172 | 4,691,172 |
| NW | 4,691,172 | 4,691,172 | 4,691,172 |

DUNS 21-740-4276
### The Sigma Group Ltd
(**Subsidiary of:** C D P Sigma Holdings Ltd)
Po 648 Bourne House, Guernsey, Channel Islands GY1 3SD
**Tel:** 01534711500 **Fax:** 01534711501
**Web:** http://sigmaci.com
**Reg No:** 0000460J **Estd:** 1927 Private Limited Company
**Line of Business:** Stationery suppliers
**Trading Style:** Collins
**Issued Capital:** £40,000
**Principals:** A Royle (Managing), M Allen (Financial)
**Responsibilities**
**Senior:** Mick Dorey (Warehouse Manager)
**Marketing:** Chris Stuart (Sales & Marketing Manager)
**Sales:** Amanda Overland (Business Development Manager), Chris Stuart (Sales & Marketing Manager)
**IT:** Dave Sands (IT Manager)
**HR:** Lisa Ingrouille (Human Resources Manager)
**Health & Safety:** Lisa Ingrouille (Human Resources Manager)
**Facilities:** Lisa Ingrouille (Human Resources Manager)
**Branches:** Sigma Group, Guernsey Office, Po Box 302, Sigma Group Complex, Braye Road, Guernsey GY3 5XB Vale
**US SIC:** 5942, 5999, 5732
**UK SIC:** 65300, 65600, 64800
**Bankers:** HSBC Bank plc (40-25-34)
**Employees:** 70

DUNS 21-158-2518
### Sigma Grp Ltd
Unit 9b Alpine Court, Glasshoughton, Castleford, West Yorkshire WF10 4TL
**Tel:** 0845 521 0258
**Web:** www.sigmagrp.co.uk
**Reg No:** 6856861 **Estd:** 2009 Private Limited Company
**Line of Business:** Management activities of other non-financial holding companies not elsewhere classified
**Issued Capital:** £100
**Director:** J Haigh

**US SIC:** 6711 **UK SIC:** 83962
**Auditors:** Walter Dawson & Son

|  | 31-12-13 | 31-12-12 | 31-12-11 |
|---|---|---|---|
| TO | 9,193,028 | 11,596,624 | N/A |
| P/L | 941,991 | 982,688 | 340,000 |
| NW | 461,843 | 1,174,813 | 100 |
| WC | 254,864 | 914,198 | (161,252) |
| Emp. | 93 | 92 | N/A |

DUNS 22-634-9629 **Imp**
### Sigma Holdings Ltd
273-283 Bath Road, Slough, Berkshire SL1 5PR
**Tel:** 01753554444
**Reg No:** 1723895 **Estd:** 1983 Private Limited Company
**Line of Business:** Management activities of holding companies
**Issued Capital:** £16,316
**Directors:** A Khayami, M Foroutan, M Khayami, D L Thomas, H B Peters
**US SIC:** 6711, 7392
**UK SIC:** 83962, 83951
**Auditors:** Hartley Fowler LLP
**Bankers:** HSBC Bank plc (40-18-30)

|  | 31-12-13 | 31-12-12 | 31-12-11 |
|---|---|---|---|
| TO | 80,053,337 | 67,822,258 | 63,773,907 |
| P/L | 767,854 | 491,678 | 452,617 |
| NW | 2,799,384 | 2,272,506 | 1,921,238 |
| WC | (3,568,496) | (1,416,692) | (1,656,661) |
| Emp. | 206 | 194 | 193 |

DUNS 22-611-6937 **Imp-Exp**
### Sigma Pharmaceuticals Plc
Unit 1-7, Colonial Way, Watford, Hertfordshire WD24 4YR
**Tel:** 01923444999 **Fax:** 01923 444998
**Web:** www.sigmaplc.co.uk
**Reg No:** 1561802 **VAT No:** 225928057
**Estd:** 1981 Public Limited Company
**Line of Business:** Wholesale of pharmaceutical goods
**Export Markets:** Kenya; Middle East
**Export Sales:** £26,132,855
**Issued Capital:** £10,000,000
**Principals:** B K Shah (Chairman and Managing), R B Shah, H D Shah, Mrs K M Shah, Mrs J B Shah, B M Shah, P K Shah, K H Shah
**Co. Secretary:** Manish Shah
**Responsibilities**
**Senior:** Hatul Shah (Financial Director), Cammel Shah (Manager)
**Finance:** Hatul Shah (Financial Director)
**Marketing:** Hatul Shah (Financial Director)
**IT:** Bhavik Patel (IT Manager), Ajay Vyas (IT Director)
**HR:** Hatul Shah (Financial Director)
**Health & Safety:** Hatul Shah (Financial Director)
**Facilities:** Hatul Shah (Financial Director)
**Purchasing:** Bhargav Gorr (Purchasing Coordinator)
**US SIC:** 5122, 7399
**UK SIC:** 61800, 83954
**Auditors:** King & King
**Bankers:** The Royal Bank Of Scotland Plc (15-10-00)

|  | 31-08-13 | 31-08-12 | 31-08-11 |
|---|---|---|---|
| TO | 214,903,208 | 177,124,619 | 213,017,541 |
| P/L | 1,740,300 | 1,055,358 | 1,875,716 |
| NW | 26,974,899 | 26,035,806 | 25,187,398 |
| WC | 29,976,139 | 31,095,245 | 33,262,249 |
| Emp. | 270 | 260 | 250 |

DUNS 73-580-7385
### Sigma Sport Ltd
37-43 High Street, Kingston-Upon-Thames, Surrey KT1 4DA
**Tel:** 02089434443 **Fax:** 020-8943-2226
**Web:** www.sigmasport.co.uk
**Reg No:** 4842265 **Estd:** 1992 Private Limited Company
**Line of Business:** Retail sale of sports goods, games and toys, stamps and coins
**Issued Capital:** £1,000,008
**Directors:** C E Cavell-Taylor, J B Turner, A H Noel
**Co. Secretary:** Ian Whittingham
**US SIC:** 5941, 5699
**UK SIC:** 65400, 64500
**Auditors:** Duncan & Toplis
**Bankers:** Lloyds TSB Bank plc (30-94-77)

|  | 31-05-13 | 31-05-12 | 31-05-11 |
|---|---|---|---|
| TO | 7,568,779 | N/A | N/A |
| P/L | 113,978 | N/A | N/A |
| NW | 1,878,723 | 1,800,867 | 1,618,602 |
| WC | 611,999 | 559,360 | 317,805 |
| Emp. | 59 | N/A | N/A |

DUNS 29-862-2515 **Imp-Exp**
### Sigmatex (U K) Ltd
Manor Farm Road, Runcorn, Cheshire WA7 1TE
**Tel:** 01928570050 **Fax:** 01928790074
**Web:** www.sigmatex.com
**Reg No:** 2065467 **VAT No:** 453245754
**Estd:** 1986 Private Limited Company
**Line of Business:** Carbon products
**Export Markets:** E U
**Export Sales:** £26,593,473
**Issued Capital:** £225,000

**Principals:** E D Ehnimb (Chairman), S J Tolson, H M Braddell, J C Coleman
**Co. Secretary:** Anthony Eaden
**Responsibilities**
**HR:** Diana Russell (Human Resources Manager), Helen Simons (Human Resources Manager)
**Health & Safety:** Scott Travis (Health & Safety Officer)
**Engineering:** Scott Goodson (Production Manager)
**US SIC:** 2392, 2824
**UK SIC:** 45550, 26000
**Auditors:** Christian Douglass LLP
**Bankers:** National Westminster Bank Plc (01-08-38)

|  | 31-12-13 | 31-12-12 | 31-12-11 |
|---|---|---|---|
| TO | 50,650,131 | 51,812,342 | 48,983,418 |
| P/L | 1,865,252 | 2,372,097 | 2,047,831 |
| NW | 9,766,461 | 8,846,166 | 7,657,101 |
| WC | 6,714,168 | 5,513,685 | 3,922,632 |
| Emp. | 176 | 173 | 145 |

DUNS 77-868-2096
### Sigmatic Ltd
(**Subsidiary of:** Drg Uk Holdco Ltd)
6 Talisman Road, Bicester, Oxfordshire OX26 6HR
**Tel:** 01869-241281
**Web:** www.abacusint.com
**Reg No:** 3034965 **Estd:** 1995 Private Limited Company
**Line of Business:** Management and business consultants
**Export Sales:** £2,081,225
**Trading Style:** Abacus International
**Issued Capital:** £92
**Directors:** J Lang, A Gupta, J M Sandler, K Bettigole
**Co. Secretary:** Kyle Bettigole
**Responsibilities**
**Senior:** Ian Belinsky (Manager), Peter Hoenigsberg (Manager)
**Sales:** Christie Harper (Sales Director)
**US SIC:** 7392 **UK SIC:** 83951
**Auditors:** Robin Wallhouse & Co

|  | 31-12-13 | 30-04-13 | 30-12-12 |
|---|---|---|---|
| TO | 4,681,698 | 6,562,483 | N/A |
| P/L | 965,065 | (186,105) | N/A |
| NW | 1,258,918 | 1,524,211 | 1,281,763 |
| WC | 1,019,353 | 1,250,936 | 1,158,396 |
| Emp. | 67 | N/A | N/A |

DUNS 23-589-9259 **Exp**
### Sign 2000 Ltd.
Deacon Trading Estate, Tonbridge, Kent TN9 1SU
**Tel:** 08452652000 **Fax:** 01732357010
**Web:** www.sign2000.co.uk
**Reg No:** 2280175 **VAT No:** 522509076
**Estd:** 1988 Private Limited Company
**Line of Business:** Manufacture of lighting equipment and electric lamps
**Export Markets:** European Union (E U)
**Issued Capital:** £20,000
**Principals:** M L Crompton (Managing), S J Spackman
**Co. Secretary:** Ralph Scott
**Responsibilities**
**Finance:** Jane Bowes (Finance Manager)
**Facilities:** Jane Bowes (Finance Manager)
**US SIC:** 3999 **UK SIC:** 49590
**Auditors:** Deeks Evans
**Bankers:** National Westminster Bank Plc (55-70-13)

|  | 31-12-13 | 31-12-12 | 31-12-11 |
|---|---|---|---|
| TA | 2,207,609 | 1,909,463 | 2,055,733 |
| NW | 363,409 | 275,251 | 233,347 |
| WC | 236,686 | 175,397 | 135,942 |

DUNS 21-924-9745 **Exp**
### Sign Specialists Ltd
19 Oxleasow Road, Redditch, Worcestershire B98 0RE
**Tel:** 01527-504250 **Fax:** 01527-504251
**Web:** www.sign-specialists.co.uk
**Reg No:** 0688806 **VAT No:** 110032750
**Estd:** 1947 Private Limited Company
**Line of Business:** Manufacturers general
**Export Sales:** £457,612
**Issued Capital:** £2,675
**Principals:** R E Tisdale (Managing), P Anelli, R M Green, V B Rowe, Ms D Tisdale, H Tisdale
**Co. Secretary:** Paul Anelli
**Responsibilities**
**Finance:** Brian Hilson (Financial Director)
**HR:** Brian Hilson (Financial Director)
**Branches:** Birmingham
**US SIC:** 2599, 3079
**UK SIC:** 46720, 48360
**Auditors:** BDO Stoy Hayward LLP
**Bankers:** The Co-Operative Bank Plc (08-90-01)

|  | 31-03-14 | 31-03-13 | 31-03-12 |
|---|---|---|---|
| TO | 8,384,654 | 7,972,402 | 9,994,288 |
| P/L | 120,988 | (139,277) | 238,419 |
| NW | 3,074,334 | 2,982,918 | 3,110,222 |
| WC | 1,177,563 | 890,486 | 1,194,054 |
| Emp. | 92 | 97 | 97 |

DUNS 73-508-2047

## Signal House Group Ltd

Cherrycourt Way, Leighton Buzzard, Bedfordshire LU7 4UH
**Tel:** 01525377477
**Reg No:** 4771284 **Estd:** 2003 Private Limited Company
**Line of Business:** Management activities of holding companies
**Export Sales:** £118,087
**Issued Capital:** £35
**Directors:** P Roberts, P Hobbs
**Co. Secretary:** John Leafe
**US SIC:** 6711 **UK SIC:** 83962
**Bankers:** Yorkshire Bank Plc (05-06-41)

| | 30-04-14 | 30-04-13 | 30-04-12 |
|---|---|---|---|
| TO | 10,473,245 | 7,141,861 | 3,525,747 |
| P/L | 254,917 | 208,721 | 36,996 |
| NW | 110,324 | (8,406) | (203,955) |
| WC | (246,764) | (30,002) | (73,233) |
| Emp. | 114 | 109 | 116 |

DUNS 51-613-9008 Exp

## Signalling Solutions Ltd

Bridgefoot House, Radlett, Hertfordshire WD7 7HT
**Tel:** 01923 635000 **Fax:** 02082075905
**Web:** www.signallingsolutions.com
**Reg No:** 5894128 **Estd:** 2006 Private Limited Company
**Line of Business:** Manufacturers of railway equipment and related system
**Issued Capital:** £1,145,130
**Directors:** S J Mclaren, I K Morgan, J Nizet
**Co. Secretary:** James Brownsword
**Responsibilities**
**Finance:** Frances Aylott *(Financial Director)*, Billy Unadkat *(Financial Director)*
**Marketing:** Bob Theaker *(Marketing Manager)*, Judy Viitanen *(Communications Officer)*
**Sales:** Maureen Mullen *(Product Sales Administrator)*
**HR:** James Thorley *(Human Resources Director)*
**Facilities:** Dale Arnold *(Facilities Manager)*
**Operations:** Mick Corner *(Operations Manager)*, Paul Filipek *(Quality Manager)*, Ian Scrawton *(Head of Operations)*
**Branches:** Signalling Solutions Ltd, Midland House, Nelson Street, Derby, DE1 2SA Derbyshire
**US SIC:** 3743 **UK SIC:** 36201
**Auditors:** Ernst & Young LLP
**Bankers:** Barclays Bank Plc (20-00-50)

| | 29-03-14 | 30-03-13 | 31-03-12 |
|---|---|---|---|
| TO | 156,824,000 | 113,353,000 | 69,701,000 |
| P/L | 2,904,000 | 4,411,000 | 4,010,000 |
| NW | 5,204,000 | 6,028,000 | 5,501,000 |
| WC | 5,906,000 | 6,434,000 | 5,347,000 |
| Emp. | 482 | 424 | 360 |

DUNS 22-076-4596

## Signature At the Miramar (Operations) Ltd

**(Subsidiary of:** Signature Senior Lifestyle Holdings Ltd)
165 Reculver Road, Herne Bay, Kent CT6 6PX
**Tel:** 01227-374488 **Fax:** 01227-374488
**Web:** www.signaturecarehomes.co.uk
**Reg No:** 4077890 **Estd:** 2001 Private Limited Company
**Line of Business:** Healthcare companies
**Issued Capital:** £150,002
**Directors:** K J Maddin, T J Ball, A G Roche, T B Newell
**Co. Secretary:** Tom Ball
**Responsibilities**
**Senior:** John Billane *(Manager)*, M Snodgraph *(General Manager)*, M Snodgraph *(General Manager)*, Tina Thomas *(Home Manager)*
**Admin:** Briony Howe *(Office Manager)*
**US SIC:** 8091, 6732
**UK SIC:** 95200, 83100
**Auditors:** PKF (UK) LLP

| | 31-12-13 | 31-12-12 | 31-12-11 |
|---|---|---|---|
| TO | 3,468,202 | 12,000 | 12,000 |
| P/L | (950,538) | (206,346) | (23,219) |
| NW | (831,524) | 119,014 | 325,360 |
| WC | 5,399,462 | 42,169 | 335,642 |

DUNS 73-556-2394 Exp

## Signature Flight Support Ltd

**(Subsidiary of:** Bba Aviation Plc)
Hangar 63, Percival Way, London Luton Airport, Luton, Bedfordshire LU2 9NT
**Tel:** 01582724182 **Fax:** 01582455453
**Web:** www.signatureflight.com
**Reg No:** 4818186 **Estd:** 2003 Private Limited Company
**Line of Business:** Regulation of and contribution to more efficient operation of business
**Trading Style:** Bba Aviation
**Issued Capital:** £65,900,001
**Directors:** D D Ruback, B Weaver, P Bouwer, Ms K King, M R Johnstone
**Responsibilities**
**Senior:** David Herlihy *(General Manager)*
**Finance:** Rachel Baker *(Senior Finance Administrator)*
**Admin:** Karen Dale *(Office Manager)*
**Branches:** Signature Flight Support Ltd, Inverness Airport, Inverness, Inverness-Shire IV2 7JB
**US SIC:** 9121 **UK SIC:** 91110
**Auditors:** Deloitte LLP

| | 31-12-13 | 31-12-12 | 31-12-11 |
|---|---|---|---|
| TA | 79,535,000 | 77,120,000 | 74,434,000 |
| P/L | 2,415,000 | 2,686,000 | 2,652,000 |
| NW | 79,535,000 | 77,120,000 | 74,434,000 |

DUNS 23-940-2048

## Signature Hotel Group Ltd

**(Subsidiary of:** Nash Sells Lp Ii)
Rugby Road, Rugby, Warwickshire CV22 6QW
**Tel:** 01788528000 **Fax:** 01788814451
**Web:** www.signaturegroup.co.uk
**Reg No:** 3929827 **Estd:** 2000 Private Limited Company
**Line of Business:** Hotels
**Trading Style:** The Mount County House Hotel, Jarvis Mount Hotel, Dunchurch Park Conference Centre
**Issued Capital:** £285,222
**Principals:** S W Gaunt *(Managing)*, M Needley
**Co. Secretary:** Graham Arksey
**Responsibilities**
**HR:** Mary Sparks *(Human Resources Manager)*
**Branches:** Signature Hotel Group Ltd, Dunchurch Park Conference Centre, Rugby Road, Dunchurch, Rugby, Warwickshire CV22 6QW
**US SIC:** 7011, 7392
**UK SIC:** 66500, 83951
**Auditors:** The Ollis Partnership Ltd
**Bankers:** Lloyds TSB Bank plc (30-13-66)

| | 30-09-13 | 30-09-12 | 30-09-11 |
|---|---|---|---|
| TO | 2,869,637 | 3,004,698 | 2,666,323 |
| P/L | 3,597 | (2,896) | (121,314) |
| NW | 2,739,331 | 2,735,732 | 2,738,630 |
| WC | (653,115) | (91,965) | (63,191) |
| Emp. | 84 | 87 | 85 |

DUNS 22-762-2339 Imp-Exp

## Signature Ltd

**(Subsidiary of:** Burelle)
Signature House, Oldbury, West Midlands B69 2NF
**Tel:** 01215570234
**Web:** www.signatureltd.com
**Reg No:** 1645551 **VAT No:** 369777577
**Estd:** 1982 Private Limited Company
**Line of Business:** Building of complete constructions or parts thereof; civil engineering
**Export Markets:** Poland; Africa; Far East
**Issued Capital:** £200,000
**Director:** R Land
**Co. Secretary:** Wayne Jones
**Responsibilities**
**Senior:** Arnaud Denolle *(Manager)*
**Marketing:** Sarah Lumley-Holmes *(Sales & Marketing Manager)*
**Sales:** Sarah Lumley-Holmes *(Sales & Marketing Manager)*
**Branches:** Signature Ltd, Signature House, Lanesfield Dr, Wolverhampton, West Midlands WV4 6UB
**US SIC:** 2599, 7399
**UK SIC:** 46720, 83954
**Auditors:** Mazars LLP
**Bankers:** Societe Generale (23-63-91)

| | 31-12-13 | 31-12-12 | 31-12-11 |
|---|---|---|---|
| TO | 12,148,082 | 10,877,667 | 10,632,189 |
| P/L | 881,392 | 1,145,159 | 1,169,508 |
| NW | 4,393,044 | 9,899,647 | 8,840,031 |
| WC | (269,692) | 2,486,947 | 1,335,871 |
| Emp. | 119 | 108 | 115 |

DUNS 39-028-3554 Imp-Exp

## Signet Armorlite Europe Ltd

**(Subsidiary of:** Essilor International)
Apollo, 1-6 Olympus Park, Gloucester, Gloucestershire GL2 4NF
**Tel:** 01452-720201 **Fax:** 01452-720004
**Web:** www.saeurope.co.uk
**Reg No:** 2108102 **VAT No:** 477776479
**Estd:** 1987 Private Limited Company
**Line of Business:** Wholesalers of optical goods
**Export Markets:** Worldwide
**Export Sales:** £4,579,132
**Issued Capital:** £1,000
**Directors:** J M Smith, P J Smith
**Co. Secretary:** Christopher Stewart
**Responsibilities**
**Senior:** Carlo Colombo *(Manager)*, Francois Glon *(Vice President)*, Mervyn McCrea *(Manager)*, Alessandro Pederzini *(Manager)*, Bruno Salvadori *(President)*
**HR:** Alison Daniels *(Human Resources Manager)*
**US SIC:** 3861, 5199
**UK SIC:** 37330, 61900
**Auditors:** Ernst & Young
**Bankers:** Lloyds TSB Bank plc (30-91-87)

| | 31-12-13 | 31-12-12 | 31-12-11 |
|---|---|---|---|
| TO | 13,757,311 | 12,886,577 | 12,188,982 |
| P/L | (1,380,926) | (1,295,178) | (160,561) |
| NW | 3,256,726 | 4,599,049 | 5,896,605 |
| WC | (1,599,675) | (734,890) | (909,757) |
| Emp. | 109 | 125 | 143 |

DUNS 23-775-6866 Imp

## Signet Trading Ltd

**(Subsidiary of:** Signet Jewelers Limited)
Hunters Road, Birmingham, West Midlands B19 1DS
**Tel:** 01216-977-400 **Fax:** 01216977913
**Web:** www.signetjewelers.com
**Reg No:** 3768979 **VAT No:** 233000924
**Estd:** 1999 Private Limited Company
**Line of Business:** Retail sale of jewellery, clocks and watches
**Trading Style:** H Samuels / H Jewellers, Ernest Jones, Leslie Davies, Signet Corporate Services
**Issued Capital:** £162,067,896
**Director:** S D Carney
**Co. Secretary:** Mark Jenkins
**Responsibilities**
**Senior:** Minna Goodman *(Manager)*, Jason Leith *(Head of Logistics)*
**Sales:** Julien Shirley *(?Director of Multichannel)*
**IT:** Alistair Fuller *(IT Director)*, Neal Griffiths *(?Head of IT Service Delivery)*
**HR:** Mike Povall *(Human Resources Director)*
**Health & Safety:** Paul Culwick *(Health & Safety Officer)*
**Fleet:** Jason Leith *(Head of Logistics)*
**Branches:** Signet Trading Limited, Management Centre, Unit 33A, London SE13 7EP
**US SIC:** 7399, 3911
**UK SIC:** 83954, 49101
**Auditors:** KPMG Audit PLC
**Bankers:** Barclays Bank Plc (20-67-59)

| | 01-02-14 | 02-02-13 | 28-02-12 |
|---|---|---|---|
| TO | 433,435,000 | 446,216,000 | 446,921,000 |
| P/L | 19,694,000 | 19,225,000 | 34,690,000 |
| NW | 239,348,000 | 228,277,000 | 234,684,000 |
| WC | 180,992,000 | 166,630,000 | 167,141,000 |
| Emp. | 3,104 | 3,156 | 3,293 |

DUNS 22-092-1543

## Signfab (U K) Ltd

Byford Road, Leicester, Leicestershire LE4 0DG
**Tel:** 01162-610104 **Fax:** 01162-612715
**Reg No:** 4093486 **Estd:** 2009 Private Limited Company
**Line of Business:** Manufacture of other office and shop furniture
**Issued Capital:** £10,000
**Directors:** P J Bartholomew, C Hodgson
**Co. Secretary:** Ms Karen Hodgson
**Responsibilities**
**HR:** Darren Lee *(Works Manager)*
**Facilities:** Darren Lee *(Works Manager)*
**Purchasing:** Tai Gokce *(Purchasing Manager)*
**US SIC:** 3499 **UK SIC:** 31694
**Auditors:** Kemp Taylor & Partners
**Bankers:** National Westminster Bank Plc (54-21-50)

| | 31-12-13 | 31-12-12 | 31-12-11 |
|---|---|---|---|
| TA | 2,303,221 | 1,342,774 | 1,993,443 |
| NW | 539,812 | 260,515 | 128,166 |
| WC | (16,920) | 378,019 | 120,094 |

DUNS 76-855-0477

## Signhealth

5 Baring Road, Beaconsfield, Buckinghamshire HP9 2NB
**Tel:** 01494687600
**Web:** www.signhealth.org.uk
**Reg No:** 2610559 **Estd:** 1986 Private Company Limited By Guarantee
**Line of Business:** Other human health activities
**Trading Style:** The Anastasia Society, Sign
**Directors:** Dr F Iqbal, Ms A M Ryan, Dr M S Gahir, R Dunford, Ms S M Bean, J Kudlick, P P Gerrard, B S Kambo
**Co. Secretary:** Stephen Powell
**Responsibilities**
**Senior:** Tyron Woolfe *(Trustee)*, Monica Wyatt *(Director)*
**Branches:** Signhealth, 100 Bowfell Rd, Manchester M41 5RR
**US SIC:** 8091, 8321
**UK SIC:** 95200, 96111
**Auditors:** H.W. Fisher & Co
**Bankers:** Barclays Bank Plc (20-02-06)

| | 31-03-14 | 31-03-13 | 31-03-12 |
|---|---|---|---|
| TO | 4,873,382 | 4,517,208 | 4,354,261 |
| P/L | (267,804) | (192,298) | 172,523 |
| NW | 3,664,775 | 3,450,684 | 3,176,045 |
| WC | 292,098 | 584,144 | 779,080 |
| Emp. | 114 | 129 | 144 |

DUNS 23-250-2534 Imp-Exp

## Signwaves Ltd

Lefevre Way, Great Yarmouth, Norfolk NR31 0NW
**Tel:** 01493419300
**Web:** www.signwaves.co.uk
**Reg No:** 2331929 **VAT No:** 521118983
**Estd:** 1989 Private Limited Company
**Line of Business:** Sign and nameplate suppliers
**Export Markets:** E U
**Export Sales:** £555,486
**Issued Capital:** £600
**Principals:** A Ford *(Chairman)*, M H Ford *(Managing)*, Mrs L C Ford, R G Brown, D N John
**Responsibilities**
**Senior:** Steven Gilbert *(Manager)*, Allan Kemp *(Manager)*
**Sales:** Cheryl Meades *(Sales Manager)*
**US SIC:** 3079 **UK SIC:** 48360
**Auditors:** Grant Thornton
**Bankers:** Lloyds TSB Bank plc (30-95-24)

| | 31-03-14 | 31-03-13 | 31-03-12 |
|---|---|---|---|
| TO | 9,258,093 | 8,651,169 | 8,662,270 |
| P/L | 674,359 | 731,460 | 802,065 |
| NW | 4,440,644 | 4,051,225 | 3,701,487 |
| WC | 2,589,561 | 2,226,469 | 2,089,163 |
| Emp. | 92 | 92 | 94 |

DUNS 22-556-5522

## Signway Supplies (Datchet) Ltd

**(Subsidiary of:** Signway (Holdings) Ltd)
Signway House, Stroudley Road, Basingstoke, Hampshire RG24 8UG
**Tel:** 01256-811-234 **Fax:** 01256-811-299
**Web:** www.signway.co.uk
**Reg No:** 1450039 **Estd:** 1979 Private Limited Company
**Line of Business:** Manufacture of other office and shop furniture
**Trading Style:** Signway Supplies
**Issued Capital:** £98
**Principals:** B J Brett *(Managing)*, C L Williams
**Co. Secretary:** Mrs Tracy Brett
**Responsibilities**
**IT:** Nick Lawes *(Head of IT)*
**US SIC:** 2599, 3499
**UK SIC:** 46720, 31694
**Bankers:** Barclays Bank Plc (20-31-06)

| | 30-09-14 | 30-09-13 | 30-09-12 |
|---|---|---|---|
| TA | 1,875,671 | 1,445,089 | 1,697,597 |
| NW | 716,553 | 603,685 | 861,527 |
| WC | 558,722 | 452,094 | 703,339 |

DUNS 21-000-4651 Imp-Exp

## Sika Ltd

**(Subsidiary of:** Schenker-Winkler Holding Ag)
Watchmead, Welwyn Garden City, Hertfordshire AL7 1BQ
**Tel:** 01707-394444
**Web:** www.sika.co.uk
**Reg No:** 0226822 **VAT No:** 197018347
**Estd:** 1927 Private Limited Company
**Line of Business:** Builders
**Export Markets:** Europe
**Export Sales:** £11,001,000
**Trading Style:** S I K A Intertol
**Issued Capital:** £3,000,000
**Directors:** Sika Ag, D E Lang, P Schuler
**Co. Secretary:** Beach Secretaries Limited
**Responsibilities**
**Senior:** Alexander Bleibler *(Manager)*, Hubert Brichambaut *(Manager)*, Christoph Ganz *(Manager)*, Sarah Grostate *(General Manager)*, Ronald Traechsel *(Manager)*
**Branches:** Sika Ltd, Bankside, 300 Peachman Way, Broadland Business Par, Norwich, Norfolk NR7 0WF
**US SIC:** 1522, 2869
**UK SIC:** 50100, 25120
**Auditors:** Ernst & Young
**Bankers:** HSBC Bank plc (40-46-08)

| | 31-12-13 | 31-12-12 | 31-12-11 |
|---|---|---|---|
| TO | 119,584,000 | 114,031,000 | 87,524,000 |
| P/L | 5,945,000 | 8,373,000 | 2,699,000 |
| NW | 13,944,000 | 9,159,000 | 4,140,000 |
| WC | 12,242,000 | 10,899,000 | 8,014,000 |
| Emp. | 376 | 352 | 237 |

DUNS 51-997-7636

## Silampos U K Ltd

**(Subsidiary of:** Silampos - Sociedade Industrial De Louça Metálica)
St Brendans Trading Estate, Avonmouth Way West, Bristol, Avon BS11 9EH
**Tel:** 01179400000 **Fax:** 01179-401100
**Reg No:** 4102311 **Estd:** 2000 Private Limited Company
**Line of Business:** Management activities of holding companies
**Export Sales:** £1,834,419
**Trading Style:** Horwood Homewares
**Issued Capital:** £84,025

**Directors:** Ms M J Campos Araujo, N Rosati, A Campos, Sociedade Industrial De Louca Me, J A Horwood
**Co. Secretary:** Nigel Hardman
**US SIC:** 6711 **UK SIC:** 83962
**Auditors:** Nexia Smith & Williamson
**Bankers:** Bank Of Scotland (12-05-77)

| | 31-12-13 | 31-12-12 | 31-12-11 |
|---|---|---|---|
| TO | 18,791,241 | 18,475,816 | 17,777,346 |
| P/L | 2,892,907 | 2,797,551 | 2,559,266 |
| NW | 9,353,953 | 7,629,098 | 6,005,164 |
| WC | 8,134,194 | 6,942,941 | 6,125,646 |
| Emp. | 51 | 50 | 48 |

DUNS 21-580-5987 **Imp-Exp**

## Silberline Ltd

(**Subsidiary of:** Silberline Manufacturing Co. Inc.)
Banbeath Road, Leven, Fife KY8 5HD
**Tel:** 01333-424734
**Web:** www.silverline.com
**Reg No:** 0055281SC **Estd:** 1974 Private Limited Company
**Line of Business:** Manufacture of paints, varnishes and similar coatings
**Export Markets:** Europe; S Africa; U S A
**Export Sales:** £22,266,530
**Issued Capital:** £100,500
**Director:** Ms L J Scheller
**Co. Secretary:** Brodies Secretarial Services Lim
**Responsibilities**
**Senior:** Peter Pearley *(Plant Manager)*
**Finance:** Stewart Blair *(Financial Director)*
**HR:** Karen Woodward *(Human Resources Manager)*
**US SIC:** 2851 **UK SIC:** 25510
**Auditors:** PricewaterhouseCoopers
**Bankers:** The Royal Bank Of Scotland Plc (83-24-24)

| | 31-12-13 | 31-12-12 | 31-12-11 |
|---|---|---|---|
| TO | 23,997,031 | 25,023,016 | 26,296,257 |
| P/L | 2,404,365 | 3,494,304 | 1,425,557 |
| NW | 16,040,174 | 15,538,448 | 18,657,506 |
| WC | 7,786,392 | 7,678,539 | 10,054,674 |
| Emp. | 133 | 130 | 155 |

DUNS 34-944-7859

## Silcock Dawson & Partners Ltd

4-5 Tower Court, Princes Risborough, Buckinghamshire HP27 0AJ
**Tel:** 01844271500 **Fax:** 01844345539
**Web:** www.silcockdawson.co.uk
**Reg No:** 5740863 **Estd:** 2006 Private Limited Company
**Line of Business:** Other engineering activities
**Issued Capital:** £100
**Directors:** P Ross, P G Lindsay, N A Purdy, C J Smart
**Co. Secretary:** John Silcock
**Responsibilities**
**Senior:** Edwin Dawson *(Manager)*
**Finance:** Allison Blue *(Finance Manager)*
**Admin:** Jackie Smart *(Fleet Administrator)*
**Fleet:** Jackie Smart *(Fleet Administrator)*
**US SIC:** 8911 **UK SIC:** 83701
**Bankers:** National Westminster Bank Plc (60-04-53)

| | 31-03-14 | 31-03-13 | 31-03-12 |
|---|---|---|---|
| TA | 1,301,143 | 950,894 | 1,108,188 |
| NW | 678,070 | 435,245 | 388,115 |
| WC | 633,117 | 435,244 | 388,114 |

DUNS 29-623-0915

## Silcock Leisure Group Ltd

Pier Forecourt Promenade, Southport, Merseyside PR8 1QX
**Tel:** 01704536733
**Web:** www.silcock-leisure.co.uk
**Reg No:** 1949537 **VAT No:** 428821049
**Estd:** 1985 Private Limited Company
**Line of Business:** Other entertainment activities not elsewhere classified
**Issued Capital:** £250,000
**Principals:** H E Silcock *(Managing)*, Mrs J Silcock, Ms P A Silcock-Callaghan, H A Silcock
**Co. Secretary:** Mark Silcock
**Responsibilities**
**Admin:** Margaret Hodkinson *(Administration Manager)*
**Branches:** Silcock Leisure Group Ltd, 16 Coronation Walk, Southport, Merseyside PR8 1RE
**US SIC:** 7999 **UK SIC:** 97913
**Auditors:** Baker Tilly
**Bankers:** The Royal Bank Of Scotland Plc (16-32-10)

| | 28-02-14 | 28-02-13 | 29-02-12 |
|---|---|---|---|
| TO | N/A | 3,008,313 | 3,282,867 |
| P/L | N/A | 72,129 | 159,184 |
| NW | 3,105,776 | 2,975,576 | 2,921,156 |
| WC | 482,068 | 503,693 | 838,228 |
| Emp. | N/A | 72 | 74 |

DUNS 21-210-3469 **Exp**

## Silcoms Ltd

(**Subsidiary of:** Bolton Engineering (Holdings) Ltd)
Victoria Mill, Piggott Street, Bolton, Lancashire BL4 9QN
**Web:** www.silcoms.co.uk
**Reg No:** 0350911 **Estd:** 1939 Private Limited Company
**Line of Business:** Manufacture of aircraft and spacecraft
**Export Markets:** Greece, Portugal, U S A, Netherlands
**Export Sales:** £8,011,445
**Issued Capital:** £546,729
**Principals:** K H Hindle *(Chairman and Managing)*, K A Harrison, J England, A C Winby, J Hill, D J Hamilton
**Co. Secretary:** John Cottam
**Responsibilities**
**Senior:** John Hynes *(Warehouse Manager)*
**Facilities:** John Hynes *(Warehouse Manager)*
**US SIC:** 3721 **UK SIC:** 36400
**Auditors:** Livesey Spottiswood
**Bankers:** The Royal Bank Of Scotland Plc (16-00-01)

| | 31-03-14 | 31-03-13 | 31-03-12 |
|---|---|---|---|
| TO | 21,688,531 | 18,247,910 | 16,723,950 |
| P/L | 215,380 | 356,637 | 552,321 |
| NW | 4,178,597 | 3,534,318 | 3,393,525 |
| WC | 2,812,350 | 2,686,241 | 2,709,412 |
| Emp. | 166 | 149 | 130 |

DUNS 21-675-6478

## Silcox Motor Coach Co Ltd

(**Subsidiary of:** Travel Centre (Midlands) Ltd)
Waterloo Garage, Waterloo, Pembroke Dock, Dyfed SA72 4RR
**Web:** www.silcoxcoaches.co.uk
**Reg No:** 0678372 **VAT No:** 122491493
**Estd:** 1882 Private Limited Company
**Line of Business:** Bus operators and stations
**Issued Capital:** £10,000
**Principals:** K W Silcox *(Managing)*, J I Silcox, Mrs M E Silcox, M R Ready, Bakerbus Ltd, Bakers Bus & Coach Ltd
**Responsibilities**
**Senior:** Doreen Miller *(Manager)*, Rosalind Silcox *(Manager)*
**Branches:** Silcox Motor Coach Co Ltd, Town Wall Arcade, Tenby, Dyfed SA70 7JE
**US SIC:** 4119 **UK SIC:** 72200
**Auditors:** Evens & Co Ltd
**Bankers:** HSBC Bank plc (40-36-24)

| | 31-08-13 | 31-08-12 | 31-08-11 |
|---|---|---|---|
| TO | N/A | N/A | 4,762,377 |
| P/L | N/A | N/A | 64,005 |
| NW | 647,045 | 767,713 | 701,813 |
| WC | (542,986) | (695,467) | (769,122) |
| Emp. | N/A | N/A | 106 |

DUNS 21-621-4064 **Imp-Exp**

## Silent Gliss Ltd

(**Subsidiary of:** Silent Gliss Holding Ag)
Poorhole Lane, Broadstairs, Kent CT10 2PT
**Tel:** 01843863571
**Web:** www.silentgliss.co.uk
**Reg No:** 0532505 **VAT No:** 201714416
**Estd:** 1954 Private Limited Company
**Line of Business:** Manufacturers of roller blind and component
**Export Markets:** Middle East, S & S E Asia
**Issued Capital:** £855,000
**Directors:** B A Bratschi, H Gage
**Co. Secretary:** Bernard Pope
**Responsibilities**
**Senior:** Sara Möckli *(Director)*
**Marketing:** Samantha Shervill *(Marketing Manager)*
**Sales:** Peter Broennimann *(Sales Director)*
**Health & Safety:** Mike McGarry *(Quality Manager)*
**Facilities:** Mike McGarry *(Quality Manager)*
**Operations:** Mike McGarry *(Quality Manager)*, Kevin Stocker *(Production Manager)*
**Engineering:** Kevin Stocker *(Production Manager)*
**Branches:** Silent Gliss Ltd, Unit 325 Business Design Centre, 52 Upper Street, London N1 0QH
**US SIC:** 2392, 8999
**UK SIC:** 45550, 83954
**Auditors:** Spain Brothers & Co
**Bankers:** National Westminster Bank Plc (52-10-19)

| | 31-12-13 | 31-12-12 | 31-12-11 |
|---|---|---|---|
| TO | 16,376,813 | 16,366,868 | 16,489,861 |
| P/L | 1,942,771 | 2,450,595 | 2,159,645 |
| NW | 6,542,048 | 6,758,736 | 6,587,930 |
| WC | 2,460,304 | 2,549,690 | 2,253,009 |
| Emp. | 97 | 91 | 94 |

DUNS 21-712-7822 **Imp**

## Silentnight Group Ltd

(**Subsidiary of:** H.I.G. Europe - Silentnight Sarl)
Long Ing Business Park, Long Ing Lane, Barnoldswick, Lancashire BB18 6BJ
**Tel:** 01282813051
**Web:** www.silentnightgroup.co.uk
**Reg No:** 7525259 **Estd:** 2011 Private Limited Company
**Line of Business:** Manufacture of other kitchen furniture
**Trading Style:** Sealy Uk
**Directors:** S Freeman, N McIlroy, M Kelly, L Laurant, A J Fawcett, R J Logan, P S Mckoen
**Responsibilities**
**Senior:** Anthony Melvin *(Head of Web Development)*
**Branches:** Silentnight Group Ltd, Station Road, Wigton, Cumbria CA7 2AS
**US SIC:** 2599, 5021, 2392
**UK SIC:** 46720, 61500, 45550
**Auditors:** Deloitte LLP
**Bankers:** Barclays Bank Plc (20-30-47)

| | 01-02-14 | 02-02-13 | 28-02-12 |
|---|---|---|---|
| TO | 109,278,000 | 98,885,000 | 72,651,000 |
| P/L | (3,163,000) | (4,479,000) | (7,196,000) |
| NW | (22,651,000) | (19,630,000) | (16,893,000) |
| WC | 11,201,000 | 8,869,000 | 5,051,000 |
| Emp. | 945 | 954 | 1,115 |

DUNS 29-625-5284 **Imp**

## Silex Ltd

Unit 4-5, Bordon, Hampshire GU35 0JX
**Tel:** 01420478820
**Web:** www.silex.fsnet.co.uk
**Reg No:** 1951973 **VAT No:** 432349855
**Estd:** 1986 Private Limited Company
**Line of Business:** Manufacturers of silicones
**Issued Capital:** £100
**Principals:** N J Soudah *(Managing)*, S J Fearn
**Co. Secretary:** Nicholas Soudah
**US SIC:** 2822 **UK SIC:** 25150
**Bankers:** National Westminster Bank Plc (60-18-01)

| | 31-10-13 | 31-10-12 | 31-10-11 |
|---|---|---|---|
| TA | 2,470,910 | 2,219,565 | 1,754,104 |
| NW | 1,485,807 | 1,214,720 | 872,739 |
| WC | 1,308,529 | 1,069,088 | 730,081 |

DUNS 76-937-8977 **Exp**

## Silflex Ltd

(**Subsidiary of:** Currie & Warner (Holdings) Ltd)
Coedcae Lane, Pontyclun, Mid Glamorgan CF72 9HJ
**Tel:** 01443-238464 **Fax:** 01443238464
**Web:** www.samcosport.com
**Reg No:** 2569811 **VAT No:** 541062482
**Estd:** 1990 Private Limited Company
**Line of Business:** Car accessories and parts
**Export Markets:** Australia; Finland; Hong Kong; European Union (E U)
**Export Sales:** £2,747,262
**Trading Style:** Silflex
**Issued Capital:** £10,000
**Principals:** M I Lloyd *(Managing)*, A W Lloyd, Mrs M E Lloyd
**Co. Secretary:** Matthew Lloyd
**US SIC:** 5531 **UK SIC:** 65100
**Auditors:** Clay Shaw Thomas Ltd
**Bankers:** Lloyds TSB Bank plc (30-00-03)

| | 31-12-13 | 31-12-12 | 31-12-11 |
|---|---|---|---|
| TO | 4,740,644 | 4,475,780 | 4,644,904 |
| P/L | 369,659 | 110,945 | 193,451 |
| NW | 2,123,447 | 2,090,965 | 2,106,517 |
| WC | 2,002,449 | 1,931,824 | 1,923,005 |
| Emp. | 103 | 125 | 135 |

DUNS 29-675-9731 **Imp**

## Silicon Graphics Ltd

(**Subsidiary of:** Silicon Graphics International Corp.)
540 Thames Valley Park Drive, Reading, Berkshire RG6 1PT
**Tel:** 08702432243 **Fax:** 01189-127505
**Web:** www.sgi.com
**Reg No:** 2002315 **VAT No:** 363359244
**Estd:** 1986 Private Limited Company
**Line of Business:** Manufacture of computers and other information processing equipment
**Trading Style:** S G I
**Issued Capital:** £8,578,021
**Directors:** R C Evans, J Abrahamsen
**Co. Secretary:** William Mitchell
**Responsibilities**
**Senior:** Timothy Pebworth *(Manager)*, Dirk Winkhaus *(Finance Director)*
**Finance:** Dirk Winkhaus *(Finance Director)*
**Branches:** Silicon Graphics Ltd, 20 Soho Sq, London W1D 3QW
**US SIC:** 3573 **UK SIC:** 33020
**Auditors:** KPMG LLP

**Bankers:** Barclays Bank Plc (20-71-03)

| | 28-06-13 | 29-06-12 | 24-06-11 |
|---|---|---|---|
| TO | 35,390,507 | 45,959,861 | 26,027,403 |
| P/L | 706,723 | 881,116 | 480,519 |
| NW | 4,409,582 | 3,853,607 | 3,237,198 |
| WC | 4,255,004 | 3,609,415 | 2,932,366 |
| Emp. | 60 | 65 | 69 |

DUNS 22-652-3397 **Imp-Exp**

## Silicone Altimex Ltd

(**Subsidiary of:** Forestcraft Ltd)
49 Pasture Road, Stapleford, Nottingham, Nottinghamshire NG9 8HR
**Fax:** 01159496890
**Web:** www.silalt.co.uk
**Reg No:** 1449832 **VAT No:** 118498639
**Estd:** 1979 Private Limited Company
**Line of Business:** Representative office
**Export Markets:** Worldwide
**Issued Capital:** £50,000
**Principals:** F W Brown *(Chairman)*, G C Ridgway *(Technical)*, C Barker
**Co. Secretary:** James Whitworth
**Responsibilities**
**IT:** Ian Minter *(IT Coordinator)*
**Health & Safety:** Andrew Pilkington *(Health & Safety Officer)*
**Facilities:** Mick Lawson *(Chief Engineer)*
**Engineering:** Mick Lawson *(Chief Engineer)*
**US SIC:** 3069 **UK SIC:** 48123
**Auditors:** Kidsons Impey
**Bankers:** National Westminster Bank Plc (56-00-61)

| | 30-09-13 | 30-09-12 | 30-09-11 |
|---|---|---|---|
| TA | 2,259,055 | 2,462,185 | 2,540,097 |
| NW | 1,570,345 | 1,806,371 | 2,064,074 |
| WC | 1,255,191 | 1,485,120 | 1,717,094 |

DUNS 42-353-3442 **Exp**

## Silicone Engineering Ltd

(**Subsidiary of:** Silicone Holdings Ltd)
Blakewater Road, Blackburn, Lancashire BB1 3HU
**Tel:** 01254-261321 **Fax:** 01254-583519
**Web:** www.silicone.co.uk
**Reg No:** 4340974 **VAT No:** 860210956
**Estd:** 2001 Private Limited Company
**Line of Business:** Manufacture of synthetic rubber in primary forms
**Export Sales:** £8,995,442
**Issued Capital:** £40,000
**Directors:** P R Kinsella, S Hadlington, A E Peel, M Patel, D P Beadman
**Responsibilities**
**Senior:** Ivor Boland *(Engineering Manager)*
**Marketing:** Melanie Bernardeau *(Sales & Marketing Director)*
**Sales:** Melanie Bernardeau *(Sales & Marketing Director)*
**HR:** Joyce Mehta *(Human Resources Manager)*
**Health & Safety:** Joyce Mehta *(Human Resources Manager)*
**Facilities:** Ivor Boland *(Engineering Manager)*
**Operations:** Melanie Bernardeau *(Sales & Marketing Director)*
**Purchasing:** Noor Moosa *(Buyer)*
**Engineering:** Ivor Boland *(Engineering Manager)*
**US SIC:** 2822, 3357
**UK SIC:** 25150, 22470
**Auditors:** RSM Tenon Audit Ltd

| | 31-12-13 | 31-12-12 | 31-12-11 |
|---|---|---|---|
| TO | 15,660,672 | 12,964,417 | 12,660,782 |
| P/L | 2,274,803 | 651,479 | 866,977 |
| NW | 2,255,621 | 1,267,223 | 1,074,734 |
| WC | 985,735 | 194,459 | 165,543 |
| Emp. | 129 | 122 | 118 |

DUNS 73-393-9990 **Imp**

## Silk Industries Ltd

Weavers Lane, Sudbury, Suffolk CO10 1BB
**Tel:** 01787-372-396
**Web:** www.vanners.com
**Reg No:** 4667190 **Estd:** 1894 Private Limited Company
**Line of Business:** Textile weaving
**Issued Capital:** £2,150,000
**Directors:** D T Brace, I R Stevenson, M J Hubert, D E Tooth, S A Nixon, M W Beck
**Co. Secretary:** Ian Stevenson
**Responsibilities**
**Senior:** Doreen Clarke *(Manager)*
**Admin:** Doreen Clarke *(Manager)*
**US SIC:** 2269 **UK SIC:** 43702
**Auditors:** Ballams

| | 30-04-14 | 30-04-13 | 30-04-12 |
|---|---|---|---|
| TO | 9,892,616 | 9,942,858 | 10,013,084 |
| P/L | 729,308 | 747,402 | 355,403 |
| NW | 1,648,045 | 901,800 | 707,100 |
| WC | 2,656,518 | 2,128,776 | 1,701,564 |
| Emp. | 157 | 155 | 158 |

DUNS 21-610-0453
## Silk Ltd
(**Subsidiary of:** Silk Industries Ltd)
Cable House, Station Road, Sheffield, South Yorkshire S20 3GT
**Tel:** 07806610319
**Web:** www.silkisoles.com
**Reg No:** 0040772 **Estd:** 2012 Private Limited Company
**Line of Business:** Beauty salons
**Issued Capital:** £787,500
**Directors:** D E Tooth, I R Stevenson
**Responsibilities**
**Senior:** Paula Stainer *(Manager)*
**Branches:** Silk Ltd, Weavers Lane, Sudbury, Suffolk CO10 1BB
**US SIC:** 7231 **UK SIC:** 98200

| | 30-04-14 | 30-04-13 | 30-04-12 |
|---|---|---|---|
| TA | 973,000 | 973,000 | 973,000 |
| NW | 787,000 | 787,000 | 787,000 |
| WC | 601,000 | 601,000 | 601,000 |

DUNS 29-755-3083
## Silklink Ltd
Gilson Road, Coleshill, Birmingham, West Midlands B46 1LJ
**Tel:** 01675-462121
**Web:** www.grimstockhotel.co.uk
**Reg No:** 2018490 **VAT No:** 418818823
**Estd:** 1986 Private Limited Company
**Line of Business:** Hotels and motels without restaurant
**Trading Style:** Grimstock Country House Hotel
**Issued Capital:** £29,629
**Principals:** M Vakil *(Managing)*, Ms J M Vakil
**Co. Secretary:** Morteza Vakil
**Responsibilities**
**Senior:** Hiliary Prince *(Marketing Director)*
**Marketing:** Hiliary Prince *(Marketing Director)*
**US SIC:** 7011 **UK SIC:** 66500
**Auditors:** Wenham Major

| | 30-06-14 | 30-06-13 | 30-06-12 |
|---|---|---|---|
| TA | 1,808,324 | 1,906,288 | 1,952,293 |
| NW | 629,125 | 524,665 | 519,655 |
| WC | (343,028) | (289,675) | (162,962) |

DUNS 21-924-9968
## Sillavan Anodes Ltd
(**Subsidiary of:** The Alumasc Group Plc)
Walsall Road, Cannock, Staffordshire WS11 9NR
**Tel:** 01543-276666 **Fax:** 01543-276418
**Web:** www.brock-metal.co.uk
**Reg No:** 1234602 **Estd:** 1975 Private Limited Company
**Line of Business:** Wholesale of metals and ores
**Issued Capital:** £100
**Director:** J D Douglas
**Co. Secretary:** Doranda Limited
**US SIC:** 7399 **UK SIC:** 83954

| | 30-06-13 | 30-06-12 | 30-06-11 |
|---|---|---|---|
| TA | 81,000 | 81,000 | 81,000 |
| NW | 81,000 | 81,000 | 81,000 |

DUNS 21-245-9757
## Silloth Nursing Home
Silloth, Wigton, Cumbria CA7 4JH
**Web:** www.sillothnursinghome.co.uk
**Estd:** 2002 Proprietorship
**Line of Business:** Medical nursing home activities
**Responsibilities**
**Senior:** Ann Blair *(Matron)*
**US SIC:** 8051 **UK SIC:** 95100
**Employees:** 60

DUNS 21-389-7008
## Sills & Betteridge
1 Ashby Road, Spilsby, Lincolnshire PE23 5DT
**Tel:** 01790752277
**Web:** www.sillslegal.co.uk
**Proprietorship**
**Line of Business:** Solicitors
**Proprietor:** J Mitchell
**US SIC:** 8111 **UK SIC:** 83500
**Employees:** 101

DUNS 42-363-2996 **Imp**
## Silvalea Ltd
Unit 1-4, Silverhills Buildings, Silverhills Road, Newton Abbot, Devon TQ12 5LZ
**Tel:** 01626-331655 **Fax:** 01626-335171
**Web:** www.silvalealtd.co.uk
**Reg No:** 4350939 **Estd:** 1991 Private Limited Company
**Line of Business:** Manufacturers of medical equipment
**Issued Capital:** £194
**Directors:** B Guilfoyle, Mrs P Guilfoyle
**Co. Secretary:** Gary Bevan
**Responsibilities**
**Marketing:** Teri Allerton *(Sales & Marketing Manager)*
**Sales:** Teri Allerton *(Sales & Marketing Manager)*
**US SIC:** 3841 **UK SIC:** 37201

| | 31-03-14 | 31-03-13 | 31-03-12 |
|---|---|---|---|
| TA | 2,196,278 | 2,718,385 | 2,683,708 |
| NW | 564,178 | 758,521 | 679,969 |
| WC | 349,185 | 510,139 | 625,564 |

DUNS 73-338-9022 **Imp**
## Silver Cross (Uk) Ltd
(**Subsidiary of:** Silver Cross Nurseries Ltd)
Silver Cross (Uk) Ltd, Micklethorn, Broughton, Broughton, Skipton, North Yorkshire BD23 3JA
**Tel:** 08458726900 **Fax:** 01756-702411
**Web:** www.silvercrossbaby.com
**Reg No:** 4611579 **Estd:** 1877 Private Limited Company
**Line of Business:** Manufacture of other games and toys not elsewhere classified
**Issued Capital:** £1,000
**Directors:** P J Taylor, N J Paxton, D A Halsall, R Best, J D Halsall
**Co. Secretary:** William Lockwood
**US SIC:** 3944 **UK SIC:** 49410
**Auditors:** Ernst & Young LLP
**Bankers:** National Westminster Bank Plc (01-67-14)

| | 31-12-13 | 31-12-12 | 31-12-11 |
|---|---|---|---|
| TO | 16,479,861 | 19,275,152 | 18,221,411 |
| P/L | 430,286 | 1,368,516 | 820,009 |
| NW | 4,796,768 | 4,460,662 | 3,235,978 |
| WC | 4,140,874 | 3,901,654 | 2,919,108 |
| Emp. | 50 | 52 | 47 |

DUNS 64-080-1494
## Silver Healthcare Ltd
The Coach House, 379b Fulwood Road, Sheffield, South Yorkshire S10 3GA
**Tel:** 01142-309988 **Fax:** 01122295640
**Web:** www.silver-healthcare.co.uk
**Reg No:** 3475391 **Estd:** 1997 Private Limited Company
**Line of Business:** Representative office
**Issued Capital:** £100
**Director:** R Young
**Branches:** Silver Healthcare Ltd, 48 Lyons Road, Sheffield, South Yorkshire S4 7EL
**US SIC:** 7399 **UK SIC:** 83954
**Bankers:** Bank Of Scotland (12-18-68)

| | 31-12-13 | 31-12-12 | 31-12-11 |
|---|---|---|---|
| TA | 4,413,682 | 4,411,664 | 4,437,268 |
| NW | 1,567,082 | 1,613,455 | 1,517,775 |
| WC | (591,152) | (813,752) | (771,544) |

DUNS 73-821-9307
## Silver Levene & Associates Ltd
(**Subsidiary of:** Warren Street Registrars Ltd)
37 Warren Street, London W1T 6AD
**Tel:** 020-7383-3200 **Fax:** 020-7383-4165
**Web:** www.silverlevene.co.uk
**Reg No:** 5077870 **Estd:** 2004 Private Limited Company
**Line of Business:** Other business activities not elsewhere classified
**Issued Capital:** £1
**Directors:** M Franks, D Ezekiel
**Co. Secretary:** Mark Gold
**US SIC:** 7399 **UK SIC:** 83954

| | 31-03-14 | 31-03-13 | 31-03-12 |
|---|---|---|---|
| TA | 44,612 | 84,228 | 126,686 |
| NW | 38 | (24,441) | (43,169) |
| WC | 38 | (24,441) | (5,293) |

DUNS 23-818-0376
## Silverbeck Rymer
Dempster Building, Atlantic Way, Brunswick Business Park, Liverpool, Merseyside L3 4UU
**Tel:** 01519060665
**Web:** www.silverbeck-rymer.co.uk
**Estd:** 1946 Partnership
**Line of Business:** Solicitors
**Trading Style:** Silverbeck Rymer
**Partners:** Ms P Ewan, J Rymer, C Rymer, Ms A Beech
**Responsibilities**
**Senior:** Joyce Duncan-Carroll *(Facilities Manager)*, Barbara Rimmer *(Financial Director)*
**Finance:** Barbara Rimmer *(Financial Director)*
**Marketing:** Joyce Duncan-Carroll *(Facilities Manager)*
**IT:** Christian Frickel *(IT Director)*
**HR:** Pam Buckley *(Training Manager)*, Alison Pearse *(Personnel Manager)*
**Health & Safety:** Joyce Duncan-Carroll *(Facilities Manager)*
**Facilities:** Joyce Duncan-Carroll *(Facilities Manager)*
**Operations:** Christian Frickel *(IT Director)*
**Purchasing:** Joyce Duncan-Carroll *(Facilities Manager)*
**Branches:** Silverbeck Rymer, Thornwood House, 102 New London Road, Chelmsford, Essex CM2 0RG
**US SIC:** 8111 **UK SIC:** 83500
**Employees:** 300

DUNS 21-034-7996
## Silverdale School
Perth Road, St Leonards-On-Sea, East Sussex TN37 7EA
**Tel:** 01424-448100
**Web:** www.silverdale.e-sussex.sch.uk
**Estd:** 1997 Proprietorship
**Line of Business:** Primary education
**Proprietor:** Mrs G Knox
**US SIC:** 8211 **UK SIC:** 93200
**Employees:** 110

DUNS 22-664-3625
## Silverdale Tours (Nottingham) Ltd
Little Tennis St South, Nottingham, Nottinghamshire NG2 4EU
**Tel:** 01159121000
**Web:** www.silverdaletours.co.uk
**Reg No:** 1325476 **VAT No:** 309254368
**Estd:** 1970 Private Limited Company
**Line of Business:** Coach and bus hire
**Issued Capital:** £341,000
**Principals:** J J Doherty *(Managing)*, S A Doherty, Mrs A M Doherty
**Co. Secretary:** Mrs Carol O'Neill
**Responsibilities**
**HR:** Coralie Matthews *(Personnel Manager)*
**Branches:** Silverdale Tours (Nottingham) Ltd, Little Tennis Street South, Nottingham, Nottinghamshire NG2 4EU
**US SIC:** 4119 **UK SIC:** 72200
**Auditors:** Cooper Parry
**Bankers:** HSBC Bank plc (40-35-19)

| | 30-09-13 | 30-09-12 | 30-09-11 |
|---|---|---|---|
| TO | 6,812,370 | 6,111,901 | 5,616,123 |
| P/L | 1,278,960 | 795,853 | 218,942 |
| NW | 8,189,757 | 7,321,736 | 6,264,992 |
| WC | 2,698,470 | 2,719,236 | 2,660,848 |
| Emp. | 90 | 97 | 99 |

DUNS 23-961-9799
## Silverdoor Ltd
(**Subsidiary of:** Eleven Heaven Holdings Ltd)
3-5 Acton Lane Dukes Gate, London W4 5DX
**Tel:** 020-8630-7200 **Fax:** 020-8630-7300
**Web:** www.silverdoor.co.uk
**Reg No:** 3950962 **Estd:** 2013 Private Limited Company
**Line of Business:** Letting agents
**Export Sales:** £414,575
**Issued Capital:** £100
**Directors:** C Gee, S Winstone
**Co. Secretary:** Marcus Angell
**Responsibilities**
**Marketing:** Louis Cooper *(Marketing Executive)*, Sacha Griffiths *(Online Strategy Manager)*, Charlotte Healey *(SEO and Web Support)*
**IT:** Charlotte Healey *(SEO and Web Support)*
**HR:** Daniel Mahony *(Head of HR)*
**US SIC:** 7021, 7999
**UK SIC:** 66500, 97913

| | 31-10-13 | 31-10-12 | 31-10-11 |
|---|---|---|---|
| TO | 3,578,633 | N/A | N/A |
| P/L | 253,191 | N/A | N/A |
| NW | 16,187 | (92,951) | 84,881 |
| WC | (708,756) | (436,595) | (194,752) |
| Emp. | 73 | N/A | N/A |

DUNS 73-740-8468 **Imp**
## Silverfield Ltd
(**Subsidiary of:** Silverfield Holdings Ltd)
Aldon Road, Poulton Industrial Estate, Poulton-Le-Fylde, Lancashire FY6 8JL
**Tel:** 01253-891733 **Fax:** 01253-894404
**Web:** www.silverfield.co.uk
**Reg No:** 2922036 **VAT No:** 636324446
**Estd:** 1994 Private Limited Company
**Line of Business:** Metal finishing and polishing services
**Issued Capital:** £1,000
**Directors:** I Fyfe, G F Berkley, C Scott
**Co. Secretary:** Joseph Southward
**Responsibilities**
**Senior:** Giles Barclay *(Manager)*
**Admin:** Gerry Smith *(Office Manager)*
**Operations:** Nick Chamberlain *(Process Planner)*, Clive Clark *(Assistant Q.A. / Planner)*, Ian Hull *(Production Controller)*, Simon Mangan *(Paint / QA Engineer)*
**Engineering:** Rob Friel *(Lab Technician)*, Bill Thornton *(Estimator / Planner)*
**US SIC:** 3499, 3398
**UK SIC:** 31694, 31380
**Auditors:** Moore & Smalley
**Bankers:** National Westminster Bank Plc (01-67-14)

| | 30-09-13 | 30-09-12 | 30-09-11 |
|---|---|---|---|
| TA | 1,620,367 | 1,532,939 | 1,175,307 |
| NW | 653,658 | 605,083 | 551,498 |
| WC | 326,515 | 280,952 | 221,193 |

DUNS 23-509-2004
## Silverlake Garage (Motor Salvage) Ltd
Botley Road, Shedfield, Southampton, Hampshire SO32 2HL
**Tel:** 01489-782537 **Fax:** 01489-788663
**Web:** www.silverlakeautoparts.co.uk
**Reg No:** 0624778 **Estd:** 1946 Private Limited Company
**Line of Business:** Car breakers
**Issued Capital:** £2,000
**Managing Director:** A W Prebble
**Co. Secretary:** Ms Denise Small
**US SIC:** 5093 **UK SIC:** 62200
**Auditors:** Johnston & Co

| | 31-03-14 | 31-03-13 | 31-03-12 |
|---|---|---|---|
| TO | 11,118,524 | 8,198,756 | 7,585,952 |
| P/L | 284,810 | 350,339 | 283,132 |
| NW | 3,189,428 | 3,046,745 | 2,825,061 |
| WC | (19,853) | 62,585 | (81,392) |
| Emp. | 80 | 69 | 63 |

DUNS 77-446-0331
## Silverleigh Ltd
(**Subsidiary of:** Cannon Care Homes Ltd)
Axminster Inn, Silver Street, Axminster, Devon EX13 5AH
**Tel:** 0129732011 **Fax:** 0129732559
**Web:** www.freenet.co.uk
**Reg No:** 2955109 **Estd:** 1994 Private Limited Company
**Line of Business:** Medical nursing home activities
**Issued Capital:** £1,000
**Director:** R G Cannon
**Co. Secretary:** Ms Jane Cannon
**Responsibilities**
**Senior:** Sarah Jennings *(General Manager)*
**Marketing:** Sarah Jennings *(General Manager)*
**HR:** Helen Anning *(Deputy Manager)*, Sarah Jennings *(General Manager)*
**Health & Safety:** Sarah Jennings *(General Manager)*
**Facilities:** Sarah Jennings *(General Manager)*
**Purchasing:** Sarah Jennings *(General Manager)*
**US SIC:** 8091, 8321
**UK SIC:** 95200, 96111
**Auditors:** Thomas Westcott Gillard Heal
**Bankers:** Abbey National Plc (09-00-24)

| | 31-03-14 | 31-03-13 | 31-03-12 |
|---|---|---|---|
| TO | 2,419,435 | 2,356,572 | N/A |
| P/L | 304,581 | 476,044 | N/A |
| NW | 6,974,082 | 262,350 | 66,159 |
| WC | 4,055,204 | 4,120,617 | (1,161,726) |
| Emp. | 95 | 92 | N/A |

DUNS 54-849-5233
## Silverline Cars
Great Western Hall, Sydenham Road, Birmingham, West Midlands B11 1DG
**Tel:** 01217736294
**Estd:** 1993 Partnership
**Line of Business:** Taxis
**Partners:** A Iqbal, Z Iqbal
**US SIC:** 4121 **UK SIC:** 72200
**Employees:** 50

DUNS 77-456-3738
## Silverline Landflight Ltd
Argent House, Vulcan Road, Solihull, West Midlands B91 2JY
**Tel:** 0121-705-5555 **Fax:** 0121-709-0556
**Web:** www.landflight.co.uk
**Reg No:** 2960695 **Estd:** 1994 Private Limited Company
**Line of Business:** Other scheduled passenger land transport not elsewhere classified
**Trading Style:** Silverline Travel Services
**Issued Capital:** £500,000
**Directors:** M E Breakwell, W J Matthews, P S Choudhry, R G Knott, A Ali
**Co. Secretary:** Alan Cakebread
**Responsibilities**
**Marketing:** Danny Matthews *(Business Development Director)*
**Sales:** Danny Matthews *(Business Development Director)*
**Facilities:** Roger Nolan *(Fleet Workshop Manager)*
**US SIC:** 4119, 4142
**UK SIC:** 72200, 72102
**Auditors:** Raftery & Co
**Bankers:** HSBC Bank plc (40-42-12)

| | 31-07-14 | 31-07-13 | 31-07-12 |
|---|---|---|---|
| TA | 2,161,047 | 2,291,422 | 1,496,947 |
| NW | 816,602 | 662,761 | 415,049 |
| WC | 252,996 | 211,577 | (23,461) |

DUNS 29-369-0749 Imp-Exp

## Silverline Office Equipment Ltd

(**Subsidiary of:** Cemar Ltd)
James Carter Road, Bury St Edmunds, Suffolk IP28 7DE
**Tel:** 01638-582700 **Fax:** 01638-715530
**Web:** www.silverline-oe.com
**Reg No:** 0901203 **VAT No:** 390597515
**Estd:** 1984 Private Limited Company
**Line of Business:** Manufacture of other office and shop furniture
**Trading Style:** Silverline Equipment
**Issued Capital:** £400,000
**Directors:** R P Ensinger, N Maydon, R C Ward
**Co. Secretary:** Richard Ward
**Responsibilities**
**Senior:** Stanley Ensinger *(Chairman)*, Norman Maiden *(Purchasing Director)*
**Finance:** Norman Maiden *(Purchasing Director)*
**US SIC:** 2599 **UK SIC:** 46720
**Auditors:** King & King
**Bankers:** Lloyds TSB Bank plc (30-95-58)

| | 31-12-13 | 31-12-12 | 31-12-11 |
|---|---|---|---|
| TO | 9,322,922 | 9,050,690 | 9,473,371 |
| P/L | 105,990 | (198,618) | 9,492 |
| NW | 355,092 | 249,102 | 447,720 |
| WC | 331,900 | 287,010 | 240,564 |
| Emp. | 88 | 95 | 120 |

DUNS 39-780-3289 Exp

## Silversands Ltd

Unit 3-5, Albany Park, Cabot Lane, Poole, Dorset BH17 7BX
**Tel:** 01202360000 **Fax:** 01202-360900
**Web:** www.silversands.co.uk
**Reg No:** 2141393 **VAT No:** 423871059
**Estd:** 1987 Private Limited Company
**Line of Business:** Computer systems and software (sales)
**Trading Style:** Silversands Computers
**Issued Capital:** £50,000
**Principals:** A Z Tosunlar *(Managing)*, Ms S Jones *(Financial)*, M Spalding
**Co. Secretary:** Ms Susan Jones
**Responsibilities**
**Senior:** Elaine Shilson *(Administrator)*
**Marketing:** Janet Churchill *(Marketing Manager)*
**Sales:** Annette Harrison *(Account Manager)*
**IT:** James Kavanagh *(IT Manager)*
**Facilities:** Neville Gerry *(Facilities Manager)*
**Operations:** Patrick Holburn *(Purchasing Manager)*
**Purchasing:** Patrick Holburn *(Purchasing Manager)*
**Fleet:** Patrick Holburn *(Purchasing Manager)*
**US SIC:** 7379 **UK SIC:** 83940
**Auditors:** Old Mill Accountancy LLP
**Bankers:** National Westminster Bank Plc (60-02-17)

| | 30-11-13 | 30-11-12 | 30-11-11 |
|---|---|---|---|
| TA | 2,925,517 | 3,651,968 | 3,148,271 |
| NW | 1,266,997 | 1,241,365 | 1,183,679 |
| WC | 591,068 | 388,773 | 205,813 |

DUNS 36-534-3649 Imp

## Silversea Cruises (Europe) Ltd

(**Subsidiary of:** Silversea Cruises (Italia) Spa)
77-79 Great Eastern Street, London EC2A 3HU
**Tel:** 08447709030 **Fax:** 0870-333-7040
**Web:** www.silversea.com
**Reg No:** 3290594 **Estd:** 1994 Private Limited Company
**Line of Business:** Activities of travel agencies
**Issued Capital:** £40,000
**Directors:** S Odell, V Visone, M J Bonner
**US SIC:** 4722 **UK SIC:** 77001
**Auditors:** BDO Stoy Hayward
**Bankers:** Bank Of America, Na (16-50-50)

| | 31-12-13 | 31-12-12 | 31-12-11 |
|---|---|---|---|
| TO | 44,621,934 | 41,149,995 | 41,585,037 |
| P/L | 479,416 | 325,113 | 134,374 |
| NW | 1,994,171 | 1,643,658 | 1,440,327 |
| WC | 1,769,540 | 1,384,148 | 1,116,121 |
| Emp. | 52 | 51 | 32 |

DUNS 64-083-3880

## Silverstar Foods Ltd

Spelmonden Farm, Spelmonden Road, Goudhurst, Cranbrook, Kent TN17 1HE
**Tel:** 01580-212818 **Fax:** 01580-212241
**Web:** www.silverstarfoods.com
**Reg No:** 4486796 **Estd:** 2004 Private Limited Company
**Line of Business:** Manufacture of other milk products
**Trading Style:** Turners Fine Foods
**Issued Capital:** £300,000
**Directors:** S G Raphael, R P Mercer
**Co. Secretary:** Toby Raphael
**Responsibilities**
**Senior:** Toby Raeheal *(Manager)*
**IT:** Christopher Stapleton *(IT Manager)*
**US SIC:** 2023 **UK SIC:** 41303
**Auditors:** Creaseys LLP

| | 30-04-14 | 30-04-13 | 30-04-12 |
|---|---|---|---|
| TO | 32,002,828 | 23,973,794 | 17,531,974 |
| P/L | 1,029,808 | 807,086 | 445,349 |
| NW | 92,643 | (115,047) | (299,204) |
| WC | (285,740) | (207,216) | (292,460) |
| Emp. | 238 | 160 | 124 |

DUNS 22-659-1089

## Silverstone Circuits Ltd

(**Subsidiary of:** British Racing Drivers Club Ltd)
Silverstone, Silverstone, Towcester, Northamptonshire NN12 8TN
**Tel:** 08704588200
**Web:** www.silverstone-circuit.co.uk
**Reg No:** 0882843 **Estd:** 1950 Private Limited Company
**Line of Business:** Motor sport preparation
**Issued Capital:** £6,550,000
**Directors:** T J Plato, J A Grant, I H Titchmarsh
**Responsibilities**
**Senior:** Edward Brookes *(Financial Director)*, Justin Elias *(Marketing Director)*
**Finance:** Edward Brookes *(Financial Director)*
**Marketing:** Justin Elias *(Marketing Director)*
**IT:** Kevin Obrien *(It Manager)*
**HR:** Vanessa Murphy *(Human Resources Manager)*
**Health & Safety:** Lesley Cox *(Environmental Health Manager)*
**Facilities:** Lee Howkins *(Operations Manager)*
**Operations:** Lesley Cox *(Environmental Health Manager)*
**Branches:** Silverstone Circuits Ltd, Towcester, Northamptonshire NN12 8TN
**US SIC:** 7999 **UK SIC:** 97913
**Auditors:** Rawlinson & Hunter
**Bankers:** HSBC Bank plc (40-05-14)

| | 31-12-13 | 31-12-12 | 31-12-11 |
|---|---|---|---|
| TO | 49,605,000 | 49,590,000 | 52,771,000 |
| P/L | (15,069,000) | (3,320,000) | (1,936,000) |
| NW | (6,477,000) | 8,592,000 | 11,912,000 |
| WC | (20,183,000) | (6,273,000) | (3,302,000) |
| Emp. | 141 | 129 | 116 |

DUNS 64-251-9078

## Silverwood Care Home

Imperial Road, Beeston, Nottingham, Nottinghamshire NG9 1FN
**Web:** www.hc-one.co.uk
**Estd:** 1994 Proprietorship
**Line of Business:** Nursing homes
**Proprietor:** R Miller
**Responsibilities**
**Senior:** Alison Jarvis *(Home Manager)*, Selina Leone *(General Manager)*, Mavis McLaughlin *(General Manager)*, Linda Sturdy *(Manager)*
**Admin:** Hazel Upton *(Administrator)*
**IT:** Hazel Upton *(Administrator)*
**HR:** Alison Jarvis *(Home Manager)*
**Health & Safety:** Alison Jarvis *(Home Manager)*
**US SIC:** 8051 **UK SIC:** 95100
**Employees:** 70

DUNS 23-385-2289

## Silverwood Enterprise Ltd

16 Silverwood Industrial Area, Silverwood Road, Lurgan, Craigavon, Co Armagh BT66 6LN
**Tel:** 028-3832-2222
**Web:** www.silverwoodenterprises.com
**Reg No:** 0051451NI **Estd:** 2004 Private Limited Company
**Line of Business:** Metal finishing and polishing services
**Issued Capital:** £20,000
**Directors:** P G Maginnis, A J Maginnis
**Co. Secretary:** Ms Heather Maginnis
**Responsibilities**
**Senior:** Ken Haslem *(Proprietor)*
**US SIC:** 3499, 3398
**UK SIC:** 31694, 31380
**Auditors:** Wm Courtney & Co

| | 31-08-13 | 31-08-12 | 31-08-11 |
|---|---|---|---|
| TA | 9,092,591 | 8,546,806 | 8,724,018 |
| NW | 7,972,431 | 7,660,332 | 7,266,144 |
| WC | 7,188,698 | 6,807,127 | 6,512,761 |

DUNS 42-431-6065 Imp

## Simarco International Ltd

(**Subsidiary of:** Simarco Holdings Ltd)
Simarco House, Crittall Road, Witham, Essex CM8 3DR
**Tel:** 01376-515397 **Fax:** 01376507950
**Web:** www.simarco.com
**Reg No:** 3341900 **VAT No:** 688528180
**Estd:** 1997 Private Limited Company
**Line of Business:** Storage and warehousing
**Trading Style:** Simarco International
**Issued Capital:** £31
**Principals:** S A Reed *(Managing)*, Ms N J Hart, C W Bentley, T Scott, D Knowles, B C Spencer
**Branches:** Simarco International Ltd, Unit 8-9, Newton Close, Wellingborough, Northamptonshire NN8 6UW
**US SIC:** 4226, 4789
**UK SIC:** 77003, 77002
**Auditors:** Lemon & Co
**Bankers:** Barclays Bank Plc (20-97-40)

| | 31-03-14 | 31-03-13 | 31-03-12 |
|---|---|---|---|
| TO | 26,300,000 | 24,120,739 | 24,622,897 |
| P/L | 1,165,724 | 853,616 | 824,768 |
| NW | 2,726,408 | 2,530,037 | 2,019,450 |
| WC | 2,361,112 | 2,284,362 | 1,763,687 |
| Emp. | 121 | 117 | 114 |

DUNS 21-919-3943 Imp-Exp

## Simbec Research Ltd

(**Subsidiary of:** Simbec-Orion Group Ltd)
Cardiff Road, Merthyr Tydfil, Mid Glamorgan CF48 4DR
**Tel:** 01443-690977 **Fax:** 01443-692499
**Web:** www.simbec.co.uk
**Reg No:** 1191772 **VAT No:** 289083321
**Estd:** 1974 Private Limited Company
**Line of Business:** Other human health activities
**Export Markets:** U S A, Japan, W Europe
**Export Sales:** £2,989,000
**Trading Style:** Simbec, S E P
**Issued Capital:** £3,733,251
**Directors:** T M Jones, C T Evans, Dr. F G Chartier, T Tanner, J R Openshaw, H R Jenkins
**Co. Secretary:** Howard Jenkins
**Responsibilities**
**Marketing:** Alan Woodward *(Sales & Marketing Manager)*
**Sales:** Alan Woodward *(Sales & Marketing Manager)*
**IT:** David Kilpatrick *(Systems Administrator)*
**HR:** Joanne Calvert *(Human Resources Manager)*
**Health & Safety:** Luke Davies *(Health & Safety Officer)*
**Operations:** Alan Woodward *(Sales & Marketing Manager)*
**US SIC:** 8091, 8922
**UK SIC:** 95200, 94000
**Auditors:** Gerald Thomas & Co

| | 30-09-13 | 30-09-12 | 30-09-11 |
|---|---|---|---|
| TO | 5,008,000 | 6,971,000 | 6,716,000 |
| P/L | (1,037,000) | (316,000) | (967,000) |
| NW | 1,447,000 | 2,675,000 | 2,851,000 |
| WC | 172,000 | (175,000) | 24,000 |
| Emp. | 87 | 92 | 100 |

DUNS 29-859-9416 Exp

## Simcorp Ltd

(**Subsidiary of:** Simcorp A/S)
2nd Floor 100 Wood Street, London EC2V 7AN
**Tel:** 02072601900 **Fax:** 02072601911
**Web:** www.simcorp-dimension.org
**Reg No:** 2063275 **VAT No:** 462744927
**Estd:** 1974 Private Limited Company
**Line of Business:** Other computer related activities
**Export Markets:** Rest of world
**Export Sales:** £9,805,027
**Trading Style:** Simcorp Treasury Solutions
**Issued Capital:** £100,000
**Directors:** Dr G V Hetrodt, K Holse, T Johansen
**Co. Secretary:** Klaus Holse
**Responsibilities**
**Senior:** Klaus Andersen *(Manager)*
**US SIC:** 7379 **UK SIC:** 83940
**Auditors:** Grant Thornton U K LLP
**Bankers:** Unibank A/s (40-48-78)

| | 31-12-13 | 31-12-12 | 31-12-11 |
|---|---|---|---|
| TO | 20,462,717 | 14,812,019 | 15,700,893 |
| P/L | 2,442,818 | (1,114,602) | 259,508 |
| NW | 590,576 | (1,370,910) | (334,160) |
| WC | 518,032 | (1,394,475) | 1,628,989 |
| Emp. | 68 | 73 | 76 |

DUNS 51-681-3029

## Simcox Quality Printers

46 Middlewich Road, Sandbach, Cheshire CW11 1HU
**Tel:** 01270762080
**Estd:** 2003 Partnership
**Line of Business:** Printers general
**Partner:** T Simcox
**Responsibilities**
**Senior:** Roger Simcox *(Proprietor)*
**US SIC:** 2752 **UK SIC:** 47544
**Employees:** 100

DUNS 22-199-0596

## Simcyp Ltd

(**Subsidiary of:** Pharsight International Uk Ltd)
Blades Enterprise Centre, John Street, Sheffield, South Yorkshire S2 4SU
**Tel:** 01142922322
**Web:** www.simcyp.com
**Reg No:** 4217235 **Estd:** 2001 Private Limited Company
**Line of Business:** Computer software (development)
**Issued Capital:** £9,082
**Directors:** J Munn, D A Deieso, M A Schemick
**Co. Secretary:** Alan Lefkowitz
**Responsibilities**
**Senior:** Richard Birtles *(Manager)*, Stephen Toon *(Manager)*, John Yingling *(Manager)*
**US SIC:** 7379, 8922, 7372
**UK SIC:** 83940, 94000
**Auditors:** BDO LLP

| | 31-12-13 | 31-12-12 | 29-12-12 |
|---|---|---|---|
| TO | 7,772,000 | 5,306,282 | N/A |
| P/L | 3,457,733 | 1,788,225 | N/A |
| NW | 6,453,503 | 5,469,070 | 4,425,919 |
| WC | 6,348,530 | 5,394,206 | 4,339,991 |
| Emp. | 58 | 58 | N/A |

DUNS 34-613-3051 Imp

## Simm Tronic Ltd

Waterside, Hoddesdon, Hertfordshire EN11 0QR
**Tel:** 01992-450126
**Web:** www.simmtronic.com
**Reg No:** 2750770 **VAT No:** 594992959
**Estd:** 1992 Private Limited Company
**Line of Business:** Manufacturers of control panels
**Issued Capital:** £3,750
**Directors:** G Russo, R A Vos, V Russo, S T Goskie
**Co. Secretary:** Mario Costanzo
**Responsibilities**
**Senior:** Alison Hosmer *(Personal Assistant)*
**Facilities:** John Gayle *(Commissioning Manager)*
**Operations:** John Gayle *(Commissioning Manager)*
**US SIC:** 3679 **UK SIC:** 34542
**Auditors:** BDO Stoy Hayward
**Bankers:** National Westminster Bank Plc (60-11-14)

| | 30-09-13 | 30-09-12 | 30-09-11 |
|---|---|---|---|
| TO | 8,776,118 | 7,329,262 | 7,509,976 |
| P/L | 260,500 | 115,985 | 548,331 |
| NW | 4,109,112 | 4,081,944 | 4,140,006 |
| WC | 3,640,421 | 3,644,683 | 3,853,253 |
| Emp. | 78 | 77 | 74 |

DUNS 22-861-9169 Imp

## Simmal Ltd

Units 479, 479-480 Walton Summit Centre Ranglet, Road, Preston, Lancashire PR5 8AR
**Tel:** 01772-324277
**Web:** www.simmal.co.uk
**Reg No:** 1741450 **VAT No:** 379856772
**Estd:** 1983 Private Limited Company
**Line of Business:** Aluminium stockholders
**Issued Capital:** £40,000
**Principals:** P G Simmons *(Chairman)*, J G Simmons *(Managing)*, Ms S Simmons *(Financial)*, Ms M Coop
**Co. Secretary:** Ms Mary Simmons
**Responsibilities**
**Senior:** Edward Mitchell *(Warehouse Manager)*
**Marketing:** Frank Power *(Sales Director)*
**Sales:** Frank Power *(Sales Director)*
**HR:** Lucia Westhead *(Office Manager)*
**Purchasing:** Chris Lever *(Purchasing Manager)*
**Branches:** Simmal Ltd, Syke Ing, Syke Lane, Dewsbury, West Yorkshire WF12 8HX
**US SIC:** 5051 **UK SIC:** 61200
**Auditors:** Douglass Grange
**Bankers:** National Westminster Bank Plc (01-67-14)

| | 30-09-13 | 30-09-12 | 30-09-11 |
|---|---|---|---|
| TO | 8,298,099 | 8,259,863 | 9,512,044 |
| P/L | 309,859 | 289,582 | 245,268 |
| NW | 2,691,755 | 2,606,560 | 2,606,043 |
| WC | 1,755,253 | 1,696,621 | 1,675,526 |
| Emp. | 50 | 50 | 45 |

DUNS 23-653-3381 Imp

## Simmons & Company International Ltd

Simmons House, 22 Waverley Place, Aberdeen, Aberdeenshire AB10 1XP
**Tel:** 01224-202300 **Fax:** 01224202303
**Web:** www.simmonsco-intl.com
**Reg No:** 0190220SC **Estd:** 1998 Private Limited Company
**Line of Business:** Accounting and auditing activities
**Issued Capital:** £975,174
**Directors:** M E Frazier, E J Leigh, C I Welsh, D M Beveridge, A P Banham
**Co. Secretary:** Colin Donald
**Responsibilities**
**Senior:** Mike Beveridge *(Manager)*, Nick Dalgarno *(Manager)*, Matthew Simmons *(Manager)*
**Finance:** Jeff Corray *(Head of Simmons Private Equity)*
**Marketing:** Emma Anderson *(Marketing Manager)*
**Sales:** Robert Muse *(Head of European Sales)*
**US SIC:** 8931 **UK SIC:** 83600
**Auditors:** Deloitte & Touche LLP

**Bankers:** Bank Of Scotland (80-05-14)

| | 30-06-14 | 30-06-13 | 30-06-12 |
|---|---|---|---|
| TO | 18,792,128 | 15,026,895 | 11,388,169 |
| P/L | 2,953,667 | 427,715 | 314,630 |
| NW | 5,401,024 | 3,662,003 | 3,435,669 |
| WC | 9,041,748 | 6,849,309 | 5,924,081 |
| Emp. | 57 | 55 | 49 |

DUNS 21-661-6279

## Simmons & Simmons Llp

Citypoint, 1 Ropemaker Street, London EC2Y 9HT

**Tel:** 020-7628-2020

**Web:** www.simmons-simmons.com
**Reg No:** 0352713OC **Estd:** 1896 Limited Partnership
**Line of Business:** Legal services
**Responsibilities**
**Senior:** Charlie Agnoli (Partner), Jeremy Arscott (Partner), Charles Bankes (Partner), Romeo Battigaglia (Partner), Jayne Bentham (Partner), Joel Bentsur (Partner), Nick Benwell (Partner), Colin Bole (Partner), Christopher Boresjo (Partner), Patrick Boylan (Partner), James Bresslaw (Partner), Sean Bulmer (Partner), Adrian Cole (Non-designated Limited Liabili), Adam Cooper (Partner), Nick Cronkshaw (Partner), Ed Crosse (Partner), Ali Crosthwaite (Partner), Willaim Cullen (Non-designated Limited Liabili), Ian Cullen (Partner), Jason Daniel (Non-designated Limited Liabili), Carlos De Laiglesia (Partner), Pedro De Sousa (Board Member), Thomas Deegan (Non-designated Limited Liabili), Giles Dennison (Non-designated Limited Liabili), Mark Dewar (Non-designated Limited Liabili), Marc Doring (Non-Designated Limited Liabili), Geoffrey Durell (Partner), Richard Dyton (Partner), Stuart Evans (Partner), Andrea Finn (Partner), Filippo Fioretti (Non-designated Limited Liabili), Darren Fox (Non-designated Limited Liabili), Rowan Freeland (Partner), Dale Gabbart (Partner), Alan Gar (Partner), Clive Garner (Partner), Michael Gavey (Partner), Janet Gaymer (Partner), Stephen Gentle (Partner), Gerhard Gispen (Non-designated Limited Liabili), Thierry Gontard (Partner), Sandra Gowrie (Executive), Helen Hancock (Partner), Rolfe Hayden (Partner), Jan-Mathijs Hermans (Non-designated Limited Liabili), Mark Hewland (Non-designated Limited Liabili), Bob Jones (Partner), Sarah Keech (Manager), John Kelsey (Partner), Paul Li (Partner; Country Head - China), Alyson Lockett (Partner), Fiona Loughrey (Partner), Charles Mayo (Partner), Simon Middleton (Partner), James Pollock (Partner), Juliet Reingold (Partner), Simon Schiff (Partner), Charlotte Stalin (Partner), Philip Vaughan (Non-designated Limited Liabili), Leo Verhoeff (Partner), Michael Wyman (Partner)
**Finance:** David McLaughlin (Finance Director)
**Marketing:** Daniela Conte (Media and Public Relations)
**Admin:** Amy Clatworthy (Secretary), Jayne Cook (Personal Assistant), Dominique Geldermans (Personal Assistant), Jennie Godfrey (Legal Secretary), Ellie Hare (Legal Secretary), Ann-Marie Jones (Legal Secretary), Dawn Luxford (Legal Secretary), Emer Such (Secretary)
**IT:** Peter Attwood (Network, Security Manager), Lorna Goulding (Manager, Information Systems a), Stuart Rowlands (IT Director)
**HR:** David Denman (Human Resources Manager), Dan Flint (Human Resources Director)
**Operations:** Loren Harper (Head of Practice Support)
**Branches:** Simmons & Simmons Llp, Temple Quay House, 2 Temple Quay, Bristol, Avon BS1 6PN
**US SIC:** 8111 **UK SIC:** 83500
**Auditors:** PricewaterhouseCoopers LLP

| | 30-04-14 | 30-04-13 | 30-04-12 |
|---|---|---|---|
| TO | 268,601,000 | 250,491,000 | 251,726,000 |
| P/L | 64,951,000 | 58,299,000 | 46,825,000 |
| NW | 46,599,000 | 30,558,000 | 29,579,000 |
| WC | 98,683,000 | 42,152,000 | 97,470,000 |
| Emp. | 1,428 | 1,363 | 1,234 |

DUNS 21-616-4061

## Simmons (Bakers) Ltd

(Subsidiary of: Hatfield Trading Ltd)
2 The Parade, Hatfield, Hertfordshire AL10 0EY

**Tel:** 01707263232 **Fax:** 01707-274329
**Web:** www.simmons-bakers.com
**Reg No:** 0421255 **VAT No:** 539937588
**Estd:** 1989 Private Limited Company
**Line of Business:** Manufacture of bread; manufacture of fresh pastry goods and cakes
**Issued Capital:** £3,369
**Principals:** I D Matthews (Managing), Ms G M Ewing, R J Matthews, P J Williams, Ms P A Matthews
**Co. Secretary:** Neal Tuson
**Responsibilities**
**HR:** Jill Ewing (Human Resources Manager)

**Branches:** Simmons (Bakers) Ltd, 129 Birchwood Avenue, Hatfield, Hertfordshire AL10 0PT
**US SIC:** 2051, 6711
**UK SIC:** 41960, 83962
**Auditors:** Barron & Barron
**Bankers:** National Westminster Bank Plc (60-10-18)

| | 30-03-14 | 31-03-13 | 31-03-12 |
|---|---|---|---|
| TO | 14,983,833 | N/A | N/A |
| P/L | 1,269,968 | 597,505 | 367,919 |
| NW | 5,393,255 | 4,430,077 | 3,975,119 |
| WC | 1,333,514 | 614,728 | 497,245 |
| Emp. | 311 | 282 | 272 |

DUNS 29-580-8166                                          Imp-Exp

## Simmons Bedding Group Plc

(Subsidiary of: Mattress Holding)
Knight Road, Rochester, Kent ME2 2BP
**Tel:** 01634-723-557 **Fax:** 01634-290-257
**Web:** www.simmons-group.co.uk
**Reg No:** 1942625 **VAT No:** 701911276
**Estd:** 1923 Public Limited Company
**Line of Business:** Manufacture of mattresses
**Export Markets:** E U, other
**Export Sales:** £837,074
**Trading Style:** Nestledown, Sleepeezee, Cumfilux
**Issued Capital:** £1,801,000
**Directors:** G Silberman, G B Raingold, H G Wilson, M Bender, Ms C Deschaumes, K H Foulstone
**Co. Secretary:** Colin Cousins
**Responsibilities**
**Marketing:** Peter Ruddle (Sales & Marketing Director)
**Sales:** Peter Ruddle (Sales & Marketing Director)
**Health & Safety:** George Hawthorn (Health & Safety Officer)
**Engineering:** Mick Fenton (Production Manager)
**Branches:** Simmons Bedding Group Plc, 1-8 Hulbert Industrial Estate, Cinder Bank, Dudley, West Midlands DY2 9AD
**US SIC:** 2515 **UK SIC:** 46715
**Auditors:** Mazars LLP
**Bankers:** National Westminster Bank Plc (60-60-08)

| | 31-12-13 | 31-12-12 | 31-12-11 |
|---|---|---|---|
| TO | 28,740,644 | 29,544,665 | 32,007,736 |
| P/L | 219,412 | 967,739 | (2,409,611) |
| NW | 6,221,784 | 5,794,716 | 6,556,982 |
| WC | 3,289,265 | 3,575,647 | 3,512,907 |
| Emp. | 293 | 284 | 329 |

DUNS 77-495-2717                                                 Exp

## Simmons Edeco Europe Ltd

(Subsidiary of: Simmons Edeco Inc)
Unit D2 Maple Road, Derby, Derbyshire DE74 2UT
**Tel:** 01332-850060
**Web:** www.simmonsedeco.com
**Reg No:** 2977551 **Estd:** 1994 Private Limited Company
**Line of Business:** Oil and gas extraction
**Export Sales:** £827,148
**Issued Capital:** £3,750,000
**Directors:** J B Simmons, D K Crowshaw, V H Redekop
**Responsibilities**
**Senior:** Steve Rogan (Manager)
**Branches:** Simmons Edeco Europe Ltd, Unit 5 Kirton Ave, Aberdeen, Aberdeenshire AB21 0DP
**US SIC:** 1311 **UK SIC:** 13000
**Auditors:** Cooper Parry Group Ltd
**Bankers:** HSBC Bank plc (40-19-15)

| | 31-12-13 | 31-12-12 | 31-12-11 |
|---|---|---|---|
| TO | 6,271,827 | 8,884,074 | 13,309,168 |
| P/L | (128,606) | (761,640) | 505,574 |
| NW | 1,622,928 | 1,751,534 | 2,391,604 |
| WC | 1,084,038 | 513,026 | 1,584,763 |
| Emp. | 86 | 100 | 111 |

DUNS 73-280-6893

## Simmons Gainsford Llp

7-10 Chandos Street, London W1G 9DQ
**Tel:** 02074479000
**Web:** www.sgllp.co.uk
**Reg No:** 0303127OC **Estd:** 1997
**Line of Business:** Accounting activities
**Responsibilities**
**Senior:** Phillip Austin (Manager), Daryush Farshchi-Heidari (Designated Limited Liability P), Jeffrey Goldman (Designated Limited Liability P), Darren Hersey (Designated Limited Liability P), Shilen Manek (Designated Limited Liability P), David Pumfrey (Designated Limited Liability P), Christopher Stebbing (Designated Limited Liability P), Steven Strauss (Designated Limited Liability P), Hua Sze (Designated Limited Liability P), Rajiv Thakerar (Designated Limited Liability P)
**US SIC:** 8931 **UK SIC:** 83600

**Auditors:** Ivan Sopher & Co

| | 31-03-14 | 31-03-13 | 31-03-12 |
|---|---|---|---|
| TO | 9,383,788 | 8,850,867 | 9,016,136 |
| P/L | 118,341 | 72,036 | N/A |
| NW | (95,323) | (134,083) | (173,544) |
| WC | 2,054,065 | 2,100,879 | 2,122,587 |
| Emp. | 96 | 91 | 90 |

DUNS 29-559-7512                                                 Imp

## Simmonsigns Ltd

(Subsidiary of: Salop Holdings Ltd)
Stafford Park 5, Telford, Shropshire TF3 3AS
**Tel:** 01952-293333
**Web:** www.simmonsigns.co.uk
**Reg No:** 1923947 **VAT No:** 433910270
**Estd:** 1985 Private Limited Company
**Line of Business:** Traffic administration and management systems
**Export Sales:** £72,788
**Trading Style:** Alpha
**Issued Capital:** £1,000
**Principals:** K R Simmons (Managing), M G Sturgess, M Simmons, M R Farley, P Simmons, D S Panton, M A Wood
**Responsibilities**
**Sales:** Steve Keary (Sales Manager), Neil Whaites (Senior Sales manager), Eric Woodhouse (Export Sales Manager)
**Fleet:** Eric Woodhouse (Export Sales Manager)
**US SIC:** 7399 **UK SIC:** 83954
**Auditors:** Price Pearson
**Bankers:** Lloyds TSB Bank plc (30-18-55)

| | 30-06-13 | 30-06-12 | 30-06-11 |
|---|---|---|---|
| TO | 7,540,089 | 6,641,852 | 7,600,562 |
| P/L | 304,930 | (79,666) | 176,151 |
| NW | 1,211,949 | 920,079 | 974,746 |
| WC | 1,201,889 | 866,526 | 899,044 |
| Emp. | 73 | 70 | 73 |

DUNS 21-580-1570

## Simmtronic

Unit A3, Lingard Court, Lingard Lane, Stockport, Cheshire SK6 2QU
**Tel:** 08445617489
**Web:** www.simmtronic.com
**Estd:** 2005 Proprietorship
**Line of Business:** Lighting consultants
**Proprietor:** D Little
**Responsibilities**
**Senior:** David Gillingham (Northern Divisional Manager)
**US SIC:** 8911 **UK SIC:** 83701
**Employees:** 51

DUNS 42-394-8848                                                 Imp

## Simoco Emea Ltd

(Subsidiary of: Gresham 4a)
Field House, Uttoxeter Old Road, Derby, Derbyshire DE1 1NH
**Tel:** 01332-375500
**Web:** www.simocogroup.com
**Reg No:** 4382515 **Estd:** 1902 Private Limited Company
**Line of Business:** Radio equipment
**Export Sales:** £6,873,000
**Issued Capital:** £1
**Directors:** M S Norfield, A P Woodhall, P E Williams, I Carr
**Co. Secretary:** Philip Williams
**Responsibilities**
**Marketing:** Elizabeth Addison (Marketing Manager)
**Sales:** Carlos Chajin (Business Development Manager)
**Purchasing:** Lea Bareham (Procurement Manager)
**US SIC:** 3662 **UK SIC:** 34430
**Auditors:** PricewaterhouseCoopers LLP
**Bankers:** HSBC Bank plc (40-27-15)

| | 30-04-14 | 30-04-13 | 30-04-12 |
|---|---|---|---|
| TO | 12,709,000 | 11,916,000 | 8,733,000 |
| P/L | 1,737,000 | 1,128,000 | 318,000 |
| NW | 977,000 | 5,648,000 | 5,487,000 |
| WC | (440,000) | 4,236,000 | 4,106,000 |
| Emp. | 77 | 70 | 64 |

DUNS 21-681-9391                                                 Exp

## Simon & Schuster (U K) Ltd

The First Floor, London WC1X 8HB
**Tel:** 020-7316-1900 **Fax:** 020-7316-0332
**Web:** http://biz.simonandschuster.co.uk
**Reg No:** 0714516 **Estd:** 1987 Private Limited Company
**Line of Business:** Publishing of books
**Export Markets:** Europe, Australasia, U S A, Africa, Asia
**Export Sales:** £14,495,000
**Issued Capital:** £5,200
**Directors:** M D Ollard, I S Chapman
**Co. Secretary:** Mitre Secretaries Limited
**Responsibilities**
**Senior:** I Churtman (Proprietor)
**Marketing:** James Horobin (Group Sales, Marketing & Brand)
**Sales:** Gemma Hamerton (Head of International Sales), James Horobin (Group Sales, Marketing & Brand)
**Admin:** Lorna James (Office Manager)
**HR:** Lorna James (Office Manager)

**Health & Safety:** Lorna James (Office Manager)
**Operations:** Julia Marshall (Production Director)
**Purchasing:** Lorna James (Office Manager)
**Engineering:** Julia Marshall (Production Director)
**Branches:** Simon & Schuster (U K) Ltd, 88 Recent Street, 64 Maids Causeway, Cambridge, Cambridgeshire CB5 8DD
**US SIC:** 2731 **UK SIC:** 47532
**Auditors:** PricewaterhouseCoopers LLP
**Bankers:** Barclays Bank Plc (20-39-07)

| | 31-12-13 | 31-12-12 | 31-12-11 |
|---|---|---|---|
| TO | 45,689,000 | 43,434,000 | 43,016,000 |
| P/L | (2,094,000) | 2,598,000 | 1,223,000 |
| NW | 23,738,000 | 25,375,000 | 22,676,000 |
| WC | 23,231,000 | 24,654,000 | 21,828,000 |
| Emp. | 99 | 103 | 89 |

DUNS 39-820-8975

## Simon Bailes Ltd

Northallerton Snooker Club, 2/3 Tannery Lane, Northallerton, North Yorkshire DL7 8DS
**Tel:** 01609-780888
**Web:** www.simonbailes.co.uk
**Reg No:** 2218953 **VAT No:** 329546435
**Estd:** 1988 Private Limited Company
**Line of Business:** Car dealers (new & used)
**Issued Capital:** £129,740
**Principals:** S D Bailes (Managing), Mrs T R Sanderson, Mrs J Kirby, Mrs B A Charlton
**Co. Secretary:** Simon Bailes
**Responsibilities**
**Health & Safety:** Jim Singers (Health & Safety Officer)
**Branches:** Simon Bailes Ltd, 36-38 Redcar Road, Guisborough, Cleveland TS14 6DB
**US SIC:** 5511, 5521, 5531
**UK SIC:** 65100
**Auditors:** Grant Thornton
**Bankers:** Barclays Bank Plc (20-61-46)

| | 31-12-13 | 31-12-12 | 31-12-11 |
|---|---|---|---|
| TO | 48,992,947 | 45,127,746 | 42,761,501 |
| P/L | 1,177,992 | 428,219 | 311,584 |
| NW | 3,333,670 | 2,435,294 | 2,172,294 |
| WC | 1,004,038 | 319,207 | 648,600 |
| Emp. | 99 | 100 | 103 |

DUNS 21-558-5849

## Simon Bellow

8 Barnwell House, Barnwell Drive, Cambridge, Cambridgeshire CB5 8UU
**Web:** www.abacuscare.co.uk
**Estd:** 2010 Proprietorship
**Line of Business:** Other human health activities
**Proprietor:** S Bellow
**US SIC:** 8091 **UK SIC:** 95200
**Bankers:** The Co-Operative Bank Plc (08-92-50)
**Employees:** 50

DUNS 21-572-9224

## Simon Boyd Fabric Superstore

Gresford Industrial Park, Chester Road, Wrexham, Clwyd LL12 8LX
**Tel:** 01978-854777
**Web:** www.simonboyd.com
**Estd:** 1972 Partnership
**Line of Business:** Soft furnishings Retailer
**Partners:** Mrs M Grymes, P Grymes
**Branches:** Simon Boyd Fabric Superstore, Smithfield Road, Shrewsbury, Shropshire SY1 1PB
**US SIC:** 5719 **UK SIC:** 64700
**Bankers:** National Westminster Bank Plc (55-81-42)
**Employees:** 50

DUNS 23-996-1311

## Simon Community Northern Ireland

49-57 Fitzroy Avenue, Belfast BT7 1HT
**Tel:** 028-9023-2882 **Fax:** 028-9032-6839
**Web:** www.simoncommunity.org
**Reg No:** 0017466NI **Estd:** 1971 Private Company Limited By Guarantee
**Line of Business:** Social work activities without accommodation
**Directors:** M E Torrans, J A Johnston, F Smyth, J Tully, I O'Doherty, Mrs K Thomson, Ms A Kilpatrick, Mrs F Mccormick
**Co. Secretary:** Jason Johnston
**Responsibilities**
**Senior:** Hugh Connor (Director), Joanne Grant (Director), Deidre Ward (Manager), Suzanne Wylie (Director)
**Marketing:** Lisa Hamilton (Marketing Manager)
**Branches:** Simon Community Northern Ireland, 49-57 Fitzroy Avenue, Belfast, Belfast BT7 1HT
**US SIC:** 7399 **UK SIC:** 83954
**Auditors:** PricewaterhouseCoopers LLP

**Bankers:** Northern Bank Ltd (95-01-01)

| | 31-03-14 | 31-03-13 | 31-03-12 |
|---|---|---|---|
| TO | 8,553,886 | 7,198,876 | 6,635,015 |
| P/L | (813,033) | (165,954) | 45,698 |
| NW | 3,101,709 | 3,914,742 | 4,080,696 |
| WC | 2,275,040 | 3,059,072 | 3,271,217 |
| Emp. | 247 | 220 | 206 |

DUNS 21-876-9913

## Simon Elvin Holdings Ltd

Thomas Road, Woodburn Industrial Park, Woodburn Green, High Wycombe, Buckinghamshire HP10 0PE
**Tel:** 01628526711
**Web:** www.simonelvin.com
**Reg No:** 8104049 **Estd:** 2012 Private Limited Company
**Line of Business:** Greeting card publishers and suppliers
**Export Sales:** £3,542,064
**Issued Capital:** £100,000
**Directors:** J P Elvin, S P Elvin, J C Elvin, J E Elvin, S Mckay
**Co. Secretary:** Mark Blundell
**US SIC:** 6711 **UK SIC:** 83962

| | 31-12-13 | 31-12-12 |
|---|---|---|
| TO | 23,379,823 | 23,847,631 |
| P/L | 947,488 | (1,058,574) |
| NW | 34,437,043 | 33,320,434 |
| WC | 12,935,602 | 12,190,414 |
| Emp. | 146 | 157 |

DUNS 73-269-2582

## Simon Gibson Transport Ltd

Unit 1 A. W. Nielsen Road, Goole, North Humberside DN14 6UE
**Tel:** 01405780459 **Fax:** 01405768870
**Web:** www.simongibsontransport.com
**Reg No:** 4542964 **Estd:** 2002 Private Limited Company
**Line of Business:** Road haulage and transport services
**Export Sales:** £173,580
**Issued Capital:** £1
**Co. Secretary:** Simon Gibson
**Responsibilities**
**Marketing:** Andrea Lewis *(Sales & Marketing Manager)*
**Sales:** Andrea Lewis *(Sales & Marketing Manager)*
**US SIC:** 4789 **UK SIC:** 77002

| | 31-12-13 | 31-12-12 | 31-12-11 |
|---|---|---|---|
| TO | 10,916,955 | 6,390,322 | N/A |
| P/L | 1,019,746 | 524,114 | N/A |
| NW | 1,932,620 | 1,385,166 | 1,145,352 |
| WC | (1,084,616) | (361,282) | (412,071) |
| Emp. | 118 | 73 | N/A |

DUNS 71-939-9110 **Imp**

## Simon Hegele Logistics & Service Ltd

**(Subsidiary of:** Simon Hegele Gesellschaft Für Logistik Und Service)
161 Milton Park, Milton, Abingdon, Oxfordshire OX14 4SD
**Tel:** 01235833015 **Fax:** 01235833016
**Web:** www.hegele.de
**Reg No:** 5320609 **Estd:** 2005 Private Limited Company
**Line of Business:** Freight transport by road not elsewhere classified
**Export Sales:** £2,218,302
**Issued Capital:** £400,000
**Directors:** C Sitzer, J K Hoeflinger, C Dorf
**Co. Secretary:** Dr Sybille Steiner
**Responsibilities**
**Senior:** Sharon Grossmann *(Manager)*, Christopher Leima *(Manager)*
**US SIC:** 4213, 7399
**UK SIC:** 72300, 83954
**Auditors:** Menzies LLP

| | 31-12-13 | 31-12-12 | 31-12-11 |
|---|---|---|---|
| TO | 4,593,416 | 5,216,035 | 4,424,440 |
| P/L | 186,826 | 327,362 | 334,328 |
| NW | 1,269,537 | 1,126,711 | 884,064 |
| WC | 1,199,429 | 1,039,589 | 731,330 |
| Emp. | 62 | 66 | 56 |

DUNS 21-724-7113 **Exp**

## Simon Holdings Plc

The Clock Tower, Bridge Street, Walton-On-Thames, Surrey KT12 1AY
**Tel:** 01932-230850 **Fax:** 01932230950
**Web:** www.simonholdings.com
**Reg No:** 0908438 **VAT No:** 222821004
**Estd:** 1967 Public Limited Company
**Line of Business:** Holding companies management activities
**Export Markets:** Europe
**Export Sales:** £8,884,766
**Issued Capital:** £50,000
**Principals:** P F Murphy *(Chairman and Managing)*, M R Harmes *(Managing)*, S J Murphy
**Co. Secretary:** Graham Harmes
**Responsibilities**
**Marketing:** Jenna Affleck *(Group Marketing Administrator)*
**Branches:** Simon Holdings Plc, 189A London Rd, Reading, Berkshire RG1 3NU
**US SIC:** 6711, 7361
**UK SIC:** 83962, 83954
**Auditors:** Parker Cavendish
**Bankers:** HSBC Bank plc (40-47-02)

| | 31-12-13 | 31-12-12 | 31-12-11 |
|---|---|---|---|
| TO | 34,929,688 | 37,170,850 | 35,020,841 |
| P/L | 146,830 | (184,107) | 208,562 |
| NW | 9,187,267 | 9,433,569 | 10,443,310 |
| WC | 3,918,015 | 4,130,553 | 3,874,891 |
| Emp. | 123 | 147 | 150 |

DUNS 21-330-9867 **Imp-Exp**

## Simon Jersey Ltd

**(Subsidiary of:** Uniform Brands Ltd)
Sykeside Drive, Altham Business Park, Altham, Accrington, Lancashire BB5 5YE
**Tel:** 01282-772555 **Fax:** 01282771603
**Web:** www.simonjersey.com
**Reg No:** 1006047 **VAT No:** 174749917
**Estd:** 1971 Private Limited Company
**Line of Business:** Manufacture of other wearing apparel and accessories not elsewhere classified
**Export Markets:** Worldwide
**Export Sales:** £991,867
**Issued Capital:** £190,000
**Directors:** N P Teagle, J R Saunders
**Co. Secretary:** Miss Bridget Kight
**Responsibilities**
**Senior:** Martin Andersen *(Manager)*, Shane Bray *(Manager)*, Anders Pedersen *(Manager)*, Thomas Rokke *(Manager)*
**US SIC:** 2389 **UK SIC:** 45393
**Auditors:** KPMG LLP
**Bankers:** National Westminster Bank Plc (01-00-04)

| | 30-09-14 | 31-12-13 | 31-09-12 |
|---|---|---|---|
| TO | 16,863,726 | 28,892,570 | 39,521,685 |
| P/L | 7,017,752 | (7,665,727) | (1,300,490) |
| NW | 1,927,231 | (10,090,521) | (2,530,199) |
| WC | 14,240,023 | (19,410,802) | (12,063,105) |
| Emp. | 152 | 179 | 217 |

DUNS 21-558-5278

## Simon Smith Group

P O Box 328, Northleach, Cheltenham, Gloucestershire GL54 3XS
**Tel:** 01451 861824
**Web:** www.simonsmithgroup.co.uk
**Estd:** 1972 Partnership
**Line of Business:** Petrol service stations
**Trading Style:** Simon Smith Retail Ltd
**Partner:** B Tew
**US SIC:** 5541, 5399
**UK SIC:** 65200, 65600
**Employees:** 110

DUNS 50-014-6386

## Simonds of Botesdale Ltd

Roswald House, Oak Drive, Diss, Norfolk IP22 4GX
**Tel:** 01379-647300 **Fax:** 01379898910
**Web:** www.simonds.co.uk
**Reg No:** 2299468 **VAT No:** 102982777
**Estd:** 1988 Private Limited Company
**Line of Business:** Coach and bus hire
**Issued Capital:** £829,076
**Principals:** M S Simonds *(Managing)*, R S Simonds, A Tant
**Co. Secretary:** Martyn Simonds
**Responsibilities**
**Senior:** Carl Lummis *(Transport Manager)*, Denis Simonds *(Manager)*
**Admin:** Ros Simonds *(Administration Coordinator)*
**Purchasing:** Ros Simonds *(Administration Coordinator)*
**Fleet:** Carl Lummis *(Transport Manager)*
**US SIC:** 4119, 7539, 4722
**UK SIC:** 72200, 67100, 77001
**Auditors:** BKR Haines Watts
**Bankers:** Barclays Bank Plc (20-26-34)

| | 31-10-13 | 31-10-12 | 31-10-11 |
|---|---|---|---|
| TO | 5,103,344 | 5,328,038 | 5,203,109 |
| P/L | (48,334) | 165,436 | 211,605 |
| NW | 933,116 | 1,095,384 | 1,086,329 |
| WC | (322,216) | (323,059) | (334,974) |
| Emp. | 88 | 91 | 90 |

DUNS 21-738-5338

## Simons Muirhead & Burton Ltd

8-9 Frith Street, London W1D 3JB
**Tel:** 02032062700 **Fax:** 02032062800
**Web:** www.smab.co.uk
**Reg No:** 7722006 **Estd:** 2011 Private Limited Company
**Line of Business:** Management activities of other non-financial holding companies not elsewhere classified
**Issued Capital:** £60
**Directors:** S M Goldberg, L Charalambous, R Mireskandari, M I Javaid
**US SIC:** 6711 **UK SIC:** 83962

| | 31-03-14 | 31-03-13 | 31-03-12 |
|---|---|---|---|
| TA | 1,298,424 | 917,192 | 813,002 |
| NW | 451,355 | (1,500) | 1 |

DUNS 73-310-7580

## Simonstone Motor Group Plc

**(Subsidiary of:** Cameo Investment Ltd)
803-805 Bath Road, Brislington, Bristol, Avon BS4 5NL
**Tel:** 01179711311 **Fax:** 01173009133
**Web:** www.simonstonemotorgroup.co.uk
**Reg No:** 4584537 **Estd:** 2002 Private Limited Company
**Line of Business:** Sale of new motor vehicles
**Issued Capital:** £415,000
**Directors:** J Keen, P J Pearce, M W Hooper, M Keen
**Co. Secretary:** Stephen Sowerby
**Responsibilities**
**Senior:** Steve Southard *(Parts Supervisor)*
**US SIC:** 5511, 5521, 7539, 5531
**UK SIC:** 65100, 67100
**Bankers:** Bank Of Scotland (12-05-77)

| | 31-12-13 | 31-12-12 | 31-12-11 |
|---|---|---|---|
| TO | 17,842,277 | 17,995,817 | 19,887,196 |
| P/L | 103,903 | 71,410 | (182,027) |
| NW | 47,571 | (28,093) | (173,668) |
| WC | (145,870) | (108,666) | (416,930) |
| Emp. | 61 | 60 | 59 |

DUNS 23-377-0056 **Imp**

## Simple Simon Foods Ltd

Unit 421 Centennial Avenue Centennial, Park, Borehamwood, Hertfordshire WD6 3TN
**Tel:** 02082365300 **Fax:** 020-8200-9569
**Web:** www.simplesimon.co.uk
**Reg No:** 2733621 **Estd:** 1980 Private Limited Company
**Line of Business:** Distribution service providers
**Trading Style:** S S F
**Issued Capital:** £10,000
**Principals:** J A Lessons *(Managing)*, A W Lessons
**Co. Secretary:** Julian Lessons
**Responsibilities**
**Finance:** Bimal Niak *(Financial Director)*
**IT:** Jonathan Milne *(Purchasing Manager)*, Bimal Niak *(Financial Director)*
**Purchasing:** Jonathan Milne *(Purchasing Manager)*
**Branches:** Simple Simon Foods Ltd, Unit 9, Capitol Way, London NW9 0EQ
**US SIC:** 4712 **UK SIC:** 77002
**Auditors:** Mehta & Co
**Bankers:** Barclays Bank Plc (20-69-17)

| | 31-08-13 | 31-08-12 | 31-08-11 |
|---|---|---|---|
| TO | 17,757,483 | 13,038,602 | 10,892,276 |
| P/L | 17,931 | 200,695 | 40,075 |
| NW | 117,563 | 206,733 | 163,142 |
| WC | (114,802) | (56,265) | (121,507) |
| Emp. | 71 | 59 | 55 |

DUNS 42-351-5456

## Simplicity Marketing Ltd

**(Subsidiary of:** Flash Topco Ltd)
5th Floor 19-22 Rathbone Place, Rathbone Place, London W1T 1HY
**Tel:** 02076372213
**Web:** www.flashtalking.com
**Reg No:** 4339257 **Estd:** 2001 Private Limited Company
**Line of Business:** Advertising
**Export Sales:** £14,227,784
**Issued Capital:** £100
**Directors:** P L Cunningham, D Freeman, J W Meeks
**Co. Secretary:** Ms Sheila Cunningham
**US SIC:** 7311 **UK SIC:** 83800

| | 31-12-13 | 31-12-12 | 31-12-11 |
|---|---|---|---|
| TO | 19,803,492 | 15,781,025 | N/A |
| P/L | 5,981,721 | 6,848,685 | N/A |
| NW | 13,152,167 | 9,382,468 | 3,348,068 |
| WC | 13,322,492 | 9,946,822 | 3,276,695 |
| Emp. | 140 | 51 | N/A |

DUNS 21-908-7215

## Simplify Digital Ltd

1 Riverside, Manbre Road, London W6 9WA
**Tel:** 02087356200
**Web:** www.simplifydigital.co.uk
**Reg No:** 6095563 **VAT No:** 898781928
**Estd:** 2007 Private Limited Company
**Line of Business:** Other non-store retail sale
**Issued Capital:** £2,137
**Directors:** The Hon C A Ponsonby, J P Hornby, D J Lee, J C Botts
**Co. Secretary:** Lawrence Bleach
**Responsibilities**
**Senior:** Paul Henry *(Head Of Customer Service)*
**US SIC:** 5963 **UK SIC:** 65600
**Auditors:** Deloitte LLP
**Bankers:** Barclays Bank Plc (20-00-00)

| | 31-01-14 | 31-01-13 | 31-01-12 |
|---|---|---|---|
| TO | 15,518,740 | 7,064,459 | 5,193,229 |
| P/L | 2,356,640 | 959,960 | (11,372) |
| NW | 3,676,709 | 2,221,821 | 832,801 |
| WC | 3,436,701 | 1,488,436 | 827,022 |
| Emp. | 78 | 43 | 24 |

DUNS 64-115-2116

## Simply Biz Ltd

Stadium Way, Huddersfield, West Yorkshire HD1 6PG
**Tel:** 01484-439100 **Fax:** 01484-439101
**Web:** www.simplybiz.co.uk
**Reg No:** 4518535 **Estd:** 2002 Private Limited Company
**Line of Business:** Financial services
**Issued Capital:** £80,278
**Directors:** S R Braidford, K E Davy, M L Timmins, Mrs S C Turvey, N M Stevens, T H Trotter, G J Kershaw, D R Kershaw
**Co. Secretary:** Mrs Rebecca Butcher
**Responsibilities**
**Senior:** Andrew Bradbury *(Manager)*
**Marketing:** Michelle Hare *(Marketing Manager)*
**Sales:** Akinola Fashola *(?Strategic Relationship Execut)*, Carly Robinson *(?Strategic Relationship Execut)*, Lisa Worthington *(?Strategic Relationship Manage)*
**Admin:** Rachel Harvey *(Personal Assistant)*
**HR:** Sharon Johnson *(Group HR Manager)*
**US SIC:** 7399 **UK SIC:** 83954
**Auditors:** Revell Ward LLP
**Bankers:** Yorkshire Bank Plc (05-04-69)

| | 31-12-13 | 31-12-12 | 31-12-11 |
|---|---|---|---|
| TO | 17,582,446 | 16,207,053 | 13,890,723 |
| P/L | 3,433,327 | 2,956,584 | 2,523,309 |
| NW | 775,134 | 13,489,009 | 12,727,710 |
| WC | 12,201,791 | 11,764,443 | 9,099,309 |
| Emp. | 165 | 148 | 148 |

DUNS 21-391-1354

## Simply Business

29 St Katherines Street, Northampton, Northamptonshire NN1 2QZ
**Tel:** 01604824300
**Web:** www.simplybusiness.co.uk
**Estd:** 2012
**Line of Business:** Insurance brokers
**Responsibilities**
**Senior:** David Summers *(Contact Centre Manager)*
**US SIC:** 6311 **UK SIC:** 82002
**Employees:** 100

DUNS 51-581-2316

## Simply Cartons Ltd

**(Subsidiary of:** Simply Cartons Holdings Ltd)
Perry Road, Nottingham, Nottinghamshire NG5 1GQ
**Tel:** 01159-422112
**Web:** www.simplycartons.co.uk
**Reg No:** 5862327 **VAT No:** 886377855
**Estd:** 2006 Private Limited Company
**Line of Business:** Packaging activities
**Export Sales:** £77,539
**Issued Capital:** £20,000
**Director:** G Gisborne
**Co. Secretary:** Craig Mather
**Responsibilities**
**Senior:** Pat Guerin *(Warehouse Manager)*
**IT:** Brendon Flanagan *(Computer Manager)*
**US SIC:** 7399, 2752
**UK SIC:** 83954, 47544
**Auditors:** UHY Hacker Young LLP

| | 31-07-14 | 31-07-13 | 30-07-12 |
|---|---|---|---|
| TO | 15,057,356 | 16,005,718 | 17,145,432 |
| P/L | 1,121,078 | 1,803,318 | 2,181,399 |
| NW | 4,477,672 | 4,137,722 | 3,617,044 |
| WC | 1,906,601 | 1,404,913 | 799,878 |
| Emp. | 120 | 118 | 115 |

DUNS 21-315-6946 **Imp**

## Simply Fresh Foods Ltd

**(Subsidiary of:** Wm Morrison Supermarkets P L C)
Chaddock Lane, Worsley, Manchester M28 1DR
**Tel:** 01617037023
**Web:** www.morrisons.com
**Reg No:** 1355438 **Estd:** 1978 Private Limited Company
**Line of Business:** Manufacturers of food products
**Trading Style:** Morrisons
**Issued Capital:** £1,004
**Directors:** M Harrison, J Lill, A Pleasance
**Co. Secretary:** Mark Amsden
**Responsibilities**
**Senior:** Nigel Boyle *(General Manager)*, Kenneth Butt *(Manager)*
**Finance:** Colin Haydock *(Finance Director)*
**Branches:** Simply Fresh Foods Ltd, Bowerbank, Penrith, Cumbria CA10 2NG
**US SIC:** 2099 **UK SIC:** 42399
**Auditors:** CLB Coopers
**Bankers:** National Westminster Bank Plc (60-13-04)

| | 02-02-14 | 03-02-13 | 29-02-12 |
|---|---|---|---|
| TO | 35,772,000 | 36,037,000 | 32,847,000 |
| P/L | 4,936,000 | 4,288,000 | 3,523,000 |
| NW | 13,481,000 | 9,641,000 | 6,336,000 |
| WC | 2,695,000 | (1,932,000) | (4,994,000) |
| Emp. | 262 | 280 | 269 |

## DUNS 42-353-8185    Imp
### Simply Pleasure Ltd
**(Subsidiary of:** Abs Wholesale Ltd)
Stirling Business Park, 6 Nimr, Wimborne,
Dorset BH21 7SH
**Tel:** 01202-868511 **Fax:** 01202868536
**Web:** www.simplypleasure.com
**Reg No:** 4341488 **VAT No:** 797821569
**Estd:** 2001 Private Limited Company
**Line of Business:** Other retail sale in
specialised stores not elsewhere classified
**Trading Style:** Simplypleasure.Com
**Issued Capital:** £165,000
**Directors:** S J Reeves, T M Hemming,
K Hodgson-Egan, T T Branston
**Co. Secretary:** Toby Branston
**Responsibilities**
**Senior:** Kate Hodgson-Ekan *(Director)*
**US SIC:** 5999 **UK SIC:** 65600
**Bankers:** National Westminster Bank Plc
(56-00-35)

| | 31-01-14 | 31-01-13 | 31-01-12 |
|---|---|---|---|
| TO | 10,983,553 | 11,177,902 | 9,994,063 |
| P/L | 835,596 | 952,084 | 264,248 |
| NW | (11,734) | (760,180) | (1,646,529) |
| WC | 1,890,189 | 1,789,583 | 1,205,958 |
| Emp. | 103 | 106 | 108 |

## DUNS 21-066-4670
### Simply Scrumptious
101 Main Street, Bingley, West Yorkshire
BD16 2HT
**Estd:** 1995 Proprietorship
**Line of Business:** Cafes and snack bars
**Proprietor:** Mrs P West
**Responsibilities**
**Senior:** Patricia West *(Proprietor)*
**US SIC:** 5812 **UK SIC:** 66110
**Employees:** 51

## DUNS 73-353-6853
### The Simply Smart Group Ltd
**(Subsidiary of:** Graysons Hospitality Ltd)
Devon House Anchor Street, Chelmsford,
Essex CM2 0GD
**Tel:** 01323580597 **Fax:** 020-8336-7377
**Web:** www.simply-smart-group.com
**Reg No:** 4627313 **Estd:** 2003 Private
Limited Company
**Line of Business:** Catering
**Issued Capital:** £3,481,071
**Directors:** Sir F H Mackay, B H Watson
**Co. Secretary:** Barnaby Watson
**Branches:** The Simply Smart Group Ltd, 11
Keswick Rd, London SW15 2HZ
**US SIC:** 5812 **UK SIC:** 66110

| | 30-06-13 | 30-06-12 | 30-06-11 |
|---|---|---|---|
| TO | N/A | N/A | 500,000 |
| P/L | (94,000) | N/A | 4,675,559 |
| NW | 678,000 | 773,000 | 772,513 |
| WC | (1,003,000) | N/A | (908,325) |
| Emp. | N/A | N/A | 3 |

## DUNS 23-923-7188
### Simply.Com Ltd
**(Subsidiary of:** Marchmont Limited)
Acton House, Perdiswell Park, Worcester,
Worcestershire WR3 7GD
**Fax:** 01684-578346
**Web:** www.simply.com
**Reg No:** 3913788 **Estd:** 1997 Private
Limited Company
**Line of Business:** Data processing
**Trading Style:** Simply.Com Ltd
**Issued Capital:** £1
**Directors:** Miss S L Bratchell, C Patel
**US SIC:** 7374 **UK SIC:** 83940
**Auditors:** Grant Thornton UK LLP
**Bankers:** HSBC Bank plc (40-47-17)

| | 31-12-12 | 31-12-11 |
|---|---|---|
| TA | 1 | 1 |
| NW | 1 | 1 |

## DUNS 22-557-7147
### Simplyhealth Access
**(Subsidiary of:** Simplyhealth Group Ltd)
Hambleden House, Waterloo Court,
Andover, Hampshire SP10 1LQ
**Tel:** 0844-579-2257
**Web:** www.simplyhealth.co.uk
**Reg No:** 0183035 **VAT No:** 631727153
**Estd:** 1922 Private Unlimited Company
**Line of Business:** Other human health
activities
**Trading Style:** Simplyheatlhcare, L H F
Healthplan, H S A Healthcare
**Issued Capital:** £1
**Directors:** J A Wilson, M A Hall, R J Harris,
K S Piggott, B D Kent, Ms R Abdin,
T T Brooke
**Co. Secretary:** James Glover
**Branches:** Simplyhealth Access, Riverside
House, 7 Canal Wharf, Leeds, West
Yorkshire LS11 5WA
**US SIC:** 8091, 6311
**UK SIC:** 95200, 82002
**Auditors:** Deloitte LLP

**Bankers:** National Westminster Bank Plc
(60-01-17)

| | 31-12-13 | 31-12-12 | 31-12-11 |
|---|---|---|---|
| TO | 393,300,000 | 397,000,000 | 333,400,000 |
| P/L | 18,800,000 | (4,300,000) | (700,000) |
| NW | 153,100,000 | 137,600,000 | 148,400,000 |
| WC | 109,300,000 | 118,300,000 | 96,000,000 |
| Emp. | 1,349 | 1,326 | 1,239 |

## DUNS 34-639-7875
### Simplyhealth Group Ltd
Hambleden House, Waterloo Court,
Andover, Hampshire SP10 1LQ
**Tel:** 08009807920 **Fax:** 01264-333650
**Web:** www.simplyhealth.co.uk
**Reg No:** 5445654 **Estd:** 2005 Private
Company Limited By Guarantee
**Line of Business:** Mobility equipment
**Directors:** Ms R Abdin, K S Piggott,
J A Wilson, B D Kent, R J Harris, T T Brooke,
M A Hall
**Co. Secretary:** James Glover
**Responsibilities**
**Senior:** Caroline Lakeman *(PR Manager)*,
Hollie Swift *(Manager)*
**Marketing:** Nicola Bareham *(Digital
Marketing Manager)*, Caroline Lakeman *(PR
Manager)*
**IT:** Caroline Lakeman *(PR Manager)*
**Branches:** Simplyhealth Group Ltd, Alan
Child House, Borden Gates, Andover,
Hampshire SP10 2RT
**US SIC:** 8091, 6399
**UK SIC:** 95200, 82001
**Auditors:** Deloitte & Touche LLP

| | 31-12-13 | 31-12-12 | 31-12-11 |
|---|---|---|---|
| TO | 393,300,000 | 397,000,000 | 333,400,000 |
| P/L | 16,100,000 | 4,300,000 | (5,600,000) |
| NW | 160,400,000 | 138,700,000 | 131,200,000 |
| WC | 113,400,000 | 114,100,000 | 67,000,000 |
| Emp. | 1,715 | 1,668 | 1,275 |

## DUNS 23-827-3366
### Simplyhealth Ltd
**(Subsidiary of:** Simplyhealth Group Ltd)
Hambleden House, Waterloo Court,
Andover, Hampshire SP10 1LQ
**Tel:** 08001380764 **Fax:** 01264333650
**Web:** www.totallyactive.co.uk
**Reg No:** 3819304 **Estd:** 1914 Private
Limited Company
**Line of Business:** Other human health
activities
**Issued Capital:** £1
**Directors:** B D Kent, Mrs R Abdin,
J A Wilson
**Co. Secretary:** James Gloveer
**US SIC:** 8091 **UK SIC:** 95200

| | 31-12-13 | 31-12-12 | 31-12-11 |
|---|---|---|---|
| TA | 1 | 1 | 1 |
| NW | 1 | 1 | 1 |

## DUNS 34-750-3364
### Simplyhealth People Ltd
**(Subsidiary of:** Simplyhealth Group Ltd)
Hambleden House, Waterloo Court,
Andover, Hampshire SP10 1LQ
**Tel:** 01264343525
**Reg No:** 5551895 **Estd:** 2005 Private
Limited Company
**Line of Business:** Other human health
activities
**Issued Capital:** £1
**Directors:** Ms R Abdin, J A Wilson, B D Kent
**Co. Secretary:** James Glover
**US SIC:** 8091 **UK SIC:** 95200
**Bankers:** National Westminster Bank Plc
(53-70-32)

| | 31-12-13 | 31-12-12 | 31-12-11 |
|---|---|---|---|
| TO | 49,785,330 | 46,735,390 | 41,899,392 |
| P/L | 253,388 | (9,347,843) | (11,493,692) |
| NW | (18,538,919) | (18,675,216) | (9,237,170) |
| WC | (17,300,902) | (18,675,216) | (9,188,698) |
| Emp. | 1,393 | 1,358 | 1,265 |

## DUNS 22-227-7795
### Simpsinns Ltd
152a High Street, Irvine, Ayrshire KA12 8AN
**Tel:** 01294212632
**Web:** www.firststepsirvine.co.uk
**Reg No:** 0220884SC **Estd:** 2001 Private
Limited Company
**Line of Business:** Hotels
**Issued Capital:** £2
**Director:** M G Simpson
**Co. Secretary:** Ms Karen Simpson
**US SIC:** 7011 **UK SIC:** 66500
**Bankers:** Allied Irish Bank (gb) (83-91-06)

| | 31-07-13 | 31-07-12 | 31-07-11 |
|---|---|---|---|
| TO | 4,745,002 | 4,011,302 | 2,514,890 |
| P/L | 88,031 | 461,965 | 441,569 |
| NW | 2,942,993 | 2,643,482 | 2,298,855 |
| WC | (675,679) | (533,474) | 38,515 |
| Emp. | 181 | 143 | 99 |

## DUNS 23-622-6379
### Simpson & Marwick
Albany House, 58 Albany Street, Edinburgh,
Midlothian EH1 3QR
**Tel:** 0131-557-1545
**Web:** www.simpmarllp.com
**Estd:** 1886 Partnership
**Line of Business:** Solicitors
**Partners:** R Loudan, Ms A Kentish, B Smith,
A Cowan
**Branches:** Simpson & Marwick, 19B Howe
Street, EH3 6TE Edinburgh
**US SIC:** 8111 **UK SIC:** 83500
**Auditors:** Baker Tilly Business Services Ltd

| | 30-04-13 |
|---|---|
| TO | 21,229,551 |
| P/L | 9,237,449 |
| NW | 6,325,126 |
| WC | 5,391,511 |
| Emp. | 160 |

## DUNS 34-828-0194
### Simpson Highview Ltd
Simpsons Garden Centre, Inshes, Inverness,
Inverness-Shire IV2 5BA
**Web:** www.simpsonsgardencentre.co.uk
**Reg No:** 0293358SC **Estd:** 2005 Private
Limited Company
**Line of Business:** Other retail sale in
specialised stores not elsewhere classified
**Issued Capital:** £1
**Director:** A I Simpson
**US SIC:** 5999 **UK SIC:** 65600
**Auditors:** Johnston Carmichael

| | 31-10-13 | 31-10-12 | 31-10-11 |
|---|---|---|---|
| TO | 4,465,929 | 3,940,019 | 3,514,375 |
| P/L | 264,909 | 245,865 | 202,980 |
| NW | 2,296,377 | 550,832 | 395,359 |
| WC | (523,305) | (727,554) | (573,084) |
| Emp. | 85 | 79 | 65 |

## DUNS 21-566-1307    Imp-Exp
### The Simpson Label Co Ltd
**(Subsidiary of:** Nsd International Operations
B.V.)
Mayfield Industrial Estate, Dalkeith,
Midlothian EH22 4AF
**Tel:** 01316-542800
**Web:** www.nsdintemational.co.uk
**Reg No:** 0009731SC **VAT No:** 268867590
**Estd:** 2010 Private Limited Company
**Line of Business:** Labelling stamping and
imprinting equipment
**Export Markets:** Europe
**Trading Style:** Nsd International
**Issued Capital:** £400,000
**Director:** A Visser
**Co. Secretary:** Maclay Murray & Spens Llp
**Responsibilities**
**Senior:** Euan Martin *(Manager)*, Neil Mills
*(Manager)*
**Finance:** Euan Martin *(Manager)*
**Marketing:** Euan Martin *(Manager)*
**Sales:** Euan Martin *(Manager)*
**IT:** Ron Bagnall *(Systems Manager)*
**Health & Safety:** Neil Briggs *(Production
Manager)*
**Facilities:** Euan Martin *(Manager)*
**Purchasing:** Neil Briggs *(Production
Manager)*
**Engineering:** Neil Briggs *(Production
Manager)*
**US SIC:** 3551, 2752
**UK SIC:** 32441, 47544
**Auditors:** BDO LLP
**Bankers:** Bank Of Scotland (80-06-29)

| | 31-12-13 | 31-12-12 | 31-12-11 |
|---|---|---|---|
| TA | 4,125,970 | 3,877,821 | 3,777,405 |
| NW | 1,746,064 | 1,598,609 | 1,572,426 |
| WC | 1,002,505 | 1,311,101 | 1,241,806 |

## DUNS 39-687-6914    Exp
### Simpson Mahoney Parrock Ltd
Castle House, Tunbridge Wells, Kent TN1
1DB
**Tel:** 01892-548282 **Fax:** 01892-538996
**Web:** www.smp.uk.com
**Reg No:** 2145924 **Estd:** 1983 Private
Limited Company
**Line of Business:** Business and
management consultancy activities not
elsewhere classified
**Export Markets:** Europe.
**Trading Style:** S M P
**Issued Capital:** £91
**Principals:** C J Simpson *(Managing)*,
S N Mahoney *(Managing)*, C Carter,
M Shellaker
**Co. Secretary:** Simon Mahoney
**US SIC:** 7392 **UK SIC:** 83951
**Auditors:** Leigh Carr
**Bankers:** National Westminster Bank Plc
(56-00-33)

| | 31-03-14 | 30-09-12 | 30-03-11 |
|---|---|---|---|
| TO | 7,442,338 | 7,876,598 | 6,623,277 |
| P/L | 158,816 | 273,907 | 559,730 |
| NW | 3,016,550 | 3,062,092 | 2,570,227 |
| WC | 2,960,579 | 2,983,101 | 2,675,803 |
| Emp. | 47 | 44 | 48 |

## DUNS 34-689-4939
### Simpson Millar Llp
27 St Pauls Street, Leeds, West Yorkshire
LS1 2JG
**Tel:** 08708551200
**Web:** www.simpsonmillar.co.uk
**Reg No:** 0313936OC **VAT No:** 235934940
**Estd:** 1880
**Line of Business:** Solicitors
**Trading Style:** Simpson Millar Solicitors
**Responsibilities**
**Senior:** Emma Costin *(Partner - Head of
Industrial D)*, Alex Dunne *(Partner -
Commercial Law)*, Adrian Fawden *(Partner -
Personal Injury)*, Ben Gent *(Partner -
Medical Negligence C)*, Liz Higgins *(General
Manager)*, Ruth Magee *(Partner - Personal
Injury Clai)*, Bryan Nott *(Partner - Personal
Injury)*, Emma Pearmaine *(Partner - Head of
Family Law)*, Lisa Sheldon *(Partner -
Personal Injury Clai)*
**Finance:** Hanah Dickinson *(Senior Finance
Administrator)*, Anthony Elston *(Partner,
Finance Director)*
**Sales:** Deborah Powell *(Partner -
Commercial Property)*
**Branches:** Simpson Millar Llp, 20 Church
Road, Bristol, Avon BS5 9JA
**US SIC:** 8111 **UK SIC:** 83500
**Auditors:** Sagars Accountants Ltd
**Bankers:** Yorkshire Bank Plc (05-00-20)

| | 30-06-13 | 30-06-12 | 30-06-11 |
|---|---|---|---|
| TO | 16,926,363 | 16,960,600 | 14,633,103 |
| P/L | N/A | 96,327 | 49,358 |
| NW | (20,743) | (11,750) | (58,750) |
| WC | 5,944,235 | 4,853,742 | 3,554,057 |
| Emp. | 249 | 254 | 253 |

## DUNS 28-872-4057
### Simpson Print Ltd
Rutherford Road, Stephenson Industrial
Estate, Washington, Tyne and Wear NE37
3HX
**Tel:** 01914161579 **Fax:** 01914-198-660
**Web:** www.simpsonprint.com
**Reg No:** 1061464 **VAT No:** 177205854
**Estd:** 1972 Private Limited Company
**Line of Business:** Printers general
**Trading Style:** Simpson Group
**Issued Capital:** £364,473
**Principals:** M W Simpson *(Managing)*,
J Reithinger, W M Mcnally
**Co. Secretary:** John Quinn
**Responsibilities**
**Purchasing:** Ray McNally *(Purchasing
Manager)*
**US SIC:** 2794, 7399
**UK SIC:** 47545, 83954
**Auditors:** KPMG LLP

| | 31-10-13 | 31-10-12 | 31-10-11 |
|---|---|---|---|
| TO | 12,157,011 | 12,697,151 | 12,967,410 |
| P/L | 550,163 | 79,572 | 328,913 |
| NW | 904,753 | 441,727 | 439,127 |
| WC | (1,898,881) | (2,431,239) | (2,283,993) |
| Emp. | 148 | 159 | 147 |

## DUNS 21-242-5870    Imp-Exp
### Simpson Ready Foods Ltd
Stretford Road, Urmston, Manchester M41
9WH
**Tel:** 0161-865-2241
**Web:** www.simpsonsfoods.co.uk
**Reg No:** 0114121 **VAT No:** 146501976
**Estd:** 1911 Private Limited Company
**Line of Business:** Manufacture of other food
products not elsewhere classified
**Export Markets:** European Union (E U);
Canada
**Export Sales:** £28,062
**Issued Capital:** £775,000
**Principals:** W J Simpson *(Managing)*,
D A Page, M W Simpson, L M Simpson
**Co. Secretary:** Andrew Simpson
**Responsibilities**
**IT:** Craig Simpson *(IT Manager)*
**Purchasing:** Alex Pembroke *(Buyer)*
**US SIC:** 2099, 5149
**UK SIC:** 42399, 61700
**Auditors:** Hacker Young
**Bankers:** National Westminster Bank Plc
(01-08-52)

| | 31-12-12 | 31-12-11 | 31-12-10 |
|---|---|---|---|
| TO | 11,275,552 | 15,965,570 | 12,617,353 |
| P/L | (317,041) | (173,351) | 171,695 |
| NW | 2,104,772 | 2,413,591 | 2,585,396 |
| WC | 462,362 | 607,783 | 486,504 |
| Emp. | 101 | 98 | 98 |

## DUNS 23-733-9635    Imp-Exp
### Simpson Strong-Tie International Inc
**(Subsidiary of:** Simpson Manufacturing Co.
Inc.)
Cardinal Point, Winchester Road, Tamworth,
Staffordshire B78 3HG
**Tel:** 01827-255600 **Fax:** 01827-255616
**Web:** www.strongtie.com
**Reg No:** 0017716FC **VAT No:** 642822150
**Estd:** 1998 Foreign Company

**Line of Business:** Manufacture of other wearing apparel and accessories not elsewhere classified
**Directors:** B Simpson, M Herbert, Ms K Colonias, P Kingsfather, B Magstadt
**Co. Secretary:** Thomas Fitzmyers
**Responsibilities**
**Senior:** phillip park (Manager)
**Branches:** Montrose Ho, Montrose Rd (Tel No: 01245-450450, Fax No: 01245-461850), Chelmsford
**US SIC:** 3999 **UK SIC:** 49590

DUNS 23-639-3625     Imp
## Simpson Thacher & Bartlett
Citypoint, 1 Ropemaker Street, Moorgate, London EC2Y 9HU
**Web:** www.stblaw.com
**Estd:** 1878 Partnership
**Line of Business:** Solicitors
**Trading Style:** S T B
**Principals:** A Clein, D R Brand, G Conway (Partner), M Wolfson (Partner), W Looney (Partner), W Dougherty (Partner)
**Responsibilities**
**Senior:** Karleen Rainey (Office Manager)
**US SIC:** 8111 **UK SIC:** 83500
**Employees:** 85

DUNS 73-714-6340
## Simpson (York) Holdings Ltd
10 Hassacarr Close, York, North Yorkshire YO19 5SN
**Tel:** 01904562400 **Fax:** 01904-562462
**Web:** www.simpsonyork.co.uk
**Reg No:** 2916899 **Estd:** 1994 Private Limited Company
**Line of Business:** Other construction work involving special trades
**Issued Capital:** £500,000
**Principals:** R C Gatenby (Chairman and Managing), I R Hildreth, A Gatenby
**Co. Secretary:** John Pursehouse
**Responsibilities**
**Senior:** Beryl Gatenby (Manager)
**Finance:** Matthew Skelhorn (IT & Accounts Manager)
**Marketing:** Stephanie Burns (Marketing Coordinator)
**IT:** Matthew Skelhorn (IT & Accounts Manager)
**HR:** Sarah Wetton (HR Manager)
**US SIC:** 1799, 1541
**UK SIC:** 50000, 50100
**Auditors:** Armstrong Watson
**Bankers:** HSBC Bank plc (40-27-15)

| | 31-12-13 | 31-12-12 | 31-12-11 |
|---|---|---|---|
| TO | 73,656,363 | 93,315,815 | 73,492,950 |
| P/L | 897,855 | 2,180,635 | 1,960,014 |
| NW | 7,633,609 | 7,312,695 | 6,740,954 |
| WC | 6,211,039 | 5,929,128 | 6,165,410 |
| Emp. | 186 | 200 | 209 |

DUNS 50-442-9481
## Simpsons Estate Agents Ltd
Wix Hill House, Epsom Road, West Horsley, Leatherhead, Surrey KT24 6DY
**Web:** www.curchods.com
**Reg No:** 2430843 **Estd:** 1960 Private Limited Company
**Line of Business:** Real estate agencies
**Trading Style:** Curchods, Curchods Estate Agents, Burns & Webber, Curchods Land & New Homes Department
**Issued Capital:** £85,000
**Director:** A C Dewar
**Co. Secretary:** John Slatter
**Branches:** Simpsons Estate Agents Ltd, 12 Bishopsmead Parade, East Horsley, Leatherhead, Surrey KT24 6RT
**US SIC:** 6531 **UK SIC:** 83400
**Auditors:** Kingston Smith LLP
**Bankers:** Lloyds TSB Bank plc (30-99-09)

| | 30-04-14 | 30-04-13 | 30-04-12 |
|---|---|---|---|
| TO | 14,131,662 | N/A | 10,786,664 |
| P/L | 3,020,746 | 1,650,743 | 1,616,163 |
| NW | 1,995,586 | 959,752 | (280,039) |
| WC | 1,712,636 | 535,969 | (689,194) |
| Emp. | 130 | 143 | 149 |

DUNS 29-761-3093
## Simpsons Garage (Gt. Yarmouth) Ltd
Suffolk Road, Great Yarmouth, Norfolk NR31 0LN
**Tel:** 01493-601696 **Fax:** 01493-657447
**Web:** www.simpsonsmotorgroup.com
**Reg No:** 2022816 **VAT No:** 442959226
**Estd:** 1986 Private Limited Company
**Line of Business:** Sale of new motor vehicles
**Trading Style:** Simpsons Motor Caravan Centre
**Issued Capital:** £2,000
**Directors:** Ms P F Woodgreaves, Ms B J Crick, A D Aldis
**Co. Secretary:** Mark Mummery
**Branches:** Simpsons Garage (Gt. Yarmouth) Ltd, Unit 1, Suffolk Road, Great Yarmouth, Norfolk NR31 0LN

**US SIC:** 5511, 7539
**UK SIC:** 65100, 67100
**Auditors:** Tubbs Son Giles & Co
**Bankers:** HSBC Bank plc (40-30-28)

| | 31-12-13 | 31-12-12 | 31-12-11 |
|---|---|---|---|
| TO | 11,997,842 | 11,615,598 | 11,123,469 |
| P/L | 46,227 | 9,878 | 21,036 |
| NW | 2,664,495 | 2,629,233 | 2,622,263 |
| WC | 1,979,956 | 1,951,228 | 1,944,372 |
| Emp. | 47 | 46 | 43 |

DUNS 21-258-1540     Imp-Exp
## Simpsons Malt Ltd
Tweed Valley Maltings, Tweedside Trading Estate, Berwick-Upon-Tweed, Northumberland TD15 2UZ
**Web:** www.simpsonsmalt.co.uk
**Reg No:** 0153026 **Estd:** 1919 Private Limited Company
**Line of Business:** Agricultural service activities; landscape gardening
**Export Markets:** Western Europe, Norway, Germany, Malaysia, Cameroon, Thailand, Japan, Africa.
**Export Sales:** £9,676,000
**Issued Capital:** £1,386,300
**Principals:** S B Simpson (Chairman), R E Simpson, S C Rowley, P L Simpson, T R Mccreath, D R Mccreath, P S Walsh, Sir J J Good
**Co. Secretary:** Graeme Hogg
**Responsibilities**
**Senior:** Janet Simpson (Director)
**Branches:** Simpsons Malt Ltd, Ferrybridge Rd, Pontefract, West Yorkshire WF8 2NU
**US SIC:** 0729, 2099, 6711
**UK SIC:** 01003, 42399, 83962
**Auditors:** PricewaterhouseCoopers LLP
**Bankers:** Bank Of Scotland (12-12-57)

| | 31-12-13 | 31-12-12 | 31-12-11 |
|---|---|---|---|
| TO | 157,891,000 | 157,570,000 | 134,596,000 |
| P/L | 7,467,000 | 9,048,000 | 8,810,000 |
| NW | 54,425,000 | 49,377,000 | 43,919,000 |
| WC | 32,818,000 | 33,707,000 | 31,914,000 |
| Emp. | 205 | 207 | 207 |

DUNS 52-553-6140
## Sims Group Uk Ltd
(**Subsidiary of:** Sims Metal Management Limited)
Long Marston, Stratford-Upon-Avon, Warwickshire CV37 8AQ
**Tel:** 01252334078 **Fax:** 01789720940
**Web:** www.simsmm.co.uk
**Reg No:** 3242331 **VAT No:** 655132744
**Estd:** 1996 Private Limited Company
**Line of Business:** Wholesale of waste and scrap
**Export Sales:** £495,447,000
**Trading Style:** Sims Metal Management, Sims Recycling Solutions
**Issued Capital:** £145,397,871
**Directors:** P M Wright, P R Bird, S M Skurnac, D M Williams
**Co. Secretary:** David Williams
**Responsibilities**
**Sales:** Kevin Fitzpatrick (Commercial Manager)
**IT:** Peter Barclay (ICT Director)
**Branches:** Sims Group Uk Ltd, Birchwood Lane, Somercotes, Alfreton, Derbyshire DE55 4NE
**US SIC:** 5093, 7379
**UK SIC:** 62200, 83940
**Auditors:** PricewaterhouseCoopers LLP
**Bankers:** Barclays Bank Plc (20-60-58)

| | 30-06-14 | 30-06-13 | 30-06-12 |
|---|---|---|---|
| TO | 684,376,000 | 747,708,000 | 824,810,000 |
| P/L | (68,365,000) | (98,134,000) | (83,483,000) |
| NW | 34,071,000 | 15,430,000 | 109,257,000 |
| WC | (49,519,000) | (128,201,000) | (30,799,000) |
| Emp. | 1,106 | 1,285 | 1,346 |

DUNS 21-607-2713
## Sims Recycling Solutions Billingham Weee Recycling Plant
Macklin Avenue, Cowpen Lane Industrial Estate, Billingham, Cleveland TS23 4BY
**Tel:** 01642373080
**Web:** www.simsrecycling.co.uk
**Estd:** 2011 Proprietorship
**Line of Business:** Recycling
**Proprietor:** P Thorman
**US SIC:** 3031 **UK SIC:** 48123
**Employees:** 65

DUNS 21-879-5006
## Sims Recycling Solutions Newport Weee Recycling Plant
Alexandra Docks South Dock, Newport, Gwent NP20 2WE
**Tel:** 01633261959
**Web:** www.simsrecyclingsolutions.co.uk
**Estd:** 2012
**Line of Business:** Recycling
**Responsibilities**
**Senior:** Paul Wake (Regional Manager)
**US SIC:** 3031 **UK SIC:** 48123
**Employees:** 100

DUNS 34-629-6445     Imp-Exp
## Sims Recycling Solutions Uk Ltd
(**Subsidiary of:** Sims Metal Management Limited)
Lochside Industrial Estate, Irongray Road, Dumfries, Dumfriesshire DG2 0NR
**Tel:** 01387-723000
**Web:** www.simsmm.com
**Reg No:** 0141132SC **VAT No:** 612483654
**Estd:** 1992 Private Limited Company
**Line of Business:** Recycling
**Export Markets:** Worldwide
**Issued Capital:** £250,000
**Director:** D M Williams
**Co. Secretary:** David Williams
**Responsibilities**
**Senior:** Graham Davy (Manager)
**Marketing:** Caroline McDonald (Marketing Manager)
**IT:** Caird Hay (IT Manager)
**Facilities:** Tom Weems (Facilities Manager)
**US SIC:** 3341, 3031
**UK SIC:** 22470, 48123
**Auditors:** PricewaterhouseCoopers LLP
**Bankers:** The Royal Bank Of Scotland Plc (83-18-07)

| | 30-06-14 | 30-06-13 | 30-06-12 |
|---|---|---|---|
| TA | 1,334,000 | 1,334,000 | 1,334,000 |
| NW | 1,334,000 | 1,334,000 | 1,334,000 |

DUNS 28-914-7894     Imp
## Simulation Systems Ltd
Unit 12 Market Industrial Estate, Yatton, Bristol, Avon BS49 4RF
**Tel:** 01934-838803
**Web:** www.simulation-systems.co.uk
**Reg No:** 1439838 **VAT No:** 303008717
**Estd:** 1979 Private Limited Company
**Line of Business:** Manufacturers of pcs
**Issued Capital:** £1,944
**Principals:** A W Griffin (Managing), L C Thompson
**Co. Secretary:** Mrs Deborah Derebag
**Responsibilities**
**Finance:** Debbie Thompson (Finance Director)
**Marketing:** Dave Harris (Sales & Marketing Manager)
**Sales:** Dave Harris (Sales & Marketing Manager)
**HR:** Sharon Adams (Human Resources Manager)
**Health & Safety:** Tony Brook (Health & Safety Officer)
**US SIC:** 3573 **UK SIC:** 33020
**Auditors:** David Cottrell & Co
**Bankers:** Barclays Bank Plc (20-94-74)

| | 31-03-14 | 31-03-13 | 31-03-12 |
|---|---|---|---|
| TO | 11,762,011 | 9,641,775 | 6,638,086 |
| P/L | 863,451 | 252,213 | 488,704 |
| NW | 958,958 | 1,639,137 | 1,215,806 |
| WC | 1,451,231 | 1,673,458 | 2,303,099 |
| Emp. | 127 | 113 | 114 |

DUNS 21-607-8360     Imp-Exp
## Sinclair & Rush Ltd
(**Subsidiary of:** Sinclair & Rush Inc.)
Unit 11-13, Twenty Twenty Industrial Estate St, Laurence Avenue, Maidstone, Kent ME16 0LL
**Tel:** 01622-693200 **Fax:** 01622-693201
**Web:** www.sinclair-rush.co.uk
**Reg No:** 0679110 **VAT No:** 203581884
**Estd:** 1960 Private Limited Company
**Line of Business:** Manufacturers of plastic products
**Export Markets:** Europe
**Trading Style:** Stockcap, Gripworks
**Issued Capital:** £560
**Directors:** P A Boulton, J J Henry, B Philip, P T Gardner
**Responsibilities**
**Senior:** Shane Bone (Works Manager), Vincent Gorguze (Manager)
**IT:** Shane Bone (Works Manager)
**Health & Safety:** Shane Bone (Works Manager)
**Facilities:** Shane Bone (Works Manager)
**Operations:** Shane Bone (Works Manager)
**Engineering:** Shane Bone (Works Manager)
**Branches:** Sinclair & Rush Ltd, 102-120 North La, Aldershot, Hampshire GU12 4QN
**US SIC:** 2821 **UK SIC:** 25140
**Auditors:** Reeves & Co Llp
**Bankers:** National Westminster Bank Plc (53-81-51)

| | 31-10-13 | 31-10-12 | 31-10-11 |
|---|---|---|---|
| TA | 1,269,470 | 1,148,367 | 1,151,739 |
| NW | 972,625 | 701,111 | 491,339 |
| WC | 906,996 | 909,774 | 921,545 |

DUNS 42-449-2838     Imp-Exp
## Sinclair Animal & Household Care Ltd
(**Subsidiary of:** Stichting Administratiekantoor Beaphar Beheer)
Ropery Road, Gainsborough, Lincolnshire DN21 2QB
**Tel:** 01427-810231 **Fax:** 01427-810837
**Web:** www.sinclair-sahc.com
**Reg No:** 4436927 **Estd:** 2002 Private Limited Company
**Line of Business:** Manufacture of basic pharmaceutical products
**Export Sales:** £687,723
**Issued Capital:** £435,523
**Directors:** D Aa, J H Aa
**Co. Secretary:** Johannes Rodijk
**Responsibilities**
**Senior:** Giles Sullivan (Warehouse Manager)
**HR:** Kieron Dunne (Operations Manager)
**Operations:** Kieron Dunne (Operations Manager)
**Purchasing:** Kieron Dunne (Operations Manager)
**Engineering:** Kieron Dunne (Operations Manager)
**US SIC:** 2834, 3999
**UK SIC:** 25700, 49590
**Bankers:** Lloyds TSB Bank plc (30-97-44)

| | 31-12-13 | 31-12-12 | 31-12-11 |
|---|---|---|---|
| TO | 7,410,141 | 11,658,095 | 12,636,451 |
| P/L | 631,382 | 837,693 | 476,954 |
| NW | 4,619,542 | 4,612,935 | 3,994,513 |
| WC | 2,627,542 | 2,570,291 | 1,839,959 |
| Emp. | 77 | 81 | 79 |

DUNS 21-232-9007
## Sinclair Collis Ltd
(**Subsidiary of:** Imperial Tobacco Group Plc)
Four Ashes, Wolverhampton, West Midlands WV10 7DZ
**Tel:** 01902797272
**Web:** www.sinclaircollis.co.uk
**Reg No:** 0107677 **VAT No:** 176042667
**Estd:** 1856 Private Limited Company
**Line of Business:** Tobacconists' suppliers
**Issued Capital:** £250,000
**Principals:** K R Pascall (Financial), P Prasad, E Walsh, M Goodall, T M Williams, G W Wood, Mrs J Bacon
**Responsibilities**
**HR:** Wendy Howard (Human Resources Manager)
**Branches:** Sinclair Collis Ltd, Unit 20, Knightsridge East, Livingston, West Lothian EH54 8RA
**US SIC:** 5194, 5963
**UK SIC:** 61700, 65600
**Auditors:** PricewaterhouseCoopers
**Bankers:** National Westminster Bank Plc (56-00-40)

| | 30-09-13 | 30-09-12 | 30-09-11 |
|---|---|---|---|
| TO | 27,491,000 | 15,937,000 | 23,063,000 |
| P/L | (4,582,000) | (5,595,000) | (3,591,000) |
| NW | (3,152,000) | 1,629,000 | 7,370,000 |
| WC | (5,501,000) | (536,000) | 6,169,000 |
| Emp. | 95 | 127 | 141 |

DUNS 28-938-6393
## Sinclair Garages (Bridgend) Ltd
(**Subsidiary of:** Sinclair Motor Holdings Ltd)
Celtic Court, Tremains Road, Bridgend, Mid Glamorgan CF31 1TZ
**Tel:** 01656664241
**Web:** www.sinclairgroup.co.uk
**Reg No:** 1567551 **Estd:** 1984 Private Limited Company
**Line of Business:** Car dealers (new & used)
**Issued Capital:** £100
**Principals:** G S Sinclair (Managing), A J Sinclair, A G Potts, J M Sinclair
**Co. Secretary:** Mrs Eleanora Sinclair
**Responsibilities**
**Senior:** Craig Godfrey (Branch Manager)
**Marketing:** Katie Mills (Marketing Manager)
**Branches:** Sinclair Garages (Bridgend) Ltd, Tremains Road, Bridgend, Mid Glamorgan CF31 1TZ
**US SIC:** 5511 **UK SIC:** 65100
**Auditors:** HWCA Ltd
**Bankers:** Barclays Bank Plc (20-84-41)

| | 31-12-13 | 31-12-12 | 31-12-11 |
|---|---|---|---|
| TO | 36,079,244 | 30,373,709 | 28,145,213 |
| P/L | 451,324 | 276,999 | 237,099 |
| NW | 3,991,747 | 3,690,416 | 3,448,066 |
| WC | 1,163,543 | 906,150 | 704,241 |
| Emp. | 63 | 73 | 74 |

DUNS 22-761-3122
## Sinclair Garages Ltd
(**Subsidiary of:** Sinclair Motor Holdings Ltd)
Gorseinon Road, Penllergaer, Swansea, West Glamorgan SA4 9GW
**Web:** www.sinclairgroup.co.uk
**Reg No:** 1342890 **Estd:** 2002 Private Limited Company
**Line of Business:** Garage related services
**Trading Style:** Sinclair Volkswogan

**Issued Capital:** £100
**Principals:** G S Sinclair (*Chairman and Managing*), A J Sinclair, J M Sinclair, A G Potts
**Co. Secretary:** Mrs Eleanora Sinclair
**Responsibilities**
**IT:** Stewart Chatman (*IT Manager*)
**HR:** Judith Sadler (*Human Resources Manager*)
**Facilities:** Clive Hopkins (*Brand Manager*)
**Branches:** Sinclair Garages Ltd, Gorseinon Road, Swansea, West Glamorgan SA4 9GW
**US SIC:** 5511, 7539
**UK SIC:** 65100, 67100
**Auditors:** BKR Mullens Robinson
**Bankers:** Barclays Bank Plc (20-84-41)

|  | 31-12-13 | 31-12-12 | 31-12-11 |
|---|---|---|---|
| TO | 96,039,536 | 82,467,750 | 67,076,015 |
| P/L | 1,546,108 | 343,022 | (78,453) |
| NW | 7,167,942 | 5,876,981 | 5,634,392 |
| WC | 937,695 | 724,415 | 689,486 |
| Emp. | 197 | 190 | 186 |

**DUNS 50-573-1786**
## Sinclair Garages (Newport) Ltd.
(**Subsidiary of:** Sinclair Motor Holdings Ltd)
Mulberry Drive, Cardiff Gate Business Park, Pontprennau, Cardiff, South Glamorgan CF23 8RS
**Tel:** 02920542400
**Web:** www.mercedes.co.uk
**Reg No:** 2521128　**Estd:** 1993 Private Limited Company
**Line of Business:** Car dealers (used)
**Trading Style:** S G Newport
**Issued Capital:** £1,200,000
**Principals:** G S Sinclair (*Managing*), A G Potts, A J Sinclair, Mrs E K Sinclair
**Responsibilities**
**Senior:** Nick Payne (*Dual Principal*)
**Marketing:** Dean Adams (*Marketing Manager*)
**Branches:** Sinclair Garages (Newport) Ltd., Pentwyn Road, Pontypool, Sheffield, Gwent CF2 7XH
**US SIC:** 5511, 7539
**UK SIC:** 65100, 67100
**Auditors:** Mullens Robinson
**Bankers:** Barclays Bank Plc (20-84-41)

|  | 31-12-13 | 31-12-12 | 31-12-11 |
|---|---|---|---|
| TO | 103,073,497 | 98,720,549 | 79,768,215 |
| P/L | 1,048,201 | 1,740,516 | 1,304,994 |
| NW | 9,221,935 | 8,461,588 | 7,463,990 |
| WC | 5,710,171 | 4,232,659 | 1,775,319 |
| Emp. | 142 | 166 | 177 |

**DUNS 76-987-6582**　　　　　　**Exp**
## Sinclair International Ltd
(**Subsidiary of:** Gulftech International Inc)
Bowthorpe Employment Area Jarrold Way, Norwich, Norfolk NR5 9JD
**Tel:** 01603-726400　**Fax:** 01603-726401
**Web:** www.sinclair-intl.com
**Reg No:** 2645817　**Estd:** 1992 Private Limited Company
**Line of Business:** Labelling stamping and imprinting equipment
**Export Markets:** Africa, North America, South America
**Issued Capital:** £1,000
**Directors:** W F Hallier, M Flug, G T Gordon, J Flug, D C Burall, D M Bejarano, E I Teranchi, M F Dacey
**Co. Secretary:** Andrew Crowe
**Responsibilities**
**Senior:** Mark Lancy (*Vice President Of Manufacturin*)
**US SIC:** 3551　**UK SIC:** 32441
**Auditors:** Deloitte & Touche
**Bankers:** Barclays Bank Plc (20-00-00)

|  | 31-12-13 | 31-12-12 | 31-12-11 |
|---|---|---|---|
| TO | 37,138,000 | 37,113,000 | 36,878,000 |
| P/L | 8,561,000 | 8,136,000 | 8,466,000 |
| NW | 12,746,000 | 11,911,000 | 10,001,000 |
| WC | 5,346,000 | 5,526,000 | 4,569,000 |
| Emp. | 133 | 132 | 136 |

**DUNS 23-824-5901**　　　　　　**Imp**
## Sinclair Is Pharma Plc
Whitfield Court, 1st Floor, London W1T 2RQ
**Tel:** 02074676920　**Fax:** 02074676930
**Web:** www.sinclairispharma.com
**Reg No:** 3816616　**Estd:** 1999 Private Limited Company
**Line of Business:** Wholesale of pharmaceutical goods
**Export Sales:** £53,559,000
**Issued Capital:** £4,349,148
**Directors:** J Tschudin, C P Spooner, C Foucher, J S Thompson, G Cook
**Co. Secretary:** Miss Jayne Burrell
**Responsibilities**
**Senior:** Natalie Dristoll (*Office Manager*), Stephen Redman (*Manager*)
**Sales:** Nairn McMaster (*Business Development Director*)
**US SIC:** 5122　**UK SIC:** 61800
**Auditors:** PricewaterhouseCoopers LLP

**Bankers:** Barclays Bank Plc (20-53-30)

|  | 30-06-14 | 30-06-13 | 30-06-12 |
|---|---|---|---|
| TO | 63,559,000 | 55,378,000 | 51,424,000 |
| P/L | (4,441,000) | (16,977,000) | (9,774,000) |
| NW | (123,624,000) | (10,821,000) | (15,347,000) |
| WC | 12,893,000 | 5,817,000 | 6,190,000 |
| Emp. | 161 | 144 | 132 |

**DUNS 52-004-5741**
## Sinclair Knight Merz (Europe) Ltd
(**Subsidiary of:** Jacobs Australia Holdings Company Pty. Ltd.)
Metro, 33 Trafford Road, Salford, Lancashire M5 3NN
**Tel:** 02077592600　**Fax:** 02077592601
**Web:** www.skmconsulting.com
**Reg No:** 3371550　**Estd:** 2011 Private Limited Company
**Line of Business:** Other engineering activities
**Trading Style:** S K M En, S K M
**Issued Capital:** £62,606,968
**Directors:** C A Wildermuth, L Power, R S Duff, J C Doyle, J R Pike
**Co. Secretary:** Michael Norris
**Responsibilities**
**Senior:** Shahram Hemmati (*Manager*), Gunninder Katari (*Manager*), Geoffrey Linke (*Manager*), Santo Rizzuto (*Manager*)
**Admin:** Nicola Carr (*Office Manager*)
**Operations:** Tim Boyle (*Chief Operations Officer*)
**Branches:** Sinclair Knight Merz (Europe) Ltd, Alberton Ho, 30 St Marys Parsonage, Manchester M3 2WJ
**US SIC:** 8911　**UK SIC:** 83701
**Auditors:** KPMG LLP

|  | 23-06-13 | 24-06-12 | 26-06-11 |
|---|---|---|---|
| TO | 72,475,000 | 69,087,000 | 48,400,000 |
| P/L | (5,051,000) | (2,219,000) | (5,825,000) |
| NW | (485,000) | 1,185,000 | (571,000) |
| WC | 4,112,000 | (8,690,000) | 6,753,000 |
| Emp. | 788 | 782 | 601 |

**DUNS 50-323-7992**
## Sinclair Ltd
37 Warren Street, London W1T 6AD
**Tel:** 01452840771　**Fax:** 01452-840315
**Web:** www.sinclairoptical.co.uk
**Reg No:** 2348610　**Estd:** 1989 Private Limited Company
**Line of Business:** Accounting and auditing activities
**Issued Capital:** £100
**Director:** E C Rouse
**US SIC:** 7399　**UK SIC:** 83954

|  | 31-07-13 | 31-07-12 | 31-07-11 |
|---|---|---|---|
| TA | 25,783 | 64,041 | 82,890 |
| NW | (20,072) | (22,246) | (24,059) |
| WC | (22,137) | (24,753) | (27,008) |

**DUNS 42-445-3673**
## Sinfonia of London Ltd
25 Grove Road, Beaconsfield, Buckinghamshire HP9 1UR
**Tel:** 01494-677934
**Reg No:** 4433025　**Estd:** 2002 Private Limited Company
**Line of Business:** Artistic and literary creation and interpretation
**Issued Capital:** £1
**Director:** P Willison
**US SIC:** 7999　**UK SIC:** 97913

|  | 31-05-14 | 31-05-13 | 31-05-12 |
|---|---|---|---|
| TA | 19,861 | 16,225 | 16,653 |
| NW | (46,138) | (53,450) | (50,680) |
| WC | (62,319) | (69,447) | (66,724) |

**DUNS 71-935-7845**
## Sing Kee Group Ltd
30-36 Cross Stamford Street, Leeds, West Yorkshire LS7 1BA
**Tel:** 01132468838
**Web:** www.singkeefoods.co.uk
**Reg No:** 5316616　**Estd:** 2004 Private Limited Company
**Line of Business:** Other letting of own property
**Issued Capital:** £367
**Director:** Mrs M Ly
**Co. Secretary:** Quoc Ly
**US SIC:** 6519　**UK SIC:** 85000
**Auditors:** B.M. Howarth
**Bankers:** Bank Of China (40-51-46)

|  | 31-08-13 | 31-08-12 | 31-08-11 |
|---|---|---|---|
| TO | 16,791,627 | 16,909,918 | 17,094,996 |
| P/L | 455,345 | 300,551 | 240,362 |
| NW | 2,324,175 | 2,011,630 | 1,796,148 |
| WC | (1,512,936) | (1,452,584) | (1,626,104) |
| Emp. | 49 | 49 | 45 |

**DUNS 21-618-7690**　　　　　　**Imp**
## Singer & James Ltd
33 Roebuck Road, Hainault Business Park, Ilford, Essex IG6 3TZ
**Web:** www.singerandjames.co.uk
**Reg No:** 1283801　**VAT No:** 360892830
**Estd:** 1976 Private Limited Company
**Line of Business:** Production of ornamental metalwork

**Issued Capital:** £241,000
**Directors:** J E Bell, G S James
**Co. Secretary:** Gregory Taylor
**Responsibilities**
**Senior:** David Elbourn (*Works Manager*)
**Health & Safety:** David Elbourn (*Works Manager*)
**Facilities:** David Elbourn (*Works Manager*)
**Operations:** David Elbourn (*Works Manager*)
**Engineering:** David Elbourn (*Works Manager*)
**US SIC:** 3442　**UK SIC:** 31420
**Auditors:** Granite Morgan Smith
**Bankers:** Barclays Bank Plc (20-44-22)

|  | 31-12-13 | 31-12-12 | 31-12-11 |
|---|---|---|---|
| TA | 2,151,568 | 2,006,516 | 2,314,421 |
| NW | 1,623,846 | 1,597,304 | 1,857,357 |
| WC | 244,543 | 229,980 | 207,230 |

**DUNS 28-973-0970**
## The Single Homeless Project
245 Gray?s Inn Road, London WC1X 8QY
**Tel:** 02075208660
**Web:** www.shp.org.uk
**Reg No:** 1741926　**Estd:** 1977 Private Company Limited By Guarantee
**Line of Business:** Social work activities
**Trading Style:** Redbridge Night Shelter, S H P
**Directors:** J R Wong, J Senker, A J Downes, Ms A L Clark, D J Braverman, Ms J C Cockcroft, P J Gillespie, Dr N S Byrne
**Co. Secretary:** Ms Elizabeth Rutherfoord
**Responsibilities**
**Senior:** Toby Williamson (*Manager*)
**Finance:** Virginia Grace (*Director of Finance*), Lookman Kazeem (*Head of Finance*)
**Admin:** Olufemi Odogwu-Okonyia (*Personal Assistant*)
**HR:** Howard Rosenthal (*Director of HR and Organisatio*), Bjoern Schlonski (*Human Resources Manager*)
**Facilities:** Thomas Stiff (*Facilities Manager*)
**Operations:** Toni Warner (*Director of Services*)
**Branches:** The Single Homeless Project, 284 Coldharbour La, London SW9 8SE
**US SIC:** 7399, 8321
**UK SIC:** 83954, 96111
**Auditors:** Lewis Jordan Ltd
**Bankers:** National Westminster Bank Plc (50-42-28)

|  | 31-03-14 | 31-03-13 | 31-03-12 |
|---|---|---|---|
| TO | 18,063,014 | 18,050,219 | 15,757,198 |
| P/L | 301,256 | 343,330 | (302,271) |
| NW | 4,597,628 | 4,296,372 | 3,953,042 |
| WC | 4,536,001 | 4,198,155 | 3,781,123 |
| Emp. | 395 | 381 | 296 |

**DUNS 22-266-4786**　　　　　　**Imp**
## Single Source Ltd
(**Subsidiary of:** Süddeutsche Zuckerrübenverwertungs-Genossenschaft)
Stafford Park 6, Telford, Shropshire TF3 3AT
**Web:** www.singlesourceportions.com
**Reg No:** 4284442　**VAT No:** 806618820
**Estd:** 1901 Private Limited Company
**Line of Business:** Food packers
**Export Sales:** £3,266,070
**Trading Style:** A P Sachet
**Issued Capital:** £1,068,738
**Directors:** A J Glabgen, I S Nicholson, G P Nota, P R Mainwaring, J M Thelwell
**Co. Secretary:** John Wardle
**US SIC:** 2099　**UK SIC:** 42399
**Auditors:** Saffery Champness
**Bankers:** The Co-Operative Bank Plc (08-90-00)

|  | 28-02-14 | 28-02-13 | 29-02-12 |
|---|---|---|---|
| TO | 22,781,095 | 25,574,173 | 23,932,830 |
| P/L | 1,189,595 | 2,505,452 | 2,056,195 |
| NW | 3,842,691 | 4,223,125 | 4,063,617 |
| WC | 2,524,056 | 2,920,696 | 2,664,111 |
| Emp. | 132 | 142 | 139 |

**DUNS 23-398-8372**
## Singleton Agriculture
P O Box 6628, Grantham, Lincolnshire NG31 8TR
**Web:** www.singletonagri.co.uk
**Estd:** 2000 Partnership
**Line of Business:** Agricultural service provider- supplier of plastics used for agriculture
**Partners:** R Mcardle, B Herbert
**Responsibilities**
**Senior:** Robert McArdle (*Partner*)
**US SIC:** 5083　**UK SIC:** 61490
**Employees:** 49

**DUNS 21-880-6834**　　　　　　**Imp-Exp**
## Singleton Birch Ltd
Melton Ross Quarries, Barnetby, South Humberside DN38 6AE
**Tel:** 01652686000　**Fax:** 01652-686081
**Web:** www.singletonbirch.co.uk
**Reg No:** 0009433　**Estd:** 1815 Private Limited Company

**Line of Business:** Other mining and quarrying not elsewhere classified
**Export Sales:** £2,254,000
**Issued Capital:** £536,800
**Directors:** S R Counsell, M J Gardiner, R M Stansfield, M D Haworth
**Co. Secretary:** Mrs Ellen Tatterton
**Responsibilities**
**Senior:** Kye Brown (*Manager*), Peter Widdowson (*Distribution Manager*)
**Finance:** Vanetta Coy (*Credit Controller*)
**Sales:** Alistair Foreman (*Lime Sales Manager*)
**IT:** Martin Howarth (*Technical Director*)
**Health & Safety:** Martin Howarth (*Technical Director*)
**Operations:** Martin Howarth (*Technical Director*), Oliver Whelpton (*Lime Production Manager*)
**Engineering:** Christian Fletcher (*Engineering Manager*), Mark Sacker (*Quarry & Engineering Services*)
**Branches:** Singleton Birch Ltd, South Thoresby, Alford, Lincolnshire LN13 0AR
**US SIC:** 1429, 2819
**UK SIC:** 23102, 25110
**Auditors:** Grant Thornton UK LLP
**Bankers:** HSBC Bank plc (40-13-30)

|  | 31-03-14 | 31-03-13 | 31-03-12 |
|---|---|---|---|
| TO | 36,529,000 | 34,657,000 | 31,260,000 |
| P/L | (283,000) | (307,000) | 2,150,000 |
| NW | 13,595,000 | 16,795,000 | 16,394,000 |
| WC | 2,923,000 | 3,785,000 | 3,282,000 |
| Emp. | 117 | 113 | 104 |

**DUNS 64-744-2607**
## Singleton Nursing Home
Hoxton Close, Ashford, Kent TN23 5LB
**Tel:** 01233666768
**Web:** http://singleton-nursing-home.co.uk
**Estd:** 1991 Partnership
**Line of Business:** Nursing homes
**Partners:** Dr V Setty, M Shah
**Responsibilities**
**Senior:** Julie Laidlaw (*Registered Manager*), Elaine Richmond (*Deputy Manager*)
**Admin:** Anette Hazell (*Administrator*)
**US SIC:** 8051　**UK SIC:** 95100
**Employees:** 60

**DUNS 21-696-1828**
## Singleton's Dairy 2010 Ltd
Mill Farm, Preston Road, Longridge, Preston, Lancashire PR3 3AN
**Tel:** 01772782112
**Web:** www.singletons.uk.com
**Reg No:** 7422049　**Estd:** 2010 Private Limited Company
**Line of Business:** Farming of cattle, dairy farming
**Export Sales:** £11,134,545
**Issued Capital:** £1,000
**Director:** Ms T M Carefoot
**US SIC:** 8999　**UK SIC:** 83954
**Bankers:** National Westminster Bank Plc (01-67-14)

|  | 31-03-14 | 31-03-13 | 31-03-12 |
|---|---|---|---|
| TO | 17,278,819 | 15,908,774 | 16,178,017 |
| P/L | 1,473,326 | 376,015 | 175,228 |
| NW | 3,782,869 | 2,342,690 | 3,686,529 |
| WC | 2,827,882 | 3,364,054 | 3,394,154 |
| Emp. | 83 | 84 | 83 |

**DUNS 22-625-9372**
## Singlewell Manor Hotel Ltd
(**Subsidiary of:** Syndicated Holdings Ltd)
Wishing Well, Hever Court Road, Gravesend, Kent DA12 5UQ
**Tel:** 01474-353100　**Fax:** 01474-354978
**Web:** www.bestwestern.co.uk
**Reg No:** 1682623　**VAT No:** 702694538
**Estd:** 1982 Private Limited Company
**Line of Business:** Hotels
**Issued Capital:** £130
**Directors:** M V Rossi, N Wilde
**Co. Secretary:** Ms Janet Rossi
**Responsibilities**
**Senior:** Danny Clarke (*Food & Beverage Manager*)
**US SIC:** 7011　**UK SIC:** 66500
**Auditors:** Barnes Roffe
**Bankers:** National Westminster Bank Plc (60-09-10)

|  | 31-03-14 | 31-03-13 | 31-03-12 |
|---|---|---|---|
| TA | 597,860 | 588,483 | 514,541 |
| NW | 328,942 | 322,413 | 230,172 |
| WC | 219,647 | 198,453 | 109,402 |

**DUNS 23-607-8796**　　　　　　**Imp-Exp**
## Siniat Ltd
(**Subsidiary of:** Etex Group Sa)
Marsh Lane, Easton-In-Gordano, Bristol, Avon BS20 0NF
**Tel:** 01275377773
**Web:** www.siniat.co.uk
**Reg No:** 2163844　**VAT No:** 479678760
**Estd:** 1987 Private Limited Company
**Line of Business:** Manufacture of plaster products for construction purposes
**Export Markets:** E U

**Export Sales:** £5,641,000
**Issued Capital:** £60,000,000
**Directors:** Ms J E Maycock, N A Ash, R G Buxton
**Co. Secretary:** Clive Ellwood
**Responsibilities**
**Senior:** Bernard Lekien *(Manager)*
**Engineering:** Dave Pearce *(Production Manager)*
**Branches:** Siniat Ltd, 3 West Bank Road, Belfast, Belfast BT3 9JL
**US SIC:** 3275 **UK SIC:** 24370
**Auditors:** Deloitte LLP
**Bankers:** Barclays Bank Plc (20-23-97)

| | 31-12-13 | 31-12-12 | 31-12-11 |
|---|---|---|---|
| TO | 122,873,000 | 119,734,000 | 118,983,000 |
| P/L | 15,223,000 | 14,010,000 | 5,970,000 |
| NW | 91,301,000 | 90,294,000 | 80,315,000 |
| WC | 23,162,000 | 26,245,000 | 17,532,000 |
| Emp. | 408 | 420 | 379 |

DUNS 22-113-3007
## Sintecmedia Global Ltd
**(Subsidiary of:** Sintec Media Ltd)
19th Floor, Wembley, Middlesex HA9 6DE
**Tel:** 02087 820700
**Web:** www.pilats.com
**Reg No:** 4132467 **Estd:** 2000 Private Limited Company
**Line of Business:** Other software consultancy and supply
**Export Sales:** £24,602,000
**Trading Style:** Sintec Media
**Issued Capital:** £3,118,175
**Directors:** J Parks, T Smach, A Yarden
**Co. Secretary:** Elad Lustig
**Responsibilities**
**Senior:** Ron Barlev *(Executive Vice President, Prod)*, Or Elovitch *(Manager)*, Avraham Engel *(Manager)*, Micha Moses *(Vice President)*, Seema Shah *(Manager)*
**Marketing:** Ron Barlev *(Executive Vice President, Prod)*
**Sales:** Yuval Tori *(Vice President, Sales EMEA)*
**Admin:** Cathy Sharp *(Office Manager)*
**HR:** Catherine Paige *(Health & Safety Director)*, Seema Shah *(Manager)*
**Health & Safety:** Catherine Paige *(Health & Safety Director)*
**US SIC:** 7379 **UK SIC:** 83940
**Auditors:** Baker Tilly UK Audit LLP

| | 31-12-13 | 31-12-12 | 31-12-11 |
|---|---|---|---|
| TO | 27,728,000 | 23,483,000 | 22,526,000 |
| P/L | 2,519,000 | 1,982,000 | (974,000) |
| NW | 20,375,000 | 18,176,000 | 15,176,000 |
| WC | 19,593,000 | 17,666,000 | 14,793,000 |
| Emp. | 263 | 234 | 218 |

DUNS 73-670-0266
## Sintons Llp
The Cube, Arngrove Court, Barrack Road, Newcastle-Upon-Tyne, Tyne and Wear NE4 6DB
**Tel:** 01912267878
**Web:** www.sintons.co.uk
**Reg No:** 0305764OC **Estd:** 2003
**Line of Business:** Solicitors
**Responsibilities**
**Senior:** Matthew Collen *(Designated Limited Liability P)*, Suzanne Davidson *(Non-designated Limited Liabili)*, Philip Davison *(Non-designated Limited Liabili)*, Katherine Jenkins *(Partner)*, Keith Land *(Partner)*, Alok Loomba *(Non-designated Limited Liabili)*, Suzanne Maddison *(Partner)*, James Mccabe *(Designated Limited Liability P)*, Paul Nickalls *(Non-designated Limited Liabili)*, Hilary Parker *(Designated Limited Liability P)*, Phil Ridley *(Practice Director)*
**Finance:** Stacey Stronach *(Accounts Assistant)*, Helen Walia *(Accounts Manager)*
**Marketing:** Charles Penn *(Marketing Manager)*
**Sales:** Julie Fawcett *(Solicitor)*, Charles Penn *(Marketing Manager)*
**Admin:** Iona Sweeney *(Secretary)*
**HR:** Louise Dack *(Training Manager)*, Louise Ledger *(Human Resources Manager)*
**Health & Safety:** Louise Dack *(Training Manager)*
**Facilities:** Phil Ridley *(Practice Director)*
**Operations:** Charles Penn *(Marketing Manager)*
**US SIC:** 8111 **UK SIC:** 83500
**Auditors:** Ryecroft Glenton

| | 31-01-14 | 31-01-13 | 31-01-12 |
|---|---|---|---|
| TO | 15,795,509 | 14,087,686 | N/A |
| P/L | 4,640,793 | N/A | N/A |
| NW | N/A | 2,636,758 | 1,924,935 |
| WC | 5,253,017 | 4,935,903 | 3,487,287 |
| Emp. | 224 | 181 | 177 |

DUNS 21-899-9761 **Imp-Exp**
## S.I.P.(Industrial Products)Ltd
**(Subsidiary of:** Trident 2020 Ltd)
Unit 5 Gelders Hall Road Loughborough, Motorway Trading Estate, Loughborough, Leicestershire LE12 9NH
**Tel:** 01509500300 **Fax:** 01509503153
**Web:** www.sip-group.com
**Reg No:** 0942287 **Estd:** 1968 Private Limited Company
**Line of Business:** Engineers (general)
**Export Markets:** E U; Africa; Middle East
**Export Sales:** £1,318,508
**Issued Capital:** £2,449,908
**Directors:** Mrs A Ippaso, R C Povoas
**Co. Secretary:** Paul Ippaso
**Responsibilities**
**Senior:** M Burandt *(Partner)*, Edy Ippaso *(Manager)*, Marco Ippaso *(Manager)*, Adrianna Ippaso *(Managing Director)*
**Finance:** Graham Gittus *(Finance Director)*
**IT:** Lee Hancox *(IT Manager)*
**US SIC:** 5199, 3563, 3545
**UK SIC:** 61900, 32831, 32223
**Auditors:** Baldwins (Ashby) Ltd
**Bankers:** HSBC Bank plc (40-28-06)

| | 31-12-13 | 31-12-12 | 31-12-11 |
|---|---|---|---|
| TO | 11,109,471 | 9,718,813 | 9,426,259 |
| P/L | 1,025,044 | 1,053,473 | 540,101 |
| NW | 2,543,721 | 1,518,677 | 215,204 |
| WC | 1,753,227 | 802,944 | (446,310) |
| Emp. | 63 | 60 | 56 |

DUNS 55-050-5227
## Sir Gabriel Woods Mariners' Home
67 Newark Street, Greenock, Renfrewshire PA16 7TQ
**Web:** www.sirgabrielwoods-marinershome.org
**Estd:** 1907
**Line of Business:** Residential care establishments
**Manager:** G Johnston
**US SIC:** 8699, 6732
**UK SIC:** 96902, 83100
**Employees:** 60

DUNS 21-876-4399
## Sir Harry Smith Academy Trust
Sir Harry Smith Academy, Eastrea Road, Whittlesey, Peterborough, Cambridgeshire PE7 1XB
**Tel:** 01733703991
**Web:** www.sirharrysmith.cambs.sch.uk
**Reg No:** 8006711 **Estd:** 2012 Private Limited Company
**Line of Business:** General secondary education
**Directors:** T J Beebe, J H Donnachie, J King, Mrs D M Hyland-Jeffery, J Digby
**US SIC:** 8211 **UK SIC:** 93200

| | 31-08-14 | 31-08-13 |
|---|---|---|
| TO | 5,821,493 | 26,039,749 |
| P/L | 171,524 | 16,447,505 |
| NW | 15,886,029 | 16,195,505 |
| WC | 1,151,190 | 494,590 |
| Emp. | 113 | 150 |

DUNS 21-260-0951 **Imp-Exp**
## Sir Jacob Behrens & Sons Ltd
Unit 4 Marshall Stevens Way, Trafford Park, Manchester M17 1PP
**Tel:** 016187-21444 **Fax:** 01617871144
**Web:** www.francisprice.co.uk
**Reg No:** 0454323 **VAT No:** 179446029
**Estd:** 1834 Private Limited Company
**Line of Business:** Textile merchants
**Export Markets:** Worldwide
**Trading Style:** Francis Price, Frank Preston Textiles, Dewhurst Dent Textiles
**Issued Capital:** £24,500
**Principals:** C D Hughes *(Managing)*, J S Behrens
**Co. Secretary:** Christopher Hughes
**Responsibilities**
**Senior:** Charles Behrens *(Manager)*
**US SIC:** 2392 **UK SIC:** 45550
**Auditors:** Deloitte LLP
**Bankers:** National Westminster Bank Plc (01-10-01)

| | 31-12-13 | 31-12-12 | 31-12-11 |
|---|---|---|---|
| TA | 16,412,717 | 17,129,874 | 18,113,906 |
| P/L | 696,501 | 1,387,778 | 1,266,833 |
| NW | 11,794,243 | 11,667,634 | 11,368,502 |
| WC | 10,758,602 | 10,363,440 | 9,694,616 |
| Emp. | 47 | 45 | 45 |

DUNS 21-164-9830
## Sir John Deane's College
Monarch Drive, Northwich, Cheshire CW9 8AF
**Tel:** 01606-810020
**Web:** www.sjd.ac.uk
**Estd:** 2003 Partnership
**Line of Business:** Post-graduate level higher education
**Director:** A Jones

**Responsibilities**
**Senior:** Kerry Kirkwood *(Principal)*
**US SIC:** 8221 **UK SIC:** 93100
**Employees:** 140

DUNS 21-232-2176
## Sir John Fitzgerald Ltd
**(Subsidiary of:** Sir John Fitzgerald (Holdings) Ltd)
Cafe Royal Buildings, Newcastle-Upon-Tyne, Tyne and Wear NE1 5AW
**Web:** www.sjf.co.uk
**Reg No:** 0214158 **VAT No:** 176117463
**Estd:** 1926 Private Limited Company
**Line of Business:** Representative office
**Issued Capital:** £13,652
**Principals:** D Horgan *(Managing)*, Mrs I Horgan-Briggs, Miss L Horgan
**Co. Secretary:** David Ridley
**Responsibilities**
**Senior:** Philip Denton *(Manager)*, david horgan *(Managing Director)*
**Marketing:** Rachel Gilbert *(Marketing and Development Mana)*
**IT:** Dean Woods *(IT Manager)*
**Branches:** Sir John Fitzgerald,Ltd, 14 Southfield Road, Middlesbrough, Cleveland TS1 3BZ
**US SIC:** 5411 **UK SIC:** 64100
**Auditors:** PricewaterhouseCoopers
**Bankers:** Barclays Bank Plc (20-59-42)

| | 31-01-14 | 31-01-13 | 31-01-12 |
|---|---|---|---|
| TO | 17,564,379 | 17,547,304 | 17,832,004 |
| P/L | 166,050 | 337,004 | (411,202) |
| NW | 21,060,891 | 21,111,999 | 19,506,245 |
| WC | 116,471 | 700,640 | 3,221,528 |
| Emp. | 529 | 528 | 541 |

DUNS 21-804-0892
## Sir John Port and John Osbourne Almshouses
Main Street, Etwall, Derby, Derbyshire DE65 6LU
**Tel:** 01283734111
**Web:** www.educationderbyshire.co.uk
**Estd:** 1983
**Line of Business:** Schools (local authority)
**Proprietor:** Mrs W Sharp
**US SIC:** 8211 **UK SIC:** 93200
**Employees:** 192

DUNS 21-879-1810
## Sir John Thursby Community College
Eastern Avenue, Burnley, Lancashire BB10 2AT
**Tel:** 01282682313
**Web:** www.sirjohnthursby.lancs.sch.uk
**Estd:** 2012
**Line of Business:** Schools (local authority)
**US SIC:** 8211 **UK SIC:** 93200
**Employees:** 400

DUNS 23-635-9626
## Sir Jonathan North
Knighton Lane East, Leicester, Leicestershire LE2 6FU
**Tel:** 01162-708116
**Web:** www.sjncc.leicester.sch.uk
**Estd:** 1937
**Line of Business:** Schools (foundation)
**Director:** Mrs J Collins
**Responsibilities**
**Senior:** Ian Dunmore *(Operations Manager)*, Alison Merrills *(Principal)*
**IT:** Ian Dunmore *(Operations Manager)*
**HR:** Ian Dunmore *(Operations Manager)*
**US SIC:** 8211 **UK SIC:** 93200
**Employees:** 130

DUNS 64-269-1570
## Sir Josiah Mason's Trust
Hillborough Road, Birmingham, West Midlands B27 6PF
**Tel:** 01212451081
**Estd:** 1967 Proprietorship
**Line of Business:** Residential care establishments
**US SIC:** 8321 **UK SIC:** 96111
**Employees:** 58

DUNS 21-250-9063
## Sir Philip Game Ctr
38 Morland Avenue, Croydon, Surrey CR0 6EA
**Tel:** 02086625752
**Web:** www.spgcentre.co.uk
**Estd:** 1945
**Line of Business:** Committee managed organisations
**Responsibilities**
**Senior:** Sue O'flynn *(Administrator)*
**US SIC:** 8699 **UK SIC:** 96902
**Employees:** 49

DUNS 21-780-9488
## Sir Robert Woodard Academy
Upper Boundstone Lane, Lancing, West Sussex BN15 9QY
**Tel:** 01903767434
**Web:** www.srwa.co.uk
**Estd:** 2002 Partnership
**Line of Business:** General secondary education
**Partners:** Mrs C Bailey, Miss Y Willams
**Responsibilities**
**Senior:** P Midwinter *(Principal)*
**US SIC:** 8211 **UK SIC:** 93200
**Employees:** 198

DUNS 21-157-0465
## Sir Roger Manwood's Grammar School
Manwood Road, Sandwich, Kent CT13 9JX
**Tel:** 01304613286
**Web:** www.srms.kent.sch.uk
**Estd:** 1560
**Line of Business:** Schools (local authority)
**Chairman:** A Kilbee
**US SIC:** 8211 **UK SIC:** 93200
**Employees:** 100

DUNS 37-811-8418
## Sir William Perkins's School
Guildford Road, Chertsey, Surrey KT16 9BN
**Tel:** 01932562161
**Web:** www.swps.org.uk
**Reg No:** 3298142 **Estd:** 1996 Private Limited Company
**Line of Business:** General secondary education
**Directors:** T J Hillier, N P Day, Ms S A Jamison, D J Wareham, P W Kennedy, P I Roberts, Mrs C Bannister, I R Fulton
**Responsibilities**
**Senior:** Helen Archibald *(Director)*, Anne Byard *(Director)*, Katherine Clemo *(Board Member)*, Susan Dadlani *(Director)*, Nick Moughtin *(Curriculum Deputy Head)*, F Roff *(Head Teacher)*, Diana Stainbank *(Board Member)*, Geoffrey Want *(Director)*
**Finance:** Alexander Gallie *(Bursar)*
**Marketing:** F Blyther *(Matron, Charities)*, Sheila Hallsworth *(Marketing Manager)*
**Sales:** Dick Beresford *(School Business Director)*
**IT:** I Barnsley *(IT Director)*, Julie McRobb *(Senior IT Technician)*
**Health & Safety:** Alexander Gallie *(Bursar)*
**Facilities:** Alexander Gallie *(Bursar)*
**Purchasing:** Alexander Gallie *(Bursar)*
**US SIC:** 8211 **UK SIC:** 93200
**Employees:** 120

DUNS 21-778-0476
## Sir William Ramsay School
Rose Avenue, Hazlemere, High Wycombe, Buckinghamshire HP15 7UB
**Tel:** 01494815211
**Web:** www.sirwilliamramsay.bucks.sch.uk
**Estd:** 1990 Proprietorship
**Line of Business:** General secondary education
**Proprietor:** Mrs G Comber
**US SIC:** 8211 **UK SIC:** 93200
**Employees:** 80

DUNS 21-735-3803
## Sir William Ramsay School Academy Trust
Rose Avenue, High Wycombe, Buckinghamshire HP15 7UB
**Tel:** 01494256141
**Web:** www.swr.bucks.sch.uk
**Reg No:** 7697618 **Estd:** 2011 Private Company Limited By Guarantee
**Line of Business:** General secondary education
**Directors:** N Waldron, M Cherret, Mrs E Beukes, J P Bajina, M Clark, S Carter, M J Mayne, Professor J Knowles
**Responsibilities**
**Senior:** Christine Davis-Foster *(Director)*, Steven Warner *(Director)*
**US SIC:** 8211 **UK SIC:** 93200
**Bankers:** HSBC Bank plc (40-09-29)

| | 31-08-14 | 31-08-13 | 31-08-12 |
|---|---|---|---|
| TO | 5,817,629 | 5,807,784 | 31,154,921 |
| P/L | (476,057) | (340,309) | 23,951,841 |
| NW | 22,539,151 | 23,326,208 | 23,760,841 |
| WC | 429,114 | 437,682 | 397,598 |
| Emp. | 138 | 131 | 122 |

DUNS 23-082-9751
## Sir William Robertson High School
Main Road, Welbourn, Lincoln, Lincolnshire LN5 0PA
**Tel:** 01400-272422
**Web:** www.swracademy.org
**Estd:** 1970

**Line of Business:** Schools (foundation)
**Director:** I Wright
**US SIC:** 8211 **UK SIC:** 93200
**Employees:** 100

DUNS 21-734-9900
## Sir William Romney's School
Lowfield Road, Tetbury, Gloucestershire GL8 8AE
**Tel:** 01666502378
**Web:** www.sirwilliamromneys.gloucs.sch.uk
**Reg No:** 7694641 **Estd:** 2011 Private Company Limited By Guarantee
**Line of Business:** Schools (local authority)
**Directors:** J E Green, J G Morgan, M J Hodge, S Mackay, Ms K M Turner, B D Gibbs, Mrs R Goodwin, Ms D J Potts
**Co. Secretary:** Ms Deborah Anderson-Dixon
**Responsibilities**
**Senior:** Natalie Morley *(Director)*, Susan Townsend *(Director)*, Mark Wallington *(Director)*
**US SIC:** 8211 **UK SIC:** 93200

| | 31-08-13 | 31-08-12 |
|---|---|---|
| TO | 2,715,262 | 9,359,754 |
| P/L | (210,702) | 6,340,554 |
| NW | 6,081,852 | 6,275,554 |
| WC | 77,630 | 179,631 |
| Emp. | 52 | 49 |

DUNS 34-768-1012 **Imp-Exp**
## Sira Test & Certification Ltd
(**Subsidiary of:** Canadian Standards Association)
Rake Lane, Eccleston, Chester, Chester, Cheshire CH4 9JN
**Tel:** 01244-670900
**Web:** www.siracertification.com
**Reg No:** 5569145 **Estd:** 1981 Private Limited Company
**Line of Business:** Technical testing and analysis
**Export Sales:** £3,967,000
**Issued Capital:** £1
**Directors:** I Rippin, R E Schunk, M O'Leary, E De Bernardis, A K Sahi
**Co. Secretary:** Robert Falconi
**Responsibilities**
**Senior:** Magali Depras *(Manager)*, Stephen Lower *(Manager)*, Gordon Martin *(Manager)*, Dana Parmentar *(Manager)*, Stephen Pickering *(Manager)*, Mike Shearman *(Manager)*, S Shearman *(General Manager)*
**Marketing:** Adam Garner *(Sales & Marketing Manager)*
**Sales:** Adam Garner *(Sales & Marketing Manager)*
**Health & Safety:** Stewart Finch *(Health & Safety Officer)*
**US SIC:** 8621 **UK SIC:** 96311
**Bankers:** Bank Of Scotland (80-09-29)

| | 31-12-12 | 31-12-11 | 31-12-10 |
|---|---|---|---|
| TO | 7,772,000 | 6,653,000 | 5,385,000 |
| P/L | 1,732,000 | 1,247,000 | 885,000 |
| NW | 3,443,000 | 1,951,000 | 921,000 |
| WC | 3,064,000 | 1,688,000 | 762,000 |
| Emp. | 76 | 64 | 49 |

DUNS 64-103-0593 **Imp**
## Sirane Ltd
Stafford Park 6, Telford, Shropshire TF3 3AT
**Fax:** 01952-210065
**Web:** www.sirane.com
**Reg No:** 4506513 **Estd:** 2002 Private Limited Company
**Line of Business:** Manufacturers of packaging materials
**Issued Capital:** £9,900
**Director:** S N Balderson
**Co. Secretary:** Andrew Willis
**US SIC:** 2654, 2645
**UK SIC:** 47280
**Auditors:** Hughes & Co (Shropshire) Ltd
**Bankers:** HSBC Bank plc (40-44-50)

| | 31-12-13 | 31-12-12 | 31-12-11 |
|---|---|---|---|
| TO | 7,838,283 | 7,394,672 | 7,463,376 |
| P/L | 478,206 | 442,047 | 939,142 |
| NW | 558,170 | 1,076,195 | 1,035,642 |
| WC | (98,213) | 320,524 | 601,913 |
| Emp. | 79 | 82 | 71 |

DUNS 23-986-9626 **Imp**
## Sirdar Spinning Ltd
(**Subsidiary of:** Sirdar Holdings Ltd)
Flanshaw Lane, Wakefield, West Yorkshire WF2 9ND
**Tel:** 01924369666
**Web:** www.sirdar.co.uk
**Reg No:** 3975238 **VAT No:** 170376272
**Estd:** 2000 Private Limited Company
**Line of Business:** Textile merchants
**Export Sales:** £7,908,000
**Issued Capital:** £8,000,000
**Principals:** R P Morris *(Managing)*, S Havis, Miss E L Mychajlowskyj
**Co. Secretary:** Ian Stead
**Responsibilities**
**Facilities:** Bob Taylor *(maintenance manager)*

**US SIC:** 5133 **UK SIC:** 61600
**Auditors:** RSM Tenon Audit Ltd
**Bankers:** National Westminster Bank Plc (55-70-23)

| | 30-06-13 | 30-06-12 | 30-06-11 |
|---|---|---|---|
| TO | 21,730,000 | 21,066,000 | 19,055,000 |
| P/L | 3,037,000 | 3,512,000 | 2,394,000 |
| NW | 15,854,000 | 13,973,000 | 11,854,000 |
| WC | 14,987,000 | 13,204,000 | 10,996,000 |
| Emp. | 129 | 124 | 120 |

DUNS 21-113-8877
## Sirius Academy
296 Anlaby Park Road South, Hull, North Humberside HU4 7JB
**Tel:** 01482352939 **Fax:** 01482569982
**Web:** www.siriusacademy.org.uk
**Reg No:** 6545396 **Estd:** 2008 Private Company Limited By Guarantee
**Line of Business:** General secondary education
**Directors:** A K Bell, G A Towse, S Allen, Mrs P A Tomlinson, A N Sutton, Dr C J Taylor, L J Gomm, Mrs J C Wright
**Co. Secretary:** Tim Priestley
**US SIC:** 8211 **UK SIC:** 93200
**Bankers:** The Co-Operative Bank Plc (08-90-72)

| | 31-08-14 | 31-08-13 | 31-08-12 |
|---|---|---|---|
| TO | 10,515,000 | 9,881,000 | 8,452,000 |
| P/L | 482,000 | 647,000 | 221,000 |
| NW | 1,692,000 | 1,581,000 | 833,000 |
| WC | 2,304,000 | 1,925,000 | 1,267,000 |
| Emp. | 189 | 182 | 163 |

DUNS 73-386-5799
## Sirius Engineering Group Ltd
Suite 2 Russell House, Mill Road Langley Moor, Durham, County Durham DH7 8HJ
**Tel:** 01913789972 **Fax:** 01913-781537
**Web:** www.thesiriusgroup.com
**Reg No:** 4660007 **Estd:** 2003 Private Limited Company
**Line of Business:** Management activities of holding companies
**Issued Capital:** £200
**Directors:** P E Kane, P J Taylor, M J Powell
**Co. Secretary:** Douglas Mill
**US SIC:** 6711 **UK SIC:** 83962
**Auditors:** Anderson Barrowcliff LLP

| | 31-12-13 | 31-12-12 | 31-12-11 |
|---|---|---|---|
| TO | 20,577,391 | 19,541,500 | 14,564,383 |
| P/L | 647,935 | 581,149 | (54,751) |
| NW | 2,769,404 | 2,264,665 | 1,931,215 |
| WC | 2,533,731 | 1,966,785 | 1,689,302 |
| Emp. | 137 | 128 | 111 |

DUNS 23-225-7894
## Sirius International
3 Minster Court, London EC3R 7DD
**Tel:** 02076174900
**Web:** www.siriusgroup.com
**Estd:** 1999 Partnership
**Line of Business:** Insurance services
**Principals:** M Dashfield, S Davies *(Partner)*, Ms S Allen *(Partner)*, M Dashfield *(Partner)*
**Responsibilities**
**Senior:** Gregory Smart *(Manager)*
**Branches:** Sirius International, The London Underwriting Centre, Mincing La, London EC3R 7DD
**US SIC:** 6411 **UK SIC:** 83200
**Employees:** 50

DUNS 73-689-4341
## Sirius Minerals Plc
7-10 Manor Court, Manor Garth, Scarborough, North Yorkshire YO11 3TU
**Tel:** 01723-470-010
**Web:** www.siriusminerals.com
**Reg No:** 4948435 **Estd:** 2003 Public Limited Company
**Line of Business:** Mining of chemicals and fertiliser minerals, specialising in potash development.
**Issued Capital:** £3,353,958
**Directors:** P J Woods, S G Pycroft, R J Scrimshaw, K E Clarke, C N Fraser, Lord H O Hutton Of Furness, C J Catlow
**Co. Secretary:** Nicholas King
**US SIC:** 1474 **UK SIC:** 23960
**Auditors:** PricewaterhouseCoopers LLP
**Bankers:** The Royal Bank Of Scotland Plc (15-10-00)

| | 31-03-14 | 31-03-13 | 31-03-12 |
|---|---|---|---|
| TA | 144,380,000 | 94,522,000 | 104,169,000 |
| P/L | (10,129,000) | (14,572,000) | (63,110,000) |
| NW | 42,059,000 | 15,496,000 | 48,248,000 |
| WC | 39,943,000 | 15,229,000 | 54,623,000 |
| Emp. | 61 | 51 | 21 |

DUNS 77-874-0837
## Sirocom Ltd
(**Subsidiary of:** Warden Holdco Ltd)
205 Brooklands Road, Weybridge, Surrey KT13 0BG
**Tel:** 01932-264700 **Fax:** 01932-264888
**Web:** www.sirocom.com
**Reg No:** 3036244 **Estd:** 1995 Private Limited Company
**Line of Business:** Internet services

**Issued Capital:** £13,780
**Directors:** S Andrews, A N Marshall
**Responsibilities**
**Marketing:** Nicola Lidgett *(Head of Marketing)*
**IT:** Mike Ramsden *(Group IT Director)*
**US SIC:** 4899 **UK SIC:** 79020
**Auditors:** PricewaterhouseCoopers LLP
**Employees:** 97

DUNS 21-880-1718
## Sirona Care & Health
Charlton House, Hawthorns Lane, Keynsham, Bristol, Avon BS31 1BF
**Tel:** 01225396600
**Web:** www.sirona-cic.org.uk
**Estd:** 2012
**Line of Business:** Social work activities
**Responsibilities**
**Senior:** Sue Breakah *(Manager)*
**US SIC:** 8321 **UK SIC:** 96111
**Employees:** 50

DUNS 21-720-5877
## Sirona Care & Health C.I.C.
59 Sedgemoor Road, Bath, Avon BA2 5PL
**Tel:** 01225837092
**Web:** www.sirona-cic.org.uk
**Reg No:** 7585003 **Estd:** 2012 Private Company Limited By Guarantee
**Line of Business:** Other human health activities
**Directors:** L Morgan-Brinkhurst Mbe, Mrs J C Walker, Mrs J Theed, D J Purdon, Miss J Rowse, R Tarring, M S Knighton
**Responsibilities**
**Senior:** Sue Barrow *(Manager)*, Shirley Reynolds *(Manager)*
**US SIC:** 8091, 8321
**UK SIC:** 95200, 96111
**Bankers:** The Co-Operative Bank Plc (08-01-00)

| | 31-03-14 | 31-03-13 |
|---|---|---|
| TO | 57,590,000 | 82,059,000 |
| P/L | (299,000) | 929,000 |
| NW | (87,000) | (2,426,000) |
| WC | (97,000) | 663,000 |
| Emp. | 1,770 | 1,713 |

DUNS 73-760-4681 **Imp**
## Sirus Automotive Ltd
Unit 2 Trident Drive Britannia Park, Wednesbury, West Midlands WS10 7XB
**Web:** www.sirusautomotive.com
**Reg No:** 5017846 **Estd:** 2004 Private Limited Company
**Line of Business:** Manufacture of other transport equipment not elsewhere classified
**Issued Capital:** £150,000
**Director:** R Venvil
**Co. Secretary:** Simon Pearson
**Responsibilities**
**IT:** Dean Peasley *(IT Manager)*
**US SIC:** 3799 **UK SIC:** 36502

| | 30-09-13 | 30-09-12 | 30-09-11 |
|---|---|---|---|
| TO | 6,379,082 | 6,516,714 | N/A |
| P/L | (440,423) | 42,138 | N/A |
| NW | (325,142) | 20,084 | 34,212 |
| WC | (304,523) | 230,238 | (66,606) |
| Emp. | 52 | 65 | N/A |

DUNS 29-818-5281
## Sirva Relocation (No.1) Ltd
(**Subsidiary of:** Sirva Inc.)
Mulberry, Kembrey Street, Swindon, Wiltshire SN2 8UY
**Tel:** 0179 361 9555 **Fax:** 0179 353 4839
**Web:** www.sirva.co.uk
**Reg No:** 2036610 **VAT No:** 648401635
**Estd:** 2014 Private Limited Company
**Line of Business:** Activities of other transport agencies
**Issued Capital:** £100
**Directors:** Mrs D Balli, Ms V E Wakeham, S D Marshall
**Co. Secretary:** Sirva Relocation (No.2) Limited
**Responsibilities**
**Senior:** Kathryn Cassidy *(Manager)*
**IT:** David Margrave *(IT Director)*
**Branches:** Sirva Relocation (NO.1) Ltd, Arborfield Belmont, Wantage, Oxfordshire OX12 9AS
**US SIC:** 4712 **UK SIC:** 77002
**Auditors:** Monahans
**Bankers:** HSBC Bank plc (40-05-20)

| | 31-12-13 | 31-12-12 | 31-12-11 |
|---|---|---|---|
| TO | 21,588,266 | 18,611,750 | 17,867,443 |
| P/L | (471,559) | (724,458) | 7,141,042 |
| NW | 2,360,645 | 2,832,204 | 3,555,819 |
| WC | 2,154,452 | 2,586,954 | 3,475,907 |
| Emp. | 63 | 67 | 59 |

DUNS 28-884-7106
## Sirva Relocation (No.3) Ltd
Unit 3, Sirva House Apple Walk, Kembrey Park, Swindon, Wiltshire SN2 8BL
**Tel:** 01793619555 **Fax:** 01793-534839
**Web:** www.sirva.com
**Reg No:** 1219485 **Estd:** 1992 Private Limited Company
**Line of Business:** Relocation services
**Trading Style:** Rowan Simmons
**Issued Capital:** £1
**Directors:** S D Marshall, Mrs D Balli, Mrs V E Wakeham
**Co. Secretary:** Sirva Relocation (No.2) Limited
**Responsibilities**
**Senior:** Glen Bansor *(Manager)*
**Branches:** Sirva Relocation (NO.3) Ltd, Deale House, 16 Lavant Street, Petersfield, Hampshire GU32 3EW
**US SIC:** 6711 **UK SIC:** 83962
**Auditors:** Monahans
**Bankers:** The Royal Bank Of Scotland Plc (16-00-30)

| | 31-12-13 | 31-12-12 | 31-12-11 |
|---|---|---|---|
| TA | 480,497 | 480,497 | 480,497 |
| NW | 480,497 | 480,497 | 480,497 |

DUNS 21-106-8071
## Sis Outside Broadcasts Ltd
(**Subsidiary of:** Satellite Information Services (Holdings) Ltd)
17-21 Corsham Street, London N1 6DR
**Tel:** 01616626700
**Web:** www.sis.tv
**Reg No:** 6490756 **Estd:** 2008 Private Limited Company
**Line of Business:** Television activities
**Issued Capital:** £1
**Director:** G J Smith
**Co. Secretary:** Sis Cosec Limited
**Responsibilities**
**Senior:** David Holdgate *(Chief Executive)*
**US SIC:** 7399, 4833
**UK SIC:** 83954, 97411

| | 31-03-14 | 31-03-13 | 31-03-12 |
|---|---|---|---|
| TO | 41,555,000 | 66,203,000 | 57,648,000 |
| P/L | (1,777,000) | (2,438,000) | (1,535,000) |
| NW | (17,562,000) | (17,274,000) | (17,315,000) |
| WC | 1,793,000 | (2,524,000) | (8,805,000) |
| Emp. | 215 | 238 | 334 |

DUNS 23-323-6764
## Sis Plastic Recyclers
Blue House Point Road, Stockton-On-Tees, Cleveland TS18 2PW
**Tel:** 01642613628
**Web:** www.sisplasticrecyclers.co.uk
**Estd:** 2003 Proprietorship
**Line of Business:** Recycling
**Proprietor:** Mrs J Walsh
**Responsibilities**
**Senior:** Glenn Walsh *(Proprietor)*
**US SIC:** 3031 **UK SIC:** 48123
**Employees:** 50

DUNS 22-932-2565 **Imp**
## Sisk Healthcare (Uk) Ltd
(**Subsidiary of:** Sisk Healthcare Holdings (Uk) Ltd)
Unit 2-3, Hawthorne House, 6 Wildflower Way, Belfast BT12 6TA
**Tel:** 028 9066 9000 **Fax:** 028 9068 7100
**Web:** www.cardiac-services.com
**Reg No:** 0018037NI **Estd:** 1984 Private Limited Company
**Line of Business:** Medical equipment maintenance
**Trading Style:** Cardiac Services
**Issued Capital:** £50,000
**Directors:** M Reid, J Osborne
**Co. Secretary:** Bernard Power
**Responsibilities**
**Senior:** Liam Nagle *(Director)*, Gerard Penny *(Manager)*
**Finance:** Gary McGovern *(Financial Manager)*
**HR:** Deirdre Breen *(Human Resources Manager)*
**Facilities:** Chris Hawthorn *(Engineer)*
**Branches:** Sisk Healthcare (Uk) Ltd, Market Drayton, Shropshire TF9 4JG
**US SIC:** 3841 **UK SIC:** 37201
**Auditors:** PricewaterhouseCoopers
**Bankers:** The Bank Of Ireland (90-02-95)

| | 31-12-13 | 31-12-12 | 31-12-11 |
|---|---|---|---|
| TO | 23,370,000 | 22,745,004 | 17,311,066 |
| P/L | 2,478,000 | 2,474,650 | 125,957 |
| NW | 6,159,000 | 7,023,210 | 5,091,826 |
| WC | 6,162,000 | 7,055,987 | 6,803,075 |
| Emp. | 46 | 46 | 48 |

DUNS 23-500-3485
## Sisley U K Ltd
55-57 Brompton Road, London SW3 1DP
**Fax:** 02074912766
**Web:** www.sisley-paris.com
**Reg No:** 3499639 **Estd:** 1996 Private Limited Company

**Line of Business:** Wholesale of perfume and cosmetics
**Issued Capital:** £5,000
**Directors:** P D'Ornano, Ms L Fiori
**Co. Secretary:** Ms Christine D'Ornano
**Responsibilities**
**Senior:** Hubert Ornano *(President)*
**Marketing:** Anna Mosek *(Assistant Marketing and Design)*
**US SIC:** 5122 **UK SIC:** 61800
**Auditors:** Mazars Neville Russell

| | 31-12-13 | 31-12-12 | 31-12-11 |
|---|---|---|---|
| TO | 11,988,755 | 10,165,336 | 7,217,912 |
| P/L | 391,947 | 770,709 | 565,369 |
| NW | 1,341,604 | 1,063,122 | 491,237 |
| WC | 935,057 | 719,704 | 141,398 |
| Emp. | 247 | 239 | 211 |

DUNS 21-008-3132
## Sisterly Care Ltd
Denvilles House, 33 Emsworth Road, Havant, Hampshire PO9 2SN
**Tel:** 023-9245-4222
**Web:** www.sisterlycare.co.uk
**Reg No:** 6323486 **Estd:** 2007 Private Limited Company
**Line of Business:** Activities of households as employers of domestic staff
**Issued Capital:** £100
**Director:** F L Hussain-Shah
**Co. Secretary:** Ms Julie Ronson
**US SIC:** 8811 **UK SIC:** 99000

| | 31-07-13 | 31-07-12 | 31-07-11 |
|---|---|---|---|
| TA | 73,857 | 105,473 | 94,105 |
| NW | 10,396 | 30,570 | 25,193 |
| WC | 5,217 | 29,035 | 30,876 |

DUNS 23-635-2449
## Sisters of Charity of St Vincent De Paul
The Marillac, Eagle Way, Warley, Brentwood, Essex CM13 3BL
**Tel:** 01277220276
**Web:** www.marillac.co.uk
**Line of Business:** Charitable organisation
**US SIC:** 7231 **UK SIC:** 98200
**Employees:** 120

DUNS 21-066-0562
## Sita
South Street, Rochford, Essex SS4 1BL
**Tel:** 01702533880
**Web:** www.sita.co.uk
**Proprietorship**
**Line of Business:** Waste disposal
**Proprietor:** T Blige
**Responsibilities**
**Senior:** James Goodwin *(Contract Manager)*
**US SIC:** 4953 **UK SIC:** 92110
**Employees:** 65

DUNS 22-521-4360 Exp
## Sita Advanced Travel Solutions Ltd
London Works, 252-254 Blyth Road, Hayes, Middlesex UB3 1BW
**Tel:** 020-8756-8000
**Web:** www.sita.aero
**Reg No:** 1391626 **VAT No:** 572415838
**Estd:** 1978 Private Limited Company
**Line of Business:** Airports & flying fields
**Export Markets:** U S A, E U, Australia, Far East
**Issued Capital:** £4,227,185
**Directors:** F Violante, R G Watkins, C S O'Higgins
**Co. Secretary:** Alain Brodeur
**Branches:** Sita Advanced Travel Solutions Ltd, Thornbrook House, Catteshall Lane, Godalming, Surrey GU7 1XE
**US SIC:** 4582, 7379
**UK SIC:** 76400, 83940
**Auditors:** Deloitte LLP
**Bankers:** HSBC Bank plc (40-05-30)

| | 31-12-13 | 31-12-12 | 31-12-11 |
|---|---|---|---|
| TO | 65,325,116 | 37,147,700 | 28,845,669 |
| P/L | 3,886,988 | 2,792,603 | 2,083,180 |
| NW | (4,658,682) | (4,426,211) | (6,646,235) |
| WC | (10,268,584) | (11,550,877) | (14,229,084) |
| Emp. | 108 | 103 | 112 |

DUNS 64-080-4803
## Sita Holdings Uk Ltd
**(Subsidiary of:** Suez Environnement Company)
Sita House 13 35, Grenfell Road, Maidenhead, Berkshire SL6 1ES
**Tel:** 01628513100
**Reg No:** 3475737 **Estd:** 1997 Private Limited Company
**Line of Business:** Management activities of holding companies
**Export Sales:** £4,601,000
**Issued Capital:** £150,000,000
**Directors:** C Cros, C A Chapron, D Palmer-Jones
**Co. Secretary:** Mark Thompson
**Responsibilities**
**Senior:** Graham Mayes *(Coo)*
**Operations:** Graham Mayes *(Coo)*
**Branches:** Sita Holdings Uk Ltd, Burnhills Landfill Site, Longridge Road, Blaydon-On-Tyne, Tyne and Wear NE21 4SW
**US SIC:** 6711 **UK SIC:** 83962
**Auditors:** Mazars LLP

| | 31-12-13 | 31-12-12 | 31-12-11 |
|---|---|---|---|
| TO | 632,584,000 | 597,508,000 | 601,546,000 |
| P/L | 12,603,000 | 7,832,000 | 15,388,000 |
| NW | 331,900,000 | 310,114,000 | 302,190,000 |
| WC | 135,779,000 | 112,385,000 | 110,049,000 |
| Emp. | 5,277 | 5,553 | 5,913 |

DUNS 51-988-2208 Imp
## Sita Information Networking Computing Uk Ltd
**(Subsidiary of:** Sita N.V.)
1 London Gate, Hayes, Middlesex UB3 1HA
**Tel:** 02087561124 **Fax:** 020-8756-8100
**Web:** www.sita.aero
**Reg No:** 3995063 **Estd:** 1949 Private Limited Company
**Line of Business:** Pre-press activities
**Trading Style:** Sita
**Directors:** R G Watkins, F Violante, C S O'Higgins
**Co. Secretary:** Alain Brodeur
**Responsibilities**
**HR:** Michele Bowers *(Human Resources Manager)*
**Health & Safety:** Daphnie Bray *(Health & Safety Officer)*
**Branches:** Sita Information Networking Computing Uk Ltd, Waterway Business Park, Unit 1, Hayes, Middlesex UB3 1EY
**US SIC:** 7399, 7379
**UK SIC:** 83954, 83940
**Auditors:** Deloitte LLP
**Bankers:** HSBC Bank plc (40-25-01)
**Employees:** 415
**Turnover:** £143,778,762

DUNS 64-102-3056
## Sita (Kirklees) Ltd
**(Subsidiary of:** Suez Environnement Company)
Diamond Street, Hillhouse, Huddersfield, West Yorkshire HD1 6BZ
**Tel:** 01484541355 **Fax:** 01484447800
**Web:** www2.kirklees.gov.uk
**Reg No:** 3497105 **Estd:** 1998 Private Limited Company
**Line of Business:** Collection and treatment of other waste
**Trading Style:** Sita (Kirklees) Ltd
**Issued Capital:** £8,839,378
**Directors:** J J Scanlon, G Mayson, M R Gordon, C A Chapron, C Scott, T Otley, A Brice, D Palmer-Jones
**Co. Secretary:** Mark Thompson
**Responsibilities**
**Senior:** Julie Craigie *(General Manager)*, Barry Walter *(Communications Manager)*
**Health & Safety:** Kate Brown *(Health & Safety Manager)*
**Branches:** Sita (Kirklees) Ltd, 1 Park Rd, Dewsbury, West Yorkshire WF13 4LQ
**US SIC:** 4953 **UK SIC:** 92110
**Auditors:** Fraser Russell
**Bankers:** National Westminster Bank Plc (53-61-07)

| | 31-12-13 | 31-12-12 | 31-12-11 |
|---|---|---|---|
| TO | 17,720,000 | 18,244,000 | 18,706,000 |
| P/L | 395,000 | 910,000 | (1,088,000) |
| NW | 3,168,000 | 2,653,000 | 1,893,000 |
| WC | 23,329,000 | 25,500,000 | 26,943,000 |
| Emp. | 123 | 132 | 139 |

DUNS 23-973-5603
## Sita South Gloucestershire Ltd
**(Subsidiary of:** Suez Environnement Company)
Dean Road, Yate, Bristol, Avon BS37 5ND
**Tel:** 01454333300
**Web:** www.sita.co.uk
**Reg No:** 3962228 **Estd:** 2000 Private Limited Company
**Line of Business:** Collection and treatment of other waste
**Issued Capital:** £2,400,002
**Directors:** C A Chapron, D Palmer-Jones
**Co. Secretary:** Mark Thompson
**Responsibilities**
**Marketing:** Sarah Ottaway *(Marketing Manager)*
**HR:** Sue Jacques *(Human Resources Manager)*
**Branches:** Sita South Gloucestershire Ltd, Pyke Quarry, Stroud, Gloucestershire GL6 0QA
**US SIC:** 4953 **UK SIC:** 92110
**Bankers:** National Westminster Bank Plc (52-21-32)

| | 31-12-13 | 31-12-12 | 31-12-11 |
|---|---|---|---|
| TO | 20,453,000 | 19,463,000 | 20,467,000 |
| P/L | 3,831,000 | 4,427,000 | 5,180,000 |
| NW | 16,726,000 | 13,882,000 | 10,406,000 |
| WC | 18,897,000 | 15,479,000 | 11,529,000 |
| Emp. | 256 | 255 | 246 |

DUNS 77-053-9872
## Sita Tees Valley Ltd
**(Subsidiary of:** Suez Environnement Company)
Haverton Hill Road, Billingham, Cleveland TS23 1PY
**Tel:** 01642-202300 **Fax:** 01642-202301
**Web:** www.sita.co.uk
**Reg No:** 2669578 **Estd:** 1995 Private Limited Company
**Line of Business:** Collection and treatment of other waste
**Issued Capital:** £5,964,976
**Directors:** P T Jackson, J M Kay, J J Scanlon, C A Chapron, G Mayson, T Otley, M R Gordon, D Palmer-Jones
**Co. Secretary:** Mark Thompson
**Responsibilities**
**Senior:** Peter Gillatt *(Manager)*, John Granger *(Partner)*, Per Hjort *(Manager)*, Graham Mayes *(Manager)*
**HR:** Kate Brown *(Health & Safety Officer)*
**Facilities:** Trevor Gowland *(Maintenance Manager)*
**Branches:** Sita Tees Valley Ltd, Haverton Hill Rd, Billingham, Cleveland TS23 1PY
**US SIC:** 4953, 4959
**UK SIC:** 92110
**Auditors:** Ernst & Young LLP
**Bankers:** National Westminster Bank Plc (60-15-08)

| | 31-12-13 | 31-12-12 | 31-12-11 |
|---|---|---|---|
| TO | 36,427,000 | 25,315,000 | 19,348,000 |
| P/L | 7,363,000 | 2,496,000 | (3,249,000) |
| NW | 40,500,000 | 34,195,000 | 31,939,000 |
| WC | (14,380,000) | (23,776,000) | (28,811,000) |
| Emp. | 130 | 96 | 103 |

DUNS 21-773-3003
## Sita Uk
Benedict Wharf, Mitcham, Surrey CR4 3BQ
**Tel:** 02086482288
**Web:** www.sita.co.uk
**Estd:** 2011 Proprietorship
**Line of Business:** Collection and treatment of other waste
**Proprietor:** N Jones
**US SIC:** 4953 **UK SIC:** 92110
**Employees:** 100

DUNS 21-812-1972
## Sita Uk Limited Qhb-151
Unit 15-16 Bootham Lane Industrial, Estate, Bootham Lane, Dunscroft, Doncaster, South Yorkshire DN7 4JU
**Tel:** 07528971665
**Web:** www.sita.co.uk
**Estd:** 2012
**Line of Business:** Manufacture of pulp
**Responsibilities**
**Senior:** Danny Kelly *(Manager)*, Darren Steele *(Supervisor)*
**US SIC:** 2611 **UK SIC:** 47101
**Employees:** 70

DUNS 21-036-7773
## Site and Field Services
1 Freeman Way, Ashington, Northumberland NE63 0YB
**Tel:** 01670-522522
**Web:** www.safs.co.uk
**VAT No:** 746523032 **Estd:** 2004 Partnership
**Line of Business:** Engineers (general)
**Partners:** B Carr, B Karr
**Responsibilities**
**Senior:** Stewart Wild *(Manager)*
**US SIC:** 3549, 8911
**UK SIC:** 32212, 83701
**Employees:** 52

DUNS 21-811-2981
## Site Confidence
Kings Court, 41-51 Kingston Road, Leatherhead, Surrey KT22 7SL
**Tel:** 01372383800
**Web:** www.nccgroup.com
**Estd:** 2005
**Line of Business:** Computer software sales
**Responsibilities**
**Senior:** Bob Dowson *(Manager)*
**US SIC:** 7379 **UK SIC:** 83940
**Employees:** 60

DUNS 76-511-6850
## Site Engineering Surveys Ltd
**(Subsidiary of:** Fastway Management Ltd)
10-16 Tiller Road, London E14 8PX
**Tel:** 020-7538-0870
**Web:** www.sesltd.uk.com
**Reg No:** 2568539 **VAT No:** 629692006
**Estd:** 1990 Private Limited Company
**Line of Business:** Land surveying activities
**Issued Capital:** £10,000
**Director:** J W Gaffney
**Co. Secretary:** Ms Sandra Warner
**Responsibilities**
**Senior:** Joel Phillips *(Resources Manager)*
**Marketing:** Gavin Perry *(Senior Marketing Executive)*
**Purchasing:** Joel Phillips *(Resources Manager)*
**US SIC:** 1541 **UK SIC:** 50100
**Auditors:** Dickinsons
**Bankers:** Lloyds TSB Bank plc (30-97-73)

| | 31-01-14 | 31-01-13 | 31-01-12 |
|---|---|---|---|
| TO | 9,361,325 | N/A | N/A |
| P/L | 1,829,277 | N/A | N/A |
| NW | 2,580,746 | 1,449,923 | 1,160,654 |
| WC | 2,351,543 | 1,338,974 | 1,039,288 |
| Emp. | 137 | N/A | N/A |

DUNS 21-722-9855
## Sitec Engineering Ltd
**(Subsidiary of:** Sitec Holdings Ltd)
Church House, Church Road, Filton, Bristol, Avon BS34 7BD
**Tel:** 01179792396
**Web:** www.sitecgroup.com
**Reg No:** 1059352 **VAT No:** 639584100
**Estd:** 2012 Private Limited Company
**Line of Business:** Employment and recruitment companies and consultants
**Trading Style:** G E D, Sitec Group
**Issued Capital:** £30,000
**Principals:** D J Medlock *(Managing)*, J Buick, K W Barnes
**Co. Secretary:** Antony Ambridge
**Responsibilities**
**Senior:** Ian Bascombe *(Non-Executive Director)*
**Branches:** Sitec Engineering Ltd, 382 Kenton Rd, Harrow, Middlesex HA3 8DP
**US SIC:** 8911 **UK SIC:** 83701
**Auditors:** Bishop Fleming
**Bankers:** Lloyds TSB Bank plc (30-90-54)

| | 31-07-14 | 31-07-13 | 31-07-12 |
|---|---|---|---|
| TO | 63,284,393 | 62,351,201 | 62,718,668 |
| P/L | 5,965,302 | 3,542,248 | 3,984,510 |
| NW | 20,222,262 | 20,022,746 | 16,862,729 |
| WC | 19,938,473 | 19,499,278 | 16,988,953 |
| Emp. | 247 | 259 | 289 |

DUNS 21-592-4406
## Sitel
Balliol Business Park, Benton Lane, Newcastle-Upon-Tyne, Tyne and Wear NE12 8EW
**Tel:** 01913502000
**Estd:** 2011 Proprietorship
**Line of Business:** Contract furnishers
**Proprietor:** T Wilson
**US SIC:** 1799 **UK SIC:** 50000
**Employees:** 200

DUNS 34-618-8907
## Sitel Europe Ltd
**(Subsidiary of:** Onex Corporation)
5 Hercules Way, Leavesden, Watford, Hertfordshire WD25 7GS
**Tel:** 01923 689 600
**Web:** www.sitel.com
**Reg No:** 2756274 **VAT No:** 685108619
**Estd:** 1992 Private Limited Company
**Line of Business:** Telecommunications
**Issued Capital:** £50,000,000
**Directors:** J Kellett, K V Brough, P L De Castro, N Benbekhti
**Co. Secretary:** John Hayward
**Responsibilities**
**Senior:** Joann Passingham *(Manager)*, Timothy Schuh *(Manager)*
**Sales:** Joann Passingham *(Manager)*
**IT:** Dawn Baker *(IT Manager)*
**Branches:** Sitel Europe Ltd, South Bar House, South Bar Street, Banbury, Oxfordshire OX16 9AD
**US SIC:** 4899, 6711
**UK SIC:** 79020, 83962
**Auditors:** PricewaterhouseCoopers LLP
**Bankers:** The Royal Bank Of Scotland Plc (16-13-18)

| | 31-12-13 | 31-12-12 | 31-12-11 |
|---|---|---|---|
| TO | 20,390,000 | 19,878,000 | 9,745,000 |
| P/L | 551,000 | (5,599,000) | (4,484,000) |
| NW | (27,854,000) | (26,636,000) | (21,561,000) |
| WC | (20,551,000) | (19,455,000) | (20,680,000) |
| Emp. | 131 | 130 | 113 |

DUNS 53-645-3665
## Sitel Uk Ltd
**(Subsidiary of:** Onex Corporation)
Sitel House, Timothys Bridge Road, Stratford Enterprise Park, Stratford-Upon-Avon, Warwickshire CV37 9HY
**Tel:** 01789299622
**Web:** www.sitel.co.uk
**Reg No:** 3450786 **Estd:** 1997 Private Limited Company
**Line of Business:** Telecommunications
**Issued Capital:** £28,500,000
**Directors:** J Kellett, K V Brough, N Benbekhti, P L De Castro
**Co. Secretary:** John Hayward
**Responsibilities**
**Senior:** Joann Passingham *(Manager)*
**Finance:** Liz Williams *(Financial Controller)*

**Marketing:** Michelle Anderson *(Marketing Manager)*
**HR:** Samantha Miller *(Human Resources Manager)*
**Branches:** Sitel Uk Ltd, Sitel House, Timothys Bridge Road, Stratford-Upon-Avon, Warwickshire CV37 9HY
**US SIC:** 4899, 7399
**UK SIC:** 79020, 83954
**Auditors:** KPMG LLP

| | 31-12-13 | 31-12-12 | 31-12-11 |
|---|---|---|---|
| TO | 60,846,000 | 57,513,000 | 60,326,000 |
| P/L | 3,043,000 | 1,207,000 | (503,000) |
| NW | 9,915,000 | 6,872,000 | 5,665,000 |
| WC | 9,630,000 | 6,999,000 | 6,009,000 |
| Emp. | 1,709 | 1,389 | 1,602 |

DUNS 23-880-2099
## Sitemaker Software Ltd
One Reading Central, Forbury Road, Reading, Berkshire RG1 3YL
**Tel:** 02075804155
**Reg No:** 3871424 **Estd:** 1999 Private Limited Company
**Line of Business:** Other software consultancy and supply
**Issued Capital:** £2,040
**Director:** P Russo
**Co. Secretary:** Christian Wells
**Responsibilities**
**Senior:** Matt Casey *(Operations Director)*, David Eckert *(Director)*
**Operations:** Matt Casey *(Operations Director)*
**US SIC:** 7379, 7374
**UK SIC:** 83940
**Auditors:** Mazars LLP

| | 31-03-14 | 31-03-13 | 31-03-11 |
|---|---|---|---|
| TO | 4,760,000 | 5,243,000 | N/A |
| P/L | (1,805,000) | (399,000) | N/A |
| NW | (2,026,000) | (637,000) | 227,784 |
| WC | (1,975,000) | (747,000) | (88,333) |
| Emp. | 82 | 47 | N/A |

DUNS 23-927-8638
## Sito Recruitment Ltd
Security House, Barbourne Road, Worcester, Worcestershire WR1 1RS
**Tel:** 08450750111
**Web:** www.skillsforsecurity.org.uk
**Reg No:** 3917802 **Estd:** 2000 Private Limited Company
**Line of Business:** Labour recruitment and provision of personnel
**Issued Capital:** £2
**Director:** J D Kelly
**Responsibilities**
**Senior:** Alex Carmichael *(Director)*
**HR:** Louise Lowe *(Operations Manager)*
**Health & Safety:** John Stanton *(Health & Safety Officer)*
**US SIC:** 7361, 7399
**UK SIC:** 83954

| | 31-12-13 | 31-12-12 | 31-12-11 |
|---|---|---|---|
| TA | 2 | 2 | 2 |
| NW | 2 | 2 | 2 |

DUNS 28-870-6401
## Sittingbourne & Kemsley Light Railway Ltd
Po Box 300, Kemsley, Sittingbourne, Kent ME10 2DZ
**Tel:** 0871-222-1568
**Reg No:** 1036616 **Estd:** 1971 Private Limited Company
**Line of Business:** Other scheduled passenger land transport not elsewhere classified
**Directors:** R Newcombe, J R Fuller, D J Pritchard, Mrs E M Fuller, P Best, E E Tombs
**Co. Secretary:** Nicholas Widdows
**US SIC:** 4119 **UK SIC:** 72200
**Bankers:** The Co-Operative Bank Plc (08-90-23)

| | 28-02-14 | 28-02-13 | 29-02-12 |
|---|---|---|---|
| TO | 67,312 | 53,967 | 51,500 |
| P/L | (9,153) | (5,213) | (11,954) |
| NW | 30,405 | 39,558 | 44,771 |
| WC | 30,351 | 39,492 | 44,690 |

DUNS 21-031-9742
## Sitwell Arms Hotel
39 Station Road, Renishaw, Sheffield, South Yorkshire S21 3WF
**Tel:** 01246435226
**Web:** www.sitwellarms.com
**Proprietorship**
**Line of Business:** Hotels
**Partners:** Mrs G Selby, J Selby
**Responsibilities**
**Senior:** Joanne Oldfield *(Partner)*
**US SIC:** 7011 **UK SIC:** 66500
**Employees:** 50

DUNS 50-395-9314 **Imp-Exp**
## Siv/Uk Ltd
**(Subsidiary of:** Nippon Sheet Glass Company Limited)
Lathom, Ormskirk, Lancashire L40 5UF
**Tel:** 01214513901 **Fax:** 024-7663-6912
**Web:** www.siv.co.uk
**Reg No:** 2402437 **VAT No:** 544881713
**Estd:** 1989 Private Limited Company
**Line of Business:** Glass producers and distributors.
**Export Markets:** Germany
**Trading Style:** S I V, Sicursiv
**Issued Capital:** £850,000
**Director:** Miss J A Brown
**Co. Secretary:** Iain Smith
**Branches:** Siv/Uk Ltd, Unit 29, Sutton Park Avenue, Reading, Berkshire RG6 1AZ
**US SIC:** 3211 **UK SIC:** 24710
**Auditors:** Coopers & Lybrand
**Bankers:** National Westminster Bank Plc (56-00-45)
**Employees:** 165

DUNS 22-602-1723 **Exp**
## Siva Holdings Ltd
Spitfire House, Hazel Road, Woolston, Southampton, Hampshire SO19 7GB
**Tel:** 02380-448838
**Web:** www.sivagroup.co.uk
**Reg No:** 1439398 **Estd:** 1979 Private Limited Company
**Line of Business:** Manufacture of plastic packing goods
**Export Sales:** £16,507,307
**Issued Capital:** £50,000
**Principals:** G S Mehta *(Managing)*, V S Mehta, T P Mehta, V P Mehta
**Co. Secretary:** Preet Athwal
**Responsibilities**
**Senior:** Babna Athwal *(Manager)*
**Finance:** Babna Athwal *(Manager)*
**US SIC:** 3079 **UK SIC:** 48360
**Auditors:** Atkinsons
**Bankers:** Lloyds TSB Bank plc (30-99-87)

| | 31-10-13 | 31-10-12 | 31-10-11 |
|---|---|---|---|
| TO | 52,397,034 | 48,160,385 | 45,266,663 |
| P/L | 1,473,819 | 2,199,087 | 1,880,109 |
| NW | 8,732,221 | 8,219,547 | 7,853,777 |
| WC | (4,501,548) | (3,196,596) | (3,125,718) |
| Emp. | 197 | 179 | 182 |

DUNS 39-671-6466
## Six Bells Ltd
44b High Street, Sevenoaks, Kent TN13 1JG
**Tel:** 01732743665
**Reg No:** 2137767 **Estd:** 1987 Private Limited Company
**Line of Business:** Licensed restaurants
**Issued Capital:** £118,007
**Director:** A Ginzler
**Co. Secretary:** Ms Gillian Ginzler
**Branches:** Six Bells Ltd, Speldhurst Hill, Tunbridge Wells, Kent TN3 0NN
**US SIC:** 5812 **UK SIC:** 66110
**Auditors:** Moores Rowland
**Bankers:** Lloyds TSB Bank plc (30-97-49)

| | 30-09-13 | 30-09-12 | 30-09-11 |
|---|---|---|---|
| TA | 1,293,381 | 1,461,940 | 1,503,082 |
| NW | 493,456 | 636,716 | 690,425 |
| WC | (125,482) | (151,132) | (115,929) |

DUNS 21-702-8116
## Six Degrees Technology Group Ltd
**(Subsidiary of:** Tosca Penta Exodus Lp)
Commodity Quay, St Katharine Docks, London E1W 1AZ
**Tel:** 02078584700
**Web:** www.6dg.co.uk
**Reg No:** 7473012 **Estd:** 2010 Private Limited Company
**Line of Business:** Telecommunications
**Export Sales:** £910,000
**Issued Capital:** £624,375
**Directors:** P R Bamford, S Scott, R W Smith, A R Mills, S Maine, W T Macnaughton
**Co. Secretary:** Andrew Booth
**Responsibilities**
**Senior:** Mike Ing *(Group Business Operations Dire)*, Daniel Lowe *(Managing Director - Six Degree)*, Michael Shanks *(Chief Technical Officer)*, Campbell Williams *(Group Strategy & Marketing Dir)*
**Marketing:** Campbell Williams *(Group Strategy & Marketing Dir)*
**Sales:** Namuli Katumba *(Head of Account Management and)*
**Operations:** Mike Ing *(Group Business Operations Dire)*
**Engineering:** Michael Shanks *(Chief Technical Officer)*
**US SIC:** 4899 **UK SIC:** 79020
**Bankers:** Clydesdale Bank Plc (82-20-00)

| | 31-03-14 | 31-03-13 | 31-03-12 |
|---|---|---|---|
| TO | 68,927,000 | 51,507,000 | 20,181,000 |
| P/L | (6,653,000) | (6,169,000) | (5,602,000) |
| NW | (88,854,000) | (86,239,000) | (47,064,000) |
| WC | (10,965,000) | (12,041,000) | 709,000 |
| Emp. | 250 | 218 | 93 |

DUNS 73-689-8326
## Six Town Housing Ltd
Point Blue, Moor Street, Bury, Lancashire BL9 5AQ
**Web:** www.sixtownhousing.org
**Reg No:** 4948846 **Estd:** 2011 Private Company Limited By Guarantee
**Line of Business:** Management of real estate on a fee or contract basis
**Directors:** Mrs A T Foster, D L Gunther, D Howell, Mrs B P Park, H Broadbent, Mrs S M Smith, Mrs S Mccambridge, Ms S J Southworth
**Co. Secretary:** Ms Ailsa Dunn
**Responsibilities**
**Senior:** Ann Fitzwalter *(Director)*, Anthony Gerrard *(Director)*, Sharon Mc Caimbridge *(Chief Executive Officer)*, Brett Nelson *(Manager)*, Anthony Noblet *(Director)*, Philip Saxton *(Director)*, Norman Tooth *(Director)*
**US SIC:** 6531 **UK SIC:** 83400
**Auditors:** PKF (U K) LLP
**Bankers:** The Co-Operative Bank Plc (08-90-00)

| | 31-03-14 | 31-03-13 | 31-03-12 |
|---|---|---|---|
| TO | 14,895,665 | 14,469,917 | 14,249,323 |
| P/L | (645,374) | (60,745) | 274,996 |
| NW | (1,557,969) | (2,006,157) | (172,856) |
| WC | 257,339 | 825,775 | (790,079) |
| Emp. | 207 | 210 | 199 |

DUNS 21-809-3623
## Sixt Kenning Ltd
**(Subsidiary of:** Sixt Se)
1 Chase Road, Epsom, Surrey KT19 8TL
**Tel:** 01372722227 **Fax:** 01246506134
**Web:** www.sixt.co.uk
**Reg No:** 0440897 **Estd:** 1947 Private Limited Company
**Line of Business:** Vehicle rental (car)
**Trading Style:** Sixt Rent A Car
**Issued Capital:** £4,000,000
**Directors:** I J Feast, Dr J Z Putlitz, I W Lawrence, P I Voegerl
**Co. Secretary:** Miss Wai-Yan Fung
**Responsibilities**
**Senior:** Catherine Hope *(Marketing Director)*
**HR:** Felicity Ball *(Training Manager)*
**Branches:** Sixt Kenning Ltd, Gate Ho, Hallwood Rd, Workington, Cumbria CA14 4JR
**US SIC:** 7512 **UK SIC:** 84801
**Auditors:** Jeffreys Henry
**Bankers:** Barclays Bank Plc (20-07-71)

| | 31-12-13 | 31-12-12 | 31-12-11 |
|---|---|---|---|
| TO | 41,420,000 | 36,243,000 | 32,663,000 |
| P/L | 5,713,000 | 2,068,000 | 3,147,000 |
| NW | 16,558,000 | 10,791,000 | 8,273,000 |
| WC | (25,883,000) | (27,311,000) | (26,767,000) |
| Emp. | 310 | 272 | 226 |

DUNS 21-581-6238
## Sixth Form Centre Grammar School
Les Varendes, St Andrew, Guernsey, Channel Islands GY6 8TD
**Tel:** 01481256571
**Web:** www.grammar.sch.gg
**Estd:** 2011 Proprietorship
**Line of Business:** Schools (local authority)
**Proprietor:** J Smith
**US SIC:** 8211 **UK SIC:** 93200
**Employees:** 110

DUNS 23-168-9238
## The Sixth Form College Farnborough
Prospect Avenue, Farnborough, Hampshire GU14 8JX
**Tel:** 01252-688200
**Web:** www.farnborough.ac.uk
**Estd:** 2003
**Line of Business:** Further education schools and colleges
**Director:** Dr J Guy
**Responsibilities**
**Finance:** Alison Mc Kenzie *(Finance Manager)*
**IT:** Kevin Balenzuela *(Network Manager)*
**US SIC:** 8221 **UK SIC:** 93100
**Employees:** 380

DUNS 23-680-6972
## The Sixth Form College Solihull
Widney Manor Road, Solihull, West Midlands B91 3WR
**Tel:** 0121-704-2581
**Web:** www.solihullsfc.ac.uk
**Estd:** 1974
**Line of Business:** Colleges (higher education)
**Directors:** Ms P Scrivenner, J M Korzeniewski
**US SIC:** 8221 **UK SIC:** 93100
**Auditors:** Chantrey Vellacott DFK LLP
**Bankers:** National Westminster Bank Plc (55-50-15)

| | 31-07-12 | 31-07-07 |
|---|---|---|
| TO | 12,642,000 | 12,225,000 |
| P/L | 954,000 | 320,000 |
| NW | 11,186,000 | 11,252,000 |
| WC | 7,724,000 | 2,268,000 |
| Emp. | 220 | 226 |

DUNS 22-053-4155
## S.J. Clarke's Construction (I.O.W.) Ltd
Rew Street, Cowes, Isle of Wight PO31 8NN
**Tel:** 01983299908
**Reg No:** 4055426 **Estd:** 2000 Private Limited Company
**Line of Business:** Building of complete constructions or parts thereof; civil engineering
**Issued Capital:** £3
**Director:** S J Clarke
**Responsibilities**
**Senior:** Keith Traves *(Manager)*
**US SIC:** 1541, 1711
**UK SIC:** 50100, 50300
**Bankers:** National Westminster Bank Plc (50-31-29)

| | 30-06-13 | 30-06-12 | 30-06-11 |
|---|---|---|---|
| TA | 332,556 | 335,632 | 338,958 |
| NW | 303,830 | 302,246 | 300,962 |
| WC | 242,361 | 223,020 | 187,266 |

DUNS 73-556-9423
## Sjb Corporate Ltd
**(Subsidiary of:** Manpowergroup Inc.)
6 New Bridge Street, London EC4V 6AB
**Tel:** 02078321960
**Web:** www.thesjbgroup.com
**Reg No:** 4818906 **Estd:** 2003 Private Limited Company
**Line of Business:** Labour recruitment and provision of personnel
**Issued Capital:** £100
**Directors:** D P Whitham, G Smith, B Doltis
**Co. Secretary:** Damian Whitham
**Responsibilities**
**Senior:** Chris Pickford *(Chief Executive Officer)*
**US SIC:** 7361 **UK SIC:** 83954

| | 31-12-13 | 31-12-12 | 31-12-11 |
|---|---|---|---|
| TO | 4,751,069 | N/A | N/A |
| P/L | 2,282,187 | N/A | N/A |
| NW | 1,906,007 | 3,094,312 | 1,851,820 |
| WC | 1,876,811 | 3,042,666 | 1,767,515 |
| Emp. | 24 | N/A | N/A |

DUNS 21-330-3076
## S.J.Bargh Ltd
Hornby Road, Caton, Lancaster, Lancashire LA2 9JA
**Tel:** 01524-770439 **Fax:** 01524-770487
**Web:** www.sjbargh.co.uk
**Reg No:** 0532272 **Estd:** 1954 Private Limited Company
**Line of Business:** Other supporting land transport activities
**Issued Capital:** £2,548
**Principals:** S Cornthwaite *(Managing)*, J M Renaghan, Ms H E Lloyd, A R Finlayson-Green, Miss R M Towers, Mrs R K Thomas, M J Sidley
**Co. Secretary:** James Renaghan
**Responsibilities**
**Senior:** Mary Bargh *(Manager)*, Robert Parr *(Manager)*
**Branches:** Cloughton, Lancaster Lancs
**US SIC:** 4789 **UK SIC:** 77002
**Auditors:** Scott & Wilkinson
**Bankers:** Barclays Bank Plc (20-47-61)

| | 30-04-14 | 30-04-13 | 30-04-12 |
|---|---|---|---|
| TO | 32,457,654 | 29,456,453 | 29,401,665 |
| P/L | 1,809,133 | 841,442 | 1,118,694 |
| NW | 14,827,527 | 13,628,691 | 13,277,951 |
| WC | 5,951,303 | 4,968,892 | 6,631,423 |
| Emp. | 354 | 341 | 339 |

DUNS 52-011-0214
## Sjc 15 Ltd
4 Carlton Street, Nottingham, Nottinghamshire NG1 1NN
**Reg No:** 3377811 **Estd:** 1997 Private Limited Company
**Line of Business:** Business services
**Issued Capital:** £771,458
**Director:** G H Akins
**Co. Secretary:** Sean Akins
**US SIC:** 7399, 7999
**UK SIC:** 83954, 97913
**Auditors:** Robt A Page Krik Cree Jepson

| | 31-12-13 | 31-12-12 | 31-12-11 |
|---|---|---|---|
| TO | 17,238,000 | 18,257,000 | 15,626,000 |
| P/L | 2,334,000 | 871,000 | 1,304,000 |
| NW | 26,086,000 | 26,267,000 | 26,947,000 |
| WC | (18,477,000) | (22,932,000) | 666,000 |
| Emp. | 313 | 268 | 260 |

## Sjd Group Ltd

DUNS 23-817-2717

(**Subsidiary of:** Sjd Accountancy Ltd)
S J D, Hemel Hempstead, Hertfordshire HP2
4AA
**Tel:** 01442-232700
**Web:** www.sjdaccountancy.com
**Reg No:** 3809453 **Estd:** 1999 Private
Limited Company
**Line of Business:** Accounting and auditing
activities
**Issued Capital:** £99,100
**Directors:** K J Budge, S J Curry
**Responsibilities**
**Senior:** Claire Canadas (Manager)
**US SIC:** 8931 **UK SIC:** 83600

|      | 31-10-13   | 31-10-12   | 31-10-11  |
|------|------------|------------|-----------|
| TO   | 13,294,556 | 13,212,134 | 9,610,625 |
| P/L  | 3,340,270  | 6,488,870  | 3,801,417 |
| NW   | 4,262,598  | 2,282,615  | 2,023,135 |
| WC   | 2,104,128  | 57,516     | 241,127   |
| Emp. | 86         | 83         | N/A       |

## S.J.Dixon & Son Ltd

DUNS 21-834-7235    Imp

(**Subsidiary of:** S.J. Dixon & Son (Holdings)
Ltd)
Old Heath Road, Wolverhampton, West
Midlands WV1 2BF
**Tel:** 01619683061
**Web:** www.sjdixon.co.uk
**Reg No:** 0284920 **Estd:** 1854 Private
Limited Company
**Line of Business:** Holding companies
management activities
**Issued Capital:** £230,250
**Principals:** B J Dixon (Chairman),
D E Swingwood (Managing), R A Campbell
(Sales), T J Dixon
**Co. Secretary:** Colin Aston
**Branches:** S.j.dixon & Son Limited, 549/551
Moseley Rd, Birmingham, West Midlands
B12 9BT
**US SIC:** 6711, 5074, 5999
**UK SIC:** 83962, 61300, 65600
**Auditors:** J W Hinks LLP
**Bankers:** HSBC Bank plc (40-11-17)

|     | 31-12-13  | 31-12-12  | 31-12-11  |
|-----|-----------|-----------|-----------|
| TO  | N/A       | 4,071,633 | N/A       |
| P/L | N/A       | (126,307) | N/A       |
| NW  | 1,010,035 | 1,061,732 | 1,718,039 |
| WC  | 944,013   | 606,584   | 1,257,842 |

## S.Jennings Ltd

DUNS 21-231-5519

(**Subsidiary of:** S. Jennings Group Ltd)
Newcastle Road, South Shields, Tyne and
Wear NE34 9PQ
**Tel:** 01670501400
**Web:** www.jenningsmotorgroup.co.uk
**Reg No:** 0120996 **VAT No:** 555910824
**Estd:** 1912 Private Limited Company
**Line of Business:** Sale of new motor
vehicles
**Trading Style:** Jennings Ford, Jennings of
Morpeth, Jennings Motor Group
**Issued Capital:** £658,827
**Principals:** N A Khan (Sales), Mrs N N Khan,
S Khan
**Branches:** S.jennings Ltd, Eslington Park,
Gateshead, Tyne and Wear NE8 2TZ
**US SIC:** 5511, 5521, 7539, 5531
**UK SIC:** 65100, 67100
**Auditors:** Ernst & Young LLP
**Bankers:** HSBC Bank plc (40-33-20)

|      | 31-12-13    | 31-12-12    | 31-12-11    |
|------|-------------|-------------|-------------|
| TO   | 145,875,120 | 124,301,038 | 128,985,721 |
| P/L  | 925,240     | 2,803,386   | (1,079,147) |
| NW   | 11,577,092  | 10,181,455  | 10,479,480  |
| WC   | 3,709,230   | 4,370,438   | (1,806,365) |
| Emp. | 389         | 412         | 454         |

## Sjg International Ltd

DUNS 21-882-6543    Imp-Exp

Tything Road, Arden Forest Industrial Estate,
Alcester, Warwickshire B49 6ES
**Tel:** 01789764547 **Fax:** 01789764070
**Web:** www.sjginternational.com
**Reg No:** 0974659 **VAT No:** 110641523
**Estd:** 1969 Private Limited Company
**Line of Business:** Other manufacturing not
elsewhere classified
**Export Markets:** Europe
**Export Sales:** £213,438
**Issued Capital:** £1,000
**Directors:** R James, D G Horsley
**Co. Secretary:** Michael James
**US SIC:** 3999 **UK SIC:** 49590
**Auditors:** Thomas & Young
**Bankers:** Barclays Bank Plc (20-07-82)

|      | 30-09-13  | 30-09-12  | 30-09-11  |
|------|-----------|-----------|-----------|
| TO   | 5,212,248 | 6,019,178 | 5,352,111 |
| P/L  | 104,401   | 170,594   | 118,201   |
| NW   | 1,644,875 | 1,572,303 | 1,775,455 |
| WC   | (228,554) | (30,727)  | (13,722)  |
| Emp. | 56        | 56        | 56        |

## S.K. Chilled Foods Ltd

DUNS 22-848-0414

(**Subsidiary of:** Entrepreneurial Food Group
Llc)
Wellington House, Wynyard Avenue,
Wynyard, Stockton-On-Tees, Cleveland
TS22 5TB
**Tel:** 01740646878 **Fax:** 0845 337 3035
**Web:** www.skfoods.co.uk
**Reg No:** 2052519 **Estd:** 1986 Private
Limited Company
**Line of Business:** Processing and
preserving of fruit and vegetables not
elsewhere classified
**Issued Capital:** £7,367
**Principals:** L Bell (Chairman), D R Roberts,
D Hodgson, D Graham, J D Faulkner,
A Harvey
**Co. Secretary:** Richard Shippee
**Branches:** S.k. Chilled Foods Ltd, Nelson
Street, Middlesbrough, Cleveland TS6 6BJ
**US SIC:** 2033 **UK SIC:** 41473
**Auditors:** Wingrave Yeats Partnership LLP
**Bankers:** National Westminster Bank Plc
(54-10-04)

|      | 30-09-13   | 30-09-12   | 30-09-11   |
|------|------------|------------|------------|
| TO   | 53,630,000 | 45,347,000 | 44,705,000 |
| P/L  | 1,252,000  | 528,000    | 22,000     |
| NW   | (8,771,000)| (10,023,000)| (12,108,000)|
| WC   | (1,396,000)| (1,921,000)| (2,649,000)|
| Emp. | 578        | 519        | 545        |

## S.K.A. Textiles Ltd

DUNS 21-313-0669    Imp-Exp

(**Subsidiary of:** Ska Holdings Ltd)
Empress Works, St Thomas's Road,
Huddersfield, West Yorkshire HD1 3LJ
**Tel:** 01484-539225 **Fax:** 01484423593
**Web:** www.skatextiles.co.uk
**Reg No:** 1939918 **VAT No:** 526045955
**Estd:** 1985 Private Limited Company
**Line of Business:** Manufacture of other
wearing apparel and accessories not
elsewhere classified
**Export Sales:** £1,091,661
**Issued Capital:** £93,340
**Directors:** A Pervaiz, S Pervaiz,
Mrs Y Pervaiz, S Pervaiz
**Co. Secretary:** Khalid Pervaiz
**Responsibilities**
**Senior:** Martin Littlewood (Warehouse
Manager)
**Finance:** Glenn Devons (Accounts Manager)
**US SIC:** 2389 **UK SIC:** 45393
**Auditors:** Clough & Co LLP
**Bankers:** Yorkshire Bank Plc (05-02-32)

|      | 31-08-13  | 31-08-12  | 31-08-11  |
|------|-----------|-----------|-----------|
| TO   | 6,877,832 | 8,057,766 | 7,878,672 |
| P/L  | 9,894     | 42,729    | 210,094   |
| NW   | 1,240,773 | 1,236,519 | 1,065,733 |
| WC   | (132,533) | 197,505   | 404,523   |
| Emp. | 48        | 44        | 45        |

## Skadden Arps Slate Meagher & Flom Ltd

DUNS 76-953-9743

40 Bank Street, London E14 5DS
**Tel:** 020-7519-7000 **Fax:** 020-7519-7070
**Web:** www.skadden.com
**Reg No:** 2622169 **Estd:** 1991 Private
Limited Company
**Line of Business:** Legal services
**Issued Capital:** £100
**Directors:** M E Hatchard, P Trivedi
**Responsibilities**
**Senior:** Gurdeep Rai (Manager)
**US SIC:** 8111 **UK SIC:** 83500

|    | 31-12-13 | 31-12-12 | 31-12-11 |
|----|----------|----------|----------|
| TA | 100      | 100      | 100      |
| NW | 100      | 100      | 100      |

## Skan Group Holdings Ltd

DUNS 21-827-9305    Imp

Skan House 425 433, Stratford Road,
Shirley, Solihull, West Midlands B90 4AB
**Tel:** 0121-733-3003
**Web:** www.skan.co.uk
**Reg No:** 0657598 **Estd:** 1960 Private
Limited Company
**Line of Business:** Management activities of
holding companies
**Export Sales:** £651,745
**Issued Capital:** £10,000
**Principals:** R J Skan (Managing),
Ms C Skan, Ms J M Skan
**Co. Secretary:** Richard Skan
**US SIC:** 6711, 5199
**UK SIC:** 83962, 61900
**Auditors:** KPMG
**Bankers:** Barclays Bank Plc (20-08-44)

|      | 30-09-13   | 30-09-12   | 30-09-11  |
|------|------------|------------|-----------|
| TO   | 10,362,248 | 13,789,900 | 8,600,615 |
| P/L  | (327,440)  | 514,880    | (273,430) |
| NW   | 8,204,622  | 8,632,238  | 8,230,207 |
| WC   | 5,814,023  | 5,977,858  | 5,633,409 |
| Emp. | 88         | 99         | 58        |

## Skandinaviska Enskilda Ltd

DUNS 22-728-3520

(**Subsidiary of:** Skandinaviska Enskilda
Banken Ab)
1 Carter Lane, London EC4V 5ER
**Fax:** 020-7588-0929
**Web:** www.seb.co.uk
**Reg No:** 1618680 **Estd:** 1982 Private
Limited Company
**Line of Business:** Financial intermediation
not elsewhere classified
**Trading Style:** S E B, Enskilda Securities
**Issued Capital:** £49,300,000
**Directors:** Ms K C Berry, A J Hennebery,
M K Crow, M B Krejcir
**Responsibilities**
**Senior:** Kenneth Berglund (Manager),
Debbie McDermott (Manager)
**IT:** Gary Bartlett (Project Manager)
**HR:** Judy Elmes (Human Resources
Manager)
**US SIC:** 6111 **UK SIC:** 81501
**Auditors:** PricewaterhouseCoopers
**Bankers:** National Westminster Bank Plc
(50-00-00)

|     | 31-12-13   | 31-12-12   | 31-12-11   |
|-----|------------|------------|------------|
| TA  | 52,486,290 | 53,460,137 | 53,619,798 |
| P/L | 44,189     | 3,108,401  | 65,695     |
| NW  | 52,349,784 | 53,328,833 | 50,360,905 |
| WC  | 17,729,777 | 18,708,826 | 15,740,898 |

## Skanem Delta Label Systems Ltd

DUNS 29-294-2794    Exp

(**Subsidiary of:** Skanem As)
Unit 9 Bassendale Road, Croft Business
Park, Bromborough, Wirral, Merseyside
CH62 3QL
**Tel:** 0151-482-3800
**Web:** www.skanem.com
**Reg No:** 1646571 **VAT No:** 387225039
**Estd:** 1983 Private Limited Company
**Line of Business:** Manufacture of paper
stationery
**Export Markets:** Lithuania; Saudi Arabia;
Europe
**Trading Style:** Skanem Delta Label Systems
Ltd
**Issued Capital:** £1,012,265
**Director:** O Rugland
**Co. Secretary:** Duncan Raper
**US SIC:** 2648 **UK SIC:** 47231
**Auditors:** Deloitte & Touche
**Bankers:** Barclays Bank Plc (20-51-01)

|    | 31-12-13  | 31-12-12  | 31-12-11  |
|----|-----------|-----------|-----------|
| TA | 1,050,000 | 1,012,265 | 1,050,000 |
| NW | 1,050,000 | 1,012,265 | 1,050,000 |

## Skanska Rashleigh Weatherfoil Ltd

DUNS 21-198-6468

(**Subsidiary of:** Skanska Ab)
Hollywood House, Church Street East,
Woking, Surrey GU21 6HJ
**Tel:** 01923722700 **Fax:** 01932791810
**Web:** www.skanska.co.uk
**Reg No:** 0798550 **Estd:** 1964 Private
Limited Company
**Line of Business:** Electrical engineers
**Trading Style:** Skanska Facilities Services,
Bedford Fabrications
**Issued Capital:** £5,000,000
**Directors:** P Chandler, M G Neeson
**Co. Secretary:** Steven Leven
**Responsibilities**
**Senior:** Derek Hickling (Partner), Owen
Wood (Partner)
**Health & Safety:** Mike Graystone (Safety
Manager)
**Facilities:** Phil Russell (Facilities Director)
**Branches:** Skanska Rashleigh Weatherfoil
Ltd, 120 Aldersgate Street, London EC1A
4JQ
**US SIC:** 8911, 1711
**UK SIC:** 83701, 50300
**Auditors:** KPMG LLP
**Bankers:** Barclays Bank Plc (20-00-00)

|      | 31-12-13    | 31-12-12    | 31-12-11    |
|------|-------------|-------------|-------------|
| TO   | 252,948,000 | 242,672,000 | 290,949,000 |
| P/L  | 9,731,000   | 10,902,000  | 10,078,000  |
| NW   | 57,944,000  | 49,729,000  | 36,234,000  |
| WC   | 69,948,000  | 58,430,000  | 49,882,000  |
| Emp. | 930         | 1,016       | 1,222       |

## Skanska Uk Plc

DUNS 21-713-8551

(**Subsidiary of:** Skanska Ab)
Maple Cross House, Rickmansworth,
Hertfordshire WD3 9SW
**Tel:** 01656869659 **Fax:** 01932791810
**Web:** www.skanska.co.uk
**Reg No:** 0784752 **VAT No:** 378403142
**Estd:** 1963 Public Limited Company
**Line of Business:** Building construction
contractors
**Export Sales:** £1,435,000
**Issued Capital:** £165,000,000
**Directors:** H J Francis, R F Bayliss,
M C Putnam, P Chandler, W J Hocking

**Co. Secretary:** Mark Galloway
**Responsibilities**
**Senior:** Anna Mann (Head Of
Communications), Deirdre Murphy
(Manager), Ray Phillips (Regional Director),
Mats Williamson (Executive Vice President)
**Finance:** Narinder Shergill (Head of Finance
Business Suppo), Philippa Smith (Head of
Pensions)
**Marketing:** Eva Harris (Communications
Business Partne), Anna Mann (Head Of
Communications), Lizzie Sparrow (Head of
Marketing Communicatio)
**Sales:** Mark Boden (Business System
Manager), Steve Cooper (Development
Director), Alex MacLeod (Business
Development Director)
**Operations:** John Crawley (Operations
Director), Chris Grodzicki (Project Director),
Brian Parke (Pre-Construction Director),
Geoff Prudhoe (Operations Manager), Mark
Snell (Director - Project Delivery), Malcolm
Stagg (Project Manager), Bill Thicknes
(Project Director)
**Purchasing:** N McIver (Head of
Procurement)
**Engineering:** Jim Mellish (Technical
Engineering Director), Brian Parke (Pre-
Construction Director), Gordon Sims
(Engineering Projects Manager)
**Branches:** Skanska Uk Plc, Lowton Way,
Rotherham, South Yorkshire S66 8RY
**US SIC:** 1522, 8911
**UK SIC:** 50100, 83701
**Auditors:** KPMG LLP
**Bankers:** Skandinaviska Enskilda Banken
Ab (publ) (40-48-65)
Following financial data are in thousands

|      | 31-12-13  | 31-12-12  | 31-12-11  |
|------|-----------|-----------|-----------|
| TO   | 1,120,676 | 1,092,326 | 1,166,808 |
| P/L  | 44,189    | 43,446    | 44,943    |
| NW   | 212,663   | 223,050   | 171,301   |
| WC   | 264,746   | 268,038   | 212,638   |
| Emp. | 4,360     | 3,823     | 4,194     |

## Skar Precision Mouldings Ltd

DUNS 21-912-3460    Imp

(**Subsidiary of:** Aspire Plastics Ltd)
Lady Lane, Ipswich, Suffolk IP7 6AZ
**Tel:** 01473-828000
**Web:** www.skar.co.uk
**Reg No:** 0949310 **VAT No:** 103512232
**Estd:** 1969 Private Limited Company
**Line of Business:** Precision engineers
**Issued Capital:** £1,000
**Principals:** G M Mclellan (Managing),
B G Mclellan, P Denny, Ms K D Gant, P M Hill
**Co. Secretary:** Ms Karen Gant
**US SIC:** 3079 **UK SIC:** 48360
**Auditors:** Edwards
**Bankers:** Barclays Bank Plc (20-44-51)

|    | 31-12-13  | 31-12-12  | 31-12-11  |
|----|-----------|-----------|-----------|
| TA | 4,566,473 | 3,059,100 | 2,940,909 |
| NW | 1,856,223 | 1,472,012 | 1,233,202 |
| WC | 1,100,338 | 830,647   | 614,998   |

## S.Kaye & Son Ltd

DUNS 21-739-8825

6-8 East Street, Newquay, Cornwall TR7
1BH
**Tel:** 01637-870011 **Fax:** 01637-875040
**Web:** www.kayeschemist.co.uk
**Reg No:** 0973958 **Estd:** 1970 Private
Limited Company
**Line of Business:** Chemists dispensing
**Trading Style:** R B A V Kaye Limited
**Issued Capital:** £800
**Directors:** N R Kaye, Dr L G Kersh
**Responsibilities**
**Senior:** Amy Kaye (Manager)
**US SIC:** 5912, 5812
**UK SIC:** 64300, 66110
**Auditors:** Winter Rule
**Bankers:** HSBC Bank plc (40-34-30)

|    | 31-01-14 | 31-01-13 | 31-01-12 |
|----|----------|----------|----------|
| TA | 640,734  | 796,514  | 729,246  |
| NW | 398,665  | 378,129  | 265,530  |
| WC | 347,425  | 332,696  | 214,373  |

## Skea Egg Farms Ltd

DUNS 42-364-1711

146 Pomeroy Road, Dungannon, Co Tyrone
BT70 2TZ
**Tel:** 028-8776-1252 **Fax:** 028-8776-7049
**Web:** www.4ni.co.uk
**Reg No:** 0031124NI **Estd:** 1972 Private
Limited Company
**Line of Business:** Egg merchants
**Issued Capital:** £510
**Directors:** M S Hayes, Mrs M D Hayes,
H Richmond, M Hayes
**Co. Secretary:** Mrs Jacqueline Mcconnell
**Responsibilities**
**Health & Safety:** Kenneth Greer (Health &
Safety Officer)
**Facilities:** Roy Burnside (Facilities Manager)
**US SIC:** 5199 **UK SIC:** 61900
**Auditors:** PricewaterhouseCoopers

**Bankers:** Northern Bank Ltd (95-03-02)

|     | 31-12-13 | 31-12-12 | 31-12-11 |
|-----|----------|----------|----------|
| TO  | 57,775,833 | 51,637,860 | 45,053,477 |
| P/L | 2,158,564 | 2,417,996 | 1,490,030 |
| NW  | 8,922,267 | 7,546,020 | 5,509,538 |
| WC  | 5,057,881 | 3,379,004 | 1,564,352 |
| Emp.| 92 | 94 | 89 |

DUNS 22-054-2463                          Imp
### Skechers Usa Ltd.
(**Subsidiary of:** Skechers S.À R.L.)
Kathrine House, 9-11 Wyllyotts Place,
Potters Bar, Hertfordshire EN6 2JD
**Tel:** 01707-655955 **Fax:** 01707-647986
**Web:** www.skechers.com
**Reg No:** 4056244 **Estd:** 2000 Private
Limited Company
**Line of Business:** Representative office
**Issued Capital:** £1
**Directors:** D Weinberg, M Greenberg
**Co. Secretary:** Philip Paccione
**Responsibilities**
**Marketing:** Delilah Atkinson (Senior
Marketing Executive), Brett Worth (Trade
Marketing Executive UK &)
**Branches:** Skechers Usa Ltd., 153 Regent
Crescent, Manchester M17 8AR
**US SIC:** 3149, 5661
**UK SIC:** 45100, 64600
**Auditors:** KPMG LLP

|     | 31-12-13 | 31-12-12 | 31-12-11 |
|-----|----------|----------|----------|
| TO  | 45,214,000 | 42,712,000 | 45,363,000 |
| P/L | 645,000 | 609,000 | 917,000 |
| NW  | 1,566,000 | 1,162,000 | 714,000 |
| WC  | 6,304,000 | (410,000) | (1,207,000) |
| Emp.| 158 | 152 | 147 |

DUNS 23-082-9744
### Skegness Grammar School
Vernon Road, Skegness, Lincolnshire PE25
2QS
**Tel:** 01754-610000
**Web:** www.skegnessgrammar.lincs.sch.uk
**Estd:** 1933
**Line of Business:** General secondary
education
**Director:** A Rigby
**Responsibilities**
**Senior:** Roy Ballantyne (Head Teacher),
Simon Spraigue (Head Teacher)
**US SIC:** 8211 **UK SIC:** 93200
**Employees:** 80

DUNS 21-771-5566
### Skelton in Cleveland Primary School
Station Lane, Saltburn-By-The-Sea,
Cleveland TS12 2LR
**Tel:** 01287650689
**Web:** www.skeltonprimaryschool.co.uk
**Estd:** 1996 Partnership
**Line of Business:** Schools (foundation)
**Partner:** Ms S Walker
**US SIC:** 8211 **UK SIC:** 93200
**Employees:** 75

DUNS 21-585-0165
### Skene Group Ltd
Viewfield, Glenrothes, Fife KY6 2RD
**Tel:** 01592-632230 **Fax:** 01592744997
**Web:** www.skene-group.co.uk
**Reg No:** 0065071SC **VAT No:** 300783388
**Estd:** 1962 Private Limited Company
**Line of Business:** Demolition contractors
**Issued Capital:** £19,600
**Principals:** D Skene (Managing), N Skene
**Co. Secretary:** Ms Jill Mason
**Branches:** Skene Group Ltd, Banknock,
Bonnybridge, Stirlingshire FK4 1TX
**US SIC:** 1795, 3271, 3273
**UK SIC:** 50000, 24370, 24360
**Auditors:** Carters
**Bankers:** Barclays Bank Plc (20-29-23)

|     | 30-06-13 | 30-06-12 | 30-06-11 |
|-----|----------|----------|----------|
| TO  | 22,258,188 | 19,617,359 | 23,472,843 |
| P/L | 1,341,041 | 953,073 | 1,431,896 |
| NW  | 7,779,245 | 6,733,259 | 5,969,056 |
| WC  | (898,556) | (602,493) | 130,080 |
| Emp.| 128 | 127 | 128 |

DUNS 21-589-3678
### Skene Investments (Aberdeen) Ltd
Skene Investments, Aberdeen,
Aberdeenshire AB15 4AL
**Tel:** 01224-326221 **Fax:** 01224-310037
**Web:** www.skene-house.co.uk
**Reg No:** 0057524SC **VAT No:** 430122907
**Estd:** 1975 Private Limited Company
**Line of Business:** Building services
**Issued Capital:** £1,573,248
**Principals:** C P Skene (Chairman),
I S Mcarthur (Managing), Ms J M Lindsay,
Miss M J Gilchrist, R M Skene,
Ms P C Norris, A J Skene
**Co. Secretary:** Ledingham Chalmers Llp
**Branches:** Skene Investments (Aberdeen)
Ltd, 7 Queens Gardens, Aberdeen,
Aberdeenshire AB15 4YD

**US SIC:** 6552, 7011, 6711
**UK SIC:** 85000, 66500, 83962
**Auditors:** Ernst & Young LLP
**Bankers:** Bank Of Scotland (80-73-30)

|     | 31-01-14 | 31-01-13 | 31-01-12 |
|-----|----------|----------|----------|
| TO  | 7,401,648 | 6,823,457 | 5,516,185 |
| P/L | 1,928,850 | 1,997,617 | 835,855 |
| NW  | 25,817,954 | 24,277,317 | 22,827,060 |
| WC  | 6,097,110 | 4,512,096 | 3,198,276 |
| Emp.| 207 | 205 | 192 |

DUNS 21-811-9781
### Skene Medical Group
Discovery Drive, Arnhall Business Park,
Westhill, Aberdeenshire AB32 6FG
**Estd:** 2012
**Line of Business:** Doctors
**Responsibilities**
**Senior:** Babs Thomson (Practice Manager)
**US SIC:** 8011 **UK SIC:** 95300
**Employees:** 49

DUNS 21-771-2955
### Sketchley Hill Primary School
Sketchley Road, Burbage, Hinckley,
Leicestershire LE10 2DY
**Tel:** 01455238640
**Web:** www.sketchleyhill.leics.sch.uk
**Estd:** 1976 Proprietorship
**Line of Business:** Schools (local authority)
**Proprietor:** Mrs S Lees
**Responsibilities**
**Senior:** Scott Sewster (Head Teacher)
**US SIC:** 8211 **UK SIC:** 93200
**Employees:** 50

DUNS 42-436-2874
### Skf. Lo (Chemists) Ltd
1 Bankfield Lane, Huddersfield, West
Yorkshire HD5 0JE
**Reg No:** 4423982 **Estd:** 2002 Private
Limited Company
**Line of Business:** Dispensing chemists
**Issued Capital:** £1
**Director:** S K Lo
**Co. Secretary:** Mrs Iris Lo
**Responsibilities**
**Senior:** Chris Donaldson (Manager)
**US SIC:** 5912 **UK SIC:** 64300
**Bankers:** HSBC Bank plc (40-09-12)

|     | 31-03-14 | 31-03-13 | 31-03-12 |
|-----|----------|----------|----------|
| TO  | 11,437,595 | 8,746,971 | 9,857,704 |
| P/L | 465,581 | 247,136 | 392,792 |
| NW  | (6,987,185) | (4,134,214) | (4,759,770) |
| WC  | (1,181,589) | (984,540) | (1,474,543) |
| Emp.| 96 | 90 | 84 |

DUNS 21-620-5948                          Imp-Exp
### Skf (U.K) Ltd
(**Subsidiary of:** Ab Skf)
Sundon Park Road, Luton, Bedfordshire LU3
3BL
**Tel:** 01582-490049
**Web:** www.skf.com
**Reg No:** 0107367 **VAT No:** 467264914
**Estd:** 1910 Private Limited Company
**Line of Business:** Manufacture of bearings,
gears, gearing and driving elements
**Export Markets:** Sweden
**Issued Capital:** £37,200,000
**Principals:** Ms S L Smith (Financial),
R Makhija, B O Hansson, R J Law
**Co. Secretary:** Mrs Paula Owen
**Responsibilities**
**Senior:** Brian Willin (Purchasing Manager),
Maria Worby (Support Administrator)
**Marketing:** Phil Burge (Marketing Manager)
**Facilities:** Yvonne Holden (Maintenance
Manager)
**Operations:** Mike Abbott (Environmental
Manager)
**Purchasing:** Brian Willin (Purchasing
Manager)
**Engineering:** Paul Dysiewicz (Engineering
Manager), Heike Sengstschmid (Production
Manager)
**Branches:** Skf (U.k) Ltd, 2 Michaelson
Square, Livingston, West Lothian EH54 7DP
**US SIC:** 3568, 3398, 3559
**UK SIC:** 32613, 31380, 32863
**Auditors:** KPMG LLP
**Bankers:** Skandinaviska Enskilda Banken
Ab (publ) (40-48-65)

|     | 31-12-13 | 31-12-12 | 31-12-11 |
|-----|----------|----------|----------|
| TO  | 254,617,000 | 239,999,000 | 250,635,000 |
| P/L | 42,273,000 | 48,222,000 | 54,105,000 |
| NW  | 74,245,000 | 75,387,000 | 68,300,000 |
| WC  | 83,784,000 | 91,619,000 | 82,836,000 |
| Emp.| 1,000 | 981 | 946 |

DUNS 29-510-6827                          Exp
### Ski Bound Ltd
(**Subsidiary of:** Tui Ag)
Olivier House, 18 Marine Parade, Brighton,
East Sussex BN2 1TL
**Tel:** 01273244570 **Fax:** 01273244501
**Web:** http://skibound.co.uk
**Reg No:** 1873956 **Estd:** 1984 Private
Limited Company

**Line of Business:** Activities of travel
organisers
**Export Markets:** France, Belgium, Austria,
Italy, U S A, Netherlands, Germany, Spain,
Bulgaria
**Trading Style:** Travelbound European Tours,
Club Ski Bound
**Issued Capital:** £3,250,003
**Directors:** N K Rust, M Froggatt,
B G Robinson, B D Jones
**Co. Secretary:** Mrs Joyce Walter
**Branches:** Ski Bound Ltd, Olivier House, 18
Marine Parade, Brighton, East Sussex BN2
1TL
**US SIC:** 8999 **UK SIC:** 83954
**Auditors:** KPMG Audit Plc
**Bankers:** Bank Of Scotland (12-12-68)

|     | 30-09-13 | 30-09-12 | 30-09-11 |
|-----|----------|----------|----------|
| TO  | 25,535,000 | 25,925,000 | 22,650,000 |
| P/L | 1,163,000 | (6,479,000) | (4,168,000) |
| NW  | (5,048,000) | (7,002,000) | (1,317,000) |
| WC  | (7,944,000) | (8,433,000) | (16,574,000) |
| Emp.| 100 | 120 | 144 |

DUNS 21-810-2696
### Ski Kings
Sterling House, 20 Renfield Street, Glasgow,
Lanarkshire G2 5AP
**Tel:** 08456018993
**Web:** www.skikings.co.uk
**Estd:** 2012
**Line of Business:** Travel agency activities
**Responsibilities**
**Senior:** Sean Semple (Department
Manager)
**US SIC:** 4722 **UK SIC:** 77001
**Employees:** 50

DUNS 50-554-7257                          Imp
### Skibo Ltd
(**Subsidiary of:** Scytherbolle Limited)
Skibo Castle, Dornoch, Sutherland IV25 3RQ
**Tel:** 01862-894600
**Web:** www.skibo.com
**Reg No:** 0125259SC **VAT No:** 552440463
**Estd:** 1990 Private Limited Company
**Line of Business:** Hotels
**Issued Capital:** £6,720,744
**Principals:** P Crome (Managing), S Bath,
P Andersson
**Co. Secretary:** Martin Lynch
**Responsibilities**
**Senior:** Wilson Guthrie (Manager)
**Branches:** Skibo Ltd, 69 Cadogan Gardens,
London SW3 2RB
**US SIC:** 7011, 7999
**UK SIC:** 66500, 97913
**Auditors:** KPMG LLP
**Bankers:** The Royal Bank Of Scotland Plc
(83-23-10)

|     | 31-03-14 | 31-03-13 | 31-03-12 |
|-----|----------|----------|----------|
| TO  | 8,647,000 | 8,024,000 | 8,350,000 |
| P/L | (636,000) | (1,217,000) | (743,000) |
| NW  | 10,276,000 | 10,880,000 | 12,181,000 |
| WC  | (12,390,000) | (538,000) | (12,700,000) |
| Emp.| 203 | 175 | 179 |

DUNS 34-904-6958
### Skill Capital Holdings Ltd
25 Bedford Street, London WC2E 9ES
**Tel:** 02077620000
**Web:** www.skillcapital.co.uk
**Reg No:** 5701911 **Estd:** 2006 Private
Limited Company
**Line of Business:** Management activities of
holding companies
**Export Sales:** £5,696,184
**Issued Capital:** £1,000
**Directors:** Mrs M G Bucci, T G Macready,
B Poulter
**Co. Secretary:** Adrian Lamb
**US SIC:** 6711 **UK SIC:** 83962

|     | 31-12-13 | 31-12-12 | 31-12-11 |
|-----|----------|----------|----------|
| TO  | 10,367,075 | 10,874,698 | 9,701,843 |
| P/L | (2,490,376) | 168,418 | 2,133,859 |
| NW  | 3,106,362 | 5,247,150 | 5,811,657 |
| WC  | 3,060,386 | 4,870,154 | 5,844,311 |
| Emp.| 61 | 40 | N/A |

DUNS 23-700-1151
### Skill Scaffolding Ltd
Skill House, Andes Road, Nursling,
Southampton, Hampshire SO16 0YZ
**Tel:** 023-8077-7750
**Web:** www.skillscaffolding.co.uk
**Reg No:** 2758962 **VAT No:** 631592052
**Estd:** 1992 Private Limited Company
**Line of Business:** Other construction work
involving special trades
**Issued Capital:** £1,000
**Principals:** Mrs J L Skilton (Managing),
P Skilton (Managing), Mrs A J Rogers,
S G Cerasoli, A D Skilton
**Co. Secretary:** Paul Skilton
**Branches:** Skill Scaffolding Ltd, Unit 3,
Fyfield Road, Andover, Hampshire SP11
8HU
**US SIC:** 1799 **UK SIC:** 50000
**Auditors:** Menzies LLP

**Bankers:** HSBC Bank plc (40-42-21)

|     | 31-03-14 | 31-03-13 | 31-03-12 |
|-----|----------|----------|----------|
| TA  | 1,804,331 | 1,717,385 | 1,923,638 |
| NW  | 899,495 | 806,664 | 962,714 |
| WC  | 159,544 | 71,937 | 269,502 |

DUNS 21-581-9771
### Skill Solutions
17-19 Whitworth St West, Manchester M1
5WG
**Tel:** 01612332600
**Web:** www.economic-solutions.co.uk
**Estd:** 2000 Proprietorship
**Line of Business:** Training providers
**Proprietor:** M Harkmeff
**Responsibilities**
**Senior:** Gary Addison (Manager)
**US SIC:** 8299 **UK SIC:** 93300
**Employees:** 100

DUNS 77-914-5064
### Skilled International (Uk) Ltd
(**Subsidiary of:** Skilled Group Uk Ltd)
Marine House, Aberdeen, Aberdeenshire
AB10 1XE
**Tel:** 01224628555 **Fax:** 01224-645446
**Web:** www.omsuk.co.uk
**Reg No:** 0302432SC **Estd:** 2006 Private
Limited Company
**Line of Business:** Employment and
recruitment companies and consultants
**Issued Capital:** £300
**Directors:** K A Smith, Ms S Page, A R Mckay
**Co. Secretary:** Ms Sharyn Page
**Responsibilities**
**Senior:** Terence Janes (Manager), Stewart
MacRae (Company Director), Timothy Paine
(Manager)
**US SIC:** 7361 **UK SIC:** 83954
**Bankers:** HSBC Bank plc (40-01-25)

|     | 30-06-14 | 30-06-13 | 30-06-12 |
|-----|----------|----------|----------|
| TO  | 11,565,000 | 8,745,694 | 8,844,705 |
| P/L | 986,000 | 786,705 | 610,902 |
| NW  | 2,732,000 | 1,962,119 | 1,366,619 |
| WC  | 2,705,000 | 1,933,273 | 1,353,535 |
| Emp.| 125 | 104 | 100 |

DUNS 73-285-6815
### Skillnet Ltd
(**Subsidiary of:** Apprenticeship Careers Ltd)
Unit 4 Field End Road Eastcote, Industrial
Estate, Ruislip, Middlesex HA4 9XG
**Tel:** 02084297320 **Fax:** 02084-297222
**Web:** www.skillnet.org.uk
**Reg No:** 4559473 **VAT No:** 922736129
**Estd:** 2002 Private Limited Company
**Line of Business:** Adult and other education
not elsewhere classified
**Trading Style:** Skillnet Automotive Academy
**Issued Capital:** £200
**Managing Director:** L Acton
**US SIC:** 8299 **UK SIC:** 93300

|     | 31-07-14 | 31-07-13 | 31-07-12 |
|-----|----------|----------|----------|
| TO  | 11,962,713 | 11,596,186 | 10,174,565 |
| P/L | 1,356,690 | 1,621,206 | 1,418,318 |
| NW  | 2,672,474 | 2,166,620 | 1,551,191 |
| WC  | 2,407,925 | 1,970,926 | 1,376,184 |
| Emp.| 107 | 94 | 82 |

DUNS 73-387-5384
### Skills Active Uk.
6 Graphite Square, Vauxhall Walk, London
SE11 5EE
**Web:** www.skillsactive.com
**Reg No:** 4661021 **Estd:** 2003 Private
Company Limited By Guarantee
**Line of Business:** Other business activities
not elsewhere classified
**Directors:** P W Rowley, Mrs S Gosling,
S S Kalirai, Mrs J A Amies, S Baddeley,
Dr A L Brown, Ms A A Cacchioli, R A Ward
**Co. Secretary:** Dr Sally East
**Responsibilities**
**Senior:** Marguerite Hunter Blair (Director),
Mark Lavington (Director)
**Branches:** Skills Active Uk., 37 The Quay,
Newcastle, Co Down BT33 0LS
**US SIC:** 7399, 8249, 7392, 7999
**UK SIC:** 83954, 93300, 83951, 97913
**Auditors:** Shipleys LLP
**Bankers:** Barclays Bank Plc (20-71-74)

|     | 30-09-13 | 30-09-12 | 30-09-11 |
|-----|----------|----------|----------|
| TO  | 7,521,314 | 11,679,744 | 31,116,428 |
| P/L | (381,345) | (1,074,922) | (248,036) |
| NW  | 637,103 | 1,018,448 | 1,758,117 |
| WC  | 304,621 | 574,491 | 1,272,779 |
| Emp.| 74 | 91 | 135 |

DUNS 21-595-8599
### Skills Development Scotland
Saltire House, Pentland Park, Glenrothes,
Fife KY6 2AL
**Estd:** 2011
**Line of Business:** Career information
services
**Responsibilities**
**Senior:** Heather Tytler (Area Manager)
**US SIC:** 7361 **UK SIC:** 83954
**Employees:** 50

## The Skills Development Scotland Co. Ltd

DUNS 23-908-9118

Careers Scotland, 12 Rivergate Centre, Irvine, Ayrshire KA12 8EH
Tel: 01506826365 Fax: 0141-285-6001
Web: www.skillsdevelopmentscotland.co.uk
Reg No: 0202659SC VAT No: 927112639
Estd: 1997 Private Limited Company
Line of Business: Adult and other education not elsewhere classified
Trading Style: Skills Development Scotland
Directors: Mrs C J Stuart, D Yeates, G Waddell, G T Smith, R Crawford, D J Boyd, W Mackie, Ms S M Mackinnon
Co. Secretary: Andrew Livingstone
Responsibilities
Senior: Alan Mcgregor (Board Member)
Marketing: Taylor Stewart (Sales & Marketing Manager)
Sales: Taylor Stewart (Sales & Marketing Manager)
HR: Sue Woodhead (Human Resources Manager)
Health & Safety: Lesley Kelly (Health & Safety Manager)
Facilities: Colin McCrae (Facilities Manager)
US SIC: 8249, 8299
UK SIC: 93300
Auditors: KPMG LLP
Bankers: Bank Of Scotland (80-11-80)

| | 31-03-14 | 31-03-13 | 31-03-12 |
|---|---|---|---|
| TO | 201,369,000 | 200,342,000 | 225,085,000 |
| P/L | (9,924,000) | 3,170,000 | 12,716,000 |
| NW | (15,420,000) | 367,000 | 4,055,000 |
| WC | 19,121,000 | 25,035,000 | 21,253,000 |
| Emp. | 1,128 | 1,068 | 1,175 |

## Skills for Care

DUNS 21-787-6691

Lynton House, 7-12 Tavistock Square, London WC1H 9LT
Tel: 02073838910
Web: www.skillsforcare.org.uk
Estd: 2011
Line of Business: Training providers
Responsibilities
Senior: Edith Ifekwuna (Office Manager)
Admin: Bernadette Butler (Office Manager)
US SIC: 8999 UK SIC: 83954
Employees: 200

## Skills for Care Ltd

DUNS 23-875-3342

West Gate, Grace Street, Leeds, West Yorkshire LS1 2RP
Tel: 01132-451716
Web: www.skillsforcare.org.uk
Reg No: 3866683 Estd: 2000 Private Company Limited By Guarantee
Line of Business: Adult and other education not elsewhere classified
Directors: Mrs H M Wilcox, B M Walsh, D A Sutton, Ms A Astle, Mrs D A Mckenzie, Ms F A Mills, M W Lauerman, P G Hodkinson
Co. Secretary: David Towns
Responsibilities
Senior: Peter Beresford (Director), Gary Kent (Director), Nina Osborne (Director), Stephen Sloss (Director), Francis Ursell (Director)
Marketing: Nicola Devereux (Marketing Manager)
IT: Rachel Clapham (Head of IT)
HR: Ruth Dickler (Head of Human Resources), Melissa Smith (Head of Human Resources)
Branches: Skills For Care Ltd, 44 High Street, Addlestone, Surrey KT15 1TR
US SIC: 8249 UK SIC: 93300
Auditors: Wyatt & Co
Bankers: The Royal Bank Of Scotland Plc (16-23-37)

| | 31-03-14 | 31-03-13 | 31-03-12 |
|---|---|---|---|
| TO | 34,720,595 | 29,432,638 | 32,494,022 |
| P/L | 801,273 | (11,371,297) | 1,857,271 |
| NW | 22,934,373 | 17,801,771 | 27,593,015 |
| WC | 12,900,524 | 13,746,075 | 24,601,418 |
| Emp. | 206 | 186 | 183 |

## Skills for Health Ltd

DUNS 21-683-3600

Goldsmiths House, Broad Plain, Bristol, Avon BS2 0JP
Tel: 0117 922 1155
Web: www.skillsforhealth.org.uk
Reg No: 7333911 Estd: 2010 Private Company Limited By Guarantee
Line of Business: Adult and other education not elsewhere classified
Trading Style: Skills for Health Ltd
Directors: H H Mccaughey, Ms C M Hannah, R Abberley, Mrs F M Calnan, Miss S M Taber, G R Davies, Ms A J Williams, Mrs D J Morris
Co. Secretary: Mrs Denise Morris
Responsibilities
Senior: Kathleen Fallon (Director), Samuel Gallaher (Director), Christina Pond (Director)

---

Marketing: Kate Smith (Marketing Manager)
US SIC: 8249, 9121
UK SIC: 93300, 91110
Auditors: Bishop Fleming
Bankers: HSBC Bank plc (40-14-13)

| | 30-09-13 | 30-09-12 | 30-09-11 |
|---|---|---|---|
| TO | 15,524,757 | 2,952,359 | 2,255,145 |
| P/L | 7,321,770 | 1,335,942 | 1,793,177 |
| NW | 10,450,889 | 3,129,119 | 1,793,177 |
| WC | 10,450,889 | 3,129,119 | 1,793,176 |
| Emp. | 83 | 14 | N/A |

## Skills for Justice (Enterprises) Ltd

DUNS 21-167-3461

(Subsidiary of: Jssc)
Centre Court Building, 26a Atlas Way, Sheffield, South Yorkshire S4 7QQ
Web: www.sfjuk.com
Reg No: 6926458 Estd: 2009 Private Limited Company
Line of Business: Charities and charitable organisations
Issued Capital: £1
Directors: N Savage, D L Wood, W J Macgowan
Co. Secretary: Mrs Catherine Woollen
US SIC: 8699, 8249
UK SIC: 96902, 93300
Bankers: National Westminster Bank Plc (56-00-09)

| | 31-03-14 | 31-03-13 | 31-03-12 |
|---|---|---|---|
| TO | 845,328 | 435,071 | 346,541 |
| P/L | (35,708) | (206,473) | 1 |
| NW | (242,180) | (206,472) | 1 |
| WC | (242,180) | (206,472) | 1 |

## Skills for Living (Leicestershire) Ltd

DUNS 21-956-4726

Quorn House, 21 Station Road, Lichfield, Staffordshire
Tel: 01455-615061 Fax: 01455440980
Web: www.skillsforliving.co.uk
Reg No: 6138004 Estd: 2007 Private Limited Company
Line of Business: Home care and help services
Issued Capital: £100
Directors: K W Roberts, A Winning
Co. Secretary: Philip Sealey
Responsibilities
Senior: Paula Burton (Manager), Lucelle Hogg (Manager)
US SIC: 8811, 8321
UK SIC: 99000, 96111

| | 31-03-14 | 31-03-13 | 31-03-12 |
|---|---|---|---|
| TA | 1,185,757 | 1,025,426 | 739,024 |
| NW | 476,670 | 336,415 | 133,714 |
| WC | 467,530 | 323,280 | 120,270 |

## Skills Training U K Ltd

DUNS 23-718-3657

Wembley Point, Wembley, Middlesex HA9 6DE
Tel: 02089034713 Fax: 02088487900
Web: www.skillstraininguk.com
Reg No: 3713193 Estd: 1999 Private Limited Company
Line of Business: Technical and vocational secondary education
Issued Capital: £1,098
Principals: S L Gotch (Managing), S J Crawley, G Q Clarke, M Shah, S Mitchell, S Gotch, M D Dunford, S R Jafery
Co. Secretary: Susan Gotch
Responsibilities
Finance: Avtar Sahi (Finance Director)
Branches: Skills Training U K Ltd, Unit 11-17, Price St, Birkenhead, Merseyside CH41 4JQ
US SIC: 8249 UK SIC: 93300
Auditors: Leigh Philip & Partners

| | 30-09-14 | 30-09-13 | 30-09-12 |
|---|---|---|---|
| TO | 8,434,555 | 3,676,206 | 19,416,322 |
| P/L | 555,264 | (1,036,831) | 7,275,197 |
| NW | 1,003,325 | 380,440 | 443,687 |
| WC | 749,092 | 169,978 | 174,990 |
| Emp. | 76 | 46 | 88 |

## Skillsoft U.K. Ltd

DUNS 29-848-4387 Imp

(Subsidiary of: Skillsoft Ltd)
Compass House 2nd Floor, Camberley, Surrey GU15 3EY
Tel: 01276401994
Web: www.skillsoft.com
Reg No: 2051729 Estd: 1986 Private Limited Company
Line of Business: Training providers
Issued Capital: £2
Directors: A P Amato, K T Young
Co. Secretary: Intertrust (Uk) Limited
Responsibilities
HR: Chris Free (Human Resources Manager)
Health & Safety: Chris Free (Human Resources Manager)
Purchasing: Chris Free (Human Resources Manager)

---

Branches: Skillsoft U.k. Ltd, 1 Beech Rd, Winscombe, Avon BS25 1SA
US SIC: 8299 UK SIC: 93300
Auditors: RSM Farrell Grant Sparks
Bankers: The Bank Of Ireland (30-16-07)

| | 31-01-14 | 31-01-13 | 31-01-12 |
|---|---|---|---|
| TO | 25,022,928 | 21,739,868 | 19,834,192 |
| P/L | 517,299 | 531,750 | 438,693 |
| NW | 3,173,994 | 2,724,689 | 2,233,103 |
| WC | 1,946,863 | 1,510,091 | 1,450,529 |
| Emp. | 92 | 91 | 93 |

## Skinner Construction Ltd

DUNS 76-429-3890

(Subsidiary of: R W & J Skinner Ltd)
Station Works, Station Road, Sidmouth, Devon EX10 8NN
Tel: 01395516566
Web: www.skinner-construction.com
Reg No: 2561328 VAT No: 141535982
Estd: 1990 Private Limited Company
Line of Business: Building construction contractors
Issued Capital: £380,000
Principals: C Mayor (Managing), Mrs D C Tucker, P E Tucker, Ms L V Mayor, A Sturgess
Co. Secretary: Ms Ann Mayor
Responsibilities
Senior: Colin Farnsworth (Partner), Richard Isaac (Manager), Ray Parsons (Buyer)
Facilities: Ray Parsons (Buyer)
Purchasing: Ray Parsons (Buyer)
US SIC: 1522 UK SIC: 50100
Auditors: Francis Clark
Bankers: National Westminster Bank Plc (55-50-06)

| | 30-09-13 | 30-09-12 | 30-09-11 |
|---|---|---|---|
| TA | 1,559,129 | 1,566,740 | 2,112,353 |
| NW | 530,887 | 525,028 | 772,997 |
| WC | 427,159 | 416,086 | 401,378 |

## Skipton Building Society

DUNS 22-805-4185

The Bailey, Skipton, North Yorkshire BD23 1DN
Tel: 01756705000 Fax: 01756705700
Web: www.skipton.co.uk
Reg No: 0000518IP Estd: 1853 Friendly Society
Line of Business: Building societies
Principals: B Braithwaite-Exley (Chairman), R J Mccormick (Financial), J A Scotter (Sales), J B Rawlings, H G Fell, A R Aspinall, R H Robinson, J R Skae
Co. Secretary: John Dawson
Responsibilities
Senior: John Goodfellow (Chief Executive Officer), R Stockdale (Vice Chairperson), Judith Summersgill (Finance Manager)
Finance: Ronald McCormick (Financial Director), Helen McGinty (Financial Director)
Marketing: Tracy Fletcher (Head of Corporate Communicatio), Rachel Ramsden (Head of Marketing)
Sales: Paul Darwin (Head of Intermediary Sales)
Admin: Elwyn Horton (Office Services Manager)
IT: Duncan Ratcliffe (Head of IT), Henry Varney (General Manager of IT)
HR: Chris Worts (Human Resources Director)
Facilities: Sarah Dyke (Property Services Manager), Steve Fielding (Building Services Manager)
Operations: Henry Varney (General Manager of IT)
Purchasing: Elwyn Horton (Office Services Manager)
Branches: Skipton Building Society, 54A High Street, Royston, Hertfordshire SG8 9AW
US SIC: 6111 UK SIC: 81501
Auditors: KPMG Audit PLC
Following financial data are in thousands

| | 31-12-12 | 31-12-11 | 31-12-10 |
|---|---|---|---|
| TA | 13,760,200 | 13,910,300 | 13,739,500 |
| P/L | 36,400 | 22,200 | 35,000 |
| NW | 637,500 | 617,000 | 627,100 |
| WC | 3,722,700 | 3,369,800 | 4,125,700 |
| Emp. | 8,438 | 8,169 | 8,233 |

## Skipton General Hospital

DUNS 21-774-0768

Keighley Road, Skipton, North Yorkshire BD23 2RJ
Web: www.nyypct.nhs.uk
Estd: 2002 Partnership
Line of Business: Hospitals
Partners: Mrs T Balderson, Miss H Halliwell, Miss A Wooller
Responsibilities
Senior: Trudie Balderson (CEO, Managing Director), Rebecca Malin (Deputy Director of Strategy an)
Sales: Rebecca Malin (Deputy Director of Strategy an)
US SIC: 8062 UK SIC: 95100
Employees: 50

---

## Skiworld Ltd

DUNS 23-091-2826 Exp

3 Vencourtplace, London W6 9NU
Web: www.skiworld.co.uk
Reg No: 2874579 VAT No: 677988149
Estd: 1982 Private Limited Company
Line of Business: Activities of travel organisers
Export Markets: France
Issued Capital: £50,333
Principals: Ms S J Searson (Managing), Ms D S Palumbo, I D Coleby
Co. Secretary: Gerald Faulds
Responsibilities
Senior: Ryan Chitty (Marketing Executive)
Marketing: Georgina Adair (Online Marketing Executive - S), Ryan Chitty (Marketing Executive)
IT: John Barco (IT Manager)
US SIC: 4722 UK SIC: 77001
Auditors: A.S. Zanettos & Co
Bankers: Barclays Bank Plc (20-35-90)

| | 30-04-13 | 30-04-12 | 30-04-11 |
|---|---|---|---|
| TO | 21,705,855 | 19,063,162 | 19,018,757 |
| P/L | 609,354 | 521,088 | 611,650 |
| NW | 6,427,517 | 6,059,865 | 5,672,520 |
| WC | 1,832,870 | 1,390,332 | 1,107,792 |
| Emp. | 211 | 253 | 242 |

## Sknl

DUNS 21-422-0354

19-20 Berners Street, London W1T 3LW
Tel: 02079087777
Estd: 2010 Proprietorship
Line of Business: Menswear retail
Proprietor: M Morris
US SIC: 5611 UK SIC: 64500
Employees: 50

## Skoda Sales Service Parts

DUNS 21-595-8743

396-414 London Road, Isleworth, Middlesex TW7 5AG
Tel: 02085686300
Web: www.marlborough-chryslergroup.co.uk
Estd: 2011
Line of Business: Sale of new motor vehicles
Proprietor: W Thompson
US SIC: 5511 UK SIC: 65100
Employees: 50

## Skopos Design Ltd

DUNS 21-118-6721 Imp-Exp

(Subsidiary of: Web Circle Ltd)
Providence Mills, Syke Lane, Dewsbury, West Yorkshire WF12 8HT
Tel: 01924-465191
Web: www.skoposdesignltd.com
Reg No: 1157536 Estd: 1974 Private Limited Company
Line of Business: Design consultants
Export Markets: Australia; Far East; Middle East; European Union (E U); Europe
Trading Style: Skopos Design, Providence Printing
Issued Capital: £614,881
Principals: Ms F S Spurgeon (Managing), J H Hopkinson (Financial), J F Ronan, Mrs R E Carr, Ms D Ronan, I Kirby
Responsibilities
Senior: Pat Perry (Personnel Manager)
Marketing: Teresa Barber (Marketing Manager)
HR: Pat Perry (Personnel Manager)
Facilities: Simon Ledger (Maintenance Manager)
Branches: Skopos Design Ltd, Salts Mill, Victoria Rd, Saltaire, Shipley, West Yorkshire BD18 3LF
US SIC: 2392, 7399
UK SIC: 45550, 83954
Auditors: Simpson Wood
Bankers: HSBC Bank plc (40-25-10)

| | 31-12-13 | 31-12-12 | 31-12-11 |
|---|---|---|---|
| TO | 5,349,368 | 5,939,275 | 7,291,833 |
| P/L | (47,797) | (105,842) | (26,756) |
| NW | 304,859 | 345,808 | 436,205 |
| WC | 554,241 | 1,146,558 | 1,220,764 |
| Emp. | 89 | 94 | 105 |

## Skrill Ltd

DUNS 22-242-8638

(Subsidiary of: Mb Acquisitions Ltd)
Floor 27 25 Canada Square, London E14 5LQ
Tel: 02035145562 Fax: 08709223274
Web: https://www.skrill.com
Reg No: 4260907 Estd: 2001 Private Limited Company
Line of Business: Financial intermediation not elsewhere classified
Trading Style: Skrill Ltd
Issued Capital: £320,665
Directors: D G Clarke, G W Von Brevern, D V Sear

**Responsibilities**
**Finance:** Fayyaz Ansari *(Financial Controller)*, Nilesh Pandya *(Chief Finance Officer)*
**US SIC:** 6111, 7374
**UK SIC:** 81501, 83940
**Auditors:** PricewaterhouseCoopers LLP

| | 31-12-13 | 31-12-12 | 31-12-11 |
|---|---|---|---|
| TA | 420,686,000 | 393,710,000 | 297,157,000 |
| P/L | 27,224,000 | 22,480,000 | 17,747,000 |
| NW | 101,273,000 | 71,334,000 | 55,158,000 |
| WC | 92,871,000 | 65,942,000 | 50,420,000 |
| Emp. | 107 | 102 | 85 |

DUNS 21-129-9988
## Sky Blues in the Community
Ricoh Arena, Coventry, Coventry, West Midlands CV6 6GE
**Tel:** 02476786349
**Reg No:** 6642112 **Estd:** 2008 Private Company Limited By Guarantee
**Line of Business:** Sports coaching
**Directors:** S Waggott, N E Newbold, A M Shaw, Ms S Garlick, Mrs E Neale, J Street, D J Busst
**US SIC:** 7999 **UK SIC:** 97913
**Bankers:** The Co-Operative Bank Plc (08-92-28)

| | 31-12-13 | 31-12-12 | 31-12-11 |
|---|---|---|---|
| TO | 711,875 | 612,609 | 439,720 |
| P/L | 21,965 | 18,443 | 4,970 |
| NW | 149,534 | 127,569 | 109,126 |
| WC | 134,776 | 114,232 | 97,067 |
| Emp. | 46 | 37 | 37 |

DUNS 21-745-8232
## Sky Handling Partner Uk Ltd
**(Subsidiary of:** Groupe Crit 92 A 98)
6th Floor, Lesley Tower, 42-46 Fountain Street, Belfast BT1 5EF
**Tel:** 02076460700
**Web:** www.shplcy.co.uk
**Reg No:** 0609088NI **Estd:** 2011 Private Limited Company
**Line of Business:** Aviation consultants
**Issued Capital:** £250,000
**Directors:** D Maloney, M Lemaitre, C Guedj
**US SIC:** 4582 **UK SIC:** 76400
**Bankers:** The Bank Of Ireland (90-02-95)

| | 30-09-13 | 30-09-12 |
|---|---|---|
| TO | 2,688,621 | 2,429,658 |
| P/L | 426,311 | 388,776 |
| NW | 895,245 | 555,421 |
| WC | 443,991 | 484,889 |
| Emp. | 84 | 84 |

DUNS 23-905-7651
## Sky High Technology Ltd
**(Subsidiary of:** Tracsis Plc)
12-14 Westgate, Tadcaster, North Yorkshire LS24 9AB
**Tel:** 01937833933
**Web:** www.skyhighplc.co.uk
**Reg No:** 3896384 **Estd:** 1982 Private Limited Company
**Line of Business:** Traffic administration and management systems
**Issued Capital:** £1,362,216
**Directors:** K Stewart, M C Prowse, G Wilson, A Johnson, J C Mcarthur, P R Jackson, M J Cawthra, M A Mattison
**Co. Secretary:** Alexander Johnson
**Responsibilities**
**Senior:** Kenneth Mackay *(Manager)*
**Health & Safety:** Stan Howard *(Health & Safety Officer)*
**US SIC:** 7399, 7539
**UK SIC:** 83954, 67100
**Auditors:** RSM Tenon Audit Ltd
**Bankers:** National Westminster Bank Plc (60-12-51)

| | 31-07-13 | 31-03-12 | 31-07-11 |
|---|---|---|---|
| TO | 12,817,000 | 5,779,000 | 4,757,000 |
| P/L | 620,000 | 80,000 | (250,000) |
| NW | 1,979,000 | 1,477,000 | 789,000 |
| WC | 1,078,000 | 617,000 | 241,000 |
| Emp. | 189 | 458 | 322 |

DUNS 22-813-8699
## Sky in-Home Service Ltd
**(Subsidiary of:** Sky Plc)
Carnegie Campus, Dunfermline, Fife KY11 8GH
**Tel:** 01383-814000 **Fax:** 01383-814355
**Web:** www.sky.com
**Reg No:** 2067075 **VAT No:** 171160788
**Estd:** 1973 Private Limited Company
**Line of Business:** Take-away food shops
**Export Sales:** £2,622,000
**Issued Capital:** £1,576,000
**Directors:** C J Taylor, A J Griffith
**Co. Secretary:** Christopher Taylor
**Responsibilities**
**Senior:** Jermery Darroch *(Head of Finance)*, David Gormley *(Manager)*, Yvonne McFarlane *(Facilities Manager)*
**Finance:** Jermery Darroch *(Head of Finance)*
**HR:** Debbie Baker *(Human Resources Manager)*
**Health & Safety:** Helen Copland *(Health & Safety Advisor)*
**Facilities:** Yvonne McFarlane *(Facilities Manager)*
**Branches:** Sky In-Home Service Ltd, 31 Stapledon Rd, Peterborough, Cambridgeshire PE2 6TD
**US SIC:** 5812 **UK SIC:** 66110
**Auditors:** Deloitte LLP
**Bankers:** Lloyds TSB Bank plc (30-93-91)

| | 30-06-14 | 30-06-13 | 30-06-12 |
|---|---|---|---|
| TO | 677,348,000 | 684,232,000 | 759,111,000 |
| P/L | 60,609,000 | 56,950,000 | 63,108,000 |
| NW | 68,372,000 | 56,011,000 | 150,971,000 |
| WC | 67,764,000 | 41,339,000 | 141,881,000 |
| Emp. | 3,048 | 2,466 | 2,604 |

DUNS 21-672-1112
## Sky Iq Ltd
**(Subsidiary of:** Sky Plc)
Site Office, Grant Way Centaurs Business Centre, Isleworth, Middlesex TW7 5QD
**Tel:** 01727421000 **Fax:** 02070 322 679
**Web:** www.skyiq.com
**Reg No:** 7246069 **Estd:** 2010 Private Limited Company
**Line of Business:** Data processing
**Issued Capital:** £100
**Directors:** C J Taylor, C R Jones
**Co. Secretary:** Christopher Taylor
**Responsibilities**
**Senior:** Taseer Khan *(Manager)*
**Branches:** Sky Iq Ltd, 4 Victoria Square, Victoria Street, St. Albans, Hertfordshire AL1 3TF
**US SIC:** 7374 **UK SIC:** 83940
**Auditors:** Deloitte LLP

| | 30-06-14 | 30-06-13 | 30-06-12 |
|---|---|---|---|
| TO | 31,886,000 | 31,233,000 | 31,562,000 |
| P/L | (3,913,000) | 2,094,000 | 3,154,000 |
| NW | 323,000 | 4,207,000 | 1,634,000 |
| WC | (2,857,000) | (300,000) | (1,382,000) |
| Emp. | 375 | 334 | 268 |

DUNS 39-934-3466
## Sky Plc
7 Grant Way, Centaurs Business Centre, Isleworth, Middlesex TW7 5QD
**Tel:** 03331000333 **Fax:** 02077053060
**Web:** www.sky.com
**Reg No:** 2247735 **Estd:** 1988 Public Limited Company
**Line of Business:** Television and radio station operators
**Issued Capital:** £795,899,667
**Directors:** D F Devoe, A Siskind, A J Griffith, A J Sukawaty, N E Ferguson, Mrs T J Clarke, D J Lewis, D J Darroch
**Co. Secretary:** Christopher Taylor
**Responsibilities**
**Senior:** Adine Axen *(Director)*, Leon Bennett *(Manager)*, Barney Francis *(Managing Director, Sky Sports)*, Simon Gawthorne *(Manager)*, Andy Higginson *(Non-Executive Director)*, Steven Liddell *(Manager)*, Matthieu Pigasse *(Non-Executive Director)*, Daniel Rimer *(Director)*, Rebecca Segal *(Senior Vice President)*, Neil Tingley *(Manager)*, Alun Webber *(Managing Director, Product Des)*, Richard Wilson Of Dinton *(Non executive director)*
**Finance:** Andy Higginson *(Non-Executive Director)*
**Marketing:** Samantha Crow *(Marketing Assistant)*, Graham Mcwilliam *(Director, Corporate Affairs)*, Kathryn Wilson *(Retail Marketing Executive)*
**Sales:** Mai Fyfield *(Group Director of Strategy and)*, Tara Green *(Recruitment Account Manager)*, Kate Rosser *(Commercial Development Manager)*, Rebecca Segal *(Senior Vice President)*, Ricardo Simard *(Commercial Manager - Sky Broad)*
**IT:** Didier Lebrat *(Chief Technology Officer)*
**HR:** Poonam Chopra *(Talent Resources)*, Tara Green *(Recruitment Account Manager)*
**Facilities:** Gavin Haggart *(Facilities Manager)*
**Operations:** Adrian Pilkington *(Director of Partnership)*
**Purchasing:** Tony Sturcke *(Head of Procurement)*
**Engineering:** Del Fowler *(Engineer)*
**Branches:** Sky Plc, Great West House, Great West Road, Brentford, Middlesex TW8 9DF
**US SIC:** 6711, 4833
**UK SIC:** 83962, 97411
**Auditors:** Deloitte LLP
**Bankers:** Barclays Bank Plc (20-78-98)
**Following financial data are in thousands**

| | 30-06-14 | 30-06-13 | 30-06-12 |
|---|---|---|---|
| TO | 7,632,000 | 7,235,000 | 6,791,000 |
| P/L | 1,082,000 | 1,257,000 | 1,189,000 |
| NW | (757,000) | (705,000) | (535,000) |
| WC | 54,000 | 252,000 | 177,000 |
| Emp. | 20,841 | 19,413 | 17,937 |

DUNS 23-813-9620 **Imp**
## Sky Subscribers Services Ltd
**(Subsidiary of:** Sky Plc)
Po Box 43, Livingston, West Lothian EH54 7DD
**Tel:** 08442411653
**Web:** www.sky.com
**Reg No:** 2340150 **VAT No:** 440627467
**Estd:** 1989 Private Limited Company
**Line of Business:** Other service activities not elsewhere classified
**Trading Style:** British Sky Broadcasting Group, Sky Business Division
**Issued Capital:** £3
**Directors:** C J Taylor, A J Griffith
**Co. Secretary:** Christopher Taylor
**Responsibilities**
**Senior:** David Gormley *(Manager)*
**Branches:** Sky Subscribers Services Ltd, Carnegie Campus, Dunfermline, Fife KY11 8GH
**US SIC:** 8999, 4899
**UK SIC:** 83954, 79020
**Auditors:** Deloitte LLP

| | 30-06-14 | 30-06-13 | 30-06-12 |
|---|---|---|---|
| TO | 535,315,000 | 502,042,000 | 494,141,000 |
| P/L | 55,014,000 | 52,111,000 | 48,224,000 |
| NW | 213,157,000 | 175,692,000 | 135,084,000 |
| WC | 173,627,000 | 128,881,000 | 79,570,000 |
| Emp. | 7,332 | 7,398 | 7,240 |

DUNS 57-195-2944
## Sky Telecommunications Services Ltd
**(Subsidiary of:** Sky Plc)
Chancellor House, 5 Thomas More Street, London E1W 1YY
**Tel:** 02070325200 **Fax:** 020-7032-5335
**Web:** www.easynet.com
**Reg No:** 2883980 **Estd:** 1993 Private Limited Company
**Line of Business:** Other business activities not elsewhere classified
**Issued Capital:** £5,821,764
**Directors:** C J Taylor, A J Griffith
**Co. Secretary:** Christopher Taylor
**US SIC:** 7399 **UK SIC:** 83954
**Auditors:** Deloitte LLP
**Bankers:** HSBC Bank plc (40-00-00)
**Following financial data are in thousands**

| | 30-06-14 | 30-06-13 | 30-06-12 |
|---|---|---|---|
| TO | 1,090,915 | 952,906 | 861,056 |
| P/L | 172,814 | 172,591 | 82,220 |
| NW | 390,034 | 276,240 | 184,016 |
| WC | 179,405 | 57,482 | 221,853 |

DUNS 21-412-7087
## Skycaps Reservations
D'Albiac House, Cromer Road, Hounslow, Middlesex TW6 1SD
**Tel:** 020-87456011
**Web:** www.skycaps.com
**Estd:** 2004 Proprietorship
**Line of Business:** Airline related services
**Proprietor:** S Dindall
**Responsibilities**
**Senior:** Berwyn Morgan *(Manager)*
**US SIC:** 4582 **UK SIC:** 76400
**Employees:** 100

DUNS 29-184-5683
## Skyepharma Plc
46-48 Grosvenor Gardens, London SW1W 0EB
**Web:** www.skyepharma.com
**Reg No:** 0107582 **Estd:** 1910 Public Limited Company
**Line of Business:** Manufacture of basic pharmaceutical products
**Export Sales:** £52,100,000
**Issued Capital:** £120,676,637
**Directors:** Dr T Werner, P W Grant, M A Derodra, F C Condella, J Tschudin, J A Biles
**Co. Secretary:** John Murphy
**Responsibilities**
**Senior:** Jeremy Scudamore *(Manager)*
**Sales:** John Buckle *(Executive Vice President of Sa)*
**US SIC:** 2834, 7391
**UK SIC:** 25700, 94000
**Auditors:** Ernst & Young LLP
**Bankers:** HSBC Bank plc (40-05-20)

| | 31-12-13 | 31-12-12 | 31-12-11 |
|---|---|---|---|
| TO | 62,600,000 | 49,900,000 | 55,200,000 |
| P/L | (1,000,000) | (10,400,000) | (1,000,000) |
| NW | (69,900,000) | (71,100,000) | (87,500,000) |
| WC | 7,300,000 | 1,200,000 | (7,900,000) |
| Emp. | 79 | 85 | 158 |

DUNS 29-760-0181
## Skyforce Ltd
7-9 Grove Way, Mansfield, Nottinghamshire NG19 8BW
**Tel:** 08003899025
**Web:** www.skyforce.co.uk
**Reg No:** 2023097 **VAT No:** 439650233
**Estd:** 1987 Private Limited Company
**Line of Business:** Aerial erectors and suppliers
**Trading Style:** Action Aerials
**Issued Capital:** £53
**Managing Director:** C T Dutton
**Co. Secretary:** Ms Shirley Dutton
**Responsibilities**
**Operations:** Parvis Taylor *(Operations Manager)*
**US SIC:** 4833, 3662
**UK SIC:** 97411, 34430
**Auditors:** Grant Thornton UK LLP
**Bankers:** National Westminster Bank Plc (60-14-03)

| | 31-07-13 | 31-07-12 | 31-07-11 |
|---|---|---|---|
| TO | N/A | N/A | 4,109,966 |
| P/L | N/A | N/A | 173,244 |
| NW | 43,948 | 34,024 | (132,542) |
| WC | (278,075) | (331,584) | (489,665) |

DUNS 22-278-2562
## Skyland Hotels Ltd
102 Moorgate Road, Rotherham, South Yorkshire S60 2BG
**Tel:** 01709-849955 **Fax:** 01709-368960
**Web:** www.carltonparkhotel.com
**Reg No:** 4296182 **Estd:** 2001 Private Limited Company
**Line of Business:** Hotels
**Trading Style:** Carlton Park Hotel
**Issued Capital:** £2
**Principals:** M B Moon *(Managing)*, C D Moon
**Co. Secretary:** Mark Moon
**Responsibilities**
**Senior:** Steve Gibbon *(CEO, Managing Director)*, Kevin Saville *(General Manager)*
**Finance:** James Umpleby *(Financial Controller)*
**Marketing:** Jason Gossop *(Sales & Marketing Manager)*
**Sales:** Jason Gossop *(Sales & Marketing Manager)*
**IT:** Kevin Saville *(General Manager)*
**HR:** Kevin Saville *(General Manager)*
**Health & Safety:** Kevin Saville *(General Manager)*
**Purchasing:** Kevin Saville *(General Manager)*
**US SIC:** 7011 **UK SIC:** 66500
**Auditors:** Clay Shaw Thomas Ltd

| | 31-01-14 | 31-01-13 | 31-01-12 |
|---|---|---|---|
| TA | 832,966 | 886,695 | 941,251 |
| NW | 484,538 | 263,922 | 166,012 |
| WC | (4,253) | (106,382) | (94,098) |

DUNS 23-705-4358
## Skyland Investments Ltd
Castle Mona Hotel, Central Promenade Douglas, Douglas, Isle of Man IM2 4LY
**Tel:** 01624624540
**Reg No:** 0057730M **Estd:** 1992 Private Limited Company
**Line of Business:** 2 star 98 bedroom hotel with 14 lane bowling centre & nightclub
**Trading Style:** Castle Mona Hotel, Super Bowl
**Issued Capital:** £4
**Principals:** Ms P M Donegan, W T Tickle, W T Tickle
**US SIC:** 7011, 7999, 5813
**UK SIC:** 66500, 97913, 66200
**Bankers:** Barclays Bank Plc (20-26-74)
**Employees:** 80

DUNS 34-523-9276
## Skyline Roofing Group Ltd
The Waterside Trading Centre, Trumpers Way, London W7 2QD
**Tel:** 02088138000
**Reg No:** 5334548 **Estd:** 2005 Private Limited Company
**Line of Business:** Management activities of other non-financial holding companies not elsewhere classified
**Issued Capital:** £410
**Directors:** R J Revell, W R Revell
**Co. Secretary:** Stephen Revell
**Branches:** Skyline Roofing Group Ltd, 227 Burnt Oak Broadway, Edgware, Middlesex HA8 5EG
**US SIC:** 6711 **UK SIC:** 83962

| | 30-06-14 | 30-06-13 | 30-06-12 |
|---|---|---|---|
| TO | 16,263,790 | 14,070,437 | N/A |
| P/L | 455,385 | 223,819 | N/A |
| NW | 2,214,697 | 1,856,899 | 100 |
| WC | 1,932,957 | 1,655,443 | N/A |
| Emp. | 76 | 69 | N/A |

DUNS 39-710-7632 **Imp-Exp**
## Skymark Packaging International Ltd
Manners Avenue, Manners Industrial Estate, Ilkeston, Derbyshire DE7 8EF
**Tel:** 01159302020
**Web:** www.skymark.co.uk
**Reg No:** 2160777 **VAT No:** 762763212
**Estd:** 1987 Private Limited Company
**Line of Business:** Manufacture of other plastic products

**Export Markets:** Continental Europe, Africa, America's and Asia
**Export Sales:** £13,112,788
**Trading Style:** Skymark
**Issued Capital:** £816,666
**Principals:** M Toofanian *(Chairman)*, J Turner *(Managing)*
**Co. Secretary:** Mehrdad Toofanian
**Responsibilities**
**Senior:** Julia Lambert *(Board Member)*, Jason Martin *(Warehouse Manager)*, Paul Neath *(Board Member)*, Graham Pilliner *(Group Manager)*
**Finance:** Karen Greenwood *(Account Executive)*, Natasha Mee *(Accounts Assistant)*, Caroline Mordecai *(Accounts Supervisor)*, Elisa Taylor *(Account Executive)*
**Sales:** Claire Hields *(Sales Coordinator)*
**Admin:** Lisa Revill *(Management Suport Assistant)*
**Facilities:** Alan Heappey *(Site Manager)*
**Fleet:** Karen Ablett *(Logistics & Accounts Manager)*, Karen Kernon *(Logistics & Accounts Manager)*
**US SIC:** 3079 **UK SIC:** 48360
**Auditors:** BDO LLP
**Bankers:** Barclays Bank Plc (20-39-64)

| | 31-12-13 | 31-12-12 | 31-12-11 |
|---|---|---|---|
| TO | 35,111,065 | 31,008,296 | 33,921,682 |
| P/L | 706,515 | 624,528 | 840,996 |
| NW | 18,758,516 | 18,000,001 | 17,399,473 |
| WC | 4,100,439 | 4,510,158 | 6,698,345 |
| Emp. | 243 | 233 | 234 |

DUNS 34-559-4878 **Exp**

## Skynet Worldwide Express Ltd

Unit 8-9, Maple Grove Business Centre, Lawrence Road, Hounslow, Middlesex TW4 6DR
**Tel:** 02085381900 **Fax:** 02085381921
**Web:** www.skynetworldwide.com
**Reg No:** 5369177 **Estd:** 2004 Private Limited Company
**Line of Business:** Couriers
**Trading Style:** Skynet Worldwide Express Ltd
**Issued Capital:** £100
**Director:** B Al Sawan
**Responsibilities**
**Senior:** M Devries *(Manager)*, Diane Larsen *(Manager)*
**IT:** Darwish Fawaz *(IT Manager)*
**Facilities:** Helen Bergin *(Operations Manager)*
**US SIC:** 4213 **UK SIC:** 72300

| | 28-02-14 | 28-02-13 | 28-02-12 |
|---|---|---|---|
| TA | 2 | 2 | 2 |
| NW | 2 | 2 | 2 |

DUNS 22-199-3335

## Skyscanner Ltd

(**Subsidiary of:** Skyscanner Holdings Ltd)
Quartermile One, 15 Lauriston Place, Edinburgh, Midlothian EH3 9EN
**Tel:** 01312-525-719
**Web:** www.skyscanner.net
**Reg No:** 4217916 **VAT No:** 774428503
**Estd:** 2001 Private Limited Company
**Line of Business:** Computer software (development)
**Issued Capital:** £16,091
**Directors:** M Logan, G J Williams, Ms M F RIce-Jones, J Pancholi, B J Smith, C M Paterson
**Co. Secretary:** Shane Corstorphine
**Branches:** Skyscanner Limited, 40 Princes Street, Edinburgh, Midlothian EH2 2BY
**US SIC:** 7379, 7399, 4722
**UK SIC:** 83940, 83954, 77001
**Auditors:** Deloitte LLP
**Bankers:** The Royal Bank Of Scotland Plc (83-00-01)

| | 31-12-13 | 31-12-12 | 31-12-11 |
|---|---|---|---|
| TO | 64,758,000 | 33,479,000 | 12,520,000 |
| P/L | 22,019,000 | 11,016,000 | 2,380,000 |
| NW | 32,379,000 | 16,571,000 | 4,654,000 |
| WC | 22,084,000 | 11,792,000 | 4,174,000 |
| Emp. | 246 | 158 | 127 |

DUNS 73-373-3773

## Skyventure International (Uk) Ltd

Xscape, 602 Marlborough Gate, Milton Keynes, Buckinghamshire MK9 3XS
**Tel:** 01908247770
**Web:** www.airkix.com
**Reg No:** 4647357 **Estd:** 2003 Private Limited Company
**Line of Business:** Other business activities not elsewhere classified
**Issued Capital:** £65,591
**Directors:** S C Ward, D S Yeager, A Metni
**Co. Secretary:** Harrison Clark (Secretarial) Ltd
**Responsibilities**
**Marketing:** Trevor Haines *(Sales and Marketing Manager)*
**Sales:** Trevor Haines *(Sales and Marketing Manager)*
**US SIC:** 7399 **UK SIC:** 83954

**Auditors:** Hazlewoods LLP

| | 31-12-13 | 31-12-12 | 31-12-11 |
|---|---|---|---|
| TO | 5,116,021 | 4,717,195 | 3,451,556 |
| P/L | 1,436,397 | 214,526 | 1,429,140 |
| NW | 6,987,388 | 5,764,864 | 7,277,692 |
| WC | (2,472,928) | (815,950) | 1,270,348 |
| Emp. | 66 | 58 | 50 |

DUNS 21-815-6743 **Imp-Exp**

## Slack & Parr (Investments) Ltd

Long Lane, Kegworth, Derby, Derbyshire DE74 2FL
**Tel:** 01509-672306 **Fax:** 01509-673357
**Web:** www.slackandparr.com
**Reg No:** 0147954 **Estd:** 1908 Private Limited Company
**Line of Business:** Manufacture of machinery for textile, apparel and leather production
**Export Markets:** U S A, Europe, Poland, S Africa, Russia, Hungary, Japan, Korea, Taiwan, China
**Export Sales:** £14,061,000
**Issued Capital:** £102,000
**Directors:** T B Barrington, E P Barrington, S L Barrington, R E Hallsworth
**Co. Secretary:** Raymond Howard
**Responsibilities**
**Senior:** Norris Hallsworth *(Non-executive Director)*
**US SIC:** 3552, 3542
**UK SIC:** 32300, 32212
**Auditors:** KPMG LLP
**Bankers:** National Westminster Bank Plc (56-00-61)

| | 31-03-14 | 31-03-13 | 31-03-12 |
|---|---|---|---|
| TO | 16,440,000 | 13,050,000 | 11,000,000 |
| P/L | 284,000 | 633,000 | 989,000 |
| NW | 8,519,000 | 9,148,000 | 9,607,000 |
| WC | 6,210,000 | 6,826,000 | 6,376,000 |
| Emp. | 223 | 215 | 230 |

DUNS 50-328-6379

## Slaley Hall Ltd

(**Subsidiary of:** Starwood Capital Group Global L.P.)
Slaley Hall, Hexham, Northumberland NE47 0BX
**Tel:** 01434673350
**Web:** www.devere-hotels.co.uk
**Reg No:** 2353375 **Estd:** 1989 Private Limited Company
**Line of Business:** Hotels
**Issued Capital:** £500
**Directors:** M E Purtill, B Palmer, I Goulding, H M Taylor
**Responsibilities**
**Senior:** Shaun Boyce *(Resort Director)*
**US SIC:** 7011 **UK SIC:** 66500
**Auditors:** Ernst & Young LLP

| | 31-12-13 | 31-12-12 | 31-12-11 |
|---|---|---|---|
| TO | 8,374,000 | 8,271,000 | 7,878,000 |
| P/L | (703,000) | 304,000 | (10,413,000) |
| NW | 1,868,000 | 2,592,000 | 2,288,000 |
| WC | (5,777,000) | (5,908,000) | (6,413,000) |
| Emp. | 180 | 164 | 170 |

DUNS 21-816-4750

## Slater & Gordon (Uk) Llp

50-52 Chancery Lane, London WC2A 1HL
**Tel:** 020-7657-1555
**Web:** www.slatergordon.co.uk
**Reg No:** 0371153OC **Estd:** 2012 Private Limited Company
**Line of Business:** Solicitors
**Responsibilities**
**Senior:** Jennifer Ainscough *(Non-Designated Limited Liabili)*, Harriet Bowtwell *(Non-designated Limited Liabili)*, Paul Cheetham *(Non-Designated Limited Liabili)*, Alasdair Cochran *(Non-designated Limited Liabili)*, Nicolas Collins *(Non-designated Limited Liabili)*, Elizabeth Dux *(Non-designated Limited Liabili)*, Susan Freeburn *(Non-designated Limited Liabili)*, Lorraine Harvey *(Non-designated Limited Liabili)*, Nicholas Holroyd *(Non-designated Limited Liabili)*, Alison Kerr *(Non-designated Limited Liabili)*, Paul Kitson *(Non-designated Limited Liabili)*, Craig Mcadam *(Non-designated Limited Liabili)*
**Branches:** Slater & Gordon (Uk) Llp, 20F Mclaren Building, 46 Priory Queensway, Birmingham, West Midlands B4 7LR
**US SIC:** 8111 **UK SIC:** 83500
**Auditors:** Baker Tilly UK Audit LLP

| | 30-06-14 | 30-06-13 |
|---|---|---|
| TO | 90,376,586 | 49,075,724 |
| NW | (63,433,756) | (32,462,099) |
| WC | 61,138,726 | 17,387,796 |

DUNS 21-806-7924 **Exp**

## Slater Harrison & Co.Ltd

(**Subsidiary of:** L.S.Dixon Group Ltd)
Lowerhouse Mill, Bollington, Macclesfield, Cheshire SK10 5HW
**Tel:** 01625-578900
**Web:** www.slater-harrison.co.uk
**Reg No:** 0374230 **Estd:** 1942 Private Limited Company
**Line of Business:** Manufacture of other articles of paper and paperboard not elsewhere classified
**Export Markets:** Europe, Asia, Other
**Export Sales:** £1,954,642
**Issued Capital:** £167,500
**Principals:** C S Dixon *(Chairman)*, M Braddock *(Managing)*, J M Braddock, C Smallwood
**Co. Secretary:** Timothy Hughes
**Responsibilities**
**Senior:** Robert Bogie *(Manager)*
**Health & Safety:** Nick Murphy *(Health & Safety Officer)*
**Operations:** Nick Murphy *(Health & Safety Officer)*
**Branches:** Slater Harrison & Co.ltd, Lowerhouse Mill, Macclesfield, Cheshire SK10 5HW
**US SIC:** 2649 **UK SIC:** 47280
**Auditors:** RSM Tenon Audit Ltd
**Bankers:** National Westminster Bank Plc (01-05-41)

| | 31-12-13 | 31-12-12 | 31-12-11 |
|---|---|---|---|
| TO | 7,616,096 | 8,302,697 | 9,045,004 |
| P/L | (125,161) | (8,873) | 37,526 |
| NW | 2,696,590 | 3,004,661 | 3,236,727 |
| WC | 2,421,248 | 2,524,560 | 2,574,438 |
| Emp. | 78 | 86 | 88 |

DUNS 21-115-8423

## Slater Menswear

165 Howard Street, Glasgow, Lanarkshire G1 4HF
**Tel:** 01415527171
**Web:** www.slaters.co.uk
**Reg No:** 0052746SC **VAT No:** 264553156
**Estd:** 1973 Private Unlimited Company
**Line of Business:** Menswear retail
**Trading Style:** Slaters
**Issued Capital:** £4,000
**Principals:** P S Slater *(Managing)*, C Mckenna *(Sales)*, Ms S Rose, G Ferguson
**Co. Secretary:** Paul Rose
**Responsibilities**
**Senior:** Tommy Swan *(Warehouse Manager)*
**IT:** William Mould *(IT Manager)*
**HR:** Stephen Suttie *(Human Resources Manager)*
**Health & Safety:** Stephen Suttie *(Human Resources Manager)*
**Branches:** Slater Menswear, Slater Menswear Ltd, 184 High Street, Ayr, Ayrshire KA7 1RQ
**US SIC:** 5611, 5661, 5621
**UK SIC:** 64500, 64600
**Bankers:** The Royal Bank Of Scotland Plc (83-41-00)
**Employees:** 318

DUNS 21-203-2312 **Imp-Exp**

## Slaters Electricals Ltd

Scotswood Bridge Works, Blaydon-On-Tyne, Tyne and Wear NE21 5TE
**Tel:** 01914-142-916
**Web:** www.slaters-electricals.com
**Reg No:** 0424830 **VAT No:** 177116950
**Estd:** 1946 Private Limited Company
**Line of Business:** Electrical engineers
**Export Markets:** Worldwide
**Export Sales:** £156,774
**Trading Style:** Slater Drive Systems, Boler S E, Slaters Group
**Issued Capital:** £82,200
**Principals:** D H Slater *(Managing)*, Ms F M Slater, D P Slater, S F Riddell, P J Slater
**Responsibilities**
**Senior:** Mark Simblett *(General Manager)*
**Branches:** Slaters Electricals Limited, Unit 6A Dukes Way, Low Prudhoe Industrial Est, Prudhoe, Northumberland NE42 6DA
**US SIC:** 8911, 3643
**UK SIC:** 83701, 34203
**Auditors:** Baker Tilly UK Audit LLP
**Bankers:** Barclays Bank Plc (20-33-51)

| | 31-01-14 | 31-01-13 | 31-01-12 |
|---|---|---|---|
| TO | 9,154,713 | 9,027,748 | 9,823,850 |
| P/L | 373,050 | 129,998 | 549,763 |
| NW | 5,195,346 | 5,023,862 | 4,951,067 |
| WC | 4,624,864 | 4,490,361 | 4,439,245 |
| Emp. | 81 | 85 | 80 |

DUNS 21-709-8698

## Slaters of Abergele Ltd

Market Street, Abergele, Clwyd LL22 7AL
**Tel:** 01745-828282 **Fax:** 01745-825390
**Web:** www.slaters.com
**Reg No:** 0488334 **Estd:** 1920 Private Limited Company
**Line of Business:** New & used motor vehicle dealers
**Issued Capital:** £31,400
**Principals:** C R Knowlson *(Managing)*, P R Martindale *(Financial)*, Ms E E Knowlson
**Co. Secretary:** Ms Patricia Knowlson
**Responsibilities**
**Senior:** Nigel Knowlson *(Manager)*, Colin Olson *(Chairman)*, Paul Taverner *(Manager)*
**Sales:** Nigel Knowlson *(Manager)*
**US SIC:** 5511, 5521, 7539, 5531
**UK SIC:** 65100, 67100
**Auditors:** Sage & Co

**Bankers:** Barclays Bank Plc (20-20-46)

| | 31-12-13 | 30-09-12 | 30-12-11 |
|---|---|---|---|
| TO | 67,659,515 | 55,186,618 | 66,340,577 |
| P/L | (535,366) | (723,032) | (420,113) |
| NW | 1,092,907 | 2,039,106 | 3,052,610 |
| WC | (1,116,224) | (1,376,019) | (1,755,450) |
| Emp. | 148 | 154 | 209 |

DUNS 28-854-8605

## Slaughter & May Services Co

1 Bunhill Row, London EC1Y 8YY
**Tel:** 020-7600-1200
**Web:** www.slaughterandmay.com
**Reg No:** 0785646 **Estd:** 1996 Private Unlimited Company
**Line of Business:** Solicitors
**Issued Capital:** £2
**Directors:** A J Mcclean, S J Cooke, R J Clark, C F Saul, Ms S J Luder, A G Ryde, M J Tobin, D A Wittmann
**Co. Secretary:** Trusec Limited
**Responsibilities**
**Senior:** Deborah Finkler *(Director)*, Robin Ogle *(Director)*
**US SIC:** 8111 **UK SIC:** 83500
**Auditors:** Morison Stoneham
**Bankers:** National Westminster Bank Plc (50-10-18)
**Employees:** 1,054
**Turnover:** £53,700,633

DUNS 21-232-7547

## Slc Solicitors

Westgate House, Shrewsbury, Shropshire SY1 1QU
**Tel:** 08451700700
**Web:** www.slcsolicitors.com
**Estd:** 2010 Proprietorship
**Line of Business:** Solicitors
**Proprietor:** N Shearing
**Responsibilities**
**Finance:** Claire France *(Account Manager)*, Laura Gregory *(Account Manager)*, Karen Hart *(Legal Cashier)*, Mami Laird *(Junior Accounts Assistant)*, Jess Lloyd-Butler *(Accounts Manager)*, Lawri Potts *(Account Manager)*
**Marketing:** Karen Bolland *(Marketing Manager)*, Sian Roberts *(Head of Marketing)*
**Admin:** Caroline Hammond *(PA to Principal Solicitor)*, Deirdre Mavin *(Secretarial Support)*, Mariyana Radoslavova Stefanova *(General Office Assistant)*
**Facilities:** Jan Woodland *(Head of Property)*
**US SIC:** 8111 **UK SIC:** 83500
**Employees:** 60

DUNS 53-610-7998 **Imp**

## Slc Turnberry Ltd

(**Subsidiary of:** D.W. Director 1 Ltd)
Maidens Road, Girvan, Ayrshire KA26 9LT
**Tel:** 01655-331000 **Fax:** 01655-331706
**Web:** www.luxurycollection.com
**Reg No:** 0177810SC **Estd:** 1997 Private Limited Company
**Line of Business:** Hotels
**Trading Style:** Turnberry Luxury Collection Resort
**Issued Capital:** £2
**Directors:** I Trump, E Trump, D Trump Jr., D Trump
**Co. Secretary:** Ms Rhona Graff-Riccio
**Responsibilities**
**Senior:** Elio Abruzzo *(Senior IT Executive)*, Ankit Airon *(Finance Director)*, Celia Fox *(Chief Executive)*, Hamza Mustafa *(Manager)*, Stewart Selbie *(Manager)*, Mark Troy *(Manager)*, Michael Wale *(Manager)*
**Finance:** Ankit Airon *(Finance Director)*
**IT:** Elio Abruzzo *(Senior IT Executive)*
**HR:** Kirstie Mackenzie *(HR Manager)*
**Purchasing:** Malika Foudad *(Purchasing Manager)*
**US SIC:** 7011, 7999, 7231, 7299
**UK SIC:** 66500, 97913, 98200, 98902
**Auditors:** Ernst & Young LLP
**Bankers:** Bank Of Scotland (80-06-96)

| | 31-12-13 | 31-12-12 | 31-12-11 |
|---|---|---|---|
| TO | 12,605,000 | 13,058,000 | 11,779,000 |
| P/L | (6,377,000) | (4,613,000) | (21,886,000) |
| NW | (33,849,000) | (83,046,000) | (78,433,000) |
| WC | (38,554,000) | (91,032,000) | (86,353,000) |
| Emp. | 249 | 286 | 256 |

DUNS 21-733-8458 **Imp-Exp**

## S.L.E. Ltd

Twin Bridges Business Park, 232 Selsdon Road, South Croydon, Surrey CR2 6PL
**Tel:** 02086-811414 **Fax:** 02086-498570
**Web:** www.sle.co.uk
**Reg No:** 1649988 **VAT No:** 372542552
**Estd:** 1982 Private Limited Company
**Line of Business:** Representative office
**Export Markets:** worldwide
**Trading Style:** Baccialised Laboratory Equipment
**Issued Capital:** £26,900
**Principals:** D P Nelligan *(Chairman)*, B J Nelligan *(Managing)*, M D Donovan *(Technical)*, M J Pearcy, P M Richards

**Co. Secretary:** Ms Susan Nelligan
**Responsibilities**
**Marketing:** Chris Worrell (*Marketing Manager*)
**Admin:** Charlene Fauska (*Customer Service Administrator*), Rachel Stride (*Customer Service Administrator*)
**IT:** Stewart Jacobs (*Senior IT Executive*)
**Health & Safety:** Wayne Iddon (*quality Assurance manager*)
**US SIC:** 3841, 5122
**UK SIC:** 37201, 61800
**Auditors:** Kingston Smith LLP
**Bankers:** National Westminster Bank Plc (50-10-29)

|  | 31-07-13 | 31-07-12 | 31-07-11 |
|---|---|---|---|
| TO | 15,658,834 | 13,355,676 | 12,593,018 |
| P/L | 1,594,574 | 2,063,396 | 736,446 |
| NW | 7,534,909 | 6,122,609 | 4,278,494 |
| WC | 6,501,109 | 5,887,853 | 4,495,181 |
| Emp. | 94 | 88 | 77 |

**DUNS 21-783-7128**
## Sleaford Church Lane Primary School
Church Lane, Sleaford, Lincolnshire NG34 7DF
**Tel:** 01529302696
**Web:** www.sleafordchurchlane.lincs.sch.uk
**Estd:** 2011 Proprietorship
**Line of Business:** Schools (local authority)
**Proprietor:** Ms H Fulcher
**US SIC:** 8211 **UK SIC:** 93200
**Employees:** 50

**DUNS 21-890-6758**    Imp
## Sleaford Quality Foods Ltd
(**Subsidiary of:** Jisl Overseas Limited)
Woodbridge Road, Sleaford, Lincolnshire NG34 7JX
**Tel:** 01529-305000 **Fax:** 01529-413720
**Web:** www.sleafordqf.com
**Reg No:** 0943156 **Estd:** 1968 Private Limited Company
**Line of Business:** Manufacture of other food products not elsewhere classified
**Export Sales:** £1,381,370
**Issued Capital:** £170,000
**Directors:** A Jain, A B Jain, S K Sharma, J P Arnold
**Co. Secretary:** Paul Lawlor
**Responsibilities**
**Senior:** Yvette Ashman (*HR Manager*), Paul Lawler (*Finance Director*)
**Finance:** Paul Lawler (*Finance Director*)
**Marketing:** Laura Pearson (*Marketing Manager*), Bridget Priestley (*Marketing Manager*)
**HR:** Yvette Ashman (*HR Manager*), Bridget Priestley (*Marketing Manager*)
**Facilities:** Chris Chew (*Operations Manager*)
**US SIC:** 2099, 5146
**UK SIC:** 42399, 61700
**Auditors:** PKF (UK) LLP

|  | 31-03-14 | 31-03-13 | 31-03-12 |
|---|---|---|---|
| TO | 40,117,953 | 36,654,816 | 39,061,967 |
| P/L | 553,695 | 400,145 | 340,831 |
| NW | 6,252,773 | 5,694,078 | 5,287,792 |
| WC | 3,615,454 | 3,107,778 | 2,618,877 |
| Emp. | 106 | 102 | 90 |

**DUNS 21-580-1610**
## The Sledmere Estate
Estate Office, Driffield, North Humberside YO25 3XQ
**Web:** www.sledmerehouse.com
**Estd:** 2011 Proprietorship
**Line of Business:** Places of interest
**Partners:** Sir T Sykes, S Greenfeld
**Responsibilities**
**Senior:** Stephen Greenfield (*Estate Manager*)
**US SIC:** 4311 **UK SIC:** 79010
**Employees:** 70

**DUNS 21-055-9904**
## Sledmere House
Sledmere, Driffield, North Humberside YO25 3XG
**Tel:** 01377-236637
**Web:** www.sledmerehouse.com
**Estd:** 2002 Proprietorship
**Line of Business:** Historic houses & gardens
**Proprietor:** T Sykes
**Responsibilities**
**Senior:** Stephen Greenfield (*Land Agent*)
**Admin:** Sarah Flather (*House Secretary*)
**US SIC:** 8411 **UK SIC:** 97700
**Employees:** 65

**DUNS 23-509-3973**
## Sleep Scotland
8 Hope Park Square, Edinburgh, Midlothian EH8 9NW
**Tel:** 0131-651-1392 **Fax:** 01316511391
**Web:** www.sleepscotland.org
**Reg No:** 0182935SC **Estd:** 1998 Private Unlimited Company

**Line of Business:** Residential care establishments
**Directors:** Ms S Smith, Ms R D Hendery, Mrs S C Mitchell, Dr M Boot, Mrs J K Mcdonald
**Co. Secretary:** Ms Sheila Ansell
**Responsibilities**
**Senior:** Ruth Gebbie (*Manager*), Anne Hand (*Manager*)
**US SIC:** 7399 **UK SIC:** 83954
**Auditors:** Danzig & Co
**Bankers:** The Royal Bank Of Scotland Plc (83-19-19)

|  | 31-03-14 | 31-03-13 | 31-03-12 |
|---|---|---|---|
| TO | 938,677 | 657,523 | 545,101 |
| P/L | 198,472 | 24,583 | (35,960) |
| NW | 420,043 | 221,571 | 196,987 |
| WC | 338,903 | 220,917 | 195,815 |
| Emp. | 52 | 52 | 52 |

**DUNS 21-136-6923**
## Sleeperz Hotels Ltd
15 Westgate Road, Newcastle-Upon-Tyne, Tyne and Wear NE1 1SE
**Tel:** 01912616171
**Web:** http://sleeperz.com
**Reg No:** 6696269 **Estd:** 2008 Private Limited Company
**Line of Business:** Hotels
**Issued Capital:** £1,542,101
**Directors:** D Myers, A J Handford, W B Kendall, B J Dale, N D Gillis
**Co. Secretary:** Ian Rollason
**US SIC:** 7011 **UK SIC:** 66500

|  | 28-02-14 | 28-02-13 | 29-02-12 |
|---|---|---|---|
| TO | 4,131,090 | 2,972,187 | N/A |
| P/L | (1,386,685) | (826,627) | (237,136) |
| NW | 3,861,758 | 136,879 | 1,302,598 |
| WC | (562,747) | (494,516) | 1,243,570 |
| Emp. | 82 | 65 | N/A |

**DUNS 21-720-7971**
## Sleieve Na Mon
Tircur Road, Omagh, Co Tyrone BT79 7TY
**Tel:** 02882251132
**Web:** www.slievenamon.co.uk
**Estd:** 2004 Proprietorship
**Line of Business:** Hairdressers (unisex)
**Proprietor:** B Mcdonald
**Responsibilities**
**Senior:** Joan Mc Laughlin (*General Manager*)
**Branches:** Brendon Mcdonnald, 12 Hospital Road, Omagh, Co Tyrone BT79 0AN
**US SIC:** 8051 **UK SIC:** 95100
**Employees:** 60

**DUNS 76-962-4404**
## Slick Stitch Embroidery Co Ltd
(**Subsidiary of:** Slick Stitch Holdings Ltd)
Unit 2-3 Villiers Trading Estate, Marston Road, Wolverhampton, West Midlands WV2 4LA
**Tel:** 01902-313368
**Web:** www.slickstitch.com
**Reg No:** 2627116 **VAT No:** 559548783
**Estd:** 1991 Private Limited Company
**Line of Business:** Embroiderers
**Export Sales:** £103,569
**Issued Capital:** £20,000
**Directors:** G M Jain, I M Jain
**Co. Secretary:** Mrs Vanita Jain
**US SIC:** 2269 **UK SIC:** 43702
**Bankers:** Barclays Bank Plc (20-97-78)

|  | 31-03-14 | 31-03-13 | 31-03-12 |
|---|---|---|---|
| TO | 6,040,358 | 5,034,035 | 4,068,241 |
| P/L | 1,249,012 | 1,363,133 | 1,173,966 |
| NW | 3,241,653 | 2,761,804 | 2,537,046 |
| WC | 1,452,439 | 1,475,881 | 1,710,484 |
| Emp. | 112 | 96 | 77 |

**DUNS 42-464-5039**
## Sliders (Uk) Ltd.
232 Walton Summit Centre Oldfield Road, Preston, Lancashire PR5 8BG
**Tel:** 01772-698222 **Fax:** 01772698333
**Web:** www.sliders-uk.com
**Reg No:** 4452168 **VAT No:** 807061159
**Estd:** 2002 Private Limited Company
**Line of Business:** Manufacturers of domestic doors
**Issued Capital:** £230
**Directors:** I G Longbottom, S P Mines, D F Brady
**Co. Secretary:** Michael Spain
**Responsibilities**
**Fleet:** Mark Sherlock (*Transport Manager*)
**US SIC:** 2431, 3079, 2421
**UK SIC:** 46300, 48360, 46101

|  | 31-10-14 | 31-10-13 | 31-10-12 |
|---|---|---|---|
| TO | 9,706,079 | 7,551,514 | 6,456,993 |
| P/L | 820,001 | 303,330 | 244,054 |
| NW | 629,780 | 233,597 | 155,543 |
| WC | 214,186 | (227,655) | (211,274) |
| Emp. | 75 | 64 | 59 |

**DUNS 33-988-0759**
## Slieve Donard Hotel
Downs Road, Newcastle, Co Down BT33 0AH
**Tel:** 028-4372-1066
**Web:** www.hastingshotels.com
**Estd:** 2002 Proprietorship
**Line of Business:** Hotels
**Proprietor:** J Toner
**Responsibilities**
**Senior:** Jackie Cartwright (*Reservations Manager*), Stephen Meldrom (*General Manager*)
**IT:** Claire Atkinson (*Reservations Manager*)
**Health & Safety:** Kieran Murtagh (*Assistant General Manager*)
**Facilities:** Nicky Poland (*Maintenance Manager*)
**Operations:** Claire Atkinson (*Reservations Manager*)
**US SIC:** 7011 **UK SIC:** 66500
**Employees:** 126

**DUNS 76-903-7102**
## Slim Holdings Ltd
3 Trinity, 161 Old Christchurch Road, Bournemouth, Dorset BH1 1JW
**Tel:** 01202555233
**Web:** www.nscclinics.co.uk
**Reg No:** 2284712 **Estd:** 1981 Private Limited Company
**Line of Business:** Clinics private
**Trading Style:** National Slimming Centres
**Issued Capital:** £1,055,000
**Directors:** J A Baker, Mrs M D Nicholls
**Co. Secretary:** Robert Houtman
**Responsibilities**
**Senior:** Janine Stamp (*Manager*)
**Branches:** Slim Holdings Ltd, 39 Charles Street, Cardiff, South Glamorgan CF10 2GB
**US SIC:** 6711, 7999
**UK SIC:** 83962, 97913
**Auditors:** K W G Ltd

|  | 30-04-13 | 30-04-12 | 30-04-11 |
|---|---|---|---|
| TA | 2,830,707 | 2,655,251 | 2,353,441 |
| NW | 2,758,485 | 2,575,939 | 2,305,180 |
| WC | 866,125 | 683,579 | 570,108 |

**DUNS 77-932-9119**
## Slimming World Field Area A Ltd
Clover Nook Road, Clover Nook Industrial Park, Somercotes, Alfreton, Derbyshire DE55 4SW
**Tel:** 0844-897-8000
**Reg No:** 3045478 **Estd:** 1995 Private Limited Company
**Line of Business:** Healthcare companies
**Issued Capital:** £10,000
**Directors:** Mrs M G Miles Bramwell, Mrs J Boxshall, Mrs L Salmon, Ms C E Richards
**Co. Secretary:** David Rathbone
**Branches:** Slimming World Field Area "A" Ltd, Allport La, Wirral, Merseyside CH62 6DD
**US SIC:** 8091 **UK SIC:** 95200
**Auditors:** Grant Thornton
**Bankers:** Barclays Bank Plc (20-20-50)

|  | 30-04-14 | 30-04-13 | 30-04-12 |
|---|---|---|---|
| TA | 2,065,015 | 1,747,135 | 1,333,977 |
| NW | 890,530 | 844,366 | 330,298 |
| WC | 594,740 | 436,797 | 20,469 |

**DUNS 77-933-0679**
## Slimming World Field Area C Ltd
Clover Nook Road, Clover Nook Industrial Estate, Somercotes, Somercotes, Alfreton, Derbyshire DE55 4RF
**Tel:** 08448920400
**Reg No:** 3045639 **Estd:** 1995 Private Limited Company
**Line of Business:** Other human health activities
**Issued Capital:** £10,000
**Principals:** Ms C E Richards (*Managing*), Mrs M G Miles Bramwell, Mrs J Boxshall, Mrs L Salmon
**Co. Secretary:** David Rathbone
**Branches:** Slimming World Field Area "C" Ltd, St Francis Of Assissi Church Hall, Ruxley La, Epsom, Surrey KT19 9JU
**US SIC:** 8091 **UK SIC:** 95200
**Auditors:** Grant Thornton
**Bankers:** Barclays Bank Plc (20-20-50)

|  | 30-04-14 | 30-04-13 | 30-04-12 |
|---|---|---|---|
| TA | 526,319 | 230,822 | 205,215 |
| NW | 216,086 | 154,280 | 148,578 |
| WC | 135,176 | 83,340 | 91,629 |

**DUNS 34-883-9408**
## Slindon College Ltd
Slindon House, Top Road, Slindon, Arundel, West Sussex BN18 0RH
**Web:** www.slindoncollege.co.uk
**Reg No:** 2823749 **Estd:** 1993 Private Limited Company
**Line of Business:** Schools

**Trading Style:** Slindon College Headmaster & Office
**Directors:** G H Matthews, M E Emmerson, J R Palmer, M J Withers, S J Lawrance, A J Smith, R K Iremonger, Mrs L P Haycock
**Co. Secretary:** Mrs Lyndsey Kite
**Responsibilities**
**Senior:** Rosemary Grindle (*Manager*), Mary Hamilton (*Manager*), David Slee (*Director*)
**US SIC:** 8211, 8249
**UK SIC:** 93200, 93300
**Auditors:** Spofforths
**Bankers:** Lloyds TSB Bank plc (30-00-00)

|  | 31-08-13 | 31-08-12 | 31-08-11 |
|---|---|---|---|
| TO | 1,843,846 | 1,836,081 | 1,651,406 |
| P/L | (56,075) | 72,439 | (85,245) |
| NW | 944,292 | 1,000,367 | 927,928 |
| WC | 259,404 | 336,100 | 268,617 |
| Emp. | 60 | 54 | 51 |

**DUNS 22-856-1650**    Imp-Exp
## Slingco Ltd
(**Subsidiary of:** Slingco Holdings Ltd)
Station Road, Facit, Rochdale, Lancashire OL12 8LJ
**Tel:** 01706-855558 **Fax:** 01706855559
**Web:** www.slingco.com
**Reg No:** 1471936 **VAT No:** 306112708
**Estd:** 1979 Private Limited Company
**Line of Business:** Manufacturers cable and wire equipment
**Export Markets:** Worldwide
**Issued Capital:** £100
**Principals:** C F Dykins (*Managing*), Mrs B Dykins, M S Dykins
**Co. Secretary:** Nicholas Dykins
**Responsibilities**
**Operations:** Dave Diggle (*Operations Manager*)
**US SIC:** 3357, 3496
**UK SIC:** 22470, 31694
**Auditors:** Wyatt Morris Golland & Co
**Bankers:** Yorkshire Bank Plc (05-05-65)

|  | 31-03-14 | 31-03-13 | 31-03-12 |
|---|---|---|---|
| TA | 2,785,877 | 2,095,361 | 1,787,293 |
| NW | 1,970,658 | 1,578,297 | 1,228,747 |
| WC | 1,808,717 | 1,497,728 | 1,172,113 |

**DUNS 22-222-2072**
## Sloane Aviation Ltd
Unit 12, Edgemead Close, Northampton, Northamptonshire NN3 8RG
**Tel:** 01604671043
**Web:** www.sloaneaviation.com
**Reg No:** 4240174 **Estd:** 1972 Private Limited Company
**Line of Business:** Other retail sale in non-specialised stores
**Issued Capital:** £1
**Directors:** W J Awenat, D A George
**Co. Secretary:** Arthur Barlow
**US SIC:** 5399 **UK SIC:** 65600
**Auditors:** Macintyre Hudson
**Bankers:** National Westminster Bank Plc (55-70-37)

|  | 31-12-13 | 31-12-12 | 31-12-11 |
|---|---|---|---|
| TA | 207,668 | 254,963 | 348,795 |
| NW | (1,470,580) | (1,438,877) | (1,245,812) |
| WC | (1,487,552) | (1,465,965) | (1,278,962) |

**DUNS 50-322-2531**    Imp-Exp
## Sloane Helicopters Ltd
Sywell Airport Business Park, Wellingborough Road, Sywell, Northampton, Northamptonshire NN6 0BN
**Web:** www.sloanehelicopters.com
**Reg No:** 2347024 **VAT No:** 536332064
**Estd:** 1991 Private Limited Company
**Line of Business:** Manufacture of aircraft and spacecraft
**Export Markets:** Europe
**Issued Capital:** £1,841,000
**Principals:** D A George (*Managing*), W J Awenat
**US SIC:** 3721, 5084
**UK SIC:** 36400, 61490
**Auditors:** MacIntyre Hudson LLP
**Bankers:** National Westminster Bank Plc (55-70-37)

|  | 31-12-13 | 31-12-12 | 31-12-11 |
|---|---|---|---|
| TO | 12,108,911 | 16,785,541 | 14,126,910 |
| P/L | 124,620 | 17,393 | 79,085 |
| NW | 1,613,019 | 1,488,399 | 1,471,006 |
| WC | (307,197) | (1,101,354) | (2,249,669) |
| Emp. | 48 | 45 | 52 |

**DUNS 73-985-7634**
## Sloane Robinson Llp
Nordic Bank House, 20 St Dunstan's Hill, London EC3R 8ND
**Tel:** 02076216900
**Web:** www.sloanerobinson.com
**Reg No:** 0309313OC **Estd:** 2004
**Line of Business:** Activities auxiliary to financial intermediation not elsewhere classified
**Trading Style:** Sloane Robinson Investment Services

**Responsibilities**
**Senior:** Edward Butchart *(Designated Limited Liability P)*, Charles Cartledge *(Designated Limited Liability P)*, Richard Chenevix-Trench *(Designated Limited Liability P)*, David Gale *(Designated Limited Liability P)*, Scott Kydd *(Designated Limited Liability P)*, Christopher Morrell *(Designated Limited Liability P)*, Hugh Sloane *(Designated Limited Liability P)*
**US SIC:** 7399 **UK SIC:** 83954
**Auditors:** Rees Pollock
**Bankers:** HSBC Bank plc (40-00-04)

| | 31-03-14 | 31-03-13 | 31-03-12 |
|---|---|---|---|
| TO | 13,061,886 | 13,223,304 | 33,948,602 |
| P/L | 12,538,124 | 13,508,783 | 34,063,457 |
| NW | 3,210,021 | 3,705,356 | 8,794,925 |
| WC | 4,597,209 | 8,253,685 | 18,563,917 |

DUNS 73-745-1679
## Sloane Square Hotel Ltd
7-12 Sloane Square, London SW1W 8EG
**Tel:** 020-7896-9988 **Fax:** 020-7824-8381
**Web:** www.sloanesquarehotel.co.uk
**Reg No:** 5002899 **Estd:** 2003 Private Limited Company
**Line of Business:** Hotels and motels without restaurant
**Issued Capital:** £275,000
**Directors:** J H Lewis, A D Stalbow, C D Pugh, Ms S F Lewis, J C Tham, J V Tham, B R Lewis
**Co. Secretary:** David Cond
**Responsibilities**
**Senior:** Christopher Pass *(Manager)*
**Finance:** Jerome Delliard *(Accounts Manager)*
**HR:** Desko Portic *(Operations Manager)*
**Health & Safety:** Desko Portic *(Operations Manager)*
**Facilities:** Desko Portic *(Operations Manager)*
**US SIC:** 7011, 6531
**UK SIC:** 66500, 83400
**Auditors:** Rothman Pantall LLP

| | 31-12-13 | 31-12-12 | 31-12-11 |
|---|---|---|---|
| TO | 9,034,901 | 6,962,776 | 7,435,776 |
| P/L | 718,484 | (231,078) | 1,352,111 |
| NW | 320,164 | 1,876 | 233,204 |
| WC | (807,802) | (975,004) | (657,601) |
| Emp. | 70 | 75 | 95 |

DUNS 21-028-7727
## Sloping Off
1 Jubilee Street, Brighton, East Sussex BN1 1GE
**Tel:** 01273-648200
**Web:** www.equity.co.uk
**Estd:** 2010 Proprietorship
**Line of Business:** Tour operators
**Proprietor:** I Foxall
**US SIC:** 7999 **UK SIC:** 97913
**Employees:** 100

DUNS 21-102-7123
## Slough Borough Council
St Martins Place, 51 Bath Road, Slough, Berkshire SL1 3UF
**Tel:** 01753 475111 **Fax:** 01621810507
**Web:** www.slough.gov.uk
**Estd:** 2011 Incorporate By Act Of Parliament
**Line of Business:** Local government
**Principals:** R H Head *(Financial)*, Mrs C Coppell, L K Rawlings, B P Hurrell, D Brooking
**Responsibilities**
**Purchasing:** Trevor Roffe *(Assets & Contractors Manager)*
**Branches:** Slough Borough Council, Dennis Way, Slough, Berkshire SL1 5JP
**US SIC:** 9121 **UK SIC:** 91110
**Employees:** 4,500

DUNS 54-863-2892
## Slough Central Library
Slough Central Library, 85 High Street, Slough, Berkshire SL1 1EA
**Tel:** 01753-535166
**Web:** www.sloughlibrary.org.uk
**Estd:** 1977 Incorporate By Act Of Parliament
**Line of Business:** Libraries
**Responsibilities**
**Senior:** Liz Macmillan *(Branch Manager)*
**US SIC:** 8231 **UK SIC:** 97700
**Bankers:** The Co-Operative Bank Plc (08-92-18)
**Employees:** 85

DUNS 21-765-7064
## Slough Federation of Licensed Car Drivers
Brunel Way, Slough, Berkshire SL1 1XW
**Tel:** 01753531725
**Estd:** 2011
**Line of Business:** Taxis and private hire vehicles

**Responsibilities**
**Senior:** Ray Aldridge *(Manager)*
**US SIC:** 4121 **UK SIC:** 72200
**Employees:** 105

DUNS 28-830-4728
## Slough Heat & Power Ltd
**(Subsidiary of:** Sse Plc)
342 Edinburgh Avenue, Slough, Berkshire SL1 4TU
**Tel:** 01753213200 **Fax:** 01753-213213
**Web:** www.sloughheatandpower.co.uk
**Reg No:** 0174142 **Estd:** 1990 Private Limited Company
**Line of Business:** Recycling
**Issued Capital:** £90,507,200
**Directors:** P R Smith, M R Hayward
**Co. Secretary:** Ms Sally Fairbairn
**Responsibilities**
**Senior:** Antony Brydon *(Manager)*, Lawrence Donnelly *(Manager)*, James Sidey *(Station Manager)*
**HR:** Rhonda Murray *(Personnel Officer)*
**Health & Safety:** Derick Mercer *(Health & Safety Officer)*
**US SIC:** 4911 **UK SIC:** 16101
**Auditors:** PricewaterhouseCoopers LLP
**Bankers:** Barclays Bank Plc (20-78-58)

| | 31-03-14 | 31-03-13 | 31-03-12 |
|---|---|---|---|
| TO | 10,600,000 | 13,200,000 | 13,500,000 |
| P/L | (5,800,000) | (7,600,000) | (4,600,000) |
| NW | (36,400,000) | (29,400,000) | (22,000,000) |
| WC | (21,200,000) | 21,800,000 | 13,600,000 |
| Emp. | 42 | 81 | 00 |

DUNS 64-239-9190
## Slow Boat Chinese Take Away
5 Risca Road, Newport, Gwent NP20 4HX
**Tel:** 01633259071
**Estd:** 2002 Proprietorship
**Line of Business:** Take away meal outlets
**US SIC:** 5812 **UK SIC:** 66110
**Employees:** 71

DUNS 23-889-4708
## Slr Consulting Ltd
**(Subsidiary of:** Slr Management Ltd)
7 Wornal Park, Aylesbury, Buckinghamshire HP18 9PH
**Tel:** 01844-337-380
**Web:** www.slrconsulting.com
**Reg No:** 3880506 **Estd:** 1999 Private Limited Company
**Line of Business:** Environmental consultants
**Export Sales:** £1,694,899
**Issued Capital:** £100
**Directors:** S M Metcalf, J N Smith, D J Sandbrook, N C Penhall, P R Mackellar, A Forster, A J Sheppard, T Paul
**Co. Secretary:** John Green
**Responsibilities**
**IT:** Matthew Daw *(IT Manager)*
**Branches:** Slr Consulting Ltd, 1 Upper Bristol Road, Kelso Place, Bath, Avon BA1 3AU
**US SIC:** 8911, 7399
**UK SIC:** 83701, 83954
**Auditors:** BDO LLP

| | 01-11-13 | 02-11-12 | 28-11-11 |
|---|---|---|---|
| TO | 24,929,610 | 25,399,226 | 25,032,280 |
| P/L | 2,424,496 | 3,116,228 | 2,972,145 |
| NW | 19,331,804 | 17,236,090 | 14,501,405 |
| WC | 19,331,804 | 17,236,090 | 14,501,405 |
| Emp. | 282 | 276 | 293 |

DUNS 21-112-9070
## Slr Management Ltd
Unit 25 Menmarsh Road Wornal Park, Aylesbury, Buckinghamshire HP18 9PH
**Tel:** 01844339993 **Fax:** 01844339996
**Web:** www.quantumproduction.co.uk
**Reg No:** 6538090 **Estd:** 2008 Private Limited Company
**Line of Business:** Engineering related scientific and technical consulting activities
**Export Sales:** £78,892,215
**Issued Capital:** £62,665
**Directors:** P J Wilson, K G Rattue, M R Cook, J C Cook, J R Crabtree, N C Penhall, G C Love
**Co. Secretary:** John Green
**Responsibilities**
**Senior:** Adela Thornton Wood *(Financial Director)*
**Finance:** Adela Thornton Wood *(Financial Director)*
**US SIC:** 8911, 7399
**UK SIC:** 83701, 83954

| | 01-11-13 | 02-11-12 | 28-11-11 |
|---|---|---|---|
| TO | 102,761,226 | 92,810,162 | 83,302,442 |
| P/L | (558,501) | 1,220,762 | 854,134 |
| NW | (21,362,361) | (21,998,078) | (23,983,469) |
| WC | 11,768,946 | 11,572,635 | 7,439,603 |
| Emp. | 1,018 | 942 | 857 |

DUNS 21-601-9972
## Slug and Lettuce Bournemouth
Richmond Hill, Bournemouth, Dorset BH2 6DT
**Tel:** 01202317686
**Web:** www.slugandlettuce.co.uk
**Estd:** 2002
**Line of Business:** Restaurants
**Proprietor:** Miss E Horan
**US SIC:** 5812 **UK SIC:** 66110
**Employees:** 50

DUNS 21-004-6920
## Slug & Lettuce Co Ltd
**(Subsidiary of:** Stonegate Pub Company Limited)
Porter Tun House, 500 Capability Green, Luton, Bedfordshire LU1 3LS
**Tel:** 08451262944 **Fax:** 08451-262920
**Web:** www.slugandlettuce.co.uk
**Reg No:** 6295354 **Estd:** 2007 Private Limited Company
**Line of Business:** Public house
**Issued Capital:** £1,001
**Directors:** Ms S L Baker, S D Longbottom, D A Ross
**Co. Secretary:**
Mazars Company Secretaries Limit
**US SIC:** 5813 **UK SIC:** 66200

| | 30-09-13 | 30-09-12 | 25-09-11 |
|---|---|---|---|
| TO | 81,726,000 | 82,152,000 | 44,134,000 |
| P/L | 3,065,000 | 4,124,000 | 1,836,000 |
| NW | 23,819,000 | 21,512,000 | 18,653,000 |
| WC | 31,627,000 | 29,308,000 | 27,326,000 |
| Emp. | 1,791 | 1,655 | 1,520 |

DUNS 21-446-2434
## S.M. Bayne & Company Ltd
Orwell Bakery, Loanhead Avenue, Lochore, Lochgelly, Fife KY5 8DD
**Web:** www.baynesthefamilybakers.co.uk
**Reg No:** 0030423SC **VAT No:** 268515436
**Estd:** 1954 Private Limited Company
**Line of Business:** Bakers & baked goods retailers
**Issued Capital:** £16,855
**Principals:** S M Bayne *(Managing)*, A D Bayne, J S Bayne
**Co. Secretary:** Ms Linda Bayne
**Responsibilities**
**Senior:** Danielle Butler *(Manager)*, Lynn Ferguson *(Despatch Manager)*
**Marketing:** Claire Lugton *(Senior Marketing Executive)*
**Sales:** Mike Hall *(Sales Manager)*
**Admin:** Lynn Petrie *(Office Manager)*
**HR:** Alison McNeil *(Personnel Manager)*
**Health & Safety:** Alison McNeil *(Personnel Manager)*
**Facilities:** Ian Laidlaw *(Engineering Manager)*
**Engineering:** Ian Laidlaw *(Engineering Manager)*
**Branches:** S.m. Bayne & Company Ltd, 100 Stirling Street, Alva, Clackmannanshire FK12 5EH
**US SIC:** 5462, 0214, 2051, 5423
**UK SIC:** 64100, 01001, 41960
**Auditors:** Condie & Co
**Bankers:** The Royal Bank Of Scotland Plc (83-33-00)

| | 31-03-14 | 31-03-13 | 31-03-12 |
|---|---|---|---|
| TO | 15,382,599 | 14,516,022 | 13,822,639 |
| P/L | 933,667 | 915,096 | 549,530 |
| NW | 14,328,701 | 13,577,564 | 12,944,726 |
| WC | 1,735,774 | 914,880 | 556,016 |
| Emp. | 470 | 452 | 390 |

DUNS 21-147-4430
## Sma Vehicle Remarketing Ltd
Cross Green Business Park, Pontefract Lane, Cross Green, Leeds, West Yorkshire LS9 0PS
**Tel:** 01132941111
**Web:** www.smaleeds.co.uk
**Reg No:** 6774529 **Estd:** 2008 Private Limited Company
**Line of Business:** Sale of used motor vehicles
**Issued Capital:** £300
**Directors:** D J Seabridge, M A Stewart, M V Rijkse, R J Anderson, N M Richards
**US SIC:** 5521 **UK SIC:** 65100

| | 31-10-13 | 31-10-12 | 31-10-11 |
|---|---|---|---|
| TO | 23,467,676 | 11,448,366 | 10,496,369 |
| P/L | 1,506,657 | 827,347 | 639,149 |
| NW | 2,156,098 | 1,421,480 | 636,630 |
| WC | (2,238,741) | (1,178,323) | 2,368,731 |
| Emp. | 493 | 145 | 154 |

DUNS 21-881-4754 **Imp-Exp**
## S.Macneillie & Son Ltd
Stockton Close, Walsall, West Midlands WS2 8LD
**Fax:** 01922720916
**Web:** www.macneillie.co.uk
**Reg No:** 0434529 **Estd:** 1912 Private Limited Company

**Line of Business:** Maintenance and repair of motor vehicles
**Export Markets:** E U, Canada
**Export Sales:** £134,288
**Issued Capital:** £240
**Directors:** G D Leeming, K R Thomas, I S Urquhart, B M Stancliffe, N Misell
**Co. Secretary:**
Babcock Corporate Secretaries Li
**Responsibilities**
**Senior:** Suzanne Beatty *(Director)*, David Beatty *(Director)*, Irene Bradley *(Director)*, Nigel Rowley *(Commercial Director)*
**Marketing:** Nigel Rowley *(Commercial Director)*
**Sales:** Nigel Rowley *(Commercial Director)*
**Admin:** Christine Clark *(PA to Commercial Dept)*
**HR:** Steve Cartwright *(Health Safety & Environmental)*, Helene Welth *(Human Resources Manager)*
**Health & Safety:** Steve Cartwright *(Health Safety & Environmental)*
**Operations:** Steve Cartwright *(Health Safety & Environmental)*
**Purchasing:** Richard Gibbons *(Buyer)*, Nigel Rowley *(Commercial Director)*
**Branches:** Walsall
**US SIC:** 7399, 3629
**UK SIC:** 83954, 34350
**Auditors:** Bakers
**Bankers:** Barclays Bank Plc (20-90-08)

| | 31-03-14 | 31-03-13 | 31-03-12 |
|---|---|---|---|
| TO | 34,606,783 | 33,539,470 | 29,859,919 |
| P/L | 7,067,061 | 3,551,940 | 3,148,560 |
| NW | 21,349,527 | 16,323,750 | 13,051,001 |
| WC | 17,927,715 | 12,997,872 | 10,330,928 |
| Emp. | 312 | 318 | 322 |

DUNS 50-054-0760
## Smailes Goldie Ltd
Regents Court, Princess Street, Hull, North Humberside HU2 8BA
**Tel:** 01482-326916
**Web:** www.smailesgoldie.co.uk
**Reg No:** 2314590 **Estd:** 1988 Private Limited Company
**Line of Business:** Accounting activities
**Issued Capital:** £8
**Directors:** J N Allison, P D Duffield, M Overfield, Ms N Shipley, J M Sharpley, S T Bramall
**Co. Secretary:** Ian Lamb
**US SIC:** 8931 **UK SIC:** 83600

| | 31-03-14 | 31-03-13 | 31-03-12 |
|---|---|---|---|
| TA | 8 | 8 | 8 |
| NW | 8 | 8 | 8 |

DUNS 21-819-6871
## Small & Co. (Engineering) Ltd
**(Subsidiary of:** Whitbread Plc)
The Dry Dock, 50 Commercial Road, Lowestoft, Suffolk NR32 2TE
**Tel:** 01502-585709
**Web:** www.smallandco.co.uk
**Reg No:** 0616719 **VAT No:** 106273789
**Estd:** 1958 Private Limited Company
**Line of Business:** Ships building and repairing
**Issued Capital:** £1,250,000
**Directors:** Whitbread Directors 1 Limited, Whitbread Directors 2 Limited, D C Lowry
**Co. Secretary:**
Whitbread Secretaries Limited
**US SIC:** 8911 **UK SIC:** 83701
**Bankers:** National Westminster Bank Plc (53-81-16)

| | 27-02-14 | 28-02-13 | 01-02-12 |
|---|---|---|---|
| TA | 936,074 | 936,074 | 936,074 |
| NW | 927,074 | 927,074 | 927,074 |
| WC | 927,074 | 927,074 | 927,074 |

DUNS 42-376-8936
## Small Heath School
Waverley Road, Birmingham, West Midlands B10 0EG
**Tel:** 01214645650
**Web:** www.smallheathschool.org.uk
**Estd:** 2002
**Line of Business:** Schools (local authority)
**Director:** C Knight
**Responsibilities**
**Finance:** Lynnette Perkins *(Financial Officer)*
**Admin:** Sue Page *(Administration Officer)*
**HR:** Tinderjit Khatkar *(Head of Human Resources)*
**Health & Safety:** Sue Page *(Administration Officer)*
**Facilities:** Sue Page *(Administration Officer)*
**US SIC:** 8211 **UK SIC:** 93200
**Employees:** 180

DUNS 34-598-0119
## Small World Financial Services Group Ltd
Sycamore Court, Royal Oak Yard, London SE1 3TQ
**Tel:** 02078638816 **Fax:** 02079-003-810
**Web:** www.smallworldfs.com
**Reg No:** 5405279 **Estd:** 2005 Private Limited Company
**Line of Business:** Financial intermediation not elsewhere classified
**Export Sales:** £49,577,154
**Trading Style:** Small World, Small World Fs
**Issued Capital:** £5,255
**Directors:** C Arnhold Simoes, A Learoyd, D G Walker, F S Knox, N H Page, H W Sallitt, N Day, K A Neuschatz
**Co. Secretary:** Antonio Inesta
**US SIC:** 6111 **UK SIC:** 81501
**Auditors:** BDO LLP

| | 30-06-13 | 30-06-12 | 30-06-11 |
|---|---|---|---|
| TA | 35,795,548 | 31,934,298 | 24,132,398 |
| P/L | (1,617,172) | (2,099,988) | (3,888,955) |
| NW | (4,749,149) | (4,219,743) | (4,023,218) |
| WC | 1,934,350 | 842,922 | (125,219) |
| Emp. | 454 | 456 | 493 |

DUNS 85-606-6944
## Smart Care Ltd
Old Bakery, Parkside Court, Weybridge, Surrey KT13 8AG
**Fax.** 0870-770-1209
**Web:** www.smartcareuk.com
**Reg No:** 6243608 **Estd:** 2007 Private Limited Company
**Line of Business:** Other human health activities
**Issued Capital:** £100
**Director:** A Van Oortmerssen
**Co. Secretary:** Ms Jan Van Oortmerssen
**Responsibilities**
**Senior:** Alex Oortmerssen *(Manager)*, Jan Oortmerssen *(Manager)*
**US SIC:** 8091 **UK SIC:** 95200

| | 31-05-14 | 31-05-13 | 31-05-12 |
|---|---|---|---|
| TA | 488,274 | 450,002 | 304,127 |
| NW | 396,839 | 344,757 | 212,005 |
| WC | 366,735 | 322,502 | 198,311 |

DUNS 21-597-0854
## Smart Centre
133 Grange Loan, Edinburgh, Midlothian EH9 2HB
**Web:** www.smart.scot.nhs.uk
**Estd:** 2011
**Line of Business:** Rehabilitation centres
**US SIC:** 3841 **UK SIC:** 37201
**Employees:** 50

DUNS 21-812-6842
## Smart Clean
Unit 5 Taverner Trading Estate, Newport, Gwent NP18 1BU
**Tel:** 01633759232
**Web:** www.smartclean.net
**VAT No:** 990092017 **Estd:** 2006 Partnership
**Line of Business:** Carpet and upholstery cleaners
**Partners:** S Ali, S Ali
**US SIC:** 7219 **UK SIC:** 98110
**Employees:** 50

DUNS 73-382-3186
## The Smart Cube Ltd
Elsinore House 77 Fulham Palac, London W6 8JA
**Tel:** 02033013940
**Web:** www.thesmartcube.com
**Reg No:** 4655800 **Estd:** 2003 Private Limited Company
**Line of Business:** Business and management consultancy activities not elsewhere classified
**Export Sales:** £6,518,000
**Issued Capital:** £3
**Directors:** O Abdullah, S Walia, J C Hewett, J Mayo
**Co. Secretary:** Gautam Singh
**US SIC:** 7392 **UK SIC:** 83951
**Auditors:** Sinclairs

| | 31-03-14 | 31-03-13 | 31-03-12 |
|---|---|---|---|
| TO | 10,585,000 | 8,767,000 | 7,385,000 |
| P/L | 672,000 | 1,566,000 | 1,270,000 |
| NW | 4,802,000 | 4,719,000 | 3,584,000 |
| WC | 4,044,000 | 3,891,000 | 2,957,000 |
| Emp. | 455 | 369 | 278 |

DUNS 23-410-4268
## Smart Education Ltd
Innovate Office, Lake View Drive, Annesley, Nottingham, Nottinghamshire NG15 0DT
**Web:** www.smartteachers.co.uk
**Reg No:** 5497433 **Estd:** 2005 Private Limited Company
**Line of Business:** Labour recruitment and provision of personnel
**Export Sales:** £1,738,241
**Issued Capital:** £584,617
**Directors:** G Lennox, D J Taylor
**Co. Secretary:** Richard Fielding
**US SIC:** 7361 **UK SIC:** 83954

| | 31-12-13 | 31-12-12 | 31-12-11 |
|---|---|---|---|
| TO | 13,214,801 | 12,791,522 | N/A |
| P/L | 791,568 | 1,062,046 | N/A |
| NW | 377,559 | (145,351) | (1,488,053) |
| WC | 565,507 | 56,865 | 1,334,632 |
| Emp. | 63 | 62 | N/A |

DUNS 21-626-0494
## Smart Metering Systems Plc
2nd Floor, Glasgow, Lanarkshire G2 5TS
**Tel:** 01412-493-850
**Web:** www.sms-plc.com
**Reg No:** 0367563SC **Estd:** 2009 Public Limited Company
**Line of Business:** Other business activities not elsewhere classified
**Trading Style:** Sms
**Issued Capital:** £833,397
**Directors:** D W Macdiarmid, G Murray, P B Dollman, A H Foy, Ms M V Greenwood
**Co. Secretary:** Glen Murray
**Responsibilities**
**Senior:** Irene Chalmers *(Head of Finance)*
**Finance:** Irene Chalmers *(Head of Finance)*
**Sales:** Stan Chaloner *(Group Sales Director)*
**US SIC:** 7399, 7374, 7392
**UK SIC:** 83954, 83940, 83951
**Auditors:** Baker Tilly UK Audit LLP

| | 31-12-13 | 31-12-12 | 31-12-11 |
|---|---|---|---|
| TO | 27,916,000 | 21,029,000 | 15,964,000 |
| P/L | 7,471,000 | 5,227,000 | 3,311,000 |
| NW | 20,574,000 | 14,680,000 | 10,571,000 |
| WC | (1,932,000) | (605,000) | 975,000 |
| Emp. | 96 | 68 | 42 |

DUNS 21-226-1951
## Smart of Coventry
Wheler Road, Coventry, West Midlands CV3 4LA
**Tel:** 02476518130
**Web:** www.smartofcoventry.co.uk
**Estd:** 1993 Proprietorship
**Line of Business:** Car dealers (new & used)
**Proprietor:** N Ward
**Responsibilities**
**Senior:** Barry Crooks *(General Manager)*, Sarah Middleton *(Sales Director)*
**Sales:** Sarah Middleton *(Sales Director)*
**US SIC:** 5511 **UK SIC:** 65100
**Employees:** 86

DUNS 21-029-7697
## Smart of Sheffield
Sheffield Road, Sheffield, South Yorkshire S9 2FZ
**Tel:** 08448443447
**Web:** www.jct600.co.uk
**Estd:** 2010 Proprietorship
**Line of Business:** Car dealers (new & used)
**US SIC:** 5511 **UK SIC:** 65100
**Employees:** 70

DUNS 21-584-8826
## Smart of Southend
15 Stephenson Road, Leigh-On-Sea, Essex SS9 5LY
**Tel:** 01702910225
**Web:** www.mercedes-benzofsouthend.co.uk
**Estd:** 2012 Proprietorship
**Line of Business:** Car dealers (new & used)
**Responsibilities**
**Senior:** Simon Kempton *(Manager)*
**US SIC:** 5511, 7539
**UK SIC:** 65100, 67100
**Employees:** 80

DUNS 77-267-3000
## Smart Parking Ltd
South Inch Business Centre, Shore Road, Perth, Perthshire PH2 8BW
**Tel:** 01738-440933 **Fax:** 01738-442994
**Web:** www.townandcityparking.co.uk
**Reg No:** 0138255SC **Estd:** 1994 Private Limited Company
**Line of Business:** Other supporting land transport activities
**Issued Capital:** £2,408,104
**Directors:** B R Johnson, P Gillespie, R Ludbrook
**Responsibilities**
**Senior:** Bernard Dickson *(Manager)*, Malcolm Holland *(Manager)*, Charlie Leiper *(Manager)*, Elaine Montgomery *(Manager)*
**Branches:** Smart Parking Ltd, Lyric House 6B, St. Andrew Street, Hertford, Hertfordshire SG14 1JA
**US SIC:** 7399 **UK SIC:** 83954
**Auditors:** BDO LLP

| | 30-06-14 | 30-06-13 | 30-06-12 |
|---|---|---|---|
| TO | 11,311,459 | 12,509,943 | 14,949,660 |
| P/L | (1,728,566) | (1,239,727) | (1,919,361) |
| NW | (3,992,179) | (2,283,942) | (864,174) |
| WC | (821,757) | (813,003) | (1,646,696) |
| Emp. | 393 | 553 | 569 |

DUNS 21-623-4503
## Smart Sec Solutions Ltd
Smart Sec House Unit 6a, 14 Bull Lane, London N18 1SX
**Tel:** 02030029121 **Fax:** 02088031781
**Web:** www.smartsecsolutions.com
**Reg No:** 7036995 **Estd:** 2009 Private Limited Company
**Line of Business:** Security and related activities
**Issued Capital:** £300
**Directors:** F Ahmad, D Nicolaou
**US SIC:** 7393 **UK SIC:** 83954

| | 31-10-13 | 31-10-12 | 31-10-11 |
|---|---|---|---|
| TA | 640,128 | 458,568 | 158,993 |
| NW | 166,679 | 138,270 | 11,560 |
| WC | 121,360 | 108,202 | 8,879 |

DUNS 21-097-8877
## Smart Solutions (Recruitment) Ltd
Unit 4 Langstone Park Langstone Business, Village, Newport, Gwent NP18 2LH
**Tel:** 01633415600 **Fax:** 01495760363
**Web:** www.smartsr.co.uk
**Reg No:** 6421189 **Estd:** 2007 Private Limited Company
**Line of Business:** Labour recruitment and provision of personnel
**Issued Capital:** £26,667
**Directors:** C Raybould, P R Ragan, J C Price, J F Hope-Dell, J P Jonoo
**Co. Secretary:** Nathan Bowles
**Responsibilities**
**Senior:** David Callaghan *(Manager)*
**Sales:** Zainab Latif *(Commercial Manager)*
**Branches:** Smart Solutions (Recruitment) Ltd, 19 Crane Street, Pontypool, Gwent NP4 6LY
**US SIC:** 7361 **UK SIC:** 83954
**Bankers:** Lloyds TSB Bank plc (30-92-49)

| | 31-07-13 | 31-07-12 | 31-07-11 |
|---|---|---|---|
| TO | 41,999,527 | 38,914,676 | 27,582,032 |
| P/L | 1,223,129 | 1,247,647 | 1,077,999 |
| NW | 1,357,819 | 951,127 | 994,497 |
| WC | 1,012,986 | 621,905 | 723,195 |
| Emp. | 104 | 89 | 62 |

DUNS 23-820-3579 Imp
## Smart Stabilizer Systems Ltd
**(Subsidiary of:** Weatherford International Ltd)
Unit 600, Ashchurch Business Centre, Alexandra Way, Tewkesbury, Gloucestershire GL20 8TD
**Tel:** 01684-853860
**Web:** www.weatherford.com
**Reg No:** 3812469 **Estd:** 2002 Private Limited Company
**Line of Business:** Oil and gas exploration services
**Issued Capital:** £125,000
**Directors:** E R Prentice, N A Macleod, D Stroud, Ms J M Thomson
**Co. Secretary:** Mrs Gemma Rose-Garvie
**Responsibilities**
**Senior:** Brian Moncur *(Manager)*
**Admin:** Sharon Hall *(Office Manager)*
**Health & Safety:** Sharon Hall *(Office Manager)*
**Facilities:** Sharon Hall *(Office Manager)*
**US SIC:** 1389, 7379
**UK SIC:** 13000, 83940
**Auditors:** KPMG LLP
**Bankers:** HSBC Bank plc (40-17-10)

| | 31-12-13 | 31-12-12 | 31-12-11 |
|---|---|---|---|
| TO | 48,840,000 | 30,038,000 | 28,740,000 |
| P/L | (6,410,000) | (26,242,000) | (3,853,000) |
| NW | (64,722,000) | (56,554,000) | (29,073,000) |
| WC | 23,180,000 | 47,142,000 | 73,735,000 |
| Emp. | 97 | 83 | 73 |

DUNS 21-735-6807 Imp-Exp
## Smart Systems Ltd
**(Subsidiary of:** Plu Holding)
Arnolds Way, Yatton, Bristol, Avon BS49 4QN
**Tel:** 01934-876100
**Web:** www.smartsystems.co.uk
**Reg No:** 1314601 **Estd:** 1977 Private Limited Company
**Line of Business:** Manufacturers of aluminium
**Export Markets:** Netherlands; U S A
**Export Sales:** £515,000
**Issued Capital:** £10,000
**Principals:** E A Robinson *(Managing)*, J P Verstrepen, True Colours Bvba, W Flo
**Co. Secretary:** Edward Robinson
**Responsibilities**
**Senior:** Adrian Ellis *(Distribution Manager)*, Eggie Robinson *(Manager)*
**Finance:** Geof Frankham *(Financial Director)*
**IT:** Adam Hann *(IT Manager)*
**HR:** Debbie Rigby *(Human Resources Manager)*, Mark Walford *(Training Manager)*
**Facilities:** Adrian Ellis *(Distribution Manager)*
**US SIC:** 3334, 5051
**UK SIC:** 22451, 61200
**Auditors:** KPMG LLP
**Bankers:** Lloyds TSB Bank plc (30-00-01)

| | 31-12-13 | 31-12-12 | 31-12-11 |
|---|---|---|---|
| TO | 51,992,000 | 44,962,108 | 38,536,922 |
| P/L | 12,000,000 | 7,292,894 | 5,083,931 |
| NW | 36,505,000 | 27,025,295 | 21,063,847 |
| WC | 23,711,000 | 13,665,776 | 7,179,429 |
| Emp. | 183 | 147 | 138 |

DUNS 23-947-6364
## Smart Transactions Group Ltd
**(Subsidiary of:** Acre 1144 Ltd)
John Loftus House, Summer Road, Thames Ditton, Surrey KT7 0QQ
**Tel:** 02083392151
**Web:** www.smarttransactionsgroup.com
**Reg No:** 3937066 **Estd:** 2000 Private Limited Company
**Line of Business:** Other software consultancy and supply
**Export Sales:** £151,000
**Issued Capital:** £2,221,156
**Directors:** D Mcneil, A C Smith, G Watts, J M Holland, P N Matthews, J P Montanana
**Co. Secretary:** Thomas Newton
**US SIC:** 7379, 7392
**UK SIC:** 83940, 83951

| | 31-12-13 | 31-12-12 | 31-12-11 |
|---|---|---|---|
| TO | 8,562,000 | 7,791,000 | 7,494,000 |
| P/L | (896,000) | (1,334,000) | (1,333,000) |
| NW | (552,000) | (369,000) | 255,000 |
| WC | 301,000 | (254,000) | (20,000) |
| Emp. | 121 | 121 | 104 |

DUNS 51-568-4723
## Smart Tv Broadcasting Ltd
3rd Floor 233 High Holborn, London WC1V 7DN
**Tel:** 08002798510
**Web:** www.smartlivegaming.com
**Reg No:** 5849825 **Estd:** 2007 Private Limited Company
**Line of Business:** Television activities
**Trading Style:** Smart Gaming Group
**Issued Capital:** £7,000,000
**Director:** Mrs A Hopstein
**Responsibilities**
**Finance:** Selma Aslan *(Fraud & Payments Executive)*
**US SIC:** 4833, 7999
**UK SIC:** 97411, 97913

| | 31-08-13 | 31-08-12 | 31-08-11 |
|---|---|---|---|
| TA | 1,565,609 | 1,768,712 | 2,390,695 |
| NW | (998,257) | (841,101) | 327,016 |
| WC | 53,573 | (1,160,296) | (180,207) |

DUNS 22-183-7003
## Smart Voucher Ltd
The Counting House, 3rd Floor, 53 Tooley Street, London SE1 2QN
**Tel:** 020-7089-4067 **Fax:** 020-7089-4702
**Web:** www.smartvoucher.com
**Reg No:** 4202050 **Estd:** 2001 Private Limited Company
**Line of Business:** Activities auxiliary to financial intermediation not elsewhere classified
**Trading Style:** Ukash
**Issued Capital:** £2,868,793
**Directors:** D J Hunter, G Millner, J R Lulham, S Rubin, M V Pamensky, S A Parento, G E Naylor, A P Murray
**Co. Secretary:** Roger Hand
**Responsibilities**
**Senior:** Ashley Head *(Director)*, Anthony Moshal *(Manager)*
**US SIC:** 6111, 7399
**UK SIC:** 81501, 83954
**Auditors:** Lewis Golden & Co
**Bankers:** National Westminster Bank Plc (56-00-20)

| | 31-05-14 | 31-05-13 | 31-05-12 |
|---|---|---|---|
| TA | 46,785,000 | 45,660,000 | 33,990,741 |
| P/L | 5,116,000 | 4,926,000 | 2,850,971 |
| NW | 11,696,000 | 11,685,000 | 7,877,134 |
| WC | 9,798,000 | 8,563,000 | 4,368,204 |
| Emp. | 120 | 92 | 55 |

DUNS 23-918-0081
## SmART421 Ltd
**(Subsidiary of:** Kcom Group Plc)
48 Felaw Street, Ipswich, Suffolk IP2 8PN
**Tel:** 01473-421421
**Web:** www.smart421.com
**Reg No:** 3908235 **Estd:** 2001 Private Limited Company
**Line of Business:** Holding companies management activities
**Trading Style:** Smart421 Ltd
**Issued Capital:** £2,000,001
**Directors:** P S Simpson, W G Halbert
**Co. Secretary:** Mrs Katharine Smith
**Responsibilities**
**Senior:** Andy Budd *(Director of Operations)*, Andrew Haskell *(Human Resources Director)*, Neil Miles *(Manager)*
**Marketing:** Martin Brazill *(Director of Sales & Marketing)*
**Sales:** Martin Brazill *(Director of Sales & Marketing)*

**HR:** Andrew Haskell *(Human Resources Director)*
**Health & Safety:** Claire Stuttaford *(Health & Safety Officer)*
**Facilities:** Claire Stuttaford *(Health & Safety Officer)*
**Operations:** Andy Budd *(Director of Operations)*, Andrew Haskell *(Human Resources Director)*, Graham Masterson *(Director of Operational Govern)*
**Engineering:** Robin Meehan *(Chief Technology Officer and D)*
**US SIC:** 7379 **UK SIC:** 83940
**Auditors:** Ensors
**Bankers:** Lloyds TSB Bank plc (30-99-31)

| | 31-03-14 | 31-03-13 | 31-03-12 |
|---|---|---|---|
| TO | 30,005,000 | 27,763,000 | 27,438,000 |
| P/L | 2,729,000 | 2,227,000 | 2,287,000 |
| NW | 17,665,000 | 15,185,000 | 13,024,000 |
| WC | 17,411,000 | 15,267,000 | 13,062,000 |
| Emp. | 143 | 155 | 150 |

DUNS 21-036-3999
## Smartcare Training
2 Hillbury Road, Wrexham, Clwyd LL13 7ET
**Web:** www.smartcaretraining.com
**Proprietorship**
**Line of Business:** Adult and other education not elsewhere classified
**Responsibilities**
**Senior:** Mario Krest *(Owner)*
**US SIC:** 8249 **UK SIC:** 93300
**Employees:** 520

DUNS 73-533-7888
## Smartcitizen Ltd
Unit 3, Building B, Truro Business Park Green Court, Truro, Cornwall TR4 9LF
**Tel:** 01872250161
**Web:** www.smartcitizen.net
**Reg No:** 4796316 **Estd:** 2003 Private Limited Company
**Line of Business:** Computer software (development)
**Issued Capital:** £79
**Directors:** S Bennetts, O P Mclaughlin, Mrs S Bennetts
**Co. Secretary:** Christopher Poulton
**Responsibilities**
**Senior:** Stewart Elkin *(Manager)*
**US SIC:** 7379 **UK SIC:** 83940

| | 30-09-13 | 30-09-12 | 30-09-11 |
|---|---|---|---|
| TA | 347,223 | 331,837 | 296,629 |
| NW | 235,192 | 226,000 | 165,758 |
| WC | 218,880 | 210,082 | 152,559 |

DUNS 51-987-7612 **Imp**
## Smartestenergy Ltd
(**Subsidiary of:** Marubeni Corporation)
Dashwood House, 69 Old Broad Street, London EC2M 1QS
**Tel:** 02074-480900 **Fax:** 02074480987
**Web:** www.smartestenergy.com
**Reg No:** 3994598 **Estd:** 2000 Private Limited Company
**Line of Business:** Electricity companies
**Issued Capital:** £6,000,000
**Directors:** M Omoto, H Tachigami, N Ito, H Sawada, R S Groves, J A Clarke, R Noyama
**Co. Secretary:** Kentaro Yamasaki
**Responsibilities**
**Sales:** Justin Fley *(Account Manager)*, Matt Neve *(Business Development Manager)*
**Admin:** Julia Byford-Smith *(Personal Assistant)*
**Branches:** Smartestenergy Ltd, Grafton House, 15-17 Russell Road, Ipswich, Suffolk IP1 2DE
**US SIC:** 4911, 4932
**UK SIC:** 16101, 16200
**Auditors:** Ernst & Young LLP
**Bankers:** The Dai-Ichi Kangyo Bank, Ltd. (70-06-35)

**Following financial data are in thousands**

| | 31-03-14 | 31-03-13 | 31-03-12 |
|---|---|---|---|
| TO | 1,030,525 | 1,413,031 | 1,016,593 |
| P/L | 10,517 | 8,566 | 14,534 |
| NW | 48,495 | 40,471 | 41,507 |
| WC | 48,341 | 35,472 | 37,603 |
| Emp. | 123 | 125 | 102 |

DUNS 21-721-0127
## Smartfocus Holdings Ltd
(**Subsidiary of:** Francisco Partners Ii (Cayman) L.P)
Lynton House, 7-12 Tavistock Square, London WC1H 9LT
**Tel:** 02075544500
**Web:** www.emailvision.co.uk
**Reg No:** 7588241 **Estd:** 2011 Private Limited Company
**Line of Business:** Internet publishers
**Issued Capital:** £143,285,927
**Directors:** A M Boisvert, N P Heys, R Mullen, N M Garfinkel, D Shah, M T Everett
**Co. Secretary:** Manoj Paul
**Responsibilities**
**Senior:** Rob Marlon *(Manager)*
**US SIC:** 7379 **UK SIC:** 83940
**Auditors:** Ernst & Young LLP
**Bankers:** The Royal Bank Of Scotland Plc (16-01-01)

| | 31-12-13 | 31-12-12 | 31-12-11 |
|---|---|---|---|
| TO | 55,432,000 | 63,211,000 | 54,289,000 |
| P/L | (27,873,000) | (40,207,000) | (18,783,000) |
| NW | (2,479,000) | 7,699,000 | (3,480,000) |
| WC | 131,000 | 9,244,000 | 2,126,000 |
| Emp. | 499 | 594 | 607 |

DUNS 22-114-2834
## Smartgo Ltd
Flat 6 Henderson Court, 6 Myers Lane, London SE14 5RX
**Tel:** 01914194990
**Reg No:** 4133473 **Estd:** 2000 Private Limited Company
**Line of Business:** Other computer related activities
**Issued Capital:** £2
**Director:** T P Jones
**Co. Secretary:** Ms Edith Jones
**US SIC:** 7379, 7374
**UK SIC:** 83940
**Auditors:** Straughans

| | 31-12-13 | 31-12-12 | 31-12-11 |
|---|---|---|---|
| TA | 170,817 | 186,466 | 138,664 |
| NW | 86,702 | 83,298 | 65,329 |
| WC | N/A | 76,892 | 58,416 |

DUNS 73-853-4358
## Smartodds Ltd
Unit 531 Highgate Studios, 53 - 79 Highgate Road, London NW5 1TL
**Tel:** 02074820077
**Web:** www.smartodds.co.uk
**Reg No:** 5108548 **Estd:** 2004 Private Limited Company
**Line of Business:** Other business activities not elsewhere classified
**Export Sales:** £833,872
**Issued Capital:** £1
**Director:** M A Benham
**Co. Secretary:** Philip Whall
**US SIC:** 7399 **UK SIC:** 83954

| | 31-03-14 | 31-03-13 | 30-03-12 |
|---|---|---|---|
| TO | 9,169,544 | 6,148,214 | 8,230,460 |
| P/L | 446,109 | 289,097 | 351,397 |
| NW | 948,256 | 613,318 | 364,765 |
| WC | 511,297 | 84,082 | (324,437) |
| Emp. | 92 | 81 | 66 |

DUNS 39-997-4120
## Smartstream Technologies Ltd
(**Subsidiary of:** Government of Dubai)
St Helen's, London EC3A 8EE
**Tel:** 02078980600 **Fax:** 02078980601
**Web:** www.smartstream-stp.com
**Reg No:** 2285524 **VAT No:** 727468504
**Estd:** 1988 Private Limited Company
**Line of Business:** Computer software (development)
**Export Sales:** £27,286,000
**Issued Capital:** £10,000,000
**Directors:** Ms K Schrolnberger, P T Chambadal, S P Thomas
**Co. Secretary:** Ms Katharina Schrolnberger
**Responsibilities**
**Senior:** Katharina Zimmermann *(Manager)*
**IT:** Ian MacLauchlan *(Computer Manager)*
**HR:** Tom Sutherland *(Human Resources Manager)*
**Health & Safety:** Tom Sutherland *(Human Resources Manager)*
**US SIC:** 7379 **UK SIC:** 83940
**Auditors:** Deloitte & Touche LLP
**Bankers:** The Royal Bank Of Scotland Plc (16-00-32)

| | 31-12-13 | 31-12-12 | 31-12-11 |
|---|---|---|---|
| TO | 36,642,000 | 35,138,000 | 29,266,000 |
| P/L | 8,091,000 | 7,339,000 | 2,545,000 |
| NW | 70,294,000 | 59,708,000 | 50,241,000 |
| WC | 64,277,000 | 53,568,000 | 43,834,000 |
| Emp. | 126 | 129 | 150 |

DUNS 73-880-1554
## Smartwater Ltd
26-28 Goodall Street, Walsall, West Midlands WS1 1QL
**Tel:** 08000436733
**Web:** www.bakerandco.net
**Reg No:** 2935281 **Estd:** 1994 Private Limited Company
**Line of Business:** Research and laboratory based activities
**Issued Capital:** £156
**Directors:** K M Mcgrigor, F N Mattinson, P A Cleary, M Cleary, M J Hawker
**Co. Secretary:** Florian Mattinson
**US SIC:** 7391 **UK SIC:** 94000
**Auditors:** Ernst & Young

| | 30-06-13 | 30-06-12 | 30-06-11 |
|---|---|---|---|
| TO | 5,617,405 | 5,926,684 | N/A |
| P/L | 331,917 | 414,421 | N/A |
| NW | 1,869,064 | 1,506,671 | 1,183,466 |
| WC | 1,785,907 | 2,691,119 | 1,183,361 |
| Emp. | 61 | 64 | N/A |

DUNS 22-189-1257
## Smartwork.Com Ltd
Whitefriars, Lewins Mead, Bristol, Avon BS1 2NT
**Tel:** 08004346446 **Fax:** 01173-763737
**Web:** www.smartwork.com
**Reg No:** 4207299 **Estd:** 2001 Private Limited Company
**Line of Business:** Payroll services
**Export Sales:** £243,792
**Issued Capital:** £1,000
**Director:** P J Koria
**Responsibilities**
**Senior:** Neil Kane *(Business Operations Manager)*
**Branches:** Smartwork.com Ltd, 18 Soho Square, London W1D 3QL
**US SIC:** 8931 **UK SIC:** 83600
**Auditors:** John Davis & Co

| | 31-10-13 | 31-10-12 | 31-10-11 |
|---|---|---|---|
| TO | 19,762,579 | 20,448,530 | 20,712,322 |
| P/L | 9,647 | 38,895 | 15,607 |
| NW | 54,670 | 40,693 | 2,533 |
| WC | 53,404 | 40,693 | 2,533 |
| Emp. | 415 | 425 | 370 |

DUNS 22-605-1092
## S.M.B. (Exeter) Ltd
(**Subsidiary of:** Helston Garages Group Ltd)
Matford Park Road, Marsh Barton Trading Estate, Exeter, Devon EX2 8FD
**Tel:** 01392-822555 **Fax:** 01392-822580
**Web:** www.westerlyexeterbmw.co.uk
**Reg No:** 1223102 **Estd:** 1982 Private Limited Company
**Line of Business:** Sale of new motor vehicles
**Trading Style:** Westerley
**Issued Capital:** £5,000
**Directors:** D S Carr, Mrs B V Carr, A J Barrett, J C Glanville
**Co. Secretary:** Paul Mitchell
**Responsibilities**
**Senior:** Kirk Broome *(Dealer Principal)*, Timothy Downer *(Manager)*
**US SIC:** 5511, 7539
**UK SIC:** 65100, 67100
**Auditors:** Kitchen & Brown
**Bankers:** HSBC Bank plc (40-20-30)

| | 31-12-13 | 31-12-12 | 31-12-11 |
|---|---|---|---|
| TO | 44,883,000 | 46,047,000 | 50,876,000 |
| P/L | 682,000 | 1,323,000 | 1,260,000 |
| NW | 9,716,000 | 11,421,000 | 10,401,000 |
| WC | 4,118,000 | 6,763,000 | 5,986,000 |
| Emp. | 78 | 76 | 73 |

DUNS 50-425-8948 **Exp**
## Smbc Nikko Capital Markets Ltd
(**Subsidiary of:** Sumitomo Mitsui Financial Group Inc.)
1 New Change, London EC4M 9AF
**Tel:** 02035277000 **Fax:** 020-3527-7500
**Web:** www.smbcnikko-cm.com
**Reg No:** 2418137 **Estd:** 2012 Private Limited Company
**Line of Business:** Investment consultants
**Export Markets:** Worldwide
**Trading Style:** Smbc Nikko
**Directors:** T Yazawa, M Oshima, H Oiwa, M Okumura, K Hosomi, Y Hayashi, Y Ohmi, A Yates
**Co. Secretary:** Jonathan Avery
**Responsibilities**
**Senior:** Ryo Suzuki *(Manager)*
**US SIC:** 6211 **UK SIC:** 83100
**Auditors:** Ernst & Young LLP
**Bankers:** The Sumitomo Bank, Ltd (40-51-25)
**Employees:** 40

DUNS 23-784-5602
## Smc (Exeter) Ltd
Clarke Centre, Exeter, Devon EX2 8NJ
**Tel:** 01392-457700
**Web:** www.smcgaragegroup.com
**Reg No:** 3777614 **Estd:** 1999 Private Limited Company
**Line of Business:** Car dealers (new & used)
**Issued Capital:** £1,000
**Director:** Mrs D M Dart
**Co. Secretary:** David Dart
**US SIC:** 5511, 5521
**UK SIC:** 65100

| | 31-03-14 | 31-03-13 | 31-03-12 |
|---|---|---|---|
| TO | N/A | 16,472,263 | 13,503,837 |
| P/L | N/A | 136,996 | 791 |
| NW | 861,874 | 790,557 | 730,089 |
| WC | 755,196 | 511,354 | 438,754 |
| Emp. | N/A | 46 | 46 |

DUNS 22-623-1819 **Imp-Exp**
## Smc Pneumatics (U.K.) Ltd
(**Subsidiary of:** Smc Corporation)
Vincent Avenue, Crownhill, Milton Keynes, Buckinghamshire MK8 0AN
**Tel:** 01908563888
**Web:** www.smcpneumatics.co.uk
**Reg No:** 1352967 **Estd:** 1978 Private Limited Company
**Line of Business:** Pneumatic systems and equipment
**Export Markets:** Worldwide
**Issued Capital:** £14,500,000
**Principals:** S E Bangs *(Managing)*, I Usui, Y Takada, K P O'Carroll
**Co. Secretary:** Kevin O'Carroll
**Responsibilities**
**Marketing:** Peter Humphries *(Marketing Manager)*
**Sales:** Nick Pittwood *(Sales Manager)*
**HR:** Hailey Walker *(Human Resources Manager)*
**Health & Safety:** Bob Farr *(Facilities Manager)*
**Facilities:** Bob Farr *(Facilities Manager)*
**Operations:** Bob Farr *(Facilities Manager)*
**Purchasing:** Peter Noble *(Procurement Manager)*
**Branches:** Smc Pneumatics (U.k.) Ltd, Vincent Avenue, Milton Keynes, Buckinghamshire MK8 0AN
**US SIC:** 3563 **UK SIC:** 32831
**Auditors:** Everett Collins & Loosley

| | 31-03-14 | 31-03-13 | 31-03-12 |
|---|---|---|---|
| TO | 47,071,598 | 42,528,866 | 41,677,272 |
| P/L | 11,489,440 | 8,805,953 | 6,131,900 |
| NW | 61,757,632 | 52,844,728 | 46,203,902 |
| WC | 47,287,987 | 42,427,858 | 36,494,837 |
| Emp. | 241 | 247 | 259 |

DUNS 76-946-8646
## Sme Group Plc
The Runway, Ruislip, Middlesex HA4 6SE
**Tel:** 02088390740 **Fax:** 020-8839-9706
**Web:** www.smegroup.co.uk
**Reg No:** 2243425 **Estd:** 1988 Public Limited Company
**Line of Business:** Management activities of holding companies
**Trading Style:** Kentucky Fried Chicken
**Issued Capital:** £500,000
**Director:** A Esmail
**Co. Secretary:** Mrs Sushma Esmail
**Responsibilities**
**Senior:** Fitzroy Licorish *(General Manager)*
**Branches:** Sme Group Plc, Oakley Road, Corby, Northamptonshire NN17 1NE
**US SIC:** 6711, 5812
**UK SIC:** 83962, 66110
**Auditors:** KLSA
**Bankers:** The Royal Bank Of Scotland Plc (16-20-38)

| | 31-03-14 | 31-03-13 | 01-03-12 |
|---|---|---|---|
| TO | 64,356,022 | 59,636,423 | 54,091,404 |
| P/L | 3,567,458 | 3,346,659 | 3,299,914 |
| NW | 33,473,412 | 26,457,695 | 23,211,107 |
| WC | (10,680,522) | (11,028,128) | (7,877,165) |
| Emp. | 1,680 | 1,808 | 1,616 |

DUNS 23-805-8221
## Sme Insurance Services Ltd
Chantrell House, The Calls, Leeds, West Yorkshire LS2 7HA
**Tel:** 08448554660 **Fax:** 0870-126-1201
**Web:** www.smeinsurance.com
**Reg No:** 3798294 **Estd:** 1999 Private Limited Company
**Line of Business:** Insurance brokers
**Issued Capital:** £10,000
**Directors:** J Webber, L Tetley, R Snowden, J P Gandy
**Co. Secretary:** Jonathan Webber
**Responsibilities**
**Senior:** Brian Trent *(Manager)*
**Sales:** Stuart Knowles *(Business Development Manager)*
**IT:** Nick Apkinson *(Senior IT Executive)*, Paul Corbett *(IT Manager)*
**US SIC:** 6411 **UK SIC:** 83200
**Auditors:** Mazars LLP
**Bankers:** Yorkshire Bank Plc (05-00-20)

| | 31-12-13 | 31-12-12 | 31-12-11 |
|---|---|---|---|
| TO | 5,032,615 | 4,458,142 | 5,508,863 |
| P/L | 778,492 | 767,920 | 826,239 |
| NW | 1,181,437 | 1,026,994 | 575,163 |
| WC | 1,110,566 | 1,002,947 | 573,471 |
| Emp. | 96 | 87 | 79 |

DUNS 22-108-7146
## Sme (Pizza) Ltd
(**Subsidiary of:** Sme Group Plc)
43c Buckingham Street, Aylesbury, Buckinghamshire HP20 2NQ
**Tel:** 07903564014
**Web:** www.sme.in
**Reg No:** 4128014 **Estd:** 2000 Private Limited Company
**Line of Business:** Unlicensed restaurants and cafes
**Issued Capital:** £100

**Co. Secretary:** Mrs Sushma Esmail
**US SIC:** 5812 **UK SIC:** 66110
**Bankers:** The Royal Bank Of Scotland Plc
(16-20-38)

| | 31-03-14 | 31-03-13 | 01-03-12 |
|---|---|---|---|
| TO | 10,667,049 | 11,120,525 | 8,323,267 |
| P/L | 122,004 | 93,381 | (356,711) |
| NW | (1,453,661) | (1,800,901) | (2,046,933) |
| WC | (3,434,946) | (3,267,847) | (2,994,162) |
| Emp. | 458 | 450 | 410 |

DUNS 50-345-7459 **Imp**
### Smeg (U K) Ltd
(**Subsidiary of:** Smeg Spa)
3 Milton Road, Abingdon, Oxfordshire OX14
4BP
**Tel:** 01235828300 **Fax:** 08445579337
**Web:** www.smeg.com
**Reg No:** 2365886 **VAT No:** 539121945
**Estd:** 1989 Private Limited Company
**Line of Business:** Manufacture of other
electrical equipment not elsewhere classified
**Issued Capital:** £700,000
**Directors:** C Manotti, M Giddings,
Ms R Boccazzi, V E Treves, V Bertazzoni,
E J Ireland
**Co. Secretary:**
Capita Company Secretarial Servi
**Responsibilities**
**Sales:** Aimee Drury (Key Account Manager)
**IT:** Simon Jarvis (IT Manager)
**US SIC:** 3620 **UK SIC:** 34350
**Auditors:** Arthur Andersen
**Bankers:** National Westminster Bank Plc
(60-22-31)

| | 31-12-13 | 31-12-12 | 31-12-11 |
|---|---|---|---|
| TO | 35,636,261 | 31,807,485 | 29,583,022 |
| P/L | 1,381,988 | 973,962 | 1,583,202 |
| NW | 8,314,272 | 7,276,347 | 6,566,130 |
| WC | 8,962,275 | 7,943,555 | 7,226,123 |
| Emp. | 82 | 78 | 76 |

DUNS 73-675-4255
### Smerdon Tree Services (Sts) Ltd
1 Station Road, Bargoed, Mid Glamorgan
CF81 9AL
**Tel:** 01443-710313 **Fax:** 01443-710313
**Reg No:** 4934812 **VAT No:** 790792683
**Estd:** 2005 Private Limited Company
**Line of Business:** Tree surgeons
**Issued Capital:** £1
**Director:** D A Smerdon
**Co. Secretary:** Ms Jennifer James
**US SIC:** 0851 **UK SIC:** 02000
**Auditors:** Watts Gregory LLP

| | 31-03-14 | 31-03-13 | 31-03-12 |
|---|---|---|---|
| TO | 7,038,264 | N/A | N/A |
| P/L | 34,280 | N/A | N/A |
| NW | 728,035 | 707,334 | 806,952 |
| WC | 585,864 | 918,553 | 370,628 |
| Emp. | 105 | N/A | N/A |

DUNS 21-884-5188 **Exp**
### Smethwick Maintenance Co Ltd
336 Spon Lane South, West Bromwich, West
Midlands B70 6AZ
**Tel:** 0121-553-3941
**Web:** www.sis-group.co.uk
**Reg No:** 0598051 **Estd:** 2010 Private
Limited Company
**Line of Business:** Builders
**Export Markets:** Worldwide
**Export Sales:** £6,145
**Issued Capital:** £500,005
**Directors:** G M Cooper, M L Cooper
**Co. Secretary:** Ms Sandra Cox
**Responsibilities**
**Marketing:** Neil Kannell (sales Coordinator)
**Health & Safety:** Neil Kannell (sales
Coordinator)
**US SIC:** 6711 **UK SIC:** 83962
**Auditors:** J W Hinks
**Bankers:** Barclays Bank Plc (20-93-15)

| | 30-11-13 | 30-11-12 | 30-11-11 |
|---|---|---|---|
| TO | 6,968,782 | 6,105,237 | 6,055,953 |
| P/L | 20,893 | (381,883) | (771,068) |
| NW | 4,315,753 | 4,374,599 | 4,779,757 |
| WC | 2,174,159 | 2,241,116 | 2,576,160 |
| Emp. | 77 | 88 | 85 |

DUNS 34-756-9522
### Smg Europe Holdings Ltd
(**Subsidiary of:** Smg Holdings Inc.)
Hunts Bank, Manchester M99 1SA
**Tel:** 01619505000
**Web:** www.bridgewater-hall.co.uk
**Reg No:** 5558259 **Estd:** 2005 Private
Limited Company
**Line of Business:** Management activities of
holding companies
**Export Sales:** £7,833,000
**Issued Capital:** £6,425,400
**Directors:** H Westley, J Burns
**Co. Secretary:** John Burns
**US SIC:** 6711 **UK SIC:** 83962
**Auditors:** PricewaterhouseCoopers LLP

**Bankers:** National Westminster Bank Plc
(56-00-06)

| | 31-12-13 | 31-12-12 | 31-12-11 |
|---|---|---|---|
| TO | 43,647,000 | 40,510,000 | 44,158,000 |
| P/L | 6,707,000 | 5,659,000 | 6,410,000 |
| NW | 20,460,000 | 18,897,000 | 17,573,000 |
| WC | 6,933,000 | 8,673,000 | 7,216,000 |
| Emp. | 1,228 | 1,126 | 1,166 |

DUNS 77-507-6938
### Smg Theatres Ltd
(**Subsidiary of:** Smg Holdings Inc.)
Bridgewater Hall, Great Bridgewater Street,
Manchester M1 5HA
**Tel:** 01619500000
**Web:** www.bridgewater-hall.co.uk
**Reg No:** 2982105 **VAT No:** 628738894
**Estd:** 1995 Private Limited Company
**Line of Business:** Theatres & concert halls
**Trading Style:** (The) Bridgewater Hall
**Issued Capital:** £1,000
**Directors:** J F Burns, H Westley
**Co. Secretary:** John Burns
**Responsibilities**
**Senior:** Nick Reed (Chief Executive)
**HR:** Sandra Perrott (Operations Manager)
**Health & Safety:** Sandra Perrott (Operations
Manager)
**Operations:** Sandra Perrott (Operations
Manager), Marco Tedde (Head Chef)
**US SIC:** 5812, 7999
**UK SIC:** 66110, 97913
**Auditors:** RSM Robson Rhodes LLP
**Bankers:** The Co-Operative Bank Plc
(08-90-00)

| | 31-12-13 | 31-12-12 | 31-12-11 |
|---|---|---|---|
| TA | 275,274 | 318,591 | 356,850 |
| P/L | N/A | 333,610 | N/A |
| NW | 275,274 | 275,274 | 23,240 |
| WC | N/A | 275,274 | 23,240 |

DUNS 73-252-7986
### Smh Fleet Solutions Ltd
Old Brickworks, Church Lane, Norton,
Worcester, Worcestershire WR5 2PR
**Tel:** 01905-829400
**Web:** www.smhfleet.com
**Reg No:** 4526612 **Estd:** 2003 Private
Limited Company
**Line of Business:** Renting of automobiles
**Issued Capital:** £66,666
**Directors:** G B Sinclair, M J Mcauley,
D Greenfield
**Co. Secretary:** Gateley Secretaries Limited
**Responsibilities**
**Senior:** Susan Field (Delivery Manager),
Jessica Holder (Administration Coordinator),
Debbie Holt (Manager), Elizabeth Mcauley
(Director), Vivienne Sinclair (Director)
**Finance:** Jeremy McGilvray (Financial
Controller)
**Admin:** Jessica Holder (Administration
Coordinator)
**HR:** Jessica Holder (Administration
Coordinator)
**Health & Safety:** Susan Field (Delivery
Manager)
**Facilities:** Susan Field (Delivery Manager)
**Branches:** Smh Fleet Solutions Ltd, Horwich
Business Park, Chorley New Road, Bolton,
Lancashire BL6 5UE
**US SIC:** 7399 **UK SIC:** 83954
**Auditors:** PKF

| | 31-12-13 | 31-12-12 | 31-12-11 |
|---|---|---|---|
| TO | 22,665,421 | 18,794,329 | 16,501,727 |
| P/L | 2,751,031 | 1,005,110 | 1,979,322 |
| NW | 5,245,019 | 3,227,452 | 3,857,862 |
| WC | 2,274,639 | 797,562 | 1,446,477 |
| Emp. | 235 | 233 | 197 |

DUNS 21-775-1597
### Smiddybrae House
Vetquoy Road, Orkney KW17 2HH
**Tel:** 01856771100
**Estd:** 2011
**Line of Business:** Social work activities
**US SIC:** 6732 **UK SIC:** 83100
**Employees:** 60

DUNS 21-605-6051
### Smile Stores Ltd
(**Subsidiary of:** McColl's Retail Group Plc)
46-48 Moorland Road, Bath, Avon BA2 3PN
**Tel:** 01225424843 **Fax:** 01179506777
**Reg No:** 0641258 **Estd:** 1959 Private
Limited Company
**Line of Business:** Convenience stores
**Trading Style:** Newshop, Smile
**Issued Capital:** £650,100
**Director:** J Lancaster
**Co. Secretary:** Simon Miller
**Branches:** Smile Stores Ltd, 85 Bradford
Road, Bath, Avon BA2 5BP
**US SIC:** 5411, 5993
**UK SIC:** 64100, 64200
**Auditors:** Deloitte LLP

**Bankers:** National Westminster Bank Plc
(60-24-37)

| | 24-11-13 | 25-11-12 | 27-11-11 |
|---|---|---|---|
| TO | 57,903,000 | 57,221,000 | 55,526,000 |
| P/L | 1,672,000 | 1,700,000 | 2,438,000 |
| NW | 5,570,000 | 3,366,000 | 754,000 |
| WC | 737,000 | (1,757,000) | (4,479,000) |
| Emp. | 1,252 | 956 | 944 |

DUNS 64-083-9148
### Smilechildcare
17 Calder Grove, Edinburgh, Midlothian
EH11 4LZ
**Tel:** 0131-476-7800
**Web:** www.smilechildcare.co.uk
**Reg No:** 0181428SC **Estd:** 1997 Private
Unlimited Company
**Line of Business:** Charities and charitable
organisations
**Directors:** Ms J H Ducreux, J Tindell,
Mrs G Mcintyre, Ms B B Stirling,
Miss L B Elliot
**Responsibilities**
**Senior:** Jacquie McCulloch (Financial
Manager), Donna Rodger (Manager)
**Finance:** Jacquie McCulloch (Financial
Manager)
**US SIC:** 8211 **UK SIC:** 93200
**Auditors:** Scott-Moncrieff
**Bankers:** Bank Of Scotland (12-21-52)

| | 31-03-14 | 31-03-13 | 31-03-12 |
|---|---|---|---|
| TO | 924,954 | 929,411 | 914,241 |
| P/L | (17,682) | 29,832 | 82,111 |
| NW | 261,036 | 278,718 | 248,886 |
| WC | 231,944 | 254,599 | 236,191 |
| Emp. | 55 | 46 | 44 |

DUNS 23-287-2528
### Smiley Monroe Holdings Ltd
23 Ferguson Drive, Lisburn, Co Antrim BT28
2EX
**Tel:** 028-9267-3777 **Fax:** 028-9266-3666
**Web:** www.smileymonroe.com
**Reg No:** 0042483NI **Estd:** 2002 Private
Limited Company
**Line of Business:** Other letting of own
property
**Export Sales:** £4,640,219
**Issued Capital:** £8,251
**Director:** D V Monroe
**Co. Secretary:** Mrs Mary Monroe
**US SIC:** 6519 **UK SIC:** 85000
**Auditors:** ASM (B) Ltd
**Bankers:** Northern Bank Ltd (95-03-61)

| | 31-12-13 | 31-12-12 | 31-12-11 |
|---|---|---|---|
| TO | 16,160,076 | 16,342,044 | 14,387,420 |
| P/L | 1,169,909 | 996,775 | 687,594 |
| NW | 3,629,445 | 2,920,897 | 2,187,705 |
| WC | 1,998,554 | 1,438,293 | 917,579 |
| Emp. | 95 | 96 | 84 |

DUNS 73-712-5646
### Smisby Day Nursery Ltd
The Byre, Main Street, Ashby-De-La-Zouch,
Leicestershire LE65 2TY
**Web:** www.smisbydaynursery.co.uk
**Reg No:** 4971196 **Estd:** 2003 Private
Limited Company
**Line of Business:** Primary education
**Issued Capital:** £20
**Director:** I Higginbotham
**Co. Secretary:** Ms Sheila Higginbotham
**US SIC:** 8321 **UK SIC:** 96111

| | 30-04-14 | 30-04-13 | 30-04-12 |
|---|---|---|---|
| TA | 60,555 | 62,182 | 60,625 |
| NW | 36,387 | 40,987 | 42,046 |
| WC | 15,153 | 15,535 | 13,364 |

DUNS 29-860-5791
### Smit International (Scotland) Ltd
(**Subsidiary of:** Smit Ship Management (U
K) Ltd)
Westminster House Crompton Way,
Segensworth West, Fareham, Hampshire
PO15 5SS
**Tel:** 02074807648 **Fax:** 01489 578588
**Web:** www.smit.com
**Reg No:** 2063791 **VAT No:** 456403454
**Estd:** 1986 Private Limited Company
**Line of Business:** Labour recruitment and
provision of personnel
**Issued Capital:** £1,000,000
**Directors:** H H Wevers, R V Richards
**Co. Secretary:** Raymond Richards
**Responsibilities**
**Senior:** Eva Dixon (Manager), Edwin Ros
(Manager), Mark Van Den Akker (Manager),
Willem Vogelaar (Director)
**HR:** Claire Summerill (Human Resources
Manager)
**Branches:** Smit International (Scotland) Ltd,
Flotta Terminal, Stromness, Orkney KW16
3NP
**US SIC:** 7361, 7392
**UK SIC:** 83954, 83951
**Auditors:** KPMG LLP

**Bankers:** Clydesdale Bank Plc (82-44-04)

| | 31-12-13 | 31-12-12 | 31-12-11 |
|---|---|---|---|
| TO | 9,675,000 | 10,425,000 | 10,762,000 |
| P/L | 639,000 | 741,000 | 790,000 |
| NW | 1,500,000 | 2,443,000 | 2,008,000 |
| WC | 1,685,000 | 2,669,000 | 1,818,000 |
| Emp. | 56 | 55 | 65 |

DUNS 21-221-9349 **Imp**
### Smith & Bateson Ltd
(**Subsidiary of:** Smith Bateson Holdings Ltd)
Stronghold House, Kitling Road, Prescot,
Merseyside L34 9HQ
**Tel:** 01515-471-801 **Fax:** 01515-477-171
**Web:** www.smithbateson.co.uk
**Reg No:** 0523345 **VAT No:** 927342519
**Estd:** 2002 Private Limited Company
**Line of Business:** Sppliers of bags various
types
**Issued Capital:** £20,000
**Principals:** S V Mckuhen (Managing),
A M Kennerley, P J Smith
**Co. Secretary:** Graeme Hurst
**US SIC:** 5199, 2651, 3079
**UK SIC:** 61900, 47253, 48360
**Auditors:** Baker Tilly UK Audit LLP
**Bankers:** National Westminster Bank Plc
(50-30-20)

| | 31-03-14 | 31-03-13 | 31-03-12 |
|---|---|---|---|
| TO | 28,429,416 | 27,722,644 | 28,093,929 |
| P/L | 656,710 | 646,472 | 675,766 |
| NW | 6,203,111 | 5,702,986 | 5,223,672 |
| WC | 5,965,997 | 5,745,899 | 5,250,939 |
| Emp. | 49 | 50 | 50 |

DUNS 22-524-2247
### Smith & Byford Ltd
St George House, Sutton, Surrey SM2 7AT
**Tel:** 020-8643-1080 **Fax:** 02086-434653
**Web:** www.smithandbyford.com
**Reg No:** 1074356 **VAT No:** 217078371
**Estd:** 1972 Private Limited Company
**Line of Business:** Electrical contractors and
electricians
**Issued Capital:** £50,012
**Principals:** W Smith (Managing),
Ms M Dorey, Mrs H R Smith, W Smith,
B Grove
**Co. Secretary:** Ms Paula Mclachlan
**Responsibilities**
**Senior:** Paula Mclichlin (Human Resources
Manager)
**HR:** Paula Mclichlin (Human Resources
Manager)
**Branches:** Smith & Byford Ltd, Unit 9,
Leatherhead Road, Chessington, Surrey KT9
2QL
**US SIC:** 1731 **UK SIC:** 50300
**Auditors:** Wesley Cooper Ltd
**Bankers:** HSBC Bank plc (40-17-07)

| | 31-03-14 | 31-03-13 | 31-03-11 |
|---|---|---|---|
| TO | 24,064,450 | 29,943,255 | 17,272,219 |
| P/L | 733,338 | 2,362,243 | 601,198 |
| NW | 6,811,985 | 6,151,861 | 5,503,147 |
| WC | 3,659,585 | 3,710,604 | 2,901,159 |
| Emp. | 272 | 252 | 235 |

DUNS 21-834-4901
### Smith & Holbourne (Holdings) Ltd
(**Subsidiary of:** Lamb-Weston/Meijer V.O.F.)
Weasenham Lane, Wisbech,
Cambridgeshire PE13 2RN
**Tel:** 01945468800 **Fax:** 01945468841
**Web:** www.lambweston.com
**Reg No:** 0369200 **VAT No:** 688857450
**Estd:** 1936 Private Limited Company
**Line of Business:** Management activities of
holding companies
**Issued Capital:** £11,794
**Directors:** B Albas, S H Van Wouwe
**Co. Secretary:** Simon Van Wouwe
**US SIC:** 6711 **UK SIC:** 83962
**Auditors:** Stephenson Smart & Co
**Bankers:** Lloyds TSB Bank plc (30-99-77)

| | 14-07-13 | 15-07-12 | 17-07-11 |
|---|---|---|---|
| TO | 52,675,263 | 56,285,260 | 53,209,317 |
| P/L | 2,414,097 | 2,495,636 | 2,464,504 |
| NW | 17,761,791 | 15,736,128 | 13,910,128 |
| WC | 6,104,300 | 3,801,787 | 9,075,516 |
| Emp. | 131 | 127 | 132 |

DUNS 21-734-3771
### Smith & Jewell Ltd
Leigh Road, Chichester, West Sussex PO19
8UF
**Tel:** 01243-784741 **Fax:** 01243-533646
**Web:** www.smithandjewell.co.uk
**Reg No:** 1158658 **VAT No:** 582825121
**Estd:** 1974 Private Limited Company
**Line of Business:** Manufacture of other
fabricated metal products not elsewhere
classified
**Issued Capital:** £2,286
**Chairman and Managing Director:** C Glass
**Co. Secretary:** Jeremy Stuart-Smith
**Responsibilities**
**Senior:** George Barton (Works Manager)
**HR:** George Barton (Works Manager)
**Health & Safety:** George Barton (Works
Manager)

**Facilities:** George Barton *(Works Manager)*
**Purchasing:** Martin Bilham *(Buyer)*
**Engineering:** George Barton *(Works Manager)*
**Branches:** Smith & Jewell Ltd, Leigh Road, Lineside Industrial Estate, Chichester, West Sussex PO19 8UF
**US SIC:** 3499 **UK SIC:** 31694
**Auditors:** Casson Beckman
**Bankers:** Lloyds TSB Bank plc (77-25-08)

| | 30-06-13 | 30-06-12 | 30-06-11 |
|---|---|---|---|
| TA | 950,316 | 1,344,670 | 1,126,868 |
| NW | 313,241 | 306,501 | 241,074 |
| WC | (156,105) | (180,480) | (286,201) |

DUNS 42-418-9855 Imp-Exp

## Smith & McLaurin Ltd

(**Subsidiary of:** Smith & McLaurin Holdings Ltd)
Cartside Mill, Johnstone, Renfrewshire PA10 2AF
**Tel:** 01505-707700
**Web:** www.smcl.co.uk
**Reg No:** 0229817SC **VAT No:** 797030511
**Estd:** 2002 Private Limited Company
**Line of Business:** Manufacturers of tag labels
**Export Markets:** Europe, Australia, Southern Ireland
**Export Sales:** £7,827,000
**Trading Style:** Smith & McLaurin Limited
**Issued Capital:** £50,000
**Directors:** J Radford, A C Mclaughlin, Mrs R Mackay, C Loudon, R S Easton, G A Oxburgh
**Co. Secretary:** Allan Mclaughlin
**Responsibilities**
**Senior:** Colin Gault *(Manager)*
**US SIC:** 2392 **UK SIC:** 45550
**Auditors:** Johnston Carmichael

| | 31-07-13 | 31-07-12 | 31-07-11 |
|---|---|---|---|
| TO | 25,947,000 | 23,545,000 | 25,013,000 |
| P/L | 735,000 | 1,273,000 | 1,228,000 |
| NW | 3,890,000 | 4,111,000 | 3,064,000 |
| WC | 928,000 | 1,272,000 | 190,000 |
| Emp. | 91 | 87 | 88 |

DUNS 21-299-2622

## Smith & Nephew Healthcare Ltd

(**Subsidiary of:** Smith & Nephew Plc)
Health House, Grange Park Lane, Hull, North Humberside HU10 6DT
**Tel:** 01482-222200 **Fax:** 01482-222211
**Web:** www.smithnephew.com
**Reg No:** 0156031 **Estd:** 1919 Private Limited Company
**Line of Business:** Other human health activities
**Issued Capital:** £45,050
**Directors:** Mrs S M Swabey, H T Waters, I C Melling
**Co. Secretary:** Smith & Nephew Nominee Services
**Responsibilities**
**Senior:** Peter Van Tiggelen *(Manager)*
**Marketing:** Andy Boyes *(Senior Vice President Strategi)*, Rod Hulme *(?Customer Insights Specialist)*, Lee Taylor *(Senior Finance Administrator)*
**HR:** Jane Brodie *(Hr Manager - Strategic Project)*, Vanessa Lucas *(Human Resources Director)*
**Engineering:** Zoe Fowler *(Packaging Technology Leader)*, David Gillis *(Technical Project Manager)*
**Branches:** Smith & Nephew Healthcare Ltd, Healthcare House, Goulton Street, Hull, North Humberside HU3 4DJ
**US SIC:** 8091 **UK SIC:** 95200

| | 31-12-13 | 31-12-12 | 31-12-11 |
|---|---|---|---|
| TA | 31,298 | 31,298 | 31,298 |
| NW | 31,298 | 31,298 | 31,298 |

DUNS 21-027-2498 Exp

## Smith & Nephew Plc

15 Adam Street, Charing Cross, London WC2N 6LA
**Tel:** 02074017646 **Fax:** 020-7930-3353
**Web:** www.smith-nephew.com
**Reg No:** 0324357 **VAT No:** 577156412
**Estd:** 1961 Public Limited Company
**Line of Business:** Pharmaceutical preparation manufacturers
**Export Markets:** U K, Continental Europe, America, Africa, Asia, Australasia
**Trading Style:** Corporate Affairs
**Directors:** Baroness V H Bottomley, M A Friedman, I E Barlow, V Bali, J Papa, R Quarta, Mrs J B Brown, E Engstrom
**Co. Secretary:** Ms Susan Swabey
**Responsibilities**
**Senior:** Rodrigo Bianchi *(President, IRAMEA)*, Olivier Bohuon *(Director)*, Diogo Correia Moreira-Rato *(President, Europe & Canada)*, Cynthia Ford *(Executive)*, Michael Frazzette *(President, Advanced Surgical D)*, Shauntell Harper *(Configuration Management and P)*, Leon Hoare *(President Asia Pacific)*, Noel Kendrick *(International Business Manager)*, Brian Larcombe *(Director)*, Jonathan Logan *(Manager)*, Tesha Saulsberry *(Board Member)*, Stacey Stadler *(Manager)*, Glenn Warner *(President, Advanced Wound Mana)*, Laura Whitsitt *(General Manager)*
**Finance:** Helen Casey *(Finance Manager)*, Maggie West *(Finance Manager)*
**Marketing:** Beth Bentley *(Brand Development Manager: Com)*, Erika Burgos *(Customer Service Manager)*, Susan Myers *(Communications Manager)*, Cyrille Petit *(Chief Corporate Development Of)*, Stacy Wygant *(Internal Communication Manager)*
**Sales:** Christian Burkhardt *(Corporate Development Director)*, Rasmus Platz *(?VP Business Development)*, John Telford *(?New Business Development Mana)*, Sarah Tuttle *(Commercial Manager)*
**Admin:** Ian Chalmers *(Human Resources Manager)*, Michael Gilson *(Administrator)*, Debbie Holm *(Admin Assistant)*, Trish Rybak *(Administrator)*
**IT:** Terry Dunn *(Compensation & Benefits Manage)*, David Farrar *(Technology Manager)*
**HR:** Ian Chalmers *(Human Resources Manager)*, Lauren Dyer *(National Training Manager)*, Elga Lohler *(Vice President Human Resources)*, Helen Maye *(Chief Human Resources Officer)*, Len Pendle *(Human Resources Director)*
**Health & Safety:** Ian Chalmers *(Human Resources Manager)*
**Facilities:** Ian Chalmers *(Human Resources Manager)*
**Operations:** Ian Chalmers *(Human Resources Manager)*, Lisa Chambliss *(Head of Information Technology)*, Harold Combs *(Security Executive)*, Margie Herring *(Manager)*, Phil Kane *(Senior Quality Engineer)*, Carl Saxby *(Advanced Wound Devices Project)*, Noel Waters *(Vice President Operations)*
**Purchasing:** Joseph Kirchner *(Brand Supply Manager)*, Catherina Lim *(Purchasing Director)*, John Siekierski *(Purchasing Director)*
**Engineering:** Ken Krause *(Engineer)*, Janaki Penmetsa *(Engineer)*, Ros Rivaz *(Chief Technology Officer)*, Robert Roberti *(Manufacturing Engineer)*, Jason Strachota *(Engineer)*, Ken Woodland *(Engineer)*
**Branches:** Smith & Nephew Plc, Cardinal Park, Endoscopy House Unit 5-6, Huntingdon, Cambridgeshire PE29 2SN
**US SIC:** 2834, 3841, 6711
**UK SIC:** 25700, 37201, 83962
**Auditors:** Ernst & Young LLP
**Bankers:** National Westminster Bank Plc (60-23-07)
**Employees:** 10,743
**Turnover:** £4,351,000,000

DUNS 64-092-6770

## Smith & Pinching Financial Services Ltd

(**Subsidiary of:** The Smith + Pinching Group Ltd)
295 Aylsham Road, Norwich, Norfolk NR3 2RY
**Tel:** 01603789966
**Web:** www.mortgages4me.co.uk
**Reg No:** 3487726 **Estd:** 1973 Private Limited Company
**Line of Business:** Insurance brokers
**Issued Capital:** £441,000
**Principals:** D W Hughff *(Managing)*, J W Simpson, D V Pring
**Co. Secretary:** Scott Pinching
**Branches:** Smith & Pinching Financial Services Ltd, 6 Middle Street, Thetford, Norfolk IP25 6AG
**US SIC:** 6111, 6411
**UK SIC:** 81501, 83200
**Auditors:** Sexty & Co
**Bankers:** Barclays Bank Plc (20-62-68)

| | 30-06-14 | 30-06-13 | 30-06-12 |
|---|---|---|---|
| TA | 1,816,025 | 1,373,482 | 1,324,662 |
| NW | 1,176,849 | 686,252 | 614,821 |
| WC | 1,434,116 | 995,431 | 918,302 |

DUNS 21-623-2652

## Smith & Sons (Bletchington) Ltd

Enslow, Kidlington, Oxfordshire OX5 3AY
**Fax:** 01869331734
**Web:** www.smithsbletchington.co.uk
**Reg No:** 0430620 **Estd:** 1911 Private Limited Company
**Line of Business:** Builders merchants
**Issued Capital:** £320,000
**Principals:** A W Smith *(Managing)*, S C Smith *(Managing)*, D J Smith
**Co. Secretary:** Andrew Smith
**Responsibilities**
**Senior:** Tim Norridge *(Workshop Manager)*
**IT:** Ann-marie Paddock *(IT Manager)*
**Fleet:** Paul Needle *(Transport Manager)*
**Engineering:** Tim Norridge *(Workshop Manager)*
**Branches:** Smith & Sons (Bletchington) Ltd, Broadway Quarry, Broadway, Worcestershire WR12 7HD
**US SIC:** 5039, 1429, 1499, 3341
**UK SIC:** 61300, 23102, 23960, 22470
**Auditors:** Wenn Townsend
**Bankers:** Barclays Bank Plc (20-98-48)

| | 31-03-14 | 31-03-13 | 31-03-12 |
|---|---|---|---|
| TO | 14,899,685 | 12,519,173 | 13,015,926 |
| P/L | 1,089,486 | 447,869 | 1,427,902 |
| NW | 18,204,953 | 16,815,286 | 16,800,233 |
| WC | 3,751,264 | 3,869,223 | 4,042,950 |
| Emp. | 100 | 97 | 98 |

DUNS 38-585-5416

## Smith & Western (Chichester) Ltd

(**Subsidiary of:** Smith & Western Restaurants Ltd)
North Parade, Horsham, West Sussex RH12 2QR
**Tel:** 01403-264927
**Web:** www.smith-western.co.uk
**Reg No:** 3340223 **Estd:** 1997 Private Limited Company
**Line of Business:** Restaurant - american
**Issued Capital:** £2
**Directors:** T H Cox, T Cox, J Cox, Miss S A Cox
**Co. Secretary:** Ms Victoria Cox
**Branches:** Smith & Western (Chichester) Ltd, Boxhill Road, Tadworth, Surrey KT20 7LB
**US SIC:** 5812 **UK SIC:** 66110

| | 30-06-14 | 30-06-13 | 30-06-12 |
|---|---|---|---|
| TA | 901,737 | 780,850 | 770,484 |
| NW | 605,457 | 477,314 | 399,666 |
| WC | 454,373 | 428,542 | 444,717 |

DUNS 23-986-2337

## Smith & Williamson Group

1 Walnut Tree Close Bishops Wharf, Guildford, Surrey GU1 4RA
**Tel:** 01483-407100
**Web:** www.smith.williamson.co.uk
**Estd:** 1993 Partnership
**Line of Business:** Accounting activities
**Partners:** N Bolt, G Healy
**Responsibilities**
**Senior:** David Blenkarn *(Partner - Restructuring & reco)*, Maggie Lowe *(Regional Director)*, Claire Perrett *(Partner-Tax services to busine)*
**HR:** Theresa Luck *(Employee Benefits Manager)*
**Operations:** Janice Clay *(Technical, Production Manager)*
**US SIC:** 8931, 8999, 6371, 7392
**UK SIC:** 83600, 83954, 82002, 83951
**Employees:** 70

DUNS 73-260-1443

## Smith & Williamson Holdings Ltd

25 Moorgate, London EC2R 6AY
**Tel:** 020-7131-4000 **Fax:** 020-7631-0741
**Web:** www.smith.williamson.co.uk
**Reg No:** 4533948 **Estd:** 2002 Private Limited Company
**Line of Business:** Financial intermediation not elsewhere classified
**Issued Capital:** £5,988,806
**Directors:** P F Hazell, K P Stopps, H C Strutt, A F Sykes, J T Boadle, R J Bogart, B C Goldring, P L Fernandes
**Co. Secretary:** Ms Deborah Saunders
**Responsibilities**
**Senior:** William Cameron *(Manager)*, David Cobb *(Director)*, Sue Dignum *(Manager)*, Gareth Pearce *(chairman)*
**US SIC:** 6111, 6012
**UK SIC:** 81501, 81402
**Auditors:** Grant Thornton UK LLP
**Bankers:** The Royal Bank Of Scotland Plc (16-00-55)

| | 30-04-14 | 30-04-13 | 30-04-12 |
|---|---|---|---|
| TA | 614,560,000 | 517,045,000 | 679,116,000 |
| P/L | 33,984,000 | 25,768,000 | 20,351,000 |
| NW | 96,833,000 | 82,151,000 | 65,727,000 |
| WC | 93,551,000 | 74,610,000 | 66,305,000 |
| Emp. | 1,406 | 1,432 | 1,410 |

DUNS 51-992-5114 Imp

## Smith Anderson Group Ltd

Rosslyn Commerce Park, Kirkcaldy, Fife KY1 3NA
**Tel:** 01592-657057 **Fax:** 01337855550
**Web:** www.smithanderson.com
**Reg No:** 0207391SC **VAT No:** 268406344
**Estd:** 1959 Private Limited Company
**Line of Business:** Manufacturers of packaging materials
**Export Sales:** £3,505,603
**Issued Capital:** £590,000
**Directors:** D W Wood, M J Longstaffe, J E Verden-Anderson, Ms F M Partridge, K E Verden-Anderson, D S Robertson, E D Murray, W G Verden-Anderson
**Branches:** Smith Anderson Group Ltd, Townsend Indstl Est, Portland Clo, Houghton Regis, Dunstable, Bedfordshire LU5 5AW
**US SIC:** 2654 **UK SIC:** 47280
**Auditors:** Carters Accountants LLP

| | 30-09-13 | 30-09-12 | 30-09-11 |
|---|---|---|---|
| TO | 21,268,131 | 20,316,732 | 19,859,279 |
| P/L | 557,857 | 977,311 | 238,931 |
| NW | 5,300,126 | 7,248,969 | 6,811,658 |
| WC | 3,228,655 | 3,147,001 | 2,463,789 |
| Emp. | 201 | 202 | 201 |

DUNS 21-209-6705

## Smith Bros (Caerconan) Wholesale Ltd

Greyfriars House, Sidings Court, Doncaster, South Yorkshire DN4 5NU
**Tel:** 01302-366922
**Web:** www.smithbrosuk.co.uk
**Reg No:** 0267023 **VAT No:** 181321294
**Estd:** 1932 Private Limited Company
**Line of Business:** Electrical wholesalers
**Issued Capital:** £230,400
**Principals:** P C Jervis *(Managing)*, M P Jervis, Mrs A Sheach, R Bielenica
**Co. Secretary:** Michael Andrews
**Responsibilities**
**Sales:** Richard Bielenica *(Sales Director)*
**Admin:** Nancy Sheach *(Office Manager)*
**US SIC:** 5074 **UK SIC:** 61300
**Auditors:** Hart Shaw LLP
**Bankers:** National Westminster Bank Plc (56-00-66)

| | 31-12-13 | 31-12-12 | 31-12-11 |
|---|---|---|---|
| TO | 31,356,005 | 30,026,420 | 31,107,000 |
| P/L | 1,413,595 | 1,451,123 | 657,040 |
| NW | 12,009,975 | 11,720,105 | 11,137,971 |
| WC | 11,417,398 | 11,123,772 | 10,579,216 |
| Emp. | 64 | 64 | 69 |

DUNS 21-818-2707 Imp-Exp

## Smith Brothers (Leicester) Ltd

295 Aylestone Road, Leicester, Leicestershire LE2 7PB
**Tel:** 01162-833581 **Fax:** 01162-837311
**Web:** www.airplants.co.uk
**Reg No:** 0091566 **Estd:** 1907 Private Limited Company
**Line of Business:** Manufacture of other fabricated metal products not elsewhere classified
**Export Markets:** Middle East; Far East
**Export Sales:** £40,568
**Issued Capital:** £52,000
**Principals:** P C Fletcher *(Managing)*, J G Smith, S R White, Mrs M J Beasley, A D Smith, J T Wilkinson, S R Smith, C J Smith
**Co. Secretary:** Peter Fletcher
**Branches:** Smith Brothers (Leicester) Ltd, Brimscombe, Stroud, Gloucestershire GL5 2SH
**US SIC:** 3499 **UK SIC:** 31694
**Auditors:** Thomas May & Co
**Bankers:** National Westminster Bank Plc (56-00-55)

| | 30-09-13 | 30-09-12 | 30-09-11 |
|---|---|---|---|
| TO | 54,801,427 | 48,264,073 | 43,171,930 |
| P/L | 4,851,960 | 3,931,934 | 2,422,302 |
| NW | 35,815,485 | 31,961,785 | 28,622,782 |
| WC | 25,569,225 | 21,522,333 | 18,789,489 |
| Emp. | 258 | 212 | 191 |

DUNS 52-537-3809

## Smith Brothers Marine Ltd

30 Crescent Road, Fareham, Hampshire PO16 0HG
**Tel:** 01329230317
**Web:** www.smithbrothersflooring.co.uk
**Reg No:** 3240923 **Estd:** 1987 Private Limited Company
**Line of Business:** Floor or wall covering
**Issued Capital:** £200
**Principals:** R Smith *(Managing)*, R Smith
**Co. Secretary:** Ms Lauren Harris
**Branches:** Smith Brothers Marine Ltd, 206 West Street, Fareham, Hampshire PO16 9XQ
**US SIC:** 1752 **UK SIC:** 50400
**Bankers:** Barclays Bank Plc (20-30-89)

| | 31-08-13 | 31-08-12 | 31-08-11 |
|---|---|---|---|
| TA | 2,168,021 | 1,818,691 | 1,815,985 |
| NW | 941,985 | 723,755 | 773,978 |
| WC | 564,878 | 334,195 | 522,360 |

DUNS 23-291-9220 Imp

## Smith Global Ltd

344 Floor, 2 Chiswick High Road, London W4 1TH
**Fax:** 020-8987-4300
**Web:** www.mrandmrssmith.com
**Reg No:** 4438845 **VAT No:** 802561850
**Estd:** 2002 Private Limited Company
**Line of Business:** Other publishing
**Export Sales:** £528,479
**Trading Style:** Mr & Mrs Smith
**Issued Capital:** £147,006
**Directors:** E G Orr, J A Lohan, Dr M C Witt, Ms T Lohan, Mrs S J Balcombe
**Co. Secretary:** Ms Natasha Shafi
**US SIC:** 2741, 4722

**UK SIC:** 47541, 77001
**Bankers:** Barclays Bank Plc (20-00-06)

| | 31-12-13 | 31-12-12 | 31-12-11 |
|---|---|---|---|
| TO | 6,710,168 | 5,863,989 | 4,362,364 |
| P/L | (979,182) | (1,359,586) | 343,110 |
| NW | (3,012,906) | (2,239,291) | 1,460,287 |
| WC | (1,649,855) | (1,227,724) | 826,328 |
| Emp. | 91 | 89 | N/A |

DUNS 50-594-9792 **Imp**

## Smith International (North Sea) Ltd

(**Subsidiary of:** Schlumberger N.V.)
Badentoy Avenue, Badentoy Industrial Estate, Portlethen, Aberdeen, Aberdeenshire AB12 4YB
**Tel:** 01224334700
**Web:** www.smith.com
**Reg No:** 2533968 **Estd:** 1972 Private Limited Company
**Line of Business:** Service activities incidental to oil and gas extraction excluding surveying
**Issued Capital:** £1,250,843
**Directors:** J Mcgachie, Mrs K A Hoeing-Cosentino, R A Kidd
**Co. Secretary:** Ms Pauline Droy Moore
**Branches:** Smith International (North Sea) Ltd, Units 9-10 Murcar Indstl Est, Denmore Rd, Bridge Of Don, Aberdeen, Aberdeenshire AB23 8JW
**US SIC:** 1389, 8911, 7391
**UK SIC:** 13000, 83701, 94000
**Auditors:** Deloitte & Touche LLP
**Bankers:** The Royal Bank Of Scotland Plc (83-49-40)

| | 31-12-13 | 31-12-12 | 31-12-11 |
|---|---|---|---|
| TO | 77,040,000 | 78,159,000 | 60,486,000 |
| P/L | 7,519,000 | 5,184,000 | 1,803,000 |
| NW | 46,620,000 | 43,536,000 | 41,795,000 |
| WC | 27,502,000 | 21,863,000 | 26,996,000 |
| Emp. | 302 | 340 | 313 |

DUNS 21-168-9136

## Smith Jones (Solicitors) Ltd

Towneley House Kingsway, Burnley, Lancashire BB11 1BJ
**Tel:** 01282855455
**Web:** www.smithjonessolicitors.co.uk
**Reg No:** 6938570 **Estd:** 2009 Private Limited Company
**Line of Business:** Solicitors
**Trading Style:** Smith Jones (Solicitors) Limited
**Issued Capital:** £80,000
**Directors:** A J Graham, P A Jones, P J Smith, D C Woodhead, C S Bibby
**Responsibilities**
**Senior:** Beverley Bellas *(Finance Director)*
**Finance:** Beverley Bellas *(Finance Director)*
**US SIC:** 8111 **UK SIC:** 83500
**Bankers:** The Royal Bank Of Scotland Plc (16-14-32)

| | 31-08-13 | 31-08-12 | 31-08-11 |
|---|---|---|---|
| TO | 3,377,693 | 4,334,624 | 4,376,629 |
| P/L | 243,287 | 1,271,389 | 1,295,163 |
| NW | (891,309) | (957,211) | (1,694,079) |
| WC | (284,529) | 623,216 | 277,418 |
| Emp. | 56 | 54 | 56 |

DUNS 29-026-9851

## Smith Knight Fay Ltd

(**Subsidiary of:** Inchcape Plc)
Gee Cross Service Station, Stockport Road, Hyde, Cheshire SK14 5ET
**Tel:** 01618259565 **Fax:** 01613678648
**Web:** www.smithknightfay.com
**Reg No:** 0702018 **Estd:** 1961 Private Limited Company
**Line of Business:** Car dealers (new & used)
**Trading Style:** Smith Knight Fay, Knightsbridge Mazda, Knightsbridge Toyota, Bolton Audi
**Issued Capital:** £1
**Directors:** R Mccluskey, M P Wheatley, C Mccormack
**Co. Secretary:** Inchcape Uk Corporate Management
**Responsibilities**
**Senior:** Barry Morrison *(Brand Manager)*
**Branches:** Smith Knight Fay Ltd, Green Lane, Stockport, Cheshire SK4 2JN
**US SIC:** 5511, 7539
**UK SIC:** 65100, 67100
**Auditors:** PricewaterhouseCoopers LLP
**Bankers:** The Royal Bank Of Scotland Plc (16-15-33)

| | 31-12-13 | 31-12-11 |
|---|---|---|
| TA | 1 | N/A |
| P/L | N/A | (2,000) |
| NW | 1 | N/A |
| Emp. | N/A | 4 |

DUNS 21-302-9064

## Smith News

Unit 6, Gateshead, Tyne and Wear NE11 0QD
**Tel:** 08451225010
**Web:** www.smithsnews.co.uk
**Estd:** 1987 Partnership
**Line of Business:** Newspaper distributors
**Proprietor:** E Lambe
**Responsibilities**
**Senior:** Ian Rockwell *(CEO, Managing Director)*
**Branches:** Smith News, Regus House, 33 Clarendon Dock, Belfast, Belfast BT1 3BW
**US SIC:** 7393 **UK SIC:** 83954
**Employees:** 80

DUNS 21-811-4452 **Imp**

## Smith of Derby Group Ltd

112 Alfreton Road, Little Eaton, Derby, Derbyshire DE21 5DE
**Tel:** 01332-831912
**Reg No:** 0135728 **VAT No:** 125677259
**Estd:** 1956 Private Limited Company
**Line of Business:** Fabricated metal products
**Export Sales:** £444,705
**Issued Capital:** £4,503
**Principals:** J N Smith *(Chairman)*, J G Smith, J J Bowler, Ms M H Whitworth, J H Smith, Ms J V Millar
**Co. Secretary:** Peter Barry
**Branches:** Smith Of Derby Group Ltd, Station Road, Whitchurch, Shropshire SY13 1RD
**US SIC:** 3441, 3873
**UK SIC:** 32042, 37400
**Auditors:** Rogers Spencer
**Bankers:** National Westminster Bank Plc (60-12-01)

| | 31-12-13 | 31-12-12 | 31-12-11 |
|---|---|---|---|
| TO | 3,131,727 | 4,329,814 | 3,713,928 |
| P/L | (234,828) | (28,919) | (386,316) |
| NW | 2,374,885 | 2,652,449 | 2,677,289 |
| WC | 480,916 | 730,213 | 836,257 |
| Emp. | 55 | 56 | 64 |

DUNS 21-820-4818

## Smith of Derby (Int) Ltd

(**Subsidiary of:** Smith of Derby Group Ltd)
112 Alfreton Road, Derby, Derby, Derbyshire DE21 4AU
**Tel:** 01332345569
**Web:** www.smithofderby.com
**Reg No:** 7925100 **Estd:** 2012 Private Limited Company
**Line of Business:** Manufacture of watches and clocks
**Issued Capital:** £1
**Director:** R Betts
**Co. Secretary:** Peter Barry
**US SIC:** 3873 **UK SIC:** 37400

| | 31-01-14 | 31-01-13 |
|---|---|---|
| TA | 1 | 1 |
| NW | 1 | 1 |

DUNS 64-262-5040

## Smith Partnership

4th Floor Celtic House, Friary Street, Derby, Derbyshire DE1 1LS
**Tel:** 01332225225
**Web:** www.smithpartnership.co.uk
**Estd:** 1987 Partnership
**Line of Business:** Law Firm
**Partners:** P Smith, Ms A Hutchins, G Dean, S Rowley
**Branches:** Smith Partnership, 88-90 The Strand, Stoke-On-Trent, Staffordshire ST3 2PB
**US SIC:** 8111 **UK SIC:** 83500
**Employees:** 250

DUNS 23-010-6911

## Smithbrewer Ltd

22 Bolton Close, Highbridge, Somerset TA9 4JR
**Tel:** 01934-642642
**Web:** www.smithbrewer.co.uk
**Reg No:** 3777353 **VAT No:** 655537219
**Estd:** 1995 Private Limited Company
**Line of Business:** Sign and nameplate suppliers
**Export Sales:** £1,203,571
**Issued Capital:** £63,000
**Managing Director:** S R Smith
**Co. Secretary:** Michael Brewer
**US SIC:** 2599, 3079
**UK SIC:** 46720, 48360
**Auditors:** Keith Willis Associates Ltd

| | 31-05-13 | 31-05-12 | 31-05-11 |
|---|---|---|---|
| TO | 9,721,300 | 8,299,755 | 6,677,860 |
| P/L | 740,295 | 427,530 | 204,483 |
| NW | 2,611,350 | 2,221,527 | 1,965,927 |
| WC | 872,246 | 553,752 | 322,048 |
| Emp. | 60 | 53 | 55 |

DUNS 73-898-9321 **Imp**

## Smithers-Oasis Europe Ltd

Crowther Road, Crowther Industrial Estate, Washington, Tyne and Wear NE38 0AQ
**Tel:** 01914175595
**Web:** http://souk.oasisfloral.com
**Reg No:** 5152689 **Estd:** 1938 Private Limited Company
**Line of Business:** Manufacture of other plastic products
**Export Sales:** £37,320,000
**Issued Capital:** £5,516,284
**Directors:** J Stull, R M Kilbride, S K Short, E Kremer
**Co. Secretary:** Paul Southwick
**Responsibilities**
**Senior:** Stephen Garrett *(Manager)*
**IT:** Peter Rising *(UK IT Manager)*
**US SIC:** 3079 **UK SIC:** 48360

| | 31-03-14 | 31-03-13 | 31-03-12 |
|---|---|---|---|
| TO | 49,776,000 | 48,730,000 | 49,552,000 |
| P/L | (877,000) | (1,491,000) | (2,010,000) |
| NW | (8,778,000) | (8,361,000) | (8,493,000) |
| WC | 12,241,000 | 10,254,000 | 11,285,000 |
| Emp. | 342 | 336 | 345 |

DUNS 34-965-7994 **Exp**

## Smithers Rapra & Smithers Pira Ltd

(**Subsidiary of:** The Smithers Group Inc)
Shawbury, Shrewsbury, Shropshire SY4 4NR
**Tel:** 01939-250383
**Web:** www.rapra.net
**Reg No:** 5761324 **Estd:** 2006 Private Limited Company
**Line of Business:** Research and laboratory based activities
**Export Sales:** £3,050,000
**Issued Capital:** £2
**Directors:** J L Dowey, J M Hochschwender
**Responsibilities**
**Senior:** Jcooo Roock *(Manager)*
**Finance:** Steve Ankers *(Accountant)*
**Marketing:** Louisa Gauld-Crichton *(Marketing Manager, Europe)*, Rebecca Leigh *(Marketing Director Europe)*
**Sales:** Helena Griffiths *(Sales Coordinator)*
**IT:** Paul Spragg *(Technical Manager)*
**Health & Safety:** Paul Spragg *(Technical Manager)*
**Facilities:** Paul Spragg *(Technical Manager)*
**Operations:** Paul Spragg *(Technical Manager)*
**US SIC:** 7391 **UK SIC:** 94000

| | 31-12-13 | 31-12-12 | 31-12-11 |
|---|---|---|---|
| TO | 10,139,000 | 9,051,000 | 7,466,157 |
| P/L | 1,004,000 | 389,000 | (541,008) |
| NW | (142,000) | (1,172,000) | (1,577,375) |
| WC | 412,000 | 1,227,000 | (7,539) |
| Emp. | 149 | 141 | 114 |

DUNS 39-158-8654

## Smithfield Murray Ltd

(**Subsidiary of:** Smithfield Poultry Ltd)
Kings Park, Mosley Road, Trafford Park, Manchester M17 1QA
**Tel:** 01618768111
**Web:** www.smithfieldmurray.com
**Reg No:** 2110715 **VAT No:** 468112547
**Estd:** 1987 Private Limited Company
**Line of Business:** Production of meat products
**Trading Style:** Wignall Food
**Issued Capital:** £40,131
**Principals:** D N Murray *(Managing)*, M T Grady
**US SIC:** 2013 **UK SIC:** 41223
**Auditors:** Cowgill Holloway LLP
**Bankers:** Barclays Bank Plc (20-55-34)

| | 01-04-14 | 01-04-13 | 01-04-12 |
|---|---|---|---|
| TO | 18,669,361 | 13,252,711 | 15,699,575 |
| P/L | 314,687 | 332,492 | 575,119 |
| NW | 1,710,709 | 1,756,220 | 1,728,837 |
| WC | 1,150,931 | 1,050,416 | 1,313,797 |
| Emp. | 56 | 53 | 52 |

DUNS 29-487-4516 **Imp**

## Smithpack Ltd

(**Subsidiary of:** Index Pack Ltd)
Unit 8 Butterly Avenue, Questor, Dartford, Kent DA1 1JG
**Fax:** 01322-351770
**Web:** www.smithpack.co.uk
**Reg No:** 1850712 **Estd:** 2010 Private Limited Company
**Line of Business:** Manufacturers of packaging materials
**Trading Style:** Storepak Ltd
**Issued Capital:** £5,000
**Directors:** K N Allwood, Miss D L Williams, R P Green, T A Coverdale
**Responsibilities**
**Senior:** Andrew Brigstock *(Manager)*, Martin Canty *(Manager)*, Paul Constant *(Plant Manager)*, Kevin Orwood *(Manager)*
**Health & Safety:** Paul Constant *(Plant Manager)*
**Facilities:** Paul Constant *(Plant Manager)*
**Operations:** Paul Constant *(Plant Manager)*
**Engineering:** Paul Constant *(Plant Manager)*
**Branches:** Smithpack Ltd, Building 55A, Second Avenue, Kingswinford, West Midlands DY6 7XL
**US SIC:** 7399, 3999, 2752
**UK SIC:** 83954, 49590, 47544
**Auditors:** Baker Tilly
**Bankers:** National Westminster Bank Plc (60-15-28)

| | 30-04-14 | 30-04-13 | 30-04-12 |
|---|---|---|---|
| TO | N/A | N/A | 5,895,444 |
| P/L | N/A | N/A | 174,807 |
| NW | 737,598 | 724,529 | 774,672 |
| WC | 572,216 | 572,596 | 560,885 |
| Emp. | N/A | N/A | 48 |

DUNS 21-614-3669 **Imp-Exp**

## Smiths Aerospace Gloucester Ltd

(**Subsidiary of:** Smiths Group Plc)
Cheltenham Road East Anson Business Park, Gloucester, Gloucestershire GL2 9QN
**Tel:** 01452 716000
**Web:** www.ge.com
**Reg No:** 0312083 **Estd:** 1936 Private Limited Company
**Line of Business:** Aeronautical engineers
**Export Markets:** Europe; Middle East; Africa; Australasia
**Trading Style:** Dowty Propellers, Dowty Aerospace Hydraulics, Smiths Aerospace Actuation Systems
**Issued Capital:** £66,010,000
**Directors:** N R Burdett, Ms A Ralph
**Co. Secretary:** Miss Fiona Gillespie
**Responsibilities**
**Senior:** Richard Bishop *(Despatch Manager)*, David Penn *(Manager)*
**Finance:** Helen Russell *(Financial Director)*
**Fleet:** Richard Bishop *(Despatch Manager)*
**Branches:** Smiths Aerospace Gloucester Ltd, Arle Court, Cheltenham, Gloucestershire GL51 0TP
**US SIC:** 8911, 3721
**UK SIC:** 83701, 36400
**Bankers:** HSBC Bank plc (40-17-10)

| | 31-07-13 | 31-07-12 | 31-07-11 |
|---|---|---|---|
| TA | 70,151,000 | 70,151,000 | 70,151,000 |
| NW | 70,151,000 | 70,151,000 | 70,151,000 |

DUNS 21-623-2660 **Exp**

## Smiths Concrete Ltd

Southam Road, Banbury, Oxfordshire OX16 2RR
**Web:** www.smithsconcrete.co.uk
**Reg No:** 0580634 **VAT No:** 194784510
**Estd:** 2002 Private Limited Company
**Line of Business:** Manufacture of ready-mixed concrete
**Issued Capital:** £40,000
**Principals:** D J Smith *(Chairman)*, A W Smith, J A Claydon, S C Smith, C A Stubbs
**Co. Secretary:** Roger Tyson
**Responsibilities**
**Senior:** Claire Gilkes *(Operations Manager)*
**HR:** Claire Gilkes *(Operations Manager)*
**Health & Safety:** Claire Gilkes *(Operations Manager)*
**Facilities:** Claire Gilkes *(Operations Manager)*
**Operations:** Claire Gilkes *(Operations Manager)*
**Engineering:** Claire Gilkes *(Operations Manager)*
**Branches:** Smiths Concrete Ltd, Industrial Estate, Stratford-Upon-Avon, Warwickshire CV37 8BJ
**US SIC:** 3273, 3275, 4959
**UK SIC:** 24360, 24370, 92110
**Auditors:** Wenn Townsend
**Bankers:** Barclays Bank Plc (20-98-48)

| | 31-12-13 | 31-12-12 | 31-12-11 |
|---|---|---|---|
| TO | 11,087,549 | 10,850,573 | 11,739,668 |
| P/L | 368,193 | 251,405 | 730,244 |
| NW | 7,712,042 | 7,718,904 | 7,510,890 |
| WC | 5,008,371 | 5,147,573 | 4,755,106 |
| Emp. | 58 | 56 | 55 |

DUNS 21-674-8053 **Exp**

## Smiths Detection-Watford Ltd

(**Subsidiary of:** Smiths Group Plc)
459 Park Avenue, Bushey, Hertfordshire WD23 2BW
**Fax:** 01923-240285
**Web:** www.smithsdetection.com
**Reg No:** 0480992 **Estd:** 1950 Private Limited Company
**Line of Business:** Manufacturers of security equipment suppliers and
**Export Markets:** E U, W Europe, S & S E Asia, U S A
**Export Sales:** £17,266,000
**Trading Style:** Smiths Detection-Watford Limited
**Issued Capital:** £76,771
**Directors:** A P Lee, Ms L Liu
**Co. Secretary:** Ms Lili Liu
**Responsibilities**
**Senior:** Stuart Grisdale *(Warehouse Manager)*, Mal Maginnis *(Manager)*
**Finance:** Nicola Pinder *(Head of Finance)*
**IT:** Dennis Parker *(IT Manager)*
**Branches:** Smiths Detection-Watford Limited, Unit 3, St. Albans Road, Watford, Hertfordshire WD24 7RY
**US SIC:** 3829, 7397
**UK SIC:** 37100, 83702

**Auditors:** PricewaterhouseCoopers LLP
**Bankers:** Barclays Bank Plc (20-77-67)

| | 31-07-14 | 31-07-13 | 31-07-12 |
|---|---|---|---|
| TO | 38,368,000 | 46,599,000 | 52,299,000 |
| P/L | (7,014,000) | (489,000) | (919,000) |
| NW | (3,486,000) | 3,163,000 | 4,366,000 |
| WC | (9,489,000) | (3,135,000) | (2,070,000) |
| Emp. | 218 | 238 | 270 |

DUNS 76-852-2591 **Imp-Exp**

## Smith's Environmental Products Ltd

Unit 1-2, Hamberts Road Blackall Industrial Estate, Chelmsford, Essex CM3 5UW
**Tel:** 01245-324900 **Fax:** 01245-324422
**Web:** www.smiths-env.com
**Reg No:** 2607831 **VAT No:** 594612223
**Estd:** 1991 Private Limited Company
**Line of Business:** Manufacture of central heating radiators and boilers
**Export Markets:** Australia; Israel; Europe; U S A
**Issued Capital:** £1,000
**Directors:** J E Swan, P Wheat, P E Jenkinson, T J Swan Iii, D L Mason
**Co. Secretary:** David Mason
**Responsibilities**
**Senior:** Phil Cross *(Works Manager)*, Darren Rolston *(Accountant)*, Gary Webster *(Managing Director)*
**Finance:** Darren Rolston *(Accountant)*
**Sales:** Marianne Hall *(Sales Supervisor)*
**IT:** Brian Cochrane *(IT Manager)*
**HR:** Phil Cross *(Works Manager)*, L Townsend *(Purchaser)*
**Health & Safety:** Phil Cross *(Works Manager)*
**Purchasing:** Belinda Townsend *(Purchasing Manager)*
**US SIC:** 5074, 3639
**UK SIC:** 61300, 34600
**Auditors:** Pearlman Rose
**Bankers:** Barclays Bank Plc (20-29-86)

| | 31-12-13 | 31-12-12 | 31-12-11 |
|---|---|---|---|
| TA | 2,314,339 | 2,119,880 | 2,633,871 |
| NW | 1,552,439 | 1,342,433 | 1,615,655 |
| WC | 1,388,501 | 1,135,029 | 1,358,984 |

DUNS 73-791-9352

## Smiths Equipment Hire (Holdings) Ltd

Whitegate Drive, Blackpool, Lancashire FY3 9JW
**Tel:** 01253696109
**Web:** www.smithshire.com
**Reg No:** 5048553 **Estd:** 2004 Private Limited Company
**Line of Business:** Management activities of holding companies
**Issued Capital:** £610
**Directors:** D W Smith, T G Smith
**US SIC:** 6711 **UK SIC:** 83962

| | 28-02-14 | 28-02-13 | 29-02-12 |
|---|---|---|---|
| TO | 7,247,058 | 6,143,468 | 5,870,132 |
| P/L | 1,066,287 | 655,600 | 780,497 |
| NW | 3,896,746 | 3,376,292 | 3,064,066 |
| WC | (1,380,297) | (1,324,008) | (1,211,876) |
| Emp. | 103 | 91 | 87 |

DUNS 22-001-2905

## Smith's (Gloucester) Ltd

Allkerton Court, Alkerton, Eastington, Stonehouse, Gloucestershire GL10 3AQ
**Tel:** 01453822227
**Web:** www.smiths-gloucester.co.uk
**Reg No:** 4004654 **VAT No:** 753631138
**Estd:** 1995 Private Limited Company
**Line of Business:** Demolition and wrecking of buildings; earth moving
**Issued Capital:** £100
**Directors:** A R Smith, Ms A Smith
**Co. Secretary:** Ms Pamela Broomfield
**Responsibilities**
**Admin:** Lynne Mowles *(Administrator)*
**IT:** Zbigniew Socha *(IT Manager)*, Ziggy socha *(IT Manager)*
**US SIC:** 1795, 1541, 4213
**UK SIC:** 50000, 50100, 72300
**Auditors:** Griffiths Marshall
**Bankers:** Barclays Bank Plc (20-19-95)

| | 31-03-14 | 31-03-13 | 31-03-12 |
|---|---|---|---|
| TO | 45,007,126 | 39,604,326 | 38,208,332 |
| P/L | 741,322 | 295,243 | 711,825 |
| NW | 2,400,187 | 1,788,273 | 1,123,579 |
| WC | (3,318,616) | (3,711,245) | (4,250,926) |
| Emp. | 407 | 411 | 412 |

DUNS 29-539-2989

## Smiths Gore Administration Ltd

**(Subsidiary of:** Smiths Gore Commercial Property Llp)
Stuart House, Peterborough, Cambridgeshire PE1 1QF
**Tel:** 01733567231
**Web:** www.smithsgore.co.uk
**Reg No:** 1906197 **Estd:** 1885 Private Limited Company
**Line of Business:** Management activities of holding companies
**Issued Capital:** £1,026
**Directors:** A R Harle, P S Coles, S F Knight
**Co. Secretary:** Keith Strong
**Branches:** Smiths Gore Administration Ltd, Alan Ho, 48 Bootham, York, North Yorkshire YO30 7WZ
**US SIC:** 8911 **UK SIC:** 83701
**Auditors:** Moore Stephens

| | 31-03-14 | 31-03-13 | 31-03-12 |
|---|---|---|---|
| TA | 26,532 | 26,532 | 26,532 |
| NW | 5,048 | 5,048 | 5,048 |

DUNS 21-027-3256

## Smiths Group Plc

80 Victoria Street, London SW1E 5JL
**Fax:** 02078085544
**Web:** www.smiths.com
**Reg No:** 0137013 **Estd:** 1914 Public Limited Company
**Line of Business:** Management activities of holding companies
**Export Sales:** £2,832,600,000
**Issued Capital:** £147,415,579
**Directors:** Ms A C Quinn, D J Challen, P A Turner, B F Angelici, W C Seeger Jr., Sir K R Tebbit, Ms T D Fratto, Sir G W Buckley
**Co. Secretary:** Ms Zillah Stone
**Responsibilities**
**Senior:** Phillip Bowman *(Chief Executive Officer)*, Mike Bullen *(Office Manager)*, William Seeger *(Director)*
**Finance:** Neil Parkin *(Treasurer)*
**Marketing:** Colin McSeveny *(Head of Group Media, PR and Ev)*
**Sales:** Neil Dupres *(Director, Business & Technolog)*, Eric Lakin *(Corporate Development Director)*, Pascale Philis *(Business Development Manager)*
**HR:** Dee Reandi *(HR Business Partner)*
**Branches:** Smiths Group Plc, Crossbow Ho,Liverpool Rd, Slough Indstl Est, Slough, Berkshire SL1 4QZ
**US SIC:** 6711, 5199
**UK SIC:** 83962, 61900
**Auditors:** PricewaterhouseCoopers LLP
**Bankers:** Lloyds TSB Bank plc (30-00-02)
**Following financial data are in thousands**

| | 31-07-14 | 31-07-13 | 31-07-12 |
|---|---|---|---|
| TO | 2,951,600 | 3,108,600 | 3,030,100 |
| P/L | 302,000 | 441,800 | 365,900 |
| NW | (306,200) | (260,000) | (744,300) |
| WC | 656,000 | 733,500 | 488,800 |
| Emp. | 23,200 | 23,250 | 23,200 |

DUNS 21-615-6794 **Imp-Exp**

## Smith's (Harlow) Ltd

Barrows Road, Harlow, Essex CM19 5AT
**Tel:** 01279425641
**Web:** www.smiths-harlow.co.uk
**Reg No:** 0549932 **VAT No:** 213979053
**Estd:** 1995 Private Limited Company
**Line of Business:** Other engineering activities
**Issued Capital:** £33,712
**Director:** J M Tennison
**Co. Secretary:** Ian Knightley
**Responsibilities**
**Health & Safety:** Nick Hatch *(Facilities Manager)*
**Facilities:** Nick Hatch *(Facilities Manager)*
**Operations:** Nick Hatch *(Facilities Manager)*
**Engineering:** Paul Platt *(Works Manager)*
**US SIC:** 8911 **UK SIC:** 83701
**Auditors:** Bird Luckin
**Bankers:** Lloyds TSB Bank plc (30-96-64)

| | 31-03-14 | 31-03-13 | 31-03-12 |
|---|---|---|---|
| TO | 8,350,468 | 7,688,407 | 7,606,388 |
| P/L | (124,651) | (41,060) | 88,123 |
| NW | 3,309,935 | 3,361,610 | 3,321,596 |
| WC | 1,309,347 | 1,172,521 | 1,050,713 |
| Emp. | 88 | 85 | 78 |

DUNS 21-043-0706 **Exp**

## Smiths Medical

1500 Eureka Park, Lower Pemberton, Kennington, Ashford, Kent TN25 4BF
**Tel:** 01233722199
**Web:** www.smiths-medical.com
**Estd:** 2007 Proprietorship
**Line of Business:** Hearing aid suppliers
**Proprietor:** M Sassone
**Responsibilities**
**Senior:** Vipin Magdani *(Logistics Manager)*
**Sales:** Vipin Magdani *(Logistics Manager)*
**HR:** Simon Wilde *(Human Resources Manager)*
**Operations:** Lynda Avison *(Production Manager)*, Vipin Magdani *(Logistics Manager)*
**Fleet:** Vipin Magdani *(Logistics Manager)*
**Engineering:** Lynda Avison *(Production Manager)*
**US SIC:** 3841 **UK SIC:** 37201
**Employees:** 150

DUNS 21-618-4630 **Imp-Exp**

## Smiths Medical International Ltd

**(Subsidiary of:** Smiths Group Plc)
1500 Eureka Park, Lower Pemberton, Kennington, Ashford, Kent TN25 4BF
**Tel:** 01233722351 **Fax:** 01233722153
**Web:** www.smiths-medical.com
**Reg No:** 0362847 **Estd:** 1940 Private Limited Company
**Line of Business:** Manufacture of other plastic products
**Export Markets:** Worldwide
**Export Sales:** £207,551,000
**Trading Style:** Smiths Medical International Ltd
**Issued Capital:** £63,217
**Directors:** I J Harper, S A Eggleston, Ms S R Hardy
**Co. Secretary:** Ms Roisin Bennett
**Responsibilities**
**Senior:** Matthew Sassone *(Manager)*
**Marketing:** Matthieu Leclerc *(Marketing Manager)*
**Branches:** Smiths Medical International Ltd, Unit K2 Lyntown Trading Estate, Eccles, Manchester M30 9QG
**US SIC:** 3079 **UK SIC:** 48360
**Auditors:** PricewaterhouseCoopers LLP
**Bankers:** Lloyds TSB Bank plc (30-00-02)

| | 31-07-14 | 31-07-13 | 31-07-12 |
|---|---|---|---|
| TO | 246,884,000 | 238,797,000 | 235,215,000 |
| P/L | 31,075,000 | 31,755,000 | 20,494,000 |
| NW | 111,254,000 | 118,089,000 | 78,051,000 |
| WC | 91,095,000 | 97,944,000 | 56,450,000 |
| Emp. | 754 | 762 | 765 |

DUNS 64-090-7853 **Imp**

## Smiths Metal Centres Ltd

Stratton Business Park, London Road, Biggleswade, Bedfordshire SG18 8QB
**Tel:** 01767604604
**Web:** www.smithshp.com
**Reg No:** 3485838 **VAT No:** 706158151
**Estd:** 1997 Private Limited Company
**Line of Business:** Representative office
**Export Sales:** £5,572,500
**Trading Style:** Smiths
**Issued Capital:** £2,500
**Principals:** H A Dye *(Managing)*, M O Mckenna, P W Hawkins, D A Adams, J M Booth
**Co. Secretary:** Mrs Morag Hale
**Responsibilities**
**Senior:** Martin Underhill *(branch manager)*
**HR:** Debbie Pryor *(Human Resources Manager)*
**Fleet:** John Milicevic *(Transport Manager)*
**Branches:** Smiths Metal Centres Ltd, Dingley Dell, Old Bristol Road, Highbridge, Somerset TA9 4HU
**US SIC:** 5051 **UK SIC:** 61200
**Auditors:** Grant Thornton UK LLP
**Bankers:** HSBC Bank plc (40-30-32)

| | 31-12-13 | 31-12-12 | 31-12-11 |
|---|---|---|---|
| TO | 58,962,203 | 62,138,025 | 44,932,819 |
| P/L | 3,033,176 | 2,785,391 | 1,886,890 |
| NW | 11,976,973 | 9,537,598 | 7,416,329 |
| WC | 11,626,885 | 9,131,094 | 6,954,993 |
| Emp. | 266 | 269 | 272 |

DUNS 23-709-2916

## Smiths of Smithfield Ltd

**(Subsidiary of:** Longlac Holdings Limited)
67-77a Charterhouse Street, London EC1M 6HJ
**Tel:** 02072517950 **Fax:** 02072365666
**Web:** www.smithsofsmithfield.co.uk
**Reg No:** 3704349 **VAT No:** 735925705
**Estd:** 1999 Private Limited Company
**Line of Business:** Restaurants
**Issued Capital:** £6,482
**Directors:** H V Williams, R P Smithson, R H Munding, J R Ratcliffe
**Responsibilities**
**Senior:** Lauren Kaswell *(Manager)*, John Torode *(Manager)*
**Finance:** John Torode *(Manager)*
**Marketing:** John Torode *(Manager)*
**US SIC:** 5812, 5813
**UK SIC:** 66110, 66200
**Auditors:** Moore Stephens LLP
**Bankers:** National Westminster Bank Plc (50-41-01)

| | 31-05-13 | 31-05-12 | 31-05-11 |
|---|---|---|---|
| TO | 8,325,759 | 9,312,109 | 9,809,583 |
| P/L | 272,822 | 81,402 | 261,246 |
| NW | 1,555,277 | 1,305,027 | 1,238,779 |
| WC | (838,756) | (1,094,145) | (1,046,969) |
| Emp. | 192 | 198 | 215 |

DUNS 21-791-5399

## Smiths of Tower Bridge

22 Wapping High Street, London E1W 1NJ
**Tel:** 02074883456
**Web:** www.smithsrestaurants.com
**Estd:** 2011 Proprietorship
**Line of Business:** Restaurant - english
**Proprietor:** Miss R Watson
**Responsibilities**
**Senior:** Greg Molan *(Manager)*
**US SIC:** 5812 **UK SIC:** 66110
**Employees:** 50

DUNS 21-780-8946

## Smith's Wood Sports College

Windward Way, Birmingham, West Midlands B36 0UE
**Tel:** 01217884100
**Web:** www.smithswood.co.uk
**Estd:** 2011 Proprietorship
**Line of Business:** Primary education
**Proprietor:** R Hawkins
**US SIC:** 7399 **UK SIC:** 83954
**Employees:** 150

DUNS 23-655-2779 **Imp**

## Sml Europe Ltd

Unit 1 Arkwright Road, Corby, Northamptonshire NN17 5AE
**Tel:** 01536408408 **Fax:** 01536-408381
**Web:** www.sml.com
**Reg No:** 3650355 **VAT No:** 708416636
**Estd:** 1998 Private Limited Company
**Line of Business:** Distribution service providers
**Trading Style:** S M L Gresham
**Issued Capital:** £500,000
**Director:** K W Ho
**Co. Secretary:** Chin Mak
**Responsibilities**
**Senior:** Hau Cheung *(Manager)*, Shane Clarke *(Manager)*, Denis Durgin *(Manager)*, Lee O'Donaghue *(Manager)*, Bo Tiu *(Manager)*
**HR:** Arlene Barnes *(Buyer)*
**US SIC:** 2752, 2389
**UK SIC:** 47544, 45393
**Auditors:** PricewaterhouseCoopers LLP
**Bankers:** HSBC Bank plc (40-27-15)

| | 31-12-13 | 31-12-12 | 31-12-11 |
|---|---|---|---|
| TO | 27,336,000 | 24,097,000 | 27,969,000 |
| P/L | 2,687,000 | 3,309,000 | 3,661,000 |
| NW | (14,342,000) | (15,792,000) | (18,837,000) |
| WC | (17,105,000) | (17,361,000) | (21,916,000) |
| Emp. | 199 | 159 | 303 |

DUNS 21-328-0118

## Smokies Entertainments Ltd

**(Subsidiary of:** Edgeman Ltd)
Ashton Road, Oldham, Lancashire OL8 3HX
**Tel:** 01617855000 **Fax:** 0161-785-5010
**Web:** www.bestwestern.co.uk
**Reg No:** 1230998 **Estd:** 1975 Private Limited Company
**Line of Business:** Hotels and motels without restaurant
**Trading Style:** Hotel Smokies Park
**Issued Capital:** £5,000
**Directors:** N Chawla, M R Chawla
**Co. Secretary:** Mrs Saroj Chawla
**Responsibilities**
**Senior:** Vicky Haynes *(Food & Beverage Manager)*, Brent Hutchins *(General)*
**Marketing:** Natalie Barton *(Sales & Marketing Manager)*
**Sales:** Natalie Barton *(Sales & Marketing Manager)*
**Operations:** Brent Hutchins *(General)*
**US SIC:** 7011 **UK SIC:** 66500
**Auditors:** Hardy & Co
**Bankers:** Lloyds TSB Bank plc (30-93-71)

| | 31-03-14 | 31-03-13 | 31-03-12 |
|---|---|---|---|
| TO | 1,928,240 | 1,805,196 | 1,543,620 |
| P/L | 199,316 | 182,389 | 16,344 |
| NW | 2,907,116 | 2,777,747 | 2,380,270 |
| WC | 844,656 | 771,307 | 410,317 |
| Emp. | 62 | 58 | 54 |

DUNS 21-742-0507

## Smonk Consultants Ltd

3 Owen Place, Carterton, Oxfordshire OX18 1BS
**Tel:** 01993845754
**Web:** www.mha.org.uk
**Reg No:** 7748834 **Estd:** 2012 Private Limited Company
**Line of Business:** Business and management consultancy activities not elsewhere classified
**Issued Capital:** £1
**Director:** S Monk
**Co. Secretary:** Miss Sophie Monk
**US SIC:** 7392 **UK SIC:** 83951

| | 31-08-14 | 31-08-13 | 31-08-12 |
|---|---|---|---|
| TA | 11,629 | 8,981 | 4,023 |
| NW | 559 | 552 | 281 |
| WC | (662) | (784) | (617) |

DUNS 21-782-6330

## Smooth Radio

Laser House, Salford, Lancashire M50 3XW
**Tel:** 08448005533
**Web:** www.smoothradio.co.uk
**Estd:** 2011 Proprietorship
**Line of Business:** Aerial erectors and suppliers
**Proprietor:** S Kilvy

**Responsibilities**
**Marketing:** Chris Dunne *(Marketing Manager)*
**US SIC:** 4833 **UK SIC:** 97411
**Employees:** 170

DUNS 22-280-3095 **Imp**
## Smoothwall Ltd
1 John Charles Way, Leeds, West Yorkshire LS12 6QA
**Tel:** 08701999500
**Web:** www.smoothwall.net
**Reg No:** 4298247 **Estd:** 2001 Private Limited Company
**Line of Business:** Computer security
**Issued Capital:** £86
**Directors:** D B Barron, I C Parrett, M Marks, Ms G Lungley, J G Logan, Mrs N J Sharp
**Co. Secretary:** Mrs Sarah Lungley
**Responsibilities**
**Sales:** Bill Flowers *(Account Manager)*
**IT:** Lawrence Manning *(Senior Developer)*
**Operations:** Tom Newton *(Product Manager)*
**US SIC:** 7379 **UK SIC:** 83940

| | 31-12-13 | 31-10-12 | 31-12-11 |
|---|---|---|---|
| TO | 8,387,269 | N/A | N/A |
| P/L | (1,716,485) | N/A | N/A |
| NW | (3,053,735) | (404,526) | (1,032) |
| WC | (220,892) | 1,139,643 | 612,113 |
| Emp. | 104 | N/A | N/A |

DUNS 23-065-6253 **Imp**
## Smp Partners Ltd
Po Box 227 Clinch's House, Douglas, Isle of Man IM99 1RZ
**Tel:** 01624696600 **Fax:** 01624 612624
**Web:** www.smppartners.com
**Reg No:** 0028731M **Estd:** 2005 Private Limited Company
**Line of Business:** Security broking and related activities
**Trading Style:** Smp
**Issued Capital:** £100,000
**Principals:** D Lavin *(Managing)*, A P Hollingsworth, S E Mcgowan, M W Denton, Ms J D Bates, M Cundy, J A Steinhart, Bruncaster Ltd
**Co. Secretary:** Paul Eckersley
**Responsibilities**
**Senior:** PAUL ECKERSLEY *(Financial Director)*, Stephen McGowan *(Director)*
**Finance:** PAUL ECKERSLEY *(Financial Director)*
**US SIC:** 6211 **UK SIC:** 83100
**Employees:** 130

DUNS 23-913-8352 **Imp**
## Smr Automotive Mirrors Uk Ltd
(**Subsidiary of:** Motherson Sumi Systems Limited)
Portchester 2, Castle Trading Estate, Fareham, Hampshire PO16 9SD
**Tel:** 02392210022 **Fax:** 023 9253 9522
**Web:** www.smr-automotive.com
**Reg No:** 3904201 **VAT No:** 750389225
**Estd:** 1935 Private Limited Company
**Line of Business:** Manufacture of other transport equipment not elsewhere classified
**Export Sales:** £37,788,000
**Issued Capital:** £2
**Directors:** A Heuser, C Zawadzinski, L V Sehgal
**Co. Secretary:** Mrs Angela Whiting
**US SIC:** 3229 **UK SIC:** 24791
**Auditors:** PricewaterhouseCoopers LLP
**Bankers:** HSBC Bank plc (40-11-02)

| | 31-03-14 | 31-03-13 | 31-03-12 |
|---|---|---|---|
| TO | 123,331,000 | 114,736,000 | 102,884,000 |
| P/L | 1,326,000 | 3,125,000 | 3,021,000 |
| NW | 7,359,000 | 23,474,000 | 19,971,000 |
| WC | 3,377,000 | 19,394,000 | 16,124,000 |
| Emp. | 525 | 501 | 485 |

DUNS 64-092-6643 **Imp-Exp**
## Sms Electronics Ltd
1f Block, Technology Drive Beeston Business Park, Nottingham, Nottinghamshire NG9 1AD
**Tel:** 01159431616 **Fax:** 01159-575758
**Web:** www.smselectronics.co.uk
**Reg No:** 4496144 **VAT No:** 804541944
**Estd:** 2002 Private Limited Company
**Line of Business:** Electronic equipment (assembly)
**Export Sales:** £20,515,000
**Issued Capital:** £250,000
**Principals:** M W Harby *(Managing)*, A Maddock, R Pitchford, C Taylor, G Shaw, R W Bridges, J Wyles, C Hunt
**Co. Secretary:** Mark Goldby
**Responsibilities**
**HR:** Hayley Aldread *(HR Manager)*
**US SIC:** 3679, 3661
**UK SIC:** 34542, 34410

**Auditors:** KPMG LLP

| | 27-09-13 | 28-09-12 | 30-09-11 |
|---|---|---|---|
| TO | 29,284,000 | 32,039,000 | 50,369,000 |
| P/L | 854,000 | 1,701,000 | 3,550,000 |
| NW | 5,248,000 | 5,509,000 | 5,736,000 |
| WC | 4,626,000 | 4,812,000 | 4,833,000 |
| Emp. | 154 | 149 | 135 |

DUNS 73-253-3679
## Sms Towage Ltd
Ocean House Unit 6 Waterside Park, Livingstone Road, Hessle, North Humberside HU13 0EG
**Tel:** 01482-350999 **Fax:** 01482-648284
**Web:** www.smstowage.com
**Reg No:** 4527156 **Estd:** 1995 Private Limited Company
**Line of Business:** Operation of habours and ports
**Issued Capital:** £500,000
**Principals:** P Escreet *(Managing)*, P L Lyon, G P Escreet
**Co. Secretary:** Michael Kemish
**US SIC:** 4469, 4441
**UK SIC:** 76300, 72603
**Bankers:** National Westminster Bank Plc (56-00-06)

| | 31-03-14 | 31-03-13 | 31-03-12 |
|---|---|---|---|
| TO | 10,107,080 | 8,769,477 | 7,573,530 |
| P/L | 1,192,808 | 410,369 | 2,801 |
| NW | 14,832,211 | 13,193,408 | 12,094,956 |
| WC | 1,721,270 | 1,020,407 | 283,791 |
| Emp. | 105 | 91 | 84 |

DUNS 21-608-0598
## Smurfit Corrugated Uk Ltd
(**Subsidiary of:** Smurfit Kappa Group Public Limited Company)
Smurfit Corrugated (Scotland) Ltd, Old Edinburgh Road, Tannochside, Glasgow, Lanarkshire G71 6PQ
**Tel:** 01698812901
**Web:** http://corrugated.smurfitkappa.co.uk
**Reg No:** 0700242 **VAT No:** 312486963
**Estd:** 1900 Private Limited Company
**Line of Business:** Manufacture of other containers
**Issued Capital:** £1
**Directors:** Mrs N Pritchard, P Mcneill
**Co. Secretary:** Mrs Nicola Pritchard
**Branches:** Smurfit Corrugated Uk Ltd, Occupation Lane, Pudsey, West Yorkshire LS28 8HL
**US SIC:** 2654, 2651
**UK SIC:** 47280, 47253
**Bankers:** National Westminster Bank Plc (60-00-08)

| | 31-12-13 | 31-12-12 | 31-12-11 |
|---|---|---|---|
| TA | 102,160,978 | 102,160,978 | 102,160,978 |
| NW | 9,097,978 | 9,097,978 | 9,097,978 |

DUNS 21-317-9229 **Exp**
## Smurfit Kappa Uk Ltd
(**Subsidiary of:** Smurfit Kappa Group Public Limited Company)
3rd Floor, Liverpool, Merseyside L3 1SF
**Tel:** 0870-240-0361 **Fax:** 0151-802-1724
**Web:** www.smurfitkappa.co.uk
**Reg No:** 1017013 **VAT No:** 344020796
**Estd:** 1971 Private Limited Company
**Line of Business:** Manufacture of corrugated paper and paperboard, sacks and bags
**Export Sales:** £29,557,000
**Trading Style:** Smurfit Kappa Shared Services, Smurfit Kappa Recycling
**Issued Capital:** £32,265,319
**Directors:** M O Riordan, C Shepherd, C Bowers, J Hiscock, P Mcneill, C Allen, K Byrne
**Co. Secretary:** Mrs Nicola Pritchard
**Responsibilities**
**Senior:** Andy Burrows *(Plant Director)*
**Marketing:** Nick Bagshaw *(Sales Director)*
**Sales:** Nick Bagshaw *(Sales Director)*
**IT:** Wayne Rumley *(IT Manager)*
**Operations:** Diane Chilton *(Quality Manager)*
**Branches:** Smurfit Kappa Uk Ltd, Campbell Street, Preston, Lancashire PR1 5LX
**US SIC:** 2645, 2651
**UK SIC:** 47280, 47253
**Auditors:** PricewaterhouseCoopers LLP

| | 31-12-13 | 31-12-12 | 31-12-11 |
|---|---|---|---|
| TO | 546,422,000 | 534,157,000 | 568,024,000 |
| P/L | (19,984,000) | 18,050,000 | 6,508,000 |
| NW | 130,537,000 | 147,261,000 | 144,491,000 |
| WC | 31,791,000 | 78,308,000 | 79,590,000 |
| Emp. | 2,880 | 2,899 | 2,719 |

DUNS 57-838-6625 **Imp**
## Smurfit Ward Ltd
(**Subsidiary of:** Smurfit Kappa Group Public Limited Company)
Unit 91 Clydesdale Place, Preston, Lancashire PR26 7QS
**Tel:** 01772454225 **Fax:** 01772-622389
**Reg No:** 2891814 **VAT No:** 636276327
**Estd:** 1994 Private Limited Company
**Line of Business:** Manufacture of corrugated paper and paperboard, sacks and bags
**Trading Style:** Bags of Choice
**Issued Capital:** £3,077,695
**Directors:** P Mcneill, Mrs N Pritchard
**Co. Secretary:** Mrs Nicola Pritchard
**US SIC:** 2645 **UK SIC:** 47280
**Auditors:** Unknown
**Bankers:** Lloyds TSB Bank plc (30-96-85)

| | 31-12-13 | 31-12-12 | 31-12-11 |
|---|---|---|---|
| NW | (5,045,800) | (5,045,800) | (5,045,800) |

DUNS 21-600-2687
## Smursitkappa
Old Nixon Estate, Winterstoke Road, Weston-Super-Mare, Avon BS24 9BH
**Tel:** 01934428600
**Web:** www.smurfitkappa.co.uk
**Estd:** 1994 Partnership
**Line of Business:** Manufacturers and filling of aerosols
**Partners:** D Moynihan, C Neophytou, M Chan
**Responsibilities**
**Senior:** F Dowehord *(Manager)*
**US SIC:** 3999 **UK SIC:** 49590
**Employees:** 160

DUNS 45-859-8299
## Smw Ltd
(**Subsidiary of:** Iberdrola Sociedad Anonima)
Daldowie Fuel Plant, Glasgow, Lanarkshire G71 7RX
**Reg No:** 0165988SC **VAT No:** 659372008
**Estd:** 2010 Private Limited Company
**Line of Business:** Disposal of sewage
**Issued Capital:** £2
**Directors:** Mrs H Chalmers White, H O Finlay
**Co. Secretary:** Alistair Orr
**Responsibilities**
**Senior:** Jim Connolly *(Operations Manager)*, Dylan Hughes *(Plant Manager)*
**US SIC:** 2999, 4952
**UK SIC:** 11150, 92120
**Auditors:** PricewaterhouseCoopers LLP

| | 31-12-13 | 31-12-12 | 31-12-11 |
|---|---|---|---|
| TO | 19,000,000 | 18,500,000 | 18,500,000 |
| P/L | 1,700,000 | 2,500,000 | 7,200,000 |
| NW | 7,400,000 | 4,800,000 | 10,100,000 |
| WC | (30,600,000) | (34,300,000) | (30,900,000) |
| Emp. | 70 | 61 | 68 |

DUNS 21-457-3487
## Smyth Patterson Ltd
18 Market Square, Lisburn, Co Antrim BT28 1AG
**Tel:** 028 9266 2707 **Fax:** 028 9260 1367
**Web:** www.smythpatterson.co.uk
**Reg No:** 0001910NI **VAT No:** 251872847
**Estd:** 1936 Private Limited Company
**Line of Business:** Departmental stores
**Trading Style:** J C Patterson
**Issued Capital:** £250
**Directors:** C W Patterson, Mrs J N Patterson
**Co. Secretary:** William Rogan
**Responsibilities**
**Senior:** Donald Frazer *(Despatch Manager)*
**US SIC:** 5399, 5719
**UK SIC:** 65600, 64700
**Auditors:** Fitch Audit Ltd
**Bankers:** Ulster Bank Ltd (98-09-60)

| | 31-01-14 | 31-01-13 | 31-01-12 |
|---|---|---|---|
| TA | 1,492,877 | 1,389,146 | 1,519,561 |
| NW | 880,083 | 838,583 | 835,202 |
| WC | 516,671 | 462,086 | 514,719 |

DUNS 22-925-7373 **Exp**
## Smyth Steel Ltd
Anvil Works, 15 Gorran Road, Garvagh, Coleraine, Co Londonderry BT51 4HA
**Web:** www.smyth-steel.co.uk
**Reg No:** 0014105NI **Estd:** 1980 Private Limited Company
**Line of Business:** Steel fabricators
**Export Markets:** Republic of Ireland
**Issued Capital:** £25,100
**Directors:** Ms M E Smyth, S E Laverty, J I Smyth, D S Kerr, S F Lindsay
**Co. Secretary:** Mrs Margaret Smyth
**Responsibilities**
**Senior:** Mervin Gilmore *(Warehouse Manager)*
**US SIC:** 1622 **UK SIC:** 50200
**Auditors:** E & M Associates
**Bankers:** Northern Bank Ltd (95-03-38)

| | 30-04-14 | 30-04-13 | 30-04-12 |
|---|---|---|---|
| TA | 4,663,265 | 3,713,355 | 4,041,905 |
| NW | 3,466,774 | 3,104,688 | 2,929,401 |
| WC | 2,723,280 | 2,332,666 | 2,098,303 |

DUNS 67-221-8190
## Smyths Toys Uk Ltd
(**Subsidiary of:** Smyths Toys Hq Iom Limited)
65 Carter Lane, London EC4V 5HF
**Tel:** 02037640823
**Web:** www.smythstoys.com
**Reg No:** 6051517 **Estd:** 2007 Private Limited Company
**Line of Business:** Retail sale of sports goods, games and toys, stamps and coins
**Issued Capital:** £3,000,100
**Directors:** T Smyth, P Smyth, L Smyth
**Co. Secretary:** Anthony Smyth
**US SIC:** 5941 **UK SIC:** 65400
**Auditors:** PricewaterhouseCoopers
**Bankers:** Allied Irish Bank (gb) (23-84-00)

| | 31-12-13 | 31-12-12 | 31-12-11 |
|---|---|---|---|
| TO | 185,779,932 | 152,541,791 | 97,356,512 |
| P/L | 2,786,699 | 2,288,127 | 2,433,913 |
| NW | 8,512,328 | 6,369,441 | 4,714,478 |
| WC | 21,100,698 | 15,484,331 | 10,066,757 |
| Emp. | 924 | 789 | 543 |

DUNS 50-455-4759
## Sn Systems Ltd
1st Floor - Hartwell House, 55-61 Victoria Street, Bristol, Avon BS1 6AD
**Tel:** 01179299733
**Web:** www.snsys.com
**Reg No:** 2436957 **Estd:** 1989 Private Limited Company
**Line of Business:** Other computer related activities
**Export Sales:** £7,400,065
**Issued Capital:** £4
**Directors:** J G Ryan, T Yutaka
**Co. Secretary:** Paul Dent Young Holman
**Responsibilities**
**Senior:** Andrew Beveridge *(Manager)*, Masayuki Chatani *(Manager)*, Martin Day *(Joint Managing Director)*
**US SIC:** 7379 **UK SIC:** 83940
**Auditors:** PricewaterhouseCoopers LLP
**Bankers:** National Westminster Bank Plc (60-17-12)

| | 31-03-14 | 31-03-13 | 31-03-12 |
|---|---|---|---|
| TO | 7,400,065 | 12,348,810 | 11,383,180 |
| P/L | 179,222 | 508,547 | 471,634 |
| NW | 8,559,638 | 8,459,979 | 8,039,804 |
| WC | 8,040,382 | 7,938,889 | 7,381,340 |
| Emp. | 85 | 84 | 78 |

DUNS 23-309-2449
## Sn Tuition Ltd
(**Subsidiary of:** Swimming Nature Ltd)
843 Finchley Road, London NW11 8NA
**Web:** www.swimmingnature.com
**Reg No:** 4560195 **Estd:** 2002 Private Limited Company
**Line of Business:** Activities of private training providers
**Issued Capital:** £1,316
**Director:** E Ferre
**Co. Secretary:** Mrs Jacquee Ferre
**US SIC:** 7399 **UK SIC:** 83954

| | 30-09-13 | 30-09-12 | 31-09-11 |
|---|---|---|---|
| TO | N/A | N/A | 2,576,098 |
| P/L | N/A | N/A | 77,128 |
| NW | (394,998) | (235,869) | (414,427) |
| WC | (420,864) | (151,280) | (268,651) |

DUNS 64-139-8656
## Snack-Away
7 Plant Lane Business Park, Plant Lane, Burntwood, Staffordshire WS7 3GN
**Tel:** 01543274811
**Web:** www.snackaway.co.uk
**Estd:** 1997 Proprietorship
**Line of Business:** Manufacturers and suppliers of pies
**Proprietor:** Ms S Wadley
**US SIC:** 2099 **UK SIC:** 42399
**Bankers:** HSBC Bank plc (40-17-60)
**Employees:** 50

DUNS 21-042-5276
## Snacks Direct
Unit 5 Broadfield Court, Sheffield, South Yorkshire S8 0XF
**Tel:** 01142-688200
**Web:** www.palmerharvey.co.uk
**Estd:** 1984 Proprietorship
**Line of Business:** Distribution service providers
**Proprietor:** C Adams
**Responsibilities**
**Senior:** Andrew McKelvie *(Manager)*, Jim Newsome *(Manager)*
**US SIC:** 4712 **UK SIC:** 77002
**Employees:** 258

DUNS 21-954-2839
## Snacktime Plc
Unit 17, London SW18 4RL
**Tel:** 08455190919
**Web:** www.integer-vbd.co.uk
**Reg No:** 6135746 **Estd:** 2012 Public Limited Company

**Line of Business:** Vending machines sale, rental and supply
**Trading Style:** Snacktime Public Limited Company
**Issued Capital:** £326,980
**Directors:** T H James, J J Hamer, S Kornienko, Ms G L White, M E Jackson, M J Stone, B Belotserkovsky
**Co. Secretary:** Timothy James
**Responsibilities**
**Senior:** Blair Jenkins *(Chief Executive Officer)*, Michiel Slinkert *(Manager)*
**Branches:** Snacktime Plc, Unit 1 Bradley House Moston Road, Manchester M24 1SE
**US SIC:** 5963, 6711
**UK SIC:** 65600, 83962
**Auditors:** BDO LLP

| | 31-03-14 | 31-03-13 | 31-03-12 |
|---|---|---|---|
| TO | 18,810,814 | 20,506,042 | 22,190,524 |
| P/L | (8,537,680) | (8,254,895) | (732,179) |
| NW | 789,607 | 1,371,251 | 3,776,254 |
| WC | (2,878,154) | (2,109,264) | 743,465 |
| Emp. | 228 | 260 | 275 |

DUNS 22-624-4135 Imp-Exp

## Snap-on Business Solutions Ltd

**(Subsidiary of:** Snap-on Incorporated)
Imperium, Reading, Berkshire RG2 0TD
**Fax:** 01189-357778
**Web:** www.sbs.snapon.com
**Reg No:** 1402893 **VAT No:** 314259082
**Estd:** 1971 Private Limited Company
**Line of Business:** Financial services
**Export Markets:** USA, Germany, Austria, Switzerland, Spain Portuagal, France and Belgium Italy, Other
**Export Sales:** £24,386,141
**Issued Capital:** £335,526
**Directors:** P R Wyeth, G Heinz, D I Stott
**Co. Secretary:** Gordon Garrett
**Responsibilities**
**IT:** Garry Argrave *(Senior IT Executive)*, Paul Glenister *(IS Analyst)*
**Branches:** Snap-On Business Solutions Ltd, Alexandra Ho, 103 London Rd, Reading, Berkshire RG1 5BY
**US SIC:** 7379, 7374
**UK SIC:** 83940
**Auditors:** Deloitte LLP
**Bankers:** Lloyds TSB Bank plc (30-96-96)

| | 31-12-13 | 31-12-12 | 31-12-11 |
|---|---|---|---|
| TO | 30,318,577 | 27,836,786 | 38,407,780 |
| P/L | 4,675,786 | 4,779,222 | 8,111,941 |
| NW | 19,614,637 | 16,032,811 | 12,310,417 |
| WC | 17,805,177 | 14,568,879 | 10,600,303 |
| Emp. | 110 | 116 | 122 |

DUNS 76-994-2582

## Snap-on U.K. Holdings Ltd

**(Subsidiary of:** Snap-on Incorporated)
Telford Way Industrial Estate, Kettering, Northamptonshire NN16 8SN
**Tel:** 01536413800 **Fax:** 01536413900
**Web:** www.snapon.com
**Reg No:** 2648720 **Estd:** 1991 Private Limited Company
**Line of Business:** Manufacture of other special purpose machinery not elsewhere classified
**Trading Style:** Snap on Diagnostics, Snap on Tools
**Issued Capital:** £10,452,144
**Directors:** P J Clarke, B J Young, W Brown, A Rodi
**Responsibilities**
**Senior:** David Ellingen *(Manager)*, Constance Johnsen *(Manager)*, Paul Tredrea *(Recruitment Manager)*
**Finance:** Michael Ebrey *(Finance Director)*
**Branches:** Snap-On U.k. Holdings Ltd, Unit 8, Trafalgar Way, Camberley, Surrey GU15 3BN
**US SIC:** 3423, 3629
**UK SIC:** 31612, 34350
**Auditors:** Deloitte LLP
**Bankers:** Barclays Bank Plc (20-46-65)

| | 31-12-13 | 31-12-12 | 31-12-11 |
|---|---|---|---|
| TO | 147,487,914 | 137,849,187 | 138,716,629 |
| P/L | 12,391,965 | 11,837,167 | 6,577,484 |
| NW | 64,668,634 | 55,198,264 | 44,418,763 |
| WC | 65,555,552 | 55,084,286 | 45,268,177 |
| Emp. | 529 | 527 | 498 |

DUNS 22-521-9963

## Snap Surveys Ltd

Unit 4-5 Mead Court, Cooper Road, Thornbury, Bristol, Avon BS35 3UW
**Tel:** 01454-280800
**Web:** www.snapsurveys.com
**Reg No:** 1672722 **Estd:** 1982 Private Limited Company
**Line of Business:** Market research organisations
**Issued Capital:** £10,000
**Principals:** P A Wills *(Managing)*, S G Jenkins
**Co. Secretary:** Stephen Szabo
**Branches:** Snap Surveys Ltd, Mead Court, Unit 4-5, Bristol, Avon BS35 3UW
**US SIC:** 7392, 7374
**UK SIC:** 83951, 83940
**Auditors:** Solomon Hare Llp
**Bankers:** Barclays Bank Plc (20-13-34)

| | 30-06-14 | 30-06-13 | 30-06-12 |
|---|---|---|---|
| TA | 2,473,143 | 2,495,505 | 2,406,985 |
| NW | 1,585,961 | 1,562,587 | 1,474,466 |
| WC | 899,200 | 1,184,564 | 1,080,370 |

DUNS 23-364-3857

## Snappy Tomato Pizza Ltd

260-260a, Hipswell Highway, Coventry, West Midlands CV2 5FS
**Tel:** 02476457171
**Web:** www.snappytomatopizza.co.uk
**Reg No:** 2854777 **Estd:** 1993 Private Limited Company
**Line of Business:** Take away meal outlets
**Issued Capital:** £50,000
**Director:** J C Wilson
**Co. Secretary:** Ms Amanda Spaven
**Responsibilities**
**Senior:** Stef Anos *(Proprietor)*
**Branches:** Snappy Tomato Pizza Ltd, 5 Timberley Lane, Birmingham, West Midlands B34 7ED
**US SIC:** 5812 **UK SIC:** 66110
**Auditors:** MCT Partnership

| | 31-03-14 | 31-03-13 | 31-03-12 |
|---|---|---|---|
| TA | 92,588 | 88,898 | 87,741 |
| NW | 18,238 | 29,681 | 29,344 |
| WC | 51,913 | 74,681 | 74,344 |

DUNS 29-842-8632 Imp-Exp

## Snc-Lavalin Uk Ltd

**(Subsidiary of:** Groupe Snc-Lavalin Inc)
Knollys House, 17 Addiscombe Road, Croydon, Surrey CR0 6SR
**Tel:** 020-8681-4250 **Fax:** 020-8681-4299
**Web:** www.snclavalin.com
**Reg No:** 2046233 **VAT No:** 452229756
**Estd:** 1986 Private Limited Company
**Line of Business:** Engineering design activities for industrial process and production
**Export Markets:** Canada, Norway
**Issued Capital:** £537,046
**Director:** S Khoury
**Co. Secretary:** Gary Whitney
**Responsibilities**
**Senior:** Hafez Aghili-Kermani *(Director)*, Karen Okka *(Office Manager)*
**HR:** Debbie Pivoriunas *(Human Resources Manager)*
**Operations:** Christian Jacqui *(Executive Vice-President Globa)*
**US SIC:** 8911, 7397
**UK SIC:** 83701, 83702
**Auditors:** Deloitte LLP
**Bankers:** National Westminster Bank Plc (60-50-01)

| | 31-12-13 | 31-12-12 | 31-12-11 |
|---|---|---|---|
| TO | 28,959,155 | 44,420,009 | 31,756,645 |
| P/L | 6,655,031 | (2,814,305) | (11,862,158) |
| NW | (4,833,204) | (10,536,938) | (9,245,252) |
| WC | (4,982,434) | (10,844,278) | (9,755,188) |
| Emp. | 175 | 225 | 205 |

DUNS 21-120-0232 Exp

## Snell Corporation Ltd

**(Subsidiary of:** Quantel Holdings Ltd)
Hartman House, Danehill, Reading, Berkshire RG6 4PB
**Tel:** 01189-866123
**Web:** www.snellgroup.com
**Reg No:** 6592512 **Estd:** 1974 Private Limited Company
**Line of Business:** Manufacturers general
**Issued Capital:** £119,756
**Directors:** R Cross, K P Leggett, I Cooper, D C Eales, M Mulligan
**Responsibilities**
**Senior:** Simon Derry *(Chief Executive Officer)*, Steve Hufflett *(Manufacturing Manager)*, Neil Maycock *(Manager)*, Peter Mayhead *(Manager)*
**HR:** Lynne Lewis *(Human Resources Manager)*
**Operations:** David Creed *(Engineering Director)*
**Engineering:** David Creed *(Engineering Director)*
**US SIC:** 3662, 7399
**UK SIC:** 34430, 83954
**Auditors:** Ernst & Young LLP

| | 28-12-13 | 29-12-12 | 31-12-11 |
|---|---|---|---|
| TO | 64,424,000 | 71,450,000 | 69,356,000 |
| P/L | (23,191,000) | (7,703,000) | (7,567,000) |
| NW | (51,791,000) | (65,233,000) | (59,712,000) |
| WC | (8,018,000) | 10,669,000 | 12,260,000 |
| Emp. | 443 | 439 | 457 |

DUNS 22-607-0027 Imp

## Snell Ltd

**(Subsidiary of:** Quantel Holdings Ltd)
Southleigh Park House, Eastleigh Road, Havant, Hampshire PO9 2PE
**Web:** www.snellgroup.com
**Reg No:** 1160119 **VAT No:** 927557881
**Estd:** 1974 Private Limited Company
**Line of Business:** Audio visual equipment
**Issued Capital:** £5,032,707
**Directors:** S D Rogers, M Mulligan, I Cooper, R Cross
**Responsibilities**
**Senior:** Sandy Kellagher *(Software, Applications Manager)*, Roderick Snell *(President)*, simon derry *(CEO)*
**IT:** Reece Percival *(Senior IT Executive)*
**Engineering:** Simon Auty *(Technical Executive)*
**Branches:** Snell Ltd, Chroma House, Shire Hill, Saffron Walden, Essex CB11 3AQ
**US SIC:** 7379, 3662
**UK SIC:** 83940, 34430
**Auditors:** Ernst & Young LLP

| | 28-12-13 | 29-12-12 | 31-12-11 |
|---|---|---|---|
| TO | 59,425,000 | 66,145,000 | 63,422,000 |
| P/L | (295,000) | 5,610,000 | 3,285,000 |
| NW | 14,652,000 | 19,809,000 | 14,052,000 |
| WC | 10,730,000 | 14,779,000 | 9,328,000 |
| Emp. | 372 | 368 | 387 |

DUNS 21-724-2653

## Snellings Ltd

Blofield Corner Blofield, Norwich, Norfolk NR13 4SQ
**Tel:** 01603712202
**Reg No:** 7613036 **Estd:** 2011 Private Limited Company
**Line of Business:** Management activities of holding companies
**Issued Capital:** £5
**Directors:** R A Cogman, N R Savory, S Phillips, S J Phillips
**Co. Secretary:** Rowland Cogman
**US SIC:** 6711 **UK SIC:** 83962
**Bankers:** Lloyds TSB Bank plc (30-96-17)

| | 30-04-14 | 30-04-13 | 30-04-12 |
|---|---|---|---|
| TO | 7,703,197 | 6,704,842 | 6,639,093 |
| P/L | (44,861) | 340,755 | 289,184 |
| NW | 7,350,586 | 7,274,733 | 6,971,935 |
| WC | 2,804,624 | 2,744,262 | 3,224,711 |
| Emp. | 57 | 53 | 54 |

DUNS 34-884-2647

## Snelsons Ltd

Nat Lane, Winsford, Cheshire CW7 3BS
**Tel:** 01606-553580
**Web:** www.snelsons.co.uk
**Reg No:** 5682186 **Estd:** 1965 Private Limited Company
**Line of Business:** Aluminium fabricators
**Trading Style:** Snelsons Ltd
**Issued Capital:** £1,000
**Directors:** Mrs L J Booth, D A Harding, Mrs G Harding
**Co. Secretary:** David Harding
**Responsibilities**
**Senior:** David Finlay *(Sales & Marketing Director)*
**Finance:** Leslie Hartley *(Manager)*
**Marketing:** David Finlay *(Sales & Marketing Director)*
**Sales:** David Finlay *(Sales & Marketing Director)*
**HR:** Leslie Hartley *(Manager)*
**Operations:** Leslie Hartley *(Manager)*
**US SIC:** 2891, 3499
**UK SIC:** 25620, 31694

| | 31-01-14 | 31-01-13 | 31-01-12 |
|---|---|---|---|
| TA | 1,979,799 | 1,924,157 | 2,045,035 |
| NW | 1,028,407 | 1,012,859 | 965,007 |
| WC | 102,326 | 143,663 | 123,912 |

DUNS 23-586-0918 Imp

## S.N.G. Barratt Group Ltd

The Heritage Building, Stourbridge Road, Bridgnorth, Shropshire WV15 6AP
**Tel:** 01746-765432
**Web:** www.sngbarratt.com
**Reg No:** 3583719 **Estd:** 1998 Private Limited Company
**Line of Business:** Classic car dealers and specialists
**Export Sales:** £10,217,556
**Issued Capital:** £3
**Principals:** Ms H M Barratt *(Managing)*, J G Barratt, S N Barratt
**Co. Secretary:** Julian Barratt
**Responsibilities**
**IT:** James Griffin *(IT Manager)*, Edward Tart *(IT Support)*
**US SIC:** 5531 **UK SIC:** 65100
**Bankers:** National Westminster Bank Plc (60-02-46)

| | 31-12-13 | 31-12-12 | 31-12-11 |
|---|---|---|---|
| TO | 14,508,998 | 13,847,916 | 12,663,847 |
| P/L | 1,644,029 | 1,484,245 | 1,122,550 |
| NW | 3,308,627 | 2,985,336 | 1,856,809 |
| WC | 2,317,981 | 2,150,598 | 1,174,710 |
| Emp. | 83 | 76 | 68 |

DUNS 73-769-8618

## Snm Pipelines Ltd

Crossley Park Industrial Estate, Crossley Road, Heaton Chapel, Stockport, Cheshire SK4 5BF
**Tel:** 0161-975-9009
**Web:** www.snmpipelines.co.uk
**Reg No:** 5026948 **Estd:** 2004 Private Limited Company
**Line of Business:** Civil engineers
**Issued Capital:** £10,100
**Directors:** L Russell, S N Morgan, T Morgan, N Morgan
**Co. Secretary:** Lee Russell
**Branches:** Snm Pipelines Ltd, Sandfold La, Manchester M19 3BJ
**US SIC:** 8911, 1622
**UK SIC:** 83701, 50200

| | 31-03-14 | 31-03-13 | 30-03-12 |
|---|---|---|---|
| TO | N/A | 3,649,024 | 10,725,772 |
| P/L | N/A | (157,143) | 270,939 |
| NW | (84,029) | (164,922) | (67,859) |
| WC | (410,325) | (519,980) | (501,873) |
| Emp. | N/A | 50 | 63 |

DUNS 21-142-8335

## Snorkel Europe Ltd

Vigo Centre, Birtley Road, Washington, Tyne and Wear NE38 9DA
**Tel:** 0845-1550-057 **Fax:** 0845-1557-756
**Web:** www.snorkellift.com
**Reg No:** 6735397 **Estd:** 2008 Private Limited Company
**Line of Business:** Access equipment
**Trading Style:** Snorkel Uk
**Issued Capital:** £1
**Directors:** D S Kell, B J Campbell
**Co. Secretary:** Charles Brooks
**US SIC:** 3531 **UK SIC:** 32541
**Auditors:** Baker Tilly UK Audit LLP
**Bankers:** The Royal Bank Of Scotland Plc (16-26-21)

| | 31-12-13 | 31-12-12 | 31-12-11 |
|---|---|---|---|
| TO | 13,607,000 | 20,808,000 | 20,283,000 |
| P/L | (366,000) | 15,716,000 | (6,263,000) |
| NW | 3,572,000 | 3,179,000 | (25,158,000) |
| WC | 2,486,000 | (1,600,000) | (26,767,000) |
| Emp. | 137 | 132 | 108 |

DUNS 73-901-2396 Imp

## Snow & Rock Sports Ltd

**(Subsidiary of:** Snow+rock Group Holdings Ltd)
The Rock, 2 Thornberry Way, Slyfield Industrial Estate, Guildford, Surrey GU1 1QB
**Tel:** 01483445335
**Web:** www.snowandrock.com
**Reg No:** 5154934 **VAT No:** 341020521
**Estd:** 2004 Private Limited Company
**Line of Business:** Representative office
**Export Sales:** £1,216,000
**Trading Style:** Snow & Rock
**Issued Capital:** £11,118,908
**Directors:** D Kohn, J Ulloa, I M Gibson, H A Mansbridge, R Cotter
**Responsibilities**
**Senior:** Richard Crotter *(Managing Director)*
**IT:** Shiva Kumar *(IT Manager)*
**Branches:** Snow & Rock Sports Ltd, 14-16 The Priory Queensway, Birmingham, West Midlands B4 6BS
**US SIC:** 5941 **UK SIC:** 65400
**Auditors:** Deloitte LLP
**Bankers:** Bank Of Scotland (80-02-34)

| | 01-09-13 | 02-09-12 | 28-09-11 |
|---|---|---|---|
| TO | 42,005,000 | 42,595,000 | 42,324,000 |
| P/L | (830,000) | 1,111,000 | (109,000) |
| NW | 26,670,000 | 26,889,000 | 25,008,000 |
| WC | 10,055,000 | 6,876,000 | (2,202,000) |
| Emp. | 396 | 386 | 372 |

DUNS 21-589-9153

## Snow Bar

Colorado Way, Castleford, West Yorkshire WF10 4TA
**Tel:** 01977523100
**Web:** www.snowzoneuk.com
**Estd:** 2011
**Line of Business:** Licensed restaurants
**Responsibilities**
**Senior:** Zoe Fenner *(General Manager)*
**US SIC:** 5812 **UK SIC:** 66110
**Employees:** 250

DUNS 73-883-9906 Imp

## Snow Factor Ltd

**(Subsidiary of:** Ice Factor International Ltd.)
Xscape, Kings Inch Road, Renfrew, Renfrewshire PA4 8XQ
**Tel:** 08712225672
**Web:** www.snozoneuk.com
**Reg No:** 5138159 **Estd:** 2004 Private Limited Company
**Line of Business:** Operation of sports arenas and stadiums
**Trading Style:** Sno!zone
**Issued Capital:** £3
**Directors:** J A Stanners, J W Smith
**Co. Secretary:** Scott Mclauchlan
**Branches:** SNO!zone Xscape 602 Marlborough Gate Central Milton Keynes MK9 3XS
**US SIC:** 7941, 7999
**UK SIC:** 97911, 97913
**Auditors:** Deloitte LLP
**Bankers:** HSBC Bank plc (40-22-47)

| | 30-11-13 | 30-11-12 | 16-11-11 |
|---|---|---|---|
| TO | 2,224,699 | 2,578,852 | 2,797,188 |
| P/L | 44,477 | 19,859 | (450,318) |
| NW | 27,347 | (5,750) | N/A |
| WC | (368,629) | (299,017) | (80,534) |
| Emp. | N/A | N/A | 74 |

DUNS 21-587-8412
## Snow Hill Police Station
Snow Hill Police Station, 5 Snow Hill, London EC1A 2DP
**Estd:** 2011
**Line of Business:** Police forces
**US SIC:** 9221 **UK SIC:** 91300
**Employees:** 100

DUNS 23-568-5617
## Snow White Laundries
69 The Highway, New Inn, Pontypool, Gwent NP4 0PN
**Tel:** 01495764652
**Web:** www.swlaundries.co.uk
**VAT No:** 133459178 **Estd:** 1967 Partnership
**Line of Business:** Linen hire
**Partners:** B D Milling, S J Milling, T O Milling
**Branches:** Snow White Laundries, Dumballs Road, Cardiff, South Glamorgan CF10 5FE
**US SIC:** 7219 **UK SIC:** 98110
**Bankers:** HSBC Bank plc (40-37-07)
**Employees:** 80

DUNS 21-864-4195
## Snowbird Foods Ltd
(**Subsidiary of:** Snowbird Foods Holdings Ltd)
Wharf Road, Enfield, Middlesex EN3 4TA
**Tel:** 02088059222
**Web:** www.snowbirdfoods.co.uk
**Reg No:** 8257747 **Estd:** 2012 Private Limited Company
**Line of Business:** Production of meat and poultry meat products
**Issued Capital:** £1
**Directors:** P J Paul, A Mcgovern, R M Anderson
**Co. Secretary:** Albert Mcgovern
**US SIC:** 2013 **UK SIC:** 41223

| | 26-04-14 | 31-03-13 |
|---|---|---|
| TO | 12,930,476 | N/A |
| P/L | 389,806 | N/A |
| NW | 330,952 | 1 |
| WC | 189,403 | N/A |

DUNS 23-825-3806 **Imp**
## Snowdome Ltd
(**Subsidiary of:** Snowdome Holdings Ltd)
Leisure Island, Tamworth, Staffordshire B79 7ND
**Tel:** 08448000011
**Web:** www.snowdome.co.uk
**Reg No:** 3817394 **Estd:** 1999 Private Limited Company
**Line of Business:** Leisure centres
**Issued Capital:** £1
**Directors:** M J Coats, G S Baker
**Co. Secretary:** Martin Smith
**US SIC:** 7999 **UK SIC:** 97913

| | 30-09-13 | 30-09-12 | 30-09-11 |
|---|---|---|---|
| TO | 5,076,092 | 5,126,133 | 4,893,430 |
| P/L | 1,056,973 | 1,254,602 | 315,737 |
| NW | 3,870,709 | 3,021,985 | 2,042,281 |
| WC | 4,564,206 | 3,456,286 | 2,331,731 |
| Emp. | 131 | 134 | 80 |

DUNS 22-152-7968
## Snowdonia Cheese Co Ltd
Unit 14 Cefndy Road Cefndy Road, Employment Park, Rhyl, Clwyd LL18 2HJ
**Tel:** 01745357070
**Web:** www.snowdoniacheese.co.uk
**Reg No:** 4171512 **Estd:** 2001 Private Limited Company
**Line of Business:** Liquid milk and cream production
**Issued Capital:** £60,250
**Directors:** I R Wynne, W J Newton-Jones
**Responsibilities**
**Finance:** Suzette Barritt *(Bookkeeper, Administrator)*
**Sales:** Michael Mort *(Business Development Manager)*, Richard Newton-Jones *(Commercial Director)*
**Admin:** Suzette Barritt *(Bookkeeper, Administrator)*
**US SIC:** 2026, 5143
**UK SIC:** 41301, 61700
**Bankers:** HSBC Bank plc (40-10-11)

| | 31-03-14 | 31-03-13 | 31-03-12 |
|---|---|---|---|
| TA | 1,266,559 | 1,119,867 | 902,438 |
| NW | 614,009 | 343,615 | 291,821 |
| WC | 288,868 | 72,310 | 59,029 |

DUNS 42-396-8411
## Snowdonia National Park Authority
National Park Offices, Penrhyndeudraeth, Gwynedd LL48 6LF
**Tel:** 01766770274
**Web:** www.eryri-npa.gov.uk
**Estd:** 1995 Incorporate By Act Of Parliament
**Line of Business:** Representative office
**Principals:** A Hughes *(Financial)*, I Huws, H Thomas
**Responsibilities**
**Senior:** Alun Gruffydd *(Head Of Communications & Educa)*, Naomi Jones *(Head Of Information Services)*, Aneurin Phillips *(Chief Executive)*, Emyr Williams *(Manager)*
**Finance:** Emyr Roberts *(Financial Manager)*
**Marketing:** Alun Gruffydd *(Head Of Communications & Educa)*
**IT:** Nia Roberts *(IT Manager)*
**HR:** Jo Worrall *(Personnel Manager)*
**Health & Safety:** Jo Worrall *(Personnel Manager)*
**Facilities:** Peter Trumper *(Property Manager)*
**Purchasing:** Jo Worrall *(Personnel Manager)*
**Branches:** Snowdonia National Park Authority, Isallt, Church St, Blaenau Ffestiniog, Gwynedd LL41 3HD
**US SIC:** 7399 **UK SIC:** 83954
**Employees:** 150

DUNS 21-926-3100
## Snowdonia (Windows & Doors) Ltd
(**Subsidiary of:** Wall Lag (Wales) Ltd)
Bromfield Lane, Mold, Clwyd CH7 1HA
**Tel:** 01352758812 **Fax:** 01352755643
**Web:** www.snowdoniawindows.co.uk
**Reg No:** 1450509 **Estd:** 1976 Private Limited Company
**Line of Business:** Conservatories
**Issued Capital:** £25,000
**Director:** R C Griffiths
**Co. Secretary:** Alan Wheatley
**Responsibilities**
**Senior:** Beverley Griffiths *(Buyer)*, Alex Kirkland *(Accountant)*
**Finance:** Alex Kirkland *(Accountant)*
**Sales:** Graham Dawson *(Sales Manager)*, Beverley Griffiths *(Buyer)*
**Purchasing:** Beverley Griffiths *(Buyer)*
**Branches:** Snowdonia (Windows & Doors) Ltd, Bromfield Lane, Mold, Clwyd CH7 1HA
**US SIC:** 3441 **UK SIC:** 32042
**Bankers:** Lloyds TSB Bank plc (30-99-95)

| | 31-03-14 | 31-03-13 | 31-03-12 |
|---|---|---|---|
| TA | 285,690 | 285,690 | 285,690 |
| NW | 285,690 | 285,690 | 285,690 |

DUNS 76-995-3431 **Exp**
## Snowdrop Systems Ltd
(**Subsidiary of:** The Sage Group Plc.)
4 Witan Way, Witney, Oxfordshire OX28 6FF
**Tel:** 01993709100
**Web:** www.sage.com
**Reg No:** 2649780 **VAT No:** 596241320
**Estd:** 1991 Private Limited Company
**Line of Business:** Publishing of software
**Issued Capital:** £29,890
**Directors:** A J Mitchell, B P Flattery
**Co. Secretary:** Mark Parry
**Responsibilities**
**Senior:** Louise Hall *(Manager)*
**Marketing:** Rebecca Barnett *(Marketing Manager)*
**Branches:** Snowdrop Systems Ltd, 102 Hope Street, Glasgow, Lanarkshire G2 6PH
**US SIC:** 7372, 7379
**UK SIC:** 83940
**Auditors:** PricewaterhouseCoopers LLP
**Bankers:** Lloyds TSB Bank plc (30-99-78)

| | 30-09-13 | 30-09-12 | 30-09-11 |
|---|---|---|---|
| TA | 197,000 | 197,000 | 197,000 |
| NW | 197,000 | 197,000 | 197,000 |

DUNS 22-608-5405
## Snows Business Forms Ltd
(**Subsidiary of:** Bondco 667 Ltd)
Manor House, Southampton, Hampshire SO15 0DF
**Tel:** 02380777711 **Fax:** 02356344330
**Web:** www.snowsbf.co.uk
**Reg No:** 1700975 **VAT No:** 382608048
**Estd:** 1975 Private Limited Company
**Line of Business:** Printers general
**Issued Capital:** £181,000
**Directors:** M Middleton, Mrs L A Cutts
**Responsibilities**
**Senior:** Stuart Bartons *(Warehouse Manager)*, Grahame Cutts *(Manager)*
**Marketing:** Angela Rawlings *(Purchasing Manager)*
**HR:** Angela Rawlings *(Purchasing Manager)*
**Health & Safety:** Angela Rawlings *(Purchasing Manager)*
**Operations:** Angela Rawlings *(Purchasing Manager)*
**Purchasing:** Angela Rawlings *(Purchasing Manager)*
**Engineering:** Steve Lake *(Production Director)*
**US SIC:** 2794, 2752
**UK SIC:** 47545, 47544
**Auditors:** Fiander Tovell LLP
**Bankers:** Lloyds TSB Bank plc (30-12-05)

| | 31-10-13 | 31-10-12 | 31-10-11 |
|---|---|---|---|
| TO | 4,049,968 | 4,383,705 | 4,974,164 |
| P/L | (48,312) | (87,737) | 54,603 |
| NW | 2,194,503 | 2,251,572 | 2,336,750 |
| WC | 1,680,772 | 1,788,937 | 1,970,094 |
| Emp. | 54 | 58 | 67 |

DUNS 29-429-6595
## Snows Business Holdings Ltd
Snows House, Second Avenue, Southampton, Hampshire SO15 0BT
**Tel:** 01202974024
**Web:** www.kingsvolvo.co.uk
**Reg No:** 1535815 **Estd:** 1983 Private Limited Company
**Line of Business:** Management activities of holding companies
**Issued Capital:** £926,522
**Principals:** M A Trapani *(Managing)*, Mrs E Snow, S P Snow, S J Gates, N R Mccue, Mrs J Snow, G S Snow, P C Maddison
**Branches:** Snows Business Holdings Ltd, Churchfields House, Telford Road, Salisbury, Wiltshire SP2 7PH
**US SIC:** 6711 **UK SIC:** 83962
**Auditors:** Burnett Swayne
**Bankers:** National Westminster Bank Plc (56-00-68)

| | 31-12-13 | 31-12-12 | 31-12-11 |
|---|---|---|---|
| TO | 174,305,467 | 130,232,920 | 116,288,840 |
| P/L | 1,123,495 | 603,651 | 787,832 |
| NW | 6,947,307 | 6,965,263 | 6,410,826 |
| WC | (2,485,028) | (2,571,457) | (236,619) |
| Emp. | 489 | 383 | 340 |

DUNS 21-040-6152
## Snowtrax
Matchams Lane, Hurn, Christchurch, Dorset BH23 6AW
**Tel:** 01202-499155
**Web:** www.snowtrax.eu
**Proprietorship**
**Line of Business:** Children's activity playcentres
**Proprietor:** N Warne
**Responsibilities**
**Senior:** Colin Izzard *(Senior Customer Services Execu)*, Trevor Izzard *(CEO, Managing Director)*
**US SIC:** 7999 **UK SIC:** 97913
**Employees:** 100

DUNS 21-595-8967
## Snozone
Colorado Way, Castleford, West Yorkshire WF10 4TA
**Tel:** 01977523090
**Web:** www.snozoneuk.com
**Estd:** 2011 Proprietorship
**Line of Business:** Ski slopes
**Proprietor:** J Gallifant
**US SIC:** 7999 **UK SIC:** 97913
**Employees:** 150

DUNS 23-999-9159
## Snozone Ltd
(**Subsidiary of:** Capital & Regional Plc)
Terminal House, 52 Grosvenor Gardens, London SW1W 0AU
**Tel:** 0871-222-5670
**Web:** www.snozoneuk.com
**Reg No:** 3988044 **Estd:** 2000 Private Limited Company
**Line of Business:** Building services
**Trading Style:** Exscape
**Issued Capital:** £1,000
**Directors:** K C Ford, C A Staveley
**Co. Secretary:** Stuart Wetherly
**Responsibilities**
**Senior:** Falguni Desai *(Manager)*
**Branches:** Castleford, Leeds
**US SIC:** 6552 **UK SIC:** 85000
**Auditors:** Deloitte & Touche LLP

| | 31-12-13 | 31-12-12 | 31-12-11 |
|---|---|---|---|
| TO | 8,922,561 | 9,932,278 | 9,635,286 |
| P/L | 1,462,524 | 1,926,257 | 1,057,260 |
| NW | 1,793,848 | 8,635,887 | 6,724,707 |
| WC | 1,268,299 | 8,140,725 | 6,311,696 |
| Emp. | 147 | 165 | 175 |

DUNS 21-734-8861 **Imp-Exp**
## Snuggledown of Norway (U K) Ltd
(**Subsidiary of:** John Cotton Group Ltd)
Beaver Court, Lockett Road, South Lancashire Industrial Estate, Wigan, Lancashire WN4 8DE
**Tel:** 01942721771 **Fax:** 01942402661
**Web:** www.snuggledown.co.uk
**Reg No:** 0987104 **VAT No:** 197848392
**Estd:** 1975 Private Limited Company
**Line of Business:** The Notes to the accounts for the period ending 03.03.2013 state that the subject acts as an agent for Northern Feather (Home Furnishings) Ltd.
**Export Markets:** Eire, France, Germany
**Issued Capital:** £200,000
**Director:** M A Cotton
**Co. Secretary:** Stephen Swalwell
**Responsibilities**
**Senior:** Mark Cunliff *(Warehouse Manager)*, Andrew Starkey *(Manager)*
**Health & Safety:** Pam Lythgoe *(Factory Manager)*
**US SIC:** 2211, 2392
**UK SIC:** 43220, 45550
**Auditors:** Mazars LLP
**Bankers:** HSBC Bank plc (40-25-10)

| | 02-03-14 | 03-03-13 | 26-03-12 |
|---|---|---|---|
| TA | 82,000 | 82,000 | 82,000 |
| NW | 82,000 | 82,000 | 82,000 |
| WC | N/A | 82,000 | 82,000 |
| Emp. | N/A | 55 | 55 |

DUNS 21-325-0561
## Snydale
New Road, Old Snydale, Pontefract, West Yorkshire WF7 6HD
**Tel:** 01924-895517
**Web:** www.snydalecarehome.co.uk
**Estd:** 1993 Proprietorship
**Line of Business:** Residential care establishments
**Proprietor:** Mrs T Holroyd
**Responsibilities**
**Senior:** Tracey Miller *(Manager)*
**US SIC:** 8321 **UK SIC:** 96111
**Bankers:** National Westminster Bank Plc (54-30-64)
**Employees:** 50

DUNS 51-998-8146
## So Clean Cleaning & Support Services Ltd
Exhibition House, 4 Wellbrook Road, Orpington, Kent BR6 7AB
**Tel:** 01689853366 **Fax:** 01689869371
**Web:** www.soclean.co.uk
**Reg No:** 4103369 **Estd:** 1995 Private Limited Company
**Line of Business:** Traditional cleaning activities
**Issued Capital:** £2
**Directors:** N M Gasson, S L Gasson
**Co. Secretary:** Ms Christine Gasson
**Responsibilities**
**Finance:** Wendy Carne *(Senior Finance Administrator)*
**Admin:** Wendy Carne *(Senior Finance Administrator)*
**US SIC:** 7349 **UK SIC:** 92300
**Auditors:** J.H. Thompson & Co
**Bankers:** Barclays Bank Plc (20-14-33)

| | 31-01-14 | 31-01-13 | 31-01-12 |
|---|---|---|---|
| TA | 754,610 | 791,557 | 499,722 |
| NW | 96,575 | 116,614 | 53,307 |
| WC | 40,853 | 75,107 | 10,826 |

DUNS 21-697-2692 **Imp**
## Soapworks Ltd
Block 8, Glasgow, Lanarkshire G33 4JD
**Web:** www.soapworksltd.co.uk
**Reg No:** 0388292SC **Estd:** 1988 Private Limited Company
**Line of Business:** Beauty products
**Export Sales:** £2,459,849
**Issued Capital:** £48,656
**Directors:** M Cook, B Cumming, Ms C Caddis, S Seddon, J Zadruzynski
**Responsibilities**
**Senior:** Sophie Gasperment *(Manager)*, Catherine Lambert *(Manager)*, Stuart Seddan *(Financial Director)*
**Finance:** Stuart Seddan *(Financial Director)*
**HR:** Margaret Milne *(Human Resources Manager)*
**Operations:** Chris Kyriacou *(Technical, Production Manager)*
**US SIC:** 2841, 5122, 2844
**UK SIC:** 25810, 61800, 25820
**Auditors:** French Duncan LLP
**Bankers:** Barclays Bank Plc (20-33-70)

| | 27-12-13 | 29-12-12 | 31-12-11 |
|---|---|---|---|
| TO | 14,684,311 | 12,245,168 | 11,970,214 |
| P/L | 375,562 | (162,863) | 661,759 |
| NW | 755,003 | 445,691 | 532,922 |
| WC | 349,479 | 759,713 | 895,440 |
| Emp. | 104 | 102 | 100 |

DUNS 73-804-3897
## Soar Community
14 Knutton Road, Sheffield, South Yorkshire S5 9NU
**Tel:** 01142134065
**Web:** www.soarcommunity.org.uk
**Reg No:** 5060698 **Estd:** 2004 Private Company Limited By Guarantee
**Line of Business:** Activities of other membership organisations not elsewhere classified
**Directors:** Miss C M Lane, M Ellaby, A C Whiting, J E Bradley, Mrs H M Shepherd, Ms E M White, P Price, Mrs E J Houlston
**Co. Secretary:** Ms Sally Whittaker

**Responsibilities**
Senior: Ian Drayton (Partnership Manager),
Lynne Hilson (Director), Alan Law (Director),
Sioned Richards (Director), Hannah Twyford
(Director), Benjamin West (Director)
US SIC: 8699 UK SIC: 96902
Bankers: The Co-Operative Bank Plc
(08-90-75)

|  | 31-03-14 | 31-03-13 | 31-03-12 |
|---|---|---|---|
| TO | 1,015,534 | 766,232 | 2,498,243 |
| P/L | (172,257) | (291,808) | 1,430,515 |
| NW | 4,299,244 | 4,471,501 | 4,854,809 |
| WC | 452,384 | 364,250 | 718,517 |
| Emp. | 53 | 53 | 23 |

DUNS 21-605-9981
## Soar Valley Leisure Centre
Kingfisher Road, Mountsorrel,
Loughborough, Leicestershire LE12 7FG
Tel: 01162375267
Web: www.fusion-lifestyle.com
Estd: 2004
Line of Business: Leisure centres
Proprietor: M Welsh
**Responsibilities**
Senior: Darren Williamson (General
Manager)
US SIC: 7999 UK SIC: 97913
Employees: 77

DUNS 64-146-8806
## Sobell House Hospice Charity
Unit 1, Swinford Farm, Swinford, Witney,
Oxfordshire OX29 4BA
Tel: 01993844632
Web: www.sobellhospicecharity.org.uk
Estd: 1986
Line of Business: Charities and voluntary
organisations
Trading Style: Charity Shop
Branches: Sobell House Hospice Charity, 21
The Square, Oxford, Oxfordshire OX2 9LJ
US SIC: 6732 UK SIC: 83100
Employees: 50

DUNS 21-584-3334
## Social Action for Health
Unit A Ment House, 1b Mentmore Terrace,
London E8 3DQ
Tel: 02085101970
Web: www.sash.org.uk
Estd: 2011 Proprietorship
Line of Business: Charities and charitable
organisations
Proprietor: Miss P Facey
US SIC: 8699 UK SIC: 96902
Employees: 50

DUNS 21-012-8456
## Social Care & Education Ltd
P.O Box 8849, Oadby, Leicester,
Leicestershire LE21 4BF
Tel: 07912568109
Web: www.scesocialcare.co.uk
Reg No: 6358794 VAT No: 913236645
Estd: 2007 Private Limited Company
Line of Business: Nursing agencies
Issued Capital: £2
Director: H V Tailor
Co. Secretary: Mrs Natasha Sheffield
US SIC: 8091, 8211, 6732, 8321
UK SIC: 95200, 93200, 83100, 96111
Auditors: David Harris

|  | 31-08-12 | 31-08-11 | 31-08-11 |
|---|---|---|---|
| TA | 872,352 | 685,152 | 379,466 |
| NW | 575,376 | 278,082 | 141,436 |
| WC | 530,364 | 253,867 | 108,084 |

DUNS 21-360-9213
## Social Care & Health
Priory House, Abbey Road, Pity Me, Durham,
County Durham DH1 5RR
Tel: 0191-3835151
Estd: 1998
Line of Business: Adoption and fostering
services
Proprietor: Mrs R Shimmin
US SIC: 8321 UK SIC: 96111
Employees: 72

DUNS 21-576-2936
## Social Care & Social Work Improvement Scotland
Compass House, 11 Riverside Drive,
Dundee, Angus DD1 4NY
Tel: 01382207200
Web: www.hollandandbarrett.com
Line of Business: Charities and charitable
organisations
Trading Style: Care Inspectorate
**Responsibilities**
Senior: Andrew Sloane (Regional Manager)
Branches: Social Care & Social Work
Improvement Scotland, Castle St, Hamilton,
Lanarkshire ML3 6BU
US SIC: 6732 UK SIC: 83100
Employees: 90

DUNS 21-584-2970
## Social Care and Social Work Improvement Scotland
450 Argyle Street, Glasgow, Lanarkshire G2
8LG
Tel: 01412420455
Estd: 2011 Proprietorship
Line of Business: The dss
Proprietor: Mrs N Hawthorn
US SIC: 8321 UK SIC: 96111
Employees: 200

DUNS 73-253-0311
## Social Care in Action
Amplevine House, Dukes Road,
Southampton, Hampshire SO14 0ST
Tel: 02380366663
Web: www.scagroup.co.uk
Reg No: 4526806 Estd: 2002 Private
Company Limited By Guarantee
Line of Business: Other human health
activities
Directors: M W Morgan, A Brooker,
Mrs W Hughes, D Lodge, R Hallett, L Judd,
M Robson, P G Dibben
Co. Secretary: Peter Dibben
**Responsibilities**
Senior: Manoj Patel (Director)
US SIC: 8091, 8249
UK SIC: 95200, 93300
Bankers: The Royal Bank Of Scotland Plc
(16-00-55)

|  | 31-03-14 | 31-03-13 | 31-03-12 |
|---|---|---|---|
| TO | 9,646,334 | 10,669,420 | 11,075,241 |
| P/L | 19,278 | (75,238) | 149,681 |
| NW | 797,005 | 767,701 | 832,942 |
| WC | 293,858 | 235,095 | 197,341 |
| Emp. | 391 | 447 | 564 |

DUNS 22-271-8665
## Social Care Institute for Excellence
206-216 Marylebone Road, London NW1
6AQ
Tel: 02075350900 Fax: 02075350901
Web: www.scie.org.uk
Reg No: 4289790 Estd: 2001 Private
Company Limited By Guarantee
Line of Business: Social work activities
without accommodation
Directors: Ms S Warren, Ms M Mckenna,
Lord M G Bichard, D Archibald,
Ms F Mcandrew, Ms S Kaur-Stubbs,
T Moran, M Kreft
Co. Secretary: Stephen Goulder
**Responsibilities**
Senior: Tina Coldham (Director), Amanda
Edwards (Deputy Chief Executive), Ann
Macfarlane (Director), Bev Searle (Director)
Marketing: Kim Rutter (Marketing and
Communications M), Iris Steen (Director,
Communications)
Admin: Andrea Allen (Administrator)
IT: Nishal Rooplal (Facilities Manager)
Operations: Shirley Ewart-Boyle (Practice
Development Manager), Pete Fleischmann
(Head of Participation)
US SIC: 8321, 8999
UK SIC: 96111, 83954
Auditors: Buzzacott LLP
Bankers: Barclays Bank Plc (20-00-00)

|  | 31-03-14 | 31-03-13 | 31-03-12 |
|---|---|---|---|
| TO | 6,567,908 | 5,433,603 | 9,277,685 |
| P/L | (1,616,871) | (4,104,288) | (5,332,121) |
| NW | 3,373,950 | 2,629,821 | 6,478,109 |
| WC | 6,697,214 | 7,854,671 | 11,665,220 |
| Emp. | 59 | 72 | 85 |

DUNS 21-409-6017
## Social Care Reception
Merrion House, 110 Merrion Centre, Leeds,
West Yorkshire LS2 8QB
Tel: 01132224401
Estd: 2002 Proprietorship
Line of Business: The dss
Proprietor: Mrs G Bell
US SIC: 8321 UK SIC: 96111
Employees: 300

DUNS 29-575-8767
## Social Enterprise Kent Cic
Kent Enterprise House, 1 The Links, Herne
Bay, Kent CT6 7GQ
Tel: 01227844464 Fax: 01227200120
Web: www.sekgroup.org.uk
Reg No: 1937728 Estd: 2007 Private
Company Limited By Guarantee
Line of Business: Activities of business and
employers organisations
Trading Style: Canterbury & District
Enterprise Trust
Directors: Mrs R A Smith, Ms E A Bailey,
G Langfield, Ms C C Sykes
**Responsibilities**
Senior: Philip Lennard (Manager),
Bernadette Morgan (Manager)
Branches: Social Enterprise Kent Cic, Pats
Cottage, 24 Linton Hill, Maidstone, Kent
ME17 4AS

US SIC: 8611, 8321
UK SIC: 96312, 96111
Auditors: Reeves & Co LLP
Bankers: HSBC Bank plc (40-46-29)

|  | 31-03-14 | 31-03-13 | 31-03-12 |
|---|---|---|---|
| TO | 4,487,234 | 5,445,460 | 4,850,779 |
| P/L | 32,311 | 159,780 | (294,659) |
| NW | 154,726 | 131,697 | 6,706 |
| WC | 146,582 | 183,551 | 131,941 |

DUNS 21-018-4188
## Social Finance Ltd
131-151 Great Titchfield Street, London
W1W 5BB
Tel: 02076676370
Web: www.socialfinance.org.uk
Reg No: 6402143 Estd: 2007 Private
Limited Company
Line of Business: Financial management
Issued Capital: £1,000,013
Directors: D Hutchison, A E Law,
C G Devane, R Gillespie, B Bailey,
D A Hutchison, D Anderson, Ms P A Newman
Co. Secretary: Ms Fiona Miller Smith
**Responsibilities**
Senior: Toby Eccles (Director), Bernard
Horn (Director)
US SIC: 7392 UK SIC: 83951

|  | 30-09-14 | 30-09-13 | 30-09-12 |
|---|---|---|---|
| TO | 3,254,115 | 1,973,583 | 833,388 |
| P/L | (232,207) | 697,725 | 304,795 |
| NW | 986,902 | 1,166,518 | 537,126 |
| WC | 1,662,438 | 1,478,824 | 857,018 |

DUNS 23-973-5199
## The Social Resource Centre Ltd
Dean & Chapter Industrial Estat, Ferryhill,
County Durham DL17 8LH
Tel: 01740658880 Fax: 01740658889
Web: www.durhamsrc.co.uk
Reg No: 3962187 Estd: 2000 Private
Limited Company
Line of Business: Charities and charitable
organisations
Directors: A Clements, J Davison, I Brown,
Mrs K Conroy, Mrs M Kearsley, R A Grinter,
A Munro, Mrs S Little
Co. Secretary: John Davison
**Responsibilities**
Senior: Margaret Meek (Director), Linda
Tyman (Director)
US SIC: 8091, 8999
UK SIC: 95200, 83954
Bankers: National Westminster Bank Plc
(52-41-38)

|  | 31-03-14 | 31-03-13 | 31-03-12 |
|---|---|---|---|
| TO | 3,089,638 | 3,553,048 | 3,644,462 |
| P/L | 2,879 | 86,860 | 55,014 |
| NW | 662,544 | 659,665 | 572,805 |
| WC | 524,703 | 527,915 | 442,669 |
| Emp. | 174 | 198 | 260 |

DUNS 21-391-1715
## Social Services
Invicta House, Maidstone, Kent ME14 1XX
Tel: 03000416161
Web: www.kent.gov.uk
Estd: 2010 Proprietorship
Line of Business: The dss
Proprietor: Mrs P Wallace
US SIC: 8321 UK SIC: 96111
Employees: 51

DUNS 21-232-4476
## Social Services & Health Dept
Welsman, Princes Street, Bristol, Avon BS2
9JA
Tel: 0117-9036500
Web: www.bristolcity.gov.uk
Estd: 1998 Proprietorship
Line of Business: The dss
Proprietor: Mrs M Bowen Hall
**Responsibilities**
Senior: Maxine Bowen-Hall (Manager),
Linda Fraiser (Manager)
US SIC: 8321 UK SIC: 96111
Employees: 100

DUNS 21-782-4308
## Social Services Department
27 Upper Bond Street, Hinckley,
Leicestershire LE10 1RH
Tel: 01455636964
Web: www.leics.gov.uk
Estd: 2002
Line of Business: The dss
**Responsibilities**
Senior: Rosemary Deacon (Office Manager)
US SIC: 8321 UK SIC: 96111
Employees: 120

DUNS 21-781-4026
## Social Work Department Coatbridge
122 Bank Street, Coatbridge, Lanarkshire
ML5 1ET
Tel: 01236622100
Web: www.northlanarkshire.gov.uk
Estd: 2011
Line of Business: The dss
US SIC: 8321 UK SIC: 96111
Employees: 150

DUNS 23-599-2935
## Societe Generale Equipment Finance Ltd
(Subsidiary of: Societe Generale)
5 Kew Road, Richmond, Surrey TW9 2PR
Tel: 020-8940-9888 Fax: 020-8940-8333
Web: www.sgef.co.uk
Reg No: 3596854 Estd: 1998 Private
Limited Company
Line of Business: Financial services
Issued Capital: £100
Principals: G Turner (Managing),
J A Bensen, S J Bowden, S W Symons,
D L Hughes
Co. Secretary: David Yates-Mercer
**Responsibilities**
Senior: Kay Goodenough (Customer
Services Manager), Tracy Mills (Manager)
Health & Safety: Ben Rybinski (operations
Manager)
Operations: Kay Goodenough (Customer
Services Manager)
Purchasing: Ben Rybinski (operations
Manager)
US SIC: 6111 UK SIC: 81501
Auditors: Ernst & Young LLP

|  | 31-12-13 | 31-12-12 | 31-12-11 |
|---|---|---|---|
| TA | 645,006,000 | 642,827,000 | 665,667,000 |
| P/L | 16,322,000 | 8,074,000 | 10,095,000 |
| NW | 27,130,000 | 25,293,000 | 19,335,000 |
| WC | 355,293,000 | 362,462,000 | 384,402,000 |
| Emp. | 66 | 69 | 66 |

DUNS 21-119-3735
## Societe Generale Investments (U.K.) Ltd
(Subsidiary of: Societe Generale)
S G House, 41 Tower Hill, London EC3N
4SG
Tel: 02076766000
Web: www.sgcib.com
Reg No: 0223382 Estd: 1927 Private
Limited Company
Line of Business: Banks and financial
institutions
Trading Style: S G Corporate Investment
Banking
Issued Capital: £142,945,001
Directors: P J Robeyns, P A Morra,
I J Fisher, M A Nimmo
Co. Secretary:
Ms Catherine Balinska-Jundzill
**Responsibilities**
Senior: Justine Bouyssou (Finance
Administrator), Thierry Garcia (Manager),
David Ishoo-Mirzayoo (Manager), Martine
Jonghi (Manager), Roberto Simon
(Managing Director - Head of Pr)
Finance: Justine Bouyssou (Finance
Administrator), Alexander Krolick (Director,
Energy Project Finan), Olivier Musset
(Deputy Global Head, Energy Pro), Phyllis
Papadavid (Foreign Exchange Manager),
Tony Venutolo (Global Head of Credit
Structur)
Fleet: Jonathan Wober (Co-Head, Transport
Research)
Branches: Societe Generale Investments
(U.k.) Ltd, Po Box 179, Leeds, West
Yorkshire LS2 8BJ
US SIC: 6111 UK SIC: 81501
Auditors: Ernst & Young LLP
Bankers: Societe Generale (23-63-91)
Following financial data are in thousands

|  | 31-12-13 | 31-12-12 | 31-12-11 |
|---|---|---|---|
| TA | 3,971,015 | 3,904,696 | 3,775,556 |
| P/L | 47,643 | (2,802) | (32,886) |
| NW | 189,208 | 175,496 | 184,115 |
| WC | 485,535 | 55,457 | 1,158,273 |

DUNS 34-600-2996          Imp
## Societe Generale Newedge Uk Ltd
(Subsidiary of: Societe Generale)
10 Bishops Square, London E1 6EG
Tel: 02076768300
Web: www.newedgegroup.com
Reg No: 5407520 Estd: 2005 Private
Limited Company
Line of Business: Financial intermediation
not elsewhere classified
Issued Capital: £483,755,202
Directors: P M Cirier, D H Escoffier,
Mrs T C Castell, B J Pearce, R S Wilson,
G A Wolens, I J Fisher
Co. Secretary: Gerard De Lambilly

**Responsibilities**
**Senior:** Malcolm Basing *(Manager)*, Amaury De Villemandy *(Manager)*, Mathieu Giovachini *(Director)*, Craig Healy *(Manager)*, Michael Schulz *(Director)*
**US SIC:** 6111 **UK SIC:** 81501
**Auditors:** Ernst & Young LLP
**Following financial data are in thousands**

| | 31-12-13 | 31-12-12 | 31-12-11 |
|---|---|---|---|
| TA | 12,171,132 | 12,854,073 | 18,677,832 |
| P/L | (24,918) | 11,324 | 6,708 |
| NW | 465,265 | 463,389 | 457,567 |
| WC | 637,475 | 631,162 | 619,721 |
| Emp. | 722 | 769 | 754 |

DUNS 29-011-2945 **Exp**
### Society for Endocrinology
Unit 22, Apex Court, Woodlands, Bristol, Avon BS32 4JT
**Web:** www.endocrinology.org
**Reg No:** 0349408 **VAT No:** 173842449
**Estd:** 1939 Private Company Limited By Guarantee
**Line of Business:** Publishing of journals and periodicals
**Export Markets:** Worldwide
**Export Sales:** £3,002,685
**Trading Style:** Bio-Scientifica
**Directors:** Professor N A Hanley, Professor A White, Professor J R Seckl, Professor D Ray, Dr M Gibson, Professor W S Dhillo, Professor C J Mccabe, Professor A P Weetman
**Co. Secretary:** Leon Heward-Mills
**Responsibilities**
**Senior:** Eleanor Davies *(Director)*, Marta Korbonits *(Manager)*, Stephen O'Rahilly *(Director)*, Kirsty Withers *(Personal Assistant)*
**Marketing:** Jennie Evans *(Media & Press Officer)*, Rebecca Ramsden *(Public & Media Relations Execu)*, Laura Udakis *(Communications Manager)*, Fiona Williams *(Marketing Assistant)*
**Facilities:** Christopher Wolfe *(Facilities Manager)*
**Operations:** Julie Cragg *(?Society Services Manager)*
**US SIC:** 2721, 8249, 8699
**UK SIC:** 47522, 93300, 96902
**Auditors:** Chantrey Vellacott DFK LLP
**Bankers:** National Westminster Bank Plc (55-61-38)

| | 31-07-14 | 31-07-13 | 31-07-12 |
|---|---|---|---|
| TO | 4,922,435 | 4,755,526 | 4,733,738 |
| P/L | (733,730) | (350,574) | 55,703 |
| NW | 5,822,986 | 6,540,166 | 6,239,103 |
| WC | 104,206 | 335,873 | 972,298 |
| Emp. | 60 | 55 | 50 |

DUNS 22-704-0011 **Exp**
### Society of Chemical Industry
14-15 Belgrave Square, London SW1X 8PS
**Tel:** 020-7598-1500 **Fax:** 020-7598-1545
**Web:** www.soci.org
**Reg No:** 0000565RC **Estd:** 1907 Incorporate By Act Of Parliament
**Line of Business:** Charities and charitable organisations
**Trading Style:** S C I
**Principals:** V Carlarco *(President)*, R Denyer
**Responsibilities**
**Senior:** Hamza Ali *(Financial Director)*, Juliet Corbett *(Chief Executive)*, Manon Frost *(Manager)*, Joanne Lyall *(Executive Director)*
**Finance:** Hamza Ali *(Financial Director)*
**Marketing:** Reshna Radiven *(Marketing Manager)*
**US SIC:** 8699 **UK SIC:** 96902
**Auditors:** Haysmacintyre
**Bankers:** HSBC Bank plc (40-03-17)
**Employees:** 25
**Turnover:** £2,986,000

DUNS 38-765-0732
### The Society of Friends
434 Penn Road, Wolverhampton, West Midlands WV4 4DH
**Tel:** 01902-341203
**Web:** www.woodlandsquakerhome.org
**Estd:** 1950
**Line of Business:** Non-charitable social work activities with accommodation
**Trading Style:** Woodlands Quaker Home for Older People
**US SIC:** 8321 **UK SIC:** 96111
**Employees:** 59

DUNS 22-729-8270 **Imp**
### The Society of Lloyd's
One Lime Street, London EC3M 7HA
**Tel:** 02073-276-809 **Fax:** 02076-262-389
**Web:** www.lloyds.com
**Estd:** 1871 Incorporate By Act Of Parliament
**Line of Business:** Insurance
**Trading Style:** Lloyd's, The Corporation of Lloyd's
**Principals:** Lord P Levene *(Chairman)*, R Ward, A Lovell, R Atkin, D Shipley, G White, Mrs J Hanratty, D O'Donohoe
**Responsibilities**
**Senior:** Celia Denton *(Principal)*, Anna Dimdore *(Manager)*, Nigel Hanbury *(Principal)*, Chriptopher Harman *(Principal)*, Bill Knight *(Vice Chairperson)*, Philip Lader *(Principal)*, Barbara Merry *(Principal)*, Dermot O'Donohoe *(Principal)*, Andreas Prindl *(Principal)*, Anthony Townsend *(Principal)*
**Branches:** The Society Of Lloyd's, Lloyds Building, 1 Lime St, London EC3M 7HL
**US SIC:** 6411 **UK SIC:** 83200
**Auditors:** Ernst & Young LLP
**Bankers:** National Westminster Bank Plc (60-00-01)
**Employees:** 912
**Turnover:** £1.810E + 10

DUNS 22-717-1154
### Society of London Theatre
32 Rose Street, Covent Garden, London WC2E 9ET
**Web:** www.solt.co.uk
**Reg No:** 0527227 **VAT No:** 242280292
**Estd:** 1953 Private Company Limited By Guarantee
**Line of Business:** Associations
**Trading Style:** Society of London Theatres, S O L T
**Directors:** Ms E R Lloyd, M T Goucher, A P Spiegel, R M Fox, J R Bierman, N Salmon, R F Noble, Ms K V Horton
**Co. Secretary:** Julian Bird
**Responsibilities**
**Senior:** Kim Poster *(Director)*, Mark Rubinstein *(Director)*, Edward Snape *(Director)*
**Branches:** Society of London Theatre, 40 Leicester Square, London WC2H 7LP
**US SIC:** 8631 **UK SIC:** 96313
**Auditors:** Nyman Libson Paul
**Bankers:** Coutts & Co (18-00-02)

| | 31-12-13 | 31-12-12 | 31-12-11 |
|---|---|---|---|
| TO | 6,215,762 | 6,285,721 | 6,120,169 |
| P/L | 248,086 | (59,204) | (236,967) |
| NW | 528,346 | 347,931 | 415,135 |
| WC | (1,258,294) | (1,490,996) | (1,480,237) |
| Emp. | 64 | 65 | 62 |

DUNS 22-703-3958 **Imp-Exp**
### The Society of Motor Manufacturers & Traders Ltd
71 Great Peter Street, London SW1P 2BN
**Tel:** 020-7235-7000 **Fax:** 020-7235-7112
**Web:** www.smmt.co.uk
**Reg No:** 0074359 **Estd:** 1902 Private Company Limited By Guarantee
**Line of Business:** Activities of professional organisations
**Trading Style:** S M M T
**Directors:** P D Price, J Davies, J A King, G P Jones, M Rosher, H Kirner, Mrs P H Randall, P Crossman
**Co. Secretary:** Seftton Samuels
**Responsibilities**
**Senior:** Timothy Abbott *(Director)*, Paddy Hopkirk *(Director)*, Stuart McCullough *(Manager)*, Martin Spencer *(Director)*
**Finance:** Paul Christian *(Financial Director)*
**Sales:** Luke Hampton *(Business Development Manager)*
**IT:** Geoff Major *(IT Coordinator)*, Vinny Phul *(Senior IT Executive)*
**Purchasing:** Geoff Major *(IT Coordinator)*
**Branches:** The Society Of Motor Manufacturers & Traders Ltd, Unit 2410, The Crescent, Birmingham, West Midlands B37 7YE
**US SIC:** 7399 **UK SIC:** 83954
**Auditors:** Baker Tilly UK Audit LLP

| | 31-12-13 | 31-12-12 | 31-12-11 |
|---|---|---|---|
| TO | 15,136,000 | 16,844,164 | 15,415,094 |
| P/L | 2,092,000 | 2,108,729 | 32,540,742 |
| NW | 30,943,000 | 27,693,157 | 25,879,381 |
| WC | 23,000 | 690,854 | 7,975,450 |
| Emp. | N/A | 129 | 132 |

DUNS 77-738-5386
### The Society of St. James
125 Albert Road South, Southampton, Hampshire SO14 3FR
**Web:** www.ssj.org.uk
**Reg No:** 3009700 **Estd:** 1995 Private Limited Company
**Line of Business:** Charities and charitable organisations
**Directors:** Mrs J Dawes, T M Rogerson, N Cato, M P Day, Mrs J M Lovelock, G W Barwick, D Blake, G Ward
**Co. Secretary:** Trevor Pickup
**Responsibilities**
**Senior:** Jonathan Diaper *(Director)*, Brian Hooper *(Manager)*
**Branches:** The Society Of St. James, 72 Howard Rd, Southampton, Hampshire SO15 5BJ
**US SIC:** 8321 **UK SIC:** 96111
**Auditors:** BDO Stoy Hayward
**Bankers:** Bank Of Scotland (12-09-61)

| | 31-03-14 | 31-03-13 | 31-03-12 |
|---|---|---|---|
| TO | 7,594,098 | 6,542,142 | 6,133,403 |
| P/L | 52,284 | 54,718 | 169,086 |
| NW | 1,785,800 | 1,700,300 | 1,608,671 |
| WC | 330,609 | 280,773 | 449,294 |
| Emp. | 227 | 177 | 137 |

DUNS 21-784-8948
### The Society of the Holy Child Jesus
35 Oatlands Drive, Harrogate, North Yorkshire HG2 8JT
**Tel:** 01423885101
**Estd:** 2011
**Line of Business:** Other human health activities
**Trading Style:** Appley Grange
**US SIC:** 8091 **UK SIC:** 95200
**Employees:** 51

DUNS 76-971-0963
### The Society of Trust & Estate Practitioners Ltd
Artillery House (South), 11 - 19 Artillery Row, London SW1P 1RT
**Tel:** 02078393886
**Web:** www.step.org
**Reg No:** 2632423 **Estd:** 1991 Private Limited Company
**Line of Business:** Adult and other education not elsewhere classified
**Directors:** J M Lawrence, Dr A M Venardos, G Lyall, E J Buckland, N D Jacob, D J Harvey, P J Seal, Mrs P M Wass
**Co. Secretary:** Ms Jessica Holifield
**US SIC:** 8249, 8621
**UK SIC:** 93300, 96311
**Auditors:** AGN Shipleys
**Bankers:** Barclays Bank Plc (20-03-53)

| | 31-03-14 | 31-03-13 | 31-03-12 |
|---|---|---|---|
| TO | 8,511,216 | 8,021,855 | 7,225,260 |
| P/L | 384,339 | 324,648 | 212,336 |
| NW | 4,129,560 | 3,971,824 | 3,587,463 |
| WC | 3,793,579 | 3,889,392 | 3,457,453 |
| Emp. | 47 | 46 | 46 |

DUNS 22-433-4032
### Sodexho Prestige
Civic Centre, Chesterfield Road South, Mansfield, Nottinghamshire NG19 7BH
**Tel:** 01623-656766
**Web:** www.youreventinmansfield.co.uk
**Estd:** 1986 Proprietorship
**Line of Business:** Conference related services
**Proprietor:** Mrs P Potter
**Responsibilities**
**Senior:** Darrell Farmsworth *(General Manager)*, Kaylee Mills *(General Manager)*
**US SIC:** 6531 **UK SIC:** 83400
**Employees:** 50

DUNS 77-517-7637
### Sodexo Holdings Ltd
**(Subsidiary of:** Sodexo)
One Southampton Row, London WC1B 5HA
**Tel:** 02074040110 **Fax:** 02031164563
**Web:** www.sodexo.com
**Reg No:** 2987170 **Estd:** 1994 Private Limited Company
**Line of Business:** Management activities of holding companies
**Issued Capital:** £513,646,471
**Directors:** Mrs L C Mawdsley, A L Leech, S A Carter, Ms D J White
**Co. Secretary:** Gareth John
**Branches:** Sodexo Holdings Ltd, Forestview, Purdy's Lane, Belfast, Belfast BT8 7AR
**US SIC:** 6711, 7392
**UK SIC:** 83962, 83951
**Auditors:** KPMG LLP

| | 31-08-13 | 31-08-12 | 31-08-11 |
|---|---|---|---|
| TA | 931,250,000 | 923,646,000 | 910,399,000 |
| P/L | 51,054,000 | 35,809,000 | 31,784,000 |
| NW | 542,714,000 | 533,991,000 | 534,907,000 |
| WC | (360,189,000) | (335,986,000) | (330,070,000) |

DUNS 50-422-8024
### Sodexo Land Technology Ltd
**(Subsidiary of:** Sodexo)
Bucks Cops Depot, Barcombe Road, Wokingham, Berkshire RG41 2RD
**Tel:** 01925639263 **Fax:** 01189-770050
**Reg No:** 2415051 **Estd:** 1990 Private Limited Company
**Line of Business:** Other service activities not elsewhere classified
**Trading Style:** Primary Management
**Issued Capital:** £984
**Directors:** S A Carter, Sodexo Corporate Services (No.1)
**Co. Secretary:**
Sodexo Corporate Services (No 2)
**Branches:** Sodexo Land Technology Ltd, Haydon Hall, Southill La, Pinner, Middlesex HA5 2EG
**US SIC:** 8999 **UK SIC:** 83954
**Auditors:** KPMG LLP
**Bankers:** National Westminster Bank Plc (60-17-21)

| | 31-08-13 | 31-08-12 | 31-08-11 |
|---|---|---|---|
| TA | 19,986 | 19,986 | 19,986 |
| NW | 19,986 | 19,986 | 19,986 |

DUNS 77-103-6464
### Sodexo Motivation Solutions U.K. Ltd
**(Subsidiary of:** Sodexo)
1 Southampton Row, London WC1B 5HA
**Tel:** 01276-687000 **Fax:** 01276-687005
**Web:** www.sodexomotivation.co.uk
**Reg No:** 2680629 **Estd:** 1992 Private Limited Company
**Line of Business:** Corporate promotional products
**Issued Capital:** £500,000
**Directors:** S R De Tramasure, I K Mcmath, D J Sandoz, D P Machuel
**Co. Secretary:**
Sodexo Corporate Services (No.2)
**US SIC:** 7399, 5182
**UK SIC:** 83954, 61700
**Auditors:** KPMG LLP

| | 31-08-13 | 31-08-12 | 31-08-11 |
|---|---|---|---|
| TO | 6,268,000 | 6,221,000 | 7,085,000 |
| P/L | 642,000 | 725,000 | 1,324,000 |
| NW | 606,000 | 581,000 | 918,000 |
| WC | 318,000 | 205,000 | 428,000 |
| Emp. | 76 | 80 | 72 |

DUNS 21-581-5820 **Exp**
### Sodexo Remote Sites Scotland Ltd
**(Subsidiary of:** Sodexo)
5th Floor Exchange Tower No 2, Aberdeen, Aberdeenshire AB11 5PJ
**Tel:** 01224-324388 **Fax:** 01224-324425
**Web:** www.sodexo.com
**Reg No:** 0059276SC **VAT No:** 735254829
**Estd:** 1976 Private Limited Company
**Line of Business:** Management and business consultants
**Export Markets:** Europe
**Export Sales:** £7,334,266
**Issued Capital:** £30,932
**Directors:** L G Tocher, N A Japy, S L Roger
**Co. Secretary:**
Raeburn Christie Clark & Wallace
**Responsibilities**
**Senior:** Jane Bristow *(Manager)*, Rebecca Herbert Jones *(Manager)*, Merit Teigiand *(Vice President, Gulf of Mexico)*
**Finance:** Bruno Reneville *(Finance Director)*
**Purchasing:** E McLcean *(Purchasing Manager)*
**Branches:** Sodexo Remote Sites Scotland Ltd, 5 Queens Ter, Aberdeen, Aberdeenshire AB10 1XL
**US SIC:** 7392 **UK SIC:** 83951
**Auditors:** PricewaterhouseCoopers LLP
**Bankers:** The Royal Bank Of Scotland Plc (83-49-40)

| | 31-08-13 | 31-08-12 | 31-08-11 |
|---|---|---|---|
| TO | 90,674,259 | 85,703,526 | 75,125,470 |
| P/L | 5,391,552 | 5,255,037 | 4,766,442 |
| NW | 5,740,735 | 5,039,440 | 5,139,992 |
| WC | 5,740,735 | 5,039,440 | 5,139,992 |
| Emp. | 425 | 296 | 272 |

DUNS 34-571-7557 **Exp**
### Sodexo Services Group Ltd
**(Subsidiary of:** Sodexo)
Solar House, Stevenage Leisure Park, Kings Way, Stevenage, Hertfordshire SG1 2UA
**Tel:** 01438341400 **Fax:** 01438341541
**Web:** www.sodexo.com
**Reg No:** 2721707 **Estd:** 1992 Private Limited Company
**Line of Business:** Management activities of holding companies
**Issued Capital:** £2,367,710
**Directors:**
Sodexo Corporate Services (No.1), S A Carter
**Co. Secretary:**
Sodexo Corporate Services (No 2)
**Responsibilities**
**Senior:** Jane Bristow *(Managing Director, Corporate S)*
**Branches:** Sodexo Services Group Ltd, Po Box 437, Sheffield, South Yorkshire S4 7WP
**US SIC:** 6711, 7399
**UK SIC:** 83962, 83954
**Auditors:** KPMG LLP

| | 31-08-13 | 31-08-12 | 31-08-11 |
|---|---|---|---|
| TA | 307,141,000 | 304,120,000 | 300,790,000 |
| P/L | 3,021,000 | 3,330,000 | 2,947,000 |
| NW | 264,807,000 | 262,498,000 | 260,006,000 |
| WC | 264,807,000 | 262,498,000 | 260,006,000 |

DUNS 34-650-8356

## Sofa Brands International Ltd

5 Ash Tree Court, Woodsy Close, Cardiff Gate Business Park, Pontprennau, Cardiff, South Glamorgan CF23 8RW
**Tel:** 02920730840 **Fax:** 02920730841
**Web:** www.sofabrands.com
**Reg No:** 5456332 **Estd:** 2005 Private Limited Company
**Line of Business:** Management activities of holding companies
**Issued Capital:** £106,303,941
**Directors:** I Oliver, D S Malvenan, B Stitfall
**Co. Secretary:** Ms Emma Jones
**Responsibilities**
**Senior:** Vincent Mc Ginlay *(Director)*
**US SIC:** 6711 **UK SIC:** 83962

| | 30-06-13 | 30-06-12 | 30-06-11 |
|---|---|---|---|
| TO | 71,236,000 | 66,280,000 | 67,894,000 |
| P/L | 4,756,000 | 2,781,000 | 4,236,000 |
| NW | (160,000) | (5,520,000) | (8,737,000) |
| WC | 4,114,000 | (3,721,000) | 4,311,000 |
| Emp. | 885 | 873 | 870 |

DUNS 73-971-6723

## Sofa.Com Ltd

Unit 33-35 Fairview Industrial Estate, Clayton Road, Hayes, Middlesex UB3 1AX
**Fax:** 02073-512-299
**Web:** www.sofa.com
**Reg No:** 5222498 **Estd:** 2004 Private Limited Company
**Line of Business:** Retail sale of furniture lighting equipment and household articles not elsewhere classified
**Export Sales:** £1,595,302
**Issued Capital:** £100
**Directors:** G A Williams, P L Woodhouse
**Responsibilities**
**Senior:** Rohan Blacker *(Director)*, Mac Eberhart *(Manager)*
**US SIC:** 5719 **UK SIC:** 64700
**Auditors:** Shipleys LLP

| | 28-02-14 | 28-02-13 | 29-02-12 |
|---|---|---|---|
| TO | 21,767,800 | 17,645,997 | 12,961,247 |
| P/L | 2,838,855 | 1,611,483 | 1,400,426 |
| NW | 3,694,441 | 1,588,313 | 1,282,111 |
| WC | 3,105,020 | 1,150,011 | 834,627 |
| Emp. | 109 | 89 | 67 |

DUNS 29-472-0776 Imp

## Sofaworks Ltd

**(Subsidiary of:** Brian Tyldesley Ltd)
Golborne Point, Ashton Road, Golborne, Warrington, Cheshire WA3 3UL
**Tel:** 08444818054 **Fax:** 01942-296475
**Web:** www.csl-furniture.co.uk
**Reg No:** 1778734 **VAT No:** 375404451
**Estd:** 1983 Private Limited Company
**Line of Business:** Furniture retail outlets
**Trading Style:** Csl
**Issued Capital:** £2,100
**Principals:** B E Tyldesley *(Managing)*, Ms A T Fadil, J Tyldesley
**Co. Secretary:** Mrs Margaret Tyldesley
**Branches:** Sofaworks Ltd, Oxford Square, Blackpool, Lancashire FY4 4DP
**US SIC:** 5719 **UK SIC:** 64700
**Auditors:** Moore & Smalley LLP
**Bankers:** Barclays Bank Plc (20-09-72)

| | 31-12-13 | 31-12-12 | 31-12-11 |
|---|---|---|---|
| TO | 101,312,010 | 89,167,877 | 63,662,774 |
| P/L | 460,428 | 2,503,417 | 200,718 |
| NW | 6,302,603 | 7,367,044 | 5,854,975 |
| WC | 299,312 | 2,055,423 | 830,660 |
| Emp. | 750 | 679 | 529 |

DUNS 39-931-8229

## Sofidel Uk Ltd

Waterside Road, Leicester, Leicestershire LE5 1TZ
**Tel:** 01162-460888 **Fax:** 01162-460222
**Web:** www.sofidel.com
**Reg No:** 2245657 **VAT No:** 565705718
**Estd:** 1979 Private Limited Company
**Line of Business:** Paper and pulp mills
**Export Sales:** £37,164,000
**Issued Capital:** £250,000
**Directors:** L Lazzareschi, E Stefani
**Co. Secretary:** Mrs Angela Helm-Davies
**Responsibilities**
**Senior:** Shirazali Dharamshi *(Manager)*, Amirali Tejani *(Manager)*, Salim Tejani *(Manager)*
**Finance:** Richard Miner *(Financial Director)*
**Branches:** Sofidel Uk Ltd, Lpc Afh Division, Park Ho Crossgate Rd Park Farm Indstl Est, Redditch, Worcestershire B98 7SN
**US SIC:** 2631, 6711
**UK SIC:** 47017, 83962
**Auditors:** Ernst & Young LLP
**Bankers:** Lloyds TSB Bank plc (30-18-69)

| | 31-12-13 | 31-12-12 | 31-12-11 |
|---|---|---|---|
| TO | 259,658,000 | 230,080,000 | 90,470,000 |
| P/L | 40,740,000 | 34,026,000 | 90,224,000 |
| NW | 161,174,000 | 131,843,000 | 105,146,000 |
| WC | 43,864,000 | 17,373,000 | 28,839,000 |
| Emp. | 493 | 506 | 591 |

DUNS 21-222-7967

## Sofitel Hotel

6 Pall Mall, London SW1Y 5NG
**Tel:** 02077472200
**Web:** www.sofitelstjames.com
**Proprietorship**
**Line of Business:** Hotels
**Proprietor:** H Jaquier
**US SIC:** 7011 **UK SIC:** 66500
**Employees:** 180

DUNS 21-027-3801

## Sofnol Ltd

Tonbridge Road, Maidstone, Kent ME18 5AF
**Tel:** 01622-814063
**Web:** www.turfsoil.co.uk
**Reg No:** 0122152 **Estd:** 1904 Private Limited Company
**Line of Business:** Agricultural service activities; landscape gardening
**Issued Capital:** £44,890
**Principals:** J O Newton *(Chairman and Managing)*, Mrs J M Newton, Mrs L J Bellhouse
**Co. Secretary:** Mrs Nina Wheat
**Responsibilities**
**Senior:** Michael Tolhurst *(Manager)*
**Branches:** Sofnol Ltd, Danson Park, Bexleyheath, Kent DA6 8HL
**US SIC:** 0729 **UK SIC:** 01003
**Auditors:** Peter Hodgson & Co
**Bankers:** National Westminster Bank Plc (60-60-08)

| | 28-02-14 | 28-02-13 | 29-02-12 |
|---|---|---|---|
| TO | 3,567,133 | 4,525,791 | 4,450,067 |
| P/L | 39,832 | 211,761 | 24,137 |
| NW | 4,741,307 | 4,712,232 | 4,526,594 |
| WC | 4,082,143 | 3,865,820 | 3,463,597 |
| Emp. | 92 | 92 | 97 |

DUNS 21-937-6723

## Softbox Systems Holdings Ltd

**(Subsidiary of:** Softbox (Topco) Ltd)
Units 11 Ridgeway, Drakes Drive Long Crendon, Aylesbury, Buckinghamshire HP18 9BF
**Tel:** 01844201793
**Reg No:** 8494918 **Estd:** 2013 Private Limited Company
**Line of Business:** Holding companies management activities
**Export Sales:** £8,298,567
**Issued Capital:** £134,087
**Directors:** E F Tattam, M Hammond, R W Jones, M De Rijk
**Co. Secretary:** Mrs Gillian Hills
**US SIC:** 6711 **UK SIC:** 83962

| | 31-12-13 |
|---|---|
| TO | 10,772,932 |
| P/L | 1,180,703 |
| NW | 1,880,756 |
| WC | 883,787 |
| Emp. | 103 |

DUNS 49-145-7404 Imp

## Softbox Systems Ltd

**(Subsidiary of:** Softbox (Topco) Ltd)
Unit 1-2 Ridgeway, Drakes Drive, Long Crendon, Aylesbury, Buckinghamshire HP18 9BF
**Tel:** 01844203560 **Fax:** 01844-203570
**Web:** www.softboxsystems.co.uk
**Reg No:** 3112875 **Estd:** 1995 Private Limited Company
**Line of Business:** Manufacturers of packaging materials
**Export Sales:** £9,090,050
**Issued Capital:** £209,077
**Directors:** M De Rijk, E F Tattam, R W Jones, M Hammond
**Co. Secretary:** Mrs Gillian Hills
**US SIC:** 2654, 2653
**UK SIC:** 47280, 47251
**Auditors:** Accounting & Executive Controls

| | 31-12-13 | 31-12-12 | 31-12-11 |
|---|---|---|---|
| TO | 13,148,933 | 12,462,765 | 11,640,063 |
| P/L | 2,523,042 | 1,195,241 | 1,227,837 |
| NW | 4,200,917 | 2,919,856 | 1,705,542 |
| WC | 3,397,869 | 2,211,249 | 1,248,548 |
| Emp. | 59 | 96 | 84 |

DUNS 39-733-3253 Imp

## Softcat Ltd

Fieldhouse Lane, Marlow, Buckinghamshire SL7 1TB
**Tel:** 01628403403 **Fax:** 08448-008182
**Web:** www.softcat.com
**Reg No:** 2174990 **VAT No:** 491848503
**Estd:** 1993 Private Limited Company
**Line of Business:** Computer services
**Issued Capital:** £93,324
**Directors:** C W Brown, M J Hellawell, B Wallace, P D Kelly, R A Lecoutre
**Co. Secretary:** William Kenny
**Responsibilities**
**Senior:** Jamie Burke *(Public Sector Director)*
**Marketing:** Rory Watts *(Partner Marketing Manager)*, Catherine Woodward *(Marketing Executive)*
**Sales:** Amy Roberts *(Sales Support Manager)*, Lance Williams *(Symantec Business Manager)*
**Admin:** G Wakefield *(Administration Manager)*
**IT:** Chow Tamana *(Technical Manager)*
**HR:** Shelley Ferrigno *(Recruitment Manager)*
**US SIC:** 7379 **UK SIC:** 83940
**Auditors:** Rayner Essex LLP
**Bankers:** HSBC Bank plc (40-32-19)

| | 31-07-14 | 31-07-13 | 31-07-12 |
|---|---|---|---|
| TO | 504,797,009 | 395,755,868 | 307,504,992 |
| P/L | 35,630,315 | 27,587,153 | 22,730,986 |
| NW | 71,776,412 | 48,358,531 | 41,691,056 |
| WC | 64,634,386 | 41,733,645 | 37,410,815 |
| Emp. | 602 | 488 | 387 |

DUNS 21-923-8912 Imp

## Software A G (U K) Ltd

**(Subsidiary of:** Software Ag)
Locomotive Way, Pride Park, Derby, Derbyshire DE24 8PU
**Tel:** 01332611000 **Fax:** 01332 611222
**Web:** www.softwareag.com
**Reg No:** 1310740 **Estd:** 1977 Private Limited Company
**Line of Business:** Hardware consultancy
**Export Sales:** £1,913,000
**Issued Capital:** £8,250,000
**Directors:** M Slater, A Zinnhardt
**Co. Secretary:** Tim Fox
**Branches:** Software A G (U K) Ltd, London House, London Road, Bracknell, Berkshire RG12 2UT
**US SIC:** 7070 **UK SIC:** 00040
**Auditors:** BDO LLP
**Bankers:** Lloyds TSB Bank plc (30-92-59)

| | 31-12-13 | 31-12-12 | 31-12-11 |
|---|---|---|---|
| TO | 48,315,000 | 36,273,000 | 29,912,000 |
| P/L | 9,254,000 | 10,108,000 | 2,600,000 |
| NW | (354,000) | 14,167,000 | 9,679,000 |
| WC | 13,012,000 | 14,549,000 | 25,022,000 |
| Emp. | 197 | 167 | 133 |

DUNS 39-029-4056 Imp

## Software Box Ltd

**(Subsidiary of:** Hocomm Ltd)
Greenpark Business Centre, Goose Lane, York, North Yorkshire YO61 1ET
**Tel:** 01347812100
**Web:** www.softbox.co.uk
**Reg No:** 2109168 **VAT No:** 734245248
**Estd:** 1989 Private Limited Company
**Line of Business:** Other computer related activities
**Export Sales:** £374,000
**Issued Capital:** £100
**Directors:** C J Williams, D Hoban
**Co. Secretary:** Brynmor Roberts
**US SIC:** 7379, 5081
**UK SIC:** 83940, 61490
**Auditors:** Grant Thornton U K LLP
**Bankers:** HSBC Bank plc (40-47-31)

| | 31-08-14 | 31-08-13 | 31-08-12 |
|---|---|---|---|
| TO | 128,083,000 | 112,196,000 | 87,969,000 |
| P/L | 2,698,000 | 2,947,000 | 2,275,000 |
| NW | 6,225,000 | 5,853,000 | 5,247,000 |
| WC | 5,732,000 | 5,512,000 | 4,954,000 |
| Emp. | 101 | 94 | 93 |

DUNS 34-889-4163

## The Software Bureau Ltd

5 White Oak Square, Swanley, Kent BR8 7AG
**Tel:** 08707359536
**Web:** www.thesoftwarebureau.com
**Reg No:** 2826490 **Estd:** 1993 Private Limited Company
**Line of Business:** Other software consultancy and supply
**Trading Style:** Dps Direct Mail
**Issued Capital:** £200
**Directors:** M C Dobson, D J Murray, P A Callow, P Morgan, M G Rides
**Co. Secretary:** David Carter
**US SIC:** 7379 **UK SIC:** 83940
**Auditors:** BDO Stoy Hayward
**Bankers:** National Westminster Bank Plc (60-16-03)

| | 30-09-13 | 30-09-12 | 30-09-11 |
|---|---|---|---|
| TA | 1,035,883 | 881,297 | 786,902 |
| NW | 582,457 | 504,800 | 430,503 |
| WC | 577,623 | 499,178 | 433,764 |

DUNS 73-934-3119

## Software of Excellence United Kingdom Ltd

**(Subsidiary of:** Software of Excellence Uk Holdings Ltd)
Medcare South, Bailey Drive, Gillingham Business Park, Gillingham, Kent ME8 0PZ
**Tel:** 08453455767 **Fax:** 01580893338
**Web:** www.softwareofexcellence.co.uk
**Reg No:** 2940919 **Estd:** 1994 Private Limited Company
**Line of Business:** Computer software sales
**Trading Style:** Software of Excellence
**Issued Capital:** £112,250
**Directors:** B W Weatherly, G B Stanley, M Zack, R N Minowitz
**Co. Secretary:** James Ludlow
**Responsibilities**
**Senior:** Bryce Donnell *(Manager)*, Ben Flewett *(General Manager)*
**Branches:** Software Of Excellence United Kingdom Ltd, 16 Inchbrakie Dr, Crieff, Perthshire PH7 3SS
**US SIC:** 7379 **UK SIC:** 83940
**Auditors:** Baker Tilly
**Bankers:** National Westminster Bank Plc (60-60-08)

| | 28-12-13 | 29-12-12 | 31-12-11 |
|---|---|---|---|
| TO | 19,487,777 | 18,413,676 | 18,425,463 |
| P/L | 2,661,561 | 2,600,343 | 3,207,605 |
| NW | 14,855,678 | 12,192,458 | (424,464) |
| WC | 4,816,663 | 2,868,380 | 997,262 |
| Emp. | 160 | 146 | 142 |

DUNS 34-654-2355 Imp

## Software Radio Technology Plc

Wireless House, First Avenue, Westfield Industrial Estate, Midsomer Norton, Bath, Avon BA3 4BS
**Tel:** 01761-409500
**Web:** www.softwarerad.com
**Reg No:** 5459678 **VAT No:** 869556264
**Estd:** 2002 Public Limited Company
**Line of Business:** Management activities of holding companies
**Export Sales:** £5,814,791
**Issued Capital:** £115,920
**Directors:** S F Rogers, A C Lapping, R Hurd, S R Tucker, N Peniket
**Co. Secretary:** Mitre Secretaries Limited
**Responsibilities**
**IT:** Clive Hunt *(IT Manager)*
**US SIC:** 6711 **UK SIC:** 83962
**Auditors:** Nexia Smith & Williamson LLP
**Bankers:** The Royal Bank Of Scotland Plc (83-07-06)

| | 31-03-14 | 31-03-13 | 31-03-12 |
|---|---|---|---|
| TO | 6,110,359 | 10,011,185 | 6,171,697 |
| P/L | (1,506,374) | 1,187,071 | 174,643 |
| NW | 5,243,979 | 7,097,344 | 3,887,379 |
| WC | 5,058,582 | 6,966,714 | 3,733,390 |
| Emp. | 46 | 42 | 39 |

DUNS 52-572-1163

## Software Stationery Holdings Ltd

**(Subsidiary of:** Evo Business Supplies Ltd)
Wheatfield Way, Hinckley, Leicestershire LE10 1YG
**Tel:** 01455615564 **Fax:** 01455-616246
**Web:** www.accessplus.co.uk
**Reg No:** 3255699 **Estd:** 1996 Private Limited Company
**Line of Business:** Other business activities not elsewhere classified
**Issued Capital:** £244,707
**Directors:** R R Baldrey, A P Gale
**Responsibilities**
**Health & Safety:** Jane Bartlett *(Customer Services Officer)*
**Operations:** Jane Bartlett *(Customer Services Officer)*
**US SIC:** 7399, 5199
**UK SIC:** 83954, 61900
**Auditors:** Ernst & Young
**Bankers:** HSBC Bank plc (40-14-13)

| | 31-12-11 |
|---|---|
| TA | 3,075,185 |
| NW | 284,089 |
| WC | 284,089 |

DUNS 23-783-7765 Exp

## Software Warehouse Holdings Ltd

**(Subsidiary of:** Home Retail Group Plc)
489-499 Avebury Boulevard, Milton Keynes, Buckinghamshire MK9 2NW
**Tel:** 01908690333 **Fax:** 01675-468343
**Reg No:** 3776853 **Estd:** 1999 Private Limited Company
**Line of Business:** Computer hardware & software wholesaler
**Export Markets:** Australia
**Issued Capital:** £50,000
**Directors:** D W Adams, G A Bentley
**Co. Secretary:** Miss Deborah Hamilton
**Responsibilities**
**Senior:** Penelope Mckelvey *(Manager)*
**US SIC:** 7372 **UK SIC:** 83940
**Auditors:** PricewaterhouseCoopers
**Employees:** 301

DUNS 23-832-8434

## Softwire Technology Ltd

Highgate Studios 53 79, London NW5 1TL
**Tel:** 020-7485-7500
**Web:** www.softwire.com
**Reg No:** 3824658 **Estd:** 1999 Private Limited Company
**Line of Business:** Computer software (development)
**Trading Style:** Softwire
**Issued Capital:** £2,000

**Directors:** T K Steer, M W Richards, A I Thomas, Ms Z F Cunningham, P Kenny, P A Marsden
**Co. Secretary:** Daniel Shavick
**US SIC:** 7379 **UK SIC:** 83940
**Auditors:** Richard Anthony & Co
**Bankers:** The Royal Bank Of Scotland Plc (16-00-23)

| | 31-12-13 | 31-12-12 | 31-12-11 |
|---|---|---|---|
| TA | 2,789,569 | 2,443,559 | 2,105,201 |
| NW | 1,363,910 | 1,283,620 | 911,675 |
| WC | 1,000,775 | 995,615 | 631,964 |

DUNS 21-638-3877 **Imp-Exp**
## Sogefi Filtration Ltd
**(Subsidiary of:** Cir Spa Compagnie Industriali Riunite)
Unit 1 Crown Business Park, Tredegar, Gwent NP22 4EF
**Tel:** 0149 5712740 **Fax:** 0149 5712799
**Web:** www.sogefigroup.com
**Reg No:** 0693949 **VAT No:** 285854608
**Estd:** 1961 Private Limited Company
**Line of Business:** Manufacture of other transport equipment not elsewhere classified
**Export Markets:** Worldwide
**Trading Style:** Coopers Division, Fram Division
**Issued Capital:** £5,126,737
**Principals:** K D Drew *(Financial)*, C Jones, G M Bocelli
**Co. Secretary:** Jonathan Thomas
**Responsibilities**
**Senior:** Emanuele Bosio *(Manager)*, John Bressington *(Despatch Manager)*
**Finance:** Alison Treharne-Jones *(Financial Director)*
**Branches:** Sogefi Filtration Ltd, Crown Avenue, Tredegar, Gwent NP22 4EF
**US SIC:** 3799 **UK SIC:** 36502
**Auditors:** Deloitte LLP
**Bankers:** Barclays Bank Plc (20-18-27)

| | 31-12-13 | 31-12-12 | 31-12-11 |
|---|---|---|---|
| TO | 59,156,000 | 63,680,000 | 75,628,000 |
| P/L | 3,231,000 | (9,848,000) | (8,754,000) |
| NW | (7,727,000) | (10,554,000) | 5,005,000 |
| WC | (11,154,000) | (12,755,000) | (3,448,000) |
| Emp. | 341 | 451 | 662 |

DUNS 22-249-9845
## Sogeti Uk Ltd
**(Subsidiary of:** Cap Gemini)
85 London Wall, London EC2M 7AD
**Tel:** 02070148900
**Web:** www.sogeti.com
**Reg No:** 4268004 **Estd:** 2001 Private Limited Company
**Line of Business:** Computer support & services
**Issued Capital:** £3,132
**Directors:** J P Van Waayenburg, P Grangeon, B E Shea, P Y Cros
**Co. Secretary:** Ms Julie Mangan
**Responsibilities**
**Senior:** Julie Pereira *(Manager)*, Ben Visser *(Senior Consultant)*, Barry Weston *(Solutions Director)*
**Finance:** Edouard Paule *(Financial Director)*
**Admin:** Chelsea Mason *(Office Manager)*, Molly Matthews *(Office Coordinator)*
**US SIC:** 7379 **UK SIC:** 83940
**Auditors:** KPMG LLP

| | 31-12-13 | 31-12-12 | 31-12-11 |
|---|---|---|---|
| TO | 29,102,171 | 32,374,947 | 19,477,099 |
| P/L | 965,528 | 1,089,886 | 591,630 |
| NW | 3,094,200 | 2,442,080 | 1,677,887 |
| WC | 2,989,496 | 2,301,049 | 1,615,258 |
| Emp. | 315 | 320 | 203 |

DUNS 21-240-1496
## Soha Housing Ltd
Royal Scot House, 99 Station Road, Didcot, Oxfordshire OX11 7NN
**Tel:** 01235-515900
**Web:** www.soha.co.uk
**Reg No:** 0028410IP **Estd:** 1997 Friendly Society
**Line of Business:** Non-charitable social work activities with accommodation
**Trading Style:** Soha Housing
**Directors:** Mrs C Hall, Mrs R Bowyer, C Heapy, R Peacock
**Responsibilities**
**Senior:** Janette Harbour *(Neighbourhood Officer)*
**Finance:** Paul Rennard *(Director of Finance)*
**Sales:** Mark Giddins *(Sales Executive)*
**IT:** Paul Rennard *(Director of Finance)*
**HR:** Katie Legg *(Human Resources Manager)*
**Health & Safety:** Penny Gotch *(Services Manager)*
**Facilities:** Penny Gotch *(Services Manager)*
**Purchasing:** Paul Rennard *(Director of Finance)*
**Branches:** Soha Housing Ltd, Marymead, Wallingford, Oxfordshire OX10 9PQ
**US SIC:** 8321 **UK SIC:** 96111
**Auditors:** BDO Stoy Hayward LLP
**Bankers:** National Westminster Bank Plc (60-16-07)

| | 31-03-12 | 31-03-11 | 31-03-10 |
|---|---|---|---|
| TO | 29,617,000 | 31,108,000 | 28,996,000 |
| P/L | 7,550,000 | 3,453,000 | 3,971,000 |
| NW | 182,303,000 | 180,541,000 | 177,088,000 |
| WC | 1,086,000 | 2,883,000 | 8,217,000 |
| Emp. | 95 | 104 | 110 |

DUNS 21-667-0304
## Sohal Health Llp
288-290 Ipswich Road, Colchester, Essex CO4 0ES
**Reg No:** 0353700OC **Estd:** 2010
**Line of Business:** Residential care services.
**US SIC:** 8361 **UK SIC:** 96112
**Auditors:** LMDB Accountants

| | 31-03-14 | 31-03-13 | 31-03-12 |
|---|---|---|---|
| TO | 4,027,347 | 4,078,015 | 4,015,375 |
| NW | (907,900) | (972,750) | (1,037,600) |
| WC | (736,724) | (546,937) | (138,584) |
| Emp. | 144 | 140 | 138 |

DUNS 57-007-8998 **Imp**
## Soho House Uk Ltd
**(Subsidiary of:** Abertarff Limited)
40 Greek Street, London W1D 4EB
**Tel:** 02077345188
**Web:** www.sohohouselondon.com
**Reg No:** 2864389 **Estd:** 1995 Private Limited Company
**Line of Business:** Licensed restaurants
**Trading Style:** Boheme Kitchen and Bar
**Issued Capital:** £1,995
**Managing Director:** N K Jones
**Co. Secretary:** Guy Williams
**Responsibilities**
**Marketing:** Jamie Caring *(Chief Marketing Officer)*
**IT:** Simon Monday *(IT Manager)*
**Branches:** Soho House Uk Ltd, 19-21 Old Compton Street, London W1D 5JJ
**US SIC:** 5812, 5813
**UK SIC:** 66110, 66200
**Auditors:** BDO LLP

| | 29-12-13 | 30-12-12 | 01-12-12 |
|---|---|---|---|
| TO | 73,346,615 | 65,339,275 | 63,944,961 |
| P/L | (2,230,797) | 1,280,776 | 6,071,183 |
| NW | 15,725,450 | 16,226,480 | 13,396,809 |
| WC | (1,881,320) | (9,386,406) | 6,534,771 |
| Emp. | 1,303 | 1,247 | 1,201 |

DUNS 28-879-0371
## Soho Theatre Co Ltd
21 Dean Street, Soho, London W1D 3NE
**Tel:** 02072875060
**Web:** www.sohotheatre.com
**Reg No:** 1151823 **Estd:** 1969 Private Company Limited By Guarantee
**Line of Business:** Artistic and literary creation and interpretation
**Directors:** O Agboluaje, R C Wingate, Ms B H Hollond, H Farsi, Ms S Robertson, N Mendoza, C Yu, Ms C J Ward
**Co. Secretary:** Mark Godfrey
**Responsibilities**
**Senior:** David Aukin *(Director)*, Shaparak Khorsandi *(Director)*, Lynne Kirwin *(Director)*, Catherine Mc Kinney *(general manager)*, Michael Naughton *(Manager)*
**US SIC:** 7999 **UK SIC:** 97913
**Auditors:** Marcusfield Dodia & Company
**Bankers:** The Royal Bank Of Scotland Plc (16-00-30)

| | 31-03-14 | 31-03-13 | 31-03-12 |
|---|---|---|---|
| TO | 5,150,502 | 3,908,581 | 3,645,824 |
| P/L | 20,326 | (61,007) | (18,468) |
| NW | 4,832,353 | 4,812,027 | 4,873,034 |
| WC | 329,568 | 194,030 | 120,971 |
| Emp. | 60 | 56 | 52 |

DUNS 50-703-2878
## Soho's Original Book Shop
12 Brewer Street, London W1F 0SF
**Tel:** 020-7494-1615
**Web:** www.sohobooks.co.uk
**Estd:** 1995 Proprietorship
**Line of Business:** Book retailers
**Proprietor:** A Poulton
**Responsibilities**
**Senior:** Nick Poulton *(Manager)*
**US SIC:** 5942 **UK SIC:** 65300
**Bankers:** Barclays Bank Plc (20-36-47)
**Employees:** 60

DUNS 28-835-9193
## The Soil Association Ltd
South Plaza, Marlborough Street, Bristol, Avon BS1 3NX
**Web:** www.soilassociation.org
**Reg No:** 0409726 **Estd:** 1946 Private Company Limited By Guarantee
**Line of Business:** Charities and charitable organisations
**Trading Style:** The Soil Association, Food for Life Partnership
**Directors:** D K Overton, G R Matravers, O H Dowding, J E Mccormick, J N Woodhouse, O G Ni Chionna, Ms A S Allott, N A Canetty-Clarke
**Co. Secretary:** Geoffrey Truscott
**Responsibilities**
**Senior:** Henen Browning *(Chief Executive)*, Clare Owens *(Director)*, Gabriel Scally *(Director)*, Charles Weston *(Director)*
**Sales:** Mike King *(Business Development Manager)*
**US SIC:** 8699 **UK SIC:** 96902
**Auditors:** Baker Tilly UK Audit LLP
**Bankers:** HSBC Bank plc (40-14-13)

| | 31-03-14 | 31-03-13 | 31-03-12 |
|---|---|---|---|
| TO | 11,349,179 | 8,922,361 | 9,865,701 |
| P/L | 926,147 | 552,569 | (61,212) |
| NW | 3,971,075 | 4,967,221 | 4,409,354 |
| WC | 1,712,417 | 1,002,413 | 448,434 |
| Emp. | 193 | 164 | 182 |

DUNS 22-809-6954 **Imp-Exp**
## Soil Machine Dynamics Ltd
**(Subsidiary of:** Specialist Machine Developments (Smd) Ltd)
Turbinia Works, Wallsend, Tyne and Wear NE28 6UZ
**Tel:** 0191-234-2222
**Web:** http://smd.co.uk
**Reg No:** 1028571 **VAT No:** 499947648
**Estd:** 1971 Private Limited Company
**Line of Business:** Manufacturers and designers of marine electronic equipment
**Export Markets:** U S A, Japan, E U
**Export Sales:** £23,818,790
**Trading Style:** Smd Hydrovision
**Issued Capital:** £100
**Principals:** J P Reece *(Managing)*, A Hodgson, A D Sims, C J Gill, P R Atkinson, M T Jones
**Co. Secretary:** Richard Howarth
**Responsibilities**
**Senior:** Michelle Christer *(Office Manager)*
**Admin:** Michelle Christer *(Office Manager)*
**HR:** Michelle Christer *(Office Manager)*
**Operations:** Steve Shoulder *(Chief Operating Officer)*
**Branches:** Soil Machine Dynamics Ltd, Davy Bank, Wallsend, Tyne and Wear NE28 6UZ
**US SIC:** 3811, 3549, 3643
**UK SIC:** 37100, 32212, 34203
**Auditors:** Ernst & Young LLP
**Bankers:** Barclays Bank Plc (20-59-42)

| | 31-12-13 | 31-12-12 | 31-12-11 |
|---|---|---|---|
| TO | 73,935,054 | 127,017,963 | 95,037,625 |
| P/L | 2,752,097 | 6,292,581 | 8,711,349 |
| NW | 43,013,057 | 40,170,504 | 35,480,887 |
| WC | 38,541,912 | 35,539,201 | 32,342,895 |
| Emp. | 308 | 328 | 228 |

DUNS 21-027-3868
## Soil Mechanics Ltd
**(Subsidiary of:** Inspicio Environmental Services Group Ltd)
Askern Road, Carcroft, Doncaster, South Yorkshire DN6 8DG
**Tel:** 01302723456 **Fax:** 01302-725240
**Web:** www.esg.co.uk
**Reg No:** 0384108 **Estd:** 1943 Private Limited Company
**Line of Business:** Site investigation services
**Issued Capital:** £1,250,000
**Directors:** A C Bolter, I Sparks
**Responsibilities**
**Senior:** Kevin Goldbury-West *(Manager)*, Karen Lomax *(Facilities Manager)*, Rebecca Savage *(Marketing)*, Alexander Sleeth *(Manager)*, Kevan West *(Manager)*
**Marketing:** Rebecca Savage *(Marketing)*
**IT:** Jerry Lane *(Computer Manager)*
**Facilities:** Jacky Foley *(Facilities Manager)*, Karen Lomax *(Facilities Manager)*
**Branches:** Soil Mechanics Ltd, Geotechnical House, Unit 18, Deeside, Clwyd CH5 2LR
**US SIC:** 8911 **UK SIC:** 83701
**Bankers:** National Westminster Bank Plc (50-00-00)

| | 31-12-13 | 31-12-12 | 31-12-11 |
|---|---|---|---|
| TA | 1,250,000 | 1,250,000 | 1,250,000 |
| NW | 1,250,000 | 1,250,000 | 1,250,000 |

DUNS 34-616-1185 **Imp-Exp**
## Sojitz Europe Plc
7th Floor, The Northern & Shell Building, 10 Lower Thames Street, London EC3R 6EQ
**Tel:** 02073377800
**Web:** www.sojitz.com
**Reg No:** 2753531 **VAT No:** 396971386
**Estd:** 1992 Public Limited Company
**Line of Business:** Fish merchants (wholesale)
**Issued Capital:** £1.331E+10
**Directors:** S Dantani, T Yoshimura, I Konno
**Co. Secretary:** John Emmerson
**Responsibilities**
**Senior:** Tetsuya Konoda *(Manager)*, Hirofumi Suganuma *(Manager)*
**US SIC:** 5146, 5052, 5161, 5199
**UK SIC:** 61700, 61200, 61900
**Auditors:** KPMG Audit PLC

| | 31-03-14 | 31-03-13 | 31-03-12 |
|---|---|---|---|
| TO | 380,171,000 | 425,407,000 | 604,186,000 |
| P/L | 4,795,000 | (763,000) | 5,639,000 |
| NW | 157,481,000 | 159,712,000 | 161,282,000 |
| WC | 151,636,000 | 142,014,000 | 141,623,000 |
| Emp. | 217 | 220 | 226 |

DUNS 21-016-9698
## Sojourn Hotels Llp
Haydon House 296 Joel Street, Pinner, Middlesex HA5 2PY
**Tel:** 02084299946 **Fax:** 02088682945
**Web:** www.sojournhotels.co.uk
**Reg No:** 0331910OC **Estd:** 2007 Private Limited Company
**Line of Business:** Hotels
**Responsibilities**
**Senior:** Clive Viner *(Designated Limited Liability P)*
**US SIC:** 7011 **UK SIC:** 66500

| | 30-04-14 | 30-04-13 | 30-04-12 |
|---|---|---|---|
| TO | 14,868,524 | 10,975,662 | 4,376,880 |
| P/L | (536,186) | (1,363,877) | (1,131,236) |
| NW | (4,626,331) | (3,285,937) | (1,814,687) |
| WC | (9,659,762) | (12,324,927) | 283,248 |
| Emp. | 284 | 268 | 98 |

DUNS 23-572-2654 **Imp**
## Solar Century Holdings Ltd
50 Great Sutton Street, London EC1V 0DF
**Tel:** 020-7549-1000 **Fax:** 020-7549-1001
**Web:** www.solarcentury.com
**Reg No:** 3570325 **VAT No:** 743874893
**Estd:** 1999 Private Limited Company
**Line of Business:** Other construction work involving special trades
**Export Sales:** £5,460,000
**Trading Style:** Solarcentury
**Issued Capital:** £36,463
**Directors:** G Le Sueur, Dr P Comberg, Ms P Splinter, S S Salty, F H Van Den Heuvel, N G Perry, A M Eggenberg, S M Hansen
**Co. Secretary:** John Faulks
**Responsibilities**
**Senior:** Ronald McCullagh *(Manager)*
**Sales:** Susannah Wood *(Sales Director)*
**HR:** Helen Roper *(Training Manager)*
**Branches:** Solar Century Holdings Ltd, Cologne Court, Block E, Unit E1, Sunbury-On-Thames, Middlesex TW16 7EB
**US SIC:** 3643, 1711
**UK SIC:** 34203, 50300
**Auditors:** Deloitte LLP
**Bankers:** National Westminster Bank Plc (60-50-06)

| | 31-03-14 | 31-03-13 | 31-03-12 |
|---|---|---|---|
| TO | 109,192,000 | 80,472,274 | 61,761,369 |
| P/L | 3,428,000 | 1,864,330 | 788,852 |
| NW | 19,786,000 | 17,984,667 | 15,161,475 |
| WC | 20,837,000 | 16,055,779 | 13,580,852 |
| Emp. | 132 | 118 | 125 |

DUNS 21-585-7133
## Solar Co-Op Supermarkets
9 Market Hill, Framlingham, Woodbridge, Suffolk IP13 9AL
**Tel:** 01728621415
**Estd:** 2011
**Line of Business:** Supermarkets
**Proprietor:** A Kerry
**US SIC:** 5411 **UK SIC:** 64100
**Employees:** 100

DUNS 50-131-9487
## Solar Communications Ltd
**(Subsidiary of:** Solar Communications Group Ltd)
Sheldon Business Park, Chippenham, Wiltshire SN14 0SQ
**Tel:** 08450730001 **Fax:** 08450730002
**Web:** www.solar.co.uk
**Reg No:** 2319958 **VAT No:** 520127009
**Estd:** 1988 Private Limited Company
**Line of Business:** Telecommunications
**Issued Capital:** £1,000
**Directors:** B L Marnham, M Colquhoun, S M Lewis
**Co. Secretary:** John Colquhoun
**US SIC:** 4899, 1731
**UK SIC:** 79020, 50300
**Auditors:** Target Consulting Ltd
**Bankers:** Lloyds TSB Bank plc (30-92-13)

| | 31-12-13 | 31-12-12 | 31-12-11 |
|---|---|---|---|
| TO | 9,210,740 | 9,361,226 | 8,590,427 |
| P/L | 676,141 | 685,712 | 512,014 |
| NW | 1,297,258 | 940,168 | 549,700 |
| WC | 1,133,598 | 857,802 | 462,766 |
| Emp. | 56 | 47 | N/A |

DUNS 73-966-8999
## Solar Fusion Ltd.
**(Subsidiary of:** Lanesborough Holdings Ltd)
Oxford House, Bournemouth, Dorset BH8 8HA
**Tel:** 01202208208
**Web:** www.solarfusionltd.co.uk
**Reg No:** 5217797 **Estd:** 2004 Private Limited Company
**Line of Business:** Manufacture of electronic valves and tubes and other electronic components
**Issued Capital:** £100
**Directors:** A M Tyler, M J Byrne, Mrs A Edge, K Edge, M J Byrne
**US SIC:** 3999, 1731

**UK SIC:** 49590, 50300

| | 31-08-13 | 31-08-12 | 31-08-11 |
|---|---|---|---|
| TO | 5,602,152 | 11,762,076 | 12,705,480 |
| P/L | 7,021 | 2,128,523 | 3,389,844 |
| NW | 1,565,544 | 2,257,672 | 1,628,934 |
| WC | 1,444,813 | 2,126,552 | 1,567,509 |
| Emp. | 76 | 77 | 50 |

---

**DUNS 77-101-8108**

## Solar Windows Ltd

Unit 15b Bedwas House Industrial Estate, Bedwas, Caerphilly, Mid Glamorgan CF83 8DW

**Tel:** 029-2085-8989 **Fax:** 029-2085-8960
**Web:** www.solarwindows.co.uk
**Reg No:** 2678809 **VAT No:** 484468308
**Estd:** 1992 Private Limited Company
**Line of Business:** Manufacturers and suppliers of pvc based products
**Issued Capital:** £100
**Director:** C P Lewis
**Co. Secretary:** Mrs Carol Lewis
**US SIC:** 3079, 3211
**UK SIC:** 48360, 24710
**Auditors:** Neil Hodge & Co Ltd
**Bankers:** Barclays Bank Plc (20-10-26)

| | 31-10-13 | 31-10-12 | 31-10-11 |
|---|---|---|---|
| TO | 10,217,984 | 10,235,712 | 10,592,176 |
| P/L | 440,678 | 1,404,783 | 1,567,371 |
| NW | 6,027,786 | 5,849,892 | 4,995,106 |
| WC | 5,654,754 | 5,353,229 | 4,633,537 |
| Emp. | 66 | 64 | 62 |

---

**DUNS 23 076 0887**

## Solaraid

17-19 Oval Way, London SE11 5RR

**Tel:** 02072780400
**Web:** www.solar-aid.org
**Reg No:** 3867741 **Estd:** 2006 Private Company Limited By Guarantee
**Line of Business:** Other business activities not elsewhere classified
**Directors:** P D Angier, D J Newman, J K Leggett
**Co. Secretary:** Ms Ruth Dobson
**Responsibilities**
**Senior:** Gerrard Graf (Manager)
**US SIC:** 7399 **UK SIC:** 83954
**Auditors:** Appleby & Wood
**Bankers:** The Co-Operative Bank Plc (08-90-99)

| | 31-03-14 | 31-03-13 | 31-03-12 |
|---|---|---|---|
| TO | 6,332,904 | 3,590,476 | 2,696,752 |
| P/L | 305,249 | (890,897) | (660,593) |
| NW | 915,204 | 600,970 | 1,328,556 |
| WC | 1,039,819 | 607,626 | 1,328,556 |
| Emp. | 101 | 81 | 44 |

---

**DUNS 21-153-9344** **Imp**

## Solarcrown Uk Ltd

(**Subsidiary of:** Green Performance Ltd)
112b Cornwall St South, Glasgow, Lanarkshire G41 1AA

**Tel:** 01416118698
**Web:** www.solarkinguk.com
**Reg No:** 6689728 **Estd:** 2008 Private Limited Company
**Line of Business:** Manufacture of electronic valves and tubes and other electronic components
**Trading Style:** Solarking Uk
**Issued Capital:** £100
**Director:** A Mikhail
**Responsibilities**
**Senior:** Ezra Winnstone (Regional Manager)
**Branches:** Solarcrown Uk Ltd T/A Solarking Uk, Britannia House, Prince Of Wales Rd, NR1 1BL Norwich
**US SIC:** 3999, 5065, 1731
**UK SIC:** 49590, 61500, 50300
**Auditors:** RSM Tenon Audit Ltd

| | 30-11-13 | 31-03-13 | 31-11-12 |
|---|---|---|---|
| TO | 11,776,315 | 10,071,952 | N/A |
| P/L | 1,741,159 | (902,223) | N/A |
| NW | 642,651 | (562,963) | 3,293,639 |
| WC | 959,118 | (412,662) | 2,810,343 |
| Emp. | 160 | 95 | N/A |

---

**DUNS 42-453-6899** **Imp**

## Solarflare Communications Ltd

Block 7 Westbrook Centre, Milton Road, Cambridge, Cambridgeshire CB4 1YG

**Web:** www.solarflare.com
**Reg No:** 4441386 **Estd:** 2014 Private Limited Company
**Line of Business:** Research and laboratory based activities
**Issued Capital:** £10,500
**Directors:** C W Cotton, Ms M J Abalos
**Co. Secretary:** Dr Derek Roberts
**US SIC:** 7391 **UK SIC:** 94000
**Auditors:** PricewaterhouseCoopers LLP

| | 31-12-13 | 31-12-12 | 31-12-11 |
|---|---|---|---|
| TO | 7,289,306 | 6,254,633 | 4,665,242 |
| P/L | 662,329 | 546,249 | 427,314 |
| NW | 3,245,447 | 2,480,154 | 1,898,859 |
| WC | 2,854,537 | 2,029,619 | 1,475,891 |
| Emp. | 70 | 51 | 41 |

---

**DUNS 22-201-8454** **Imp-Exp**

## Solartron Metrology Ltd

(**Subsidiary of:** Ametek European Holdings Ltd)
Steyning Way, Bognor Regis, West Sussex PO22 9SB

**Tel:** 01243833300
**Web:** www.solartronmetrology.com
**Reg No:** 4220056 **Estd:** 1993 Private Limited Company
**Line of Business:** Manufacture of electronic instruments and appliances for measuring, checking, testing, navigating and other purposes, except industrial process control equipment
**Issued Capital:** £12,000,001
**Directors:** B P Wilson, T C Bache
**Co. Secretary:** David Coley
**Responsibilities**
**Finance:** Karen Pearce (Financial Director)
**Marketing:** Mark Claxton (Sales and Marketing Director)
**Sales:** Mark Claxton (Sales and Marketing Director)
**IT:** Michael Cocker (IT Manager)
**Purchasing:** Natalie Pullen (Supply Chain Manager)
**Engineering:** Nick Deadman (Engineering Director)
**US SIC:** 3829 **UK SIC:** 37100
**Bankers:** National Westminster Bank Plc (56-00-55)

| | 31-12-13 | 31-12-12 | 31-12-11 |
|---|---|---|---|
| TO | 18,681,000 | 19,970,000 | 21,857,000 |
| P/L | 5,773,000 | 6,600,000 | 7,002,000 |
| NW | 16,410,000 | 16,846,000 | 16,194,000 |
| WC | 13,930,000 | 14,526,000 | 13,947,000 |
| Emp. | 139 | 139 | 134 |

---

**DUNS 21-324-3421**

## Solarwall Ltd

Green Lane Trading Estate, Clifton, York, North Yorkshire YO30 5PY

**Tel:** 01904-690824
**Web:** www.solarwall.co.uk
**Reg No:** 1340753 **VAT No:** 313442985
**Estd:** 1977 Private Limited Company
**Line of Business:** Other building installation
**Issued Capital:** £1,550
**Directors:** Ms S P Lamb, Mrs R Partridge
**Co. Secretary:** Grant Henderson
**Responsibilities**
**Health & Safety:** Dean Abbott (Health & Safety Director)
**US SIC:** 1796, 1799
**UK SIC:** 50400, 50000
**Bankers:** National Westminster Bank Plc (55-81-11)

| | 30-09-14 | 30-09-13 | 30-09-12 |
|---|---|---|---|
| TA | 982,716 | 860,865 | 1,034,622 |
| NW | (126,470) | (185,723) | (61,752) |
| WC | (352,874) | (327,378) | (180,162) |

---

**DUNS 77-044-7654**

## Soldata Ltd

Unit 9 Spectrum West, St Laurence Avenue, 20/20 Business Estate, Maidstone, Kent ME16 0LL

**Tel:** 01622-609920 **Fax:** 01622-609950
**Web:** www.soldata.co.uk
**Reg No:** 2667726 **Estd:** 2000 Private Limited Company
**Line of Business:** Other construction work involving special trades
**Export Sales:** £121,745
**Issued Capital:** £20,000
**Directors:** J G La Fonta, M L Beth, P J Hines, G J Trafford
**Co. Secretary:** Graham Trafford
**US SIC:** 1799 **UK SIC:** 50000
**Auditors:** KPMG LLP
**Bankers:** Barclays Bank Plc (20-02-53)

| | 31-12-13 | 31-12-12 | 31-12-11 |
|---|---|---|---|
| TO | 7,788,000 | 8,391,993 | 7,164,322 |
| P/L | 107,577 | 295,890 | 112,303 |
| NW | 1,641,365 | 1,458,998 | 1,637,898 |
| WC | 1,641,365 | 1,458,998 | 1,637,898 |
| Emp. | 68 | 58 | 48 |

---

**DUNS 21-804-4704**

## Soldiers' Sailors' and Airmen's Families Association (Warwi

3 Rugby Road, Weston Under Wetherley, Leamington Spa, Warwickshire CV33 9BW

**Web:** www.nivus.com
**Estd:** 2012
**Line of Business:** Charities and charitable organisations
**US SIC:** 6732 **UK SIC:** 83100
**Employees:** 120

---

**DUNS 21-736-6574**

## Solent Body Builders & Repairs Ltd

4 Cockerell Close, Fareham, Hampshire PO15 5SR

**Tel:** 01489-575611 **Fax:** 01489-578780
**Web:** www.solentbodybuilders.co.uk
**Reg No:** 1006087 **Estd:** 1971 Private Limited Company
**Line of Business:** Van and truck bodybuilders and repairers
**Trading Style:** Solent Body Builders & Repairs Ltd
**Issued Capital:** £2,802
**Director:** M D Sainsbury
**Co. Secretary:** Kevin Sainsbury
**Responsibilities**
**Health & Safety:** Philip Sprack (Quality Manager)
**Branches:** Solent Body Builders & Repairs Ltd, The I O Centre, Unit 5, Fareham, Hampshire PO15 5RU
**US SIC:** 3713, 7539
**UK SIC:** 35201, 67100
**Auditors:** Wettone Matthews Ltd
**Bankers:** HSBC Bank plc (40-42-58)

| | 31-03-14 | 31-03-13 | 31-03-12 |
|---|---|---|---|
| TA | 1,113,931 | 971,698 | 1,023,095 |
| NW | 371,553 | 338,028 | 414,790 |
| WC | 297,794 | 267,964 | 341,577 |

---

**DUNS 29-503-5695**

## Solent Butchers Ltd

2 Dundas Lane, Portsmouth, Hampshire PO3 5SD

**Tel:** 023-9266-9228 **Fax:** 023-9266-9227
**Web:** www.solentbutchers.co.uk
**Reg No:** 1866754 **VAT No:** 381009179
**Estd:** 1984 Private Limited Company
**Line of Business:** Meat wholesalers
**Issued Capital:** £207
**Director:** S Cristofoli
**Co. Secretary:** Mark Cristofoll
**US SIC:** 5147 **UK SIC:** 61700
**Auditors:** CW Fellowes Ltd
**Bankers:** Barclays Bank Plc (20-69-34)

| | 31-01-14 | 31-01-13 | 31-01-12 |
|---|---|---|---|
| TO | 8,037,992 | 7,370,489 | 7,081,974 |
| P/L | 197,552 | 60,647 | (44,665) |
| NW | 554,328 | 480,772 | 436,704 |
| WC | 85,534 | 80,857 | 42,943 |
| Emp. | 64 | 55 | 53 |

---

**DUNS 23-791-3111**

## Solent Cliffs Nursing Home Ltd

2 Cliff Road, Fareham, Hampshire PO14 3JS

**Tel:** 01329662047 **Fax:** 01329665429
**Web:** www.brookvalehealthcare.co.uk
**Reg No:** 3784089 **Estd:** 2000 Private Limited Company
**Line of Business:** Medical nursing home activities
**Issued Capital:** £25,000
**Directors:** A Asaria, M Allana
**Co. Secretary:** Mrs Sheila Asaria
**Responsibilities**
**Senior:** Helen Davison (Manager)
**Branches:** Solent Cliffs Nursing Home Ltd, 2 Cliff Road, Fareham, Hampshire PO14 3JS
**US SIC:** 8051 **UK SIC:** 95100

| | 30-06-13 | 30-06-12 | 30-06-11 |
|---|---|---|---|
| TA | 1,760,129 | 1,633,302 | 1,564,168 |
| NW | 509,805 | 362,973 | 318,615 |
| WC | 263,497 | 304,836 | 280,132 |

---

**DUNS 22-001-1428**

## Solent Mind

28 The Avenue, Southampton, Hampshire SO17 1XN

**Tel:** 02380334977 **Fax:** 023-8020-8902
**Web:** www.solentmind.org.uk
**Reg No:** 4004500 **Estd:** 2000 Private Company Limited By Guarantee
**Line of Business:** Social work activities
**Directors:** Mrs C I Duncan, C J Martin, R I Cassy, M York, A A Beg, B Palmer, Dr P R Hanlon, Ms P A Shirley
**Co. Secretary:** Richard Barritt
**Responsibilities**
**IT:** Sebastian Rupik (IT Manager)
**US SIC:** 7399, 8321
**UK SIC:** 83954, 96111
**Auditors:** Sheen Stickland LLP
**Bankers:** Unity Trust Bank Plc (08-60-01)

| | 31-03-14 | 31-03-13 | 31-03-12 |
|---|---|---|---|
| TO | 4,673,107 | 4,345,883 | 3,975,527 |
| P/L | 56,691 | 56,208 | 116,300 |
| NW | 2,149,526 | 2,105,183 | 2,090,095 |
| WC | 1,235,218 | 1,126,630 | 1,086,778 |
| Emp. | 127 | 112 | 96 |

---

**DUNS 21-661-5945**

## Solex Legal Services Ltd

(**Subsidiary of:** Legal Investments Ltd)
The Ground Floor, 1 Elmfield Park, Bromley, Kent BR1 1LU

**Tel:** 02084602237
**Web:** www.solexlegalservices.com
**Reg No:** 7171613 **Estd:** 2010 Private Limited Company
**Line of Business:** Solicitors
**Issued Capital:** £1,001
**Directors:** J C Walker, M Taylor, D R Green
**Co. Secretary:** Nigel Burgess
**Responsibilities**
**Senior:** Caroline Havers (Manager)
**US SIC:** 8111 **UK SIC:** 83500

| | 31-12-12 | 31-12-11 | 30-12-11 |
|---|---|---|---|
| TA | 1,514,195 | 1,854,802 | 2,031,873 |
| NW | 1,252,101 | 505,124 | 644,314 |
| WC | 1,205,042 | 1,449,864 | 1,577,342 |

---

**DUNS 21-120-9642**

## The Solicitors Regulation Authority

Ipsley Court, Berrington Close, Redditch, Worcestershire B98 0TD

**Tel:** 03706062555
**Web:** www.fleindia.com
**Estd:** 2011
**Line of Business:** Trade assoc & regulatory bodies
**Responsibilities**
**Senior:** Antony Townsend (Chief Executive)
**Marketing:** Angeline Burton (Director of Communications)
**US SIC:** 8111 **UK SIC:** 83500
**Employees:** 300

---

**DUNS 23-661-7663** **Imp**

## Solid Solutions Management Ltd

Innovation Centre, Warwick, Warwickshire CV34 6UW

**Tel:** 01926623160
**Web:** www.solidsolutions.co.uk
**Reg No:** 3656695 **Estd:** 1999 Private Limited Company
**Line of Business:** Computer consumables suppliers
**Trading Style:** Solid Solutions
**Issued Capital:** £100
**Directors:** A J Sampson, S C Turner
**Co. Secretary:** Mrs Katharine Sampson
**Responsibilities**
**Senior:** Karen Aston (Manager), John Perrin (Manager)
**Branches:** Solid Solutions Management Ltd, E-Volve Centre, Cygnet Way, Rainton Bridge Business Park South, Houghton Le Spring, Tyne and Wear DH4 5QY
**US SIC:** 7339, 7379
**UK SIC:** 83954, 83940
**Auditors:** Cooper Adams Ltd

| | 31-03-14 | 31-03-13 | 31-03-12 |
|---|---|---|---|
| TO | 14,859,950 | 12,538,086 | 12,044,672 |
| P/L | 2,405,705 | 1,929,620 | 1,552,504 |
| NW | 2,635,010 | 2,293,681 | 1,893,706 |
| WC | 2,502,939 | 2,193,427 | 1,734,965 |
| Emp. | 66 | 59 | 51 |

---

**DUNS 21-734-8846**

## Solid State Plc

Ravensbank Business Park, Redditch, Worcestershire B98 9EY

**Tel:** 01527830800 **Fax:** 01527830801
**Web:** www.sssplc.com
**Reg No:** 0771335 **Estd:** 1963 Public Limited Company
**Line of Business:** Manufacturers and distributors of electronic components
**Export Sales:** £3,826,633
**Issued Capital:** £359
**Principals:** G S Marsh (Managing), J L Macmichael, J M Lavery, A B Frere
**Co. Secretary:** Peter Haining
**Responsibilities**
**Senior:** Gordon Comben (Director)
**Branches:** Solid State Plc, 111-117 Regent St, Kingswood, Bristol, Avon BS15 8LJ
**US SIC:** 6711 **UK SIC:** 83962
**Auditors:** Haysmacintyre
**Bankers:** HSBC Bank plc (40-44-20)

| | 31-03-14 | 31-03-13 | 31-03-12 |
|---|---|---|---|
| TO | 32,085,432 | 31,494,977 | 25,874,151 |
| P/L | 2,153,709 | 1,770,433 | 1,599,144 |
| NW | 5,471,603 | 3,884,331 | 2,680,588 |
| WC | 4,817,470 | 3,020,810 | 1,917,221 |
| Emp. | 138 | 114 | 96 |

---

**DUNS 21-810-6474** **Exp**

## Solid Swivel Co Ltd

Porters Field Road, Cradley Heath, West Midlands B64 7BL

**Tel:** 01384-636421
**Web:** www.solidswivel.co.uk
**Reg No:** 0487248 **VAT No:** 277222063
**Estd:** 1910 Private Limited Company
**Line of Business:** Blacksmiths

**Export Markets:** W Europe, Middle East, U S A, Africa, Australasia, Canada#
**Issued Capital:** £10,667
**Principals:** W G Perry *(Managing)*, Ms E P Perry
**Co. Secretary:** Peter Killey
**US SIC:** 3534, 3568
**UK SIC:** 32553, 32613
**Auditors:** Moore Stephens
**Bankers:** Barclays Bank Plc (20-27-17)

| | 31-03-14 | 31-03-13 | 31-03-12 |
|---|---|---|---|
| TA | 2,304,841 | 2,382,504 | 2,365,605 |
| NW | 1,564,211 | 1,462,340 | 1,392,602 |
| WC | 1,131,695 | 1,008,346 | 947,001 |

DUNS 76-680-8273 **Imp-Exp**

### Solideal U K Ltd

(**Subsidiary of:** Camso Holding Luxembourg Sa)
Unit 35a, Cowbridge, South Glamorgan CF71 7PF
**Tel:** 01446-774914 **Fax:** 01446-775410
**Web:** www.solidealuk.com
**Reg No:** 2589003 **VAT No:** 587917671
**Estd:** 1991 Private Limited Company
**Line of Business:** Sale of motor vehicle parts and accessories
**Export Markets:** Europe
**Issued Capital:** £909,312
**Directors:** J V Howe, F J Augnet
**Co. Secretary:** Ms Ann Barnaby
**Branches:** Solideal U K Ltd, Unit B3, Walter Leigh Way, Moss Industrial Estate, Leigh, Lancashire WN7 3PT
**US SIC:** 5531 **UK SIC:** 65100
**Auditors:** Ernst & Young LLP
**Bankers:** National Westminster Bank Plc (51-81-29)

| | 31-03-14 | 31-03-13 | 31-03-12 |
|---|---|---|---|
| TO | 18,924,265 | 18,623,577 | 20,468,616 |
| P/L | 329,069 | 610,500 | 1,410,417 |
| NW | 3,893,795 | 3,642,531 | 3,181,004 |
| WC | 3,504,137 | 3,255,147 | 2,806,648 |
| Emp. | 76 | 72 | 71 |

DUNS 34-627-5196

### Solidor Ltd

(**Subsidiary of:** Passivdor Ltd)
Solidor House Smithpool Road, Fenton, Stoke-On-Trent, Staffordshire ST4 4PW
**Tel:** 01782847300
**Web:** www.solidor.co.uk
**Reg No:** 5433881 **Estd:** 2005 Private Limited Company
**Line of Business:** Manufacture of other plastic products
**Trading Style:** Nice Doors Panel
**Issued Capital:** £125
**Directors:** P Mifsud, L Williams, G A Mobley, J Martoccia
**Co. Secretary:** Carlton Hopley
**US SIC:** 3442, 3999
**UK SIC:** 31420, 49590
**Auditors:** Dean Statham LLP

| | 31-03-14 | 31-03-13 | 31-03-12 |
|---|---|---|---|
| TA | 5,789,391 | 3,244,808 | 2,106,354 |
| NW | 3,462,437 | 1,763,412 | 930,805 |
| WC | 2,568,200 | 1,265,156 | 665,753 |

DUNS 64-092-2621 **Imp**

### Solidworks R & D Ltd

(**Subsidiary of:** Dassault Systemes)
2 Quayside, Cambridge, Cambridgeshire CB5 8AB
**Web:** www.solidworks.co.uk
**Reg No:** 3487323 **Estd:** 1997 Private Limited Company
**Line of Business:** Other software consultancy and supply
**Export Sales:** £7,847,500
**Issued Capital:** £234,755
**Directors:** G Norrie, S J Chadwick
**Co. Secretary:** Mark Neil
**Responsibilities**
**Senior:** Austin O'Malley *(Manager)*
**Finance:** Sally Dowding *(Financial Director)*
**IT:** Emma Condon *(IT Manager)*
**HR:** Sally Dowding *(Financial Director)*
**Health & Safety:** Sally Dowding *(Financial Director)*
**US SIC:** 7379 **UK SIC:** 83940
**Auditors:** B Z Alexander

| | 31-12-13 | 31-12-12 | 31-12-11 |
|---|---|---|---|
| TO | 7,847,500 | 7,544,299 | 9,013,900 |
| P/L | 377,717 | 359,264 | 429,222 |
| NW | 3,629,825 | 3,207,700 | 2,765,041 |
| WC | 3,425,899 | 2,946,103 | 2,554,437 |
| Emp. | 71 | 68 | 67 |

DUNS 22-741-5817

### Solihull College

Blossomfield Road, Solihull, West Midlands B91 1SB
**Web:** www.solihull.ac.uk
**VAT No:** 614122194 **Estd:** 1993
**Line of Business:** Further education schools and colleges
**Principals:** T Moir *(Financial)*, C Flint, Ms A Myers, P Luscombe
**Responsibilities**
**Senior:** Brenda Sheils *(Principal)*, Brenda Shields *(Principal)*
**Marketing:** Dave Cooper *(Marketing Director)*
**IT:** Tony Lavelle *(IT Security Manager)*
**Health & Safety:** Lindsworth Mckenzie *(Health & Safety Officer)*
**Branches:** Solihull College, Keepers Lodge, Chelmsley Rd, Birmingham, West Midlands B37 7RS
**US SIC:** 9121, 8221
**UK SIC:** 91110, 93100
**Bankers:** National Westminster Bank Plc (55-50-15)
**Employees:** 750

DUNS 77-777-5586

### Solihull Community Care Trust

Olton Wharf, Richmond Road, Solihull, West Midlands B92 7RN
**Tel:** 0121-706-3630
**Web:** www.scct.co.uk
**Reg No:** 3023650 **Estd:** 1995 Private Limited Company
**Line of Business:** Social work activities without accommodation
**Director:** D C Mattocks
**Co. Secretary:** Dennis Lawrence
**US SIC:** 8321 **UK SIC:** 96111
**Auditors:** Advance 2001
**Bankers:** Lloyds TSB Bank plc (30-97-78)
**Employees:** 70

DUNS 42-474-9542

### Solihull Community Housing Ltd

Endeavour House, Meriden Drive, Birmingham, West Midlands B37 6BX
**Fax:** 0121-779-8820
**Web:** www.solihullcommunityhousing.org.uk
**Reg No:** 4462630 **Estd:** 2002 Private Company Limited By Guarantee
**Line of Business:** Other letting of own property
**Directors:** C J Horrocks, A M Mackiewicz, Ms D A Evans, J W Potts, Mrs B A Maynard, C A Williams, Ms N A Drayson, Dr A G Lane
**Co. Secretary:** Mary Moroney-Barnett
**Responsibilities**
**Senior:** Wendy Blackburn *(Director)*, Steven Boyd *(Chief Executive)*, Stephen Partridge *(Education Audiologist)*
**HR:** Sheena Heaton *(Human Resources Coordinator)*
**US SIC:** 6519 **UK SIC:** 85000
**Auditors:** Grant Thornton UK LLP
**Bankers:** Barclays Bank Plc (20-07-71)

| | 31-03-14 | 31-03-13 | 31-03-12 |
|---|---|---|---|
| TO | 36,889,000 | 32,393,000 | 30,432,000 |
| P/L | (2,032,000) | (280,000) | 424,000 |
| NW | (4,768,000) | (10,696,000) | (5,800,000) |
| WC | 1,319,000 | 1,948,000 | 1,753,000 |
| Emp. | 300 | 306 | 335 |

DUNS 21-585-7908

### Solihull Fire Station

Fire Station, Solihull, West Midlands B91 1QY
**Web:** www.wmfs.net
**Estd:** 2011 Proprietorship
**Line of Business:** Fire stations
**Proprietor:** B Diamond
**US SIC:** 9224 **UK SIC:** 91400
**Employees:** 60

DUNS 42-422-8807

### Solihull Healthcare N H S Trust

Friars Gate 1011 Stratford Road, Solihull, West Midlands B90 4BN
**Tel:** 01217138399
**Web:** www.solihullccg.nhs.uk
**Estd:** 1994
**Line of Business:** Nhs clinics
**Principals:** Ms C Griffiths *(Chairman)*, P Ashton
**Branches:** Solihull Healthcare N H S Trust, 3 Marston Drive, Birmingham, West Midlands B37 6BD
**US SIC:** 8091 **UK SIC:** 95200
**Employees:** 1,250

DUNS 22-987-6230

### Solihull Metropolitan Borough Council

Central Depot, Solihull, West Midlands B91 2LW
**Web:** www.solihull.gov.uk
**VAT No:** 111979171 **Estd:** 2011
**Line of Business:** Driver and vehicle licensing agency
**Trading Style:** Smbc, Smbc Property Services, Solihull Council
**Principals:** D Howson *(Financial)*, J Wilson, D Nixon, Dr N Perry, M Hake *(Partner)*, J O'Callaghan *(Partner)*
**Responsibilities**
**Senior:** Anne Bettison *(Team Leader)*
**Branches:** Solihull Metropolitan Borough Council, Waterloo Avenue Chelmsley Wood, Birmingham, West Midlands B37 6QQ
**US SIC:** 9121 **UK SIC:** 91110
**Bankers:** National Westminster Bank Plc (55-50-15)
**Employees:** 3,000

DUNS 67-215-7943

### Solihull Moors Football Club (2007) Ltd

Damson Parkway, Solihull, West Midlands B91 2PP
**Tel:** 01217056770 **Fax:** 01217114045
**Web:** www.solihullmoorsfc.co.uk
**Reg No:** 6045572 **Estd:** 1970 Private Company Limited By Guarantee
**Line of Business:** Sports clubs
**Directors:** S M Hawker, S R Shipway, G G Davison, T Stevens
**Co. Secretary:** Ms Margaret Smith
**Responsibilities**
**Senior:** John Bignell *(Manager)*, Raymond Bird *(Manager)*, Nigel Collins *(Chairman)*, Terence Evans *(Manager)*, Godfrey George *(Manager)*
**US SIC:** 7999 **UK SIC:** 97913

| | 30-06-13 | 30-06-12 | 30-06-11 |
|---|---|---|---|
| TA | 107,190 | 76,624 | 85,049 |
| NW | (136,958) | (94,041) | (102,217) |
| WC | (109,504) | (124,495) | (133,480) |

DUNS 21-879-9818

### Solihull Police Station

Homer Road, Solihull, West Midlands B91 3QL
**Tel:** 01217126018
**Estd:** 2012
**Line of Business:** Police Force Services
**Responsibilities**
**Senior:** Deborah Hetherington *(Team Manager)*
**US SIC:** 9221 **UK SIC:** 91300
**Employees:** 550

DUNS 21-010-0816

### Solihull School

793 Warwick Road, 793 Warwick Road, Solihull, West Midlands B91 3DJ
**Tel:** 01217055803
**Web:** www.solsch.org.uk
**Reg No:** 6337650 **Estd:** 2007 Private Company Limited By Guarantee
**Line of Business:** Primary education
**Directors:** J A Shackleton, Ms L J Lunt, M A Cutler, M C Morris, Dr H M Gay, Mrs A L Lavery, M T Hopton, D J Kelly
**Co. Secretary:** Richard Bate
**Responsibilities**
**Senior:** Catherine Gilbert *(Director)*, Philip Griffiths *(Headmaster)*, Tristram Jones-Parry *(Director)*, Paul Mantle *(Director)*, Apollo Mulira *(Director)*
**Finance:** Christopher Warren *(Bursar)*
**Admin:** Lorraine Johnson *(Office Manager)*, Lisa Lese *(Office Manager)*
**US SIC:** 8211 **UK SIC:** 93200
**Bankers:** Lloyds TSB Bank plc (30-97-78)

| | 31-08-14 | 31-08-13 | 31-08-12 |
|---|---|---|---|
| TO | 11,298,578 | 11,108,312 | 10,630,302 |
| P/L | 424,655 | 801,238 | 666,294 |
| NW | 47,332,088 | 43,163,248 | 41,295,667 |
| WC | 6,428,857 | 2,757,653 | 1,809,649 |
| Emp. | 172 | 168 | 165 |

DUNS 21-232-0744

### Solihull Social Services

West Mall, Chelmsley Wood Shopping Centre, Birmingham, West Midlands B37 5TN
**Tel:** 0121-7884300
**Web:** www.solihull.gov.uk
**Proprietorship**
**Line of Business:** The dss
**Proprietor:** Mrs J Wilton
**Responsibilities**
**Senior:** Tina Russell *(Sector Manager)*
**US SIC:** 8321 **UK SIC:** 96111
**Employees:** 100

DUNS 73-639-4912

### Solitaire Homecare Services Ltd

Halesfield House, Birmingham, West Midlands B44 8NS
**Tel:** 0121-605-0084
**Web:** www.solitairehomecare.co.uk
**Reg No:** 4899791 **Estd:** 1994 Private Limited Company
**Line of Business:** Home care service providers
**Issued Capital:** £100
**Directors:** Ms S L Webster, G Webster
**Co. Secretary:** Ms Amy Webster
**US SIC:** 8811 **UK SIC:** 99000

| | 31-07-13 | 31-07-12 | 31-07-11 |
|---|---|---|---|
| TA | 157,621 | 153,359 | 110,720 |
| NW | 11,072 | 11,613 | 11,683 |
| WC | 9,874 | 10,696 | 10,992 |

DUNS 73-931-3802

### Soll Leisure Group

Abbey Close, Abingdon, Oxfordshire OX14 3JD
**Tel:** 01235530678
**Web:** www.soll-leisure.co.uk
**Reg No:** 5184388 **Estd:** 2004 Private Limited Company
**Line of Business:** Operation of swimming pools
**Directors:** F P Sambrook, R Booker, N K Robinson, P A Turner, T A Hampson
**Co. Secretary:** Mark Jaggers
**US SIC:** 7999 **UK SIC:** 97913

| | 31-03-13 | 31-03-12 | 31-03-11 |
|---|---|---|---|
| TA | 20,599 | 26,020 | 41,700 |
| NW | (50,358) | (15,066) | (9,551) |
| WC | (50,358) | (15,066) | (9,552) |

DUNS 73-931-3604

### Soll (Vale)

17 Milton Park, Milton, Abingdon, Oxfordshire OX14 4RS
**Tel:** 01235206777
**Web:** www.soll-leisure.co.uk
**Reg No:** 5184368 **Estd:** 2004 Private Company Limited By Guarantee
**Line of Business:** Other sporting activities not elsewhere classified
**Directors:** P Sambrook, R D Booker, N K Robinson, P A Turner, T A Hampson
**Co. Secretary:** Mark Jaggers
**Responsibilities**
**Senior:** Dave Morrell *(General Manager)*
**US SIC:** 7999 **UK SIC:** 97913

| | 31-03-14 | 31-03-13 | 31-03-12 |
|---|---|---|---|
| TO | 5,776,001 | 4,320,437 | 3,275,160 |
| P/L | 175,456 | 409,431 | 241,077 |
| NW | 687,692 | 470,900 | 170,730 |
| WC | 57,591 | 126,873 | (27,055) |
| Emp. | 158 | 105 | 73 |

DUNS 22-531-7452 **Imp-Exp**

### Sollatek(U.K.) Ltd

Unit 10, Newlands Drive, Colnbrook, Slough, Berkshire SL3 0DX
**Tel:** 01753-688300
**Web:** www.sollatek.com
**Reg No:** 1704907 **VAT No:** 365559026
**Estd:** 1984 Private Limited Company
**Line of Business:** Manufacture of other electrical equipment not elsewhere classified
**Export Markets:** E U, Africa, Middle East, U.S.A.
**Export Sales:** £6,761,674
**Issued Capital:** £180,279
**Principals:** M B Allos *(Managing)*, Dr J E Allos *(Financial)*, Doctor M J Allos
**Co. Secretary:** Manhal Allos
**Branches:** Sollatek(U.k.) Ltd, 3 Kilrue La, Walton-On-Thames, Surrey KT12 5BN
**US SIC:** 3629 **UK SIC:** 34350
**Auditors:** Lubbock Fine
**Bankers:** National Westminster Bank Plc (56-00-18)

| | 31-12-13 | 31-12-12 | 30-12-11 |
|---|---|---|---|
| TO | 8,041,505 | 12,067,665 | 8,543,178 |
| P/L | 254,458 | 385,819 | 324,187 |
| NW | 3,150,077 | 2,872,435 | 2,453,272 |
| WC | 3,841,416 | 4,551,796 | 2,126,260 |
| Emp. | 50 | 47 | 41 |

DUNS 21-700-5543

### Solo Cup Finance Ltd

St Peter's Industrial Park, Tower Close, Huntingdon, Cambridgeshire PE18 7BZ
**Tel:** 01480459413 **Fax:** 01480459274
**Reg No:** 7455611 **Estd:** 2010 Private Limited Company
**Line of Business:** Manufacture plastic cups bowls & cultery
**Export Sales:** £29,968,000
**Issued Capital:** £5
**Directors:** J D Lammers, Ms C T Dart, A F Waters, T L Jewell, G H Jenkins, R C Dart
**Co. Secretary:** Pinsent Masons Secretarial Limit
**US SIC:** 2821 **UK SIC:** 25140
**Auditors:** KPMG LLP

| | 31-12-13 | 31-12-12 | 25-12-11 |
|---|---|---|---|
| TO | 84,935,000 | 12,994,000 | N/A |
| P/L | (6,323,000) | 154,000 | 448,718 |
| NW | 4,820,000 | 10,740,000 | 13,057,468 |
| WC | 18,340,000 | (8,064,000) | N/A |
| Emp. | 525 | 91 | N/A |

DUNS 73-768-7900

### Solo Life Opportunities

38 Walnut Close, Birmingham, West Midlands B37 7PU
**Tel:** 01217793865
**Web:** www.solihullsolo.org
**Reg No:** 5025939 **Estd:** 2004 Private Limited Company
**Line of Business:** Social work activities without accommodation
**Trading Style:** Solihull Life Opportunities
**Directors:** Mrs L Crompton, Ms S Russell, J Prior, O Simjee, R Stuart, Mrs S Stocks, Ms G Penny, Mrs H Partridge

**Co. Secretary:** Ms Janet Down
**Responsibilities**
**Senior:** Roger Derwent *(Manager)*, Mark Hinsley *(Manager)*, Wendy Magee *(Manager)*, Linda Nugent *(Director)*
**US SIC:** 8321 **UK SIC:** 96111
**Bankers:** Abbey National Plc (09-00-00)

| | 31-03-14 | 31-03-13 | 31-03-12 |
|---|---|---|---|
| TO | 930,991 | 701,878 | 577,623 |
| P/L | 65,154 | (7,726) | (49,555) |
| NW | 334,884 | 269,730 | 277,456 |
| WC | 186,100 | 253,730 | 255,456 |
| Emp. | 152 | 144 | 19 |

DUNS 76-962-0550

## Solo Service Group Ltd

Axis Court, Riverside Business Park Mallard Way, Swansea, West Glamorgan SA7 0AJ
**Tel:** 01792-793021 **Fax:** 01792793137
**Web:** www.soloservicegroup.com
**Reg No:** 2626708 **Estd:** 1989 Private Limited Company
**Line of Business:** Cleaning contracting commercial
**Issued Capital:** £254,634
**Directors:** Mrs C M Cooper, Ms C J Sypliwtchak, Ms J E Rees, S L Hammett
**Co. Secretary:** Clive Hammett
**Responsibilities**
**HR:** Carli Kennedy *(Human Resources Administrator)*
**Branches:** Solo Service Group Ltd, Axis Court, Axis 3, Swansea, West Glamorgan SA7 0AJ
**US SIC:** 7349 **UK SIC:** 92300
**Auditors:** Willis Jones

| | 31-07-14 | 31-07-13 | 31-07-12 |
|---|---|---|---|
| TO | 30,020,787 | 27,346,386 | 27,075,300 |
| P/L | 1,315,226 | 2,042,525 | 1,580,063 |
| NW | 7,038,699 | 5,972,982 | 4,373,151 |
| WC | 3,935,527 | 2,703,712 | 1,726,827 |
| Emp. | 4,191 | 4,276 | 3,932 |

DUNS 21-785-7659

## Solomon Commercials

Carrs Industrial Estate, Commerce Street, Haslingden, Rossendale, Lancashire BB4 5JT
**Tel:** 01706237090
**Web:** www.solocom.co.uk
**Estd:** 2011 Proprietorship
**Line of Business:** Manufacturers of refrigeration equipment
**Proprietor:** M Solomon
**Responsibilities**
**Senior:** Jonathan Patchick *(Manager)*
**US SIC:** 3585 **UK SIC:** 32841
**Employees:** 160

DUNS 21-327-6330 **Imp**

## Solomon Commercials Ltd

(**Subsidiary of:** Solcomm Ltd)
Knowsley Road, Knowsley Road Industrial Estate, Hasling, Rossendale, Lancashire BB4 4RX
**Fax:** 01706-831518
**Web:** www.solomoncommercials.co.uk
**Reg No:** 1555887 **Estd:** 1981 Private Limited Company
**Line of Business:** Van and truck bodybuilders and repairers
**Export Sales:** £2,218,501
**Issued Capital:** £25,500
**Principals:** R Solomon *(Managing)*, M J Solomon, Mrs S E Solomon, M C Solomon
**Co. Secretary:** Michael Solomon
**Responsibilities**
**Senior:** Jonathan Patchick *(Works Director)*, Solomon Vehicle *(Proprietor)*
**Finance:** Barrie Rawstron *(Financial Director)*
**HR:** Jonathan Patchick *(Works Director)*
**Health & Safety:** Jonathan Patchick *(Works Director)*
**Engineering:** Jonathan Patchick *(Works Director)*
**US SIC:** 3713 **UK SIC:** 35201
**Auditors:** Marsden & Co
**Bankers:** National Westminster Bank Plc (01-07-29)

| | 30-04-14 | 30-04-13 | 30-04-12 |
|---|---|---|---|
| TO | 53,292,145 | 43,200,477 | 36,969,620 |
| P/L | 4,258,305 | 8,009,864 | 3,753,861 |
| NW | 7,094,958 | 7,360,606 | 515,323 |
| WC | 5,080,970 | 5,708,584 | 4,464,190 |
| Emp. | 306 | 271 | 231 |

DUNS 22-987-9192

## Solomon Hare

Portwall Place, Portwall Lane, Bristol, Avon BS1 6NA
**Tel:** 01173-762000
**Web:** www.smith.williamson.co.uk
**Estd:** 1867 Partnership
**Line of Business:** Accounting and auditing activities
**Trading Style:** Smith & Williamson Solomon Hare
**Principals:** J D Lewis, T J Chapple, D A Robinson, P Engel *(Partner)*, R F Mannion *(Partner)*, A J Hards *(Partner)*, T Keeley *(Partner)*, R Chant *(Partner)*
**Responsibilities**
**Senior:** Richard Bunker *(Partner)*, Steven Butt *(Partner)*, Jerry Garland *(Partner)*, Mike Lee *(Manager)*, Roy McFarlane *(Partner)*, Philip Moody *(Partner)*, Dave Mouncey *(Partner)*
**Finance:** Fiona Brewer *(Finance Director)*
**Branches:** Solomon Hare, 4 St Pauls Churchyard, London EC4M 8AY
**US SIC:** 8931, 7392
**UK SIC:** 83600, 83951
**Employees:** 250

DUNS 22-281-0579

## Solor Care Group Ltd

(**Subsidiary of:** Voyage Mezzco Ltd)
Carriage Court, 25 Circus Mews, Bath, Avon BA1 2PW
**Web:** www.robinia.co.uk
**Reg No:** 4299004 **Estd:** 2001 Private Limited Company
**Line of Business:** Residential care establishments
**Trading Style:** Robinia
**Issued Capital:** £8,000,000
**Directors:** P A Sealey, A Winning
**Co. Secretary:** Philip Sealey
**Responsibilities**
**Senior:** Kit Doleman *(Chief Executive Officer)*, Julie Moran *(Business Development Manager)*
**Finance:** Benjamin McGinn *(Financial Director)*
**Branches:** Solor Care Group Ltd, Bilton Industrial Estate, Humber Avenue, Coventry, West Midlands CV3 1JL
**US SIC:** 8321 **UK SIC:** 96111
**Auditors:** Deloitte & Touche LLP
**Bankers:** Bank Of Scotland (80-20-19)

| | 31-03-14 | 31-03-13 | 31-03-12 |
|---|---|---|---|
| TO | 21,808,000 | 23,119,000 | 17,285,115 |
| P/L | 1,013,000 | 2,245,000 | 1,621,333 |
| NW | 18,316,000 | 17,525,000 | 22,842,444 |
| WC | 64,448,000 | 29,336,000 | 10,207,542 |
| Emp. | 789 | 821 | 735 |

DUNS 21-136-4409

## Solsbury Solutions Ltd

109 Chiswick High Road, London W4 2ED
**Tel:** 02088148903
**Web:** www.solsburysolutions.com
**Reg No:** 6692690 **Estd:** 2008 Private Limited Company
**Line of Business:** Employment and recruitment companies and consultants
**Issued Capital:** £100
**Director:** J N Wolfe
**US SIC:** 7361 **UK SIC:** 83954

| | 31-12-13 | 31-12-12 | 31-12-11 |
|---|---|---|---|
| TO | 13,252,987 | 12,479,489 | N/A |
| P/L | (84,174) | (248,985) | N/A |
| NW | (444,546) | (386,550) | (167,547) |
| WC | (453,273) | (391,413) | (171,672) |
| Emp. | 865 | 414 | N/A |

DUNS 39-792-8185 **Imp**

## Soltech Systems Ltd

Unit 10 Boyn Valley Road Boyn Valley, Industrial Estate, Maidenhead, Berkshire SL6 4EJ
**Tel:** 01628776488 **Fax:** 01628-776781
**Web:** www.soltech.uk.com
**Reg No:** 2205072 **VAT No:** 491885985
**Estd:** 1988 Private Limited Company
**Line of Business:** Blinds and canopies
**Issued Capital:** £100
**Principals:** N J Colbourn *(Managing)*, Ms S Colbourn, C G Fowler
**Co. Secretary:** Nicholas Colbourn
**Responsibilities**
**Finance:** Craig Thorne *(Financial Director)*
**US SIC:** 2392 **UK SIC:** 45550
**Bankers:** Barclays Bank Plc (20-78-58)

| | 31-03-14 | 31-03-13 | 31-03-12 |
|---|---|---|---|
| TA | 1,539,201 | 1,759,188 | 1,400,524 |
| NW | 756,691 | 766,243 | 594,553 |
| WC | 529,739 | 528,678 | 412,331 |

DUNS 21-773-9257

## Solus Coaches

Lovell, Apollo, Lichfield Road Industrial Estate, Tamworth, Staffordshire B79 7TA
**Web:** www.soluscoaches.co.uk
**Estd:** 2011 Proprietorship
**Line of Business:** Coach and bus hire
**Proprietor:** B Edwards
**US SIC:** 4119 **UK SIC:** 72200
**Employees:** 55

DUNS 49-068-3653

## Solus (London) Ltd

(**Subsidiary of:** Aviva Plc)
1-9 Chase Road, London NW10 6LX
**Tel:** 020-8453-3100
**Web:** www.solusgl.com
**Reg No:** 3078842 **Estd:** 1997 Private Limited Company
**Line of Business:** Car body repairers
**Trading Style:** Solus
**Issued Capital:** £1,000
**Directors:** J S Price, A J Morrish, A Caldwell, R I Townend
**Co. Secretary:** Aviva Company Secretarial Servic
**Responsibilities**
**Senior:** Dominic Clayden *(Manager)*, Robert Florence *(Manager)*, Alison Wilford *(Manager)*
**Marketing:** Jacci Marcus *(Head of Marketing)*
**Sales:** May Philpott *(Sales Director)*
**Health & Safety:** Mike Burt *(Health & Safety Officer)*
**Branches:** Solus (London) Ltd, North Hyde House, North Hyde Wharf, Hayes Road, Southall, Middlesex UB2 5NS
**US SIC:** 7539 **UK SIC:** 67100
**Auditors:** Ernst & Young LLP

| | 31-12-13 | 31-12-12 | 31-12-11 |
|---|---|---|---|
| TO | 69,547,000 | 70,568,000 | 71,803,000 |
| P/L | 10,893,000 | 11,567,000 | 10,862,000 |
| NW | 9,275,000 | 42,918,000 | 34,147,000 |
| WC | (4,061,000) | (11,106,000) | (6,404,000) |
| Emp. | 615 | 628 | 655 |

DUNS 71-885-7290

## Solus Tile Co Ltd

Unit 1, Cole River Park, 285 Warwick Road, Birmingham, West Midlands B11 2QX
**Web:** www.solustilestudio.com
**Reg No:** 5268096 **Estd:** 2004 Private Limited Company
**Line of Business:** Other retail sale in specialised stores not elsewhere classified
**Issued Capital:** £200
**Directors:** P A Bentley, K A Dixon, S P Baker, G Hogan
**Co. Secretary:** Marcus Bentley
**US SIC:** 5999 **UK SIC:** 65600

| | 31-03-14 | 31-03-13 | 31-03-12 |
|---|---|---|---|
| TO | 11,243,227 | 11,386,642 | 10,394,309 |
| P/L | 1,243,790 | 1,353,855 | 1,225,926 |
| NW | 1,997,598 | 1,664,760 | 470,643 |
| WC | (168,716) | (234,072) | (1,069,004) |
| Emp. | 59 | 51 | 42 |

DUNS 23-620-7887

## Solutia U K Holdings Ltd

(**Subsidiary of:** Eastman Chemical Company)
Corporation Road, Newport, Gwent NP19 4XF
**Tel:** 01633-278221
**Reg No:** 3617925 **Estd:** 1998 Private Limited Company
**Line of Business:** Manufacture of other organic basic chemicals
**Trading Style:** Solutia U K Holdings Ltd
**Issued Capital:** £70,814
**Directors:** S N Westhead, W J Van Rooijen
**Responsibilities**
**Senior:** Jan Derycke *(Manager)*
**US SIC:** 2869 **UK SIC:** 25120
**Auditors:** Deloitte LLP
**Bankers:** Citibank Na (08-60-71)

| | 31-12-13 | 31-12-12 | 31-12-11 |
|---|---|---|---|
| TA | 183,488,000 | 179,169,000 | 173,782,000 |
| P/L | (881,000) | (3,771,000) | (3,467,000) |
| NW | 28,702,000 | 31,385,000 | 35,327,000 |
| WC | 58,389,000 | 55,965,000 | 20,998,000 |

DUNS 50-969-9856 **Imp-Exp**

## Solutia U K Ltd

(**Subsidiary of:** Eastman Chemical Company)
Corporation Road, Newport, Gwent NP19 4XF
**Tel:** 01633278221
**Web:** www.eastman.co.uk
**Reg No:** 3295486 **Estd:** 1996 Private Limited Company
**Line of Business:** Manufacture of other chemical products not elsewhere classified
**Trading Style:** Solutia, C P Films
**Issued Capital:** £70,814
**Directors:** S N Westhead, M R Deal, S Hampson
**Responsibilities**
**Senior:** Keith McIlquham *(Purchasing Manager)*
**Purchasing:** Keith McIlquham *(Purchasing Manager)*
**Branches:** Solutia U K Ltd, Chadwick Rd, Astmoor Indstl Est, Runcorn, Cheshire WA7 1PW
**US SIC:** 2899 **UK SIC:** 25670
**Auditors:** Deloitte & Touche LLP
**Bankers:** HSBC Bank plc (40-34-27)

| | 31-12-13 | 31-12-12 | 31-12-11 |
|---|---|---|---|
| TO | 115,769,000 | 117,185,000 | 120,974,000 |
| P/L | 13,541,000 | 7,406,000 | 14,480,000 |
| NW | 127,735,000 | 117,876,000 | 109,598,000 |
| WC | 117,966,000 | 120,910,000 | 117,540,000 |
| Emp. | 217 | 221 | 222 |

DUNS 21-102-5930

## Solution Eu Ltd

5 Apollo Court, ., ., Buckingham, Buckinghamshire MK18 4DF
**Tel:** 01280878268
**Web:** www.koko-innovates.com
**Reg No:** 6457657 **Estd:** 2007 Private Limited Company
**Line of Business:** Manufacture of other plastic products
**Issued Capital:** £8
**Director:** T G Mckenna
**Co. Secretary:** Mark Mcloughlin
**US SIC:** 3079 **UK SIC:** 48360

| | 31-12-13 | 31-12-12 | 31-12-11 |
|---|---|---|---|
| TA | 2,476,808 | 1,849,572 | 844,603 |
| NW | 519,406 | 201,829 | 141,002 |
| WC | 508,228 | 191,771 | 132,402 |

DUNS 22-208-2625

## Solutions 4 Cleaning Ltd

Unit 3 Sandall Stones Road, Kirk Sandall Industrial Estate, Doncaster, South Yorkshire DN3 1QR
**Tel:** 01302761633
**Web:** www.solutionsforcleaning.co.uk
**Reg No:** 4226397 **Estd:** 2012 Private Limited Company
**Line of Business:** Cleaning contracting commercial
**Trading Style:** Solutions 4 Cleaning
**Issued Capital:** £2
**Director:** K B Kerley
**Co. Secretary:** Ms Samantha Kerley
**Responsibilities**
**Senior:** Tracey Dudley *(Managing Manager)*
**US SIC:** 7349 **UK SIC:** 92300
**Auditors:** Broderick & Leslie

| | 31-03-14 | 31-03-13 | 31-03-12 |
|---|---|---|---|
| TA | 361,477 | 390,077 | 336,676 |
| NW | 27,614 | 25,759 | 5,630 |
| WC | 22,595 | 37,822 | 43,877 |

DUNS 21-104-8388

## Solutions 4 Health Ltd

200 Brook Drive Green Park, Reading, Berkshire RG2 6UB
**Tel:** 08445831111
**Web:** www.solution1.co.uk
**Reg No:** 6475161 **VAT No:** 939378273
**Estd:** 2006 Private Limited Company
**Line of Business:** Other human health activities
**Issued Capital:** £1,000
**Directors:** Ms L Sankia, K Sankla
**Co. Secretary:** Ms Leena Sankla
**Responsibilities**
**Senior:** William Ginn *(Manager)*
**US SIC:** 8091 **UK SIC:** 95200

| | 31-12-13 | 31-12-12 | 31-12-11 |
|---|---|---|---|
| TO | N/A | 3,073,091 | 1,981,063 |
| P/L | N/A | 5,317 | 57,492 |
| NW | (109,008) | 71,592 | 67,339 |
| WC | 160,115 | 152,977 | 107,197 |

DUNS 23-191-7998 **Imp**

## Solutions Inc. Ltd

255 Old Shoreham Road, Hove, East Sussex BN3 7ED
**Tel:** 01273200800 **Fax:** 01273889030
**Web:** www.solutions-inc.co.uk
**Reg No:** 2994117 **Estd:** 1994 Private Limited Company
**Line of Business:** Other retail sale in specialised stores not elsewhere classified
**Issued Capital:** £100
**Directors:** A T Bowen, S G Birch, S Upton, R J Furber, M P Harmer
**Co. Secretary:** John Parvin
**US SIC:** 5999 **UK SIC:** 65600
**Auditors:** Cardens Accountants LLP

| | 30-06-13 | 30-06-12 | 30-06-11 |
|---|---|---|---|
| TO | 16,225,038 | 15,778,787 | 15,777,268 |
| P/L | 274,398 | 265,341 | (184,225) |
| NW | 1,127,226 | 1,021,484 | 829,973 |
| WC | 570,132 | 470,126 | 289,516 |
| Emp. | 73 | 77 | 80 |

DUNS 51-563-1815

## Solutions Sk Ltd

(**Subsidiary of:** Stockport Metropolitan Borough Council)
Enterprise House, Office Bird Hall Lane, Stockport, Cheshire SK3 0XT
**Tel:** 01614745584
**Web:** www.solutionssk.co.uk
**Reg No:** 5844684 **Estd:** 2006 Private Limited Company
**Line of Business:** Misc special bldg trade contractors
**Issued Capital:** £2
**Directors:** G R Aitken, N A Masom, D A Teale, S Jallands, S P Morris

**Co. Secretary:** Stephen Jallands
**Responsibilities**
**Senior:** Iain Skelton *(Manager)*
**US SIC:** 1799, 1611, 7393
**UK SIC:** 50000, 50200, 83954
**Auditors:** PKF (UK) LLP
**Bankers:** The Co-Operative Bank Plc (08-90-24)

| | 31-03-14 | 31-03-13 | 31-03-12 |
|---|---|---|---|
| TO | 35,944,000 | 39,738,000 | 35,366,000 |
| P/L | 231,000 | 20,000 | (5,318,000) |
| NW | (7,208,000) | (9,525,000) | (6,446,000) |
| WC | (1,503,000) | (2,530,000) | (2,371,000) |
| Emp. | 876 | 978 | 937 |

DUNS 23-255-2716
## Solutions Uk
Oakhurst Drive, Stockport, Cheshire SK3 0XT
**Tel:** 01614745584
**Web:** www.solutionssk.co.uk
**Estd:** 2006 Proprietorship
**Line of Business:** Recycling
**Responsibilities**
**Senior:** Barry Jennings *(Manager)*
**US SIC:** 9121 **UK SIC:** 91110
**Employees:** 100

DUNS 21-194-9698 **Imp-Exp**
## Solvay Interox Ltd
**(Subsidiary of:** Solvay Sa)
Baronet Works, Baronet Road, Warrington, Cheshire WA4 6HA
**Web:** www.solvaychemicals.com
**Reg No:** 1005238 **VAT No:** 582237729
**Estd:** 1971 Private Limited Company
**Line of Business:** Manufacture of other inorganic basic chemicals
**Export Markets:** E U; U S A; Australia; Africa; Asia
**Export Sales:** £2,771,000
**Trading Style:** Solvay Caprolactone, Solvay Chemicals
**Issued Capital:** £30,000,000
**Directors:** L Sharpe, S A Webb
**Co. Secretary:** Melvin Dawes
**Responsibilities**
**Senior:** Vincent Cuyper *(Manager)*, Eric Mignonat *(Manager)*
**IT:** John Wharne *(Systems Analyst)*
**Operations:** J McDonagh *(Environmental Coordinator)*
**Branches:** Solvay Interox Ltd, Moorfield Rd, Cheshire Widnes
**US SIC:** 2819, 5161
**UK SIC:** 25110, 61200
**Auditors:** Deloitte & Touche LLP
**Bankers:** National Westminster Bank Plc (56-00-68)

| | 31-12-13 | 31-12-12 | 31-12-11 |
|---|---|---|---|
| TO | 33,210,000 | 31,374,000 | 30,952,000 |
| P/L | 4,594,000 | 5,012,000 | 10,343,000 |
| NW | 34,124,000 | 35,404,000 | 33,320,000 |
| WC | 32,907,000 | 31,237,000 | 29,127,000 |
| Emp. | 110 | 112 | 116 |

DUNS 21-000-5179
## Solvay Solutions Uk Ltd
**(Subsidiary of:** Solvay Sa)
Oak House, Reeds Crescent, Watford, Hertfordshire WD24 4QP
**Tel:** 01923485868
**Web:** www.solvay.com
**Reg No:** 0036833 **VAT No:** 730994808
**Estd:** 1863 Private Limited Company
**Line of Business:** Manufacturers of chemicals
**Export Sales:** £69,075,000
**Trading Style:** Rhodia Perfumery Performance Argo
**Issued Capital:** £33,304,391
**Directors:** J Berthiaume, M N Holland, Dr T Dutton, B Downward, G L Peron
**Co. Secretary:** Mrs Alison Murphy
**Responsibilities**
**Senior:** John Hamnett *(Manager)*, Barry Milner *(Manager)*
**Branches:** Solvay Solutions Uk Ltd, Trinity Street, Oldbury, West Midlands B69 4LN
**US SIC:** 2899 **UK SIC:** 25670
**Auditors:** Deloitte LLP
**Bankers:** Barclays Bank Plc (20-07-82)

| | 31-12-13 | 31-12-12 | 31-12-11 |
|---|---|---|---|
| TO | 106,701,000 | 115,064,000 | 112,564,000 |
| P/L | (15,529,000) | 4,022,000 | (48,292,000) |
| NW | (525,273,000) | (498,276,000) | (433,765,000) |
| WC | (42,983,000) | (15,252,000) | (26,467,000) |
| Emp. | 385 | 387 | 378 |

DUNS 22-120-0921
## Solventia Ltd
2 Normay Rise, Newbury, Berkshire RG14 6RY
**Web:** www.relyoncleaningservices.co.uk
**Reg No:** 4139123 **Estd:** 2001 Private Limited Company
**Line of Business:** Traditional cleaning activities
**Issued Capital:** £99
**Director:** P T Bennellick
**Co. Secretary:** Ms Carol Spencer
**US SIC:** 7349 **UK SIC:** 92300

| | 31-01-14 | 31-01-13 | 31-01-12 |
|---|---|---|---|
| TA | 222,969 | 224,627 | 362,452 |
| NW | 79,029 | 47,275 | 239,561 |
| WC | 101,988 | 81,146 | 265,423 |

DUNS 73-799-6108
## Solway Foods Holdings Ltd
**(Subsidiary of:** Boparan Holdco Ltd)
3 Godwin Walk, Northampton, Northamptonshire NN5 7RW
**Tel:** 01536464400 **Fax:** 01536403227
**Web:** www.solway.com
**Reg No:** 2930016 **Estd:** 1994 Private Limited Company
**Line of Business:** Management activities of holding companies
**Trading Style:** Northern Foods
**Issued Capital:** £1,034,903
**Directors:** D S Morgan, S P Leadbeater
**Responsibilities**
**Senior:** Veepul Patel *(Manager)*, Huan Quayle *(Manager)*
**US SIC:** 6711, 2033
**UK SIC:** 83962, 41473
**Auditors:** Deloitte & Touche LLP
**Bankers:** Banque Nationale De Paris Plc (23-46-35)

| | 27-07-13 | 28-07-12 | 02-07-11 |
|---|---|---|---|
| TA | 10,174,000 | 10,174,000 | 10,174,000 |
| NW | 10,174,000 | 10,174,000 | 10,174,000 |

DUNS 39-749-2760
## Solway Foods Ltd
**(Subsidiary of:** Boparan Holdco Ltd)
Godwin Road, Corby, Northamptonshire NN17 4DS
**Tel:** 01536401400
**Web:** www.solway.com
**Reg No:** 2189139 **VAT No:** 486261817
**Estd:** 1988 Private Limited Company
**Line of Business:** Manufacture of other food products not elsewhere classified
**Issued Capital:** £117,866,999
**Directors:** J A Dunsford, S P Leadbeater, Ms S Amin, D S Morgan, S J Wookey, C D Smith, R S Boparan, L J Feeley
**Responsibilities**
**Senior:** Clare Arostegui *(Manager)*, Dean Carr *(Despatch Manager)*, Huan Quayle *(Manager)*
**HR:** Emma Welch *(Human Resources Manager)*
**Operations:** David Rafferty *(Environmental Manager)*
**Fleet:** Dean Carr *(Despatch Manager)*
**Branches:** Solway Foods Ltd, Manton Wood Enterprise Park, Worksop, Nottinghamshire S80 2RS
**US SIC:** 2099 **UK SIC:** 42399
**Auditors:** Deloitte LLP
**Bankers:** Barclays Bank Plc (20-45-77)

| | 27-07-13 | 28-07-12 | 02-07-11 |
|---|---|---|---|
| TO | 368,633,000 | 369,240,000 | 176,845,000 |
| P/L | 3,321,000 | 28,131,000 | 16,467,000 |
| NW | 36,917,000 | 38,937,000 | 18,448,000 |
| WC | (6,212,000) | (4,926,000) | 1,013,000 |
| Emp. | 3,606 | 2,649 | 1,735 |

DUNS 76-941-6132
## Solway Veg Ltd.
**(Subsidiary of:** Jewel Associates Ltd)
Gretna Industrial Estate, Empire Way, Gretna, Cumbria
**Tel:** 01461-337239 **Fax:** 01461338436
**Web:** www.parripak.co.uk
**Reg No:** 0091729SC **Estd:** 1980 Private Limited Company
**Line of Business:** Processing and preserving of fruit and vegetables not elsewhere classified
**Trading Style:** Parripak Foods
**Issued Capital:** £100,000
**Directors:** N P Gale, N G Soutar, Wjs Executives Limited
**Co. Secretary:** Gary Urmston
**Responsibilities**
**Purchasing:** Ady Taylor *(Purchasing Manager)*
**US SIC:** 2033 **UK SIC:** 41473
**Auditors:** Dodd & Co
**Bankers:** Clydesdale Bank Plc (82-43-03)

| | 26-04-14 | 27-04-13 | 28-04-12 |
|---|---|---|---|
| TA | 6,000 | 6,000 | 6,000 |
| NW | 6,000 | 6,000 | 6,000 |

DUNS 21-312-4969
## Solway Vehicle Distributors Ltd
Ministry Of Transport, Carlisle, Cumbria CA3 0HA
**Tel:** 01228544686
**Web:** www.solwaydaf.co.uk
**Reg No:** 1393710 **VAT No:** 288267901
**Estd:** 1969 Private Limited Company
**Line of Business:** Van and truck dealers
**Trading Style:** Solway Daf
**Issued Capital:** £28,000
**Principals:** P Fullelove *(Managing)*, E W Coulthard
**Co. Secretary:** John O'Mahony
**Responsibilities**
**Finance:** Steve O'Mahony *(Financial Controller)*
**IT:** Steve O'Mahony *(Financial Controller)*
**Health & Safety:** Steve O'Mahony *(Financial Controller)*
**Branches:** Solway Vehicle Distributors Ltd, Stoneykirk Road, Stranraer, Wigtownshire DG9 7BT
**US SIC:** 5511, 7539, 5531
**UK SIC:** 65100, 67100
**Auditors:** Torgersens
**Bankers:** Lloyds TSB Bank plc (30-93-71)

| | 31-01-14 | 31-01-13 | 31-01-12 |
|---|---|---|---|
| TO | 20,956,025 | 21,391,325 | 19,987,173 |
| P/L | 765,788 | 708,823 | 667,624 |
| NW | 5,675,050 | 5,176,558 | 4,705,707 |
| WC | 2,783,974 | 3,056,877 | 2,407,415 |
| Emp. | 76 | 78 | 78 |

DUNS 34-616-8099
## Soma Healthcare Ltd
Euro House 131 133, Ballards Lane, London N3 1GR
**Tel:** 02083710116 **Fax:** 02077358020
**Web:** www.somahealthcare.co.uk
**Reg No:** 2754194 **Estd:** 1992 Private Limited Company
**Line of Business:** Other human health activities
**Issued Capital:** £190,380
**Director:** Dr A A Akinola
**Co. Secretary:** Mrs Oluwayemisi Gibbons
**Responsibilities**
**Senior:** Yetunde Akinola *(Manager)*, Janet Akinola *(Manager)*, Oluwakayode Akinola *(Manager)*, Abiola Okubanjo *(Manager)*
**US SIC:** 8091, 8321
**UK SIC:** 95200, 96111
**Auditors:** H.W. Fisher & Co
**Bankers:** Barclays Bank Plc (20-37-16)

| | 31-03-14 | 31-03-13 | 31-03-12 |
|---|---|---|---|
| TO | 3,178,664 | 3,521,359 | 3,647,914 |
| P/L | (604,351) | (629,390) | (37,874) |
| NW | 599,385 | 1,225,892 | 1,942,731 |
| WC | 555,920 | 1,788,294 | 1,869,043 |
| Emp. | 155 | 172 | 208 |

DUNS 76-925-3782
## Somerhill Charitable Trust Ltd
Somerhill, Tonbridge, Kent TN11 0NJ
**Tel:** 01732352124
**Web:** www.schools.somerhill.com
**Reg No:** 2331296 **Estd:** 1988 Private Company Limited By Guarantee
**Line of Business:** Primary education
**Trading Style:** Somerhill Pre-Prep
**Directors:** M A Norrie, C J Warner, C D Kinloch, Mrs K C Lewis, Miss H P Tebay, D R Walsh, P C Braggins, J C Hills
**Co. Secretary:** Michael Scragg
**Responsibilities**
**Senior:** John Coakley *(Principal)*, Nicholas Heroys *(Director)*, Diane Huntingford *(Director)*, Catherine Mayhew *(Director)*, Jill Milner *(Director)*
**IT:** Mark Tompkins *(Computer Manager)*
**US SIC:** 8211 **UK SIC:** 93200
**Auditors:** NSP Chartered Accountants
**Bankers:** National Westminster Bank Plc (55-70-13)

| | 31-08-13 | 31-08-12 | 31-08-11 |
|---|---|---|---|
| TO | 6,613,339 | 6,460,519 | 6,300,871 |
| P/L | 1,026,072 | 1,058,102 | 947,514 |
| NW | 15,926,868 | 14,900,796 | 13,842,694 |
| WC | 1,473,041 | 1,242,711 | 129,344 |
| Emp. | 131 | 126 | 129 |

DUNS 21-861-5664 **Imp-Exp**
## Somers Forge Ltd
**(Subsidiary of:** Folkes Forgings Acquisition Ltd)
Forge House, Stourbridge, West Midlands DY9 8EL
**Tel:** 01384424242
**Web:** www.folkesgroup.plc.uk
**Reg No:** 0468767 **Estd:** 1946 Private Limited Company
**Line of Business:** Forging, pressing, stamping and roll forming of metal; powder metallurgy
**Export Markets:** Europe, U S A, Asia, Middle East, Africa and others
**Export Sales:** £3,313,781
**Issued Capital:** £1,000,023
**Principals:** C J Folkes *(Chairman)*, Miss A A Folkes, Ms T Inglis, P M Turner, Miss C L Folkes, J Warr, P V Mitchel, S J Folkes
**Co. Secretary:** Paul Tomlinson
**Responsibilities**
**Finance:** John Monkton *(Property Finance Director)*
**US SIC:** 3469 **UK SIC:** 31200
**Auditors:** Ernst & Young LLP
**Bankers:** HSBC Bank plc (40-43-17)

| | 31-12-13 | 31-12-12 | 31-12-11 |
|---|---|---|---|
| TO | 20,723,580 | 18,463,902 | 22,202,370 |
| P/L | 2,164,410 | 550,046 | 1,543,203 |
| NW | 18,869,721 | 17,062,494 | 9,300,199 |
| WC | 12,322,307 | 10,144,869 | 4,229,405 |
| Emp. | 138 | 124 | 142 |

DUNS 77-894-3048
## Somerset Activity & Sports Partnership
1st Floor Offices, Castle Business Centre, Castle Road, Chelston Business Park, Wellington, Somerset TA21 9JQ
**Tel:** 01823666640
**Reg No:** 5798066 **Estd:** 2006 Private Company Limited By Guarantee
**Line of Business:** Sports clubs
**Directors:** A B Lees, G Jones, A F Gloak, K J Freedman
**Co. Secretary:** Colin Johnson
**US SIC:** 7999 **UK SIC:** 97913
**Auditors:** D.I. Wicks
**Bankers:** National Westminster Bank Plc (60-14-30)

| | 31-03-14 | 31-03-13 | 31-03-12 |
|---|---|---|---|
| TO | 1,270,824 | 1,690,749 | 207,329 |
| P/L | 2,313 | 502,299 | 97,731 |
| NW | 382,125 | 490,812 | 116,513 |
| WC | 634,713 | 607,919 | 115,879 |
| Emp. | 53 | 57 | 4 |

DUNS 21-790-0716
## Somerset Cancer Care
Heron Drive, Bishops Hull, Taunton, Somerset TA1 5HA
**Tel:** 01823346952
**Web:** www.st-margarets-hospice.org.uk
**Estd:** 2009
**Line of Business:** Information services
**Responsibilities**
**Senior:** Jon Andrews *(Chief Executive)*
**US SIC:** 8699 **UK SIC:** 96902
**Employees:** 90

DUNS 76-334-4355
## Somerset Care Ltd
2nd Floor Equity House, Blackbrook Park Avenue, Taunton, Somerset TA1 2PX
**Web:** www.somerset-chamber.co.uk
**Reg No:** 2548025 **VAT No:** 586323128
**Estd:** 1995 Private Company Limited By Guarantee
**Line of Business:** Chambers of commerce
**Directors:** C J Wall, E C Keogh, Mrs H Strawbridge, Dr J Townson Philpott, J C Iles, R J Barnfield, Mrs A L Martin, J R Davies
**Co. Secretary:** Christopher Wall
**Responsibilities**
**Senior:** Rupert Cox *(Chief Executive Officer)*
**Branches:** Somerset Care Ltd, 92 High St, Ryde, Isle Of Wight PO33 4PR
**US SIC:** 8621, 8051, 8321
**UK SIC:** 96311, 95100, 96111
**Auditors:** Dixon Walsh
**Bankers:** Lloyds TSB Bank plc (30-12-21)

| | 31-03-14 | 31-03-13 | 31-03-12 |
|---|---|---|---|
| TO | 80,781,179 | 80,526,530 | 77,675,554 |
| P/L | 4,535,382 | 5,000,290 | 4,321,421 |
| NW | 16,105,874 | 11,473,050 | 9,241,511 |
| WC | 2,406,138 | 131,945 | (3,027,913) |
| Emp. | 4,441 | 4,547 | 4,372 |

DUNS 23-997-5352
## Somerset College Arts and Technology
Wellington Road, Taunton, Somerset TA1 5AX
**Tel:** 01823-366366
**Web:** www.somerset.ac.uk
**Estd:** 1971
**Line of Business:** Adult education locations
**Trading Style:** Somerset College
**Director:** Ms A Scott
**Responsibilities**
**Senior:** Claire Merchant-Jones *(Executive)*
**Finance:** Liz Hurst *(Finance Manager)*
**IT:** Liz Hurst *(Finance Manager)*
**HR:** Sheena Murphy-Collett *(Human Resources Manager)*
**Health & Safety:** Jon Peters *(Health & Safety Officer)*
**Facilities:** Gael Burns *(Estates Manager)*
**Branches:** Somerset College Arts and Technology, Victoria Ho, Victoria St, Taunton, Somerset TA1 3FA
**US SIC:** 8221, 8249
**UK SIC:** 93100, 93300
**Employees:** 300

DUNS 21-122-9406 **Imp**
## Somerset County Council
County Hall, Taunton, Somerset TA1 4DY
**Tel:** 08453459122
**Web:** www.somerset.gov.uk
**Estd:** 2000 Incorporate By Act Of Parliament
**Line of Business:** Community networks
**Trading Style:** South West Parent Partnership
**Principals:** H Hubhouse *(Chairman)*, Dr G Court, J Whitcutt, B M Tanner, Ms M Treharne, D Dawson

**Responsibilities**
**Senior:** Catherine Bakewell (Chairman), Julia Bayley (Training Director), John Edney (Chairman), Mike Gillingham (Manager), Karen Horsfield (Manager), Kevin Nacey (Head of Finance), Deborah Porter (Deputy Head of Communications), Sheila Wheeler (Chief Executive)
**Finance:** Kevin Nacey (Head of Finance)
**Marketing:** Nick Graham (Web Manager), Peter Harnett (Councillor), Karen Kral (Group Manager - Children's Soc), Deborah Porter (Deputy Head of Communications)
**Sales:** Steve Aelberry (Business Development Manager), Emma Kennedy (Business Development Group Man), Adrienne Parry (Group Manager - Business Devel)
**Admin:** Karen Higgs (Personal Assistant), Jamie Jackson (Community Governance Admin Sup), Sarah Stirland (Personal Assistant), Annabelle Taylor (Administrator)
**HR:** Julia Bayley (Training Director), Angie Davies (Driver Training Manager), Kaye Elston (Inter Agency Trainer), Martin Walsh (HR Policy Manager)
**Facilities:** Heidi Boyle (Facilities Manager)
**Operations:** Carrie Blogg (Project Manager), Jo Boyland (Operations Manager), Eileen Coombes (Production and Operations Mana), Steve Dury (Project Manager)
**Purchasing:** Caroline Adams (Procurement Manager)
**Branches:** Somerset County Council, Laburnum Dr, Somerton, Somerset TA11 6LN
**US SIC:** 9121, 7397
**UK SIC:** 91110, 83702
**Employees:** 8,749

---

DUNS 34-734-6525
### Somerset Creameries Group Ltd
Nottingham Road, Cropwell Bishop, Nottingham, Nottinghamshire NG12 3BQ
**Tel:** 01159894504
**Reg No:** 5536799  **Estd:** 2005 Private Limited Company
**Line of Business:** Butter and cheese production
**Export Sales:** £3,737,259
**Issued Capital:** £8,968
**Directors:** Mrs P G Sykes, I M Skailes, D S Skailes
**Co. Secretary:** John Poland
**US SIC:** 2021  **UK SIC:** 41302

| | 31-03-14 | 31-03-13 | 31-03-12 |
|---|---|---|---|
| TO | 10,969,300 | 10,375,299 | 9,203,018 |
| P/L | 270,474 | 51,410 | 104,882 |
| NW | 4,119,201 | 3,945,874 | 3,944,994 |
| WC | 1,670,591 | 1,415,570 | 841,545 |
| Emp. | 91 | 94 | 95 |

---

DUNS 29-820-8281
### Somerset Creameries Ltd
(**Subsidiary of:** Somerset Creameries Group Ltd)
Nottingham Road, Nottingham, Nottinghamshire NG12 3BQ
**Tel:** 01159-892350
**Web:** www.cropwellbishopstilton.com
**Reg No:** 0366174  **Estd:** 1941 Private Limited Company
**Line of Business:** Manufacture of other milk products
**Trading Style:** Cropwell Bishop Creameries
**Issued Capital:** £105
**Managing Directors:** D S Skailes, I M Skailes
**Co. Secretary:** John Poland
**US SIC:** 2023  **UK SIC:** 41303
**Auditors:** Cooper-Parry

| | 31-03-14 | 31-03-13 | 31-03-12 |
|---|---|---|---|
| TA | 928 | 928 | 928 |
| NW | 928 | 928 | 928 |

---

DUNS 52-021-5724  **Imp**
### Somerset House Trust
Somerset House, Strand, London WC2R 1LA
**Tel:** 02078872992
**Web:** www.somerset-house.org.uk
**Reg No:** 3388137  **Estd:** 1997 Private Limited Company
**Line of Business:** Places of interest
**Issued Capital:** £2
**Directors:** Ms L Woodhouse, L I Green, R A Gillespie, M A Pain, Ms C J Michel, M J Lyon, A M Elliott, Ms J B Pitman
**Co. Secretary:** Mark Stuart-Smith
**Responsibilities**
**Senior:** George Collum (Visitor Communications), Malcolm Grant (Director), Jeremy Hardie (Director), Mark Potter (Director), Nitin Sawhney (Director)
**Marketing:** George Collum (Visitor Communications)
**US SIC:** 6519, 8999, 8411
**UK SIC:** 85000, 83954, 97700
**Auditors:** Binder Hamlyn

---

**Bankers:** National Westminster Bank Plc (60-05-07)

| | 31-03-14 | 31-03-13 | 31-03-12 |
|---|---|---|---|
| TO | 10,863,771 | 18,334,795 | 11,800,422 |
| P/L | (2,828,526) | 6,293,048 | 1,392,003 |
| NW | 87,711,394 | 90,543,960 | 84,250,912 |
| WC | 2,402,610 | 7,555,012 | 3,158,310 |
| Emp. | 47 | 39 | 35 |

---

DUNS 21-039-2852
### Somerset Nuffield Hospital
Staplegrove, Taunton, Somerset TA2 6AN
**Tel:** 01823-286991
**Web:** www.nuffieldhospitals.org.uk
**Estd:** 2002 Proprietorship
**Line of Business:** Hospitals
**Proprietor:** P Eke
**Responsibilities**
**Senior:** Sasha Burns (Hospital Director)
**US SIC:** 8062  **UK SIC:** 95100
**Employees:** 145

---

DUNS 64-253-1594
### Somerset Partnership Nhs Foundation Trust
2nd Floor Mallard Court, Bridgwater, Somerset TA6 4RN
**Tel:** 01278-432000
**Web:** www.sompar.nhs.uk
**Line of Business:** Public sector hospital activities, including nhs trusts
**Trading Style:** Somerset Partnership Nhs & Social Care Trust
**Issued Capital:** £1
**Directors:** J Hepple, Ms D Rowe, E Colgan, I Halsey, R How, P Watts, Ms A Hill, Ms D Rowe
**Responsibilities**
**Senior:** Mick Hill (Director)
**Branches:** Somerset Partnership Nhs Foundation Trust, Park Gate House, East Reach, Taunton, Somerset TA1 3ES
**US SIC:** 8062  **UK SIC:** 95100
**Auditors:** PricewaterhouseCoopers LLP

| | 31-03-14 | 31-03-13 | 31-03-12 |
|---|---|---|---|
| TO | 158,499,000 | 149,655,000 | 140,502,000 |
| P/L | (11,828,000) | 568,000 | 501,000 |
| NW | 108,288,000 | 32,566,000 | 33,084,000 |
| WC | 955,000 | (1,774,000) | (1,079,000) |
| Emp. | 3,084 | 3,120 | 3,039 |

---

DUNS 36-517-6887
### Somerset Primary Care Trust
Wynford House, Lufton Way, Yeovil, Somerset BA22 8HR
**Tel:** 01935384000
**Web:** www.somersetpct.nhs.uk
**Estd:** 2006
**Line of Business:** Public sector hospital activities, including nhs trusts
**Principals:** Ms J Barrie (Chairman), I Tipney, L Evans, A Govier, Ms L Simons, D Wood, P Jackson
**Responsibilities**
**Marketing:** Paul Courtney (Communication Manager), Anita Trout (Communications Manager)
**IT:** Nigel Painter (Senior Technical Analyst), Matthew Rawles (Senior IT Executive)
**Branches:** Somerset Primary Care Trust, 95 Locks Hill, Frome, Somerset BA11 1NG
**US SIC:** 8062  **UK SIC:** 95100
**Employees:** 1,500

---

DUNS 22-069-8018
### Somerset Redstone Trust
Gatchell House, Trull, Taunton, Somerset TA3 7EG
**Tel:** 01823-270694
**Web:** www.srtrust.co.uk
**Reg No:** 4071304  **Estd:** 2007 Private Company Limited By Guarantee
**Line of Business:** Social work activities
**Directors:** W M Waddington, Mrs J V Barter, Mrs P A Walker, J Baker, Mrs L A Hayes, Ms L E Darts, A Cooper, C J Spencer
**Co. Secretary:** Gordon Lester
**Responsibilities**
**Senior:** Emma Hardwick (HR Director), Richard Macey (Manager), Brian Parkes (Manager), Paul Raine (Manager), Paula Willis (Manager)
**Branches:** Somerset Redstone Trust, 7 Bodenham Rd, Hereford, Herefordshire HR1 2TN
**US SIC:** 7399  **UK SIC:** 83954
**Auditors:** Albert Goodman
**Bankers:** Lloyds TSB Bank plc (30-98-45)

| | 31-03-14 | 31-03-13 | 31-03-12 |
|---|---|---|---|
| TO | 8,480,615 | 6,026,834 | 5,610,017 |
| P/L | (592,599) | (1,410,709) | (324,122) |
| NW | 13,584,262 | 15,090,879 | 16,501,588 |
| WC | (1,961,740) | 2,114,634 | 5,290,885 |
| Emp. | 303 | 279 | 246 |

---

DUNS 21-604-9501
### Somerset Support Services
8 Buckland Road, Pen Mill Trading Estate, Yeovil, Somerset BA21 5EA
**Tel:** 01935476130
**Web:** www.somerset.gov.uk
**Estd:** 2011
**Line of Business:** Education services
**US SIC:** 8299  **UK SIC:** 93300
**Employees:** 75

---

DUNS 73-518-9255
### Somerston Hotels (Investments) Ltd
(**Subsidiary of:** Somerston Hotels U K Ltd)
Bridgeway House Bridgeway, Stratford-Upon-Avon, Warwickshire CV37 6YX
**Tel:** 01789415015
**Web:** www.somerstonhotels.co.uk
**Reg No:** 4781745  **Estd:** 2003 Private Limited Company
**Line of Business:** Hotels
**Issued Capital:** £1,000
**Directors:** K I Griffiths, S Robinson
**Co. Secretary:** Christopher Byrd
**Responsibilities**
**Marketing:** Lesley-Ann Cardow (group Marketing Manager)
**Admin:** Phillippa Brendon (administration manager)
**Health & Safety:** Phillippa Brendon (administration manager)
**Branches:** Somerston Hotels (Investments) Ltd, Worcester Road, Droitwich, Worcestershire WR9 7PA
**US SIC:** 7011  **UK SIC:** 66500
**Auditors:** KPMG LLP
**Bankers:** Bank Of Scotland (80-20-19)

| | 31-12-12 | 31-12-11 | 31-12-10 |
|---|---|---|---|
| TO | 9,117,104 | 8,711,281 | 8,718,655 |
| P/L | (414,249) | (12,559,130) | 9,208,652 |
| NW | (25,404,643) | (24,990,394) | (11,677,997) |
| WC | (47,679,370) | (47,490,394) | (46,670,172) |
| Emp. | 94 | 94 | 95 |

---

DUNS 23-767-7724
### Somerston Hotels (Properties) Ltd
(**Subsidiary of:** Somerston Hotels U K Ltd)
Ryon Hill House, Ryon Hill Park, Warwick Road, Stratford-Upon-Avon, Warwickshire CV37 0UX
**Tel:** 08719021621  **Fax:** 08704445189
**Web:** www.expresshammersmith.co.uk
**Reg No:** 3761275  **Estd:** 1999 Private Limited Company
**Line of Business:** Hotels
**Issued Capital:** £2
**Directors:** K I Griffiths, S Robinson
**Co. Secretary:** Christopher Byrd
**Branches:** Somerston Hotels (Properties) Ltd, 120-124 King Street, London W6 0QU
**US SIC:** 7011  **UK SIC:** 66500
**Auditors:** KPMG LLP
**Bankers:** The Royal Bank Of Scotland Plc (83-07-06)

| | 31-12-12 | 31-12-11 | 31-12-10 |
|---|---|---|---|
| TO | 6,880,015 | 7,162,472 | 6,855,190 |
| P/L | 1,523,959 | 1,730,315 | 2,534,509 |
| NW | 19,838,424 | 24,272,029 | 29,505,718 |
| WC | (9,822,466) | (12,127,973) | (14,458,559) |
| Emp. | 56 | 58 | 54 |

---

DUNS 23-720-6990
### Somerton Homes Ltd
(**Subsidiary of:** P & F McDonnell Ltd)
47 Somerton Road, Belfast BT15 3LH
**Tel:** 028-9077-2483  **Fax:** 02890371044
**Reg No:** 0022766NI  **Estd:** 1989 Private Limited Company
**Line of Business:** Nursing homes
**Issued Capital:** £1
**Directors:** B M Mcdonnell, F Mcdonnell
**Co. Secretary:** Fergal Mcdonnell
**Responsibilities**
**Senior:** Brian McDonald (Proprietor)
**Finance:** Brian McDonald (Proprietor)
**Marketing:** Brian McDonald (Proprietor)
**Sales:** Brian McDonald (Proprietor)
**IT:** Brian McDonald (Proprietor)
**HR:** Brian McDonald (Proprietor)
**Health & Safety:** Brian McDonald (Proprietor)
**Purchasing:** Brian McDonald (Proprietor)
**US SIC:** 8051, 8321
**UK SIC:** 95100, 96111
**Auditors:** Duffy & Co (A & T) Ltd
**Bankers:** Northern Bank Ltd (95-01-26)

| | 31-05-14 | 31-05-13 | 31-05-12 |
|---|---|---|---|
| TA | 823,119 | 866,747 | 907,828 |
| NW | 609,223 | 657,345 | 655,393 |
| WC | (41,888) | (10,298) | (27,109) |

---

DUNS 21-775-9983
### Somerville Primary School
Northbrook Road, Wallasey, Merseyside CH44 9AR
**Tel:** 01516385074
**Web:** www.somerville.wirral.sch.uk
**Estd:** 2011 Proprietorship
**Line of Business:** Schools (local authority)
**Proprietor:** Mrs A Ellison
**US SIC:** 8211  **UK SIC:** 93200
**Employees:** 70

---

DUNS 77-011-7265
### Somethin' Else Sound Directions Ltd
(**Subsidiary of:** Loudwater Investment Partners Ltd)
20-26 Brunswick Place, London N1 6DZ
**Tel:** 020-7250-5500  **Fax:** 02072500937
**Web:** www.somethinelse.com
**Reg No:** 2661600  **VAT No:** 564375814
**Estd:** 1991 Private Limited Company
**Line of Business:** Television activities
**Export Sales:** £152,071
**Trading Style:** X Y Network
**Issued Capital:** £3,752,744
**Directors:** J F Sanderson, P R Bennun, T H Barnicoat, S L Ackerman, J Nelson
**Co. Secretary:** Stuart Smith
**Responsibilities**
**Senior:** Sunita Alleyene (Manager), Trevor Klein (General Manager), Jez Nelson (Chief Executive Officer), Ian Sharpe (General Manager), Other Talent (Executive)
**Finance:** Barry Lee (General Finance Manager)
**HR:** Richard Howells (Talent Manager)
**Operations:** Joby Waldman (Radio Producer)
**US SIC:** 4833, 4832
**UK SIC:** 97411
**Auditors:** KPMG
**Bankers:** National Westminster Bank Plc (60-07-31)

| | 31-03-14 | 31-03-13 | 31-03-12 |
|---|---|---|---|
| TO | 5,517,239 | 6,194,951 | 8,245,283 |
| P/L | (225,186) | (745,709) | 37,196 |
| NW | 1,952,100 | 2,106,043 | 2,770,281 |
| WC | 1,767,554 | 1,895,143 | 549,994 |
| Emp. | 66 | 64 | 90 |

---

DUNS 21-115-5173
### Somme Nursing Home
Hollywood Road, 121 Circular Road, Belfast BT4 2NA
**Tel:** 028-9076-3044
**Web:** www.thesommenursinghome.co.uk
**Reg No:** 0068709NI  **Estd:** 2008 Private Company Limited By Guarantee
**Line of Business:** Social work activities with accommodation
**Directors:** S J Phillips, Mrs E A Robinson, Mrs H M Johnston, J C Stanley, J I Davies, D W Twigg, S M Elder, E R Telford
**Co. Secretary:** Charles Kitson
**Responsibilities**
**Senior:** Patricia Browne (Director), George Gardiner (Director)
**US SIC:** 8321  **UK SIC:** 96111
**Bankers:** Ulster Bank Ltd (98-01-25)

| | 31-03-14 | 31-03-13 | 31-03-12 |
|---|---|---|---|
| TO | 1,442,889 | 1,405,158 | N/A |
| P/L | (100,268) | (106,164) | N/A |
| NW | 2,031,982 | 2,132,250 | 2,238,414 |
| WC | (60,131) | (58,017) | (88,715) |
| Emp. | 55 | 60 | N/A |

---

DUNS 21-669-0726
### Somo Global Ltd
18th Floor, Portland House, Bressenden Place, London SW1E 5RS
**Tel:** 02033973550
**Reg No:** 7222754  **Estd:** 2010 Private Limited Company
**Line of Business:** Management activities of holding companies
**Issued Capital:** £4,841
**Directors:** R D Langston, D W Evans, N A Hynes, M W Opzoomer, T Schulz, C S Uminski, S M Taylor, S S Edelstyn
**Co. Secretary:** Richard Langston
**US SIC:** 6711  **UK SIC:** 83962

| | 31-12-13 | 31-12-12 | 31-12-11 |
|---|---|---|---|
| TO | 23,066,912 | N/A | N/A |
| P/L | (2,299,236) | N/A | N/A |
| NW | (4,086,122) | (918,547) | (1,347,755) |
| WC | (4,068,254) | (930,387) | (1,347,755) |
| Emp. | 106 | N/A | N/A |

---

DUNS 56-956-1491
### Sompo Japan Nipponkoa Insurance Co of Europe Ltd
(**Subsidiary of:** Sompo Japan Nipponkoa Holdings Inc.)
1st Floor, London EC2M 4YE
**Web:** www.sjeurope.com
**Reg No:** 2846429  **Estd:** 1993 Private Limited Company
**Line of Business:** Insurance brokers
**Issued Capital:** £173,700,000

**Directors:** S Ehara, P J Standish, A D Page, K Uehara, P B Wakefield, D M Broome, T Yoshino, S Takahashi
**Co. Secretary:** John Bithell
**Responsibilities**
**Senior:** Masahide Naito (Manager), Antony Pinsent (Manager), Hans Verstraete (Director), Tomoyuki Yoshida (Manager)
**US SIC:** 6411 **UK SIC:** 83200
**Auditors:** Ernst & Young LLP
**Bankers:** The Dai-Ichi Kangyo Bank, Ltd. (40-50-69)

|  | 31-12-13 | 31-12-12 | 31-12-11 |
|---|---|---|---|
| TO | 14,475,000 | N/A | 14,593,000 |
| P/L | 1,333,000 | (12,061,000) | (5,747,000) |
| NW | 90,456,000 | 88,070,000 | 56,215,000 |
| WC | 28,108,000 | 16,931,000 | 10,682,000 |
| Emp. | 124 | 106 | 105 |

DUNS 49-090-3671
### Son Dacre & Hartley Ltd
1-5 The Grove, Ilkley, West Yorkshire LS29 9HS
**Tel:** 01943600655
**Web:** www.dacres.co.uk
**Reg No:** 3090769 **Estd:** 1995 Private Limited Company
**Line of Business:** Estate agents
**Trading Style:** Son Dacre & Hartley Ltd
**Issued Capital:** £98,231
**Principals:** J J Isles (Managing), S Potts, I J Bradbury, J Shaw, T Usherwood, P F Leadbeater, P J Mccutcheon, D J Scarborough
**Co. Secretary:** John Skinner
**Responsibilities**
**Senior:** Andrew Peacock (Director), John Phillip (Director)
**HR:** Sarah Elliott (Human Resources Manager)
**Branches:** Dacre,Son & Hartley Ltd, 8 Westgate, Shipley, West Yorkshire BD17 5EJ
**US SIC:** 6531, 8911
**UK SIC:** 83400, 83701
**Auditors:** KPMG

|  | 31-10-13 | 31-10-12 | 31-10-11 |
|---|---|---|---|
| TO | 6,839,565 | 6,699,017 | 6,470,809 |
| P/L | 148,304 | (198,027) | 66,009 |
| NW | 2,552,496 | 2,601,523 | 2,810,678 |
| WC | 1,857,092 | 1,857,099 | 2,130,904 |
| Emp. | 111 | 127 | 127 |

DUNS 23-799-6025
### Sonali Bank (U K) Ltd
(Subsidiary of: Ministry of Finance Bangladesh)
29-33 Osborn Street, London E1 6TD
**Tel:** 01617858216
**Web:** www.sonali-bank.co.uk
**Reg No:** 3792250 **Estd:** 1999 Private Limited Company
**Line of Business:** Financial services
**Issued Capital:** £25,000,000
**Directors:** P K Dutta, A R Prodhan, D Blackmore, A Alam, M A Chowdhury
**Co. Secretary:** Ataur Prodhan
**Responsibilities**
**Senior:** Khondoker Iqbal (Manager), Mohammed Iqbal-Khandaker (General Manager)
**IT:** Fred Kok (IT Manager)
**HR:** Aya Davies (Human Resources Manager), Amaya Mugica-Davies (Human Resources Manager)
**Facilities:** Abdul Hannan (Operations Manager)
**Branches:** Sonali Bank (U K) Ltd, 84 Manningham Lane, Bradford, West Yorkshire BD1 3ES
**US SIC:** 6012 **UK SIC:** 81402
**Auditors:** Mazars Neville Russell

|  | 31-12-13 | 31-12-12 | 31-12-11 |
|---|---|---|---|
| TA | 214,046,471 | 180,762,639 | 73,428,983 |
| P/L | 3,958,273 | 1,027,787 | 569,973 |
| NW | 29,549,765 | 26,926,412 | 12,733,238 |
| WC | 27,784,866 | 25,035,326 | 11,001,580 |
| Emp. | 63 | 64 | 64 |

DUNS 21-781-0182
### Sonali Gardens
79 Tarling Street, London E1 0AT
**Tel:** 02072659211
**Web:** www.sthildas.org.uk
**Estd:** 2006 Proprietorship
**Line of Business:** Home care service providers
**Proprietor:** R Williams
**US SIC:** 8091 **UK SIC:** 95200
**Employees:** 50

DUNS 29-642-1993
### Sonardyne Group Ltd
Ocean House, Saxony Way, Blackbushe Business Park, Yateley, Hampshire GU46 6GD
**Tel:** 01252872288
**Web:** www.sonardyne.com
**Reg No:** 1968550 **Estd:** 1985 Private Limited Company

**Line of Business:** Manufacture of electronic instruments and appliances for measuring, checking, testing, navigating and other purposes, except industrial process control equipment
**Export Sales:** £47,963,036
**Issued Capital:** £99,995
**Principals:** C J Partridge (Managing), Mrs B F Partridge
**Co. Secretary:** Charles Partridge
**Responsibilities**
**Senior:** Simon Partridge (Manager)
**Engineering:** Simon Partridge (Manager)
**US SIC:** 3829 **UK SIC:** 37100
**Auditors:** Pridie Brewster
**Bankers:** Lloyds TSB Bank plc (30-93-32)

|  | 31-03-14 | 31-03-13 | 31-03-12 |
|---|---|---|---|
| TO | 61,951,177 | 50,276,087 | 43,848,849 |
| P/L | 18,595,626 | 8,409,566 | 8,474,554 |
| NW | 70,135,282 | 53,486,296 | 46,209,907 |
| WC | 59,414,519 | 44,405,554 | 39,646,479 |
| Emp. | 308 | 290 | 267 |

DUNS 29-634-8774  **Imp-Exp**
### Sonatest Nde Ltd
Dickens Road, Milton Keynes, Buckinghamshire MK12 5QQ
**Tel:** 01908-316345
**Web:** www.sonatest.com
**Reg No:** 1961000 **VAT No:** 443721462
**Estd:** 1986 Private Limited Company
**Line of Business:** Measuring instruments and appliances
**Export Markets:** Worldwide
**Export Sales:** £7,374,000
**Issued Capital:** £131,543
**Directors:** N Ng, P C Husarek, Dr A A Aikman
**US SIC:** 3829 **UK SIC:** 37100
**Auditors:** Grant Thornton UK LLP
**Bankers:** National Westminster Bank Plc (60-20-34)

|  | 31-12-13 | 31-12-12 | 31-12-11 |
|---|---|---|---|
| TO | 10,581,000 | 10,593,000 | 10,427,000 |
| P/L | 849,000 | 1,449,000 | 2,994,000 |
| NW | 6,727,000 | 6,559,000 | 5,805,000 |
| WC | 6,308,000 | 6,079,000 | 5,580,000 |
| Emp. | 84 | 79 | 71 |

DUNS 23-606-4965  **Imp**
### Sondex Wireline Ltd
(Subsidiary of: General Electric Company)
Ford Lane, Hook, Hampshire RG27 0RH
**Fax:** 01189-326704
**Web:** www.sondex.com
**Reg No:** 3603786 **VAT No:** 806617823
**Estd:** 1998 Private Limited Company
**Line of Business:** Service activities incidental to oil and gas extraction excluding surveying
**Issued Capital:** £1,671,430
**Directors:** K H Taleghani, D D Kleckner
**Co. Secretary:** Oakwood Corporate Secretary Limi
**Responsibilities**
**Senior:** James Junker (Director)
**US SIC:** 1389, 3829
**UK SIC:** 13000, 37100
**Auditors:** Ernst & Young LLP

|  | 31-12-13 | 31-12-12 | 31-12-11 |
|---|---|---|---|
| TO | 64,313,000 | 65,152,000 | 49,455,000 |
| P/L | 6,771,000 | 18,978,000 | 12,728,000 |
| NW | 97,253,000 | 45,755,000 | 28,662,000 |
| WC | 58,384,000 | 43,209,000 | 26,256,000 |
| Emp. | 208 | 209 | 191 |

DUNS 21-676-5064
### Sone Products Ltd
(Subsidiary of: Sone Products Holdings Ltd)
Unit R, Tanfield Lea Industrial Estate South, Ta, Stanley, County Durham DH9 9QX
**Tel:** 01207-288150 **Fax:** 01207-288190
**Web:** www.sone-products.co.uk
**Reg No:** 7279763 **Estd:** 2010 Private Limited Company
**Line of Business:** Manufacture of basic pharmaceutical products
**Issued Capital:** £9
**Directors:** W Schmidt, H R Stork, R Oliver
**Responsibilities**
**Senior:** Lisa Fletcher (Administration Assistant)
**US SIC:** 2834 **UK SIC:** 25700
**Bankers:** The Royal Bank Of Scotland Plc (16-26-19)

|  | 31-07-13 | 31-07-12 | 31-07-11 |
|---|---|---|---|
| TO | 8,443,761 | 7,223,854 | 8,409,284 |
| P/L | 752,212 | 962,598 | 1,465,701 |
| NW | 2,453,600 | 1,819,060 | 1,075,878 |
| WC | 1,630,591 | 1,481,064 | 917,434 |
| Emp. | 122 | 125 | 133 |

DUNS 73-786-7627
### Songbird Estates Plc.
One Canada Square, London E14 5AA
**Tel:** 02074182312 **Fax:** 02074771001
**Web:** www.songbirdestates.com
**Reg No:** 5043352 **Estd:** 2004 Public Limited Company
**Line of Business:** Other business activities not elsewhere classified

**Issued Capital:** £349,037,461
**Directors:** K S Al-Rabban, J S Haick, M B Al-Thani, R Clark, K J Costa, B W Kingston
**Co. Secretary:** John Garwood
**Responsibilities**
**Senior:** Faisal Al-Hamadi (Manager), Peter Harned (Director), Shmuel Levinson (Director), Alexander Midgen (Director), Brian Niles (Director)
**US SIC:** 7399 **UK SIC:** 83954
**Auditors:** Deloitte LLP
**Bankers:** The Royal Bank Of Scotland Plc (16-04-00)
Following financial data are in thousands

|  | 31-12-13 | 31-12-12 | 31-12-11 |
|---|---|---|---|
| TO | 379,900 | 361,600 | 352,300 |
| P/L | 1,036,700 | 201,500 | (212,800) |
| NW | 1,746,700 | 1,133,000 | 1,042,200 |
| WC | (144,900) | 397,800 | 664,100 |
| Emp. | 973 | 942 | 926 |

DUNS 23-196-2882
### Soni Ltd
(Subsidiary of: Department of Public Expenditure and Reform)
Castlereagh House 12 Manse Road, Belfast BT6 9RT
**Tel:** 028 90794336 **Fax:** 028 90707560
**Web:** www.soni.ltd.uk
**Reg No:** 0038715NI **Estd:** 2000 Private Limited Company
**Line of Business:** Transmission of electricity
**Issued Capital:** £2
**Directors:** F C Slye, R Mccormick, A Cooke, M P Walsh, A Skelly
**Co. Secretary:** Ms Niamh Cahill
**US SIC:** 4911 **UK SIC:** 16101
**Auditors:** Deloitte & Touche
**Bankers:** The Bank Of Ireland (90-21-27)

|  | 30-09-13 | 30-09-12 | 30-09-10 |
|---|---|---|---|
| TO | 131,403,000 | 105,259,000 | 91,201,000 |
| P/L | 16,224,000 | (4,205,000) | 1,589,000 |
| NW | 14,041,000 | 1,065,000 | 449,000 |
| WC | 6,295,000 | (1,489,000) | (1,568,000) |
| Emp. | 112 | 106 | 80 |

DUNS 21-126-9372
### Sonia Heway Care Agency Ltd
1a Pickford Road, Bexleyheath, Kent DA7 4AT
**Tel:** 02083014565 **Fax:** 02083016714
**Web:** www.soniaheway.co.uk
**Reg No:** 6618771 **Estd:** 2008 Private Limited Company
**Line of Business:** Home care and help services
**Issued Capital:** £1,000
**Director:** K Fawole
**Responsibilities**
**Senior:** Caroline Fawole (Deputy Manager)
**US SIC:** 8811, 8321
**UK SIC:** 99000, 96111

|  | 30-06-13 | 30-06-12 | 30-06-11 |
|---|---|---|---|
| TO | N/A | N/A | 32,325 |
| P/L | N/A | N/A | 2,456 |
| NW | 42,910 | 9,281 | 1,663 |
| WC | 26,325 | 4,770 | (4,838) |

DUNS 21-914-8319  **Imp-Exp**
### Sonic Communications (International) Ltd
(Subsidiary of: Bowmer and Kirkland Limited)
Birmingham International Park, Birmingham, West Midlands B37 7HB
**Tel:** 0121-781-4400
**Web:** www.sonic-comms.com
**Reg No:** 1248257 **VAT No:** 113242718
**Estd:** 1977 Private Limited Company
**Line of Business:** Manufacture of other special purpose machinery not elsewhere classified
**Export Markets:** Worldwide
**Trading Style:** Soncell International Group
**Issued Capital:** £100,000
**Directors:** M R Wilbraham, N Barker, M S Sheldon, M J Beale
**Responsibilities**
**Senior:** Robert Bowmer (Manager)
**Sales:** Colin Bentley (Regional Sales Manager), Stephen Cherry (Sales Manager), Marcus Twomlow (Regional Sales Manager)
**US SIC:** 7399, 3651
**UK SIC:** 83954, 34541
**Auditors:** RSM Tenon Audit Ltd
**Bankers:** Barclays Bank Plc (20-08-98)

|  | 31-08-13 | 31-08-12 | 31-08-11 |
|---|---|---|---|
| TO | 7,784,783 | 7,663,431 | 13,176,694 |
| P/L | 933,889 | 213,411 | 3,689 |
| NW | 11,136,708 | 10,702,315 | 10,546,518 |
| WC | 8,884,913 | 8,396,096 | 8,117,232 |
| Emp. | 86 | 84 | 114 |

DUNS 54-845-3109
### Sonic Couriers
2 Mortimer Lane, Freckenham, Bury St Edmunds, Suffolk IP28 8JD
**Web:** www.newtaxtaxis.co.uk
**Estd:** 1993 Proprietorship
**Line of Business:** Couriers

**Proprietor:** P Polley
**Responsibilities**
**Senior:** Philip Polley (Proprietor)
**US SIC:** 4213 **UK SIC:** 72300
**Employees:** 50

DUNS 52-033-9961
### Sonic Rail Services Ltd
Unit 15 Springfield Industrial Estate, Springfield Road, Southminster, Essex CM0 8UA
**Tel:** 01621784688
**Web:** www.sonicrail.co.uk
**Reg No:** 3400496 **Estd:** 1997 Private Limited Company
**Line of Business:** Public works contractors
**Issued Capital:** £10,050
**Directors:** S Robinson, Ms A L Robinson
**US SIC:** 8911 **UK SIC:** 83701
**Auditors:** Robertson Milroy Ltd

|  | 31-07-13 | 31-07-12 | 31-07-11 |
|---|---|---|---|
| TO | 11,876,225 | 15,371,889 | 18,065,489 |
| P/L | 904,001 | (178,063) | 4,356,980 |
| NW | 5,499,223 | 4,831,682 | 5,328,393 |
| WC | 3,822,141 | 3,735,707 | 4,189,568 |
| Emp. | 54 | 50 | 56 |

DUNS 21-914-1553  **Imp-Exp**
### Sonifex Ltd
61 Station Road, Irthlingborough, Wellingborough, Northamptonshire NN9 5QE
**Web:** www.sonifex.co.uk
**Reg No:** 1717864 **VAT No:** 119853252
**Estd:** 1969 Private Limited Company
**Line of Business:** Sound recording apparatus and equipment
**Export Markets:** Worldwide
**Issued Capital:** £801,600
**Principals:** P Brooke (Chairman), M H Brooke (Managing), A Q Brooke, C A Stills, P A Schofield
**Co. Secretary:** Ms Vivien Chettle
**Responsibilities**
**Senior:** Gareth Laughton (Production Manager)
**Sales:** Richard Butlin (Sales Manager)
**IT:** Daniel Sore (IT Manager)
**Purchasing:** richard Amey (Purchasing Manager)
**Engineering:** Gareth Laughton (Production Manager)
**US SIC:** 3651 **UK SIC:** 34541
**Auditors:** Mark S Hollyman & Co
**Bankers:** HSBC Bank plc (40-46-03)

|  | 31-07-13 | 31-07-12 | 31-07-11 |
|---|---|---|---|
| TA | 2,688,062 | 2,708,068 | 2,641,332 |
| NW | 1,950,907 | 2,119,497 | 2,110,105 |
| WC | 1,599,578 | 1,855,545 | 1,918,153 |

DUNS 22-864-4134  **Exp**
### Sonoco Ltd
(Subsidiary of: Sonoco Products Company)
Station Road Milnrow, Rochdale, Lancashire OL16 4HQ
**Tel:** 01706641661 **Fax:** 01706 649630
**Web:** www.sonoco.com
**Reg No:** 0082196 **VAT No:** 566809694
**Estd:** 1904 Private Limited Company
**Line of Business:** Manufacture of paper and paperboard
**Export Markets:** Rest of Europe, Africa, America, Middle East, Australia and far East
**Export Sales:** £7,546,000
**Trading Style:** Sonoco Alcore, Harland Machine Division, Sonoco Triident, Sonoco Capseals Trident Uk
**Issued Capital:** £15,849
**Directors:** A Wood, R F Carroll, C D Beck, T J Nash, Ms A Clayton
**Co. Secretary:** David Collins
**Responsibilities**
**Senior:** Kostantinos Kiriakopoulos (Manager), Kevin Mahoney (Manager)
**IT:** Ian Mcneil (IT Manager)
**Branches:** Sonoco Ltd, 4 Wenlock Road, Craigavon, Co Armagh BT66 8QW
**US SIC:** 2631 **UK SIC:** 47017
**Auditors:** PricewaterhouseCoopers LLP

|  | 31-12-13 | 31-12-12 | 31-12-11 |
|---|---|---|---|
| TO | 39,184,000 | 37,613,000 | 32,538,000 |
| P/L | (1,079,000) | 1,021,000 | 1,563,000 |
| NW | (13,744,000) | (16,829,000) | (9,741,000) |
| WC | (6,716,000) | 2,103,000 | 6,659,000 |
| Emp. | 546 | 448 | 460 |

DUNS 73-640-4398  **Imp-Exp**
### Sonomatic Ltd
(Subsidiary of: Entech Holding Group Ltd)
Dornoch House, Kelvin Close, Birchwood, Warrington, Cheshire WA3 7PB
**Web:** www.sonomatic.com
**Reg No:** 4900658 **Estd:** 2003 Private Limited Company
**Line of Business:** Engineering services
**Export Sales:** £5,164,833
**Issued Capital:** £1,000
**Principals:** R Cesan (Managing), Dr C Becht Iv

**Responsibilities**
**Senior:** Charles Becht IV *(Director)*, Sandra Minshull *(Human Resources Manager)*
**Finance:** Anne Crompton *(Financial Director)*
**US SIC:** 8911 **UK SIC:** 83701

| | 31-10-13 | 31-10-12 | 31-10-11 |
|---|---|---|---|
| TO | 19,297,448 | 13,583,568 | 14,643,248 |
| P/L | 3,815,649 | 1,685,881 | 1,963,560 |
| NW | 6,849,676 | 3,955,298 | 2,860,178 |
| WC | 4,677,217 | 2,474,755 | 2,143,820 |
| Emp. | 92 | 82 | 76 |

DUNS 21-605-4189
## Sons & Co. Gardiner Ltd
(**Subsidiary of:** Gardiner (Holdings) Ltd)
Straight Street, Bristol, Avon BS2 0JP
**Tel:** 01179292288
**Web:** www.gardinerhaskins.co.uk
**Reg No:** 0039402 **Estd:** 1893 Private Limited Company
**Line of Business:** Other retail sale in non-specialised stores
**Trading Style:** Gardiner Homecentre, Gardiner Haskins Homecentre
**Issued Capital:** £1,262,661
**Directors:** S D Butcher, A P Webb, S D Whitcombe, J A Dursley, A G Allen
**Co. Secretary:** John Watson
**Responsibilities**
**Senior:** Mike Burridge *(Transport Manager)*
**HR:** Karen Bush *(Head of Training)*
**Fleet:** Mike Burridge *(Transport Manager)*
**Branches:** Sons & Co. Gardiner Ltd, Gardiner Homecentre, 00-72 Dyer Street, Cirencester, Gloucestershire GL7 2PF
**US SIC:** 5399, 5251
**UK SIC:** 65600, 64800
**Auditors:** PricewaterhouseCoopers LLP
**Bankers:** The Royal Bank Of Scotland Plc (16-14-25)

| | 31-12-13 | 31-12-12 | 31-12-11 |
|---|---|---|---|
| TO | 15,123,498 | 15,763,484 | 16,328,799 |
| P/L | 1,500,216 | 1,709,274 | 1,940,423 |
| NW | 10,763,281 | 10,839,133 | 10,740,703 |
| WC | 3,806,011 | 3,916,959 | 3,692,880 |
| Emp. | 135 | 135 | 141 |

DUNS 21-240-9122 **Imp-Exp**
## Sons Bell & Co (Druggists) Ltd
(**Subsidiary of:** Marksans Pharma Limited)
Cheshire House, Gorsey Lane, Widnes, Cheshire WA8 0RP
**Tel:** 0151 422 1200
**Web:** www.bells-healthcare.com
**Reg No:** 0351951 **VAT No:** 163464952
**Estd:** 1939 Private Limited Company
**Line of Business:** Manufacturers of pharmaceutical products
**Export Markets:** East & West Africa & Middle East
**Trading Style:** Bells Healthcare
**Issued Capital:** £6,334
**Directors:** B T Gulliver, M B Saldanha
**Co. Secretary:** David Barlow
**Branches:** Bell,Sons & Co.(Druggists) Ltd, Bell Sons & Co (Druggists) Ltd, Gifford House, Southport, Merseyside PR9 9AL
**US SIC:** 2834, 5122
**UK SIC:** 25700, 61800
**Auditors:** PKF (UK) LLP
**Bankers:** Barclays Bank Plc (20-51-01)

| | 31-03-14 | 31-03-13 | 31-03-12 |
|---|---|---|---|
| TO | 16,911,972 | 15,541,954 | 13,970,880 |
| P/L | 931,361 | 931,543 | 612,096 |
| NW | 6,227,457 | 8,498,220 | 7,838,868 |
| WC | 3,389,050 | 5,570,844 | 4,776,402 |
| Emp. | 175 | 157 | 144 |

DUNS 50-743-2995
## The Sons of Devine Providence
25 Lower Teddington Road, Kingston-Upon-Thames, Surrey KT1 4HB
**Web:** www.sonsofdivineprovidence.org
**Estd:** 1952
**Line of Business:** Social work activities
**Trading Style:** Molesey Horticultural Day Centre, Orione House, Fatima House
**Principals:** J C Perrotta *(Chairman)*, R Grady, H Parry, R Simionato, A Lanza, F Meade, J Mcardle, J Vallauri
**Branches:** The Sons Of Devine Providence, Holiday Homes Gradwells Farm, Moor Rd, Leyland, Lancashire PR26 9HP
**US SIC:** 6732, 6531, 8321
**UK SIC:** 83100, 83400, 96111
**Auditors:** H W Fisher & Co
**Bankers:** HSBC Bank plc (40-05-20)
**Employees:** 156

DUNS 23-268-4394
## The Sons of Divine Providence
13 Lower Teddington Road, Kingston-Upon-Thames, Surrey KT1 4EU
**Tel:** 02089770105
**Web:** www.sonsofdivine.org
**Reg No:** 4249759 **Estd:** 2001 Private Limited Company
**Line of Business:** Other letting of own property
**Directors:** C P Kehoe, Rev J Perrotta, Rev M A Moss, S P Beale, Ms B M Griffin, Mrs U H Harrison
**Co. Secretary:** Michael Healy
**Branches:** The Sons Of Divine Providence, 38 Palace Rd, London SW2 3NJ
**US SIC:** 6519, 8091, 8661
**UK SIC:** 85000, 95200, 96600
**Bankers:** HSBC Bank plc (40-05-20)

| | 31-03-14 | 31-03-13 | 31-03-12 |
|---|---|---|---|
| TO | 3,378,549 | 3,229,551 | 3,234,764 |
| P/L | (86,766) | (445,575) | (719,572) |
| NW | 7,716,262 | 7,808,183 | 7,872,613 |
| WC | 2,082,176 | 2,133,215 | 2,605,282 |
| Emp. | 114 | 114 | 112 |

DUNS 21-700-2427
## Son(South Quick & West)Ltd
St Michaels House, Severn Road, Hallen, Bristol, Avon BS10 7SA
**Tel:** 01179-591959
**Web:** www.quicksons.co.uk
**Reg No:** 0810448 **VAT No:** 139484145
**Estd:** 1964 Private Limited Company
**Line of Business:** Painting & decorating contractors
**Trading Style:** Quick Sons
**Issued Capital:** £4,000
**Principals:** M Quick *(Managing)*, Ms M Quick
**Co. Secretary:** Ms Susan Hopkins
**Responsibilities**
**Senior:** Alex Quick *(Property Surveyor)*, Karl Quick *(Manager)*
**Branches:** Quick,Son(South & West)ltd, Whiteway Ct, Cirencester, Gloucestershire GL7 7BA
**US SIC:** 1721, 1761
**UK SIC:** 50400
**Auditors:** Stone & Co
**Bankers:** Lloyds TSB Bank plc (30-00-01)

| | 30-04-14 | 30-04-13 | 30-04-12 |
|---|---|---|---|
| TA | 1,296,571 | 748,561 | 1,321,199 |
| NW | 430,743 | 168,358 | 383,967 |
| WC | 350,835 | 100,530 | 305,745 |

DUNS 23-974-7574 **Imp**
## Sonus Networks Ltd
(**Subsidiary of:** Sonus Networks Inc.)
Edison House, Edison Road, Dorcan, Swindon, Wiltshire SN3 5JX
**Tel:** 01793601400
**Web:** www.sonusnet.com
**Reg No:** 3963438 **Estd:** 2000 Private Limited Company
**Line of Business:** Telecommunications
**Export Sales:** £4,369,499
**Issued Capital:** £100
**Directors:** J Snider, M T Greenquist
**Co. Secretary:** John Mellor
**Responsibilities**
**Senior:** Maurice Castonguay *(Manager)*, Jill Marshall *(Office Manager)*
**Admin:** Jill Marshall *(Office Manager)*
**Health & Safety:** Jill Marshall *(Office Manager)*
**Facilities:** Jill Marshall *(Office Manager)*
**US SIC:** 4899 **UK SIC:** 79020

| | 31-12-13 | 31-12-12 | 31-12-11 |
|---|---|---|---|
| TO | 8,204,818 | 8,741,947 | 10,282,747 |
| P/L | (193,740) | (49,754) | 124,962 |
| NW | 3,787,780 | 3,764,778 | 3,668,078 |
| WC | 2,213,412 | 2,077,506 | 3,812,620 |
| Emp. | 58 | 66 | 60 |

DUNS 34-841-7382 **Imp**
## Sony Dadc Uk Ltd
(**Subsidiary of:** Sony Corporation)
Worthing Road Southwater Business Park, Horsham, West Sussex RH13 9YT
**Tel:** 01403739600 **Fax:** 01403-739601
**Web:** www.sonydadc.com
**Reg No:** 5640889 **VAT No:** 882212630
**Estd:** 2005 Private Limited Company
**Line of Business:** Manufacturers of cd's record and cassette
**Export Sales:** £15,983,000
**Issued Capital:** £1,000,000
**Directors:** D Daum, R D Taylor
**Co. Secretary:** Russell Taylor
**Responsibilities**
**Senior:** Colin Lammie *(General Manager)*
**Branches:** Sony Dadc Uk Ltd, 6 Solar Way, Enfield, Middlesex EN3 7XY
**US SIC:** 3651, 7819, 3679, 4226
**UK SIC:** 34541, 97111, 34542, 77003
**Auditors:** PricewaterhouseCoopers LLP
**Bankers:** National Westminster Bank Plc (60-02-20)

| | 31-03-13 | 31-03-12 | 31-03-11 |
|---|---|---|---|
| TO | 49,459,000 | 60,030,000 | 57,193,000 |
| P/L | 158,000 | 1,489,000 | 2,442,000 |
| NW | 1,153,000 | 1,300,000 | 603,000 |
| WC | (15,580,000) | (7,772,000) | (12,379,000) |
| Emp. | 383 | 351 | 337 |

DUNS 50-434-7444 **Imp**
## Sony Europe Ltd
(**Subsidiary of:** Sony Corporation)
The Heights, Brooklands, Weybridge, Surrey KT13 0XW
**Tel:** 01932-816000 **Fax:** 01932-817000
**Web:** www.sony.co.uk
**Reg No:** 2422874 **VAT No:** 636110080
**Estd:** 1968 Private Limited Company
**Line of Business:** Manufacture of television and radio receivers, sound or video recording or reproducing apparatus and associated goods
**Export Sales:** £3,426,304,000
**Trading Style:** Sony Computer Peripherals & Components Europe, Sony Semiconductor & Electronic Solutions, Sony Manufacturing Co Uk, Sony Business Europe Sony Professional Solutions
**Issued Capital:** £56,596,321
**Directors:** A Kobayashi, M Tamagawa, R Londema, G Pelliet
**Co. Secretary:** Nicholas Langhorne
**Responsibilities**
**Senior:** Steven Dowdle *(Manager)*, Kazuhiko Takeda *(Manager)*
**Health & Safety:** Phil Crowhurst *(Divisional Director)*
**Purchasing:** Phil Crowhurst *(Divisional Director)*
**Branches:** Sony Europe Ltd, Bridgend Plant, Bridgend, Mid Glamorgan CF31 3YH
**US SIC:** 3651, 3861, 5064, 5081
**UK SIC:** 34541, 37330, 61500, 61490
**Auditors:** PricewaterhouseCoopers LLP

**Following financial data are in thousands**

| | 31-03-14 | 31-03-13 | 31-03-12 |
|---|---|---|---|
| TO | 3,915,851 | 3,827,777 | 4,892,166 |
| P/L | (265,781) | (292,233) | (605,796) |
| NW | (1,276,343) | (945,650) | (588,028) |
| WC | (457,817) | (852,763) | 116,704 |
| Emp. | 3,944 | 4,593 | 5,062 |

DUNS 22-239-0820 **Imp**
## Sony Mobile Communications Management Ltd
(**Subsidiary of:** Sony Corporation)
202 Hammersmith Road, London W6 7DN
**Tel:** 02087625880 **Fax:** 02087625881
**Web:** www.sonymobile.com
**Reg No:** 4257114 **Estd:** 2001 Private Limited Company
**Line of Business:** Business information services
**Issued Capital:** £100,000
**Directors:** J E Pearl, A H Van Schie, Y Oshima
**Co. Secretary:** Jonathan Pearl
**Responsibilities**
**Senior:** Erik Ahlgren *(Executive)*, Darrell Brauner *(Manager)*, Peter Crowell *(Manager)*, Drew Crowell *(Spokesman)*, Stacy Doster *(Manager)*, Mats Ekstrand *(Vice President)*, Farhad Esmail *(Executive)*, Martin Essl *(Partner)*, Steffen Grosch *(Manager)*, Mattias Holm *(Spokesman)*, Bjorn Kilburn *(Manager)*, Aldo Liguori *(Manager)*, Katsunori Miura *(Manager)*, Takahiro Miyake *(Manager)*, Eva Nilsson *(Senior Manager)*, Albin Olofsson *(Manager)*, Idris Omerovic *(Executive)*, Ken Schmidt *(General Manager)*, Vijay Sharan *(Executive)*, Laura Sharples *(Sales Director)*, Rikard Skogberg *(Category Manager)*, Koutarou Takahashi *(Executive)*, Masaki Takeuchi *(Manager)*, Ryosuke Takeuchi *(Executive)*, Masaki Tashiro *(Manager)*, Gen Tsuchikawa *(Director)*, Mats Wolf *(Executive)*, Alex Wong *(General Manager)*, Merran Wrigley *(Vice President)*, Chikashi Yajima *(Manager)*
**Finance:** Tayo Ogundipe *(Head of Finance)*
**Marketing:** Herve Baurez *(Marketing Director)*, Amitabh Bhatnagar *(Business Manager)*, Boris Borenko *(Product Marketing Manager)*, Jennifer Bromley *(Marketing Director)*, Helene Browall *(Head of Product and Technology)*, David Chapon *(Marketing Director)*, Catherine Cherry *(Market Business Manager)*, Richard Dorman *(Marketing Manager)*, Dee Dutta *(Senior Marketing Executive)*, Sandra Echeverri *(Marketing Manager)*, Rosa Fernandez *(Product Marketing Manager)*, Mattias Jarlevi *(Digital Campaign Manager)*, Anurag Kontu *(Marketing Director)*, Calum Macdougall *(Marketing Director)*, Sumit Malhotra *(Marketing Manager)*, Jenny Maltesson *(Marketing Manager)*, Edgar Martinez *(Marketing Manager)*, David Mignot *(Marketing Director)*, Michael Ning *(Media and Public Relations)*, Zorayda Pedersen *(Global Marketing Manager)*, Linda Schori *(Marketing Manager)*, Peggy Schulz *(Marketing Director)*
**Sales:** Rahul Goel *(Sales Director)*, Fabio Ito *(Business Development Manager)*, Emeka Nkpa *(National Accounts Manager)*, Erik Sandsmark *(Account Manager)*, Laura Sharples *(Sales Director)*, John Wareby *(Senior Sales Executive)*
**Admin:** Julie Conner *(Assistant)*, Julia Persson *(Administrator)*
**IT:** Richard Camacho *(Software Project Manager)*, Ib Green *(IT Manager)*, Hubert Lin *(Information Technology Manager)*, Carl-Eric Mols *(Director, Software Strategies)*, Patrik Olsson *(IT Manager)*, Chris Sganga *(Head of Information Systems)*, Anders Westin *(Manager Software Development)*
**HR:** Bernstad Bernstad *(Head of Human Resources)*, Julie Gonzalez *(Human Resources)*, Jennifer Mertz *(Human Resources)*
**Operations:** Sachin Anand *(Senior Product Manager)*, Jan Fredander *(Product Manager)*, Mamatha Gopal *(Project Manager)*, Wang Lin *(Operations Director)*, Mike Sink *(Senior Project Manager)*, Kristian Tarnhed *(Production and Operations Mana)*, Endre Vaitzner *(Product Manager)*
**Purchasing:** Catherine Chuang *(Procurement Officer)*, Patrik Jansson *(Purchasing Director)*, Nina Rohrt *(SAP Solution Manager Supply Ch)*, Leanne Tolsma *(Procurement Officer)*
**Fleet:** Lars Jarmander *(Director, Global Logistics)*, Alan Pendleton *(Contract Manager)*
**Engineering:** Srdan Boskovic *(Software Engineer)*, Mark Clemens *(Software Engineer)*, Dera Gray *(Engineer)*, Priyanka Sharma *(Software Engineer)*, Keita Sugawara *(Software Engineer)*, Zhenfeng Sun *(Engineer)*, Magnus Wallin *(Software Engineer)*, Daniel Zhang *(Engineer)*
**US SIC:** 7399 **UK SIC:** 83954
**Auditors:** Scodie Deyong LLP

| | 31-03-14 | 31-03-13 | 31-03-11 |
|---|---|---|---|
| TO | 34,996,027 | 31,178,199 | 30,039,833 |
| P/L | 2,677,723 | 2,694,837 | 2,986,889 |
| NW | 6,130,317 | 4,082,983 | 2,816,717 |
| WC | 5,927,314 | 4,289,275 | 4,413,475 |
| Emp. | 103 | 76 | 59 |

DUNS 22-954-2295 **Imp-Exp**
## Sony Music Entertainment Uk Ltd
(**Subsidiary of:** Sony Corporation)
9 Derry Street, Kensington, London W8 5HY
**Tel:** 02073618000 **Fax:** 020 7371 9298
**Web:** www.sonymusic.com
**Reg No:** 1471066 **Estd:** 1980 Private Limited Company
**Line of Business:** Other publishing
**Export Markets:** E U; North America
**Export Sales:** £58,924,000
**Trading Style:** R C A/Ariola, Arista Records, B M G Distribution (Uk)
**Issued Capital:** £5,250,902
**Directors:** E Berger, W P Rowe, M A Smith, S Bondell, Ms J Swidler
**Co. Secretary:** Simon Jenkins
**Responsibilities**
**Senior:** Gerald Doherty *(Manager)*
**Branches:** Sony Music Entertainment Uk Ltd, Unit 24, Crystal Drive, Smethwick, West Midlands B66 1QG
**US SIC:** 2741, 5065
**UK SIC:** 47541, 61500
**Auditors:** PricewaterhouseCoopers LLP

| | 31-03-14 | 31-03-13 | 31-03-12 |
|---|---|---|---|
| TO | 238,676,000 | 205,578,000 | 191,104,503 |
| P/L | 22,247,000 | 16,114,000 | 15,150,087 |
| NW | 202,014,000 | 225,329,000 | 208,765,075 |
| WC | 28,434,000 | 46,169,000 | 35,198,438 |
| Emp. | 310 | 301 | 324 |

DUNS 53-625-9955
## Sony/Atv Music Publishing (Uk) Ltd
(**Subsidiary of:** Sony/Atv Music Publishing Llc)
30 Golden Square, London W1F 9LD
**Tel:** 02032062501
**Web:** www.sonyatv.com
**Reg No:** 3431011 **Estd:** 1997 Private Limited Company
**Line of Business:** Other publishing
**Export Sales:** £16,736,000
**Issued Capital:** £1,000
**Directors:** J S Puzio, M N Bandier, G K Moot, G R Henderson
**Co. Secretary:** Abogado Nominees Limited
**Responsibilities**
**Senior:** Jane Moriai *(Manager)*
**Sales:** Melanie Johnson *(Business Development Director)*
**US SIC:** 2741 **UK SIC:** 47541
**Auditors:** PricewaterhouseCoopers

| | 31-03-14 | 31-03-13 | 31-03-12 |
|---|---|---|---|
| TO | 45,961,000 | 38,880,000 | 37,001,000 |
| P/L | 4,631,000 | 4,168,000 | 4,060,000 |
| NW | 4,446,000 | 1,830,000 | 1,575,000 |
| WC | 4,439,000 | 1,830,000 | 1,575,000 |

DUNS 28-857-7968
## Soothills Ltd
(**Subsidiary of:** Soothills Bakeries Ltd)
1 East Street, Fareham, Hampshire PO16 0BW
**Tel:** 01329-232570
**Reg No:** 0834357 **Estd:** 1965 Private Limited Company

**Line of Business:** Retail sale of bread, cakes, flour confectionery and sugar confectionery
**Issued Capital:** £13,000
**Managing Director:** A R Jenkins
**Co. Secretary:** Ms Angela Moyse
**Branches:** Soothills Ltd, Centre Way, Locks Heath, Southampton, Hampshire SO31 6DX
**US SIC:** 5462 **UK SIC:** 64100
**Bankers:** National Westminster Bank Plc (52-41-32)

| | 30-11-13 | 30-11-12 | 30-11-11 |
|---|---|---|---|
| TA | 500,091 | 443,974 | 458,369 |
| NW | 366,530 | 342,459 | 371,034 |
| WC | 119,440 | 173,183 | 205,692 |

DUNS 45-880-1537 **Exp**

## Sopheon P L C
Unit 61 Surrey Technology Centre, Surrey Research Park, Guildford, Surrey GU2 7YG
**Fax:** 01483883050
**Web:** www.sopheon.com
**Reg No:** 3217859 **Estd:** 1996 Public Limited Company
**Line of Business:** Other computer related activities
**Export Markets:** Netherlands & USA
**Trading Style:** Sopheon P L C
**Issued Capital:** £7,279,000
**Directors:** S A Silcock, B K Mence, D Metzger, A L Michuda, B P Al
**Co. Secretary:** Arif Karimjee
**US SIC:** 7379 **UK SIC:** 83940
**Auditors:** BDO LLP
**Bankers:** Lloyds TSB Bank plc (30-97-84)

| | 31-12-13 | 31-12-12 | 31-12-11 |
|---|---|---|---|
| TO | 13,276,000 | 12,663,000 | 10,276,000 |
| P/L | 341,000 | 281,000 | 104,000 |
| NW | 123,000 | (258,000) | (666,000) |
| WC | 1,892,000 | 1,654,000 | 819,000 |
| Emp. | 114 | 102 | 92 |

DUNS 21-033-3797

## Sophie's Steak House & Bar
311-313 Fulham Road, London SW10 9QH
**Tel:** 020-7352-0088
**Web:** www.sophiessteakhouse.com
**Estd:** 2002 Proprietorship
**Line of Business:** Restaurant - english
**Proprietor:** M Coulcon
**Responsibilities**
**Senior:** Johan Jager (Manager)
**US SIC:** 5812 **UK SIC:** 66110
**Employees:** 50

DUNS 21-585-1769

## Sophies Steak House & Bar
29-31 Wellington Street, London WC2E 7DB
**Tel:** 02078368836
**Web:** www.sophiessteakhouse.co.uk
**Estd:** 2010 Proprietorship
**Line of Business:** Restaurants
**Proprietor:** M Belcher
**US SIC:** 5812 **UK SIC:** 66110
**Employees:** 80

DUNS 29-893-6147 **Imp-Exp**

## Sophos Ltd
(**Subsidiary of:** Apax Partners Europe Managers Ltd)
The Pentagon, Abingdon, Oxfordshire OX14 3YP
**Tel:** 01235559933
**Web:** www.sophos.com
**Reg No:** 2096520 **VAT No:** 348387320
**Estd:** 1987 Private Limited Company
**Line of Business:** Other software consultancy and supply
**Export Sales:** £114,699,000
**Directors:** S B Fillingham, Mrs J M Onslow, N P Bray
**Responsibilities**
**Senior:** Bryan Barney (Senior Vice President & Genera), Hazem Gacem (Manager), Edwin Gillis (Board Member), Peter Gyenes (Board Member), Kristof Hagerman (Chief Executive Officer), Jan Hruska (Board Member), Peter Lammer (Co-Founder), Stephen Munford (Chief Executive), Salim Nathoo (Board Member)
**Finance:** Jeff Babka (Chief Financial Officer), Sharon Collins (Financial Controller)
**Marketing:** Andrea Collins (Head of Marketing), Matt Fairbanks (Chief Marketing Officer), Alexandra Light (Marketing Manager), Chris Weeds (Director of Product Marketing)
**Sales:** Ari Buchler (Senior Vice President, Corpora), Michael Mcguiness (SVP, Worldwide Sales and Field), Cieron Rafferty (Sales Manager), Michael Valentine (Senior Vice President, Sales)
**IT:** Bryan Barney (Senior Vice President & Genera), Tom Elger (IT Manager), Bill Luchini (Senior Vice President & Genera), Dan Schiappa (Senior Vice President & Genera), Mary Winfield (Senior Vice President, Global)

**HR:** Edie Givens (Senior Vice President, Human R)
**Health & Safety:** Simon Pedrazzini (Facilities Manager)
**Facilities:** Simon Pedrazzini (Facilities Manager)
**Branches:** Sophos Ltd, 9 Muir Wood Crescent, Currie, Midlothian EH14 5HD
**US SIC:** 7399, 7379
**UK SIC:** 83954, 83940
**Auditors:** KPMG LLP
**Bankers:** Lloyds TSB Bank plc (30-96-35)

| | 31-03-14 | 31-03-13 | -03- |
|---|---|---|---|
| TO | 128,194,000 | 113,993,000 | N/A |
| P/L | 72,719,000 | 16,644,000 | N/A |
| NW | 152,962,000 | 138,596,000 | N/A |
| WC | (71,554,000) | (48,274,000) | N/A |
| Emp. | 450 | 452 | 1,648 |

DUNS 22-627-6343 **Exp**

## Sopra Banking Software Ltd
Ground Floor The Arenson Centre, Dunstable, Bedfordshire LU5 5UL
**Tel:** 01582889700 **Fax:** 01582668442
**Web:** www.soprabanking.com
**Reg No:** 1454835 **VAT No:** 600649759
**Estd:** 1979 Private Limited Company
**Line of Business:** Miscellaneous computer services
**Export Markets:** Worldwide
**Export Sales:** £2,082,912
**Issued Capital:** £2,340,000
**Directors:** P Commanay, E Howard, H M Heiskanen
**Responsibilities**
**Finance:** Paul Jameson (Financial Director)
**Health & Safety:** Caroline Rollo (Facilities Specialist)
**Facilities:** Caroline Rollo (Facilities Specialist)
**Branches:** Sopra Banking Software Ltd, Eastleigh House, Upper Market Street, Eastleigh, Hampshire SO50 9FD
**US SIC:** 7379, 7399
**UK SIC:** 83940, 83954
**Auditors:** PricewaterhouseCoopers LLP
**Bankers:** National Westminster Bank Plc (60-18-11)

| | 31-12-13 | 31-12-12 | 31-12-11 |
|---|---|---|---|
| TO | 23,588,956 | 21,653,076 | 23,950,599 |
| P/L | 4,112,081 | 4,635,823 | 4,811,299 |
| NW | 10,928,131 | 7,892,321 | 4,124,543 |
| WC | 16,256,726 | 7,313,658 | 7,862,627 |
| Emp. | 163 | 158 | 206 |

DUNS 22-076-5411 **Imp-Exp**

## Sopra Steria Ltd
(**Subsidiary of:** Sopra Group)
Three Cherry Trees Lane, Hemel Hempstead, Hertfordshire HP2 7AH
**Tel:** 08706004466
**Web:** www.steria.com
**Reg No:** 4077975 **VAT No:** 207950855
**Estd:** 2001 Private Limited Company
**Line of Business:** Computer systems and software (sales)
**Issued Capital:** £48,150,185
**Directors:** S C Dangu, J J Moran, D S Ahluwalia, J P Torrie, L P Lemaire
**Co. Secretary:** Peter Cashmore
**Responsibilities**
**Senior:** Franois Enaud (Group CEO), Peter Jawanda (Executive), Jean-Bernard Rampini (Development Director), Hilary Robertson (Group Director, Business Proce), Anthony Singleton (Aerospace General Manager)
**Finance:** Lynn Millar (Head of Payments Transformatio)
**Marketing:** Michael Harding (e-Business Marketing Manager), Kathryn Howe (Marketing Manager), Patricia Langrand (Director of Business Developme)
**Sales:** Delphine Arnaud (Responsible Commercial), Andrew Bradburn (Sales Manager), Joanna Collis (Account Manager), Tim Difford (Business Solutions Director), Patricia Langrand (Director of Business Developme), Malcolm Little (Sales Director)
**Admin:** Ekta Agarwal (Personal Assistant)
**IT:** Paul Dhillon (IT Director)
**HR:** Bipasha Batheja (India Resource Business Partne), Hannebicque Hannebicque (Human Resources)
**Operations:** Kenneth Mikkelsen (Service Manager)
**Engineering:** Kristian Lindvik (Engineer)
**Branches:** Steria Ltd, Pavilions Office Park, Kinnegar Drive, Co Down Broadstairs
**US SIC:** 7379 **UK SIC:** 83940
**Auditors:** Ernst & Young LLP
**Bankers:** Barclays Bank Plc (20-00-00)

| | 31-12-13 | 31-12-12 | 31-12-11 |
|---|---|---|---|
| TO | 442,662,000 | 473,717,000 | 484,733,000 |
| P/L | 24,193,000 | 24,266,000 | 35,017,000 |
| NW | 105,002,000 | 48,737,000 | 2,575,000 |
| WC | 227,753,000 | 220,746,000 | 108,181,000 |
| Emp. | 3,206 | 3,392 | 3,538 |

DUNS 77-164-9936

## Sopra Steria Services Ltd
(**Subsidiary of:** Sopra Group)
Three Cherry Trees Lane, Hemel Hempstead, Hertfordshire HP2 7AH
**Tel:** 08706004466
**Web:** www.steria.com
**Reg No:** 2706218 **VAT No:** 207950855
**Estd:** 1969 Private Limited Company
**Line of Business:** Other computer related activities
**Issued Capital:** £94,721,513
**Directors:** D S Ahluwalia, L P Lemaire, Ms S C Dangu, J J Moran, J P Torrie
**Co. Secretary:** Peter Cashmore
**Branches:** Steria Services Ltd, Avenue Ct, Victoria Ave, Camberley, Surrey GU15 3HX
**US SIC:** 7379 **UK SIC:** 83940
**Auditors:** Ernst & Young LLP
**Bankers:** National Westminster Bank Plc (60-03-23)

| | 31-12-13 | 31-12-12 | 31-12-11 |
|---|---|---|---|
| TA | 243,336,000 | 243,336,000 | 143,336,000 |
| NW | 143,336,000 | 143,336,000 | 143,336,000 |

DUNS 21-002-7585

## Sorbic International Plc
3rd Floor, London SW1A 2BX
**Tel:** 02079308888
**Web:** www.sorbicinternational.com
**Reg No:** 6280431 **Estd:** 2007 Public Limited Company
**Line of Business:** Manufacture of other chemical products not elsewhere classified
**Export Sales:** £14,619,913
**Issued Capital:** £3,429,273
**Directors:** Y T Wang, J Newman, J N Mclean
**Co. Secretary:** Nigel Cartwright
**US SIC:** 2899 **UK SIC:** 25670
**Auditors:** Crowe Clark Whitehill LLP

| | 30-09-13 | 30-09-12 | 30-09-11 |
|---|---|---|---|
| TO | 14,619,913 | 16,780,832 | 14,737,545 |
| P/L | (6,129,650) | (144,406) | 270,851 |
| NW | 8,208,823 | 12,122,821 | 11,899,639 |
| WC | 2,207,752 | 1,068,786 | 2,734,065 |
| Emp. | 262 | 264 | 265 |

DUNS 23-651-7152

## Sorbon Homes Ltd
Sorbon Aylesbury End, Beaconsfield, Buckinghamshire HP9 1LW
**Tel:** 01494685800
**Web:** www.michaelshanly.co.uk
**Reg No:** 3646926 **Estd:** 1998 Private Limited Company
**Line of Business:** Property developers
**Issued Capital:** £30,100,000
**Directors:** M J Shanly, T J Potter, N M Trott, D A Tucker, Mrs T M Booth
**Co. Secretary:** Paul Giles
**Responsibilities**
**Finance:** Louise Franey (Credit Control Manager)
**Facilities:** Tom Gormley (Senior Estates Manager), Jonathan Gould (Senior Estates Manager), Melanie Wills (Senior Estates Manager)
**US SIC:** 6552, 6519
**UK SIC:** 85000
**Auditors:** PricewaterhouseCoopers LLP

| | 31-12-13 | 31-12-12 | 31-12-11 |
|---|---|---|---|
| TO | 136,985,722 | 104,381,111 | 41,252,731 |
| P/L | 33,334,138 | 25,889,586 | 7,913,723 |
| NW | 133,140,073 | 88,410,617 | 66,897,355 |
| WC | 160,877,923 | 113,710,226 | 91,247,258 |
| Emp. | 148 | 130 | 118 |

DUNS 21-596-7933

## Soreen Bakery
Marshall Stevens Way, Trafford Park, Manchester M17 1PP
**Tel:** 01618744100
**Web:** www.soreen.com
**Estd:** 2010
**Line of Business:** Bakers and confectioners supplies
**Responsibilities**
**Senior:** Paul Tripp (Manager)
**US SIC:** 2051 **UK SIC:** 41960
**Employees:** 100

DUNS 21-621-1672 **Exp**

## Sorex Ltd
(**Subsidiary of:** Basf Se)
St Michaels Industrial Estate, Widnes, Cheshire WA8 8TJ
**Tel:** 0151-420-7151
**Web:** www.pestcontrol.basf.co.uk
**Reg No:** 0469788 **VAT No:** 439193331
**Estd:** 1949 Private Limited Company
**Line of Business:** Manufacture of other inorganic basic chemicals
**Export Markets:** Other EU Countries, Rest of the World
**Trading Style:** Network, Sorex International
**Issued Capital:** £100
**Directors:** S Hatton, T Urwin
**Co. Secretary:** Stephen Hatton

**Responsibilities**
**Senior:** Mark Downing (Operations Manager)
**Sales:** Shirley Wilson (Commercial Manager)
**IT:** Terry Loftus (IT Manager)
**HR:** Paula Chatterton (Human Resources Manager)
**Health & Safety:** Alan Vincent (Environmental Manager)
**Facilities:** Stephen Browne (Site Manager)
**Operations:** Mark Downing (Operations Manager), Alan Vincent (Environmental Manager)
**US SIC:** 2819, 2899
**UK SIC:** 25110, 25670
**Auditors:** Baker Tilly
**Bankers:** National Westminster Bank Plc (01-09-17)

| | 31-12-13 | 31-12-12 | 31-12-11 |
|---|---|---|---|
| TA | 2,125 | 893,663 | 794,697 |
| P/L | (18,660) | (7,939) | (32,198) |
| NW | 237 | 18,897 | 19,597 |
| WC | 237 | 161,977 | 162,677 |

DUNS 73-911-2683 **Imp**

## Sorin Group Uk Ltd
(**Subsidiary of:** Sorin Spa)
1370 Montpellier Court, Gloucester, Gloucestershire GL3 4AH
**Web:** www.sorin.com
**Reg No:** 5164704 **VAT No:** 040945320
**Estd:** 2004 Private Limited Company
**Line of Business:** Wholesale of pharmaceutical goods
**Issued Capital:** £1
**Directors:** G Cordano, K J Tuite, Mrs D M Carroll
**Co. Secretary:** Mrs Sharon Ayres
**Responsibilities**
**Senior:** Steven Adamson (Country Leader), Brian Sheridan (Manager)
**US SIC:** 5122, 8999
**UK SIC:** 61800, 83954
**Auditors:** Ernst & Young LLP
**Bankers:** Fortis Bank London Bch (formerly Generale Bk) (40-52-62)

| | 31-12-13 | 31-12-12 | 31-12-11 |
|---|---|---|---|
| TO | 20,811,992 | 19,592,224 | 19,478,342 |
| P/L | 2,735,955 | 1,395,764 | 643,973 |
| NW | 8,914,078 | 6,914,312 | 5,875,204 |
| WC | 8,086,818 | 6,212,690 | 4,998,362 |
| Emp. | 50 | 53 | 55 |

DUNS 22-077-1690

## Sortium Ltd
P O Box 2280, Brighton, East Sussex BN2 6WU
**Tel:** 01273307501
**Web:** www.sortium.com
**Reg No:** 4078641 **Estd:** 2000 Private Limited Company
**Line of Business:** Business and management consultancy activities not elsewhere classified
**Issued Capital:** £1
**Managing Director:** J A Smith
**Co. Secretary:** Ms Rosemary Smith
**US SIC:** 7392, 8249
**UK SIC:** 83951, 93300

| | 30-09-14 | 30-09-13 | 30-09-12 |
|---|---|---|---|
| TA | 11,856 | 5,950 | 7,280 |
| NW | 8,136 | (1,218) | (9,857) |
| WC | 7,855 | (1,218) | (9,857) |

DUNS 21-001-6782 **Imp**

## Sos Metals (Uk) Ltd
(**Subsidiary of:** Sos Metals (Europe) Holdings Ltd)
Unit 5 Berristow Lane, Alfreton, Derbyshire DE55 2EG
**Tel:** 01773862611
**Web:** www.sosmetals.com
**Reg No:** 6272151 **Estd:** 2007 Private Limited Company
**Line of Business:** Scrap metal dealers
**Directors:** S C Blackmore, D L Rose, Mrs S R Hagel, R P Becker, Ms R A Beyer, Ms S A Lacks
**Co. Secretary:** Paul Edelstyn
**Responsibilities**
**Senior:** Dave Mccafferty (Production Manager)
**US SIC:** 5093 **UK SIC:** 62200
**Employees:** 25
**Turnover:** £9,043,608

DUNS 21-909-2087

## Sotham Engineering Services Ltd
(**Subsidiary of:** Sotham Group Ltd)
The Granary, Home End, Fulbourn, Cambridge, Cambridgeshire CB21 5BS
**Tel:** 01223-881081
**Web:** www.sotham.co.uk
**Reg No:** 0874533 **VAT No:** 665858087
**Estd:** 1966 Private Limited Company
**Line of Business:** Engineering services
**Trading Style:** Sotham Engineering Services Ltd

**Issued Capital:** £100,000
**Managing Director:** P R Kerrison
**Co. Secretary:** Benjamin Sloan
**Branches:** Sotham Engineering Services Ltd, Unit G-H, Iceni Court, Delft Way, Norwich, Norfolk NR6 6BB
**US SIC:** 8911, 1711, 1796, 1799
**UK SIC:** 83701, 50300, 50400, 50000
**Auditors:** Price Bailey LLP
**Bankers:** Lloyds TSB Bank plc (30-12-18)

| | 31-12-13 | 31-12-12 | 31-12-11 |
|---|---|---|---|
| TO | 7,904,649 | 5,326,410 | 9,807,257 |
| P/L | 82,703 | 170,354 | 303,676 |
| NW | 1,030,143 | 1,088,364 | 1,080,962 |
| WC | 971,072 | 1,068,856 | 1,057,173 |
| Emp. | 63 | 63 | 67 |

DUNS 21-027-4452 **Imp-Exp**

## Sotheby's

(**Subsidiary of:** Sotheby's)
34-35 New Bond Street, London W1S 2RT
**Tel:** 02072935000
**Web:** www.sothebys.com
**Reg No:** 0874867 **VAT No:** 512549263
**Estd:** 1966 Private Unlimited Company
**Line of Business:** Auctioneers and valuers
**Export Sales:** £1,138,000
**Issued Capital:** £19,110,000
**Directors:** M Cornell, I M Fleming, C G Lord
**Co. Secretary:** Miss Antonia Scott
**Responsibilities**
**Senior:** George Bailey *(Manager)*, Alexander Bell *(Board Member)*, Thomas Christophoroon *(Manager)*, William Ruprecht *(CEO, Managing Director)*, William Sheridan *(Manager)*, Serena Sutcliffe *(Manager)*, Patrick Van Maris Van Dijk *(Manager)*, Robin Woodhead *(Vice President)*
**Marketing:** Giulia Costantini *(Chief Marketing Officer)*
**Sales:** George Bailey *(Manager)*
**IT:** Karen Hubbard *(IT Director)*
**Facilities:** Chloe Carpenter *(Head of Facilities)*
**Branches:** Sotheby's, 222 Bethnal Green Road, London E2 0AA
**US SIC:** 7399 **UK SIC:** 83954
**Auditors:** Deloitte LLP
**Bankers:** Barclays Bank Plc (20-67-59)

| | 31-12-13 | 31-12-12 | 31-12-11 |
|---|---|---|---|
| TO | 149,145,000 | 144,855,000 | 152,641,000 |
| P/L | 35,999,000 | 38,891,000 | 50,595,000 |
| NW | 193,157,000 | 179,101,000 | 157,834,000 |
| WC | 141,323,000 | 136,907,000 | 110,611,000 |
| Emp. | 515 | 508 | 489 |

DUNS 23-281-0523

## Soughton Hall Hotel

Hall Lane, Sychdyn, Mold, Clwyd CH7 6AD
**Tel:** 01352-840811
**Web:** www.soughtonhall.co.uk
**Estd:** 1987 Partnership
**Line of Business:** Hotels
**Partners:** J E Rodenhurst, Mrs R B Rodenhurst
**Responsibilities**
**Senior:** Annette Gallop *(Manager)*
**US SIC:** 7011 **UK SIC:** 66500
**Bankers:** National Westminster Bank Plc (54-10-10)
**Employees:** 50

DUNS 21-232-9480

## Soul Cafe Bar

333 Union Street, Aberdeen, Aberdeenshire AB11 6BS
**Tel:** 01224-211150
**Web:** www.pbdevco.com
**Estd:** 2004 Proprietorship
**Line of Business:** Clubs social and associations
**Proprietor:** Y Adebowale
**US SIC:** 5813 **UK SIC:** 66200
**Employees:** 58

DUNS 21-324-1078 **Imp-Exp**

## Sound Leisure Ltd

Sandleas Way, Leeds, West Yorkshire LS15 8AR
**Tel:** 08452301775 **Fax:** 0845-230-1776
**Web:** www.soundleisure.com
**Reg No:** 1342898 **VAT No:** 313514105
**Estd:** 1978 Private Limited Company
**Line of Business:** Juke box suppliers and renovators
**Export Markets:** Worldwide
**Issued Capital:** £5,100
**Principals:** A J Black *(Chairman and Managing)*, C J Black, M J Black, K E Moss
**Co. Secretary:** David Cross
**Responsibilities**
**Purchasing:** Allan Hick *(Buyer)*
**Engineering:** Jim Boyle *(Engineer)*
**US SIC:** 3651 **UK SIC:** 34541
**Auditors:** Mazars Neville Russell
**Bankers:** Lloyds TSB Bank plc (77-14-01)

| | 30-04-14 | 30-04-13 | 30-04-12 |
|---|---|---|---|
| TO | 5,787,405 | 4,365,025 | 5,848,796 |
| P/L | 92,200 | 59,588 | 59,913 |
| NW | 3,460,826 | 3,489,179 | 3,480,774 |
| WC | 1,270,954 | 1,420,185 | 1,510,312 |
| Emp. | 110 | 106 | 107 |

DUNS 21-306-6360

## Sound Performance

Halesfield 14, Telford, Shropshire TF7 4QR
**Tel:** 01952680131
**Web:** www.soundperformance.co.uk
**Proprietorship**
**Line of Business:** Multimedia publishers and producers
**Proprietor:** C Garbett
**US SIC:** 3679 **UK SIC:** 34542
**Employees:** 80

DUNS 34-737-8031

## Sound Performance Holdings Ltd

Unit 2-3 Block A, Greenwich Quay, Clarence Road, London SE8 3EY
**Tel:** 02086912121 **Fax:** 020-8691-3144
**Web:** www.superperformance.co.uk
**Reg No:** 5539753 **Estd:** 2005 Private Limited Company
**Line of Business:** Other letting of own property
**Export Sales:** £1,108,423
**Issued Capital:** £100
**Director:** C P Marksberry
**Co. Secretary:** Ms Nicola Marksberry
**US SIC:** 6519, 7372
**UK SIC:** 85000, 83940

| | 28-02-13 | 29-02-12 | 28-02-11 |
|---|---|---|---|
| TO | 9,473,697 | 12,874,047 | 11,858,852 |
| P/L | (228,528) | (79,632) | (61,708) |
| NW | 89,924 | 360,777 | 519,400 |
| WC | (1,163,322) | (961,473) | (883,202) |
| Emp. | 100 | 119 | 134 |

DUNS 50-655-3155

## Soup Kitchen

2 Church Lane, Stafford, Staffordshire ST16 2AW
**Web:** www.thesoupkitchen.co.uk
**Proprietorship**
**Line of Business:** Licensed restaurants
**Proprietor:** D Sandy
**US SIC:** 5812 **UK SIC:** 66110
**Employees:** 47

DUNS 21-833-7517 **Imp-Exp**

## Source Bioscience Plc

1 Nottingham Business Park Orchard Place, Nottingham, Nottinghamshire NG8 6PX
**Tel:** 01159-739012
**Web:** www.sourcebioscience.com
**Reg No:** 0079136 **Estd:** 1903 Public Limited Company
**Line of Business:** Management activities of holding companies
**Export Markets:** E U, Europe, The Americas, Africa, Asia, Other
**Export Sales:** £3,741,000
**Trading Style:** Vindon Healthcare Plc
**Issued Capital:** £4,095,665
**Directors:** L A Turnbull, Dr N I Leaves, Dr S Foden, T C Metcalfe, Mrs P Liversidge
**Co. Secretary:** Dr Nicholas Ash
**Responsibilities**
**Senior:** Robert Bakewell *(Financial Controller)*, Robin Slinger *(Manager)*
**Finance:** Robert Bakewell *(Financial Controller)*
**Marketing:** Robin Bodicoat *(Marketing Manager)*, Sarah Dyas *(Marketing Manager)*
**HR:** Eileen Barrett *(Legal Manager)*
**US SIC:** 6711, 5081
**UK SIC:** 83962, 61490
**Auditors:** KPMG Audit PLC
**Bankers:** HSBC Bank plc (40-05-30)

| | 31-12-13 | 31-12-12 | 31-12-11 |
|---|---|---|---|
| TO | 19,525,000 | 16,431,000 | 15,192,000 |
| P/L | (1,137,000) | 963,000 | (2,967,000) |
| NW | 5,669,000 | 7,008,000 | 3,160,000 |
| WC | 722,000 | 1,451,000 | 1,237,000 |
| Emp. | 140 | 119 | 127 |

DUNS 57-014-3727

## Source Insurance Ltd

Drake House, Plymouth Road, South Glamorgan, Penarth, South Glamorgan CF64 3TP
**Tel:** 02920265265 **Fax:** 02920704455
**Web:** www.sourcesoftware.co.uk
**Reg No:** 2864963 **Estd:** 1993 Private Limited Company
**Line of Business:** Insurance companies and agents
**Issued Capital:** £2,000
**Directors:** G L Davidson, K R Paterson, A A Masters, M R Cairns
**Responsibilities**
**Sales:** Brian Coulton *(Head of Sales)*
**Branches:** Source Insurance Ltd, Titan House, Cardiff Bay Business Centre, Titan Road, Cardiff, South Glamorgan CF24 5BS
**US SIC:** 6411 **UK SIC:** 83200
**Auditors:** John Price & Co
**Bankers:** National Westminster Bank Plc (54-21-33)

| | 31-12-13 | 31-12-12 | 31-12-11 |
|---|---|---|---|
| TO | 9,451,419 | 9,763,234 | 9,528,789 |
| P/L | 469,778 | 435,937 | 707,846 |
| NW | 859,654 | 861,787 | 664,132 |
| WC | 851,299 | 944,025 | 311,286 |
| Emp. | 60 | 65 | 65 |

DUNS 73-852-6289

## Source Personnel Ltd

(**Subsidiary of:** Source Personnel Holdings Ltd)
Wessex House Teign Road, Newton Abbot, Devon TQ12 4AA
**Tel:** 02031160000
**Web:** www.sourcepersonnel.co.uk
**Reg No:** 5107695 **Estd:** 2004 Private Limited Company
**Line of Business:** Labour recruitment and provision of personnel
**Issued Capital:** £1,002
**Directors:** Mrs N T Plinston, Ms B Fleming, A Dickinson, Ms A De Friend
**Co. Secretary:** Jonathan Lindon
**Branches:** Source Personnel Ltd, Colonial Buildings, 59 Hatton Garden, London EC1N 8LS
**US SIC:** 7361 **UK SIC:** 83954
**Bankers:** HSBC Bank plc (40-02-17)

| | 31-12-13 | 31-12-12 | 30-12-12 |
|---|---|---|---|
| TO | 10,987,819 | 5,517,094 | 8,897,612 |
| P/L | 373,317 | 189,082 | 117,171 |
| NW | 315,774 | 162,994 | 76,733 |
| WC | 183,667 | 102,722 | 142,557 |
| Emp. | 64 | 71 | 76 |

DUNS 76-375-5717

## Sourcecircle Ltd

Swan Lake Glass Works, Upperton Road, Leicester, Leicestershire LE2 7AY
**Tel:** 01162-541373
**Reg No:** 2553229 **Estd:** 1990 Private Limited Company
**Line of Business:** Holding companies management activities
**Export Sales:** £1,286,029
**Trading Style:** Source Circle Ltd
**Issued Capital:** £100
**Managing Director:** D A King
**Co. Secretary:** Mrs Jennifer King
**US SIC:** 3229, 3832
**UK SIC:** 24791, 37320
**Auditors:** John F Mould & Co Ltd
**Bankers:** Barclays Bank Plc (20-49-11)

| | 31-03-14 | 31-03-13 | 31-03-12 |
|---|---|---|---|
| TO | 9,361,186 | 9,563,582 | 11,267,981 |
| P/L | 898,844 | 894,413 | 1,241,461 |
| NW | 6,140,271 | 5,637,356 | 5,000,487 |
| WC | 3,904,217 | 3,440,935 | 2,939,399 |
| Emp. | 74 | 78 | 87 |

DUNS 22-021-3636

## Souters Sports Ltd

2 South Wardpark Court, Wardpark South, Cumbernauld, Glasgow, Lanarkshire G67 3EH
**Fax:** 01236731062
**Web:** www.souterssports.co.uk
**Reg No:** 0208665SC **VAT No:** 774639877
**Estd:** 2000 Private Limited Company
**Line of Business:** Building of complete constructions or parts thereof; civil engineering
**Issued Capital:** £100
**Principals:** S C Aird *(Managing)*, Mrs J A Aird, Mrs J Aird
**Co. Secretary:** Ms Jane Aird
**Responsibilities**
**Senior:** Una Bolton *(Manager)*
**Branches:** Souters Sports Ltd, Kell Green Farm, Kell Green Lane, Knutsford, Cheshire WA16 7SL
**US SIC:** 1541 **UK SIC:** 50100
**Auditors:** Macfarlane Gray Ltd
**Bankers:** The Royal Bank Of Scotland Plc (83-48-00)

| | 31-12-13 | 31-12-12 | 31-12-11 |
|---|---|---|---|
| TO | 7,209,214 | N/A | 7,349,474 |
| P/L | 109,352 | N/A | 205,058 |
| NW | 257,787 | 282,507 | 375,621 |
| WC | (116,223) | (218,274) | (298,413) |
| Emp. | 65 | N/A | 63 |

DUNS 42-374-6049

## South and City College Birmingham

Digbeth Campus, Birmingham, West Midlands B5 5SU
**Tel:** 01216945000
**Web:** www.sbc.ac.uk
**Estd:** 1998
**Line of Business:** Training centres
**Trading Style:** South & City College Birmingham, Sccb
**Responsibilities**
**Senior:** Margaret Watkinson *(Assistant Principal)*
**Marketing:** Dawn Cockcroft *(Head of Marketing)*, Claire Wainwright *(PR Manager)*
**Sales:** PAul Leahy *(Sales Manager)*
**HR:** Omar Khan *(International Recruitment Mana)*
**Engineering:** Kevin Osman *(Technical Engineer)*
**Branches:** South and City College Birmingham, Cole Bank Road, Birmingham, West Midlands B28 8ES
**US SIC:** 8221 **UK SIC:** 93100
**Employees:** 300

DUNS 21-783-5977

## South & West Devon Personalised Learning Service

Shinners Bridge, Totnes, Devon TQ9 6JD
**Tel:** 01803865580
**Web:** www.swdpls.devon.sch.uk
**Estd:** 2011 Proprietorship
**Line of Business:** Schools (special)
**Proprietor:** Mrs S Acland
**US SIC:** 8299 **UK SIC:** 93300
**Employees:** 53

DUNS 23-295-8934

## South Anglia Housing Ltd

Unit 5 Raynham Close, Bishops Stortford, Hertfordshire CM23 5PJ
**Tel:** 01270 711711 **Fax:** 01270 711700
**Web:** www.circleanglia.org
**Reg No:** 0028100IP **Estd:** 1995 Friendly Society
**Line of Business:** Housing associations societies trusts & co-operatives
**Issued Capital:** £2
**Principals:** R Parker *(Chairman)*, H Smith, D Jacob, N Marks, J Spenceley, J Farrow, H Davis, M Hayman
**Co. Secretary:** Peter Lewis
**Responsibilities**
**Senior:** E Flatt *(Director)*, J Overy *(Director)*, Kim Sell *(Personal Assistant)*, J Winzer *(Director)*, G Wonnacott *(Director)*
**Marketing:** Katrina Robinson *(Sales & Marketing Officer)*
**Sales:** Katrina Robinson *(Sales & Marketing Officer)*
**US SIC:** 8321 **UK SIC:** 96111
**Auditors:** KPMG LLP

| | 31-03-12 | 31-03-11 | 31-03-10 |
|---|---|---|---|
| TO | 39,594,000 | 37,891,000 | 42,060,000 |
| P/L | (1,525,000) | (1,150,000) | (823,000) |
| NW | (5,926,000) | (4,737,000) | (3,647,000) |
| WC | (306,298,000) | (294,932,000) | (293,714,000) |
| Emp. | 84 | 75 | 72 |

DUNS 42-402-2226

## South Ayrshire Council

County Buildings, Wellington Square, Ayr, Ayrshire KA7 1DR
**Tel:** 01292612381
**Web:** www.south-ayrshire.gov.uk
**Estd:** 2011
**Line of Business:** Central government
**Principals:** T Cairns *(Financial)*, G Thorley
**Responsibilities**
**Senior:** Eileen Howat *(Network, Security Manager)*
**Marketing:** Aileen Paul *(Senior Marketing Executive)*
**IT:** Phil Gatt *(Assistant IT Support Analist)*, Eileen Howat *(Network, Security Manager)*
**Branches:** South Ayrshire Council, Sandgate House, 43 Sandgate, Ayr, Ayrshire KA7 1DA
**US SIC:** 9121 **UK SIC:** 91110
**Employees:** 12

DUNS 22-988-7922

## South Bank Centre

Belvedere Road Southbank Centre, London SE1 8XX
**Tel:** 02079280681
**Web:** www.southbankcentre.co.uk
**VAT No:** 494234433 **Estd:** 1986
**Line of Business:** Art centres
**Principals:** P Mason *(Financial)*, E Bernerd *(Commercial)*, M Mccart *(Marketing)*, Sir C Marshall, Lady P Harlech, R Hambro, Weidenfeld, S Jenkins
**Responsibilities**
**Senior:** Victor Garland *(Vice Chairperson)*, Brent Hansen *(Board Member)*, Ying Man *(Manager)*, David Michel *(Office Manager)*, Julian Webber *(Board Member)*
**Marketing:** Libby Binks *(Press Officer)*, NicolaHarriet Black *(Press Coordinator)*, Sim Eldem *(Press Manager)*, Nicola Jeffs *(Press Officer)*, Michael McCart *(Marketing Director)*, Patricia O'Connor *(Head of Press)*, Khadeen O'Donnell *(Corporate Development Manager)*, Helena Zedig *(Deputy Head of Press)*
**Sales:** Matthew Holt *(Head of Corporate Development)*

**Admin:** Pam Chowhan (*Head of Planning & Administrat*), Janet Sinha (*Administrator*)
**HR:** Sarita Godber (*Human Resources Manager*)
**Facilities:** Hilton Wells (*Project Manager*)
**Branches:** South Bank Centre, Belvedere Road, London SE1 8XT
**US SIC:** 8699, 7922
**UK SIC:** 96902, 97412
**Auditors:** T J Burr
**Bankers:** Lloyds TSB Bank plc (77-30-30)
**Employees:** 407
**Turnover:** £51,979,000

## DUNS 45-816-9588
## The South Bank Foundation Ltd

(**Subsidiary of:** Southbank Centre Ltd)
Belvedere Road Southbank Centre, London SE1 8XX
**Tel:** 02079210600 **Fax:** 08701633896
**Web:** www.southindianbank.com
**Reg No:** 3174667 **Estd:** 1951 Private Limited Company
**Line of Business:** Other service activities not elsewhere classified
**Trading Style:** Royal Festival Hall, The South Centre
**Issued Capital:** £100
**Director:** A J Bishop
**Co. Secretary:** Timothy Deane
**US SIC:** 8999 **UK SIC:** 83954
**Auditors:** Grant Thornton UK LLP
**Bankers:** Lloyds TSB Bank plc (30-94-04)

|    | 31-03-14 | 31-03-13 | 31-03-12 |
|----|----------|----------|----------|
| TA | 100      | 100      | 100      |
| NW | 100      | 100      | 100      |

## DUNS 23-219-5870
## South Belfast Sure Start

Second Floor, 9 Lower Crescent, Belfast BT7 1NR
**Tel:** 028-9094-2525 **Fax:** 028-9094-2727
**Web:** www.surestart.co.uk
**Reg No:** 0040060NI **Estd:** 2001 Private Company Limited By Guarantee
**Line of Business:** Community networks
**Directors:** Ms E M Jordan, Ms N Johnston, E Westerhuis, Ms N Brennan, Ms T Adair, Ms J Mcgovern, Ms E Mansfield, N Houston
**Responsibilities**
**Senior:** Glenda Davies (*Manager*), Katie Hanlon (*Director*), William Olphert (*Director*), Joy Poots (*Manager*), Ruth Pritchard (*Director*), Bernie Reid (*Director*)
**US SIC:** 8321 **UK SIC:** 96111
**Auditors:** Lynn, Drake & Co
**Bankers:** First Trust Bank (aib Group (uk) Plc) (93-84-24)

|     | 31-03-14  | 31-03-13 | 31-03-12 |
|-----|-----------|----------|----------|
| TO  | 1,135,279 | 869,475  | 858,760  |
| P/L | 172,952   | (3,903)  | (3,821)  |
| NW  | 211,479   | 38,527   | 42,430   |
| WC  | 46,715    | 38,527   | 42,430   |
| Emp.| 53        | N/A      | N/A      |

## DUNS 21-161-7027
## South Benfleet Foundation Primary School

High Road, Benfleet, Essex SS7 5HA
**Tel:** 01268-793276
**Estd:** 2003
**Line of Business:** Primary education
**Principals:** Mrs E French (*Chairman*), Ms C Batty, J Hibbitt, Ms L Carlane
**Responsibilities**
**Senior:** Jayne Hartland (*Secretary*)
**US SIC:** 8211 **UK SIC:** 93200
**Employees:** 50

## DUNS 34-602-2668
## South Birmingham College Ltd

Cole Bank Road, Hall Green, Birmingham, West Midlands B28 8ES
**Tel:** 01216945034 **Fax:** 01217021037
**Web:** www.sccb.ac.uk
**Reg No:** 2743773 **Estd:** 2012 Private Limited Company
**Line of Business:** Primary education
**Issued Capital:** £2
**Director:** A Howey
**Co. Secretary:** Michael Hopkins
**Responsibilities**
**Senior:** Elizabeth Beard (*Nursery Manager*)
**Health & Safety:** Dawn Ward (*Health & Safety Officer*)
**US SIC:** 8211 **UK SIC:** 93200
**Bankers:** National Westminster Bank Plc (60-02-35)

|    | 31-07-13 | 31-07-12 | 31-07-11 |
|----|----------|----------|----------|
| TA | 2        | 2        | 2        |
| NW | 2        | 2        | 2        |

## DUNS 23-288-3210
## South Birmingham Primary Care Trust

Alcester Road, Birmingham, West Midlands B13 8JL
**Tel:** 01214666000
**Web:** www.sbpct.nhs.uk
**VAT No:** 654415832 **Estd:** 2002
**Line of Business:** Nhs clinics
**Issued Capital:** £1
**Principals:** Prof D Cox (*Chairman*), Dr S Singh (*Chairman*), Mrs T Taylor (*Managing*), Ms R Hardy (*Financial*), M Harris, Dr C Spencer-Jones, Ms M Dumma, Mrs B Webster
**Responsibilities**
**Senior:** Professor Beider (*Non-Executive Director*), Sandra Cooper (*Non-Executive Director*), Ruth Dukes (*Regional Manager*), Denise McLellan (*Chief Executive Officer*), Christine Parkinson (*Non-Executive Director*), Chris Spencer-jones (*Director*)
**Operations:** Denise Price (*Director of Nursing and Qualit*)
**Branches:** South Birmingham Primary Care Trust, 324 Holly La, Birmingham, West Midlands B24 9LN
**US SIC:** 9121, 8011
**UK SIC:** 91110, 95300
**Employees:** 3,229

## DUNS 23-326-1846
## South Bucks District Council

Capswood, Oxford Road, Denham, Uxbridge, Middlesex UB9 4LH
**Tel:** 01895837200
**Web:** www.southbucks.gov.uk
**Line of Business:** House building contractors
**Principals:** F T Bowater (*Chairman*), C Furness
**Responsibilities**
**Senior:** Jim Burness (*Director of Resources*)
**Finance:** Jim Burness (*Director of Resources*)
**IT:** Linda Grange (*Head of IT*)
**HR:** Jackie Hills (*Human Resources Manager*)
**Branches:** South Bucks District Council, Flat Farnham Park Golf Course, Park Road, Stoke Poges, Slough, Berkshire SL2 4PJ
**US SIC:** 9121 **UK SIC:** 91110
**Employees:** 200

## DUNS 21-641-4417                                    Imp-Exp
## South Caernarvon Creameries Ltd

Chwilog, Pwllheli, Gwynedd LL53 6SB
**Tel:** 01766-810251 **Fax:** 01766810178
**Web:** www.dragonwales.co.uk
**Reg No:** 0012227IP **Estd:** 1937 Friendly Society
**Line of Business:** Dairy produce merchants
**Trading Style:** South Caernarvon Creameries
**Principals:** R T Lewis (*Chairman*), G Jenkins, W J Hughes, A Roberts, D M Roberts, W H Thomas, A Owen, G Evans
**Co. Secretary:** Alan Jones
**Responsibilities**
**Senior:** R Elmitt (*Manager*), Rhisiart Lewis (*Farmer Director*), Darwlyn Roberts (*Export Manager*)
**IT:** Ffion Morris (*IT Manager*)
**HR:** Elwin Jones (*Human Resources Officer*)
**Facilities:** Ioan Jones (*Engineer*)
**Operations:** Mark Beavon (*Operations Director*), Julian Durrant (*Quality Manager*)
**Fleet:** Darwlyn Roberts (*Export Manager*)
**US SIC:** 5199 **UK SIC:** 61900
**Auditors:** Bryn Afon
**Bankers:** HSBC Bank plc (40-37-30)
**Employees:** 129
**Turnover:** £27,081,737

## DUNS 23-636-9484
## South Cambridgeshire Dist Cncl

South Cambridgeshire Hall, Cambridge, Cambridgeshire CB23 6EA
**Tel:** 03450450500
**Web:** www.scambs.gov.uk
**Line of Business:** Local government
**Trading Style:** South Cambridgeshire Dist Cncl
**Principals:** E W Bullman (*Chairman*), J Ballantine, J W Townend
**Responsibilities**
**Finance:** Alex Colyer (*Chief Finance Officer*), Sean Missin (*Procurement Officer*), Lee Phanco (*Financial Director*)
**Marketing:** Kelly Quigley (*Communications Manager*)
**IT:** Steve Rayment (*IT Manager*)
**Operations:** Kelly Quigley (*Communications Manager*)

**Purchasing:** Sean Missin (*Procurement Officer*)
**Branches:** South Cambridgeshire Dist Cncl, 1 Quinion Close, Peterborough, Cambridgeshire PE7 1TG
**US SIC:** 9121 **UK SIC:** 91110
**Employees:** 350

## DUNS 21-028-2642
## South Central Ambulance Service Nhs Foundation Trust

7-8 Talisman Road, Bicester, Oxfordshire OX26 6HR
**Tel:** 01869365000
**Web:** www.southcentralambulance.nhs.uk
**Estd:** 2002
**Line of Business:** Hospitals
**Principals:** C Porter (*Financial*), Ms F Thompson, P Clarke, J Nichols, W Hancock, D Burke, J Black
**Responsibilities**
**Senior:** Mike Kerrigin (*Estates Manager*)
**Sales:** Rafael Cicci (*Sales Manager*)
**Facilities:** Arthur Kennedy (*Estates Manager*)
**US SIC:** 8062 **UK SIC:** 95100
**Auditors:** Maria Grindley

|     | 29-02-12    |
|-----|-------------|
| TO  | 121,203,000 |
| P/L | 2,595,000   |
| NW  | 60,053,000  |
| WC  | 9,305,000   |
| Emp.| 2,500       |

## DUNS 23-293-4641
## South Central Strategic Health Authority

(**Subsidiary of:** Department of Health)
Newbury Business Park, Newbury, Berkshire RG14 2PZ
**Tel:** 01635-275500
**Web:** www.ntda.nhs.uk
**Estd:** 2006
**Line of Business:** Other human health activities
**Issued Capital:** £1
**Principals:** G Harris (*Chairman*), Dr G Harris (*Chairman*), B Lloyd (*Financial*), P Newton, Ms K Fenton, Ms A Young, T Jones, C Le Fevre
**Responsibilities**
**Senior:** Alyson Coates (*Non-Executive Director*), Joe McLoone (*Non Executive Member*)
**Finance:** Bob Alexander (*Director of Finance*)
**Branches:** South Central Strategic Health Authority, 22 Carisbrooke High Street, Newport, Isle Of Wight PO30 1NR
**US SIC:** 9121, 8062
**UK SIC:** 91110, 95100
**Employees:** 3,000

## DUNS 42-397-0466
## South Cheshire College

Dane Bank Avenue, Crewe, Cheshire CW2 8AB
**Tel:** 01270-654654 **Fax:** 01270-651515
**Web:** www.scc.ac.uk
**Estd:** 1850 Incorporate By Act Of Parliament
**Line of Business:** Further education schools and colleges
**Trading Style:** Dane Bank Travel Centre, The College Shop
**Principals:** Dr D Collins, S Cowell
**Responsibilities**
**Senior:** Dhesi Jafbir (*Principal*)
**Branches:** South Cheshire College, Middlewich Rd, Sandbach, Cheshire CW11 3NT
**US SIC:** 8221, 8249, 8211
**UK SIC:** 93100, 93300, 93200
**Bankers:** National Westminster Bank Plc (60-06-23)
**Employees:** 380

## DUNS 42-358-9951
## South Cheshire Model Engineering Society

11 Davidson Avenue, Congleton, Cheshire CW12 2EQ
**Tel:** 01260-273036
**Reg No:** 3161547 **Estd:** 1996 Private Limited Company
**Line of Business:** Other entertainment activities not elsewhere classified
**Directors:** L J Riley, S J Daw, D A Craig, C J Mansell, A R Malpas, P J Vidler, D Potts
**Co. Secretary:** Michael Smith
**Responsibilities**
**Senior:** Kenneth Tweats (*Manager*)
**US SIC:** 7999 **UK SIC:** 97913

|     | 30-09-13 | 30-09-12 | 30-09-11 |
|-----|----------|----------|----------|
| TO  | 7,842    | 6,351    | 6,380    |
| P/L | (2,845)  | (215)    | 963      |
| NW  | 29,539   | 27,679   | 27,245   |

## DUNS 28-899-3413
## South Coast Nursing Homes Ltd

34 Crescent Road, Worthing, West Sussex BN11 1RL
**Tel:** 01903-210612
**Web:** www.scnh.co.uk
**Reg No:** 1337123 **Estd:** 1977 Private Limited Company
**Line of Business:** Medical nursing home activities
**Issued Capital:** £24,792
**Directors:** Ms C Blackburn, Ms S M Hazell, J Colville, Ms A Scott
**Co. Secretary:** Patrick Colville
**Responsibilities**
**Senior:** Katherine Blackburn (*Director*)
**Branches:** South Coast Nursing Homes Ltd, 42 Shelley Road, Worthing, West Sussex BN11 4DA
**US SIC:** 7399, 6732
**UK SIC:** 83954, 83100
**Auditors:** Hartley Fowler
**Bankers:** National Westminster Bank Plc (60-60-08)

|     | 31-10-14    | 31-10-13    | 31-10-12    |
|-----|-------------|-------------|-------------|
| TO  | 13,400,075  | 11,977,211  | 9,472,232   |
| P/L | 1,841,104   | 1,236,140   | 662,026     |
| NW  | 7,391,024   | 6,141,317   | 5,354,812   |
| WC  | (1,251,963) | (1,530,634) | (1,136,958) |
| Emp.| 573         | 524         | 434         |

## DUNS 23-856-0374
## South Coast Port Services Ltd

(**Subsidiary of:** Canute Management Services Ltd)
Canute Chambers, Ocean Way, Southampton, Hampshire SO14 3TU
**Tel:** 023-8023-7051
**Web:** www.portskills.co.uk
**Reg No:** 3847838 **Estd:** 1999 Private Limited Company
**Line of Business:** Stevedoring
**Issued Capital:** £1
**Directors:** M Eardley, P A Drake
**Co. Secretary:** Steven Pearce
**US SIC:** 4469, 4712
**UK SIC:** 76300, 77002
**Bankers:** National Westminster Bank Plc (52-30-23)

|     | 31-12-13  | 31-12-12  | 31-12-11  |
|-----|-----------|-----------|-----------|
| TA  | 1,608,529 | 1,288,737 | 963,849   |
| P/L | 496,771   | 146,281   | 29,235    |
| NW  | 644,769   | 27,504    | (175,655) |
| WC  | 321,447   | 139,206   | 31,691    |
| Emp.| 642       | 646       | 551       |

## DUNS 23-216-8666                                    Imp
## South Devon College

Vantage Point, Paignton, Devon TQ4 7EJ
**Tel:** 08000380123
**Web:** www.southdevon.ac.uk
**Estd:** 2010
**Line of Business:** Further education schools and colleges
**Director:** Dr I Bentley
**Co. Secretary:** Mrs Karen Chapman
**Responsibilities**
**Finance:** Emma Cox (*Financial Director*)
**Marketing:** Pat Denham (*Assistant Principal*), Karen Tew (*Marketing Manager*)
**Admin:** Cheryl Davies (*Administrator*), Sara Reddish (*Administrator Services, Inform*), Jenny Tostevin (*Administrator*)
**IT:** Kelly Cassidy (*Computer Operations Manager*), Christopher Vincenti (*IT Manager*), Joy Wood (*IT Manager*)
**HR:** Peta Harper (*Human Resources Manager*)
**Branches:** South Devon College, Belgrave Ho, 73 Mutley Plain, Plymouth, Devon PL4 6JJ
**US SIC:** 8221 **UK SIC:** 93100
**Employees:** 800

## DUNS 23-265-8034
## South Devon Healthcare Nhs Foundation Trust

Torbay Hospital, Newton Road, Torquay, Devon TQ2 7AA
**Tel:** 01803-614-567
**Web:** www.sdhct.nhs.uk
**VAT No:** 654941219 **Estd:** 1991
**Line of Business:** Local government healthcare autority overseeing hospitals, health services and some pharmaceutical manufacture.
**Trading Style:** Torbay Hospital, Torbay Pharmaceutical Manufacturing Unit (P.M.U.), Sdhct
**Issued Capital:** £1
**Principals:** P Cooper (*Financial*), J Lowes, Ms A Murphy, Ms P Vasco-Knight, Ms L Childs, P Mears
**Responsibilities**
**Senior:** Gaynor Raisey (*Catering Manager*)
**IT:** Gary Hotine (*Computer Manager*)
**Branches:** South Devon Healthcare Nhs Foundation Trust, Newton Abbot Hospital, 64 East Street, Newton Abbot, Devon TQ12 4PT

**US SIC:** 9121, 8062, 2834, 8091
**UK SIC:** 91110, 95100, 25700, 95200
**Auditors:** PricewaterhouseCoopers LLP

| | 31-03-14 | 31-03-13 | 31-03-12 |
|---|---|---|---|
| TO | 240,989,000 | 231,667,000 | 191,779,000 |
| P/L | (1,527,000) | (1,161,000) | (10,255,000) |
| NW | 90,475,000 | 89,574,000 | 91,797,000 |
| WC | 8,316,000 | 11,137,000 | 8,763,000 |
| Emp. | 3,647 | 3,472 | 3,313 |

DUNS 54-428-1181
## The South Devon Holiday Parks Ltd
(**Subsidiary of:** Caledonia Investments P L C)
Coghurst Cottage Farm, Ivyhouse Lane, Hastings, East Sussex TN35 4NP
**Tel:** 08458159775
**Web:** www.parkholidays.com
**Reg No:** 3274393 **Estd:** 1996 Private Limited Company
**Line of Business:** Holiday parks and camps
**Trading Style:** Waterside Holiday Park
**Issued Capital:** £440,000
**Directors:** J A Sills, A N Clish
**Co. Secretary:** Alasdair Loch
**Responsibilities**
**Finance:** Darren Permaul *(Finance Director)*
**IT:** Kevin Padgen *(IT Director)*
**US SIC:** 7032 **UK SIC:** 66702
**Auditors:** Ernst & Young LLP
**Bankers:** Barclays Bank Plc (20-60-88)

| | 31-03-14 | 31-12-12 | 31-03-11 |
|---|---|---|---|
| TA | 0,100,700 | 11,250,000 | 12,964,132 |
| P/L | 6,940 | 1,234 | 684 |
| NW | 6,347,953 | 8,219,417 | 9,809,520 |
| WC | (3,111,995) | N/A | N/A |

DUNS 29-231-0935
## South Devon Railway Trust
The Station, The Station, Buckfastleigh, Devon TQ11 0DZ
**Tel:** 01364642338
**Web:** www.southdevonrailway.org
**Reg No:** 1157099 **Estd:** 1974 Private Company Limited By Guarantee
**Line of Business:** Rail transport services
**Issued Capital:** £119,149
**Directors:** A L Taylor, J Keohane, D J Lemar, N W Smith, A R Cash, J K Morton, R J Elliott, D A Woodward
**Co. Secretary:** Charles Haslam
**Responsibilities**
**Senior:** John Crownshaw *(Manager)*, Philip Parratt *(Director)*, Peter Treglown *(Director)*
**Branches:** South Devon Railway Trust, Railway Station, Buckfastleigh, Devon TQ11 0DZ
**US SIC:** 4011 **UK SIC:** 71000
**Auditors:** Spence Robert Pethick

| | 31-12-13 | 31-12-12 | 31-12-11 |
|---|---|---|---|
| TO | 2,343,130 | 2,147,546 | 2,168,794 |
| P/L | 195,613 | 28,660 | 65,318 |
| NW | 2,892,772 | 2,694,400 | 2,662,981 |
| WC | 245,970 | 104,844 | (1,374) |
| Emp. | 60 | 57 | 55 |

DUNS 49-497-9883
## South Doc Services Ltd
15 Katie Road, Birmingham, West Midlands B29 6JG
**Tel:** 01214152090
**Web:** http://southdocservices.co.uk
**Reg No:** 3160204 **Estd:** 1996 Private Limited Company
**Line of Business:** Medical practice activities
**Issued Capital:** £612
**Directors:** Dr S J Watkins, Dr N Chauhan
**Co. Secretary:** Dr Ashok Vora
**US SIC:** 8011 **UK SIC:** 95300
**Auditors:** S Pabari & Co
**Bankers:** National Westminster Bank Plc (60-15-26)

| | 31-03-14 | 31-03-13 | 31-03-12 |
|---|---|---|---|
| TO | 2,504,784 | 2,308,099 | 2,217,121 |
| P/L | 471,200 | 415,317 | 516,038 |
| NW | 2,089,634 | 1,719,268 | 1,393,397 |
| WC | 1,711,353 | 1,321,246 | 1,014,038 |

DUNS 22-270-1885
## South Downs Capital Ltd
West Street, Havant, Hampshire PO9 1LG
**Tel:** 02392-499888
**Web:** www.portsmouthwater.co.uk
**Reg No:** 4288161 **Estd:** 2001 Private Limited Company
**Line of Business:** Holding companies management activities
**Trading Style:** Portsmouth Water Plc
**Issued Capital:** £100
**Directors:** N Smith, R C Porteous
**Co. Secretary:** Christopher Hardyman
**US SIC:** 6711 **UK SIC:** 83962
**Auditors:** Saffery Champness
**Bankers:** National Westminster Bank Plc (57-00-00)

| | 31-03-14 | 31-03-13 | 31-03-12 |
|---|---|---|---|
| TO | 37,109,000 | 36,282,000 | 36,665,000 |
| P/L | (795,000) | 737,000 | 92,000 |
| NW | 19,083,000 | 17,762,000 | 12,452,000 |
| WC | (2,125,000) | (7,230,000) | (4,211,000) |
| Emp. | 238 | 232 | 223 |

DUNS 21-127-9611
## South Downs Care Ltd
Reservoir Lane, Petersfield, Hampshire GU32 2HX
**Tel:** 01730710710
**Web:** www.southdownscare.co.uk
**Reg No:** 6626394 **Estd:** 2008 Private Limited Company
**Line of Business:** Representative office
**Issued Capital:** £100
**Director:** P A Rogers
**Co. Secretary:** Marja Rogers
**US SIC:** 7399 **UK SIC:** 83954

| | 30-06-13 | 30-06-12 | 30-06-11 |
|---|---|---|---|
| TA | 100 | 100 | 100 |
| NW | 100 | 100 | 100 |

DUNS 54-896-9658
## The South Downs College
College Road, Purbrook, Waterlooville, Hampshire PO7 8AA
**Web:** www.southdowns.ac.uk
**Estd:** 1974
**Line of Business:** Further education schools and colleges
**Trading Style:** South Downs College
**Directors:** M Oakes, Z J Mach
**Responsibilities**
**Senior:** Paula Humby *(Manager)*, Lyn Surgeon *(Principal)*
**Admin:** Ben Read *(Applications Administrator)*
**HR:** Kirby Berger *(Training Director)*
**Engineering:** Martin Crook *(Engineer)*
**Branches:** The South Downs College, 14A Greywell Road, Havant, Hampshire PO9 5AL
**US SIC:** 8221 **UK SIC:** 93100
**Employees:** 1,200

DUNS 21-781-3024
## South Downs Community Special School
Shinewater Lane, Eastbourne, East Sussex BN23 8AT
**Tel:** 01323761061
**Web:** www.south.downs.e-sussex.sch.uk
**Estd:** 1959 Proprietorship
**Line of Business:** Schools (special)
**Proprietor:** R Palladino
**US SIC:** 8299 **UK SIC:** 93300
**Employees:** 105

DUNS 34-550-6328
## South Downs Real Estate Ltd
(**Subsidiary of:** Nyetimber Wines Ltd)
The Granary Studio, Nyetimber Vineyard, Pulborough, West Sussex RH20 2HH
**Web:** www.nyetimber.com
**Reg No:** 5360623 **Estd:** 2005 Private Limited Company
**Line of Business:** Growing of other fruit, nuts and spice crops; growing of other beverage crops
**Issued Capital:** £22,593,776
**Director:** E N Heerema
**Co. Secretary:** Robert Macdonald Watson
**US SIC:** 0179, 5182, 6531
**UK SIC:** 01002, 61700, 83400
**Auditors:** Spofforthe LLP

| | 31-12-13 | 31-12-12 | 31-12-11 |
|---|---|---|---|
| TA | 33,026,986 | 29,042,143 | 29,300,396 |
| NW | 15,158,518 | 15,262,637 | 15,003,817 |
| WC | 5,740,394 | 1,856,841 | 6,453,853 |

DUNS 21-007-4831
## The South Downs Special School Trust
Beechy Avenue, Eastbourne, East Sussex BN20 8NU
**Tel:** 01323-730302
**Web:** www.southdowns-lindfield.com
**Reg No:** 6317107 **Estd:** 1930 Private Company Limited By Guarantee
**Line of Business:** Schools (local authority)
**Directors:** Ms S J Fuller, Ms J Compton, R T Palladino
**Co. Secretary:** Ms Judith Compton
**Responsibilities**
**Senior:** E Gidlow *(Head Teacher)*
**US SIC:** 8299 **UK SIC:** 93300
**Bankers:** Lloyds TSB Bank plc (30-92-86)

| | 31-07-14 | 31-07-13 | 31-07-12 |
|---|---|---|---|
| TO | 2,929 | 3,832 | 803 |
| P/L | 1,099 | 2,491 | (9) |
| NW | 118,310 | 116,171 | 107,273 |
| WC | 74,308 | 73,209 | 70,718 |

DUNS 21-041-5148
## South East Coast Ambulance Service Nhs Foundation Trust
The Horseshoe, Banstead, Surrey SM7 2AS
**Tel:** 01737-353333
**Web:** www.secamb.nhs.uk
**Estd:** 1995
**Line of Business:** Activities of other membership organisations not elsewhere classified
**Proprietor:** P Sutton
**Responsibilities**
**Senior:** Katrina Herren *(Director Medical)*, Jeff Jones *(Executive)*, Louise Massen *(Senior Manager)*, Nigel Penny *(Non-Executive Director)*, Tony Thorne *(Board Member)*, Justin Wand *(Director of Support Services)*, Trevor Willington *(Non-Executive Director)*
**Finance:** Graham Colbert *(Senior Vice President Finance)*
**Marketing:** Liz Spiers *(Media Relations Officer)*
**HR:** Isobel Allen *(Membership Manager)*, Warwick Avery *(Learning and Development Lead)*, Sandie Gibson *(Assistant Director of HR)*, Verity Snook *(Training Director)*
**Health & Safety:** Justin Wand *(Director of Support Services)*
**Facilities:** Justin Wand *(Director of Support Services)*
**Operations:** Glenn Borthwick *(Hailsham Clinical Operations M)*, James Pavey *(Senior Operations Manager)*, Kath Start *(Director of Workforce Developm)*
**Purchasing:** Justin Wand *(Director of Support Services)*
**Engineering:** Rachel Pratt *(Ambulance Technician)*
**US SIC:** 7399 **UK SIC:** 83954
**Auditors:** Paul Grady

| | 31-03-14 | 31-03-13 | 31-03-12 |
|---|---|---|---|
| TO | 187,147,000 | 172,243,000 | 168,171,000 |
| P/L | 117,000 | 3,055,000 | 5,655,000 |
| NW | 90,541,000 | 86,337,000 | 82,447,000 |
| WC | 20,712,000 | 19,546,000 | 18,337,000 |
| Emp. | 3,608 | 3,150 | 3,023 |

DUNS 21-713-0444
## South East Essex Academy Trust
Kenilworth Gardens, Westcliff-On-Sea, Essex SS0 0BS
**Tel:** 01702476026
**Reg No:** 7527304 **Estd:** 2011 Private Company Limited By Guarantee
**Line of Business:** General secondary education
**Directors:** L B Campbell, Ms J Harding, W Hill, Ms S A Schofield, A C Howe, M D Wilson, Dr P B Hayman, Ms S Worthington
**Responsibilities**
**Senior:** Omash Aggarwal *(Governor)*, Anthony Cains *(Teacher)*, Murray Foster *(Director)*, Michael Lambert *(Director)*
**US SIC:** 8211 **UK SIC:** 93200
**Bankers:** Barclays Bank Plc (20-70-93)

| | 31-08-13 | 31-08-12 | 31-08-11 |
|---|---|---|---|
| TO | 5,887,315 | 5,720,719 | 20,183,927 |
| P/L | (125,079) | (155,721) | 17,191,137 |
| NW | 15,672,551 | 15,873,630 | 16,026,137 |
| WC | 668,273 | 519,453 | 362,593 |
| Emp. | 143 | 136 | N/A |

DUNS 42-327-7342
## South East Essex College
Southend Campus, Southend-On-Sea, Essex SS1 1ND
**Tel:** 08455212345
**Web:** www.southessex.ac.uk
**Estd:** 2003
**Line of Business:** Further education schools and colleges
**Director:** Ms J Hodges
**Responsibilities**
**Senior:** Anthony McGarel *(Financial Director)*, Susan Murray *(Manager)*, Angela Odonaghue *(Principal)*
**Finance:** Anthony McGarel *(Financial Director)*
**IT:** Craig Willcocks *(IT Manager)*
**HR:** Nicola Rees *(Personnel Manager)*
**Branches:** South East Essex College, Runnymede Chase, Benfleet, Essex SS7 3DB
**US SIC:** 8221 **UK SIC:** 93100
**Bankers:** National Westminster Bank Plc (55-50-28)
**Employees:** 600

DUNS 36-517-6820
## South East Essex Primary Care Trust
Suffolk House, Southend-On-Sea, Essex SS2 6HZ
**Web:** www.see.nhs.uk
**Estd:** 2006
**Line of Business:** Local government
**Principals:** Ms K Kirk *(Chairman)*, Ms J Garbutt, Mrs B Furr, Mrs G Hind, J Bermon, Dr H Hillier, T L Masurier
**Responsibilities**
**Senior:** Wendy George *(General Manager)*, Tony Le Masurier *(Non Executive Member)*, Corinne Woods-Taylor *(Executive)*
**Marketing:** Johanne Springett *(Communications Manager)*
**Sales:** Viv Barnes *(Assistant Director - Clinical)*
**Admin:** Anne Davey *(Receptionist)*, Elizabeth Rawlinson *(Secretary)*, Jean Thraves *(Office Manager)*, Pamela Turnnidge *(Secretary)*
**IT:** Della Cain *(Manager)*, Eve Passey *(Manager)*
**US SIC:** 9121, 8062
**UK SIC:** 91110, 95100
**Employees:** 850

DUNS 49-493-7907
## South East London Doctors Co Operative Ltd
Dulwich Hospital, East Dulwich Grove, London SE22 8QF
**Tel:** 02082992619
**Web:** www.seldoc.co.uk
**Reg No:** 3156031 **Estd:** 1996 Private Limited Company
**Line of Business:** Medical practice activities
**Directors:** D G Witt, Dr E J Rowley -Conwy, Dr B Coker, Dr M Uti, S H Dewar, P D Ruthen, Dr P Heenan, Dr R Rastogi
**Responsibilities**
**Senior:** Riaz Jetha *(Director)*, Charlene Sables *(Director)*, Kishor Vasant *(Director)*
**US SIC:** 8011 **UK SIC:** 95300

| | 31-03-14 | 31-03-13 | 31-03-12 |
|---|---|---|---|
| TO | 5,020,094 | 4,363,304 | 3,981,667 |
| P/L | 29,292 | 89,393 | 33,523 |
| NW | 3,207,927 | 3,179,805 | 3,196,370 |
| WC | 2,993,580 | 2,996,539 | 2,981,675 |
| Emp. | 68 | 78 | 75 |

DUNS 77-106-8343
## South East Water Ltd
(**Subsidiary of:** Hdf (Uk) Holdings Ltd)
South East Water, Snodland, Kent ME6 5AH
**Tel:** 03330002244
**Web:** www.southeastwater.co.uk
**Reg No:** 2679874 **VAT No:** 844278604
**Estd:** 1981 Public Limited Company
**Line of Business:** Water authorities
**Issued Capital:** £1,291,548
**Directors:** J P Ouellet, P Butler, G W Maxwell, C F Girling, O Fortin, P A Rich, G H Setterfield, Ms J E Stimpson
**Co. Secretary:** Nicolas Truillet
**Responsibilities**
**Senior:** Charlotte Gilthorpe *(Director)*, Steven Rankine *(Non Executive Director)*, Valeria Rosati *(Non Executive Director)*, Paul Seeley *(Director)*
**Marketing:** Jane Gould *(Communications Manager)*
**Sales:** Jane Gould *(Communications Manager)*
**IT:** David Chung *(Computer Manager)*
**HR:** Stuart Capeling *(Training Officer)*
**Health & Safety:** Stuart Capeling *(Training Officer)*
**Branches:** South East Water Ltd, Barcombe Mills, Lewes, East Sussex BN8 5BU
**US SIC:** 4941 **UK SIC:** 17000
**Auditors:** Deloitte LLP

| | 31-03-14 | 31-03-13 | 31-03-12 |
|---|---|---|---|
| TO | 213,588,000 | 207,887,000 | 200,067,000 |
| P/L | 51,427,000 | 41,740,000 | 42,353,000 |
| NW | 267,895,000 | 240,007,000 | 239,896,000 |
| WC | 20,826,000 | 55,952,000 | (7,444,000) |
| Emp. | 789 | 749 | 730 |

DUNS 23-989-9917
## South Eastern Education and Library Board
Grahams Bridge Road, Belfast BT16 2HS
**Tel:** 028-9056-6200
**Web:** www.seelb.org.uk
**Estd:** 1972
**Line of Business:** Education agencies and authorities
**Trading Style:** S E E L B, Clintclay Primary School
**Director:** J B Fitzsimmons
**Responsibilities**
**Senior:** Neil Coates *(Executive)*, Richard Herron *(Chairman)*, Cecil Lee *(Manager)*, Dolores Mcardle *(Manager)*, Dorothy Morrow *(Area Manager)*, Alberta Park *(Executive)*, Trevor Quinn *(Executive)*
**Finance:** Nadine Bell *(Accounts Officer)*, Myles Boyle *(Accounts Officer)*
**Admin:** Lisa Cross *(Administrator)*, Cyril King *(Advisor)*, Diane Mckee *(Administrator)*, Brenda Montgomery *(Advisor)*
**HR:** Paula Beers *(Human Resources Officer)*, Angela Campbell *(Human Resources Recruitment)*, Bronagh Murray *(Human Resources Recruitment)*, John Shivers *(Training Director)*
**Facilities:** Jim Adams *(Maintenance Officer)*, Brian Booth *(Grounds and Maintenance Manage)*, Brian Forsythe *(Facilities Manager)*
**Operations:** Jim Dunbar *(Project Coordinator)*
**Purchasing:** Marjorie Stanfield *(Purchasing Officer)*

**Branches:** South Eastern Education and Library Board, Clandeboye Road, Bangor, Co Down BT20 3JW
**US SIC:** 8299 **UK SIC:** 93300
**Employees:** 400

DUNS 22-636-2945
## South Eastern Electrical Plc
(**Subsidiary of:** The South Eastern Group of Companies Ltd)
South Eastern House, Ilford, Essex IG6 3UT
**Tel:** 020-8502-6900 **Fax:** 0870-300-0333
**Web:** www.southeastern.co.uk
**Reg No:** 1579718 **VAT No:** 360921660
**Estd:** 1981 Public Limited Company
**Line of Business:** Installation of electrical wiring and fittings
**Issued Capital:** £50,000
**Principals:** N P Davey *(Chairman)*, P N Davey, C J Harding, J A Saunders, C Phillips, J P Davey
**Co. Secretary:** Rajesh Patel
**Responsibilities**
**Senior:** Sidney Osbourn *(Financial Director)*
**Finance:** Sidney Osbourn *(Financial Director)*
**IT:** Darren O'Hara *(Head of IT)*, Sidney Osbourn *(Financial Director)*
**Branches:** South Eastern Electrical Plc, 2117 Coventry Rd, Birmingham, West Midlands B26 3EA
**US SIC:** 1731, 1711
**UK SIC:** 50300
**Auditors:** Fisher Michael
**Bankers:** Barclays Bank Plc (20-29-86)

| | 31-03-14 | 31-03-13 | 31-03-12 |
|---|---|---|---|
| TO | 31,599,837 | 34,549,396 | 29,721,068 |
| P/L | 1,190,661 | 1,245,012 | (646,769) |
| NW | 3,888,921 | 3,520,642 | 3,368,400 |
| WC | 2,848,706 | 2,967,591 | 2,074,995 |
| Emp. | 178 | 154 | 147 |

DUNS 23-339-2518 Imp
## South England Conference of Seventh Day Adventists
25 St Johns Road, Watford, Hertfordshire WD17 1PZ
**Tel:** 01923-232728
**Web:** www.adventist.org.uk
**Estd:** 1995
**Line of Business:** Religious organisations and places of worship
**Principals:** S Davis *(President)*, J Redman, J Phillips, I Williams, B Kavaloh, A Vontzalides, M Martin, J Wong
**Responsibilities**
**Senior:** G Abbequaye *(Principal)*, N Bonnie *(Principal)*, Jacqui Crawford *(Human Resources Manager)*, J Gittens *(Principal)*, D McFarlene *(Reverend)*, M Ndebele *(Principal)*, B Nysschen *(Principal)*, B Sabadin *(Principal)*, D St Marie *(Principal)*, K Sterling *(Principal)*
**Finance:** Victor Pilmoor *(Treasurer)*, E Ramharacksingh *(Treasurer)*
**Admin:** P Lockham *(Secretary)*
**US SIC:** 8661 **UK SIC:** 96600
**Auditors:** Colledge Redfern

| | 31-12-13 | 31-12-12 | 31-12-11 |
|---|---|---|---|
| TO | 22,137,931 | 22,023,835 | 17,988,572 |
| P/L | 2,484,499 | 2,877,141 | 545,969 |
| NW | 27,924,248 | 25,528,503 | 23,713,573 |
| WC | 12,633,399 | 10,521,274 | 11,360,270 |
| Emp. | 182 | 214 | 175 |

DUNS 73-523-7682
## South Essex Commercial Services Ltd
Luker Road, Southend-On-Sea, Essex SS1 1ND
**Tel:** 01702220598 **Fax:** 01702-432320
**Web:** www.southend.ac.uk
**Reg No:** 4786472 **Estd:** 2003 Private Limited Company
**Line of Business:** Licensed restaurants
**Issued Capital:** £1
**Directors:** Mrs A M O'Donoghue, J Hayles, R N Launder, A D Mcgarel
**Co. Secretary:** Robert Millea
**US SIC:** 5812, 6531
**UK SIC:** 66110, 83400

| | 31-07-13 | 31-07-12 | 31-07-11 |
|---|---|---|---|
| TO | 636,148 | 584,508 | 603,219 |
| NW | 1 | 1 | 1 |
| WC | (55,695) | (17,839) | (19,462) |

DUNS 21-161-5580
## South Essex Gymnastics Club Ltd
Gloucester Park North, Cranes Farm Road, Basildon, Essex SS14 3GR
**Tel:** 01268295985
**Web:** www.southessexgym.co.uk
**Reg No:** 6882268 **Estd:** 2009 Private Company Limited By Guarantee
**Line of Business:** Other sporting activities not elsewhere classified
**Directors:** S D Smith, N Inns, R Harper, R D Short, Ms J A Hickton
**Co. Secretary:** Ms Susan Hibbitt
**US SIC:** 7999 **UK SIC:** 97913
**Auditors:** Michael Letch & Partners LLP

| | 31-05-14 | 31-05-13 | 31-05-12 |
|---|---|---|---|
| TO | 1,047,372 | 940,676 | 799,999 |
| P/L | 138,680 | 199,810 | 123,773 |
| NW | 792,101 | 653,421 | 453,611 |
| WC | 604,112 | 456,406 | 218,904 |
| Emp. | 64 | 51 | 45 |

DUNS 34-648-0093
## South Essex Homes Ltd
Cheviot House 70 Baxter Avenue, Southend-On-Sea, Essex SS2 6HZ
**Tel:** 08000234057
**Web:** www.southessexhomes.co.uk
**Reg No:** 5453601 **Estd:** 2005 Private Company Limited By Guarantee
**Line of Business:** Other letting of own property
**Directors:** M Assenheim, P Goldsmith, Ms J Mcmahon, Ms C Haycock, Mrs M Betson, A C Churton, Mrs M Butler, Ms W M Greenberg
**Co. Secretary:** Mrs Beverley Gallacher
**Responsibilities**
**Senior:** Elizabeth Mansfield *(Director)*
**US SIC:** 6519 **UK SIC:** 85000
**Bankers:** Barclays Bank Plc (20-04-96)

| | 31-03-14 | 31-03-13 | 31-03-12 |
|---|---|---|---|
| TO | 10,339,000 | 10,710,000 | 10,364,000 |
| P/L | (323,000) | 1,066,000 | 164,000 |
| NW | (4,581,000) | (6,207,000) | (7,153,000) |
| WC | 1,985,000 | 1,861,000 | 1,173,000 |
| Emp. | 200 | 184 | 190 |

DUNS 21-007-5074
## South Essex Insurance Brokers Ltd
(**Subsidiary of:** Allchurches Trust Ltd)
South Essex House, North Road, South Ockendon, Essex RM15 5BE
**Tel:** 0170850000
**Web:** www.seib.co.uk
**Reg No:** 6317314 **Estd:** 2007 Private Limited Company
**Line of Business:** Insurance - other
**Trading Style:** Lansdown Insurance Brokers
**Issued Capital:** £250
**Directors:** M C Hews, B Thaker, B Fehler, Mrs S J Middleton, K S Jones
**Co. Secretary:** Ms Rachael Hall
**Responsibilities**
**Marketing:** Nicky Mackenzie *(Marketing Manager)*
**Sales:** Suzy Titcombe *(Commercial Premises Manager)*
**Branches:** South Essex Insurance Brokers Ltd, Lansdown House, Pittville Circus Road, Cheltenham, Gloucestershire GL52 2QE
**US SIC:** 6399 **UK SIC:** 82001
**Auditors:** Kingston Smith LLP

| | 31-12-13 | 31-12-12 | 31-12-11 |
|---|---|---|---|
| TO | 7,299,143 | 7,175,507 | 6,628,584 |
| P/L | 2,456,404 | 2,506,280 | 2,151,604 |
| NW | 7,672,477 | 5,737,343 | 5,572,520 |
| WC | 7,521,172 | 5,512,120 | 5,339,510 |
| Emp. | 62 | 64 | 61 |

DUNS 21-722-4104 Imp
## South Essex Stockholders Ltd
Metalstock House, Vanguard Way, Shoeburyness, Southend-On-Sea, Essex SS3 9RE
**Tel:** 01702-296-922
**Web:** www.industrialmetal.co.uk
**Reg No:** 1219136 **Estd:** 1975 Private Limited Company
**Line of Business:** Steel stockholders
**Trading Style:** Industrial Metal Services, Ims
**Issued Capital:** £350,000
**Principals:** R J Eyre *(Managing)*, A T Large *(Sales)*, R J Rout
**Co. Secretary:** Darren Hills
**Responsibilities**
**Senior:** Neil Simson *(Manager)*
**Sales:** Stephen Castleton *(Office Manager)*
**Admin:** Stephen Castleton *(Office Manager)*
**IT:** Terry Halls *(IT Manager)*
**HR:** Mark Ardron *(Health & Safety Officer)*
**Health & Safety:** Mark Ardron *(Health & Safety Officer)*
**US SIC:** 5051, 5199
**UK SIC:** 61200, 61900
**Auditors:** BDO LLP
**Bankers:** National Westminster Bank Plc (55-50-28)

| | 31-07-13 | 31-07-12 | 31-07-11 |
|---|---|---|---|
| TO | 62,562,300 | 66,284,159 | 61,138,123 |
| P/L | 1,105,148 | 1,430,521 | 2,642,515 |
| NW | 7,668,628 | 7,957,335 | 7,701,192 |
| WC | (381,370) | 1,388,928 | 1,871,281 |
| Emp. | 248 | 236 | 210 |

DUNS 64-223-4181
## South Forest Leisure Centre
Clipstone Road, Mansfield, Nottinghamshire NG21 9JF
**Tel:** 01623823866
**Web:** www.southforestcomplex.co.uk
**Estd:** 1997 Proprietorship
**Line of Business:** Leisure centres
**Proprietor:** R Bowring
**US SIC:** 5813 **UK SIC:** 66200
**Employees:** 50

DUNS 23-644-5300
## South Glamorgan Area Health Authority
Community Headquarters, Sanatorium Road, Cardiff, South Glamorgan CF11 8PL
**Tel:** 02920233651
**Estd:** 1974 Incorporate By Act Of Parliament
**Line of Business:** Health authority.
**Principals:** D Lewis, G Harry *(General Manager)*
**Branches:** South Glamorgan Area Health Authority, Churchill Way Dental Practice, 4A Churchill Way, Cardiff, South Glamorgan CF10 2DW
**US SIC:** 8062 **UK SIC:** 95100
**Bankers:** National Westminster Bank Plc (56-00-41)
**Employees:** 300

DUNS 42-429-1482
## South Gloucestershire Council
Civic Centre, High Street, Kingswood, Bristol, Avon BS15 0DS
**Tel:** 01454 868 000
**Web:** www.southglos.gov.uk
**Estd:** 1996
**Line of Business:** General (overall) public service activities
**Director:** Ms A Deeks
**Responsibilities**
**Senior:** Liz Allison *(Executive)*, Kenny Braidwood *(Board Lead Officer)*, Brian Gardner *(Senior Manager)*, Cllr Godwin *(Executive Member, External Aff)*, John Godwin *(Director of Partnerships)*, Marlynne Grant *(Manager)*, Emily Greentree *(Manager)*, Richard Hanks *(Training Director)*, Pat Hockey *(Vice Chair)*, Cathy McKeown *(Executive)*, Kay Palmer *(Member of the Board)*, Mark Pullin *(General manager)*, Nigel Shipley *(Senior Manager)*, Rebecca Tomms *(Services Manager)*, Sarah Tucker *(Executive)*, Anita Walker *(Representative)*
**Finance:** Janet Faire *(Finance Manager)*, Mike Hayesman *(Head of Finance and Customer S)*
**Marketing:** Kate Batchelor *(Senior Marketing Officer)*, Kate Champion *(Spokeswoman)*, Sarah Hudspith *(Spokeswoman)*, Marian Jones *(Community Engagement Officer)*, Clare Nelmes *(Community Consultation Officer)*, Jane Sheppard *(Marketing Manager)*, Julie Vince *(Head of Strategic Communicatio)*
**Sales:** Liz Townend *(Business Development Director)*
**Admin:** Jane Antrobus *(Administrator)*, Leanne Cook *(Administrator)*
**IT:** Andreas Burt *(IT Manager)*, David Dawkins *(ICT Customer Services Manager)*
**HR:** Julie Embury *(Training Director)*, Guy Halley *(Training Director)*, Richard Hanks *(Training Director)*, Claire Kerswill *(Head of Human Resources)*, Holly Magson *(Executive)*, Sue Rice *(Teacher)*, Liz Thomas *(Training Director)*
**Health & Safety:** Charlotte Musgrove *(Healthy Eating Coordinator)*
**Facilities:** Rebecca Tomms *(Services Manager)*
**Operations:** Karen Hayes *(Senior Planning Officer)*
**Fleet:** Chris Sane *(Strategic Head of Transport)*
**Engineering:** Rhodri Briggs *(Technical Engineer)*, Vicky Gent *(Street Works Coordinator)*, Nichola Winstone *(Technical Engineer)*
**Branches:** South Gloucestershire Council, Stephens Drive, Longwell Grn, Bristol, Avon BS30 7JB
**US SIC:** 9121 **UK SIC:** 91110
**Employees:** 200

DUNS 42-342-3099
## South Green Park Ltd
(**Subsidiary of:** Poultec Ltd)
48 South Green, Mattishall, Dereham, Norfolk NR20 3JY
**Tel:** 01362-857100 **Fax:** 01362858983
**Web:** www.southgreenpark.co.uk
**Reg No:** 4330014 **Estd:** 2003 Private Limited Company
**Line of Business:** Letting of conference and exhibition centres
**Issued Capital:** £1
**Directors:** N Mcardle, E J Bales
**Co. Secretary:** Ms Nicola Guy
**US SIC:** 7399 **UK SIC:** 83954

| | 31-07-14 | 31-07-13 | 31-07-12 |
|---|---|---|---|
| TA | 2,522,868 | 2,528,491 | 2,556,399 |
| NW | 276,401 | 142,458 | 89,748 |
| WC | (520,296) | (532,673) | (360,450) |

DUNS 21-821-2095
## South Hampstead High School
1-3 Maresfield Gardens, London NW3 5SS
**Tel:** 020-7435-2899
**Web:** www.gdst.net
**Estd:** 1995
**Line of Business:** General secondary education
**Proprietor:** Mrs J Stephens
**Responsibilities**
**Senior:** Elisabeth Nicholas *(Acting Head Teacher)*, Jenny Stephen *(Principal)*
**Finance:** Beverly Quilantang *(Financial Manager)*
**Marketing:** Stacy Street *(Marketing Manager)*
**HR:** Jenny Stephen *(Principal)*
**Health & Safety:** Helen Kaye *(Estates Manager)*
**Facilities:** Helen Kaye *(Estates Manager)*
**US SIC:** 8211 **UK SIC:** 93200
**Employees:** 81

DUNS 23-644-5342
## South Hams District Council
Follaton House, Plymouth Road, Totnes, Devon TQ9 5NE
**Web:** www.southhams.gov.uk
**VAT No:** 142204125 **Estd:** 1974
**Line of Business:** Central government
**Director:** P G West
**Responsibilities**
**Senior:** Richard Gage *(Planning Officer)*, David Incoll *(Chief Executive)*, Richard Sheard *(Chief Executive)*
**Finance:** Michael Tithecott *(Chief Accountant)*
**Marketing:** Kate Hamp *(Customer Services Manager)*, Ian Rowden *(Communications Officer)*, Alison Stoneham *(Communications Manager)*
**Admin:** Liz Tucker *(Administrator)*
**IT:** Robin Barlow *(Non-PC Systems Manager)*
**HR:** Reg Hambly *(Head of Personnel)*
**Facilities:** Kate Cassar *(Head of Assets)*
**Branches:** South Hams District Council, Ashwood, South Brent, Devon TQ10 9PH
**US SIC:** 9121 **UK SIC:** 91110
**Bankers:** HSBC Bank plc (40-44-24)
**Employees:** 350

DUNS 55-070-9398
## South Haven Lodge
69-73 Portsmouth Road, Southampton, Hampshire SO19 9BE
**Tel:** 023-8068-5606
**Estd:** 1989 Proprietorship
**Line of Business:** Nursing homes
**Proprietor:** Mrs S Badells
**Responsibilities**
**Senior:** Rebecca Jarvis *(Manager)*, Max Whatman *(Manager)*
**US SIC:** 8051 **UK SIC:** 95100
**Employees:** 54

DUNS 21-917-0552
## South Hereford Garages Ltd
(**Subsidiary of:** Shg Holdings Ltd)
Centurion Way, Hereford, Herefordshire HR1 1LQ
**Tel:** 01600890235
**Web:** www.southherefordvolkswagen.co.uk
**Reg No:** 1111864 **Estd:** 1973 Private Limited Company
**Line of Business:** Car dealers (new & used)
**Issued Capital:** £51,720
**Directors:** S Powell, C J Richards, C Barker
**Co. Secretary:** Ian Phillips
**Responsibilities**
**HR:** Carol Dawson *(Human Resources Manager)*
**Branches:** South Hereford Garages Ltd, Greenacres, Marsh Lane, Coleford, Gloucestershire GL16 7NA
**US SIC:** 5511 **UK SIC:** 65100
**Auditors:** Kidsons Impey
**Bankers:** HSBC Bank plc (40-33-11)

| | 31-12-13 | 31-12-12 | 31-12-11 |
|---|---|---|---|
| TO | 66,153,829 | 54,274,365 | 51,745,458 |
| P/L | 1,417,644 | 935,684 | 834,460 |
| NW | 10,487,637 | 9,618,032 | 8,772,225 |
| WC | 9,683,565 | 9,008,819 | 8,403,624 |
| Emp. | 158 | 149 | 154 |

DUNS 21-129-0007
## South Herts Golf Club
Links Drive, London N20 8QU
**Tel:** 02084452035
**Web:** www.southhertsgolfclub.co.uk
**Estd:** 2010
**Line of Business:** Golf clubs
**Proprietor:** D Bujicic
**Branches:** South Herts Golf Club, Links Drive, London N20 8QU
**US SIC:** 5812 **UK SIC:** 66110
**Employees:** 800

DUNS 28-875-5697
**South Hill Park Trust Ltd**
South Hill Park Mansion, Ringmead, Bracknell, Berkshire RG12 7PA
**Tel:** 01344484123
**Web:** www.southhillpark.org.uk
**Reg No:** 1104422 **VAT No:** 200169025
**Estd:** 1973 Private Company Limited By Guarantee
**Line of Business:** Arts centres
**Trading Style:** South Hill Park Arts Centre
**Directors:** G H Taylor, Mrs V A O'Riordan, Mrs H Hyde, R Angell, C Titley, W Davison, J Mills, D Morton
**Co. Secretary:** Ronald Mcallister
**Responsibilities**
**Senior:** Chas Baily *(Director)*, Dorothy Hayes *(Director)*, Jennie Mccracken *(Director)*, Jade Potter *(Director)*
**US SIC:** 7911, 7832
**UK SIC:** 97913, 97113
**Auditors:** BDO Stoy Hayward
**Bankers:** Lloyds TSB Bank plc (30-91-11)

| | 31-03-14 | 31-03-13 | 31-03-12 |
|---|---|---|---|
| TO | 1,888,930 | 1,893,584 | 2,013,644 |
| P/L | (109,149) | (99,679) | (22,344) |
| NW | 3,073,890 | 2,960,039 | 3,141,718 |
| WC | 240,485 | 205,926 | 140,761 |
| Emp. | 66 | 72 | 81 |

DUNS 23-644-5383
**South Holland District Council**
Council Offices, Priory Road, Spalding, Lincolnshire PE11 2XE
**Tel:** 01775761161
**Web:** www.sholland.gov.uk
**Estd:** 1974
**Line of Business:** Local government
**Principals:** J R Pearl *(Chairman)*, J Clark *(Financial)*, Councillor Neil Judge
**Co. Secretary:** Ms Natalie Warren
**Responsibilities**
**Senior:** Christian Mycock *(Executive)*, Amanda Puttick *(Chair)*, Vicky Thompson *(Assistant Director - Democrati)*
**Finance:** Colin Wyatt *(Finance Manager)*
**HR:** Kelly Sooben *(Human Resources Manager)*
**Health & Safety:** Nick Kendrick *(Health & Safety Officer)*, Tony Lascelles *(Head of human resources)*
**Engineering:** Michael Charlton *(Principal Surveyor)*, Vikki Humphries *(Technical Engineer)*
**Branches:** South Holland District Council, Lyndis Walk, Holbeach, Spalding, Lincolnshire PE12 7DF
**US SIC:** 9121 **UK SIC:** 91110
**Bankers:** Lloyds TSB Bank plc (30-97-95)
**Employees:** 320

DUNS 73-723-8316
**South Hook Lng Terminal Co Ltd.**
Dale Road, Herbrandston, Milford Haven, Dyfed SA73 3SU
**Fax:** 01437-782-201
**Web:** www.southhooklng.co.uk
**Reg No:** 4982132 **Estd:** 2003 Private Limited Company
**Line of Business:** Manufacture of gas
**Issued Capital:** £300,000,000
**Directors:** Y S Al-Jaidah, N K Al-Jaidah, N J Poulteney, A J Al-Kuwari, J P Chaplin, A G Routledge
**Co. Secretary:** Ms Linda Pszon
**Responsibilities**
**Senior:** Mohammed Al-Naimi *(general Manager)*, Bradley Corson *(Manager)*, Gunnar Olsen *(Manager)*, Mandy Tilling *(Proprietor)*
**Marketing:** Mariam Dalziel *(Media Relations Officer)*
**Operations:** Hamad Al Samra *(Operations Manager)*
**Branches:** SOUTH HOOK LNG TERMINAL COMPANY LTD - 2 London Bridge, London, SE1 9RA.
**US SIC:** 4925 **UK SIC:** 25670
**Auditors:** Ernst & Young LLP
**Bankers:** Citibank Na (18-50-08)

| | 31-12-13 | 31-12-12 | 31-12-11 |
|---|---|---|---|
| TO | 63,998,000 | 64,912,000 | 68,806,000 |
| P/L | 115,641,000 | 112,841,000 | 109,326,000 |
| NW | 486,279,000 | 463,646,000 | 377,403,000 |
| WC | 22,691,000 | 32,420,000 | 18,495,000 |
| Emp. | 95 | 95 | 90 |

DUNS 22-747-0747
**South Kesteven District Council**
Council Offices, St Peters Hill, Grantham, Lincolnshire NG31 6PZ
**Tel:** 01476406080
**Web:** www.southkesteven.gov.uk
**Estd:** 2002
**Line of Business:** Local government
**Director:** C Farmer
**Responsibilities**
**Senior:** Beverley Agass *(Chief Executive)*, Mandy Braithwaite *(Legal Team Manager)*, Carol Drury *(Director of Partnerships)*, Rob Howbrook *(Chairman)*, Blake Hutchinson *(Senior Manager)*, Jo Toomey *(General Manager)*
**Finance:** Jeanette Strutt *(Revenues Manager)*, Richard Wyles *(Head of Finance)*
**Marketing:** Debbie Wyles *(Business Management Officer)*
**IT:** Gary Andrew *(Senior IT Executive)*, Kevin Munford *(IT Support Officer)*, Andy Nix *(Computer Manager)*
**HR:** Sue Griffiths *(Head of People, Projects and P)*
**Health & Safety:** Sandy Kavanagh *(Health and Safety Executive)*, Christian Polzin *(Food Health and Safety Officer)*, Rachael Smith *(Community Health Walks Officer)*
**Facilities:** Liz Banner *(Property Manager)*, Neil Cucksey *(Property Development Manager)*, S McCahon *(Facilities Manager)*, Sandra Mullin *(Estate Supervisor)*
**Operations:** Lucy Bonshor *(Performance Officer)*, Steve Cullington *(Supported Housing Service Mana)*, Mandy Gee *(Partnerships and Project Offic)*, David Lambley *(Fraud Investigator)*, Daren Turner *(Strategic Director Finance Pro)*, Ian Yates *(Operations Director, Environme)*
**Branches:** South Kesteven District Council, Stamford Arts Centre, 27 St. Marys Street, Stamford, Lincolnshire PE9 2DL
**US SIC:** 9121 **UK SIC:** 91110
**Bankers:** National Westminster Bank Plc (60-09-09)
**Employees:** 350

DUNS 23-644-5466
**South Lakeland District Council**
Lowther Street, Kendal, Cumbria LA9 4UQ
**Tel:** 08450504434
**Web:** www.southlakeland.gov.uk
**Estd:** 2002
**Line of Business:** Local government
**Trading Style:** Birthwaite 1
**Directors:** M Jayne, B Parkinson, F Rae, A Crooks
**Responsibilities**
**Senior:** Lawrence Conway *(Chief Executive)*, Peter Ridgway *(Chief Executive)*
**Branches:** South Lakeland District Council, Town Hall, Highgate, Kendal, Cumbria LA9 4DL
**US SIC:** 9121 **UK SIC:** 91110
**Bankers:** HSBC Bank plc (40-26-02)
**Employees:** 600

DUNS 23-275-0893
**South Lanarkshire College**
College Way, East Kilbride, Glasgow, Lanarkshire G75 0NE
**Tel:** 01355-807780
**Web:** www.south-lanarkshire-college.ac.uk
**Estd:** 1927
**Line of Business:** Further education schools and colleges
**Principals:** Mrs S Moore *(Chairman)*, G Robbins, N Glenask
**Responsibilities**
**Senior:** Craig Ferguson *(Head of Facilities)*, Stewart Mckillop *(Principal)*
**Finance:** Keith Mcallister *(Financial Director)*
**Marketing:** Lisa Brown *(Marketing Manager)*
**IT:** Chris Sumner *(IT Technical Support Superviso)*, Linda Young *(IT Manager)*
**HR:** Kirsten Oswald *(Personnel Manager)*
**Health & Safety:** Sharon McCarroll *(Facilities Manager)*
**Facilities:** Craig Ferguson *(Head of Facilities)*, Sharon McCarroll *(Facilities Manager)*
**Branches:** 86/88 Main St, East Kilbride, Glasgow
**US SIC:** 8221, 8249
**UK SIC:** 93100, 93300
**Bankers:** Clydesdale Bank Plc (82-61-18)
**Employees:** 350

DUNS 23-641-2490
**South Lanarkshire Council**
46 South Vennel, Lanark, Lanarkshire ML11 7JT
**Tel:** 01555667600
**Web:** www.southlanarkshire.gov.uk
**VAT No:** 262287747 **Estd:** 2010
**Line of Business:** Accounting activities
**Principals:** D S Anderson *(Financial)*, T Harding, R Russell, W G U'Ren
**Branches:** South Lanarkshire Council, Carlisle Road, Lanark, Lanarkshire ML11 9SB
**US SIC:** 9121 **UK SIC:** 91110
**Bankers:** The Royal Bank Of Scotland Plc (83-24-12)
**Employees:** 200

DUNS 42-343-8050
**South Lanarkshire Council**
Council Offices, Almada Street, Hamilton, Lanarkshire ML3 0AA
**Tel:** 03031231015
**Web:** www.southlanarkshire.gov.uk
**Estd:** 1992
**Line of Business:** Local government
**Director:** M Docherty
**Responsibilities**
**Marketing:** Tom Little *(Head of Corporate Communicatio)*
**Sales:** Scott Nimmo *(Development Officer)*
**IT:** Martin Low *(Senior IT Executive)*
**HR:** Geraldine McCann *(Human Resources Manager)*
**Health & Safety:** Neil Addie *(Health & Safety Officer)*, Tracy Blake *(RTI Team Leader)*
**Branches:** South Lanarkshire Council, Carlisle Rd, Biggar, Lanarkshire ML12 6SD
**US SIC:** 9121 **UK SIC:** 91110
**Bankers:** Clydesdale Bank Plc (82-70-03)
**Employees:** 2,000

DUNS 42-341-4163
**South Lanarkshire Leisure & Culture Ltd**
1st Floor North Stand, Cadzow Avenue, Hamilton, Lanarkshire ML3 0LX
**Web:** www.slleisureandculture.co.uk
**Reg No:** 0225702SC **Estd:** 2011 Private Company Limited By Guarantee
**Line of Business:** Operation of other sports arenas and stadiums not elsewhere classified
**Trading Style:** Strathclyde Park Golf Course
**Directors:** C Mcdowall, G J Docherty, A D Morrison, Ms A L Beggan, D W Watson, L Freeland, A R Mcgown, J Steele
**Co. Secretary:** Alison Dougall
**Responsibilities**
**Senior:** Elaine Bernard *(Marketing Manager)*, Jerry Campbell *(Manager)*, Gerry Convery *(Director)*, Robert Craig *(Director)*, Joan Gibson *(Director)*, Stephen Smellie *(Director)*, Lois Tenant *(Line Manager)*
**Marketing:** Sarah Mcphie *(Marketing Officer)*
**Branches:** South Lanarkshire Leisure & Culture Ltd, Forth Library, Main Street, Lanark, Lanarkshire ML11 8AE
**US SIC:** 7399, 8231, 7941
**UK SIC:** 83954, 97700, 97911
**Auditors:** KPMG LLP
**Bankers:** The Royal Bank Of Scotland Plc (83-22-26)

| | 31-03-14 | 31-03-13 | 31-03-12 |
|---|---|---|---|
| TO | 41,438,000 | 39,384,000 | 39,855,000 |
| P/L | (658,000) | 281,000 | 640,000 |
| NW | (5,968,000) | (2,294,000) | 2,012,000 |
| WC | 2,026,000 | 1,904,000 | 2,238,000 |
| Emp. | 865 | 866 | 859 |

DUNS 21-773-1817
**South Lanarkshire Lifestlye - Fairhill**
Neilsland Road, Hamilton, Lanarkshire ML3 8HJ
**Tel:** 01698456350
**Web:** www.southlanarkshire.gov.uk
**Estd:** 2011 Proprietorship
**Line of Business:** Other sporting activities not elsewhere classified
**Proprietor:** Mrs E Davidson
**Responsibilities**
**Senior:** Jo Gillies *(Centre Manager)*
**US SIC:** 7999 **UK SIC:** 97913
**Employees:** 50

DUNS 28-849-6292
**South Lee School Ltd**
Nowton Road, Bury St Edmunds, Suffolk IP33 2BT
**Tel:** 01284-754654
**Web:** www.southlee.co.uk
**Reg No:** 0698102 **Estd:** 1961 Private Company Limited By Guarantee
**Line of Business:** Schools (independent)
**Directors:** K F Watson, Ms C Godfrey, Mrs M Gilkes, R W Hatch, Mrs D M Legge, Mrs L K Heymoz, D E Barker, Mrs I M Finbow
**Co. Secretary:** Derek Whipp
**Responsibilities**
**Senior:** Heather Bentley *(Manager)*, Stephen Honeywood *(Director)*, Derek Wilding *(Manager)*
**IT:** Tim Bright *(Head of IT)*
**US SIC:** 8211 **UK SIC:** 93200
**Auditors:** Whiting & Partners
**Bankers:** Lloyds TSB Bank plc (30-91-49)

| | 31-08-14 | 31-08-13 | 31-08-12 |
|---|---|---|---|
| TO | 2,015,902 | 2,061,067 | 2,082,400 |
| P/L | (29,067) | 98,500 | 67,790 |
| NW | 2,950,443 | 2,979,510 | 2,881,009 |
| WC | 84,555 | 257,203 | 1,534,140 |
| Emp. | 47 | 47 | 48 |

DUNS 73-935-2813
**South Leicestershire College Enterprises Ltd**
Blaby Road, Wigston, Leicestershire LE18 4PH
**Fax:** 01162775578
**Web:** www.slcollege.ac.uk
**Reg No:** 2941883 **Estd:** 1994 Private Limited Company
**Line of Business:** Steam and hot water supply
**Trading Style:** South Leicestershire College
**Issued Capital:** £180,000
**Directors:** Mrs M G Plant, Ms T E Fazaeli
**Co. Secretary:** Ms Sally Brook Shanahan
**Responsibilities**
**Senior:** Christine Bullock *(Manager)*, Ann Height *(Manager)*
**Finance:** Hari Khurmi *(Finance Director)*
**Marketing:** Katie Phelan *(Senior Marketing Coordinator)*
**IT:** Dhirajlal Chauhan *(IT Team Leader)*
**US SIC:** 4961, 8249
**UK SIC:** 16300, 93300
**Auditors:** RSM Tenon Audit Ltd

| | 31-07-13 | 31-07-12 | 31-07-11 |
|---|---|---|---|
| TO | N/A | N/A | 20,526 |
| P/L | 37 | 42 | (6,547) |
| NW | 212,173 | 212,136 | 212,093 |
| WC | 217,173 | 154,270 | 154,227 |

DUNS 23-551-6403
**South Liverpool Housing Ltd**
South Liverpool Housing, Parklands, Conleach Road, Liverpool, Merseyside L24 0TY
**Fax:** 01512845679
**Web:** www.slhgroup.co.uk
**Reg No:** 0031210I **Estd:** 1998 Friendly Society
**Line of Business:** Housing associations societies trusts & co-operatives
**Directors:** C Strickland, Ms B Southern, Ms L Skerry, M Birkett, Mrs B Southern, T Smith, R A Brown, L S Dack
**Co. Secretary:** Anthony Russell
**Responsibilities**
**Senior:** Ruth Stott *(Director)*
**Finance:** Michael Whitehead *(Head of Finance)*
**Marketing:** Michelle Bloore *(Sales & Marketing Manager)*, Claire Ryan *(Head of Business Excellence)*
**Sales:** Michelle Bloore *(Sales & Marketing Manager)*
**Operations:** Wayne Gales *(Executive Director, Operations)*
**Branches:** South Liverpool Housing Ltd, 10 Speke Rd, Liverpool, Merseyside L19 2PA
**US SIC:** 8699 **UK SIC:** 96902
**Auditors:** PKF (UK) LLP
**Bankers:** National Westminster Bank Plc (60-13-19)
**Employees:** 91
**Turnover:** £15,008,000

DUNS 21-810-8658
**South Liverpool Probation Centre**
Liverpool Community Probation Centre, 180 Falkner Street, Liverpool, Merseyside L8 7SX
**Tel:** 01517066600
**Estd:** 2012
**Line of Business:** Probation services
**US SIC:** 9121 **UK SIC:** 91110
**Employees:** 100

DUNS 21-233-9166
**South London & Maudsley Nhs Foundation Trust**
Addictions Resource Centre 63-65, Denmark Hill, London SE5 8RS
**Tel:** 02032283381
**Web:** www.national.slam.nhs.uk
**Estd:** 2013
**Line of Business:** Hospitals
**Principals:** M Long *(Chairman)*, G Heafield *(Financial)*, S Bell Cbe, K Jacob, E Taylor, C Bland, P Clare, Ms H Mccallion
**Responsibilities**
**Senior:** Stuart Bell CBE *(Chief Executive Officer)*
**US SIC:** 8321 **UK SIC:** 96111
**Auditors:** Jon Hayes
**Employees:** 5,456
**Turnover:** £311,337,000

DUNS 23-641-6632
**South London and Maudsley Nhs Foundation Trust**
Monks Orchard Road, Beckenham, Kent BR3 3BX
**Tel:** 020-3228-6000
**Web:** www.slam.nhs.uk
**Estd:** 1975
**Line of Business:** Public sector hospital activities, including nhs trusts

**Trading Style:** York Clinic, Bethlem Royal Hospital, Maudsley Hospital
**Issued Capital:** £1
**Directors:** S Bell, G Heafield
**Responsibilities**
**Admin:** Mafo Kamama *(Personal Assistant)*
**IT:** Michael Denis *(IT Director)*
**Health & Safety:** Jane Moody *(Health & Safety Officer)*
**Facilities:** Hugh Barter *(Estates Manager)*
**Branches:** South London and Maudsley Nhs Foundation Trust, Lennard Lodge, 3 Lennard Road, Croydon, Surrey CR0 2UL
**US SIC:** 8062 **UK SIC:** 95100
**Auditors:** Deloitte LLP

| | 31-03-14 | 31-03-13 | 31-03-12 |
|---|---|---|---|
| TO | 363,219,000 | 370,750,000 | 364,840,000 |
| P/L | 5,857,000 | 2,301,000 | 4,785,000 |
| NW | 404,745,000 | 293,156,000 | 295,408,000 |
| WC | 32,655,000 | 44,879,000 | 39,982,000 |
| Emp. | 5,093 | 5,190 | 4,000 |

DUNS 28-831-4891

## The South London Church Fund & Southwark Diocesan Board of Finance

Trinity House, 4 Chapel Court, London SE1 1HW
**Tel:** 02079399400
**Web:** www.southwark.anglican.org
**Reg No:** 0236594 **Estd:** 1929 Private Company Limited By Guarantee
**Line of Business:** Activities of religious organisations
**Directors:** S P Gates, R L Hickson, S R Kingston, The Reverend N J Peacock, C J Glasson, P H Siggs, C P Clementi, Ms B A Truttero
**Co. Secretary:** Ms Ruth Martin
**Responsibilities**
**Senior:** Ian Akhurst *(Director)*, Philip Bladen *(Director)*, William Campen *(Director)*, Martin Day *(Director)*, Jeremy Garton *(Director)*, Christian Hansen *(Director)*, John Henson *(Director)*, Roger Hird *(Director)*, Daniel Kajumba *(Director)*, John Kempsell *(Director)*, Jane Kustner *(Director)*, Barry Nichols *(Director)*, David Plummer *(Director)*, Christopher Skilton *(Director)*, John Thewlis *(Director)*
**Branches:** The South London Church Fund & Southwark Diocesan Board of Finance, St. James's Church, Sussex Gardens, London W2 3UD
**US SIC:** 6732 **UK SIC:** 83100
**Auditors:** BDO Stoy Hayward

| | 31-12-13 | 31-12-12 | 31-12-11 |
|---|---|---|---|
| TO | 21,165,000 | 20,566,000 | 19,928,000 |
| P/L | (3,171,000) | (3,335,000) | (4,918,000) |
| NW | 226,561,000 | 224,105,000 | 222,372,000 |
| WC | 5,094,000 | 6,775,000 | 6,217,000 |
| Emp. | 46 | 390 | 47 |

DUNS 21-795-7503

## South London College

10 Woolwich New Road, London SE18 6AB
**Tel:** 02083058698
**Web:** www.southlondoncollege.co.uk
**Estd:** 2011
**Line of Business:** Further education schools and colleges
**US SIC:** 8221 **UK SIC:** 93100
**Employees:** 70

DUNS 22-734-9966

## South London Nursing Homes Ltd

**(Subsidiary of:** Mhl Holdco Ltd)
Knowle Lane, Cranleigh, Surrey GU6 8JL
**Tel:** 01483-275432
**Web:** www.caringhomes.org
**Reg No:** 1587431 **Estd:** 1982 Private Limited Company
**Line of Business:** Nursing homes
**Trading Style:** Knowle Park Nursing Home
**Issued Capital:** £1
**Directors:** P A Jeffery, P M Hill
**Co. Secretary:** Nigel Schofield
**Responsibilities**
**Senior:** Netra Longhurst *(Home Manager)*
**Marketing:** Netra Longhurst *(Home Manager)*
**HR:** Netra Longhurst *(Home Manager)*
**Health & Safety:** Netra Longhurst *(Home Manager)*
**Operations:** Netra Longhurst *(Home Manager)*
**Purchasing:** Netra Longhurst *(Home Manager)*
**Branches:** South London Nursing Homes Ltd, Knowle La, Cranleigh, Surrey GU6 8JL
**US SIC:** 8051 **UK SIC:** 95100
**Auditors:** Macintyre Hudson
**Bankers:** Barclays Bank Plc (20-24-61)

| | 31-03-14 | 31-03-13 | 31-03-12 |
|---|---|---|---|
| TO | 2,434,609 | 3,294,445 | 8,048,182 |
| P/L | 740,263 | 1,238,764 | 1,816,424 |
| NW | 5,269,358 | 4,470,908 | 30,185,141 |
| WC | 5,098,058 | 4,318,252 | 6,209,596 |
| Emp. | 63 | 216 | 171 |

DUNS 21-782-6667

## South London Press

2-4 Leigham Court Road, London SW16 2PG
**Tel:** 02087688680
**Web:** www.southlondonpress.co.uk
**Estd:** 2011 Partnership
**Line of Business:** Newspapers publishing
**Partners:** Ms N Rodgers, M Brown
**US SIC:** 2711 **UK SIC:** 47512
**Employees:** 112

DUNS 73-534-0049

## South London Ymca

8th Floor Marco Polo House, Croydon, Surrey CR0 2BX
**Tel:** 020-7101-9960 **Fax:** 0120 7501 8005
**Web:** www.slymca.org.uk
**Reg No:** 4796537 **Estd:** 2003 Private Company Limited By Guarantee
**Line of Business:** Hostels
**Trading Style:** South London Ymca
**Directors:** Mrs S R Twerdochlib, D E Shrimpton, D A Ford, R F Howgego, Ms V Perrault Sri Chandrasekera, Miss S Y Lewis, A J Hudson, Ms P M Thomas
**Co. Secretary:** Dennis Simmonds
**Responsibilities**
**Senior:** Jeremy Grey *(Chief Executive)*, Hilary Knight *(Director)*
**US SIC:** 7021 **UK SIC:** 66500
**Auditors:** PKF (UK) LLP
**Bankers:** HSBC Bank plc (40-18-30)

| | 31-03-14 | 31-03-13 | 31-03-12 |
|---|---|---|---|
| TO | 8,482,246 | 8,246,998 | 7,110,621 |
| P/L | 452,233 | 296,223 | 267,746 |
| NW | 12,833,783 | 12,183,430 | 11,887,207 |
| WC | 776,376 | 2,849,867 | 3,158,463 |
| Emp. | 107 | 98 | 109 |

DUNS 50-595-5336 **Imp-Exp**

## South Marston D C Ltd

**(Subsidiary of:** Honda Motor Co. Ltd.)
Unit 2 Keypoint, Thornhill Road, South Marston, Swindon, Wiltshire SN3 4RY
**Tel:** 01793827015
**Web:** www.sdc.co.uk
**Reg No:** 2534528 **VAT No:** 584228620
**Estd:** 1990 Private Limited Company
**Line of Business:** Warehouses
**Export Markets:** Japan & E U
**Export Sales:** £132,207
**Issued Capital:** £5,000,000
**Directors:** Y Tanaka, T Hashimoto, S Hashimoto
**Co. Secretary:** Akira Nagashima
**Responsibilities**
**Senior:** Yoshiki Ishida *(Manager)*, Tomoyuki Kishi *(Manager)*, Eiichi Murashima *(Manager)*, Nobuhiro Nakamura *(Manager)*
**Finance:** Patrick Earner *(Financial Manager)*
**IT:** Patrick Earner *(Financial Manager)*
**HR:** Brian Harris *(Facilities Manager)*
**Health & Safety:** Brian Harris *(Facilities Manager)*, Michael Rorks *(Health and Safety Manager)*
**Facilities:** Brian Harris *(Facilities Manager)*
**US SIC:** 4226 **UK SIC:** 77003
**Auditors:** KPMG LLP
**Bankers:** The Bank Of Tokyo-Mitsubishi, Ltd (60-01-09)

| | 31-03-14 | 31-03-13 | 31-03-12 |
|---|---|---|---|
| TO | 28,046,698 | 34,765,207 | 24,870,211 |
| P/L | 2,635,196 | 3,392,446 | 2,335,165 |
| NW | 11,071,136 | 10,109,145 | 8,261,844 |
| WC | 9,030,321 | 7,285,425 | 4,806,430 |
| Emp. | 738 | 835 | 539 |

DUNS 23-181-4377

## South Midlands Co-Op Society

8 Hall Grove, Welwyn Garden City, Hertfordshire AL7 4PH
**Tel:** 01707323380
**Web:** www.co-operative.coop
**Line of Business:** Retail sale in non-specialised stores (excluding ctns) holding an alcohol licence with food, beverages or tobacco predominating
**Trading Style:** Enfield & St Albans Co-Operative Society Cws
**Branches:** South Midlands Co-Op Society, 14 Bushland Road, Northampton, Northamptonshire NN3 2NS
**US SIC:** 5199, 5699
**UK SIC:** 61900, 64500
**Employees:** 473

DUNS 21-629-7242 **Imp-Exp**

## South Midlands Communications Ltd

South Midlands House, School Close, Eastleigh, Hampshire SO53 4BY
**Tel:** 023-8024-6200 **Fax:** 023-8024-6206
**Web:** www.smc-comms.com
**Reg No:** 0603500 **VAT No:** 329904829
**Estd:** 1958 Private Limited Company
**Line of Business:** Radio equipment
**Export Sales:** £4,994,586
**Issued Capital:** £1,150,000
**Principals:** B D Gardner *(Chairman)*, J Lightfoot *(Managing)*, Mrs S Brown, G Griffin, S Hey, Mrs S Nutbrown, M Gardner, N S Hopkins
**Co. Secretary:** Ms Daphne Gardner
**Responsibilities**
**Senior:** Jillian Diamond *(Director)*, Sheila Spacagna *(Manager)*
**Marketing:** Nick Deabill *(Sales & Marketing Manager)*
**Sales:** Nick Deabill *(Sales & Marketing Manager)*
**IT:** Chris Lorek *(Chief Engineer)*
**HR:** Gordon Mackenzie *(Quality Manager)*
**Health & Safety:** Gordon Mackenzie *(Quality Manager)*
**Facilities:** Malcolm Peaty *(Facilities Manager)*
**Operations:** Chris Lorek *(Chief Engineer)*
**Engineering:** Chris Lorek *(Chief Engineer)*
**Branches:** South Midlands Communications Ltd, 6 Royal Pde, London W5 1ET
**US SIC:** 3662 **UK SIC:** 34430
**Auditors:** Martin & Co
**Bankers:** Barclays Bank Plc (20-79-25)

| | 30-06-13 | 30-06-12 | 30-06-11 |
|---|---|---|---|
| TO | 6,410,735 | 5,708,286 | 5,413,715 |
| P/L | 258,255 | 166,065 | 189,269 |
| NW | 6,247,667 | 6,011,442 | 6,075,500 |
| WC | 3,801,459 | 3,507,088 | 3,344,968 |
| Emp. | 56 | 56 | 60 |

DUNS 21-768-6246

## South Molton Community College

Alswear Old Road, South Molton, Devon EX36 4LA
**Tel:** 01769572129
**Web:** www.smcc.devon.sch.uk
**Estd:** 1955 Proprietorship
**Line of Business:** Schools (local authority)
**Proprietor:** Mrs J Glover
**Responsibilities**
**Senior:** Jenny Glevor *(Head Teacher)*
**Finance:** Cowel Huckle *(Senior Finance Administrator)*, Pat Huckle *(Senior Finance Administrator)*, Jeff Lawson *(Caretaker)*
**IT:** Hazel Carter *(IT Executive)*, James Pullin *(Network, Security Manager)*
**US SIC:** 8211 **UK SIC:** 93200
**Employees:** 70

DUNS 23-260-5717

## South Norfolk District Council

South Norfolk House, Norwich, Norfolk NR15 2XE
**Tel:** 01508533633
**Web:** www.south-norfolk.gov.uk
**Estd:** 1974
**Line of Business:** Local government
**Directors:** G Rivers, S Shortman, T Mobbs, K N Barnes
**Responsibilities**
**Senior:** Sandra Dinneen *(Chief Executive)*, Councillor Kemp *(Member)*
**HR:** Serena Bremner *(Human Resources Manager)*
**Health & Safety:** Carolyn James *(Senior Health and Safety Manag)*
**Branches:** South Norfolk District Council, Sheltered Housing Schemes, Brooke, Churchill Place, Norwich, Norfolk NR15 1LQ
**US SIC:** 9121 **UK SIC:** 91110
**Bankers:** Barclays Bank Plc (20-26-34)
**Employees:** 300

DUNS 23-259-6460

## South Northants Council

Council Offices, Springfields, Towcester, Northamptonshire NN12 6AE
**Tel:** 01327322322
**Web:** www.southnorthants.gov.uk
**Estd:** 2002 Incorporate By Act Of Parliament
**Line of Business:** Local government
**Trading Style:** South Northamptonshire Council
**Director:** K Whitehead
**Responsibilities**
**Finance:** Karen Curtin *(Finance)*, Martin Henry *(Head of Finance)*
**HR:** Gina Thomas *(Human Resources Manager)*
**Health & Safety:** Dave Bennet *(Health & Safety Officer)*
**Facilities:** Duncan Wigley *(Property Services Manager)*
**Purchasing:** Richard Sterling *(Purchasing Manager)*
**Branches:** South Northants Council, Waynslete Ave, Brackley, Northamptonshire NN13 5EE
**US SIC:** 9121 **UK SIC:** 91110
**Employees:** 250

DUNS 21-122-2213

## South Northants Homes Ltd

Katherines House, Dunstable Street, Ampthill, Bedford, Bedfordshire MK45 2JP
**Tel:** 08454606888
**Web:** www.southnorthantshomes.co.uk
**Reg No:** 0030387IP **VAT No:** 746212838
**Line of Business:** Other letting of own property
**US SIC:** 7399 **UK SIC:** 83954
**Bankers:** National Westminster Bank Plc (60-01-16)

| | 31-03-12 | 31-03-11 | 31-03-10 |
|---|---|---|---|
| TO | 14,059,000 | 12,095,000 | 11,953,000 |
| P/L | 180,000 | (3,971,000) | (4,135,000) |
| NW | 17,576,000 | 11,725,000 | 7,962,000 |
| WC | 27,554,000 | 33,685,000 | 42,083,000 |
| Emp. | 85 | 82 | 92 |

DUNS 21-601-1021

## South Nottingham College

Charnwood Centre, Farnborough Road, Nottingham, Nottinghamshire NG11 8LU
**Tel:** 01159146300
**Web:** www.snc.ac.uk
**Estd:** 1973
**Line of Business:** Further education schools and colleges
**Trading Style:** Central College Nottingham
**Principals:** D Drury *(Marketing)*, Ms D Stewart, A Beazeley, P Wilson, Ms D Fortescue, Ms G Coult, Ms J Drury, D Buckley
**Responsibilities**
**Senior:** Alison Asbury *(head of school)*, Jason Folkett *(Director)*, Neil Fowkes *(Director)*, Sharon Townes *(head of school)*
**Operations:** Eric Braham *(Operations Director)*
**Branches:** South Nottingham College,West Bridgford Centre,Greythorn Drive, NG2 7GAnottingham
**US SIC:** 8221 **UK SIC:** 93100
**Employees:** 86

DUNS 22-847-2965

## South Oxfordshire District Council

Council Offices, Benson Lane, Wallingford, Oxfordshire OX10 1ZY
**Tel:** 01491823000
**Web:** www.southoxon.gov.uk
**Estd:** 2002
**Line of Business:** Local government
**Directors:** R Watson, R Watson, P Benney, M J Butt
**Responsibilities**
**Finance:** William Jacobs *(Head of Finance)*, Michael Jaques *(Strategic Director Finance)*
**Marketing:** Shona Ware *(Publicity Manager)*
**HR:** Jillian Pidgeon *(Performance Officer HR, IT & C)*, Michelle Yankah *(Senior Human Resources Busines)*
**Operations:** Shona Ware *(Publicity Manager)*
**Branches:** South Oxfordshire District Council, Green Furlong, Berinsfield, Wallingford, Oxfordshire OX10 7NR
**US SIC:** 9121 **UK SIC:** 91110
**Bankers:** Lloyds TSB Bank plc (30-99-03)
**Employees:** 300

DUNS 21-778-4906

## South Parade Primary School

South Parade, Grimsby, South Humberside DN31 1TX
**Tel:** 01472231659
**Web:** www.osparade.co.uk
**Estd:** 1935 Proprietorship
**Line of Business:** Primary education
**Proprietor:** Mrs S Holmes
**US SIC:** 8211 **UK SIC:** 93200
**Employees:** 80

DUNS 21-581-2375

## South Park Nursing Home

Gale Lane, York, North Yorkshire YO24 3HX
**Tel:** 01904784198
**Web:** www.fshc.co.uk
**Estd:** 2011 Proprietorship
**Line of Business:** Nursing homes
**Proprietor:** Ms S Paskett
**Responsibilities**
**Senior:** Sam Cuppusamy *(Home Manager)*, Vikki Hamblin *(Deputy Manageress)*
**US SIC:** 8051 **UK SIC:** 95100
**Employees:** 90

DUNS 21-781-8992

## South Parks House

63 Napier Road, Glenrothes, Fife KY6 1DS
**Tel:** 01592583456
**Estd:** 2011 Proprietorship
**Line of Business:** Social work activities
**Proprietor:** Mrs S Mccloud
**US SIC:** 6732 **UK SIC:** 83100
**Employees:** 50

DUNS 21-783-3217
## South Petherton Hospital
South Petherton Hospital, Bernard Way, South Petherton, Somerset TA13 5EF
**Tel:** 01460243000
**Web:** www.sompar.nhs.uk
**Estd:** 2011 Proprietorship
**Line of Business:** Hospitals
**Proprietor:** Ms J Brown
**US SIC:** 8062 **UK SIC:** 95100
**Employees:** 300

DUNS 23-644-9096
## South Ribble Borough Council
Civic Centre, West Paddock, Preston, Lancashire PR25 1DH
**Tel:** 01772-421491
**Web:** www.southribble.gov.uk
**Estd:** 1991
**Line of Business:** Local government
**Directors:** C Monk, J Dalton, P Halsall, M Nicholls
**Responsibilities**
**Senior:** Greig Clark *(Executive)*, Steve Nugent *(Head of Human Resources)*, Mike Nuttall *(Chief Executive)*
**Finance:** Carol Eddleston *(Democratic Services Officer)*
**Admin:** Trudy Quinn *(Admin Office)*
**HR:** Steve Nugent *(Head of Human Resources)*
**Health & Safety:** Mike Nuttall *(Chief Executive)*
**Branches:** South Ribble Borough Council, Worden Park, Leyland, Lancashire PR25 1DJ
**US SIC:** 9121 **UK SIC:** 91110
**Bankers:** HSBC Bank plc (40-28-17)
**Employees:** 420

DUNS 23-208-9060
## South Shields Catholic Mens Club Ltd
Westoe Road, South Shields, Tyne and Wear NE33 2RL
**Tel:** 01914241717
**Web:** www.southtyneside.info
**Reg No:** 0015850IP **Estd:** 1961 Friendly Society
**Line of Business:** Community networks
**Chairman:** B Brewer
**US SIC:** 5813 **UK SIC:** 66200
**Employees:** 86

DUNS 67-206-4680
## South Somerset Association for Voluntary & Community Action Ltd
Unit 5 Yeovil Small Business Centre, Houndstone Business Park, Yeovil, Somerset BA22 8WA
**Tel:** 01935411572
**Web:** www.ssvca.org.uk
**Reg No:** 6014757 **Estd:** 2006 Private Company Limited By Guarantee
**Line of Business:** Activities of other membership organisations not elsewhere classified
**Directors:** P A Gane, I M Speight, M H Jenkins, N S Engert, M R Batchelor, A J Lennox
**Co. Secretary:** Brian Maxwell
**Responsibilities**
**Senior:** Samantha Best *(Chief Executive Officer)*
**US SIC:** 7399 **UK SIC:** 83954

| | 31-03-14 | 31-03-13 | 31-03-12 |
|---|---|---|---|
| TO | 740,338 | 810,621 | 801,431 |
| P/L | (26,340) | (54,324) | (119,676) |
| NW | 210,022 | 236,362 | 290,686 |
| WC | 191,461 | 211,939 | 234,390 |
| Emp. | 67 | 68 | 72 |

DUNS 23-985-0811
## South Somerset District Council
The Council Offices, Brympton Way, Yeovil, Somerset BA20 2HT
**Tel:** 01935-462462
**Web:** www.southsomerset.gov.uk
**Estd:** 1974
**Line of Business:** Local government
**Principals:** Mrs G M Coleshill *(Chairman)*, M Usher, R W Mills
**Responsibilities**
**Finance:** Donna Parham *(Financial Director)*
**HR:** Mike Holliday *(Human Resources Manager)*
**Health & Safety:** Gary Russ *(Procurement & Risk Manager)*
**Purchasing:** Gary Russ *(Procurement & Risk Manager)*
**Fleet:** Nigel Collins *(Transport Strategic Manager)*
**Branches:** South Somerset District Council, Petters House, Petters Way, Yeovil, Somerset BA20 1AS
**US SIC:** 9121 **UK SIC:** 91110
**Auditors:** K Marston (Audit Manager)
**Bankers:** National Westminster Bank Plc (60-24-37)
**Employees:** 400

DUNS 21-775-2066
## South Staffordshire & Shropshire Health Care Nhs Foundation Trust
Mellor House, Corporation Street, Stafford, Staffordshire ST16 3SR
**Tel:** 01785257888
**Web:** www.sssft.nhs.uk
**Estd:** 2002 Proprietorship
**Line of Business:** Hospitals
**Proprietor:** N Carr
**US SIC:** 8062 **UK SIC:** 95100
**Employees:** 3,000

DUNS 23-182-2060
## South Staffordshire and Shropshire Healthcare Nhs Foundation Trust
4 Parish Lane, London SE20 7LH
**Tel:** 01785252233
**Web:** www.southstaffsandshropshealthcar-eft.nhs.uk
**Estd:** 2011
**Line of Business:** Hospitals
**Trading Style:** South Staffordshire Health Informatics Services
**Principals:** S Jones *(Chairman)*, N Carr, P Woolrich, Ms E Chumley-Roberts, R Craven, Ms S Green, R Evans, Ms J Deaville
**Responsibilities**
**Senior:** Stuart Poynor *(Chief Executive Officer)*, John Whicks *(Manager)*
**Operations:** Richard Beeken *(Director Operations)*
**Branches:** South Staffordshire and Shropshire Healthcare Nhs Foundation Trust, 161 Eccleshall Road, Stafford, Staffordshire ST16 1PD
**US SIC:** 8062 **UK SIC:** 95100
**Auditors:** PricewaterhouseCoopers LLP

| | 31-03-14 | 31-03-13 | 31-03-12 |
|---|---|---|---|
| TO | 178,507,000 | 171,889,000 | 167,009,000 |
| P/L | 3,992,000 | (20,807,000) | (531,000) |
| NW | 81,536,000 | 77,216,000 | 96,897,000 |
| WC | 21,263,000 | 4,771,000 | 10,241,000 |
| Emp. | 3,236 | 3,153 | 12 |

DUNS 21-705-4740
## South Staffordshire College
The Green, Cannock, Staffordshire WS11 1UE
**Tel:** 01543462200
**Web:** www.southstaffs.ac.uk
**VAT No:** 947331904 **Estd:** 2012
**Line of Business:** Further education schools and colleges
**Director:** G Morley
**Responsibilities**
**IT:** Gary Booth *(Chief Technical Engineer)*
**Branches:** South Staffordshire College, Croft Street, Tamworth, Staffordshire B79 8AE
**US SIC:** 8221 **UK SIC:** 93100
**Employees:** 1,000

DUNS 76-923-1747 **Exp**
## South Staffordshire Freight Services Ltd
Lynn Lane, Shenstone, Lichfield, Staffordshire WS14 0ED
**Tel:** 01543480888 **Fax:** 01543481773
**Web:** www.dhl.co.in
**Reg No:** 2139958 **VAT No:** 478248603
**Estd:** 1987 Private Limited Company
**Line of Business:** Other letting of own property
**Export Markets:** Germany and France.
**Issued Capital:** £100
**Principals:** B R Whorton *(Managing)*, N C Whorton
**Co. Secretary:** Mrs Irene Whorton
**US SIC:** 6519 **UK SIC:** 85000
**Auditors:** A J Leedham
**Bankers:** Barclays Bank Plc (20-84-13)

| | 31-07-14 | 31-07-13 | 31-07-12 |
|---|---|---|---|
| TA | 475,078 | 462,596 | 515,399 |
| NW | 408,593 | 429,428 | 467,364 |
| WC | 408,593 | 429,428 | 458,607 |

DUNS 21-225-4456
## South Staffordshire Health Care Nhs Trust
Queens Hospital, Belvedere Road, Burton-On-Trent, Staffordshire DE13 0RB
**Tel:** 01283505300
**Web:** www.nationshealthcare.com
**Estd:** 1995
**Line of Business:** Nhs clinics
**Proprietor:** K Price
**Responsibilities**
**Senior:** Paul Bowers *(Ward Manager)*
**US SIC:** 8062 **UK SIC:** 95100
**Employees:** 120

DUNS 21-229-0771
## South Staffordshire Healthcare Nhs Trust
12 Park Road, Park House, Cannock, Staffordshire WS11 1JN
**Tel:** 01543431576
**Web:** www.southstaffsandshropshealthcar-eft.nhs.uk
**Proprietorship**
**Line of Business:** Other human health activities
**Proprietor:** Mrs A Pickard
**US SIC:** 8091 **UK SIC:** 95200
**Employees:** 63

DUNS 21-413-1532
## South Staffordshire Pct
Anglesey Court, Towers Plaza, Wheelhouse Road, Rugeley, Staffordshire WS15 1UL
**Tel:** 01785252233
**Web:** www.southstaffordshirepct.nhs.uk
**Estd:** 2006 Proprietorship
**Line of Business:** Local government
**Proprietor:** Miss K Brunbridge
**US SIC:** 8062 **UK SIC:** 95100
**Employees:** 100

DUNS 22-277-4346 **Imp**
## South Staffordshire Plc
(**Subsidiary of:** Kkr & Co. L.P.)
Green Lane, Walsall, West Midlands WS2 7PD
**Tel:** 01922618009 **Fax:** 01922723631
**Web:** www.busybeeschildcare.co.uk
**Reg No:** 4295398 **Estd:** 1991 Public Limited Company
**Line of Business:** Nursery schools
**Issued Capital:** £5,448,439
**Directors:** R Ammoun, J O Clavijo, A P Page, R S Kumar
**Co. Secretary:** Jason Goodwin
**Responsibilities**
**Senior:** Liz Swarbrick *(Manager)*
**US SIC:** 4941 **UK SIC:** 17000
**Auditors:** Deloitte LLP
**Bankers:** HSBC Bank plc (40-11-02)

| | 31-03-14 | 31-03-13 | 31-03-12 |
|---|---|---|---|
| TO | 224,701,000 | 205,027,000 | 188,551,000 |
| P/L | 35,085,000 | 29,663,000 | 23,096,000 |
| NW | 29,930,000 | 10,404,000 | (161,000) |
| WC | 88,986,000 | 33,509,000 | 8,917,000 |
| Emp. | 2,370 | 2,193 | 2,083 |

DUNS 77-027-2342
## South Staffordshire Water Plc
(**Subsidiary of:** Kkr & Co. L.P.)
Green Lane, Walsall, West Midlands WS2 7PD
**Tel:** 01922-638282 **Fax:** 01922723631
**Web:** www.south-staffordshire.com
**Reg No:** 2662742 **Estd:** 1991 Public Limited Company
**Line of Business:** Water authorities
**Issued Capital:** £2,123,210
**Principals:** A P Page *(Financial)*, R S Kumar, P C Newland, S B Kay, Sir J F Perowne, J O Clavijo, M A Hughes
**Co. Secretary:** Jason Goodwin
**Responsibilities**
**Senior:** David Baldwin Sankey *(Executive Chairman)*, Rachel Barber *(Manager)*, Simon Rigall *(Non-Executive Director)*, Elizabeth Swarbrick *(Management Director)*
**IT:** Colin Wayper *(Director of Network Management)*
**HR:** Marcella Nash *(Human Resources Manager)*
**Operations:** Rachel Barber *(Manager)*
**US SIC:** 4941 **UK SIC:** 17000
**Auditors:** Deloitte LLP
**Bankers:** HSBC Bank plc (40-11-18)

| | 31-03-14 | 31-03-13 | 31-03-12 |
|---|---|---|---|
| TO | 122,504,000 | 94,732,000 | 91,060,000 |
| P/L | 22,783,000 | 14,670,000 | 12,622,000 |
| NW | 10,466,000 | 2,991,000 | 3,849,000 |
| WC | 22,137,000 | 20,997,000 | 27,342,000 |
| Emp. | 511 | 397 | 406 |

DUNS 21-783-8826
## South Stoke Pct
Meir Health Centre, Saracen Way, Stoke-On-Trent, Staffordshire ST3 7DS
**Tel:** 03001231452
**Estd:** 1967 Proprietorship
**Line of Business:** Hospitals
**Proprietor:** Mrs M Hilton
**US SIC:** 8062 **UK SIC:** 95100
**Employees:** 50

DUNS 34-791-5915
## South Suffolk Leisure
Stonehouse Road, Ipswich, Suffolk IP7 5BH
**Tel:** 01473823470
**Web:** www.ssleisure.co.uk
**Reg No:** 5592081 **Estd:** 2005 Private Company Limited By Guarantee
**Line of Business:** Sports clubs
**Directors:** B L Lazenby, C Vickers, T B Mutum, J R Blatch, Mrs J Janas, Mrs M C Mills, C Moss, M O Munson
**Co. Secretary:** Zack Gilbert
**Responsibilities**
**Senior:** Leigh Alston *(Director)*, Janetta Byrne *(Director)*, Mick Packer *(Contract Manager)*, Rodney Sharp *(Director)*, John Turnbull *(Director)*
**US SIC:** 7941 **UK SIC:** 97911
**Bankers:** The Co-Operative Bank Plc (08-90-83)

| | 31-03-14 | 31-03-13 | 31-03-12 |
|---|---|---|---|
| TO | 2,044,663 | 1,857,550 | 1,424,159 |
| P/L | 134,363 | 151,456 | (102,349) |
| NW | 309,559 | 175,196 | 23,740 |
| WC | 248,789 | 69,660 | (6,808) |
| Emp. | 119 | 107 | 88 |

DUNS 21-248-2623
## South Suffolk Leisure Trust
Kingfisher Leisure Centre, Station Road, Sudbury, Suffolk CO10 2SU
**Tel:** 01787375656
**Web:** www.ssleisure.co.uk
**Line of Business:** Amusement and gaming machines
**Trading Style:** Kingfisher Leisure Centre
**Responsibilities**
**Senior:** Tracy Loynds *(Manager)*
**US SIC:** 7941 **UK SIC:** 97911
**Employees:** 80

DUNS 23-265-9776
## South Tees Hospital Nhs Foundation Trust
The James Cook University Hospital, Middlesbrough, Cleveland TS4 3TA
**Tel:** 01642850850
**Web:** www.southtees.nhs.uk
**Estd:** 2012
**Line of Business:** Disability services
**Trading Style:** Middlesborough General Hospital
**Issued Capital:** £1
**Principals:** Ms D Jenkins *(Chairman)*, J Roebuck *(Financial)*, Ms J Moulton, Ms S Watson, S Pleydell, D Kirby, M Bramble, Ms T Hart
**Responsibilities**
**Senior:** Joanne Deewer *(Senior IT Executive)*, Cristine Willans *(Manager)*
**Marketing:** Amanda Marksby *(Senior Marketing Executive)*
**IT:** Joanne Deewer *(Senior IT Executive)*
**Branches:** South Tees Hospital Nhs Foundation Trust, Bullamoor Road, Northallerton, North Yorkshire DL6 1LP
**US SIC:** 8062 **UK SIC:** 95100
**Auditors:** PricewaterhouseCoopers LLP

| | 31-03-14 | 31-03-13 | 31-03-12 |
|---|---|---|---|
| TO | 550,547,000 | 532,252,000 | 522,789,000 |
| P/L | (4,385,000) | (2,876,000) | (4,792,000) |
| NW | 116,732,000 | 104,353,000 | 108,218,000 |
| WC | 7,787,000 | 6,619,000 | 5,113,000 |
| Emp. | 7,718 | 7,549 | 7,000 |

DUNS 23-215-7362
## South Thames College
Wandsworth High Street, London SW18 2PP
**Tel:** 02089187777
**Web:** www.south-thames.ac.uk
**Estd:** 2002
**Line of Business:** Further education schools and colleges
**Principals:** Ms L De Courcy *(Financial)*, Ms J Scribbins, C Carter, Ms L Wilson
**Responsibilities**
**Senior:** Andrew Beardall *(Manager)*, Marianne Boivandii *(Centre Manager)*, Maggie Moore *(Executive)*
**Marketing:** Katie Burrell *(Head of Marketing and Communic)*, Maria Kearney *(Marketing Manager)*, Howard Thomas *(Marketing Manager)*
**Sales:** Nicola Moore *(Account Manager)*
**Admin:** Natalie Watt *(Clerk to the Corporation)*
**IT:** Carolyne Cheeseman *(Computer Operations Manager)*
**HR:** Mary Segovia *(Human Resources Director)*
**Facilities:** Marianne Boivandii *(Centre Manager)*
**Branches:** South Thames College, South Thames College, Tooting Centre, 71 Tooting High Street, To, London SW17 0TQ
**US SIC:** 8221 **UK SIC:** 93100
**Bankers:** Barclays Bank Plc (20-90-69)
**Employees:** 600

**DUNS 64-262-5164**
## South Trafford College
Talbot Road, Manchester M32 0XH
**Web:** www.northtrafford.ac.uk
**Estd:** 1930
**Line of Business:** Further education schools and colleges
**Directors:** Dr R S Baker, B Moorcroft
**Responsibilities**
**Sales:** Jannet Gathercole (Sectory)
**Branches:** Sale Centre, Manor Ave, Sale, Cheshire M33 5JX
**US SIC:** 8221  **UK SIC:** 93100
**Bankers:** The Bank Of Ireland (30-15-14)
**Employees:** 340

**DUNS 21-233-4351**
## South Tyneside Homecare
Wawn Street, South Shields, Tyne and Wear NE33 4EB
**Tel:** 0191-4967857
**Web:** www.sunderlandhomecare.co.uk
**Estd:** 2007
**Line of Business:** Accommodation advice
**Proprietor:** Mrs J Hutchinson
**US SIC:** 8091  **UK SIC:** 95200
**Employees:** 80

**DUNS 22-820-9391**
## South Tyneside Metropolitan Borough Council
Town Hall, Westoe Road, South Shields, Tyne and Wear NE33 2RL
**Tel:** 01914277000
**Web:** www.southtyneside.info
**VAT No:** 178177329 **Estd:** 2013 Incorporate By Act Of Parliament
**Line of Business:** Local government
**Trading Style:** Central Library South Tyneside Early Years Excellence Centrea, John Right Day Care Centre, Hillpark Community Centre
**Director:** M Swales
**Responsibilities**
**Finance:** Philip Glasgow (Principal Accountant)
**Admin:** Lisa Charlton (Senior Administration Officer)
**HR:** Steffani Smith (Staff Development Officer For)
**Health & Safety:** Lisa Charlton (Senior Administration Officer)
**Facilities:** Graham Whitehead (Education Building Team Leader)
**Branches:** South Tyneside Metropolitan Borough Council, Town Hall, Grange Road, Jarrow, Tyne and Wear NE32 3LE
**US SIC:** 9121, 6732, 4712, 7399, 8211
**UK SIC:** 91110, 83100, 77002, 83954, 93200
**Employees:** 1,000

**DUNS 23-208-4223**
## South Tyneside Nhs Foundation Trust
Harton Lane, South Shields, Tyne and Wear NE34 0PL
**Tel:** 01914041000
**Web:** www.stft.nhs.uk
**Estd:** 2010
**Line of Business:** Hospitals
**Issued Capital:** £1
**Principals:** P Davidson (Chairman), E Brennan, Ms L Lambert, V Elsy, D Fleetwood, Ms M Hamilton, A Brewster, P Melia
**Responsibilities**
**Senior:** Ian Frame (Manager), Steve Jamieson (Director of Service Reform and)
**IT:** Kent Thomson (Senior IT Executive)
**HR:** Ian Frame (Manager)
**Branches:** South Tyneside Nhs Foundation Trust, Boker Lane Health Centre, Boker Lane, East Boldon, Tyne and Wear NE36 0RY
**US SIC:** 8091  **UK SIC:** 95200
**Auditors:** PricewaterhouseCoopers LLp

|      | 31-03-14      | 31-03-13      | 31-03-12      |
|------|---------------|---------------|---------------|
| TO   | 214,762,000   | 217,479,000   | 217,662,000   |
| P/L  | (1,926,000)   | (2,641,000)   | 1,623,000     |
| NW   | 100,900,000   | 99,408,000    | 103,665,000   |
| WC   | 9,832,000     | 10,776,000    | 13,586,000    |
| Emp. | 4,044         | 4,090         | 3,000         |

**DUNS 21-756-2102**
## South Tyneside Primary Care Trust
Monkton Lane, Jarrow, Tyne and Wear NE32 5NN
**Tel:** 01912831903
**Web:** www.stpct.nhs.uk
**Estd:** 2010
**Line of Business:** Hospitals
**Trading Style:** South Tyneside Clinical Commissioning Group
**Principals:** C Macklin (Financial), R Barker, Dr J Thomas, Mrs B Atkinson, Mrs V Taylor, Dr M Prentice, Mrs J Forster, Dr G Stephenson

**Responsibilities**
**Senior:** Margaret Kennedy (Assistant director), Kim Mansfield (Facilities Manager), Karen Straughair (Chief Executive Officer)
**US SIC:** 8062  **UK SIC:** 95100
**Employees:** 200

**DUNS 34-840-4492**
## South Tyneside Training Services Ltd
(**Subsidiary of:** South Tyneside College)
Westoe Campus, St Georges Avenue, South Shields, Tyne and Wear NE34 6ET
**Tel:** 0191-427-3500
**Web:** www.stc.ac.uk
**Reg No:** 2803965  **Estd:** 1993 Private Limited Company
**Line of Business:** Adult and other education not elsewhere classified
**Issued Capital:** £2,500
**Directors:** Ms L J Whiterod, Ms H Beaton
**Co. Secretary:** Stephen Chittenden
**Responsibilities**
**Senior:** Joanne Harris (Manager), Robert Jacques (Manager)
**US SIC:** 8249  **UK SIC:** 93300
**Auditors:** Ernst & Young
**Bankers:** National Westminster Bank Plc (54-10-31)

|      | 31-07-13 | 31-07-12 | 31-07-11 |
|------|----------|----------|----------|
| TO   | 14,428   | N/A      | N/A      |
| P/L  | (775)    | N/A      | N/A      |
| NW   | 1,279    | 2,054    | 2,054    |
| WC   | 1,279    | 2,054    | 2,054    |

**DUNS 50-691-6568**
## The South Wales Autistic Society
Longford Court, Neath, West Glamorgan SA10 7HN
**Tel:** 01792-326820
**Web:** www.nas.org.uk
**Estd:** 2002
**Line of Business:** Rest and retirement homes
**Proprietor:** Mrs J Thomas
**Responsibilities**
**Senior:** Pauline Collins (Manager)
**Branches:** The South Wales Autistic Society, Lonlas Village Workshops, Unit 4, Neath, West Glamorgan SA10 6RP
**US SIC:** 8699, 6732
**UK SIC:** 96902, 83100
**Employees:** 50

**DUNS 21-808-9064**
## South Wales Chamber of Commerce
Suite 2, Vivian Court, Llys Felin Newydd, Swansea, West Glamorgan SA7 9FG
**Tel:** 01792793686
**Web:** www.southwaleschamber.co.uk
**Estd:** 2012
**Line of Business:** Chambers of commerce
**US SIC:** 8621  **UK SIC:** 96311
**Employees:** 80

**DUNS 42-316-1785**
## South Warwickshire Combined Care
Guys Cliffe Avenue, Leamington Spa, Warwickshire CV32 6NB
**Tel:** 01789263464
**Web:** www.stagecoach.co.uk
**Line of Business:** Drama schools
**Trading Style:** Royal Leamington Spa Rehabilitation Hospital, Alcester Hospital, Ellen Badger Hospital, Inspect A Gadget
**Director:** Mrs M Black
**Branches:** South Warwickshire Combined Care, Cape Road, Warwick, Warwickshire CV34 4JP
**US SIC:** 8299  **UK SIC:** 93300
**Employees:** 900

**DUNS 54-864-0176**
## South Warwickshire Nhs Foundation Trust
Lakin Road, Warwick, Warwickshire CV34 5BW
**Tel:** 01926-495321
**Web:** www.swft.nhs.uk
**Line of Business:** Public sector hospital activities, including nhs trusts
**Trading Style:** Warwick Hospital
**Issued Capital:** £1
**Principals:** Ms J Blacklay, G Burley, Ms V Cotterill, G Murrell, A Harrison, T Boorman, D Derbyshire, D Moon
**Responsibilities**
**Senior:** Ernie Macefield (Manager)
**Finance:** Nicky Lloyd (Director of Finance), Colin Reeves (Finance Manager)
**IT:** Susan Hartshorn (IT Manager), Danny Roberts (Chief Technology Officer)
**HR:** Ann Pope (HR Director)

**Operations:** Jane Ives (Director of Operations)
**Branches:** South Warwickshire Nhs Foundation Trust, Physiotherapy Dept, Pde, Leamington Spa, Warwickshire CV31 3JH
**US SIC:** 8062  **UK SIC:** 95100
**Auditors:** De3loitte LLP

|      | 31-03-14     | 31-03-13     | 31-03-12     |
|------|--------------|--------------|--------------|
| TO   | 208,068,000  | 215,445,000  | 187,419,000  |
| P/L  | 4,037,000    | 2,303,000    | 4,877,000    |
| NW   | 98,367,000   | 72,003,000   | 71,076,000   |
| WC   | (3,136,000)  | (79,000)     | (1,721,000)  |
| Emp. | 3,730        | 3,585        | 2,200        |

**DUNS 34-595-8297**
## South West Airports Ltd
Bristol International Airport, Bristol, Avon BS48 3DY
**Tel:** 01275-475-206
**Web:** www.bristolairport.co.uk
**Reg No:** 5403045  **Estd:** 2001 Private Limited Company
**Line of Business:** Other supporting air transport activities
**Issued Capital:** £50,000,003
**Directors:** L E Bugeja, Mrs J C Kong
**Co. Secretary:** James Mcauliffe
**Responsibilities**
**Senior:** Nigel Mclochlin (Station Engineer)
**US SIC:** 4582  **UK SIC:** 76400
**Auditors:** PricewaterhouseCoopers LLP

|      | 31-12-13      | 31-12-12      | 31-12-11      |
|------|---------------|---------------|---------------|
| TO   | 65,100,000    | 60,720,000    | 58,393,000    |
| P/L  | (12,898,000)  | (8,256,000)   | (8,689,000)   |
| NW   | (299,170,000) | (285,835,000) | (277,180,000) |
| WC   | (30,670,000)  | (21,055,000)  | (1,517,000)   |
| Emp. | 215           | 205           | 213           |

**DUNS 22-265-2336**
## South West Care Homes Ltd
Unit 317 I T T C Building, 1 Tamar Science Park, Plymouth, Devon PL6 8BX
**Tel:** 01752764466
**Web:** www.southwestcarehomes.co.uk
**Reg No:** 4283187  **Estd:** 2001 Private Limited Company
**Line of Business:** Other business activities not elsewhere classified
**Issued Capital:** £1,000
**Director:** A A Beale
**Co. Secretary:** Ms Sharon Beale
**US SIC:** 8321  **UK SIC:** 96111
**Bankers:** HSBC Bank plc (40-20-29)

|      | 31-01-14    | 31-01-13    | 31-01-12    |
|------|-------------|-------------|-------------|
| TO   | 5,904,411   | 5,683,850   | 5,245,096   |
| P/L  | 714,990     | 613,893     | 454,311     |
| NW   | (1,489,899) | (1,829,944) | (2,213,673) |
| WC   | (1,785,120) | (1,490,449) | (1,209,659) |
| Emp. | 191         | 207         | 227         |

**DUNS 34-839-6933**
## South West Communications Group Holdings Ltd
Moor Lane, Exeter, Devon EX2 7JF
**Fax:** 01392360011
**Web:** www.swcomms.co.uk
**Reg No:** 5638837  **Estd:** 1984 Private Limited Company
**Line of Business:** Management activities of holding companies
**Export Sales:** £39,773
**Issued Capital:** £1,956
**Directors:** B Lodge, A G Rowe, Ms S E Tadd, D H Langley, Mrs S Flowers
**Co. Secretary:** Mrs Sharon Rowe
**US SIC:** 6711  **UK SIC:** 83962

|      | 31-12-13    | 31-12-12    | 31-12-11    |
|------|-------------|-------------|-------------|
| TO   | 19,098,318  | 18,910,497  | 19,005,115  |
| P/L  | 524,037     | 781,810     | 944,111     |
| NW   | 5,160,786   | 4,942,546   | 4,340,065   |
| WC   | (1,064,678) | (1,368,302) | (2,037,357) |
| Emp. | 147         | 141         | 146         |

**DUNS 21-682-1009**
## South West Environmental Parks Ltd
Totnes Road, Paignton, Devon TQ4 7EU
**Tel:** 08444742222 **Fax:** 01803523457
**Web:** www.southwestzoo.org.uk
**Reg No:** 0792877 **VAT No:** 141291006
**Estd:** 1964 Private Limited Company
**Line of Business:** Fair and amusement park activities
**Issued Capital:** £10,000
**Directors:** Ms S J Greinig, P M Stevens, M C Proctor, Dr P R Chanin, A C Cooper, Mrs S Barr, Mrs R Hill, R W Ford
**Co. Secretary:** Christopher Pyne
**Responsibilities**
**Senior:** Henry Elliot (Director), Judy Ravenscroft (Director)
**IT:** Jason Pace (IT Supervisor)
**US SIC:** 7996  **UK SIC:** 97913
**Auditors:** Francis Clark
**Bankers:** Barclays Bank Plc (20-60-88)

|      | 31-10-13   | 31-10-12   | 31-10-11   |
|------|------------|------------|------------|
| TO   | 11,607,417 | 10,590,584 | 10,055,638 |
| P/L  | 1,038,684  | 341,554    | (239,572)  |
| NW   | 6,451,607  | 5,378,769  | 5,003,061  |
| WC   | 2,843,309  | 1,954,140  | 1,701,882  |
| Emp. | 255        | 257        | 266        |

**DUNS 77-774-0887**
## South West Highways Ltd
Rockbeare Hill, Rockbeare, Exeter, Devon EX5 2HB
**Tel:** 01404-821500 **Fax:** 01404-821501
**Web:** www.swhltd.co.uk
**Reg No:** 3021985  **Estd:** 1995 Private Limited Company
**Line of Business:** Civil engineers
**Issued Capital:** £200,200
**Principals:** B Pyle (Managing), D N Binding, D Lee, S L Struthers, M D Overton, G C Batut, L Rushbrooke, S A Wardrop
**Co. Secretary:** Graham Stanton
**Responsibilities**
**Senior:** Adrian Sheppard (Manager), Richard Weddle (Manager)
**Marketing:** Glynn Bramwell (Commercial Manager)
**Health & Safety:** Tim Pegler (Health & Safety Manager)
**Purchasing:** Graham Archer (Fleet Controller)
**Branches:** South West Highways Ltd, Gas Lane, Torrington, Devon EX38 7BB
**US SIC:** 1611  **UK SIC:** 50200
**Auditors:** KPMG LLP
**Bankers:** National Westminster Bank Plc (56-00-49)

|      | 31-12-13   | 31-12-12   | 31-12-11   |
|------|------------|------------|------------|
| TO   | 82,067,000 | 85,627,000 | 77,551,000 |
| P/L  | 3,718,000  | 2,761,000  | 1,793,000  |
| NW   | 2,641,000  | 2,813,000  | 3,272,000  |
| WC   | 832,000    | 755,000    | 738,000    |
| Emp. | 612        | 606        | 588        |

**DUNS 23-957-3251**
## South West Lakes Trust
Brompton Regis, Dulverton, Somerset TA22 9AW
**Tel:** 01398371116
**Web:** www.swlakestrust.org.uk
**Reg No:** 3946529  **Estd:** 2000 Private Company Limited By Guarantee
**Line of Business:** Forestry and logging
**Directors:** Ms M S Read, D B Robertson, Ms D A Nichols, Mrs L Jones, M E Bell, J A Lee, R D Preston, Ms J A Edwards
**Co. Secretary:** Matthew Boyer
**Responsibilities**
**Senior:** Peter Briens (Director)
**Branches:** South West Lakes Trust, Roadford Reservoir, Broadwoodwidger, Okehampton, Devon EX20 4QS
**US SIC:** 0851, 0729, 8249, 7999
**UK SIC:** 02000, 01003, 93300, 97913
**Auditors:** Francis Clark LLP
**Bankers:** Lloyds TSB Bank plc (77-18-00)

|      | 31-01-14  | 31-01-13  | 31-01-12  |
|------|-----------|-----------|-----------|
| TO   | 3,543,715 | 3,414,367 | 4,223,957 |
| P/L  | (58,213)  | (211,482) | 724,065   |
| NW   | 3,657,716 | 3,715,929 | 3,927,411 |
| WC   | 306,910   | 78,359    | 424,458   |
| Emp. | 66        | 68        | 67        |

**DUNS 54-864-4756**
## South West London & St Georges Mental Health N H S Trust
Springfield Hospital, 61 Glenburnie Road, Tooting, London SW17 7DJ
**Web:** www.swlstg-tr.nhs.uk
**Line of Business:** Administration of the state and the economic and social policy of the community
**Trading Style:** Springfield University
**Issued Capital:** £1
**Principals:** P Cardell (Financial), S Gillett (Personnel), Ms J Wilson, Dr B Nereli, Ms K Goddard, Ms M Ness
**Responsibilities**
**Senior:** Emma Witcher (Medical Director)
**Branches:** South West London & St Georges Mental Health N H S Trust, 313-315 Cortis Road, London SW15 6XG
**US SIC:** 9121, 8051
**UK SIC:** 91110, 95100
**Employees:** 3,000

**DUNS 21-880-4756**
## South West London & St Georges Mental Health Nhs Trust
Kew Foot Road, Richmond, Surrey TW9 2TE
**Tel:** 02035133282
**Estd:** 2012
**Line of Business:** Mental health centres
**US SIC:** 8091  **UK SIC:** 95200
**Employees:** 100

DUNS 39-932-4292 **Imp**

### South West Metal Finishing Ltd

**(Subsidiary of:** E.I.C. Group Ltd)
Unit 9a, Limber Road, Yeovil, Somerset BA22 8RR
**Tel:** 01935429881
**Web:** www.eicgroup.co.uk
**Reg No:** 2246273 **VAT No:** 510626581
**Estd:** 1988 Private Limited Company
**Line of Business:** Manufacture of other fabricated metal products not elsewhere classified
**Export Sales:** £159,005
**Issued Capital:** £300,000
**Directors:** K Baker, M Jacobs, P Jacobs
**Co. Secretary:** Ms Jacqueline Jacobs
**Responsibilities**
**Senior:** Stuart Hallett *(Works Manager)*, Alan Prouse *(Works Manager)*
**Facilities:** Stuart Hallett *(Works Manager)*, Alan Prouse *(Works Manager)*
**Purchasing:** Stuart Hallett *(Works Manager)*, Alan Prouse *(Works Manager)*
**Engineering:** Stuart Hallett *(Works Manager)*, Alan Prouse *(Works Manager)*
**Branches:** South West Metal Finishing Ltd, Yeovil, 9A Limber Road,Lufton Trading Estate, BA22 8RRyeovil
**US SIC:** 3499 **UK SIC:** 31694
**Auditors:** Thompson Jenner LLP
**Bankers:** Lloyds TSB Bank plc (30-93-14)

| | 31-03-14 | 31-03-13 | 31-03-12 |
|---|---|---|---|
| TO | 6,000,304 | 5,575,382 | 4,762,224 |
| P/L | 353,747 | 512,633 | 235,920 |
| NW | 2,938,098 | 2,988,938 | 2,549,334 |
| WC | 1,282,276 | 1,442,097 | 1,210,849 |
| Emp. | 100 | 100 | 89 |

DUNS 21-116-0070

### South West News Service Ltd

Media Centre Abbey Wood Business Park, Emma Chris Way, Filton, Bristol, Avon BS34 7JU
**Web:** www.contactpress.co.uk
**Reg No:** 6561578 **Estd:** 1988 Private Limited Company
**Line of Business:** News agency activities
**Issued Capital:** £100
**Directors:** P M Walters, M A Winter, N A Iskander, A W Young
**Co. Secretary:** Andrew Young
**Responsibilities**
**Senior:** Anne Heald *(Manager)*
**US SIC:** 7351 **UK SIC:** 83954

| | 31-03-14 | 31-03-13 | 31-03-12 |
|---|---|---|---|
| TA | 2,386,789 | 2,176,062 | 1,987,898 |
| NW | 366,664 | (476,291) | (872,507) |
| WC | (48,035) | (613,231) | (993,118) |

DUNS 21-879-4737

### South West Surrey Reablement Service

Old Church, Bridge Street, Godalming, Surrey GU7 1HY
**Tel:** 01483518351
**Web:** www.surreycc.gov.uk
**Estd:** 2012
**Line of Business:** Home care service providers
**Responsibilities**
**Senior:** Sue Coburn *(South West Manager)*
**US SIC:** 8091 **UK SIC:** 95200
**Employees:** 200

DUNS 73-927-7572

### South West Trains Ltd

**(Subsidiary of:** Stagecoach Group Plc)
41-45 Blackfriars Road, London SE1 8NZ
**Tel:** 0870-000-5151
**Web:** www.southwesttrains.co.uk
**Reg No:** 2938995 **VAT No:** 435757819
**Estd:** 1994 Private Limited Company
**Line of Business:** Urban and suburban passenger transportation by underground, metro and similar systems
**Issued Capital:** £15,842,000
**Director:** R J Paterson
**Co. Secretary:** Andrew West
**Responsibilities**
**Senior:** Roger Rampling *(Purchasing Manager)*
**Purchasing:** Roger Rampling *(Purchasing Manager)*
**Branches:** South West Trains Ltd, South West Trains Ltd, Central Railway Station, Southampton, Hampshire SO15 1AL
**US SIC:** 4011 **UK SIC:** 71000
**Auditors:** PricewaterhouseCoopers LLP
**Bankers:** The Royal Bank Of Scotland Plc (16-04-00)

| | 26-04-14 | 27-04-13 | 28-04-12 |
|---|---|---|---|
| TA | 16,752,000 | 16,752,000 | 16,764,000 |
| P/L | N/A | (1,000) | (1,000) |
| NW | 16,709,000 | 16,709,000 | 16,710,000 |
| WC | 16,709,000 | 16,709,000 | 16,710,000 |

DUNS 21-691-7849

### South West Wales Newspapers Ltd

**(Subsidiary of:** Gannett Co. Inc.)
Fishguard Road, Tangiers, Haverfordwest, Dyfed SA62 4BU
**Tel:** 01437765100 **Fax:** 01646693941
**Web:** www.milfordmercury.co.uk
**Reg No:** 0493370 **Estd:** 1993 Private Limited Company
**Line of Business:** Newspapers publishing
**Issued Capital:** £31,896
**Directors:** P A Hunter, H K Faure Walker
**Co. Secretary:** Neil Carpenter
**Responsibilities**
**Senior:** Dean Merrick *(Manager)*, Nigel Whites *(Manager)*
**US SIC:** 2711 **UK SIC:** 47512
**Employees:** 50

DUNS 23-615-7459 **Imp**

### South West Water Ltd

**(Subsidiary of:** Pennon Group Plc)
Peninsula House, Rydon Lane, Exeter, Devon EX2 7HR
**Tel:** 01392446688 **Fax:** 01392423792
**Web:** www.southwestwater.co.uk
**Reg No:** 2366665 **VAT No:** 540465165
**Estd:** 1989 Private Limited Company
**Line of Business:** Collection, purification and distribution of water
**Trading Style:** Pennon Group
**Issued Capital:** £150,950,000
**Directors:** Mrs L F Rowe, Ms M S Read, D G Ingram, K G Harvey, S Johnson, C Loughlin, M O Taylor, Dr S C Bird
**Co. Secretary:** Miss Karen Gale
**Responsibilities**
**Senior:** Debbie Cross *(Facilities Manager)*, Martin Hagen *(Director)*
**Marketing:** Alan Hyde *(Communications Manager)*
**Sales:** Les Metcalfe *(Commercial Manager)*
**IT:** Kevin Nankivell *(IS Manager)*, Andrew Willicott *(Senior IT Executive)*
**Health & Safety:** Buster Brown *(Head of Health and safety)*
**Operations:** Mike Walton *(Project Manager)*
**Branches:** South West Water Ltd, Bridge Road, Exeter, Devon EX2 7AA
**US SIC:** 4941, 4952
**UK SIC:** 17000, 92120
**Auditors:** PricewaterhouseCoopers LLP
**Bankers:** Lloyds TSB Bank plc (30-00-02)

| | 31-03-14 | 31-03-13 | 31-03-12 |
|---|---|---|---|
| TO | 521,500,000 | 500,100,000 | 474,700,000 |
| P/L | 162,200,000 | 164,500,000 | 141,400,000 |
| NW | 586,900,000 | 480,100,000 | 494,100,000 |
| WC | 161,600,000 | 126,600,000 | 183,300,000 |
| Emp. | 1,169 | 1,163 | 1,182 |

DUNS 54-864-0291

### South West Yorkshire Partnership Nhs Foundation Trust

Fieldhead, Ouchthorpe Lane, Wakefield, West Yorkshire WF1 3SP
**Tel:** 01924-327-000
**Web:** www.southwestyorkshire.nhs.uk
**VAT No:** 654948785 **Estd:** 2002
**Line of Business:** Healthcare companies
**Principals:** I Black *(Chairman)*, A Davis, Ms K Taylor, S Rayner, Ms A Basford, Ms D Stephenson, A Berry, S Michael
**Responsibilities**
**Senior:** Peter Aspinall *(Non-Executive Director)*, Alex Farrell *(Deputy Chief Executive Officer)*, Bernard Fee *(Non-Executive Director)*, Bronwyn Gill *(Head of Communications and Cus)*, Jai Tout *(Chairman)*, Helen Wollaston *(Chairman)*, alan davies *(Head of Human Resources)*
**Admin:** Kim Hibbert *(Office Manager)*
**HR:** Bronwyn Gill *(Head of Communications and Cus)*, alan davies *(Head of Human Resources)*
**Health & Safety:** Angela O'Connor *(Health & Safety Officer)*
**Branches:** Southwest Yorkshire Partnership Nhs Foundation Trust, Queensway House, 2ND Floor, Southend-On-Sea, Essex SS1 2NY
**US SIC:** 8091, 7399
**UK SIC:** 95200, 83954
**Auditors:** Deloitte LLP

| | 31-03-14 | 31-03-13 | 31-03-12 |
|---|---|---|---|
| TO | 235,755,000 | 232,446,000 | 219,361,000 |
| P/L | 3,693,000 | 6,301,000 | 6,320,000 |
| NW | 112,730,000 | 74,873,000 | 69,204,000 |
| WC | 13,415,000 | 9,625,000 | 8,328,000 |
| Emp. | 4,394 | 4,402 | 4,434 |

DUNS 21-589-9078

### South Western Amb Service Trust

The Concept Centre, Innovation Close, Poole, Dorset BH12 4QD
**Web:** www.swast.nhs.uk
**Estd:** 2011 Proprietorship
**Line of Business:** Ambulance and medical transportation services
**Proprietor:** Mrs N Storey
**US SIC:** 8091 **UK SIC:** 95200
**Employees:** 60

DUNS 54-864-1356 **Imp**

### South Western Ambulance Service Nhs Foundation Trust

Eagle Way, Sowton Industrial Estate, Exeter, Devon EX2 7HY
**Web:** www.swast.nhs.uk
**Estd:** 1999
**Line of Business:** Other human health activities
**Trading Style:** Wells Community Responders
**Issued Capital:** £1
**Principals:** Ms J Kingston *(Financial)*, K Wenman
**Responsibilities**
**Marketing:** Sue Steen *(Director of Human Resources)*
**HR:** Lizzie Ryan *(Training Manager)*, Sue Steen *(Director of Human Resources)*
**Branches:** South Western Ambulance Service Nhs Foundation Trust, Chinon Court, Unit 3, Tiverton, Devon EX16 6SS
**US SIC:** 7399 **UK SIC:** 83954
**Auditors:** PricewaterhouseCoopers LLP

| | 31-03-14 | 31-03-13 | 31-03-12 |
|---|---|---|---|
| TO | 225,618,000 | 147,210,000 | N/A |
| P/L | 333,000 | 1,878,000 | 1,645,000 |
| NW | 84,845,000 | 80,428,000 | 42,534,000 |
| WC | 10,044,000 | 4,711,000 | (60,000) |
| Emp. | 4,073 | 2,655 | 2,338 |

DUNS 21-234-0527

### South Western Magistrates

176a Lavender Hill, London SW11 1JU
**Tel:** 020-78051445
**Estd:** 1964 Proprietorship
**Line of Business:** Courts
**Proprietor:** Ms J Hartnett
**US SIC:** 9211 **UK SIC:** 91200
**Employees:** 70

DUNS 21-101-1754

### South Western Regional Health Authority

King Square House, 26-27 King Square, Bristol, Avon BS2 8EE
**Tel:** 01179423271
**Web:** www.swrha.co.tt
**Line of Business:** Regional health authority, responsible for the provision and administration of health care facilities for the local community.
**Principals:** Ms R Macdonald *(Financial)*, J Le Vay, A Mason
**US SIC:** 8091 **UK SIC:** 95200
**Bankers:** National Westminster Bank Plc (56-00-05)
**Employees:** 1,100

DUNS 36-521-4670

### South Western Staffordshire Pct

Mellor House, Corporation Street, Stafford, Staffordshire ST16 3SR
**Tel:** 01785220004
**Estd:** 2004 Proprietorship
**Line of Business:** Primary Care Trust
**Principals:** Mrs J Cornes *(Chairman)*, W Price
**Branches:** 10 Browning St, Stafford, ST16 3AT, Staffordshire
**US SIC:** 9121, 8062
**UK SIC:** 91110, 95100
**Employees:** 1,500

DUNS 21-764-5553

### South Westminster Centre

St Georges House, 82 Vincent Square, London SW1P 2PF
**Tel:** 02087465704
**Web:** www.westminsterdoctors.co.uk
**Estd:** 2011
**Line of Business:** Doctors
**US SIC:** 8011 **UK SIC:** 95300
**Employees:** 70

DUNS 21-558-5015

### South Wolverhampton & Bilston Academy

Dudley Street, Bilston, West Midlands WV14 0LN
**Web:** www.swbacademy.org.uk
**Estd:** 2003
**Line of Business:** Schools (local authority)
**Trading Style:** S W B Academy
**Proprietor:** Mrs K Incker
**Responsibilities**
**IT:** Pete Hardiman *(IT Executive)*
**US SIC:** 8211, 8299
**UK SIC:** 93200, 93300
**Bankers:** Lloyds TSB Bank plc (30-99-83)
**Employees:** 170

DUNS 21-783-5211

### South Woodford Health Centre

114 High Road, London E18 2QS
**Tel:** 02084913333
**Web:** www.queenmarypractice.nhs.uk
**Estd:** 1984 Proprietorship
**Line of Business:** Health centres
**Proprietor:** Mrs N Pollard
**Responsibilities**
**Senior:** Rhoda Jewiss *(Clinic Manager)*
**US SIC:** 8091 **UK SIC:** 95200
**Employees:** 48

DUNS 55-061-0919

### South Worcestershire College

Davies Road, Evesham, Worcestershire WR11 1LP
**Tel:** 01386712690
**Web:** www.sworcs.ac.uk
**VAT No:** 589514101 **Estd:** 1970
**Line of Business:** Colleges (higher education)
**Director:** D Blades
**Responsibilities**
**Finance:** Virginia McKay *(Head of Finance)*
**Admin:** Tracey Hodgkins *(Office Manager)*
**HR:** Maria Arkell *(Training Manager)*
**Facilities:** Gordon Powell *(Premises Manager)*
**Purchasing:** Virginia McKay *(Head of Finance)*
**Branches:** South Worcestershire College, Davies Road, Evesham, Worcestershire WR11 1LP
**US SIC:** 8221 **UK SIC:** 93100
**Bankers:** Lloyds TSB Bank plc (30-93-11)
**Employees:** 500

DUNS 22-814-6098

### South Yorkshire Housing Association Ltd

43-47 Wellington Street, Sheffield, South Yorkshire S1 4HF
**Tel:** 01142900200
**Web:** www.syha.co.uk
**Reg No:** 0020165IP **VAT No:** 471352556
**Estd:** 1972 Private Limited Company
**Line of Business:** Non-charitable social work activities with accommodation
**Trading Style:** Syha
**Directors:** D Walker, D Hunt, J Steinke, C Rogers, D Reid, V Killen, L Greenwood, P Lamberton
**Responsibilities**
**Senior:** A Damms *(Director)*, Lindsay Greenwood *(Board Member)*, Maggie Riley *(Vice Chair)*
**Finance:** Beverly Carr *(Finance Manager)*
**HR:** Rebecca White *(Human Resources Manager)*
**Branches:** South Yorkshire Housing Association Ltd, 2A Basegreen Road, Sheffield, South Yorkshire S12 3FH
**US SIC:** 8321 **UK SIC:** 96111
**Auditors:** Mazars LLP
**Bankers:** The Co-Operative Bank Plc (08-90-75)

| | 31-03-12 | 31-03-11 | 31-03-10 |
|---|---|---|---|
| TO | 45,157,000 | 46,702,000 | 46,714,000 |
| P/L | 2,626,000 | 1,990,000 | 1,496,000 |
| NW | 22,521,000 | 19,614,000 | 17,420,000 |
| WC | (6,495,000) | (1,150,000) | 4,229,000 |
| Emp. | 395 | 410 | 48 |

DUNS 49-129-7651

### South Yorkshire Newspapers Ltd

**(Subsidiary of:** Johnston Press Plc)
39 Printing Office Street, Doncaster, South Yorkshire DN1 1TN
**Tel:** 01302819111 **Fax:** 01302348529
**Web:** www.doncasterfreepress.co.uk
**Reg No:** 3103977 **Estd:** 1995 Private Limited Company
**Line of Business:** Newspapers publishing
**Trading Style:** Doncaster Free Press, Doncaster Courier Doncaster Advertiser, South Yorkshire Times, Goole Courier
**Issued Capital:** £82
**Directors:** J Bills, A G Highfield, D J King
**Co. Secretary:** Peter Mccall
**Responsibilities**
**Senior:** Johns Bills *(Managing Director)*
**Finance:** Simon Lilley *(Finance Director)*
**Sales:** Eve Hansan *(Sales Manager)*
**HR:** Jean Gardner *(Personnel Manager)*
**Fleet:** Mark Morrison *(Transport Manager)*
**Branches:** South Yorkshire Newspapers Ltd, Market Place, Gainsborough, Lincolnshire DN21 2BP
**US SIC:** 2711, 2721
**UK SIC:** 47512, 47522
**Auditors:** Deloitte LLP

**Bankers:** The Royal Bank Of Scotland Plc (83-06-08)

| | 28-12-13 | 29-12-12 | 01-12-11 |
|---|---|---|---|
| TO | 1,757,000 | 2,413,000 | 2,930,000 |
| P/L | (641,000) | (141,000) | (582,000) |
| NW | (6,786,000) | (7,251,000) | (7,251,000) |
| WC | (6,786,000) | N/A | N/A |
| Emp. | 75 | 93 | 132 |

DUNS 23-285-9843

## South Yorkshire Passenger Transport Authority

P O Box 37, Barnsley, South Yorkshire S70 2PQ
**Tel:** 01226772803 **Fax:** 01226-772877
**Web:** www.southyorks.gov.uk
**Estd:** 1986 Incorporate By Act Of Parliament
**Line of Business:** Strategic passenger transport committe for bus and rail passengers.
**Directors:** W J Wilkinson, J M Hoare, R Johnstone
**Co. Secretary:** Ms Maureen Oades
**US SIC:** 9121 **UK SIC:** 91110
**Bankers:** The Co-Operative Bank Plc (08-90-88)
**Employees:** 60

DUNS 22-814-2311

## South Yorkshire Passenger Transport Executive

11 Road St West, Sheffield, South Yorkshire S1 2BQ
**Tel:** 01142-767575
**Web:** www.sypte.co.uk
**VAT No:** 599912961 **Estd:** 1952 Incorporate By Act Of Parliament
**Line of Business:** Public relations consultants
**Directors:** P J Haywood, A F Ritchie, T D Hoskinton
**Responsibilities**
**Senior:** Lorraine Gandy *(Manager)*, Nicola Macguire *(Manager)*, Helen Plummer *(Project Manager - Trams and Tr)*
**Marketing:** Victoria Butterworth *(Communications Officer)*, Richard Pilgrim *(Marketing Manager - Projects)*, Tanya Shildrick *(Marketing Manager)*
**Operations:** Nathan Broadhead *(Senior Public Transport Operat)*, Helen Plummer *(Project Manager - Trams and Tr)*
**Fleet:** Nathan Broadhead *(Senior Public Transport Operat)*, Roy Mitchell *(Principal Public Transport Man)*, Stephen Skeet *(Trams and Trains Manager)*
**Engineering:** Helen Plummer *(Project Manager - Trams and Tr)*
**Branches:** South Yorkshire Passenger Transport Executive, Mexborough Bus Station, John Street, Mexborough, South Yorkshire S64 9HS
**US SIC:** 7392, 4119
**UK SIC:** 83951, 72200
**Bankers:** The Royal Bank Of Scotland Plc (16-00-08)
**Employees:** 250

DUNS 23-256-8295

## South Yorkshire Pensions Auth

18 Regent Street, Barnsley, South Yorkshire S70 2HG
**Tel:** 01226772923
**Web:** www.southyorks.org.uk
**Estd:** 2005
**Line of Business:** General (overall) public service activities
**Director:** R Johnston
**Responsibilities**
**Senior:** John Hattersley *(Fund Manager)*
**Finance:** John Hattersley *(Fund Manager)*
**IT:** A Ramsbottom *(IT Manager)*
**HR:** Vicki Jackson *(Training & Development Manager)*
**Health & Safety:** Vicki Jackson *(Training & Development Manager)*
**US SIC:** 9121 **UK SIC:** 91110
**Employees:** 50

DUNS 23-261-8355 **Imp**

## South Yorkshire Police

Sheffield Parkway Nunnery Square, Sheffield, South Yorkshire S2 5DH
**Tel:** 01142197219 **Fax:** 01142197012
**Web:** www.southyorks.police.uk
**Estd:** 1974 Incorporate By Act Of Parliament
**Line of Business:** Public security, law and order activities
**Director:** R Wells
**Responsibilities**
**Senior:** Benjamin Outram *(Software, Applications Manager)*
**Branches:** South Yorkshire Police, 5-15 Market Place, Sheffield, South Yorkshire S1 2GH
**US SIC:** 9221 **UK SIC:** 91300
**Bankers:** The Co-Operative Bank Plc (08-90-88)
**Employees:** 1,000

DUNS 50-456-9963

## Southampton Cargo Handling Ltd

(**Subsidiary of:** Independent Port Handling Ltd)
Pathfinder House, Southampton, Hampshire SO40 2RW
**Tel:** 02380820300
**Web:** www.schplc.com
**Reg No:** 2439620 **VAT No:** 566519020
**Estd:** 1989 Public Limited Company
**Line of Business:** Cargo handling
**Issued Capital:** £426,002
**Directors:** Miss D Mckay, I Morrison, K Hulme, I R Dighe, S W Burgess, L J Rawles
**Responsibilities**
**Senior:** Anthony Mac Donald *(Sales & Marketing Officer)*
**Marketing:** Anthony Mac Donald *(Sales & Marketing Officer)*
**Sales:** Anthony Mac Donald *(Sales & Marketing Officer)*
**Admin:** Karen Kirwan *(Office Manager)*
**Branches:** Southampton Cargo Handling Ltd, Herbert Walker Avenue, Southampton, Hampshire SO15 1HJ
**US SIC:** 4712 **UK SIC:** 77002
**Auditors:** PricewaterhouseCoopers
**Bankers:** National Westminster Bank Plc (56-00-68)

| | 31-12-13 | 31-12-12 | 31-12-12 |
|---|---|---|---|
| TO | 14,291,092 | 12,737,113 | 14,693,554 |
| P/L | 250,317 | 373,475 | 274,150 |
| NW | 1,681,037 | 1,507,223 | 1,255,603 |
| WC | 1,168,859 | 1,013,649 | 769,076 |
| Emp. | 194 | 253 | 244 |

DUNS 23-212-4727

## Southampton City College

St Mary Street, Southampton, Hampshire SO14 1AR
**Tel:** 02380484848
**Web:** www.southampton-city.ac.uk
**VAT No:** 631533367 **Estd:** 1955
**Line of Business:** Further education schools and colleges
**Directors:** G Collyer, Ms S Brakewell, M Rhowbotham, Ms A Bundy, J Bridge, F Stanley, P Gibson
**Responsibilities**
**Sales:** Ivan Gregory *(Vice Principal Curriculum Desi)*
**Operations:** Liz Thornhill *(Production and Operations Mana)*
**Purchasing:** Jackie Nicholas *(Purchasing Coordinator)*
**Engineering:** Colin Willott *(Technical Engineer)*
**Branches:** Southampton City College, 135 St Mary Street, Southampton, Hampshire SO14 1NX
**US SIC:** 8221 **UK SIC:** 93100
**Bankers:** Barclays Bank Plc (20-79-25)
**Employees:** 600

DUNS 21-692-7475 **Imp**

## Southampton City Council

Civic Centre, Southampton, Hampshire SO14 7LY
**Web:** www.southampton.gov.uk
**Estd:** 1974
**Line of Business:** General (overall) public service activities
**Trading Style:** The Euro Info Centre, Southampton Ski Centre, Fairisle Infant School
**Directors:** D Marlow, B Roynon, M D Smith
**Responsibilities**
**Senior:** Christine Rawnsley *(Learning Manager)*, Clive Webster *(Executive Director, Children'S)*
**IT:** Kevin Foley *(Computer Manager)*, Gisela Hoppe *(It Manager)*
**Operations:** Loretta Emery *(Production and Operations Mana)*
**Branches:** Southampton City Council, Town Hall Centre, Eastleigh, Hampshire SO50 9DE
**US SIC:** 9121 **UK SIC:** 91110
**Bankers:** National Westminster Bank Plc (56-00-68)
**Employees:** 9,000

DUNS 21-781-6108

## Southampton City Council - Road Safety

1 Guildhall Square, Southampton, Hampshire SO14 7FP
**Web:** www.southampton.gov.uk
**Estd:** 2011 Proprietorship
**Line of Business:** The dss
**Proprietor:** Miss C Bagshaw
**US SIC:** 9121 **UK SIC:** 91110
**Employees:** 450

DUNS 34-636-4805

## Southampton City Leisure Ltd

Central Library, Southampton, Hampshire SO14 7LW
**Web:** www.southampton.gov.uk
**Reg No:** 2766116 **Estd:** 1992 Private Company Limited By Guarantee
**Line of Business:** Libraries
**Directors:** D J Burke, M D Smith
**Co. Secretary:** Mark Heath
**US SIC:** 8231 **UK SIC:** 97700
**Employees:** 6,000

DUNS 42-443-8302

## Southampton Container Logistics Ltd

(**Subsidiary of:** Forest Lodge Investments Ltd)
Unit 11, Nursling Industrial Estate, Oriana Way, Nursling, Southampton, Hampshire SO16 0YU
**Tel:** 023-8074-3510 **Fax:** 023-8055-9191
**Web:** www.sclltd.co.uk
**Reg No:** 4431548 **Estd:** 2002 Private Limited Company
**Line of Business:** Freight transport by road not elsewhere classified
**Issued Capital:** £93
**Principals:** G J Roberts *(Managing)*, D Carse
**Responsibilities**
**Operations:** John Leath *(Operations Director)*
**US SIC:** 4213 **UK SIC:** 72300

| | 31-03-14 | 31-03-13 | 31-03-12 |
|---|---|---|---|
| TA | 2,263,213 | 1,731,506 | 1,876,420 |
| NW | 216,187 | 212,208 | 149,182 |
| WC | (145,591) | 130,617 | 76,247 |

DUNS 29-634-4005 **Imp**

## Southampton Container Terminals Ltd

(**Subsidiary of:** Dubai World Corporation)
Greenmoor Road, Nuneaton, Warwickshire CV11 4HH
**Tel:** 02476383684
**Web:** www.sct.uk.com
**Reg No:** 1960484 **VAT No:** 568401531
**Estd:** 1985 Private Limited Company
**Line of Business:** Agents involved in the sale of timber and building materials
**Trading Style:** S C T, Dp World Southampton
**Issued Capital:** £3,725,000
**Principals:** R B Woods *(Chairman)*, F Dalgaard, A M Bin Damithan Alqmzi, N J Ridehalgh, G S Bull, Ms J E Douglas, J N Cooper, F C Lewis
**Co. Secretary:** Nicholas Loader
**Responsibilities**
**Senior:** Sean Brophy *(Purchasing Officer)*
**Marketing:** Lynsey Haynes *(Marketing Manager)*
**Purchasing:** Sean Brophy *(Purchasing Officer)*
**US SIC:** 5072, 4712
**UK SIC:** 61500, 77002
**Auditors:** KPMG LLP
**Bankers:** Lloyds TSB Bank plc (30-00-02)

| | 31-12-13 | 31-12-12 | 31-12-11 |
|---|---|---|---|
| TO | 101,066,000 | 96,561,000 | 99,687,000 |
| P/L | 3,781,000 | (1,595,000) | 10,351,000 |
| NW | 77,035,000 | 71,806,000 | 75,750,000 |
| WC | 13,199,000 | 12,550,000 | 12,637,000 |
| Emp. | 566 | 578 | 579 |

DUNS 21-584-1069

## Southampton Council

City Depot, First Avenue, Southampton, Hampshire SO15 0LJ
**Web:** www.southampton.gov.uk
**Estd:** 2011
**Line of Business:** Fleet management
**Proprietor:** D Bone
**US SIC:** 9121 **UK SIC:** 91110
**Employees:** 200

DUNS 21-706-1290

## Southampton Football Club Ltd

(**Subsidiary of:** St Mary's Football Group Ltd)
The Friends Provident, St Marys Stadium Britannia Road, Southampton, Hampshire SO14 5FP
**Tel:** 08456889448
**Web:** www.saintsfc.co.uk
**Reg No:** 0053301 **Estd:** 1885 Private Limited Company
**Line of Business:** Operation of other sports arenas and stadiums not elsewhere classified
**Issued Capital:** £500,000
**Directors:** Ms K M Liebherr, L A Reed, G Rogers, D E Bence
**Co. Secretary:** Mrs Karenjit Dhaliwal
**Responsibilities**
**Senior:** Nicola Cortese *(Manager)*
**Finance:** M Fenn *(Financial Director)*
**Marketing:** Kate Tarry *(Marketing Director)*
**Sales:** Becky Sivier *(Sales Manager)*
**Branches:** Southampton Football Club Ltd, 145 Wilton Rd, Southampton, Hampshire SO15 5JU
**US SIC:** 7999 **UK SIC:** 97913
**Auditors:** BDO Stoy Hayward LLP
**Bankers:** Barclays Bank Plc (20-79-25)

| | 30-06-13 | 30-06-12 | 30-06-11 |
|---|---|---|---|
| TO | 69,412,667 | 21,030,782 | 13,372,915 |
| P/L | (5,302,567) | (8,357,168) | (11,737,713) |
| NW | (56,431,132) | (49,794,007) | (28,748,540) |
| WC | (46,140,734) | (16,178,851) | (1,755,182) |
| Emp. | 210 | 177 | 170 |

DUNS 21-231-6720

## Southampton Gym Club

On Redbridge School Site, Cuckmere Lane, Southampton, Hampshire SO16 9AR
**Tel:** 023-80529952
**Web:** www.sotongym.co.uk
**Estd:** 2006
**Line of Business:** Other sporting activities not elsewhere classified
**Proprietor:** Mrs K Lyons
**US SIC:** 8999 **UK SIC:** 83954
**Employees:** 60

DUNS 21-629-7283

## Southampton Isle of Wight & South of England Royal Mail Steam Packet Company Ltd

(**Subsidiary of:** Infracapital Partners Lp)
12 Bugle Street, Southampton, Hampshire SO14 2JY
**Tel:** 02380248500 **Fax:** 02380248501
**Web:** www.redfunnel.co.uk
**Reg No:** 0002404 **VAT No:** 902873131
**Estd:** 1861 Private Limited Company
**Line of Business:** Ferry operators
**Trading Style:** Red Funnel, Red Funnel
**Issued Capital:** £5,245,129
**Directors:** L R Hudson, P R Winter, A M Carter, K A George, S K Nelson, M D Helmore, J M Slawson, Mrs S A Anderson
**Responsibilities**
**Finance:** Kate Irvine *(Management Accountant)*
**Marketing:** Tom Pell-Stevens *(Head of Marketing)*
**Sales:** Geoff Crouch *(Account Manager)*, Paula Lewis *(Account Manager)*
**Admin:** Carole Harding *(Administration Manager)*
**IT:** Shaun Bradley *(Systems & Development Manager)*
**HR:** Debbie Reed *(Human Resources Manager)*
**Health & Safety:** Richard Watts *(Health & Safety Officer)*
**Operations:** David Nevin *(Southampton Terminal Operation)*
**Fleet:** Sarah Drackford *(Freight Travel Centre Manager)*, Alwyn Rees *(Head of Fleet Operations)*
**US SIC:** 4452, 4411
**UK SIC:** 74002, 74001
**Auditors:** Grant Thornton UK LLP
**Bankers:** HSBC Bank plc (40-42-18)

| | 31-12-13 | 31-12-12 | 31-12-11 |
|---|---|---|---|
| TO | 40,290,000 | 39,326,000 | 38,254,000 |
| P/L | 5,849,000 | 7,983,000 | 9,049,000 |
| NW | 39,391,000 | 37,958,000 | 29,803,000 |
| WC | 17,089,000 | 50,928,000 | 42,383,000 |
| Emp. | 383 | 394 | 400 |

DUNS 21-588-0607

## Southampton Itec

St Mary Street, Southampton, Hampshire SO14 1AR
**Tel:** 02380577404
**Web:** www.southampton-city.ac.uk
**Estd:** 1955
**Line of Business:** Further education schools and colleges
**Responsibilities**
**Senior:** Lindsay Noble *(Head Teacher)*
**US SIC:** 8221 **UK SIC:** 93100
**Employees:** 400

DUNS 28-967-1265

## The Southampton Nuffield Theatre Trust

University Road, Southampton, Hampshire SO17 1TR
**Tel:** 02380315500
**Web:** www.nuffieldtheatre.co.uk
**Reg No:** 1711502 **Estd:** 1964 Private Company Limited By Guarantee
**Line of Business:** Artistic and literary creation and interpretation
**Directors:** D J Burke, C R Carter, Ms H M Keall, E J Rochead, Professor A S Dean, L M Norris, Professor R C King, S W Barnes-Andrews
**Co. Secretary:** Gathorne Gough

**Responsibilities**
**Senior:** Adrian Jackson *(Director)*, Jeremy Meadow *(Director)*, Maria Mills *(Director)*
**US SIC:** 7999 **UK SIC:** 97913
**Auditors:** Fiander Tovell & Co
**Bankers:** Barclays Bank Plc (20-79-25)

| | 31-03-14 | 31-03-13 | 31-03-12 |
|---|---|---|---|
| TO | 1,885,995 | 1,788,289 | 1,968,471 |
| P/L | 23,078 | (96,843) | (166,597) |
| NW | 442,459 | 419,381 | 516,224 |
| WC | 3,292 | (12,586) | 45,690 |
| Emp. | 43 | 49 | 53 |

DUNS 33-989-8371
## Southampton Park Hotel
Southampton Park Hotel, Southampton, Hampshire SO15 2WY
**Tel:** 023-8034-3343
**Web:** www.stjameshotels.co.uk
**Proprietorship**
**Line of Business:** Other tourist assistance activities not elsewhere classified
**Proprietor:** R Collins
**Responsibilities**
**Senior:** Sue Leidecker *(General Manager)*
**HR:** Sue Leidecker *(General Manager)*
**Health & Safety:** Sue Leidecker *(General Manager)*
**Facilities:** Sue Leidecker *(General Manager)*
**US SIC:** 7999, 5812, 5813
**UK SIC:** 97913, 66110, 66200
**Employees:** 55

DUNS 21-577-7686
## Southbank Child Centre
207 Old Rutherglen Road, Glasgow, Lanarkshire G5 0RE
**Tel:** 0141-201-0914
**Estd:** 1965 Proprietorship
**Line of Business:** Nhs clinics
**Proprietor:** Mrs M Brewer
**Responsibilities**
**Senior:** Lee Urquhart *(Clinical Service Manager)*
**US SIC:** 8062 **UK SIC:** 95100
**Employees:** 55

DUNS 21-777-0001
## Southbury Leisure Centre Fusion Lifestyle
192 Southbury Road, Enfield, Middlesex EN1 1YP
**Web:** www.fusion-lifestyle.com
**Estd:** 2011 Partnership
**Line of Business:** Leisure centres
**Partners:** P Kay, K Biggs
**US SIC:** 7999 **UK SIC:** 97913
**Employees:** 117

DUNS 22-778-7686 **Imp-Exp**
## Southco Europe Ltd.
(**Subsidiary of:** South Chester Tube Company)
Touch Point, Wainwright Road, Warndon, Worcester, Worcestershire WR4 9FA
**Tel:** 01905-346500 **Fax:** 01905 346501
**Web:** www.southco.com
**Reg No:** 1844833 **VAT No:** 396121055
**Estd:** 1983 Private Limited Company
**Line of Business:** Manufacture of locks and hinges
**Export Markets:** Europe, Asia
**Issued Capital:** £100
**Directors:** Ms S L Harding, A L Eisen
**Co. Secretary:** Quintin Potgieter
**Responsibilities**
**Senior:** Phil Kempson *(General Manager)*, David Montgomery Iii *(Manager)*
**Marketing:** Petra Reichle *(Marketing Manager)*
**Admin:** Phil Kempson *(General Manager)*
**Purchasing:** Roy Kitchen *(Purchasing Manager)*
**US SIC:** 8999, 7399
**UK SIC:** 83954
**Bankers:** National Westminster Bank Plc (55-81-36)

| | 31-12-13 | 31-12-12 | 31-12-11 |
|---|---|---|---|
| TA | 101 | 101 | 101 |
| NW | 101 | 101 | 101 |

DUNS 42-340-3307 **Exp**
## Southco Manufacturing Ltd
(**Subsidiary of:** South Chester Tube Company)
Shire Business Park, Wainwright Road, Worcester, Worcestershire WR4 9FA
**Tel:** 01905-751000
**Web:** www.southco.com
**Reg No:** 4328069 **Estd:** 1996 Private Limited Company
**Line of Business:** Manufacture of locks and hinges
**Export Sales:** £57,908,000
**Issued Capital:** £15,000,200
**Directors:** P Brown, P Testeil, Ms S L Harding, A L Eisen
**Co. Secretary:** Quintin Potgieter
**Responsibilities**
**Senior:** Susan Austin *(Manager)*
**Marketing:** Petra Reichle *(Marketing Manager)*
**Branches:** Southco Manufacturing Ltd, 12 Balloch Road, Alexandria, Dunbartonshire G83 8SR
**US SIC:** 3429 **UK SIC:** 31694
**Auditors:** Grant Thornton UK LLP
**Bankers:** The Royal Bank Of Scotland Plc (15-00-00)

| | 31-12-13 | 31-12-12 | 31-12-11 |
|---|---|---|---|
| TO | 69,486,000 | 65,400,000 | 71,918,000 |
| P/L | 6,901,000 | 4,370,000 | 6,812,000 |
| NW | 19,126,000 | 14,362,000 | 12,238,000 |
| WC | 20,781,000 | 12,482,000 | 13,790,000 |
| Emp. | 336 | 346 | 331 |

DUNS 21-630-5490 **Imp**
## Southcombe Brothers Ltd
Great Field Lane, Stoke-Sub-Hamdon, Somerset TA14 6QD
**Tel:** 01935-823567
**Web:** www.southcombe.co.uk
**Reg No:** 0372391 **VAT No:** 186283043
**Estd:** 1847 Private Limited Company
**Line of Business:** Manufacturers of gloves
**Issued Capital:** £621,850
**Principals:** R M Southcombe *(Chairman)*, D M Southcombe
**Co. Secretary:** David Evans
**Responsibilities**
**Senior:** W Ings *(Production Manager)*
**Admin:** Glenda Wright *(Office)*
**IT:** Aleister Ford *(IT Engineer)*, Alaistair Ford *(IT Engineer)*
**HR:** W Ings *(Production Manager)*
**Health & Safety:** W Ings *(Production Manager)*
**Facilities:** P Gaines *(Maintenance Manager)*
**Operations:** W Ings *(Production Manager)*
**Engineering:** P Gaines *(Maintenance Manager)*, W Ings *(Production Manager)*
**Branches:** Southcombe Brothers Ltd, Wincombe Lane, Shaftesbury, Dorset SP7 8PJ
**US SIC:** 2389 **UK SIC:** 45393
**Auditors:** Wilkins Kennedy
**Bankers:** Lloyds TSB Bank plc (30-99-98)

| | 31-12-13 | 31-12-12 | 31-12-11 |
|---|---|---|---|
| TA | 1,909,627 | 2,336,569 | 2,856,500 |
| NW | 1,456,850 | 1,815,720 | 2,234,021 |
| WC | 570,297 | 921,370 | 1,334,176 |

DUNS 36-517-2233
## Southcote Primary School
Silchester Road, Reading, Berkshire RG30 3EJ
**Tel:** 01189375533
**Web:** www.southcote.reading.sch.uk
**Estd:** 1959
**Line of Business:** Schools (local authority)
**Director:** Ms L Green
**Responsibilities**
**Senior:** Lisa Telling *(Head Teacher)*
**US SIC:** 8211 **UK SIC:** 93200
**Employees:** 50

DUNS 21-781-2733
## Southcraig Campus
38 Belmont Avenue, Ayr, Ayrshire KA7 2ND
**Estd:** 1997 Proprietorship
**Line of Business:** Schools (special)
**Proprietor:** Mrs L Stobie
**US SIC:** 8299 **UK SIC:** 93300
**Employees:** 65

DUNS 21-772-0680
## Southcrest Nursing Home
215 Mount Pleasant, Redditch, Worcestershire B97 4JG
**Tel:** 01527-550-720
**Estd:** 1988 Partnership
**Line of Business:** Nursing homes
**Partners:** Mrs K Ananthram, Dr S Ananthram
**Responsibilities**
**Senior:** Vanessa House *(Manager)*
**US SIC:** 8051 **UK SIC:** 95100
**Employees:** 30

DUNS 23-621-7670
## Southdale Ltd
(**Subsidiary of:** Southdale Holdings Ltd)
Westholme Road, Halifax, West Yorkshire HX1 4JF
**Tel:** 01422-380090
**Web:** www.southdale-homes.co.uk
**Reg No:** 3618913 **Estd:** 1988 Private Limited Company
**Line of Business:** Residential property developers
**Issued Capital:** £127,840
**Principals:** C Harris *(Chairman)*, P R Moore *(Managing)*, R Greenwood, J J O Hara, D F Mchugh, S B Allison, Ms T Mccormick
**Co. Secretary:** Guy Pearson
**Responsibilities**
**IT:** Lee Argyle *(IT Manager)*
**US SIC:** 6552, 1541
**UK SIC:** 85000, 50100
**Auditors:** Clough & Co LLP

| | 30-06-13 | 30-06-12 | 30-06-11 |
|---|---|---|---|
| TO | 32,895,343 | 48,821,539 | 59,033,739 |
| P/L | (1,225,986) | (645,170) | (893,679) |
| NW | 2,068,418 | 3,258,704 | 3,780,457 |
| WC | 1,644,647 | 2,802,872 | 3,302,615 |
| Emp. | 124 | 137 | 186 |

DUNS 21-224-6069
## Southdowns Holiday Village
South Downs Holiday Village, Bracklesham Lane, Chichester, West Sussex PO20 8JE
**Tel:** 01243-673683
**Web:** www.richardsonsholidayvillages.co.uk
**Estd:** 1998 Proprietorship
**Line of Business:** Holiday parks and camps
**Proprietor:** A Hawkes
**Responsibilities**
**Senior:** Anthony Hawkes *(Managing Director)*
**Health & Safety:** Anthony Hawkes *(Managing Director)*, Jane Reid *(House Manager)*
**Facilities:** Anthony Hawkes *(Managing Director)*, Jane Reid *(House Manager)*
**US SIC:** 7021 **UK SIC:** 66500
**Employees:** 80

DUNS 23-259-5939
## Southend Care Ltd
(**Subsidiary of:** Johnson Care Ltd)
Chestnut Way, Brightlingsea, Colchester, Essex CO7 0UH
**Tel:** 01206-303311
**Web:** www.southendcare.com
**Reg No:** 4241958 **Estd:** 2001 Private Limited Company
**Line of Business:** Social work activities with accommodation
**Issued Capital:** £1,004
**Directors:** S J Vive-Kananda, Dr D S Vive Kananda
**Branches:** Southend Care Ltd, Chestnut Way, Colchester, Essex CO7 0UH
**US SIC:** 8321 **UK SIC:** 96111
**Auditors:** Dutchmans

| | 31-12-13 | 31-12-12 | 31-12-11 |
|---|---|---|---|
| TO | 5,180,307 | 5,143,603 | 4,985,663 |
| P/L | (126,797) | (2,534,064) | (187,460) |
| NW | 6,476,804 | 6,603,601 | 7,739,729 |
| WC | 840,877 | 449,411 | 925,935 |
| Emp. | 249 | 274 | 281 |

DUNS 21-704-4492
## Southend High School for Boys Academy Trust
Southend High School For Boys, Prittlewell Chase, Southend-On-Sea, Essex SS0 0RG
**Tel:** 01702343074
**Reg No:** 7485584 **Estd:** 2011 Private Company Limited By Guarantee
**Line of Business:** General secondary education
**Directors:** S R Baldwin, A J Barrett, R G Maddison, P K Richards
**Responsibilities**
**Senior:** Robin Bevin *(Manager)*
**US SIC:** 8211 **UK SIC:** 93200

| | 31-08-14 | 31-08-13 | 31-08-12 |
|---|---|---|---|
| TO | 6,599,683 | 6,252,436 | 6,032,815 |
| P/L | 197,592 | 246,959 | 65,959 |
| NW | 9,663,164 | 9,381,572 | 9,189,613 |
| WC | 456,306 | 278,469 | 164,162 |
| Emp. | 106 | 94 | 109 |

DUNS 21-706-7263
## Southend-on-Sea Borough Council
The Tickfield Centre, Tickfield Industrial Estate, Tickfield A, Southend-On-Sea, Essex SS2 6LL
**Tel:** 01702215000
**Web:** www.southend.gov.uk
**VAT No:** 352173473 **Estd:** 1892
**Line of Business:** General (overall) public service activities
**Directors:** D Andrews, D Moulson
**Responsibilities**
**Senior:** Laurence Cops *(Head of ICT)*, Peter Geraghty *(Chairman)*, Dean Hermitage *(Manager)*
**Marketing:** Joanna Ruffle *(Head of Communications)*
**IT:** Laurence Cops *(Head of ICT)*
**HR:** Karen Melville *(Human Resources Manager)*, Joanna Ruffle *(Head of Communications)*
**Health & Safety:** Richard Potticary *(Health & Safety Officer)*
**Operations:** Nick Corrigan *(Head of Customer Services)*, Janice Lyons *(Production and Operations Mana)*
**Branches:** Southend-On-Sea Borough Council, 49 Tailors Court, Southend-On-Sea, Essex SS2 5SX
**US SIC:** 9121, 8211
**UK SIC:** 91110, 93200
**Employees:** 1,250

DUNS 22-568-1261
## Southend-on-Sea Bowling Club Ltd
7 Tunbridge Road, Southend-On-Sea, Essex SS2 6LT
**Tel:** 01702467073
**Web:** www.sovereignfoods.co.za
**Reg No:** 0105819 **Estd:** 1910 Private Limited Company
**Line of Business:** Other sporting activities not elsewhere classified
**Issued Capital:** £1,994
**Directors:** D A Fowler, B S Tattoo, Mrs J D Jenner, G W Fincham, M A Cohen, J R Horner, P H Maley
**Co. Secretary:** John Vile
**Branches:** Southend-On-Sea Bowling Club Ltd, 7 Tunbridge Road, Southend-On-Sea, Essex SS2 6LT
**US SIC:** 7399 **UK SIC:** 83954
**Auditors:** Alan Kitson & Co
**Bankers:** Lloyds TSB Bank plc (30-97-84)

| | 31-12-13 | 31-12-12 | 31-12-11 |
|---|---|---|---|
| TO | 129,836 | 125,671 | 128,214 |
| P/L | 5,472 | 9,829 | 8,379 |
| NW | 279,964 | 274,492 | 264,663 |
| WC | 85,382 | 75,591 | 77,572 |

DUNS 22-643-4652
## The Southend United Football Club Ltd
(**Subsidiary of:** Mezcal Investments Limited)
Roots Hall, Victoria Avenue, Southend-On-Sea, Essex SS2 6NQ
**Tel:** 01702351117
**Web:** www.shrimpers-clubshop.co.uk
**Reg No:** 0089767 **Estd:** 1906 Private Limited Company
**Line of Business:** Sports goods retailers
**Issued Capital:** £169,508
**Principals:** G King *(Financial)*, F Van Wezel, R Martin, S A Kavanagh, D M Markscheffel, G J Lockett
**Co. Secretary:** Mrs Helen Norbury
**Responsibilities**
**Senior:** Tom Brooks *(Manager)*, Jessika Hilaire *(Manager)*
**Branches:** The Southend United Football Club Ltd, Roots Hall Football Ground, Victoria Avenue, Southend-On-Sea, Essex SS2 6NQ
**US SIC:** 7999 **UK SIC:** 97913
**Auditors:** WMT
**Bankers:** Lloyds TSB Bank plc (30-97-84)

| | 31-07-13 | 31-07-12 | 31-07-11 |
|---|---|---|---|
| TO | 4,279,479 | 3,785,300 | 3,164,383 |
| P/L | (614,180) | (1,176,459) | (1,159,693) |
| NW | (11,264,876) | (10,652,771) | (9,470,030) |
| WC | (11,350,970) | (10,744,499) | (9,576,155) |
| Emp. | 123 | 132 | 123 |

DUNS 54-864-0887
## Southend University Hospital Nhs Foundation Trust
Prittlewell Chase, Westcliff-On-Sea, Essex SS0 0RY
**Tel:** 01702-435-555
**Web:** www.southend.nhs.uk
**Estd:** 1932
**Line of Business:** Public sector hospital activities, including nhs trusts
**Principals:** J Bruce *(Chairman)*, B Shipley *(Financial)*, Ms S Le Blanc *(Personnel)*, Ms S Hardy, M Mcfrederick, Ms J Totterdell, Ms C Dobie, Ms M Parsons
**Responsibilities**
**Senior:** Yusuf Goolamali *(Non-Executive Director)*, Malcolm McFrederick *(Director)*, David Parkins *(Non-Executive Director)*, Neil Rothnie *(Medical Director)*, Nigel Towler *(Non-Executive Director)*
**Finance:** James O'Sullivan *(Chief Financial Officer)*
**Admin:** Jenny Gates *(Hospital Administrator)*
**Facilities:** Jan China *(Director of Estates and Facili)*
**Branches:** Southend University Hospital Nhs Foundation Trust, Long Road, Canvey Island, Essex SS8 0JA
**US SIC:** 8062 **UK SIC:** 95100
**Auditors:** Ernst & Young Statutory

| | 31-03-14 | 31-03-13 | 31-03-12 |
|---|---|---|---|
| TO | 270,682,000 | 257,747,000 | 230,042,000 |
| P/L | (1,523,000) | 792,000 | 267,000 |
| NW | 152,730,000 | 148,288,000 | 145,695,000 |
| WC | 4,343,000 | 4,589,000 | 1,610,000 |
| Emp. | 4,068 | 4,146 | 4,099 |

DUNS 22-542-0678
## The Southern & South East England Tourist Board
40 Chamberlayne Road, Eastleigh, Hampshire SO50 5JH
**Tel:** 02380625400
**Web:** www.tourismsoutheast.com
**Reg No:** 1345038 **Estd:** 1977 Private Company Limited By Guarantee
**Line of Business:** Tourist information offices

**Directors:** Mrs S Barnes-Keywood, C M Smith, Ms L J Bibbings, S Munn, A H Mellins, J A Bates, C A White, P J Colling
**Co. Secretary:** Paul Oliver
**Responsibilities**
**Senior:** Sandra Barnes-keywood *(Non-Executive Director)*, Terry Boswell *(Director)*, David Philip *(Director)*, Kenneth Robinson *(Director)*
**Finance:** Matthew Feldwick *(Finance Assistant)*, Lin Lancefield *(Finance Manager)*
**Marketing:** Fran Downton *(International Marketing Manage)*
**Sales:** Sergi Jarques *(Business Development and Resea)*
**Branches:** The Southern & South East England Tourist Board, 86A Pingle Drive, Bicester, Oxfordshire OX26 6WD
**US SIC:** 7999 **UK SIC:** 97913
**Auditors:** Burnett Swayne
**Bankers:** Lloyds TSB Bank plc (30-92-94)

| | 31-03-14 | 31-03-13 | 31-03-12 |
|---|---|---|---|
| TO | 2,077,378 | 2,229,338 | 2,906,896 |
| P/L | (47,142) | (287,023) | (282,917) |
| NW | (2,651,409) | (2,538,267) | (2,412,244) |
| WC | 310,273 | 422,309 | 677,798 |
| Emp. | N/A | N/A | 70 |

DUNS 42-335-5085
## Southern Business Technologies Ltd
(**Subsidiary of:** Southern Communications Holdings Ltd)
Glebe Farm, Down Street, Dummer, Basingstoke, Hampshire RG25 2AD
**Tel:** 0845-056-7765
**Web:** www.southern-comms.co.uk
**Reg No:** 4323164 **Estd:** 2001 Private Limited Company
**Line of Business:** Telecom consultants
**Issued Capital:** £50,000
**Directors:** J N Wilson, M O Kirk, P J Bradford, A J Moody, D C Phillips
**Co. Secretary:** James Wilson
**Branches:** Southern Business Technologies Ltd, Hassocks Workshops, Unit 11, Basingstoke, Hampshire RG24 8UQ
**US SIC:** 4899, 6711
**UK SIC:** 79020, 83962

| | 31-03-14 | 31-03-13 | 31-03-12 |
|---|---|---|---|
| TO | 18,136,147 | 15,560,646 | 12,393,538 |
| P/L | 1,172,535 | 860,881 | 299,776 |
| NW | (189,354) | (886,473) | 50,598 |
| WC | (528,876) | (585,168) | (247,035) |
| Emp. | 124 | 94 | 86 |

DUNS 21-761-7607
## Southern Co-Operatives Ltd
1000 Lakeside, Western Road, North Harbour, Portsmouth, Hampshire PO6 3FE
**Tel:** 02392-222500 **Fax:** 02392-222650
**Web:** www.thesouthernco-operative.co.uk
**Reg No:** 0001591IP **Estd:** 1873 Friendly Society
**Line of Business:** Retail sale in non-specialised stores with food, beverages or tobacco predominating
**Principals:** D J Blowe *(Chairman)*, M S Smith, M K Hastilow, P Lympany, S L Toone, G Heath, F A Hobson, A Vincent-Prior
**Responsibilities**
**Senior:** T Blair *(Principal)*, N Blanchard *(Principal)*
**US SIC:** 7399 **UK SIC:** 83954
**Auditors:** Deloitte LLP
**Bankers:** The Co-Operative Bank Plc (08-90-81)

| | 25-01-14 | 26-01-13 | 28-01-12 |
|---|---|---|---|
| TO | 326,716,000 | 303,106,000 | 281,442,000 |
| P/L | 11,790,000 | 7,748,000 | 9,826,000 |
| NW | 86,555,000 | 85,704,000 | 79,697,000 |
| WC | 2,054,000 | 11,030,000 | 16,546,000 |
| Emp. | 3,982 | 3,744 | N/A |

DUNS 21-916-8620
## Southern Communications Holdings Ltd
Glebe Farm, Down Street, Dummer, Basingstoke, Hampshire RG25 2AD
**Tel:** 01256391000
**Web:** www.southern-comms.co.uk
**Reg No:** 8413599 **Estd:** 2013 Private Limited Company
**Line of Business:** Telecom consultants
**Issued Capital:** £1
**Directors:** P J Bradford, M O Kirk, A J Moody, J N Wilson, D C Phillips
**Co. Secretary:** James Wilson
**US SIC:** 4899 **UK SIC:** 79020

| | 31-03-14 |
|---|---|
| TO | 18,313,353 |
| P/L | 676,882 |
| NW | (3,202,948) |
| WC | (968,191) |
| Emp. | 124 |

DUNS 39-808-1299
## Southern Counties Care Ltd
Heathcote, Station Road, Heathfield, East Sussex TN21 8DR
**Tel:** 01435-862952
**Web:** www.southerncountycare.co.uk
**Reg No:** 2213016 **Estd:** 2007 Private Limited Company
**Line of Business:** Medical equipment maintenance
**Issued Capital:** £300,000
**Director:** S Jeebun
**Co. Secretary:** Mrs Zainah Jeebun
**Responsibilities**
**Senior:** David Harmar *(Manager)*
**Admin:** Hayley Lavender *(Administrator)*
**US SIC:** 3841 **UK SIC:** 37201
**Auditors:** Hazlewoods LLP
**Bankers:** Barclays Bank Plc (20-00-00)

| | 31-12-13 | 31-12-12 | 31-12-11 |
|---|---|---|---|
| TO | 3,674,320 | 4,081,741 | 4,215,230 |
| P/L | 584,770 | 87,700 | 747,100 |
| NW | 7,366,273 | 6,869,084 | 6,319,535 |
| WC | 1,847,437 | 1,428,717 | 725,937 |
| Emp. | 157 | 158 | 162 |

DUNS 42-381-5695
## Southern Counties Fresh Foods Ltd
(**Subsidiary of:** Rwm Food Group Holdings Ltd)
The Abbatoir, Muchelney Road Huish Episcopi, Langport, Somerset TA10 9HG
**Tel:** 01458-254545
**Web:** www.rwmfoodgroup.com
**Reg No:** 3239694 **Estd:** 1946 Private Limited Company
**Line of Business:** Meat wholesalers
**Trading Style:** Rwm Food Group
**Issued Capital:** £1
**Directors:** T J Kirwan, J M Burton, P J Finnerty
**Co. Secretary:** John Mclaughlin
**Responsibilities**
**Senior:** Jason Channing *(Manager)*, Graham Heffer *(Chief Executive)*
**US SIC:** 5147, 2013
**UK SIC:** 61700, 41223
**Auditors:** Milsted Langdon
**Bankers:** National Westminster Bank Plc (60-03-27)

| | 30-03-14 | 31-03-13 | 01-03-12 |
|---|---|---|---|
| TO | N/A | 70,893,000 | 43,341,000 |
| P/L | N/A | 12,440,000 | 3,629,000 |
| NW | 5,000 | 5,000 | 10,351,000 |
| WC | N/A | 5,000 | 6,558,000 |
| Emp. | N/A | 75 | 88 |

DUNS 21-690-4276 Exp
## Southern Counties Fuels Ltd
(**Subsidiary of:** Dcc Plc)
Colwood Lane, Warninglid, Haywards Heath, West Sussex RH17 5UE
**Tel:** 08456004006
**Web:** www.southerncountiesfuels.co.uk
**Reg No:** 0903234 **VAT No:** 191223188
**Estd:** 1967 Private Limited Company
**Line of Business:** Manufacture of gas
**Export Markets:** W Indies
**Issued Capital:** £51
**Directors:** P T Vian, I Mackie, D Murphy, C J Murphy
**Co. Secretary:** Ian Mackie
**Responsibilities**
**Senior:** None Available *(None Available)*
**Sales:** Ruth Everett *(Sales Manager)*
**Health & Safety:** Ruth Everett *(Sales Manager)*
**Facilities:** Yvette Ferguson *(Facilities Manager)*
**Branches:** Southern Counties Fuels Ltd, 43 Springfield Rd, Horsham, West Sussex RH12 2PG
**US SIC:** 4925 **UK SIC:** 25670
**Auditors:** Deloitte & Touche
**Bankers:** National Westminster Bank Plc (60-06-20)

| | 31-03-14 | 31-03-13 | 31-03-12 |
|---|---|---|---|
| TA | 20,188,600 | 20,188,600 | 20,188,600 |
| NW | 20,188,600 | 20,188,600 | 20,188,600 |

DUNS 21-609-9929
## Southern Counties Garages Ltd
(**Subsidiary of:** Minelock Ltd)
Discovery House, 13-15 London Road, Crawley, West Sussex RH10 8JG
**Tel:** 01293-520191 **Fax:** 01293-530131
**Web:** www.gatwick-honda.co.uk
**Reg No:** 0413361 **Estd:** 2003 Private Limited Company
**Line of Business:** Car dealers (new & used)
**Trading Style:** Southern Counties Honda
**Issued Capital:** £38,747
**Directors:** A B Donald, N S Donald
**Co. Secretary:** Ms Jennifer Liddle
**Responsibilities**
**Sales:** Steve Peters *(Business Manager)*
**Operations:** Craig Curtis *(Service Manager)*

**US SIC:** 5511, 5541
**UK SIC:** 65100, 65200

| | 31-12-13 | 31-12-12 | 31-12-11 |
|---|---|---|---|
| TA | 2,300,000 | 2,500,000 | 2,500,000 |
| NW | 1,131,344 | 1,197,298 | 1,038,558 |

DUNS 53-657-3108
## Southern Cranes & Access Ltd
The Business Park, Maydwell Avenue, Slinfold, Horsham, West Sussex
**Fax:** 01403 339116
**Web:** www.southerncranes.co.uk
**Reg No:** 3462517 **VAT No:** 704383352
**Estd:** 1970 Private Limited Company
**Line of Business:** Crane sales, service and hire
**Issued Capital:** £112
**Directors:** M P Sadler, K Prince, R Sadler, C S Sadler
**Co. Secretary:** Ms Angela Sadler
**US SIC:** 7394 **UK SIC:** 84000
**Auditors:** Lewis Brownlee (Chichester) Ltd
**Bankers:** National Westminster Bank Plc (60-16-27)

| | 30-04-14 | 30-04-13 | 30-04-12 |
|---|---|---|---|
| TO | 11,527,360 | 8,389,078 | 8,077,110 |
| P/L | 1,738,471 | 165,807 | (142,679) |
| NW | 3,408,106 | 1,756,272 | 1,746,363 |
| WC | (294,172) | (390,064) | (532,597) |
| Emp. | 80 | 74 | 73 |

DUNS 77-979-4473
## Southern Dental Ltd
Innovation House, Crawley, West Sussex RH10 9TF
**Tel:** 01293-522835 **Fax:** 01293515566
**Web:** www.southerndental.co.uk
**Reg No:** 5947797 **Estd:** 1990 Private Limited Company
**Line of Business:** Dentists
**Issued Capital:** £2,000
**Directors:** Dr A Eyrumlu, Dr M Eyrumlu, Dr H S Shakir
**Co. Secretary:** Neal Hendrie
**Responsibilities**
**Senior:** Lesley Stadnes *(Practice Manager)*
**US SIC:** 8021 **UK SIC:** 95400
**Bankers:** Abbey National Plc (09-00-21)

| | 31-03-14 | 31-03-13 | 31-03-12 |
|---|---|---|---|
| TO | 34,492,551 | 26,419,791 | 19,556,867 |
| P/L | 1,962,363 | 1,162,299 | 214,650 |
| NW | (25,836,045) | (18,980,473) | (16,359,841) |
| WC | (2,027,710) | (3,096,906) | (4,287,697) |
| Emp. | 385 | 223 | 241 |

DUNS 22-741-1279
## Southern Education Authority
3 Charlemont Place, Armagh, Co Armagh BT61 9AX
**Tel:** 028-3751-2200
**Web:** www.feld.org
**Line of Business:** Schools & educational services
**Directors:** Ms H Mcclenaghan, Mrs K Wilkinson
**Responsibilities**
**Senior:** Helen McClenaghan *(Chief Executive Officer)*, Ron McMurray *(Stores Officer)*
**Facilities:** Sam Berry *(Facilities Manager)*
**Branches:** Southern Education Authority, 77 Dundalk Road, Newry, Co Down BT35 9HP
**US SIC:** 8299 **UK SIC:** 93300
**Employees:** 300

DUNS 22-093-0080
## Southern Electric Power Distribution Plc
(**Subsidiary of:** Sse Plc)
Inveralmond House, 200 Dunkeld Road, Perth, Perthshire PH1 3AQ
**Tel:** 0845-600-2006
**Reg No:** 4094290 **Estd:** 2000 Public Limited Company
**Line of Business:** Electricity companies
**Issued Capital:** £7,850,000
**Directors:** G C Steel, S A Kennedy, F M Alexander, Dr A E Mcleod, D Rutherford, Mrs C C Nicol, S J Hogarth, D Gardner
**Co. Secretary:** Ms Helen Gettinby
**Responsibilities**
**Senior:** Lilian Manderson *(Manager)*
**US SIC:** 4911 **UK SIC:** 16101
**Auditors:** KPMG Audit PLC

| | 31-03-14 | 31-03-13 | 31-03-12 |
|---|---|---|---|
| TO | 659,600,000 | 663,800,000 | 578,800,000 |
| P/L | 253,500,000 | 282,600,000 | 198,400,000 |
| NW | 867,200,000 | 688,200,000 | 846,300,000 |
| WC | (28,200,000) | (7,800,000) | (102,700,000) |
| Emp. | 1,467 | 1,421 | 1,361 |

DUNS 45-846-7156
## Southern England Farms Ltd
Lambo, Fraddam Road, Leedstown, Hayle, Cornwall TR27 5PF
**Web:** www.cabbage-online.co.uk
**Reg No:** 3193422 **Estd:** 1996 Private Limited Company
**Line of Business:** Packaging activities
**Issued Capital:** £100

**Director:** G N Richards
**Co. Secretary:** Ms Jane Richards
**US SIC:** 7399 **UK SIC:** 83954

| | 31-10-13 | 31-10-12 | 31-10-11 |
|---|---|---|---|
| TO | 12,861,265 | 13,378,896 | 12,231,991 |
| P/L | (862,861) | 821,667 | 1,208,171 |
| NW | 2,032,351 | 2,556,237 | 1,927,344 |
| WC | (711,053) | 154,446 | (443,944) |
| Emp. | 219 | 179 | 180 |

DUNS 73-913-5890
## Southern Gas Networks Plc
(**Subsidiary of:** Scotia Gas Networks Ltd)
Scotia Gas Networks, 55 Vastern Road, Reading, Berkshire RG1 8BU
**Tel:** 08450703497
**Web:** www.sgn.co.uk
**Reg No:** 5167021 **Estd:** 2004 Public Limited Company
**Line of Business:** Distribution and trade of gaseous fuels through mains
**Issued Capital:** £160,174,772
**Directors:** F M Alexander, P R Jeffrey, J Mcphillimy, J J Mcmanus, G G Juggins, S B Sherman, Ms O P Steedman, Ms N M Flageul
**Co. Secretary:** Ms Nicola Shand
**Branches:** Southern Gas Networks Plc, North Close, GU12 4DF Aldershot
**US SIC:** 4932, 6711
**UK SIC:** 16200, 83962
**Auditors:** Deloitte LLP

| | 31-03-14 | 31-03-13 | 31-03-12 |
|---|---|---|---|
| TO | 765,700,000 | 657,100,000 | 635,800,000 |
| P/L | 139,600,000 | 23,000,000 | 27,700,000 |
| NW | 63,900,000 | (69,400,000) | (99,500,000) |
| WC | 468,700,000 | 254,500,000 | 216,600,000 |
| Emp. | 882 | 943 | 1,001 |

DUNS 21-580-1637
## Southern Grill & Gate
Unit 4, Eagle Trading Estate, Mitcham, Surrey CR4 4UY
**Tel:** 02086409989
**Web:** www.sgg-ltd.co.uk
**Estd:** 1995 Proprietorship
**Line of Business:** Manufacture of locks and hinges
**Proprietor:** A Nurse
**US SIC:** 3429 **UK SIC:** 31694
**Employees:** 46

DUNS 21-705-9663
## Southern Health & Social Care Trust
Lurgan Road, Portadown, Craigavon, Co Armagh BT63 5QQ
**Tel:** 02838334444
**Web:** www.southerntrust.hscni.net
**Estd:** 2007
**Line of Business:** Hospitals
**Trading Style:** Craigavon Area Hospital, Southern Health & Social Care Trust (A&D), Southern Health & Social Care Trust (Chld D), Southern Health & Social Care Trust (N&M)
**Principals:** Mrs R Brownlee *(Chairman)*, Ms A Balmer *(Chairman)*, B Dornan *(Managing)*, Ms P Clarke *(Managing)*, S Mcnally *(Financial)*, Ms A Mcveigh, Ms A Mcveigh, Ms M Mcalinden
**Responsibilities**
**Senior:** Kieran Donaghy *(General Manager)*, Mairead McAlinden *(Chief Executive Officer)*, Angela McVeigh *(Director)*
**Finance:** Stephen McNally *(Financial Director)*
**Branches:** Southern Health & Social Care Trust, 68 Lurgan Road, Craigavon, Co Armagh BT63 5QQ
**US SIC:** 8062 **UK SIC:** 95100
**Auditors:** JM Dowdall CB
**Employees:** 1,500

DUNS 21-557-9444
## Southern Health Nhs Foundation Trust
Tatchbury Mount, Southampton, Hampshire SO40 2RZ
**Tel:** 023 8087 4000
**Web:** www.southernhealth.nhs.uk
**Estd:** 2011
**Line of Business:** Public sector hospital activities, including nhs trusts
**Principals:** M Brooks *(Financial)*, Ms K Percy, Ms K Percy *(Partner)*
**Responsibilities**
**HR:** Sandra Grant *(Human Resources Manager)*
**Branches:** Southern Health Nhs Foundation Trust, Forest Road, Bordon, Hampshire GU35 0XT
**US SIC:** 8062 **UK SIC:** 95100
**Auditors:** PricewaterhouseCoopers LLP

| | 31-03-14 | 31-03-13 | 31-03-11 |
|---|---|---|---|
| TO | 353,918,000 | 332,601,000 | 165,043,000 |
| P/L | 50,000 | 1,534,000 | (1,180,000) |
| NW | 199,006,000 | 140,568,000 | 123,160,000 |
| WC | 5,214,000 | 5,739,000 | 5,486,000 |
| Emp. | 7,250 | 6,491 | 4,073 |

DUNS 22-210-4791
## Southern Healthcare (Wessex) Ltd
Sefton Hall, Dawlish, Devon EX7 9DS
**Web:** www.southernhealthcare.co.uk
**Reg No:** 4228592 **Estd:** 2001 Private Limited Company
**Line of Business:** Other human health activities
**Issued Capital:** £525,000
**Directors:** Miss S R Coyte, C G Crocker, D Cox, Ms K A Bolt, J C Coyte, Miss T Cox, J R Cox, G D Cox
**Responsibilities**
**Senior:** Susan Mosedale *(Administrator)*
**US SIC:** 8091 **UK SIC:** 95200

| | 31-08-13 | 31-08-12 | 31-08-11 |
|---|---|---|---|
| TO | 4,809,223 | 4,714,302 | 4,715,425 |
| P/L | 250,182 | 195,581 | 45,361 |
| NW | 1,020,031 | 1,149,405 | 1,037,982 |
| WC | 477,632 | 593,805 | 705,145 |
| Emp. | 212 | 216 | 203 |

DUNS 21-209-5397
## Southern House
18 Water Street, Abergele, Clwyd LL22 7SH
**Tel:** 01745-833600
**Web:** www.chestnuthealthcaregroup.com
**Estd:** 1987 Proprietorship
**Line of Business:** Nursing homes
**Proprietor:** D Southern
**Responsibilities**
**Senior:** Pauline Evans *(Home Manager)*, Sandeep Gupta *(Proprietor)*
**Finance:** Pauline Evans *(Home Manager)*
**Marketing:** Pauline Evans *(Home Manager)*
**Health & Safety:** Pauline Evans *(Home Manager)*
**Facilities:** Pauline Evans *(Home Manager)*
**US SIC:** 8051 **UK SIC:** 95100
**Employees:** 46

DUNS 21-705-8738
## Southern Housing Group Ltd
Fleet House, 59-61 Clerkenwell Road, London EC1M 5LA
**Tel:** 084 5612 0021
**Web:** www.shgroup.org.uk
**Reg No:** 0031055IP **Estd:** 2002 Friendly Society
**Line of Business:** Housing associations societies trusts & co-operatives
**Principals:** A Mcintyre *(Chairman)*, A Mcintyre *(Chairman)*, D Kelly, T Bourne, P Rao, M Groves, Ms L Oyedele, J Hitch
**Responsibilities**
**Senior:** John Castleberg *(Director)*, Jonathan Cavanagh *(Manager)*, Tom Dacey *(CEO, Managing Director)*, Peter Goodacre *(Director)*, Linne Griffin *(Executive)*, Jane Hives *(Director)*, Duncan Howard *(Regional Director - London)*, Georgia Jerram *(Head Of Communications)*, Dionne Johnson *(Executive)*, Suzanne Kay *(Manager)*, Elisa Vaughan *(Manager)*
**Finance:** Phillippa Caine *(Finance Director)*
**Marketing:** Georgia Jerram *(Head Of Communications)*
**HR:** Brian Benneyworth *(HR Manager)*
**Facilities:** Paul Wenham *(Director, Property Services an)*
**Operations:** Marisa Ling *(Regional Operations Manager)*, James Mark *(Operations Project Manager)*, Dale Meredith *(Development Director)*
**Engineering:** Kevan Allaway *(Manager)*
**Branches:** Southern Housing Group Limited, 39 High Street, Reading, Berkshire RG7 5AH
**US SIC:** 8321, 6531
**UK SIC:** 96111, 83400
**Bankers:** National Westminster Bank Plc (56-00-20)

| | 31-03-12 | 31-03-11 | 31-03-10 |
|---|---|---|---|
| TO | 135,138,000 | 136,723,000 | 133,731,000 |
| P/L | 18,178,000 | 21,116,000 | 8,246,000 |
| NW | 277,097,000 | 261,651,000 | 236,338,000 |
| WC | 164,997,000 | 114,620,000 | 7,484,000 |
| Emp. | 766 | 795 | 811 |

DUNS 28-967-1174
## Southern Monitoring Services Ltd
212 218 London Road, Waterlooville, Hampshire PO7 7AJ
**Tel:** 08448712223 **Fax:** 0870-243-3330
**Web:** www.smon.co.uk
**Reg No:** 1711464 **Estd:** 1983 Private Limited Company
**Line of Business:** Security activities
**Issued Capital:** £111
**Principals:** B M Christie *(Chairman and Managing)*, S B Kimber *(Managing)*, Mrs G Gardner, A P Christie
**Co. Secretary:** Ms Janet Christie
**Responsibilities**
**IT:** Glen Morgan *(Technical Support Manager)*
**Facilities:** Glen Morgan *(Technical Support Manager)*
**US SIC:** 7393 **UK SIC:** 83954

**Auditors:** Wheatley Pearce
**Bankers:** HSBC Bank plc (40-18-15)

| | 30-09-13 | 30-09-12 | 30-09-11 |
|---|---|---|---|
| TO | 8,954,468 | 9,157,994 | 8,976,534 |
| P/L | 289,104 | 517,327 | 561,947 |
| NW | 436,595 | 839,711 | 457,406 |
| WC | (712,799) | (451,469) | (877,224) |
| Emp. | 103 | 98 | 95 |

DUNS 21-724-4771
## The Southern Motor Group Ltd
22 Lansdowne Road, Croydon, Surrey CR0 2BD
**Tel:** 02086800300 **Fax:** 02086497577
**Web:** www.smgvans.co.uk
**Reg No:** 0905101 **VAT No:** 676067604
**Estd:** 1984 Private Limited Company
**Line of Business:** Van hire
**Trading Style:** M V Trucks Kent, Hitgift Hire, S M G Chessington, M V T Gatwick
**Issued Capital:** £24,000
**Principals:** D J Marsh *(Managing)*, M C Gough, P J Price
**Co. Secretary:** Stephen Price
**Responsibilities**
**Senior:** Shirley Price *(Manager)*
**IT:** Michael Creech *(IT Manager)*
**Branches:** The Southern Motor Group Ltd, Peartree Hill, Brenhurst Rd, Salfords, Redhill, Surrey RH1 5EG
**US SIC:** 7513, 7512
**UK SIC:** 84802, 84801
**Auditors:** Menzies LLP
**Bankers:** The Royal Bank Of Scotland Plc (16-00-53)

| | 31-12-13 | 31-12-12 | 31-12-11 |
|---|---|---|---|
| TO | 52,791,265 | 50,126,121 | 47,020,056 |
| P/L | 236,865 | 203,933 | 291,315 |
| NW | 3,966,069 | 3,725,870 | 3,589,373 |
| WC | (1,029,808) | (1,028,457) | (532,697) |
| Emp. | 150 | 162 | 171 |

DUNS 21-117-7331
## Southern Railway Ltd
**(Subsidiary of:** The Go-Ahead Group Plc)
3rd Floor, Newcastle-Upon-Tyne, Tyne and Wear NE1 6EE
**Tel:** 02089298600
**Web:** www.southernrailway.com
**Reg No:** 6574965 **Estd:** 2008 Private Limited Company
**Line of Business:** Operators of railway
**Issued Capital:** £10,000,000
**Directors:** N L Vandevyver, C S Horton, A D Scorey, Mrs W M Allan, M R Rimmer, D A Brown, A J Gordon, K Down
**Co. Secretary:** Ms Carolyn Ferguson
**Responsibilities**
**Senior:** Alex Foulds *(Operations Director)*
**Health & Safety:** Steve Enright *(Health & Safety Officer)*
**Facilities:** Paul Trevett *(Facilities Manager)*
**Operations:** Alex Foulds *(Operations Director)*
**US SIC:** 4011 **UK SIC:** 71000
**Auditors:** Ernst & Young LLP
**Bankers:** The Royal Bank Of Scotland Plc (16-00-38)

| | 29-06-13 | 30-06-12 | 02-06-11 |
|---|---|---|---|
| TO | 704,709,000 | 665,079,000 | 610,993,000 |
| P/L | 22,234,000 | 18,828,000 | 22,176,000 |
| NW | 24,543,000 | 19,116,000 | 18,599,000 |
| WC | 48,593,000 | 48,960,000 | 39,667,000 |
| Emp. | 4,016 | 4,067 | 4,039 |

DUNS 21-034-7078
## Southern Regional College
Patrick Street, Newry, Co Down BT35 8DN
**Tel:** 02830261071
**Web:** www.src.ac.uk
**Estd:** 1902
**Line of Business:** Education services
**Principals:** Ms H Shields *(Financial)*, J Edwards, G Devlin, F Caherty, D Vint, J O'Hagan, J Mckinney, Ms M Connolly
**Responsibilities**
**Senior:** Brian Doran *(Chief Executive Officer)*, Jasper McKinney *(Director)*
**US SIC:** 8221 **UK SIC:** 93100
**Employees:** 1,100

DUNS 21-595-9239
## Southern Regional College
Londsdale Street, Armagh, Co Armagh BT61 7HN
**Tel:** 02837522205
**Web:** www.src.ac.uk
**Estd:** 1906
**Line of Business:** Further education schools and colleges
**Trading Style:** Southern Regional College
**Proprietor:** Miss M Miller
**Responsibilities**
**Senior:** Steven Balzell *(PC Manager)*
**HR:** Jim Cunningham *(Training Director)*
**US SIC:** 8221 **UK SIC:** 93100
**Employees:** 1,100

DUNS 29-648-3837
## Southern Salads Ltd
1-6 Cannon Lane, Tonbridge, Kent TN9 1PP
**Tel:** 01732-362444
**Web:** www.southernsalads.com
**Reg No:** 1974678 **Estd:** 1985 Private Limited Company
**Line of Business:** Pizza suppliers
**Issued Capital:** £100
**Managing Director:** R Boakes
**Co. Secretary:** Andrew Boakes
**Responsibilities**
**Sales:** Lorna Proops *(Business Development Manager)*
**US SIC:** 5812 **UK SIC:** 66110
**Auditors:** Landau Morley LLP
**Bankers:** Barclays Bank Plc (20-65-63)

| | 31-03-14 | 31-03-13 | 31-03-12 |
|---|---|---|---|
| TO | 28,216,814 | 27,319,859 | 31,190,609 |
| P/L | 613,909 | (120,359) | (412,040) |
| NW | 2,176,198 | 1,616,627 | 1,736,986 |
| WC | (2,943,964) | (3,471,147) | (3,533,241) |
| Emp. | 199 | 180 | 170 |

DUNS 21-093-7397
## Southern Syringe Services Ltd
**(Subsidiary of:** Bunzl Plc)
George House, Unit 6, Delta Park Industrial Estate, Millmarsh Lane, Enfield, Middlesex EN3 7QJ
**Tel:** 02084437800 **Fax:** 02084437843
**Web:** www.bunzlhealthcare.co.uk
**Reg No:** 0000000 **Estd:** 1961 Private Limited Company
**Line of Business:** Other wholesale
**Trading Style:** 3s Healthcare
**Issued Capital:** £12,500
**Directors:** A J Ball, B M May
**Co. Secretary:** Paul Hussey
**Responsibilities**
**HR:** Paula Eavis *(Human Resources Manager)*
**Branches:** Southern Syringe Services Ltd, Unit K2 Lynwell Road, Manchester M30 9AL
**US SIC:** 5199 **UK SIC:** 61900
**Bankers:** Lloyds TSB Bank plc (30-12-34)

| | 31-12-14 | 31-12-13 | 31-12-12 |
|---|---|---|---|
| TA | 12,500 | 12,500 | 12,500 |
| NW | 12,500 | 12,500 | 12,500 |

DUNS 39-742-8376
## Southern Testing Laboratories Ltd
**(Subsidiary of:** Stl (Holdings) Ltd)
Keeble House, Stuart Way, East Grinstead, West Sussex RH19 4QA
**Tel:** 01604500020 **Fax:** 01342-410321
**Web:** www.southerntesting.co.uk
**Reg No:** 2183217 **Estd:** 1967 Private Limited Company
**Line of Business:** Architectural and engineering activities and related technical consultancy
**Trading Style:** Southern Testing
**Issued Capital:** £400,000
**Principals:** J M Hickmott *(Managing)*, A J Timms, Dr L D Mockett, M W Stevenson, R C Smith, D T Vooght, J J Kelly
**Co. Secretary:** Anthony Gurney
**Responsibilities**
**IT:** Chris Lennard *(Head of IT)*
**HR:** Tim Heywood *(Health & Safety Manager)*
**Operations:** Neil Burrows *(Director of Operations)*
**Branches:** Southern Testing Laboratories Ltd, Unit 20A Durkins Road, East Grinstead, West Sussex RH19 2RW
**US SIC:** 8911, 7397
**UK SIC:** 83701, 83702
**Auditors:** Place Campbell
**Bankers:** Barclays Bank Plc (20-23-97)

| | 31-03-14 | 31-03-13 | 31-03-12 |
|---|---|---|---|
| TA | 1,789,746 | 1,784,381 | 1,566,372 |
| NW | 895,726 | 801,254 | 800,526 |
| WC | 566,753 | 397,629 | 446,716 |

DUNS 51-690-6369
## Southern Timber Frame
Unit 1-4 Longdown Estate Yard, Southampton, Hampshire SO40 4UH
**Tel:** 023-8029-3062
**Web:** www.southerntimberframe.com
**VAT No:** 189289986 **Estd:** 1995 Partnership
**Line of Business:** Timber constructed buildings
**Partners:** F Burgess, Mrs M Burgess
**Responsibilities**
**Senior:** Sean Burgess *(Contracts Manager and Partner)*, Eric Dorrell *(Manager)*
**Finance:** Sean Burgess *(Contracts Manager and Partner)*
**US SIC:** 1541 **UK SIC:** 50100
**Bankers:** National Westminster Bank Plc (55-70-05)
**Employees:** 50

DUNS 22-526-4449 **Imp-Exp**
## Southern Tyre Co Ltd
Unit 7, Hackhurst Lane, Hailsham, East Sussex BN27 4BW
**Tel:** 01323-449-889
**Web:** www.setyres.co.uk
**Reg No:** 0615334 **VAT No:** 461752543
**Estd:** 1999 Private Limited Company
**Line of Business:** Tyre dealers
**Trading Style:** Setyres
**Issued Capital:** £495,000
**Principals:** J E Sattin *(Managing)*, J E Sattin, S A Sattin, Ms K A Sattin, A M Sattin
**Co. Secretary:** Joseph Sattin
**Responsibilities**
**Senior:** Chris Ashdown *(Branch Manager)*, John Ashdown *(Manager)*
**US SIC:** 5531 **UK SIC:** 65100
**Auditors:** Friend-James Ltd
**Bankers:** National Westminster Bank Plc (01-01-23)

| | 31-03-14 | 31-03-13 | 31-03-12 |
|---|---|---|---|
| TO | 56,756,000 | 58,282,000 | 60,333,000 |
| P/L | 1,983,000 | 1,828,000 | 1,502,000 |
| NW | 13,162,000 | 11,822,000 | 10,645,000 |
| WC | 3,313,000 | 2,814,000 | 2,377,000 |
| Emp. | 248 | 249 | 231 |

DUNS 29-192-4470
## Southern United Ltd
**(Subsidiary of:** A D Wright Ltd)
The Old Brewery, Skipton, North Yorkshire BD23 5PS
**Tel:** 01273-418636
**Web:** www.sunited.co.uk
**Reg No:** 0477349 **Estd:** 1935 Private Limited Company
**Line of Business:** Other manufacturing not elsewhere classified
**Issued Capital:** £2,000
**Director:** A D Wright
**Responsibilities**
**Senior:** Ian Malby *(Manager)*
**US SIC:** 3999 **UK SIC:** 49590
**Auditors:** R.C.A. Andrews
**Bankers:** National Westminster Bank Plc (60-03-33)

| | 31-03-14 | 31-12-12 | 31-03-11 |
|---|---|---|---|
| TA | 419,084 | 328,540 | 347,984 |
| NW | 304,917 | 236,755 | 234,946 |
| WC | 299,825 | 220,219 | 204,746 |

DUNS 21-700-0975
## The Southern Vectis Omnibus Company Ltd
**(Subsidiary of:** The Go-Ahead Group Plc)
Nelson Road, Newport, Isle of Wight PO30 1RD
**Tel:** 01983827000 **Fax:** 01983-568234
**Web:** www.southernvectis.com
**Reg No:** 0241973 **Estd:** 1986 Private Limited Company
**Line of Business:** Other scheduled passenger land transport not elsewhere classified
**Issued Capital:** £515,000
**Directors:** K Down, N J Woods, D A Brown, E Wills, S J Hamilton, A R Wickham
**Co. Secretary:** Ms Carolyn Ferguson
**Responsibilities**
**Senior:** Marc Morgan-Huws *(Divisional Director)*
**Branches:** The Southern Vectis Omnibus Company Ltd, Quay Street, Yarmouth, Isle Of Wight PO41 0PB
**US SIC:** 4119 **UK SIC:** 72200
**Bankers:** National Westminster Bank Plc (54-10-34)

| | 29-06-13 | 30-06-12 | 02-06-11 |
|---|---|---|---|
| TA | 896,000 | 896,000 | 896,000 |
| NW | 896,000 | 896,000 | 896,000 |

DUNS 23-616-7748 **Imp**
## Southern Water Services Ltd
**(Subsidiary of:** Slag Systems (Glasgow) Ltd)
Southern House, Yeoman Road, Worthing, West Sussex BN13 3NX
**Tel:** 08452720845 **Fax:** 01903693068
**Web:** www.southernwater.co.uk
**Reg No:** 2366670 **VAT No:** 543900063
**Estd:** 1989 Private Limited Company
**Line of Business:** Water companies
**Trading Style:** Southern Water Services
**Issued Capital:** £317,500
**Principals:** R A Jennings *(Chairman)*, P J Moy, D Golden, B L Somes, W Tame, M Carmedy, A J Truscott, M A Walters
**Co. Secretary:** Kevin Hall
**Responsibilities**
**Senior:** Peter Antolik *(Director)*, Susan Gibbs *(Facilities Manager)*, Geoff Loader *(Director of Communications)*
**Marketing:** Geoff Loader *(Director of Communications)*
**IT:** Geoff Loader *(Director of Communications)*
**HR:** Mandy Dowden *(Development Manager)*

**Health & Safety:** Susan Gibbs (*Facilities Manager*)
**Facilities:** Susan Gibbs (*Facilities Manager*)
**Purchasing:** Graham Aldred (*Purchasing Manager*)
**Branches:** Southern Water Services Ltd, Southern House, Yeoman Road, Worthing, West Sussex BN13 3NX
**US SIC:** 4941, 4952, 7397
**UK SIC:** 17000, 92120, 83702
**Auditors:** PricewaterhouseCoopers LLP
**Bankers:** National Westminster Bank Plc (60-24-31)

Following financial data are in thousands

|      | 31-03-14 | 31-03-13 | 31-03-12 |
|------|----------|----------|----------|
| TO   | 806,200  | 778,700  | 716,200  |
| P/L  | 139,500  | 179,100  | 84,900   |
| NW   | 1,085,000| 960,700  | 854,600  |
| WC   | 847,200  | 864,400  | 802,500  |
| Emp. | 2,026    | 1,938    | 1,742    |

DUNS 21-552-3791
## Southerness Golf Club
Southerness, Kirkbean, Dumfries, Dumfriesshire DG2 8AZ
**Tel:** 01387271050
**Web:** www.parkdeanholidays.com
**Estd:** 1959
**Line of Business:** Holiday parks and camps
**Principals:** J Handley, J Handley
**Co. Secretary:** Ian Robbin
**Responsibilities**
**Senior:** Kaz Mortimer (*Manager*)
**US SIC:** 7021 **UK SIC:** 66500
**Employees:** 50

DUNS 29-380-2203     Exp
## Southernprint Ltd
(**Subsidiary of:** Walstead Investments Ltd)
Unit 17-21, Factory Road Upton Industrial Estate, Poole, Dorset BH16 5SN
**Tel:** 01202-628300 **Fax:** 01202-632403
**Web:** www.wyndeham.co.uk
**Reg No:** 1085192 **VAT No:** 504339860
**Estd:** 1972 Private Limited Company
**Line of Business:** Printing not elsewhere classified
**Issued Capital:** £6,000,000
**Directors:** R C Fookes, P G Utting, R E Kingston, Mrs D Read
**Co. Secretary:** Mrs Zoe Repman
**Responsibilities**
**HR:** Shauna Reynolds (*Human Resources Manager*)
**Operations:** David Scovell (*Planning & Production Manager*)
**US SIC:** 2752 **UK SIC:** 47544
**Auditors:** Ernst & Young LLP
**Bankers:** Lloyds TSB Bank plc (30-91-08)

|      | 31-12-13  | 31-12-12  | 31-12-11  |
|------|-----------|-----------|-----------|
| TO   | 21,961,000| 20,711,000| 20,354,000|
| P/L  | 348,000   | 312,000   | (2,502,000)|
| NW   | (838,000) | (1,186,000)| (1,498,000)|
| WC   | (5,373,000)| (4,884,000)| (3,734,000)|
| Emp. | 191       | 166       | 186       |

DUNS 21-782-2374
## Southfield Special School
Gipsy Lane, Wokingham, Berkshire RG40 2HR
**Tel:** 01189771293
**Web:** www.southfield.wokingham.sch.uk
**Estd:** 2011 Proprietorship
**Line of Business:** Schools (local authority)
**Proprietor:** M Pedley
**Responsibilities**
**Senior:** Dominic Geraghty (*Head Teacher*)
**US SIC:** 8299 **UK SIC:** 93300
**Employees:** 50

DUNS 21-009-2873
## Southgates Ltd
278 Weyhill Road, Andover, Hampshire SP10 3LS
**Web:** www.southgategroup.co.uk
**Reg No:** 6331214 **Estd:** 2007 Private Limited Company
**Line of Business:** Business services
**Issued Capital:** £100
**Director:** A Rookes
**Co. Secretary:** Ms Maria Rookes
**US SIC:** 7399, 5521
**UK SIC:** 83954, 65100

|    | 31-05-14 | 31-05-13 | 31-05-12 |
|----|----------|----------|----------|
| TA | 100      | 100      | 100      |
| NW | 100      | 100      | 100      |

DUNS 64-251-9375
## Southlands Nursing Home
13 Wetherby Road, Leeds, West Yorkshire LS8 2JU
**Tel:** 01132-655876
**Web:** www.westwardcare.co.uk
**Estd:** 1987 Partnership
**Line of Business:** Nursing homes
**Partners:** Mrs J A Adamson, N Adamson

**Responsibilities**
**Senior:** Angela Randell (*Manager*)
**US SIC:** 8051 **UK SIC:** 95100
**Employees:** 50

DUNS 21-386-8222
## Southmead Nursing Home
Porthcawl Road, South Cornelly, Bridgend, Mid Glamorgan CF33 4RE
**Web:** www.nbt.nhs.uk
**Estd:** 1992 Partnership
**Line of Business:** Medical nursing home activities
**Trading Style:** Sevencross Health Care
**Partners:** Mrs D Walls, D Tibbit
**Responsibilities**
**Senior:** Deborah South (*Manager*)
**Sales:** Sasha Karakusevic (*Director of Strategy and Trans*)
**US SIC:** 8051 **UK SIC:** 95100
**Employees:** 62

DUNS 21-996-2151
## The Southover Partnership Ltd
322 Ballards Lane, London N12 0EY
**Tel:** 020-8446-0300 **Fax:** 020-8446-0430
**Web:** www.southoverpartnership.com
**Reg No:** 6177629 **Estd:** 2001 Private Limited Company
**Line of Business:** Education services
**Issued Capital:** £1
**Director:** Mrs C Frankl
**Co. Secretary:** Maurice Balfe
**US SIC:** 8299 **UK SIC:** 93300

|    | 31-08-13 | 31-05-12 | 31-08-11 |
|----|----------|----------|----------|
| TA | 584,742  | 661,174  | 594,957  |
| NW | 320,893  | 230,262  | 158,715  |
| WC | 192,349  | 246,299  | 203,749  |

DUNS 50-435-3830
## Southpaw Communications Ltd
(**Subsidiary of:** Hakuhodo Dy Holdings Incorporated)
Multimedia House, Hill Street, Tunbridge Wells, Kent TN1 2BY
**Tel:** 01892-517-777
**Web:** www.nexush.com
**Reg No:** 2423405 **Estd:** 1989 Private Limited Company
**Line of Business:** Advertising
**Export Sales:** £1,171,000
**Trading Style:** Media by Desgin
**Issued Capital:** £184,000
**Directors:** S Ito, N Mizuno, K Kitagawa, D F Ham, Y R Fukumoto, T G Poynter
**Co. Secretary:** David Ham
**US SIC:** 7311 **UK SIC:** 83800
**Auditors:** KPMG LLP
**Bankers:** Lloyds TSB Bank plc (30-98-77)

|      | 31-12-13  | 31-12-12  | 31-12-11  |
|------|-----------|-----------|-----------|
| TO   | 6,290,000 | 8,060,000 | 12,784,000|
| P/L  | (997,000) | (447,000) | 208,000   |
| NW   | 368,000   | 1,743,000 | 2,137,000 |
| WC   | (686,000) | 44,000    | 1,269,000 |
| Emp. | 51        | 54        | 64        |

DUNS 54-864-0051
## Southport & Formby Community Health
Services Nhs Trust, Hesketh Centre, Albert Road, Southport, Merseyside PR9 0LT
**Tel:** 01704535093
**Line of Business:** Healthcare companies
**Director:** F Robertson
**Branches:** Southport & Formby Community Health, Town Lane, Southport, Merseyside PR8 6PN
**US SIC:** 8091 **UK SIC:** 95200
**Employees:** 200

DUNS 23-293-3200
## Southport College
Mornington Road, Southport, Merseyside PR9 0TT
**Web:** www.southport-college.ac.uk
**VAT No:** 582289213 **Estd:** 2010
**Line of Business:** Further education schools and colleges
**Principals:** B Mitchell, J Pickering, R Thorpe, Dr D Mark, Ms W Moorcroft (*Manager*)
**Co. Secretary:** Miss Jannet Leachman
**Responsibilities**
**Senior:** Gill Kitchen (*Chairman*), Marion Mak (*Executive*)
**Finance:** Andrew Winrow (*Head of Finance*)
**Marketing:** David Rad (*Marketing Manager*), Elizabeth Rushton (*Marketing Manager*)
**IT:** Christine Bampton (*IT Manager*), Polly Robinson (*Support Coordinator*)
**HR:** Jill Kelly (*Human Resources Manager*)
**Health & Safety:** Eric Todd (*Premises Manager*)
**Facilities:** Eric Todd (*Premises Manager*)
**Purchasing:** Andrew Winrow (*Head of Finance*)
**Branches:** Southport College, Ormonde Dr, Liverpool, Merseyside L31 7AW

**US SIC:** 8221 **UK SIC:** 93100
**Bankers:** The Royal Bank Of Scotland Plc (16-32-10)
**Employees:** 650

DUNS 23-677-2559
## Southport Promenade Hotels Ltd
The Promenade, Southport, Merseyside PR8 1RB
**Tel:** 01704-533771
**Web:** www.mellorscatering.co.uk
**Reg No:** 3671820 **Estd:** 1998 Private Limited Company
**Line of Business:** Hotels
**Trading Style:** Royal Clifton Hotel
**Issued Capital:** £2
**Directors:** K Timmerman, M J Timmerman
**Co. Secretary:** Mark Timmerman
**Responsibilities**
**Senior:** Pamela Wall (*Manager*)
**US SIC:** 7011 **UK SIC:** 66500
**Auditors:** Tenon Audit Ltd
**Bankers:** The Royal Bank Of Scotland Plc (16-32-10)

|      | 30-04-14  | 30-04-13  | 30-04-12  |
|------|-----------|-----------|-----------|
| TO   | 2,904,598 | 2,859,373 | 2,580,581 |
| P/L  | 120,550   | 40,527    | 53,503    |
| NW   | 1,082,836 | 978,618   | 954,394   |
| WC   | (720,044) | (715,112) | (935,407) |
| Emp. | 99        | 101       | 97        |

DUNS 23-080-1565
## Southside Partnership
31-33 Lumiere Court, 209 Balham High Road, London SW17 7BQ
**Tel:** 020 8772 6222 **Fax:** 02087726222
**Web:** www.certitude.org.uk
**Reg No:** 2599171 **Estd:** 1991 Private Company Limited By Guarantee
**Line of Business:** Charities and charitable organisations
**Trading Style:** Southside Partnership
**Directors:** S L Plant, Ms C ( James, S G Maingot, G A Venus, Ms S Wickerson
**Co. Secretary:** Aisling Duffy
**Responsibilities**
**Senior:** Patricia Connell Julien (*Manager*), Yasmin Miller (*Manager*), Caroline Pillay (*Manager*)
**Sales:** Marianne Selby-Boothroyd (*Director of Development*)
**HR:** Mark Ospedale (*Human Resources Director*), Percilla Robinson (*Human Resources Manager*)
**Facilities:** Sam Mason (*Office & Facilities Manager*)
**Branches:** Southside Partnership, Cavendish House, 25-27 Dulwich Road, London SE24 0NJ
**US SIC:** 8811 **UK SIC:** 99000
**Auditors:** Beever & Struthers
**Bankers:** Barclays Bank Plc (20-21-78)

|      | 31-03-14  | 31-03-13  | 31-03-12  |
|------|-----------|-----------|-----------|
| TO   | 10,648,000| 10,834,226| 10,793,279|
| P/L  | 231,000   | 287,797   | 106,941   |
| NW   | 5,820,000 | 4,842,269 | 4,554,472 |
| WC   | 1,877,000 | 2,603,569 | 2,276,216 |
| Emp. | 369       | 352       | 292       |

DUNS 23-742-0062
## Southview Leisure Park
Burgh Road, Skegness, Lincolnshire PE25 2LA
**Tel:** 01754896000
**Web:** www.park-resorts.com
**Estd:** 1979 Partnership
**Line of Business:** Leisure centres
**Trading Style:** Southview Leisure Park
**Partners:** C J Vernon, D J Vernon, Mrs P C Vernon, J M Vernon
**Responsibilities**
**Senior:** Bob Walker (*Hotel Manager*)
**Finance:** Lucille Rust (*Financial Controller*)
**Marketing:** Bob Walker (*Hotel Manager*)
**US SIC:** 7999 **UK SIC:** 97913
**Employees:** 70

DUNS 77-968-1167
## Southview Leisure Park Ltd
(**Subsidiary of:** Regent Topco Ltd)
3 Bunhill Row, London EC1Y 8YZ
**Tel:** 08433088765
**Web:** www.southviewparkhotel.co.uk
**Reg No:** 5936854 **Estd:** 2006 Private Limited Company
**Line of Business:** Holiday centres and holiday villages
**Issued Capital:** £3
**Directors:** M Clark, D Boden, A Castledine, N D Brewster
**Co. Secretary:** T&H Secretarial Services (Park R
**US SIC:** 7032 **UK SIC:** 66702

|      | 31-03-14    | 31-03-13    | 30-03-11    |
|------|-------------|-------------|-------------|
| TO   | 8,041,927   | 9,877,469   | 5,903,305   |
| P/L  | 533,254     | (424,591)   | 195,486     |
| NW   | (17,779,693)| (18,312,571)| (17,887,980)|
| WC   | (39,956,479)| (41,090,368)| (40,972,652)|
| Emp. | 135         | 107         | 122         |

DUNS 21-715-9982
## Southview Park Hotel
Burgh Road, Skegness, Lincolnshire PE25 2LA
**Tel:** 01754896060
**Web:** www.southviewparkhotel.co.uk
**Estd:** 2004 Proprietorship
**Line of Business:** Hotels
**Proprietor:** J M Vernon
**US SIC:** 7011 **UK SIC:** 66500
**Employees:** 48

DUNS 50-325-3536
## Southwark Disablement Association
2 Bradenham Close, London SE17 2QB
**Tel:** 020-7701-1391
**Web:** www.sda.dircon.co.uk
**Reg No:** 2350180 **Estd:** 1988 Private Company Limited By Guarantee
**Line of Business:** Social work activities without accommodation
**Trading Style:** S D A
**Principals:** D K Stock (*Managing*), Mrs D L Mace, Mrs A M Carden, Miss J V Jackson, Ms M E Grossett, P Horan, Miss M P Brock, Ms G P Nicholson
**Co. Secretary:** David Stock
**Responsibilities**
**Senior:** Alan Cain (*Manager*), Mark Duke (*Director*), Eric Segoh (*Director*)
**US SIC:** 8321 **UK SIC:** 96111
**Auditors:** Godwin Nede & Co
**Bankers:** Barclays Bank Plc (20-80-57)

|      | 31-03-14 | 31-03-13 | 31-03-12 |
|------|----------|----------|----------|
| TO   | 1,000,341| 1,023,847| 1,142,077|
| P/L  | (60,669) | 9,683    | 81,831   |
| NW   | 178,800  | 239,469  | 229,786  |
| WC   | 178,800  | 239,469  | 229,786  |
| Emp. | 68       | 69       | 68       |

DUNS 21-583-9137
## Southwark Primary Care Trust
Rehabilitation Centre, Bowley Close, London SE19 1SZ
**Tel:** 02030497700
**Estd:** 2009 Proprietorship
**Line of Business:** Rehabilitation centres
**Proprietor:** Mrs A Mcrae
**US SIC:** 8062 **UK SIC:** 95100
**Employees:** 80

DUNS 73-778-1141
## Southwater Event Group Ltd
Tic St Quentin Gate, Telford, Shropshire TF3 4JH
**Tel:** 01952425000
**Web:** www.southwatereventgroup.com
**Reg No:** 5034924 **Estd:** 2004 Private Limited Company
**Line of Business:** Management activities of holding companies
**Issued Capital:** £14,675,800
**Director:** T E Gray
**Co. Secretary:** Mark Lloyd
**US SIC:** 6711 **UK SIC:** 83962
**Bankers:** HSBC Bank plc (40-45-19)

|      | 31-03-14   | 31-03-13   | 31-03-12   |
|------|------------|------------|------------|
| TO   | 14,571,524 | 14,256,945 | 13,069,108 |
| P/L  | 1,772,435  | 1,441,963  | 1,645,159  |
| NW   | 27,388,246 | 26,113,041 | 25,102,103 |
| WC   | (913,818)  | (1,008,192)| (1,813,400)|
| Emp. | 455        | 429        | 409        |

DUNS 21-557-9427
## Southway Housing Trust (Manchester) Ltd
Aspen House, Manchester M20 2SN
**Tel:** 01614-484200
**Web:** www.southwayhousing.co.uk
**Reg No:** 0030348IP **Estd:** 2007
**Line of Business:** Housing associations societies trusts & co-operatives
**Responsibilities**
**Senior:** Natalie Lewis (*Central Services Manager*)
**US SIC:** 8321 **UK SIC:** 96111
**Auditors:** Grant Thornton UK LLP

|      | 31-03-12   | 31-03-11    | 31-03-10    |
|------|------------|-------------|-------------|
| TO   | 23,702,000 | 25,636,000  | 28,911,000  |
| P/L  | 3,902,000  | (11,902,000)| (10,533,000)|
| NW   | 28,251,000 | (27,965,000)| (34,793,000)|
| WC   | 14,021,000 | 8,255,000   | 1,055,000   |
| Emp. | 168        | 154         | 154         |

DUNS 21-879-4031
## Southway Primary School
South Way, Bognor Regis, West Sussex PO21 5EZ
**Tel:** 01243810200
**Web:** www.southwayprimary.co.uk
**Estd:** 1957
**Line of Business:** Schools (local authority)
**Responsibilities**
**Senior:** Michael Westgarth (*Head Teacher*), Matthew Westgarth (*Head Teacher*)
**US SIC:** 8211 **UK SIC:** 93200
**Employees:** 100

DUNS 21-589-5068
## Soutlands Resource Centre
Church Road, Port St Mary, Douglas, Isle of Man IM9 5NL
**Tel:** 01624831831
**Estd:** 2011 Proprietorship
**Line of Business:** Non-charitable social work activities with accommodation
**Proprietor:** Mrs R Dooley
**Responsibilities**
**Senior:** Paula Beattie *(Manager)*, Helen Booth *(Manager)*
**US SIC:** 8321 **UK SIC:** 96111
**Employees:** 70

DUNS 21-657-9172
## Soutwoods Nursing Home
28 Thirsk Road, Northallerton, North Yorkshire DL6 1PH
**Tel:** 01609-780362
**Web:** www.southwoodatnorwell.com
**Estd:** 2003 Proprietorship
**Line of Business:** Medical nursing home activities
**Proprietor:** S Dhanji
**Responsibilities**
**Senior:** Theresa Watkins *(Home Manager)*
**US SIC:** 8051 **UK SIC:** 95100
**Employees:** 50

DUNS 23-649-9351
## Sova
1st Floor Cil Offices, London WO1D 0DO
**Tel:** 02078336733
**Web:** www.sova.org.uk
**Reg No:** 3645143 **Estd:** 1998 Private Company Limited By Guarantee
**Line of Business:** Social work activities without accommodation
**Directors:** D J Gregson, R Perkin, Ms H M Jackson
**Responsibilities**
**Senior:** Helen Cantrell *(Chief Executive)*, Paul Fulton *(Manager)*, Randeep Kular *(Manager)*, Martine Laffan *(Manager)*, Sharon Lowrie *(Financial Director)*, Sarah Mallender *(Interim Chief Executive)*, Lorna Ryan *(Manager)*, Tony Savage *(Computer Manager)*
**Finance:** Sharon Lowrie *(Financial Director)*
**IT:** Tony Savage *(Computer Manager)*
**HR:** Junr Graham *(Head of Human Resources)*
**Branches:** Sova, 1 Craven Pk, London NW10 8SX
**US SIC:** 7399 **UK SIC:** 83954
**Auditors:** Blinkhorns
**Bankers:** Lloyds TSB Bank plc (30-16-85)

| | 31-03-14 | 31-03-13 | 31-03-12 |
|---|---|---|---|
| TO | 4,099,825 | 4,991,034 | 8,116,117 |
| P/L | 30,438 | (477,636) | 24,825 |
| NW | 62,833 | 32,395 | 537,371 |
| WC | 56,174 | 6,384 | 534,898 |
| Emp. | 120 | N/A | 218 |

DUNS 77-527-8104
## Sovereign Business Integration Group Plc
1a Chalk Lane, Cockfosters, Barnet, Hertfordshire EN4 9JQ
**Web:** www.sovereign-plc.co.uk
**Reg No:** 2991219 **Estd:** 1994 Public Limited Company
**Line of Business:** Computer support & services
**Export Sales:** £39,055
**Trading Style:** Sovereign Business Integration Group Plc
**Issued Capital:** £463,158
**Directors:** A G Riddick, K J Doran, D I Stratton, M P Rutherford, R D Barker, Ms J C Sedley-Burke, M H Williams
**Co. Secretary:** Ms Heather Barker
**Responsibilities**
**Senior:** Joanna Burke *(Manager)*, Gary O'Sullivan *(Manager)*
**Finance:** Andy Cristin *(Financial Commercial Director)*
**Marketing:** Andy Cristin *(Financial Commercial Director)*
**US SIC:** 7379, 7374
**UK SIC:** 83940
**Auditors:** Baker Tilly UK Audit LLP
**Bankers:** Allied Irish Bank (gb) (23-84-85)

| | 31-03-14 | 31-03-13 | 31-03-12 |
|---|---|---|---|
| TO | 8,688,253 | 8,600,939 | 8,074,560 |
| P/L | (418,550) | (473,065) | (181,136) |
| NW | 3,794,001 | 4,210,634 | 4,674,131 |
| WC | 386,523 | 810,668 | 1,714,851 |
| Emp. | 66 | 72 | 62 |

DUNS 21-660-1202
## Sovereign Care Ltd
Filsam Lodge Nursing Home, 137 Bar 141 South Road, Hailsham, East Sussex BN27 3NN
**Tel:** 01323844008
**Web:** www.southgategroup.co.uk
**Reg No:** 7160239 **Estd:** 2010 Private Limited Company
**Line of Business:** Other human health activities
**Issued Capital:** £100
**Directors:** Mrs R Ravichandran, T Ravichandran
**US SIC:** 8091, 8321
**UK SIC:** 95200, 96111

| | 31-03-14 | 31-03-13 | 31-03-12 |
|---|---|---|---|
| TO | 2,519,255 | 2,471,610 | N/A |
| P/L | (48,446) | 54,558 | N/A |
| NW | (1,526,106) | (1,682,954) | (1,920,547) |
| WC | (4,238,153) | (4,312,495) | (391,783) |
| Emp. | 113 | 113 | N/A |

DUNS 55-052-4045
## Sovereign Centre
Royal Parade, Eastbourne, East Sussex BN22 7LQ
**Tel:** 01323738822
**Web:** www.serco.com
**Estd:** 1977 Proprietorship
**Line of Business:** Leisure centres
**Proprietor:** P Matthews
**Responsibilities**
**Senior:** Jamie Bryant *(CEO, Managing Director)*
**US SIC:** 7999 **UK SIC:** 97913
**Employees:** 90

DUNS 37-973-9246
## Sovereign Chemicals Ltd
**(Subsidiary of:** Total Sa)
Park Road Industrial Estate, Park Road, Barrow-In-Furness, Cumbria LA14 4EQ
**Tel:** 01229-870800 **Fax:** 01229-870850
**Web:** www.sovchem.co.uk
**Reg No:** 3281228 **Estd:** 1996 Private Limited Company
**Line of Business:** Manufacture of other chemical products not elsewhere classified
**Export Sales:** £71,000
**Issued Capital:** £15,000,000
**Directors:** C O'Driscoll, J Walker, B Williams, R Albers
**Co. Secretary:** Paul Hudson
**Responsibilities**
**Senior:** Philip Derby *(Manager)*
**Finance:** Allan Pitcher *(Accountant)*
**Sales:** Simon Thurstan *(Sales Director)*
**IT:** Allan Pitcher *(Accountant)*
**US SIC:** 2899 **UK SIC:** 25670
**Auditors:** KPMG LLP

| | 31-12-13 | 31-12-12 | 31-12-11 |
|---|---|---|---|
| TO | 9,948,000 | 9,832,000 | 9,515,000 |
| P/L | 370,000 | 434,000 | 226,000 |
| NW | 13,586,000 | 13,840,000 | 13,318,000 |
| WC | 13,639,000 | 13,818,000 | 13,258,000 |
| Emp. | 68 | 70 | 67 |

DUNS 23-331-0833
## Sovereign Design Play Systems Ltd
40 Towerfield Road, Shoeburyness, Southend-On-Sea, Essex SS3 9QT
**Tel:** 01702291129
**Web:** www.sovereignplayequipment.co.uk
**Reg No:** 5024016 **VAT No:** 832510264
**Estd:** 2004 Private Limited Company
**Line of Business:** Manufacture of sports goods
**Issued Capital:** £100
**Directors:** D Hine, M Fernandes, Mrs J J Humphreys
**Co. Secretary:** Maxwell Fernandes
**Responsibilities**
**Senior:** Michelle Tuvey *(Manager)*
**IT:** R Pearcey *(IT Manager)*
**US SIC:** 3999, 5941
**UK SIC:** 49590, 65400
**Auditors:** Burgis & Bullock

| | 31-12-13 | 31-12-12 | 31-12-11 |
|---|---|---|---|
| TO | 7,909,564 | 8,334,470 | 7,820,210 |
| P/L | 65,966 | 60,965 | (146,476) |
| NW | 21,239 | (26,422) | 15,003 |
| WC | (287,671) | (353,640) | (334,275) |
| Emp. | 73 | 75 | 79 |

DUNS 45-840-0389
## Sovereign Executive Cars (London) Ltd
**(Subsidiary of:** Sovereign London Ltd)
Unit 28-29 The Highway Trading Centre, Heckford Street, London E1W 3HR
**Tel:** 020-7987-2007 **Fax:** 020-7538-2383
**Web:** www.sovereign-london.co.uk
**Reg No:** 3190223 **Estd:** 1996 Private Limited Company
**Line of Business:** Other passenger land transport not elsewhere classified
**Issued Capital:** £100
**Directors:** K Hussain, G M Greene, M Hughes
**US SIC:** 4141 **UK SIC:** 72102

| | 30-06-13 | 30-06-12 | 30-06-11 |
|---|---|---|---|
| TA | 1,353,703 | 1,129,277 | 1,129,605 |
| NW | 686,453 | 414,945 | 335,564 |
| WC | 643,808 | 361,190 | 286,005 |

DUNS 53-640-3009
## Sovereign Fm Ltd
Sovereign, 32 Southwark Bridge Road, London SE1 9EU
**Tel:** 020-7202-2640 **Fax:** 01329-288811
**Web:** www.sovereignfm.org
**Reg No:** 3445836 **Estd:** 1997 Private Limited Company
**Line of Business:** Specialised building trade contractors
**Issued Capital:** £90
**Directors:** S Spencer, S Mckeown
**Co. Secretary:** Keith Webster
**Responsibilities**
**Senior:** Julie Welch *(Office Manager)*
**Admin:** Julie Welch *(Office Manager)*
**US SIC:** 1731, 1711, 1799
**UK SIC:** 50300, 50000
**Auditors:** taylorcocks

| | 31-12-13 | 31-12-12 | 31-12-11 |
|---|---|---|---|
| TA | 1,488,246 | 1,456,363 | 1,719,485 |
| NW | 605,815 | 478,939 | 491,429 |
| WC | 458,463 | 354,022 | 381,514 |

DUNS 21-322-4975
## Sovereign Group Ltd
**(Subsidiary of:** Austhall Holdings Ltd)
Vale St Mill, Nelson, Lancashire BB9 0TA
**Web:** www.sov-group.co.uk
**Reg No:** 1089940 **VAT No:** 546492028
**Estd:** 1973 Private Limited Company
**Line of Business:** Painting and glazing
**Issued Capital:** £30,000
**Principals:** A J Mackie *(Financial)*, D J Fitton, K Manning, Ms F A Austin, J Park-Davies, A Craig, J S Hall
**Co. Secretary:** Miss Lorraine Kluczniak
**Responsibilities**
**Senior:** Glenn Taylor *(Manager)*
**US SIC:** 1721, 3442
**UK SIC:** 50400, 31420
**Auditors:** Pierce C.A. Ltd
**Bankers:** Barclays Bank Plc (20-15-70)

| | 31-12-13 | 31-12-12 | 31-12-11 |
|---|---|---|---|
| TO | 20,753,662 | 19,211,600 | 16,803,147 |
| P/L | 758,917 | 727,229 | 316,032 |
| NW | 2,554,264 | 2,219,059 | 1,691,798 |
| WC | 2,384,115 | 2,082,364 | 1,491,595 |
| Emp. | 168 | 177 | 164 |

DUNS 29-184-3845
## Sovereign Health Care
Royal Standard House, Bradford, West Yorkshire BD1 3DN
**Tel:** 01274-729472
**Web:** www.sovereignhealthcare.co.uk
**Reg No:** 0085588 **Estd:** 1873 Private Company Limited By Guarantee
**Line of Business:** Health insurance services
**Trading Style:** Sovereign Health Care
**Directors:** S M Cummings, C M Hudson, M S Bower, R S Piper, D Child, Dr R E Dugdale, M Austin
**Co. Secretary:** Ms Katherine Robb-Webb
**Responsibilities**
**Marketing:** Tom Pratt *(Digital Marketing Manager)*
**US SIC:** 6399 **UK SIC:** 82001
**Auditors:** Naylor Wintersgill
**Bankers:** Barclays Bank Plc (20-11-81)

| | 31-12-13 | 31-12-12 | 31-12-11 |
|---|---|---|---|
| TO | 10,082,436 | 9,595,985 | 8,920,075 |
| P/L | 6,923,485 | 2,777,088 | (1,670,911) |
| NW | 50,459,328 | 44,953,982 | 42,592,795 |
| WC | 11,064,375 | 9,195,708 | 6,334,557 |
| Emp. | 50 | 49 | 49 |

DUNS 76-907-8007
## Sovereign Housing Association Ltd
17-24 Bartholomew Street, Newbury, Berkshire RG14 5LL
**Tel:** 08457125530
**Web:** www.sovereign.org.uk
**Reg No:** 0026480IP **Estd:** 1988 Friendly Society
**Line of Business:** Housing associations societies trusts & co-operatives
**Principals:** Ms Norrie *(Chairman)*, Ms B Ridley *(Managing)*, M Huckerby *(Financial)*, Ms J Ince *(Personnel)*, H Harrison, J Mole, S Tagg, N Fleming
**Co. Secretary:** Ms Betty Ridley
**Responsibilities**
**Senior:** Chris Trigwell *(Principal)*, Brian Uzzell *(Principal)*
**HR:** Lynn Hanford-Day *(Manager)*
**Branches:** Sovereign Housing Association Ltd, Windmill Rd, Reading, Berkshire RG7 3RL
**US SIC:** 6531 **UK SIC:** 83400
**Auditors:** KPMG LLP
**Bankers:** National Westminster Bank Plc (60-15-07)

**Following financial data are in thousands**

| | 31-03-13 | 31-03-12 |
|---|---|---|
| TO | 197,869 | 180,078 |
| P/L | 31,967 | 27,960 |
| NW | 1,177,811 | 1,107,700 |
| WC | 1,900 | 10,783 |
| Emp. | 958 | 982 |

DUNS 21-175-9095
## Sovereign Housing Capital Plc
**(Subsidiary of:** Sovereign Housing Association Ltd)
17-24 Bartholomew Street, Newbury, Berkshire RG14 5LL
**Tel:** 01635572220
**Web:** www.sovereign.org.uk
**Reg No:** 6992513 **Estd:** 2009 Public Limited Company
**Line of Business:** Financial intermediation not elsewhere classified
**Issued Capital:** £50,000
**Directors:** J N Simpson, Ms A J Santry, M Hattersley
**Co. Secretary:** Ms Valerie Lynch
**Responsibilities**
**Senior:** Steve Abbott *(Board member)*, Lee Bambridge *(Board member)*, Alan Hickmore *(Resident Board member)*, Ronald Manley *(Board member)*, Verity Murricane *(Board member)*, John Rees-Evans *(Board member)*, Matthew Sands *(Board member)*
**Marketing:** Tim Abbott *(Head of Corporate Affairs)*, Debbie Down *(Communications Officer)*, Wendy Drinkwater *(People and Communications Dire)*, Lisa Moran *(Head of Sales & Marketing)*, Roy Probert *(Public Relations Manager)*, Phil Stephens *(Development and Commercial Dir)*
**Sales:** Gary Bremner *(Head of Sales Delivery)*, Sarah Griffin *(Regional Head of Development)*, Lisa Moran *(Head of Sales & Marketing)*, Phil Stephens *(Development and Commercial Dir)*
**Admin:** Helen Stapley *(PA to CEO)*, Jane Whitfield *(PA)*
**HR:** Lynn Hanford-Day *(Manager)*
**Facilities:** Heather Bowman *(Housing and Communities Direct)*
**Purchasing:** Micky Cummins *(Purchasing manager)*
**US SIC:** 6111 **UK SIC:** 81501
**Bankers:** National Westminster Bank Plc (60-15-07)

| | 31-03-14 | 31-03-13 | 31-03-12 |
|---|---|---|---|
| TA | 429,518,000 | 429,749,000 | 175,683,000 |
| NW | 13,000 | 7,000 | 13,000 |
| WC | 425,013,000 | 425,007,000 | 175,013,000 |

DUNS 73-929-6098 **Imp**
## Sovereign Rotating Machines Ltd
Unit 1-2, Christie Place, Bognor Regis, West Sussex PO22 9RT
**Tel:** 01243833420
**Web:** www.sovereignltd.co.uk
**Reg No:** 5182619 **Estd:** 2004 Private Limited Company
**Line of Business:** Manufacturers of vehicle components
**Issued Capital:** £100
**Directors:** G W Ubsdell, D Moul, J Sween
**Co. Secretary:** Richard Welland
**Responsibilities**
**IT:** Peter Copland *(Computer Manager)*, John Twine *(IT Director)*
**US SIC:** 3714 **UK SIC:** 35300

| | 31-12-13 | 31-10-12 | 31-12-11 |
|---|---|---|---|
| TO | 9,488,588 | 7,236,719 | N/A |
| P/L | (444,079) | 216,316 | N/A |
| NW | (12,167) | 337,197 | 177,231 |
| WC | 699,050 | 955,807 | 750,711 |
| Emp. | 111 | 118 | N/A |

DUNS 73-324-8970
## Sovex Ltd
2 Prenton Way, Prenton, Merseyside CH43 3EA
**Tel:** 01516 082323 **Fax:** 01516 082929
**Web:** www.sovexsystems.com
**Reg No:** 4598802 **VAT No:** 806510653
**Estd:** 2002 Private Limited Company
**Line of Business:** Manufacture of lifting and handling equipment
**Export Sales:** £5,278,115
**Issued Capital:** £116,160
**Directors:** M Dooley, M Dematteis, N R Owen, R C Leung, D A Lindfield
**Co. Secretary:** Michele Dematteis
**Branches:** Sovex Ltd, Harris Ho, Moorbridge Rd, Bingham, Nottingham, Nottinghamshire NG13 8GG
**US SIC:** 3534 **UK SIC:** 32553
**Auditors:** Grant Thornton UK LLP
**Bankers:** Barclays Bank Plc (20-51-01)

| | 31-12-13 | 31-12-12 | 31-12-11 |
|---|---|---|---|
| TO | 20,417,126 | 13,130,790 | 8,592,116 |
| P/L | 649,347 | 556,743 | 282,964 |
| NW | (985,299) | (262,560) | (733,412) |
| WC | (646,370) | (468,111) | (624,485) |
| Emp. | 149 | 87 | N/A |

DUNS 21-719-0024 **Imp**
## Sovrin Plastics Ltd
697 Stirling Road, Slough, Berkshire SL1 4ST
**Tel:** 01753-825155
**Web:** www.sovrin.com
**Reg No:** 0958135 **VAT No:** 208120608
**Estd:** 1965 Private Limited Company

**Line of Business:** Plastic injection moulding
**Export Sales:** £2,082,660
**Issued Capital:** £2,550
**Principals:** P Joiner *(Managing)*, K Rawlinson, A J Rankin
**Co. Secretary:** Peter Joiner
**Responsibilities**
**Marketing:** Peter Wigmore *(Sales & Marketing Manager)*
**Sales:** Peter Wigmore *(Sales & Marketing Manager)*
**IT:** James Joiner *(IT Manager)*
**Health & Safety:** Arthur Mumkley *(Health & Safety Officer)*
**Operations:** Urik Swiatek *(Production Manager)*
**Engineering:** Urik Swiatek *(Production Manager)*
**US SIC:** 3079, 8911
**UK SIC:** 48360, 83701
**Auditors:** Chhaya Hare Wilson Ltd
**Bankers:** Lloyds TSB Bank plc (30-97-73)

| | 31-12-13 | 31-12-12 | 31-12-11 |
|---|---|---|---|
| TO | 9,597,306 | 7,833,337 | 8,644,245 |
| P/L | 518,665 | 124,481 | (133,898) |
| NW | 8,439,289 | 8,094,318 | 8,009,076 |
| WC | 8,211,323 | 7,492,136 | 7,437,908 |
| Emp. | 118 | 125 | 136 |

DUNS 21-394-4222
## Sowerbutts
Odiham Road, Winchfield, Hook, Hampshire RG27 8BS
**Tel:** 01252-842763
**Estd:** 1991
**Line of Business:** Residential care establishments
**Proprietor:** Mrs J Swinsted
**Responsibilities**
**Senior:** Fran Sowerbutts *(Proprietor)*, Janis Swinstead *(Manager)*
**US SIC:** 8321 **UK SIC:** 96111
**Employees:** 53

DUNS 22-657-3673
## S.P. Fabrications (Ollerton) Ltd
Maun Way Ollerton, Newark, Nottinghamshire NG22 9ZD
**Tel:** 01623-863607 **Fax:** 01623-862879
**Web:** www.spfabrications.co.uk
**Reg No:** 1890345 **VAT No:** 379184802
**Estd:** 1985 Private Limited Company
**Line of Business:** Manufacture of metal structures and parts of structures
**Issued Capital:** £10,000
**Principals:** S Adlington *(Managing)*, Mrs K Adlington
**Co. Secretary:** Mrs Kay Adlington
**Responsibilities**
**Admin:** Ian Starbrook *(Office Manager)*
**Branches:** Unit 120-121, Boughton Ind Est, Ollerton, Newark Notts
**US SIC:** 3441 **UK SIC:** 32042
**Auditors:** Page Kirk

| | 30-09-13 | 30-09-12 | 30-09-11 |
|---|---|---|---|
| TA | 1,207,736 | 1,220,321 | 1,108,897 |
| NW | 408,045 | 387,540 | 606,531 |
| WC | (98,093) | (96,722) | 111,160 |

DUNS 21-137-8904
## Sp Holding Group Ltd
Upper Coalmoor Farm, Moreton Coppice, Telford, Shropshire TF4 2PX
**Tel:** 01952501155
**Web:** www.spholding.co.uk
**Reg No:** 6705293 **Estd:** 2008 Private Limited Company
**Line of Business:** Management activities of holding companies
**Export Sales:** £303,328
**Issued Capital:** £100
**Director:** S P Holding
**US SIC:** 6711 **UK SIC:** 83962

| | 31-03-13 | 31-03-12 | 31-03-11 |
|---|---|---|---|
| TO | 12,747,356 | 10,924,013 | 5,773,233 |
| P/L | 308,787 | 710,701 | 602,008 |
| NW | 3,824,987 | 3,648,581 | 3,093,779 |
| WC | (1,111,369) | (433,062) | (764,437) |
| Emp. | 90 | 71 | 64 |

DUNS 22-272-1255
## Sp Network Connections Ltd
**(Subsidiary of:** Iberdrola Sociedad Anonima)
Chadwick House, Warrington Road, Warrington, Cheshire WA3 6AE
**Tel:** 01925512600 **Fax:** 01925 512610
**Web:** www.spnetwork.com
**Reg No:** 4290066 **VAT No:** 659372008
**Estd:** 2002 Private Limited Company
**Line of Business:** Other construction work involving special trades
**Issued Capital:** £2,000,000
**Director:** F Mitchell
**Co. Secretary:** Seumus O'Gorman
**Responsibilities**
**Sales:** Sybil Hughes *(Business Development Manager)*
**Branches:** Sp Network Connections Ltd, Grove House, 1 Kilmartin Place, Uddingston, Glasgow, Lanarkshire G71 5PH
**US SIC:** 4911, 1622
**UK SIC:** 16101, 50200
**Auditors:** Ernst & Young LLP
**Bankers:** The Royal Bank Of Scotland Plc (83-07-06)

| | 31-12-13 | 31-12-12 | 31-12-11 |
|---|---|---|---|
| TO | 2,600,000 | 8,300,000 | 13,900,000 |
| P/L | 300,000 | (200,000) | 300,000 |
| NW | 2,700,000 | 2,500,000 | 2,700,000 |
| WC | 2,600,000 | 2,400,000 | 2,500,000 |

DUNS 22-142-7110
## Sp Power Systems Ltd
**(Subsidiary of:** Iberdrola Sociedad Anonima)
1 Atlantic Quay, Robertson Street, Glasgow, Lanarkshire G2 8SP
**Tel:** 01412488200
**Web:** www.sppowersystems.co.uk
**Reg No:** 0215841SC **Estd:** 2013 Private Limited Company
**Line of Business:** Representative office
**Issued Capital:** £11,247,000
**Directors:** J Sutherland, G C Jefferson
**Co. Secretary:** Seumus O'Gorman
**Branches:** Sp Power Systems Ltd, 3 Prenton Way, Prenton, Merseyside CH43 3ET
**US SIC:** 7399 **UK SIC:** 83954
**Auditors:** Ernst & Young LLP

| | 31-12-13 | 31-12-12 | 31-12-11 |
|---|---|---|---|
| TO | 717,300,000 | 583,000,000 | 557,700,000 |
| P/L | 29,200,000 | 26,800,000 | 24,200,000 |
| NW | 33,000,000 | 23,300,000 | 19,900,000 |
| WC | 16,500,000 | 12,500,000 | 8,200,000 |
| Emp. | 2,810 | 2,697 | 2,682 |

DUNS 50-564-4369
## S.P. Shutler Associates Ltd
Unit 5, Loomer Road Industrial Estate, Loomer Road, Newcastle, Staffordshire ST5 7LB
**Tel:** 01782-576590 **Fax:** 01782-576599
**Web:** www.shieldon-siteservices.com
**Reg No:** 2512180 **VAT No:** 462516943
**Estd:** 1987 Private Limited Company
**Line of Business:** Architectural and engineering activities and related technical consultancy
**Trading Style:** Shield On-Site Services
**Issued Capital:** £118
**Director:** S S Gibbs
**Responsibilities**
**Admin:** D Tunicliffe *(Administration Manager)*
**IT:** Mark Booth *(Technical Manager)*
**Health & Safety:** Mark Booth *(Technical Manager)*
**Operations:** Mark Booth *(Technical Manager)*
**US SIC:** 8911 **UK SIC:** 83701
**Bankers:** National Westminster Bank Plc (54-10-27)

| | 31-03-14 | 31-03-13 | 31-03-12 |
|---|---|---|---|
| TA | 894,000 | 894,000 | 894,000 |
| NW | 894,000 | 894,000 | 894,000 |

DUNS 22-630-2271
## The Spa Hotel (Tunbridge Wells) Ltd
**(Subsidiary of:** Scragg Hotels Ltd)
Mount Ephraim, Tunbridge Wells, Kent TN4 8XJ
**Tel:** 01892-520331 **Fax:** 01892-510575
**Web:** www.spahotel.co.uk
**Reg No:** 0884883 **VAT No:** 339981113
**Estd:** 1966 Private Limited Company
**Line of Business:** Hotels
**Trading Style:** The Spa Hotel (Tunbridge Wells) Ltd
**Issued Capital:** £265,000
**Directors:** C D Scragg, J P Cotter
**Co. Secretary:** Ms Anne Collins
**Responsibilities**
**Senior:** Harry Armstrong *(Partner)*, Livi Cabuderra *(Food & Beverage Manager)*, Peter Devnay *(Partner)*
**Facilities:** Greg Moon *(Maintenance Manager)*
**Branches:** The Spa Hotel (Tunbridge Wells) Ltd, Langton Road, Tunbridge Wells, Kent TN4 8XH
**US SIC:** 7011, 6531
**UK SIC:** 66500, 83400
**Auditors:** Alliotts
**Bankers:** HSBC Bank plc (40-01-13)

| | 31-03-14 | 31-03-13 | 31-03-12 |
|---|---|---|---|
| TO | 4,372,465 | 4,586,876 | 4,449,924 |
| P/L | 212,296 | 411,731 | 349,634 |
| NW | 792,729 | 630,334 | 318,024 |
| WC | (2,216,769) | (2,495,999) | (3,002,426) |
| Emp. | 107 | 108 | 100 |

DUNS 23-207-0854
## Spa Housing Association Ltd
The Royal Exchange, 9 Queen Street, Droitwich, Worcestershire WR9 8LA
**Tel:** 01905-823100
**Web:** www.spahousing.org
**Reg No:** 0027787IP **Estd:** 1993 Friendly Society
**Line of Business:** Housing associations societies trusts & co-operatives
**Trading Style:** Festival Housing Ltd
**Principals:** Ms J Weir *(Chairman)*, J Kelly, M Jones, Ms E Hope, R Brighton, H Coward, R Foster, Ms C Jackson
**Responsibilities**
**Senior:** Lyudmila Kayne *(Senior Customer Service)*, Don Lawney *(Vice Chairperson)*
**HR:** Lyudmila Kayne *(Senior Customer Service)*
**Branches:** Spa Housing Association Ltd, 16 Doverdale Close, Droitwich, Worcestershire WR9 8JR
**US SIC:** 8321 **UK SIC:** 96111
**Auditors:** Mazars Neville Russell
**Bankers:** Barclays Bank Plc (20-98-61)

| | 31-03-12 | 31-03-11 | 31-03-10 |
|---|---|---|---|
| TO | 17,369,000 | 15,933,000 | 15,312,000 |
| P/L | 2,530,000 | 1,460,000 | 2,173,000 |
| NW | N/A | 56,669,000 | 53,173,000 |
| WC | N/A | 642,000 | 3,096,000 |
| Emp. | 95 | 84 | 76 |

DUNS 21-313-8001
## Spa Laminates Ltd
59 Pepper Road, Leeds, West Yorkshire LS10 2TH
**Tel:** 01132-718311 **Fax:** 01132-703968
**Web:** www.spalaminates.co.uk
**Reg No:** 1188511 **VAT No:** 171718166
**Estd:** 1974 Private Limited Company
**Line of Business:** Manufacturers of veneer sheets
**Issued Capital:** £1,501
**Directors:** Mrs R Bradley, M Forster, D Forster, T Bradley, P Sunter
**Co. Secretary:** Ms Angela Williamson
**Branches:** 59 Pepper Road, Leeds, West Yorkshire LS10 2TH
**US SIC:** 2435 **UK SIC:** 46201
**Auditors:** Watson Buckle LLP
**Bankers:** National Westminster Bank Plc (56-00-54)

| | 31-10-13 | 31-10-12 | 31-10-11 |
|---|---|---|---|
| TA | 2,488,374 | 1,595,747 | 1,674,081 |
| NW | 1,588,462 | 1,242,770 | 1,395,279 |
| WC | 306,342 | 927,969 | 1,106,309 |

DUNS 23-281-2784
## Spa Nursing Homes Ltd
77-79 Grove Road, Ballynahinch, Co Down BT24 8PW
**Tel:** 02897561898
**Reg No:** 0026058NI **Estd:** 2010 Private Limited Company
**Line of Business:** Nursing homes
**Issued Capital:** £77,867
**Directors:** E S Johnston, G W Beattie, Mrs L H Johnston, C Johnston
**Co. Secretary:** David Ross
**Responsibilities**
**Senior:** Ellen Hughes *(Manager)*, Jocelyn Leyson *(Home Manager)*
**Branches:** Spa Nursing Homes Ltd, 2A Graham Gardens, Belfast, Belfast BT6 9FB
**US SIC:** 8091, 8999
**UK SIC:** 95200, 83954
**Auditors:** GoldBlatt McGuigan
**Bankers:** The Bank Of Ireland (90-22-58)

| | 30-11-13 | 30-11-12 | 30-11-11 |
|---|---|---|---|
| TO | 3,806,589 | 3,865,437 | 3,844,836 |
| P/L | (2,353,911) | (29,382) | 293,832 |
| NW | (798,578) | 1,574,662 | 1,955,078 |
| WC | (2,104,498) | 211,906 | 96,694 |
| Emp. | 170 | 188 | 185 |

DUNS 22-502-6913 Imp
## Space Airconditioning P L C
Willway Court, 1 Deacon Field Guildford Industrial, Estate, Guildford, Surrey GU2 8YT
**Tel:** 01483-504883
**Web:** www.spaceair.co.uk
**Reg No:** 1313460 **VAT No:** 689285468
**Estd:** 1980 Public Limited Company
**Line of Business:** Other wholesale
**Export Sales:** £1,304,067
**Issued Capital:** £410,800
**Principals:** N H Afram *(Managing)*, M S Nankivell
**Co. Secretary:** Mark Houghton
**Responsibilities**
**Senior:** Mervyn Burby *(Financial Director)*, Barry Stone *(Technical Services Director)*
**Finance:** Mervyn Burby *(Financial Director)*
**HR:** Bridget Fernandez *(Human Resources Manager)*
**Health & Safety:** Barry Stone *(Technical Services Director)*
**Facilities:** Barry Stone *(Technical Services Director)*
**Purchasing:** Barry Stone *(Technical Services Director)*
**Fleet:** Barry Stone *(Technical Services Director)*
**Branches:** Space Airconditioning P L C, Duckworth House, Talbot Road, Stretford, Manchester M32 0FP
**US SIC:** 5199 **UK SIC:** 61900
**Auditors:** Baker Tilly
**Bankers:** Lloyds TSB Bank plc (30-93-74)

| | 31-12-13 | 31-12-12 | 31-12-11 |
|---|---|---|---|
| TO | 15,344,866 | 16,842,339 | 18,753,873 |
| P/L | (332,857) | (324,639) | (418,731) |
| NW | 881,401 | 1,234,258 | 1,486,034 |
| WC | 169,667 | 457,842 | 841,337 |
| Emp. | 98 | 97 | 101 |

DUNS 73-401-6038
## Space Architecture (Europe) Ltd
**(Subsidiary of:** Space Group (Europe) Ltd)
Spaceworks Benton Park Road, Newcastle-Upon-Tyne, Tyne and Wear NE7 7LX
**Tel:** 01912 236600 **Fax:** 01912 236610
**Web:** www.spacegroup.co.uk
**Reg No:** 4674960 **VAT No:** 848107812
**Estd:** 1957 Private Limited Company
**Line of Business:** Architectural activities
**Trading Style:** _space
**Issued Capital:** £200,000
**Directors:** A R Roberts, R J Charlton
**Co. Secretary:** Andrew Roberts
**Responsibilities**
**Senior:** Christopher Alete *(Financial Director)*
**Finance:** Christopher Alete *(Financial Director)*
**Branches:** Space Architecture (Europe) Ltd, 1 Brewery Place, Brewery Wharf, Leeds, West Yorkshire LS10 1NE
**US SIC:** 8911 **UK SIC:** 83701
**Auditors:** unw LLP
**Bankers:** Girobank Plc (72-00-00)

| | 30-06-13 | 30-06-12 | 30-06-11 |
|---|---|---|---|
| TO | 4,832,990 | 4,263,880 | 6,761,684 |
| P/L | 1,029,298 | 251,504 | 651,787 |
| NW | 1,384,838 | 996,956 | 1,015,129 |
| WC | 691,128 | 463,342 | 723,166 |
| Emp. | 61 | 74 | 114 |

DUNS 71-939-3840
## Space Cooling Systems Holdings Ltd
**(Subsidiary of:** Space Cooling Topco Ltd)
Causeway Central, Pioneer Park, Bristol, Avon BS4 3QB
**Reg No:** 5320054 **Estd:** 2004 Private Limited Company
**Line of Business:** Management activities of holding companies
**Export Sales:** £2,719,224
**Issued Capital:** £1,964,435
**Directors:** D E Nouch, C M Murphy, M B Woods
**Co. Secretary:** Charles Murphy
**Responsibilities**
**Senior:** Barry Stevenson *(Manager)*
**US SIC:** 6711 **UK SIC:** 83962
**Bankers:** National Westminster Bank Plc (01-01-55)

| | 31-03-14 | 31-03-13 | 31-03-12 |
|---|---|---|---|
| TO | 110,538,944 | 104,067,568 | 114,014,309 |
| P/L | 2,136,414 | 353,301 | (1,461,139) |
| NW | 5,168,238 | 2,035,615 | 220,203 |
| WC | 3,986,052 | 907,449 | (587,617) |
| Emp. | 597 | 608 | 751 |

DUNS 34-648-8919 Imp
## Space Nk Ltd
Brunswick Centre, Brunswick Square, London WC1N 1AW
**Tel:** 02078332622 **Fax:** 0207 299 4998
**Web:** http://uk.spacenk.com
**Reg No:** 2773985 **VAT No:** 606138363
**Estd:** 1992 Private Limited Company
**Line of Business:** Manufacture of perfumes and toilet preparations
**Export Sales:** £7,483,835
**Issued Capital:** £3,038,444
**Directors:** C Garek, W S Fisher, A K Smith
**Co. Secretary:** Tom Mackney
**Responsibilities**
**Senior:** Nicola Kinnaird *(Joint Managing Director)*
**Finance:** M Giffin *(Financial Director)*
**Marketing:** Nicola Kinnaird *(Joint Managing Director)*
**Sales:** Nicola Kinnaird *(Joint Managing Director)*
**HR:** Hazel Caesari *(Human Resources Manager)*
**Health & Safety:** Hazel Caesari *(Human Resources Manager)*
**Branches:** Space Nk Ltd, 109-125 Knightsbridge, London SW1X 7RJ
**US SIC:** 2844, 5999
**UK SIC:** 25820, 65600
**Auditors:** Mazars LLP

**Bankers:** National Westminster Bank Plc (56-00-27)

| | 29-03-14 | 31-03-13 | 31-03-12 |
|---|---|---|---|
| TO | 70,076,060 | 58,541,425 | 53,940,902 |
| P/L | 2,368,788 | 776,231 | 975,911 |
| NW | 12,791,258 | 11,393,407 | 11,112,753 |
| WC | 7,992,032 | 7,305,097 | 7,681,684 |
| Emp. | 471 | 447 | 409 |

DUNS 84-692-1898

## Space Solutions (Scotland) Ltd

Bishop House, Aberdeen, Aberdeenshire AB10 1UP
**Tel:** 01224-218500
**Web:** www.spacesolutions.info
**Reg No:** 0322119SC **Estd:** 2007 Private Limited Company
**Line of Business:** Architectural activities
**Issued Capital:** £181,540
**Directors:** K Cope, S C Judge, D M Binnie, J G Barrack, M Wilson
**Co. Secretary:** Stronachs Secretaries Limited
**US SIC:** 4953, 6552, 1752
**UK SIC:** 92110, 85000, 50400

| | 30-06-14 | 30-06-13 | 30-06-12 |
|---|---|---|---|
| TO | 38,315,259 | 33,960,373 | 22,781,845 |
| P/L | 1,588,040 | 2,052,178 | 870,505 |
| NW | 3,039,032 | 2,061,860 | 882,037 |
| WC | 2,709,690 | 1,904,055 | 820,964 |
| Emp. | 229 | 193 | 161 |

DUNS 23-707-4963

## SpACE4 Ltd

(**Subsidiary of:** Persimmon Plc)
Tameside Drive, Castle Vale, Birmingham, West Midlands B35 7AG
**Tel:** 0121-748-8383 **Fax:** 01217667369
**Web:** www.space4.co.uk
**Reg No:** 3702606 **VAT No:** 412116509
**Estd:** 2000 Private Limited Company
**Line of Business:** Construction of domestic buildings
**Issued Capital:** £27,720,769
**Directors:** M H Killoran, J Fairburn, G N Francis, N P Greenaway
**Co. Secretary:** Miss Tracy Davison
**Responsibilities**
**Senior:** Michael Farley *(Chief Executive)*, Chris Hagan *(Manager)*
**IT:** David Powis *(Technical Manager)*
**US SIC:** 1522 **UK SIC:** 50100
**Auditors:** KPMG Audit PLC

| | 31-12-13 | 31-12-12 | 31-12-11 |
|---|---|---|---|
| TO | 24,917,000 | 23,910,000 | 24,864,000 |
| P/L | 2,376,000 | 1,549,000 | 752,000 |
| NW | 15,324,000 | 13,203,000 | 11,579,000 |
| WC | 10,696,000 | 8,539,000 | 6,721,000 |
| Emp. | 91 | 93 | 93 |

DUNS 22-094-5302

## Spaceandpeople Plc

2nd Floor, Glasgow, Lanarkshire G2 2QD
**Tel:** 01413531215 **Fax:** 08450518645
**Web:** www.spaceandpeople.com
**Reg No:** 0212277SC **Estd:** 2000 Public Limited Company
**Line of Business:** Advertising related services
**Issued Capital:** £194,411
**Directors:** R A Chadwick, A P Stirling, W G Watt, S R Curtis, G R Dunlay, Ms N J Cullen, C G Hammond, M J Bending
**Co. Secretary:** Gregor Dunlay
**Responsibilities**
**Sales:** Nick Hill *(Sales Director)*
**US SIC:** 7319 **UK SIC:** 83800
**Auditors:** Campbell Dallas LLP
**Bankers:** The Royal Bank Of Scotland Plc (83-00-81)

| | 31-12-13 | 31-12-12 | 31-12-11 |
|---|---|---|---|
| TO | 14,567,000 | 13,055,000 | 10,660,000 |
| P/L | 2,439,000 | 2,274,000 | 1,588,000 |
| NW | 1,781,000 | 490,000 | (347,000) |
| WC | 198,000 | 45,000 | (755,000) |
| Emp. | 139 | 99 | 81 |

DUNS 21-670-7349 **Imp**

## Spacelabs Healthcare Ltd

1-4 Harforde Court, John Tate Road, Hertford, Hertfordshire SG13 7NW
**Tel:** 01992-507700 **Fax:** 01992-501213
**Web:** www.spacelabshealthcare.com
**Reg No:** 0570647 **VAT No:** 573274135
**Estd:** 1967 Private Limited Company
**Line of Business:** Manufacture of medical and surgical equipment and orthopaedic appliances
**Export Sales:** £849,039
**Issued Capital:** £425,000
**Directors:** R Lines, M J Barkham, A I Mutch
**Co. Secretary:** Gravitas Company Secretarial Ser
**Responsibilities**
**Senior:** Karita Salokangas *(Manager)*
**Finance:** Karita Lassila *(Finance Director)*
**HR:** Sarah Rayner *(Human Resources Manager)*
**Health & Safety:** Sarah Rayner *(Human Resources Manager)*
**Branches:** Spacelabs Healthcare Ltd, Chiltern Court, Unit 3, Chesham, Buckinghamshire HP5 2PX
**US SIC:** 3841, 5122
**UK SIC:** 37201, 61800
**Auditors:** Mazars LLP
**Bankers:** Bank Of America, Na (30-16-35)

| | 30-06-13 | 30-06-12 | 30-06-11 |
|---|---|---|---|
| TO | 10,196,878 | 10,308,581 | 9,682,695 |
| P/L | 3,074,257 | 2,422,951 | 1,915,059 |
| NW | 9,813,176 | 7,420,840 | 5,524,653 |
| WC | 11,986,631 | 9,571,302 | 7,668,204 |
| Emp. | 110 | 110 | 115 |

DUNS 23-668-8433 **Exp**

## Spacemaker Furniture Ltd

Westgate Chambers, Pinner, Middlesex HA5 3LA
**Tel:** 01268472020
**Web:** www.spacemakerfurniture.co.uk
**Reg No:** 3663679 **Estd:** 1998 Private Limited Company
**Line of Business:** The Notes to the accounts for the period ending 31.08.2013 state that the subject acts as an agent for a person.
**Issued Capital:** £2
**Directors:** J Harrison, W Harrison
**Co. Secretary:** Ms Laura Harrison
**Branches:** Spacemaker Furniture Ltd, 29-31 High Street, Ruislip, Middlesex HA4 7AU
**US SIC:** 2599, 2517
**UK SIC:** 46720, 46714

| | 31-08-13 | 31-08-11 | 31-08-10 |
|---|---|---|---|
| TA | 2 | 2 | 2 |
| NW | 2 | 2 | 2 |
| WC | 2 | N/A | N/A |
| Emp. | 70 | N/A | N/A |

DUNS 64-071-1974

## Spacemaker Group Ltd

Westgate Chambers, 8a Elm Park Road, Pinner, Middlesex HA5 3LA
**Tel:** 01708473020
**Reg No:** 3466673 **Estd:** 1997 Private Limited Company
**Line of Business:** Management activities of holding companies
**Issued Capital:** £50,080
**Directors:** W Harrison, M J Harrison, J Harrison
**Co. Secretary:** Ms Laura Harrison
**Branches:** Spacemaker Group Ltd, 160-162 Hornchurch Road, Hornchurch, Essex RM11 1QH
**US SIC:** 6711 **UK SIC:** 83962
**Auditors:** Morgan Berkeley Ltd
**Bankers:** Barclays Bank Plc (20-46-57)

| | 31-07-13 | 31-07-12 | 31-07-11 |
|---|---|---|---|
| TO | 7,612,507 | 7,937,187 | 7,885,420 |
| P/L | 303,527 | 685,143 | 739,500 |
| NW | 3,640,336 | 3,327,993 | 2,827,429 |
| WC | 668,031 | 234,669 | (337,539) |
| Emp. | 93 | 93 | 90 |

DUNS 21-126-8006 **Imp-Exp**

## Spaceright Europe Ltd

38 Tollpark Road, Wardpark East, Cumbernauld, Glasgow, Lanarkshire G68 0LW
**Tel:** 01236-853120 **Fax:** 01923237546
**Web:** www.spacerighteurope.com
**Reg No:** 0344257SC **VAT No:** 935524810
**Estd:** 1980 Private Limited Company
**Line of Business:** Other manufacturing not elsewhere classified
**Trading Style:** Spaceright Europe Limited
**Issued Capital:** £7,350
**Directors:** A Houstoun, A W Symon, S R Ashton, J J Nettleton
**Co. Secretary:** Mbm Secretarial Services Limited
**Responsibilities**
**Senior:** Sandy Abercrombie *(Works Manager)*, Bruno Baillavoine *(Manager)*, William Mccoll *(Sales Manager)*
**Sales:** William Mccoll *(Sales Manager)*
**Health & Safety:** Sandy Abercrombie *(Works Manager)*
**Facilities:** Sandy Abercrombie *(Works Manager)*
**Operations:** Sandy Abercrombie *(Works Manager)*
**Purchasing:** Sandy Abercrombie *(Works Manager)*
**Engineering:** Sandy Abercrombie *(Works Manager)*
**US SIC:** 3999, 3579
**UK SIC:** 49590, 33010
**Auditors:** Scott- Moncrieff
**Bankers:** Clydesdale Bank Plc (82-69-09)

| | 31-10-13 | 31-10-12 | 31-10-11 |
|---|---|---|---|
| TA | 2,927,783 | 2,436,672 | 2,254,848 |
| NW | 293,209 | 165,067 | 444,100 |
| WC | 829,425 | 578,185 | 789,155 |

DUNS 34-872-0298

## Spaghetti House Restaurants Group Ltd

24 Cranbourn Street, London WC2H 7AB
**Tel:** 02073950390
**Reg No:** 5670290 **Estd:** 2006 Private Limited Company
**Line of Business:** Management activities of other non-financial holding companies not elsewhere classified
**Issued Capital:** £88,000
**Directors:** Ms S Lavarini, L Lavarini
**Co. Secretary:** Riccardo Lavarini
**US SIC:** 6711 **UK SIC:** 83962
**Auditors:** BKB Sears Morgan

| | 31-03-13 | 01-04-12 | 03-03-11 |
|---|---|---|---|
| TO | 14,476,586 | 12,326,115 | 11,967,128 |
| P/L | (771,877) | (166,505) | 446,238 |
| NW | 401,539 | 847,059 | 2,489,936 |
| WC | (1,771,765) | (1,364,208) | 573,115 |
| Emp. | 319 | 293 | 252 |

DUNS 21-771-0309

## Spalding Area Social Services

The Vista, Spalding, Lincolnshire PE11 2RA
**Tel:** 01775725751
**Estd:** 2011 Proprietorship
**Line of Business:** The dss
**Proprietor:** Ms J Mcintyre
**US SIC:** 8321 **UK SIC:** 96111
**Employees:** 200

DUNS 21-919-5230

## Spalding Grammar School

Priory Road, Spalding, Lincolnshire PE11 2XH
**Tel:** 01775724646 **Fax:** 01775756801
**Web:** www.spaldinggrammar.lincs.sch.uk
**Reg No:** 8357352 **Estd:** 2013 Private Company Limited By Guarantee
**Line of Business:** General secondary education
**Directors:** N Meekins, K J Bean, A J Faulkner, M F Morris, K C Casswell, H R Johnson, Mrs J Smith, B Chappell
**Co. Secretary:** Shaun Barton
**Responsibilities**
**Senior:** Jonathon Bradley *(Governor)*, Adrian Cunnington *(Director)*, Ruth Fuggle *(Governor)*, Debra Haslam *(Governor)*, Sharon Hoult *(Director)*, Nigel Ryan *(Director)*
**IT:** David Ellen *(Head of IT)*
**US SIC:** 8211 **UK SIC:** 93200

| | 31-08-13 |
|---|---|
| TO | 20,544,065 |
| P/L | 17,631,546 |
| NW | 16,900,546 |
| WC | 755,253 |
| Emp. | 106 |

DUNS 29-280-0885 **Imp-Exp**

## Spaldings Ltd

(**Subsidiary of:** Marubeni Corporation)
25-35 Sadler Road, Lincoln, Lincolnshire LN6 3XJ
**Tel:** 01522-500600
**Web:** www.spaldings.co.uk
**Reg No:** 1558147 **VAT No:** 389012442
**Estd:** 1981 Private Limited Company
**Line of Business:** Agricultural machinery sales service and repair
**Export Markets:** Worldwide
**Export Sales:** £1,157,000
**Trading Style:** Spaldings Ltd
**Issued Capital:** £1,000,000
**Principals:** D A Fox *(Marketing)*, H Shimada, T Masuyama, Y Ishii
**Co. Secretary:** John Sorby
**Responsibilities**
**Senior:** Roger Chase *(agricultural Sales Director)*, Steve Constable *(Operations Director)*, Sid Deaton *(Senior Customer Services Execu)*, Catherine Locking *(groundcare sales Director)*
**Sales:** Roger Chase *(agricultural Sales Director)*, Catherine Locking *(groundcare sales Director)*
**Operations:** Steve Constable *(Operations Director)*
**US SIC:** 0729, 5083
**UK SIC:** 01003, 61490
**Auditors:** Streets Audit LLP
**Bankers:** Barclays Bank Plc (20-50-21)

| | 31-03-14 | 31-03-13 | 31-03-11 |
|---|---|---|---|
| TO | 26,676,000 | 31,097,000 | 23,662,155 |
| P/L | 2,916,000 | 3,430,000 | 2,529,320 |
| NW | 14,087,000 | 11,849,000 | 9,254,690 |
| WC | 13,671,000 | 11,433,000 | 8,534,844 |
| Emp. | 157 | 146 | 146 |

DUNS 28-946-1089

## Spanclad Roofing Ltd

(**Subsidiary of:** Spanclad Holdings Ltd)
337 Heath Street, Smethwick, West Midlands B66 2QY
**Tel:** 0121-558-2131
**Web:** www.spanclad.com
**Reg No:** 1603473 **Estd:** 1979 Private Limited Company
**Line of Business:** Erection of roof covering and frames
**Trading Style:** Spanclad Roofing and Construction Ltd
**Issued Capital:** £2
**Directors:** J B Glover, C J Jackson, S P Morgan, J Mcdonald-Roberts
**Co. Secretary:** Brian Johnston
**Responsibilities**
**Senior:** Jake McDonald-Roberts *(Director)*
**Admin:** Virginia Bomber *(Office Administrator)*
**US SIC:** 1761 **UK SIC:** 50400

| | 31-12-13 | 31-12-12 | 31-12-11 |
|---|---|---|---|
| TA | 54 | 54 | 54 |
| NW | (1,657) | (1,657) | (1,657) |
| WC | (1,657) | (1,657) | (1,657) |

DUNS 21-733-7625 **Imp-Exp**

## Spandex Ltd

(**Subsidiary of:** Spandex Holding Ii Ag)
1600 Park Avenue, Bristol, Avon BS32 4UA
**Tel:** 01454-616444 **Fax:** 01454-616777
**Web:** www.spandex.co.uk
**Reg No:** 1266024 **VAT No:** 771345919
**Estd:** 2010 Private Limited Company
**Line of Business:** Sign and nameplate equipment
**Export Sales:** £13,882,000
**Issued Capital:** £3,249,532
**Directors:** R W Larson, R W Jackson
**Co. Secretary:** Mrs Beverley Meredith
**Responsibilities**
**Senior:** Kerry Mcgeown *(Sales Manager)*
**Marketing:** Gabi Paris *(Marketing Manager)*, Debbie Parish *(Senior Marketing Executive)*
**Sales:** Phil McMullin *(Business Manager)*, Kerry Mcgeown *(Sales Manager)*
**Admin:** Anita Nelson *(Office Manager)*
**IT:** Andy Burgess *(IT Manager)*
**HR:** Kerry Bennett *(Training Officer)*
**Health & Safety:** Mike Coates *(Facilities Manager)*
**Facilities:** Mike Coates *(Facilities Manager)*
**Purchasing:** Tania Coates *(Purchasing Manager)*, Anita Nelson *(Office Manager)*
**Fleet:** Anita Nelson *(Office Manager)*
**Branches:** Spandex Ltd, 21 Portland Sq, Bristol, Avon BS2 8SJ
**US SIC:** 5199 **UK SIC:** 61900
**Auditors:** PricewaterhouseCoopers LLP
**Bankers:** Lloyds TSB Bank plc (30-00-01)

| | 30-04-14 | 30-04-13 | 30-04-12 |
|---|---|---|---|
| TO | 34,767,000 | 32,151,000 | 32,188,000 |
| P/L | 2,630,000 | 1,523,000 | 45,363,000 |
| NW | 47,982,000 | 60,545,000 | 59,070,000 |
| WC | 48,756,000 | 66,530,000 | 68,152,000 |
| Emp. | 118 | 116 | 122 |

DUNS 22-964-0180

## Spanish Embassy

39 Chesham Place, London SW1X 8SB
**Tel:** 08700056975
**Web:** www.maec.es
**Estd:** 1992
**Line of Business:** Embassies
**Trading Style:** Spanish Nursery, The Spanish Embassy, Spanish Commercial Office
**Director:** F P La Morena
**Responsibilities**
**Senior:** Felipe la Morena *(Principal)*
**Branches:** Spanish Embassy, 20 Peel Street, London W8 7PD
**US SIC:** 9121 **UK SIC:** 91110
**Employees:** 60

DUNS 21-896-3833 **Imp-Exp**

## Spanset Ltd

(**Subsidiary of:** Spanset Inter Ag)
Telford Way, Middlewich Business Industrial, Middlewich, Cheshire CW10 0HX
**Tel:** 01606-737494
**Web:** www.spanset.co.uk
**Reg No:** 0960688 **VAT No:** 160851865
**Estd:** 1969 Private Limited Company
**Line of Business:** Manufacture of household textiles
**Export Markets:** E E C, Middle East, Far East, Africa, North America
**Export Sales:** £1,189,538
**Issued Capital:** £500,000
**Principals:** E D Ehnimb *(Chairman)*, A J Eaden *(Managing)*, P J Ward
**Co. Secretary:** Mrs Jane Freeley
**Responsibilities**
**Marketing:** Eunice Williams *(Marketing Manager)*
**HR:** Simon Mitchell *(Training Manager)*
**Health & Safety:** Bob Murdoch *(Manager, Height Safety)*
**Branches:** Spanset Ltd, Barton Park, Richmond, North Yorkshire DL10 6NF
**US SIC:** 2392, 3534
**UK SIC:** 45550, 32553
**Auditors:** Christian Douglass LLP

**Bankers:** National Westminster Bank Plc (01-08-38)

| | 31-12-13 | 31-12-12 | 31-12-11 |
|---|---|---|---|
| TO | 8,086,675 | 7,634,184 | 7,273,381 |
| P/L | 556,889 | 240,255 | 136,803 |
| NW | 2,803,243 | 2,576,676 | 2,818,951 |
| WC | 1,346,059 | 1,011,561 | 1,233,521 |
| Emp. | 79 | 83 | 85 |

DUNS 49-712-5146

## Spar

100 Main Street, Cullybackey, Ballymena, Co Antrim BT42 1BW
**Tel:** 02825881995
**Web:** www.spar.co.uk
**Estd:** 1995 Partnership
**Line of Business:** Convenience stores
**Partners:** L Wiseman, Mrs R Wiseman
**Responsibilities**
**Senior:** Laura Mclean (Manager)
**US SIC:** 5411  **UK SIC:** 64100
**Bankers:** The Bank Of Ireland (90-20-55)
**Employees:** 50

DUNS 28-846-0140  Imp

## Spar (Uk) Ltd

(**Subsidiary of:** Spar Food Distributors Ltd)
Hygeia Building 66-68, College Road, Harrow, Middlesex HA1 1BE
**Tel:** 02084-263-700 **Fax:** 02084-263-701
**Web:** www.spar.co.uk
**Reg No:** 0634226  **VAT No:** 726447913
**Estd:** 1959 Private Limited Company
**Line of Business:** Misc grocery wholesalers
**Issued Capital:** £51
**Principals:** R R Hill (Financial), M S Keeley, Mrs S J Darbyshire, C W Lewis, Ms D M Robinson
**Co. Secretary:** Philip Marchant
**Responsibilities**
**Admin:** Paul Coombes (Office Manager)
**US SIC:** 5149, 5431, 5499
**UK SIC:** 61700, 64100
**Auditors:** Baker Tilly UK Audit LLP
**Bankers:** National Westminster Bank Plc (60-10-10)

| | 26-04-14 | 27-04-13 | 28-04-12 |
|---|---|---|---|
| TO | 62,636,235 | 64,805,994 | 66,987,826 |
| P/L | 386,000 | 317,000 | 335,000 |
| NW | (1,526,141) | (2,204,586) | (1,654,006) |
| WC | (435,140) | (458,787) | (340,761) |
| Emp. | 68 | 62 | 61 |

DUNS 21-318-0573  Exp

## Spare Ipg 21 Ltd

(**Subsidiary of:** Procoman Ltd)
Po Box 9, Salt Meadows, Gateshead, Tyne and Wear NE8 1SW
**Tel:** 01914772271 **Fax:** 01912010438
**Reg No:** 1342505  **Estd:** 1870 Private Limited Company
**Line of Business:** Manufacture of lifting and handling equipment
**Export Markets:** Worldwide
**Trading Style:** Wellman Booth, Clarke Chapman Engineering Services, Stothert & Pitt
**Issued Capital:** £100
**Director:** R A Bell
**Branches:** Spare Ipg 21 Ltd, Unit 15 Planetary Industrial Estate, Planetary Road, Willenhall, West Midlands WV13 3XA
**US SIC:** 3534, 5084
**UK SIC:** 32553, 61490
**Auditors:** KPMG Audit PLC
**Bankers:** National Westminster Bank Plc (54-10-27)

| | 31-12-13 | 31-12-12 | 31-12-11 |
|---|---|---|---|
| TA | 100 | 100 | 100 |
| NW | 100 | 100 | 100 |

DUNS 21-671-1267  Imp-Exp

## Sparex Ltd

(**Subsidiary of:** Agco Corporation)
Exeter Airport, Exeter, Devon EX5 2LJ
**Tel:** 01392-368892 **Fax:** 01392-369904
**Web:** www.sparex.com
**Reg No:** 0841771  **VAT No:** 754819987
**Estd:** 1965 Private Limited Company
**Line of Business:** Wholesale of agricultural machinery and accessories and implements, including tractors
**Export Markets:** Worldwide
**Trading Style:** Sparex Uk
**Issued Capital:** £261,612
**Directors:** J Burgess, P W De Brissac Bernard, M A Doggrell
**Co. Secretary:** Mark Doggrell
**Responsibilities**
**Senior:** Boris Schoepplein (Manager), Theunis Stortenbeker (Manager)
**Admin:** Boris Schoepplein (Manager)
**IT:** Martin Mclaren (Senior IT Executive), Neill Robson (Computer Operations Manager)
**Branches:** Sparex Ltd, 56 Seskanore Road, Omagh, Co Tyrone BT78 1RW
**US SIC:** 5083, 3523
**UK SIC:** 61490, 32113
**Auditors:** KPMG LLP

---

**Bankers:** The Royal Bank Of Scotland Plc (16-04-00)

| | 31-12-13 | 31-12-12 | 31-12-11 |
|---|---|---|---|
| TO | 31,621,670 | 31,915,169 | 30,436,115 |
| P/L | 1,454,521 | 3,420,954 | 5,210,606 |
| NW | 37,005,266 | 35,576,167 | 32,174,736 |
| WC | 32,541,521 | 31,224,287 | 28,228,640 |
| Emp. | 174 | 187 | 180 |

DUNS 23-939-0979  Exp

## Spargonet Consulting Plc

Spargonet House, 188 High Street, Egham, Surrey TW20 9ED
**Tel:** 01784-223000 **Fax:** 01784-223050
**Web:** www.spargonet.com
**Reg No:** 3928751  **Estd:** 2000 Public Limited Company
**Line of Business:** Computer software (development)
**Issued Capital:** £116,660
**Directors:** W A Spargo, T Russell, I C Chandler, A L Morton
**Co. Secretary:** Tony Russell
**Responsibilities**
**HR:** Chris Whent (Human Resources Manager)
**US SIC:** 7379, 7374
**UK SIC:** 83940
**Auditors:** KPMG LLP

| | 28-02-14 | 28-02-13 | 29-02-12 |
|---|---|---|---|
| TO | 13,010,000 | 13,409,000 | 14,102,000 |
| P/L | 1,235,000 | 1,231,000 | 1,443,000 |
| NW | 1,957,000 | 1,963,000 | 1,744,000 |
| WC | 903,000 | 952,000 | 810,000 |
| Emp. | 101 | 108 | 128 |

DUNS 21-834-4116

## Spark Ecommerce Group Ltd

Follingsby Avenue, Follingsby Park, Gateshead, Tyne and Wear NE10 8HQ
**Tel:** 01914959999
**Web:** www.sparkresponse.com
**Reg No:** 8030236  **Estd:** 2012 Private Limited Company
**Line of Business:** Management activities of holding companies
**Issued Capital:** £3,000,000
**Directors:** N C Lambert, P B Slee, B A Stiefel
**Co. Secretary:** Peter Slee
**US SIC:** 6711  **UK SIC:** 83962
**Bankers:** Guinness Mahon Guernsey Ltd (40-48-15)

| | 30-06-14 | 30-06-13 | 30-06-12 |
|---|---|---|---|
| TO | 13,709,269 | 13,271,056 | 12,840,293 |
| P/L | 483,557 | 493,976 | 418,184 |
| NW | (1,220,229) | (1,523,407) | (2,015,672) |
| WC | 1,578,209 | 1,815,202 | 2,094,789 |
| Emp. | 184 | 173 | 189 |

DUNS 34-995-8210

## Spark Energy Ltd

Etterick Riverside, Dunsdale Road, Selkirk, Selkirkshire TD7 5EB
**Tel:** 08450 347474
**Web:** www.sparkenergy.co.uk
**Reg No:** 0301188SC  **VAT No:** 927164711
**Estd:** 2006 Private Limited Company
**Line of Business:** Management activities of holding companies
**Issued Capital:** £1,211
**Directors:** J H Paget, C Gauld, C G Fletcher, T P Noble, H Osborne, N J Leeming
**Co. Secretary:**
Mbm Secretarial Services Limited
**US SIC:** 6711, 7399
**UK SIC:** 83962, 83954
**Auditors:** Johnston Carmichael LLP

| | 30-06-14 | 30-06-13 | 30-06-12 |
|---|---|---|---|
| TO | 83,066,691 | 40,778,132 | 18,026,714 |
| P/L | 1,265,062 | 337,469 | (3,265,800) |
| NW | 355,605 | (1,796,595) | (4,016,702) |
| WC | 823,645 | (1,180,309) | (3,910,250) |
| Emp. | 190 | 140 | 99 |

DUNS 21-011-5573

## Sparkle Cleaning & Maintenance Services Ltd

(**Subsidiary of:** Saxon Point Ltd)
Unit 6, Wansdyke Business Centre, Oldfield Lane, Bath, Avon BA2 3LY
**Tel:** 01225-421129
**Web:** www.sparklecleaningbath.co.uk
**Reg No:** 6348889  **Estd:** 2007 Private Limited Company
**Line of Business:** Cleaning activities not elsewhere classified
**Issued Capital:** £1
**Director:** P F Lidgitt
**Responsibilities**
**Senior:** Simro Lewis (Proprietor)
**US SIC:** 7349  **UK SIC:** 92300

| | 31-10-13 | 31-10-12 | 31-10-11 |
|---|---|---|---|
| TA | 175,869 | 179,310 | 248,718 |
| NW | 32,459 | (9,239) | (33,311) |
| WC | 30,970 | (10,729) | (34,584) |

---

DUNS 64-223-4413

## Sparkle Cleaning Co

27 Wilhelmina Avenue, Coulsdon, Surrey CR5 1NL
**Tel:** 01737-555837
**Web:** www.sparklecleaningltd.com
**Estd:** 1991 Proprietorship
**Line of Business:** Cleaning contracting commercial
**Proprietor:** Ms M J Hamilton
**Responsibilities**
**Senior:** Richard Hamilton (Manager)
**US SIC:** 7349  **UK SIC:** 92300
**Employees:** 98

DUNS 21-114-2758

## Sparkles Scotland Ltd

Elgin House, Elgin Street, Dunfermline, Fife KY12 7SD
**Tel:** 01383-728200 **Fax:** 01383-873186
**Reg No:** 0340475SC  **Estd:** 2001 Private Limited Company
**Line of Business:** Commercial premises cleaning
**Issued Capital:** £3
**Directors:** Ms L Mclure, Ms L Leslie
**Co. Secretary:** David Mclure
**US SIC:** 7349  **UK SIC:** 92300

| | 31-03-14 | 31-03-13 | 31-03-12 |
|---|---|---|---|
| TA | 332,118 | 378,397 | 369,670 |
| NW | 172,827 | 162,322 | 152,405 |
| WC | 89,251 | 72,831 | 113,702 |

DUNS 22-735-8546

## Sparks Catering Butchers Ltd

Unit 3 Millmarsh Lane Delta Park, Industrial Estate, Enfield, Middlesex EN3 7QJ
**Fax:** 020-8443-9349
**Web:** www.sparkscatering.co.uk
**Reg No:** 1202108  **VAT No:** 221833391
**Estd:** 1975 Private Limited Company
**Line of Business:** Catering food and drink suppliers
**Trading Style:** Sparks Catering Butchers Ltd
**Issued Capital:** £100
**Principals:** J W Sparks (Managing), A D Sparks, Mrs S J Wells, M Mordsley
**Co. Secretary:** Mrs Catherine Sparks
**Responsibilities**
**Senior:** Sarah Fisher (Director)
**US SIC:** 5149  **UK SIC:** 61700
**Auditors:** FMCB
**Bankers:** The Bank Of Ireland (30-16-07)

| | 30-09-13 | 30-09-12 | 30-09-11 |
|---|---|---|---|
| TO | 12,668,098 | 12,563,779 | 11,222,164 |
| P/L | 282,699 | 630,135 | 475,889 |
| NW | 2,146,754 | 2,061,826 | 1,743,076 |
| WC | 1,318,650 | 1,208,140 | 930,284 |
| Emp. | 61 | 60 | 55 |

DUNS 21-705-1310

## Sparks Managed Services Ltd

(**Subsidiary of:** Sheffield College)
City College, Granville Road, Sheffield, South Yorkshire S2 2RL
**Fax:** 01142602100
**Web:** www.sparkssheffcol.ac.uk
**Reg No:** 7490897  **Estd:** 1974 Private Limited Company
**Line of Business:** Restaurants
**Issued Capital:** £1
**Directors:** D Tidmarsh, Mrs H Macdonald, J Pepper
**Responsibilities**
**Senior:** Anne Townsend (Manager)
**US SIC:** 5812  **UK SIC:** 66110
**Bankers:** Barclays Bank Plc (20-59-42)

| | 31-07-13 | 31-07-12 | 31-07-12 |
|---|---|---|---|
| TO | N/A | 349,037 | 52,447 |
| NW | N/A | 1 | 1 |
| WC | N/A | (9,999) | (13,332) |

DUNS 29-880-7249

## Spark's Mechanical Services Ltd

(**Subsidiary of:** Bkf Twenty-Seven Ltd)
Broadfold Road, Aberdeen, Aberdeenshire AB23 8EY
**Tel:** 01224-704448 **Fax:** 01224-703864
**Web:** www.sparksms.co.uk
**Reg No:** 0102458SC  **Estd:** 1987 Private Limited Company
**Line of Business:** Manufacture of non-domestic cooling and ventilation equipment
**Issued Capital:** £25
**Principals:** C C Argo (Managing), R Delday, R Burnett, D A Kirk, P A Goodchild
**Co. Secretary:** Mrs Lesley Forrest
**Responsibilities**
**Senior:** Grigor Watt (Manager)
**Branches:** Spark's Mechanical Services Ltd, 27 29 Nelson Street, Nottingham, Nottinghamshire NG1 1DR
**US SIC:** 3585, 5074
**UK SIC:** 32841, 61300
**Auditors:** Tawse & Partners

---

**Bankers:** Clydesdale Bank Plc (82-69-23)

| | 31-12-13 | 31-12-12 | 31-12-11 |
|---|---|---|---|
| TO | 16,090,908 | 13,195,356 | 15,573,679 |
| P/L | (176,455) | 72,266 | 628,211 |
| NW | 2,584,677 | 2,979,641 | 3,106,384 |
| WC | 2,043,820 | 2,454,245 | 2,726,605 |
| Emp. | 171 | 150 | 154 |

DUNS 22-186-1219

## Sparring Partners Ltd

(**Subsidiary of:** Sparring Partners Holdings Ltd)
25 Garrick Street, London WC2E 9AX
**Tel:** 02073379790
**Web:** www.sparringpartners.co.uk
**Reg No:** 4204345  **Estd:** 2001 Private Limited Company
**Line of Business:** Other sporting activities not elsewhere classified
**Issued Capital:** £1,206,535
**Directors:** D Cooper, R S Hilton, M D Diaper, S Vernon
**Responsibilities**
**Senior:** Lynda Head (Manager), Gem Williamson (Manager)
**Branches:** Sparring Partners Ltd, High Holborn, London WC1V 6RD
**US SIC:** 7999  **UK SIC:** 97913
**Auditors:** Deloitte & Touche LLP
**Bankers:** HSBC Bank plc (40-18-22)

| | 31-10-13 | 31-10-12 | 31-10-11 |
|---|---|---|---|
| TO | 9,120,163 | 7,493,617 | 6,433,836 |
| P/L | 1,986,369 | 296,344 | 528,231 |
| NW | 3,073,933 | 0,263,602 | 2,359,775 |
| WC | (3,462,106) | (2,713,487) | (343,790) |
| Emp. | 59 | 58 | 41 |

DUNS 73-675-9072

## Sparrows Fluid Power Ltd

Unit 12-13, Murcar Commercial Park, Denmore Road, Aberdeen, Aberdeenshire AB23 8JW
**Tel:** 01224-826888
**Web:** www.sparrowsgroup.com
**Reg No:** 0257776SC  **Estd:** 2003 Private Limited Company
**Line of Business:** Other business activities not elsewhere classified
**Issued Capital:** £1
**Directors:** N A Johnson, S A Mitchell
**Co. Secretary:**
Pinsent Masons Secretarial Limit
**Responsibilities**
**Senior:** Steven Ord (Manager)
**US SIC:** 7399, 1389
**UK SIC:** 83954, 13000
**Auditors:** Deloitte LLP
**Bankers:** Riyad Bank Europe Ltd (60-91-84)

| | 31-12-13 | 31-12-12 | 31-12-11 |
|---|---|---|---|
| TO | 9,122,000 | 8,794,000 | 7,933,000 |
| P/L | 1,748,000 | 1,014,000 | (90,000) |
| NW | 1,648,000 | (172,000) | (1,486,000) |
| WC | 667,000 | (1,097,000) | (2,445,000) |
| Emp. | 51 | 57 | 65 |

DUNS 21-855-3075

## Sparrows Offshore Group Ltd

(**Subsidiary of:** Hawk Caledonia Lp)
Seton House, Murcar Industrial Estate, Denmore Road, Bridge Of Don, Aberdeen, Aberdeenshire AB23 8JW
**Tel:** 01224704868 **Fax:** 01224825191
**Reg No:** 0431036SC  **Estd:** 2012 Private Limited Company
**Line of Business:** Other business activities not elsewhere classified
**Export Sales:** £105,186,000
**Issued Capital:** £57,174
**Directors:** N A Johnson, B A Mccluskie, A J Hoffman, A W Wilkinson, P W Soldatos, D A Sedge, S A Mitchell, B W Connolly
**Co. Secretary:**
Pinset Masons Secretarial Limite
**US SIC:** 7399  **UK SIC:** 83954
**Bankers:** The Royal Bank Of Scotland Plc (83-00-78)

| | 31-12-13 | 31-12-12 |
|---|---|---|
| TO | 211,669,000 | 32,850,000 |
| P/L | (625,000) | (372,000) |
| NW | (116,776,000) | (104,119,000) |
| WC | 20,746,000 | 36,592,000 |
| Emp. | 1,855 | 1,751 |

DUNS 22-593-5519

## Sparshatts Holdings Ltd

Unit 10 Castle Road Eurolink Industrial, Centre, Sittingbourne, Kent ME10 3RN
**Tel:** 01795-479571
**Web:** www.sparshatts.co.uk
**Reg No:** 1559196  **Estd:** 1985 Private Limited Company
**Line of Business:** Sale of new motor vehicles
**Issued Capital:** £460,759
**Principals:** R C Sparshatt (Chairman), D R Jones (Managing), A Sparshatt, Ms H C Jones, M Sparshatt
**Co. Secretary:** Colin Hayward
**Responsibilities**
**HR:** Donna Berllaque (Human Resources Manager)

**Health & Safety:** Donna Berllaque *(Human Resources Manager)*
**US SIC:** 5511, 7539
**UK SIC:** 65100, 67100
**Auditors:** Jones Avens

| | 31-12-13 | 31-12-12 | 31-12-11 |
|---|---|---|---|
| TO | 97,862,630 | 66,210,621 | 57,581,761 |
| P/L | 1,369,747 | 889,379 | 774,971 |
| NW | 8,706,838 | 8,104,754 | 7,680,908 |
| WC | 1,615,834 | 109,759 | 1,009,281 |
| Emp. | 175 | 170 | 178 |

DUNS 52-026-9788

### Sparshatts of Botley Ltd

Newgate Lane, Fareham, Hampshire PO14 1AL
**Tel:** 01489785111 **Fax:** 01329 828182
**Web:** www.sparshattsgroup.co.uk
**Reg No:** 3393853 **Estd:** 1996 Private Limited Company
**Line of Business:** Car dealers (used)
**Trading Style:** Sparshatts of Botley, Sparshatts of Fareham, Sparshatts of Havant, Sparshatts of Hedge End
**Issued Capital:** £1,383,333
**Principals:** L Jones *(Managing)*, N Roberts, S Prebble
**Co. Secretary:** Brian Prebble
**Branches:** Sparshatts Of Botley Ltd, Broad Oak Garage, Broad Oak, Botley, Southampton, Hampshire SO30 2EU
**US SIC:** 5521, 7539
**UK SIC:** 65100, 67100
**Auditors:** BDO LLP

| | 31-10-13 | 31-10-12 | 31-10-11 |
|---|---|---|---|
| TO | 30,018,084 | 25,787,232 | 21,111,174 |
| P/L | 167,204 | 14,415 | 20,932 |
| NW | 2,103,961 | 1,977,078 | 1,468,003 |
| WC | 388,167 | 262,928 | (18,579) |
| Emp. | 77 | 72 | 74 |

DUNS 21-392-4212

### Sparshatts of Kent Dartford

Unit H, Acorn Industrial Park, Crayford Road, Dartford, Kent DA1 4FL
**Tel:** 01322520030
**Web:** www.sparshatts.co.uk
**Estd:** 2010 Proprietorship
**Line of Business:** Commercial vehicle servicing repairs parts & accessories
**US SIC:** 5511 **UK SIC:** 65100
**Employees:** 50

DUNS 23-434-3549

### Sparsholt College

Ivy Cottage, Westley Close, Winchester, Hampshire SO22 5LA
**Web:** www.sparsholt.ac.uk
**VAT No:** 631546452 **Estd:** 1997
**Line of Business:** Training services
**Trading Style:** Wessex Conference Centre, Sparsholt College
**Responsibilities**
**Senior:** Len Norman *(Manager)*
**Finance:** Richard Devonshire *(Finance Director)*, Steve Handford *(Financial Director)*
**HR:** Stewart Cameron *(Personnel Manager)*
**Branches:** Sparsholt College, Charlton Rd, Andover, Hampshire SP10 1EJ
**US SIC:** 8221 **UK SIC:** 93100
**Bankers:** National Westminster Bank Plc (55-81-26)
**Employees:** 600

DUNS 22-513-4683 **Imp**

### Spartal Ltd

**(Subsidiary of:** Spartal Holdings Ltd)
Unit 69 Northwick Business Centre, Northwick Park, Blockley, Moreton-In-Marsh, Gloucestershire GL56 9RF
**Tel:** 01386700898
**Web:** www.spartal.co.uk
**Reg No:** 1551538 **Estd:** 1981 Private Limited Company
**Line of Business:** Other manufacturing not elsewhere classified
**Issued Capital:** £2,700
**Co. Secretary:** Richard Evans
**Responsibilities**
**Marketing:** Stewart Philips *(Sales & Marketing)*
**Sales:** Stewart Philips *(Sales & Marketing)*
**US SIC:** 3999 **UK SIC:** 49590
**Auditors:** Oliver H Smith & Co
**Bankers:** Barclays Bank Plc (20-18-15)

| | 31-03-14 | 31-03-13 | 31-03-12 |
|---|---|---|---|
| TA | 721,791 | 653,004 | 654,770 |
| NW | 358,887 | 339,323 | 263,633 |
| WC | 309,491 | 310,720 | 231,146 |

DUNS 21-105-2425

### Spartan Services Uk Ltd

Woodland Court, Gillhams Lane, Haslemere, Surrey GU27 3ND
**Web:** www.spartanservices.co.uk
**Reg No:** 6478271 **Estd:** 2008 Private Limited Company
**Line of Business:** Security activities
**Issued Capital:** £100

**Director:** S A Hatchard
**Co. Secretary:** Daniel Howden
**US SIC:** 7393 **UK SIC:** 83954

| | 31-01-14 | 31-01-13 | 31-01-12 |
|---|---|---|---|
| TA | 24,658 | 28,417 | 27,906 |
| NW | 11,396 | 13,146 | 13,228 |
| WC | 10,181 | 11,168 | 11,428 |

DUNS 22-121-3098 **Imp**

### Spartan Uk Ltd

**(Subsidiary of:** Scm Holdings Limited)
Ropery Road, Gateshead, Tyne and Wear NE8 2RD
**Tel:** 0191-460-4245 **Fax:** 0191-460-0567
**Web:** www.spartan.metinvestholding.com
**Reg No:** 4140355 **Estd:** 1984 Private Limited Company
**Line of Business:** Manufacture of basic iron and steel and of ferro-alloys
**Issued Capital:** £2,500,000
**Directors:** A Kutepov, A Pogozhev, B Spotorno
**Co. Secretary:** Beach Secretaries Limited
**Responsibilities**
**Senior:** Igor Golchenko *(Manager)*, Neil Locker *(Plant Manager)*, Sergiy Novikov *(Manager)*
**US SIC:** 3325 **UK SIC:** 31110
**Auditors:** PricewaterhouseCoopers LLP

| | 31-12-13 | 31-12-12 | 31-12-11 |
|---|---|---|---|
| TO | 92,125,660 | 78,982,678 | 89,363,971 |
| P/L | (2,517,848) | (8,211,887) | 1,338,914 |
| NW | 30,559,701 | 32,499,187 | 38,565,288 |
| WC | 18,374,918 | 19,688,132 | 25,947,984 |
| Emp. | 116 | 117 | 114 |

DUNS 21-281-6086

### Spaw Engineering Ltd

**(Subsidiary of:** Adrem Enterprises Ltd)
Unit 4 Turner St Dowry Park Industrial, Estate, Oldham, Lancashire OL4 3NU
**Tel:** 01617855100 **Fax:** 01616652335
**Web:** www.spaw.co.uk
**Reg No:** 0852576 **Estd:** 1965 Private Limited Company
**Line of Business:** Manufacture of parts and accessories for motor vehicles and their engines
**Trading Style:** The Spaw Engineering Co
**Issued Capital:** £250
**Principals:** A D Rayner *(Managing)*, P Hardy, H L Rayner
**Co. Secretary:** Andrew Rayner
**Responsibilities**
**Senior:** Roy Hubball *(Operations Director)*
**Facilities:** Roy Hubball *(Operations Director)*
**Operations:** Roy Hubball *(Operations Director)*
**Purchasing:** Tony Heaton *(Purchasing Manager)*
**Engineering:** Roy Hubball *(Operations Director)*
**US SIC:** 3714 **UK SIC:** 35300
**Auditors:** Samuel Slater & Sons
**Bankers:** Barclays Bank Plc (20-64-12)

| | 30-06-13 | 30-06-12 | 30-06-11 |
|---|---|---|---|
| TO | 10,553,296 | 10,492,442 | 11,148,458 |
| P/L | 171,122 | (218,375) | 556,185 |
| NW | 633,548 | 485,804 | 681,128 |
| WC | 544,116 | 405,148 | 596,607 |
| Emp. | 129 | 134 | 131 |

DUNS 22-097-3452

### Spc Europe Ltd

Cory Way, Westbury, Wiltshire BA13 4BR
**Tel:** 01373-866-020 **Fax:** 01373-866-045
**Web:** www.spcuk.com
**Reg No:** 4098629 **VAT No:** 772359015
**Estd:** 2001 Private Limited Company
**Line of Business:** Manufacturers of rubber products
**Export Sales:** £16,050,539
**Trading Style:** Spc Uk
**Issued Capital:** £100
**Principals:** S Hallas *(Managing)*, P M Hallas
**Co. Secretary:** Ms Marilyn Hallas
**US SIC:** 3069 **UK SIC:** 48123
**Auditors:** Brosnans
**Bankers:** Lloyds TSB Bank plc (77-71-73)

| | 31-03-14 | 31-03-13 | 31-03-12 |
|---|---|---|---|
| TO | 28,026,078 | 20,112,853 | 18,324,098 |
| P/L | 1,544,584 | 430,451 | 2,232,441 |
| NW | 4,776,218 | 3,678,679 | 3,444,226 |
| WC | 950,234 | 2,007,650 | 2,506,561 |
| Emp. | 137 | 53 | 54 |

DUNS 67-224-6188

### Spd Development Co Ltd

**(Subsidiary of:** Spd Swiss Precision Diagnostics Gmbh)
Priory Business Park, Stannard Way, Bedford, Bedfordshire MK44 3UP
**Tel:** 01234835000 **Fax:** 01234835006
**Web:** www.clearplan.com
**Reg No:** 6032177 **Estd:** 2006 Private Limited Company
**Line of Business:** Research and experimental development on natural sciences and engineering
**Issued Capital:** £11,404,179

**Directors:** S Wilson, Mrs F J Clancy, Dr S Alaluf, S C Hart
**Co. Secretary:** Allstair Davis
**Responsibilities**
**Senior:** Joanne Winfield *(Manager)*
**US SIC:** 7391 **UK SIC:** 94000
**Bankers:** HSBC Bank plc (40-22-04)

| | 30-06-13 | 30-06-12 | 30-06-11 |
|---|---|---|---|
| TO | 13,529,000 | 13,946,000 | 15,163,000 |
| P/L | 895,000 | 920,000 | 973,000 |
| NW | 4,531,000 | 4,547,000 | 4,283,000 |
| WC | 4,908,000 | 4,346,000 | 4,436,000 |
| Emp. | 133 | 136 | 133 |

DUNS 39-925-6858

### Spdns Nurse Care Community Interest Co

Spdns House, 449 London Road, Westcliff, Westcliff-On-Sea, Essex SS0 9LG
**Web:** www.spdnsnursecare.co.uk
**Reg No:** 2239798 **Estd:** 1988
**Line of Business:** Other human health activities
**Issued Capital:** £2
**Directors:** Miss R M Clark, Mrs G M Booth, Mrs A Cherry, C M Kirby
**Responsibilities**
**Senior:** Nicola Sweeny *(Manager)*
**US SIC:** 8091 **UK SIC:** 95200
**Auditors:** Segrave & Partners

| | 29-09-13 | 30-09-12 | 25-09-11 |
|---|---|---|---|
| TO | N/A | N/A | 2,646,515 |
| P/L | N/A | N/A | 24,301 |
| NW | 417,153 | 379,313 | 304,122 |
| WC | 399,239 | 354,718 | 298,318 |

DUNS 21-231-2394

### Speach & Language Therapy

Plant Hill Clinic, Plant Hill Road, Manchester M9 8LX
**Tel:** 0161-7402186
**Web:** www.cmft.nhs.uk
**Estd:** 1978 Proprietorship
**Line of Business:** Accommodation advice
**Proprietor:** Mrs A Gordon
**Responsibilities**
**Senior:** Elizabeth Figg *(Team Coordinator for Paediatri)*
**US SIC:** 8091 **UK SIC:** 95200
**Employees:** 50

DUNS 38-549-3366

### Speakerbus Group Plc

Fourways House, Ware Road, Hoddesdon, Hertfordshire EN11 9RS
**Web:** www.speakbus.com
**Reg No:** 3330946 **Estd:** 1997 Public Limited Company
**Line of Business:** Management activities of holding companies
**Export Sales:** £6,202,045
**Issued Capital:** £715,750
**Directors:** S J Grave, S J Patey, A Wodhams, I N Hamilton
**US SIC:** 6711 **UK SIC:** 83962
**Auditors:** Moore Stephens

| | 31-05-14 | 31-05-13 | 31-05-12 |
|---|---|---|---|
| TO | 9,538,676 | 10,108,152 | 12,045,240 |
| P/L | 17,870 | (631,660) | (283,228) |
| NW | 631,558 | 600,921 | 1,141,042 |
| WC | 478,398 | (720,629) | (414,948) |
| Emp. | 99 | 110 | 120 |

DUNS 23-715-3767 **Imp**

### Spear Europe Ltd

**(Subsidiary of:** Sgh (No. 2) Ltd)
Christopher Grey Court, Lakeside, Llantarnam Industrial Park, Cwmbran, Gwent NP44 3SE
**Tel:** 01633-627600 **Fax:** 01633-627601
**Web:** www.spearsystem.com
**Reg No:** 3710253 **VAT No:** 741547434
**Estd:** 1999 Private Limited Company
**Line of Business:** Manufacture of plastic packing goods
**Issued Capital:** £113,503
**Directors:** M J Henry, R F Spear, R Spear
**Co. Secretary:** Michael Hill
**US SIC:** 2752 **UK SIC:** 47544
**Auditors:** Deloitte LLP
**Bankers:** Barclays Bank Plc (20-60-58)

| | 31-12-13 | 31-12-12 | 31-12-11 |
|---|---|---|---|
| TO | 36,447,000 | 34,972,000 | 36,031,000 |
| P/L | 615,000 | 3,497,000 | 4,991,000 |
| NW | 15,938,000 | 14,618,000 | 11,531,000 |
| WC | 7,322,000 | 6,807,000 | 3,251,000 |
| Emp. | 145 | 141 | 149 |

DUNS 73-672-0504

### Spear Publishing Ltd

**(Subsidiary of:** Progressive Media International Ltd)
John Carpenter House, John Carpenter Street, London EC4Y 0AN
**Tel:** 02079366445
**Web:** www.spearswms.com
**Reg No:** 4931527 **Estd:** 2003 Private Limited Company
**Line of Business:** Publishing of journals and periodicals

**Issued Capital:** £1
**Directors:** P Danson, W R Cash
**Responsibilities**
**Senior:** Kenneth Appiah *(Manager)*
**US SIC:** 2721 **UK SIC:** 47522

| | 31-12-13 | 31-12-12 | 31-12-11 |
|---|---|---|---|
| TA | 866,973 | 305,116 | 257,000 |
| NW | (1,132,838) | (952,576) | (655,000) |
| WC | (1,134,523) | (955,533) | (657,000) |

DUNS 22-657-9498 **Exp**

### Spearhead International Ltd

Compass House, Chivers Way, Cambridge, Cambridgeshire CB24 9AD
**Tel:** 01223257900
**Web:** www.spearheadinternational.co.uk
**Reg No:** 1056769 **VAT No:** 432130896
**Estd:** 1972 Private Limited Company
**Line of Business:** Farming (mixed)
**Export Markets:** Germany
**Issued Capital:** £3,050,979
**Principals:** T M Green *(Managing)*, R J Clothier, M N Thomas, O Zahn, D Gray, S W Turley, T J Zdziebkowski
**Co. Secretary:** Charles Morgan
**Branches:** Spearhead International Ltd, 50 High St, Ely, Cambridgeshire CB7 5HE
**US SIC:** 6711 **UK SIC:** 83962
**Auditors:** Deloitte LLP
**Bankers:** Barclays Bank Plc (20-17-19)

| | 31-12-13 | 31-12-12 | 31-12-11 |
|---|---|---|---|
| TO | 152,050,000 | 133,292,000 | 139,356,000 |
| P/L | 17,032,000 | 16,401,000 | 20,812,000 |
| NW | 129,545,000 | 120,356,000 | 107,590,000 |
| WC | 73,346,000 | 75,620,000 | 66,194,000 |
| Emp. | 1,423 | 1,257 | 1,236 |

DUNS 21-019-5434 **Imp-Exp**

### Spearmark International Ltd

**(Subsidiary of:** Spearmark Holdings Ltd)
Howard Road, St Neots, Cambridgeshire PE19 8GA
**Tel:** 01480-213633 **Fax:** 01480-217048
**Web:** www.spearmark.co.uk
**Reg No:** 0242587 **VAT No:** 456014859
**Estd:** 1908 Private Limited Company
**Line of Business:** Manufacturers and suppliers of tableware
**Export Markets:** Europe and worldwide
**Issued Capital:** £40,000
**Principals:** T A Bloom *(Managing)*, A S Bloom, A S Bloom, M J Withers, M Fitzjohn, A Turner, R M Bloom
**Co. Secretary:** Darren Price
**Responsibilities**
**Finance:** Katherine Dent *(Credit Controller)*
**Marketing:** Becky Griffiths *(Marketing Coordinator)*
**HR:** Katherine Dent *(Credit Controller)*
**US SIC:** 3421 **UK SIC:** 31621
**Auditors:** Grant Thornton UK LLP
**Bankers:** Lloyds TSB Bank plc (30-94-47)

| | 31-12-13 | 31-12-12 | 31-12-11 |
|---|---|---|---|
| TO | N/A | N/A | 3,730,972 |
| P/L | N/A | N/A | (349,998) |
| NW | 652,610 | 512,704 | 281,078 |
| WC | 551,212 | 435,609 | 209,097 |
| Emp. | N/A | N/A | 61 |

DUNS 23-923-9770

### Spearmint Rhino Ventures (Uk) Ltd

161 Tottenham Court Road, London W1T 7NN
**Tel:** 02072094488
**Reg No:** 3914051 **Estd:** 2000 Private Limited Company
**Line of Business:** Management activities of holding companies
**Issued Capital:** £1,000
**Directors:** Ms K Vercher, J R Specht
**Co. Secretary:** Spearmint Rhino Secretarial Serv
**Branches:** Spearmint Rhino Ventures (Uk) Ltd, 120 High St, Uxbridge, Middlesex UB8 1JT
**US SIC:** 6711 **UK SIC:** 83962

| | 31-12-13 | 31-12-12 | 31-12-11 |
|---|---|---|---|
| TO | 7,701,465 | 8,500,046 | 9,920,229 |
| P/L | 551,217 | (307,701) | (2,090,746) |
| NW | (1,675,133) | (2,042,369) | (1,348,262) |
| WC | (3,868,385) | (5,030,341) | (4,737,894) |
| Emp. | 127 | 139 | 162 |

DUNS 34-521-6642 **Imp**

### Specflue Ltd

8-9 Curzon Road, Sudbury, Suffolk CO10 2XW
**Tel:** 01787880333 **Fax:** 01787-880555
**Web:** www.specflue.com
**Reg No:** 2716331 **VAT No:** 594925880
**Estd:** 1992 Private Limited Company
**Line of Business:** Chimney builders
**Issued Capital:** £3
**Principals:** J Fry *(Managing)*, Mrs J Fry, Ms S E Williams
**Responsibilities**
**Finance:** Antony Williams *(Finance Director)*
**US SIC:** 1799 **UK SIC:** 50000
**Auditors:** Kneill & Co

Bankers: HSBC Bank plc (40-43-23)

| | 31-12-13 | 31-12-12 | 31-12-11 |
|---|---|---|---|
| TO | 20,289,454 | 16,530,034 | 15,957,733 |
| P/L | 1,762,886 | 1,347,394 | 1,403,209 |
| NW | 5,260,491 | 3,894,684 | 5,232,001 |
| WC | 3,524,557 | 3,111,249 | 3,411,537 |
| Emp. | 83 | 77 | 72 |

DUNS 29-519-6067                                    Exp
## The Special Carrier Ltd
Express House, Dover, Kent CT16 3NX
Web: www.specialcarrier.com
Reg No: 1882764 VAT No: 316654751
Estd: 1985 Private Limited Company
Line of Business: Road haulage and transport services
Export Markets: Europe
Trading Style: Nightingale Special Carrier
Issued Capital: £69
Directors: S P Herman, S K Williams
Co. Secretary: Phillip Henley
Branches: Birmingham
US SIC: 4789 UK SIC: 77002
Auditors: McCabe Ford Williams
Bankers: Barclays Bank Plc (20-02-62)

| | 30-09-14 | 30-09-13 | 30-09-12 |
|---|---|---|---|
| TA | 925,016 | 794,574 | 764,062 |
| NW | 394,315 | 375,544 | 350,560 |
| WC | 388,425 | 365,756 | 336,595 |

DUNS 29-199-0166                                    Exp
## Special Contingency Risks Ltd
(Subsidiary of: Willis Group Holdings Public Limited Company)
30 Fenchurch Avenue, London EC3M 5AD
Tel: 020-7088-9100 Fax: 020-7208-5223
Web: www.scr-ltd.co.uk
Reg No: 0617667 Estd: 1958 Private Limited Company
Line of Business: Insurance - commercial
Export Sales: £7,377,000
Issued Capital: £750,000
Directors: D R Milne, Ms J Timms-Mitchell, P A Owens, Ms J R Holliday
Co. Secretary: Alistair Peel
Responsibilities
Senior: Jenner Fitzgerald (Executive Assistant)
Finance: Matthew Wignall (Head Of Accounts)
HR: Emma Baker (Personnel Manager)
US SIC: 6411 UK SIC: 83200
Auditors: Deloitte & Touche LLP

| | 31-12-13 | 31-12-12 | 31-12-11 |
|---|---|---|---|
| TO | 8,265,000 | 7,495,000 | 7,123,000 |
| P/L | 2,485,000 | 1,414,000 | 2,626,000 |
| NW | 8,030,000 | 6,117,000 | 11,081,000 |
| WC | 13,354,000 | 6,513,000 | 11,796,000 |
| Emp. | 46 | 34 | 34 |

DUNS 21-582-9008
## Special E U Programmes Body
7th Floor 2 Clarence St West, Belfast BT2 7GP
Tel: 028-9026-6660
Web: www.seupb.eu
Estd: 2007
Line of Business: Financial services
Proprietor: P Colgan
Branches: Special E U Programmes Body, EU Ho, 11 Kevlin Rd, Omagh - BT78 1LB.
US SIC: 6111, 7399
UK SIC: 81501, 83954
Bankers: The Bank Of Ireland (90-21-27)
Employees: 50

DUNS 21-814-4277                               Imp-Exp
## Special Metals Wiggin Ltd
(Subsidiary of: Precision Castparts Corp.)
Holmer Road, Hereford, Herefordshire HR4 9SL
Tel: 01432-382200 Fax: 01432-264030
Web: www.specialmetals.com
Reg No: 0036721 VAT No: 135070108
Estd: 1835 Private Limited Company
Line of Business: Other non-ferrous metal production
Issued Capital: £770,090
Directors: K B Smith, Ms R A Beyer, R S Pattee, S C Blackmore, Mrs S R Hagel, P A Groves, R P Becker, K D Buck
Co. Secretary: Paul Edelstyn
Responsibilities
Sales: Tracey Holmes (Sales Manager), Claire Reynolds (Sales Manager)
Operations: Bob Meredith (Environmental Officer)
Branches: Special Metals Wiggin Ltd, Unit 6 Regal Rd, Stratford-Upon-Avon, Warwickshire CV37 0AZ
US SIC: 3339, 3496
UK SIC: 22470, 31694
Auditors: Deloitte & Touche LLP
Bankers: HSBC Bank plc (40-31-24)

| | 30-03-14 | 31-03-13 | 01-03-12 |
|---|---|---|---|
| TO | 133,437,000 | 146,817,000 | 155,912,000 |
| P/L | 20,634,000 | 25,430,000 | 18,532,000 |
| NW | 127,928,000 | 110,310,000 | 88,439,000 |
| WC | 101,565,000 | 86,120,000 | 66,662,000 |
| Emp. | 569 | 600 | 630 |

DUNS 21-130-6423
## Special Offer Supplies
Stores Road, East Midlands, Derby, Derbyshire DE21 4BD
Tel: 01332 361761
Web: www.specialoffersupplies.com
VAT No: 507829723 Estd: 2002 Partnership
Line of Business: Cash and carry wholesalers
Trading Style: Sos
Partners: S I Beckett, M Beckett
Branches: Special Offer Supplies, 128 West Street, Barnsley, South Yorkshire S74 9DU
US SIC: 5199 UK SIC: 61900
Bankers: National Westminster Bank Plc (60-12-01)
Employees: 70

DUNS 21-634-4459
## Special People Partnership Ltd
Laundry Club Sparsholt Road, London N19 4EL
Tel: 02076862488
Web: http://specialpeople.org.uk
Reg No: 7121508 Estd: 2010 Private Limited Company
Line of Business: Social work activities without accommodation
Issued Capital: £1
Director: Ms J L Skinner
US SIC: 8321 UK SIC: 96111

| | 31-03-14 | 31-03-13 | 31-03-12 |
|---|---|---|---|
| TA | 325,858 | 240,166 | 298,456 |
| NW | 107,820 | 37,073 | 36,272 |
| WC | 102,108 | 32,275 | 36,272 |

DUNS 21-964-6079
## Special Piping Materials (Holdings) Ltd
Unit 26, Globe Lane Industrial Estate, Dukinfield, Cheshire SK16 4UU
Tel: 01613437005
Reg No: 8699508 Estd: 2013 Private Limited Company
Line of Business: Wholesale of metals and ores
Issued Capital: £5
Directors: Mrs M L Buckley, L Buckley
Co. Secretary: Ms Anne King
US SIC: 5051 UK SIC: 61200

| | 31-12-13 |
|---|---|
| TO | 27,834,561 |
| P/L | 2,646,117 |
| NW | 17,140,007 |
| WC | 14,193,911 |
| Emp. | 55 |

DUNS 29-659-2405                                    Imp
## Special Quality Alloys Ltd
(Subsidiary of: Special Steel Co. Ltd)
Continental Works, Sheffield, South Yorkshire S9 3XN
Tel: 01142-434366
Web: www.specialqualityalloys.com
Reg No: 1985443 VAT No: 438951417
Estd: 1986 Private Limited Company
Line of Business: Manufacture of other fabricated metal products not elsewhere classified
Export Sales: £13,538,064
Issued Capital: £100,000
Principals: A K Beardshaw (Managing), S G Marshall, D M Pryce, B J Beardshaw, R Wood, R L Stevens
Responsibilities
Senior: Dean Matthews (Works Director)
Finance: Mike Greensmith (Accounts)
US SIC: 3499, 3325
UK SIC: 31694, 31110
Auditors: Barber Harrison & Platt
Bankers: National Westminster Bank Plc (56-00-09)

| | 31-05-14 | 31-05-13 | 31-05-12 |
|---|---|---|---|
| TO | 31,127,706 | 32,634,578 | 31,842,545 |
| P/L | 3,045,918 | 4,222,659 | 6,161,477 |
| NW | 18,770,719 | 18,349,237 | 16,912,365 |
| WC | 16,799,357 | 16,965,866 | 15,634,046 |
| Emp. | 61 | 59 | 58 |

DUNS 22-802-0749
## Special Testing Ltd
(Subsidiary of: Special Steel Co. Ltd)
Bacon Lane, Sheffield, South Yorkshire S9 3NH
Tel: 01142-441061
Web: www.specialtesting.co.uk
Reg No: 0355744 Estd: 1939 Private Limited Company
Line of Business: Technical testing and analysis
Trading Style: Special Testing Ltd
Issued Capital: £100,000
Principals: A K Beardshaw (Managing), B J Beardshaw, D Cundy
US SIC: 7397 UK SIC: 83702
Auditors: Barber Harrison & Platt

Bankers: Barclays Bank Plc (20-76-89)

| | 31-05-14 | 31-05-13 | 31-05-12 |
|---|---|---|---|
| TA | 1,512,479 | 1,480,493 | 1,117,120 |
| NW | 218,154 | 361,056 | 316,705 |
| WC | (79,498) | 83,807 | 102,118 |

DUNS 23-944-9507
## Specialised Automotive
West End Road, High Wycombe, Buckinghamshire HP11 2QB
Web: www.motshop.biz
VAT No: 208691943 Estd: 1972 Proprietorship
Line of Business: Garage related services
Proprietor: N Rogers
US SIC: 7539 UK SIC: 67100
Bankers: Barclays Bank Plc (20-40-71)
Employees: 49

DUNS 50-384-1165                                    Imp
## Specialised Belting Supplies Ltd
26-32 Brunel Way, Thetford, Norfolk IP24 1HP
Tel: 01842-754392
Web: www.sbsbelting.com
Reg No: 2393041 VAT No: 571099428
Estd: 1984 Private Limited Company
Line of Business: Conveyor belts and systems
Trading Style: Specialised Belting Supplies
Issued Capital: £490
Director: M Welp
Co. Secretary: Barry Mills
Responsibilities
Senior: Steve Farmer (Works Manager), Geoff Toft (Manager)
Health & Safety: Michael Bax (Health & Safety Officer)
US SIC: 3534, 3069
UK SIC: 32553, 48123
Auditors: Lovewell Blake LLP
Bankers: Lloyds TSB Bank plc (30-91-49)

| | 31-12-13 | 31-12-12 | 31-12-11 |
|---|---|---|---|
| TO | N/A | 5,991,685 | N/A |
| P/L | N/A | 23,429 | N/A |
| NW | 2,345,114 | 2,323,976 | 2,303,884 |
| WC | 1,706,430 | 1,261,588 | 1,363,661 |
| Emp. | N/A | 52 | N/A |

DUNS 21-770-9052
## Specialised Commission Team
Quayside Building Bruntwood Site, Greenalls Avenue, Warrington, Cheshire WA4 6HL
Tel: 01925406000
Web: www.cmha.nhs.uk
Estd: 2011 Proprietorship
Line of Business: Health authorities
Proprietor: A Spours
Responsibilities
Senior: John Devling (Chief Executive)
US SIC: 8062 UK SIC: 95100
Employees: 150

DUNS 77-543-2602
## Specialised Orthotic Services Ltd
127-128 Fauld Industrial Park, Fauld, Tutbury, Tutbury, Burton-On-Trent, Staffordshire DE13 9HS
Tel: 01283-520400 Fax: 01283-520401
Web: www.specialisedorthoticservices.co.uk
Reg No: 2996918 VAT No: 616975309
Estd: 1994 Private Limited Company
Line of Business: Manufacture of medical and surgical equipment and orthopaedic appliances
Export Sales: £9,009
Issued Capital: £2
Principals: G Mcquilton (Managing), M T Waine, R J Mcgleenan
Co. Secretary: Michael Waine
US SIC: 3841, 8091
UK SIC: 37201, 95200
Auditors: Bates Weston

| | 31-12-13 | 31-12-12 | 31-12-11 |
|---|---|---|---|
| TO | 5,585,994 | N/A | N/A |
| P/L | 522,023 | N/A | N/A |
| NW | 3,217,294 | 2,846,743 | 2,380,209 |
| WC | 1,068,037 | 1,177,381 | 846,812 |
| Emp. | 89 | N/A | N/A |

DUNS 76-854-6756                               Imp-Exp
## Specialised Petroleum Manufacturing Ltd
(Subsidiary of: The Weir Group Plc)
S P M House Badentoy Crescent, Badentoy Crescent Industrial Estate, Portlethen, Aberdeen, Aberdeenshire AB12 4YD
Tel: 01224-783666
Web: www.weiroilandgas.com
Reg No: 0131809SC VAT No: 553228941
Estd: 1991 Private Limited Company
Line of Business: Oil and gas exploration services
Export Markets: Europe and Central America
Trading Style: Weir Spm

Issued Capital: £1,000
Directors: D A Paradis, C B Mcgregor, J P Zeller, A Mcdonald
Co. Secretary: Colin Mcgregor
Responsibilities
Senior: Alasdair Murray (General Manager), Alistair Robb (Manager)
Marketing: Raymond Thomson (Sales & Marketing Engineer)
Sales: Raymond Thomson (Sales & Marketing Engineer)
HR: Alistair Robb (Manager)
Health & Safety: Alistair Robb (Manager)
Facilities: Alistair Robb (Manager)
US SIC: 1389, 7394
UK SIC: 13000, 84000
Auditors: Ernst & Young LLP
Bankers: The Royal Bank Of Scotland Plc (83-07-06)

| | 03-01-14 | 28-12-12 | 30-01-11 |
|---|---|---|---|
| TO | 25,471,000 | 24,706,000 | 18,284,000 |
| P/L | 2,661,000 | 4,656,000 | 3,455,000 |
| NW | 26,797,000 | 24,761,000 | 21,008,000 |
| WC | 23,599,000 | 22,131,000 | 18,422,000 |
| Emp. | 53 | 48 | 46 |

DUNS 22-902-8345
## Specialised Petroleum Services International Ltd
(Subsidiary of: Schlumberger N.V.)
Endeavour Drive, Westhill, Aberdeenshire AB32 6UF
Tel: 01224-742200 Fax: 01224-742288
Web: www.miswaco.com
Reg No: 0071516SC VAT No: 297389096
Estd: 1991 Private Limited Company
Line of Business: Drilling and boring equipment
Trading Style: Mi Sweco Specialised Tools
Issued Capital: £250,000
Directors: R A Kidd, I Jack
Co. Secretary: Ms Pauline Droy Moore
Responsibilities
Sales: Ron Evett (Senior Sales Executive)
Health & Safety: Maureen Phyfer (Quality Manager)
US SIC: 3531 UK SIC: 32541
Auditors: Deloitte LLP
Bankers: The Royal Bank Of Scotland Plc (83-49-40)

| | 31-12-13 | 31-12-12 | 31-12-11 |
|---|---|---|---|
| TA | 33,854,000 | 33,934,000 | 33,446,000 |
| P/L | 34,000 | N/A | N/A |
| NW | 10,005,000 | 10,051,000 | 10,379,000 |
| WC | 10,005,000 | 10,051,000 | 10,379,000 |

DUNS 50-386-2583                               Imp-Exp
## Specialised Wiring Accessories Ltd
Charfield Road Kingswood, Wotton-Under-Edge, Gloucestershire GL12 8RL
Tel: 01453844333 Fax: 01453-842224
Web: www.s-w-a.co.uk
Reg No: 2395173 VAT No: 484766494
Estd: 1989 Private Limited Company
Line of Business: Electrical wholesalers
Export Markets: E.E.C.
Export Sales: £644,969
Trading Style: S W A
Issued Capital: £6
Directors: G E Ray, B Hands
Co. Secretary: Garry Ray
Responsibilities
Senior: Warren Gibbons (Office Manager)
Admin: Warren Gibbons (Office Manager)
HR: Warren Gibbons (Office Manager)
Operations: Warren Gibbons (Office Manager)
Purchasing: Paul Pring (Purchasing Manager)
US SIC: 5074 UK SIC: 61300
Auditors: Davies Williams
Bankers: Barclays Bank Plc (20-33-83)

| | 30-06-14 | 30-06-13 | 30-06-12 |
|---|---|---|---|
| TO | 9,324,605 | 8,346,007 | 9,197,152 |
| P/L | 518,206 | 489,452 | 321,426 |
| NW | 1,582,479 | 1,372,782 | 1,577,593 |
| WC | 1,236,128 | 1,025,255 | 1,247,402 |
| Emp. | 54 | 53 | 54 |

DUNS 22-868-5822                               Imp-Exp
## Specialist Anodising Co Ltd
(Subsidiary of: Lendlock Group Limited)
New Hall Works, Elm Street, Burnley, Lancashire BB10 1NY
Tel: 01282-412500
Web: www.sacoltd.com
Reg No: 1849981 VAT No: 375474521
Estd: 1984 Private Limited Company
Line of Business: Anodisers
Export Markets: U S A; Europe
Export Sales: £11,427,673
Trading Style: S A C O
Issued Capital: £6
Director: Mrs V A Duffell
Co. Secretary: Michael Duffell

**Responsibilities**
**Senior:** Roy Barlow *(Manager)*, Richard Bilo *(Anodising Director)*, Andrea Clarking *(Manufacturing Manager)*, Graham Logue *(General Manager)*
**Operations:** Andrea Clarking *(Manufacturing Manager)*
**Engineering:** Mark Gwinnet *(Engineering Manager)*
**US SIC:** 3398 **UK SIC:** 31380
**Auditors:** Wilson Henry LLP
**Bankers:** National Westminster Bank Plc (60-16-22)

| | 31-07-13 | 31-07-12 | 31-07-11 |
|---|---|---|---|
| TO | 14,060,884 | 12,570,300 | 12,314,234 |
| P/L | 3,222,696 | 2,812,121 | 2,120,689 |
| NW | 11,560,521 | 9,113,116 | 7,027,604 |
| WC | 8,274,420 | 7,028,553 | 4,964,507 |
| Emp. | 220 | 213 | 200 |

DUNS 34-825-8146 **Imp**

## Specialist Aviation Services Ltd

Gloucestershire Airport, Staverton, Cheltenham, Gloucestershire GL51 6SS
**Tel:** 01452857999
**Web:** www.eurojet.co.uk
**Reg No:** 2799272 **Estd:** 1984 Private Limited Company
**Line of Business:** Police forces
**Export Sales:** £9,714,000
**Trading Style:** Helicopter (Uk), Medical Aviation Services, Police Aviation Services
**Issued Capital:** £5,373,083
**Directors:** K R Van Den Nieuwenhuijzen, J F Van Den Nieuwenhuitzen, A H Schaeken, Ms P S Walker
**Co. Secretary:** Pinsent Masons Secretarial Limit
**Responsibilities**
**Senior:** Michael Hayle *(Manager)*, Thomas Piron *(Manager)*, Henk Schaeken *(Manager)*
**Marketing:** Nigel Lemon *(Sales & Marketing Manager)*
**Sales:** Nigel Lemon *(Sales & Marketing Manager)*
**Purchasing:** Kasthuri Fraser *(Purchasing Manager)*
**US SIC:** 4582, 3714
**UK SIC:** 76400, 35300
**Auditors:** Hazlewoods LLP
**Bankers:** National Westminster Bank Plc (52-41-27)

| | 31-12-13 | 31-12-12 | 31-12-11 |
|---|---|---|---|
| TO | 25,988,000 | 23,491,000 | 22,113,000 |
| P/L | 2,518,000 | 1,785,000 | 1,837,000 |
| NW | 14,479,000 | 13,462,000 | 11,015,000 |
| WC | 1,578,000 | 4,133,000 | 3,445,000 |
| Emp. | 166 | 142 | 135 |

DUNS 21-744-5345

## Specialist Building Products Ltd

**(Subsidiary of:** Epwin Group Plc)
Apollo, Lichfield Road Industrial Estate, Tamworth, Staffordshire B79 7TA
**Tel:** 0182754422 **Fax:** 01724-280-241
**Web:** www.scp-uk.com
**Reg No:** 1268689 **VAT No:** 864450710
**Estd:** 2002 Private Limited Company
**Line of Business:** Manufacture of other plastic products
**Export Sales:** £14,559,000
**Trading Style:** Kestrel
**Issued Capital:** £101,000
**Directors:** C A Empson, J A Bednall
**Co. Secretary:** Epwin Secretaries Limited
**Responsibilities**
**Senior:** Mark Dodds *(Works Manager)*, Sean Rice *(Manager)*
**Marketing:** Greg Wilde *(Marketing Manager)*
**Branches:** Specialist Building Products Ltd, Dart Sensors Ltd, Elm House, Exeter, Devon EX4 3BA
**US SIC:** 3079, 1761
**UK SIC:** 48360, 50400
**Auditors:** KPMG LLP
**Bankers:** National Westminster Bank Plc (56-00-49)

| | 31-12-13 | 31-12-12 | 31-12-11 |
|---|---|---|---|
| TO | 238,794,000 | 177,310,000 | 177,004,000 |
| P/L | 8,649,000 | 6,520,000 | 7,552,000 |
| NW | 16,390,000 | 10,931,000 | 4,245,000 |
| WC | 28,018,000 | 12,993,000 | 8,001,000 |
| Emp. | 1,953 | 1,645 | 1,732 |

DUNS 22-562-5433

## Specialist Cars

Gunnels Wood Road, Stevenage, Hertfordshire SG1 2BT
**Tel:** 01438760200
**Web:** www.specialistcars.co.uk
**Estd:** 1971 Partnership
**Line of Business:** Sale of motor vehicles
**Partners:** M Donavon, C Fletcher
**US SIC:** 5511 **UK SIC:** 65100
**Employees:** 150

DUNS 29-556-2904

## Specialist Cars (Aberdeen) Ltd

**(Subsidiary of:** John Clark (Holdings) Ltd)
53 Abbotswell Road, Aberdeen, Aberdeenshire AB12 3AD
**Tel:** 01224400500 **Fax:** 01224-336895
**Web:** www.john-clark.co.uk
**Reg No:** 0093775SC **Estd:** 1985 Private Limited Company
**Line of Business:** Sale of new motor vehicles
**Issued Capital:** £100,000
**Principals:** J H Clark *(Managing)*, C J Clark, R S North, M H Shaw
**Co. Secretary:** Ms Deirdre Clark
**Responsibilities**
**Operations:** Julie Stewart *(Operations Manager)*
**Branches:** Specialist Cars (Aberdeen) Ltd, Abbotswell Rd West Tullos, Aberdeen, Aberdeenshire AB12 3AD
**US SIC:** 5511, 5521, 7539, 5531
**UK SIC:** 65100, 67100
**Auditors:** KPMG Audit PLC
**Bankers:** Bank Of Scotland (80-05-14)

| | 31-12-13 | 31-12-12 | 31-12-11 |
|---|---|---|---|
| TO | 253,785,980 | 203,513,157 | 180,840,751 |
| P/L | 6,124,195 | 4,234,359 | 3,869,563 |
| NW | 10,500,466 | 7,063,390 | 5,089,584 |
| WC | 8,558,622 | 5,261,132 | 3,199,270 |
| Emp. | 478 | 447 | 435 |

DUNS 67-217-9079

## Specialist Cars Holdings Ltd

C/O Specialist Cars Ltd, Arlington Business Park, Stevenage, Hertfordshire SG1 2BE
**Tel:** 08455394966
**Reg No:** 6047694 **Estd:** 2007 Private Limited Company
**Line of Business:** Management activities of holding companies
**Issued Capital:** £100,000
**Directors:** C M Fletcher, M J Donovan
**Co. Secretary:** Clive James
**US SIC:** 6711 **UK SIC:** 83962
**Bankers:** Barclays Bank Plc (20-03-80)

| | 31-12-13 | 31-12-12 | 31-12-11 |
|---|---|---|---|
| TO | 155,062,034 | 136,673,015 | 130,650,954 |
| P/L | 1,147,073 | 1,124,661 | 1,001,286 |
| NW | 11,295,488 | 11,197,260 | 10,107,404 |
| WC | 4,731,826 | 4,969,564 | 4,171,233 |
| Emp. | 289 | 271 | 268 |

DUNS 21-041-6359

## Specialist Cars Volkswagen

Craigshaw Crescent, West Tullos Industrial Estate, Aberdeen, Aberdeenshire AB12 3AW
**Tel:** 01224384000
**Web:** www.voltswagenaberdeen.co.uk
**Estd:** 2005 Proprietorship
**Line of Business:** Car dealers (new & used)
**Proprietor:** M Shaw
**US SIC:** 5511 **UK SIC:** 65100
**Employees:** 70

DUNS 21-929-5870

## Specialist Computer Services Ltd

**(Subsidiary of:** Rigby Group (Rg) Plc)
James House, Warwick Road, Birmingham, West Midlands B11 2LE
**Tel:** 01217411230 **Fax:** 01217733986
**Web:** www.scc.com
**Reg No:** 0893138 **Estd:** 1986 Private Limited Company
**Line of Business:** Hardware consultancy
**Trading Style:** S C S
**Issued Capital:** £50,000
**Principals:** Sir P Rigby *(Chairman and Managing)*, J P Rigby, Mrs P A Rigby, T Markham
**Branches:** Specialist Computer Services Ltd, Lady Bay Retail Park, Meadow Lane, Nottingham, Nottinghamshire NG2 3GZ
**US SIC:** 7379 **UK SIC:** 83940
**Auditors:** Deloitte LLP
**Bankers:** HSBC Bank plc (40-46-04)

| | 31-03-14 | 31-03-13 | 31-03-12 |
|---|---|---|---|
| TO | 3,903,000 | 3,858,000 | 3,984,000 |
| P/L | 383,000 | 403,000 | 437,000 |
| NW | 1,602,000 | 1,927,000 | 1,416,000 |
| WC | 1,322,000 | 1,516,000 | 1,254,000 |
| Emp. | 69 | 70 | 74 |

DUNS 22-093-5741

## Specialist Crafts Ltd

Hamilton House, 21 Mountain Road, Leicester, Leicestershire LE4 9HQ
**Tel:** 01162697711 **Fax:** 01162-697722
**Web:** www.craftsuperstore.co.uk
**Reg No:** 4094887 **Estd:** 2000 Private Limited Company
**Line of Business:** Other wholesale
**Issued Capital:** £2,000,000
**Directors:** Miss L Beavon, N Beavon
**Co. Secretary:** Alan Beavon
**Responsibilities**
**Finance:** Angela Raynor *(Finance Director)*
**Sales:** Chris Burch *(Sales Manager)*
**Branches:** Specialist Crafts Ltd, Unit 2 Wanlip Road, Leicester, Leicestershire LE7 1PD
**US SIC:** 5961 **UK SIC:** 65600
**Auditors:** Grant Thornton UK LLP
**Bankers:** Lloyds TSB Bank plc (30-16-93)

| | 31-08-14 | 31-08-13 | 31-08-12 |
|---|---|---|---|
| TO | 11,073,052 | 10,052,393 | 9,644,216 |
| P/L | 705,998 | 382,742 | 133,274 |
| NW | 1,548,414 | 1,213,518 | 1,060,679 |
| WC | 1,151,639 | 816,350 | 789,990 |
| Emp. | 63 | 61 | 63 |

DUNS 37-849-3001

## Specialist Engineering Services Ltd

**(Subsidiary of:** Ses (Specialist Engineering) Group Ltd)
S E S House Harworth Park Blyth Road, Doncaster, South Yorkshire DN11 8DB
**Tel:** 01302756800
**Web:** www.ses-holdings.com
**Reg No:** 3300301 **VAT No:** 847719091
**Estd:** 1997 Private Limited Company
**Line of Business:** Civil engineers
**Trading Style:** Ses
**Issued Capital:** £15,400
**Directors:** W T Shinkins, Ms J Shinkins, D Hyland
**Responsibilities**
**Senior:** Carl Abraitis *(Manager)*, Susan Hirst *(Manager)*
**Branches:** Specialist Engineering Services Ltd, Daw Mill Colliery, Daw Mill Lane, Coventry, West Midlands CV7 8HS
**US SIC:** 8911, 1622
**UK SIC:** 83701, 50200
**Auditors:** Child & Co
**Bankers:** Barclays Bank Plc (20-37-13)

| | 31-03-14 | 31-03-13 | 31-03-12 |
|---|---|---|---|
| TO | 15,671,245 | 13,070,846 | 8,263,728 |
| P/L | 259,178 | (75,247) | 30,872 |
| NW | (340,790) | (556,218) | (417,876) |
| WC | (538,194) | (747,152) | (574,923) |
| Emp. | 46 | 60 | 63 |

DUNS 21-293-8567 **Imp**

## Specialist Group Ltd

Guiness Circle, Manchester M17 1EB
**Tel:** 01618720626 **Fax:** 0161-873-7778
**Web:** www.specialistgr.com
**Reg No:** 0985943 **VAT No:** 145419763
**Estd:** 1969 Private Limited Company
**Line of Business:** Photographic activities not elsewhere classified
**Export Sales:** £228,615
**Trading Style:** Specialist Group Ltd
**Issued Capital:** £7,092
**Principals:** J P Franks *(Managing)*, A L Bracken *(Sales)*, Miss D R Franks, Mrs M I Franks
**Co. Secretary:** Ms Lynne Hackett
**Responsibilities**
**Senior:** Josh Benson *(Proprietor)*
**Branches:** Specialist Group Ltd, Premier Ho, 2 Grayton Rd, Harrow, Middlesex HA1 2XU
**US SIC:** 5199 **UK SIC:** 61900
**Auditors:** Percy Westhead & Co
**Bankers:** Bank Of Scotland (12-08-95)

| | 28-02-14 | 28-02-13 | 29-02-12 |
|---|---|---|---|
| TO | 6,511,557 | 5,811,082 | 5,773,021 |
| P/L | 123,543 | 108,293 | (12,970) |
| NW | 1,810,550 | 1,818,251 | 1,876,569 |
| WC | 1,824,986 | 1,715,760 | 1,739,014 |
| Emp. | 56 | 52 | 55 |

DUNS 21-909-6385 **Imp-Exp**

## Specialist Heat Exchangers Ltd

**(Subsidiary of:** Dynamic Technologies Spa)
Freeman Road, North Hykeham, Lincoln, Lincolnshire LN6 9AP
**Web:** www.specheat.co.uk
**Reg No:** 0936014 **VAT No:** 911526646
**Estd:** 1968 Private Limited Company
**Line of Business:** Manufacture of non-domestic cooling and ventilation equipment
**Export Markets:** Worldwide
**Export Sales:** £5,067,000
**Trading Style:** S H E
**Issued Capital:** £500,000
**Directors:** I C Sheriff, G Berti
**Co. Secretary:** Walter Zonta
**Branches:** Lincoln
**US SIC:** 3585, 8911
**UK SIC:** 32841, 83701
**Auditors:** Deloitte LLP
**Bankers:** National Westminster Bank Plc (60-12-01)

| | 31-12-13 | 31-12-12 | 31-12-11 |
|---|---|---|---|
| TO | 8,694,000 | 9,524,000 | 9,899,000 |
| P/L | 724,000 | 1,029,000 | 1,263,000 |
| NW | 3,989,000 | 3,381,000 | 4,300,000 |
| WC | 1,364,000 | 625,000 | 1,386,000 |
| Emp. | 120 | 120 | 115 |

DUNS 42-426-1522

## The Specialist Hire Group Ltd

Hinckley Fields Industrial Estate, Barleyfield, Hinckley, Leicestershire LE10 1YE
**Tel:** 01388-770700
**Web:** www.specialisthiregroup.co.uk
**Reg No:** 4413747 **Estd:** 2002 Private Limited Company
**Line of Business:** Management activities of holding companies
**Issued Capital:** £496,830
**Directors:** G Holyland, G Farquhar, Mrs J Loke, P Cosgrove, Nova General Partner (Guernsey), J Chappell
**Co. Secretary:** Ms Lynn Cosgrove
**US SIC:** 6711 **UK SIC:** 83962
**Auditors:** Mitchell Gordon LLP

| | 31-08-13 | 31-08-12 | 31-08-11 |
|---|---|---|---|
| TO | 28,746,308 | 28,853,510 | 23,465,810 |
| P/L | 1,995,491 | 1,778,858 | 794,234 |
| NW | 7,245,716 | 6,276,573 | 4,892,779 |
| WC | (2,814,107) | (3,891,108) | (4,438,284) |
| Emp. | 236 | 241 | 236 |

DUNS 22-693-1236

## Specialist Holidays Ltd

**(Subsidiary of:** Tui Ag)
St Marks Hill, Wood Street, Surbiton, Surrey KT6 4BH
**Tel:** 02089395035 **Fax:** 08708487031
**Web:** www.specialistholidays.com
**Reg No:** 1976915 **VAT No:** 492493022
**Estd:** 1986 Private Limited Company
**Line of Business:** Tour operators
**Export Sales:** £87,000
**Trading Style:** Crystal Holidays
**Issued Capital:** £1,100,000
**Director:** M R Prior
**Co. Secretary:** Mrs Joyce Walter
**Responsibilities**
**Senior:** Samantha Clapton *(Head of Sales)*
**Sales:** Samantha Clapton *(Head of Sales)*
**IT:** Paul Sebry *(Computer Support Manager)*
**Facilities:** Keith Gillard *(Facilities Manager)*
**Operations:** Samantha Clapton *(Head of Sales)*
**US SIC:** 7999, 7399, 5961
**UK SIC:** 97913, 83954, 65600
**Auditors:** PricewaterhouseCoopers LLP
**Bankers:** Lloyds TSB Bank plc (30-98-77)

| | 30-09-13 | 30-09-12 | 30-09-11 |
|---|---|---|---|
| TO | 87,000 | 88,000 | 119,000 |
| P/L | 464,000 | 55,000 | 721,000 |
| NW | 4,764,000 | 4,163,000 | 4,131,000 |
| WC | 2,033,000 | 1,421,000 | 1,356,000 |

DUNS 21-783-5384

## Specialist Inclusion Division

Ash Way, Newcastle, Staffordshire ST5 3UB
**Tel:** 01782297524
**Web:** www.staffordshire.gov.uk
**Proprietorship**
**Line of Business:** Adult and other education not elsewhere classified
**Proprietor:** F Morgan
**US SIC:** 8249 **UK SIC:** 93300
**Employees:** 60

DUNS 23-273-3477 **Exp**

## Specialist Joinery Fittings Ltd

100 Coleraine Road, Maghera, Co Londonderry BT46 5BP
**Tel:** 028-7964-3021
**Web:** www.sjg.co.uk
**Reg No:** 0022906NI **VAT No:** 432791937
**Estd:** 1989 Private Limited Company
**Line of Business:** Manufacture of builders carpentry and joinery
**Export Markets:** EU, Middle East, North America
**Issued Capital:** £180,000
**Directors:** C J Campbell, M P Collins, S P O'Hagan, D H O'Hagan, Mrs T O'Hagan, Miss P Mccloskey, J B O'Hagan, C P O'Hagan
**Co. Secretary:** Mrs Teresa O'Hagan
**Responsibilities**
**Senior:** Teresa O' Hagan *(Director)*
**US SIC:** 2517 **UK SIC:** 46714
**Bankers:** Northern Bank Ltd (95-03-81)

| | 30-04-14 | 30-04-13 | 30-04-12 |
|---|---|---|---|
| TO | 8,619,544 | 6,923,036 | N/A |
| P/L | 152,416 | 162,551 | N/A |
| NW | 1,672,499 | 1,546,191 | 1,119,650 |
| WC | 438,854 | 524,826 | 715,736 |
| Emp. | 90 | 82 | N/A |

DUNS 21-112-3244

## Specialist Machine Developments (Smd) Ltd

The Outlook, Ling Road, Tower Park, Poole, Dorset BH12 4PY
**Tel:** 01912348585
**Web:** www.smdltd.co.uk
**Reg No:** 6533623 **Estd:** 1971 Private Limited Company

**Line of Business:** Manufacture of other special purpose machinery not elsewhere classified
**Export Sales:** £25,782,042
**Issued Capital:** £1,198,544
**Directors:** A Hodgson, A D Sims, C J Gill, Mrs C A Richards, A D Caffyn, T Smallbone, J P Reece
**Co. Secretary:** Richard Howarth
**Responsibilities**
IT: Paul Cavern (IT Manager)
**US SIC:** 3999, 3519
**UK SIC:** 49590, 32811
**Auditors:** Ernst & Young LLP
**Bankers:** Barclays Bank Plc (20-00-30)

|     | 31-12-13 | 31-12-12 | 31-12-11 |
|-----|----------|----------|----------|
| TO  | 76,041,237 | 128,765,586 | 95,931,172 |
| P/L | (6,974,251) | (4,699,518) | (2,524,628) |
| NW  | (68,189,436) | (64,618,285) | (62,167,094) |
| WC  | 3,233,913 | 2,469,152 | 4,255,575 |
| Emp. | 330 | 352 | 244 |

DUNS 50-498-1713
## Specialist Mortgage Services Ltd
(Subsidiary of: Computershare Limited)
Prospect House, Po Box 72, Scarborough, North Yorkshire YO11 3WW
**Tel:** 01723504390 **Fax:** 01723-586817
**Web:** www.scarboroughms.co.uk
**Reg No:** 2466320 **Estd:** 1991 Private Limited Company
**Line of Business:** Financial intermediation not elsewhere classified
**Issued Capital:** £2
**Directors:** P M Costigan, A P Freeley, A N Jones, J T Hood, Dr J M Pattison, N Sarkar
**Co. Secretary:** Jonathan Dolbear
**US SIC:** 6111 **UK SIC:** 81501
**Auditors:** KPMG Audit Plc
**Bankers:** HSBC Bank plc (40-40-22)

|     | 31-12-13 | 31-12-12 | 31-12-11 |
|-----|----------|----------|----------|
| TA  | 2,276,000 | 2,199,000 | 1,915,000 |
| P/L | 151,000 | 296,000 | 84,000 |
| NW  | 2,185,000 | 2,069,000 | 1,846,000 |
| WC  | 2,185,000 | 2,069,000 | 1,846,000 |
| Emp. | N/A | N/A | 4 |

DUNS 22-048-8147
## Specialist Power Engineering Contracts Ltd
Unit 5, Eagle Point, Telford Way, Wakefield, West Yorkshire WF2 0XW
**Tel:** 01924871558
**Web:** www.spec-ltd.com
**Reg No:** 4051023 **Estd:** 2000 Private Limited Company
**Line of Business:** Electrical engineers
**Export Sales:** £614,579
**Trading Style:** S P E C
**Issued Capital:** £150
**Director:** C A Wright
**Co. Secretary:** Ian Needham
**Branches:** Specialist Power Engineering Contracts Ltd, Victoria Wks Albert Rd, Halifax, West Yorkshire HX2 0BY
**US SIC:** 8911, 1731
**UK SIC:** 83701, 50300
**Bankers:** Barclays Bank Plc (20-04-65)

|     | 31-03-14 | 31-03-13 | 31-03-12 |
|-----|----------|----------|----------|
| TO  | 10,751,001 | 8,608,420 | 7,102,901 |
| P/L | 1,371,179 | 895,390 | 929,613 |
| NW  | 3,170,610 | 2,624,930 | 2,041,693 |
| WC  | 2,475,940 | 2,027,377 | 1,447,973 |
| Emp. | 62 | 53 | 65 |

DUNS 23-080-8891
## Specialist Risk Underwriters Ltd
(Subsidiary of: Charles Taylor Plc)
Minster House, 42 Mincing Lane, London EC3R 7AE
**Tel:** 02074599200
**Web:** www.londonspecialrisks.com
**Reg No:** 2792127 **Estd:** 1994 Private Limited Company
**Line of Business:** Insurance brokers
**Issued Capital:** £500,000
**Directors:** I J Keane, H A Game
**Co. Secretary:**
Charles Taylor Administration Se
**US SIC:** 7399 **UK SIC:** 83954
**Auditors:** PricewaterhouseCoopers

|     | 31-12-13 | 31-12-12 | 31-12-11 |
|-----|----------|----------|----------|
| TA  | 210,104 | 210,104 | 210,104 |
| NW  | 210,104 | 210,104 | 210,104 |

DUNS 21-677-0956
## Specialist Software Services Ltd
(Subsidiary of: Specialist Software Holdings Ltd)
Rose Kiln Lane, Kilnbrook House, Reading, Berkshire RG2 0BY
**Tel:** 0845-634-5170
**Web:** www.ssh-group.com
**Reg No:** 7284243 **Estd:** 2010 Private Limited Company

**Line of Business:** Hardware consultancy
**Trading Style:** Livingstone
**Issued Capital:** £20,000
**Directors:** J Allaway, D Ward, S Leuty, E Mond
**US SIC:** 7379 **UK SIC:** 83940
**Auditors:** taylorcocks

|     | 31-12-13 | 31-12-12 | 31-12-11 |
|-----|----------|----------|----------|
| TA  | 1,523,968 | 1,463,471 | 951,018 |
| NW  | (180,476) | (35,233) | 72,804 |
| WC  | (98,071) | (261,809) | (148,003) |

DUNS 21-000-1621
## Specialist Waste Recycling Ltd
4th Floor 115 George Street, Edinburgh, Midlothian EH2 4JN
**Tel:** 01925214745
**Reg No:** 0324466SC **Estd:** 2007 Private Limited Company
**Line of Business:** Recycling
**Issued Capital:** £1,711,963
**Directors:** J D Maxwell, A M Butler, A F Macdonald, R L Pennant-Rea, S P Cameron, R T Kanter
**Co. Secretary:** Andrew Butler
**Branches:** Specialist Waste Recycling Ltd, Aaron Road, Peterborough, Cambridgeshire PE7 2EX
**US SIC:** 3341 **UK SIC:** 22470
**Bankers:** The Royal Bank Of Scotland Plc (16-20-30)

|     | 31-12-13 | 31-12-12 | 31-12-11 |
|-----|----------|----------|----------|
| TO  | 13,018,473 | 10,389,602 | 8,246,398 |
| P/L | (460,729) | (202,381) | (738,855) |
| NW  | 2,861,591 | 1,335,324 | 1,512,864 |
| WC  | 2,123,856 | 2,492,760 | 2,612,539 |
| Emp. | 83 | 78 | 72 |

DUNS 45-811-9286
## Speciality Breads Ltd
(Subsidiary of: Central Restaurant & Catering Co Ltd)
Unit N1 Westwood Industrial Estate, Enterprise Road, Margate, Kent CT9 4JA
**Tel:** 01843297074
**Web:** www.specialitybreads.co.uk
**Reg No:** 3169637 **Estd:** 2002 Private Limited Company
**Line of Business:** Bakers and confectioners supplies
**Issued Capital:** £245,000
**Directors:** Ms C W Macleod, F A Markland, P R Millen
**Co. Secretary:**
Empyraen Secretaries Limited
**Responsibilities**
Admin: Val Preston (Administrator)
**US SIC:** 2051 **UK SIC:** 41960
**Auditors:** Lewis Rowell & Co
**Bankers:** Barclays Bank Plc (20-00-52)

|     | 31-12-13 | 31-12-12 | 31-12-11 |
|-----|----------|----------|----------|
| TA  | 1,587,675 | 1,507,583 | 878,414 |
| NW  | 1,258,277 | 933,735 | 622,400 |
| WC  | 895,579 | 604,069 | 348,011 |

DUNS 42-461-5131 **Imp**
## Speciality Drinks Ltd
Unit 7, Space Business Park, Abbey Road, London NW10 7SU
**Tel:** 02088389444 **Fax:** 02088389366
**Web:** www.thewhiskyexchange.com
**Reg No:** 4449145 **VAT No:** 735785005
**Estd:** 2002 Private Limited Company
**Line of Business:** Wholesalers of beer and spirits
**Issued Capital:** £100
**Director:** R S Sawhney
**Co. Secretary:** Sukhinder Sawhney
**US SIC:** 5182, 5961
**UK SIC:** 61700, 65600

|     | 30-06-13 | 30-06-12 | 30-06-11 |
|-----|----------|----------|----------|
| TO  | 34,802,513 | 30,000,638 | 24,792,916 |
| P/L | 5,995,298 | 4,834,478 | 4,301,136 |
| NW  | 14,704,012 | 10,258,993 | 6,993,029 |
| WC  | 11,131,317 | 10,175,210 | 7,376,193 |
| Emp. | 61 | 55 | 41 |

DUNS 21-904-1423 **Exp**
## Speciality Fibres & Materials Ltd
(Subsidiary of: Lohmann & Rauscher International Gmbh & Co Kg)
101 Lockhurst Lane, Coventry, West Midlands CV6 5SF
**Tel:** 02476708200
**Web:** www.specialityfibres.com
**Reg No:** 0267936 **Estd:** 1932 Private Limited Company
**Line of Business:** Medical equipment leasing and rental
**Export Markets:** Countries worldwide
**Export Sales:** £5,630,000
**Trading Style:** Courtaulds Exports
**Issued Capital:** £225,500
**Directors:** T Menitz, Ms T S Thomas, C Ludford, W G Suessle, M D Stratton, H Maegdefrau
**Co. Secretary:**
Reed Smith Corporate Services Li
**Responsibilities**
Senior: Alan Tinklin (General Manager)

**Branches:** Speciality Fibres & Materials Ltd, Po Box 111, Coventry, West Midlands CV6 5RS
**US SIC:** 2297 **UK SIC:** 43992
**Auditors:** PricewaterhouseCoopers LLP
**Bankers:** Barclays Bank Plc (20-00-00)

|     | 31-12-13 | 31-12-12 | 31-12-11 |
|-----|----------|----------|----------|
| TO  | 7,413,000 | 7,685,000 | N/A |
| P/L | 1,632,000 | 1,350,000 | N/A |
| NW  | 5,747,000 | 4,450,000 | 3,407,000 |
| WC  | 3,775,000 | 2,386,000 | 1,710,000 |
| Emp. | 53 | 52 | N/A |

DUNS 21-036-2692
## Speciality Food Merchant Gourmet Uk
2 Rollins Street, London SE15 1EW
**Tel:** 08007313549
**Web:** www.merchant-gourmet.com
**Proprietorship**
**Line of Business:** Postal service
**US SIC:** 5812 **UK SIC:** 66110
**Employees:** 200

DUNS 52-007-8049
## Specialized Fabrications Ltd
Unit 4b Heritage Business Park, Heritage Way, Gosport, Hampshire PO12 4BG
**Web:** www.specfabs.co.uk
**Reg No:** 3374710 **VAT No:** 699178069
**Estd:** 1997 Private Limited Company
**Line of Business:** Production of ornamental metalwork
**Issued Capital:** £1,000
**Directors:** A C Dunn, T M World
**Co. Secretary:** Tony World
**Responsibilities**
HR: Graham Samuda (Production Manager)
Health & Safety: Nigel Spencer (Health & Safety Officer)
Facilities: Graham Samuda (Production Manager)
Purchasing: Martin World (Buyer)
Engineering: Graham Samuda (Production Manager)
**Branches:** Specialized Fabrications Ltd, Unit B1, Heritage Way, Gosport, Hampshire PO12 4BG
**US SIC:** 3442 **UK SIC:** 31420
**Auditors:** Compass Accountants Ltd
**Bankers:** Lloyds TSB Bank plc (30-93-17)

|     | 31-05-13 | 31-05-12 | 31-05-11 |
|-----|----------|----------|----------|
| TO  | N/A | 3,945,201 | 3,687,646 |
| P/L | N/A | 11,392 | (6,259) |
| NW  | 417,739 | 406,787 | 397,673 |
| WC  | 504,900 | 286,109 | 264,276 |
| Emp. | N/A | 69 | 69 |

DUNS 23-777-4596 **Imp**
## The Specials Laboratory Ltd
(Subsidiary of: Pcca (Uk) Holdings Ltd)
Unit 1 Regents Drive, Prudhoe, Northumberland NE42 6PX
**Tel:** 01661831811 **Fax:** 01661-831097
**Web:** www.specialslab.co.uk
**Reg No:** 3770732 **Estd:** 2003 Private Limited Company
**Line of Business:** Manufacture of basic pharmaceutical products
**Export Sales:** £160,710
**Issued Capital:** £200,000
**Directors:** L D Sparks, J R Smith, Ms S Griffiths
**Responsibilities**
Finance: Kris Todd (Head of Finance)
Marketing: Jan Armstrong (Head of Marketing)
Sales: Kevin Patterson (Head of Sales)
Health & Safety: Tony Robson (Facilities Manager)
Facilities: Tony Robson (Facilities Manager)
Operations: Lee Craig (Head of Operations)
**US SIC:** 2834 **UK SIC:** 25700
**Auditors:** Tait Walker
**Bankers:** Lloyds TSB Bank plc (30-93-71)

|     | 30-09-13 | 30-09-12 | 30-09-11 |
|-----|----------|----------|----------|
| TO  | 12,256,390 | 14,622,536 | 15,860,226 |
| P/L | 877,346 | 2,179,999 | 3,745,036 |
| NW  | 4,311,369 | 4,127,549 | 4,131,128 |
| WC  | 3,045,444 | 2,982,233 | 3,198,004 |
| Emp. | 108 | 122 | 133 |

DUNS 21-678-9459
## Specialty Powders Holdings Ltd
Unit 7 Monkswell Park, Manse Lane, Knaresborough, North Yorkshire HG5 8NQ
**Tel:** 01423868411
**Web:** www.aggtech.co.uk
**Reg No:** 7298437 **Estd:** 2010 Private Limited Company
**Line of Business:** Manufacturers of food products
**Export Sales:** £20,945,399
**Issued Capital:** £61,142
**Directors:** S J Howarth, D Corbishley, M J Kirby, C M Terry, Mrs L Bagley, J Nagle
**Co. Secretary:** Christopher Terry
**Responsibilities**
Senior: Neil Dyer (Director)

**US SIC:** 2099 **UK SIC:** 42399
**Bankers:** The Royal Bank Of Scotland Plc (16-10-15)

|     | 31-12-13 | 31-12-12 | 31-12-11 |
|-----|----------|----------|----------|
| TO  | 43,592,915 | 27,321,017 | 21,495,612 |
| P/L | 151,087 | 330,364 | 403,227 |
| NW  | (1,237,119) | (1,582,318) | 729,725 |
| WC  | (2,093,060) | (1,980,968) | (376,841) |
| Emp. | 153 | 100 | 47 |

DUNS 21-109-4231
## Specific Media International Ltd
(Subsidiary of: Interactive Media Holdings Inc.)
4th Floor 16 Dufour's Place, London W1F 7SP
**Tel:** 02072276370
**Web:** www.specificmedia.co.uk
**Reg No:** 6511065 **Estd:** 2008 Private Limited Company
**Line of Business:** Advertising related services
**Export Sales:** £18,830,000
**Issued Capital:** £5,152,224
**Director:** C J Vanderhook
**Co. Secretary:** Timothy Vanderhook
**Responsibilities**
Senior: Paul Oronoz (Manager)
**US SIC:** 7319 **UK SIC:** 83800
**Auditors:** Deloitte LLP

|     | 31-12-13 | 31-12-12 | 31-12-11 |
|-----|----------|----------|----------|
| TO  | 28,838,000 | 41,094,000 | 52,856,000 |
| P/L | (11,549,000) | (5,276,000) | (2,704,000) |
| NW  | (25,207,000) | (16,471,000) | (10,522,000) |
| WC  | (5,853,000) | 545,000 | 3,459,000 |
| Emp. | 166 | 226 | 221 |

DUNS 23-231-7805
## Specsavers Finance (Guernsey) Ltd
(Subsidiary of: Specsavers International Healthcare Limited)
Lane Villiaze Street Andrews, Guernsey, Channel Islands GY6 8YP
**Tel:** 03452020241
**Web:** www.specsavers.com
**Reg No:** 0025466G **Estd:** 1992 Private Limited Company
**Line of Business:** Opticians
**Issued Capital:** £100
**Directors:** T P Blatchford, J F Southwell, M B White, D J Perkins
**US SIC:** 5999 **UK SIC:** 65600
**Employees:** 500

DUNS 76-837-8622
## Specsavers Healthcall Ltd
(Subsidiary of: Specsavers International Healthcare Limited)
Unit 5 Laporte Way Titan Court, Luton, Bedfordshire LU4 8EF
**Web:** www.healthcalloptical.co.uk
**Reg No:** 2604077 **Estd:** 1991 Private Limited Company
**Line of Business:** Manufacture of photographic and cinematographic equipment
**Issued Capital:** £2
**Directors:** G S Edmonds, Mrs M L Perkins, Mrs J B Rawlinson, Mrs D E Roberts
**Co. Secretary:**
Specsavers Optical Group Limited
**US SIC:** 3861 **UK SIC:** 37330
**Auditors:** Grant Thornton UK LLP
**Bankers:** National Westminster Bank Plc (50-42-27)

|     | 28-02-14 | 31-10-12 | 31-02-11 |
|-----|----------|----------|----------|
| TO  | 9,925,285 | 8,624,709 | 9,537,497 |
| P/L | 299,268 | (481,869) | 462,050 |
| NW  | 1,454,399 | 156,986 | 731,973 |
| WC  | 1,112,190 | (44,719) | 410,908 |
| Emp. | 186 | 200 | 204 |

DUNS 22-613-3858
## Specsavers Optical Group Ltd
(Subsidiary of: Specsavers International Healthcare Limited)
Lane Villiaze, Guernsey, Channel Islands GY6 8YP
**Tel:** 01481236000
**Web:** www.specsavers.com
**Reg No:** 0012294G **Estd:** 1998 Private Limited Company
**Line of Business:** Retail sale by opticians
**Trading Style:** Chepstow News
**Issued Capital:** £10,000
**Principals:** D J Perkins (Managing), S Freear (Financial), P Watson, C Johansen, S Keough, Ms M L Perkins, R Murray
**Co. Secretary:** Ms Leonie Mozezierski
**Responsibilities**
Senior: Dennis Midgeley (Distribution Manager)
IT: Helen Carre (IT Manager)
HR: Nicole Morrow (Training Manager)
Health & Safety: Nick James (Health & Safety Officer)

**Branches:** Specsavers Optical Group Limited, 7 Market Place, Driffield, North Humberside YO25 6AP
**US SIC:** 7399 **UK SIC:** 83954
**Bankers:** National Westminster Bank Plc (60-09-20)
**Employees:** 442

DUNS 29-461-2015 **Imp**
## Specsavers Optical Superstores Ltd
(**Subsidiary of:** Specsavers International Healthcare Limited)
Forum 6 Parkway, Solent Business Park, Whiteley, Fareham, Hampshire PO15 7PA
**Fax:** 0818 275 665
**Web:** www.specsavers.co.uk
**Reg No:** 1721624 **Estd:** 1983 Private Limited Company
**Line of Business:** Development and selling of real estate
**Trading Style:** Corporate Eyecare
**Issued Capital:** £2
**Principals:** D J Perkins *(Managing)*, P B Fussey, J D Perkins, D Dyson, H D Lord, P F Carroll, Mrs M L Perkins, C C Howarth
**Co. Secretary:** Specsavers Optical Group Limited
**Branches:** Specsavers Optical Superstores Ltd, Unit 18A, 18C Dalston Cross Shopping Centre, London E8 2LX
**US SIC:** 6552, 5999
**UK SIC:** 85000, 65600
**Auditors:** BDO LLP
**Bankers:** HSBC Bank plc (40-22-25)

| | 28-02-14 | 28-02-13 | 29-02-12 |
|---|---|---|---|
| TO | 392,606,000 | 346,739,000 | 378,438,000 |
| P/L | 18,533,000 | 15,349,000 | 21,265,000 |
| NW | 73,847,000 | 100,290,000 | 94,909,000 |
| WC | 70,238,000 | 96,085,000 | 88,719,000 |
| Emp. | 3,369 | 3,316 | 2,993 |

DUNS 22-719-8207 **Exp**
## The Spectator (1828) Ltd
(**Subsidiary of:** May Corporation Ltd)
22 Old Queen Street, London SW1H 9HP
**Tel:** 02079610200 **Fax:** 02079610101
**Web:** www.spectator.co.uk
**Reg No:** 1232804 **Estd:** 1828 Private Limited Company
**Line of Business:** Publishers
**Export Markets:** W Europe, S America, U S A, Canada, Africa, Australia, Far East
**Export Sales:** £613,000
**Trading Style:** The Spectator
**Issued Capital:** £1,403,968
**Directors:** A S Barclay, H M Barclay, R K Mowatt, P L Peters, M Seal
**Responsibilities**
**Senior:** Ben Greenish *(Manager)*, Andrew Neil *(Chairman)*, Fraser Nelson *(Editor)*
**US SIC:** 2731 **UK SIC:** 47532
**Auditors:** PricewaterhouseCoopers LLP
**Bankers:** The Royal Bank Of Scotland Plc (16-00-38)

| | 31-12-13 | 31-12-12 | 31-12-11 |
|---|---|---|---|
| TO | 9,828,000 | 9,275,000 | 9,591,000 |
| P/L | 567,000 | (916,000) | 448,000 |
| NW | 8,604,000 | 8,037,000 | 8,893,000 |
| WC | 8,375,000 | 7,806,000 | 8,715,000 |
| Emp. | 47 | 50 | 48 |

DUNS 23-339-6261
## Spectra Analysis Services Ltd
Unit 2 Paycocke Road Olympic Business, Centre, Basildon, Essex SS14 3EX
**Tel:** 01268-534380 **Fax:** 01268-272985
**Web:** www.spectra-analysis.co.uk
**Reg No:** 4664619 **Estd:** 2003 Private Limited Company
**Line of Business:** Asbestos products & removal
**Issued Capital:** £2
**Directors:** N Chinnery, D J Yon, G Hudson, D Deakin, D Chinnery
**Co. Secretary:** Perry Winch
**US SIC:** 1799, 8911
**UK SIC:** 50000, 83701
**Auditors:** Keith English & Co

| | 31-03-14 | 31-03-13 | 31-03-12 |
|---|---|---|---|
| TA | 1,203,923 | 1,567,693 | 1,439,979 |
| NW | 856,669 | 945,638 | 949,643 |
| WC | 477,265 | 509,448 | 490,994 |

DUNS 21-008-3589
## Spectra Packaging Solutions Ltd
Antonine Way, Sparrowhawk Road, Halesworth, Suffolk IP19 8RX
**Tel:** 01986834190
**Web:** www.spectra-packaging.co.uk
**Reg No:** 6323869 **Estd:** 2007 Private Limited Company
**Line of Business:** Plastic injection moulding
**Issued Capital:** £100
**Directors:** C Bridges, Ms C J Maynard, G Chenery, J Powell, J E Maynard
**Co. Secretary:** Joseph Maynard
**US SIC:** 3079 **UK SIC:** 48360

| | 31-12-13 | 31-12-12 | 31-12-11 |
|---|---|---|---|
| TO | 5,902,922 | 3,942,904 | N/A |
| P/L | 342,360 | (304,950) | N/A |
| NW | (2,294,983) | (3,154,957) | (2,850,007) |
| WC | 1,653,293 | 706,064 | 626,312 |
| Emp. | 72 | 59 | N/A |

DUNS 39-414-7342
## Spectra Specialist Engineering Ltd
31d Link Road, West Wilts Trading Estate, Westbury, Wiltshire BA13 4JB
**Tel:** 01373-865548
**Web:** www.spectra.uk.net
**Reg No:** 2121500 **VAT No:** 452838823
**Estd:** 1987 Private Limited Company
**Line of Business:** Van and truck bodybuilders and repairers
**Issued Capital:** £2,500
**Directors:** R Hayes, A J Pearce, S Allberry, N J Brown
**Responsibilities**
**Senior:** Czeslaw Ziemniak *(Manager)*
**Health & Safety:** Richard Joseph *(Engineering Manager)*
**Facilities:** Richard Joseph *(Engineering Manager)*
**Purchasing:** Russell Kirkham *(Purchasing Manager)*
**Engineering:** Richard Joseph *(Engineering Manager)*
**US SIC:** 3713 **UK SIC:** 35201
**Auditors:** Advance Business Consultants Ltd
**Bankers:** National Westminster Bank Plc (52-21-30)

| | 31-05-14 | 31-05-13 | 31-05-12 |
|---|---|---|---|
| TA | 1,733,911 | 1,386,857 | 1,771,831 |
| NW | 414,907 | 324,829 | 350,045 |
| WC | 351,330 | 255,547 | 127,881 |

DUNS 21-584-4552
## Spectrex Inc
6 Applecross Road, Kirkintilloch, Glasgow, Lanarkshire G66 3TJ
**Web:** www.spectrex-inc.com
**Estd:** 2011 Proprietorship
**Line of Business:** Safety equipment suppliers
**Proprietor:** I Buchanan
**US SIC:** 5999 **UK SIC:** 65600
**Employees:** 120

DUNS 29-761-9090 **Imp-Exp**
## Spectris Plc
Heritage House, Church Road, Egham, Surrey TW20 9QD
**Web:** www.spectris.com
**Reg No:** 2025003 **VAT No:** 453063174
**Estd:** 1986 Public Limited Company
**Line of Business:** Management activities of holding companies
**Export Markets:** Worldwide
**Export Sales:** £1,162,100,000
**Issued Capital:** £6,250,256
**Directors:** Mrs L A Davis, J L Hughes, U Quellmann, Mrs M B Wyrsch, P A Chambre, J E O'Higgins, C G Watson, W C Seeger Jr.
**Co. Secretary:** Roger Stephens
**Responsibilities**
**Senior:** Anthony Reading *(Manager)*, William Seeger *(Director)*, James Webster *(Manager)*
**Marketing:** Sue Wadham *(Communications Manager)*
**Sales:** Sue Wadham *(Communications Manager)*
**US SIC:** 6711, 3829
**UK SIC:** 83962, 37100
**Auditors:** KPMG Audit PLC
**Bankers:** National Westminster Bank Plc (50-00-00)

**Following financial data are in thousands**

| | 31-12-13 | 31-12-12 | 31-12-11 |
|---|---|---|---|
| TO | 1,202,000 | 1,230,800 | 1,106,200 |
| P/L | 271,700 | 186,700 | 166,000 |
| NW | 145,600 | (27,100) | (146,200) |
| WC | 177,300 | 71,100 | 134,400 |
| Emp. | 7,344 | 7,361 | 6,447 |

DUNS 21-778-1944
## Spectrum
Merton Drive, Redmoor, Milton Keynes, Buckinghamshire MK6 4AG
**Tel:** 01908689600
**Estd:** 2002 Partnership
**Line of Business:** Distribution service providers
**Partners:** P Clarke, S Turner, K Lunn, Ms J Bate, M Scriven, Ms S Walker
**Responsibilities**
**Senior:** Jackie Hughes *(General Manager)*
**US SIC:** 4712 **UK SIC:** 77002
**Employees:** 320

DUNS 50-385-6882 **Imp-Exp**
## Spectrum Brands (Uk) Ltd
(**Subsidiary of:** Harbinger Group Inc.)
Regent Mill, Fir Street, Failsworth, Manchester M35 0HS
**Tel:** 0161 947 3000 **Fax:** 01914-178-390
**Web:** www.eu.spectrumbrands.com
**Reg No:** 2394603 **VAT No:** 532783437
**Estd:** 1989 Private Limited Company
**Line of Business:** Manufacture of accumulators, primary cells and primary batteries
**Export Markets:** Europe and other countries worldwide
**Trading Style:** Black&Decker Remington, Rayovac George Foreman Russell Hobbs, United Pet Group, United Industries
**Issued Capital:** £78,456,823
**Directors:** Ms A Krueger, A D Streets, T J Wright, A Rouve, C Berry
**Co. Secretary:** Andrew Streets
**Branches:** Spectrum Brands (Uk) Ltd, Beaumont Way, Newton Aycliffe, County Durham DL5 6SN
**US SIC:** 5199 **UK SIC:** 61900
**Auditors:** KPMG LLP
**Bankers:** National Westminster Bank Plc (54-10-27)

| | 30-09-13 | 30-09-12 | 30-09-11 |
|---|---|---|---|
| TO | 167,836,000 | 149,675,000 | 114,866,000 |
| P/L | 27,740,000 | 18,090,000 | 13,886,000 |
| NW | 127,358,000 | 99,629,000 | 85,930,000 |
| WC | (62,377,000) | 26,824,000 | 11,124,000 |
| Emp. | 420 | 368 | 292 |

DUNS 21-679-1614
## Spectrum Community Health C.I.C.
White Rose House, West Parade, Wakefield, West Yorkshire WF1 1LT
**Tel:** 01924-311-400 **Fax:** 01924-782-076
**Web:** www.spectrumhealth.org.uk
**Reg No:** 7300133 **Estd:** 2010 Private Limited Company
**Line of Business:** Other human health activities
**Issued Capital:** £1
**Directors:** Mrs S P Hardcastle, R M Grasby, Mrs J Fleetwood, P G Morris, Dr L D Harris, A M Griggs, Mrs L E Johnson, Mrs C E Morris
**Co. Secretary:** Mrs Sharon Hardcastle
**US SIC:** 8091 **UK SIC:** 95200
**Auditors:** Sadofskys Chartered Accountants
**Bankers:** Unity Trust Bank Plc (08-60-01)

| | 31-03-14 | 31-03-13 | 31-03-12 |
|---|---|---|---|
| TO | 12,556,613 | 8,471,633 | 8,661,594 |
| P/L | 308,822 | 328,301 | 373,151 |
| NW | 961,993 | 727,414 | 477,713 |
| WC | 775,672 | 625,668 | 381,393 |
| Emp. | 271 | 189 | 119 |

DUNS 50-029-3659 **Exp**
## Spectrum Computer Supplies Ltd
Spectrum House, Bradford, West Yorkshire BD1 5RJ
**Tel:** 01274-308188
**Web:** www.spectrumltd.co.uk
**Reg No:** 2306938 **VAT No:** 500322420
**Estd:** 1982 Private Limited Company
**Line of Business:** Computer systems and software (sales)
**Export Markets:** Ireland, France, Germany, Netherlands, Denmark, Sweden
**Export Sales:** £14,214
**Trading Style:** Spectrum Computer Supplies Limited
**Issued Capital:** £50,000
**Director:** R A Thaxter
**Co. Secretary:** Michael Buckley
**Responsibilities**
**Marketing:** Steven Teale *(Tele Marketing Manager)*
**US SIC:** 5081 **UK SIC:** 61490
**Auditors:** Baker Tilly UK Audit LLP
**Bankers:** Lloyds TSB Bank plc (30-91-12)

| | 31-10-13 | 31-10-12 | 31-10-11 |
|---|---|---|---|
| TO | 50,980,342 | 50,833,479 | 49,936,214 |
| P/L | 3,046,416 | 3,086,622 | 3,027,277 |
| NW | 13,515,358 | 11,177,683 | 9,819,050 |
| WC | 12,272,025 | 9,890,155 | 9,750,146 |
| Emp. | 83 | 89 | 90 |

DUNS 39-477-7502 **Imp**
## Spectrum Franchising Ltd
(**Subsidiary of:** Iss A/S)
Spectrum House, Lower Oakham Way, Mansfield, Nottinghamshire NG18 5BY
**Tel:** 01623675100 **Fax:** 01623-422466
**Web:** www.rainbow-int.co.uk
**Reg No:** 2130421 **VAT No:** 458198602
**Estd:** 2002 Private Limited Company
**Line of Business:** Carpet and upholstery cleaners
**Trading Style:** Rainbow International
**Issued Capital:** £850,000
**Directors:** B Wallage, P M Else, M E Brabin, R I Sykes
**Responsibilities**
**Senior:** Phill Elf *(Manager)*, Ronald Hutton *(Manager)*
**Finance:** Christopher Roche *(Finance Director)*
**Marketing:** Paul Mastin *(Sales & Marketing Manager)*
**Sales:** Paul Mastin *(Sales & Marketing Manager)*
**Branches:** Spectrum Franchising Ltd, 28-29 Kingsland Grange, Tatton Court, Warrington, Cheshire WA1 4RR
**US SIC:** 7399 **UK SIC:** 83954
**Auditors:** KPMG LLP
**Bankers:** HSBC Bank plc (40-32-01)

| | 31-12-13 | 31-12-12 | 31-12-11 |
|---|---|---|---|
| TO | 4,173,482 | 5,391,570 | 6,666,382 |
| P/L | 1,688,414 | 2,177,185 | 2,476,425 |
| NW | 21,848,662 | 20,559,221 | 18,902,605 |
| WC | 21,588,274 | 20,272,880 | 18,661,544 |
| Emp. | 62 | 62 | 76 |

DUNS 29-653-0603 **Exp**
## Spectrum Geo Ltd
(**Subsidiary of:** Spectrum Asa)
Dukes Court, Duke Street, Woking, Surrey GU21 5BH
**Tel:** 01483-730-201
**Web:** www.spectrumasa.com
**Reg No:** 1979422 **VAT No:** 413612783
**Estd:** 1986 Private Limited Company
**Line of Business:** Business services
**Export Markets:** E U, Africa, Middle East, Australasia, & Far East
**Directors:** Dr N A Hodgson, G P Mayhew
**Co. Secretary:** Keith Watt
**Responsibilities**
**IT:** John Lyons *(IT Manager)*
**HR:** Liza Ludovici *(Personnel Manager)*
**Branches:** Spectrum Geo Limited, 374-376 Gilmerton Rd, Edinburgh, Midlothian EH17 7QS
**US SIC:** 7399, 1389
**UK SIC:** 83954, 13000
**Auditors:** Ernst & Young LLP
**Bankers:** National Westminster Bank Plc (60-24-20)

| | 31-12-12 | 31- -11 |
|---|---|---|
| TO | 23,287,109 | 16,224,165 |
| P/L | 5,031,477 | 3,215,710 |
| NW | 15,502,372 | 10,446,668 |
| WC | 3,039,839 | 7,412,834 |
| Emp. | 61 | 56 |

DUNS 21-121-1270
## Spectrum Housing Group Ltd
Signpost House, 15 Higher Shaftesbury Road Sunrise, Business Park, Blandford Forum, Dorset DT11 8SA
**Tel:** 03001113600
**Web:** www.spectrumhousing.co.uk
**Reg No:** 0028960R **VAT No:** 744882008
**Estd:** 2007
**Line of Business:** Associations
**Principals:** D Wells *(Chairman)*, M Lucas *(Financial)*, A Wildeman *(Personnel)*, M Pearl, J Takhar, J Wright, P Bryan, R Morris
**Co. Secretary:** J Clarke
**Responsibilities**
**Senior:** Craig Francis *(Area Development Manager)*, Rob Webber *(Director of Operations)*
**Marketing:** Tina Partridge *(Marketing Manager)*
**Branches:** Spectrum Housing Group Limited, Signpost Ho 15 Sunrise Business Pk, Higher Shaftesbury Rd, Blandford Forum, Dorset DT11 8SA
**US SIC:** 8699, 6732
**UK SIC:** 96902, 83100
**Auditors:** KPMG Audit LLP
**Bankers:** National Westminster Bank Plc (56-00-35)
**Employees:** 1,000
**Turnover:** £88,998,000

DUNS 42-452-7880
## Spectrum Interactive Ltd
(**Subsidiary of:** Arqiva Broadcast Holdings Ltd)
One Park Lane, Hemel Hempstead, Hertfordshire HP2 4YJ
**Tel:** 01442-205500 **Fax:** 01442-261001
**Web:** www.arqiva.com
**Reg No:** 4440500 **Estd:** 2002 Private Limited Company
**Line of Business:** Management activities of holding companies
**Trading Style:** Arqiva
**Issued Capital:** £293,528
**Directors:** P D Moses, J H Cresswell, N F Ott
**Co. Secretary:** William Giles
**Responsibilities**
**Senior:** Jim Stobo *(Financial Director)*, Nigel Styne *(Operations Director)*
**Finance:** Jim Stobo *(Financial Director)*
**Operations:** Nigel Styne *(Operations Director)*
**US SIC:** 6711, 1731

**UK SIC:** 83962, 50300
**Auditors:** Deloitte LLP

| | 30-06-14 | 30-06-13 | 30-06-12 |
|---|---|---|---|
| TO | N/A | N/A | 13,505,395 |
| P/L | N/A | (1,390,011) | (3,386,325) |
| NW | (560,846) | (560,846) | 2,170,088 |
| WC | N/A | N/A | (1,085,813) |
| Emp. | N/A | N/A | 71 |

DUNS 73-606-5038
## Spectrum Premier Homes Ltd
Spectrum House, Grange Road, Christchurch, Dorset BH23 4GE
**Tel:** 01425283600 **Fax:** 01425-283555
**Web:** www.westernchallenge.co.uk
**Reg No:** 2914932 **Estd:** 2005 Private Limited Company
**Line of Business:** Construction of domestic buildings
**Directors:** R J Avon, N J Dyer, Ms L J Cousins, N E Morrow, B J Neaves, R J Morrissey, Ms C A Turner
**Co. Secretary:** Ms Claire Mckenna
**Responsibilities**
**Senior:** Barbara Compton *(Principal)*, H Milroy *(Principal)*
**Branches:** Spectrum Premier Homes Ltd, Dallimore Mead, Frome, Somerset BA11 4NB
**US SIC:** 1522 **UK SIC:** 50100
**Auditors:** KPMG LLP

| | 31-03-14 | 31-03-13 | 31-03-12 |
|---|---|---|---|
| TO | 14,907,000 | 2,010,000 | N/A |
| P/L | 193,000 | (151,000) | N/A |
| NW | 34,000 | (115,000) | 1,278 |
| WC | 4,634,000 | 500,000 | N/A |

DUNS 21-972-3372
## Spectrum Property Care Ltd
**(Subsidiary of:** Spectrum Housing Group)
Spectrum House Grange Road, Christchurch, Dorset BH23 4GE
**Tel:** 08007837837
**Web:** www.spectrumhousing.co.uk
**Reg No:** 8758536 **Estd:** 2013 Private Limited Company
**Line of Business:** Management of real estate on a fee or contract basis
**Directors:** P Bryan, Spectrum Housing Group, S Lindley, J Templeton, P D Dean, Mrs T M Peters, R Davies, C I Garland
**Co. Secretary:** Claire-Marie Mckenna
**US SIC:** 6531 **UK SIC:** 83400

| | 31-03-14 |
|---|---|
| TO | 31,550,000 |
| P/L | 376,000 |
| NW | 2,083,000 |
| WC | 1,835,000 |
| Emp. | 361 |

DUNS 50-376-8848 **Imp-Exp**
## Spectrum Technologies P L C
Western Avenue, Bridgend Industrial Estate, Bridgend, Mid Glamorgan CF31 3RT
**Tel:** 01656655437
**Web:** www.spectrumtech.com
**Reg No:** 2385991 **VAT No:** 530146388
**Estd:** 1989 Public Limited Company
**Line of Business:** Manufacturers cable and wire equipment
**Export Markets:** Worldwide
**Export Sales:** £7,378,421
**Issued Capital:** £705,273
**Principals:** Dr P H Dickinson *(Managing)*, M A Reason, M Lewis, B Thomas
**Co. Secretary:** Matthew Lewis
**Responsibilities**
**IT:** Adam Leyshon *(Computer Manager)*
**Purchasing:** Lee Hopkins *(Purchasing Manager)*
**US SIC:** 3357, 3662
**UK SIC:** 22470, 34430
**Auditors:** Grant Thornton UK LLP
**Bankers:** Lloyds TSB Bank plc (30-91-18)

| | 31-03-14 | 31-03-13 | 31-03-12 |
|---|---|---|---|
| TO | 7,605,820 | 8,838,887 | 8,423,544 |
| P/L | 318,410 | 479,202 | 808,540 |
| NW | 4,487,835 | 4,303,774 | 3,768,777 |
| WC | 4,271,826 | 4,051,055 | 3,602,803 |
| Emp. | 79 | 80 | 74 |

DUNS 21-315-0212 **Imp-Exp**
## Spectrum Yarns Ltd
Spa Mill, Huddersfield, West Yorkshire HD7 5BB
**Web:** www.glenbraegolf.com
**Reg No:** 1142407 **VAT No:** 184415361
**Estd:** 1973 Private Limited Company
**Line of Business:** Wholesale suppliers of yarn
**Export Markets:** Worldwide
**Issued Capital:** £9,000
**Managing Director:** R K Brown
**Co. Secretary:** Ian Porter
**Responsibilities**
**Senior:** Phillip Jefferson *(Warehouse Manager)*
**HR:** Debra Taylor *(Human Resources Manager)*
**Health & Safety:** Debra Taylor *(Human Resources Manager)*
**Operations:** Phillip Jefferson *(Warehouse Manager)*
**Engineering:** Mick Cresswell *(Production Manager)*
**US SIC:** 2299, 5133
**UK SIC:** 43992, 61600
**Auditors:** Bamforth & Co
**Bankers:** Lloyds TSB Bank plc (30-94-43)

| | 31-03-14 | 31-03-13 | 31-03-12 |
|---|---|---|---|
| TO | 16,429,993 | 16,236,548 | 15,380,936 |
| P/L | (180,409) | 40,599 | 354,140 |
| NW | 3,769,144 | 3,949,553 | 3,908,954 |
| WC | 5,530,250 | 5,609,800 | 5,107,405 |
| Emp. | 157 | 149 | 145 |

DUNS 21-123-1816 **Exp**
## Specwood Ltd
**(Subsidiary of:** Mayroy Sa)
190 Bath Road, Slough, Berkshire SL1 3XE
**Tel:** 01753627777
**Reg No:** 1146287 **Estd:** 1973 Private Limited Company
**Line of Business:** Pharmaceutical products manufacturers
**Export Markets:** U S A
**Issued Capital:** £1
**Directors:** E A Booth, J H Barnsley
**Co. Secretary:** Edward Booth
**US SIC:** 2834 **UK SIC:** 25700
**Bankers:** National Westminster Bank Plc (60-17-21)

| | 31-12-13 | 31-12-12 | 31-12-11 |
|---|---|---|---|
| TA | 1 | 1 | 1 |
| NW | 1 | 1 | 1 |

DUNS 49-485-5588
## Spedivet Ltd
**(Subsidiary of:** Genus Plc)
Unit 28, Slough Business Park, 94 Farnham Road, Slough, Berkshire SL1 3FQ
**Tel:** 08454562223 **Fax:** 08454562122
**Web:** www.ersmedical.co.uk
**Reg No:** 3150464 **Estd:** 2012 Private Limited Company
**Line of Business:** Ambulance and medical transportation services
**Trading Style:** Procare Dental, Mediforce
**Issued Capital:** £2,333,334
**Directors:** D Noonan, K Bitar, S D Wilson
**Co. Secretary:** Ms Cara Crichton
**Responsibilities**
**Senior:** Sam Stanley *(Business Process Manager)*
**Branches:** Spedivet Ltd, 135-141, 1 Stamford Street, Glasgow, Lanarkshire G31 4AW
**US SIC:** 5199 **UK SIC:** 61900
**Auditors:** Ernst & Young
**Bankers:** Barclays Bank Plc (20-99-56)

| | 30-06-13 | 30-06-12 | 30-06-11 |
|---|---|---|---|
| TA | 2,896,000 | 2,896,000 | 2,896,000 |
| NW | 2,896,000 | 2,896,000 | 2,896,000 |

DUNS 51-627-2023
## Speechly Bircham Llp
6 New St Square, London EC4A 3LX
**Tel:** 02074276400
**Web:** www.speechlybircham.co.uk
**Reg No:** 0321620OC **Estd:** 1800
**Line of Business:** Solicitors
**Responsibilities**
**Senior:** John Avery Jones *(Partner)*, Jonathan Bayliss *(Partner)*, William Begley *(Partner)*, Bill Bidder *(Partner)*, Alison Broadberry *(Partner)*, Elizabeth Budd *(Partner)*, Kenneth Calcutt *(Partner)*, Anthony Cartmell *(Partner)*, Penny Cogher *(Partner and Head of Pensions)*, Kevin Forsyth *(Partner)*, William Garner *(Partner)*, Charles Gothard *(Partner)*, William Granger *(Non-designated Limited Liabili)*, Robin Grove *(Partner)*, Paul Henty *(Partner)*, Nicholas Ivey *(Partner)*, Nick Janmohamed *(Partner)*, Micheal Janney *(Partner)*, Alan Julyan *(Designated Limited Liability P)*, Paul Kay *(Partner)*, Ashley Kopitko *(Partner)*, Dominic Lawrance *(Partner)*, Jon Leggett *(Partner)*, John Liddington *(Partner)*, Graham Ling *(Partner)*, Malcom MacDougall *(Partner)*, James Meakin *(Partner)*, Nathalie Moreno *(Partner)*, Matthew Newing *(Partner)*, Rhys Novak *(Partner)*, Tim Raper *(Partner)*, Daniel Rosenberg *(Partner)*, Duncan Salmon *(Partner)*, Richard Schmidt *(Partner)*, Sanjvee Shah *(Partner)*, Thomas Shaw *(Designated Limited Liability P)*, Daniel Sullivan *(Partner)*, Timothy Voake *(Partner)*
**Finance:** Chokri Bouzidi *(Head of Tax)*, Elizabeth Budd *(Partner)*, Thomas Shaw *(Designated Limited Liability P)*
**Admin:** Julie Patmore *(Administrator)*
**IT:** Robert Cohen *(IT Director)*
**US SIC:** 8111 **UK SIC:** 83500
**Auditors:** Grant Thornton UK LLP
**Bankers:** The Royal Bank Of Scotland Plc (15-00-00)

| | 30-04-14 | 30-04-13 | 30-04-12 |
|---|---|---|---|
| TO | 56,618,000 | 57,019,000 | 57,577,000 |
| P/L | 17,484,000 | 18,411,000 | 20,007,000 |
| NW | 16,475,000 | 17,647,000 | 19,451,000 |
| WC | 24,025,000 | 24,930,000 | 25,552,000 |
| Emp. | 380 | 370 | 386 |

DUNS 23-568-5778
## Speed Medical Examination Services Ltd
16 Eaton Avenue, Chorley, Lancashire PR7 7NA
**Tel:** 08444129333 **Fax:** 08444129334
**Web:** www.speedmedical.com
**Reg No:** 3566725 **Estd:** 1998 Private Limited Company
**Line of Business:** Medical practice activities
**Issued Capital:** £1,000
**Directors:** G Pulford, Ms S Henry, C J Chatterton
**Co. Secretary:** Ms Debra Grant
**Responsibilities**
**Finance:** George Ogungbola *(Finance Director)*
**Marketing:** Daniel Chesney *(Group Marketing Manager)*
**Sales:** Faye Catley *(National Sales Manager)*, Dylan Riley *(Business Development Manager)*
**Branches:** Speed Medical Examination Services Ltd, Albion House, Farington Business Park, Leyland, Lancashire PR25 3GG
**US SIC:** 8011, 8111
**UK SIC:** 95300, 83500

| | 31-05-13 | 31-05-12 | 31-05-11 |
|---|---|---|---|
| TO | 38,684,345 | 35,147,634 | 52,723,991 |
| P/L | 4,927,869 | 2,160,587 | 4,134,012 |
| NW | 4,446,228 | 2,483,662 | 1,559,433 |
| WC | 6,006,625 | 4,000,047 | 680,787 |
| Emp. | 144 | 146 | 146 |

DUNS 23-927-8448
## Speed Six (Citroen) Ltd
**(Subsidiary of:** Cameo Investment Ltd)
100 Barbirolli Square, Manchester M2 3AB
**Tel:** 01978311777
**Reg No:** 3917782 **Estd:** 2000 Private Limited Company
**Line of Business:** Sale of new motor vehicles
**Issued Capital:** £5,000
**Director:** M Keen
**Co. Secretary:** Stephen Sowerby
**US SIC:** 5511, 7539
**UK SIC:** 65100, 67100
**Auditors:** Afford Astbury Bond LLP
**Bankers:** National Westminster Bank Plc (54-10-10)

| | 31-12-13 | 31-12-12 | 31-12-11 |
|---|---|---|---|
| NW | (285,763) | (285,763) | (285,763) |

DUNS 39-933-6973
## Speedbird Developments Ltd
**(Subsidiary of:** Etchecan Ltd)
Thistle Aberdeen Airport, Aberdeen, Aberdeenshire AB21 0AF
**Web:** www.speedbirdinns.co.uk
**Reg No:** 0110805SC **Estd:** 1988 Private Limited Company
**Line of Business:** Hotels
**Issued Capital:** £400,000
**Directors:** W Paisley, A Higgins, Ms S F Valentine, J A Brown, B Hutchison
**Co. Secretary:** Hbjg Secretarial Limited
**US SIC:** 7011 **UK SIC:** 66500
**Auditors:** Williamson & Dunn
**Bankers:** Bank Of Scotland (80-29-01)

| | 26-01-14 | 27-01-13 | 29-01-12 |
|---|---|---|---|
| TO | 6,044,000 | 5,562,000 | 5,032,000 |
| P/L | 1,653,000 | 1,331,000 | 1,137,000 |
| NW | 5,293,000 | 5,416,000 | 5,467,000 |
| WC | 4,869,000 | 5,014,000 | 4,917,000 |
| Emp. | 74 | 71 | 68 |

DUNS 22-666-0017 **Exp**
## Speedibake Ltd
**(Subsidiary of:** Wittington Investments Ltd)
Colinsway, Wakefield, West Yorkshire WF2 9RJ
**Tel:** 01924231900 **Fax:** 08708307401
**Web:** www.speedibake.co.uk
**Reg No:** 0046991 **Estd:** 1984 Private Limited Company
**Line of Business:** Bakers shops
**Export Markets:** E U
**Issued Capital:** £300,000
**Directors:** D S Barton, S P Hawkins
**Co. Secretary:** Mrs Rosalyn Schofield
**Responsibilities**
**HR:** Kelly Hepworth *(Head of Human Resources)*
**Facilities:** Bert Walker *(Operations Director)*
**Engineering:** Bert Walker *(Operations Director)*
**Branches:** Speedibake Ltd, 6 Cross Lane, Bradford, West Yorkshire BD4 0SG
**US SIC:** 3357, 2033
**UK SIC:** 22470, 41473

| | 14-09-13 | 15-09-12 | 17-09-11 |
|---|---|---|---|
| TA | 300,000 | 300,000 | 300,000 |
| NW | 300,000 | 300,000 | 300,000 |
| WC | 300,000 | 300,000 | N/A |
| Emp. | 400 | 400 | N/A |

DUNS 22-850-0344
## Speedier Scaffolding Ltd
Manchester Road, Westhoughton, Bolton, Lancashire BL5 3QH
**Tel:** 01942-841-919 **Fax:** 01942-841-918
**Web:** www.speedierscaffolding.com
**Reg No:** 1609213 **VAT No:** 163308087
**Estd:** 1990 Private Limited Company
**Line of Business:** Other construction work involving special trades
**Issued Capital:** £1,108,100
**Directors:** J Bate, J Salkeld
**Co. Secretary:** John Kazer
**Branches:** Speedier Scaffolding Ltd, 19A Hamil Road, Stoke-On-Trent, Staffordshire ST6 1AB
**US SIC:** 1799 **UK SIC:** 50000
**Auditors:** Jackson Stephen LLP
**Bankers:** Barclays Bank Plc (20-96-37)

| | 31-03-14 | 31-03-13 | 31-03-12 |
|---|---|---|---|
| TA | 3,130,126 | 2,753,841 | 2,466,339 |
| NW | 2,484,243 | 2,293,069 | 2,048,034 |
| WC | 2,433,332 | 2,224,297 | 1,984,964 |

DUNS 85-604-1301
## Speedline Taxi Ltd
Unit 2 Centec Court, Towcester Road, Old Stratford, Milton Keynes, Buckinghamshire MK19 6AQ
**Tel:** 01908-260260
**Web:** www.speedlinetaxis.com
**Reg No.** 0241050 **Estd:** 2007 Private Limited Company
**Line of Business:** Taxis and private hire vehicles
**Issued Capital:** £90
**Directors:** A Siddiq, M I Siddiq
**Co. Secretary:** Mohammad Siddiq
**Responsibilities**
**Senior:** Mohammed Sadiq *(Manager)*
**US SIC:** 4121 **UK SIC:** 72200

| | 31-03-14 | 31-03-13 | 31-03-12 |
|---|---|---|---|
| TA | 1,334,484 | 1,135,560 | 1,172,335 |
| NW | 477,669 | 427,662 | 302,123 |
| WC | (499,171) | (426,071) | (565,149) |

DUNS 34-612-7579
## Speedlink Travel & Freight Ltd
710 High Road, Tottenham, London N17 0AE
**Tel:** 020-8885-2122
**Web:** www.speedlinkltd.co.uk
**Reg No:** 5419418 **Estd:** 2005 Private Limited Company
**Line of Business:** Cargo handling
**Issued Capital:** £1
**Director:** S Williams
**Co. Secretary:** Evelyn Essel
**US SIC:** 4712 **UK SIC:** 77002
**Auditors:** NSK & Co

| | 30-04-14 | 30-04-13 | 30-04-12 |
|---|---|---|---|
| TA | 30,666 | 30,035 | 36,938 |
| NW | (16,309) | (17,310) | (16,169) |
| WC | (32,092) | (45,992) | 4,353 |

DUNS 21-277-3469
## Speeds of Blackpool Ltd
**(Subsidiary of:** Speeds Ltd)
1 Ashworth Road, Blackpool, Lancashire FY4 5LP
**Tel:** 01253798282 **Fax:** 01253-798199
**Web:** www.mercedes-benzofblackpool.co.uk
**Reg No:** 0913893 **Estd:** 1965 Private Limited Company
**Line of Business:** Sale of new motor vehicles
**Issued Capital:** £250,000
**Principals:** G E Speed *(Managing)*, K E Strawson, J B Flanders, Ms T Haggas, M Speed
**Co. Secretary:** Ms Pauline Speed
**Branches:** Blackpool.
**US SIC:** 5511, 7539
**UK SIC:** 65100, 67100
**Auditors:** Pannell Kerr Forster
**Bankers:** Barclays Bank Plc (20-20-50)

| | 31-12-13 | 31-12-12 | 31-12-11 |
|---|---|---|---|
| TA | 250,000 | 250,000 | 250,000 |
| NW | 250,000 | 250,000 | 250,000 |

DUNS 21-157-0617
## Speedy Asset Services Ltd
**(Subsidiary of:** Speedy Hire Plc)
Unit 14 Paxman Road, King's Lynn, Norfolk PE30 4NE
**Tel:** 01553761199 **Fax:** 01942720077
**Web:** www.speedyhire.plc.uk
**Reg No:** 6847930 **VAT No:** 151629570
**Estd:** 2009 Private Limited Company
**Line of Business:** Renting of other machinery and equipment not elsewhere classified
**Trading Style:** Speedy Hire
**Issued Capital:** £1
**Directors:** Ms T M Atkin, M Rogerson, A Bennett
**Co. Secretary:** James Blair
**Responsibilities**
**Senior:** Steven Corcoran *(Chief Executive)*, John Hickson *(Facilities Manager)*

**Facilities:** John Hickson *(Facilities Manager)*
**Branches:** Speedy Asset Services Ltd, 3 Enterprise Centre, Skipton Road, Keighley, West Yorkshire BD20 7BX
**US SIC:** 7394 **UK SIC:** 84000

| | 31-03-14 | 31-03-13 | 31-03-12 |
|---|---|---|---|
| TO | 323,394,000 | 318,082,000 | 311,893,000 |
| P/L | 8,436,000 | 25,672,000 | 23,619,000 |
| NW | 35,592,000 | 27,264,000 | 1,127,000 |
| WC | (142,127,000) | (142,902,000) | (172,209,000) |
| Emp. | 3,115 | 3,128 | 3,236 |

DUNS 21-719-3838

## Speedy Hire Direct Ltd

**(Subsidiary of:** Speedy Hire Plc)
Newmarket House, 20 The Parks, Newton-Le-Willows, Merseyside WA12 0JQ
**Tel:** 01942277000
**Web:** www.speedyservices.com
**Reg No:** 0974324 **Estd:** 1970 Private Limited Company
**Line of Business:** Plant and tool hire
**Trading Style:** Speedy Northern
**Issued Capital:** £100
**Directors:** M Rogerson, A Bennett, Ms T M Atkin
**Co. Secretary:** James Blair
**Responsibilities**
**Senior:** John Horsley *(Operations Director)*
**Branches:** Speedy Hire Direct Ltd, Park Road, Gateshead, Tyne and Wear NE8 3HL
**US SIC:** 7394 **UK SIC:** 84000
**Auditors:** KPMG Audit PLC
**Bankers:** Barclays Bank Plc (20-35-81)

| | 31-03-14 | 31-03-13 | 31-03-12 |
|---|---|---|---|
| TA | 3,420,000 | 3,420,000 | 3,420,000 |
| NW | 3,420,000 | 3,420,000 | 3,420,000 |

DUNS 21-244-0515 **Imp**

## Speedy Hire Plc

Chase House, 16 The Parks, Newton-Le-Willows, Merseyside WA12 0JQ
**Tel:** 01234353148 **Fax:** 01942 327198
**Web:** www.speedyhire.plc.uk
**Reg No:** 0927680 **Estd:** 1968 Public Limited Company
**Line of Business:** Tool hire services
**Export Sales:** £26,800,000
**Issued Capital:** £25,912,329
**Directors:** C Masters, J Morley, M Rogerson, J G Astrand, M C Averill
**Co. Secretary:** James Blair
**Responsibilities**
**Senior:** Steven Corcoran *(Chief Executive)*
**Marketing:** Jackie Cuthbert *(Group Head of Marketing)*
**HR:** Duncan Lawrence *(Human Resources Manager)*
**Health & Safety:** Mark Turnbull *(Health & Safety Officer)*
**Facilities:** Alex Trigg *(Property Director)*
**Purchasing:** Julie Sherriff *(Supply Chain & IT Manager)*
**Fleet:** Ian Leonard *(Fleet Manager)*
**Branches:** Speedy Hire Plc, Firth Road, Houstoun Industrial Estate, Livingston, West Lothian EH54 5DJ
**US SIC:** 7394, 5082, 5084
**UK SIC:** 84000, 61490
**Auditors:** KPMG Audit PLC
**Bankers:** Barclays Bank Plc (20-96-37)

| | 31-03-14 | 31-03-13 | 31-03-12 |
|---|---|---|---|
| TO | 349,700,000 | 340,400,000 | 329,300,000 |
| P/L | 7,000,000 | 12,800,000 | 3,200,000 |
| NW | 188,000,000 | 182,800,000 | 171,500,000 |
| WC | 27,100,000 | 24,500,000 | 19,600,000 |
| Emp. | 3,729 | 3,776 | 3,844 |

DUNS 22-851-7967 **Imp-Exp**

## Speedy Products Ltd

Speedy House, Cheltenham Street, Salford, Lancashire M6 6WY
**Tel:** 0161-737-1001
**Web:** www.speedy-products.co.uk
**Reg No:** 1242000 **VAT No:** 150911100
**Estd:** 1976 Private Limited Company
**Line of Business:** Blinds and canopies
**Export Markets:** Worldwide
**Export Sales:** £1,522,775
**Issued Capital:** £56,400
**Managing Director:** I H Seddon
**Co. Secretary:** Dean Seddon
**Responsibilities**
**Senior:** Lorraine Perry *(Administrator)*
**Marketing:** Michelle Belcher *(Head of Marketing)*
**Sales:** Sandra Dooley *(Sales Director)*, Lorraine Perry *(Administrator)*
**Admin:** Eleanor Bursk *(Administrator)*, Lorraine Perry *(Administrator)*
**HR:** May Houghton *(Personnel Officer)*
**Health & Safety:** May Houghton *(Personnel Officer)*
**Purchasing:** Derick Bailey *(Purchasing Manager)*
**US SIC:** 3499 **UK SIC:** 31694
**Auditors:** Campbell Woolley LLP

**Bankers:** The Royal Bank Of Scotland Plc (16-00-02)

| | 31-12-13 | 31-12-12 | 31-12-12 |
|---|---|---|---|
| TO | 11,075,905 | 11,042,321 | 10,392,488 |
| P/L | 452,709 | 257,327 | 186,555 |
| NW | 4,225,459 | 3,894,719 | 4,000,079 |
| WC | 2,012,607 | 1,900,628 | 2,023,450 |
| Emp. | 63 | 59 | 60 |

DUNS 21-617-2019

## Speedy Pumps

37 Downiebrae Road, Rutherglen, Glasgow, Lanarkshire G73 1PW
**Tel:** 01416133546
**Web:** www.speedyhire.com
**Estd:** 2011 Proprietorship
**Line of Business:** Baby goods hire
**Proprietor:** J Cassiday
**US SIC:** 7394 **UK SIC:** 84000
**Employees:** 50

DUNS 29-683-5119

## Speirs & Jeffrey Ltd

George House, 50 George Square, Glasgow, Lanarkshire G2 1EH
**Fax:** 01415527175
**Web:** www.speirsjeffrey.co.uk
**Reg No:** 0098335SC **Estd:** 2002 Private Limited Company
**Line of Business:** Stockbrokers
**Issued Capital:** £68,300
**Directors:** A A Waddell, M J Wilson, C C Baxter, G H Waddell, T M Brown, R L Crichton, W G Dickie, J R Mcculloch
**Co. Secretary:** Steven Mathieson
**Responsibilities**
**Senior:** Barry Fullarton *(Associate Director)*, Alastair Hunt *(Associate Director)*, Catherine Nicholl *(Manager)*, Gavin Paterson *(Associate Director)*, Stuart Summers *(Manager)*
**US SIC:** 6211 **UK SIC:** 83100
**Auditors:** KPMG Audit PLC
**Bankers:** Bank Of Scotland (80-11-80)

| | 10-05-14 | 10-05-13 | 13-05-12 |
|---|---|---|---|
| TA | 33,125,000 | 39,243,000 | 31,192,000 |
| P/L | 7,313,000 | 6,026,000 | 4,853,000 |
| NW | 9,629,000 | 7,880,000 | 6,778,000 |
| WC | 8,776,000 | 7,667,000 | 6,498,000 |
| Emp. | 129 | 130 | 118 |

DUNS 28-826-5259

## Speirs Gumley Property Management

194 Bath Street, Glasgow, Lanarkshire G2 4LE
**Tel:** 01413329225 **Fax:** 0141-332-7899
**Web:** www.speirsgumley.com
**Reg No:** 0078921SC **VAT No:** 353733551
**Estd:** 1850 Private Unlimited Company
**Line of Business:** Management of real estate on a fee or contract basis
**Issued Capital:** £100
**Directors:** J Neil, B J Mcmanus, C W Adams, I J Friel, A Lawrie
**Co. Secretary:** Messrs Speirs Gumley
**Responsibilities**
**Senior:** Peter McConnell *(Senior Partner)*
**Marketing:** Alan Lapsley *(Partner)*
**HR:** Jim McManus *(Partner)*
**Health & Safety:** Peter McConnell *(Senior Partner)*
**Branches:** Speirs Gumley Property Management, 30 Gordon St, Paisley, Renfrewshire PA1 1XA
**US SIC:** 6531 **UK SIC:** 83400
**Employees:** 70

DUNS 21-142-3969

## Speller Metcalfe Ltd

Maple Road, Malvern, Worcestershire WR14 1GQ
**Tel:** 01684571200 **Fax:** 01684-571220
**Web:** www.spellermetcalfe.com
**Reg No:** 6740881 **Estd:** 2002 Private Limited Company
**Line of Business:** Other construction work involving special trades
**Issued Capital:** £100,000
**Directors:** A J Metcalfe, S R Speller
**Co. Secretary:** Michael Clarke
**US SIC:** 1799 **UK SIC:** 50000
**Bankers:** Svenska Handelsbanken Ab (publ) (40-53-59)

| | 31-03-14 | 31-03-13 | 31-03-12 |
|---|---|---|---|
| TO | 77,319,882 | 56,495,752 | 71,570,339 |
| P/L | 363,282 | 221,202 | 61,804 |
| NW | 1,451,605 | 1,257,911 | 1,186,232 |
| WC | 717,353 | 994,165 | 852,926 |
| Emp. | 154 | 134 | 152 |

DUNS 34-784-7605

## Spellman & Walker Direct Ltd

Graphica House, Chase Way, Bradford, West Yorkshire BD5 8SW
**Tel:** 01274760160
**Web:** www.spellman.co.uk
**Reg No:** 5585420 **Estd:** 2005 Private Limited Company
**Line of Business:** Printers general

**Issued Capital:** £1
**Directors:** M O Hirst, N S Risby
**Co. Secretary:** Nigel Risby
**US SIC:** 6711 **UK SIC:** 83962
**Bankers:** National Westminster Bank Plc (56-00-36)

| | 31-12-13 | 31-12-12 | 31-12-11 |
|---|---|---|---|
| TO | 5,056,094 | N/A | N/A |
| P/L | 558,875 | N/A | N/A |
| NW | 1,563,440 | 1 | 1 |
| WC | 1,140,289 | N/A | N/A |
| Emp. | 104 | N/A | N/A |

DUNS 21-205-5933

## Spellman & Walker Ltd

**(Subsidiary of:** Spellman & Walker Direct Ltd)
Graphica House, Chase Way, Bradford, West Yorkshire BD5 8SW
**Tel:** 01274722555
**Web:** www.spellman.co.uk
**Reg No:** 0686106 **VAT No:** 179483708
**Estd:** 1947 Private Limited Company
**Line of Business:** Printing not elsewhere classified
**Issued Capital:** £3,840
**Directors:** N S Risby, M O Hirst
**Co. Secretary:** Nigel Risby
**Responsibilities**
**Finance:** Andrew Beaumont *(Senior Account Manager)*, Darren Childerson *(Accounts Manager)*, Lena Depledge *(Accounts Manager)*, Louisa Whitaker *(Accounts Manager)*
**Marketing:** Michael Vaiksaar *(Marketing Manager)*, Melanie Vauvelle-Don *(Business Development Manager)*
**US SIC:** 2752 **UK SIC:** 47544
**Auditors:** MGI Watson Buckle LLP
**Bankers:** National Westminster Bank Plc (56-00-36)

| | 31-12-13 | 31-12-12 | 31-12-11 |
|---|---|---|---|
| TO | 12,068,020 | 13,052,739 | 15,907,066 |
| P/L | 1,597,612 | 1,079,175 | 2,117,498 |
| NW | 1,956,727 | 3,733,642 | 3,904,345 |
| WC | 1,902,823 | 2,796,364 | 2,710,048 |
| Emp. | 105 | 116 | 118 |

DUNS 50-150-9095 **Imp-Exp**

## Spellman High Voltage Electronics Ltd.

**(Subsidiary of:** Spellman High Voltage Electronics Corporation)
Unit 14 Broomers Hill Lane Broomers Hill, Park, Pulborough, West Sussex RH20 2RY
**Web:** www.spellmanhv.com
**Reg No:** 2329112 **Estd:** 1947 Private Limited Company
**Line of Business:** Manufacture of electronic valves and tubes and other electronic components
**Export Sales:** £15,696,094
**Issued Capital:** £250,000
**Directors:** Ms J Collyer, L R Skeist, N Hogan, R D Adam, D Bay, M Ford
**Co. Secretary:**
Cargil Management Services Limit
**Responsibilities**
**HR:** Hazel Reed *(Human Resources Manager)*
**Health & Safety:** Adrian Bamforth *(Quality Manager)*
**Facilities:** K Allum *(Logistics Manager)*
**Operations:** Adrian Bamforth *(Quality Manager)*
**Purchasing:** K Allum *(Logistics Manager)*
**Fleet:** K Allum *(Logistics Manager)*
**US SIC:** 3679, 3661, 3629, 4899
**UK SIC:** 34542, 34410, 34350, 79020
**Auditors:** Clark McBride
**Bankers:** HSBC Bank plc (40-17-16)

| | 31-03-14 | 31-03-13 | 31-03-12 |
|---|---|---|---|
| TO | 20,263,816 | 18,813,835 | 19,141,080 |
| P/L | 1,285,103 | 1,593,123 | 1,602,561 |
| NW | 6,778,071 | 6,476,386 | 6,115,554 |
| WC | 4,741,441 | 4,497,573 | 4,613,479 |
| Emp. | 105 | 104 | 98 |

DUNS 21-117-7332

## Spelthorne Borough Council

Council Offices, Knowle Green, Staines, Middlesex TW18 1XB
**Tel:** 01784-451499
**Web:** www.spelthorne.gov.uk
**Estd:** 1974
**Line of Business:** Local government
**Principals:** P G Harding *(Financial)*, V Conduit *(Technical)*, A Walker, M B Taylor
**Responsibilities**
**Senior:** J Chilton *(Partner)*, Heather Morgan *(Partner)*, Sandy Muirhead *(Partner)*, S Surgeon *(Partner)*, Roberto Tambini *(Manager)*
**Finance:** Terry Collier *(Head of Financial Services)*, S Surgeon *(Partner)*
**IT:** Alistair Corkish *(Deputy ICT Manager)*, Helen Dunn *(Head of IT)*
**Health & Safety:** Stuart Mann *(Health & Safety Officer)*
**Facilities:** Lawrence Crossam *(Facilities Manager)*

**Operations:** Lee O'Neil *(Environmental Manager)*
**Branches:** Spelthorne Borough Council, Knowle Green, Staines, Middlesex TW18 1AJ
**US SIC:** 9121 **UK SIC:** 91110
**Bankers:** The Co-Operative Bank Plc (08-90-34)
**Employees:** 350

DUNS 23-230-2539

## Spelthorne Housing Association Ltd

Spelthorne House, Thames Street, Staines, Middlesex TW18 4TA
**Tel:** 01784456756 **Fax:** 01784-449063
**Reg No:** 0027312IP **Estd:** 1991 Friendly Society
**Line of Business:** Property developers
**Trading Style:** Apex Group
**Principals:** J White-Jones *(Chairman)*, H Hughes, R D Treadway, S Shackel, B J Sheppard, R Edwards, N Hutchins, A Walker
**Branches:** Spelthorne Housing Association Ltd, Elizabeth Gdns, Sunbury-On-Thames, Middlesex TW16 5LQ
**US SIC:** 6531 **UK SIC:** 83400
**Bankers:** Lloyds TSB Bank plc (30-00-09)
**Employees:** 60
**Turnover:** £15,490,000

DUNS 28-959-5472

## Spenborough Abattoir Ltd

**(Subsidiary of:** Bullcliff Ltd)
Headlands Road, Liversedge, West Yorkshire WF15 6PR
**Tel:** 01924-402261 **Fax:** 01924-402261
**Reg No:** 1672626 **Estd:** 1982 Private Limited Company
**Line of Business:** Abattoirs
**Issued Capital:** £1,500
**Principals:** R A Gawthorpe *(Financial)*, D A Gawthorpe, J R Worsley
**Co. Secretary:** Ms Margaret Worsley
**US SIC:** 2013 **UK SIC:** 41223
**Auditors:** Malcolm Jones & Co

| | 30-11-13 | 30-11-12 | 30-11-11 |
|---|---|---|---|
| TA | 1,637,666 | 1,694,683 | 1,336,001 |
| NW | 885,214 | 932,847 | 747,183 |
| WC | (172,786) | (135,964) | (7,692) |

DUNS 21-618-8956

## Spencer & Arlington

221-223 Chingford Mount Road, London E4 8LP
**Tel:** 02085239090
**Web:** www.spencerandarlington.co.uk
**Estd:** 2000 Proprietorship
**Line of Business:** Home care service providers
**Proprietor:** Z Ali
**US SIC:** 8091 **UK SIC:** 95200
**Employees:** 120

DUNS 76-911-0065 **Exp**

## Spencer Coatings Group Ltd

6 York Street, Aberdeen, Aberdeenshire AB11 5DD
**Tel:** 01224288780 **Fax:** 01224-648116
**Web:** www.spencercoatings.co.uk
**Reg No:** 0123258SC **Estd:** 1990 Private Limited Company
**Line of Business:** Management activities of holding companies
**Issued Capital:** £31,580
**Principals:** P A Buck *(Managing)*, J A Stokes
**Co. Secretary:** Graham Stronach
**US SIC:** 6711, 3398
**UK SIC:** 83962, 31380
**Auditors:** Ritson Smith
**Bankers:** The Royal Bank Of Scotland Plc (83-30-00)

| | 30-09-13 | 31-03-12 | 31-09-11 |
|---|---|---|---|
| TO | 16,791,998 | 6,710,694 | 6,309,034 |
| P/L | 3,872,715 | 700,914 | 455,560 |
| NW | 724,350 | (925,095) | (1,217,302) |
| WC | 2,799,113 | 341,176 | 205,569 |
| Emp. | 87 | 55 | 55 |

DUNS 21-584-1942

## Spencer Grove Care Home

Springwood Gardens, Belper, Derbyshire DE56 1JR
**Tel:** 01773599349
**Web:** www.milfordcare.co.uk
**Estd:** 2011 Proprietorship
**Line of Business:** Nursing homes
**Proprietor:** Mrs S Brown
**Responsibilities**
**Senior:** Donna Annable *(Home Manager)*
**US SIC:** 8051 **UK SIC:** 95100
**Employees:** 50

DUNS 21-831-4680  **Imp-Exp**
## Spencer Manufacturing Ltd
(**Subsidiary of:** Spencer Manufacturing Holdings Ltd)
Orleton Road, Ludlow Business Park, Ludlow, Shropshire SY8 1XF
**Tel:** 01584-877333 **Fax:** 01584-872444
**Web:** www.spencermanufacturing.co.uk
**Reg No:** 0500155 **VAT No:** 589336586
**Estd:** 1951 Private Limited Company
**Line of Business:** Manufacturers of wire products
**Export Markets:** Europe, U S A, Canada
**Issued Capital:** £2,568
**Principals:** G W Hawkins (Managing), S J Hughes, D G Hawkins
**Co. Secretary:** Richard Philips
**Responsibilities**
**IT:** Jolyon Partridge (Production Manager)
**HR:** Kelly Angel (Human Resources Coordinator)
**Health & Safety:** Jolyon Partridge (Production Manager)
**Facilities:** Chris Meek (Purchasing Manager)
**Operations:** Jolyon Partridge (Production Manager)
**Purchasing:** Chris Meek (Purchasing Manager)
**Engineering:** Jolyon Partridge (Production Manager)
**US SIC:** 3357, 3469
**UK SIC:** 22470, 31200
**Auditors:** Grant Thornton
**Bankers:** HSBC Bank plc (40-43-19)

|    | 31-12-13 | 31-12-12 | 31-12-11 |
|----|----------|----------|----------|
| TA | 3,010,682 | 2,254,000 | 2,153,805 |
| NW | 982,161 | 1,027,449 | 1,046,485 |
| WC | 777,174 | 877,674 | 824,892 |

DUNS 21-174-2202
## Spencer Ogden Ltd
33 Charlotte Street, London W1T 1RR
**Tel:** 02072689300 **Fax:** 02072689301
**Web:** www.spencer-ogden.com
**Reg No:** 6979438 **Estd:** 2011 Private Limited Company
**Line of Business:** Manufacture of electricity distribution and control apparatus
**Export Sales:** £36,318,721
**Issued Capital:** £990
**Directors:** P J Ogden, D Spencer-Percival
**Co. Secretary:** Stephen Segel
**Responsibilities**
**Sales:** James Pipe (Global Business Manager - Ener)
**US SIC:** 7361 **UK SIC:** 83954
**Auditors:** KPMG LLP

|     | 31-12-13 | 31-12-12 | 31-12-11 |
|-----|----------|----------|----------|
| TO  | 51,382,275 | 32,257,305 | 18,668,121 |
| P/L | 1,537,663 | 831,432 | 278,512 |
| NW  | 1,455,828 | 275,923 | (332,000) |
| WC  | 1,927,972 | 1,729,609 | 791,867 |
| Emp.| 237 | 154 | 65 |

DUNS 39-702-5321
## Spencer Signs Ltd
70 Scarborough Street, Hull, North Humberside HU3 4TG
**Tel:** 01482325797 **Fax:** 01482-323077
**Web:** www.spencersigns.co.uk
**Reg No:** 2155579 **VAT No:** 500785464
**Estd:** 1987 Private Limited Company
**Line of Business:** Sign and nameplate suppliers
**Issued Capital:** £18,750
**Principals:** J R Spencer (Managing), R Spencer
**Co. Secretary:** Ms Diane Spencer
**Responsibilities**
**Senior:** Paul Newlove (Manager), John Sollitt (Operations Director)
**IT:** John Sollitt (Operations Director)
**HR:** John Sollitt (Operations Director)
**Health & Safety:** John Becketts (Health & Safety Officer), Dave Dodgson (Health & Safety Officer)
**Facilities:** John Sollitt (Operations Director)
**Operations:** Paul Newlove (Manager), John Sollitt (Operations Director)
**US SIC:** 5199 **UK SIC:** 61900
**Bankers:** National Westminster Bank Plc (56-00-06)

|    | 30-04-14 | 30-04-13 | 30-04-12 |
|----|----------|----------|----------|
| TA | 2,439,604 | 2,627,607 | 2,740,027 |
| NW | 542,645 | 583,500 | 712,156 |
| WC | (15,965) | (66,379) | (101,763) |

DUNS 22-701-6482  **Imp-Exp**
## Spencer Stuart & Associates Ltd
Bain House, 16 Connaught Place, London W2 2ED
**Fax:** 020-7298-3388
**Web:** www.spencerstuart.co.uk
**Reg No:** 0703962 **VAT No:** 239669904
**Estd:** 1961 Private Limited Company
**Line of Business:** Management and business consultants

**Trading Style:** Stuart Spencer Management Consultants, Selector Europe
**Issued Capital:** £7,002,000
**Directors:** E R Speed, H M Thorneycroft, P J Hynes
**Co. Secretary:** Keith Winter
**Responsibilities**
**Senior:** Mark Broer (Board Member), Will Dawkins (Board Member), Carolyn Eadie (Manager), Mark Stroyan (Manager), James Stroyan (Manager)
**Finance:** Hilary Attenborough (Finance), Kevin Connelly (CEO), Mark Eban (Finance Consultant), David Juster (Finance Consultant)
**Marketing:** Alastair Rolfe (Marketing Manager)
**Sales:** Alastair Rolfe (Marketing Manager)
**Branches:** Spencer Stuart & Associates Ltd, Equinox 3, Audby Lane, Wetherby, West Yorkshire LS22 7RD
**US SIC:** 7392 **UK SIC:** 83951
**Auditors:** Deloitte LLP

|     | 30-09-13 | 30-09-12 | 30-09-11 |
|-----|----------|----------|----------|
| TO  | 33,894,751 | 33,788,529 | 34,630,732 |
| P/L | 387,337 | (727,134) | 601,888 |
| NW  | 7,467,792 | 7,318,949 | 7,967,830 |
| WC  | 5,049,892 | 4,248,527 | 4,238,139 |
| Emp.| 111 | 113 | 120 |

DUNS 23-561-9702
## Spencers Ltd
(**Subsidiary of:** Carrs (Holdings) Ltd)
Thetford Road, Fornham St Martin, Bury St Edmunds, Suffolk IP31 1SX
**Tel:** 01284-752525 **Fax:** 01284-750751
**Web:** www.carrsbmw.co.uk
**Reg No:** 3560193 **Estd:** 2010 Private Limited Company
**Line of Business:** Car dealers (new & used)
**Trading Style:** Carrs of Bury St. Edmunds
**Issued Capital:** £100,000
**Managing Director:** N A Spencer
**Co. Secretary:** Ms Christine Spencer
**US SIC:** 5511, 7539
**UK SIC:** 65100, 67100
**Auditors:** BDO Stoy Hayward
**Bankers:** Barclays Bank Plc (20-62-68)

|     | 31-12-13 | 31-12-12 | 31-12-11 |
|-----|----------|----------|----------|
| TO  | 40,552,165 | 34,001,449 | 28,338,861 |
| P/L | 139,402 | 599,058 | 413,375 |
| NW  | 1,839,733 | 1,932,509 | 1,672,903 |
| WC  | 2,887,362 | 3,628,284 | 1,047,551 |
| Emp.| 54 | 53 | 52 |

DUNS 21-743-9314  **Imp-Exp**
## Spenco Engineering Co. Ltd
(**Subsidiary of:** Agco Corporation)
Station Road, Whimple, Exeter, Devon EX5 2QH
**Tel:** 01392-369795 **Fax:** 01392-364439
**Web:** www.spenco.co.uk
**Reg No:** 1242155 **Estd:** 1976 Private Limited Company
**Line of Business:** Manufacture of metal structures and parts of structures
**Export Markets:** Worldwide
**Issued Capital:** £10,000
**Directors:** M Doggrell, J Burgess, P W De Brissac Bernard
**Co. Secretary:** Mark Doggrell
**Responsibilities**
**Senior:** Gary Lomas (Operations Director), Pierre Nadeau (Manager)
**Health & Safety:** Gary Lomas (Operations Director)
**US SIC:** 3441, 8911
**UK SIC:** 32042, 83701
**Auditors:** PricewaterhouseCoopers
**Bankers:** Lloyds TSB Bank plc (30-00-03)

|     | 31-12-13 | 31-12-12 | 31-12-11 |
|-----|----------|----------|----------|
| TO  | 3,655,085 | 3,395,250 | 3,551,794 |
| P/L | 247,491 | 157,306 | 277,720 |
| NW  | 5,308,628 | 5,065,486 | 4,916,169 |
| WC  | 5,067,591 | 4,803,350 | 4,718,058 |
| Emp.| 46 | 44 | 41 |

DUNS 64-077-6662
## Spencross Ltd
(**Subsidiary of:** Sedale Investments Limited)
46 Fountain Street, Manchester M2 2BE
**Tel:** 01618352858
**Reg No:** 3472901 **Estd:** 1997 Private Limited Company
**Line of Business:** Management activities of holding companies
**Issued Capital:** £1,000,000
**Directors:** Dr D J Clayton, R Roberts
**Co. Secretary:** Nathan Chuwen
**US SIC:** 6711, 7339
**UK SIC:** 83962, 83954
**Auditors:** Finlay Robertson

|     | 30-09-13 | 30-09-12 | 30-09-11 |
|-----|----------|----------|----------|
| TO  | 8,235,406 | 8,562,535 | 8,419,511 |
| P/L | 131,960 | (26,946) | (117,701) |
| NW  | 822,401 | 1,225,203 | 1,483,437 |
| WC  | 1,093,818 | 901,867 | 1,255,043 |
| Emp.| 102 | 100 | 94 |

DUNS 21-454-9883
## Spendlove C. Jebb
(**Subsidiary of:** Travis Perkins Plc)
107-127 Grosvenor Road, Belfast BT12 4GT
**Tel:** 02890027192 **Fax:** 028-9043-9903
**Web:** www.spendlovecjebbbelfast.co.uk
**Reg No:** 0007345NI **Estd:** 1946 Private Unlimited Company
**Line of Business:** Bathroom fixtures and fittings
**Issued Capital:** £100
**Directors:** J P Carter, A D Buffin, Tp Directors Ltd
**Responsibilities**
**Senior:** Carl Hegley (General Manager), Ken Kead (CEO, Managing Director)
**Finance:** Keira Breen (Senior Finance Director)
**Branches:** Spendlove C. Jebb, Ballinderry Industrial Estate, Unit 1, Lisburn, Co Antrim BT28 2SA
**US SIC:** 3499 **UK SIC:** 31694
**Auditors:** PricewaterhouseCoopers LLP
**Bankers:** Ulster Bank Ltd (98-00-90)

|    | 31-12-13 | 31-12-12 | 31-12-11 |
|----|----------|----------|----------|
| TA | 6,967,114 | 6,967,114 | 6,967,114 |
| NW | 19,994 | 19,994 | 19,994 |
| WC | 19,994 | 19,994 | 19,994 |

DUNS 73-468-0262
## The Speratus Group Ltd
Blenheim House, Fountainhall Road, Aberdeen, Aberdeenshire AB15 4DT
**Tel:** 01316563108
**Web:** www.thesperatusgroup.com
**Reg No:** 0247778SC **Estd:** 2003 Private Limited Company
**Line of Business:** Bars
**Issued Capital:** £3,252,400
**Directors:** N J Wood, G R Wood, M A Brown, G Good
**Co. Secretary:** Mrs Lindsay Mckenzie
**US SIC:** 5813 **UK SIC:** 66200

|     | 31-10-13 | 31-10-12 | 31-10-11 |
|-----|----------|----------|----------|
| TO  | 3,623,607 | N/A | N/A |
| P/L | 323,568 | N/A | N/A |
| NW  | 1,109,230 | 771,319 | 537,556 |
| WC  | 4,833,444 | 4,766,122 | 1,181,373 |
| Emp.| 94 | N/A | N/A |

DUNS 21-148-7828  **Imp-Exp**
## Sperling Retail Ltd
6 Manor Road, Haverhill, Suffolk CB9 0EP
**Tel:** 01440707088 **Fax:** 01440-704152
**Web:** www.sperlingretail.com
**Reg No:** 6784789 **Estd:** 2009 Private Limited Company
**Line of Business:** Manufacture of other fabricated metal products not elsewhere classified
**Issued Capital:** £241,000
**Directors:** D A Gillett, A W Lean, C J Fellows, P N Ince
**Responsibilities**
**Senior:** Shirley Barber (Manager), Glyndwr Thomas (Managing Director, Director)
**Finance:** Shirley Barber (Manager)
**IT:** Shirley Barber (Manager)
**US SIC:** 3499, 2599
**UK SIC:** 31694, 46720

|    | 31-12-13 | 31-12-12 | 31-12-11 |
|----|----------|----------|----------|
| TA | 1,841,253 | 2,040,579 | 1,366,782 |
| NW | 643,869 | 865,270 | 575,651 |
| WC | 699,133 | 952,821 | 778,887 |

DUNS 22-925-1079  **Exp**
## Sperrin Holdings Ltd
Cahore Road, Draperstown, Magherafelt, Co Londonderry BT45 7AP
**Tel:** 02879-628362 **Fax:** 028-7962-8972
**Web:** www.sperrin-metal.com
**Reg No:** 0014144NI **Estd:** 1980 Private Limited Company
**Line of Business:** Management activities of holding companies
**Issued Capital:** £100
**Directors:** Ms C Gormley, P Gormley
**Co. Secretary:** Patrick Mcallister
**Responsibilities**
**Senior:** Patrick Mc Allister (Financial Director), Jimmy Trainor (Operations Manager)
**Finance:** Patrick Mc Allister (Financial Director)
**Marketing:** Caroline McKenna (Marketing Manager)
**Sales:** Paul Gormley (Sales Manager), Patrick Mc Allister (Financial Director)
**IT:** Gerad Scullion (IT Manager)
**HR:** Jimmy Trainor (Operations Manager)
**Health & Safety:** Tom Cassidy (Health & Safety Officer)
**Facilities:** Jimmy Trainor (Operations Manager)
**Operations:** Peter Gormley (Operations Manager), Jimmy Trainor (Operations Manager)
**Purchasing:** Peter Gormley (Operations Manager)

**Engineering:** Noel Stewart (Installations Manager)
**US SIC:** 6711, 3443
**UK SIC:** 83962, 32051
**Auditors:** PricewaterhouseCoopers
**Bankers:** Northern Bank Ltd (95-03-81)

|     | 31-12-13 | 31-12-12 | 31-12-11 |
|-----|----------|----------|----------|
| TO  | 12,685,031 | 12,982,055 | 13,353,530 |
| P/L | 215,976 | 440,845 | 216,364 |
| NW  | 5,104,023 | 5,127,009 | 4,674,507 |
| WC  | 3,486,469 | 3,267,660 | 2,949,703 |
| Emp.| 147 | 144 | 146 |

DUNS 23-260-4400
## Sperrin Integrated College Ltd
39 Pound Road, Magherafelt, Co Londonderry BT45 6NR
**Tel:** 028-7963-4177
**Web:** www.sperrin.magherafelt.ni.sch.uk
**Reg No:** 0041342NI **Estd:** 2001 Private Limited Company
**Line of Business:** General secondary education
**Directors:** Mrs F T Ferson, F Symington, Dr A I Mccullough, D Herron, R J Mckeown, R Dougan, Mrs I C Porte, Ms H Keys
**Co. Secretary:** Mrs Mona Houston
**Responsibilities**
**Senior:** Alastair Rowan (Principal)
**US SIC:** 8211 **UK SIC:** 93200
**Bankers:** The Bank Of Ireland (90-49-82)

|     | 31-03-14 | 31-03-13 | 31-03-12 |
|-----|----------|----------|----------|
| TO  | 16,930 | 2,307 | 44,054 |
| P/L | 9,120 | (3) | (283) |
| NW  | 9,857 | 737 | 740 |
| WC  | 9,857 | 737 | 740 |

DUNS 42-387-1560  **Imp**
## Sperry Rail (International) Ltd
(**Subsidiary of:** Rockwood Service Corporation)
Trent House, Derby, Derbyshire DE24 8UP
**Tel:** 01332-262565
**Web:** www.sperryrail.com
**Reg No:** 4374749 **Estd:** 2002 Private Limited Company
**Line of Business:** Engineering services
**Export Sales:** £2,762,308
**Issued Capital:** £1
**Director:** J Stroud
**Co. Secretary:** Ms Bridgette Murphy
**Responsibilities**
**Senior:** Peter Scannell (Manager)
**Engineering:** Duncan Grant (Mechanical Design Engineer)
**US SIC:** 8911 **UK SIC:** 83701

|     | 31-12-13 | 31-12-12 | 31-12-11 |
|-----|----------|----------|----------|
| TO  | 10,188,393 | 10,113,599 | 9,574,870 |
| P/L | 2,236,711 | 2,030,077 | 2,082,935 |
| NW  | 8,517,167 | 12,820,752 | 11,293,132 |
| WC  | 7,794,159 | 11,884,300 | 9,933,909 |
| Emp.| 72 | 68 | 68 |

DUNS 21-161-3709
## Spex Services Ltd
Dunnottar House, Howe Moss Drive, Kirkhill Industrial Estate, Dyce, Aberdeen, Aberdeenshire AB21 0FN
**Tel:** 01224727840
**Web:** www.spexservices.com
**Reg No:** 0358360SC **Estd:** 2009 Private Limited Company
**Line of Business:** Service activities incidental to oil and gas extraction excluding surveying
**Export Sales:** £5,126,349
**Issued Capital:** £157
**Directors:** R K Strachan, N Mahjoub, J G Oag, G F Coutts, M A Sibson, C Smith, J Fox
**Co. Secretary:** Blackwood Partners Llp
**Responsibilities**
**Senior:** Andrew Pettitt (Manager)
**Sales:** Sidney Johnston (VP - Innovation and Strategy)
**US SIC:** 3999 **UK SIC:** 49590
**Auditors:** Johnston Carmichael LLP

|     | 31-12-13 | 31-12-12 | 31-12-11 |
|-----|----------|----------|----------|
| TO  | 9,746,795 | 13,934,563 | 7,195,441 |
| P/L | (1,646,948) | 2,949,004 | 1,052,738 |
| NW  | 2,081,280 | 3,238,342 | 908,959 |
| WC  | 1,318,677 | 2,248,553 | (53,115) |
| Emp.| 71 | 80 | 44 |

DUNS 22-079-8024
## Speyfruit Ltd
5 Chanonry Road South, Elgin, Morayshire IV30 6NG
**Tel:** 01343-547733
**Web:** www.speyfruit.co.uk
**Reg No:** 0211546SC **VAT No:** 762139824
**Estd:** 2000 Private Limited Company
**Line of Business:** Wholesalers of fruit and vegetable
**Issued Capital:** £62,002
**Director:** I R Taylor
**Co. Secretary:** Ms Jane Taylor
**US SIC:** 5148 **UK SIC:** 61700
**Auditors:** J.F. Hornby & Co

**Bankers:** The Royal Bank Of Scotland Plc (83-20-06)

| | 31-10-13 | 31-10-12 | 31-10-11 |
|---|---|---|---|
| TA | 1,757,656 | 1,704,909 | 1,607,647 |
| NW | 537,557 | 605,009 | 685,277 |
| WC | (279,013) | (205,726) | (145,833) |

DUNS 21-406-5211 **Imp-Exp**

## Speymalt Whisky Distributors Ltd

58-60 South Street, Elgin, Morayshire IV30 1JY
**Web:** www.gordonandmacphail.com
**Reg No:** 0037522SC **VAT No:** 266070562
**Estd:** 1895 Private Limited Company
**Line of Business:** Wholesale of wine, beer, spirits and other alcoholic beverages
**Export Markets:** W Europe, Canada, S & S E Asia, Australasia, U S A
**Export Sales:** £6,704,115
**Trading Style:** Gordon & Macphail
**Issued Capital:** £190,000
**Principals:** M G Urquhart *(Financial)*, D A Urquhart *(Marketing)*, J P Curran, I M Chapman, N Ross, S A Rankin, E C Mackintosh, Mrs S A Bearne
**Co. Secretary:** Norman Ross
**Responsibilities**
**Senior:** Rosemary Rankin *(Manager)*
**HR:** Maureen Henderson *(Human Resources Manager)*
**Purchasing:** Maureen Henderson *(Human Resources Manager)*
**Engineering:** Callum McCasserly *(Production Manager)*
**US SIC:** 5182, 5921
**UK SIC:** 61700, 64200
**Auditors:** Grant Thornton UK LLP
**Bankers:** Clydesdale Bank Plc (82-63-07)

| | 28-02-14 | 28-02-13 | 29-02-12 |
|---|---|---|---|
| TO | 24,761,748 | 21,550,054 | 22,333,295 |
| P/L | 3,247,644 | 2,620,706 | 3,034,051 |
| NW | 22,199,202 | 20,251,357 | 18,989,531 |
| WC | 17,535,132 | 16,175,929 | 15,657,581 |
| Emp. | 138 | 133 | 137 |

DUNS 21-458-9855 **Imp-Exp**

## Speyside Cooperage Ltd

**(Subsidiary of:** Sas La Demigniere)
Dufftown Road, Craigellachie, Aberlour, Banffshire AB38 9RS
**Tel:** 01340881264
**Web:** www.speysidecooperage.co.uk
**Reg No:** 0041812SC **Estd:** 1965 Private Limited Company
**Line of Business:** Manufacturers and suppliers of drums and barrel
**Export Markets:** Spain; France; Germany
**Export Sales:** £6,037,860
**Trading Style:** Broxburn Cooperage
**Issued Capital:** £18,944
**Principals:** W H Taylor *(Managing)*, J J Francois, W Jamieson, F J Witasse
**Co. Secretary:** Grigor & Young
**Branches:** Speyside Cooperage Ltd, Macdonald House, 18 Westerton Road, Broxburn, West Lothian EH52 5AQ
**US SIC:** 2449 **UK SIC:** 46402
**Auditors:** Ritsons
**Bankers:** The Royal Bank Of Scotland Plc (83-23-17)

| | 30-04-14 | 30-04-13 | 30-04-12 |
|---|---|---|---|
| TO | 39,290,797 | 30,045,621 | 22,432,087 |
| P/L | 4,498,675 | 2,473,466 | 1,526,012 |
| NW | 13,206,249 | 10,283,013 | 8,390,660 |
| WC | 9,635,070 | 7,289,272 | 6,848,148 |
| Emp. | 82 | 81 | 75 |

DUNS 55-067-1127

## Speyside Residential Care

11 Conval Drive, Aberlour, Banffshire AB38 9QE
**Tel:** 01340871640
**Estd:** 1988
**Line of Business:** Social work activities with accommodation
**Partners:** Miss A Robertson, Miss A Robertdon
**Responsibilities**
**Senior:** Glen Erskine *(Manager)*, Allison Robertson *(Manager)*
**US SIC:** 8321 **UK SIC:** 96111
**Employees:** 50

DUNS 21-719-2172

## Spf Private Clients Holdings Ltd

25 Finsbury Circus, London EC2M 7EE
**Tel:** 08709007762
**Reg No:** 7574553 **Estd:** 2011 Private Limited Company
**Line of Business:** Activities auxiliary to financial intermediation not elsewhere classified
**Issued Capital:** £1,075
**Directors:** J L Rodea, M E Harris, C A Rose, M R Boles, D A Yeadon, N J Moore, A L King
**US SIC:** 6111 **UK SIC:** 81501

**Bankers:** Barclays Bank Plc (20-00-50)

| | 31-12-13 | 31-12-12 | 31-12-11 |
|---|---|---|---|
| TA | 9,426,000 | 7,139,000 | 7,836,000 |
| P/L | 2,220,000 | 707,000 | 1,049,000 |
| NW | (791,000) | (1,290,000) | (1,754,000) |
| WC | 110,000 | (1,139,000) | 1,131,000 |
| Emp. | 89 | 95 | 99 |

DUNS 39-735-5934 **Imp**

## Spg Ltd

**(Subsidiary of:** Spg (Blue) Ltd)
9 Little End Road, Eaton Socon, St Neots, Cambridgeshire PE19 8JH
**Tel:** 01480-403099 **Fax:** 01480-406638
**Web:** www.spgltd.co.uk
**Reg No:** 2177320 **VAT No:** 491012867
**Estd:** 1987 Private Limited Company
**Line of Business:** Manufacture of non-domestic cooling and ventilation equipment
**Export Sales:** £643,937
**Issued Capital:** £397
**Directors:** A David, S Leach, G M Smith
**Co. Secretary:** Harry Rees
**Responsibilities**
**HR:** Natalie Allen *(Accounts Manager)*
**Branches:** Spg Ltd, Unit 1 The Airfield, Bedford, Bedfordshire MK44 2BN
**US SIC:** 3585 **UK SIC:** 32841
**Auditors:** HLB AV Audit PLC
**Bankers:** Barclays Bank Plc (20-91-79)

| | 31-03-14 | 31-03-13 | 31-03-12 |
|---|---|---|---|
| TO | 12,012,663 | 12,423,235 | 17,083,957 |
| P/L | (219,426) | 158,654 | 105,066 |
| NW | 4,221,417 | 4,553,843 | 4,373,510 |
| WC | 4,216,503 | 4,394,106 | 4,229,712 |
| Emp. | 117 | 117 | 126 |

DUNS 22-160-9386 **Imp**

## Sphere Medical Holding Plc

Harston Mill, Royston Road, Harston, Cambridge, Cambridgeshire CB22 7GG
**Tel:** 01223875222
**Web:** www.spheremedical.com
**Reg No:** 4179503 **Estd:** 2001 Public Limited Company
**Line of Business:** Research and experimental development on natural sciences and engineering
**Export Sales:** £37,000
**Issued Capital:** £368,056
**Directors:** M F Schmidt, Dr A F Martin, W Rencken, F M Hall, S H Mahle, J H Gregory, Dr D R Martyr
**Co. Secretary:** Frank Hall
**US SIC:** 7391, 6711
**UK SIC:** 94000, 83962
**Auditors:** Grant Thornton UK LLP

| | 31-12-13 | 31-12-12 | 31-12-11 |
|---|---|---|---|
| TO | 40,000 | 46,000 | 40,000 |
| P/L | (5,523,000) | (7,759,000) | (6,326,000) |
| NW | 8,718,000 | 4,823,000 | 11,658,000 |
| WC | 8,495,000 | 4,572,000 | 11,567,000 |
| Emp. | 67 | 54 | 45 |

DUNS 34-965-9388

## Spi (Gb) Ltd

Morley Carr Business Centre, Morley Carr Road, Low Moor, Bradford, West Yorkshire BD12 0RA
**Tel:** 01274691777 **Fax:** 01274693832
**Web:** www.styrene.biz
**Reg No:** 5761472 **Estd:** 2006 Private Limited Company
**Line of Business:** Manufacture of other articles of paper and paperboard not elsewhere classified
**Issued Capital:** £100
**Director:** M Edge
**Co. Secretary:** Joseph Edge
**US SIC:** 7399 **UK SIC:** 83954

| | 31-03-14 | 31-03-13 | 31-03-12 |
|---|---|---|---|
| TA | 100 | 100 | 100 |
| NW | 100 | 100 | 100 |

DUNS 28-870-9926 **Imp-Exp**

## Spi Global Play Ltd

Unit C, Spectrum Business Park, Wrexham Industrial Estate, Wrexham, Clwyd LL13 9QA
**Tel:** 01978-664456 **Fax:** 01978-664416
**Web:** www.spiplay.com
**Reg No:** 1041364 **VAT No:** 219070579
**Estd:** 1972 Private Limited Company
**Line of Business:** Manufacture of sports goods
**Export Markets:** European Union (E U); Poland
**Export Sales:** £3,622,279
**Trading Style:** The Play Co
**Issued Capital:** £200
**Directors:** M Wettergren, S Johansson
**Responsibilities**
**Senior:** Alexander Ramos *(Manager)*
**IT:** Gerraint Pritchard *(Computer Manager)*
**HR:** Sue Hughes *(Human Resources Manager)*
**US SIC:** 3999 **UK SIC:** 49590
**Auditors:** Conways

**Bankers:** Barclays Bank Plc (20-25-76)

| | 31-12-13 | 31-12-12 | 31-12-11 |
|---|---|---|---|
| TO | 5,460,997 | N/A | N/A |
| P/L | 97,801 | N/A | N/A |
| NW | 608,996 | 531,699 | 424,236 |
| WC | 267,580 | 217,779 | 237,783 |

DUNS 36-534-3805 **Imp**

## Spi Lasers Uk Ltd

**(Subsidiary of:** Trumpf Gmbh + Co. Kg)
6 Wellington Park, Southampton, Hampshire SO30 2QU
**Tel:** 01489-779696
**Web:** www.spilasers.com
**Reg No:** 3290610 **Estd:** 2010 Private Limited Company
**Line of Business:** Manufacture of other metalworking machine tools
**Trading Style:** S P I
**Issued Capital:** £101,417
**Directors:** T Reinauer, Dr S R Norman
**Co. Secretary:** Dr Malcolm Varnham
**Responsibilities**
**Sales:** Audrey Bourriez *(Sales Director)*, Jack Gabzdyl *(Product Line Manager)*, John Tinson *(VP of Sales)*
**Operations:** Don Riddell *(Director, Manufacturing)*
**US SIC:** 3999 **UK SIC:** 49590
**Auditors:** KPMG LLP
**Bankers:** HSBC Bank plc (40-42-18)

| | 30-06-14 | 30-06-13 | 30-06-12 |
|---|---|---|---|
| TO | 38,668,000 | 35,260,000 | 23,236,000 |
| P/L | (4,548,000) | (5,579,000) | (10,617,000) |
| NW | 23,709,000 | 3,227,000 | 6,775,000 |
| WC | 17,909,000 | (1,577,000) | 5,369,000 |
| Emp. | 251 | 256 | 248 |

DUNS 21-033-0095

## Spice Lodge

E S L (Cheltenham) Ltd, Eagle Tower, Montpellier Drive, Cheltenham, Gloucestershire GL50 1TA
**Tel:** 01242-226300
**Web:** www.spicelodge.com
**Estd:** 2005 Proprietorship
**Line of Business:** Restaurant - indian
**Proprietor:** D Wood
**Responsibilities**
**Senior:** Mohammad Rahman *(Manager)*
**US SIC:** 5812 **UK SIC:** 66110
**Employees:** 501

DUNS 21-027-0588

## Spice of Life

41 Gateside Street, Hamilton, Lanarkshire ML3 7JG
**Tel:** 01698-282272
**Estd:** 1989 Partnership
**Line of Business:** Take-away food shops
**Partners:** A Mohammed, I Mohammed
**US SIC:** 5812 **UK SIC:** 66110
**Bankers:** Airdrie Savings Bank (80-36-06)
**Employees:** 80

DUNS 21-442-8559 **Imp-Exp**

## Spicemanns Ltd

55-59 Kelvin Avenue, Glasgow, Lanarkshire G52 4LR
**Tel:** 01418 834797 **Fax:** 01418 105242
**Web:** www.kerry.com
**Reg No:** 0023225SC **Estd:** 1879 Private Limited Company
**Line of Business:** Manufacture of condiments and seasonings
**Export Markets:** West Europe
**Trading Style:** Inc Kerry
**Issued Capital:** £8,000
**Directors:** S Mccarthy, B C Mehigan, F Healy
**Co. Secretary:** Brian Durran
**Responsibilities**
**Senior:** Isabelle McLaughlin *(Finance Director)*
**Finance:** Isabelle McLaughlin *(Finance Director)*
**Purchasing:** Rachel Johnson *(Supply Chain Manager)*
**US SIC:** 2099 **UK SIC:** 42399
**Bankers:** National Westminster Bank Plc (60-80-08)

| | 31-12-13 | 31-12-12 | 31-12-11 |
|---|---|---|---|
| TA | 3,796,781 | 3,796,781 | 3,796,781 |
| NW | 3,796,781 | 3,796,781 | 3,796,781 |

DUNS 21-043-1741

## Spicerhaart

Newfield House, Vicarage Lane, Blackpool, Lancashire FY4 4EW
**Tel:** 01253-603000
**Web:** www.spicerhaart.co.uk
**Estd:** 2012
**Line of Business:** Estate agents
**Responsibilities**
**Senior:** Mark Pilling *(Manager)*
**US SIC:** 6531 **UK SIC:** 83400
**Employees:** 100

DUNS 22-080-2230

## Spicerhaart Group Ltd

Colwyn House, Sheepen Place, Colchester, Essex CO3 3LD
**Tel:** 01206765599
**Web:** www.spicerhaart.co.uk
**Reg No:** 4081664 **Estd:** 2000 Private Limited Company
**Line of Business:** Real estate agencies
**Issued Capital:** £4,030
**Directors:** J A Spence, R Jervis, A R Benn
**Co. Secretary:** Paul Smith
**Responsibilities**
**Senior:** Nesta Anderson *(Branch Manager)*, Warren Brandon *(Branch Manager)*, Scott Cave *(Branch Manager)*, Marcus Dowding *(Branch Manager)*, Tracey Dumont *(Branch Manager)*, Melissa Glenister *(Branch Manager)*, Tamara Greener *(Branch Manager)*, Simon Haart *(General Manager)*, Jason Harvey *(Branch Manager)*, Clare Hempson *(Branch Manager)*, Michelle Humphreys *(Branch Manager)*, Sharon James *(Branch Manager)*, Ann Law *(Branch Manager)*, Nina Maltby *(Branch Manager)*, Jackie Martin *(Branch Manager)*, Michelle Mason *(Branch Manager)*, Trevor Mills *(Branch Manager)*, Gary Morton *(Branch Manager)*, Anna Mylonas *(Branch Manager)*, Kelly Nicholls *(Branch Manager)*, Emma O'Neill *(Branch Manager)*, Yvonne Oakley *(Branch Manager)*, Daryl Parr *(Branch Manager)*, Janet Pavely *(Branch Manager)*, Joanne Pennells *(Branch Manager)*, Steve Shore *(Branch Manager)*, Kate Stearman *(Branch Manager)*, Vicky Tevan *(Branch Manager)*, Annette Thompson *(General Manager)*, Caroline Toll *(Branch Manager)*
**Branches:** Spicerhaart Group Ltd, 375 Walderslade Road, Chatham, Kent ME5 9LL
**US SIC:** 7399 **UK SIC:** 83954
**Auditors:** Dixon Wilson
**Bankers:** National Westminster Bank Plc (60-06-06)

| | 31-12-13 | 31-12-12 | 31-12-11 |
|---|---|---|---|
| TO | 107,313,029 | 92,263,074 | 88,789,516 |
| P/L | 8,581,655 | 6,394,717 | 1,759,576 |
| NW | 17,100,027 | 10,275,614 | 3,793,491 |
| WC | 11,282,637 | 6,679,073 | 7,230,194 |
| Emp. | 1,765 | 1,687 | 1,531 |

DUNS 22-745-1747

## Spicers

Pilsworth Road, Heywood, Lancashire OL10 2TA
**Tel:** 08442380077
**Web:** www.spicers.co.uk
**Estd:** 1978
**Line of Business:** Wholesale of other household goods not elsewhere classified
**US SIC:** 5199 **UK SIC:** 61900
**Employees:** 1,000

DUNS 21-615-4120 **Exp**

## Spicers Ltd

**(Subsidiary of:** Becap Spicers (Uk) Ltd)
Building 1000, Waterbeach, Cambridge, Cambridgeshire CB25 9PD
**Tel:** 0844-238-0000
**Web:** www.spicers.co.uk
**Reg No:** 0425809 **Estd:** 2006 Private Limited Company
**Line of Business:** Wholesale of other office machinery and equipment
**Export Sales:** £9,088,000
**Trading Style:** Spicers Furniture
**Issued Capital:** £10,005,400
**Directors:** J M Whiteway, G J Michael, A M Skinner, A G Mobbs
**Co. Secretary:** Richard Warwick-Saunders
**Responsibilities**
**Senior:** alan ball *(chief executive)*
**Marketing:** jeanette brisetz *(marketing director)*
**Branches:** Spicers Ltd, Banks Rd, Aylesbury, Buckinghamshire HP17 8EE
**US SIC:** 5081 **UK SIC:** 61490
**Auditors:** Deloitte LLP
**Bankers:** National Westminster Bank Plc (60-00-01)

| | 30-04-13 | 30-04-12 | 30-04-11 |
|---|---|---|---|
| TO | 240,287,000 | 389,066,000 | 480,741,000 |
| P/L | 1,379,000 | 31,281,000 | 6,511,000 |
| NW | 85,125,000 | 83,092,000 | 57,921,000 |
| WC | 63,928,000 | 67,452,000 | 39,018,000 |
| Emp. | 614 | 1,091 | 1,366 |

DUNS 51-653-5262 **Imp**

## Spie Fs Northern Uk Ltd

**(Subsidiary of:** Cdr Bounce (Cayman) Partners L.P.)
Hochtief House, Warrington, Cheshire WA1 1RL
**Tel:** 01925-404-500 **Fax:** 01925-404-598
**Web:** www.spie.com
**Reg No:** 5970050 **VAT No:** 910316862
**Estd:** 2006 Private Limited Company
**Line of Business:** Management of real estate on a fee or contract basis
**Trading Style:** Spie
**Issued Capital:** £1,500,000

**Directors:** J O Thoden Van Velzen, G H Restall
**Co. Secretary:** Christopher Rowe
**Responsibilities**
**Senior:** Guido Hilgers *(Chief executive officer)*
**Finance:** Guido Hilgers *(Chief executive officer)*
**Sales:** Grace Deegan *(Contract Manager)*
**Admin:** Sarah Nuttall *(Personal Assistant)*
**IT:** Philip Critchley *(IT Manager)*
**Purchasing:** Sheila Hendrick *(Procurement Manager)*
**US SIC:** 6531, 7399
**UK SIC:** 83400, 83954
**Auditors:** Deloitte LLP
**Bankers:** Citibank Na (08-60-71)

| | 31-12-13 | 31-12-12 | 31-12-11 |
|---|---|---|---|
| TO | 39,336,299 | 37,732,797 | 33,615,831 |
| P/L | 607,030 | 148,572 | (144,882) |
| NW | 3,991,342 | 3,318,121 | 3,109,618 |
| WC | 5,914,953 | 4,223,227 | 3,966,210 |
| Emp. | 953 | 902 | 881 |

DUNS 21-002-1263
## Spie Ltd
**(Subsidiary of:** Cdr Bounce (Cayman) Partners L.P.)
33 Gracechurch Street, London EC3V 0BT
**Tel:** 02071052300
**Web:** www.spiematthewhall.com
**Reg No:** 6275653 **VAT No:** 945781189
**Estd:** 1961 Private Limited Company
**Line of Business:** Mechanical engineering general
**Trading Style:** Spie Whs, Spie Group, Spie Industrial Services
**Issued Capital:** £30,000,000
**Directors:** J O Thoden Van Velzen, G H Restall, T J Atherton
**Co. Secretary:** Christopher Rowe
**Responsibilities**
**Senior:** Gary Mcclellan *(Manager)*, Kevin Morgan *(Manager)*
**HR:** Kate Marchant *(Human Resources Manager)*
**Branches:** Spie Ltd, 71 Firhill Road, Glasgow, Lanarkshire G20 7BE
**US SIC:** 8911, 7399
**UK SIC:** 83701, 83954
**Auditors:** PricewaterhouseCoopers LLP
**Bankers:** Societe Generale (23-63-91)

| | 31-12-13 | 31-12-12 | 31-12-11 |
|---|---|---|---|
| TO | 165,625,000 | 182,542,000 | 263,765,000 |
| P/L | (13,524,000) | (17,385,000) | (23,004,000) |
| NW | (6,695,000) | (8,455,000) | (6,354,000) |
| WC | (9,753,000) | (8,526,000) | 1,529,000 |
| Emp. | 1,304 | 1,610 | 1,849 |

DUNS 22-021-8551 Imp
## Spiecapag Uk Ltd
46 West Bar Street, Banbury, Oxfordshire OX16 9RZ
**Tel:** 01295220330 **Fax:** 01295220339
**Web:** www.spiecapag.com
**Reg No:** 4024580 **Estd:** 2000 Private Limited Company
**Line of Business:** Building construction contractors
**Issued Capital:** £250,000
**Directors:** S J Hancock, G Durand, J C Van De Wiele
**Co. Secretary:** Mrs Julie Shackleton
**Responsibilities**
**Senior:** Francois Billard *(Manager)*, Dominique Bouvier *(Manager)*, Nicholas Dansette *(Manager)*, Martyn James *(Business Development Manager)*, Bruno Roussiere *(Manager)*
**Marketing:** Martyn James *(Business Development Manager)*
**Sales:** Martyn James *(Business Development Manager)*
**Health & Safety:** Stuart Hosegood *(Health & Safety Manager)*
**Branches:** Spiecapag Uk Ltd, Annat Ho, South Quay, Montrose, Angus DD10 9UG
**US SIC:** 1522 **UK SIC:** 50100
**Auditors:** Bourner Bullock
**Bankers:** The Royal Bank Of Scotland Plc (16-28-17)

| | 31-12-13 | 31-12-12 | 31-12-11 |
|---|---|---|---|
| TO | 17,670,399 | 8,095,085 | 17,888,157 |
| P/L | (1,307,995) | (3,364,976) | (4,123,318) |
| NW | (7,646,114) | (5,923,939) | (3,164,330) |
| WC | (7,697,159) | (6,084,103) | (3,389,008) |
| Emp. | 74 | 30 | 90 |

DUNS 22-777-7869
## Spiers & Hartwell Ltd
Station Road, Evesham, Worcestershire WR11 8YH
**Tel:** 01386-833633 **Fax:** 01386833667
**Reg No:** 1037540 **VAT No:** 589484273
**Estd:** 1972 Private Limited Company
**Line of Business:** Road haulage and transport services
**Export Sales:** £37,415
**Issued Capital:** £1,047
**Principals:** C A Hartwell *(Managing)*, Ms D A Hartwell
**Responsibilities**
**Senior:** Peter Hiles *(Workshop Manager)*
**Finance:** Rodney Willoughby *(Office Manager)*
**Admin:** Rodney Willoughby *(Office Manager)*
**HR:** Roy Pritchard *(Human Resources Officer)*
**Health & Safety:** Roy Pritchard *(Human Resources Officer)*
**Facilities:** Rodney Willoughby *(Office Manager)*
**Operations:** Roy Pritchard *(Human Resources Officer)*
**Purchasing:** Rodney Willoughby *(Office Manager)*
**Engineering:** Peter Hiles *(Workshop Manager)*
**US SIC:** 4789, 7399
**UK SIC:** 77002, 83954
**Auditors:** Clement Rabjohns
**Bankers:** National Westminster Bank Plc (60-08-44)

| | 28-02-14 | 28-02-13 | 29-02-12 |
|---|---|---|---|
| TO | 13,699,342 | 10,525,231 | 9,039,170 |
| P/L | 537,982 | 612,040 | (131,235) |
| NW | 6,251,768 | 6,481,110 | 6,028,846 |
| WC | 1,171,842 | 1,070,966 | 993,891 |
| Emp. | 154 | 131 | 106 |

DUNS 29-846-7283
## Spillers of Chard Ltd
**(Subsidiary of:** Croscard Ltd)
Leach Road, Chard Business Park, Chard, Somerset TA20 1FA
**Web:** www.cookercentre.com
**Reg No:** 2049497 **Estd:** 1986 Private Limited Company
**Line of Business:** Retail sale of electrical household appliances and radio and television goods
**Trading Style:** Spillers of Chard Ltd
**Issued Capital:** £10,000
**Principals:** Ms C Durie *(Managing)*, R A Durie, R A Durie
**Co. Secretary:** David Mears
**Responsibilities**
**Senior:** Andrew Durie *(Director)*
**US SIC:** 5732, 1751
**UK SIC:** 64800, 50400
**Auditors:** A C Mole & Sons
**Bankers:** Barclays Bank Plc (20-85-26)

| | 30-09-13 | 30-09-12 | 30-09-11 |
|---|---|---|---|
| TA | 3,181,155 | 2,775,261 | 2,881,711 |
| NW | 1,722,580 | 1,662,365 | 1,276,153 |
| WC | 254,957 | 46,218 | (23,034) |

DUNS 45-817-5098
## Spinal Injuries Association
Sia House, Milton Keynes, Buckinghamshire MK6 2HH
**Tel:** 08456786633 **Fax:** 08450706911
**Web:** www.spinal.co.uk
**Reg No:** 3175203 **Estd:** 1996 Private Limited Company
**Line of Business:** Social work activities without accommodation
**Directors:** M F Williams, P J Hamilton, M R Mcclelland, J R Robinson, Ms M Howard, Mrs C J Dyson, Dr R T Earl, M L Pollard
**Co. Secretary:** Martin Pollard
**Responsibilities**
**Senior:** Margaret Deane *(Director)*, John Dongen *(Manager)*, Jonathan Fogerty *(Director)*, Peter Hanley *(Executive)*, Nicola Iannelli-Popham *(Director)*, Judith Jeskey *(Director)*, Greg Judge *(Director)*, Frances Porter *(General Manager Member & Clien)*, Raquel Siganporia *(Director)*, Jonathan Wilkes *(Finance Director)*
**Finance:** John Illankovan *(Head of Fiance)*, Julie Patton *(Finance Assistant)*, Bhanji Solanki *(Finance Assistant)*, Jonathan Wilkes *(Finance Director)*, Elizabeth Wright *(Community Fundraising Manager)*
**Marketing:** Dan Burden *(Head of Public Affairs)*, Helen Chapman *(Communications & Marketing Off)*, Breda Duggan *(Publications Manager)*, Mick Hutchins *(Public Affairs Officer)*, Catherine Stribling *(Public Affairs Communications)*, Elizabeth Wright *(Community Fundraising Manager)*
**Sales:** Rebecca Garrard *(Business Development Officer)*, Sarah Tennent *(Business Development Manager)*
**Admin:** Maureen Hampson *(PA to the Chief Executive Offi)*, Bernie Murphy *(Head of Administration)*, Chris Pinches *(Office Administrator)*
**HR:** Bernie Murphy *(Head of Administration)*
**Facilities:** Chris Pinches *(Office Administrator)*
**Operations:** Jamie Rhind *(Outreach Services Manager, Out)*
**US SIC:** 7399 **UK SIC:** 83954
**Auditors:** Binder Hamlyn
**Bankers:** Barclays Bank Plc (20-87-43)

| | 05-04-14 | 05-04-13 | 05-04-12 |
|---|---|---|---|
| TO | 2,151,617 | 2,929,455 | 1,812,314 |
| P/L | (64,368) | 823,074 | 54,379 |
| NW | 3,444,891 | 3,509,259 | 2,686,185 |
| WC | 1,628,158 | 1,752,419 | 943,857 |
| Emp. | 50 | 42 | 38 |

DUNS 21-232-5732 Exp
## Spincraft Etg Ltd
**(Subsidiary of:** Standex International Corporation)
Shelley Road, Newcastle-Upon-Tyne, Tyne and Wear NE15 9RT
**Web:** www.spincraft-etg.com
**Reg No:** 0556473 **VAT No:** 175806245
**Estd:** 1955 Private Limited Company
**Line of Business:** Manufacture of other fabricated metal products not elsewhere classified
**Export Markets:** European Union (E U)
**Export Sales:** £3,702,000
**Trading Style:** Metal Spinners Group Limited
**Issued Capital:** £150,000
**Directors:** Ms D A Rosen, L Paolillo, D A Dunbar
**Co. Secretary:** Halco Secretaries Limited
**Responsibilities**
**Senior:** Brian Batcholor *(Manager)*, Douglas Brookes *(Manager)*, Roger Fix *(Manager)*, Fred Patrickson *(Production Manager)*, Malcolm Shaw *(Manager)*
**Purchasing:** Stephen Webber *(Purchasing Manager)*
**Branches:** Spincraft Etg Limited, Whitehouse Works, Clough Road, Manchester M9 4FP
**US SIC:** 3499, 8911
**UK SIC:** 31694, 83701
**Auditors:** KPMG LLP
**Bankers:** Allied Irish Bank (gb) (23-92-82)

| | 30-06-13 | 30-06-12 | 30-06-11 |
|---|---|---|---|
| TO | 11,737,000 | 16,496,000 | 3,930,000 |
| P/L | 1,931,000 | 4,986,000 | 816,000 |
| NW | 9,668,000 | 9,900,000 | 6,192,000 |
| WC | 8,621,000 | 8,670,000 | 5,523,000 |
| Emp. | 82 | 91 | 91 |

DUNS 42-382-1474 Imp-Exp
## Spink & Son Ltd
**(Subsidiary of:** Capital 1818 Pte. Ltd.)
67-69 Southampton Row, London WC1B 4ET
**Tel:** 020-7563-4000 **Fax:** 020-7563-4066
**Web:** www.spink.com
**Reg No:** 4369748 **Estd:** 2002 Private Limited Company
**Line of Business:** Coins and medals
**Trading Style:** Spink
**Issued Capital:** £1,101,000
**Principals:** T S Hirsch *(Managing)*, O D Stocker, A F Spink
**Co. Secretary:** Alison Bennet
**Responsibilities**
**IT:** Segun Magbagbeola *(Computer Manager)*
**US SIC:** 5941 **UK SIC:** 65400
**Auditors:** Deloitte & Touche LLP
**Bankers:** The Royal Bank Of Scotland Plc (16-00-79)

| | 31-01-14 | 31-01-13 | 31-01-12 |
|---|---|---|---|
| TO | 19,700,974 | 21,004,826 | 21,260,462 |
| P/L | 1,162,636 | 1,287,105 | 983,172 |
| NW | 3,180,877 | 4,680,736 | 3,734,331 |
| WC | 3,369,772 | 4,679,238 | 3,584,999 |
| Emp. | 62 | 69 | 65 |

DUNS 22-213-3980
## Spinko Ltd
Westland Road, Leeds, West Yorkshire LS11 5SN
**Tel:** 01132-055200
**Reg No:** 4231536 **Estd:** 2001 Private Limited Company
**Line of Business:** Manufacture of mattresses
**Export Sales:** £1,857,457
**Issued Capital:** £101,000
**Directors:** P D Spinks, S P Spinks
**Co. Secretary:** Ms Amanda Shea
**US SIC:** 2515, 5133
**UK SIC:** 46715, 61600

| | 30-06-13 | 30-06-12 | 30-06-11 |
|---|---|---|---|
| TO | 28,218,418 | 24,843,867 | 25,209,079 |
| P/L | 2,757,084 | 2,925,584 | 3,355,632 |
| NW | 19,879,825 | 17,610,683 | 15,079,468 |
| WC | 5,213,295 | 5,575,662 | 6,793,828 |
| Emp. | 314 | 291 | 279 |

DUNS 50-568-9380 Imp-Exp
## Spinnaker International Ltd
**(Subsidiary of:** Staysail Ltd)
Saltash Parkway, Saltash, Cornwall PL12 6LF
**Tel:** 01752-850300
**Web:** www.spinnakerinternational.com
**Reg No:** 2516654 **Estd:** 1992 Private Limited Company
**Line of Business:** Manufacture of electronic valves and tubes and other electronic components
**Export Markets:** E U, U S A, South Africa, Far East, Norway and Iceland
**Export Sales:** £7,410,078
**Issued Capital:** £120
**Principals:** J A Yandell *(Chairman)*, C G Yandell, A R Westington, Ms V L Yandell
**Co. Secretary:** Martin Pascoe
**Responsibilities**
**IT:** Stuart Deakin *(IT Manager)*
**HR:** Anne Temple *(Personnel Manager)*
**Health & Safety:** Mike Wing *(Facilities Manager)*
**Facilities:** Mike Wing *(Facilities Manager)*
**Purchasing:** Tony Gullis *(Purchasing Manager)*
**US SIC:** 3679, 7391
**UK SIC:** 34542, 94000
**Auditors:** Nicklin LLP
**Bankers:** Lloyds TSB Bank plc (30-96-68)

| | 30-04-14 | 30-04-13 | 30-04-12 |
|---|---|---|---|
| TO | 10,332,549 | 10,608,645 | 11,021,778 |
| P/L | 1,238,418 | 1,415,041 | 801,708 |
| NW | 938,993 | 2,792,851 | 1,604,701 |
| WC | 737,818 | 2,864,877 | 1,391,935 |
| Emp. | 104 | 104 | 103 |

DUNS 64-263-0057
## The Spinney
21 Forest View, London E4 7AU
**Tel:** 020-8524-2200
**Web.** www.carebase.org.uk
**Estd:** 1998 Partnership
**Line of Business:** Residential care establishments
**Partners:** R Fry, Ms B Fry
**Responsibilities**
**Senior:** Juliette Oates *(Home Manager)*
**US SIC:** 8321 **UK SIC:** 96111
**Employees:** 64

DUNS 21-784-1200
## Spinney Hill Primary School
Ventnor Street, Leicester, Leicestershire LE5 5EZ
**Tel:** 01162737047
**Web:** www.spinneyhill.leicester.sch.uk
**Estd:** 2011 Proprietorship
**Line of Business:** Schools (local authority)
**Proprietor:** M Stoves
**Responsibilities**
**Senior:** Bernie Ranzetta *(Head Teacher)*
**US SIC:** 8211 **UK SIC:** 93200
**Employees:** 110

DUNS 21-226-6866
## Spinneyfields Specialist Care Centre
H E Bates Way, Rushden, Northamptonshire NN10 9YP
**Tel:** 01933352840
**Web:** www.shaw.co.uk
**Estd:** 2004 Proprietorship
**Line of Business:** Rehabilitation centres
**Proprietor:** Mrs S Thompson
**Responsibilities**
**Senior:** Robert Hollins *(Home Manager)*
**US SIC:** 8062 **UK SIC:** 95100
**Employees:** 64

DUNS 50-698-1026
## Spinning Wheel Inn
The Esplanade, Paignton, Devon TQ4 6ED
**Tel:** 01803-555000
**Web:** www.spinny.com
**Estd:** 1980 Partnership
**Line of Business:** Managed public houses and bars
**Partners:** D Thompson, M Thompson
**US SIC:** 5813 **UK SIC:** 66200
**Employees:** 49

DUNS 21-873-0469
## Spiral Academies Trust
Mandeville Primary School, Mandeville Drive, St Albans, Hertfordshire AL1 2LE
**Tel:** 01727774098
**Web:** www.spiral.herts.sch.uk
**Reg No:** 8322127 **Estd:** 2012 Private Company Limited By Guarantee
**Line of Business:** Primary education
**Directors:** Mrs T G Sutton, Mrs K E Burton, Prof A J Mayo, K A Baldwin, Ms A J Godfrey, B P Evans, Mrs E Murphy, Mrs S L Othen
**Co. Secretary:** Ms Elizabeth Allpress
**US SIC:** 8211 **UK SIC:** 93200
**Bankers:** Lloyds TSB Bank plc (30-97-25)

| | 31-08-14 | 31-08-13 |
|---|---|---|
| TO | 2,806,931 | 11,470,583 |
| P/L | 96,612 | 9,558,583 |
| NW | 9,622,195 | 9,541,583 |
| WC | 587,018 | 441,762 |
| Emp. | 130 | 106 |

DUNS 23-269-4406

## Spiral Construction Ltd

12 The Broadway, St Ives, Cambridgeshire PE27 5BN
**Tel:** 01480301102
**Web:** www.spiral.uk.com
**Reg No:** 1888016 **VAT No:** 418210387
**Estd:** 2002 Private Limited Company
**Line of Business:** Building construction contractors
**Trading Style:** Spiral Construction Limited
**Issued Capital:** £90
**Directors:** E Nicholls, Mrs C R Nicholls
**Co. Secretary:** Craig Coull
**Responsibilities**
**Senior:** Jason Bullen *(Manager)*, Matt Chambers *(Despatch Manager)*
**US SIC:** 1522 **UK SIC:** 50100
**Auditors:** Paul & Maundrell
**Bankers:** Lloyds TSB Bank plc (30-94-07)

| | 30-06-13 | 30-06-12 | 30-06-11 |
|---|---|---|---|
| TA | 2,225,229 | 2,343,968 | 2,625,644 |
| NW | 1,898,327 | 1,694,565 | 2,131,960 |
| WC | 959,331 | 919,727 | 1,063,931 |

DUNS 23-557-5888 **Imp**

## Spiral Software Ltd

(**Subsidiary of:** Schneider Electric Sa)
St Andrews House, Cambridge, Cambridgeshire CB4 1DL
**Web:** www.spiralsoft.co.uk
**Reg No:** 3555875 **Estd:** 1998 Private Limited Company
**Line of Business:** Computer software (development)
**Export Sales:** £9,209,423
**Issued Capital:** £10,050
**Directors:** T Lambeth, S Thorogood, K C Smith
**Co. Secretary:** Invensys Secretaries Limited
**Responsibilities**
**Senior:** Dawn Oakley *(Director of Corporaste Adminis)*, Ali Webster *(CEO)*
**US SIC:** 7379 **UK SIC:** 83940
**Auditors:** Deloitte LLP

| | 31-03-14 | 31-03-13 | 30-03-12 |
|---|---|---|---|
| TO | 10,172,019 | 6,925,337 | 9,442,573 |
| P/L | 1,239,511 | (725,067) | 2,276,949 |
| NW | 4,319,457 | 3,070,159 | 3,548,345 |
| WC | 2,244,998 | 414,220 | 926,505 |
| Emp. | 70 | 54 | 46 |

DUNS 21-608-4236 **Exp**

## Spirax-Sarco Engineering P L C

Charlton House, Cheltenham, Gloucestershire GL53 8ER
**Tel:** 01242-521-361
**Web:** www.spiraxsarco.com
**Reg No:** 0596337 **VAT No:** 274210483
**Estd:** 1958 Public Limited Company
**Line of Business:** Manufacture of pumps
**Export Markets:** W Europe, E Europe, Canada, S America, Africa, S & SE Asia, Australasia, U S A, Middle East
**Trading Style:** Spirax Sarco Engineering
**Issued Capital:** £19,565,123
**Principals:** D J Meredith *(Financial)*, Dr G E Schoolenberg, C G Watson, W H Whiteley, Doctor K Rajagopal, J L Whalen, J R Pike, N H Daws
**Co. Secretary:** Andrew Robson
**Responsibilities**
**Senior:** Jay Whalen *(Executive Director)*
**Marketing:** Suzanne Beadnell *(Market Intelligence Analyst)*, Mark Crompton *(Group Strategic Marketing Mana)*, Eve Fullwood *(Marketing Advisor)*, Sharon Graves *(Head of UK Marketing Communica)*
**Admin:** Anne Collette *(Office Manager)*
**IT:** Tim Dewson *(?IT Services Manager)*
**HR:** Sally OConnell *(Training Manager)*
**Operations:** Francisco Pedrosa *(Head of Product Management- Cl)*
**Engineering:** Tammy Lillie *(Head of Engineering - Capabili)*, Frank Milloy *(Senior Contracts Manager)*
**Branches:** Spirax-Sarco Engineering P L C, 18 Duncombe Avenue, Clydebank, Dunbartonshire G81 6PW
**US SIC:** 3561, 3519
**UK SIC:** 32870, 32811
**Auditors:** KPMG Audit PLC
**Bankers:** Barclays Bank Plc (20-20-15)

| | 31-12-13 | 31-12-12 | 31-12-11 |
|---|---|---|---|
| TO | 689,388,000 | 661,723,000 | 649,991,000 |
| P/L | 145,714,000 | 127,652,000 | 132,341,000 |
| NW | 312,374,000 | 346,185,000 | 314,081,000 |
| WC | 245,971,000 | 249,290,000 | 196,380,000 |
| Emp. | 4,725 | 4,706 | 4,683 |

DUNS 77-910-5027

## Spire Automotive Ltd

1083 High Road, London N20 0QA
**Tel:** 08447016972 **Fax:** 01707 277870
**Web:** www.m25audi.co.uk
**Reg No:** 5813758 **Estd:** 2006 Private Limited Company
**Line of Business:** Car dealers (used)
**Issued Capital:** £250,000
**Director:** D Guiver
**Co. Secretary:** Kim Richardson
**Responsibilities**
**Senior:** Justin Howard *(Head of Business)*
**HR:** Elle Gates *(Human Resources Manager)*
**US SIC:** 5521, 7539, 5531
**UK SIC:** 65100, 67100
**Auditors:** Deloitte LLP
**Bankers:** Girobank Plc (72-16-00)

| | 31-12-13 | 31-12-12 | 31-12-11 |
|---|---|---|---|
| TO | 251,483,594 | 166,392,394 | 151,541,581 |
| P/L | 4,972,466 | 4,653,598 | 4,291,513 |
| NW | 13,341,013 | 12,526,805 | 8,863,176 |
| WC | 107,473 | 2,729,102 | 1,134,503 |
| Emp. | 386 | 291 | 276 |

DUNS 21-584-0969

## Spire Harpenden Hospital

Harpenden Hospital, Ambrose Lane, Harpenden, Hertfordshire AL5 4BP
**Tel:** 0800585112
**Web:** www.aspirehealthcare.com
**Estd:** 2002 Proprietorship
**Line of Business:** Clinics private
**Proprietor:** Mrs J Salmon
**US SIC:** 8062 **UK SIC:** 95100
**Employees:** 300

DUNS 22-630-2081 **Imp**

## Spire Healthcare Ltd

(**Subsidiary of:** Spire Healthcare Holdings 1)
3 Dorset Rise, London EC4Y 8EN
**Tel:** 08001691777
**Web:** www.spirehealthcare.com
**Reg No:** 1522532 **Estd:** 1980 Private Limited Company
**Line of Business:** Hospital activities
**Issued Capital:** £43,137
**Directors:** R Roger, S Gordon, Dr J J De Gorter
**Co. Secretary:** Daniel Toner
**Responsibilities**
**Senior:** Jean-Jacques De Gorter *(Clinical Services Director)*, Tina Waters *(P A To Chief Executive Officer)*
**Sales:** Mitra Abtahi *(Business Development Director)*, Neil McCullough *(Director of Business Improveme)*
**Admin:** Michael Soo *(Head Office Administrator)*
**IT:** Marc O'Brien *(IT Director)*, Phil Peplow *(IT Manager)*
**Health & Safety:** Michael Savva *(Health & Safety Officer)*
**Branches:** Spire Healthcare Ltd, B U P A, 118 Corstorphine Road, Edinburgh, Midlothian EH12 6TU
**US SIC:** 8062, 8051
**UK SIC:** 95100
**Auditors:** Ernst & Young LLP
**Following financial data are in thousands**

| | 31-12-13 | 31-12-12 | 31-12-11 |
|---|---|---|---|
| TO | 595,880 | 580,827 | 537,304 |
| P/L | 155,679 | 134,698 | 138,098 |
| NW | 1,820,760 | 1,701,691 | 1,606,336 |
| WC | 1,603,326 | 1,572,030 | 1,467,000 |
| Emp. | 5,373 | 5,263 | 4,966 |

DUNS 42-407-2408

## Spire Homes Ltd

44a Storforth Lane Trading Estate, Chesterfield, Derbyshire S41 0QR
**Tel:** 03001236611
**Web:** www.spire-homes.org
**Reg No:** 4394887 **Estd:** 2002 Private Limited Company
**Line of Business:** Engineers (structural)
**Issued Capital:** £8
**Co. Secretary:** John Nightingale
**US SIC:** 8911 **UK SIC:** 83701

| | 31-10-13 | 31-10-12 | 31-10-11 |
|---|---|---|---|
| TA | 38,452 | 46,021 | 20,865 |
| NW | (36,971) | (35,077) | (13,786) |
| WC | N/A | (54,318) | (13,786) |

DUNS 21-605-6302

## Spire Hospital

Fordcombe Road, Fordcombe, Tunbridge Wells, Kent TN3 0RD
**Tel:** 01892740047
**Web:** www.spirehealthcare.com
**Estd:** 1989 Proprietorship
**Line of Business:** Hospitals
**Proprietor:** A Connolly
**US SIC:** 8062 **UK SIC:** 95100
**Employees:** 109

DUNS 21-777-4412

## Spire Midlands Rdc

Unit 101 Stonebridge Cross Business Park, Droitwich, Worcestershire WR9 0LW
**Tel:** 01905823002
**Web:** www.spirehealthcare.com
**Estd:** 2011 Proprietorship
**Line of Business:** Healthcare companies
**Proprietor:** R Wise
**US SIC:** 8091 **UK SIC:** 95200
**Employees:** 200

DUNS 21-731-7315

## Spire Payments Ltd

Unit 3-6, Milford Trading Estate, Blakey Road, Salisbury, Wiltshire SP1 2UD
**Tel:** 01722332255
**Web:** www.spirepayments.com
**Reg No:** 7669734 **Estd:** 2011 Private Limited Company
**Line of Business:** Manufacture of computers and other information processing equipment
**Issued Capital:** £1
**Directors:** M K Aminaee Chatroodi, G Klein, A Fernando-Santana
**US SIC:** 3573, 5199
**UK SIC:** 33020, 61900

| | 31-12-13 | 31-12-12 | 31-12-11 |
|---|---|---|---|
| TO | 16,322,000 | 25,227,000 | 9,640,000 |
| P/L | 740,000 | 1,608,000 | 1,493,000 |
| NW | 1,914,000 | 2,146,000 | 913,000 |
| WC | (1,508,000) | (684,000) | (2,282,000) |
| Emp. | 162 | 166 | 143 |

DUNS 23-255-6485

## Spire Southampton Hospital

Southampton Hospital, Chalybeate Close, Southampton, Hampshire SO16 6UY
**Tel:** 02380775544
**Web:** www.spirehealthcare.com
**Estd:** 1986 Proprietorship
**Line of Business:** Hospitals
**Proprietor:** N Clarke
**Responsibilities**
**Senior:** Laura Geer *(Operations Manager)*, Claire Oatridge *(Business Development Manager)*, Jane Whitney-Smith *(Hospital Director)*
**Marketing:** Claire Oatridge *(Business Development Manager)*
**HR:** Sue Haywood *(Health & Safety Manager)*, Sue vivian *(Health & Safety Manager)*
**Health & Safety:** Sue Haywood *(Health & Safety Manager)*, Sue vivian *(Health & Safety Manager)*
**Facilities:** Dennis O'Shea *(Engineering Manager)*
**US SIC:** 8091 **UK SIC:** 95200
**Employees:** 300

DUNS 21-111-2197

## Spire Thames Valley Hospital Ltd

(**Subsidiary of:** Spire Healthcare Holdings 1)
3 Dorset Rise, London EC4Y 8EN
**Tel:** 01753665404
**Reg No:** 6526032 **Estd:** 2008 Private Limited Company
**Line of Business:** Hospital activities
**Issued Capital:** £3,000,001
**Directors:** S Gordon, Dr J J De Gorter, R Roger
**Co. Secretary:** Daniel Toner
**Responsibilities**
**Senior:** Parm Sandhu *(Hospital Director)*
**US SIC:** 8062 **UK SIC:** 95100

| | 31-12-13 | 31-12-12 | 31-12-11 |
|---|---|---|---|
| TO | 12,989,797 | 12,710,033 | 12,056,745 |
| P/L | 1,325,663 | 744,084 | 354,709 |
| NW | (284,120) | (1,438,119) | (2,272,195) |
| WC | (11,421,994) | (12,104,491) | (13,066,593) |
| Emp. | 120 | 122 | 117 |

DUNS 21-670-8404 **Imp**

## Spirent Communications Plc

Northwood Park, Crawley, West Sussex RH10 9XN
**Tel:** 01293767676 **Fax:** 01293-767-677
**Web:** www.spirent.com
**Reg No:** 0470893 **VAT No:** 209799810
**Estd:** 1949 Public Limited Company
**Line of Business:** Telecom services
**Principals:** E G Hutchinson *(Financial)*, D J Lewis, Ms S Swenson, I Brindle, A Walker, Mrs R E Whiting, T J Maxwell
**Co. Secretary:** Angus Iveson
**Responsibilities**
**Marketing:** Mike McKernan *(Product Marketing Manager)*, John Pottle *(Marketing Director)*, Frances Simm *(Public Relations Manager)*, Sailaja Tennati *(Relations Manager)*, Ken Van Orman *(Marketing Manager)*
**Sales:** Dharen Ells *(Business Development Manager)*, James Mcmath *(Sales Executive)*
**Admin:** Diane DeMatteis *(Personal Assistant)*
**IT:** E Owusu *(IT Manager)*
**Operations:** Steve Hickling *(Product Manager)*
**Engineering:** Edward Nakamoto *(Director, Engineering)*, Wayne Wang *(Engineer)*
**Branches:** Spirent Communications Plc, Aspen Way, Paignton, Devon TQ4 7QR
**US SIC:** 4899, 6711
**UK SIC:** 79020, 83962
**Auditors:** Ernst & Young LLP
**Bankers:** HSBC Bank plc (40-18-22)
**Employees:** 1,460
**Turnover:** £413,500,000

DUNS 39-984-0024

## Spirent Systems No 2 Ltd

(**Subsidiary of:** Spirent Communications Plc)
Unit 10 Priory Industrial Park, Airspeed Road, Christchurch, Dorset BH23 4HD
**Tel:** 01425-271444 **Fax:** 01425-272655
**Web:** www.pgdt.com
**Reg No:** 2279804 **Estd:** 1974 Private Limited Company
**Line of Business:** Manufacturers and suppliers of disbility equipment
**Issued Capital:** £10,000
**Directors:** Mrs R E Whiting, E G Hutchinson
**Co. Secretary:** Angus Iveson
**Responsibilities**
**Senior:** Christian Howe *(Proprietor)*, Rachel Whitin *(Director)*
**Finance:** Tom Murray *(Financial Director)*
**Sales:** Collin Penny *(Sales Manager)*
**HR:** Sharon Green-Buckley *(Personnel Manager)*
**Health & Safety:** Matthew Whicher *(Health & Safety Manager)*
**Operations:** Matthew Whicher *(Health & Safety Manager)*
**US SIC:** 3799 **UK SIC:** 36502
**Auditors:** Ernst & Young LLP

| | 31-12-13 | 31-12-12 | 31-12-11 |
|---|---|---|---|
| TA | 10,100 | 10,100 | 10,000 |
| P/L | N/A | 100 | N/A |
| NW | 10,100 | 10,100 | 10,000 |
| WC | 10,100 | 10,100 | N/A |
| Emp. | N/A | 180 | N/A |

DUNS 85-613-5744

## Spires Academy

Bredlands Lane, Westbere, Canterbury, Kent CT2 0HD
**Tel:** 01227-710392
**Web:** www.spiresacademy.com
**Reg No:** 6207067 **Estd:** 1993 Private Company Limited By Guarantee
**Line of Business:** General secondary education
**Directors:** Mrs A Watson, G W Ward, Mrs U D Fuller, Mrs D K Everitt, G N Pack
**Co. Secretary:** David Mckivett
**Responsibilities**
**Senior:** Nicki Mattin *(Head Teacher)*
**US SIC:** 8211 **UK SIC:** 93200
**Bankers:** Barclays Bank Plc (20-03-80)

| | 31-08-14 | 31-08-13 | 31-08-12 |
|---|---|---|---|
| TO | 3,609,000 | 3,304,000 | 17,386,000 |
| P/L | (644,000) | (752,000) | 13,888,000 |
| NW | 12,059,000 | 13,222,000 | 13,982,000 |
| WC | 138,000 | 174,000 | 256,000 |
| Emp. | 73 | 70 | 75 |

DUNS 21-037-3637

## Spires of Oxford

P.O.Box 24, Oxford, Oxfordshire OX33 1RA
**Tel:** 01865-875539
**Web:** www.spiresofoxford.co.uk
**Proprietorship**
**Line of Business:** Caravan dealers
**Proprietor:** D Clarke
**US SIC:** 7033 **UK SIC:** 66701
**Employees:** 50

DUNS 34-864-2567 **Imp**

## Spirit Aerosystems (Europe) Ltd

(**Subsidiary of:** Spirit Aerosystems Holdings Inc.)
Building 2, Prestwick, Ayrshire KA9 2RW
**Tel:** 01292672312 **Fax:** 01292-479703
**Web:** www.spiritaero.com
**Reg No:** 5663660 **Estd:** 2002 Private Limited Company
**Line of Business:** Manufacture of aircraft and spacecraft
**Export Sales:** £62,149,000
**Issued Capital:** £100
**Directors:** M J Suchinski, T H Cowan, S Mclarty
**Co. Secretary:** Jamie Lewis
**Responsibilities**
**Senior:** Jonathan Greenberg *(Manager)*, Paul Holtappel *(Engineering Director)*, Scott Mclarthy *(Managing Director)*, Michelle Russell *(Senior Vice President/General)*, Freddie Swart *(Head Of Engineering Global Ope)*
**Finance:** Andy Shact *(Vice President of Taxation)*
**Operations:** Scott Mclarthy *(Managing Director)*, Steven Watson *(Manufacturing Systems Engineer)*
**Engineering:** Stevie Brown *(Lead Engineer)*, Paul Holtappel *(Engineering Director)*, Shaun Jennings *(Design Assurance Team Leader)*, Freddie Swart *(Head Of Engineering Global Ope)*
**US SIC:** 3721, 5084
**UK SIC:** 36400, 61490
**Auditors:** PricewaterhouseCoopers LLP

**Bankers:** Citibank Na (18-50-08)

| | 31-12-13 | 31-12-12 | 31-12-11 |
|---|---|---|---|
| TO | 443,603,000 | 347,878,000 | 334,808,000 |
| P/L | 47,272,000 | 17,708,000 | (5,674,000) |
| NW | 81,390,000 | 55,921,000 | 37,583,000 |
| WC | 77,858,000 | 49,573,000 | 35,841,000 |
| Emp. | 956 | 927 | 913 |

DUNS 73-406-3881     Imp-Exp

## Spirit Circuits Ltd
22-24 Aston Road, Waterlooville, Hampshire PO7 7XJ
**Tel:** 02392243000
**Web:** www.spiritcircuits.com
**Reg No:** 4679779   **Estd:** 2003 Private Limited Company
**Line of Business:** Manufacture of electronic valves and tubes and other electronic components
**Issued Capital:** £100,000
**Directors:** L M Lloyd, S C Driver
**Co. Secretary:** Steven Wiggins
**Branches:** Spirit Circuits Ltd, Aston Road, Waterlooville, Hampshire PO7 7XJ
**US SIC:** 3679   **UK SIC:** 34542

| | 30-11-13 | 30-11-12 | 25-11-11 |
|---|---|---|---|
| TO | 8,246,356 | N/A | N/A |
| P/L | 12,310 | N/A | N/A |
| NW | 118,074 | 103,948 | 121,608 |
| WC | (229,728) | (217,260) | (367,095) |

DUNS 21-760-0272

## Spirit Pub Company Plc
Sunrise House, Ninth Avenue, Burton-On-Trent, Staffordshire DE14 3JZ
**Tel:** 01283-498-400 **Fax:** 01283-498-250
**Web:** www.spiritpubcompany.com
**Reg No:** 7662835   **Estd:** 2011 Private Limited Company
**Line of Business:** Other business activities not elsewhere classified
**Issued Capital:** £6,602,794
**Directors:** P J Gallagher, M A Pain, I Dyson, M E Tye, C Bell, M E Tye, W G Boyd, M E Tye
**Co. Secretary:** Ian Powell
**Responsibilities**
**Finance:** Paddy Gallagher (Finance Director)
**Sales:** Clive Briscoe (Commercial Director)
**IT:** Bob Broadbridge (IT Director)
**HR:** Debbie Moore (HR Director)
**Operations:** Alan Morgab (Chief Operating Officer)
**Branches:** Spirit Pub Company Plc, 8-14 Prince Of Wales Road, Norwich, Norfolk NR1 1LB
**US SIC:** 7399   **UK SIC:** 83954
**Auditors:** KPMG LLP
**Bankers:** Barclays Bank Plc (20-10-03)

| | 23-08-14 | 17-08-13 | 18-08-12 |
|---|---|---|---|
| TO | 800,900,000 | 758,200,000 | 760,000,000 |
| P/L | 110,200,000 | 71,700,000 | (588,900,000) |
| NW | 447,700,000 | 302,100,000 | 239,200,000 |
| WC | (17,100,000) | (62,100,000) | (60,300,000) |
| Emp. | 16,461 | 16,800 | 17,234 |

DUNS 23-994-2274

## Spirit (Sgl) Ltd
(**Subsidiary of:** Spirit Pub Company Plc)
107 Station Street, Burton-On-Trent, Staffordshire DE14 1SR
**Tel:** 01524410724
**Web:** www.spiritgroup.com
**Reg No:** 3982443   **Estd:** 2000 Private Limited Company
**Line of Business:** Bars
**Trading Style:** Wacky Warehouse
**Issued Capital:** £3
**Directors:** Ms L J Bell, J R Langford, D A Kelly, P J Gallagher
**Co. Secretary:** Henry Jones
**Responsibilities**
**Senior:** Lee Dolphin (Licensee Of The Station)
**Branches:** Spirit (Sgl) Ltd, 19 St. Edmund Street, Weymouth, Dorset DT4 8AR
**US SIC:** 5813   **UK SIC:** 66200
**Auditors:** Ernst & Young
**Bankers:** Barclays Bank Plc (20-07-71)

| | 23-08-14 | 17-08-13 | 18-08-12 |
|---|---|---|---|
| TA | 248,203,000 | 246,507,000 | 246,907,000 |
| P/L | (42,000) | (60,000) | (63,000) |
| NW | 233,412,000 | 235,978,000 | 238,785,000 |
| WC | 197,402,000 | 198,534,000 | 201,389,000 |
| Emp. | 4 | N/A | N/A |

DUNS 73-763-7673     Imp

## Spirotech Srd Group Ltd
(**Subsidiary of:** Srd Holdings Ltd)
Brookside Industrial Estate, Sawtry, Huntingdon, Cambridgeshire PE28 5SB
**Tel:** 0148-783-2053
**Web:** www.spirotechgroup.co.uk
**Reg No:** 5021065   **Estd:** 2004 Private Limited Company
**Line of Business:** Construction of civil engineering constructions
**Issued Capital:** £100
**Directors:** R M Gadsby, C L Dennis, S K Moore, D J Gadsby

**Responsibilities**
**Senior:** Stewart Darlow (Manager)
**US SIC:** 1622   **UK SIC:** 50200
**Auditors:** Edwards

| | 30-06-14 | 30-06-13 | 30-06-12 |
|---|---|---|---|
| TO | N/A | N/A | 4,026,088 |
| P/L | N/A | N/A | 206,169 |
| NW | 1,150,949 | 575,774 | 302,518 |
| WC | (62,566) | (443,402) | (639,074) |

DUNS 23-740-5357

## Spitalfields Crypt Trust
116-118 Shoreditch High Street, London E1 6JN
**Web:** www.sct.org.uk
**Reg No:** 3734793   **Estd:** 1999 Private Company Limited By Guarantee
**Line of Business:** Charitable social work activities with accommodation
**Directors:** Mrs A Walker, A D Enga, J R Brown, D C Ely, P J Young
**Co. Secretary:** Mrs Janice Taylor
**Branches:** Spitalfields Crypt Trust, 116-118 Shoreditch High Street, London E1 6JN
**US SIC:** 8321   **UK SIC:** 96111
**Auditors:** Griffin Stone Moscrop & Co
**Bankers:** HSBC Bank plc (40-02-33)

| | 31-03-14 | 31-03-13 | 31-03-12 |
|---|---|---|---|
| TO | 2,313,808 | 2,055,989 | 1,735,486 |
| P/L | 110,460 | 32,527 | 74,178 |
| NW | 1,231,846 | 1,121,386 | 1,088,859 |
| WC | 445,178 | 267,823 | 319,179 |
| Emp. | 56 | 53 | 46 |

DUNS 39-809-2411

## Spitfire Technology Group Ltd
The Print Works, 139 Clapham Road, London SW9 0HP
**Tel:** 02075013333
**Web:** www.spitfire.co.uk
**Reg No:** 2213640   **VAT No:** 801976621
**Estd:** 1991 Private Limited Company
**Line of Business:** Management activities of holding companies
**Trading Style:** Spitfire Network Services Ltd
**Issued Capital:** £241,388
**Managing Director:** J R Orde
**Co. Secretary:** Henry Bowlby
**Responsibilities**
**Senior:** Nirosh Wijewardene (Chief Executive Officer)
**Marketing:** Susie Ward (Operations Director)
**Sales:** Tom Fellowes (Sales Director), Hannah Minns (Account Manager), Susie Ward (Operations Director)
**Admin:** Jane Layzell (Administrator)
**IT:** Graham Lewis (IT Manager)
**HR:** Susie Ward (Operations Director)
**Health & Safety:** Susie Ward (Operations Director)
**Facilities:** Susie Ward (Operations Director)
**US SIC:** 6711, 4899
**UK SIC:** 83962, 79020
**Auditors:** SPW (UK) LLP
**Bankers:** HSBC Bank plc (40-07-30)

| | 31-03-14 | 31-03-13 | 31-03-12 |
|---|---|---|---|
| TO | 21,369,851 | 19,950,547 | 18,866,191 |
| P/L | 1,395,737 | 1,350,365 | 1,372,151 |
| NW | 4,013,781 | 3,462,960 | 2,843,623 |
| WC | 2,016,178 | 1,323,154 | 1,722,454 |
| Emp. | 99 | 101 | 97 |

DUNS 23-904-4584

## Spl Powerlines Uk Ltd
(**Subsidiary of:** Gilde Buy-Out Management Holding B.V.)
Unit 3a, Coatbridge, Lanarkshire ML5 4BS
**Tel:** 01236-424666 **Fax:** 01236424444
**Web:** www.powerlines-group.com
**Reg No:** 0202412SC **VAT No:** 743310759
**Estd:** 1999 Private Limited Company
**Line of Business:** Railway wagons and stock
**Trading Style:** Border Rail & Plant
**Issued Capital:** £60,000
**Directors:** G Kielmayer, M Hawley
**Co. Secretary:** Guenter Kielmayer
**Responsibilities**
**Senior:** Gerhard Ehringer (Manager), Scott Kernachan (Manager)
**Finance:** Janet McCrae (Accountant)
**HR:** Scott Kernachan (Manager)
**US SIC:** 3743   **UK SIC:** 36201
**Auditors:** Deloitte LLP
**Bankers:** Lloyds TSB Bank plc (30-13-53)

| | 31-03-14 | 31-03-13 | 31-03-12 |
|---|---|---|---|
| TO | 9,702,348 | 2,874,353 | 5,934,109 |
| P/L | 307,367 | (672,686) | 130,546 |
| NW | 391,429 | (1,111,642) | (438,956) |
| WC | 113,648 | (1,257,968) | (620,484) |
| Emp. | 83 | N/A | N/A |

DUNS 23-709-1301

## Splash Project Management
Timberwharf 16/22, Urban Splash (Developments) Ltd, Sales Office, Worsley Street, Manchester M15 4LD
**Tel:** 0161-237-9546
**VAT No:** 588698939   **Estd:** 1993 Partnership
**Line of Business:** Building services

**Trading Style:** Urban Splash
**Partners:** J Falkingham, T Bloxham
**Branches:** Concert Sq, 24-34 Wood St, Liverpool Merseyside L1 4AQ (Tel: 0151-709-8211).
**US SIC:** 1622   **UK SIC:** 50200
**Bankers:** HSBC Bank plc (40-31-24)
**Employees:** 50

DUNS 21-600-9796

## Splashes Leisure Pool
Bloors Lane, Rainham, Gillingham, Kent ME8 7EG
**Tel:** 01634333977
**Estd:** 1990 Proprietorship
**Line of Business:** Operation of swimming pools
**Proprietor:** Miss J Dearlove
**US SIC:** 7999   **UK SIC:** 97913
**Employees:** 97

DUNS 21-771-8932

## Splott Clinic
The Core, The Corby Cube, Parkland Gateway, George Street, Corby, Northamptonshire NN17 1QG
**Tel:** 01536464643
**Estd:** 2011 Proprietorship
**Line of Business:** Nhs clinics
**Proprietor:** Ms J Williams
**US SIC:** 8062 **UK SIC:** 95100
**Employees:** 50

DUNS 22-061-9089

## Spm Plastics U.K. Ltd
(**Subsidiary of:** Aurora Capital Partners L.P.)
Cwm Cynon Industrial Estate, Cwm Cynon Business Park, Mountain Ash, Mid Glamorgan CF45 4ER
**Tel:** 01443-471200
**Web:** www.upgintl.com
**Reg No:** 4063696   **Estd:** 2000 Private Limited Company
**Line of Business:** Manufacture of other plastic products
**Export Sales:** £13,342,000
**Trading Style:** Upg
**Issued Capital:** £100
**Directors:** H Faig, C A Brickman
**Co. Secretary:** Robert Ospalik
**Responsibilities**
**HR:** Alison Dacey (Human Resources Manager)
**US SIC:** 3079   **UK SIC:** 48360
**Auditors:** Ernst & Young LLP
**Bankers:** Bank Of America, Na (16-50-50)

| | 31-12-13 | 31-12-12 | 31-12-11 |
|---|---|---|---|
| TO | 17,261,000 | 16,457,000 | 21,728,000 |
| P/L | (1,141,000) | 3,049,000 | (3,434,000) |
| NW | (64,089,000) | (63,542,000) | (65,192,000) |
| WC | (34,064,000) | (32,692,000) | (30,623,000) |
| Emp. | 291 | 238 | 363 |

DUNS 21-033-2746

## Spofforths
1 Jubilee Street, Brighton, East Sussex BN1 1GE
**Web:** www.sofforths.co.uk
**Estd:** 1900
**Line of Business:** Accounting activities
**US SIC:** 8931   **UK SIC:** 83600
**Employees:** 190

DUNS 34-805-7527

## Spofforths Llp
Donnington Park, 85 Birdham Road, Chichester, West Sussex PO20 7DU
**Web:** www.spofforths.co.uk
**Reg No:** 0315867OC **Estd:** 2006
**Line of Business:** Accounting activities
**Responsibilities**
**Senior:** Ian Burrows (Non-designated Limited Liabili), Sarah Ediss (Non-designated Limited Liabili), Chay Took (Non-designated Limited Liabili)
**Branches:** Spofforths Llp, Spofforths, Yeoman Gate, Worthing, West Sussex BN13 3QZ
**US SIC:** 8931   **UK SIC:** 83600

| | 31-12-13 | 31-12-12 | 31-12-11 |
|---|---|---|---|
| TO | 8,953,000 | 9,203,000 | 8,882,000 |
| P/L | 712,000 | 125,000 | 114,000 |
| NW | 638,000 | 149,000 | 75,000 |
| WC | 1,814,000 | 1,541,000 | 1,194,000 |
| Emp. | 183 | 189 | 186 |

DUNS 21-712-8491

## Sponne School
Brackley Road, Towcester, Northamptonshire NN12 6DJ
**Tel:** 01327350284
**Web:** www.sponne.org.uk
**Reg No:** 7525820   **Estd:** 1953 Private Company Limited By Guarantee
**Line of Business:** Schools (local authority)
**Directors:** Mrs S M Wagstaff, J Clarke, M Holmes, P S Williams, S M Marshall, Mrs P A Brearley, Ms J D Higgs, T M Foster
**Co. Secretary:** Mrs Coral Bird

**Responsibilities**
**Senior:** Joanne Chitty (Director), Ronnie Clucas (PTA), Nicholas Orrin (Director), Graham Rees (Director)
**US SIC:** 8211   **UK SIC:** 93200

| | 31-08-13 | 31-08-12 | 31-08-11 |
|---|---|---|---|
| TO | 6,561,859 | 7,268,895 | 15,123,018 |
| P/L | (63,623) | 580,134 | 11,930,780 |
| NW | 12,281,291 | 12,285,914 | 11,924,780 |
| WC | 1,203,000 | 1,300,591 | 512,933 |
| Emp. | 152 | 154 | 138 |

DUNS 21-215-4314     Imp-Exp

## Spooner Industries Ltd
(**Subsidiary of:** Aegeus Industries Ltd)
Lower Railway Road, Ilkley, West Yorkshire LS29 8JB
**Fax:** 01943-603190
**Web:** www.spooner.co.uk
**Reg No:** 0643047 **VAT No:** 427828818
**Estd:** 1959 Private Limited Company
**Line of Business:** Representative office
**Export Sales:** £11,504,000
**Issued Capital:** £1,060,931
**Principals:** M J Brook (Managing), S P Newell, Dr A D Marson, B J Lawrence, R T Proctor, R A Summers, Dr R D Summers
**Co. Secretary:** John Muggleston
**Responsibilities**
**Purchasing:** Joanne Luccock (Buyer)
**US SIC:** 3567, 3585, 3554
**UK SIC:** 32452, 32841, 32754
**Auditors:** PricewaterhouseCoopers LLP
**Bankers:** National Westminster Bank Plc (56-00-34)

| | 30-06-14 | 30-06-13 | 30-06-12 |
|---|---|---|---|
| TO | 20,720,000 | 29,161,000 | 22,264,000 |
| P/L | 1,041,000 | 1,384,000 | 1,174,000 |
| NW | 8,525,000 | 7,777,000 | 6,339,000 |
| WC | 6,835,000 | 6,088,000 | 4,670,000 |
| Emp. | 144 | 140 | 127 |

DUNS 42-467-5890

## Spoor & Fisher (Jersey)
Africa House, Jersey, Channel Islands JE2 3RP
**Tel:** 01534-838000
**Web:** www.spoor.com
**Estd:** 1977 Partnership
**Line of Business:** Legal services
**Partners:** W R Spence, M F Sevant, M Costard, W B Meiring, Mrs J Hughes
**Responsibilities**
**Senior:** Mike Berry (Chief Operating Officer), Wayne Meiring (Managing Director), Mike Sevant (Partner), Mack Spence (Associate)
**Finance:** Jo Manby (Finance Manager)
**Sales:** Olivia O'Mahony (Business Development Manager)
**Operations:** Mike Berry (Chief Operating Officer)
**US SIC:** 8111   **UK SIC:** 83500
**Bankers:** Lloyds TSB Bank (Jersey) Ltd (30-94-61)
**Employees:** 70

DUNS 22-570-2083

## Sport & Ski
Chiltern Park Industrial Estate, Boscombe Road, Dunstable, Bedfordshire LU5 4LT
**Tel:** 01582691504
**VAT No:** 349116453   **Estd:** 1982 Proprietorship
**Line of Business:** Sports goods retailers
**Proprietor:** M J Ashley
**Branches:** Sport Soccer, Unit 142A, The Harlequin, Watford, Hertfordshire WD17 2TL
**US SIC:** 5941   **UK SIC:** 65400
**Bankers:** National Westminster Bank Plc (60-04-53)
**Employees:** 3,500

DUNS 21-589-7893

## Sportech Plc
101 Wigmore Street, London W1U 1QU
**Tel:** 02072-682400 **Fax:** 01315-578177
**Web:** www.sportechplc.com
**Reg No:** 0069140SC   **Estd:** 1979 Public Limited Company
**Line of Business:** Online gaming
**Export Sales:** £66,700,000
**Issued Capital:** £99,405,151
**Directors:** P W Williams, I R Penrose, R D Withers, D Mckeith, J C Baty, R C Roberts
**Co. Secretary:** Robert Mercer
**Responsibilities**
**Finance:** Cliff Baty (Chief Financial Officer)
**Marketing:** Christian Heap (Director of International Busi)
**Branches:** Sportech Plc, Sportech Racing Ireland,Unit 2, Creevaghbeg, Ballymahon, Co.Longford, Ireland
**US SIC:** 7999   **UK SIC:** 97913
**Auditors:** PricewaterhouseCoopers LLP

**Bankers:** Bank Of Scotland (80-08-09)

| | 31-12-13 | 31-12-12 | 31-12-11 |
|---|---|---|---|
| TO | 110,300,000 | 112,000,000 | 118,200,000 |
| P/L | 5,200,000 | 2,100,000 | 8,000,000 |
| NW | (56,100,000) | (65,400,000) | (66,800,000) |
| WC | (10,900,000) | (19,700,000) | (27,900,000) |
| Emp. | 795 | 801 | 849 |

DUNS 23-679-6640

### Sportif Ltd

Park Street, Stock Lake, Aylesbury, Buckinghamshire HP20 1DN
**Tel:** 01296415155 **Fax:** 01296-439850
**Web:** www.sportifaylesbury.citroen.co.uk
**Reg No:** 3674220 **Estd:** 1998 Private Limited Company
**Line of Business:** Car dealers (new & used)
**Issued Capital:** £100,000
**Director:** J P Miskin
**Co. Secretary:** John Boardman
**Branches:** Sportif Ltd, Park Street, Stocklake, Aylesbury, Buckinghamshire HP20 1DN
**US SIC:** 6711 **UK SIC:** 83962

| | 31-12-13 | 31-12-12 | 31-12-11 |
|---|---|---|---|
| TO | 21,228,913 | 17,220,709 | 16,260,134 |
| P/L | 136,178 | 87,383 | (57,388) |
| NW | 636,765 | 600,916 | 630,469 |
| WC | (337,932) | (354,089) | (272,874) |
| Emp. | 66 | 67 | 66 |

DUNS 23-884-3762

### Sporting Club St. Helens Ltd

Site Office, Langtree Park Mcmanus Drive, St Helens, Merseyside WA9 3AL
**Tel:** 01744455050 **Fax:** 01744455055
**Web:** www.sportingclubsthelens.co.uk
**Reg No:** 3875497 **Estd:** 2011 Private Limited Company
**Line of Business:** Sports clubs
**Issued Capital:** £332,502
**Directors:** J A Hartley, R K Mccormack, M Coleman, K J Marren, E Mcmanus, J Nicholl
**Co. Secretary:** Paul Kitchen
**Responsibilities**
**Senior:** Anthony Colquitt *(Manager)*
**US SIC:** 5999 **UK SIC:** 65600

| | 31-10-13 | 31-10-12 | 31-10-11 |
|---|---|---|---|
| TO | 5,383,158 | 5,798,309 | 4,399,220 |
| P/L | (2,411,945) | (1,685,141) | (2,542,979) |
| NW | 16,853,858 | 19,265,803 | 20,400,949 |
| WC | (1,201,840) | (6,021,621) | (4,903,169) |
| Emp. | 478 | 145 | 139 |

DUNS 23-777-2442 **Imp**

### The Sporting Exchange Ltd

(**Subsidiary of:** Betfair Group Plc)
Chancellors Road, London W6 9HP
**Tel:** 020-8834-8000 **Fax:** 02088348000
**Web:** www.betfair.com
**Reg No:** 3770548 **Estd:** 2000 Private Limited Company
**Line of Business:** Other computer related activities
**Trading Style:** Betfair
**Issued Capital:** £104,136
**Directors:** B T Corcoran, A Gersh
**Co. Secretary:** Ms Fiona Russell
**Responsibilities**
**Senior:** Martin Cruddace *(Manager)*
**US SIC:** 7379, 7999
**UK SIC:** 83940, 97913
**Auditors:** KPMG Audit PLC

| | 30-04-14 | 30-04-13 | 30-04-12 |
|---|---|---|---|
| TA | 358,739,000 | 660,957,000 | 652,535,000 |
| P/L | 30,256,000 | (10,400,000) | 27,163,000 |
| NW | 36,998,000 | 274,987,000 | 286,347,000 |
| WC | (50,279,000) | (66,132,000) | (65,244,000) |

DUNS 21-034-1414

### Sporting Lodge Inns

Low Lane, Thornaby, Stockton-On-Tees, Cleveland TS17 9LW
**Tel:** 01642-578100
**Web:** www.sportinglodgeinns.co.uk
**Estd:** 2004 Proprietorship
**Line of Business:** Hotels
**Proprietor:** P Nixon
**Responsibilities**
**Senior:** Daniel Kirkham *(General Manager)*, Mark Lammiman *(Manager)*, Lousie Waters *(Manager)*
**Finance:** Shirley Hesp *(Financial Controller)*
**IT:** Shirley Hesp *(Financial Controller)*
**Health & Safety:** Daniel Kirkham *(General Manager)*
**US SIC:** 7011, 6531
**UK SIC:** 66500, 83400
**Employees:** 80

DUNS 73-963-3936

### Sportingbet (It Services) Ltd

(**Subsidiary of:** Sportingbet Holdings Ltd)
Gvc 3rd Floor, 45 Moorfields, London EC2Y 9AE
**Tel:** 02072513801 **Fax:** 020 7184 1810
**Web:** www.finsbury.com
**Reg No:** 5214498 **Estd:** 2004 Private Limited Company
**Line of Business:** Public relations activities
**Issued Capital:** £1
**Directors:** R Q Cooper, K J Alexander
**Co. Secretary:** Daniel Talisman
**US SIC:** 7399 **UK SIC:** 83954
**Auditors:** Grant Thornton UK LLP

| | 31-12-13 | 31-07-12 | 31-12-11 |
|---|---|---|---|
| TO | 18,707,000 | 12,990,000 | 12,158,000 |
| P/L | (13,870,000) | (13,008,000) | 273,000 |
| NW | (13,720,000) | 150,000 | 13,153,000 |
| WC | (13,922,000) | (6,904,000) | (284,000) |
| Emp. | 66 | 75 | 90 |

DUNS 22-057-5224

### The Sports & Leisure Group Ltd

(**Subsidiary of:** Civil Services Sports Council Ltd)
Wilford Lane, Nottingham, Nottinghamshire NG2 7RN
**Tel:** 01159823276
**Web:** www.sportsleisuregroup.com
**Reg No:** 4059485 **Estd:** 2000 Private Limited Company
**Line of Business:** Stadiums and sports grounds
**Issued Capital:** £2,319,643
**Directors:** B Hunter, R J Haskell, R B Simpson, Ms M Holmes
**Co. Secretary:** Nigel Maglione
**Branches:** The Sports & Leisure Group Ltd, Wilford Lane, West Bridgford, Nottingham, Nottinghamshire NG2 7RN
**US SIC:** 7941 **UK SIC:** 97911
**Auditors:** BDO Stoy Hayward LLP
**Bankers:** Allied Irish Bank (gb) (23-83-96)

| | 31-12-13 | 31-12-12 | 31-12-11 |
|---|---|---|---|
| TO | 16,240,116 | 14,645,375 | 14,932,319 |
| P/L | 99,891 | (104,939) | (3,470,759) |
| NW | 899,894 | 1,224,173 | (3,587,523) |
| WC | (2,137,570) | (2,628,198) | (3,656,016) |
| Emp. | 310 | 277 | 287 |

DUNS 39-791-8590

### Sports & Leisure Management Ltd

(**Subsidiary of:** Castle View Ventures Ltd)
Open House, Sketchley Meadows, Hinckley, Leicestershire LE10 3EY
**Tel:** 01455-890508 **Fax:** 01455-890512
**Web:** www.everyoneactive.com
**Reg No:** 2204085 **VAT No:** 485469690
**Estd:** 1987 Private Limited Company
**Line of Business:** Operation of sports arenas and stadiums
**Issued Capital:** £108,000
**Principals:** D J Bibby *(Financial)*, J M Drysdale
**Co. Secretary:** Martin Bell
**Responsibilities**
**Senior:** David Brougham *(It Manager)*, Stephen Hulme *(Managing Director, Director)*
**Finance:** Tim Stooks *(Financial Controller)*
**IT:** David Brougham *(It Manager)*
**Branches:** Sports & Leisure Management Ltd, Hinckley Leisure Centre, Coventry Road, Hinckley, Leicestershire LE10 0JR
**US SIC:** 7941 **UK SIC:** 97911
**Auditors:** Ernst & Young LLP
**Bankers:** National Westminster Bank Plc (60-11-06)

| | 31-03-14 | 31-03-13 | 31-03-12 |
|---|---|---|---|
| TO | 95,854,445 | 84,164,936 | 71,799,630 |
| P/L | 4,015,521 | 3,748,266 | 2,387,623 |
| NW | 9,876,817 | 11,073,919 | 8,382,276 |
| WC | 1,963,148 | 5,632,373 | 1,633,538 |
| Emp. | 3,779 | 2,952 | 2,509 |

DUNS 21-607-4883

### Sports Cafe

239-240 Broad Street, Birmingham, West Midlands B1 2HG
**Tel:** 01216334000
**Web:** www.thesportscafe.com
**Estd:** 1999
**Line of Business:** Eating Establishments
**Proprietor:** M Murphy
**US SIC:** 5812 **UK SIC:** 66110
**Employees:** 100

DUNS 22-535-0941

### The Sports Council

3rd Floor Victoria House, Bloomsbury Square, London WC13 4SE
**Tel:** 02072731500
**Web:** www.uksport.gov.uk
**Reg No:** 0000578RC **Estd:** 1972 Incorporate By Act Of Parliament
**Line of Business:** Sports council. The principal activities are the continuation of programes of sport; the promotion of a general understanding of the social importance and value of sports and physical recreation; provision of new sports facilities; the encouragementof wider participation in sport and physical recreation as a means of enjoying leisure; the raising of standards of performance.
**Trading Style:** British College of Sport
**Principals:** Sir P G Yarranton *(Chairman)*, D Pickup, J Birch, D G Casey, D Mason, D Westgarth, Prof R Miquel, Ms M E Peters
**Branches:** The Sports Council, Grove Ho, Bridgford Rd, West Bridgford, Nottingham, Nottinghamshire NG2 6AP
**US SIC:** 7941 **UK SIC:** 97911
**Bankers:** Barclays Bank Plc (20-77-67)
**Employees:** 434

DUNS 23-399-3208

### Sports Council for Northern Ireland

House Of Sport, 2a Upper Malone Road, Belfast BT9 5LA
**Tel:** 028-9038-1222
**Web:** www.sportni.net
**Estd:** 1973 Incorporate By Act Of Parliament
**Line of Business:** Sports clubs
**Trading Style:** Sport Ni, Sport Northern Ireland
**Responsibilities**
**Senior:** Nick Harkness *(Acting CEO)*, Noleen Lennon *(Development Assistant)*, Roisin Mallon *(Board Member)*, Antoinette McKeown *(CEO)*, Eamonn Mccartan *(Chief Executive)*, Shane Mccullough *(Board Member)*, Joe Mckearney *(Executive)*, Hilary Mclain *(Executive)*
**Finance:** Louise Clarke *(Finance Manager)*, Marion Greenan *(Finance Officer)*, Colm Jennings *(Finance Officer)*, Rachael McDowell *(Finance Manager)*, Andrea McKittrick *(Performance and Finance Monito)*, Claire Mclister *(Grants Officer)*, James Rowlinson *(Finance Officer)*, Tracy Smyth *(Finance Manager)*, Ian Weir *(Finance Manager)*
**Marketing:** Clare Adair *(Development Officer)*, Helena Blair *(Development Assistant)*, Helen Donnelly *(Development Officer)*, Dawn Flynn *(Publications Officer / Website)*, Joanne Hullock *(Development Assistant)*, Richard McCormick *(Advocacy and Communications Ma)*, Catherine McKeown *(Communications Officer)*, Julie Mccann *(Development Officer)*, Patrick O' Toole *(Development Assistant)*
**Sales:** Aidan Creamer *(Development Assistant)*, Jolene Mccarney *(Development Assistant)*, Damien Mcconville *(Development Assistant)*
**Admin:** Lisa Beattie *(PA to CEO)*, Liz Cunningham *(Receptionist)*, Marie-Therese Higgins *(Administrative Assistant)*, Louise Mcatamney *(Personal Assistant)*, Jennifer Redmond *(Administrator)*, Jackie Stevenson *(GIS Database Administrator)*
**IT:** Margaret Mcclintock *(Information Systems Officer)*
**HR:** Emma Bohill *(Human Resources Manager)*, Conor Cunning *(Development Assistant (Coach E)*, Leslie Dewart *(Human Resources Manager)*, Robin Gregg *(Talent id systems Manager)*, Sinead McErlain *(Human Resources Manager)*, Kieran O' Hara *(Trainer)*, Kristine Telford *(Human Resources Business Partn)*
**Facilities:** Anne Lowden *(Development Assistant, Facilit)*, Sean O' Hare *(Development Assistant, Sports)*, Shaun Ogle *(Director of Performance)*
**Operations:** Mike Mcclure *(Development Officer Countrysid)*, Laura Trainor *(Capital Monitoring Officer)*
**Engineering:** Sean O' Hare *(Development Assistant, Sports)*, Carl Southern *(Architect and Technical Manage)*
**US SIC:** 9121 **UK SIC:** 91110
**Employees:** 100

DUNS 42-440-1206

### The Sports Council for Wales

Welsh Institute Of Sport, Sophia Gardens, Cardiff, South Glamorgan CF11 9SW
**Tel:** 0300 3003111
**Web:** www.sportwales.org.uk
**Reg No:** 0000579RC **Estd:** 1972
**Line of Business:** Sports coaching
**Chairman:** G Davies
**Responsibilities**
**Senior:** Malcolm Zaple *(Facilities Manager)*
**Finance:** Dawn French *(Finance Controller)*
**IT:** Simon Napper *(IT Manager)*
**HR:** Kerry Chown *(Human Resources Manager)*
**Facilities:** Malcolm Zaple *(Facilities Manager)*
**Branches:** The Sports Council For Wales, 240 Whitchurch Rd, Cardiff, South Glamorgan CF14 3ND
**US SIC:** 7999 **UK SIC:** 97913
**Employees:** 190

DUNS 21-802-4146

### Sports Direct

Unit 7 Spires Retail Park, Moy Road, Armagh, Co Armagh BT61 8DB
**Tel:** 08443325357
**Web:** www.sportsdirect.com
**Estd:** 2011
**Line of Business:** Sports goods retailers
**US SIC:** 5941 **UK SIC:** 65400
**Employees:** 60

DUNS 67-205-1005

### Sports Direct International Plc

(**Subsidiary of:** Mash Holdings Ltd)
Unit D, Brook Park Meadow Lane, Shirebrook, Mansfield, Nottinghamshire NG20 8RY
**Tel:** 08443325058 **Fax:** 08451229201
**Web:** www.sportsdirect.com
**Reg No:** 6035106 **VAT No:** 898439743
**Estd:** 2012 Public Limited Company
**Line of Business:** Management activities of holding companies
**Export Sales:** £642,234,000
**Trading Style:** Sports Direct
**Issued Capital:** £64,060,237
**Directors:** M J Ashley, D M Forsey, D Singleton, Ms C E Jenkins, S A Bentley, Dr. K Hellawell
**Co. Secretary:** Cameron Olsen
**Responsibilities**
**Senior:** Jamie Towyl *(Branch Manager)*
**Finance:** Bob Mellors *(Finance Director)*
**IT:** Mark Macaulay *(IT Director)*
**Branches:** Sports Direct International Plc, Unit 57, Charter Way, Braintree, Essex CM77 8YH
**US SIC:** 6711 **UK SIC:** 83962
**Auditors:** Grant Thornton UK LLP
**Bankers:** Bank Of Scotland (12-20-10)

**Following financial data are in thousands**

| | 27-04-14 | 28-04-13 | 29-04-12 |
|---|---|---|---|
| TO | 2,705,958 | 2,185,580 | 1,835,756 |
| P/L | 239,452 | 207,226 | 151,498 |
| NW | 565,983 | 404,511 | 247,240 |
| WC | 44,627 | 276,124 | 147,566 |
| Emp. | 17,165 | 14,076 | 12,145 |

DUNS 34-820-9557

### Sports Leaders Uk Ltd

23-25 Linford Forum, Rockingham Drive, Linford Wood, Milton Keynes, Buckinghamshire MK14 6LY
**Web:** www.sportsleaders.org
**Reg No:** 5620594 **Estd:** 2005 Private Limited Company
**Line of Business:** Other sporting activities not elsewhere classified
**Issued Capital:** £2
**Director:** Miss L C Plowright
**Co. Secretary:** William Firth
**US SIC:** 7999 **UK SIC:** 97913

| | 31-03-14 | 31-03-13 | 31-03-12 |
|---|---|---|---|
| TA | 2 | 2 | 2 |
| NW | 2 | 2 | 2 |

DUNS 23-570-6244

### Sports Vision Presents Ltd

(**Subsidiary of:** Sports Vision (International) Ltd)
1st 2nd & 3rd Floors, 37 Shelton Street, London WC2H 9HN
**Tel:** 02036176000
**Web:** www.visionninehq.com
**Reg No:** 3568741 **Estd:** 1998 Private Limited Company
**Line of Business:** Other entertainment activities not elsewhere classified
**Issued Capital:** £1,572
**Directors:** A J Topham, J A Topham
**Co. Secretary:** Lee Bater
**Responsibilities**
**Senior:** Alan Crofton *(Manager)*
**US SIC:** 7999 **UK SIC:** 97913
**Auditors:** The Barnbrook Sinclair Partnership LLP

| | 31-12-13 | 31-12-12 | 31-12-11 |
|---|---|---|---|
| TA | 767,230 | 1,470,802 | 2,645,392 |
| NW | 242,961 | 197,811 | 114,974 |
| WC | 237,474 | 291,006 | 214,439 |

DUNS 21-580-5817

### Sportscotland

Templeton Business Centre, 62 Templeton Street, Glasgow, Lanarkshire G40 1DA
**Tel:** 01415346500
**Web:** www.sportscotland.org.uk
**Estd:** 1999 Proprietorship
**Line of Business:** Sports clubs
**US SIC:** 7999 **UK SIC:** 97913
**Employees:** 100

DUNS 23-800-5081 **Imp**

### Sportswear International Ltd

Fairoak Lane, Whitehouse Industrial Estate, Runcorn, Cheshire WA7 3DU
**Tel:** 08455190099 **Fax:** 01928-571452
**Web:** www.swi.co.uk
**Reg No:** 3793118 **Estd:** 1999 Private Limited Company
**Line of Business:** Wholesale of textiles
**Issued Capital:** £103
**Directors:** D Plant, P Walker, A Poynton, H Baird, G Rooney, K F Robertson
**US SIC:** 5641, 5611

**UK SIC:** 64500

| | 31-12-13 | 31-12-12 | 31-12-11 |
|---|---|---|---|
| TO | 8,831,544 | 8,903,740 | 8,293,051 |
| P/L | 143,367 | 372,529 | 311,994 |
| NW | 1,395,673 | 1,422,283 | 1,243,605 |
| WC | 1,098,045 | 1,068,346 | 885,459 |
| Emp. | 60 | 57 | 51 |

DUNS 64-098-2666 Imp

## Sportswift Ltd

(**Subsidiary of:** Cf Topco Ltd)
Century House, Brunel Road, Wakefield 41 Industrial Estate, Wakefield, West Yorkshire WF2 0XG
**Tel:** 01924-839150 **Fax:** 01924-839160
**Web:** www.cardfactory.eu.com
**Reg No:** 3493972 **Estd:** 1997 Private Limited Company
**Line of Business:** Retail
**Trading Style:** The Card Factory, Rosecards Distribution
**Issued Capital:** £1,539
**Principals:** R Hayes *(Financial)*, A D Barraclough, T J Lloyd, D Bryant, C R Beck
**Co. Secretary:** Shiv Sibal
**Responsibilities**
**Senior:** Andrew Longstaffe *(Manager)*
**Branches:** Sportswift Ltd, 9A Lagrange Arcade, St. Helens, Merseyside WA10 1BN
**US SIC:** 5399, 5942
**UK SIC:** 65600, 65300
**Auditors:** KPMG LLP

| | 31-01-14 | 31-01-13 | 31-01-12 |
|---|---|---|---|
| TO | 313,182,000 | 285,957,000 | 254,346,000 |
| P/L | 69,243,000 | 66,111,000 | 56,206,000 |
| NW | 215,073,000 | 180,674,000 | 130,318,000 |
| WC | 182,434,000 | 152,215,000 | 105,628,000 |
| Emp. | 8,428 | 7,820 | 6,774 |

DUNS 23-132-2061

## Spot Service Station

171 Sutherland Road, Stoke-On-Trent, Staffordshire ST3 1HZ
**Tel:** 01283521493
**Web:** www.esso.co.uk
**VAT No:** 823557228 **Estd:** 1992 Proprietorship
**Line of Business:** Petrol filling station
**Proprietor:** A Hussain
**Branches:** Spot Service Station, Leek Rd, Stoke-On-Trent, Staffordshire ST9 9BA
**US SIC:** 5541 **UK SIC:** 65200
**Bankers:** Habib Bank Limited (70-14-59)
**Employees:** 50

DUNS 21-034-1412

## Spotless Commercial Cleaning

51 Sandilands Street, Glasgow, Lanarkshire G32 0HT
**Tel:** 0141-778-7673
**Web:** www.spotlessclean.co.uk
**Proprietorship**
**Line of Business:** Cleaning contracting commercial
**Proprietor:** Mrs M Lamb
**US SIC:** 7349 **UK SIC:** 92300
**Employees:** 300

DUNS 49-492-6934

## Spotless Commercial Cleaning Ltd

Llan Coed Court, Darcy Business Park, Llandarcy, Neath, West Glamorgan SA10 6FG
**Tel:** 08451122322 **Fax:** 0131-622-8540
**Web:** www.spotlessclean.co.uk
**Reg No:** 0163138SC **Estd:** 1988 Private Limited Company
**Line of Business:** Traditional cleaning activities
**Issued Capital:** £122,397
**Directors:** Ms F Thomson, Mrs P Manson, Ms M Lamb, R B Green, N J Moffat, R R Leach, Miss O C Bennett
**Co. Secretary:** Ms Joanna Green
**Responsibilities**
**Senior:** Trisha Aanson *(Operations Director)*
**Operations:** Trisha Aanson *(Operations Director)*
**Branches:** Spotless Commercial Cleaning Ltd, Douglas Court, Unit 16, Gateshead, Tyne and Wear NE11 0JY
**US SIC:** 7349 **UK SIC:** 92300
**Auditors:** French Duncan LLP
**Bankers:** The Royal Bank Of Scotland Plc (83-06-08)

| | 06-10-13 | 07-10-12 | 09-10-11 |
|---|---|---|---|
| TO | 10,134,462 | 10,302,617 | 9,714,810 |
| P/L | 241,502 | 981,846 | 247,545 |
| NW | 739,198 | 750,207 | 117,184 |
| WC | 685,787 | 735,122 | 100,887 |
| Emp. | 1,064 | 1,086 | 959 |

DUNS 21-009-0171 Imp-Exp

## Spotless Punch Ltd

(**Subsidiary of:** Spotless Punch Ireland Ltd)
57-65 Station Road, Redhill, Surrey RH1 1DL
**Tel:** 01737781300 **Fax:** 02083-020647
**Web:** www.spotlesspunch.com
**Reg No:** 0352454 **VAT No:** 927303140
**Estd:** 1939 Private Limited Company
**Line of Business:** Consumer organisations
**Export Markets:** Europe, Middle East, Canada, S America, Africa, S & S E Asia, Australasia, U S A
**Export Sales:** £6,412,000
**Issued Capital:** £1,000
**Directors:** M Petrelli, D J Toms, I J Hamilton, P D Budden, D J Luther, C A Stubbs, G Mountford, J Keeley
**Co. Secretary:** Iain Hamilton
**Branches:** Spotless Punch Ltd, Lower Farm Road, Northampton, Northamptonshire NN3 6XF
**US SIC:** 3999 **UK SIC:** 49590
**Auditors:** Ernst & Young
**Bankers:** Barclays Bank Plc (20-00-00)

| | 31-12-13 | 31-12-12 | 31-12-11 |
|---|---|---|---|
| TO | 27,547,000 | 26,104,000 | 26,117,000 |
| P/L | 4,144,000 | 2,165,000 | 1,413,000 |
| NW | 7,165,000 | 5,989,000 | 9,477,000 |
| WC | 4,425,000 | 2,504,000 | 3,626,000 |
| Emp. | 47 | 49 | 49 |

DUNS 28 868 0755

## Spratton Hall School Trust Ltd

Smith Street, Northampton, Northamptonshire NN6 8HP
**Tel:** 01604-847292
**Web:** www.sprattonhall.com
**Reg No:** 1013863 **Estd:** 1971 Private Limited Company
**Line of Business:** General secondary education
**Directors:** Mrs N Pert, Ms S A Bennett, J Beynon, R V Peel, A S Gough, Ms P M Long, R Green, J Belbin
**Co. Secretary:** William Coley
**Responsibilities**
**Senior:** Roger Outwin Flinders *(Director)*
**Facilities:** Andrew Harte *(Maintenance Manager)*
**US SIC:** 8211 **UK SIC:** 93200
**Auditors:** Grant Thornton
**Bankers:** Lloyds TSB Bank plc (30-96-09)

| | 31-08-13 | 31-08-12 | 31-08-11 |
|---|---|---|---|
| TO | 4,230,082 | 4,089,513 | 3,890,154 |
| P/L | 163,932 | 73,700 | (29,053) |
| NW | 4,485,488 | 4,321,556 | 4,247,856 |
| WC | 630,193 | 151,133 | 313,507 |
| Emp. | 82 | 77 | 75 |

DUNS 23-703-6702

## Spread Asset Management Ltd

Martello Court, Guernsey, Channel Islands GY1 2HR
**Tel:** 01481751551 **Fax:** 01481-724723
**Web:** www.intertrustgroup.com
**Reg No:** 0021077J **Estd:** 1989 Private Limited Company
**Line of Business:** Financial services
**Trading Style:** B G L Reads Asset Management, Spread International
**Issued Capital:** £7
**Principals:** T Pearson *(Managing)*, K Lycett, M J Quarrington, D Warr, A Pollock
**US SIC:** 7392, 6211
**UK SIC:** 83951, 83100
**Bankers:** HSBC Bank plc (40-22-25)
**Employees:** 250

DUNS 23-544-3889

## Spreadex Com Ltd

Ziggurat House, 25 Grosvenor Road, St Albans, Hertfordshire AL1 3AW
**Tel:** 01727-895000 **Fax:** 01727895102
**Web:** www.spreadex.com
**Reg No:** 3542879 **Estd:** 2000 Private Limited Company
**Line of Business:** Gambling and betting activities
**Issued Capital:** £12,548,640
**Directors:** C D Allen, T W Harris, J G Hufford
**Co. Secretary:** Jonathan Hufford
**US SIC:** 7999 **UK SIC:** 97913

| | 31-05-14 | 31-05-13 | 31-05-12 |
|---|---|---|---|
| TO | 35,441,988 | 29,397,489 | 25,695,780 |
| P/L | 18,506,950 | 14,401,111 | 11,509,029 |
| NW | 50,743,898 | 41,434,121 | 34,178,794 |
| WC | 49,929,461 | 41,345,845 | 33,928,031 |
| Emp. | 98 | 93 | 85 |

DUNS 21-783-4385

## Spring Cottage Primary School

Dressay Grove, Hull, North Humberside HU8 9JH
**Tel:** 01482794183
**Web:** www.springcottage.hull.sch.uk
**Estd:** 2011 Proprietorship
**Line of Business:** Primary education
**Proprietor:** A Rhodes
**US SIC:** 8211 **UK SIC:** 93200
**Employees:** 50

DUNS 21-597-1088

## Spring Lighting

132-134 Grafton Road, London NW5 4BA
**Tel:** 02072678735
**Web:** www.springstudios.com
**Estd:** 2011
**Line of Business:** Photographic studios
**Responsibilities**
**Senior:** Jean Harris *(Manager)*
**US SIC:** 7333 **UK SIC:** 83953
**Employees:** 200

DUNS 21-033-3609

## Spring Meadow Infant & Nursery School

High Banks, Pen Y Waun, Cardiff, South Glamorgan CF15 9SJ
**Tel:** 01353-664742
**Web:** www.springmeadowschool.co.uk
**Estd:** 1995 Proprietorship
**Line of Business:** General secondary education
**Proprietor:** Mrs S Harbour
**Responsibilities**
**Senior:** Sheila Sands *(Head Teacher)*
**US SIC:** 8211 **UK SIC:** 03200
**Employees:** 50

DUNS 42-355-3135

## Spring Petroleum Co Ltd

Unit 53, Batley, West Yorkshire WF17 6ER
**Tel:** 01924-446040
**Web:** www.ctpetro.com
**Reg No:** 4342974 **Estd:** 2001 Private Limited Company
**Line of Business:** Retail sale of automotive fuel
**Issued Capital:** £300
**Directors:** J Sheth, M D Patel
**Co. Secretary:** Farook Asmal
**Branches:** Spring Petroleum Co Ltd, Total Service Station, Cardigan Road, Leeds, West Yorkshire LS6 1QL
**US SIC:** 5541 **UK SIC:** 65200
**Auditors:** HW Chartered Accountants
**Bankers:** National Westminster Bank Plc (52-30-29)

| | 31-03-14 | 31-03-13 | 31-03-12 |
|---|---|---|---|
| TO | 35,612,061 | 34,737,318 | 36,946,691 |
| P/L | 372,175 | 242,333 | 273,347 |
| NW | 10,759,607 | 10,425,275 | 10,293,556 |
| WC | 43,430 | 122,591 | 113,867 |
| Emp. | 114 | 123 | 196 |

DUNS 52-530-9043 Imp

## Spring Studios Ltd

Spring House, 10 Spring Place, Kentish Town, London NW5 3BH
**Tel:** 020-7267-8383
**Web:** www.springstudios.com
**Reg No:** 3235594 **Estd:** 1996 Private Limited Company
**Line of Business:** Photographic studios
**Export Sales:** £13,282,791
**Issued Capital:** £120
**Directors:** F Costa, H Uberoi, M N Loy, J M Moffat
**Responsibilities**
**Senior:** Martin Butcher *(Manager)*, Godfrey Jillings *(Manager)*
**US SIC:** 7333 **UK SIC:** 83953
**Auditors:** Cohen Arnold

| | 31-12-13 | 31-12-12 | 31-12-11 |
|---|---|---|---|
| TO | 29,587,065 | 23,073,576 | 15,800,959 |
| P/L | (2,312,940) | 1,559,571 | 1,019,531 |
| NW | (3,404,696) | 3,085,926 | 1,920,826 |
| WC | (4,374,735) | (1,464,405) | (2,166,914) |
| Emp. | 177 | 158 | 115 |

DUNS 21-778-5753

## Springbank

Mill Hayes Road, Knypersley, Stoke-On-Trent, Staffordshire ST8 7PS
**Tel:** 01782516889
**Web:** www.springbank.co.uk
**Estd:** 1988 Partnership
**Line of Business:** Nursing homes
**Partners:** Mrs J Collier, Ms S Sharp
**US SIC:** 8051 **UK SIC:** 95100
**Employees:** 50

DUNS 49-426-9152

## Springbank Community Care Ltd

(**Subsidiary of:** C&C Bidco Ltd)
Unit 12 Moorland Road Burslem Enterprise, Centre, Stoke-On-Trent, Staffordshire ST6 1JQ
**Tel:** 01782-839023
**Web:** www.eur-ist.com
**Reg No:** 3141583 **Estd:** 1995 Private Limited Company
**Line of Business:** Home care and help services
**Issued Capital:** £100
**Directors:** M A Harrison, C Rushton
**Co. Secretary:** Mark Harrison
**Responsibilities**
**Senior:** Hayley Goodchild *(Maintenance Manager)*
**IT:** Derek Monty *(Head of IT)*
**Facilities:** Amanda Bowler *(Maintenance Manager)*
**US SIC:** 8811 **UK SIC:** 99000
**Auditors:** Robert Hayden & Co
**Bankers:** The Royal Bank Of Scotland Plc (16-24-32)

| | 31-03-13 | 31-03-12 | 31-03-10 |
|---|---|---|---|
| TO | 1,952,686 | 2,590,493 | N/A |
| P/L | 552,619 | 761,012 | N/A |
| NW | 1,155,423 | 602,591 | 58,483 |
| WC | 1,155,423 | 602,591 | 57,013 |
| Emp. | 116 | 105 | N/A |

DUNS 50-708-0208

## Springbank Nursing Home

Neuadd Went, College Road, Barry, South Glamorgan CF62 8HS
**Tel:** 01446-740190
**Web:** www.springbankcare.co.uk
**Estd:** 2000 Proprietorship
**Line of Business:** Nursing homes
**Proprietor:** J Llewellyn
**Responsibilities**
**Senior:** Julia McCarthy *(General Manager)*, Simon Trehearne-Teague *(Home Manager)*
**US SIC:** 8051 **UK SIC:** 95100
**Employees:** 150

DUNS 22-716-7897

## Springboard Housing Association Ltd

Springboard House, 2 Claughton Road, London E13 9PN
**Tel:** 020-8475-0033
**Web:** www.genesisha.org.uk
**Reg No:** 0020015IP **Estd:** 1971 Friendly Society
**Line of Business:** Housing associations societies trusts & co-operatives
**Directors:** H Savill, Miss J Seymour, D Burton, A Entecott, Mrs P Mason, H Ashton, G Reynolds, Dr D Abrahams
**Co. Secretary:** Lady K Avebury
**Responsibilities**
**Senior:** N Osbourne *(Director)*, R Shail *(Director)*
**US SIC:** 8699 **UK SIC:** 96902
**Auditors:** KPMG LLP
**Bankers:** Barclays Bank Plc (20-57-06)
**Employees:** 1,383
**Turnover:** £41,959,000

DUNS 39-414-8886

## Springboard Sunderland Trust

147 Roker Avenue, Sunderland, Tyne and Wear SR6 0BS
**Tel:** 0191-564-0291
**Web:** www.springboard-ne.org
**Reg No:** 2121694 **Estd:** 1987 Private Company Limited By Guarantee
**Line of Business:** Adult and other education not elsewhere classified
**Directors:** T J Robinson, J Nicholson, Dr M H Thurlbeck, B J Moore, W Jackson
**Co. Secretary:** Ms Denise Wilson
**Responsibilities**
**Senior:** Joseph Surtees *(Manager)*
**Branches:** Springboard Sunderland Trust, Tanfield Road, Hartlepool, Cleveland TS25 5DD
**US SIC:** 8249, 6732
**UK SIC:** 93300, 83100
**Auditors:** Deloitte & Touche LLP
**Bankers:** National Westminster Bank Plc (55-61-11)

| | 31-07-14 | 31-07-13 | 31-07-12 |
|---|---|---|---|
| TO | 7,197,487 | 10,953,413 | 6,013,795 |
| P/L | (779,009) | 24,776 | 178,469 |
| NW | 2,105,314 | 2,884,323 | 2,859,547 |
| WC | 550,612 | 717,874 | 781,104 |
| Emp. | 103 | 105 | 93 |

DUNS 21-100-5772 Imp-Exp

## Springbrook Ltd

(**Subsidiary of:** Cloverbrook Holdings Ltd)
Peel Mill, Burnley, Lancashire BB12 6JJ
**Tel:** 01282-712000 **Fax:** 01282-457723
**Web:** www.springbrook.ca
**Reg No:** 0947534 **VAT No:** 174328164
**Estd:** 1969 Private Limited Company
**Line of Business:** Wholesale of textiles
**Export Markets:** Scandinavia; U S A; E U
**Trading Style:** Cloverbrook
**Issued Capital:** £29,000
**Managing Director:** S Chippendale
**Co. Secretary:** John Wilkinson
**Branches:** Riversid Mill, Lune St, Padiham Lancashire BB12 8dg, Padiham
**US SIC:** 5133, 7399
**UK SIC:** 61600, 83954

**Auditors:** PM&M
**Bankers:** HSBC Bank plc (40-15-17)

| | 01-04-14 | 01-04-13 | 01-04-12 |
|---|---|---|---|
| TA | 8,459,348 | 8,459,348 | 8,459,348 |
| NW | 8,459,348 | 8,459,348 | 8,459,348 |

DUNS 21-226-2537
## Springburn Fire Station
47 Midton Street, Glasgow, Lanarkshire G21 4RS
**Tel:** 0141-5582223
**Web:** www.scottishfireandrescueservice.com
**Estd:** 1986 Proprietorship
**Line of Business:** Fire service activities
**Proprietor:** H Mullin
**Responsibilities**
**Senior:** Billy Lang *(Station Commander)*
**US SIC:** 9224 **UK SIC:** 91400
**Employees:** 60

DUNS 22-278-9849
## Springcare Ltd
Whitchurch Business Park, Shakespeare Way, Whitchurch, Shropshire SY13 1LJ
**Tel:** 01948661400 **Fax:** 01948-661401
**Web:** www.springcare.org.uk
**Reg No:** 4296959 **Estd:** 2010 Private Limited Company
**Line of Business:** Medical nursing home activities
**Trading Style:** Springcare Ltd
**Issued Capital:** £140,000
**Director:** L D Cox
**Co. Secretary:** Ms Helen Cox
**Responsibilities**
**Senior:** Sharon Whitfield *(Personal Assistant To Managing)*
**US SIC:** 7399, 8321
**UK SIC:** 83954, 96111
**Auditors:** McLintocks

| | 31-12-13 | 31-12-12 | 31-12-11 |
|---|---|---|---|
| TO | 11,983,418 | 11,399,951 | 10,664,766 |
| P/L | 718,941 | 1,396,300 | 856,515 |
| NW | 14,256,642 | 7,916,270 | 6,891,621 |
| WC | 211,912 | 609,394 | (3,315) |
| Emp. | 514 | 444 | 480 |

DUNS 29-045-1491
## Springdene Nursing & Care Homes Ltd
55 Oakleigh Park North, London N20 9NH
**Tel:** 020-8446-2117
**Web:** www.thephysiotherapysite.co.uk
**Reg No:** 0994783 **Estd:** 1970 Private Limited Company
**Line of Business:** Other human health activities
**Issued Capital:** £500
**Directors:** M J Williams, Dr M Powell, J Balcombe, Ms A Rosen, Dr R Powell, A Powell, Ms S L Balcombe
**Co. Secretary:** Ms June Powell
**Branches:** Springdene Nursing & Care Homes Ltd, Springview Retirement Home, Crescent Road, Enfield, Middlesex EN2 7BL
**US SIC:** 8091 **UK SIC:** 95200
**Auditors:** Ramsay Brown & Partners
**Bankers:** Barclays Bank Plc (20-80-78)

| | 31-01-14 | 31-01-13 | 31-01-12 |
|---|---|---|---|
| TO | 8,696,419 | 8,794,158 | 8,540,725 |
| P/L | 439,705 | 789,670 | 882,564 |
| NW | 16,911,425 | 16,589,425 | 16,005,565 |
| WC | (2,576,492) | (2,783,312) | (2,531,770) |
| Emp. | 289 | 293 | 296 |

DUNS 77-125-1352
## Springdew Ltd
Unit 9-10, Woodlands Business Park, Swansea, West Glamorgan SA9 1JW
**Tel:** 01639849676 **Fax:** 01639-845662
**Web:** www.springdew.co.uk
**Reg No:** 2697495 **Estd:** 1992 Private Limited Company
**Line of Business:** Packagers
**Issued Capital:** £187,501
**Principals:** D H Evans *(Managing)*, P N Evans
**Co. Secretary:** Donald Evans
**Responsibilities**
**Health & Safety:** Rachel Evans *(Health & Saftety Officer)*
**Facilities:** Simon Dugay *(Engineering Manager)*
**Engineering:** Simon Dugay *(Engineering Manager)*
**US SIC:** 7399 **UK SIC:** 83954
**Auditors:** Clay Shaw Thomas
**Bankers:** Barclays Bank Plc (20-58-72)

| | 31-05-14 | 31-05-13 | 31-05-12 |
|---|---|---|---|
| TA | 3,164,460 | 3,413,065 | 3,597,637 |
| NW | 819,955 | 793,055 | 653,158 |
| WC | 29,660 | (46) | (31,818) |

DUNS 23-680-0462 Exp
## Springfarm Architectural Mouldings Ltd
Greystone Road, Antrim, Co Antrim BT41 2QN
**Tel:** 028-9442-8288 **Fax:** 028-9442-8244
**Web:** www.sammouldings.co.uk
**Reg No:** 0024953NI **VAT No:** 516777223
**Estd:** 1990 Private Limited Company
**Line of Business:** Architectural woodwork
**Export Markets:** Republic of Ireland
**Export Sales:** £2,102,830
**Trading Style:** Sam Mouldings
**Issued Capital:** £441,000
**Directors:** G Wilson, M Kirkpatrick, R Holmes, T Patton, Ms J M Mccrea, S J Mccrea
**Co. Secretary:** Ms Julienne Mc Crea
**Responsibilities**
**HR:** Grace Cahoon *(HR Manager)*
**US SIC:** 8911 **UK SIC:** 83701
**Auditors:** Muir & Addy
**Bankers:** First Trust Bank (aib Group (uk) Plc) (93-81-57)

| | 28-02-14 | 28-02-13 | 29-02-12 |
|---|---|---|---|
| TO | 15,531,096 | 13,509,274 | 12,520,552 |
| P/L | (237,692) | 40,654 | (468,619) |
| NW | 4,113,816 | 4,288,318 | 4,221,128 |
| WC | 32,639 | 441,041 | (206,050) |
| Emp. | 121 | 101 | 89 |

DUNS 21-228-2913
## Springfield Care Centre
20 Springfield Drive, Ilford, Essex IG2 6PS
**Tel:** 020-85189270
**Web:** www.lifestylecare.co.uk
**Estd:** 2000 Proprietorship
**Line of Business:** Nursing homes
**Proprietor:** Mrs M Oniah
**Responsibilities**
**Senior:** Mary Ng'ambi *(Manager)*
**US SIC:** 8051 **UK SIC:** 95100
**Employees:** 49

DUNS 39-934-6030
## Springfield Cars Ltd
3 Crowther Road, Washington, Tyne and Wear NE38 0AQ
**Tel:** 01914172677 **Fax:** 0191-417-3314
**Web:** www.springfieldmotorcars.co.uk
**Reg No:** 2248011 **VAT No:** 708582223
**Estd:** 1989 Private Limited Company
**Line of Business:** Car dealers (new & used)
**Trading Style:** Springfield Motor Group
**Issued Capital:** £144,000
**Principals:** R Price *(Managing)*, M Price, K W Turner, G Price
**Co. Secretary:** Ms Linda Price
**Responsibilities**
**Finance:** M Fantin *(Senior Finance Administrator)*
**IT:** Kevin Ellengworth *(IT Manager)*
**Branches:** Springfield Cars Ltd, Middle Engine La Abbey Rd, Silverlink Business Pk, Newcastle-Upon-Tyne, Tyne and Wear NE28 9NZ
**US SIC:** 5511 **UK SIC:** 65100
**Auditors:** Trevor Jones
**Bankers:** Lloyds TSB Bank plc (30-93-43)

| | 31-12-13 | 31-12-12 | 31-12-11 |
|---|---|---|---|
| TO | 43,210,007 | 74,030,391 | 66,392,604 |
| P/L | 463,430 | 1,096,506 | 622,840 |
| NW | 6,964,318 | 7,098,255 | 6,415,650 |
| WC | 2,248,043 | 634,018 | 74,135 |
| Emp. | 86 | 174 | 196 |

DUNS 55-067-1259
## Springfield Cottage Residential Home
Preston New Road, Blackburn, Lancashire BB2 6PS
**Web:** www.springfield-cottage.com
**Estd:** 1994 Proprietorship
**Line of Business:** Residential care establishments
**Proprietor:** D Martin
**Responsibilities**
**Senior:** Lindsey Spencer *(Registered Manager)*
**US SIC:** 8321 **UK SIC:** 96111
**Employees:** 50

DUNS 21-728-7762
## Springfield Country Hotel (Stoborough) Ltd
Grange Road, Wareham, Dorset BH20 5AL
**Tel:** 01929-552177 **Fax:** 01929-551862
**Web:** www.springfield-country-hotel.co.uk
**Reg No:** 1165188 **Estd:** 1974 Private Limited Company
**Line of Business:** Hotels
**Trading Style:** Springfield Country Hotel & Country Club
**Issued Capital:** £90
**Directors:** P G Alford, Ms J M Alford
**Co. Secretary:** John Alford
**Responsibilities**
**Senior:** John Osmond *(General Manager)*
**Finance:** Andrea Alford *(Financial Director)*
**HR:** John Osmond *(General Manager)*
**US SIC:** 7011 **UK SIC:** 66500
**Auditors:** Carter & Coley
**Bankers:** National Westminster Bank Plc (60-07-01)

| | 28-02-14 | 28-02-13 | 29-02-12 |
|---|---|---|---|
| TA | 8,116,427 | 7,782,716 | 7,181,263 |
| NW | 4,452,649 | 4,237,193 | 4,112,158 |
| WC | 2,347,532 | 2,199,751 | 2,075,904 |

DUNS 50-327-0704
## Springfield Court Ltd
Springfield Road, Aughton, Ormskirk, Lancashire L39 6ST
**Tel:** 01695424344
**Web:** www.springfieldcourt.org
**Reg No:** 2351770 **Estd:** 1989 Private Limited Company
**Line of Business:** Medical nursing home activities
**Issued Capital:** £285,720
**Directors:** Ms L G Burrows, Mrs M Pollitt, R Pollitt, Mrs W M Wilkinson
**Co. Secretary:** Colin Wilkinson
**US SIC:** 8051 **UK SIC:** 95100
**Auditors:** Rustons
**Bankers:** National Westminster Bank Plc (01-00-85)

| | 30-11-13 | 30-11-12 | 30-11-11 |
|---|---|---|---|
| TO | 1,707,492 | 1,710,438 | 1,711,384 |
| P/L | 128,396 | 156,407 | 170,903 |
| NW | 877,673 | 1,606,736 | 1,582,965 |
| WC | (84,133) | (278,239) | (258,429) |
| Emp. | 82 | 84 | 81 |

DUNS 23-591-1372
## Springfield (Durham) Ltd
**(Subsidiary of:** Springfield Cars Ltd)
Durham Road, Gateshead, Tyne And, Gateshead, Tyne and Wear NE8 4AP
**Tel:** 01914772323
**Web:** www.drivespringfield.com
**Reg No:** 3588707 **Estd:** 1998 Private Limited Company
**Line of Business:** Sale of new motor vehicles
**Trading Style:** Springfield Cars
**Issued Capital:** £250,000
**Director:** R Price
**Co. Secretary:** Ms Linda Price
**Responsibilities**
**IT:** Kevin Illingworth *(IT Manager)*
**US SIC:** 5511, 7539
**UK SIC:** 65100, 67100
**Auditors:** Illegible
**Bankers:** Barclays Bank Plc (20-00-00)

| | 31-12-13 | 31-12-12 | 31-12-11 |
|---|---|---|---|
| TA | 370,202 | 370,202 | 370,202 |
| NW | 370,202 | 370,202 | 370,202 |

DUNS 23-748-4089
## Springfield Home Care Services Ltd
2 Fusion Court, Aberford Road, Leeds, West Yorkshire LS25 2GH
**Tel:** 01132876789 **Fax:** 01132-876800
**Web:** www.springfieldhealthcaregroup.com
**Reg No:** 3742352 **Estd:** 1999 Private Limited Company
**Line of Business:** Home care service providers
**Issued Capital:** £19,591
**Directors:** R D Taylor, M R Beadle, G S Lee, P R Phillips
**Responsibilities**
**Senior:** Harriet Thresh *(Financial Director)*
**Finance:** Harriet Thresh *(Financial Director)*
**US SIC:** 8091 **UK SIC:** 95200
**Auditors:** Grants
**Bankers:** National Westminster Bank Plc (56-00-36)

| | 31-03-14 | 31-03-13 | 31-03-12 |
|---|---|---|---|
| TO | 11,487,815 | 9,209,478 | 8,427,002 |
| P/L | 92,167 | 124,158 | 422,298 |
| NW | (977,066) | (475,640) | (358,400) |
| WC | 24,918 | 391,232 | (130,197) |
| Emp. | 855 | 723 | 615 |

DUNS 21-593-1321
## Springfield Hospital
Lawn Lane, Chelmsford, Essex CM1 7GU
**Tel:** 01245234000
**Web:** www.ramsayhealth.co.uk
**Estd:** 1989 Proprietorship
**Line of Business:** Hospitals
**Proprietor:** J Frame
**US SIC:** 8062 **UK SIC:** 95100
**Employees:** 300

DUNS 21-226-1196
## Springfield House Business Centre
Hilltop, Whitehouse Lane, Leeds, West Yorkshire LS26 8BJ
**Tel:** 01132387203
**Web:** www.springfieldhouse-leeds.com
**Estd:** 2004 Proprietorship
**Line of Business:** Business and commerce centres
**Proprietors:** Ms D Mcguire, Ms D Mcguire
**Responsibilities**
**Senior:** Adrian Howe *(CEO, Managing Director)*
**US SIC:** 7392 **UK SIC:** 83951
**Employees:** 50

DUNS 21-213-7041
## Springfield Park Nursing Home
Springfield Park, Rochdale, Lancashire OL11 4RE
**Tel:** 01706-646333
**Web:** www.hallmarkhealthcare.co.uk
**Estd:** 2002 Proprietorship
**Line of Business:** Nursing homes
**Proprietor:** P Mellor
**Responsibilities**
**Senior:** Fay Royale *(General Manager)*
**US SIC:** 8051 **UK SIC:** 95100
**Employees:** 85

DUNS 21-032-9669
## Springfield Primary School
Nursery Road, Sunbury-On-Thames, Middlesex TW16 6LY
**Tel:** 01932-782815
**Web:** www.springfield.surrey.sch.uk
**Estd:** 1943 Proprietorship
**Line of Business:** Primary education
**Proprietor:** Miss T Lewis
**Responsibilities**
**Senior:** Peta Fain *(Acting Head Teacher)*, Bethan Smith *(Head Teacher)*
**US SIC:** 8211 **UK SIC:** 93200
**Employees:** 50

DUNS 21-777-1095
## Springfield Private Old Peoples Home
1-3 Lowther Avenue, Garforth, Leeds, West Yorkshire LS25 1EP
**Tel:** 01132863415
**Web:** www.springfieldhealthcaregroup.com
**Estd:** 2003 Proprietorship
**Line of Business:** Children's homes
**Proprietor:** Mrs G Lawson
**US SIC:** 8321 **UK SIC:** 96111
**Employees:** 60

DUNS 28-821-8969
## Springfield Properties Plc
8 Southfield Drive, Elgin, Morayshire IV30 6GR
**Tel:** 01343552550
**Web:** www.springfield.co.uk
**Reg No:** 0031286SC **Estd:** 2010 Private Limited Company
**Line of Business:** Property developers
**Trading Style:** Springfield Properties
**Issued Capital:** £57,175
**Directors:** R Macleod, J Adam, A W Adam, R J Eddie, Mrs A F Adam, Ms M H Motion, M J Benson
**Co. Secretary:** Innes Smith
**Responsibilities**
**Senior:** Sandy Anderson *(Manager)*, John Main *(Manager)*
**Marketing:** Jane Innes *(Sales & Marketing Manager)*
**Sales:** Jane Innes *(Sales & Marketing Manager)*
**IT:** Kevin Gunn *(IT Manager)*
**US SIC:** 1799, 1522
**UK SIC:** 50000, 50100
**Auditors:** Johnston Carmichael LLP
**Bankers:** Bank Of Scotland (80-06-66)

| | 31-05-14 | 31-05-13 | 31-05-12 |
|---|---|---|---|
| TO | 74,042,277 | 46,633,219 | 53,485,953 |
| P/L | 4,134,543 | 3,459,514 | 3,940,454 |
| NW | 21,919,704 | 17,037,294 | 14,368,326 |
| WC | 34,985,371 | 17,234,830 | 13,309,094 |
| Emp. | 339 | 233 | 230 |

DUNS 21-782-2038
## Springfield School
Cedar Drive, Witney, Oxfordshire OX28 1AR
**Tel:** 01993703963
**Web:** www.springfield.oxon.sch.uk
**Estd:** 1970 Proprietorship
**Line of Business:** Schools (local authority)
**Proprietor:** Mrs E Lawley
**US SIC:** 8299 **UK SIC:** 93300
**Employees:** 82

DUNS 28-898-2242
## Springfield Solutions Ltd
**(Subsidiary of:** Westrhode Ltd)
Unit 1-7 Acorn Industrial Estate, Thomas Street, Hull, North Humberside HU9 1EH
**Tel:** 01482484700 **Fax:** 01482-225269
**Web:** www.springfieldsolutions.co.uk
**Reg No:** 1331331 **Estd:** 1977 Private Limited Company

**Line of Business:** Labels finishing and supply
**Issued Capital:** £1,392,942
**Principals:** A W Dass *(Managing)*, M Dass, D Ebeltoft, S G Forster
**Co. Secretary:** Albert Dass
**US SIC:** 2752 **UK SIC:** 47544
**Auditors:** RSM Robson Rhodes
**Bankers:** HSBC Bank plc (40-25-16)

| | 31-12-13 | 31-12-12 | 31-12-11 |
|---|---|---|---|
| TA | 3,883,668 | 3,683,598 | 3,256,689 |
| NW | 2,071,779 | 2,000,946 | 1,634,250 |
| WC | 1,495,892 | 1,598,984 | 1,250,170 |

DUNS 21-581-1148

## Springfields

Gatehouse, High Street, Northampton, Northamptonshire NN6 8PU
**Tel:** 01858575006
**Estd:** 2008 Proprietorship
**Line of Business:** Representative office
**Proprietor:** R Holyland
**US SIC:** 5411 **UK SIC:** 64100
**Employees:** 50

DUNS 23-866-2774 **Imp**

## Springfields Fuels Ltd

**(Subsidiary of:** Toshiba Corporation)
Salwick, Preston, Lancashire PR4 0XJ
**Tel:** 01772 762 000
**Web:** www.westinghousenuclear.com
**Reg No:** 3857770 **VAT No:** 892219895
**Estd:** 2002 Private Limited Company
**Line of Business:** Processing of nuclear fuel
**Export Sales:** £34,290,000
**Trading Style:** Westinghouse
**Issued Capital:** £15,000,000
**Directors:** D S Peacock, M R Gornall, Ms T S Evans, Ms K Armer, Ms J Leybourne, S R Hart
**Co. Secretary:** Ms Fiona Houghton
**Responsibilities**
**Senior:** Peter Groom *(Stores Manager)*, Neil Longfellow *(General Manager)*
**Marketing:** Steve Whitehead *(Marketing Manager)*
**IT:** Steve Hawley *(Senior IT Executive)*
**HR:** Keith Tidmarsh *(Training Manager)*
**Health & Safety:** Karen Fishwick *(health & safety manager)*
**Facilities:** Arnold Leasdale *(Facilities Manager)*
**Operations:** Peter Bleasdale *(Head of Research)*, Dave Watson *(Environmental Officer)*
**Engineering:** Ian Curran *(Chief Engineer)*
**US SIC:** 2869, 4911
**UK SIC:** 25120, 16101
**Auditors:** Ernst & Young LLP
**Bankers:** National Westminster Bank Plc (01-10-01)

| | 31-03-14 | 31-03-13 | 31-03-12 |
|---|---|---|---|
| TO | 191,981,000 | 169,954,000 | 175,895,000 |
| P/L | 30,255,000 | 16,661,000 | 23,755,000 |
| NW | 39,057,000 | 42,270,000 | 33,803,000 |
| WC | 25,286,000 | 30,401,000 | 19,507,000 |
| Emp. | 1,178 | 1,239 | 1,270 |

DUNS 29-543-9111

## Springfields Ltd

Rectory Road, Copford, Colchester, Essex CO6 1DH
**Tel:** 01206-211065
**Web:** www.springfieldsatcopford.co.uk
**Reg No:** 1910644 **Estd:** 1985 Private Limited Company
**Line of Business:** Residential care establishments
**Issued Capital:** £2,000
**Principals:** R L Gilbart *(Managing)*, V H Jones
**US SIC:** 8321 **UK SIC:** 96111
**Auditors:** Baker Chapman & Bussey
**Bankers:** Barclays Bank Plc (20-22-67)

| | 31-08-14 | 31-08-13 | 31-08-12 |
|---|---|---|---|
| TA | 3,024,587 | 3,006,280 | 2,277,177 |
| NW | 2,840,583 | 2,894,573 | 2,155,897 |
| WC | 312,739 | 321,618 | 109,901 |

DUNS 39-969-6731

## Springhealth Leisure Ltd

**(Subsidiary of:** Thistledown Developments Ltd)
Pools On The Park, Twickenham Road, Richmond, Surrey TW9 2SF
**Tel:** 020-8940-0561 **Fax:** 020-8332-2345
**Web:** www.springhealth.net
**Reg No:** 2194104 **Estd:** 1987 Public Limited Company
**Line of Business:** Operation of sports arenas and stadiums
**Issued Capital:** £193,625
**Director:** A C Anderson
**Co. Secretary:** Jason Melrose
**Responsibilities**
**HR:** Natalie Freeman *(Human Resources Manager)*, Kelvin Mills *(Human Resources Manager)*
**Branches:** Springhealth Leisure Ltd, Warley Gap, Brentwood, Essex CM13 3DP

**US SIC:** 7941, 7999
**UK SIC:** 97911, 97913
**Auditors:** BDO Stoy Hayward LLP
**Bankers:** S G Hambros Bank & Trust Ltd (40-48-58)

| | 31-08-13 | 31-08-12 | 31-08-11 |
|---|---|---|---|
| TO | 4,315,458 | 4,273,903 | 4,210,395 |
| P/L | 197,353 | 288,336 | 282,459 |
| NW | (160,995) | (488,500) | (884,074) |
| WC | (728,555) | (1,147,000) | (1,641,302) |
| Emp. | 190 | 189 | 186 |

DUNS 23-581-2349

## Springhill Care Group Ltd

11 Cannon Street, Accrington, Lancashire BB5 1NJ
**Web:** www.springhillcare.com
**Reg No:** 3578977 **Estd:** 2003 Private Limited Company
**Line of Business:** Business services
**Issued Capital:** £300
**Principals:** K A Nolan *(Managing)*, Ms D M Briggs *(Financial)*, M J Nolan, L A Nolan
**Co. Secretary:** Ms Nicola Nolan
**US SIC:** 6711, 6732
**UK SIC:** 83962, 83100
**Auditors:** Pierce
**Bankers:** The Royal Bank Of Scotland Plc (16-18-18)

| | 31-07-13 | 31-01-13 | 31-07-11 |
|---|---|---|---|
| TO | 3,798,102 | 10,238,440 | 6,669,863 |
| P/L | (43,837) | (91,353) | 115,961 |
| NW | (1,619,188) | (1,580,586) | 1,458,538 |
| WC | (603,766) | (42,913) | 269,046 |
| Emp. | 322 | 309 | 295 |

DUNS 50-147-7822

## Springhill Hospice (Rochdale)

Broad Lane, Rochdale, Lancashire OL16 4PZ
**Tel:** 01706649920
**Web:** www.springhill.org.uk
**Reg No:** 2325905 **Estd:** 1988 Private Company Limited By Guarantee
**Line of Business:** Doctors
**Directors:** Dr J A Ransome, Reverend M Davies, S Ali, S C Price, R Mukherjee, J F Dafforne, R Clegg, S Beckwith
**Co. Secretary:** Ian Anderton
**Responsibilities**
**Senior:** Diane Bailey Ginever *(Manager)*, Ian Sandiford *(Director)*
**US SIC:** 8011 **UK SIC:** 95300
**Bankers:** The Royal Bank Of Scotland Plc (83-00-01)

| | 31-03-14 | 31-03-13 | 31-03-12 |
|---|---|---|---|
| TO | 3,461,367 | 3,425,723 | 2,907,550 |
| P/L | 160,237 | 460,672 | 218,555 |
| NW | 6,178,084 | 6,043,644 | 5,582,972 |
| WC | 2,974,547 | 3,708,073 | 3,156,893 |
| Emp. | 112 | 87 | 83 |

DUNS 29-972-8741

## Springhill House (Accrington) Ltd

**(Subsidiary of:** Springhill Care Group Ltd)
Fairfield Street, Accrington, Lancashire BB5 0LD
**Tel:** 01254381719
**Web:** www.springhillcare.com
**Reg No:** 2106218 **Estd:** 1987 Private Limited Company
**Line of Business:** Medical nursing home activities
**Issued Capital:** £100
**Directors:** K A Nolan, Mrs D M Briggs, Ms K A Parkinson
**Co. Secretary:** Ms Nicola Nolan
**US SIC:** 8051, 8321
**UK SIC:** 95100, 96111
**Bankers:** National Westminster Bank Plc (01-00-04)

| | 31-07-13 | 31-01-13 | 31-07-11 |
|---|---|---|---|
| TO | 1,527,038 | 3,171,515 | 1,884,416 |
| P/L | 56,023 | (261,841) | 18,265 |
| NW | 102,158 | 37,097 | 1,692,959 |
| WC | (218,751) | 57,170 | 140,850 |
| Emp. | 132 | 102 | 92 |

DUNS 23-383-4667 **Imp**

## Springisland Supermarket Ltd

**(Subsidiary of:** Springisland Investments Ltd)
2 Washingbay Road, Coalisland, Dungannon, Co Tyrone BT71 4ND
**Tel:** 02887747272
**Web:** www.springislandsupermarket.co.uk
**Reg No:** 0051615NI **Estd:** 1997 Private Limited Company
**Line of Business:** Supermarkets
**Issued Capital:** £4
**Director:** P Rice
**Co. Secretary:** Mrs Roisin Rice
**Responsibilities**
**Senior:** Maria Cushnahan *(Senior Finance Administrator)*, Austin Kelly *(Manager)*

**US SIC:** 5411 **UK SIC:** 64100

| | 30-09-13 | 30-09-12 | 30-09-11 |
|---|---|---|---|
| TA | 2,086,728 | 2,104,614 | 2,070,806 |
| NW | 1,378,762 | 1,293,255 | 1,190,351 |
| WC | 526,311 | 464,632 | 439,646 |

DUNS 22-765-3383 **Imp-Exp**

## Springmasters Ltd

55 Arthur Street, Redditch, Worcestershire B98 8LF
**Tel:** 01527-521000 **Fax:** 01527-528866
**Web:** www.springmasters.com
**Reg No:** 0897155 **VAT No:** 112262912
**Estd:** 1967 Private Limited Company
**Line of Business:** Manufacturers of springs
**Export Markets:** Europe & South Africa
**Export Sales:** £1,432,159
**Issued Capital:** £6,311
**Principals:** I R Whitehead *(Managing)*, D C Clarke *(Sales)*, D N Cartwright, Mrs E Whitehead, J R Hewitt
**Co. Secretary:** Ms Catherine Roberts
**Responsibilities**
**Senior:** Barry Bott *(Warehouse Manager)*, Brian Roberts *(Works Manager)*
**Facilities:** Brian Roberts *(Works Manager)*
**Engineering:** Brian Roberts *(Works Manager)*
**Branches:** Springmasters Ltd, 23 Camus Rd East, Edinburgh, Midlothian EH10 6RE
**US SIC:** 3452 **UK SIC:** 31371
**Auditors:** Rigbey Harrison
**Bankers:** HSBC Bank plc (40-38-07)

| | 31-05-14 | 31-05-13 | 31-05-12 |
|---|---|---|---|
| TO | 7,702,133 | 7,267,395 | 7,219,441 |
| P/L | 1,272,068 | 1,042,806 | 1,325,133 |
| NW | 8,444,758 | 7,623,762 | 6,841,881 |
| WC | 5,084,298 | 5,049,484 | 4,176,708 |
| Emp. | 119 | 115 | 115 |

DUNS 21-774-6822

## Springmead Primary School

Hilly Fields, Welwyn Garden City, Hertfordshire AL7 2HB
**Tel:** 01707331508
**Web:** www.springmead.herts.sch.uk
**Estd:** 1990 Proprietorship
**Line of Business:** Schools (local authority)
**Proprietor:** Ms J Sumner
**US SIC:** 8211 **UK SIC:** 93200
**Employees:** 70

DUNS 77-960-1590

## The Springs Hotel (Thames Valley) Ltd

**(Subsidiary of:** Asus Ag)
1 Wallingford Road, Wallingford, Oxfordshire OX10 6BE
**Tel:** 01491836687
**Web:** www.thespringshotel.com
**Reg No:** 3063541 **Estd:** 1998 Private Limited Company
**Line of Business:** Hotels
**Trading Style:** The Springs Hotel (Thames Valley) Ltd
**Issued Capital:** £575,000
**Directors:** C Bultmann, P E Franklin
**Co. Secretary:** Mrs Svenia Franklin
**Responsibilities**
**Senior:** Ssvenia Franklin *(Director)*
**US SIC:** 7011 **UK SIC:** 66500
**Auditors:** Shaw & Co
**Bankers:** The Royal Bank Of Scotland Plc (16-29-25)

| | 31-03-14 | 31-03-13 | 31-03-12 |
|---|---|---|---|
| TO | N/A | 922,953 | 905,993 |
| P/L | N/A | (109,000) | (87,518) |
| NW | (859,977) | (739,017) | (632,001) |
| WC | (230,464) | (215,658) | (174,957) |

DUNS 21-692-1049 **Exp**

## Springtech Ltd

**(Subsidiary of:** Market+ Ltd)
Unit 1 Fairview Estate, Beech Road, High Wycombe, Buckinghamshire HP11 1RY
**Tel:** 01346518061
**Web:** www.springs.co.uk
**Reg No:** 0915764 **VAT No:** 207931468
**Estd:** 1967 Private Limited Company
**Line of Business:** Manufacture of wire products
**Export Markets:** Europe
**Trading Style:** Springtech Ltd
**Issued Capital:** £52,000
**Directors:** Ms M F Turner, A Turner
**Responsibilities**
**Senior:** Frank Goodall *(General Manager)*, Stuart Montrose *(Group General Manager)*
**Facilities:** Ian Green *(Maintenance Manager)*
**Branches:** Springtech Ltd, Watermill Road, Fraserburgh, Aberdeenshire AB43 9BU
**US SIC:** 3496, 8911, 3469
**UK SIC:** 31694, 83701, 31200
**Auditors:** Eastmond & Co Ltd

**Bankers:** The Royal Bank Of Scotland Plc (16-21-29)

| | 31-12-13 | 31-12-12 | 30-12-11 |
|---|---|---|---|
| TA | 2,713,341 | 2,273,438 | 2,336,836 |
| NW | 1,819,313 | 1,405,838 | 1,218,073 |
| WC | 991,048 | 952,664 | 774,357 |

DUNS 23-976-5659

## Springtown Resourcing Ltd

20 Millhouse Road, Birmingham, West Midlands B25 8QH
**Tel:** 0121-628-5644
**Web:** www.springtown.ltd.uk
**Reg No:** 3965184 **Estd:** 2000 Private Limited Company
**Line of Business:** Other construction work involving special trades
**Issued Capital:** £100
**Director:** J P Smith
**Responsibilities**
**Finance:** Veronica Smith *(Finance Director)*
**US SIC:** 1799 **UK SIC:** 50000
**Auditors:** R K Thomas & Co
**Bankers:** National Westminster Bank Plc (60-06-37)

| | 31-03-14 | 31-03-13 | 31-03-12 |
|---|---|---|---|
| TA | 601,178 | 563,240 | 548,899 |
| NW | 507,521 | 486,521 | 392,973 |
| WC | 165,728 | 178,916 | 288,745 |

DUNS 21-456-4767 **Imp-Exp**

## Springvale Eps Ltd

**(Subsidiary of:** Brand New Co (444) Ltd)
75 Springvale Road, Doagh, Ballyclare, Co Antrim BT39 0SS
**Tel:** 02893340203 **Fax:** 0191 21712129
**Web:** www.springvale.com
**Reg No:** 0001043NI **VAT No:** 422242692
**Estd:** 1996 Private Limited Company
**Line of Business:** Plastic injection moulding
**Export Markets:** Republic of Ireland
**Issued Capital:** £10,000
**Directors:** M S Gilholme, A France
**Co. Secretary:** Neil Tebbutt
**Responsibilities**
**Senior:** Pamela Mccabe *(Manager)*
**Branches:** Springvale Eps Ltd, Dinting Vale Works, Dinting Vale Business Park, Glossop, Derbyshire SK13 6LG
**US SIC:** 3079 **UK SIC:** 48360
**Auditors:** Ernst & Young LLP
**Bankers:** Northern Bank Ltd (95-02-27)

| | 30-06-13 | 30-06-12 | 30-06-11 |
|---|---|---|---|
| TO | 18,688,505 | 14,764,167 | 7,848,313 |
| P/L | 1,579,988 | 1,144,027 | 274,945 |
| NW | 4,138,050 | 2,964,115 | 2,231,741 |
| WC | 3,071,280 | 1,814,603 | 1,106,201 |
| Emp. | 85 | 71 | 91 |

DUNS 42-466-3057 **Imp**

## Springvale Leisure Ltd

711 Manners Avenue, Ilkeston, Derbyshire DE7 8EF
**Tel:** 01159-444533
**Web:** www.springvaleleisure.co.uk
**Reg No:** 4453971 **VAT No:** 797057579
**Estd:** 2001 Private Limited Company
**Line of Business:** Caravan accessories
**Issued Capital:** £165
**Directors:** Ms C Duffield, S J Duffield, J Duffield, Mrs L C Page
**Co. Secretary:** John Hill
**Responsibilities**
**Senior:** Mick Eaves *(Factory Manager)*
**US SIC:** 3792 **UK SIC:** 35230

| | 30-06-14 | 30-06-13 | 30-06-12 |
|---|---|---|---|
| TO | 9,537,491 | 8,140,646 | N/A |
| P/L | 634,211 | 554,441 | N/A |
| NW | 1,061,686 | 916,642 | 623,415 |
| WC | 882,925 | 747,724 | 444,294 |
| Emp. | 129 | 119 | N/A |

DUNS 42-313-1317

## Springvale Training Ltd

200 Springfield Road, Belfast BT12 7DR
**Tel:** 028-9024-2362
**Web:** www.springvalelearning.com
**Reg No:** 0026947NI **Estd:** 1992 Private Limited Company
**Line of Business:** Labour recruitment and provision of personnel
**Issued Capital:** £2
**Directors:** G Mcmahon, Ms T Mckernan, A J Mcferran, E Malone, S O'Prey, Ms N A Wright, S Kennedy
**Co. Secretary:** Kieran Mcconville
**Responsibilities**
**Senior:** Aidan Sloane *(Financial Manager)*
**Finance:** Aidan Sloane *(Financial Manager)*
**HR:** Aidan Sloane *(Financial Manager)*
**Health & Safety:** Aidan Sloane *(Financial Manager)*
**Facilities:** Aidan Sloane *(Financial Manager)*
**Branches:** Springvale Training Ltd, 200 Springfield Road, Belfast, Belfast BT12 7DR
**US SIC:** 7361, 8249
**UK SIC:** 83954, 93300
**Auditors:** BDO Stoy Hayward

**Bankers:** Northern Bank Ltd (95-01-26)

| | 31-03-14 | 31-03-13 | 31-03-12 |
|---|---|---|---|
| TO | 6,649,212 | 5,677,871 | 8,487,597 |
| P/L | 213,133 | (180,922) | 823,442 |
| NW | 3,020,226 | 2,807,093 | 2,988,015 |
| WC | 1,840,953 | 2,343,823 | 2,594,109 |
| Emp. | 83 | 87 | 85 |

DUNS 21-462-6405
## Springwater Lodge
10 Smithy View, Nottingham,
Nottinghamshire NG14 6FA
**Web:** www.hc-one.co.uk
**Estd:** 1995
**Line of Business:** Nursing homes
**Partners:** Mrs S Graham, Mrs S Wright
**US SIC:** 8051 **UK SIC:** 95100
**Employees:** 47

DUNS 21-579-0666
## Springwell Park Community Primary School
Menai Road, Bootle, Merseyside L20 6PG
**Tel:** 01512886054
**Web:** www.springwellparkprimary.co.uk
**Estd:** 2011 Proprietorship
**Line of Business:** Schools (local authority)
**Proprietor:** D Stubbs
**US SIC:** 8211 **UK SIC:** 93200
**Employees:** 50

DUNS 21-500-0404
## Springwood Day Centre
Ransom Drive, Nottingham, Nottinghamshire
NG3 5LR
**Tel:** 01159622611
**Estd:** 1972 Proprietorship
**Line of Business:** Pre school education
**Proprietor:** Ms M Lonergan
**US SIC:** 8321 **UK SIC:** 96111
**Employees:** 60

DUNS 21-688-5500
## Sprint Digital Ltd
4th Floor Salt Quay House, 6 North East
Quay, Sutton Harbour, Plymouth, Devon PL4
0HP
**Tel:** 01209714473
**Web:** www.sprint-digital.com
**Reg No:** 7363157 **VAT No:** 997715452
**Estd:** 2010 Private Limited Company
**Line of Business:** Management and
business consultants
**Issued Capital:** £24
**Directors:** Mrs E M Thomas, J D Williams
**Responsibilities**
**Senior:** Jonathan Duval (Manager)
**US SIC:** 7392 **UK SIC:** 83951

| | 31-07-13 | 31-07-12 | 31-07-11 |
|---|---|---|---|
| TA | 28,498 | 45,407 | 44,813 |
| NW | 19,549 | 1,606 | 7,997 |
| WC | 18,416 | 1,293 | 7,997 |

DUNS 23-940-4135 **Imp**
## Sprintlink U K Ltd
(**Subsidiary of:** Softbank Corp.)
Grand Building, 1-3 Strand, London WC2N
5EJ
**Tel:** 02071521500
**Web:** www.sprint.com
**Reg No:** 3930041 **Estd:** 2000 Private
Limited Company
**Line of Business:** Telecommunications
**Issued Capital:** £2
**Director:** S K Schnopp
**US SIC:** 4899 **UK SIC:** 79020
**Auditors:** KPMG

| | 31-03-14 | 31-12-12 | 31-03-11 |
|---|---|---|---|
| TO | 22,929,197 | 17,617,397 | 19,407,766 |
| P/L | 477,142 | 364,460 | 455,781 |
| NW | (3,478,813) | (3,840,552) | (4,047,369) |
| WC | 9,095,480 | 8,473,119 | 10,366,590 |
| Emp. | 55 | 52 | 49 |

DUNS 21-118-8100
## Sprite Consultancy Ltd
(**Subsidiary of:** Boss Projects Llp)
Oak House Shackleford Road, Elstead,
Godalming, Surrey GU8 6LB
**Tel:** 08456430600 **Fax:** 01189560380
**Web:** www.sprite-services.com
**Reg No:** 6583204 **Estd:** 1995 Private
Limited Company
**Line of Business:** Business and
management consultancy activities not
elsewhere classified
**Issued Capital:** £666
**Directors:** P M Squire, Ms S L Crinson,
B J Sitch-Oliver
**Co. Secretary:** Benjamin Sitch-Oliver
**Responsibilities**
**Senior:** James Gregg (Manager)
**US SIC:** 8931 **UK SIC:** 83600

**Auditors:** Faust Loveday Bell LLP

| | 31-03-14 | 31-05-13 | 31-03-12 |
|---|---|---|---|
| TO | 32,826,339 | 41,227,005 | 43,167,169 |
| P/L | 545,314 | 45,563 | 210,686 |
| NW | 502,983 | 201,091 | 164,399 |
| WC | 502,983 | 201,091 | 164,399 |
| Emp. | 1,412 | 1,466 | 1,509 |

DUNS 51-984-4703 **Imp**
## Sprue Aegis Plc
The Techno Centre, Coventry University
Technology Park, Puma Way, Coventry,
West Midlands CV1 2TS
**Tel:** 02476323232 **Fax:** 024-7623-6603
**Web:** www.fireangel.co.uk
**Reg No:** 3991353 **Estd:** 2000 Public Limited
Company
**Line of Business:** Wholesale of radio and
television goods; wholesale of electrical
household appliances not elsewhere
classified
**Issued Capital:** £773,707
**Directors:** A V Silverton, G R Whitworth,
N A Rutter, P J Lawrence, J R Gahan,
T J Russo
**Co. Secretary:** William Payne
**US SIC:** 5064, 5732
**UK SIC:** 61500, 64800
**Auditors:** Baker Tilly UK Audit LLP

| | 31-12-13 | 31-12-12 | 31-12-11 |
|---|---|---|---|
| TO | 48,357,000 | 37,214,000 | 33,275,000 |
| P/L | 4,872,000 | 3,177,000 | 3,422,000 |
| NW | 11,530,000 | 9,327,000 | 7,972,000 |
| WC | 12,430,000 | 9,570,000 | 8,546,000 |
| Emp. | 112 | 85 | 73 |

DUNS 29-583-9823 **Imp-Exp**
## Sps Aerostructures Ltd
(**Subsidiary of:** S P S Technologies Ltd)
Unit 21a Willow Drive, Annesley, Nottingham,
Nottinghamshire NG15 0DP
**Tel:** 01159-880000
**Web:** www.spstech.com
**Reg No:** 1945689 **VAT No:** 697448470
**Estd:** 1986 Private Limited Company
**Line of Business:** Manufacture of metal
structures and parts of structures
**Export Markets:** U S A
**Export Sales:** £4,248,000
**Issued Capital:** £1,960,484
**Directors:** Ms R A Beyer, J Snowden,
A V Masterman, R S Pattee, R P Becker,
S C Blackmore, Mrs S R Hagel
**Co. Secretary:** Mrs Monika Bailey
**Responsibilities**
**Senior:** Monika Frankow (Manager), Mike
Quinn (Manager)
**HR:** bob crowley (Human resources
manager)
**US SIC:** 3441 **UK SIC:** 32042
**Auditors:** Deloitte LLP

| | 31-03-14 | 31-03-13 | 31-03-12 |
|---|---|---|---|
| TO | 100,376,000 | 91,401,000 | 83,049,000 |
| P/L | 19,614,000 | 16,762,000 | 12,751,000 |
| NW | 49,860,000 | 33,805,000 | 20,933,000 |
| WC | 31,218,000 | 13,909,000 | 2,150,000 |
| Emp. | 637 | 644 | 559 |

DUNS 50-000-0740
## Sps Doorguard Ltd
296 St Vincent Street, Glasgow, Lanarkshire
G2 5RU
**Tel:** 01412432424 **Fax:** 0141-243-2221
**Web:** www.spsdoorguard.com
**Reg No:** 0113186SC **Estd:** 1988 Private
Limited Company
**Line of Business:** Property maintenance
services
**Issued Capital:** £5,000
**Directors:** Ms S J Duffus, R Gilliland,
A M Duffus, J Mcbride
**Co. Secretary:** Ms Gail Morrison
**Responsibilities**
**Senior:** Arthur Cronan (Marketing Manager)
**Branches:** Sps Doorguard Ltd, 14 Colville
Court, Warrington, Cheshire WA2 8QT
**US SIC:** 1799 **UK SIC:** 50000
**Auditors:** Bannerman Johnstone Maclay
**Bankers:** Lloyds Tsb Scotland Plc (30-18-05)

| | 30-06-13 | 30-06-12 | 30-06-11 |
|---|---|---|---|
| TO | 5,848,341 | 6,194,011 | 6,416,641 |
| P/L | 214,351 | 117,214 | 192,023 |
| NW | 5,185,738 | 5,023,981 | 4,954,746 |
| WC | 4,178,725 | 4,120,925 | 3,967,012 |
| Emp. | 80 | 88 | 84 |

DUNS 50-570-1508 **Imp**
## Sps (Eu) Ltd
(**Subsidiary of:** Gateley Llp)
Neptune House, Blackpool, Lancashire FY4
3RL
**Tel:** 01253340400 **Fax:** 01253-340401
**Web:** www.sps-eu.co.uk
**Reg No:** 2518132 **Estd:** 1990 Private
Limited Company
**Line of Business:** Clothing retailers
**Export Sales:** £1,544,000
**Trading Style:** Supreme, Supreme Plastics
**Issued Capital:** £1,000,000
**Directors:** Ms S J Brownley, Ms D Anderton,
R M Wildsmith, P J Morgan
**Co. Secretary:** Ms Sharon Brownley

**US SIC:** 5699, 3861
**UK SIC:** 64500, 37330
**Auditors:** PricewaterhouseCoopers LLP
**Bankers:** HSBC Bank plc (40-12-06)

| | 28-12-13 | 29-12-12 | 31-12-11 |
|---|---|---|---|
| TO | 16,911,000 | 15,517,000 | 14,221,000 |
| P/L | 116,000 | 593,000 | (3,832,000) |
| NW | 3,480,000 | 3,378,000 | 2,705,000 |
| WC | 3,134,000 | 1,919,000 | 1,611,000 |
| Emp. | 214 | 199 | 193 |

DUNS 34-594-5778
## Sps Security Ltd
(**Subsidiary of:** Millwood Investments Ltd)
Neptune House, Omega Business Park,
Neptune Street, Hull, North Humberside HU3
2BP
**Tel:** 01482-226570 **Fax:** 01482215528
**Web:** www.sps-security.com
**Reg No:** 2738677 **Estd:** 1992 Private
Limited Company
**Line of Business:** Security activities
**Trading Style:** S P S Security
**Issued Capital:** £80,000
**Directors:** J R Beharrell, A J Ford,
A J Beharrell
**Responsibilities**
**Senior:** Lesley Beharrell (Manager)
**US SIC:** 7393 **UK SIC:** 83954
**Auditors:** Dutton Moore Atkin Gilbert

| | 31-01-14 | 31-01-13 | 31-01-12 |
|---|---|---|---|
| TA | 2,402,934 | 2,171,066 | 2,456,891 |
| NW | 810,672 | 731,610 | 659,053 |
| WC | 751,878 | 723,630 | 691,279 |

DUNS 21-727-1871 **Imp-Exp**
## Spts Technologies Group Ltd
(**Subsidiary of:** Orbotech Ltd.)
Coed Rhedyn, Ringland Way, Newport,
Gwent NP18 2TA
**Tel:** 01633 414000 **Fax:** 01633 414141
**Web:** www.spts.com
**Reg No:** 7635249 **Estd:** 2011 Private
Limited Company
**Line of Business:** Manufacture of other
electrical equipment not elsewhere classified
**Trading Style:** Spts
**Directors:** A Steimberg, K T Crofton, A Levy,
D Abramovitch, R J Rees
**Co. Secretary:** Richard Craven
**US SIC:** 3629 **UK SIC:** 34350
**Auditors:** Ernst & Young LLP
**Employees:** 472
**Turnover:** £155,709,000

DUNS 52-532-9645
## Spudulike Group Ltd
9 Central Business Centre, Great Central
Way, London NW10 0UR
**Tel:** 020-8830-2424
**Web:** www.spudulike.com
**Reg No:** 3237548 **Estd:** 1996 Private
Limited Company
**Line of Business:** Restaurant - ethiopian
**Trading Style:** Spud U Like
**Issued Capital:** £5,000
**Managing Director:** A P Schlesinger
**Co. Secretary:** Peter Banks
**Branches:** Spudulike Group Ltd, The Food
Court, 5 Royal Victoria Place Shopping
Centre, Tunbridge Wells, Kent TN1 2SP
**US SIC:** 5812 **UK SIC:** 66110
**Auditors:** Nexia Audit Ltd

| | 02-01-14 | 27-12-12 | 29-01-11 |
|---|---|---|---|
| TO | 14,944,253 | 15,660,071 | 16,981,266 |
| P/L | (733,492) | (284,546) | 247,653 |
| NW | 3,692,269 | 4,298,107 | 4,455,020 |
| WC | 514,724 | 897,268 | 783,178 |
| Emp. | 437 | 461 | 476 |

DUNS 50-468-5942
## Spur Lodge Ltd
Avonmore Mansions, Avonmore Road,
London W14 8RN
**Tel:** 02076006837
**Reg No:** 2447537 **Estd:** 1989 Private
Limited Company
**Line of Business:** Investment consultants
**Issued Capital:** £2
**Directors:** Mrs J Reeves, A Reeves
**Co. Secretary:** Eldine Wilson
**US SIC:** 7399, 7361
**UK SIC:** 83954
**Auditors:** Kingston Smith

| | 31-12-13 | 31-12-12 | 31-12-11 |
|---|---|---|---|
| TO | N/A | N/A | 74,969 |
| P/L | N/A | N/A | 5,651 |
| NW | 160,814 | 235,337 | 284,967 |
| WC | 129,980 | 197,969 | 208,779 |

DUNS 51-983-5461
## Spurgeons
74 Wellingborough Road, Rushden,
Northamptonshire NN10 9TY
**Tel:** 01933412412
**Web:** www.spurgeons.org
**Reg No:** 3990460 **Estd:** 1967 Private
Company Limited By Guarantee
**Line of Business:** Social work activities
without accommodation

**Trading Style:** Footsteps Nursery
**Directors:** S Beresford, Mrs N T Cronin,
J Singlehurst, T M Elgar, Mrs C A Russell,
S J Cornwell, Mrs C Burns, A R Gilbert
**Co. Secretary:** Andrew Owst
**Responsibilities**
**Senior:** Ruth Vincent (Director)
**Branches:** Spurgeons, 55 Silver Street,
Manchester M44 6HT
**US SIC:** 8321 **UK SIC:** 96111
**Auditors:** Haysmacintyre

| | 31-03-14 | 31-03-13 | 31-03-12 |
|---|---|---|---|
| TO | 17,115,000 | 18,161,000 | 13,678,000 |
| P/L | 179,000 | (2,000) | (1,245,000) |
| NW | 13,310,000 | 8,891,000 | 8,465,000 |
| WC | 2,074,000 | 2,037,000 | 1,083,000 |
| Emp. | 456 | 703 | 420 |

DUNS 22-069-9230
## Spw Secretaries Ltd
Gable House, 239 Regents Park Road,
London N3 3LF
**Tel:** 02083715000
**Web:** www.spwca.com
**Reg No:** 4071431 **Estd:** 1945 Private
Limited Company
**Line of Business:** Accounting activities
**Trading Style:** Spw
**Issued Capital:** £1
**Directors:** Ms C R Shah, S A Shah,
D L Platt, P J Winter
**Co. Secretary:** Harold Sorsky
**Responsibilities**
**Admin:** Linda Fletcher (Office Manager)
**US SIC:** 8931 **UK SIC:** 83600

| | 30-09-13 | 30-09-12 | 30-09-11 |
|---|---|---|---|
| TA | 1 | 1 | 1 |
| NW | 1 | 1 | 1 |

DUNS 21-727-2194 **Imp-Exp**
## Spx Flow Technology Crawley Ltd
(**Subsidiary of:** Spx Corporation)
Unit 3 Wheatstone Close, Crawley, West
Sussex RH10 9UA
**Tel:** 01293527777
**Web:** www.spx.com
**Reg No:** 0068014 **Estd:** 1900 Private
Limited Company
**Line of Business:** Manufacture of machinery
for food, beverage and tobacco processing
**Export Markets:** Africa; Australasia; W
Europe; S & S E Asia; U S A; Canada; S
America
**Export Sales:** £423,000
**Trading Style:** Spx Flow Technology,
Invensys Apv
**Issued Capital:** £52,644,443
**Directors:** K L Lilly, M A Reilly, J W Smeltser
**Co. Secretary:** Eversecretary Limited
**Responsibilities**
**Senior:** Patrick O'leary (Executive Vice
President), Barbara Pitts (Operations
Manager)
**Branches:** Spx Flow Technology Crawley
Ltd, Bernic Security Ltd, 22 Lorn St,
Birkenhead, Merseyside CH41 6AR
**US SIC:** 3551 **UK SIC:** 32441
**Auditors:** Deloitte LLP
**Bankers:** Lloyds TSB Bank plc (30-00-02)

| | 31-12-13 | 31-12-12 | 31-12-11 |
|---|---|---|---|
| TO | 29,462,000 | 26,096,000 | 20,214,000 |
| P/L | 1,520,000 | 2,413,000 | (1,692,000) |
| NW | 10,235,000 | 8,715,000 | 6,302,000 |
| WC | 12,141,000 | 10,085,000 | 7,651,000 |
| Emp. | 50 | 43 | 43 |

DUNS 34-857-2496 **Imp-Exp**
## Spx Flow Technology Ltd
(**Subsidiary of:** Spx International Eg)
Ironstone Way, Brixworth, Northampton,
Northamptonshire NN6 9UD
**Tel:** 01604-880-751 **Fax:** 01604-880-145
**Web:** www.spxprocessequipment.com
**Reg No:** 2813467 **VAT No:** 119163381
**Estd:** 1966 Private Limited Company
**Line of Business:** Manufacture of electronic
instruments and appliances for measuring,
checking, testing, navigating and other
purposes, except industrial process control
equipment
**Export Markets:** Europe, Africa, America,
Asia, Australasia
**Export Sales:** £23,227,000
**Issued Capital:** £200,001
**Directors:** J Fisher, M A Reilly, K L Lilly,
J W Smeltser
**Co. Secretary:** Eversecretary Limited
**Responsibilities**
**Senior:** Neil Prapp (Team Leader)
**IT:** Joe Knapman (Vice President Information
Tec)
**Operations:** Stuart Muffit (Technical,
Production Manager)
**Branches:** Spx Flow Technology Limited, 8-
14 Earl Haig Road, Glasgow, Lanarkshire
G52 4JN
**US SIC:** 3829, 3561
**UK SIC:** 37100, 32870
**Auditors:** Deloitte LLP

**Bankers:** HSBC Bank plc (40-35-46)

| | 31-12-13 | 31-12-12 | 31-12-11 |
|---|---|---|---|
| TO | 46,888,000 | 33,336,000 | 40,157,000 |
| P/L | 2,736,000 | 1,378,000 | 2,539,000 |
| NW | 21,881,000 | 19,191,000 | 18,737,000 |
| WC | 21,512,000 | 18,914,000 | 18,162,000 |
| Emp. | 143 | 141 | 143 |

DUNS 21-804-2315 **Imp-Exp**

## Spx International Ltd

**(Subsidiary of:** Spx Corporation)
Plenty House, Hambridge Road, Newbury, Berkshire RG14 5TR
**Tel:** 0163542363 **Fax:** 01635497583
**Web:** www.spxft.com
**Reg No:** 0517486 **VAT No:** 765367006
**Estd:** 1924 Private Limited Company
**Line of Business:** Manufacture of instruments and appliances for measuring, checking, testing, navigating and other purposes, except industrial process control equipment
**Export Markets:** E U, Middle East, Africa, N & S America, Far East, Australasia and Asia.
**Export Sales:** £40,153,000
**Trading Style:** S P X Flow Technology, Copes-Vulcan, G D Engineering, Airpel Plenty Filters Plenty Process Filtration
**Issued Capital:** £301,538
**Directors:** B Sohal, M E Shanahan, J W Smeltser
**Co. Secretary:** Kevin Lilly
**Branches:** Spx International Ltd, Unit 7 Thames Gateway Choats Road, Dagenham, Essex RM9 6RJ
**US SIC:** 3999 **UK SIC:** 49590
**Auditors:** Deloitte LLP
**Bankers:** Bank Of America, Na (16-50-50)

| | 31-12-13 | 31-12-12 | 31-12-11 |
|---|---|---|---|
| TO | 71,815,000 | 77,926,000 | 57,500,000 |
| P/L | 15,607,000 | 14,377,000 | 8,113,000 |
| NW | 106,719,000 | 89,895,000 | 76,230,000 |
| WC | 92,409,000 | 75,155,000 | 60,664,000 |
| Emp. | 269 | 270 | 265 |

DUNS 50-020-5067

## Spz Holdings Ltd

8-10 Basing Street, London W11 1DG
**Tel:** 02072291229
**Web:** www.spz.com
**Reg No:** 2301116 **Estd:** 1988 Private Limited Company
**Line of Business:** Performing arts management and promotion
**Issued Capital:** £100,000
**Directors:** A Horn, T C Horn, Ms A J Horn
**Responsibilities**
**Senior:** Julie Bateman *(Manager)*
**Finance:** Julian Lyons *(Financial Director)*
**Engineering:** Vicky Ball *(Production Manager)*
**US SIC:** 8999, 7399
**UK SIC:** 83954
**Auditors:** Kingston Smith
**Bankers:** Coutts & Co (18-00-12)

| | 31-10-13 | 31-10-12 | 31-10-11 |
|---|---|---|---|
| TO | 5,524,238 | 5,991,629 | 6,230,630 |
| P/L | (556,763) | (374,528) | (362,420) |
| NW | (2,074,189) | (1,707,269) | (1,370,596) |
| WC | 547,744 | 1,069,554 | (1,529,053) |
| Emp. | N/A | 38 | 59 |

DUNS 22-051-6111

## Sq Computer Personnel Ltd

1 Cresswell Park, London SE3 9RD
**Tel:** 020-8463-0555 **Fax:** 020-8463-0444
**Web:** www.sqcp.com
**Reg No:** 4053700 **Estd:** 2000 Private Limited Company
**Line of Business:** Labour recruitment and provision of personnel
**Issued Capital:** £1,700
**Directors:** J Fay, Homes Management Group Limited, D Ward, Miss C S Cooke
**Co. Secretary:** Bernard Potton
**Responsibilities**
**Senior:** Polyana Lenkic *(Partner)*
**Finance:** Jodie Moriarty *(Accounts Assistant)*, Ashley Nowell *(Financial Analyst)*, Stacey Rhodes *(Accounts Assistant)*
**Marketing:** Anthony Gardiner *(Manager)*
**Sales:** Matt Chesterman *(Senior Account Manager)*, William Chu *(Account Manager)*, Cliff Eton *(Recruitment Consultant)*, Marc Gumbrell *(Business Development Manager)*, Tessa Heywood *(Sales Executive)*, Nikki Leinster *(Resources)*, Jodie Moriarty *(Accounts Assistant)*, Ashley Nowell *(Financial Analyst)*, Jenny Probert *(Account Manager)*, Stacey Rhodes *(Accounts Assistant)*, Jamie Sears *(Sales Manager)*, Peter Springett *(Account Manager)*
**Admin:** Sarah Crane *(Administrative Assistant)*, Guy Green *(Administrative Assistant, Info)*, Chris Mortlock *(Administrative Assistant, Info)*, Jack Sharp *(Administrator)*
**IT:** Rian Pachonick *(IT Manager)*
**HR:** Louise Banyton *(Recruitment Consultant)*, Cliff Eton *(Recruitment Consultant)*, Nikki Leinster *(Resources)*, Gemma McDonald *(Recruitment Consultant)*
**US SIC:** 7361 **UK SIC:** 83954
**Auditors:** Haines Watts
**Bankers:** National Westminster Bank Plc (60-08-46)

| | 31-10-13 | 31-10-12 | 31-10-11 |
|---|---|---|---|
| TO | 20,278,854 | 23,226,272 | 26,479,290 |
| P/L | 67,809 | 276,907 | (1,089,118) |
| NW | 259,535 | 131,930 | (218,172) |
| WC | 215,090 | 71,339 | (299,391) |
| Emp. | 50 | 52 | 54 |

DUNS 23-866-3699

## Sqs Group Ltd

**(Subsidiary of:** Sqs Software Quality Systems Ag)
Basildon House, 7-11 Moorgate, London EC2R 6AF
**Tel:** 07795114053 **Fax:** 020-7448-4651
**Web:** www.sqs.com
**Reg No:** 3857864 **Estd:** 1999 Private Limited Company
**Line of Business:** It consultants
**Export Sales:** £5,394,619
**Trading Style:** Sqs Group Ltd
**Issued Capital:** £173,241
**Directors:** R F Gillessen, Ms C A Truyens, P J Codd, R Gawron, P N Tomblin
**Co. Secretary:** Ms Deborah Futcher
**Responsibilities**
**Senior:** Stephen Fice *(Manager)*
**IT:** Phil Jack *(IT Manager)*
**HR:** Kirsty Parnell *(Training Manager)*, Julie Wells *(Operations Manager)*
**Health & Safety:** Julie Wells *(Operations Manager)*
**Facilities:** Julie Wells *(Operations Manager)*
**US SIC:** 7379 **UK SIC:** 83940
**Auditors:** Grant Thornton UK LLP
**Bankers:** Lloyds TSB Bank plc (30-95-74)

| | 31-12-13 | 31-12-12 | 31-12-11 |
|---|---|---|---|
| TO | 44,646,604 | 43,989,958 | 44,526,000 |
| P/L | 957,615 | 2,194,457 | 2,513,000 |
| NW | 6,342,718 | 7,423,217 | 7,507,000 |
| WC | 6,106,659 | 7,165,342 | 7,130,000 |
| Emp. | 481 | 480 | 463 |

DUNS 34-558-3020

## Squad Security Ltd

1 Kings Park, Primrose Hill, King's Langley, Hertfordshire WD4 8ST
**Tel:** 02033-845-387 **Fax:** 01923-220-801
**Web:** www.squadsecurity.co.uk
**Reg No:** 5368069 **Estd:** 2005 Private Limited Company
**Line of Business:** Security and related activities
**Export Sales:** £4,828,679
**Trading Style:** Bespoke Security Solutions
**Issued Capital:** £100
**Director:** M Sapraicone
**Co. Secretary:** John Bullimore
**Responsibilities**
**Senior:** Dave Herbert *(Business Manager)*
**US SIC:** 7393 **UK SIC:** 83954
**Auditors:** A. Mitra & Co

| | 31-12-13 | 31-12-12 | 31-12-11 |
|---|---|---|---|
| TO | 7,052,924 | 9,204,771 | N/A |
| P/L | 1,019,093 | 1,985,494 | N/A |
| NW | 1,267,099 | 1,303,785 | 595,190 |
| WC | 907,324 | 950,312 | 353,098 |
| Emp. | 86 | 109 | N/A |

DUNS 49-072-0455 **Imp**

## Squadron Medical Ltd

**(Subsidiary of:** Dcc Plc)
Greaves Close, Markham Vale, Chesterfield, Derbyshire S44 5FB
**Tel:** 01246822822 **Fax:** 01246-284030
**Web:** www.squadronmedical.co.uk
**Reg No:** 3081982 **VAT No:** 646606034
**Estd:** 2012 Private Limited Company
**Line of Business:** Take-away food shops
**Trading Style:** Squadron Medical Limited
**Issued Capital:** £670,000
**Directors:** R Mcevoy, C Costigan, P Tracey, K Pritchard
**Co. Secretary:** Leslie Deacon
**Responsibilities**
**Senior:** Andrew O' Connell *(Manager)*, Ian O' Donovan *(Manager)*
**Operations:** Andrew Luczko *(Operations Project Manager)*
**US SIC:** 5812, 5122
**UK SIC:** 66110, 61800
**Auditors:** PricewaterhouseCoopers LLP
**Bankers:** National Westminster Bank Plc (56-00-09)

| | 31-03-14 | 31-03-13 | 31-03-12 |
|---|---|---|---|
| TO | 54,250,000 | 53,002,000 | 51,749,000 |
| P/L | 652,000 | 259,000 | 282,000 |
| NW | 5,834,000 | 5,340,000 | 5,179,000 |
| WC | 2,077,000 | 1,408,000 | 947,000 |
| Emp. | 69 | 71 | 71 |

DUNS 76-999-2256

## Square Deal Motors Ltd

Ladysmill, Falkirk, Stirlingshire FK2 9AU
**Tel:** 01324635935
**Web:** www.sdm-group.co.uk
**Reg No:** 0134473SC **Estd:** 1965 Private Limited Company
**Line of Business:** Car accessories and parts
**Trading Style:** S D M Group, S D M Mazda, S D M Toyota, S D M Hyundi
**Issued Capital:** £986,000
**Directors:** B Aitken, Ms H Aitken, C A Clark, D Aitken
**Co. Secretary:** Colin Clark
**Responsibilities**
**Senior:** Raymond Dempsey *(Centre Principal)*, Alastair Elrick *(Manager)*, Peter Mcgregor *(Parts Manager)*
**Branches:** Square Deal Motors Ltd, 4 Middlefield Industrial Estate, Middlefield Road, Falkirk, Stirlingshire FK2 9ZD
**US SIC:** 5531, 5521
**UK SIC:** 65100
**Auditors:** Grant Thornton
**Bankers:** The Royal Bank Of Scotland Plc (83-20-32)

| | 31-12-13 | 31-12-12 | 31-12-11 |
|---|---|---|---|
| TO | 26,810,406 | 26,726,380 | 23,749,248 |
| P/L | 102,849 | 187,074 | 68,644 |
| NW | 5,810,632 | 6,776,506 | 6,689,688 |
| WC | 1,923,869 | 1,826,356 | 1,655,920 |
| Emp. | 94 | 98 | 100 |

DUNS 22-730-6925 **Imp-Exp**

## Square Enix Ltd

**(Subsidiary of:** Square Enix Holdings Co. Ltd.)
240 Blackfriars Road, London SE1 8NW
**Tel:** 02086-363-000 **Fax:** 02086-383-001
**Web:** www.square-enix.com
**Reg No:** 1804186 **Estd:** 1984 Private Limited Company
**Line of Business:** Computer software (development)
**Export Markets:** Worldwide
**Export Sales:** £130,591,000
**Issued Capital:** £111,902,082
**Directors:** P T Rogers, M Sherlock
**Co. Secretary:** Ms Charlotte Osborne
**Responsibilities**
**Senior:** Robert Brent *(Manager)*, Hans-juergen Goeldner *(Manager)*
**Marketing:** Ben Cusack *(Marketing Director)*, Chris Glover *(?Vice President Communications)*, Sarah Hoeksma *(VP Brand & Marketing - Live Di)*
**Sales:** Fabien Rossini *(Group Strategic Planning Direc)*
**Branches:** Square Enix Ltd, Unit 2, 4 Holford Way, Birmingham, West Midlands B6 7AX
**US SIC:** 2741 **UK SIC:** 47541
**Auditors:** Ernst & Young LLP
**Bankers:** Lloyds TSB Bank plc (30-00-08)

| | 31-03-13 | 31-03-12 | 31-03-11 |
|---|---|---|---|
| TO | 171,743,000 | 63,799,000 | 56,199,000 |
| P/L | (39,930,000) | (20,546,000) | (10,655,000) |
| NW | (218,637,000) | (178,678,000) | (158,110,000) |
| WC | (269,393,000) | (230,031,000) | (209,022,000) |
| Emp. | 207 | 189 | 192 |

DUNS 21-714-3969

## Square One Law Llp

Anson House Fleming Business Centre, Burdon Terrace, Newcastle-Upon-Tyne, Tyne and Wear NE2 3AE
**Tel:** 08432247900
**Web:** www.squareonelaw.com
**Reg No:** 0362083OC **Estd:** 2011
**Line of Business:** Solicitors
**Responsibilities**
**Senior:** Francesca Angelucci *(Non-designated Limited Liabili)*, Anita Swift *(Head Of Client Services)*, Simon Winskell *(Designated Limited Liability P)*
**US SIC:** 8999 **UK SIC:** 83954

| | 30-04-14 | 30-04-13 | 30-04-12 |
|---|---|---|---|
| TA | 1,682,736 | 1,300,797 | 818,635 |
| NW | 516,751 | 587,500 | 402,300 |
| WC | 945,029 | 753,659 | 559,250 |

DUNS 49-141-0288 **Exp**

## Square One Resources Ltd

**(Subsidiary of:** Square One Holdings Ltd)
6 Devonshire Square, London EC2M 4YE
**Tel:** 020-7208-2828 **Fax:** 020-7208-2838
**Web:** www.squareoneresources.com
**Reg No:** 3110911 **VAT No:** 661856118
**Estd:** 1995 Private Limited Company
**Line of Business:** Employment and recruitment companies and consultants
**Export Markets:** European Union (E U)
**Export Sales:** £22,254,000
**Issued Capital:** £1,608
**Principals:** P S Hanikene *(Managing)*, M R Rush, T J Harlow, S Walker
**Co. Secretary:** Gavin Gaskin
**Responsibilities**
**Marketing:** Lisa Fynch *(Marketing Manager)*
**Sales:** Adam Breacher *(Sales Manager)*, Jonathan Brewer *(SAP Sales Consultant)*
**IT:** Danny Cater *(IT Manager)*, Tariq Raheman *(Senior Infrastructure Consulta)*
**US SIC:** 7361 **UK SIC:** 83954
**Auditors:** Grant Thornton UK LLP
**Bankers:** Lloyds TSB Bank plc (30-93-23)

| | 30-06-14 | 30-06-13 | 30-06-12 |
|---|---|---|---|
| TO | 64,400,000 | 66,977,000 | 70,765,000 |
| P/L | 1,310,000 | 1,601,000 | 1,635,000 |
| NW | 4,813,000 | 4,911,000 | 4,709,000 |
| WC | 3,840,000 | 3,810,000 | 3,432,000 |
| Emp. | 104 | 105 | 106 |

DUNS 21-152-3063

## Squibb Group Ltd

62 River Road, Barking, Essex IG11 0DS
**Tel:** 02085947143
**Web:** www.squibbgroup.co.uk
**Reg No:** 1058215 **VAT No:** 247271655
**Estd:** 2010 Private Limited Company
**Line of Business:** Demolition contractors
**Issued Capital:** £50,000
**Principals:** L Squibb *(Managing)*, P W Hamilton, L M Smith, P G Ashfield, W J Squibb, M J Luchford, R S Parcell, J E Symons
**Co. Secretary:** Leslie Squibb
**Responsibilities**
**Senior:** Paul Blanks *(General Manager)*
**Branches:** Squibb Group Ltd, 62 River Rd, Barking, Essex IG11 0DS
**US SIC:** 1795, 1541
**UK SIC:** 50000, 50100
**Auditors:** ESW Ltd
**Bankers:** National Westminster Bank Plc (60-06-33)

| | 31-01-14 | 31-01-13 | 31-01-12 |
|---|---|---|---|
| TO | 30,049,418 | 22,639,469 | 22,520,226 |
| P/L | 1,530,038 | 536,981 | 653,087 |
| NW | 8,144,803 | 7,163,828 | 6,907,349 |
| WC | 2,158,287 | 2,322,945 | 2,259,911 |
| Emp. | 177 | 167 | 146 |

DUNS 45-805-0424

## Squid Ltd

Trafalgar Way, Cambridge, Cambridgeshire CB23 8TU
**Fax:** 01954-782874
**Web:** www.domino-printing.com
**Reg No:** 3163001 **Estd:** 1978 Private Limited Company
**Line of Business:** Manufacture of other electrical equipment not elsewhere classified
**Trading Style:** Domino Printing Sciences
**Issued Capital:** £2
**Director:** A C Herbert
**Co. Secretary:** Richard Pryn
**US SIC:** 3629 **UK SIC:** 34350

| | 31-10-13 | 31-10-12 | 31-10-11 |
|---|---|---|---|
| TA | 2 | 30,282,844 | 30,282,844 |
| P/L | (30,369,768) | (312,209) | (439,646) |
| NW | (31,121,621) | (751,853) | (439,644) |
| WC | (31,121,621) | (31,034,695) | (30,722,486) |

DUNS 21-597-5967

## Squire Furneaux

Petersfield Avenue, Slough, Berkshire SL2 5EF
**Tel:** 01753-523031
**Web:** www.squirefurneaux.co.uk
**Estd:** 1980 Partnership
**Line of Business:** Car dealers (new & used)
**Partner:** M Squires
**Responsibilities**
**Senior:** Mark Squire *(Dealer Principal)*, Steve Stone *(Sales Manager)*
**Sales:** Franco Longorbadi *(Sales Manager)*, Steve Stone *(Sales Manager)*
**Health & Safety:** Tim Fairminer *(After Sales Manager)*
**Operations:** Tim Fairminer *(After Sales Manager)*
**US SIC:** 5511 **UK SIC:** 65100
**Employees:** 50

DUNS 21-615-5721

## Squire Furneaux Cobham Ltd

**(Subsidiary of:** Grafise Holdings Ltd)
Riverdene Business Park, Molesey Road, Hersham, Walton-On-Thames, Surrey KT12 4RG
**Tel:** 01932222382
**Web:** www.squirefurneaux.co.uk
**Reg No:** 0457299 **Estd:** 1948 Private Limited Company
**Line of Business:** Car dealers (new & used)
**Issued Capital:** £37,200
**Directors:** P Nott, C A Slaughter
**Responsibilities**
**Senior:** Nigel Furneaux *(Manager)*, Lionel Squire *(Managing Director, Director)*, Andy Stone *(Service Manager)*, Brian Watts *(Parts Manager)*
**Finance:** Lesley Richardson *(Accountant)*
**IT:** Jeff Seaman *(IT Manager)*
**Facilities:** Brian Higgin *(Workshop Manager)*
**Operations:** Andy Stone *(Service Manager)*
**Engineering:** Brian Higgin *(Workshop Manager)*
**Branches:** Squire Furneaux Cobham Ltd, 87 Portsmouth Rd, Cobham, Surrey KT11 1JH

**US SIC:** 5511 **UK SIC:** 65100
**Auditors:** Mark Holt & Co Ltd
**Bankers:** National Westminster Bank Plc (60-23-34)

| | 31-12-13 | 31-12-12 | 31-12-11 |
|---|---|---|---|
| TO | 29,517,317 | 31,899,970 | 33,466,314 |
| P/L | 447,606 | 545,894 | 608,235 |
| NW | 2,693,720 | 2,346,041 | 1,927,755 |
| WC | 1,345,836 | 1,063,630 | 697,507 |
| Emp. | 87 | 87 | 87 |

DUNS 21-781-6905
## Squire Furneaux Leatherhead
7 Barnett Wood Lane, Leatherhead, Surrey KT22 7DL
**Tel:** 08442097998
**Web:** www.squirefurneaux.co.uk
**Estd:** 2001 Partnership
**Line of Business:** Sale of new motor vehicles
**Partners:** R Emerson, M Brior
**Responsibilities**
**Senior:** Nigel Furneaux *(Manager)*
**US SIC:** 5511 **UK SIC:** 65100
**Employees:** 89

DUNS 21-620-8520
## Squire Furneaux Maidenhead Ltd
(**Subsidiary of:** Grafise Holdings Ltd)
80 Norden Road, Maidenhead, Berkshire SL6 4BD
**Tel:** 01628680066
**Web:** www.squirefurneaux.co.uk
**Reg No:** 0623743 **Estd:** 1956 Private Limited Company
**Line of Business:** Sale of new motor vehicles
**Issued Capital:** £10,000
**Directors:** C A Slaughter, P Nott
**Responsibilities**
**Senior:** Nigel Furneaux *(Financial Director)*
**Finance:** Nigel Furneaux *(Financial Director)*
**Facilities:** Richard Cleary *(Service Director)*
**Branches:** Squire Furneaux Maidenhead Ltd, London Rd, Aylesbury, Buckinghamshire HP22 5HQ
**US SIC:** 5511, 7539
**UK SIC:** 65100, 67100
**Auditors:** Mark Holt & Co Ltd
**Bankers:** National Westminster Bank Plc (60-23-34)

| | 31-12-13 | 31-12-12 | 31-12-11 |
|---|---|---|---|
| TO | 17,819,767 | 18,841,402 | 20,020,032 |
| P/L | 338,038 | 300,715 | (463,077) |
| NW | 1,030,643 | 772,223 | 555,800 |
| WC | 903,461 | 603,989 | 340,061 |
| Emp. | 50 | 57 | 59 |

DUNS 21-112-4137
## Squire Patton Boggs (Uk) Llp
7 Devonshire Square, London EC2M 4YH
**Web:** www.squiresanders.com
**Reg No:** 0335584OC **Estd:** 2004
**Line of Business:** Solicitors
**Export Sales:** £19,072,000
**Trading Style:** Sanders Squire & Hammonds
**Responsibilities**
**Senior:** John Alderton *(Non-designated Limited Liabili)*, Nick Allen *(Partner - Corporate Strategy &)*, Robin Baillie *(Non-designated Limited Liabili)*, Kirsty Bartlett *(Partner)*, Olivia Bateman *(Partner - Construction)*, Robert Bray *(Partner - Private Equity and V)*, Jane Bullen *(Partner - Labor and Employment)*, Matthew Byford *(Associate)*, Victoria Camfield *(Non-designated Limited Liabili)*, Jesus Carrasco *(Non-designated Limited Liabili)*, Tomas Cerdan *(Partner)*, Philippa Chadwick *(Partner)*, Giles Chesher *(Non-designated Limited Liabili)*, Lucci Dammone *(Partner - Litigation Mancheste)*, Carol Dick *(Partner)*, Giles Distin *(Partner - Corporate Transactio)*, Matthew Doughty *(Partner)*, Massimo Galli *(Non-designated Limited Liabili)*, Simon Garbett *(Non-designated Limited Liabili)*, Bernhard Gilbey *(Partner)*, James Hennigan *(Partner)*, Tim Hewens *(Partner)*, Benjamin Holland *(Non-designated Limited Liabili)*, Wendy Hunter *(Partner)*, Trevor Ingle *(Partner)*, Paula Laird *(Partner)*, Janette Lucas *(Partner)*, Annabel Mace *(Partner)*, Joseph Markoski *(Partner)*, James McKay *(Partner)*, Kai Mertens *(Personal Assistant)*, Ramez Moussa *(Non-designated Limited Liabili)*, Paul Muscutt *(Partner)*, Dharmendra Nair *(Partner)*, Caroline Noblet *(Partner)*, Mark Norris *(Partner)*, Gary Paddison *(Non-designated Limited Liabili)*, Geoffrey Perry *(Non-designated Limited Liabili)*, Gerry Peyton *(Director of HR)*, Carl Rohsler *(Partner)*, Diarmuid Ryan *(Partner)*, Stephen Sampson *(Partner - Sports)*, Laura Sayer *(Partner)*, Claire Scott-Priestley *(Partner)*, Supinder Sian *(Partner)*, Clifford Sims *(Partner)*, Andrew Stones *(Non-designated Limited Liabili)*, Gareth Timms *(Non-designated Limited Liabili)*, Florian Traub *(Partner)*, George Von Mehren *(Partner)*, Robert Wegenek *(Partner)*, Carol Welu *(Partner)*, Cathryn Williams *(Partner)*
**Finance:** Malcolm Gunn *(Tax Consultant)*
**Admin:** Stephanie Dare *(Legal Assistant)*
**IT:** Craig Morgan *(IT Director)*
**HR:** Gerry Peyton *(Director of HR)*
**US SIC:** 8111 **UK SIC:** 83500
**Auditors:** PricewaterhouseCoopers LLP

| | 30-04-14 | 30-04-13 | 30-04-12 |
|---|---|---|---|
| TO | 119,957,000 | 119,639,000 | 130,906,000 |
| P/L | 32,069,000 | 32,376,000 | 35,503,000 |
| NW | 10,916,000 | 9,574,000 | 9,508,000 |
| WC | 27,604,000 | 24,512,000 | 24,613,000 |
| Emp. | 942 | 1,085 | 1,165 |

DUNS 34-890-1570
## Squires Executive Ltd
Market Hall, New Market, Maidenhead, Berkshire SL6 1DS
**Tel:** 01628625240 **Fax:** 01628625240
**Reg No:** 2827213 **Estd:** 1993 Private Limited Company
**Line of Business:** Taxi operation
**Trading Style:** U Want Taxes
**Issued Capital:** £1,001
**Director:** M Azam
**Co. Secretary:** Ms Erika Seekings
**US SIC:** 4121 **UK SIC:** 72200
**Bankers:** National Westminster Bank Plc (60-13-35)

| | 30-06-13 | 30-06-12 | 30-06-11 |
|---|---|---|---|
| TA | 4,423 | 3,909 | 5,913 |
| NW | 1,092 | 1,251 | 2,761 |
| WC | 1,092 | 596 | 1,511 |

DUNS 21-776-9592 **Imp**
## Squires Garden Centre
Badshot Lea Road, Badshot Lea, Farnham, Surrey GU9 9JX
**Tel:** 01252333666
**Web:** www.squires-garden.co.uk
**Estd:** 2007 Proprietorship
**Line of Business:** Garden centres
**Proprietor:** R Mcewan
**Responsibilities**
**Senior:** Ross McEwan *(Proprietor)*
**US SIC:** 5999 **UK SIC:** 65600
**Employees:** 450

DUNS 21-771-8524
## Squirrels Heath Infants School
Salisbury Road, Romford, Essex RM2 5TP
**Tel:** 01708446476
**Web:** www.squirrelsheath.com
**Estd:** 1911 Proprietorship
**Line of Business:** Schools (local authority)
**Proprietor:** Mrs C Drew
**US SIC:** 8211 **UK SIC:** 93200
**Employees:** 50

DUNS 73-554-4939
## Squiz Uk Ltd
(**Subsidiary of:** Squiz Pty Ltd)
Zetland House, 109 - 123 Clifton Street, London EC2A 4LD
**Tel:** 02071018300 **Fax:** 0870 112 3394
**Web:** www.squiz.net
**Reg No:** 4816468 **Estd:** 2003 Private Limited Company
**Line of Business:** Other computer related activities
**Issued Capital:** £100
**Directors:** J P Syriatowicz, S M Barker
**Co. Secretary:** Stephen Morgan
**US SIC:** 7379 **UK SIC:** 83940
**Auditors:** Hughes Spencer

| | 30-06-13 | 30-06-12 | 30-06-11 |
|---|---|---|---|
| TO | 5,000,754 | N/A | N/A |
| P/L | 966,907 | N/A | N/A |
| NW | 601,130 | 30,947 | 80,015 |
| WC | 407,628 | (41,686) | 45,815 |

DUNS 73-688-2262
## Sqw Group Ltd
43 Chalton Street, London NW1 1JD
**Tel:** 01223-209400 **Fax:** 01223209401
**Web:** www.sqw.co.uk
**Reg No:** 4947276 **Estd:** 2003 Private Limited Company
**Line of Business:** Business and management consultancy activities not elsewhere classified
**Export Sales:** £728,254
**Issued Capital:** £22,220
**Directors:** C C Green, M E Hay, R E Quince, M T Lyons, I M Laing, M V Hess
**Co. Secretary:** Malcolm Hay
**US SIC:** 7399 **UK SIC:** 83954
**Bankers:** HSBC Bank plc (40-05-16)

| | 31-03-14 | 31-03-13 | 31-03-12 |
|---|---|---|---|
| TO | 26,379,757 | 22,335,456 | 12,676,524 |
| P/L | 1,126,879 | 801,238 | (710,606) |
| NW | 2,226,719 | 1,630,890 | 970,081 |
| WC | 2,116,879 | 1,523,559 | 920,638 |
| Emp. | 209 | 185 | 160 |

DUNS 21-727-6652
## The Sr Group (Uk) Ltd
(**Subsidiary of:** The Sr Group Holding Co Ltd)
95 Queen Victoria Street, London EC4V 4HN
**Tel:** 02074150050
**Web:** www.careerswiththesrgroup.com
**Reg No:** 7638893 **Estd:** 2011 Private Limited Company
**Line of Business:** Labour recruitment and provision of personnel
**Issued Capital:** £1
**Directors:** M P Brewer, N P Root, A C Calcutt
**US SIC:** 7361 **UK SIC:** 83954

| | 31-12-13 | 29-11-12 | 31-12-11 |
|---|---|---|---|
| TO | 20,581,027 | N/A | N/A |
| P/L | 184,781 | N/A | N/A |
| NW | (23,589,653) | 1 | 1 |
| WC | (24,070,733) | N/A | N/A |
| Emp. | 122 | N/A | N/A |

DUNS 21-610-7813 **Imp-Exp**
## Sr Technics Uk Ltd
(**Subsidiary of:** Takeoff Luxco 3 Sarl)
Diamond Hangar, Long Border Road, London Stansted Airport, London Stansted Airpo, Stansted, Essex CM24 1RE
**Tel:** 01279680068 **Fax:** 020888311245
**Web:** www.srtechnique.com
**Reg No:** 0154604 **VAT No:** 538226147
**Estd:** 1960 Private Limited Company
**Line of Business:** Airline related services
**Trading Style:** Sr Technics
**Issued Capital:** £395,811,926
**Directors:** A M Thurnheer, A Wall
**Co. Secretary:** David Venus & Company Llp
**Responsibilities**
**Senior:** Andy Gilby *(Despatch Manager)*, Zeljko Raisic *(Site Manager)*
**Finance:** Sarah Firth *(Financial Manager)*
**Admin:** Maureen Pearce *(Administrator)*
**Fleet:** Andy Gilby *(Despatch Manager)*
**Branches:** Sr Technics Uk Ltd, Hanger 1,Western Maintenance Area, Manchester Intrntnl Airport Rt, Manchester M90 5FL
**US SIC:** 4582 **UK SIC:** 76400
**Auditors:** KPMG LLP
**Bankers:** HSBC Bank plc (40-16-08)

| | 31-12-13 | 31-12-12 | 31-12-11 |
|---|---|---|---|
| TO | 15,856,000 | N/A | 23,362,000 |
| P/L | (1,466,000) | (6,787,000) | (9,603,000) |
| NW | (104,998,000) | (108,535,000) | (101,908,000) |
| WC | 20,488,000 | 41,320,000 | (8,665,000) |
| Emp. | 255 | 235 | 232 |

DUNS 45-889-5968
## Srcl Ltd
(**Subsidiary of:** Stericycle Inc.)
2nd Floor Apex House, Gravesend, Kent DA11 9PD
**Tel:** 08451609292
**Web:** www.srcl.com
**Reg No:** 3226910 **VAT No:** 702461079
**Estd:** 1996 Private Limited Company
**Line of Business:** Waste disposal
**Issued Capital:** £8,707,388
**Directors:** C A Alutto, D Ginnetti, J P Johnston
**Responsibilities**
**Senior:** Andy Wenham *(Manager)*
**Marketing:** Jonathan Cliff *(Marketing Manager)*
**Sales:** Mark Greenhalgh *(Sales Manager)*
**IT:** David Copland *(IT Director)*, Emma Peace *(IT Director)*
**Operations:** Simon Hadfield *(Operations Manager)*
**Branches:** Srcl Ltd, Avonmouth Terminal, Holesmouth, Bristol, Avon BS11 9BN
**US SIC:** 8091 **UK SIC:** 95200
**Auditors:** Ernst & Young LLP
**Bankers:** Bank Of Scotland (12-11-03)

| | 31-12-12 | 31-12-11 | 31-12-10 |
|---|---|---|---|
| TO | 90,664,000 | 86,864,000 | 86,591,000 |
| P/L | 4,276,000 | 10,234,000 | 12,507,000 |
| NW | 4,256,000 | 13,521,000 | 9,371,000 |
| WC | (15,766,000) | (13,442,000) | (14,008,000) |
| Emp. | 1,143 | 980 | 856 |

DUNS 22-226-5147 **Imp**
## Srixon Sports Europe Ltd
(**Subsidiary of:** Sumitomo Rubber Industries Ltd.)
Grove Park, Alton, Hampshire GU34 2QG
**Tel:** 01420-541709
**Web:** www.srixon.co.uk
**Reg No:** 4244454 **Estd:** 2001 Private Limited Company
**Line of Business:** Golf equipment
**Export Sales:** £12,120,313
**Issued Capital:** £7,542,902
**Directors:** K K Matsubara, L D Hepsworth, M Yasumoto, M G Powell
**Co. Secretary:** Julian Palmer
**Responsibilities**
**Senior:** M Ashiono *(Manager)*, Gregory Hopkins *(Manager)*, Kazuo Kinameri *(Manager)*, Keiji Okada *(Manager)*
**Marketing:** Kaisa Jokelainen *(Marketing Manager Continental)*
**US SIC:** 5199, 5941
**UK SIC:** 61900, 65400
**Auditors:** KPMG LLP

| | 31-12-13 | 31-12-12 | 31-12-11 |
|---|---|---|---|
| TO | 23,895,774 | 24,164,775 | 26,774,113 |
| P/L | 339,205 | (2,205,823) | 827,946 |
| NW | 508,181 | 359,132 | 2,128,951 |
| WC | 186,370 | (185,645) | 1,761,240 |
| Emp. | 88 | 87 | 81 |

DUNS 76-919-5488
## Srk Consulting (Uk) Ltd
Churchill House, 17 Churchill Way, Cardiff Do, Cardiff, South Glamorgan CF10 2HH
**Web:** www.srk.co.uk
**Reg No:** 1575403 **VAT No:** 508657231
**Estd:** 1989 Private Limited Company
**Line of Business:** Engineering, architectural, & surveying
**Export Sales:** £16,611,024
**Trading Style:** S R K
**Issued Capital:** £32,769
**Directors:** Dr I Humphreys, A J Barrett, M F Pittuck, Dr M G Armitage, R C Oldcorn, Ms F M Cessford - Le Roux, P D Jenkins
**Co. Secretary:** Philip Jenkins
**Responsibilities**
**Senior:** Alan McCracken *(Chief Executive)*
**US SIC:** 8911, 7399
**UK SIC:** 83701, 83954
**Auditors:** Guilfoyle Sage & Co

| | 31-03-14 | 31-03-13 | 31-03-12 |
|---|---|---|---|
| TO | 23,070,867 | 25,244,353 | 22,334,298 |
| P/L | [illegible] | [illegible] | [illegible] |
| NW | 8,030,277 | 8,138,638 | 6,789,612 |
| WC | 6,669,957 | 6,609,484 | 5,916,849 |
| Emp. | 202 | 186 | 157 |

DUNS 22-071-0706
## S.R.K. Scaffolding Ltd
Durston Forestry Yard, Taunton, Somerset TA3 5AG
**Web:** www.srkscaffold.co.uk
**Reg No:** 4072540 **Estd:** 1999 Private Limited Company
**Line of Business:** Other construction work involving special trades
**Issued Capital:** £30,000
**Directors:** S R Trott, R K Trott
**Co. Secretary:** Shawn Trott
**US SIC:** 1799 **UK SIC:** 50000

| | 31-05-14 | 31-05-13 | 31-05-12 |
|---|---|---|---|
| TA | 1,629,527 | 1,090,241 | 1,298,471 |
| NW | 277,731 | 50,551 | 33,062 |
| WC | (280,417) | (230,192) | (213,268) |

DUNS 29-892-3392 **Exp**
## Sruc
King's Buildings, West Mains Road Ashworth Laboratories, Edinburgh, Midlothian EH9 3JT
**Tel:** 0131-535-4000 **Fax:** 01316672601
**Web:** www.sruc.ac.uk
**Reg No:** 0103046SC **VAT No:** 435882817
**Estd:** 1987 Private Company Limited By Guarantee
**Line of Business:** Other sporting activities not elsewhere classified
**Trading Style:** Greens of Scotland, Edinburgh Genetics, S A C, Environmental Consultancy Services
**Directors:** A D Bell, R J Dinning, Professor D M Mckenzie, J R Cumming, Miss B Dall, W M Marshall, Lord J R Lindsay, Professor S Mcdaid
**Co. Secretary:** Ms Janet Swadling
**Responsibilities**
**Senior:** Luke Borwick *(Director)*, Grahame Bulfield *(Director)*, Patrick Machray *(Director)*, Geoffrey Simm *(Director)*, Bob Webb *(Principal)*
**HR:** Alix Malcolm *(Training Manager)*
**Engineering:** John Moisey *(Technician)*
**Branches:** Sruc, Caledonean Maps, Stirling, Stirlingshire FK7 7LS
**US SIC:** 7399, 0741, 8211
**UK SIC:** 83954, 95601, 93200
**Auditors:** Ernst & Young LLP
**Bankers:** Bank Of Scotland (80-02-24)

| | 31-03-14 | 31-03-13 | 31-03-12 |
|---|---|---|---|
| TO | 84,068,000 | 67,241,000 | 54,540,000 |
| P/L | 3,285,000 | 4,290,000 | (765,000) |
| NW | 51,943,000 | 55,722,000 | 44,923,000 |
| WC | 2,620,000 | 312,000 | (5,238,000) |
| Emp. | 1,133 | 1,097 | 819 |

DUNS 39-734-0159
## S.S. White Manufacturing
(**Subsidiary of:** A D Burs Ltd)
Unit E, Stephenson Drive, Gloucester, Gloucestershire GL2 2HA
**Tel:** 01452-307171 **Fax:** 01452-307187
**Web:** www.primadental.com
**Reg No:** 2175700 **Estd:** 1987 Private Unlimited Company
**Line of Business:** Manufacture of medical and surgical equipment and orthopaedic appliances
**Trading Style:** Dental Manufacturing Engineering
**Issued Capital:** £1

**Directors:** R O Muller, C Ashkin, M W Caputo
**Co. Secretary:** Ms Annette John
**US SIC:** 3841, 6711
**UK SIC:** 37201, 83962
**Auditors:** Hazelwoods LLP
**Bankers:** Barclays Bank Plc (20-33-83)

| | 31-12-13 | 31-12-12 | 31-12-11 |
|---|---|---|---|
| TA | 3 | 3 | 1,100,001 |
| NW | 3 | 3 | 1,100,001 |

DUNS 21-840-1015
## Ssat (The Schools Network) Ltd
5th Floor Central House, 142 Central Street, London EC1V 8AR
**Tel:** 02078022300
**Web:** www.ssatuk.co.uk
**Reg No:** 8073410 **Estd:** 2012 Private Limited Company
**Line of Business:** Primary education
**Issued Capital:** £150,000
**Directors:** Mrs S M Williamson, Mrs S M Williamson, J G Chin
**Responsibilities**
**Senior:** Neil Hopkin *(Board Member)*
**IT:** Jessica Nash *(Head of Special Schools Networ)*
**Operations:** Sylvia Paddock *(Operations Director)*, Bill Watkin *(Operations Director)*
**US SIC:** 8211, 8249
**UK SIC:** 93200, 93300
**Bankers:** Barclays Bank Plc (20-00-50)

| | 31-08-14 | 31-08-13 |
|---|---|---|
| TO | 5,721,013 | 7,393,338 |
| P/L | 738,834 | 531,230 |
| NW | 1,095,941 | 535,585 |
| WC | 906,606 | 500,101 |
| Emp. | 66 | 61 |

DUNS 21-688-0432
## Ssc Holdings (Uk) Ltd
Kemp House 152 160, City Road, London EC1V 2DW
**Tel:** 08009996999
**Web:** www.student-support.co.uk
**Reg No:** 7360013 **Estd:** 2010 Private Limited Company
**Line of Business:** Management activities of holding companies
**Issued Capital:** £1,000
**Directors:** R M Wilman, A C Lee
**US SIC:** 6711 **UK SIC:** 83962

| | 31-08-13 | 31-08-12 | 31-08-11 |
|---|---|---|---|
| TO | 19,434,458 | 12,163,403 | 10,477,614 |
| P/L | 1,663,936 | 47,578 | (2,838,396) |
| NW | (3,038,383) | (5,685,865) | (5,739,211) |
| WC | (3,822,851) | (5,881,459) | (5,645,605) |
| Emp. | 90 | 92 | 91 |

DUNS 21-724-9424 **Exp**
## Ssd Drives Ltd
**(Subsidiary of:** Parker-Hannifin Corporation)
New Courtwick Lane, Wick, Littlehampton, West Sussex BN17 7RZ
**Tel:** 01903-737000 **Fax:** 01903-737100
**Web:** www.parker.com
**Reg No:** 1159876 **VAT No:** 792445306
**Estd:** 1974 Private Limited Company
**Line of Business:** Electricity generating equipment
**Trading Style:** Parker Ssd Drives
**Issued Capital:** £350,000
**Director:** J A Elsey
**Co. Secretary:** Graham Ellinor
**Responsibilities**
**Senior:** Brian Hurley *(Manager)*, Peter Vos *(Manager)*
**HR:** Kate Rogers *(Human Resources Manager)*
**Health & Safety:** Tony Woodward *(Health & Safety Manager)*
**Facilities:** Roy Broadhurst *(Engineering Manager)*
**Engineering:** Roy Broadhurst *(Engineering Manager)*, Steve Jay *(Production Manager)*
**Branches:** Ssd Drives Ltd, Armstrong Ho, Washington, Tyne and Wear NE37 1PR
**US SIC:** 3643 **UK SIC:** 34203
**Auditors:** Grant Thornton (UK) LLP
**Bankers:** HSBC Bank plc (40-28-23)

| | 30-06-13 | 30-06-12 | 30-06-11 |
|---|---|---|---|
| TA | 111,337,000 | 111,337,000 | 111,337,000 |
| NW | 24,422,000 | 24,422,000 | 24,777,000 |
| WC | 24,422,000 | 24,422,000 | 24,777,000 |

DUNS 22-149-5596
## Sse Audio Group Holdings Ltd
Burnt Meadow House, Burnt Meadow Road, Moons Moat North Industrial Esta, Moons Moat, Redditch, Worcestershire B98 9PA
**Web:** www.sseaudiogroup.com
**Reg No:** 4168340 **Estd:** 2001 Private Limited Company
**Line of Business:** Management activities of holding companies
**Export Sales:** £8,281,137
**Issued Capital:** £332
**Directors:** J L Penn, T Tranchant, A J Penn, S J Beard, I T Bidmead, I D Stile
**Co. Secretary:** Ms Heather Penn
**US SIC:** 6711, 7922
**UK SIC:** 83962, 97412
**Bankers:** The Royal Bank Of Scotland Plc (16-13-18)

| | 31-12-13 | 31-12-12 | 31-12-11 |
|---|---|---|---|
| TO | 19,958,873 | 12,542,212 | 10,643,618 |
| P/L | 1,168,082 | 952,829 | 530,502 |
| NW | 4,761,940 | 4,917,636 | 4,466,943 |
| WC | (2,290,650) | (1,126,355) | (932,962) |
| Emp. | 132 | 81 | 75 |

DUNS 28-933-8014 **Imp-Exp**
## Sse Audio Group Ltd
**(Subsidiary of:** Sse Audio Group Holdings Ltd)
Unit 3 Cumberland Avenue, London NW10 7RX
**Web:** www.sseaudiogroup.com
**Reg No:** 1542797 **VAT No:** 352900862
**Estd:** 2010 Private Limited Company
**Line of Business:** Hire and rental of television goods
**Export Markets:** Worldwide
**Export Sales:** £1,302,918
**Issued Capital:** £450
**Principals:** J L Penn *(Managing)*, A J Penn, S J Beard, Ms E S Bigg, I T Bidmead, M R Spratt, I D Stile
**Co. Secretary:** Ms Heather Penn
**Responsibilities**
**Senior:** Emma Barwell *(Manager)*
**US SIC:** 7394 **UK SIC:** 84000
**Auditors:** Bloomer Heaven Ltd
**Bankers:** Barclays Bank Plc (20-71-45)

| | 31-12-13 | 31-12-12 | 31-12-11 |
|---|---|---|---|
| TO | 9,845,985 | 8,879,023 | 7,274,769 |
| P/L | 743,451 | 835,871 | 535,887 |
| NW | 3,304,272 | 2,738,162 | 2,098,246 |
| WC | (128,328) | (578,023) | (578,194) |
| Emp. | 66 | 58 | 56 |

DUNS 50-056-5262
## Sse Contracting Ltd
**(Subsidiary of:** Sse Plc)
55 Vastern Road, Reading, Berkshire RG1 8BU
**Tel:** 01954213550
**Web:** www.ssecontracting.co.uk
**Reg No:** 2317133 **VAT No:** 570118464
**Estd:** 2012 Private Limited Company
**Line of Business:** Electrical contractors and electricians
**Trading Style:** Sse Electric
**Issued Capital:** £4,000,002
**Directors:** D Mullineaux, B D Sharma, J Mcphillimy, C M Hillman, S J Chapman, M C Rough
**Co. Secretary:** Brian Sharma
**Responsibilities**
**Senior:** Elizabeth Tanner *(Head of Legal Services Directo)*
**Marketing:** Claire Dance *(Marketing Manager)*, Hannah Thame *(Sales & Marketing Manager)*
**Sales:** Barry Clothier *(Business Development Manager)*, Hannah Thame *(Sales & Marketing Manager)*
**Facilities:** Annette Bennett *(Facilities Manager)*
**Branches:** Sse Contracting Ltd, Benett Street, Ryde, Isle Of Wight PO33 2BJ
**US SIC:** 1731, 8911
**UK SIC:** 50300, 83701
**Auditors:** KPMG Audit PLC
**Bankers:** National Westminster Bank Plc (60-17-21)

| | 31-03-14 | 31-03-13 | 31-03-12 |
|---|---|---|---|
| TO | 490,138,000 | 489,667,000 | 457,892,000 |
| P/L | 3,928,000 | 20,841,000 | 24,954,000 |
| NW | 76,182,000 | 112,306,000 | 94,459,000 |
| WC | 117,963,000 | 132,086,000 | 109,764,000 |
| Emp. | 4,262 | 4,462 | 4,506 |

DUNS 21-985-2238
## Sse Metering Ltd
**(Subsidiary of:** Sse Plc)
Inveralmond House, 200 Dunkeld Road, Perth, Perthshire PH1 3AQ
**Tel:** 0800117116
**Web:** www.sse.com
**Reg No:** 0318950SC **Estd:** 2007 Private Limited Company
**Line of Business:** Other business activities not elsewhere classified
**Issued Capital:** £1
**Directors:** W K Morris, S A Forbes
**Co. Secretary:** Peter Lawns
**US SIC:** 7399 **UK SIC:** 83954

| | 31-03-14 | 31-03-13 | 31-03-12 |
|---|---|---|---|
| TO | 98,000,000 | 95,900,000 | 94,100,000 |
| P/L | 9,400,000 | 4,900,000 | (4,700,000) |
| NW | 29,900,000 | 43,500,000 | 36,600,000 |
| WC | (17,000,000) | (17,900,000) | (11,800,000) |
| Emp. | 1,772 | 1,846 | 1,788 |

DUNS 23-617-2573
## Sse Plc
Inveralmond House, 200 Dunkeld Road, Perth, Perthshire PH1 3AQ
**Tel:** 01738456000 **Fax:** 01738-456-137
**Web:** www.sse.com
**Reg No:** 0117119SC **VAT No:** 553769603
**Estd:** 2005 Public Limited Company
**Line of Business:** Management activities of holding companies
**Export Sales:** £857,100,000
**Trading Style:** Scottish Hydro Electric, Southern Electric, Swalec, Scottish & Southern Energy
**Issued Capital:** £479,190,106
**Directors:** P J Lynas, J Beeton, F M Alexander, T L Kelvin, K Bickerstaffe, P M Phillips-Davies, Mrs S M Bruce, R D Gillingwater
**Co. Secretary:** Ms Sally Fairbairn
**Responsibilities**
**Senior:** Lawrence Donnelly *(Manager)*
**Sales:** Alistair Davies *(Sales Director)*
**Branches:** Sse Plc, Scottish & Southern Energy, Fiddlers Ferry Power Station, Warrington, Cheshire WA5 2UT
**US SIC:** 6711 **UK SIC:** 83962
**Auditors:** KPMG LLP
**Bankers:** The Royal Bank Of Scotland Plc (83-06-08)
**Following financial data are in thousands**

| | 31-03-14 | 31-03-13 | 31-03-12 |
|---|---|---|---|
| TO | 30,585,000 | 28,304,600 | 31,723,900 |
| P/L | 575,300 | 600,900 | 268,500 |
| NW | 4,230,200 | 2,444,100 | 3,737,800 |
| WC | (386,600) | (855,400) | (23,600) |
| Emp. | 19,890 | 19,769 | 19,647 |

DUNS 21-680-0110 **Imp**
## Ssi Schaefer Ltd
**(Subsidiary of:** Fritz Schäfer Gmbh & Co Kg Einrichtungssysteme)
83-84 Livingstone Road Walwort, Andover, Hampshire SP10 5QZ
**Tel:** 01264-386600 **Fax:** 01264-386611
**Web:** www.ssi-schaefer.co.uk
**Reg No:** 0676451 **VAT No:** 198976375
**Estd:** 1960 Private Limited Company
**Line of Business:** Material handling equipment
**Export Sales:** £538,003
**Issued Capital:** £4,000,000
**Directors:** G Schaefer, R Keller
**Co. Secretary:** Shailen Shah
**Responsibilities**
**Marketing:** Debbie Griffiths *(Marketing Coordinator)*
**Branches:** Ssi Schaefer Ltd, 3 Bury Hill, Towcester, Northamptonshire NN12 8EG
**US SIC:** 2599, 5399
**UK SIC:** 46720, 65600
**Auditors:** Wilkins Kennedy
**Bankers:** HSBC Bank plc (40-09-18)

| | 31-12-13 | 31-12-12 | 31-12-11 |
|---|---|---|---|
| TO | 64,028,451 | 80,772,635 | 62,322,320 |
| P/L | 163,090 | 131,568 | (128,851) |
| NW | 5,104,577 | 4,939,449 | 4,848,851 |
| WC | 3,786,419 | 2,239,527 | 1,911,516 |
| Emp. | 121 | 91 | 77 |

DUNS 22-216-4738
## Ssp Ltd
**(Subsidiary of:** H&F Sensor Lux 2 Sarl)
2nd Floor G Mill, Dean Clough, Halifax, West Yorkshire HX3 5AX
**Web:** www.ssp-worldwide.com
**Reg No:** 4234499 **Estd:** 1901 Private Limited Company
**Line of Business:** Other software consultancy and supply
**Issued Capital:** £251
**Directors:** J M Davey, L J Walker, S P Cargill, S M Lathrope
**Co. Secretary:** Richard Forrest
**Responsibilities**
**Senior:** Steven Bow *(Manager)*
**Branches:** Ssp Ltd, Fountain House, Halesowen, West Midlands B63 3BL
**US SIC:** 7379, 7374
**UK SIC:** 83940
**Auditors:** Deloitte LLP
**Bankers:** Barclays Bank Plc (20-88-40)

| | 31-03-14 | 31-03-13 | 31-03-12 |
|---|---|---|---|
| TO | 65,710,000 | 59,465,000 | 59,403,000 |
| P/L | 6,897,000 | 5,494,000 | (1,384,000) |
| NW | 12,700,000 | 3,047,000 | (5,313,000) |
| WC | 60,786,000 | 55,629,000 | 52,259,000 |
| Emp. | 433 | 468 | 465 |

DUNS 28-983-9763 **Exp**
## Ssp Sirius Ltd
**(Subsidiary of:** H&F Sensor Lux 2 Sarl)
Fearnley Mill, Dean Clough Mills, Halifax, West Yorkshire HX3 5AX
**Fax:** 01217798401
**Web:** www.ssp-uk.com
**Reg No:** 1792078 **VAT No:** 405217489
**Estd:** 1984 Private Limited Company
**Line of Business:** Other computer related activities
**Export Markets:** Worldwide
**Issued Capital:** £1
**Directors:** L J Walker, S P Cargill
**Co. Secretary:** Richard Forrest
**Responsibilities**
**Senior:** Nicholas Bate *(Manager)*
**US SIC:** 7379 **UK SIC:** 83940
**Auditors:** Deloitte LLP
**Bankers:** Bank Of Scotland (12-05-65)

| | 31-03-14 | 31-03-13 | 31-03-12 |
|---|---|---|---|
| TA | 22,920,000 | 22,920,000 | 22,920,000 |

DUNS 21-700-4883
## Ssr Site Solutions Ltd
Offices 4b & 4c 572 Ipswich Road, Colchester, Essex CO4 9HB
**Tel:** 01206862402
**Web:** www.ssrsitesolutionsltd.co.uk
**Reg No:** 7455053 **Estd:** 2010 Private Limited Company
**Line of Business:** Employment and recruitment companies and consultants
**Issued Capital:** £1
**Directors:** S Jacobs, M Ridgers
**Responsibilities**
**Senior:** Scott Ridgers *(Manager)*
**US SIC:** 7361 **UK SIC:** 83954

| | 31-01-14 | 31-01-13 | 31-01-12 |
|---|---|---|---|
| TO | N/A | N/A | 1,064,169 |
| P/L | N/A | N/A | 54,198 |
| NW | 156,477 | 99,299 | 43,540 |
| WC | 117,473 | 56,151 | 36,233 |

DUNS 34-892-8529
## Ssuk Ltd
45 Queen Elizabeth Avenue, Hillington Park, Glasgow, Lanarkshire G52 4NQ
**Tel:** 01418104111
**Web:** www.ssuk.co.uk
**Reg No:** 0296269SC **Estd:** 2009 Private Limited Company
**Line of Business:** Audio/visual production services
**Issued Capital:** £100
**Directors:** K J Forbes, S Maitland, S A Mccahill, A Adleigh
**Co. Secretary:** Keith Forbes
**US SIC:** 7819 **UK SIC:** 97111

| | 31-12-13 | 31-03-13 | 31-12-12 |
|---|---|---|---|
| TA | 983,788 | 1,228,821 | 1,189,078 |
| NW | 312,865 | 436,501 | 322,397 |
| WC | 297,753 | 394,982 | 271,718 |

DUNS 50-342-3907
## Ssy Shipping Services Ltd
**(Subsidiary of:** Simpson Spence & Young Ltd)
Lloyds Chambers, 1 Portsoken Street, London E1 8PH
**Tel:** 02079777400
**Reg No:** 2362585 **Estd:** 1989 Private Limited Company
**Line of Business:** Shipping companies
**Trading Style:** S S Y
**Issued Capital:** £100
**Director:** J A Welham
**Co. Secretary:** David Soutter
**US SIC:** 4411 **UK SIC:** 74001

| | 31-12-13 | 31-12-12 | 31-12-11 |
|---|---|---|---|
| TA | 248,207 | 248,207 | 248,207 |
| NW | 100 | 100 | 100 |
| WC | (248,007) | (248,007) | (248,007) |

DUNS 21-224-9987
## St Aidan Lodge
Front Street, Framwellgate Moor, Durham, County Durham DH1 5BL
**Web:** www.staidanlodge.com
**Estd:** 2000
**Line of Business:** Residential care establishments
**Proprietor:** Mrs C Shannon
**Responsibilities**
**Senior:** Virginia Lowrey *(Manager)*
**US SIC:** 8321, 6732
**UK SIC:** 96111, 83100
**Employees:** 55

DUNS 21-981-2851
## St Aidan's Church of England Academy Ltd
Hundens Lane, Darlington, County Durham DL1 1LL
**Tel:** 01325373770
**Web:** www.staidansacademy.org.uk
**Reg No:** 6162865 **Estd:** 2007 Private Company Limited By Guarantee
**Line of Business:** Schools (local authority)
**Directors:** M A Banks, Reverend S C Williamson, M E Crossland, Rev S Bamber, Mrs J Marriner, Ms C A Mccoy
**Co. Secretary:** Ms Alison Gent
**Responsibilities**
**Senior:** Alison Appleyard *(Principal)*
**US SIC:** 8211 **UK SIC:** 93200

| | 31-08-13 | 31-08-12 | 31-08-11 |
|---|---|---|---|
| TO | 4,851,000 | 4,851,000 | 21,066,000 |
| P/L | (932,000) | (4,737,000) | 15,633,000 |
| NW | 10,925,000 | 11,817,000 | 16,785,000 |
| WC | 776,000 | 1,007,000 | 1,291,000 |
| Emp. | 97 | 94 | 88 |

DUNS 21-730-9760
## St Aidan's Church of England High School
Oatlands Drive, Harrogate, North Yorkshire HG2 8JR
**Tel:** 01423885814
**Web:** www.staidans.co.uk
**Reg No:** 7663935 **Estd:** 2011 Private Company Limited By Guarantee
**Line of Business:** General secondary education
**Directors:** Ms P M Robinson, D J Fisher, M Park, Ms C Rose, J Birch, Ms P B Young, Mrs J Wicks, Miss M Chanter
**Co. Secretary:** Christopher Burt
**Responsibilities**
**Senior:** Dorothy Boyd *(Director)*, John Bushell *(Director)*, Sheina Demain *(Director)*, Claire Dowson *(Bursar)*, John Garnett *(Director)*, Claire Kelley *(Director)*, Canon Shepherd *(Director)*
**Finance:** Claire Dowson *(Bursar)*
**US SIC:** 8211 **UK SIC:** 93200

| | 31-08-14 | 31-08-13 | 31-08-12 |
|---|---|---|---|
| TO | 11,662,572 | 12,105,096 | 26,102,968 |
| P/L | 681,263 | 1,473,250 | 13,113,772 |
| NW | 15,671,587 | 14,460,022 | 12,908,772 |
| WC | 4,334,647 | 3,533,122 | 2,158,480 |
| Emp. | 254 | 273 | 209 |

DUNS 21-771-5339
## St Albans Academy
Angelina Street, Birmingham, West Midlands B12 0UU
**Tel:** 01214461300
**Web:** www.stalbansacademy.org
**Estd:** 2011 Proprietorship
**Line of Business:** Schools (local authority)
**Proprietor:** D Gould
**US SIC:** 8211 **UK SIC:** 93200
**Employees:** 100

DUNS 21-121-9934
## St Albans Catholic Primary School
St Albans R C School Priory Lane, Macclesfield, Cheshire SK10 3HJ
**Tel:** 01625-425905
**Web:** www.stalbansprimarymacclesfield.co.uk
**Estd:** 2004 Proprietorship
**Line of Business:** Primary education
**Proprietor:** Mrs M Johnstone
**Responsibilities**
**Senior:** Theresa Cooke *(Principal)*
**US SIC:** 8211 **UK SIC:** 93200
**Employees:** 50

DUNS 21-790-5004
## St Albans City Hospital
Waverley Road, St Albans, Hertfordshire AL3 5PN
**Tel:** 01727866122
**Web:** www.stalbans.gov.uk
**Estd:** 2002
**Line of Business:** Hospitals
**Proprietor:** Mrs S Walker
**US SIC:** 8062 **UK SIC:** 95100
**Employees:** 1,000

DUNS 21-231-6142
## St Albans Fire Station
Fire Station, 153 London Road, St Albans, Hertfordshire AL1 1TQ
**Tel:** 01727818919
**Web:** www.hertsdirect.org
**Estd:** 2002 Partnership
**Line of Business:** Fire stations
**Partners:** I Markwell, T Morrison
**Responsibilities**
**Senior:** Trevor' Brown *(Station Commander)*
**US SIC:** 9224 **UK SIC:** 91400
**Employees:** 50

DUNS 21-738-1519
## St Albans Girls' School
Sandridgebury Lane, St Albans, Hertfordshire AL3 6DB
**Tel:** 01727853134
**Web:** www.stags.herts.sch.uk
**Reg No:** 7719076 **Estd:** 2011 Private Company Limited By Guarantee
**Line of Business:** General secondary education
**Directors:** Miss P Randerson, Mrs J M Jenkins, Mrs C F Barnard, M G Federici, Ms M C Chapman, P O Webster, Dr D Houlihan, A P Snook
**Co. Secretary:** Paul Lerwill
**Responsibilities**
**Senior:** Amanda Jefferies *(Director)*, Elizabeth Kilborn *(Director)*, C Murrell *(Head Teacher)*, William Parish *(Director)*
**US SIC:** 8211 **UK SIC:** 93200

| | 31-08-14 | 31-08-13 | 31-08-12 |
|---|---|---|---|
| TO | 6,477,377 | 6,431,769 | 23,952,309 |
| P/L | (215,935) | 34,544 | 17,593,302 |
| NW | 16,710,911 | 17,058,846 | 16,993,302 |
| WC | 624,007 | 724,070 | 522,977 |
| Emp. | 108 | 109 | 106 |

DUNS 23-517-5130
## St Albans High School for Girls
Townsend Avenue, St Albans, Hertfordshire AL1 3SW
**Tel:** 01727-853800
**Web:** www.stahs.org.uk
**Reg No:** 0321911 **Estd:** 1908 Private Company Limited By Guarantee
**Line of Business:** General secondary education
**Directors:** D M Roe, R E Allnutt, Mrs J Ross, B R Kettle, Ms R K Musgrave, Mrs M K Wellens, D M Alterman, Ms J Woolley
**Co. Secretary:** Archibald Campbell
**Responsibilities**
**Senior:** Catherine Callegari *(Director)*, Elizabeth Curtis *(Manager)*, Eleanor De Galleani *(Director)*, Andrew Follows *(Director)*, Heather Greatrex *(Director)*, Dorothy Henderson *(Director)*, Jeffrey John *(Director)*, Theodore Pencier *(Manager)*, Jennifer Stroud *(Governor)*
**Marketing:** Helen Monighan *(Director of Communication)*, Gene Ross *(Senior Marketing Executive)*
**Sales:** Sarah Nicholls *(Registrar)*
**IT:** Carole Wright *(Head of IT)*
**HR:** Sarah Nicholls *(Registrar)*
**Purchasing:** Sarah Nicholls *(Registrar)*
**US SIC:** 8211 **UK SIC:** 93200
**Auditors:** Messrs Mereer & Hole

| | 31-08-14 | 31-08-13 | 31-08-12 |
|---|---|---|---|
| TO | 13,726,000 | 12,469,000 | 11,319,000 |
| P/L | 2,138,000 | 980,000 | 612,000 |
| NW | 17,109,000 | 14,971,000 | 13,991,000 |
| WC | 1,281,000 | (636,000) | (575,000) |
| Emp. | 161 | 161 | 156 |

DUNS 64-251-9631
## St Albans Nursing Home
Swinton Street, Cardiff, South Glamorgan CF24 2NT
**Tel:** 029-2047-2161
**Web:** www.crusadermedicalcare.com
**Estd:** 1989 Proprietorship
**Line of Business:** Nursing homes
**Proprietor:** M Ashley
**Responsibilities**
**Senior:** Vincent Ashley *(Proprietor)*
**US SIC:** 8051 **UK SIC:** 95100
**Employees:** 58

DUNS 21-121-0776
## St Albans Rc High School
Park Road, Pontypool, Gwent NP4 6XG
**Tel:** 01495765800
**Web:** http://joomla.stalbans-pontypool.org.uk
**Estd:** 1985 Proprietorship
**Line of Business:** General secondary education
**Proprietor:** M Coady
**Responsibilities**
**IT:** Peter Olearczk *(Head of IT)*
**US SIC:** 8211 **UK SIC:** 93200
**Employees:** 110

DUNS 42-412-5107
## St Albans School
Abbey Gateway, St Albans, Hertfordshire AL3 4HB
**Tel:** 01727-855521
**Web:** www.st-albans.herts.sch.uk
**Reg No:** 4400125 **Estd:** 2005 Private Company Limited By Guarantee
**Line of Business:** Schools (independent)
**Directors:** A L Dalwood, A M Woodgate, Professor R J Munton, S J Majumdar, Miss L M Ainsworth, Mrs C Leach, S P Eames, Ms J M Mark
**Co. Secretary:** Derek Todd
**Responsibilities**
**Senior:** Richard Blossom *(Director)*, Anne Hurst *(Director)*, Chris Mcintyre *(Director)*, Michael Pegg *(Director)*
**Admin:** Michelle Clinch *(Administration Manager)*
**US SIC:** 8211 **UK SIC:** 93200
**Bankers:** Barclays Bank Plc (20-39-07)

| | 31-08-13 | 31-08-12 | 31-08-11 |
|---|---|---|---|
| TO | 14,059,254 | 13,146,406 | 12,120,247 |
| P/L | 281,519 | 819,198 | 506,150 |
| NW | 10,864,315 | 10,445,964 | 9,563,749 |
| WC | (2,327,324) | (262,498) | 1,288,880 |
| Emp. | 146 | 138 | 129 |

DUNS 21-226-3704
## St Andreqws Healthcare
Pound Lane, North Benfleet, Wickford, Essex SS12 9JP
**Tel:** 01268723800
**Web:** www.standrewshealthcare.co.uk
**Estd:** 2002 Proprietorship
**Line of Business:** Hospitals
**Proprietor:** P Brierley
**Responsibilities**
**Senior:** Sue Green *(Manager)*, Ron Gutu *(Hospital Director)*, A Phurlby *(Manager)*, Alex Thurlby *(Manager)*
**US SIC:** 8062 **UK SIC:** 95100
**Employees:** 150

DUNS 21-777-1503
## St Andrew Halls of Residence
189 Hills Road, Cambridge, Cambridgeshire CB2 8RN
**Estd:** 2011 Proprietorship
**Line of Business:** Student accommodation
**Proprietor:** M Martin
**Responsibilities**
**Senior:** Hannah Clayton *(Manager)*
**US SIC:** 6531 **UK SIC:** 83400
**Employees:** 100

DUNS 21-779-7867
## St Andrew's C of E Infant School
Winchelsea Road, Eastbourne, East Sussex BN22 7PP
**Web:** www.st-andrews-inf.e-sussex.sch.uk
**Estd:** 1953 Partnership
**Line of Business:** General secondary education
**Partners:** Mrs C Meakins, Mrs K Meakins
**US SIC:** 8211 **UK SIC:** 93200
**Employees:** 50

DUNS 21-781-3538
## St Andrews C of E Primary School
Tulketh Road, Preston, Lancashire PR2 1EQ
**Tel:** 01772726729
**Web:** www.st-andrews23.lancsngfl.ac.uk
**Estd:** 2011 Proprietorship
**Line of Business:** Schools (local authority)
**Proprietor:** Mrs S Hesketh
**US SIC:** 8211 **UK SIC:** 93200
**Employees:** 50

DUNS 21-157-2081
## St Andrews Catholic Primary School
Polworth Road, London SW16 2ET
**Tel:** 020-8769-4980
**Web:** www.st-andrewsrc.lambeth.sch.uk
**Estd:** 2002 Proprietorship
**Line of Business:** Primary education
**Proprietor:** Mrs D Assid
**US SIC:** 8211 **UK SIC:** 93200
**Employees:** 50

DUNS 21-041-5277
## St Andrew's Christian Bookshop
61-65 High Street, Great Missenden, Buckinghamshire HP16 0AA
**Web:** www.standrewsbookshop.co.uk
**Estd:** 1977 Proprietorship
**Line of Business:** Book retailers
**Proprietor:** S Barnett
**Responsibilities**
**Marketing:** Andrew Bray *(Marketing Manager)*
**US SIC:** 5942 **UK SIC:** 65300
**Employees:** 3,040

DUNS 21-584-7924
## St Andrews Community Hospital
Largo Road, St Andrews, Fife KY16 8NJ
**Tel:** 01334465656
**Estd:** 2011 Proprietorship
**Line of Business:** Public sector hospital activities, including nhs trusts
**Proprietor:** Mrs K Nolan
**US SIC:** 8062 **UK SIC:** 95100
**Employees:** 300

DUNS 73-923-8413
## St Andrew's Healthcare
Billing Road, Northampton, Northamptonshire NN1 5DG
**Tel:** 01604616000 **Fax:** 01604-232325
**Web:** www.stah.org
**Reg No:** 5176998 **Estd:** 2004 Private Company Limited By Guarantee
**Line of Business:** Other human health activities
**Directors:** M Kersey, Dr F L Mason, P B Ellwood, S J Richmond Watson, T R Harris, W Irving, Mrs F M Jackson, G Baldwin
**Co. Secretary:** Ms Clare Auty
**Responsibilities**
**Senior:** Jane Forman Hardy *(Director)*, Sue Green *(Manager)*, James Mackaness *(Manager)*, Jo Nairn *(Manager)*, Hereward Wake *(Governor)*, Peter Winslow *(Director)*
**Admin:** Lesley Collins *(Service Director)*, Tina Connelly *(Administrator)*
**HR:** Clare Allen *(Human Resources Director)*
**US SIC:** 8091, 8062
**UK SIC:** 95200, 95100
**Auditors:** PricewaterhouseCoopers LLP

| | 31-03-14 | 31-03-13 | 31-03-12 |
|---|---|---|---|
| TO | 189,400,000 | 178,000,000 | 168,733,000 |
| P/L | 20,500,000 | 16,800,000 | 13,187,000 |
| NW | 211,500,000 | 191,300,000 | 174,060,000 |
| WC | 24,300,000 | 9,200,000 | (14,025,000) |
| Emp. | 3,188 | 3,142 | 3,152 |

DUNS 21-206-9145
## St Andrews Hospice
1 Henderson Street, Airdrie, Lanarkshire ML6 6DJ
**Web:** www.st-andrews-hospice.com
**Estd:** 2006
**Line of Business:** Hospice registered charity
**Director:** C Egan
**Responsibilities**
**Senior:** Tom Gault *(Chief Executive)*, Geoff Sage *(Chief Executive)*
**HR:** Catherine Lavery *(Human Resources Officer)*
**Health & Safety:** Catherine Lavery *(Human Resources Officer)*
**Branches:** St Andrews Hospice, 228 Main Street, Bellshill, Lanarkshire ML4 1AB
**US SIC:** 8062 **UK SIC:** 95100
**Bankers:** The Royal Bank Of Scotland Plc (83-15-11)
**Employees:** 100

DUNS 77-189-3013
## St Andrew's Hospice Ltd
Peaks Lane, Grimsby, South Humberside DN32 9RP
**Tel:** 01472-350908
**Web:** www.standrewshospice.com
**Reg No:** 2710865 **Estd:** 1992 Private Limited Company
**Line of Business:** Hospices
**Directors:** Ms A P Turner, L Jones, Ms R Brewin, G E Hirst, C Ellis, B P Wallis, D J Everatt, A K North
**Co. Secretary:** Stephen Oldridge
**Responsibilities**
**Senior:** David Hatfield *(Director)*
**Marketing:** Jane Whenham-White *(Operations Manager)*
**US SIC:** 8091 **UK SIC:** 95200
**Auditors:** Jemmett Burn
**Bankers:** The Co-Operative Bank Plc (08-90-71)

| | 31-03-14 | 31-03-13 | 31-03-12 |
|---|---|---|---|
| TO | 4,279,035 | 3,072,698 | 2,979,811 |
| P/L | 326,706 | 110,184 | 126,524 |
| NW | 8,038,034 | 7,717,339 | 7,616,642 |
| WC | 5,929,519 | 4,675,273 | 4,625,981 |
| Emp. | 122 | 112 | 109 |

DUNS 21-595-9908
## St Andrews House
St Andrews House, 1 James Foulis Court, St Andrews, Fife KY16 8SY
**Web:** www.standrewshouse.co.uk
**Estd:** 2003
**Line of Business:** Nursing homes
**Proprietor:** Mrs L Thompson
**Responsibilities**
**Senior:** Linda Thomtson *(CEO, Managing Director)*
**US SIC:** 8051 **UK SIC:** 95100
**Employees:** 80

DUNS 49-130-2949
## St Andrew's Insurance Plc
**(Subsidiary of:** Lloyds Banking Group Plc)
Old Broad Street, London EC2N 1HZ
**Tel:** 08706005000 **Fax:** 02089-421875
**Reg No:** 3104671 **Estd:** 1995 Public Limited Company
**Line of Business:** Non-life insurance
**Issued Capital:** £158,000,000
**Directors:** Dr N M Bryson, V Maru, T E Strauss, N E Prettejohn, M G Culmer, C J Thornton, D J Oldfield, R L Wohanka
**Co. Secretary:** Mrs Joanne Jolly
**Responsibilities**
**Senior:** Jeremy Goford *(Director)*
**US SIC:** 6399 **UK SIC:** 82001
**Auditors:** KPMG Audit PLC

| | 31-12-13 | 31-12-12 | 31-12-11 |
|---|---|---|---|
| TO | 454,665,000 | 471,234,000 | 521,752,000 |
| P/L | 147,114,000 | 172,279,000 | 183,419,000 |
| NW | 276,359,000 | 290,343,000 | 170,701,000 |
| WC | 328,511,000 | 721,183,000 | (355,701,000) |
| Emp. | N/A | 33 | 52 |

DUNS 49-130-2931
## St Andrew's Life Assurance Plc
(Subsidiary of: Lloyds Banking Group Plc)
St Andrews House, Portsmouth Road, Esher, Surrey KT10 9SA
Tel: 08453002456

Web: www.st-andrews.co.uk
Reg No: 3104670  Estd: 1995 Public Limited Company
Line of Business: Life insurance
Issued Capital: £360,000,000
Directors: D J Oldfield, N E Prettejohn, T E Strauss, A M Parsons, R L Wohanka, M Christophers, C J Thornton, M G Culmer
Co. Secretary: Mrs Joanne Jolly
Responsibilities
Senior: Jeremy Goford (Director)
US SIC: 6311  UK SIC: 82002
Auditors: KPMG Audit PLC
Following financial data are in thousands

|  | 31-12-13 | 31-12-12 | 31-12-11 |
|---|---|---|---|
| TO | 110,000 | 332,000 | 504,000 |
| P/L | 119,000 | 114,000 | 47,000 |
| NW | 741,000 | 714,000 | 614,000 |
| WC | 675,000 | 7,117,000 | (10,575,000) |

DUNS 23-814-4393                                Imp
## St Andrews Links Golf Shops Ltd
Pilmour House, St Andrews, Fife KY16 9SF
Tel: 01334466694  Fax: 01334479555
Web: www.standrews.org.uk
Reg No: 0198094SC  Estd: 1999 Private Limited Company
Line of Business: Sports coaching
Issued Capital: £500,000
Directors: K D Stewart, Mrs I Morrison, D J Campbell, Mrs G G Kirkwood, W E Loudon
Co. Secretary: Euan Macgregor
Responsibilities
Senior: Paul Kirkcaldy (Golf Practice Centre Manager), Euan Loudon (Chief Executive Officer)
US SIC: 5699  UK SIC: 64500
Auditors: Henderson Black & Co

|  | 31-12-13 | 31-12-12 | 31-12-11 |
|---|---|---|---|
| TA | 1,672,775 | 1,445,095 | 1,185,111 |
| NW | 1,127,890 | 273,425 | 198,619 |
| WC | 784,291 | 141,425 | 87,639 |

DUNS 21-223-1668
## St Andrews Lodge
Riber Crescent, Nottingham, Nottinghamshire NG5 1LP
Tel: 0115-9245467
Web: www.mha.org.uk
Estd: 2002 Proprietorship
Line of Business: Medical nursing home activities
Proprietor: Mrs H Wilson
Responsibilities
Senior: Emmeline Bingham (Home Manager)
US SIC: 8051  UK SIC: 95100
Employees: 111

DUNS 21-213-7074
## St Andrews Nursing & Residential Home
Church Bank, Stanley, County Durham DH9 0DU
Web: www.mpscaregroup.co.uk
Estd: 1988 Proprietorship
Line of Business: Nursing homes
Proprietor: Dr V P Pillei
Responsibilities
Senior: Anna Clift (Home Manager), Janis Watson (Manager)
US SIC: 8051  UK SIC: 95100
Employees: 47

DUNS 21-205-6548
## St Andrews Nursing Home
Stirches, Hawick, Roxburghshire TD9 7NS
Tel: 01450-372360
Estd: 1926
Line of Business: Nursing homes
Proprietor: Miss A Barr
Responsibilities
Facilities: Johnny Thomson (Maintenance)
US SIC: 8051  UK SIC: 95100
Employees: 55

DUNS 28-849-7829
## St Andrews (Pangbourne) School Trust Ltd
Buckhold, Pangbourne, Reading, Berkshire RG8 8QA
Tel: 01189744276
Web: www.standrewspangbourne.co.uk
Reg No: 0700881  Estd: 1934 Private Company Limited By Guarantee
Line of Business: Schools (independent)
Trading Style: Bere Court Nursery School, St Andrews School

Directors: Mrs J M Wood, P N Waite, Mrs F M Rutland, R W Obbard, O G Dereham, Mrs J D Kingsland, H C Jones, Mrs R S Dent
Co. Secretary: Mrs Penelope Franklin
Responsibilities
Senior: David Livingstone (Headmaster), Neil Mcintosh (Director), Nicholas Sampson (Manager), Philip Seymour (Director)
Marketing: Carolyn Reeves (Registrar)
US SIC: 8211  UK SIC: 93200
Auditors: Ernest Francis
Bankers: Lloyds TSB Bank plc (30-91-31)

|  | 31-08-13 | 31-08-12 | 31-08-11 |
|---|---|---|---|
| TO | 3,341,763 | 3,103,892 | 2,959,516 |
| P/L | 132,799 | 57,373 | 107,386 |
| NW | 2,677,391 | 2,544,592 | 2,487,219 |
| WC | (16,250) | (265,407) | 6,930 |
| Emp. | 72 | 66 | 61 |

DUNS 21-781-7938
## St Andrew's Secondary School
47 Torphin Crescent, Glasgow, Lanarkshire G32 6SF
Tel: 01415820240
Web: www.st-andrews-sec.glasgow.sch.uk
Estd: 2011 Proprietorship
Line of Business: Schools (local authority)
Proprietor: B Malone
Responsibilities
Senior: Gerry Lyons (Head Teacher)
US SIC: 8211  UK SIC: 93200
Employees: 120

DUNS 39-715-5276
## St Andrew's Tutorial Services Ltd
13 Station Road, Cambridge, Cambridgeshire CB1 2JB
Web: www.standrews.demon.co.uk
Reg No: 1835460  Estd: 1984 Private Limited Company
Line of Business: Schools (independent)
Issued Capital: £8,068
Directors: Ms H Martin, N J Claydon, D R Martin, Ms H L Claydon
Co. Secretary: Mervyn Martin
Responsibilities
Senior: Martin Robert (Manager)
Finance: Heather Black (Bursar)
Marketing: Heather Black (Bursar)
Admin: D Lassman (College Secretary)
IT: David Mcewan-Cox (IT Director)
HR: Ashley Collins (Principal)
Health & Safety: David Mcewan-Cox (IT Director)
Facilities: Ashley Collins (Principal)
US SIC: 8211  UK SIC: 93200
Auditors: Lakin Rose
Bankers: Lloyds TSB Bank plc (30-91-56)

|  | 30-06-14 | 30-06-13 | 30-06-12 |
|---|---|---|---|
| TO | 5,956,872 | 5,119,294 | 5,444,354 |
| P/L | 680,746 | 274,001 | 150,714 |
| NW | 5,938,045 | 3,918,037 | 3,715,907 |
| WC | (37,747) | (879,867) | (1,047,293) |
| Emp. | 95 | 92 | 97 |

DUNS 21-782-0246
## St Anne's Anchor Nursing Home
60 Durham Road, London N7 7DL
Web: www.anchor.org.uk
Estd: 2011
Line of Business: Medical nursing home activities
Responsibilities
Senior: Azaad Sauntally (Manager)
US SIC: 8051  UK SIC: 95100
Employees: 58

DUNS 50-019-0863
## St Anne's Community Services
6 St Marks Avenue, Leeds, West Yorkshire LS2 9BN
Tel: 01765606151
Web: www.st-annes.org.uk
Reg No: 1089026  Estd: 2012 Private Company Limited By Guarantee
Line of Business: Other letting of own property
Directors: J Tait, Ms S Nazir, T Moran, S Durham, Mrs S J Frier, Ms A M Legg, I Mcintosh, R Craven
Co. Secretary: Henry Baczkowski
Responsibilities
Senior: Jennifer Hanrahan (Home Manager), Michael Ludlum (Director), Julie Ronbinson (Chief Executive), Peter Shillito (Director)
Admin: Janette Care (Senior Administrator)
HR: Roy Fawcett (Learning & Development Manager)
Purchasing: Janette Care (Senior Administrator)
Branches: St Anne's Community Services, 10 Albany Road, Oxfield Court, Huddersfield, West Yorkshire HD5 9UZ

US SIC: 6519, 8091, 8321
UK SIC: 85000, 95200, 96111
Auditors: Grant Thornton UK LLP
Bankers: HSBC Bank plc (40-27-29)

|  | 31-03-14 | 31-03-13 | 31-03-12 |
|---|---|---|---|
| TO | 40,208,000 | 36,396,000 | 34,182,000 |
| P/L | 47,000 | 195,000 | 2,473,000 |
| NW | 6,307,000 | 1,002,000 | 473,000 |
| WC | 8,041,000 | 7,689,000 | 7,721,000 |
| Emp. | 1,324 | 1,487 | 1,151 |

DUNS 21-040-1731
## St Annes Convent
Windsor Gardens, Musselburgh, Midlothian EH21 7LP
Tel: 01316655591
Estd: 1912 Proprietorship
Line of Business: Residential care establishments
Proprietor: Mrs A Taylor
US SIC: 8321  UK SIC: 96111
Employees: 48

DUNS 23-679-2552
## St Annes Convent School
Carlton Road, Southampton, Hampshire SO15 2WZ
Tel: 023-8032-8200
Web: www.st-annes.southampton.sch.uk
Estd: 1904
Line of Business: Schools (local authority)
Directors: Miss C A Hargaden, M Hilton
Responsibilities
Senior: Bernadette Barrett-John (Deputy Head), Mike Cave (Site Manager), Beverley Murtagh (Headmistress)
Finance: Qing Bradbury (Finance Officer), Kate Cruse (Finance & Admin Manager), Donna Shorter (Finance Manager)
Marketing: Anne Murphy (Business Manager)
Admin: Kate Cruse (Finance & Admin Manager), Beverly Trueick (Administration Manager)
IT: Anne Allin (IT Technician), Matthew Dear (Network Manager)
US SIC: 8211  UK SIC: 93200
Bankers: The Bank Of Ireland (30-15-73)
Employees: 100

DUNS 21-774-1436
## St Anne's R C School
Underwood Road, London E1 5AW
Tel: 02072476327
Web: www.stannesschool.org.uk
Estd: 1976 Proprietorship
Line of Business: Schools (local authority)
Proprietor: Mrs J Sheehan
Responsibilities
Senior: Sheila Mouna (Head Teacher)
US SIC: 8211  UK SIC: 93200
Employees: 60

DUNS 21-032-2570
## St Ann's Hospice
Peel Lane, Manchester M28 0FE
Web: www.sah.org.uk
Estd: 2002 Proprietorship
Line of Business: Activities of other membership organisations not elsewhere classified
Proprietor: Mrs J Foley
Responsibilities
Health & Safety: Jane Close (Health & Safety Officer)
US SIC: 8699  UK SIC: 96902
Employees: 50

DUNS 22-504-1920
## St Anthonys Hospital
North Cheam House, Sutton, Surrey SM3 9DW
Tel: 020-8337-6691
Web: www.stanthonys.org.uk
Estd: 1894 Private Company Limited By Guarantee
Line of Business: Hospitals
Principals: S F Cope (Financial), P R Cook (Marketing), B M Clarke, D Of Cross (Proprietor)
Responsibilities
Senior: brian clarke (hospital director), Daughters of Cross (Proprietor)
IT: John Groom (Network, Security Manager), John Mcgurk (IT Manager)
Facilities: Myriame Lawley (Intensive Care Manager), Steve Leverington (Site Services Manager)
Purchasing: Julie Wale (Purchasing Manager)
Branches: St Anthonys Hospital, 81 Banstead Road, Carshalton, Surrey SM5 3NP
US SIC: 8062  UK SIC: 95100
Bankers: Barclays Bank Plc (20-65-82)
Employees: 500

DUNS 54-905-1159
## St Anthony's Primary School
Tullygally Road, Legahory, Craigavon, Co Armagh BT65 5BL
Tel: 028-3834-1569
Web: www.stanthonysprimaryschool.com
Estd: 1970
Line of Business: General secondary education
Proprietor: S Mcmorrow
Responsibilities
Senior: Sean McMorrow (Proprietor)
US SIC: 8211  UK SIC: 93200
Employees: 60

DUNS 23-644-7850
## St Augustine Home
Firfield House, Simplemarsh Road, Addlestone, Surrey KT15 1QR
Tel: 01932842254
Web: www.sistershospitallers.org
Estd: 2002 Proprietorship
Line of Business: Non-charitable social work activities with accommodation
Proprietor: P Davies
Responsibilities
Senior: Isabel Canton (Manager)
US SIC: 8321  UK SIC: 96111
Employees: 49

DUNS 50-646-7252
## St Austell Educational Foundation
John Keay House, Tregonissey Road, St Austell, Cornwall PL25 4DJ
Tel: 01726226226
Web: www.cornwall.ac.uk
Estd: 2003
Line of Business: First-degree level higher education
Responsibilities
HR: Jayne Ninnes (Staff Development Manager)
Facilities: Malcolm Palin (Estates Manager)
US SIC: 8221  UK SIC: 93100
Employees: 500

DUNS 45-808-1031
## St Barnabas Hospice Trust (Lincolnshire)
36 Nettleham Road, Lincoln, Lincolnshire LN2 1RE
Tel: 01522511566
Web: www.stbarnabashospice.co.uk
Reg No: 3166056  Estd: 1996 Private Limited Company
Line of Business: Hospital activities
Trading Style: St Barnabas Lincolnshire Hospice
Directors: Mrs S P Glaister, D Libiszewski, A J Maltby, E G Hale, Mrs J S Smith, Mrs A Daulton, R F Neilans, P J Jordan
Co. Secretary: Thomas Murray
Responsibilities
Senior: Noel Baumber (trustee), Keith Darwin (Director)
Branches: St Barnabas Hospice Trust (Lincolnshire), 24 New Road, Spalding, Lincolnshire PE12 9RA
US SIC: 8062, 8011
UK SIC: 95100, 95300
Bankers: National Westminster Bank Plc (60-13-15)

|  | 31-03-14 | 31-03-13 | 31-03-12 |
|---|---|---|---|
| TO | 10,708,236 | 8,465,580 | 7,714,666 |
| P/L | 2,020,674 | 640,899 | 206,014 |
| NW | 15,114,695 | 12,929,265 | 12,025,265 |
| WC | 4,175,538 | 2,549,996 | 2,364,158 |
| Emp. | 207 | 204 | 184 |

DUNS 23-506-3682
## St Barnabas Hospices (Sussex) Ltd
St Barnabas House, 2 Titnore Lane, Worthing, West Sussex BN12 6NZ
Tel: 01903706300  Fax: 01903706398
Web: www.stbarnabas-hospice.org.uk
Reg No: 0930107  Estd: 1966 Private Company Limited By Guarantee
Line of Business: Hospices
Directors: T V Wolstenholme, Mrs M Chowen, Mrs P Woolgar, P J Seear, M Carroll, G A Jeffs, Dr R H Eve, C G Clinch
Co. Secretary: Max Caunhye
Responsibilities
Senior: Jean Baumann (Director), David Bunce (Director), Graham Hunton (Director), Hugh Lowson (Chief Executive), Elizabeth Orford (Director), Michael Rymer (Director)
Marketing: Stephanie Smith (Marketing Director)
HR: David Gayler (Personnel Manager)
Health & Safety: Sheila Leach (Health & Safety Officer)
Branches: St Barnabas Hospices (Sussex) Ltd, 11 Broadwater Street West, Cricketers Parade, Worthing, West Sussex BN14 9DB

US SIC: 8091  UK SIC: 95200
Auditors: Carpenter Box
Bankers: National Westminster Bank Plc
(60-03-38)

| | 31-03-14 | 31-03-13 | 31-03-12 |
|---|---|---|---|
| TO | 15,420,000 | 12,866,000 | 12,681,000 |
| P/L | 1,762,000 | 204,000 | 789,000 |
| NW | 38,776,000 | 36,686,000 | 35,725,000 |
| WC | 6,768,000 | 4,143,000 | 3,574,000 |
| Emp. | 262 | 253 | 228 |

DUNS 64-251-9805
## St Bartholomew's C of E Primary School
Bredon Avenue, Binley, Coventry, West Midlands CV3 2LP
Tel: 024-7645-8960
Web: www.stbarthprimaryschool.com
Estd: 1970
Line of Business: Primary education
Director: Mrs J Steane
Responsibilities
Senior: Hillary Perry (Head Teacher)
US SIC: 8211, 6732
UK SIC: 93200, 83100
Employees: 50

DUNS 42-429-4718
## St Bartholomews Medical College
Room 205c, Department Of General Practice, Charterhouse Square, London EC1M 4BQ
Tel: 02078823850
Estd: 2012
Line of Business: Technical and industrial schools
Trading Style: Wolfson Institute of Prevent Medicine
Responsibilities
Senior: Cheryl Mason (Institute Manager)
US SIC: 8249  UK SIC: 93300
Employees: 100

DUNS 21-738-4699
## St Bartholomew's School
St Bartholomew's School, Andover Road, Newbury, Berkshire RG14 6JP
Tel: 01635576372
Web: www.stbarts.co.uk
Reg No: 7721470  Estd: 2011 Private Company Limited By Guarantee
Line of Business: General secondary education
Directors: K A Astill, I J Peddie, Ms M Howes, D G Brown, N Fleming, Ms J A Mortimore, R Deal, S M Foyle
Responsibilities
Senior: Rajan Bhandari (Director), Ahmad Bhatti (Director), Jeanette Clifford (Director), Nicola Ostinelli (Director), Patricia Ray (Director), Karen Sadler (Director), Bruce Steiner (Director), Stephen Uden (Director)
US SIC: 8211  UK SIC: 93200
Bankers: Lloyds TSB Bank plc (30-95-89)

| | 31-08-14 | 31-08-13 | 31-08-12 |
|---|---|---|---|
| TO | 9,136,235 | 9,252,577 | 49,360,462 |
| P/L | (776,546) | (341,115) | 38,681,355 |
| NW | 36,637,694 | 37,395,240 | 37,832,355 |
| WC | 1,905,407 | 2,254,814 | 1,751,035 |
| Emp. | 179 | 184 | 184 |

DUNS 23-975-7292
## St Basil's
Heath Mill Lane, Birmingham, West Midlands B9 4AX
Tel: 0121-772-2483
Web: www.stbasils.org.uk
Reg No: 3964376  Estd: 1982 Private Company Limited By Guarantee
Line of Business: Other tourist or short-stay accommodation
Directors: C J Hutchings, A Mccann, Ms M C Bunker, T J Parr, Ms S Fowler, J H Templeton, Ms S A Thompson, D A Leigh
Co. Secretary: Brian Adams
Responsibilities
Senior: Harris Beider (Director), Jonathan Broome (trustee), Patricia Brown Richards (trustee), Kathryn Halliday (Director), Sue Southern (Director)
Marketing: Ellie Jones (Marketing and Communications O)
IT: Mandy Blizard (ICT Manager)
Operations: Lorna Esien (Director of Operations)
Branches: St Basil's, 110 St. Andrews Road, Birmingham, West Midlands B9 4NA
US SIC: 8699, 6732
UK SIC: 96902, 83100
Bankers: Lloyds TSB Bank plc (30-13-66)

| | 31-03-14 | 31-03-13 | 31-03-12 |
|---|---|---|---|
| TO | 8,307,042 | 8,414,351 | 8,307,572 |
| P/L | (70,879) | 69,528 | 405,081 |
| NW | 3,899,236 | 3,965,213 | 3,999,859 |
| WC | 2,007,554 | 2,259,516 | 2,331,013 |
| Emp. | 205 | 185 | 166 |

DUNS 21-748-8053
## St Bede's Catholic College
Long Cross, Lawrence Weston, Bristol, Avon BS11 0SU
Web: www.stbedescc.org
Reg No: 7798550  Estd: 2011 Private Company Limited By Guarantee
Line of Business: General secondary education
Directors: C M Stevens, M J Hibbert, Ms A B Pilkington, A D Edmonds, M Mcandrew, Ms M A Hendricks, Rev T Finnergan, J T Bees
Co. Secretary: Ms Charmaine Lander
Responsibilities
Senior: Kevin Magner (Director), Amanda Parsons (Director)
US SIC: 8211  UK SIC: 93200

| | 31-08-14 | 31-08-13 | 31-08-12 |
|---|---|---|---|
| TO | 17,498,899 | 5,087,959 | 8,035,274 |
| P/L | 12,163,203 | 246,451 | 4,201,747 |
| NW | 16,504,647 | 4,561,444 | 4,101,747 |
| WC | 2,342,885 | 2,483,600 | 1,918,563 |
| Emp. | 97 | 99 | 94 |

DUNS 21-772-7970
## St Bede's Catholic Grammar School
Heaton, Bradford, West Yorkshire BD9 4BQ
Tel: 01274941941
Web: www.sbsj.co.uk
Estd: 1904 Proprietorship
Line of Business: Schools (local authority)
Proprietor: P Martin
Responsibilities
Senior: Frank Ashcroft (Head Teacher), Lawerence Bentley (Head Teacher)
Finance: Gabriele Barrett (Senior Finance Administrator)
HR: Lena Matthews (HR Manager)
US SIC: 8211  UK SIC: 93200
Employees: 120

DUNS 21-362-9971
## St Bendicts College
5 Craigstown Road, Randalstown, Antrim, Co Antrim BT41 2AF
Tel: 028-94472411
Web: www.stbenedictscollege.co.uk
Estd: 1969
Line of Business: Schools (foundation)
Trading Style: St Bendicts College
Partners: S Mcneil, S Mcauley
Responsibilities
IT: Dermot Shivers (Senior IT Executive)
US SIC: 8211  UK SIC: 93200
Employees: 60

DUNS 21-600-4760
## St Benedict's High School
Bridge Of Weir Road, Johnstone, Renfrewshire PA5 8EX
Tel: 01505327500
Web: www.oraetlabora.co.uk
Estd: 2002 Proprietorship
Line of Business: Schools (local authority)
Proprietor: Mrs M Monroe
US SIC: 8211  UK SIC: 93200
Employees: 120

DUNS 21-776-2219
## St Benedict's Infant School
St Benedicts Road, Birmingham, West Midlands B10 9DP
Tel: 01214646420
Web: www.stbendic.bham.sch.uk
Estd: 2011 Proprietorship
Line of Business: Schools (local authority)
Proprietor: Mrs A Williams
US SIC: 8211  UK SIC: 93200
Employees: 75

DUNS 23-083-2334
## St Benedict's Junior School
5 Montpelier Avenue, Ealing, London W5 2XP
Web: www.stbenedicts.org.uk
Estd: 1902
Line of Business: Schools (independent)
Director: D Mcsweeney
Responsibilities
Senior: Dennis McSweeney (Principal)
US SIC: 8211  UK SIC: 93200
Employees: 50

DUNS 21-206-9160
## St Benedicts Nursing Home
Benedict Street, Glastonbury, Somerset BA6 9NB
Tel: 01458833275
Web: www.stbens.co.uk
Estd: 1985 Partnership
Line of Business: Nursing homes
Partner: D White

Branches: St Benedicts Nursing Home, 1 Hitchen Lane, Shepton Mallet, Somerset BA4 5TZ
US SIC: 8051  UK SIC: 95100
Employees: 52

DUNS 22-832-3143
## St Benedicts School
54 Eaton Rise, Ealing, London W5 2ES
Web: www.stbenedicts.org.uk
Estd: 1902
Line of Business: Schools (independent)
Trading Style: St. Benedict's School
Responsibilities
Senior: Christopher Cleugh (Principal)
US SIC: 8211  UK SIC: 93200
Auditors: Buzzacott
Employees: 100
Turnover: £9,324,206

DUNS 21-842-7241
## St Benedict's School Ealing
54 Eaton Rise, Ealing, London W5 2ES
Tel: 02089981066
Web: www.stbenedicts.org.uk
Reg No: 8093330  Estd: 2012 Private Company Limited By Guarantee
Line of Business: Schools (independent)
Directors: J P Walsh, C W Field, Rev M G Shipperlee, Dr P A Hopley, Ms M Doyle, Rev A J Hughes, B A Taylor, J J Dilger
Co. Secretary: Ms Catherine De Cintra
Responsibilities
Senior: Michael Ainslie (Director), Jonathan Berger (Director), Mary Codrington (Director), Patrick Murphy-O'Connor (Director), Tony Shilling (Director), Susan Vale (Director)
US SIC: 8211  UK SIC: 93200
Bankers: Allied Irish Bank (gb) (23-83-94)

| | 31-08-13 |
|---|---|
| TO | 14,277,296 |
| P/L | 1,570,109 |
| NW | 1,570,109 |
| WC | 1,556,555 |
| Emp. | 260 |

DUNS 21-206-9178
## St Benet's Nursing Home
32a College Road, Newton Abbot, Devon TQ12 1EQ
Tel: 01626-354069
Web: www.devoncaregroup.co.uk
Estd: 1984 Partnership
Line of Business: Rest and retirement homes
Partners: B Harstead, Mrs G Harstead
Responsibilities
Senior: Nikki Rogers (Partner)
US SIC: 8321  UK SIC: 96111
Employees: 51

DUNS 45-847-0655
## St Bernards Residential Care Home Ltd
76 St Bernards Road, Solihull, West Midlands B92 7BP
Tel: 0121-708-0177
Web: www.stbernardscare.co.uk
Reg No: 3193755  Estd: 1996 Private Limited Company
Line of Business: Residential care establishments
Issued Capital: £100
Director: P B Byrne
Co. Secretary: Ms Claire Byrne
US SIC: 8321  UK SIC: 96111
Auditors: Hlb Kidsons

| | 31-10-13 | 31-10-12 | 31-10-11 |
|---|---|---|---|
| TA | 2,804,001 | 2,605,723 | 2,458,109 |
| NW | 2,120,385 | 1,833,835 | 1,561,457 |
| WC | 346,776 | 320,363 | 145,950 |

DUNS 21-527-7919
## St Beuno's
Tremeirchion, St Asaph, Clwyd LL17 0AS
Tel: 01745-583444
Web: www.beunos.com
Line of Business: Religious organisations and places of worship
Chairman: T Mcguinness
Responsibilities
Senior: Nick Hawkins (Minister), Tom McGuinness (Chairperson)
US SIC: 8661  UK SIC: 96600
Employees: 50

DUNS 23-280-6638
## St Brelades Bay Hotel
Lane Route De Lane Baie, St Brelade, Jersey, Channel Islands JE3 8EF
Tel: 01534-746141 Fax: 01534-747278
Web: www.stbreladesbayhotel.com
Reg No: 0002770J  Estd: 1967 Private Limited Company
Line of Business: Hotels
Issued Capital: £3

Principals: R D Colley (Managing), Mrs M J Colley
Co. Secretary: L Phillips
Responsibilities
Senior: Leo Basil (Restaurant Manager), Robert Colley (Proprietor), Emerson Colley (Proprietor), David Whalen (Proprietor)
Finance: Robert Colley (Proprietor), David Whalen (Proprietor)
Marketing: Robert Colley (Proprietor), David Whalen (Proprietor)
Sales: Margriet Barnes (General Manager)
IT: Robert Colley (Proprietor), David Whalen (Proprietor)
HR: Margriet Barnes (General Manager)
Health & Safety: Robert Colley (Proprietor), David Whalen (Proprietor)
Facilities: Robert Colley (Proprietor)
US SIC: 7011  UK SIC: 66500
Bankers: HSBC Bank plc (40-25-34)
Employees: 90

DUNS 22-269-1847
## St Brelades Retirement Homes Ltd
2 The Links, Herne Bay, Kent CT6 7GQ
Tel: 01227375301
Reg No: 4287163  Estd: 2001 Private Limited Company
Line of Business: Social work activities with accommodation
Issued Capital: £1,000
Directors: Mrs C M Chuck, E F Chuck
Responsibilities
Senior: Catherine Mcneill (Manager)
US SIC: 8321, 6732
UK SIC: 96111, 83100
Bankers: National Westminster Bank Plc (60-10-37)

| | 31-03-14 | 31-03-13 | 31-03-12 |
|---|---|---|---|
| TA | 500,411 | 689,886 | 608,074 |
| NW | 276,404 | 286,313 | 304,705 |
| WC | 199,355 | (95,993) | (79,552) |

DUNS 42-470-0037
## St Brendans Sixth Form College
Broomhill Road, Bristol, Avon BS4 5RQ
Tel: 01179-777766
Web: www.stbrn.ac.uk
Estd: 1897
Line of Business: Further education schools and colleges
Principals: K C Maloney (Financial), P G Bradshaw
Responsibilities
Senior: Ann Barrow (Principal), Michael Jaffrain (Principal)
Finance: Christine Hart (Financial Officer)
Marketing: Christine Hayward (Marketing Manager)
IT: Derek Durrant (IT Manager), Mitchell Gardner (IT Manager)
Health & Safety: Paul Connors (Premises Manager)
Facilities: Paul Connors (Premises Manager)
US SIC: 8221  UK SIC: 93100
Bankers: National Westminster Bank Plc (56-00-05)
Employees: 120

DUNS 21-033-9681
## St Bridget's C of E Controlled Primary School
St Bridgets Lane, Wirral, Merseyside CH48 3JT
Tel: 0151-625-7652
Web: www.stbridgets.wirral.sch.uk
Line of Business: Schools (local authority)
Responsibilities
Senior: Neil Feuvre (Head Teacher)
US SIC: 8211  UK SIC: 93200
Employees: 50

DUNS 28-976-2098
## St Catherine's - Speech & Language
Grove Road, Ventnor, Isle of Wight PO38 1TT
Tel: 01983-852722
Web: www.stcatherines.org.uk
Reg No: 1757474  Estd: 1983 Private Company Limited By Guarantee
Line of Business: Schools (special)
Directors: Ms P S James, Ms P Collyer, J P Metcalfe, Mrs C Daish-Miller, A J Flower, Mrs I M Pratley, J C Pulsford, P J Rudd
Co. Secretary: Ms Rachel Thomson
Responsibilities
Senior: Anthony Bicknell (Manager), Felicity Raines (Manager), Samantha Rooney (Director), Susan Scoccia (Director), G Shipley (Headmaster), Lawrence Tutton (Manager), Kim Williams (Director)
US SIC: 8211  UK SIC: 93200
Auditors: Harrison Black

**Bankers:** National Westminster Bank Plc (54-41-31)

|     | 31-08-13 | 31-08-12 | 31-08-11 |
| --- | --- | --- | --- |
| TO | 2,598,054 | 2,543,946 | 2,583,375 |
| P/L | 208,564 | 27,221 | (80,137) |
| NW | 1,869,125 | 1,359,561 | 1,623,340 |
| WC | 903,926 | 417,345 | 358,947 |
| Emp. | 87 | N/A | N/A |

DUNS 23-701-1911

## St Catherines Care Centre

East Lane, Shipton By Beningbrough, York, North Yorkshire YO30 1AH
**Tel:** 01904470644
**Web:** www.wellbum-carehomes.co.uk
**Estd:** 2001 Proprietorship
**Line of Business:** Nursing homes
**Proprietor:** Mrs B A Mcnelis
**Responsibilities**
**Senior:** Brigette McNelis (Proprietor), Judeth Scurr (Matron)
**HR:** Judeth Scurr (Matron)
**Health & Safety:** Judeth Scurr (Matron)
**Facilities:** Judeth Scurr (Matron)
**US SIC:** 8051 **UK SIC:** 95100
**Bankers:** National Westminster Bank Plc (60-12-01)
**Employees:** 70

DUNS 21-466-1410

## St Catherines Care Home

1 Queen Street, Horwich, Bolton, Lancashire BL6 5QU
**Tel:** 01204-668740
**Web:** www.fshc.co.uk
**Estd:** 1992 Partnership
**Line of Business:** Nursing homes
**Partners:** Mrs M Barker, Mrs M Barker
**Responsibilities**
**Senior:** Samantha Anyon (Home Manager)
**Facilities:** Szymon Kacperski (Maintenance Officer), Roy Tennant (Maintenance Officer)
**US SIC:** 8321 **UK SIC:** 96111
**Employees:** 53

DUNS 21-734-9817

## St Catherine's Catholic School

Watling Street, Bexleyheath, Kent DA6 7QJ
**Tel:** 02083031466
**Web:** www.stagecoach.co.uk
**Reg No:** 7694573 **Estd:** 2011 Private Company Limited By Guarantee
**Line of Business:** General secondary education
**Directors:** M T Totman, V Fanawopo, Mrs T Grant, Mrs M R Redgrave, Dr G Houghton-Boyle, Mrs B A Aleppo, M I Ross, R C Fernandez
**Responsibilities**
**Senior:** Barry Connell (Director), Paul Gannaway (Director), Karen Laponder (Director), Patricia Slonecki (Director), Yvonne Uttley Wright (Director), Sandra Wheeler (Director)
**US SIC:** 8211 **UK SIC:** 93200
**Bankers:** Lloyds TSB Bank plc (30-00-00)

|     | 31-08-14 | 31-08-13 | 31-08-12 |
| --- | --- | --- | --- |
| TO | 6,083,000 | 6,025,000 | 15,379,000 |
| P/L | 186,000 | (205,000) | 9,665,000 |
| NW | 9,483,000 | 9,431,000 | 9,547,000 |
| WC | 1,435,000 | 970,000 | 902,000 |
| Emp. | 106 | 102 | 105 |

DUNS 21-328-8827

## St Catherines Hospice

Throxenby Lane, Scarborough, North Yorkshire YO12 5RE
**Tel:** 01723351421
**Web:** www.stcatherineshospice-nyorks.org
**Estd:** 2003 Proprietorship
**Line of Business:** Other human health activities
**Proprietor:** Mrs L Barker
**Responsibilities**
**Senior:** Diane Flint (Manager), James Garnett (Manager), Ian Westmoreland (Manager)
**Admin:** Jan Sharp (Office Administrator)
**IT:** Jan Sharp (Office Administrator)
**HR:** Gordon Queen (Personnel Officer)
**Health & Safety:** Sandra Bewell-Frost (Health & Safety Officer)
**Purchasing:** Jan Sharp (Office Administrator)
**Branches:** St Catherines Hospice, 28C Ramshill Road, Scarborough, North Yorkshire YO11 2QF
**US SIC:** 8091 **UK SIC:** 95200
**Employees:** 113

DUNS 23-083-1583

## St Catherine's R C School for Girls

Watling Street, Bexleyheath, Kent DA6 7QJ
**Tel:** 01322-556333
**Web:** www.stccg.co.uk
**Estd:** 1944
**Line of Business:** Schools (local authority)
**Director:** Miss S Powell

**Responsibilities**
**Senior:** Patricia Slonecki (Head Teacher)
**Finance:** Kulbinder Singh (Finance Assistant)
**Marketing:** Jack Hayter (Media Resources Officer)
**Admin:** Jane Lenihan (PA, Office Manager)
**IT:** David Burls (Network Administrator), Adam Young (Communication Information Syst)
**Facilities:** Brian Sims (Premises Officer)
**Operations:** Gino Carrano (Site Manager)
**US SIC:** 8211 **UK SIC:** 93200
**Employees:** 50

DUNS 22-506-3973

## St Catherines School

Station Road, Bramley, Guildford, Surrey GU5 0AY
**Tel:** 01483893363
**Web:** www.stcatherines.info
**VAT No:** 211497382 **Estd:** 1998
**Line of Business:** Schools (local authority)
**Chairman:** R Lilley
**Responsibilities**
**Senior:** Alice Phillips (Principal)
**Finance:** Chris Silver (Bursar)
**Marketing:** Gill David (Marketing Manager)
**Admin:** Laura Tong (Office Manager)
**IT:** Jennifer Obaditch (Head of IT)
**HR:** Alice Phillips (Principal)
**Health & Safety:** Chris Silver (Bursar)
**Facilities:** Tim Brett (Facilities Manager)
**Operations:** Gill David (Marketing Manager)
**Purchasing:** Chris Silver (Bursar)
**US SIC:** 8211 **UK SIC:** 93200
**Bankers:** Lloyds TSB Bank plc (30-93-74)
**Employees:** 171

DUNS 77-104-5515

## St Catherine's School Twickenham

Cross Deep, Cross Deep, Twickenham, Middlesex TW1 4QJ
**Web:** www.stcatherineschool.co.uk
**Reg No:** 2681512 **Estd:** 1992 Private Limited Company
**Line of Business:** Drama schools
**Directors:** A Perrier, W Skehan, Ms L M Mcdonald, Ms C M Rushton, E C Sparrow, S Skehan, P L Clifford, S Jefferson
**Co. Secretary:** Ian Stewart
**Responsibilities**
**Senior:** Graham Elkes (Director), Beryl Lane (Director), Edward Latham (Manager)
**IT:** Munir Hassen (Computer Manager)
**Health & Safety:** All Hall (Facilities Manager)
**US SIC:** 8299, 8211
**UK SIC:** 93300, 93200
**Bankers:** National Westminster Bank Plc (60-22-03)

|     | 31-07-13 | 31-07-12 | 31-07-11 |
| --- | --- | --- | --- |
| TO | 4,565,663 | 4,225,669 | 3,944,323 |
| P/L | 382,407 | 189,181 | 504,114 |
| NW | 5,111,592 | 4,729,185 | 4,540,004 |
| WC | 518,795 | 305,491 | 624,781 |
| Emp. | 67 | 66 | 61 |

DUNS 23-684-0294

## St Cenydd Comprehensive School

St Cenydd Road, Caerphilly, Mid Glamorgan CF83 2RP
**Tel:** 02920852504
**Web:** http://learn.caerphilly.org.uk
**Estd:** 1973
**Line of Business:** Schools (local authority)
**Directors:** D Eynon, Mrs M Lewis
**Co. Secretary:** Mrs Maureen Lewis
**Responsibilities**
**Senior:** Rebecca Collins (Head Teacher), Ian Kilcoyne (Head Teacher)
**US SIC:** 8211 **UK SIC:** 93200
**Employees:** 120

DUNS 21-038-1057

## St Chads C . E . Primary School

Crackley Bank, Newcastle, Staffordshire ST5 7AB
**Web:** www.st-chads-newcastle.staffs.sch.uk
**Estd:** 1963
**Line of Business:** Schools (local authority)
**Proprietor:** G Davis
**Responsibilities**
**Senior:** Samantha Clarke (Head Teacher)
**US SIC:** 8211 **UK SIC:** 93200
**Employees:** 55

DUNS 22-963-1353

## St Christopher School (Letchworth) Ltd

Barrington Road, Letchworth, Hertfordshire SG6 3JZ
**Tel:** 01462650850
**Web:** www.stchris.co.uk
**Reg No:** 0535836 **Estd:** 2012 Private Limited Company
**Line of Business:** Schools (local authority)
**Issued Capital:** £40
**Directors:** Dr D R Macgregor, J Simmonds, P M De Voil, Ms S J Kilcoyne, R W Middleton, M A Leigh, Mrs J A Bolter, P Mcmeekin
**Co. Secretary:** William Hawkes
**Responsibilities**
**Senior:** Thomas Routh (Director)
**US SIC:** 8211 **UK SIC:** 93200
**Auditors:** Horwath Clark Whitehill
**Bankers:** Barclays Bank Plc (20-41-12)

|     | 31-08-13 | 31-08-12 | 31-08-11 |
| --- | --- | --- | --- |
| TO | 7,120,720 | 7,066,166 | 7,774,301 |
| P/L | (33,421) | 11,038 | 549,337 |
| NW | 9,224,901 | 8,918,998 | 8,907,960 |
| WC | (409,251) | (371,158) | (280,072) |
| Emp. | 142 | 138 | 137 |

DUNS 64-718-4746

## St Christophers Playgroup

Allesley Old Road, Coventry, West Midlands CV5 8GB
**Tel:** 02476675017
**Web:** www.st-christopher.coventry.sch.uk
**Estd:** 1953
**Line of Business:** Schools (local authority)
**Co. Secretary:** Ms Mandy Aynsworth
**Responsibilities**
**Senior:** Clair Robinson (Head Teacher)
**US SIC:** 8211 **UK SIC:** 93200
**Employees:** 80

DUNS 21-780-6903

## St Christophers School

Stockwell Grove, Wrexham, Clwyd LL13 7BW
**Tel:** 01978346910
**Web:** www.stcfootball.co.uk
**Estd:** 2002 Partnership
**Line of Business:** Schools (special)
**Partners:** Mrs M Pittaway, Mrs M Grant
**Responsibilities**
**Finance:** Tracy Fornstone (Senior Finance Administrator)
**Admin:** Tracy Fornstone (Senior Finance Administrator)
**IT:** Phil Pumfort (IT Manager)
**US SIC:** 8299 **UK SIC:** 93300
**Employees:** 147

DUNS 28-837-6940

## St Christopher's School (Bristol)

Carisbrooke Lodge, Westbury Park, Bristol, Avon BS6 7JE
**Tel:** 01179736875
**Web:** www.st-christophers.bristol.sch.uk
**Reg No:** 0462901 **Estd:** 1945 Private Company Limited By Guarantee
**Line of Business:** Schools (special)
**Directors:** C M Tolman, B D Willerton, L A Melarickas, G D Meyer, M T Underwood
**Co. Secretary:** Omer Paker
**Responsibilities**
**Senior:** Orna Matz (Head of Education), Omer Packer (Head of Resources)
**Finance:** Omer Packer (Head of Resources)
**HR:** Orna Matz (Head of Education), Omer Packer (Head of Resources)
**Health & Safety:** Omer Packer (Head of Resources)
**Facilities:** Omer Packer (Head of Resources)
**Purchasing:** Omer Packer (Head of Resources)
**US SIC:** 8299, 8211
**UK SIC:** 93300, 93200
**Auditors:** PricewaterhouseCoopers
**Bankers:** Bank Of Scotland (12-05-77)

|     | 31-08-13 | 31-08-12 | 31-08-11 |
| --- | --- | --- | --- |
| TO | 8,809,034 | 9,274,443 | 8,979,173 |
| P/L | (264,347) | 53,527 | 456,468 |
| NW | 12,082,617 | 12,333,891 | 12,263,882 |
| WC | (1,739,808) | (1,527,255) | (1,512,632) |
| Emp. | 369 | 418 | 385 |

DUNS 55-067-1929

## St Christopher's Trust

Redcourt, Hollincross Lane, Glossop, Derbyshire SK13 8JH
**Tel:** 01457852687
**Web:** www.stchristophers.org.uk
**Estd:** 1953
**Line of Business:** Staff (domestic)
**Chairman:** Mrs J Thomson
**Responsibilities**
**Senior:** Susan Hammond (Care Manager)
**US SIC:** 8091 **UK SIC:** 95200
**Employees:** 50

DUNS 21-779-1749

## St Clair Centre

Bank Street, Kirkcaldy, Fife KY1 3DT
**Tel:** 01592583338
**Estd:** 2011
**Line of Business:** Non-charitable social work activities without accommodation
**Responsibilities**
**Senior:** Maureen Sebcebney (Manager)
**US SIC:** 8321 **UK SIC:** 96111
**Employees:** 50

DUNS 42-441-4266

## St Clare West Essex Hospice Care Trust

St Clare Hospice Centre, Hastingwood Road, Hastingwood, Harlow, Essex CM17 9JX
**Tel:** 01279773700
**Web:** www.stclare-hospice.co.uk
**Reg No:** 3398955 **Estd:** 1990 Private Company Limited By Guarantee
**Line of Business:** Other human health activities
**Directors:** Dr R F Morgan, P A Quincey, P C Foster, Mrs J A Minihane, D F Thomson, R E Cattell, B G Moore, J Frazer
**Co. Secretary:** Philip Quincey
**Responsibilities**
**Senior:** Debbie Bodhanya (Director)
**US SIC:** 8091 **UK SIC:** 95200
**Auditors:** Kingston Smith
**Bankers:** HSBC Bank plc (40-23-10)

|     | 31-03-14 | 31-03-13 | 31-03-12 |
| --- | --- | --- | --- |
| TO | 4,901,870 | 3,950,015 | 4,018,918 |
| P/L | 3,528,770 | 2,628,141 | 373,792 |
| NW | 5,731,993 | 4,878,684 | 4,651,261 |
| WC | 3,155,083 | 2,725,134 | 2,372,428 |
| Emp. | 98 | 90 | 90 |

DUNS 21-878-9672

## St Clare's Care Home

Ditchling Road St Georges Park, Burgess Hill, West Sussex RH15 0GU
**Web:** www.anh.org.uk
**Estd:** 2012
**Line of Business:** Residential care establishments
**Responsibilities**
**Senior:** Elenita Haban (Manager), Devendra Lallchand (Manager)
**US SIC:** 8321 **UK SIC:** 96111
**Employees:** 110

DUNS 21-877-5022

## St Cleres Co-Operative Academy Trust

St Clere's School, Butts Lane, Stanford-Le, Stanford-Le-Hope, Essex SS17 0NW
**Web:** www.st-cleres.thurrock.sch.uk
**Reg No:** 7703865 **Estd:** 2011 Private Limited Company
**Line of Business:** Primary education
**Directors:** K M Willett, B A Martin, R L Osborne, C Fegan, Mrs D M Mummery, G J Mack, Ms S D Walker, Mrs A C Gaywood
**Co. Secretary:** Mrs Kathryn Draper
**Responsibilities**
**Senior:** Michael Fall (Director), Joy Leader (Director), Brian Moss (Director)
**US SIC:** 8211 **UK SIC:** 93200
**Bankers:** Lloyds TSB Bank plc (30-13-51)

|     | 31-08-14 | 31-08-13 | 31-08-12 |
| --- | --- | --- | --- |
| TO | 15,260,000 | 26,304,000 | 26,689,486 |
| P/L | (407,000) | 13,474,000 | 18,844,387 |
| NW | 28,715,000 | 31,468,000 | 18,464,387 |
| WC | 1,798,000 | 1,646,000 | 926,637 |
| Emp. | 342 | 317 | 232 |

DUNS 21-163-3537

## St Cleres School

Butts Lane, Stanford-Le-Hope, Essex SS17 0NW
**Tel:** 01375-641001
**Web:** www.st-cleres.thurrock.sch.uk
**Estd:** 1978
**Line of Business:** Schools (foundation)
**Director:** P Griffiths
**Responsibilities**
**Senior:** Ashley Hughes (Head Teacher)
**Finance:** R Chaston (Finance Officer)
**IT:** Ravi Chagger (Head of ICT)
**Facilities:** J Nyland (Business Manager)
**US SIC:** 8211 **UK SIC:** 93200
**Employees:** 98

DUNS 21-328-5385

## St Colman's College

46 Armagh Road, Newry, Co Down BT35 6PP
**Tel:** 028-3026-2451
**Web:** www.stcolmans.org.uk
**Estd:** 2002 Partnership
**Line of Business:** Schools (local authority)
**Proprietor:** C Mckinney
**Responsibilities**
**Senior:** Cormack McKinney (Proprietor)

**IT:** Claire Hollywood (Senior IT Executive)
**US SIC:** 8211 **UK SIC:** 93200
**Employees:** 100

DUNS 21-842-1542
## St Columba's Catholic Boys' School
Halcot Avenue, Bexleyheath, Kent DA6 7QB
**Tel:** 01322553236 **Fax:** 01322522471
**Web:** www.st-columbas.bexley.sch.uk
**Reg No:** 8088957 **Estd:** 1993 Private
Company Limited By Guarantee
**Line of Business:** Schools (local authority)
**Directors:** Mrs S M Biggs, R M Gillespie,
N W Fisher, J Spencer, Ms J P Johnson,
S A Middleton, P Strub, K M Kelly
**Co. Secretary:** Mrs Jacqueline Hobbs
**Responsibilities**
**Senior:** Philip Clemas (Chairperson), Chloe
Natali (Director)
**Finance:** Jay Hobbs (Senior Finance
Administrator)
**Admin:** Jay Hobbs (Senior Finance
Administrator)
**IT:** Lewis Williams (IT Executive)
**US SIC:** 8211 **UK SIC:** 93200
**Bankers:** Lloyds TSB Bank plc (30-90-76)

| | 31-08-14 | 31-08-13 |
|---|---|---|
| TO | 5,424,000 | 5,737,000 |
| P/L | 55,000 | 910,000 |
| NW | 941,000 | 971,000 |
| WC | 395,000 | 420,000 |
| Emp. | 86 | 94 |

DUNS 21-781-0146
## St Columba's Catholic Primary School
Tong Street, Bradford, West Yorkshire BD4 9PY
**Web:** www.stcolumbas.bradford.sch.uk
**Estd:** 1930 Proprietorship
**Line of Business:** Schools (local authority)
**Proprietor:** P Spillane
**US SIC:** 8211 **UK SIC:** 93200
**Employees:** 50

DUNS 21-333-0694
## St Columba's College
8-10 King Harry Lane, St Albans,
Hertfordshire AL3 4AW
**Tel:** 01727862616
**Web:** www.stcolumbascollege.com
**Estd:** 2001
**Line of Business:** Schools (local authority)
**Trading Style:** St Columba's
**Director:** S Darlington
**Responsibilities**
**Senior:** Robert Croteau (Manager),
Raymond Hetu (Manager), Mark Hilton
(Manager), Daniel St Jacques (Manager)
**Finance:** W Gerrard (Finance Manager)
**Marketing:** Rebecca Nansoz (Marketing and
Development)
**IT:** J Twyman (Head of It)
**US SIC:** 8211 **UK SIC:** 93200
**Employees:** 100

DUNS 21-782-8223
## St Columba's Nursing Home
1 Logie Street, Dundee, Angus DD2 2QF
**Web:** www.priority-care.co.uk
**Estd:** 2011 Proprietorship
**Line of Business:** Residential care
establishments
**Proprietor:** Mrs A Percival
**Responsibilities**
**Senior:** Claire Garven (Manager)
**US SIC:** 8321 **UK SIC:** 96111
**Employees:** 55

DUNS 23-933-7608
## St Columba's School (Developments) Ltd
(**Subsidiary of:** St. Columba's School Ltd)
St Colms, Duchal Road, Kilmacolm,
Renfrewshire PA13 4AY
**Tel:** 01505872238 **Fax:** 01505-873995
**Web:** www.st-columbas.org
**Reg No:** 0203853SC **Estd:** 1897 Private
Limited Company
**Line of Business:** Schools (independent)
**Issued Capital:** £2
**Directors:** P Yacoubian, H M Currie
**Responsibilities**
**Senior:** David Girdwood (Headmaster)
**Marketing:** Nichola McKay (Head of
Marketing)
**IT:** Stuart MacDonald (Network, Security
Manager)
**HR:** David Girdwood (Headmaster)
**Facilities:** Alex Galbraith (Maintenance
Manager)
**US SIC:** 8211 **UK SIC:** 93200
**Bankers:** The Royal Bank Of Scotland Plc
(83-21-08)

| | 31-07-14 | 31-07-13 | 31-07-12 |
|---|---|---|---|
| NW | (266,615) | (266,615) | (266,615) |

DUNS 21-283-5456
## St Columbs College
23 Buncrana Road, Londonderry, Co
Londonderry BT48 8NH
**Tel:** 028-71285000
**Web:** www.stcolumbs.com
**Estd:** 1879 Proprietorship
**Line of Business:** Schools (independent)
**Proprietor:** S Mcginty
**Responsibilities**
**Senior:** Finbar Madden (Principal)
**Finance:** Fedelma Hegarty (Senior Finance
Administrator)
**IT:** Damian Boast (Network, Security
Manager), Joe Stewart (IT Director)
**US SIC:** 8211 **UK SIC:** 93200
**Employees:** 300

DUNS 22-842-9239
## St Cuthberts Care
St Cuthberts House, West Road, Newcastle-
Upon-Tyne, Tyne and Wear NE15 7PY
**Web:** www.stcuthbertscare.org.uk
**Reg No:** 1645917 **VAT No:** 556244437
**Estd:** 1982 Private Company Limited By
Guarantee
**Line of Business:** Social work activities
**Directors:** M G Dickson, N A Gilbert,
Rev M J Campion, Mrs P C Wager,
J R Devine, A M Russell, F D Relton,
P B Moran
**Co. Secretary:** Ms Moira Ashman
**Responsibilities**
**Senior:** Jeremiah Kelliher (Director), Elsie
Robson (Manager)
**IT:** Mary Nicholson (Head of IT)
**Branches:** St Cuthberts Care, West Denton
Hall, St. Vincents Home, Newcastle Upon
Tyne, Tyne and Wear NE15 7LT
**US SIC:** 7399, 8091, 8321
**UK SIC:** 83954, 95200, 96111
**Auditors:** PricewaterhouseCoopers LLP
**Bankers:** National Westminster Bank Plc
(54-10-31)

| | 31-03-14 | 31-03-13 | 31-03-12 |
|---|---|---|---|
| TO | 9,304,250 | 8,182,430 | 7,538,006 |
| P/L | 55,258 | (241,867) | 156,289 |
| NW | 4,998,649 | 4,943,391 | 5,185,258 |
| WC | 427,241 | 419,569 | 745,494 |
| Emp. | 347 | 334 | 287 |

DUNS 21-034-4598
## St Cuthberts Catholic Community College
Berrys Lane, St Helens, Merseyside WA9 3HE
**Tel:** 01744-678123
**Web:** www.stcuthberts.com
**Partnership**
**Line of Business:** Schools (local authority)
**Partners:** Mrs M Gallimore, D Cairnes
**US SIC:** 8211 **UK SIC:** 93200
**Employees:** 69

DUNS 21-354-4534
## St Cyres G M Comprehensive School
St Cyres Road, Penarth, South Glamorgan CF64 2XP
**Tel:** 029-2070-8708
**Web:** www.stcyres.glamorgan.sch.uk
**Estd:** 2002 Proprietorship
**Line of Business:** Schools (foundation)
**Proprietor:** Dr J Hicks
**Responsibilities**
**Finance:** Nicola Reese (Senior Finance
Administrator)
**US SIC:** 8211 **UK SIC:** 93200
**Employees:** 130

DUNS 21-607-4947
## St Dallans Primary School
Clonallon Road, Warrenpoint, Newry, Co
Down BT34 3RP
**Tel:** 02841752655
**Web:** www.stdallans.com
**Estd:** 2011 Proprietorship
**Line of Business:** Schools (local authority)
**Proprietor:** Mrs P Quinn
**US SIC:** 8211 **UK SIC:** 93200
**Employees:** 50

DUNS 21-322-5654
## St Davids Catholic Sixth Form College
Ty-Gwyn Road, Penylan, Cardiff, South
Glamorgan CF23 5QD
**Web:** www.st-davids-coll.ac.uk
**Estd:** 2002 Proprietorship
**Line of Business:** Post-graduate level
higher education
**Proprietor:** M Leighfields
**US SIC:** 8221 **UK SIC:** 93100
**Employees:** 100

DUNS 21-228-7279
## St Davids Church
The Vicarage, Glanyrafon Road, Ystalyfera,
Swansea, West Glamorgan SA9 2EP
**Estd:** 1996
**Line of Business:** Places of worship
**Proprietor:** Reverend T Hewitts
**US SIC:** 8661 **UK SIC:** 96600
**Employees:** 55

DUNS 73-744-0347
## St David's Hospice
Abbey Road, Llandudno, Gwynedd LL30 2EN
**Tel:** 01492879058
**Web:** www.stdavidshospice.org.uk
**Reg No:** 2922828 **Estd:** 1993 Private
Limited Company
**Line of Business:** Hospices
**Directors:** Ms V M Macdonald, R Drinkwater,
A M Thomas, Ms G Harrison, A H Neville,
D R Thomas, C J Davies, M G Mason
**Co. Secretary:** John Jones
**Responsibilities**
**Senior:** Doreen Atkinson (Manager),
Amanda Hughes (Director), Jack Moffett
(Trustee), Nefyn Williams (Manager)
**Facilities:** Janet Magill (Hospice Manager)
**Fleet:** Jack Moffett (Trustee)
**Branches:** St David's Hospice, 19 Mostyn
Ave, Llandudno, Gwynedd LL30 1YS
**US SIC:** 8091, 6732
**UK SIC:** 95200, 83100
**Auditors:** Harold Smith

| | 31-12-13 | 31-12-12 | 31-12-11 |
|---|---|---|---|
| TO | 2,698,477 | 2,823,572 | 3,221,063 |
| P/L | (215,800) | 63,305 | 511,223 |
| NW | 4,619,406 | 4,490,164 | 4,349,821 |
| WC | 1,106,500 | 1,113,721 | 2,065,189 |
| Emp. | 97 | 72 | 70 |

DUNS 23-253-2809
## St Davids Nursing Home
12 Castlebar Hill, London W5 1TE
**Tel:** 02089975121
**Web:** www.stdavidshome.org
**Estd:** 1918
**Line of Business:** Nursing homes
**Chairman:** J Poland
**Responsibilities**
**Senior:** Jane McAuley (Manager)
**US SIC:** 8051 **UK SIC:** 95100
**Employees:** 80

DUNS 21-493-0534
## St Dominics Nursing Home
71 Filsham Road, St Leonards-On-Sea, East
Sussex TN38 0PA
**Tel:** 01424436140
**Web:** www.asterhealthcare.co.uk
**Estd:** 2002 Proprietorship
**Line of Business:** Nursing homes
**Proprietor:** B Roarty
**Responsibilities**
**Senior:** Beverley Therese (Manager)
**US SIC:** 8051 **UK SIC:** 95100
**Employees:** 50

DUNS 21-717-7751
## St Dominic's Priory School (Stone)
Station Road, Stone, Staffordshire ST15 8EN
**Tel:** 01785814181
**Web:** www.stdominicspriory.co.uk
**Reg No:** 7563439 **Estd:** 2011 Private
Company Limited By Guarantee
**Line of Business:** Primary education
**Directors:** A Ashton, M B Hughes,
G Cunningham, Ms C D Gill, Mrs G Brian,
Ms J S Francis, M C Burton, G Gibson
**Co. Secretary:**
Velocity Company Secretarial Ser
**Responsibilities**
**Senior:** Jennifer Leech (Manager), Enid
Mackie (Manager)
**US SIC:** 8211 **UK SIC:** 93200
**Bankers:** Barclays Bank Plc (20-36-43)

| | 31-08-13 | 31-08-12 |
|---|---|---|
| TO | 1,512,581 | 1,558,529 |
| P/L | (69,901) | (348,490) |
| NW | (418,391) | (348,490) |
| WC | (45,203) | (31,218) |
| Emp. | 67 | 60 |

DUNS 21-493-6770
## St Dominics School
Hambledon, Godalming, Surrey GU8 4DX
**Tel:** 01428684693
**Web:** www.stdominicsschool.org.uk
**Estd:** 1929
**Line of Business:** Schools (special)
**Director:** G Chapman
**Responsibilities**
**Senior:** Angela Drayton (Principal)
**Finance:** Debbie Louw (School Business
Manager)
**Sales:** Debbie Louw (School Business
Manager)

**Health & Safety:** Ginny Willis (Head of
Inclusion, Safeguardin)
**Facilities:** Dave Ward (Site Manager)
**US SIC:** 8299 **UK SIC:** 93300
**Employees:** 100

DUNS 21-812-6336
## St Dominic's Sixth Form College
Mount Park Avenue, Harrow-On-The-Hill,
Harrow, Middlesex HA1 3HX
**Tel:** 020-8422-8084
**Web:** www.stdoms.ac.uk
**Estd:** 1979
**Line of Business:** Further education schools
and colleges
**US SIC:** 8211 **UK SIC:** 93200
**Employees:** 100

DUNS 23-630-6957
## St Dunstans
St Dunstans, Ian Fraser House, Brighton,
East Sussex BN2 7BS
**Tel:** 01273-307811
**Web:** www.st-dunstans.org.uk
**Estd:** 2003
**Line of Business:** Charities and charitable
organisations
**Trading Style:** Blind Veterans
**Director:** D Bray
**Responsibilities**
**Senior:** Helen Emmerson (General
Manager), Lesley Garven (Centre Manager),
Jackie Greer (Manager)
**Finance:** Paul Sheard (Financial Manager)
**HR:** Melinda Dixon (Training Manager)
**Health & Safety:** Adrian Elliott (Health &
Safety Officer)
**Branches:** St Dunstans, 29 Devon Rd,
Smethwick, West Midlands B67 5EL
**US SIC:** 8699 **UK SIC:** 96902
**Employees:** 200

DUNS 21-777-6146
## St Ebbas Hospital
4 Ethel Bailey Close, Epsom, Surrey KT19 8NQ
**Tel:** 03005555222
**Web:** www.sabp.nhs.uk
**Estd:** 2011 Partnership
**Line of Business:** Hospitals
**Partners:** Mrs F Edwards, Mrs M Somekh
**US SIC:** 8062 **UK SIC:** 95100
**Employees:** 200

DUNS 36-491-0419
## St Edmunds College
Old Hall Green, Ware, Hertfordshire SG11 1DS
**Tel:** 01920-821504
**Web:** www.stedmundscollege.org
**Estd:** 2003
**Line of Business:** Schools (independent)
**Principals:** P J Mitton (Chairman),
B A Tomlinson (Financial), C P Long,
Mrs M Lynch, Dr J Sweeney, N Ransley,
J Sinclair, Mrs P Newton
**Responsibilities**
**Senior:** Leonard Blom (Head Teacher), M
Brockie (Partner), Steven Cartwright (Head
Teacher), Paulo Duran (Headmaster), F
MacIntosh (Manager), Ron Wrega
(Groundsman)
**Finance:** Roger Pettit (Accounts Manager)
**IT:** Karl Fry (Director IT/Computing and e-le),
Stuart Winfield (IT Manager)
**Health & Safety:** Ron Wrega (Groundsman)
**US SIC:** 8211 **UK SIC:** 93200
**Auditors:** Peters Elworthy & Moore
**Employees:** 171
**Turnover:** £11,828,449

DUNS 23-083-2300
## St Edmund's R C School
Arundel Street, Portsmouth, Hampshire PO1 1RX
**Tel:** 023-9282-3766
**Web:** http://st-edmunds.wajoomla.com
**Estd:** 2002
**Line of Business:** Schools (local authority)
**Director:** B M Wright
**Responsibilities**
**Finance:** K Shipp (Finance Assistant)
**IT:** Robin Holman (Assistant Network
Manager)
**US SIC:** 8211 **UK SIC:** 93200
**Employees:** 100

DUNS 23-644-7975
## St Edmundsbury Borough Council
West Suffolk House, Bury St Edmunds,
Suffolk IP33 3YU
**Tel:** 01284763233 **Fax:** 01284757375
**Web:** www.westsuffolk.gov.uk
**Estd:** 2011 Incorporate By Act Of Parliament

**Line of Business:** Local government
**Trading Style:** Environmental Health & Housing, Town Hall Art Centre
**Principals:** D Addy (Financial), G R Toft, S Cook, D J Albon, E G Spooner, B Coley, Ms L Aisbett, J Aspland
**Responsibilities**
**Senior:** Neil Anthony (Head of Leisure, Culture & Com), Micheal Dawson (Partner), Ian Gallin (CEO, Managing Director), Jerry Massey (Partner), Steven Palframan (Principal), Angela Rushen (Council)
**Finance:** Andrea Mayley (Head of Economic Development &)
**Marketing:** Sally Easton (Communications Officer), Sharon Fairweather (Market Development Officer), Davina Howes (Head of Policy, Strategy, Comm), Marianne Hulland (Corporate Communications Manag), Ian Poole (Planning Manager)
**Sales:** Andrea Mayley (Head of Economic Development &)
**IT:** James Wager (ICT Manager)
**HR:** Karen Points (HR Manager)
**Health & Safety:** Martin Hosker (Health and Safety Manager), Helen Lindfield (Community Safety Officer)
**Facilities:** Simon Phelan (Head of Housing)
**Operations:** Chris Silverwood (Operations Manager)
**Purchasing:** Ziaul Quader (Procurement Manager)
**Fleet:** Ian Poole (Planning Manager)
**Branches:** St Edmundsbury Borough Council, Withersfield Road, Haverhill, Suffolk CB9 9HE
**US SIC:** 9121　**UK SIC:** 91110
**Bankers:** Lloyds TSB Bank plc (30-91-49)
**Employees:** 800

DUNS 23-082-7839
## St Edwards College
North Drive, Liverpool, Merseyside L12 1LF
**Tel:** 01512811999
**Web:** www.st-edwards.co.uk
**Estd:** 1845
**Line of Business:** General secondary education
**Director:** J E Waszek
**Responsibilities**
**Senior:** John Waszek (Principal)
**Marketing:** Emma Quayle (Communications Manager)
**Admin:** Jane Whitfield (Administration Manager)
**IT:** David Armbsey (Senior IT Executive), Christian Williams (IT Support Assistant)
**HR:** Susan Maher (HR Manager)
**US SIC:** 8211　**UK SIC:** 93200
**Employees:** 100

DUNS 23-083-2672
## St Edwards Junior School Runnymede
North Drive, Sandfield Park, Liverpool, Merseyside L12 1LE
**Tel:** 0151-281-2300
**Web:** www.runnymede-school.org.uk
**Estd:** 1900
**Line of Business:** Schools (independent)
**Director:** P Sweeney
**Responsibilities**
**Senior:** Bradley Slater (Head Teacher)
**US SIC:** 8211　**UK SIC:** 93200
**Employees:** 150

DUNS 64-262-5784
## St Edwards School
Cirencester Road, Charlton Kings, Cheltenham, Gloucestershire GL53 8EY
**Tel:** 01242-538600
**Web:** www.stedwards.co.uk
**Estd:** 1985 Proprietorship
**Line of Business:** General secondary education
**Proprietor:** Dr A Nash
**Responsibilities**
**Senior:** Pat Playfield (Head Teacher)
**Admin:** Alison Scarboro (Office Manager)
**IT:** Jonathan Todd (IT Manager)
**Health & Safety:** Stuart Jeal (Estates Manager)
**Facilities:** Stuart Jeal (Estates Manager)
**US SIC:** 8211　**UK SIC:** 93200
**Employees:** 100

DUNS 38-782-9880
## St Elizabeth's School & Home
Perry Green, Much Hadham, Hertfordshire SG10 6EF
**Tel:** 01279-843451
**Web:** www.stelizabeths.org.uk
**Line of Business:** Schools (special)
**Proprietor:** B Sainsburys
**Responsibilities**
**Finance:** Annette Clemets (Finance Director)

**HR:** Sandra Evans Kerr (Director of HR)
**US SIC:** 8699, 8321, 8211
**UK SIC:** 96902, 96111, 93200
**Employees:** 600

DUNS 55-045-8434
## St Enoch Hotel
44 Howard Street, Glasgow, Lanarkshire G1 4EE
**Tel:** 0141-221-2400
**Web:** www.glasgowbudgethotels.co.uk
**Estd:** 1994 Partnership
**Line of Business:** Hotels and motels without restaurant
**Partners:** I Shirley, Mrs G Shirley
**Responsibilities**
**Senior:** Ikram Hussain (Proprietor)
**US SIC:** 7011, 5812
**UK SIC:** 66500, 66110
**Employees:** 150

DUNS 21-780-5657
## St Fagans National History Museum
St Fagans, Cardiff, South Glamorgan CF5 6XB
**Tel:** 02920573500
**Web:** www.museumwales.ac.uk
**Estd:** 2011 Proprietorship
**Line of Business:** Museums
**Proprietor:** Ms B Lewis
**US SIC:** 8411　**UK SIC:** 97700
**Employees:** 100

DUNS 64-255-1246
## St Faiths
6 Trumpington Road, Cambridge, Cambridgeshire CB2 8AG
**Tel:** 01223-352073
**Web:** www.stfaiths.com
**Estd:** 1987
**Line of Business:** Schools (independent)
**Director:** Ms C Smith
**Responsibilities**
**Senior:** Nigel Helliwell (Head Teacher)
**US SIC:** 8211　**UK SIC:** 93200
**Employees:** 120

DUNS 21-777-6846
## St Francesca Cabrini R C Primary School
Honor Oak Park, London SE23 3LE
**Tel:** 02086998862
**Web:** www.stfrancescacabrini.com
**Estd:** 2002 Proprietorship
**Line of Business:** Schools (local authority)
**Proprietor:** Mrs J Martin
**US SIC:** 8211　**UK SIC:** 93200
**Employees:** 60

DUNS 21-813-1309
## St Francis Catholic and Church of England Primary School
Newport Road, Ventnor, Isle of Wight PO38 1BQ
**Web:** www.stfrancisventnor.co.uk
**Estd:** 2013
**Line of Business:** Primary School
**US SIC:** 8211　**UK SIC:** 93200
**Employees:** 66

DUNS 28-969-6692
## St Francis' College Trust
Broadway, Letchworth, Hertfordshire SG6 3PJ
**Web:** www.st-francis.herts.sch.uk
**Reg No:** 1724197　**Estd:** 1933 Private Company Limited By Guarantee
**Line of Business:** Schools (independent)
**Trading Style:** St Francis' College
**Directors:** H M Garavelli, Ms S Boardman, Dr V A Mcnicholas, C G Nott, J Procter, A W Goodwin, Ms P J Barlow, Professor D S Freeth
**Co. Secretary:** Ms Eileen Ismay
**Responsibilities**
**Senior:** Dorothy Macginty (Principal), Rosamund Rainey (Director), George Ritchie (Director)
**Marketing:** Dorothy Macginty (Principal)
**HR:** Dorothy Macginty (Principal)
**US SIC:** 8211, 7021
**UK SIC:** 93200, 66500
**Auditors:** MacIntyre & Co
**Bankers:** Clydesdale Bank Plc (82-04-03)

| | 31-08-13 | 31-08-12 | 31-08-11 |
|---|---|---|---|
| TO | 5,395,475 | 4,932,532 | 4,898,383 |
| P/L | 16,710 | (233,655) | (221,131) |
| NW | 3,244,505 | 3,227,795 | 3,461,450 |
| WC | 244,103 | 64,475 | 329,092 |
| Emp. | 109 | 121 | 241 |

DUNS 21-774-5917
## St Francis De Sales Catholic Junior Mixed School
Hale Road, Walton, Liverpool, Merseyside L4 3RL
**Tel:** 01515257602
**Web:** www.st-francis-de-sales.co.uk
**Estd:** 2011 Proprietorship
**Line of Business:** Schools (local authority)
**Proprietor:** Mrs E Seymour
**US SIC:** 8211　**UK SIC:** 93200
**Employees:** 50

DUNS 76-913-4784
## St Francis Ltd
(Subsidiary of: Vts Buying Services Ltd)
Meadowside & St Francis Care Centre, Plymouth, Devon PL7 4LE
**Tel:** 01752347774
**Web:** www.sfcs.org.uk
**Reg No:** 2617906　**Estd:** 1991 Private Limited Company
**Line of Business:** Veterinary activities
**Trading Style:** Meadowside & St Francis Care Centre
**Issued Capital:** £100
**Directors:** K A Willis, A White, J B Hodgkin, D G Whittaker, N R Park, S P Stephenson
**Co. Secretary:** Simon Stephenson
**Responsibilities**
**Senior:** Sarah Hodgkin (Manager), Gina Patterson (Home Manager)
**Finance:** Sandy Kellaway (Administrator)
**Marketing:** Gina Patterson (Home Manager)
**Sales:** Gina Patterson (Home Manager)
**Admin:** Sandy Kellaway (Administrator)
**HR:** Gina Patterson (Home Manager)
**Health & Safety:** Gina Patterson (Home Manager)
**Facilities:** Gina Patterson (Home Manager)
**US SIC:** 0741, 6732
**UK SIC:** 95601, 83100

| | 30-09-13 | 30-09-12 | 30-09-11 |
|---|---|---|---|
| TA | 3,560,916 | 3,802,574 | 3,280,468 |
| NW | 653,887 | 887,948 | 1,042,625 |
| WC | 633,787 | 863,039 | 1,017,839 |

DUNS 64-259-5763
## St Francis Nursing Home
54 Merryland Street, Glasgow, Lanarkshire G51 2QE
**Tel:** 01414451118
**Estd:** 1996
**Line of Business:** Medical nursing home activities
**Proprietor:** C Cawley
**Responsibilities**
**Senior:** Lisette Prele (Manager)
**US SIC:** 8051　**UK SIC:** 95100
**Employees:** 50

DUNS 21-783-7158
## St Francis R C Primary School
Merchiston Avenue, Falkirk, Stirlingshire FK2 7JS
**Estd:** 2011 Proprietorship
**Line of Business:** Schools (local authority)
**Proprietor:** F Doran
**Responsibilities**
**Senior:** Tina O'neil (Head Teacher)
**US SIC:** 8211　**UK SIC:** 93200
**Employees:** 50

DUNS 21-607-4995
## St Francis School
Wickenby Crescent, Lincoln, Lincolnshire LN1 3TJ
**Tel:** 01522526498
**Web:** www.st-francis.lincs.sch.uk
**Estd:** 1996
**Line of Business:** Schools (special)
**Proprietor:** Mrs A Hoffman
**Responsibilities**
**Senior:** Ann Hoffmann (Head Teacher)
**US SIC:** 8299　**UK SIC:** 93300
**Employees:** 80

DUNS 21-318-6328
## St Francis Xavier 6TH Form College
Malwood Road, London SW12 8EN
**Tel:** 020-8772-6000
**Web:** www.sfx.ac.uk
**Estd:** 1985
**Line of Business:** Sixth form colleges
**Director:** B Borland
**US SIC:** 8221　**UK SIC:** 93100
**Employees:** 130

DUNS 23-082-9710
## St Francis Xaviers College
Beaconsfield Road, Liverpool, Merseyside L25 6EG
**Tel:** 0151-288-1000
**Web:** www.sfx.liverpool.sch.uk
**Estd:** 1842
**Line of Business:** Schools (local authority)
**Director:** B Francis
**Responsibilities**
**Senior:** Joanne Deane (Manager), David Delaney (Manager), Kenneth Glover (Manager), Patricia Goodall (Manager), Mark Helme (Manager), Andrew Keeley (Manager), Harold King (Manager), Sharon O'Driscoll (Manager), Nicholas O'Hare (Manager), Amanda Oliver (Manager), Mark Ord (Manager), Francis Patterson (Manager), Mark Power (Manager), Lisa Riccio-Jones (Manager), Leslie Rippon (Manager), Neal Summers (Manager), Eileen Tedford (Manager)
**US SIC:** 8211　**UK SIC:** 93200
**Bankers:** HSBC Bank plc (40-29-39)
**Employees:** 120

DUNS 21-516-0883
## St Gabriel's Convent
The Ridge, Cold Ash, Thatcham, Berkshire RG18 9HU
**Tel:** 01635864161
**Estd:** 2002 Proprietorship
**Line of Business:** Activities of religious organisations
**Proprietor:** M Donnelly
**Responsibilities**
**Senior:** Sister Condon (Manager)
**US SIC:** 8661　**UK SIC:** 96600
**Employees:** 61

DUNS 21-607-4966
## St Gabriel's R C High School
Bridge Road, Bury, Lancashire BL9 0TZ
**Tel:** 01617643186
**Web:** http://st-gabriels.org.uk
**Estd:** 2011 Proprietorship
**Line of Business:** Schools (local authority)
**Proprietor:** E Robinson
**Responsibilities**
**IT:** Nicky Latham (IT Teacher)
**US SIC:** 8211　**UK SIC:** 93200
**Employees:** 60

DUNS 21-665-7879
## St Genevieve S High School for Girls
87 Stewartstown Road, Belfast BT11 9JP
**Tel:** 028-9092-5670
**Web:** www.stgenevieves.org.uk
**Estd:** 1992
**Line of Business:** Schools (local authority)
**Responsibilities**
**Purchasing:** Linda Draine (Purchasing Manager)
**US SIC:** 8211　**UK SIC:** 93200
**Employees:** 120

DUNS 57-846-1105
## St George (North London) Ltd
(Subsidiary of: The Berkeley Group Holdings Plc)
Hendon Project Offices, Aerodrome Road, London NW9 5JJ
**Tel:** 02085118600
**Web:** www.stgeorgeplc.com
**Reg No:** 2899017　**VAT No:** 564207841
**Estd:** 1995 Private Limited Company
**Line of Business:** Construction of commercial buildings
**Trading Style:** St George (North London) Construction Co
**Issued Capital:** £2
**Directors:** N A Hutchings, P J Hunt, N G Simpkin, C J Carson, J R Faragher, A W Pidgley, G J Fry, M R Elgar
**Co. Secretary:** Stuart Luck
**Responsibilities**
**Senior:** Heston Attwell (Director), Neil Bowron (Director)
**US SIC:** 1541　**UK SIC:** 50100
**Bankers:** Barclays Bank Plc (20-90-56)

| | 30-04-13 | 30-04-12 | 30-04-10 |
|---|---|---|---|
| TA | 2 | 2,000 | 2 |
| NW | 2 | 2,000 | 2 |
| WC | 2 | 2,000 | N/A |
| Emp. | 80 | 80 | N/A |

DUNS 76-687-6213
## St George Plc
(Subsidiary of: The Berkeley Group Holdings Plc)
Ratcliffe Road, Leicester, Leicestershire LE2 3TE
**Tel:** 01162745115
**Web:** www.heron-view.co.uk
**Reg No:** 2590468　**Estd:** 2012 Public Limited Company

**Line of Business:** Management activities of holding companies
**Trading Style:** Platinum Hotline
**Issued Capital:** £6,035,862
**Principals:** G J Fry *(Commercial)*, J R Faragher, N G Simpkin, Ms J M Salomon, I Dobie, M P Griffiths, A W Pidgley, N A Hutchings
**Co. Secretary:** Stuart Luck
**Responsibilities**
**Senior:** Maureen Murray *(Manager)*
**Marketing:** Christine Tiernan *(Sales & Marketing Director)*
**Sales:** Christine Tiernan *(Sales & Marketing Director)*
**Branches:** St George Plc, Warren House, Flat 185, London W14 8TR
**US SIC:** 6711, 1522
**UK SIC:** 83962, 50100
**Auditors:** KPMG LLP
**Bankers:** Barclays Bank Plc (20-90-56)

| | 30-04-14 | 30-04-13 | 30-04-12 |
|---|---|---|---|
| TO | 121,979,495 | 339,366,978 | 322,553,511 |
| P/L | 20,603,096 | 76,819,303 | 92,169,169 |
| NW | 368,163,881 | 429,740,061 | 134,848,153 |
| WC | 365,668,445 | 547,845,253 | 146,751,986 |
| Emp. | 278 | 196 | 163 |

DUNS 23-083-2656
## St George's C of E School
Westwood Road, Broadstairs, Kent CT10 2LH
**Tel:** 01843861696
**Web:** www.saintgeorgescofe.kent.sch.uk
**Estd:** 1830
**Line of Business:** Schools (foundation)
**Director:** K Rumblo
**Responsibilities**
**Senior:** Kim Stoner *(Principal)*
**US SIC:** 8211 **UK SIC:** 93200
**Employees:** 150

DUNS 21-600-4617
## St Georges College Junior School
Thames Street, Weybridge, Surrey KT13 8NL
**Tel:** 01932839400
**Web:** www.st-georges-college.co.uk
**Estd:** 1904 Proprietorship
**Line of Business:** General secondary education
**Proprietor:** A Hudson
**Responsibilities**
**IT:** Angela Disher *(Librarian & Information Office)*
**HR:** Suzanne Knights *(Career Development Manager)*
**Health & Safety:** Catherine Peuleve *(Child Protection Liaison Offic)*
**US SIC:** 8211 **UK SIC:** 93200
**Employees:** 76

DUNS 21-774-0911
## St Georges Community Health Centre
Winter Street, Sheffield, South Yorkshire S3 7ND
**Tel:** 01142716920
**Web:** www.shsc.nhs.uk
**Estd:** 2002 Proprietorship
**Line of Business:** Clinics private
**Proprietor:** C Singleton
**Responsibilities**
**Senior:** Diane Allen *(Manager)*
**US SIC:** 8062 **UK SIC:** 95100
**Employees:** 100

DUNS 21-746-2178
## St George's Crypt
St Georges Crypt, Great George Street, Leeds, West Yorkshire LS1 3BR
**Tel:** 01132451335
**Web:** www.stgeorgescrypt.org.uk
**Reg No:** 7780402 **Estd:** 2011 Private Company Limited By Guarantee
**Line of Business:** Social work activities without accommodation
**Directors:** P F Walker, J Battle, D Gladman, Dr N Bishop, Mrs T A Greig, Ms R Weldon, P D Hooper, J J Clark
**Responsibilities**
**Senior:** Christopher Burford *(Director)*
**US SIC:** 8321 **UK SIC:** 96111
**Bankers:** HSBC Bank plc (40-27-15)

| | 31-03-14 | 31-03-13 | 31-03-12 |
|---|---|---|---|
| TO | 1,749,783 | 1,641,976 | 1,515,822 |
| P/L | 74,079 | 271,822 | 268,555 |
| NW | 3,031,348 | 2,956,794 | 2,683,982 |
| WC | 844,862 | 747,308 | 489,918 |
| Emp. | 49 | 46 | 49 |

DUNS 23-680-5466
## St George's Estates Ltd
**(Subsidiary of:** St George's Hospital Medical School)
Cranmer Terrace, Tooting, London SW17 0RE
**Tel:** 02082666853
**Web:** www.intranet.sgul.ac.uk
**Reg No:** 3675065 **Estd:** 1998 Private Limited Company
**Line of Business:** Other letting of own property
**Issued Capital:** £2
**Directors:** J W Unsworth, Mrs A Whittle
**Co. Secretary:** John Unsworth
**US SIC:** 6519, 6531
**UK SIC:** 85000, 83400
**Auditors:** KPMG

| | 31-07-13 | 31-07-12 | 31-07-11 |
|---|---|---|---|
| TA | 2 | 2 | 2 |
| NW | 2 | 2 | 2 |

DUNS 21-031-6834
## St George's Hall
Middleton St George Hospital Site, Durham Tees Valley Airport, Darlington, County Durham DL2 1TS
**Tel:** 01325335425
**Web:** www.orchardcarehomes.com
**Estd:** 2006 Proprietorship
**Line of Business:** Residential care establishments
**Proprietor:** Ms L Morehead
**Responsibilities**
**Senior:** Emma Hardy *(Home Manager)*
**US SIC:** 8321 **UK SIC:** 96111
**Employees:** 84

DUNS 54-864-0119 Imp
## St Georges Healthcare Nhs Trust
Blackshaw Road, Tooting, London SW17 0QT
**Tel:** 020-8672-1255
**Web:** www.stgeorges.nhs.uk
**Estd:** 1980
**Line of Business:** Charities and charitable organisations
**Trading Style:** St Georges Hospital Nhs Trust
**Principals:** N Coker *(Chairman)*, P Murphy, Ms E Gilthorpe, G Hibbert, P Hilton, M Rappolt, Ms M Nangle, M Bailey
**Responsibilities**
**Senior:** Richard Eley *(Nursing Director)*, Miles Scott *(Chief Executive)*
**IT:** John-Joe Campbell *(IT Manager)*
**Health & Safety:** Peter McDermott *(Health & Safety Officer)*
**Branches:** St Georges Healthcare Nhs Trust, Copse Hill, London SW20 0NQ
**US SIC:** 8062 **UK SIC:** 95100
**Employees:** 7,000

DUNS 28-869-9457
## St George's Hill Lawn Tennis Club Ltd
St Georges Hill, Warreners Lane, Weybridge, Surrey KT13 0LL
**Tel:** 01932-843541
**Web:** www.stghltc.co.uk
**Reg No:** 1026986 **Estd:** 1971 Private Company Limited By Guarantee
**Line of Business:** Operation of sports arenas and stadiums
**Directors:** P S Hammond, T C Catton, N F Fleming, Dr P F Loveday, P N Jamieson, Mrs T Sheperdigian, R T Sowerby, K J Springall
**Co. Secretary:** Miles Hill
**Responsibilities**
**Senior:** Gilly Chapman *(Personal Assistant)*
**Finance:** Ann Percival *(accounts manager)*
**Operations:** Susanna Pegram *(Operations Manager)*
**US SIC:** 7941 **UK SIC:** 97911
**Auditors:** Rawlinson & Hunter

| | 31-03-14 | 31-03-13 | 31-03-12 |
|---|---|---|---|
| TO | 4,012,630 | 3,545,208 | 3,050,764 |
| P/L | 107,044 | 81,168 | 76,161 |
| NW | 4,264,121 | 4,157,728 | 4,077,097 |
| WC | (904,722) | (985,665) | (768,155) |
| Emp. | 84 | 87 | 79 |

DUNS 23-216-7098
## St George's Hospital Medical School
Cranmer Terrace, London SW17 0RE
**Tel:** 020-8672-9944
**Web:** www.sgul.ac.uk
**VAT No:** 562044464 **Estd:** 1755
**Line of Business:** Hospitals
**Trading Style:** St George's University of London
**Principals:** M Bery *(Financial)*, J Duffy, Sir W Asscher, H Jones, Prof M Farthing, M Smith, Prof G Griffe, Prof S Hilton
**Responsibilities**
**Senior:** Jan Annan *(Associate Director)*, Wilfred Carneiro *(Manager)*, Alicia Erauncetamurguil *(Senior Manager)*, Rosalind Given-Wilson *(Medical Director)*, Jeremy Turk *(Manager)*
**Finance:** Raquel Evans *(Accounts Assistant)*, Ravi Visaga *(Accountant)*
**Marketing:** Helena Clay *(Senior Press Officer)*, Rachel MacBeath *(Communications Officer)*, Jean-Pierre Moser *(Director, Communications)*, Samuel Ridge *(Head of Communications)*, Howard Wheeler *(Senior Communications Officer)*, Liz Woods *(Head of Fundraising and Charit)*
**Sales:** Chris Conneely *(Development Manager)*
**Admin:** Lynda Carter *(Admission Officer)*, Debbie Matthias *(Administrator)*, Jayshree Morjaria *(Joint Research Office Administ)*, Faye Nicholls *(Medical Secretary)*, Michilla Regan *(MBBS Admissions Officer)*
**IT:** Dave Iveson *(Support Systems Restructuring)*, Andrew Judycki *(Head of Management IS project)*
**HR:** Kim Brett *(IT Training Administrator)*, Mary Luckiram *(Human Resources Manager)*, Terry Poulton *(Associate Dean and Head of the)*
**Facilities:** Andrea Wright *(Facilities Manager)*
**US SIC:** 8221 **UK SIC:** 93100
**Auditors:** KPMG LLP
**Bankers:** National Westminster Bank Plc (60-21-29)
**Employees:** 899
**Turnover:** £90,281,000

DUNS 21-780-6113
## St Georges Market
12-20 East Bridge Street, Town Centre, Belfast BT1 3NQ
**Tel:** 02890435704
**Web:** www.belfastcity.gov.uk
**Estd:** 2011 Proprietorship
**Line of Business:** Retail sale via stalls and markets
**Proprietor:** I Carmichael
**US SIC:** 5963 **UK SIC:** 65600
**Employees:** 1

DUNS 21-192-9471
## St Georges Nursing Home
42 Kneesworth Street, Royston, Hertfordshire SG8 5AQ
**Tel:** 01763-242243
**Web:** www.stgeorgescare.com
**Estd:** 2002 Partnership
**Line of Business:** Clinics private
**Partners:** Mrs E Newton, R Newton
**Responsibilities**
**Senior:** Jane Collis *(Registered Manager)*
**US SIC:** 8051 **UK SIC:** 95100
**Employees:** 65

DUNS 23-014-3265
## St Georges Nursing Homes Ltd
Kenn Road, Bristol, Avon BS5 7PD
**Tel:** 01179541234
**Web:** www.caringhomes.org
**Reg No:** 3032346 **Estd:** 1995 Private Limited Company
**Line of Business:** Nursing homes
**Trading Style:** St Georges Care Centre
**Issued Capital:** £1
**Director:** J D Farkas
**Co. Secretary:**
Sanne Group Secretaries (Uk) Lim
**Responsibilities**
**Senior:** Garland King *(Manager)*, Keith Priestnall *(Manager)*, Mathieu Streiff *(Director)*
**Admin:** Gill Hatherell *(Office Manager)*
**Facilities:** Gill Hatherell *(Office Manager)*
**US SIC:** 8051, 8091
**UK SIC:** 95100, 95200
**Auditors:** Target DNP
**Bankers:** National Westminster Bank Plc (60-06-39)

| | 31-03-13 | 31-12-12 |
|---|---|---|
| TA | 1 | 1 |
| NW | 1 | 1 |

DUNS 21-167-4721
## St George's R C Primary School
Gordon Road, Enfield, Middlesex EN2 0QA
**Tel:** 020-8363-3729
**Web:** www.st-georges.enfield.sch.uk
**Estd:** 1906 Proprietorship
**Line of Business:** Schools (local authority)
**Proprietor:** Mrs P Alder
**US SIC:** 8211 **UK SIC:** 93200
**Employees:** 50

DUNS 64-255-1295
## St Georges Residential Home
St Georges Road, Millom, Cumbria LA18 4JE
**Tel:** 01229-773959
**Web:** www.stgeorgesmillom.org
**Estd:** 1992 Proprietorship
**Line of Business:** Non-charitable social work activities with accommodation
**Proprietor:** S Bilsland
**Responsibilities**
**Senior:** Frederick Bilsland *(Manager)*, Janet Bosanko *(Manager)*, Gaynor Jordan *(Manager)*
**US SIC:** 8321 **UK SIC:** 96111
**Bankers:** Barclays Bank Plc (20-04-68)
**Employees:** 50

DUNS 64-264-6954
## St George's School
Wells Lane, Ascot, Berkshire SL5 7DZ
**Web:** www.stgeorges-ascot.org.uk
**Estd:** 1953
**Line of Business:** Schools (independent)
**Proprietor:** Mrs C Jordan
**Responsibilities**
**Finance:** Kate Nicholson *(Bursar)*
**IT:** Kate Nicholson *(Bursar)*
**HR:** Kate Nicholson *(Bursar)*
**Health & Safety:** Kate Nicholson *(Bursar)*
**Facilities:** Matt Heather *(Facilities Manager)*
**Operations:** Kate Nicholson *(Bursar)*
**Purchasing:** Kate Nicholson *(Bursar)*
**US SIC:** 8211 **UK SIC:** 93200
**Employees:** 100

DUNS 23-870-0384
## St George's School Edgbaston
St Georges School, Birmingham, West Midlands B15 1RX
**Tel:** 0121-625-0398
**Web:** www.sgse.co.uk
**Reg No:** 3861455 **Estd:** 1999 Private Company Limited By Guarantee
**Line of Business:** Schools (independent)
**Directors:** K A George, K Hawkins, Miss J Parkes, J Dickens, W D Weir, Sir R Dowling, J Watkins
**Co. Secretary:** Mrs Maureen Fahy
**Responsibilities**
**Senior:** Colin Goodier *(Manager)*, Howard Mainwaring *(Manager)*, Gary Neal *(Head Teacher)*, Rosemary Plevey *(Manager)*
**IT:** Julie Glover *(Computer Manager)*
**US SIC:** 8211 **UK SIC:** 93200
**Auditors:** Bloomr Heaven
**Bankers:** HSBC Bank plc (40-11-18)

| | 31-08-13 | 31-08-12 | 31-08-11 |
|---|---|---|---|
| TO | 4,797,856 | 3,980,350 | 3,791,861 |
| P/L | 450,741 | 338,330 | 199,284 |
| NW | 1,422,507 | 971,766 | 633,436 |
| WC | 482,080 | 267,727 | 120,001 |
| Emp. | 123 | 102 | 94 |

DUNS 28-821-0867
## St George's School for Girls
Garscube Terrace, Edinburgh, Midlothian EH12 6BG
**Tel:** 0131-311-8000 **Fax:** 0131-311-8120
**Web:** www.st-georges.edin.sch.uk
**Reg No:** 0008667SC **Estd:** 1913 Private Company Limited By Guarantee
**Line of Business:** Schools (independent)
**Directors:** Mrs J M Montgomery, R J Wylie, Dr E Duvall, S E Woolman, Ms R J Wood, Professor J E Simmons, Ms L M Ruxton, Dr E D Mccall-Smith
**Co. Secretary:** Jeremy Chittleburgh
**Responsibilities**
**Senior:** Stephanie Cowie *(Director)*, Lindsay Duguid *(Director)*, Isabella Miller *(Director)*
**Marketing:** John Hammell *(Communications Manager)*, Ali Lawrence *(Marketing Manager)*
**Sales:** Ali Lawrence *(Marketing Manager)*
**IT:** Ed Dias *(IT Manager)*
**Health & Safety:** Margaret Imlah *(Facilities Director)*
**Facilities:** Margaret Imlah *(Facilities Director)*
**Operations:** Ali Lawrence *(Marketing Manager)*
**Purchasing:** Margaret Imlah *(Facilities Director)*
**Branches:** St George's School For Girls, Lansdowne House, Coltbridge Terrace, Edinburgh, Midlothian EH12 6AG
**US SIC:** 8211 **UK SIC:** 93200
**Auditors:** KPMG
**Bankers:** The Royal Bank Of Scotland Plc (83-51-00)

| | 31-07-13 | 31-07-12 | 31-07-11 |
|---|---|---|---|
| TO | 9,283,421 | 9,525,205 | 9,624,244 |
| P/L | 210,703 | 478,630 | 445,155 |
| NW | 7,721,380 | 7,438,501 | 6,960,612 |
| WC | 605,317 | 672,879 | 426,710 |
| Emp. | 192 | 194 | 200 |

## DUNS 73-278-8406
### St Georges School (Harpenden) Lettings Ltd
(**Subsidiary of:** St Georges School (Harpenden) Ltd)
St Georges School, Sun Lane, Harpenden, Hertfordshire AL5 4TD
**Tel:** 01582765477
**Web:** www.stgeorges.herts.sch.uk
**Reg No:** 4552567 **Estd:** 2002 Private Limited Company
**Line of Business:** Other entertainment activities not elsewhere classified
**Issued Capital:** £1
**Director:** K R Parsons
**Co. Secretary:** Mrs Jane Jukes
**US SIC:** 7999 **UK SIC:** 97913
**Auditors:** Kingston Smith LLP
**Bankers:** National Westminster Bank Plc (60-10-07)

|     | 31-03-14 | 31-03-13 | 31-03-12 |
| --- | --- | --- | --- |
| TO | 154,969 | 132,695 | 105,177 |
| NW | 1 | 1 | 1 |
| WC | (12,270) | (1,628) | (3,259) |

## DUNS 23-082-9405
### St Georges School Windsor Castle
Windsor Castle, Windsor, Berkshire SL4 1QF
**Web:** www.stgwindsor.co.uk
**Line of Business:** Schools (independent)
**Responsibilities**
**Senior:** Hueston Finlay (Manager), John Ovenden (Manager)
**US SIC:** 8211 **UK SIC:** 93200
**Employees:** 55

## DUNS 64-264-0551
### St George's Veterinary Clinic
8-10 St Georges Parade, Wolverhampton, West Midlands WV2 1BD
**Tel:** 01902-425262
**Web:** www.stgeorgesvets.co.uk
**Estd:** 2003 Partnership
**Line of Business:** Veterinary activities
**Partners:** D Franklin, J Goulding, A Crane, Mrs H Franklin
**Responsibilities**
**Senior:** Julie Clements (Group Manager)
**Branches:** St George's Veterinary Clinic, 29 Station Road, Wolverhampton, West Midlands WV7 3QH
**US SIC:** 0741 **UK SIC:** 95601
**Employees:** 70

## DUNS 34-803-8886
### St George's Weybridge
St Georges College, Addlestone, Surrey KT15 2QS
**Tel:** 01932839300
**Web:** www.st-georges-college.co.uk
**Reg No:** 2789023 **Estd:** 1900 Private Company Limited By Guarantee
**Line of Business:** Primary education
**Directors:** D J Anderson, K L Jones, Prof A H Muggeridge, J M Lewin, C T Jansen, Mrs K L Patterson, M Farmer, D Bicarregui
**Co. Secretary:** Gregory Cole
**Responsibilities**
**Senior:** Kevin Alexander (Manager), Lisa Burrell (Director), Michael Davie (Director), Diane Ewart (Director), Phillip Fletcher (Manager), Catherine Mccormick (Director), Joe Peake (Principal), Charles Prescott (Director), Kathleen Quint (Manager), John Rourke (Director)
**US SIC:** 8211 **UK SIC:** 93200
**Auditors:** Haysmacintyre

|     | 31-07-13 | 31-07-12 | 31-07-11 |
| --- | --- | --- | --- |
| TO | 20,775,477 | 19,040,403 | 18,007,863 |
| P/L | 2,643,810 | 1,950,968 | 1,539,783 |
| NW | 24,028,306 | 21,384,496 | 19,433,528 |
| WC | 3,216,556 | 1,500,230 | 205,803 |
| Emp. | 281 | 276 | 263 |

## DUNS 77-444-6892
### St Giles Hotel Ltd
Central London, London WC1B 3GH
**Tel:** 02073003000
**Web:** www.stgiles.com
**Reg No:** 2954321 **Estd:** 1994 Private Limited Company
**Line of Business:** Hotels
**Export Sales:** £14,954,000
**Issued Capital:** £555,420
**Directors:** Ms A H Tan, C B Oh, S H Noar, R C Tan, S Y Chua
**Co. Secretary:** Boodle Hatfield Secretarial Limi
**Responsibilities**
**Senior:** Victoria Millbank (General Manager), Salvatori Verardi (Food & Beverage Manager)
**Marketing:** Anit Popat (Sales Manager)
**Sales:** Anit Popat (Sales Manager)
**IT:** Jaz Mehmi (IT Manager)
**HR:** Darrell Murphy (Human Resources Manager)

**Health & Safety:** Darrell Murphy (Human Resources Manager)
**US SIC:** 7399 **UK SIC:** 83954
**Auditors:** Blueprint Audit Ltd
**Bankers:** National Westminster Bank Plc (51-50-14)

|     | 31-12-13 | 31-12-12 | 31-12-11 |
| --- | --- | --- | --- |
| TO | 34,683,000 | 29,593,000 | 32,806,000 |
| P/L | 807,000 | (3,374,000) | (661,000) |
| NW | 7,115,000 | 7,377,000 | 11,987,000 |
| WC | (4,666,000) | (4,501,000) | 1,179,000 |
| Emp. | 330 | 362 | 436 |

## DUNS 28-843-9375
### St Giles Schools of Languages Ltd
154 Southampton Row, London WC1B 5JX
**Tel:** 02078370404 **Fax:** 020-7837-4099
**Web:** www.stgiles.co.uk
**Reg No:** 0596651 **Estd:** 1955 Private Limited Company
**Line of Business:** Technical and vocational secondary education
**Export Sales:** £9,932,467
**Trading Style:** St Giles College London Central
**Issued Capital:** £3,000
**Principals:** M A Lindsay (Managing), P C Lindsay (Managing), Ms D A Lindsay
**Co. Secretary:** Mark Lindsay
**Responsibilities**
**Marketing:** Hannah Lindsay (Marketing Manager)
**Admin:** Martha Raczynski (Administration)
**HR:** Garth Cadden (Teacher Training)
**Branches:** St Giles Schools Of Languages Ltd, 13 Silverdale Road, Eastbourne, East Sussex BN20 7AJ
**US SIC:** 8249 **UK SIC:** 93300
**Auditors:** W Rowlands Fry & Son

|     | 31-12-13 | 31-12-12 | 31-12-11 |
| --- | --- | --- | --- |
| TO | 30,229,547 | 28,882,252 | 25,708,871 |
| P/L | 2,310,139 | 2,404,131 | 2,120,669 |
| NW | 12,302,590 | 11,216,680 | 9,897,272 |
| WC | 2,961,659 | 1,708,962 | 3,461,076 |
| Emp. | 396 | 378 | 317 |

## DUNS 39-733-4814
### St Giles Trust
Georgian House, 64-68 Camberwell Church Street, Camberwe, London SE5 8JB
**Tel:** 02077037000
**Web:** www.stgilestrust.org.uk
**Reg No:** 2175146 **Estd:** 1987 Private Limited Company
**Line of Business:** Charities and charitable organisations
**Directors:** Lady L Gibbings, Sir A A Greener, D J Pinto-Duschinsky, Mrs D N Jagger, Ms J Rice, H Bansil, Ms J Bateman, C H Pitts-Tucker
**Co. Secretary:** Robert Owen
**Responsibilities**
**Senior:** David Adade (Manager), Maria Mcnicholl (Senior Manager), Christopher Priestley (Manager), Louise Shepherd Evans (trustee), Philip Wheatley (Director), Penny White (General Manager)
**Marketing:** Sean McFadden (Head of Fund Raising)
**IT:** Shirley Redwood (Senior IT Executive)
**HR:** Victoria Bryan (Head of Human Resources), Maggie Cramb (Head of Employment & Training)
**Operations:** Andy Cross (Director of Services)
**Branches:** St Giles Trust, The Maidstone Community Support, Marsham Street, Maidstone, Kent ME14 1HH
**US SIC:** 8699, 6732
**UK SIC:** 96902, 83100
**Auditors:** Macintyre & Co
**Bankers:** Barclays Bank Plc (20-66-51)

|     | 31-03-14 | 31-03-13 | 31-03-12 |
| --- | --- | --- | --- |
| TO | 7,792,915 | 5,413,129 | 4,712,380 |
| P/L | 1,324,525 | 482,000 | 45,134 |
| NW | 3,398,351 | 2,069,902 | 1,583,729 |
| WC | 2,287,812 | 1,074,296 | 597,299 |
| Emp. | 137 | 99 | 102 |

## DUNS 21-605-3994
### St Gregory's Catholic College
Combe Hay Lane, Bath, Avon BA2 8PA
**Tel:** 01225832873
**Web:** www.st-gregorys.bathnes.sch.uk
**Estd:** 1986
**Line of Business:** Schools (local authority)
**Proprietor:** R Friel
**Responsibilities**
**Senior:** Karen Howard (Executive Bursar)
**Finance:** Karen Howard (Executive Bursar)
**IT:** Stuart Hodder (Network Manager), Sue Hughes (IT Coordinator)
**Operations:** Julie Trings (ICT trainer)
**US SIC:** 8211 **UK SIC:** 93200
**Employees:** 55

## DUNS 89-652-4709
### St Gregory's Homecare Ltd
46 Market Street, Carnforth, Lancashire LA5 9LB
**Tel:** 01539730343
**Web:** www.sgh-homecare.co.uk
**Reg No:** 3320408 **Estd:** 2010 Private Limited Company
**Line of Business:** Home care and help services
**Issued Capital:** £100
**Principals:** R H Ellwood (Managing), Mrs M F Wellock, C A Weatherill, Mrs C Ellwood
**Co. Secretary:** Raymond Ellwood
**Responsibilities**
**Senior:** Carl Witherill (Manager)
**US SIC:** 8811 **UK SIC:** 99000
**Auditors:** Thompson & Co

|     | 30-09-13 | 30-09-12 | 30-09-11 |
| --- | --- | --- | --- |
| TA | 497,122 | 494,753 | 486,815 |
| NW | 231,359 | 178,764 | 184,578 |
| WC | 290,404 | 169,971 | 182,637 |

## DUNS 64-083-5471
### St Gresham Ltd
99 Holdenhurst Road, Bournemouth, Dorset BH8 8DY
**Tel:** 01202-550000
**Web:** www.goadsby.com
**Reg No:** 4486958 **Estd:** 2002 Private Limited Company
**Line of Business:** Management activities of holding companies
**Trading Style:** Goadsby
**Issued Capital:** £1,535
**Directors:** N Price, R Craven, D Huck
**Co. Secretary:** David Errington
**US SIC:** 6711 **UK SIC:** 83962

|     | 30-06-13 | 30-06-12 | 30-06-11 |
| --- | --- | --- | --- |
| TO | 10,426,971 | 10,655,854 | 10,857,746 |
| P/L | 242,702 | 310,088 | 889,560 |
| NW | 630,185 | 306,399 | (9,258) |
| WC | (1,068,238) | (1,372,751) | (1,267,850) |
| Emp. | 265 | 275 | 264 |

## DUNS 21-818-8719
### St Helena School
Sheepen Road, Colchester, Essex CO3 3LE
**Tel:** 01206572253
**Reg No:** 7912930 **Estd:** 2012 Private Company Limited By Guarantee
**Line of Business:** General secondary education
**Directors:** Mrs J D Archard, B T Avis, Ms S J Cullis, A H Stevens, C K Jeggo, Ms E Maclean, M R Jordan, Mrs C Fritz
**Co. Secretary:** Mrs Sarah Caven-Atack
**Responsibilities**
**Senior:** Geoffrey Davison (Director), Eleanor Phillips (Bursar)
**US SIC:** 8211 **UK SIC:** 93200
**Bankers:** Lloyds TSB Bank plc (30-92-16)

|     | 31-08-14 | 31-08-13 | 31-08-12 |
| --- | --- | --- | --- |
| TO | 6,183,165 | 6,350,164 | 7,182,313 |
| P/L | 564,419 | 318,986 | 4,340,746 |
| NW | 5,145,151 | 4,467,732 | 4,231,746 |
| WC | 1,456,959 | 762,342 | 478,245 |
| Emp. | 114 | 112 | 115 |

## DUNS 54-864-0473
### St Helens & Knowsley Teaching Hospitals Nhs Trust
Whiston Hospital, Warrington Road, Prescot, Merseyside L35 5DR
**Tel:** 0151-426-1600
**Web:** www.sthk.nhs.uk
**VAT No:** 654943996 **Estd:** 1991
**Line of Business:** Hospitals
**Issued Capital:** £1
**Principals:** L Howell (Chairman), D Finn (Financial), Ms A Marie-Stretch (Personnel), I Stewardson, P Williams, N Darvill, Ms A Marr, Ms D Mclaughlin
**Branches:** St Helens & Knowsley Teaching Hospitals Nhs Trust, Irwin Road Centre, Irwin Road, St. Helens, Merseyside WA9 3UG
**US SIC:** 8091, 8062
**UK SIC:** 95200, 95100
**Employees:** 4,500

## DUNS 21-780-1601
### St Helen's Catholic Primary School
Chargeable Lane, London E13 8DW
**Web:** www.st-helens.newham.sch.uk
**Estd:** 2003 Proprietorship
**Line of Business:** Schools (local authority)
**Proprietor:** Mrs G Hicks
**US SIC:** 8211 **UK SIC:** 93200
**Employees:** 70

## DUNS 50-479-2631
### St Helens Chamber Ltd
Salisbury Street, Off Chalon Way, St Helens, Merseyside WA10 1FY
**Tel:** 01744742000
**Web:** www.sthelenschamber.com
**Reg No:** 2453212 **VAT No:** 534847718

**Estd:** 1989 Private Company Limited By Guarantee
**Line of Business:** Chambers of commerce
**Trading Style:** St Helens Chamber
**Directors:** G Charlton, Ms K E Boullen, N T Taylor, R C Young, S M Gange, A M Harrison, R Mccauley, D N Buxton
**Co. Secretary:** Ms Clare Gravener
**Responsibilities**
**Senior:** Patricia Bacon (board member), Jackie Mafi (Director), Andrew Mcminnis (Director), Neil Reid (board member), Grace Tabern (board member), William Worsley (board member)
**HR:** Debbie Brown (Director of Training Services), Pauline Devine (Director of Employment Service)
**Purchasing:** Gillian Warburton (Purchasing Manager)
**US SIC:** 8621, 8249, 8611
**UK SIC:** 96311, 93300, 96312
**Auditors:** Baker Tilly
**Bankers:** National Westminster Bank Plc (60-70-08)

|     | 31-03-14 | 31-03-13 | 31-03-12 |
| --- | --- | --- | --- |
| TO | 4,949,655 | 4,409,876 | 4,937,309 |
| P/L | 48,638 | 27,536 | 1,592 |
| NW | 5,748,789 | 5,842,323 | 5,978,822 |
| WC | 187,041 | 272,796 | 370,676 |
| Emp. | 110 | 108 | 116 |

## DUNS 23-455-6819
### St Helens College
Brook Street, St Helens, Merseyside WA10 1PZ
**Tel:** 01744 733766
**Web:** www.sthelens.ac.uk
**Estd:** 1896
**Line of Business:** Institutes
**Director:** Dr J Burford
**Branches:** St Helens College, Water Street, St. Helens, Merseyside WA10 1PP
**US SIC:** 8621 **UK SIC:** 96311
**Employees:** 800

## DUNS 22-864-5594
### St Helens Metropolitan Borough Council
Wesley House, Corporation Street, St Helens, Merseyside WA10 1HF
**Tel:** 01744456789
**Web:** www.sthelens.gov.uk
**Estd:** 1974
**Line of Business:** Day and care centres
**Directors:** Ms C Hudson, P Yates
**Responsibilities**
**Senior:** Malcolm Clough (Manager), Chris Dove (Facilities Manager), Carole Fletcher (Manager), Joanne Griffiths (Manager), Donna Hardiman (Manager), Rachel Horrocks (Manager), Damian Keegan (Manager), Brian Malcolm (Manager), Sonia Neighbour (Manager), Tom Neylon (Manager), Carmen Nunez (Manager), Cath Shea (Chairman), Kirsty Watkinson (Manager), Darrell Wilson (Chief Trading Standards Office)
**Marketing:** Lorraine Simpson (Marketing Manager)
**Sales:** Dave Boocock (Business Development Manager), Gary Maddock (Business Development Manager), Steve Sharples (Business Development Manager)
**Admin:** Mary Dixon (Administrator), Marie Kendrick (Administrator)
**HR:** Brendan Farrell (Human Resources Manager), Melanie Latham (Principal Training Officer), Phil Leach (Personnel Manager), Grace Tatlock (Training Director), Vicki Wignall (HR)
**Health & Safety:** Andy Dempsey (Health & Safety Officer), Liz Gaulton (Director of Public Health)
**Facilities:** Chris Dove (Facilities Manager)
**Branches:** St Helens Metropolitan Borough Council, Elton Head Road, St. Helens, St. Helens, Merseyside WA9 5AU
**US SIC:** 9121 **UK SIC:** 91110
**Employees:** 809

## DUNS 21-811-0822
### St Helens P C C
4 Upper Packington Road, Ashby-De-La-Zouch, Leicestershire LE65 1EF
**Estd:** 2012
**Line of Business:** Activities of religious organisations
**US SIC:** 8661 **UK SIC:** 96600
**Employees:** 100

## DUNS 23-703-1539
### St Helier International Ltd
99 Old St Johns Road, Jersey, Channel Islands JE2 3LG
**Tel:** 01534766366
**Web:** www.shyc.je
**Reg No:** 0001624J **Estd:** 1966 Private Limited Company
**Line of Business:** Clubs social and associations

**Issued Capital:** £15,000
**Principals:** R L Weston (Managing), N J Weston, Ms E Weston
**Co. Secretary:** Alan Weston
**Responsibilities**
**Senior:** Helen Marquand (Manager), Chris Parlett (Club Manager)
**US SIC:** 5813, 6111
**UK SIC:** 66200, 81501
**Employees:** 100

DUNS 23-083-2649
### St Hilda's C of E High School
Croxteth Drive, Liverpool, Merseyside L17 3AL
**Tel:** 01517332709
**Web:** www.st-hildas.com
**Estd:** 1995
**Line of Business:** General secondary education
**Director:** J C Yates
**US SIC:** 8211 **UK SIC:** 93200
**Employees:** 94

DUNS 34-872-2195
### St Hugh's Conferences Ltd
(**Subsidiary of:** University of Oxford)
St Margarets Road, Oxford, Oxfordshire OX2 6LE
**Web:** www.st-hughs.ox.ac.uk
**Reg No:** 5670486 **Estd:** 2006 Private Limited Company
**Line of Business:** Catering
**Issued Capital:** £1
**Directors:** Dame E F Angiolini, Ms V Stott
**Co. Secretary:** Ms Victoria Stott
**Responsibilities**
**Senior:** Roy Westbrook (Director)
**US SIC:** 5812 **UK SIC:** 66110
**Auditors:** Critchleys

|  | 31-07-14 | 31-07-13 | 31-07-12 |
|---|---|---|---|
| TA | 149,132 | 95,153 | 37,327 |
| NW | 1 | 1 | 1 |
| WC | 1 | 1 | 1 |

DUNS 21-776-2312
### St Hughs Hospital
Peaks Lane, Grimsby, South Humberside DN32 9RP
**Tel:** 01472251100
**Web:** www.sthughshospital.co.uk
**Estd:** 1994 Proprietorship
**Line of Business:** Public sector hospital activities, including nhs trusts
**Proprietor:** Miss D Read
**Responsibilities**
**Senior:** Angela Breeze (Personal Assistant)
**US SIC:** 8062 **UK SIC:** 95100
**Employees:** 100

DUNS 21-504-5829
### St Hugh's School
Cromwell Avenue, Woodhall Spa, Lincolnshire LN10 6TQ
**Tel:** 01526-352169
**Web:** www.st-hughs.lincs.sch.uk
**Estd:** 1918
**Line of Business:** Schools (independent)
**Director:** S Greenish
**US SIC:** 8211 **UK SIC:** 93200
**Employees:** 50

DUNS 21-283-5764
### St Itas Primary School
4 Alderwood Hill, Belfast BT8 6YY
**Tel:** 028-90798811
**Web:** www.stitas.co.uk
**Estd:** 2006 Proprietorship
**Line of Business:** Schools (local authority)
**Proprietor:** Mrs J Brown
**Responsibilities**
**Senior:** Joanne Browne (Principal)
**US SIC:** 8211 **UK SIC:** 93200
**Employees:** 60

DUNS 21-777-2146
### St Ives
Trenwith Burrows, St Ives, Cornwall TR26 1HB
**Tel:** 01736797006
**Web:** www.tempusleisure.org.uk
**Estd:** 2001 Proprietorship
**Line of Business:** Leisure centres
**Proprietor:** C Perry
**US SIC:** 7999 **UK SIC:** 97913
**Employees:** 60

DUNS 21-162-0067
### St Ives Plc
One Tudor Street, London EC4Y 0AH
**Tel:** 02079 288 844 **Fax:** 02079 026 375
**Web:** www.st-ives.co.uk
**Reg No:** 1552113 **VAT No:** 233250991
**Estd:** 1964 Public Limited Company
**Line of Business:** Management activities of holding companies
**Issued Capital:** £11,982,637
**Directors:** M R Armitage, J B Gordon, R Stillwell, Ms H C Stevenson, P B Gray, M G Butterworth
**Co. Secretary:** Philip Harris
**Responsibilities**
**Sales:** Tony Ayles (Sales Director)
**IT:** David Greenbury (Technical Manager)
**Health & Safety:** David Greenbury (Technical Manager)
**Facilities:** David Greenbury (Technical Manager)
**Branches:** St Ives Plc, Unit 1-2 Backfields, Bristol, Avon BS2 8QP
**US SIC:** 6711, 2721
**UK SIC:** 83962, 47522
**Auditors:** Deloitte LLP
**Bankers:** National Westminster Bank Plc (50-41-01)

|  | 01-08-14 | 02-08-13 | 27-08-12 |
|---|---|---|---|
| TO | 330,684,000 | 322,679,000 | 329,459,000 |
| P/L | 11,883,000 | 7,060,000 | 14,908,000 |
| NW | (22,918,000) | 24,723,000 | 27,581,000 |
| WC | (846,000) | 6,608,000 | 20,965,000 |
| Emp. | 2,943 | 3,031 | 2,894 |

DUNS 21-736-1758
### St Ivo School
High Leys, St Ives, Cambridgeshire PE27 6RR
**Tel:** 01480375400
**Web:** www.stivoschool.org
**Reg No:** 7703797 **Estd:** 2011 Private Company Limited By Guarantee
**Line of Business:** General secondary education
**Directors:** S J Grey, M R Sanderson, C Hillsdon, Ms C A Darnell, D J Mead, R D King, J P Andrews, C W Glanville
**Co. Secretary:** Ms Jane Jest
**Responsibilities**
**Senior:** Judith Barnes (Director), Howard Gilbert (Head Teacher), Claire Lynn (Director), Jewel Meichan (Principal), Francis Newton (Director), James Stavrou (Director), Tricia Tacconi (Manager)
**Finance:** Sue Weston (finance manager)
**US SIC:** 8211 **UK SIC:** 93200
**Bankers:** Lloyds TSB Bank plc (77-72-19)

|  | 31-08-14 | 31-08-13 | 31-08-12 |
|---|---|---|---|
| TO | 10,043,179 | 9,991,801 | 24,659,381 |
| P/L | 262,504 | 346,635 | 14,384,789 |
| NW | 14,380,928 | 14,658,424 | 14,196,789 |
| WC | 1,334,183 | 1,510,320 | 949,862 |
| Emp. | 205 | 272 | 270 |

DUNS 21-778-6767
### St James C of E Primary School
Shelsley Avenue, Oldbury, West Midlands B69 1BG
**Tel:** 01215525491
**Web:** www.st-james-pri.sandwell.sch.uk
**Estd:** 1969 Proprietorship
**Line of Business:** Primary education
**Proprietor:** P Longden
**US SIC:** 8211 **UK SIC:** 93200
**Employees:** 60

DUNS 42-442-3945
### St James Catholic High School
Great Strand, London NW9 5PE
**Tel:** 020-8358-2800
**Web:** www.st-james.barnet.sch.uk
**Estd:** 1934
**Line of Business:** Schools (local authority)
**Principals:** Ms A M Colvin (Financial), K Macsharry
**Responsibilities**
**Senior:** Kevin MacSharry (Principal), Sean McGowan (Manager), Anne O'Shea (Head Teacher)
**Finance:** Brian Alcock (Senior Finance Administrator)
**HR:** Donna Marco (Head Teacher)
**US SIC:** 8211 **UK SIC:** 93200
**Bankers:** Allied Irish Bank (gb) (23-84-88)
**Employees:** 65

DUNS 21-506-9373
### St James Clinic
Extons Road, King's Lynn, Norfolk PE30 5NU
**Tel:** 01553668500
**Web:** www.norfolk.nhs.uk
**Estd:** 2002 Partnership
**Line of Business:** Nhs clinics
**Partners:** Mrs S Palmer, Mrs S Palmer
**Responsibilities**
**HR:** Vicky Naylor (Staff Development Manager)
**US SIC:** 8091 **UK SIC:** 95200
**Employees:** 200

DUNS 45-839-8807
### St James Group Ltd
(**Subsidiary of:** The Berkeley Group Holdings Plc)
St James House, Leatherhead, Surrey KT22 8BZ
**Tel:** 01372-364-500
**Web:** www.berkeleygroup.co.uk
**Reg No:** 3190056 **Estd:** 1996 Private Limited Company
**Line of Business:** Development and selling of real estate
**Trading Style:** Berkeley Group
**Issued Capital:** £20,000
**Directors:** N G Simpkin, P Kemkers, Miss A J Dowsett, R C Perrins, A W Pidgley, P I Hopkins, S Ellis, C N Walter
**Co. Secretary:** Ms Elaine Driver
**Responsibilities**
**Senior:** Alastair Bradshaw (Manager), Dean Summers (Manager)
**Marketing:** Lana Hunt (Marketing Executive)
**Admin:** Georgina McHugh (Personal Assistant)
**US SIC:** 6552 **UK SIC:** 85000
**Auditors:** PricewaterhouseCoopers LLP

|  | 30-04-14 | 30-04-13 | 30-04-12 |
|---|---|---|---|
| TO | 177,257,000 | 321,452,000 | 261,553,000 |
| P/L | 88,748,000 | 120,843,000 | 91,408,000 |
| NW | 356,348,000 | 434,086,000 | 151,490,000 |
| WC | 411,695,000 | 437,703,000 | 148,965,000 |
| Emp. | 275 | 237 | 221 |

DUNS 55-071-0115
### St James School
22 Bargate, Grimsby, South Humberside DN34 4SY
**Web:** www.saintjamesschool.co.uk
**Estd:** 2003 Proprietorship
**Line of Business:** Schools (independent)
**Proprietor:** Mrs S Isaac
**US SIC:** 8211 **UK SIC:** 93200
**Employees:** 70

DUNS 21-242-4613
### St James's Club
7 Park Place, London SW1A 1LS
**Tel:** 02073161600
**Web:** www.stjameshotelandclub.com
**Estd:** 1975
**Line of Business:** Hotels
**Principals:** C Stein (Chairman), Sir H Solomon, Ms K Lempe
**Responsibilities**
**Senior:** Henrik Muehler (Manager)
**Marketing:** Kate Dixon (Sales & Marketing Director)
**Sales:** Kate Dixon (Sales & Marketing Director)
**Admin:** blanche Devon (Secretary)
**Branches:** St James's Club, 43 Pall Mall, London SW1Y 5JG
**US SIC:** 7011 **UK SIC:** 66500
**Employees:** 60

DUNS 22-721-3196
### St John Ambulance
27 St Johns Lane, London EC1M 4BU
**Web:** www.sja.org.uk
**Reg No:** 3866129 **VAT No:** 564553916
**Estd:** 1999 Private Limited Company
**Line of Business:** Teaching and practice of first aid
**Trading Style:** St John Ambulance Association, St John Ambulance Brigade, Order of St John of Jerusalem, St John Ambulance Commercial Training Divison(North East Regio
**Directors:** M Messinger, M R Patten, R A Green, The Very Reverend N A Frayling, S G Russell, Miss A Jarvie, Ms S C Ellen, P M Holland
**Co. Secretary:** Gary Maydon
**Responsibilities**
**Senior:** Colin Imray (Principal), A Mellows (Principal), The Of Gloucester (Principal), James Remnant (Principal), sue killen (chief exec)
**Branches:** St John Ambulance, 310 Goswell Road, London EC1V 7LW
**US SIC:** 8091 **UK SIC:** 95200
**Auditors:** Grant Thornton UK LLP
**Bankers:** National Westminster Bank Plc (60-05-37)

|  | 31-12-13 | 31-12-05 |
|---|---|---|
| TO | 91,300,000 | 71,273,000 |
| P/L | (5,700,000) | 9,087,000 |
| NW | 113,500,000 | 150,636,000 |
| WC | 11,800,000 | 36,346,000 |
| Emp. | 1,682 | 1,516 |

DUNS 23-083-1567
### St John Fisher Catholic School
Ordnance Street, Chatham, Kent ME4 6SG
**Tel:** 01634335757
**Web:** www.st-johnfisher.medway.sch.uk
**Estd:** 1990
**Line of Business:** Schools (local authority)
**Director:** K Findlay

**Responsibilities**
**Finance:** Carole Oliver (Finance Officer)
**US SIC:** 8211 **UK SIC:** 93200
**Employees:** 85

DUNS 23-016-4758
### St John Fisher Roman Catholic High School
Oxford Road, Dewsbury, West Yorkshire WF13 4LL
**Web:** www.stjohnfisher.org.uk
**Estd:** 2002 Proprietorship
**Line of Business:** Schools (local authority)
**Proprietor:** K Higgins
**US SIC:** 8211 **UK SIC:** 93200
**Employees:** 98

DUNS 21-163-3990
### St John Houghton Catholic Secondary School
Abbot Road, Ilkeston, Derbyshire DE7 4HX
**Web:** www.st-johnhoughton.derbyshire.sch.uk
**Estd:** 1974
**Line of Business:** Schools (local authority)
**Director:** B Monaghan
**Responsibilities**
**Senior:** Joan Mccarthy (Head Teacher)
**Finance:** Debbie Vallis (Bursar)
**Health & Safety:** Debbie Vallis (Bursar)
**US SIC:** 8211 **UK SIC:** 93200
**Employees:** 80

DUNS 23-082-9026
### St John Rigby College
Gathurst Road, Orrell, Wigan, Lancashire WN5 0LJ
**Tel:** 01942-214797
**Web:** www.sjr.ac.uk
**Estd:** 1985
**Line of Business:** Further education schools and colleges
**Director:** J A Crowley
**Responsibilities**
**Senior:** Peter Mc Gee (Principal)
**US SIC:** 8211 **UK SIC:** 93100
**Employees:** 140

DUNS 23-082-9389
### St John Vianney School
Rye Bank Road, Firswood, Manchester M16 0EX
**Tel:** 0161-881-7843
**Web:** www.stjohnvianneyschool.co.uk
**Estd:** 1990
**Line of Business:** Schools (special)
**Director:** J Cusick
**Responsibilities**
**Senior:** Eileen Mcmorrow (Head Teacher)
**US SIC:** 8299 **UK SIC:** 93300
**Employees:** 60

DUNS 64-252-0027
### St John's C of E Primary School
Dawson Lane, Bradford, West Yorkshire BD4 6JF
**Web:** www.stjohnsceprimary.co.uk
**Estd:** 2003
**Line of Business:** Schools (foundation)
**Proprietor:** Mrs E Lawley
**Responsibilities**
**Senior:** Elizabeth Lawley (Head Teacher)
**US SIC:** 8211 **UK SIC:** 93200
**Bankers:** Yorkshire Bank Plc (05-03-03)
**Employees:** 46

DUNS 21-775-4215
### St John's Catholic Primary School
Rochester Road, Gravesend, Kent DA12 2SY
**Tel:** 01474361609
**Web:** www.stjohnsprimary.kent.sch.uk
**Estd:** 1947 Proprietorship
**Line of Business:** Schools (local authority)
**Proprietor:** Mrs A Ratcliffe
**Responsibilities**
**Senior:** Jonathan Shields (Head Teacher)
**US SIC:** 8211 **UK SIC:** 93200
**Employees:** 65

DUNS 22-878-0722
### St Johns Catholic School
Church Street, Boston Spa, Wetherby, West Yorkshire LS23 6DF
**Web:** www.stjohns.org.uk
**Estd:** 1870
**Line of Business:** Schools (special)
**Directors:** T Wrynne, Rev D Harrison
**Branches:** St Johns Catholic School, Church Street, Wetherby, West Yorkshire LS23 6DF
**US SIC:** 8299 **UK SIC:** 93300
**Bankers:** HSBC Bank plc (40-46-21)
**Employees:** 80

**DUNS 21-229-3233**

## St John's Church of England
The Vicarage, Romsey Road, Lockerley, Romsey, Hampshire SO51 0JF
**Estd:** 2005 Proprietorship
**Line of Business:** Places of worship
**Proprietor:** Reverend J Pitkin
**US SIC:** 8661  **UK SIC:** 96600
**Employees:** 100

**DUNS 21-919-2232**

## St John's Church of England Middle School Academy
Watt Close, Bromsgrove, Worcestershire B61 7DH
**Tel:** 01527832376
**Web:** www.st-johns-bromsgrove.worcs.sch.uk
**Reg No:** 8355037  **Estd:** 2013 Private Company Limited By Guarantee
**Line of Business:** Primary education
**Directors:** Mrs D K Matharu, P Andrews, A Elwell-Thomas, Ms R S Shorter, R Powell, S Reeves, P J Norris, Ms R Sumner
**Co. Secretary:** Ms Janet Perrey
**Responsibilities**
**Senior:** Karen Baxter (Director), Valerie Clarke (Director), Melanie Ireland (Director), Adele Lee (Director), Sara Pemberton (Director)
**US SIC:** 8211  **UK SIC:** 93200

|      | 31-08-14  | 31-08-13  |
|------|-----------|-----------|
| TO   | 2,507,000 | 5,647,000 |
| P/L  | (58,000)  | 4,317,000 |
| NW   | 4,260,000 | 4,327,000 |
| WC   | 272,000   | 423,000   |
| Emp. | 74        | 67        |

**DUNS 21-866-0649**

## St John's Church of England Primary School Sparkhill
Stratford Road, Birmingham, West Midlands B11 4EA
**Tel:** 01216751469
**Web:** www.st-johns-pri.bham.sch.uk
**Reg No:** 8270275  **Estd:** 2012 Private Company Limited By Guarantee
**Line of Business:** Primary education
**Directors:** Dr S Raashid Latif, Dr A R Maher, S K Shah, Rev J A Self, Rev A B Samy, D L Heard, Mrs L Bradbury, Miss L J Poole
**Co. Secretary:** Darren Forth
**Responsibilities**
**Senior:** Pravina Bhardwa (Director), Lewis Coley (Director), Keith May (Director)
**Finance:** Lewis Coley (Director)
**US SIC:** 8211  **UK SIC:** 93200
**Bankers:** Lloyds TSB Bank plc (30-00-03)

|      | 31-08-14  | 31-08-13  |
|------|-----------|-----------|
| TO   | 2,250,963 | 4,390,233 |
| P/L  | (135,471) | 2,914,887 |
| NW   | 2,799,416 | 2,965,887 |
| WC   | 109,206   | 151,716   |
| Emp. | 52        | 49        |

**DUNS 23-213-1545**

## St Johns College
Grove Road South, Southsea, Hampshire PO5 3QW
**Web:** www.stjohnscollege.co.uk
**Estd:** 1998
**Line of Business:** Nursery schools
**Responsibilities**
**Senior:** Jeanette Mynhardt (Nursery Leader)
**IT:** G Burwood (Computer Manager), Osmond Glodic (It Manager)
**US SIC:** 8211  **UK SIC:** 93200
**Employees:** 120

**DUNS 21-449-8177**                                  **Imp**

## St John's College Cambridge
St Johns Street, Cambridge, Cambridgeshire CB2 1TP
**Web:** www.joh.cam.ac.uk
**VAT No:** 636861316  **Estd:** 1511 Incorporate By Act Of Parliament
**Line of Business:** First-degree level higher education
**Directors:** C Dobson, C Ewbank
**US SIC:** 8221  **UK SIC:** 93100
**Auditors:** Deloitte LLP
**Bankers:** Barclays Bank Plc (20-17-19)

|      | 30-06-13    | 30-06-12    | 30-06-11    |
|------|-------------|-------------|-------------|
| TO   | 32,518,000  | 32,841,000  | 27,846,000  |
| P/L  | (602,000)   | (401,000)   | (592,000)   |
| NW   | 625,293,000 | 601,791,000 | 587,649,000 |
| WC   | 8,636,000   | 20,943,000  | 6,361,000   |
| Emp. | 451         | 454         | 450         |

**DUNS 23-082-8498**

## St John's College Oxford
Porters Lodge, St Giles, Oxford, Oxfordshire OX1 3JP
**Web:** www.sjc.ox.ac.uk
**Reg No:** 0000603RC  **Estd:** 2002
**Line of Business:** University
**Principals:** Dr A Boyce (President), Sir M Scholar
**Responsibilities**
**Finance:** Sally Layburn (Financial Bursar)

**Health & Safety:** Sally Layburn (Financial Bursar)
**Purchasing:** Murray Goodes (Purchasing Manager)
**Branches:** St John's College Oxford, St. Giles, Oxford, Oxfordshire OX1 3JP
**US SIC:** 8221  **UK SIC:** 93100
**Auditors:** Ernst & Young LLP
**Employees:** 50
**Turnover:** £12,116,201

**DUNS 21-039-2228**

## St Johns College School
73 Grange Road, Cambridge, Cambridgeshire CB3 9AB
**Tel:** 01223 353532
**Web:** www.sjcs.co.uk
**Estd:** 2004
**Line of Business:** Schools (independent)
**Proprietor:** K Spurway
**Responsibilities**
**Marketing:** Alex Loria (Marketing Manager)
**IT:** Graham Hastings (Senior IT Executive)
**HR:** Linda Hague (Director of Studies)
**Facilities:** Andy Bainbridge (Facilities Manager)
**US SIC:** 8211  **UK SIC:** 93200
**Employees:** 150

**DUNS 50-703-6838**

## St Johns Health Centre
Lightowler Road, Halifax, West Yorkshire HX1 5NB
**Tel:** 01422-341611
**Estd:** 1997 Proprietorship
**Line of Business:** Public sector hospital activities, including nhs trusts
**Proprietor:** Mrs H Webster-Mair
**US SIC:** 8062  **UK SIC:** 95100
**Employees:** 70

**DUNS 21-022-7272**

## St Johns Home
St Marys Road, Oxford, Oxfordshire OX4 1QE
**Web:** www.stjohnshome.org.uk
**Estd:** 2002 Proprietorship
**Line of Business:** Residential care establishments
**Proprietor:** Miss M Burns
**Responsibilities**
**Senior:** Mollie Burns (Home Manager), Joyce Roachford (Manager)
**Finance:** Brian Pike (Bursar)
**Health & Safety:** Derek Meadham (Assistant Manager)
**Facilities:** Derek Meadham (Assistant Manager)
**US SIC:** 8321  **UK SIC:** 96111
**Employees:** 50

**DUNS 23-217-6354**

## St Johns Hospital
4-5 Chapel Court, Bath, Avon BA1 1SQ
**Tel:** 01225486410
**Web:** www.stjohnsbath.org.uk
**Estd:** 1984
**Line of Business:** Sheltered housing accommodation
**Responsibilities**
**Finance:** James Money-Kyrle (Director of Support Services)
**IT:** Sarah Exton (IT Manager)
**HR:** Teresa Cross (Human Resources Manager)
**Health & Safety:** James Money-Kyrle (Director of Support Services)
**US SIC:** 8321  **UK SIC:** 96111
**Auditors:** Monahans
**Employees:** 65
**Turnover:** £521,000

**DUNS 42-394-3778**

## St Johns Hospital
**(Subsidiary of:** Scottish Government)
St Johns Hospital, Howden Road West, Livingston, West Lothian EH54 6PP
**Web:** www.nhslothian.scot.nhs.uk
**Estd:** 1989
**Line of Business:** Building construction contractors
**Trading Style:** St Johns Hospital
**Issued Capital:** £1
**Responsibilities**
**Finance:** Cindy Macleod (Financial Director)
**IT:** John Sturgeon (IS Director)
**Health & Safety:** Shona Cameron (Health & Safety Officer)
**Branches:** St Johns Hospital, Dedridge Medical Group, Nigel Rise, Livingston, West Lothian EH54 6QQ
**US SIC:** 8062, 9121
**UK SIC:** 95100, 91110
**Employees:** 3,500

**DUNS 21-591-8158**

## St Johns Nursing Home
St Peters Walk, Droitwich, Worcestershire WR9 8EX
**Tel:** 01905794506
**Web:** www.shaw.co.uk
**Estd:** 2011
**Line of Business:** Nursing homes
**Responsibilities**
**Senior:** Catherine Sandy (Home Manager)
**Admin:** Eleanor Hannah (Administrator)
**US SIC:** 8051  **UK SIC:** 95100
**Employees:** 70

**DUNS 28-846-5404**

## St John's-on-the-Hill & Brightlands School Trust Ltd
Castleford Hill, Tutshill, Chepstow, Gwent NP16 7LE
**Tel:** 01291-622045  **Fax:** 01291-623932
**Web:** www.stjohnsonthehill.co.uk
**Reg No:** 0643994  **Estd:** 1959 Private Company Limited By Guarantee
**Line of Business:** Schools (foundation)
**Directors:** S J Willis, Ms C M Hopkinson, Mrs E Taylor, R Lister, Mrs K Maguire
**Co. Secretary:** Miss Louise Strange
**Responsibilities**
**Senior:** Judy Brown (Governor), Teresa Cash (Manager), Paul Stickler (Governor), Albert Vaux (Manager), Trent Ward (Manager)
**Finance:** Richard Blight (Bursar)
**US SIC:** 8211  **UK SIC:** 93200
**Auditors:** KPMG
**Bankers:** The Bank Of Ireland (30-15-17)

|      | 31-08-13    | 31-08-12    | 31-08-11    |
|------|-------------|-------------|-------------|
| TO   | 4,053,853   | 4,307,594   | 4,221,151   |
| P/L  | (284,644)   | (198,850)   | (217,826)   |
| NW   | (140,984)   | 143,660     | 342,510     |
| WC   | (4,287,583) | (4,148,391) | (4,098,893) |
| Emp. | 113         | 119         | 122         |

**DUNS 21-584-8705**

## St Johns R C High School
Harefield Road, Dundee, Angus DD3 6EY
**Web:** www.stjohnshigh.ea.dundeecity.sch.uk
**Estd:** 2011 Proprietorship
**Line of Business:** Schools (local authority)
**Proprietor:** G Haggarty
**Responsibilities**
**Senior:** Fiona Mclagan (Head Teacher)
**US SIC:** 8211  **UK SIC:** 93200
**Employees:** 80

**DUNS 21-532-1477**

## St Johns R C School
Turpins Lane, Woodford Green, Essex IG8 8AX
**Tel:** 020-8504-1818
**Web:** www.stjohnsrc.org.uk
**Estd:** 1989
**Line of Business:** Schools (special)
**Partners:** B Sainsbury, Ms J Sheehy
**Responsibilities**
**Senior:** Susan Burnside (Head Teacher)
**IT:** Poraig Drugan (Senior IT Executive)
**US SIC:** 8299, 8211
**UK SIC:** 93300, 93200
**Employees:** 75

**DUNS 21-229-6502**

## St Johns Rectory
Lower Church Road, Weston-Super-Mare, Avon BS23 2AQ
**Tel:** 01934-623399
**Estd:** 2005 Proprietorship
**Line of Business:** Places of worship
**Proprietor:** Reverend R Taylor
**US SIC:** 8661  **UK SIC:** 96600
**Employees:** 200

**DUNS 21-589-3329**

## St John's Residential Home
Saumarez Park, Lane Route De Saumarez, Castel, Guernsey, Channel Islands GY5 7UJ
**Tel:** 01481256865
**Estd:** 2011
**Line of Business:** Rest and retirement homes
**Responsibilities**
**Senior:** Susan Fleming (Matron)
**US SIC:** 8321  **UK SIC:** 96111
**Employees:** 60

**DUNS 34-705-9581**

## St John's School
47-49 Stock Road, Billericay, Essex CM12 0AR
**Tel:** 01277623070
**Web:** www.stjohnsleatherhead.co.uk
**Reg No:** 5510138  **Estd:** 1982 Private Unlimited Company
**Line of Business:** Schools (independent)
**Issued Capital:** £100
**Directors:** Ms S Green, Ms J A Osen

**Co. Secretary:** Gideon Osen
**Responsibilities**
**Senior:** Fiona Armour (Headmistress)
**Marketing:** Sue Philpott (Marketing Coordinator)
**Health & Safety:** Jeff Summers (Health & Safety Officer)
**Branches:** St John's School, La Rue De Lane Mare Ballam, St John, Jersey, Channel Islands JE3 4EJ
**US SIC:** 8211  **UK SIC:** 93200
**Employees:** 60

**DUNS 37-852-6552**

## St John's School & College
Walpole Road, Brighton, East Sussex BN2 0AF
**Tel:** 01273-244000
**Web:** www.st-johns.co.uk
**Reg No:** 3303549  **Estd:** 1886 Private Limited Company
**Line of Business:** Misc schools & educational services
**Directors:** C N Harrison, W C Catchpole, R A Stewart, G P Holden, L A Parkyn, Mrs A Braunston, Ms P M Foster, Ms J E Gray
**US SIC:** 8299, 8211, 8221, 8249
**UK SIC:** 93300, 93200, 93100
**Auditors:** Friend James Ltd
**Bankers:** Barclays Bank Plc (20-12-75)

|      | 31-08-13  | 31-08-12  | 31-08-11  |
|------|-----------|-----------|-----------|
| TO   | 0,040,431 | 6,606,198 | 6,339,332 |
| P/L  | (164,654) | (703,186) | (699,787) |
| NW   | 3,398,957 | 3,563,891 | 4,266,800 |
| WC   | 202,130   | 413,936   | 1,113,564 |
| Emp. | 186       | 195       | 197       |

**DUNS 21-255-5127**

## St Johns Social Club
192 Cooper Lane, Bradford, West Yorkshire BD6 3NS
**Tel:** 01274671012
**Estd:** 1990
**Line of Business:** Social Club
**Principals:** Ms L Towley, G O-Hara
**US SIC:** 8641  **UK SIC:** 96902
**Employees:** 200

**DUNS 21-742-2180**

## St John's Special School & College
Austin Canons, Bedford Road, Kempston, Bedford, Bedfordshire MK42 8AA
**Tel:** 01234345565
**Web:** www.st-johns-school.co.uk
**Reg No:** 7750051  **Estd:** 2011 Private Company Limited By Guarantee
**Line of Business:** Adult and other education not elsewhere classified
**Directors:** M Zand, Ms F J Coniam, M W Bonney, R L Babbage, Ms J C Jones, K H Green, B A Cooper, Ms P K Rimmer
**Co. Secretary:** Ms Valerie Pendall
**Responsibilities**
**Senior:** Gina Duffield (Director), Karen Kent (Director), Keith Mulliner (Director), Amanda Rizzo (Director), David Sawford (Director), Laura Sherwood King (Director)
**US SIC:** 8249  **UK SIC:** 93300
**Auditors:** Duncan & Toplis
**Bankers:** National Westminster Bank Plc (60-12-45)

|      | 31-08-13  | 31-08-12  |
|------|-----------|-----------|
| TO   | 3,303,005 | 5,800,987 |
| P/L  | 89,047    | 2,967,005 |
| NW   | 2,874,052 | 2,775,005 |
| WC   | 599,428   | 534,747   |
| Emp. | 112       | 117       |

**DUNS 21-328-4701**

## St John's Upper School
Granham Hill, Marlborough, Wiltshire SN8 4AX
**Web:** www.stjohns.wilts.sch.uk
**Estd:** 2012
**Line of Business:** Schools (foundation)
**Responsibilities**
**Senior:** Patrick Hazlewood (Manager), Sue Watson (Director, Impact and Innovatio)
**Finance:** Valeria Kendrick (Accounts Payable), Alison O'Shaughnessy (Finance Manager)
**Sales:** Kate Hunter (Development Officer)
**Admin:** Brigid Jones (Administration Manager)
**HR:** Anne Stokes (Training Director)
**US SIC:** 8211  **UK SIC:** 93200
**Employees:** 200

**DUNS 22-906-5263**

## The St Johnstone Football Club Ltd
Mcdiarmid Park, Crieff Road, Perth, Perthshire PH1 2SJ
**Tel:** 01738-459090  **Fax:** 01738-625771
**Web:** www.perthstjohnstonefc.co.uk
**Reg No:** 0007629SC  **Estd:** 1884 Private Limited Company

**Line of Business:** Sports clubs
**Trading Style:** The St Johnstone Football Club Ltd
**Issued Capital:** £157,500
**Directors:** J Mcdougall, S Brown, S Y Harris, C W Fraser
**Co. Secretary:** Albert Ramsay
**Responsibilities**
**Senior:** Stuart Hutton (General manager)
**US SIC:** 7999 **UK SIC:** 97913
**Auditors:** Condie & Co
**Bankers:** Bank Of Scotland (80-91-28)

|    | 31-05-14 | 31-05-13 | 31-05-12 |
|----|----------|----------|----------|
| TA | 2,519,843 | 2,652,032 | 2,711,012 |
| NW | 1,825,127 | 1,551,722 | 1,748,489 |
| WC | 1,166,671 | 912,882 | 1,104,422 |

DUNS 21-581-8073
**St Joseph Rc Sec School**
Harrington Road, Workington, Cumbria CA14 3EE
**Tel:** 01900873290
**Web:** www.st-josephs.cumbria.sch.uk
**Estd:** 2011 Proprietorship
**Line of Business:** Schools (local authority)
**Proprietor:** Mrs S Worthsly
**US SIC:** 8211 **UK SIC:** 93200
**Employees:** 70

DUNS 21-542-4487
**St Joseph S R C School**
Goodson Road, London NW10 9LS
**Tel:** 020-8965-5651
**Estd:** 1952 Proprietorship
**Line of Business:** Schools (local authority)
**Proprietor:** Mrs S Riley
**Responsibilities**
**Senior:** Dawn Titus (Head Teacher)
**US SIC:** 8211 **UK SIC:** 93200
**Employees:** 60

DUNS 21-166-0811
**St Joseph's**
14 Cumnock Road, Glasgow, Lanarkshire G33 1QT
**Tel:** 01415585114
**Line of Business:** Social work activities with accommodation
**Responsibilities**
**Senior:** Sis Agnes (Manager)
**US SIC:** 8321 **UK SIC:** 96111
**Employees:** 70

DUNS 49-427-8187
**St Joseph's College Ltd**
Belstead Road, Ipswich, Suffolk IP2 9DR
**Tel:** 01473-690281
**Web:** www.stjos.co.uk
**Reg No:** 3142500 **Estd:** 1995 Private Limited Company
**Line of Business:** Schools (local authority)
**Directors:** R C Stace, J M Button, Mrs J E Lea, P Clement, Mrs R A Chester, M A Earl, P D Glading, P J Dennis
**Responsibilities**
**Senior:** Deborah Baber (Bursar), Joanna Carrick (Director), Penny Cavenagh (Director), Danielle Clarke (Principal), Andrew Goulborn (Director), James Hehir (Manager), Marc Howes (Director), Chris Lumb (Principal), Anthony Newman (Director), Matthew Potter (Director)
**Finance:** Deborah Baber (Bursar)
**IT:** Kerian Orris (IT Manager)
**Purchasing:** Deborah Baber (Bursar)
**US SIC:** 8211 **UK SIC:** 93200
**Auditors:** Baker Tilly UK Audit LLP
**Bankers:** Barclays Bank Plc (20-44-51)

|      | 31-07-14 | 31-07-13 | 31-07-12 |
|------|----------|----------|----------|
| TO   | 7,417,933 | 7,549,884 | 7,308,742 |
| P/L  | 303,644 | 152,787 | 161,947 |
| NW   | 2,369,127 | 2,065,483 | 1,912,696 |
| WC   | (1,644,197) | (219,127) | 261,442 |
| Emp. | 135 | 136 | 151 |

DUNS 42-414-6348
**St Josephs Convent Grammar School**
58 Castlecaulfield Road, Dungannon, Co Tyrone BT70 3HE
**Web:** www.stjosephs.donaghmore.ni.sch.uk
**Estd:** 2010
**Line of Business:** Schools (foundation)
**Director:** Mrs H Mccrory
**Responsibilities**
**Senior:** Enda Cullen (Head Teacher), Geraldine Donnelly (Head Teacher), Helen McCrory (Principal)
**US SIC:** 8211 **UK SIC:** 93200
**Bankers:** First Trust Bank (aib Group (uk) Plc) (93-82-89)
**Employees:** 70

DUNS 21-224-3225
**St Josephs Convent Nursing Home**
Lichfield Road, Stafford, Staffordshire ST17 4LG
**Tel:** 01785251577
**Estd:** 1991
**Line of Business:** Nursing homes
**Partners:** Mrs S Jaggers, Y Kelly
**US SIC:** 8051 **UK SIC:** 95100
**Employees:** 80

DUNS 23-082-9371
**St Josephs High School**
Beresford Avenue, Coleraine, Co Londonderry BT52 1HJ
**Tel:** 028-7034-3009
**Estd:** 1962
**Line of Business:** Schools (local authority)
**Chairmen:** F Rogan, F Donnelly
**US SIC:** 8211 **UK SIC:** 93200
**Employees:** 60

DUNS 23-082-7730
**St Joseph's Home**
71 Queens Park Road, Birmingham, West Midlands B32 2LB
**Tel:** 0121-427-2486
**Estd:** 1907
**Line of Business:** Residential care establishments
**Trading Style:** Little Sisters of the Poor
**Directors:** S Gasinta, S Helen
**Responsibilities**
**Senior:** Charles Banner (Head Chef), Isabella Donnelly (Manager), Frances Field (Home Manager)
**Finance:** Marie Rodgers (Financial Administrator)
**HR:** Frances Field (Home Manager), Anne Lardin (Training Manager)
**Health & Safety:** David Colborn (Health & Safety Officer)
**Facilities:** Frances Field (Home Manager)
**Purchasing:** Frances Field (Home Manager)
**US SIC:** 8321 **UK SIC:** 96111
**Employees:** 90

DUNS 21-185-9058
**St Josephs Home**
Seaview, Warrenpoint, Newry, Co Down BT34 3NH
**Tel:** 02841753572
**Web:** www.kilmoreycare.com
**Estd:** 1938
**Line of Business:** Nursing homes
**Proprietor:** Mrs J Rooney
**US SIC:** 8051 **UK SIC:** 95100
**Employees:** 75

DUNS 22-249-6304
**St Joseph's Hospice Association**
Ince Road, Thornton, Liverpool, Merseyside L23 4UE
**Tel:** 01519243812
**Web:** www.jospice.co.uk
**Reg No:** 4267625 **Estd:** 2001 Private Company Limited By Guarantee
**Line of Business:** Retail sale of other second-hand goods in stores
**Trading Style:** St Josephs Hospice
**Directors:** G Foster, J R Pedley, Ms T Owen, Dr J A Welch, B H Mcloughlin, D J Bricknell, Ms Y E Atkinson, Mrs J H Daly
**Co. Secretary:** Keith Cawdron
**Responsibilities**
**Senior:** Catherine Caddick (Director)
**US SIC:** 5931, 7339
**UK SIC:** 65400, 83954
**Bankers:** HSBC Bank plc (40-31-33)

|      | 31-03-14 | 31-03-13 | 31-03-12 |
|------|----------|----------|----------|
| TO   | 3,304,317 | 3,420,875 | 2,553,946 |
| P/L  | 312,208 | 565,861 | (198,931) |
| NW   | 3,225,057 | 2,909,338 | 2,343,265 |
| WC   | 731,276 | 938,586 | 402,941 |
| Emp. | 106 | N/A | 112 |

DUNS 34-709-8605
**St Joseph's Hospice Hackney**
St Josephs Hospice, Mare Street, London E8 4SA
**Tel:** 02085256026
**Web:** www.stjh.org.uk
**Reg No:** 5513914 **Estd:** 2005 Private Company Limited By Guarantee
**Line of Business:** Social work activities with accommodation
**Directors:** M E Astarita, M Byrne, A Browne, R Dawson, Dr C F Phillips, C L Manners, A P Graham, F C Bourne
**Co. Secretary:** Ms Emma Snow
**Responsibilities**
**Senior:** Christopher Hamill (Director), Gerard Mahaffey (Director), Geraldine O'Connor (Director)
**US SIC:** 8321 **UK SIC:** 96111

**Bankers:** The Co-Operative Bank Plc (08-02-28)

|    | 31-03-14 | 31-03-13 |
|----|----------|----------|
| TO | 13,135,000 | 13,879,000 |
| P/L | (1,093,000) | (43,000) |
| NW | 36,026,000 | 36,872,000 |
| WC | 5,958,000 | 7,835,000 |
| Emp. | 271 | 255 |

DUNS 21-036-3217
**St Josephs Hospital**
Harding Avenue, Newport, Gwent NP20 6ZE
**Tel:** 01633820321
**Web:** www.stjosephshospital.org.uk
**Estd:** 1950
**Line of Business:** Hospitals
**Responsibilities**
**Finance:** A Byard (Finance Director)
**US SIC:** 8062, 6732
**UK SIC:** 95100, 83100
**Employees:** 300

DUNS 34-615-2874
**St Joseph's in the Park School**
St Marys Lane, Hertingfordbury, Hertford, Hertfordshire SG14 2LX
**Tel:** 01992-581378 **Fax:** 01992505202
**Web:** www.stjosephsinthepark.co.uk
**Reg No:** 5422009 **Estd:** 2005 Private Limited Company
**Line of Business:** Schools (independent)
**Directors:** Ms E H Bartholomew, Mrs J Kemp, Ms A P Bayford, Ms C E May, Mrs J R Goldsmith, A J Head, Mrs P A Maile, A Wodhams
**Co. Secretary:** Ms Claire Sharp
**Responsibilities**
**Senior:** Louisa Finlay (Manager), Jarmaine Haddon (Manager), Andrew Holden (Director), Margaret Lidgett (Manager), Jennifer Longbourne (Director)
**US SIC:** 8211 **UK SIC:** 93200
**Auditors:** R.M. Chancellor & Co Ltd
**Bankers:** Barclays Bank Plc (20-05-74)

|      | 31-08-13 | 31-08-12 | 31-08-11 |
|------|----------|----------|----------|
| TO   | 1,791,422 | 1,748,324 | 1,721,004 |
| P/L  | 59,802 | 136,086 | 93,639 |
| NW   | 708,478 | 645,178 | 505,594 |
| WC   | 210,625 | 218,997 | 155,816 |
| Emp. | 48 | 50 | 50 |

DUNS 23-529-8044
**St Joseph's Ltd**
(**Subsidiary of:** Esquire Pearl Realty Ltd)
Manor House, Gay Bowers Road, Danbury, Chelmsford, Essex CM3 4JQ
**Tel:** 01245-223367
**Web:** www.europeancare.co.uk
**Reg No:** 3528683 **Estd:** 1947 Private Limited Company
**Line of Business:** Nursing homes
**Issued Capital:** £100
**Directors:** J A Pickstock, D L Manson, A E Smith
**Co. Secretary:** John Pickstock
**US SIC:** 8051 **UK SIC:** 95100
**Auditors:** Maynard Heady
**Employees:** 90

DUNS 21-193-6641
**St Joseph's Primary School**
15 Glenavy Road, Belfast BT29 4LA
**Tel:** 02894422345
**Web:** www.stjosephscrumlin.co.uk
**Estd:** 1998
**Line of Business:** Primary education
**Director:** Mrs C Wegwermer
**US SIC:** 8211 **UK SIC:** 93200
**Employees:** 60

DUNS 21-780-2226
**St Joseph's R C High School**
Edgware Road The Hyde, London NW9 6LS
**Web:** www.sjhs.org.uk
**Estd:** 2011 Proprietorship
**Line of Business:** Schools (local authority)
**Proprietor:** Miss S Jenkins
**Responsibilities**
**IT:** Alex Guest (Database Manager)
**HR:** Mark Rowlands (Human Resources Manager)
**US SIC:** 8211 **UK SIC:** 93200
**Employees:** 120

DUNS 21-180-1290
**St Joseph's School**
St Stephens Hill, Launceston, Cornwall PL15 8HN
**Tel:** 01566-772580
**Web:** www.stjosephscornwall.co.uk
**Estd:** 1983 Proprietorship
**Line of Business:** Schools (independent)
**Proprietor:** G Garret
**Responsibilities**
**Senior:** Sue Rowe (Head Teacher)
**US SIC:** 8211 **UK SIC:** 93200
**Employees:** 50

DUNS 23-613-9648
**St Josephs School**
Amlets Lane, Cranleigh, Surrey GU6 7DH
**Tel:** 01483-272449
**Web:** www.st-josephscranleigh.surrey.sch.uk
**Estd:** 2002
**Line of Business:** Schools (special)
**Director:** A Lowry
**Responsibilities**
**Senior:** Gerry Willmer (Site Manager)
**IT:** Sue Collins (School Business Manager, Finan), Vlad Kolev (Senior IT Executive)
**US SIC:** 8299 **UK SIC:** 93300
**Employees:** 120

DUNS 21-600-0610
**St Judes C E Primary School**
Paget Road, Wolverhampton, West Midlands WV6 0DT
**Tel:** 01902558848
**Web:** www.stjudes.wolverhampton.sch.uk
**Estd:** 1913 Proprietorship
**Line of Business:** Schools (foundation)
**Proprietor:** Mrs C Gould
**Responsibilities**
**Senior:** Denise Dalton (Head Teacher)
**US SIC:** 8211 **UK SIC:** 93200
**Employees:** 65

DUNS 37-766-9528
**St Jude's Laundry**
7a Loaning Road, Edinburgh, Midlothian EH7 6JE
**Tel:** 01316618090
**Web:** www.stjudeslaundry.co.uk
**Estd:** 2002
**Line of Business:** Day and care centres
**Proprietor:** Ms C Mcalpin
**Responsibilities**
**Senior:** Joyce Manson (Branch Manager), Carole McAlpin (Proprietor)
**US SIC:** 7219 **UK SIC:** 98110
**Employees:** 50

DUNS 21-211-8702
**St Judes Nursing & Residential Home**
31 Mayfield Road, Sutton, Surrey SM2 5DU
**Tel:** 020-8643-1335
**Web:** www.stjudesnursinghome.co.uk
**Estd:** 1978 Proprietorship
**Line of Business:** Nursing homes
**Proprietor:** Mrs A Manji
**Responsibilities**
**Senior:** Amyna Manji (Proprietor), Anne McCormack (Home Manager), Mary Rose (Manager)
**US SIC:** 8051 **UK SIC:** 95100
**Employees:** 50

DUNS 55-067-2398
**St Katharine's House**
Ormond Road, Wantage, Oxfordshire OX12 8EA
**Web:** www.goldcarehomes.com
**Estd:** 2004
**Line of Business:** Residential care establishments
**Directors:** Commander R House, Commander R House
**Responsibilities**
**Senior:** Carol Dwyer (Home Manager)
**US SIC:** 8321 **UK SIC:** 96111
**Employees:** 100

DUNS 21-473-4894
**St Kevins Boys & Girls Primary School**
446 Falls Road, Belfast BT12 6EN
**Tel:** 028-9032-6791
**Web:** www.stkevinsprimaryschool.org
**Estd:** 2002
**Line of Business:** Schools (local authority)
**Co. Secretary:** Mrs Elian Burg
**Responsibilities**
**Senior:** Fiona Keegan (Head Teacher)
**US SIC:** 8211 **UK SIC:** 93200
**Employees:** 50

DUNS 21-879-5525
**St Kilda Community Support Centre**
15 Drew Street, Brixham, Devon TQ5 9JU
**Tel:** 01803853158
**Estd:** 2012
**Line of Business:** Community centres
**Responsibilities**
**Senior:** Sue Cohen (Manager)
**US SIC:** 8321 **UK SIC:** 96111
**Employees:** 200

**DUNS 21-606-3063**
## St Lawrence Academy
Doncaster Road, Scunthorpe, South
Humberside DN15 7DF
**Tel:** 01724842447
**Web:** www.thestlawrenceacademy.co.uk
**Estd:** 1965
**Line of Business:** Schools (local authority)
**Proprietor:** Mrs J Barnes
**US SIC:** 8211  **UK SIC:** 93200
**Employees:** 65

**DUNS 34-763-5190**
## St Leger Homes of Doncaster Ltd
St Leger Court, White Rose Way, Doncaster,
South Yorkshire DN4 5ND
**Tel:** 01302-862862
**Web:** www.stlegerhomes.co.uk
**Reg No:** 5564649  **Estd:** 2005 Private
Company Limited By Guarantee
**Line of Business:** Management of real
estate on a fee or contract basis
**Directors:** Mrs M Tennison, R D Mayo,
S P Wray, Ms S J Jordan, J Blackham,
Mrs L D Christon, R A Jones, R L Haldenby
**Co. Secretary:** Miss Julie Crook
**Responsibilities**
**Senior:** Mandy Chippindale (Director),
Emma Roots (Senior Communications
Officer), Alan Tolhurst (Director)
**Marketing:** Emma Roots (Senior
Communications Officer)
**Health & Safety:** Diane Marshall (Health &
Safety advisor)
**Branches:** St Leger Homes Of Doncaster
Ltd, G19-G20 Mexborough Business Centre,
College Road, Mexborough, South Yorkshire
S64 9JP
**US SIC:** 6531, 6519
**UK SIC:** 83400, 85000
**Auditors:** Beever & Struthers
**Bankers:** The Co-Operative Bank Plc
(08-90-00)

|     | 31-03-14 | 31-03-13 | 31-03-12 |
|-----|----------|----------|----------|
| TO  | 35,502,000 | 34,203,000 | 34,891,000 |
| P/L | (10,157,000) | 4,992,000 | 1,233,000 |
| WC  | 44,000 | 180,000 | 185,000 |
| Emp.| 630 | 635 | 642 |

**DUNS 21-879-6132**
## St Leonards Health Centre
St Leonards Hospital, Kingsland Road,
London N1 5LZ
**Tel:** 02076834367
**Estd:** 1998
**Line of Business:** Dentists
**Responsibilities**
**Senior:** Nicola Pearson (Clinical Director)
**US SIC:** 8062  **UK SIC:** 95100
**Employees:** 110

**DUNS 21-161-8538**
## St Louise's (G M) Comprehensive College
468 Falls Road, Belfast BT12 6EN
**Tel:** 02890325631
**Web:** www.stlouises.org.uk
**Estd:** 2003
**Line of Business:** Schools (local authority)
**Trading Style:** St Louise's Comprehensive
College
**Proprietor:** Mrs C Mccartan
**Responsibilities**
**Senior:** Mary Mchenry (Head Teacher)
**US SIC:** 8211  **UK SIC:** 93200
**Employees:** 240

**DUNS 21-231-2655**
## St Lukes
Palacefields Avenue, Palacefields, Runcorn,
Cheshire WA7 2SU
**Tel:** 01928-791552
**Web:** www.c-i-c.co.uk
**Estd:** 1991
**Line of Business:** Medical nursing home
activities
**Proprietor:** Mrs I Marston
**Responsibilities**
**Senior:** Sue Ashcroft (Manager)
**US SIC:** 8051  **UK SIC:** 95100
**Employees:** 100

**DUNS 21-600-6621**
## St Luke's C of E Primary School
66 Church Road, Tiptree, Colchester, Essex
CO5 0SU
**Tel:** 01621815456
**Web:** www.stlukeschurch-cp.essex.sch.uk
**Estd:** 2001 Proprietorship
**Line of Business:** General secondary
education
**Proprietor:** Mrs W Enguell

**Responsibilities**
**Senior:** Gordon Malcolm (Head Teacher)
**US SIC:** 8211  **UK SIC:** 93200
**Employees:** 60

**DUNS 28-996-4181**
## St Luke's (Cheshire) Hospice
Grosvenor House, Queensway, Winsford,
Cheshire CW7 1BH
**Tel:** 01606551246
**Web:** www.stlukeshospice.co.uk
**Reg No:** 1846186  **Estd:** 1988 Private
Limited Company
**Line of Business:** Hospices
**Principals:** Ms L R Robertson (Financial),
Dr R E Pugh, J Colclough, A Roberts,
J D Baldwin, R P Parker, Mrs A Davies,
Mrs A J Holland
**Responsibilities**
**Senior:** Boo Edleston (Director), Andrea
Jackson (Director of Business), Julia
Timpson (Director)
**Marketing:** Andrea Jackson (Director of
Business)
**IT:** Andrea Jackson (Director of Business)
**HR:** Andrea Jackson (Director of Business)
**Operations:** Andrea Jackson (Director of
Business)
**Purchasing:** Andrea Jackson (Director of
Business)
**Branches:** St Luke's (Cheshire) Hospice, 76
Wheelock Street, Middlewich, Cheshire
CW10 9AB
**US SIC:** 8091  **UK SIC:** 95200
**Auditors:** Howard Worth
**Bankers:** National Westminster Bank Plc
(60-15-29)

|     | 31-12-13 | 31-12-12 | 31-12-11 |
|-----|----------|----------|----------|
| TO  | 4,891,789 | 4,443,586 | 4,148,673 |
| P/L | 246,657 | 62,930 | (2,895) |
| NW  | 7,417,803 | 6,567,388 | 6,219,196 |
| WC  | 1,003,417 | 703,368 | 875,658 |
| Emp.| 150 | 131 | 136 |

**DUNS 21-121-9940**
## St Lukes Cofe Primary School
New Penkridge Road, Cannock,
Staffordshire WS11 1HN
**Tel:** 01543-510230
**Web:** www.st-lukes-cannock.staffs.sch.uk
**Proprietorship**
**Line of Business:** Schools (local authority)
**Proprietor:** Ms J Roberts
**Responsibilities**
**Senior:** Shaun Miles (Head Teacher)
**US SIC:** 8211  **UK SIC:** 93200
**Employees:** 50

**DUNS 64-243-5879**
## St Lukes Hospice Shop
706 Abbeydale Road, Sheffield, South
Yorkshire S7 2BL
**Tel:** 01142507474
**Web:** www.stlukeshospice.org.uk
**Estd:** 1992 Proprietorship
**Line of Business:** Adoption and fostering
services
**Proprietor:** Mrs V Plant
**Branches:** St Lukes Hospice Shop, 700-704
Chesterfield Road, Sheffield, South
Yorkshire S8 0SD
**US SIC:** 8321  **UK SIC:** 96111
**Employees:** 50

**DUNS 21-779-2799**
## St Luke's Primary School
Grange Lane North, Scunthorpe, South
Humberside DN16 1BN
**Tel:** 01724844560
**Web:** www.stlukes.northlincs.yhgfl.net
**Estd:** 2011 Proprietorship
**Line of Business:** Schools (special)
**Proprietor:** R Ashdown
**Responsibilities**
**Senior:** Robert Ashdown (Head Teacher),
Alastair Sutherland (Head Teacher)
**US SIC:** 8299  **UK SIC:** 93300
**Employees:** 100

**DUNS 21-585-6426**
## St Lukes Primary School
Queens Park Rise, Brighton, East Sussex
BN2 9ZF
**Tel:** 01273675080
**Web:** www.stlukes.brighton-hove.sch.uk
**Estd:** 2011 Proprietorship
**Line of Business:** Primary education
**Proprietor:** J Cooper
**US SIC:** 8211  **UK SIC:** 93200
**Employees:** 75

**DUNS 21-163-4212**
## St Macnissi's College
25 Tower Road, (Carnlough, Ballymena, Co
Antrim BT44 0JS
**Tel:** 028-2888-5202
**Web:** www.stkillianscollege.org.uk
**Estd:** 1951

**Line of Business:** Schools (local authority)
**Director:** S Doherty
**Co. Secretary:** Mrs Gramia Delargy
**Responsibilities**
**Senior:** Jonny Brady (Head Teacher)
**Facilities:** Mark McKinbridge (Maintenance
Manager)
**US SIC:** 8211  **UK SIC:** 93200
**Employees:** 70

**DUNS 21-773-3857**
## St Malachy's College
36 Antrim Road, Belfast BT15 2AE
**Tel:** 02890748285
**Web:** www.stmalachys.com
**Estd:** 2003 Proprietorship
**Line of Business:** General secondary
education
**Proprietor:** Dr J Moorn
**Responsibilities**
**Senior:** David Lambon (Principal), Paul Mc
Bride (Head Teacher)
**US SIC:** 8211  **UK SIC:** 93200
**Employees:** 300

**DUNS 21-338-6111**
## St Malachys High School
3 Dublin Road, Castlewellan, Co Down BT31
9AG
**Tel:** 02843778255
**Web:** www.stmalachys.org.uk
**Estd:** 1965
**Line of Business:** Schools (local authority)
**Proprietor:** Mrs N Cunningham
**Responsibilities**
**Senior:** Joan Mccombe (Principal)
**Finance:** Sharon O' Hare (Senior Finance
Administrator)
**Admin:** Sharon O' Hare (Senior Finance
Administrator)
**IT:** Eamonn O' Hare (Senior IT Executive)
**US SIC:** 8211  **UK SIC:** 93200
**Employees:** 80

**DUNS 34-566-1156**
## St Margaret of Scotland Hospice
East Barns Street, Clydebank,
Dunbartonshire G81 1EG
**Tel:** 01419521141  **Fax:** 01419514206
**Web:** www.smh.org.uk
**Reg No:** 0280689SC  **Estd:** 2005 Private
Company Limited By Guarantee
**Line of Business:** Hospices
**Directors:** Professor L Martin,
E B Mcguigan, S W Barnett, Miss L A Millar,
Mrs J L English, D C Mccrea, R Dawson,
Professor M T Fallon
**Co. Secretary:** Ms Clare Murphy
**Responsibilities**
**Senior:** Guy Haworth (Executive), Ellen
Mcgarvie (Executive), Sheila Morrow
(Director)
**IT:** John Mclinton (Network, Security
Manager)
**US SIC:** 8091  **UK SIC:** 95200
**Bankers:** Bank Of Scotland (80-06-14)

|     | 31-03-14 | 31-03-13 | 31-03-12 |
|-----|----------|----------|----------|
| TO  | 5,862,268 | 4,808,911 | 5,317,465 |
| P/L | 652,679 | (168,132) | 591,545 |
| NW  | 9,658,364 | 9,005,685 | 9,173,817 |
| WC  | 2,111,374 | 1,196,364 | 1,454,887 |
| Emp.| 145 | 142 | 136 |

**DUNS 21-213-0442**
## St Margarets
20 Twiss Avenue, Hythe, Kent CT21 5NU
**Tel:** 01303-267557
**Web:** www.stmargarets.com
**Estd:** 1985 Partnership
**Line of Business:** Nursing homes
**Partners:** J Dean, Mrs M Dean
**US SIC:** 8051  **UK SIC:** 95100
**Employees:** 47

**DUNS 23-083-1989**
## St Margaret's C of E High School
Aigburth Road, Liverpool, Merseyside L17
6AB
**Tel:** 01514271825
**Web:** www.stmargaretsacademy.com
**Estd:** 1960
**Line of Business:** General secondary
education
**Director:** Mrs M Griffiths-Parr
**Responsibilities**
**Senior:** Stephen Brierley (Principal)
**US SIC:** 8211  **UK SIC:** 93200
**Employees:** 130

**DUNS 21-280-2016**
## St Margaret's Ce Junior School
Orchard Street, Gillingham, Kent ME8 9AE
**Tel:** 01634230998
**Web:** www.stmargarets.org.uk
**Estd:** 2002
**Line of Business:** General secondary
education
**Principals:** Mrs J Clarke (Chairman),
P Gabbett, Mrs J Thompson, J Ennis,
P Gabbett, Mrs P Cordingley, Mrs R Gray,
R Meacham
**Responsibilities**
**Senior:** J Boughton (Principal), Paul Gabbett
(Head Teacher), C Pavey (Principal), D
Unter (Principal)
**US SIC:** 8211  **UK SIC:** 93200
**Employees:** 60

**DUNS 21-320-5177**
## St Margarets Nursing Home
Little Coates Road, Grimsby, South
Humberside DN34 4NQ
**Tel:** 01472-241780
**Estd:** 2002 Partnership
**Line of Business:** Medical nursing home
activities
**Partners:** Mrs S Ford-Williams,
B Ford-Williams
**Responsibilities**
**Senior:** Debbie Cousins (Manager)
**US SIC:** 8051  **UK SIC:** 95100
**Employees:** 75

**DUNS 64-264-7028**
## St Margarets Preparatory School
Gosfield Hall Park, Gosfield, Halstead, Essex
CO9 1SE
**Tel:** 01787-472134
**Web:** www.stmargaretsprep.com
**Estd:** 1996 Proprietorship
**Line of Business:** Schools (independent)
**Proprietor:** Mrs B Boyton
**Responsibilities**
**Senior:** Bernice Boyton Corbett (Principal),
Bernice Corbett (Head Teacher), Elaine
Powling (Head Teacher)
**Finance:** Bernice Boyton Corbett (Principal)
**Marketing:** Bernice Boyton Corbett
(Principal)
**Sales:** Bernice Boyton Corbett (Principal)
**Health & Safety:** Bernice Boyton Corbett
(Principal)
**US SIC:** 8211  **UK SIC:** 93200
**Employees:** 50

**DUNS 21-460-5516**
## St Margarets School
Merry Hill Road, Bushey, Hertfordshire
WD23 1DT
**Tel:** 02084164400
**Web:** www.stmargaretsbushey.co.uk
**Estd:** 1996
**Line of Business:** Schools (independent)
**Partners:** Mrs M Rudland,
C Maunder Taylor, Ms J Herbert, K Young,
Mrs K Bower, P Faulkner, Mrs L Crighton
**Responsibilities**
**Senior:** Lynne Crighton (Principal), Rose
Hardy (Head Mistress)
**IT:** Martin Raver (Head of IT)
**Operations:** Lynne Crighton (Principal)
**US SIC:** 8211  **UK SIC:** 93200
**Employees:** 100

**DUNS 21-344-5112**
## St Marks C of E Secondary School
Bay Tree Road, Bath, Avon BA1 6ND
**Tel:** 01225-312661
**Web:** www.st-marks.bathnes.sch.uk
**Estd:** 1995
**Line of Business:** Schools (local authority)
**Proprietor:** Ms C Pope
**Responsibilities**
**Senior:** Cherril Pope (Head Teacher)
**US SIC:** 8211  **UK SIC:** 93200
**Employees:** 50

**DUNS 51-594-7419**
## St Mark's Church of England Academy Trust
Acacia Road, Mitcham, Surrey CR4 1SF
**Tel:** 020-8648-6627
**Web:** www.stmarksacademy.com
**Reg No:** 5875416  **Estd:** 1994 Private
Company Limited By Guarantee
**Line of Business:** General secondary
education
**Directors:** S C Surtees, Dr M G Hutchinson,
S L Hallal, R B Hughes, J Cavalcanti,
Ms R Millington, Ms W J Tansey, A Boaten
**Senior:** P Belmour (Head Teacher)

**Finance:** Esther Holland *(Director and Company Secretary)*
**IT:** Eduart Taylor *(Network, Security Manager)*, Wayne Vance *(IT Network Technician)*
**US SIC:** 8211  **UK SIC:** 93200
**Auditors:** Buzzacott LLP
**Bankers:** The Co-Operative Bank Plc (08-92-50)

|      | 31-08-14  | 31-08-13  | 31-08-12  |
|------|-----------|-----------|-----------|
| TO   | 6,214,000 | 6,321,000 | 6,402,000 |
| P/L  | (634,000) | (430,000) | 113,000   |
| NW   | 9,260,000 | 10,079,000| 10,505,000|
| WC   | 1,370,000 | 1,126,000 | 992,000   |
| Emp. | 110       | 112       | 108       |

DUNS 21-327-6723
### St Martin in the Fields C of E Secondary School
155 Tulse Hill, London SW2 3UP
**Tel:** 02086745594
**Web:** www.stmartins.lambeth.sch.uk
**Estd:** 1935 Partnership
**Line of Business:** Schools (local authority)
**Partner:** Mrs L Morrison
**US SIC:** 8211  **UK SIC:** 93200
**Employees:** 100

DUNS 23-691-5435
### St Martin of Tours Housing Association
318 320 St Pauls Road, Highbury, London N1 2LF
**Tel:** 02077043820
**Web:** www.stmartinoftours.org
**Reg No:** 0022546IP  **Estd:** 1979 Friendly Society
**Line of Business:** Children's homes
**Principals:** D A Bartley *(Chairman)*, K Ogunmuyiwa, S Paterson, C Mccaffrey, S C Mcerlean, M G Brown, A Bartlett, B Shodeke
**Co. Secretary:** A Lally
**Responsibilities**
**Senior:** Simon Bartley *(Director)*, James Crockhart *(Home Manager)*, Nick Howard *(Director)*, Chris McCaffrey *(Director)*, Doreen McCollin *(Director)*, S McErlean *(Director)*, Annabel Palmer *(Chairman)*, Nick Purchase *(Chairman)*, Geoffrey Rimmer *(Director)*, Henry Salvatierra *(Manager)*
**Finance:** Philip Bowles *(Director of Finance and Compan)*, Mayan Shah *(Treasurer)*
**Operations:** Vimala Uttarkar *(Director of Operations)*
**Branches:** St Martin Of Tours Housing Association, 14 Rutford Road, London SW16 2DH
**US SIC:** 8321  **UK SIC:** 96111
**Auditors:** Bentley Jennison

|      | 31-03-12  | 31-03-11  | 31-03-10  |
|------|-----------|-----------|-----------|
| TO   | 3,951,905 | 3,960,491 | 4,187,825 |
| P/L  | 82,553    | 82,157    | 156,544   |
| NW   | 3,646,932 | 4,409,047 | 4,824,187 |
| WC   | 476,320   | 2,628,171 | 3,084,533 |
| Emp. | 82        | 86        | 92        |

DUNS 21-774-4131
### St Martins
Hillside, Caerphilly, Mid Glamorgan CF83 1UW
**Tel:** 02920858050
**Web:** www.stmartins.caerphilly.sch.uk
**Estd:** 2003 Proprietorship
**Line of Business:** Schools (local authority)
**Proprietor:** Mrs K Davies
**US SIC:** 8211  **UK SIC:** 93200
**Employees:** 80

DUNS 23-690-5253
### St Martins Garage (Guernsey) Ltd
Flat Guernsey Telecoms, Lane Grande Rue, St Martin, Guernsey, Channel Islands GY4 6LQ
**Tel:** 01481239432  **Fax:** 01481-230236
**Web:** www.motor-mall.co.uk
**Reg No:** 0020202J  **Estd:** 1984 Private Limited Company
**Line of Business:** Motor dealers. Subject operates Volkeswagen, Audi and Porch and franchises.
**Trading Style:** Jacksons
**Managing Director:** J Falla
**Branches:** St Martins Garage (Guernsey) Ltd, Bailiffs Cross, St Andrews, Fife GY6 8TU
**US SIC:** 5511  **UK SIC:** 65100
**Bankers:** National Westminster Bank Plc (60-09-20)
**Employees:** 60

DUNS 50-381-3438
### St Martins Housing Trust
35 Bishopgate, Norwich, Norfolk NR1 4AA
**Tel:** 01603667706
**Web:** www.stmartinshousing.org.uk
**Reg No:** 2390375  **Estd:** 1989 Private Company Limited By Guarantee

**Line of Business:** Charities and charitable organisations
**Directors:** J S Richards, C R Bland, D Brief, P Downes, Mrs K ( Daynes, Dr J Blyth, N Williams, K E Long
**Co. Secretary:** Miss Tracy Yates
**Responsibilities**
**Senior:** David Hoy *(Director)*, Madelaine Light *(Manager)*
**Finance:** David Goodwin *(Finance Manager)*
**Marketing:** Ursula Harte *(Administration Officer)*
**Sales:** David Goodwin *(Finance Manager)*
**Admin:** David Goodwin *(Finance Manager)*, Ursula Harte *(Administration Officer)*
**IT:** David Goodwin *(Finance Manager)*
**HR:** Ursula Harte *(Administration Officer)*
**Health & Safety:** Bob Stainton *(Health & Safety Officer)*
**Branches:** St Martins Housing Trust, 1-1A St. Faiths Lane, Norwich, Norfolk NR1 1NN
**US SIC:** 7021, 6732
**UK SIC:** 66500, 83100
**Auditors:** Lovewell Blake
**Bankers:** Barclays Bank Plc (20-62-68)

|      | 31-03-14  | 31-03-13  | 31-03-12  |
|------|-----------|-----------|-----------|
| TO   | 3,495,356 | 3,107,818 | 2,929,462 |
| P/L  | 291,882   | 127,864   | 66,560    |
| NW   | 4,377,896 | 4,086,014 | 3,958,150 |
| WC   | 1,057,329 | 672,634   | 634,114   |
| Emp. | 83        | 77        | 89        |

DUNS 21-777-3789
### St Martins School
40 Moor Park Road, Northwood, Middlesex HA6 2DJ
**Tel:** 01923825740
**Web:** www.stmartins.essex.sch.uk
**Estd:** 2011 Proprietorship
**Line of Business:** Schools (local authority)
**Proprietor:** D Tidmarsh
**Responsibilities**
**Senior:** Simon Pithers *(Manager)*
**IT:** Brendan Kenny *(Head of IT)*
**US SIC:** 8211  **UK SIC:** 93200
**Employees:** 100

DUNS 21-783-6731
### St Mary & St John Catholic Primary School
Kingsmere Remand Unit, 18 Gravelly Hill North, Birmingham, West Midlands B23 6BQ
**Tel:** 01213731702
**Web:** www.stmryjon.bham.sch.uk
**Estd:** 2011
**Line of Business:** Schools (local authority)
**Responsibilities**
**Senior:** Veronica Fenlon *(Head Teacher)*
**US SIC:** 8211  **UK SIC:** 93200
**Employees:** 50

DUNS 23-082-9363
### St Mary & St Joseph's School
Chislehurst Road, Sidcup, Kent DA14 6BP
**Tel:** 02083097700
**Web:** www.smsj.bexley.lgsl.net
**Estd:** 2004
**Line of Business:** Social work activities with accommodation
**Director:** A Sogell
**US SIC:** 8321  **UK SIC:** 96111
**Employees:** 64

DUNS 21-559-0124
### St Mary Magdalene Academy
Liverpool Road, London N7 8PG
**Tel:** 020-7697-0123
**Web:** www.smmacademy.com
**Estd:** 2012
**Line of Business:** Schools (foundation)
**US SIC:** 8211  **UK SIC:** 93200
**Bankers:** Allied Irish Bank (gb) (23-83-97)
**Employees:** 162

DUNS 21-775-9375
### St Mary of the Angels R C Primary School
Shrewsbury Road, London W2 5PR
**Tel:** 02076414482
**Web:** www.stmaryangels.co.uk
**Estd:** 1986 Proprietorship
**Line of Business:** Schools (local authority)
**Proprietor:** Mrs H Connolly
**US SIC:** 8211  **UK SIC:** 93200
**Employees:** 50

DUNS 21-774-9305
### St Mary Queen of Martyrs R C Primary School
Nidderdale, Hull, North Humberside HU7 4BS
**Tel:** 01482825625
**Web:** www.stmaryqom.co.uk
**Estd:** 2011 Proprietorship
**Line of Business:** Schools (local authority)
**Proprietor:** Mrs S Barron

**Responsibilities**
**Senior:** Patrica Graham *(Head Teacher)*
**US SIC:** 8211  **UK SIC:** 93200
**Employees:** 60

DUNS 21-182-9408
### St Mary's Boys Primary School
48 Melmount Road, Strabane, Co Tyrone BT82 9EF
**Tel:** 028-7138-2422
**Web:** www.stmarysboysprimaryschool.co.uk
**Estd:** 1965
**Line of Business:** Schools (local authority)
**Responsibilities**
**Senior:** Sandra O'doherty *(Principal)*
**US SIC:** 8211  **UK SIC:** 93200
**Employees:** 60

DUNS 21-318-4380
### St Marys C of E High School
Downage, London NW4 1AB
**Tel:** 020-8203-2827
**Web:** www.stmaryshigh.barnet.lgfl.net
**Estd:** 2002 Proprietorship
**Line of Business:** Schools (local authority)
**Proprietor:** Mrs K Roskell
**US SIC:** 8211  **UK SIC:** 93200
**Employees:** 102

DUNS 21-584-8394
### St Mary's Care Centres
Beverley Road, Anlaby, Hull, North Humberside HU10 7BQ
**Tel:** 01482307593
**Web:** www.wecareforyou.co.uk
**Estd:** 2011 Proprietorship
**Line of Business:** Residential care establishments
**Proprietor:** P Bignell
**US SIC:** 8321  **UK SIC:** 96111
**Employees:** 60

DUNS 21-041-2083
### St Marys Catholic College
St Walburgas Road, Blackpool, Lancashire FY3 7EQ
**Tel:** 01253-396286
**Web:** www.st-mary.blackpool.sch.uk
**Estd:** 2002 Proprietorship
**Line of Business:** General secondary education
**Proprietor:** S Tierney
**Responsibilities**
**IT:** Paul Flook *(IT Manager)*, Simon Preston *(Network, Security Manager)*
**Health & Safety:** David Flack *(Centre Manager)*
**Facilities:** David Flack *(Centre Manager)*
**US SIC:** 8211  **UK SIC:** 93200
**Employees:** 57

DUNS 21-844-5705
### St Mary's Catholic High School Academy Trust
Newbold Road, Chesterfield, Derbyshire S41 8AG
**Tel:** 01246201191
**Web:** www.st-maryshigh.derbyshire.sch.uk
**Reg No:** 8107212  **Estd:** 2012 Private Company Limited By Guarantee
**Line of Business:** Schools (local authority)
**Directors:** Ms D Thompson, P J Clancy, Reverend M G Mcmanus, A T Topley, J O Cox, W O'Connell, W Hayes, M Molloy
**Co. Secretary:** Ms Julie Sims
**Responsibilities**
**Senior:** Patricia Armstrong-Read *(Director)*, Marie Beaulieu *(Director)*, Tracy Carroll *(Director)*, Elizabeth Cruise *(Director)*, Margaret Curley *(Director)*, Margaret Kilkey *(Director)*, Sean Mcclafferty *(Director)*, Anthony O'Malley *(Director)*, Maureen Strelley *(Director)*, Catherine Thurlow *(Director)*
**US SIC:** 8211  **UK SIC:** 93200
**Bankers:** National Westminster Bank Plc (60-40-09)

|      | 31-08-14  | 31-08-13  | 31-08-12  |
|------|-----------|-----------|-----------|
| TO   | 7,099,853 | 7,023,505 | 538,008   |
| P/L  | 147,544   | 539,216   | (268,099) |
| NW   | (323,470) | (442,014) | (268,099) |
| WC   | 976,432   | 947,144   | 287,401   |
| Emp. | 222       | 248       | 202       |

DUNS 21-781-7339
### St Marys Catholic Primary School
Ford Green Road, Stoke-On-Trent, Staffordshire ST6 8EZ
**Tel:** 01782234820
**Web:** www.stmarysstoke.co.uk
**Estd:** 1994 Partnership
**Line of Business:** Schools (local authority)
**Partner:** I Beardmore
**US SIC:** 8211  **UK SIC:** 93200
**Employees:** 50

DUNS 23-641-6012
### St Mary's Christian Brothers (Voluntary) Grammar School
147a Glen Road, Belfast BT11 8NR
**Tel:** 02890294000
**Web:** www.stmaryscbgs.com
**Estd:** 1929
**Line of Business:** Schools (local authority)
**Principals:** K Burke, D Finnegan
**Responsibilities**
**Senior:** Jim Sheerin *(Principal)*
**Finance:** Maria Morris *(Finance Officer)*
**IT:** Oonagh Convery *(Senior IT Executive)*
**Branches:** Barrack St, Belfast
**US SIC:** 8211  **UK SIC:** 93200
**Bankers:** First Trust Bank  (aib Group (uk) Plc) (93-80-92)
**Employees:** 149

DUNS 23-295-7415
### St Marys College
Shear Brow, Blackburn, Lancashire BB1 8DX
**Tel:** 01254580464
**Web:** www.stmarysblackburn.ac.uk
**Line of Business:** Religious organisations and places of worship
**US SIC:** 8221  **UK SIC:** 93100
**Employees:** 165

DUNS 23-970-6935
### St Mary's Convent & Nursing Home (Chiswick)
Burlington Lane, London W4 2QE
**Tel:** 020-8994-4641
**Web:** www.stmaryscnh.org.uk
**Reg No:** 3959483  **Estd:** 1904 Private Unlimited Company
**Line of Business:** Nursing homes
**Trading Style:** St Mary's Convent & Nursing Home
**Directors:** Ms C F Boreham, J B Randle, Ms J A Goodeve, C M Mackay, Miss R M Browne, Sir G Morgan, Miss P Groombridge, R I Turner
**Co. Secretary:** Ms Catharine Owst
**US SIC:** 8051  **UK SIC:** 95100
**Bankers:** National Westminster Bank Plc (50-00-00)

|      | 31-03-14  | 31-03-13  | 31-03-12  |
|------|-----------|-----------|-----------|
| TO   | 2,560,263 | 2,356,020 | 2,346,837 |
| P/L  | 37,561    | (125,751) | (46,139)  |
| NW   | 5,013,070 | 4,907,141 | 4,898,909 |
| WC   | 869,228   | 621,258   | 678,557   |
| Emp. | 102       | 97        | 72        |

DUNS 23-083-2540
### St Mary's Home
Margaret Street, Stone, Staffordshire ST15 8EJ
**Tel:** 01785-813894
**Estd:** 1979
**Line of Business:** Nursing homes
**Proprietor:** M Conleth
**US SIC:** 8051, 8091
**UK SIC:** 95100, 95200
**Employees:** 60

DUNS 42-394-4636
### St Mary's Hospital N H S Trust - (Isle of Wight Acute)
St Marys Hospital, Parkhurst Road, Newport, Isle of Wight PO30 5TG
**Tel:** 01983-524081
**Web:** www.iow.nhs.uk
**Estd:** 1991 Incorporate By Act Of Parliament
**Line of Business:** Human health activities
**Trading Style:** Isle of Wight Hospital Radio, Isle of Wight House Care N H S Trust
**Principals:** B Livesey *(Chairman)*, M Powell
**Responsibilities**
**Senior:** Karen Baker *(Acting CEO)*, Mark Pugh *(Medical Director)*
**Marketing:** Andy Hollebon *(Head of Communication)*
**IT:** Bill Johnston *(IT Technical Engineer Speciali)*, Mark Pugh *(Medical Director)*
**Health & Safety:** Connie Wendes *(Health & Safety Officer)*
**Facilities:** Kevin Bolan *(Estates Manager)*
**Operations:** Mark Pugh *(Medical Director)*
**US SIC:** 8091  **UK SIC:** 95200
**Employees:** 3,200

DUNS 21-584-8550
### St Marys Nhs Treatment Centre
C/O Care Uk, Milton Road, Portsmouth, Hampshire PO3 6AD
**Tel:** 03332001822
**Web:** www.stmarystreatmentcentre.nhs.uk
**Estd:** 2011 Proprietorship
**Line of Business:** Nhs clinics
**Proprietor:** N Wilkinson
**Responsibilities**
**Senior:** Penny Daniels *(General Manager)*

**Admin:** Louise Mccombie (Administration Manager)
**US SIC:** 8062 **UK SIC:** 95100
**Employees:** 80

DUNS 21-596-0124
## St Mary's Nursing Home
Penny Lane, Collins Green, Warrington, Cheshire WA5 4DS
**Tel:** 01925294850
**Web:** www.stmaryscarecentre.co.uk
**Estd:** 2011 Proprietorship
**Line of Business:** Residential care establishments
**Proprietor:** Mrs M Mungins
**Responsibilities**
**Senior:** Paul Ikin (Home Manager)
**US SIC:** 8321 **UK SIC:** 96111
**Employees:** 100

DUNS 23-213-5165
## St Marys Nursing Home
Montilo Lane, Harborough Magna, Rugby, Warwickshire CV23 0HF
**Tel:** 01788-832589
**Estd:** 1985 Partnership
**Line of Business:** Nursing homes
**Partners:** S Northover, S Northover, S Northover
**Responsibilities**
**Senior:** Ann Manklow (Home Manager), Chrissie Phelan (General Manager)
**US SIC:** 8051 **UK SIC:** 95100
**Employees:** 50

DUNS 54-900-9710
## St Marys Radcliffe Primary School
Windmill Close, Bristol, Avon BS3 4DP
**Tel:** 01173534760
**Web:** www.bristol-city.gov.uk
**Estd:** 1966
**Line of Business:** Schools (local authority)
**Director:** J Bishop
**Responsibilities**
**Senior:** Emma Payne (Head Teacher)
**US SIC:** 8211, 8299
**UK SIC:** 93200, 93300
**Employees:** 50

DUNS 28-995-9629
## St Mary's School Ascot
St Marys School, Ascot, Berkshire SL5 9JF
**Tel:** 01344623721
**Web:** www.st-marys-ascot.co.uk
**Reg No:** 1844327 **Estd:** 1984 Private Limited Company
**Line of Business:** Schools (independent)
**Directors:** Ms O Berry, Mrs C E Colacicchi, D A Power, Mrs A Ayton, P Gaynor, G V Thompson, A M Robinson, E F Horswell
**Co. Secretary:** Giles Brand
**Responsibilities**
**Senior:** Aoga Association (Development Director), Charles Hemphill (Director), George Jerjian (Director)
**Finance:** Andrew Tidd (Accountant)
**Admin:** Shelia Hickmott (Receptionist)
**IT:** Barbara Hudson-Reed (IT Director)
**Facilities:** Trevor Clark (Estates Manager)
**US SIC:** 8211, 7021
**UK SIC:** 93200, 66500
**Auditors:** Hlb Kidsons
**Bankers:** Lloyds TSB Bank plc (30-90-24)

| | 31-08-13 | 31-08-12 | 31-08-11 |
|---|---|---|---|
| TO | 12,771,000 | 12,038,000 | 11,644,000 |
| P/L | 1,147,000 | 980,000 | 1,037,000 |
| NW | 20,366,000 | 19,219,000 | 18,239,000 |
| WC | (1,185,000) | (243,000) | (365,000) |
| Emp. | 178 | 173 | 165 |

DUNS 21-812-8820
## St Marys School Gerrard Cross Ltd
Packhorse Road, Gerrards Cross, Buckinghamshire SL9 8JQ
**Tel:** 01753-883370
**Web:** www.stmarysschool.co.uk
**Estd:** 1944
**Line of Business:** General secondary education
**Proprietor:** Mrs J Ross
**Responsibilities**
**Admin:** C Pearcey (Office Manager)
**IT:** Ravi Manohar (IT Manager)
**US SIC:** 8211 **UK SIC:** 93200
**Employees:** 65

DUNS 23-644-1143
## St Marys University College
191 Falls Road, Belfast BT12 6FE
**Tel:** 028-9032-7678
**Web:** www.stmarys-belfast.ac.uk
**Estd:** 1900
**Line of Business:** University
**Trading Style:** St Mary's University College
**Chairman:** M O'Callaghan

**Responsibilities**
**Finance:** Brian Mcfall (Bursar)
**Sales:** Frank Hennessey (Head of Business Development), Brian Mcfall (Bursar)
**Admin:** Trevor Abbott (Admissions Officer), Briege Ellis (Lecturer), Anne Farren (Administrative Assistant), Brian Mcfall (Bursar), Peggy O'Neill (Office Manager)
**HR:** Clodagh Hanna (Human Resources Manager)
**Facilities:** Gary Murphy (Facilities Manager)
**US SIC:** 8221 **UK SIC:** 93100
**Employees:** 200
**Turnover:** £8,221,000

DUNS 67-136-7084
## St Mary's University Twickenham
Waldegrave Road, Strawberry Hill, Twickenham, Middlesex TW1 4SX
**Tel:** 02082404000 **Fax:** 020-8240-4255
**Web:** www.smuc.ac.uk
**Reg No:** 5977277 **Estd:** 2006 Private Company Limited By Guarantee
**Line of Business:** First-degree level higher education
**Directors:** A F Arbour, Mrs S K Handley Jones, D A Hartnett, Mrs H P Frostick, J S Dixon, F M Campbell, Dr T Walsh, S G Kemp
**Co. Secretary:** Graham Fice
**Responsibilities**
**Senior:** Victoria Armstrong (Programme Director Education a), Paula Askew (Academic Director for CPD), Janet Clegg (Programme Directors), Jeffery Cottle (Director), Lise Georgesonma (Programme Director), Maureen Glackin (Director), Mark Glaister (Programme Director), Gill Horgan (Programme Director), Chris Hull (Teaching Fellow and Academic D), Nancy John (Director), Ryan Jones (Director), Charles Moth (Director), June Mulroy (Director), Stuart Oliver (Programme Director), Andrew Reid-Smith (Director of Sport), Peter Tyler (Programme Director), Simon Uttley (Director)
**Finance:** Sheela Patel (Finance Officer)
**Marketing:** Marina Boor (Senior PR and Marketing Office), Cindy Croucher-Wright (School Business Manager), Ruth Mellor (Marketing Manager)
**Sales:** Annie Recuerda (Business Development and Event)
**Admin:** Mariann Baker (Head of International Office), Samantha Chant (School Administrator), Sarah Cheshire (Administrator), Vickie Coles (Continuing Professional Develo), Liz Everett (Administrator), Jason Harcourt (School Data Administrator), Celine James (Education Administrator), Sarah Marshall (Administrator), Sarah Middleton (Administrator), Louise Mooney (School Administrator), Sabina Nardell (Programme Administrator), Tracey Penny (Administrator), Natalie Turner (Graduate Assistant), Margaret Waddell (Administrator)
**IT:** Janet Clegg (Programme Directors), Paul Dancy (Programme Director), Lise Georgesonma (Programme Director), Mark Glaister (Programme Director), Jason Harcourt (School Data Administrator), Gill Horgan (Programme Director), Moeen Muzaffar (Assistant IT Director), Stuart Oliver (Programme Director), Martin Scarrott (Director of Information Servic), Peter Tyler (Programme Director), Stacy Winter (Programme Director)
**HR:** Rachel Bowles (Senior Recruitment Officer), Rachel Trippitt (Senior Recruitment Officer)
**Operations:** Alexandra King (Programme Director), Rik Mellor (Programme Director)
**Engineering:** Lucy Banham (Technician), Sarah Catling (Performance Arts & Design Tech), Jack Lineham (Technician), Damian O' Byrne (Technical and Learning Support), Michelle Penrice (English Technician), James Simms (Technical Support Manager)
**US SIC:** 8221 **UK SIC:** 93100
**Bankers:** HSBC Bank plc (40-05-20)

| | 31-07-13 | 31-07-12 | 31-07-11 |
|---|---|---|---|
| TO | 38,670,000 | 36,901,000 | 34,805,000 |
| P/L | 2,845,000 | 4,224,000 | 2,084,000 |
| NW | 35,460,000 | 29,456,000 | 27,837,000 |
| WC | 7,437,000 | 3,313,000 | 871,000 |
| Emp. | 549 | 517 | 493 |

DUNS 21-580-8584
## St Mathias & Dr Bells C of E Primary School
Fishponds Road, Fishponds, Bristol, Avon BS16 3UH
**Tel:** 01179030491
**Web:** www.fishpondschurchacademy.bristol.sch.uk
**Estd:** 2011 Proprietorship
**Line of Business:** General secondary education
**Proprietor:** Ms M Phipps

**Responsibilities**
**Senior:** Michael Eatwell (Head Teacher)
**US SIC:** 8211 **UK SIC:** 93200
**Employees:** 60

DUNS 73-890-5681
## The St Matthew Academy Ltd
St Josephs Vale, London SE3 0XX
**Tel:** 02088536250 **Fax:** 020-8318-0103
**Web:** www.stmatthewacademy.co.uk
**Reg No:** 5144640 **Estd:** 2004 Private Company Limited By Guarantee
**Line of Business:** Schools (local authority)
**Directors:** Mrs M Boley, N J Rothon, M Barry, J A Egan, C Garvey, Ms M Key-Lewis, A P Mclean, T J Mullally
**Co. Secretary:** Richard Lambert
**Responsibilities**
**Senior:** Monica Cross (Principal), Helena Green (Director), Anthony Halmos (Director), Peter Worden (Director)
**IT:** Douglas Wallace (Networks Manager)
**Facilities:** Guy Buckland (Premises Officer)
**US SIC:** 8211 **UK SIC:** 93200
**Bankers:** Allied Irish Bank (gb) (23-84-82)

| | 31-08-13 | 31-08-12 | 31-08-11 |
|---|---|---|---|
| TO | 9,359,000 | 10,260,000 | 9,672,000 |
| P/L | (346,000) | 507,000 | (146,000) |
| NW | 29,147,000 | 29,473,000 | 29,233,000 |
| WC | (328,000) | 93,000 | (164,000) |
| Emp. | 179 | 175 | 175 |

DUNS 21-780-0385
## St Matthews C of E Primary School
Linkfield Lane, Redhill, Surrey RH1 1JF
**Tel:** 01737762080
**Web:** www.stmatthewsredhill.org.uk
**Estd:** 1987
**Line of Business:** Schools (local authority)
**US SIC:** 8211 **UK SIC:** 93200
**Employees:** 100

DUNS 21-771-9888
## St Matthews Health & Community Centre
Prince Philip House, Leicester, Leicestershire LE1 2NZ
**Tel:** 01162954600
**Web:** www.nhs.uk
**Estd:** 2011 Proprietorship
**Line of Business:** Nhs clinics
**Proprietor:** Mrs S Skidmore
**Responsibilities**
**Senior:** Victoria Wightman (Building Premises Assurance Of)
**US SIC:** 8062 **UK SIC:** 95100
**Employees:** 101

DUNS 73-337-6813
## St Matthews Ltd
(**Subsidiary of:** St Matthews Holdings Ltd)
29-31 St Matthews Parade, Northampton, Northamptonshire NN2 7HF
**Fax:** 01604716526
**Web:** www.stmatthewshealthcare.com
**Reg No:** 4611507 **Estd:** 2002 Private Limited Company
**Line of Business:** Activities of religious organisations
**Issued Capital:** £1,000
**Managing Director:** N S Sidhu Brar
**Co. Secretary:** Mrs Kanwaljit Sandhu
**US SIC:** 7399 **UK SIC:** 83954

| | 31-08-13 | 31-08-12 | 31-08-11 |
|---|---|---|---|
| TO | 9,027,727 | 8,739,443 | 7,844,986 |
| P/L | 1,432,089 | 1,456,936 | 721,455 |
| NW | 1,060,489 | (505,299) | (2,041,426) |
| WC | 2,581,234 | 1,261,744 | 2,674,848 |
| Emp. | 280 | 272 | 236 |

DUNS 21-780-5737
## St Michaels C of E Primary School
South Lawn Terrace, Exeter, Devon EX1 2SN
**Tel:** 01392256669
**Web:** www.st-michaels-exeter.devon.sch.uk
**Estd:** 1997 Proprietorship
**Line of Business:** Schools (local authority)
**Proprietor:** Mrs C Pawley
**Responsibilities**
**Senior:** Gill Kendrick (Head Teacher)
**US SIC:** 8211 **UK SIC:** 93200
**Employees:** 50

DUNS 21-121-9932
## St Michael's Cofe Primary School
Bothel, Wigton, Cumbria CA7 2HN
**Tel:** 01697-320632
**Line of Business:** Primary education
**US SIC:** 8211 **UK SIC:** 93200
**Employees:** 90

DUNS 23-629-4252
## St Michaels Convent & Convalescent Home
93 Marine Parade East, Clacton-On-Sea, Essex CO15 6JW
**Tel:** 01255-423688
**Estd:** 1908
**Line of Business:** Residential care establishments
**Trading Style:** St. Michaels Care Home
**Directors:** M Z Butler, E O'Brian
**Responsibilities**
**Senior:** Angela Barton (Manager)
**US SIC:** 8321, 6732
**UK SIC:** 96111, 83100
**Bankers:** Barclays Bank Plc (20-21-73)
**Employees:** 50

DUNS 73-556-5590
## St Michael's Fellowship
136 Streatham High Road, London SW16 1BW
**Tel:** 02088359570
**Web:** www.stmichaelsfellowship.org.uk
**Reg No:** 2914273 **Estd:** 2010 Private Limited Company
**Line of Business:** Charities and charitable organisations
**Directors:** Mrs M A Gibson, Mrs P J Alford, Ms C F Roskill, Mrs C Forman, W W Anderson, Mrs P M Owen, Ms S B Smith, C C Lindsay
**Responsibilities**
**Senior:** Bernard Bindman (Director), Stephen Hair (Director), Sue Pettigrew (Manager)
**US SIC:** 8699, 8321
**UK SIC:** 96902, 96111
**Auditors:** Sayer Vincent
**Bankers:** National Westminster Bank Plc (60-18-05)

| | 31-03-14 | 31-03-13 | 31-03-12 |
|---|---|---|---|
| TO | 2,074,384 | 2,330,926 | 2,912,655 |
| P/L | (170,956) | (162,421) | 158,429 |
| NW | 905,124 | 1,076,080 | 1,238,501 |
| WC | 854,076 | 1,013,028 | 1,158,450 |
| Emp. | 50 | 56 | 61 |

DUNS 28-980-4270
## St Michael's Hospice Hastings & Rother
St Michaels Hospice, St Leonards-On-Sea, East Sussex TN38 0LB
**Tel:** 01424-445177
**Web:** www.stmichaelshospice.org
**Reg No:** 1776496 **Estd:** 1983 Private Company Limited By Guarantee
**Line of Business:** Medical nursing home activities
**Directors:** S Barnes, B D Hibbs, N A Gaymer, Dr R Guy, S P Corello, Mrs I O Dibben, M J Foster, C J Rowe
**Co. Secretary:** Richard Ostle
**Responsibilities**
**Senior:** Angela Chivers (Director), Charles Everett (Director), Bryan Sagar (Manager), Clifford Wallis (Director)
**Marketing:** Peridita Chamberlain (Head of Fundraising)
**HR:** Leanne Goodsell (Human Resources Manager)
**Facilities:** Timothy Faulkes (Maintenance Manager)
**Branches:** St Michael's Hospice Hastings & Rother, 484 Old London Road, Hastings, East Sussex TN35 5BG
**US SIC:** 8051 **UK SIC:** 95100
**Auditors:** Phipps & Co
**Bankers:** Lloyds TSB Bank plc (30-97-66)

| | 31-03-14 | 31-03-13 | 31-03-12 |
|---|---|---|---|
| TO | 5,757,493 | 5,018,310 | 5,655,145 |
| P/L | 550,602 | (152,658) | 884,698 |
| NW | 8,847,880 | 8,264,078 | 8,287,155 |
| WC | 4,625,111 | 5,387,018 | 6,257,393 |
| Emp. | 136 | 126 | 121 |

DUNS 29-292-3737
## St Michael's Hospice (Incorporating the Freda Pearce Foundation)
Bartestree, Hereford, Herefordshire HR1 4HA
**Tel:** 01432-851000 **Fax:** 01432851022
**Web:** www.st-michaels-hospice.org.uk
**Reg No:** 1634942 **Estd:** 1982 Private Limited Company
**Line of Business:** Hospital activities
**Directors:** M E Greene, D T Hammond, Dr R G Miller, A J Walshe, D R Teague, G B Nairn, D J Campion, Dr J J Kramer
**Co. Secretary:** Miss Susan Newbould
**Responsibilities**
**Senior:** John Dalziel (Director), Kathleen Garlick (Director), Patricia Greenwood (Director), Tristram Jenkins (Director), Carol Winney (Director)

**Branches:** St Michael's Hospice (Incorporating The Freda Pearce Foundation), 7 George Place, Gloucester Road, Ross-On-Wye, Herefordshire HR9 5BS
**US SIC:** 8062, 8321
**UK SIC:** 95100, 96111
**Auditors:** HLB Kidsons
**Bankers:** National Westminster Bank Plc (53-50-41)

| | 31-03-14 | 31-03-13 | 31-03-12 |
|---|---|---|---|
| TO | 8,511,020 | 4,665,692 | 3,963,392 |
| P/L | 4,145,247 | 427,987 | (114,309) |
| NW | 12,750,568 | 8,584,949 | 7,980,504 |
| WC | 1,184,142 | 111,107 | 183,053 |
| Emp. | 96 | 88 | 86 |

DUNS 76-678-4896
## St Michael's Hospice (North Hampshire)
Aldermaston Road, Basingstoke, Hampshire RG24 9NB
**Tel:** 01256844744
**Web:** www.stmichaelshospice.org.uk
**Reg No:** 2588395 **Estd:** 1991 Private Company Limited By Guarantee
**Line of Business:** Hospices
**Directors:** Dr M E Ashworth, A W Chancellor, A J Soundy, Mrs S C Scott-Malden, M A Lane, A Holden, D G Fairley, Dr M J Reynolds
**Co. Secretary:** Mark Lane
**Responsibilities**
**Senior:** Christian De Ferranti *(Director)*, Joy Macandrew *(Manager)*, Anthony Marten *(Director)*, David Monkman *(Chief Executive)*, Margaret Stebbing *(Director)*
**HR:** Dorothy Atwood *(Senior Sister)*
**Operations:** Dorothy Atwood *(Senior Sister)*
**Purchasing:** Gill Drury *(Head of Purchasing)*
**US SIC:** 8091, 8062
**UK SIC:** 95200, 95100
**Auditors:** BKL Blueprint
**Bankers:** Lloyds TSB Bank plc (30-90-53)

| | 31-03-14 | 31-03-13 | 31-03-12 |
|---|---|---|---|
| TO | 4,551,322 | 4,064,311 | 3,589,455 |
| P/L | 300,855 | 83,197 | (202,165) |
| NW | 4,497,972 | 4,146,227 | 3,814,280 |
| WC | 244,695 | 520,965 | 251,991 |
| Emp. | 91 | 117 | 82 |

DUNS 23-623-2476
## St Michaels Manor Nursing Home
Springwood Avenue, Woolton, Liverpool, Merseyside L25 7UW
**Tel:** 0151-427-9419
**Web:** www.liverpoolcare.co.uk
**Estd:** 1989 Partnership
**Line of Business:** Nursing homes
**Trading Style:** St. Micheal Manor
**Partners:** M Hanlon, J Mutch
**Responsibilities**
**Senior:** Steve Gartsive *(Manager)*, James Mutch *(Partner)*, Philip Sargeant *(General Manager)*
**Marketing:** Philip Sargeant *(General Manager)*
**IT:** Philip Sargeant *(General Manager)*
**HR:** Philip Sargeant *(General Manager)*
**Health & Safety:** Philip Sargeant *(General Manager)*
**Operations:** Philip Sargeant *(General Manager)*
**US SIC:** 8051, 8091, 6732
**UK SIC:** 95100, 95200, 83100
**Employees:** 50

DUNS 21-043-0418
## St Michaels Mount
St Michaels Mount, Marazion, Cornwall TR17 0HS
**Tel:** 01736710265
**Web:** www.stmichaelsmount.co.uk
**Estd:** 2002 Proprietorship
**Line of Business:** Places of interest
**Proprietor:** R Abbernady
**Responsibilities**
**Senior:** Charlotte Somers *(Head Of Marketing & Public Rel)*
**Marketing:** Charlotte Somers *(Head Of Marketing & Public Rel)*
**US SIC:** 8411 **UK SIC:** 97700
**Employees:** 65

DUNS 21-772-2814
## St Michaels Nursing Home
9 Chesterfield Road, Brimington, Chesterfield, Derbyshire S43 1AB
**Tel:** 01246558828
**Web:** www.suncarehomes.com
**Estd:** 1992 Partnership
**Line of Business:** Medical nursing home activities
**Partners:** Mrs C Wignall, B Choli
**US SIC:** 8051 **UK SIC:** 95100
**Employees:** 48

DUNS 21-589-3395
## St Michael's Preparatory School
Lane Rue De Lane Houguette, St Saviour, Jersey, Channel Islands JE2 7UG
**Tel:** 01534856904
**Web:** www.stmichaelsschool.je
**Estd:** 2011
**Line of Business:** Schools (independent)
**Responsibilities**
**Senior:** Richard Figueiredo *(Headmaster)*
**Admin:** Claire Taylor *(Office Manager)*
**US SIC:** 8211 **UK SIC:** 93200
**Employees:** 80

DUNS 54-905-0318
## St Michael's School
Otford Court, St Michaels Drive, Otford, Sevenoaks, Kent TN14 5SA
**Tel:** 01959522137
**Web:** www.stmichaels.kent.sch.uk
**Estd:** 1996
**Line of Business:** Schools (independent)
**Director:** Dr P Rootes
**Responsibilities**
**Senior:** Jill Aisher *(Head Teacher)*
**Marketing:** Judith Yarnold *(Director of Marketing)*
**US SIC:** 8211 **UK SIC:** 93200
**Employees:** 80

DUNS 21-328-2705
## St Michaels School
Harts Lane, Burghclere, Newbury, Berkshire RG20 9JW
**Web:** www.sspx.co.uk
**Estd:** 1997
**Line of Business:** Schools (independent)
**Director:** J Emily
**Responsibilities**
**Senior:** F Kurtz *(Principal)*, Patrick Summers *(Principal)*
**US SIC:** 8221 **UK SIC:** 93100
**Employees:** 49

DUNS 34-854-7774
## St Moritz Hotel & Garden Villas Ltd
**(Subsidiary of:** St Moritz (Holdings) Ltd)
St Moritz Villas Court, Trebetherick, Wadebridge, Cornwall PL27 6SD
**Web:** www.stmoritzvillas.co.uk
**Reg No:** 5653512 **Estd:** 2005 Private Limited Company
**Line of Business:** Other tourist or short-stay accommodation
**Issued Capital:** £2
**Directors:** S Ridgway, F Whyte
**Co. Secretary:** Hugh Ridgway
**US SIC:** 7021 **UK SIC:** 66500

| | 31-03-14 | 31-03-13 | 31-03-12 |
|---|---|---|---|
| TO | 3,541,694 | 3,480,495 | 3,396,360 |
| P/L | 196,819 | 89,333 | 17,680 |
| NW | 2,401,815 | 2,227,013 | 882,275 |
| WC | 755,141 | 663,642 | 667,364 |
| Emp. | 89 | 87 | 83 |

DUNS 21-860-2136
## St Mungo Community Housing Association
Griffin House, London W6 8BS
**Tel:** 02087625500 **Fax:** 02079288444
**Web:** www.mungos.org
**Reg No:** 8225808 **Estd:** 2012 Private Company Limited By Guarantee
**Line of Business:** Charitable social work activities with accommodation
**Directors:** Ms G Nanda, Sir L W Lewis, Ms J Williams, A J Keir, A Kumar, Ms G M Charlesworth, M G Foster, J Maxted
**Co. Secretary:** Michael Mccall
**Responsibilities**
**Senior:** Rod Cullen *(Group Manager)*, Miles Davis *(Area Manager)*, Paul Doe *(Director)*, Cliff Dymond *(Area Manager)*, Timothy Gadd *(Director)*, Judith Higgin *(General Manager)*, Edwin Hilliard *(Director)*, Angela Manners *(Manager)*, Alexia Murphy *(Director of New Business)*, Howard Sinclair *(Chief Executive Officer)*
**Marketing:** Amy Macconnachie *(Public Affairs Officer)*, Rebecca Sycamore *(Executive Director of Fundrais)*
**Operations:** Matt Catlow *(Production and Operations Mana)*
**Branches:** St Mungo Community Housing Association, 155 Tufnell Park Road, London N7 0PU
**US SIC:** 8321 **UK SIC:** 96111
**Bankers:** HSBC Bank plc (40-03-05)

| | 31-03-14 | 31-03-13 |
|---|---|---|
| TO | 53,832,000 | 49,120,000 |
| P/L | 657,000 | 1,251,000 |
| NW | 21,135,000 | 20,478,000 |
| WC | 10,150,000 | 12,066,000 |
| Emp. | 1,219 | 1,112 |

DUNS 21-106-6362
## St Neots Holdings Ltd
**(Subsidiary of:** Sun Capital Partners Inc.)
7 Howard Road, Eaton Socon, Eaton Socon, St Neots, Cambridgeshire PE19 8ET
**Web:** www.fastfoodpackaging.com
**Reg No:** 6489426 **Estd:** 2008 Private Limited Company
**Line of Business:** Financial management
**Export Sales:** £2,546,000
**Trading Style:** Coveris
**Issued Capital:** £8,509,023
**Directors:** K Bostock, M E Lapping
**Responsibilities**
**Senior:** Michael Kearns *(Manager)*, Alan Pealling *(Manager)*
**US SIC:** 7392 **UK SIC:** 83951
**Auditors:** Grant Thornton UK LLP
**Bankers:** HSBC Bank plc (40-40-10)

| | 30-06-13 | 30-06-12 | 30-06-11 |
|---|---|---|---|
| TO | 33,140,000 | 32,166,000 | 30,287,000 |
| P/L | 2,677,000 | 283,000 | (3,030,000) |
| NW | (1,218,000) | (3,778,000) | (4,525,000) |
| WC | (922,000) | (4,364,000) | (4,785,000) |
| Emp. | 211 | 167 | 140 |

DUNS 21-464-3541
## St Neots Preparatory Lower School
St Neots Road, Eversley, Hook, Hampshire RG27 0PN
**Web:** www.stneotsschool.ik.org
**Estd:** 1989 Proprietorship
**Line of Business:** Schools (independent)
**Proprietor:** R Thorp
**Responsibilities**
**IT:** Mark Kenton *(Computer Manager)*
**HR:** Debbie Berger-North *(PA to Principal)*
**US SIC:** 8211 **UK SIC:** 93200
**Employees:** 50

DUNS 50-635-1241
## St Nicholas Catholic High Scho
Greenbank Lane, Hartford, Northwich, Cheshire CW8 1JW
**Tel:** 01606706000
**Proprietorship**
**Line of Business:** General secondary education
**Proprietor:** K Kelly
**Responsibilities**
**Senior:** Kieren Kelly *(Schools - Principal)*
**US SIC:** 8211 **UK SIC:** 93200
**Employees:** 114

DUNS 21-780-2228
## St Nicholas' School
Reedham Old Lodge Lane, Purley, Surrey CR8 4DN
**Tel:** 02086604861
**Web:** www.st-nicholas.croydon.sch.uk
**Estd:** 1970 Proprietorship
**Line of Business:** Schools (special)
**Proprietor:** Mrs J Melton
**US SIC:** 8299 **UK SIC:** 93300
**Employees:** 55

DUNS 22-702-5111
## St Nicholas' Training Centre for the Montessori Method of Education Ltd
23 Princes Gate, London SW7 1PT
**Tel:** 020-7225-1277 **Fax:** 02076297808
**Web:** www.stnicholasprep.co.uk
**Reg No:** 0531204 **VAT No:** 240478470
**Estd:** 1954 Private Company Limited By Guarantee
**Line of Business:** Primary education
**Trading Style:** St Nicholas" Propeparitoy School, Montessori St Nicholas School
**Directors:** Ms A J Newman, Mrs G M Nester-Smith, K R Coyne, A J Ling, W Callaway, Dr A C Parmley, W B Sketchley, Miss C Hobey-Hamsher
**Co. Secretary:** Christopher Marke
**Responsibilities**
**Senior:** Gill Aisher *(Head Teacher)*, Catherine Hobey-hamsher *(Director)*, Felicity Marrian *(Director)*, Rees Rawlings *(Director)*
**Finance:** Coomar Jayadeva *(Bursar)*
**Branches:** St Nicholas' Training Centre For The Montessori Method Of Education Lt, 6 Melior St, London SE1 3QP
**US SIC:** 8211, 8249
**UK SIC:** 93200, 93300
**Auditors:** Dixon Wilson
**Bankers:** The Royal Bank Of Scotland Plc (16-00-42)

| | 31-08-13 | 31-08-12 | 31-08-11 |
|---|---|---|---|
| TO | 3,244,868 | 2,320,219 | 13,868,315 |
| P/L | (514,184) | 241,482 | 11,515,480 |
| NW | 15,886,751 | 15,488,183 | 15,246,701 |
| WC | 4,381,390 | 6,698,028 | 7,570,365 |
| Emp. | 61 | 26 | 28 |

DUNS 21-778-2801
## St Ninians Health Centre
Mayfield Street, Stirling, Stirlingshire FK7 0BS
**Tel:** 01786479555
**Estd:** 1979 Partnership
**Line of Business:** Public sector hospital activities, including nhs trusts
**Partners:** Mrs C Perk, Miss C Park
**Responsibilities**
**Senior:** Christopher Hunter *(Senior Partner)*
**US SIC:** 8062 **UK SIC:** 95100
**Employees:** 50

DUNS 21-327-6962
## St Olaves Preparatory School
106-110 Southwood Road, London SE9 3QS
**Tel:** 020-8294-8930
**Web:** www.stolaves.org.uk
**Estd:** 2000 Proprietorship
**Line of Business:** Schools (independent)
**Proprietor:** Mrs C Fisher
**Responsibilities**
**Senior:** James Tilly *(Head Teacher)*
**US SIC:** 8211 **UK SIC:** 93200
**Employees:** 50

DUNS 21-839-1596
## St Osmund's Ce Middle School
Barnes Way, Dorchester, Dorset DT1 2DZ
**Tel:** 01305262897
**Web:** www.stosmunds.dorset.sch.uk
**Reg No.** 8000279 **Estd.** 2012 Private Company Limited By Guarantee
**Line of Business:** Schools (local authority)
**Directors:** Mrs C Pugh, Mrs L J Bainbridge, Mrs J White, T M Woodhouse, A J Gannon, Mrs J M Lang, Ms S A Wilson, D E Bowen
**Co. Secretary:** Ms Valerie Ray
**Responsibilities**
**Senior:** Philip Browne *(Director)*, Julia Denham *(Director)*, Anthony Holt *(Director)*, Joanna Jeffery *(Director)*, Nicolas Power *(Director)*, Jeremy Williams *(Director)*
**US SIC:** 8211 **UK SIC:** 93200
**Auditors:** Rothmans Audit LLP
**Bankers:** Lloyds TSB Bank plc (30-92-69)

| | 31-08-14 | 31-08-13 |
|---|---|---|
| TO | 2,679,954 | 4,665,000 |
| P/L | (73,139) | 864,000 |
| NW | 562,861 | 699,000 |
| WC | 129,073 | 144,000 |
| Emp. | 35 | 60 |

DUNS 21-600-2731
## St Oswald's C of E Primary School
Cross Lane, Bradford, West Yorkshire BD7 3JT
**Tel:** 01274573396
**Web:** www.stoswalds.bradford.sch.uk
**Estd:** 1904 Partnership
**Line of Business:** Schools (foundation)
**Partner:** Mrs E Davison
**US SIC:** 8211 **UK SIC:** 93200
**Employees:** 80

DUNS 21-600-3281
## St Oswald's Hospital
Clifton Road, Ashbourne, Derbyshire DE6 1DR
**Tel:** 01335230000
**Estd:** 1966 Proprietorship
**Line of Business:** Rehabilitation centres
**Proprietor:** Mrs P Arnold
**Responsibilities**
**Senior:** Maggie Barrett *(Locality Manager)*, L Stockton *(Practice Manager)*
**US SIC:** 8062 **UK SIC:** 95100
**Employees:** 100

DUNS 21-585-1574
## St Pancras Grand Restaurant & Champagne Bar
Hertford Street, Coventry, West Midlands CV1 1JT
**Web:** www.searcyschampagnebars.co.uk
**Estd:** 2011 Proprietorship
**Line of Business:** Bars
**Proprietor:** Miss M Cartwright
**Responsibilities**
**Senior:** Peter Alderin *(General Manager)*
**US SIC:** 5813 **UK SIC:** 66200
**Employees:** 70

DUNS 21-600-0727
## St Patrick's Academy
Ballinderry Road, Lisburn, Co Antrim BT28 1TD
**Tel:** 02892664877
**Web:** www.stpatsni.co.uk
**Estd:** 1962 Proprietorship
**Line of Business:** Schools (local authority)
**Proprietor:** S Quinn
**US SIC:** 8211 **UK SIC:** 93200
**Employees:** 60

**DUNS 21-783-2694**
## St Patrick's College
Business Depot, Killymeal Road, Dungannon, Co Tyrone BT71 6LJ
**Tel:** 02887722934
**Estd:** 1975 Partnership
**Line of Business:** Bus operators and stations
**Partners:** Mrs R O'Neill, Mrs R O'Neil
**Responsibilities**
**Senior:** Dale Hanna (Manager)
**US SIC:** 8221 **UK SIC:** 93100
**Employees:** 67

**DUNS 21-600-0706**
## St Patricks College
38 Scarva Road, Banbridge, Co Down BT32 3AS
**Tel:** 02840662309
**Web:** www.stpatrickscollege.org.uk
**Estd:** 1960 Proprietorship
**Line of Business:** Sixth form colleges
**Proprietor:** P Carlin
**Responsibilities**
**Senior:** Tracy Diamond (Executive Director), Anne Mallon (Head Teacher)
**IT:** Finnuala Hartigan (Senior IT Executive)
**US SIC:** 8221 **UK SIC:** 93100
**Employees:** 50

**DUNS 23-082-9355**
## St Patricks (G M) Boys School
Bearnageeha House, Belfast BT15 4DZ
**Tel:** 028-9077-0011
**Web:** www.stpatrickscollege.net
**Estd:** 2004
**Line of Business:** Educational training
**Director:** P J O'Grady
**Responsibilities**
**IT:** Martin Mccoy (Senior IT Executive)
**US SIC:** 8211 **UK SIC:** 93200
**Employees:** 70

**DUNS 23-083-2615**
## St Patricks Grammar School
Cathedral Road, Armagh, Co Armagh BT61 7QZ
**Tel:** 028-3752-2018
**Web:** www.stpatricksarmagh.com
**Estd:** 1973
**Line of Business:** Schools (local authority)
**Directors:** L S Kelly, L S Kelly
**Responsibilities**
**Senior:** Kevin Donaghy (Head Teacher), Kevin Donoghue (Head Teacher)
**IT:** Damian Mullen (Network, Security Manager)
**US SIC:** 8211 **UK SIC:** 93200
**Employees:** 72

**DUNS 21-165-1877**
## St Pauls Cathedral School
2 New Change, London EC4M 9AD
**Tel:** 020-7248-5156
**Web:** www.spcslondon.com
**Estd:** 2002
**Line of Business:** Schools (independent)
**Co. Secretary:** Ms Claire Morgan
**Responsibilities**
**Senior:** Neil Chippington (Principal)
**US SIC:** 8211 **UK SIC:** 93200
**Employees:** 70

**DUNS 21-353-3487**
## St Pauls Catholic College
The Ridings, Green Street, Sunbury-On-Thames, Middlesex TW16 6NX
**Tel:** 01932783811
**Web:** www.stpaulscatholiccollege.co.uk
**Estd:** 2003
**Line of Business:** Schools (local authority)
**Principals:** J Wright (Chairman), C Hobday
**Responsibilities**
**Senior:** Carrie Bacon (Head Teacher), Mattthew Bennett (CEO, Managing Director), Simon Uttley (Head Teacher)
**Finance:** Shelaith Aldridge (Senior Finance Administrator)
**US SIC:** 8211 **UK SIC:** 93200
**Employees:** 1,000

**DUNS 21-960-4068**
## St Paul's Girls' School
Brook Green Hammersmith, London W6 7BS
**Tel:** 020-7603-2288
**Web:** www.spgs.org
**Reg No:** 6142007 **Estd:** 2007 Private Company Limited By Guarantee
**Line of Business:** General secondary education
**Directors:** P N Chisholm, Professor C M Roueche, M C Aspinall, Professor H K Harrison, The Hon T J Palmer, Miss C A Palmer, D H Hodson, Ms J S Portrait
**Co. Secretary:** Mrs Nicki Goodfellow

**Responsibilities**
**Senior:** Helen Alexander (Director), Kate Bingham (Director), Pauline Davies (Director), Clarissa Farr (CEO, Managing Director), Alice Hohler (Director), Julia Riley (Director)
**Finance:** Susannah Parsons (Senior Finance Administrator)
**Admin:** Susannah Parsons (Senior Finance Administrator)
**IT:** Miriam Brizuela (Database Manager), Sebastian Cerazy (Network, Security Manager), Lee Kwunman (Network, Security Manager)
**HR:** Urszula Bereza (Human Resources Manager)
**Operations:** Rosemary Torrington (Technical, Production Manager)
**US SIC:** 8211 **UK SIC:** 93200
**Auditors:** Crowe Clark Whitehill LLP
**Bankers:** Allied Irish Bank (gb) (23-84-82)

|  | 31-08-14 | 31-08-13 | 31-08-12 |
|---|---|---|---|
| TO | 17,751,000 | 16,800,000 | 15,056,000 |
| P/L | 2,237,000 | 2,030,000 | 1,077,000 |
| NW | 27,557,000 | 25,524,000 | 22,282,000 |
| WC | 12,899,000 | 10,211,000 | 8,049,000 |
| Emp. | 174 | 169 | 161 |

**DUNS 21-765-2096**
## St Paul's Medical Centre
Dickson Road, Blackpool, Lancashire FY1 2HH
**Tel:** 01253623896
**Web:** www.stpaulspcc.co.uk
**Estd:** 1995
**Line of Business:** Doctors
**Responsibilities**
**Senior:** Nicolaas Klerk (General Practitioner)
**US SIC:** 8011 **UK SIC:** 95300
**Employees:** 55

**DUNS 23-083-1948**
## St Paul's R C (A) Primary School
Bourne Road, Portsmouth, Hampshire PO6 4JD
**Web:** www.st-pauls.portsmouth.sch.uk
**Estd:** 1959
**Line of Business:** Schools (local authority)
**Director:** Mrs E M Pescots
**Responsibilities**
**Senior:** Brenda Schouller (Head Teacher)
**US SIC:** 8211 **UK SIC:** 93200
**Employees:** 50

**DUNS 21-585-3223**
## St Pauls R C Academy
Gillburn Road, Dundee, Angus DD3 0EH
**Estd:** 2002 Proprietorship
**Line of Business:** Schools (local authority)
**Proprietor:** Mrs M Leck
**US SIC:** 8211 **UK SIC:** 93200
**Employees:** 150

**DUNS 42-345-1111**
## St Paul's School
Lonsdale Road, London SW13 9JT
**Tel:** 020-8748-9162
**Web:** www.stpaulsschool.org.uk
**Estd:** 1509
**Line of Business:** Adult and other education not elsewhere classified
**Director:** D Loveridge
**US SIC:** 8249, 8299
**UK SIC:** 93300
**Employees:** 260

**DUNS 49-454-8258**
## St Peter & St James Hospice Shops Ltd
North Common Road, Lewes, East Sussex BN8 4ED
**Tel:** 01444471598
**Web:** www.stpeter-stjames.org.uk
**Reg No:** 3146736 **Estd:** 1996 Private Limited Company
**Line of Business:** Retail sale of other second-hand goods in stores
**Issued Capital:** £90,000
**Directors:** P B Boyse, C D Burgess, D C Crudge
**Responsibilities**
**Finance:** Sue Adams (Director of Fundraising & Mark), Jody Sharp (Finance Director)
**Sales:** Brian Paddock (Retail Area Manager), Therese Wilson (Head of Retail)
**HR:** Julia Vokes (HR Administrator)
**Branches:** St Peter & St James Hospice Shops Ltd, 58 High Street, Lewes, East Sussex BN7 1XE
**US SIC:** 5931 **UK SIC:** 65400
**Auditors:** Keymer Haslam & Co

**Bankers:** Barclays Bank Plc (20-49-76)

|  | 31-03-14 | 31-03-13 | 31-03-12 |
|---|---|---|---|
| TO | 704,985 | 530,429 | 591,616 |
| P/L | 2,632 | 1,898 | 3,444 |
| NW | 100,774 | 98,142 | 96,244 |
| WC | 24,541 | 23,401 | 37,082 |

**DUNS 21-511-5144**
## St Peter and St Paul's Church
St Alphege Road, Dover, Kent CT16 2PU
**Web:** www.broadhamcare.co.uk
**Estd:** 2011
**Line of Business:** Residential care establishments
**Responsibilities**
**Senior:** Sandra Paine (Manager)
**US SIC:** 8321 **UK SIC:** 96111
**Employees:** 49

**DUNS 21-778-3376**
## St Peter in Thanet Junior School
Grange Road, Broadstairs, Kent CT10 3EP
**Tel:** 01843-861430
**Web:** www.st-peters-broadstairs.kent.sch.uk
**Estd:** 2002
**Line of Business:** Schools (local authority)
**Proprietor:** Mrs S Irvine
**Responsibilities**
**Senior:** Tim Huner-Whitehouse (Head Teacher), Hunter Whitehouse (Head Teacher)
**IT:** Debbie Spirgin (Senior IT Executive)
**US SIC:** 8211 **UK SIC:** 93200
**Employees:** 60

**DUNS 23-082-8183**
## St Peter's C of E Primary School
Eaves Lane, Chorley, Lancashire PR6 0DX
**Tel:** 01257-262625
**Web:** www.stpeters.lancs.sch.uk
**Estd:** 1966
**Line of Business:** Schools (local authority)
**Trading Style:** Saint Peter's Primary School
**Director:** J Gray
**US SIC:** 8211 **UK SIC:** 93200
**Employees:** 50

**DUNS 21-033-0219**
## St Peters Collegiate School
Compton Park, Compton Road West, Wolverhampton, West Midlands WV3 9DU
**Tel:** 01902-558600
**Web:** www.speters.org.uk
**Estd:** 2002 Proprietorship
**Line of Business:** Schools (local authority)
**Proprietor:** A Richards
**Responsibilities**
**IT:** Marie Spencer (Senior IT Executive)
**Health & Safety:** Mike Cook (Caretaker)
**Facilities:** Mike Cook (Caretaker)
**US SIC:** 8211 **UK SIC:** 93200
**Employees:** 149

**DUNS 28-882-1820**
## St Peter's Hospice
Charlton Road, Brentry, Bristol, Avon BS10 6NL
**Tel:** 01179-159400
**Web:** www.stpetershospice.org.uk
**Reg No:** 1191227 **Estd:** 1974 Private Company Limited By Guarantee
**Line of Business:** Charities and charitable organisations
**Trading Style:** St Peter''s Hospice
**Directors:** Dr N P Goyder, P B Montague, Ms K N Ward, D P Walker, M Plummeridge, Professor K Forbes, Ms H C Staines, Mrs S S Chaudhry
**Co. Secretary:** Stephen Melling
**Responsibilities**
**Senior:** Arthur Bonham (Manager), Robert Bourns (Chairman), Simon Carassi (Chief Executive), Martin Mohan (Director), Alison Moon (Director)
**Health & Safety:** Ian Trigg (Facilities Manager)
**Facilities:** Ian Trigg (Facilities Manager)
**Branches:** St Peter's Hospice, St. Saviours House, St. Agnes Avenue, Bristol, Avon BS4 2DU
**US SIC:** 8091, 8249, 8011
**UK SIC:** 95200, 93300, 95300
**Auditors:** KPMG
**Bankers:** National Westminster Bank Plc (56-00-05)

|  | 31-03-14 | 31-03-13 | 31-03-12 |
|---|---|---|---|
| TO | 13,645,000 | 11,942,000 | 11,794,000 |
| P/L | 1,551,000 | 118,000 | 2,000 |
| NW | 20,193,000 | 13,696,000 | 12,879,000 |
| WC | 6,668,000 | 705,000 | 402,000 |
| Emp. | 297 | 283 | 282 |

**DUNS 21-774-7162**
## St Peters House Residential Home
29 Out Risbygate, Bury St Edmunds, Suffolk IP33 3RJ
**Tel:** 01284706603
**Web:** www.countycarehomes.co.uk
**Estd:** 1985 Partnership
**Line of Business:** Residential care establishments
**Partners:** Mrs M Clare, Mrs M Clare
**US SIC:** 8321 **UK SIC:** 96111
**Employees:** 49

**DUNS 23-752-3084**
## St Peter's Lasallian School Trust
St Catherines Road, Bournemouth, Dorset BH6 4AH
**Tel:** 01202-421141
**Web:** www.st-peters.bournemouth.sch.uk
**Reg No:** 3746203 **Estd:** 1999 Private Company Limited By Guarantee
**Line of Business:** Schools (local authority)
**Trading Style:** St Peters School
**Directors:** R J Belcher, P Kazmierczak, Miss R S Dixon, B Hayward
**Co. Secretary:** Mrs Janet Lasham
**US SIC:** 8211 **UK SIC:** 93200
**Auditors:** Moore Stephens
**Bankers:** Lloyds TSB Bank plc (77-83-17)

|  | 31-03-13 | 31-03-12 | 31-03-11 |
|---|---|---|---|
| TO | 74,812 | 139,731 | 300,986 |
| P/L | 10,156 | (26,888) | 28,719 |
| NW | 125,790 | 115,634 | 142,522 |
| WC | 125,790 | 115,634 | 142,522 |

**DUNS 21-778-1420**
## St Peter's R C Primary School
Dunbar Street, Aberdeen, Aberdeenshire AB24 3UJ
**Tel:** 01224485611
**Web:** www.st-peters.aberdeen.sch.uk
**Estd:** 1982 Partnership
**Line of Business:** General secondary education
**Partners:** Mrs J Martin, Mrs J Martin
**US SIC:** 8211 **UK SIC:** 93200
**Employees:** 60

**DUNS 21-749-9495**
## St Peter's Rc High School
142 Kirkmanshulme Lane, Manchester M12 4WB
**Tel:** 0161-248-1550
**Web:** www.st-petershigh.manchester.sch.uk
**Estd:** 2003
**Line of Business:** Schools (local authority)
**Director:** J Mcnerney
**US SIC:** 8211 **UK SIC:** 93200
**Employees:** 180

**DUNS 23-083-2235**
## St Peters School
Clifton, York, North Yorkshire YO30 6AB
**Tel:** 01904527416
**Web:** www.stolavesyork.org.uk
**Estd:** 1986
**Line of Business:** General secondary education
**Director:** T Mulryne
**Responsibilities**
**Senior:** Stewart Howman (Purchasing Manager), Leo Winkley (Headmaster)
**Finance:** Penny Lacy (Bursar)
**Marketing:** Erica Town (Director of Marketing)
**IT:** Christopher Lawrie (Head of IT)
**HR:** Penny Lacy (Bursar)
**Health & Safety:** Graham Dentith (Deputy Bursar)
**Facilities:** Graham Fennell (Estates Manager)
**Purchasing:** Stewart Howman (Purchasing Manager)
**US SIC:** 8211 **UK SIC:** 93200
**Employees:** 80

**DUNS 21-167-4145**
## St Peter's School York
Clifton, York, North Yorkshire YO30 6AB
**Tel:** 01904527304
**Web:** www.cliftonprep.york.sch.uk
**Reg No:** 6927030 **Estd:** 2009 Private Company Limited By Guarantee
**Line of Business:** Adult and other education not elsewhere classified
**Directors:** W R Woolley, P Hilling, Ms P Kaur, A R Lees, D Salter, J E Burdass, J R Coles, M D Matravers
**Co. Secretary:** Ms Kathryn Hodges
**Responsibilities**
**Senior:** Daryl Hayward (Director), Stephen Town (Director)
**US SIC:** 8249 **UK SIC:** 93300

**Bankers:** Yorkshire Bank Plc (05-09-94)

|     | 31-08-13 | 31-08-12 |
| --- | --- | --- |
| TO | 14,404,902 | 14,720,753 |
| P/L | 885,861 | 1,788,849 |
| NW | 17,685,040 | 16,650,402 |
| WC | 1,415,748 | 517,508 |
| Emp. | 259 | 245 |

DUNS 21-390-1711
## St Peters Youth
Dean Street, Ashton-Under-Lyne, Lancashire OL6 7HD
**Web:** www.stpeterspartnerships.com
**Estd:** 2009 Proprietorship
**Line of Business:** Youth centres and associations
**Proprietor:** C Kelsall
**US SIC:** 8699  **UK SIC:** 96902
**Employees:** 60

DUNS 21-774-7678
## St Petrocs Church of England Primary School
Athelstan Park, Bodmin, Cornwall PL31 1DS
**Tel:** 0120872526
**Web:** www.st-petrocs.org
**Estd:** 1990 Proprietorship
**Line of Business:** Schools (local authority)
**Proprietor:** S Renshaw
**Responsibilities**
**Senior:** Sue Green (Head Teacher)
**US SIC:** 8211  **UK SIC:** 93200
**Employees:** 65

DUNS 21-600-9542
## St Philips C of E Primary School
Whitby Terrace, Bradford, West Yorkshire BD8 9JL
**Tel:** 01274546496
**Web:** www.stphilipsbradford.org.uk
**Estd:** 2004 Proprietorship
**Line of Business:** Schools (local authority)
**Proprietor:** Mrs J Bey
**US SIC:** 8211  **UK SIC:** 93200
**Employees:** 50

DUNS 64-262-6519
## St Philips School
Main St Plains, Airdrie, Lanarkshire ML6 7SF
**Tel:** 01236750407
**Web:** www.cora.org.uk
**Estd:** 1990 Proprietorship
**Line of Business:** Schools (local authority)
**Proprietor:** B Harold
**Responsibilities**
**Senior:** John Bremner (Proprietor)
**US SIC:** 8211  **UK SIC:** 93200
**Employees:** 120

DUNS 21-605-6171
## St Pierre Park Hotel
Rohais, St Peter Port, Guernsey, Channel Islands GY1 1FD
**Tel:** 01481-728282
**Web:** www.stpierrepark.co.uk
**Proprietorship**
**Line of Business:** Hotels
**Proprietor:** Mrs D Leelacheur
**Responsibilities**
**Finance:** Richard Stockton (Accounts Manager)
**Marketing:** Julia Zaddersare (Sales& Marketing Manager)
**US SIC:** 7011  **UK SIC:** 66500
**Employees:** 100

DUNS 21-031-9016
## St Raphael's Hospice
801 London Road, Sutton, Surrey SM3 9DX
**Tel:** 02080997777
**Web:** www.straphaels.org.uk
**Estd:** 2005 Partnership
**Line of Business:** Hospices
**Partners:** Mrs M Ford, P Cook
**Responsibilities**
**Senior:** Marie Joseph (Manager), Mike Roycroft (Chief Executive Officer)
**US SIC:** 8091  **UK SIC:** 95200
**Employees:** 100

DUNS 21-566-5467
## St Raphaels Nursing Home
Church Lane, Danehill, Haywards Heath, West Sussex RH17 7EZ
**Estd:** 1951 Partnership
**Line of Business:** Nursing homes
**Proprietor:** C Basil
**US SIC:** 8051  **UK SIC:** 95100
**Employees:** 58

DUNS 21-391-6815
## St Richard's R C Primary School
Marfleet Lane, Hull, North Humberside HU9 5TE
**Tel:** 01482-781928
**Web:** www.st-richards.hull.sch.uk
**Estd:** 2001
**Line of Business:** Schools (local authority)
**Responsibilities**
**Senior:** Sharon Melia-Craven (Head Teacher)
**US SIC:** 8211  **UK SIC:** 93200
**Employees:** 50

DUNS 21-810-6833
## St Rita's Care Home
Ditchling Road St Georges Park, Burgess Hill, West Sussex RH15 0GT
**Web:** www.anh.org.uk
**Estd:** 2012
**Line of Business:** Residential care establishments
**Responsibilities**
**Senior:** Emma Monaghan (Manager)
**US SIC:** 8321  **UK SIC:** 96111
**Employees:** 80

DUNS 53-614-5378
## St Ronan's School (Hawkhurst)
Water Lane Gun Green, Cranbrook, Kent TN18 5DJ
**Tel:** 01580-752271
**Web:** www.saintronans.co.uk
**Reg No:** 3419744  **Estd:** 1997 Private Limited Company
**Line of Business:** General secondary education
**Directors:** R Dalton Holmes, Dr S P Bulter-Gallie, Professor K Dacre, Dr R J Blundell, N Phillis, J C Lucas, C C Willis, S P Davies
**Co. Secretary:** John Buckles
**Responsibilities**
**Senior:** Charles Langer (Director), Bruce Seton (Director), William Trelawny-Vernon (Registrar)
**Marketing:** William Trelawny-Vernon (Registrar)
**IT:** Ben Clarke (Head of IT)
**HR:** William Trelawny-Vernon (Registrar)
**US SIC:** 8211  **UK SIC:** 93200
**Auditors:** HLB Kidsons
**Bankers:** Allied Irish Bank (gb) (23-84-84)

|     | 31-07-14 | 31-07-13 | 31-07-12 |
| --- | --- | --- | --- |
| TO | 4,634,509 | 3,967,022 | 3,983,712 |
| P/L | 499,835 | 54,483 | 141,721 |
| NW | 1,609,781 | 1,109,946 | 1,055,463 |
| WC | 266,368 | (168,521) | (301,076) |
| Emp. | 67 | 66 | 61 |

DUNS 21-771-3901
## St Rose's Dominican College
Beechmount Avenue, Belfast BT12 7NA
**Tel:** 02890240937
**Web:** www.stroses.belfast.ni.sch.uk
**Estd:** 2011 Proprietorship
**Line of Business:** Schools (local authority)
**Proprietor:** Ms T Mcnamee
**Responsibilities**
**Senior:** Michele Mcgurran (Head Teacher)
**US SIC:** 8211  **UK SIC:** 93200
**Employees:** 60

DUNS 23-082-7706
## St Saviour's C of E Junior School
Elm Grove, Westgate-On-Sea, Kent CT8 8LD
**Tel:** 01843-831707
**Web:** www.stsavioursjunior.com
**Estd:** 1995
**Line of Business:** Schools (local authority)
**Director:** A Andreo
**Responsibilities**
**Senior:** Nick Bonell (Head Teacher)
**US SIC:** 8211  **UK SIC:** 93200
**Employees:** 50

DUNS 33-990-0649
## St Simeon
38 Harrington Gardens, South Kensington, London SW7 4LT
**Tel:** 020-7373-0505
**Web:** www.st-simeonhotel.co.uk
**Estd:** 1977 Partnership
**Line of Business:** Hotels and motels without restaurant
**Partners:** R Gojkovic, J Gojkovic
**Responsibilities**
**Senior:** George Gojkovic (Manager)
**US SIC:** 7011  **UK SIC:** 66500
**Employees:** 51

DUNS 23-082-9314
## St Simon Stock School
Oakwood Park, Maidstone, Kent ME16 0JP
**Tel:** 01622-754551
**Web:** www.st-simon-stock.kent.sch.uk
**Estd:** 1988
**Line of Business:** Schools (local authority)
**Director:** E Mulheard
**Responsibilities**
**Senior:** J McParland (Head Teacher), Brendan Wall (Head Teacher)
**Admin:** Cindy Theisen (Clerk to Governors)
**IT:** Aiden McGee (Head of IT)
**US SIC:** 8211  **UK SIC:** 93200
**Employees:** 101

DUNS 21-779-8406
## St Stephens Centre Management
110 Ferensway, Hull, North Humberside HU2 8LN
**Tel:** 01482313960
**Web:** www.ststephens-hull.com
**Estd:** 2011 Proprietorship
**Line of Business:** Shopping centres
**Proprietor:** J Harris
**US SIC:** 6531  **UK SIC:** 83400
**Employees:** 1,500

DUNS 21-596-0265
## St Stephens Health Centre
William Place, London E3 5ED
**Tel:** 02089801760
**Estd:** 2001 Partnership
**Line of Business:** Public sector hospital activities, including nhs trusts
**Partner:** A Ross
**Responsibilities**
**Senior:** Balvinder Kullar (Practice Manager)
**US SIC:** 8062  **UK SIC:** 95100
**Employees:** 31

DUNS 21-782-6617
## St Teresa's Catholic Primary School
Easthampstead Road, Wokingham, Berkshire RG40 2EB
**Tel:** 01189784310
**Web:** www.st-teresas.wokingham.sch.uk
**Estd:** 1991 Proprietorship
**Line of Business:** Schools (local authority)
**Proprietor:** Mrs L Adams
**Responsibilities**
**Senior:** Nikki Peters (Acting Head)
**US SIC:** 8211  **UK SIC:** 93200
**Employees:** 60

DUNS 21-773-6419
## St Teresas Catholic Primary School
Kingsbury Drive, Nottingham, Nottinghamshire NG8 3EP
**Tel:** 01159155762
**Web:** www.stteresasprimaryschool.co.uk
**Estd:** 1992 Proprietorship
**Line of Business:** Schools (foundation)
**Proprietor:** W Milburn
**Responsibilities**
**Senior:** Ann Glynne-Jones (Head Teacher)
**US SIC:** 8211  **UK SIC:** 93200
**Employees:** 50

DUNS 21-596-0268
## St Teresa's Hospice
The Woodlands, 91 Woodland Road, Darlington, County Durham DL3 7UA
**Tel:** 01325254321
**Web:** www.darlingtonhospice.org.uk
**Estd:** 1997 Proprietorship
**Line of Business:** Charities and charitable organisations
**Proprietor:** I Rose
**US SIC:** 8091  **UK SIC:** 95200
**Employees:** 50

DUNS 64-262-6568
## St Teresa's School
Effingham Hill, Dorking, Surrey RH5 6ST
**Web:** www.stteresasschool.com
**Estd:** 1997
**Line of Business:** General secondary education
**Co. Secretary:** Mrs M Prescott
**Responsibilities**
**Senior:** Natalie Blackwell (P A To Head Teacher)
**US SIC:** 8211  **UK SIC:** 93200
**Employees:** 80

DUNS 21-205-6712
## St Theresas Care Centre
St Therese Close, Callington, Cornwall PL17 7QF
**Tel:** 01579-383488
**Web:** www.sttheresas.co.uk
**Estd:** 1986 Proprietorship
**Line of Business:** Medical nursing home activities
**Proprietor:** M Freeland
**Responsibilities**
**Senior:** Carol Meakin (Manager)
**US SIC:** 8051, 6732
**UK SIC:** 95100, 83100
**Bankers:** National Westminster Bank Plc (56-00-63)
**Employees:** 50

DUNS 21-778-4139
## St Theresa's Catholic Primary School
Barwick Road, Leeds, West Yorkshire LS15 8RQ
**Tel:** 01132930240
**Web:** www.st-theresas.leeds.sch.uk
**Estd:** 1953 Partnership
**Line of Business:** Schools (local authority)
**Partners:** J Hutchinson, J Hutchenson
**US SIC:** 8211  **UK SIC:** 93200
**Employees:** 70

DUNS 21-778-7314
## St Thomas Aquinas Secondary School
112 Mitre Road, Glasgow, Lanarkshire G14 9PP
**Tel:** 01415820280
**Web:** www.st-thomasaquinas-sec.glasgow.sch.uk
**Estd:** 2011 Proprietorship
**Line of Business:** Schools (local authority)
**Proprietor:** A Mcsorley
**US SIC:** 8211  **UK SIC:** 93200
**Employees:** 110

DUNS 21-159-1511
## St Thomas Moor R C High School
Lynn Road, North Shields, Tyne and Wear NE29 8LF
**Tel:** 01912588340
**Web:** www.stmschool.org.uk
**Line of Business:** Schools (foundation)
**Director:** J Marshall
**Responsibilities**
**Finance:** Anthony Gollings (Director of Finance and Resour)
**Admin:** Linda McArdle (Head Pa)
**IT:** Anna Merchant (Head of IT)
**HR:** Anthony Gollings (Director of Finance and Resour)
**US SIC:** 8211  **UK SIC:** 93200
**Employees:** 100

DUNS 21-353-3198
## St Thomas Moore Catholic Comphrensive G M School
Darlaston Lane, Bilston, West Midlands WV14 7BL
**Tel:** 01902-368798
**Web:** www.st-thomasmore.walsall.sch.uk
**Estd:** 1971
**Line of Business:** Schools (local authority)
**Proprietor:** S Flynn
**Responsibilities**
**Senior:** Peter Mayland (Head Teacher)
**IT:** Gary Wood (Head of IT)
**US SIC:** 8211  **UK SIC:** 93200
**Employees:** 137

DUNS 21-772-6171
## St Thomas More R C Va High School
Danebank Avenue, Crewe, Cheshire CW2 8AE
**Tel:** 01270568014
**Web:** www.st-thomasmore.cheshire.sch.uk
**Estd:** 1997 Partnership
**Line of Business:** General secondary education
**Partners:** E Mchugh, P Walters
**Responsibilities**
**Senior:** Edward McHugh (Partner)
**US SIC:** 8211  **UK SIC:** 93200
**Employees:** 50

DUNS 42-366-8391
## St Thomas of Canterbury P T A
Horeshoe Lane West, Merrow, Guildford, Surrey GU1 2SX
**Web:** www.st-thomas.surrey.sch.uk
**Proprietorship**
**Line of Business:** Elementary & Secondary Schools

**Proprietor:** K Gawley
**US SIC:** 8211 **UK SIC:** 93200
**Employees:** 52

DUNS 22-449-0933
## St Thomas the Apostle College
Hollydale Road, London SE15 2EB
**Tel:** 020-7639-0106
**Web:** www.stac.uk.com
**Estd:** 1973 Proprietorship
**Line of Business:** Schools (local authority)
**Proprietor:** Dr F Tope
**US SIC:** 8211 **UK SIC:** 93200
**Employees:** 100

DUNS 45-816-9653
## St Vincent De Paul Society (England & Wales)
9 Larcom Street, London SE17 1RX
**Tel:** 02077033030
**Web:** www.svp-tyne.org.uk
**Reg No:** 3174679 **Estd:** 2005 Private Company Limited By Guarantee
**Line of Business:** Activities of professional organisations
**Trading Style:** The St Vincent De Paul
**Directors:** M Reynolds, P A Greenidge, M Walmsley, D Ion, Mrs A Harris, M Brady, I L Mawdsley, A G Abel
**Responsibilities**
**Senior:** Richard Palmi *(Director)*, Ingrid Phillips *(Director)*
**Branches:** St Vincent De Paul Society (England & Wales), 51 Mill Dam, South Shields, Tyne and Wear NE33 1EQ
**US SIC:** 7399 **UK SIC:** 83954
**Auditors:** Kingston Smith
**Bankers:** HSBC Bank plc (40-29-08)

| | 31-03-14 | 31-03-13 | 31-03-12 |
|---|---|---|---|
| TO | 8,440,091 | 8,156,447 | 7,895,033 |
| P/L | 239,882 | (288,725) | 197,033 |
| NW | 8,750,069 | 8,518,823 | 8,279,578 |
| WC | 4,799,470 | 4,593,352 | 4,331,772 |
| Emp. | 162 | 159 | 132 |

DUNS 21-163-5128
## St Vincents College
Mill Lane, Gosport, Hampshire PO12 4QA
**Tel:** 023-9258-8311
**Web:** www.stvincent.ac.uk
**Estd:** 1994
**Line of Business:** Further education schools and colleges
**Director:** Mrs L Lee
**Responsibilities**
**Senior:** Steven Wain *(Principal)*
**Admin:** Chris Bilton *(Office Manager)*
**IT:** Rob Ackroyd *(IT Network Manager)*
**US SIC:** 8299, 8249
**UK SIC:** 93300
**Employees:** 200

DUNS 21-206-9541
## St Vincent's Hospice
Midtown Road, Johnstone, Renfrewshire PA9 1AF
**Tel:** 01505705635
**Web:** www.svh.co.uk
**Estd:** 1988
**Line of Business:** Hospices
**Trading Style:** S V H Trading
**Partners:** A Watson, Mrs J Young, S Carr, J Mooney
**Responsibilities**
**Senior:** Kate Lennon *(Chief Executive Officer)*, Jackie Young *(Managing Director)*
**Purchasing:** Wilma Jamieson *(Purchasing Manager)*
**Branches:** St Vincent's Hospice, 26 Cochrane Street, Glasgow, Lanarkshire G78 1RF
**US SIC:** 8091 **UK SIC:** 95200
**Bankers:** Bank Of Scotland (80-16-53)
**Employees:** 61

DUNS 34-571-8563
## St Vincent's Hospital
Wiltshire Lane, Pinner, Middlesex HA5 2NB
**Tel:** 02088724900 **Fax:** 020-8866-6512
**Web:** www.svnh.co.uk
**Reg No:** 2721809 **Estd:** 1992 Private Limited Company
**Line of Business:** Medical nursing home activities
**Directors:** F G Davern, A J Edmondson, N G Ransley, Ms J A Scott, J C Steinitz
**Co. Secretary:** Jonathan Lipscomb
**Responsibilities**
**Senior:** Shiria Halsey *(Home Manager)*
**US SIC:** 8051 **UK SIC:** 95100
**Auditors:** Kingston Smith

**Bankers:** Barclays Bank Plc (20-03-80)

| | 31-03-14 | 31-03-13 | 31-03-12 |
|---|---|---|---|
| TO | 3,024,127 | 2,980,739 | 2,926,385 |
| P/L | 282,095 | 270,253 | 254,444 |
| NW | 8,284,259 | 8,014,312 | 7,725,431 |
| WC | 735,607 | 927,071 | 702,282 |
| Emp. | 82 | 82 | 82 |

DUNS 21-358-8697
## St Vincents Housing Association
Metropolitan House, 20 Brindley Road, Manchester M16 9HQ
**Tel:** 01617722120
**Web:** www.svha.co.uk
**Estd:** 2011
**Line of Business:** Housing associations societies trusts & co-operatives
**Director:** P Smith
**Responsibilities**
**Senior:** Charlotte Norman *(Manager)*
**Finance:** Annie Huang *(Financial Director)*
**Branches:** St Vincents Homecare and Repair, 41 Bury Road, Haslingden, BB4 5PG Lancashire
**US SIC:** 6531, 7399
**UK SIC:** 83400, 83954
**Auditors:** Grant Thornton UK LLP

| | 31-12-13 | 31-12-10 |
|---|---|---|
| TO | 18,668,639 | 14,769,245 |
| P/L | 2,020,132 | 2,381,154 |
| NW | 14,288,243 | 15,978,063 |
| WC | (170,119) | (993,839) |
| Emp. | 129 | 149 |

DUNS 23-174-0341
## St Vincents Housing Association Ltd
1st Floor Metropolitan House, Manchester M16 9HQ
**Tel:** 08456066565 **Fax:** 01617722121
**Web:** www.svha.co.uk
**Reg No:** 0019947IP **VAT No:** 603740763
**Estd:** 1999 Friendly Society
**Line of Business:** Housing associations societies trusts & co-operatives
**Principals:** L Egan *(Chairman)*, C J Harris, G Pelham, A Sudlow, Mrs P Diskin, P Cusack, E Birch, A Stephenson
**Co. Secretary:** Hugh Barrett
**Responsibilities**
**Senior:** James Alker *(Director)*, Campbell Benjamin *(Director)*, Sarah Mansfield *(Board Member)*, Charlie Norman *(Chief Executive Officer)*, Geoffrey Tarpey *(Director)*, John Towers *(Chairman)*
**Finance:** Claire Harris *(Finance/IT Director)*, Annie Huang *(Financial Manager)*
**Marketing:** Damien Mason *(Development Manager)*
**IT:** Joanne Tucker *(Project Manager)*
**Operations:** Maria Crompton *(Production and Operations Mana)*, Asif Iqbal *(Operations Director)*
**Branches:** St Vincents Housing Association Ltd, Charles Forbes Court, Mersey Street, Warrington, Cheshire WA1 2BH
**US SIC:** 8699 **UK SIC:** 96902
**Auditors:** Mitchel Charlesworth
**Bankers:** The Royal Bank Of Scotland Plc (16-14-17)
**Employees:** 150
**Turnover:** £15,568,912

DUNS 21-770-9431
## St Vincent's Rc Primary School
Edenfield Road, Rochdale, Lancashire OL12 7QL
**Tel:** 01706642469
**Web:** www.st-vincents.rochdale.sch.uk
**Estd:** 2011 Proprietorship
**Line of Business:** Schools (local authority)
**Proprietor:** S Callaghan
**Responsibilities**
**Senior:** Stephen Callaghan *(Head Teacher)*
**US SIC:** 8211 **UK SIC:** 93200
**Employees:** 50

DUNS 21-159-1602
## St Vincents School for the Blind & Partially Sighted
Yew Tree Lane, Liverpool, Merseyside L12 9HN
**Tel:** 0151-228-9968
**Web:** www.stvin.com
**Estd:** 1997
**Line of Business:** Schools (special)
**Principals:** A Macquarrie, S Robberts, Mrs L Caroll
**Responsibilities**
**Senior:** A MacQuarrie *(Principal)*
**US SIC:** 8299, 8211
**UK SIC:** 93300, 93200
**Employees:** 60

DUNS 21-731-9445
## St Wilfrid's Church of England Academy
Duckworth Street, Blackburn, Lancashire BB2 2JR
**Tel:** 01254604000
**Web:** www.saintwilfrids.co.uk
**Reg No:** 7671404 **Estd:** 2011 Private Company Limited By Guarantee
**Line of Business:** General secondary education
**Directors:** Mrs M E Haworth, V M Edge, M A Hodson, Mrs S Pitman, J H Venables, M Stanley, J Leigh, Mrs A Orme
**Co. Secretary:** Ms Caroline Holt
**Responsibilities**
**Senior:** Christopher Armstrong *(Director)*, Aileen Cross *(Director)*, Heather Henderson *(Director)*, Catherine Huddleston *(Director)*, Gordon Moulding *(Director)*, Janet Vials *(Director)*
**US SIC:** 8211 **UK SIC:** 93200
**Bankers:** The Royal Bank Of Scotland Plc (16-13-26)

| | 31-08-13 | 31-08-12 |
|---|---|---|
| TO | 9,835,558 | 35,665,040 |
| P/L | 682,210 | 24,699,950 |
| NW | 25,237,160 | 24,492,950 |
| WC | 3,127,158 | 1,883,057 |
| Emp. | 232 | 222 |

DUNS 28-944-1685
## St Wilfrid's Hospice (Eastbourne)
2-4 Mill Gap Road, Eastbourne, East Sussex BN21 2FF
**Tel:** 01323644500 **Fax:** 01323530587
**Web:** www.st-wilfrids.co.uk
**Reg No:** 1594410 **Estd:** 1987 Private Company Limited By Guarantee
**Line of Business:** Hospices
**Directors:** Mrs K L Planterose, A D Bodkin, A Breeze, Mrs R Ross, N A Elphick, Mrs M Carter-Lee
**Co. Secretary:** Ms Kara Bishop
**Branches:** St Wilfrid's Hospice (Eastbourne), 11 Broad Street, Seaford, East Sussex BN25 1LS
**US SIC:** 8091 **UK SIC:** 95200
**Auditors:** Price & Co
**Bankers:** Barclays Bank Plc (20-27-91)

| | 31-03-14 | 31-03-13 | 31-03-12 |
|---|---|---|---|
| TO | 5,709,529 | 5,485,255 | 5,363,220 |
| P/L | 526,659 | 1,077,219 | 1,481,423 |
| NW | 13,440,515 | 12,913,856 | 11,836,637 |
| WC | 1,579,998 | 2,295,166 | 6,720,655 |
| Emp. | 143 | 131 | 119 |

DUNS 57-840-4253 **Exp**
## Sta International Ltd
(**Subsidiary of:** Sta Credit Corp)
Colman House, King Street, Maidstone, Kent ME14 1DN
**Tel:** 01622914967 **Fax:** 01622-600396
**Web:** www.stainternational.com
**Reg No:** 2893487 **VAT No:** 646003171
**Estd:** 1994 Private Limited Company
**Line of Business:** Credit reporting and collection agency activities
**Trading Style:** Sta Credit Corporation, Sta Graydon
**Issued Capital:** £333,333
**Directors:** C D Thomas, J Tulchin
**Co. Secretary:** Matthew Quinn
**Responsibilities**
**Sales:** Miles Wybourn *(Sales Manager)*
**US SIC:** 7321 **UK SIC:** 83954
**Auditors:** Perrys

| | 30-06-14 | 30-06-13 | 30-06-12 |
|---|---|---|---|
| TA | 1,371,751 | 1,488,540 | 1,421,402 |
| NW | 826,889 | 787,558 | 710,182 |
| WC | 796,579 | 743,371 | 661,992 |

DUNS 22-714-3708 **Exp**
## Sta Travel Ltd
(**Subsidiary of:** Diethelm Keller Holding Ag)
Priory House, 6 Wrights Lane, Kensington, London W8 6TA
**Tel:** 08701606070 **Fax:** 02073680075
**Web:** www.statravel.co.uk
**Reg No:** 1263330 **VAT No:** 577018231
**Estd:** 1976 Private Limited Company
**Line of Business:** Activities of travel agencies
**Export Markets:** France; Italy; S America
**Issued Capital:** £5,305,100
**Directors:** J Constable, S A Jenkins, P J Maine
**Branches:** Sta Travel Ltd, Bradbury House, 12 Shakespeare Street, Nottingham, Nottinghamshire NG1 4FQ
**US SIC:** 4722 **UK SIC:** 77001
**Auditors:** PricewaterhouseCoopers LLP
**Bankers:** HSBC Bank plc (40-04-07)

| | 31-12-13 | 31-12-12 | 31-12-11 |
|---|---|---|---|
| TO | 25,231,000 | 23,394,000 | 23,390,000 |
| P/L | 35,000 | 26,000 | 276,000 |
| NW | 10,714,000 | 10,993,000 | 10,787,000 |
| WC | 9,117,000 | 9,575,000 | 9,194,000 |
| Emp. | 462 | 450 | 484 |

DUNS 42-433-9765
## The Stable Family Home Trust
Bisterne, Ringwood, Hampshire BH24 3BN
**Tel:** 01425-478043
**Web:** www.stablefamilies.co.uk
**Reg No:** 4421606 **Estd:** 2002 Private Company Limited By Guarantee
**Line of Business:** Charities and charitable organisations
**Directors:** Ms S Pepper, S F Farrow, F L Tucker, G M Mills, D A Rule, B J Rothwell, C A Clifford
**Responsibilities**
**Senior:** Jan Mills *(CEO)*, David Mowinski *(Day Service Manager)*
**Finance:** Sam Atter *(Finance Manager)*
**Marketing:** Gen Mills *(Manager)*
**Admin:** Nathan Andrews *(Head of HR and Administration)*
**HR:** Nathan Andrews *(Head of HR and Administration)*
**Health & Safety:** Ben Swan *(Service Manager - Health & Wel)*
**Operations:** David Mowinski *(Day Service Manager)*, Colin Waters *(Operations Director)*
**US SIC:** 8321 **UK SIC:** 96111
**Bankers:** Lloyds TSB Bank plc (30-13-42)

| | 31-03-14 | 31-03-13 | 31-03-12 |
|---|---|---|---|
| TO | 2,140,546 | 2,112,567 | 2,079,345 |
| P/L | (70,322) | (55,258) | (22,287) |
| NW | 1,830,454 | 1,900,776 | 1,956,034 |
| WC | 598,667 | 644,612 | 644,404 |
| Emp. | 67 | 67 | 64 |

DUNS 22-647-0946
## Stace
271-273 High Street, Epping, Essex CM16 4DA
**Tel:** 01992565565
**Web:** www.stace.co.uk
**Estd:** 1960 Partnership
**Line of Business:** Technical testing and analysis
**Trading Style:** Stace Quantity Surveying
**Principals:** D A Harrison, D A Ward *(Partner)*, B D Sheppard *(Partner)*, M Dick *(Partner)*, G Crawley *(Partner)*, R Bassett *(Partner)*, G J Fletcher *(Partner)*, R C Gough *(Partner)*
**Responsibilities**
**Senior:** P Stratton *(Partner)*
**Branches:** Stace, Rose House, 80 East Street, Leeds, West Yorkshire LS9 8EE
**US SIC:** 7397 **UK SIC:** 83702
**Bankers:** Barclays Bank Plc (20-82-94)
**Employees:** 150

DUNS 22-188-4062
## Stacey's Coaches Ltd
Millrace Road, Carlisle, Cumbria CA2 5RS
**Tel:** 01228511127 **Fax:** 0128524467
**Web:** www.staceys-coaches.co.uk
**Reg No:** 4206635 **Estd:** 2001 Private Limited Company
**Line of Business:** Bus operators and stations
**Issued Capital:** £100
**Director:** Ms C Barnes
**Co. Secretary:** Barrie Barnes
**Responsibilities**
**Senior:** Carroll Barnes *(Proprietor)*
**US SIC:** 4119 **UK SIC:** 72200
**Bankers:** The Royal Bank Of Scotland Plc (16-15-47)

| | 31-08-13 | 31-08-12 | 31-08-11 |
|---|---|---|---|
| TA | 1,348,746 | 1,792,837 | 2,368,951 |
| NW | 70,435 | 79,735 | 402,752 |
| WC | (530,519) | (650,681) | (510,125) |

DUNS 21-719-3110
## Stackhouse Fisher Ltd
New House Bedford Road, Guildford, Surrey GU1 4SJ
**Tel:** 01483407440
**Web:** www.stackhouse.co.uk
**Reg No:** 7575168 **Estd:** 2011 Private Limited Company
**Line of Business:** Activities auxiliary to insurance and pension funding
**Issued Capital:** £200
**Directors:** J M Cary, D W Breger, A R Parfitt, S A Scahill, J I Agnew
**Co. Secretary:** Christopher Milam
**US SIC:** 6411 **UK SIC:** 83200

| | 31-12-13 | 31-12-12 | 31-12-11 |
|---|---|---|---|
| TO | 136,567 | 42,386 | 20,138 |
| P/L | 30,794 | (8,425) | (44,947) |
| NW | (22,378) | (53,172) | (44,747) |
| WC | (22,378) | (53,172) | (44,747) |
| Emp. | N/A | 1 | 2 |

DUNS 22-263-3724

## Stackhouse Poland Holdings Ltd

Exchange House, 33 Station Road, Liphook, Hampshire GU30 7DW
**Tel:** 01462725388
**Web:** www.stackhouse.co.uk
**Reg No:** 4281378 **Estd:** 2001 Private Limited Company
**Line of Business:** Insurance companies and agents
**Issued Capital:** £406,093
**Directors:** T D Johnson, J I Agnew, J M Cary
**Co. Secretary:** Christopher Milam
**Responsibilities**
**Senior:** Caroline Ellicott *(Manager)*, Keith Hester *(Manager)*
**US SIC:** 6411 **UK SIC:** 83200
**Bankers:** Bank Of Scotland (12-09-69)

| | 31-12-13 | 31-12-12 | 31-12-11 |
|---|---|---|---|
| TO | 14,785,768 | 10,124,024 | 9,279,394 |
| P/L | 1,822,576 | 1,875,493 | 1,473,265 |
| NW | (6,493,265) | (134,148) | (1,516,016) |
| WC | 359,628 | 1,104,379 | 351,666 |
| Emp. | 161 | 106 | 105 |

DUNS 21-843-2825

## Stackright North West Ltd

West Gillibrands Industrial Esta, Gardiners Place, Skelmersdale, Lancashire WN8 9SP
**Tel:** 01005455000
**Reg No:** 8097420 **Estd:** 2012 Private Limited Company
**Line of Business:** Management activities of other non-financial holding companies not elsewhere classified
**Issued Capital:** £100
**Directors:** D Jones, M Monnelly
**Co. Secretary:** Mrs Deborah Jones
**US SIC:** 6711 **UK SIC:** 83962
**Bankers:** National Westminster Bank Plc (60-70-08)

| | 31-01-14 | 31-01-13 |
|---|---|---|
| TO | 8,370,287 | N/A |
| P/L | 1,586,391 | N/A |
| NW | 1,423,269 | 100 |
| WC | 498,820 | N/A |
| Emp. | 80 | N/A |

DUNS 21-827-1666 **Imp-Exp**

## Stadco Ltd

**(Subsidiary of:** Stadco Automotive Ltd)
Harlescott Lane, Harlescott, Shrewsbury, Shropshire SY1 3AS
**Tel:** 01743462227 **Fax:** 01743447709
**Web:** www.stadco.co.uk
**Reg No:** 0008614 **VAT No:** 160468272
**Estd:** 1864 Private Limited Company
**Line of Business:** Manufacture of other special purpose machinery not elsewhere classified
**Export Markets:** E U
**Export Sales:** £5,891,000
**Issued Capital:** £3,030,020
**Directors:** C P Fisher, M R Hawkin, G I Macleod
**Co. Secretary:** Michael Hayhurst
**Responsibilities**
**Senior:** Dermot Sterne *(Manager)*
**IT:** Chas Parker *(IT Manager)*, Karen Shepherd *(IT Service Manager)*
**HR:** Stan Meiklem *(Human Resources Director)*
**Health & Safety:** Nigel Disney *(Health & Safety Manager)*
**Facilities:** Martin Noblet *(Maintenance Manager)*
**Engineering:** Heather Quigley *(Senior Quality Engineering Man)*
**Branches:** Stadco Ltd, Queensway, Hortonwood Industrial Estate, Telford, Shropshire TF1 7LL
**US SIC:** 3713 **UK SIC:** 35201
**Auditors:** PricewaterhouseCoopers LLP
**Bankers:** Bank Of Scotland (12-05-65)

| | 31-12-13 | 31-12-12 | 31-12-11 |
|---|---|---|---|
| TO | 166,744,000 | 172,202,000 | 149,971,000 |
| P/L | 12,991,000 | 9,417,000 | 7,304,000 |
| NW | 30,709,000 | 21,066,000 | 14,232,000 |
| WC | 35,348,000 | 18,087,000 | 10,886,000 |
| Emp. | 902 | 884 | 829 |

DUNS 21-566-1369

## Stademos Hotel

42 Park Road, London N8 8TD
**Tel:** 02083484334
**Proprietorship**
**Line of Business:** Hotels
**Proprietor:** S Demosthenous
**Responsibilities**
**Senior:** Kyriakos Pyrillos *(Manager)*
**US SIC:** 7011 **UK SIC:** 66500
**Employees:** 60

DUNS 21-043-8410

## Stadium Cars

27 St Johns Road, Wembley, Middlesex HA9 7HU
**Tel:** 02089-001111
**Web:** www.angelcars.com
**Estd:** 1990 Proprietorship
**Line of Business:** Taxi operation
**Proprietor:** S Shan
**Responsibilities**
**Senior:** Sabaratnam Shanmuganathan *(Proprietor)*
**US SIC:** 4121, 7512
**UK SIC:** 72200, 84801
**Employees:** 50

DUNS 21-612-6649 **Imp-Exp**

## Stadium Group Plc

Stephen House, Brenda Road Tofts Farm Industrial Estate, West, Hartlepool, Cleveland TS25 2BQ
**Tel:** 01429-852500 **Fax:** 01429852798
**Web:** www.stadium-electronics.com
**Reg No:** 0236394 **Estd:** 1929 Public Limited Company
**Line of Business:** Electronic equipment (assembly)
**Export Markets:** European Union (E U); U S A
**Export Sales:** £13,393,000
**Trading Style:** Stadium Electronic Controls
**Issued Capital:** £1,477,870
**Directors:** N P Brayshaw, C S Peppiatt, Ms J E Estell, C J Gill
**Co. Secretary:** Ms Joanne Estell
**Responsibilities**
**Senior:** Antony Inskip *(Manager)*, Ken Leung *(Manager)*, Stephen Phipson *(Proprietor)*
**Marketing:** Stacey Vinther *(Marketing Manager)*
**Operations:** Stewart Walton *(Customer Services Manager)*
**Purchasing:** Katrina Hickey *(Purchasing Manager)*
**Branches:** Stadium Group Plc, Bryant Ave, Romford, Essex RM3 0AP
**US SIC:** 3643 **UK SIC:** 34203
**Auditors:** PKF (UK) LLP
**Bankers:** Bank Of Scotland (12-11-03)

| | 31-12-13 | 31-12-12 | 31-12-11 |
|---|---|---|---|
| TO | 42,215,000 | 40,989,000 | 44,938,000 |
| P/L | 430,000 | 1,770,000 | 3,960,000 |
| NW | 2,836,000 | 2,777,000 | 7,448,000 |
| WC | 7,253,000 | 8,147,000 | 9,485,000 |
| Emp. | 792 | 885 | 881 |

DUNS 21-622-4299 **Imp**

## Stadium United Wireless Ltd

28 Hardwick Grange Melford Court, Warrington, Cheshire WA1 4RZ
**Tel:** 01925838300
**Web:** www.unitedems.co.uk
**Reg No:** 7030729 **Estd:** 2009 Private Limited Company
**Line of Business:** Manufacture of electronic valves and tubes and other electronic components
**Trading Style:** United E M S
**Issued Capital:** £2,000
**Directors:** C S Peppiatt, A J Mcfadden, Ms J E Estell, C A Helm
**Co. Secretary:** Ms Joanne Estell
**US SIC:** 3679 **UK SIC:** 34542

| | 30-09-13 | 30-09-12 | 30-09-11 |
|---|---|---|---|
| TA | 2,250,470 | 2,000,249 | 1,050,427 |
| NW | 313,919 | 251,718 | 141,222 |
| WC | 102,204 | (73,535) | (97,734) |

DUNS 29-666-5151

## Staff Management Ltd

**(Subsidiary of:** August Equity Partners Ii A)
1 Suffolk Way, Sevenoaks, Kent TN13 1YL
**Tel:** 01732-779353
**Web:** www.activeassistance.com
**Reg No:** 1992626 **Estd:** 1986 Private Limited Company
**Line of Business:** Other human health activities
**Trading Style:** Active Assistance
**Issued Capital:** £200
**Directors:** E M Nabi, S M Booty, D Jackson
**US SIC:** 8091, 8321
**UK SIC:** 95200, 96111
**Auditors:** Hazlewoods LLP
**Bankers:** HSBC Bank plc (40-00-00)

| | 31-03-14 | 31-03-13 | 31-03-12 |
|---|---|---|---|
| TO | 21,766,398 | 18,714,715 | 16,220,943 |
| P/L | 4,609,336 | 4,379,816 | 3,339,129 |
| NW | 3,962,192 | 2,833,204 | 1,763,265 |
| WC | 8,756,724 | 7,473,933 | 4,219,801 |
| Emp. | 731 | 615 | 572 |

DUNS 73-849-1054

## Staffcare Ltd

Leatherhead House, Station Road, Leatherhead, Surrey KT22 7FG
**Tel:** 08706001296
**Web:** www.staffcare.net
**Reg No:** 5104223 **Estd:** 2004 Private Limited Company
**Line of Business:** Corporate promotional products
**Issued Capital:** £600,164
**Directors:** G Jarvis, M L Timmins, Mrs S C Turvey, N M Stevens, R A Sieber, P J Hollingdale
**Co. Secretary:** Mrs Rebecca Butcher
**Responsibilities**
**Senior:** Andrew Thorn *(Manager)*
**US SIC:** 7379 **UK SIC:** 83940
**Bankers:** Barclays Bank Plc (20-29-90)

| | 31-12-13 | 30-06-13 | 30-12-12 |
|---|---|---|---|
| TO | 2,528,370 | 5,628,265 | 5,663,029 |
| P/L | 191,285 | 1,334,565 | 1,061,144 |
| NW | 1,757,784 | 925,450 | (409,115) |
| WC | 2,073,728 | 827,861 | 1,345,997 |
| Emp. | 55 | N/A | N/A |

DUNS 21-751-3344

## Staffgroup Ltd

First Floor 135 Park Street, London SE1 9EA
**Tel:** 02078030606
**Web:** www.staffgroup.com
**Reg No:** 7817905 **Estd:** 2011 Private Limited Company
**Line of Business:** Labour recruitment and provision of personnel
**Export Sales:** £35,609,415
**Issued Capital:** £7,260
**Directors:** P J Flynn, M S Znowski
**Co. Secretary:** Mark Znowski
**US SIC:** 7361 **UK SIC:** 83954
**Auditors:** Baker Tilly UK Audit LLP

| | 31-12-13 | 31-12-12 |
|---|---|---|
| TO | 42,487,771 | 34,230,329 |
| P/L | 2,343,584 | 2,180,731 |
| NW | 3,742,872 | 2,614,782 |
| WC | 3,670,532 | 2,515,993 |
| Emp. | 99 | 83 |

DUNS 77-898-0313

## The Staffing Group Ltd

Forster House, Hatherton Road, Walsall, West Midlands WS1 1XZ
**Tel:** 01922-615488
**Web:** www.extrapersonnel.com
**Reg No:** 5801688 **Estd:** 2006 Private Limited Company
**Line of Business:** Labour recruitment and provision of personnel
**Issued Capital:** £9,001,000
**Directors:** S P Price, J C Mcgrail, R Robinson
**Co. Secretary:** Mrs Carole Price
**US SIC:** 7361, 7399
**UK SIC:** 83954
**Auditors:** Baldwins (Walsall) Ltd

| | 30-11-13 | 30-11-12 | 30-11-11 |
|---|---|---|---|
| TO | 130,676,771 | 103,870,648 | 94,943,460 |
| P/L | 932,162 | 522,017 | 507,554 |
| NW | 1,618,924 | 600,868 | 23,457 |
| WC | 169,897 | (393,470) | (579,800) |
| Emp. | 218 | 191 | 181 |

DUNS 71-886-2464

## Staffline Group Plc

19 - 20 The Triangle, Nottingham, Nottinghamshire NG2 1AE
**Tel:** 01582414092
**Web:** www.staffline.co.uk
**Reg No:** 5268636 **Estd:** 2012 Public Limited Company
**Line of Business:** Employment and recruitment companies and consultants
**Trading Style:** Staffline Group
**Issued Capital:** £2,287,723
**Directors:** Dame C Braddock, A J Hogarth, J R Crabtree, Mrs D J Martyn, E Barker, P N Ledgard
**Co. Secretary:** Phillip Ledgard
**Responsibilities**
**Senior:** Mark Bagshaw *(Manager)*, Matthew Breed *(Regional Manager)*
**Finance:** Dan Carpenter *(Account Manager)*, Terri Peebles *(Account Manager)*, Adrian Walsh *(Accountant)*
**Sales:** Craig Brittain *(Sales Executive)*
**Branches:** Staffline Group Plc, 237 Queens Garden Business Centre, 31 Iron Markey, Newcastle-Under-Lyme, Newcastle, Staffordshire ST5 1RP
**US SIC:** 7361 **UK SIC:** 83954
**Auditors:** Grant Thornton UK LLP
**Bankers:** Bank Of Scotland (12-09-26)

| | 31-12-13 | 31-12-12 | 31-12-11 |
|---|---|---|---|
| TO | 416,193,000 | 366,980,000 | 288,303,000 |
| P/L | 8,564,000 | 8,521,000 | 7,534,000 |
| NW | 10,774,000 | 5,847,000 | 1,056,000 |
| WC | 18,582,000 | 11,639,000 | 5,120,000 |
| Emp. | 807 | 693 | 498 |

DUNS 23-608-9020

## Stafforce Personnel Ltd

**(Subsidiary of:** Nicholas Associates Ltd)
Reginald Arthur House, 2-8 Percy Street, Rotherham, South Yorkshire S65 1ED
**Tel:** 01709-377177 **Fax:** 01709370037
**Web:** www.stafforce.co.uk
**Reg No:** 3606174 **Estd:** 1984 Private Limited Company
**Line of Business:** Employment and recruitment companies and consultants
**Trading Style:** Stafforce Recruitment
**Issued Capital:** £1,004
**Directors:** N Cragg, P M Brammer, B J Allen, A N Boorman
**Co. Secretary:** Mrs Marie Cragg
**Responsibilities**
**Senior:** Nick Clark *(Chairman)*
**Branches:** Stafforce Personnel Ltd, 17 Whitefriargate, Hull, North Humberside HU1 2ER
**US SIC:** 7392, 7361
**UK SIC:** 83951, 83954
**Auditors:** BDO Stoy Hayward

| | 31-12-13 | 31-12-12 | 31-12-11 |
|---|---|---|---|
| TO | 52,387,609 | 51,674,125 | 43,218,415 |
| P/L | (369,182) | 559,678 | 111,321 |
| NW | 1,855,350 | 2,053,462 | 1,296,699 |
| WC | 609,895 | 838,072 | 15,862 |
| Emp. | 3,376 | 4,594 | 3,806 |

DUNS 21-615-7665

## The Stafford

Blue Ball Yard, St James's, London SW1A 1ND
**Tel:** 08719713361
**Estd:** 2011
**Line of Business:** Hotels
**Responsibilities**
**Senior:** Christine Hodder *(Manager)*
**US SIC:** 7011 **UK SIC:** 66500
**Employees:** 120

DUNS 21-749-8794

## Stafford & Rural Homes

1 Parker Court, Staffordshire Technology Park, Stafford, Staffordshire ST18 0WP
**Tel:** 08001114554
**Web:** www.sarh.co.uk
**Estd:** 2005
**Line of Business:** Non-charitable social work activities with accommodation
**Principals:** J Kemp *(Chairman)*, Mrs P Evans-Nixon *(Chairman)*, Ms K Armitage
**Responsibilities**
**Health & Safety:** Clive Gill *(Facilities Manager)*, Kathryn Ing *(Facilities Manager)*
**Facilities:** Clive Gill *(Facilities Manager)*, Kathryn Ing *(Facilities Manager)*
**US SIC:** 8321 **UK SIC:** 96111
**Employees:** 80

DUNS 22-747-6934

## Stafford Borough Council

Civic Centre, Riverside, Stafford, Staffordshire ST16 3AQ
**Tel:** 01785619000 **Fax:** 01785619119
**Web:** www.staffordbc.gov.uk
**Estd:** 1974 Incorporate By Act Of Parliament
**Line of Business:** Pest control
**Trading Style:** Longhope House Sheltered Housing, Kingston Resource & Development Centre
**Principals:** I Thompson, M Heenan
**Responsibilities**
**Senior:** Howard Thomas *(head service)*
**Marketing:** Will Conaghan *(Communications Manager)*
**Operations:** Ted Manders *(Head of Planning and Regenerat)*
**Branches:** Stafford Borough Council, Burton Upon Trent Registry Office, Rangemoor House, Burton-On-Trent, Staffordshire DE14 2ED
**US SIC:** 9121 **UK SIC:** 91110
**Bankers:** National Westminster Bank Plc (01-08-32)
**Employees:** 5

DUNS 23-635-7125

## Stafford College

Earl Street, Stafford, Staffordshire ST16 2QR
**Tel:** 01785223800
**Web:** www.staffordcoll.ac.uk
**VAT No:** 592710236 **Estd:** 1975
**Line of Business:** Further education schools and colleges
**Trading Style:** Stafford College
**Directors:** Ms C Megson, P Jenkins
**Responsibilities**
**IT:** Darren Rollason *(Computer Manager)*
**Health & Safety:** Kim Mantle *(Health & Safety Officer)*
**Facilities:** Paul Hanlon *(Facilities Manager)*
**Branches:** Stafford College, Malt Mill Lane, Salter Street, Stafford, Staffordshire ST16 2JU

**US SIC:** 8221 **UK SIC:** 93100
**Bankers:** Barclays Bank Plc (20-81-00)
**Employees:** 900

DUNS 21-227-3220
## Stafford Group Managers Office
The Combined Court Centre, Victoria Square, Stafford, Staffordshire ST16 2QQ
**Tel:** 01785-610730
**Proprietorship**
**Line of Business:** Justice and judicial activities
**Proprietor:** D Bennett
**Responsibilities**
**Senior:** Jake Greenwood *(Court Manager)*
**US SIC:** 9211 **UK SIC:** 91200
**Employees:** 50

DUNS 28-924-1275 **Imp**
## The Stafford Hotel Ltd
(**Subsidiary of:** Britannia Hospitality Ltd)
St James's Place, London SW1A 1NJ
**Tel:** 020-7493-0111
**Web:** www.kempinski.com
**Reg No:** 1491604 **VAT No:** 325984821
**Estd:** 1980 Private Limited Company
**Line of Business:** Hotels
**Trading Style:** Kempinski, Aztec Hotel, Cottons Hotel
**Issued Capital:** £100,000
**Directors:** M H Bakr-Ibrahim, M L Armitstead
**Co. Secretary:**
Tmf Corporate Administration Ser
**Responsibilities**
**Senior:** Katerina Esakova *(Front of House Manager)*
**Branches:** The Stafford Hotel Ltd, Church Lane, Blackburn, Lancashire BB2 7JL
**US SIC:** 7011 **UK SIC:** 66500
**Auditors:** PricewaterhouseCoopers LLP
**Bankers:** The Royal Bank Of Scotland Plc (16-13-26)

| | 31-12-13 | 31-12-12 | 31-12-11 |
|---|---|---|---|
| TO | 12,354,000 | 12,249,000 | 10,239,000 |
| P/L | (440,000) | (140,000) | (1,205,000) |
| NW | 34,792,000 | 35,141,000 | 35,770,000 |
| WC | (1,162,000) | (3,570,000) | (1,897,000) |
| Emp. | 120 | 128 | 121 |

DUNS 28-847-2400
## Stafford House School of English Ltd
(**Subsidiary of:** Camelot Interco Ltd)
68 New Dover Road, Canterbury, Kent CT1 3LQ
**Tel:** 01227866540
**Web:** www.staffordhouse.com
**Reg No:** 0656294 **Estd:** 1960 Private Limited Company
**Line of Business:** Colleges (higher education)
**Issued Capital:** £1,000
**Directors:** F S Brownlee, Ms R K Fenton, H V Shah
**Co. Secretary:** Mark Stanton
**Branches:** Stafford House School Of English Ltd, 19 New Dover Road, Canterbury, Kent CT1 3AS
**US SIC:** 8249 **UK SIC:** 93300
**Auditors:** Imray & Co
**Bankers:** National Westminster Bank Plc (60-04-27)

| | 31-08-13 | 31-08-12 | 31-08-11 |
|---|---|---|---|
| TO | 5,108,249 | 3,203,694 | 4,098,913 |
| P/L | 157,350 | (355,154) | 117,203 |
| NW | (20,075) | (126,540) | 163,456 |
| WC | (445,315) | (602,464) | (5,243) |
| Emp. | 69 | 67 | 48 |

DUNS 29-757-6837
## Stafford Long & Partners Ltd
107-111 Fleet Street, London EC4A 2AB
**Web:** www.staffordlong.com
**Reg No:** 2020715 **VAT No:** 440476852
**Estd:** 1986 Private Limited Company
**Line of Business:** Employment and recruitment companies and consultants
**Issued Capital:** £6,841
**Managing Director:** P A Stafford
**Co. Secretary:** Miss Barbara Kelly
**US SIC:** 7361 **UK SIC:** 83954
**Auditors:** Gallagher & Co
**Bankers:** Lloyds TSB Bank plc (30-92-45)

| | 30-06-13 | 30-06-12 | 30-06-11 |
|---|---|---|---|
| TA | 1,227,534 | 1,002,249 | 815,153 |
| NW | 541,400 | 497,120 | 454,548 |
| WC | 536,905 | 484,678 | 447,448 |

DUNS 21-616-4087 **Imp-Exp**
## Stafford-Miller Ltd
Broadwater House, 45 Broadwater Road, Welwyn Garden City, Hertfordshire AL7 3AX
**Tel:** 01707356100
**Web:** www.biopark.co.uk
**Reg No:** 0318499 **Estd:** 1936 Private Limited Company
**Line of Business:** Manufacture of perfumes and toilet preparations
**Export Markets:** Europe, Africa, Middle East, Austrailia, Asia and rest of world
**Issued Capital:** £4,599,800
**Directors:** P F Blackburn, Glaxo Group Limited, Edinburgh Pharmaceutical Industr
**Co. Secretary:** Ms Victoria Whyte
**Branches:** Stafford-Miller Ltd, Tamar House, Thornbury Road, Plymouth, Devon PL6 7PP
**US SIC:** 2844, 3841
**UK SIC:** 25820, 37201
**Auditors:** PricewaterhouseCoopers LLP

| | 31-12-13 | 31-12-12 | 31-12-11 |
|---|---|---|---|
| TA | 5,085,000 | 5,071,000 | 5,160,000 |
| P/L | 9,000 | 14,000 | 15,000 |
| NW | 5,075,000 | 5,068,000 | 5,061,000 |
| WC | 5,075,000 | 5,068,000 | 5,061,000 |

DUNS 21-318-3924 **Imp**
## Staffords Ltd
Overbrook Court, Overbrook Lane, Knowsley, Prescot, Merseyside L34 9FB
**Tel:** 01519070027 **Fax:** 0159070028
**Web:** www.staffords.ltd.uk
**Reg No:** 1311369 **Estd:** 1918 Private Limited Company
**Line of Business:** Other manufacturing not elsewhere classified
**Issued Capital:** £5,000
**Principals:** P W Stafford *(Chairman)*, M E Barnett, D Latham
**Co. Secretary:** Mrs Elizabeth Stafford
**Responsibilities**
**Senior:** Dave Brown *(Parts Coordinator)*
**Purchasing:** Dave Brown *(Parts Coordinator)*
**Branches:** Staffords Ltd, 120 Stanstead Rd, London SE23 1BX
**US SIC:** 7379, 7629
**UK SIC:** 83940, 67301
**Auditors:** Michell Charlesworth
**Bankers:** Barclays Bank Plc (20-51-01)

| | 30-06-14 | 30-06-13 | 30-06-12 |
|---|---|---|---|
| TA | 1,346,596 | 1,264,459 | 1,348,171 |
| NW | 747,389 | 695,015 | 659,922 |
| WC | 306,960 | 243,640 | 206,047 |

DUNS 21-580-3530
## Staffordshire and West Midlands Community Rehabilitation Company
5 St Philips Place, Birmingham, West Midlands
**Tel:** 01216-341-300
**Web:** www.swmprobation.gov.uk
**Estd:** 2006 Incorporate By Act Of Parliament
**Line of Business:** Probation services
**Trading Style:** Swm Probation
**Principals:** Dr A Harrison *(Chairman)*, M Madden, P Singh, K James, Mrs B Thomas, Ms H Kemshall, J Ryan, P Singh
**Responsibilities**
**Senior:** Jonathon Parkes *(Senior Probation Officer)*
**Branches:** Staffordshire & Westmidlands Probation Trust, Sheriffs Court, Coventry CV1 3RY 12 Greyfriars Road
**US SIC:** 9121 **UK SIC:** 91110
**Employees:** 2,142

DUNS 21-704-5582
## Staffordshire County Council
1 Staffordshire Place, Stafford, Staffordshire ST16 2LP
**Web:** www.staffordshire.gov.uk
**Estd:** 1900
**Line of Business:** Administration of the state and the economic and social policy of the community
**Principals:** I Lawson *(Chairman)*, P Hunter, I Parry, F Chapman, J Tradewell
**Responsibilities**
**Senior:** Philip Atkins *(Council Chairman)*, Nick Bell *(Chief Executive Officer)*, Julie Castree-Denton *(Manager)*, Alfia Cox *(General Manager)*, Jane Dodd *(General Manager)*, Debbie Holihead *(Manager)*, Jonathan Vining *(Chairman)*
**Finance:** Lee Assiter *(Finance Manager)*
**Marketing:** Louise Clayton *(School Crossing Patrol)*, Mike Grundy *(Manager - Planning, Policy & D)*, Jacqui McKinlay *(Director of Strategy and Custo)*
**Sales:** Donna Barley *(Senior Sales Executive)*
**Admin:** Josephine Bowen *(Administration)*, Sheila Manning *(Superintendent Registrar)*
**IT:** Tim Billings *(IT Manager)*, Vic Falcus *(Head of ICT)*, Becky Fuller *(Network Manager)*, Brian Hawkins *(Senior IT Executive)*, Sander Kristel *(Director of ICT and Chief Info)*
**HR:** Dave Wisher *(Human Resources Manager)*
**Health & Safety:** Clare Hardie *(Community Safety Manager)*, Kevin Wilcox *(Road Safety Officer)*, Irene Williamson *(Road Safety Manager)*
**Facilities:** Becky Murphy *(Safer Communities Development)*, Rosie O'Doherty *(Bidding Housing Manager)*, Michelle Ryan *(Group Manager, Cleaning and Gr)*
**Operations:** John Commins *(Project Manager)*, Dominic Davidson *(Production and Operations Mana)*
**Purchasing:** Chris Ballance *(Procurement Manager - Highways)*, Gail Stephens *(Procurement Officer)*
**Fleet:** Nick Dawson *(Group Manager, Transport Plann)*, Nicola Swinnerton *(Rural Development Manager)*
**Engineering:** Ali Glaisher *(Principal Ecologist)*
**Branches:** Staffordshire County Council, Wedgwood Buildings, Tipping St, Stafford, Staffordshire ST16 2DH
**US SIC:** 9121, 8211, 8091
**UK SIC:** 91110, 93200, 95200
**Bankers:** The Co-Operative Bank Plc (08-90-08)
**Employees:** 615

DUNS 23-260-0577
## Staffordshire Fire & Rescue Services
Pirehill House, Pirehill, Stone, Staffordshire ST15 0BS
**Tel:** 0845-122-1155 **Fax:** 01785898395
**Web:** www.staffordshirefire.gov.uk
**Estd:** 1974 Incorporate By Act Of Parliament
**Line of Business:** Representative office
**Director:** A Doig
**Responsibilities**
**Senior:** Peter Dartford *(Chief Fire Officer)*
**Marketing:** Phillip Gillingham *(Media Manager)*
**HR:** Tim Wareham *(Training Manager)*
**Facilities:** Jeff Spruce *(Maintenance Manager)*
**Branches:** Staffordshire Fire & Rescue Services, Northern Division Headquarters, Lower Bethesda St, Stoke-On-Trent, Staffordshire ST1 3RP
**US SIC:** 9224 **UK SIC:** 91400
**Employees:** 150

DUNS 23-993-7998
## Staffordshire Housing Association Ltd
308 London Road, Stoke-On-Trent, Staffordshire ST4 5AB
**Tel:** 01782744533
**Web:** www.staffshousing.org.uk
**Reg No:** 0017093IP **Estd:** 1988 Friendly Society
**Line of Business:** Housing associations societies trusts & co-operatives
**Principals:** F W James *(Chairman)*, S M Shaw, R A Kirby, J Baxter, D P Johnstone, D Small, Ms M Hopley, S Russell
**Responsibilities**
**Sales:** Barry Pitts *(Business Development Director)*
**Operations:** Joanne Betts *(Project Manager)*
**US SIC:** 8321 **UK SIC:** 96111
**Auditors:** Neville Russell
**Bankers:** The Co-Operative Bank Plc (08-90-09)
**Employees:** 7
**Turnover:** £13,425,000

DUNS 22-762-6322
## Staffordshire Meats Ltd
New House Farm, Werrington Road, Bucknell, Stoke-On-Trent, Staffordshire ST2 9AL
**Tel:** 01782274515 **Fax:** 01782202695
**Web:** www.staffordshiremeatpackers.co.uk
**Reg No:** 1603491 **Estd:** 1981 Private Limited Company
**Line of Business:** Wholesale of meat and meat products
**Issued Capital:** £1,000
**Director:** H James
**Co. Secretary:** Mrs Dorothy James
**US SIC:** 5147 **UK SIC:** 61700
**Auditors:** Illegible
**Bankers:** National Westminster Bank Plc (01-03-69)

| | 31-03-14 | 31-03-13 | 31-03-12 |
|---|---|---|---|
| TA | 5,075 | 5,075 | 5,075 |
| NW | 5,075 | 5,075 | 5,075 |

DUNS 21-777-9304
## Staffordshire Moorlands Children's Centre
Albert Street, Stoke-On-Trent, Staffordshire ST8 6DT
**Tel:** 01782297970
**Web:** www.staffordshire.gov.uk
**Estd:** 2011 Proprietorship
**Line of Business:** Childcare services
**Proprietor:** Mrs S Bloor
**US SIC:** 8321 **UK SIC:** 96111
**Employees:** 50

DUNS 23-693-4477
## Staffordshire Moorlands District Council
Moorlands House, Stockwell Street, Leek, Staffordshire ST13 6HQ
**Tel:** 03456053010
**Web:** www.staffsmoorlands.gov.uk
**Estd:** 2002
**Line of Business:** Local government
**Trading Style:** Environment & Leisure
**Directors:** A Stokes, B Preedy
**Responsibilities**
**Senior:** Michelle Costello *(Executive)*, Mark Trillo *(Manager)*
**HR:** Julie Grime *(Human Resources Manager)*
**Operations:** Vicki Ellis *(Production and Operations Mana)*
**Branches:** Staffordshire Moorlands District Council, Blythe Bridge Library, Uttoxeter Road, Stoke-On-Trent, Staffordshire ST11 9JR
**US SIC:** 6732 **UK SIC:** 83100
**Employees:** 250

DUNS 23-274-9775
## Staffordshire Moorlands Primary Care Trust
Newspaper House, Brook Street, Leek, Staffordshire ST13 5JE
**Web:** www.homeinstead.co.uk
**Estd:** 2012
**Line of Business:** Home care and help services
**Trading Style:** Leek Moorlands Hospital, Staffordshire Moorlands Pct
**Issued Capital:** £1
**Principals:** Mrs P Ryan *(Financial)*, P Da'Silva
**Branches:** Staffordshire Moorlands Primary Care Trust, Mount Road, Stoke-On-Trent, Staffordshire ST7 4AY
**US SIC:** 8062, 9121
**UK SIC:** 95100, 91110
**Employees:** 740

DUNS 76-948-5426
## Staffordshire North & Stoke-on-Trent Citizens Advice Bureaux
Advice House Cheapside Hanley Street, Stoke-On-Trent, Staffordshire ST1 1HL
**Tel:** 01782408600
**Web:** www.royalvoluntaryservice.org.uk
**Reg No:** 2402902 **Estd:** 1989 Private Limited Company
**Line of Business:** Social work activities without accommodation
**Directors:** N Holloway, Mrs J J Seaman, R J Pemberton, B C Lawton, Ms J Durose, J E Davies, R J Holt, Dr A Mlouk
**Co. Secretary:** Simon Harris
**Responsibilities**
**Senior:** Lesley Haines *(Director)*, Madelaine Lovatt *(Director)*, Emor Porteous *(Director)*, Trevor Watkins *(Director)*, Angela Wilshaw *(Director)*
**US SIC:** 8321 **UK SIC:** 96111
**Bankers:** Barclays Bank Plc (20-36-43)

| | 31-03-14 | 31-03-13 | 31-03-12 |
|---|---|---|---|
| TO | 2,454,447 | 2,202,556 | 2,041,906 |
| P/L | (42,561) | 337,529 | 66,347 |
| NW | 1,153,218 | 1,195,779 | 858,250 |
| WC | 595,848 | 845,510 | 482,098 |
| Emp. | 101 | 78 | 78 |

DUNS 23-211-7291
## Staffordshire Police
3 Acton Hill Cottages, Cannock Road, Stafford, Staffordshire ST17 0QN
**Tel:** 03001234455
**Web:** www.staffordshire.police.uk
**Estd:** 1961 Incorporate By Act Of Parliament
**Line of Business:** Police forces
**Director:** J W Giffard
**Responsibilities**
**Senior:** Faye Lewis *(Manager)*
**Health & Safety:** John Axon *(Health And Safety Officer)*
**Branches:** Staffordshire Police, Police Station, Fountain Street, Leek, Staffordshire ST13 6QT
**US SIC:** 9221 **UK SIC:** 91300
**Employees:** 110

DUNS 23-983-5010 **Imp**
## Staffordshire University
College Road, Stoke-On-Trent, Staffordshire ST4 2DE
**Tel:** 01782-294000
**Web:** www.staffs.ac.uk
**VAT No:** 488832293
**Incorporate By Act Of Parliament**

**Line of Business:** Post-graduate level higher education
**Trading Style:** Union Travel Centre
**Principals:** I Starkie *(Financial)*, Prof C E King
**Responsibilities**
**Senior:** Francesca Francis *(Dean of Students)*
**Operations:** Janet Weaver *(Head of Customer Services)*
**Branches:** Staffordshire University, Unit 19 Hollies Avenue, Cannock, Staffordshire WS11 1DW
**US SIC:** 8221 **UK SIC:** 93100
**Auditors:** KPMG LLP
**Bankers:** Lloyds TSB Bank plc (30-98-00)
**Employees:** 2,000
**Turnover:** £118,524,000

DUNS 21-736-2028
### Staffordshire University Academy
Marston Road, Cannock, Staffordshire WS12 4JH
**Tel:** 01543512415
**Web:** www.staffordshireuniversityacademy.org.uk
**Reg No:** 7704020 **Estd:** 2011 Private Company Limited By Guarantee
**Line of Business:** Schools (foundation)
**Directors:** Dr M Lowe, P H Richards, Mrs L A Rollason, T Ramgopal, Ms C L Heywood, J K Capper, A Howells
**Responsibilities**
**Senior:** Diane Crook *(Manager)*, Kenneth Sproston *(Manager)*
**US SIC:** 8211 **UK SIC:** 93200
**Bankers:** Lloyds TSB Bank plc (30-91-58)

| | 31-08-13 | 31-08-12 |
|---|---|---|
| TO | 4,056,000 | 4,393,000 |
| P/L | 700,000 | 899,000 |
| NW | 852,000 | 140,000 |
| WC | 1,633,000 | 920,000 |
| Emp. | 73 | 72 |

DUNS 21-810-3551
### Staffordshire University Halls of Residence
Stafford Court, Stafford, Staffordshire ST18 0AB
**Tel:** 01785353595
**Web:** www.staffs.ac.uk
**Estd:** 2012
**Line of Business:** Student accommodation
**Responsibilities**
**Senior:** Judy Ryder *(Manager)*
**US SIC:** 6531 **UK SIC:** 83400
**Employees:** 2,000

DUNS 76-915-9989
### The Staffordshire Wildlife Trust Ltd
The Wolseley Centre, Wolseley Bridge, Stafford, Staffordshire ST17 0WT
**Tel:** 01889-880100
**Web:** www.staffordshirewildlife.org.uk
**Reg No:** 0959609 **Estd:** 1969 Private Limited Company
**Line of Business:** Charities and charitable organisations
**Directors:** B Dore, N A Young, B A Price, R C Higgs, Dr R Green, H V Clark, Miss S M Carr, V D Smith
**Co. Secretary:** Bernard Price
**Responsibilities**
**Senior:** Patricia Callaghan *(Manager)*, Guy Corbett-Marshall *(Board Member)*, Guy Corbett-Moss *(Chief Executive)*, Keith Gracie *(Manager)*, Dave Haslam *(Chairman)*, Peter Shirley *(Manager)*
**US SIC:** 8699, 0971
**UK SIC:** 96902, 01003
**Bankers:** National Westminster Bank Plc (60-21-59)

| | 31-12-13 | 31-12-12 | 31-12-11 |
|---|---|---|---|
| TO | 2,799,000 | 2,816,000 | 2,514,000 |
| P/L | 238,000 | 306,000 | 117,000 |
| NW | 5,655,000 | 5,322,000 | 4,965,000 |
| WC | 1,023,000 | 1,287,000 | 916,000 |
| Emp. | 59 | 52 | 54 |

DUNS 77-777-2021
### Stag Brewing Company Ltd
**(Subsidiary of:** Anheuser-Busch Inbev Sa)
Lower Richmond Road, Mortlake, London SW14 7ET
**Tel:** 02083925400
**Web:** www.abinbev.com
**Reg No:** 3023279 **Estd:** 1995 Private Limited Company
**Line of Business:** Brewers
**Trading Style:** Budweiser
**Issued Capital:** £5,000,000
**Directors:** Ms A E Tolley, Mrs C Lake, P Mirant-Borde, R Mclellan
**Co. Secretary:** Kayleigh Wilshaw
**Branches:** Stag Brewing Company Limited, 50 Lower Richmond Rd, London SW15 1JT
**US SIC:** 2082, 5182
**UK SIC:** 42702, 61700

**Auditors:** PricewaterhouseCoopers LLP

| | 31-12-13 | 31-12-12 | 31-12-11 |
|---|---|---|---|
| TO | 31,417,000 | 36,475,000 | 40,154,000 |
| P/L | 4,817,000 | (88,000) | 76,000 |
| NW | 45,274,000 | 44,963,000 | 51,001,000 |
| WC | 53,291,000 | 51,549,000 | 48,180,000 |
| Emp. | 93 | 96 | 102 |

DUNS 21-117-1184
### Stag Group Ltd
1 Lyon Road, Walton-On-Thames, Surrey KT12 3PU
**Tel:** 01932251560
**Web:** www.stag-aerospace.com
**Reg No:** 6570222 **Estd:** 2008 Private Limited Company
**Line of Business:** Management activities of other non-financial holding companies not elsewhere classified
**Export Sales:** £11,968,622
**Issued Capital:** £100,000
**Director:** T M De Bouillane
**Co. Secretary:** Colin Davis
**US SIC:** 6711 **UK SIC:** 83962

| | 31-12-13 | 31-12-12 | 31-12-11 |
|---|---|---|---|
| TO | 23,610,402 | 24,096,041 | 20,637,188 |
| P/L | 885,005 | 523,178 | 450,822 |
| NW | 5,605,632 | 5,213,036 | 4,964,925 |
| WC | 6,074,168 | 5,985,639 | 5,031,463 |
| Emp. | 95 | 116 | 110 |

DUNS 21-775-3705
### Stage Coach London
Pettman Crescent, London SE28 0BJ
**Tel:** 02088559022
**Web:** www.stagecoachbus.com
**Estd:** 2008 Proprietorship
**Line of Business:** Bus operators and stations
**Proprietor:** B Daly
**US SIC:** 4119 **UK SIC:** 72200
**Employees:** 500

DUNS 45-866-7565                    Imp
### Stage Electrics Partnership Ltd
Third Way, Avonmouth, Bristol, Avon BS11 9YL
**Tel:** 01895834106
**Web:** www.stage-electrics.co.uk
**Reg No:** 3209293 **VAT No:** 793883661
**Estd:** 1979 Private Limited Company
**Line of Business:** Other retail sale in specialised stores not elsewhere classified
**Export Sales:** £1,970,650
**Trading Style:** Stage Electrics
**Issued Capital:** £295,756
**Directors:** G J Irvine, J S Laycock, T Smallwood, G K Wood, Mrs A M Western, D V Aldridge, R J Smith
**Co. Secretary:** Quayseco Limited
**Responsibilities**
**Senior:** Jennifer Agu *(Marketing)*, Adam Blaxill *(Head of Marketing)*
**Finance:** Christine Hatfield *(Credit Control Manager)*, Lynda Shaw *(Financial Controller)*
**Marketing:** Jennifer Agu *(Marketing)*, Adam Blaxill *(Head of Marketing)*
**Sales:** Darren Beckley *(Divisional Sales Manager)*, Davie Bell *(Divisional Sales Manager)*, Stephen Bray *(Branch Sales Manager)*, Paul Roughton *(Business Development Manager)*
**Admin:** Christine Cheeseman *(HR Administrator)*
**HR:** Christine Cheeseman *(HR Administrator)*, Annabelle Jordan *(HR Manager)*
**Health & Safety:** Liz Brathwaite *(Health & Safety Manager)*, Liz Reed *(Health and Safety Manager)*
**Operations:** Nick Broad *(Production and Operations Mana)*, Chris Merriman *(Production and Operations Mana)*, Richard Phare *(Projects Operations Manager)*
**Purchasing:** Marc Ferris *(Supply Chain Manager)*
**Fleet:** Pete Toogood *(Fleet Manager)*
**Engineering:** Adrian Searle *(Head of Technical and Hire)*
**Branches:** Stage Electrics Partnership Ltd, 175 Long Lane, London SE1 4PN
**US SIC:** 5999 **UK SIC:** 65600
**Auditors:** KPMG LLP
**Bankers:** Barclays Bank Plc (20-00-00)

| | 31-01-14 | 31-01-13 | 31-01-12 |
|---|---|---|---|
| TO | 29,432,570 | 30,392,496 | 29,911,599 |
| P/L | 844,537 | 813,391 | 907,177 |
| NW | 7,823,384 | 6,711,281 | 6,712,928 |
| WC | 2,496,671 | 464,711 | 78,412 |
| Emp. | 227 | 232 | 239 |

DUNS 85-611-2644
### Stage Ltd
**(Subsidiary of:** Stage Holdings Ltd)
Hesketh House, 43-45 Portman Square, London W1H 6HN
**Tel:** 02079692703
**Web:** www.stageconsultancy.com
**Reg No:** 6204831 **Estd:** 2009 Private Limited Company
**Line of Business:** It consultants
**Issued Capital:** £1,000
**Co. Secretary:** Ms Toni Kendall-Troughton
**Responsibilities**
**Senior:** Christine Ansell *(Manager)*
**Sales:** David Southey *(Account Manager)*
**Operations:** Julie Pickrell *(Delivery Manager)*
**US SIC:** 7379 **UK SIC:** 83940
**Auditors:** MHA MacIntyre Hudson
**Bankers:** Barclays Bank Plc (20-00-50)

| | 31-03-14 | 31-03-13 | 31-03-12 |
|---|---|---|---|
| TO | 10,668,603 | 10,940,748 | 11,583,924 |
| P/L | 307,318 | 325,385 | 52,538 |
| NW | (306,170) | (526,681) | (878,775) |
| WC | 177,049 | 132,857 | (197,742) |
| Emp. | 49 | 56 | 60 |

DUNS 49-485-5307                    Imp-Exp
### Stage One Creative Services Ltd
**(Subsidiary of:** Stage One Creative Services Companies Ltd)
Unit 88 Marston Moor Business Pa, Tockwith, York, North Yorkshire YO26 7QF
**Web:** www.stageone.co.uk
**Reg No:** 3150434 **Estd:** 1996 Private Limited Company
**Line of Business:** Other manufacturing not elsewhere classified
**Export Sales:** £23,901,797
**Issued Capital:** £75
**Directors:** M N Johnson, J W Tinsley
**Co. Secretary:** Richard Fagg
**Responsibilities**
**HR:** Julie Schofield *(Human Resources Coordinator)*
**US SIC:** 3999, 3648
**UK SIC:** 49590, 34702
**Auditors:** Clive Owen & Co LLP

| | 30-06-14 | 31-12-12 | 31-06-11 |
|---|---|---|---|
| TO | 32,216,077 | 14,573,927 | 10,996,925 |
| P/L | 813,870 | 960,776 | 46,643 |
| NW | (401,213) | 1,267,903 | 525,836 |
| WC | (1,939,464) | 495,869 | 73,082 |
| Emp. | 103 | 91 | 87 |

DUNS 77-460-6016
### Stage Technologies Ltd
**(Subsidiary of:** Rich Forwarding Ltd)
9 Falcon Park Industrial Estate, London NW10 1RZ
**Web:** www.stagetech.com
**Reg No:** 2962782 **VAT No:** 649725006
**Estd:** 1994 Private Limited Company
**Line of Business:** Engineering & scientific equipment mfrs
**Export Sales:** £9,114,496
**Issued Capital:** £70,000
**Principals:** M A Ager *(Managing)*, T E Guhl, Ms N J Scott, D C Bernstein, A D Davis
**Co. Secretary:** David Colbert
**Responsibilities**
**Senior:** Kenneth Golding *(Manager)*
**Sales:** Matthew Tonks *(Business Development Manager)*
**US SIC:** 3811, 3559, 7999
**UK SIC:** 37100, 32863, 97913
**Auditors:** Reeves & Co LLP
**Bankers:** National Westminster Bank Plc (56-00-29)

| | 31-12-13 | 31-03-13 | 31-12-12 |
|---|---|---|---|
| TO | 11,448,464 | 15,368,028 | 12,924,863 |
| P/L | 594,683 | 1,072,339 | 204,131 |
| NW | 3,316,316 | 2,871,819 | 2,984,363 |
| WC | 2,477,466 | 1,326,777 | 1,983,184 |
| Emp. | 79 | 79 | 82 |

DUNS 21-773-9737
### Stagecoach Bluebird
Business Station, Guild Street, Aberdeen, Aberdeenshire AB11 6NA
**Tel:** 01224591381
**Web:** www.stagecoachbus.com
**Estd:** 1990 Proprietorship
**Line of Business:** Bus operators and stations
**Proprietor:** R Jarvis
**Responsibilities**
**Operations:** Bob Hall *(Technical, Production Manager)*
**US SIC:** 4119 **UK SIC:** 72200
**Employees:** 250

DUNS 21-812-1893
### Stagecoach Bus Merseyside
East Lancashire Road, Liverpool, Merseyside L11 0BB
**Tel:** 01513306200
**Web:** www.stagecoachbus.com
**Estd:** 2012
**Line of Business:** Bus operators and stations
**Responsibilities**
**Senior:** Les Burton *(Operations Director)*
**US SIC:** 4119 **UK SIC:** 72200
**Employees:** 490

DUNS 29-846-5758                    Imp
### Stagecoach Group Plc
10 Dunkeld Road, Perth, Perthshire PH1 5TW
**Tel:** 01738-442111
**Web:** www.stagecoach.com
**Reg No:** 0100764SC **Estd:** 1980 Public Limited Company
**Line of Business:** Bus operators and stations
**Issued Capital:** £3,168,550
**Principals:** Sir B Souter *(Chairman)*, Ms A H Gloag *(Managing)*, E Brown, W E Whitehorn, R J Paterson, M A Griffiths, F M Alexander, Ms H Mahy
**Co. Secretary:** Michael Vaux
**Responsibilities**
**HR:** June Ashton *(Human Resources Manager)*, Matthew Darroch *(Training Manager)*
**Health & Safety:** Graham Whitelocks *(Health & Safety Officer)*
**Facilities:** Brendan MacKinven *(Group Construction Manager)*
**Purchasing:** Jim Crompton *(Purchasing Manager)*
**Branches:** Stagecoach Group Plc, Plumstead Bus Garage, Pettman Crescent, London SE28 0BJ
**US SIC:** 4119, 6711
**UK SIC:** 72200, 83962
**Auditors:** PricewaterhouseCoopers LLP
**Bankers:** Bank Of Scotland (12-21-91)
Following financial data are in thousands

| | 30-04-14 | 30-04-13 | 30-04-12 |
|---|---|---|---|
| TO | 2,930,000 | 2,804,800 | 2,590,700 |
| P/L | 158,000 | 195,800 | 239,800 |
| NW | (55,700) | (173,800) | (156,700) |
| WC | (213,700) | (240,500) | (175,100) |
| Emp. | 35,470 | 35,506 | 32,906 |

DUNS 21-605-4169
### Stagecoach in Fife
Dunfermline Business Station, Queen Anne Street, Dunfermline, Fife KY12 7BA
**Tel:** 01383621249
**Estd:** 2011 Proprietorship
**Line of Business:** Bus operators and stations
**Proprietor:** W Renton
**Responsibilities**
**Senior:** Gary Stuart *(Manager)*
**US SIC:** 4119 **UK SIC:** 72200
**Employees:** 150

DUNS 21-590-1458
### Stagecoach in Huntingdonshire
Cambridge Road, Fenstanton, Huntingdon, Cambridgeshire PE28 9JB
**Tel:** 01480309080
**Web:** www.stagecoachbus.com
**Estd:** 2011 Proprietorship
**Line of Business:** Bus operators and stations
**Proprietor:** T Mead
**US SIC:** 4119 **UK SIC:** 72200
**Employees:** 100

DUNS 21-572-8408
### Stagecoach Midland Red
Railway Terrace, Rugby, Warwickshire CV21 3HS
**Tel:** 01788562036
**Web:** www.stagecoachbus.com
**Estd:** 2002 Proprietorship
**Line of Business:** Bus operators and stations
**Partners:** S Burd, S Burd, W Simpson, A Rideout
**US SIC:** 4119 **UK SIC:** 72200
**Employees:** 120

DUNS 22-956-1527
### Stagecoach (South) Ltd
**(Subsidiary of:** Stagecoach Group Plc)
19-20 Marine Parade, Worthing, West Sussex BN11 3PT
**Tel:** 01903237661 **Fax:** 01903211719
**Web:** www.stagecoachbus.com
**Reg No:** 1673542 **Estd:** 1919 Private Limited Company
**Line of Business:** Bus operators and stations

**Trading Style:** Hampshire Bus Co, Stagecoach Hants & Surrey United Counties, Stagecoach Coastline Buses, South Coast Buses
**Issued Capital:** £495,000
**Directors:** R Montgomery, A W Dyer, R G Andrew, G J Nolan, S D Greer, C Brown
**Co. Secretary:** Michael Vaux
**Responsibilities**
**Senior:** Colin Ashcroft (Manager), Steve Venables (Manager)
**Branches:** Stagecoach (South) Ltd, Beaufort Road, St Leonards-On-Sea, St. Leonards-On-Sea, East Sussex TN37 6PL
**US SIC:** 4119  **UK SIC:** 72200
**Auditors:** PricewaterhouseCoopers LLP
**Bankers:** Bank Of Scotland (80-11-00)

|  | 30-04-14 | 30-04-13 | 30-04-12 |
|---|---|---|---|
| TO | 83,741,000 | 93,251,000 | 92,551,000 |
| P/L | 11,243,000 | 13,599,000 | 13,518,000 |
| NW | 4,009,000 | 4,028,000 | 4,188,000 |
| WC | (35,228,000) | (26,687,000) | (29,691,000) |
| Emp. | 1,658 | 1,867 | 1,902 |

DUNS 21-812-2102
### Stagecoach South West Trains
Clapham Junction Railway Station, Clapham Junction Approach, London SW11 2QP
**Tel:** 02079229920
**Web:** www.swtrains.co.uk
**Estd:** 2012
**Line of Business:** Freight services
**Responsibilities**
**Senior:** Damon Ede (Station Manager), Tim Keen (Manager)
**US SIC:** 4011  **UK SIC:** 71000
**Employees:** 60

DUNS 34-799-5727
### Stagecoach South Western Trains Ltd
(**Subsidiary of:** Stagecoach Group Plc)
Friars Bridge Court, London SE1 8NZ
**Web:** www.southwesttrains.co.uk
**Reg No:** 5599788  **Estd:** 2005 Private Limited Company
**Line of Business:** Transport via railways
**Trading Style:** South West Trains
**Issued Capital:** £200
**Directors:** M A Griffiths, C Roth, T C Shoveller, J H Kelly, R J Paterson
**Co. Secretary:** Andrew West
**US SIC:** 4011  **UK SIC:** 71000
**Auditors:** PricewaterhouseCoopers LLP

|  | 26-04-14 | 27-04-13 | 28-04-12 |
|---|---|---|---|
| TO | 910,145,000 | 866,837,000 | 815,372,000 |
| P/L | 29,678,000 | 23,719,000 | 48,608,000 |
| NW | 10,317,000 | 4,209,000 | 4,792,000 |
| WC | 4,821,000 | 956,000 | 1,696,000 |
| Emp. | 4,610 | 4,562 | 4,424 |

DUNS 22-846-1919
### Stagecoach Supertram Maintenance Ltd.
(**Subsidiary of:** Stagecoach Group Plc)
Nunnery Depot, Woodbourn Road, Sheffield, South Yorkshire S9 3LS
**Tel:** 01142-759888
**Web:** www.supertram.com
**Reg No:** 2032602  **Estd:** 1994 Private Limited Company
**Line of Business:** Manufacture of other transport equipment not elsewhere classified
**Trading Style:** Stagecoach Supertram Maintenance Ltd.
**Issued Capital:** £2
**Directors:** Mrs M P Kay, N Wragg, T D Bilby, K Wright, Ms C Ansley, M A Griffiths
**Co. Secretary:** Michael Vaux
**Responsibilities**
**Marketing:** Julia Shaw (Commercial Manager)
**HR:** Julia Shaw (Commercial Manager), David Skirrow (Training Officer)
**Purchasing:** Julia Shaw (Commercial Manager)
**US SIC:** 3799  **UK SIC:** 36502
**Auditors:** PricewaterhouseCoopers LLP

|  | 30-04-14 | 30-04-13 | 30-04-12 |
|---|---|---|---|
| TO | 8,129,000 | 5,886,000 | 9,626,000 |
| P/L | 329,000 | (56,000) | 1,421,000 |
| NW | 2,501,000 | 1,786,000 | 1,808,000 |
| WC | 2,326,000 | 1,580,000 | 1,522,000 |
| Emp. | 66 | 52 | 56 |

DUNS 73-757-7122
### Stagecoach Theatre Arts Ltd
(**Subsidiary of:** Lifeskills Education Holdings Ltd)
Elm Grove, Hersham Road, Walton-On-Thames, Surrey KT12 1LZ
**Tel:** 01932254333
**Web:** www.stagecoach.co.uk
**Reg No:** 2924719  **Estd:** 1994 Private Limited Company
**Line of Business:** Other business activities not elsewhere classified
**Trading Style:** Stagecoach Theatre Arts Ltd - Walton
**Issued Capital:** £500,000

**Directors:** Mrs S A Kelly, H M Meikle, S Gandhi
**Co. Secretary:** Miss Julia Early
**Responsibilities**
**Marketing:** Zeena Hicks (Marketing Manager)
**Admin:** Carol Newton (Office Manager)
**IT:** Mike Cowan (IT Manager)
**HR:** Carol Newton (Office Manager)
**Health & Safety:** Carol Newton (Office Manager)
**Facilities:** Carol Gwilliams (Facilities Manager)
**Operations:** Zeena Hicks (Marketing Manager)
**Branches:** Stagecoach Theatre Arts Ltd, 1 Brooklands Rd, Bedford, Bedfordshire MK44 1EE
**US SIC:** 7399, 8999
**UK SIC:** 83954
**Auditors:** KPMG Audit PLC
**Bankers:** Barclays Bank Plc (20-46-73)

|  | 31-05-13 | 31-05-12 | 31-05-11 |
|---|---|---|---|
| TO | 5,827,000 | 5,574,000 | 5,987,000 |
| P/L | 353,000 | 108,000 | 650,000 |
| NW | 3,209,000 | 2,827,000 | 2,697,000 |
| WC | 2,703,000 | 2,318,000 | 2,592,000 |
| Emp. | 50 | 52 | 55 |

DUNS 21-869-3500
### Stagecoach Yorkshire
Dale Road, Rawmarsh, Rotherham, South Yorkshire S62 5AL
**Tel:** 01709524323
**Web:** www.stagecoachbus.com
**Estd:** 1990 Partnership
**Line of Business:** Bus operators and stations
**Partners:** P Hill, M Adamson, N Cooke, T Cox, C Mullen
**Responsibilities**
**Senior:** D Broadhead (Manager), Paul Sylvester (Operations Manager)
**US SIC:** 4119, 4142, 4722
**UK SIC:** 72200, 72102, 77001
**Employees:** 2,087

DUNS 22-710-1318
### Stagetruck Ltd
(**Subsidiary of:** Speed 1971 Ltd)
Larkwhistle Farm Works, Larkwhistle Farm Road, Winchester, Hampshire SO21 3BG
**Web:** www.stagetruck.com
**Reg No:** 1478729  **VAT No:** 689476165
**Estd:** 1980 Private Limited Company
**Line of Business:** Road haulage and transport services
**Export Sales:** £3,837,713
**Issued Capital:** £100
**Principals:** R Hewett (Managing), Ms J A Hewett
**Co. Secretary:** Robert Hewett
**Responsibilities**
**Health & Safety:** Jackie Wise (Health & Safety Officer)
**US SIC:** 4213  **UK SIC:** 72300
**Auditors:** Coulthards Mackenzie

|  | 31-03-14 | 31-03-13 | 31-03-12 |
|---|---|---|---|
| TO | 10,660,315 | 6,852,996 | 6,312,266 |
| P/L | 1,101,788 | 392,349 | 272,623 |
| NW | 1,971,791 | 1,120,084 | 815,546 |
| WC | 1,942,940 | 1,113,075 | 802,560 |
| Emp. | 90 | N/A | N/A |

DUNS 21-775-4077
### Stainburn School
Stainburn Road, Workington, Cumbria CA14 4EB
**Tel:** 01900873926
**Web:** www.stainburn.cumbria.sch.uk
**Estd:** 2011 Proprietorship
**Line of Business:** Schools (foundation)
**Proprietor:** C Mcgrath
**Responsibilities**
**Senior:** David Dawes (Interim Head Teacher), Chris McGrath (Proprietor)
**US SIC:** 8211  **UK SIC:** 93200
**Employees:** 100

DUNS 39-229-8618
### Staines Preparatory School Trust
3 Gresham Road, Staines, Middlesex TW18 2BT
**Tel:** 01784-450909
**Web:** www.stainesprep.co.uk
**Reg No:** 2114440  **Estd:** 1935 Private Company Limited By Guarantee
**Line of Business:** General secondary education
**Directors:** Ms W J Ransom, M R Hall, R H Chadburn, Dr. R Shaunak, Ms M Robinson, M Bannister, R F Adams, M J Graham
**Co. Secretary:** Ms Susan Rogers
**Responsibilities**
**Senior:** Penelope Austin (Director), Jennifer Sice (Director), Thomas Spencer (Director)
**Marketing:** Natasha Tait (Marketing Director)

**US SIC:** 8211  **UK SIC:** 93200
**Auditors:** Bolton Colby
**Bankers:** Barclays Bank Plc (20-42-73)

|  | 31-08-13 | 31-08-12 | 31-08-11 |
|---|---|---|---|
| TO | 3,044,719 | 2,854,151 | 2,723,531 |
| P/L | 89,302 | 227,288 | 118,750 |
| NW | 3,753,912 | 3,664,610 | 3,437,322 |
| WC | (579,294) | 210,510 | 647,767 |
| Emp. | 87 | 81 | 143 |

DUNS 29-634-8717    Exp
### Stainless Threaded Fasteners Ltd
(**Subsidiary of:** Marlowe Holdings Ltd)
7 Beldray Road Beldray Park, Bilston, West Midlands WV14 7NH
**Tel:** 01902499200
**Web:** www.stffasteners.co.uk
**Reg No:** 1960994  **VAT No:** 431461774
**Estd:** 1986 Private Limited Company
**Line of Business:** Production of non ferrous metals
**Trading Style:** S T F
**Issued Capital:** £805
**Directors:** R D Goddard, D S Jackson, S Davies, K Harrison
**Co. Secretary:** William Woof
**Responsibilities**
**IT:** Kevin Benton (IT Manager)
**HR:** David Stilton (Director General Manager)
**US SIC:** 3339, 5084
**UK SIC:** 22470, 61490
**Bankers:** Bank Of Wales Plc (12-23-00)

|  | 31-12-13 | 31-12-12 | 31-12-11 |
|---|---|---|---|
| TA | 61,030 | 61,030 | 61,030 |
| NW | 61,030 | 61,030 | 61,030 |

DUNS 21-042-7632
### Stainton Way Care Home
Hemlington, Middlesbrough, Cleveland TS8 9LX
**Tel:** 01642599157
**Estd:** 2006 Partnership
**Line of Business:** Residential care establishments
**Partners:** R Duggart, T Chopra
**Responsibilities**
**Senior:** Beverley Stubbs (Home Manager)
**Finance:** Carole Saunders (Administrator)
**Marketing:** Dave Bell (Marketing Manager)
**Health & Safety:** Beverley Stubbs (Home Manager)
**US SIC:** 8321  **UK SIC:** 96111
**Employees:** 67

DUNS 56-962-5429
### Stairways (Holdings) Ltd
Bescot Crescent, Walsall, West Midlands WS1 4ND
**Tel:** 01922-728600
**Web:** www.stairways.co.uk
**Reg No:** 2851575  **VAT No:** 592757982
**Estd:** 1993 Private Limited Company
**Line of Business:** Management activities of holding companies
**Issued Capital:** £1,000
**Director:** N C Stevens
**Co. Secretary:** Ms Karen Wood
**Responsibilities**
**Senior:** Barry Slack (Finance Director)
**Finance:** Barry Slack (Finance Director)
**Branches:** Stairways (Holdings) Ltd, Sydenham Industrial Estate, Leamington Spa, Warwickshire CV31 1PS
**US SIC:** 6711  **UK SIC:** 83962
**Auditors:** The Southill Partnership
**Bankers:** Barclays Bank Plc (20-65-18)

|  | 31-12-13 | 31-12-12 | 31-12-11 |
|---|---|---|---|
| TO | 7,980,785 | 6,967,694 | 7,466,810 |
| P/L | 596,071 | 353,595 | 749,379 |
| NW | 5,354,422 | 5,076,503 | 5,566,131 |
| WC | 3,527,330 | 3,170,421 | 3,108,231 |
| Emp. | 95 | 101 | 99 |

DUNS 21-828-4396    Exp
### Stalham Engineering Co Ltd
Stalham, Norwich, Norfolk NR12 9QG
**Tel:** 01692-580513  **Fax:** 01692-581770
**Web:** www.stalhameng.co.uk
**Reg No:** 0759472  **VAT No:** 104714993
**Estd:** 1963 Private Limited Company
**Line of Business:** Miscellaneous vehicle repair
**Trading Style:** Nicholsons
**Issued Capital:** £50,000
**Principals:** M G Nicholson (Managing), D G Nicholson, A W Nicholson, G H Nicholson, P Nicholson, A R Nicholson, T J Nicholson
**Co. Secretary:** Malcolm Nicholson
**Responsibilities**
**Senior:** Roger Nicholson (Facilities Manager)
**Facilities:** Roger Nicholson (Facilities Manager)
**Purchasing:** Roger Nicholson (Facilities Manager)
**US SIC:** 7539, 5531
**UK SIC:** 67100, 65100

**Auditors:** Sexty & Co
**Bankers:** Barclays Bank Plc (20-99-21)

|  | 30-06-14 | 30-06-13 | 30-06-12 |
|---|---|---|---|
| TO | 14,333,176 | 15,380,069 | 12,387,263 |
| P/L | 40,065 | 74,189 | 65,392 |
| NW | 1,068,912 | 1,037,882 | 979,157 |
| WC | 363,189 | 367,898 | 337,512 |
| Emp. | 50 | 49 | 49 |

DUNS 29-580-0288
### Stalkers Transport Services Ltd
Townfoot Industrial Estate, Brampton, Cumbria CA8 1SW
**Tel:** 01697-73699
**Web:** www.stalkerstransport.co.uk
**Reg No:** 1941795  **Estd:** 1985 Private Limited Company
**Line of Business:** Road haulage and transport services
**Issued Capital:** £275,100
**Directors:** D Stalker, Mrs D J Elliott, Ms K Stalker
**Co. Secretary:** Ms Karen Stalker
**Responsibilities**
**Senior:** Gerald Stalker (Manager), Karen Vernon (Human Resources Manager)
**HR:** Karen Vernon (Human Resources Manager)
**US SIC:** 4789  **UK SIC:** 77002
**Auditors:** Blueprint Audit Ltd
**Bankers:** HSBC Bank plc (40-13-19)

|  | 30-09-14 | 30-09-13 | 30-09-12 |
|---|---|---|---|
| TO | N/A | N/A | 5,690,085 |
| P/L | N/A | N/A | 34,993 |
| NW | 230,970 | 175,984 | 77,258 |
| WC | (539,908) | (785,644) | (865,793) |
| Emp. | N/A | N/A | 71 |

DUNS 55-067-1473
### Stallcombe House
Sanctuary Lane, Exeter, Devon EX5 1EX
**Web:** www.stallcombehouse.co.uk
**Estd:** 1981
**Line of Business:** Residential care establishments
**Chairman:** J Morris
**Responsibilities**
**Senior:** Stanley Brown (Manager), Lisa Humphries (Manager), Ann Liverton (Manager), Christopher Retallack (Manager), David Retallack (Manager), John Sillett (Manager), Christopher Thistle (General Manager)
**IT:** Christopher Thistle (General Manager)
**HR:** Tom Roncraelli (Health & Safety Officer)
**Health & Safety:** Tom Roncraelli (Health & Safety Officer)
**Facilities:** Christopher Thistle (General Manager)
**Branches:** Stallcombe House, 43 Cranford Ave, Exmouth, Devon EX8 2QD
**US SIC:** 8321  **UK SIC:** 96111
**Employees:** 49

DUNS 33-980-6465
### Stamco Timber
Churchfields Mill, St Leonards-On-Sea, East Sussex TN38 9TG
**Tel:** 01424856800
**Web:** www.stamco.co.uk
**Estd:** 2007 Proprietorship
**Line of Business:** Timber merchants
**Proprietor:** L Shepherdson
**Responsibilities**
**Health & Safety:** Ian Doxford (Health & Safety Manager)
**Facilities:** Ian Doxford (Health & Safety Manager)
**US SIC:** 5072, 5039
**UK SIC:** 61500, 61300
**Bankers:** National Westminster Bank Plc (60-10-15)
**Employees:** 100

DUNS 36-488-8979
### Stamford Endowed Schools
Brazenose House, St Pauls Street, Stamford, Lincolnshire PE9 2BE
**Tel:** 01780750310
**Web:** www.ses.lincs.sch.uk
**Estd:** 1966
**Line of Business:** General secondary education
**Principals:** Dr P R Mason (Chairman), N Chedd
**Responsibilities**
**Senior:** David Laventure (Director, Sport), Will Phelan (Head Teacher)
**US SIC:** 8211  **UK SIC:** 93200
**Employees:** 160

DUNS 76-965-1878

## Stamford Endowed Schools Enterprises Ltd

(**Subsidiary of:** Stamford Endowed Schools Trustee Ltd)
16 St Pauls Street, Stamford, Lincolnshire PE9 2BE
**Tel:** 01780750302
**Web:** www.ses.lincs.sch.uk
**Reg No:** 2629879 **Estd:** 1991 Private Limited Company
**Line of Business:** General secondary education
**Issued Capital:** £2
**Directors:** M J Cockerill, T Hindmarch, I D Moss
**Co. Secretary:** Ms Emma Crossland
**Responsibilities**
**Senior:** Michael Deoraj *(Markietng Director)*
**Marketing:** Michael Deoraj *(Markietng Director)*
**IT:** Nick Fox *(Senior IT Executive)*
**US SIC:** 8211 **UK SIC:** 93200
**Auditors:** Crowe Clark Whitehill LLP
**Bankers:** Barclays Bank Plc (20-01-96)

| | 30-09-14 | 30-09-13 | 30-09-12 |
|---|---|---|---|
| TA | 691,027 | 598,000 | 516,843 |
| NW | 55,875 | 55,875 | 55,877 |
| WC | 55,873 | 55,872 | 55,874 |

DUNS 22-952-3626 Imp-Exp

## The Stamford Group Ltd

(**Subsidiary of:** Navagator Ltd)
Stamford Mill, Bayley Street, Stalybridge, Cheshire SK15 1QQ
**Tel:** 01613306511
**Web:** www.stamford-group.co.uk
**Reg No:** 1647353 **Estd:** 1981 Private Limited Company
**Line of Business:** Management activities of holding companies
**Export Markets:** Worldwide
**Export Sales:** £5,015,000
**Issued Capital:** £1,035,000
**Directors:** Mrs K J Ferris, S Dubyl, A Reay
**Co. Secretary:** Stephen Picot
**Responsibilities**
**Senior:** Colin Hesketh *(Manager)*, Stephen Mckenna *(Manager)*
**Sales:** Allison Seabourne *(Sales Director)*
**US SIC:** 3079 **UK SIC:** 48360
**Auditors:** Beever & Struthers
**Bankers:** The Royal Bank Of Scotland Plc (16-12-17)

| | 30-09-13 | 30-09-12 | 30-09-11 |
|---|---|---|---|
| TO | 16,014,000 | 16,213,000 | 61,180,000 |
| P/L | (1,155,000) | 2,916,000 | 3,326,000 |
| NW | 7,443,000 | 10,786,000 | 15,643,000 |
| WC | 4,765,000 | 7,274,000 | 4,982,000 |
| Emp. | 202 | 206 | 352 |

DUNS 23-251-8188

## Stamford High School for Girls

St Martins, St Martins, Stamford, Lincolnshire PE9 2LL
**Tel:** 01780484200
**Web:** www.ses.lincs.sch.uk
**Estd:** 2002
**Line of Business:** Schools (independent)
**Director:** Mrs P Clark
**Responsibilities**
**Senior:** Yvonne Powell *(Headmistress)*
**IT:** Nick Faux *(Computer Manager)*, Scott Slocombe *(Head of IT Services)*
**US SIC:** 8211 **UK SIC:** 93200
**Employees:** 200

DUNS 23-214-4613

## Stamford Junior School

Kettering Road, Stamford, Lincolnshire PE9 2LR
**Tel:** 01780484400
**Web:** www.ses.lincs.sch.uk
**Estd:** 1997 Proprietorship
**Line of Business:** Schools (independent)
**Director:** Mrs E Smith
**Responsibilities**
**HR:** Sally Brittain *(Human Resources Manager)*
**US SIC:** 8211 **UK SIC:** 93200
**Employees:** 70

DUNS 21-872-3318

## Stamp Jackson & Procter Llp

5 Parliament Street, Hull, North Humberside HU1 2AZ
**Tel:** 01482324591
**Web:** www.sjplaw.co.uk
**Reg No:** 0380705OC **Estd:** 2001 Private Limited Company
**Line of Business:** Solicitors
**US SIC:** 8999 **UK SIC:** 83954

| | 30-04-14 |
|---|---|
| TA | 4,462,665 |
| NW | 911,159 |
| WC | 3,188,493 |

DUNS 21-931-2873 Imp-Exp

## Stampiton Labels Ltd

(**Subsidiary of:** Klimax A/S)
Bingswood Industrial Estate, Whaley Bridge, High Peak, Derbyshire SK23 7SP
**Tel:** 01663-733535
**Web:** www.stampiton.co.uk
**Reg No:** 1290334 **VAT No:** 565532333
**Estd:** 1976 Private Limited Company
**Line of Business:** Labelling stamping and imprinting equipment
**Export Markets:** Far East, Western Europe, Scandinavia, Australasia and Middle East
**Export Sales:** £412,409
**Issued Capital:** £2,505,000
**Directors:** B Petersen, T J Pattison, A D Worthington, A P Woodhouse, B Kluge
**Responsibilities**
**Senior:** Derek Maskell *(Manager)*, Bent-age Petersen *(Director)*, Rene Van Leeuwen *(Manager)*
**Sales:** Derek Maskell *(Manager)*, Darren Turford *(Sales Account Manager)*
**Facilities:** Tony Saunders *(Engineering Manager)*
**Engineering:** Tony Saunders *(Engineering Manager)*
**Branches:** Customark Label Solution, Unit 4 City Est, Congreaves Rd, Cradley Heath
**US SIC:** 3551, 2752
**UK SIC:** 32441, 47544
**Auditors:** Allens Accountants Ltd
**Bankers:** National Westminster Bank Plc (01-05-41)

| | 31-12-13 | 31-12-12 | 31-12-11 |
|---|---|---|---|
| TO | 12,048,237 | 11,351,350 | 11,001,589 |
| P/L | 871,399 | 1,002,562 | 258,993 |
| NW | 4,528,754 | 3,669,195 | 2,670,715 |
| WC | 4,028,112 | 3,088,212 | 1,898,220 |
| Emp. | 65 | 61 | 64 |

DUNS 21-710-1831 Imp

## Stan Brouard Ltd

Landes Du Marche, Vale, Guernsey, Channel Islands GY6 8DE
**Tel:** 01481-252521 **Fax:** 01481-256556
**Web:** www.sbproducts.co.uk
**Reg No:** 0001660G **Estd:** 1882 Private Limited Company
**Line of Business:** Agricultural consultants
**Issued Capital:** £27,000
**Managing Director:** R Brouard
**Responsibilities**
**Senior:** Bridgette Foss *(Financial Director)*
**Finance:** Bridgette Foss *(Financial Director)*, John Le Page *(Director and Company Secretary)*
**IT:** Bridgette Foss *(Financial Director)*
**US SIC:** 0729 **UK SIC:** 01003
**Employees:** 60

DUNS 21-157-6004 Imp-Exp

## Stan Chem International Ltd

4 Kings Road, Reading, Berkshire RG1 3AA
**Tel:** 01189-580-247 **Fax:** 01189-500-460
**Web:** www.biotechnica.co.uk
**Reg No:** 1336946 **VAT No:** 242278664
**Estd:** 1977 Private Limited Company
**Line of Business:** Chemicals distribution and wholesale
**Export Markets:** Africa; Far East; U S A
**Export Sales:** £10,622,810
**Trading Style:** Inovia International
**Issued Capital:** £65
**Directors:** P Rohof, L R Litwinowicz, T Engelen
**Responsibilities**
**Senior:** Vivian Freeman *(Manager)*, Paul Styles *(Manager)*
**Branches:** Stan Chem International Ltd, Gapton Hall, Viking Road, Great Yarmouth, Norfolk NR31 0NU
**US SIC:** 5161, 2834
**UK SIC:** 61200, 25700
**Auditors:** Rayner Essex LLP
**Bankers:** Barclays Bank Plc (20-71-03)

| | 31-10-13 | 31-10-12 | 31-10-11 |
|---|---|---|---|
| TO | 22,226,100 | 21,452,883 | 19,764,918 |
| P/L | 2,021,292 | 1,789,711 | 1,895,668 |
| NW | 7,609,643 | 6,059,616 | 4,801,518 |
| WC | 6,951,971 | 5,408,554 | 4,205,092 |
| Emp. | 79 | 77 | 68 |

DUNS 21-927-0980

## Stan Robinson Group Ltd

Ladfordfields, Stafford, Staffordshire ST18 9QE
**Tel:** 01785-282501 **Fax:** 01785-282843
**Web:** www.stanrobinson.com
**Reg No:** 1211657 **Estd:** 1970 Private Limited Company
**Line of Business:** Storage and warehousing
**Issued Capital:** £39,440
**Directors:** I G Robinson, M S Robinson, Mrs F E Robinson
**Co. Secretary:** Mrs Pauline Wilson
**Branches:** Stan Robinson Group Ltd, Drumhead Rd, Glasgow East Investment Pk, Glasgow, Lanarkshire G32 8EX
**US SIC:** 4226, 4213
**UK SIC:** 77003, 72300
**Auditors:** Bdo Stoy Hayward
**Bankers:** Yorkshire Bank Plc (05-09-26)

| | 31-05-14 | 31-05-13 | 31-05-12 |
|---|---|---|---|
| TO | 23,402,803 | 23,151,475 | 21,653,348 |
| P/L | 387,802 | 4,004 | 225,247 |
| NW | 12,041,060 | 11,748,334 | 11,771,052 |
| WC | 1,510,882 | 1,802,136 | 1,549,656 |
| Emp. | 326 | 327 | 329 |

DUNS 21-912-3585 Imp

## Stanair Industrial Door Services Ltd

Unit 2 Henson Way, Telford Way Industrial Estate, Kettering, Northamptonshire NN16 8PX
**Tel:** 01536482187
**Web:** www.stanair.co.uk
**Reg No:** 1180826 **VAT No:** 121807693
**Estd:** 1974 Private Limited Company
**Line of Business:** Doors & shutters retails and installers
**Issued Capital:** £3,250
**Principals:** M A Markham *(Managing)*, J T Standoloft, J Standoloft, M J Wall, D A Wood, Mrs L M Voss, Ms M H Hill, D Martin
**Co. Secretary:** Mrs Sheena Markham
**Branches:** Stanair Industrial Door Services Ltd, 5 Fairweather Court, Peterborough, Cambridgeshire PE1 5UN
**US SIC:** 1751 **UK SIC:** 50400
**Auditors:** Moore Stephens
**Bankers:** HSBC Bank plc (40-10-02)

| | 31-08-13 | 31-08-12 | 31-08-11 |
|---|---|---|---|
| TA | 2,534,390 | 2,479,351 | 2,179,843 |
| NW | 1,412,920 | 1,386,744 | 1,238,651 |
| WC | 491,908 | 510,754 | 460,123 |

DUNS 21-779-6647

## The Stanborough Beefeater & Travel Inn

Stanborough, Stanborough Road, Welwyn Garden City, Hertfordshire AL8 6DQ
**Tel:** 01707391345
**Web:** www.beefeater.co.uk
**Estd:** 2011
**Line of Business:** Licensed restaurants
**US SIC:** 5812 **UK SIC:** 66110
**Employees:** 75

DUNS 54-905-1217

## Stanborough Secondary School

Stanborough Park, Watford, Hertfordshire WD25 9JT
**Tel:** 01923-673268
**Web:** www.stanboroughprimary.org.uk
**Estd:** 1923 Partnership
**Line of Business:** Schools (independent)
**Partners:** R Murphy, R Murphy
**Responsibilities**
**Senior:** Lorraine Dixon *(Principal)*
**US SIC:** 8211 **UK SIC:** 93200
**Employees:** 80

DUNS 76-964-1374

## Stanbridge Group Ltd

Wessex House Cadland Road Hardle, Hythe, Southampton, Hampshire SO45 3NY
**Tel:** 02380898054 **Fax:** 023-8089-8055
**Reg No:** 2628793 **VAT No:** 580274244
**Estd:** 1992 Private Limited Company
**Line of Business:** Building services
**Issued Capital:** £10,000
**Principals:** D R Fairchild *(Managing)*, B C Fairchild, R J Fairchild, Ms S J Fairchild
**Co. Secretary:** Lee Tybinkowski
**US SIC:** 6552 **UK SIC:** 85000
**Auditors:** Ward Goodman
**Bankers:** Lloyds TSB Bank plc (30-94-90)

| | 31-12-13 | 31-12-12 | 31-12-11 |
|---|---|---|---|
| TO | 143,419,119 | 133,516,040 | 116,501,479 |
| P/L | 1,668,278 | 935,966 | 440,319 |
| NW | 4,635,116 | 3,301,754 | 2,595,452 |
| WC | 1,452,831 | 1,160,560 | 1,176,779 |
| Emp. | 100 | 88 | 74 |

DUNS 29-489-3979

## Stanbridge Homes Ltd

Unit 6 Denbigh Hall Industrial Estate, Denbigh Hall, Bletchley, Milton Keynes, Buckinghamshire MK3 7QT
**Reg No:** 1852791 **Estd:** 1946 Private Limited Company
**Line of Business:** Other letting of own property
**Issued Capital:** £100
**Director:** Mrs S J Worrall
**Co. Secretary:** Allen Worrall
**US SIC:** 6519, 1541
**UK SIC:** 85000, 50100
**Auditors:** R A & D A Thompson

| | 31-12-13 | 31-12-12 | 31-12-11 |
|---|---|---|---|
| TA | 103,382 | 105,668 | 100,010 |
| NW | (117,341) | (120,741) | (123,315) |
| WC | (184,341) | (187,741) | (190,315) |

DUNS 73-773-2961

## Stanbridge School Trading Ltd

Stanbridge Earls, Romsey, Hampshire SO51 0ZS
**Tel:** 01794-529400
**Web:** www.stanbridgeearls.co.uk
**Reg No:** 5030273 **Estd:** 2004 Private Limited Company
**Line of Business:** Other tourist or short-stay accommodation
**Trading Style:** Stanbridge Earl School
**Issued Capital:** £1
**Directors:** J A Chandler, P C Goodship, D R Du Croz
**Responsibilities**
**IT:** Russell Dearlove *(Computer Manager)*, dean williams *(computer manager)*
**US SIC:** 7021 **UK SIC:** 66500

| | 31-08-13 | 31-08-12 | 31-08-11 |
|---|---|---|---|
| TO | 57,664 | 62,559 | 57,650 |
| P/L | (7,437) | N/A | N/A |
| NW | 1 | 7,438 | 7,438 |
| WC | 1 | 7,438 | 7,438 |

DUNS 21-586-6915

## Stanchester Community School

East Stoke, Stoke-Sub-Hamdon, Somerset TA14 6UG
**Tel:** 01935823200
**Web:** www.stanchester-academy.co.uk
**Estd:** 2011 Proprietorship
**Line of Business:** Schools (local authority)
**Proprietor:** Mrs J Mcblain
**Responsibilities**
**Senior:** Jason Beardmore *(Principal)*
**Finance:** Hellen Cole *(Senior Finance Administrator)*
**HR:** Liz Joynes *(Human Resources Manager)*
**US SIC:** 8211 **UK SIC:** 93200
**Employees:** 120

DUNS 21-732-7039

## Stanchester Community School Academy

East Stoke, Stoke-Sub-Hamdon, Somerset TA14 6UG
**Tel:** 01935827247
**Web:** www.stanchester-academy.co.uk
**Reg No:** 7677142 **Estd:** 2011 Private Company Limited By Guarantee
**Line of Business:** General secondary education
**Directors:** Ms J Watson, S G Barrow, Ms R Atkinson, D Ryan, Ms M Todd, S D Crabb, Ms S Collard, G Mcwilliams
**Responsibilities**
**Senior:** Jason Beardmore *(Director)*, Lynn Benfield *(Director)*, Susan Chant *(Director)*, Simon Darley *(Director)*, Andrew Draper *(Director)*, Helen Green *(Director)*, Charlotte Hall *(Director)*, Nicola Holt *(Director)*, Tim Olivey *(Director)*
**US SIC:** 8211 **UK SIC:** 93200

| | 31-08-14 | 31-08-13 | 31-08-12 |
|---|---|---|---|
| TO | 4,226,681 | 4,569,090 | 13,032,509 |
| P/L | 22,603 | 197,227 | 8,392,518 |
| NW | 8,155,348 | 8,058,745 | 7,918,518 |
| WC | 894,443 | 620,585 | 432,087 |
| Emp. | 84 | 84 | 93 |

DUNS 21-633-5628

## Standard & Poor's Credit Market Services Europe Ltd

20 Canada Square, London E14 5LH
**Tel:** 020-7176-3800 **Fax:** 020-7176-3690
**Web:** www.standardandpoors.com
**Reg No:** 7114748 **Estd:** 2009 Private Limited Company
**Line of Business:** Other business activities not elsewhere classified
**Issued Capital:** £1,000
**Directors:** J F Penrose, J G Strubel, N Sahai, E C Meister, Y Le Pallec, A H Schuman
**Co. Secretary:** Ms Catherine Shelley
**US SIC:** 7399 **UK SIC:** 83954
**Auditors:** Ernst & Young LLP

| | 31-12-13 | 31-12-12 | 31-12-11 |
|---|---|---|---|
| TO | 281,827,000 | 229,158,000 | 195,762,000 |
| P/L | 63,944,000 | 30,143,000 | 15,249,000 |
| NW | (172,222,000) | (197,738,000) | (223,341,000) |
| WC | 96,884,000 | 67,916,000 | 36,578,000 |
| Emp. | 718 | 706 | 620 |

DUNS 39-949-4673

## Standard Bank London Holdings Ltd

20 Gresham Street, London EC2V 7JE
**Tel:** 02078153022 **Fax:** 020 3189 5000
**Web:** www.standardbank.com
**Reg No:** 2255588 **Estd:** 1837 Private Limited Company
**Line of Business:** Financial intermediation not elsewhere classified
**Trading Style:** Stanbic Bank
**Directors:** D C Munro, S P Ridley, T J Lancaster, Mrs S C Smollett, G M Vogel

**Co. Secretary:** Ms Susan Smollett
**Responsibilities**
**Senior:** David Duffy (Manager), Dennis Dugmore (Director), Grant Joyce (Director), Jennifer Knott (Manager), Robert Leith (Manager), Marc Van Der Spuy (Director)
**US SIC:** 6111, 6012
**UK SIC:** 81501, 81402
**Auditors:** KPMG Audit PLC
**Bankers:** National Westminster Bank Plc (50-00-00)
**Employees:** 778

DUNS 23-351-6991
## Standard Bank of South Africa Ltd
(**Subsidiary of:** Standard Bank Group Ltd)
One Circular Road, Douglas, Isle of Man IM1 1SB
**Tel:** 01624643643
**Web:** www.standardbankoffshorezone.com
**Reg No:** 0002373Q **Estd:** 1996 Foreign Company
**Line of Business:** Bankers and Trust Company
**US SIC:** 6111 **UK SIC:** 81501

DUNS 22-142-5056
## Standard Brands (Uk) Ltd
Cleeve Court, 4 Cleeve Road, Leatherhead, Surrey KT22 7SD
**Tel:** 01372-360833 **Fax:** 01372-360996
**Web:** www.standard-brands.com
**Reg No:** 4161375 **Estd:** 1924 Private Limited Company
**Line of Business:** Manufacturer of domestic fire products - firelighters, firelogs, BBQ fuels, and ancillary products.
**Issued Capital:** £1,000
**Directors:** R Harris, G Mcdonnell, M I Escolme, D Mccourt, M J Boxford
**Co. Secretary:** Terry Coates
**US SIC:** 2899 **UK SIC:** 25670
**Auditors:** Deloitte & Touche
**Bankers:** Lloyds TSB Bank plc (30-16-83)

| | 31-12-13 | 31-12-12 | 31-12-11 |
|---|---|---|---|
| TO | 23,862,042 | 22,166,099 | 19,883,568 |
| P/L | (16,003) | (154,473) | (805,406) |
| NW | (9,992,706) | (9,830,614) | (10,452,175) |
| WC | (1,458,554) | 2,692,766 | 1,757,372 |
| Emp. | 96 | 98 | 97 |

DUNS 21-370-6917
## Standard Business Investment Group
Unit 3 Meridian Centre, Vulcan Way, New Addington, Croydon, Surrey CR0 9UG
**Tel:** 01689809844
**Web:** www.standard-holdings.co.uk
**Estd:** 2009 Proprietorship
**Line of Business:** Holding companies management activities
**Proprietor:** T Lally
**US SIC:** 6711 **UK SIC:** 83962
**Employees:** 55

DUNS 28-994-7152
## Standard Chartered Equitor Ltd
(**Subsidiary of:** Standard Chartered Plc)
1 Aldermanbury Square, London EC2V 7SB
**Tel:** 02031455000
**Reg No:** 1839037 **Estd:** 1984 Private Limited Company
**Line of Business:** Other business activities not elsewhere classified
**Directors:** P S Chambers, Mrs B A Mcall, T Lord
**Co. Secretary:** Sc (Secretaries) Limited
**US SIC:** 7399 **UK SIC:** 83954
**Auditors:** KPMG Audit Plc
**Bankers:** Standard Chartered Bank (60-91-06)
**Employees:** 250

DUNS 21-738-4551
## Standard Chartered (Jersey) Ltd
(**Subsidiary of:** Standard Chartered Plc)
P O Box 80, Jersey, Channel Islands JE4 8PT
**Tel:** 01534-704000 **Fax:** 01534704600
**Web:** www.standardchartered.com
**Reg No:** 0002170J **Estd:** 1966 Private Limited Company
**Line of Business:** Banks
**Issued Capital:** £3,633,333
**Managing Director:** C Dickinson
**Co. Secretary:** G Buckland
**Responsibilities**
**Senior:** Alison McFadyen (Manager)
**US SIC:** 6012, 7399
**UK SIC:** 81402, 83954
**Bankers:** National Westminster Bank Plc (60-12-03)
**Employees:** 150

DUNS 21-196-6312    **Imp-Exp**
## Standard Chartered Plc
1 Basinghall Avenue, London EC2V 5DD
**Tel:** 020-7885-8888 **Fax:** 02078859999
**Web:** www.standardchartered.com
**Reg No:** 0966425 **Estd:** 1858 Public Limited Company
**Line of Business:** Financial intermediation not elsewhere classified
**Trading Style:** Standard Chartered Bank
**Directors:** A N Halford, O P Bhatt, L C Cheung, Sir J W Peace, Dr K M Campbell, Ms R Markland, Dr S Han, J S Bindra
**Co. Secretary:** Ms Annemarie Durbin
**Responsibilities**
**Senior:** Richard Delbridge (Non-Executive Director), Seung-soo Han (Non-Executive Director), Alun Rees (Director), Peter Sands (Chief Executive), Viswanathan Shankar (Director), Paul Skinner (Director), Lars Thunell (Director)
**Health & Safety:** Courtney Joseph (Health & Safety Officer)
**Facilities:** Alan Bridges (Property Manager)
**US SIC:** 6111 **UK SIC:** 81501
**Auditors:** KPMG Audit PLC
**Bankers:** Bank Of England (10-00-00)
**Employees:** 2,000

DUNS 21-120-8036
## Standard Life Assurance Company
Standard Life House, 30 Lothian Road, Edinburgh, Midlothian EH1 2DH
**Tel:** 01312252552 **Fax:** 01312458390
**Web:** www.standardlife.co.uk
**Reg No:** 0000038 **Estd:** 1997 Private Limited Company
**Line of Business:** Representative office
**Principals:** J Trott (Chairman), The Hon R Maclaren, N Lessels, S Crombie, H Stevenson, B Beamish, S Bell, B Stewart
**Responsibilities**
**Senior:** Jean Delorme (Vice Chairperson), Claude Garcia (Director), Francis Kirwan (Manager), Roy MacLaren (Director), Alison Mitchell (Director), David Newlands (Director), Nathan Parnaby (Manager), Jim Stretton (Director)
**US SIC:** 6399 **UK SIC:** 82001
**Employees:** 1,400

DUNS 23-717-9432
## Standard Life Client Management Ltd
(**Subsidiary of:** Standard Life Plc)
Dundas House, 20 Brandon Street, Edinburgh, Midlothian EH3 5PP
**Tel:** 08452726600
**Web:** www.slpcm.com
**Reg No:** 0193444SC **Estd:** 1999 Private Limited Company
**Line of Business:** Life insurance
**Issued Capital:** £4,000,000
**Directors:** S L Ingledew, Ms N M Riding, J E Gill, F A O'Dwyer
**Co. Secretary:** Ms Gillian Mcgovern
**Responsibilities**
**Sales:** James Brunning (Sales Manager), Angela Smith (Sales Manager)
**US SIC:** 6311 **UK SIC:** 82002
**Auditors:** Professional Tax Management Ltd

| | 31-12-13 | 31-12-12 | 31-12-11 |
|---|---|---|---|
| TO | 34,813,000 | 15,144,000 | 27,072,000 |
| P/L | 21,504,000 | 1,900,000 | 2,113,000 |
| NW | 20,775,000 | 5,685,000 | 5,957,000 |
| WC | 20,775,000 | 5,685,000 | 5,957,000 |
| Emp. | 121 | 128 | 160 |

DUNS 50-506-4394
## Standard Life Investments Ltd
(**Subsidiary of:** Standard Life Plc)
3 George Street, Edinburgh, Midlothian EH2 2PA
**Tel:** 01312252345 **Fax:** 01312 201534
**Web:** www.standardlife.com
**Reg No:** 0123321SC **Estd:** 1990 Private Limited Company
**Line of Business:** Management activities of holding companies
**Issued Capital:** £32,440,000
**Directors:** G Stern, D T Cumming, A S Acheson, C R Walklin, N K Skeoch, W R Littleboy, R A Charnock, Ms J Martin
**Co. Secretary:** David Burns
**Responsibilities**
**Senior:** Roger Renaud (Director), Michael Tumilty (Director)
**US SIC:** 6711 **UK SIC:** 83962
**Auditors:** PricewaterhouseCoopers LLP

| | 31-12-13 | 31-12-12 | 31-12-11 |
|---|---|---|---|
| TO | 452,670,000 | 363,093,000 | 308,777,000 |
| P/L | 120,329,000 | 104,290,000 | 82,078,000 |
| NW | 142,616,000 | 135,301,000 | 143,516,000 |
| WC | 99,329,000 | 92,751,000 | 97,500,000 |
| Emp. | 912 | 822 | 791 |

DUNS 34-690-6592    **Imp**
## Standard Life Plc
Standard Life House, 30 Lothian Road, Edinburgh, Midlothian EH1 2DH
**Tel:** 08456060100 **Fax:** 01312 457 990
**Web:** www.standardlife.com
**Reg No:** 0286832SC **Estd:** 1825 Public Limited Company
**Line of Business:** Management activities of holding companies
**Export Sales:** £6,057,000,000
**Issued Capital:** £237,636,307
**Directors:** Mrs I F Hudson, K A Parry, D T Nish, N K Skeoch, M S Pike, C Gillies, P Danon, L Savage
**Co. Secretary:** Kenneth Gilmour
**Responsibilities**
**Senior:** Gerald Grimstone (Director), Margaret McDonagh (Manager), John Paynter (Director), Jocelyn Proteau (Manager)
**US SIC:** 6711, 6371 **UK SIC:** 83962, 82002
**Auditors:** PricewaterhouseCoopers LLP
Following financial data are in thousands

| | 31-12-13 | 31-12-12 | 31-12-11 |
|---|---|---|---|
| TO | 20,545,000 | 19,185,000 | 3,245,000 |
| P/L | 801,000 | 996,000 | 595,000 |
| NW | 3,927,000 | 4,141,000 | 3,761,000 |
| WC | (4,128,000) | (5,810,000) | 15,345,000 |
| Emp. | 8,224 | 8,458 | 8,789 |

DUNS 21-884-2219    **Imp-Exp**
## Standard Motor Products Europe Ltd
Little Oak Drive, Nottingham, Nottinghamshire NG15 6DR
**Tel:** 01623-886410 **Fax:** 01623886500
**Web:** www.smpeurope.co.uk
**Reg No:** 0955888 **Estd:** 1967 Private Limited Company
**Line of Business:** Manufacture of parts and accessories for motor vehicles and their engines
**Export Markets:** U.S.A., E U, Africa, Middle East, Far East
**Issued Capital:** £6,150,883
**Directors:** S T Hall, I L Turner
**Co. Secretary:** Sukhjinder Chahal
**Responsibilities**
**Senior:** Les Kershaw (Senior Sales Executive)
**Sales:** Les Kershaw (Senior Sales Executive)
**Branches:** Standard Motor Products Europe Ltd, Occupation Rd, Nottingham, Nottinghamshire NG15 6DZ
**US SIC:** 3714 **UK SIC:** 35300
**Auditors:** Grant Thornton UK LLP
**Bankers:** The Royal Bank Of Scotland Plc (16-26-32)

| | 31-12-13 | 31-12-12 | 31-12-11 |
|---|---|---|---|
| TO | 27,747,041 | 27,839,774 | 21,211,436 |
| P/L | 2,120,960 | 2,104,992 | 1,339,655 |
| NW | 7,195,444 | 8,832,659 | 8,510,386 |
| WC | 4,482,856 | 8,540,209 | 7,799,148 |
| Emp. | 168 | 169 | 131 |

DUNS 29-027-6690    **Imp-Exp**
## Standard Wool (U K) Ltd
Carlton Buildings, Bradford, West Yorkshire BD8 7DB
**Tel:** 01274495511
**Web:** www.standard-wool.co.uk
**Reg No:** 0713917 **Estd:** 1962 Private Limited Company
**Line of Business:** Hair and wool
**Export Markets:** Worldwide
**Export Sales:** £30,409,878
**Trading Style:** Mainz, Thomas Chadwick & Sons
**Issued Capital:** £2,552,030
**Principals:** P T Hughes (Managing), I R Marwood, P S Hughes, M V Willis, M Andrews
**Responsibilities**
**Senior:** Nicholas Maddams (Financial Director), Martin Springthorpe (Manager)
**Finance:** Nicholas Maddams (Financial Director), Martin Springthorpe (Manager)
**US SIC:** 5133 **UK SIC:** 61600
**Auditors:** Grant Thornton UK LLP
**Bankers:** National Westminster Bank Plc (56-00-36)

| | 31-03-14 | 31-03-13 | 31-03-12 |
|---|---|---|---|
| TO | 50,992,815 | 49,578,539 | 56,285,308 |
| P/L | 1,042,236 | 570,094 | 1,433,543 |
| NW | 8,714,415 | 8,011,775 | 7,784,638 |
| WC | 7,357,731 | 8,488,420 | 8,414,371 |
| Emp. | 82 | 81 | 73 |

DUNS 73-803-0209
## Standard Wool Uk (Holdings) Ltd
Standard House, Trevor Foster Way, Bradford, West Yorkshire BD5 8HB
**Tel:** 01274756600
**Reg No:** 5059381 **Estd:** 2004 Private Limited Company
**Line of Business:** Preparation and spinning of textile fibres

**Export Sales:** £32,040,890
**Issued Capital:** £100,000
**Directors:** M V Willis, P T Hughes
**Responsibilities**
**Senior:** Nicholas Maddams (Director)
**US SIC:** 2299, 5199
**UK SIC:** 43992, 61900

| | 31-03-14 | 31-03-13 | 31-03-12 |
|---|---|---|---|
| TO | 52,623,827 | 51,782,496 | 58,365,909 |
| P/L | 788,302 | 911,220 | 1,205,940 |
| NW | 6,230,507 | 5,794,550 | 5,250,579 |
| WC | 5,595,935 | 6,795,651 | 6,114,574 |
| Emp. | 154 | 152 | 144 |

DUNS 21-778-5556
## Standards & Learning Effectiveness Service
St Marks House, 14 Upperton Road, Eastbourne, East Sussex BN21 1EP
**Tel:** 01323466810
**Web:** www.eastsussex.gov.uk
**Estd:** 1995 Partnership
**Line of Business:** Education services
**Partners:** M Dunkley, B Little
**Responsibilities**
**Senior:** Fiona Wright (Manager)
**US SIC:** 8299 **UK SIC:** 93300
**Employees:** 72

DUNS 29-506-4471
## Standby Pest Control Ltd
(**Subsidiary of:** Iss A/S)
I S S Pest Control, I S S House, Woking, Surrey GU21 5RW
**Tel:** 08450576271 **Fax:** 02087421310
**Web:** www.standbypest-control.co.uk
**Reg No:** 1869679 **Estd:** 1985 Private Limited Company
**Line of Business:** Commercial pest control contractors
**Issued Capital:** £1,000
**Directors:** M E Brabin, R I Sykes
**US SIC:** 7342 **UK SIC:** 92110
**Auditors:** CLB
**Bankers:** HSBC Bank plc (40-35-32)

| | 31-12-13 | 31-12-12 | 31-12-11 |
|---|---|---|---|
| TA | 1,000 | 1,000 | 1,000 |
| NW | 1,000 | 1,000 | 1,000 |

DUNS 22-297-9432    **Exp**
## Standen Engineering Ltd
Hereward Works, Station Road, Ely, Cambridgeshire CB7 4BP
**Tel:** 01353666200
**Web:** www.standen.co.uk
**Reg No:** 4315838 **VAT No:** 432243682
**Estd:** 1987 Private Limited Company
**Line of Business:** Agricultural engineers
**Export Sales:** £1,605,654
**Trading Style:** Standen-Reflex
**Issued Capital:** £8,155
**Directors:** R A Holmes, A J Winter, D P Wilson, A C Bone
**Co. Secretary:** Owen Blake
**Responsibilities**
**Senior:** Douglas Carter (Production Director)
**HR:** Douglas Carter (Production Director)
**Health & Safety:** Douglas Carter (Production Director)
**Facilities:** Douglas Carter (Production Director)
**Operations:** Douglas Carter (Production Director)
**Engineering:** Douglas Carter (Production Director)
**US SIC:** 3559 **UK SIC:** 32863
**Auditors:** Whiting & Partners
**Bankers:** The Royal Bank Of Scotland Plc (16-08-05)

| | 30-11-13 | 30-11-12 | 30-11-11 |
|---|---|---|---|
| TO | 13,436,556 | 11,116,343 | 11,856,235 |
| P/L | 673,370 | 324,393 | 514,528 |
| NW | 1,800,600 | 796,724 | 1,270,842 |
| WC | 3,086,340 | 2,754,577 | 2,655,683 |
| Emp. | 87 | 87 | 88 |

DUNS 21-304-7624
## Standish Engineering Co. Ltd
(**Subsidiary of:** Standish Engineering Holdings Ltd)
Mayflower Works, Bradley Lane, Standish, Wigan, Lancashire WN6 0XF
**Tel:** 01257422838
**Web:** www.standishengineering.co.uk
**Reg No:** 0696880 **VAT No:** 152230216
**Estd:** 1961 Private Limited Company
**Line of Business:** Precision engineers
**Issued Capital:** £4,000
**Principals:** C J Kindon (Financial), N J Kindon
**Co. Secretary:** Ms Joanna Kindon
**US SIC:** 8911 **UK SIC:** 83701
**Auditors:** Fairhurst
**Bankers:** National Westminster Bank Plc (60-24-02)

| | 31-07-14 | 31-07-13 | 31-07-12 |
|---|---|---|---|
| TA | 1,941,379 | 2,321,188 | 2,044,091 |
| NW | 1,225,376 | 1,176,126 | 1,089,885 |
| WC | 608,462 | 558,777 | 466,681 |

DUNS 55-059-8684

## Stanely Park Residential Home

Stanely Road, Paisley, Renfrewshire PA2 6HJ
**Tel:** 01418847617
**Web:** www.pacificcare.co.uk
**Estd:** 1992 Proprietorship
**Line of Business:** Residential care establishments
**Proprietor:** J Brawley
**Responsibilities**
**Senior:** Karen Armstrong *(Manager)*, Elizabeth Caunter *(Manager)*
**US SIC:** 8321 **UK SIC:** 96111
**Employees:** 50

DUNS 77-902-5936

## Stanfield Nursing Home (Holdings) Ltd

Stanfield Nursing Home, Worcester, Worcestershire WR2 5SU
**Tel:** 01905-420459
**Web:** www.stanfieldnursing.co.uk
**Reg No:** 5807763 **Estd:** 2006 Private Limited Company
**Line of Business:** Medical nursing home activities
**Issued Capital:** £100
**Director:** R L White
**Co. Secretary:** Timothy Sherwood
**US SIC:** 6711 **UK SIC:** 83962
**Bankers:** The Royal Bank Of Scotland Plc (10-10-13)

| | 03-04-14 | 05-04-13 | 03-04-12 |
|---|---|---|---|
| TA | 2,057,800 | 2,070,433 | 2,175,155 |
| NW | 455,793 | 363,319 | 298,300 |
| WC | (551,275) | (502,325) | (517,264) |

DUNS 21-730-5548

## The Stanford & Corringham Schools Trust

Southend Road, Corringham, Stanford-Le-Hope, Essex SS17 8JT
**Tel:** 01375400800
**Web:** www.gablehall.com
**Reg No:** 7660783 **Estd:** 2011 Private Company Limited By Guarantee
**Line of Business:** Schools (local authority)
**Directors:** Mrs J Seymour, C R Georgiou, Mrs G A Clark, R P Harman, S Nash, R W Barr, Mrs S A Feeney, Dr S Asong
**Co. Secretary:** Des Shillingford
**Responsibilities**
**Senior:** Mark Allinson *(Governor)*, Lindsay Bayfield *(Governor)*, Philip Edgar *(Director)*, Philomena Yeldham *(Director)*
**Finance:** Jenny Turner *(Financial Administrator)*
**Admin:** Mary Gay *(Secretary)*
**IT:** Richard Bowles *(Senior It Executive)*
**US SIC:** 8211 **UK SIC:** 93200

| | 31-08-13 | 31-08-12 |
|---|---|---|
| TO | 10,457,000 | 16,422,000 |
| P/L | 2,515,000 | 7,779,000 |
| NW | 9,701,000 | 7,364,000 |
| WC | 2,057,000 | 1,729,000 |
| Emp. | 142 | 139 |

DUNS 50-502-0651

## Stanford Industrial Concrete Flooring Ltd

5 Richmond St South, West Bromwich, West Midlands B70 0DG
**Tel:** 01215-222220
**Web:** www.stanford-flooring.co.uk
**Reg No:** 2470129 **VAT No:** 559313429
**Estd:** 1988 Private Limited Company
**Line of Business:** Other construction work involving special trades
**Export Sales:** £123,136
**Issued Capital:** £199
**Principals:** C G Stanford *(Managing)*, Mrs B A Stanford *(Financial)*, K Louch
**Co. Secretary:** David Booth
**US SIC:** 1799 **UK SIC:** 50000
**Auditors:** AGS Accountants & Business Advisors Ltd
**Bankers:** The Royal Bank Of Scotland Plc (16-18-41)

| | 31-03-14 | 31-03-13 | 31-03-12 |
|---|---|---|---|
| TO | 19,690,275 | 15,227,959 | 12,148,538 |
| P/L | 319,554 | 132,640 | 115,079 |
| NW | 2,383,563 | 2,267,094 | 2,215,340 |
| WC | 1,306,115 | 1,281,122 | 1,794,387 |
| Emp. | 48 | 56 | 54 |

DUNS 21-900-3597

## Stanford Marsh Ltd

Buckholt Drive, Worcester, Worcestershire WR4 9ND
**Tel:** 01905-458000 **Fax:** 01905-754057
**Web:** www.stanfordmarsh.co.uk
**Reg No:** 0838089 **Estd:** 1968 Private Limited Company
**Line of Business:** Office furniture and equipment suppliers
**Export Sales:** £154,240
**Trading Style:** Cadspec
**Issued Capital:** £1,180
**Principals:** C S Marsh *(Chairman and Managing)*, A Painter, J S Marsh, M Perkins
**Co. Secretary:** Jonathan Marsh
**Responsibilities**
**Finance:** Robb Jones *(Senior Finance Administrator)*, Andrew Potts *(Finance Director)*
**Marketing:** Clemency Evans *(Marketing Manager)*, James McCourt *(Telemarketing/ Telesales Manage)*
**Sales:** James McCourt *(Telemarketing/ Telesales Manage)*, Nadine Staples *(Business Development Manager)*
**IT:** Andrew Potts *(Finance Director)*
**Branches:** Stanford Marsh Ltd, Amber Ho, 15 Mundy St, Heanor, Derbyshire DE75 7EB
**US SIC:** 2599, 7379
**UK SIC:** 46720, 83940
**Auditors:** BDWM
**Bankers:** National Westminster Bank Plc (55-81-36)

| | 31-01-14 | 31-01-13 | 31-01-12 |
|---|---|---|---|
| TO | 12,762,652 | 12,396,068 | 11,356,675 |
| P/L | 388,555 | 374,779 | (50,416) |
| NW | 4,061,515 | 3,773,003 | 3,512,138 |
| WC | 1,413,124 | 1,557,464 | 1,361,486 |
| Emp. | 86 | 78 | 79 |

DUNS 21-779-1237

## Stanford Primary School

Chilmark Road, London SW16 5HB
**Tel:** 02087643892
**Web:** www.stanford.merton.sch.uk
**Estd:** 2011 Proprietorship
**Line of Business:** General secondary education
**Responsibilities**
**Senior:** Keran Currie *(Head Teacher)*, Patricia Millanaise *(Business Manager)*
**US SIC:** 8211 **UK SIC:** 93200
**Employees:** 55

DUNS 45-834-8570

## Stanford Scaffolding Ltd

(**Subsidiary of:** Stanford Management Services Ltd)
Redburn House, 2 Tonbridge Road, Romford, Essex RM3 8QE
**Tel:** 01708-343427 **Fax:** 01708-343428
**Web:** www.stanfordscaffolding.co.uk
**Reg No:** 3185593 **Estd:** 1996 Private Limited Company
**Line of Business:** Scaffolds and work platform erectors
**Issued Capital:** £100
**Managing Director:** J A Readings
**Co. Secretary:** Stephen Readings
**US SIC:** 1799 **UK SIC:** 50000
**Auditors:** Thornton Springer LLP
**Bankers:** Barclays Bank Plc (20-72-89)

| | 28-02-14 | 28-02-13 | 29-02-12 |
|---|---|---|---|
| TO | N/A | N/A | 5,468,440 |
| P/L | N/A | N/A | 74,762 |
| NW | 576,839 | 831,543 | 759,393 |
| WC | 515,063 | 772,816 | 750,440 |

DUNS 56-938-7277

## Stangs Ltd

P O Box 231, Shipley, West Yorkshire BD17 7AS
**Tel:** 01274-531828
**Reg No:** 2838257 **Estd:** 1993 Private Limited Company
**Line of Business:** Printing not elsewhere classified
**Issued Capital:** £56,596
**Directors:** A K Chapman, J H Chapman, J G Chapman, K Chapman, Ms E S Lammas
**Co. Secretary:** Ms Ann Chapman
**US SIC:** 2752 **UK SIC:** 47544
**Auditors:** Burton & Co
**Bankers:** Barclays Bank Plc (20-11-81)

| | 31-03-14 | 31-03-13 | 31-03-12 |
|---|---|---|---|
| TO | 8,977,232 | 9,605,918 | 8,844,739 |
| P/L | (10,374) | (413,035) | (1,044,730) |
| NW | 3,830,029 | 3,905,473 | 4,280,497 |
| WC | 1,261,392 | 1,087,796 | 1,320,138 |
| Emp. | 121 | 106 | 113 |

DUNS 73-850-9061

## Stanhope Capital Llp

35 Portman Square, London W1H 6LR
**Tel:** 02077251877
**Web:** www.stanhopecapital.com
**Reg No:** 0307719OC **Estd:** 2004 Private Limited Company
**Line of Business:** Activities of venture and development capital companies
**Responsibilities**
**Senior:** Ivo Coulson *(Partner)*, Edward Jewson *(Manager)*, Simon Paul *(Designated Limited Liability P)*
**US SIC:** 7399, 6111
**UK SIC:** 83954, 81501
**Auditors:** Ernst & Young LLP
**Bankers:** Coutts & Co (18-00-09)

| | 31-12-13 | 31-12-12 | 31-12-11 |
|---|---|---|---|
| TA | 7,115,255 | 5,271,711 | 4,963,029 |
| P/L | 4,798,953 | 2,582,829 | 1,319,477 |
| NW | 5,012,920 | 3,259,215 | 3,069,229 |
| WC | 4,588,662 | 2,818,513 | 2,549,609 |
| Emp. | 51 | 46 | 42 |

DUNS 73-840-4065

## Stanhope Capital Management Ltd

35 Portman Square, London W1H 6LR
**Tel:** 02077251800
**Reg No:** 5095816 **Estd:** 2004 Private Limited Company
**Line of Business:** Financial intermediation not elsewhere classified
**Issued Capital:** £7,400,000
**Directors:** J A Bell, D E Pinto
**Co. Secretary:** Julien Sevaux
**US SIC:** 6111 **UK SIC:** 81501
**Bankers:** Coutts & Co (18-00-09)

| | 31-12-13 | 31-12-12 | 31-12-11 |
|---|---|---|---|
| TA | 6,540,705 | 5,743,260 | 6,269,916 |
| P/L | 4,442,682 | 2,170,045 | 1,204,678 |
| NW | 391,492 | (212,414) | 257,500 |
| WC | 2,580,677 | 1,314,685 | 1,352,515 |
| Emp. | 52 | 48 | 44 |

DUNS 34-968-7496

## Stanhope Group Holdings Ltd

Norfolk House, 31 St Jamess Square, London SW1Y 4JJ
**Tel:** 02071701700
**Web:** www.stanhopeplc.com
**Reg No:** 5764165 **Estd:** 2006 Private Limited Company
**Line of Business:** Development and selling of real estate
**Issued Capital:** £7,027,921
**Directors:** O H Stocken, D J Camp, M Dal Bello, H Yamada
**Co. Secretary:** Ms Clare Pagan
**US SIC:** 6552 **UK SIC:** 85000

| | 31-03-14 | 31-03-13 | 31-03-12 |
|---|---|---|---|
| TO | 21,539,000 | 27,241,000 | 13,614,000 |
| P/L | 6,896,000 | 5,139,000 | 1,958,000 |
| NW | 23,779,000 | 19,150,000 | 3,858,000 |
| WC | 18,542,000 | 18,788,000 | 13,139,000 |
| Emp. | 46 | 45 | 43 |

DUNS 21-612-3752 **Imp-Exp**

## Stanhope-Seta Ltd

London Street, Chertsey, Surrey KT16 8AP
**Tel:** 01932-564391
**Web:** www.stanhope-seta.co.uk
**Reg No:** 0361699 **VAT No:** 211438404
**Estd:** 1940 Private Limited Company
**Line of Business:** Business and management consultancy activities not elsewhere classified
**Export Markets:** Worldwide
**Issued Capital:** £1,000,100
**Principals:** G Verity *(Managing)*, M Verity *(Financial)*
**Co. Secretary:** Ms Maureen Richardson
**Responsibilities**
**Senior:** Bryan Powell *(Works Manager)*
**Finance:** Ian Denby *(Accounts Manager)*
**Marketing:** Stephen Zeal *(Marketing Director)*
**Branches:** Stanhope-Seta Ltd, London Street, Chertsey, Surrey KT16 8AP
**US SIC:** 7399 **UK SIC:** 83954
**Auditors:** Shipleys LLP
**Bankers:** The Royal Bank Of Scotland Plc (15-10-00)

| | 31-07-14 | 31-07-13 | 31-07-12 |
|---|---|---|---|
| TO | 13,237,407 | 12,829,086 | 12,700,765 |
| P/L | 1,026,517 | 900,642 | 779,038 |
| NW | 5,741,515 | 5,150,998 | 4,700,511 |
| WC | 4,748,785 | 4,137,802 | 3,654,235 |
| Emp. | 80 | 78 | 73 |

DUNS 21-593-0810

## Staniforth Hkb

Eastwood Industrial Estate, Chesterton Way, Eastwood Trading Estate, Rotherham, South Yorkshire S65 1ST
**Tel:** 01709789272
**Web:** www.barrettengsteel.com
**Estd:** 2000 Partnership
**Line of Business:** Steel stockholders
**Partners:** J Barrett, P Chasney, Miss T Waters, J Childs
**Responsibilities**
**Senior:** John Hagyard *(Manager)*
**US SIC:** 5051 **UK SIC:** 61200
**Employees:** 50

DUNS 21-294-1330

## Staniforths (Rawmarsh) Ltd

106-108 Broad Street, Rotherham, South Yorkshire S62 6EN
**Tel:** 01709-522171 **Fax:** 01709-525374
**Web:** www.staniforths-rawmarsh.co.uk
**Reg No:** 0774484 **Estd:** 1963 Private Limited Company
**Line of Business:** Manufacture of bread; manufacture of fresh pastry goods and cakes
**Trading Style:** Staniforths
**Issued Capital:** £20,000
**Directors:** Ms D Moorcroft, S J Staniforth, I R Staniforth
**Co. Secretary:** Lindsay Hans
**Responsibilities**
**Facilities:** Chris Mullins *(Engineer)*
**Purchasing:** Michael Dukes *(Stores Manager)*
**Engineering:** Chris Mullins *(Engineer)*
**Branches:** Staniforths (Rawmarsh) Ltd, 938 Ecclesall Road, Sheffield, South Yorkshire S11 8TR
**US SIC:** 2051 **UK SIC:** 41960
**Auditors:** Allotts
**Bankers:** Yorkshire Bank Plc (05-07-32)

| | 30-09-14 | 30-09-13 | 30-09-12 |
|---|---|---|---|
| TA | 1,402,900 | 1,466,701 | 1,628,883 |
| NW | 1,171,964 | 1,263,773 | 1,393,243 |
| WC | 591,862 | 733,948 | 834,454 |

DUNS 29-846-2375 **Imp**

## Stanjames (Abingdon) Ltd

(**Subsidiary of:** Stan James (Gibraltar) Plc)
Downsview Road, Wantage, Oxfordshire OX12 9FN
**Tel:** 01235777007 **Fax:** 01235-777001
**Web:** www.stanjamesshops.com
**Reg No:** 2050734 **Estd:** 1986 Private Limited Company
**Line of Business:** Representative office
**Issued Capital:** £124
**Directors:** S D Fisher, E Mccormick, Ms A P Fisher, I Blackburn
**Co. Secretary:** Ian Blackburn
**Branches:** Stanjames (Abingdon) Ltd, 18 High Street, Hungerford, Berkshire RG17 0DN
**US SIC:** 7399 **UK SIC:** 83954
**Auditors:** James Cowper LLP
**Bankers:** HSBC Bank plc (40-32-07)

| | 31-12-13 | 31-12-12 | 31-12-11 |
|---|---|---|---|
| TO | 128,712,409 | 117,874,153 | 102,487,318 |
| P/L | (2,564,526) | (1,472,683) | (1,831,454) |
| NW | 9,067,022 | 10,540,222 | 14,655,543 |
| WC | 4,224,045 | 7,820,146 | 9,242,305 |
| Emp. | 438 | 348 | 302 |

DUNS 29-754-2441

## Stanley Brothers (Tippers) Ltd

Spring Court, Great Harwood, Blackburn, Lancashire BB6 7UL
**Tel:** 01254-887030
**Web:** www.sbtippers.co.uk
**Reg No:** 2017365 **VAT No:** 444828038
**Estd:** 1972 Private Limited Company
**Line of Business:** Plant hire and leasing
**Issued Capital:** £5,002
**Principals:** C Stanley *(Managing)*, G P Stanley *(Managing)*, G W Bolton, S Bolton, S P Stanley
**Co. Secretary:** Christopher Stanley
**Responsibilities**
**Admin:** Julie Hollin *(Office Manager)*
**US SIC:** 4789, 7394
**UK SIC:** 77002, 84000
**Auditors:** Bishop & Partners
**Bankers:** The Royal Bank Of Scotland Plc (16-13-26)

| | 31-03-14 | 31-03-13 | 31-03-12 |
|---|---|---|---|
| TA | 2,534,067 | 2,506,744 | 2,889,925 |
| NW | 1,064,706 | 868,878 | 990,125 |
| WC | 144,048 | (61,929) | 121,533 |

DUNS 50-416-9079

## Stanley Davis Group Ltd

41 Chalton Street, London NW1 1JD
**Tel:** 02075542222
**Web:** www.stanleydavis.co.uk
**Reg No:** 2413680 **Estd:** 1989 Private Limited Company
**Line of Business:** Business and management consultancy activities not elsewhere classified
**Export Sales:** £2,792,794
**Issued Capital:** £530,908
**Directors:** N J Dolby, S H Davis, A S Davis, N Lindsay Fynn
**Co. Secretary:** David Kaye
**Responsibilities**
**Purchasing:** Susan Yew *(Buyer)*
**US SIC:** 7392 **UK SIC:** 83951
**Auditors:** Armstrong Watson
**Bankers:** HSBC Bank plc (40-05-30)

| | 30-06-14 | 30-06-13 | 30-06-12 |
|---|---|---|---|
| TO | 9,601,106 | 7,547,992 | 6,545,419 |
| P/L | 1,565,962 | 1,016,220 | 948,847 |
| NW | 2,109,410 | 1,199,298 | 2,634,638 |
| WC | 1,897,271 | 1,073,473 | (364,572) |
| Emp. | 147 | 135 | 107 |

DUNS 21-033-8325

## Stanley Fyffe Associates

3 Panton Street, London SW1Y 4DL
**Tel:** 03453700744
**Estd:** 2003 Proprietorship
**Line of Business:** Engineers (structural)
**Proprietor:** S Fyffe
**Responsibilities**
**Senior:** Stanley Fyffe *(Proprietor)*
**US SIC:** 8911 **UK SIC:** 83701
**Employees:** 70

DUNS 22-602-2697 Exp

## The Stanley Gibbons Group Plc

18 Hill Street, St Helier, Jersey, Channel Islands JE2 4UA
**Tel:** 01534-766711 **Fax:** 01534-766177
**Web:** www.stanleygibbons.com
**Reg No:** 0013177J **Estd:** 1977 Private Limited Company
**Line of Business:** Collectors items
**Issued Capital:** £9
**Principals:** D P Duff *(Financial)*, J Byfield, M Hall
**Co. Secretary:** R Purkis
**Responsibilities**
**Senior:** John Byfield *(Manager)*, Winston Cunningham *(Operations Manager)*
**Marketing:** Alex Hanrahan *(Sales & Marketing Manager)*
**Sales:** Alex Hanrahan *(Sales & Marketing Manager)*
**Health & Safety:** Winston Cunningham *(Operations Manager)*
**Facilities:** Winston Cunningham *(Operations Manager)*
**Purchasing:** Winston Cunningham *(Operations Manager)*
**US SIC:** 5931, 2731
**UK SIC:** 65400, 47532
**Auditors:** Nexia Smith & Williamson
**Employees:** 50
**Turnover:** £35,704,000

DUNS 22-951-4997

## Stanley Gibbons Holdings Ltd

399 Strand, London WC2R 0LX
**Tel:** 02075574436
**Web:** www.stanleygibbons.com
**Reg No:** 1124806 **Estd:** 1973 Private Limited Company
**Line of Business:** Management activities of other non-financial holding companies not elsewhere classified
**Export Sales:** £5,115,000
**Issued Capital:** £3,289,099
**Directors:** A M Gee, K A Heddle
**Co. Secretary:** Richard Purkis
**US SIC:** 6711 **UK SIC:** 83962
**Auditors:** Nexia Smith & Williamson

| | 31-03-14 | 31-12-12 | 31-03-11 |
|---|---|---|---|
| TO | 19,004,000 | 15,728,000 | 16,974,000 |
| P/L | (1,146,000) | 1,322,000 | 1,280,000 |
| NW | 6,995,000 | 7,932,000 | 9,508,000 |
| WC | 7,081,000 | 7,902,000 | 7,942,000 |
| Emp. | 88 | 92 | 109 |

DUNS 21-580-4822

## Stanley Park

Wear Road, Stanley, County Durham DH9 6AH
**Tel:** 01207290800
**Web:** www.careuk.com
**Estd:** 2006 Proprietorship
**Line of Business:** Residential care establishments
**Proprietor:** Ms T Webbster
**Responsibilities**
**Senior:** Karen Morrison *(Manager)*
**US SIC:** 8321 **UK SIC:** 96111
**Employees:** 60

DUNS 21-603-1427

## Stanley Pond Ltd

Pond House, Blandford Heights, Blandford Forum, Dorset DT11 7TF
**Tel:** 01258456095 **Fax:** 01258456095
**Reg No:** 0550006 **VAT No:** 186124363
**Estd:** 1955 Private Limited Company
**Line of Business:** Property leasing
**Issued Capital:** £9,244
**Directors:** Ms B Pond, Mrs H Pond
**Co. Secretary:** Timothy Pond
**Branches:** Stanley Pond Ltd, West St, Salisbury, Wiltshire SP2 0DG
**US SIC:** 6519 **UK SIC:** 85000
**Auditors:** Rothman Pantall & Co
**Bankers:** Lloyds TSB Bank plc (30-90-92)

| | 31-12-13 | 31-12-12 | 31-12-11 |
|---|---|---|---|
| TA | 387,494 | 412,692 | 398,417 |
| NW | 346,194 | 346,909 | 353,739 |
| WC | (13,424) | (14,499) | (9,459) |

DUNS 21-003-3742 Exp

## Stanley Security Solutions Ltd

**(Subsidiary of:** Stanley Black & Decker Inc.)
Stanley House, Bramble Road, Techno Trading Estate, Swindon, Wiltshire SN2 8ER
**Tel:** 01793-692401 **Fax:** 01793618147
**Web:** www.stanleysecuritysolutions.co.uk
**Reg No:** 0181585 **VAT No:** 232244695
**Estd:** 1960 Private Limited Company
**Line of Business:** Radio & tv equip mfrs, ex communication
**Issued Capital:** £1,000,000
**Directors:** Ms S Stubbs, A S Lord, M R Smiley, A K Sood
**Co. Secretary:** Steven Costello
**Responsibilities**
**Senior:** Robin Brice *(Operations Director)*, Fred Hayhurst *(Manager)*, John Tripp *(Financial Director)*
**Finance:** John Tripp *(Financial Director)*
**Facilities:** Tracey Hayward *(Facilities Coordinator)*
**Branches:** Stanley Security Solutions Ltd, Unit 69, 1 Balloo Link, Bangor, Co Down BT19 7HJ
**US SIC:** 3651, 7399, 7394, 7393
**UK SIC:** 34541, 83954, 84000
**Auditors:** Ernst & Young LLP
**Bankers:** The Royal Bank Of Scotland Plc (16-08-05)

| | 31-12-13 | 31-12-12 | 31-12-11 |
|---|---|---|---|
| TO | 62,021,000 | 54,957,000 | 43,261,000 |
| P/L | 1,739,000 | 1,137,000 | (96,000) |
| NW | 34,792,000 | 32,654,000 | 31,031,000 |
| WC | 38,003,000 | 37,276,000 | 33,211,000 |
| Emp. | 575 | 578 | 411 |

DUNS 21-770-9365

## Stanley Steamer

Highfield, 27 Mount Nebo, Taunton, Somerset TA1 4HG
**Web:** www.stanleysteamer.co.uk
**Estd:** 2011 Proprietorship
**Line of Business:** Carpet and upholstery cleaners
**Proprietor:** S Steamer
**US SIC:** 1799 **UK SIC:** 50000
**Employees:** 100

DUNS 21-775-7500

## Stanley Taxis

Taxi Office Stanley Business Interchange, Mary Street, Stanley, County Durham DH9 0NQ
**Estd:** 1961 Proprietorship
**Line of Business:** Taxis and private hire vehicles
**Proprietor:** A Scott
**US SIC:** 4121 **UK SIC:** 72200
**Employees:** 172

DUNS 53-613-9397

## Stanley Tee Nominees Ltd

**(Subsidiary of:** Tees Financial Ltd)
High Street, Bishops Stortford, Hertfordshire CM23 2LU
**Tel:** 01279-755200 **Fax:** 01279-758400
**Web:** www.stanleytee.co.uk
**Reg No:** 3419141 **Estd:** 1997 Private Limited Company
**Line of Business:** Solicitors
**Trading Style:** Tees Law
**Issued Capital:** £1
**Directors:** M G Henry, D I Redfern, G P Bramley, Ms C M Izzard, Ms L P Glaister, J R Tee
**US SIC:** 6711 **UK SIC:** 83962

| | 31-03-14 | 31-03-13 | 31-03-12 |
|---|---|---|---|
| TA | 1 | 1 | 1 |
| NW | 1 | 1 | 1 |

DUNS 23-904-8841

## Stanley U K Services Ltd

**(Subsidiary of:** Black & Decker International Finance 3)
3 Europa Court, Europa Link, Sheffield Airport Business Park, Sheffield, South Yorkshire S9 1XU
**Tel:** 08701630630
**Web:** www.bostitch.co.uk
**Reg No:** 3895529 **Estd:** 1991 Private Limited Company
**Line of Business:** Other business activities not elsewhere classified
**Issued Capital:** £2
**Directors:** M R Smiley, A K Sood, Ms S Stubbs
**Co. Secretary:** Steven Costello
**US SIC:** 7399 **UK SIC:** 83954
**Auditors:** Ernst & Young LLP
**Bankers:** Barclays Bank Plc (20-00-06)

| | 31-12-13 | 31-12-12 | 31-12-11 |
|---|---|---|---|
| TO | 9,325,000 | 9,235,000 | 9,999,000 |
| P/L | (5,852,000) | (13,749,000) | 162,000 |
| NW | (18,452,000) | (12,772,000) | 1,315,000 |
| WC | (29,623,000) | (30,189,000) | 2,594,000 |
| Emp. | 58 | 47 | 50 |

DUNS 21-311-8151 Imp-Exp

## Stanley Vickers Ltd

Snowdon Road, Middlesbrough, Cleveland TS2 1LG
**Tel:** 01642-247353 **Fax:** 01642-231571
**Web:** www.sv-ltd.co.uk
**Reg No:** 0562792 **VAT No:** 258212467
**Estd:** 1956 Private Limited Company
**Line of Business:** Engineers (general)
**Export Markets:** Germany; Denmark; Switzerland; Netherlands
**Issued Capital:** £3,500
**Principals:** H H Zarei *(Managing)*, Mrs S M Phillips
**Responsibilities**
**Senior:** Dave Ford *(Works Manager)*
**US SIC:** 3079 **UK SIC:** 48360
**Auditors:** Chipchase Manners & Co
**Bankers:** National Westminster Bank Plc (54-10-04)

| | 31-03-14 | 31-03-13 | 31-03-12 |
|---|---|---|---|
| TA | 3,754,436 | 3,338,962 | 2,844,958 |
| NW | 1,655,294 | 1,463,589 | 1,258,796 |
| WC | 1,303,266 | 1,097,955 | 875,693 |

DUNS 21-811-7797

## Stanley Wilson Lodge

Four Acres, Saffron Walden, Essex CB11 3JE
**Tel:** 01799529189
**Web:** www.excelcareholdings.com
**Estd:** 2012
**Line of Business:** Rest and retirement homes
**Responsibilities**
**Senior:** Sue Clayden *(Manager)*
**US SIC:** 8321 **UK SIC:** 96111
**Employees:** 90

DUNS 21-239-6931 Imp-Exp

## The Stanley Works Ltd

**(Subsidiary of:** Black & Decker International Finance 3)
Europa Court, Sheffield, South Yorkshire S9 1XE
**Tel:** 01142-448883 **Fax:** 01142-739038
**Web:** www.stanleytools.com
**Reg No:** 0170466 **VAT No:** 530201905
**Estd:** 1863 Private Limited Company
**Line of Business:** Manufacture of tools
**Export Markets:** W Europe; Middle East; Africa; U S A; Canada
**Trading Style:** Stanley Tools, Stanley Hydraulic Tools, Stanley Tools Europe, Stanley Air Tools
**Issued Capital:** £144,156
**Directors:** Ms S Stubbs, A K Sood, M R Smiley
**Co. Secretary:** Steven Costello
**Responsibilities**
**Health & Safety:** Nick Knightley *(health & Safety Manager)*
**Branches:** The Stanley Works Ltd, Hellaby La, Rotherham, South Yorkshire S66 8HN
**US SIC:** 3423, 3546
**UK SIC:** 31612, 32852
**Auditors:** Ernst & Young LLP
**Bankers:** Barclays Bank Plc (20-76-89)

| | 31-12-13 | 31-12-12 | 31-12-11 |
|---|---|---|---|
| TO | 8,110,000 | 7,900,000 | 12,682,000 |
| P/L | 552,000 | (734,000) | 4,685,000 |
| NW | (3,084,000) | 5,601,000 | 9,091,000 |
| WC | 209,000 | (3,898,000) | 5,080,000 |
| Emp. | 150 | 144 | 143 |

DUNS 64-088-9023

## Stanleybet International Ltd

**(Subsidiary of:** Stanleybet Holdings Ltd)
201-210 Mercury Court, Tithebarn Street, Liverpool, Merseyside L2 2QP
**Tel:** 0151-235-2000 **Fax:** 0151-235-2100
**Web:** www.stanleybetcorporate.com
**Reg No:** 4492320 **Estd:** 2002 Private Limited Company
**Line of Business:** Management activities of holding companies
**Trading Style:** Stanleybet
**Issued Capital:** £125,000
**Directors:** W L Bland, J S Whittaker, G Garrisi
**US SIC:** 6711 **UK SIC:** 83962
**Auditors:** PricewaterhouseCoopers LLP

| | 31-12-13 | 31-12-12 | 31-12-11 |
|---|---|---|---|
| TO | 3,495,000 | 3,355,892 | 3,379,350 |
| P/L | 2,480,000 | (34,567) | 2,246,723 |
| NW | 1,474,000 | (78,524) | 286,884 |
| WC | (447,000) | (2,706,727) | (3,668,204) |

DUNS 38-783-6604

## Stanley's

17 East Bond Street, Leicester, Leicestershire LE1 4SX
**Tel:** 01162625036
**Proprietorship**
**Line of Business:** Private members night clubs
**US SIC:** 5813 **UK SIC:** 66200
**Employees:** 50

DUNS 34-617-1705

## Stanmore Contractors Ltd

**(Subsidiary of:** Akaal Group Plc)
Stanmore House, Erith, Kent DA8 1DE
**Tel:** 01322-446446 **Fax:** 01322-448448
**Web:** www.stanmoreltd.co.uk
**Reg No:** 2754550 **VAT No:** 625560641
**Estd:** 1992 Private Limited Company
**Line of Business:** Plastering and related building services
**Trading Style:** Stanmore
**Issued Capital:** £23,000
**Co. Secretary:** Rajbir Manak
**Responsibilities**
**Senior:** Tanya Barracks *(Computer Manager)*, Raybir Singh Manak *(Managing Director)*
**US SIC:** 1742 **UK SIC:** 50400
**Auditors:** Perrys Accountants Ltd

| | 31-03-14 | 31-03-13 | 31-03-12 |
|---|---|---|---|
| TO | 87,559,941 | 58,234,591 | 52,004,859 |
| P/L | 10,088,980 | 7,773,166 | 3,779,950 |
| NW | 23,508,506 | 16,386,792 | 11,328,853 |
| WC | 22,384,750 | 15,542,219 | 10,588,319 |
| Emp. | 158 | 122 | 112 |

DUNS 49-498-9502

## Stanmore Implants Worldwide Ltd

**(Subsidiary of:** Siw Holdings Ltd)
210 Centennial Avenue, Centennial Park, Elstree, Borehamwood, Hertfordshire WD6 3SJ
**Tel:** 02082386500 **Fax:** 02089530617
**Web:** www.stanmoreimplants.com
**Reg No:** 3161085 **VAT No:** 778136495
**Estd:** 1996 Private Limited Company
**Line of Business:** Manufacture of medical and surgical equipment and orthopaedic appliances
**Export Sales:** £3,404,000
**Trading Style:** Stanmore Implants Worldwide Ltd
**Issued Capital:** £129,607
**Directors:** M F Garner, E S Dodd
**Co. Secretary:** Eric Dodd
**Responsibilities**
**Senior:** Brian Steer *(Executive chairman)*, Paul Unwin *(Managing Director)*
**Marketing:** Rory Heaslip *(Product Development Manager)*, Sudha Shunmugam *(Product Development Manager)*
**Sales:** Priya Amin *(Sales Business Manager)*
**IT:** Paul Unwin *(Managing Director)*
**HR:** Julie Campbell *(Human Resources Manager)*
**Facilities:** Paul Unwin *(Managing Director)*
**Engineering:** Aditi Augustine *(Mechanical Design Engineering)*, Pamela Bennett *(Manufacturing/Validation Engin)*, Abtin Eshraghi *(Senior Design Engineering Mana)*, Shaaz Ghouse *(Additive Layer Manufacturing E)*, Paul Unwin *(Managing Director)*
**US SIC:** 3841 **UK SIC:** 37201
**Auditors:** PricewaterhouseCoopers LLP
**Bankers:** Barclays Bank Plc (20-17-19)

| | 31-12-13 | 31-12-12 | 31-12-11 |
|---|---|---|---|
| TO | 10,184,000 | 9,572,000 | 7,734,835 |
| P/L | (4,210,000) | (2,378,000) | (2,934,086) |
| NW | (6,499,000) | (4,632,000) | (3,143,178) |
| WC | (10,743,000) | (8,878,000) | (6,111,530) |
| Emp. | 91 | 82 | 65 |

DUNS 52-534-1103

## Stanmore Quality Surfacing Ltd

Brent Terrace, London NW2 1LR
**Tel:** 01727857077
**Web:** www.sqsltd.co.uk
**Reg No:** 3238593 **Estd:** 1996 Private Limited Company
**Line of Business:** Other business activities not elsewhere classified
**Issued Capital:** £100
**Director:** M A O'Connor
**Co. Secretary:** Ms Caterina O'Connor
**Responsibilities**
**Senior:** Caterina O' Connor *(Manager)*
**Branches:** Stanmore Quality Surfacing Ltd, Scratchwood Service Area, London NW7 3JA
**US SIC:** 7399 **UK SIC:** 83954
**Auditors:** BDO Northern Ireland
**Bankers:** Barclays Bank Plc (20-00-00)

| | 31-08-13 | 31-08-12 | 31-08-11 |
|---|---|---|---|
| TO | 31,598,585 | 25,957,786 | 26,219,759 |
| P/L | 988,274 | 826,261 | 1,325,570 |
| NW | 3,245,022 | 3,245,669 | 3,183,711 |
| WC | 2,219,847 | 2,687,008 | 2,677,387 |
| Emp. | 186 | 148 | 134 |

DUNS 34-898-2141

## Stanmore Training Co Ltd

Elm Park, Stanmore, Middlesex HA7 4BQ
**Tel:** 020-8420-7700 **Fax:** 020-8420-6502
**Web:** www.stanmore.ac.uk
**Reg No:** 2829132 **Estd:** 1993 Private Limited Company
**Line of Business:** Colleges (higher education)
**Issued Capital:** £2
**Directors:** Ms C A Bednell, Ms J D Mace
**Responsibilities**
**Senior:** Urmila Rasan *(Manager)*
**US SIC:** 8221 **UK SIC:** 93100
**Auditors:** MacIntyre Hudson

| | 31-07-13 | 31-07-12 | 31-07-11 |
|---|---|---|---|
| TA | 2 | 2 | 2 |
| NW | 2 | 2 | 2 |

DUNS 22-721-4715

## Stannah Lift Services Ltd

(**Subsidiary of:** Stannah Lifts Holdings Ltd)
6850 Daresbury Park, Warrington, Cheshire WA4 4GE
**Tel:** 01614773344 **Fax:** 0161-477-3377
**Web:** www.stannahlifts.co.uk
**Reg No:** 1189799 **Estd:** 1974 Private Limited Company
**Line of Business:** Miscellaneous repair services
**Issued Capital:** £100
**Directors:** J N Stannah, A D Stannah, B L Stannah, A N Stannah, N D Stannah, P G Stannah
**Co. Secretary:** Ms Deborah Coveney
**Responsibilities**
**Senior:** Carl Bramhall *(Branch Manager)*, L Raftery *(Branch Manager)*
**Branches:** Stannah Lift Services Ltd, Unit 4, Boundary Road, Brackley, Northamptonshire NN13 7ES
**US SIC:** 7699, 8911
**UK SIC:** 67303, 83701
**Auditors:** PricewaterhouseCoopers
**Bankers:** National Westminster Bank Plc (51-50-03)

| | 31-12-13 | 31-12-12 | 31-12-11 |
|---|---|---|---|
| TO | 92,564,000 | 90,343,000 | 84,117,000 |
| P/L | 1,713,000 | 1,462,000 | 191,000 |
| NW | 13,345,000 | 13,096,000 | 12,163,000 |
| WC | 13,072,000 | 12,627,000 | 12,146,000 |
| Emp. | 732 | 693 | 692 |

DUNS 21-191-0864 **Exp**

## Stannah Lifts Holdings Ltd

Anton Mill, Anton Mill Lane, Andover, Hampshire SP10 2NX
**Tel:** 01264339090 **Fax:** 01264350617
**Web:** www.stannahlifts.co.uk
**Reg No:** 0686996 **Estd:** 1961 Private Limited Company
**Line of Business:** Other letting of own property
**Export Sales:** £97,673,000
**Issued Capital:** £2,001,000
**Principals:** A N Stannah *(Managing)*, B L Stannah, Mrs J C Stannah, J N Stannah, P G Stannah, A D Stannah, Mrs J M Stannah, Ms H L Stirrup
**Co. Secretary:** Ms Deborah Coveney
**Responsibilities**
**Senior:** Peter Gilbert *(Marketing Director)*
**Marketing:** Peter Gilbert *(Marketing Director)*, Joanne Monro *(Head of Commercial Marketing)*, Fiona Neil *(Head of Marketing)*
**Sales:** Mike Howe *(Senior Sales Executive)*, Joanne Monro *(Head of Commercial Marketing)*, Denise Munday *(Supplier Account Manager)*, Larry Power *(Sales Manager)*
**IT:** Martin Carter *(Operations Director)*, Andy Porter *(Network, Security Manager)*
**Operations:** Steve Leathley *(Engineering Director)*, Kim Saville *(Technical, Production Manager)*
**Purchasing:** Sarah Riglar *(?Purchasing Coordinator)*
**Engineering:** Steve Leathley *(Engineering Director)*
**Branches:** Stannah Lifts Holdings Ltd, 48 Bleak Hill Way, Mansfield, Nottinghamshire NG18 5EZ
**US SIC:** 6519, 6711
**UK SIC:** 85000, 83962
**Auditors:** PricewaterhouseCoopers LLP
**Bankers:** National Westminster Bank Plc (51-50-03)

| | 31-12-13 | 31-12-12 | 31-12-11 |
|---|---|---|---|
| TO | 211,406,000 | 201,670,000 | 195,937,000 |
| P/L | 11,768,000 | 11,091,000 | 9,969,000 |
| NW | 95,663,000 | 89,925,000 | 82,628,000 |
| WC | 63,315,000 | 56,659,000 | 47,101,000 |
| Emp. | 1,771 | 1,708 | 1,753 |

DUNS 21-136-0008

## Stan's Fish & Burger Bar

2 High Street, Bilston, West Midlands WV14 0EH
**Tel:** 01902409476
**Proprietorship**
**Line of Business:** Take-away food shops
**Proprietor:** S Menicou
**US SIC:** 5812 **UK SIC:** 66110
**Bankers:** Bank Of Cyprus (london) Ltd (30-03-17)
**Employees:** 50

DUNS 22-763-9184

## Stans Superstore

Overton Road, St Martins, Oswestry, Shropshire SY11 3AY
**Web:** www.stans-superstore.co.uk
**VAT No:** 159893404 **Estd:** 1947 Partnership
**Line of Business:** Supermarkets
**Trading Style:** Stans Superstore
**Partners:** A Faulkeas, Mrs V M Faulks, P C Faulks, R A Faulks
**US SIC:** 5411 **UK SIC:** 64100
**Bankers:** HSBC Bank plc (40-35-32)
**Employees:** 185

DUNS 21-680-1571

## Stansell Ltd

(**Subsidiary of:** Morgan Sindall Group Plc)
24 Garrett Road, Lynx Trading Estate, Yeovil, Somerset BA20 2TJ
**Tel:** 01935-403700
**Web:** www.morgansindall.com
**Reg No:** 0422058 **VAT No:** 667115920
**Estd:** 1943 Private Limited Company
**Line of Business:** Construction of domestic buildings
**Trading Style:** Morgan Sindall
**Issued Capital:** £2,749,750
**Directors:** J C Morgan, S P Crummett
**Co. Secretary:** Ms Clare Sheridan
**Responsibilities**
**Senior:** T Cscofield *(Commercial Director)*, Isobel Nettleship *(Manager)*, Mike Pinney *(General Manager)*
**Admin:** Mike Pinney *(General Manager)*
**Branches:** Stansell Ltd, Stoke Damerel Business Centre, Unit 3, Plymouth, Devon PL3 4DT
**US SIC:** 1522 **UK SIC:** 50100
**Bankers:** Lloyds TSB Bank plc (30-00-02)

| | 31-12-13 | 31-12-12 | 31-12-11 |
|---|---|---|---|
| TA | 2,749,750 | 2,749,750 | 2,749,750 |
| NW | 2,749,750 | 2,749,750 | 2,749,750 |

DUNS 21-775-2242

## Stanshawes Nursing Home

11 Stanshawes Drive, Yate, Bristol, Avon BS37 4ET
**Tel:** 01454850005
**Estd:** 1995 Proprietorship
**Line of Business:** Nursing homes
**Proprietor:** Mrs L Corner
**Responsibilities**
**Senior:** Evangeline Williams *(Manager)*
**US SIC:** 8051 **UK SIC:** 95100
**Employees:** 70

DUNS 21-414-5547

## Stansty House Nursing Home

34 Stansty Road, Wrexham, Clwyd LL11 2BU
**Web:** www.minstercaregroup.co.uk
**Estd:** 1988 Partnership
**Line of Business:** Residential care establishments
**Partners:** Mrs R Roberts, A Roberts
**US SIC:** 8321 **UK SIC:** 96111
**Employees:** 100

DUNS 50-568-3151

## Stantec Ltd

88 Gray's Inn Road, London WC1X 8AA
**Tel:** 02074925700 **Fax:** 01242-520342
**Web:** www.stantec.com
**Reg No:** 2516029 **VAT No:** 575944785
**Estd:** 2011 Private Limited Company
**Line of Business:** Architectural services
**Issued Capital:** £2,100,000
**Directors:** J Wilson, J P Stone, R K Allen, B Musselmann, D Martin
**Responsibilities**
**Senior:** Aaron Taylor *(Principal)*
**Branches:** Stantec Ltd, 131 Gt Titchfield St, London W1P 8AE
**US SIC:** 8911 **UK SIC:** 83701
**Auditors:** Whyatt Pakeman Partners

| | 31-12-13 | 31-12-12 | 31-12-11 |
|---|---|---|---|
| TA | 2,669,216 | 2,037,065 | 1,741,378 |
| NW | (3,917,636) | (3,438,872) | (2,207,121) |
| WC | (4,200,070) | (3,739,652) | (2,507,223) |

DUNS 39-963-6315 **Imp-Exp**

## Stanton Bonna Concrete Ltd

Littlewell Lane, Stanton-By-Dale, Ilkeston, Derbyshire DE7 4QW
**Tel:** 01159-441448 **Fax:** 01159-441466
**Web:** www.stanton-bonna.co.uk
**Reg No:** 2263795 **VAT No:** 520584365
**Estd:** 1988 Private Limited Company
**Line of Business:** Manufacture of concrete products for construction purposes
**Export Markets:** France
**Issued Capital:** £3,334,000
**Principals:** B Wilson *(Financial)*, J L Perron, N Yatzimirsky, P M Brousse
**Responsibilities**
**Senior:** Vincent Guelfucci *(Manager)*, Philippe Milliet *(Manager)*, Glyn Woolley *(Chief Executive Officer)*
**Finance:** Jean Guillou *(Finance Director)*
**Marketing:** Jeanette Edwards *(Marketing Executive)*, Neil O'Sullivan *(Marketing Manager)*
**Sales:** Daniel Cross *(Commercial Coordinator)*
**Admin:** Jayne Hawley *(Senior Secretary)*
**Health & Safety:** Glen Paul *(Health & Safety Officer)*
**Operations:** Robert Fifer *(Operations Director)*, Steve Hallam *(Operations Support Manager)*
**US SIC:** 3271, 3272
**UK SIC:** 24370
**Auditors:** Deloitte LLP
**Bankers:** HSBC Bank plc (40-35-18)

| | 31-12-13 | 31-12-12 | 31-12-11 |
|---|---|---|---|
| TO | 19,547,000 | 18,928,000 | 17,509,000 |
| P/L | 1,388,000 | 986,000 | 494,000 |
| NW | 5,114,000 | 3,155,000 | 2,688,000 |
| WC | 4,402,000 | 3,409,000 | 2,581,000 |
| Emp. | 126 | 125 | 123 |

DUNS 29-631-6110

## Stanton Consultancy Ltd

(**Subsidiary of:** Stanton Consultancy International Ltd)
Park Gate 161-163, 161-163 Preston Road, Brighton, East Sussex BN1 6AU
**Tel:** 01273666616
**Web:** www.scluk.com
**Reg No:** 1957652 **Estd:** 1985 Private Limited Company
**Line of Business:** It consultants
**Trading Style:** S C L
**Issued Capital:** £100
**Directors:** R J Stanton, J C Turner
**Co. Secretary:** George Chapman
**Responsibilities**
**Marketing:** Fiona Honeyman *(Marketing executive)*
**US SIC:** 7379 **UK SIC:** 83940
**Bankers:** HSBC Bank plc (40-19-22)

| | 31-12-13 | 31-12-12 | 31-12-11 |
|---|---|---|---|
| TA | 984,446 | 1,016,061 | 882,846 |
| NW | 451,390 | 368,796 | 394,562 |
| WC | 376,510 | 314,705 | 337,140 |

DUNS 21-478-8940

## Stanton Court Nursing Home

Bromley Road, Stanton Drew, Bristol, Avon BS39 4ER
**Estd:** 2012 Partnership
**Line of Business:** Medical nursing home activities
**Partner:** P Townsend
**Responsibilities**
**Senior:** Diane Piekarski *(Home Manager)*
**US SIC:** 8051 **UK SIC:** 95100
**Employees:** 60

DUNS 53-572-6632

## Stanton Hall Retirement Home

22-28 Trinity Road, Darlington, County Durham DL3 7AZ
**Tel:** 01325-488399
**Web:** www.supremecarehomes.co.uk
**Estd:** 2011 Proprietorship
**Line of Business:** Medical nursing home activities
**Trading Style:** The Terrace Retirement Home, Ventress Hall
**Proprietor:** G M Pickersgill
**Responsibilities**
**Senior:** Donna Dobe *(Manager)*, Jude Goode *(Manager)*, Judy Wray *(Manager)*
**US SIC:** 8051 **UK SIC:** 95100
**Employees:** 100

DUNS 21-777-7117

## Stanton Vale Special Needs School

Thoresby Road, Long Eaton, Nottingham, Nottinghamshire NG10 3NP
**Web:** www.stantonvale.derbyshire.sch.uk
**Estd:** 1974 Proprietorship
**Line of Business:** Schools (special)
**Proprietor:** Ms J Wells
**US SIC:** 8299 **UK SIC:** 93300
**Employees:** 90

DUNS 21-319-0783

## The Stanway School

Winstree Road, Stanway, Colchester, Essex CO3 0QA
**Tel:** 01206575488
**Web:** www.stanway.essex.sch.uk
**Estd:** 2003
**Line of Business:** Schools (local authority)
**Director:** J Tippett
**Responsibilities**
**Senior:** Paul Bickmore *(Manager)*, Andrew Davenall *(Manager)*, Dominic Davies *(Manager)*, Valerie Endean *(Manager)*, Lisa French *(general)*, Dave Harris *(Manager)*, Claire Holmes *(Manager)*, Julian Lamb *(Manager)*, Frances Long *(Manager)*, Marc Mabbott *(Manager)*, Sarah Neal *(Manager)*, Valerie Pratt *(Manager)*, John Spademan *(Manager)*, Mark Walter *(Manager)*, Claire Wheeler *(Manager)*, Barry Wild *(Manager)*, Barbara Williamson *(Manager)*
**IT:** Garry Robinson *(Senior IT Executive)*
**US SIC:** 8211 **UK SIC:** 93200
**Employees:** 100

DUNS 51-640-2968

## Stapely Jewish Care Home Ltd

North Mossley Hill Road, Liverpool, Merseyside L18 8BR
**Tel:** 0151-724-3260
**Reg No:** 5957410 **Estd:** 2006 Private Company Limited By Guarantee
**Line of Business:** Medical nursing home activities
**Directors:** Dr E Toke, Ms C Wiseman, P S Ettinger, R J Ettinger
**US SIC:** 8051, 8091
**UK SIC:** 95100, 95200

| | 31-03-14 | 31-03-13 |
|---|---|---|
| TO | 1,468,242 | 1,312,625 |
| P/L | 76,497 | (422,617) |
| NW | (346,120) | (422,617) |
| WC | (366,671) | (424,672) |
| Emp. | 64 | 64 |

DUNS 22-600-8316 **Imp**

## Stapleford Flying Club Ltd

Stapleford Aerodrome, Stapleford Tawney, Romford, Essex RM4 1SJ
**Web:** www.flysfc.com
**Reg No:** 0967895 **VAT No:** 246272364
**Estd:** 1969 Private Limited Company
**Line of Business:** Driving school activities
**Trading Style:** Stapleford Flight Centre
**Issued Capital:** £100
**Managing Director:** J H Chicken
**Co. Secretary:** Mrs Tania Chicken
**US SIC:** 8999, 7999
**UK SIC:** 83954, 97913
**Auditors:** Raffingers
**Bankers:** Lloyds TSB Bank plc (30-97-13)

| | 31-12-13 | 31-12-12 | 31-12-11 |
|---|---|---|---|
| TA | 2,847,921 | 2,356,457 | 2,458,704 |
| NW | 1,471,959 | 747,271 | 748,446 |
| WC | (749,256) | (807,360) | (780,742) |

DUNS 64-268-4427

## Stapleford Health Centre

1a Sandiacre Road, Nottingham, Nottinghamshire NG9 8EX
**Tel:** 01159396699
**Web:** www.staplefordmot.co.uk
**Estd:** 2009 Partnership
**Line of Business:** Maintenance and repair of motor vehicles
**Partners:** Dr P A Jones, Dr K F Winterbottom, Dr L Wercholа, Dr C D Perko
**Branches:** Stapleford Health Centre, 205 Russell Dr, Nottingham, Nottinghamshire NG8 2BD
**US SIC:** 7539 **UK SIC:** 67100
**Employees:** 50

DUNS 29-622-0668 **Imp**

## Stapleford Park Ltd

(**Subsidiary of:** Arlaform Ltd)
Stapleford Road, Melton Mowbray, Leicestershire LE14 2SF
**Tel:** 01572-787522 **Fax:** 01572-787651
**Web:** www.staplefordpark.co.uk
**Reg No:** 1948599 **VAT No:** 394880696
**Estd:** 1988 Private Limited Company
**Line of Business:** Hotels and motels without restaurant
**Trading Style:** Carnegie Link, London Outpost
**Issued Capital:** £3,798,067
**Director:** M S Hussain
**Co. Secretary:** Renold Tang
**Responsibilities**
**Finance:** Manoj Mistry *(Financial Director)*
**US SIC:** 7011, 5812
**UK SIC:** 66500, 66110
**Auditors:** Grant Thornton
**Bankers:** Bank Of Scotland (80-20-00)

| | 31-12-13 | 31-12-12 | 31-12-11 |
|---|---|---|---|
| TO | N/A | 4,296,301 | 4,410,665 |
| P/L | N/A | 5,095,925 | (787,900) |
| NW | (4,795,793) | (3,405,210) | (8,495,135) |
| WC | (1,340,404) | (1,369,213) | (1,215,014) |
| Emp. | N/A | 180 | 175 |

DUNS 45-837-6126

## Staplehurst Transits Ltd

Staplehurst Road, Marden, Tonbridge, Kent TN12 9BT
**Tel:** 01580-893714 **Fax:** 01580-892695
**Web:** www.staplehursttransits.co.uk
**Reg No:** 3187836 **VAT No:** 204253606
**Estd:** 1973 Private Limited Company
**Line of Business:** Other supporting land transport activities
**Issued Capital:** £1,000
**Director:** M C Goldup
**Co. Secretary:** Ms Susan Goldup
**Responsibilities**
**Senior:** Darren Goldup *(Assistant Manager)*
**US SIC:** 4789 **UK SIC:** 77002
**Auditors:** Nash Harvey

**Bankers:** National Westminster Bank Plc (60-60-08)

| | 31-12-13 | 31-12-12 | 31-12-11 |
|---|---|---|---|
| TO | 5,407,300 | 4,916,515 | N/A |
| P/L | 600,091 | 598,323 | N/A |
| NW | 3,334,195 | 2,556,338 | 2,178,838 |
| WC | 500,655 | 1,011,786 | 1,015,563 |
| Emp. | 60 | 55 | N/A |

DUNS 21-915-9522 Imp-Exp

## Staples Disposables Ltd

(**Subsidiary of:** Staples Holdings Ltd)
Hurlingham Business Park, Fulbeck Heath, Grantham, Lincolnshire NG32 3HL
**Tel:** 01400262800 **Fax:** 01400262811
**Web:** www.staplesdisposables.com
**Reg No:** 1576051 **VAT No:** 648024344
**Estd:** 1981 Private Limited Company
**Line of Business:** Disposable products
**Export Markets:** Cyprus; Iceland; W Europe
**Export Sales:** £1,918,778
**Issued Capital:** £75,000
**Principals:** A Staples *(Managing)*, R Staples, B P Molloy, R Haslam
**Co. Secretary:** Richard Leatherland
**Responsibilities**
**Senior:** Antony Clifton *(Warehouse Manager)*
**Finance:** Roy Gater *(Financial Controller)*
**Facilities:** Steven Kemp *(Engineering Manager)*
**Purchasing:** Anthony Boseley *(Purchasing Manager)*
**US SIC:** 2647 **UK SIC:** 47220
**Auditors:** haysmacintyre
**Bankers:** National Westminster Bank Plc (55-50-11)

| | 29-03-14 | 30-03-13 | 31-03-12 |
|---|---|---|---|
| TO | 33,463,876 | 32,948,982 | 31,046,976 |
| P/L | 6,845 | 3,019,628 | (1,352,416) |
| NW | 9,658,870 | 9,612,484 | 6,566,729 |
| WC | 5,795,930 | 5,998,540 | 3,042,456 |
| Emp. | 376 | 346 | 330 |

DUNS 21-743-5993

## Stapleton's (Retail) Ltd

(**Subsidiary of:** Itochu Corporation)
Unit 2 3, Manford Busines Park, Luton, Bedfordshire LU4 8EN
**Tel:** 01582 561389
**Web:** www.tyrecity.co.uk
**Reg No:** 7760510 **Estd:** 2011 Private Limited Company
**Line of Business:** Maintenance and repair of motor vehicles
**Trading Style:** Tire City
**Issued Capital:** £1
**Directors:** S C Parker, K Murai, P H Lambert, M Slade, P Boulton
**Co. Secretary:** Ian Ellis
**Branches:** Stapleton's (Retail) Ltd, Madford Retail Park, Unit 2-3, Luton, Bedfordshire LU4 8DN
**US SIC:** 7539 **UK SIC:** 67100

| | 31-03-14 | 31-03-13 | 31-03-12 |
|---|---|---|---|
| TO | 64,471,343 | 65,453,212 | 28,777,231 |
| P/L | (147,634) | 1,630,632 | 790,295 |
| NW | (2,907,673) | (3,904,340) | (5,766,603) |
| WC | (6,077,199) | (7,128,220) | (9,320,261) |
| Emp. | 621 | 1,176 | 766 |

DUNS 21-634-1586 Exp

## Stapleton's (Tyre Services) Ltd

(**Subsidiary of:** Itochu Corporation)
Fourth Avenue, Letchworth, Hertfordshire SG6 2TT
**Tel:** 01462659528 **Fax:** 01462-488707
**Web:** www.stapletons-tyres.co.uk
**Reg No:** 0332098 **VAT No:** 419065062
**Estd:** 1937 Private Limited Company
**Line of Business:** Sale of motor vehicle parts and accessories
**Export Markets:** E U, worldwide
**Issued Capital:** £230,179
**Directors:** Y Kimbara, M Slade
**Co. Secretary:** Ian Ellis
**Responsibilities**
**Senior:** Ashley Croft *(Manager)*
**Marketing:** Stephen Childs *(Marketing Manager)*
**IT:** Andy Scaplehorn *(IT Manager)*
**Branches:** Stapleton's (Tyre Services) Ltd, Eastgate, 76-80 Moorbridge Rd, Maidenhead, Berkshire SL6 8GE
**US SIC:** 5531 **UK SIC:** 65100
**Auditors:** PricewaterhouseCoopers LLP
**Bankers:** Barclays Bank Plc (20-53-30)

| | 31-03-14 | 31-03-13 | 31-03-12 |
|---|---|---|---|
| TO | 376,962,000 | 342,447,000 | 463,028,000 |
| P/L | 12,348,000 | 7,075,000 | 8,808,000 |
| NW | 7,709,000 | 24,520,000 | 30,258,000 |
| WC | (31,088,000) | (10,561,000) | (15,069,000) |
| Emp. | 1,100 | 1,262 | 766 |

DUNS 21-714-0369

## Staploe Education Trust

Sand Street, Soham, Ely, Cambridgeshire CB7 5AA
**Tel:** 01353724100
**Web:** www.sohamcollege.org.uk
**Reg No:** 7534901 **Estd:** 1996 Private Company Limited By Guarantee
**Line of Business:** Other adult and other education not elsewhere classified
**Directors:** Mrs C P Littlewood, Ms N Close, Reverend T M Alban Jones, D J Waller, Mrs G E Greet, Mrs R M Mcnaughton, Dr J S Humphrey, J Keyworth
**Co. Secretary:** Mrs Anna Jarvis
**Responsibilities**
**Senior:** William Bateson *(Manager)*
**US SIC:** 8299, 8211
**UK SIC:** 93300, 93200
**Bankers:** The Co-Operative Bank Plc (08-90-43)

| | 31-08-14 | 31-08-13 | 31-08-12 |
|---|---|---|---|
| TO | 15,440,375 | 8,570,043 | 6,953,109 |
| P/L | 6,859,606 | 658,946 | (98,457) |
| NW | 29,961,601 | 23,838,995 | 23,083,049 |
| WC | 941,077 | 993,539 | 766,120 |
| Emp. | 169 | 157 | 137 |

DUNS 73-902-7634

## Star Brands (Holdings) Ltd

Unit East, Millshaw Business Living, Global Avenue, Leeds, West Yorkshire LS11 8PR
**Tel:** 01133855610 **Fax:** 01132-666690
**Web:** www.wizzproducts.co.uk
**Reg No:** 5156476 **Estd:** 2004 Private Limited Company
**Line of Business:** Manufacture of soap and detergents
**Export Sales:** £998,445
**Issued Capital:** £1,000
**Directors:** T Robertshaw, P G Siddall
**Co. Secretary:** Mrs Diane Makin
**US SIC:** 2841, 2842
**UK SIC:** 25810, 25990

| | 31-08-13 | 31-08-12 | 31-08-11 |
|---|---|---|---|
| TO | 12,575,575 | 10,439,663 | 9,496,805 |
| P/L | 433,027 | 315,695 | 165,208 |
| NW | 405,329 | 24,308 | (273,106) |
| WC | (339,646) | 178,139 | (102,241) |
| Emp. | 63 | 55 | 53 |

DUNS 21-596-0331

## Star Cabs

17 Strabane Old Road, Londonderry, Co Londonderry BT47 2DL
**Tel:** 02871311366
**Estd:** 2011 Proprietorship
**Line of Business:** Taxis and private hire vehicles
**Proprietor:** P Beale
**US SIC:** 4121 **UK SIC:** 72200
**Employees:** 60

DUNS 29-507-4447

## Star Cargo Plc

Star Cargo House, Thompson Close, Harpenden, Hertfordshire AL5 4SB
**Tel:** 01582469933
**Web:** www.starcargo.co.uk
**Reg No:** 1870657 **Estd:** 1984 Public Limited Company
**Line of Business:** Road haulage and transport services
**Trading Style:** Star Cargo Public Limited Company
**Issued Capital:** £56,454
**Principals:** J G James *(Chairman and Managing)*, C R Howell, T G James, A J Caldwell
**Co. Secretary:** Richard Edgell
**Responsibilities**
**Admin:** Debby Wild *(PA to Chairman)*
**Health & Safety:** daryl king-lee *(Health & Safety Manager)*
**Branches:** Star Cargo Plc, The Freight Terminal, Lydden Hill, Dover, Kent CT15 7JW
**US SIC:** 6711, 4712
**UK SIC:** 83962, 77002
**Auditors:** Arthur Andersen
**Bankers:** National Westminster Bank Plc (60-04-27)

| | 30-09-14 | 30-09-13 | 30-09-12 |
|---|---|---|---|
| TO | 79,732,740 | 74,570,778 | 73,591,884 |
| P/L | 3,226,160 | 3,219,169 | 3,188,632 |
| NW | 12,000,777 | 10,348,426 | 9,825,299 |
| WC | 5,835,563 | 5,193,321 | 4,911,524 |
| Emp. | 213 | 207 | 195 |

DUNS 77-537-4440

## Star Cars Ltd

5 Plantagenet Road, Barnet, Hertfordshire EN5 5JG
**Tel:** 020-8447-1980 **Fax:** 02084471984
**Web:** www.starcars.co.uk
**Reg No:** 2993937 **Estd:** 1994 Private Limited Company
**Line of Business:** Other passenger land transport
**Trading Style:** Star Cars Limited
**Issued Capital:** £100,000
**Directors:** K Parkinson, A Parkinson
**Co. Secretary:** Carl Parkinson
**Branches:** Star Cars Ltd, 255 Hoxton St, London N1 5LG
**US SIC:** 4141 **UK SIC:** 72102
**Auditors:** EA Associates

| | 31-07-13 | 31-07-12 | 31-07-11 |
|---|---|---|---|
| TA | 1,107,351 | 1,427,081 | 1,360,877 |
| NW | 310,920 | 300,170 | 445,670 |
| WC | (306,093) | (329,407) | (48,559) |

DUNS 22-536-0593

## Star Computers Ltd

(**Subsidiary of:** Blayhall Ltd)
Building 3, Hatters Lane, Watford, Hertfordshire WD18 8YG
**Tel:** 01923246414
**Web:** www.starplc.com
**Reg No:** 1553154 **Estd:** 1981 Private Limited Company
**Line of Business:** Hardware consultancy
**Export Sales:** £543,940
**Issued Capital:** £2
**Directors:** C C Bennett, Ms J N Blechner, B Skalla, R Blechner
**Co. Secretary:** Dylan Evans
**Responsibilities**
**Admin:** Alison Kallsen *(Office Manager)*
**Health & Safety:** Jackie Baer *(Health & Safety Officer)*
**Facilities:** Alison Kallsen *(Office Manager)*
**Branches:** Star Computers Ltd, Po Box 834, Oxford, Oxfordshire OX2 6FH
**US SIC:** 7379 **UK SIC:** 83940
**Auditors:** Nexia Audit Ltd
**Bankers:** Bank Of Scotland (12-11-03)

| | 30-06-13 | 30-06-12 | 30-06-11 |
|---|---|---|---|
| TO | 11,066,092 | 8,095,187 | 5,258,245 |
| P/L | 6,007,464 | 1,077,173 | 893,633 |
| NW | 5,200,572 | 2,741,392 | 2,143,421 |
| WC | 7,312,409 | 6,546,617 | 5,071,302 |
| Emp. | 63 | 61 | 54 |

DUNS 21-584-0441

## The Star Foundation

Astrum House, Nightingale Close, Rotherham, South Yorkshire S60 2AB
**Tel:** 01709834000
**Estd:** 2011 Proprietorship
**Line of Business:** Other human health activities
**Proprietor:** T Payne
**US SIC:** 8091 **UK SIC:** 95200
**Employees:** 60

DUNS 73-903-8664 Imp

## Star Global Trading Ltd

(**Subsidiary of:** Marimba Holdings Ltd)
Unit 6 Dallas Court, Salford, Lancashire M50 2GF
**Tel:** 0161 8771222
**Web:** www.starperfumes.com
**Reg No:** 5157558 **Estd:** 1999 Private Limited Company
**Line of Business:** Wholesale of perfume and cosmetics
**Trading Style:** Star Perfumes
**Issued Capital:** £3,751,100
**Managing Directors:** N A Barron, D M Thakrar
**Co. Secretary:** Mrs Rachana Thakrar
**Responsibilities**
**HR:** Kim Pemberton *(Human Resources Manager)*
**Health & Safety:** Kim Pemberton *(Human Resources Manager)*
**Operations:** Tony Christian *(Operations Manager)*
**US SIC:** 5122, 5621
**UK SIC:** 61800, 64500
**Auditors:** RSM Tenon Audit Ltd

| | 28-02-13 | 29-02-12 | 11-02-11 |
|---|---|---|---|
| TO | 68,015,423 | 66,201,555 | 69,723,816 |
| P/L | 113,721 | 140,170 | 126,829 |
| NW | 780,052 | 732,463 | 623,742 |
| WC | 27,093,955 | 23,216,367 | 21,887,347 |
| Emp. | 151 | 129 | 128 |

DUNS 23-342-2539

## Star Instruments Ltd

(**Subsidiary of:** Dunellen Group Ltd)
Waterfront Plaza, 8 Laganbank Road, St Neots, Cambridgeshire PE19 8ER
**Web:** www.star-instruments.co.uk
**Reg No:** 0047049NI **Estd:** 2003 Private Limited Company
**Line of Business:** Manufacture of non-electronic instruments and appliances for measuring, checking, testing, navigating and other purposes, except industrial process control equipment
**Issued Capital:** £43,800
**Directors:** Ms S Donnelly, H Bicker, S Donnelly
**Co. Secretary:** Mrs Shauna Donnelly
**Branches:** Star Instruments Ltd, 12 Colmworth Business Park, Eaton Court Road, St. Neots, Cambridgeshire PE19 8ER
**US SIC:** 3811 **UK SIC:** 37100
**Auditors:** Trevor Jones & Co

| | 31-07-13 | 31-07-12 | 31-07-11 |
|---|---|---|---|
| TA | 1,716,180 | 1,785,798 | 1,742,206 |
| NW | 1,548,403 | 1,551,209 | 1,523,247 |
| WC | 1,488,680 | 1,450,653 | 1,427,826 |

DUNS 64-083-8863

## Star Medical Ltd

4 Upper Bristol Road Kelso Place, Bath, Avon BA1 3AU
**Tel:** 01225336335 **Fax:** 01225326398
**Web:** www.starmedical.co.uk
**Reg No:** 4487307 **Estd:** 2002 Private Limited Company
**Line of Business:** Employment and recruitment companies and consultants
**Issued Capital:** £1,000
**Directors:** Mrs L O'Neill, T E Webster
**Responsibilities**
**Senior:** Aaron Payne *(Manager)*, Lucy Randle *(Manager)*, Steve Waller *(Senior Manager)*
**Finance:** Martin Levoir *(Financial Director)*, Sarah Rumball *(Financial Controller)*
**Marketing:** Archie Austin *(Marketing Manager)*, Kate Hosker *(Business Support Coordinator)*
**Sales:** Carly Edwards *(Brand Manager)*, Carly Hill *(Sales Executive)*
**HR:** Stewart Musselle *(Recruitment Manager)*
**US SIC:** 7361 **UK SIC:** 83954
**Bankers:** HSBC Bank plc (40-09-19)

| | 30-09-13 | 30-09-12 | 30-09-11 |
|---|---|---|---|
| TO | 10,501,492 | N/A | 1,524,857 |
| P/L | 107,562 | N/A | 145,565 |
| NW | 210,568 | 167,345 | 94,587 |
| WC | 29,938 | 1,208 | (19,923) |
| Emp. | 106 | N/A | N/A |

DUNS 73-531-6742

## Star Pubs & Bars Ltd

(**Subsidiary of:** L'Arche Green N.V.)
3-4 South Gyle Broadway Broadway Park, Edinburgh, Midlothian EH12 9JZ
**Tel:** 01315282700
**Web:** www.starpubs.co.uk
**Reg No:** 0250925SC **Estd:** 2003 Private Limited Company
**Line of Business:** Bars
**Issued Capital:** £1
**Directors:** J P Van Der Burg, C J Moore, C M Jowsey, D M Forde
**Co. Secretary:** Graeme Colquhoun
**Responsibilities**
**Senior:** Anne Oliver *(Manager)*
**Branches:** Star Pubs & Bars Ltd, Old Grey Mare, 331 Oldham Road, Oldham, Lancashire OL2 6AB
**US SIC:** 7399 **UK SIC:** 83954
**Auditors:** KPMG LLP

| | 31-12-13 | 31-12-12 | 31-12-11 |
|---|---|---|---|
| TO | 67,399,000 | 81,819,000 | 92,445,680 |
| P/L | 7,762,000 | 10,095,000 | (26,478,619) |
| NW | 6,506,000 | 641,000 | (5,098,297) |
| WC | (6,992,000) | (12,871,000) | (18,271,471) |
| Emp. | 73 | 73 | 95 |

DUNS 21-564-2935 Imp-Exp

## Star Refrigeration Ltd

Unit 4, Thornliebank Industrial Estate, Nitshill Road, Glasgow, Lanarkshire G46 8JW
**Tel:** 0141-638-7916
**Web:** www.star-ref.co.uk
**Reg No:** 0048005SC **VAT No:** 260412890
**Estd:** 1970 Private Limited Company
**Line of Business:** Air conditioning contractors
**Export Markets:** Middle East; W Europe; Australia
**Export Sales:** £4,483,000
**Issued Capital:** £940,362
**Principals:** A H Brown *(Chairman)*, Dr S F Pearson *(Chairman)*, G D Stuart *(Financial)*, Dr R A Lamb, J R Rowell, Dr A B Pearson, C J Fraser
**Co. Secretary:** James Bolster
**Responsibilities**
**IT:** Collin Wright *(IT Manager)*
**Facilities:** Derek Barclay *(Production Manager)*
**Operations:** Derek Barclay *(Production Manager)*
**Branches:** Star Refrigeration Ltd, 13 Charles Wood Road, Dereham, Norfolk NR19 1SX
**US SIC:** 1711 **UK SIC:** 50300
**Auditors:** Ernst & Young LLP
**Bankers:** The Royal Bank Of Scotland Plc (83-21-42)

| | 31-12-13 | 31-12-12 | 31-12-11 |
|---|---|---|---|
| TO | 40,806,000 | 38,553,000 | 38,484,000 |
| P/L | (704,000) | (139,000) | (488,000) |
| NW | 4,763,000 | 4,882,000 | 4,999,000 |
| WC | 3,329,000 | 3,295,000 | 3,326,000 |
| Emp. | 322 | 343 | 361 |

DUNS 73-673-0016
## Star Scaffolding Ltd
(**Subsidiary of:** Star Scaffolding Holdings Ltd)
Unit 6 Western Way, Wednesbury, West Midlands WS10 7BW
**Tel:** 01215056366 **Fax:** 01215056377
**Web:** www.star-scaffolding.co.uk
**Reg No:** 4932413 **Estd:** 2010 Private Limited Company
**Line of Business:** Scaffolds and work platform erectors
**Issued Capital:** £3
**Directors:** M I Chard, S Bunn
**Co. Secretary:** Stephen Kettle
**US SIC:** 7394, 1799
**UK SIC:** 84000, 50000

| | 31-10-13 | 31-10-12 | 31-10-11 |
|---|---|---|---|
| TA | 863,282 | 1,003,838 | 562,765 |
| NW | 480,268 | 459,887 | 302,073 |
| WC | 158,415 | 107,410 | 103,318 |

DUNS 23-162-7589
## Star Taxis
162-164 Canterbury Street, Gillingham, Kent ME7 5UB
**Tel:** 01634-575656
**Web:** www.startaxismedway.co.uk
**Estd:** 2010 Partnership
**Line of Business:** Taxis and private hire vehicles
**Partner:** D Sandhu
**Responsibilities**
**Senior:** Bob Sandhu *(Partner)*
**US SIC:** 4121 **UK SIC:** 72200
**Employees:** 80

DUNS 49-064-3723
## Star Technology Services Ltd
(**Subsidiary of:** Claranet Internet Holdings Ltd)
Brighouse Court, Barnett Way, Barnwood, Gloucester, Gloucestershire GL4 3RT
**Tel:** 08001384443 **Fax:** 01285880044
**Web:** www.crm.star.co.uk
**Reg No:** 3077786 **Estd:** 1995 Private Limited Company
**Line of Business:** Other computer related activities
**Issued Capital:** £4,001,000
**Directors:** C Nasser, M Robert, N Fairhurst
**Branches:** Star Technology Services Ltd, 40 Whitfield Street, London W1T 2RH
**US SIC:** 7379 **UK SIC:** 83940
**Auditors:** Ernst & Young LLP
**Bankers:** Lloyds TSB Bank plc (30-92-06)

| | 30-06-13 | 31-07-12 | 31-06-11 |
|---|---|---|---|
| TO | 46,857,000 | 50,045,000 | 45,941,000 |
| P/L | 599,000 | 933,000 | (88,000) |
| NW | 6,636,000 | 6,534,000 | 5,459,000 |
| WC | 1,597,000 | (1,125,000) | (2,195,000) |
| Emp. | 223 | 243 | 245 |

DUNS 23-354-9414
## Star Trac Europe Ltd
(**Subsidiary of:** Core Industries Inc.)
4 The Gateway Centre, Coronation Road, Cressex Business Park, High Wycombe, Buckinghamshire HP12 3SU
**Tel:** 01494-688260
**Reg No:** 4969159 **Estd:** 2000 Private Limited Company
**Line of Business:** Fitness equipment
**Issued Capital:** £2
**Director:** D L Grosz
**Responsibilities**
**Senior:** George Baxter *(Manager)*, John Gamble *(Manager)*, Steven Nero *(Manager)*, Matthew Pengelly *(Manager)*, Gregory Sherman *(Chief Executive)*
**US SIC:** 5941 **UK SIC:** 65400

| | 31-12-13 | 31-12-12 | 31-12-11 |
|---|---|---|---|
| TA | 2 | 2 | 2 |
| NW | 2 | 2 | 2 |

DUNS 22-661-2372
## Star Transport & Warehousing Ltd
Star House, Brunel Way, Thetford, Norfolk IP24 1HP
**Tel:** 01842752603
**Web:** www.star-transport.co.uk
**Reg No:** 1620450 **VAT No:** 334121502
**Estd:** 1963 Private Limited Company
**Line of Business:** Road haulage and transport services
**Issued Capital:** £135,328
**Principals:** N P Marriott *(Chairman)*, M P Marriott, J R Marriott, H S Marriott
**Co. Secretary:** Neville Marriott
**Responsibilities**
**Senior:** Rob Borrer *(Warehouse Manager and Administ)*
**Finance:** Sally Neave *(Credit Control Manager)*
**Admin:** Rob Borrer *(Warehouse Manager and Administ)*, Lisa Holmes *(Receptionist)*
**Fleet:** Rob Borrer *(Warehouse Manager and Administ)*
**US SIC:** 4789, 4226
**UK SIC:** 77002, 77003
**Auditors:** BDO Stoy Hayward
**Bankers:** HSBC Bank plc (40-09-10)

| | 31-12-13 | 31-12-12 | 31-12-11 |
|---|---|---|---|
| TO | 7,890,342 | 7,419,651 | 7,444,529 |
| P/L | 283,202 | 95,027 | 207,613 |
| NW | 2,591,776 | 2,265,063 | 2,194,594 |
| WC | 831,502 | 569,048 | 435,777 |
| Emp. | 86 | 83 | 82 |

DUNS 73-888-1551
## Starbank Holdings Ltd
20-22 Anglezarke Road, Newton-Le-Willows, Merseyside WA12 8DJ
**Tel:** 01925-223965
**Web:** www.starbankpanelproducts.com
**Reg No:** 5142333 **Estd:** 2004 Private Limited Company
**Line of Business:** Holding companies management activities
**Issued Capital:** £251,000
**Directors:** Ms W K Elsworthy, P G Darbyshire, G Darbyshire
**Co. Secretary:** Ms Mary Darbyshire
**US SIC:** 6711 **UK SIC:** 83962

| | 30-11-13 | 30-11-12 | 30-11-11 |
|---|---|---|---|
| TO | 8,869,959 | 8,582,440 | 7,559,765 |
| P/L | 509,105 | 375,405 | 291,606 |
| NW | 2,804,313 | 2,395,792 | 2,227,034 |
| WC | (37,526) | (211,995) | (157,045) |
| Emp. | 89 | 86 | 80 |

DUNS 77-453-3913
## Starbucks Coffee Co (U K) Ltd
(**Subsidiary of:** Starbucks Corporation)
Building 4, London W4 5YE
**Tel:** 02088345000 **Fax:** 02089943733
**Web:** http://starbucks.co.uk
**Reg No:** 2959325 **Estd:** 2006 Private Limited Company
**Line of Business:** Coffee shops
**Issued Capital:** £316,985
**Directors:** C J Carter, N B Williams, M W Fox, A Thurston
**Co. Secretary:** Adrian Thurston
**Responsibilities**
**Senior:** Philip Broad *(Manager)*, Kris Engskov *(Manager)*, Roger Skeete *(Manager)*
**Marketing:** Ian Cranna *(Vice President Marketing & Cat)*, Liz Forte *(Head of Marketing ?Head of Mar)*, Brian Wareing *(Sales & Marketing Manager)*
**Sales:** Dale Calcutt *(VP of Store Development)*, Brian Wareing *(Sales & Marketing Manager)*
**IT:** Robert Teagle *(EMEA IT Director)*
**HR:** Sandra Porter *(Human Resources Director)*
**Health & Safety:** Samantha Edge *(Health & Safety Officer)*
**Facilities:** Kiernan Lynch *(Head of Constructions)*
**Operations:** Rhys Iley *(Vice President Licensed Operst)*
**Branches:** Starbucks Coffee Co (U K) Ltd, The Plaza, 120 Oxford Street, London W1D 1LT
**US SIC:** 5812 **UK SIC:** 66110
**Auditors:** Deloitte LLP
**Bankers:** National Westminster Bank Plc (60-00-01)

| | 28-09-14 | 29-09-13 | 30-09-12 |
|---|---|---|---|
| TO | 408,721,070 | 399,405,183 | 413,392,826 |
| P/L | 1,056,196 | (20,465,123) | (30,403,907) |
| NW | 35,513,082 | 43,838,060 | 51,975,514 |
| WC | (9,289,314) | (15,531,296) | (10,513,618) |
| Emp. | 7,345 | 7,726 | 8,739 |

DUNS 28-965-8981
## Starburger Ltd
Unit 6-8, Priestley Way Forest Trading Estate, London E17 6AL
**Tel:** 020-8527-2666 **Fax:** 020-8503-2029
**Web:** www.starcateringsupplies.co.uk
**Reg No:** 1704664 **Estd:** 1983 Private Limited Company
**Line of Business:** Non-specialised wholesale of food, beverages and tobacco
**Issued Capital:** £2,200
**Principals:** A Gultekin *(Managing)*, A Munir
**Co. Secretary:** Altan Gultekin
**Branches:** Starburger Ltd, 7 High Street, Grays, Essex RM17 6NB
**US SIC:** 5149 **UK SIC:** 61700
**Auditors:** Haj & Co
**Bankers:** HSBC Bank plc (40-06-20)

| | 31-03-14 | 31-03-13 | 31-03-12 |
|---|---|---|---|
| TO | 48,381,108 | 43,723,734 | N/A |
| P/L | 1,559,212 | 527,837 | 143,000 |
| NW | 2,922,259 | 1,951,729 | 465,741 |
| WC | 1,712,371 | 644,567 | N/A |
| Emp. | 195 | 191 | 2 |

DUNS 21-017-8584
## Starcare Ltd
Richmond Place, 125 Boughton, Chester, Cheshire CH3 5BH
**Tel:** 01244313576
**Web:** www.starcare.co
**Reg No:** 6397723 **Estd:** 2007 Private Limited Company
**Line of Business:** Home care service providers
**Issued Capital:** £152
**Director:** J P Ellison
**Co. Secretary:** Mrs Paula Pedlow
**US SIC:** 8811 **UK SIC:** 99000

| | 31-10-13 | 31-10-12 | 31-10-11 |
|---|---|---|---|
| TA | 109,075 | 66,627 | 64,030 |
| NW | 26,809 | 11,142 | 4,278 |
| WC | 18,611 | 2,647 | (7,052) |

DUNS 76-388-6926
## Starcom Worldwide Ltd
(**Subsidiary of:** Publicis Groupe S.A.)
83-89 Whitfield Street, London W1T 4HQ
**Tel:** 02071908000 **Fax:** 02076365280
**Web:** www.smgtalent.co.uk
**Reg No:** 2555573 **Estd:** 1990 Private Limited Company
**Line of Business:** Advertising, radio, tv and other media
**Trading Style:** Starcom Mediavest
**Issued Capital:** £10,000
**Principals:** C D Locke *(Managing)*, I B Jacob, Ms P Glucklich, S Parker
**Co. Secretary:** Mrs Sarah Dailey
**Branches:** Starcom Worldwide Ltd, 83-89 Whitfield Street, London W1T 4HQ
**US SIC:** 7311, 7319
**UK SIC:** 83800
**Auditors:** Mazars LLP

| | 31-12-13 | 31-12-12 | 31-12-11 |
|---|---|---|---|
| TA | 10,000 | 10,000 | 10,000 |
| NW | 10,000 | 10,000 | 10,000 |
| WC | 10,000 | 10,000 | 10,000 |
| Emp. | 110 | 110 | 110 |

DUNS 42-418-3015
## Starcounty Textile Services Ltd
Aerial Road, Llay Industrial Estate, Llay, Wrexham, Clwyd LL12 0TU
**Tel:** 01978859070
**Web:** www.starcounty.co.uk
**Reg No:** 4405925 **Estd:** 2006 Private Limited Company
**Line of Business:** Linen hire
**Issued Capital:** £115,000
**Director:** P S O'Sullivan
**Co. Secretary:** Maurice Salvoni
**US SIC:** 7219 **UK SIC:** 98110

| | 30-06-13 | 30-06-12 | 30-06-11 |
|---|---|---|---|
| TA | 2,844,334 | 2,920,027 | 2,902,311 |
| NW | 669,774 | 543,879 | 497,492 |
| WC | (115,572) | (109,516) | (86,927) |

DUNS 28-967-4848
## Stardust Leisure Ltd
5 Eastern Promenade, Porthcawl, Mid Glamorgan CF36 5TS
**Tel:** 01656-785911
**Web:** www.cottagefieldstables.co.uk
**Reg No:** 1713293 **Estd:** 1983 Private Limited Company
**Line of Business:** Fair and amusement park activities
**Issued Capital:** £500,862
**Director:** L J Crole
**Co. Secretary:** John Crole
**Branches:** Stardust Leisure Ltd, 52 Plymouth Street, Swansea, West Glamorgan SA1 3QQ
**US SIC:** 7399 **UK SIC:** 83954
**Auditors:** Bartons Ltd
**Bankers:** Barclays Bank Plc (20-12-25)

| | 31-05-14 | 31-05-13 | 31-05-12 |
|---|---|---|---|
| TO | 1,939,107 | 1,637,219 | 1,724,771 |
| P/L | 172,493 | (127,938) | (300,359) |
| NW | 1,358,499 | 1,302,119 | 1,644,185 |
| WC | (863,972) | (919,228) | (575,739) |
| Emp. | 55 | 56 | 51 |

DUNS 34-649-2671
## Starglaze Windows & Conservatories Ltd
(**Subsidiary of:** Conarie International Ltd)
Unit 5 Waterside South, Lincoln, Lincolnshire LN5 7JD
**Tel:** 01522512020
**Web:** www.starglaze-windows.com
**Reg No:** 2774368 **Estd:** 2002 Private Limited Company
**Line of Business:** Painting and glazing
**Issued Capital:** £100
**Directors:** M E Parczuk, S J Parczuk, M J Cashmore
**Co. Secretary:** Mrs Barbara Parczuk
**Responsibilities**
**Senior:** Laura Wiltshire *(Retail Manager)*
**Finance:** Richard Cripps *(Finance Director)*
**HR:** Shelley Bloom *(HR Manager)*
**Purchasing:** Shaun Cannon *(Purchasing Manager)*
**Engineering:** Keith McCarthy *(Factory Manager)*
**US SIC:** 1721 **UK SIC:** 50400
**Auditors:** PKF
**Bankers:** Lloyds TSB Bank plc (30-95-05)

| | 31-12-13 | 31-12-12 | 31-12-11 |
|---|---|---|---|
| TO | 12,312,829 | 10,406,464 | 11,352,558 |
| P/L | 926,237 | 569,747 | 555,078 |
| NW | 1,608,942 | 1,612,025 | 1,800,589 |
| WC | 1,272,336 | 1,070,846 | 1,070,359 |
| Emp. | 121 | 117 | 126 |

DUNS 73-461-0314 **Imp**
## Stark Software International Ltd.
Sentinel House, Horley, Surrey RH6 7DE
**Tel:** 01293-776747
**Web:** www.stark.co.uk
**Reg No:** 2911704 **Estd:** 1994 Private Limited Company
**Line of Business:** Energy conservation consultants
**Issued Capital:** £950
**Directors:** Mrs A E Hauser, J D Stark, H P Stark
**Co. Secretary:** Mrs Johanna Stark
**Responsibilities**
**Senior:** Dave Goodfellow *(Sales Manager)*
**Finance:** Iain Kelly *(Senior Finance Administrator)*
**IT:** Sara Naguleswaran *(Computer Manager)*
**US SIC:** 7392 **UK SIC:** 83951
**Auditors:** Jack Ross & Co

| | 31-05-13 | 31-05-12 | 31-05-11 |
|---|---|---|---|
| TO | 8,827,605 | 8,411,769 | N/A |
| P/L | 777,727 | 1,154,864 | N/A |
| NW | 1,584,224 | 2,362,025 | 1,324,606 |
| WC | 1,356,668 | 2,153,552 | 1,087,659 |
| Emp. | 97 | 88 | N/A |

DUNS 77-119-4933 **Exp**
## Starkey Laboratories Ltd
(**Subsidiary of:** Starkey Laboratories Inc.)
William F Austin House, Pepper Road, Hazel Grove, Stockport, Cheshire SK7 5BX
**Tel:** 01614832200 **Fax:** 0161-483-9833
**Web:** www.starkey.co.uk
**Reg No:** 2691952 **Estd:** 1992 Private Limited Company
**Line of Business:** Hearing aid suppliers
**Export Markets:** Europe, Rest of the World
**Export Sales:** £3,499,193
**Issued Capital:** £50,100
**Director:** W Austin
**Co. Secretary:** Roger Lewin
**Responsibilities**
**HR:** Lindsay Fulcher *(General Manager)*
**Health & Safety:** Lindsay Fulcher *(General Manager)*
**Facilities:** Tony Bower *(Maintenance Engineer)*
**Purchasing:** Angela Cooper *(Purchasing Manager)*
**Engineering:** Tony Bower *(Maintenance Engineer)*
**Branches:** Starkey Laboratories Ltd, Greenham Lodge, Pigeons Farm Rd, Thatcham, Berkshire RG19 8XA
**US SIC:** 3841 **UK SIC:** 37201
**Auditors:** Ernst & Young LLP
**Bankers:** National Westminster Bank Plc (01-10-01)

| | 31-12-13 | 31-12-12 | 31-12-11 |
|---|---|---|---|
| TO | 13,410,182 | 14,253,553 | 14,970,714 |
| P/L | 638,372 | 309,500 | 844,414 |
| NW | 9,260,067 | 7,288,033 | 6,845,438 |
| WC | 7,091,328 | 6,039,314 | 5,485,267 |
| Emp. | 172 | 199 | 212 |

DUNS 21-724-1868 **Imp**
## Starkstrom Ltd
(**Subsidiary of:** Progility Plc)
256 Field End Road, Ruislip, Middlesex HA4 9LT
**Tel:** 02088-683-732 **Fax:** 02088-683-736
**Web:** www.starkstrom.com
**Reg No:** 1013256 **VAT No:** 223011140
**Estd:** 1971 Private Limited Company
**Line of Business:** Specialised building trade contractors
**Trading Style:** S-Equip
**Issued Capital:** £35,199
**Directors:** J J Mcintosh, N Jackson, D J Stewart
**Co. Secretary:** John Mcintosh
**Responsibilities**
**Senior:** Scott Pickering *(Manager)*, Brenda Tabibi *(Manager)*
**Branches:** Starkstrom Limited, 350 Melton Road, Leicester, Leicestershire LE4 7SL
**US SIC:** 1799, 5999, 8091
**UK SIC:** 50000, 65600, 95200
**Auditors:** Ashley Associates
**Bankers:** HSBC Bank plc (40-18-22)

| | 31-05-13 | 31-05-12 | 31-05-11 |
|---|---|---|---|
| TO | 11,574,548 | 10,467,012 | 8,686,475 |
| P/L | 1,634,110 | 1,244,674 | 945,448 |
| NW | 3,846,735 | 3,558,872 | 3,009,381 |
| WC | 3,296,012 | 3,224,876 | 2,781,391 |
| Emp. | 83 | N/A | N/A |

DUNS 23-515-8073 **Imp**

## Starlab (Uk) Ltd

(**Subsidiary of:** Aceg Beteiligungsges. Mbh)
4 Tanners Drive, Blakelands, Milton Keynes, Buckinghamshire MK14 5NA
**Tel:** 01908-283800 **Fax:** 01908-283802
**Web:** www.starlab.co.uk
**Reg No:** 3514931 **Estd:** 1998 Private Limited Company
**Line of Business:** Laboratory supplies
**Issued Capital:** £600,000
**Director:** Ms D Fane De Salis
**Responsibilities**
**Senior:** Klaus Ambos *(Manager)*, Heinz-Jorn Peplow *(Manager)*, Jorg Richter *(Manager)*
**US SIC:** 5199 **UK SIC:** 61900
**Auditors:** Arthur Andersen

| | 31-12-13 | 31-12-12 | 31-12-11 |
|---|---|---|---|
| TA | 3,811,640 | 3,247,215 | 3,346,755 |
| NW | 3,060,795 | 2,303,116 | 1,777,476 |
| WC | 2,708,070 | 1,984,429 | 1,414,492 |

DUNS 28-851-0209

## Starlanes Bowling Ltd

8 Gate Lane, Sutton Coldfield, West Midlands B73 5TT
**Tel:** 01213552330
**Web:** www.allstarlanes.co.uk
**Reg No:** 0720734 **Estd:** 1962 Private Limited Company
**Line of Business:** Other sporting activities not elsewhere classified
**Issued Capital:** £10,000
**Director:** T W Clarke
**Co. Secretary:** Stephen Clarke
**US SIC:** 7999 **UK SIC:** 97913
**Auditors:** Moore Stephens

| | 30-06-13 | 30-06-12 | 30-06-11 |
|---|---|---|---|
| TA | 1,341,819 | 1,938,276 | 1,808,335 |
| NW | 912,808 | 1,183,170 | 1,433,464 |
| WC | (108,962) | (177,836) | 136,973 |

DUNS 23-597-7191

## Starley Hall School Ltd

Starleyhall, Burntisland, Fife KY3 0AG
**Tel:** 01383-860314
**Web:** www.starleyhall.co.uk
**Reg No:** 0187499SC **Estd:** 1998 Private Limited Company
**Line of Business:** Schools (special)
**Issued Capital:** £500,000
**Director:** P Barton
**Co. Secretary:** Ms Judith Barton
**US SIC:** 8299 **UK SIC:** 93300
**Auditors:** Niller McIntyre & Gellanty
**Bankers:** The Royal Bank Of Scotland Plc (83-16-23)

| | 31-08-13 | 31-08-12 | 31-08-11 |
|---|---|---|---|
| TA | 2,961,843 | 2,751,887 | 2,191,977 |
| NW | 1,875,281 | 1,639,797 | 1,476,149 |
| WC | 223,920 | 11,744 | 455,745 |

DUNS 42-370-6741

## Starline Taxis Ltd

6 Royal Well Place, Cheltenham, Gloucestershire GL50 3DN
**Tel:** 01242250250
**Reg No:** 4358341 **Estd:** 2002 Private Limited Company
**Line of Business:** Taxis
**Issued Capital:** £100
**Director:** L R Jackson
**Co. Secretary:** Robert Bates
**Branches:** Starline Taxis Ltd, 10 Ambrose Street, Cheltenham, Gloucestershire GL50 3LG
**US SIC:** 4121 **UK SIC:** 72200

| | 31-01-14 | 31-01-13 | 31-01-12 |
|---|---|---|---|
| TA | 166,028 | 160,348 | 177,475 |
| NW | 74,832 | 66,747 | 11,724 |
| WC | (39,875) | (50,460) | (91,640) |

DUNS 21-196-9043 **Exp**

## Starna Ltd

52 / 54 Fowler Road, Ilford, Essex IG6 3UT
**Tel:** 02085995115 **Fax:** 02085990707
**Web:** www.starnaindustries.co.uk
**Reg No:** 1032938 **VAT No:** 246560163
**Estd:** 1971 Private Limited Company
**Line of Business:** Other business activities not elsewhere classified
**Export Markets:** Countries worldwide
**Issued Capital:** £100,000
**Principals:** A K Hulme *(Chairman and Managing)*, N R Hulme
**Co. Secretary:** Nathan Hulme
**Responsibilities**
**Senior:** Angela Hares *(Manager)*
**Finance:** Angela Hares *(Manager)*
**US SIC:** 7399 **UK SIC:** 83954
**Auditors:** Kingston Smith
**Bankers:** Barclays Bank Plc (20-29-23)

| | 30-04-14 | 30-04-13 | 30-04-12 |
|---|---|---|---|
| TO | 5,073,942 | 5,029,089 | 4,969,120 |
| P/L | 604,045 | 547,770 | 399,266 |
| NW | 3,728,687 | 3,342,758 | 3,129,080 |
| WC | 3,368,641 | 3,059,823 | 2,864,537 |
| Emp. | 101 | 99 | 96 |

DUNS 23-718-2522 **Imp**

## Starplan Furniture Ltd

173 Killyman Road, Dungannon, Co Tyrone BT71 6LN
**Tel:** 02887723663
**Web:** www.starplanbedrooms.com
**Reg No:** 0017138NI **VAT No:** 454608343
**Estd:** 1976 Private Limited Company
**Line of Business:** Furniture retail outlets
**Issued Capital:** £180,000
**Directors:** D Wilson, I Mccreery, M Wilson
**Co. Secretary:** Ms Lynda Boyd
**Branches:** Starplan Furniture Ltd, Unit 2, 605 Stratford Road, Solihull, West Midlands B90 4BP
**US SIC:** 5719, 2517
**UK SIC:** 64700, 46714
**Auditors:** PricewaterhouseCoopers LLP
**Bankers:** Northern Bank Ltd (95-03-02)

| | 30-04-14 | 30-04-13 | 30-04-12 |
|---|---|---|---|
| TO | 17,001,381 | 17,161,180 | 16,314,078 |
| P/L | 77,580 | 523,452 | 329,348 |
| NW | 12,907,847 | 12,822,024 | 13,070,109 |
| WC | (3,888,561) | (3,926,538) | (3,666,799) |
| Emp. | 222 | 229 | 226 |

DUNS 23-724-3761 **Imp**

## Starr Underwriting Agents Ltd

(**Subsidiary of:** Starr International Company Inc.)
140 Leadenhall Street, London EC3V 4QT
**Tel:** 020-7337-3550
**Web:** www.starrcompanies.com
**Reg No:** 2973661 **Estd:** 1994 Private Limited Company
**Line of Business:** Underwriting
**Issued Capital:** £900,000
**Directors:** G J Broughton, Lord P K Levene, D Stewart, S G Blakey
**Co. Secretary:** Adrian Missen
**Responsibilities**
**Senior:** Ralph Bull *(Manager)*, Eliasch Johan *(Manager)*, Richard Shaak *(Manager)*
**IT:** Ben Robins *(IT Manager)*
**Health & Safety:** Giuseppe Salcaggio *(Health & Safety Officer)*
**US SIC:** 6411 **UK SIC:** 83200
**Auditors:** Mazars LLP

| | 31-12-13 | 31-12-12 | 31-12-11 |
|---|---|---|---|
| TO | 25,535,089 | 26,108,439 | 42,593,924 |
| P/L | (1,221,770) | (1,927,137) | 11,047,869 |
| NW | 4,755,619 | 5,061,935 | 6,508,913 |
| WC | 8,994,822 | 8,883,031 | 10,422,489 |
| Emp. | 134 | 138 | 158 |

DUNS 45-883-1435

## Start Fresh Ltd

26-32 Miall Street, Nottingham, Nottinghamshire NG7 2AQ
**Tel:** 01159-244039 **Fax:** 01159-424403
**Web:** www.startfresh.co.uk
**Reg No:** 3220725 **Estd:** 1992 Private Limited Company
**Line of Business:** Wholesale of fruit and vegetables
**Issued Capital:** £200
**Principals:** Mrs N Crommer *(Managing)*, A A Mahjouri, K Mahjouri
**Co. Secretary:** Andre Mahjouri
**Responsibilities**
**Senior:** Kaz Mahjouri *(Manager)*
**Finance:** Sabah Umar *(Financial Director)*
**Marketing:** Kaz Mahjouri *(Manager)*
**Sales:** Kaz Mahjouri *(Manager)*
**US SIC:** 5148 **UK SIC:** 61700
**Auditors:** Tenon Ltd
**Bankers:** Barclays Bank Plc (20-63-25)

| | 30-06-13 | 30-06-12 | 30-06-11 |
|---|---|---|---|
| TA | 2,196,530 | 2,205,243 | 1,901,005 |
| NW | 1,019,469 | 1,148,081 | 976,565 |
| WC | 355,095 | 502,382 | 578,646 |

DUNS 22-144-5914 **Imp**

## Start Ltd

The Tea Building, 56 Shoreditch High Street, London E1 6JJ
**Tel:** 020-7269-0101 **Fax:** 02072690102
**Web:** www.startjg.com
**Reg No:** 4163386 **Estd:** 1995 Private Limited Company
**Line of Business:** Engineering design activities for industrial process and production
**Export Sales:** £8,282,238
**Trading Style:** Start Creative Ltd
**Issued Capital:** £60,000
**Directors:** M H Curtis, J R Kydd
**Co. Secretary:** Darren Whittingham
**Responsibilities**
**Senior:** Kevin Gill *(Manager)*, Jennifer Mcaleer *(Manager)*, Martin Muir *(Creative Director)*
**HR:** Polly Barnes *(Human Resources director)*
**US SIC:** 8911, 7311
**UK SIC:** 83701, 83800

| | 31-03-14 | 31-03-13 | 31-03-12 |
|---|---|---|---|
| TO | 15,524,198 | 13,873,327 | 12,330,872 |
| P/L | (437,452) | (47,763) | (666,170) |
| NW | 2,947,065 | 3,369,738 | 3,441,475 |
| WC | 3,015,527 | 3,593,875 | 3,581,353 |
| Emp. | 146 | 114 | 135 |

DUNS 42-439-9640

## StART360 Ltd

Hildon House, 30-34 Hill Street, Belfast BT1 2LB
**Tel:** 02890435810
**Web:** www.opportunity-youth.org
**Reg No:** 0033207NI **Estd:** 1993 Private Company Limited By Guarantee
**Line of Business:** Adult and other education not elsewhere classified
**Directors:** B J Higgins, J Mccormick, J Mccorry, Mrs G Hobson, J I Lopes, A F Hennessey, A J Ledlie, Ms M M Marken
**Responsibilities**
**Senior:** Michele Marken O B E *(Chairman)*, Shadd Maruna *(Board Member)*, John McCormick *(Board Member)*, John McCorry *(Board Member)*, Cara McHugh *(Corporate Services Manager)*, Anne Mcclure *(Manager)*, Orlagh Mckearney *(Opportunity Youth Team Manager)*, Eamonn Molloy *(Manager)*
**Finance:** Clare O'Reilly *(Finance Manager)*
**Marketing:** Zoe Anderson *(Communications Manager)*
**Branches:** StaRT360 Ltd, Hildon House, 30-34 Hill Street, Belfast, Belfast BT1 2LB
**US SIC:** 8249 **UK SIC:** 93300
**Auditors:** Goldblatt McGuigan
**Bankers:** Ulster Bank Ltd (98-00-50)

| | 31-03-14 | 31-03-13 | 31-03-12 |
|---|---|---|---|
| TO | 3,166,688 | 2,893,602 | 2,752,924 |
| P/L | 129,833 | 164,974 | 25,000 |
| NW | 972,368 | 842,535 | 677,561 |
| WC | 932,497 | 798,290 | 602,748 |
| Emp. | 81 | 75 | 77 |

DUNS 22-769-6010

## Startin Group Ltd

(**Subsidiary of:** Freeman Junior Ltd)
Farmoor Lane, Redditch, Worcestershire B98 0SD
**Tel:** 01527883800 **Fax:** 01527529944
**Web:** www.startingroup.co.uk
**Reg No:** 0543964 **VAT No:** 580710745
**Estd:** 2002 Private Limited Company
**Line of Business:** Car dealers (new & used)
**Trading Style:** Startins of Birmingham (Vauxhall), Startins of Worcester (Rover), Startins of Redditch (Rover)
**Issued Capital:** £116,000
**Directors:** B P Winslow, G P Freeman, M A Geobey
**Co. Secretary:** Ms Elizabeth Freeman
**Branches:** Startin Group Ltd, Bromyard Road, Worcester, Worcestershire WR2 5YJ
**US SIC:** 5511 **UK SIC:** 65100
**Auditors:** Moore Stephens
**Bankers:** National Westminster Bank Plc (60-07-41)

| | 31-12-13 | 31-12-12 | 31-12-11 |
|---|---|---|---|
| TO | N/A | 8,673,052 | 11,314,586 |
| P/L | N/A | (336,053) | (972,551) |
| NW | (188,095) | (334,332) | 9,563 |
| WC | (247,867) | (189,671) | 202,649 |
| Emp. | N/A | 22 | 27 |

DUNS 23-211-8849

## Starwood Holdings Ltd

Millennium House, 46 Athol Street, Douglas, Douglas, Isle of Man IM1 1JB
**Tel:** 01624613979 **Fax:** 01624-615462
**Web:** www.mayerton.com
**Reg No:** 0070955M **Estd:** 1996 Private Limited Company
**Line of Business:** Investment holding company
**Directors:** J Beckmann, J A Cowan
**Co. Secretary:** Roger Barrs
**US SIC:** 6799 **UK SIC:** 81502
**Turnover:** £89,121,000

DUNS 21-027-9774 **Imp**

## State Bank of India

(**Subsidiary of:** State Bank of India)
15-17 King St The City, London EC2V 8EA
**Tel:** 02074544300 **Fax:** 02074544334
**Web:** www.sbiuk.com
**Reg No:** 0004460FC **Estd:** 2012 Foreign Company
**Line of Business:** Banks and financial institutions
**Principals:** D Basu *(Chairman)*, P Bhattacharjee *(Managing)*, Dr S Ramani, Y Rashid, Anila R Dholakia, Dr K Kanungo, Dr R K Chakrabarti, S K Purnachandra Rao
**Co. Secretary:** R Guptar
**Responsibilities**
**Senior:** Chaman Anand *(Director)*, David Attree *(Financial Officer)*, Mast Awasthi *(Director)*, Shri Chatterjee *(Director)*, Smt Dholakia *(Director)*, R Janakiraman *(Director)*, Parmpal Mann *(Director)*, Kumar Rajat Chakrabarti *(Director)*, Kuchimanchi Rao *(Director)*, JK Shivan *(Chief Executive)*, Singh Shrui Parmal Mann *(Director)*, Rashid Shrui Yawai *(Director)*, Umed Singh *(Director)*
**IT:** Mishra Debasish *(System IT Manager)*
**HR:** Terry Derbridge *(Human Resources Manager)*, Ritu Parihar *(Personnel Manager)*
**Health & Safety:** Terry Harrison *(Health & Safety Officer)*
**Facilities:** Shyan Vatsa *(Facilities Manager)*
**Operations:** Oliver Conaty *(Technical, Production Manager)*
**Purchasing:** Shyan Vatsa *(Facilities Manager)*
**US SIC:** 6012 **UK SIC:** 81402
**Bankers:** HSBC Bank plc (40-05-30)

DUNS 23-666-2565

## State Hospital Board

110 Lampits Road, Carstairs Junction, Carstairs, Lanark, Lanarkshire ML11 8RP
**Web:** www.tsh.scot.nhs.uk
**Estd:** 2003
**Line of Business:** Public sector hospital activities, including nhs trusts
**Principals:** A Hewitt *(Chairman)*, D Manson *(General Manager)*
**Responsibilities**
**Senior:** Andreana Abminson *(Manager)*, Andreana Adamson *(Chief Executive)*
**Finance:** Hazel Robertson *(Financial Director)*
**IT:** Thomas Best *(Infrastructure Operations Mana)*
**HR:** Rebecca Chalmers *(Human Resources Manager)*
**Health & Safety:** Tom Kerr *(Health & Safety Officer)*
**Facilities:** Martin Henry *(Facilities Manager)*
**US SIC:** 8062 **UK SIC:** 95100
**Employees:** 500

DUNS 42-345-3021

## State of Flux Ltd

The Outer Temple, 222 Strand, London WC2R 1BA
**Tel:** 020-7842-0600 **Fax:** 02078420601
**Web:** www.stateofflux.co.uk
**Reg No:** 4332999 **Estd:** 1998 Private Limited Company
**Line of Business:** Miscellaneous computer services
**Trading Style:** State of Flux Ltd
**Issued Capital:** £100
**Director:** A E Day
**Co. Secretary:** Patrice Day
**US SIC:** 7379, 7374, 7399, 7392
**UK SIC:** 83940, 83954, 83951

| | 31-12-13 | 31-12-12 | 31-12-11 |
|---|---|---|---|
| TA | 966,971 | 906,900 | 1,293,432 |
| NW | 519,146 | 456,584 | 927,425 |
| WC | 317,110 | 256,233 | 847,532 |

DUNS 23-228-3064

## State of Jersey Police

Po Box 789, Jersey, Channel Islands JE4 8ZD
**Tel:** 01534 612612
**Web:** www.jersey.police.uk
**Estd:** 1853
**Line of Business:** Public security, law and order activities
**Director:** G Power
**Responsibilities**
**Senior:** Mike Bowron *(Chief Officer)*
**US SIC:** 7399, 9221
**UK SIC:** 83954, 91300
**Employees:** 326

DUNS 53-608-4890 **Imp**

## State Street Bank Europe Ltd

(**Subsidiary of:** State Street Corporation)
20 Churchill Place, Canary Wharf, London E14 5HG
**Tel:** 02033952500
**Web:** www.ssga.com
**Reg No:** 3413759 **Estd:** 1997 Private Limited Company
**Line of Business:** Financial intermediation not elsewhere classified
**Export Sales:** £2,636,000
**Trading Style:** Globallink
**Issued Capital:** £10,000,000
**Directors:** P O'Neill, S J Craig, Ms K N Chebator, R Shah, D Arnum, H Fairweather
**Co. Secretary:** Mikko Nahkuri
**Responsibilities**
**Senior:** James Caccivio *(Director)*, Karen Keenan *(Director)*
**US SIC:** 6111 **UK SIC:** 81501

**Auditors:** Ernst & Young LLP

| | 31-12-13 | 31-12-12 | 31-12-11 |
|---|---|---|---|
| TA | 405,908,000 | 358,185,000 | 544,426,000 |
| P/L | 7,791,000 | 35,439,000 | (338,000) |
| NW | 183,115,000 | 181,864,000 | 160,673,000 |
| WC | 183,302,000 | 186,124,000 | 160,263,000 |
| Emp. | 135 | 126 | 116 |

DUNS 50-558-7097 **Exp**

## State Street Global Advisors Ltd

(**Subsidiary of:** State Street Corporation)
20 Churchill Place, London E14 5HJ
**Tel:** 020-3395-6000 **Fax:** 02076986350
**Web:** www.ssga.com
**Reg No:** 2509928 **Estd:** 1990 Private Limited Company
**Line of Business:** Bureau de change
**Export Markets:** U.S.A.
**Export Sales:** £61,809,924
**Issued Capital:** £77,000,000
**Directors:** M J Karpik, A J Castle, J Kearney, W D Street
**Co. Secretary:** Vathoulla Sullivan
**Responsibilities**
**Senior:** Amy Armstrong *(Human Resources Business Partn)*, Jess Conway *(CEO, Managing Director)*, Kanesh Lakhakni *(Manager)*, Scott Powers *(President and CEO)*, Lee Reeve *(Vice President)*, Alasdair Reid *(Head of Asset Owner)*
**Finance:** Patrick Waller *(Manager)*
**Sales:** Wade McDoland *(Sales Director)*
**IT:** Lynn Blake *(CIO, Global Equity Beta Soluti)*, Kevin Gough *(Non PC Systems Manager)*, Michael Krupsdahl *(Head of IT Operation)*, Keith Lau *(IT Manager)*
**HR:** Amy Armstrong *(Human Resources Business Partn)*, Hazel Keating *(Human Resources Manager)*
**Health & Safety:** Hazel Keating *(Human Resources Manager)*
**Purchasing:** Peter Condon *(Buyer)*
**US SIC:** 6111, 6371
**UK SIC:** 81501, 82002
**Auditors:** Ernst & Young LLP
**Bankers:** The Royal Bank Of Scotland Plc (15-10-00)

| | 31-12-13 | 31-12-12 | 31-12-11 |
|---|---|---|---|
| TA | 184,791,422 | 145,797,697 | 122,340,565 |
| P/L | 50,563,027 | 16,506,462 | 19,321,044 |
| NW | 148,197,990 | 107,084,404 | 93,048,402 |
| WC | 149,247,416 | 111,647,515 | 92,498,105 |
| Emp. | 320 | 322 | 324 |

DUNS 29-571-0909

## State Street London Ltd

(**Subsidiary of:** State Street Corporation)
1 Canada Square, London E14 5AF
**Tel:** 02074162500 **Fax:** 020-7915-7230
**Web:** www.statestreet.com
**Reg No:** 1932894 **Estd:** 1985 Private Limited Company
**Line of Business:** Financial intermediation not elsewhere classified
**Issued Capital:** £250,000
**Directors:** Ms C Sunderland, S J Craig
**US SIC:** 6111 **UK SIC:** 81501
**Auditors:** Ernst & Young LLP
**Bankers:** The Royal Bank Of Scotland Plc (15-10-00)

| | 31-12-13 | 31-12-12 | 31-12-11 |
|---|---|---|---|
| TA | 2,205,917 | 1,935,493 | 1,757,083 |
| P/L | 318,314 | 208,217 | 111,138 |
| NW | 2,192,817 | 1,924,993 | 1,749,583 |
| WC | 1,739,827 | 1,472,003 | 1,296,593 |

DUNS 28-933-7651

## State Street Nominees Ltd

(**Subsidiary of:** State Street Corporation)
525 Ferry Road, Edinburgh, Midlothian EH5 2AW
**Tel:** 01313152000
**Web:** www.statestreet.com
**Reg No:** 1542561 **Estd:** 1981 Private Limited Company
**Line of Business:** Investment consultants
**Issued Capital:** £100
**Directors:** K J Hummerstone, S J Olford, Ms D A Summers
**Responsibilities**
**HR:** Gillian Campbell *(Training Manager)*
**Health & Safety:** Emma Waugh *(Premises Manager)*
**Facilities:** Emma Waugh *(Premises Manager)*
**US SIC:** 6111 **UK SIC:** 81501
**Bankers:** Coutts & Co (18-00-91)

| | 31-12-13 | 31-12-12 | 31-12-11 |
|---|---|---|---|
| TA | 100 | 100 | 100 |
| NW | 100 | 100 | 100 |

DUNS 77-508-5350

## State Street Trustees Ltd

(**Subsidiary of:** State Street Corporation)
20 Churchill Place, London E14 5HJ
**Tel:** 02033952500
**Web:** www.statestreet.com
**Reg No:** 2982384 **Estd:** 1997 Private Limited Company
**Line of Business:** Financial intermediation not elsewhere classified
**Issued Capital:** £100
**Directors:** G Stark, G A Adams, B S Allis, M Westwell
**Co. Secretary:** Gerard Paterson
**Responsibilities**
**Senior:** Darren Banks *(Manager)*
**Engineering:** Donald Conover *(Production Manager)*
**Branches:** State Street Trustees Ltd, 25 Ferry Road, Edinburgh, Midlothian EH6 4AD
**US SIC:** 6111 **UK SIC:** 81501
**Auditors:** Ernst & Young LLP

| | 31-12-13 | 31-12-12 | 31-12-11 |
|---|---|---|---|
| TA | 45,637,416 | 38,053,610 | 34,073,785 |
| P/L | 9,457,337 | 5,726,699 | 4,471,743 |
| NW | 43,393,395 | 36,180,017 | 30,724,478 |
| WC | 43,393,395 | 36,180,017 | 30,786,140 |
| Emp. | 53 | 53 | 48 |

DUNS 21-303-0513 **Imp-Exp**

## Statebourne (Cryogenic) Ltd

19 Parsons Road, Washington, Tyne and Wear NE37 1EZ
**Tel:** 0191-416-4104
**Web:** www.statebourne.com
**Reg No:** 0952351 **Estd:** 1969 Private Limited Company
**Line of Business:** Manufacturers of containers
**Export Markets:** E U
**Issued Capital:** £54,297
**Principals:** D Haley *(Managing)*, J C Haley *(Managing)*, B Makepeace
**Co. Secretary:** John Short
**Responsibilities**
**Purchasing:** Ray Stobbs *(Purchasing Manager)*
**Branches:** Statebourne (Cryogenic) Ltd, 6-7 Parsons Road, Washington, Tyne and Wear NE37 1HB
**US SIC:** 3999 **UK SIC:** 49590
**Auditors:** Mitchells
**Bankers:** National Westminster Bank Plc (60-22-52)

| | 31-03-14 | 31-03-13 | 31-03-12 |
|---|---|---|---|
| TO | 7,614,128 | 7,050,769 | 8,666,109 |
| P/L | 513,112 | 520,996 | 451,298 |
| NW | 2,518,740 | 2,290,184 | 1,888,057 |
| WC | 1,606,096 | 1,598,376 | 1,420,053 |
| Emp. | 64 | 62 | 65 |

DUNS 21-695-1483

## Stately-Albion Ltd

Unit 20 Prince Of Wales Industrial, Estate Darren Drive, Newport, Gwent NP11 5AR
**Tel:** 01495-244472 **Fax:** 01495-248939
**Web:** www.stately-albion.co.uk
**Reg No:** 0790270 **VAT No:** 135069378
**Estd:** 1964 Private Limited Company
**Line of Business:** Mobile homes
**Issued Capital:** £14,500
**Principals:** D J Hurd *(Managing)*, Mrs D Phillips *(Financial)*
**Co. Secretary:** David Hurd
**Responsibilities**
**HR:** Yvonne Hurd *(Human Resources Manager)*
**Health & Safety:** Clive Gadd *(Health & Safety Manager)*
**Purchasing:** Cary Golding *(Purchasing Manager)*
**US SIC:** 7033 **UK SIC:** 66701
**Auditors:** Evans & Partners
**Bankers:** National Westminster Bank Plc (56-00-59)

| | 31-07-13 | 31-07-12 | 31-07-11 |
|---|---|---|---|
| TO | 22,899,000 | 23,284,000 | 22,196,294 |
| P/L | (322,000) | 335,000 | (280,853) |
| NW | 8,179,000 | 8,446,000 | 8,187,509 |
| WC | 4,987,000 | 5,121,000 | 4,781,627 |
| Emp. | 208 | 195 | 182 |

DUNS 22-613-4971

## States of Guernsey Recreation Committee

Amherst, St Peter Port, Guernsey, Channel Islands GY1 2DL
**Tel:** 01481747200
**Web:** www.beausejour.gg
**Estd:** 1977
**Line of Business:** Other sporting activities not elsewhere classified
**Trading Style:** Beau Sejour Centre
**Principals:** D Chilton, D Ferguson *(Manager)*
**Responsibilities**
**Senior:** Martyn Bourgaize *(Manager)*, Nathan Dicker *(Manager)*, Debbie Le Noury *(Manager)*
**Marketing:** Peter Falla *(Senior Marketing Executive)*
**IT:** Mike Blanchard *(Senior IT Executive)*
**US SIC:** 7999 **UK SIC:** 97913
**Bankers:** National Westminster Bank Plc (60-09-20)
**Employees:** 140

DUNS 22-845-3429

## States of Jersey

Cyril Le Marquand House, St Helier, Jersey, Channel Islands JE4 8QT
**Tel:** 01534-445-500
**Web:** www.gov.je
**Line of Business:** Local government
**Trading Style:** Health & Social Services, Official Analysts Lab, States of Jersey Tourism
**Directors:** V A Tomes, J R Lecornu
**Responsibilities**
**Senior:** Sue Cordwell *(Proprietor)*, Ian Gorst *(Chief Executive)*
**Finance:** Laura Rowley *(Treasurer of the States)*
**Marketing:** Cathy Keir *(Communications Manager)*
**IT:** Mark Leschery *(Network, Security Manager)*
**Branches:** States Of Jersey, South Hill, Jersey, Channel Islands JE2 4US
**US SIC:** 9121 **UK SIC:** 91110
**Employees:** 350

DUNS 50-443-7872 **Imp**

## Stateside Foods Ltd

(**Subsidiary of:** Süddeutsche Zuckerrübenverwertungs-Genossenschaft)
Great Bank Road, Bolton, Lancashire BL5 3XU
**Tel:** 01942-841200
**Web:** www.statesidefoods.co.uk
**Reg No:** 2431656 **VAT No:** 633874419
**Estd:** 1988 Private Limited Company
**Line of Business:** Manufacture of other food products not elsewhere classified
**Export Sales:** £512,000
**Issued Capital:** £6,824,134
**Principals:** J A Lucas *(Managing)*, R Marnell, G R Harrow, S Weber, O C Heinisch, H D Schulz, M I Kent, U Berndt
**Co. Secretary:** Timothy Jones
**Branches:** Stateside Foods Ltd, 5-7 Priorswood Place, Skelmersdale, Lancashire WN8 9QB
**US SIC:** 2099, 5149
**UK SIC:** 42399, 61700
**Auditors:** Grant Thornton UK LLP
**Bankers:** Lloyds TSB Bank plc (30-90-87)

| | 28-02-14 | 28-02-13 | 29-02-12 |
|---|---|---|---|
| TO | 110,831,000 | 100,560,000 | 94,365,236 |
| P/L | 1,983,000 | 6,271,000 | 3,372,489 |
| NW | 8,709,000 | 11,635,000 | 19,237,148 |
| WC | 14,839,000 | 17,419,000 | 2,461,285 |
| Emp. | 632 | 576 | 573 |

DUNS 21-120-9382

## Statesman Travel Ltd

(**Subsidiary of:** Statesman Travel Group Ltd)
Norman House 105 109, Strand, London WC2R 0AA
**Tel:** 01730711016
**Web:** www.statesman-travel.co.uk
**Reg No:** 1055301 **VAT No:** 494688282
**Estd:** 1975 Private Limited Company
**Line of Business:** Activities of travel agencies
**Issued Capital:** £100,000
**Directors:** E E Brannan, J M Langley, K Paschalis, Miss S E Bark
**Co. Secretary:** Mervyn Williamson
**Branches:** Statesman Travel Ltd, Business Travel Norman Ho, 105-109 Strand, London WC2R 0AA
**US SIC:** 4722 **UK SIC:** 77001
**Auditors:** Oury Clark
**Bankers:** Lloyds TSB Bank plc (30-00-08)

| | 31-12-13 | 31-12-12 | 31-12-11 |
|---|---|---|---|
| TO | 93,672,797 | 7,464,283 | 46,194,884 |
| P/L | 740,889 | 1,076,931 | 823,673 |
| NW | (2,163,233) | (3,009,962) | (4,083,673) |
| WC | 431,655 | 414,536 | 1,256,427 |
| Emp. | 126 | 120 | 79 |

DUNS 22-715-3178

## Statesman Travel Services Ltd

(**Subsidiary of:** Statesman Travel Group Ltd)
244 Vauxhall Bridge Road, London SW1V 1AU
**Tel:** 02074207333 **Fax:** 02036671019
**Web:** www.masterfare.co.uk
**Reg No:** 1480303 **VAT No:** 340337878
**Estd:** 1980 Private Limited Company
**Line of Business:** Travel agency activities
**Trading Style:** Statesman Travel, Masterfare
**Issued Capital:** £550,000
**Directors:** J M Langley, M J Williamson
**Co. Secretary:** Mervyn Williamson
**Responsibilities**
**Senior:** Jyoti Dasani *(Manager)*
**Sales:** Jyoti Dasani *(Manager)*
**Branches:** Statesman Travel Services Ltd, 177 Shaftesbury Avenue, London WC2H 8JR
**US SIC:** 4722 **UK SIC:** 77001

**Auditors:** Price Bailey LLP

| | 31-12-13 | 31-12-12 | 31-12-11 |
|---|---|---|---|
| TO | 24,665,154 | 36,479,491 | 45,430,110 |
| P/L | 239,512 | 1,073,263 | 802,964 |
| NW | 2,221,965 | 2,019,660 | 1,171,675 |
| WC | 2,108,304 | 1,994,953 | 1,155,721 |
| Emp. | N/A | 32 | 62 |

DUNS 22-614-3386

## Stateworks

Lane Hure Mare, Vale, Guernsey, Channel Islands GY3 5UD
**Tel:** 01481-246263
**Web:** www.statesworks.com
**Estd:** 1970
**Line of Business:** Public works contractors
**General Manager:** D Parish
**Responsibilities**
**Senior:** Malcolm Cleal *(Senior Manager Services)*, Nigel Legg *(Stores Coordinator)*, Paul Lickley *(General Manager)*
**Finance:** Helen Bourgaize *(Client Accounts Assistant)*, Dave Bradshaw *(Accounts Manager)*, Joanne Duquemin *(Client Accounts Assistant)*, Hugh Keyho *(Assistant Manager Accounts Adm)*, Sue Midgley *(Supplier Accounts Assistant)*, Nicola Nicholson *(Financial Controller)*
**Admin:** Hugh Keyho *(Assistant Manager Accounts Adm)*, June Stevens *(Staff Administration Coordinat)*
**HR:** Dave Bradshaw *(Accounts Manager)*
**Fleet:** Dave Correia *(Manager Cleansing & Waste Mana)*, Robin Coutanche *(Fleet manager)*
**Engineering:** Joe Beard *(Manager Highways & Drainage)*, Tony Booth *(Building manager)*, Kevin Dowinton *(Technical Manager)*, Graham Elwin *(Estimator Technical Support)*, Bob Fisher *(Manager Landfill & Recycling)*, Phil Merrien *(Manager Grounds Maintenance)*, Nick Nicolle *(Senior Technical manager)*, Stuart Price *(Part Time Assistant Sewage)*, Roger Sarre *(Sewage Department)*
**US SIC:** 9121 **UK SIC:** 91110
**Bankers:** National Westminster Bank Plc (60-09-20)
**Employees:** 232

DUNS 57-829-6535

## Statex Press (Northern) Ltd

Unit 6 Airport Industrial Estate, Newcastle-Upon-Tyne, Tyne and Wear NE3 2EF
**Tel:** 0191-245-7200 **Fax:** 0191-245-7300
**Web:** www.statex.co.uk
**Reg No:** 2887894 **Estd:** 1994 Private Limited Company
**Line of Business:** Printers general
**Trading Style:** Statex Colour Print
**Issued Capital:** £250,000
**Directors:** Mrs K Minett, S A Miller, G Minett, J E Dark, N R Macray, C N Nellist
**Co. Secretary:** Ms Susan Maitland
**Responsibilities**
**Senior:** Stuart Melville *(Manager)*
**US SIC:** 2794, 7399
**UK SIC:** 47545, 83954
**Auditors:** Thomas R Dixon & Co
**Bankers:** Lloyds TSB Bank plc (30-90-50)

| | 28-02-14 | 28-02-13 | 29-02-12 |
|---|---|---|---|
| TO | 5,438,950 | 5,153,299 | 5,586,432 |
| P/L | 112,338 | 199,086 | 155,187 |
| NW | 769,204 | 838,469 | 839,550 |
| WC | (125,872) | 51,105 | (37,506) |
| Emp. | 82 | 79 | 84 |

DUNS 56-990-9336 **Imp**

## Static Control Components (Europe) Ltd

(**Subsidiary of:** Static Control Components Inc)
Unit 30, Reading, Berkshire RG2 0TG
**Tel:** 01189-238-800 **Fax:** 01189-238-811
**Web:** www.scceurope.co.uk
**Reg No:** 2858337 **VAT No:** 614888019
**Estd:** 1993 Private Limited Company
**Line of Business:** Distribution service providers
**Export Sales:** £61,369,000
**Issued Capital:** £5,749,749
**Directors:** M L Swartz, W K Swartz, W London
**Co. Secretary:** Simon Barrett
**Responsibilities**
**Senior:** S Wheedon *(Chief Executive)*
**Sales:** Simon Grimes *(Global Sales Manager - Eastern)*
**IT:** Tony Weston *(Senior IT Executive)*
**Fleet:** Sophie Lillie *(Distribution Manager)*
**US SIC:** 5199 **UK SIC:** 61900
**Auditors:** Chantrey Vellacott DFK LLP

| | 31-12-13 | 31-12-12 | 31-12-11 |
|---|---|---|---|
| TO | 66,774,000 | 68,349,000 | 67,269,000 |
| P/L | 476,000 | 577,000 | 361,000 |
| NW | 2,260,000 | 1,273,000 | 664,000 |
| WC | 4,715,000 | 3,666,000 | 2,686,000 |
| Emp. | 269 | 255 | 205 |

DUNS 21-925-1691 **Imp-Exp**

## Static Systems Group Plc

**(Subsidiary of:** Static Systems Holdings Ltd)
Heath Mill Road, Wombourne, Wolverhampton, West Midlands WV5 8AN
**Tel:** 01902-895551 **Fax:** 01902-324969
**Web:** www.staticsystems.co.uk
**Reg No:** 1331299 **VAT No:** 101859681
**Estd:** 1964 Public Limited Company
**Line of Business:** Manufacture of radio and electronic capital goods
**Export Markets:** Middle East, Far East, South Africa, Nigeria
**Export Sales:** £824,964
**Issued Capital:** £300,095
**Principals:** L F Turner *(Chairman)*, P C Garbett, P C Marsh, G M Cardew, A Turner, A C Turner, P J Wade
**Co. Secretary:** John Owen
**Responsibilities**
**Senior:** Stuart Squire *(Operations Director)*
**Operations:** Stuart Squire *(Operations Director)*
**US SIC:** 3662 **UK SIC:** 34430
**Auditors:** AGS Accountants & Business Advisors Ltd
**Bankers:** Barclays Bank Plc (20-97-78)

| | 31-12-13 | 31-12-12 | 31-12-11 |
|---|---|---|---|
| TO | 18,830,844 | 16,434,822 | 17,728,000 |
| P/L | 503,861 | (166,259) | (697,967) |
| NW | 3,864,842 | 3,433,213 | 5,277,406 |
| WC | 2,577,006 | 2,278,790 | 3,257,041 |
| Emp. | 238 | 250 | 289 |

DUNS 29-632-1656 **Imp**

## The Station Hotel (Newcastle) Ltd

31-40 West Parade, Newcastle-Upon-Tyne, Tyne and Wear NE4 7LB
**Tel:** 01912725788
**Web:** www.cairnhotelgroup.com
**Reg No:** 1958222 **Estd:** 1985 Private Limited Company
**Line of Business:** Hotels
**Trading Style:** The Cairn Group
**Issued Capital:** £100,000
**Principals:** A Handa *(Managing)*, R L Handa, A Handa
**Co. Secretary:** Handa Aran
**Branches:** The Station Hotel (Newcastle) Ltd, The Mount, York, North Yorkshire YO24 1GE
**US SIC:** 7399 **UK SIC:** 83954
**Auditors:** Deloitte & Touche LLP
**Bankers:** HSBC Bank plc (40-34-45)

| | 30-04-14 | 30-04-13 | 30-04-12 |
|---|---|---|---|
| TO | 40,606,000 | 34,263,000 | 29,569,000 |
| P/L | 2,358,000 | (13,758,000) | 357,000 |
| NW | 10,532,000 | 8,913,000 | 21,411,000 |
| WC | (8,810,000) | (33,038,000) | (31,366,000) |
| Emp. | 731 | 730 | 696 |

DUNS 77-937-5633

## The Stationery Office Ltd

**(Subsidiary of:** Deutsche Post Ag)
St Crispins, Norwich, Norfolk NR3 1PD
**Tel:** 01603622211 **Fax:** 01603696506
**Web:** www.tso.co.uk
**Reg No:** 3049649 **VAT No:** 676834780
**Estd:** 1786 Private Limited Company
**Line of Business:** Book publishers
**Trading Style:** Tso
**Issued Capital:** £19,200,001
**Directors:** S D Trood, M A Pierleoni, Ms A Lattimore, S J Faulkner, R S Coward
**Co. Secretary:** Exel Secretarial Services Limite
**Responsibilities**
**Senior:** Mike Toulson-Clarke *(Chairman)*
**Marketing:** Jeremy Hook *(Sales & Marketing Director)*
**Sales:** Lisa Hallett *(Business Development Services)*, Jeremy Hook *(Sales & Marketing Director)*
**Admin:** Nicky Hargraves *(Personal Assistant)*
**HR:** Sandy Rodwell *(Human Resources Manager)*, Stephen Walmsley *(Training Manager)*
**Health & Safety:** Stephen Walmsley *(Training Manager)*
**Engineering:** Terry Blake *(Technical Services Director)*
**Branches:** The Stationery Office Ltd, 71-73 Lothian Rd, Edinburgh, Midlothian EH3 9AZ
**US SIC:** 2731, 2741
**UK SIC:** 47532, 47541
**Auditors:** PricewaterhouseCoopers LLP
**Bankers:** Bank Of Scotland (80-20-00)

| | 31-12-13 | 31-12-12 | 31-12-11 |
|---|---|---|---|
| TO | 52,400,000 | 55,200,000 | 59,600,000 |
| P/L | 14,500,000 | 18,600,000 | 20,800,000 |
| NW | 113,100,000 | 102,400,000 | 138,300,000 |
| WC | 119,100,000 | 109,100,000 | 145,900,000 |
| Emp. | 323 | 332 | 350 |

DUNS 22-628-9403 **Imp-Exp**

## Statoil (U.K.) Ltd

**(Subsidiary of:** Statoil Asa)
One Kingdom Street, London W2 6BD
**Tel:** 020-3204-3200 **Fax:** 02032043600
**Web:** www.statoil.com
**Reg No:** 1285743 **VAT No:** 290677036
**Estd:** 1976 Private Limited Company
**Line of Business:** Petroleum product producers
**Export Markets:** Republic of Ireland
**Export Sales:** £141,239,000
**Issued Capital:** £370,000,000
**Directors:** S Skeie, R S Adams, C Andrews, G Breivik, Ms G B Haaland
**Co. Secretary:** Anthony Saul
**Responsibilities**
**Senior:** Knut Aanstad *(Manager)*, Tor Anfinnsen *(Manager)*, Eystein Eikesdal *(Vice President, Global Strateg)*, Helge Halstead *(Manager)*, Kjetil Johnson *(Manager)*, Irini Katsiani *(Manager)*, Helge Lund *(Chief Executive Officer)*, Jan Oyvind Oftedal *(Manager)*, Torgrim Reitan *(Chief Financial Officer)*, Ottar Rekdal *(Manager)*, Grete Tveit *(Manager)*
**Finance:** Torgrim Reitan *(Chief Financial Officer)*
**Marketing:** Stian Vere *(Business Development Unconvent)*
**Sales:** Dana Bernstein *(Business Development Leader)*, Julio Dalpoz *(Senior Business Analyst)*, Eystein Eikesdal *(Vice President, Global Strateg)*, Mark Purdy *(Business Development Manager -)*, Fawad Quraishi *(VP, Commercial and Negotiation)*
**Facilities:** Laura Mossa *(Facilities Manager)*
**Operations:** Nick Maden *(Senior Vice President Internat)*, Morten Ruud *(Executive Vice President for P)*
**Purchasing:** Laura Mossa *(Facilities Manager)*
**Engineering:** Andrea Scarabello *(Senior Process Engineer - Upst)*
**US SIC:** 2999 **UK SIC:** 11150
**Auditors:** Ernst & Young LLP
**Bankers:** Citibank Na (18-50-08)

| | 31-12-13 | 31-12-12 | 31-12-11 |
|---|---|---|---|
| TO | 755,214,000 | 813,505,000 | 774,389,000 |
| P/L | 298,745,000 | (87,765,000) | 16,103,000 |
| NW | 522,198,000 | 305,056,000 | 142,542,000 |
| WC | 101,308,000 | (25,341,000) | (25,239,000) |
| Emp. | 302 | 280 | 230 |

DUNS 73-460-4895 **Imp**

## Statpro Group Plc

Mansel Court, London SW19 4AA
**Tel:** 02084109876
**Web:** www.statpro.com
**Reg No:** 2910629 **VAT No:** 645464228
**Estd:** 1994 Public Limited Company
**Line of Business:** Other computer related activities
**Trading Style:** Compass, Atlas
**Issued Capital:** £677,037
**Principals:** J M Wheatley *(Managing)*, M Adorian, Ms J E Tozer, C R Bacon, S J Clark, A M Fabian
**Co. Secretary:** Andrew Fabian
**Responsibilities**
**Senior:** Laurent Laclaverie *(CEO / Managing Director - Asia)*
**Marketing:** Daryl Peddar *(Senior Vice President Client S)*
**Sales:** Joey Cozens-Smith *(Business Development Manager)*, Harriet Downing *(Business Development Manager)*, Saherish Khan *(Business Development Manager)*, Michel Lempicki *(European Sales Director)*, Simon Stillwell *(North American Sales Director)*
**Operations:** Dario Cintioli *(Products Director)*, Andrew Peddar *(Group Chief Operating Officer)*
**US SIC:** 7379, 6111
**UK SIC:** 83940, 81501
**Auditors:** Ernst & Young LLP
**Bankers:** The Royal Bank Of Scotland Plc (15-10-00)

| | 31-12-13 | 31-12-12 | 31-12-11 |
|---|---|---|---|
| TA | 66,304,000 | 70,947,000 | 71,109,000 |
| P/L | 3,113,000 | 3,782,000 | 3,863,000 |
| NW | (6,616,000) | (8,063,000) | (15,215,000) |
| WC | (8,202,000) | (9,252,000) | (10,651,000) |
| Emp. | 249 | 253 | 266 |

DUNS 23-511-4456 **Imp**

## Stats (Uk) Ltd.

Stats House Tofthills Way, Inverurie, Aberdeenshire AB51 0QG
**Tel:** 01224-772461
**Web:** www.statsgroup.com
**Reg No:** 0183018SC **VAT No:** 845243919
**Estd:** 1998 Private Limited Company
**Line of Business:** Engineers (consulting)
**Export Sales:** £14,652,376
**Issued Capital:** £1,081
**Directors:** S Munro, P A Duguid, W Herron, D M Shand, L J Howarth, R D Anderson, G F Coutts, A Bowie
**Co. Secretary:** Ms Lorraine Porter
**Responsibilities**
**Senior:** Garry Allan *(Manager)*
**Sales:** Scott Garner *(Technical Sales Engineer)*
**HR:** Louise Thomson *(Human Resources Manager)*
**Operations:** Scott McNae *(Projects Manager)*
**Engineering:** Scott Garner *(Technical Sales Engineer)*, Ashley Thomas *(Contract/ Proposals Engineer)*
**US SIC:** 8911 **UK SIC:** 83701
**Auditors:** Anderson Anderson & Brown LLP
**Bankers:** Bank Of Scotland (80-06-60)

| | 31-12-13 | 31-12-12 | 31-12-11 |
|---|---|---|---|
| TO | 26,437,024 | 18,341,603 | 15,055,048 |
| P/L | 1,105,662 | (183,475) | 808,594 |
| NW | 1,498,568 | 297,570 | 437,227 |
| WC | 3,921,191 | 2,510,320 | (2,692,356) |
| Emp. | 189 | 144 | 131 |

DUNS 21-907-8847

## Status Heating Ltd

James House, Birmingham, West Midlands B47 5QB
**Tel:** 08452570799
**Web:** www.statusheating.co.uk
**Reg No:** 1104666 **VAT No:** 111852695
**Estd:** 1973 Private Limited Company
**Line of Business:** Central heating systems (installation and servicing)
**Issued Capital:** £150
**Principals:** R Skillett *(Managing)*, L R Skillett *(Financial)*, R W Bone, Ms S J Skillett, L R Skillett, R W Bone, R Skillett, Mrs A V Neely
**Co. Secretary:** Mrs Aimee Neely
**Responsibilities**
**Senior:** Matt Eustace *(Team Leader)*, Valerie Woolmore *(General Manager)*
**Admin:** Michelle Crates *(Administration Manager)*
**Engineering:** Heath Elliot *(Installations Manager)*
**US SIC:** 1711 **UK SIC:** 50300
**Auditors:** Prime
**Bankers:** National Westminster Bank Plc (60-19-14)

| | 31-03-14 | 31-03-13 | 31-03-12 |
|---|---|---|---|
| TA | 2,274,913 | 2,294,174 | 2,281,608 |
| NW | 1,335,628 | 1,271,409 | 1,259,418 |
| WC | 580,740 | 518,263 | 540,025 |

DUNS 76-429-6141 **Imp**

## Status International (U K) Ltd

Pennine House, Mortimer Street, Cleckheaton, West Yorkshire BD19 5AR
**Tel:** 01274-852200 **Fax:** 01274-852217
**Web:** www.statusinternationaluk.co.uk
**Reg No:** 2561562 **VAT No:** 525963228
**Estd:** 1990 Private Limited Company
**Line of Business:** Food import and exporters and agents
**Export Sales:** £1,173,678
**Trading Style:** Status International (Uk) Ltd
**Issued Capital:** £100,000
**Principals:** P B Mcveigh *(Managing)*, A Myatt, J M Sheard
**Co. Secretary:** Nicholas Mcveigh
**Responsibilities**
**Health & Safety:** Richard Dennison *(Health & Safety Officer)*
**Branches:** Status International (U K) Ltd, Marsh Mills, Dewsbury Road, Cleckheaton, West Yorkshire BD19 5BQ
**US SIC:** 4712 **UK SIC:** 77002
**Auditors:** Walter Dawson & Son
**Bankers:** National Westminster Bank Plc (52-30-29)

| | 30-07-14 | 31-07-13 | 31-07-12 |
|---|---|---|---|
| TO | 28,956,987 | 28,705,712 | 26,394,641 |
| P/L | 3,032,891 | 3,661,113 | 3,721,785 |
| NW | 15,242,550 | 14,012,921 | 12,225,004 |
| WC | 12,548,488 | 11,316,688 | 9,598,705 |
| Emp. | 63 | 62 | 60 |

DUNS 76-929-8266

## Status Investments Ltd

Abbeydale Hall, Abbeydale Road South, Dore, Sheffield, South Yorkshire S17 3LJ
**Tel:** 01142-621662 **Fax:** 01142-621980
**Web:** www.77entertainment.com
**Reg No:** 2338635 **Estd:** 1990 Private Limited Company
**Line of Business:** Bars
**Issued Capital:** £88
**Director:** R D Law
**Responsibilities**
**Senior:** Geoffrey Sleight *(Manager)*
**Finance:** Geoffrey Sleight *(Manager)*
**Branches:** Status Investments Ltd, 2A Edward Street, Stockport, Cheshire SK1 3DQ
**US SIC:** 5813, 6711
**UK SIC:** 66200, 83962
**Auditors:** H Hebblethwaite & Co
**Bankers:** The Royal Bank Of Scotland Plc (16-00-08)

| | 30-09-13 | 01-10-12 | 30-09-11 |
|---|---|---|---|
| TA | 5,757,511 | 5,818,843 | 5,780,004 |
| NW | 1,594,473 | 1,391,318 | 1,229,325 |
| WC | (153,984) | (3,303,782) | (3,357,622) |

DUNS 39-934-0017

## Status Scientific Controls Ltd

**(Subsidiary of:** Richbloom Holdings Ltd)
6 Hermitage Lane Inudst Estate, Kings Mill Way, Mansfield, Nottinghamshire NG18 5ER
**Tel:** 01623651381
**Web:** www.status-scientific.com
**Reg No:** 2231611 **Estd:** 1988 Private Limited Company
**Line of Business:** Gas safety testing & inspection
**Export Sales:** £929,975
**Issued Capital:** £2
**Principals:** W R Baxter *(Managing)*, Ms L Baxter
**Co. Secretary:** Mrs Karen Kowalski
**Responsibilities**
**Senior:** Robert Atkins *(Works Manager)*
**Sales:** Katie Foster *(Sales Manager)*, Katie Stewart *(Sales manager)*
**IT:** Frank Kups *(IT Manager)*
**Operations:** Katie Foster *(Sales Manager)*
**Branches:** Status Scientific Controls Ltd, 12 Westgate, Peterborough, Cambridgeshire PE1 1RA
**US SIC:** 3829 **UK SIC:** 37100
**Auditors:** PKF

| | 31-12-13 | 31-12-12 | 31-12-11 |
|---|---|---|---|
| TO | 1,859,950 | 1,813,604 | 2,215,104 |
| P/L | 434,664 | 369,106 | 506,820 |
| NW | 812,690 | 412,951 | 371,905 |
| WC | 798,385 | 398,301 | 358,435 |

DUNS 50-542-2238 **Imp**

## Stauff Uk Ltd

**(Subsidiary of:** Lukad Holding Gmbh & Co. Kg)
500 Carlisle St East, Sheffield, South Yorkshire S4 8BS
**Tel:** 01142-518-518
**Web:** www.stauff.co.uk
**Reg No:** 2496544 **VAT No:** 599884050
**Estd:** 1990 Private Limited Company
**Line of Business:** Hydraulic equipment & accessories - sales & service
**Export Sales:** £2,424,517
**Issued Capital:** £4,912,600
**Directors:** J P Morris, K Menshen
**Co. Secretary:** Nicholas Deeks
**Responsibilities**
**Senior:** Heinz Toelle *(Manager)*
**Engineering:** Ian Medlock *(Production Manager)*
**Branches:** Stauff Uk Limited, 3 Rennie Place, Glasgow, Lanarkshire G74 5HD
**US SIC:** 3999, 3494, 3452
**UK SIC:** 49590, 32880, 31371
**Auditors:** Holmes Widlake Ltd
**Bankers:** Yorkshire Bank Plc (05-08-03)

| | 31-12-13 | 31-12-12 | 31-12-11 |
|---|---|---|---|
| TO | 27,472,279 | 25,170,186 | 25,308,657 |
| P/L | 602,984 | 463,024 | 217,729 |
| NW | 4,405,518 | 3,802,534 | 3,339,510 |
| WC | 1,882,675 | 1,391,442 | 1,072,721 |
| Emp. | 190 | 179 | 166 |

DUNS 21-313-5254

## Staveley 2005 No 3 Ltd

**(Subsidiary of:** Guinness Peat Group Plc)
Oak House, Littleton Road, Ashford, Middlesex TW15 1TZ
**Tel:** 01784425949 **Fax:** 01753-833434
**Web:** www.hkfire.co.uk
**Reg No:** 0488428 **Estd:** 2010 Private Limited Company
**Line of Business:** Engineering services
**Trading Style:** Hall & Kay Fire Engineering
**Issued Capital:** £250,000
**Directors:** R Howes, Allied Mutual Insurance Services
**Co. Secretary:** Allied Mutual Insurance Services
**Responsibilities**
**Senior:** Bernice Davey *(Personal Assistant)*
**US SIC:** 8911 **UK SIC:** 83701
**Employees:** 60

DUNS 22-806-4671

## Staveley's Eggs Ltd

Coppull Moor Farm, 244 Preston Road, Coppull, Coppull, Chorley, Lancashire PR7 5EB
**Tel:** 01257-791595
**Web:** www.staveleyseggs.co.uk
**Reg No:** 1399727 **VAT No:** 294996285
**Estd:** 1978 Private Limited Company
**Line of Business:** Egg merchants
**Trading Style:** Staveley"s Eggs Ltd
**Issued Capital:** £100
**Principals:** K T Staveley *(Managing)*, D J Staveley, Mrs M Staveley
**Co. Secretary:** Ms Helen Staveley
**Responsibilities**
**Senior:** Keith Staveley *(Manager)*
**Finance:** Jenny Lacey *(Payroll)*
**US SIC:** 5199, 5143
**UK SIC:** 61900, 61700
**Auditors:** Abrams Ashton

**Bankers:** The Royal Bank Of Scotland Plc (16-17-18)

| | 30-11-13 | 30-11-12 | 30-11-11 |
|---|---|---|---|
| TO | 18,526,470 | 14,481,470 | 11,331,694 |
| P/L | 1,094,544 | 1,497,906 | 179,579 |
| NW | 3,900,277 | 3,205,940 | 2,259,803 |
| WC | 2,796,653 | 2,011,403 | 1,109,219 |
| Emp. | 130 | 121 | 121 |

DUNS 21-159-0613
## Staverton (Uk) Ltd
Micklebring Way, Hellaby, Rotherham, South Yorkshire S66 8QD
**Tel:** 08442257474
**Web:** www.staverton.co.uk
**Reg No:** 6863140 **Estd:** 2009 Private Limited Company
**Line of Business:** Manufacture of other office and shop furniture
**Export Sales:** £107,939
**Issued Capital:** £300,000
**Directors:** M J Gardner, P Edward, A P Cole, S J Watts
**Responsibilities**
**Marketing:** James Barke *(Product Designer)*, Roger Holt *(Product Designer)*
**Sales:** Andrew Cloggie *(Sales Manager)*, Cameron Struthers *(Business Development Manager)*, Jamie Wilson *(Business Development Manager)*
**Operations:** Kelvin Staniforth *(Works Manager)*
**US SIC:** 2599, 1799
**UK SIC:** 46720, 50000
**Auditors:** BDO LLP
**Bankers:** The Royal Bank Of Scotland Plc (16-00-38)

| | 30-09-13 | 30-09-12 | 30-09-11 |
|---|---|---|---|
| TO | 5,556,882 | 6,340,774 | 6,025,089 |
| P/L | (153,566) | 83,893 | (501,779) |
| NW | (660,908) | (583,329) | (668,995) |
| WC | 363,141 | 379,785 | 260,286 |
| Emp. | 52 | 55 | 61 |

DUNS 21-784-2115
## Stax Leeds
Howley Park Road East, Morley, Leeds, West Yorkshire LS27 0SW
**Tel:** 01133936600
**Web:** www.staxtradecentres.co.uk
**Estd:** 2011 Proprietorship
**Line of Business:** Retail sale of hardware, paints and glass
**Proprietor:** S Holmes
**US SIC:** 5251 **UK SIC:** 64800
**Employees:** 65

DUNS 39-911-1178 Imp
## Stax Trade Centres Plc
Holloway Drive, Wardley Industrial Estat, Worsley, Manchester M28 2LA
**Tel:** 01617288000
**Web:** www.staxtradecentres.co.uk
**Reg No:** 2235950 **Estd:** 1988 Public Limited Company
**Line of Business:** Cash and carry wholesalers
**Issued Capital:** £105,176
**Principals:** D G Hibbert *(Managing)*, E J Brady, T Ball, Ms D Butler, Mrs A Hibbert, S J Wright, Ms H L Mayers, Mrs A Gardiner
**Co. Secretary:** David Hibbert
**Responsibilities**
**Senior:** Mark Duff *(Branch Manager)*
**HR:** Paula Ellis *(Human Resources Manager)*
**Branches:** Stax Trade Centres Plc, Unit 2 3, Express Industl Est, Widnes, Cheshire WA8 8RB
**US SIC:** 5199, 5065
**UK SIC:** 61900, 61500
**Auditors:** Alexander & Co
**Bankers:** HSBC Bank plc (40-31-23)

| | 31-08-13 | 01-09-12 | 27-08-11 |
|---|---|---|---|
| TO | 98,011,348 | 100,822,426 | 95,791,455 |
| P/L | 1,064,019 | 2,009,226 | 2,572,757 |
| NW | 17,932,721 | 18,047,112 | 16,826,377 |
| WC | 7,396,491 | 6,959,552 | 6,269,881 |
| Emp. | 543 | 543 | 503 |

DUNS 34-666-8622
## Stayathome Ltd
Unit 2 Chenoweth Business Park, Ruan High Lanes, Truro, Cornwall TR2 5JT
**Tel:** 01872500052
**Reg No:** 5471922 **Estd:** 2005 Private Limited Company
**Line of Business:** Other human health activities
**Issued Capital:** £100
**Director:** Mrs B E Rounsevell
**Co. Secretary:** David Rounsevell
**US SIC:** 8091 **UK SIC:** 95200

| | 31-08-13 | 31-08-12 | 31-08-11 |
|---|---|---|---|
| TA | 805,215 | 636,395 | 343,450 |
| NW | 391,805 | 423,181 | 202,181 |
| WC | 292,747 | 400,866 | 191,808 |

DUNS 21-413-6268
## Staybridge Suites
21 Keel Wharf, Liverpool, Merseyside L3 4FN
**Tel:** 0151-7039700
**Web:** www.staybridge.com
**Estd:** 2010 Proprietorship
**Line of Business:** Hotels
**Responsibilities**
**Senior:** Asli Kutlucan *(General Manager)*
**US SIC:** 7011 **UK SIC:** 66500
**Employees:** 50

DUNS 28-922-2978 Imp-Exp
## Staystrip Group Ltd
11-16 Eyre Street, Birmingham, West Midlands B18 7AA
**Tel:** 0121 455 0111
**Web:** www.staystrip.co.uk
**Reg No:** 1481306 **VAT No:** 559193994
**Estd:** 1956 Private Limited Company
**Line of Business:** Other manufacturing not elsewhere classified
**Export Markets:** E U and U S A
**Export Sales:** £113,700
**Trading Style:** Staystrip
**Issued Capital:** £664,782
**Principals:** D Myers *(Chairman and Managing)*, P A Leadbeater *(Managing)*, D A Shorthouse, L W Myers
**Co. Secretary:** John Haynes
**Responsibilities**
**Senior:** Sonia Myers *(Manager)*
**IT:** Lynne Myers *(IT Manager)*
**Health & Safety:** Richard Carrier *(Quality Manager)*
**US SIC:** 3999, 3315
**UK SIC:** 49590, 22340
**Auditors:** Grant Thornton UK LLP
**Bankers:** Barclays Bank Plc (20-07-71)

| | 31-12-13 | 31-12-12 | 31-12-11 |
|---|---|---|---|
| TO | 5,110,682 | 5,504,760 | 6,361,099 |
| P/L | (72,343) | (194,275) | (90,058) |
| NW | 1,692,882 | 1,765,255 | 1,943,164 |
| WC | 1,432,663 | 1,478,690 | 1,696,543 |
| Emp. | 48 | 50 | 50 |

DUNS 73-887-9811
## Staysure.Co.Uk Ltd
Mcgowan House, Waterside The Lakes Bedford Road, Northampton, Northamptonshire NN4 7XD
**Tel:** 08446928444
**Web:** www.staysure.co.uk
**Reg No:** 5142148 **Estd:** 2004 Private Limited Company
**Line of Business:** Insurance - car and automotive
**Issued Capital:** £1,000
**Directors:** L D Howsam, J R Cattle, R C Howsam, R A Savelli
**Responsibilities**
**Senior:** Michele Goodman *(Manager)*
**US SIC:** 6411 **UK SIC:** 83200

| | 31-12-13 | 31-12-12 | 31-12-11 |
|---|---|---|---|
| TO | 19,545,790 | 14,933,355 | N/A |
| P/L | 770,920 | 1,928,599 | N/A |
| NW | 1,637,280 | 1,469,719 | 1,003,540 |
| WC | 1,943,529 | 1,364,358 | 944,987 |
| Emp. | 207 | 165 | N/A |

DUNS 73-358-7823
## Stc Packers Ltd.
Church Farm, Church Lane, Cannock, Staffordshire WS11 1RR
**Tel:** 01543574444 **Fax:** 01543-574066
**Web:** www.churchfarmgroup.com
**Reg No:** 4632310 **Estd:** 2003 Private Limited Company
**Line of Business:** Animal husbandry service activities, except veterinary activities, not elsewhere classified
**Trading Style:** Stc Packers
**Issued Capital:** £100
**Directors:** J R Corbett, S T Corbett
**Responsibilities**
**Finance:** Keith Burson *(Financial Director)*
**US SIC:** 0751 **UK SIC:** 01003

| | 31-03-14 | 31-03-13 | 31-03-12 |
|---|---|---|---|
| TA | 2,910,108 | 2,898,951 | 3,213,157 |
| NW | 331,295 | 319,294 | 308,561 |
| WC | (898,127) | (1,098,628) | (1,033,548) |

DUNS 22-769-3108 Imp
## S.T.D. Pharmaceutical Products Ltd
Plough Lane, Hereford, Herefordshire HR4 0EL
**Tel:** 01432-373555
**Web:** www.stdpharm.co.uk
**Reg No:** 0905546 **VAT No:** 134376178
**Estd:** 1967 Private Limited Company
**Line of Business:** Pharmaceutical suppliers and wholesalers
**Export Sales:** £837,853
**Issued Capital:** £1,039
**Principals:** R N Gardiner *(Managing)*, Ms N E Leach, Ms M F Gardiner, A J Leach, B M Gardiner
**Co. Secretary:** Christopher Smith

**Responsibilities**
**Finance:** N Monday *(Accounts Manager)*
**US SIC:** 5122, 5999
**UK SIC:** 61800, 65600
**Auditors:** Thorne Widgery
**Bankers:** Barclays Bank Plc (20-39-64)

| | 30-04-14 | 30-04-13 | 30-04-12 |
|---|---|---|---|
| TO | 3,460,389 | N/A | N/A |
| P/L | 106,715 | N/A | N/A |
| NW | 2,723,427 | 2,677,536 | 2,598,167 |
| WC | 2,421,394 | 2,386,072 | 2,289,663 |
| Emp. | 59 | N/A | N/A |

DUNS 23-588-4876
## Stead McAlpin & Company Ltd
Cummersdale Print Works, Cummersdale, Carlisle, Cumbria CA2 6BT
**Tel:** 01228 525 224 **Fax:** 01228 512 070
**Web:** www.steadmcalpin.co.uk
**Reg No:** 3586119 **Estd:** 1999 Private Limited Company
**Line of Business:** Finishing of textiles
**Issued Capital:** £45,000
**Directors:** C R Soper, J A Jones, B D Soper, Ms S Magee
**Co. Secretary:** Jack Simpson
**Responsibilities**
**Finance:** Aidan Queen *(Finance Director)*
**HR:** Bill Bulman *(Training Manager)*, Elaine Watson *(Human Resources Manager)*
**US SIC:** 2269 **UK SIC:** 43702
**Auditors:** Whitehead & Howarth
**Bankers:** National Westminster Bank Plc (01 00 01)

| | 31-01-14 | 31-01-13 | 31-01-12 |
|---|---|---|---|
| TO | 11,053,192 | 11,680,983 | 9,296,489 |
| P/L | 242,655 | 201,085 | 241,986 |
| NW | 779,230 | 581,356 | 435,514 |
| WC | 769,170 | (268,311) | (678,649) |
| Emp. | 127 | 124 | 109 |

DUNS 28-973-0392
## Steadfast Cleaning Co Ltd
Unit 7 Bircholt Road Target Business, Centre, Maidstone, Kent ME15 9YY
**Tel:** 01622-692235
**Web:** www.steadfastcleaning.co.uk
**Reg No:** 1741651 **Estd:** 1983 Private Limited Company
**Line of Business:** Cleaning activities not elsewhere classified
**Issued Capital:** £6,400
**Managing Director:** K A Miller
**Co. Secretary:** Robert Humphrey
**US SIC:** 7349 **UK SIC:** 92300
**Auditors:** Nash Harvey
**Bankers:** National Westminster Bank Plc (53-81-51)

| | 31-07-14 | 31-07-13 | 31-07-12 |
|---|---|---|---|
| TA | 715,488 | 714,975 | 710,910 |
| NW | 373,083 | 370,864 | 341,328 |
| WC | 366,766 | 363,028 | 333,482 |

DUNS 21-919-9015 Imp-Exp
## Steadfast Engineering Co Ltd
2a Broadway, Hyde, Cheshire SK14 4GA
**Tel:** 0161-368-3636 **Fax:** 0161-368-3646
**Web:** www.steadfast.co.uk
**Reg No:** 1410223 **VAT No:** 151568660
**Estd:** 1979 Private Limited Company
**Line of Business:** Manufacturers of bolts and fixings
**Export Sales:** £1,198,649
**Issued Capital:** £140,625
**Principals:** K Sharp *(Managing)*, S A Sharp
**Responsibilities**
**Senior:** Rafik Mansour *(Manager)*, Gary Saxon *(Stores Manager)*, Andrea Sharp *(Manager)*
**US SIC:** 3452 **UK SIC:** 31371
**Auditors:** Edwards Veeder (Oldham) LLP
**Bankers:** Barclays Bank Plc (20-10-71)

| | 31-03-14 | 31-03-13 | 31-03-12 |
|---|---|---|---|
| TO | 14,501,242 | 16,307,041 | 14,689,318 |
| P/L | 1,633,583 | 1,840,726 | 1,106,333 |
| NW | 2,474,544 | 1,698,518 | 2,410,047 |
| WC | 2,083,690 | 1,333,064 | 2,113,579 |
| Emp. | 95 | 80 | 76 |

DUNS 23-814-5119
## Steamer Trading Ltd
(**Subsidiary of:** Steamer Properties Ltd)
20-21 High Street, Lewes, East Sussex BN7 2LN
**Tel:** 01273487230
**Web:** www.steamer.co.uk
**Reg No:** 3806750 **Estd:** 1999 Private Limited Company
**Line of Business:** Kitchenware
**Issued Capital:** £760,002
**Directors:** B S Phillips, Ms E A Phillips
**Co. Secretary:** David Phillips
**Branches:** Steamer Trading Ltd, Saffron Bldg Soc, Saffron House, Saffron Walden, Essex CB10 1HX
**US SIC:** 5199 **UK SIC:** 61900

**Auditors:** Swindells Gentry & Hutchinson

| | 31-12-13 | 31-12-12 | 31-12-11 |
|---|---|---|---|
| TO | 18,847,052 | 17,474,579 | 15,924,275 |
| P/L | 1,233,665 | 1,003,281 | 1,069,825 |
| NW | 8,706,479 | 7,785,889 | 7,178,603 |
| WC | 649,112 | 644,572 | 783,069 |
| Emp. | 336 | 298 | 269 |

DUNS 23-864-1679 Imp
## Steamship Insurance Management Services Ltd
Aquatical House, 39 Bell Lane, Whitechapel, London E1 7LU
**Tel:** 020-7247-5490 **Fax:** 020-7377-2912
**Web:** www.steamshipmutual.com
**Reg No:** 3855693 **Estd:** 1909 Private Limited Company
**Line of Business:** Insurance services
**Issued Capital:** £1,271,718
**Directors:** S A Ward, J Kim, S J Martin, B Dyer, M A Shelmerdine, S T Alfrey, G M Field, M Underhill
**Co. Secretary:** Richard Harrison
**Responsibilities**
**Senior:** Christian Ahrenkiel *(Manager)*, Jonathan Andrews *(Director)*, Adrian Benham *(Director)*, Chris Durrant *(Company Director)*, Isabella Grimaldi *(Manager)*, Rupert Harris *(Director)*, Michael Hird *(Director)*, Alan Marchisotto *(Manager)*, David Ragan *(Director)*, Gary Rynsard *(Director)*, Mohammad Souri *(Manager)*
**US SIC:** 6411 **UK SIC:** 83200
**Auditors:** Deloitte LLP

| | 20-02-14 | 20-02-13 | 20-02-12 |
|---|---|---|---|
| TO | 16,494,224 | 15,402,005 | 17,514,002 |
| P/L | 298,210 | 319,087 | 895,565 |
| NW | (3,623,226) | 1,540,722 | 1,398,198 |
| WC | (291,954) | (507,532) | (688,674) |
| Emp. | 152 | 151 | 148 |

DUNS 21-824-2725 Exp
## Stearn Electric Company Ltd
(**Subsidiary of:** Newbury Investments B.V.)
The Vo-Tec Centre, Hambridge Lane, Newbury, Berkshire RG14 5TN
**Tel:** 01635279370 **Fax:** 01489797370
**Web:** www.stearn.co.uk
**Reg No:** 0201097 **VAT No:** 927202736
**Estd:** 1924 Private Limited Company
**Line of Business:** Manufacture of other electrical equipment not elsewhere classified
**Issued Capital:** £48,000
**Directors:** N J Palmer, D J Schofield
**Co. Secretary:** Steven Westbrook
**Branches:** Stearn Electric Company Ltd, 1 Olympic Way, Bootle, Merseyside L30 1RD
**US SIC:** 3629 **UK SIC:** 34350
**Auditors:** Grant Thornton UK LLP
**Bankers:** National Westminster Bank Plc (60-15-07)

| | 31-12-13 | 31-12-12 | 31-12-11 |
|---|---|---|---|
| TO | 92,878,000 | 85,962,000 | 81,689,000 |
| P/L | 7,579,000 | 7,601,000 | 8,038,000 |
| NW | 45,591,000 | 40,201,000 | 35,636,000 |
| WC | 44,974,000 | 40,667,000 | 35,416,000 |
| Emp. | 330 | 307 | 303 |

DUNS 23-634-2721
## Stebon Primary School
Wallwood Street, London E14 7AD
**Tel:** 020-7987-4237
**Web:** www.stebon.org.uk
**Estd:** 1990
**Line of Business:** General secondary education
**Director:** Mrs P Sehmi
**Responsibilities**
**Senior:** Alyson Brewer *(Head Teacher)*, Jo Franklin *(Head Teacher)*
**US SIC:** 8211 **UK SIC:** 93200
**Employees:** 60

DUNS 21-810-7380
## Stebonheath C P School
Brynallt Terrace, Llanelli, Dyfed SA15 1NB
**Tel:** 01554758603
**Web:** www.stebonheath.amdro.org.uk
**Estd:** 2012
**Line of Business:** Primary education
**Responsibilities**
**Senior:** Jay Littler *(Head Teacher)*, Julian Littler *(Head Teacher)*
**US SIC:** 8211 **UK SIC:** 93200
**Employees:** 50

DUNS 21-890-8424 Imp
## Steel & Alloy Processing Ltd
(**Subsidiary of:** Cartera Gonvarri Sl)
Trafalgar Works, Union Street, West Bromwich, West Midlands B70 6BZ
**Tel:** 01215535292
**Web:** www.steelalloy.co.uk
**Reg No:** 0944053 **VAT No:** 705330473
**Estd:** 1997 Private Limited Company
**Line of Business:** Management activities of other non-financial holding companies not elsewhere classified
**Export Sales:** £853,493
**Issued Capital:** £210,000

**Principals:** M T Cooper *(Sales)*, M R Coleman, R D Riberas, J C Moreira, J M Mera, F B Gonzalez, P J Whitehouse, M R Escribano
**Co. Secretary:** Mario Escribano
**Responsibilities**
**Senior:** Simon Ashwell *(Manager)*, James Ashwell *(Manager)*
**Finance:** Paul O' Hagan *(Finance Manager)*
**Sales:** Dave Barnett *(Sales Manager, Shaped Blanks)*, Simon Dean *(General Sales Manager)*
**Admin:** Vickie Reynolds *(Managing Director PA)*
**IT:** Graham Jewkes *(IT Manager)*
**HR:** Marie Fleetwood *(Human Resources Manager)*
**Health & Safety:** George Parkes *(Health & Safety Manager)*
**Facilities:** John Boggild *(Maintenance Manager)*
**Operations:** Jackie Bradnick *(Materials Control Manager)*, Andy Hickman *(Production Manager)*, Geoff Straw *(Manufacturing Manager)*
**Engineering:** John Boggild *(Maintenance Manager)*
**Branches:** Steel & Alloy Processing Ltd, Bridge Street North, The Bridge Trading Estate, Smethwick, West Midlands B66 2BA
**US SIC:** 3325  **UK SIC:** 31110
**Auditors:** PricewaterhouseCoopers LLP
**Bankers:** Barclays Bank Plc (20-97-78)

| | 31-12-13 | 31-12-12 | 31-12-12 |
|---|---|---|---|
| TO | 153,484,135 | 109,896,052 | 156,472,207 |
| P/L | 3,188,318 | 2,387,189 | (4,146,374) |
| NW | 26,119,832 | 23,653,677 | 22,007,488 |
| WC | 21,413,146 | 18,840,669 | 16,726,080 |
| Emp. | 178 | 172 | 163 |

**DUNS 22-181-6130**
## Steel Business Briefing Ltd
Peek House, 20 Eastcheap, London EC3M 1EB
**Tel:** 02076260600 **Fax:** 020-7929-4666
**Web:** www.knowledgeview.co.uk
**Reg No:** 4199965 **Estd:** 2001 Private Limited Company
**Line of Business:** Publishers
**Issued Capital:** £1.753E + 11
**Directors:** L P Neal, S K Randall, K Wise, A Goodwin, H R Thomas, P J Sansom
**Co. Secretary:** Anthony Montague
**Responsibilities**
**Senior:** Hollie Sheriff *(Manager)*
**US SIC:** 2731, 2741
**UK SIC:** 47532, 47541

| | 31-12-13 | 31-12-12 | 31-12-11 |
|---|---|---|---|
| TO | N/A | 2,562,490 | 5,465,722 |
| P/L | 14,261,000 | (6,438,890) | (3,075,167) |
| NW | 217,428,000 | 203,166,864 | (2,816,703) |
| WC | 7,239,000 | (6,988,957) | (2,932,455) |
| Emp. | N/A | 16 | 75 |

**DUNS 29-332-0909**
## Steel Fence Supplies Ltd
*(Subsidiary of: Hadley Industries Plc)*
Downing Street, Smethwick, West Midlands B66 2PA
**Tel:** 01215551430
**Web:** www.hadleygroup.co.uk
**Reg No:** 1843612 **Estd:** 1984 Private Limited Company
**Line of Business:** Metal merchants
**Issued Capital:** £2
**Co. Secretary:** Stewart Towe
**Branches:** "Corrugated Sheets and Profiles" Units 9 & 10, Wednesbury Trad Est, Wednesbury
**US SIC:** 3315  **UK SIC:** 22340
**Bankers:** HSBC Bank plc (40-46-13)

| | 30-04-14 | 30-04-13 | 30-04-12 |
|---|---|---|---|
| TA | 1,228,668 | 1,228,668 | 1,228,668 |
| NW | 1,228,668 | 1,228,668 | 1,228,668 |

**DUNS 39-952-4867**
## Steel Services (Great Yarmouth) Ltd
*(Subsidiary of: Steel Services Holding Co Ltd)*
Unit A, Harman Buildings, South Denes Road, Great Yarmouth, Norfolk NR30 3PF
**Tel:** 01493-856180 **Fax:** 01493859844
**Web:** www.steelservices.co.uk
**Reg No:** 2258323 **VAT No:** 511036700
**Estd:** 1971 Private Limited Company
**Line of Business:** Other engineering activities
**Export Sales:** £2,489,625
**Issued Capital:** £85,000
**Principals:** B E Duffy *(Chairman and Managing)*, K G Chilvers
**Responsibilities**
**Senior:** Charlie Andrews *(Stores Manager)*
**US SIC:** 8911  **UK SIC:** 83701
**Auditors:** P K F

**Bankers:** National Westminster Bank Plc (55-81-45)

| | 31-07-14 | 31-07-13 | 31-07-12 |
|---|---|---|---|
| TO | 8,278,770 | 8,008,414 | 7,294,426 |
| P/L | 915,418 | 1,140,391 | 883,094 |
| NW | 3,270,633 | 2,802,650 | 2,055,744 |
| WC | 2,280,685 | 2,095,227 | 1,550,271 |
| Emp. | 72 | 67 | 62 |

**DUNS 73-767-4668**                                    **Imp-Exp**
## Steelcase (South - East) Ltd
*(Subsidiary of: Steelcase Inc.)*
77-79 Farringdon Road, London EC1M 3JU
**Tel:** 020 7421 9000 **Fax:** 020 7421 9001
**Web:** www.steelcase-solutions.co.uk
**Reg No:** 5024679 **VAT No:** 744114555
**Estd:** 2004 Private Limited Company
**Line of Business:** Manufacture of other office and shop furniture
**Trading Style:** Steelcase Solutions
**Issued Capital:** £2,000,000
**Directors:** L Morison, M R Spragg, Ms J Mccallion
**Responsibilities**
**Senior:** Yvan Stehly *(Manager)*
**Marketing:** Nikof Liapis *(Sales & Marketing Director)*
**Sales:** Nikof Liapis *(Sales & Marketing Director)*
**Health & Safety:** Gerry Kavanagh *(Health & Safety Officer)*
**Branches:** Steelcase (South - East) Ltd, Booth Street, Manchester M2 4AW
**US SIC:** 2599, 1721
**UK SIC:** 46720, 50400
**Auditors:** Deloitte LLP
**Bankers:** HSBC Bank plc (40-43-04)

| | 28-02-13 | 29-02-12 | 28-02-11 |
|---|---|---|---|
| TO | 35,445,000 | 35,334,000 | 28,707,000 |
| P/L | (613,000) | (411,000) | (70,000) |
| NW | 5,349,000 | 662,000 | 1,073,000 |
| WC | 5,484,000 | 829,000 | 1,746,000 |
| Emp. | 92 | 88 | 75 |

**DUNS 34-573-8090**
## Steele Davis Ltd
Unit 18 Devizes Trade Centre, Hopton Road, Devizes, Wiltshire SN10 2EH
**Tel:** 01380728738
**Web:** www.steeledavis.co.uk
**Reg No:** 2723666 **VAT No:** 576395884
**Estd:** 1992 Private Limited Company
**Line of Business:** Builders
**Issued Capital:** £15,000
**Principals:** A L Steele-Davis *(Chairman)*, M D Gingell *(Managing)*, J M Steele Davis
**Co. Secretary:** Ms Mary Steele-Davis
**Responsibilities**
**Senior:** Anne Saunders *(Finance Manager)*
**Finance:** Anne Saunders *(Finance Manager)*
**Branches:** Steele Davis Ltd, 18 Devizes Trade Centre, Hopton Park Industrial Estate, Devizes, Wiltshire SN10 2EH
**US SIC:** 1522  **UK SIC:** 50100
**Auditors:** Monahans
**Bankers:** Barclays Bank Plc (20-84-58)

| | 30-09-14 | 30-09-13 | 30-09-12 |
|---|---|---|---|
| TO | 9,715,609 | 9,555,713 | 8,795,453 |
| P/L | 303,410 | 275,096 | 193,720 |
| NW | 724,391 | 544,714 | 395,108 |
| WC | 569,131 | 387,409 | 180,121 |
| Emp. | 55 | 54 | 58 |

**DUNS 34-543-5718**
## Steele Raymond Llp
Richmond Point, 43 Richmond Hill, Bournemouth, Dorset BH2 6LR
**Tel:** 01202-294566
**Web:** www.steeleraymond.co.uk
**Reg No:** 0311376OC **Estd:** 2001
**Line of Business:** Tour operators
**Responsibilities**
**Senior:** Robert Bajaj *(Partner)*, Paul Longland *(Designated Limited Liability P)*
**US SIC:** 7999  **UK SIC:** 97913

| | 31-03-14 | 31-03-13 | 31-03-12 |
|---|---|---|---|
| TA | 2,030,164 | 1,917,754 | 2,000,947 |
| WC | 845,260 | 781,639 | 575,721 |

**DUNS 73-684-5020**
## Steeles (Law) Llp
2-3 Norwich Business Park, Whiting Road, Norwich, Norfolk NR4 6DJ
**Tel:** 01603 598 000
**Web:** www.steeleslaw.co.uk
**Reg No:** 0305891OC
**Proprietorship**
**Line of Business:** Solicitors
**Responsibilities**
**Senior:** Michael Berriman *(Manager)*, Julian Charles *(Manager)*, Peter Hastings *(Manager)*, Victoria Swetman *(Manager)*, James Tarling *(Manager)*
**Marketing:** Sarah Monk *(Marketing Manager)*
**US SIC:** 8111  **UK SIC:** 83500
**Auditors:** Scrutton Bland

| | 30-04-14 | 30-04-13 | 30-04-12 |
|---|---|---|---|
| TO | 1,587,834 | 2,925,000 | 3,406,000 |
| NW | N/A | N/A | 319,000 |
| WC | N/A | 648,000 | 749,000 |
| Emp. | 48 | 54 | 54 |

**DUNS 64-087-9128**
## Steelfields (Holdings) Ltd
Owens Way, Gads Hill, Gillingham, Kent ME7 2RT
**Tel:** 01634-280135 **Fax:** 01634280689
**Web:** www.steelfields.com
**Reg No:** 3483012 **Estd:** 1998 Private Limited Company
**Line of Business:** Construction of civil engineering constructions
**Issued Capital:** £50
**Director:** P Polhill
**Co. Secretary:** Hadley Polhill
**US SIC:** 1622  **UK SIC:** 50200
**Auditors:** McCabe Ford Williams

| | 30-06-14 | 30-06-13 | 30-06-12 |
|---|---|---|---|
| TA | 1,782,574 | 1,744,355 | 1,497,508 |
| NW | 1,757,570 | 1,391,583 | 1,359,425 |
| WC | 407,197 | N/A | N/A |

**DUNS 22-765-9539**                                    **Imp-Exp**
## Steelite International Plc
Orme Street, Stoke-On-Trent, Staffordshire ST6 3RB
**Tel:** 01782821000 **Fax:** 01782-819926
**Web:** www.steelite.com
**Reg No:** 1697123 **VAT No:** 792414517
**Estd:** 1983 Public Limited Company
**Line of Business:** Manufacturers and suppliers of tableware
**Export Markets:** Worldwide
**Issued Capital:** £1,000,000
**Principals:** R E Poole *(Financial)*, K G Oakes *(Sales)*
**Co. Secretary:** Philip Ray
**Responsibilities**
**Facilities:** Dave Arrowsmith *(Maintenance Manager)*
**Engineering:** Bernard Matthews *(Production Director)*
**US SIC:** 3421  **UK SIC:** 31621
**Auditors:** KPMG LLP
**Bankers:** The Royal Bank Of Scotland Plc (16-26-19)

| | 31-12-13 | 31-12-12 | 31-12-11 |
|---|---|---|---|
| TO | 89,681,000 | 70,273,000 | 66,251,000 |
| P/L | 8,424,000 | 7,200,000 | 7,914,000 |
| NW | 47,862,000 | 45,477,000 | 43,724,000 |
| WC | 47,476,000 | 46,621,000 | 43,065,000 |
| Emp. | 1,044 | 823 | 790 |

**DUNS 21-164-9291**
## Steelmark Ltd
*(Subsidiary of: Temple Secretaries Limited)*
Hud Hey Industrial Estate, Hud Hey Road, Haslingden, Rossendale, Lancashire BB4 5JH
**Tel:** 01706212111
**Web:** www.cppfs.com
**Reg No:** 6908086 **Estd:** 1988 Private Limited Company
**Line of Business:** Bookbinding
**Issued Capital:** £1
**Directors:** M A Hargreaves, J R Sayer, Ms J C Timlin
**US SIC:** 2789  **UK SIC:** 47545

| | 31-10-13 | 31-10-12 | 31-10-11 |
|---|---|---|---|
| TA | 574,566 | 493,309 | 574,297 |
| NW | 104,323 | 113,281 | 169,321 |
| WC | (11,440) | 18,704 | 18,045 |

**DUNS 21-775-3486**
## Steelphalt
The Ickles, Rotherham, South Yorkshire S60 1DP
**Tel:** 01709300500
**Web:** www.multiservegroup.com
**Estd:** 2011 Proprietorship
**Line of Business:** Asphalt & macadam supply
**Proprietor:** D Raynor
**US SIC:** 7399  **UK SIC:** 83954
**Employees:** 50

**DUNS 73-534-8000**                                    **Imp**
## Steelstrip Services Ltd
*(Subsidiary of: Essar Steel Coöperatief U.A.)*
Pensnett Road, Dudley, West Midlands DY1 2HA
**Fax:** 01384-471370
**Web:** www.servosteel.com
**Reg No:** 4797346 **VAT No:** 825425729
**Estd:** 2003 Private Limited Company
**Line of Business:** Manufacturers of steel
**Trading Style:** Servosteel
**Issued Capital:** £4,913,954
**Director:** P E Guest
**Co. Secretary:** Mark Anderson
**Responsibilities**
**Senior:** David Fabb *(Chairman, Managing Director)*
**Sales:** Sarah Ostins *(Accounts Manager)*
**Admin:** Jennifer Lee *(Order Entry)*
**Operations:** Wayne Kettley *(Production Supervisor)*, Mick Pickett *(Decoiling Planner)*
**Engineering:** Martin Skidmore *(Engineering Manager)*

**US SIC:** 3325  **UK SIC:** 31110
**Auditors:** Deloitte LLP
**Bankers:** HSBC Bank plc (40-43-17)

| | 31-03-14 | 31-03-13 | 31-03-12 |
|---|---|---|---|
| TO | 9,691,726 | 16,250,878 | 31,138,741 |
| P/L | 130,701 | (1,523,697) | (1,505,345) |
| NW | 2,893,573 | 2,798,208 | 3,057,444 |
| WC | 2,132,204 | 375,368 | 598,086 |
| Emp. | 75 | 93 | 101 |

**DUNS 23-881-7873**                                    **Exp**
## Steelway Fensecure Ltd
*(Subsidiary of: Steelway Holdings Ltd)*
Queensgate Works, Bilston Road, Wolverhampton, West Midlands WV2 2NJ
**Tel:** 01902451733
**Web:** www.steelway.co.uk
**Reg No:** 3872973 **Estd:** 1999 Private Limited Company
**Line of Business:** Fabricated metal products
**Export Sales:** £162,895
**Issued Capital:** £200,000
**Directors:** W Karpynec, D C Houghton
**Branches:** Steelway Fensecure Ltd, Brickhouse Lane, West Bromwich, West Midlands B70 0DY
**US SIC:** 3441, 3079
**UK SIC:** 32042, 48360
**Auditors:** Grant Thornton UK LLP
**Bankers:** National Westminster Bank Plc (01-00-90)

| | 30-06-13 | 30-06-12 | 30-06-11 |
|---|---|---|---|
| TO | 10,806,703 | 11,358,278 | 11,874,662 |
| P/L | 99,602 | 326,528 | 222,157 |
| NW | 655,175 | 587,929 | 353,298 |
| WC | 319,132 | 261,615 | 77,214 |
| Emp. | 160 | 150 | 150 |

**DUNS 42-343-4380**
## Steelweld Fabrications Ltd
3 Ballyreagh Business Park, Cookstown, Co Tyrone BT80 9AR
**Tel:** 028-8676-6495 **Fax:** 028-8676-6496
**Web:** www.steelweld.co.uk
**Reg No:** 0025337NI **Estd:** 1988 Private Limited Company
**Line of Business:** Fabricators
**Issued Capital:** £2
**Director:** D Crilly
**Co. Secretary:** Mrs Tracey Hill
**Responsibilities**
**Senior:** Dominic Crilley *(Manager)*, Mary Orr *(Manager)*
**HR:** Bronagh Graham *(Human Resources Manager)*
**US SIC:** 5084  **UK SIC:** 61490
**Auditors:** G Marley & Co
**Bankers:** The Bank Of Ireland (90-48-19)

| | 31-08-13 | 31-08-12 | 31-08-11 |
|---|---|---|---|
| TO | 6,668,050 | 7,195,154 | N/A |
| P/L | 60,304 | 285,496 | N/A |
| NW | 1,913,289 | 1,868,835 | 1,917,755 |
| WC | (490,641) | (497,626) | (175,201) |
| Emp. | 128 | 133 | N/A |

**DUNS 21-702-2060**
## The Steeplechase Company (Cheltenham) Ltd
*(Subsidiary of: The Jockey Club)*
Evesham Road, Cheltenham, Gloucestershire GL50 4SH
**Tel:** 01242-513014
**Web:** www.cheltenham.co.uk
**Reg No:** 0096124 **VAT No:** 190487834
**Estd:** 1967 Private Limited Company
**Line of Business:** Racecourses and racetracks
**Trading Style:** Cheltenham Racecourse
**Issued Capital:** £40,000
**Directors:** I R Renton, N J Truesdale, P Fisher
**Co. Secretary:** Mrs Sheila Handley
**Responsibilities**
**Admin:** Paula Griffin *(Administration Manager)*
**HR:** Paula Griffin *(Administration Manager)*
**Health & Safety:** Paula Griffin *(Administration Manager)*
**Facilities:** Tim Partridge *(Facilities Manager)*
**Purchasing:** Ian Sidgwick *(Group Purchasing Director)*
**Branches:** The Steeplechase Company (Cheltenham) Ltd, Cheltenham Racecourse, Prestbury Pk, Cheltenham, Gloucestershire GL50 4SH
**US SIC:** 7999, 7941
**UK SIC:** 97913, 97911
**Bankers:** HSBC Bank plc (40-03-22)

| | 31-12-13 | 31-12-12 | 31-12-11 |
|---|---|---|---|
| TA | 40,000 | 40,000 | 40,000 |
| NW | 40,000 | 40,000 | 40,000 |

**DUNS 29-520-6247**                                    **Exp**
## Steer Davies & Gleave Ltd
26-32 Upper Ground, London SE1 9PD
**Tel:** 02079105000 **Fax:** 02079105001
**Web:** www.steerdaviesgleave.com
**Reg No:** 1883830 **Estd:** 1978 Private Limited Company
**Line of Business:** Freight forwarders

**Export Markets:** South and Central America, Europe, Middle and Far East
**Issued Capital:** £50,583
**Directors:** Ms C L Clark, W Pike, S Hewitt, J K Steer, J L Lawrence, H Jones
**Co. Secretary:** Mrs Victoria Dorrington
**Responsibilities**
**Senior:** Francesco Dionori *(Chairman)*, Ian Druce *(Chairman)*
**Marketing:** Holly Cheung *(Marketing and Communications M)*, Nadine Kayser *(Marketing Manager)*
**Sales:** Fred Beltrandi *(Executive Director)*
**Operations:** Freddy Gangemi *(Operations Manager)*
**Engineering:** Paul Belsham *(Senior Infrastructure Engineer)*, Julian Sindall *(Head of Engineering)*, Paul Zanna *(Development Officer)*
**Branches:** Steer Davies & Gleave Ltd, Ingram House, 3rd Floor, Glasgow, Lanarkshire G1 1DA
**US SIC:** 4712 **UK SIC:** 77002
**Auditors:** BDO LLP
**Bankers:** National Westminster Bank Plc (51-50-03)

| | 31-03-14 | 31-03-13 | 31-03-12 |
|---|---|---|---|
| TO | 37,493,975 | 31,568,561 | 28,934,444 |
| P/L | 2,435,679 | 1,418,875 | 1,090,591 |
| NW | 12,992,435 | 11,586,475 | 13,221,528 |
| WC | 13,994,508 | 12,710,066 | 13,179,332 |
| Emp. | 338 | 313 | 304 |

DUNS 28-915-7042 **Imp**
## Steerpike Ltd
35 Endell Street, London WC2H 9BA
**Tel:** 02074510600
**Reg No:** 1444906 **Estd:** 1979 Private Limited Company
**Line of Business:** Live theatrical presentation
**Export Sales:** £7,111,528
**Issued Capital:** £100
**Directors:** T S Oakes, Mrs F C Fowler, G M Sumner
**Co. Secretary:** Ms Trudie Styler Sumner
**US SIC:** 7922 **UK SIC:** 97412
**Auditors:** MRI Moores Rowland
**Bankers:** Lloyds TSB Bank plc (30-90-59)

| | 31-12-13 | 31-12-12 | 31-12-11 |
|---|---|---|---|
| TO | 12,337,578 | 8,869,392 | 9,946,191 |
| P/L | 2,380,461 | 729,545 | 5,287,375 |
| NW | (42,360,181) | (45,537,846) | (46,684,992) |
| WC | (44,464,027) | (47,635,232) | (48,473,472) |
| Emp. | 64 | 29 | 10 |

DUNS 22-070-0442
## Steetley Dolomite Ltd
(**Subsidiary of:** Cleb Holdings Ltd)
Southfield Lane, Whitwell, Worksop, Nottinghamshire S80 3LJ
**Tel:** 01909 726 100
**Reg No:** 4071554 **VAT No:** 852921321
**Estd:** 2010 Private Limited Company
**Line of Business:** Manufacture of refractory ceramic products
**Export Sales:** £15,560,000
**Issued Capital:** £15,243,001
**Directors:** L L De Mot, D Donck, J W Carlill, C J De Vicq De Cumptich
**Co. Secretary:** Dirk Donck
**Responsibilities**
**Sales:** Ian Houldsworth *(Sales Manager)*
**Facilities:** Jim Bowman *(Plant Manager)*
**US SIC:** 3269, 3241, 3275
**UK SIC:** 24894, 24200, 24370
**Auditors:** BDO LLP
**Bankers:** Yorkshire Bank Plc (05-08-80)

| | 31-12-13 | 31-12-12 | 31-12-11 |
|---|---|---|---|
| TO | 36,036,000 | 34,280,000 | 32,907,000 |
| P/L | 3,395,000 | 2,549,000 | 1,550,000 |
| NW | 21,525,000 | 20,144,000 | 19,168,000 |
| WC | 12,283,000 | 14,510,000 | 15,426,000 |
| Emp. | 125 | 121 | 120 |

DUNS 21-587-5670
## Steeton Court Nursing Home
Steeton Hall Gardens, Steeton, Keighley, West Yorkshire BD20 6SW
**Tel:** 01535-656124
**Web:** www.steetoncourt.co.uk
**Estd:** 1990 Partnership
**Line of Business:** Nursing homes
**Partners:** Mrs R Spellman, A Spellman
**Responsibilities**
**Senior:** Joanne Alton *(Manager)*, Steven Spellman *(Manager)*, Michael Spellman *(Manager)*
**Finance:** Rachel Holdsworth *(Senior Finance Administrator)*
**US SIC:** 8051 **UK SIC:** 95100
**Employees:** 85

DUNS 21-631-2896
## Stefanini International Holdings Ltd
Jubilee House 3 The Drive, Brentwood, Essex CM13 3FR
**Tel:** 02086223058
**Reg No:** 7097325 **Estd:** 2009 Private Limited Company
**Line of Business:** Hardware consultancy
**Directors:** A C Moreira Junior, Ms M D Stefanini, M A Stefanini
**Responsibilities**
**Senior:** Antonio Moreira *(Director)*
**US SIC:** 7379 **UK SIC:** 83940
**Employees:** 4,237
**Turnover:** £280,163,000

DUNS 21-593-0721
## Steiner Acadmey Hereford
Church Farm, Hereford, Herefordshire HR2 8DL
**Tel:** 01981540221
**Web:** www.steineracademyhereford.eu
**Estd:** 1982 Partnership
**Line of Business:** Nursery schools
**Partners:** Miss K Rogers, C Mayers, Miss E Davies
**US SIC:** 8211 **UK SIC:** 93200
**Employees:** 60

DUNS 28-843-1570 **Imp-Exp**
## Steiner Training Ltd
Steiner Group, 92 Uxbridge Road, Harrow, Middlesex HA3 6DQ
**Tel:** 02089546121
**Web:** www.str.co.uk
**Reg No:** 0580061 **Estd:** 1957 Private Limited Company
**Line of Business:** Other adult and other education not elsewhere classified
**Export Sales:** £3,698,360
**Issued Capital:** £2
**Directors:** R B Schaverien, L I Fluxman
**Co. Secretary:** Mrs Melanie Casey
**US SIC:** 7361, 8249
**UK SIC:** 83954, 93300
**Auditors:** Arthur Andersen
**Bankers:** The Royal Bank Of Scotland Plc (15-00-00)

| | 31-12-13 | 31-12-12 | 31-12-11 |
|---|---|---|---|
| TO | 4,352,626 | 4,626,577 | 4,535,469 |
| P/L | 170,251 | 185,936 | 174,325 |
| NW | 2,036,574 | 1,903,395 | 1,656,042 |
| WC | 1,829,311 | 1,651,939 | 1,344,616 |
| Emp. | 56 | 57 | 54 |

DUNS 21-005-3500
## Steinhoff Uk Retail Ltd
(**Subsidiary of:** Steinhoff International Holdings Ltd)
Support Centre, Thame, Oxfordshire OX9 3HD
**Tel:** 08443329000
**Web:** www.cargohomeshop.com
**Reg No:** 0040754 **VAT No:** 506331284
**Estd:** 1894 Private Limited Company
**Line of Business:** Household stores
**Trading Style:** Cargo Homeshop, Carpenters, Bensons for Beds
**Issued Capital:** £734,418
**Directors:** F J Nel, P J Dieperink, S Summers, S J Grobler, H Odendaal, M J Jooste
**Co. Secretary:** John Robins
**Responsibilities**
**Senior:** Richard Cowley *(Manager)*, Clive Gilbert *(Manager)*, Daniël Van Der Merwe *(Director)*
**IT:** Steven Rooks *(IT Manager)*
**Purchasing:** Lauren Revill *(Purchasing Manager)*
**Branches:** Steinhoff Uk Retail Ltd, Cargo Homeshop, 12-16 Market Place, Henley-On-Thames, Oxfordshire RG9 2AH
**US SIC:** 5399, 5719
**UK SIC:** 65600, 64700
**Auditors:** Deloitte LLP
**Bankers:** HSBC Bank plc (40-03-27)

| | 29-06-13 | 30-06-12 | 25-06-11 |
|---|---|---|---|
| TO | 449,215,000 | 433,868,000 | 230,157,000 |
| P/L | 15,324,000 | 19,389,000 | 9,527,000 |
| NW | 59,443,000 | 51,672,000 | 40,853,000 |
| WC | 17,097,000 | 32,851,000 | 173,918,000 |
| Emp. | 2,623 | 3,061 | 1,828 |

DUNS 29-931-4419 **Imp**
## Steljes Ltd
(**Subsidiary of:** Steljes Holdings Ltd)
Bagshot Manor, Green Lane, Bagshot, Surrey GU19 5NL
**Tel:** 08450-758-758 **Fax:** 08450-261-500
**Web:** www.steljes.com
**Reg No:** 2100043 **VAT No:** 480686418
**Estd:** 1987 Private Limited Company
**Line of Business:** Wholesalers and distributors of audio visual equipment
**Export Sales:** £1,841,227
**Issued Capital:** £48,000
**Principals:** N F Steljes *(Managing)*, M I Large *(Financial)*, M M Mason, I Goodhind, Ms S K Sugden, Ms N A Harris Briggs, Ms S D Baker
**Co. Secretary:** Ms Shelley Sugden
**Responsibilities**
**HR:** Eva Ringer *(Human Resources Manager)*
**Health & Safety:** Alex Blackmun *(Facilities Manager)*
**Facilities:** Alex Blackmun *(Facilities Manager)*
**Branches:** Steljes Ltd, 16 Cairnburn Ave, Belfast, Belfast BT4 2HT
**US SIC:** 3662 **UK SIC:** 34430
**Auditors:** KPMG LLP
**Bankers:** HSBC Bank plc (40-02-13)

| | 30-06-13 | 30-06-12 | 30-06-11 |
|---|---|---|---|
| TO | 56,699,741 | 60,649,651 | 58,895,777 |
| P/L | 2,782,513 | 1,110,098 | 624,532 |
| NW | 4,133,243 | 2,909,100 | 2,013,626 |
| WC | 2,685,724 | 2,221,542 | 1,079,142 |
| Emp. | 144 | 155 | 164 |

DUNS 22-151-1962 **Imp**
## Stella McCartney Ltd
3 Olaf Street, London W11 4BE
**Tel:** 02078982710 **Fax:** 020-7518-3101
**Web:** www.stellamccartney.com
**Reg No:** 4169969 **Estd:** 2003 Private Limited Company
**Line of Business:** Clothing retailers
**Issued Capital:** £201
**Directors:** M Bizzarri, Ms S N Mccartney, A J Willis, Ms H Newman, F H Pinault, Ms H Newman
**Responsibilities**
**Senior:** Alexis Babeau *(Manager)*, Michel Friocourt *(Director)*
**Branches:** Stella Mccartney, London W1J 6QR 30BRuton St
**US SIC:** 5699 **UK SIC:** 64500
**Auditors:** KPMG LLP
**Bankers:** HSBC Bank plc (40-05-01)

| | 31-12-13 | 31-12-12 | 31-12-11 |
|---|---|---|---|
| TO | 28,415,712 | 25,771,742 | 20,987,352 |
| P/L | 4,880,614 | 4,575,206 | 3,296,418 |
| NW | 11,881,505 | 11,086,599 | 10,064,033 |
| WC | 3,349,763 | 2,590,805 | 7,715,636 |
| Emp. | 84 | 69 | 63 |

DUNS 71-880-7055
## Stella Travel Services (Uk) Ltd
Glendale House Glendale Park, Glendale Avenue, Sandycroft Industrial Estate, Sandycroft, Deeside, Clwyd CH5 2DL
**Tel:** 08448264567
**Reg No:** 5263204 **Estd:** 2004 Private Limited Company
**Line of Business:** Activities of travel organisers
**Issued Capital:** £1,000,000
**Directors:** I C Andrew, Mrs A Pollard, A H Parkar, A I Botterill
**Co. Secretary:** Jens Penny
**US SIC:** 4722, 6711
**UK SIC:** 77001, 83962
**Auditors:** PricewaterhouseCoopers LLP

| | 30-06-14 | 30-06-13 | 30-06-12 |
|---|---|---|---|
| TO | 192,794,000 | 165,825,000 | 132,924,000 |
| P/L | 3,529,000 | 1,333,000 | 722,000 |
| NW | 4,565,000 | (4,243,000) | (6,010,000) |
| WC | 5,484,000 | (1,815,000) | (3,551,000) |
| Emp. | 302 | 375 | 370 |

DUNS 34-617-5651
## Stellar Diamonds Plc
20 + 22 Bedford Row, London, London WC1R 4JS
**Tel:** 08000073500
**Web:** www.stellar-diamonds.com
**Reg No:** 5424214 **Estd:** 1995 Public Limited Company
**Line of Business:** Quarries
**Directors:** S J Poulton, Lord P G Daresbury, L Meran, N K Smithson, Dr. M Elsasser, L G Da Silva
**Co. Secretary:** Philip Knowles
**US SIC:** 1499 **UK SIC:** 23960
**Auditors:** Deloitte & Touche
**Employees:** 153

DUNS 21-068-9743
## Stellar Europe Llc
(**Subsidiary of:** Stellar Global Inc.)
4 Symington Place, Riverside Business Park, Irvine, Ayrshire KA11 5DE
**Tel:** 01294-225300 **Fax:** 01294-225301
**Web:** www.stellarbpo.co.uk
**Reg No:** 0000890SF **VAT No:** 803632456
**Estd:** 2002 Foreign Company
**Line of Business:** Call centres
**Directors:** R Jensen, J Hollingsworth, J Jensen, A T Huxtable, S Morphett, S Letier, D Zeleznik
**Co. Secretary:** Stephen Fuller
**Responsibilities**
**Senior:** Mary Graham *(Chief Executive)*, Michael Lumsden *(CEO)*
**Marketing:** Vanessa O'Brien *(Sales & Marketing Director)*
**Sales:** Vanessa O'Brien *(Sales & Marketing Director)*
**Health & Safety:** Brian McKee *(Health & Safety Officer)*
**US SIC:** 4899, 7392
**UK SIC:** 79020, 83951
**Bankers:** The Royal Bank Of Scotland Plc (83-07-06)

DUNS 21-630-1887 **Imp-Exp**
## Stellison Ltd
14 Manor Trading Estate Parsons Road, Benfleet, Essex SS7 4PY
**Tel:** 01268756276 **Fax:** 01268638050
**Web:** www.stellisonltd.co.uk
**Reg No:** 0743883 **Estd:** 1964 Private Limited Company
**Line of Business:** Retail sale of electrical household appliances and radio and television goods
**Export Markets:** Russia
**Trading Style:** Stellison Kitchen Centre
**Issued Capital:** £20,000
**Directors:** M R Scogings, S A Scogings
**Co. Secretary:** Ms Brenda Scogings
**Branches:** Stellison Ltd, 350 Harwich Road, Colchester, Essex CO4 3HP
**US SIC:** 5732, 5064
**UK SIC:** 64800, 61500
**Auditors:** MacIntyre Hudson
**Bankers:** Barclays Bank Plc (20-70-93)

| | 30-09-13 | 30-09-12 | 30-09-11 |
|---|---|---|---|
| TO | 10,171,015 | 9,609,642 | 10,497,520 |
| P/L | 291,874 | 533,995 | 473,267 |
| NW | 6,195,130 | 6,102,414 | 5,706,366 |
| WC | 2,426,226 | 2,692,244 | 2,773,228 |
| Emp. | 91 | 83 | 82 |

DUNS 21-014-8011 **Imp-Exp**
## Stena Drilling Ltd
(**Subsidiary of:** Stena Ab)
Ullevi House, Aberdeen, Aberdeenshire AB12 3BG
**Tel:** 01224-401180 **Fax:** 01224-097009
**Web:** www.stena-drilling.com
**Reg No:** 0061135 **VAT No:** 605170867
**Estd:** 1899 Private Limited Company
**Line of Business:** Oil and gas exploration services
**Export Markets:** Europe, Australia
**Directors:** D S Olsson, A Jansson, C W Hagman, G F Coutts, T P Welo, Dr C E Fay, P Claesson
**Co. Secretary:** Stuart Wyness
**Responsibilities**
**Marketing:** Elrik Relnertsen *(Marketing and Contracts Manage)*
**IT:** Alex Cawthorne *(Project Manager)*, Damien Shine *(SPS Project Manager)*
**Health & Safety:** Malcolm Rattray *(Health & Safety Officer)*
**Operations:** Nick Anders *(Rig Manager)*, Stuart Greer *(Operations Manager)*
**Engineering:** Erik Ronsberg *(Engineering Manager)*
**Branches:** Stena Drilling Ltd, Bucksburn House, Howes Road, Bucksburn, Aberdeen, Aberdeenshire AB21 9PD
**US SIC:** 1389 **UK SIC:** 13000
**Auditors:** KPMG LLP
**Bankers:** Svenska Handelsbanken Ab (publ) (40-51-62)
**Employees:** 200
**Turnover:** £63,281,000

DUNS 23-242-9550
## Stena Line Freight
Victoria Business Park 9 West Bank Road, Belfast BT3 9JL
**Tel:** 02890884080
**Web:** www.stenalinefreight.com
**Reg No:** 0003572NF **Estd:** 2001 Private Limited Company
**Line of Business:** Freight forwarders
**Director:** Details Held At Cardiff
**Co. Secretary:** Details Held At Cardiff
**US SIC:** 4213 **UK SIC:** 72300

DUNS 21-153-9465 **Imp**
## Stena Line Ltd
(**Subsidiary of:** Stena Ab)
Stena House, Station Approach, Holyhead, Gwynedd LL65 1DQ
**Tel:** 01407606666
**Web:** www.stenaline.com
**Reg No:** 1402237 **Estd:** 1989 Private Limited Company
**Line of Business:** Ferry operators
**Trading Style:** Stena Line
**Issued Capital:** £198,000,001
**Directors:** K Macleod, Ms A M Denrenstrand, U N Martensson
**Co. Secretary:** Leslie Stracey
**Responsibilities**
**Senior:** John Akerlund *(Board Member)*, Gunnar Blomdahl *(Chief Executive Officer)*, Dermot Cairns *(General Manager)*, Nick Flanagan *(Acd Manager Stena Line)*, Eamonn Hewitt *(Spokesman)*, Win Parry *(Port Manager)*, Bo Severed *(Manager)*, Inger Sund *(Manager)*
**Finance:** Ben Boers *(Specialist)*, Svante Carlsson *(Financial Director)*
**Marketing:** Olle Melin *(Port Development Manager)*, Orla Noonan *(Marketing Manager)*, Tiffany Tate *(Marketing Executive)*, Jesper Waltersson *(Communications Manager)*

**Sales:** Mikael Leveau (*Key Account Manager*), Richard Rigby (*Senior Account Manager*)
**IT:** Vic Goodwin (*Computer Operations Manager*), Win Parry (*Port Manager*), Gareth Simpson (*IT Manager*)
**HR:** Robert Akerlund (*Human Resources and Technical*), Michael Ambrose (*Head of HR*), Joanne Clowes (*HR Manager*), Jim Gaffney (*Training Director*), Lana McMullan (*Training Officer*), Sean Mcbride (*Human Resources Manager*)
**Health & Safety:** Garth Halanen (*Group Safety Advisor*)
**Purchasing:** Sue Bowers (*Purchasing Manager*), Ray Lacey (*Purchasing Manager*)
**Engineering:** Robert Akerlund (*Human Resources and Technical*), Dick Van Der Ent (*Engineer*)
**Branches:** Stena Line Ltd, Corry Rd, Belfast, Belfast BT3 9SS
**US SIC:** 4452 **UK SIC:** 74002
**Auditors:** KPMG LLP
**Bankers:** Barclays Bank Plc (20-00-00)

| | 31-12-13 | 31-12-12 | 31-12-11 |
|---|---|---|---|
| TO | 217,700,000 | 208,700,000 | 202,800,000 |
| P/L | (18,400,000) | (31,100,000) | (25,900,000) |
| NW | 17,000,000 | 2,400,000 | 26,500,000 |
| WC | 47,500,000 | 58,400,000 | 49,600,000 |
| Emp. | 1,167 | 1,227 | 1,568 |

DUNS 71-939-1083
## Stens (Uk) Ltd
5 Ridge House, Ridgehouse Drive, Stoke-On-Trent, Staffordshire ST1 5SJ
**Tel:** 01782262121
**Reg No:** 5319856 **Estd:** 2004 Private Limited Company
**Line of Business:** Other letting of own property
**Issued Capital:** £1,000
**Director:** Ms M Thommes
**Co. Secretary:** Slyvia Grundy
**US SIC:** 6519 **UK SIC:** 85000

| | 31-12-13 | 31-12-12 | 31-12-11 |
|---|---|---|---|
| TO | 25,862,629 | 23,942,998 | 25,355,582 |
| P/L | 8,763,157 | 7,230,210 | 6,863,742 |
| NW | 32,173,629 | 25,253,426 | 28,125,097 |
| WC | 17,467,183 | 10,039,584 | 12,515,219 |
| Emp. | 91 | 93 | 87 |

DUNS 76-381-3672
## Step by Step Ltd
(*Subsidiary of:* Findel P.L.C.)
2 Gregory Street, Hyde, Cheshire SK14 4HR
**Tel:** 0161-367-2000
**Web:** www.findell-education.co.uk
**Reg No:** 2553408 **VAT No:** 576000951
**Estd:** 1991 Private Limited Company
**Line of Business:** Mail order houses
**Trading Style:** Findel Educational, Hope Education, Premier Educational Supplies
**Issued Capital:** £995
**Directors:** P B Maudsley, T J Kowalski, R W Siddle
**Co. Secretary:** Mark Ashcroft
**Branches:** Step By Step Ltd, 2 Gregory Street, Hyde, Cheshire SK14 4HR
**US SIC:** 5961 **UK SIC:** 65600
**Bankers:** Barclays Bank Plc (20-63-25)

| | 28-03-14 | 29-03-13 | 30-03-12 |
|---|---|---|---|
| NW | (84,254) | (84,254) | (84,254) |

DUNS 54-377-0812    **Imp-Exp**
## Stepan U K Ltd
(*Subsidiary of:* Stepan Company)
Bridge House, Stalybridge, Cheshire SK15 1PH
**Tel:** 0161-338-5511 **Fax:** 0161-303-2991
**Web:** www.stepan.com
**Reg No:** 3264997 **VAT No:** 677582285
**Estd:** 1963 Private Limited Company
**Line of Business:** Manufacturers of chemicals
**Export Markets:** Worldwide
**Export Sales:** £13,208,000
**Trading Style:** Manro
**Issued Capital:** £3
**Director:** A Martin
**Co. Secretary:** Iain Davies
**Responsibilities**
**Senior:** John Langton (*Manager*)
**US SIC:** 2841, 2899
**UK SIC:** 25810, 25670
**Auditors:** Deloitte LLP
**Bankers:** HSBC Bank plc (40-31-24)

| | 31-12-13 | 31-12-12 | 31-12-11 |
|---|---|---|---|
| TO | 67,774,000 | 67,182,000 | 81,357,000 |
| P/L | 583,000 | 1,964,000 | 2,224,000 |
| NW | 21,500,000 | 19,792,000 | 19,619,000 |
| WC | 8,291,000 | 9,202,000 | 9,206,000 |
| Emp. | 118 | 115 | 114 |

DUNS 42-354-3383
## Stephen Austin (Holdings) Ltd
(*Subsidiary of:* S A Printing Group Ltd)
Caxton Hill, Hertford, Hertfordshire SG13 7LU
**Tel:** 01992584955 **Fax:** 01992-500021
**Web:** www.stephenaustin.co.uk
**Reg No:** 4341989 **Estd:** 2001 Private Limited Company
**Line of Business:** Management activities of production holding companies
**Issued Capital:** £3,014,800
**Directors:** R J Fowler, M Chitson, P G Fowler
**Co. Secretary:** Ian Angus
**Responsibilities**
**Sales:** Marcel Van Den Voogaard (*Sales Manager*)
**US SIC:** 6711 **UK SIC:** 83962
**Bankers:** HSBC Bank plc (40-24-13)

| | 30-09-13 | 30-09-12 | 30-09-11 |
|---|---|---|---|
| TO | 15,978,000 | 14,370,000 | 13,803,707 |
| P/L | 603,000 | 951,000 | 646,955 |
| NW | 5,038,000 | 4,617,000 | 4,275,678 |
| WC | 2,905,000 | 3,366,000 | 3,636,640 |
| Emp. | 145 | 145 | 132 |

DUNS 23-693-8130
## Stephen George & Partners
166-170 London Road, Leicester, Leicestershire LE2 1ND
**Tel:** 01162-470557
**Web:** www.stephengeorge.co.uk
**Estd:** 1971 Partnership
**Line of Business:** Architects
**Trading Style:** Stephen George & Partners
**Principals:** P Overton (*Partner*), M Barker (*Partner*), S Richardson (*Partner*), D Taylor
**Responsibilities**
**Senior:** Stephen Armitage (*Manager*), Nick Austin (*Practice Manager*), Kanti Chhapi (*Manager*), Alexander Daw (*Manager*), Vladislav Dechev (*Manager*), Chris Halligan (*Manager*), Tihomir Kazakov (*Manager*), Marcus Madden-Smith (*Manager*), John Morfey (*Partner*), Micheal Smith (*Proprietor*), Richard Smyth (*Manager*), Ian Yallop (*Partner*)
**Finance:** Justine Chamberlain (*Financial Controller*)
**IT:** Andrew Langton (*CAD Manager*), Kenji Matthews (*IT Manager*)
**Engineering:** Clive Watterson (*Director-Architectural*)
**Branches:** Stephen George & Partners, 25 Courtland Terrace, Merthyr Tydfil, Mid Glamorgan CF47 0DT
**US SIC:** 8911 **UK SIC:** 83701
**Bankers:** HSBC Bank plc (40-28-04)
**Employees:** 60

DUNS 21-278-1835
## Stephen H Smith Garden & Leisure
Pool Road, Otley, West Yorkshire LS21 1DY
**Tel:** 01943850050
**Web:** www.shrubs.co.uk
**VAT No:** 168844126 **Estd:** 1967 Partnership
**Line of Business:** Garden centres
**Partners:** S H Smith, C S Smith
**Responsibilities**
**Health & Safety:** Mark Waite (*Facilities Manager*)
**Facilities:** Mark Waite (*Facilities Manager*)
**Branches:** Stephen H Smith Garden & Leisure, Radcliffe Moor Road, Bolton, Lancashire BL2 6RF
**US SIC:** 5999, 0161
**UK SIC:** 65600, 01001
**Bankers:** Barclays Bank Plc (20-37-13)
**Employees:** 60

DUNS 21-582-9304
## Stephen James
Maidstone Road, Sidcup, Kent DA14 5BG
**Tel:** 02083026431
**Web:** www.stephenjames.co.uk
**Estd:** 2011 Proprietorship
**Line of Business:** Car dealers (new & used)
**Proprietor:** D Coleman
**Responsibilities**
**Senior:** Des Campbell (*Dealer Principal*), Jim O'donnell (*Dealer Principal*)
**US SIC:** 5511 **UK SIC:** 65100
**Employees:** 50

DUNS 67-215-3843
## Stephen James Group Trading Llp
Unit 1 Martinbridge Indutl Estate, Estate Lincoln Road, Enfield, Middlesex EN1 1SP
**Tel:** 08432161051
**Web:** www.stephenjamesenfieldbmw.co.uk
**Reg No:** 0325235OC **VAT No:** 898690442
**Estd:** 2007
**Line of Business:** Automotive repair services

**Responsibilities**
**Senior:** Paul Ballard (*Non-designated Limited Liabili*), Desmond Campbell (*Non-designated Limited Liabili*), Gordon Down (*Non-designated Limited Liabili*), Jason Draper (*Non-designated Limited Liabili*), Alan Jenks (*Non-designated Limited Liabili*), Gayle Kelly (*Non-designated Limited Liabili*), Gary Lovejoy (*Non-designated Limited Liabili*), Matthew Meager (*Non-designated Limited Liabili*), Ryan O'Sullivan (*Non-designated Limited Liabili*)
**Branches:** Stephen James Group Trading Llp, 208 Lincoln Road, Enfield, Middlesex EN1 1SW
**US SIC:** 7699 **UK SIC:** 67303
**Auditors:** Lubbock Fine
**Bankers:** National Westminster Bank Plc (60-14-55)

| | 31-12-13 | 31-12-12 | 31-12-11 |
|---|---|---|---|
| TO | 177,647,000 | 157,620,000 | 145,310,000 |
| P/L | 1,504,000 | 1,205,000 | 1,017,000 |
| NW | 5,744,000 | 5,682,000 | 5,620,000 |
| WC | 9,037,000 | 4,973,000 | 5,177,000 |
| Emp. | 293 | 290 | 301 |

DUNS 21-154-6809
## Stephen James Ltd
(*Subsidiary of:* Dc Management Services Ltd)
Lincoln Road, Enfield, Middlesex EN1 1SW
**Tel:** 02083440900 **Fax:** 02084430901
**Web:** www.stephenjames.co.uk
**Reg No:** 1089649 **Estd:** 1972 Private Limited Company
**Line of Business:** Car dealers (new & used)
**Trading Style:** Stephen James
**Issued Capital:** £1,012,075
**Principals:** D P Collins (*Managing*), Mrs S C Collins, B J Collins, S Breese
**Co. Secretary:** Steve Breese
**Responsibilities**
**Senior:** Ben Saul (*Marketing Manager*)
**Finance:** Lee Camp (*Financial Director*)
**Marketing:** Sue Coates (*Senior Marketing Executive*), Ben Saul (*Marketing Manager*)
**Sales:** Gayle Kelly (*Dealer Principal*)
**IT:** Martin Hamlin (*Computer Manager*)
**HR:** Gayle Kelly (*Dealer Principal*)
**Branches:** Stephen James Ltd, Old Orchard, Bickley Road, Bromley, Kent BR1 2NE
**US SIC:** 5511, 5531
**UK SIC:** 65100
**Auditors:** Mazars Neville Russell
**Bankers:** Barclays Bank Plc (20-95-61)

| | 31-12-13 | 31-12-12 | 31-12-11 |
|---|---|---|---|
| TA | 1,012,075 | 7,241,940 | 6,711,376 |
| NW | 1,012,075 | 6,503,395 | 6,467,434 |
| WC | N/A | 1,258,983 | 1,223,022 |

DUNS 50-513-4320
## Stephen Joseph Theatre Enterprises Ltd
Westborough, Scarborough, North Yorkshire YO11 1JW
**Web:** www.sjt.uk.com
**Reg No:** 2481307 **Estd:** 1990 Private Limited Company
**Line of Business:** Retail sale of books, newspapers and stationery
**Issued Capital:** £15,000
**Directors:** J G Armistead, N R Taylor, C Groom
**Co. Secretary:** Ian Wyatt
**US SIC:** 5942, 5812
**UK SIC:** 65300, 66110
**Auditors:** Coulsons
**Bankers:** HSBC Bank plc (40-40-22)

| | 31-03-14 | 31-03-13 | 31-03-12 |
|---|---|---|---|
| TA | 12,041 | 12,044 | 73,531 |
| NW | 12,041 | 12,041 | 11,930 |
| WC | N/A | 12,041 | 2,689 |

DUNS 21-924-4568
## The Stephen Perse Foundation
Union Road, Cambridge, Cambridgeshire CB2 1HF
**Tel:** 01223454700
**Web:** www.stephenperse.com
**Reg No:** 6113565 **Estd:** 2013 Private Company Limited By Guarantee
**Line of Business:** Schools (independent)
**Directors:** Mrs A M Powell, Mrs K A Ollerenshaw, Dr M T Calaresu, Dr G R Sutherland, B J Schwieger, Professor S Peacock, Dr C Y Barlow, S D Galbraith
**Co. Secretary:** Mrs Jennifer Neild
**Responsibilities**
**Senior:** Harriet Allen (*Director*), Joanna Burch (*Director*), Anthony Crouch (*Director*), John Dix (*Director*), Gordon Johnson (*Director*), Carl Watkins (*Director*)
**US SIC:** 8211 **UK SIC:** 93200
**Bankers:** Barclays Bank Plc (20-17-22)

| | 31-08-14 | 31-08-13 | 31-08-12 |
|---|---|---|---|
| TO | 16,631,679 | 10,677,136 | 10,270,054 |
| P/L | 3,329,930 | 357,147 | 316,293 |
| NW | 12,151,481 | 9,006,937 | 8,375,681 |
| WC | (405,280) | 50,734 | (69,921) |
| Emp. | 205 | 159 | 164 |

DUNS 21-139-2716
## Stephen Rimmer Llp
28-30 Hyde Gardens, Eastbourne, East Sussex BN21 4PX
**Tel:** 01323644222
**Web:** www.stephenrimmer.com
**Reg No:** 0340622OC **VAT No:** 350975439
**Estd:** 1981 Private Limited Company
**Line of Business:** Solicitors
**Responsibilities**
**Senior:** Stephen Rimmer (*Commercial Partner*)
**Finance:** Stephen Rimmer (*Commercial Partner*)
**IT:** Diane Ash (*Computer Manager*)
**Facilities:** Stephen Rimmer (*Commercial Partner*)
**US SIC:** 8111 **UK SIC:** 83500
**Bankers:** The Royal Bank Of Scotland Plc (16-19-15)

| | 31-03-14 | 31-03-13 | 31-03-12 |
|---|---|---|---|
| TA | 1,783,870 | 1,616,674 | 1,195,921 |
| WC | 1,039,151 | 1,021,502 | 636,072 |

DUNS 22-658-9679
## Stephen Sanderson Transport Ltd
(*Subsidiary of:* Stephen Sanderson Transport Holdings Ltd)
Units 1&2, Market Harborough, Leicestershire LE16 7PT
**Tel:** 01858466499
**Web:** www.sandersontransport.com
**Reg No:** 2063681 **VAT No:** 121889949
**Estd:** 2010 Private Limited Company
**Line of Business:** Road haulage and transport services
**Issued Capital:** £100,050
**Principals:** S Sanderson (*Managing*), E H Sanderson, C C Sanderson
**Co. Secretary:** Mrs Janice Sanderson
**Responsibilities**
**Senior:** Don McCulloch (*Warehouse Manager*)
**Operations:** Don McCulloch (*Warehouse Manager*)
**US SIC:** 4789 **UK SIC:** 77002
**Auditors:** Berry & Co
**Bankers:** Lloyds TSB Bank plc (30-95-47)

| | 31-12-13 | 31-12-12 | 31-12-11 |
|---|---|---|---|
| TO | 9,879,284 | 8,399,001 | 7,795,463 |
| P/L | 496,655 | 307,524 | 141,377 |
| NW | 3,690,516 | 3,358,508 | 3,201,936 |
| WC | 508,922 | 493,757 | 789,761 |
| Emp. | 74 | 70 | 71 |

DUNS 21-830-9193    **Imp-Exp**
## Stephen Walters & Sons Ltd
(*Subsidiary of:* Walters Holdings Ltd)
Sudbury Silk Mills, Sudbury, Suffolk CO10 2XB
**Web:** www.stephenwalters.co.uk
**Reg No:** 0060209 **VAT No:** 102022651
**Estd:** 1899 Private Limited Company
**Line of Business:** Textile weaving
**Export Markets:** Worldwide
**Issued Capital:** £32,466
**Principals:** D J Walters (*Chairman and Managing*), R Heap, B R Crabtree, M C James, J D Walters
**Co. Secretary:** Miss Nicola Currie
**Responsibilities**
**Senior:** Clive Golding (*Warehouse Manager*)
**Health & Safety:** Clive Golding (*Warehouse Manager*)
**Facilities:** John Maisey (*Engineering Manager*)
**Operations:** Clive Golding (*Warehouse Manager*)
**Engineering:** John Maisey (*Engineering Manager*)
**US SIC:** 2269 **UK SIC:** 43702
**Auditors:** Grant Thornton
**Bankers:** Lloyds TSB Bank plc (30-98-31)

| | 31-03-14 | 31-03-13 | 31-03-12 |
|---|---|---|---|
| TO | 8,566,155 | 8,073,824 | 8,258,015 |
| P/L | 441,580 | 211,623 | 326,213 |
| NW | 3,680,590 | 3,338,990 | 3,181,551 |
| WC | 2,817,756 | 2,364,857 | 2,114,418 |
| Emp. | 109 | 109 | 113 |

DUNS 23-743-8127    **Imp**
## Stephen Webster Ltd
(*Subsidiary of:* Delltrade Ltd)
24 Albemarle Street, London W1S 4HT
**Tel:** 08455391800 **Fax:** 020-7486-6439
**Web:** www.stephenwebster.com
**Reg No:** 3738018 **Estd:** 2001 Private Limited Company
**Line of Business:** Retail sale of jewellery, clocks and watches
**Export Sales:** £3,991,000
**Issued Capital:** £229,719
**Directors:** E Renwick, S Webster
**Co. Secretary:** David Webster
**Responsibilities**
**Senior:** Harry Patel (*Chief Financial Officer*)
**Finance:** Harry Patel (*Chief Financial Officer*)
**US SIC:** 5944 **UK SIC:** 65400

**Auditors:** PricewaterhouseCoopers LLP
**Bankers:** HSBC Bank plc (40-05-30)

| | 31-03-13 | 31-03-12 | 31-03-11 |
|---|---|---|---|
| TO | 6,977,000 | 6,997,000 | 7,048,000 |
| P/L | (424,000) | (664,000) | 796,000 |
| NW | (4,139,000) | (3,708,000) | (3,484,000) |
| WC | (4,237,000) | (3,902,000) | (3,844,000) |
| Emp. | 54 | 52 | 43 |

DUNS 21-641-4813 **Exp**

## Stephens & George Ltd

Goat Mill Road, Merthyr Tydfil, Mid Glamorgan CF48 3TD
**Tel:** 01685385678 **Fax:** 01685388888
**Web:** www.stephensandgeorge.co.uk
**Reg No:** 0411176 **Estd:** 1912 Private Limited Company
**Line of Business:** Commercial lithographic printers
**Export Markets:** U S A; Switzerland
**Trading Style:** Stephens & George Magazines, S G C Printing, Pelican Print Finishing
**Issued Capital:** £48,300
**Principals:** A L Jones *(Managing)*, D J Debattista, S Davies, N A Pressling
**Co. Secretary:** Clive Mathias
**Responsibilities**
**Marketing:** Ben Powell *(Marketing Executive)*
**Engineering:** Paul Enoch *(Production Manager)*
**US SIC:** 2752, 2789, 2753
**UK SIC:** 47544, 47545
**Auditors:** KTS
**Bankers:** Bank Of Wales Plc (12-23-11)

| | 31-03-14 | 31-03-13 | 31-03-12 |
|---|---|---|---|
| TO | 23,012,278 | 22,840,350 | 23,556,399 |
| P/L | 1,242,439 | 818,257 | 998,709 |
| NW | 9,124,792 | 8,456,520 | 8,460,977 |
| WC | 2,110,278 | 850,380 | 1,280,390 |
| Emp. | 207 | 211 | 219 |

DUNS 21-583-3559 **Imp-Exp**

## Stephens Catering Equipment Co Ltd

205 Carnalbanagh Road, Broughshane, Ballymena, Co Antrim BT42 4NY
**Tel:** 02825861711 **Fax:** 02825-862006
**Web:** www.stephens-catering.com
**Reg No:** 0011092NI **VAT No:** 286304745
**Estd:** 1973 Private Limited Company
**Line of Business:** Catering equipment
**Export Markets:** Republic of Ireland
**Trading Style:** Donegal & Cater-Quipment
**Issued Capital:** £10,000
**Directors:** T P Caves, T S Caves, Ms P J Morrissey
**Co. Secretary:** Ms Elizabeth Caves
**Responsibilities**
**Senior:** Cargin McKeown *(Warehouse Manager)*
**Finance:** Thompson McCullough *(Financial Director)*
**Marketing:** George Long *(Sales & Marketing Manager)*
**Sales:** George Long *(Sales & Marketing Manager)*
**IT:** Leonard Craig *(Computer Manager)*
**HR:** Thompson McCullough *(Financial Director)*
**Facilities:** Cargin McKeown *(Warehouse Manager)*
**US SIC:** 3551 **UK SIC:** 32441
**Auditors:** Stevenson & Wilson
**Bankers:** Ulster Bank Ltd (98-01-80)

| | 30-04-14 | 30-04-13 | 30-04-12 |
|---|---|---|---|
| TO | 11,989,052 | 13,355,855 | 13,493,228 |
| P/L | 116,909 | 107,716 | 216,214 |
| NW | 2,961,847 | 2,868,498 | 2,790,750 |
| WC | 2,232,159 | 2,092,955 | 1,998,361 |
| Emp. | 87 | 90 | 91 |

DUNS 21-682-0534

## Stephens Scown Llp

Curzon House, Southernhay West, Exeter, Devon EX1 1RS
**Tel:** 01392210700
**Web:** www.stephensandscown.co.uk
**Reg No:** 0356696OC **Estd:** 2000 Partnership
**Line of Business:** Solicitors
**Responsibilities**
**Senior:** Sonya Bedford *(Partner and Head of Renewable)*, Robert Brightley *(Non-designated Limited Liabili)*, David Corsellis *(Non-designated Limited Liabili)*, Phillip Gregory *(Non-designated Limited Liabili)*, Simon Harding *(Partner)*, Jonathan Hoggett *(Partner)*, Andrew Knox *(Associate)*, Catherine Mathews *(Non-designated Limited Liabili)*, Laura McFadyen *(Associate)*, Scott Mitchell *(Non-designated Limited Liabili)*, Philip Mogridge *(Non-designated Limited Liabili)*, Susie Murray *(Partner)*, Philip Reed *(Non-designated Limited Liabili)*, Andy Steele *(Chief Executive)*, Matthew Wald *(Partner)*, Christian Wilson *(Non-designated Limited Liabili)*
**Finance:** Andy Steele *(Chief Executive)*
**Marketing:** Mandy Reynolds *(Marketing Manager)*
**Admin:** Jamie Thornton *(Office Manager)*
**IT:** Dean Mostert *(IT Manager)*
**HR:** Jamie Thornton *(Office Manager)*
**Health & Safety:** Jamie Thornton *(Office Manager)*
**Facilities:** Jamie Thornton *(Office Manager)*
**Purchasing:** Jamie Thornton *(Office Manager)*
**Engineering:** Philip Mogridge *(Non-designated Limited Liabili)*
**US SIC:** 8111 **UK SIC:** 83500

| | 30-04-14 | 30-04-13 | 30-04-12 |
|---|---|---|---|
| TO | 13,643,504 | 12,049,807 | 11,359,263 |
| NW | (110,500) | N/A | N/A |
| WC | 4,386,698 | 4,099,977 | 3,619,236 |
| Emp. | 205 | 187 | 177 |

DUNS 23-981-5004

## Stephenson College

Thornborough Road, Coalville, Leicestershire LE67 3TN
**Tel:** 01530836136
**Web:** www.stephensoncoll.ac.uk
**VAT No:** 616951917 **Estd:** 1920
**Line of Business:** Further education schools and colleges
**Directors:** Ms C Peach, D J Rathe, Mrs F E Chatfield
**Responsibilities**
**Senior:** Martin Concannon *(Estates Manager)*, Cheryl Duncan-Ratcliff *(Senior Manager)*
**Finance:** Tom Bill *(Finance Manager)*
**Facilities:** Martin Concannon *(Estates Manager)*
**Branches:** Stephenson College, Easter Park, Unit 8, Nottingham, Nottinghamshire NG7 2PX
**US SIC:** 8221, 8249
**UK SIC:** 93100, 93300
**Employees:** 300

DUNS 21-830-2756 **Imp**

## Stephenson Harwood Llp

1 Finsbury Circus, London EC2M 7SH
**Tel:** 020-7329-4422
**Web:** www.shlegal.com
**Reg No:** 0373597OC **VAT No:** 243393954
**Estd:** 1994
**Line of Business:** Solicitors
**Responsibilities**
**Senior:** Alan Bercow *(Non-designated Limited Liabili)*, Nigel Bowen-Morris *(Non-designated Limited Liabili)*, Catherine Brearley *(Non-designated Limited Liabili)*, Stephanie Salou *(Non-designated Limited Liabili)*, Maryanna Sharrock *(Non-designated Limited Liabili)*, Appa Shunmugam *(Non-designated Limited Liabili)*, James Tinworth *(Non-designated Limited Liabili)*, Jonathon Wilkes *(Non-designated Limited Liabili)*, Langdon Young *(Non-designated Limited Liabili)*, Hongkai Zhou *(Non-designated Limited Liabili)*, Charalampos Zografakis *(Non-designated Limited Liabili)*
**US SIC:** 8111 **UK SIC:** 83500
**Auditors:** KPMG LLP

| | 30-04-14 | 30-04-13 |
|---|---|---|
| TO | 122,000,000 | 113,300,000 |
| P/L | 43,800,000 | 37,300,000 |
| NW | 49,100,000 | 40,600,000 |
| WC | 64,200,000 | 56,200,000 |
| Emp. | 725 | 702 |

DUNS 21-102-7441

## Stephenson Smart & Co

22-26 King Street, King's Lynn, Norfolk PE30 1HJ
**Tel:** 01553774104
**Web:** www.stephenson-smart.com
**Estd:** 2009 Partnership
**Line of Business:** Accounting activities
**Partner:** A E Wilkinson
**Responsibilities**
**Senior:** Clive Dodds *(Senior Partner)*
**Finance:** Derek Donaldson *(Office Manager)*
**Marketing:** Derek Donaldson *(Office Manager)*
**Sales:** Derek Donaldson *(Office Manager)*
**Admin:** Derek Donaldson *(Office Manager)*
**Health & Safety:** Derek Donaldson *(Office Manager)*
**Branches:** Stephenson Smart & Co, Stephenson Smart & Co, 11 Oak Street, Fakenham, Norfolk NR21 9DX
**US SIC:** 8931 **UK SIC:** 83600
**Employees:** 50

DUNS 73-989-4447

## Stephenson Smart Ltd

**(Subsidiary of:** Rns Business Solutions Ltd)
36 Tyndall Court Commerce Road, Lynchwood, Peterborough, Cambridgeshire PE2 6LR
**Tel:** 01733-343275
**Web:** www.stephensonsmart.com
**Reg No:** 5239986 **Estd:** 2004 Private Limited Company
**Line of Business:** Accounting activities primarily bookkeeping
**Issued Capital:** £5
**Director:** P H Evans
**Co. Secretary:** Garry Wiles
**Responsibilities**
**Senior:** Tina Newstead *(Administration Manager)*
**Finance:** Tina Newstead *(Administration Manager)*
**Marketing:** Tina Newstead *(Administration Manager)*
**Sales:** Tina Newstead *(Administration Manager)*
**IT:** Tina Newstead *(Administration Manager)*
**HR:** Ivan Walker *(Partner)*
**Health & Safety:** Ivan Walker *(Partner)*
**Facilities:** Tina Newstead *(Administration Manager)*
**Operations:** Tina Newstead *(Administration Manager)*
**Purchasing:** Tina Newstead *(Administration Manager)*
**US SIC:** 8931 **UK SIC:** 83600

| | 30-09-14 | 30-09-13 | 30-09-12 |
|---|---|---|---|
| TA | 5 | 5 | 5 |
| NW | 5 | 5 | 5 |

DUNS 21-730-8070

## The Stephenson Studio School Trust

Thornborough Road, Coalville, Leicestershire LE67 3TN
**Tel:** 01530519099
**Web:** www.stephensonstudioschool.co.uk
**Reg No:** 7662709 **Estd:** 2011 Private Company Limited By Guarantee
**Line of Business:** General secondary education
**Directors:** Mrs G M Laird, G D Gudger, G Tacey, M Anderson, S Forbes, W S Devitt, N W Leigh, S A Kibble
**Co. Secretary:** Miss Sylvia Royle
**Responsibilities**
**Senior:** Rachel Gordon *(Executive Head Teacher)*
**US SIC:** 8211 **UK SIC:** 93200
**Bankers:** Lloyds TSB Bank plc (30-00-03)

| | 31-08-14 | 31-08-13 | 31-08-12 |
|---|---|---|---|
| TO | 1,074,000 | 1,397,000 | 1,471,000 |
| P/L | (88,000) | 107,000 | 396,000 |
| NW | 415,000 | 503,000 | 396,000 |
| WC | 180,000 | 326,000 | 202,000 |
| Emp. | 18 | 61 | 19 |

DUNS 23-251-0537

## Stephensons

26 Union Street, Leigh, Lancashire WN7 1AT
**Web:** www.stephensons.co.uk
**Estd:** 1978 Partnership
**Line of Business:** Solicitors
**Partners:** A Wemyss, C J Stephenson, T Bridge, N Boldand, M Carr, O Williams, N Yates, B Trainor
**Responsibilities**
**Finance:** Jim Thirkettle *(Operations Director)*
**Marketing:** Sarah Boustouller *(Marketing Manager)*
**Purchasing:** Jim Thirkettle *(Operations Director)*
**Branches:** Stephensons, Stephensons Solicitors Llp, 95-101 Corporation Street, St. Helens, Merseyside WA10 1SX
**US SIC:** 8111 **UK SIC:** 83500
**Bankers:** HSBC Bank plc (40-28-10)
**Employees:** 100

DUNS 51-641-1738

## Stephensons Solicitors Llp

24 - 34 Lord Street, Leigh, Lancashire WN7 1AB
**Tel:** 03333444772 **Fax:** 01942774383
**Web:** www.stephensons.co.uk
**Reg No:** 0322962OC **VAT No:** 294832719
**Estd:** 1983 Private Limited Company
**Line of Business:** Solicitors
**Responsibilities**
**Senior:** Karen Atkins *(Non-designated Limited Liabili)*, Sarah Boustouller *(Marketing Manager & Partner)*, Louise Griffiths *(Non-designated Limited Liabili)*, Thomas Hodson *(Non-designated Limited Liabili)*, Linda Kirk *(Non-designated Limited Liabili)*, Andrew Leakey *(Non-designated Limited Liabili)*, Liam Waine *(Partner)*
**Finance:** Anne-Marie McCann *(Accounts Manager)*
**Marketing:** Lianne Tracey *(Public Relations Manager)*
**Sales:** Mark Fenning *(Business Development Manager)*
**Operations:** Jim Thirkettle *(Director of Operations)*
**Branches:** Stephensons Solicitors Llp, Sefton House, Northgate Close, Bolton, Lancashire BL6 6PQ
**US SIC:** 8111 **UK SIC:** 83500
**Auditors:** Jackson Stephen LLP
**Bankers:** The Royal Bank Of Scotland Plc (16-17-26)

| | 14-04-14 | 14-04-13 | 14-04-12 |
|---|---|---|---|
| TO | 17,691,704 | 16,323,299 | 14,388,274 |
| NW | 1,280,216 | 1,767,464 | 2,166,107 |
| WC | 5,401,440 | 5,700,227 | 4,811,154 |
| Emp. | 392 | 378 | 356 |

DUNS 21-147-7602

## Stepnell Holdings Ltd

Lawford Road, Rugby, Warwickshire CV21 2UU
**Tel:** 01788574511
**Web:** www.stepnell.co.uk
**Reg No:** 6776973 **Estd:** 2008 Private Limited Company
**Line of Business:** Management activities of holding companies
**Issued Capital:** £9,999,200
**Directors:** P G Wakeford, T B Wakeford, J R Wakeford, M R Wakeford
**Co. Secretary:** Thomas Wakeford
**US SIC:** 6711 **UK SIC:** 83962
**Bankers:** National Westminster Bank Plc (52-30-21)

| | 31-03-13 | 31-03-12 | 31-03-11 |
|---|---|---|---|
| TO | 66,886,932 | 81,977,785 | 76,447,633 |
| P/L | 3,269,306 | 8,786,784 | 6,404,508 |
| NW | 60,170,714 | 37,356,115 | 30,253,374 |
| WC | 46,662,757 | 49,097,323 | 45,709,211 |
| Emp. | 307 | 308 | 311 |

DUNS 76-993-1700

## Stepping Stone Projects

Redfearn House, Ings Avenue, Rochdale, Lancashire OL12 7LH
**Tel:** 01706526296
**Web:** www.stepping-stone.org.uk
**Reg No:** 2647645 **Estd:** 1991 Private Limited Company
**Line of Business:** Hostels
**Directors:** Miss P R Du Plessis, D Berry, Ms K Owen, J Woodham, Mrs J A Allen, D Andrew, Miss S V Ashby, B Courtney
**Co. Secretary:** Ms Kathleen Barlow
**Responsibilities**
**Senior:** Clare Lewis *(Compliance and HR Manager)*, Paula Plessis *(Manager)*
**HR:** Clare Lewis *(Compliance and HR Manager)*
**Operations:** Ben Courtney *(Service Manager)*
**Branches:** Stepping Stone Projects, Parkside House, Bowness Road, Middleton, Manchester M24 4WT
**US SIC:** 7021 **UK SIC:** 66500
**Auditors:** BDO Stoy Hayward
**Bankers:** The Royal Bank Of Scotland Plc (16-29-34)

| | 31-03-14 | 31-03-13 | 31-03-12 |
|---|---|---|---|
| TO | 2,574,786 | 2,637,513 | 2,924,652 |
| P/L | (62,053) | (271,434) | 93,542 |
| NW | 1,105,788 | 1,167,841 | 1,439,275 |
| WC | 882,472 | 905,206 | 1,093,755 |
| Emp. | 61 | 64 | 72 |

DUNS 50-037-0937

## Stepping Stones for Families

Unit 3003a, Abbey Mill Business Centre, 12 Seedhill Road, Paisley, Renfrewshire PA1 1JS
**Tel:** 0141-849-6333 **Fax:** 0141-331-1191
**Web:** www.ssff.org.uk
**Reg No:** 0114228SC **Estd:** 1988 Private Company Limited By Guarantee
**Line of Business:** Charities and charitable organisations
**Directors:** Miss C M Mcghie, Ms C O'Neill, C Webster, D Mcgarrigle, E D Milligan
**Co. Secretary:** Ms Isobel Lawson
**Branches:** Stepping Stones For Families, Calvay Young Families Centre, 7 Calvay Cres, Glasgow, Lanarkshire G33 4RG
**US SIC:** 8321 **UK SIC:** 96111
**Auditors:** French Duncan
**Bankers:** Bank Of Scotland (80-07-14)

| | 31-03-14 | 31-03-13 | 31-03-12 |
|---|---|---|---|
| TO | 1,282,997 | 1,637,208 | 1,607,372 |
| P/L | 63,115 | (22,976) | (98,968) |
| NW | 334,358 | 271,243 | 294,219 |
| WC | 334,358 | 271,243 | 294,219 |
| Emp. | 80 | 105 | 119 |

DUNS 23-744-1071

## Steps to Work (Walsall) Ltd

10 Hatherton Road, Walsall, West Midlands WS1 1XS
**Fax:** 01922-622133
**Web:** www.cooptravelshop.co.uk
**Reg No:** 3738249 **Estd:** 1999 Private Limited Company
**Line of Business:** Labour recruitment and provision of personnel
**Trading Style:** Steps to Work (Walsall) Ltd
**Directors:** Ms V M Birch, M S Jhooty, P H Newland, Ms S Wakeman, Mrs S M Wood, S J Preston, R M Thomas, Ms C D Wildman
**Co. Secretary:** John Brewer

**Responsibilities**
**Senior:** Thomas Ansell *(Manager)*, David Bassett *(Director)*, Mary Clarke-Mortiboys *(Manager)*, Mandy Holcroft *(Manager)*, Ravinder Sahota *(Director)*
**Finance:** Sue Brooks *(Finance Director)*
**IT:** Sue Brooks *(Finance Director)*
**US SIC:** 7361, 8249
**UK SIC:** 83954, 93300
**Bankers:** National Westminster Bank Plc (60-22-22)

| | 31-03-14 | 31-03-13 | 31-03-12 |
|---|---|---|---|
| TO | 15,257,936 | 13,038,481 | 11,461,509 |
| P/L | (66,213) | 398,572 | 321,073 |
| NW | 1,954,418 | 1,354,631 | 1,170,059 |
| WC | 2,731,506 | 2,949,983 | 2,429,247 |
| Emp. | 90 | 86 | 88 |

DUNS 23-329-8467 **Imp**
## Steptoe & Johnson
99 Gresham Street, London EC2V 7NG
**Web:** www.steptoe.com
**Partnership**
**Line of Business:** Solicitors
**Partners:** S Moury, M Thompson
**Responsibilities**
**Senior:** Andrew Bloom *(Partner)*, Matthew Coleman *(Partner)*, Simon Collis *(Partner)*, Jeffrey Cottle *(Partner)*, Matthew Farmer *(Partner)*, Paul Marcuse *(Chief Executive)*, Brendan Patterson *(Senior Partner)*, M Shank *(Partner)*
**Finance:** Neil Diment *(Accounts Administrator)*, Julie Reeves *(Accounts Administrator)*
**HR:** Annie Swan *(HR / Personnel)*
**US SIC:** 8111 **UK SIC:** 83500
**Employees:** 65

DUNS 89-692-4826
## Ster Century (U K) Ltd
**(Subsidiary of:** Allen & Overy Llp)
Ster Century (Uk) Ltd, Granite House, 55-61 High Street, Frimley, Camberley, Surrey GU16 7HJ
**Tel:** 08702408984 **Fax:** 01276-605600
**Web:** www.stercentury.co.uk
**Reg No:** 3347110 **VAT No:** 695741194
**Estd:** 1997 Private Limited Company
**Line of Business:** Cinemas
**Issued Capital:** £24,793,740
**Directors:** S J Knibbs, A E Mcnair, J T Richards
**US SIC:** 7832 **UK SIC:** 97113
**Auditors:** PricewaterhouseCoopers LLP
**Bankers:** The Royal Bank Of Scotland Plc (16-23-15)

| | 28-11-13 | 29-11-12 | 24-11-11 |
|---|---|---|---|
| TO | 35,347,000 | 39,354,000 | 41,278,000 |
| P/L | (2,129,000) | 2,861,000 | 4,139,000 |
| NW | 35,327,000 | 37,004,000 | 35,089,000 |
| WC | 29,670,000 | 27,935,000 | 25,254,000 |
| Emp. | 369 | 377 | 420 |

DUNS 21-109-5529 **Imp**
## Sterilin Ltd
**(Subsidiary of:** Thermo Fisher Scientific Inc.)
Pen-Y-San Industrial Estate, Newport, Gwent NP11 3EF
**Fax:** 01495242242
**Web:** www.thermofisher.com
**Reg No:** 6512031 **Estd:** 2008 Private Limited Company
**Line of Business:** Manufacture of other plastic products
**Export Sales:** £7,928,000
**Issued Capital:** £5,376
**Directors:** K N Wheeler, Ms L M Grant, Ms K R Wright
**Co. Secretary:** Oakwood Corporate Secretary Limi
**Responsibilities**
**Senior:** Dilwyn Harris *(Warehouse Coordinator)*
**Admin:** Sharon Lambeth *(IS Administrator)*
**IT:** Paul Beattie *(IT Manager)*, Sharon Lambeth *(IS Administrator)*
**US SIC:** 3079 **UK SIC:** 48360
**Auditors:** PricewaterhouseCoopers LLP
**Bankers:** HSBC Bank plc (40-38-04)

| | 31-12-13 | 31-12-12 | 31-12-11 |
|---|---|---|---|
| TO | 21,500,000 | 20,993,000 | 26,074,000 |
| P/L | (1,456,000) | (2,102,000) | (4,681,000) |
| NW | 10,207,000 | 10,255,000 | (6,864,000) |
| WC | (1,757,000) | 1,576,000 | 4,157,000 |
| Emp. | 256 | 264 | 258 |

DUNS 21-590-3952
## The Sterilization & Disinfection Unit
Odstock Road, Salisbury, Wiltshire SP2 8BJ
**Tel:** 01722429213
**Web:** www.salisbury.nhs.uk
**Estd:** 2011
**Line of Business:** Hygiene and cleaning services
**Responsibilities**
**Senior:** Robert Warburton *(Manager)*
**US SIC:** 5199 **UK SIC:** 61900
**Employees:** 50

DUNS 34-637-5280 **Imp**
## Steris Ltd
**(Subsidiary of:** Steris Corporation)
Steris House, Jays Close, Viables, Basingstoke, Hampshire RG22 4AX
**Tel:** 01256840400
**Web:** www.sterislifesciences.com
**Reg No:** 2767165 **Estd:** 1987 Private Limited Company
**Line of Business:** Other wholesale
**Export Sales:** £7,208,785
**Issued Capital:** £2
**Directors:** R E Snyder, M J Tokich
**Co. Secretary:** Dennis Patton
**Responsibilities**
**Senior:** Carla Cerchio *(European Customer Svc Director)*
**Operations:** Carla Cerchio *(European Customer Svc Director)*
**Branches:** Steris Ltd, Steris House, Jays Close, Basingstoke, Hampshire RG22 4AX
**US SIC:** 5199, 3841
**UK SIC:** 61900, 37201
**Auditors:** Ernst & Young LLP
**Bankers:** Abn Amro Bank Nv (40-50-30)

| | 31-03-14 | 31-03-13 | 31-03-12 |
|---|---|---|---|
| TO | 19,552,437 | 18,440,927 | 21,282,533 |
| P/L | 641,097 | 872,420 | 228,586 |
| NW | 5,339,050 | 4,854,596 | 4,049,749 |
| WC | 5,104,454 | 4,647,030 | 3,775,365 |
| Emp. | 89 | 98 | 114 |

DUNS 21-113-8600
## Sterling 2000 (Holdings) Ltd
Sterling House, 810 Mandarin Court, Warrington, Cheshire WA1 1GG
**Tel:** 08449411111
**Reg No:** 6545164 **Estd:** 2008 Private Limited Company
**Line of Business:** Management activities of holding companies
**Issued Capital:** £400
**Directors:** I A Black, S A Mclean
**Co. Secretary:** Mrs Janene Rudge
**US SIC:** 6711 **UK SIC:** 83962
**Bankers:** The Royal Bank Of Scotland Plc (16-33-33)

| | 31-03-14 | 31-03-13 | 31-03-12 |
|---|---|---|---|
| TO | 155,503,244 | 144,419,205 | 162,458,331 |
| P/L | (166,558) | 962,341 | 1,784,587 |
| NW | 342,177 | 1,083,876 | 1,068,325 |
| WC | (1,541,855) | (240,181) | (55,349) |
| Emp. | 1,254 | 1,096 | 2,117 |

DUNS 45-805-2487 **Exp**
## Sterling Commerce (U K) Ltd
**(Subsidiary of:** International Business Machines Corporation)
3 Furzeground Way, Stockley Park, Uxbridge, Middlesex UB11 1EZ
**Tel:** 02088678000
**Web:** www.sterlingcommerce.com
**Reg No:** 3163427 **Estd:** 1996 Private Limited Company
**Line of Business:** Computer aided design
**Issued Capital:** £133
**Director:** S M Bond
**Co. Secretary:** Alison Sullivan
**Responsibilities**
**Finance:** Joseph Auman *(Financial Director)*
**US SIC:** 7379 **UK SIC:** 83940
**Auditors:** Ernst & Young
**Bankers:** Lloyds TSB Bank plc (30-91-31)

| | 30-06-13 | 30-06-12 | 30-06-11 |
|---|---|---|---|
| TO | N/A | N/A | 43,758,019 |
| P/L | N/A | N/A | 2,279,521 |
| NW | 1,835,442 | 1,835,442 | 1,835,442 |
| WC | N/A | N/A | 1,246,396 |
| Emp. | N/A | N/A | 121 |

DUNS 21-783-2150
## Sterling Exchange
45 Ludgate Hill, London EC4M 7JU
**Tel:** 02073299977
**Web:** www.sterlingexchange.co.uk
**Estd:** 2011 Partnership
**Line of Business:** Miscellaneous Financial Institutions
**Partner:** K Gunning
**US SIC:** 6111 **UK SIC:** 81501
**Employees:** 50

DUNS 39-976-7672
## Sterling Financial Print Ltd
63 Queen Victoria Street, London EC4N 4UA
**Tel:** 02076344900 **Fax:** 02077867043
**Web:** www.sterlingfp.com
**Reg No:** 2273286 **VAT No:** 524572449
**Estd:** 1988 Private Limited Company
**Line of Business:** Printing not elsewhere classified
**Issued Capital:** £409
**Principals:** J E Mccormick *(Managing)*, G M Keating, A J Moore, S W Pearson Miles, L Skyner
**Responsibilities**
**Operations:** Duncan Myers *(Production Manager)*
**US SIC:** 2752, 7399
**UK SIC:** 47544, 83954

**Auditors:** Baker Tilly UK Audit LLP
**Bankers:** The Royal Bank Of Scotland Plc (16-29-25)

| | 30-04-14 | 30-04-13 | 30-04-12 |
|---|---|---|---|
| TO | 9,019,351 | 6,881,489 | 18,264,001 |
| P/L | 1,157,116 | (391,712) | 640,733 |
| NW | 1,418,692 | 474,072 | 815,730 |
| WC | 1,244,437 | 496,506 | 627,533 |
| Emp. | 76 | 79 | 139 |

DUNS 21-582-1109 **Imp**
## Sterling Furniture Group Ltd
76 Moss Road, Tillicoultry, Clackmannanshire FK13 6NS
**Tel:** 01259-750655 **Fax:** 01259-752463
**Web:** www.sterlingfurniture.co.uk
**Reg No:** 0054090SC **VAT No:** 271464067
**Estd:** 1973 Private Limited Company
**Line of Business:** Furniture retail outlets
**Trading Style:** Sterling Furniture
**Issued Capital:** £133,699
**Directors:** Mrs I M Knowles, L A Graham, Ms S Howarth, G S Knowles
**Co. Secretary:** Gordon Mearns
**Responsibilities**
**Senior:** John Copeland *(General Manager)*
**Branches:** Sterling Furniture Group Ltd, Sterling Furniture Group Ltd, 1 Station Road, Cupar, Fife KY14 7DP
**US SIC:** 5719, 5732
**UK SIC:** 64700, 64800
**Auditors:** French Duncan LLP
**Bankers:** Bank Of Scotland (80-91-29)

| | 28-02-14 | 28-02-13 | 29-02-12 |
|---|---|---|---|
| TO | 44,891,243 | 41,151,721 | 41,721,152 |
| P/L | 808,314 | 1,101,507 | 34,544 |
| NW | 18,096,326 | 17,533,967 | 16,736,571 |
| WC | 352,643 | 921,383 | 144,982 |
| Emp. | 523 | 470 | 460 |

DUNS 21-610-1378 **Exp**
## Sterling Industries Plc
**(Subsidiary of:** Caledonia Investments P L C)
George Smith Way, Yeovil, Somerset BA22 8QR
**Tel:** 01237472339
**Web:** www.dlgroup.co.uk
**Reg No:** 0299644 **Estd:** 1935 Public Limited Company
**Line of Business:** Management activities of holding companies
**Export Markets:** U K, Rest of Europe, North America, Other countries
**Export Sales:** £55,460,000
**Trading Style:** Dl Group Building, Huntley & Sparks, Thermo
**Issued Capital:** £1,109,310
**Directors:** C H Edwards, J M Weeks, D G Hussey, M Paver, Ms S D Flanagan
**Co. Secretary:** Michael Paver
**US SIC:** 6711, 3494
**UK SIC:** 83962, 32880
**Auditors:** Deloitte LLP
**Bankers:** Barclays Bank Plc (20-99-40)

| | 31-03-14 | 31-03-13 | 31-03-12 |
|---|---|---|---|
| TO | 75,396,000 | N/A | N/A |
| P/L | 5,809,000 | 2,236,576 | (98,563) |
| NW | 21,852,000 | 8,020,756 | 8,882,566 |
| WC | 17,079,000 | (4,127,035) | (2,043,554) |
| Emp. | 444 | 4 | 4 |

DUNS 29-349-7442
## Sterling Insurance Co Ltd
**(Subsidiary of:** Sterling Insurance Group Ltd)
50 Kings Hill Avenue, Kings Hill, West Malling, Kent ME19 4JX
**Tel:** 08452711300 **Fax:** 08452711466
**Web:** www.sterlinginsurancegroup.com
**Reg No:** 0498605 **Estd:** 1952 Private Limited Company
**Line of Business:** Non-life insurance
**Issued Capital:** £25,500,000
**Principals:** E P Penollar *(Financial)*, S A Clarke, A Pritchard, J G Blundell, D K Sweeney, P E Thompson, Mrs L J Randall, S D Williams
**Co. Secretary:** Graham Rivers-Moore
**Responsibilities**
**Senior:** Brett Mcwilliam *(Director)*
**Branches:** Room 119, Il L U Building, 49 Leadenhall St, EC3A 2BE, London
**US SIC:** 6399 **UK SIC:** 82001
**Auditors:** PricewaterhouseCoopers
**Bankers:** Bank Of Scotland (12-01-03)

| | 31-12-13 | 31-12-12 | 31-12-11 |
|---|---|---|---|
| TO | 91,238,000 | 67,081,000 | 69,180,000 |
| P/L | 5,130,000 | 3,904,000 | 6,203,000 |
| NW | 33,836,000 | 35,379,000 | 35,630,000 |
| WC | 59,117,000 | 45,701,000 | 45,665,000 |

DUNS 77-467-8403
## Sterling Insurance Group Ltd
Ambassador House, Paradise Road, Richmond Upon Thames, Richmond, Surrey TW9 1SQ
**Tel:** 08702242424 **Fax:** 08702242446
**Web:** www.sterlinginsurancegroup.com
**Reg No:** 2966506 **Estd:** 1994 Private Limited Company
**Line of Business:** Management activities of holding companies
**Trading Style:** Sterling Insurance Group
**Issued Capital:** £20,450,620
**Directors:** E P Penollar, J G Blundell, J B Alexander, N Cooper, Mrs P J Cooper
**Co. Secretary:** Graham Rivers-Moore
**US SIC:** 6711 **UK SIC:** 83962
**Auditors:** PricewaterhouseCoopers LLP

| | 31-12-13 | 31-12-12 | 31-12-11 |
|---|---|---|---|
| TO | 138,642,000 | 101,006,000 | 101,768,000 |
| P/L | 7,420,000 | 5,443,000 | 4,163,000 |
| NW | 42,130,000 | 42,471,000 | 38,103,000 |
| WC | 49,625,000 | 41,466,000 | 96,602,000 |
| Emp. | 423 | 404 | 347 |

DUNS 21-925-1866
## Sterling International Brokers Ltd
**(Subsidiary of:** Bgc International Lp)
Colechurch House, London SE1 2SS
**Tel:** 02079629960 **Fax:** 02074035377
**Web:** www.sterling-int.co.uk
**Reg No:** 8400226 **Estd:** 1992 Private Limited Company
**Line of Business:** Insurance companies and agents
**Issued Capital:** £1
**Directors:** M A Cooper, A G Sadler
**US SIC:** 6211 **UK SIC:** 83100

| | 31-12-13 |
|---|---|
| TA | 1 |
| NW | 1 |

DUNS 21-824-6353 **Exp**
## Sterling International Technology Ltd
**(Subsidiary of:** Government of Dubai)
Colliery Lane, Exhall, Coventry, West Midlands CV7 9NW
**Tel:** 02476-645252 **Fax:** 02476-645312
**Web:** www.doncasters.com
**Reg No:** 0093897 **Estd:** 1907 Private Limited Company
**Line of Business:** Production of non ferrous metals
**Trading Style:** Doncaster Sterling
**Issued Capital:** £425,000
**Directors:** D Hinks, M J Schurch
**Co. Secretary:** Ian Molyneux
**Responsibilities**
**Senior:** Brendan Haffner *(General Manager)*, john mcilvenny *(Purchasing manager)*
**Finance:** K Blocksidge *(Financial Controller)*
**Sales:** john mcilvenny *(Purchasing manager)*
**US SIC:** 3339 **UK SIC:** 22470
**Bankers:** Barclays Bank Plc (20-97-78)

| | 31-12-13 | 31-12-12 | 31-12-11 |
|---|---|---|---|
| TA | 425,000 | 425,000 | 425,000 |
| NW | 425,000 | 425,000 | 425,000 |

DUNS 21-597-5493
## Sterling Motor Group
491-499 Hall Road, Norwich, Norfolk NR4 6ET
**Tel:** 01603219951
**Web:** www.busseys.co.uk
**Estd:** 1994
**Line of Business:** Car dealers (new & used)
**US SIC:** 5511 **UK SIC:** 65100
**Employees:** 50

DUNS 22-953-6701
## Sterling Pension Management Ltd
**(Subsidiary of:** Spm Employee Benefits Ltd)
City Reach, London E14 9NN
**Tel:** 02075376930 **Fax:** 02079877487
**Web:** www.sterlingpensions.co.uk
**Reg No:** 0811724 **Estd:** 1964 Private Limited Company
**Line of Business:** Insurance services
**Issued Capital:** £450,000
**Directors:** Ms S G Higgins, M Owen, R A Hulland
**Co. Secretary:** Ms Susan Giles
**US SIC:** 6411 **UK SIC:** 83200
**Auditors:** Baker Tilly
**Bankers:** Barclays Bank Plc (20-00-00)

| | 31-10-12 | 31-10-11 |
|---|---|---|
| TA | 9,729 | 17,995 |
| NW | 1,729 | 3,090 |
| WC | 1,729 | 3,090 |

DUNS 50-377-6874
## Sterling Press Ltd
**(Subsidiary of:** Seckloe 297 Ltd)
Sterling House, Kettering Parkway, Kettering Venture Park, Kettering, Northamptonshire NN15 6XU
**Tel:** 08700842100 **Fax:** 08700842099
**Web:** www.sterlingsolutions.co.uk
**Reg No:** 2386753 **VAT No:** 678826766
**Estd:** 1990 Private Limited Company
**Line of Business:** Lithographic printers
**Issued Capital:** £40,000

**Principals:** S D Pizzey (Managing), J F Pizzey
**Co. Secretary:** Steven Pizzey
**Responsibilities**
**HR:** Daniella Giammarco (Human Resources Manager)
**Health & Safety:** Jay Worsfold (Health & Safety Officer)
**Branches:** Sterling Press Ltd, Demagio Ltd, Wellingborough, Northamptonshire NN8 6UF
**US SIC:** 2752 **UK SIC:** 47544
**Auditors:** Hawsons
**Bankers:** National Westminster Bank Plc (55-70-37)

| | 31-03-14 | 31-03-13 | 31-03-12 |
|---|---|---|---|
| TO | 23,864,098 | 22,502,042 | 21,250,490 |
| P/L | 442,213 | 202,048 | 660,398 |
| NW | 2,747,485 | 2,331,715 | 2,140,689 |
| WC | (543,608) | (1,682,552) | (2,358,161) |
| Emp. | 209 | 200 | 195 |

DUNS 21-619-9310
### Sterling Ship Services
Shed, Alexandra Dock, Hull, North Humberside HU9 1TA
**Tel:** 01482326877
**Web:** www.global-shipping.co.uk
**Estd:** 2002 Partnership
**Line of Business:** Activities of other transport agencies
**Trading Style:** Sterling Ship Services
**Partner:** T Russell
**US SIC:** 4712, 4226
**UK SIC:** 77002, 77003
**Bankers:** Lloyds TSB Bank plc (30-94-44)
**Employees:** 50

DUNS 22-643-5220    Imp-Exp
### Sterling Thermal Technology Ltd
**(Subsidiary of:** Caledonia Investments P L C)
Brunel Road, Rabans Lane, Aylesbury, Buckinghamshire HP19 8TD
**Tel:** 01296-487171
**Web:** www.pcc-sterling.co.uk
**Reg No:** 1335179 **VAT No:** 564509918
**Estd:** 1924 Private Limited Company
**Line of Business:** Manufacturers of heat exchangers
**Export Markets:** Worldwide
**Trading Style:** Argo Flare Services
**Issued Capital:** £250,000
**Principals:** C R Armitage (Managing), D Stojkovic, N J Wilson, M Paver
**Co. Secretary:** Mrs Sandra Saganowski
**Responsibilities**
**Senior:** David Blunn (Manager)
**Finance:** David Blunn (Manager)
**Sales:** Steven Gomm (Sales Project Manager)
**Facilities:** Alan Crook (Production Manager)
**Operations:** Alan Crook (Production Manager)
**Engineering:** Alan Crook (Production Manager)
**Branches:** Sterling Thermal Technology Ltd, A5, Maple Road, Derby, Derbyshire DE74 2UT
**US SIC:** 3567, 5084
**UK SIC:** 32452, 61490
**Auditors:** KPMG Audit PLC
**Bankers:** Barclays Bank Plc (20-99-40)

| | 31-03-14 | 31-03-13 | 31-03-12 |
|---|---|---|---|
| TO | 16,187,945 | 20,717,231 | 14,729,444 |
| P/L | 1,066,789 | 2,890,950 | 1,450,972 |
| NW | 5,431,180 | 6,569,219 | 6,417,075 |
| WC | 3,532,520 | 4,683,087 | 4,272,022 |
| Emp. | 146 | 163 | 96 |

DUNS 50-696-2471
### Sterling Window Blinds
1 Butts Court, Leigh, Lancashire WN7 3AW
**Tel:** 01942608449
**VAT No:** 534649232 **Estd:** 2002 Partnership
**Line of Business:** Blinds and canopies
**US SIC:** 2499 **UK SIC:** 46500
**Employees:** 49

DUNS 21-925-9231
### Stermat Hardware (Gwynedd) Ltd
Holyhead Road, Gaerwen, Gwynedd LL60 6BL
**Tel:** 01248-421674
**Reg No:** 1379735 **Estd:** 1978 Private Limited Company
**Line of Business:** Other retail sale in non-specialised stores
**Issued Capital:** £1,475
**Principals:** L Ellis (Managing), Ms C W Ellis, L E Ellis, D E Ellis
**Co. Secretary:** Ms Rita Ellis
**Branches:** Stermat Hardware (Gwynedd) Ltd, London Road, Valley, Holyhead, Gwynedd LL65 3DP
**US SIC:** 5399, 5541, 5999
**UK SIC:** 65600, 65200
**Auditors:** Williams Denton Cyf

**Bankers:** HSBC Bank plc (40-09-03)

| | 31-12-13 | 31-12-12 | 31-12-11 |
|---|---|---|---|
| TO | 10,062,823 | N/A | 9,725,154 |
| P/L | 312,460 | 266,380 | 42,697 |
| NW | 2,947,701 | 2,722,286 | 2,607,571 |
| WC | 442,152 | 243,850 | 104,514 |
| Emp. | 136 | 130 | 141 |

DUNS 21-772-0617
### Sternberg & Co Solicitors
102 South Street, Romford, Essex RM1 1RX
**Web:** www.sternberg-reed.co.uk
**Estd:** 1990 Proprietorship
**Line of Business:** Solicitors
**Proprietor:** D Charnley
**US SIC:** 8111 **UK SIC:** 83500
**Employees:** 100

DUNS 23-225-5570
### Sternberg Reed
Focal House, 12-18 Station Parade, Barking, Essex IG11 8DN
**Web:** www.sternberg-reed.co.uk
**VAT No:** 283942233 **Estd:** 1984 Partnership
**Line of Business:** Solicitors
**Partners:** G Sternberg, M Gill, R Sharma, N Jeffs, J Abraham, C Redley, G Reed, Ms A Nunn
**Responsibilities**
**Senior:** Frances Anderson (Partner), Elizabeth Bendall (Partner), Colette Kelly (Partner), Soulla Kokkinos (Partner), Damian Stuart (Partner)
**US SIC:** 8111 **UK SIC:** 83500
**Bankers:** Barclays Bank Plc (20-95-61)
**Employees:** 140

DUNS 23-764-1712
### Stertil Koni (Uk) Ltd
**(Subsidiary of:** Stichting Administratiekantoor Citadel Enterprises)
Stertil House, Northampton, Northamptonshire NN4 7PW
**Tel:** 01604662049
**Web:** www.koni.stertil.co.uk
**Reg No:** 3757764 **Estd:** 1999 Private Limited Company
**Line of Business:** Garage equipment
**Trading Style:** Stertil Koni, Stertil Uk
**Issued Capital:** £2
**Director:** U Bijlsma
**Co. Secretary:** William Macsweeney
**Responsibilities**
**Marketing:** Anthony Edge (Marketing Director), Andrew Georgiou (Marketing Director)
**IT:** Nick Stewart (IT Manager)
**Purchasing:** Maria Kelly (Purchasing Manager)
**US SIC:** 3559 **UK SIC:** 32863

| | 31-12-13 | 31-12-12 | 31-12-11 |
|---|---|---|---|
| TA | 2 | 2 | 2 |
| NW | 2 | 2 | 2 |

DUNS 21-726-5206    Imp-Exp
### Stertil U K Ltd
**(Subsidiary of:** Stichting Administratiekantoor Citadel Enterprises)
Stertil House, Northampton, Northamptonshire NN4 7PW
**Tel:** 08707700471 **Fax:** 01604-765181
**Web:** www.stertiluk.com
**Reg No:** 1103855 **VAT No:** 223567566
**Estd:** 1969 Private Limited Company
**Line of Business:** Manufacturers of industrial doors
**Export Markets:** Jordan, Bahrain & Saudi Arabia
**Issued Capital:** £1,002
**Directors:** M A Paynter, U Bijlsma
**Co. Secretary:** William Macsweeney
**Responsibilities**
**Sales:** Matt Rowley (Area Sales Manager), Tim Venn (Sales Office Manager), Tracy Williamson-Graff (After Sales Manager)
**Admin:** Maria Kelly (Office Manager)
**Branches:** Stertil U K Ltd, 34 Taylor Way, Oldbury, West Midlands B69 1JP
**US SIC:** 3534, 7699, 5084
**UK SIC:** 32553, 67303, 61490
**Auditors:** Ernst & Young LLP
**Bankers:** HSBC Bank plc (40-08-19)

| | 31-12-13 | 31-12-12 | 31-12-11 |
|---|---|---|---|
| TO | 15,157,948 | 13,854,386 | 16,088,827 |
| P/L | 865,155 | 806,376 | 589,140 |
| NW | 3,126,649 | 2,471,328 | 1,868,514 |
| WC | 3,060,883 | 2,368,996 | 1,739,891 |
| Emp. | 56 | 55 | 55 |

DUNS 23-284-2633
### Steve Benton Transport
Garretts Green Industrial Estate, Bannerley Road, Birmingham, West Midlands B33 0SL
**Tel:** 0121-783-7400
**Web:** www.stevebentontransport.co.uk
**VAT No:** 580417053 **Estd:** 1999 Partnership
**Line of Business:** Road haulage and transport services
**Partners:** Mrs J Benton, S Benton

**Responsibilities**
**Senior:** Hayley Benton (Manager)
**Finance:** Sue Farmer (Accounts Manager)
**IT:** Sue Farmer (Accounts Manager)
**Health & Safety:** Anne Devin (Facilities Manager)
**Facilities:** Anne Devin (Facilities Manager)
**Branches:** Steve Benton Transport, Lanes End, Aspley Heath La, Solihull, West Midlands B94 5HU
**US SIC:** 4789 **UK SIC:** 77002
**Bankers:** National Westminster Bank Plc (51-70-30)
**Employees:** 50

DUNS 23-840-6750
### Steve Caunce Ltd
Trafalgar House, Collins Industrial Estate, Merton Bank R, St Helens, Merseyside WA9 1HY
**Tel:** 01744-746860 **Fax:** 01744746861
**Web:** www.stevecaunce.co.uk
**Reg No:** 3832338 **VAT No:** 748315028
**Estd:** 1999 Private Limited Company
**Line of Business:** Drainage contractors
**Issued Capital:** £2
**Directors:** Ms L Caunce, S R Caunce
**Responsibilities**
**Senior:** Sheila Frodsham (Manager)
**US SIC:** 4952 **UK SIC:** 92120

| | 31-05-14 | 31-05-13 | 31-05-12 |
|---|---|---|---|
| TA | 902,818 | 881,704 | 855,075 |
| NW | 439,575 | 418,269 | 409,978 |
| WC | 128,386 | 109,874 | 87,745 |

DUNS 49-109-1914
### Steve Hoskin Construction Ltd
Pensilva Industrial Estate, St Ive Road, Liskeard, Cornwall PL14 5RE
**Tel:** 01579362630
**Web:** www.shc-ltd.co.uk
**Reg No:** 3096602 **Estd:** 1995 Private Limited Company
**Line of Business:** Civil engineers
**Issued Capital:** £2
**Principals:** S R Hoskin (Managing), N Hoskin, Mrs C Worden
**Co. Secretary:** Mrs Charlotte Worden
**US SIC:** 8911, 1611
**UK SIC:** 83701, 50200
**Auditors:** Dawe Hawken & Dodd

| | 30-09-13 | 30-09-12 | 30-09-11 |
|---|---|---|---|
| TO | 25,494,550 | 17,635,204 | 15,831,676 |
| P/L | 1,925,198 | 883,702 | 852,328 |
| NW | 4,794,422 | 3,370,101 | 2,764,615 |
| WC | 2,343,135 | 1,090,676 | 1,171,797 |
| Emp. | 175 | 138 | 121 |

DUNS 22-925-3125    Imp-Exp
### Steve Orr Ltd
1 Banbridge Road Quillyburn Business, Park, Dromore, Co Down BT25 1BY
**Tel:** 028-9269-9020
**Web:** www.upuindustries.com
**Reg No:** 0012419NI **VAT No:** 681445719
**Estd:** 1977 Private Limited Company
**Line of Business:** Ropes and cables
**Export Markets:** Europe and Far East
**Trading Style:** Steve Orr Ltd
**Issued Capital:** £44,175
**Directors:** P S Orr, Ms D Orr, A Leatham, C S Orr
**Co. Secretary:** Brian Doyle
**Responsibilities**
**Marketing:** Tony Foran (Senior Marketing Executive)
**IT:** Mark Leesom (Senior IT Executive)
**HR:** Steven Hoakes (Human Resources Manager), Carrie Nesbitt (Human Resources Manager)
**US SIC:** 2298 **UK SIC:** 43960
**Auditors:** Coopers & Lybrand
**Bankers:** Northern Bank Ltd (95-01-47)

| | 30-09-14 | 30-09-13 | 30-09-12 |
|---|---|---|---|
| TO | 15,783,079 | 17,845,938 | 18,555,706 |
| P/L | 764,108 | 1,378,172 | 1,363,359 |
| NW | 11,660,718 | 11,715,451 | 12,415,102 |
| WC | 5,861,459 | 5,660,154 | 5,693,841 |
| Emp. | 101 | 108 | 104 |

DUNS 50-338-1410    Exp
### Steve Porter Transport Ltd
**(Subsidiary of:** Sph (Iw) Ltd)
Dallimore House, Somerton Industrial Par, Cowes, Isle of Wight PO31 8PB
**Tel:** 01983291732
**Web:** www.steveportertransport.com
**Reg No:** 2362199 **Estd:** 1981 Private Limited Company
**Line of Business:** Activities of other transport agencies
**Export Markets:** E E C countries.
**Issued Capital:** £500
**Principals:** S P Porter (Managing), T P Porter
**Co. Secretary:** Malcolm Gibson
**Responsibilities**
**Senior:** Mark Breakey (Depot Manager), David Groves (Depot General Manager)

**Sales:** Nick Kirkby (Business Development Manager)
**Branches:** Steve Porter Transport Ltd, Unit 2, Jackson Close, Portsmouth, Hampshire PO6 1UR
**US SIC:** 4712, 4226
**UK SIC:** 77002, 77003
**Auditors:** Ken Baugh
**Bankers:** Barclays Bank Plc (20-60-55)

| | 30-04-14 | 30-04-13 | 30-04-12 |
|---|---|---|---|
| TO | 8,097,476 | 7,245,015 | 7,789,637 |
| P/L | 145,437 | 68,668 | (57,243) |
| NW | 884,688 | 774,454 | 720,386 |
| WC | 844,927 | 735,821 | 659,743 |
| Emp. | 56 | 62 | 72 |

DUNS 23-271-0876
### Steve Soult Ltd
Byron Avenue, Lowmoor Business Park, Kirkby-, Kirkby-In-Ashfield, Sutton-In-Ashfield, Nottinghamshire NG17 7LA
**Web:** www.stevesoult.com
**Reg No:** 4342885 **Estd:** 2002 Private Limited Company
**Line of Business:** Funeral directors
**Issued Capital:** £200
**Directors:** G Soult, S B Soult
**Co. Secretary:** Mrs Anthea Henshaw
**Responsibilities**
**Senior:** Steven Bingley (Manager)
**US SIC:** 2499 **UK SIC:** 46500

| | 30-11-13 | 30-11-12 | 30-11-11 |
|---|---|---|---|
| TA | 844,544 | 741,493 | 688,083 |
| NW | 172,232 | 120,194 | 63,134 |
| WC | 93,895 | 49,032 | 10,399 |

DUNS 73-850-9210
### Steve Walker Bodyshop Ltd.
13 Inchmuir Road, Whitehill Industrial Estate, Bathgate, West Lothian EH48 2EP
**Web:** www.stevewalkersbodyshop.com
**Reg No:** 0266708SC **VAT No:** 416016391
**Estd:** 2004 Private Limited Company
**Line of Business:** Car body repairers
**Issued Capital:** £2
**Managing Director:** G S Walker
**Co. Secretary:** Jean Walker
**US SIC:** 7539 **UK SIC:** 67100

| | 31-05-14 | 31-05-13 | 31-05-12 |
|---|---|---|---|
| TA | 211,115 | 251,353 | 255,734 |
| NW | 79,949 | 117,264 | 98,964 |
| WC | 57,469 | 89,831 | 75,866 |

DUNS 23-344-8997    Imp
### Steven Cavanagh
48 Lynch Lane, Weymouth, Dorset DT4 9DN
**Tel:** 08006350021
**Web:** www.treds.co.uk
**Estd:** 1996 Proprietorship
**Line of Business:** Retail sale of footwear
**Proprietor:** S Cavanagh
**Branches:** Steven Cavanagh, 24 King St, Truro, Cornwall TR1 2RQ
**US SIC:** 5661 **UK SIC:** 64600
**Bankers:** National Westminster Bank Plc (60-23-35)
**Employees:** 100

DUNS 21-042-1936
### Steven Eagell Toyota
Merton Drive, Milton Keynes, Buckinghamshire MK6 4AG
**Tel:** 01908248888
**Web:** www.steveneagelltoyota.co.uk
**Estd:** 2002 Proprietorship
**Line of Business:** Car dealers (new & used)
**Proprietor:** D Sheriff
**Responsibilities**
**Senior:** Aaron Henry (Parts Manager)
**Sales:** Ishfaq Hussain (Sales Manager)
**US SIC:** 5511 **UK SIC:** 65100
**Employees:** 70

DUNS 23-644-0186
### Stevenage Borough Council
Daneshill House, Danestrete, Stevenage, Hertfordshire SG1 1HN
**Tel:** 01438242242
**Web:** www.stevenage.gov.uk
**Estd:** 1975
**Line of Business:** Local government
**Principals:** D Cook (Financial), I Paske, H Miller, M Mccardle, N Parry, I Paske, G Johnstone, G Johnstone
**Responsibilities**
**Senior:** Michael McCardle (Principal), Deborah Walters (Children's Centre Manager)
**Finance:** Carolyn Keil (Admin and Finance Officer)
**Marketing:** Henry Lewis (IT Manager), Karen Swift (?Head of Strategy)
**Admin:** Karen Bryce (Administrator), Sue Crane (Administrator), Carolyn Keil (Admin and Finance Officer)
**IT:** Henry Lewis (IT Manager), Peter Wain (Senior IT Executive)
**HR:** Dee Williams (Head of Personnel)
**Purchasing:** Zoe Harriss (Purchasing Manager)

**Branches:** Stevenage Borough Council, 2-6 The Hyde, Stevenage, Hertfordshire SG2 9SE
**US SIC:** 9121 **UK SIC:** 91110
**Employees:** 500

DUNS 21-812-2073
## Stevenage Delivery Office
London Road, Stevenage, Hertfordshire SG1 1AA
**Tel:** 01438767025
**Web:** www.royalmail.com
**Estd:** 2012
**Line of Business:** Goods delivery services
**Trading Style:** Royal Mail
**Responsibilities**
**Senior:** Simon Reat (Manager), Derick Remington (General Manager)
**US SIC:** 4213 **UK SIC:** 72300
**Employees:** 350

DUNS 21-601-1268
## Stevenage Fire Station
St Georges Way, Stevenage, Hertfordshire SG1 1HS
**Tel:** 01438202500
**Web:** www.hertscc.gov.uk
**Estd:** 1967 Partnership
**Line of Business:** Fire stations
**Partners:** I Parkhouse, T Robinson
**US SIC:** 9224 **UK SIC:** 91400
**Employees:** 60

DUNS 53-640-6499
## Stevenage Leisure Ltd
Stevenage Leisure Centre, Lytton Way, Stevenage, Hertfordshire SG1 1LZ
**Tel:** 01438242267 **Fax:** 01438-242675
**Web:** www.stevenage-leisure.co.uk
**Reg No:** 3446357 **Estd:** 1998 Private Limited Company
**Line of Business:** Leisure centres
**Directors:** Ms Y Rugg, S Crudgington, I L Morton, I D Paske, D M Williams, Mrs J M Salisbury, Ms J L Ransom
**Responsibilities**
**Senior:** Roselyn Hawkes (Manager), Allan Prescott (Operations Manager), Paul Raine (Board member)
**Finance:** Natalie Bennett (Financial Director)
**Marketing:** Paul Russ (Marketing Manager)
**HR:** Donna Radics (Human Resources Manager)
**Branches:** Stevenage Leisure Ltd, Fairlands Valley Sailing Centre, Six Hills Way, Stevenage, Hertfordshire SG2 0BL
**US SIC:** 7999, 6531
**UK SIC:** 97913, 83400
**Auditors:** Wagstaffs
**Bankers:** HSBC Bank plc (40-43-36)

|     | 31-03-14 | 31-03-13 | 31-03-12 |
|-----|---------|---------|---------|
| TO | 18,035,668 | 17,411,121 | 15,637,303 |
| P/L | 51,209 | 86,917 | 120,187 |
| NW | 306,261 | 504,052 | (1,368,865) |
| WC | (976,270) | (1,094,454) | (718,449) |
| Emp. | 914 | 910 | 839 |

DUNS 34-740-6613
## Stevenage Sheet Metal Co. Ltd
Unit 1 Jubilee Road Jubilee Trade Centre, Letchworth, Hertfordshire SG6 1SP
**Tel:** 01462674794 **Fax:** 01462-481132
**Web:** www.stevenagesheetmetal.net
**Reg No:** 2782093 **VAT No:** 632352170
**Estd:** 1993 Private Limited Company
**Line of Business:** Manufacture of metal structures and parts of structures
**Issued Capital:** £1,000
**Directors:** Ms M A Byatt, G M Byatt
**Co. Secretary:** Wkh Company Services Limited
**US SIC:** 3499 **UK SIC:** 31694
**Auditors:** Asley Clarke & Associates Ltd
**Bankers:** Barclays Bank Plc (20-41-12)

|     | 31-01-14 | 31-01-13 | 31-01-12 |
|-----|---------|---------|---------|
| TA | 2,421,615 | 2,731,605 | 3,025,378 |
| NW | 1,561,303 | 1,496,509 | 1,369,336 |
| WC | 404,499 | 376,005 | 323,412 |

DUNS 73-790-6698
## Stevens & Bolton Llp
Wey House, Farnham Road, Guildford, Surrey GU1 4YD
**Tel:** 01483-302264
**Web:** www.stevens-bolton.co.uk
**Reg No:** 0306955OC **Estd:** 1870 Limited Partnership
**Line of Business:** Solicitors
**Trading Style:** Stevens & Bolton Llp
**Responsibilities**
**Senior:** Joseph Bedford (Non-designated Limited Liabili), Helen Boddy (Non-designated Limited Liabili), Garry Brett (Partner), Nicola Broadhurst (Partner), Andrew Bussy (Partner), Tim Carter (Partner), Stephanie Dale (Non-designated Limited Liabili), Gustaf Duhs (Non-designated Limited Liabili), Beverley Flynn (Partner), Kerry Garcia-Deleito (Non-

designated Limited Liabili), Caroline Gordon Smith (Non-designated Limited Liabili), Nicola Harries (Non-designated Limited Liabili), Paul Lambdin (Non-designated Limited Liabili), Howard Lupton (Non-designated Limited Liabili), Richard Mumford (Non-designated Limited Liabili), Jennifer Robertson (Non-designated Limited Liabili), James Waddell (Non-designated Limited Liabili)
**Marketing:** Laura Reynolds (Marketing Manager)
**Sales:** Laura Reynolds (Marketing Manager)
**IT:** A Robins (IT Manager)
**Operations:** Adrian Bourne (Chief Operating Officer)
**US SIC:** 8111 **UK SIC:** 83500
**Auditors:** Nexia Smith & Williamson
**Bankers:** HSBC Bank plc (40-22-26)

|     | 30-04-14 | 30-04-13 | 30-04-12 |
|-----|---------|---------|---------|
| TO | 19,801,000 | 17,974,000 | 17,614,000 |
| P/L | 4,638,000 | 4,087,000 | 3,923,000 |
| NW | 5,156,000 | 4,523,000 | 4,300,000 |
| WC | 7,730,000 | 7,343,000 | 7,657,000 |
| Emp. | 173 | 124 | 158 |

DUNS 21-694-4504
## Stevens & Carlotti Ltd
Pembroke Works, Ramsgate Road, Sandwich, Kent CT13 9ST
**Fax:** 01304-614-636
**Web:** www.stevens-and-carlotti.co.uk
**Reg No:** 0916841 **VAT No:** 201405824
**Estd:** 2003 Private Limited Company
**Line of Business:** Fabricated metal products
**Export Sales:** £398,381
**Issued Capital:** £100,000
**Directors:** C Johnston, S P Carlotti
**Co. Secretary:** Marco Carlotti
**Responsibilities**
**Senior:** Giancarlo Carlotti (Joint Managing Director)
**Finance:** Franco Carlotti (Finance Director)
**IT:** Giancarlo Carlotti (Joint Managing Director)
**Health & Safety:** Ann Carlotti (Joint Managing Director)
**Purchasing:** Giancarlo Carlotti (Joint Managing Director)
**US SIC:** 3441 **UK SIC:** 32042
**Auditors:** Reeves & Co LLP
**Bankers:** National Westminster Bank Plc (60-18-34)

|     | 30-09-13 | 30-09-12 | 30-09-11 |
|-----|---------|---------|---------|
| TO | 6,052,979 | 9,000,716 | 7,755,817 |
| P/L | 446,645 | 1,481,287 | 1,309,043 |
| NW | 3,409,206 | 3,487,561 | 2,778,221 |
| WC | 2,521,108 | 2,362,826 | 1,545,057 |
| Emp. | 99 | 96 | 83 |

DUNS 22-512-9253
## Stevens Drake
117-119 High Street, Crawley, West Sussex RH10 1DD
**Tel:** 01293527855
**Web:** www.stevensdrake.com
**VAT No:** 315704968 **Estd:** 1780 Partnership
**Line of Business:** Solicitors
**Trading Style:** Ststevens Drake Solicitors
**Partners:** J Drake, G Penn, A Mitchell
**US SIC:** 8111 **UK SIC:** 83500
**Bankers:** Barclays Bank Plc (20-23-97)
**Employees:** 90

DUNS 22-502-1393     Imp
## Stevens-Hatherley Holdings Ltd
212 Hatherley Road, Cheltenham, Gloucestershire GL51 6ET
**Tel:** 01242240700 **Fax:** 01242-240750
**Web:** www.simplybetterlaundry.com
**Reg No:** 1055871 **VAT No:** 366209839
**Estd:** 1972 Private Limited Company
**Line of Business:** Laundries
**Trading Style:** Paragon Laundry, Westgate Motors
**Issued Capital:** £21,420
**Directors:** J R Stevens, Ms C E Williamson, Mrs A C Edwards, D I Stevens, R A Stevens
**Co. Secretary:** Anthony Priestley
**Responsibilities**
**Marketing:** Richard Taverner (Sales & Marketing Director)
**Sales:** Richard Taverner (Sales & Marketing Director)
**HR:** David Munday (Human Resources Manager)
**Health & Safety:** Richard Langhorn (Health & Safety Officer)
**Branches:** Stevens-Hatherley Holdings Ltd, Netherton Road, Ross-On-Wye, Herefordshire HR9 7QQ
**US SIC:** 7219 **UK SIC:** 98110
**Auditors:** Pitt Godden & Taylor
**Bankers:** Lloyds TSB Bank plc (30-91-87)

|     | 28-09-13 | 29-09-12 | 01-09-11 |
|-----|---------|---------|---------|
| TO | 29,317,248 | 27,199,846 | 25,225,031 |
| P/L | 917,529 | 939,856 | 1,571,217 |
| NW | 10,478,520 | 10,135,576 | 9,334,054 |
| WC | 1,655,189 | 1,142,467 | 623,444 |
| Emp. | 656 | 618 | 600 |

DUNS 55-079-3996
## Stevens Hewlett & Perkins
1 St Augustines Place, Bristol, Avon BS1 4UD
**Tel:** 01179-226007
**Web:** www.shandp.com
**Estd:** 1989 Partnership
**Line of Business:** Activities of patent and copyright agents
**Partners:** A D Marples, I Smith, S Wilkinson
**Responsibilities**
**Senior:** David Marles (Partner)
**IT:** Tony Acres (IT Manager)
**HR:** Sian Orchard (Human Resources Manager)
**US SIC:** 7399, 8111
**UK SIC:** 83954, 83500
**Employees:** 50

DUNS 21-568-1925
## Stevens (Scotland) Ltd
Denburn Way, Brechin, Angus DD9 7DW
**Tel:** 01356625111 **Fax:** 01356623755
**Web:** www.stevensscotland.co.uk
**Reg No:** 0066731SC **VAT No:** 296966481
**Estd:** 1969 Private Limited Company
**Line of Business:** Blinds and canopies
**Trading Style:** Chris Craft, Sun Vista
**Issued Capital:** £42,000
**Principals:** G W Stevens (Managing), Mrs P M Stevens
**Responsibilities**
**Senior:** Angie Johnson (Warehouse Manager)
**Marketing:** Ray Elsworth (Marketing Manager)
**Sales:** Karl Burn (Area sales manager), Anita Burnett (Sales Manager), Ray Elsworth (Marketing Manager), Damon Elsworth (Area sales manager), Michelle Hagen (Area Sales Manager), Tim Wise (Area Sales Manager)
**IT:** Gordon Livingstone (IT Manager), Wayne Owen (Computer Manager)
**Operations:** Angie Johnson (Warehouse Manager)
**Branches:** Stevens (Scotland) Ltd, Unit 5 Govan Workspace, 6 Harmony Row, Glasgow, Lanarkshire G51 3BA
**US SIC:** 2599, 5719
**UK SIC:** 46720, 64700
**Auditors:** Henderson Loggie
**Bankers:** Bank Of Scotland (80-12-66)

|     | 31-12-13 | 31-12-12 | 31-12-11 |
|-----|---------|---------|---------|
| TO | 6,646,187 | N/A | N/A |
| P/L | 308,068 | N/A | N/A |
| NW | 2,401,798 | 2,316,232 | 2,079,814 |
| WC | 1,426,025 | 1,699,288 | 1,493,904 |
| Emp. | 97 | N/A | N/A |

DUNS 21-659-9775
## Stevensdrake Ltd
117-119 High Street, Crawley, West Sussex RH10 1DD
**Tel:** 01293596900 **Fax:** 01293596968
**Web:** www.stevensdrake.com
**Reg No:** 7159192 **Estd:** 2010 Private Limited Company
**Line of Business:** Solicitors
**Trading Style:** Stevensdrake Ltd
**Issued Capital:** £48
**Directors:** J P Lovatt, I M Price, G J Pickering, M K Patel, A G Mitchell, G P Penn
**Co. Secretary:** Stevensdrake Company Secretaries
**Responsibilities**
**Senior:** Mark O' Halloran (Partner)
**US SIC:** 8111 **UK SIC:** 83500

|     | 31-03-14 | 31-03-13 | 31-03-12 |
|-----|---------|---------|---------|
| TA | 2,394,815 | 1,949,480 | 1,970,184 |
| NW | 29,363 | 35,814 | (95,811) |
| WC | 675,896 | 73,681 | (410,695) |

DUNS 21-582-3378
## Stevenson Bros.(Avonbridge)Ltd
Blackstone Road, Falkirk, Stirlingshire FK1 2NB
**Tel:** 01324861331
**Web:** www.stevensonbros.co.uk
**Reg No:** 0060051SC **VAT No:** 272032393
**Estd:** 1948 Private Limited Company
**Line of Business:** Freight transport by road not elsewhere classified
**Issued Capital:** £329,591
**Principals:** J Stevenson (Managing), W D Stevenson, Mrs J C Hunter, W Stevenson
**Co. Secretary:** Ms Jennifer Hunter
**Responsibilities**
**Marketing:** Jackie Mccall (IT Manager)
**Admin:** Ena Stevenson (Office Manager)
**IT:** Jackie Mccall (IT Manager)
**Health & Safety:** Ena Stevenson (Office Manager)
**Operations:** Jackie Mccall (IT Manager)
**US SIC:** 4213 **UK SIC:** 72300
**Auditors:** A S Fisher & Co

**Bankers:** The Royal Bank Of Scotland Plc (83-20-32)

|     | 31-12-13 | 31-12-12 | 31-12-11 |
|-----|---------|---------|---------|
| TO | 9,387,434 | 9,032,258 | 8,867,638 |
| P/L | 91,005 | 239,520 | 113,263 |
| NW | 556,503 | 536,511 | 367,491 |
| WC | (64,632) | (97,390) | (64,968) |
| Emp. | 88 | 83 | 79 |

DUNS 23-217-1736
## Stevenson College
Bankhead Avenue, Edinburgh, Midlothian EH11 4DE
**Tel:** 01315354600
**Web:** www.stevenson.ac.uk
**Estd:** 1974
**Line of Business:** Further education schools and colleges
**Trading Style:** Edinburgh College
**Directors:** Ms S Bird, M Leech
**Responsibilities**
**Senior:** Mandy Axley (Principal), Ian McKay (Chairman)
**Admin:** Heather Sutherland (Head of Section, Administratio)
**IT:** Iain Summers (PC Manager)
**HR:** Sheena Cunningham (Training Manager)
**Facilities:** Dave Keen (Estates Manager)
**Branches:** Stevenson College, 4 Duncan Place, Edinburgh, Midlothian EH6 8HW
**US SIC:** 8221, 8249
**UK SIC:** 93100, 93300
**Auditors:** Scott Moncrieff
**Bankers:** The Royal Bank Of Scotland Plc (83-03-10)
**Employees:** 600
**Turnover:** £17,891,000

DUNS 34-679-5706
## Stevenswood Ltd
14 Grange Road, Houstoun Industrial Estate, Livingston, West Lothian EH54 5DE
**Tel:** 01506438111
**Web:** www.stevenswood.co.uk
**Reg No:** 0286404SC **Estd:** 2005 Private Limited Company
**Line of Business:** Manufacturers of window frames
**Issued Capital:** £100
**Directors:** D W Taylor, D Murray, M Mcgarvie, D P Pearson, P Graham, M Linden
**Co. Secretary:** Ronald Hepburn
**Responsibilities**
**IT:** Alan Weir (IT Manager)
**Branches:** Stevenswood Ltd, Unit 1 Glencairn Industrial Estate, Kilmarnock, Ayrshire KA1 4BD
**US SIC:** 3442, 3079
**UK SIC:** 31420, 48360

|     | 31-10-13 | 31-10-12 | 31-10-11 |
|-----|---------|---------|---------|
| TO | 9,885,593 | N/A | N/A |
| P/L | 594,050 | N/A | N/A |
| NW | 854,898 | 596,145 | 459,139 |
| WC | (421,913) | (109,512) | (189,383) |
| Emp. | 93 | N/A | N/A |

DUNS 36-816-2806
## Steves Private Hire
49 Market Square, St Neots, Cambridgeshire PE19 2AR
**Web:** www.stevescarsales.co.uk
**Estd:** 1996 Proprietorship
**Line of Business:** Taxis and private hire vehicles
**Proprietor:** S Woodham
**US SIC:** 4121, 5521, 7539
**UK SIC:** 72200, 65100, 67100
**Bankers:** Barclays Bank Plc (20-43-63)
**Employees:** 100

DUNS 21-014-5053
## Steve's Taxis
27 High Street, Huntingdon, Cambridgeshire PE29 3TA
**Tel:** 01480413222
**Estd:** 2002 Proprietorship
**Line of Business:** Taxis and private hire vehicles
**Proprietor:** S Woodham
**Responsibilities**
**Senior:** Vicky Woodham (Manager)
**US SIC:** 4121 **UK SIC:** 72200
**Employees:** 60

DUNS 21-129-2766
## Stevro Ltd
Dewsbury Mills, Thornhill Road, Dewsbury, West Yorkshire WF12 9QE
**Tel:** 01924666633 **Fax:** 08447365731
**Web:** www.jaybe.com
**Reg No:** 6636595 **Estd:** 2008 Private Limited Company
**Line of Business:** Manufacturers of household furnishings
**Trading Style:** Jaybe
**Issued Capital:** £100

**Directors:** S M Durrans, R E Durrans, Mrs R E Durrans
**Co. Secretary:** Mrs Rosemary Durrans
**Responsibilities**
**Senior:** Gregory Durrans *(Director)*
**HR:** Gregory Durrans *(Director)*
**US SIC:** 2517 **UK SIC:** 46714

| | 24-08-13 | 25-08-12 | 27-08-11 |
|---|---|---|---|
| TO | 6,444,557 | 6,097,338 | N/A |
| P/L | 591,141 | 447,235 | N/A |
| NW | 365,446 | 265,621 | (107,822) |
| WC | 72,309 | 96,203 | 109,634 |

DUNS 21-579-4116 Imp-Exp

## Stewart-Buchanan Gauges Ltd

Burnside Industrial Estate 7 Garden, Glasgow, Lanarkshire G65 9JX
**Tel:** 01236-821533
**Web:** www.stewarts-group.com
**Reg No:** 0021724SC **VAT No:** 552546146
**Estd:** 1870 Private Limited Company
**Line of Business:** Manufacture of non-electronic instruments and appliances for measuring, checking, testing, navigating and other purposes, except industrial process control equipment
**Export Markets:** Worldwide
**Issued Capital:** £17,002
**Principals:** F Phair *(Managing)*, H B Service, C J Phair, S Nicol, J J Borsos, J O'Donnell, Miss L P Kelman
**Co. Secretary:** Miss Lynne Kelman
**Responsibilities**
**Senior:** Catherine Phair *(Manager)*, Stuart Tominey *(Director)*, Eddie Weldon *(Purchasing Manager)*
**IT:** Robert Baird *(IT Manager)*
**HR:** Jim Hamilton *(Human Resources Manager)*
**Health & Safety:** Jim Hamilton *(Human Resources Manager)*
**Operations:** Jim Hamilton *(Human Resources Manager)*
**Purchasing:** Eddie Weldon *(Purchasing Manager)*
**US SIC:** 3829, 3494
**UK SIC:** 37100, 32880
**Auditors:** Scott-Moncrieff
**Bankers:** The Royal Bank Of Scotland Plc (83-54-60)

| | 31-12-13 | 31-12-12 | 31-12-11 |
|---|---|---|---|
| TO | 10,596,821 | 8,719,763 | 7,456,662 |
| P/L | 813,338 | 697,689 | 370,607 |
| NW | 5,490,534 | 2,707,243 | 2,147,076 |
| WC | 3,172,110 | 2,398,056 | 2,296,972 |
| Emp. | 159 | 152 | 149 |

DUNS 21-585-9803

## The Stewart Community Mental Health Team

5 Ardencraig Road, Glasgow, Lanarkshire G45 0EQ
**Tel:** 01416345430
**Estd:** 2011 Proprietorship
**Line of Business:** Health authorities
**Proprietor:** Ms S Pettigrew
**Responsibilities**
**Senior:** Audrey Mcann *(Manager)*
**US SIC:** 9121 **UK SIC:** 91110
**Employees:** 50

DUNS 21-011-0433 Imp-Exp

## Stewart Fraser Ltd

Stewart Fraser Ltd, Henwood Industrial Estate, Ashford, Kent TN24 8DT
**Web:** www.stewartfraser.com
**Reg No:** 0392490 **VAT No:** 201170336
**Estd:** 1945 Private Limited Company
**Line of Business:** Manufacture of builders carpentry and joinery of metal
**Export Markets:** Europe
**Export Sales:** £42,695
**Issued Capital:** £340,900
**Principals:** A S Fraser *(Managing)*, D J Hale, P Saint, C Brimson, Ms J C Fraser
**Co. Secretary:** Clive Croucher
**US SIC:** 3442, 3534
**UK SIC:** 31420, 32553
**Auditors:** Spain Brothers & Co
**Bankers:** Lloyds TSB Bank plc (30-90-28)

| | 31-03-14 | 31-03-13 | 31-03-12 |
|---|---|---|---|
| TO | 5,669,906 | 4,833,949 | 5,702,581 |
| P/L | 116,289 | 36,079 | (587,780) |
| NW | 1,865,622 | 1,701,701 | 1,622,439 |
| WC | 877,133 | 298,952 | 239,421 |
| Emp. | 68 | 66 | 61 |

DUNS 29-280-9530

## Stewart Longton Caravans Ltd

Friday Street, Chorley, Lancashire PR6 0AH
**Tel:** 01257279921 **Fax:** 01257-241877
**Web:** www.stewartlongton.co.uk
**Reg No:** 1563648 **VAT No:** 350085578
**Estd:** 1971 Private Limited Company
**Line of Business:** Sale of new motor vehicles
**Trading Style:** Longton Stewart (Chorley)caravans, Longton Stewart Aprilia
**Issued Capital:** £10,000
**Principals:** W A Hall *(Chairman)*, G D Hall *(Managing)*, S W Hall, P C Hall
**Co. Secretary:** Mrs Linda Smith
**Branches:** Stewart Longton Caravans Ltd, Bengal Street, Chorley, Lancashire PR7 1SA
**US SIC:** 5511, 5999, 6711
**UK SIC:** 65100, 65600, 83962
**Auditors:** Haworth Moore
**Bankers:** Yorkshire Bank Plc (05-02-57)

| | 31-01-14 | 31-01-13 | 31-01-12 |
|---|---|---|---|
| TO | 13,395,990 | 13,142,274 | 13,218,124 |
| P/L | 257,143 | 205,113 | 128,270 |
| NW | 2,785,411 | 2,720,757 | 2,633,347 |
| WC | 1,119,323 | 1,048,218 | 946,888 |
| Emp. | 60 | 61 | 61 |

DUNS 22-885-2885 Imp

## Stewart McConnell Ltd

10-12 William Street, Cookstown, Co Tyrone BT80 8NB
**Tel:** 02886-762341 **Fax:** 02886-766611
**Reg No:** 0019414NI **VAT No:** 252432485
**Estd:** 1884 Private Limited Company
**Line of Business:** Footwear retailers
**Trading Style:** McConnells Stores
**Issued Capital:** £333
**Directors:** Ms D R Mcconnell, J Mcconnell
**Branches:** Stewart Mcconnell Ltd, 16-18 William Street, Cookstown, Co Tyrone BT80 8NB
**US SIC:** 5661, 5699
**UK SIC:** 64600, 64500
**Bankers:** Northern Bank Ltd (95-02-82)

| | 30-04-14 | 30-04-13 | 30-04-12 |
|---|---|---|---|
| TA | 872,524 | 953,951 | 916,058 |
| NW | 470,850 | 467,726 | 498,707 |
| WC | 47,646 | 33,153 | 48,425 |

DUNS 21-583-7022

## Stewart McNee (Dunoon) Ltd

20 Highland Avenue Sandbank Business, Park, Dunoon, Argyll PA23 8PB
**Tel:** 01369-702578 **Fax:** 01369706318
**Web:** www.stewartmcnee.com
**Reg No:** 0080175SC **VAT No:** 264719144
**Estd:** 1973 Private Limited Company
**Line of Business:** Development and selling of real estate
**Issued Capital:** £30,000
**Director:** Ms A B Mcnee
**Co. Secretary:** Ian Mcnee
**Responsibilities**
**Senior:** Ian McNee *(Managing Director)*
**Finance:** Ian McNee *(Managing Director)*
**Health & Safety:** Ian McNee *(Managing Director)*
**Facilities:** Ian McNee *(Managing Director)*
**US SIC:** 6552 **UK SIC:** 85000
**Auditors:** Campbell Dallas LLP
**Bankers:** Bank Of Scotland (80-91-27)

| | 30-06-14 | 31-12-13 | 30-06-12 |
|---|---|---|---|
| TO | 2,415,689 | 5,245,270 | 5,909,651 |
| P/L | 172,378 | (436,322) | 176,645 |
| NW | 827,604 | 717,926 | 1,268,864 |
| WC | 968,489 | 590,060 | 884,800 |
| Emp. | 55 | 64 | 70 |

DUNS 21-454-0858

## Stewart Miller & Sons Ltd

40 Main Street, Bangor, Co Down BT20 5AG
**Tel:** 02891270108 **Fax:** 028-9127-0108
**Web:** www.toymaster.co.uk
**Reg No:** 0007419NI **VAT No:** 252211115
**Estd:** 1917 Private Limited Company
**Line of Business:** Retail of games and toys
**Trading Style:** Stewart Miller
**Issued Capital:** £46,667
**Directors:** Ms S Jackson, Ms S M Leeming, R V Weatherup, P S Miller, M S Miller, S Miller
**Co. Secretary:** Ms Susan Jackson
**Branches:** Stewart Miller & Sons Ltd, Flagship Centre, Main Street, Bangor, Co Down BT20 5AU
**US SIC:** 5941, 5942
**UK SIC:** 65400, 65300
**Auditors:** Opus
**Bankers:** Northern Bank Ltd (95-02-52)

| | 28-02-14 | 28-02-13 | 29-02-12 |
|---|---|---|---|
| TA | 1,865,041 | 2,053,720 | 2,179,481 |
| NW | 1,424,680 | 1,519,079 | 1,602,720 |
| WC | 237,265 | 293,310 | 330,020 |

DUNS 21-581-7818

## Stewart Milne Group Ltd

Peregrine House, Mosscroft Avenue, Westhill Industrial Estate, Westhill, Aberdeenshire AB32 6JQ
**Tel:** 01224747000
**Web:** www.stewartmilne.com
**Reg No:** 0057709SC **VAT No:** 296869477
**Estd:** 1975 Private Limited Company
**Line of Business:** Construction of commercial buildings
**Issued Capital:** £180,400
**Principals:** S Milne *(Chairman and Managing)*, G F Allison *(Financial)*, J Slater Fearn, J C Irvine, A Goodfellow
**Co. Secretary:** Scott Martin
**Responsibilities**
**Senior:** Stuart Oag *(Manager)*
**Marketing:** Mike Cowie *(Group Sales & Marketing Manage)*
**Sales:** Mike Cowie *(Group Sales & Marketing Manage)*
**IT:** Nigel Reid *(IT Manager)*
**HR:** Karen Catto *(Human Resources Manager)*
**Branches:** Stewart Milne Group Ltd, Station Bank, Edinburgh Rd, Peebles, Peeblesshire EH45 8EJ
**US SIC:** 1541, 6711
**UK SIC:** 50100, 83962
**Auditors:** KPMG LLP
**Bankers:** Bank Of Scotland (80-07-60)

| | 30-06-14 | 30-06-13 | 30-06-12 |
|---|---|---|---|
| TO | 209,731,000 | 211,121,000 | 268,116,000 |
| P/L | 3,010,000 | (5,667,000) | 486,000 |
| NW | 101,259,000 | 98,780,000 | 102,688,000 |
| WC | 276,365,000 | 80,193,000 | 86,758,000 |
| Emp. | 696 | 724 | 838 |

DUNS 21-780-7188

## Stewart Park

The Stables, Stewart Park, Middlesbrough, Cleveland TS7 8AR
**Tel:** 01642515654
**Web:** www.middlesbrough.gov.uk
**Estd:** 2011 Proprietorship
**Line of Business:** Preservation of historical sites and buildings
**Proprietor:** D Miller
**US SIC:** 8411 **UK SIC:** 97700
**Employees:** 50

DUNS 21-730-8998 Imp-Exp

## Stewart Plastics Ltd

**(Subsidiary of:** Eci Partners Llp)
Stewart House, Croydon, Surrey CR9 4HS
**Tel:** 02086862231 **Fax:** 02086883515
**Web:** www.stewartcompany.co.uk
**Reg No:** 0399253 **Estd:** 1945 Private Limited Company
**Line of Business:** Plastic injection moulding
**Export Markets:** Europe and Worldwide
**Export Sales:** £917,000
**Trading Style:** Stewart Co
**Issued Capital:** £5,000,000
**Directors:** P Horton, A Burns
**Co. Secretary:** Paul Horton
**Responsibilities**
**Senior:** Phil Haslam *(Warehouse Manager)*, Paul Keeney *(Production Manager)*, Graham Morbin *(Warehouse Manager)*, Lee Mowle *(Manager)*, Shirley O' connell *(General Manager)*
**Finance:** Lee Mowle *(Manager)*
**Marketing:** Alan Slack *(Senior Marketing Executive)*
**Sales:** Shirley O' connell *(General Manager)*
**HR:** Shirley O' connell *(General Manager)*
**Health & Safety:** Paul Keeney *(Production Manager)*
**Facilities:** Geoff Tanner *(Maintenance Manager)*
**Operations:** Paul Keeney *(Production Manager)*
**Purchasing:** Paul Keeney *(Production Manager)*
**Engineering:** Paul Keeney *(Production Manager)*, Geoff Tanner *(Maintenance Manager)*
**US SIC:** 3079 **UK SIC:** 48360
**Auditors:** Baker Tilly UK Audit LLP
**Bankers:** Lloyds TSB Bank plc (30-96-07)

| | 30-09-13 | 30-09-12 | 30-09-11 |
|---|---|---|---|
| TO | 12,052,000 | 12,670,000 | 12,831,000 |
| P/L | (912,000) | (319,000) | 2,238,000 |
| NW | 5,077,000 | 5,886,000 | 6,175,000 |
| WC | 2,193,000 | 4,041,000 | 5,023,000 |
| Emp. | 115 | 88 | 81 |

DUNS 34-645-0125

## Stewart Title Ltd

**(Subsidiary of:** Stewart Information Services Corporation)
6 Henrietta Street, London WC2E 8PS
**Tel:** 02070107820 **Fax:** 01392-680690
**Web:** www.stewarttitle.co.uk
**Reg No:** 2770166 **Estd:** 1993 Private Limited Company
**Line of Business:** Underwriting
**Export Sales:** £5,886,637
**Issued Capital:** £330,000
**Directors:** L P Thompson, D W Chalmers, S Morris, S Lessack, J L Killea
**Co. Secretary:** Ms Katja Huitikka
**Responsibilities**
**Senior:** Stephen Smyth *(Country Manager)*, John Welling *(Manager)*, Donovan Woodcroft *(Head Of Sales And Marketing)*, jonathan woodcraft *(sales manager)*
**Marketing:** Sally Knowles *(Sales Manager)*
**Sales:** Sally Knowles *(Sales Manager)*
**Branches:** Stewart Title Ltd, Phoenix House, Phoenix Crescent, Strathclyde Business Park, Bellshill, Lanarkshire ML4 3NJ
**US SIC:** 6411 **UK SIC:** 83200
**Auditors:** KPMG Audit PLC

| | 31-12-13 | 31-12-12 | 31-12-11 |
|---|---|---|---|
| TO | 11,621,856 | 8,131,000 | 8,200,081 |
| P/L | 1,549,343 | 1,433,289 | 3,670,315 |
| NW | 22,808,810 | 22,489,660 | 21,088,532 |
| WC | 5,833,319 | 4,439,582 | 2,108,415 |
| Emp. | 47 | 37 | 38 |

DUNS 28-826-8899

## Stewart Travel Centre Ltd

7 Main Street, Prestwick, Ayrshire KA9 1AA
**Tel:** 01292-476721 **Fax:** 01292-671320
**Web:** www.stewarttravel.co.uk
**Reg No:** 0081104SC **Estd:** 1972 Private Limited Company
**Line of Business:** Travel agency activities
**Issued Capital:** £100
**Director:** Ms J P Stewart
**Co. Secretary:** William Stewart
**Responsibilities**
**Senior:** Donna Bicker *(Office Manager)*
**IT:** Debbie Hay *(Senior IT Executive)*
**US SIC:** 4722 **UK SIC:** 77001

| | 30-04-14 | 30-04-13 | 30-04-12 |
|---|---|---|---|
| TA | 220,505 | 188,730 | 1,113,388 |
| NW | 70,328 | 33,202 | (337,991) |
| WC | 69,707 | 32,270 | (337,991) |

DUNS 21-067-7564

## Stewartery Archaeological Trust

Kingston, Rhonehouse, Castle Douglas, Kirkcudbrightshire DG7 1SA
**Web:** www.sat.org.uk
**Estd:** 1999 Proprietorship
**Line of Business:** Archaeologists
**Proprietor:** A Penman
**Responsibilities**
**Senior:** Alistair Penman *(Consultant)*, Lizzy Penman *(Proprietor)*
**US SIC:** 7391 **UK SIC:** 94000
**Employees:** 47

DUNS 21-782-9997

## Stewarton Academy

Cairnduff Place, Stewarton, Kilmarnock, Ayrshire KA3 5QF
**Tel:** 01560482342
**Web:** www.stewartonacademy.co.uk
**Estd:** 1986 Proprietorship
**Line of Business:** Schools (local authority)
**Proprietor:** Mrs S Leslie
**US SIC:** 8211 **UK SIC:** 93200
**Employees:** 130

DUNS 21-507-1122

## Stewartry Care

92 King Street, Castle Douglas, Kirkcudbrightshire DG7 1AD
**Tel:** 01556504699
**Estd:** 1995 Proprietorship
**Line of Business:** Care for the Elderly in their own Homes.
**Proprietor:** Mrs J Young
**US SIC:** 8091 **UK SIC:** 95200
**Employees:** 130

DUNS 21-007-1694

## Stewarts Law Llp

5 New St Square, London EC4A 3BF
**Web:** www.stewartslaw.com
**Reg No:** 0329883OC **Estd:** 2007
**Line of Business:** Solicitors
**Export Sales:** £9,171,048
**Responsibilities**
**Senior:** Mohan Bhaskaran *(Non-designated Limited Liabili)*, Deborah Chism *(Non-designated Limited Liabili)*, Stewart Dench *(Partner and Head of Business D)*, Nichola Fosler *(Non-designated Limited Liabili)*, Kevin Grealis *(Non-designated Limited Liabili)*, Emma Hatley *(Non-designated Limited Liabili)*, James Healy Pratt *(Non-designated Limited Liabili)*, Daniel Herman *(Non-designated Limited Liabili)*, Warren Maxwell *(Non-designated Limited Liabili)*, Richard Nicolle *(Non-designated Limited Liabili)*, David Pickstone *(Non-designated Limited Liabili)*, Scott Rigby *(Non designated Limited Liabili)*, Lucy Robinson *(Non-designated Limited Liabili)*, Nicola Wager *(Non-designated Limited Liabili)*
**Marketing:** Stewart Dench *(Partner and Head of Business D)*, Alon Riza *(Senior Marketing Manager and H)*
**Sales:** Elaina Bailes *(Solicitor in the Commercial Li)*
**Admin:** Philip Studd *(Head of Administration)*
**HR:** Angela Melia *(HR Manager)*
**US SIC:** 8111 **UK SIC:** 83500

| | 30-04-14 | 30-04-13 | 30-04-12 |
|---|---|---|---|
| TO | 46,353,572 | 44,659,721 | 34,903,583 |
| P/L | 23,836,271 | 22,097,586 | 18,524,025 |
| NW | 16,025,956 | 17,007,321 | 14,557,801 |
| WC | 23,267,359 | 18,648,652 | 15,709,833 |
| Emp. | 227 | 215 | 179 |

DUNS 23-854-1101

## Stewarts of Tayside (Holdings) Ltd.

Tofthill, Glencarse, Perth, Perthshire PH2 7LS
**Tel:** 01738-860370
**Web:** www.stewartsoftayside.co.uk
**Reg No:** 0200086SC **Estd:** 1999 Private Limited Company
**Line of Business:** Growing of vegetables, horticultural specialities and nursery products
**Issued Capital:** £9,389
**Director:** J C Stewart
**Co. Secretary:** Ms Mary Stewart
**Responsibilities**
**Finance:** Fraser Gibson *(Financial Director)*
**US SIC:** 0161 **UK SIC:** 01001

| | 31-05-13 | 31-05-12 | 31-05-11 |
|---|---|---|---|
| TO | 20,414,022 | 18,792,413 | 18,645,572 |
| P/L | 2,103,704 | 293,476 | 497,491 |
| NW | 4,293,551 | 3,037,532 | 2,929,496 |
| WC | 1,057,463 | (834,023) | (700,248) |
| Emp. | 248 | 246 | 248 |

DUNS 77-008-7559

## Stewarts Plumbing & Heating Ltd

(**Subsidiary of:** Stewarts Holdings (Uk) Ltd)
Stewart House, Elmdon Road, Acocks Green, Birmingham, West Midlands B27 6LJ
**Tel:** 0121-707-8118 **Fax:** 0121-628-8484
**Web:** www.stewartsplumbing.co.uk
**Reg No:** 2659028 **VAT No:** 580411757
**Estd:** 1991 Private Limited Company
**Line of Business:** Plumbing
**Issued Capital:** £100,000
**Directors:** S N Angus, I S Jamison, M Tipper
**Co. Secretary:** Mrs Brenda Jamison
**Branches:** Stewarts Plumbing & Heating Ltd, 43 Leicester Road, Coalville, Leicestershire LE67 6HN
**US SIC:** 1711 **UK SIC:** 50300
**Auditors:** Rochesters Audit Services Ltd
**Bankers:** Barclays Bank Plc (20-07-84)

| | 30-04-14 | 30-04-13 | 30-04-12 |
|---|---|---|---|
| TO | 10,585,101 | 8,963,811 | 9,947,475 |
| P/L | 159,220 | (55,769) | 101,529 |
| NW | 765,438 | 639,018 | 682,628 |
| WC | 612,788 | 505,175 | 582,284 |
| Emp. | 112 | 84 | 76 |

DUNS 22-223-8458

## Steyne Hotels Ltd

Chatsworth House, Chatsworth Road, Worthing, West Sussex BN11 1LY
**Tel:** 01903-236103
**Web:** www.steynehotel.com
**Reg No:** 4241783 **Estd:** 2001 Private Limited Company
**Line of Business:** Hotels
**Issued Capital:** £1,000
**Directors:** M J Clinch, Mrs G M Clinch, Mrs L J Dopson, N Clinch, P M Clinch, J A Dopson
**Co. Secretary:** David Langridge
**US SIC:** 7011 **UK SIC:** 66500

| | 30-04-14 | 30-04-13 | 30-04-12 |
|---|---|---|---|
| TO | 3,354,326 | N/A | N/A |
| P/L | (113,768) | N/A | N/A |
| NW | 3,378,335 | 3,470,096 | 3,348,287 |
| WC | (642,091) | (804,349) | (315,939) |
| Emp. | 113 | N/A | N/A |

DUNS 23-635-8461

## Steyning Grammar School

Upper School, Shooting Field, Steyning, West Sussex BN44 3RX
**Tel:** 01903814555
**Web:** www.sgs.uk.net
**Estd:** 2012
**Line of Business:** General secondary education
**Directors:** P J Senior, C Taylor, Mrs M E Seal
**Responsibilities**
**Finance:** Jo Burroughs *(Senior Finance Administrator)*
**US SIC:** 8211 **UK SIC:** 93200
**Employees:** 250

DUNS 34-668-8042

## Sth Ltd

(**Subsidiary of:** Claranet Internet Holdings Ltd)
Brighouse Court, Barnett Way, Barnwood, Gloucester, Gloucestershire GL4 3RT
**Tel:** 01452-631000
**Web:** www.sth-ltd.co.uk
**Reg No:** 5473890 **Estd:** 2005 Private Limited Company
**Line of Business:** Management activities of holding companies
**Issued Capital:** £405,000
**Directors:** N Fairhurst, C Nasser, M Robert
**Responsibilities**
**Senior:** David Leese *(Finance Director)*
**Finance:** David Leese *(Finance Director)*
**US SIC:** 6711, 7379
**UK SIC:** 83962, 83940
**Auditors:** Dovedale Dean Ltd

| | 30-06-13 | 31-07-12 | 31-06-11 |
|---|---|---|---|
| TO | 22,702 | 50,045,000 | 45,941,000 |
| P/L | 5,366 | (3,342,000) | (3,695,000) |
| NW | 1,324 | (21,819,000) | (18,617,000) |
| WC | 1,103 | (10,924,000) | (7,371,000) |
| Emp. | N/A | 246 | 248 |

DUNS 23-813-7009

## Sthree Plc

5th Floor, London W1W 5PN
**Tel:** 02072686000 **Fax:** 02072686001
**Web:** www.sthree.com
**Reg No:** 3805979 **Estd:** 1986 Public Limited Company
**Line of Business:** Employment and recruitment companies and consultants
**Export Sales:** £491,144,000
**Issued Capital:** £1,233,941
**Directors:** T Ward, E J Hughes, Ms A B Lesniak, C M Brendish, A Smith, S M Quinn, N Zahawi, G P Elden
**Co. Secretary:** Steven Hornbuckle
**Responsibilities**
**Senior:** Natasha Clarke *(Director, Strategic Capability)*, Fiona Macleod *(Director)*, Dave Rees *(Managing Director SThree DACH)*, Sunil Wickremeratne *(Non-Executive Director)*
**Marketing:** Natasha Clarke *(Director, Strategic Capability)*, Gemma Reyes *(Brand Manager)*, Henok Zeratzion *(Brand Manager)*
**IT:** Lance Fisher *(Chief Information Officer)*, Paul Smerkinich *(Infrastructure Manager)*
**US SIC:** 7361 **UK SIC:** 83954
**Auditors:** PricewaterhouseCoopers LLP

| | 30-11-14 | 01-12-13 | 25-11-12 |
|---|---|---|---|
| TO | 746,924,000 | 634,297,000 | 577,457,000 |
| P/L | 23,985,000 | 15,522,000 | 25,267,000 |
| NW | 40,266,000 | 39,582,000 | 47,673,000 |
| WC | 36,218,000 | 36,208,000 | 39,525,000 |
| Emp. | 2,487 | 2,228 | 2,234 |

DUNS 22-250-9700 **Imp**

## Sti Line Ltd

(**Subsidiary of:** Stabernack Holding Gmbh)
Pentland House, Saracen Close, Gillingham Business Park, Gillingham, Kent ME8 0QN
**Tel:** 01634377590 **Fax:** 01634377560
**Web:** www.linepackaging.co.uk
**Reg No:** 4268941 **VAT No:** 780185422
**Estd:** 1981 Private Limited Company
**Line of Business:** Manufacturers of packaging materials
**Export Sales:** £2,437,195
**Issued Capital:** £930,548
**Directors:** A Stojanovic, P M Clarke
**Co. Secretary:** Dr Tom Giessler
**Responsibilities**
**Finance:** Mandi Harris *(Accounts Manager)*, Caroline Reid *(Accounts Manager)*
**US SIC:** 2654, 8911
**UK SIC:** 47280, 83701
**Auditors:** Glazers

| | 31-12-13 | 31-12-12 | 31-12-11 |
|---|---|---|---|
| TO | 13,777,461 | 16,213,053 | 19,998,069 |
| P/L | (662,905) | 326,505 | (336,911) |
| NW | 1,105,072 | 1,767,977 | 626,623 |
| WC | 1,115,534 | 2,066,977 | 1,963,100 |
| Emp. | 129 | 138 | 154 |

DUNS 73-360-0725

## Stickyeyes Ltd

West One, Leeds, West Yorkshire LS1 1BA
**Tel:** 01133-912929 **Fax:** 01133-912939
**Web:** www.stickyeyes.com
**Reg No:** 4633595 **Estd:** 1998 Private Limited Company
**Line of Business:** Marketing consultants
**Issued Capital:** £820
**Co. Secretary:** Andrew Chalmers
**Responsibilities**
**Senior:** Phil Kissane *(Manager)*
**Finance:** Tom Howard *(Chief Financial Officer)*, Percy Vear *(Finance Director)*
**Marketing:** Heather Healy *(Creative Communications Direct)*, Phil McGuin *(Head of Insight & Data Analyti)*, Lisa Wisniowski *(Marketing Executive)*
**Sales:** Glen Conybeare *(Chief Commercial Officer)*, Daniel Donoghue *(Senior Business Development Ma)*
**US SIC:** 7392 **UK SIC:** 83951
**Bankers:** National Westminster Bank Plc (60-12-39)

| | 31-03-14 | 31-03-13 | 31-03-12 |
|---|---|---|---|
| TO | 15,128,526 | 8,987,672 | N/A |
| P/L | 1,636,327 | 1,035,167 | N/A |
| NW | 4,899,156 | 3,229,407 | 3 |
| WC | 4,639,929 | 3,140,161 | N/A |
| Emp. | 117 | 104 | N/A |

DUNS 21-567-8284

## Stiff Kitten

1 Bankmore Square, Belfast BT7 1DH
**Tel:** 028-9023-8700
**Web:** www.thestiffkitten.com
**Estd:** 2005 Partnership
**Line of Business:** Bars
**Partner:** P Donaldson
**Responsibilities**
**Senior:** Phil Donaldson *(Partner)*, Orla Ferguson *(Manager)*, Ben Simms *(Owner)*
**US SIC:** 5813 **UK SIC:** 66200
**Employees:** 50

DUNS 55-078-2502

## Stilecroft Residential Home

51 Stainburn Road, Stainburn, Workington, Cumbria CA14 1SS
**Tel:** 01900603776
**Estd:** 1983 Partnership
**Line of Business:** Non-charitable social work activities with accommodation
**Partners:** J C Fox, Mrs D M Fox
**Responsibilities**
**Senior:** Annette Daniel *(Manager)*
**US SIC:** 8321 **UK SIC:** 96111
**Employees:** 50

DUNS 37-892-5655

## Stiles Harold Williams Ltd

6 Babmaes Street, London SW1Y 6HD
**Tel:** 02073891501
**Web:** www.shw.co.uk
**Reg No:** 3311644 **VAT No:** 692771690
**Estd:** 1997 Private Limited Company
**Line of Business:** Real estate agencies
**Issued Capital:** £473,894
**Principals:** R D Stiles *(Chairman)*, C Richardson, N Mcguinness, P K Spruce, P S Coldbreath, R E Markham, R H Stapleton, M S Mcfadden
**Co. Secretary:** Andrew Scholefield
**Responsibilities**
**Senior:** Trudi Allen-Shalless *(Director)*, Nicholas Bradbeer *(Director)*, Robert Bradley Smith *(Director)*, Ian Coomber *(Director)*, Howard Cox *(Manager)*, David Marcelline *(Director)*, Haydon Murton *(Manager)*, Richard Pyne *(Director)*, Mark Skelton *(Director)*, Paul Wade *(Director)*
**Branches:** Stiles Harold Williams Ltd, Ivy House, 3 Ivy Terrace, Eastbourne, East Sussex BN21 4QU
**US SIC:** 6531 **UK SIC:** 83400
**Auditors:** Mazars LLP
**Bankers:** National Westminster Bank Plc (60-30-09)

| | 31-03-14 | 31-03-13 | 30-03-12 |
|---|---|---|---|
| TO | 10,821,000 | 8,806,000 | 8,745,000 |
| P/L | 3,964,000 | 2,318,000 | (230,000) |
| NW | 5,639,000 | 3,815,000 | 1,858,000 |
| WC | 5,265,000 | 3,554,000 | 1,586,000 |
| Emp. | 157 | 128 | 146 |

DUNS 45-825-4141

## Stiller Warehousing & Distribution Ltd

Ridgeway, Aycliffe Business Park, Newton Aycliffe, County Durham DL5 6SP
**Tel:** 01325-313-140 **Fax:** 01325-304-096
**Web:** www.stiller.co.uk
**Reg No:** 3178500 **Estd:** 1954 Private Limited Company
**Line of Business:** Road haulage and transport services
**Export Sales:** £149,198
**Issued Capital:** £4
**Directors:** P W Stiller, A B Winney
**Co. Secretary:** Andrew Winney
**Responsibilities**
**Admin:** Julie Monaghan *(Office Manager)*
**US SIC:** 4226, 4712
**UK SIC:** 77003, 77002
**Auditors:** Tait Walker LLP
**Bankers:** Yorkshire Bank Plc (05-02-27)

| | 31-12-13 | 31-12-12 | 31-12-11 |
|---|---|---|---|
| TO | 9,539,327 | 8,187,446 | 7,321,452 |
| P/L | 98,733 | 162,104 | 601,532 |
| NW | 1,276,727 | 1,197,010 | 1,071,644 |
| WC | 930,879 | 950,675 | 950,723 |
| Emp. | 104 | 99 | 99 |

DUNS 53-634-3924

## Stink Ltd

(**Subsidiary of:** Stillking Film Holdings Limited)
5-23 Old Street, London EC1V 9HL
**Tel:** 020-7462-4000 **Fax:** 020-7462-4001
**Web:** www.stink.tv
**Reg No:** 3439238 **VAT No:** 707600948
**Estd:** 1997 Private Limited Company
**Line of Business:** Tv and film producers and directors
**Export Sales:** £59,954,977
**Issued Capital:** £9,217
**Directors:** D Bergmann, I Zacharias
**Co. Secretary:** Dylan Davies
**Responsibilities**
**Senior:** Georgia Eyres *(Executive Assistant)*, Martin Forbes *(Director)*
**Finance:** Peter Meaklim *(Group Financial Controller)*
**Marketing:** Lacyn Clarke *(Director Representative)*
**Admin:** Alice Nutt *(Office Manager)*
**Operations:** Nell Jordan *(Head of Production)*, Blake Powell *(Executive Producer)*
**US SIC:** 7819 **UK SIC:** 97111
**Auditors:** Kingston Smith LLP

| | 31-12-13 | 31-12-12 | 31-12-11 |
|---|---|---|---|
| TO | 79,208,274 | 71,847,674 | 37,686,461 |
| P/L | 2,723,335 | 1,531,499 | 888,507 |
| NW | 3,463,812 | 3,414,019 | 1,812,801 |
| WC | 3,993,611 | 3,740,879 | 1,315,810 |
| Emp. | 132 | 125 | 48 |

DUNS 22-759-8133 **Imp**

## Stirchley Bacon Co. Ltd

(**Subsidiary of:** Stirchley Bacon Holdings Ltd)
Units 36-37 Cossgate Road, Park Farm Industrial Estate, Redditch, Worcestershire B98 7SN
**Tel:** 01527-500140
**Web:** http://stirchleybacon.com
**Reg No:** 1634794 **VAT No:** 338087930
**Estd:** 1982 Private Limited Company
**Line of Business:** Other meat and poultry meat processing
**Issued Capital:** £6,600
**Principals:** Mrs N S Pollard *(Managing)*, B C Pollard
**Co. Secretary:** Mrs Natalie Pollard
**Responsibilities**
**Finance:** Carole Smith *(Human Resources Manager)*
**Sales:** Bob Evans *(Sales Managers)*
**Admin:** Carole Smith *(Human Resources Manager)*
**HR:** Carole Smith *(Human Resources Manager)*
**Operations:** Tommy Gillan *(Dispatch Manager)*
**Engineering:** Tommy Gillan *(Dispatch Manager)*
**US SIC:** 2013, 5147
**UK SIC:** 41223, 61700
**Auditors:** P J Doyle & Co
**Bankers:** National Westminster Bank Plc (60-06-37)

| | 31-03-14 | 31-03-13 | 31-03-12 |
|---|---|---|---|
| TO | 15,608,647 | N/A | N/A |
| P/L | 480,568 | N/A | N/A |
| NW | 1,757,014 | 1,506,142 | 1,387,314 |
| WC | 553,637 | 437,956 | 502,586 |
| Emp. | 46 | N/A | N/A |

DUNS 45-848-2676

## Stirland Paterson (Printers) Ltd

(**Subsidiary of:** Stirland Paterson (Holdings) Ltd)
Tom Olivia Court, Merlin Way, Quarry Hill Industrial Estate, Ilkeston, Derbyshire DE7 4RA
**Tel:** 01159-447600
**Web:** www.stirlandpaterson.co.uk
**Reg No:** 3194946 **VAT No:** 660607249
**Estd:** 1996 Private Limited Company
**Line of Business:** Printers general
**Issued Capital:** £102
**Directors:** J Paterson, S Stirland
**Co. Secretary:** Philip Wilson
**US SIC:** 2752 **UK SIC:** 47544
**Auditors:** Gregory Priestley & Stewart
**Bankers:** Yorkshire Bank Plc (05-06-38)

| | 30-09-13 | 30-09-12 | 30-09-11 |
|---|---|---|---|
| TA | 1,685,646 | 1,661,472 | 1,660,682 |
| NW | 191,213 | 218,944 | 232,078 |
| WC | 86,310 | 120,320 | 138,830 |

DUNS 39-029-6895

## Stirling Ackroyd Ltd

36-42 New Inn Yard, London EC2A 3EY
**Tel:** 02077493838
**Web:** www.stirlingackroyd.com
**Reg No:** 2109457 **Estd:** 1987 Private Limited Company
**Line of Business:** Estate agents
**Issued Capital:** £1,000
**Managing Director:** A J Goff
**Co. Secretary:** Guy Ellis
**Responsibilities**
**Senior:** Nick Davies *(Head of Residential Developmen)*
**Finance:** Rebecca Gove *(Accounts Assistance)*, Paul Larke *(Financial Controller)*
**Sales:** Jack Gibson *(Sales Neogotiator)*, Mark Oneil *(COMMERCIAL SALES, Acquisitions)*, Brett Sullings *(COMMERCIAL SALES, Acquisitions)*, Michael Woolley *(Sales Manager)*
**HR:** Leanne Darwin *(Company Coordinator)*
**Facilities:** Andrew Blythe *(Lettings Manager)*, Georgina Lewis *(Head of Short Lets)*, Scott Murrary *(Senior Lettings Manager)*, Mark Oneil *(COMMERCIAL SALES, Acquisitions)*, Brett Sullings *(COMMERCIAL SALES, Acquisitions)*
**Branches:** Stirling Ackroyd Ltd, 106 St. John Street, London EC1M 4EH
**US SIC:** 6531 **UK SIC:** 83400
**Auditors:** Simsoft Jones

**Bankers:** National Westminster Bank Plc (60-80-01)

| | 31-03-13 | 31-03-12 | 31-03-11 |
|---|---|---|---|
| TO | 4,828,521 | 4,251,161 | 4,197,024 |
| P/L | 210,894 | (248,689) | (566,720) |
| NW | 647,110 | 196,006 | 505,958 |
| WC | 380,733 | 180,843 | (301,355) |
| Emp. | 67 | 62 | 64 |

DUNS 21-749-5097
## Stirling Audi
Unit 8/1, Craig Leith Road, Stirling, Stirlingshire FK7 7LQ
**Tel:** 01786446888
**Web:** www.stirlingaudi.com
**Estd:** 1997 Proprietorship
**Line of Business:** Car dealers (new & used)
**Proprietor:** G Proll
**Responsibilities**
**Senior:** Stephen Marchetti *(Head Of Business)*
**Sales:** Sandy Fleming *(After Sales Manager)*
**US SIC:** 5511 **UK SIC:** 65100
**Employees:** 50

DUNS 22-906-4696
## Stirling Council
Viewforth 14-20 Pitt Terrace, Stirling, Stirlingshire FK8 2ET
**Tel:** 02868658357
**Web:** www.stirling.gov.uk
**Estd:** 1975 Incorporate By Act Of Parliament
**Line of Business:** Community centres
**Trading Style:** Rainbow Slides Leisure Centre Ochill Community Hall, St Ninians Primary School, Adult Carers Education
**Principals:** K Yates *(Chairman)*, W Dixon *(Financial)*
**Responsibilities**
**Senior:** John Coyle *(Chairperson)*
**Finance:** John Risk *(Financial Manager)*
**IT:** Mark Tye *(Corporate IT Manager)*
**HR:** Susan Duffus *(Employee Development Advisor)*
**Health & Safety:** Nicholas Sabo *(Health & Safety Coordinator)*
**Fleet:** Gavin Hutton *(Fleet Manager)*
**Branches:** Stirling Council, Broomhill Road, Bonnybridge, Stirlingshire FK4 2AN
**US SIC:** 9121 **UK SIC:** 91110
**Bankers:** Clydesdale Bank Plc (82-68-05)
**Employees:** 2,000

DUNS 29-889-0823 **Imp**
## Stirling Dynamics Ltd
26-28 Regent Street, Bristol, Avon BS8 4HG
**Tel:** 01179741195
**Web:** www.stirling-dynamics.com
**Reg No:** 2092114 **VAT No:** 464655129
**Estd:** 1987 Private Limited Company
**Line of Business:** Engineers (consulting)
**Export Sales:** £3,326,740
**Issued Capital:** £10,521
**Directors:** Ms M Raven, A P Dannatt, M A Cook, C Cormack, A L Pfeil
**Co. Secretary:** Stephen Judd
**Responsibilities**
**Senior:** Maragaret Smith *(Manager)*, Bob Stirling *(President)*
**Branches:** Stirling Dynamics Ltd, Brabazon Business Park, Golf Course La, Bristol, Avon BS34 7PZ
**US SIC:** 8911, 7372
**UK SIC:** 83701, 83940
**Auditors:** Nexia Smith & Williamson LLP
**Bankers:** National Westminster Bank Plc (60-17-12)

| | 30-06-14 | 30-06-13 | 30-06-12 |
|---|---|---|---|
| TO | 7,804,146 | 7,460,573 | 7,691,960 |
| P/L | (805,347) | 91,391 | 336,689 |
| NW | (520,185) | 559,189 | 521,188 |
| WC | (450,207) | 550,767 | 500,898 |
| Emp. | 145 | 141 | 120 |

DUNS 73-256-7552 **Imp**
## Stirling Lloyd Plc
Union Bank, 127 King Street, Knutsford, Cheshire WA16 6EF
**Tel:** 01565-633111
**Web:** www.stirlinglloyd.com
**Reg No:** 4530488 **Estd:** 2002 Public Limited Company
**Line of Business:** Management activities of holding companies
**Issued Capital:** £50,000
**Directors:** D Lloyd, J S Lloyd, J A Volpicelli
**Co. Secretary:** Colin Baxter
**Responsibilities**
**IT:** Simon Ignotus *(IT Manager)*
**US SIC:** 6711, 2851
**UK SIC:** 83962, 25510
**Bankers:** Lloyds TSB Bank plc (30-12-51)

| | 31-03-14 | 31-03-13 | 31-03-12 |
|---|---|---|---|
| TO | 15,442,983 | 19,973,420 | 22,246,970 |
| P/L | 507,011 | 2,597,567 | 3,134,713 |
| NW | 8,866,043 | 8,391,392 | 6,803,041 |
| WC | 6,809,286 | 6,402,772 | 4,452,863 |
| Emp. | 98 | 96 | 92 |

DUNS 42-447-5668
## Stirling Park Llp
24 Saint Enoch Square, Glasgow, Lanarkshire G1 4DB
**Tel:** 0141-565-5765
**Web:** www.stirlingpark.co.uk
**Reg No:** 0300097SO **Estd:** 1921 Partnership
**Line of Business:** Police forces
**Responsibilities**
**Senior:** Kevin Dillon *(Non-designated Limited Liabili)*, Ronald Murison *(Non-designated Limited Liabili)*
**IT:** Alan Mc Dougall *(Senior IT Executive)*
**HR:** Jennifer Erunlu *(Human Resource Manager)*
**Branches:** Stirling Park Llp, 16 Nelson Street, Kilmarnock, Ayrshire KA1 1BD
**US SIC:** 9221 **UK SIC:** 91300
**Auditors:** PricewaterhouseCoopers LLP
**Bankers:** The Royal Bank Of Scotland Plc (83-00-40)

| | 31-12-13 | 31-12-12 | 31-12-11 |
|---|---|---|---|
| TA | 3,158,082 | 3,025,738 | 2,809,475 |
| WC | 787,414 | 1,093,508 | 1,090,937 |

DUNS 23-222-2885
## Stirling Royal Infirmary
Livilands Gate, Stirling, Stirlingshire FK8 2AU
**Tel:** 01786-434000
**Web:** www.nhsforthvalley.com
**Estd:** 1919 Proprietorship
**Line of Business:** Nhs clinics
**Trading Style:** Orchard House Day Care Hospital, Nhs Forth Valley
**Financial Director:** D Pedan
**Responsibilities**
**Senior:** D Bremner *(Manager)*, Jane Curry *(Chief Executive)*, Dan Docherty *(Estate Manager)*, Angela Wallace *(Director of Nursing)*
**Finance:** Jonathan Procter *(Financial Director)*
**IT:** S Jaffery *(Network Analyst)*, Scott Jaffray *(Head of IT)*
**HR:** A Cairney *(Personnel Officer)*, Ann McPherson *(Human Resources Manager)*
**Facilities:** Dan Docherty *(Estate Manager)*, Charley Donald *(Estates Manager)*
**Purchasing:** Dan Docherty *(Estate Manager)*
**Branches:** Stirling Royal Infirmary, Park Drive, Larbert, Stirlingshire FK5 3BB
**US SIC:** 8062 **UK SIC:** 95100
**Employees:** 1,000

DUNS 23-673-9251
## Stirling Solutions Ltd
8 Bakewell Street, Coalville, Leicestershire LE67 3BA
**Tel:** 01530811000 **Fax:** 01530510241
**Web:** www.stirlingsolutions.co.uk
**Reg No:** 3668581 **Estd:** 1993 Private Limited Company
**Line of Business:** Other computer related activities
**Issued Capital:** £119
**Directors:** P A Hall, A Razak, V K Ball, J M Ball
**Responsibilities**
**Senior:** Philip Sturdy *(Manager)*, Andrew Whitby *(Manager)*
**Finance:** Linda Heap *(Accountant)*
**US SIC:** 7379, 7399
**UK SIC:** 83940, 83954

| | 31-12-13 | 31-12-12 | 31-12-11 |
|---|---|---|---|
| TO | N/A | N/A | 109,450 |
| P/L | N/A | N/A | 66,996 |
| NW | 257,073 | 368,677 | 272,280 |
| WC | 98,788 | 316,273 | 197,933 |

DUNS 21-027-4510
## Stl Technologies Ltd
**(Subsidiary of:** Capita Plc)
Equis House, Bury St Edmunds, Suffolk IP32 7AB
**Tel:** 01284778600 **Fax:** 01284-778778
**Web:** www.capita.co.uk
**Reg No:** 0832098 **VAT No:** 213742488
**Estd:** 1965 Private Limited Company
**Line of Business:** Other software consultancy and supply
**Trading Style:** Capita
**Issued Capital:** £36,612
**Directors:** S J Maynard, S A Massey, M P Collier, Capita Corporate Director Limite, C H Rodgerson
**Co. Secretary:** Capita Group Secretary Limited
**Responsibilities**
**IT:** Roy Bird *(IT Manager)*
**Branches:** Stl Technologies Ltd, Riverside House, 6 Horne Lane, Bedford, Bedfordshire MK40 1PY
**US SIC:** 7379 **UK SIC:** 83940
**Auditors:** Grant Thornton UK LLP

**Bankers:** The Royal Bank Of Scotland Plc (15-10-00)

| | 31-12-13 | 30-09-12 | 30-12-11 |
|---|---|---|---|
| TO | 9,187,025 | 7,509,331 | 9,448,020 |
| P/L | 1,215,153 | (22,663) | 1,318,634 |
| NW | 7,875,808 | 8,589,903 | 8,854,697 |
| WC | 7,810,324 | 7,322,897 | 7,533,693 |
| Emp. | 106 | 113 | 115 |

DUNS 23-293-1100
## Stm Group Plc
Clinches House Po Box 227, Douglas, Isle of Man IM1 4LN
**Tel:** 01179-858-989 **Fax:** 01179-858-979
**Web:** www.stmgroupplc.com
**Reg No:** 0005398M **Estd:** 2005 Public Limited Company
**Line of Business:** Financial Institution.
**Principals:** J P Telling *(Chairman)*, A R Kentish, C D Porter
**Responsibilities**
**Finance:** Therese Neish *(Chief Financial Officer)*
**US SIC:** 6111, 7399
**UK SIC:** 81501, 83954
**Employees:** 129

DUNS 77-950-4260
## Stm Packaging Group Ltd
21-23 Concorde Road, Norwich, Norfolk NR6 6BJ
**Tel:** 01603-404217 **Fax:** 01603483944
**Web:** www.transmail.co.uk
**Reg No:** 5919785 **Estd:** 2006 Private Limited Company
**Line of Business:** Manufacture of other articles of paper and paperboard not elsewhere classified
**Issued Capital:** £10
**Directors:** P Wilson, G E Hough, Mrs E K Evans, M T Biddulph
**Co. Secretary:** Graham Hough
**Responsibilities**
**Senior:** Peter Opperman *(Manager)*
**US SIC:** 2649, 5942
**UK SIC:** 47280, 65300
**Auditors:** Lovewell Blake

| | 31-05-13 | 31-05-12 | 30-05-11 |
|---|---|---|---|
| TO | 5,502,633 | 2,939,257 | 2,974,282 |
| P/L | 127,719 | 152,636 | (289,323) |
| NW | 75,353 | (36,107) | (222,959) |
| WC | (288,114) | (218,814) | (329,945) |
| Emp. | 49 | 48 | 33 |

DUNS 34-661-5524
## Stm Security Group (Uk) Ltd
3rd Floor Heraldic House, Ilford, Essex IG1 4LX
**Tel:** 02085-189682 **Fax:** 02085-180679
**Web:** www.stmsecurity.com
**Reg No:** 5466873 **VAT No:** 863540715
**Estd:** 2005 Private Limited Company
**Line of Business:** Security and related activities
**Issued Capital:** £2,000
**Directors:** H Shahzad, P B Simpson
**Co. Secretary:** Zainab Shahzad
**US SIC:** 7393 **UK SIC:** 83954
**Auditors:** GB & Co

| | 31-07-14 | 31-07-13 | 31-07-12 |
|---|---|---|---|
| TO | 15,294,443 | 12,693,113 | 11,161,197 |
| P/L | 338,254 | 372,621 | 372,045 |
| NW | 690,605 | 490,166 | 436,085 |
| WC | 463,753 | 292,564 | 387,460 |
| Emp. | 580 | 453 | 453 |

DUNS 21-052-3916
## Stmicroelectronics (Research & Development) Ltd
**(Subsidiary of:** Stmicroelectronics N.V.)
Planar House, Parkway, Marlow, Buckinghamshire SL7 1YL
**Tel:** 01628-890800
**Reg No:** 0714719 **Estd:** 1962 Private Limited Company
**Line of Business:** Research and experimental development on natural sciences and engineering
**Issued Capital:** £1,150,000
**Directors:** Ms P De Martini, P Morris, L A Grant, Ms A Talpo
**Co. Secretary:** Andrew Smith
**Responsibilities**
**Senior:** Hubert Chevrinais *(Manager)*, Loic Lietar *(Manager)*
**US SIC:** 5064 **UK SIC:** 61500
**Auditors:** PricewaterhouseCoopers LLP
**Bankers:** Barclays Bank Plc (20-05-00)

| | 31-12-13 | 31-12-12 | 31-12-11 |
|---|---|---|---|
| TO | 28,139,000 | 27,024,000 | 24,940,000 |
| P/L | (9,334,000) | 1,296,000 | 146,000 |
| NW | (7,983,000) | 3,799,000 | 4,753,000 |
| WC | 947,000 | 2,754,000 | 3,716,000 |
| Emp. | 281 | 277 | 267 |

DUNS 21-754-7111
## Stobart Group Ltd
Unit 10 Langford Way Stretton Green, Distribution Park, Warrington, Cheshire WA4 4TZ
**Tel:** 01925605400
**Web:** www.stobartgroup.co.uk
**Reg No:** 0039117G **Estd:** 1970 Private Limited Company
**Line of Business:** Road haulage and transport services
**Export Sales:** £5,839,000
**Directors:** W Stobart, N M Watts, B M Whawell, N K Rawlings, W A Tinkler, M A Kayser, R C Burrell, R P Baker-Bates
**Responsibilities**
**Senior:** Kevin Simpson *(Regional Operations Manager)*
**US SIC:** 4789, 4213, 4226
**UK SIC:** 77002, 72300, 77003

| | 28-02-14 |
|---|---|
| TO | 99,179,000 |
| P/L | (10,187,000) |
| NW | 349,232,000 |
| WC | 258,810,000 |

DUNS 34-882-3717
## Stobart Rail Ltd
**(Subsidiary of:** Stobart Group Ltd)
Kingmoor Business Centre, Carlisle, Cumbria CA6 4BY
**Fax:** 01228882301
**Web:** www.stobartgroup.co.uk
**Reg No:** 2821207 **VAT No.** 022105004
**Estd:** 1993 Private Limited Company
**Line of Business:** Construction of commercial buildings
**Issued Capital:** £37,600
**Directors:** B M Whawell, K A Taylor, D Garner, A Richardson, K A Winnery, W A Tinkler
**Co. Secretary:** Richard Butcher
**Responsibilities**
**Senior:** Stephen Harker *(Project Manager)*, Liam Martin *(Manager)*
**IT:** Vince Sparks *(IT Director)*
**US SIC:** 1541, 4011
**UK SIC:** 50100, 71000
**Auditors:** Ernst & Young LLP
**Bankers:** HSBC Bank plc (40-26-18)

| | 28-02-14 | 28-02-13 | 29-02-12 |
|---|---|---|---|
| TO | 28,786,954 | 30,861,964 | 57,357,663 |
| P/L | 1,868,818 | 2,711,339 | 4,614,947 |
| NW | 18,437,881 | 16,868,262 | 14,596,406 |
| WC | 15,998,608 | 14,405,362 | 12,044,850 |
| Emp. | 181 | 177 | 197 |

DUNS 21-205-6204 **Imp-Exp**
## Stobarts (Bradford) Ltd
Carr Lane, Low Moor, Bradford, West Yorkshire BD12 0QU
**Tel:** 01274-676282
**Web:** www.stobarts.co.uk
**Reg No:** 0723776 **Estd:** 1867 Private Limited Company
**Line of Business:** Manufacturers of food products
**Issued Capital:** £100,002
**Managing Directors:** A I Stobart, N K Stobart
**Co. Secretary:** Philip Stobart
**US SIC:** 2099 **UK SIC:** 42399
**Auditors:** Stirk Lambert & Co
**Bankers:** Barclays Bank Plc (20-45-14)

| | 30-09-14 | 30-09-13 | 30-09-12 |
|---|---|---|---|
| TA | 1,905,381 | 1,798,941 | 1,620,266 |
| NW | 1,299,619 | 1,111,694 | 995,610 |
| WC | 792,144 | 636,787 | 470,937 |

DUNS 21-580-7270
## Stobartt Chilled
Brunel Drive, Newark, Nottinghamshire NG24 2EG
**Tel:** 01636703034
**Web:** www.stobartgroup.com
**Estd:** 2005 Proprietorship
**Line of Business:** Frozen food processors and distributors
**Proprietor:** K Smith
**US SIC:** 5149 **UK SIC:** 61700
**Employees:** 100

DUNS 21-772-4192
## Stobhill Care Home
70 Stobhill Road, Glasgow, Lanarkshire G21 3TX
**Tel:** 01415588500
**Web:** www.fshc.co.uk
**Estd:** 1997 Proprietorship
**Line of Business:** Medical nursing home activities
**Proprietor:** Ms K Cartright
**Responsibilities**
**Senior:** Karen Cartwright *(Manager)*
**US SIC:** 8051 **UK SIC:** 95100
**Employees:** 58

DUNS 29-820-7887

### Stobo Castle Health Spa Ltd

Stobo Castle, Peebles, Peeblesshire EH45 8NY
**Tel:** 01721-725300 **Fax:** 01721-760294
**Web:** www.stobocastle.co.uk
**Reg No:** 0100188SC **VAT No:** 446473825
**Estd:** 1986 Private Limited Company
**Line of Business:** Hairdressing and other beauty treatment
**Issued Capital:** £44,444
**Principals:** S M Winyard *(Managing)*, Mrs P Winyard, Mrs A Winyard, J S Ward Obe
**Co. Secretary:** As Company Services Limited
**Responsibilities**
**Senior:** Mark Wick *(Facilities Manager)*
**Finance:** Morag Roper *(Accounts Manager)*
**IT:** Morag Roper *(Accounts Manager)*
**Health & Safety:** Morag Roper *(Accounts Manager)*
**Facilities:** Malcom Bruce *(Facilities Employee)*, Mark Wick *(Facilities Manager)*
**Purchasing:** Morag Roper *(Accounts Manager)*
**US SIC:** 7231 **UK SIC:** 98200
**Auditors:** KPMG
**Bankers:** Bank Of Scotland (80-09-33)

| | 31-12-13 | 31-12-12 | 31-12-11 |
|---|---|---|---|
| TO | 5,924,394 | 5,603,581 | 5,629,138 |
| P/L | 482,400 | 508,517 | 538,548 |
| NW | 4,971,246 | 4,985,374 | 4,898,097 |
| WC | (180,485) | (253,905) | (1,562,400) |
| Emp. | 170 | 168 | 174 |

DUNS 50-597-1663 **Imp**

### Stock Brook Manor (Golf Club) Ltd

(**Subsidiary of:** Peachey (Basildon) Group Ltd)
Queens Park Avenue, Billericay, Essex CM12 0SP
**Tel:** 01277653616
**Web:** www.stockbrook.com
**Reg No:** 2535759 **Estd:** 1990 Private Limited Company
**Line of Business:** Golf clubs
**Trading Style:** Stock Brook Manor Golf & Country Club
**Issued Capital:** £10,000
**Directors:** T B Peachey, M R Peachey, Mrs J S Gunn, G P Peachey
**Co. Secretary:** Ms Karen Anderson
**US SIC:** 7999 **UK SIC:** 97913
**Auditors:** Littlestone Martin Glenton
**Bankers:** Lloyds TSB Bank plc (30-10-52)

| | 29-09-13 | 30-09-12 | 25-09-11 |
|---|---|---|---|
| TO | 6,188,542 | 6,416,288 | 5,987,624 |
| P/L | 328,429 | 569,385 | 206,036 |
| NW | 1,881,234 | 1,629,039 | 1,206,047 |
| WC | 1,689,842 | 1,527,131 | 1,154,061 |
| Emp. | 294 | 292 | 286 |

DUNS 73-666-0080 **Imp-Exp**

### Stock Redler Ltd

(**Subsidiary of:** Schenck Process Uk Holding Ltd)
Redler House, Stroud, Gloucestershire GL5 3EY
**Tel:** 01453704300 **Fax:** 01453-763582
**Web:** www.redler.com
**Reg No:** 4925560 **VAT No:** 806633925
**Estd:** 2003 Private Limited Company
**Line of Business:** Manufacture of lifting and handling equipment
**Trading Style:** Schenck Process Uk Limited
**Issued Capital:** £1,900,000
**Directors:** N P Jones, R G Ellis
**Co. Secretary:** Nicholas Jones
**Responsibilities**
**Senior:** Ian Woolf *(Manager)*, Andrew Workman *(Sales Director)*
**Marketing:** Brendan Glover *(Senior Marketing Executive)*, Andrew Workman *(Sales Director)*
**Sales:** Julie Precious *(Sales Manager)*, Andrew Workman *(Sales Director)*
**IT:** Alex Chestnutt *(Senior IT Executive)*
**HR:** Sharon Macrae *(Personnel Department)*
**Purchasing:** Claire Wells *(Purchasing Manager)*
**US SIC:** 3534 **UK SIC:** 32553
**Auditors:** Deloitte LLP

| | 31-12-13 | 31-12-12 | 31-12-11 |
|---|---|---|---|
| TO | 327,875 | 199,225 | 246,785 |
| P/L | (17,318) | (514,025) | (246,584) |
| NW | 2,010,567 | 1,811,438 | 2,036,985 |
| WC | 3,930,499 | 3,731,370 | 4,112,662 |

DUNS 85-598-5283

### Stock Register Office

Town Hall, John Street Entrance, Stockport, Cheshire SK1 3XE
**Tel:** 01612176007
**Web:** www.stockport.gov.uk
**Estd:** 2012
**Line of Business:** Births, marriage & deaths registration offices
**Responsibilities**
**Senior:** John Pasieczmik *(Media Public Relations Officer)*, John Schultz *(Chief Executive)*
**HR:** Phil Badley *(Director of Personnel)*
**US SIC:** 9121 **UK SIC:** 91110
**Employees:** 16

DUNS 22-000-4933

### Stock Spirits Group Plc

Solar House, Mercury Park, Wooburn Green, High Wycombe, Buckinghamshire HP10 0HH
**Tel:** 01628648500
**Web:** www.stockspirits.com
**Reg No:** 8687223 **Estd:** 2013 Public Limited Company
**Line of Business:** Management activities of holding companies
**Issued Capital:** £1
**Directors:** J R Nicolson, C Heath, V L Jackson, A G Cripps, J M Keenan, D O Maloney
**Co. Secretary:** Ms Elisa Gomez De Bonilla Gonzalez
**US SIC:** 6711 **UK SIC:** 83962
**Auditors:** Ernst & Young LLP

| | 31-12-13 |
|---|---|
| TO | 296,847,000 |
| P/L | (7,566,000) |
| NW | (29,781,000) |
| WC | 71,775,000 |
| Emp. | 962 |

DUNS 21-228-2307

### Stockburns

12 Hatton Close, Northfleet, Gravesend, Kent DA11 8SD
**Tel:** 01474-745508
**Proprietorship**
**Line of Business:** Plastering and related building services
**Proprietor:** M Stockburn
**US SIC:** 1742 **UK SIC:** 50400
**Employees:** 46

DUNS 21-580-1715

### Stockdales

47 Ashton Lane, Sale, Cheshire M33 5PA
**Tel:** 01619620978
**Web:** www.stockdales.org.uk
**Estd:** 1978 Proprietorship
**Line of Business:** Residential care establishments
**Proprietor:** Mrs E Morris
**US SIC:** 8321 **UK SIC:** 96111
**Employees:** 91

DUNS 28-907-2688

### Stockdales of Sale Altrincham & District Ltd

34 Harboro Road, Sale, Cheshire M33 5AH
**Tel:** 01619693527
**Web:** www.stockdales.org.uk
**Reg No:** 1392344 **Estd:** 1957 Private Company Limited By Guarantee
**Line of Business:** Children's homes
**Trading Style:** Stockdales, S A A D S S
**Directors:** A S Gresty, Ms D A Watkins, Ms R Kasaven, P V Wall, Mrs W A Carstairs, N P Mather
**Co. Secretary:** Tony Gresty
**Responsibilities**
**Senior:** Lesley Grant *(Assistant Chief Executive)*
**Finance:** Mary Cox *(Accounts Administrator)*
**Branches:** Stockdales Of Sale Altrincham & District Ltd, Hayling Road, Sale, Cheshire M33 6GN
**US SIC:** 8091, 7999, 8999
**UK SIC:** 95200, 97913, 83954
**Auditors:** Kevin H Rourke & Co
**Bankers:** National Westminster Bank Plc (01-07-71)

| | 05-04-14 | 05-04-13 | 05-04-12 |
|---|---|---|---|
| TO | 2,219,233 | 2,061,943 | 2,041,729 |
| P/L | (71,243) | (136,188) | (142,307) |
| NW | 2,747,835 | 2,865,187 | 2,985,616 |
| WC | 234,263 | 215,188 | 1,076,645 |
| Emp. | 114 | 115 | 99 |

DUNS 21-774-3741

### Stockingford Early Years Centre

St Pauls Road, Nuneaton, Warwickshire CV10 8HW
**Tel:** 02476383708
**Web:** www.stockingford-earlyyears.co.uk
**Estd:** 2011 Proprietorship
**Line of Business:** Creches
**Proprietor:** Mrs A Clay
**US SIC:** 8211 **UK SIC:** 93200
**Employees:** 60

DUNS 23-269-8212

### Stockley Academy

Park View Road, Uxbridge, Middlesex UB8 3GA
**Tel:** 01895-430066
**Web:** www.stockleyacademy.com
**Reg No:** 4302474 **Estd:** 2001 Private Company Limited By Guarantee
**Line of Business:** Schools (local authority)
**Directors:** J Howlett, L Jarrett, Mrs M Gibbons, D J Boden, A Ahmed, P Stevenson, G Bennett, Ms M Russell
**Co. Secretary:** Karam Bhogal
**Responsibilities**
**Senior:** Alexander Biddle *(Director)*, Eric Blaire *(Director)*, Karam Boghal *(Director of Finance)*, Jane Grant *(Director)*, Kripali Manek *(Director)*, Anita Mark *(Director)*, Ian Storey *(Principal)*
**Finance:** Karam Boghal *(Director of Finance)*
**HR:** Ian Storey *(Principal)*
**Health & Safety:** Karam Boghal *(Director of Finance)*
**US SIC:** 8211 **UK SIC:** 93200
**Bankers:** HSBC Bank plc (40-24-18)

| | 31-08-14 | 31-08-13 | 31-08-12 |
|---|---|---|---|
| TO | 7,603,654 | 7,505,675 | 7,625,211 |
| P/L | (797,475) | (575,210) | (203,815) |
| NW | 24,093,743 | 25,288,218 | 25,772,428 |
| WC | 1,007,338 | 1,152,002 | 1,247,158 |
| Emp. | 144 | 144 | 165 |

DUNS 21-156-9816

### Stockleys Sweets Ltd

(**Subsidiary of:** Morris & Son (Holdings) Ltd)
11 Park Place, Leeds, West Yorkshire LS1 2RU
**Web:** www.stockleys-sweets.co.uk
**Reg No:** 6847256 **Estd:** 2009 Private Limited Company
**Line of Business:** Manufacture of sugar confectionery
**Issued Capital:** £1
**Directors:** S M Roberts, A D Needham
**Branches:** Stockleys Sweets Ltd, Cartwright Street, Cleckheaton, West Yorkshire BD19 5LY
**US SIC:** 2065 **UK SIC:** 42142

| | 31-07-13 | 31-07-12 | 31-07-11 |
|---|---|---|---|
| TO | N/A | N/A | 2,608,006 |
| P/L | N/A | N/A | 25,231 |
| NW | 52,942 | 36,111 | 12,334 |
| WC | (291,387) | (330,763) | (413,253) |
| Emp. | N/A | N/A | 51 |

DUNS 21-283-8561

### Stockport Audi

101 Brinksway, Stockport, Cheshire SK3 0HX
**Tel:** 08451226547
**Web:** www.anyaudi.co.uk
**Estd:** 1999
**Line of Business:** Sale of new motor vehicles
**Proprietor:** R Clough
**US SIC:** 5511 **UK SIC:** 65100
**Employees:** 80

DUNS 23-082-7243

### Stockport College

Horseshoe Cottage, Town Fold, Stockport, Cheshire SK6 5BT
**Tel:** 01619583100
**Web:** www.stockport.ac.uk
**Estd:** 1989
**Line of Business:** Creches
**Trading Style:** Stockport College
**Director:** Dr R Evans
**Responsibilities**
**Senior:** Sharon Dymond-Muller *(Nursery Manager)*, Lee Gregory *(Training Manager)*
**US SIC:** 8211 **UK SIC:** 93200
**Employees:** 1,000

DUNS 23-275-8909

### Stockport Grammar School

Buxton Road, Stockport, Cheshire SK2 7AF
**Tel:** 01614192405
**Web:** www.stockportgrammar.co.uk
**Line of Business:** Independent grammar school
**Director:** I Mellor
**US SIC:** 8211 **UK SIC:** 93200
**Employees:** 100

DUNS 77-946-9592

### Stockport Grammar School (2007) Ltd

Buxton Road, Stockport, Cheshire SK2 7AF
**Tel:** 01614569000
**Web:** www.stockportgrammar.co.uk
**Reg No:** 3053242 **Estd:** 1995 Private Company Limited By Guarantee
**Line of Business:** General secondary education
**Directors:** Mrs S Lansbury, P L Giblin, P A Cuddy, Dr R Shah, F A Booth, C F Dunn, D J Bills, K Lansdale
**Co. Secretary:** Christopher Watson
**Responsibilities**
**Senior:** Philip Britton *(Director)*, Anthony Carr *(Director)*, Sarah Carroll *(Director)*, John Dainton *(Director)*, Paul Milner *(Director)*, Laura Wolfe *(Director)*
**IT:** Jonathan Quinn *(System Manager)*
**US SIC:** 8211 **UK SIC:** 93200
**Employees:** 250

DUNS 64-118-0091

### Stockport Homes Ltd

1 St Peters Square, Stockport, Cheshire SK1 1NZ
**Tel:** 01612181840
**Web:** www.stockporthomes.org
**Reg No:** 4521257 **Estd:** 2002 Private Limited Company
**Line of Business:** Housing associations societies trusts & co-operatives
**Directors:** J Bowker, Mrs C Woolridge, D Wright, D R Beckett, Mrs J T Hague, P V Porgess, Mrs A H Vine, R Phillips
**Responsibilities**
**Senior:** Thomas Dotchin *(Director)*, Helen McHale *(Chief Executive Officer)*, Maureen Rowles *(Board Member)*
**Finance:** Carmel Chambers *(Head of Financial Services)*
**Marketing:** Nicola Green *(Relations Executive)*, Rebecca Mcavoy *(Relations Executive)*, Nicola Poulter *(Marketing Executive)*, Jane Ratcliff *(Marketing and Communications M)*
**US SIC:** 6531 **UK SIC:** 83400
**Auditors:** PKF (UK) LLP
**Bankers:** The Co-Operative Bank Plc (08-90-24)

| | 31-03-14 | 31-03-13 | 31-03-12 |
|---|---|---|---|
| TO | 37,189,000 | 33,936,000 | 31,022,000 |
| P/L | 166,000 | 1,168,000 | 1,137,000 |
| NW | (2,414,000) | (2,136,000) | (725,000) |
| WC | 4,780,000 | 4,685,000 | 3,945,000 |
| Emp. | 476 | 433 | 397 |

DUNS 21-249-7835

### Stockport Met Borough Council

Enterprise House, Bird Hall Lane, Stockport, Cheshire SK3 0XS
**Tel:** 01614745710
**Web:** www.solutionssk.co.uk
**Line of Business:** Retail sale of sports goods, games and toys, stamps and coins
**Responsibilities**
**IT:** Simon Winter *(IT Manager)*
**Health & Safety:** Peter Clifton *(Health & Safety Officer)*
**US SIC:** 5941 **UK SIC:** 65400
**Employees:** 1,500

DUNS 54-864-0770

### Stockport Nhs Foundation Trust

Stepping Hill Hospital, Poplar Grove, Stockport, Cheshire SK2 7JE
**Tel:** 01614831010
**Web:** www.stockport.nhs.uk
**Estd:** 1995
**Line of Business:** Hospitals
**Issued Capital:** £1
**Principals:** Dr R Shah *(Chairman)*, W Gregory *(Financial)*, Ms N Reucroft *(Personnel)*, Ms J Morris, Ms C Spencer, Dr C Burke, Ms G Easson, Ms C Prowse
**Responsibilities**
**Senior:** John McGuire *(Non-Executive Director)*, Michelle Mullender *(Manager)*, Les Wilcox *(Non Executive Chairperson)*
**Operations:** Jayne Shaw *(Director of Workforce & Organi)*
**Branches:** Stockport Nhs Foundation Trust, Marple Library, Memorial Park, Stockport, Cheshire SK6 6BA
**US SIC:** 8062, 6732
**UK SIC:** 95100, 83100
**Auditors:** Jackie Bellard ACA

| | 31-03-14 | 31-03-13 | 31-03-12 |
|---|---|---|---|
| TO | 293,744,000 | 290,194,000 | 231,060,000 |
| P/L | 943,000 | 2,619,000 | 3,041,000 |
| NW | 142,826,000 | 139,132,000 | 136,368,000 |
| WC | 28,053,000 | 28,349,000 | 25,939,000 |
| Emp. | 5,063 | 4,997 | 4,348 |

DUNS 22-286-6951

### Stockport Sports Trust

4th Floor Landmark House, Station Road Cheadle Hulme, Cheadle, Cheshire SK8 7BS
**Tel:** 01614774242 **Fax:** 0161-491-3816
**Web:** www.lifeleisure.net
**Reg No:** 4304674 **Estd:** 2001 Private Company Limited By Guarantee
**Line of Business:** Other business activities not elsewhere classified
**Directors:** N H Walker, A C Thompson, A D Hopkins, M J Pomfret, S H Mccombe, M Atkinson, G N Lawrence, Ms V J Cottam
**Co. Secretary:** Philip Vibrans
**Responsibilities**
**Senior:** Andrew Smithson *(Director)*

**Branches:** Stockport Sports Trust, Gorton Rd, Stockport, Cheshire SK5 6RL
**US SIC:** 7399 **UK SIC:** 83954
**Bankers:** The Co-Operative Bank Plc (08-90-00)

| | 31-03-14 | 31-03-13 | 31-03-12 |
|---|---|---|---|
| TO | 11,521,684 | 11,015,990 | 9,699,727 |
| P/L | 223,738 | 256,415 | 327,638 |
| NW | 1,652,196 | 978,458 | 851,043 |
| WC | 699,687 | 554,657 | 726,143 |
| Emp. | 472 | 480 | 425 |

DUNS 64-108-7478
### Stocks Group Ltd
18 Woodhouse Road, Scunthorpe, South Humberside DN16 1BD
**Tel:** 01724-281811
**Web:** www.stocksgroup.co.uk
**Reg No:** 4512220 **Estd:** 2002 Private Limited Company
**Line of Business:** Renting of other machinery and equipment not elsewhere classified
**Trading Style:** Stocks Group Ltd
**Issued Capital:** £100
**Directors:** C J Claypole, D Stocks, S D Stocks, Mrs S M Stocks
**Co. Secretary:** Ms Anne Short
**US SIC:** 7394 **UK SIC:** 84000

| | 31-03-14 | 31-03-13 | 31-03-12 |
|---|---|---|---|
| TO | 10,970,696 | 9,429,657 | 10,624,040 |
| P/L | 753,576 | (302,071) | 115,228 |
| NW | 2,415,509 | 1,919,092 | 2,164,320 |
| WC | 1,738,197 | 932,330 | 53,511 |
| Emp. | 198 | 184 | 241 |

DUNS 39-733-1729
### Stocks Hall Care Homes Ltd
50c White Moss Road, Skelmersdale, Lancashire WN8 8BL
**Tel:** 01695556996 **Fax:** 01695-557100
**Web:** www.stockshall-care.co.uk
**Reg No:** 2174831 **VAT No:** 548799371
**Estd:** 1987 Private Limited Company
**Line of Business:** Rest and retirement homes
**Trading Style:** Stocks Hall Residential, Stocks Homecare & Nursing Services
**Issued Capital:** £200
**Principals:** Mrs S E Lace (Managing), S H Lace, R A Jones, G B Jones
**Co. Secretary:** Mrs Susan Lace
**Branches:** Stocks Hall Care Homes Ltd, 251 Liverpool Road South, Ormskirk, Lancashire L40 7RE
**US SIC:** 8321, 6732
**UK SIC:** 96111, 83100
**Auditors:** BDO Stoy Hayward
**Bankers:** National Westminster Bank Plc (01-06-45)

| | 31-10-13 | 31-10-12 | 31-10-11 |
|---|---|---|---|
| TO | 10,117,532 | 9,867,088 | 9,739,367 |
| P/L | 706,418 | 874,539 | 815,688 |
| NW | 5,553,491 | 5,216,546 | 4,827,245 |
| WC | 1,064,028 | 186,203 | (152,988) |
| Emp. | 561 | 528 | 500 |

DUNS 64-805-9434
### Stocks Hall Residential Rest Home
76 Nursery Avenue, Ormskirk, Lancashire L39 2DZ
**Tel:** 01695579842
**Web:** www.stockshall-care.co.uk
**Estd:** 1988 Partnership
**Line of Business:** Other human health activities
**Partners:** S Lace, Mrs S Lace
**Responsibilities**
**Senior:** Sandra Donaldson (Home Manager)
**US SIC:** 8321 **UK SIC:** 96111
**Employees:** 46

DUNS 21-605-4191
### Stocks Homecare & Nursing Services
86 Sandy Lane, Skelmersdale, Lancashire WN8 8LQ
**Tel:** 01695722211
**Web:** www.stockshall-care.co.uk
**Estd:** 2011 Proprietorship
**Line of Business:** Home care service providers
**Proprietor:** Miss C Bradley
**US SIC:** 8091 **UK SIC:** 95200
**Employees:** 75

DUNS 21-462-3584
### Stocksbridge High School
Shay House Lane, Sheffield, South Yorkshire S36 1FD
**Tel:** 01142883410
**Web:** www.stocksbridgehigh.co.uk
**Proprietorship**
**Line of Business:** Schools (local authority)
**Proprietor:** Mrs J Featherstone
**US SIC:** 8211 **UK SIC:** 93200
**Employees:** 150

DUNS 21-227-2476
### Stocksbridge Neuro Rehab Centre
2a Haywood Lane, Sheffield, South Yorkshire S36 2QE
**Tel:** 0114-2837200
**Web:** www.huntercombe.co.uk
**Estd:** 1997 Proprietorship
**Line of Business:** Nursing homes
**Proprietor:** A Murrey
**Responsibilities**
**Senior:** Jill Salmon (Business Manager)
**US SIC:** 8051 **UK SIC:** 95100
**Employees:** 95

DUNS 73-797-2005
### Stockton & District Advice & Information Service
Bath Lane, Stockton-On-Tees, Cleveland TS18 2DS
**Tel:** 01642607445
**Web:** www.stockton-cab.co.uk
**Reg No:** 5053647 **Estd:** 1993 Private Company Limited By Guarantee
**Line of Business:** Counselling & advice services
**Directors:** T Stephenson, Ms S Jarvis, Ms F J Webb, N B Rodrigues, Ms B G Kirby, Ms A M Mccoy, R Cains, B R Cooper
**Co. Secretary:** Ian Bartlett
**Responsibilities**
**Senior:** Victoria Cooper (Director), Kathryn Hobson (Director)
**US SIC:** 8321 **UK SIC:** 96111
**Auditors:** Draycott & Kirk
**Bankers:** National Westminster Bank Plc (55-61-00)

| | 31-03-14 | 31-03-13 | 31-03-12 |
|---|---|---|---|
| TO | 1,291,606 | 1,357,700 | 1,314,218 |
| P/L | 26,532 | 24,386 | (42,694) |
| NW | 162,706 | 191,854 | 167,468 |
| WC | 132,797 | 174,457 | 147,167 |
| Emp. | 52 | 59 | 62 |

DUNS 21-791-3925
### Stockton Heath Primary School Pta
West Avenue, Warrington, Cheshire WA4 6HX
**Tel:** 01925215640
**Web:** www.stocktonheathprimary.com
**Estd:** 2002
**Line of Business:** Schools (local authority)
**Proprietor:** Mrs L Carnes
**Responsibilities**
**Senior:** Dan Harding (Head Teacher)
**US SIC:** 8211 **UK SIC:** 93200
**Employees:** 50

DUNS 23-644-0467
### Stockton-on-Tees Borough Council
Stockton-On-Tees Borough Council, Po Box 11, Stockton-On-Tees, Cleveland TS18 1LD
**Tel:** 01642393939
**Web:** www.stockton.gov.uk
**Estd:** 1996
**Line of Business:** General (overall) public service activities
**Trading Style:** Ash Trees School; Oaktree Primary School, St John the Evangalist R C School, Care for Your Area; St Patrick R.C. Primary School
**Directors:** Ms J Danks, P Dobson, D Bond, Ms J Humphreys, N Schneider
**Responsibilities**
**Health & Safety:** Derek MacDonald (Health & Safety Officer)
**Purchasing:** Angela Lench (Procurement Officer)
**Branches:** Stockton-On-Tees Borough Council, Baysdale Road, Stockton-On-Tees, Cleveland TS17 9DF
**US SIC:** 9121 **UK SIC:** 91110
**Bankers:** National Westminster Bank Plc (55-61-00)
**Employees:** 7,710

DUNS 23-635-9741
### Stockton Riverside College
Harvard Avenue, Stockton-On-Tees, Cleveland TS17 6FB
**Fax:** 01642865537
**Web:** www.stockton.ac.uk
**VAT No:** 602240207 **Estd:** 1950 Incorporate By Act Of Parliament
**Line of Business:** Further education schools and colleges
**Principals:** A Pilkington (Financial), Mrs M Armstrong, F Mccrindle
**Responsibilities**
**Senior:** Martin Copley (Team Leader), Pat Lawton (Senior Manager)
**Finance:** Ron Booth (Army Bursary Coordinator)
**Marketing:** Kate Nicholson (Career Development Manager)
**Admin:** Elaine Collier (Office Manager)

**IT:** Neville Dart (IS Manager)
**HR:** Paul Hiser (Head of HR Management and Effi)
**Facilities:** Jason Faulkner (Head of Faculty - Creative and), Mark Grosvenor (Facilities Manager)
**Operations:** Gillian Hutchinson (Production and Operations Mana)
**Branches:** Stockton Riverside College, Oxbridge Ave, Stockton-On-Tees, Cleveland TS18 4QA
**US SIC:** 8221 **UK SIC:** 93100
**Bankers:** National Westminster Bank Plc (51-70-17)
**Employees:** 300

DUNS 76-944-2039
### Stockvale Ltd
(Subsidiary of: Stockvale Investments Ltd)
Sunken Gardens, Western Esplanade, Southend-On-Sea, Essex SS1 1EE
**Tel:** 01702-443400 **Fax:** 01702443400
**Web:** www.adventureisland.co.uk
**Reg No:** 1253715 **VAT No:** 251485560
**Estd:** 2002 Private Limited Company
**Line of Business:** Amusement park activities
**Trading Style:** Adventure Island
**Issued Capital:** £10,000
**Principals:** M J Miller (Chairman), P A Miller (Chairman and Managing), Ms M K Bean, A Renton, J Miller
**Co. Secretary:** Marc Miller
**Responsibilities**
**IT:** Martyn Bailey (Head of Information Technology)
**US SIC:** 7996 **UK SIC:** 97913
**Auditors:** Rickard Keen
**Bankers:** Barclays Bank Plc (20-79-73)

| | 31-12-13 | 31-12-12 | 31-12-11 |
|---|---|---|---|
| TO | 6,628,654 | 7,057,685 | 7,962,698 |
| P/L | 653,005 | 148,370 | 668,615 |
| NW | 14,854,636 | 15,516,771 | 15,182,223 |
| WC | 7,394,217 | 8,200,506 | 8,959,565 |
| Emp. | 226 | 279 | 305 |

DUNS 21-596-0713
### Stockwell Primary School
Dodswell Grove, Hull, North Humberside HU9 5HY
**Tel:** 01482782122
**Web:** www.stockwell.hull.sch.uk
**Estd:** 2011
**Line of Business:** Primary education
**Responsibilities**
**Senior:** Christopher Coulter (Head Teacher)
**US SIC:** 8211 **UK SIC:** 93200
**Employees:** 50

DUNS 73-762-0703
### Stok Uk Ltd
5 Sopwith Park Royce Close, Andover, Hampshire SP10 3TS
**Tel:** 01264335117
**Web:** www.stokuk.com
**Reg No:** 5019402 **Estd:** 2013 Private Limited Company
**Line of Business:** Hospital equipment
**Issued Capital:** £100
**Directors:** S Glaeser, T Winkelmann, P D Wilkinson
**Co. Secretary:** Ms Lianne Branton
**Branches:** Stok Uk Ltd, 6 Campus 5, Letchworth Garden City, Hertfordshire SG6 2JF
**US SIC:** 5199, 7399
**UK SIC:** 61900, 83954

| | 30-06-14 | 30-06-13 | 30-06-12 |
|---|---|---|---|
| TO | 4,374,390 | N/A | N/A |
| P/L | 705,510 | N/A | N/A |
| NW | 884,551 | 391,730 | 135,846 |
| WC | 690,174 | 128,910 | (90,189) |

DUNS 21-028-6706
### Stoke Audi
Charon Way, Westbrook, Warrington, Cheshire WA5 7YD
**Web:** www.stokeaudi.co.uk
**Estd:** 2011 Proprietorship
**Line of Business:** Car dealers (new & used)
**Proprietor:** J Coppock
**US SIC:** 5511 **UK SIC:** 65100
**Employees:** 60

DUNS 28-874-9559
### The Stoke by Nayland Club Ltd.
(Subsidiary of: The Boxford Group Ltd.)
Keepers Lane, Leavenheath, Colchester, Essex CO6 4PZ
**Tel:** 01206-262836
**Web:** www.stokebynaylandclub.co.uk
**Reg No:** 1095790 **VAT No:** 103314726
**Estd:** 1973 Private Limited Company
**Line of Business:** Physical well-being activities
**Issued Capital:** £1,443,090
**Principals:** Ms S P Rendall (Managing), Ms T C Unwin, A W Cracknell

**Co. Secretary:** Jonathan Loshak
**Responsibilities**
**Senior:** Gordon Duckenfield (Accounts Admin), Winstone Loshak (Wright), Matthew Manning (General Manager), Keith Prichard (Manager)
**Sales:** Debbie Hynard (Sales Manager)
**HR:** Moira Carr (Human Resources Manager)
**Health & Safety:** Matthew Manning (General Manager)
**US SIC:** 7299 **UK SIC:** 98902
**Auditors:** Deloitte & Touche
**Bankers:** HSBC Bank plc (40-43-23)

| | 31-03-14 | 31-03-13 | 31-03-12 |
|---|---|---|---|
| TO | 5,893,690 | 5,619,111 | 5,491,853 |
| P/L | 87,573 | 37,160 | 176,371 |
| NW | 4,719,688 | 4,144,042 | 4,115,382 |
| WC | (316,610) | (337,717) | (523,742) |
| Emp. | 155 | 152 | 154 |

DUNS 21-314-8971
### Stoke City Football Club
The Britannia Stadium, Stanley Matthews Way, Stoke-On-Trent, Staffordshire ST4 4EG
**Tel:** 01782592234
**Web:** www.stokecityfc.com
**Proprietorship**
**Line of Business:** Conference related services
**Proprietor:** T Scholes
**US SIC:** 6531 **UK SIC:** 83400
**Employees:** 291

DUNS 28-829-4507
### Stoke City Football Club Ltd
(Subsidiary of: Bet365 Group Limited)
The Britannia Stadium, Stanley Matthews Way, Stoke-On-Trent, Staffordshire ST4 4EG
**Tel:** 01782367598 **Fax:** 01782599210
**Web:** www.stokecityfc.com
**Reg No:** 0099885 **Estd:** 1908 Private Limited Company
**Line of Business:** Sports clubs
**Issued Capital:** £35,843,345
**Principals:** P Coates (Chairman), R K Smith, K A Humphreys, A J Scholes
**Co. Secretary:** Martin Goodman
**Responsibilities**
**Senior:** Andrew Billingham (Sales & Marketing Manager), Eddie Harrison (Club Secretary), Philip Rawlins (Manager)
**Marketing:** Andrew Billingham (Sales & Marketing Manager), Lewis Carroll (Marketing Executive - CRM Data), Paul Lakin (Sales & Marketing Manager), Mark Mothershaw (Website & Magazine Editor), Fraser Nicholson (Head of Media & Communications)
**Sales:** Andrew Billingham (Sales & Marketing Manager), Paul Lakin (Sales & Marketing Manager), Rob Pass (Sales Executive)
**IT:** Mark Mothershaw (Website & Magazine Editor)
**HR:** Margaret Stringer (Human Resources Manager), Gary Worthington (Kit Manager)
**Health & Safety:** Rob Killingworth (Health & Safety Manager), Ravi Sharma (Head of Health & Safety)
**Facilities:** Craig Jepson (Head of Facilities), Nick Robinson (Head of Facilities)
**Purchasing:** Lucy Basnett (Purchasing Manager)
**Branches:** Stoke City Football Club Ltd, Stafford Street, Stoke-On-Trent, Staffordshire ST1 1SA
**US SIC:** 7999 **UK SIC:** 97913
**Auditors:** Deloitte & Touche
**Bankers:** Barclays Bank Plc (20-36-43)

| | 31-05-14 | 31-05-13 | 31-05-12 |
|---|---|---|---|
| TO | 98,318,000 | 66,516,000 | 70,734,000 |
| P/L | 3,786,000 | (31,119,000) | (9,529,000) |
| NW | (49,734,000) | (63,540,000) | (34,053,000) |
| WC | (46,851,000) | (57,664,000) | (25,278,000) |
| Emp. | 264 | 251 | 235 |

DUNS 21-163-4550
### Stoke College
Stoke By Clare, Sudbury, Suffolk CO10 8JE
**Tel:** 01787-278141
**Web:** www.stokecollege.co.uk
**Estd:** 1950
**Line of Business:** Schools (independent)
**Principals:** C Trewhella (Chairman), Ms C Burne, D Pillar
**Responsibilities**
**Senior:** Angela Austen (Manager), Susan Caddock (Manager), Mary Fitch (Manager), Simon Packford (Manager), John Parcell (Manager)
**IT:** Dean Moss (IT Coordinator)
**Health & Safety:** Steve Ager (Head of Maintenance)
**Facilities:** Steve Ager (Head of Maintenance)
**Branches:** Stoke College, Stoke By Clare, Sudbury, Suffolk CO10 8JE

**US SIC:** 8221 **UK SIC:** 93100
**Bankers:** Lloyds TSB Bank plc (30-98-31)
**Employees:** 63

DUNS 21-717-0191
### Stoke Damerel Community College
Somerset Place, Plymouth, Devon PL3 4BD
**Tel:** 01752556065 **Fax:** 01752562323
**Web:** www.sdcc.net
**Reg No:** 7557634 **Estd:** 2011 Private Company Limited By Guarantee
**Line of Business:** General secondary education
**Directors:** Ms M Baines, Ms P J Gregory, W H Blagdon, D J Stark, Ms C Hannaford, S W Cornwell, K Martin, R G Gilley
**Co. Secretary:** Martyn Cox
**Responsibilities**
**Senior:** Lisa Beachem *(Director)*, Janice Cole *(Director)*, Gordon Cryer *(Director)*, Colin Searls *(Director)*, Joanna Ware *(Director)*
**US SIC:** 8211 **UK SIC:** 93200
**Bankers:** Lloyds TSB Bank plc (30-96-68)

| | 31-08-14 | 31-08-13 | 31-08-12 |
|---|---|---|---|
| TO | 9,443,000 | 9,488,000 | 22,836,000 |
| P/L | (260,000) | 339,000 | 10,670,000 |
| NW | 8,597,000 | 8,984,000 | 8,755,000 |
| WC | 272,000 | 482,000 | 396,000 |
| Emp. | 214 | 192 | 176 |

DUNS 21-414-9028
### Stoke House Nursing Home
24-26 Stoke Lane, Gedling, Nottingham, Nottinghamshire NG4 2QP
**Tel:** 01159400635
**Web:** www.stokehouse.com
**Estd:** 1985 Partnership
**Line of Business:** Nursing Homes
**Partners:** Ms C Russell, D Brett
**Responsibilities**
**Senior:** David Brett *(Partner)*, Deirdre Gibbs *(Manager)*
**Finance:** Amanda Clarke *(Senior Finance Administrator)*
**US SIC:** 8051 **UK SIC:** 95100
**Employees:** 50

DUNS 28-862-2277
### Stoke-on-Trent & North Staffordshire Theatre Trust Ltd
Etruria Road, Newcastle, Staffordshire ST5 0JG
**Web:** www.newvictheatre.org.uk
**Reg No:** 0911924 **Estd:** 1967 Private Limited Company
**Line of Business:** Artistic and literary creation and interpretation
**Directors:** M Holt, Dr I M Jones, J M Shepherd, I M Parry, Ms S L Williams, B C Carnes, Ms S V Honeyands, C I Barcroft
**Co. Secretary:** Ms Andrea Wallace
**Responsibilities**
**Senior:** Rosemary Crehan *(Director)*, Brian Fender *(Director)*, Terence Follows *(Director)*
**US SIC:** 7999 **UK SIC:** 97913
**Auditors:** KPMG
**Bankers:** National Westminster Bank Plc (60-21-59)

| | 31-03-14 | 31-03-13 | 31-03-12 |
|---|---|---|---|
| TO | 3,617,233 | 3,285,950 | 3,194,891 |
| P/L | 197,401 | 83,103 | 104,991 |
| NW | 2,247,845 | 2,050,444 | 1,967,341 |
| WC | 1,402,764 | 1,164,816 | 1,049,859 |
| Emp. | 118 | 111 | 116 |

DUNS 21-600-9136
### Stoke on Trent College
Tunstall Neighbourhood College, Stoke-On-Trent, Staffordshire ST6 4JU
**Tel:** 01782835032
**Web:** www.stokeontrentlocksmiths.com
**Estd:** 2004
**Line of Business:** Universities, Colleges, Prof. Schools
**US SIC:** 8221 **UK SIC:** 93100
**Employees:** 47

DUNS 23-033-5911
### Stoke-on-Trent College
Cauldon Campus, Stoke Road, Stoke-On-Trent, Staffordshire ST4 2DG
**Tel:** 01782-208208
**Web:** www.stokecoll.ac.uk
**Estd:** 1993 Incorporate By Act Of Parliament
**Line of Business:** Colleges (higher education)
**Principals:** B Taylor *(Financial)*, G Moor
**Responsibilities**
**Finance:** Colin Briley *(Financial Director)*, Bryan Taylor *(Financial Director)*
**IT:** Steve Anesbury *(IT Manager)*, Dave Phillips *(Computer Operations Manager)*
**Branches:** Stoke-On-Trent College, Market Square, Stoke-On-Trent, Staffordshire ST1 1PS
**US SIC:** 8221 **UK SIC:** 93100
**Employees:** 1,200

DUNS 21-558-5814
### Stoke on Trent Community Health Services
Stoke On Trent Longton Cottage Hospital, Upper Belgrave Road, Stoke-On-Trent, Staffordshire ST3 4QX
**Web:** www.stokepct.nhs.uk
**Estd:** 2006
**Line of Business:** Community Health Services
**US SIC:** 8091 **UK SIC:** 95200
**Employees:** 1,200

DUNS 34-587-9571
### Stoke Park Ltd
(**Subsidiary of:** International Group Ltd)
Park Road, Slough, Berkshire SL2 4PG
**Tel:** 01753717171 **Fax:** 01753-717181
**Web:** www.theoldstationnursery.co.uk
**Reg No:** 2732069 **VAT No:** 578564779
**Estd:** 2012 Private Limited Company
**Line of Business:** Nursery schools
**Trading Style:** Stoke Park Hotel, Stoke Park Golf Club
**Issued Capital:** £1,000
**Principals:** H M King *(Managing)*, C M King *(Financial)*, W M King, R M King
**Co. Secretary:** Hertford King
**Branches:** Stoke Park Ltd, Hertford Pl, Rickmansworth, Hertfordshire WD3 9HG
**US SIC:** 8211, 7941
**UK SIC:** 93200, 97911
**Auditors:** KPMG LLP
**Bankers:** National Westminster Bank Plc (60-19-28)

| | 31-12-13 | 31-12-12 | 31-12-11 |
|---|---|---|---|
| TO | 13,839,000 | 13,413,000 | 12,674,000 |
| P/L | 661,000 | 527,000 | 28,000 |
| NW | 19,991,000 | 19,330,000 | 18,941,000 |
| WC | (7,659,000) | (7,624,000) | (8,216,000) |
| Emp. | 190 | 196 | 192 |

DUNS 22-665-0489
### Stoke Rochford Management Ltd
Stoke Rochford, Grantham, Lincolnshire NG33 5EJ
**Tel:** 01476530337 **Fax:** 01476-530534
**Web:** www.stokerochfordhall.co.uk
**Reg No:** 1361390 **Estd:** 1978 Private Limited Company
**Line of Business:** Hotels
**Issued Capital:** £1,163,673
**Directors:** E J Glazier, I Murch, I Grayson, R King, Ms C Blower, D Brinson, I Leaver, Ms M Harrop
**Co. Secretary:** Ms Audrey Allen-Chitwa
**Responsibilities**
**Senior:** Barry Clark *(General Manager)*, Mike Loveridge *(Head Chef)*, Jackie Robinson *(Manager)*, Neill Walker *(General Manager)*
**Finance:** Nicola Burridge *(Financial Manager)*
**Admin:** Nicky Griffin *(Administration Manager)*
**IT:** Nicola Burridge *(Financial Manager)*
**HR:** Nicky Griffin *(Administration Manager)*
**Health & Safety:** David Frampton *(Health & Safety Officer)*
**Facilities:** Jim Burne *(Project Manager)*
**Purchasing:** Nicky Griffin *(Administration Manager)*
**US SIC:** 7011, 8999
**UK SIC:** 66500, 83954
**Auditors:** Knox Cropper

| | 31-12-13 | 31-12-12 | 31-12-11 |
|---|---|---|---|
| TO | 2,509,897 | 2,443,919 | 2,277,855 |
| P/L | (905,696) | (889,688) | (944,473) |
| NW | 12,182,146 | 13,092,757 | 13,943,693 |
| WC | (131,211) | 332,263 | 315,411 |
| Emp. | 55 | 53 | 97 |

DUNS 21-227-2229
### Stoke Town Hall
Civic Centre, Glebe Street, Stoke-On-Trent, Staffordshire ST4 1HH
**Tel:** 01782-232631
**Web:** www.stoke.gov.uk
**Estd:** 2002 Proprietorship
**Line of Business:** Community networks
**Proprietor:** J Vandelaarshot
**Responsibilities**
**Senior:** John Van De Laarschot *(Chief Executive)*
**US SIC:** 9121 **UK SIC:** 91110
**Employees:** 2,000

DUNS 21-233-9204 **Imp**
### Stokers Ltd
(**Subsidiary of:** Stokers Holdings Ltd)
277 Wennington Road, Southport, Merseyside PR9 7TW
**Tel:** 01704500028 **Fax:** 01704-501119
**Web:** www.stokers.co.uk
**Reg No:** 0307357 **VAT No:** 165868124
**Estd:** 1899 Private Limited Company
**Line of Business:** Furniture retail outlets
**Issued Capital:** £431,709
**Director:** S G Schofield
**Co. Secretary:** Jonathan Stoker
**Branches:** Stokers Ltd, 9 Regent Street, Leeds, West Yorkshire LS2 7QN
**US SIC:** 5719, 5713
**UK SIC:** 64700
**Auditors:** McMillan & Co
**Bankers:** HSBC Bank plc (40-35-29)

| | 30-04-14 | 30-04-13 | 30-04-12 |
|---|---|---|---|
| TO | 31,212,611 | 27,911,390 | 25,676,143 |
| P/L | 2,141,603 | 1,525,487 | 1,044,436 |
| NW | 7,906,122 | 6,508,509 | 5,513,287 |
| WC | 7,240,073 | 5,916,937 | 4,851,945 |
| Emp. | 173 | 167 | 160 |

DUNS 76-497-9621
### Stokes Group Ltd
Po Box 18, Dudley, West Midlands DY2 0SE
**Tel:** 01384342550 **Fax:** 01384342551
**Web:** www.stokesforging.com
**Reg No:** 2567976 **VAT No:** 928799941
**Estd:** 1990 Private Limited Company
**Line of Business:** Manufacture of parts and accessories for motor vehicles and their engines
**Export Sales:** £2,701,671
**Trading Style:** Stokes Forgings, Mahindra Forgings
**Issued Capital:** £1,547,731
**Directors:** P G Morgan, H H Luthra
**Co. Secretary:** Lee Seville
**Responsibilities**
**Senior:** Alan Ledbury *(Manager)*
**HR:** Catherine Thornton *(Human Resources Manager)*
**Health & Safety:** Catherine Thornton *(Human Resources Manager)*
**Branches:** Stokes Group Ltd, Vine St, Brierley Hill, West Midlands DY5 1JE
**US SIC:** 3714 **UK SIC:** 35300
**Auditors:** Grant Thornton UK LLP
**Bankers:** Lloyds TSB Bank plc (30-99-06)

| | 31-12-13 | 31-03-13 | 31-12-12 |
|---|---|---|---|
| TO | 12,759,328 | 16,817,811 | 21,666,928 |
| P/L | (67,708) | (1,129,571) | 791,723 |
| NW | (3,388,753) | (3,308,295) | (2,161,723) |
| WC | (630,379) | (230,163) | (4,809,362) |
| Emp. | 159 | 159 | 178 |

DUNS 63-452-2932
### The Stokes Partnership Solicitors
Kingfisher House, Market Square, Crewkerne, Somerset TA18 7LH
**Tel:** 01460-279279
**Web:** www.stokespartners.co.uk
**Partnership**
**Line of Business:** Solicitors
**Trading Style:** The Stokes Partnership Solicitors
**Partners:** J Stokes, D Stokes, M Williams
**US SIC:** 8111 **UK SIC:** 83500
**Employees:** 80

DUNS 55-084-2827
### Stokesley Community Education Centre
Station Road, Stokesley, Middlesbrough, Cleveland TS9 5AL
**Tel:** 01642710050
**Line of Business:** Committee managed organisations
**US SIC:** 8699 **UK SIC:** 96902
**Employees:** 52

DUNS 77-496-5321
### Stollers Furniture World Ltd
(**Subsidiary of:** Stollers Stores (Barrow))
Walney Road, Barrow-In-Furness, Cumbria LA14 5UN
**Tel:** 01229-820679 **Fax:** 01229-870152
**Web:** www.stollers.co.uk
**Reg No:** 2978393 **VAT No:** 621491263
**Estd:** 1905 Private Limited Company
**Line of Business:** Furniture retail outlets
**Issued Capital:** £2
**Principals:** D M Stoller *(Managing)*, D Clamp *(Financial)*, L D Stoller
**Branches:** Stollers Furniture World Ltd, Lapstone Rd, Millom, Cumbria LA18 4BZ
**US SIC:** 5719 **UK SIC:** 64700
**Auditors:** RST Accountants Ltd
**Bankers:** National Westminster Bank Plc (01-00-61)

| | 31-08-13 | 31-08-12 | 31-08-11 |
|---|---|---|---|
| TO | 4,966,441 | 4,945,531 | 4,933,964 |
| P/L | 335,856 | 200,011 | 1,326,017 |
| NW | 3,501,503 | 3,308,833 | 3,178,795 |
| WC | 929,212 | 635,690 | 409,756 |
| Emp. | 69 | 76 | N/A |

DUNS 23-706-5818 **Imp-Exp**
### Stolzle Flaconnage Ltd
(**Subsidiary of:** Cag Handels-Gmbh & Co.Kg)
Weeland Road, Knottingley, West Yorkshire WF11 8AP
**Tel:** 01977-607124 **Fax:** 01977-672879
**Web:** www.stoelzle.com
**Reg No:** 2973822 **VAT No:** 642788896
**Estd:** 1994 Private Limited Company
**Line of Business:** Manufacturers of bottles
**Export Markets:** France; U S A; Germany; Scandinavia; Poland
**Issued Capital:** £2,350,000
**Directors:** P S Grumett, J W Schick
**Co. Secretary:** Jason Malloy
**US SIC:** 3221 **UK SIC:** 24780
**Auditors:** KPMG LLP
**Bankers:** Barclays Bank Plc (20-89-68)

| | 31-12-13 | 31-12-12 | 31-12-11 |
|---|---|---|---|
| TO | 63,658,236 | 68,842,927 | 60,288,654 |
| P/L | 3,059,415 | 2,536,819 | 3,359,226 |
| NW | 12,994,742 | 10,598,878 | 8,738,218 |
| WC | 3,653,521 | 3,148,228 | (1,279,127) |
| Emp. | 334 | 327 | 317 |

DUNS 28-881-5822
### Ston Easton Park Investments Ltd
The Old Pump House, Eastdown Road, Bath, Avon BA3 3DN
**Tel:** 01761-241631
**Web:** www.stoneaston.co.uk
**Reg No:** 1184260 **Estd:** 1974 Private Limited Company
**Line of Business:** Hotels and motels without restaurant
**Issued Capital:** £2
**Director:** Lady G Rees Mogg
**Co. Secretary:** Thomas Meadows
**US SIC:** 7011 **UK SIC:** 66500

| | 05-04-14 | 05-04-13 | 05-04-12 |
|---|---|---|---|
| TA | 2 | 2 | 2 |
| NW | 2 | 2 | 2 |

DUNS 22-639-1068
### Stonbury Ltd
(**Subsidiary of:** Stonbury Group Ltd)
187c High Street, Cranfield, Bedford, Bedfordshire MK43 0JB
**Tel:** 01234750924 **Fax:** 01482868457
**Web:** www.stonbury.com
**Reg No:** 1721842 **VAT No:** 382286532
**Estd:** 1983 Private Limited Company
**Line of Business:** Other construction work involving special trades
**Issued Capital:** £40,000
**Principals:** P M Stonor *(Managing)*, J W Perryman, I Mellor, N W Simpson, J A Stonor, J M Featherstone
**Co. Secretary:** Ms Sarah Stonor
**Responsibilities**
**IT:** Camran Liaqat
**Branches:** Stonbury Ltd, Unit 4, Oldbeck Road, Beverley, North Humberside HU17 0JW
**US SIC:** 1799, 1761
**UK SIC:** 50000, 50400
**Auditors:** Gallaghers
**Bankers:** National Westminster Bank Plc (60-24-19)

| | 30-06-14 | 30-06-13 | 30-06-12 |
|---|---|---|---|
| TO | 12,465,610 | 14,034,922 | N/A |
| P/L | 382,122 | 708,835 | N/A |
| NW | 1,046,948 | 1,657,327 | 1,114,755 |
| WC | 821,517 | 1,507,188 | 962,724 |
| Emp. | 77 | N/A | N/A |

DUNS 21-392-7195
### Stone Eden Nursery School
Wheelbarrow Hall, Aglionby, Carlisle, Cumbria CA4 8AD
**Tel:** 01228599400
**Web:** www.stoneedennursery.co.uk
**Estd:** 2008 Proprietorship
**Line of Business:** Nursery schools
**Proprietor:** D Farrell
**US SIC:** 8211 **UK SIC:** 93200
**Employees:** 50

DUNS 39-729-6195
### Stone Hardy Ltd
18-19 Saddleback Road, Westgate Industrial Estate, Northampton, Northamptonshire NN5 5HL
**Tel:** 01604591359 **Fax:** 01604-683529
**Web:** www.stonehardy.co.uk
**Reg No:** 2171820 **Estd:** 1987 Private Limited Company
**Line of Business:** Maintenance and repair of motor vehicles

**Issued Capital:** £2
**Directors:** G W Ford, P Clark, Mrs S Whitmore, J E Ratcliff
**Co. Secretary:** Mark Ivinson
**Responsibilities**
**Senior:** Stephen Mulvaney (Manager)
**Branches:** Stone Hardy Ltd, London House, Chittening Industrial Estate, Bristol, Avon BS11 0YB
**US SIC:** 7539 **UK SIC:** 67100
**Auditors:** Deloitte & Touche
**Bankers:** National Westminster Bank Plc (60-23-07)

| | 31-12-13 | 31-12-12 | 31-12-11 |
|---|---|---|---|
| TO | 9,678,026 | 8,862,836 | 8,673,797 |
| P/L | 546,870 | (128,627) | (657,762) |
| NW | 594,338 | 450 | 115,750 |
| WC | (820) | (559,861) | (363,517) |
| Emp. | 133 | 133 | N/A |

DUNS 52-018-0001

### Stone Manor Hotels Ltd
Stone, Stone, Chaddesley Corbett, Kidderminster, Worcestershire DY10 4PJ
**Tel:** 01562-777555 **Fax:** 01562777834
**Web:** www.stonemanorhotel.co.uk
**Reg No:** 3384578 **VAT No:** 711184566
**Estd:** 1999 Private Limited Company
**Line of Business:** Hotels
**Issued Capital:** £51,004
**Directors:** Mrs L D Winkle, M C Dunn, C W Dunn, R C Dunn, Miss D J Dunn
**Co. Secretary:** Robert Dunn
**Responsibilities**
**Senior:** James Rich (general manager)
**Branches:** Stone Manor Hotels Ltd, Stonechaddesley Corbett, Kidderminster, Worcestershire DY10 4PJ
**US SIC:** 7011 **UK SIC:** 66500
**Auditors:** Hoadley & Weavers Ltd
**Bankers:** Bank Of Scotland (80-20-19)

| | 30-09-13 | 30-09-12 | 30-09-11 |
|---|---|---|---|
| TO | 2,276,218 | 2,216,581 | 2,078,608 |
| P/L | (34,930) | (73,246) | (100,929) |
| NW | 3,571,532 | 3,871,426 | 3,650,505 |
| WC | 239,359 | 204,078 | (24,094) |
| Emp. | 149 | 149 | 152 |

DUNS 21-624-5305

### Stone Rowe Brewer Llp
12-13 Church Street, Twickenham, Middlesex TW1 3NJ
**Tel:** 02088916141
**Web:** www.srb.co.uk
**Reg No:** 0349339OC **Estd:** 2009
**Line of Business:** Solicitors
**Responsibilities**
**Senior:** Gillian Giblin (Office Manager)
**Admin:** Gillian Giblin (Office Manager), Sue Seymour (Personal Assistant)
**US SIC:** 8111 **UK SIC:** 83500

| | 31-03-14 | 31-03-13 | 31-03-12 |
|---|---|---|---|
| TA | 2,038,460 | 1,663,927 | 1,663,306 |
| NW | (31,201) | (35,101) | N/A |
| WC | 459,464 | 548,512 | 333,256 |

DUNS 21-114-0619

### Stone Topco Ltd
Omega House, Emerald Way, Stone Business Park, Stone, Staffordshire ST15 0SR
**Tel:** 01785812100
**Reg No:** 6546702 **Estd:** 2008 Private Limited Company
**Line of Business:** Computer services
**Issued Capital:** £1,000,000
**Directors:** M G Weavis, Ms J Williams, S R Harbridge, J E Dillon, S Constantinides
**Co. Secretary:** Sotos Constantinides
**US SIC:** 6711, 7399
**UK SIC:** 83962, 83954
**Auditors:** BDO LLP

| | 31-12-13 | 31-12-12 | 31-12-11 |
|---|---|---|---|
| TO | 77,274,000 | 73,812,808 | 65,516,205 |
| P/L | (5,225,000) | (2,987,062) | (2,361,300) |
| NW | (29,755,000) | (27,097,567) | (24,954,946) |
| WC | 4,031,000 | 3,932,535 | 4,189,850 |
| Emp. | 229 | 231 | 222 |

DUNS 50-635-3684

### Stoneacre
Stoneacre, Plas Acton Road, Wrexham, Clwyd LL11 2UB
**Tel:** 01978311666
**Web:** www.stoneacre.co.uk
**Estd:** 2008 Proprietorship
**Line of Business:** Sale of new motor vehicles
**Proprietor:** R Teatum
**Responsibilities**
**Finance:** Alex Dutton (Business Manager)
**Sales:** Simon McKeane (Sales Manager)
**US SIC:** 5511 **UK SIC:** 65100
**Employees:** 50


DUNS 21-573-6278

### Stoneacre Motor Group
Barnby Dun Road, Doncaster, South Yorkshire DN2 4QP
**Tel:** 01302327111
**Web:** www.stoneacre.co.uk
**Estd:** 1999 Proprietorship
**Line of Business:** Car dealers (new & used)
**Proprietor:** R Leetham
**Responsibilities**
**Senior:** Phil Ainsworth (Manager), Jason Holt (Service Manager), John Lam (Proprietor), Darren Laverick (General Manager)
**HR:** Kevin Harrington (Facilities Manager)
**Health & Safety:** Kevin Harrington (Facilities Manager)
**Facilities:** Kevin Harrington (Facilities Manager)
**Operations:** Jason Holt (Service Manager)
**US SIC:** 5511 **UK SIC:** 65100
**Employees:** 100

DUNS 21-818-9702

### Stonebow Wholesale Co Ltd
Pelham House, Canwick Road, Lincoln, Lincolnshire LN5 8HG
**Tel:** 01522511115
**Web:** www.jacksonbc.co.uk
**Reg No:** 0666044 **Estd:** 1960 Private Limited Company
**Line of Business:** Agents involved in the sale of timber and building materials
**Trading Style:** Jobs & Buildings Centre
**Issued Capital:** £100
**Principals:** S Jackson (Managing), Mrs S A Knight (Financial), Mrs K Wishart, S C Knight, Ms F C Jackson, Ms K M Jackson, C M Jackson, I Wishart
**Co. Secretary:** Michael Bishop
**Responsibilities**
**Purchasing:** Paul Bullivant (Purchasing Manager)
**US SIC:** 5072 **UK SIC:** 61500
**Bankers:** National Westminster Bank Plc (60-13-15)

| | 31-12-13 | 31-12-12 | 31-12-11 |
|---|---|---|---|
| TA | 3,530 | 3,530 | 3,530 |
| NW | 3,530 | 3,530 | 3,530 |

DUNS 73-921-3176

### Stonebridge Holdings Ltd
Unit 4 Launton Business Centre, Bicester, Oxfordshire OX26 4PL
**Tel:** 01869-357800 **Fax:** 01869357801
**Web:** www.stonebridge-ltd.com
**Reg No:** 5174535 **Estd:** 2004 Private Limited Company
**Line of Business:** Management activities of holding companies
**Trading Style:** Stonebridge Holdings Ltd
**Issued Capital:** £2,000
**Directors:** J L Green, A A Green, P J Green
**Co. Secretary:** Leslie Green
**US SIC:** 6711 **UK SIC:** 83962

| | 30-11-13 | 30-11-12 | 30-11-11 |
|---|---|---|---|
| TO | 2,709,141 | 2,802,644 | 2,764,704 |
| P/L | 367,194 | 256,237 | 313,374 |
| NW | 3,223,203 | 3,168,147 | 3,198,590 |
| WC | 925,787 | 816,442 | 797,266 |
| Emp. | 59 | 60 | 61 |

DUNS 21-206-9467

### Stonebridge Nursing Home
178-180 Birchfield Road, Redditch, Worcestershire B97 4NA
**Tel:** 01527542170
**Web:** www.stonebridgenursinghome.co.uk
**Estd:** 1986 Proprietorship
**Line of Business:** Residential care establishments
**Proprietor:** Mrs J Jones
**Responsibilities**
**Senior:** Julia Foley (Manager)
**US SIC:** 8051 **UK SIC:** 95100
**Employees:** 50

DUNS 49-120-1133      Imp

### Stoneforce Ltd
Unit 2c, Shakespeare Street Shakespeare, Industrial Estate, Watford, Hertfordshire WD24 5RR
**Tel:** 08450702861 **Fax:** 08450702861
**Web:** www.stoneforce.co.uk
**Reg No:** 3099713 **Estd:** 1995 Private Limited Company
**Line of Business:** Shopfitting contractors
**Issued Capital:** £55
**Directors:** P Smith, G Teden, D R Harvey
**Co. Secretary:** Ms Nina Smith
**US SIC:** 1796, 1799
**UK SIC:** 50400, 50000
**Auditors:** Hillier Hopkins LLP
**Bankers:** Barclays Bank Plc (20-39-07)

| | 31-12-13 | 31-12-12 | 31-12-11 |
|---|---|---|---|
| TO | 14,911,973 | 20,410,224 | 13,437,586 |
| P/L | 202,171 | 304,064 | 582,250 |
| NW | 712,336 | 609,105 | 510,171 |
| WC | 178,563 | 223,755 | 346,967 |
| Emp. | 47 | 47 | 35 |


DUNS 21-297-3135

### Stonegate 1434
17-19 Stonegate, York, North Yorkshire YO1 8ZW
**Tel:** 01904-620736
**Web:** www.mulberryhall.co.uk
**Reg No:** 0842884 **VAT No:** 170096181
**Estd:** 1965 Private Unlimited Company
**Line of Business:** China glass and crystalware shops
**Trading Style:** Mulberry Hall
**Issued Capital:** £158,500
**Principals:** A M Sinclair (Managing), J M Burnett, Ms V M Rose, M D Sinclair, Ms J M Sinclair
**Co. Secretary:** Adam Sinclair
**Branches:** Stonegate 1434, 14 Montpellier Parade, Harrogate, North Yorkshire HG1 2TG
**US SIC:** 5719 **UK SIC:** 64700
**Employees:** 70

DUNS 21-111-1924

### Stonegate Holdings Ltd
The Old Sidings, Corsham Road, Lacock, Chippenham, Wiltshire SN15 2LZ
**Tel:** 01249732230
**Web:** www.stonegate.co.uk
**Reg No:** 6525806 **Estd:** 2008 Private Limited Company
**Line of Business:** Poultry farmers
**Issued Capital:** £4,000,000
**Directors:** R G Corbett, Ms P J Corbett
**Responsibilities**
**Senior:** Nick Rogers (Manager)
**US SIC:** 0259 **UK SIC:** 01001
**Bankers:** Lloyds TSB Bank plc (30-00-02)

| | 28-09-13 | 29-09-12 | 01-09-11 |
|---|---|---|---|
| TO | 112,298,000 | 131,058,000 | 122,642,000 |
| P/L | 5,939,000 | 3,446,000 | 72,000 |
| NW | 8,152,000 | 2,684,000 | 1,326,000 |
| WC | (6,423,000) | (10,878,000) | (8,941,000) |
| Emp. | 466 | 443 | 469 |

DUNS 21-707-3983

### Stonegate Pub Co Ltd
(**Subsidiary of:** Codan Trust Company (Cayman) Limited)
Porter Tun House, 500 Capability Green, Luton, Bedfordshire LU1 3LS
**Tel:** 08451262944
**Web:** www.stonegatepubs.com
**Reg No:** 0029833FC **Estd:** 2010 Foreign Company
**Line of Business:** Public house management services
**Directors:** P Rowland, M Gudmundsson, M Dale, S D Longbottom, B J Magnus, I T Payne, D A Ross
**Co. Secretary:** Codan Trust Company (Cayman) Lim
**Responsibilities**
**Senior:** Maureen Heffernan (Public Relations Manager)
**US SIC:** 5813 **UK SIC:** 66200
**Auditors:** Unknown

DUNS 22-713-0051      Imp

### Stonehage Ltd
(**Subsidiary of:** Stonehage Financial Services Holdings Limited)
21 Dartmouth Street, London SW1H 9BP
**Tel:** 02070870000
**Web:** www.stonehage.com
**Reg No:** 1234340 **VAT No:** 524489135
**Estd:** 1975 Private Limited Company
**Line of Business:** Management activities of holding companies
**Issued Capital:** £2,702,000
**Directors:** A R Nolan, E Sofer, D F Fletcher, A H Sternberg
**Co. Secretary:** Miss Carmella Troise
**Responsibilities**
**Senior:** Aris Tatos (Director)
**US SIC:** 6711 **UK SIC:** 83962
**Auditors:** PricewaterhouseCoopers LLP
**Bankers:** National Westminster Bank Plc (60-40-02)

| | 31-03-14 | 31-03-13 | 31-03-12 |
|---|---|---|---|
| TO | 14,316,038 | 12,793,206 | 13,571,822 |
| P/L | 279,017 | (418,929) | 203,412 |
| NW | 3,074,603 | 2,765,085 | 2,272,647 |
| WC | 2,541,059 | 2,239,605 | 1,623,461 |
| Emp. | 63 | 59 | 60 |

DUNS 50-585-9421

### Stoneham Construction Ltd
Station Road, Havenstreet, Ryde, Isle of Wight PO33 4DT
**Web:** www.stonehamconstruction.co.uk
**Reg No:** 2528618 **VAT No:** 615138558
**Estd:** 1939 Private Limited Company
**Line of Business:** Construction of commercial buildings
**Trading Style:** Stoneham Construction Limited
**Issued Capital:** £250,000
**Directors:** D A Harris, A J Corbin, Ms L Corbin, Ms A R Harris


**Co. Secretary:** David Harris
**Responsibilities**
**Senior:** Ian Groves (Joint Managing Director), Alan Loaring (Manager), Michael Munns (Joint Managing Director)
**Finance:** Michael Munns (Joint Managing Director)
**US SIC:** 1522, 1799
**UK SIC:** 50100, 50000
**Auditors:** Casson Beckman
**Bankers:** Lloyds TSB Bank plc (30-95-99)

| | 30-09-14 | 30-09-13 | 07-09-12 |
|---|---|---|---|
| TO | N/A | N/A | 6,861,049 |
| P/L | N/A | N/A | (393,563) |
| NW | 211,041 | 82,466 | 174,322 |
| WC | 103,394 | (24,626) | 67,415 |

DUNS 21-686-7622      Imp-Exp

### Stoneham Plc
Powerscroft Road, Sidcup, Kent DA14 5DZ
**Tel:** 02083008181
**Web:** www.stoneham-kitchens.co.uk
**Reg No:** 0321764 **VAT No:** 205302030
**Estd:** 1936 Public Limited Company
**Line of Business:** Kitchen planners and installers
**Export Markets:** Europe
**Trading Style:** Stoneham Designed Kitchens, Stoneham Kitchens
**Issued Capital:** £100,000
**Principals:** E G Stoneham (Managing), H N Stoneham, A J Stoneham, M P Stoneham
**Co. Secretary:** Edward Stoneham
**Responsibilities**
**Senior:** Monica Stoneham (Manager)
**Finance:** Monica Stoneham (Manager)
**HR:** Corrine Fleming (Human Resources Manager)
**US SIC:** 7399, 2599, 5719
**UK SIC:** 83954, 46720, 64700
**Auditors:** McBrides
**Bankers:** HSBC Bank plc (40-42-01)

| | 31-12-13 | 31-12-12 | 31-12-11 |
|---|---|---|---|
| TO | 5,149,548 | 5,577,389 | 5,771,949 |
| P/L | 98,894 | 97,447 | 124,586 |
| NW | 1,564,458 | 1,486,787 | 1,433,387 |
| WC | 1,038,888 | 919,813 | 841,041 |
| Emp. | 69 | 68 | 67 |

DUNS 21-458-5150      Exp

### Stonehatch Ltd
Obins Avenue, Craigavon, Co Armagh BT62 1DF
**Tel:** 02838333215
**Reg No:** 0001108NI **Estd:** 1898 Private Limited Company
**Line of Business:** Furniture (fitted)
**Export Markets:** Republic of Ireland
**Issued Capital:** £74,000
**Directors:** T S Mcdonagh, Ms D L Mcdonagh
**Co. Secretary:** John Mcdonagh
**US SIC:** 6519 **UK SIC:** 85000
**Auditors:** R P Nichol & Associates
**Bankers:** Northern Bank Ltd (95-04-11)

| | 31-12-13 | 31-12-12 | 31-12-11 |
|---|---|---|---|
| TA | 1,063,657 | 1,096,932 | 1,137,014 |
| NW | 1,039,438 | 1,059,604 | 1,083,508 |
| WC | (18,639) | 399,226 | 395,336 |

DUNS 21-811-2598

### Stonehaven Community Education Centre
Bath Street, Stonehaven, Kincardineshire AB39 2DH
**Web:** www.stonehavencommunitycentre.org
**Estd:** 1973
**Line of Business:** Education agencies and authorities
**Responsibilities**
**Senior:** Leslie Murison (Senior Community Worker)
**US SIC:** 8299 **UK SIC:** 93300
**Employees:** 82

DUNS 23-655-1011

### Stonehaven (Healthcare) Ltd
Mardle House, Mardle Way, Buckfastleigh, Devon TQ11 0NS
**Web:** www.stone-haven.co.uk
**Reg No:** 3650153 **Estd:** 1996 Private Limited Company
**Line of Business:** Social work activities with accommodation
**Issued Capital:** £28,000
**Directors:** Ms D S Stone, R H Stone, N S Stone
**Co. Secretary:** Stephen Stone
**US SIC:** 8321 **UK SIC:** 96111

| | 30-04-14 | 30-04-13 | 30-04-12 |
|---|---|---|---|
| TO | 5,275,486 | 4,551,088 | 3,682,163 |
| P/L | 702,537 | 382,524 | 330,070 |
| NW | (24,435) | (454,857) | (615,103) |
| WC | 356,164 | 95,766 | 154,895 |
| Emp. | 204 | 193 | 154 |

**DUNS 21-630-5714**   *Exp*
## Stonehouse Paper & Bag Mills Ltd
Lower Mills, Stonehouse, Gloucestershire GL10 2BD
**Tel:** 01453-822173
**Web:** www.stonehousepaper.co.uk
**Reg No:** 0182580 **Estd:** 1922 Private Limited Company
**Line of Business:** Sppliers of bags various types
**Export Markets:** Greece, West Indies, Singapore and Hong Kong.
**Issued Capital:** £39,075
**Principals:** Mrs G M Daniels (Chairman), J H Daniels (Managing), Miss J G Daniels
**Co. Secretary:** Jonathan Daniels
**US SIC:** 2645 **UK SIC:** 47280
**Auditors:** Griffiths Marshall
**Bankers:** Barclays Bank Plc (20-33-83)

|    | 31-03-14 | 31-03-13 | 31-03-12 |
|----|----------|----------|----------|
| TA | 1,058,239 | 991,516 | 1,058,365 |
| NW | 783,533 | 718,623 | 798,377 |
| WC | 553,898 | 518,931 | 520,843 |

**DUNS 55-067-2752**
## Stonehouse Residential Home
55-57 Cheyney Road, Chester, Cheshire CH1 4BR
**Tel:** 01244-375015
**Web:** www.stonehousecarehome.co.uk
**Estd:** 1987 Proprietorship
**Line of Business:** Residential care establishments
**Proprietor:** H Kyzar
**Responsibilities**
**Senior:** Harry Keyzor (Proprietor), Lisa Wilford (Manager)
**US SIC:** 8321, 6732
**UK SIC:** 96111, 83100
**Employees:** 48

**DUNS 73-260-9438**   *Imp*
## Stonemanor Ltd
Unit 2 49-50 Eagle Wharf Road, London N1 7ED
**Tel:** 0207-253-6000
**Web:** www.apricotonline.co.uk
**Reg No:** 4534724 **Estd:** 2013 Private Limited Company
**Line of Business:** Armed service outfitters
**Export Sales:** £5,927,002
**Trading Style:** Apricot
**Issued Capital:** £1,000
**Director:** P M Chaimo
**Co. Secretary:** Hugh Kelly
**Branches:** Stonemanor Ltd, 1-2 Union Street, Bath, Avon BA1 1RP
**US SIC:** 5621 **UK SIC:** 64500
**Auditors:** Donald Jacobs & Partners

|      | 28-02-14 | 28-02-13 | 29-02-12 |
|------|----------|----------|----------|
| TO   | 30,124,447 | 28,365,731 | 39,931,546 |
| P/L  | 1,096,874 | 361,886 | 620,569 |
| NW   | 4,229,063 | 3,668,328 | 3,500,628 |
| WC   | 3,397,631 | 3,112,457 | 3,198,192 |
| Emp. | 177 | 150 | 127 |

**DUNS 42-442-3952**
## Stonemarket Concrete
Old Gravel Quarry, Oxford Road, Ryton On Dunsmore, Kenilworth, Warwickshire CV8 3EJ
**Tel:** 08453020603
**Web:** www.stonemarket.co.uk
**VAT No:** 669564576 **Estd:** 1980 Proprietorship
**Line of Business:** Manufacture of concrete products for construction purposes
**Proprietor:** J E Douglass
**US SIC:** 3271, 3281
**UK SIC:** 24370, 24503
**Bankers:** Bank Of Scotland (12-20-26)
**Employees:** 50

**DUNS 21-412-7633**
## Stonepillow
St Josephs, Hunston Road, Chichester, West Sussex PO20 1NP
**Web:** www.stonepillow.org.uk
**Estd:** 1990 Proprietorship
**Line of Business:** Activities of other membership organisations not elsewhere classified
**Proprietor:** Ms S Johnston
**US SIC:** 8699 **UK SIC:** 96902
**Employees:** 50

**DUNS 29-226-2201**
## Stonepit Nurseries Ltd
1 Cutlers Croft, Nep Town Road, Henfield, West Sussex BN5 9EL
**Tel:** 01273492682
**Web:** www.landscaperswestsussex.com
**Reg No:** 1081428 **Estd:** 1972 Private Limited Company
**Line of Business:** Landscape contractors
**Issued Capital:** £100
**Director:** N D Johnson

**Co. Secretary:** Mrs Jean Johnson
**Branches:** Stonepit Nurseries Ltd, Stone Pit Lane, Henfield, West Sussex BN5 9QU
**US SIC:** 0729 **UK SIC:** 01003

|    | 31-10-14 | 31-10-13 | 31-10-12 |
|----|----------|----------|----------|
| TA | 8,600 | 11,610 | 11,377 |
| NW | (33,548) | (35,630) | (15,183) |
| WC | (37,148) | (40,430) | (21,560) |

**DUNS 34-582-3421**   *Imp-Exp*
## Stoneridge Electronics Ltd
Charles Bowman Avenue, Claverhouse Industrial Park, Dundee, Angus DD4 9UB
**Tel:** 01382866400 **Fax:** 0870-704-0002
**Web:** www.stoneridge.com
**Reg No:** 0139213SC **VAT No:** 607474730
**Estd:** 1992 Private Limited Company
**Line of Business:** Manufacture of electrical equipment for engines and vehicles not elsewhere classified
**Export Markets:** Europe, U.S.A. and South Africa
**Export Sales:** £14,066,000
**Issued Capital:** £250,000
**Directors:** J C Corey, P Kruk, Ms A B Robertson
**Co. Secretary:** George Strickler
**Responsibilities**
**Facilities:** Doug MacDonald (Maintenance Manager)
**US SIC:** 3999, 5065
**UK SIC:** 49590, 61500
**Auditors:** Arthur Andersen
**Bankers:** Bank Of Scotland (80-73-31)

|      | 31-12-13 | 31-12-12 | 31-12-11 |
|------|----------|----------|----------|
| TO   | 18,072,000 | 17,705,000 | 19,328,000 |
| P/L  | (52,000) | (626,000) | 132,000 |
| NW   | 1,404,000 | 1,099,000 | 1,697,000 |
| WC   | 3,344,000 | 3,022,000 | 3,668,000 |
| Emp. | 130 | 137 | 132 |

**DUNS 50-415-4204**
## Stonewall Equality Ltd
The Tower Building, 11 York Road, London SE1 7NX
**Tel:** 020-7593-1850
**Web:** www.stonewall.org.uk
**Reg No:** 2412299 **Estd:** 1997 Private Limited Company
**Line of Business:** Activities of other membership organisations not elsewhere classified
**Directors:** S Mills, Ms J M Gooding, O Rowe, T J Toulmin, P R Havelock, Ms S Milne, Ms L Pinney, Ms P Opoku - Gyimah
**Co. Secretary:** Miss Cathryn Wright
**Responsibilities**
**Senior:** Ruth Hunt (Chief Executive Officer), Laura Mcallister (Non-Executive Director), Ewan Rintoul (Executive)
**Finance:** Catherine Bosworth (Director Fundraising)
**Admin:** Roy Peterson (Office Manager)
**IT:** Alex Little (IT Manager)
**HR:** Simon Feeke (Head of Workplace)
**Operations:** Sam Dick (Director of Campaigns)
**Branches:** Stonewall Equality Ltd, Windsor House, Windsor Lane, Cardiff, South Glamorgan CF10 3DE
**US SIC:** 8699, 6732
**UK SIC:** 96902, 83100
**Auditors:** Hacker Young
**Bankers:** National Westminster Bank Plc (60-40-04)

|      | 30-09-14 | 30-09-13 | 30-09-12 |
|------|----------|----------|----------|
| TO   | 5,387,006 | 4,334,054 | 4,016,778 |
| P/L  | 243,367 | 129,458 | 174,260 |
| NW   | 3,250,679 | 3,007,312 | 2,877,854 |
| WC   | 3,250,679 | 3,000,226 | 2,838,554 |
| Emp. | 75 | 64 | 64 |

**DUNS 22-617-8267**
## Stonewater Ltd
Suite C, Lancaster House, Grange Business Park, Enderby Road Whetstone, Leicester, Leicestershire LE8 6EP
**Fax:** 01202 665091
**Web:** www.stonewater.org
**Reg No:** 0020558IP **VAT No:** 619915805
**Estd:** 1973 Friendly Society
**Line of Business:** Housing associations societies trusts & co-operatives
**Directors:** D Francis, P Burton, J James, G H Cross, R Tomlins, J Grant, I K Andrews, C Mitchell
**Co. Secretary:** Anthony Seabright
**Responsibilities**
**Senior:** Kate Greenway (Director), Beryl Maxwell (Director), Sylvia Tidy (Director)
**US SIC:** 8699, 6732
**UK SIC:** 96902, 83100
**Auditors:** KPMG Audit LLP
**Bankers:** Barclays Bank Plc (20-68-79)

|      | 31-03-12 | 31-03-11 | 31-03-10 |
|------|----------|----------|----------|
| TO   | 57,023,000 | 54,972,000 | 54,179,000 |
| P/L  | 4,616,000 | 1,134,000 | 45,000 |
| NW   | 54,756,000 | 33,796,000 | 31,741,000 |
| WC   | 3,283,000 | (5,283,000) | 994,000 |
| Emp. | 336 | 358 | 345 |

**DUNS 50-148-9868**
## Stonewell Property Co Ltd
Brockholes Pavilion, Claughton Industrial Estate, Brockholes Way, Claughton-On-Brock, Preston, Lancashire PR3 0PZ
**Tel:** 01995-640690 **Fax:** 01995640771
**Web:** www.worthingtons.co.uk
**Reg No:** 2327137 **Estd:** 1988 Private Limited Company
**Line of Business:** Development and selling of real estate
**Issued Capital:** £52,002
**Directors:** J M Worthington, J S Worthington, G M Worthington, Mrs A V Worthington, R E Worthington
**Co. Secretary:** Stephen Smith
**US SIC:** 6552, 6711, 6519, 1541
**UK SIC:** 85000, 83962, 50100
**Auditors:** Towers & Gornall
**Bankers:** Lloyds TSB Bank plc (30-16-79)

|      | 31-12-13 | 31-12-12 | 31-12-11 |
|------|----------|----------|----------|
| TO   | 25,110,205 | 34,486,362 | 27,258,453 |
| P/L  | 690,260 | 1,694,255 | 1,716,320 |
| NW   | 9,816,021 | 9,033,186 | 7,724,648 |
| WC   | 1,918,456 | 3,157,461 | 72,021 |
| Emp. | 77 | 91 | 67 |

**DUNS 21-655-4804**
## Stonewest Ltd
(Subsidiary of: Stone Control Ltd)
67 Westow Street, London SE19 3RW
**Tel:** 02086846646 **Fax:** 02086849323
**Web:** www.stonewest.co.uk
**Reg No:** 7124696 **Estd:** 1994 Private Limited Company
**Line of Business:** Stone and exterior cleaning
**Issued Capital:** £100
**Directors:** L Livramento, J C Sherwen, A M Tuck
**Responsibilities**
**Senior:** Graham Bright (Manager)
**US SIC:** 1799 **UK SIC:** 50000
**Auditors:** Chelepis Watson Ltd

|    | 30-09-13 | 30-09-12 | 30-09-11 |
|----|----------|----------|----------|
| TO | N/A | 13,846,568 | 1,063,225 |
| P/L | N/A | 227,217 | 146,335 |
| NW | 372,286 | 286,529 | 120,227 |
| WC | 737,374 | 840,894 | 1,028,357 |

**DUNS 22-219-9528**
## Stonewood Builders Ltd
(Subsidiary of: Stonewood Properties Ltd)
West Yatton Lane, Chippenham, Wiltshire SN14 7EY
**Web:** www.stonewoodbuilders.co.uk
**Reg No:** 4237944 **Estd:** 1901 Private Limited Company
**Line of Business:** Property refurbishment contractors
**Issued Capital:** £2
**Director:** M Aitkenhead
**Co. Secretary:** Benjamin Lang
**Responsibilities**
**Senior:** Neill Aitkenhead (Manager)
**US SIC:** 1799 **UK SIC:** 50000
**Bankers:** National Westminster Bank Plc (52-21-30)

|      | 30-09-13 | 01-10-12 | 30-09-11 |
|------|----------|----------|----------|
| TO   | 7,406,950 | N/A | N/A |
| P/L  | 128,240 | N/A | N/A |
| NW   | 350,596 | 340,504 | 312,165 |
| WC   | 237,709 | 233,896 | 204,610 |
| Emp. | 71 | N/A | N/A |

**DUNS 22-658-3292**   *Imp-Exp*
## Stoney Cove Marine Trials Ltd
(Subsidiary of: Stoney Cove Marine Centre Ltd)
Stoney Cove, Sapcote Road, Leicester, Leicestershire LE9 4DW
**Web:** www.stoneycove.com
**Reg No:** 1365450 **VAT No:** 566075327
**Estd:** 1978 Private Limited Company
**Line of Business:** Public house
**Export Markets:** Germany
**Trading Style:** Stoney Cove, Underwater World, Nemos Bar and Diner, Hydrotech
**Issued Capital:** £100
**Principals:** A C King (Chairman), R D Crouch, C D Baggott, M C Woodward
**Co. Secretary:** Ms Beverley Forman
**Responsibilities**
**Senior:** Sue Woodward (Licensee)
**Branches:** Stoney Cove Marine Trials Ltd, 78 Oldbury Rd, Rowley Regis, West Midlands B65 0JS
**US SIC:** 3811, 5199, 5999, 7399
**UK SIC:** 37100, 61900, 65600, 83954
**Auditors:** Newby Castleman
**Bankers:** National Westminster Bank Plc (60-60-06)

|    | 30-11-13 | 30-11-12 | 30-11-11 |
|----|----------|----------|----------|
| TA | 2,170,679 | 2,098,567 | 2,117,038 |
| NW | 1,563,763 | 1,545,617 | 1,520,892 |
| WC | 1,263,849 | 1,346,152 | 1,347,966 |

**DUNS 28-847-2814**
## Stoneygate School Ltd
6 London Road, Leicester, Leicestershire LE8 9DJ
**Tel:** 01162-592282
**Web:** www.stoneygateschool.co.uk
**Reg No:** 0656816 **Estd:** 1957 Private Limited Company
**Line of Business:** Schools (independent)
**Issued Capital:** £10,675
**Director:** J Josephs
**Co. Secretary:** Ms Ann Josephs
**US SIC:** 8211 **UK SIC:** 93200
**Auditors:** Grant Thornton
**Bankers:** Lloyds TSB Bank plc (30-16-93)

|    | 22-04-14 | 22-04-13 | 22-04-12 |
|----|----------|----------|----------|
| TA | 3,113,168 | 3,104,728 | 3,050,586 |
| NW | 2,510,080 | 2,409,381 | 2,307,301 |
| WC | 578,139 | 475,370 | 359,783 |

**DUNS 21-128-7114**
## Stonyhurst
Stonyhurst, Clitheroe, Lancashire BB7 9PZ
**Tel:** 01254-827015
**Web:** www.stonyhurst.ac.uk
**Reg No:** 6632303 **Estd:** 2007 Private Company Limited By Guarantee
**Line of Business:** Sports clubs
**Directors:** A M Chitnis, M R Riley, Dr M A Guzkowska, P Willcocks, C Whitehead, M Walsh, R F Brumby, M J Power
**Co. Secretary:** Julian Ridley
**Responsibilities**
**Senior:** Mark Belderboss (Director), William Boylan (Manager), Carl Riley (Manager), Anthony Verity (Director)
**US SIC:** 7999, 8211
**UK SIC:** 97913, 93200
**Bankers:** National Westminster Bank Plc (01-05-31)

|      | 31-08-13 | 31-08-12 | 31-08-11 |
|------|----------|----------|----------|
| TO   | 13,859,102 | 13,396,533 | 14,377,679 |
| P/L  | (825,271) | (1,287,932) | (426,756) |
| NW   | 64,639,293 | 62,956,776 | 62,531,109 |
| WC   | (3,456,999) | (3,755,480) | (2,571,328) |
| Emp. | 306 | 293 | 290 |

**DUNS 21-736-9842**   *Imp*
## Stop-Choc Ltd
(Subsidiary of: Total Sa)
Banbury Avenue, Slough, Berkshire SL1 4LR
**Tel:** 01753-533223
**Web:** www.stop-choc.co.uk
**Reg No:** 1286216 **VAT No:** 234891348
**Estd:** 1976 Private Limited Company
**Line of Business:** Aircraft - services for
**Issued Capital:** £70,000
**Directors:** R W Steer, L F Poirier, M J Smith, M G Walker, Ms C F Souchet
**Co. Secretary:** Marian Raszpla
**Responsibilities**
**Senior:** Eric Antolin (Manager), Arnaud Vaz (Manager)
**US SIC:** 4582, 3629
**UK SIC:** 76400, 34350
**Auditors:** Ernst & Young LLP
**Bankers:** HSBC Bank plc (40-42-09)

|      | 31-12-13 | 31-12-12 | 31-12-11 |
|------|----------|----------|----------|
| TO   | 15,874,293 | 15,664,082 | 15,161,810 |
| P/L  | 3,726,043 | 3,662,831 | 3,551,641 |
| NW   | 6,849,610 | 6,715,735 | 31,852,217 |
| WC   | 8,422,316 | 8,193,038 | 33,342,496 |
| Emp. | 80 | 78 | 75 |

**DUNS 23-048-1124**
## Stop Gap Ltd
Goodwin House, 5 Union Court, Richmond, Surrey TW9 1AA
**Tel:** 02083327656
**Web:** www.stopgap.co.uk
**Estd:** 1999 Partnership
**Line of Business:** Labour recruitment and provision of personnel
**Partners:** Ms G Egon, Ms C Adam
**Responsibilities**
**Finance:** Andrew Morpeth (Financial Director)
**HR:** Rowan Lawrence (Personnel Manager)
**US SIC:** 7361 **UK SIC:** 83954
**Bankers:** Lloyds TSB Bank plc (30-97-06)
**Employees:** 63

**DUNS 42-372-1948**
## Stopgap Group Ltd
Goodwin House, 5 Union Court, Richmond, Surrey TW9 1AA
**Tel:** 020-8332-7656
**Web:** www.stopgap.co.uk
**Reg No:** 4359844 **Estd:** 1999 Private Limited Company
**Line of Business:** Employment and recruitment companies and consultants
**Export Sales:** £2,188,724
**Issued Capital:** £9,000
**Director:** Ms C M Owen
**Co. Secretary:** William Reid

**US SIC:** 7361 **UK SIC:** 83954

| | 30-04-14 | 30-04-13 | 30-04-12 |
|---|---|---|---|
| TO | 11,386,866 | 11,992,692 | 12,777,843 |
| P/L | 402,288 | 275,951 | 420,021 |
| NW | 4,345,436 | 4,356,940 | 4,201,335 |
| WC | 2,830,386 | 2,903,839 | 2,587,135 |
| Emp. | 71 | 70 | 77 |

DUNS 29-074-0281

## Stor-A-File Ltd

(**Subsidiary of:** Stor-A-File Group Ltd)
Unit 5 Wanlip Road Industrial Estate, Leicester, Leicestershire LE7 1PD
**Fax:** 01162742392
**Web:** www.storafile.co.uk
**Reg No:** 1316362 **VAT No:** 887139281
**Estd:** 2012 Private Limited Company
**Line of Business:** Image processing services
**Issued Capital:** £104
**Principals:** S Cockbill *(Managing)*, Ms H Cockbill
**Responsibilities**
**Senior:** Gavin Prior *(General Manager)*
**Branches:** Stor-A-File Ltd, 26 Wenlock Way, Leicester, Leicestershire LE4 9HU
**US SIC:** 3579 **UK SIC:** 33010
**Auditors:** Clear & Lane
**Bankers:** National Westminster Bank Plc (60-13-39)

| | 30-06-14 | 30-06-13 | 30-06-12 |
|---|---|---|---|
| TO | 4,571,183 | 3,454,222 | 3,255,880 |
| P/L | 849,938 | 565,465 | 713,496 |
| NW | 2,395,865 | 1,685,789 | 2,591,093 |
| WC | 1,517,370 | 1,010,020 | 2,071,706 |
| Emp. | 83 | 76 | 72 |

DUNS 22-620-3750

## Stora Enso U K Ltd

(**Subsidiary of:** Stora Enso Oyj)
1 Kingfisher House, Crayfields Business Park, New Mill Road, Orpington, Kent BR5 3QG
**Tel:** 01689883220 **Fax:** 01689-897290
**Web:** www.storaenso.com
**Reg No:** 1294742 **Estd:** 1977 Private Limited Company
**Line of Business:** Manufacture of paper and paperboard
**Issued Capital:** £1,000
**Directors:** J Kaarlehto, J F Barr, O M Nuottamo, S Von Holst
**Co. Secretary:** James Barr
**Responsibilities**
**Senior:** Antti Huttunen *(Manager)*
**Branches:** Stora Enso U K Ltd, G4 Ash Tree Court, Nottingham Business Park, Nottingham, Nottinghamshire NG8 6PY
**US SIC:** 2631 **UK SIC:** 47017
**Auditors:** PricewaterhouseCoopers LLP
**Bankers:** S G Hambros Bank & Trust Ltd (40-48-58)

| | 31-12-13 | 31-12-12 | 31-12-11 |
|---|---|---|---|
| TO | 8,139,000 | 5,782,000 | 6,104,000 |
| P/L | 282,000 | 726,000 | (8,000) |
| NW | 2,016,000 | 1,111,000 | 390,000 |
| WC | 3,317,000 | 3,075,000 | 3,352,000 |
| Emp. | 56 | 55 | 56 |

DUNS 21-777-3663

## Storage Centre

1 R B F Business Centre, Pontymister Industrial Estate, Risca, Newport, Gwent NP11 6NP
**Tel:** 01633615600
**Estd:** 2011 Proprietorship
**Line of Business:** Warehouses
**Proprietor:** Mrs J Jamieson
**US SIC:** 4226 **UK SIC:** 77003
**Employees:** 70

DUNS 21-706-1327

## Storage Data Uk

28 Melville House, Sparta Street, London SE10 8DP
**Tel:** 08432890439
**Web:** www.storagedata.co.uk
**VAT No:** 925793389 **Estd:** 2006 Partnership
**Line of Business:** Reseller of data storage and other I T components, offering outsourced hardware and software support services
**Partners:** B Owens, A Williams
**US SIC:** 7379 **UK SIC:** 83940
**Bankers:** Lloyds TSB Bank plc (77-91-36)
**Employees:** 60

DUNS 21-809-0471

## Store 21

Central Boulevard, Solihull, West Midlands B90 8AH
**Tel:** 01217467013
**Web:** www.storetwentyone.co.uk
**Estd:** 2012
**Line of Business:** Representative office
**US SIC:** 5699 **UK SIC:** 64500
**Employees:** 100

DUNS 21-370-0051

## Store Invasion

Suite 40 Basepoint Business Centre, Little High Street, Shoreham-By-Sea, West Sussex BN43 5EG
**Tel:** 01273467512
**Web:** www.zappies.com
**Proprietorship**
**Line of Business:** Accounting and auditing activities
**Proprietor:** Ms C Smith
**Responsibilities**
**Senior:** Andrew Hardwich *(Manager)*
**US SIC:** 5199 **UK SIC:** 61900
**Employees:** 68

DUNS 39-761-7754

## Storer Refrigeration & Catering Manufacturers Ltd

(**Subsidiary of:** Storer Holdings Ltd)
Newstead Industrial Estate, Brookfield Road, Arnold, Arnold, Nottingham, Nottinghamshire NG5 7ER
**Tel:** 01159-200329 **Fax:** 01159-670676
**Web:** www.storersltd.com
**Reg No:** 2198808 **VAT No:** 450190380
**Estd:** 1987 Private Limited Company
**Line of Business:** Ventilation systems
**Trading Style:** Storer Refrigeration
**Issued Capital:** £100
**Managing Director:** G W Storer
**Co. Secretary:** Mrs Helen Storer-Smith
**US SIC:** 3551 **UK SIC:** 32441
**Auditors:** Ashgates Corporate Services Ltd
**Bankers:** National Westminster Bank Plc (54-21-51)

| | 31-03-14 | 31-03-13 | 31-03-12 |
|---|---|---|---|
| TO | 8,013,259 | 6,711,490 | N/A |
| P/L | 146,967 | 75,579 | N/A |
| NW | 551,558 | 408,500 | 350,388 |
| WC | 352,939 | 208,443 | 121,693 |
| Emp. | 65 | 64 | N/A |

DUNS 73-455-1547 **Imp**

## Storetec Services Ltd

Unit 4 Sidings Business Park, Freightliner Road, Hull, North Humberside HU3 4XA
**Tel:** 01482-608630 **Fax:** 01482-608639
**Web:** www.storetec.net
**Reg No:** 4719444 **Estd:** 2003 Private Limited Company
**Line of Business:** Activities of exhibition and fair organisers
**Issued Capital:** £100
**Director:** D Wilkinson
**Co. Secretary:** Neil Robson
**US SIC:** 7399 **UK SIC:** 83954
**Auditors:** Townends

| | 31-03-14 | 31-03-13 | 31-03-12 |
|---|---|---|---|
| TA | 1,197,591 | 1,091,598 | 1,290,875 |
| NW | 179,895 | 149,149 | 129,226 |
| WC | 218,054 | 211,972 | 306,737 |

DUNS 23-125-2917

## Storey

The Street, Corton, Lowestoft, Suffolk NR32 5HN
**Tel:** 01502730317
**Web:** www.warnerbreaks.co.uk
**Estd:** 2002 Partnership
**Line of Business:** Managed public houses and bars
**Trading Style:** Corton Hutt
**Partners:** S Crawshaw, Mrs P Simmons, Mrs C Fletcher, I Gyte
**US SIC:** 5813 **UK SIC:** 66200
**Employees:** 200

DUNS 21-241-9980

## Storey Carpets Ltd

(**Subsidiary of:** Carpetright Plc)
Bob Watts Building, Bolton Road Nova Scotia Wharf, Blackburn, Lancashire BB2 3GE
**Tel:** 01914175100
**Web:** www.storeycarpets.co.uk
**Reg No:** 1148245 **VAT No:** 178567117
**Estd:** 1921 Private Limited Company
**Line of Business:** Retail sale of floor coverings
**Issued Capital:** £45,913
**Directors:** N L Page, J A Sampson
**Branches:** Storey Carpets Ltd, Armstrong, Washington, Tyne and Wear NE37 1QW
**US SIC:** 5713 **UK SIC:** 64700
**Auditors:** Ernst & Young LLP
**Bankers:** Lloyds TSB Bank plc (30-98-34)

| | 30-04-14 | 30-04-13 | 30-04-12 |
|---|---|---|---|
| TA | 4,044,000 | 4,044,000 | 4,044,000 |
| NW | 4,044,000 | 4,044,000 | 4,044,000 |

DUNS 56-962-4505

## The Storey Group Ltd

1-3 Call Lane, Leeds, West Yorkshire LS1 7DH
**Tel:** 01132-423567
**Web:** www.thestorygroup.co.uk
**Reg No:** 2851474 **Estd:** 1993 Private Limited Company
**Line of Business:** Amusement park activities
**Issued Capital:** £100
**Director:** G S Storey
**Co. Secretary:** Ms Maureen Hatton
**Branches:** The Storey Group Ltd, 10 Fish Street, Leeds, West Yorkshire LS1 6DB
**US SIC:** 7996 **UK SIC:** 97913
**Auditors:** Thomas Coombs & Son

| | 30-09-13 | 30-09-12 | 30-09-11 |
|---|---|---|---|
| TO | 2,514,970 | 2,698,549 | N/A |
| P/L | (377,534) | 958,692 | 2,623,491 |
| NW | 11,868,023 | 14,378,111 | 13,609,729 |
| WC | 2,358,798 | 4,754,191 | 4,029,663 |
| Emp. | 52 | 58 | 58 |

DUNS 23-779-8400

## Storeys Amusements

1-3 Call Lane, Leeds, West Yorkshire LS1 7DH
**Tel:** 01132455406
**Line of Business:** Amusement and gaming machines
**Branches:** Storeys Amusements, 9 Peel Sq, Barnsley, South Yorkshire S70 2QT
**US SIC:** 7996 **UK SIC:** 97913
**Employees:** 70

DUNS 21-750-9229

## Storeys Edward Symmons Ltd

Higham House, New Bridge St West, Newcastle-Upon-Tyne, Tyne and Wear NE1 8AU
**Tel:** 01912326291
**Web:** www.storeys-es.com
**Reg No:** 7814732 **Estd:** 2011 Private Limited Company
**Line of Business:** Real estate agencies
**Issued Capital:** £50,000
**Directors:** P H Easton, N C Boyd, M Lytollis, P J Proctor, S T Gilroy, W G Lynn
**Co. Secretary:** Paul Griffiths
**US SIC:** 6531 **UK SIC:** 83400

| | 30-04-14 | 30-04-13 | 30-04-12 |
|---|---|---|---|
| TO | 4,395,000 | 4,509,000 | 1,580,000 |
| P/L | 208,000 | 236,000 | 121,000 |
| NW | 290,000 | 325,000 | 142,000 |
| WC | 364,000 | 182,000 | 436,000 |
| Emp. | 68 | 68 | 88 |

DUNS 73-971-3795

## Stork Technical Services (Holdings) Ltd

(**Subsidiary of:** Coöperatieve Centrale Raiffeisen-Boerenleenbank B.)
Norfolk House, Pitmedden Road, Dyce, Aberdeen, Aberdeenshire AB21 0DP
**Tel:** 01224-722888
**Web:** www.storktechnicalservices.com
**Reg No:** 0272959SC **Estd:** 2004 Private Limited Company
**Line of Business:** Labour recruitment and provision of personnel
**Export Sales:** £42,851,000
**Trading Style:** Stork Technical Services (Holdings) Ltd
**Issued Capital:** £5,302
**Directors:** C C Watson, S Sharma
**Co. Secretary:** Colin Watson
**US SIC:** 7361 **UK SIC:** 83954
**Auditors:** PricewaterhouseCoopers LLP
**Bankers:** Bank Of Scotland (80-05-14)

| | 31-12-13 | 31-12-12 | 31-12-11 |
|---|---|---|---|
| TO | 378,154,000 | N/A | 322,082,000 |
| P/L | 11,954,000 | (2,469,000) | 3,823,000 |
| NW | 79,107,000 | (4,873,000) | 22,312,000 |
| WC | 60,423,000 | 9,576,000 | 58,145,000 |
| Emp. | 3,675 | N/A | 3,892 |

DUNS 23-817-0117

## Stork Technical Services (Sts) Ltd

(**Subsidiary of:** London Acquisition Luxco Sarl)
Unit 21 24, Slaidburn Industrial Estate, Slaidburn Crescent, Southport, Merseyside PR9 9YF
**Fax:** 01704215601
**Web:** www.storktechnicalservices.com
**Reg No:** 3809192 **VAT No:** 732364348
**Estd:** 1999 Private Limited Company
**Line of Business:** Heat treatment (metals)
**Issued Capital:** £4
**Directors:** Stork Technical Services Holding, C C Watson
**Co. Secretary:** Colin Watson
**Responsibilities**
**Senior:** Nigel Bleackley *(Manager)*
**Health & Safety:** Tony Duckworth *(Health & Safety Officer)*
**Facilities:** Tony Duckworth *(Health & Safety Officer)*
**Branches:** Stork Technical Services (Sts) Ltd, 3-4 Links Court, Bo'ness, West Lothian EH51 9UD
**US SIC:** 3398 **UK SIC:** 31380
**Auditors:** KPMG LLP
**Bankers:** Barclays Bank Plc (20-80-33)

| | 31-12-13 | 31-12-12 | 31-12-11 |
|---|---|---|---|
| TO | N/A | 15,933,000 | 9,007,000 |
| P/L | N/A | 3,476,000 | 514,000 |
| NW | 6,186,000 | 3,425,000 | 6,216,000 |
| WC | N/A | 2,531,000 | 2,569,000 |
| Emp. | N/A | 183 | 131 |

DUNS 73-978-7302 **Imp**

## Storm Aviation Ltd

(**Subsidiary of:** Avia Solutions Group Ab)
Capability Green, Luton, Bedfordshire LU1 3LU
**Fax:** 01582-480-455
**Web:** www.fltechnicsline.com
**Reg No:** 5229468 **Estd:** 2004 Private Limited Company
**Line of Business:** Other supporting air transport activities
**Export Sales:** £2,215,780
**Issued Capital:** £173,265
**Directors:** P Akstinas, T Buckley, Z Lapinskas
**Co. Secretary:** Mh Secretaries Limited
**Responsibilities**
**Senior:** Jonas Butautis *(Manager)*
**US SIC:** 4582, 7539
**UK SIC:** 76400, 67100
**Auditors:** Baker Tilly UK Audit LLP

| | 31-12-13 | 31-12-12 | 31-12-11 |
|---|---|---|---|
| TO | 6,884,995 | 7,746,149 | 6,381,101 |
| P/L | (32,800) | (2,039,813) | (625,708) |
| NW | (2,453,086) | (2,565,107) | (1,303,577) |
| WC | (1,413,250) | (2,778,610) | (478,934) |
| Emp. | 52 | 65 | 75 |

DUNS 51-991-6048 **Imp**

## Storm Technologies Ltd

Unit 41 Park House Greenhill Crescent, Watford, Hertfordshire WD18 8PH
**Tel:** 01923-801080 **Fax:** 01923-252106
**Web:** www.storm-technologies.co.uk
**Reg No:** 3998372 **VAT No:** 760609235
**Estd:** 2000 Private Limited Company
**Line of Business:** Hardware consultancy
**Export Sales:** £3,883,936
**Issued Capital:** £77
**Principals:** J R Brooker *(Managing)*, G Ware, N M Umney, T J Nickolls
**Co. Secretary:** Mrs Soraya Brooker
**Responsibilities**
**Sales:** Simon Dearn *(Sales Director)*
**Health & Safety:** Simon Vick *(Health & Safety Officer)*
**US SIC:** 7379 **UK SIC:** 83940
**Auditors:** Newlyn Ware
**Bankers:** Lloyds TSB Bank plc (30-00-09)

| | 31-12-13 | 31-12-12 | 31-12-11 |
|---|---|---|---|
| TO | 56,316,899 | 50,892,615 | 56,649,376 |
| P/L | 2,100,633 | 1,142,004 | 2,358,567 |
| NW | 2,252,890 | 1,975,361 | 1,615,566 |
| WC | 1,462,819 | 982,542 | 501,419 |
| Emp. | 91 | 95 | 75 |

DUNS 23-845-5385

## Stormdfx Ltd

Unit 1 The Office Village Keypoint, Keys Road, Alfreton, Derbyshire DE55 7FQ
**Tel:** 01773 546724 **Fax:** 01773823052
**Web:** www.designfx.com
**Reg No:** 3837594 **Estd:** 1999 Private Limited Company
**Line of Business:** Printing not elsewhere classified
**Issued Capital:** £101
**Directors:** Ms T A Mcveigh, T G Wilson
**US SIC:** 2752 **UK SIC:** 47544
**Bankers:** HSBC Bank plc (40-17-15)

| | 31-12-13 | 31-12-12 | 31-12-11 |
|---|---|---|---|
| TO | 8,191,808 | N/A | N/A |
| P/L | 1,130,399 | N/A | N/A |
| NW | 1,406,001 | 1,208,726 | 1,153,345 |
| WC | 896,758 | 799,980 | 847,327 |
| Emp. | 126 | N/A | N/A |

DUNS 77-966-7950

## Stormfront Retail Ltd

(**Subsidiary of:** Professional Reseller Group Ltd)
Newton Centre Thorverton Road, Exeter, Devon EX2 8GN
**Tel:** 01392823700
**Web:** www.stormfront.co.uk
**Reg No:** 5935581 **Estd:** 2006 Private Limited Company
**Line of Business:** It consultants
**Issued Capital:** £1,120,000
**Directors:** Mrs T W Slack, M D Fleming, J S Collard-Jenkins
**Co. Secretary:** Ms Catherine Chapman
**Responsibilities**
**Senior:** Henry Gordon Clark *(Manager)*

**US SIC:** 5946    **UK SIC:** 65400

| | 30-09-13 | 30-09-12 | 30-09-11 |
|---|---|---|---|
| TO | 52,390,412 | 39,690,863 | 22,803,774 |
| P/L | (552,519) | 411,797 | 346,318 |
| NW | 813,218 | 1,470,958 | 1,129,291 |
| WC | (287,113) | 576,419 | 919,070 |
| Emp. | 212 | 177 | 99 |

DUNS 21-906-6073        **Imp-Exp**

## Stormguard Sills
Regency Mill, Chester Road, Macclesfield, Cheshire SK11 8HR
**Tel:** 01625613311
**Web:** www.stormguard.co.uk
**Estd:** 1965 Partnership
**Line of Business:** Draughtproofing installers
**Export Markets:** U.S.A.
**Trading Style:** Stormguard
**Partners:** P J Allmand-Smith, Ms H M Allmand-Smith
**Responsibilities**
**Senior:** Oliver Allmand-Smith (Manager), Martin Reader (Despatch Manager)
**Sales:** Michelle Bradley (Office Manager)
**Admin:** Michelle Bradley (Office Manager)
**IT:** Martin Reader (Despatch Manager)
**HR:** Oliver Allmand-Smith (Manager)
**Health & Safety:** Oliver Allmand-Smith (Manager)
**US SIC:** 1742, 5039
**UK SIC:** 50400, 61300
**Bankers:** The Royal Bank Of Scotland Plc (16-24-32)
**Employees:** 90

DUNS 21-156-1863
## Stormharbour Securities Llp
10 Old Burlington Street, London W1S 3AG
**Tel:** 02073555750
**Web:** www.stormharbour.com
**Reg No:** 0343890OC   **Estd:** 2009 Private Limited Company
**Line of Business:** Banks and financial institutions
**Export Sales:** £11,625,241
**Responsibilities**
**Senior:** Amanda Alcock (Head of HR), Antonio Cacorino (Manager), Mounir Guessous (Principal and Managing Directo)
**Finance:** Stephane Marchi (Public Finance/Infrastructure), Salvatore Ruocco (Chief Financial Officer)
**HR:** Amanda Alcock (Head of HR)
**Engineering:** Ingrid Weston (Partner - Infrastructure)
**US SIC:** 6111   **UK SIC:** 81501
**Auditors:** PricewaterhouseCoopers LLP
**Bankers:** The Chase Manhattan Bank (60-91-41)

| | 31-12-13 | 31-12-12 | 31-12-11 |
|---|---|---|---|
| TA | 13,032,109 | 8,664,861 | 10,957,977 |
| P/L | 2,451,485 | (2,210,847) | N/A |
| NW | 7,766,681 | 5,720,085 | 8,795,932 |
| WC | 7,684,018 | 5,614,496 | 8,563,971 |
| Emp. | 73 | 59 | 70 |

DUNS 21-156-2687
## Stormharbour Securities Uk Ltd
10 Old Burlington Street, London W1S 3AG
**Tel:** 02072929820
**Reg No:** 6841751   **Estd:** 2009 Private Limited Company
**Line of Business:** Financial intermediation not elsewhere classified
**Export Sales:** £13,973,667
**Issued Capital:** £10,803,586
**Directors:** R D Atkinson, T L Keeley, A M De Freitas Cacorino Dias
**US SIC:** 6111   **UK SIC:** 81501
**Bankers:** The Chase Manhattan Bank (60-91-41)

| | 31-12-13 | 31-12-12 | 31-12-11 |
|---|---|---|---|
| TA | 14,073,287 | 14,268,776 | 14,563,621 |
| P/L | 8,354,934 | 281,750 | 1,432,006 |
| NW | 8,077,856 | 9,605,591 | 11,063,960 |
| WC | 8,597,962 | 10,424,119 | 10,783,313 |
| Emp. | 76 | 62 | 72 |

DUNS 22-785-1763
## Stormking Plastics Ltd
Sandy Way, Amington Industrial Estate, Tamworth, Staffordshire B77 4ED
**Tel:** 01827311100
**Web:** www.stormking.co.uk
**Reg No:** 1714695   **VAT No:** 425328169
**Estd:** 1985 Private Limited Company
**Line of Business:** Glass fibre materials and tools
**Issued Capital:** £100
**Principals:** G J King (Managing), B Whitehall, Ms C D King, Ms M Whitehall
**Co. Secretary:** Gary King
**Responsibilities**
**Senior:** Tony Hardman (Manufacturing Manager)
**HR:** Robert Satherley (Human Resources Manager)
**Health & Safety:** Tony Hardman (Manufacturing Manager)

**Facilities:** Tony Hardman (Manufacturing Manager)
**Operations:** Tony Hardman (Manufacturing Manager)
**Purchasing:** Roy Stafford (Purchasing Manager)
**Engineering:** Tony Hardman (Manufacturing Manager)
**Branches:** Tamworth
**US SIC:** 3229   **UK SIC:** 24791
**Auditors:** KPMG LLP
**Bankers:** Lloyds TSB Bank plc (30-95-04)

| | 28-02-14 | 28-02-13 | 29-02-12 |
|---|---|---|---|
| TO | 19,082,461 | 14,075,015 | 13,760,211 |
| P/L | 1,309,623 | 1,207,826 | 1,974,266 |
| NW | 6,487,039 | 5,413,965 | 4,403,529 |
| WC | 6,324,448 | 5,216,835 | 4,184,234 |
| Emp. | 190 | 168 | 157 |

DUNS 22-155-2693
## Stormont Truck & Van Ltd
(Subsidiary of: Knaresborough Investments Ltd)
London Road, Hildenborough, Tonbridge, Kent TN11 8NN
**Tel:** 01732-833005
**Web:** www.stormonttruckandvan.com
**Reg No:** 4173907   **Estd:** 2002 Private Limited Company
**Line of Business:** Motor factors
**Issued Capital:** £105,000
**Directors:** W J Sangster, A C Smith, S N Parkin, P A Latham, S E Fahey, D A Hodkin
**Co. Secretary:** Paul White
**Responsibilities**
**Senior:** Simon O'Shea (Stores Manager)
**Finance:** Michael Blackmore (Finance Director)
**Sales:** Simon O'Shea (Stores Manager)
**IT:** Daniel Kennedy (IT Manager)
**HR:** Sally Levitt (Human Resources Manager)
**Health & Safety:** Nick Hawkins (Health & Safety Officer)
**Branches:** Stormont Truck & Van Ltd, Jackdaw Close, Northampton, Northamptonshire NN3 9ER
**US SIC:** 5531, 7539
**UK SIC:** 65100, 67100
**Auditors:** Grant Thornton UK LLP

| | 30-04-14 | 30-04-13 | 30-04-12 |
|---|---|---|---|
| TO | 10,294,000 | 34,187,000 | 38,570,000 |
| P/L | 1,833,000 | 12,000 | 147,000 |
| NW | 130,000 | 2,679,000 | 2,684,000 |
| WC | N/A | 2,346,000 | 2,037,000 |
| Emp. | 40 | 172 | 188 |

DUNS 23-388-7228
## Storrington Industries Ltd
Unit 1 Cottons Yard, Water Lane, Pulborough, West Sussex RH20 3EA
**Tel:** 01903743941
**Web:** www.lbsstone.co.uk
**Reg No:** 5357031   **Estd:** 2005 Private Limited Company
**Line of Business:** Holding companies management activities
**Issued Capital:** £168,878
**Directors:** Dr J C Ramage, Professor S Williamson
**Co. Secretary:** Dr Michael Begg
**Responsibilities**
**Senior:** Steven Cheshire (Sales Manager)
**US SIC:** 6711   **UK SIC:** 83962

| | 28-02-14 | 28-02-13 | 29-02-12 |
|---|---|---|---|
| TO | 37,284,000 | 41,393,000 | 40,761,000 |
| P/L | 4,979,000 | 5,561,000 | 6,104,000 |
| NW | 20,953,000 | 16,670,000 | 11,032,000 |
| WC | 13,056,000 | 11,804,000 | 8,691,000 |
| Emp. | 374 | 379 | 379 |

DUNS 21-724-4537
## Storth Post Office
Storth Road, Storth, Milnthorpe, Cumbria LA7 7HT
**Tel:** 01539-563392
**Web:** www.postoffice.co.uk
**Estd:** 1990 Proprietorship
**Line of Business:** National post activities
**Proprietor:** R Crompton
**Responsibilities**
**Senior:** Rob Crompton (Postmaster)
**US SIC:** 7399, 5411
**UK SIC:** 83954, 64100
**Bankers:** Alliance & Leicester Plc (72-60-00)
**Employees:** 46

DUNS 21-811-8697
## Storthes Hall Park
Storthes Hall Student Village, Storthes Hall Lane, Kirkburton, Huddersfield, West Yorkshire HD8 0WA
**Tel:** 01484488805
**Estd:** 2012
**Line of Business:** Other retail sale of food, beverages and tobacco in specialised stores
**Proprietor:** W Brook
**US SIC:** 5499   **UK SIC:** 64100
**Employees:** 50

DUNS 23-714-8924
## Story Contracting Ltd
Marconi Road, Burgh Road Industrial Estate, Carlisle, Cumbria CA2 7NA
**Tel:** 01228-640880 **Fax:** 01228640881
**Web:** www.storyrail.co.uk
**Reg No:** 3709861   **Estd:** 1999 Private Limited Company
**Line of Business:** Industrial building contractors
**Issued Capital:** £1,000
**Directors:** J F Story, M S Halliday, P S Stybelski, A Cook, N F Story, A L Grant
**Co. Secretary:** Roger Gass
**US SIC:** 1541, 1611
**UK SIC:** 50100, 50200
**Auditors:** UNW LLP
**Bankers:** The Royal Bank Of Scotland Plc (16-15-25)

| | 31-03-14 | 31-03-13 | 31-03-12 |
|---|---|---|---|
| TO | 52,404,076 | 36,613,182 | 17,336,789 |
| P/L | 5,496,408 | 2,304,149 | 608,227 |
| NW | 8,561,692 | 6,811,951 | 6,406,572 |
| WC | 781,358 | 2,237,157 | 5,232,743 |
| Emp. | 309 | 256 | 107 |

DUNS 39-979-1649
## Story Homes Ltd
Marconi Road, Burgh Road Industrial Estate, Carlisle, Cumbria CA2 7NA
**Tel:** 01228590444 **Fax:** 01228593359
**Web:** www.storycontracting.com
**Reg No:** 2275441   **VAT No:** 514333577
**Estd:** 1988 Private Limited Company
**Line of Business:** Building construction contractors
**Trading Style:** Story Contracting
**Issued Capital:** £131,957
**Directors:** P S Stybelski, N F Story, Ms V J Story, S Errington
**Co. Secretary:** Stuart Marshall
**Responsibilities**
**Senior:** Sharon Benson (Human Resources Director), Malcolm Lamount (Manager), Ian Sewell (Manager), Mark Thom (Operations Manager)
**Admin:** Jane Roe (Administration Officer)
**HR:** Angela Jeffries (Human Resources Director), Jane Roe (Administration Officer)
**Facilities:** Mark Thom (Operations Manager)
**Branches:** Story Homes Ltd, Marconi Road, Carlisle, Cumbria CA2 7NA
**US SIC:** 1522   **UK SIC:** 50100
**Auditors:** UNW LLP
**Bankers:** Bank Of Scotland (12-05-94)

| | 31-03-14 | 31-03-13 | 31-03-12 |
|---|---|---|---|
| TO | 47,891,095 | 57,677,494 | 59,372,125 |
| P/L | 7,662,020 | 4,116,273 | 3,223,616 |
| NW | 43,545,276 | 45,931,273 | 43,469,146 |
| WC | 42,712,428 | 40,192,977 | 39,142,128 |
| Emp. | 141 | 373 | 322 |

DUNS 22-451-4633
## Stotfold Bowls Club
Brook Street, Stotfold, Hitchin, Hertfordshire SG5 4JT
**Tel:** 01462734891
**Estd:** 1939 Proprietorship
**Line of Business:** Clubs social and associations
**Proprietor:** S Cooper
**Responsibilities**
**Senior:** Molly Jennings (Chairman)
**US SIC:** 7999   **UK SIC:** 97913
**Employees:** 98

DUNS 23-272-8501
## Stothers (M. & E.) Ltd
(Subsidiary of: J E H Ltd)
Radiant Works, 23 Sunwich Street, Ravenhill Avenue, Belfast BT6 8HR
**Tel:** 02890 450821 **Fax:** 02890 458342
**Web:** www.stothersm-e.co.uk
**Reg No:** 0024313NI   **VAT No:** 517271750
**Estd:** 1957 Private Limited Company
**Line of Business:** Miscellaneous business services
**Issued Capital:** £25,000
**Directors:** C Cherry, J Marley, B Megarry, D Monaghan, Ms H A Ellis, G E Preston
**Co. Secretary:** David Conlon
**Responsibilities**
**Senior:** Chris McErlean (Stores Manager)
**Admin:** Billy Crean (Office Manager)
**IT:** Billy Crean (Office Manager)
**Facilities:** Chris McErlean (Stores Manager)
**Branches:** Stothers (M. & E.) Ltd, 151 West George St, Glasgow, Lanarkshire G2 2JJ
**US SIC:** 7399, 1711
**UK SIC:** 83954, 50300
**Auditors:** Flanagan W.L. & Co
**Bankers:** Northern Bank Ltd (95-01-14)

| | 30-06-14 | 30-06-13 | 30-06-12 |
|---|---|---|---|
| TO | 18,514,826 | 19,424,676 | 23,084,258 |
| P/L | 516,625 | 348,019 | 801,595 |
| NW | 4,499,550 | 4,342,510 | 4,003,790 |
| WC | 4,392,621 | 4,177,856 | 3,838,379 |
| Emp. | 61 | 68 | 68 |

DUNS 21-175-2507
## Stott & May Professional Search Ltd
5 Aldermanbury Square, London EC2V 7HR
**Tel:** 02074963650
**Web:** www.stottandmay.com
**Reg No:** 6987598   **Estd:** 2009 Private Limited Company
**Line of Business:** Employment and recruitment companies and consultants
**Export Sales:** £5,792,410
**Issued Capital:** £3,597,750
**Directors:** G Daniels, S P Stott
**Co. Secretary:** Laurence Rosen
**US SIC:** 7361   **UK SIC:** 83954
**Auditors:** Rayner Essex LLP

| | 31-12-13 | 31-12-12 | 31-12-11 |
|---|---|---|---|
| TO | 21,645,014 | 19,336,450 | 10,320,692 |
| P/L | 170,769 | 109,277 | 11,094 |
| NW | 385,260 | 271,820 | 191,518 |
| WC | 336,277 | 204,113 | 115,690 |
| Emp. | 50 | N/A | N/A |

DUNS 21-669-5835
## Stour Valley Educational Trust Ltd
Cavendish Road, Clare, Sudbury, Suffolk CO10 8PJ
**Tel:** 01787279342
**Web:** www.stourvalleycommunityschool.org
**Reg No:** 7226557   **Estd:** 2010 Private Company Limited By Guarantee
**Line of Business:** Schools (foundation)
**Directors:** Mrs G A Lovejoy, R M Smith, Miss K J Terry, Mrs S A Nicoll, C G Hawkins, K Haisman, G Brown, Mrs C Inchley
**Responsibilities**
**Senior:** Derek Blake (Director), Penny Hurrell (Director), Philip Stanbury-Jones (Director), Katharine Waghorn (Director)
**US SIC:** 8211   **UK SIC:** 93200
**Bankers:** Lloyds TSB Bank plc (30-98-31)

| | 31-08-14 | 31-08-13 | 31-08-12 |
|---|---|---|---|
| TO | 9,700,891 | 2,438,690 | 2,381,470 |
| P/L | 6,713,203 | (75,239) | 350,286 |
| NW | 6,911,969 | 302,766 | 375,005 |
| WC | 222,688 | 167,734 | 188,700 |
| Emp. | 57 | 53 | 35 |

DUNS 23-607-7095
## Stourbridge College
Hagley Road Centre, Stourbridge, West Midlands DY8 1QU
**Tel:** 01384-344344
**Web:** www.stourbridge.ac.uk
**VAT No:** 632131779   **Estd:** 1990
**Line of Business:** Colleges (higher education)
**Directors:** Ms S Walton, D Toeman
**Responsibilities**
**Senior:** Lynette Cutting (Principal)
**Finance:** Debbie Hingley (Accountant)
**Marketing:** Derek Danks (Head of Marketing), Mags Winthrope (Communications Officer)
**Facilities:** Craig Blake (Facilities Manager)
**Purchasing:** Corinna Marsh (Financial Coordinator)
**Branches:** Stourbridge College, Bromley La, Kingswinford, West Midlands DY6 8QG
**US SIC:** 8221   **UK SIC:** 93100
**Bankers:** HSBC Bank plc (40-43-17)
**Employees:** 500

DUNS 77-825-8954
## Stourgarden Ltd
Boxted Road, Great Horkesley, Great Horkesley, Colchester, Essex CO6 4AP
**Web:** www.stourgarden.com
**Reg No:** 3031052   **Estd:** 1995 Private Limited Company
**Line of Business:** Packagers
**Issued Capital:** £200
**Principals:** W H Rix (Managing), J G Rix, S J Rix, G P Rix
**Co. Secretary:** Gerald Farrow
**Responsibilities**
**Facilities:** Mick Patterson (Facilities Manager)
**US SIC:** 5148   **UK SIC:** 61700
**Auditors:** HLB Kidsons
**Bankers:** Lloyds TSB Bank plc (30-92-16)

| | 31-07-13 | 31-07-12 | 31-07-11 |
|---|---|---|---|
| TO | 24,128,450 | 22,011,364 | 22,586,693 |
| P/L | 978,792 | 878,181 | 939,041 |
| NW | 7,081,532 | 6,358,706 | 5,729,047 |
| WC | 6,539,906 | 5,721,486 | 5,065,575 |
| Emp. | 89 | 87 | 91 |

DUNS 34-751-8573
## Stourport Nursing & Home Care Ltd
Hernes Nest House, 7 Hernes Nest, Bewdley, Worcestershire DY12 2ET
**Tel:** 01299-403353
**Web:** www.stourportnursingandhomecare.co.uk
**Reg No:** 2784388   **Estd:** 1993 Private Limited Company

**Line of Business:** Home care service providers
**Trading Style:** Hernes Nest House
**Issued Capital:** £100
**Co. Secretary:** Ms Stella Gurney
**Responsibilities**
**Senior:** Lesley Jones *(Manager)*, Rebecca Lathe *(Manager)*
**US SIC:** 8091 **UK SIC:** 95200
**Auditors:** PKF

| | 30-04-14 | 30-04-13 | 30-04-12 |
|---|---|---|---|
| TA | 934,642 | 930,745 | 927,439 |
| NW | 894,642 | 885,882 | 867,147 |
| WC | 817,053 | 806,105 | 785,895 |

DUNS 21-870-0884
## Stovax Heating Group Ltd
(**Subsidiary of:** Nibe Industrier Ab)
Falcon Road, Sowton Industrial Estate, Exeter, Devon EX2 7LF
**Tel:** 01392474000
**Reg No:** 8299613 **Estd:** 2012 Private Limited Company
**Line of Business:** Management activities of holding companies
**Issued Capital:** £1
**Directors:** A D Walker, S H Axelsson, D F Nilsson, M A Sage, B O Gunnarsson, R J Crabb
**Co. Secretary:** Andrew Walker
**US SIC:** 6711 **UK SIC:** 83962
**Auditors:** Deloitte LLP

| | 31-12-13 | 31-01-13 |
|---|---|---|
| TO | 39,143,104 | 26,487,387 |
| P/L | 5,607,830 | 4,965,918 |
| NW | 18,563,001 | 14,267,592 |
| WC | 18,316,010 | 14,076,516 |
| Emp. | 268 | 255 |

DUNS 22-607-8996 **Imp-Exp**
## Stovax Ltd
(**Subsidiary of:** Nibe Industrier Ab)
Falcon Road, Sowton Industrial Estate, Exeter, Devon EX2 7LF
**Tel:** 01392-474011
**Web:** www.stovax.com
**Reg No:** 1572550 **VAT No:** 675762883
**Estd:** 1981 Private Limited Company
**Line of Business:** Fireplaces
**Export Markets:** Worldwide
**Issued Capital:** £190,347
**Principals:** M A Sage *(Financial)*, R J Crabb *(Sales)*, M Oram, E G Henry
**Co. Secretary:** Andrew Walker
**Responsibilities**
**IT:** Garren Moorhouse *(Senior IT Executive)*
**Branches:** Falcon Road, Falcon Indstl Est, Exeter, Devon EX2 7LF
**US SIC:** 3251, 3999
**UK SIC:** 24100, 49590
**Auditors:** PricewaterhouseCoopers
**Bankers:** HSBC Bank plc (40-20-30)

| | 31-12-13 | 31-01-13 | 31-12-12 |
|---|---|---|---|
| TO | 24,250,633 | 16,884,010 | 24,569,624 |
| P/L | 4,560,648 | 3,976,098 | 5,782,751 |
| NW | 12,043,001 | 8,536,669 | 7,972,334 |
| WC | 11,802,189 | 8,304,818 | 7,788,431 |
| Emp. | 132 | 122 | 122 |

DUNS 22-609-0652
## Stover School Association
Stover, Newton Abbot, Devon TQ12 6QG
**Web:** www.stover.co.uk
**Reg No:** 0565995 **Estd:** 1996 Private Company Limited By Guarantee
**Line of Business:** General secondary education
**Directors:** Ms L J Jones, R D Hourahane, D Wilson, Ms B L Atkinson, Ms J Milstead, M G Roberts, Ms M Batten, B J Key
**Co. Secretary:** Stuart Drabble
**Responsibilities**
**Senior:** Penelope Key *(Manager)*, Stewart Killick *(Director)*
**Finance:** Henry Cummins *(Bursar)*
**Marketing:** Felicity White *(Marketing Manager)*
**Admin:** Jackie Warrender *(Office Manager)*
**IT:** Elaine Machin *(Computer Manager)*
**HR:** Henry Cummins *(Bursar)*, Karen Veal *(Training Coordinator)*
**Health & Safety:** Henry Cummins *(Bursar)*, Hazel Goodwin *(Health & Safety Officer)*
**Facilities:** Henry Cummins *(Bursar)*
**Purchasing:** Ginny Hanbury *(Purchasing Manager)*
**US SIC:** 8211 **UK SIC:** 93200
**Auditors:** Francis Clark
**Bankers:** Lloyds TSB Bank plc (30-96-06)

| | 31-07-13 | 31-07-12 | 31-07-11 |
|---|---|---|---|
| TO | 4,904,056 | 4,827,075 | 4,854,569 |
| P/L | 71,155 | 74,544 | 122,247 |
| NW | 1,044,535 | 973,380 | 898,836 |
| WC | (1,119,082) | (909,602) | (863,795) |
| Emp. | 132 | 138 | 136 |

DUNS 23-217-6222
## Stow College
43 Shamrock Street, Glasgow, Lanarkshire G4 9LD
**Tel:** 01413321786 **Fax:** 0141-332-5207
**Web:** www.stow.ac.uk
**Estd:** 1934 Incorporate By Act Of Parliament
**Line of Business:** Colleges (higher education)
**Principals:** P Rea *(Financial)*, J Chown, R Miller, J Mcgreggor, R Mcgrory, R Mcgrory, I M Smith
**Responsibilities**
**Senior:** Alan Sherry *(Principal)*
**Branches:** Stow College, 43 Shamrock Street, Glasgow, Lanarkshire G4 9LD
**US SIC:** 8221 **UK SIC:** 93100
**Bankers:** Clydesdale Bank Plc (82-64-24)
**Employees:** 300

DUNS 34-930-4308
## Stowcare Holdings Ltd
Chilton Court, Gainsborough Road, Stowmarket, Suffolk IP14 1LL
**Tel:** 01449-675426
**Web:** www.stowcare.co.uk
**Reg No:** 5726917 **Estd:** 2006 Private Limited Company
**Line of Business:** Social work activities with accommodation
**Issued Capital:** £5,000
**Director:** B S Gibbs
**Co. Secretary:** Ms Hilary Gibbs
**US SIC:** 8321, 6732
**UK SIC:** 96111, 83100

| | 31-03-14 | 31-03-13 | 31-03-12 |
|---|---|---|---|
| TO | 347,005 | 1,824,974 | 1,652,364 |
| P/L | 279,956 | 342,511 | 338,752 |
| NW | 2,165,142 | 2,504,690 | 2,352,805 |
| WC | 936,419 | (167,250) | (175,514) |
| Emp. | 5 | 95 | 98 |

DUNS 22-635-4934
## Stowe School Ltd
Stowe, Buckingham, Buckinghamshire MK18 5EH
**Tel:** 01280-818000 **Fax:** 01280818131
**Web:** www.stowe.co.uk
**Reg No:** 0187251 **Estd:** 1923 Private Company Limited By Guarantee
**Line of Business:** General secondary education
**Directors:** Mrs E M Phillips, Lady J A Stringer, Reverend P M Ackroyd, J R Arkwright, D W Hudson, Mrs J E Hastie-Smith, Ms J C Brunskill, Mrs A K Johnson
**Co. Secretary:** Michael Porter
**Responsibilities**
**Senior:** Jonathan Bewes *(Director)*, James Burnell Nugent *(Director)*, John Cluff *(Chairman)*, Simon Creedy Smith *(Director)*, Christopher Honeyman Brown *(Director)*, George Magan *(Director)*, Juliet Shepherd-Smith *(Director)*, Christopher Tate *(Director)*, Marten Veen *(Manager)*, Susan Veen *(Manager)*, Edmund Verney *(Manager)*
**Finance:** Janis Hill *(Financial Director)*
**Marketing:** Tori Roddy *(Marketing Manager)*, T Scarff *(Marketing Manager)*
**IT:** David Meadows *(Database & Gift Administrator)*
**Facilities:** Frank Byrne *(Maintenance Manager)*
**Branches:** Stowe School,Ltd, Stowe, Buckingham, Buckinghamshire MK18 5DF
**US SIC:** 8211 **UK SIC:** 93200
**Auditors:** Binder Hamlyn
**Bankers:** Barclays Bank Plc (20-57-40)

| | 31-07-13 | 31-07-12 | 31-07-11 |
|---|---|---|---|
| TO | 24,499,730 | 21,644,032 | 19,996,886 |
| P/L | 5,337,169 | 3,142,429 | 2,155,058 |
| NW | 29,952,911 | 24,491,080 | 21,073,200 |
| WC | 717,119 | 878,075 | 418,109 |
| Emp. | 449 | 440 | 441 |

DUNS 53-571-1550
## Stowe Veterinary Group
54 Bury Road, Stowmarket, Suffolk IP14 1JF
**Tel:** 01449613130
**Web:** www.stowevets.co.uk
**Estd:** 1984 Partnership
**Line of Business:** Veterinary activities
**Partners:** J Mackinnon, R Harvey, R Kelly, I Kennedy, M Barrow, J M Webster
**Branches:** Stowe Veterinary Group, Coddenham Rd, Needham Mkt, Ipswich, Suffolk IP6 8NU
**US SIC:** 9121 **UK SIC:** 91110
**Employees:** 200

DUNS 21-581-7455
## The Stowe Youth Centre
258 Harrow Road, London W2 5ES
**Tel:** 02072668220
**Estd:** 2011 Proprietorship
**Line of Business:** Activities of other membership organisations not elsewhere classified
**Proprietor:** Miss J Rosenberg
**US SIC:** 8699 **UK SIC:** 96902
**Employees:** 50

DUNS 21-211-8751
## Stowlangtoft Hall Nursing Home
Kiln Lane, Stowlangtoft, Bury St Edmunds, Suffolk IP31 3JY
**Tel:** 01359-230216
**Web:** www.stowlangtoftestate.co.uk
**Estd:** 1996 Proprietorship
**Line of Business:** Nursing homes
**Partners:** Mrs H Macdonald, I Macdonald
**Responsibilities**
**Senior:** Roger Catchpole *(Proprietor)*, Ian MacDonald *(Partner)*, Hilary MacDonald *(Partner)*
**Admin:** n/a Catchpole *(Owner)*
**US SIC:** 8051 **UK SIC:** 95100
**Employees:** 55

DUNS 21-779-3260
## Stowlawn Primary School
Green Park Avenue, Bilston, West Midlands WV14 6EH
**Tel:** 01902558048
**Estd:** 2011 Proprietorship
**Line of Business:** Schools (local authority)
**Proprietor:** Mrs S Vaughan
**US SIC:** 8211 **UK SIC:** 93200
**Employees:** 220

DUNS 21-783-8377
## Stowmarket Middle School
Walnut Tree Walk, Stowmarket, Suffolk IP14 1JP
**Tel:** 01449742510
**Web:** www.stowmarketmiddle.suffolk.sch.uk
**Estd:** 2011 Proprietorship
**Line of Business:** Schools (local authority)
**Proprietor:** Mrs S Holmes
**Responsibilities**
**Senior:** Sally Holmes *(Head Teacher)*, Tim Odgers *(Head Teacher)*
**US SIC:** 8211 **UK SIC:** 93200
**Employees:** 62

DUNS 22-062-5961
## Str Ltd
(**Subsidiary of:** Str Group Ltd)
Unit1 & 2 Quay Point Northarbour Road, Portsmouth, Hampshire PO6 3TD
**Tel:** 02392374444
**Web:** www.strgroup.co.uk
**Reg No:** 4064332 **Estd:** 2004 Private Limited Company
**Line of Business:** Employment and recruitment companies and consultants
**Issued Capital:** £99
**Directors:** D J Wilson, C J Hutchings, S A Saunders, B Stephens
**Co. Secretary:** Richard Crawley
**US SIC:** 7361 **UK SIC:** 83954
**Auditors:** Rothmans LLP
**Bankers:** HSBC Bank plc (40-18-15)

| | 31-12-13 | 31-12-12 | 31-12-11 |
|---|---|---|---|
| TO | 20,947,624 | 17,299,298 | 8,751,633 |
| P/L | 328,653 | 204,586 | 419,062 |
| NW | 1,414,716 | 1,175,942 | 1,073,416 |
| WC | 1,341,791 | 1,084,003 | 969,098 |
| Emp. | 102 | 78 | 79 |

DUNS 22-935-8502
## Strabane District Council
Office 47, Derry Road, Strabane, Co Tyrone BT82 8DY
**Tel:** 028-7138-2204
**Web:** www.strabanedc.com
**Estd:** 2002
**Line of Business:** Local government
**Trading Style:** Sperrin Heritage Centre
**Principals:** J O'Kane *(Chairman)*, J Mckinney, Ms M Britton
**Responsibilities**
**Senior:** Derek Hussey *(Vice Chairman)*, J McKinney *(Principal)*, Daniel McSorley *(Chief Executive)*, Kieran Mcguire *(Chairman)*
**Marketing:** Rachel Craig *(Senior Marketing Executive)*, Sharon Maxwell *(Business Manager)*
**IT:** Sean Mullen *(IT Executive)*
**Health & Safety:** Catherine Collins *(Health and Safety Executive)*
**Operations:** Heather Torrens *(Project Officer)*
**Purchasing:** Sharon Maxwell *(Business Manager)*
**Branches:** Strabane District Council, 31 Longland Road, Strabane, Co Tyrone BT82 0PH
**US SIC:** 9121 **UK SIC:** 91110
**Bankers:** Ulster Bank Ltd (98-14-40)
**Employees:** 100

DUNS 21-579-5561
## Stracathro Hospital
By Brechin, Angus, Brechin, Angus DD9 7QA
**Tel:** 01356647291
**Web:** www.nhstayside.scot.nhs.uk
**Estd:** 2011
**Line of Business:** Hospitals
**Proprietor:** J Marr
**Responsibilities**
**Senior:** Bill Thomson *(Support Services Manager)*
**Branches:** Stracathro Hospital, Supplies Dept, Angus DD9 7QA Brechin
**US SIC:** 8062 **UK SIC:** 95100
**Employees:** 202

DUNS 77-915-4280
## Strachan Holdings Ltd
2 Dolphin Court, Stanningley Road, Bramley, Leeds, West Yorkshire LS13 4UN
**Tel:** 0800212637
**Web:** www.strachan.co.uk
**Reg No:** 5818607 **Estd:** 2006 Private Limited Company
**Line of Business:** Management activities of holding companies
**Issued Capital:** £57,874
**Director:** D G Strachan
**Co. Secretary:** Adam Strachan
**US SIC:** 6711 **UK SIC:** 83962
**Bankers:** Bank Of Scotland (80-20-00)

| | 30-06-13 | 30-06-12 | 30-06-11 |
|---|---|---|---|
| TO | 6,432,673 | 6,189,416 | 7,269,397 |
| P/L | [illegible] | 477,700 | [illegible] |
| NW | 3,375,792 | 3,233,631 | 3,167,345 |
| WC | 1,711,661 | 1,659,850 | 1,595,063 |
| Emp. | 73 | 74 | 81 |

DUNS 21-447-9503 **Imp**
## Strachans Ltd
(**Subsidiary of:** Ow Lux Sarl)
54 Windmill Street, Peterhead, Aberdeenshire AB42 1UE
**Tel:** 01779485300
**Web:** www.strachans.co.uk
**Reg No:** 0062092SC **VAT No:** 604814948
**Estd:** 1977 Private Limited Company
**Line of Business:** Food import and exporters and agents
**Issued Capital:** £83,000
**Principals:** J G Strachan *(Managing)*, S W Morrice, A Skipper, R S Kledal
**Co. Secretary:** Masson & Glennie
**Responsibilities**
**Finance:** Brenda Forsyth *(Finance Manager)*
**Marketing:** Stewart Patience *(E-Business Strategist)*
**Facilities:** Shona Niven *(Facilities Manager)*
**Branches:** Strachans Ltd, Admiralty Road, Great Yarmouth, Norfolk NR30 3PU
**US SIC:** 5149, 5143
**UK SIC:** 61700
**Auditors:** Deloitte LLP
**Bankers:** Clydesdale Bank Plc (82-67-12)

| | 31-12-13 | 31-12-12 | 31-12-11 |
|---|---|---|---|
| TO | 67,763,000 | 60,020,587 | 42,560,711 |
| P/L | 5,917,000 | 6,380,743 | 4,525,341 |
| NW | 10,274,000 | 9,881,300 | 8,976,889 |
| WC | 9,764,000 | 9,344,308 | 8,490,918 |
| Emp. | 180 | 160 | 155 |

DUNS 21-090-4975
## Stradbrook Holdings Ltd
(**Subsidiary of:** Pegasus Nominees Ltd.)
1 Canada Square, London E14 5AP
**Tel:** 02072932001
**Web:** www.sundaymirror.co.uk
**Reg No:** 0168660 **Estd:** 1920 Private Limited Company
**Line of Business:** Post offices
**Trading Style:** Sunday Mirror, The Racing Post
**Issued Capital:** £4,000
**Directors:** P Crowley, N Hughes, A Byrne
**Co. Secretary:** Mark Francis
**Branches:** Stradbrook Holdings Ltd, Easter Road Stadium, South Stand, Albion Rd, Edinburgh, Midlothian EH7 5QY
**US SIC:** 2711 **UK SIC:** 47512
**Auditors:** Deloitte & Touche LLP
**Bankers:** National Westminster Bank Plc (60-00-01)

| | 29-12-13 | 24-12-12 | 25-12-11 |
|---|---|---|---|
| TA | 172,619,000 | 172,619,000 | 172,619,000 |
| NW | 170,119,000 | 170,119,000 | 170,119,000 |

DUNS 21-540-3044
## The Stradey Park Hotel
Furnace, Llanelli, Dyfed SA15 4HA
**Tel:** 01554-758171
**Web:** www.stradeyparkhotel.com
**Estd:** 1995 Proprietorship
**Line of Business:** Hotels
**Proprietor:** Miss A Saunders
**Responsibilities**
**Senior:** Bronwyn Lanham *(Joint Managing Director)*
**HR:** Lesley Morgan *(Health & Safety Officer)*

**Health & Safety:** Lesley Morgan *(Health & Safety Officer)*
**Purchasing:** Bronwyn Lanham *(Joint Managing Director)*
**US SIC:** 7011 **UK SIC:** 66500
**Employees:** 70

DUNS 22-815-4928

## Straight Line Construction Co Ltd

Unit 2, Sandison Court, Brunswick Industrial Estate, Newcastle-Upon-Tyne, Tyne and Wear NE13 7BA
**Tel:** 01912170733
**Web:** www.straightlineconstruction.co.uk
**Reg No:** 1482191 **VAT No:** 297927684
**Estd:** 1980 Private Limited Company
**Line of Business:** Builders
**Issued Capital:** £14,100
**Principals:** R P Gilbert *(Managing)*, S C Reay *(Financial)*, K Newbegin
**Co. Secretary:** Mrs Lorna Gilbert
**Responsibilities**
**Senior:** Tony Dunlop *(Site Supervisor)*, Raymond Gilbert *(Chairman)*
**Health & Safety:** Chris Oxnard *(Health & Safety Officer)*
**US SIC:** 1522, 1541
**UK SIC:** 50100
**Auditors:** Stokoe Rodger
**Bankers:** Lloyds TSB Bank plc (30-91-50)

| | 31-03-14 | 31-03-13 | 31-03-12 |
|---|---|---|---|
| TO | N/A | N/A | 5,401,453 |
| P/L | N/A | N/A | 227,543 |
| NW | 307,616 | 172,714 | 180,333 |
| WC | (817,810) | (544,935) | (157,917) |
| Emp. | N/A | N/A | 53 |

DUNS 73-744-3317 Imp

## Straight Ltd

**(Subsidiary of:** One Fifty One Plc)
1 Whitehall Riverside, Leeds, West Yorkshire LS1 4BN
**Tel:** 01132-452244 **Fax:** 08435570011
**Web:** www.straight.co.uk
**Reg No:** 2923140 **Estd:** 1994 Private Limited Company
**Line of Business:** Recycling
**Export Sales:** £1,309,000
**Issued Capital:** £118,993
**Directors:** P R Murdoch, A Walsh, P Dalton
**Co. Secretary:** Ms Susan Holburn
**Responsibilities**
**IT:** Zap Voffey-Brittain *(IT Manager)*
**HR:** Carol Gough *(Human Resources Manager)*
**Health & Safety:** Carol Gough *(Human Resources Manager)*
**Purchasing:** Paul Crayton *(Production & Supply Chain Mana)*
**US SIC:** 3031 **UK SIC:** 48123
**Auditors:** Ernst & Young LLP
**Bankers:** The Royal Bank Of Scotland Plc (16-23-17)

| | 31-12-13 | 31-12-12 | 31-12-11 |
|---|---|---|---|
| TO | 26,097,000 | 27,822,000 | 27,974,000 |
| P/L | (133,000) | (1,629,000) | (790,000) |
| NW | 1,685,000 | 1,576,000 | 2,928,000 |
| WC | (2,881,000) | (3,843,000) | (3,209,000) |
| Emp. | 114 | 124 | 146 |

DUNS 73-720-2429

## Straight Talking Peer Education

Siddeley House, 50 Canbury Park Road, Kingston-Upon-Thames, Surrey KT2 6LX
**Web:** www.straighttalking.org
**Reg No:** 4978681 **Estd:** 2003 Private Company Limited By Guarantee
**Line of Business:** Charities and charitable organisations
**Directors:** P Glynne, Ms P Katsaouni, G Casley, J Botterill, Ms S N Kingsley
**Co. Secretary:** Ms Hilary Pannack
**Responsibilities**
**Senior:** Heather Owens *(Manager)*, Stephen Pugsley *(Manager)*
**US SIC:** 7392 **UK SIC:** 83951
**Bankers:** Lloyds TSB Bank plc (30-98-62)

| | 31-07-13 | 31-07-12 | 31-07-11 |
|---|---|---|---|
| TO | 318,726 | 325,236 | 233,137 |
| P/L | (25,025) | 59,517 | (28,901) |
| NW | 72,814 | 97,839 | 38,322 |
| WC | 72,083 | 97,125 | 37,692 |
| Emp. | 63 | 65 | 79 |

DUNS 39-757-3205 Imp-Exp

## Straightset Ltd

Stadium Close, Dukeries Industrial Estate, Worksop, Nottinghamshire S81 7BT
**Tel:** 01909-480055 **Fax:** 0190950128
**Web:** www.straightset.co.uk
**Reg No:** 2196324 **VAT No:** 471061472
**Estd:** 1987 Private Limited Company
**Line of Business:** Engineers (consulting)
**Export Markets:** Cyprus, Saudi Arabia
**Trading Style:** Straightset Engineering Services
**Issued Capital:** £22,210
**Principals:** P Bates *(Chairman and Managing)*, N Hopwood, T Hornsby
**Co. Secretary:** Stephen Bates
**Responsibilities**
**Engineering:** Mike Devilliers *(Service Manager)*
**US SIC:** 1799, 5999
**UK SIC:** 50000, 65600
**Auditors:** Allotts
**Bankers:** HSBC Bank plc (40-41-13)

| | 31-12-13 | 31-12-12 | 31-12-11 |
|---|---|---|---|
| TO | 7,382,124 | 6,066,631 | 7,466,312 |
| P/L | 457,099 | 433,689 | 578,006 |
| NW | 4,729,746 | 4,374,339 | 4,094,941 |
| WC | 3,741,801 | 3,380,570 | 3,417,961 |
| Emp. | 71 | 71 | 74 |

DUNS 22-040-5497 Exp

## Strainstall U K Ltd

**(Subsidiary of:** James Fisher & Sons Plc)
7-10 Mariners Way, Cowes, Isle of Wight PO31 8PD
**Tel:** 01983-203600
**Web:** www.strainstall.com
**Reg No:** 4042929 **VAT No:** 760192441
**Estd:** 1970 Private Limited Company
**Line of Business:** Engineers (structural)
**Issued Capital:** £1
**Directors:** M D Smith, S A Everett, J M Lambrechts, N P Henry, S C Kilpatrick, J G St Leger, R D Burmeister, A Coventry
**Co. Secretary:** Jonathan Vick
**Responsibilities**
**Senior:** Matthew Anderson *(Director)*, Raymond Leach *(Production Director)*, Karen Lucas *(Manager)*, Mike Shields *(Manager)*, Shennon Slade *(Marketing Manager)*, Justin Tyler *(Manager)*
**IT:** David Vodden *(Technical Director)*
**Health & Safety:** Raymond Leach *(Production Director)*
**Facilities:** Raymond Leach *(Production Director)*
**Purchasing:** Joel Mather *(Purchasing Officer)*
**Engineering:** Raymond Leach *(Production Director)*, Alan Owens *(Technical Director)*, David Vodden *(Technical Director)*
**US SIC:** 3829, 7397
**UK SIC:** 37100, 83702
**Auditors:** Blueprint Audit Ltd

| | 31-12-13 | 31-12-12 | 31-12-11 |
|---|---|---|---|
| TO | 13,516,158 | 10,388,988 | 10,940,472 |
| P/L | 708,456 | 400,299 | 1,645,345 |
| NW | 1,751,145 | 1,589,546 | 1,414,378 |
| WC | 1,452,487 | 1,243,664 | 1,118,856 |
| Emp. | 116 | 92 | 82 |

DUNS 22-955-1163 Imp-Exp

## Stralfors Plc

**(Subsidiary of:** Stralfors U K Ltd)
Cardrew Way, Cardrew Industrial Estate, Redruth, Cornwall TR15 1SH
**Tel:** 01209312800
**Web:** www.stralfors.co.uk
**Reg No:** 1626027 **Estd:** 1986 Public Limited Company
**Line of Business:** Pre-press activities
**Export Markets:** Scandinavia
**Issued Capital:** £610,000
**Directors:** U Skold, P J Samuelson, A J Plummer
**Co. Secretary:** Robin Olver
**Branches:** Stralfors Plc, Unit 10, Capstan Court, Dartford, Kent DA2 6QG
**US SIC:** 2794, 5199
**UK SIC:** 47545, 61900
**Auditors:** Ernst & Young LLP
**Bankers:** Barclays Bank Plc (20-87-94)

| | 31-12-13 | 31-12-12 | 31-12-11 |
|---|---|---|---|
| TO | 18,876,000 | 19,478,000 | 18,713,000 |
| P/L | (901,000) | (2,102,000) | (2,548,000) |
| NW | 1,894,000 | 2,513,000 | 1,596,000 |
| WC | (1,174,000) | (948,000) | (3,114,000) |
| Emp. | 102 | 127 | 159 |

DUNS 45-807-9100

## Strand Palace Hotel & Restaurants Ltd

**(Subsidiary of:** London & Regional Guarantee Co Ltd)
372 Strand, London WC2R 0JJ
**Tel:** 02078368080
**Web:** www.strandpalacehotel.co.uk
**Reg No:** 3165882 **Estd:** 1996 Private Limited Company
**Line of Business:** Hotels
**Issued Capital:** £46,978,326
**Director:** R J Livingstone
**Co. Secretary:** Richard Luck
**Responsibilities**
**IT:** Ben Chapman *(IT Manager)*
**Branches:** Strand Palace Hotel & Restaurants Ltd, Maidstone Road, Chatham, Kent ME5 9SF
**US SIC:** 7011, 6531
**UK SIC:** 66500, 83400
**Auditors:** UHY Hacker Young

| | 30-09-14 | 30-09-13 | 30-09-12 |
|---|---|---|---|
| TO | 33,309,000 | 30,401,000 | 29,909,000 |
| P/L | 9,549,000 | 2,731,000 | 9,880,000 |
| NW | 54,879,000 | 54,799,000 | 54,521,000 |
| WC | 8,698,000 | 7,456,000 | 7,796,000 |
| Emp. | 228 | 228 | 236 |

DUNS 22-632-0802 Imp

## Strandhaven Ltd

600 High Road, Ilford, Essex IG3 8BS
**Tel:** 020-8599-4436
**Web:** www.somexpharma.com
**Reg No:** 1413692 **VAT No:** 250007515
**Estd:** 1980 Private Limited Company
**Line of Business:** Chemists - wholesale
**Trading Style:** Pharmaram Chemists, Somex Pharma
**Issued Capital:** £100,000
**Managing Director:** D Somaiya
**Co. Secretary:** Harsha Somaiya
**Branches:** Strandhaven Ltd, Ilford Lane, Ilford, Essex IG1 2JZ
**US SIC:** 5122 **UK SIC:** 61800
**Auditors:** Ashfords Partnership LLP
**Bankers:** Barclays Bank Plc (20-05-75)

| | 31-07-13 | 31-07-12 | 31-07-11 |
|---|---|---|---|
| TO | 9,138,092 | 9,716,856 | 8,618,899 |
| P/L | 429,111 | 58,122 | 207,076 |
| NW | 2,534,149 | 2,122,058 | 2,008,713 |
| WC | 1,991,730 | 2,002,222 | 1,840,528 |
| Emp. | 46 | N/A | 40 |

DUNS 23-242-6135

## Strangford College

Abbey Road, Carrowdore, Newtownards, Co Down BT22 2GB
**Tel:** 028-9186-1199 **Fax:** 028-9186-3900
**Web:** www.strangfordcollege.net
**Reg No:** 0032886NI **Estd:** 1997 Private Company Limited By Guarantee
**Line of Business:** General secondary education
**Trading Style:** Strangford College
**Directors:** Ms F Moffett, Ms L Totton, B Small, Ms M Berry, Ms A D Morrow, Ms L Calvin, P J Mcintyre, B Ireland
**Co. Secretary:** Scroggie Trevor
**Responsibilities**
**Senior:** Jackie Anderson *(Governor)*, Susan Mackie *(Director)*, Raymond Murray *(Governor)*, Trevor Scroggie *(Director)*
**US SIC:** 8211 **UK SIC:** 93200
**Auditors:** FGS McClure Watters
**Bankers:** The Bank Of Ireland (90-23-46)

| | 31-03-14 | 31-03-13 | 31-03-12 |
|---|---|---|---|
| TO | 2,979,282 | 22,630 | N/A |
| P/L | (136,331) | 21,509 | N/A |
| NW | 5,100,773 | 43,344 | 21,835 |
| WC | 364,424 | N/A | N/A |
| Emp. | 72 | N/A | N/A |

DUNS 22-937-8112 Imp

## Stranmillis University College

Stranmillis Road, Belfast BT9 5DY
**Tel:** 028-9038-1271
**Web:** www.stran.ac.uk
**Estd:** 1922
**Line of Business:** Further education schools and colleges
**Principals:** Dr R Mcminn, N C Halliday
**Responsibilities**
**Senior:** Hilary Quigley *(General Manager)*, Charlie Reid *(Head Of I.T)*, Hugh Storey *(Secretary)*
**Finance:** Jo O' Boyle *(Corporate Affairs Director)*
**Marketing:** Jo O' Boyle *(Corporate Affairs Director)*
**Admin:** Rae Gibson *(Administrative Officer)*, Louise Macnamee *(Administrative Officer)*
**HR:** Jo O' Boyle *(Corporate Affairs Director)*
**Purchasing:** Donna Castles *(Purchasing Manager)*
**US SIC:** 8221 **UK SIC:** 93100
**Bankers:** Ulster Bank Ltd (98-00-00)
**Employees:** 200
**Turnover:** £11,002,000

DUNS 21-780-3614

## Stranraer Academy

Mcmasters Road, Stranraer, Wigtownshire DG9 8AX
**Tel:** 01776706484
**Web:** www.stranraeracademy.org.uk
**Estd:** 2002 Partnership
**Line of Business:** General secondary education
**Partner:** N Dawson
**Responsibilities**
**Finance:** Graham Clyne *(Senior Finance Administrator)*
**Admin:** Graham Clyne *(Senior Finance Administrator)*
**US SIC:** 8211 **UK SIC:** 93200
**Employees:** 130

DUNS 49-130-7534

## Strapack Uk Ltd

**(Subsidiary of:** Strapack Corporation)
Gordian House, Brunel Road, Basingstoke, Hampshire RG21 6XX
**Tel:** 01256394400
**Reg No:** 3104788 **Estd:** 1995 Private Limited Company
**Line of Business:** Management activities of holding companies
**Export Sales:** £3,843,118
**Issued Capital:** £1,100,000
**Directors:** K Yamamoto, T Shimojima
**Co. Secretary:** Andrew Lea
**US SIC:** 6711 **UK SIC:** 83962
**Auditors:** Haines Watts
**Bankers:** The Bank Of Tokyo-Mitsubishi, Ltd (60-01-09)

| | 31-12-13 | 31-12-12 | 31-12-11 |
|---|---|---|---|
| TO | 10,488,860 | 10,755,090 | 10,576,916 |
| P/L | 430,078 | 304,976 | 390,358 |
| NW | 4,776,505 | 4,476,234 | 4,307,889 |
| WC | 4,395,607 | 4,267,194 | 3,965,379 |
| Emp. | 47 | 43 | 41 |

DUNS 45-865-6030

## Strapex Holdings Ltd

Lambton St Industrial Estate, Shildon, County Durham DL4 1PX
**Tel:** 01388774061
**Web:** www.strapex.com
**Reg No:** 3208188 **Estd:** 1996 Private Limited Company
**Line of Business:** Manufacture of other plastic products
**Trading Style:** Wilsonart
**Issued Capital:** £7,100,002
**Directors:** H Kaiser, O Streit, N Stenger
**US SIC:** 3079 **UK SIC:** 48360
**Auditors:** Deloitte LLP
**Bankers:** Barclays Bank Plc (20-95-61)

| | 31-12-13 | 31-12-12 | 31-12-11 |
|---|---|---|---|
| TA | 453,846,656 | 23,177,812 | 23,241,488 |
| P/L | 15,578,119 | (1,542,081) | (1,656,541) |
| NW | 417,063,331 | (35,840,625) | (34,675,509) |
| WC | (35,225,569) | (18,550,625) | (17,385,509) |

DUNS 22-815-0561

## Strata Homes Ltd

Quaypoint, Lakeside Boulevard, Doncaster, South Yorkshire DN4 5PL
**Tel:** 01302308508
**Web:** www.strata.co.uk
**Reg No:** 1709069 **Estd:** 1983 Private Limited Company
**Line of Business:** Builders
**Issued Capital:** £43,700
**Principals:** R I Weaver *(Chairman)*, J N Davis, J J Wren, M Rosindale, A R Weaver
**Co. Secretary:** Julian Davis
**Responsibilities**
**Health & Safety:** Vicky Chwalczyk *(Facilities Manager)*
**Facilities:** Vicky Chwalczyk *(Facilities Manager)*
**Branches:** Strata Homes Ltd, Old Rd, Churwell, Leeds, West Yorkshire LS27 7RS
**US SIC:** 1522, 6711
**UK SIC:** 50100, 83962
**Auditors:** Allotts
**Bankers:** Yorkshire Bank Plc (05-04-14)

| | 31-12-13 | 31-12-12 | 31-12-11 |
|---|---|---|---|
| TO | 80,388,000 | 36,902,000 | 39,142,000 |
| P/L | 8,788,000 | 775,000 | (440,000) |
| NW | 39,171,000 | 32,298,000 | 30,068,000 |
| WC | 38,437,000 | 32,147,000 | 32,521,000 |
| Emp. | 115 | 107 | 92 |

DUNS 39-232-6690 Imp-Exp

## Strata Products Ltd

Brookhill Industrial Estate, Pinxton, Nottingham, Nottinghamshire NG16 6NS
**Tel:** 01773-510520
**Web:** www.strataproducts.co.uk
**Reg No:** 2117372 **VAT No:** 494666394
**Estd:** 1989 Private Limited Company
**Line of Business:** Manufacture of plastics in primary forms
**Issued Capital:** £450,000
**Principals:** M A Ilsen *(Managing)*, J Ilsen
**Responsibilities**
**IT:** Terri Cartledge *(Buyer)*, James Cavanagh *(Production Manager)*
**Health & Safety:** James Cavanagh *(Production Manager)*
**Facilities:** James Cavanagh *(Production Manager)*
**Purchasing:** Terri Cartledge *(Buyer)*
**Engineering:** James Cavanagh *(Production Manager)*
**US SIC:** 2821, 3079
**UK SIC:** 25140, 48360
**Auditors:** Nyman Libson Paul

**Bankers:** National Westminster Bank Plc (60-17-33)

| | 31-12-13 | 31-12-12 | 31-12-11 |
|---|---|---|---|
| TO | 18,515,739 | 16,738,840 | 15,737,094 |
| P/L | 1,608,935 | 2,014,925 | 1,134,149 |
| NW | 9,257,792 | 8,030,158 | 6,485,669 |
| WC | 3,628,383 | 3,027,049 | 1,850,989 |
| Emp. | 112 | 107 | 91 |

DUNS 23-825-8367

## Strata Security & Combined Services Ltd

(**Subsidiary of:** Iss A/S)
Strata House, Strata House, Stockport, Cheshire SK3 0DT
**Tel:** 0161-480-6565
**Web:** www.stratagroupplc.com
**Reg No:** 3817833 **Estd:** 1999 Private Limited Company
**Line of Business:** Detective agencies
**Issued Capital:** £1,000
**Directors:** M E Brabin, R I Sykes
**Responsibilities**
**Senior:** Steven Stonehouse *(Finance Director)*
**US SIC:** 7393, 7349
**UK SIC:** 83954, 92300
**Auditors:** KPMG LLP
**Bankers:** Barclays Bank Plc (20-20-46)

| | 31-12-13 | 31-12-12 | 31-12-11 |
|---|---|---|---|
| TA | 1,000 | 1,000 | 1,000 |
| NW | 1,000 | 1,000 | 1,000 |

DUNS 21-100-0223

## Strategic Team Group Ltd

Strategic Business Centre, Blue Ridge Park, Thunderhead Ridge, Castleford, West Yorkshire WF10 4UA
**Tel:** 01977555550
**Web:** www.strategicteamgroup.com
**Reg No:** 6437711 **Estd:** 2007 Private Limited Company
**Line of Business:** Construction of commercial buildings
**Issued Capital:** £108,405
**Directors:** A R Watson, L Robinson, G Taylor, S M Ashton, A M Coates, C N Tweed
**Co. Secretary:** Simon Lazenby
**US SIC:** 1541 **UK SIC:** 50100
**Auditors:** PKF (UK) LLP

| | 30-09-14 | 30-09-13 | 31-09-13 |
|---|---|---|---|
| TO | 56,958,926 | 26,002,917 | 56,009,017 |
| P/L | 24,067 | (30,985) | (5,473,572) |
| NW | (7,243,616) | (7,930,851) | (8,231,450) |
| WC | (7,376,299) | (8,076,251) | (8,120,581) |
| Emp. | 169 | 185 | 206 |

DUNS 21-789-0728

## Strategic Thoughts

1 Grenfell Road, Maidenhead, Berkshire SL6 1HN
**Tel:** 01628582500
**Estd:** 2011
**Line of Business:** Business services
**Trading Style:** Strategic Thoughts
**US SIC:** 7399 **UK SIC:** 83954
**Employees:** 100

DUNS 34-800-9056

## Stratex International Plc

180 Piccadilly, London W1J 9HF
**Tel:** 0207 830 9650
**Web:** www.stratexinternational.com
**Reg No:** 5601091 **Estd:** 2005 Public Limited Company
**Line of Business:** Mining of metals
**Issued Capital:** £4,667,582
**Directors:** R P Foster, C R Hall, J Cole-Baker, G P Addison, Ms E K Priestley
**Co. Secretary:** Perry Ashwood
**US SIC:** 1099 **UK SIC:** 21000
**Auditors:** PKF Littlejohn LLP
**Bankers:** Lloyds TSB Bank plc (77-49-17)

| | 31-12-13 | 31-12-12 | 31-12-11 |
|---|---|---|---|
| TA | 24,370,338 | 28,513,520 | 10,699,835 |
| P/L | (3,830,681) | 9,696,795 | (517,377) |
| NW | 13,455,087 | 18,251,856 | 2,918,693 |
| WC | 10,377,388 | 16,969,442 | 2,573,221 |
| Emp. | 55 | 45 | 45 |

DUNS 23-628-5107

## Stratfield Saye Estates Management Co Ltd

(**Subsidiary of:** Wellington Country Park Ltd)
The Estate Office, Stratfield Saye, Reading, Berkshire RG7 2BT
**Tel:** 01256882694
**Reg No:** 3625576 **Estd:** 1815 Private Limited Company
**Line of Business:** Other business activities not elsewhere classified
**Trading Style:** Stratfield Saye Estates, Stratfield Farms, Stratfield Saye House
**Issued Capital:** £2
**Directors:**
The Honourable A C Wellesley The Marquess Of Douro,
The Honourable A E Wellesley The Marchioness Of Dou, J F Hare

**US SIC:** 7399 **UK SIC:** 83954
**Auditors:** B K L Weeks Green

| | 31-03-14 | 31-03-13 | 31-03-12 |
|---|---|---|---|
| TA | 174 | 174 | 188 |
| NW | 174 | 174 | 188 |

DUNS 21-211-8769

## The Stratford Bentley Nursing Home

Saffron Meadow, Stratford-Upon-Avon, Warwickshire CV37 6GD
**Tel:** 01789-414078
**Estd:** 1988 Proprietorship
**Line of Business:** Clinics private
**Proprietor:** Dr P Bellamy
**Responsibilities**
**Senior:** Lucy Burr *(Manager)*
**US SIC:** 8051 **UK SIC:** 95100
**Employees:** 48

DUNS 21-618-0812

## Stratford Circus

Theatre Square, London E15 1BX
**Tel:** 08443572625
**Web:** www.stratford-circus.com
**Estd:** 1998 Proprietorship
**Line of Business:** Theatres & concert halls
**Proprietor:** A Brizman
**Responsibilities**
**Senior:** Clare Connor *(Manager)*
**US SIC:** 7911 **UK SIC:** 97913
**Employees:** 49

DUNS 21-728-5952

## Stratford Girls' Grammar School

Shottery, Shottery, Stratford-Upon-Avon, Warwickshire CV37 9HA
**Web:** www.sggs.org.uk
**Reg No:** 7646003 **Estd:** 2011 Private Company Limited By Guarantee
**Line of Business:** General secondary education
**Directors:** J R Downes, Mrs V Harper, S Ewing, Ms D Precious, Mrs H Bendle, R N Cox, Ms A Harvey, Ms C Watt
**Co. Secretary:** Paul Day
**Responsibilities**
**Senior:** Kate Barnett *(Director)*, Brian Follett *(Director)*, Steve Gee *(Director)*, John Millett *(Director)*, David Morse *(Director)*, Lynda Organ *(Director)*, Diana Woods *(Director)*
**US SIC:** 8211 **UK SIC:** 93200
**Bankers:** Lloyds TSB Bank plc (30-98-26)

| | 31-08-14 | 31-08-13 | 31-08-12 |
|---|---|---|---|
| TO | 4,213,000 | 4,822,000 | 14,468,588 |
| P/L | 139,000 | 767,000 | 10,036,054 |
| NW | 10,833,000 | 10,674,000 | 9,858,054 |
| WC | 464,000 | 400,000 | 639,751 |
| Emp. | 95 | 96 | 88 |

DUNS 21-782-9004

## Stratford Holiday Inn

Bridgefoot, Stratford-Upon-Avon, Warwickshire CV37 6YR
**Tel:** 01789279988
**Web:** www.holidayinn.co.uk
**Estd:** 2011 Partnership
**Line of Business:** Hotels
**Partners:** M Abellam, M Abellan Van Kan
**US SIC:** 7011 **UK SIC:** 66500
**Employees:** 100

DUNS 22-845-0144

## Stratford-upon-Avon College

Alcester Road, Stratford-Upon-Avon, Warwickshire CV37 9DH
**Tel:** 01789-266245
**Web:** www.stratford.ac.uk
**Estd:** 1970
**Line of Business:** Further education schools and colleges
**Directors:** N Briggs, Ms J Bluteau
**Responsibilities**
**Finance:** Norman MacDonald *(Head of Finance)*
**Marketing:** Natalie Corcoran *(Marketing Manager)*
**HR:** Kay Taylor *(Vice Principal)*
**Health & Safety:** Alex Patterson *(Health & Safety Officer)*
**Facilities:** Karen Rees *(Facilities Manager)*, Hazel Skwirzynska *(Vice Principal & Estates Manag)*
**Branches:** Stratford-Upon-Avon College, Alcester Road, Stratford-Upon-Avon, Warwickshire CV37 9QR
**US SIC:** 8249 **UK SIC:** 93300
**Employees:** 500

DUNS 22-747-3881

## Stratford upon Avon District Council

Elizabeth House, Church Street, Stratford-Upon-Avon, Warwickshire CV37 6HX
**Tel:** 01789267575
**Web:** www.stratford-dc.gov.uk
**Estd:** 2011
**Line of Business:** Local government
**Principals:** M Henwood *(Financial)*, I B Prosser
**Responsibilities**
**Senior:** Julia Aratoon *(Senior Manager)*, Charles Bates *(Executive)*, Pauline Day *(Chairman)*, Gary Fisher *(Manager)*, Serena James *(Relations Manager)*, Claire Johnson *(Chairman's Secretary)*, Paul Lankester *(Chief Executive)*, Ruth Mounstephen *(Senior Manager)*, Colin Staves *(Manager)*, Darren Whitney *(Executive)*, Lucy Workman *(Executive)*
**Finance:** Sarah Pittaway *(Finance Manager)*
**Marketing:** Serena James *(Relations Manager)*, Rachael Mckinlay *(Relations Manager)*
**Admin:** Tina Brain *(Administrator)*, Morag Haymes *(Administrator)*
**IT:** James Deeley *(Information Security Manager)*, Balvinder Heran *(IT Support Manager)*
**HR:** Laila Cherry *(Personnel Officer)*, Laila Doman *(Human Resources Manager)*, Bharti Quinn *(Executive)*
**Health & Safety:** Robert Weeks *(Head of Environmental)*
**Facilities:** Matthew Austin *(Environment Maintenance Office)*, Nick Cadd *(Housing and Communities Manage)*, Shree Johansen *(Project Officer-Empty Homes)*
**Operations:** Yvette Saunders *(CCTV Manager)*, Robert Weeks *(Head of Environmental)*, Yvette Widdowfield *(CCTV Services Manager)*
**Branches:** Stratford Upon Avon District Council, Erme Court, Leonards Road, Ivybridge, Devon PL21 0SZ
**US SIC:** 9121 **UK SIC:** 91110
**Employees:** 250

DUNS 21-770-8115

## Strathallan Primary School

Strathallan Drive, Kirkcaldy, Fife KY2 5YP
**Tel:** 01592583434
**Estd:** 2011 Proprietorship
**Line of Business:** Primary education
**Proprietor:** Mrs I Mcbain
**US SIC:** 8211 **UK SIC:** 93200
**Employees:** 300

DUNS 23-645-4252

## Strathallan School

Forgandenny, Perth, Perthshire PH2 9EG
**Tel:** 01738-812546 **Fax:** 01738-812549
**Web:** www.strathallan.co.uk
**Reg No:** 0044822SC **Estd:** 1915 Private Company Limited By Guarantee
**Line of Business:** Schools (independent)
**Trading Style:** Strathallan School
**Directors:** A M Wilkinson, Professor J Cleland, Mrs P A Milne, Mrs K J Dunn, K C Dinsmore, Mrs E Lister, J G Barrack, Miss R Sandison
**Co. Secretary:** Anthony Glasgow
**Responsibilities**
**Senior:** Jean Cachia *(Director)*, Stephen Hay *(Director)*, Trevor Hoey *(Director)*, Neil Houston *(Director)*, Jeremy Huggett *(Governor)*, Ellen Lane *(Manager)*, Jonathan Leiper *(Manager)*, Richard Linton *(Director)*, Pauline Lockhart *(Director)*
**IT:** Glyn Gardiner *(Head of IT)*, Billy Greig *(IT Manager)*, Adam Streatfeild-James *(Senior IT manager)*
**HR:** Alison Chartres *(Human Resources Manager)*
**US SIC:** 8211 **UK SIC:** 93200
**Auditors:** Ernst & Young
**Bankers:** Clydesdale Bank Plc (82-67-11)

| | 31-07-14 | 31-07-13 | 31-07-12 |
|---|---|---|---|
| TO | 11,914,935 | 11,707,340 | 11,278,550 |
| P/L | 663,594 | 626,695 | 876,641 |
| NW | 11,945,237 | 11,279,648 | 10,654,345 |
| WC | 2,148,966 | 1,818,911 | 1,570,595 |
| Emp. | 225 | 244 | 192 |

DUNS 21-782-3339

## Strathaven Academy

Bowling Green Road, Strathaven, Lanarkshire ML10 6DP
**Tel:** 01357524040
**Web:** www.strathaven.s-lanark.sch.uk
**Estd:** 2011 Proprietorship
**Line of Business:** Schools (local authority)
**Proprietor:** Ms M Irvine
**Responsibilities**
**Senior:** Stewart Nicolson *(Head Teacher)*
**US SIC:** 8211 **UK SIC:** 93200
**Employees:** 90

DUNS 28-824-9584

## Strathcarron Hospice

Randolph Hill, Denny, Stirlingshire FK6 5HJ
**Tel:** 01324-826222
**Web:** www.strathcarronhospice.org
**Reg No:** 0068503SC **Estd:** 1980 Private Limited Company
**Line of Business:** Hospices
**Trading Style:** Strathcarron Hospice
**Directors:** Mrs R C Davidson, M Mcmonagle, S J Teahan, E Toal, D Mcgregor, Mrs C J Mckinlay, Ms E M Hallam, S Reid
**Co. Secretary:** William Andrew
**Responsibilities**
**Senior:** Michael Fyall *(Director)*, Colin Mather *(Director)*, Elizabeth Millar *(Director)*, Tom Ogilvie *(Director)*
**Branches:** Strathcarron Hospice, 61 High Street, Tillicoultry, Clackmannanshire FK13 6AA
**US SIC:** 8091 **UK SIC:** 95200
**Auditors:** R A Scott Wheelan & Co
**Bankers:** Clydesdale Bank Plc (82-63-12)

| | 31-03-14 | 31-03-13 | 31-03-12 |
|---|---|---|---|
| TO | 5,852,825 | 5,921,740 | 5,611,835 |
| P/L | (327,532) | (9,776) | 159,027 |
| NW | 1,593,461 | 2,235,537 | 2,209,762 |
| WC | 246,133 | 213,834 | 106,914 |
| Emp. | 115 | 114 | 143 |

DUNS 21-583-3246

## Strathclyde Fire & Rescue

Greenfaulds Road, Cumbernauld, Glasgow, Lanarkshire G67 2DH
**Tel:** 01236729797
**Web:** www.strathclydefire.org
**Estd:** 2011 Proprietorship
**Line of Business:** Fire service activities
**Proprietor:** J Mcshane
**Responsibilities**
**Senior:** Graham Binning *(Station Commander)*, John McShane *(Proprietor)*
**US SIC:** 9224 **UK SIC:** 91400
**Employees:** 60

DUNS 21-782-2559

## Strathclyde Graduate Business School

199 Cathedral Street, Glasgow, Lanarkshire G4 0QU
**Tel:** 01415536000
**Web:** www.gsb.strath.ac.uk
**Estd:** 2002 Proprietorship
**Line of Business:** University
**Proprietor:** Mrs S Hart
**US SIC:** 8221 **UK SIC:** 93100
**Employees:** 60

DUNS 22-905-7567 **Imp**

## Strathclyde Partnership for Transport

Consort House, West George Street, Glasgow, Lanarkshire G2 1HN
**Tel:** 01413326811
**Web:** www.spt.co.uk
**Estd:** 1980
**Line of Business:** Non-charitable social work activities with accommodation
**Trading Style:** Spt
**Principals:** J Pow, G Maclennan, Ms V Davidson
**Responsibilities**
**Senior:** Gordon MacLennan *(Chief Executive)*, Shona Seymour *(Executive)*, Clare Strain *(Executive)*
**Finance:** Stuart Paul *(Chief Accountant)*, Neil Wylie *(Head of Finance)*
**Marketing:** Bruce Kiloh *(Head of Transport Planning)*, Michelle Watt *(Communications Manager)*
**Admin:** Elaine Campbell *(Assistant)*
**IT:** Donald Baddon *(IT Manager)*, Clive Farron *(Service Support Team Leader)*
**HR:** Audrey Kelly *(Human Resources Manager)*, Debbie Mackie *(HR Operations Manager)*, Neil Wylie *(Head of Finance)*
**Health & Safety:** Martin Conroy *(Health & Safety Officer)*
**Fleet:** Bruce Kiloh *(Head of Transport Planning)*
**Engineering:** Neil Gatenby *(Infrastructure Engineer)*
**Branches:** Strathclyde Partnership For Transport, The Paisley Centre, Unit 35B, Paisley, Renfrewshire PA1 1UN
**US SIC:** 8321 **UK SIC:** 96111
**Bankers:** Bank Of Scotland (80-54-01)
**Employees:** 600

DUNS 22-741-7748 **Imp**

## Strathclyde Police

House 8 94 Elm Bank Street, 173 Pitt Street, Glasgow, Lanarkshire G2 4JS
**Tel:** 01415322000
**Web:** www.strathclyde.police.uk
**Estd:** 1968

**Line of Business:** Public security, law and order activities
**Director:** J Orr
**Responsibilities**
**Finance:** Allan MacLeod *(Head of Finance)*
**Marketing:** Gillian Main *(Marketing Manager)*
**Admin:** Gordon McGrath *(Administration Manager)*
**IT:** Fiona O'Hare *(Computer Services Manager)*
**HR:** John Gillies *(Human Resources Director)*
**Health & Safety:** Frederick Cullum *(Senior Force Safety Officer)*
**Facilities:** Ian McCracken *(Property Services Manager)*
**Purchasing:** Gordon McGrath *(Administration Manager)*
**Branches:** Strathclyde Police, Police Station, 1 Caledonia Road, Shotts, Lanarkshire ML7 4DU
**US SIC:** 9221 **UK SIC:** 91300
**Employees:** 10,700

DUNS 50-440-8451 **Imp**
## Strathclyde Tyre Services Ltd
6 Rankine Street, Johnstone, Renfrewshire PA5 8BA
**Tel:** 01505-324891
**Web:** www.strathclydetyres.co.uk
**Reg No:** 0120607SC **VAT No:** 554304754
**Estd:** 1989 Private Limited Company
**Line of Business:** Tyre dealers
**Issued Capital:** £132,480
**Managing Director:** B Tracey
**Co. Secretary:** Jaine Chisholm
**Branches:** Strathclyde Tyre Services Ltd, 106 Main Street, Coatbridge, Lanarkshire ML5 3BJ
**US SIC:** 7539 **UK SIC:** 67100
**Auditors:** Campbell Dallas LLP
**Bankers:** Clydesdale Bank Plc (82-65-23)

| | 30-09-13 | 30-09-12 | 30-09-11 |
|---|---|---|---|
| TO | 7,960,586 | N/A | N/A |
| P/L | 296,479 | N/A | N/A |
| NW | 656,621 | 499,607 | 430,004 |
| WC | 265,030 | 176,078 | 223,478 |
| Emp. | 65 | N/A | N/A |

DUNS 21-597-7508
## Strathearn Community Campus
Pittenzie Road, Crieff, Perthshire PH7 3JN
**Tel:** 01764657700
**Web:** www.pkc.gov.uk
**Estd:** 2011 Proprietorship
**Line of Business:** Schools (local authority)
**Proprietor:** T Rae
**Responsibilities**
**Senior:** Christine Ross *(Campus Leader)*
**US SIC:** 8211 **UK SIC:** 93200
**Employees:** 200

DUNS 23-640-4570
## Strathearn Leisure Parks Ltd
Seafield Road, Seahouses, Northumberland NE68 7SP
**Tel:** 01665-720628
**Web:** www.seafieldpark.co.uk
**Reg No:** 0631554 **VAT No:** 297865973
**Estd:** 1959 Private Limited Company
**Line of Business:** Caravan parks
**Trading Style:** Seafield Caravan Park
**Issued Capital:** £144
**Directors:** S I Manners, J K Britton, J D Stuart
**Co. Secretary:** William Cunningham
**Responsibilities**
**Senior:** Carolyn Britton *(Proprietor)*, Ken Britton *(proprietor)*
**US SIC:** 7033 **UK SIC:** 66701
**Auditors:** Byers & Co

| | 31-10-13 | 31-10-12 | 31-10-11 |
|---|---|---|---|
| TA | 4,340,441 | 3,782,830 | 3,591,347 |
| NW | 1,708,274 | 1,415,673 | 992,770 |
| WC | (1,572,791) | (1,223,076) | (1,433,906) |

DUNS 42-471-8187
## Strathearn School Belfast
Strathearn School, Belfast BT4 2AU
**Tel:** 02890471595 **Fax:** 028-9065-0555
**Web:** www.strathearn.org
**Reg No:** 0020602NI **Estd:** 1929 Private Company Limited By Guarantee
**Line of Business:** Schools (local authority)
**Directors:** Mrs C Meredith, D Manning, N Crawford, I C Noad, Dr K S Gibson, Ms C Auchmuty, Mrs L Mallon, N Mckeown
**Co. Secretary:** Mrs Ann Flannigan
**Responsibilities**
**Senior:** Rosemary Bailie *(Director)*, William Caldwell *(Director)*, Susan Dermott *(Director)*, Diane Eakin *(Director)*, Thomas Forde *(Director)*, George Mcgowan *(Director)*, Ann O'Dwyer *(Director)*, Evelyn Rodgers *(Director)*, Patricia Stewart *(Director)*, Patrick White *(Director)*
**US SIC:** 8211 **UK SIC:** 93200

**Auditors:** Moore Stephens
**Bankers:** Ulster Bank Ltd (98-01-30)

| | 31-03-14 | 31-03-13 | 31-03-12 |
|---|---|---|---|
| TO | 4,334,977 | 4,356,872 | 4,165,698 |
| P/L | 9,475 | 113,691 | 57,991 |
| NW | 2,755,242 | 2,635,415 | 2,396,878 |
| WC | 397,343 | 889,530 | 1,054,155 |
| Emp. | 225 | 125 | 224 |

DUNS 73-762-0174
## Strathmore Care Ltd
58-60 Avenue Road, Westcliff-On-Sea, Essex SS0 7PJ
**Tel:** 01702433335
**Web:** www.strathmorecare.com
**Reg No:** 5019344 **Estd:** 2004 Private Limited Company
**Line of Business:** Individual & Family Social Services
**Issued Capital:** £1
**Director:** Dr D S Vive Kananda
**US SIC:** 8321 **UK SIC:** 96111

| | 31-01-14 | 31-01-13 | 31-01-12 |
|---|---|---|---|
| TA | 1 | 1 | 1 |
| NW | 1 | 1 | 1 |

DUNS 21-582-7692
## Strathmore Foods Ltd
Carsview Road, Forfar, Angus DD8 3NG
**Tel:** 01307-462333
**Web:** www.strathmore-foods.com
**Reg No:** 0053180SC **VAT No:** 269286218
**Estd:** 1973 Private Limited Company
**Line of Business:** Manufacturers of food products
**Trading Style:** Strathmore Foods Ltd
**Issued Capital:** £158,355
**Principals:** C S Nisbet *(Managing)*, I H Clarke, Ms J E Nisbet, D J Nisbet
**Co. Secretary:** Dain Egan
**Responsibilities**
**Admin:** Gail Low *(Office Manager)*
**US SIC:** 2099 **UK SIC:** 42399
**Auditors:** Henderson Loggie
**Bankers:** Clydesdale Bank Plc (82-64-20)

| | 30-06-13 | 30-06-12 | 30-06-11 |
|---|---|---|---|
| TO | 12,078,685 | 11,097,456 | 11,640,861 |
| P/L | 843,044 | 472,588 | 232,037 |
| NW | 3,402,125 | 2,768,961 | 2,404,981 |
| WC | 1,408,204 | 949,370 | 651,357 |
| Emp. | 136 | 132 | 152 |

DUNS 76-386-2786
## Strathmore Hotels Ltd
**(Subsidiary of:** Strathmore Hotels (Scotland) Ltd)
116-120 Strathmore House, Glasgow, Lanarkshire G74 1LF
**Tel:** 01355266886 **Fax:** 01355260782
**Web:** www.strathmorehotels.com
**Reg No:** 0128215SC **VAT No:** 556665700
**Estd:** 1994 Private Limited Company
**Line of Business:** Bus operators and stations
**Issued Capital:** £250,000
**Directors:** Mrs L G Hamill, Ms B Rickard, L J Cormack, C L Rickard
**Branches:** Strathmore Hotels Ltd, Argyll Square, Oban, Argyll PA34 4BE
**US SIC:** 4119 **UK SIC:** 72200
**Auditors:** PricewaterhouseCoopers
**Bankers:** The Royal Bank Of Scotland Plc (83-28-13)

| | 31-12-13 | 31-12-12 | 31-12-11 |
|---|---|---|---|
| TO | 13,306,944 | 13,034,629 | 12,934,533 |
| P/L | 584,046 | 822,959 | 1,023,316 |
| NW | 17,394,059 | 16,795,856 | 16,127,769 |
| WC | 2,317,188 | 2,377,098 | 1,878,883 |
| Emp. | 398 | 398 | 385 |

DUNS 22-928-5309 **Exp**
## Strathroy Dairy Ltd
Shergrim, Omagh, Co Tyrone BT79 7JD
**Tel:** 028-8224-0948
**Web:** www.strathroydairy.com
**Reg No:** 0019798NI **Estd:** 1923 Private Limited Company
**Line of Business:** Dairies
**Export Markets:** Republic of Ireland
**Issued Capital:** £100,000
**Directors:** E D Cunningham, R J Cunningham, Mrs K L Mcmahon, P Cunningham, A D Mccarron
**Co. Secretary:** James Mc Cann
**US SIC:** 2026 **UK SIC:** 41301
**Auditors:** McElholm & Co
**Bankers:** Northern Bank Ltd (95-04-07)

| | 31-07-14 | 31-07-13 | 31-07-12 |
|---|---|---|---|
| TO | 56,604,312 | 48,518,735 | 44,267,184 |
| P/L | 160,496 | 199,179 | 215,997 |
| NW | 4,332,536 | 4,191,386 | 3,541,176 |
| WC | (1,538,023) | (1,631,542) | (1,725,527) |
| Emp. | 152 | 131 | 135 |

DUNS 73-919-9813
## Stratmin Global Resources Plc
30 Percy Street, London W1T 2DB
**Tel:** 02076365639
**Web:** www.ipt-ltd.co.uk
**Reg No:** 5173250 **Estd:** 2004 Public Limited Company

**Line of Business:** Management activities of holding companies
**Issued Capital:** £2,621,383
**Directors:** J R Marvin, D R Premraj, M G Yannaghas, J L Hunter, M J Pienaar
**Co. Secretary:** Manoli Yannaghas
**US SIC:** 6711 **UK SIC:** 83962
**Auditors:** Welbeck Associates
**Bankers:** Barclays Bank Plc (20-37-75)

| | 31-12-13 | 31-12-12 | 31-12-11 |
|---|---|---|---|
| TO | 46,000 | N/A | N/A |
| P/L | (2,507,000) | (1,244,000) | (234,000) |
| NW | 130,000 | 1,074,000 | 865,000 |
| WC | (672,000) | 97,000 | 286,000 |
| Emp. | 70 | 2 | 1 |

DUNS 21-385-2079
## Stratstone
Paragon House, Citadel Way Citadel Trading Park, Hull, North Humberside HU9 1TQ
**Web:** www.stratstone.com
**Estd:** 1990
**Line of Business:** Car dealers (new & used)
**Responsibilities**
**Senior:** Daniel Shores *(Dealer Principal)*
**Finance:** Dave Petch *(Financial Manager)*
**US SIC:** 5511 **UK SIC:** 65100
**Employees:** 50

DUNS 21-034-2500
## Stratstone Mini
Eastside Park, East Side Road, Chesterfield, Derbyshire S41 9BH
**Tel:** 01246208681
**Web:** www.stratstonederbymini.co.uk
**Estd:** 1976 Proprietorship
**Line of Business:** Car dealers (new & used)
**Partners:** M Casha, D Forsyth, R Maloney, T Finn, Ms H Sykes
**US SIC:** 5511, 5521
**UK SIC:** 65100
**Employees:** 162

DUNS 22-415-7755
## Stratton Bowling Club
Poundfield, Stratton, Bude, Cornwall EX23 9AX
**Tel:** 01288-354936
**Estd:** 1945 Proprietorship
**Line of Business:** Sports clubs
**Proprietor:** B Peardon
**Responsibilities**
**Senior:** Bruce Peaden *(Secretary)*
**US SIC:** 7999 **UK SIC:** 97913
**Employees:** 87

DUNS 21-748-8144
## Stratton Education Trust
Eagle Farm Road, Biggleswade, Bedfordshire SG18 8JB
**Tel:** 01767317268
**Web:** www.stratton.beds.sch.uk
**Reg No:** 7798627 **Estd:** 2011 Private Company Limited By Guarantee
**Line of Business:** Adult and other education not elsewhere classified
**Directors:** N G Lillywhite, Ms M A Russell, J M Booth, A G Field, R H Watson
**Co. Secretary:** Gary Waghorn
**US SIC:** 8249 **UK SIC:** 93300
**Bankers:** Lloyds TSB Bank plc (30-90-79)

| | 31-08-13 | 31-08-12 |
|---|---|---|
| TO | 8,803,237 | 14,044,391 |
| P/L | 196,082 | 9,029,473 |
| NW | 9,220,555 | 9,022,473 |
| WC | 905,999 | 826,512 |
| Emp. | 258 | 262 |

DUNS 21-710-7217
## Stratus (Holdings) Ltd
91 Brick Lane, London E1 6QL
**Tel:** 02070537684
**Reg No:** 7509461 **Estd:** 2011 Private Limited Company
**Line of Business:** Management activities of holding companies
**Issued Capital:** £54,609
**Directors:** Ms C E Morley, G Clarke, A Chamberlain, D E Bredahl, A W Kilgour, P S Male
**Co. Secretary:** Ian Burrell
**US SIC:** 6711 **UK SIC:** 83962
**Bankers:** The Royal Bank Of Scotland Plc (15-00-00)

| | 31-12-13 | 31-12-12 | 31-12-11 |
|---|---|---|---|
| TO | 30,274,500 | 30,215,648 | 20,411,905 |
| P/L | (7,542,174) | (7,140,659) | (5,459,793) |
| NW | (55,595,866) | (53,333,388) | (50,720,686) |
| WC | 2,635,555 | 1,910,984 | 2,430,959 |
| Emp. | 207 | 193 | 196 |

DUNS 76-987-8455 **Imp**
## Straumann Ltd
**(Subsidiary of:** Straumann Holding Ag)
3 Pegasus Place, Crawley, West Sussex RH10 9AY
**Tel:** 01293651230
**Web:** www.straumann.com
**Reg No:** 2646013 **VAT No:** 583857782

**Estd:** 1991 Private Limited Company
**Line of Business:** Dental technicians
**Issued Capital:** £300,000
**Directors:** G Daniellot, T Dressendorfer, Dr A Meier
**Co. Secretary:** Hexagon Tds Limited
**Responsibilities**
**Senior:** John Finnis *(Financial Controller)*, Marco Gadola *(CEO)*
**Finance:** John Finnis *(Financial Controller)*
**Marketing:** Frank Hemm *(Head Customer Solutions & Mark)*, Sandro Matter *(Head Strategic Projects & Alli)*
**Sales:** Alexander Ochsner *(Head Sales APAC)*
**HR:** Raul Perez *(Human Resources Manager)*
**Health & Safety:** John Finnis *(Financial Controller)*
**US SIC:** 8021, 8091
**UK SIC:** 95400, 95200
**Auditors:** Ernst & Young
**Bankers:** National Westminster Bank Plc (60-30-06)

| | 31-12-13 | 31-12-12 | 31-12-11 |
|---|---|---|---|
| TO | 12,930,389 | 13,083,948 | 12,208,319 |
| P/L | 414,444 | 405,048 | 430,138 |
| NW | 918,561 | 919,157 | 913,616 |
| WC | 633,337 | 528,353 | 394,388 |
| Emp. | 52 | 57 | 58 |

DUNS 22-251-3900
## Strawson Ltd
Featherstone House Farm, Mickledale Lane, Bilsthorpe, Newark, Nottinghamshire NG22 8RD
**Tel:** 01623870421 **Fax:** 01623-870502
**Web:** www.strawsons.com
**Reg No:** 4269401 **Estd:** 2001 Private Limited Company
**Line of Business:** Growing of cereals and other crops not elsewhere classified
**Issued Capital:** £5,000
**Director:** Mrs J Strawson
**Co. Secretary:** Robert Strawson
**Responsibilities**
**Finance:** Gwen Shreeve *(Financial Controller)*
**Admin:** Gwen Shreeve *(Financial Controller)*
**IT:** Jake Rice *(General Manager)*
**Health & Safety:** Gemma Williams *(Health & Safety Manager)*
**Facilities:** Jake Rice *(General Manager)*
**US SIC:** 0119 **UK SIC:** 01001
**Auditors:** Wright Vigar Ltd

| | 31-12-13 | 31-12-12 | 31-12-11 |
|---|---|---|---|
| TO | 34,516,235 | 33,796,532 | 30,945,843 |
| P/L | (386,996) | 668,433 | 1,075,082 |
| NW | 8,066,273 | 8,504,119 | 7,990,934 |
| WC | 4,648,871 | 5,004,432 | 5,237,071 |
| Emp. | 80 | 77 | 79 |

DUNS 23-777-7276 **Imp**
## Streamfoods Ltd
**(Subsidiary of:** Lydian Capital Partners L.P.)
5 Broadend Road, Wisbech, Cambridgeshire PE14 7BQ
**Tel:** 01945-580280
**Web:** www.fruit-bowl.com
**Reg No:** 3771000 **Estd:** 1999 Private Limited Company
**Line of Business:** Manufacturers of food products
**Export Sales:** £17,000
**Issued Capital:** £188,002
**Directors:** M J Lane, G V Magee
**Co. Secretary:** Mark Lane
**Responsibilities**
**Senior:** Jon Hather *(Manager)*
**HR:** David Willgress *(Production Manager)*
**Health & Safety:** Julie Churchyard *(Health & Safety Officer)*
**Operations:** Jean Hale *(Customer Services Manager)*
**Purchasing:** Jean Hale *(Customer Services Manager)*
**Engineering:** David Willgress *(Production Manager)*
**US SIC:** 2099 **UK SIC:** 42399
**Auditors:** Ernst & Young LLP

| | 31-12-13 | 31-12-12 | 31-12-11 |
|---|---|---|---|
| TO | 14,010,000 | 11,337,000 | 13,172,000 |
| P/L | 1,592,000 | 866,000 | 2,333,000 |
| NW | 10,727,000 | 9,529,000 | 8,886,000 |
| WC | 9,454,000 | 8,274,000 | 7,505,000 |
| Emp. | 84 | 73 | 78 |

DUNS 34-573-8363
## Streamline (Kent) Ltd
Station Approach, Maidstone, Kent ME16 8RJ
**Tel:** 01622-750000 **Fax:** 01622752978
**Web:** www.streamline.travel
**Reg No:** 2723694 **Estd:** 1938 Private Limited Company
**Line of Business:** Taxis
**Issued Capital:** £78,250
**Managing Director:** R C Parker
**Co. Secretary:** Ms Angela Parker
**Responsibilities**
**Finance:** Aileen Jeffrey *(financial controller)*

**Branches:** Streamline (Kent) Ltd, Camden House, North Farm Road, Tunbridge Wells, Kent TN2 3DH
**US SIC:** 4121, 4141
**UK SIC:** 72200, 72102
**Auditors:** Trevor Aldridge

| | 30-04-14 | 30-04-13 | 30-04-12 |
|---|---|---|---|
| TA | 1,315,529 | 1,056,398 | 967,947 |
| NW | 359,356 | 292,401 | 224,333 |
| WC | (171,059) | (153,117) | (167,333) |

DUNS 29-497-9059
## Streamline Press Ltd
(Subsidiary of: Mlak Ltd)
11 Boston Road, Leicester, Leicestershire LE4 1AA
**Tel:** 01162-355003 **Fax:** 01162-355004
**Web:** www.streamlinepress.co.uk
**Reg No:** 1861186 **VAT No:** 371815056
**Estd:** 1984 Private Limited Company
**Line of Business:** Printing not elsewhere classified
**Issued Capital:** £500
**Director:** M A Lockley
**Responsibilities**
**Finance:** Yvonne Allen (Accounts Manager)
**US SIC:** 2752 **UK SIC:** 47544
**Auditors:** Curo Professional Services Ltd
**Bankers:** Barclays Bank Plc (20-49-08)

| | 30-11-13 | 30-11-12 | 30-11-11 |
|---|---|---|---|
| TO | 4,207,903 | 3,575,382 | 5,187,329 |
| P/L | (306,061) | (86,398) | 45,848 |
| NW | 536,773 | 784,496 | 853,466 |
| WC | (568,274) | (429,043) | (291,865) |
| Emp. | 49 | 46 | 56 |

DUNS 76-894-1270
## Streamline Shipping Group Ltd
Streamline Terminal, Blaikies Quay, Aberdeen, Aberdeenshire AB11 5PU
**Tel:** 01224-211506
**Web:** www.streamlineshippinggroup.com
**Reg No:** 0131956SC **VAT No:** 605086948
**Estd:** 1991 Private Limited Company
**Line of Business:** Management activities of holding companies
**Issued Capital:** £500,000
**Principals:** E S Roberts (Managing), A Mitchell (Financial)
**Co. Secretary:** Maclay Murray & Spens Llp
**US SIC:** 6711 **UK SIC:** 83962
**Auditors:** Gray McDonald & Dinnic
**Bankers:** Bank Of Scotland (80-05-11)

| | 31-12-13 | 31-12-12 | 31-12-11 |
|---|---|---|---|
| TO | 36,924,915 | 26,048,214 | 21,535,865 |
| P/L | 2,907,824 | 613,825 | 70,236 |
| NW | 2,928,894 | 1,298,647 | 1,140,713 |
| WC | (378,562) | (1,220,667) | (1,219,245) |
| Emp. | 214 | 202 | 202 |

DUNS 28-833-8395
## Streamline Supply Co Ltd
(Subsidiary of: Brighton & Hove Streamline Taxis Ltd)
5 Clifton Hill, Brighton, East Sussex BN1 3HL
**Tel:** 01273729403 **Fax:** 01273-327328
**Web:** www.brighton-streamline.com
**Reg No:** 0339057 **Estd:** 2007 Private Limited Company
**Line of Business:** Taxis and private hire vehicles
**Issued Capital:** £680
**Directors:** J Streeter, D Smith
**Co. Secretary:** John Streeter
**US SIC:** 4121 **UK SIC:** 72200
**Auditors:** Friend-James

| | 31-10-14 | 31-10-13 | 31-10-12 |
|---|---|---|---|
| TA | 226,923 | 226,923 | 226,923 |
| NW | 184,611 | 184,611 | 184,611 |

DUNS 76-497-1636
## Streamline Taxis (York) Ltd
Cromwell House, 7 Cumberland Street, York, North Yorkshire YO1 9SW
**Tel:** 01904638833
**Web:** www.streamline-taxis-york.co.uk
**Reg No:** 2567228 **Estd:** 1937 Private Limited Company
**Line of Business:** Taxi operation
**Trading Style:** Streamline Taxis
**Issued Capital:** £36
**Directors:** M A Robertson Moss, A P Murray, S Dunn, G Rollinson, C J North, S H Cooper, M A Burbidge, D Leeke
**Co. Secretary:** Mark Wilson
**Responsibilities**
**Senior:** Peter Aspinall (Director), Dionysis Bekators (Director), Raymond Close (Director), Michael Dowson (Director), Kevin Drinkeld (Director), Gary Fernie (Director), Neil Sollitt (Director), Martin Trueman (Director), Tracey Yeomans (Director)
**US SIC:** 4121, 4119
**UK SIC:** 72200
**Bankers:** Barclays Bank Plc (20-99-56)

| | 31-12-13 | 31-12-12 | 31-12-11 |
|---|---|---|---|
| TA | 1,356,772 | 1,500,805 | 702,562 |
| NW | 336,133 | 340,578 | 280,970 |
| WC | (16,953) | 7,915 | (6,252) |

DUNS 21-927-1194 Exp
## Streason Ltd
Chapel-En-Le-Frith, High Peak, Derbyshire SK23 0PH
**Tel:** 01298-812456
**Web:** www.streetcrane.co.uk
**Reg No:** 0733435 **Estd:** 1962 Private Limited Company
**Line of Business:** Management activities of holding companies
**Export Markets:** Worldwide
**Export Sales:** £15,746,397
**Trading Style:** Street Crane Company
**Issued Capital:** £1,467
**Director:** S J Eastwood
**Co. Secretary:** Martin Street
**Responsibilities**
**Senior:** Andrew Pimblett (Manager)
**Marketing:** GUS Zona (Sales & Marketing Director)
**Sales:** GUS Zona (Sales & Marketing Director)
**IT:** Terry Partridge (IT Manager), Ian Wing (Technical Director)
**Engineering:** Ian Wing (Technical Director)
**US SIC:** 6711 **UK SIC:** 83962
**Auditors:** Barber Harrison & Platt
**Bankers:** The Royal Bank Of Scotland Plc (16-12-24)

| | 31-03-14 | 31-03-13 | 31-03-12 |
|---|---|---|---|
| TO | 28,267,457 | 28,195,959 | 24,353,383 |
| P/L | 1,139,527 | 1,839,907 | 1,135,160 |
| NW | 8,278,404 | 7,122,201 | 5,522,763 |
| WC | 5,726,452 | 5,576,023 | 4,253,679 |
| Emp. | 175 | 166 | 156 |

DUNS 23-281-7952
## The Streat
79 Dublin Road, Belfast BT2 7HF
**Estd:** 1998 Partnership
**Line of Business:** Restaurants
**Partners:** M Mcquillian, Ms N Mcquillian
**Responsibilities**
**Senior:** Nikki McQuillian (Partner), Michael McQuillian (Partner)
**Branches:** The Streat, The Odyessy Pavilion, Queens Road, Belfast, Belfast BT3 9DT
**US SIC:** 5812 **UK SIC:** 66110
**Employees:** 65

DUNS 23-222-3599
## Streatham & Clapham High School
42 Abbotswood Road, Streatham, London SW16 1AW
**Web:** www.schs.gdst.net
**Estd:** 1994
**Line of Business:** Schools (independent)
**Responsibilities**
**Finance:** Samantha Lucas (Receptionist Administrative/Fi), Catherine O'Neill (School Business Manager)
**Marketing:** Lynda Sale (Marketing Officer)
**Admin:** Samantha Lucas (Receptionist Administrative/Fi), Catherine O'Neill (School Business Manager)
**IT:** Jatinder Rela (Network Manager)
**Health & Safety:** Catherine O'Neill (School Business Manager)
**Facilities:** Mary Kpobie (Facilities Manager)
**Purchasing:** Catherine O'Neill (School Business Manager)
**US SIC:** 8211 **UK SIC:** 93200
**Employees:** 70

DUNS 21-581-6119
## Streatham Hill & Clapham High Preparatory School
Wavertree Road, London SW2 3SR
**Tel:** 02086746912
**Web:** www.schs.gdst.net
**Estd:** 2011 Proprietorship
**Line of Business:** Schools (independent)
**Proprietor:** Miss L Astley
**Responsibilities**
**Senior:** Elizabeth Astley (Head Teacher), Rachael Paynter (Acting Head Teacher)
**US SIC:** 8211 **UK SIC:** 93200
**Employees:** 150

DUNS 21-634-0658
## Street Cars
29-31 Sackville Street, Manchester M1 3LZ
**Tel:** 01612287878
**Web:** www.streetcarsmanchester.co.uk
**Estd:** 2002 Proprietorship
**Line of Business:** Taxi operation
**Proprietor:** N Arshad
**Responsibilities**
**Senior:** A Arshad (Manager)
**US SIC:** 4121 **UK SIC:** 72200
**Employees:** 180

DUNS 73-716-0809
## Street League
Unit 3.05 Canterbury Court 1-3, Brixton Road, London SW9 6DE
**Web:** www.streetleague.co.uk
**Reg No:** 4974643 **Estd:** 2003 Private Company Limited By Guarantee
**Line of Business:** Social work activities without accommodation
**Directors:** M Parker, D J Lloyd, A A Hubbard, T Kiddell, A M Ransom, J Mcmanus, Mrs S Zindel
**Co. Secretary:** Mrs Melanie Davies
**Responsibilities**
**Senior:** Damien Hatten (Chief Executive), Nasima Khanam (Manager), Sally Marsh (operations manager), Matt Stevenson-dodd (CEO Managing Director)
**Marketing:** Dougie' Stevenson (Chief Operating Officer)
**US SIC:** 8321 **UK SIC:** 96111
**Auditors:** haysmacintyre
**Bankers:** Cater Allen Ltd (10-60-05)

| | 31-03-14 | 31-03-13 | 31-03-12 |
|---|---|---|---|
| TO | 3,420,407 | 2,665,716 | 2,349,432 |
| P/L | 7,579 | (28,818) | 99,219 |
| NW | 540,860 | 533,281 | 562,099 |
| WC | 626,301 | 500,523 | 538,610 |
| Emp. | 79 | 64 | 38 |

DUNS 21-769-9444
## Street Pride
15 Stores Road, Derby, Derbyshire DE21 4BD
**Tel:** 03332006981
**Web:** www.derby.gov.uk
**Estd:** 2011 Proprietorship
**Line of Business:** Community networks
**Proprietor:** T Knight
**Responsibilities**
**Senior:** Tim Clegg (Manager)
**US SIC:** 8699 **UK SIC:** 96902
**Employees:** 50

DUNS 21-605-4027
## Street Scene
Stockton Concrete Garages, Portrack Grange Road, Stockton-On-Tees, Cleveland TS18 2PH
**Tel:** 01642670332
**Estd:** 2003
**Line of Business:** Road Construction
**US SIC:** 1611 **UK SIC:** 50200
**Employees:** 48

DUNS 63-458-8487
## Streeter Marshall Solicitors
74 High Street, Croydon, Surrey CR9 2UU
**Tel:** 02086802638
**Web:** www.streetermarshall.com
**Estd:** 2001 Partnership
**Line of Business:** Solicitors
**Trading Style:** Streeter Marshall Solicitors
**Proprietor:** D Moore
**Responsibilities**
**Senior:** Dianne Moore (Finance Director), Mark Smeed (Proprietor)
**Finance:** Dianne Moore (Finance Director)
**Branches:** Streeter Marshall Solicitors, 416 Limpsfield Road, Warlingham, Surrey CR6 9LA
**US SIC:** 7399 **UK SIC:** 83954
**Employees:** 50

DUNS 23-592-9635
## Streetfacts Target Marketing & Mailing Ltd
Unit 5 Batten Road, Salisbury, Wiltshire SP5 3HU
**Tel:** 01725515000
**Web:** www.priority.co.uk
**Reg No:** 2324765 **VAT No:** 504479055
**Estd:** 1989 Private Limited Company
**Line of Business:** Direct mail service providers
**Trading Style:** Priority Mailing
**Issued Capital:** £489,682
**Principals:** T A Turner (Managing), Mrs S Turner, K Poore, P E Butcher
**Co. Secretary:** Terence Turner
**Responsibilities**
**Sales:** Dave Lee (Sales Manager)
**IT:** Claire Whatley (Data Manager)
**HR:** Sheila Merton-Jones (Health & Safety Officer)
**Health & Safety:** Sheila Merton-Jones (Health & Safety Officer)
**US SIC:** 7319 **UK SIC:** 83800
**Auditors:** Gibson Booth
**Bankers:** Lloyds TSB Bank plc (30-97-41)

| | 31-12-13 | 31-12-12 | 31-12-11 |
|---|---|---|---|
| TA | 2,525,286 | 2,548,445 | 2,502,524 |
| NW | 1,970,164 | 1,852,054 | 1,718,662 |
| WC | 467,629 | 362,842 | 264,381 |

DUNS 21-161-9171
## The Streetly School
Queslett Road East, Sutton Coldfield, West Midlands B74 2EX
**Tel:** 0121-353-2709
**Web:** www.streetly.walsall.sch.uk
**Estd:** 1992 Proprietorship
**Line of Business:** Schools (foundation)
**Proprietor:** B Downie
**Responsibilities**
**Senior:** Billy Downie (Head Teacher)
**Finance:** Sally Whittington (School Business Manager)
**IT:** James Pheasant (Computer Operations Manager)
**HR:** Sally Whittington (School Business Manager)
**US SIC:** 8211 **UK SIC:** 93200
**Employees:** 127

DUNS 22-845-2090
## Streets
Tower House, Lucy Tower Street, Lincoln, Lincolnshire LN1 1XW
**Web:** www.streetsweb.co.uk
**Estd:** 1988 Partnership
**Line of Business:** Book-keeping activities
**Partners:** R Godley, R Millett, N Kirk, B Picksley, R Myland, S Sargent, R Hair, P Hennell
**Responsibilities**
**Senior:** Paul Tutin (Partner)
**Branches:** Streets, 33 Churchgate, Retford, Nottinghamshire DN22 6PA
**US SIC:** 8931 **UK SIC:** 83600
**Bankers:** HSBC Bank plc (40-28-20)
**Employees:** 100

DUNS 39-693-4556
## Streets Ahead (Borders)
Streets Ahead, Hawick, Roxburghshire TD9 0AE
**Tel:** 01450-377924
**Web:** www.streetsahead.org.uk
**Reg No:** 0105923SC **Estd:** 1987 Private Limited Company
**Line of Business:** Charities and charitable organisations
**Directors:** R Chlopas, A K Maule, G Mooney, Ms P A Hunter, S F Scott, J Middlemass, Ms M Middlemass, R M Johnson
**Co. Secretary:** George Young
**Responsibilities**
**Senior:** Pam Collinson (Company Development Manager), Gordon Robb (Manager)
**Admin:** Aileen Rafferty (Office Manager)
**Health & Safety:** Aileen Rafferty (Office Manager)
**US SIC:** 8321, 8999
**UK SIC:** 96111, 83954
**Auditors:** Welch & Co
**Bankers:** Bank Of Scotland (80-16-22)

| | 30-09-13 | 30-09-12 | 30-09-11 |
|---|---|---|---|
| TO | 2,619,161 | 2,771,097 | 2,502,076 |
| P/L | 16,962 | 206,499 | 17,642 |
| NW | 606,060 | 589,098 | 382,599 |
| WC | 350,565 | 328,670 | 373,937 |
| Emp. | 142 | 140 | 134 |

DUNS 73-989-7168
## Streets Audit Llp
Tower House, Lucy Tower Street, Lincoln, Lincolnshire LN1 1XW
**Web:** www.streetsweb.co.uk
**Reg No:** 0309381OC **Estd:** 1988
**Line of Business:** Accounting, Auditing, Bookkeeping Svcs
**US SIC:** 8931 **UK SIC:** 83600

| | 30-06-13 | 30-06-12 | 30-06-11 |
|---|---|---|---|
| TA | 583,732 | 578,461 | 625,237 |
| WC | 25,733 | 26,630 | 72,097 |

DUNS 77-124-6865
## Streetwise Couriers Ltd
Unit 8 Beverley Way Shannon Commercial, Centre, New Malden, Surrey KT3 4PT
**Tel:** 02083361444
**Web:** www.streetwisecouriers.com
**Reg No:** 2697026 **Estd:** 1992 Private Limited Company
**Line of Business:** Couriers
**Issued Capital:** £3
**Directors:** Mrs D G Russell, Mrs R A Russell
**Co. Secretary:** Martin Russell
**Branches:** Streetwise Couriers Ltd, Unit 2 Collins Road, Heathcote Industrial Estate, Warwick, Warwickshire CV34 6TF
**US SIC:** 4311, 4712
**UK SIC:** 79010, 77002
**Auditors:** Michael Burke & Co

| | 30-11-13 | 30-11-12 | 30-11-11 |
|---|---|---|---|
| TO | N/A | 1,036,302 | 910,283 |
| P/L | N/A | 98,953 | 77,304 |
| NW | 5,320 | 26,947 | 2,873 |
| WC | 138 | 24,031 | 1,873 |

DUNS 21-777-8522
## Streetwork
The Cowgate Centre, 22 Holyrood Road, Edinburgh, Midlothian EH8 8AF
**Web:** www.streetwork.org.uk
**Estd:** 1998 Proprietorship
**Line of Business:** Charities and charitable organisations
**Proprietor:** Miss C Gibson
**US SIC:** 8321 **UK SIC:** 96111
**Employees:** 70

DUNS 73-500-1534
## Streetwork Uk
18 South Bridge, Edinburgh, Midlothian EH1 1LL
**Tel:** 01313440825
**Web:** www.streetwork.org.uk
**Reg No:** 0249435SC **Estd:** 2003 Private Company Limited By Guarantee
**Line of Business:** Accommodation advice
**Directors:** G S Pearson, G S Davis, Mrs N A Wilson, M M Wood, C R Maclean, Miss K E Lamont
**Co. Secretary:** Gordon Watson
**Responsibilities**
**Senior:** Jan Williamson *(Manager)*
**US SIC:** 8091 **UK SIC:** 95200
**Bankers:** Bank Of Scotland (80-11-00)

| | 31-03-14 | 31-03-13 | 31-03-12 |
|---|---|---|---|
| TO | 1,727,175 | 1,000,914 | 1,790,900 |
| P/L | (19,815) | 29,588 | (24,639) |
| NW | 575,830 | 589,645 | 548,057 |
| WC | 99,676 | 111,824 | 157,757 |
| Emp. | 54 | 47 | 52 |

DUNS 21-780-8244
## Strelley Health Centre
116 Strelley Road, Nottingham, Nottinghamshire NG8 6LN
**Tel:** 01158833300
**Web:** www.nottinghamcitycare.nhs.uk
**Estd:** 1982 Proprietorship
**Line of Business:** Nhs clinics
**Proprietor:** Mrs J Clifford
**Responsibilities**
**Senior:** Victoria Hinchley *(Manager)*, Lyn Webster *(Manager)*
**US SIC:** 8062 **UK SIC:** 95100
**Employees:** 54

DUNS 21-882-0645 Imp
## Stressline Ltd
**(Subsidiary of:** Stressline Holdings Ltd)
Station Road, Leicester, Leicestershire LE9 4LX
**Tel:** 01455-272457 **Fax:** 01455-274564
**Web:** www.stressline.ltd.uk
**Reg No:** 0819180 **VAT No:** 114668665
**Estd:** 1964 Private Limited Company
**Line of Business:** Concrete products
**Issued Capital:** £4,700
**Principals:** D K Fox *(Managing)*, S R Fox *(Managing)*, C P Fox
**Co. Secretary:** Stephen Fox
**Responsibilities**
**HR:** Jodie Fox *(Human Resources Manager)*
**Facilities:** David Stratham *(Production Manager)*
**Engineering:** Terry Hensley *(Production Manager)*, David Stratham *(Production Manager)*
**US SIC:** 3271, 3499, 1796
**UK SIC:** 24370, 31694, 50400
**Auditors:** Knight Arnold Wall
**Bankers:** The Royal Bank Of Scotland Plc (16-23-21)

| | 31-12-13 | 31-12-12 | 31-12-11 |
|---|---|---|---|
| TA | 3,021,838 | 2,406,041 | 2,492,900 |
| P/L | 138,253 | (156,545) | 62,717 |
| NW | 889,827 | 781,382 | 910,927 |
| WC | 773,961 | 651,379 | 813,532 |
| Emp. | 85 | 90 | 84 |

DUNS 22-189-2123 Imp
## Stretchline (U K) Ltd
Sherston, Malmesbury, Wiltshire SN16 0NG
**Tel:** 01666842100
**Web:** www.stretchline.com
**Reg No:** 4207389 **VAT No:** 771849195
**Estd:** 2004 Private Limited Company
**Line of Business:** Elastic based products
**Issued Capital:** £81,556
**Principals:** C S Tubbs *(Financial)*, P M Allen, B N Collier
**Branches:** Stretchline (U K) Ltd, Babdown Industrial Estate, Unit 7, Tetbury, Gloucestershire GL8 8YL
**US SIC:** 2299, 5133
**UK SIC:** 43992, 61600
**Auditors:** Alliotts
**Bankers:** Bank Of Scotland (12-05-77)

| | 31-12-13 | 31-12-12 | 31-12-11 |
|---|---|---|---|
| TO | 5,487,039 | 5,058,000 | 5,633,000 |
| P/L | (149,473) | 2,251,000 | 797,000 |
| NW | 7,459,381 | 9,117,000 | 6,866,000 |
| WC | 1,731,942 | 3,463,000 | 1,151,000 |
| Emp. | 101 | 100 | 86 |

DUNS 21-013-0712 Imp
## Stretton Hills Mineral Water Co Ltd
**(Subsidiary of:** Mitsubishi Corporation)
Shrewsbury Road, Church Stretton, Shropshire SY6 6HD
**Tel:** 01694722935 **Fax:** 01694724318
**Web:** www.wellwellwell.co.uk
**Reg No:** 0564125 **Estd:** 1956 Private Limited Company
**Line of Business:** Non-specialised wholesale of food, beverages and tobacco
**Issued Capital:** £75,625
**Director:** K D Critchley
**Co. Secretary:** Manabu Oda
**Responsibilities**
**Facilities:** Dennis Duppa *(Factory Engineer)*
**US SIC:** 5149 **UK SIC:** 61700

| | 31-03-14 | 31-03-13 | 31-03-12 |
|---|---|---|---|
| TA | 11,386,000 | 11,386,000 | 11,386,000 |
| NW | 3,290,000 | 3,290,000 | 3,290,000 |
| WC | 3,290,000 | 3,290,000 | 3,290,000 |

DUNS 21-205-6704
## Stretton Nursing Home
Manor Fields, Burghill, Hereford, Herefordshire HR4 7RR
**Tel:** 01432761066
**Web:** www.strettonnursinghome.co.uk
**Estd:** 2006 Proprietorship
**Line of Business:** Nursing homes
**Proprietor:** P Lewis
**Responsibilities**
**Senior:** Libby Knight *(Manager)*, Amarjit Sehmi *(Proprietor)*
**US SIC:** 8051 **UK SIC:** 95100
**Employees:** 60

DUNS 28-832-1862
## Strettons Ltd
**(Subsidiary of:** Strettons Group Ltd)
Central House, 189-203 Hoe Street, London E17 3SZ
**Tel:** 02085209911
**Web:** www.strettons.co.uk
**Reg No:** 0268552 **VAT No:** 549203641
**Estd:** 1931 Private Limited Company
**Line of Business:** Estate agents
**Issued Capital:** £32,893
**Principals:** P G Tobin *(Managing)*, G R Slyper, P Tobin, Ms G M Mariner, M H Shaw, P J Waterfield, N A Matthews, F C Hunter
**Co. Secretary:** Benjamin Tobin
**Responsibilities**
**Senior:** Mark Iliffe *(Director)*, Simon Tilsiter *(Director)*
**Finance:** Kirit Jethwa *(Financial Controller)*
**Branches:** Strettons Ltd, 41 Artillery Lane, London E1 7LD
**US SIC:** 8911, 6531
**UK SIC:** 83701, 83400
**Auditors:** Goodman Jones
**Bankers:** National Westminster Bank Plc (60-00-01)

| | 30-04-14 | 30-04-13 | 30-04-12 |
|---|---|---|---|
| TO | 7,723,908 | 7,086,686 | 6,944,120 |
| P/L | 24,728 | 24,793 | 10,043 |
| NW | 807,956 | 799,341 | 784,852 |
| WC | 834,312 | 488,300 | 551,237 |
| Emp. | 105 | 97 | 90 |

DUNS 64-082-7309 Imp
## Strickland Tracks Ltd
Heath Park B4084 Near Cropthorne, Pershore, Worcestershire WR10 3NE
**Tel:** 01386862800
**Web:** www.stricklandtracks.co.uk
**Reg No:** 3477947 **Estd:** 1997 Private Limited Company
**Line of Business:** Other service activities not elsewhere classified
**Issued Capital:** £400,000
**Directors:** C J Hopcroft, M O'Neill, S Taylor, H P Dooey
**Co. Secretary:** Aidan O'Neill
**Responsibilities**
**Senior:** Donna James *(Manager)*, Martin O' Neill *(Director)*, Aidan O' Neill *(Manager)*
**US SIC:** 8999, 5511
**UK SIC:** 83954, 65100
**Auditors:** Davies Mayers Barnett LLP
**Bankers:** Ulster Bank Ltd (98-00-10)

| | 31-12-13 | 31-07-12 | 31-12-11 |
|---|---|---|---|
| TO | 66,906,872 | 51,062,642 | 35,600,879 |
| P/L | 3,628,578 | 2,550,948 | 1,590,704 |
| NW | 8,695,785 | 6,792,147 | 4,845,166 |
| WC | 8,600,103 | 7,761,386 | 4,964,669 |
| Emp. | 54 | 49 | 38 |

DUNS 28-876-8773
## Stride Ltd
**(Subsidiary of:** Stride Holdings (Chichester) Ltd)
Birch House Parklands Business P, Forest Road, Denmead, Waterlooville, Hampshire PO7 6XP
**Tel:** 08003899949
**Web:** www.computerquoteinsurance.com
**Reg No:** 1122247 **Estd:** 1989 Private Limited Company
**Line of Business:** Insurance services
**Trading Style:** Computer Quote
**Issued Capital:** £9,999
**Directors:** R W Lovegrove, J Walker, M Stride, A G Davies
**Co. Secretary:** David Woods
**Responsibilities**
**HR:** Justin Ward *(Regional Manager)*
**Branches:** Stride Ltd, 40 Jewry St, Winchester, Hampshire SO23 8RY
**US SIC:** 6411 **UK SIC:** 83200
**Auditors:** Hughes Spencer

| | 31-12-13 | 31-12-12 | 31-12-11 |
|---|---|---|---|
| TA | 5,174,338 | 5,321,583 | 5,173,038 |
| NW | 1,695,395 | 1,553,823 | 1,363,021 |
| WC | 1,585,595 | 1,502,929 | 1,293,571 |

DUNS 53-659-3734
## Stride Treglown Group Plc
Promenade House, Bristol, Avon BS8 3NE
**Tel:** 01179743271 **Fax:** 01179-745207
**Web:** www.stridetreglown.co.uk
**Reg No:** 3464501 **VAT No:** 609371536
**Estd:** 1990 Public Limited Company
**Line of Business:** Architectural activities
**Export Sales:** £434,340
**Issued Capital:** £106,898
**Directors:** R J Sargent, D P Wilkins, M R Tarling, J A Wright, G D Tero, D J Hunter, D A Steele, C T Saxon
**Co. Secretary:** Kevin Mcdonald
**Responsibilities**
**Senior:** Kieran Lilley *(Divisional Director)*, Caroline Mayes *(Divisional Director)*, Gary Milliner *(Director)*, Dominic Wells *(Director)*
**Finance:** Penny Burgess *(Financial Controller)*
**Sales:** Daniel Van Luttmer *(Director-Retail)*
**IT:** Jason Pitchers *(Head of IT)*
**Facilities:** John Franklin *(Head of Building Surveying)*
**Operations:** Peter Badger *(Sustainability Assessment Mana)*
**US SIC:** 8911 **UK SIC:** 83701
**Auditors:** Grant Thornton

| | 31-12-13 | 31-12-12 | 31-12-11 |
|---|---|---|---|
| TO | 14,431,257 | 13,681,758 | 12,936,657 |
| P/L | 590,149 | 345,639 | 199,294 |
| NW | 4,626,705 | 4,600,106 | 4,407,189 |
| WC | 3,075,904 | 3,348,291 | 3,378,496 |
| Emp. | 252 | 242 | 249 |

DUNS 29-887-3548
## Stringfellow Restaurants Ltd
16-19 Upper St Martin's Lane, London WC2H 9EF
**Tel:** 020-7240-5534 **Fax:** 020-7379-3570
**Web:** www.stringfellows.co.uk
**Reg No:** 2090397 **VAT No:** 577390600
**Estd:** 1992 Private Limited Company
**Line of Business:** Licensed restaurants
**Issued Capital:** £500,000
**Principals:** P J Stringfellow *(Managing)*, C S Silver *(Financial)*
**Co. Secretary:**
B. H. Company Secretarial Servic
**Responsibilities**
**Senior:** Roger Howe *(Operations Director)*
**Marketing:** Pat Jay *(Sales & Marketing Manager)*
**Sales:** Pat Jay *(Sales & Marketing Manager)*
**Admin:** Chrissie Kiernan *(Office Manager)*
**HR:** Roger Howe *(Operations Director)*
**Health & Safety:** Roger Howe *(Operations Director)*
**Facilities:** Steve Beauchamp *(Maintenance Manager)*
**Operations:** Roger Howe *(Operations Director)*
**Purchasing:** Roger Howe *(Operations Director)*
**US SIC:** 5812, 5813, 7999
**UK SIC:** 66110, 66200, 97913
**Auditors:** West & Foster
**Bankers:** Barclays Bank Plc (20-03-53)

| | 31-12-13 | 31-12-12 | 30-12-11 |
|---|---|---|---|
| TO | 8,050,208 | 12,720,187 | 9,434,580 |
| P/L | (229,960) | (73,915) | 480,096 |
| NW | 3,189,233 | 3,332,336 | 3,480,177 |
| WC | 2,001,383 | 1,889,081 | 1,601,728 |
| Emp. | 135 | 135 | 135 |

DUNS 23-794-1724
## Stripestar Ltd
**(Subsidiary of:** Pendragon Plc)
Loxley House, 2 Oakwood Crt, Little Oak Drive, Nottingham, Nottinghamshire NG15 0DR
**Tel:** 01482324234
**Reg No:** 3786959 **Estd:** 1999 Private Limited Company
**Line of Business:** Car dealers (used)
**Issued Capital:** £8,700,000
**Directors:** T G Finn, M S Casha, Pendragon Management Services Li, T P Holden
**Co. Secretary:** Ms Hilary Sykes
**Branches:** Stripestar Ltd, Treforest Industrial Estate, Pontypridd, Mid Glamorgan CF37 5YA
**US SIC:** 5521, 5511
**UK SIC:** 65100
**Auditors:** KPMG Audit PLC

| | 31-12-13 | 31-12-12 | 31-12-11 |
|---|---|---|---|
| TO | 864,435,000 | 786,420,000 | 838,368,000 |
| P/L | 7,759,000 | 3,056,000 | 1,535,000 |
| NW | 4,386,000 | (10,127,000) | (12,467,000) |
| WC | (16,808,000) | (25,824,000) | (27,688,000) |
| Emp. | 1,865 | 1,845 | 1,937 |

DUNS 21-215-5097 Imp-Exp
## Strix Ltd
**(Subsidiary of:** Sula Ltd)
Forrest House, Ronalds Way, Ballasalla, Douglas, Isle of Man IM9 2RG
**Tel:** 01624-829829
**Web:** www.strix.com
**Reg No:** 0001259M **Estd:** 1951 Private Limited Company
**Line of Business:** Manufacturers and distributors of electronic components
**Export Markets:** Worldwide
**Issued Capital:** £308,739
**Directors:** E Davies, B L Amey, M J Scott, J M Brodie, P B Snowden
**Co. Secretary:** Gary Lamb
**Responsibilities**
**Senior:** Ailsa Evans *(Trade Marketing Manager)*, David Trustrum *(Global Materials & Logistics M)*
**Finance:** Gerry Gray *(Finance Director)*, Keith Hadley *(Accounts Manager)*
**IT:** Andy Moony *(IT Manager)*
**Operations:** Andrew Hewins *(Approvals Manager)*
**Fleet:** David Trustrum *(Global Materials & Logistics M)*
**Branches:** Strix Ltd, Gladstone Park Industrial Estate, Isle Of Man, Isle Of Man IM8 2LA
**US SIC:** 3679, 3829
**UK SIC:** 34542, 37100
**Bankers:** Barclays Bank Plc (20-26-74)
**Employees:** 50

DUNS 28-835-8534
## Strode Park Foundation for People With Disablities
Strode Park House, Lower Herne Road, Herne, Herne Bay, Kent CT6 7NE
**Tel:** 01227-373292
**Web:** www.strodepark.org.uk
**Reg No:** 0407697 **Estd:** 1946 Private Company Limited By Guarantee
**Line of Business:** Other human health activities
**Directors:** N P Swift, Mrs J Clifford, Mrs M Mcdonagh, Dr M O Rake, Mrs B Todd, B Dale, Mrs R A Giles, M E Conybeare
**Co. Secretary:** Paul Montgomery
**Responsibilities**
**Senior:** Ray Cordell *(Director)*, Virginia Mccarthy *(Director)*, Dennis Rose *(Director)*, Michael Vaile *(Director)*
**Finance:** Tim Cheshire *(Financial Director)*
**Marketing:** Tracy Barden *(Marketing Manager)*
**IT:** Tim Cheshire *(Financial Director)*
**HR:** David Dye *(Human Resources Director)*
**Facilities:** Paul Clayson *(Facilities Manager)*
**Branches:** Strode Park Foundation For People With Disablities, 29 William Street, Herne Bay, Kent CT6 5EG
**US SIC:** 8091, 8321, 8999
**UK SIC:** 95200, 96111, 83954
**Auditors:** McCabe Ford Williams
**Bankers:** National Westminster Bank Plc (60-10-37)

| | 31-03-14 | 31-03-13 | 31-03-12 |
|---|---|---|---|
| TO | 8,109,269 | 6,197,371 | 6,365,958 |
| P/L | 233,061 | 23,957 | 188,713 |
| NW | 4,489,450 | 4,261,306 | 4,235,297 |
| WC | 919,599 | 848,578 | 958,490 |
| Emp. | 336 | 295 | 302 |

DUNS 23-232-5766
## Strodes College
High Street, Egham, Surrey TW20 9DR
**Tel:** 01784437506
**Web:** www.strodes.ac.uk
**Estd:** 2013 Proprietorship
**Line of Business:** Schools (local authority)

**Proprietor:** Dr F Botham
**Responsibilities**
**Senior:** Anne Fielding Smith *(Principal)*
**IT:** Rob Disbury *(Director - IT)*
**US SIC:** 8221, 8249
**UK SIC:** 93100, 93300
**Employees:** 200

DUNS 29-341-3704
## Stroke Association
240 City Road, London EC1V 2PR
**Tel:** 020-7566-0300
**Web:** www.stroke.org.uk
**Reg No:** 0061274 **Estd:** 1967 Private Company Limited By Guarantee
**Line of Business:** Charities and charitable organisations
**Directors:** J P Leacy, I Black, P Rawlinson, Professor P J Tyrrell, Doctor M A James, Mrs H E Boyd, Dr A Gordon, Ms S M Duncan
**Co. Secretary:** Ms Holly Bowden
**Responsibilities**
**Senior:** Myra Barker *(Senior Manager)*, Michael Cornbleet *(Director)*, Robert Empson *(Director)*, Jacqueline Fowler *(Director)*, Eleanor Freeman *(Director)*, Damien Jenkinson *(Director)*, Tom Richardson *(Director, Northern Ireland)*, Thompson Robinson *(Trustee)*, Niraj Shah *(Director)*, Paula Souza *(Manager)*, Robert Stout *(Director)*, Peter Troy *(Director)*
**Finance:** Louise Kay *(Regional Fundraising Manager)*, Louise Quarendon *(Fundraiser (South East))*, Roy Quiddington *(Financial Director)*
**Marketing:** Katie Chatburn *(Communications Manager)*, Laura Dart *(?Deputy Director of External A)*, Nikki Hill *(Communications Director)*, Joe Korner *(Communications Director)*, Pat Storey *(Communications Support Manager)*, Maria Wilkinson *(Communications Manager)*
**Sales:** Azizah Aziz *(?Head of Legacy Development)*, Chari Hingorani *(Head of Legacies)*
**Admin:** Lynne Messenger *(Office Manager)*
**HR:** Mike Jenkins *(Learning & Development Manager)*, Martin Margrie *(Human Resources Manager)*, Valerie McGlinchey *(Human Resources Director)*
**Operations:** Kate Rogalska *(Administrative Assistant and O)*
**Engineering:** Carla Mccabe *(Senior Technical & IT Database)*
**Branches:** Stroke Association, Ryecroft Pl, Walsall, West Midlands WS3 1SN
**US SIC:** 8321, 8299
**UK SIC:** 96111, 93300
**Auditors:** Buzzacott
**Bankers:** National Westminster Bank Plc (60-80-07)

| | 31-03-14 | 31-03-13 | 31-03-12 |
|---|---|---|---|
| TO | 33,546,000 | 31,051,000 | 30,587,000 |
| P/L | 1,616,000 | (399,000) | (1,923,000) |
| NW | 22,989,000 | 20,363,000 | 18,396,000 |
| WC | 936,000 | (694,000) | (654,000) |
| Emp. | 635 | 755 | 634 |

DUNS 71-873-8789 **Imp**
## Stroma Developments Ltd
(**Subsidiary of:** Mysing No 1 Ltd)
Unit 4, Pioneer Way, Castleford, West Yorkshire WF10 5QU
**Tel:** 08456211111
**Web:** www.stroma.com
**Reg No:** 5256474 **Estd:** 2004 Private Limited Company
**Line of Business:** Management activities of holding companies
**Export Sales:** £558,455
**Issued Capital:** £400
**Directors:** R J Coxon, M J Ferguson, J Higgins
**US SIC:** 6711, 7392
**UK SIC:** 83962, 83951

| | 31-03-14 | 31-03-13 | 31-03-12 |
|---|---|---|---|
| TO | 13,137,117 | 10,768,066 | 10,571,215 |
| P/L | 2,445,985 | 857,123 | 1,774,774 |
| NW | 5,376,308 | 3,944,195 | 3,548,576 |
| WC | 2,236,889 | 856,825 | 515,654 |
| Emp. | 207 | 187 | 164 |

DUNS 21-579-5574
## Stromness Academy
Cairston Road, Stromness, Orkney KW16 3JS
**Tel:** 01856850660
**Web:** www.stromnessacademy.orkney.sch.uk
**Estd:** 1988 Proprietorship
**Line of Business:** Schools (local authority)
**Proprietor:** Miss H Learmonts
**Responsibilities**
**Senior:** Stephen Crawford *(Business Manager)*, Helda Learmonth *(Head Teacher)*
**Finance:** Stephen Crawford *(Business Manager)*
**US SIC:** 8211 **UK SIC:** 93200
**Employees:** 104

DUNS 23-123-7475
## Strong Inns Ltd
630 Antrim Road, Newtownabbey, Co Antrim BT36 4RH
**Tel:** 02890844925 **Fax:** 028-9084-4352
**Web:** www.chimneycorner.co.uk
**Reg No:** 0035190NI **Estd:** 1871 Private Limited Company
**Line of Business:** Hotels and motels without restaurant
**Trading Style:** Chimney Corner
**Issued Capital:** £2
**Director:** C Wicklow
**Co. Secretary:** Mrs Ann Wicklow
**Responsibilities**
**Senior:** Monica Quinn *(General Manager)*
**US SIC:** 7011 **UK SIC:** 66500
**Auditors:** Daniel G. Walsh & Co
**Bankers:** Ulster Bank Ltd (98-00-40)

| | 31-10-13 | 31-10-12 | 31-10-11 |
|---|---|---|---|
| TA | 1,346,607 | 1,404,897 | 1,432,197 |
| NW | (46,225) | 79,204 | (1,210,259) |
| WC | (107,802) | (93,439) | (88,440) |

DUNS 21-689-5805 **Imp**
## Stronghold International Ltd
Unit A, Nicholson Court, Hoddesdon, Hertfordshire EN11 0NE
**Tel:** 01992479470 **Fax:** 01992-479471
**Web:** www.stronghold.co.uk
**Reg No:** 0867533 **VAT No:** 220706602
**Estd:** 1965 Private Limited Company
**Line of Business:** Manufacture of other transport equipment not elsewhere classified
**Trading Style:** Stronghold, Eurobuckle
**Issued Capital:** £1,900
**Principals:** A T Rowell *(Chairman)*, D L Green, A A Westwood, Ms R Rowell
**Co. Secretary:** Ms Linda Rowell
**Responsibilities**
**Senior:** Alan Skipp *(Manager)*
**US SIC:** 3799 **UK SIC:** 36502
**Auditors:** Thickbroom Coventry
**Bankers:** Barclays Bank Plc (20-20-37)

| | 30-06-14 | 30-06-13 | 30-06-12 |
|---|---|---|---|
| TA | 2,316,471 | 2,325,916 | 2,379,727 |
| NW | 1,275,059 | 1,240,606 | 1,293,812 |
| WC | 115,790 | 43,451 | 66,660 |

DUNS 21-556-6583
## Strood Academy
Carnation Road, Rochester, Kent ME2 2SX
**Tel:** 01634717121
**Web:** www.stroodacademy.org
**Reg No:** 6914263 **Estd:** 2009
**Line of Business:** General secondary education
**Directors:** Mrs K Gunn, Mrs J N Greenleaf, D V Mead, R C Moreton, Mrs W Millar, Professor M A Hunt, G Down, S G Vadher
**Co. Secretary:** Mrs Tracey Damerum
**Responsibilities**
**Senior:** Fred Davies *(Director)*, Steven Munday *(Director)*, Francine Norris *(Director)*, Angela Prodger *(Director)*
**Finance:** Tracy Dimon *(Finance Administrator)*
**IT:** Richard Bowery *(Senior IT Executive)*
**US SIC:** 8211 **UK SIC:** 93200
**Bankers:** Lloyds TSB Bank plc (77-95-13)

| | 31-08-14 | 31-08-13 | 31-08-12 |
|---|---|---|---|
| TO | 8,147,000 | 7,901,000 | 35,947,000 |
| P/L | (851,000) | (1,593,000) | 27,813,000 |
| NW | 26,567,000 | 28,131,000 | 29,695,000 |
| WC | 3,515,000 | 3,032,000 | 3,193,000 |
| Emp. | 215 | 216 | 193 |

DUNS 55-067-3065
## Stroud College
Stroud Campus, Stroud, Gloucestershire GL5 4AH
**Tel:** 01453763424
**Web:** www.sgscol.ac.uk
**Estd:** 2002
**Line of Business:** Further education schools and colleges
**Directors:** G R Kirk, K T Wright, M E Hendley, G Morris
**Responsibilities**
**Senior:** Rachel Fleetwood *(Board member)*, Carole Garfield *(Board member)*, Marie-Annick Gournet *(Board member)*, Mike Guest *(Board member)*, Kevin Hamblin *(Principal)*, Moyra Pascoe *(Board member)*, Mandy Robertson *(PA of CEO)*
**Admin:** Chloe Thompson *(PA)*, Sandie Vaughan *(PA)*
**HR:** Katie Harrington *(Human Resources Manager)*
**Branches:** Stroud College, Drake House, Drake Lane, Dursley, Gloucestershire GL11 4HH
**US SIC:** 8221 **UK SIC:** 93100
**Auditors:** Deloitte & Touche
**Employees:** 120

DUNS 34-588-8911
## Stroud Court Community Trust Ltd
Longfords, Minchinhampton, Stroud, Gloucestershire GL6 9AN
**Web:** www.stroudcourt.org.uk
**Reg No:** 2733012 **Estd:** 1982 Private Company Limited By Guarantee
**Line of Business:** Residential care establishments
**Directors:** G Slade, Ms J Lewis, Mrs J Lewis, Mrs J W Lusty, G R Kirk, A D Bateson, Mrs V J Fenwick, Mrs M L Bruton-Cox
**Co. Secretary:** Simon Bruton
**Responsibilities**
**Senior:** Chris Atkins *(Executive Director)*, Paul Cadle *(Director)*
**Facilities:** Adrian Palmer *(Facilities Manager)*
**US SIC:** 8321 **UK SIC:** 96111
**Auditors:** Bank & Partners
**Bankers:** Lloyds TSB Bank plc (30-98-29)

| | 31-03-14 | 31-03-13 | 31-03-12 |
|---|---|---|---|
| TO | 2,364,483 | 2,369,823 | 2,377,507 |
| P/L | (79,456) | 181,192 | 98,158 |
| NW | 2,070,026 | 2,149,482 | 1,968,290 |
| WC | 1,414,335 | 1,278,059 | 1,062,599 |
| Emp. | 86 | 83 | 80 |

DUNS 23-257-6363
## Stroud District Council
Ebley Mill, Ebley Wharf, Stroud, Gloucestershire GL5 4UB
**Tel:** 01453-766321
**Web:** www.stroud.gov.uk
**Estd:** 1974 Incorporate By Act Of Parliament
**Line of Business:** Central government
**Directors:** R Ollin, M J Harwood
**Responsibilities**
**Senior:** Gideon Darley *(Board Member)*, David Hagg *(Chief Executive Officer)*, Carlos Novoth *(Public Space Service Manager)*, Cllr Pearson *(Deputy Leader)*, Suzie Phelps *(Board Member)*
**Marketing:** Jane Bullows *(Sport Development Officer)*, Hannah Drew *(Development Officer)*, Jackie Haines *(Senior Business Support Office)*, Krista Harris *(Regeneration Officer)*, John Longmuir *(Development Control Manager)*, Kam Mistry *(Spokesman)*, Eka Nowakowska *(Principal Policy Officer)*
**Sales:** Phil Park *(Commercial Service Manager)*
**Admin:** Shaun Butler *(Benefits Service Manager)*, Abigail Large *(Administrator)*
**IT:** Pauline Bird *(Infrastructure Manager)*
**Health & Safety:** Cllr Forbes *(Cabinet Member for Community S)*, Paul Helbrow *(Community Safety Manager)*
**Facilities:** Kelly Headley *(Performance and Improvement Of)*
**Operations:** Phil Drew *(Warden)*
**Engineering:** Carlos Novoth *(Public Space Service Manager)*
**Branches:** Stroud District Council, Rednock Drive, Dursley, Gloucestershire GL11 4BX
**US SIC:** 9121 **UK SIC:** 91110
**Bankers:** National Westminster Bank Plc (55-61-08)
**Employees:** 300

DUNS 21-781-5055
## Stroud General Hospital
Trinity Road, Stroud, Gloucestershire GL5 2HY
**Tel:** 03004218080
**Estd:** 2002 Partnership
**Line of Business:** Hospitals
**Partner:** Mrs K Haughton
**Responsibilities**
**Senior:** Michelle Smith *(Administrator)*
**US SIC:** 8062 **UK SIC:** 95100
**Employees:** 300

DUNS 28-824-9204
## Struan Motors Ltd
Crieff Road, Perth, Perthshire PH1 2SJ
**Web:** www.struans.co.uk
**Reg No:** 0068088SC **Estd:** 1979 Private Limited Company
**Line of Business:** Sale of new motor vehicles
**Trading Style:** Struan Motor Centre
**Issued Capital:** £135,900
**Principals:** J A Robertson *(Managing)*, S D Robertson
**Co. Secretary:** John Robertson
**Responsibilities**
**Marketing:** Julie Eglinton *(Marketing Manager)*
**Branches:** Struan Motors Ltd, 102 Scott Street, Perth, Perthshire PH2 8LU
**US SIC:** 5511, 7399
**UK SIC:** 65100, 83954
**Auditors:** Bell & Co

**Bankers:** The Royal Bank Of Scotland Plc (83-47-00)

| | 31-03-14 | 31-03-13 | 31-03-12 |
|---|---|---|---|
| TO | 29,475,156 | 27,521,874 | 27,854,917 |
| P/L | 320,920 | 215,436 | 308,397 |
| NW | 6,159,942 | 5,920,892 | 5,752,084 |
| WC | 2,505,715 | 3,243,331 | 4,152,016 |
| Emp. | 97 | 94 | 97 |

DUNS 22-718-2029
## Structadene Ltd
9 White Lion Street, London N1 9PD
**Tel:** 020-7843-3788
**Web:** www.structadene.co.uk
**Reg No:** 1397642 **Estd:** 1978 Private Limited Company
**Line of Business:** Buying and selling of own real estate
**Trading Style:** Structadene Group
**Issued Capital:** £1,954,496
**Principals:** D A Pearlman *(Managing)*, N A Watson *(Marketing)*, M R Goldberger, G M Patel, P A Colvin
**Co. Secretary:** Howard Pearlman
**Responsibilities**
**Senior:** Daniel Parnes *(Director, Central London Acqui)*
**Branches:** Structadene Ltd, Ensign Ct, London E1 8JQ
**US SIC:** 6531 **UK SIC:** 83400
**Auditors:** UHY Hacker Young

| | 30-09-13 | 30-09-12 | 30-09-11 |
|---|---|---|---|
| TO | 64,219,231 | 60,354,161 | 64,316,973 |
| P/L | 24,851,481 | 5,552,618 | 5,558,647 |
| NW | 166,732,955 | 135,268,521 | 116,824,961 |
| WC | (337,111,951) | (194,079,063) | (63,054,851) |
| Emp. | 76 | 84 | 80 |

DUNS 50-544-9926
## Structura Uk Ltd
Unit 1 Oakcroft Road, Chessington, Surrey KT9 1RH
**Tel:** 020-8397-4361 **Fax:** 020-8391-5805
**Web:** www.structura-uk.com
**Reg No:** 2499497 **VAT No:** 564012274
**Estd:** 1990 Private Limited Company
**Line of Business:** Curtain walling
**Issued Capital:** £1,500
**Directors:** P A Mackett, R Sanders, D Rickman
**Co. Secretary:** Manish Patel
**Branches:** Structura Uk Ltd, Eden Business Centre, Unit 3, Ashford, Kent TN23 7RS
**US SIC:** 1799 **UK SIC:** 50000
**Auditors:** David Rich
**Bankers:** HSBC Bank plc (40-45-22)

| | 31-05-13 | 31-05-12 | 31-05-11 |
|---|---|---|---|
| TO | 6,770,660 | 7,445,661 | 7,954,558 |
| P/L | (88,484) | 304,538 | 944,580 |
| NW | 2,329,302 | 2,758,361 | 2,953,140 |
| WC | 2,105,514 | 2,496,765 | 2,751,889 |
| Emp. | 63 | 66 | 65 |

DUNS 57-830-0394
## Structural Fabrications Ltd
(**Subsidiary of:** Structural Properties Ltd)
2 Castings Road, Derby, Derbyshire DE23 8YL
**Tel:** 01332-747400 **Fax:** 01332-747447
**Web:** www.structural-fabrications.co.uk
**Reg No:** 2888263 **VAT No:** 616769311
**Estd:** 1994 Private Limited Company
**Line of Business:** Steel fabricators
**Issued Capital:** £586
**Principals:** S S Kang *(Managing)*, M J Simpson
**Co. Secretary:** Sukhjit Kang
**US SIC:** 1622, 3421
**UK SIC:** 50200, 31621
**Auditors:** BW Business Services Ltd
**Bankers:** Barclays Bank Plc (20-25-85)

| | 31-01-14 | 31-01-13 | 31-01-12 |
|---|---|---|---|
| TA | 1,394,567 | 991,476 | 1,287,667 |
| NW | 353,600 | 248,915 | 323,154 |
| WC | (37,115) | (154,317) | (96,561) |

DUNS 23-562-3472
## Structural Metal Decks Ltd
(**Subsidiary of:** Smd 2013 Ltd)
The Outlook, Ling Road, Poole, Dorset BH12 4PY
**Tel:** 01202-718898 **Fax:** 01202-714980
**Web:** www.smdltd.co.uk
**Reg No:** 3560591 **VAT No:** 717571621
**Estd:** 1998 Private Limited Company
**Line of Business:** Steel constructed buildings
**Issued Capital:** £100,000
**Directors:** B Pratten, J F Turner, D S Williams, R T Firth
**Co. Secretary:** Benedict Pratten
**Responsibilities**
**Senior:** Sid Pratten *(Manager)*
**Finance:** Sid Pratten *(Manager)*
**Admin:** Penny Bayford *(Office Manager)*
**US SIC:** 3441 **UK SIC:** 32042
**Auditors:** Andrew Pollock

**Bankers:** Bank Of Scotland (12-09-49)

|     | 31-07-13 | 31-07-12 | 31-07-11 |
|-----|----------|----------|----------|
| TO  | 13,449,137 | 13,541,079 | 13,886,026 |
| P/L | 63,493 | (41,738) | 460,460 |
| NW  | 5,234,602 | 5,529,879 | 5,834,026 |
| WC  | 4,291,184 | 4,538,536 | 4,796,380 |
| Emp.| 101 | 77 | 69 |

DUNS 21-655-3879
## Structural Steelwork Ltd
Unit 33, Thornleigh Trading Estate, Dudley, West Midlands DY2 8UB
**Tel:** 01384258400
**Web:** www.ssteelwork.co.uk
**Reg No:** 7123920 **Estd:** 2010 Private Limited Company
**Line of Business:** Manufacture of basic iron and steel and of ferro-alloys
**Issued Capital:** £500
**Directors:** Ms L S Micklewright, S J Micklewright, A C Micklewright
**US SIC:** 3325 **UK SIC:** 31110
**Auditors:** Nicklin LLP

|     | 31-01-14 | 31-01-13 | 31-01-12 |
|-----|----------|----------|----------|
| TA  | 1,608,591 | 785,378 | 500 |
| NW  | 312,059 | 227,357 | 500 |
| WC  | 312,059 | 227,357 | N/A |

DUNS 21-718-0249                                    Imp-Exp
## Structure-Flex Ltd
(**Subsidiary of:** Resolute Corporate Holdings Ltd)
Peacock Way, Melton Constable, Norfolk NR24 2AZ
**Tel:** 01263-863100
**Web:** www.structure-flex.co.uk
**Reg No:** 0981555 **Estd:** 1970 Private Limited Company
**Line of Business:** Manufacture of household textiles
**Export Markets:** Worldwide
**Export Sales:** £3,410,744
**Issued Capital:** £20,000
**Principals:** I S Doughty (Managing), J P Wallace-King, P J Reeve
**Co. Secretary:** Mrs Sarah Davis
**Responsibilities**
**Senior:** Kate Reeve (Human Resources Manager and Co)
**Finance:** Kate Doughty (Manager), Bill Wallace-King (Senior Finance Administrator)
**HR:** Kate Reeve (Human Resources Manager and Co)
**Health & Safety:** Kate Doughty (Manager)
**Facilities:** Mick High (Maintenance Officer)
**Purchasing:** Alan Willey (Purchasing Manager)
**Branches:** Structure-Flex Ltd, 19 Bowthorpe Employment Area, Francis Way, Norwich, Norfolk NR5 9JA
**US SIC:** 2392, 3999
**UK SIC:** 45550, 49590
**Auditors:** Larking Gowen
**Bankers:** National Westminster Bank Plc (53-50-73)

|     | 31-08-14 | 31-08-13 | 31-08-12 |
|-----|----------|----------|----------|
| TO  | 6,403,545 | 10,243,599 | 10,532,610 |
| P/L | 626,382 | 3,436,041 | 3,850,484 |
| NW  | 5,425,173 | 6,413,651 | 4,805,004 |
| WC  | 3,032,021 | 5,616,765 | 3,846,582 |
| Emp.| 70 | 84 | 85 |

DUNS 21-223-8069
## Structured Networks Solutions
The Old Coach House, 211 Canterbury Road, Birchington, Kent CT7 9AH
**Web:** www.snsuk.co.uk
**Proprietorship**
**Line of Business:** Other computer related activities
**Proprietor:** B Green
**US SIC:** 7399 **UK SIC:** 83954
**Employees:** 47

DUNS 22-101-0668
## Structuretone International Ltd
(**Subsidiary of:** Structure-Tone Inc.)
1a Aylesbury Street, London EC1R 0ST
**Tel:** 020-7204-7000
**Web:** www.structuretone.com
**Reg No:** 4120482 **Estd:** 1990 Private Limited Company
**Line of Business:** Management activities of holding companies
**Export Sales:** £44,229,679
**Issued Capital:** £2,000,000
**Directors:** I G Phillpot, D Manning, J Donaghy, A Carvette Iii
**US SIC:** 6711 **UK SIC:** 83962
**Auditors:** Deloitte LLP
**Bankers:** National Westminster Bank Plc (60-13-14)

|     | 31-12-13 | 31-12-12 | 31-12-11 |
|-----|----------|----------|----------|
| TO  | 151,931,793 | 104,746,813 | 78,127,469 |
| P/L | 764,449 | (1,558,524) | 1,016,075 |
| NW  | (1,872,669) | (2,187,113) | (278,300) |
| WC  | (2,073,518) | (2,476,050) | (587,959) |
| Emp.| 151 | 126 | 106 |

DUNS 21-919-3491
## Strukta Group Ltd
22 Cherry Orchard Lane, Churchfields Industrial Estate, Salisbury, Wiltshire SP2 7LD
**Tel:** 01722414011
**Web:** www.strukta.co.uk
**Reg No:** 8356072 **Estd:** 2013 Private Limited Company
**Line of Business:** Builders merchants
**Issued Capital:** £1
**Directors:** K Diffey, M Diffey, B Diffey, M S Moggach, S M Diffey, P Moggach, A Diffey, M Moggach
**Responsibilities**
**Senior:** David Moggach (Director), Lauren Moggach (Director)
**US SIC:** 5072 **UK SIC:** 61500

|     | 30-06-14 |
|-----|----------|
| TO  | 11,840,256 |
| P/L | 476,266 |
| NW  | (4,202,250) |
| WC  | 849,234 |
| Emp.| 70 |

DUNS 21-685-1048
## Strutt & Parker (Farms) Ltd
Whitbreads Farm, Chatham Green, Chelmsford, Essex CM3 3LQ
**Web:** www.spfarms.co.uk
**Reg No:** 0151618 **VAT No:** 102936981
**Estd:** 1918 Private Limited Company
**Line of Business:** Representative office
**Issued Capital:** £3,459,034
**Principals:** D A Nutting (Chairman), S R Wallis, C O Fillingham, C Maton, The Right Honourable L De Ramsey, A J Buxton, D J Harden
**Co. Secretary:** Peter Wood
**Responsibilities**
**Senior:** Vincent Lewis (Manager), Fiona Macleod (Manager)
**Branches:** Strutt & Parker (Farms) Ltd, Lawn Hall Farm, Lawn Hall Chase, Dunmow, Essex CM6 3PN
**US SIC:** 0291 **UK SIC:** 01001
**Auditors:** Deloitte & Touche
**Bankers:** Barclays Bank Plc (20-97-40)

|     | 31-03-14 | 31-03-13 | 31-03-12 |
|-----|----------|----------|----------|
| TO  | 11,976,000 | 11,590,000 | 10,136,000 |
| P/L | 3,249,000 | 3,511,000 | 4,901,000 |
| NW  | 32,189,000 | 26,200,000 | 25,128,000 |
| WC  | 1,495,000 | 4,643,000 | 6,171,000 |
| Emp.| 66 | 55 | 49 |

DUNS 23-674-5621                                    Imp
## Stryker U K Ltd
(**Subsidiary of:** Stryker Corporation)
Stryker House, Hambridge Road, Newbury, Berkshire RG14 5AW
**Tel:** 01635-262400
**Web:** www.stryker.com
**Reg No:** 3669454 **Estd:** 1998 Private Limited Company
**Line of Business:** Medical equipment leasing and rental
**Issued Capital:** £11,645,306
**Directors:** L Hipkin, M S Davison
**Co. Secretary:** Tony Mckinney
**Responsibilities**
**Senior:** David Grice (Facilities Manager), Diljit Khalsa (It Manager)
**IT:** Diljit Khalsa (It Manager)
**HR:** Charlotte Henderson (Human Resources Manager), Wendy Perry (Human Resources Manager)
**Facilities:** David Grice (Facilities Manager)
**Branches:** Stryker U K Ltd, Po Box 5946, Newbury, Berkshire RG14 5EG
**US SIC:** 7394 **UK SIC:** 84000
**Auditors:** Ernst & Young LLP
**Bankers:** Barclays Bank Plc (20-00-00)

|     | 31-12-13 | 31-12-12 | 31-12-11 |
|-----|----------|----------|----------|
| TO  | 192,482,000 | 183,321,000 | 177,890,000 |
| P/L | 9,976,000 | 5,674,000 | 10,356,000 |
| NW  | 31,268,000 | 49,308,000 | 59,960,000 |
| WC  | 11,180,000 | 27,621,000 | 21,977,000 |
| Emp.| 362 | 367 | 350 |

DUNS 45-846-5994                                    Imp-Exp
## Sts Defence Ltd
(**Subsidiary of:** Key Technologies Ltd)
Mumby Road, Gosport, Hampshire PO12 1AF
**Tel:** 02392 584222 **Fax:** 02392 529598
**Web:** www.sts-defence.com
**Reg No:** 3193298 **Estd:** 1996 Private Limited Company
**Line of Business:** Aeronautical engineers
**Export Sales:** £612,608
**Issued Capital:** £164,000
**Directors:** K Hilton, T Middleton, R Papanicolaou
**Co. Secretary:** Kevin Hilton
**Responsibilities**
**Sales:** Kevin Boorn (Sales Manager)
**IT:** J Thompkinson (IT Manager)
**HR:** K Chamberlin (Personnel Manager)
**Purchasing:** Sharon Denness (Purchasing Manager)

**Branches:** Sts Defence Ltd, 12-20 Sharlands Rd, Fareham, Hampshire PO14 1RD
**US SIC:** 8911, 3357
**UK SIC:** 83701, 22470
**Auditors:** Baker Tilly Audit Ltd
**Bankers:** Lloyds TSB Bank plc (30-90-34)

|     | 30-06-13 | 30-06-12 | 30-06-11 |
|-----|----------|----------|----------|
| TO  | 10,981,694 | 12,164,683 | 12,196,060 |
| P/L | 1,583,311 | 1,046,729 | 2,057,864 |
| NW  | 4,759,458 | 3,991,276 | 5,870,408 |
| WC  | 4,423,392 | 3,578,465 | 5,447,341 |
| Emp.| 142 | 149 | 130 |

DUNS 54-372-5329
## Sts Flooring Distributors Ltd
(**Subsidiary of:** Stair Tread Holdings Ltd)
Orpington Trade Centre, Orpington, Kent BR5 3SS
**Tel:** 08454341000
**Web:** www.stsflooring.co.uk
**Reg No:** 3260566 **Estd:** 1973 Private Limited Company
**Line of Business:** Wholesale of furniture
**Issued Capital:** £531,250
**Principals:** C E Wallman (Managing), R J Colgate, B Pitt, S M Gay, J C Flockhart
**Co. Secretary:** Raymond Colegate
**Branches:** Sts Flooring Distributors Ltd, Unit 13, Beddington Farm Road, Croydon, Surrey CR0 4WP
**US SIC:** 5021, 5199
**UK SIC:** 61500, 61900
**Auditors:** Spokes & Co
**Bankers:** Lloyds TSB Bank plc (30-98-63)

|     | 31-12-13 | 31-12-12 | 31-12-11 |
|-----|----------|----------|----------|
| TO  | 20,701,990 | 21,345,296 | 18,553,071 |
| P/L | 187,214 | 323,382 | 293,406 |
| NW  | 5,968,528 | 5,812,906 | 5,553,115 |
| WC  | 5,184,682 | 5,034,060 | 4,804,994 |
| Emp.| 92 | 89 | 89 |

DUNS 50-190-8149
## Sts Industrial Ltd
Raventhorpe Lodge, Brigg Road, Scunthorpe, South Humberside DN16 3RJ
**Tel:** 01724-281175 **Fax:** 01724854675
**Web:** www.stindustries.com
**Reg No:** 2330164 **VAT No:** 555531833
**Estd:** 1982 Private Limited Company
**Line of Business:** Freight forwarders
**Issued Capital:** £300,100
**Principals:** A Skelton (Managing), S A Smith, M J Swan
**Co. Secretary:** Andrew Skelton
**US SIC:** 4712 **UK SIC:** 77002
**Bankers:** HSBC Bank plc (40-25-20)

|     | 31-10-13 | 31-10-12 | 31-10-11 |
|-----|----------|----------|----------|
| TA  | 470,180 | 353,475 | 422,259 |
| NW  | 271,389 | 193,065 | 225,668 |
| WC  | 252,962 | 160,250 | 192,189 |

DUNS 89-672-3632
## Sts School Travel Service Ltd
(**Subsidiary of:** Eatg (Debtco) Ltd)
Jubilee Street, Brighton, East Sussex BN1 1GE
**Tel:** 0870-240-6828 **Fax:** 01273693116
**Web:** www.skiplan.co.uk
**Reg No:** 3323339 **Estd:** 1991 Private Limited Company
**Line of Business:** Tour operators
**Trading Style:** Equity
**Issued Capital:** £1,600,002
**Directors:** J Bentley, N D Goodwin
**Responsibilities**
**HR:** Ruth Cornford (Human Resources Manager)
**US SIC:** 4722 **UK SIC:** 77001
**Auditors:** Grant Thornton
**Bankers:** National Westminster Bank Plc (01-01-23)

|     | 31-10-13 | 31-07-12 | 31-10-11 |
|-----|----------|----------|----------|
| TO  | 17,387,000 | 14,992,000 | 14,794,000 |
| P/L | 649,000 | 1,240,000 | 633,000 |
| NW  | 5,552,000 | 5,390,000 | 4,224,000 |
| WC  | 5,462,000 | 5,296,000 | 4,106,000 |

DUNS 45-846-6018                                    Exp
## Sts Switchgear Ltd
(**Subsidiary of:** Prime Endeavour Ltd)
Douton Road, Cradley Heath, Cradley Heath, West Midlands B64 5QB
**Tel:** 01384-567755
**Web:** www.sts-switchgear.co.uk
**Reg No:** 3193301 **Estd:** 1996 Private Limited Company
**Line of Business:** Manufacture of electronic valves and tubes and other electronic components
**Export Sales:** £297,713
**Trading Style:** Sts Motors, Sts Signals
**Issued Capital:** £10,002
**Directors:** D F Parkinson, S C Hall, A G Ansari
**US SIC:** 3679, 3621
**UK SIC:** 34542, 34201
**Auditors:** HLB AV Audit Plc

**Bankers:** Barclays Bank Plc (20-07-71)

|     | 31-12-13 | 30-06-12 | 30-12-11 |
|-----|----------|----------|----------|
| TO  | 5,670,720 | 5,057,759 | 4,428,831 |
| P/L | (120,547) | 65,161 | 106,221 |
| NW  | 410,190 | 1,738,287 | 1,731,554 |
| WC  | 212,244 | 1,642,852 | 1,520,845 |
| Emp.| N/A | 45 | 47 |

DUNS 21-172-4788
## Sts Uk Holdco Ii Ltd
(**Subsidiary of:** Europe Voyager Nv)
Glendale Park, Sandycroft Industrial Estate Glendale, Avenue, Deeside, Clwyd CH5 2DL
**Tel:** 0844 826 2600
**Web:** www.stellatravel.co.uk
**Reg No:** 6966146 **Estd:** 2009 Private Limited Company
**Line of Business:** Travel clinics
**Trading Style:** Stella Travel Service
**Issued Capital:** £12,223,604
**Directors:** A D Cummins, A I Botterill, J L Penny
**US SIC:** 4722, 6711
**UK SIC:** 77001, 83962
**Auditors:** PricewaterhouseCoopers LLP
**Bankers:** Barclays Bank Plc (20-30-47)

|     | 30-06-13 | 30-06-12 | 30-06-11 |
|-----|----------|----------|----------|
| TO  | 165,825,000 | 132,924,000 | 114,773,000 |
| P/L | 566,000 | 189,000 | 269,000 |
| NW  | (4,698,000) | (6,161,000) | (7,248,000) |
| WC  | 3,229,000 | (3,702,000) | (7,365,000) |
| Emp.| 375 | 370 | 368 |

DUNS 21-778-3558
## Stuart Crescent Health Centre
Stuart Crescent Hthctr, 8 Stuart Crescent, London N22 5NJ
**Tel:** 02036971760
**Estd:** 1980 Proprietorship
**Line of Business:** Doctors
**Proprietor:** Mrs B Dave
**Responsibilities**
**Senior:** MAHENDRA DAVE (Doctor)
**US SIC:** 8062 **UK SIC:** 95100
**Employees:** 80

DUNS 39-230-0521                                    Imp-Exp
## Stuart Group Ltd
Stuart House, Crowshall Lane, Attleborough, Norfolk NR17 1AD
**Tel:** 01953454540
**Web:** www.stuartgroup.co.uk
**Reg No:** 2114643 **VAT No:** 451328466
**Estd:** 2010 Private Limited Company
**Line of Business:** Pipework contractors
**Export Markets:** European Union (E U); Africa
**Trading Style:** Stuart Well Services, Stuart Pumps, Stuart Plant, Millar's Wellpoint
**Issued Capital:** £2,675
**Principals:** S Sayer (Managing), A P Sayer, N T Hood, R Tregent, R J Tebble
**Co. Secretary:** John Sayer
**Branches:** Stuart Group Ltd, Unit 9A3, Carcroft Enterprise Park, Carcroft, Doncaster, South Yorkshire DN6 8DD
**US SIC:** 7394, 5199
**UK SIC:** 84000, 61900
**Auditors:** Larking Gowen
**Bankers:** Lloyds TSB Bank plc (30-98-58)

|     | 31-10-13 | 31-10-12 | 31-10-11 |
|-----|----------|----------|----------|
| TO  | 9,302,454 | 9,780,973 | 10,338,319 |
| P/L | 170,002 | 63,619 | 131,119 |
| NW  | 2,125,004 | 2,075,986 | 2,071,213 |
| WC  | 944,941 | 979,215 | 632,835 |
| Emp.| 70 | 73 | 75 |

DUNS 21-740-4524                                    Imp
## Stuart Jones Ltd
Artex Avenue, Rustington, Littlehampton, West Sussex BN16 3LN
**Web:** www.stuartjones.co.uk
**Reg No:** 1321838 **VAT No:** 194149247
**Estd:** 1977 Private Limited Company
**Line of Business:** Bedroom furnishers and planners
**Trading Style:** Jones Stuart Collection
**Issued Capital:** £10,000
**Principals:** P Kerssemakers (Commercial), A G Bennett
**Co. Secretary:** Panayis Panayi
**Responsibilities**
**Senior:** Bob Mitchell (Manager)
**Finance:** s Panayi (Finance Director)
**HR:** Bob Mitchell (Manager)
**Health & Safety:** Bob Mitchell (Manager)
**Facilities:** Bob Mitchell (Manager)
**Engineering:** Bob Mitchell (Manager)
**US SIC:** 2517 **UK SIC:** 46714
**Auditors:** Spiers & Co
**Bankers:** Barclays Bank Plc (20-20-62)

|     | 31-10-13 | 31-10-12 | 31-10-11 |
|-----|----------|----------|----------|
| TA  | 1,297,213 | 1,444,428 | 1,526,142 |
| NW  | 109,344 | 279,926 | 264,380 |
| WC  | 152,198 | 267,436 | 274,115 |

DUNS 21-109-6555
## Stuart Lyons Ltd
**(Subsidiary of:** Lyons Group Holdings Ltd)
Hitchcock House Hilltop Park, Devizes Road, Salisbury, Wiltshire SP3 8UF
**Tel:** 01243555536
**Reg No:** 6512892 **Estd:** 2008 Private Limited Company
**Line of Business:** Other business activities not elsewhere classified
**Issued Capital:** £2
**Director:** S D Lyons
**Co. Secretary:** Mrs Marcia Lyons
**US SIC:** 7399 **UK SIC:** 83954

| | 31-03-14 | 31-03-13 | 31-03-12 |
|---|---|---|---|
| TA | 2 | 2 | 2 |
| NW | 2 | 2 | 2 |

DUNS 28-962-7267
## Stuart Marsh Shoes Ltd
Hennock Court Hennock Road Marsh Barton, Exeter, Devon EX2 8RU
**Tel:** 01392207061
**Reg No:** 1689153 **VAT No:** 631054283
**Estd:** 1990 Private Limited Company
**Line of Business:** Manufacturers of footwear
**Export Sales:** £3,334,777
**Issued Capital:** £1,000
**Principals:** S Marsh *(Managing)*, Ms M L Marsh, P B Marsh, R P Marsh
**Co. Secretary:** Richard Rudling
**US SIC:** 6711, 3149
**UK SIC:** 83962, 45100
**Auditors:** Francis Clark

| | 31-07-13 | 31-07-12 | 31-07-11 |
|---|---|---|---|
| TO | 9,075,127 | 10,007,498 | 10,599,611 |
| P/L | 246,779 | 374,930 | 476,305 |
| NW | 2,935,035 | 2,862,032 | 2,667,764 |
| WC | 2,043,199 | 1,898,238 | 1,675,967 |
| Emp. | 59 | 69 | 73 |

DUNS 22-708-2088 **Imp-Exp**
## Stuart Peters Ltd
**(Subsidiary of:** Stuart Peters (Holdings) Ltd)
184-192 Drummond Street, London NW1 3HP
**Tel:** 020-7554-8440
**Web:** www.speters.co.uk
**Reg No:** 1617684 **VAT No:** 371156366
**Estd:** 1982 Private Limited Company
**Line of Business:** Clothing wholesale and suppliers
**Export Markets:** E U
**Issued Capital:** £500,000
**Directors:** K Crump, J D Peters
**Co. Secretary:** Mrs Erica Peters
**US SIC:** 5136 **UK SIC:** 61600
**Auditors:** M.J. Golz & Co
**Bankers:** The Royal Bank Of Scotland Plc (15-20-25)

| | 31-03-14 | 30-06-13 | 30-03-12 |
|---|---|---|---|
| TO | 3,244,405 | 4,355,511 | 7,807,762 |
| P/L | 57,976 | 827,999 | 637,992 |
| NW | 1,643,328 | 2,835,352 | 2,143,830 |
| WC | 1,363,388 | 2,645,080 | 2,143,830 |
| Emp. | 98 | 88 | 78 |

DUNS 21-616-9888 **Imp-Exp**
## Stuart Turner Ltd
Market Place, Henley-On-Thames, Oxfordshire RG9 2AD
**Tel:** 01491-572655 **Fax:** 01491573704
**Web:** www.stuart-turner.co.uk
**Reg No:** 0088368 **VAT No:** 199098792
**Estd:** 1906 Private Limited Company
**Line of Business:** Pumps sales and servicing
**Export Markets:** European Union (E U); Australasia; Middle East
**Issued Capital:** £1,977,386
**Directors:** M Harris, M Williams, S J Lee, W S Barnard, G A Ellis, P R Manning
**Co. Secretary:** Malcolm Harris
**Responsibilities**
**Senior:** Alan Penson *(Manager)*, Naomi Thomas *(Manager)*, Rory Topping *(Manager)*, John Tugwell *(Manager)*
**US SIC:** 3563 **UK SIC:** 32831
**Auditors:** Kpmg
**Bankers:** National Westminster Bank Plc (60-10-35)

| | 30-09-13 | 30-09-12 | 30-09-11 |
|---|---|---|---|
| TO | 15,417,822 | 15,035,535 | 14,951,063 |
| P/L | 2,718,342 | 3,311,014 | 3,282,532 |
| NW | 15,383,393 | 15,122,183 | 14,495,910 |
| WC | 9,028,191 | 8,823,111 | 9,842,110 |
| Emp. | 74 | 77 | 78 |

DUNS 23-181-2140
## Stuarts Coaches
Castlehill Garage, Airdrie Road, Carluke, Lanarkshire ML8 5EP
**Tel:** 01555773533
**Web:** www.stuarts-coaches.com
**Estd:** 1987 Proprietorship
**Line of Business:** Coach tour operators.
**Proprietor:** S Shevill
**US SIC:** 4142, 4151, 4141
**UK SIC:** 72102
**Employees:** 85

DUNS 39-678-3128 **Imp**
## Stubbins Marketing Ltd
Station Approach, Waltham Cross, Hertfordshire EN8 7LY
**Tel:** 01992713200 **Fax:** 01992 763 607
**Web:** www.stubbins.com
**Reg No:** 2142565 **Estd:** 1987 Private Limited Company
**Line of Business:** Wholesalers of fruit and vegetable
**Trading Style:** Stubbins
**Issued Capital:** £300,000
**Directors:** S Difrancesco, S Turone, S M Difrancesco, P Turone
**Co. Secretary:** Salvatore Difrancesco
**Responsibilities**
**Senior:** Mario Di Francesco *(Managing Director)*, Antonio Difrancesco *(Director)*, Anthony Francesco *(Manager)*, Paolina Turone *(Director)*, Peter Turone *(Chief Executive Officer)*
**Marketing:** Mario Di Francesco *(Managing Director)*
**IT:** Paul Cantrell *(Senior IT Manager)*, Simon Redfern *(IT Manager)*
**Engineering:** Fred Sheppard *(Production Manager)*
**Branches:** Stubbins Marketing Ltd, Began Road, Old Street Mellons, Cardiff, South Glamorgan CF3 6XL
**US SIC:** 5148, 0161
**UK SIC:** 61700, 01001
**Auditors:** Thickbroom Coventry Ltd
**Bankers:** Barclays Bank Plc (20-20-37)

| | 30-06-13 | 30-06-12 | 30-06-11 |
|---|---|---|---|
| TO | 53,848,356 | 50,748,230 | 57,673,349 |
| P/L | 543,695 | 624,514 | 282,544 |
| NW | 11,263,450 | 10,727,126 | 10,188,412 |
| WC | (2,936,849) | (2,282,313) | (2,388,662) |
| Emp. | 306 | 328 | 331 |

DUNS 50-394-5115
## Student Loans Company Ltd
100 Bothwell Street, Glasgow, Lanarkshire G2 7JD
**Tel:** 01413062000 **Fax:** 01413-062005
**Web:** www.slc.co.uk
**Reg No:** 2401034 **Estd:** 1989 Private Limited Company
**Line of Business:** Loans
**Issued Capital:** £10
**Directors:** G M Breakwell, W G Gallagher, M F Laverty, R A Kennedy, C N Brodie, M G Yuille
**Co. Secretary:** John Brown
**Responsibilities**
**Marketing:** Rona Cameron *(Marketing & Communications Man)*, Eleanor Currie *(Public Relations Manager)*
**Sales:** Yvonne Harkness *(Relationship Manager, Business)*
**HR:** Taroub Zahran *(Director if People and Transfo)*
**Operations:** Eleanor Currie *(Public Relations Manager)*
**Purchasing:** Michael Mullin *(Procurement Manager)*
**Branches:** Student Loans Company Ltd, Mowden Hall, Staindrop Road, Darlington, County Durham DL3 9BG
**US SIC:** 6111 **UK SIC:** 81501
**Auditors:** KPMG LLP

| | 31-03-14 | 31-03-13 | 31-03-12 |
|---|---|---|---|
| TA | 46,317,000 | 29,239,000 | 27,722,000 |
| P/L | (312,000) | 783,000 | 2,412,000 |
| NW | (33,489,000) | (20,058,000) | (10,379,000) |
| WC | (6,795,000) | (4,243,000) | (3,999,000) |
| Emp. | 2,367 | 2,140 | 1,920 |

DUNS 21-363-2477
## Student Support Centre
Mill House, Quarry Wood Industrial Estate, Mills Road, Aylesford, Kent ME20 7NA
**Tel:** 01622792880
**Web:** www.student-support.co.uk
**Estd:** 1999 Proprietorship
**Line of Business:** Adult education locations
**Proprietor:** A Levy
**US SIC:** 8299 **UK SIC:** 93300
**Employees:** 46

DUNS 21-777-3144
## Students Union of University of Central Lancashire
Fylde Road, Preston, Lancashire PR1 2XQ
**Tel:** 01772893000
**Estd:** 1979 Partnership
**Line of Business:** Trade unions
**Partners:** P Goodwin, P Shilton-Godwin
**US SIC:** 8221 **UK SIC:** 93100
**Employees:** 50

DUNS 28-930-3976
## Students' Union Services (East Anglia) Ltd
Norwich Research Park, Earlham Road, Norwich, Norfolk NR4 7TJ
**Tel:** 01603593272
**Web:** www.ueastudent.com
**Reg No:** 1524381 **VAT No:** 353370466
**Estd:** 1980 Private Limited Company
**Line of Business:** Retail sale in non-specialised stores with food, beverages or tobacco predominating
**Trading Style:** Union of Uea Students
**Issued Capital:** £3,750,000
**Directors:** C Rand, L Mccafferty, Y Yu, C Jarvis, Ms H Staynor
**Co. Secretary:** Anthony Moore
**Responsibilities**
**Senior:** Robert Bloomer *(Finance Officer)*, Johan Bolling *(Director)*, Toby Cunningham *(Deputy Chief Executive)*, Jim Dickinson *(CEO)*, Bintu Foday *(Manager)*, Annie Grant *(Manager)*, Lesley Hanner *(Senior Finance Administrator)*, Joseph Levell *(Manager)*, Leslie Morrell *(Director)*, Paul Waugh *(Director)*
**Finance:** Robert Bloomer *(Finance Officer)*, Lesley Hanner *(Senior Finance Administrator)*, Joseph Levell *(Manager)*
**Branches:** Students' Union Services (East Anglia) Ltd, Norwich Research Park, Earlham Road, Norwich, Norfolk NR4 7TJ
**US SIC:** 5411, 5813, 4722, 7999
**UK SIC:** 64100, 66200, 77001, 97913
**Auditors:** Haines Watts
**Bankers:** Barclays Bank Plc (20-62-53)

| | 30-04-13 | 30-04-12 | 31-04-11 |
|---|---|---|---|
| TO | 7,231,666 | 6,206,726 | 7,843,855 |
| P/L | (105,145) | (79,477) | (74,496) |
| NW | 3,218,164 | 3,323,309 | 3,402,786 |
| WC | 1,173,762 | 1,117,432 | 1,052,060 |
| Emp. | 304 | 320 | 262 |

DUNS 21-386-0090
## Studio 2
198 Keyham Road, Plymouth, Devon PL2 1RD
**Web:** www.uk-vip.co.uk
**Line of Business:** Other sporting activities not elsewhere classified
**US SIC:** 7299 **UK SIC:** 98902
**Employees:** 50

DUNS 34-605-6468
## Studio Language Courses (Cambridge) Ltd
5-6 Salisbury Villas, Cambridge, Cambridgeshire CB1 2JF
**Tel:** 01223-369701
**Web:** www.studiocambridge.co.uk
**Reg No:** 2747020 **Estd:** 2012 Private Limited Company
**Line of Business:** Language schools
**Trading Style:** Studio School
**Issued Capital:** £5,000
**Director:** C B Roberts
**Responsibilities**
**Senior:** Malcolm Mottram *(Manager)*
**US SIC:** 8249, 8211
**UK SIC:** 93300, 93200
**Auditors:** Lakin Rose
**Bankers:** Barclays Bank Plc (20-17-35)

| | 31-12-13 | 31-12-12 | 31-12-11 |
|---|---|---|---|
| TO | 7,347,293 | N/A | N/A |
| P/L | 481,101 | N/A | N/A |
| NW | 564,639 | 293,254 | 338,523 |
| WC | 539,599 | 278,255 | 231,918 |
| Emp. | 111 | N/A | N/A |

DUNS 21-784-2862
## Studio Theatre
Morley Street, Bradford, West Yorkshire BD7 1AJ
**Tel:** 01274432000
**Web:** www.bradford-theatres.co.uk
**Estd:** 2003 Proprietorship
**Line of Business:** Theatres & concert halls
**Proprietor:** A Renton
**US SIC:** 6531 **UK SIC:** 83400
**Employees:** 206

DUNS 23-652-0578
## Studiocanal Ltd
**(Subsidiary of:** Vivendi)
50 Marshall Street, London W1F 9BQ
**Tel:** 020-7534-2700 **Fax:** 020-7543-2701
**Web:** www.studiocanal.co.uk
**Reg No:** 3647235 **VAT No:** 736093134
**Estd:** 1998 Private Limited Company
**Line of Business:** Distribution service providers
**Export Sales:** £1,361,000
**Issued Capital:** £1,000
**Principals:** D K Perkins *(Managing)*, O Courson, S Murphy, R M Bessi, Ms S Arnould, J Forde
**Responsibilities**
**Senior:** Hugh Spearing *(Manager)*
**US SIC:** 7829 **UK SIC:** 97112
**Auditors:** PricewaterhouseCoopers LLP

| | 31-12-13 | 31-12-12 | 31-12-11 |
|---|---|---|---|
| TO | 68,042,000 | 66,748,000 | 63,270,000 |
| P/L | 3,064,000 | (1,230,000) | 6,959,000 |
| NW | 9,708,000 | 6,072,000 | 5,285,000 |
| WC | 39,228,000 | 40,113,000 | 3,121,000 |
| Emp. | 60 | 59 | 61 |

DUNS 22-136-6680
## Studley Castle Ltd
**(Subsidiary of:** Phoenix Venture Holdings Ltd)
Castle Road, Studley, Warwickshire B80 7AJ
**Tel:** 01527853111
**Web:** www.bw-studleycastle.co.uk
**Reg No:** 4155565 **Estd:** 1968 Private Limited Company
**Line of Business:** Hotels
**Issued Capital:** £2
**Director:** P A Dillon
**Co. Secretary:** Miss Jane Ruston
**Responsibilities**
**Senior:** Peter Beale *(Manager)*, Aimi Pomeroy *(Joint Assistant Manager)*, Mark Starkey *(General Manager)*, Nicholas Stephenson *(Manager)*
**Finance:** Sam Phillips *(Accountant)*
**Marketing:** Maxine Napolitano *(Sales Manager)*
**Sales:** Maxine Napolitano *(Sales Manager)*
**Health & Safety:** Geoff Bishop *(Maintenance Manager)*
**Facilities:** Geoff Bishop *(Maintenance Manager)*
**US SIC:** 7011 **UK SIC:** 66500
**Auditors:** Deloitte & Touche LLP
**Bankers:** The Royal Bank Of Scotland Plc (15-00-00)

| | 27-06-14 | 27-06-13 | 27-06-12 |
|---|---|---|---|
| TA | 1 | 1 | 1 |
| NW | 1 | 1 | 1 |

DUNS 28-975-5217
## Studley Engineering Ltd
17 Vulcan Street, Liverpool, Merseyside L3 7BG
**Tel:** 0151-236-7825
**Web:** www.studleyengineering.co.uk
**Reg No:** 1754001 **VAT No:** 392399017
**Estd:** 1983 Private Limited Company
**Line of Business:** Other building installation
**Issued Capital:** £50,170
**Managing Directors:** N W Brierton, J Hyland
**Co. Secretary:** Mrs Frances Malone
**Responsibilities**
**Health & Safety:** Stephen Kendrick *(Health & Safety Officer)*
**Branches:** Studley Engineering Ltd, Trafford Park Road, Manchester M17 1PA
**US SIC:** 1796 **UK SIC:** 50400
**Auditors:** BKR Haines Watts
**Bankers:** HSBC Bank plc (40-45-14)

| | 31-10-13 | 31-10-12 | 31-10-11 |
|---|---|---|---|
| TO | 11,883,370 | 10,086,039 | 8,745,042 |
| P/L | 310,304 | 171,285 | 425,615 |
| NW | 656,345 | 509,458 | 465,697 |
| WC | 651,360 | 499,058 | 444,436 |
| Emp. | 140 | 132 | 114 |

DUNS 36-511-5885
## Studley High School
Crooks Lane, Studley, Warwickshire B80 7QX
**Web:** www.studleyhigh.demon.co.uk
**Proprietorship**
**Line of Business:** Schools (local authority)
**Proprietor:** Mrs E Young
**US SIC:** 8211 **UK SIC:** 93200
**Employees:** 150

DUNS 73-509-1196
## Studsvik Uk Ltd
**(Subsidiary of:** Studsvik Ab)
Unit 14, Gateshead, Tyne and Wear NE11 0NF
**Tel:** 01914-821744 **Fax:** 01914-821747
**Web:** www.studsvik.co.uk
**Reg No:** 4772229 **Estd:** 2003 Private Limited Company
**Line of Business:** Waste disposal
**Issued Capital:** £1,022,500
**Directors:** M B Skeppstedt, M Fridolfsson, S G Usher, Dr K J Dodd
**Co. Secretary:** Paul Mcdonald
**Responsibilities**
**Senior:** Jerry Ericsson *(Manager)*, Anders Jackson *(Manager)*, Paul McDonald *(Manager)*
**Branches:** Studsvik Uk Ltd, Ribble House, Meanygate, Preston, Lancashire PR5 6UP
**US SIC:** 4953 **UK SIC:** 92110
**Auditors:** PricewaterhouseCoopers LLP
**Bankers:** Svenska Handelsbanken Ab (publ) (40-53-59)

| | 31-12-13 | 31-12-12 | 31-12-11 |
|---|---|---|---|
| TO | 26,830,051 | 21,045,469 | 10,849,903 |
| P/L | 1,792,565 | 456,644 | (1,382,755) |
| NW | (6,111,918) | 7,125,919 | 5,305,157 |
| WC | 2,693,612 | 924,476 | (701,207) |
| Emp. | 88 | 89 | 80 |

DUNS 21-164-0187

## Studwelders Composite Floor Decks Ltd

**(Subsidiary of:** Studwelders Holdings Ltd)
Millennium House, Newhouse Farm Industrial Estate Severn, Link Distribution Centre, Chepstow, Gwent NP16 6UN
**Tel:** 01291-626048 **Fax:** 01291-629979
**Web:** www.studwelders.co.uk
**Reg No:** 6901006 **Estd:** 1955 Private Limited Company
**Line of Business:** Other construction work involving special trades
**Issued Capital:** £1,000
**Directors:** S J Haines, P A Smart, C W Phillips, M W Smith, N R Beatson, D J Hillier
**US SIC:** 1799 **UK SIC:** 50000

| | 31-03-14 | 31-03-13 | 31-03-12 |
|---|---|---|---|
| TA | 3,325,935 | 2,919,285 | 1,537,820 |
| NW | 270,413 | 212,957 | 130,519 |
| WC | 242,583 | 219,941 | 130,519 |

DUNS 49-137-5101

## Study Group Uk Ltd

**(Subsidiary of:** Edu Luxco Sarl)
1 Billinton Way, Brighton, East Sussex BN1 4LF
**Tel:** 01273339333
**Reg No:** 3108030 **Estd:** 1995 Private Limited Company
**Line of Business:** Primary education
**Export Sales:** £4,906,424
**Trading Style:** Study Group
**Issued Capital:** £1,596,818
**Directors:** A C Petersen, J H Pitman, T J Coope, Mrs E V Lancaster
**Co. Secretary:** Gordon Bull
**Branches:** Study Group Uk Ltd, Arbury Road, Cambridge, Cambridgeshire CB4 2JF
**US SIC:** 8211 **UK SIC:** 93200
**Auditors:** Deloitte & Touche LLP
**Bankers:** National Westminster Bank Plc (53-61-02)

| | 31-12-13 | 31-12-12 | 31-12-11 |
|---|---|---|---|
| TO | 5,713,125 | 4,642,373 | 4,703,666 |
| P/L | 47,513,747 | (22,647,261) | 25,800,238 |
| NW | 30,668,444 | 8,952,538 | 27,719,178 |
| WC | 121,177,541 | 119,310,536 | 75,538,041 |
| Emp. | 293 | 287 | 227 |

DUNS 28-885-6735

## The Study (Wimbledon) Ltd

Peek Crescent Wimbledon, London SW19 5ER
**Tel:** 02089476969 **Fax:** 020-8944-5980
**Web:** www.thestudyprep.co.uk
**Reg No:** 1229741 **Estd:** 1975 Private Company Limited By Guarantee
**Line of Business:** Schools (independent)
**Trading Style:** Study Preparatory School
**Directors:** L Jacobson, Ms J Downs, N G Brookes, C Holloway, R Healey, Mrs J C Dwyer, Mrs T A Pritchard-Drummond, K Greenhalgh
**Co. Secretary:** Mrs Hilary Hunter
**Responsibilities**
**Senior:** Brian Bennetts *(Manager)*, Christine Facon *(Director)*, Simon Pole *(Director)*
**US SIC:** 8211 **UK SIC:** 93200
**Auditors:** Arnold Hill & Co
**Bankers:** Barclays Bank Plc (20-96-89)

| | 31-08-14 | 31-08-13 | 31-08-12 |
|---|---|---|---|
| TO | 3,764,441 | 3,607,189 | 3,268,833 |
| P/L | 491,416 | 476,499 | 430,184 |
| NW | 6,110,599 | 5,619,183 | 5,142,684 |
| WC | 4,670,464 | 4,426,707 | 4,251,523 |
| Emp. | 68 | 66 | 68 |

DUNS 22-217-3218

## Stuff-Uk Ltd

Radiant House, 2 Davis Road, Chessington, Surrey KT9 1TT
**Tel:** 08702353637
**Web:** www.stuff-uk.net
**Reg No:** 4235327 **Estd:** 2001 Private Limited Company
**Line of Business:** Computer systems and software (sales)
**Issued Capital:** £50,100
**Director:** J Gordon
**Co. Secretary:** Alan Stanley
**Responsibilities**
**Finance:** annette turner *(credit controller)*
**US SIC:** 5081 **UK SIC:** 61490
**Auditors:** Howard & Co
**Bankers:** National Westminster Bank Plc (60-60-02)

| | 30-06-13 | 30-06-12 | 30-06-11 |
|---|---|---|---|
| TA | 300,118 | 214,649 | 255,730 |
| NW | 64,336 | 36,780 | 23,804 |
| WC | 18,856 | (17,971) | 144 |

DUNS 23-663-2597 Imp

## Sturrock & Robson (Uk) Ltd

**(Subsidiary of:** Sturrock and Robson International B.V.)
Nailsworth Mills Estate, Avening Road, Nailsworth, Stroud, Gloucestershire GL6 0BS
**Tel:** 01453833381
**Web:** www.sturrockandrobson.co.za
**Reg No:** 3658217 **Estd:** 1998 Private Limited Company
**Line of Business:** Management activities of holding companies
**Export Sales:** £10,114,000
**Trading Style:** Fluid Tranfer
**Issued Capital:** £100
**Directors:** T W Robson, J M Little, D G Mech, B E Purchon, J Hunter
**Co. Secretary:** Reuben Shamuyarira
**Responsibilities**
**Senior:** Charles Bignell *(Manager)*
**Finance:** Richard Iles-Caine *(Financial Controller)*
**US SIC:** 6711 **UK SIC:** 83962
**Auditors:** KPMG LLP

| | 30-06-14 | 30-06-13 | 30-06-12 |
|---|---|---|---|
| TO | 16,561,000 | 31,154,000 | 22,045,000 |
| P/L | 223,000 | 2,852,000 | 1,763,000 |
| NW | 11,388,000 | 11,402,000 | 9,285,000 |
| WC | 14,335,000 | 15,008,000 | 12,662,000 |
| Emp. | 133 | 133 | 132 |

DUNS 89-620-7727

## Stv Central Ltd

Pacific Quay, Glasgow, Lanarkshire G51 1PQ
**Tel:** 01382591005 **Fax:** 0141-300-3030
**Web:** www.stv.tv
**Reg No:** 0172149SC **Estd:** 1965 Private Limited Company
**Line of Business:** Television activities
**Issued Capital:** £2,567,001
**Principals:** R Hain *(Managing)*, W G Watt, A S Brown, P Reilly, Mrs E Partyka, R S Woodward, Ms S Burns
**Co. Secretary:** Ms Jane Tames
**US SIC:** 4833 **UK SIC:** 97411
**Auditors:** PricewaterhouseCoopers LLP
**Bankers:** Clydesdale Bank Plc (82-64-12)

| | 31-12-13 | 31-12-12 | 31-12-11 |
|---|---|---|---|
| TO | 76,277,000 | 67,347,000 | 65,415,000 |
| P/L | 8,834,000 | 4,780,000 | (4,136,000) |
| NW | 15,607,000 | 8,935,000 | 5,498,000 |
| WC | 61,757,000 | 54,161,000 | 49,288,000 |
| Emp. | 195 | 178 | 168 |

DUNS 23-933-7806 Imp-Exp

## Stv Group Plc

Pacific Quay, Glasgow, Lanarkshire G51 1DZ
**Tel:** 01413003300 **Fax:** 01413-003030
**Web:** www.stvplc.tv
**Reg No:** 0203873SC **Estd:** 2000 Public Limited Company
**Line of Business:** Management activities of holding companies
**Export Sales:** £1,200,000
**Trading Style:** Stv Central, Stv North, Solutions.Tv, Stv.Tv
**Issued Capital:** £19,525,110
**Directors:** Ms A M Cannon, D J Shearer, Baroness M Ford, J G Matheson, Ms G Shore, W G Watt, M Jackson, C Woolfenden
**Co. Secretary:** Ms Jane Tames
**Responsibilities**
**Senior:** Richard Findlay *(Chairman)*
**Marketing:** Eleanor Marshall *(PR & Communications Manager)*
**Facilities:** Tom Durham *(Facilities Manager)*
**Branches:** Stv Group Plc, Pavilion, Craigshaw Business Park, Craigshaw Road, West Tullos I, Aberdeen, Aberdeenshire AB12 3QH
**US SIC:** 4833, 4899
**UK SIC:** 97411, 79020
**Auditors:** PricewaterhouseCoopers LLP
**Bankers:** Bank Of Scotland (80-12-80)

| | 31-12-13 | 31-12-12 | 31-12-11 |
|---|---|---|---|
| TO | 112,100,000 | 102,700,000 | 102,000,000 |
| P/L | 14,300,000 | 9,100,000 | (900,000) |
| NW | (1,000,000) | (28,800,000) | (37,600,000) |
| WC | (14,200,000) | 19,400,000 | (28,500,000) |
| Emp. | 396 | 376 | 387 |

DUNS 23-116-2983

## Stv Productions Ltd

Pacific Quay, Glasgow, Lanarkshire G51 1DZ
**Tel:** 0141-300-3000
**Web:** www.stv.tv
**Reg No:** 0139254SC **Estd:** 1992 Private Limited Company
**Line of Business:** Television activities
**Issued Capital:** £1,000
**Directors:** A Clements, W G Watt, R S Woodward, P Sheehan
**Co. Secretary:** Ms Jane Tames
**US SIC:** 4833, 8999
**UK SIC:** 97411, 83954

**Auditors:** PricewaterhouseCoopers LLP

| | 31-12-13 | 31-12-12 | 31-12-11 |
|---|---|---|---|
| TO | 13,857,000 | 10,084,000 | 9,836,000 |
| P/L | (129,000) | (271,000) | 80,000 |
| NW | 469,000 | 582,000 | 854,000 |
| WC | 12,839,000 | 12,937,000 | 13,209,000 |
| Emp. | 103 | 98 | 61 |

DUNS 21-150-4063 Exp

## Stva Uk Ltd

**(Subsidiary of:** Soc Nat Des Chemins De Fer Franc)
1st Floor Street Andrews House, St Andrews Road, Avonmouth, Bristol, Avon BS11 9DQ
**Tel:** 01454-410200 **Fax:** 01454-410230
**Web:** www.stva.com
**Reg No:** 1150563 **VAT No:** 657113835
**Estd:** 1973 Private Limited Company
**Line of Business:** Transportation consultants
**Export Markets:** E U
**Issued Capital:** £3,707,329
**Directors:** J Floret, P G Tapparo, F Briand, A Ritz
**Co. Secretary:** Ian Brown
**Responsibilities**
**Senior:** Pierre Enderle *(Chairman / Executive Managing)*
**Branches:** Stva Uk Ltd, 1 26 Whitburn Road, Bathgate, West Lothian EH48 1HE
**US SIC:** 4213 **UK SIC:** 72300
**Auditors:** Ernst & Young LLP
**Bankers:** HSBC Bank plc (40-14-13)

| | 31-12-13 | 31-12-12 | 31-12-11 |
|---|---|---|---|
| TO | 34,316,000 | 30,165,000 | 26,296,000 |
| P/L | 1,210,000 | 1,700,000 | 1,592,000 |
| NW | 3,490,000 | 1,881,000 | 267,000 |
| WC | 3,760,000 | 2,563,000 | 850,000 |
| Emp. | 48 | 49 | 43 |

DUNS 21-005-8122

## Style Accessories Ltd

17 The Arcade, Westgate, Peterborough, Cambridgeshire PE1 1PY
**Fax:** 01733373325
**Web:** www.co-op.co.uk
**Reg No:** 6304072 **Estd:** 2007 Private Limited Company
**Line of Business:** Retail sale of jewellery, clocks and watches
**Issued Capital:** £100
**Director:** Ms S I Marshall
**Co. Secretary:** Barry Marshall
**Responsibilities**
**Senior:** Tuncay Korkmaz *(Operations Manager)*
**Admin:** Sugrah Bibi *(Office Manager)*
**HR:** Tuncay Korkmaz *(Operations Manager)*, Joanne Pearson *(Training Officer)*
**Health & Safety:** Joanne Pearson *(Training Officer)*
**Facilities:** Tuncay Korkmaz *(Operations Manager)*
**US SIC:** 5944, 4213
**UK SIC:** 65400, 72300

| | 30-09-13 | 30-09-12 | 30-09-11 |
|---|---|---|---|
| TA | 251,402 | 268,054 | 180,512 |
| NW | 180,019 | 200,603 | 119,808 |
| WC | 160,284 | 185,079 | 109,407 |

DUNS 21-606-3994

## Style Commercial T A Ecocleen

14 Aragon Close, Ashford, Kent TN23 5DH
**Tel:** 01233639253
**Estd:** 2011 Proprietorship
**Line of Business:** Commercial premises cleaning
**Proprietor:** P Tiltman
**US SIC:** 7349 **UK SIC:** 92300
**Employees:** 50

DUNS 23-947-9491

## Style Group U K Ltd

**(Subsidiary of:** Safestyle Uk Plc)
Style House, Eldon Place, Bradford, West Yorkshire BD1 3AZ
**Tel:** 01274-842000
**Web:** www.safestyle.co.uk
**Reg No:** 3937383 **Estd:** 2000 Private Limited Company
**Line of Business:** Management activities of holding companies
**Issued Capital:** £1,085,000
**Directors:** S J Birmingham, M J Robinson, K K Kisra
**Co. Secretary:** Richard Short
**US SIC:** 6711 **UK SIC:** 83962
**Auditors:** Baker Tilly
**Bankers:** HSBC Bank plc (40-27-15)

| | 31-12-13 | 31-12-12 | 31-12-11 |
|---|---|---|---|
| TO | 124,796,392 | 110,242,918 | 98,572,164 |
| P/L | 11,875,841 | 9,529,091 | 7,437,914 |
| NW | 18,098,884 | 21,438,635 | 14,342,161 |
| WC | 13,849,739 | 21,304,638 | 14,591,729 |
| Emp. | 625 | 583 | 548 |

DUNS 28-978-3003

## Style Motors Ltd

Wych Hill Hook Heath, Woking, Surrey GU22 0EU
**Tel:** 01252 367300
**Web:** www.smcrenault.co.uk
**Reg No:** 1766596 **VAT No:** 384399110
**Estd:** 1985 Private Limited Company
**Line of Business:** Car dealers (new & used)
**Trading Style:** S M C Renault
**Issued Capital:** £300,000
**Principals:** J N Kimber *(Managing)*, T M Golding, K P Wheeler, Ms A F Knight, S J Lillywhite
**Co. Secretary:** Andrew Smith
**Responsibilities**
**HR:** Kate Graham *(Human Resources Manager)*
**Branches:** Style Motors Ltd, Wych Hill, Woking, Surrey GU22 0EU
**US SIC:** 5511 **UK SIC:** 65100
**Auditors:** Wise & Co
**Bankers:** Barclays Bank Plc (20-35-35)

| | 31-03-14 | 31-03-13 | 31-03-12 |
|---|---|---|---|
| TO | 23,782,039 | 12,481,766 | 10,959,072 |
| P/L | 265,531 | 132,678 | (59,435) |
| NW | 752,588 | 643,774 | 609,736 |
| WC | 698,139 | 576,847 | 549,498 |

DUNS 23-508-5805

## Styles & Brown Ltd

Unit 10, Weycroft Avenue, Millwey Rise Industrial Estate, Axminster, Devon EX13 5PH
**Tel:** 03332406406
**Reg No:** 3507847 **Estd:** 1998 Private Limited Company
**Line of Business:** Other retail sale in non-specialised stores
**Export Sales:** £3,244,787
**Issued Capital:** £100,004
**Directors:** I V Styles, Mrs K J Styles, A V Styles, B G Styles
**Co. Secretary:** Andrew Thomas
**Branches:** Styles & Brown Ltd, Mcneil House, George Street, Axminster, Devon EX13 5DP
**US SIC:** 5399, 5251
**UK SIC:** 65600, 64800
**Bankers:** HSBC Bank plc (40-20-30)

| | 30-04-14 | 30-04-13 | 30-04-12 |
|---|---|---|---|
| TO | 34,303,075 | 32,867,326 | 31,492,339 |
| P/L | 478,312 | 214,472 | 390,780 |
| NW | 4,269,001 | 3,857,358 | 3,799,862 |
| WC | 984,876 | 1,043,611 | 1,023,649 |
| Emp. | 248 | 230 | 232 |

DUNS 34-822-4135

## Styles & Wood Group Plc

Aspect House, Manchester Road, West Timperley, Altrincham, Cheshire WA14 5PG
**Tel:** 0161-926-6000 **Fax:** 01619266001
**Web:** www.stylesandwood.co.uk
**Reg No:** 5622016 **Estd:** 2005 Public Limited Company
**Line of Business:** Management activities of holding companies
**Issued Capital:** £35,455,958
**Directors:** R E Hough, A S Lenehan, P Mitchell
**Co. Secretary:** Philip Lanigan
**Responsibilities**
**Senior:** Andy Byrne *(Divisional Managing Director)*, Neal Handforth *(Service & Development Director)*
**Finance:** Colin Baines *(Account Principal)*
**Marketing:** Neal Handforth *(Service & Development Director)*
**Sales:** Steve Wilton *(Head of Retail)*
**HR:** Tina Clayton *(HR Advisor)*, Karen Morley *(HR Director)*
**Operations:** Steve Ramsden *(Operations Director)*
**US SIC:** 6711 **UK SIC:** 83962
**Auditors:** PricewaterhouseCoopers LLP

| | 31-12-13 | 31-12-12 | 31-12-11 |
|---|---|---|---|
| TO | 93,983,000 | 97,937,000 | 101,011,000 |
| P/L | (515,000) | 806,000 | 479,000 |
| NW | (7,254,000) | (6,513,000) | (6,731,000) |
| WC | 1,433,000 | 2,308,000 | 2,054,000 |
| Emp. | 310 | 327 | 290 |

DUNS 76-918-4573 Imp

## Stylex Auto Products Ltd

**(Subsidiary of:** Rubicon Partners Industries Llp)
2 Atkinsons Way, Foxhills Industrial Estate, Scunthorpe, South Humberside DN15 8QJ
**Tel:** 01724272400
**Web:** www.stylex.co.uk
**Reg No:** 1378507 **VAT No:** 555421940
**Estd:** 1978 Private Limited Company
**Line of Business:** Manufacturers of transport equipment
**Export Sales:** £1,212,000
**Trading Style:** Stylex
**Issued Capital:** £9,901
**Directors:** A O Fischer, I Fisher, A C Ross, A T Fletcher
**Co. Secretary:** Jonathan Richardson

**Responsibilities**
**Purchasing:** Aurora Bateson *(Head of Purchasing)*
**Branches:** Stylex Auto Products Ltd, Stylex House, Northern Way, Bury St. Edmunds, Suffolk IP32 6NL
**US SIC:** 3711, 2279
**UK SIC:** 35101, 43852
**Auditors:** PricewaterhouseCoopers LLP
**Bankers:** Lloyds TSB Bank plc (30-97-44)

| | 31-12-13 | 31-12-12 | 31-12-11 |
|---|---|---|---|
| TO | 5,823,000 | 4,684,000 | 4,180,000 |
| P/L | 59,000 | 73,000 | 68,000 |
| NW | 1,511,000 | 1,463,000 | 1,405,000 |
| WC | 1,339,000 | 1,366,000 | 1,325,000 |
| Emp. | 55 | 54 | 35 |

DUNS 21-013-1523
## Subaqua Solutions Ltd
**(Subsidiary of:** Kkr & Co. L.P.)
Unit 1.1 Discovery House, Gemini Crescent, Dundee Technology Park, Dundee, Angus DD2 1SW
**Tel:** 01382-568462 **Fax:** 01382562055
**Web:** www.hydrosave.co.uk
**Reg No:** 0330437SC **Estd:** 2007 Private Limited Company
**Line of Business:** Irrigation systems design and development
**Trading Style:** Hydrosave (Dundee) Limited
**Issued Capital:** £990
**Directors:** S Dray, A P Page
**Co. Secretary:** Jason Goodwin
**Responsibilities**
**Senior:** Michelle Birse *(Manager)*
**US SIC:** 8999 **UK SIC:** 83954
**Auditors:** Bird Simpson & Co

| | 31-03-14 | 31-03-13 | 31-03-12 |
|---|---|---|---|
| TA | 1 | 1,000 | 1,000 |
| P/L | N/A | N/A | 247,000 |
| NW | 1 | 1,000 | 1,000 |

DUNS 22-172-5745
## Subex (Uk) Ltd
**(Subsidiary of:** Subex Limited)
Subex (Uk) Limited, 3rd Floor Finsbury Tower, 103-105 Bunhill Row, London EC1Y 8LZ
**Tel:** 02078-265-420 **Fax:** 02078-265-437
**Web:** www.subexworld.com
**Reg No:** 4190929 **Estd:** 2001 Private Limited Company
**Line of Business:** Computer programming & software services
**Export Sales:** £12,987,000
**Issued Capital:** £50,396
**Directors:** S Singh, V K Padmanabhan, G Kangeyam Venkataramanan
**Co. Secretary:** Ganesh Kangeyam Venkataramanan
**US SIC:** 7372, 4899, 7379, 7374
**UK SIC:** 83940, 79020
**Auditors:** Ensors
**Bankers:** HSBC Bank plc (40-42-08)

| | 31-03-14 | 31-03-13 | 31-03-12 |
|---|---|---|---|
| TO | 18,265,000 | 19,670,000 | 26,697,000 |
| P/L | 1,134,000 | 1,012,000 | 4,093,000 |
| NW | 13,696,000 | 12,818,000 | 12,088,000 |
| WC | 13,666,000 | 12,755,000 | 11,938,000 |
| Emp. | 63 | 71 | 91 |

DUNS 23-693-2166 Imp
## Submarine Manufacturing & Products Ltd
**(Subsidiary of:** Mss Holdings (Uk) Ltd)
Fleetwood Road, Preston, Lancashire PR4 3HD
**Tel:** 01772687775
**Web:** www.smp-ltd.co.uk
**Reg No:** 2608984 **Estd:** 1991 Private Limited Company
**Line of Business:** Diving equipment
**Issued Capital:** £100
**Principals:** P J Connolly *(Managing)*, A Scott
**Co. Secretary:** Ms Joanne Connolly
**Responsibilities**
**Senior:** David Ormsby *(Financial Director)*
**Finance:** David Ormsby *(Financial Director)*
**Marketing:** Ross Connolly *(Marketing Manager)*
**Admin:** Debbie Ellis *(Workshop & QA Coordinator)*
**HR:** David Ormsby *(Financial Director)*
**Health & Safety:** Debbie Ellis *(Workshop & QA Coordinator)*
**US SIC:** 3811 **UK SIC:** 37100
**Auditors:** Mills Adams
**Bankers:** Yorkshire Bank Plc (05-02-67)

| | 31-12-13 | 31-12-12 | 31-12-11 |
|---|---|---|---|
| TA | 4,491,078 | 4,125,014 | 4,268,690 |
| NW | 1,335,109 | 2,079,052 | 2,122,764 |
| WC | 1,076,830 | 1,925,255 | 1,979,840 |

DUNS 22-952-5258
## Subsea 7 Crewing Ltd
**(Subsidiary of:** Jarius Investments Limited)
200 Hammersmith Road, London W6 7DL
**Tel:** 020 8210 5500 **Fax:** 020 8210 5501
**Web:** www.subsea7.com
**Reg No:** 1130356 **Estd:** 1973 Private Limited Company
**Line of Business:** Other service activities not elsewhere classified
**Directors:** S A Mcneill, J A Gordon, J R Tame
**Co. Secretary:** Subsea 7 M.S. Limited
**Responsibilities**
**Senior:** Gael Cailleaux *(Manager)*
**Branches:** 16 Besselmer Way, Great Yarmouth
**US SIC:** 8999 **UK SIC:** 83954
**Auditors:** Deloitte LLP
**Bankers:** National Westminster Bank Plc (60-30-22)
**Employees:** 50
**Turnover:** £646,506,000

DUNS 22-298-8003 Imp
## Subsea 7 Ltd
**(Subsidiary of:** Jarius Investments Limited)
East Campus, Westhill, Aberdeenshire AB32 6FE
**Tel:** 01224-526-000 **Fax:** 01224-344-600
**Web:** www.subsea7.com
**Reg No:** 4316695 **VAT No:** 804143174
**Estd.** 2003 Private Limited Company
**Line of Business:** Building construction contractors
**Issued Capital:** £75,621,000
**Directors:** S G Wisely, J A Gordon, G C Sharland, S A Mcneill, S D Ellis, Ms P Murray, P J Simons
**Co. Secretary:** Ms Lorna Peace
**Responsibilities**
**Senior:** Jean Cahuzac *(Vice President)*, Oeyvind Mikaelsen *(Director)*
**Sales:** Graeme Kinnell *(UK Business Development Direct)*, Don Shaw *(Business Development Manager)*
**IT:** Gordon McCaw *(IT Manager)*
**Facilities:** Bill McDonald *(Facilities Manager)*
**Purchasing:** John Cardno *(Purchasing Manager)*, Andrew Strachan *(Purchasing Manager)*
**Branches:** Subsea 7 Ltd, Greenwell Base, Greenwell Road, Aberdeen, Aberdeenshire AB12 3AX
**US SIC:** 1629, 1381, 1382
**UK SIC:** 50000, 13000
**Auditors:** Deloitte LLP
**Bankers:** HSBC Bank plc (40-01-25)
**Following financial data are in thousands**

| | 31-12-13 | 31-12-12 | 31-12-11 |
|---|---|---|---|
| TO | 1,193,374 | 992,352 | 812,917 |
| P/L | 120,759 | 121,706 | 10,356 |
| NW | 717,301 | 705,248 | 77,572 |
| WC | 103,796 | 106,107 | 85,016 |

DUNS 22-904-6842
## Subsea 7 Pipeline Production Ltd
**(Subsidiary of:** Jarius Investments Limited)
Riverclyde House, Erskine Ferry Road, Old Kilpatrick, Glasgow, Lanarkshire G60 5EU
**Tel:** 01389801700 **Fax:** 01389801701
**Web:** www.subsea7.com
**Reg No:** 0078566SC **VAT No:** 369126239
**Estd:** 1982 Private Limited Company
**Line of Business:** Building construction contractors
**Issued Capital:** £20,500
**Directors:** K Rassouli-Saniabadi, L S Duthie, D A Wilson Cormell, J Mcconnell, J R Tame
**Responsibilities**
**IT:** Jeff Atkins *(Head of IT)*
**Branches:** Subsea 7 Pipeline Production Ltd, Riverclyde House, Erskine Ferry Road, Glasgow, Lanarkshire G60 5EU
**US SIC:** 1522, 5199
**UK SIC:** 50100, 61900
**Auditors:** PricewaterhouseCoopers LLP
**Bankers:** Clydesdale Bank Plc (82-47-07)

| | 31-12-13 | 31-12-12 | 31-12-11 |
|---|---|---|---|
| TO | 40,077,890 | 31,625,391 | 29,052,310 |
| P/L | 1,597,245 | 1,762,643 | 386,323 |
| NW | 14,191,630 | 4,122,993 | 12,271,749 |
| WC | (535,022) | (4,613,709) | 6,479,388 |

DUNS 73-843-0276
## Subsea Uk
Innovation Centre, Aberdeen, Aberdeenshire AB23 8GX
**Tel:** 08455053535
**Web:** www.subseauk.org
**Reg No:** 0266233SC **Estd:** 2004 Private Company Limited By Guarantee
**Line of Business:** Trade and business organisations
**Directors:** T N Gordon, W Edgar, J A Mair
**Co. Secretary:** Mrs Patricia Banks

**Responsibilities**
**Senior:** Trish Banks *(Manager)*
**US SIC:** 8611 **UK SIC:** 96312
**Auditors:** Simpson Forsyth

| | 31-03-14 | 31-03-13 | 31-03-12 |
|---|---|---|---|
| TA | 1,276,838 | 1,312,585 | 825,574 |
| NW | 985,696 | 787,159 | 553,475 |
| WC | 964,085 | 762,504 | 550,001 |

DUNS 21-413-6437
## Subway
53-55 Gatwick Road, Crawley, West Sussex RH10 9RD
**Tel:** 01293535605
**Web:** www.subway.com
**Estd:** 2010 Proprietorship
**Line of Business:** Take away meal outlets
**Proprietor:** S Byrne
**US SIC:** 5961 **UK SIC:** 65600
**Employees:** 100

DUNS 34-811-6422
## Successfactors Uk Ltd
**(Subsidiary of:** Sap Se)
The Oriel Sydenham Road, Guildford, Surrey GU1 3SR
**Fax:** 020-7153-1111
**Web:** www.successfactors.com
**Reg No:** 5611507 **Estd:** 2005 Private Limited Company
**Line of Business:** Hardware consultancy
**Export Sales:** £20,205,333
**Issued Capital:** £1
**Director:** Ms H B Smith
**US SIC:** 7379 **UK SIC:** 83940
**Auditors:** KPMG LLP

| | 31-12-13 | 31-12-12 | 31-12-11 |
|---|---|---|---|
| TO | 20,205,333 | 14,271,982 | 9,156,599 |
| P/L | 961,948 | 679,618 | 436,027 |
| NW | 335,461 | 15,452 | 1,335,195 |
| WC | 202,257 | (175,734) | 1,143,154 |
| Emp. | 99 | 79 | 53 |

DUNS 21-115-2012 Exp
## Sucden Financial Ltd
**(Subsidiary of:** Sucres Et Denrees)
Plantation Place South, 60 Great Tower Street, London EC3R 5AZ
**Tel:** 02032075800 **Fax:** 020 3207 5010
**Web:** www.comfinfunds.com
**Reg No:** 1095841 **Estd:** 1973 Private Limited Company
**Line of Business:** Financial services
**Export Markets:** Worldwide
**Issued Capital:** £16,500,000
**Directors:** J D Goldwyn, S E Demal, M Breillout, S Varsano, T Bourvis, M Overlander, R James
**Co. Secretary:** Jonathan Tunnell
**Responsibilities**
**Senior:** Robert Montefusco *(General Manager)*
**Marketing:** Robert Cantle *(Marketing & Communications Man)*
**Admin:** Ann Livett *(Office Manager)*
**Health & Safety:** Ann Livett *(Office Manager)*
**Facilities:** Ann Livett *(Office Manager)*
**US SIC:** 6111 **UK SIC:** 81501
**Auditors:** KPMG Audit PLC
**Bankers:** National Westminster Bank Plc (50-00-00)

| | 31-12-13 | 31-12-12 | 31-12-11 |
|---|---|---|---|
| TA | 401,084,197 | 388,953,164 | 347,068,902 |
| P/L | 13,314,378 | 42,968,739 | 12,253,803 |
| NW | 71,629,284 | 62,863,549 | 66,462,962 |
| WC | 66,974,060 | 68,468,972 | 48,047,993 |
| Emp. | 178 | 176 | 169 |

DUNS 29-500-3792 Imp
## Suckling Airways (Cambridge) Ltd
**(Subsidiary of:** Airline Investments Ltd)
Atlas House, Cambridge Place, Cambridge, Cambridgeshire CB2 1NS
**Tel:** 01223293777 **Fax:** 01223292160
**Web:** www.scotairways.co.uk
**Reg No:** 1863628 **VAT No:** 720301988
**Estd:** 1986 Private Limited Company
**Line of Business:** Scheduled passenger air transport
**Trading Style:** Suckling Airways
**Issued Capital:** £14,352,759
**Directors:** P G Preston, D A Harrison, S A Adams
**Responsibilities**
**Senior:** Marlyn Suckling *(Manager)*
**Finance:** Stuart Mott *(Financial Director)*
**Branches:** Hanger 125, Percival Way, Luton
**US SIC:** 4511 **UK SIC:** 75000
**Auditors:** Peters Elworthy & Moore
**Bankers:** The Royal Bank Of Scotland Plc (16-53-60)

| | 31-03-13 | 31-03-12 |
|---|---|---|
| TA | 4,659,719 | 5,939,282 |
| NW | 2,883,275 | 2,124,780 |
| WC | 2,873,911 | 1,800,713 |

DUNS 21-808-8210
## Suda Thai Restaurant
23 Slingsby Place, London WC2E 9AB
**Tel:** 02072408010
**Web:** www.suda-thai.com
**Estd:** 2011
**Line of Business:** Restaurant - thai
**Responsibilities**
**Senior:** Vasan Kanthont *(Manager)*, Tinna Korn *(Manager)*
**US SIC:** 5812 **UK SIC:** 66110
**Employees:** 50

DUNS 21-809-8965
## Sudbury Congregation of Jehovah's Witnesses
Kingdom Hall 6 Station Road, Sudbury, Suffolk CO10 2SP
**Tel:** 01787-880839
**Web:** www.jw.org
**Estd:** 2012
**Line of Business:** Places of worship
**US SIC:** 8661 **UK SIC:** 96600
**Employees:** 120

DUNS 22-665-3186 Imp
## Sue Ryder
King House, King Street, Sudbury, Suffolk CO10 2EG
**Tel:** 01787314205
**Web:** www.sueryder.org
**Reg No:** 0943228 **VAT No:** 927507902
**Estd:** 1968 Private Company Limited By Guarantee
**Line of Business:** Charity shops
**Trading Style:** Ryder Sue
**Directors:** Ms C Edwards, K G Cameron, Dr D M Walford, Rev D J Stoter, Ms L J Riches, J M Wythe, M C Duncanson, Ms M A Moore
**Co. Secretary:** Ms Helen Organ
**Responsibilities**
**Senior:** Michael Attwood *(Director)*, Roger Paffard *(Director)*
**HR:** Alison Cadman *(Human Resources Business Manag)*
**Facilities:** Martin Bullen *(Head of Estates Management)*
**Branches:** Sue Ryder, 86 Edinburgh Place, Cheltenham, Gloucestershire GL51 7SE
**US SIC:** 8321 **UK SIC:** 96111
**Auditors:** BDO LLP
**Bankers:** Lloyds TSB Bank plc (30-94-55)

| | 31-03-14 | 31-03-13 | 31-03-12 |
|---|---|---|---|
| TO | 90,347,000 | 83,881,000 | 78,689,000 |
| P/L | 410,000 | 1,285,000 | (3,204,000) |
| NW | 45,341,000 | 44,480,000 | 41,935,000 |
| WC | 11,563,000 | 9,870,000 | 9,165,000 |
| Emp. | 3,239 | 2,166 | 2,186 |

DUNS 21-274-2295
## Sue Ryder Care
First Floor, Kings House, Borehamgate Precinct, Sudbury, Suffolk CO10 2ED
**Tel:** 01787314200
**Web:** www.sueryder.org
**Estd:** 1968
**Line of Business:** Charity shops
**Responsibilities**
**Senior:** Caroline Stockmann *(Manager)*
**Branches:** Sue Ryder Care, 45 Connaught Ave, Frinton-On-Sea, Essex CO13 9PN
**US SIC:** 8699, 6732, 9121
**UK SIC:** 96902, 83100, 91110
**Employees:** 50

DUNS 21-033-7677
## Sue Ryder Care Wheatfields
Wood Lane Grove Road, Headingley, Leeds, West Yorkshire LS6 2AE
**Tel:** 01132-787249
**Web:** www.suerydercare.org
**Estd:** 2008 Proprietorship
**Line of Business:** Charities and charitable organisations
**Proprietor:** Mrs S Cheverton
**Responsibilities**
**Marketing:** Donna Woodman *(Fundraising Manager)*
**IT:** Alan Anslow *(Health & Safety Manager)*
**Health & Safety:** Alan Anslow *(Health & Safety Manager)*
**US SIC:** 6732 **UK SIC:** 83100
**Employees:** 110

DUNS 21-224-7219
## Suerider Care
58 High Street, Arbroath, Angus DD11 1AW
**Tel:** 01241878887
**Web:** www.suerydercare.org
**Estd:** 2003 Proprietorship
**Line of Business:** Home care service providers
**Proprietor:** G Butchart

**Responsibilities**
**Senior:** Lorraine Linton *(Care Manager)*
**US SIC:** 8699 **UK SIC:** 96902
**Employees:** 50

DUNS 23-993-3203
## Suffolk Coastal District Council
Council Offices, Melton Hill, Woodbridge, Suffolk IP12 1AU
**Tel:** 01394383789
**Web:** www.suffolkcoastal.gov.uk
**Estd:** 1974
**Line of Business:** Local government
**Principals:** P J Collicott *(Financial)*, T Griffin
**Responsibilities**
**Senior:** Liz Beighton *(Chairman)*, Jennie Catling *(Outdoor Playspace Development)*, Julia Catterwell *(Executive)*, Homira Javadi *(Financial Director)*, Rachel Nightingale *(Executive)*, Kate Rookyard *(Anti-Social Behaviour Officer)*, Sarah Shinnie *(Sports Development Officer)*, Jane Spivey *(Executive)*
**Finance:** David Ablett *(Senior Finance Administrator)*, Homira Javadi *(Financial Director)*, Alan McFarlane *(Head of Finance)*
**Marketing:** Patsy Dobson *(Development Management Team Le)*, Steve Henry *(Communications Manager)*, Viv Hotten *(Communications Manager)*, James Selby *(Councillor)*, Andy Smith *(Councillor)*, Ben Woolnough *(Senior Planning & Enforcement)*
**IT:** John Bax *(PC Manager)*
**HR:** Shani Howard *(Human Resources Manager)*
**Health & Safety:** Phil Gore *(Health & Safety Officer)*
**Branches:** Suffolk Coastal District Council, 91 Undercliff Road West, Felixstowe, Suffolk IP11 2AF
**US SIC:** 9121 **UK SIC:** 91110
**Bankers:** Barclays Bank Plc (20-98-07)
**Employees:** 200

DUNS 73-870-0231
## Suffolk Coastal Norse Ltd
(**Subsidiary of:** Norfolk Calibration Services)
Ufford Park Offices, Woodbridge, Suffolk IP13 6ET
**Tel:** 01394444000 **Fax:** 01394444042
**Web:** www.suffolkcoastalservices.co.uk
**Reg No:** 5124558 **Estd:** 2004 Private Limited Company
**Line of Business:** Collection and treatment of other waste
**Issued Capital:** £10
**Directors:** A J Nunn, A J Charvonia, P M Hawes, M T Emms, A J Merricks
**Co. Secretary:** Ms Hilary Jones
**Branches:** Suffolk Coastal Services Ltd, Ufford Park Offices, Great Yarmouth Road, Ufford, Woodbridge, Suffolk IP13 6ET
**US SIC:** 4953, 8999
**UK SIC:** 92110, 83954
**Bankers:** The Co-Operative Bank Plc (08-92-28)

| | 02-02-14 | 27-01-13 | 29-02-12 |
|---|---|---|---|
| TO | 11,926,426 | 11,616,965 | 11,318,407 |
| P/L | 280,751 | 331,830 | 286,706 |
| NW | (547,008) | (211,929) | 145,916 |
| WC | 1,140,192 | 896,541 | 659,196 |
| Emp. | 291 | 253 | 252 |

DUNS 22-747-3519
## Suffolk Constabulary
Police Headquarters, Martlesham Heath, Ipswich, Suffolk IP5 3QS
**Tel:** 01473613500
**Web:** www.suffolk.police.uk
**Estd:** 1970 Incorporate By Act Of Parliament
**Line of Business:** Representative office
**Directors:** A Coe, B Rogers
**Responsibilities**
**Senior:** Marian Graveling *(Head of HR)*, M Jelly *(Proprietor)*, Douglas Paxton *(Chief Constable)*
**Purchasing:** K Ramsey *(Buyer)*
**Branches:** Suffolk Constabulary, 34 Kings Road, Leiston, Suffolk IP16 4DA
**US SIC:** 9221 **UK SIC:** 91300
**Bankers:** Lloyds TSB Bank plc (30-94-55)
**Employees:** 400

DUNS 23-644-5243
## Suffolk County Council
Endeavour House, 8 Russell Road, Ipswich, Suffolk IP1 2BX
**Web:** www.suffolk.gov.uk
**Estd:** 1974
**Line of Business:** Local government
**Trading Style:** Rendlesham Community Primary School, Sandlings Primary School Sudbury Upper School, Hawthorn Drive Social Services Edgar Sewter Playschool, Schools' Choice
**Directors:** C Mole, M Elsey, A Pritchard, M Brown, J Owen, K Stevens, P Bye, Mrs L Holmer
**Responsibilities**
**Senior:** Gemma Adams *(Executive)*, Edward Alcock *(Elected Member - Thredling Div)*, Beth Andrews *(Executive)*, Joanne Austin *(Head Teacher)*, Sheila Bell *(Manager)*, Pam Boone *(Manager)*, Suzanne Buck *(General Manager)*, Sue Burstall *(Manager)*, Carol Carruthers *(Strategic Commissioner and Bus)*, Edwina Child *(Executive)*, Allison Coleman *(Manager)*, Claudia Costa *(Executive)*, Kerry Cozens *(Manager)*, Hannah Dunnett *(Program Manager)*, Phil Embury *(Area Manager)*, Emma Flint *(Environment Strategy Manager)*, Paul Freemind *(Manager)*, Lynn Gallant *(Executive)*, Chris Game *(Executive)*, John Godward *(Senior Manager)*, Linda Gower *(Business Support Coordinator)*, Clare Hammerton *(Senior Manager)*, Mark Hardingham *(Manager)*, Sue Hargadon *(Manager)*, Helen Heaps *(Senior Manager)*, Paul Hopfensperger *(Board Member)*, Susanna Johns *(Manager)*, Yvonne Kane *(Manager)*, Richard Kemp *(Board Member)*, Julia Kett *(Manager)*, Sue Lowndes *(Manager)*, Graeme Mateer *(General Manager)*, Sue Morgan *(Manager)*, Patricia O' Brien *(Manager)*, Ian Piddington *(Manager)*, Darrell Reeve *(General Manager)*, Ferial Rolfe *(Manager)*, Paulette Scott *(Manager)*, Caroline Sutton *(Manager)*, Jemima Thompson *(Executive)*, Julie Wilkes *(Manager)*
**Finance:** Claire Tolliday *(Head of Financial Inclusion an)*
**Marketing:** Adam Barnes *(Senior Strategic Communication)*, Helen Dodman *(Press Officer)*, Alison Dunnett *(Business Support Officer)*, Hayley Fisher *(Business Support Officer)*, Vince Gates *(Supporting People Manager ( Bu)*, Clare Good *(Business Support Manager)*, Lisa Grove *(Business Improvement Manager)*, Debbie Install *(Internal Communications Manage)*, Barrie Peers *(Commissioning Manager)*
**Sales:** Fran Toomey *(Business Development Manager)*, Dawn Turpin *(Business Development Manager)*, Kevin Wegg *(External Funding Specialist)*, Tim Wetton *(Business Partner, Strategic Bu)*
**Admin:** Nina Bettzieche *(Administrator)*, Sue Farrow *(Administrator)*, Kristiina Hope *(Administrative Officer)*, Val Lockwood *(Personal Assistant)*, Hugh Mackay *(Administrator)*, Shirley Whitwood *(PA)*
**IT:** David Grimmer *(Senior Manager)*
**HR:** Duncan Allan *(Training Director)*, Martin Bedwell *(Executive)*, Jean Cobbold *(Executive)*, Jaime Milton *(Human Resources)*, Christine Tremlett *(Executive)*
**Health & Safety:** Ian Bowell *(Community Safety Officer)*, David Daw *(Health and Safety Executive)*, Charlotte Foster *(Health and Safety Executive)*, Gary Phillips *(Chief Fire Officer)*
**Operations:** Stuart Boulter *(Production and Operations Mana)*, Allan Cadzow *(Assistant Director for Integra)*, Joanna Caruth *(Project Officer)*, Simon Cass *(Project Officer)*, Chris Dashper *(Programmes Manager)*, Rhodri Gardner *(Production and Operations Mana)*, Ruth Gillan *(Production and Operations Mana)*, Cheryl Paget *(Economic Development Project O)*, James Rolfe *(Project Officer)*, Andrew Tester *(Production and Operations Mana)*, Tina Wilson *(Head of Safeguarding)*
**Purchasing:** Ann Burton *(Purchasing Manager)*
**Fleet:** John Boutcher *(Assistant Area Manager, Transp)*, Sally Harper *(Passenger Transport Manager)*, Paul Horne *(Senior Transport Planner)*, Guy Mcgregor *(Roads And transport Director)*, Tracey Vobe *(Passenger Transport Manager)*
**Engineering:** Rachael Monk *(Assistant Archaeological Offic)*
**Branches:** Suffolk County Council, Airfield Industrial Park, Airfield Industrial Estate, Eye, Suffolk IP23 7HN
**US SIC:** 9121 **UK SIC:** 91110
**Bankers:** Lloyds TSB Bank plc (30-94-55)
**Employees:** 4,000

DUNS 21-112-5743
## Suffolk Disaster Recovery Ltd
(**Subsidiary of:** Ipplus Plc)
2 Melford Court, 2 The Havens, Ransomes Europark, Ipswich, Suffolk IP3 9SJ
**Tel:** 08444098560
**Web:** www.ancora.co.uk
**Reg No:** 6535461 **Estd:** 2012 Private Limited Company
**Line of Business:** Archive storage
**Issued Capital:** £2
**Director:** W A Catchpole
**Co. Secretary:** Robert Gordon
**Responsibilities**
**Senior:** Richard Clement *(Manager)*
**US SIC:** 4226 **UK SIC:** 77003

| | 30-06-14 | 30-06-13 | 30-06-12 |
|---|---|---|---|
| TA | 2 | 2 | 2 |
| NW | 2 | 2 | 2 |

DUNS 23-508-3370
## Suffolk Family Carers Ltd
Unit 6-8, Hillview Business Park, Old Ipswich Road, Ipswich, Suffolk IP6 0AJ
**Tel:** 01473-835400
**Web:** www.suffolk-carers.co.uk
**Reg No:** 3507600 **Estd:** 1998 Private Limited Company
**Line of Business:** Other human health activities
**Directors:** Mrs J Dillaway, Dr B Azvine, T A Ward, Mrs A Hulme, D P Johnson, Ms S Thomas, D H Weston, D P Eagles
**Responsibilities**
**Senior:** Jacqui Martin *(Chief Executive)*, Donald Mcelhinney *(Director)*, Brian Parrott *(Manager)*, Jean Zoller *(Manager)*
**US SIC:** 8091, 8321
**UK SIC:** 95200, 96111
**Auditors:** Ensors
**Bankers:** Lloyds TSB Bank plc (30-94-55)

| | 31-03-14 | 31-03-13 | 31-03-12 |
|---|---|---|---|
| TO | 2,790,811 | 2,498,839 | 1,969,722 |
| P/L | 176,945 | 290,652 | 209,202 |
| NW | 1,444,474 | 1,267,529 | 976,877 |
| WC | 1,434,062 | 1,265,285 | 973,927 |
| Emp. | 79 | 65 | 66 |

DUNS 21-581-3159
## Suffolk Fire & Rescue
Endeavour House, Russell Road, Ipswich, Suffolk IP1 2BX
**Tel:** 01473260588
**Web:** www.suffolkcc.gov.uk
**Estd:** 2007 Proprietorship
**Line of Business:** Fire stations
**Proprietor:** Mrs M Finbow
**Responsibilities**
**Senior:** M Alcock *(Principal)*, Helen Berry *(Support Services Manager)*
**US SIC:** 9224 **UK SIC:** 91400
**Employees:** 50

DUNS 29-232-7145
## Suffolk Life Pensions Ltd
(**Subsidiary of:** Legal & General Group Plc)
Suffolk Life, Ipswich, Suffolk IP1 1QJ
**Tel:** 01473213237 **Fax:** 08704148000
**Web:** www.suffolklife.co.uk
**Reg No:** 1180742 **Estd:** 2012 Private Limited Company
**Line of Business:** Pension funding
**Issued Capital:** £3,484,770
**Directors:** W A Self, Ms J A Ridgley, D P Fagan, Ms R A Chester, J M Bury, S T Lloyd, C F Jones
**Co. Secretary:** Legal & General Co Sec Limited
**Responsibilities**
**Senior:** Henry Catchpole *(Manager)*, Andrew Phipps *(Head Of Proposition)*, Nigel Rodgers *(Director)*
**Marketing:** Greg Kingston *(Head of Marketing and Proposit)*
**Sales:** Sean Osborne *(Head of Sales)*
**IT:** Nigel Rodgers *(Director)*
**Facilities:** Dominic Savage *(Property Director)*
**US SIC:** 6371, 6411
**UK SIC:** 82002, 83200
**Auditors:** PricewaterhouseCoopers LLP
**Bankers:** The Royal Bank Of Scotland Plc (16-26-30)

| | 31-12-13 | 31-12-12 | 31-12-11 |
|---|---|---|---|
| TO | 18,482,647 | 19,702,369 | 15,689,716 |
| P/L | 3,772,805 | 2,841,949 | 1,989,200 |
| NW | 11,038,055 | 8,910,387 | 8,152,076 |
| WC | 10,163,131 | 8,435,547 | 7,189,309 |
| Emp. | 210 | 205 | 205 |

DUNS 21-815-5737
## Suffolk Meat Traders Ltd
Grove Lane, Elmswell, Bury St Edmunds, Suffolk IP30 9HN
**Tel:** 01359-242500
**Web:** www.suffolkmeattradersltd.co.uk
**Reg No:** 0616304 **VAT No:** 103232533
**Estd:** 1954 Private Limited Company
**Line of Business:** Meat wholesalers
**Issued Capital:** £88
**Principals:** C J Arnold *(Chairman and Managing)*, D H Warner *(Managing)*, H C Moore, M A Hayward
**Co. Secretary:** Kurt Atwell
**Responsibilities**
**Senior:** Roy Challis *(Manager)*, Jim Craig *(General Manager)*, Gary Dedman *(Factory Manager)*
**Health & Safety:** Jim Craig *(General Manager)*
**Facilities:** Ivan Arnold *(Maintenance Manager)*
**US SIC:** 5147 **UK SIC:** 61700
**Auditors:** BDO Stoy Hayward
**Bankers:** Lloyds TSB Bank plc (30-94-55)

| | 03-01-14 | 30-12-12 | 30-01-11 |
|---|---|---|---|
| TO | 13,023,007 | 11,721,846 | 11,060,274 |
| P/L | (115,907) | (105,874) | 19,333 |
| NW | 2,546,243 | 2,662,150 | 2,767,982 |
| WC | 1,434,122 | 1,536,119 | 1,630,458 |
| Emp. | 54 | 52 | 50 |

DUNS 76-861-3663
## Suffolk Mind
Hyntle Barn, Silver Hill, Hintlesham, Ipswich, Suffolk IP8 3NJ
**Tel:** 01473652847 **Fax:** 01473-652105
**Web:** www.suffolkmind.org.uk
**Reg No:** 2611510 **Estd:** 1991 Private Limited Company
**Line of Business:** Counselling & advice services
**Directors:** A J Hanson, Dr C P Johnson, N J Suckling, J Tyndale-Biscoe, A George, Dr E K Brierly, Mrs J M Rose, D A Cocks
**Co. Secretary:** Alan Hanson
**Responsibilities**
**Senior:** David Mcquade *(Director)*, Jo Serla *(Chief Executive Officer)*
**Branches:** Suffolk Mind, The Willows, Station Approach, Saxmundham, Suffolk IP17 1BW
**US SIC:** 8321 **UK SIC:** 96111
**Auditors:** Edward Jones & Co
**Bankers:** Barclays Bank Plc (20-44-51)

| | 31-03-14 | 31-03-13 | 31-03-12 |
|---|---|---|---|
| TO | 2,153,362 | 2,836,091 | 4,756,857 |
| P/L | (272,253) | (34,470) | 24,334 |
| NW | 1,791,129 | 2,037,098 | 2,057,604 |
| WC | 620,092 | 1,174,910 | 1,160,365 |
| Emp. | 50 | 60 | 112 |

DUNS 22-845-3833
## Suffolk New College
Rope Walk, Ipswich, Suffolk IP4 1LT
**Tel:** 01473-382200 **Fax:** 01473230054
**Web:** www.suffolk.ac.uk
**Estd:** 1958 Incorporate By Act Of Parliament
**Line of Business:** Colleges (higher education)
**Director:** Professor D Miller
**Responsibilities**
**Senior:** Tracey Bailey *(Head of Marketing)*, Vikki Curtis *(Purchasing Manager)*, Dave Muller *(Principal)*
**Marketing:** Tracey Bailey *(Head of Marketing)*
**IT:** Burhan Loqueman *(Head of Network Services)*
**Facilities:** Vikki Curtis *(Purchasing Manager)*, Matthew Lake *(Facilities Manager)*
**Purchasing:** Vikki Curtis *(Purchasing Manager)*, Andrew Digby *(Purchasing Manager)*
**Branches:** Suffolk New College, 83 Main Road, Ipswich, Suffolk IP5 1AF
**US SIC:** 8221 **UK SIC:** 93100
**Employees:** 700

DUNS 21-781-8615
## Suffolk Probation Service
Dettingen Way, Bury St Edmunds, Suffolk IP33 3TU
**Tel:** 01284716600
**Web:** www.justice.gov.uk
**Estd:** 2011 Partnership
**Line of Business:** Probation services
**Partners:** Mrs K Layzel, Mrs K Layzell
**US SIC:** 9121 **UK SIC:** 91110
**Employees:** 50

DUNS 36-517-5731
## Suffolk West Primary Care Trust
Paper Mill Lane, Bramford, Ipswich, Suffolk IP8 4DE
**Tel:** 01473-770000
**Web:** www.suffolk.nhs.uk
**Estd:** 2006
**Line of Business:** Administration of the state and the economic and social policy of the community
**Trading Style:** Suffolk West Primary Care Trust, Stow Lodge Centre
**Principals:** A Mcwhirter *(Chairman)*, P Watson
**Responsibilities**
**Senior:** Alastair McWhirter *(Chairperson)*
**Health & Safety:** Lois Wreathall *(Health & Safety Coordinator)*
**Branches:** Suffolk West Primary Care Trust, Barking Road, Ipswich, Suffolk IP6 8EZ
**US SIC:** 9121, 8062
**UK SIC:** 91110, 95100
**Employees:** 160

DUNS 28-849-4578
## Suffolk Wildlife Trust Ltd
Brooke House, The Green, Ashbocking, Ipswich, Suffolk IP6 9JY
**Tel:** 01473-890089
**Web:** www.suffolkwildlifetrust.org
**Reg No:** 0695346 **Estd:** 1961 Private Limited Company
**Line of Business:** Botanical and zoological gardens and nature reserve activities
**Directors:** R Drayton, N C Farthing, S Roberts, I D Brown, A C Goymour, Ms D R Girling, J Cousins, Mrs D Goldsmith
**Co. Secretary:** James Robinson

**Responsibilities**
**Senior:** Kenneth Carlisle *(chairman)*, Mandy Emery *(Financial Manager)*, Philippa Goodwin *(Director)*, Peter Holborn *(Director)*, Terence Lock *(Manager)*, Mandy McNeill *(Financial Manager)*, Julian Roughton *(Chief Executive Officer)*
**Finance:** Mandy Emery *(Financial Manager)*, Mandy McNeill *(Financial Manager)*
**Marketing:** Chris Luxton *(Sales & Marketing Manager)*
**Sales:** Chris Luxton *(Sales & Marketing Manager)*
**Purchasing:** Carole Wilson *(Buyer)*
**Branches:** Suffolk Wildlife Trust Ltd, Saddlemakers Lane, Woodbridge, Suffolk IP12 1PP
**US SIC:** 8421 **UK SIC:** 97700
**Auditors:** Ensors
**Bankers:** Barclays Bank Plc (20-44-51)

| | 31-03-14 | 31-03-13 | 31-03-12 |
|---|---|---|---|
| TO | 3,074,000 | 2,815,000 | 2,945,000 |
| P/L | 728,000 | 712,000 | 1,143,000 |
| NW | 11,635,000 | 10,917,000 | 10,121,000 |
| WC | 4,493,000 | 3,906,000 | 3,879,000 |
| Emp. | 65 | 45 | 40 |

DUNS 21-039-5131
## Suffolk Young Enterprise
The Suffolk Enterprise Centre, Felaw Maltings, Ipswich, Suffolk IP2 8SJ
**Tel:** 01473407000
**Web:** www.nwes.org.uk
**Estd:** 2011
**Line of Business:** Serviced office facilities
**Responsibilities**
**Senior:** Edd Cottee *(Area Manager)*, Alison Morrissey *(Area Manager)*
**US SIC:** 9121 **UK SIC:** 91110
**Employees:** 100

DUNS 64-074-3233
## The Sugar Club Restaurants Ltd
13 Station Road, Finchley, London N3 2SB
**Tel:** 02089648225
**Web:** www.thegroceron.com
**Reg No:** 3469743 **Estd:** 1998 Private Limited Company
**Line of Business:** Licensed restaurants
**Trading Style:** Sugar Club Restaurants
**Issued Capital:** £100,100
**Director:** A Sumner
**Co. Secretary:** Ms Vivienne Hayman
**US SIC:** 5812 **UK SIC:** 66110

| | 30-09-13 | 30-09-12 | 30-09-11 |
|---|---|---|---|
| TA | 612,272 | 136,265 | 533,375 |
| NW | (203,470) | (163,343) | (155,244) |
| WC | (214,680) | (178,289) | (175,171) |

DUNS 21-175-1981 Imp
## Sugarich Ltd
Moorgate Road, Liverpool, Merseyside L33 7RX
**Tel:** 01515476710 **Fax:** 01515476718
**Web:** www.sugarich.co.uk
**Reg No:** 6987163 **Estd:** 1978 Private Limited Company
**Line of Business:** Mills and millers
**Issued Capital:** £100,000
**Directors:** P Latham, J S Knight, P Featherstone, D Evans, N A Keogh, A C Newton, P R Bright
**Co. Secretary:** Christopher Houghton
**Responsibilities**
**Senior:** David Jennison *(National Operations Manager)*
**Marketing:** Alex Keogh *(Commercial Director)*
**US SIC:** 2043 **UK SIC:** 42398

| | 30-04-14 | 30-04-13 | 30-04-12 |
|---|---|---|---|
| TO | 91,765,110 | 101,566,710 | 78,595,441 |
| P/L | 2,569,088 | 5,925,433 | 2,438,019 |
| NW | 3,520,753 | 1,510,082 | (2,735,285) |
| WC | (440,362) | (702,817) | (1,598,382) |
| Emp. | 168 | 158 | 131 |

DUNS 23-546-6195
## Sugarman Group Ltd
**(Subsidiary of:** Cordant Group Plc)
Fifth Floor, 120 Moorgate, London EC2M 6UR
**Tel:** 02076144250 **Fax:** 02074696898
**Web:** www.sugarman.co.uk
**Reg No:** 3545071 **Estd:** 2006 Private Limited Company
**Line of Business:** Labour recruitment and provision of personnel
**Issued Capital:** £125,313
**Directors:** J R Ullmann, S Kirkpatrick, P L Ullmann
**Co. Secretary:** Alan Connor
**Responsibilities**
**Senior:** Paul Sugarman *(Manager)*
**US SIC:** 7399, 8011
**UK SIC:** 83954, 95300
**Auditors:** Haslers

**Bankers:** HSBC Bank plc (40-02-18)

| | 30-06-14 | 30-04-13 | 30-06-12 |
|---|---|---|---|
| TO | 41,285,591 | 24,725,661 | 18,529,190 |
| P/L | 4,471,470 | 3,125,137 | 1,977,787 |
| NW | 8,337,440 | 5,078,963 | 3,049,006 |
| WC | 9,477,928 | 4,962,319 | 2,962,002 |
| Emp. | 63 | 53 | 46 |

DUNS 51-996-2666
## Suiko Ltd
Bath Brewery, Toll Bridge Road, Bath, Avon BA1 7DE
**Tel:** 01225-852400
**Web:** www.suiko.co.uk
**Reg No:** 3363376 **Estd:** 1997 Private Limited Company
**Line of Business:** Business and management consultancy activities not elsewhere classified
**Issued Capital:** £103,000
**Principals:** A D Marsh *(Managing)*, P J Austin, R C Lyle
**Co. Secretary:** Ms Sarah Kelly
**US SIC:** 7392 **UK SIC:** 83951
**Bankers:** National Westminster Bank Plc (57-00-00)

| | 30-04-14 | 30-04-13 | 30-04-12 |
|---|---|---|---|
| TA | 1,154,733 | 1,131,924 | 1,127,737 |
| NW | 592,391 | 680,433 | 613,227 |
| WC | 573,300 | 655,888 | 600,402 |

DUNS 77-117-5833
## Suites Hotel Knowsley Ltd
**(Subsidiary of:** The Bell Tower Hotel Ltd)
Ribblers Lane, Knowsley, Prescot, Merseyside L34 9HA
**Tel:** 0151-549-2222 **Fax:** 0151-549-1116
**Web:** www.suiteshotelgroup.com
**Reg No:** 2690085 **Estd:** 1992 Private Limited Company
**Line of Business:** Hotels and motels without restaurant
**Issued Capital:** £1,000,000
**Principals:** P Tyer *(Managing)*, Miss L Case, Mrs L Tyer
**Co. Secretary:** Michael Jebson
**US SIC:** 7011 **UK SIC:** 66500
**Auditors:** PKF (UK) LLP
**Bankers:** The Royal Bank Of Scotland Plc (16-24-06)

| | 31-07-13 | 31-07-12 | 31-07-11 |
|---|---|---|---|
| TO | 3,034,465 | 3,175,113 | 3,351,700 |
| P/L | 272,011 | 119,799 | 138,465 |
| NW | 2,844,461 | 2,627,927 | 2,517,732 |
| WC | (266,614) | (411,151) | (316,866) |
| Emp. | 87 | 84 | 87 |

DUNS 21-812-5629 Imp
## Sullivan & Cromwell
1 New Fetter Lane, London EC4A 1AN
**Tel:** 02079 598 900
**Web:** www.sullcrom.com
**Estd:** 2012
**Line of Business:** Other legal activities not elsewhere classified
**Proprietor:** Ms K Cambell
**Responsibilities**
**Senior:** Anthony Colletta *(Partner)*, Frederic Rich *(Partner)*
**Finance:** Janet Erington *(Senior Finance Administrator)*
**US SIC:** 8111 **UK SIC:** 83500
**Employees:** 170

DUNS 22-656-5117 Imp-Exp
## Sultans Ltd
**(Subsidiary of:** Multiplex Investments Ltd)
Burrell Way, Thetford, Norfolk IP24 3RB
**Tel:** 01842-751515 **Fax:** 01842-764269
**Web:** www.sultans.co.uk
**Reg No:** 1452181 **Estd:** 1980 Private Limited Company
**Line of Business:** Manufacturers of confectionery
**Export Markets:** Australia; China; European Union (E U)
**Export Sales:** £163,471
**Issued Capital:** £122,500
**Principals:** N Darbaz *(Chairman and Managing)*, Ms R D Darbaz, Z I Hussein
**Co. Secretary:** Kemal Darbaz
**Branches:** Sultans Ltd, 11 Wendene, Bowthorpe Main Centre, Norwich, Norfolk NR5 9HA
**US SIC:** 2065 **UK SIC:** 42142
**Auditors:** Larking Gowen
**Bankers:** HSBC Bank plc (40-35-09)

| | 31-03-14 | 31-03-13 | 31-03-12 |
|---|---|---|---|
| TO | 3,420,651 | 2,998,253 | 3,198,476 |
| P/L | (45,894) | (28,720) | (1,307,495) |
| NW | 4,922,232 | 6,121,137 | 6,068,162 |
| WC | 2,104,114 | 2,730,630 | 2,847,385 |
| Emp. | 90 | 64 | 77 |

DUNS 21-772-8685
## Sulzer Bootham Engineering
Cayton Low Road, Eastfield, Scarborough, North Yorkshire YO11 3BZ
**Tel:** 01723582621
**Web:** www.sulzer.com
**Estd:** 2011 Proprietorship
**Line of Business:** Mechanical engineering general
**Proprietor:** P Atkinson
**US SIC:** 8911 **UK SIC:** 83701
**Employees:** 52

DUNS 29-867-1553 Imp-Exp
## Sulzer Pumps (U K) Ltd
**(Subsidiary of:** Sulzer Ag)
Manor Mill Lane, Leeds, West Yorkshire LS11 8BR
**Web:** www.sulzer.com
**Reg No:** 2070346 **VAT No:** 232520015
**Estd:** 1986 Private Limited Company
**Line of Business:** Manufacturers of pump devices
**Export Markets:** France, Germany, Egypt, India & Alaska
**Trading Style:** Sulzer & Pumpcare, Sulzer Pump Care South, Sulzer U K Pumps
**Issued Capital:** £9,610,000
**Directors:** M O Streicher, R W Whiteley, Mrs T Micki
**Co. Secretary:** Miss Natalie James
**Responsibilities**
**Senior:** Keith Dowle *(Manager)*, Kim Jackson *(Manager)*, Markus Tritschler *(Finance Director)*
**Finance:** Markus Tritschler *(Finance Director)*
**Branches:** Sulzer Pumps (U K) Ltd, Unit 7 Spectrum West, 20 22 Maidstone Business Estat, Allington, Maidstone, Kent ME16 0LL
**US SIC:** 3563 **UK SIC:** 32831
**Auditors:** PricewaterhouseCoopers LLP
**Bankers:** Barclays Bank Plc (20-48-46)

| | 31-12-13 | 31-12-12 | 31-12-11 |
|---|---|---|---|
| TO | 174,492,000 | 178,927,000 | 142,696,000 |
| P/L | 21,055,000 | 20,357,000 | 16,335,000 |
| NW | 32,996,000 | 30,601,000 | 26,939,000 |
| WC | 17,828,000 | 11,943,000 | 6,436,000 |
| Emp. | 591 | 569 | 550 |

DUNS 23-091-4939 Imp-Exp
## Sulzer Wood Ltd
**(Subsidiary of:** Sulzer Ag)
Castle Street, Castlepark Industrial Estate, Ellon, Aberdeenshire AB41 9RF
**Tel:** 01358-721068
**Web:** www.sulzerwood.co.uk
**Reg No:** 0147952SC **VAT No:** 605203587
**Estd:** 1982 Private Limited Company
**Line of Business:** Pumps sales and servicing
**Export Markets:** France, Spain & Norway
**Trading Style:** Sulzer Wood Ltd
**Issued Capital:** £198,000
**Directors:** D A Stewart, A J Percy, S J Nicol, S S Nadkarni
**Co. Secretary:** Robert Brown
**Responsibilities**
**Senior:** Stuart Broadley *(Manager)*, Graham Dickie *(Manager)*, Murray Willson *(General Manager)*
**Branches:** Sulzer Wood Ltd, Coutts Yard, Unit B12, Peterhead, Aberdeenshire AB42 3LJ
**US SIC:** 5084 **UK SIC:** 61490
**Auditors:** Deloitte & Touche
**Bankers:** Clydesdale Bank Plc (82-63-10)

| | 31-12-13 | 31-12-12 | 31-12-11 |
|---|---|---|---|
| TO | 27,989,000 | 29,813,000 | 26,367,000 |
| P/L | 3,836,000 | 5,121,000 | 4,714,000 |
| NW | 5,435,000 | 4,147,000 | 4,105,000 |
| WC | 5,032,000 | 3,629,000 | 3,615,000 |
| Emp. | 93 | 95 | 89 |

DUNS 49-124-5320 Imp
## Sumac Precision Engineering Ltd
26 Cambridge Road, Weymouth, Dorset DT4 9TJ
**Tel:** 01305775535
**Web:** www.sumac.co.uk
**Reg No:** 3103369 **Estd:** 1995 Private Limited Company
**Line of Business:** Other engineering activities
**Export Sales:** £1,404,791
**Issued Capital:** £9,763
**Directors:** J A Marsh, Ms D Clothier, M A Robson
**Co. Secretary:** John Stevenson
**US SIC:** 8911 **UK SIC:** 83701
**Auditors:** Pugsley Revill

| | 30-09-13 | 30-09-12 | 30-09-11 |
|---|---|---|---|
| TO | 6,979,316 | 5,861,730 | 8,033,646 |
| P/L | 777,528 | 375,814 | 1,125,360 |
| NW | 2,940,955 | 2,601,862 | 2,286,923 |
| WC | 2,356,910 | 2,065,388 | 2,116,452 |
| Emp. | 87 | 85 | 85 |

DUNS 22-289-3856
## Sumerian Europe Ltd
Hobart House, 80 Hanover Street, Edinburgh, Midlothian EH2 1EL
**Tel:** 01312269300 **Fax:** 01412-290666
**Web:** www.sumerian.com
**Reg No:** 0224403SC **VAT No:** 801563360
**Estd:** 2001 Private Limited Company
**Line of Business:** Data processing
**Issued Capital:** £122,160
**Directors:** D J Stevens, D J Sibbald, Mrs C Sibbald, M Velasco
**Co. Secretary:** David Allan
**Responsibilities**
**Senior:** Calum Smeaton *(Manager)*
**Branches:** Sumerian Europe Ltd, Hobart House, 80 Hanover Street, Edinburgh, Midlothian EH2 1EL
**US SIC:** 7374, 7392
**UK SIC:** 83940, 83951
**Auditors:** Mazars LLP

| | 31-12-13 | 31-12-12 | 31-12-11 |
|---|---|---|---|
| TA | 1,120,377 | 2,030,941 | 1,960,703 |
| NW | 687,570 | 1,319,557 | 1,568,373 |
| WC | 654,436 | 1,227,286 | 1,027,884 |

DUNS 49-012-1555
## Sumi Agro Europe Ltd
**(Subsidiary of:** Sumitomo Corporation)
Vintners Place, 68 Upper Thames Street, London EC4V 3BJ
**Tel:** 020 7246 3600
**Web:** www.sumitomocorpeurope.com
**Reg No:** 3073407 **Estd:** 1995 Private Limited Company
**Line of Business:** Manufacture of pesticides and other agro-chemical products
**Export Sales:** £200,612,000
**Issued Capital:** £8,805,000
**Directors:** Y Okura, K Tameda, W J Wleklik, M Yugen, K Okuyama, H Ozaki
**Co. Secretary:** Steven Parrianen
**US SIC:** 2879, 6711
**UK SIC:** 25680, 83962
**Auditors:** KPMG LLP
**Bankers:** The Sumitomo Bank, Ltd (40-51-25)

| | 31-12-13 | 31-12-12 | 31-12-11 |
|---|---|---|---|
| TO | 200,788,000 | 154,521,000 | 92,568,000 |
| P/L | 16,344,000 | 10,538,000 | 7,712,000 |
| NW | 44,063,000 | 34,480,000 | 30,805,000 |
| WC | 42,521,000 | 31,589,000 | 25,453,000 |
| Emp. | 460 | 460 | 173 |

DUNS 76-711-5884 Exp
## Sumika Polymer Compounds (Europe) Ltd
**(Subsidiary of:** Sumitomo Chemical Company Limited)
28 New Lane, Havant, Hampshire PO9 2NQ
**Tel:** 02392 486350
**Reg No:** 2594323 **Estd:** 1991 Private Limited Company
**Line of Business:** Management activities of holding companies
**Export Markets:** Europe
**Export Sales:** £63,494,000
**Issued Capital:** £11,100,100
**Directors:** L S Seynave, Y Kawai, R Shibata, H Hamada, M Ogiwara, K Fuse, M Onishi
**Co. Secretary:** Paul Claydon
**US SIC:** 6711 **UK SIC:** 83962
**Auditors:** KPMG LLP

| | 31-03-14 | 31-12-12 | 31-03-11 |
|---|---|---|---|
| TO | 80,218,000 | 53,122,000 | 59,874,000 |
| P/L | 1,942,000 | (1,967,000) | (1,495,000) |
| NW | 6,537,000 | 3,189,000 | 2,992,000 |
| WC | (5,066,000) | (7,840,000) | (6,060,000) |
| Emp. | 98 | 109 | 122 |

DUNS 50-466-6389 Imp
## Sumitomo Electric Wiring Systems (Europe) Ltd
**(Subsidiary of:** Sumitomo Electric Industries Ltd.)
Prospect House, Maries Way, Silverdale Business Park, Silverdale, Newcastle, Staffordshire ST5 6PA
**Web:** www.sews-e.com
**Reg No:** 2445665 **VAT No:** 729954776
**Estd:** 1989 Private Limited Company
**Line of Business:** Manufacturers of automotive components
**Export Sales:** £393,162,000
**Trading Style:** Sews-E
**Issued Capital:** £49,335,511
**Directors:** H Kiyokawa, K Phillips, T Kato, M Ikeuchi, M J Lawson, K Urushibata, Y Ono, E Saijyo
**Co. Secretary:** Christopher Foster
**Responsibilities**
**Senior:** Junichi Iba *(Manager)*, Hiroki Ishida *(Manager)*, Masami Makido *(Director)*, Yuichi Mizutani *(Manager)*, Toshihiro Nitto *(Manager)*, Dave Whalley *(Director)*, Nigel Whittingham *(Manager)*
**IT:** Eric Handley *(IT Manager)*

**Branches:** Sumitomo Electric Wiring Systems (Europe) Ltd, Unit 1, Woodlands Business Park, Swansea, West Glamorgan SA9 1JW
**US SIC:** 3714 **UK SIC:** 35300
**Auditors:** KPMG LLP
**Bankers:** Lloyds TSB Bank plc (30-93-66)

| | 31-03-14 | 31-03-13 | 31-03-12 |
|---|---|---|---|
| TO | 536,803,000 | 471,810,000 | 473,848,000 |
| P/L | 13,539,000 | (28,510,000) | (15,305,000) |
| NW | 3,762,000 | (22,857,000) | 12,815,000 |
| WC | 116,363,000 | 101,214,000 | 101,973,000 |
| Emp. | 16,826 | 16,908 | 16,625 |

DUNS 73-410-7530
## Sumitomo Mitsui Banking Corporation Europe Ltd
(**Subsidiary of:** Sumitomo Mitsui Financial Group Inc.)
99 Queen Victoria Street, London EC4V 4EH
**Tel:** 020-7786-1000 **Fax:** 02072360049
**Web:** www.smbcgroup.com
**Reg No:** 4684034 **Estd:** 2003 Private Limited Company
**Line of Business:** Banks
**Directors:** S Mori, K Hosomi, Y Ohmi, M Oshima, D A Ross, K Nakamura, I M Jameson, T Inoue
**Co. Secretary:** Mark Bradley
**Responsibilities**
**Senior:** Mitsuhiro Akiyama *(Manager)*, Hiroyuki Iwami *(CEO)*, Yasuyuki Kawasaki *(Manager)*, Jun Mizoguchi *(Manager)*
**HR:** Valerie Palmer *(SVP of Human Resources)*
**US SIC:** 6012 **UK SIC:** 81402
**Auditors:** KPMG Audit PLC
**Employees:** 900
**Turnover:** £635,900,000

DUNS 21-155-1916 **Exp**
## Sumitomo Mitsui Trust Bank Ltd
(**Subsidiary of:** Sumitomo Mitsui Trust Holdings Inc.)
3rd Floor, London EC2M 3XU
**Tel:** 020-7945-7000 **Fax:** 020-7945-7177
**Web:** www.sumitomotrust.co.jp
**Reg No:** 0008329FC **Estd:** 1925 Foreign Company
**Line of Business:** Other credit granting not elsewhere classified
**Principals:** O Sakurai *(Chairman)*, T Watanabe *(Managing)*, M Toyoshima *(Managing)*, H Besho *(Managing)*, N Fukuda *(Managing)*, H Tsunekage, S Shinohara, R Hattori
**Responsibilities**
**Senior:** Takehiko Asakawa *(Director)*, Hiroshi Deguchi *(Principal)*, Kunihiro Fujita *(Director)*, Takaaki Hatabe *(Director)*, Yashuhiko Hatano *(Principal)*, Tamiyoshi Horikiri *(Principal)*, Toshiro Machida *(Director)*, Shunsuke Matsui *(Director)*, Takeshi Matsumoto *(Principal)*, Yukio Muto *(Director)*, Isao Nagata *(Director)*, Y Nishida *(Manager)*, Yoichi Sekino *(Principal)*, Atsushi Takahashi *(Director)*, Masayuki Tsubonoya *(Director)*, Ken Watanabe *(Director)*
**Admin:** John Shipp *(General Manager)*
**IT:** Cliff Downton *(IT Manager)*
**HR:** Dominic Grealy *(Personnel Manager)*
**Health & Safety:** John Shipp *(General Manager)*
**Facilities:** John Shipp *(General Manager)*
**US SIC:** 6111 **UK SIC:** 81501
**Bankers:** HSBC Bank plc (40-05-15)

DUNS 21-032-1435
## Summer Lane Care Home
Diamond Batch, Weston-Super-Mare, Avon BS24 7AY
**Tel:** 01934-529190
**Web:** http://countrycourtcare.co
**Estd:** 2005 Proprietorship
**Line of Business:** Residential care establishments
**Proprietor:** Mrs A Skipper
**Responsibilities**
**Senior:** Demelza James *(Manager)*, Suria Webb *(Manager)*
**US SIC:** 8321 **UK SIC:** 96111
**Employees:** 125

DUNS 33-990-0847
## Summer Lodge Hotel
9 Fore Streetevershot, Evershot, Dorchester, Dorset DT2 0JR
**Tel:** 01935-482000
**Web:** www.summerlodgehotel.co.uk
**Estd:** 1979 Proprietorship
**Line of Business:** Hotels
**Proprietor:** N S Corbett
**Responsibilities**
**Senior:** Charles Lotter *(General Manager)*, Steven Titman *(Head Chef)*
**HR:** Laura Pages *(Human Resources Manager)*
**Facilities:** Joe Layden *(Head of Maintenance)*
**Purchasing:** Charles Lotter *(General Manager)*
**US SIC:** 7011 **UK SIC:** 66500
**Employees:** 60

DUNS 73-546-9517
## Summer Lodge Management Ltd
(**Subsidiary of:** Mountbatten Ltd)
2-4 Sackville Road, Hove, East Sussex BN3 3FA
**Tel:** 01273775577
**Reg No:** 4809168 **Estd:** 2003 Private Limited Company
**Line of Business:** Nursing homes
**Issued Capital:** £1
**Directors:** J J Raggett, Ms A Tollman, Ms V O Hana
**Co. Secretary:** Simon Royce
**US SIC:** 8051 **UK SIC:** 95100

| | 31-12-13 | 31-12-12 | 31-12-11 |
|---|---|---|---|
| TO | 2,015,702 | 1,960,487 | 2,027,695 |
| P/L | (1,092,229) | (1,259,763) | (1,189,993) |
| NW | (13,208,482) | (12,327,639) | (11,533,451) |
| WC | (6,054,514) | (5,716,958) | 461,789 |
| Emp. | 57 | 61 | 62 |

DUNS 21-775-9137
## Summerbank Central Primary School
Summerbank Road, Stoke-On-Trent, Staffordshire ST6 5HA
**Tel:** 01782233611
**Estd:** 1955 Proprietorship
**Line of Business:** Primary education
**Proprietor:** R Shenton
**US SIC:** 8211 **UK SIC:** 93200
**Employees:** 50

DUNS 49-497-7994
## Summerbridge Doors Ltd
26 Springfield Way, Anlaby, Hull, North Humberside HU10 6RJ
**Tel:** 01482505566 **Fax:** 01482-503877
**Web:** www.summerbridgedoors.co.uk
**Reg No:** 3159998 **VAT No:** 551948812
**Estd:** 1996 Private Limited Company
**Line of Business:** Wooden goods other than furniture
**Issued Capital:** £1,000
**Directors:** C D Bean, L Newton, K S Bean
**Co. Secretary:** Stephen Waite
**US SIC:** 2421 **UK SIC:** 46101
**Auditors:** Graybrowne
**Bankers:** Yorkshire Bank Plc (05-05-15)

| | 31-07-13 | 31-07-12 | 31-07-11 |
|---|---|---|---|
| TO | 8,910,777 | 9,459,874 | 8,974,029 |
| P/L | 786,284 | 698,493 | 769,768 |
| NW | 2,495,825 | 2,102,667 | 1,757,196 |
| WC | 1,094,146 | 817,451 | 264,246 |
| Emp. | 96 | 102 | 96 |

DUNS 21-226-1637
## Summerdale Court Care Centre
73 Butchers Road, London E16 1PH
**Tel:** 020-75402200
**Web:** www.fshc.co.uk
**Estd:** 2002 Proprietorship
**Line of Business:** Nursing homes
**Proprietor:** Ms R Mbaki
**Responsibilities**
**Senior:** Ram Awatar *(Manager)*
**US SIC:** 8321 **UK SIC:** 96111
**Employees:** 101

DUNS 76-236-1400
## Summerfield Developments (S W) Ltd
Tauntfield, South Road, Taunton, Somerset TA1 3ND
**Web:** www.summerfield.co.uk
**Reg No:** 2539922 **VAT No:** 586305914
**Estd:** 1994 Private Limited Company
**Line of Business:** Subdividers & developers, not cemeteries
**Issued Capital:** £515,000
**Directors:** C Winter, A J Vodden, J E Holyday, R D Lloyd, N D Hounslow, T B Stapleton, R Mead
**Co. Secretary:** Mark Blackwell
**US SIC:** 6552, 1541, 1522, 6531
**UK SIC:** 85000, 50100, 83400
**Auditors:** Amherst & Shapland
**Bankers:** Lloyds TSB Bank plc (30-98-45)

| | 31-12-13 | 31-12-12 | 31-12-11 |
|---|---|---|---|
| TO | 6,639,197 | 4,732,574 | 13,169,593 |
| P/L | 397,554 | 581,356 | 494,506 |
| NW | 18,760,901 | 19,241,215 | 20,574,392 |
| WC | 7,174,238 | 7,498,820 | 8,534,827 |
| Emp. | 46 | 44 | 46 |

DUNS 21-205-6803
## Summerfields Nursing Home
54 Rock Lane West, Birkenhead, Merseyside CH42 4PA
**Tel:** 01516431503
**Estd:** 1990 Partnership
**Line of Business:** Other human health activities
**Partners:** Mrs B Fry, R Merchant, R Fry
**US SIC:** 8091 **UK SIC:** 95200
**Bankers:** Allied Irish Bank (gb) (23-85-81)
**Employees:** 50

DUNS 21-223-7722
## Summerlea House
East Street, Littlehampton, West Sussex BN17 6AJ
**Tel:** 01903-718877
**Web:** www.lrh-homes.com
**Estd:** 2000 Partnership
**Line of Business:** Nursing homes
**Partners:** B Surtees, Mrs C Boxall
**Responsibilities**
**Senior:** Dawn Davie *(Manager)*, Celia Potts *(Home Manager)*
**US SIC:** 8051 **UK SIC:** 95100
**Employees:** 75

DUNS 22-639-2322
## Summerleaze Ltd
7 Summerleaze Road, Maidenhead, Berkshire SL6 8SP
**Tel:** 01628630444
**Web:** www.summerleaze.com
**Reg No:** 1738920 **VAT No:** 385778486
**Estd:** 1983 Private Limited Company
**Line of Business:** Builders merchants
**Issued Capital:** £2,000
**Principals:** P H Prior *(Managing)*, B G Prior, M A Lowe
**Co. Secretary:** Jeremy Malkinson
**Responsibilities**
**Senior:** Jason Prior *(Manager)*
**Finance:** Jeremy Malcolmson *(Finance Director)*
**Marketing:** Stuart Hunt *(Sales & Marketing Manager)*
**Sales:** Stuart Hunt *(Sales & Marketing Manager)*
**Branches:** Summerleaze Ltd, Sandford Farm Mohawk Way, Reading, Berkshire RG5 4UE
**US SIC:** 5039, 1499, 6519
**UK SIC:** 61300, 23960, 85000
**Auditors:** BDO Stoy Hayward
**Bankers:** National Westminster Bank Plc (60-13-35)

| | 31-03-14 | 31-03-13 | 31-03-12 |
|---|---|---|---|
| TO | 20,452,661 | 15,385,070 | 15,116,378 |
| P/L | (1,956,718) | (1,424,709) | (1,230,206) |
| NW | 61,594,824 | 64,493,032 | 64,086,621 |
| WC | 16,538,814 | 18,978,315 | 20,367,908 |
| Emp. | 67 | 58 | 56 |

DUNS 21-392-7290
## Summerlee House
1 West Canal St Canal Court, Coatbridge, Lanarkshire ML5 1PE
**Tel:** 01236-433466
**Web:** www.summerleehouse.com
**Estd:** 2005 Proprietorship
**Line of Business:** Medical nursing home activities
**Proprietor:** Mrs M Mcdonald
**US SIC:** 8051 **UK SIC:** 95100
**Employees:** 120

DUNS 73-291-2980
## Summers-Inman Construction & Property Consultants L L P
62 The Drive, Gosforth, Newcastle-Upon-Tyne, Tyne and Wear NE3 4AR
**Tel:** 01912-841121
**Web:** www.summers-inman.co.uk
**Reg No:** 0303181OC **Estd:** 2002
**Line of Business:** Quantity surveyors
**Responsibilities**
**Senior:** Alan Mcevoy *(Non-designated Limited Liabili)*, Adrian Redwood *(Non-designated Limited Liabili)*, James Sneddon *(Non-designated Limited Liabili)*
**Branches:** Summers-Inman Construction & Property Consultants L L P, 18 Great King Street, Edinburgh, Midlothian EH3 6QL
**US SIC:** 7397, 7399
**UK SIC:** 83702, 83954
**Auditors:** Tait Walker

| | 30-04-14 | 30-04-13 | 30-04-12 |
|---|---|---|---|
| TO | 7,597,310 | 6,832,502 | 6,434,349 |
| P/L | 750,867 | 435,481 | 233,148 |
| NW | 69,867 | (132,519) | 53,250 |
| WC | 1,260,957 | 1,098,719 | 798,234 |
| Emp. | 90 | 90 | 89 |

DUNS 73-936-0022
## Summit Food Holdings Ltd
170 Walton Summit Centre Brierley Road, Preston, Lancashire PR5 8AH
**Tel:** 01772322153 **Fax:** 01772-628110
**Web:** www.summitfoods.co.uk
**Reg No:** 2942608 **Estd:** 1982 Private Limited Company
**Line of Business:** Management activities of holding companies
**Trading Style:** Summit Food
**Issued Capital:** £2,542
**Directors:** D R Lewis, Ms V C Lewis
**Co. Secretary:** Mrs Susan Mckeever
**US SIC:** 6711 **UK SIC:** 83962
**Auditors:** TLP Audit Ltd
**Bankers:** Lloyds TSB Bank plc (30-96-85)

| | 31-08-13 | 01-09-12 | 27-08-11 |
|---|---|---|---|
| TO | 11,700,000 | 16,488,000 | 13,026,000 |
| P/L | 1,021,000 | 559,000 | 100,000 |
| NW | 1,760,000 | 1,174,000 | 705,000 |
| WC | 1,461,000 | 984,000 | 726,000 |
| Emp. | 165 | 198 | 161 |

DUNS 21-036-3984
## Summit Media
Hmp Wolds, Everthorpe, Brough, Brough, North Humberside HU15 2JZ
**Tel:** 01430-876876
**Web:** www.summitmedia.co.uk
**Estd:** 2000 Proprietorship
**Line of Business:** Advertising activities not elsewhere classified
**Responsibilities**
**Engineering:** Tomas Honz *(Chief Technology Officer)*
**US SIC:** 7319 **UK SIC:** 83800
**Employees:** 100

DUNS 22-026-0629
## Summit Media Ltd
(**Subsidiary of:** Summit Records Ltd.)
The Wolds, Brough, North Humberside HU15 2JZ
**Tel:** 01430888031 **Fax:** 01430425808
**Web:** www.summit.co.uk
**Reg No:** 4028661 **Estd:** 2000 Private Limited Company
**Line of Business:** E-commerce
**Trading Style:** Summit Media
**Issued Capital:** £1
**Director:** H J Aylott
**Co. Secretary:** Ms Marion Aylott
**US SIC:** 7379 **UK SIC:** 83940

| | 31-01-13 | 31-01-12 | 31-01-11 |
|---|---|---|---|
| TO | 39,362,655 | 34,836,857 | 27,543,037 |
| P/L | 171,599 | 169,533 | 180,417 |
| NW | (282,009) | (267,093) | (708,121) |
| WC | (1,282,555) | (1,186,433) | (1,445,762) |
| Emp. | 108 | 82 | 77 |

DUNS 73-301-9348
## Summitskills Ltd
34 Palace Court, London W2 4HY
**Tel:** 01908303960 **Fax:** 01908303989
**Web:** www.summitskills.org.uk
**Reg No:** 4575759 **Estd:** 2008 Private Company Limited By Guarantee
**Line of Business:** Other adult and other education not elsewhere classified
**Directors:** I J Pattle, A J Honey, Ms R Devine, R J Clarke, S A Hunt, D W Smith, B G Lea
**Responsibilities**
**Senior:** Nigel Hollett *(Manager)*
**Admin:** Angela Gennery *(Office Manager)*
**Branches:** Summitskills Ltd, 9 Cotland Acres, Redhill, Surrey RH1 6JZ
**US SIC:** 8299 **UK SIC:** 93300
**Auditors:** Grant Thornton UK LLP
**Bankers:** Barclays Bank Plc (20-45-28)

| | 31-03-14 | 31-03-13 | 31-03-12 |
|---|---|---|---|
| TO | 1,498,495 | 2,094,023 | 3,683,611 |
| P/L | (735,202) | (437,742) | 263,255 |
| NW | 605,988 | 1,341,190 | 1,778,932 |
| WC | 602,625 | 1,329,913 | 1,758,030 |
| Emp. | 15 | 58 | 36 |

DUNS 73-429-4478 **Imp**
## Sumo Digital Ltd.
(**Subsidiary of:** Foundation 9 Entertainment Inc.)
Unit 32, Jessops Riverside, 800 Brightside Lane, Sheffield, South Yorkshire S9 2RX
**Tel:** 01142426766 **Fax:** 01142-426772
**Web:** www.sumo-digital.com
**Reg No:** 4703224 **Estd:** 2003 Private Limited Company
**Line of Business:** Other software consultancy and supply
**Issued Capital:** £10,000
**Directors:** D R Mills, C M Stockwell, P R Porter, C Cavers
**Co. Secretary:** Christopher Stockwell
**Responsibilities**
**Senior:** James North-Hearn *(Ceo)*, Steven Sardegna *(Manager)*
**US SIC:** 7379 **UK SIC:** 83940

**Auditors:** Hodgson & Oldfield

| | 31-12-13 | 31-12-12 | 31-12-11 |
|---|---|---|---|
| TO | 13,264,220 | 16,346,740 | 13,903,008 |
| P/L | 869,075 | 2,141,733 | 1,828,871 |
| NW | 7,091,259 | 7,206,981 | 5,575,188 |
| WC | 6,912,003 | 6,310,335 | 4,711,802 |
| Emp. | 208 | 188 | 150 |

DUNS 54-426-4104     Imp
### Sumo Uk Ltd.
Rudgate, York, North Yorkshire YO26 8AL
**Tel:** 01759-319900
**Web:** www.sumo1.com
**Reg No:** 3272544  **Estd:** 1996 Private Limited Company
**Line of Business:** Manufacture of insulated wire and cable
**Export Sales:** £658,463
**Trading Style:** Sumo
**Issued Capital:** £95,510
**Managing Director:** S Wealleans
**Co. Secretary:** Ms Karen Wealleans
**US SIC:** 3357  **UK SIC:** 22470
**Auditors:** Kirk Newsholme
**Bankers:** Lloyds TSB Bank plc (30-18-64)

| | 30-06-13 | 30-06-12 | 30-06-11 |
|---|---|---|---|
| TO | 7,705,426 | 8,551,708 | N/A |
| P/L | 510,245 | 719,289 | N/A |
| NW | 1,883,365 | 1,552,475 | 1,044,742 |
| WC | 307,509 | 604,357 | 496,159 |
| Emp. | 61 | 54 | N/A |

DUNS 22-168-6947     Imp
### Sumosan Ltd
26b Albemarle Street, London W1S 4HY
**Tel:** 020-7495-5999 **Fax:** 020-7355-1247
**Web:** www.sumosan.com
**Reg No:** 4187190  **VAT No:** 778620296
**Estd:** 1995 Private Limited Company
**Line of Business:** Restaurant - japanese
**Issued Capital:** £1,000
**Director:** Ms J Wolkow
**Co. Secretary:** Bim Wagner
**US SIC:** 5812, 6711
**UK SIC:** 66110, 83962
**Auditors:** Vantis NM LLP
**Bankers:** HSBC Bank plc (40-04-26)

| | 31-03-13 | 31-03-12 | 31-03-11 |
|---|---|---|---|
| TO | N/A | N/A | 4,358,935 |
| P/L | N/A | N/A | 113,722 |
| NW | (2,370,205) | (2,254,670) | (2,080,565) |
| WC | (2,919,795) | (2,880,260) | (2,794,508) |

DUNS 21-217-4387     Exp
### Sun Branding Solutions Ltd
**(Subsidiary of:** Sun Chemical Group Coöperatief U.A.)
Albion Mills, Albion Road, Greengates, Bradford, West Yorkshire BD10 9TQ
**Tel:** 01274-200700 **Fax:** 01274-202425
**Web:** www.sunbrandingsolutions.com
**Reg No:** 0873405  **VAT No:** 169604538
**Estd:** 1800 Private Limited Company
**Line of Business:** Speciality design activities
**Export Markets:** U S A, Western Europe, Canada
**Export Sales:** £3,980,613
**Issued Capital:** £300,065
**Principals:** P R Bean (Managing), N M Jupe (Financial), B Schrader
**Co. Secretary:** Ms Margaret Pearce
**Responsibilities**
**Senior:** Sarah Wilfred (Sales Manager)
**Sales:** Sarah Wilfred (Sales Manager)
**Branches:** Sun Branding Solutions Ltd, 12 Great Newport Street, London WC2H 7JD
**US SIC:** 7399  **UK SIC:** 83954
**Auditors:** Deloitte & Touche LLP
**Bankers:** HSBC Bank plc (40-27-15)

| | 31-12-13 | 31-12-12 | 31-12-11 |
|---|---|---|---|
| TO | 20,994,875 | 21,769,845 | 21,625,417 |
| P/L | 451,550 | 987,596 | 667,300 |
| NW | 9,406,543 | 9,042,100 | 8,360,208 |
| WC | 8,907,863 | 8,449,849 | 7,556,092 |
| Emp. | 228 | 229 | 229 |

DUNS 21-391-0501
### Sun Centre World
Ivy House, Egerton Street, Stockton Heath, Warrington, Cheshire WA4 6DT
**Tel:** 01925-601060
**Web:** www.suncentreworld.co.uk
**Proprietorship**
**Line of Business:** Hairdressing and other beauty treatment
**Proprietor:** M Dunn
**US SIC:** 7231  **UK SIC:** 98200
**Employees:** 100

DUNS 76-992-6049
### Sun Chemical Ltd
**(Subsidiary of:** Sun Chemical Group Coöperatief U.A.)
3 High View Road, Alfreton, Derbyshire DE55 2DT
**Tel:** 01773813704 **Fax:** 01773580045
**Web:** www.sunchemical.com
**Reg No:** 2647054  **VAT No:** 216018402
**Estd:** 1929 Private Limited Company

**Line of Business:** Manufacture of printing ink
**Trading Style:** Sunjet, Sun Chemical Circuit
**Issued Capital:** £11,600,005
**Directors:** A R Palmer, Mrs S A Foster, J P Law, G W Hayes, G R Jurgens, C A Heynes
**Co. Secretary:** Ms Margaret Pearce
**Responsibilities**
**Senior:** David Garahan (Site Manager), Peter Hepworth (Director)
**Marketing:** Angus Blundell (Marketing Director), Brian Crombie (Innovation Leader), V Winn (Marketing Manager)
**Sales:** Colin Colverd (Sales Director), Donald Frazer (Sales Manager)
**HR:** J Dhaliwal (Personnel Manager)
**Branches:** Sun Chemical Limited, Bradfield Road, London E16 2AX
**US SIC:** 7399, 2893
**UK SIC:** 83954, 25520
**Auditors:** Deloitte LLP
**Bankers:** Citibank Na (08-60-71)

| | 31-12-13 | 31-12-12 | 31-12-11 |
|---|---|---|---|
| TO | 252,840,000 | 262,020,000 | 276,985,000 |
| P/L | 5,346,000 | 4,056,000 | 1,610,000 |
| NW | (15,683,000) | (12,479,000) | 4,235,000 |
| WC | 14,481,000 | 13,106,000 | 16,510,000 |
| Emp. | 1,103 | 1,178 | 1,245 |

DUNS 23-248-6030
### Sun Healthcare Ltd
Wharncliffe Business Park Longfields, Court, Barnsley, South Yorkshire S71 3GN
**Tel:** 01220020670
**Web:** www.sunhealthcare.co.uk
**Reg No:** 4220821  **Estd:** 2001 Private Limited Company
**Line of Business:** Representative office
**Issued Capital:** £2
**Directors:** A J Tolan, S Garside
**Co. Secretary:** Steven Garside
**US SIC:** 7399, 8091
**UK SIC:** 83954, 95200
**Bankers:** National Westminster Bank Plc (60-08-49)

| | 30-06-13 | 30-06-12 | 30-06-11 |
|---|---|---|---|
| TO | 8,771,784 | 8,302,605 | 7,893,921 |
| P/L | 784,085 | 693,556 | 662,041 |
| NW | 8,017,449 | 7,570,588 | 7,245,740 |
| WC | 2,463 | 349,550 | 226,087 |
| Emp. | 345 | 338 | 281 |

DUNS 29-547-1650     Imp-Exp
### Sun Hydraulics Ltd
**(Subsidiary of:** Sun Hydraulics Corporation)
Wheler Road, Coventry, West Midlands CV3 4LA
**Tel:** 02476307696 **Fax:** 024-7621-7488
**Web:** www.sunhydraulics.co.uk
**Reg No:** 1914045  **VAT No:** 307583062
**Estd:** 1981 Private Limited Company
**Line of Business:** Hydraulic equipment & accessories - sales & service
**Export Markets:** Europe
**Export Sales:** £6,177,576
**Issued Capital:** £1,140,000
**Directors:** A J Carlson, S Hancox, R Glasspole, Ms T L Fulton
**Co. Secretary:**
Taylor Wessing Secretaries Limit
**Responsibilities**
**Senior:** Paul McSheffrey (Warehouse Manager)
**Finance:** Roy Glasspole (Financial Controller)
**US SIC:** 3494  **UK SIC:** 32880
**Auditors:** PricewaterhouseCoopers

| | 28-12-13 | 29-12-12 | 31-12-11 |
|---|---|---|---|
| TO | 12,393,573 | 13,982,992 | 15,831,179 |
| P/L | 2,293,180 | 2,456,414 | 2,735,112 |
| NW | 15,870,560 | 14,121,640 | 12,281,943 |
| WC | 11,504,179 | 10,749,544 | 9,139,280 |
| Emp. | 63 | 66 | 67 |

DUNS 28-865-2688
### Sun Life Assurance Company of Canada (U.K.) Ltd
**(Subsidiary of:** Slfc Assurance (Uk) Ltd)
Matrix House, Basing View, Basingstoke, Hampshire RG21 4DZ
**Tel:** 01256841414 **Fax:** 01256460067
**Web:** www.sloc.co.uk
**Reg No:** 0959082  **Estd:** 1969 Private Limited Company
**Line of Business:** Pension companies
**Trading Style:** Sun Life Financial of Canada
**Issued Capital:** £30,000,001
**Directors:** E E Anstee, D A Stewart, Ms K A Garner, H Askari, J S Moss, S M Coombes
**Co. Secretary:** Mrs Margaret Hobbs
**Responsibilities**
**Senior:** Bettina Harvey (Manager), Robert Littlejohn (Manager), Robert Sharkey (Manager), Eric Weinheimer (Manager)
**Facilities:** Graham Savage (facilities manager)
**Branches:** Sun Life Assurance Company Of Canada (U K) Ltd, 24-26 Great Victoria St, Belfast, Belfast BT2 7BA

**US SIC:** 6311, 6371
**UK SIC:** 82002
**Auditors:** Deloitte LLP
Following financial data are in thousands

| | 31-12-13 | 31-12-12 | 31-12-11 |
|---|---|---|---|
| TO | 1,324,765 | 125,765 | 54,128 |
| P/L | 61,565 | 100,446 | 53,422 |
| NW | 519,449 | 505,800 | 490,421 |
| WC | (11,089,970) | 193,376 | (10,351,211) |

DUNS 77-739-5807
### Sun Mark Ltd
Chadha Building, 428 Long Drive, Greenford, Middlesex UB6 8UH
**Tel:** 020 8575 3700 **Fax:** 020 8575 9900
**Web:** www.sunmark.co.uk
**Reg No:** 3010238  **VAT No:** 681398694
**Estd:** 1995 Private Limited Company
**Line of Business:** Agents involved in the sale of food, beverages and tobacco
**Export Sales:** £126,712,040
**Issued Capital:** £170,000
**Directors:** H S Ahuja, R S Ranger
**Co. Secretary:** Ms Renu Ranger
**Branches:** Sun Mark Ltd, 94-96 Queensbury Rd, Wembley, Middlesex HA0 1QG
**US SIC:** 5149  **UK SIC:** 61700
**Auditors:** Paul & Co
**Bankers:** Barclays Bank Plc (20-03-80)

| | 31-08-13 | 31-08-12 | 31-08-11 |
|---|---|---|---|
| TO | 143,280,701 | 142,339,717 | 109,051,969 |
| P/L | 5,624,500 | 9,762,565 | 7,375,894 |
| NW | 23,076,224 | 20,925,546 | 14,037,423 |
| WC | 17,511,829 | 15,920,867 | 9,305,039 |
| Emp. | 69 | 55 | 47 |

DUNS 23-293-4179     Imp
### Sun Microsystems Scotland Lp
Blackness Road, Linlithgow, West Lothian EH49 7SF
**Tel:** 01506672000 **Fax:** 01506672672
**Web:** www.oracle.com
**Reg No:** 0003791SL  **Estd:** 1992 Limited Partnership
**Line of Business:** Computer services
**Trading Style:** Sun Microsystems
**Responsibilities**
**Senior:** Hugh Aitken (Manager), Emma Courtney (Manager), Wolfgang Engels (Manager), Andrew Laverty (Manager)
**Finance:** Neil Mackinnon (Finance Director)
**US SIC:** 3573  **UK SIC:** 33020
**Employees:** 500

DUNS 21-686-5501
### Sun Realm Heating Co. Ltd
166 28 Camford Way, Luton, Bedfordshire LU3 3AN
**Tel:** 01582-571925 **Fax:** 01582-492803
**Web:** www.sunrealmheatingcoluton.co.uk
**Reg No:** 1202277  **Estd:** 1975 Private Limited Company
**Line of Business:** Plumbing
**Issued Capital:** £24,950
**Principals:** M J Follan (Managing), J F Montgomery, M J Follan
**Co. Secretary:** Ms Nicola Follan
**US SIC:** 1711  **UK SIC:** 50300
**Auditors:** F E Hawkes & Co
**Bankers:** Barclays Bank Plc (20-53-30)

| | 31-12-13 | 31-12-12 | 31-12-11 |
|---|---|---|---|
| TO | 7,409,545 | 4,857,373 | N/A |
| P/L | 281,462 | 116,215 | N/A |
| NW | 2,739,757 | 2,590,998 | 2,503,218 |
| WC | 2,146,882 | 2,002,006 | 1,871,648 |
| Emp. | 68 | 62 | N/A |

DUNS 21-789-4753
### The Sun Tanz Company
Unit 15 Motherwell Business Centre, Coursington Road, Motherwell, Lanarkshire ML1 1PW
**Tel:** 01698260817
**Web:** www.tanztanning.co.uk
**Estd:** 2011
**Line of Business:** Hair & Beauty Salons
**Responsibilities**
**Senior:** John Patison (Manager)
**US SIC:** 7231  **UK SIC:** 98200
**Employees:** 100

DUNS 21-818-6187     Imp-Exp
### Sun Valley Foods Ltd
**(Subsidiary of:** Cargill Uk Holdings Ltd)
Grandstand Road, Hereford, Herefordshire HR4 9PB
**Tel:** 01432352400
**Web:** www.cargill.co.uk
**Reg No:** 0678294  **VAT No:** 340592075
**Estd:** 1960 Private Limited Company
**Line of Business:** Production of meat products
**Export Markets:** E U
**Export Sales:** £51,076,000
**Trading Style:** Cargill Meats Europe
**Issued Capital:** £400,000
**Directors:** P De Braal, Ms M D Cruz Diaz, D W Marsh, J W Reed, X Hyenne

**Co. Secretary:** Mrs Dena Lo'Bue
**Responsibilities**
**Marketing:** Rebecca Webb (Marketing Manager)
**HR:** Fiona Morris (HR Manager)
**Branches:** Sun Valley Foods Ltd, Shobdon Court, Shobdon, Leominster, Herefordshire HR6 9NA
**US SIC:** 2013  **UK SIC:** 41223
**Auditors:** KPMG LLP
**Bankers:** Barclays Bank Plc (20-39-64)

| | 31-05-13 | 31-05-12 | 31-05-11 |
|---|---|---|---|
| TO | 451,218,000 | 442,501,000 | 378,150,000 |
| P/L | (8,033,000) | (14,780,000) | (25,178,000) |
| NW | (7,204,000) | 2,502,000 | 23,216,000 |
| WC | (15,971,000) | 3,108,000 | 16,534,000 |
| Emp. | 2,242 | 2,162 | 1,980 |

DUNS 21-317-6498     Imp-Exp
### Sun Valley Ltd
Georgia Avenue, Wirral, Merseyside CH62 3RD
**Tel:** 01514827100
**Web:** www.sun-valley.co.uk
**Reg No:** 0548296  **VAT No:** 163950159
**Estd:** 1950 Private Limited Company
**Line of Business:** Manufacture of other food products not elsewhere classified
**Export Markets:** Worldwide
**Export Sales:** £3,825,106
**Trading Style:** Sun Valley Nut Products, Seabrook Blanching, Jimbos
**Issued Capital:** £300,000
**Principals:** Mrs G Hacking (Chairman), G W Street (Managing), T H Hacking (Sales), Mrs F M Street, Miss C H Hacking, Mrs K A Thomas
**Co. Secretary:** James Hacking
**Responsibilities**
**Senior:** Dave Perry (Factory Manager)
**HR:** Adrian Scott (Human Resources Manager)
**Health & Safety:** Dave Perry (Factory Manager)
**Facilities:** Dave Perry (Factory Manager)
**Engineering:** Tony Finnigan (Engineering Manager)
**US SIC:** 2099  **UK SIC:** 42399
**Auditors:** Clarke Broome & Fleming
**Bankers:** HSBC Bank plc (40-10-22)

| | 31-12-13 | 31-12-12 | 31-12-11 |
|---|---|---|---|
| TO | 31,754,987 | 26,844,333 | 23,523,919 |
| P/L | 688,681 | (107,607) | (270,684) |
| NW | 9,270,974 | 8,728,899 | 8,707,339 |
| WC | 5,567,347 | 4,954,973 | 4,881,455 |
| Emp. | 137 | 125 | 114 |

DUNS 22-701-2895
### Sunbeam Group Ltd
17-21 Sunbeam Road, London NW10 6JP
**Tel:** 02083571020
**Web:** www.sunbeamgroup.co.uk
**Reg No:** 1534284  **VAT No:** 354364844
**Estd:** 1980 Private Limited Company
**Line of Business:** Management activities of holding companies
**Trading Style:** Sunbeamgroup
**Issued Capital:** £1,000
**Principals:** S D Morrison (Managing), J Morrison
**Responsibilities**
**IT:** Lloyd Patterson (Group General Manager)
**HR:** Rodney Dash (General Manager)
**Health & Safety:** Lloyd Patterson (Group General Manager)
**Facilities:** Noel Brown (Production Manager)
**Purchasing:** Noel Brown (Production Manager)
**Engineering:** Noel Brown (Production Manager)
**US SIC:** 6711, 6552
**UK SIC:** 83962, 85000
**Auditors:** Richard Anthony & Co
**Bankers:** National Westminster Bank Plc (50-41-10)

| | 31-12-13 | 31-12-12 | 31-12-11 |
|---|---|---|---|
| TA | 4,977,357 | 4,756,188 | 4,659,287 |
| NW | 2,659,306 | 2,537,653 | 2,373,463 |
| WC | 351,310 | 318,936 | 297,181 |

DUNS 21-232-8154
### Sunblest Bread Tray Recovery Service
66 South Access Road, London E17 8AX
**Tel:** 0800585223
**Proprietorship**
**Line of Business:** Bakers and confectioners supplies
**US SIC:** 2051  **UK SIC:** 41960
**Employees:** 405

DUNS 21-234-0666
### Sunborn Yacht Hotel
Excel, Royal Victoria Dock, London E16 1SL
**Tel:** 02037148111
**Web:** www.sunbornhotels.com
**Estd:** 2002 Proprietorship
**Line of Business:** Hotels

**Proprietor:** C Thompson
**US SIC:** 7011 **UK SIC:** 66500
**Employees:** 55

DUNS 36-798-2915
## Sunbury Leisure Centre
Nursery Road, Sunbury-On-Thames, Middlesex TW16 6LG
**Tel:** 01932-772287
**Web:** www.everyoneactive.com
**Estd:** 1993 Proprietorship
**Line of Business:** Leisure centres
**Proprietor:** Ms D Hazel
**US SIC:** 7999 **UK SIC:** 97913
**Employees:** 92

DUNS 54-383-8122
## Sunbury Nursing Homes Ltd
West Lodge Cottage, Sunbury-On-Thames, Middlesex TW16 6AJ
**Web:** www.sunburynursinghomes.co.uk
**Reg No:** 3268807 **Estd:** 1996 Private Limited Company
**Line of Business:** Other human health activities
**Issued Capital:** £100,000
**Principals:** J K White *(Managing)*, Ms J D Hartland, Ms N M White, C J White
**Co. Secretary:** John White
**Responsibilities**
**Senior:** Stella Rhule *(Manager)*, Ellen White *(Senior Finance Administrator)*
**Finance:** Ellen White *(Senior Finance Administrator)*
**US SIC:** 8091 **UK SIC:** 95200
**Bankers:** National Westminster Bank Plc (60-22-25)

| | 31-10-13 | 31-10-12 | 31-10-11 |
|---|---|---|---|
| TA | 2,448,718 | 2,242,923 | 2,256,028 |
| NW | 2,024,246 | 1,344,841 | 1,237,006 |
| WC | 91,180 | 63,302 | (225,577) |

DUNS 77-483-9179
## Sunclean Ltd
9 Atkinsons Buildings Trimdon Street, Sunderland, Tyne and Wear SR4 6AH
**Tel:** 0191-514-1289
**Web:** www.sunclean.co.uk
**Reg No:** 2970914 **Estd:** 1994 Private Limited Company
**Line of Business:** Cleaning contracting commercial
**Issued Capital:** £100
**Director:** C B Duddin
**Co. Secretary:** Ms Pamela Duddin
**US SIC:** 7349 **UK SIC:** 92300
**Auditors:** Laverick Walton & Co
**Bankers:** Barclays Bank Plc (20-83-69)

| | 30-09-13 | 30-09-12 | 30-09-11 |
|---|---|---|---|
| TA | 54,375 | 59,283 | 59,969 |
| NW | 27,952 | 28,701 | 31,349 |
| WC | (17,699) | (18,426) | (13,588) |

DUNS 21-319-6186
## Suncourt Nursing Home
1 Morris Street, Sheringham, Norfolk NR26 8JX
**Estd:** 1986 Partnership
**Line of Business:** Nursing homes
**Partners:** Mrs J Leadbeater, T Leadbeater
**US SIC:** 8051 **UK SIC:** 95100
**Bankers:** National Westminster Bank Plc (60-15-31)
**Employees:** 53

DUNS 21-928-2597 **Imp**
## Suncream Holdings Ltd
Unit 7d, Claymore, Tame Valley Industrial Estate, Wilnecote, Tamworth, Staffordshire B77 5DQ
**Tel:** 01827282571 **Fax:** 01827260568
**Web:** www.suncreamicecream.com
**Reg No:** 1204416 **VAT No:** 405260294
**Estd:** 1967 Private Limited Company
**Line of Business:** Management activities of holding companies
**Trading Style:** Suncream Dairies
**Issued Capital:** £5,000
**Directors:** Ms S R Manfredi, Ms S D Thirlby
**Co. Secretary:** Susan Manfredi
**US SIC:** 6711, 2023
**UK SIC:** 83962, 41303
**Bankers:** Lloyds TSB Bank plc (30-98-44)

| | 31-12-13 | 31-03-13 | 31-12-12 |
|---|---|---|---|
| TA | 2,200,499 | 1,716,696 | 1,795,654 |
| NW | 610,547 | 615,633 | 620,053 |
| WC | (339,631) | (102,534) | (162,895) |

DUNS 21-228-5370
## Sunday Post
185 Fleet Street, London EC4A 2HS
**Tel:** 02074001030
**Estd:** 2002 Proprietorship
**Line of Business:** Newspapers Publishing or Publishing & Printing
**Proprietor:** D Westmore
**US SIC:** 2711 **UK SIC:** 47512
**Employees:** 69

DUNS 21-783-6026
## The Sunday Times
Guild Hall, 57 Queen Street, Glasgow, Lanarkshire G1 3EN
**Tel:** 01414205151
**Web:** www.thesundaytimes.co.uk
**Estd:** 2002 Partnership
**Line of Business:** Publishing of newspapers
**Partners:** C Mcclatchie, D Binsmore
**Responsibilities**
**Senior:** C McClatchie *(Partner)*, Gordon Smart *(Editor)*
**US SIC:** 2711 **UK SIC:** 47512
**Employees:** 300

DUNS 28-854-8951
## The Sunday Times Ltd
**(Subsidiary of:** News Corporation)
3 Thomas More Square, London E98 1XY
**Tel:** 02077825000 **Fax:** 02077825765
**Web:** www.sunday-times.co.uk
**Reg No:** 0786069 **Estd:** 1963 Private Limited Company
**Line of Business:** Advertising, radio, tv and other media
**Issued Capital:** £2
**Directors:** C C Longcroft, M C Gill
**Responsibilities**
**Senior:** Dominic Carter *(Manager)*, Tom Mockeridge *(Chief Executive)*, James Murdock *(Chief Executive)*
**Finance:** Steven Daintes *(Senior Financial Executive)*
**Marketing:** Iain Dey *(Deputy Business Editor)*, Dominic O'Connell *(Business Editor)*, Suzi Watford *(Senior Marketing Executive)*
**IT:** Lee O'Neill *(Senior IT Executive)*
**US SIC:** 2711 **UK SIC:** 47512

| | 29-06-14 | 30-06-13 | 01-06-12 |
|---|---|---|---|
| TA | 2 | 2 | 2 |
| NW | 2 | 2 | 2 |

DUNS 22-282-0065 **Imp**
## Sundeala Ltd
Middle Mill, Cam, Dursley, Gloucestershire GL11 5LQ
**Tel:** 01453-542286 **Fax:** 01453548939
**Web:** www.sundeala.co.uk
**Reg No:** 4299962 **VAT No:** 790788571
**Estd:** 2001 Private Limited Company
**Line of Business:** Stationery suppliers
**Export Sales:** £50,520
**Issued Capital:** £70,805
**Directors:** P C Hambro, G R Steer, M Allen, P J Harper, L P Hambro
**Co. Secretary:** Ms Deborah Robson
**Responsibilities**
**Senior:** Jonathan Timpany *(Manager)*
**Marketing:** Graham Osborne *(Marketing Manager)*
**IT:** Steve Newell *(Computer Manager)*
**HR:** Sandra Lineker *(Human Resources Manager)*
**Engineering:** Jonathan Timpany *(Manager)*
**US SIC:** 5942 **UK SIC:** 65300
**Auditors:** Baker Tilly

| | 28-02-14 | 28-02-13 | 29-02-12 |
|---|---|---|---|
| TO | 5,232,735 | 5,351,614 | 4,772,899 |
| P/L | 785,538 | 730,698 | 522,209 |
| NW | 4,801,777 | 4,409,285 | 3,984,194 |
| WC | 2,545,645 | 2,138,815 | 1,718,303 |
| Emp. | 59 | 62 | 61 |

DUNS 23-538-2041
## The Sunderland Association Football Club Ltd
**(Subsidiary of:** Alchemy Business Solutions Ltd)
Stadium Of Light, Sunderland, Tyne and Wear SR5 1SU
**Tel:** 08719111200 **Fax:** 0191-551-5123
**Web:** www.safc.com
**Reg No:** 0049116 **Estd:** 1996 Private Limited Company
**Line of Business:** Sports clubs
**Issued Capital:** £30,502
**Directors:** G Hutchinson, M Byrne, P Andersson, Ms A Lowes, E Short Iv
**Co. Secretary:** Ms Margaret Byrne
**Responsibilities**
**Senior:** Lesley Callaghan *(Manager)*, David Miliband *(Vice Chairman)*
**Finance:** Roger Whitehill *(Financial Manager)*
**Marketing:** Mike Farnan *(Marketing Director)*, Christine Lindon *(Commercial Manager)*
**Sales:** Christine Lindon *(Commercial Manager)*
**IT:** Graham Stenning *(IT Manager)*
**Facilities:** Peter Weymes *(Facilities Manager)*
**Purchasing:** Peter Weymes *(Facilities Manager)*
**Fleet:** Peter Weymes *(Facilities Manager)*
**Branches:** The Sunderland Association Football Club Ltd, 34 Sandringham Ter, Sunderland, Tyne and Wear SR6 9RA
**US SIC:** 7999 **UK SIC:** 97913
**Auditors:** PricewaterhouseCoopers LLP
**Bankers:** Barclays Bank Plc (20-83-69)

| | 31-07-13 | 31-07-12 | 31-07-11 |
|---|---|---|---|
| TO | 72,026,000 | 77,042,000 | 79,326,000 |
| P/L | (13,144,000) | (31,013,000) | (6,234,000) |
| NW | (98,581,000) | (84,173,000) | (86,716,000) |
| WC | (83,897,000) | (68,330,000) | (54,695,000) |
| Emp. | 634 | 646 | 611 |

DUNS 21-962-2703
## Sunderland Care & Support Ltd
**(Subsidiary of:** Care & Support Sunderland (Holding Company) Ltd)
Civic Centre Burdon Road, Sunderland, Tyne and Wear SR2 7DN
**Tel:** 01915205000
**Web:** www.sunderlandcareandsupport.co.uk
**Reg No:** 8681649 **Estd:** 2013 Private Limited Company
**Line of Business:** Social work activities without accommodation
**Issued Capital:** £1
**Directors:** A Wilson, A Lawson, J E Fletcher
**Co. Secretary:** David Smith
**US SIC:** 8321 **UK SIC:** 96111
**Bankers:** National Westminster Bank Plc (55-61-11)

| | 31-03-14 |
|---|---|
| TO | 9,571,160 |
| P/L | 184,959 |
| NW | (4,630,280) |
| WC | 30,720 |
| Emp. | 677 |

DUNS 49-722-9559
## Sunderland College
Bede Centre, Durham Road, Sunderland, Tyne and Wear SR3 4AH
**Tel:** 01915116000
**Web:** www.citysun.ac.uk
**Estd:** 1996
**Line of Business:** Further education schools and colleges
**Trading Style:** Usworth 6th Form College
**Financial Director:** P Wyness
**Responsibilities**
**Senior:** Helen Willen *(HR Manager)*
**Health & Safety:** Phil Storey *(Health & Safety Officer)*
**Branches:** Sunderland College, Second Floor, Phoenix Ho, Union St, Sunderland, Tyne and Wear SR1 3BT
**US SIC:** 8221 **UK SIC:** 93100
**Employees:** 1,000

DUNS 22-585-4587
## Sunderland Empire Theatre Trust Ltd
Sunderland Empire, 4-5 High St West, Sunderland, Tyne and Wear SR1 3EX
**Tel:** 01915661040
**Web:** www.sunderland.gov.uk
**Reg No:** 1100887 **Estd:** 1973 Private Company Limited By Guarantee
**Line of Business:** Theatres & concert halls
**Directors:** K G Macknight, D E Snowdon, P Stewart, G Rowley, Ms N Wright, T H Wright, J Heron, Ms J Wilson
**Co. Secretary:** Dr. David Smith
**Responsibilities**
**Senior:** Ellen Ball *(Director)*, Jill Flecther *(Director)*, Cecilia Gofton *(Director)*, Dale Mordey *(Director)*, Dennis Richardson *(Director)*
**US SIC:** 8999 **UK SIC:** 83954
**Bankers:** The Co-Operative Bank Plc (08-90-22)

| | 31-03-14 | 31-03-13 | 31-03-12 |
|---|---|---|---|
| TO | 11,530 | 11,647 | 12,143 |
| P/L | 20 | 20 | 25 |
| NW | 7,134 | 7,114 | 7,094 |

DUNS 23-566-6018
## Sunderland Home Care Associates (20-20) Ltd
Hendon Co Op Centre, Sunderland, Tyne and Wear SR2 8EL
**Tel:** 0191-510-8366
**Web:** www.homecare.co.uk
**Reg No:** 3564689 **Estd:** 1994 Private Limited Company
**Line of Business:** Other human health activities
**Issued Capital:** £23,400
**Principals:** Mrs M E Elliott *(Managing)*, Ms D Byers, Ms R L Blyth, R Taylor, Mrs L J Smith, Mrs H Hepple, Mrs J M Hutchinson
**Co. Secretary:** Ms Rachael Blyth
**US SIC:** 8321 **UK SIC:** 96111

| | 31-07-13 | 31-07-12 | 31-07-11 |
|---|---|---|---|
| TA | 2,780,201 | 2,007,362 | 1,857,315 |
| NW | 2,016,185 | 1,402,622 | 1,257,404 |
| WC | 1,918,307 | 1,302,309 | 1,250,308 |

DUNS 45-839-4160 **Imp**
## Sunderland Ltd
**(Subsidiary of:** Alchemy Business Solutions Ltd)
Stadium Of Light, Sunderland, Tyne and Wear SR5 1SU
**Tel:** 0191-551-5000 **Fax:** 0191-551-5123
**Web:** www.safc.com
**Reg No:** 3189630 **Estd:** 1996 Private Limited Company
**Line of Business:** Operation of other sports arenas and stadiums not elsewhere classified
**Issued Capital:** £85,575
**Directors:** E Short Iv, P Andersson, M Byrne
**Co. Secretary:** Ms Margaret Byrne
**US SIC:** 7999 **UK SIC:** 97913
**Auditors:** PricewaterhouseCoopers LLP
**Bankers:** Halifax Plc (11-00-44)

| | 31-07-13 | 31-07-12 | 31-07-11 |
|---|---|---|---|
| TO | 75,521,000 | 77,959,000 | 79,447,000 |
| P/L | (13,023,000) | (32,298,000) | (7,838,000) |
| NW | (27,208,000) | (12,921,000) | (14,179,000) |
| WC | (83,376,000) | (73,590,000) | (56,589,000) |
| Emp. | 991 | 809 | 611 |

DUNS 22-808-4174 **Exp**
## Sunderland Marine Insurance Co Ltd
Salvus House, Aykley Heads, Durham, County Durham DH1 5TS
**Tel:** 0191-374-0400
**Web:** www.sunderlandmarine.com
**Reg No:** 0016432 **Estd:** 1882 Private Company Limited By Guarantee
**Line of Business:** Non-life insurance
**Trading Style:** Salvus Bain Management
**Directors:** J M De Groot, G C Parkinson, F J Mattera, T F Hart, P B Shirke, L B Christensen, P M Johnson, A A Wilson
**Co. Secretary:** Alan Rowland
**Responsibilities**
**Senior:** Alistair Allan *(Manager)*, Graham Darke *(Assistant Company Secretary)*, Thomas Rutter *(Manager)*, Silas Taylor *(Manager)*, Angela Vipond *(Executive Director)*
**Finance:** Alison Alden *(Finance Director)*, Steve Blake *(Corporate Treasurer)*, Janet Cook *(P&I Claims Manager)*, Bev Harrison *(Claims Adjuster)*, Linda Sant *(Premium Collection Manager)*, Paul Sowerby *(Claims Manager)*, Kathy Walker *(Senior Finance Administrator)*
**Marketing:** Laura Rippon *(Marketing Manager)*
**Admin:** Sharon Ferry *(PA to CEO and Event Coordinato)*, Kathy Walker *(Senior Finance Administrator)*
**US SIC:** 6399 **UK SIC:** 82001
**Auditors:** KPMG Audit PLC
**Bankers:** Barclays Bank Plc (20-83-69)

| | 31-12-13 | 31-12-12 | 31-12-11 |
|---|---|---|---|
| TO | 34,642,000 | 39,509,000 | 42,547,000 |
| P/L | 372,000 | (533,000) | (6,902,000) |
| NW | 30,829,000 | 31,937,000 | 31,442,000 |
| WC | 12,131,000 | 14,529,000 | 9,507,000 |
| Emp. | 156 | 171 | 175 |

DUNS 23-714-0830
## Sundial C.S.R. Ltd
12 Albert Street, Rugby, Warwickshire CV21 2RS
**Tel:** 08448-226332 **Fax:** 08448226149
**Web:** www.carewatch-southmidlands.co.uk
**Reg No:** 3709043 **Estd:** 1999 Private Limited Company
**Line of Business:** Social work activities without accommodation
**Trading Style:** Care Watch, Carewatch (South Midlands)
**Issued Capital:** £100
**Principals:** M J Garrod *(Managing)*, Ms B A Garrod
**Co. Secretary:** Michael Garrod
**Responsibilities**
**Senior:** Clare Garrod *(Director)*
**Branches:** Sundial C.s.r. Ltd, 72 Main Street, Leicester, Leicestershire LE9 6RD
**US SIC:** 8321 **UK SIC:** 96111
**Auditors:** Baldwins (Nuneaton) Ltd

| | 31-03-13 | 31-03-12 | 31-03-11 |
|---|---|---|---|
| TA | 717,890 | 1,045,364 | 617,975 |
| NW | (112,243) | (54,625) | 269,288 |
| WC | (117,544) | 72,013 | 237,619 |

DUNS 53-627-7791
## Sundial Group Ltd
Grooms Lane, Northampton, Northamptonshire NN6 8NN
**Tel:** 01604-505505 **Fax:** 01604-505656
**Web:** www.sundialgroup.com
**Reg No:** 3432674 **Estd:** 1998 Private Limited Company
**Line of Business:** Hotels
**Trading Style:** Highgate House Conference Centre, Barnet Hill Conference Centre, Woodside Conference Centre
**Issued Capital:** £200

**Directors:** Ms J E Chudley, Mrs L M Mcgibbon, T S Chudley, J P Toth, B Howes, Mrs V Darby
**Co. Secretary:** Lee Forskitt
**Responsibilities**
**Admin:** Martina Sedlakova *(Office Coordinator)*
**IT:** Peter Branson *(Maintenance Manager)*
**Health & Safety:** Peter Branson *(Maintenance Manager)*
**Facilities:** Peter Branson *(Maintenance Manager)*
**Branches:** Sundial Group Ltd, Blackheath Farm, Blackheath Lane, Guildford, Surrey GU5 0RF
**US SIC:** 7011 **UK SIC:** 66500
**Auditors:** Bentley Jennison
**Bankers:** Barclays Bank Plc (20-53-30)

| | 31-12-13 | 31-12-12 | 31-12-11 |
|---|---|---|---|
| TO | 8,723,414 | 9,223,856 | 9,039,075 |
| P/L | (560,316) | (266,591) | (3,916,008) |
| NW | 5,752,960 | 5,754,982 | 5,939,279 |
| WC | (384,069) | (13,115,905) | (819,037) |
| Emp. | 155 | 160 | 162 |

DUNS 22-086-3588     Imp
### Sundolitt Ltd
Suite A2 Stirling Agricultural Centre, Stirling, Stirlingshire FK9 4RN
**Fax:** 01786464825
**Web:** www.sundolitt.co.uk
**Reg No:** 0211936SC **Estd:** 2000 Private Limited Company
**Line of Business:** Manufacturers of packaging materials
**Issued Capital:** £3,700,000
**Directors:** K J Sunde, G Kielland, B Sunde
**Co. Secretary:** Colin Brunton
**Responsibilities**
**Senior:** Philip Cheshire *(General Manager)*, Rune Midtgaard *(Manager)*
**Branches:** Sundolitt Ltd, 72 Crombie Rd, Aberdeen, Aberdeenshire AB11 9QP
**US SIC:** 2654, 3079
**UK SIC:** 47280, 48360
**Auditors:** Ernst & Young LLP
**Bankers:** The Royal Bank Of Scotland Plc (83-07-06)

| | 31-12-13 | 31-12-12 | 31-12-11 |
|---|---|---|---|
| TO | 9,821,646 | 8,361,082 | 10,092,310 |
| P/L | 69,100 | 212,445 | 839,023 |
| NW | 545,950 | 503,500 | 368,459 |
| WC | 1,025,715 | 538,097 | 856,060 |
| Emp. | 53 | 49 | 48 |

DUNS 23-601-7091
### Sundorne Products (Willenhall) Ltd
6 High Street, Llangefni, Gwynedd LL77 7LT
**Tel:** 01248722130 **Fax:** 01922-479972
**Reg No:** 0869697 **VAT No:** 100612343
**Estd:** 1966 Private Limited Company
**Line of Business:** Retail sale in non-specialised stores with food, beverages or tobacco predominating
**Trading Style:** Spar Supermarket
**Issued Capital:** £8,000
**Principals:** A Burns *(Managing)*, Ms M Burns
**Co. Secretary:** Andrew Burns
**Branches:** Sundorne Products (Willenhall) Ltd, 202 Bocking Lane, Sheffield, South Yorkshire S8 7BP
**US SIC:** 5411 **UK SIC:** 64100
**Auditors:** Lancaster Clements Ltd
**Bankers:** Girobank Plc (72-00-00)

| | 31-03-13 | 31-03-12 | 31-03-11 |
|---|---|---|---|
| TA | 151,867 | 151,385 | 148,753 |
| NW | 7,719 | 8,907 | 7,738 |
| WC | (15,685) | (17,710) | (13,163) |

DUNS 29-534-7751
### Sundown Pets Garden Ltd
Sundown, Treswell Road, Rampton, Retford, Nottinghamshire DN22 0HX
**Tel:** 01777-248274 **Fax:** 01777-248967
**Web:** www.sundownadventureland.co.uk
**Reg No:** 1901871 **Estd:** 1985 Private Limited Company
**Line of Business:** Other recreational activities not elsewhere classified
**Issued Capital:** £600
**Principals:** Mrs A Rhodes *(Managing)*, Ms G S Corr
**Co. Secretary:** Mrs Audrey Rhodes
**US SIC:** 7999 **UK SIC:** 97913
**Auditors:** Gwilym G Hughes & Co
**Bankers:** National Westminster Bank Plc (60-17-28)

| | 31-12-13 | 31-12-12 | 31-12-11 |
|---|---|---|---|
| TO | 3,032,266 | N/A | N/A |
| P/L | 391,775 | N/A | N/A |
| NW | 4,640,240 | 4,320,186 | 4,400,601 |
| WC | 992,229 | 105,372 | 170,344 |
| Emp. | 63 | N/A | N/A |

DUNS 28-836-0530
### Sunfield Childrens Homes Ltd
Bracken Unit, Stourbridge, West Midlands DY9 9PB
**Tel:** 01562882253
**Web:** www.sunfield.org.uk
**Reg No:** 0413810 **Estd:** 1928 Private Limited Company
**Line of Business:** Training centres
**Issued Capital:** £100
**Directors:** G J Robertson, I J James, M D Brocklebank-Smith, A Parsons, Capt G P Brocklebank, M H Wood
**Co. Secretary:** Martin Wood
**Responsibilities**
**Senior:** Hilary Clement *(Manager)*
**Branches:** Sunfield Childrens Homes Ltd, The Lodge, Walton Pool Lane, Stourbridge, West Midlands DY9 9PJ
**US SIC:** 8249 **UK SIC:** 93300
**Auditors:** Mazars Neville Russell
**Bankers:** Barclays Bank Plc (20-07-71)

| | 31-03-14 | 31-03-13 | 31-03-12 |
|---|---|---|---|
| TO | 10,260,384 | 10,338,322 | 10,954,404 |
| P/L | (112,003) | (88,577) | 275,041 |
| NW | 8,812,918 | 8,810,972 | 8,502,150 |
| WC | 446,252 | 573,232 | 644,034 |
| Emp. | 323 | 321 | 340 |

DUNS 23-452-9886
### Sunfold Systems
188 Sutton Court Road, London W4 3HR
**Tel:** 02087428887
**Web:** www.sunfold.com
**Estd:** 2002 Proprietorship
**Line of Business:** Double glazing installers
**Proprietor:** M Rowlings
**US SIC:** 1721 **UK SIC:** 50400
**Employees:** 60

DUNS 23-260-9669     Imp
### Sungard Availability Services (Uk) Ltd
**(Subsidiary of:** Sungard Capital Corp.)
Forum 1 Station Road, Reading, Berkshire RG7 4RA
**Tel:** 08082388080 **Fax:** 020-8080-8999
**Web:** www.sungard.co.uk
**Reg No:** 2368123 **Estd:** 1989 Private Limited Company
**Line of Business:** Other computer related activities
**Export Sales:** £6,414,000
**Issued Capital:** £10,000
**Directors:** K Tilley, R C Singer, E C Mckeever
**Responsibilities**
**Marketing:** Richard Bewley *(Head of Online Marketing)*, Chris Ducker *(Head of Proposition Marketing)*
**IT:** Paul Labbett *(Tech Support Manager)*
**Operations:** Omar White *(Head of City Operations)*
**Engineering:** Justin Jarvis *(Head of Solutions Engineering)*
**Branches:** Sungard Availability Services (Uk) Ltd, 38-39 Clarke Road, Milton Keynes, Buckinghamshire MK1 1LG
**US SIC:** 7379 **UK SIC:** 83940
**Auditors:** PricewaterhouseCoopers LLP
**Bankers:** Barclays Bank Plc (20-00-00)

| | 31-12-13 | 31-12-12 | 31-12-11 |
|---|---|---|---|
| TO | 182,484,000 | 169,807,000 | 169,179,000 |
| P/L | 11,385,000 | 23,829,000 | 19,755,000 |
| NW | 25,138,000 | 35,402,000 | 51,539,000 |
| WC | (36,164,000) | (37,611,000) | (29,593,000) |
| Emp. | 542 | 472 | 485 |

DUNS 21-736-6418     Imp-Exp
### Sungard Sherwood Systems Group Ltd
**(Subsidiary of:** Sungard Capital Corp.)
25 Canada Square, London E14 5LQ
**Tel:** 02080812000 **Fax:** 01932-757563
**Web:** www.sungard.co.uk
**Reg No:** 0982833 **Estd:** 1970 Private Limited Company
**Line of Business:** Computer software (development)
**Export Markets:** E U, worldwide
**Export Sales:** £36,229,000
**Trading Style:** Sungard
**Issued Capital:** £60,001
**Directors:** H M Miller Jr, Ms V E Silbey, D B Gluyas, M R Boyd
**Co. Secretary:** Ms Kerin Kimber
**Responsibilities**
**Senior:** Henry Miller *(Director)*
**Branches:** Sungard Sherwood Systems Group Ltd, Sherwood House, Eastworth Road, Chertsey, Surrey KT16 8SH
**US SIC:** 7379 **UK SIC:** 83940
**Auditors:** PricewaterhouseCoopers LLP

**Bankers:** National Westminster Bank Plc (60-00-01)

| | 31-12-13 | 31-12-12 | 31-12-11 |
|---|---|---|---|
| TO | 40,517,000 | 35,538,000 | 33,977,000 |
| P/L | 9,572,000 | 7,095,000 | 3,933,000 |
| NW | 21,055,000 | 13,287,000 | 10,436,000 |
| WC | 21,382,000 | 14,758,000 | 10,409,000 |
| Emp. | 115 | 112 | 116 |

DUNS 34-963-8259
### Sunkar Resources Plc
Suite 5, Floor 2, London EC2V 6DN
**Tel:** 02073-973-730 **Fax:** 02073890199
**Web:** www.sunkarresources.com
**Reg No:** 5759399 **Estd:** 2006 Public Limited Company
**Line of Business:** Mining of chemicals and fertiliser minerals
**Directors:** S Utegen, R Abdrakhmanov
**Co. Secretary:** Maclay Murray & Spens Llp
**Responsibilities**
**Senior:** Teck Kong *(Non Executive Chairman)*, Charles de Chezelles *(Non-Executive Director)*
**US SIC:** 1474, 2873
**UK SIC:** 23960, 25130
**Auditors:** Deloitte LLP
**Bankers:** HSBC Bank plc (40-05-30)
**Employees:** 118
**Turnover:** £14,952,000

DUNS 38-586-8815
### Sunline Direct Mail Ltd
**(Subsidiary of:** Ceps Plc.)
Weldon Road Industrial Estate, Loughborough, Leicestershire LE11 5FJ
**Tel:** 01509-263434 **Fax:** 01509-264225
**Web:** www.sunlinedirect.co.uk
**Reg No:** 3341560 **Estd:** 1978 Private Limited Company
**Line of Business:** Mail order houses
**Issued Capital:** £119,601
**Directors:** J R Ellis, N T Roberts, P G Cook, R T Organ, P Teer
**Co. Secretary:** Nigel Maybury
**Responsibilities**
**IT:** Shaun Donoher *(It Manager)*
**Branches:** Sunline Direct Mail Ltd, 10 Cotton Way, Loughborough, Leicestershire LE11 5FJ
**US SIC:** 7399, 2752
**UK SIC:** 83954, 47544
**Auditors:** Grant Thornton
**Bankers:** Bank Of Scotland (12-08-81)

| | 31-12-13 | 31-12-12 | 31-12-11 |
|---|---|---|---|
| TO | 6,317,000 | 5,686,000 | 6,376,000 |
| P/L | 210,000 | (33,000) | 181,000 |
| NW | 3,064,000 | 2,791,000 | 2,822,000 |
| WC | 2,360,000 | 2,022,000 | 2,089,000 |
| Emp. | 127 | 132 | 134 |

DUNS 57-024-2073
### Sunmaster Ltd
**(Subsidiary of:** Europe Voyager Nv)
Elizabeth Street, Wyke, Bradford, West Yorkshire BD12 8PN
**Tel:** 08717000031
**Web:** www.sunmaster.co.uk
**Reg No:** 2871028 **Estd:** 1994 Private Limited Company
**Line of Business:** Travel agency activities
**Issued Capital:** £5,161
**Director:** A I Botterill
**Co. Secretary:** Jens Penny
**US SIC:** 4722 **UK SIC:** 77001
**Auditors:** Beever & Struthers
**Bankers:** Barclays Bank Plc (20-12-05)

| | 30-06-14 | 30-06-13 | 30-06-12 |
|---|---|---|---|
| TO | 10,055,000 | 8,317,000 | 6,640,000 |
| P/L | 733,000 | 710,000 | 705,000 |
| NW | 7,181,000 | 6,405,000 | 5,685,000 |
| WC | 7,130,000 | 6,586,000 | 5,622,000 |
| Emp. | 96 | 76 | 64 |

DUNS 21-580-8086
### Sunmaster Travel Agents
Bowling Mill, Dean Clough Mills, Halifax, West Yorkshire HX3 5AX
**Tel:** 01274422188
**Web:** www.sunmaster.co.uk
**Estd:** 2006 Partnership
**Line of Business:** Travel agency activities
**Partners:** P Edward, P Edwards, A Walton
**US SIC:** 4722 **UK SIC:** 77001
**Employees:** 60

DUNS 57-837-0983     Imp
### Sunnen Products Ltd
**(Subsidiary of:** Sunnen Products Company)
Centro 1, Maxted Road, Hemel Hempstead Industrial Estate, Hemel Hempstead, Hertfordshire HP2 7EF
**Tel:** 01442-393939 **Fax:** 01442-391212
**Web:** www.sunnen.com
**Reg No:** 2890320 **Estd:** 1994 Private Limited Company
**Line of Business:** Manufacturers of machine tools
**Export Sales:** £17,704,266

**Issued Capital:** £2,020,302
**Directors:** M C Haughey, J B Hooper, M Sunnen Kreider
**Co. Secretary:** Ms Yemisi Palmer
**Responsibilities**
**Senior:** Grenig Lewis *(Manager)*
**US SIC:** 3542, 5074
**UK SIC:** 32212, 61300
**Auditors:** Hacker Young
**Bankers:** HSBC Bank plc (40-40-01)

| | 31-12-13 | 31-12-12 | 31-12-11 |
|---|---|---|---|
| TO | 20,093,580 | 19,656,959 | 19,733,518 |
| P/L | 726,458 | 851,705 | 666,647 |
| NW | 5,166,764 | 4,713,260 | 3,979,899 |
| WC | 7,704,598 | 7,423,067 | 4,119,124 |
| Emp. | 86 | 83 | 78 |

DUNS 21-227-9628
### Sunny Valley
The Square, Holyhead, Gwynedd LL65 3DP
**Tel:** 01407740494
**Estd:** 2002 Proprietorship
**Line of Business:** Licensed restaurants
**Proprietor:** T Chan
**US SIC:** 5812 **UK SIC:** 66110
**Employees:** 94

DUNS 21-583-9517
### The Sunnybank Trust
Temple Road, Epsom, Surrey KT19 8HA
**Tel:** 01372749871
**Web:** www.sunnybanktrust.org
**Estd:** 2011 Proprietorship
**Line of Business:** Charities and charitable organisations
**Proprietor:** C Snell
**Responsibilities**
**Senior:** Joanna Matthews *(Fundraiser)*
**US SIC:** 8699 **UK SIC:** 96902
**Employees:** 130

DUNS 21-778-8623
### Sunnycliffe Residential Home
20-22 Broadway, Sandown, Isle of Wight PO36 9DQ
**Tel:** 01983403844
**Web:** www.stvincentcare.co.uk
**Estd:** 2007 Proprietorship
**Line of Business:** Residential care establishments
**Proprietor:** D Niles
**US SIC:** 8321 **UK SIC:** 96111
**Employees:** 50

DUNS 55-084-3114
### Sunnycroft Care Home
113-115 Fakenham Road, Taverham, Norwich, Norfolk NR8 6QB
**Tel:** 01603-261957
**Proprietorship**
**Line of Business:** Residential care establishments
**Proprietor:** Mrs P Ratan
**Responsibilities**
**Senior:** Kelly Gilham *(General Manager)*, Shereen Jesudason *(Proprietor)*
**Health & Safety:** Jean Wiltshorne *(Health & Safety Officer)*
**US SIC:** 8321 **UK SIC:** 96111
**Employees:** 60

DUNS 22-768-4362
### Sunnysands Caravan Park Ltd
Talybont, Talybont, Gwynedd LL43 2LQ
**Tel:** 01341-247301
**Web:** www.sunnysands.co.uk
**Reg No:** 0746345 **VAT No:** 161498940
**Estd:** 1963 Private Limited Company
**Line of Business:** Camping sites, including caravan sites
**Trading Style:** Moelfre View Caravan Park, Snowden View Caravan Park
**Issued Capital:** £25,000
**Principals:** C Mead *(Managing)*, J C Mead, Miss S A Mead, T R Mead, C P Mead
**Co. Secretary:** David Morgan
**Branches:** Sunnysands Caravan Park Ltd, 1 Moelfre View Caravan Site, Talybont, Gwynedd LL43 2AJ
**US SIC:** 7032 **UK SIC:** 66702
**Auditors:** Laud, Grice & Co
**Bankers:** National Westminster Bank Plc (60-20-11)

| | 31-12-13 | 31-12-12 | 31-12-11 |
|---|---|---|---|
| TA | 23,576,516 | 22,934,241 | 22,138,378 |
| NW | 21,263,946 | 20,715,149 | 19,979,978 |
| WC | 1,323,102 | 4,268,912 | 3,538,970 |

DUNS 21-781-6852
### Sunnyside Primary School
Erskine Street, Alloa, Clackmannanshire FK10 2AT
**Tel:** 01259214976
**Web:** www.sunnyside.clacks.sch.uk
**Estd:** 1905 Proprietorship
**Line of Business:** Primary education
**Proprietor:** Miss L Mcalpine

**Responsibilities**
**Senior:** Helen Finch *(Head Teacher)*, Linda McAlpine *(Proprietor)*
**US SIC:** 8211 **UK SIC:** 93200
**Employees:** 50

DUNS 21-141-2683
## Sunquest Europe Ltd
(**Subsidiary of:** Roper Industries Inc.)
Unit 6 Octagon Business Park, Hospital Road, Little Plumstead, Norwich, Norfolk NR13 5FH
**Tel:** 08455194010
**Web:** www.sunquestinfo.com
**Reg No:** 6730825 **Estd:** 1995 Private Limited Company
**Line of Business:** Management activities of other non-financial holding companies not elsewhere classified
**Issued Capital:** £3,453,204
**Directors:** D B Liner, J R Humphrey, P J Soni
**Co. Secretary:** John Bignall
**Responsibilities**
**Senior:** Vicky Nicholson *(Office Manager)*
**US SIC:** 6711 **UK SIC:** 83962

| | 31-12-13 | 31-12-12 | 31-12-12 |
|---|---|---|---|
| TA | 10,616,221 | 10,616,221 | 10,616,221 |
| P/L | 3,425,242 | 1,121,643 | 1,950,962 |
| NW | 7,597,729 | 5,933,112 | 5,380,086 |
| WC | (2,988,792) | (4,653,409) | (653,490) |

DUNS 22-259-8422 Imp
## Sunrise Brokers Llp
4 Triton Square, London NW1 3HG
**Tel:** 02076637829
**Web:** www.sunrisebrokers.com
**Reg No:** 0300626OC **Estd:** 2001 Limited Partnership
**Line of Business:** Finance brokers
**Responsibilities**
**Senior:** Anne Amar *(Non-designated Limited Liabili)*, Charly Amar *(Non-designated Limited Liabili)*, Davy Barthes *(Partner)*, Michael Benhamou *(Non-designated Limited Liabili)*, Armand Benslous *(Non-designated Limited Liabili)*, Philip Boddy *(Non-designated Limited Liabili)*, Cedric Chanoine *(Non-designated Limited Liabili)*, Hadar Finegold *(Non-designated Limited Liabili)*, Benjamin Jevons *(Non-designated Limited Liabili)*, Alexander Langham *(Non-designated Limited Liabili)*, Edward Lees *(Partner)*, David Loubaton *(Non-designated Limited Liabili)*, Zachary Morgan *(Partner)*, Gilles Ohana *(Non-designated Limited Liabili)*, Derek Wilks *(Non-designated Limited Liabili)*
**Finance:** Steven Raucher *(Equity Derivative Broker)*
**US SIC:** 6411 **UK SIC:** 83200
**Auditors:** KPMG LLP

| | 31-12-13 | 31-12-12 | 31-12-11 |
|---|---|---|---|
| TO | 31,947,000 | 31,688,000 | 34,586,000 |
| NW | 2,500,000 | 2,500,000 | 1,000,000 |
| WC | 24,885,000 | 22,310,000 | 29,963,000 |
| Emp. | 100 | 86 | 62 |

DUNS 23-572-1490 Exp
## Sunrise Medical Ltd
(**Subsidiary of:** Sunrise Medical Logistics B.V.)
Thorns Road, Brierley Hill, West Midlands DY5 2BQ
**Tel:** 08456056688
**Web:** www.sunrisemedical.com
**Reg No:** 3570204 **VAT No:** 388606802
**Estd:** 1998 Private Limited Company
**Line of Business:** Mobility equipment
**Export Sales:** £3,982,000
**Issued Capital:** £6,254,455
**Directors:** R F Smith, T J Rossnagel, E T O'Brien
**Co. Secretary:** Peter Riley
**US SIC:** 3799 **UK SIC:** 36502
**Auditors:** Deloitte LLP
**Bankers:** Barclays Bank Plc (20-97-78)

| | 30-06-13 | 29-06-12 | 01-06-11 |
|---|---|---|---|
| TO | 28,238,000 | 28,479,000 | 28,745,000 |
| P/L | 1,386,000 | 2,105,000 | 3,932,000 |
| NW | 12,148,000 | 5,463,000 | 6,850,000 |
| WC | 26,675,000 | 4,577,000 | 5,858,000 |
| Emp. | 156 | 158 | 179 |

DUNS 21-419-6001
## Sunrise of Beaconsfield
30-34 Station Road, Beaconsfield, Buckinghamshire HP9 1AB
**Tel:** 01494739600
**Web:** www.sunriseseniorliving.co.uk
**Estd:** 2011 Proprietorship
**Line of Business:** Nursing homes
**Proprietor:** T Mills
**Responsibilities**
**Senior:** Malcolm Hague *(Manager)*
**US SIC:** 8321 **UK SIC:** 96111
**Employees:** 100

DUNS 21-016-2854
## Sunrise Operations Bagshot Ii Ltd
125 London Wall, London EC2Y 5AL
**Tel:** 02380706050
**Web:** www.sunriseseniorliving.com
**Reg No:** 6385464 **Estd:** 2007 Private Limited Company
**Line of Business:** Medical nursing home activities
**Issued Capital:** £1
**Directors:** M A Crabtree, J Skiver, K Crockett, Ms E C Ibele
**Co. Secretary:** Eps Secretaries Limited
**Responsibilities**
**Senior:** Tim Dutson *(Executive Director)*
**US SIC:** 8051 **UK SIC:** 95100

| | 31-12-13 | 31-12-12 | 31-12-11 |
|---|---|---|---|
| TO | 6,046,904 | 5,358,055 | 4,833,077 |
| P/L | 572,950 | 160,829 | (56,781) |
| NW | (1,352,071) | (1,747,272) | (1,820,636) |
| WC | (1,352,071) | (1,747,272) | (1,820,636) |
| Emp. | 131 | 129 | 114 |

DUNS 21-011-7765
## Sunrise Operations Beaconsfield Ltd
(**Subsidiary of:** Dawn Opco Ii Ltd)
Lacon House, 84 Theobalds Road, London WC1X 8RW
**Tel:** 02081271774
**Reg No:** 6350633 **Estd:** 2007 Private Limited Company
**Line of Business:** Beauty salons
**Issued Capital:** £2
**Directors:** Ms E C Ibele, K Crockett, J Skiver
**Co. Secretary:** Eps Secretaries
**US SIC:** 7231 **UK SIC:** 98200

| | 31-12-13 | 31-12-12 | 31-12-11 |
|---|---|---|---|
| TO | 6,182,847 | 5,896,560 | 5,947,959 |
| P/L | 726,031 | 458,098 | 506,245 |
| NW | 1,927,929 | 1,197,844 | 739,746 |
| WC | 1,927,928 | 1,197,843 | 739,745 |
| Emp. | 113 | 116 | 111 |

DUNS 22-658-2823
## Sunrise Poultry Farms Ltd
250 Seagrave Road, Loughborough, Leicestershire LE12 7NJ
**Web:** www.sunrise-eggs.com
**Reg No:** 1135442 **VAT No:** 115925963
**Estd:** 1973 Private Limited Company
**Line of Business:** Egg merchants
**Issued Capital:** £10,000
**Directors:** Miss W M Crawley, Mrs S M Crawley, P A Crawley
**Co. Secretary:** Adian Crawley
**Responsibilities**
**Marketing:** Chris Stocks *(Sales & Marketing Manager)*
**Sales:** Chris Stocks *(Sales & Marketing Manager)*
**Purchasing:** Chris Stocks *(Sales & Marketing Manager)*
**US SIC:** 0259, 5143
**UK SIC:** 01001, 61700
**Auditors:** Newby Castleman
**Bankers:** HSBC Bank plc (40-30-24)

| | 30-06-13 | 30-06-12 | 30-06-11 |
|---|---|---|---|
| TO | 21,506,129 | 19,891,002 | 17,192,393 |
| P/L | 2,535,077 | 2,860,467 | 1,570,913 |
| NW | 11,589,155 | 9,643,169 | 7,384,895 |
| WC | 2,038,907 | 851,853 | (601,864) |
| Emp. | 78 | 75 | 72 |

DUNS 21-034-0660
## Sunrise Senior Living
21-27 Russell Hill Road, Purley, Surrey CR8 2LF
**Tel:** 020-8676-2300
**Web:** www.sunriseseniorliving.com
**Proprietorship**
**Line of Business:** Residential care establishments
**Proprietor:** Mrs E Ferris
**Responsibilities**
**Senior:** Janet Collins *(Manager)*
**US SIC:** 8321 **UK SIC:** 96111
**Employees:** 100

DUNS 53-622-2128
## Sunrise Senior Living Ltd
(**Subsidiary of:** Health Care Reit Inc.)
Sunrise House, Post Office Lane, Beaconsfield, Buckinghamshire HP9 1FN
**Tel:** 01494739000
**Web:** www.sunriseseniorliving.co.uk
**Reg No:** 3427251 **Estd:** 1997 Private Limited Company
**Line of Business:** Management of real estate on a fee or contract basis
**Issued Capital:** £2
**Directors:** M E Roder, Ms A R Scott, J M Harper, F Mestre
**Co. Secretary:**
Aa State Street Secretaries (Uk) Li

**Responsibilities**
**Senior:** Edward Burnett *(Manager)*, Laura Mcduffie *(Manager)*, Paul Milstein *(Manager)*, Chris Winkle *(Chief Executive Officer)*
**Finance:** Tirath Bansal *(Financial Director)*
**Branches:** Sunrise Senior Living Ltd, High View, Rickmansworth, Hertfordshire WD3 5TQ
**US SIC:** 8321, 6732
**UK SIC:** 96111, 83100
**Auditors:** Ernst & Young LLP
**Bankers:** Bank Of Scotland (80-29-01)

| | 31-12-13 | 31-12-12 | 31-12-11 |
|---|---|---|---|
| TO | 8,307,804 | 10,342,571 | 9,732,313 |
| P/L | (4,784,392) | (118,487) | 707,853 |
| NW | (64,083) | 3,663,776 | 3,634,549 |
| WC | (334,248) | 3,532,756 | 3,533,176 |
| Emp. | 47 | 49 | 46 |

DUNS 21-585-9725
## Sunrise Senior Living of Knowle
1270 Warwick Road, Solihull, West Midlands B93 9LQ
**Tel:** 01564732400
**Web:** www.sunriseseniorliving.com
**Estd:** 2009 Proprietorship
**Line of Business:** Rest and retirement homes
**Proprietor:** Mrs H Keatley
**Responsibilities**
**Senior:** Pauline Hunter *(Executive Director)*
**US SIC:** 8321 **UK SIC:** 96111
**Employees:** 100

DUNS 21-583-3816
## Sunrise Senior Living of Solihull
1 Worcester Way, Shirley, Solihull, West Midlands B90 4JX
**Tel:** 01217012700
**Web:** www.sunrise-care.co.uk
**Estd:** 2011 Proprietorship
**Line of Business:** Nursing homes
**Proprietor:** M Dearn
**US SIC:** 8321 **UK SIC:** 96111
**Employees:** 120

DUNS 22-613-3585 Imp-Exp
## Sunsail Worldwide Sailing Ltd
(**Subsidiary of:** Tui Ag)
The Port House, Marina Keep, Port Solent, Portsmouth, Hampshire PO6 4TH
**Tel:** 01475676000 **Fax:** 023-9221-9827
**Web:** www.sunsail.com
**Reg No:** 1658245 **Estd:** 1976 Private Limited Company
**Line of Business:** Renting of passenger water transport equipment
**Trading Style:** Sunsail Worldwide Sailing Ltd
**Issued Capital:** £2,460,400
**Directors:** C J Parselle, M R Prior, F Bauguil, S B Cross, P V Cochran
**Co. Secretary:** Joyce Walter
**Responsibilities**
**Senior:** John Wimbleton *(Director tui)*
**Branches:** Sunsail Worldwide Sailing Ltd, The Port House, Marina Keep, Portsmouth, Hampshire PO6 4TH
**US SIC:** 4469, 4722
**UK SIC:** 76300, 77001
**Auditors:** KPMG Audit Plc
**Bankers:** Barclays Bank Plc (20-96-96)

| | 30-09-13 | 30-09-12 | 30-09-11 |
|---|---|---|---|
| TO | 32,053,000 | 30,250,000 | 29,189,000 |
| P/L | (7,533,000) | (3,493,000) | 1,783,000 |
| NW | 33,600,000 | 11,727,000 | 11,483,000 |
| WC | 40,322,000 | 11,875,000 | 5,111,000 |
| Emp. | 71 | 75 | 66 |

DUNS 77-944-8187
## Sunseeker International (Holdings) Ltd
(**Subsidiary of:** Portofino Yacht Investments Limited)
27-31 West Quay Road, Poole, Dorset BH15 1HX
**Tel:** 01202-381111 **Fax:** 01202-382222
**Reg No:** 5914384 **Estd:** 2006 Private Limited Company
**Line of Business:** Management activities of holding companies
**Issued Capital:** £104,112
**Directors:** B Ding, P C Popham, M Wheeler, J Wang, S Thakrar, N Hughes, C Liu
**Co. Secretary:** Adrian Powell
**US SIC:** 6711 **UK SIC:** 83962
**Auditors:** Deloitte LLP
**Bankers:** Bank Of Scotland (12-22-91)

| | 31-12-13 | 31-07-12 | 31-12-11 |
|---|---|---|---|
| TO | 343,770,000 | 288,820,000 | 276,097,000 |
| P/L | (31,037,000) | 17,069,000 | (7,175,000) |
| NW | (44,971,000) | (41,967,000) | (62,643,000) |
| WC | (70,155,000) | (28,817,000) | (45,341,000) |
| Emp. | 2,212 | 2,170 | 2,251 |

DUNS 23-080-7737
## Sunseeker London Ltd
21-22 Grosvenor Street, London SW1X 9FE
**Tel:** 02074933441 **Fax:** 02073550985
**Web:** www.sunseekerboats.co.uk
**Reg No:** 2875114 **Estd:** 1993 Private Limited Company
**Line of Business:** Other wholesale
**Issued Capital:** £100
**Principals:** D Lewis *(Managing)*, C P Head
**Co. Secretary:** Gary Cleaverly
**US SIC:** 5199, 5941
**UK SIC:** 61900, 65400
**Auditors:** UHY Hacker Young
**Bankers:** HSBC Bank plc (40-03-17)

| | 30-11-13 | 30-11-12 | 30-11-11 |
|---|---|---|---|
| TO | 101,686,773 | 110,873,481 | 85,113,394 |
| P/L | 1,370,754 | 2,500,729 | 1,680,797 |
| NW | 10,096,945 | 9,781,312 | 8,372,472 |
| WC | 8,312,666 | 7,055,272 | 6,380,331 |
| Emp. | 53 | 53 | 51 |

DUNS 28-888-7052
## Sunset & Vine Productions Ltd
(**Subsidiary of:** Dmwsl 660 Ltd)
Elsinore House, 77 Fulham Palace Road, London W6 8JA
**Tel:** 020-7478-7300
**Web:** www.sunsetvine.co.uk
**Reg No:** 1257931 **Estd:** 1990 Private Limited Company
**Line of Business:** Television activities
**Export Sales:** £4,508,000
**Trading Style:** T V Corporation
**Issued Capital:** £2
**Principals:** J Foulser *(Managing)*, J H Leach, O G Jones, Ms J Roberts, W A Rees
**Co. Secretary:** Ms Sara Bond
**Responsibilities**
**Senior:** Gary Franses *(Executive Producer)*, David Stranks *(Executive Producer)*
**Marketing:** Nick Vance *(PR Manager)*
**Operations:** Gary Franses *(Executive Producer)*, Diana Keen *(Production Manager)*, David Stranks *(Executive Producer)*
**Engineering:** Gary Franses *(Executive Producer)*, David Stranks *(Executive Producer)*
**US SIC:** 4833 **UK SIC:** 97411
**Auditors:** KPMG Audit PLC

| | 30-09-13 | 30-09-12 | 30-09-11 |
|---|---|---|---|
| TO | 21,449,000 | 21,624,000 | 20,752,000 |
| P/L | 2,565,000 | 3,586,000 | 2,497,000 |
| NW | 2,605,000 | 1,982,000 | 614,000 |
| WC | 305,000 | (296,000) | (1,773,000) |
| Emp. | 74 | 58 | 58 |

DUNS 23-941-3847
## Sunshine Cruise Holidays Ltd
(**Subsidiary of:** Royal Caribbean Cruises Ltd.)
Falcon Court 209 211, Broadway, Salford, Lancashire M50 2UE
**Tel:** 01617721023
**Web:** www.cruise1st.co.uk
**Reg No:** 3931005 **Estd:** 1999 Private Limited Company
**Line of Business:** Activities of travel agencies
**Issued Capital:** £75,000
**Principals:** D R Townsley *(Managing)*, M Caspar, D J Paul
**Co. Secretary:** Mrs Ruth Marshall
**US SIC:** 4722 **UK SIC:** 77001
**Auditors:** KPMG Audit PLC
**Bankers:** National Westminster Bank Plc (60-60-40)

| | 31-12-13 | 31-12-12 | 31-12-11 |
|---|---|---|---|
| TO | 19,737,378 | 17,727,003 | 13,990,314 |
| P/L | 18,407 | (158,084) | (348,210) |
| NW | 1,651,990 | 900,639 | 1,159,378 |
| WC | 61,369 | (659,914) | 370,053 |
| Emp. | 62 | 60 | 52 |

DUNS 50-978-6034
## Sunshine Garden Services Ltd
Durnsford Road, London N11 2EL
**Tel:** 020-8889-4224 **Fax:** 020-8881-3818
**Web:** www.sunshinegardencentre.co.uk
**Reg No:** 3295628 **Estd:** 1996 Private Limited Company
**Line of Business:** Other retail sale in specialised stores not elsewhere classified
**Issued Capital:** £20,000
**Directors:** E Loughrey, P A Douglass
**Co. Secretary:** Mrs Stephanie Loughrey
**US SIC:** 5999 **UK SIC:** 65600
**Auditors:** Foster Lewis Stone

| | 31-12-13 | 31-12-12 | 31-12-11 |
|---|---|---|---|
| TA | 975,785 | 768,114 | 572,556 |
| NW | 388,169 | 264,312 | 165,062 |
| WC | 305,362 | 193,786 | 62,162 |

DUNS 23-021-8724
## Sunter Ltd
14 Hetton Lyons Industrial Estate, Houghton-Le-Spring, Tyne and Wear DH5 0RH
**Tel:** 0191-526-8106
**Web:** www.sunters.com
**Reg No:** 3551244 **Estd:** 1973 Private Limited Company
**Line of Business:** Plumbing
**Trading Style:** Sunter Bros Garage
**Issued Capital:** £20,100
**Principals:** T Sunter *(Managing)*, Ms M Sunter, L T Sunter, K Stubbs
**Branches:** Sunter Ltd, Unit 15 Hetton Lyons Indstl Est, Houghton Le Spring, Tyne and Wear DH5 0RH
**US SIC:** 1711 **UK SIC:** 50300
**Auditors:** J N Straughan & Co

| | 30-04-14 | 30-04-13 | 30-04-12 |
|---|---|---|---|
| TO | N/A | 5,744,047 | 8,142,278 |
| P/L | N/A | (389,122) | 394,681 |
| NW | 1,819,965 | 1,768,218 | 2,086,459 |
| WC | 1,313,817 | 1,248,388 | 1,544,575 |
| Emp. | N/A | 61 | 59 |

DUNS 21-404-8829 **Imp-Exp**
## Sunvic Controls Ltd
(**Subsidiary of:** Tayclyde Ltd)
251 Low Waters Road Cadzow Industrial, Estate, Hamilton, Lanarkshire ML3 7QN
**Tel:** 01698-812944
**Web:** www.sunvic.co.uk
**Reg No:** 0786405 **Estd:** 1964 Private Limited Company
**Line of Business:** Wholesale of hardware, plumbing and heating equipment and supplies
**Export Markets:** Worldwide
**Issued Capital:** £100
**Director:** D M Paulin
**Responsibilities**
**Senior:** Mark Broidy *(Despatch Coordinator)*
**Finance:** Colin Hamilton *(Financial Controller)*
**Sales:** Pamela Canavan *(Sales Manager)*
**HR:** Moira Campbell *(Training Manager)*, Pam Caneven *(Human Resources Manager)*
**Health & Safety:** John McGuiness *(Health & Safety Officer)*
**US SIC:** 5074 **UK SIC:** 61300
**Auditors:** FB Accountancy Services Ltd
**Bankers:** HSBC Bank plc (40-02-50)

| | 31-05-14 | 31-05-13 | 31-05-12 |
|---|---|---|---|
| TA | 1,066,214 | 1,388,249 | 1,601,688 |
| NW | 363,027 | 396,369 | 485,894 |
| WC | 304,229 | 331,825 | 449,323 |

DUNS 21-718-9117
## Sunvil International Sales Ltd
7-11 Upper Square, Isleworth, Middlesex TW7 7BJ
**Tel:** 02088473041 **Fax:** 02082329790
**Web:** www.sunvil.co.uk
**Reg No:** 0984970 **Estd:** 1997 Private Limited Company
**Line of Business:** Travel agency activities
**Trading Style:** Sunvil Travel, Sunvil Holidays, Discovery World, Greek Islands
**Issued Capital:** £288,000
**Principals:** P V Der Parthog *(Chairman and Managing)*, N C Josephides *(Managing)*, C Wright, N J Der Parthog
**Co. Secretary:** Ismet Emin
**Responsibilities**
**Senior:** June Purves *(Manager)*
**US SIC:** 4722 **UK SIC:** 77001
**Auditors:** BKR Haines Watts
**Bankers:** Lloyds TSB Bank plc (30-97-06)

| | 31-12-13 | 31-12-12 | 31-12-11 |
|---|---|---|---|
| TO | 27,479,632 | 23,738,557 | 23,802,789 |
| P/L | 270,268 | 158,297 | 35,448 |
| NW | 2,611,261 | 2,373,879 | 2,288,065 |
| WC | 770,250 | 503,943 | 399,545 |
| Emp. | 70 | 70 | 71 |

DUNS 39-230-4234
## Sunway Travel (Coaching) Ltd
(**Subsidiary of:** Tours Abroad Group Ltd)
Sunway House, West Bawtry Road Canklow Meadows, Industrial Estate, Rotherham, South Yorkshire S60 2XR
**Tel:** 01709-839839 **Fax:** 01709-833821
**Web:** www.leger.co.uk
**Reg No:** 2115045 **VAT No:** 806152749
**Estd:** 1987 Private Limited Company
**Line of Business:** Activities of travel organisers
**Trading Style:** Leger Holidays
**Issued Capital:** £183,525
**Principals:** I D Henry *(Managing)*, H D Williams, P Mctiernan, Mrs K Henry
**Co. Secretary:** Nicholas Newton
**Responsibilities**
**HR:** Michelle Ford *(Training Manager)*
**Health & Safety:** hannah scott *(health and safety director)*
**US SIC:** 4722 **UK SIC:** 77001
**Auditors:** RSM Tenon Audit Ltd
**Bankers:** National Westminster Bank Plc (60-13-15)

| | 31-12-13 | 31-12-12 | 31-12-11 |
|---|---|---|---|
| TO | 29,244,159 | 29,990,368 | 29,566,666 |
| P/L | 1,882,373 | 2,073,694 | 1,742,102 |
| NW | 1,782,021 | 1,649,849 | 1,534,959 |
| WC | 1,145,625 | 1,084,477 | 1,000,994 |
| Emp. | 103 | 103 | 107 |

DUNS 38-781-1631
## Sunyip
142-154 Sherlock Street, Birmingham, West Midlands B5 6NB
**Tel:** 0121-622-1849
**Estd:** 1997 Partnership
**Line of Business:** Cash and carry wholesalers
**Partners:** P T Yip, S Yip
**Responsibilities**
**Senior:** Chee Yip *(Manager)*
**US SIC:** 5411 **UK SIC:** 64100
**Bankers:** Bank Of China (40-51-46)
**Employees:** 49

DUNS 21-833-1211
## Supacat Group Ltd
The Airfield, Dunkeswell Airfield, Honiton, Devon EX14 4LF
**Tel:** 07785735264
**Web:** www.supacat.com
**Reg No:** 8020542 **Estd:** 2012 Private Limited Company
**Line of Business:** Management activities of holding companies
**Export Sales:** £6,199,859
**Issued Capital:** £925
**Directors:** N L Jones, R S Ames, Ms E M Jones, A S Mitchell
**Co. Secretary:** Alan Mitchell
**US SIC:** 6711 **UK SIC:** 83962
**Bankers:** The Royal Bank Of Scotland Plc (16-19-25)

| | 31-08-13 |
|---|---|
| TO | 14,824,370 |
| P/L | 994,783 |
| NW | 9,346,070 |
| WC | 9,117,015 |
| Emp. | 131 |

DUNS 29-820-0197
## Supacleen Ltd
1 Bessemer Close, Cardiff, South Glamorgan CF11 8DL
**Tel:** 02920666663 **Fax:** 0845-363-0405
**Web:** www.supacleen.co.uk
**Reg No:** 2038165 **Estd:** 1986 Private Limited Company
**Line of Business:** Traditional cleaning activities
**Issued Capital:** £150
**Director:** J C Hexter
**Co. Secretary:** Lee Hexter
**US SIC:** 7399, 7341, 7349
**UK SIC:** 83954, 91300
**Auditors:** PricewaterhouseCoopers

| | 31-07-13 | 31-07-12 | 31-07-11 |
|---|---|---|---|
| TA | 244,957 | 226,632 | 259,044 |
| NW | 47,421 | 43,578 | 39,286 |
| WC | 30,449 | 17,569 | 780 |

DUNS 21-009-6575
## Supaglaze Ltd
Shepley House Outram Road, Dukinfield, Cheshire SK16 4XE
**Tel:** 01612223131
**Reg No:** 6334186 **Estd:** 2007 Private Limited Company
**Line of Business:** Manufacture of other plastic products
**Issued Capital:** £3
**Directors:** A G Fry, D L Howard
**Co. Secretary:** Timothy Walker
**US SIC:** 3079 **UK SIC:** 48360
**Auditors:** Downham Morris & Co

| | 31-12-13 | 31-12-12 | 31-12-11 |
|---|---|---|---|
| TO | 11,468,921 | 9,580,308 | 8,576,854 |
| P/L | 1,273,288 | 874,939 | 717,986 |
| NW | 2,053,524 | 1,420,312 | 1,058,489 |
| WC | 1,712,115 | 1,171,013 | 803,418 |
| Emp. | 121 | 101 | 92 |

DUNS 22-625-1833 **Imp**
## Supaglazing Ltd
Unit 5 Deacon Trading Centre, Knight Road, Rochester, Kent ME2 2AU
**Tel:** 01634727406
**Web:** www.supaglazing.com
**Reg No:** 1559083 **VAT No:** 304360206
**Estd:** 1981 Private Limited Company
**Line of Business:** Double glazing suppliers
**Trading Style:** Supaglazing Ltd
**Issued Capital:** £1,000
**Principals:** G A Jones *(Financial)*, L A Jones, Ms K G Keen
**Co. Secretary:** Ms Elefteria Jones
**Responsibilities**
**Admin:** S Mintram *(Office Manager)*
**IT:** S Mintram *(Office Manager)*
**Branches:** Supaglazing Ltd, 13 Lowfield Street, Dartford, Kent DA1 1EN
**US SIC:** 1721 **UK SIC:** 50400
**Auditors:** E G Bellamy & Co
**Bankers:** HSBC Bank plc (40-31-06)

| | 30-06-13 | 30-06-12 | 30-06-11 |
|---|---|---|---|
| TA | 3,461,029 | 3,232,110 | 3,013,336 |
| NW | 1,107,336 | 1,252,181 | 1,224,274 |
| WC | 738,170 | 803,468 | 798,861 |

DUNS 54-382-8487
## Super Camps Ltd
(**Subsidiary of:** Cognita Topco Limited)
11c Milton Road, Abingdon, Oxfordshire OX14 4BP
**Tel:** 01235-832222 **Fax:** 01235-831991
**Web:** www.supercamps.co.uk
**Reg No:** 3267803 **Estd:** 1996 Private Limited Company
**Line of Business:** Childcare services
**Issued Capital:** £100
**Directors:** E J Hyslop, G M Ker, P Thornhill
**Co. Secretary:** Emw Secretaries Limited
**Responsibilities**
**Senior:** Gary Narunsky *(Manager)*, Mark Vingoe *(Manager)*
**US SIC:** 8321 **UK SIC:** 96111
**Auditors:** TaxAssist Direct
**Bankers:** Alliance & Leicester Plc (16-50-26)

| | 31-08-14 | 31-08-13 | 31-08-12 |
|---|---|---|---|
| TO | 3,377,000 | 3,618,000 | 3,501,000 |
| P/L | 287,000 | 236,000 | 392,000 |
| NW | 1,180,000 | 1,414,000 | 1,890,000 |
| WC | 843,000 | 1,144,000 | 1,706,000 |
| Emp. | 99 | 113 | 114 |

DUNS 23-259-8011 **Exp**
## Super Seal Window Systems Ltd
Unit B1 B2 Kilbegs Business Park, Kilbegs Road, Antrim, Co Antrim BT41 4NN
**Tel:** 028-9446-5772 **Fax:** 028-9446-5831
**Web:** www.supersealni.com
**Reg No:** 0024368NI **Estd:** 1990 Private Limited Company
**Line of Business:** Replacement window services and repairs
**Export Markets:** Republic Of Ireland
**Export Sales:** £2,257,899
**Issued Capital:** £2
**Directors:** Mrs E A Taylor, T K Taylor
**Co. Secretary:** Thomas Taylor
**Responsibilities**
**Senior:** Claire Mulholland *(General Manager)*
**Branches:** Super Seal Window Systems Ltd, Superseal Window Systems, Unit 3, Magherafelt, Co Londonderry BT45 8HN
**US SIC:** 1799, 1751
**UK SIC:** 50000, 50400
**Auditors:** Mcilveen Howard & Co
**Bankers:** The Bank Of Ireland (90-49-82)

| | 31-03-13 | 31-03-12 | 31-03-11 |
|---|---|---|---|
| TO | 8,261,216 | 7,813,242 | 6,621,622 |
| P/L | 580,066 | 254,947 | 83,303 |
| NW | 1,560,950 | 1,200,477 | 1,106,749 |
| WC | 311,549 | (61,077) | (190,317) |
| Emp. | 76 | 74 | 73 |

DUNS 21-779-7162
## Super Value
26 Newry Street, Banbridge, Co Down BT32 3HB
**Tel:** 02840622329
**Web:** www.shop.supervalu.ie
**Estd:** 2011 Proprietorship
**Line of Business:** Retail sale in non-specialised stores (excluding ctns) holding an alcohol licence with food, beverages or tobacco predominating
**Proprietor:** F Mcpolin
**Responsibilities**
**Senior:** Frank McPolin *(Proprietor)*
**US SIC:** 5199 **UK SIC:** 61900
**Employees:** 50

DUNS 22-719-0626
## Superbreak Mini-Holidays Ltd
(**Subsidiary of:** Cox and Kings Limited)
Apollo House, York, North Yorkshire YO31 7RE
**Tel:** 08712214444 **Fax:** 0871-221-3377
**Web:** www.superbreak.com
**Reg No:** 1674987 **Estd:** 1983 Private Limited Company
**Line of Business:** Travel agency activities
**Trading Style:** Goldenrail, Superbreak, Highlife
**Issued Capital:** £10,000
**Directors:** T W May, N Bali, P R Richards, Mrs J L Atkins, A Goenka, A P Menon, I D Anderson, D L Neylon
**Co. Secretary:** Timothy May
**Responsibilities**
**Marketing:** Richard Stelmach *(Website Developer)*
**US SIC:** 4722 **UK SIC:** 77001
**Auditors:** Deloitte LLP
**Bankers:** National Westminster Bank Plc (56-00-70)

| | 31-03-14 | 31-03-13 | 31-03-12 |
|---|---|---|---|
| TO | 77,305,451 | 73,100,890 | 132,479,744 |
| P/L | 5,863,313 | 6,323,089 | (6,253,363) |
| NW | 14,856,745 | 16,385,034 | 10,815,369 |
| WC | 29,939,740 | 32,199,266 | 26,661,907 |
| Emp. | 164 | 156 | 186 |

DUNS 23-737-0924
## Superclean Services Wothorpe Ltd
Unit 7, Stamford, Lincolnshire PE9 2JL
**Tel:** 01780-480016 **Fax:** 01780-480017
**Web:** www.scswothorpe.co.uk
**Reg No:** 3731435 **Estd:** 1999 Private Limited Company
**Line of Business:** Cleaning contracting commercial
**Issued Capital:** £1,000
**Director:** C R Pratt
**Co. Secretary:** Ms Pamela Pratt
**US SIC:** 7349 **UK SIC:** 92300
**Auditors:** MacIntyre Hudson LLP

| | 31-03-14 | 31-03-13 | 31-03-12 |
|---|---|---|---|
| TO | 7,942,819 | 6,697,719 | 6,262,271 |
| P/L | 28,064 | 144,129 | 78,092 |
| NW | 170,428 | 147,977 | 168,409 |
| WC | 261,341 | 60,889 | 243,060 |
| Emp. | 1,224 | 974 | 998 |

DUNS 77-952-8868
## Supercover Insurance Ltd
(**Subsidiary of:** Markerstudy Holdings Limited)
Cumberland House, 80 Scrubs Lane, Harlesden, London NW10 6RF
**Tel:** 02089604191
**Web:** www.supercoverinsurance.com
**Reg No:** 3058631 **Estd:** 1995 Private Limited Company
**Line of Business:** Activities auxiliary to insurance and pension funding
**Issued Capital:** £100,000
**Directors:** K J Barber, G Humphreys, K R Spencer
**Co. Secretary:** Mrs Susan Hayward
**Responsibilities**
**Senior:** Amanda Kerry-Wallington *(Manager)*, Carmi Korine *(Manager)*
**US SIC:** 7399, 6399
**UK SIC:** 83954, 82001
**Auditors:** Sopher & Co
**Bankers:** Bank Of Scotland (12-21-37)

| | 31-05-13 | 31-05-12 | 31-05-11 |
|---|---|---|---|
| TO | 8,754,145 | N/A | N/A |
| P/L | 1,670,692 | N/A | N/A |
| NW | 1,277,628 | 626,619 | 340,339 |
| WC | 1,201,719 | 551,829 | 262,702 |
| Emp. | 71 | N/A | N/A |

DUNS 22-518-6279 **Imp-Exp**
## Supercraft Ltd
(**Subsidiary of:** Supercraft Holdings Ltd)
Canada Road Oyster Lane, West Byfleet, Surrey KT14 7JL
**Tel:** 01932-351941 **Fax:** 01932-340807
**Web:** www.supercraft.co.uk
**Reg No:** 1624314 **VAT No:** 226033500
**Estd:** 1982 Private Limited Company
**Line of Business:** Sheet metal fabricators
**Export Markets:** Italy, Germany
**Export Sales:** £247,162
**Issued Capital:** £75,000
**Directors:** P Barber, J Riordan, G A Green, D Mcdougall
**Co. Secretary:** Jeffrey Dosser
**Responsibilities**
**Senior:** Andy Kirby *(General Manager)*
**Marketing:** Keith Middlecott *(Business Development Director)*
**IT:** I. Rashid *(IT Manager)*
**Purchasing:** Wayne Garbutt *(Purchasing Officer)*
**US SIC:** 4582, 1622
**UK SIC:** 76400, 50200
**Auditors:** Wilkins Kennedy
**Bankers:** HSBC Bank plc (40-47-08)

| | 31-03-14 | 31-03-13 | 31-03-12 |
|---|---|---|---|
| TO | 13,058,809 | 9,759,508 | 10,928,193 |
| P/L | 1,458,657 | 1,709,291 | 1,004,978 |
| NW | 2,109,200 | 1,884,642 | 1,628,168 |
| WC | 1,322,155 | 1,370,998 | 1,220,969 |
| Emp. | 129 | 108 | 99 |

DUNS 21-036-0020 **Imp**
## Superdrug Stores Plc
(**Subsidiary of:** A.S. Watson (Europe) Holdings B.V.)
118 Beddington Lane, Croydon, Surrey CR0 4TB
**Fax:** 02086-846102
**Web:** www.superdrug.com
**Reg No:** 0807043 **VAT No:** 777947160
**Estd:** 1964 Public Limited Company
**Line of Business:** Drug stores outlets
**Trading Style:** Superdrug
**Issued Capital:** £220,000,000
**Directors:** Dr A J Heaton, Ms G G Smith, P W Macnab, D K Lai
**Co. Secretary:** Ms Edith Shih

**Responsibilities**
**Senior:** Joey Watt *(Manager)*
**IT:** Bill Fitzgerald *(IT Infrastructure Services Tea)*
**Health & Safety:** Michael Courtier *(Health & Safety Officer)*
**Facilities:** Eddie Page *(Facilities Manager)*
**Branches:** Superdrug Stores Plc, Superdrug Stores Plc, 53A-54 Middle St South, Driffield, North Humberside YO25 6PS
**US SIC:** 5912, 5999
**UK SIC:** 64300, 65600
**Auditors:** PricewaterhouseCoopers LLP
**Bankers:** National Westminster Bank Plc (60-00-01)

Following financial data are in thousands

| | 28-12-13 | 29-12-12 | 31-12-11 |
|---|---|---|---|
| TO | 1,010,212 | 1,021,021 | 1,049,128 |
| P/L | 28,982 | (3,977) | 5,517 |
| NW | 122,235 | 106,905 | 124,652 |
| WC | 55,060 | 30,094 | 27,397 |
| Emp. | 6,352 | 6,580 | 7,116 |

DUNS 39-707-9351 **Imp-Exp**

## Superglass Insulation Ltd

**(Subsidiary of:** Superglass Holdings Plc)
6 Kerse Road, Stirling, Stirlingshire FK7 7QQ
**Tel:** 01786451170
**Web:** www.superglass.co.uk
**Reg No:** 2160591 **VAT No:** 864438693
**Estd:** 1987 Private Limited Company
**Line of Business:** Cladding and insulation materials
**Export Markets:** Germany, France, Denmark
**Issued Capital:** £100,000
**Directors:** C P Lea, A J Mcleod
**Co. Secretary:** Christopher Lea
**Responsibilities**
**Senior:** John Ivinson *(Operations Director)*
**Sales:** Tony Gordon *(Commercial Manager)*
**IT:** George Williamson *(IT Manager)*
**Health & Safety:** Paul Tyers *(Health & Safety Officer)*
**Operations:** John Ivinson *(Operations Director)*, Paul Tyers *(Health & Safety Officer)*
**Purchasing:** Tony Gordon *(Commercial Manager)*
**Branches:** Superglass Insulation Ltd, Thistle Industrial Estate Kerse, Stirling, Stirlingshire FK7 7QQ
**US SIC:** 3079 **UK SIC:** 48360
**Auditors:** KPMG Audit PLC
**Bankers:** Bank Of Scotland (12-09-19)

| | 31-08-13 | 31-08-12 | 31-08-11 |
|---|---|---|---|
| TO | 25,195,000 | 33,402,000 | 33,406,000 |
| P/L | (5,565,000) | (2,064,000) | (12,711,000) |
| NW | 2,831,000 | 7,733,000 | 9,040,000 |
| WC | (14,311,000) | (8,761,000) | (4,955,000) |
| Emp. | 178 | 189 | 199 |

DUNS 21-626-8418 **Imp**

## Supergroup Plc

Unit 60 The Runnings, Cheltenham, Gloucestershire GL51 9NW
**Web:** www.supergroupholdings.com
**Reg No:** 7063562 **VAT No:** 974823775
**Estd:** 2009 Public Limited Company
**Line of Business:** Wholesale of clothing and footwear
**Export Sales:** £176,100,000
**Issued Capital:** £4,011,729
**Directors:** J M Dunkerton, J Holder, T M Powell, E A Sutherland, P R Bamford, S S Wills, K Mccall, K G Edelman
**Co. Secretary:** Mrs Lindsay Beardsell
**Responsibilities**
**Senior:** Wendy Edwards *(Manager)*, Susanne Given *(Director)*, Minnow Powell *(Non-Executive Director and Cha)*, Indira Thambiah *(Non-Executive Director)*
**Finance:** Minnow Powell *(Non-Executive Director and Cha)*
**Sales:** Flemming Jensen *(Global Head of Sales)*
**Operations:** Susanne Given *(Director)*
**Branches:** Supergroup Plc, Barnwood, 4 Barnett Way, Barnwood, Gloucester, Gloucestershire GL4 3GG
**US SIC:** 5136, 5699, 5661, 5999
**UK SIC:** 61600, 64500, 64600, 65600
**Auditors:** PricewaterhouseCoopers LLP

| | 26-04-14 | 28-04-13 | 29-04-12 |
|---|---|---|---|
| TO | 430,900,000 | 360,400,000 | 313,800,000 |
| P/L | 45,200,000 | 51,800,000 | 51,400,000 |
| NW | 212,900,000 | 182,000,000 | 143,300,000 |
| WC | 145,200,000 | 116,900,000 | 75,800,000 |
| Emp. | 2,228 | 2,022 | 1,774 |

DUNS 21-233-7604

## Superide Ltd

**(Subsidiary of:** Brennan Enterprise Ltd)
Windsor Mill, Hollinwood, Oldham, Lancashire OL8 3RA
**Tel:** 01616812206
**Web:** www.fergusonpolycom.co.uk
**Reg No:** 0579444 **VAT No:** 145070884
**Estd:** 1951 Private Limited Company
**Line of Business:** Manufacturers of fabricated rubber products
**Issued Capital:** £15,000
**Director:** P G Brennan
**US SIC:** 3031 **UK SIC:** 48123

| | 31-12-13 | 31-12-12 | 31-12-11 |
|---|---|---|---|
| TA | 15,000 | 15,000 | 15,000 |
| NW | 15,000 | 15,000 | 15,000 |

DUNS 64-117-7212

## Superior Cleaning Ltd.

51 Brebner Crescent, Aberdeen, Aberdeenshire AB16 7HT
**Tel:** 01224-690069 **Fax:** 01224690210
**Web:** www.superiorcleaningltd.co.uk
**Reg No:** 0236065SC **Estd:** 2004 Private Limited Company
**Line of Business:** Cleaning contracting commercial
**Issued Capital:** £2
**Director:** S S Brown
**Co. Secretary:** Andrew Brown
**US SIC:** 7349 **UK SIC:** 92300

| | 30-09-13 | 30-09-12 | 30-09-11 |
|---|---|---|---|
| TA | 157,647 | 176,002 | 146,693 |
| NW | 84,702 | 102,984 | 71,065 |
| WC | 73,786 | 87,419 | 56,672 |

DUNS 37-762-5041

## Superior Cold Store

Riby Street, Grimsby, South Humberside DN31 3HF
**Tel:** 01472350071
**Web:** www superiorseafoods.co.uk
**Estd:** 1990 Proprietorship
**Line of Business:** Cold storage
**Proprietor:** M Eaton
**US SIC:** 4226 **UK SIC:** 77003
**Employees:** 65

DUNS 22-553-4577

## Superior Creative Services Ltd

**(Subsidiary of:** Superior G Ltd)
Hercules Way, Bowerhill, Melksham, Wiltshire SN12 6TS
**Tel:** 01225704311
**Web:** www.superior.co.uk
**Reg No:** 1248213 **Estd:** 1976 Private Limited Company
**Line of Business:** Printers general
**Issued Capital:** £40,000
**Directors:** R Blueitt, R C Masterton, M J King
**Co. Secretary:** Ian O'Connor
**Responsibilities**
**Senior:** Stewart Powell *(Print Manager)*
**Sales:** Matthew Attree *(Business Development Manager)*
**IT:** Stewart Powell *(Print Manager)*
**Facilities:** Adrian Ashdown *(Maintenance Manager)*
**Branches:** Superior Creative Services Ltd, Unit 28, Hercules Way, Melksham, Wiltshire SN12 6TS
**US SIC:** 2794, 7311
**UK SIC:** 47545, 83800
**Auditors:** Monahans
**Bankers:** HSBC Bank plc (40-32-13)

| | 31-03-14 | 31-03-13 | 31-03-12 |
|---|---|---|---|
| TO | 16,795,767 | 16,139,320 | 15,201,867 |
| P/L | 773,173 | 948,976 | 654,809 |
| NW | 4,310,731 | 3,906,736 | 4,112,511 |
| WC | 2,035,967 | 1,951,938 | 2,068,913 |
| Emp. | 146 | 137 | 128 |

DUNS 29-682-8627 **Exp**

## Superior Food Ltd

**(Subsidiary of:** India Hospitality Corp)
Unit 1 The Square, Southall Lane, Southall, Middlesex UB2 5NH
**Tel:** 08453131546 **Fax:** 02088138512
**Web:** www.adeliefoods.co.uk
**Reg No:** 2006417 **VAT No:** 673030949
**Estd:** 2000 Private Limited Company
**Line of Business:** Pizza suppliers
**Issued Capital:** £6,069,100
**Director:** G Cox
**Co. Secretary:** Gavin Cox
**Responsibilities**
**Senior:** David Guy *(Commercial Director)*, Fraser Hall *(Manager)*
**US SIC:** 5812, 2099
**UK SIC:** 66110, 42399
**Auditors:** Abbots
**Bankers:** National Westminster Bank Plc (55-50-39)

| | 29-03-14 | 30-03-13 | 01-03-11 |
|---|---|---|---|
| TO | 12,557,000 | 30,080,000 | 21,534,000 |
| P/L | (5,085,000) | (881,000) | 5,924,000 |
| NW | 2,446,000 | 1,813,000 | (3,522,000) |
| WC | 1,444,000 | 1,121,000 | 1,977,000 |
| Emp. | 234 | 335 | 353 |

DUNS 21-584-8400

## Superior Foods

Units 17 Armstrong Way, Southall, Middlesex UB2 4SD
**Tel:** 02087447933
**Web:** www.superiorfoods.co.uk
**Estd:** 2010
**Line of Business:** Manufacturers of food products
**Proprietor:** M Ballard
**US SIC:** 2099 **UK SIC:** 42399
**Employees:** 300

DUNS 21-921-8278

## Superior International Ltd

**(Subsidiary of:** Coöperatie Coforta U.A.)
Unit 2a Vantage Park, Washingley Road, Huntingdon, Cambridgeshire PE29 6SR
**Tel:** 01480422025 **Fax:** 01832-735200
**Reg No:** 0341680 **VAT No:** 486297590
**Estd:** 1938 Private Limited Company
**Line of Business:** Business services
**Issued Capital:** £5,000
**Directors:** Greenery Uk Limited, T Wortel
**Co. Secretary:** Ms Deborah Tarry
**US SIC:** 7399 **UK SIC:** 83954
**Auditors:** Grant Thornton
**Bankers:** Barclays Bank Plc (20-43-63)

| | 31-12-13 | 31-12-12 | 31-12-11 |
|---|---|---|---|
| NW | (62,542) | (62,542) | (62,542) |

DUNS 23-517-9426

## Superior Link Ltd

8 Nimrod Way, Wimborne, Dorset BH21 7PE
**Tel:** 01202890432 **Fax:** 01202890435
**Web:** www.superiorltd.com
**Reg No:** 3517020 **Estd:** 1998 Private Limited Company
**Line of Business:** Manufacturers of rubber seals
**Issued Capital:** £2
**Director:** T J Brown
**Co. Secretary:** Mark Wallis
**US SIC:** 3069 **UK SIC:** 48123

| | 31-05-14 | 31-05-13 | 31-05-12 |
|---|---|---|---|
| TA | 2 | 1 | 2 |
| NW | 2 | 1 | 2 |

DUNS 21-452-6170 **Imp**

## Superior Seals Ltd

**(Subsidiary of:** Superior Group Ltd)
East Dorset Trade Park Nimrod Way, Wimborne, Dorset BH21 7SH
**Tel:** 01202854300 **Fax:** 01202-854313
**Web:** www.superiorltd.com
**Reg No:** 0887366 **VAT No:** 186520551
**Estd:** 1998 Private Limited Company
**Line of Business:** Manufacture of other rubber products
**Export Sales:** £10,169,107
**Issued Capital:** £90
**Managing Director:** T J Brown
**Co. Secretary:** Mark Wallis
**Responsibilities**
**Senior:** Paskal Barat *(Senior Marketing Director)*
**Marketing:** Paskal Barat *(Senior Marketing Director)*
**Branches:** Superior Seals Ltd, 3 East Dorset Trade Park, Nimrod Way, Wimborne, Dorset BH21 7SH
**US SIC:** 3069 **UK SIC:** 48123
**Auditors:** Ward Goodman
**Bankers:** National Westminster Bank Plc (52-41-37)

| | 31-05-13 | 31-05-12 | 31-05-11 |
|---|---|---|---|
| TO | 20,017,333 | 20,480,832 | 18,930,975 |
| P/L | 3,985,671 | 3,758,076 | 3,600,780 |
| NW | 21,102,288 | 19,048,635 | 17,602,975 |
| WC | 16,918,394 | 15,134,282 | 12,981,657 |
| Emp. | 119 | 115 | 113 |

DUNS 23-246-4532

## Supernews Stores Ltd

**(Subsidiary of:** First Stop News Ltd)
12 Guildborne Centre, Worthing, West Sussex BN11 1LZ
**Tel:** 01903211364
**Reg No:** 4200709 **Estd:** 2001 Private Limited Company
**Line of Business:** Retail sale of tobacco products
**Issued Capital:** £5,050,000
**Directors:** A R Hargreave, M J Colley
**Co. Secretary:** Peter Hyett
**Branches:** Supernews Stores Ltd, 130 High Street, Blackwood, Gwent NP12 1AF
**US SIC:** 5993 **UK SIC:** 64200
**Auditors:** PricewaterhouseCoopers LLP
**Bankers:** National Westminster Bank Plc (60-07-06)

| | 26-07-14 | 27-07-13 | 28-07-12 |
|---|---|---|---|
| TO | 31,900,000 | 38,295,000 | 42,734,000 |
| P/L | 166,000 | (81,000) | 34,000 |
| NW | 2,517,000 | 2,362,000 | 2,399,000 |
| WC | N/A | N/A | 2,166,000 |
| Emp. | 161 | 254 | 260 |

DUNS 21-332-5020

## Supertune Automotive Ltd.

**(Subsidiary of:** McCarthy Shanks Ltd)
Oldham Central, Coulton Close Oldham Central Trading, Park, Oldham, Lancashire OL1 4EB
**Tel:** 01616263681
**Web:** www.supertune.co.uk
**Reg No:** 0932753 **VAT No:** 145403785
**Estd:** 1968 Private Limited Company
**Line of Business:** Motor factors
**Trading Style:** Supertune Automotive, Supertune Automotive (Bolton)
**Issued Capital:** £2,000
**Principals:** Miss M J Shanks *(Managing)*, C M Mccarthy *(Managing)*, C Roper
**Co. Secretary:** Christopher Mccarthy
**Branches:** Supertune Automotive Ltd., Ribble House, Bury, Lancashire BL9 0JA
**US SIC:** 2851 **UK SIC:** 25510
**Auditors:** Grundy Anderson & Kershaw
**Bankers:** Barclays Bank Plc (20-76-89)

| | 31-07-13 | 31-07-12 | 31-07-11 |
|---|---|---|---|
| TO | 13,210,508 | 12,284,959 | 9,112,134 |
| P/L | 250,785 | 152,262 | 111,047 |
| NW | 2,524,432 | 2,412,211 | 2,376,083 |
| WC | 1,888,342 | 1,733,651 | 1,754,147 |
| Emp. | 89 | 88 | 71 |

DUNS 21-782-6526

## Supervalu

30 Dungannon Road, Dungannon, Co Tyrone BT71 4HP
**Tel:** 02887746980
**Web:** www.supervalu.co.uk
**Estd:** 1994 Partnership
**Line of Business:** Retail sale of leather goods
**Partners:** K Kelly, S Murphy
**US SIC:** 5948 **UK SIC:** 64600
**Employees:** 80

DUNS 21-715-2242

## Supervalu Aughnacloy Ltd

Aughnacloy Orange Hall, 105 Moore Street, Aughnacloy, Co Tyrone BT69 6AR
**Tel:** 02885557899
**Web:** www.supervalu.co.uk
**Reg No:** 0606355NI **Estd:** 2011 Private Limited Company
**Line of Business:** Retail sale in non-specialised stores with food, beverages or tobacco predominating
**Trading Style:** Supervalu
**Issued Capital:** £2
**Directors:** Mrs M Daly, L Daly
**Co. Secretary:** Leo Daly
**US SIC:** 5411 **UK SIC:** 64100

| | 31-03-14 | 31-03-13 | 31-03-12 |
|---|---|---|---|
| TA | 489,210 | 362,614 | 170,102 |
| NW | 415,937 | 313,906 | 135,282 |
| WC | N/A | (48,706) | 135,282 |

DUNS 21-778-1451

## Supervalue

2-6 Lisburn Street, Ballynahinch, Co Down BT24 8BD
**Tel:** 02897565095
**Estd:** 2002 Proprietorship
**Line of Business:** Supermarkets
**Proprietor:** N Flynn
**US SIC:** 5411 **UK SIC:** 64100
**Employees:** 79

DUNS 21-172-1271

## Supply Chain Lincs Ltd

4 Henley Way, Doddington Road, Lincoln, Lincolnshire LN6 3QR
**Tel:** 01724734809 **Fax:** 01724292090
**Web:** www.dhl.com
**Reg No:** 6963540 **Estd:** 2009 Private Limited Company
**Line of Business:** Management and business consultants
**Issued Capital:** £1
**Director:** D Kemp
**US SIC:** 7392, 4213
**UK SIC:** 83951, 72300

| | 31-07-13 | 31-07-12 | 31-07-11 |
|---|---|---|---|
| TA | 141,574 | 179,138 | 119,285 |
| NW | 129,350 | 144,069 | 66,825 |
| WC | 127,146 | 140,256 | 63,431 |

DUNS 21-913-3691 **Imp-Exp**

## Supply Plus Ltd

**(Subsidiary of:** Supply 999 Holdings Ltd)
Unit 1 Stirling Way, Papworth Everard, Cambridge, Cambridgeshire CB23 3WA
**Tel:** 01480 832200 **Fax:** 01480 832233
**Web:** www.supplyplus.com
**Reg No:** 1047919 **Estd:** 2013 Private Limited Company
**Line of Business:** Safety equipment suppliers
**Export Markets:** Middle East, Malaysia and E U
**Export Sales:** £3,041,451
**Trading Style:** Collins Youldon
**Issued Capital:** £3,550
**Directors:** D Gotts, M Corbishley
**Co. Secretary:** Michael Corbishley
**Branches:** Supply Plus Ltd, Unit 1, Stirling Way, Cambridge, Cambridgeshire CB23 3WA
**US SIC:** 5999 **UK SIC:** 65600
**Auditors:** Grant Thornton UK LLP

**Bankers:** HSBC Bank plc (40-35-18)

| | 31-03-14 | 31-03-13 | 31-03-12 |
|---|---|---|---|
| TO | 7,746,548 | 7,135,235 | 8,239,645 |
| P/L | 747,808 | 303,038 | (723,535) |
| NW | 1,048,061 | 431,397 | 122,733 |
| WC | 994,189 | 334,074 | (12,854) |
| Emp. | 68 | 75 | 83 |

DUNS 64-099-4604
## Supply Point Systems Ltd
Units 3 & 4 Churchill Way, Leicester, Leicestershire LE8 8UD
**Tel:** 08445761247 **Fax:** 08445761248
**Web:** www.supplypointsystems.com
**Reg No:** 3495308 **Estd:** 2000 Private Limited Company
**Line of Business:** Manufacture of other special purpose machinery not elsewhere classified
**Export Sales:** £7,582,882
**Issued Capital:** £100,000
**Directors:** M Guppy, Q Potgieter, P Brown, A L Eisen
**Co. Secretary:** Andrew Evans
**Branches:** Supply Point Systems Ltd, Unit 21, Catteshall Lane, Godalming, Surrey GU7 1LG
**US SIC:** 3559 **UK SIC:** 32863
**Auditors:** W Accountancy Ltd
**Bankers:** Lloyds TSB Bank plc (30-94-97)

| | 31-08-13 | 31-08-12 | 31-08-11 |
|---|---|---|---|
| TO | 10,237,553 | N/A | N/A |
| P/L | 2,585,092 | N/A | N/A |
| NW | 6,613,477 | 5,108,643 | 3,822,149 |
| WC | 6,004,327 | 4,486,091 | 3,231,317 |
| Emp. | 57 | N/A | N/A |

DUNS 21-917-5148 Imp
## Supply Technologies (Ukgrp) Ltd
**(Subsidiary of:** Park-Ohio Holdings Corp.)
Unit 492 Holly Place, Preston, Lancashire PR5 8AX
**Tel:** 01772-339521
**Web:** www.supplytechnologies.com
**Reg No:** 0725298 **VAT No:** 174971429
**Estd:** 1880 Private Limited Company
**Line of Business:** Other business activities not elsewhere classified
**Export Sales:** £163,574
**Issued Capital:** £50,000
**Principals:** M Mchugh *(Managing)*, R D Vilsack, M J Mahon, W S Emerick, M L Justice, P E Hyland
**Co. Secretary:** Robert Vilsack
**Responsibilities**
**Senior:** Christina Mchugh *(Manager)*
**Facilities:** Phil Tetley *(Transport Manager)*
**Purchasing:** Adam Morris *(Purchasing Manager)*
**Fleet:** Phil Tetley *(Transport Manager)*
**Branches:** Supply Technologies (Ukgrp) Ltd, Unit 2, Brooklands Way, Boldon Colliery, Tyne and Wear NE35 9LZ
**US SIC:** 7399 **UK SIC:** 83954
**Auditors:** BDO LLP
**Bankers:** Bank Of Scotland (80-07-48)

| | 31-03-14 | 31-03-13 | 31-03-12 |
|---|---|---|---|
| TO | 15,867,342 | 15,678,282 | 13,789,368 |
| P/L | 2,350,528 | 1,768,164 | 1,507,657 |
| NW | 1,368,902 | 4,866,489 | 3,724,594 |
| WC | 652,128 | 4,121,917 | 3,489,432 |
| Emp. | 56 | 58 | 68 |

DUNS 23-543-6768 Imp
## Supply U K Hire Shops Ltd
Lowry House Opal Court, Manchester M14 6ZT
**Tel:** 01612244600 **Fax:** 0161-224-7200
**Web:** www.supplyuk.co.uk
**Reg No:** 3542206 **Estd:** 1998 Private Limited Company
**Line of Business:** Tool hire services
**Trading Style:** Supply U K Hire Shops Ltd
**Issued Capital:** £10,000
**Directors:** S J Mulley, R Coffey, N Topping
**Co. Secretary:** Christopher Haycocks
**Responsibilities**
**Senior:** Jim Field *(Director of Commercial)*
**Branches:** Supply U K Hire Shops Ltd, Unit 11 Marshgate Business Centre, London E15 2NH
**US SIC:** 7394 **UK SIC:** 84000
**Auditors:** Dyke Yaxley Ltd
**Bankers:** HSBC Bank plc (40-43-56)

| | 30-04-14 | 30-04-13 | 30-04-12 |
|---|---|---|---|
| TO | 15,788,864 | 14,028,300 | 11,076,707 |
| P/L | 1,273,937 | 1,254,138 | 600,733 |
| NW | 3,664,694 | 2,643,151 | 1,960,631 |
| WC | (1,304,254) | (236,945) | (1,277,306) |
| Emp. | 150 | 145 | 138 |

DUNS 23-519-2148
## Support for Ordinary Living
58-60 Albert Street, Motherwell, Lanarkshire ML1 1PR
**Tel:** 01698-276206
**Web:** www.forliving.org
**Reg No:** 0183408SC **Estd:** 2008 Private Limited Company

**Line of Business:** Social work activities without accommodation
**Directors:** S J Gibb, Ms J K Findlay, J Hoey, Ms L Shields, Ms A Bowman, J R Alexander, Ms M J Blair, I P Turner
**Co. Secretary:** Bernard Ruddy
**Responsibilities**
**Senior:** Gina Hagan *(Manager)*, Donna Thompson *(Manager)*
**Marketing:** Crawford Ross *(Operations Manager)*
**Health & Safety:** Crawford Ross *(Operations Manager)*
**Facilities:** Crawford Ross *(Operations Manager)*
**US SIC:** 8321, 7361
**UK SIC:** 96111, 83954
**Auditors:** MacMillan & Co
**Bankers:** The Co-Operative Bank Plc (83-91-26)

| | 31-03-14 | 31-03-13 | 31-03-12 |
|---|---|---|---|
| TO | 3,916,655 | 4,314,388 | 4,613,851 |
| P/L | (190,881) | (214,914) | 93,370 |
| NW | 620,879 | 811,760 | 1,026,674 |
| WC | 597,701 | 780,858 | 986,068 |
| Emp. | 221 | 245 | 241 |

DUNS 22-217-2889
## Support in Sport Group Ltd
**(Subsidiary of:** Support in Sport Group (Irl) Limited)
Glasson Industrial Estate, Maryport, Cumbria CA15 8NT
**Tel:** 01900-812796
**Web:** www.supportinsport.com
**Reg No:** 4235291 **Estd:** 2001 Private Limited Company
**Line of Business:** Construction of motorways, roads, railways, airfields and sports facilities
**Export Sales:** £1,760,502
**Issued Capital:** £45,250
**Directors:** G A Mullan, D W Kells
**Co. Secretary:** Grahame Jones
**Responsibilities**
**Senior:** Alan Wearmouth *(Manager)*
**US SIC:** 1611 **UK SIC:** 50200

| | 31-12-13 | 31-12-12 | 31-12-11 |
|---|---|---|---|
| TO | 11,658,956 | 10,528,418 | 8,846,060 |
| P/L | 159,699 | 127,500 | 16,261 |
| NW | 1,152,712 | 868,815 | 779,384 |
| WC | 928,612 | 746,751 | 236,223 |
| Emp. | 62 | 61 | 58 |

DUNS 21-596-1891
## Supporta Care
Friesian Way, King's Lynn, Norfolk PE30 4JQ
**Tel:** 01553816470
**Web:** www.supportaplc.com
**Estd:** 2011 Proprietorship
**Line of Business:** Home care service providers
**Proprietor:** Mrs K Seppings
**US SIC:** 8091 **UK SIC:** 95200
**Employees:** 150

DUNS 42-388-7871
## Supported Independence Ltd
100-102 Kings Drive, Bristol, Avon BS7 8JH
**Tel:** 01179232132 **Fax:** 01179-232132
**Web:** www.supportedindependence.co.uk
**Reg No:** 4376396 **Estd:** 2002 Private Limited Company
**Line of Business:** Residential care establishments
**Issued Capital:** £100
**Managing Director:** Ms C E Twine
**Co. Secretary:** Joseph Kelly
**Responsibilities**
**Senior:** Trudie Hill *(Manager)*
**US SIC:** 8321 **UK SIC:** 96111

| | 30-06-13 | 30-06-12 | 30-06-11 |
|---|---|---|---|
| TA | 4,118,048 | 3,255,020 | 3,244,161 |
| NW | 2,064,954 | 1,670,599 | 1,323,461 |
| WC | 2,140,540 | 1,434,720 | 1,225,690 |

DUNS 21-580-2721
## Supported Lives
Rebecca House, Rebecca Street, Bradford, West Yorkshire BD1 2RX
**Tel:** 01274377100
**Web:** www.supportedlives.co.uk
**Estd:** 2004 Partnership
**Line of Business:** Disability services
**Partners:** J Drury, J Wright
**US SIC:** 8321 **UK SIC:** 96111
**Employees:** 55

DUNS 21-880-4384
## Supported Living Service
1st Floor The Gamble Building, Victoria Square, St Helens, Merseyside WA10 1DY
**Tel:** 01744674439
**Web:** www.sthelens.gov.uk
**Estd:** 2012
**Line of Business:** Disability services

**Responsibilities**
**Senior:** Barbara Boadey *(Manager)*
**US SIC:** 8321 **UK SIC:** 96111
**Employees:** 200

DUNS 22-600-9736
## Supreme Concrete Ltd
**(Subsidiary of:** Crh Plc)
Coppingford Hall, Coppingford Road, Sawtry, Huntingdon, Cambridgeshire PE28 5GP
**Tel:** 01487833317 **Fax:** 01487833305
**Web:** www.supremeconcrete.co.uk
**Reg No:** 1410463 **Estd:** 1979 Private Limited Company
**Line of Business:** Manufacturers and distributors of concrete and mortar
**Issued Capital:** £31,000
**Principals:** R A Lee *(Financial)*, W M Sheppard, K J Sims, J K Bentley, M W Houghton, T W Wright
**Responsibilities**
**Senior:** Stephen Mascall *(Sales & Marketing Director)*, Karen Montague *(Facilities Manager)*
**Marketing:** Stephen Mascall *(Sales & Marketing Director)*
**Sales:** Stephen Mascall *(Sales & Marketing Director)*
**IT:** Sarah Everitt *(IT Systems Manager)*, James Foulkes Arnold *(IT Manager)*
**Facilities:** Karen Montague *(Facilities Manager)*
**Branches:** Supreme Concrete Ltd, Dolphin Works, Crown Quay Lane, Sittingbourne, Kent ME10 3SL
**US SIC:** 3273 **UK SIC:** 24360
**Auditors:** Moore Stephens (South) LLP
**Bankers:** The Royal Bank Of Scotland Plc (16-20-38)

| | 31-12-13 | 31-12-12 | 31-12-11 |
|---|---|---|---|
| TO | 29,294,182 | 26,217,925 | 24,452,931 |
| P/L | 4,558,335 | 3,782,604 | 2,736,925 |
| NW | 33,360,561 | 29,915,838 | 27,140,652 |
| WC | 29,520,127 | 25,927,659 | 23,068,768 |
| Emp. | 197 | 192 | 185 |

DUNS 21-784-1439
## Supreme Court of the United Kingdom
Parliament Square, London SW1P 3BD
**Tel:** 02079601900
**Web:** www.supremecourt.uk
**Estd:** 2011 Proprietorship
**Line of Business:** Courts
**Proprietor:** G Marwick
**US SIC:** 9211 **UK SIC:** 91200
**Employees:** 250

DUNS 21-877-9272
## Supreme Healthcare Services
Unit 16a, Boundary Way Boundary Business Centre, Woking, Surrey GU21 5DH
**Tel:** 01483 750 748
**Web:** www.supreme-healthcare.co.uk
**Estd:** 2004 Partnership
**Line of Business:** Healthcare companies
**Partners:** I Mukarat, Mrs C Gurajena
**US SIC:** 8091 **UK SIC:** 95200
**Employees:** 85

DUNS 71-910-3249 Imp
## Supreme Imports Ltd
4 Beacon Road, Trafford Park, Manchester M17 1AF
**Tel:** 01618-725151
**Web:** www.supreme-imports.co.uk
**Reg No:** 5292196 **VAT No:** 927173808
**Estd:** 1975 Private Limited Company
**Line of Business:** Import and export agents
**Export Sales:** £8,415,000
**Issued Capital:** £2
**Directors:** G S Chadha, Mrs A Chadha, S S Chadha
**Co. Secretary:** Michael Clinch
**Responsibilities**
**Senior:** Sandy Chadha *(Manager)*
**US SIC:** 4712, 5199
**UK SIC:** 77002, 61900
**Auditors:** Mazars LLP

| | 31-03-14 | 31-03-13 | 31-03-12 |
|---|---|---|---|
| TO | 44,648,438 | 34,201,664 | 30,606,540 |
| P/L | 3,032,081 | 2,060,773 | 1,475,604 |
| NW | 6,715,564 | 5,056,612 | 3,462,757 |
| WC | 6,525,938 | 5,016,711 | 3,396,301 |
| Emp. | 77 | 66 | 53 |

DUNS 28-945-3359 Imp
## Supreme Petfoods Ltd
**(Subsidiary of:** Supreme Pet Food Holdings Ltd)
Stone Street, Hadleigh, Ipswich, Suffolk IP7 6DN
**Tel:** 08450343330 **Fax:** 01473-824570
**Web:** www.russelrabbit.com
**Reg No:** 1599755 **Estd:** 1987 Private Limited Company
**Line of Business:** Animal feed and pet foods
**Issued Capital:** £1,800,000
**Directors:** P J Whittle, C Childs

**Co. Secretary:** Robert Baker
**Responsibilities**
**Engineering:** Adrian Cobie *(Production Manager)*
**Branches:** Supreme Petfoods Ltd, 19-23 Poplar Road Great Cornard, Sudbury, Suffolk CO10 0LH
**US SIC:** 2047, 5199
**UK SIC:** 42221, 61900
**Auditors:** Horwath Clark Whitehill LLP
**Bankers:** Barclays Bank Plc (20-44-51)

| | 31-07-14 | 31-07-13 | 31-07-12 |
|---|---|---|---|
| TO | 10,476,812 | 9,335,726 | 9,177,491 |
| P/L | (61,572) | (1,098,669) | (1,520,060) |
| NW | 770,712 | 832,284 | 328,725 |
| WC | 335,050 | 355,921 | 151,032 |
| Emp. | 59 | 59 | 57 |

DUNS 22-522-4567 Imp-Exp
## Supremia International Plc
Jubilee House, Merrion Avenue, Stanmore, Middlesex HA7 4RY
**Tel:** 020-8416-1200
**Web:** www.supremia.com
**Reg No:** 1559794 **VAT No:** 350717859
**Estd:** 1981 Public Limited Company
**Line of Business:** Corporate promotional products
**Export Sales:** £23,260,063
**Issued Capital:** £202,500
**Principals:** S Kahya *(Chairman)*, R J Thomson
**Co. Secretary:** Ms Temple Secretaries Limited
**Responsibilities**
**Finance:** Amir Soryano *(Finance Director)*
**US SIC:** 3999 **UK SIC:** 49590
**Auditors:** Dub & Co
**Bankers:** The Royal Bank Of Scotland Plc (16-10-29)

| | 31-03-14 | 31-03-13 | 31-03-12 |
|---|---|---|---|
| TO | 25,660,320 | 27,708,221 | 29,753,119 |
| P/L | (195,865) | 770,110 | 730,893 |
| NW | 6,395,943 | 6,864,081 | 6,169,830 |
| WC | 6,102,572 | 6,589,552 | 5,160,968 |
| Emp. | 51 | 57 | 58 |

DUNS 21-033-8842
## Surbiton Assembly Rooms
138 Maple Road, Surbiton, Surrey KT6 4RT
**Tel:** 02083903771
**Web:** www.surbitonassemblyrooms.com
**Estd:** 1998 Proprietorship
**Line of Business:** Hotels and motels without restaurant
**Proprietor:** Mrs S Thomas
**US SIC:** 7011 **UK SIC:** 66500
**Employees:** 150

DUNS 21-041-4957
## Surbiton High Senior School
13 Surbiton Crescent, Kingston-Upon-Thames, Surrey KT1 2JT
**Tel:** 02085465245
**Web:** www.surbitonhigh.com
**Estd:** 2006 Proprietorship
**Line of Business:** Schools (independent)
**Proprietor:** Ms C Bufton
**Responsibilities**
**Senior:** Ann Haydon *(Head Teacher)*
**US SIC:** 8211 **UK SIC:** 93200
**Employees:** 250

DUNS 21-414-3242
## Sure Care
659a Kingstanding Road, Birmingham, West Midlands B44 9RH
**Tel:** 01213548137
**Estd:** 1991 Proprietorship
**Line of Business:** Charitable social work activities without accommodation
**Proprietor:** S Ali
**US SIC:** 6732 **UK SIC:** 83100
**Employees:** 66

DUNS 23-308-1624
## Sure Guernsey Ltd
**(Subsidiary of:** Bahrain Telecommunications Company (Batelco))
Po Box 3, Upland Road, St Peter Port, Guernsey, Channel Islands GY1 3AB
**Tel:** 01481700700 **Fax:** 01481-724640
**Web:** www.surecw.com
**Reg No:** 0038694G **Estd:** 2001 Private Limited Company
**Line of Business:** Telecom consultants
**Issued Capital:** £1
**Responsibilities**
**Senior:** Eddie Saints *(Chief Executive Officer)*
**Branches:** Sure (Guernsey) Limited, Waterloo House, High Street, GY1 2JK Spp
**US SIC:** 4899 **UK SIC:** 79020
**Employees:** 200

DUNS 71-938-4518
## Sure Maintenance Group Ltd
Unit 16, The Matchworks, Speke Road, Liverpool, Merseyside L19 2RF
**Tel:** 01517285700 **Fax:** 01215029661
**Web:** www.suregroup.co.uk
**Reg No:** 5319177 **Estd:** 2004 Private Limited Company
**Line of Business:** Other manufacturing not elsewhere classified
**Issued Capital:** £174,404
**Directors:** D Cunningham, P S Cornes, N P Winks
**Responsibilities**
**IT:** Steven Marsh (Computer Operations Manager)
**US SIC:** 3999 **UK SIC:** 49590
**Bankers:** Lloyds TSB Bank plc (30-00-05)

|      | 31-12-13    | 31-12-12    | 31-12-11    |
|------|-------------|-------------|-------------|
| TO   | 21,569,000  | 16,250,294  | 16,638,199  |
| P/L  | 752,000     | (370,192)   | (1,804,293) |
| NW   | (2,763,000) | (3,571,713) | (3,569,576) |
| WC   | (636,000)   | (3,678,842) | (3,653,918) |
| Emp. | 301         | 242         | 218         |

DUNS 22-070-9948
## Sure Maintenance Ltd
The West Wing The Matchworks, Speke Road, Garston, Liverpool, Merseyside L19 2RF
**Tel:** 01514945800
**Web:** www.suregroup.co.uk
**Reg No:** 4072464 **Estd:** 2000 Private Limited Company
**Line of Business:** Gas safety testing & inspection
**Issued Capital:** £940
**Directors:** P Cornes, N P Winks, D Cunningham
**Responsibilities**
**Marketing:** Paula Campbell (Marketing Manager)
**Branches:** Sure Maintenance Ltd, Greenwood Business Centre, Regent Road, Salford, Lancashire M5 4QH
**US SIC:** 8911, 7399
**UK SIC:** 83701, 83954
**Auditors:** PricewaterhouseCoopers LLP

|      | 31-12-13   | 31-12-12   | 31-12-11   |
|------|------------|------------|------------|
| TO   | 18,534,187 | 13,721,699 | 10,491,974 |
| P/L  | 505,970    | 77,561     | (400,223)  |
| NW   | 3,506,181  | 3,024,775  | 2,947,214  |
| WC   | 3,132,786  | 2,839,995  | 2,793,480  |
| Emp. | 278        | 218        | 152        |

DUNS 50-445-5825
## Sure Plan Homes Ltd
97 Victoria Road, Waunarlwydd, Swansea, West Glamorgan SA5 4TB
**Tel:** 01792874306 **Fax:** 01474854763
**Reg No:** 2433447 **Estd:** 1982 Private Limited Company
**Line of Business:** Medical nursing home activities
**Trading Style:** Meadow House Nursing Home, Ty Victoria Nursing Home
**Issued Capital:** £111,000
**Director:**
Homes Management Group Limited
**Co. Secretary:** Paul Hudson
**Responsibilities**
**Senior:** Nicola Whitelock (Manager)
**Branches:** Sure Plan Homes Ltd, 97 Victoria Rd, Swansea, West Glamorgan SA5 4TB
**US SIC:** 8051, 8091
**UK SIC:** 95100, 95200

|      | 31-03-14    | 31-03-13    | 31-03-12    |
|------|-------------|-------------|-------------|
| TA   | 1,654,083   | 1,577,298   | 1,454,047   |
| NW   | 84,403      | 80,384      | 51,172      |
| WC   | (1,460,930) | (1,415,325) | (1,331,425) |

DUNS 36-480-2111
## Sure Start
Roehampton Centre, 166 Roehampton Lane, London SW15 4HR
**Tel:** 02087890572
**Estd:** 2011 Incorporate By Act Of Parliament
**Line of Business:** Social work activities
**Director:** Ms S Forrester
**Responsibilities**
**Senior:** Jason Terrett (Senior Premises Manager)
**US SIC:** 6732 **UK SIC:** 83100
**Employees:** 50

DUNS 21-225-5068
## Sure Start Blackburn With Darwen
Neighbourhood Centre, Pringle Street, Blackburn, Lancashire BB1 1SF
**Web:** www.blackburn.gov.uk
**Estd:** 2003
**Line of Business:** Adult education locations
**Responsibilities**
**Senior:** Heather Fergusson (Centre Manager)
**US SIC:** 8299 **UK SIC:** 93300
**Employees:** 50

DUNS 21-879-9242
## Sure Start Bridlington
Butts Close, Bridlington, North Humberside YO16 7BS
**Tel:** 01262409596
**Web:** www.eastriding.gov.uk
**Estd:** 2003
**Line of Business:** Pre school education
**Responsibilities**
**Senior:** Kay Roantree (Head Of Centre)
**US SIC:** 8211 **UK SIC:** 93200
**Employees:** 50

DUNS 85-598-5157
## Sure Start Children Centre
11a Howdon Lane, Wallsend, Tyne and Wear NE28 0AL
**Web:** www.northtyneside.co.uk
**Estd:** 2002 Proprietorship
**Line of Business:** Creches
**Proprietor:** Miss G Derby
**Responsibilities**
**Senior:** Fiona Hawker (Manager)
**US SIC:** 8211 **UK SIC:** 93200
**Employees:** 80

DUNS 21-580-1779
## Sure Start Dover
Unit 2 Poulton Close, Dover, Kent CT17 0HL
**Tel:** 01304226919
**Web:** www.kenttrustweb.org.uk
**Estd:** 2001 Proprietorship
**Line of Business:** Adult education locations
**Proprietor:** Mrs D Beale
**Responsibilities**
**Admin:** Sylvia Bywater (Administrator)
**US SIC:** 8299 **UK SIC:** 93300
**Employees:** 50

DUNS 21-778-9594
## Sure Start Great Yarmouth
The Priory Centre, Priory Plain, Great Yarmouth, Norfolk NR30 1NW
**Tel:** 01493743000
**Web:** www.priorycentre.co.uk
**Estd:** 1999 Proprietorship
**Line of Business:** Organised childrens play schemes
**Proprietor:** Ms K Harvey
**US SIC:** 8699 **UK SIC:** 96902
**Employees:** 50

DUNS 21-228-9747
## Sure Start Plus Bus Bkgs
1 Academy Gardens, Northolt, Middlesex UB5 5QN
**Tel:** 02088420220
**Estd:** 2007 Proprietorship
**Line of Business:** Children's activity playcentres
**Proprietor:** Mrs N Dada
**Responsibilities**
**Senior:** Claire Fry (Manager)
**US SIC:** 8211 **UK SIC:** 93200
**Employees:** 100

DUNS 21-414-0019
## Sure Start Tilbury
The Flagship Centre, Tilbury, Essex RM18 8EY
**Tel:** 01375858243
**Web:** www.askthurrock.org.uk
**Estd:** 1999
**Line of Business:** Organised childrens play schemes
**Partners:** Mrs L Barton, Ms L Barton
**Responsibilities**
**Senior:** Wendy Springham (General Manager)
**Branches:** Sure Start Tilbury, Overdale Community Cntr Oak Rd, Telford, Shropshire TF3 5BG
**US SIC:** 8699 **UK SIC:** 96902
**Employees:** 60

DUNS 23-297-8051
## Surecare Bristol
7 Passage Road, Bristol, Avon BS9 3HN
**Tel:** 01173-774225
**Web:** www.surecarebristol.com
**Estd:** 2000 Proprietorship
**Line of Business:** Nursing agencies
**Proprietor:** R H Pickford
**Responsibilities**
**Senior:** Phil Pickford (Manager)
**US SIC:** 8091 **UK SIC:** 95200
**Employees:** 55

DUNS 21-587-0458
## Surecare Domiciliary Services Shropshire
Merrington Road, Shrewsbury, Shropshire SY4 3PP
**Tel:** 01939291434
**Web:** www.surecare.co.uk
**Estd:** 2010 Proprietorship
**Line of Business:** Home care service providers
**Proprietor:** C Davies
**US SIC:** 8091 **UK SIC:** 95200
**Employees:** 70

DUNS 34-719-0899
## Surecare Health Link Ltd
Ifield Green, Ifield, Crawley, West Sussex RH11 0LZ
**Tel:** 01293561704 **Fax:** 01293561635
**Web:** www.shaw.co.uk
**Reg No:** 5522717 **Estd:** 2005 Private Limited Company
**Line of Business:** Dispensing chemists
**Trading Style:** Deerswood Lodge
**Issued Capital:** £1,000
**Directors:** K A Agyekum-Kwatiah, C B Agyekum-Kwatiah
**Co. Secretary:** Ms Patience Asare-Boafo
**Responsibilities**
**Senior:** Arlette Chalcraft (Home Manager), Jo Mosses (Manager)
**US SIC:** 5912 **UK SIC:** 64300
**Auditors:** Shelter Two Associate

|    | 31-07-13 | 31-07-12 | 31-07-11 |
|----|----------|----------|----------|
| TA | 135,668  | 129,976  | 120,402  |
| NW | (2,140)  | (13,433) | (40,782) |
| WC | (5,301)  | (17,457) | 11,490   |

DUNS 23-564-3918                          **Imp**
## Sureclean Ltd
Unit 10, River Drive, Teaninich Industrial Estate, Alness, Ross-Shire IV17 0PG
**Tel:** 01349-884480 **Fax:** 01349-883612
**Web:** www.sureclean.com
**Reg No:** 0185760SC **Estd:** 1998 Private Limited Company
**Line of Business:** Cleaning contracting commercial
**Export Sales:** £2,758,416
**Issued Capital:** £243,714
**Directors:** N A Challis, J M Barron, G Shor, A Harman
**Co. Secretary:** Burness Paull Llp
**Responsibilities**
**Senior:** Graham McLellan (Commercial Director), Phillip Thorn (Chairman)
**Finance:** Yasmin Overton (Finance Manager)
**Sales:** Graham McLellan (Commercial Director)
**Branches:** Sureclean Ltd, Tamala Burnside, Whitecairns, Aberdeen, Aberdeenshire AB23 8UN
**US SIC:** 7349, 7394
**UK SIC:** 92300, 84000
**Auditors:** Johnston Carmichael LLP
**Bankers:** Bank Of Scotland (80-91-26)

|      | 31-12-13   | 31-12-12   | 31-12-11   |
|------|------------|------------|------------|
| TO   | 22,777,646 | 15,910,223 | 12,347,609 |
| P/L  | 5,476,121  | 2,641,150  | 1,737,488  |
| NW   | 9,888,986  | 6,065,180  | 4,132,577  |
| WC   | 3,277,088  | 1,816,834  | 1,107,667  |
| Emp. | 164        | 154        | 121        |

DUNS 22-850-2597                       **Imp-Exp**
## Surefil Beauty Products Ltd
(Subsidiary of: Sbp Investments Ltd)
The Bedford Centre, Bedford Street, St Helens, Merseyside WA9 1PN
**Tel:** 01744-758820
**Web:** www.surefil.co.uk
**Reg No:** 1480297 **VAT No:** 582453919
**Estd:** 1980 Private Limited Company
**Line of Business:** Manufacturers of cosmetics
**Export Sales:** £3,575,394
**Issued Capital:** £100
**Directors:** J Macavoy, P B Critchley, S Loggenberg
**Co. Secretary:** Mrs Catherine Critchley
**Responsibilities**
**HR:** Celia Jackson (Human Resources Manager)
**Facilities:** Michael Critchley (Warehouse Manager), Matt Waring (Engineering Manager)
**Engineering:** Matt Waring (Engineering Manager)
**US SIC:** 2844 **UK SIC:** 25820
**Auditors:** Abrams Ashton
**Bankers:** The Royal Bank Of Scotland Plc (16-30-28)

|      | 28-02-14  | 28-02-13  | 29-02-12  |
|------|-----------|-----------|-----------|
| TO   | 5,431,809 | 4,382,490 | 5,183,770 |
| P/L  | 314,599   | 34,066    | 176,815   |
| NW   | 2,057,499 | 1,819,313 | 1,797,256 |
| WC   | 2,132,570 | 1,970,486 | 1,988,211 |
| Emp. | 103       | 80        | 80        |

DUNS 73-396-1499                          **Imp**
## Surefreight (International) Ltd
Unit 41 Hillam Road Industrial Estate, Hillam Road, Bradford, West Yorkshire BD2 1QN
**Tel:** 01274-731199 **Fax:** 01274-731114
**Web:** www.surefreight.co.uk
**Reg No:** 4669584 **Estd:** 2003 Private Limited Company
**Line of Business:** Freight forwarders
**Issued Capital:** £100
**Principals:** A Daly (Managing), V Waddell, M Briggs
**Co. Secretary:** Brian Mcmanus
**Branches:** Surefreight (International) Ltd, Derwent House, Unit A1, Bury, Lancashire BL9 7BR
**US SIC:** 4712 **UK SIC:** 77002
**Auditors:** Clough & Co LLP

|      | 31-03-14   | 31-03-13   | 31-03-12   |
|------|------------|------------|------------|
| TO   | 17,620,538 | 16,838,265 | 14,684,138 |
| P/L  | 483,798    | 265,585    | 366,651    |
| NW   | 880,902    | 826,150    | 816,439    |
| WC   | (671,719)  | (563,318)  | (280,194)  |
| Emp. | 70         | 65         | 61         |

DUNS 23-996-6773                          **Imp**
## Surefreight Ltd
4 Shepherds Drive, Carnbane Industrial Estate, Newry, Co Down BT35 6JQ
**Tel:** 02830261127 **Fax:** 02830260995
**Web:** www.surefreight.co.uk
**Reg No:** 0022809NI **Estd:** 1989 Private Limited Company
**Line of Business:** Road haulage and transport services
**Issued Capital:** £240
**Directors:** B G Mcmanus, V J Waddell
**Co. Secretary:** Brian Mcmanus
**Responsibilities**
**Senior:** Vincent Warelse (Manager)
**Finance:** Niall Smith (Finance Director)
**Branches:** Surefreight Ltd, Cardiff
**US SIC:** 4789 **UK SIC:** 77002
**Auditors:** John MacMahon & Co
**Bankers:** First Trust Bank (aib Group (uk) Plc) (93-83-78)

|      | 30-06-13   | 30-06-12   | 30-06-11   |
|------|------------|------------|------------|
| TO   | 20,011,210 | 20,910,072 | 18,014,434 |
| P/L  | (123,296)  | 622,771    | 496,981    |
| NW   | 3,266,301  | 3,358,420  | 2,960,014  |
| WC   | (434,466)  | (161,782)  | (179,646)  |
| Emp. | 184        | 183        | 162        |

DUNS 21-141-3003
## Surehaven Glasgow Ltd
(Subsidiary of: Shaw Healthcare (Group) Ltd)
3 Drumchapel Place, Glasgow, Lanarkshire G15 6BN
**Tel:** 01419443990
**Web:** www.surehaven.co.uk
**Reg No:** 6731003 **Estd:** 2010 Private Limited Company
**Line of Business:** Mental health centres
**Issued Capital:** £1,001
**Directors:** A C Savery, R S Brown, P J Nixey
**Responsibilities**
**Senior:** Garry Walker (Manager)
**US SIC:** 8091 **UK SIC:** 95200
**Bankers:** Bank Of Ireland (iom) Ltd (40-53-30)

|      | 31-03-14  | 31-03-13  | 31-03-12  |
|------|-----------|-----------|-----------|
| TO   | 3,045,118 | 2,799,941 | 1,882,568 |
| P/L  | 758,518   | 578,676   | (227,451) |
| NW   | 311,961   | (190,170) | (542,538) |
| WC   | 591,165   | 300,407   | 302,421   |
| Emp. | 66        | 64        | 56        |

DUNS 21-192-1804                       **Imp-Exp**
## Surelock McGill Ltd
26 Molly Millars Lane The Business, Centre, Wokingham, Berkshire RG41 2QY
**Tel:** 01189-772525
**Web:** www.surelock.co.uk
**Reg No:** 0684463 **VAT No:** 438497604
**Estd:** 1971 Private Limited Company
**Line of Business:** General mechanical engineering
**Export Sales:** £2,202,944
**Issued Capital:** £25,950
**Principals:** J Mcgill (Managing), M Popov, S V Bradley, D R Milne, D W Dunbar-Jones
**Co. Secretary:** Ms Annette Bambrook
**Responsibilities**
**Senior:** John McGill (Managing Director)
**Marketing:** John McGill (Managing Director)
**Sales:** John McGill (Managing Director)
**US SIC:** 8911 **UK SIC:** 83701
**Auditors:** Auker Rhodes
**Bankers:** Barclays Bank Plc (20-42-73)

|      | 31-03-14   | 31-03-13  | 31-03-12  |
|------|------------|-----------|-----------|
| TO   | 10,901,693 | 9,412,808 | 9,118,511 |
| P/L  | 245,412    | 579,686   | 813,946   |
| NW   | 3,374,895  | 3,078,253 | 3,015,573 |
| WC   | 2,814,408  | 2,872,328 | 2,532,449 |
| Emp. | 121        | 127       | 102       |

DUNS 28-944-1917
## Suremime Ltd
Edithmead, Highbridge, Somerset TA9 4HD
**Tel:** 01278-788888
**Web:** www.homefarmholidaypark.co.uk
**Reg No:** 1594544 **Estd:** 2003 Private Limited Company
**Line of Business:** Camping sites, including caravan sites
**Trading Style:** Home Farm Holiday Park
**Issued Capital:** £100
**Directors:** G Atkinson, S G Atkinson
**Co. Secretary:** Mrs Glenys Atkinson
**US SIC:** 7033 **UK SIC:** 66701
**Auditors:** Llewelyn Davis
**Bankers:** Barclays Bank Plc (20-18-41)

| | 31-12-13 | 31-12-12 | 31-12-11 |
|---|---|---|---|
| TO | 3,249,586 | 2,821,474 | N/A |
| P/L | 183,092 | 68,991 | N/A |
| NW | 5,231,619 | 5,003,875 | 4,965,990 |
| WC | (875,331) | (956,680) | (1,024,733) |
| Emp. | 55 | 58 | N/A |

DUNS 77-025-2583
## Surepak Ltd
Willow Drive, Sherwood Business Park, Annesley, Nottingham, Nottinghamshire NG15 0DP
**Web:** www.surepak.com
**Reg No:** 2665390 **VAT No:** 580991602
**Estd:** 1991 Private Limited Company
**Line of Business:** Manufacturers of packaging materials
**Issued Capital:** £999
**Directors:** P B Yorston, S A Yorston
**Co. Secretary:** David Wagstaff
**US SIC:** 2654 **UK SIC:** 47280
**Auditors:** Rogers Spencer
**Bankers:** The Royal Bank Of Scotland Plc (16-26-32)

| | 31-12-13 | 31-12-12 | 31-12-11 |
|---|---|---|---|
| TA | 2,675,886 | 2,546,722 | 2,204,182 |
| NW | 1,025,552 | 1,071,795 | 1,117,326 |
| WC | 456,199 | 361,489 | 450,789 |

DUNS 22-677-2374 **Imp-Exp**
## Surepharm Services Ltd
(**Subsidiary of:** Centaur Healthcare Ltd)
Unit 2 H Bretby Business Park, Bretby, Burton-On-Trent, Staffordshire DE15 0YZ
**Tel:** 01283-224337
**Web:** www.surepharm.com
**Reg No:** 1654137 **VAT No:** 354572444
**Estd:** 1982 Private Limited Company
**Line of Business:** Manufacture of basic pharmaceutical products
**Export Markets:** France; Netherlands; Germany; Italy
**Issued Capital:** £200
**Principals:** I C Gardner *(Managing)*, J J Richardson, A D Ingley, A Corbett, J America
**Responsibilities**
**Senior:** Margaret Thornton *(Manager)*
**Finance:** Richard Savory *(Financial Manager)*
**HR:** Martyn Priestley *(Training Officer)*, Pam Tompkins *(Human Resources Coordinator)*
**US SIC:** 2834 **UK SIC:** 25700
**Auditors:** Buckler Spencer Ltd
**Bankers:** HSBC Bank plc (40-43-30)

| | 31-10-13 | 31-10-12 | 31-10-11 |
|---|---|---|---|
| TO | 10,476,502 | 8,987,340 | 8,483,641 |
| P/L | 1,016,462 | 732,375 | 730,793 |
| NW | 3,611,734 | 3,052,256 | 2,687,640 |
| WC | 2,399,714 | 1,774,336 | 1,329,982 |
| Emp. | 127 | 121 | 113 |

DUNS 22-791-1674 **Imp-Exp**
## Suresprung Finishings
78 Clase Road, Morriston, Swansea, West Glamorgan SA6 8DZ
**Tel:** 01792-534400
**Web:** www.swansea.gov.uk
**Estd:** 1974 Proprietorship
**Line of Business:** Beds and bedding
**Principals:** P D Marr, L Tovin *(General Manager)*, L Tobin *(Proprietor)*, A G Chilcott, D F Bevan, D J Turner, T E John
**Responsibilities**
**Finance:** Susan Daw *(Senior Finance Administrator)*
**US SIC:** 2392 **UK SIC:** 45550
**Bankers:** HSBC Bank plc (40-43-31)
**Employees:** 46

DUNS 21-043-5719
## Surestart
Briercliffe, Scarborough, North Yorkshire YO12 6NS
**Tel:** 01609798700
**Line of Business:** Miscellaneous membership organisations
**US SIC:** 7032 **UK SIC:** 66702
**Employees:** 49

DUNS 21-613-4563
## Surestart Children's Centre
1a Rosebery Avenue, Clerkenwell, London EC1R 4SR
**Tel:** 02079747024
**Estd:** 2011
**Line of Business:** Other recreational activities not elsewhere classified
**Responsibilities**
**Senior:** Marilyn Sherwood-Chilton *(Nursery Centre Head)*
**US SIC:** 8999 **UK SIC:** 83954
**Employees:** 50

DUNS 21-007-2751 **Imp**
## Suretank Uk Ltd
(**Subsidiary of:** Suretank Group Limited)
Peel Road, West Pimbo, Skelmersdale, Lancashire WN8 9PT
**Tel:** 01695-555577 **Fax:** 01695-728566
**Web:** www.sntg.com
**Reg No:** 6315452 **VAT No:** 916737696
**Estd:** 2007 Private Limited Company
**Line of Business:** Fish farms
**Issued Capital:** £2
**Director:** J Fitzgerald
**Co. Secretary:** Dermot Beirne
**Responsibilities**
**Senior:** Shane Gilson *(General Manager)*, Kevin Sharratt *(General Manager)*, Alex Wilsdon *(General Manager)*
**US SIC:** 3443 **UK SIC:** 32051
**Auditors:** Kirk & Associates
**Bankers:** Ulster Bank Ltd (98-11-40)

| | 31-12-13 | 31-03-13 | 31-12-12 |
|---|---|---|---|
| TO | 4,868,515 | N/A | N/A |
| P/L | 786,862 | N/A | N/A |
| NW | 645,599 | 179,865 | 113,243 |
| WC | (295,015) | (809,708) | (651,535) |
| Emp. | 56 | N/A | N/A |

DUNS 23-339-1549 **Exp**
## Surf Bay Caravans
The Airfield, Winkleigh, Devon EX19 8DW
**Tel:** 0183783743
**Web:** www.surfbayleisure.co.uk
**VAT No:** 143550879 **Estd:** 1907 Partnership
**Line of Business:** Sale of new motor vehicles
**Export Markets:** European Union (E U)
**Partners:** Ms S Taylor, M Taylor, J E Taylor
**Branches:** Surf Bay Caravans, Central Caravan Park, Warren Road, Burnham-On-Sea, Somerset TA8 2RP
**US SIC:** 5511 **UK SIC:** 65100
**Bankers:** National Westminster Bank Plc (51-70-16)
**Employees:** 50

DUNS 21-170-2310
## Surface Finishing Equipment Group Ltd
Shakespeare House Salop Street, Bolton, Lancashire BL2 1DZ
**Tel:** 01902601312
**Web:** www.sfeg.co.uk
**Reg No:** 6948768 **Estd:** 2009 Private Limited Company
**Line of Business:** Casting of iron
**Issued Capital:** £999
**Directors:** I Francis, A J Howe, M L Stanley, N Walton
**Co. Secretary:** Ms Laura Francis
**US SIC:** 3321 **UK SIC:** 31110
**Bankers:** National Westminster Bank Plc (01-01-75)

| | 31-12-13 | 31-12-12 | 31-12-11 |
|---|---|---|---|
| TO | 8,232,595 | 8,380,032 | N/A |
| P/L | 474,391 | 630,882 | N/A |
| NW | 462,897 | 143,372 | 999 |
| WC | 79,902 | (38,115) | (556,779) |
| Emp. | 59 | 59 | N/A |

DUNS 21-037-0814
## Surface Gallery
16 Southwell Road, Nottingham, Nottinghamshire NG1 1DL
**Tel:** 01159470793
**Web:** www.surfacegallery.org
**Estd:** 2008 Proprietorship
**Line of Business:** Art gallery
**Proprietor:** Ms L Hoyle
**Responsibilities**
**Senior:** Helen De Main *(Manager)*
**US SIC:** 7911 **UK SIC:** 97913
**Employees:** 48

DUNS 50-547-5087 **Imp-Exp**
## The Surface Print Co Ltd
Clayton Works, Hill Street, Clayton Le Moors, Accrington, Lancashire BB5 5EA
**Tel:** 01254-397631 **Fax:** 01254-237410
**Web:** www.surfaceprint.com
**Reg No:** 2501973 **VAT No:** 572283238
**Estd:** 1989 Private Limited Company
**Line of Business:** Wallpapers
**Export Markets:** Scandinavia
**Export Sales:** £2,132,663
**Issued Capital:** £12,393
**Principals:** J W Watson *(Managing)*, Ms A Watson, N D Peel, A Thornton, J W Watson
**Co. Secretary:** Ms Julia Watson
**US SIC:** 2649 **UK SIC:** 47280
**Auditors:** CLB Coopers
**Bankers:** Barclays Bank Plc (20-16-08)

| | 30-09-13 | 30-09-12 | 30-09-11 |
|---|---|---|---|
| TO | 8,949,439 | 9,100,649 | 9,176,342 |
| P/L | 379,098 | 331,577 | 228,995 |
| NW | 1,637,881 | 1,459,053 | 1,351,000 |
| WC | 84,105 | 73,869 | (18,509) |
| Emp. | 91 | 91 | 87 |

DUNS 22-258-2202
## Surface Solutions International Ltd
Broadmeads, Ware, Hertfordshire SG12 9HS
**Tel:** 01920-465041
**Web:** www.werkmaster.com
**Reg No:** 4276286 **Estd:** 2001 Private Limited Company
**Line of Business:** Holding companies management activities
**Issued Capital:** £237,593
**Directors:** Mrs H B Hawkins, I D Maclellan, Mrs B A Freedman, R M Selwyn
**Co. Secretary:** Mrs Benita Freedman
**Responsibilities**
**Senior:** Benita Kapsalis *(Director)*, Yvonne Nice *(Manager)*, Ronald Petersen *(Manager)*
**HR:** Yvonne Nice *(Manager)*
**US SIC:** 6711 **UK SIC:** 83962
**Bankers:** Fortis Bank London Bch (formerly Generale Bk) (40-52-62)

| | 31-12-13 | 31-12-12 | 31-12-11 |
|---|---|---|---|
| TO | 17,727,970 | 15,957,097 | 15,648,625 |
| P/L | 1,842,366 | (286,004) | 1,232,332 |
| NW | 7,604,577 | 6,451,578 | 6,771,859 |
| WC | 6,417,290 | 5,230,024 | 5,548,815 |
| Emp. | 82 | 93 | 93 |

DUNS 50-002-0086 **Imp**
## Surface Technology International Ltd
(**Subsidiary of:** Sti Enterprises Plc)
Unit C2 Osborn Way Industrial Estate, Hook, Hampshire RG27 9HX
**Tel:** 01256-768070 **Fax:** 01256-763449
**Web:** www.sti-limited.com
**Reg No:** 2292621 **VAT No:** 537422155
**Estd:** 1988 Private Limited Company
**Line of Business:** Electronic engineers
**Export Sales:** £3,209,929
**Trading Style:** S T I
**Issued Capital:** £125,600
**Directors:** S A Best, C W Lyon, N J Davey, A J Best
**Co. Secretary:**
Reid & Co Professional Services
**Responsibilities**
**Health & Safety:** Jackie Kennedy *(Health & Safety Officer)*
**Operations:** Anthony Muise *(Technical, Production Manager)*
**US SIC:** 3661 **UK SIC:** 34410
**Auditors:** S.F. Brocklehurst & Co
**Bankers:** National Westminster Bank Plc (60-02-49)

| | 31-05-14 | 31-05-13 | 31-05-12 |
|---|---|---|---|
| TO | 41,565,564 | 36,529,478 | 50,089,338 |
| P/L | 508,294 | 1,134,784 | 3,177,326 |
| NW | 10,087,482 | 10,055,033 | 9,129,778 |
| WC | 10,817,608 | 7,674,824 | 6,262,749 |
| Emp. | 404 | 408 | 387 |

DUNS 22-861-8443 **Imp**
## Surfachem Ltd
(**Subsidiary of:** 2m Group Ltd)
2 The Embankment, Sovereign Street, Leeds, West Yorkshire LS1 4BA
**Tel:** 0113 394 9200 **Fax:** 0113 244 5910
**Web:** www.surfachem.com
**Reg No:** 1565953 **Estd:** 1981 Private Limited Company
**Line of Business:** Chemicals distribution and wholesale
**Issued Capital:** £100,000
**Directors:** Dr R J Smith, M Kessler, W Stevens, G C Barton, F Jones, S Edwards
**Co. Secretary:** Simon Edwards
**Responsibilities**
**Senior:** Philip Sumpter *(Manager)*, Ieuan Thomas *(Manager)*
**Marketing:** Nichole Hall *(Marketing Director)*
**Branches:** Surfachem Ltd, The Ainleys, Huddersfield Road, Elland, West Yorkshire HX5 0EE
**US SIC:** 5161 **UK SIC:** 61200
**Auditors:** UHY Hacker Young LLP
**Bankers:** Barclays Bank Plc (20-48-46)

| | 30-04-14 | 30-04-13 | 30-04-12 |
|---|---|---|---|
| TO | 47,828,987 | 54,375,316 | 50,245,281 |
| P/L | 4,060,731 | 4,453,811 | 4,315,956 |
| NW | 15,569,986 | 12,453,794 | 14,676,555 |
| WC | 15,386,350 | 12,267,173 | 14,463,018 |
| Emp. | 87 | 77 | 79 |

DUNS 34-849-1734
## Surfdome Shop Ltd
(**Subsidiary of:** Surfstitch Group Limited)
9th Floor York House, Empire Way, Wembley, Middlesex HA9 0PA
**Tel:** 08443571022
**Web:** www.surfdome.com
**Reg No:** 5648145 **Estd:** 2005 Private Limited Company
**Line of Business:** Retail sale of sports goods, games and toys, stamps and coins
**Export Sales:** £9,885,060
**Trading Style:** Surfdome.Com
**Issued Capital:** £1,125
**Directors:** J Lane, J P Stone
**Co. Secretary:** Ms Emma Stone
**US SIC:** 5941 **UK SIC:** 65400
**Auditors:** Constantin

| | 31-12-13 | 31-10-12 | 31-12-11 |
|---|---|---|---|
| TO | 38,709,903 | 19,777,026 | 8,547,143 |
| P/L | (482,960) | 316,930 | 52,502 |
| NW | 1,851,133 | 2,269,758 | 762,198 |
| WC | 2,412,346 | 1,152,621 | 301,968 |
| Emp. | 161 | 124 | N/A |

DUNS 23-993-4222 **Imp**
## Surfkitchen Ltd
(**Subsidiary of:** Symphony Technology Group L.L.C.)
Parkshot House, Reading, Berkshire RG2 6UB
**Fax.** 00700510111
**Web:** www.symphonyteleca.com
**Reg No:** 3981666 **Estd:** 2000 Private Limited Company
**Line of Business:** Other software consultancy and supply
**Export Sales:** £780,719
**Trading Style:** Symphonyteleca
**Issued Capital:** £6,772
**Directors:** P Chaudhry, A D Till
**US SIC:** 7379 **UK SIC:** 83940
**Auditors:** BDO LLP

| | 31-12-13 | 31-12-12 | 31-12-11 |
|---|---|---|---|
| TO | 780,719 | 3,360,719 | 4,838,495 |
| P/L | (1,896,385) | (1,282,786) | (888,002) |
| NW | (5,152,610) | (3,256,225) | (1,973,439) |
| WC | (5,152,610) | (3,261,115) | (1,988,942) |

DUNS 73-653-9011
## Surgeons Lodge Ltd
Nicolson Street, Edinburgh, Midlothian EH8 9DW
**Tel:** 01315273434
**Web:** www.surgeonshall.com
**Reg No:** 0256751SC **Estd:** 2003 Private Limited Company
**Line of Business:** Conference centres and facilities
**Issued Capital:** £100
**Directors:** R R Jeffrey, Ms E C Colingsworth, Professor G C Borthwick, L N Young, Mrs M Skinner, J L Duncan
**Co. Secretary:** Alison Rooney
**Responsibilities**
**Sales:** Scott Mitchell *(Commercial Director)*
**US SIC:** 7011 **UK SIC:** 66500

| | 31-12-13 | 31-12-12 | 31-12-11 |
|---|---|---|---|
| TA | 1,410,144 | 1,469,683 | 1,117,507 |
| NW | (106,687) | (537,382) | (1,018,514) |
| WC | (549,917) | (1,001,082) | (1,093,985) |

DUNS 50-013-3574
## Surgical Innovations Group Plc
Unit 2 Kings Meadow, Ferry Hinksey Road, Oxford, Oxfordshire OX2 0DP
**Tel:** 01132307597 **Fax:** 01865-248884
**Web:** www.surgical-innovations.co.uk
**Reg No:** 2298163 **Estd:** 1996 Public Limited Company
**Line of Business:** Manufacture of medical and surgical equipment and orthopaedic appliances
**Export Sales:** £6,212,000
**Trading Style:** Haemocell Healthcare
**Issued Capital:** £4,045,919
**Directors:** M R Thornton, D B Liversidge, Dr M J Mcmahon, C J Rea
**Co. Secretary:** Michael Thornton
**Branches:** Surgical Innovations Group Plc, 12 Napier Court, Barton Lane, Abingdon, Oxfordshire OX14 3YT
**US SIC:** 3841, 7391
**UK SIC:** 37201, 94000
**Auditors:** Grant Thornton UK LLP
**Bankers:** Barclays Bank Plc (20-59-42)

| | 31-12-13 | 31-12-12 | 31-12-11 |
|---|---|---|---|
| TO | 8,553,000 | 7,639,000 | 7,602,000 |
| P/L | 796,000 | 1,233,000 | 1,705,000 |
| NW | 7,274,000 | 7,170,000 | 7,373,000 |
| WC | 3,429,000 | 4,698,000 | 4,456,000 |
| Emp. | 93 | 107 | 104 |

DUNS 71-884-3993
## Surgical Specialties Uk Holdings Ltd
(**Subsidiary of:** Angiotech Pharmaceuticals Inc)
Tancred Street, Taunton, Somerset TA1 1RY
**Tel:** 01823253198
**Reg No:** 5266856 **Estd:** 2004 Private Limited Company
**Line of Business:** Manufacture of medical and surgical equipment and orthopaedic appliances
**Export Sales:** £15,805,000
**Issued Capital:** £2
**Director:** J Barr
**Co. Secretary:** Daniel Sutherby
**US SIC:** 3841 **UK SIC:** 37201
**Auditors:** PricewaterhouseCoopers LLP
**Bankers:** National Westminster Bank Plc (60-07-34)

| | 31-12-13 | 31-12-12 | 31-12-11 |
|---|---|---|---|
| TO | 16,709,000 | 16,061,000 | 10,485,000 |
| P/L | 9,423,000 | 9,282,000 | 5,874,000 |
| NW | 5,954,000 | 8,943,000 | 3,620,000 |
| WC | 5,305,000 | 8,338,000 | 2,966,000 |
| Emp. | 140 | 156 | 105 |

DUNS 21-233-0831
## Surgo Construction Ltd
(**Subsidiary of:** Hawkpost Ltd)
Newcastle House, Albany Court Monarch, Newcastle Business Park, Newcastle-Upon-Tyne, Tyne and Wear NE4 7YB
**Tel:** 01912733311 **Fax:** 0191-273-6620
**Web:** www.surgo.co.uk
**Reg No:** 0235552 **Estd:** 1928 Private Limited Company
**Line of Business:** Builders
**Trading Style:** Surgo Construction
**Issued Capital:** £15,022
**Directors:** J R Alexander, J G Walker, J Charlton, I Walker
**Co. Secretary:** Steven Coombes
**Responsibilities**
**Senior:** Arnold Macdonald *(Manager)*, George Stevenson *(Manager)*
**Branches:** Surgo Construction Ltd, 7 Coquet Street, Newcastle Upon Tyne, Tyne and Wear NE1 2QE
**US SIC:** 1522, 1541
**UK SIC:** 50100
**Auditors:** KPMG LLP
**Bankers:** Barclays Bank Plc (20-59-61)

| | 31-08-14 | 31-08-13 | 31-08-12 |
|---|---|---|---|
| TO | 22,463,273 | 20,872,503 | 24,116,472 |
| P/L | 391,797 | 373,616 | 460,686 |
| NW | 3,353,199 | 3,344,623 | 3,338,923 |
| WC | 1,967,184 | 1,933,814 | 1,893,866 |
| Emp. | 87 | 96 | 103 |

DUNS 21-811-1914
## Surrey & Boarders Partnership Trust
Unit A-C, Philanthropic Road Kingsfield Business, Centre, Redhill, Surrey RH1 4DP
**Tel:** 01737288288
**Estd:** 2003
**Line of Business:** Nhs clinics
**US SIC:** 8062 **UK SIC:** 95100
**Employees:** 56

DUNS 54-864-3717
## Surrey & Borders Partnership Nhs Foundation Trust
Randalls Road Mole Business Park, Leatherhead, Surrey KT22 7AD
**Tel:** 01372204000
**Web:** www.sabp.nhs.uk
**Estd:** 2005
**Line of Business:** NHS Foundation Trust over-seeing procurement & provision of health and social care services for people with mental health problems, drug and alcohol problems and learning disabilities in Surrey and North East Hampshire.
**Principals:** R Greenhalgh *(Chairman)*, Ms F Edwards
**Responsibilities**
**Finance:** Clive Field *(Director of Finance)*
**Branches:** Surrey & Borders Partnership Nhs Foundation Trust, Woodside Rd, Godalming, Surrey GU8 4QD
**US SIC:** 9121, 8062, 8091, 7399
**UK SIC:** 91110, 95100, 95200, 83954
**Auditors:** KPMG LLP

| | 31-03-14 | 31-03-13 | 31-03-12 |
|---|---|---|---|
| TO | 155,808,000 | 165,178,000 | 133,112,000 |
| P/L | 1,415,000 | (32,203,000) | (20,247,000) |
| NW | 110,114,000 | 107,167,000 | 130,729,000 |
| WC | 28,778,000 | 32,599,000 | 30,027,000 |
| Emp. | 2,512 | 2,492 | 2,551 |

DUNS 50-635-6398
## Surrey & Sussex Healthcare Nhs Trust
East Surrey Hospital, Canada Avenue, Redhill, Surrey RH1 5RH
**Tel:** 01737-768511
**Web:** www.surreyandsussex.nhs.uk
**Estd:** 2012
**Line of Business:** Hospitals
**Trading Style:** Surrey & Sussex Healthcare Nhs Trust
**Principals:** R Davies *(Chairman)*, P Simpson *(Financial)*, Ms J Woollett *(Personnel)*, Ms G Wannell, A Walker, G Curtis, Ms Y Robbins, E Cooke
**Responsibilities**
**Senior:** Eloise Clarke *(Head Of Communications)*, Richard Durban *(Non-Executive Director)*, Catherine Greenaway *(Consultant Padedrician)*, Alan McCarthy *(Chairperson)*
**Marketing:** Eloise Clarke *(Head Of Communications)*
**IT:** Peter Hodgetts *(Computer Manager)*
**HR:** Eyvonne Parker *(Director of Human Resources)*
**Health & Safety:** Diane Mahoney *(Health & Safety Officer)*
**US SIC:** 8062, 9121
**UK SIC:** 95100, 91110
**Employees:** 4,000

DUNS 22-586-4073
## Surrey Community Development Trust
1st Floor Bradmere House, Brook Way, Leatherhead, Surrey KT22 7NA
**Tel:** 01372-387100
**Web:** www.transformhousing.org.uk
**Reg No:** 1057984 **Estd:** 1972 Private Company Limited By Guarantee
**Line of Business:** Non-charitable social work activities with accommodation
**Trading Style:** Transform Housing & Support
**Directors:** Ms D A Drury, R W Mills, Ms E A Kennedy, D J Turner, D S Parmee, B J Stevens, L Harris, D W Steeds
**Co. Secretary:** Ratna Sukumaran
**Responsibilities**
**Senior:** Jane Bolton *(Director)*, Christopher Deacon *(Director)*, David Hypher *(Manager)*, Asif Khan *(Maintenance Manager)*, Colin Selvin *(Manager)*, Beverley Stone *(Manager)*
**Facilities:** Asif Khan *(Maintenance Manager)*
**Branches:** Surrey Community Development Trust, 6-9 Middle Church Lane, Farnham, Surrey GU9 7PP
**US SIC:** 8321, 9121, 6732
**UK SIC:** 96111, 91110, 83100
**Auditors:** Nexia Smith & Williamson
**Bankers:** Barclays Bank Plc (20-06-05)

| | 31-03-14 | 31-03-13 | 31-03-12 |
|---|---|---|---|
| TO | 6,404,000 | 6,597,000 | 6,384,910 |
| P/L | 661,000 | 390,000 | 463,573 |
| NW | 12,578,000 | 12,722,000 | 11,755,650 |
| WC | 3,040,000 | 3,494,000 | 4,202,253 |
| Emp. | 98 | 106 | 100 |

DUNS 21-103-6447
## Surrey County Council
Contact Centre Room 296-298, Kingston-Upon-Thames, Surrey KT1 2DN
**Tel:** 03456009009
**Web:** www.surreycc.gov.uk
**VAT No:** 216947249 **Estd:** 1889
**Line of Business:** Bus operators and stations
**Trading Style:** Surrey Health and Project Sildow Bridge Centre, Reigate School Old Dean Youth, Woodlands School
**Principals:** D Munro *(Chairman)*, T Pugh, Ms Y Rees, Ms S Kemp, Ms J Fisher, D Sargeant, N Wilson, D Mcnulty
**Responsibilities**
**Senior:** Phyllis Avory *(Secretary)*, Andy Butler *(Manager)*, Sylvia Carter *(Committee Officer)*, Marion Chapman *(Owner)*, Carole Comfort *(Executive)*, Karen Dack *(Executive)*, Peter Derrick *(Principal)*, Tim Dukes *(Owner)*, Sarah Dutton *(Manager)*, Beryl Evans *(Principal)*, Sara Faithfull *(Owner)*, Matthew Farrow *(Owner)*, Elizabeth Filby *(Senior Manager)*, Bronwen Fisher *(General Manager)*, Paul Fishwick *(Manager)*, Rachel Gabitass *(Executive)*, Cecilia Gerrard *(Chairman)*, Kay Hammond *(Board Member)*, David Harmer *(Councillor)*, Marisa Heath *(Board Member)*, David Ivison *(Member)*, Peter La Hayes *(Executive)*, Charlotte Langridge *(Business Development Manager)*, Mike Lea *(Board Member)*, Michelle Manson *(Board Member)*, Sally Marks *(Vice Chairman of the County Co)*, Katy May *(General Manager)*, Kerry Middleton *(Manager)*, Liz Moore *(Owner)*, Steve Pointer *(Manager)*, Joanne Porter *(Executive)*, Tom Quinn *(Owner)*, Penny Robinson *(Owner)*, Matthew Smyth *(Manager)*, Dave Steggles *(Area Manager)*, Malcolm Styles *(Area Manager)*, Tania Surridge *(Owner)*, Shamas Tabrez *(Board Member)*, Derek Thomas *(Chief Executive Officer)*, Val Tinney *(Member)*, Clive Whitehread *(General Manager)*, Roy Wolstenholme *(Principal)*
**Finance:** Jill Harris *(Accounts & Funding Manager)*, Sheila Little *(Chief Finance Officer)*
**Marketing:** Paul Marinko *(Relations Manager)*, Joy Ridley *(Media Officer)*
**Sales:** Charlotte Langridge *(Business Development Manager)*, Nick Roberts *(Business Development Manager)*
**Admin:** Phyllis Avory *(Secretary)*, Adele Seex *(Local Support Assistant)*
**IT:** Paul Brocklehurst *(Head of IT)*, Steve Mabey *(Messaging & Collaboration Spec)*
**HR:** Ron Critcher *(Carers Development Officer)*, Sandie Hamilton *(Skills Development Manager)*, Tom Lewis *(HR Helpdesk Adviso)*, Carmel Millar *(Head of Human Resources)*
**Health & Safety:** Michael Gosling *(Cabinet Member for Public Heal)*
**Facilities:** John Stebbings *(Chief Property Manager)*
**Operations:** John Bangs *(Carers Lead Development Worker)*, Paul Bowen *(County Operations Manager)*, Simon Harding *(Senior Team Leader)*, Sue Ryle *(Project Executive)*
**Purchasing:** Laura Langstaff *(Head of Procurement)*
**Fleet:** Clive Batchelor *(Senior Engineer)*, John Furey *(Cabinet Member for Highways, T)*
**Engineering:** Clive Batchelor *(Senior Engineer)*, Angie Boxall *(Technical Engineer)*, Nigel Woodger *(Technician)*
**Branches:** Surrey County Council, Brightwells Road, Farnham, Surrey GU9 7RF
**US SIC:** 9121, 8211, 8091
**UK SIC:** 91110, 93200, 95200
**Auditors:** Grant Thornton UK LLP
**Bankers:** HSBC Bank plc (40-05-30)

| | 31-03-14 | 31-03-93 |
|---|---|---|
| TO | 851,740,000 | N/A |
| P/L | (786,834,000) | N/A |
| NW | (246,758,000) | 65,722,000 |
| WC | (63,330,000) | 6,425,000 |
| Emp. | 692 | 18,065 |

DUNS 42-416-6916
## Surrey County Cricket Club Ltd
The Kia Oval, London SE11 5SS
**Tel:** 02078205739
**Web:** www.surreycricket.com
**Reg No:** 0027896IP **Estd:** 2013 Friendly Society
**Line of Business:** Sports clubs
**Trading Style:** Kia Oval
**Principals:** B G Downing *(Chairman)*, M J Stewart *(Chairman)*, R G Willis, M J Edwards, V J Dodds, J E Douglas, D R Gilbert, D T Watts
**Co. Secretary:** P Sheldon
**Responsibilities**
**Senior:** Rebecca Lockyer *(Executive)*
**Marketing:** Zac Toumazi *(Group Commercial Director)*
**Sales:** Charlie Hodgson *(Commercial Director)*, Zac Toumazi *(Group Commercial Director)*
**Branches:** Surrey County Cricket Club Ltd, The Kia Oval, Kennington Oval, London SE11 5SS
**US SIC:** 7999 **UK SIC:** 97913
**Auditors:** Ernst & Young
**Employees:** 66

DUNS 21-941-7784
## Surrey Crossroads
Residents House Community Walk High, Street, Esher, Surrey KT10 9RA
**Tel:** 01483447770
**Web:** www.crossroadscaresurrey.org.uk
**Reg No:** 6303805 **Estd:** 2007 Private Company Limited By Guarantee
**Line of Business:** Home care and help services
**Directors:** M Dharamsi, Ms S Hickson, B R Edwards, Ms C C Warne, A L Hunt, Professor J M Scudamore, A D Paterson, Ms B Everett
**Co. Secretary:** Professor James Scudamore
**US SIC:** 8811 **UK SIC:** 99000
**Bankers:** Barclays Bank Plc (20-11-74)

| | 31-03-14 | 31-03-13 | 31-03-12 |
|---|---|---|---|
| TO | 2,804,000 | 2,694,000 | 2,433,000 |
| P/L | (50,000) | 101,000 | 147,000 |
| NW | 1,474,000 | 1,275,000 | 1,156,000 |
| WC | 1,004,000 | 836,000 | 728,000 |
| Emp. | 110 | 107 | 110 |

DUNS 76-697-6666
## Surrey Envelopes Ltd
(**Subsidiary of:** Bong Ab)
Unit 7, Nelson Trading Estate, The Path, London SW19 3BL
**Tel:** 020-8545-0099 **Fax:** 020-8544-0832
**Web:** www.surrey-envelopes.com
**Reg No:** 2592120 **VAT No:** 574184032
**Estd:** 1991 Private Limited Company
**Line of Business:** Manufacture of paper stationery
**Export Sales:** £150,904
**Issued Capital:** £50,000
**Principals:** J Greenleaf *(Managing)*, Miss S O Bataille, H Gunnarsson, M P Lucas
**Co. Secretary:** Michael Lucas
**Responsibilities**
**Senior:** Anders Davidsson *(Manager)*
**US SIC:** 2648 **UK SIC:** 47231
**Auditors:** PricewaterhouseCoopers LLP
**Bankers:** Lloyds TSB Bank plc (30-90-44)

| | 31-12-13 | 31-12-12 | 31-12-11 |
|---|---|---|---|
| TO | 15,014,018 | 16,227,044 | 17,085,702 |
| P/L | (445,642) | (94,446) | (154,812) |
| NW | (507,378) | (61,736) | 32,753 |
| WC | 1,420,611 | 1,374,685 | 1,427,864 |
| Emp. | 106 | 104 | 106 |

DUNS 42-487-2703
## Surrey Fire & Rescue Service
Croydon Road, Reigate, Surrey RH2 0EJ
**Tel:** 01737-242444 **Fax:** 01737-222857
**Web:** www.surrey-fire.gov.uk
**Estd:** 1974 Incorporate By Act Of Parliament
**Line of Business:** Fire service activities
**Director:** M Kitchen
**Responsibilities**
**IT:** Carl Walker *(Systems Information Technology)*
**HR:** Martin Riddle *(Training Officer)*, nicky webber *(traing& development manager)*
**Health & Safety:** Michael Redman *(Health & Safety Officer)*
**Facilities:** Paul Summerton *(Facilities Manager)*
**Branches:** Surrey Fire & Rescue Service, Fire Station, 34-36 London Road, Camberley, Surrey GU15 3UH
**US SIC:** 9224 **UK SIC:** 91400
**Employees:** 200

DUNS 21-229-1469
## Surrey Hampshire Borders Nhs Trust
Farnham Road Hospital, Farnham Road, Guildford, Surrey GU2 7LX
**Proprietorship**
**Line of Business:** Drug counselling
**Proprietor:** Mrs C Marbich
**US SIC:** 8062 **UK SIC:** 95100
**Employees:** 125

DUNS 23-644-5441
## Surrey Heath Borough Council
Surrey Heath House, Knoll Road, Camberley, Surrey GU15 3HD
**Tel:** 01276-707100 **Fax:** 01276707433
**Web:** www.surreyheath.gov.uk
**Estd:** 1974 Incorporate By Act Of Parliament
**Line of Business:** Local government
**Directors:** B Catchpole, C Allen, J Silvester, M Lovelock, P Trott, D Thomson, R Collins
**Responsibilities**
**Senior:** Karen Whelan *(Chief Executive)*, Michael Willis *(Chief Executive)*
**HR:** Andrea Vincent *(Head Personnel)*
**Branches:** Surrey Heath Borough Council, Westerham Road, Oxted, Surrey RH8 0EA
**US SIC:** 9121 **UK SIC:** 91110
**Bankers:** National Westminster Bank Plc (60-04-20)
**Employees:** 289

DUNS 56-955-3845
## Surrey National Golf Club Ltd
(**Subsidiary of:** Altonwood Ltd)
Rook Lane, Chaldon, Caterham, Surrey CR3 5AA
**Tel:** 01883-344555 **Fax:** 01883-344422
**Web:** www.surreynational.co.uk
**Reg No:** 2845617 **Estd:** 1996 Private Limited Company
**Line of Business:** Other sporting activities not elsewhere classified
**Issued Capital:** £1,000
**Directors:** S Hodsdon, Mrs N L Noades, R O Noades
**Responsibilities**
**Senior:** Kelly Noades *(Manager)*, Philip Skinner *(Manager)*
**US SIC:** 7999 **UK SIC:** 97913
**Auditors:** Meyers Williams

| | 30-04-14 | 30-04-13 | 30-04-12 |
|---|---|---|---|
| TO | 1,699,563 | 1,676,082 | 1,801,938 |
| P/L | 422,581 | 389,069 | 1,598,338 |
| NW | 3,630,143 | 3,196,539 | 2,782,083 |
| WC | (2,492,308) | (2,915,351) | (3,294,617) |
| Emp. | 49 | 52 | 53 |

DUNS 21-596-1948

## Surrey Oaklands Nhs Trust

Horton Lane, Epsom, Surrey KT19 8PB
**Tel:** 01372203425
**Estd:** 2011
**Line of Business:** Hospitals
**Proprietor:** Ms S Joyce
**Responsibilities**
**Senior:** Sheila Lakey *(Matron)*, Deana Mellett *(Manager)*
**US SIC:** 8062 **UK SIC:** 95100
**Employees:** 50

DUNS 36-517-5285

## Surrey Primary Care Trust

Cedar Court Guildford Road, Leatherhead, Surrey KT22 9AE
**Tel:** 01372-201-700
**Web:** www.surreydownsccg.nhs.uk
**Estd:** 2014
**Line of Business:** Local authority for the provision and administration of healthcare services in Surrey. Part of the National Health Service.
**Trading Style:** Surrey Pct, Nhs Surrey, Fort House Surgery
**Principals:** D Robertson *(Chairman)*, C Butler
**Branches:** Surrey Primary Care Trust, Surrey Primary Care Trust, Health Centre, Woking, Surrey GU21 3LQ
**US SIC:** 9121, 8091, 8062, 8049, 8072
**UK SIC:** 91110, 95200, 95100, 95000
**Employees:** 3,383

DUNS 21-138-7552

## Surrey Security Service Ltd

137 Princess Road, Woking, Surrey GU22 8ER
**Tel:** 01483-830626 **Fax:** 01483-827857
**Web:** www.thesurreysecurity.co.uk
**Reg No:** 6711429 **VAT No:** 975924467
**Estd:** 2008 Private Limited Company
**Line of Business:** Security activities
**Issued Capital:** £100
**Director:** A Waheed
**US SIC:** 7393 **UK SIC:** 83954
**Bankers:** HSBC Bank plc (40-47-08)

| | 30-09-13 | 30-09-12 | 30-09-11 |
|---|---|---|---|
| TA | 555,572 | 453,181 | 175,057 |
| NW | 18,496 | 22,848 | 10,216 |
| WC | 449,362 | 328,321 | 102,722 |

DUNS 28-846-6113

## Surrey Wildlife Trust

School Lane, Pirbright, Woking, Surrey GU24 0JN
**Tel:** 01483795440
**Web:** www.surreywildlifetrust.org
**Reg No:** 0645176 **Estd:** 1959 Private Company Limited By Guarantee
**Line of Business:** Representative office
**Trading Style:** Surrey Wildlife Trust
**Directors:** A Curtis, Ms P J Whyman, Mrs S E Rooke, Mrs S E Scott, J W Edwards, G Muir, A Oakley, R J Pritchard
**Co. Secretary:** Mrs Susan Rooke
**Responsibilities**
**Senior:** Mary Adler *(Director)*, Heather Hawker *(Director)*, Katharine Mills *(Director)*, Gordon Vincent *(Director)*
**Health & Safety:** David Sayce *(Head of Property Services)*
**Branches:** Surrey Wildlife Trust, Nower Wood Educational Nature Reserve, Mill Way, Leatherhead, Surrey KT22 8QA
**US SIC:** 8699 **UK SIC:** 96902
**Auditors:** Menzies
**Bankers:** HSBC Bank plc (40-05-30)

| | 31-03-14 | 31-03-13 | 31-03-12 |
|---|---|---|---|
| TO | 5,203,145 | 4,723,526 | 4,538,297 |
| P/L | (9,694) | 363,920 | 127,796 |
| NW | 3,896,449 | 3,906,143 | 3,542,223 |
| WC | 1,814,564 | 1,847,843 | 1,223,791 |
| Emp. | 92 | 83 | 84 |

DUNS 21-028-6530

## Surridge Dawson (Holdings) Ltd

(**Subsidiary of:** Connect Group Plc)
Blenheim House 1 Blenheim Road, Epsom, Surrey KT19 9AP
**Tel:** 01372800466 **Fax:** 020-8774-3013
**Web:** www.it-services.co.uk
**Reg No:** 0283121 **VAT No:** 235615568
**Estd:** 2007 Private Limited Company
**Line of Business:** Computer services
**Trading Style:** Surri
**Issued Capital:** £120,000
**Directors:** M R Cashmore, N J Gresham
**Co. Secretary:** Stuart Marriner
**Branches:** Surridge Dawson (Holdings) Ltd, 39 Manor Road, Luton, Bedfordshire LU1 4EE
**US SIC:** 6711, 5199
**UK SIC:** 83962, 61900
**Auditors:** Deloitte & Touche
**Bankers:** Barclays Bank Plc (20-32-29)

| | 31-08-13 | 31-08-12 | 31-08-11 |
|---|---|---|---|
| TA | 256,000 | 256,000 | 256,000 |
| NW | 256,000 | 256,000 | 256,000 |

DUNS 39-968-0016

## Sursum Ltd

(**Subsidiary of:** R & G Quality Care Ltd)
The Retreat, Warminster, Wiltshire BA12 0SZ
**Tel:** 01483300552
**Web:** www.sursum-securities.com
**Reg No:** 2267578 **Estd:** 1988 Private Limited Company
**Line of Business:** Other human health activities
**Issued Capital:** £103
**Director:** R J Wagner
**Branches:** Sursum Ltd, Elmgrove House Nursing Home, 7 Ballifeary Road, Inverness, Inverness-Shire IV3 5PJ
**US SIC:** 8091 **UK SIC:** 95200
**Auditors:** Fletcher & Partners
**Bankers:** The Royal Bank Of Scotland Plc (16-00-19)

| | 31-03-14 | 31-03-13 | 31-03-12 |
|---|---|---|---|
| TA | 2,630,061 | 2,464,802 | 2,294,343 |
| NW | 1,353,890 | 1,347,791 | 1,429,847 |
| WC | (264,937) | (258,924) | (182,816) |

DUNS 57-055-3321

## Survey & Construction Ltd

(**Subsidiary of:** Survey & Construction Services Ltd)
Survey House, 6 Station Road, Caterham, Surrey CR3 0EP
**Tel:** 01883625215
**Web:** www.surveyroofing.co.uk
**Reg No:** 2880312 **Estd:** 1993 Private Limited Company
**Line of Business:** Other construction work involving special trades
**Issued Capital:** £100
**Directors:** M N Jones, V F Sawyer
**Responsibilities**
**Senior:** Sharon Banton *(Manager)*, Nickola Langridge *(Manager)*
**Finance:** Nickola Langridge *(Manager)*
**US SIC:** 1799, 6711
**UK SIC:** 50000, 83962
**Bankers:** National Westminster Bank Plc (60-02-12)

| | 31-08-13 | 31-08-12 | 31-08-11 |
|---|---|---|---|
| TO | 13,040,039 | 14,284,144 | 15,518,088 |
| P/L | 193,060 | 305,388 | 25,267 |
| NW | 1,343,541 | 1,332,732 | 1,263,616 |
| WC | 876,465 | 859,335 | 624,920 |
| Emp. | 96 | 87 | 86 |

DUNS 28-879-4977 **Exp**

## Survey Force Ltd

Algarve House, 140 Borden Lane, Borden, Sittingbourne, Kent ME9 8HW
**Tel:** 01795-423778
**Web:** www.touchmedway.com
**Reg No:** 1158389 **Estd:** 1974 Private Limited Company
**Line of Business:** Market research organisations
**Issued Capital:** £100
**Managing Director:** K F Lainton
**Responsibilities**
**Senior:** Edith Shaw *(Manager)*
**Finance:** Edith Shaw *(Manager)*
**Marketing:** Peter Sidlett *(Sales & Marketing Director)*
**Sales:** Peter Sidlett *(Sales & Marketing Director)*
**Operations:** Peter Sidlett *(Sales & Marketing Director)*
**US SIC:** 7392, 7311
**UK SIC:** 83951, 83800
**Bankers:** HSBC Bank plc (40-31-06)

| | 30-04-13 | 30-04-12 | 30-04-11 |
|---|---|---|---|
| TA | 33,550 | 34,997 | 36,911 |
| NW | 18,336 | 18,884 | 19,519 |
| WC | 18,167 | 18,685 | 19,285 |

DUNS 76-887-2194

## Survey Operations Ltd

(**Subsidiary of:** Survey Holdings Ltd)
Smith Street, Skelmersdale, Lancashire WN8 8LN
**Tel:** 01695-725662
**Web:** www.survops.co.uk
**Reg No:** 2614668 **Estd:** 1991 Private Limited Company
**Line of Business:** Land surveying activities
**Issued Capital:** £20,000
**Directors:** S G Popely, D J Orritt, Ms S M Birchall
**Co. Secretary:** Ms Anne Popely
**US SIC:** 8911 **UK SIC:** 83701
**Auditors:** Fairhurst
**Bankers:** Barclays Bank Plc (20-74-45)

| | 31-10-13 | 31-10-12 | 31-10-11 |
|---|---|---|---|
| TA | 1,111,673 | 801,563 | 917,205 |
| NW | 242,649 | 156,427 | 221,712 |
| WC | (200,883) | (221,392) | (161,201) |

DUNS 54-863-4203

## The Survey Shop

7 North Hermitage, Shrewsbury, Shropshire SY3 7JW
**Web:** www.thesurveyshop.com
**Estd:** 1991 Proprietorship
**Line of Business:** Market research organisations
**Proprietor:** P Gill
**US SIC:** 7392 **UK SIC:** 83951
**Employees:** 50

DUNS 21-311-2519 **Imp-Exp**

## Survey Supplies Ltd

(**Subsidiary of:** Precise Construction Instruments Ltd)
Blundellsands House, 34-44 Mersey View, Liverpool, Merseyside L22 6QB
**Tel:** 01519313161
**Web:** www.surveysupplies.co.uk
**Reg No:** 0965862 **VAT No:** 164422870
**Estd:** 1967 Private Limited Company
**Line of Business:** Surveying instruments
**Export Markets:** Worldwide
**Export Sales:** £1,063,969
**Trading Style:** Korec
**Issued Capital:** £420,200
**Directors:** A Beckerson, A C Browne, O C Brooks
**Co. Secretary:** David Hodkinson
**Responsibilities**
**HR:** Kirsten Moss *(Human Resources Manager)*
**Branches:** Survey Supplies Ltd, Po Box 270, Diss Norfolk, Diss, Norfolk IP22 5WJ
**US SIC:** 3832, 7394
**UK SIC:** 37320, 84000
**Auditors:** Saffery Champness
**Bankers:** Barclays Bank Plc (20-51-01)

| | 30-11-13 | 30-11-12 | 30-11-11 |
|---|---|---|---|
| TO | 13,541,035 | 12,067,260 | 10,783,319 |
| P/L | 174,736 | 391,750 | 54,787 |
| NW | 5,227,261 | 5,085,238 | 4,795,019 |
| WC | 2,428,661 | 3,374,967 | 4,246,142 |
| Emp. | 81 | 70 | 62 |

DUNS 29-369-2570 **Imp-Exp**

## Survitec Group Ltd

(**Subsidiary of:** Survitec Group (Cayman Islands) Limited)
Kingsway, Dunmurry, Belfast BT17 9AF
**Tel:** 02890-301531 **Fax:** 02890621765
**Web:** www.survitecgroup.com
**Reg No:** 0905173 **Estd:** 1967 Private Limited Company
**Line of Business:** Manufacture of workwear
**Export Markets:** Europe, North America, Australasia and other
**Export Sales:** £41,200,000
**Issued Capital:** £100
**Directors:** B M Stringer, C R Bates, S B Withey
**Co. Secretary:** Miss Sally Lewis
**Responsibilities**
**Senior:** Stuart Mcintosh *(Manager)*
**US SIC:** 3732 **UK SIC:** 36102
**Auditors:** PricewaterhouseCoopers LLP

| | 31-03-14 | 31-03-13 | 31-03-12 |
|---|---|---|---|
| TO | 65,440,000 | 54,356,000 | 67,162,000 |
| P/L | (40,344,000) | 7,767,000 | 19,738,000 |
| NW | 104,952,000 | 146,928,000 | 138,565,000 |
| WC | 90,203,000 | 88,307,000 | 80,277,000 |
| Emp. | 522 | 489 | 479 |

DUNS 76-836-9514 **Imp-Exp**

## Survival Craft Inspectorate Ltd

Findon Shore, Findon, Aberdeen, Aberdeenshire AB12 3RL
**Tel:** 01224-784488 **Fax:** 01224-784111
**Web:** www.survivalcraft.com
**Reg No:** 0131397SC **VAT No:** 553180750
**Estd:** 1991 Private Limited Company
**Line of Business:** Manufacture of medical and surgical equipment and orthopaedic appliances
**Export Markets:** Netherlands
**Export Sales:** £4,752
**Issued Capital:** £100
**Principals:** A Campbell *(Chairman and Managing)*, R K Hunt
**Co. Secretary:** Ms Catherine Campbell
**Branches:** Survival Craft Inspectorate Ltd, 15 Old Road, Frinton-On-Sea, Essex CO13 9DA
**US SIC:** 3841 **UK SIC:** 37201
**Auditors:** Johnston Carmichael
**Bankers:** Bank Of Scotland (80-05-21)

| | 31-05-13 | 31-05-12 | 31-05-11 |
|---|---|---|---|
| TO | 18,412,276 | 18,565,276 | 15,438,287 |
| P/L | 2,937,625 | 2,287,901 | 2,212,000 |
| NW | 8,553,124 | 6,868,654 | 6,241,577 |
| WC | 6,217,506 | 5,293,021 | 4,344,110 |
| Emp. | 148 | 141 | 126 |

DUNS 23-617-5811 **Exp**

## Survival-One Ltd

(**Subsidiary of:** Survitec Group (Cayman Islands) Limited)
Howemoss Drive, Aberdeen, Aberdeenshire AB21 0GL
**Tel:** 01224-214444
**Web:** www.multifabs-survival.co.uk
**Reg No:** 0188500SC **Estd:** 1998 Private Limited Company
**Line of Business:** Renting of passenger air transport equipment
**Export Sales:** £6,599,420
**Issued Capital:** £1,554,000
**Directors:** B M Stringer, S B Withey, C G Taylor, G R Allanach, C R Bates
**Co. Secretary:** Ms Sally Lewis
**Responsibilities**
**Senior:** Rune Veenstra *(Vice President)*
**Finance:** Louise Ramsay *(Financial Director)*
**Sales:** Jim Cook *(Sales Manager)*
**HR:** Julie Adie *(Human Resources Manager)*
**US SIC:** 7394, 2328
**UK SIC:** 84000, 45340
**Auditors:** Deloitte LLP
**Bankers:** Bank Of Scotland (80-29-01)

| | 31-03-14 | 31-03-13 | 31-03-12 |
|---|---|---|---|
| TO | 19,651,555 | 16,787,619 | 14,360,697 |
| P/L | 7,406,091 | 7,162,435 | 5,470,442 |
| NW | 10,360,488 | 7,423,777 | 6,278,329 |
| WC | 2,746,357 | 1,132,411 | 1,364,337 |
| Emp. | 196 | 169 | 177 |

DUNS 28-830-9115

## The Sussex Archaeological Society

Bull House, 92 High Street, Lewes, East Sussex BN7 1XH
**Web:** www.sussexpast.co.uk
**Reg No:** 0202795 **Estd:** 1925 Private Company Limited By Guarantee
**Line of Business:** Caterers
**Trading Style:** Sussex Past
**Directors:** C A Watson, Professor R R Milner-Gulland, P Balmer, E K Andrews, A G Howell, T Reid, Mrs L Drewett, J Manley
**Responsibilities**
**Senior:** Richard Akhurst *(chair of trustees)*, Vivienne Blandford *(Director)*, Michael Chartier *(Director)*, Lisa Fisher *(Director)*, Anne Locke *(Manager)*, Janet Oldham *(Director)*, David Rudling *(Director)*, Peter Sangster *(Manager)*, Jane Vokins *(Director)*, Peter Vos *(Director)*
**Admin:** Lorna Gartside *(Administrator)*
**Health & Safety:** James Thatcher *(Health & Safety Officer)*
**Branches:** The Sussex Archaeological Society, Salthill Road, Chichester, West Sussex PO19 3QR
**US SIC:** 7911 **UK SIC:** 97913
**Auditors:** Grant Thornton
**Bankers:** Barclays Bank Plc (20-49-76)

| | 31-12-13 | 31-12-12 | 31-12-11 |
|---|---|---|---|
| TO | 1,736,033 | 1,553,750 | 1,431,911 |
| P/L | (132,853) | (255,875) | (182,910) |
| NW | 2,466,087 | 2,491,200 | 3,043,274 |
| WC | 249,871 | 51,615 | 137,273 |
| Emp. | 106 | 94 | 85 |

DUNS 28-903-1296

## Sussex Cleaning & Care Ltd.

Unit 30 Bolney Grange Industrial Park, Haywards Heath, West Sussex RH17 5PB
**Tel:** 01444872187
**Web:** www.scc-ltd.co.uk
**Reg No:** 1362066 **Estd:** 1973 Private Limited Company
**Line of Business:** Cleaning activities not elsewhere classified
**Issued Capital:** £200
**Director:** R Morris
**Co. Secretary:** Nicholas Pitcher
**US SIC:** 7349 **UK SIC:** 92300
**Auditors:** Haines & Co
**Bankers:** Lloyds TSB Bank plc (30-18-30)

| | 31-08-14 | 31-08-13 | 31-08-12 |
|---|---|---|---|
| TA | 317,296 | 267,792 | 226,816 |
| NW | 144,526 | 114,343 | 96,693 |
| WC | 136,467 | 102,304 | 80,514 |

DUNS 42-377-6111

## Sussex Coast College Hastings

Station Approach, Hastings, East Sussex TN34 1BA
**Tel:** 01424442222
**Web:** www.sussexcoast.ac.uk
**VAT No:** 621533570 **Estd:** 2010
**Line of Business:** Further education schools and colleges
**Principals:** J Morris *(Financial)*, Mrs J Walker, C Luxford
**Responsibilities**
**Senior:** Sue Middlehurst *(Principal)*, Janak Patel *(Principal)*
**HR:** Susan Gorridge *(Human Resources Manager)*
**Facilities:** Mark Oak *(Facilities Manager)*

**Branches:** Sussex Coast College Hastings, 80 St. Saviours Road, St. Leonards-On-Sea, East Sussex TN38 0AR
**US SIC:** 8211 **UK SIC:** 93200
**Bankers:** Barclays Bank Plc (20-27-91)
**Employees:** 700

DUNS 52-021-0907

## Sussex Community Development Association Ltd

Denton Island, Newhaven, East Sussex BN9 9BA
**Fax:** 01273-612821
**Web:** www.ncda.org.uk
**Reg No:** 3387617 **Estd:** 1997 Private Limited Company
**Line of Business:** Activities of other membership organisations not elsewhere classified
**Directors:** G R Amy, Ms M G Aguilar, G S Bishop, Mrs H Macaulay, P C Foote, K J Ward, J W Cornish
**Responsibilities**
**Senior:** Emily Mottram (Manager), Penny Shimmin (Chief Executive)
**US SIC:** 8999, 8699
**UK SIC:** 83954, 96902
**Auditors:** Russell New
**Bankers:** HSBC Bank plc (40-34-35)

| | 31-03-14 | 31-03-13 | 31-03-12 |
|---|---|---|---|
| TO | 2,127,560 | 1,464,497 | 1,903,717 |
| P/L | 101,903 | (79,887) | 13,370 |
| NW | 827,799 | 726,856 | 806,743 |
| WC | 243,307 | 142,636 | 223,424 |
| Emp. | 67 | 65 | 66 |

DUNS 23-827-8944

## Sussex Community Internet Project

Community Base 113 Queens Road, Brighton, East Sussex BN1 3XG
**Tel:** 01273-234049
**Web:** www.scip.org.uk
**Reg No:** 3819836 **Estd:** 1999 Private Company Limited By Guarantee
**Line of Business:** Computer support & services
**Trading Style:** Sussex Community Internet Project
**Directors:** A Fairhall, Miss A M Hinton, M D James
**US SIC:** 7379 **UK SIC:** 83940

| | 31-03-14 | 31-03-13 | 31-03-12 |
|---|---|---|---|
| TO | 257,252 | 190,996 | 195,065 |
| P/L | 8,043 | (9,519) | 313 |
| NW | 5,061 | (2,982) | 6,537 |
| WC | 3,284 | (3,775) | 4,670 |

DUNS 22-224-7202

## Sussex County Arts Club

3 Bond St Cottages, Brighton, East Sussex BN1 1RP
**Tel:** 07708870791
**Web:** www.sussexcountyartsclub.co.uk
**Reg No:** 4242659 **Estd:** 2001 Private Limited Company
**Line of Business:** Activities of other membership organisations not elsewhere classified
**Directors:** G T Hanney, Ms M A Poluck, J N Mead, P Gluckman, W Donohoe, R D Newman
**Co. Secretary:** Ms Philippa Burley
**US SIC:** 8699 **UK SIC:** 96902
**Bankers:** HSBC Bank plc (40-14-01)

| | 31-03-14 | 31-03-13 | 31-03-12 |
|---|---|---|---|
| TO | 19,772 | 17,370 | 31,223 |
| P/L | 2,710 | 273 | 4,544 |
| NW | 25,278 | 23,075 | 23,010 |
| WC | 25,278 | 23,075 | 22,735 |

DUNS 55-049-0593

## Sussex County Cricket Club

Eaton Road, Hove, East Sussex BN3 3AN
**Tel:** 01273827100
**Web:** www.sussexcricket.co.uk
**VAT No:** 190879616 **Estd:** 1839
**Line of Business:** Sports clubs
**Principals:** D Holst (President), D Trangmar (Chairman), D Gilbert (General Manager)
**Responsibilities**
**Senior:** Dave Brooks (Chief Executive)
**Finance:** Sandra Hill (Finance Manager)
**Marketing:** Trevor Mould (Sales & Marketing Manager)
**Sales:** Trevor Mould (Sales & Marketing Manager)
**Admin:** Sarah McKee (Administrator)
**Facilities:** Ian Waring (Operations & Facilities manager)
**Purchasing:** Sarah McKee (Administrator)
**US SIC:** 7999 **UK SIC:** 97913
**Bankers:** Barclays Bank Plc (20-12-75)
**Employees:** 50

DUNS 21-232-9434

## Sussex Downs & Weald Nhs Primary Care Trust

Crowborough War Memorial Hospital, Southview Road, Crowborough, East Sussex TN6 1HB
**Tel:** 01892-669393
**Web:** www.esdw.nhs.uk
**Estd:** 2003 Proprietorship
**Line of Business:** Health authorities
**Proprietor:** Mrs E Singfield
**Responsibilities**
**Senior:** Lindsay Ransome (Estate Manager)
**US SIC:** 9121 **UK SIC:** 91110
**Employees:** 51

DUNS 42-478-8529

## Sussex Downs College

Mountfield Road, Lewes, East Sussex BN7 2XH
**Tel:** 01273-483188
**Web:** www.sussexdowns.ac.uk
**Estd:** 2010
**Line of Business:** Further education schools and colleges
**Directors:** H Ball, P Gibson
**Responsibilities**
**Senior:** Sherry Russell (Head Of Lewes)
**Finance:** John Cretts (Senior Finance Administrator)
**Sales:** Rosanna Francis (Development Learning Coordinat), Lizzie Kemp (Business Development Coordinat)
**Admin:** Jackie Bennett (Administrator), John Cretts (Senior Finance Administrator)
**Purchasing:** Sally Teague (Purchasing Manager)
**Branches:** Sussex Downs College, West St, Lewes, East Sussex BN7 2NZ
**US SIC:** 8211 **UK SIC:** 93200
**Employees:** 1,500

DUNS 22-151-7779

## Sussex Enterprise Ltd

Unit 4 Victoria Business Centre, 43 Victoria Road, Burgess Hill, West Sussex RH15 9LR
**Tel:** 08443759550 **Fax:** 01444259255
**Web:** www.sussexchamberofcommerce.co.uk
**Reg No:** 4170509 **Estd:** 2001 Private Limited Company
**Line of Business:** Chambers of commerce
**Trading Style:** Sussex Enterprise Chamber of Commerce
**Issued Capital:** £2
**Directors:** R A Clare, D Sheppard, Mrs M J Richardson, N M Handley, D A Shore, Mrs A M Christie, Mrs S D Phillips, P Hills
**Co. Secretary:** Timothy Aspinall
**Responsibilities**
**Senior:** Farid Ahmed (Director), Malcolm Bradshaw (Manager), Robert Fryatt (Manager)
**Marketing:** Mark Tilley (Marketing and IT Executive)
**Sales:** Chris Goulding (Sales Executive), Jane Phelps (International Trade Developmen)
**HR:** Mo Rasanayagam
**US SIC:** 8621 **UK SIC:** 96311
**Bankers:** Barclays Bank Plc (20-23-97)

| | 31-03-14 | 31-03-13 | 31-03-12 |
|---|---|---|---|
| TO | 776,713 | 818,876 | 1,009,946 |
| P/L | 939,495 | (179,106) | (424,306) |
| NW | (61,139) | (1,000,634) | (821,528) |
| WC | (65,826) | (1,000,634) | (784,700) |

DUNS 22-224-1478

## Sussex Enterprise Services Ltd

(**Subsidiary of:** Sussex Chamber of Commerce & Enterprise)
Greenacre Court, Station Road, Burgess Hill, West Sussex RH15 9DS
**Tel:** 01444259259 **Fax:** 01444-259255
**Web:** www.sussexenterprise.co.uk
**Reg No:** 4242100 **Estd:** 1995 Private Limited Company
**Line of Business:** Other business activities not elsewhere classified
**Issued Capital:** £100
**Directors:** D Sheppard, R A Clare, P Hills, D A Shore, N M Handley
**Co. Secretary:** Timothy Aspinall
**Responsibilities**
**Senior:** Farid Ahmed (Director)
**US SIC:** 7399, 8611
**UK SIC:** 83954, 96312
**Auditors:** RSM Robson Rhodes
**Bankers:** Barclays Bank Plc (20-71-02)

| | 31-03-14 | 31-03-13 | 31-03-12 |
|---|---|---|---|
| TA | 4 | 102 | 102 |
| P/L | (98) | N/A | N/A |
| NW | 4 | 102 | 102 |

DUNS 22-698-6735

## Sussex Health Care

Tylden House, Dorking Road, Warnham, Horsham, West Sussex RH12 3RZ
**Tel:** 01403217338
**Web:** www.sussexhealthcare.org
**Estd:** 1985 Partnership
**Line of Business:** Other human health activities
**Partners:** S Sachedina, S Boghani
**Responsibilities**
**Senior:** Pam Stuart (Home manager)
**Finance:** David Blackman (Senior Finance Administrator)
**Marketing:** Corrine Wallace (Senior Marketing Executive)
**Admin:** David Blackman (Senior Finance Administrator)
**Operations:** Corrine Wallace (Senior Marketing Executive)
**Branches:** Sussex Health Care, Plawhatch Lane, East Grinstead, West Sussex RH19 4JH
**US SIC:** 8091, 8321
**UK SIC:** 95200, 96111
**Bankers:** Barclays Bank Plc (20-66-51)
**Employees:** 750

DUNS 21-412-2722

## Sussex Newspapers

Cannon House, Chatsworth Road, Worthing, West Sussex BN11 1NA
**Tel:** 01903282382
**Web:** www.worthingherald.co.uk
**Estd:** 1988 Proprietorship
**Line of Business:** Newspapers publishing
**Proprietor:** K Deimmock
**US SIC:** 2711 **UK SIC:** 47512
**Employees:** 50

DUNS 21-596-1961

## Sussex Partnership Nhs Foundation Trust

Swandean, 85 Arundel Road, Worthing, West Sussex BN13 3EP
**Tel:** 01903843000
**Web:** www.sussexpartnership.nhs.uk
**Estd:** 2002 Proprietorship
**Line of Business:** Local government
**Proprietor:** Mrs L Rodrigues
**Responsibilities**
**Senior:** Colm Eonaghy (Chief Executive)
**US SIC:** 8062 **UK SIC:** 95100
**Auditors:** PricewaterhouseCoopers LLP

| | 31-03-14 | 31-03-13 | 31-03-12 |
|---|---|---|---|
| TO | 228,915,000 | 223,782,000 | 224,901,000 |
| P/L | 3,581,000 | 2,529,000 | (36,895,000) |
| NW | 144,899,000 | 135,760,000 | 133,285,000 |
| WC | 23,435,000 | 15,458,000 | 15,208,000 |
| Emp. | 4,321 | 4,072 | 4,038 |

DUNS 36-522-7326

## Sussex Partnership Nhs Trust

Swandean, Arundel Road, Worthing, West Sussex BN13 3EP
**Tel:** 01903843000
**Web:** www.sussexpartnership.nhs.uk
**Estd:** 2002
**Line of Business:** Public sector hospital activities, including nhs trusts
**Director:** Mrs L Rodrigues
**Responsibilities**
**Finance:** Sally Flint (Financial Director)
**Marketing:** Ranjeet Kaile (Press Officer)
**HR:** Sarah Daniel (Human Resources Manager)
**US SIC:** 7399 **UK SIC:** 83954
**Employees:** 4,000

DUNS 22-747-0903    Imp

## Sussex Police Headquarters

Malling House, Malling, Lewes, East Sussex BN7 2DZ
**Tel:** 08456070999 **Fax:** 0845404213
**Web:** www.sussex.police.uk
**Estd:** 1845 Incorporate By Act Of Parliament
**Line of Business:** Police forces
**Director:** P C Whitehouse
**Responsibilities**
**Senior:** Martin Richards (Chief Constable)
**HR:** Scott Edwards (Training Manager)
**Fleet:** Malcolm Naftel (Service Delivery Manager)
**Branches:** Sussex Police Headquarters, 13 London Road, Pulborough, West Sussex RH20 1AP
**US SIC:** 9221 **UK SIC:** 91300
**Employees:** 900

DUNS 21-683-4069

## Sussex Turnery & Moulding Co Ltd

Highfield Business Park, Highfield Drive, St Leonards-On-Sea, East Sussex TN38 9TG
**Tel:** 01424-856883 **Fax:** 01424-440505
**Web:** www.stamco.co.uk
**Reg No:** 1223584 **VAT No:** 202699367

**Estd:** 1957 Private Limited Company
**Line of Business:** Saw milling and planing of wood, impregnation of wood
**Trading Style:** Stamco Timber
**Issued Capital:** £192,622
**Principals:** R D Brightiff (Managing), M S Cullis, J Cornelius, C R Willard
**Co. Secretary:** Nicholas Wilde
**US SIC:** 2421, 5039
**UK SIC:** 46101, 61300
**Auditors:** Ogilvie Booth Coles
**Bankers:** National Westminster Bank Plc (60-10-15)

| | 31-08-14 | 31-08-13 | 31-08-12 |
|---|---|---|---|
| TO | 22,008,147 | 17,838,133 | 17,507,172 |
| P/L | 592,475 | 464,091 | 448,631 |
| NW | 4,586,144 | 4,439,439 | 4,398,779 |
| WC | 456,068 | 417,269 | 437,858 |
| Emp. | 123 | 114 | 106 |

DUNS 73-927-1070

## Sussex Waste Recycling Ltd

(**Subsidiary of:** Rabbit Waste Management Ltd)
Unit 2 Chartwell Road, Lancing, West Sussex BN15 8TU
**Tel:** 01903762020
**Web:** www.sussex-waste.co.uk
**Reg No:** 2938266 **VAT No:** 679431987
**Estd:** 1994 Private Limited Company
**Line of Business:** Collection and treatment of other waste
**Trading Style:** Rabbit Group Lancing, Rabbit Group Newhaven
**Issued Capital:** £1,000
**Directors:** Ms A Bridson, G D Blurton
**Co. Secretary:** Peter Gilmartin
**Responsibilities**
**Senior:** Dane Jordan (Partner), Josh Mitchinson (Proprietor)
**Branches:** Sussex Waste Recycling Ltd, North Quay Road, Newhaven, East Sussex BN9 0AB
**US SIC:** 4953, 8999
**UK SIC:** 92110, 83954
**Auditors:** Wilson Sandford (Brighton) Ltd
**Bankers:** Allied Irish Bank (gb) (23-85-89)

| | 30-09-13 | 30-09-12 | 30-09-11 |
|---|---|---|---|
| TO | 7,875,424 | 7,055,696 | 8,383,903 |
| P/L | 850,217 | 50,490 | (55,418) |
| NW | 1,427,791 | 880,702 | 945,558 |
| WC | (311,799) | (1,032,718) | (1,212,026) |
| Emp. | 62 | 71 | 79 |

DUNS 22-530-2173

## Sussex Wildlife Trust

Woods Mill, Shoreham Road, Henfield, West Sussex BN5 9SD
**Tel:** 01273492630
**Web:** www.sussexwildlifetrust.org.uk
**Reg No:** 0698851 **VAT No:** 191305969
**Estd:** 1961 Private Company Limited By Guarantee
**Line of Business:** Individual & family social services
**Directors:** C J Warne, Dr J Parry, Ms L M Leeson, Mrs S M Walton, R B Williams, Mrs C J Nicholson, Dr A Stewart, Ms E A Montlake
**Co. Secretary:** Mrs Susan Walton
**Responsibilities**
**Senior:** Philip Belden (Director), Alice Parfitt (Executive), David Plummer (Executive), Mike Russell (Manager), David Streeter (Director), Tony Whitbread (Chief Executive)
**Finance:** Jon Whitty (Business Manager)
**Marketing:** Jon Whitty (Business Manager)
**Sales:** Mike Murphy (Seven Sisters Schools Developm)
**IT:** Laura Bristow (Information Officer)
**HR:** Jaci Baker (Personnel Officer)
**Facilities:** Jon Whitty (Business Manager)
**Branches:** Sussex Wildlife Trust, Exceat Farm, East Dean Road, Seaford, East Sussex BN25 4AD
**US SIC:** 8321, 8211, 8299, 8699
**UK SIC:** 96111, 93200, 93300, 96902
**Auditors:** HLB Kidsons
**Bankers:** Barclays Bank Plc (20-49-76)

| | 31-03-14 | 31-03-13 | 31-03-12 |
|---|---|---|---|
| TO | 3,236,180 | 3,055,362 | 2,973,809 |
| P/L | 197,759 | 129,166 | (237,979) |
| NW | 5,301,644 | 5,103,885 | 4,974,719 |
| WC | 1,637,142 | 1,470,886 | 1,375,077 |
| Emp. | 66 | 63 | 67 |

DUNS 42-446-0389    Imp

## Sustainable Drainage Systems Ltd

(**Subsidiary of:** Sds Holdings Ltd)
Clearwater House, Castlemills, Axbridge, Somerset BS26 2RE
**Tel:** 01934-751303 **Fax:** 01934-751304
**Web:** www.sdslimited.com
**Reg No:** 4433740 **Estd:** 2002 Private Limited Company
**Line of Business:** Collection and treatment of sewage
**Issued Capital:** £100
**Directors:** S Cullen, Ms S Cullen
**Co. Secretary:** Patrick Cullen

**Responsibilities**
**Senior:** Richard Averley *(Sales Director)*
**Sales:** Richard Averley *(Sales Director)*
**US SIC:** 4952, 1622
**UK SIC:** 92120, 50200
**Auditors:** T.P. Lewis & Partners (BOS) Ltd
**Bankers:** Lloyds TSB Bank plc (30-91-84)

| | 30-11-13 | 31-05-12 | 31-11-11 |
|---|---|---|---|
| TO | 19,413,111 | 12,845,518 | 9,482,584 |
| P/L | 1,275,519 | 1,002,353 | 411,635 |
| NW | 2,138,100 | 1,160,438 | 608,652 |
| WC | 1,063,367 | (339,767) | (257,174) |
| Emp. | 64 | 58 | 52 |

DUNS 28-985-2949
## Sustrans Ltd
2 Cathedral Square, Bristol, Avon BS1 5DD
**Tel:** 01179268893
**Web:** www.sustrans.org.uk
**Reg No:** 1797726 **VAT No:** 416740656
**Estd:** 1998 Private Company Limited By Guarantee
**Line of Business:** Social work activities
**Directors:** Ms C L Addison, W L Stow, Ms A P Hyland, A G Balfour, R S Morris, Ms V A Aherne, E F Condry, J F O'Hara
**Co. Secretary:** Andrew Appleby
**Responsibilities**
**Senior:** Gina Alcock *(Executive)*, Philippa Cochrane *(Manager)*, Mark Edgell *(Director)*, Vincent Gibson *(Executive)*, Vicki Hill *(Senior Manager)*, Jim Imeson *(Executive)*, Ilanora Lewin *(Director)*, Marina Littek *(Executive)*, William Methven *(Manager)*, Susan Otty *(Manager)*, Kelly Richardson *(Executive)*, Ben Sherratt *(Manager)*, Mark Tucker *(Representative)*, Nikki Wingfield *(Area Manager)*
**Marketing:** Jess Beaton *(Senior Press Officer)*, Joanna Corfield *(Press Officer)*, Paul Dyett *(Head of Media Relations)*, Melissa Henry *(Communications Director)*, Alec James *(Press Officer)*
**Sales:** Jane Coles *(Head of Business Development)*, Susie Dunham *(Strategy Manager)*
**IT:** Martyn Brunt *(National Cycle Network Manager)*, Rory Mitchinson *(IT Manager)*
**Operations:** Natalie Gledhill *(Project Coordinator)*, Robyn Hughes *(Project Coordinator)*, Susie Lea *(Senior Manager)*, Ciaran Mullan *(Manager)*, Clare Prosser *(Production and Operations Mana)*
**Branches:** Sustrans Ltd, Rosebery House, 9 Haymarket Terrace, Edinburgh, Midlothian EH12 5EZ
**US SIC:** 7399 **UK SIC:** 83954
**Auditors:** PricewaterhouseCoopers LLP
**Bankers:** The Royal Bank Of Scotland Plc (16-14-25)

| | 31-03-14 | 31-03-13 | 31-03-12 |
|---|---|---|---|
| TO | 49,576,000 | 78,694,000 | 48,872,000 |
| P/L | 366,000 | 689,000 | 274,000 |
| NW | 10,136,000 | 9,770,000 | 9,081,000 |
| WC | 7,542,000 | 7,137,000 | 6,436,000 |
| Emp. | 210 | 450 | 348 |

DUNS 28-977-0463
## Sutcliffe Group Ltd
Unit 6 Sandbeds Trading Estate, Dewsbury Road, Ossett, West Yorkshire WF5 9ND
**Tel:** 01924273777
**Reg No:** 1761194 **Estd:** 1983 Private Limited Company
**Line of Business:** Management activities of holding companies
**Export Sales:** £971,470
**Issued Capital:** £92,400
**Principals:** D R Sutcliffe *(Chairman and Managing)*, M E Griffin, D F Brady
**Co. Secretary:** Stuart White
**Responsibilities**
**Senior:** Henry Clapham *(Proprietor)*
**US SIC:** 6711, 3069
**UK SIC:** 83962, 48123
**Auditors:** KPMG
**Bankers:** Lloyds TSB Bank plc (30-99-01)

| | 28-09-13 | 29-09-12 | 01-09-11 |
|---|---|---|---|
| TO | 6,302,052 | 6,828,584 | 8,335,017 |
| P/L | 116,782 | 125,704 | 523,222 |
| NW | 1,622,882 | 1,630,802 | 1,609,616 |
| WC | 590,683 | 721,796 | 695,300 |
| Emp. | 63 | 68 | 76 |

DUNS 23-289-1759
## Sutherland Homes
Sheringham House, Cremers Drift, Sheringham, Norfolk NR26 8HZ
**Tel:** 01263-825552
**Web:** www.sutherlandhomes.com
**Estd:** 1999 Proprietorship
**Line of Business:** Property developers
**Proprietor:** R F Davies
**US SIC:** 6531, 1541, 1522
**UK SIC:** 83400, 50100
**Employees:** 60

DUNS 21-632-1461
## The Sutton Academy
Elton Head Road, St Helens, Merseyside WA9 5AU
**Tel:** 01744678859
**Web:** www.thesuttonacademy.org.uk
**Reg No:** 7103919 **Estd:** 2009 Private Company Limited By Guarantee
**Line of Business:** Post-graduate level higher education
**Directors:** Mrs S Jee, B Dean, R Molloy, Mrs J I Burford
**Co. Secretary:** Mrs Christine Jones
**Responsibilities**
**Senior:** Steve Fullerton *(Principal)*, Karen Sudworth *(Head Teacher)*, Dave Terry *(Head Teacher)*
**US SIC:** 8221 **UK SIC:** 93100
**Auditors:** KPMG LLP
**Bankers:** Lloyds TSB Bank plc (30-00-00)

| | 31-08-13 | 31-08-12 | 31-08-11 |
|---|---|---|---|
| TO | 8,123,000 | 8,720,000 | 9,568,000 |
| P/L | 39,000 | 366,000 | 1,120,000 |
| NW | 115,000 | (2,000) | (139,000) |
| WC | 1,248,000 | 1,176,000 | 600,000 |
| Emp. | 158 | 171 | 175 |

DUNS 50-471-8636
## Sutton & East Surrey Water Plc
**(Subsidiary of:** Sumisho Osaka Gas Water Uk Ltd)
London Road, Redhill, Surrey RH1 1LJ
**Tel:** 01737-772000
**Web:** www.waterplc.com
**Reg No:** 2447875 **VAT No:** 602534967
**Estd:** 1989 Public Limited Company
**Line of Business:** Water companies
**Issued Capital:** £15,489,237
**Directors:** D J Shemmans, J R Chadwick, W Oba, J D Pelczer, S C Gilliland, A J Ferrar, J A Biles, K Kawamoto
**Co. Secretary:** John Chadwick
**Responsibilities**
**Senior:** Nick Fisher *(Manager)*, Lester Sonden *(Technical Director)*
**Admin:** Lorraine Taylor *(Personal Assistant)*
**IT:** Michael Cock *(IT Manager)*
**Health & Safety:** Karl Reid *(Health & Safety Officer)*
**Operations:** Michael Hegarty *(Operations Director)*, Nicola Houlahan *(Water Quality Director)*
**Engineering:** Lester Sonden *(Technical Director)*
**Branches:** Sutton & East Surrey Water Plc, Woodmansterne Treatment Works, Outwood Lane, Coulsdon, Surrey CR5 3NE
**US SIC:** 4941 **UK SIC:** 17000
**Auditors:** KPMG Audit PLC
**Bankers:** Lloyds TSB Bank plc (30-94-38)

| | 31-03-14 | 31-03-13 | 31-03-12 |
|---|---|---|---|
| TO | 62,253,000 | 58,841,000 | 57,161,000 |
| P/L | 7,322,000 | 6,924,000 | 4,488,000 |
| NW | 22,632,000 | 24,370,000 | 25,908,000 |
| WC | 3,865,000 | 8,013,000 | 6,907,000 |
| Emp. | 242 | 237 | 228 |

DUNS 50-467-4144
## Sutton & East Surrey Water Services Ltd
**(Subsidiary of:** Sumisho Osaka Gas Water Uk Ltd)
59 Gander Green Lane, Sutton, Surrey SM1 2EW
**Tel:** 02087-227004 **Fax:** 020-8770-3913
**Web:** www.h20services.com
**Reg No:** 2446416 **Estd:** 1989 Private Limited Company
**Line of Business:** Plumbing
**Issued Capital:** £1,000
**Directors:** A J Ferrar, J R Chadwick, N J Chapman
**Responsibilities**
**Senior:** Lester Sonden *(Engineering Director)*
**Finance:** Nicholas Fisher *(Finance Director)*, Debbie Scott *(Financial Controller)*
**Health & Safety:** Sonia Barclays *(Customer Services Manager)*
**Operations:** Sonia Barclays *(Customer Services Manager)*
**Engineering:** Lester Sonden *(Engineering Director)*
**US SIC:** 1711 **UK SIC:** 50300
**Auditors:** KPMG Audit PLC
**Bankers:** Lloyds TSB Bank plc (30-98-36)

| | 31-03-14 | 31-03-13 | 31-03-12 |
|---|---|---|---|
| TO | 4,994,999 | 4,998,660 | 6,039,518 |
| P/L | 422,783 | 397,243 | 157,935 |
| NW | 576,490 | 558,109 | 492,499 |
| WC | 376,677 | 270,316 | 216,145 |
| Emp. | 72 | 72 | 72 |

DUNS 21-390-5023
## Sutton Counselling
21a Cheam Road, Sutton, Surrey SM1 1SN
**Web:** www.suttoncounselling.co.uk
**Estd:** 2009 Proprietorship
**Line of Business:** Counselling & advice services

**Proprietor:** A Jenkins
**Responsibilities**
**Senior:** Alaistair Park *(Manager)*
**US SIC:** 8321 **UK SIC:** 96111
**Employees:** 50

DUNS 21-726-9767
## Sutton Grammar School Trust
Manor Lane, Sutton, Surrey SM1 4AS
**Tel:** 02086423821
**Web:** www.suttongrammar.sutton.sch.uk
**Reg No:** 7633715 **Estd:** 2011 Private Company Limited By Guarantee
**Line of Business:** General secondary education
**Directors:** G D Ironside, J R Edwards, P S Davis, P S Chambers, J A Stevens, R W Murrill, Miss F H Alexander, R A Pletts
**Co. Secretary:** Dr Neville Wrench
**Responsibilities**
**Senior:** Samuel Karlsson *(Director)*, Amanda Nobel *(Director)*, Mary Takeda *(Director)*, Lesley Williams *(Director)*
**Finance:** Adrian Wilder *(Finance Director)*
**US SIC:** 8211 **UK SIC:** 93200
**Bankers:** Barclays Bank Plc (27-99-00)

| | 31-08-14 | 31-08-13 | 31-08-12 |
|---|---|---|---|
| TO | 4,929,491 | 4,874,749 | 22,182,958 |
| P/L | (233,186) | (120,665) | 16,169,976 |
| NW | 15,543,125 | 15,930,311 | 16,059,976 |
| WC | 681,547 | 646,151 | 726,076 |
| Emp. | 78 | 76 | 78 |

DUNS 50-469-8416
## Sutton Group Holdings Ltd
St James House, Grosvenor Road, Twickenham, Middlesex TW1 4AJ
**Tel:** 02088914021
**Web:** www.suttonwinson.com
**Reg No:** 2448730 **Estd:** 1989 Private Limited Company
**Line of Business:** Activities auxiliary to insurance and pension funding
**Issued Capital:** £10,125
**Directors:** M B Baldwin, K Macevoy, P I Jones
**Co. Secretary:** Ms Kimberley Lyle
**US SIC:** 6411 **UK SIC:** 83200
**Auditors:** Leach & Co
**Bankers:** Barclays Bank Plc (20-36-47)

| | 31-03-14 | 31-03-13 | 31-03-12 |
|---|---|---|---|
| TO | 9,193,550 | 8,855,875 | 8,649,952 |
| P/L | 1,186,290 | 1,186,331 | 1,247,794 |
| NW | 3,260,548 | 3,190,330 | 2,975,322 |
| WC | 1,947,786 | 2,025,163 | 1,749,661 |
| Emp. | 136 | 133 | 128 |

DUNS 21-585-4250
## Sutton Hall
Commill Walkoff Sutton Lane, Sutton-In-Craven, Keighley, West Yorkshire BD20 7AJ
**Tel:** 01535635793
**Web:** www.orchardcarehomes.com
**Estd:** 2011 Proprietorship
**Line of Business:** Residential care establishments
**Proprietor:** M Hebdon
**US SIC:** 8321 **UK SIC:** 96111
**Employees:** 50

DUNS 21-779-3695
## Sutton High School
55 Cheam Road, Sutton, Surrey SM1 2AX
**Tel:** 02086420594
**Web:** www.gdst.net
**Estd:** 1994 Proprietorship
**Line of Business:** Schools (independent)
**Proprietor:** S Callaghan
**Responsibilities**
**Senior:** K Crouch *(Headmistress)*
**US SIC:** 8211 **UK SIC:** 93200
**Employees:** 150

DUNS 34-788-5035
## Sutton Housing Partnership Ltd
Sutton Gate, 1 Carshalton Road, Sutton, Surrey SM1 4LE
**Tel:** 02089152000 **Fax:** 020-8915-2238
**Web:** www.suttonhousingpartnership.org.uk
**Reg No:** 5589014 **Estd:** 2005 Private Company Limited By Guarantee
**Line of Business:** Management of real estate on a fee or contract basis
**Directors:** Ms R Scott, J Drage, J Phillips, M Baldwin, K ( Morgan (Murugavarothayan), B A Russell, Miss A M Lock, Ms T White
**Co. Secretary:** Andrew Taylor
**Responsibilities**
**Senior:** Enid Bakewell *(Manager)*, Zowie Biden *(Director)*, Samantha Bromige *(Independent Board Member)*, Findlay Macpherson *(Manager)*, Wendy Mathys *(Manager)*, Lesley O'Connell *(Manager)*, Viktorija Skudneva *(Director)*, Peter Walters *(Director)*
**HR:** Brendan Crossan *(Executive Director of Resource)*

**Operations:** Joanne Cambra *(Executive Director of Neighbou)*
**US SIC:** 6531 **UK SIC:** 83400
**Auditors:** Grant Thornton UK LLP
**Bankers:** Barclays Bank Plc (20-42-58)

| | 31-03-14 | 31-03-13 | 31-03-12 |
|---|---|---|---|
| TO | 15,700,000 | 15,179,000 | 14,295,000 |
| P/L | 162,000 | 392,000 | 264,000 |
| NW | (4,633,000) | (2,797,000) | (2,388,000) |
| WC | 1,250,000 | 1,088,000 | 773,000 |
| Emp. | 160 | 158 | 158 |

DUNS 21-494-7827
## Sutton in the Elms Private Nursing & Residential Home
34 Sutton Lane, Sutton In The Elms, Broughton Astley, Leicester, Leicestershire LE9 6QF
**Tel:** 01455286577
**Web:** www.drehealthcare.co.uk
**Estd:** 2007 Proprietorship
**Line of Business:** Residential care establishments
**Proprietor:** Ms A Lonsdale
**US SIC:** 8321, 7231
**UK SIC:** 96111, 98200
**Employees:** 65

DUNS 21-782-7683
## Sutton Lodge Residential Home
Priestsic Road, Sutton-In-Ashfield, Nottinghamshire NG17 2AH
**Tel:** 01623442073
**Web:** www.ashmere.co.uk
**Estd:** 1993 Proprietorship
**Line of Business:** Rest and retirement homes
**Proprietor:** Miss T Sheppard
**US SIC:** 8321 **UK SIC:** 96111
**Employees:** 52

DUNS 23-642-8983
## Sutton Park Garage
54 Upper Stone Street, Maidstone, Kent ME15 6HA
**Tel:** 01622766410
**Web:** www.scmf.co.uk
**Estd:** 1979 Proprietorship
**Line of Business:** Sale of motor vehicle parts and accessories
**Proprietor:** D Payne
**Responsibilities**
**Senior:** Don Harper *(Manager)*
**Branches:** Sutton Park Group, Brunswick St, Maidstone, Kent ME15 6NP
**US SIC:** 5531, 7539
**UK SIC:** 65100, 67100
**Employees:** 65

DUNS 73-709-7613
## Sutton Park Holdings Ltd
37 Lichfield Street, Burton-On-Trent, Staffordshire DE14 3RH
**Tel:** 01283-740001
**Web:** www.renault.co.uk
**Reg No:** 4968449 **Estd:** 2003 Private Limited Company
**Line of Business:** Sale of new motor vehicles
**Issued Capital:** £1,000
**Directors:** D Fulton, Mrs J Fulton, Mrs C Thomas, M P Yarwood
**Co. Secretary:** Mrs Joanne Shannon
**Responsibilities**
**Senior:** Peter Allwood *(Manager)*
**US SIC:** 5511, 5521
**UK SIC:** 65100

| | 31-12-13 | 31-12-12 | 31-12-11 |
|---|---|---|---|
| TO | 64,730,670 | 55,765,515 | 58,254,896 |
| P/L | 420,400 | 488,590 | (28,388) |
| NW | 5,807,485 | 5,563,524 | 5,165,748 |
| WC | 351,324 | 90,637 | 649,832 |
| Emp. | 141 | 160 | 160 |

DUNS 21-600-6303
## Sutton Park Motor Company
Shultern Lane, Coventry, West Midlands CV4 7AN
**Tel:** 02476693366
**Web:** www.suttonparkgroup.co.uk
**Estd:** 1991 Proprietorship
**Line of Business:** Car dealers (new & used)
**Proprietor:** D Fulton
**US SIC:** 5511 **UK SIC:** 65100
**Employees:** 47

DUNS 76-969-8200
## Sutton Services International Ltd
**(Subsidiary of:** Rkm Capital Ltd)
Breakspear Park, Breakspear Way, Hemel Hempstead, Hertfordshire HP2 4UL
**Tel:** 01418129612 **Fax:** 01418129611
**Web:** www.sutcom.co.uk
**Reg No:** 2630803 **Estd:** 2010 Private Limited Company

**Line of Business:** Engineering services
**Trading Style:** Bam Construct Uk Ltd
**Issued Capital:** £60,000
**Principals:** P Kilgour *(Managing)*,
P M Rowledge *(Managing)*, C Mccluskey,
W J Mccluskey
**Responsibilities**
**Senior:** Stephen Crossley *(Manager)*, Billy
McCluskey *(Manager)*
**Branches:** Sutton Services International Ltd,
48 Darnley St, Glasgow, Lanarkshire G41
2SE
**US SIC:** 8911  **UK SIC:** 83701
**Auditors:** Tait Walker
**Bankers:** National Westminster Bank Plc
(60-60-08)

|     | 31-05-13 | 31-05-12 | 31-05-11 |
|-----|----------|----------|----------|
| TO  | N/A | 3,368,133 | 3,112,045 |
| P/L | N/A | 172,456 | (167,270) |
| NW  | 169,739 | 441,160 | 315,214 |
| WC  | 623,825 | 357,286 | 209,027 |

DUNS 28-840-0724

## Sutton United Football Club Ltd

Borough Sports Ground, Gander Green
Lane, Sutton, Surrey SM1 2EY
**Tel:** 020-8644-4440
**Web:** www.suttonunited.net
**Reg No:** 0519334 **VAT No:** 216816759
**Estd:** 1953 Private Limited Company
**Line of Business:** Clubs social and
associations
**Issued Capital:** £178,300
**Directors:** L G Wallis, A E Holland,
B B Williams, A J Barry, B G Elliott,
G F Starns, S L Moore, P L Letts
**Co. Secretary:** Anthony Dolbear
**Responsibilities**
**Senior:** Barry Aplin *(Manager)*, Michael
Bidmead *(Director)*, David Farebrother
*(Director)*, David Gibba *(Executive)*, David
Mathers *(Director)*, Steve Prince *(Club
Steward)*
**Sales:** Barry Aplin *(Manager)*
**Admin:** Gerard Mills *(Administrator)*
**US SIC:** 7999  **UK SIC:** 97913
**Auditors:** Maurice Andrews
**Bankers:** National Westminster Bank Plc
(60-21-08)

|     | 31-05-14 | 31-05-13 | 31-05-12 |
|-----|----------|----------|----------|
| TA  | 82,540 | 68,188 | 125,375 |
| NW  | 5,878 | (9,498) | 24,507 |
| WC  | 20,426 | 9,042 | 46,709 |

DUNS 23-215-9371

## Sutton Venture Group Ltd

Sutton House, Berry Hill Road, Stoke-On-
Trent, Staffordshire ST4 2NL
**Tel:** 01782339559
**Web:** www.slimtone-products.com
**Reg No:** 4070786 **Estd:** 2000 Private
Limited Company
**Line of Business:** Electrical wholesalers
**Export Sales:** £2,464,343
**Issued Capital:** £25,100
**Directors:** Mrs S M Sutton, R Sutton
**Co. Secretary:** Ms Susan Sutton
**US SIC:** 6711  **UK SIC:** 83962
**Auditors:** DJH Accountants Ltd

|     | 30-06-13 | 30-06-12 | 30-06-11 |
|-----|----------|----------|----------|
| TO  | 54,977,467 | 37,422,337 | 33,469,608 |
| P/L | 1,632,797 | 564,924 | 85,393 |
| NW  | 5,023,534 | 3,795,640 | 3,532,568 |
| WC  | 1,907,610 | 1,056,120 | 1,040,777 |
| Emp. | 134 | 108 | 110 |

DUNS 21-558-7580

## Sutton Veny House Nursing Home

Sutton Veny, Warminster, Wiltshire BA12
7BJ
**Tel:** 01985-840224
**Web:** www.suttonvenyhouse.com
**Estd:** 1982
**Line of Business:** Nursing homes
**Responsibilities**
**Senior:** Patricia Gronow *(Home Manager)*
**US SIC:** 8051  **UK SIC:** 95100
**Employees:** 50

DUNS 29-187-1085                    **Imp-Exp**

## Suttons Consumer Products Ltd

**(Subsidiary of:** Limagrain Clermont
Limagne)
Woodview Road, Paignton, Devon TQ4 7NG
**Tel:** 01803696300 **Fax:** 01803696333
**Web:** www.suttons.co.uk
**Reg No:** 0284448 **VAT No:** 158931827
**Estd:** 1977 Private Limited Company
**Line of Business:** Agents involved in the
sale of agricultural raw materials, live
animals, textile raw materials and semi-
finished goods
**Export Markets:** Eire, Australasia, U S A,
Canada, Russia
**Export Sales:** £707,861

**Trading Style:** Suttons Seeds, Carters
Tested Seeds, Samuel Dobies Seeds, R G
Cuthbert
**Issued Capital:** £30,000
**Directors:** R Roberts, N K Woodrow,
C Ramsden, D C Robinson
**Responsibilities**
**Senior:** Francois Deloche *(Manager)*, Jean
Faure *(Manager)*, Robin Grenfell *(Manager)*,
Martin Keattch *(Financial Director)*, Gerard
Renard *(Manager)*
**Finance:** Martin Keattch *(Financial Director)*
**IT:** Morag MacKinnon *(IT Manager)*
**Branches:** Suttons Consumer Products Ltd,
Woodview Road, Paignton, Devon TQ4 7NG
**US SIC:** 5159, 5961, 5199
**UK SIC:** 61100, 65600, 61900
**Auditors:** KPMG LLP
**Bankers:** Barclays Bank Plc (20-60-88)

|     | 30-06-13 | 30-06-12 | 30-06-11 |
|-----|----------|----------|----------|
| TO  | 15,037,477 | 16,516,567 | 19,263,057 |
| P/L | (1,520,242) | (1,189,564) | (981,613) |
| NW  | (3,031,115) | (1,556,778) | 464,108 |
| WC  | (2,719,954) | (862,075) | 345,660 |
| Emp. | 181 | 195 | 204 |

DUNS 21-093-7645

## Suttons International Ltd

**(Subsidiary of:** Thomas Cradley Holdings
Ltd)
Gorsey Lane, Widnes, Cheshire WA8 0GG
**Tel:** 01514202020 **Fax:** 01514206159
**Web:** www.suttonsgroup.com
**Reg No:** 0914137 **Estd:** 1967 Private
Limited Company
**Line of Business:** Other supporting land
transport activities
**Export Sales:** £71,559,505
**Issued Capital:** £500,000
**Directors:** K Broom, I D Daines,
G W Rooney, J M Sutton, P Molyneaux
**Co. Secretary:** Christopher Orger
**Responsibilities**
**Senior:** Tony Baldwin *(Transport Manager)*
**Branches:** Suttons International Ltd, Gorsey
Lane, Widnes, Cheshire WA8 0GG
**US SIC:** 4789, 4213
**UK SIC:** 77002, 72300
**Auditors:** Jackson Stephen LLP
**Bankers:** HSBC Bank plc (40-29-08)

|     | 30-04-14 | 30-04-13 | 30-04-12 |
|-----|----------|----------|----------|
| TO  | 91,003,943 | 89,403,044 | 85,110,170 |
| P/L | 7,538,081 | 5,454,454 | 5,413,935 |
| NW  | 22,106,505 | 17,141,767 | 13,263,914 |
| WC  | 19,293,430 | 15,041,611 | 11,127,409 |
| Emp. | 131 | 131 | 129 |

DUNS 21-805-8915                    **Imp**

## Suzuki G B Plc

**(Subsidiary of:** Suzuki Motor Corporation)
Steinbeck Crescent, Snelshall West, Milton
Keynes, Buckinghamshire MK4 4AE
**Tel:** 01908336600 **Fax:** 01908336719
**Web:** www.suzuki.co.uk
**Reg No:** 0768587 **VAT No:** 644310075
**Estd:** 1963 Public Limited Company
**Line of Business:** Sale of new motor
vehicles
**Trading Style:** Suzuki Factory Racing Team
**Issued Capital:** £12,000,000
**Directors:** N Suyama, Y Abe
**Co. Secretary:** Charles O'Shea
**Responsibilities**
**Senior:** Andy Franks *(Warehouse Manager)*
**Finance:** Jeremy Leigh *(Financial Director)*
**IT:** Wayne Charters *(IT Manager)*
**US SIC:** 5511, 5531
**UK SIC:** 65100
**Auditors:** Ernst & Young LLP
**Bankers:** Lloyds TSB Bank plc (30-00-02)

|     | 31-03-14 | 31-03-13 | 31-03-12 |
|-----|----------|----------|----------|
| TO  | 366,864,307 | 290,451,156 | 253,203,212 |
| P/L | 3,179,995 | 1,490,796 | 1,286,719 |
| NW  | 34,756,373 | 32,426,733 | 31,679,091 |
| WC  | 14,239,784 | 11,968,355 | 6,855,249 |
| Emp. | 149 | 148 | 145 |

DUNS 28-985-4838

## S.V. (Leasing) Ltd

**(Subsidiary of:** Strong Vend Ltd)
8 St Marks Industrial Estate, North Woolwich
Road, London E16 2BS
**Tel:** 02075113511 **Fax:** 020-7473-0573
**Reg No:** 1798601 **Estd:** 1984 Private
Limited Company
**Line of Business:** Renting of other
machinery and equipment not elsewhere
classified
**Issued Capital:** £100
**Director:** Ms J L Strong
**Co. Secretary:** Christopher Strong
**US SIC:** 7394  **UK SIC:** 84000
**Auditors:** Bird Luckin
**Bankers:** National Westminster Bank Plc
(60-03-25)

|     | 30-06-13 | 30-06-12 | 30-06-11 |
|-----|----------|----------|----------|
| TO  | N/A | N/A | 101,915 |
| P/L | N/A | N/A | (6,241) |
| NW  | 225,444 | 209,430 | 197,156 |
| WC  | 197,665 | 185,242 | 187,702 |

DUNS 21-144-4881

## Sva Ltd

Unit 2-12 Ivanhoe Office Park, Ivanhoe Park
Way, Ashby-De-La-Zouch, Leicestershire
LE65 2AB
**Tel:** 01530561000
**Web:** www.svaltd.com
**Reg No:** 6751823 **Estd:** 2008 Private
Limited Company
**Line of Business:** Technical testing and
analysis
**Issued Capital:** £611,970
**Directors:** N M Griffiths, P M Berryman,
J Longworth, J S Williams, N M Jupe
**US SIC:** 7397  **UK SIC:** 83702

|     | 30-04-14 | 30-04-13 | 30-04-12 |
|-----|----------|----------|----------|
| TA  | 5,031,449 | 2,497,608 | 2,465,615 |
| NW  | 2,414,946 | 921,319 | 379,578 |
| WC  | 2,019,649 | 530,611 | 446,181 |

DUNS 22-522-9038                    **Imp**

## Sven Christiansen Plc

Court Farm, Littleton Lane, Guildford, Surrey
GU3 1HW
**Tel:** 01483-302-728
**Web:** www.sven-christiansen.co.uk
**Reg No:** 1428696 **VAT No:** 358679002
**Estd:** 1979 Public Limited Company
**Line of Business:** Manufacture of other
office and shop furniture
**Export Sales:** £41,452
**Issued Capital:** £50,000
**Principals:** W O'Brien *(Chairman)*, A J Ralph
*(Managing)*, P Rudge
**Co. Secretary:** Andrew Ralph
**Responsibilities**
**Senior:** William O'brien *(Chairman of the
Board and Dire)*
**Branches:** Sven Christiansen Plc, Building
21, First Avenue, Pensnett Trading Estate,
Kingswinford, West Midlands DY6 7TU
**US SIC:** 2599, 5021
**UK SIC:** 46720, 61500
**Auditors:** Roffe Swayne
**Bankers:** National Westminster Bank Plc
(60-09-21)

|     | 30-09-13 | 30-09-12 | 30-09-11 |
|-----|----------|----------|----------|
| TO  | 11,517,256 | 10,861,571 | 14,943,749 |
| P/L | (155,596) | (137,895) | (501,499) |
| NW  | 2,057,864 | 2,160,220 | 2,232,733 |
| WC  | 1,820,109 | 1,759,614 | 1,669,369 |
| Emp. | 189 | 188 | 191 |

DUNS 50-037-6827

## Svenska Property Nominees Ltd

**(Subsidiary of:** Svenska Handelsbanken
Ab)
3 Thomas More Square, London E1W 1WY
**Web:** www.handelsbanken.co.uk
**Reg No:** 2308524 **Estd:** 1988 Private
Limited Company
**Line of Business:** Banks and financial
institutions
**Trading Style:** Handels Banken
**Issued Capital:** £100
**Directors:** J C Wiklund, L C Vincent
**Co. Secretary:** Paul Symons
**Responsibilities**
**Senior:** Amjad Beg *(Manager)*, Anders
Bouvin *(Head Of Bank)*, Mikael Strom
*(Financial Director)*
**Finance:** Mikael Strom *(Financial Director)*
**Marketing:** Simon Alderson *(Head of
Corporate Communicatio)*
**IT:** Paul Fincham *(Head of IT Operations)*
**HR:** Jeremy Hollworthy *(Human Resources
Manager)*
**Health & Safety:** Jeremy Hollworthy *(Human
Resources Manager)*
**US SIC:** 6111, 6211
**UK SIC:** 81501, 83100

|     | 31-12-13 | 31-12-12 | 31-12-11 |
|-----|----------|----------|----------|
| TA  | 100 | 100 | 100 |
| NW  | 100 | 100 | 100 |

DUNS 21-813-7461                    **Exp**

## Svitzer Humber Ltd

**(Subsidiary of:** A.P. Møller - Mærsk A/S)
Triton House, Alexandra Road, Immingham
Dock, Immingham, South Humberside DN40
2LZ
**Tel:** 08456081344
**Web:** www.svitzer.com
**Reg No:** 0524008 **Estd:** 1953 Private
Limited Company
**Line of Business:** Towing services
**Issued Capital:** £8,900,000
**Directors:** N R Thulin, M R Niederer
**Co. Secretary:** David Noakes
**Responsibilities**
**Senior:** Mark Malone *(Manager)*, Jacqueline
Readman *(Manager)*
**Branches:** Sheerness Docks, Garrison Rd,
Sheerness, Kent ME12 1RX
**US SIC:** 4712, 4469
**UK SIC:** 77002, 76300
**Auditors:** Ernst & Young

**Bankers:** HSBC Bank plc (40-25-20)

|     | 31-12-13 | 31-12-12 | 31-12-11 |
|-----|----------|----------|----------|
| TO  | 18,144,000 | 18,205,000 | 18,642,000 |
| P/L | (3,347,000) | (3,213,000) | (5,314,000) |
| NW  | 8,374,000 | 11,489,000 | 12,391,000 |
| WC  | (8,717,000) | (7,155,000) | (7,984,000) |
| Emp. | 88 | 54 | 68 |

DUNS 21-024-3424                    **Imp-Exp**

## Svitzer Marine Ltd

**(Subsidiary of:** A.P. Møller - Mærsk A/S)
Tees Wharf, Dockside Road, Middlesbrough,
Cleveland TS3 6AB
**Tel:** 01642-258300 **Fax:** 01642246370
**Web:** www.svitzer.com
**Reg No:** 0069494 **VAT No:** 372859120
**Estd:** 1901 Private Limited Company
**Line of Business:** Towing services
**Issued Capital:** £3,000,000
**Directors:** N R Thulin, M R Niederer
**Co. Secretary:** David Noakes
**Responsibilities**
**Senior:** Jacqueline Readman *(Financial
Director)*
**Finance:** Jacqueline Readman *(Financial
Director)*
**HR:** Emma Sewell *(Human Resources
Manager)*
**Health & Safety:** Mark Ranson *(Safety
Manager)*
**Branches:** Svitzer Marine Ltd, 9 Duff Street,
Greenock, Renfrewshire PA15 1DB
**US SIC:** 4789, 4469
**UK SIC:** 77002, 76300
**Auditors:** Deloitte & Touche LLP
**Bankers:** Lloyds TSB Bank plc (30-00-00)

|     | 31-12-13 | 31-12-12 | 31-12-11 |
|-----|----------|----------|----------|
| TO  | 69,427,000 | 66,214,000 | 61,705,000 |
| P/L | 10,604,000 | 8,785,000 | 12,110,000 |
| NW  | 85,892,000 | 80,509,000 | 47,481,000 |
| WC  | 14,349,000 | 7,999,000 | 32,832,000 |
| Emp. | 450 | 441 | 447 |

DUNS 28-862-6138

## S.W. Durham Training Ltd

Durham Way South, Aycliffe Business Park,
Newton Aycliffe, County Durham DL5 6AT
**Fax:** 01325-318249
**Web:** www.southwestdurham.co.uk
**Reg No:** 0918178 **Estd:** 1967 Private
Company Limited By Guarantee
**Line of Business:** Training services
**Directors:** G Willis, A A Dunn, S J Rose,
A Scott
**Responsibilities**
**Senior:** Trevor Alley *(Chief Executive)*,
Stanley Cavell *(Manager)*, Charl Erasmus
*(Chief Executive)*
**US SIC:** 8299, 8221, 8249
**UK SIC:** 93300, 93100
**Auditors:** Clive Owen & Co LLP
**Bankers:** HSBC Bank plc (40-19-03)

|     | 31-08-13 | 31-08-12 | 31-08-11 |
|-----|----------|----------|----------|
| TO  | 1,863,311 | 1,514,475 | 5,097,365 |
| P/L | (630,040) | (787,950) | 2,919,204 |
| NW  | 4,877,107 | 5,420,676 | 6,189,890 |
| WC  | 103,330 | 307,521 | 401,121 |
| Emp. | 51 | 44 | 43 |

DUNS 23-589-5638

## Sw Global Resourcing Ltd

**(Subsidiary of:** Scotweld Group Services
Ltd)
270 Petershill Road, Glasgow, Lanarkshire
G21 4AY
**Tel:** 01415576138 **Fax:** 0141-557-6143
**Web:** www.sw-gr.com
**Reg No:** 0112898SC **VAT No:** 481722737
**Estd:** 2014 Private Limited Company
**Line of Business:** Protective clothing and
workwear
**Trading Style:** Specialist Industrial Supplies
**Issued Capital:** £20,000
**Principals:** G Nixon *(Chairman)*, T D Flynn
*(Managing)*, T P Larkin *(Financial)*,
Ms F Baggley *(Personnel)*
**Responsibilities**
**Engineering:** Brian Webber *(Engineering
Operations Directo)*
**Branches:** Sw Global Resourcing Ltd, 62-66
Lowther St, Carlisle, Cumbria CA3 8DP
**US SIC:** 2389  **UK SIC:** 45393
**Auditors:** Sinclair Wood & Co
**Bankers:** The Royal Bank Of Scotland Plc
(83-16-13)

|     | 31-07-13 | 31-07-12 | 31-07-11 |
|-----|----------|----------|----------|
| TO  | 14,020,425 | 16,191,205 | 13,789,962 |
| P/L | 26,551 | 390,872 | 168,157 |
| NW  | 1,999,545 | 1,972,994 | 1,582,122 |
| WC  | 1,221,450 | 1,168,299 | 687,944 |
| Emp. | 130 | 202 | 240 |

DUNS 22-149-4276

## Sw Golf Ltd

**(Subsidiary of:** Sun Capital Partners Inc.)
Europa Boulevard, Gemini Business Park,
Warrington, Cheshire WA5 7YW
**Fax:** 01279452319
**Web:** www.onlinegolf.co.uk
**Reg No:** 4168205 **Estd:** 2001 Private
Limited Company

**Line of Business:** Other retail sale in specialised stores not elsewhere classified
**Export Sales:** £4,489,526
**Issued Capital:** £2,715
**Directors:** A J Fort, Ms M D Greenland, T Walsh, Ms T D Hills
**US SIC:** 5999 **UK SIC:** 65600
**Auditors:** KPMG Audit PLC
**Bankers:** National Westminster Bank Plc (01-00-04)

| | 27-01-13 | 29-01-12 | 31-01-11 |
|---|---|---|---|
| TO | 13,847,856 | 14,648,249 | 16,300,528 |
| P/L | (1,620,138) | 856,824 | (28,236) |
| NW | (676,257) | 957,540 | 463,349 |
| WC | (596,592) | 889,112 | 418,380 |
| Emp. | 46 | 53 | 44 |

DUNS 28-839-2269
## S.W. Wreford Warehousing Company Ltd
Ransome Road, Northampton, Northamptonshire NN4 8AD
**Tel:** 01604761231
**Web:** www.swwreford.co.uk
**Reg No:** 0501479 **VAT No:** 536355635
**Estd:** 1904 Private Limited Company
**Line of Business:** Other storage and warehousing not elsewhere classified
**Issued Capital:** £19,200
**Principals:** M W Wreford *(Managing)*, M W Wreford, A M Wreford, R J Wreford
**Co. Secretary:** Michael Wreford
**Responsibilities**
**Senior:** Sydney Wreford *(Manager)*
**Finance:** Sydney Wreford *(Manager)*
**Admin:** Sydney Wreford *(Manager)*
**Facilities:** Sydney Wreford *(Manager)*
**US SIC:** 8999, 4213
**UK SIC:** 83954, 72300
**Auditors:** Moore Stephens
**Bankers:** National Westminster Bank Plc (56-00-60)

| | 31-03-14 | 31-03-13 | 31-03-12 |
|---|---|---|---|
| TA | 2,850,658 | 2,807,936 | 2,728,350 |
| NW | 1,439,888 | 1,375,605 | 1,235,042 |
| WC | 642,108 | 590,833 | 498,616 |

DUNS 21-370-4713
## Sw14 Minicab & Courier
Unit 1, Church House, 1 Hanover Street, Liverpool, Merseyside L1 3DN
**Tel:** 01517060092
**Web:** www.sw14cars.co.uk
**Estd:** 2004 Proprietorship
**Line of Business:** Licensed restaurants
**Proprietor:** K Khan
**Responsibilities**
**Senior:** Ricky Khan *(Proprietor)*
**US SIC:** 5812 **UK SIC:** 66110
**Employees:** 48

DUNS 21-787-1950
## Swad Cars
Sharpes Industrial Estate, Alexandra Road, Swadlincote, Derbyshire DE11 9AZ
**Tel:** 01283262626
**Web:** www.swadcars.co.uk
**Estd:** 2011 Proprietorship
**Line of Business:** Taxi operation
**Proprietor:** P Hackett
**Responsibilities**
**Senior:** Mohammed Afzal *(Proprietor)*
**US SIC:** 4121 **UK SIC:** 72200
**Employees:** 46

DUNS 21-332-6783
## Swadelands Centre
Maidstone Road, Lenham, Maidstone, Kent ME17 2QJ
**Tel:** 01622-858267
**Web:** www.swadelands.kent.sch.uk
**Proprietorship**
**Line of Business:** Schools (local authority)
**US SIC:** 8211 **UK SIC:** 93200
**Employees:** 100

DUNS 22-853-4210 **Exp**
## Swagelok Ltd
Millenium Park Studio B, Allafletcher Road, Douglas, Douglas, Isle of Man IM4 4QJ
**Tel:** 01624612627
**Web:** www.isoiom.com
**Reg No:** 0004168M **VAT No:** 000155645
**Estd:** 1972 Private Limited Company
**Line of Business:** Environmental consultants
**Export Markets:** Worldwide
**Issued Capital:** £100
**Principals:** R A Hastings *(Managing)*, J D Ronan *(Financial)*, T D Mackay
**Responsibilities**
**Senior:** Kevin Burnell *(Manager)*, David Hester *(Manager)*, Lee Mcclelland *(Manager)*
**HR:** Mamta Paradise *(Human Resources Manager)*
**Engineering:** Dave Parkes *(Engineering Manager)*
**US SIC:** 3721, 3494
**UK SIC:** 36400, 32880
**Bankers:** Isle Of Man Bank (55-91-00)
**Employees:** 180

DUNS 22-576-3291
## Swain & Jones (Contracts) Ltd
(**Subsidiary of:** Swain & Jones Ltd)
35-42 East Street, Farnham, Surrey GU9 7TP
**Tel:** 01252711018
**Web:** www.swainandjones-farnham.co.uk
**Reg No:** 0732099 **Estd:** 1962 Private Limited Company
**Line of Business:** Sale of new motor vehicles
**Issued Capital:** £100
**Managing Director:** A P Lewis Jones
**US SIC:** 5511, 5521, 7539, 5531
**UK SIC:** 65100, 67100
**Auditors:** Grant Thornton
**Bankers:** HSBC Bank plc (40-21-05)

| | 31-12-13 | 31-12-12 | 31-12-11 |
|---|---|---|---|
| TA | 37,015 | 37,015 | 37,015 |
| NW | 37,015 | 37,015 | 37,015 |

DUNS 49-730-2257
## Swaithe-Main Working Mens Club
Monkspring, Worsbrough, Barnsley, South Yorkshire S70 4QY
**Estd:** 1959
**Line of Business:** Clubs social and associations
**Principals:** R Dirkin *(Chairman)*, D Stables
**US SIC:** 8699 **UK SIC:** 96902
**Employees:** 50

DUNS 21-758-7329
## Swakeleys School for Girls
Clifton Gardens, Uxbridge, Middlesex UB10 0EJ
**Tel:** 01895251962
**Reg No:** 7570315 **Estd:** 2011 Private Limited Company
**Line of Business:** General secondary education
**Directors:** Dr C B Kilbride, D C Charles, D P Mclauchlan
**Co. Secretary:** Ms Helen Manwaring
**US SIC:** 8211 **UK SIC:** 93200

| | 31-08-14 | 31-08-13 | 31-08-12 |
|---|---|---|---|
| TO | 6,593,736 | 6,752,016 | 27,233,991 |
| P/L | (2,333,746) | (2,358,730) | 14,988,612 |
| NW | 9,812,137 | 12,405,882 | 14,684,612 |
| WC | 775,954 | 898,010 | 844,318 |
| Emp. | 137 | 137 | 140 |

DUNS 23-281-6744
## Swalcliffe Park School
Swalcliffe, Banbury, Oxfordshire OX15 5EP
**Tel:** 01295780302
**Web:** http://swalcliffepark-oxon.frogos.net
**Estd:** 1965
**Line of Business:** Schools (special)
**Principals:** Ms C Hutton *(Chairman)*, R Hooper
**Responsibilities**
**Senior:** Jeff Demmar *(manager)*, Kiran Hingorani *(Principal)*
**Finance:** Joyce Bond *(Bursar)*
**US SIC:** 8299, 8211
**UK SIC:** 93300, 93200
**Bankers:** Lloyds TSB Bank plc (30-90-42)
**Employees:** 70

DUNS 21-684-7489
## Swale Academies Trust
Ashdown House Johnson Road, Sittingbourne, Kent ME10 1JS
**Tel:** 01795430629
**Web:** www.westlandsnursery.org.uk
**Reg No:** 7344732 **Estd:** 2010 Private Company Limited By Guarantee
**Line of Business:** Primary education
**Directors:** Ms K A Mirams, D M Stevens, S Cox, A Barham, Ms K L Walsh, J A Fassenfelt, G R Clifton, Mrs C Wood
**Responsibilities**
**Senior:** Suzanne Dickinson *(Director)*, Richard Slee *(Director)*, Fiona Trigwell *(Director)*, Jonathan Whitcombe *(Director)*
**US SIC:** 8211 **UK SIC:** 93200
**Bankers:** HSBC Bank plc (40-42-04)

| | 31-08-13 | 31-08-12 | 31-08-11 |
|---|---|---|---|
| TO | 35,640,518 | 29,710,113 | 41,833,724 |
| P/L | 8,513,004 | 9,647,736 | 29,211,311 |
| NW | 42,065,051 | 34,370,047 | 27,230,311 |
| WC | 2,200,178 | 2,045,581 | 1,509,673 |
| Emp. | 679 | 595 | 391 |

DUNS 23-984-2768
## Swale Borough Council
Swale House, East Street, Sittingbourne, Kent ME10 3HT
**Tel:** 01795-424341 **Fax:** 01795-417141
**Web:** www.swale.gov.uk
**Estd:** 1974 Incorporate By Act Of Parliament
**Line of Business:** Local government
**Trading Style:** Borden Grammar School
**Directors:** J Stringer, I Russell, M Radford, C Edwards
**Responsibilities**
**Senior:** Geraldine Chidley *(Executive)*, Abdool Kara *(Chief Executive)*, Kieren Mansfield *(Marketing Manager)*, Nick Prior *(Executive)*, Mark Radford *(Director of Corporate Services)*, Rob Viner *(Executive)*
**Finance:** Zoe Kent *(Finance Manager)*, Amanda Lukey *(Accounts Manager)*, Nick Vickers *(Head of Finance)*
**Marketing:** Lorraine Burke *(Head of Corporate. Strategy &.)*, Kieren Mansfield *(Marketing Manager)*
**Admin:** Sharon Dormedy *(Administrator)*, Teresa Harvey *(Administration Assistant)*, Ginny Wilkinson *(Benefits Manager)*
**IT:** Andy Cole *(Head of ICT)*
**HR:** Catherine Harrison *(Training Manager)*, Filmer Wellard *(HR)*
**Facilities:** Anne Adams *(Head of Property Services)*, Amber Christou *(Head of Housing Services)*
**Operations:** Katherine Bescoby *(Head of. Organisational. Devel)*, Alan Best *(Local Planning Policy)*, Lyn Newton *(Culture Services Manager)*, Brian Planner *(Environmental Manager)*, Mark Radford *(Director of Corporate Services)*, Pete Raine *(Director of Regeneration)*, Val Wakeling *(Operations Manager)*
**Branches:** Swale Borough Council, Queenborough Library, Railway Terrace, Queenborough, Kent ME11 5AY
**US SIC:** 9121 **UK SIC:** 91110
**Bankers:** National Westminster Bank Plc (60-19-25)
**Employees:** 300

DUNS 29-685-8087
## Swale Building Services Ltd
Rushenden Road, Queenborough, Kent ME11 5HB
**Tel:** 01795-665311
**Reg No:** 2009400 **VAT No:** 445144169
**Estd:** 1986 Private Limited Company
**Line of Business:** Construction of domestic buildings
**Issued Capital:** £50,000
**Managing Director:** A R Phillips
**Co. Secretary:** Miss Susan Phillips
**US SIC:** 1522 **UK SIC:** 50100
**Auditors:** Stephen Hill Partnership Ltd
**Bankers:** National Westminster Bank Plc (60-08-37)

| | 31-08-14 | 31-08-13 | 31-08-12 |
|---|---|---|---|
| TA | 114,317 | 199,569 | 287,372 |
| NW | 11,402 | (69,519) | 32,153 |
| WC | 8,293 | (73,899) | 25,443 |

DUNS 21-722-3239
## Swale Heating Ltd
Eurolink Industrial Estate, Heard Way, Sittingbourne, Kent ME10 3SA
**Tel:** 01795-477098 **Fax:** 01795436367
**Web:** www.swaleheating.com
**Reg No:** 1076034 **Estd:** 1972 Private Limited Company
**Line of Business:** Central heating systems (installation and servicing)
**Issued Capital:** £27,500
**Principals:** I M Pierson *(Managing)*, P R Whittington, G J Fotheringham, M W Edwards, M D Pope, S J Davis, S R Brewer
**Co. Secretary:** Ian Pierson
**Responsibilities**
**Senior:** Christopher Riley *(Operations Director)*
**Sales:** Chris Link *(Sales Manager)*
**Admin:** Tracey Umpleby *(Office Coordinator)*
**HR:** Melissa Rodgers *(HR Manager)*
**Facilities:** Christopher Riley *(Operations Director)*
**Branches:** Swale Heating Ltd, 30 High Street, Sheerness, Kent ME12 1NL
**US SIC:** 1711 **UK SIC:** 50300
**Auditors:** Day, Smith & Hunter
**Bankers:** Barclays Bank Plc (20-54-11)

| | 31-03-14 | 31-03-13 | 31-03-12 |
|---|---|---|---|
| TO | 50,119,388 | 40,150,044 | 37,289,533 |
| P/L | 1,151,852 | 2,625,497 | 3,179,356 |
| NW | 18,871,391 | 19,048,497 | 17,324,407 |
| WC | 12,236,600 | 12,497,336 | 10,720,015 |
| Emp. | 425 | 337 | 331 |

DUNS 23-230-3040
## Swale Housing Association Ltd
60 Bell Road, Sittingbourne, Kent ME10 4HE
**Tel:** 01795431134
**Web:** www.swale-housing.org.uk
**Reg No:** 0026746IP **VAT No:** 530834363
**Estd:** 1989 Friendly Society
**Line of Business:** Non-charitable social work activities with accommodation
**Trading Style:** Amicushorizon
**Principals:** Mrs M Weatherhead *(Chairman)*, J Clark, Ms N Mcelhone, M Heath, Ms J Addy, Mrs H Ingham, P Wilson, S Worrall
**Co. Secretary:** Stephen Howlett
**Responsibilities**
**Senior:** Stephen Glayzer *(Director)*, Derek Hale *(Director)*, Alex Knox *(Director)*, Nuala McElhone *(Director)*, Adrian Speller *(Director)*
**Finance:** Mike Hyams *(Financial Director)*
**HR:** Alison Reading *(Human Resources Manager)*
**Health & Safety:** Lisa McCarrick *(Health & Safety Officer)*
**Facilities:** Kirsty Calvert *(Facilities Manager)*
**Branches:** Swale Housing Association Ltd, Bridge Road, Sheerness, Kent ME12 1RH
**US SIC:** 8321 **UK SIC:** 96111
**Bankers:** National Westminster Bank Plc (60-19-25)
**Employees:** 90
**Turnover:** £34,649,000

DUNS 29-767-0051
## Swale Scaffolding Ltd
Gatherley Road Industrial Estate, Brompton On Swale, Richmond, North Yorkshire DL10 7JQ
**Tel:** 01748-812777 **Fax:** 01748812234
**Web:** www.swalegroup.com
**Reg No:** 2030093 **VAT No:** 441476356
**Estd:** 1986 Private Limited Company
**Line of Business:** Renting of scaffold
**Issued Capital:** £50,000
**Directors:** P S Ward, Miss S L Richardson, Ms G Pepe
**Responsibilities**
**Senior:** Alan Shackleton *(Regional Manager)*
**US SIC:** 7394 **UK SIC:** 84000
**Bankers:** Yorkshire Bank Plc (05-07-12)

| | 31-07-13 | 31-07-12 | 31-07-11 |
|---|---|---|---|
| TA | 1,827,544 | 1,506,811 | 1,577,460 |
| NW | 1,056,768 | 966,081 | 987,001 |
| WC | 377,071 | 371,750 | 407,090 |

DUNS 22-680-7139
## Swallow Cleaning Contractors
Spa Road, Lincoln, Lincolnshire LN2 5TB
**Web:** www.swallowcleaningcontractorsln2.co.uk
**VAT No:** 310623019 **Estd:** 1975 Partnership
**Line of Business:** Cleaning contracting commercial
**Partners:** Mrs C Muggleton-Sleath, Miss C M Muggleton-Sleath
**Responsibilities**
**Senior:** Celia Sleath *(Manager)*
**US SIC:** 7349 **UK SIC:** 92300
**Bankers:** The Royal Bank Of Scotland Plc (16-23-32)
**Employees:** 149

DUNS 21-783-7291
## Swallow Hill Community College
Swallow Crescent, Leeds, West Yorkshire LS12 4RB
**Tel:** 01133368866
**Web:** www.swallowhill.leeds.sch.uk
**Estd:** 2011 Proprietorship
**Line of Business:** Schools (local authority)
**Proprietor:** Mrs L Room
**Responsibilities**
**Senior:** Gill Knutsson *(Acting Head)*
**US SIC:** 8211 **UK SIC:** 93200
**Employees:** 210

DUNS 22-841-5535
## Swallow Hilltop Hotel
Hilltop Heights London Road, Carlisle, Cumbria CA1 2NS
**Web:** www.swallow-hotels.com
**Estd:** 1997 Proprietorship
**Line of Business:** Hotels
**Proprietor:** M Gardner
**Responsibilities**
**Senior:** Jim Mingle *(General Manager)*
**Operations:** Margaret Tefler *(Conference Manager)*
**US SIC:** 7011 **UK SIC:** 66500
**Employees:** 70

DUNS 77-498-5352
## Swallow Holdings Ltd
Creamline Dairies, Mellors Road, Manchester M17 1PB
**Tel:** 01617895161
**Reg No:** 2979029 **Estd:** 1994 Private Limited Company
**Line of Business:** Dairy farmers
**Trading Style:** Cream Line Dairies
**Issued Capital:** £20,000
**Directors:** Ms H H Swallow, A D Swallow, R K Purvis
**Co. Secretary:** Christopher Swallow
**Branches:** Swallow Holdings Ltd, 56-58 Red Bank, Manchester M8 8TS

**US SIC:** 2026, 5143, 5963
**UK SIC:** 41301, 61700, 65600
**Bankers:** National Westminster Bank Plc (01-10-01)

| | 30-09-13 | 30-09-12 | 30-09-11 |
|---|---|---|---|
| TO | 21,977,634 | 19,041,330 | 19,140,047 |
| P/L | 1,186,923 | 766,206 | 833,007 |
| NW | 3,927,650 | 3,871,257 | 3,547,520 |
| WC | 1,613,510 | 3,006,104 | 2,677,121 |
| Emp. | 187 | 177 | 186 |

DUNS 22-608-9795
## Swallowcourt Ltd
(**Subsidiary of:** Swallowcourt Holdings Ltd)
Breage House, Breage, Helston, Cornwall TR13 9PW
**Tel:** 01326-565805
**Web:** www.swallowcourt.com
**Reg No:** 1748499 **Estd:** 2007 Private Limited Company
**Line of Business:** Residential care establishments
**Trading Style:** Poldhu Nursing & Residential Home, Breage House
**Issued Capital:** £80,000
**Directors:** Ms M L Murray, Ms N M Minchella, Ms D Keely, S M Keely
**Responsibilities**
**Senior:** Jon Edgecombe *(Manager)*, Ruth Stock *(Manager)*
**Branches:** Swallowcourt Ltd, Chyandour Terrace, Penzance, Cornwall TR18 3LT
**US SIC:** 8321 **UK SIC:** 96111
**Auditors:** Robinson Reed Layton

| | 31-03-14 | 31-03-13 | 31-03-12 |
|---|---|---|---|
| TO | 6,456,751 | 6,546,706 | 6,207,398 |
| P/L | (75,891) | (77,372) | 29,322 |
| NW | 7,170,878 | 9,208,437 | 9,296,809 |
| WC | (1,893,218) | (2,061,018) | (1,548,144) |
| Emp. | 227 | 263 | 253 |

DUNS 29-649-1541 Imp-Exp
## Swallowfield Plc
Swallowfield House, Station Road, Wellington, Somerset TA21 8NL
**Tel:** 01823-662-241 **Fax:** 01823-663-642
**Web:** www.swallowfield.com
**Reg No:** 1975376 **Estd:** 1986 Public Limited Company
**Line of Business:** Manufacture of perfumes and toilet preparations
**Export Sales:** £18,860,000
**Issued Capital:** £565,321
**Directors:** R S Mcdowell, F P Berrebi, E J Beale, B Hynes, C G How, M W Warren, Ms J Fletcher
**Co. Secretary:** Mark Warren
**Responsibilities**
**Senior:** Martin Hagen *(Independent Non-Executive Dire)*
**Marketing:** Mandy Meakin *(Marketing Manager)*
**IT:** Spencer Golding *(IT Manager)*
**Health & Safety:** John Portt *(Safety Officer)*
**Fleet:** Ian McKenzie *(Logistics Manager)*
**Branches:** Swallowfield Plc, Alverdiscott Road, Bideford, Devon EX39 4DA
**US SIC:** 3999, 2842
**UK SIC:** 49590, 25990
**Auditors:** Grant Thornton UK LLP
**Bankers:** Barclays Bank Plc (20-85-26)

| | 30-06-14 | 30-06-13 | 30-06-12 |
|---|---|---|---|
| TO | 50,033,000 | 48,591,000 | 57,879,000 |
| P/L | 140,000 | (1,210,000) | 1,556,000 |
| NW | 12,446,000 | 12,299,000 | 13,543,000 |
| WC | 3,718,000 | 3,307,000 | 4,668,000 |
| Emp. | 559 | 561 | 573 |

DUNS 21-208-2551
## Swallownest Nursing Home
Chesterfield Road, Swallownest, Sheffield, South Yorkshire S26 4TL
**Web:** www.hc-one.co.uk
**Estd:** 1989 Partnership
**Line of Business:** Clinics private
**Partners:** Mrs L Knowles, Mrs C Bradley
**Responsibilities**
**Senior:** Maggie Chatwyn *(General Manager)*, Jill Kilgallen *(Manager)*, Jan Myers *(Manager)*
**Finance:** Gail Morton *(Administration Manager)*
**Admin:** Gail Morton *(Administration Manager)*
**HR:** Maggie Chatwyn *(General Manager)*
**Health & Safety:** Maggie Chatwyn *(General Manager)*
**Facilities:** Mike Poulton *(Maintenance Manager)*
**Operations:** Gail Morton *(Administration Manager)*
**US SIC:** 8051 **UK SIC:** 95100
**Employees:** 65

DUNS 21-733-9043
## S.Walsh & Son Ltd
(**Subsidiary of:** S Walsh Holdings Ltd)
Tilbury Road, Brentwood, Essex CM13 3LR
**Tel:** 01277-814200 **Fax:** 01277-814201
**Web:** www.swalsh.com
**Reg No:** 1053148 **Estd:** 1972 Private Limited Company
**Line of Business:** Activities of other transport agencies
**Issued Capital:** £100
**Directors:** N S Walsh, T J Wheeler, W Mercer, R J Walsh
**Co. Secretary:** Timothy Wheeler
**Responsibilities**
**Admin:** Cindy Breeze *(Office Manager)*
**Health & Safety:** Dereck Breeze *(Transport Manager)*
**Fleet:** Dereck Breeze *(Transport Manager)*
**US SIC:** 4712, 1622
**UK SIC:** 77002, 50200
**Auditors:** Bird Luckin Ltd
**Bankers:** National Westminster Bank Plc (60-09-11)

| | 31-05-14 | 31-05-13 | 31-05-12 |
|---|---|---|---|
| TO | 31,499,158 | 29,616,734 | 19,333,359 |
| P/L | 1,217,015 | 1,232,352 | 602,855 |
| NW | 6,406,071 | 5,684,883 | 5,055,836 |
| WC | 1,037,835 | (835,330) | (1,132,610) |
| Emp. | 114 | 105 | 86 |

DUNS 21-157-5886
## The Swaminarayan School
260 Brentfield Road, London NW10 8HE
**Tel:** 02089614043
**Web:** www.swaminarayan.brent.sch.uk
**Estd:** 1991
**Line of Business:** Schools (independent)
**Director:** P Patel
**Responsibilities**
**Senior:** Nilesh Malani *(Head Teacher)*, Umesh Prep *(Head Teacher)*, Mahendra Savjani *(Head Teacher)*
**Marketing:** Mahendra Savjani *(Head Teacher)*
**HR:** Mahendra Savjani *(Head Teacher)*
**US SIC:** 8211 **UK SIC:** 93200
**Employees:** 77

DUNS 22-560-0808
## Swan
659 Eccles New Road, Salford, Lancashire M50 1AY
**Tel:** 01617877000
**Estd:** 2011 Proprietorship
**Line of Business:** Taxis and private hire vehicles
**Principals:** . Burrows, M Callaghan *(Partner)*, J Callaghan *(Partner)*
**US SIC:** 4121 **UK SIC:** 72200
**Bankers:** National Westminster Bank Plc (01-05-75)
**Employees:** 55

DUNS 21-582-7710
## The Swan At the Globe
Shakespeare Globe Trust Ltd, 21 New Globe Walk, Lambeth, London SE1 9DT
**Tel:** 02079289444
**Web:** www.loveswan.co.uk
**Estd:** 2006 Proprietorship
**Line of Business:** Restaurant - english
**Proprietor:** Miss M Semia
**US SIC:** 5812 **UK SIC:** 66110
**Employees:** 100

DUNS 21-228-7337
## Swan Hotel
The Swan Hotel, Keswick Road, Ambleside, Cumbria LA22 9RF
**Tel:** 08448799120
**Web:** www.macdonald-hotels.co.uk
**Estd:** 1954 Proprietorship
**Line of Business:** Hotels
**Proprietor:** H Harrsion
**US SIC:** 7011 **UK SIC:** 66500
**Employees:** 96

DUNS 21-596-7568
## The Swan Hotel
46 Greengate Street, Stafford, Staffordshire ST16 2JA
**Web:** www.theswanstafford.co.uk
**VAT No:** 318926044 **Estd:** 1991 Partnership
**Line of Business:** Hotels
**Trading Style:** The Moat House, Lewis Partnership
**Partners:** Ms M Lewis, J Lewis, C Lewis, A Lewis, M Lewis
**Branches:** The Swan Hotel, Lower Penkridge Road, Stafford, Staffordshire ST17 0RJ
**US SIC:** 7011 **UK SIC:** 66500
**Employees:** 60

DUNS 21-735-8600
## The Swan Hotel (Newby Bridge) Holdings Ltd
Globe Square, Globe Lane, Dunkinfield, Greater Manchester, Dukinfield, Cheshire SK16 4UY
**Tel:** 01539531917
**Web:** www.swanhotel.com
**Reg No:** 5702585 **Estd:** 2006 Private Limited Company
**Line of Business:** Hotels
**Issued Capital:** £885
**Directors:** Ms S A Bardsley, Mrs A Bardsley, S T Ramsdale, Miss A C Robertson
**Co. Secretary:** Stephen Ramsdale
**US SIC:** 7011 **UK SIC:** 66500

| | 29-06-14 | 30-06-13 | 01-06-12 |
|---|---|---|---|
| TO | 4,893,393 | 4,662,059 | 4,403,737 |
| P/L | 1,703,483 | 41,574 | (72,743) |
| NW | 1,860,018 | 585,484 | 560,551 |
| WC | (388,843) | (1,850,069) | (2,190,135) |
| Emp. | 113 | 118 | 107 |

DUNS 21-225-5978
## Swan House
Pooles Lane, Willenhall, West Midlands WV12 5HJ
**Tel:** 01922-407040
**Web:** www.schealthcare.co.uk
**Estd:** 2000
**Line of Business:** Medical nursing home activities
**Proprietor:** Miss M Cleobury
**Responsibilities**
**Senior:** Rosemary Eagleton *(Home Manager)*
**US SIC:** 8051 **UK SIC:** 95100
**Employees:** 55

DUNS 21-772-7831
## Swan House Care Home
Swan Drive New Road, Chatteris, Cambridgeshire PE16 6EX
**Tel:** 01354696644
**Web:** www.fshc.co.uk
**Estd:** 1996 Proprietorship
**Line of Business:** Residential care establishments
**Proprietor:** Mrs C Brown
**Responsibilities**
**Senior:** Anne Richmond *(Manager)*
**US SIC:** 8321 **UK SIC:** 96111
**Employees:** 60

DUNS 23-085-7943
## Swan Housing Association
Zurich House, 129 High Street, Billericay, Essex CM12 9AH
**Tel:** 03003032500 **Fax:** 01277844720
**Web:** www.swan.org.uk
**Reg No:** 0028496IP **Estd:** 1991 Friendly Society
**Line of Business:** Housing associations societies trusts & co-operatives
**Principals:** R Hines *(Chairman)*, S Wheeler, R Hall, H F Chen, T Smith, R Pearce, D Moore, R Weekley
**Responsibilities**
**Senior:** John Synnuck *(Chief Executive)*, Suzanne Wicks *(Manager)*
**Marketing:** Malcolm O'Brien *(Executive Director of People a)*
**Admin:** John Synnuck *(Chief Executive)*
**US SIC:** 6531 **UK SIC:** 83400
**Auditors:** Grant Thornton UK LLP
**Bankers:** The Royal Bank Of Scotland Plc (16-12-33)

| | 31-03-12 | 31-03-11 | 31-03-10 |
|---|---|---|---|
| TO | 106,258,000 | 76,032,000 | 13,707,000 |
| P/L | 13,094,000 | 1,061,000 | 78,000 |
| NW | 234,807,000 | 133,152,000 | 107,428,000 |
| WC | 103,869,000 | 57,510,000 | (3,188,000) |
| Emp. | 336 | 309 | N/A |

DUNS 22-640-0778
## Swan Investments Group Ltd
Hanger 6 Inflite House, First Avenue, London Stansted Airport, Stansted, Essex CM24 1RY
**Tel:** 01279-681681 **Fax:** 01279-311293
**Web:** www.inflite.co.uk
**Reg No:** 1621189 **Estd:** 1982 Private Limited Company
**Line of Business:** Management activities of holding companies
**Trading Style:** Swan Investments Group Ltd
**Issued Capital:** £396,000
**Principals:** R A Stephens *(Chairman and Managing)*, Ms P A Stephens, W C Stephens, Ms L M Stephens, Mrs P M Monksfield
**Co. Secretary:** Ms Linda Ellis
**Responsibilities**
**Senior:** Pauline Stephens *(Manager)*
**Branches:** Swan Investments Group Ltd, Unit 2 Woodside, Dunmow Road, Bishop's Stortford, Hertfordshire CM23 5RG
**US SIC:** 6711, 6111
**UK SIC:** 83962, 81501

**Auditors:** Baker Tilly
**Bankers:** HSBC Bank plc (40-12-03)

| | 31-03-14 | 31-03-13 | 31-03-12 |
|---|---|---|---|
| TA | 89,600,164 | 88,702,098 | 83,252,835 |
| P/L | 3,947,501 | (2,226,319) | 1,540,972 |
| NW | 62,525,302 | 59,498,777 | 60,965,570 |
| WC | 16,763,954 | 13,195,173 | 9,564,270 |
| Emp. | 623 | 631 | 564 |

DUNS 21-631-1472 Exp
## Swan Mill (Holdings) Ltd
10 High Street, Swanley, Kent BR8 8BE
**Tel:** 01322-665566 **Fax:** 01322-666460
**Web:** www.swantex.co.uk
**Reg No:** 0248875 **Estd:** 1892 Private Limited Company
**Line of Business:** Management activities of holding companies
**Export Sales:** £6,173,000
**Trading Style:** Swan Mill Paper, Swantex
**Issued Capital:** £198,000
**Directors:** G Rogers, R M Sanderson, J Bryan, T A Worton, D C Byk
**Responsibilities**
**Marketing:** Sally Davies *(Marketing Manager)*, Roxanna Roberts *(Trade Marketing Executive)*
**Health & Safety:** Bob Pike *(Health & Safety Manager)*
**Facilities:** Clive Calvert *(Maintenance Manager)*
**Branches:** Swan Mill (Holdings) Ltd, Hirwaun Industrial Estate, Aberdare, Mid Glamorgan CF44 9UP
**US SIC:** 6711 **UK SIC:** 83962
**Auditors:** Baker Tilly
**Bankers:** National Westminster Bank Plc (60-05-37)

| | 31-03-14 | 31-03-13 | 31-03-12 |
|---|---|---|---|
| TO | 44,370,000 | 43,635,000 | 43,205,000 |
| P/L | 3,880,000 | 4,612,000 | 4,358,000 |
| NW | 23,782,000 | 20,618,000 | 17,521,000 |
| WC | 17,515,000 | 14,910,000 | 12,223,000 |
| Emp. | 218 | 219 | 222 |

DUNS 49-313-4043
## Swan Staff Recruitment Ltd
50 High Street, Swanley, Kent BR8 8BQ
**Tel:** 01322614900
**Web:** www.swanstaff.co.uk
**Reg No:** 3121740 **Estd:** 2002 Private Limited Company
**Line of Business:** Employment and recruitment companies and consultants
**Trading Style:** Swanstaff Recruitment
**Issued Capital:** £100
**Directors:** D R Freeman, Mrs C Sanderson, Ms G J Rogers, Miss Z Bristow, S J Rogers
**Responsibilities**
**Senior:** Dan Crocombe *(Manager)*
**US SIC:** 7361, 7399
**UK SIC:** 83954
**Auditors:** A J Shah & Co

| | 31-03-14 | 31-03-13 | 31-03-12 |
|---|---|---|---|
| TO | 11,427,510 | 7,449,277 | N/A |
| P/L | 410,958 | 184,174 | N/A |
| NW | 333,620 | 127,901 | 80,203 |
| WC | (237,518) | (358,372) | (413,556) |
| Emp. | 432 | 294 | N/A |

DUNS 55-063-3309
## Swanborough House
Swanborough Drive, Brighton, East Sussex BN2 5PH
**Tel:** 01273696391
**Web:** www.raphaelmedicalcentre.co.uk
**Estd:** 1996 Proprietorship
**Line of Business:** Residential care establishments
**Proprietor:** G Florschutz
**Responsibilities**
**Senior:** Elizabeth Miles *(Manager)*
**US SIC:** 8321 **UK SIC:** 96111
**Employees:** 60

DUNS 28-866-9955
## Swanbourne House School Trust Ltd
Swanbourne, Milton Keynes, Buckinghamshire MK17 0HZ
**Tel:** 01296720264
**Web:** www.swanbournehouse.bucks.sch.uk
**Reg No:** 0984935 **Estd:** 1970 Private Company Limited By Guarantee
**Line of Business:** Primary education
**Trading Style:** Swanbourne House School
**Directors:** Mrs S L Tyler, J F Willmott, J Leggett, M J Rushton, Mrs M E Beacon, P H Rushforth, Lady N M Bonsor, J Denman
**Co. Secretary:** Paul Jochimsen
**Responsibilities**
**Senior:** Steven Goodhart *(Joint Head Teacher)*, Linda Hawes *(Supplies Coordinator)*, Simon Hitchings *(Head Teacher)*, Katherine Langston *(Director)*
**Finance:** Marilyn Aldis *(Bursar)*
**Marketing:** Julie Goodhart *(Joint Head Teacher)*
**Sales:** Julie Goodhart *(Joint Head Teacher)*
**HR:** Marilyn Aldis *(Bursar)*, Steven Goodhart *(Joint Head Teacher)*

**Health & Safety:** Julie Goodhart *(Joint Head Teacher)*
**Facilities:** Tony Fisher *(Facilities Manager)*
**Purchasing:** Julie Goodhart *(Joint Head Teacher)*
**US SIC:** 8211 **UK SIC:** 93200
**Auditors:** Haysmacintyre
**Bankers:** Barclays Bank Plc (20-03-18)

| | 31-08-14 | 31-08-13 | 31-08-12 |
|---|---|---|---|
| TO | 5,436,536 | 5,413,524 | 5,349,891 |
| P/L | 268,279 | (117,698) | (87,854) |
| NW | 4,496,508 | 4,228,229 | 4,345,927 |
| WC | 1,594,648 | 1,247,065 | 1,384,687 |
| Emp. | 124 | 134 | 122 |

DUNS 77-752-2939
## Swancote Foods Ltd
(**Subsidiary of:** Produce Investments Plc)
Hortonwood 7, Telford, Shropshire TF1 7GP
**Tel:** 01952670656 **Fax:** 0870-770-5647
**Web:** www.swancote.co.uk
**Reg No:** 3016339 **Estd:** 2010 Private Limited Company
**Line of Business:** Manufacturers of food products
**Issued Capital:** £1,300,001
**Co. Secretary:** George Macdonald
**US SIC:** 2099 **UK SIC:** 42399
**Auditors:** Baker Tilly UK Audit LLP
**Bankers:** Barclays Bank Plc (20-97-78)

| | 29-06-13 | 30-06-12 | 25-06-11 |
|---|---|---|---|
| TA | 1,300,000 | 1,300,000 | 1,300,000 |
| NW | 1,300,000 | 1,300,000 | 1,300,000 |

DUNS 39-844-1535
## Swanke Hayden Connell International Ltd
(**Subsidiary of:** Aukett Swanke Group Plc)
25 Christopher Street, London EC2A 2BS
**Tel:** 02074548200 **Fax:** 020-7454-8400
**Web:** www.shca.com
**Reg No:** 2222545 **VAT No:** 867834275
**Estd:** 1988 Private Limited Company
**Line of Business:** Architects
**Export Sales:** £3,797,000
**Trading Style:** Swanke Hayden Connell Architect
**Issued Capital:** £309,150
**Principals:** D J Hughes *(Managing)*, R Fry *(Managing)*, Mrs B A Wright, J N Thompson
**Co. Secretary:** Neil Tullis
**Responsibilities**
**Senior:** Richard Hayden *(Chairperson)*, Maryvonne Mcgetrick *(Personal Assistant)*, Julian Seward *(Manager)*
**US SIC:** 8911, 7399
**UK SIC:** 83701, 83954
**Auditors:** BDO LLP
**Bankers:** Barclays Bank Plc (20-77-67)

| | 31-12-13 | 31-12-12 | 31-12-11 |
|---|---|---|---|
| TO | 6,948,000 | 6,372,000 | 8,743,000 |
| P/L | 135,000 | (515,000) | (804,000) |
| NW | 852,000 | 485,000 | 949,000 |
| WC | 873,000 | 341,000 | 758,000 |
| Emp. | 76 | 96 | 101 |

DUNS 64-112-7626 **Imp**
## Swanline Print Ltd
(**Subsidiary of:** Leavale Properties Ltd)
Whitebridge Park, Stone, Staffordshire ST15 8LQ
**Tel:** 01785-816686
**Web:** www.swanlineprint.co.uk
**Reg No:** 4112878 **Estd:** 2000 Private Limited Company
**Line of Business:** Screen printers
**Issued Capital:** £75,001
**Directors:** R Mclellan, S C Kirby, N A Kirby, Ms J Offord
**Co. Secretary:** Richard Towers
**US SIC:** 2752, 5199
**UK SIC:** 47544, 61900

| | 31-12-13 | 31-12-12 | 31-12-11 |
|---|---|---|---|
| TO | 9,143,019 | 8,060,868 | 7,797,475 |
| P/L | 744,984 | 871,889 | 823,907 |
| NW | 1,591,911 | 1,194,864 | 859,153 |
| WC | 262,084 | 415,084 | (3,335) |
| Emp. | 92 | 86 | 78 |

DUNS 34-682-7905
## Swann Group Ltd
Windsor House, 39 King Street, London EC2V 8LL
**Tel:** 01376320100
**Web:** www.swanngroupltd.com
**Reg No:** 5487474 **Estd:** 2005 Private Limited Company
**Line of Business:** Management activities of holding companies
**Issued Capital:** £120,000
**Director:** P J Jarvis
**Co. Secretary:** Andrew Pirrie
**US SIC:** 6711 **UK SIC:** 83962
**Auditors:** Lambert Chapman LLP
**Bankers:** HSBC Bank plc (40-17-08)

| | 31-03-14 | 31-03-13 | 31-03-12 |
|---|---|---|---|
| TO | 12,986,454 | 16,705,832 | 16,624,339 |
| P/L | (96,837) | 636,616 | (69,416) |
| NW | 52,543 | 29,983 | (730,376) |
| WC | (29,299) | (402,958) | (1,171,617) |
| Emp. | 148 | 161 | 173 |

DUNS 29-533-8826
## Swansea Bakeries Ltd
(**Subsidiary of:** Hunts Bakeries Ltd)
Unit 10-11 St Davids Industrial Estate, St Davids Road, Swansea Enterprise Park, Swansea, West Glamorgan SA6 8RX
**Tel:** 01792-798042
**Reg No:** 1900945 **Estd:** 1985 Private Limited Company
**Line of Business:** Distribution service providers
**Issued Capital:** £30,000
**Managing Director:** J D Hughes
**Co. Secretary:** William Hughes
**Responsibilities**
**IT:** Lesley Thomas *(Computer Manager)*
**US SIC:** 4712 **UK SIC:** 77002
**Auditors:** Griffith & Miles
**Bankers:** Lloyds TSB Bank plc (30-12-15)

| | 31-07-13 | 31-07-12 | 31-07-11 |
|---|---|---|---|
| TA | 491,574 | 540,689 | 431,870 |
| NW | 129,215 | 258,207 | 66,852 |
| WC | 66,066 | 126,464 | (100,514) |

DUNS 22-760-8528
## The Swansea City Association Football Club Ltd
(**Subsidiary of:** Swansea City Football 2002 Ltd)
Vetch Field, Swansea, West Glamorgan SA1 3SU
**Tel:** 01792-616600 **Fax:** 01792-646120
**Web:** www.swanseacity.net
**Reg No:** 0123414 **Estd:** 1912 Private Limited Company
**Line of Business:** Other sporting activities not elsewhere classified
**Trading Style:** Swansea City F C
**Issued Capital:** £4,699,989
**Directors:** L A Dineen, D G Keefe, S R Penny, G G Joseph, H D Cooze, B L Katzen, M W Morgan, H M Jenkins
**Co. Secretary:** Alun Cowie
**Responsibilities**
**Senior:** John Van Zweden *(Director)*
**Admin:** Jackie Rockey *(Club Secretary)*
**Branches:** The Swansea City Association Football Club Ltd, 33 William Street, Swansea, West Glamorgan SA1 3QS
**US SIC:** 7999 **UK SIC:** 97913
**Auditors:** Gerald Thomas & Co
**Bankers:** Lloyds TSB Bank plc (30-95-46)

| | 31-05-14 | 31-05-13 | 31-05-12 |
|---|---|---|---|
| TO | 98,691,997 | 67,113,301 | 65,165,603 |
| P/L | 1,324,666 | 20,831,699 | 17,419,145 |
| NW | (11,153,432) | 318,656 | (3,622,672) |
| WC | (18,500,593) | (726,346) | (184,057) |
| Emp. | 246 | 208 | 192 |

DUNS 76-972-2406
## Swansea City Waste Disposal Co Ltd
(**Subsidiary of:** City & County of Swansea Council)
Unit 6 Ferry Boat Close, Swansea Enterprise Park, Swansea, West Glamorgan SA6 8QN
**Tel:** 01792796886
**Web:** www.swansea.gov.uk
**Reg No:** 2633573 **Estd:** 1991 Private Limited Company
**Line of Business:** Waste disposal
**Trading Style:** Swansea City Bailing Plant
**Issued Capital:** £4,800,000
**Directors:** R A Lloyd, M Thomas
**Co. Secretary:** Ms Beverley Hitchman
**Responsibilities**
**Senior:** Gerald Clement *(Manager)*, Richard Henchliffe *(Manager)*, Eamon Kinsella *(Manager)*, Wynn Lawrence *(Environmental/ General Manager)*, Michael Shellard *(Manager)*
**Marketing:** Wynn Lawrence *(Environmental/ General Manager)*
**IT:** Christopher Fender *(Operations Manager)*
**HR:** Christopher Fender *(Operations Manager)*, Wynn Lawrence *(Environmental/ General Manager)*
**Health & Safety:** Christopher Fender *(Operations Manager)*
**Facilities:** Wynn Lawrence *(Environmental/ General Manager)*
**Operations:** Wynn Lawrence *(Environmental/ General Manager)*
**US SIC:** 4953 **UK SIC:** 92110
**Auditors:** PricewaterhouseCoopers LLP
**Bankers:** Lloyds TSB Bank plc (30-93-53)

| | 30-09-14 | 30-09-13 | 31-09-12 |
|---|---|---|---|
| TO | N/A | 12,553,022 | 10,419,756 |
| P/L | N/A | 11,088,062 | (250,738) |
| NW | (18,208) | (172,900) | (10,509,582) |
| WC | (18,208) | (172,900) | 1,057,792 |
| Emp. | 5 | 74 | 77 |

DUNS 23-222-9286
## Swansea College
Tycoch Road, Sketty, Swansea, West Glamorgan SA2 9EB
**Tel:** 01792284000
**Web:** www.gowercollegeswansea.ac.uk
**Estd:** 1986
**Line of Business:** Universities services
**Principals:** G Hilton *(Financial)*, K Elliott
**Responsibilities**
**Marketing:** Julie Mason *(Senior Marketing Executive)*
**HR:** Elaine McCallion *(Skills for Industry & Business)*, Nichola Perkins *(Human Resources Manager)*, Sue Poole *(Training Director)*
**Branches:** Swansea College, 37 The Kingsway, Swansea, West Glamorgan SA1 5LF
**US SIC:** 8221 **UK SIC:** 93100
**Employees:** 700

DUNS 64-076-3009
## Swansea Flyers Ltd
Unit 1 Viking Way, Winch Wen Industrial Estate, Winch Wen, Swansea, West Glamorgan SA1 7DA
**Tel:** 01792775594 **Fax:** 01792784235
**Web:** www.fedex.com
**Reg No:** 3471664 **Estd:** 2012 Private Limited Company
**Line of Business:** Couriers
**Trading Style:** Sedex
**Issued Capital:** £100
**Director:** D R Lukes
**Co. Secretary:** John Lukes
**US SIC:** 4213 **UK SIC:** 72300
**Auditors:** Bevan & Buckland
**Bankers:** National Westminster Bank Plc (55-61-20)

| | 31-05-14 | 31-05-13 | 31-05-12 |
|---|---|---|---|
| TA | 373,120 | 380,470 | 318,460 |
| NW | 44,990 | 60,246 | 52,773 |
| WC | (12,590) | 4,938 | 30,406 |

DUNS 21-812-2068
## Swansea Insititute Townhill Campus
Townhill Campus, Townhill Road, Cockett, Swansea, West Glamorgan SA2 0UT
**Tel:** 01792482001
**Web:** www.smu.ac.uk
**Estd:** 2012
**Line of Business:** University
**Responsibilities**
**Senior:** Medwyn Hughes *(Vice Chancellor)*
**US SIC:** 8221 **UK SIC:** 93100
**Employees:** 200

DUNS 21-531-6733
## Swansea Magistrates Court
Grove Place, Swansea, West Glamorgan SA1 5DB
**Tel:** 01792478300
**Web:** www.magistrates-court.co.uk
**Estd:** 1998 Proprietorship
**Line of Business:** Courts
**Proprietor:** J Barron
**Responsibilities**
**Senior:** Jim Heir *(Manager)*
**US SIC:** 9211 **UK SIC:** 91200
**Employees:** 60

DUNS 23-691-3026 **Imp**
## Swansea Metropolitan University
Mount Pleasant Campus, Mount Pleasant, Swansea, West Glamorgan SA1 6ED
**Tel:** 01792-481000 **Fax:** 01792481037
**Web:** www.tsd.ac.uk
**VAT No:** 588109018 **Estd:** 1876 Incorporate By Act Of Parliament
**Line of Business:** University
**Principals:** B R Lewis *(Financial)*, Professor D A Warner, C Heycock, Professor K C Reid
**Responsibilities**
**Senior:** Medwyn Hughes *(Principal)*, Joyce Wills *(Personal Assistant)*
**Marketing:** Nadine Davies *(Marketing and Communications O)*, Cagwalldwr Tom *(Head of Marketing)*
**IT:** Chris Godsmark *(MIS Manager)*, Dean Parratt *(Network Manager)*
**Health & Safety:** John bowen *(Health & Safety Officer)*
**Facilities:** John bowen *(Health & Safety Officer)*
**Branches:** Swansea Metropolitan University, Mount Pleasant Campus, Mount Pleasant, Swansea, West Glamorgan SA1 6ED
**US SIC:** 8221 **UK SIC:** 93100
**Auditors:** Derwyn Owen
**Employees:** 200
**Turnover:** £37,071,000

DUNS 50-707-2080
## Swansea Neath Port Talbot Crossroads Care Attendant Scheme
Quall Road Clydach, Swansea, West Glamorgan SA6 5DT
**Tel:** 01792846351
**Estd:** 1983
**Line of Business:** Charity involved as residential care for elderly. Charity registration number 701835.
**Manager:** Mrs P Bates
**Branches:** Swansea Neath Port Talbot Crossroads Care Attendant Scheme, 1 High St, Swansea, West Glamorgan SA8 4HU
**US SIC:** 8699, 8361
**UK SIC:** 96902, 96112
**Employees:** 60

DUNS 23-222-7629 **Imp**
## Swansea University
Singleton Park, Swansea, West Glamorgan SA2 8PP
**Web:** www.swansea.ac.uk
**Reg No:** 0234056 **VAT No:** 123853477
**Estd:** 2010
**Line of Business:** University
**Trading Style:** Swansea University
**Directors:** Prof R B Davies, Prof I Cluckie, Sir D Williams, Ms V Sugar, B Jones
**Responsibilities**
**Marketing:** Adrian Rees *(Web Editor)*
**Admin:** Andrea Carr *(Office Manager & Events Admini)*, Anita Davies *(Administrative Assistant)*, Paul Dicks *(Administrative Assistant)*, Lynda Horgan *(Administrative Assistant)*, Shirley Jenkins *(Administrative Assistant)*, Philip Maull *(Administrator)*
**IT:** Terry Daniels *(Systems Development Officer)*, Adrian Rees *(Web Editor)*, Tinnu Sarvotham *(Network Manager)*
**HR:** Suki Collins *(Human Resources Officer)*, Sian Cushion *(Deputy Director of Human Resou)*, Sally Davies *(Human Resources Officer)*, Charlotte Morgans *(Head of Development and Traini)*, Sara Walters *(Recruitment Officer)*
**Operations:** Caroline Coleman-Davies *(Strategic Partnerships Manager)*
**US SIC:** 8221 **UK SIC:** 93100
**Auditors:** PricewaterhouseCoopers LLP
**Bankers:** Lloyds TSB Bank plc (30-95-46)
**Employees:** 3,000
**Turnover:** £158,918,000

DUNS 76-202-8249
## Swansea Young Single Homeless Project
6a Walter Road, Swansea, West Glamorgan SA1 5NF
**Tel:** 01792-537530
**Web:** www.syshp.org.uk
**Reg No:** 2538278 **Estd:** 1990 Private Limited Company
**Line of Business:** Representative office
**Trading Style:** S Y S H P
**Directors:** P Wales, A N Jones, L Davies, S Prosser, Miss L A Rees, S J Pettifer, C J Maggs, T N Devonald
**Responsibilities**
**Senior:** Owen Burt *(Director)*, Susan Hutson *(Manager)*, Susan Pritchard *(Manager)*, Liz Slade *(Manager)*
**US SIC:** 7399, 8999
**UK SIC:** 83954
**Auditors:** Bevan & Buckland
**Bankers:** Barclays Bank Plc (20-84-41)

| | 31-03-14 | 31-03-13 | 31-03-12 |
|---|---|---|---|
| TO | 1,259,624 | 1,278,201 | 1,349,594 |
| P/L | (4,091) | (81,148) | (53,038) |
| NW | 703,227 | 707,318 | 788,466 |
| WC | 383,156 | 412,865 | 708,484 |
| Emp. | 57 | 57 | 57 |

DUNS 21-632-3941
## Swansway Group Ltd
Queensway, Wrexham, Clwyd LL11 2NR
**Tel:** 01706892352
**Web:** www.swansway-honda-rochdale.com
**Reg No:** 7105886 **Estd:** 2009 Private Limited Company
**Line of Business:** Management activities of holding companies
**Issued Capital:** £1,102
**Directors:** P Smyth, J Smyth, J Holgate, D Smyth, M Smyth
**US SIC:** 6711 **UK SIC:** 83962

| | 31-12-13 | 31-12-12 | 31-12-11 |
|---|---|---|---|
| TO | 369,143,768 | 290,396,077 | 262,847,395 |
| P/L | 5,137,330 | 3,264,234 | 7,914,583 |
| NW | 15,085,943 | 12,323,739 | 11,249,857 |
| WC | 7,167,323 | 3,795,865 | 3,300,170 |
| Emp. | 626 | 546 | 520 |

DUNS 23-698-2018

## Swanswell Charitable Trust

Suite 5 Hilton House, Corporation Street, Rugby, Warwickshire CV21 2DN
**Tel:** 01788559400
**Web:** www.swanswell.org.uk
**Reg No:** 3692925 **Estd:** 1969 Private Company Limited By Guarantee
**Line of Business:** Social work activities without accommodation
**Directors:** J W Bland, J S Watkins, M G Pilgrim, T C Rutherford, Mrs R Stringfellow, Dr A M Zaghloul, C E Mitchell
**Responsibilities**
**Senior:** Ritchie Bosworth *(Manager)*
**Branches:** Swanswell Charitable Trust, 9 Lamb Street, Coventry, West Midlands CV1 4AE
**US SIC:** 8321 **UK SIC:** 96111
**Auditors:** Luckmans Duckett Parker
**Bankers:** National Westminster Bank Plc (60-02-35)

| | 31-03-14 | 31-03-13 | 31-03-12 |
|---|---|---|---|
| TO | 11,156,113 | 10,996,549 | 10,376,175 |
| P/L | 546,663 | 63,090 | 14,870 |
| NW | 1,670,175 | 1,117,845 | 1,009,025 |
| WC | 1,550,962 | 908,303 | 715,303 |
| Emp. | 303 | 286 | 263 |

DUNS 73-262-5970

## Swanton Care & Community (Autism North) Ltd

**(Subsidiary of:** Swanton Care & Community Ltd)
All Saints Vicarage, Church Road, Hetton-Le-Hole, Houghton-Le-Spring, Tyne and Wear DH5 9AJ
**Tel:** 0191-526-6326
**Web:** www.barchester.com
**Reg No:** 4536431 **Estd:** 2002 Private Limited Company
**Line of Business:** Residential care establishments
**Issued Capital:** £100
**Directors:** P E Murphy, Dr A J Rose-Quirie
**Co. Secretary:** Ms Joanne Richardson
**US SIC:** 8321 **UK SIC:** 96111
**Auditors:** Brennan Neil & Leonard
**Bankers:** The Royal Bank Of Scotland Plc (15-10-00)

| | 31-12-13 | 31-12-12 | 31-12-11 |
|---|---|---|---|
| TO | 8,836,000 | 8,878,000 | 8,703,000 |
| P/L | 2,103,000 | 2,183,000 | 2,305,000 |
| NW | 11,483,000 | 9,394,000 | 7,621,000 |
| WC | 10,881,000 | 8,833,000 | 7,068,000 |
| Emp. | 244 | 251 | 252 |

DUNS 34-994-8252

## Swanton Care & Community Ltd

Suite 201, The Chambers, Chelsea Harbour, London, London SW10 0XF
**Tel:** 02073494435
**Reg No:** 5789785 **Estd:** 2006 Private Limited Company
**Line of Business:** Hospices
**Issued Capital:** £1
**Directors:** Ms E Headon, Dr A J Rose-Quirie, G V Magee, P Murphy, Dr P Calveley, Ms B E Mcintosh
**Co. Secretary:** Ms Joanne Richardson
**Responsibilities**
**Senior:** Christine Tang *(Director)*
**US SIC:** 8091 **UK SIC:** 95200
**Bankers:** The Royal Bank Of Scotland Plc (16-04-00)

| | 31-12-13 | 31-12-12 | 31-12-11 |
|---|---|---|---|
| TO | 24,447,000 | 24,699,000 | 24,646,000 |
| P/L | 5,601,000 | 5,292,000 | 3,940,000 |
| NW | 22,639,000 | 18,426,000 | 14,478,000 |
| WC | (1,358,000) | (2,457,000) | (4,431,000) |
| Emp. | 757 | 710 | 724 |

DUNS 21-742-2633 Imp-Exp

## Swap

Alexandria Park, 1 Penner Road, Havant, Hampshire PO9 1QY
**Tel:** 02392453711 **Fax:** 023-9247-3918
**Web:** www.waspswitches.co.uk
**Reg No:** 1183279 **VAT No:** 108584755
**Estd:** 1974 Private Limited Company
**Line of Business:** Powder coating specialists
**Export Markets:** Continental, Americas, Australasia
**Trading Style:** W A S P, Wessex Advance Switching Products
**Issued Capital:** £2
**Principals:** R D Middleton *(Managing)*, W R Exton, J P Martyn
**Co. Secretary:** Hackwood Secretaries Limited
**Responsibilities**
**Sales:** Sue Austin *(Senior Sales Executive)*
**US SIC:** 3357, 3629
**UK SIC:** 22470, 34350
**Bankers:** Bank Of Scotland (12-09-61)

| | 31-12-13 | 31-12-12 | 31-12-11 |
|---|---|---|---|
| TA | 10,002 | 10,002 | 10,002 |
| NW | 2 | 2 | 2 |

DUNS 76-948-4031

## Swarco Traffic Ltd

7 Mercury Road, Gallowfields Trading Estate, Richmond, North Yorkshire DL10 4TQ
**Tel:** 01908-315-400
**Web:** www.swarcotraffic.com
**Reg No:** 2389500 **VAT No:** 499576855
**Estd:** 1989 Private Limited Company
**Line of Business:** Manufacture of other electrical equipment not elsewhere classified
**Issued Capital:** £500,000
**Directors:** C Dyer, J P Cowling
**Co. Secretary:** Mrs Berony Abraham
**Responsibilities**
**Senior:** Peter Eccleson *(Manager)*
**Finance:** Peter Eccleson *(Manager)*, Jane Lowson *(Administration Manager)*
**Admin:** Jane Lowson *(Administration Manager)*
**HR:** Peter Eccleson *(Manager)*, Jane Lowson *(Administration Manager)*
**US SIC:** 3999, 3799, 1799
**UK SIC:** 49590, 36502, 50000
**Auditors:** Clive Owen & Co LLP
**Bankers:** Barclays Bank Plc (20-25-29)

| | 31-12-13 | 31-12-12 | 31-12-11 |
|---|---|---|---|
| TO | N/A | N/A | 6,296,029 |
| P/L | N/A | N/A | (78,272) |
| NW | 659,648 | 654,151 | 126,074 |
| WC | 247,577 | 244,784 | (122,792) |

DUNS 21-090-9776 Imp

## Swarovski Uk Ltd

**(Subsidiary of:** D. Swarovski Kg)
Grand Arcade, 14 St Andrew's Street, Cambridge, Cambridgeshire CB2 3BJ
**Tel:** 01223305511
**Web:** www.swarovski.com
**Reg No:** 0835806 **Estd:** 2010 Private Limited Company
**Line of Business:** Retail sale of jewellery, clocks and watches
**Trading Style:** Swarovski Corporate Communications and Design Services
**Issued Capital:** £4,000,000
**Directors:** G R Taylor, Ms H A Quinn
**Co. Secretary:** Graham Taylor
**Responsibilities**
**Senior:** Sharon Stone *(Branch Manager)*, Jennifer Turner *(Marketing Manager)*
**Branches:** Swarovski Uk Ltd, Walmer House, 296 Regent Street, London W1B 3AW
**US SIC:** 5944 **UK SIC:** 65400
**Auditors:** PricewaterhouseCoopers LLP
**Bankers:** HSBC Bank plc (40-18-22)

| | 31-12-13 | 31-12-12 | 31-12-11 |
|---|---|---|---|
| TO | 73,610,236 | 76,615,780 | 78,455,440 |
| P/L | 2,349,312 | 1,218,656 | 2,107,135 |
| NW | 11,605,496 | 10,275,529 | 9,155,623 |
| WC | 2,007,709 | 12,765,161 | 486,907 |
| Emp. | 875 | 874 | 812 |

DUNS 21-462-7593

## Swarthmore Educational Centre

3-7 Woodhouse Square, Leeds, West Yorkshire LS3 1AD
**Tel:** 01132432210
**Web:** www.swarthmore.org.uk
**Estd:** 1909 Partnership
**Line of Business:** Training centres
**Partners:** J Arnison, Mrs M Butterworth, Miss F Chapel, P Hall, Dr H Hubbard, Miss M Belt, Ms F Matthews
**US SIC:** 8299 **UK SIC:** 93300
**Employees:** 100

DUNS 21-021-9960 Imp

## The Swatch Group (U K) Ltd

**(Subsidiary of:** The Swatch Group Sa)
Building 1000 2nd Floor East Wing, London E16 2QU
**Tel:** 08452743500 **Fax:** 0845-274-3501
**Web:** www.swatchgroup.com
**Reg No:** 0177501 **Estd:** 2003 Private Limited Company
**Line of Business:** Manufacture of watches and clocks
**Issued Capital:** £2,000,000
**Directors:** F A Nardin, Y Y Gamard, G M Vallade
**Co. Secretary:** Mrs Hajra Patel
**Responsibilities**
**Senior:** Arlette Ducommun *(Manager)*
**Branches:** The Swatch Group (U K) Ltd, Capitol Shopping Centre, Queen St, Cardiff, South Glamorgan CF10 2HQ
**US SIC:** 3873 **UK SIC:** 37400
**Auditors:** KPMG LLP
**Bankers:** Lloyds TSB Bank plc (30-92-94)

| | 31-12-13 | 31-12-12 | 31-12-11 |
|---|---|---|---|
| TO | 61,292,000 | 57,452,000 | 47,992,000 |
| P/L | 7,403,000 | 6,118,000 | 5,029,000 |
| NW | 22,047,000 | 17,040,000 | 13,780,000 |
| WC | 23,001,000 | 18,552,000 | 13,682,000 |
| Emp. | 500 | 465 | 461 |

DUNS 22-550-2103

## Swaythling Housing Society Ltd

Herbert Collins House, 5 Walnut Avenue Northleigh Corner, Southampton, Hampshire SO18 2HR
**Tel:** 02380584661 **Fax:** 023-8058-6416
**Reg No:** 0010237IP **VAT No:** 411525004
**Estd:** 1925 Friendly Society
**Line of Business:** Housing association. Subject leases private houses in approximately 18 local authority areas, including the counties of Hampshire, Dorset and Wiltshire. Member of the National and Federation of Housing Societies.
**Principals:** M J Caton *(Chairman)*, E W Forster, R Barritt, J B Rose Jp, Ms M Dorward, S Wallbridge, Ms M Holmes, N Dewey
**Responsibilities**
**Senior:** Paul Clapp *(Director)*, D Hankins *(Vice Chairman)*
**Branches:** Swaythling Housing Society Ltd, Ellen Wren Ho, 15 Westbrook Way, Southampton, Hampshire SO18 2JY
**US SIC:** 6531 **UK SIC:** 83400
**Auditors:** Deloitte LLP
**Bankers:** Lloyds TSB Bank plc (30-97-80)

| | 31-03-12 | 31-03-11 | 31-03-10 |
|---|---|---|---|
| TO | 51,717,000 | 39,735,000 | 34,684,000 |
| P/L | (1,695,000) | 11,988,000 | 10,359,000 |
| NW | 45,054,000 | 57,513,000 | 55,952,000 |
| WC | 17,445,000 | (6,750,000) | (2,592,000) |
| Emp. | 564 | 188 | 91 |

DUNS 28-865-2969

## The Swedish School Society in London

82 Lonsdale Road, London SW13 9JS
**Tel:** 020-8741-1751 **Fax:** 020-8741-9372
**Web:** www.swedishschool.org.uk
**Reg No:** 0959675 **Estd:** 1969 Private Company Limited By Guarantee
**Line of Business:** Primary education
**Directors:** S Marthinsson, A C Beaver, Ms K Andreasson, P Burman, Mrs L Smith Juntti
**Responsibilities**
**Senior:** Jan Dackenberg *(Manager)*, Annelie Gunnarsson *(Manager)*, Anna Jagverg *(Headmistress)*, Richard Jönsson *(Director)*, Annelie Krepp *(Manager)*, Sven Littorin *(Manager)*, Michael Persson *(Manager)*, Mia Touzin Leffler *(Manager)*
**US SIC:** 8211 **UK SIC:** 93200
**Auditors:** PKF
**Bankers:** HSBC Bank plc (40-25-03)

| | 30-06-13 | 30-06-12 | 30-06-11 |
|---|---|---|---|
| TO | 3,317,198 | 3,013,248 | 2,745,264 |
| P/L | 57,940 | (44,920) | (28,139) |
| NW | 1,828,295 | 1,770,355 | 1,815,275 |
| WC | 1,068,347 | 1,267,415 | 1,312,301 |
| Emp. | 47 | 46 | 39 |

DUNS 51-639-5352

## Sweeep Kuusakoski Ltd

**(Subsidiary of:** Kuusakoski Group Oy)
Gas Road, Sittingbourne, Kent ME10 2QB
**Tel:** 01795434125 **Fax:** 01795479516
**Web:** www.sweeep.co.uk
**Reg No:** 5956680 **Estd:** 2006 Private Limited Company
**Line of Business:** Recycling of non-metal waste and scrap
**Issued Capital:** £200
**Directors:** A I Kekkonen, Ms L J Salo, P Watts
**Co. Secretary:** Ms Pamela Watts
**Responsibilities**
**Senior:** Petri Halonen *(Manager)*, Mike Marais *(Plant Manager)*, Barry Walker *(Factory Manager)*
**Sales:** Justin Greenaway *(Commercial Manager)*
**Operations:** Mike Marais *(Plant Manager)*
**US SIC:** 3031 **UK SIC:** 48123
**Bankers:** Barclays Bank Plc (20-14-33)

| | 31-12-12 | 31-12-11 | 31-12-10 |
|---|---|---|---|
| TO | 11,213,777 | 9,000,457 | 6,733,107 |
| P/L | 744,345 | 1,208,921 | 341,664 |
| NW | 2,320,061 | 1,692,136 | 744,917 |
| WC | (1,121,234) | 34,377 | (287,227) |
| Emp. | 142 | 124 | N/A |

DUNS 50-136-4731 Imp

## Sweet Dreams (Nelson) Ltd

**(Subsidiary of:** Dreambase Ltd)
Primrose Mill, Martin Street, Burnley, Lancashire BB10 1SH
**Tel:** 01282-830033 **Fax:** 01282-830055
**Web:** www.sweetdreamsuk.com
**Reg No:** 2322358 **VAT No:** 525528935
**Estd:** 1989 Private Limited Company
**Line of Business:** Manufacturers of beds and mattresses
**Export Sales:** £157,404
**Issued Capital:** £20,000
**Principals:** R Ahmed *(Managing)*, A F Ahmed, M Ahmed
**Co. Secretary:** Adnan Ahmed
**Responsibilities**
**Senior:** Ghazala Ahmed *(Manager)*
**Finance:** Denise Warglewörgh *(Senior Finance Administrator)*
**HR:** Pervais Akbar *(Human Resources Manager)*
**US SIC:** 2515 **UK SIC:** 46715
**Auditors:** KM Chartered Accountants
**Bankers:** National Westminster Bank Plc (01-01-35)

| | 31-03-14 | 31-03-13 | 31-03-12 |
|---|---|---|---|
| TO | 15,282,317 | 15,708,162 | 13,800,567 |
| P/L | 157,771 | 607,919 | 488,186 |
| NW | 1,186,901 | 1,056,839 | 793,041 |
| WC | 37,052 | 216,136 | 322,908 |
| Emp. | 189 | 177 | 159 |

DUNS 29-538-3434

## Sweet Homes Ltd

28 Salisbury Road, Carshalton, Surrey SM5 3HD
**Tel:** 02086692592
**Web:** www.sweethomesltd.com
**Reg No:** 1905197 **Estd:** 1885 Private Limited Company
**Line of Business:** Nursing homes
**Trading Style:** Carshalton Nursing Home
**Issued Capital:** £100,000
**Directors:** Mrs P Joshi, A K Joshi
**Responsibilities**
**Senior:** Sudhir Jatania *(Manager)*, Anu Joshi *(Proprietor)*
**US SIC:** 8051 **UK SIC:** 95100

| | 31-03-14 | 31-03-13 | 31-03-12 |
|---|---|---|---|
| TA | 748,889 | 759,266 | 717,515 |
| NW | 251,156 | 227,195 | 195,358 |
| WC | (256,656) | (282,894) | (328,569) |

DUNS 50-378-1338

## Sweet Ventures Ltd

12 Bow Lane, London EC4M 9AL
**Tel:** 02073298988
**Web:** www.sweetpotato.co.uk
**Reg No:** 2387211 **Estd:** 1989 Private Limited Company
**Line of Business:** Other retail sale in non-specialised stores
**Trading Style:** Cards Galore, Perfect Present
**Issued Capital:** £100
**Director:** R R Shah
**Co. Secretary:** Rumit Shah
**Branches:** Sweet Ventures Ltd, 18 Devonshire Row, London EC2M 4RH
**US SIC:** 5399 **UK SIC:** 65600
**Auditors:** Ramesh Shah & Co
**Bankers:** Girobank Plc (72-00-00)

| | 31-03-14 | 31-03-13 | 31-03-12 |
|---|---|---|---|
| TO | 13,900,753 | 14,514,172 | 14,371,410 |
| P/L | 294,028 | 543,258 | 332,456 |
| NW | 1,128,484 | 925,386 | 528,051 |
| WC | 405,839 | 177,472 | (207,518) |
| Emp. | 225 | 228 | 216 |

DUNS 53-646-8382

## Sweett Group Plc

60 Gray's Inn Road, London WC1X 8AQ
**Tel:** 01752825000
**Web:** www.sweettgroup.com
**Reg No:** 3452251 **Estd:** 2012 Public Limited Company
**Line of Business:** Quantity surveyors
**Issued Capital:** £6,769,406
**Directors:** R S Mabey, D C Wilton, J Dodds, P M Sinclair, K Berry, D R Pitcher, A C Lovell
**Co. Secretary:** Philip Watt
**Responsibilities**
**Senior:** Rob Cameron *(Project Director)*, Graham Gill *(Manager)*, Martin Hadnutt *(Deputy Managing Director)*, Julian Heard *(Partner)*, Nick Jack *(Business Unit Director, Easter)*, Stuart McGee *(Regional Director)*, Nigel Mccreith *(Regional Director, Cambridge)*, Neil Mcmullen *(Regional Director)*, Tony Newberry *(Associate Director)*, Scott Ripley *(Associate Director)*
**Finance:** Christopher Goscomb *(Finance Director)*
**Marketing:** Charlotte Graimes-Goscomb *(Marketing & Proposals Manager)*, Josephine Guckian *(UK Marketing & Proposals Manag)*, Amy Hampton *(Marketing & Proposals Executiv)*, Sophie Hull *(?Head of Corporate Communicati)*, Theo Kjellberg *(Business Analysis & Communicat)*, Dima Qumsieh *(Marketing Manager)*
**IT:** Alastair Bloore *(Group Business Systems Directo)*
**HR:** Nicholas Van Dorp *(?Group Human Resources Directo)*
**Health & Safety:** Derek Sayers *(Health and Safety Manager)*
**Operations:** Paul Hollett *(Project Director)*, Alan Manuel *(Operations Director, Scotland)*, Vic Mosca *(Director, Production and Opera)*, Fergus Taylor *(Director, Project Management)*, Geoff Warke *(Joint Operations Director, Ire)*, James Wickett *(Production Manager)*
**Engineering:** Christian Oliver *(Head of Technical Due Diligenc)*

**Branches:** Sweett Group Plc, Hawarden Ho, 163 Upr Newtownards Rd, Belfast, Belfast BT4 3HZ
**US SIC:** 7397, 7392
**UK SIC:** 83702, 83951
**Auditors:** PricewaterhouseCoopers LLP
**Bankers:** Barclays Bank Plc (20-65-63)

| | 31-03-14 | 31-03-13 | 31-03-12 |
|---|---|---|---|
| TO | 89,398,000 | 80,636,000 | 72,806,000 |
| P/L | 2,826,000 | 1,775,000 | (1,021,000) |
| NW | 9,623,000 | 8,877,000 | 9,290,000 |
| WC | 14,513,000 | 10,425,000 | 4,156,000 |
| Emp. | 1,470 | 1,357 | 1,255 |

DUNS 42-399-2390
## Sweettree Home Care Services Ltd
(**Subsidiary of:** Sweettree Retirement Communities Ltd)
Coleridge House 2-3 Coleridge Gardens, London NW6 3QH
**Tel:** 020-7624-9944 **Fax:** 02076249955
**Web:** www.sweettree.co.uk
**Reg No:** 4386901 **Estd:** 2002 Private Limited Company
**Line of Business:** Home care and help services
**Issued Capital:** £1
**Director:** B J Sweetbaum
**Co. Secretary:**
St James'S Square Secretaries Li
**Responsibilities**
**Senior:** Jake Dane *(Executive)*, Magda Dyson *(Senior Manager)*, Sharon Horvath *(Executive)*
**Finance:** Abdul Ali *(Management Accountant)*, Keith Ashcroft *(Director of Finance)*, Bhanu Gorasiya *(Accountant)*
**Marketing:** Nadene Marlborough *(Communications Manager)*
**HR:** Dorota Kucala *(Human Resources Assistant)*
**Health & Safety:** Phil Bones *(facilities manager)*
**Operations:** Dela Begum *(Production and Operations Mana)*, Nicki Bones *(Director, Operations)*, Justin Burmeister *(Production and Operations Mana)*
**Engineering:** Phil Bones *(facilities manager)*
**US SIC:** 8811, 8321
**UK SIC:** 99000, 96111

| | 31-03-14 | 31-03-13 | 31-03-12 |
|---|---|---|---|
| TA | 1,751,092 | 1,439,372 | 1,359,406 |
| NW | 352,706 | 257,341 | 169,639 |
| WC | 581,240 | 323,351 | 267,473 |

DUNS 85-619-4592
## Swellfix Uk Ltd
12a Peterseat Drive, Tollgate, Chandler's Ford, Altens, Aberdeen, Aberdeenshire AB12 3HT
**Tel:** 01224896100
**Web:** www.tendeka.com
**Reg No:** 6212769 **Estd:** 2004 Private Limited Company
**Line of Business:** Service activities incidental to oil and gas extraction excluding surveying
**Directors:** G J Smart, B J Barry, A Pearson
**Co. Secretary:** Burness Paull Llp
**Responsibilities**
**Senior:** Bert Dequae *(Governor)*
**Branches:** Swellfix Uk Ltd, 12A Peterseat Drive, Aberdeen, Aberdeenshire AB12 3HT
**US SIC:** 1389 **UK SIC:** 13000
**Auditors:** PricewaterhouseCoopers LLP
**Employees:** 42
**Turnover:** £50,538,412

DUNS 73-256-6059 **Imp**
## Swemko (Uk) Ltd
29 Bonville Road, Bristol, Avon BS4 5QH
**Tel:** 08450760960 **Fax:** 01179-720470
**Web:** www.swemkoknife.com
**Reg No:** 4530324 **Estd:** 1994 Private Limited Company
**Line of Business:** Manufacturers of tools
**Issued Capital:** £1,000,199
**Director:** D J Medd
**Co. Secretary:** Ms Tammy Medd
**Responsibilities**
**Senior:** Julie Limbrick *(Manager)*, Steve Medd *(Manager)*, Raymond Medd *(Manager)*
**Finance:** Christopher Pillinger *(Financial Director)*
**Branches:** Swemko (Uk) Ltd, Rich Industrial Estate, Crimscott Street, London SE1 5TE
**US SIC:** 3423 **UK SIC:** 31612

| | 30-09-13 | 30-09-12 | 30-09-11 |
|---|---|---|---|
| TA | 877,540 | 850,583 | 1,034,035 |
| NW | 276,177 | 269,128 | 270,560 |
| WC | 131,616 | 147,833 | 134,649 |

DUNS 28-861-1924
## Swettenham Stud
(**Subsidiary of:** Sangster Group Ltd)
Manton House Estate, Marlborough, Wiltshire SN8 1PN
**Tel:** 01672-514905
**Web:** www.swettenham.com
**Reg No:** 0894186 **Estd:** 1966 Private Unlimited Company
**Line of Business:** Farming of sheep, goats, horses, asses, mules and hinnies
**Issued Capital:** £63,000,100
**Directors:** G E Sangster, B V Sangster
**Co. Secretary:** David Mccormick
**US SIC:** 0214, 7999
**UK SIC:** 01001, 97913
**Auditors:** PricewaterhouseCoopers
**Bankers:** National Westminster Bank Plc (01-10-01)

| | 31-01-13 | 31-01-12 | 31-01-11 |
|---|---|---|---|
| TO | 7,001,000 | 3,774,000 | 4,453,000 |
| P/L | (1,761,000) | (909,000) | 69,000 |
| NW | 45,469,000 | 39,713,000 | 40,813,000 |
| WC | 20,867,000 | 22,374,000 | 23,294,000 |
| Emp. | 67 | 67 | 74 |

DUNS 21-032-9687
## SwG3
100 Eastvale Place, Glasgow, Lanarkshire G3 8QG
**Tel:** 0141-357-7246
**Web:** www.swg3.tv
**Estd:** 2006 Proprietorship
**Line of Business:** Aerial photographers & surveys
**Proprietor:** A Brown
**US SIC:** 7333 **UK SIC:** 83953
**Employees:** 150

DUNS 21-390-5063
## Swgr
Unit 2, Carlisle, Cumbria CA1 2PS
**Tel:** 01228-818858
**Web:** www.sw-gr.com
**Estd:** 2009 Proprietorship
**Line of Business:** Public works contractors
**Proprietor:** P Cook
**Responsibilities**
**Senior:** Joe Carroll *(Regional Manager)*, Tony Hope *(Resource Manager)*
**US SIC:** 1522 **UK SIC:** 50100
**Employees:** 800

DUNS 71-897-1802
## Swietelsky Construction Co Ltd
Holybrook House, 63 Castle Street, Reading, Berkshire RG1 7SN
**Tel:** 01189-503380
**Web:** www.swietelsky.at
**Reg No:** 5279323 **Estd:** 2004 Private Limited Company
**Line of Business:** Construction of motorways, roads, railways, airfields and sports facilities
**Issued Capital:** £100,000
**Directors:** C S Goldie, G C Skalla
**Co. Secretary:** John Jenkins
**US SIC:** 1611 **UK SIC:** 50200

| | 31-03-14 | 31-03-13 | 31-03-12 |
|---|---|---|---|
| TO | 9,301,169 | 8,763,569 | 8,925,287 |
| P/L | 1,016,357 | 1,068,845 | 1,209,391 |
| NW | 2,171,672 | 3,179,917 | 2,375,753 |
| WC | 2,185,127 | 3,106,552 | 2,326,241 |
| Emp. | 47 | 37 | 34 |

DUNS 77-915-5857
## Swift Alarms Group Ltd
2 Crown Yard, Bedgebury Road, Goudhurst, Cranbrook, Kent TN17 2QZ
**Tel:** 08700424212
**Web:** www.swiftalarms.com
**Reg No:** 5818770 **Estd:** 2000 Private Limited Company
**Line of Business:** Management activities of other non-financial holding companies not elsewhere classified
**Issued Capital:** £15,000
**Director:** A J Smith
**Responsibilities**
**Senior:** Paul Grist *(Director)*, Roger Rawlings *(Director)*
**US SIC:** 6711, 1796, 7393
**UK SIC:** 83962, 50400, 83954
**Auditors:** Lindeyer Francis Ferguson

| | 30-09-13 | 30-09-12 | 30-09-11 |
|---|---|---|---|
| TO | 7,644,061 | N/A | N/A |
| P/L | (356,579) | N/A | N/A |
| NW | (1,053,515) | 1,205,756 | 503,742 |
| WC | (589,068) | (881,847) | (407,268) |
| Emp. | 61 | N/A | N/A |

DUNS 77-095-0681
## Swift Brickwork Contractors Ltd
Beehive Lane, Chelmsford, Essex CM2 9RX
**Tel:** 01245255000
**Web:** www.swiftbrickwork.com
**Reg No:** 2675963 **VAT No:** 609869294
**Estd:** 1992 Private Limited Company
**Line of Business:** Construction of commercial buildings
**Trading Style:** Swift Project Services, Swift Scaffolding
**Issued Capital:** £1,000
**Principals:** M Walsh *(Managing)*, N A Moye
**Co. Secretary:** Michael Walsh
**Responsibilities**
**Finance:** Sonia Fisher *(Financial Director)*
**Admin:** Nina Joel *(Receptionist)*
**Health & Safety:** Dick Peek *(Health & Safety Officer)*
**Branches:** Swift Brickwork Contractors Ltd, 3 Cable Court, Pittman Way, Preston, Lancashire PR2 9YW
**US SIC:** 1541, 1522
**UK SIC:** 50100
**Auditors:** Bird Luckin Ltd
**Bankers:** Lloyds TSB Bank plc (30-15-19)

| | 31-05-13 | 31-05-12 | 31-05-11 |
|---|---|---|---|
| TO | 21,297,864 | 16,992,364 | 14,133,518 |
| P/L | 330,649 | (123,190) | 125,378 |
| NW | 6,664,286 | 6,974,222 | 7,034,178 |
| WC | 1,724,546 | 3,152,767 | 4,289,458 |
| Emp. | 130 | 105 | 89 |

DUNS 21-500-0101
## Swift Car & Couriers
3a Winchmore Hill Road Dennis Parade, London N14 6AA
**Tel:** 02088865000
**Estd:** 2002
**Line of Business:** Taxis
**Proprietor:** S Stylianou
**US SIC:** 4121 **UK SIC:** 72200
**Employees:** 50

DUNS 57-045-3936
## Swift Dental Laboratory Ltd
Robert Street, Atherton, Manchester M46 9AS
**Tel:** 08700467000 **Fax:** 01942887404
**Web:** www.swiftdental.co.uk
**Reg No:** 2878530 **Estd:** 1980 Private Limited Company
**Line of Business:** Dental technicians
**Issued Capital:** £1,000
**Directors:** Ms S Mcgillivray, Ms J A Stevenson, M H Stevenson
**Co. Secretary:** Roy Mcgillivray
**Responsibilities**
**Senior:** Gary Halliwell *(Manager)*
**Branches:** Swift Dental Laboratory Ltd, 24 Eastern Avenue, Chase Lane, Gloucester, Gloucestershire GL4 6PH
**US SIC:** 8021 **UK SIC:** 95400
**Auditors:** Jackson Stephen

| | 31-01-14 | 31-01-13 | 31-01-12 |
|---|---|---|---|
| TA | 2,327,461 | 1,901,339 | 1,914,481 |
| NW | 1,656 | (241,993) | (267,249) |
| WC | (2,504) | (266,913) | (283,824) |

DUNS 23-241-5687
## Swift Electrical Wholesalers (S-o-T) Ltd
P O Box 141, Stoke-On-Trent, Staffordshire ST4 1EW
**Tel:** 01782854100 **Fax:** 01782441412
**Web:** www.swiftuk.co.uk
**Reg No:** 2401639 **Estd:** 1989 Private Limited Company
**Line of Business:** Retail sale of electrical household appliances and radio and television goods
**Issued Capital:** £2
**Directors:** M J Swift, J A Swift
**Co. Secretary:** Jonathan Lawson
**Responsibilities**
**HR:** Linda Dunn *(Human Resources Administrator)*
**Health & Safety:** Linda Dunn *(Human Resources Administrator)*
**Purchasing:** Neil Mason *(Head of Purchasing)*
**US SIC:** 5732 **UK SIC:** 64800
**Auditors:** Baker Tilly

| | 31-12-13 | 31-12-12 | 31-12-11 |
|---|---|---|---|
| TO | 18,310,173 | 17,974,885 | 16,868,662 |
| P/L | 240,568 | 208,335 | 33,758 |
| NW | 2,700,751 | 2,499,414 | 2,325,212 |
| WC | 2,102,171 | 1,818,650 | 1,637,197 |
| Emp. | 65 | 65 | 65 |

DUNS 22-880-0660
## Swift Fire & Security Group Plc
(**Subsidiary of:** Elvere Ltd)
Mathew Elliot House, 64 Broadway, Salford, Lancashire M50 2TS
**Tel:** 01618724240 **Fax:** 01618-772-424
**Web:** www.swiftfireandsecurity.com
**Reg No:** 1609444 **VAT No:** 344171670
**Estd:** 1982 Public Limited Company
**Line of Business:** Security activities
**Issued Capital:** £150,000
**Principals:** N K Jackson *(Chairman)*, R E Lee, Elvere Limited, P Richardson, Miss A Withnell, P Nield
**Co. Secretary:** James Smith
**Branches:** Swift Fire & Security Group Plc, 4-5 Diamond Court, Newcastle Upon Tyne, Tyne and Wear NE3 2EN
**US SIC:** 7393, 7399
**UK SIC:** 83954
**Auditors:** Cowgill Holloway LLP
**Bankers:** The Royal Bank Of Scotland Plc (16-18-26)

| | 31-05-14 | 31-05-13 | 31-05-12 |
|---|---|---|---|
| TO | 18,886,744 | 16,641,135 | 15,729,432 |
| P/L | 929,452 | 580,725 | 24,006 |
| NW | 1,692,352 | 1,602,109 | 949,703 |
| WC | 2,466,534 | 1,599,096 | 1,219,111 |
| Emp. | 231 | 198 | 195 |

DUNS 21-018-2621
## Swift Fire & Security Ltd
(**Subsidiary of:** Elvere Ltd)
Mathew Elliot House, 64 Broadway, Salford, Lancashire M50 2TS
**Tel:** 08444130177 **Fax:** 01618772424
**Web:** www.swiftfireandsecurity.com
**Reg No:** 6400926 **Estd:** 2007 Private Limited Company
**Line of Business:** Security activities
**Issued Capital:** £100
**Directors:** P Richardson, Swift Fire And Security Group Pl, N K Jackson
**Co. Secretary:** James Smith
**US SIC:** 1731, 5999
**UK SIC:** 50300, 65600

| | 31-05-14 | 31-05-13 | 31-05-12 |
|---|---|---|---|
| TA | 100 | 100 | 100 |
| NW | 100 | 100 | 100 |

DUNS 39-757-8360
## Swift Frame Ltd
(**Subsidiary of:** Swift Group Holdings Ltd)
Calcy Close, Norwich, Norfolk NR3 2BU
**Tel:** 01603-488030 **Fax:** 01603-482514
**Web:** www.swiftframe.co.uk
**Reg No:** 2196855 **VAT No:** 595438690
**Estd:** 1986 Private Limited Company
**Line of Business:** Manufacturers of window frames
**Issued Capital:** £10,525
**Directors:** T A Rush, C Clements
**Co. Secretary:** Terence Rush
**Responsibilities**
**Senior:** David Tunnicliffe *(Manager)*
**HR:** Shane Hunter *(Factory Manager)*
**US SIC:** 3442 **UK SIC:** 31420
**Auditors:** Banham Graham
**Bankers:** National Westminster Bank Plc (60-15-31)

| | 30-04-14 | 30-04-13 | 30-04-12 |
|---|---|---|---|
| TO | 6,340,613 | 5,813,773 | 6,185,669 |
| P/L | 42,730 | (195,182) | 48,629 |
| NW | (58,350) | (7,840) | 127,986 |
| WC | 897,785 | 798,118 | 1,206,192 |
| Emp. | 70 | 69 | 71 |

DUNS 21-290-2639 **Exp**
## Swift Group Ltd
(**Subsidiary of:** Swift Acquisitions Ltd)
Dunswell Road, Cottingham, North Humberside HU16 4JS
**Tel:** 01482847332 **Fax:** 01482841042
**Web:** www.swifttv.co.uk
**Reg No:** 0832994 **VAT No:** 167411467
**Estd:** 1965 Private Limited Company
**Line of Business:** Manufacturers and dealers of caravans
**Export Markets:** W Europe
**Export Sales:** £12,483,699
**Issued Capital:** £100,000
**Directors:** N J Page, C Milburn, J Turner, A Spacey, G Artley, Ms A Archer, G Raper
**Co. Secretary:** Gordon Artley
**Responsibilities**
**Senior:** Keith Brayshaw *(Manager)*
**US SIC:** 3792 **UK SIC:** 35230
**Auditors:** Ernst & Young LLP
**Bankers:** HSBC Bank plc (40-25-18)

| | 31-08-14 | 31-08-13 | 31-08-12 |
|---|---|---|---|
| TO | 199,812,429 | 186,418,000 | 189,336,000 |
| P/L | 8,235,371 | 8,026,000 | 5,431,000 |
| NW | 16,957,704 | 11,423,000 | 27,443,000 |
| WC | 19,940,775 | 12,712,000 | 29,546,000 |
| Emp. | 861 | 820 | 802 |

DUNS 21-152-3121
## Swift Office Cleaning Services (Hounslow) Ltd
439a Great West Road, Hounslow, Middlesex TW5 0BY
**Tel:** 02085773200 **Fax:** 020-8814-0849
**Web:** www.swift-cleaning.co.uk
**Reg No:** 0893357 **Estd:** 2002 Private Limited Company
**Line of Business:** Commercial premises cleaning

**Issued Capital:** £5,200
**Principals:** J S Wright *(Managing)*, D Gazdic
**Co. Secretary:** Kerrin Wright
**Responsibilities**
**Senior:** Danny Gazdic *(Manager)*
**US SIC:** 7349 **UK SIC:** 92300
**Auditors:** Goodman Jones
**Bankers:** National Westminster Bank Plc (60-07-10)

| | 31-08-13 | 31-08-12 | 31-08-11 |
|---|---|---|---|
| TA | 979,685 | 997,811 | 1,020,159 |
| NW | 760,583 | 807,276 | 788,611 |
| WC | 434,521 | 490,278 | 478,174 |

DUNS 49-486-8763
## Swift Research Ltd
**(Subsidiary of:** Sandmarten Holdings Ltd)
Concept House, Sandbeck Way, Wetherby, West Yorkshire LS22 7DN
**Tel:** 01937543600 **Fax:** 01937-543610
**Web:** www.swift-research.co.uk
**Reg No:** 3151774 **Estd:** 1996 Private Limited Company
**Line of Business:** Market research organisations
**Issued Capital:** £10,000
**Directors:** N J Mellor, M D Penfold, A M Flannery
**Co. Secretary:** Mrs Kathleen Penfold
**US SIC:** 7392, 7399
**UK SIC:** 83951, 83954
**Auditors:** Kilner Johnson Associates
**Bankers:** National Westminster Bank Plc (60-21-13)

| | 28-02-14 | 28-02-13 | 29-02-12 |
|---|---|---|---|
| TA | 996,247 | 1,108,723 | 1,145,108 |
| NW | 144,562 | 144,556 | 359,171 |
| WC | 154,964 | 116,170 | 133,086 |

DUNS 73-368-2962
## Swift Technical (Russia) Ltd
(Subsidiary of: Swift Technical Group Holdings Ltd)
Innova House Innova Business, Park Kinetic Crescent, Enfield, Middlesex EN3 7XH
**Tel:** 01992704900
**Reg No:** 4641797 **Estd:** 2003 Private Limited Company
**Line of Business:** Labour recruitment and provision of personnel
**Issued Capital:** £100
**Directors:** J H Read, J G Dymott, Miss L Katunina
**US SIC:** 7361 **UK SIC:** 83954
**Auditors:** Higgisons
**Bankers:** The Royal Bank Of Scotland Plc (16-00-35)

| | 31-12-13 | 31-12-12 | 31-12-11 |
|---|---|---|---|
| TO | 14,639,000 | 16,664,000 | 19,278,442 |
| P/L | 60,000 | (34,000) | 1,538,009 |
| NW | (152,000) | (139,000) | (104,961) |
| WC | (175,000) | (149,000) | (117,163) |
| Emp. | 47 | 47 | 50 |

DUNS 50-410-5271 **Imp**
## Swiftbase International Ltd
**(Subsidiary of:** Swiftbase Collective Ltd)
Badger Banks, Harpsden, Henley-On-Thames, Oxfordshire RG9 4HL
**Tel:** 01491-410913
**Web:** www.theclimate.co.uk
**Reg No:** 2407639 **VAT No:** 537835122
**Estd:** 1989 Private Limited Company
**Line of Business:** Other software consultancy and supply
**Issued Capital:** £100
**Principals:** R E Fiander *(Managing)*, Mrs L Fiander
**Co. Secretary:** Robert Fiander
**US SIC:** 7379, 5065
**UK SIC:** 83940, 61500
**Bankers:** National Westminster Bank Plc (60-10-35)

| | 31-10-13 | 31-10-12 | 31-10-11 |
|---|---|---|---|
| TA | 1,413,782 | 841,051 | 282,201 |
| NW | 65,485 | 462,352 | 23,683 |
| WC | 15,715 | 411,366 | 9,701 |

DUNS 23-637-3242 **Imp**
## Swiftool Precision Engineering Ltd
Brookside Way, Sutton-In-Ashfield, Nottinghamshire NG17 2NL
**Tel:** 01623-515544
**Web:** www.swiftool.co.uk
**Reg No:** 3634212 **Estd:** 1998 Private Limited Company
**Line of Business:** Precision engineers
**Issued Capital:** £200
**Director:** S J Handley
**Co. Secretary:** Peter Handley
**US SIC:** 8911 **UK SIC:** 83701
**Auditors:** Charnwood Accountants & Business Advisors LLP

| | 30-09-13 | 30-09-12 | 30-09-11 |
|---|---|---|---|
| TO | 6,509,891 | 4,571,908 | 3,358,001 |
| P/L | 413,502 | 382,508 | (101,814) |
| NW | 1,053,819 | 806,759 | 622,146 |
| WC | (75,212) | (165,166) | (166,897) |
| Emp. | 76 | 71 | 50 |

DUNS 73-783-4627 **Imp-Exp**
## Swiftpack Automation Ltd
**(Subsidiary of:** Lopam Fin Spa)
3 Arden Road, Alcester, Warwickshire B49 6HN
**Tel:** 01789-400880
**Web:** www.ima.it
**Reg No:** 5040173 **Estd:** 2004 Private Limited Company
**Line of Business:** Packaging equipment
**Export Sales:** £8,926,667
**Issued Capital:** £500,000
**Directors:** P Tampieri, A Malagoli, S Marzo, D J O'Neil
**Co. Secretary:** David Worton
**Responsibilities**
**Senior:** Wendy Shirmpton *(Shipping Controller)*
**Health & Safety:** Kevin Cokayne *(Production Manager)*
**Facilities:** Kevin Cokayne *(Production Manager)*
**Engineering:** Kevin Cokayne *(Production Manager)*
**US SIC:** 3551 **UK SIC:** 32441
**Auditors:** Horwath Clark Whitehill LLP

| | 31-12-13 | 31-12-12 | 31-12-11 |
|---|---|---|---|
| TO | 9,405,284 | 9,362,502 | 10,238,614 |
| P/L | 2,007,660 | 2,371,927 | 2,865,490 |
| NW | 3,944,184 | 4,302,003 | 4,409,732 |
| WC | 3,920,879 | 4,271,727 | 4,374,547 |
| Emp. | 54 | 55 | 52 |

DUNS 76-870-2862
## Swift's Holdings Ltd
Unit 1/9 Stanley Mill Kirkebrok Road, Bolton, Lancashire BL3 4JE
**Tel:** 01204659606
**Web:** www.circuit-tele.com
**Reg No:** 2613822 **Estd:** 1991 Private Limited Company
**Line of Business:** Holding companies management activities
**Issued Capital:** £2
**Principals:** S P Swift *(Managing)*, Mrs E Swift, Mrs E D Gilmore
**Co. Secretary:** Mrs Elaine Swift
**US SIC:** 6711, 7629
**UK SIC:** 83962, 67301
**Auditors:** Ryans
**Bankers:** Yorkshire Bank Plc (05-02-77)

| | 31-03-14 | 31-03-13 | 31-03-12 |
|---|---|---|---|
| TA | 730,875 | 954,082 | 851,100 |
| NW | 432,506 | 436,688 | 436,277 |
| WC | (181,397) | (196,985) | (37,132) |

DUNS 73-980-7092
## Swiis Foster Care Scotland Ltd
Glenlevan House Carnegie Campus South, Enterprise Way, Inverkeithing, Fife KY11 8PY
**Tel:** 01383-842284 **Fax:** 01383842288
**Web:** www.swiisfostercare.co.uk
**Reg No:** 0273400SC **Estd:** 2004 Private Company Limited By Guarantee
**Line of Business:** Adoption and fostering services
**Director:** T Notchell
**Responsibilities**
**Senior:** Sam Arnott *(Assistant Director)*, Louise Findlay *(Manager)*, Marion Geddes *(Manager)*
**Admin:** Maxine Smith *(Administrator)*
**US SIC:** 8321 **UK SIC:** 96111

| | 30-09-13 | 30-09-12 | 30-09-11 |
|---|---|---|---|
| TO | 11,574,568 | 11,193,896 | 10,600,385 |
| P/L | 316,478 | 160,795 | 207,799 |
| NW | 717,936 | 475,395 | 346,025 |
| WC | 663,681 | 417,821 | 305,134 |
| Emp. | 71 | 83 | 74 |

DUNS 64-096-3521
## Swiis International Ltd
Connaught House, London W1G 9RE
**Tel:** 02032192850 **Fax:** 02073078384
**Web:** www.swiis.com
**Reg No:** 4499819 **Estd:** 2002 Private Limited Company
**Line of Business:** Employment and recruitment companies and consultants
**Issued Capital:** £50,004
**Director:** T Notchell
**Co. Secretary:** Oliver Webber
**Responsibilities**
**Senior:** Dev Dadral *(Proprietor)*, Balvir Dadral *(Manager)*
**Branches:** Swiis International Ltd, Royal Buildings, 2 Mosley Street, Manchester M2 3AN
**US SIC:** 7361 **UK SIC:** 83954
**Auditors:** MacIntyre Hudson LLP

| | 30-09-13 | 30-09-12 | 30-09-11 |
|---|---|---|---|
| TO | 35,555,966 | 37,870,127 | 39,279,656 |
| P/L | 1,825,901 | 797,125 | 2,074,699 |
| NW | 3,081,245 | 2,663,949 | 2,126,285 |
| WC | 1,439,435 | 1,186,417 | 762,699 |
| Emp. | 222 | 265 | 257 |

DUNS 22-780-2667 **Imp**
## The Swimming Teachers Association Ltd
Anchor House, Birch Street, Walsall, West Midlands WS2 8HZ
**Fax:** 01922720628
**Web:** www.sta.co.uk
**Reg No:** 1272519 **Estd:** 1976 Private Company Limited By Guarantee
**Line of Business:** Sports coaching
**Export Sales:** £44,930
**Directors:** R Timms, Ms J C O'Sullivan, Mrs M C Robinson, H M Hall, D J Candler, R Phillips
**Co. Secretary:** Anthony Harvey
**Responsibilities**
**Senior:** Roger Millward *(Chief Executive Officer)*, Lynne Pritchard *(Course Department Manager)*
**Finance:** Zoe Cooper *(Head of Accounts)*, Stuart Tanfield *(Head of Finance)*
**Sales:** Rachel Dean *(Sales Manager)*, Leanne Husselbee *(Account Manager)*
**IT:** Brett Preston *(Head of IT)*
**HR:** Gary Seghers *(Qualifications Development Man)*
**Operations:** Claire Brisbourne *(Head of Product Services)*, Theo Millward *(Operations Director)*
**Engineering:** Richard Lamburn *(Technical Manager)*
**Branches:** The Swimming Teachers Association Ltd, 4 Firfields, Antrim, Co Antrim BT41 4DJ
**US SIC:** 7999, 8621
**UK SIC:** 97913, 96311
**Auditors:** R A Lea & Co
**Bankers:** National Westminster Bank Plc (01-09-31)

| | 31-05-14 | 31-05-13 | 31-05-12 |
|---|---|---|---|
| TO | 2,231,982 | 2,162,706 | 1,966,196 |
| P/L | 3,695 | 19,061 | 5,256 |
| NW | 970,260 | 966,436 | 926,610 |
| WC | 343,194 | 402,970 | 380,103 |
| Emp. | 51 | 48 | 48 |

DUNS 22-841-9495
## Swindells & Gentrey
New Olives, High Street, Uckfield, East Sussex TN22 1QE
**Web:** www.swindellsandgentry.co.uk
**Estd:** 1930 Partnership
**Line of Business:** Chartered accountants
**Partners:** J Terry, R Thompson, J Sweeney, J Fackler, P Moorey, I Jenkins, P Gale, A Hussey
**Branches:** Swindells & Gentrey, 20-21 Clinton Place, Seaford, East Sussex BN25 1NP
**US SIC:** 8931 **UK SIC:** 83600
**Employees:** 50

DUNS 21-122-3385
## Swindon Academy
Beech Avenue, Swindon, Wiltshire SN2 1JR
**Tel:** 01793426900
**Web:** www.swindon-academy.org
**Estd:** 2010
**Line of Business:** Schools (independent)
**Director:** Miss J Shadick
**Responsibilities**
**Senior:** Ruth Robinson *(Principal)*
**Finance:** Lynn Fletcher *(Business Manager)*
**IT:** Bev Sismey *(Computer Manager)*
**HR:** Elizabeith Page *(Human)*, Julie Ringrose *(Human Resources Manager)*
**Health & Safety:** Lynn Fletcher *(Business Manager)*
**Facilities:** Sheila Pike *(Facilities Manager)*
**US SIC:** 8211 **UK SIC:** 93200
**Employees:** 70

DUNS 21-040-7429
## Swindon Audi
Welton Road, Swindon, Wiltshire SN5 7XG
**Tel:** 01793777700
**Web:** www.inchcapeaudi.co.uk
**Estd:** 1998
**Line of Business:** Car dealers (new & used)
**Proprietor:** H Jessup
**Responsibilities**
**Senior:** Bob McGarver *(General Manager)*, Craig Strike *(General Manager)*
**Finance:** Alex Hills *(Financial Manager)*
**Facilities:** phil gadsby *(After Sales Manager)*
**Operations:** phil gadsby *(After Sales Manager)*
**US SIC:** 5511 **UK SIC:** 65100
**Employees:** 75

DUNS 21-127-8007 **Imp**
## Swindon Borough Council
Civic Offices, Euclid Street, Swindon, Wiltshire SN1 2JH
**Tel:** 01793463000
**Web:** www.swindon.gov.uk
**Estd:** 2002
**Line of Business:** Local government
**Trading Style:** Link Centre, Upland School, Oakhurst Community Primary School
**Principals:** I Thompson *(Financial)*, P Doherty
**Responsibilities**
**Senior:** Amanda Garnham *(Assessment Centre Manager)*, Peter Giles *(Team Leader)*, Peter Maksymuk *(Manager)*, Liz Matthews *(Manager)*, Sandra Pinnegar *(Proprietor)*, Anne Snelgrove *(Member)*, Ian Tuck *(Executive)*
**Marketing:** Sally Burnett *(Strategy & Development Manager)*
**Operations:** Martin Rowbotham *(Sales Manager)*
**Branches:** Swindon Borough Council, County Ground, County Road, Swindon, Wiltshire SN1 2ED
**US SIC:** 9121 **UK SIC:** 91110
**Employees:** 7,500

DUNS 73-457-7500
## Swindon Caravan Centre Ltd
Swindon Caravan Centre, Swindon, Wiltshire SN4 8EQ
**Tel:** 01793-772096
**Web:** www.swindoncaravans.com
**Reg No:** 4721969 **Estd:** 1988 Private Limited Company
**Line of Business:** Other retail sale in specialised stores not elsewhere classified
**Issued Capital:** £100
**Director:** Ms J Collister
**Co. Secretary:** Guy Collister
**Responsibilities**
**Senior:** Tom Collister *(General Manager)*
**US SIC:** 5511, 7519
**UK SIC:** 65100, 84804

| | 31-03-14 | 31-03-13 | 31-03-12 |
|---|---|---|---|
| TO | 17,274,434 | 13,101,621 | 14,824,067 |
| P/L | 478,996 | 239,942 | 330,565 |
| NW | 686,446 | 361,181 | 296,738 |
| WC | 435,262 | 200,550 | 142,156 |
| Emp. | 63 | 61 | 61 |

DUNS 23-635-7307
## Swindon College
North Star Avenue, Swindon, Wiltshire SN2 1DY
**Tel:** 01793491591
**Web:** www.swindon-college.ac.uk
**VAT No:** 618141753 **Estd:** 1950
**Line of Business:** Pre school education
**Principals:** J Swift *(Financial)*, Dr S Griffiths
**Responsibilities**
**Senior:** Kelly Stoneham *(Nursery Manager)*, Roger Whitfield *(General Manager)*
**Finance:** Karl Dorling *(Payroll Manager)*
**IT:** Philip Chaston *(Technical Analysis)*
**HR:** Penny Page *(HR Manager)*
**Health & Safety:** Meryl Hamilton *(Health & Safety Officer)*
**Branches:** Swindon College, Baileys Court, Webbs Wood Road, Bristol, Avon BS32 8EJ
**US SIC:** 8221 **UK SIC:** 93100
**Bankers:** HSBC Bank plc (40-43-34)
**Employees:** 800

DUNS 21-812-1534
## Swindon Garden Centre
Hyde Road, Swindon, Wiltshire SN2 7SE
**Tel:** 08442885112
**Web:** www.thegardencentregroup.co.uk
**Estd:** 2004
**Line of Business:** Garden centres
**Responsibilities**
**Senior:** Lewis Fox *(Store Manager)*
**US SIC:** 5999 **UK SIC:** 65600
**Employees:** 50

DUNS 23-961-8486
## Swindon Pressings Ltd
**(Subsidiary of:** Bayerische Motoren Werke Ag)
Bridge End Road, Swindon, Wiltshire SN3 4PE
**Web:** www.bmwgroup.com
**Reg No:** 3950873 **Estd:** 2000 Private Limited Company
**Line of Business:** Manufacturers of car interiors
**Issued Capital:** £1,500,002
**Directors:** F J Bachmann, J P Stoyle
**Co. Secretary:** Ms Gillian Woolley
**Responsibilities**
**Senior:** Chris Mark *(Manager)*
**Branches:** Swindon Pressings Ltd, Saltley Business Park, Cumbria Way, Saltley, Birmingham, West Midlands B8 1BH
**US SIC:** 3714 **UK SIC:** 35300
**Auditors:** KPMG LLP

| | 31-12-13 | 31-12-12 | 31-12-11 |
|---|---|---|---|
| TO | 151,532,000 | 157,467,000 | 154,371,000 |
| P/L | 7,535,000 | 5,709,000 | 13,195,000 |
| NW | 87,145,000 | 80,480,000 | 77,020,000 |
| WC | 52,258,000 | 41,293,000 | 15,987,000 |
| Emp. | 775 | 758 | 794 |

DUNS 23-293-5572
## Swindon Primary Care Trust
North Swindon District Centre, Swindon, Wiltshire SN25 2HH
**Tel:** 01793-708700 **Fax:** 01793-708701
**Web:** www.swindonpct.nhs.uk
**Incorporate By Act Of Parliament**
**Line of Business:** Social work activities
**Trading Style:** Swindon Pct
**Issued Capital:** £1
**Principals:** Ms M Howard *(Chairman)*, D Wren, I James, M Barnes, D Bignell
**Responsibilities**
**Senior:** Paul Bearman *(Executive Director)*
**Finance:** Tony Ranzetta *(Accountable Officer)*
**Branches:** Swindon Primary Care Trust, Guildford Avenue, Swindon, Wiltshire SN3 1JL
**US SIC:** 6732 **UK SIC:** 83100
**Employees:** 80

DUNS 21-772-9744
## Swingate Infant School
Sultan Road, Chatham, Kent ME5 8TJ
**Tel:** 01634863778
**Web:** www.swingate.medway.sch.uk
**Estd:** 1968 Partnership
**Line of Business:** Schools (local authority)
**Partner:** Miss K Boon
**US SIC:** 8211 **UK SIC:** 93200
**Employees:** 50

DUNS 42-407-2630
## Swinton Hall Nursing Home Ltd
(**Subsidiary of:** Ampersand Care Ltd)
188-190 Worsley Road, Manchester M27 5SN
**Tel:** 01617942236 **Fax:** 0161-281-6341
**Reg No:** 4394913 **Estd:** 2002 Private Limited Company
**Line of Business:** Nursing homes
**Issued Capital:** £3,000
**Directors:** Dr J Patel, J Patel, R Patel
**Co. Secretary:** Arvind Vashisht
**Responsibilities**
**Senior:** Umi Barwell *(Manager)*, Shirley Lawton *(matron)*
**Health & Safety:** Shirley Lawton *(matron)*
**Facilities:** Shirley Lawton *(matron)*
**US SIC:** 8051, 8091
**UK SIC:** 95100, 95200

| | 31-03-14 | 31-03-13 | 30-03-12 |
|---|---|---|---|
| TA | 1,177,793 | 1,217,394 | 1,314,317 |
| NW | 712,822 | 603,241 | 584,359 |
| WC | (144,974) | (50,541) | (3,720) |

DUNS 28-973-0913
## Swinton (Holdings) Ltd
(**Subsidiary of:** Covea)
Swinton House, Manchester M1 5SW
**Tel:** 01612361222 **Fax:** 01612363810
**Web:** www.swinton.co.uk
**Reg No:** 1741892 **Estd:** 1983 Private Limited Company
**Line of Business:** Insurance services
**Trading Style:** Swinton Insurance, Swinton Group Ltd
**Issued Capital:** £23,059,399
**Directors:** P P Forget, B Lefebvre, G J Mclarnon, D Salvy, G Normand, C C Plumer
**Co. Secretary:** Ms Annabel Wilson
**Responsibilities**
**HR:** Donna Winrow *(Human Resources Director)*
**Branches:** Swinton (Holdings) Ltd, 45 Lichfield Rd, Wolverhampton, West Midlands WV11 1TW
**US SIC:** 6411 **UK SIC:** 83200
**Auditors:** Ernst & Young LLP
**Bankers:** HSBC Bank plc (40-02-50)

| | 31-12-13 | 31-12-12 | 31-12-11 |
|---|---|---|---|
| TO | 304,768,000 | 301,584,000 | 329,295,000 |
| P/L | 23,216,000 | 25,003,000 | 50,665,000 |
| NW | 98,658,000 | 82,467,000 | 73,911,000 |
| WC | 78,510,000 | 36,988,000 | 32,271,000 |
| Emp. | 4,260 | 4,554 | 4,561 |

DUNS 23-980-9333
## Swinton Park Ltd
Swinton Park, Ripon, North Yorkshire HG4 4JH
**Tel:** 01765-680900
**Web:** www.swintonpark.com
**Reg No:** 3969380 **Estd:** 2001 Private Limited Company
**Line of Business:** Hotels and motels without restaurant
**Issued Capital:** £500,000
**Principals:** M W Cunliffe-Lister *(Financial)*, The Honourable E S Cunliffe-Lister
**Co. Secretary:** Ms Felicity Cunliffe-Lister
**US SIC:** 7011 **UK SIC:** 66500
**Auditors:** CFW

**Bankers:** HSBC Bank plc (40-32-09)

| | 31-01-14 | 31-01-13 | 31-01-12 |
|---|---|---|---|
| TO | 3,038,307 | 3,039,998 | 2,909,550 |
| P/L | 214,968 | 257,725 | 155,908 |
| NW | 1,067,049 | 885,200 | 627,475 |
| WC | (551,030) | (536,090) | (669,141) |
| Emp. | 95 | 95 | 95 |

DUNS 73-476-7192 **Imp**
## Swire Oilfield Services Ltd
(**Subsidiary of:** John Swire & Sons Ltd)
Swire House, Souter Head Road, Altens Industrial Estate, Aberdeen, Aberdeenshire AB12 3LF
**Tel:** 01224-872-707
**Web:** www.swireos.com
**Reg No:** 4740627 **Estd:** 2005 Private Limited Company
**Line of Business:** Freight transport by road not elsewhere classified
**Export Sales:** £5,378,000
**Issued Capital:** £4,300,000
**Directors:** M King, T Helgeland, R L Sell, R Burrell, Mrs S J Davie
**Co. Secretary:** Ms Brenda Kelly
**Branches:** Swire Oilfield Services Ltd, Swire House, Souter Head Road, Aberdeen, Aberdeenshire AB12 3LF
**US SIC:** 4213 **UK SIC:** 72300
**Auditors:** KPMG LLP

| | 31-12-13 | 31-12-12 | 31-12-11 |
|---|---|---|---|
| TO | 33,747,000 | 31,344,000 | 32,141,000 |
| P/L | 941,000 | (346,000) | 2,836,000 |
| NW | 5,288,000 | 5,887,000 | 6,959,000 |
| WC | 844,000 | 2,908,000 | 5,618,000 |
| Emp. | 201 | 187 | 171 |

DUNS 21-414-1005
## Swish Building Products
Pioneer House, Tamworth, Staffordshire B79 7TF
**Web:** www.swishbp.co.uk
**VAT No:** 668461107 **Estd:** 1989 Proprietorship
**Line of Business:** Plastic extruders
**Partners:** S Hanrahan, Mrs A Horne, D Matschullat
**Responsibilities**
**Senior:** Greg Wilde *(Marketing Manager)*
**Finance:** Martin Gunn *(Financial Controller)*, Diane Lichfield *(Accounting Clerk)*
**Marketing:** Greg Wilde *(Marketing Manager)*
**Admin:** Sue Patrick *(Computer Operations Manager)*
**IT:** Sue Patrick *(Computer Operations Manager)*
**Operations:** Sue Patrick *(Computer Operations Manager)*
**US SIC:** 3079 **UK SIC:** 48360
**Employees:** 111

DUNS 21-706-5590
## Swiss & Global Asset Management (Luxembourg) Sa
(**Subsidiary of:** Gam Holding Ag)
12 St James's Place, London SW1A 1NX
**Tel:** 02071668101
**Web:** www.swissglobal-am.co.uk
**Reg No:** 0029719FC **Estd:** 2010 Foreign Company
**Line of Business:** Fund management activities
**Directors:** Ms C Rion, M A Porro, P Wahle, K A Rumbelow, Ms M M Williams, Ms P E Esser-Dannhauer, M F Malpas, Ms S C Clement
**Co. Secretary:** Ewald Hamlescher
**Responsibilities**
**Senior:** Dietmar Braun *(Director)*, Christelle Dechamps *(Manager)*, Simone Grosdidier *(Manager)*, Carsten Huber *(Director)*, Martin Jufer *(Director)*, Yvon Lauret *(Director)*, David Solo *(Chief Executive)*, Melanie Ternite *(Director)*, Hugo Wheeler *(Director)*, Stephan Wiele *(Director)*
**US SIC:** 6371 **UK SIC:** 82002

DUNS 50-635-7917
## Swiss Cottage Leisure Centre
Swiss Cottage Sports Centre, Adelaide Road, London NW3 3NF
**Tel:** 02079745440
**Web:** www.camdenswimming.co.uk
**Estd:** 2011 Proprietorship
**Line of Business:** Sports coaching
**Proprietor:** D Hobbs
**Responsibilities**
**Senior:** Tim Hartley *(Head Coach)*
**US SIC:** 7999 **UK SIC:** 97913
**Employees:** 80

DUNS 21-205-6910
## Swiss Cottage Nursing Home
Plantation Road, Leighton Buzzard, Bedfordshire LU7 3JF
**Tel:** 01525-377922
**Web:** www.sevencrosshealthcare.co.uk
**Estd:** 1996 Partnership

**Line of Business:** Medical nursing home activities
**Partners:** Mrs J Acres, Mrs S Munyuki
**Responsibilities**
**Senior:** Nancy Mothojakan *(Acting Home Manager)*, Jan Sillitoe *(Manager)*
**US SIC:** 8051 **UK SIC:** 95100
**Employees:** 75

DUNS 21-808-4309
## The Swiss Laundry Ltd
149 Cherry Hinton Road, Cambridge, Cambridgeshire CB1 7BY
**Tel:** 01223247513
**Web:** www.swisslaundry.co.uk
**Reg No:** 0206893 **VAT No:** 213498857
**Estd:** 1925 Private Limited Company
**Line of Business:** Laundries
**Trading Style:** Swiss Conection
**Issued Capital:** £100,000
**Principals:** Mrs M S Turvill-Smith *(Chairman)*, G J Turvill *(Managing)*, M K Turvill, J L Turvill, W S Hammill
**Co. Secretary:** Richard Turvill
**US SIC:** 7219, 7394
**UK SIC:** 98110, 84000
**Auditors:** Whitmarsh Sterland
**Bankers:** Barclays Bank Plc (20-17-19)

| | 30-06-13 | 30-06-12 | 30-06-11 |
|---|---|---|---|
| TO | 8,203,875 | 8,092,646 | 7,269,907 |
| P/L | 440,335 | 560,512 | 588,857 |
| NW | 4,844,034 | 4,576,445 | 4,171,616 |
| WC | 706,883 | 492,794 | 61,808 |
| Emp. | 202 | 196 | 184 |

DUNS 21-829-4008
## The Swiss Partnership
Scrivener Drive, Pinewood, Ipswich, Suffolk IP8 3SU
**Tel:** 01473556600
**Web:** www.suffolkone.ac.uk
**Reg No:** 7992334 **Estd:** 2012 Private Company Limited By Guarantee
**Line of Business:** General secondary education
**Directors:** Ms S Skinner, M G Brakenbury, Ms D A Pritchard, C J Turner, Ms C M Gibson, O Doran, D Sidday, C Edwards
**Co. Secretary:** Robert Dool
**Responsibilities**
**Senior:** Janet Dickson *(Director)*, Alan Whittaker *(Director)*
**US SIC:** 8211 **UK SIC:** 93200
**Employees:** 220

DUNS 64-078-8878 **Imp**
## Swiss Post Solutions Ltd
(**Subsidiary of:** Die Schweizerische Post Ag)
Northumberland House, 15 Petersham Road, Richmond, Surrey TW10 6TP
**Tel:** 08453013708 **Fax:** 02086147601
**Web:** www.swisspost.com
**Reg No:** 4482213 **Estd:** 2005 Private Limited Company
**Line of Business:** Other business activities not elsewhere classified
**Trading Style:** Mailsource
**Issued Capital:** £7,272,000
**Directors:** G Harrold, J Vollmer
**Co. Secretary:** Adam Cater
**US SIC:** 7399 **UK SIC:** 83954
**Auditors:** KPMG LLP

| | 31-12-13 | 31-12-12 | 31-12-11 |
|---|---|---|---|
| TO | 81,720,000 | 65,239,000 | 64,369,000 |
| P/L | (1,095,000) | 28,000 | 815,000 |
| NW | (7,295,000) | (215,000) | (1,636,000) |
| WC | 17,793,000 | 11,098,000 | 10,614,000 |
| Emp. | 1,962 | 1,226 | 1,243 |

DUNS 22-156-2015 **Imp**
## Swiss Re Services Ltd
(**Subsidiary of:** Swiss Re Ag)
30 St Mary Axe, London EC3A 8EP
**Web:** www.swissre.com
**Reg No:** 4174890 **Estd:** 1863 Private Limited Company
**Line of Business:** Other business activities not elsewhere classified
**Issued Capital:** £2,190,165
**Directors:** I W Haycock, R M Higginbotham, Ms N J Parton, S Jukes
**Co. Secretary:** Ms Jennifer Gandy
**US SIC:** 8999 **UK SIC:** 83954
**Auditors:** PricewaterhouseCoopers LLP

| | 31-12-13 | 31-12-12 | 31-12-11 |
|---|---|---|---|
| TO | 220,681,000 | 224,453,000 | 233,838,000 |
| P/L | 29,279,000 | 21,103,000 | 22,682,000 |
| NW | 35,077,000 | 52,204,000 | 43,813,000 |
| WC | 46,862,000 | 52,248,000 | 45,188,000 |
| Emp. | 798 | 762 | 750 |

DUNS 34-653-1783 **Imp**
## Swisslog (Uk) Ltd.
(**Subsidiary of:** Swisslog Holding Ag)
Swisslog (Uk) Ltd, Redditch, Worcestershire B98 9DW
**Tel:** 08448002752 **Fax:** 01527 551664
**Web:** www.swisslog.com
**Reg No:** 2775102 **VAT No:** 669486665
**Estd:** 1992 Private Limited Company
**Line of Business:** Control system equipment
**Export Sales:** £441,000
**Trading Style:** Swisslog
**Issued Capital:** £250,000
**Directors:** J A Sharples, C A Schwyn, A P Manship, C Mader
**Co. Secretary:** Jeffrey Adams
**Responsibilities**
**Senior:** Ray Mercer *(Head of Projects)*
**Marketing:** Emma Daniels *(Sales And Marketing Manager)*, Emma Rawlinson *(Sales And Marketing Manager)*
**Sales:** Emma Daniels *(Sales And Marketing Manager)*, Emma Rawlinson *(Sales And Marketing Manager)*
**IT:** Stuart Phippf *(It Manager)*
**Branches:** Swisslog (Uk) Ltd., Archbold Ho, Archbold Terr, Newcastle Upon Tyne, Tyne and Wear NE2 1DB
**US SIC:** 4226 **UK SIC:** 77003
**Auditors:** Ernst & Young LLP
**Bankers:** Svenska Handelsbanken Ab (publ) (40-51-62)

| | 31-12-13 | 31-12-12 | 31-12-11 |
|---|---|---|---|
| TO | 24,752,000 | 23,228,000 | 15,872,000 |
| P/L | (486,000) | 3,200,000 | 200,000 |
| NW | (5,043,000) | (4,355,000) | (6,583,000) |
| WC | (803,000) | (396,000) | (1,034,000) |
| Emp. | 116 | 105 | 95 |

DUNS 34-566-3942 **Imp**
## Swissport Cargo Services Uk Ltd
(**Subsidiary of:** Pai Partners)
Cirrus House, Bedfont Road, Stanwell, Staines, Middlesex TW19 7NL
**Tel:** 01784266260 **Fax:** 01784-266262
**Web:** www.swissport.com
**Reg No:** 2719480 **Estd:** 1994 Private Limited Company
**Line of Business:** Cargo handling
**Issued Capital:** £4,250,000
**Directors:** T Watt, N P Knudsen, P J Foster
**Co. Secretary:** Jl Nominees Two Limited
**Responsibilities**
**Senior:** David Bermingham *(Manager)*
**Sales:** Darren Beamer *(Commercial Director)*
**HR:** Lucy Cross *(HR Manager)*
**Operations:** Simon Dickerson *(Terminal Manager)*
**US SIC:** 4712 **UK SIC:** 77002
**Auditors:** PricewaterhouseCoopers LLP
**Bankers:** Barclays Bank Plc (20-72-17)

| | 31-12-13 | 31-12-12 | 31-12-11 |
|---|---|---|---|
| TO | 21,939,000 | 24,534,568 | 30,292,727 |
| P/L | (1,867,000) | (3,297,479) | (3,039,030) |
| NW | (8,965,000) | (7,036,495) | (3,635,126) |
| WC | (10,384,000) | (8,501,423) | (4,251,590) |
| Emp. | 348 | 361 | 425 |

DUNS 23-818-8242
## Swissport Ltd
(**Subsidiary of:** Pai Partners)
Rooms 10-21 Pier 3, London Gatwick Airport, Horley, Surrey RH6 0NP
**Tel:** 01293502134
**Web:** www.swissportuk.com
**Reg No:** 3810974 **Estd:** 1999 Private Limited Company
**Line of Business:** Airline related services
**Trading Style:** Groundstar
**Issued Capital:** £23,610
**Directors:** A G Lago Di Lanzos, T Watt, P J Foster
**Co. Secretary:** Jl Nominees Two Limited
**Responsibilities**
**Senior:** Juan Alvez *(Manager)*, John Batten *(Manager)*, Nigel Cadman *(Manager)*, Richard Prince *(General Manager)*
**Branches:** Swissport Ltd, Level 3 Swissport, Newcastle Upon Tyne, Tyne and Wear NE13 8BY
**US SIC:** 4582 **UK SIC:** 76400
**Auditors:** KPMG LLP
**Bankers:** Bank Of Scotland (12-09-19)

| | 31-12-13 | 31-12-12 | 31-12-11 |
|---|---|---|---|
| TO | 68,978,000 | 61,483,000 | 62,496,000 |
| P/L | (7,356,000) | (1,462,000) | 1,377,000 |
| NW | (8,820,000) | (1,464,000) | (2,000) |
| WC | (10,181,000) | (3,032,000) | (1,590,000) |
| Emp. | 2,013 | 1,911 | 1,965 |

DUNS 21-824-2121 **Imp-Exp**
## Swisstulle Uk Ltd
(**Subsidiary of:** Cwc Textil Ag)
Perry Street Works, Factory Lane, South Chard, Chard, Somerset TA20 2NR
**Tel:** 01460220312
**Web:** www.swisstulle.co.uk
**Reg No:** 0045771 **VAT No:** 116316694
**Estd:** 1900 Public Limited Company
**Line of Business:** Textile weaving
**Export Markets:** The Americas, E C Countries, Far East, Australia
**Issued Capital:** £600,000
**Directors:** A Brugger, C Hautle
**Co. Secretary:** Carl Illi
**Responsibilities**
**Sales:** Lindsey Bristow *(Manager)*

**Branches:** Swisstulle Uk Ltd, Perry Street Works, Factory Lane, Chard, Somerset TA20 2NR
**US SIC:** 2269, 2399
**UK SIC:** 43702, 45560
**Auditors:** Smith Cooper
**Bankers:** National Westminster Bank Plc (56-00-61)

| | 31-12-13 | 31-12-12 | 31-12-11 |
|---|---|---|---|
| TA | 1,667,573 | 1,683,597 | 1,676,101 |
| NW | 1,035,529 | 1,017,656 | 882,246 |
| WC | 1,051,476 | 841,411 | 802,945 |

DUNS 76-987-0957
## Switch Communications Ltd
12-16 Addiscombe Road, Croydon, Surrey CR0 0XT
**Tel:** 020-8604-0000 **Fax:** 02086645566
**Web:** www.switchcomms.co.uk
**Reg No:** 2645307 **Estd:** 1991 Private Limited Company
**Line of Business:** Telecom services
**Issued Capital:** £6,000
**Director:** D Campanaro
**Co. Secretary:** Andrew Terry
**Branches:** Switch Communications Ltd, 216 Westward Rd, Stroud, Gloucestershire GL5 4ST
**US SIC:** 4899, 1731
**UK SIC:** 79020, 50300
**Auditors:** N Harris & Co

| | 31-12-13 | 31-12-12 | 31-12-11 |
|---|---|---|---|
| TO | 8,649,575 | 6,529,107 | 6,603,790 |
| P/L | 437,944 | 118,589 | 632,569 |
| NW | (17,044) | (71,415) | 239,205 |
| WC | 1,291,401 | 1,069,014 | 1,489,133 |

DUNS 21-137-9939
## Switch Concepts Ltd
Hounsdown House, Newmans Copse Road Hounsdown Business, Park, Southampton, Hampshire SO40 9LX
**Tel:** 0333 200 1230
**Web:** www.switchconcepts.com
**Reg No:** 6706037 **Estd:** 2008 Private Limited Company
**Line of Business:** Advertising related services
**Issued Capital:** £1,010
**Directors:** T R Barnett, Mrs J D Spector, J E Spector
**Co. Secretary:** Julian Spector
**Responsibilities**
**Admin:** Amanda Golding *(Office Manager)*
**Facilities:** Amanda Golding *(Office Manager)*
**US SIC:** 7311 **UK SIC:** 83800

| | 30-04-14 | 30-04-13 | 30-04-12 |
|---|---|---|---|
| TO | 30,674,800 | N/A | N/A |
| P/L | 1,179,763 | N/A | N/A |
| NW | 1,876,308 | 923,134 | 144,386 |
| WC | 1,033,806 | 622,902 | 56,028 |
| Emp. | 68 | N/A | N/A |

DUNS 21-778-1700
## Switch International Trailers
Station Yard, Mylen Road, Andover, Hampshire SP10 3HE
**Tel:** 01264363322
**Estd:** 2011 Partnership
**Line of Business:** Freight forwarders
**Partners:** A Thomas, F Barlow, T Taylor
**US SIC:** 4712 **UK SIC:** 77002
**Employees:** 50

DUNS 21-735-7931
## Switchgear & Instrumentation Ltd
(**Subsidiary of:** Powell Industries International B.V.)
Ripley Road, Bradford, West Yorkshire BD4 7EH
**Tel:** 01274742658
**Web:** www.powellind.com
**Reg No:** 7700827 **Estd:** 1980 Private Limited Company
**Line of Business:** Fabricators
**Issued Capital:** £2
**Directors:** M E Honeycutt, D R Madison
**Co. Secretary:** Don Madison
**Responsibilities**
**Senior:** Barbara Cowell *(Manager)*, Phil Powbrill *(Finance Director)*
**Finance:** Phil Powbrill *(Finance Director)*
**US SIC:** 5084 **UK SIC:** 61490

| | 31-07-13 | 31-07-12 |
|---|---|---|
| TA | 2 | 2 |
| NW | 2 | 2 |

DUNS 21-821-6752 **Imp-Exp**
## Swizzels Matlow Ltd
Carlton House, Albion Road, High Peak, Derbyshire SK22 3HA
**Tel:** 01663744144
**Web:** www.swizzels-matlow.com
**Reg No:** 0562269 **Estd:** 1956 Private Limited Company
**Line of Business:** Manufacturers of confectionery
**Issued Capital:** £38,252
**Principals:** M N Dee *(Managing)*, T J Matlow *(Managing)*, A C Matlow, Mrs N R Wertheim, J M Dee, J A Dee, B N Dee
**Co. Secretary:** Ian Walker
**Responsibilities**
**Senior:** Nigel Wanford *(Supply Chain Manager)*
**Marketing:** Andrew Matlow *(Marketing Manager)*
**Sales:** Mark Walter *(Sales Manager)*
**IT:** Selwyn Parry *(IT Director)*
**HR:** Nici Matlow *(Head of Personnel)*, Tony Salt *(Training Manager)*
**Health & Safety:** Mark Nadin *(Quality Assurance Manager)*
**Facilities:** Tony Bartley *(Maintenance Manager)*
**Operations:** Nigel Wanford *(Supply Chain Manager)*
**US SIC:** 2065 **UK SIC:** 42142
**Auditors:** Pricewaterhouse Coopers
**Bankers:** Barclays Bank Plc (20-36-47)

| | 31-12-13 | 31-12-12 | 31-12-11 |
|---|---|---|---|
| TO | 62,150,000 | 54,839,000 | 49,852,000 |
| P/L | 3,324,000 | 1,496,000 | 5,064,000 |
| NW | 19,839,000 | 16,707,000 | 19,093,000 |
| WC | 18,278,000 | 15,818,000 | 17,493,000 |
| Emp. | 635 | 619 | 621 |

DUNS 34-619-1500
## Sword Contracts Ltd
Brooke Lodge, Gillingham, Kent ME7 3NH
**Tel:** 01634 377078 **Fax:** 01634 366838
**Web:** www.sword-contracts.org.uk
**Reg No:** 5425778 **VAT No:** 857915968
**Estd:** 2005 Private Limited Company
**Line of Business:** Civil engineers
**Issued Capital:** £100
**Director:** F A Sword
**Co. Secretary:** Ms Lorraine Sword
**US SIC:** 8911 **UK SIC:** 83701

| | 31-03-14 | 31-03-13 | 31-03-12 |
|---|---|---|---|
| TA | 3,455,309 | 2,503,739 | 2,449,502 |
| NW | 2,774,807 | 2,134,171 | 2,286,850 |
| WC | 2,681,115 | 2,062,455 | 2,197,494 |

DUNS 23-158-0338
## Sword Security (N.I.) Ltd
68 Donegall Pass, Belfast BT7 1BU
**Tel:** 028-9050-3040 **Fax:** 028-9050-3041
**Web:** www.sword-security.co.uk
**Reg No:** 0035728NI **Estd:** 1999 Private Limited Company
**Line of Business:** Security activities
**Issued Capital:** £64
**Director:** B D Cain
**Co. Secretary:** Ms Fiona Noble
**US SIC:** 7393 **UK SIC:** 83954
**Auditors:** Money Moore
**Bankers:** The Bank Of Ireland (90-24-42)

| | 31-05-14 | 31-05-13 | 31-05-12 |
|---|---|---|---|
| TA | 1,474,458 | 1,414,757 | 1,558,018 |
| NW | 556,432 | 463,966 | 348,077 |
| WC | 325,694 | 236,503 | 134,864 |

DUNS 29-193-4222 **Imp-Exp**
## Swp Group Plc
1 Regal Lane, Soham, Ely, Cambridgeshire CB7 5BA
**Tel:** 01353723270 **Fax:** 01353725193
**Web:** www.swpgroupplc.com
**Reg No:** 0503188 **Estd:** 1952 Public Limited Company
**Line of Business:** Management activities of holding companies
**Export Markets:** Europe, SE Asia, Australasia
**Export Sales:** £12,126,000
**Issued Capital:** £1,005,625
**Principals:** J A Walker *(Financial)*, A G Smith, C A Stott, M Bell
**Co. Secretary:** David Pett
**US SIC:** 6711, 3499
**UK SIC:** 83962, 31694
**Auditors:** Crowe Clark Whitehill LLP
**Bankers:** Bank Of Scotland (80-54-01)

| | 30-06-14 | 30-06-13 | 30-06-12 |
|---|---|---|---|
| TO | 20,325,000 | 14,317,000 | 20,922,000 |
| P/L | 1,422,000 | (454,000) | 835,000 |
| NW | 7,017,000 | 5,738,000 | 6,535,000 |
| WC | 2,340,000 | 2,098,000 | 3,428,000 |
| Emp. | 113 | 116 | 148 |

DUNS 21-822-3253 **Exp**
## S.W.Wreford & Sons. Ltd
Silvanus Park, Northampton, Northamptonshire NN5 5JT
**Tel:** 01604761429
**Web:** www.swwreford.co.uk
**Reg No:** 0371161 **VAT No:** 120163429
**Estd:** 1904 Private Limited Company
**Line of Business:** Road haulage and transport services
**Export Sales:** £80,244
**Trading Style:** Wreford's Transport, Wreford's Warehousing
**Issued Capital:** £51,300
**Principals:** M W Wreford *(Managing)*, A M Wreford, I J Mayes, M W Wreford
**Co. Secretary:** Michael Wreford
**Responsibilities**
**Senior:** Sydney Wreford *(Manager)*, W Wreford *(Manager)*
**HR:** Liz Mayes *(Personnel Manager)*, Simon Waddy *(Training Manager)*
**Operations:** Simon Waddy *(Training Manager)*
**Fleet:** Simon Waddy *(Training Manager)*
**US SIC:** 4789 **UK SIC:** 77002
**Auditors:** Moore Stephens
**Bankers:** National Westminster Bank Plc (54-10-44)

| | 31-03-14 | 31-03-13 | 31-03-12 |
|---|---|---|---|
| TO | 9,109,450 | 8,751,953 | N/A |
| P/L | 219,780 | 78,395 | N/A |
| NW | 1,364,383 | 1,255,368 | 1,194,124 |
| WC | 45,542 | 59,466 | (312,447) |
| Emp. | 101 | 100 | N/A |

DUNS 39-733-5928 **Imp-Exp**
## Sybase (Uk) Ltd
(**Subsidiary of:** Sap Se)
Sybase Court, Crown Lane, Maidenhead, Berkshire SL6 8QZ
**Web:** www.sybase.co.uk
**Reg No:** 2175260 **Estd:** 1987 Private Limited Company
**Line of Business:** Computer systems and software (sales)
**Issued Capital:** £47,418
**Directors:** Ms E Shishkina, H Winkler, J D Hillman
**Co. Secretary:** Miss Helen Matthews
**Branches:** Sybase (Uk) Ltd, 4 The Embankment, 3rd Fl, Leeds, West Yorkshire LS1 4BA
**US SIC:** 7379 **UK SIC:** 83940
**Auditors:** KPMG LLP
**Bankers:** Abn Amro Bank Nv (40-50-30)

| | 31-12-13 | 31-12-12 | 31-12-11 |
|---|---|---|---|
| TO | N/A | 34,823,374 | 37,161,322 |
| P/L | N/A | 9,151,839 | 2,674,826 |
| NW | 1 | 17,656,809 | 8,864,750 |
| WC | N/A | N/A | 6,603,429 |
| Emp. | N/A | 201 | 203 |

DUNS 21-582-4641
## Sycamore Farm
Liverpool Road, Burnley, Lancashire BB12 6HH
**Tel:** 01282427101
**Web:** www.farmhouseinns.co.uk
**Estd:** 2011 Partnership
**Line of Business:** Licensed restaurants
**Partners:** Miss K Mcanon, M Worsley
**Responsibilities**
**Senior:** Katrina McAnon *(Partner)*, Katrina Mccarron *(Assistant Manager)*
**US SIC:** 5812 **UK SIC:** 66110
**Employees:** 70

DUNS 21-580-4092
## Sycamores Nursing Home
Johnson Street, Wolverhampton, West Midlands WV2 3BD
**Tel:** 01902-873750
**Estd:** 2001 Proprietorship
**Line of Business:** Medical nursing home activities
**Proprietor:** M Lakhani
**Responsibilities**
**Senior:** Amanda Morgan *(Home Manager)*
**US SIC:** 8051 **UK SIC:** 95100
**Employees:** 100

DUNS 21-722-1076
## Syd Bishop & Sons (Demolition) Ltd
(**Subsidiary of:** Watch It Come Down Ltd)
Waldens Road, Orpington, Kent BR5 4EU
**Tel:** 01689820315
**Web:** www.sydbishopdemolition.co.uk
**Reg No:** 1092292 **VAT No:** 205928169
**Estd:** 1929 Private Limited Company
**Line of Business:** Demolition contractors
**Issued Capital:** £12,000
**Principals:** T M Bishop *(Managing)*, S E Bishop, S M Bishop, T J Bishop
**Responsibilities**
**Senior:** Kathleen Arnold *(Manager)*, Peter Osmond *(Group Account Manager)*
**Sales:** Peter Osmond *(Group Account Manager)*
**US SIC:** 1795 **UK SIC:** 50000
**Auditors:** Creaseys LLP
**Bankers:** HSBC Bank plc (40-15-05)

| | 30-09-13 | 30-09-12 | 30-09-11 |
|---|---|---|---|
| TO | 14,144,696 | 13,165,066 | 12,439,822 |
| P/L | 138,479 | 29,276 | 319,990 |
| NW | 3,041,816 | 4,028,383 | 4,000,492 |
| WC | 637,849 | 1,065,610 | (1,057,853) |
| Emp. | 122 | 110 | 106 |

DUNS 21-293-7973
## Syd Brown & Sons Ltd
181-183 Preston Road, Grimsargh, Preston, Lancashire PR2 5JP
**Tel:** 01772652323 **Fax:** 01772-784617
**Reg No:** 0859366 **Estd:** 1965 Private Limited Company
**Line of Business:** Sale of new motor vehicles
**Issued Capital:** £26,500
**Managing Director:** S R Brown
**Co. Secretary:** Sydney Brown
**Branches:** Syd Brown & Sons Ltd, Park Road, Grimshaw Park, Blackburn, Lancashire BB2 3DN
**US SIC:** 5511, 7539
**UK SIC:** 65100, 67100
**Auditors:** Moore & Smalley
**Bankers:** National Westminster Bank Plc (01-05-24)

| | 31-03-14 | 31-03-13 | 31-03-12 |
|---|---|---|---|
| TA | 645,786 | 518,195 | 373,067 |
| NW | 482,827 | 411,914 | 366,938 |
| WC | 479,189 | 406,584 | 366,938 |

DUNS 23-082-7300
## Sydenham High School
19 Westwood Hill, London SE26 6BL
**Tel:** 02085577000
**Web:** www.sydenhamhighschool.gdst.net
**Estd:** 1995
**Line of Business:** Schools (independent)
**Director:** Dr D Lodge
**Responsibilities**
**Senior:** Catherine Colin *(Head Teacher)*, Philip O'Halloran *(Office Manager)*, Katherine Pullen *(Head Teacher)*
**Finance:** Philip O'Halloran *(Office Manager)*
**Marketing:** Philip O'Halloran *(Office Manager)*
**Admin:** Philip O'Halloran *(Office Manager)*
**IT:** Triston James *(Computer Manager)*
**HR:** Katherine Pullen *(Head Teacher)*
**Health & Safety:** Philip O'Halloran *(Office Manager)*
**Facilities:** Philip O'Halloran *(Office Manager)*
**Purchasing:** Philip O'Halloran *(Office Manager)*
**US SIC:** 8211 **UK SIC:** 93200
**Employees:** 72

DUNS 22-688-6596
## Sydney Mitchell & Co
Aspley House, 35 Waterloo Street, Birmingham, West Midlands B2 5TJ
**Tel:** 08081668827
**Web:** www.sydneymitchell.co.uk
**Estd:** 1994 Partnership
**Line of Business:** Solicitors
**Principals:** B E Williams *(Partner)*, R P Holland *(Partner)*, T Lewis *(Partner)*, A M Mcquire *(Partner)*, A J Williams *(Partner)*, D Singh, Ms S Moore, A Kay
**Responsibilities**
**Senior:** Simon Jobson *(Partner)*, Anthony McQuire *(Partner)*, Sydney Mitchell *(Partner)*, Leanne Schneider-Rose *(Partner)*, Mauro Vinti *(Partner)*
**Admin:** Ronald Halstead *(Secretary)*, Shelly Shorthouse *(Personal Assistant)*
**Engineering:** Tony Lynch *(Conveyancer)*
**Branches:** Sydney Mitchell & Co, Aspley House, 35 Waterloo Street, Birmingham, West Midlands B2 5TJ
**US SIC:** 8111 **UK SIC:** 83500
**Bankers:** Allied Irish Bank (gb) (23-85-82)
**Employees:** 80

DUNS 21-150-1132
## Sydney Mitchell Llp
Chattock House, 346 Stratford Road, Solihull, West Midlands B90 3DN
**Tel:** 08081668860
**Web:** www.sydneymitchell.co.uk
**Reg No:** 0342756OC **Estd:** 1991 Private Limited Company
**Line of Business:** Solicitors
**Responsibilities**
**Marketing:** Linda Heyworth *(Senior Marketing Manager)*
**US SIC:** 8111 **UK SIC:** 83500

| | 30-04-14 | 30-04-13 | 30-04-12 |
|---|---|---|---|
| TO | 5,129,953 | 5,414,929 | 5,447,020 |
| WC | 1,426,800 | 1,455,427 | 1,584,735 |
| Emp. | 84 | 86 | 88 |

DUNS 73-959-3429 **Imp**
## Sygnature Discovery Ltd
(**Subsidiary of:** Sygil Group Ltd)
Laurus Building, Biocity Nottingham, Nottingham, Nottinghamshire NG1 1GF
**Fax:** 01159-242788
**Web:** www.sygnaturediscovery.com
**Reg No:** 5210563 **Estd:** 2004 Private Limited Company
**Line of Business:** Research and laboratory based activities
**Export Sales:** £3,328,990
**Issued Capital:** £95
**Directors:** Dr P J Clewlow, Mrs V J Tabiner, Dr S C Hirst, Dr L J Nisbet, Dr J G Williams, Dr J Slack
**Co. Secretary:** Mrs Gillian Bowness
**Responsibilities**
**Senior:** Juliette Thompson *(PA)*

**US SIC:** 7391, 7397
**UK SIC:** 94000, 83702
**Auditors:** Collins Hart
**Bankers:** Barclays Bank Plc (20-63-25)

|     | 31-03-14 | 31-03-13 | 31-03-12 |
| --- | --- | --- | --- |
| TO | 8,582,245 | 6,951,533 | N/A |
| P/L | 1,149,627 | 1,153,232 | N/A |
| NW | 5,658,797 | 4,979,935 | 2,558,436 |
| WC | 3,435,207 | 3,860,999 | 1,657,456 |
| Emp. | 92 | 69 | N/A |

DUNS 23-676-4895

## Sykes Chemists Ltd
328 St Helens Road, Bolton, Lancashire BL3 3RP
**Tel:** 01204-61677
**Web:** www.sykeschemists.co.uk
**Reg No:** 3671068 **Estd:** 1998 Private Limited Company
**Line of Business:** Chemists dispensing
**Issued Capital:** £200,000
**Directors:** U G Patel, S G Patel
**Co. Secretary:** Chimanlal Patel
**Branches:** Sykes Chemists Ltd, 284 Derby Street, Bolton, Lancashire BL3 6LF
**US SIC:** 5912 **UK SIC:** 64300
**Auditors:** Warings
**Bankers:** National Westminster Bank Plc (01-30-99)

|     | 07-03-14 | 28-02-13 | 29-03-12 |
| --- | --- | --- | --- |
| TO | 13,828,912 | 12,883,982 | 12,336,712 |
| P/L | (9,816) | 107,325 | (257,187) |
| NW | (518,864) | (1,206,893) | (1,998,502) |
| WC | 470,649 | 119,551 | 211,819 |
| Emp. | 110 | 120 | 120 |

DUNS 42-481-5764

## Sykes Cottages Ltd
Lime Tree House, Hoole Lane, Chester, Cheshire CH2 3EG
**Tel:** 01244-345700
**Web:** www.sykescottages.co.uk
**Reg No:** 4469189 **Estd:** 2002 Private Limited Company
**Line of Business:** Holidays (self catering)
**Issued Capital:** £100
**Directors:** Ms L J Teasdale, M G Hill, C P Sykes
**Co. Secretary:** Simon Taylor
**Responsibilities**
**Marketing:** Mark Bissoni (Marketing Manager)
**US SIC:** 7021 **UK SIC:** 66500
**Bankers:** Lloyds TSB Bank plc (30-91-92)

|     | 30-09-13 | 30-09-12 | 30-09-11 |
| --- | --- | --- | --- |
| TO | 13,456,880 | 9,710,514 | N/A |
| P/L | 3,852,078 | 2,396,029 | N/A |
| NW | 2,546,428 | 2,685,356 | 940,783 |
| WC | 153,059 | 1,079,647 | 599,340 |
| Emp. | 159 | 110 | N/A |

DUNS 22-913-0463     Imp-Exp

## Sykes Global Services Ltd
(**Subsidiary of:** Sei International Services Sarl)
Nether Road, Galashiels, Selkirkshire TD1 3HE
**Tel:** 01896-754866
**Web:** www.sykes.com
**Reg No:** 0086519SC **Estd:** 1984 Private Limited Company
**Line of Business:** Operation of storage facilities
**Export Markets:** Worldwide
**Export Sales:** £11,949,271
**Issued Capital:** £21,621
**Directors:** P J Berendonk, D E Grimes, J T Holder, J Chapman
**Co. Secretary:** Brodies Secretarial Services Lim
**Responsibilities**
**Senior:** Douglas Watt (Senior Sales Executive)
**Finance:** Anne Dods (Assistant Finance Manager), Graeme Sandie (Finance Manager)
**Marketing:** Alan Carmichael (Sales & Marketing Manager), Gerry Moncur (Facilities Manager), Nick Sellers (Marketing Director)
**Sales:** Alan Carmichael (Sales & Marketing Manager), Douglas Watt (Senior Sales Executive)
**IT:** Stewart Mabon (IT Manager)
**HR:** Wendy Bell (Human Resources Manager), Jill Patterson (Human Resources Officer)
**Health & Safety:** Gerry Moncur (Facilities Manager)
**Facilities:** Gerry Moncur (Facilities Manager)
**Operations:** Stewart Mabon (IT Manager), Gerry Moncur (Facilities Manager)
**Purchasing:** John Goldie (?Director of Procurement), Hilary Temple (Purchasing Manager)
**Engineering:** Gerry Moncur (Facilities Manager)
**Branches:** Sykes Global Services Ltd, Sykes Global Services Ltd, Calder House, Edinburgh, Midlothian EH11 4GA
**US SIC:** 4226 **UK SIC:** 77003

---

**Auditors:** Deloitte LLP
**Bankers:** Bank Of Scotland (80-06-88)

|     | 31-12-13 | 31-12-12 | 31-12-11 |
| --- | --- | --- | --- |
| TO | 21,514,936 | 20,970,699 | 20,662,418 |
| P/L | 1,428,086 | 1,172,837 | 958,722 |
| NW | 7,486,981 | 8,290,094 | 11,840,281 |
| WC | 5,096,909 | 5,507,861 | 8,749,798 |
| Emp. | 641 | 621 | 653 |

DUNS 23-510-6247

## Sykes Seafoods Ltd
Smithfield Enterprise Estate, Whitworth Street East, Manchester M11 2NQ
**Tel:** 01612231000
**Web:** www.sykesseafoods.co.uk
**Reg No:** 3509831 **Estd:** 1998 Private Limited Company
**Line of Business:** Fish merchants (wholesale)
**Export Sales:** £1,274,269
**Issued Capital:** £3,750
**Directors:** M Sykes, J F Holloway, D Sykes, A D Dale, M J Sykes, A J Sykes
**Co. Secretary:** Mrs Patricia Sykes
**US SIC:** 5146 **UK SIC:** 61700
**Auditors:** Styles & George
**Bankers:** The Royal Bank Of Scotland Plc (16-21-25)

|     | 31-12-13 | 31-12-12 | 31-12-11 |
| --- | --- | --- | --- |
| TO | 65,939,157 | 59,408,440 | 56,021,231 |
| P/L | 1,437,122 | 654,400 | 569,345 |
| NW | 2,654,131 | 1,935,228 | 1,717,682 |
| WC | 1,060,740 | 493,187 | 423,986 |
| Emp. | 89 | 83 | 82 |

DUNS 76-576-7793

## Symantec (Uk) Ltd
(**Subsidiary of:** Symantec Corporation)
350 Brook Drive, Green Park, Reading, Berkshire RG2 6UH
**Tel:** 08702431080 **Fax:** 0870-243-1081
**Web:** www.symantec.com
**Reg No:** 2575013 **Estd:** 1991 Private Limited Company
**Line of Business:** Hardware consultancy
**Issued Capital:** £100
**Directors:** J P Seccombe, N Osumi, Mrs E J Kim
**Co. Secretary:** Abogado Nominees Limited
**Responsibilities**
**Senior:** Carolyn Herzog (Manager)
**Marketing:** Tamasin Allery (Commercial Marketing Manager -), Melanie Pracht (Marketing Assistant)
**Sales:** Neal Watkins (Technology sales)
**HR:** Janice Willis (Human Resources Manager)
**US SIC:** 7379 **UK SIC:** 83940
**Auditors:** KPMG
**Bankers:** Bank Of America, Na (16-50-50)

|     | 28-03-14 | 29-03-13 | 30-03-12 |
| --- | --- | --- | --- |
| TO | 170,221,000 | 171,230,000 | 170,476,000 |
| P/L | 4,889,000 | 4,520,000 | 3,308,000 |
| NW | 52,541,000 | 44,371,000 | 35,332,000 |
| WC | 48,007,000 | 40,447,000 | 31,195,000 |
| Emp. | 914 | 947 | 904 |

DUNS 21-328-9064

## Symes Bains Broomer
2 Park Square, Scunthorpe, South Humberside DN15 6JH
**Tel:** 01724-281616
**Web:** www.sbblaw.com
**Estd:** 1999
**Line of Business:** Solicitors
**Proprietor:** S Cranage
**Branches:** Symes Bains Broomer, 2 Park Square, Scunthorpe, South Humberside DN15 6JH
**US SIC:** 8111 **UK SIC:** 83500
**Employees:** 4

DUNS 50-585-5726

## Symington's Ltd
(**Subsidiary of:** Speedboat Holdco Ltd)
Pontefract Lane, Leeds, West Yorkshire LS9 0DN
**Tel:** 01132-706061
**Web:** www.symingtons.com
**Reg No:** 2528254 **Estd:** 1990 Private Limited Company
**Line of Business:** Manufacturers of food products
**Issued Capital:** £74,000
**Directors:** J E Kitson, H N Pade
**Co. Secretary:** David Salkeld
**Branches:** Symington's Ltd, Unit 2 Felnex Clo, Felnex Indstl Est, New Market La, Leeds, West Yorkshire LS9 0SH
**US SIC:** 2099, 2098
**UK SIC:** 42399, 42397
**Auditors:** KPMG LLP
**Bankers:** National Westminster Bank Plc (56-00-06)

|     | 23-02-14 | 24-02-13 | 25-02-12 |
| --- | --- | --- | --- |
| TO | 148,336,000 | 141,476,000 | 107,872,000 |
| P/L | 4,950,000 | 10,131,000 | 7,680,000 |
| NW | 17,905,000 | 10,075,000 | 7,563,000 |
| WC | (86,000) | (3,761,000) | 1,370,000 |
| Emp. | 776 | 694 | 537 |

---

DUNS 21-623-2785     Imp

## Symm Group Ltd
Osney Mead, Oxford, Oxfordshire OX2 0EQ
**Fax:** 01865790070
**Web:** www.symm.co.uk
**Reg No:** 0232770 **Estd:** 1815 Private Limited Company
**Line of Business:** Management activities of holding companies
**Issued Capital:** £137,778
**Directors:** Ms C M Maurice, R A Pedder, J D Pike, M Wittet, J J Axtell, A T Mortimer
**Co. Secretary:** Christopher Vane
**US SIC:** 6711, 7339
**UK SIC:** 83962, 83954
**Auditors:** Wenn Townsend
**Bankers:** National Westminster Bank Plc (60-70-03)

|     | 31-03-14 | 31-03-13 | 31-03-12 |
| --- | --- | --- | --- |
| TO | 38,008,296 | 34,777,368 | 30,779,646 |
| P/L | 363,300 | 442,890 | 394,239 |
| NW | 4,467,470 | 4,281,293 | 3,451,748 |
| WC | 3,212,936 | 3,057,617 | 2,635,000 |
| Emp. | 240 | 242 | 239 |

DUNS 21-239-7939     Imp-Exp

## Symmetry Medical Sheffield Ltd.
(**Subsidiary of:** Tecomet Inc.)
6 Beulah Road, Sheffield, South Yorkshire S6 2AN
**Tel:** 01142855881 **Fax:** 01142-336978
**Web:** www.symmetrymedical.com
**Reg No:** 0293190 **VAT No:** 471210877
**Estd:** 1890 Private Limited Company
**Line of Business:** Aviation supplies
**Export Markets:** E U, U S A, Japan & Canada
**Export Sales:** £16,601,000
**Trading Style:** Symmetry Medical Inc
**Issued Capital:** £7,996,498
**Directors:** R Rutledge, D Golde, E J Layland
**Co. Secretary:** Adrian Jones
**Responsibilities**
**Senior:** John Hynes (Chief Operating Officer), Kester Vaughan (General Manager)
**HR:** Neil Hemmingway (Personnel Manager), Steve Watters (People Performance & Developme)
**Facilities:** Dominic Herring (Works Engineer)
**Purchasing:** Michelle Senior (Purchasing Manager)
**Engineering:** Dominic Herring (Works Engineer)
**US SIC:** 3721, 3841
**UK SIC:** 36400, 37201
**Auditors:** Ernst & Young LLP
**Bankers:** Barclays Bank Plc (20-07-71)

|     | 31-12-13 | 31-12-12 | 31-12-11 |
| --- | --- | --- | --- |
| TO | 22,302,000 | 21,802,000 | 21,379,000 |
| P/L | (3,489,000) | 3,209,000 | (950,000) |
| NW | (3,480,000) | 9,000 | (4,061,000) |
| WC | 1,883,000 | 2,908,000 | (6,185,000) |
| Emp. | 255 | 256 | 296 |

DUNS 22-636-6854     Exp

## Symology Ltd
Unit 1, Vanguard House, Millfield Lane Cotswold Business Park, Luton, Bedfordshire LU1 4AJ
**Web:** www.symology.co.uk
**Reg No:** 1760502 **VAT No:** 403937556
**Estd:** 1983 Private Limited Company
**Line of Business:** Computer software (development)
**Issued Capital:** £110
**Principals:** K G Hickson (Managing), R Gordon, J Smith, S L Whipp, M J Bartlett
**Co. Secretary:** Kenneth Hickson
**Responsibilities**
**Finance:** Nick Calver (Financial Manager)
**US SIC:** 7379 **UK SIC:** 83940
**Auditors:** Holmes Peat Thorpe
**Bankers:** Lloyds TSB Bank plc (30-94-08)

|     | 31-03-14 | 31-03-13 | 31-03-12 |
| --- | --- | --- | --- |
| TO | 5,972,530 | 4,703,180 | 4,764,968 |
| P/L | 953,080 | 328,206 | 521,737 |
| NW | 5,925,823 | 5,052,192 | 4,857,196 |
| WC | 4,637,564 | 3,758,247 | 3,872,217 |
| Emp. | 82 | 79 | 75 |

DUNS 21-965-7868

## Symonds & Sampson Llp
30 High West Street, Dorchester, Dorset DT1 1UP
**Tel:** 01305-265058 **Fax:** 01305265058
**Web:** www.symondsandsampson.co.uk
**Reg No:** 0326649OC **Estd:** 2007 Private Limited Company
**Line of Business:** Estate agents

---

**Responsibilities**
**Senior:** Edward Dyke (Non-designated Limited Liabili), Rodger Excel (Compliance Officer), Mark Northcott (Non-designated Limited Liabili), James Pellow (Non-designated Limited Liabili), Michelle Powell (Manager), James Rowe (Non-designated Limited Liabili), Nigel Sheppard (Non-designated Limited Liabili), Lester Williams (Non-designated Limited Liabili), Camilla white (Partner)
**Branches:** Symonds & Sampson Llp, 2 Court Ash, Yeovil, Somerset BA20 1HG
**US SIC:** 6531, 6552
**UK SIC:** 83400, 85000
**Bankers:** Barclays Bank Plc (20-26-62)

|     | 31-03-14 | 31-03-13 | 31-03-12 |
| --- | --- | --- | --- |
| TA | 2,531,063 | 2,002,171 | 2,075,726 |
| NW | 1,123,147 | N/A | 676,250 |
| WC | 531,996 | 432,640 | 572,383 |

DUNS 21-579-5859

## Symonds Nursing & Residential Home
Symonds House, 44 Symonds Lane, Cambridge, Cambridgeshire CB21 4HY
**Tel:** 01223891237
**Web:** www.symondshouse.com
**Estd:** 2002 Partnership
**Line of Business:** Medical nursing home activities
**Partners:** V Gajjar, A Rajani, Dr M Rajani, R Indra, D Rajdev
**Responsibilities**
**Senior:** Indra Rajeevan (Manager)
**US SIC:** 8051 **UK SIC:** 95100
**Employees:** 58

DUNS 34-648-9461

## Symonds (Uk) Ltd
(**Subsidiary of:** Wanzl Gmbh & Co. Holding Kg)
Unit 2, Newport, Gwent NP10 9XX
**Tel:** 01633-892362 **Fax:** 01633-896618
**Web:** www.symondshydroclean.co.uk
**Reg No:** 2774043 **Estd:** 1993 Private Limited Company
**Line of Business:** Management of real estate on a fee or contract basis
**Issued Capital:** £10,000
**Director:** D M Rolland
**Co. Secretary:** 1846 Secretaries Limited
**Responsibilities**
**Senior:** Edward French (Manager), Barry Mitchell (Manager)
**US SIC:** 6531, 7349
**UK SIC:** 83400, 92300
**Auditors:** Deloitte LLP
**Bankers:** Barclays Bank Plc (20-18-15)

|     | 31-12-13 | 31-12-12 | 31-12-11 |
| --- | --- | --- | --- |
| TO | 17,958,785 | 20,810,204 | 24,142,127 |
| P/L | (246,912) | 204,052 | 359,466 |
| NW | 2,761,134 | 2,961,018 | 2,912,941 |
| WC | 1,903,513 | 3,451,753 | 1,884,937 |
| Emp. | 458 | 452 | 436 |

DUNS 34-601-3365

## Symphony Care Ltd
43-45 Queens Park Parade, Northampton, Northamptonshire NN2 6LP
**Tel:** 01604722772
**Web:** www.symphonycare.co.uk
**Reg No:** 5408457 **Estd:** 2005 Private Limited Company
**Line of Business:** Other human health activities
**Issued Capital:** £100
**Director:** T D Robinson
**Co. Secretary:** Mrs Anita Robinson
**Responsibilities**
**Senior:** Darren Weeks (Home Care Manager)
**US SIC:** 8091 **UK SIC:** 95200

|     | 31-03-14 | 31-03-13 | 31-03-12 |
| --- | --- | --- | --- |
| TA | 154,734 | 156,547 | 126,306 |
| NW | 73,478 | 59,228 | 25,310 |
| WC | 63,015 | 10,796 | (41,509) |

DUNS 34-731-0208

## Symphony Holdings Ltd
Pen Hill Estate, Park Spring Road, Barnsley, South Yorkshire S72 7EZ
**Tel:** 01226446000 **Fax:** 01226711185
**Web:** www.symphony-group.co.uk
**Reg No:** 5533292 **Estd:** 2005 Private Limited Company
**Line of Business:** Management activities of holding companies
**Issued Capital:** £65
**Directors:** M R Davis, G Smith, Miss K M Langellier, D S Gregory
**Co. Secretary:** Mrs Adrienne Murdoch
**Responsibilities**
**Marketing:** Claire Beaumont (Marketing Communications Manag)
**IT:** Ruth Rew (IT Manager)
**Operations:** Craig Monument (Technical Project Manager)
**US SIC:** 6711 **UK SIC:** 83962

**Bankers:** Lloyds TSB Bank plc (30-00-05)

| | 31-12-13 | 31-12-12 | 31-12-11 |
|---|---|---|---|
| TO | 130,387,000 | 117,915,000 | 105,285,000 |
| P/L | 4,205,000 | 1,681,000 | 1,392,000 |
| NW | 51,364,000 | 54,694,000 | 53,590,000 |
| WC | 20,161,000 | 17,091,000 | 15,038,000 |
| Emp. | 992 | 970 | 910 |

DUNS 21-706-4624

## Symphony Housing Group Ltd

1st Floor - Lowry Mall, Salford, Lancashire M50 3AH
**Tel:** 08456021120
**Web:** www.symphonyhousing.org.uk
**Reg No:** 0031216IP **Estd:** 2011 Private Limited Company
**Line of Business:** Housing associations societies trusts & co-operatives
**Chairman:** T Dobson
**Responsibilities**
**Senior:** Alison Birch (Communications Officer)
**Marketing:** Alison Birch (Communications Officer)
**US SIC:** 8321 **UK SIC:** 96111
**Bankers:** National Westminster Bank Plc (01-06-88)

| | 31-03-12 |
|---|---|
| TO | 149,478,000 |
| P/L | 25,620,000 |
| NW | 295,204,000 |
| WC | 62,040,000 |
| Emp. | 914 |

DUNS 21-626-1735 **Imp-Exp**

## Symrise Ltd

(Subsidiary of: Symrise Ag)
Thames Industrial Estate, Marlow, Buckinghamshire SL7 1TB
**Tel:** 01628646017 **Fax:** 01628 646016
**Web:** www.symrise.com
**Reg No:** 0868875 **VAT No:** 215910582
**Estd:** 1966 Private Limited Company
**Line of Business:** Manufacture of condiments and seasonings
**Export Markets:** Africa; Europe
**Issued Capital:** £100,000
**Directors:** B Hirsch, R C Sears-Black, M Sattler
**Co. Secretary:** Ronald Fairhead
**Responsibilities**
**Senior:** Dominique Yates (Manager)
**Branches:** Symrise Ltd, 10-12 Cockerell Road, Corby, Northamptonshire NN17 5DU
**US SIC:** 2099 **UK SIC:** 42399
**Auditors:** KPMG LLP
**Bankers:** Barclays Bank Plc (20-59-14)

| | 31-12-13 | 31-12-12 | 31-12-11 |
|---|---|---|---|
| TO | 35,513,000 | 31,275,000 | 50,504,000 |
| P/L | 4,643,000 | 3,804,000 | 4,929,000 |
| NW | 17,508,000 | 13,391,000 | 9,798,000 |
| WC | 15,863,000 | 11,663,000 | 7,905,000 |
| Emp. | 118 | 108 | 105 |

DUNS 21-720-9961

## Synaptic Trust

Rosecourt Road, Croydon, Surrey CR0 3BS
**Web:** www.westthornton.croydon.sch.uk
**Reg No:** 7588104 **Estd:** 2011 Private Company Limited By Guarantee
**Line of Business:** Primary education
**Directors:** M E George, M O Yusoof, Ms S A Rowe, K H Robinson, A S Roberts, Ms K I Dugan, L C Jones
**Co. Secretary:** London Registrars Plc
**US SIC:** 8211 **UK SIC:** 93200

| | 31-08-13 | 31-08-12 |
|---|---|---|
| TO | 3,042,000 | 12,562,923 |
| P/L | (59,000) | 9,040,868 |
| NW | 8,843,000 | 8,922,868 |
| WC | 215,000 | 247,827 |
| Emp. | 74 | 75 |

DUNS 73-807-7382

## Synarbor Plc

Sir Wilfrid Newton House, Sheffield, South Yorkshire S35 2PH
**Tel:** 01142572700 **Fax:** 01142572742
**Web:** www.synarbor.com
**Reg No:** 5064012 **VAT No:** 842592023
**Estd:** 2004 Public Limited Company
**Line of Business:** Labour recruitment and provision of personnel
**Issued Capital:** £4,510,810
**Directors:** D A Kelly, D J Hall, L O Johnson, D Urmson
**Co. Secretary:** Ms Katharine Spedding
**US SIC:** 7361 **UK SIC:** 83954
**Auditors:** PricewaterhouseCoopers LLP

| | 31-12-13 | 31-12-12 | 31-12-11 |
|---|---|---|---|
| TO | 23,618,000 | 19,695,000 | 21,440,000 |
| P/L | 1,379,000 | (3,608,000) | (621,000) |
| NW | (2,432,000) | (3,523,000) | 4,088,000 |
| WC | (1,989,000) | (2,812,000) | (2,326,000) |
| Emp. | 95 | 90 | 124 |

DUNS 21-893-2994 **Imp-Exp**

## Synatel Instrumentation Ltd

Walsall Road, Norton Canes, Cannock, Staffordshire WS11 9TB
**Tel:** 01543-277003 **Fax:** 01543-271217
**Web:** www.synatel.co.uk
**Reg No:** 1495116 **Estd:** 1980 Private Limited Company
**Line of Business:** Manufacturers of electronic equipment and components
**Export Markets:** U S A; Worldwide
**Issued Capital:** £12
**Directors:** N V Wheat, D V Wheat
**Co. Secretary:** David Wheat
**Responsibilities**
**Senior:** Varinder Bahal (Financial Director)
**Finance:** Varinder Bahal (Financial Director)
**Facilities:** Rob Winkle (Maintenance Manager)
**US SIC:** 3679 **UK SIC:** 34542
**Auditors:** RSM Tenon Ltd
**Bankers:** HSBC Bank plc (40-45-19)

| | 31-05-14 | 31-05-13 | 31-05-12 |
|---|---|---|---|
| TA | 1,542,670 | 1,407,328 | 1,387,470 |
| NW | 1,045,811 | 929,513 | 627,586 |
| WC | 934,995 | 817,942 | 687,046 |

DUNS 21-028-7868 **Imp**

## Synchemicals Ltd

Unit 2, Owen Street, Coalville, Leicestershire LE67 3DE
**Web:** www.vitax.co.uk
**Reg No:** 0368448 **Estd:** 1941 Private Limited Company
**Line of Business:** Management activities of holding companies
**Trading Style:** Vitax
**Issued Capital:** £959,000
**Principals:** P A Gooding (Financial), D Wilkinson, J W Plews
**Co. Secretary:** Ms Anja Gooding
**Branches:** Synchemicals Ltd, Old Station Yard, Tewkesbury, Gloucestershire GL20 7AN
**US SIC:** 6711 **UK SIC:** 83962
**Auditors:** PricewaterhouseCoopers LLP
**Bankers:** National Westminster Bank Plc (60-14-10)

| | 31-08-13 | 31-08-12 | 31-08-11 |
|---|---|---|---|
| TO | 22,906,000 | 24,015,000 | 22,962,000 |
| P/L | 1,206,000 | 1,053,000 | 1,457,000 |
| NW | 23,322,000 | 22,578,000 | 22,082,000 |
| WC | 17,079,000 | 16,275,000 | 16,490,000 |
| Emp. | 169 | 167 | 177 |

DUNS 22-508-1397 **Exp**

## Synchro Clutch Co Ltd

Synchro House, Park Road, Sunbury-On-Thames, Middlesex TW16 5BL
**Tel:** 01932-780644
**Reg No:** 1439359 **Estd:** 1955 Private Limited Company
**Line of Business:** Engineering services
**Export Markets:** Worldwide
**Export Sales:** £7,919,623
**Trading Style:** Synchro Clutch Co Ltd
**Issued Capital:** £99,000
**Principals:** H A Clements (Chairman and Managing), P Bizzill
**Co. Secretary:** James Neeves
**US SIC:** 6711, 3568
**UK SIC:** 83962, 32613
**Auditors:** CMB Partnership
**Bankers:** Barclays Bank Plc (20-72-17)

| | 31-12-13 | 31-12-12 | 31-12-11 |
|---|---|---|---|
| TO | 16,372,433 | 18,151,490 | 15,943,644 |
| P/L | 3,910,535 | 5,744,261 | 5,544,778 |
| NW | 57,784,853 | 55,917,803 | 51,732,201 |
| WC | 29,030,308 | 31,013,728 | 27,819,166 |
| Emp. | 56 | 42 | 40 |

DUNS 23-342-1549

## Synchronised Cabling Solutions Ltd

15 Dalewood, Armagh, Co Armagh BT61 9AU
**Tel:** 02890832777 **Fax:** 02890842077
**Web:** www.syncsolutions.co.uk
**Reg No:** 0046964NI **Estd:** 1995 Private Limited Company
**Line of Business:** Computer services
**Issued Capital:** £700
**Director:** A Smyth
**Co. Secretary:** Ms Ruth Smyth
**US SIC:** 1731, 1799
**UK SIC:** 50300, 50000

| | 31-08-13 | 31-08-12 | 31-08-11 |
|---|---|---|---|
| TA | 553,330 | 449,460 | 351,805 |
| NW | 359,559 | 344,189 | 276,780 |
| WC | 334,910 | 340,182 | 270,291 |

DUNS 28-977-1669

## Syncreon Technology (Uk) Ltd

(Subsidiary of: Syncreon Emea)
Unit 5 Logix Park, Watling Street, Hinckley, Leicestershire LE10 3BQ
**Tel:** 0145 562 2500 **Fax:** 0145 562 2685
**Web:** www.syncreon.com
**Reg No:** 1761717 **VAT No:** 437884505
**Estd:** 1987 Private Limited Company

**Line of Business:** Goods delivery services
**Trading Style:** Syncreon
**Issued Capital:** £25,000
**Directors:** S Faulkner, M J Enright, B Enright
**Co. Secretary:** Kenneth Pocius
**Responsibilities**
**IT:** Alan Lodge (IT Manager), mark partridge (IT manager)
**Branches:** Syncreon Technology (Uk) Ltd, Jumbo Distribution Centre, Cross Point Business Pk, Gielgud Way, Coventry, West Midlands CV2 2SZ
**US SIC:** 4213, 4226
**UK SIC:** 72300, 77003
**Auditors:** PricewaterhouseCoopers
**Bankers:** The Bank Of Ireland (30-14-74)

| | 31-12-13 | 31-12-12 | 31-12-11 |
|---|---|---|---|
| TO | 38,097,991 | 37,384,705 | 36,241,081 |
| P/L | 937,779 | 5,138,199 | 4,661,059 |
| NW | 16,519,273 | 15,797,046 | 15,921,344 |
| WC | 16,558,579 | 14,438,940 | 15,126,590 |
| Emp. | 265 | 274 | 266 |

DUNS 21-621-2995

## The Syndicate

15 Nelson Street, Bristol, Avon BS1 2JY
**Tel:** 01179450325
**Web:** www.thesyndicate.com
**Estd:** 2011 Proprietorship
**Line of Business:** Managed public houses and bars
**Proprietor:** C Beetham
**Responsibilities**
**Senior:** Mark Byford (Manager)
**US SIC:** 5813 **UK SIC:** 66200
**Employees:** 100

DUNS 49-483-1951

## Syne Qua Non Ltd

(Subsidiary of: Sqn Clinical Ltd)
Gostling House, Diss Business Park, Hopper Way, Sandy Lane, Diss, Norfolk IP22 4GT
**Web:** www.synequanon.com
**Reg No:** 3148610 **Estd:** 1996 Private Limited Company
**Line of Business:** Other business activities not elsewhere classified
**Issued Capital:** £1,000
**Director:** Mrs K M Grover
**Co. Secretary:** Michael Rees
**Responsibilities**
**Senior:** Tony Rees (Joint Managing Director)
**Marketing:** Tony Rees (Joint Managing Director)
**Sales:** Tony Rees (Joint Managing Director)
**IT:** Tony Rees (Joint Managing Director)
**US SIC:** 7399 **UK SIC:** 83954
**Bankers:** HSBC Bank plc (40-19-18)

| | 31-12-13 | 31-12-12 | 31-12-11 |
|---|---|---|---|
| TA | 1,632,083 | 1,319,324 | 1,622,348 |
| NW | 238,664 | (22,311) | 558,187 |
| WC | 195,991 | (101,440) | 430,253 |

DUNS 22-772-2212 **Exp**

## Synectics Plc

Studley Point, 88 Birmingham Road, Studley, Warwickshire B80 7AS
**Tel:** 01923216622
**Web:** www.synecticsplc.com
**Reg No:** 1740011 **VAT No:** 417069846
**Estd:** 1989 Public Limited Company
**Line of Business:** Management activities of holding companies
**Export Markets:** Worldwide
**Trading Style:** Synectics Plc
**Issued Capital:** £3,517,698
**Directors:** D J Coghlan, S Coggins, P M Rae, P A Webb, D Bate
**Co. Secretary:** Nigel Poultney
**Responsibilities**
**Senior:** Simon Crooks (Assistant Company Secretary)
**Branches:** Synectics Plc, Axiom Ho, 23 Sherwood Rd, Bromsgrove, Worcestershire B60 3DR
**US SIC:** 6711, 5043
**UK SIC:** 83962, 61900
**Auditors:** KPMG Audit PLC
**Bankers:** Barclays Bank Plc (20-07-71)

| | 30-11-13 | 30-11-12 | 30-11-11 |
|---|---|---|---|
| TO | 82,363,000 | 77,039,000 | 69,083,000 |
| P/L | 6,621,000 | 4,709,000 | 2,462,000 |
| NW | 16,870,000 | 14,471,000 | 7,260,000 |
| WC | 19,370,000 | 15,020,000 | 13,646,000 |
| Emp. | 512 | 474 | 428 |

DUNS 77-108-2526 **Exp**

## Synectics Solutions Ltd

Synectics House, The Brampton The Hollies, Newcastle, Staffordshire ST5 0QY
**Tel:** 01782-664000
**Web:** www.synectics-solutions.com
**Reg No:** 2685135 **VAT No:** 592436323
**Estd:** 1992 Private Limited Company
**Line of Business:** Computer consumables suppliers
**Export Sales:** £2,825,186
**Issued Capital:** £100

**Principals:** K J Shanahan (Managing), R A Moorhouse (Financial), Miss R L Shanahan, Mrs C A Shanahan, R M Wood, Mrs K M Beardmore, Mrs M K Humphreys
**Responsibilities**
**Finance:** Kate Shanahan (Financial Manager)
**IT:** Lee Bradbury (Itanager)
**Health & Safety:** Steve Sands (Facilities Manager)
**Facilities:** Steve Sands (Facilities Manager)
**US SIC:** 7379, 7374
**UK SIC:** 83940
**Auditors:** PKF
**Bankers:** Barclays Bank Plc (20-59-23)

| | 31-08-14 | 31-08-13 | 31-08-12 |
|---|---|---|---|
| TO | 11,440,870 | 10,336,063 | 8,886,309 |
| P/L | 867,812 | 732,103 | 148,232 |
| NW | 1,658,867 | 1,349,034 | 823,255 |
| WC | 2,771,257 | 1,895,003 | (488,223) |
| Emp. | 257 | 247 | 237 |

DUNS 21-110-8619

## Synergie Holdings Ltd

322 Manchester Road, Greater Manchester, Bolton, Lancashire BL3 2QS
**Tel:** 08713107381
**Web:** www.synergieholdings.com
**Reg No:** 6523149 **Estd:** 2008 Private Limited Company
**Line of Business:** Retail sale of automotive fuel
**Issued Capital:** £300
**Directors:** A I Patel, A I Patel
**Co. Secretary:** Anis Patel
**US SIC:** 5541 **UK SIC:** 65200

| | 30-04-14 | 30-04-13 | 30-04-12 |
|---|---|---|---|
| TO | 96,797,000 | 97,426,000 | 100,610,000 |
| P/L | 1,056,000 | 445,000 | 550,000 |
| NW | 8,480,000 | 7,583,000 | 640,000 |
| WC | (258,000) | (1,089,000) | (908,000) |
| Emp. | 223 | 243 | 268 |

DUNS 21-705-9065 **Imp**

## Synergy

16 Petersham Road, Richmond, Surrey TW10 6UW
**Web:** www.synergymedical.co.uk
**Estd:** 2011 Partnership
**Line of Business:** Research institutions and organisations
**US SIC:** 7391 **UK SIC:** 94000
**Employees:** 58

DUNS 34-733-5445

## Synergy Civil Engineering Ltd

Victoria House, 5 East Blackhall Street, Greenock, Renfrewshire PA15 1HD
**Tel:** 01475 807166 **Fax:** 01475 806832
**Web:** www.synergycivils.co.uk
**Reg No:** 0288879SC **VAT No:** 873567482
**Estd:** 2006 Private Limited Company
**Line of Business:** Civil engineers
**Issued Capital:** £10,000
**Director:** R Alexander
**Co. Secretary:** Kenneth Campbell
**Responsibilities**
**Senior:** Ryan Dunlop (Manager)
**US SIC:** 8911, 1622
**UK SIC:** 83701, 50200
**Auditors:** Campbell Dallas LLP
**Bankers:** Clydesdale Bank Plc (82-65-04)

| | 31-12-13 | 31-12-12 | 31-12-11 |
|---|---|---|---|
| TO | 9,403,490 | 8,446,045 | N/A |
| P/L | 488,944 | 532,158 | N/A |
| NW | 952,691 | 792,127 | 755,652 |
| WC | 811,040 | 653,750 | 666,115 |
| Emp. | 71 | 65 | N/A |

DUNS 34-941-5468

## Synergy Construction and Property Consultants Llp

8-9 Faraday Road, Guildford, Surrey GU1 1EA
**Web:** www.synergyllp.com
**Reg No:** 0318352OC **VAT No:** 235779919
**Estd:** 2006
**Line of Business:** Building services
**Responsibilities**
**Senior:** Duncan Ball (Non-designated Limited Liabili), Ron Brooker (Non-designated Limited Liabili), Robert Ebdon (Non-designated Limited Liabili), Declan Gleeson (Non-designated Limited Liabili), Paul Grinham (Non-designated Limited Liabili), David Hawtin (Non-designated Limited Liabili), Stephen Jopson (Non-designated Limited Liabili), William Khoo (Non-designated Limited Liabili), Anthony Luff (Non-designated Limited Liabili)
**Branches:** Synergy Construction and Property Consultants Llp, Alberton House, 30 St Marys Parsonage, Manchester M3 2WJ
**US SIC:** 1522, 1541
**UK SIC:** 50100
**Auditors:** Moore Stephens LLP

**Bankers:** National Westminster Bank Plc (60-60-04)

| | 31-03-14 | 31-03-13 | 31-03-12 |
|---|---|---|---|
| TO | 5,532,596 | 5,502,262 | 5,458,160 |
| P/L | 440,019 | 397,212 | 227,240 |
| NW | N/A | 442,818 | (576,782) |
| WC | 1,554,642 | 1,743,420 | 1,432,729 |
| Emp. | 63 | 61 | 62 |

DUNS 21-164-2838

## Synergy Farm Health Ltd

West Hill Barn, West Hill, Evershot, Dorchester, Dorset DT2 0LD
**Tel:** 0193583682
**Web:** www.synergyfarmhealth.com
**Reg No:** 6903100 **Estd:** 2009 Private Limited Company
**Line of Business:** Veterinary activities
**Issued Capital:** £72,500
**Directors:** J D Reader, M C Burnell, A P Adler, A R Davies, A J Hayton, A E King
**Co. Secretary:** Alan King
**Responsibilities**
**Senior:** Jereme Darke *(Manager)*
**US SIC:** 0741 **UK SIC:** 95601

| | 31-10-13 | 31-10-12 | 31-10-11 |
|---|---|---|---|
| TA | 2,787,738 | 2,879,651 | 2,738,195 |
| NW | 247,412 | 1,247 | (562,983) |
| WC | 485,893 | 392,676 | 251,525 |

DUNS 51-988-2559 **Imp**

## Synergy Health Plc

Ground Floor Stella Windmill Hill, Business Park, Whitehill Way, Swindon, Wiltshire SN5 6NX
**Tel:** 08447-280-290 **Fax:** 01793-891-892
**Web:** www.synergyhealthplc.com
**Reg No:** 3355631 **Estd:** 1970 Public Limited Company
**Line of Business:** Cleaning activities not elsewhere classified
**Export Sales:** £232,594,000
**Issued Capital:** £365,750
**Directors:** Sir D K Nichol, Dr A V Coward, B A Edwards, G Hill, Mrs C F Baroudel, Doctor R M Steeves, J F Harris
**Co. Secretary:** Jonathan Turner
**Responsibilities**
**Senior:** Nikki Mcmullen *(Personal Assistant To Chief Ex)*
**Finance:** Ivan Jacques *(Financial Director)*
**Branches:** Synergy Health Plc, Oakwood Close, Off Birdwood Avenue, Lewisham, London SE13 6TL
**US SIC:** 7349 **UK SIC:** 92300
**Auditors:** KPMG Audit PLC
**Bankers:** Barclays Bank Plc (20-20-44)

| | 30-03-14 | 31-03-13 | 01-03-12 |
|---|---|---|---|
| TO | 380,453,000 | 361,248,000 | 311,954,000 |
| P/L | 42,893,000 | 38,846,000 | 32,477,000 |
| NW | 79,406,000 | 63,694,000 | 11,908,000 |
| WC | 29,203,000 | 18,105,000 | (15,626,000) |
| Emp. | 5,107 | 5,256 | 4,399 |

DUNS 22-606-7312

## Synergy Health Sterilisation Uk Ltd

(**Subsidiary of:** Synergy Health Plc)
Ground Floor, Stella Windmill Hill Business Park, Whitehill Way, Swindon, Wiltshire SN5 6NX
**Tel:** 08456 889977 **Fax:** 08456-889978
**Web:** www.synergyhealthplc.com
**Reg No:** 1771333 **Estd:** 1970 Private Limited Company
**Line of Business:** Other business activities not elsewhere classified
**Issued Capital:** £5,430,656
**Directors:** G Hill, J P Turner, P N Santing, Doctor R M Steeves, Miss K L Somerfield, A V Coward
**Co. Secretary:** Jonathan Turner
**Branches:** Synergy Health Sterilisation Uk Ltd, Roydsdale Way, Bradford, West Yorkshire BD4 6SE
**US SIC:** 7399 **UK SIC:** 83954
**Auditors:** KPMG Audit PLC
**Bankers:** National Westminster Bank Plc (60-21-40)

| | 30-03-14 | 31-03-13 | 01-03-12 |
|---|---|---|---|
| TO | 24,473,000 | 23,290,000 | 23,857,000 |
| P/L | 10,499,000 | 9,620,000 | 9,335,000 |
| NW | 54,407,000 | 45,890,000 | 52,289,000 |
| WC | (101,000) | (8,644,000) | (1,911,000) |
| Emp. | 187 | 189 | 196 |

DUNS 23-825-2779 **Imp-Exp**

## Synergy (High Wycombe) Ltd

(**Subsidiary of:** Carbery Creameries Ltd)
Synergy House Hillbottom Road, Sands Industrial Estate, High Wycombe, Buckinghamshire HP12 4HJ
**Tel:** 01494492222
**Web:** www.synergytaste.com
**Reg No:** 2452095 **VAT No:** 370213784
**Estd:** 1996 Private Limited Company
**Line of Business:** Manufacture of condiments and seasonings
**Export Markets:** European Union (E U); U S A; Africa; Russia
**Issued Capital:** £49,639
**Principals:** C A Leen *(Financial)*, S Morgan, D J Holland, D B Macsweeney, N Corcoran
**Co. Secretary:** Ms Nicola Mcfadden
**US SIC:** 2099 **UK SIC:** 42399
**Auditors:** Ernst & Young
**Bankers:** HSBC Bank plc (40-31-05)

| | 31-12-13 | 31-12-12 | 31-12-11 |
|---|---|---|---|
| TO | 9,432,585 | 8,076,785 | N/A |
| P/L | 1,277,484 | 841,293 | N/A |
| NW | 6,428,361 | 5,717,550 | 5,212,655 |
| WC | 2,820,186 | 3,169,515 | 2,781,112 |
| Emp. | 56 | 53 | N/A |

DUNS 21-762-0117

## Synergy Housing Ltd

Link House, West Street, Poole, Dorset BH15 1LD
**Tel:** 01202308600 **Fax:** 08451728080
**Web:** www.synergyhousing.co.uk
**Reg No:** 0031447IP **Estd:** 2011 Friendly Society
**Line of Business:** Non-charitable social work activities with accommodation
**US SIC:** 8321 **UK SIC:** 96111
**Bankers:** The Royal Bank Of Scotland Plc (16-31-28)

| | 31-03-12 |
|---|---|
| TO | 42,409,000 |
| P/L | (335,000) |
| NW | 175,051,000 |
| WC | (1,631,000) |
| Emp. | 380 |

DUNS 53-654-2970

## Synergy Technology Ltd

The Theatre, Manchester Road, Carrington, Manchester M31 4DD
**Tel:** 0845-456-0050 **Fax:** 084545600449
**Web:** www.synergytechnology.co.uk
**Reg No:** 3459600 **Estd:** 1997 Private Limited Company
**Line of Business:** Miscellaneous computer services
**Issued Capital:** £2,000
**Directors:** A G Hughes, A B Poole
**Responsibilities**
**Senior:** Bronwen Wilkinson *(Manager)*
**Branches:** Synergy Technology Ltd, Unit J Black Lane, Preston, Lancashire PR3 0LH
**US SIC:** 7379, 7374
**UK SIC:** 83940
**Auditors:** S. Samuels & Co
**Bankers:** Bank Of Scotland (12-08-95)

| | 31-12-13 | 31-12-12 | 31-12-11 |
|---|---|---|---|
| TA | 379,165 | 381,371 | 577,903 |
| NW | (43,775) | (76,198) | (100,312) |
| WC | (72,389) | (76,903) | (51,294) |

DUNS 23-722-8965

## Synertec Ltd

Unit 2 Castle Road, Chelston Business Park, Wellington, Somerset TA21 9JQ
**Tel:** 01823-652360
**Web:** www.synertec.co.uk
**Reg No:** 3717583 **Estd:** 1999 Private Limited Company
**Line of Business:** Image processing services
**Issued Capital:** £1,000
**Directors:** G A Jordan, M W Cleave, S Nester, M R Baldock, M Hasnip
**US SIC:** 3579, 5081
**UK SIC:** 33010, 61490
**Auditors:** Lentells Ltd

| | 31-03-14 | 31-03-13 | 31-03-12 |
|---|---|---|---|
| TO | 19,925,649 | 17,463,170 | 14,605,820 |
| P/L | 1,550,485 | 1,166,337 | 684,344 |
| NW | 3,766,374 | 2,607,468 | 2,274,575 |
| WC | 149,658 | (367,268) | (15,309) |
| Emp. | 117 | 106 | 97 |

DUNS 64-097-0117 **Exp**

## Synetrix (Holdings) Ltd

(**Subsidiary of:** Capita Plc)
49-51 Victoria Road, Farnborough, Hampshire GU14 7PA
**Tel:** 01252405600
**Web:** www.synetrix.co.uk
**Reg No:** 3491956 **VAT No:** 776125907
**Estd:** 1998 Private Limited Company
**Line of Business:** Telecommunication networks
**Issued Capital:** £2
**Directors:** Capita Corporate Director Limite, R J Shearer
**Co. Secretary:** Capita Group Secretary Limited
**Responsibilities**
**Senior:** A Merelie *(Manager)*
**Marketing:** A Tertzakian *(Marketing Manager)*
**HR:** S Whittam *(Human Resources Manager)*
**Branches:** Synetrix (Holdings) Ltd, 40 Princess Street, Manchester M1 6DE
**US SIC:** 7379 **UK SIC:** 83940
**Auditors:** KPMG Audit PLC
**Bankers:** The Royal Bank Of Scotland Plc (16-20-30)

| | 31-12-13 | 31-12-12 | 31-12-11 |
|---|---|---|---|
| TO | N/A | 10,258,832 | 19,538,801 |
| P/L | N/A | 19,899,605 | 4,285,340 |
| NW | 13,418,960 | 13,418,960 | 11,170,752 |
| WC | 13,418,960 | 13,418,960 | (29,238,408) |
| Emp. | N/A | 72 | 84 |

DUNS 34-775-0809 **Imp**

## Synexus Clinical Research Ltd

(**Subsidiary of:** Synexus Clinical Research Finance Ltd)
Sandringham House, Ackhurst Business Park, Foxhole Road, Chorley, Lancashire PR7 1NY
**Tel:** 01257230723 **Fax:** 01257231981
**Web:** www.synexus.com
**Reg No:** 5575991 **Estd:** 2005 Private Limited Company
**Line of Business:** Research and experimental development on natural sciences and engineering
**Export Sales:** £19,978,000
**Trading Style:** Synexus Ltd
**Issued Capital:** £2,364,335
**Directors:** C Berthoux, P M Chambers
**Responsibilities**
**Senior:** Malcolm Cantor *(Business Information Manager)*
**HR:** Wendy Ingham *(Group Human Resources Director)*
**US SIC:** 7399 **UK SIC:** 83954
**Auditors:** KPMG LLP

| | 31-12-13 | 31-12-12 | 31-12-11 |
|---|---|---|---|
| TO | 37,145,000 | 29,656,000 | 16,972,000 |
| P/L | 3,189,000 | 1,844,000 | (7,723,000) |
| NW | (4,711,000) | (7,008,000) | (9,474,000) |
| WC | (7,897,000) | (9,515,000) | (11,606,000) |
| Emp. | 489 | 406 | 339 |

DUNS 23-729-6590

## Synexus Ltd

(**Subsidiary of:** Synexus Clinical Research Finance Ltd)
Sandringham House, Ackhurst Business Park, Foxhole Road, Chorley, Lancashire PR7 1NY
**Tel:** 01257237438 **Fax:** 01257-231981
**Web:** www.synexus.com
**Reg No:** 3724238 **Estd:** 1999 Private Limited Company
**Line of Business:** Research and experimental development on natural sciences and engineering
**Issued Capital:** £4,297,324
**Directors:** C Berthoux, P M Chambers
**Branches:** Synexus Ltd, Burlington House, Crosby Road North, Liverpool, Merseyside L22 0LG
**US SIC:** 7399 **UK SIC:** 83954
**Auditors:** KPMG LLP

| | 31-12-13 | 31-12-12 | 31-12-11 |
|---|---|---|---|
| TO | 18,176,416 | 15,198,233 | 8,431,852 |
| P/L | 420,379 | (381,638) | (6,470,829) |
| NW | (682,750) | (1,308,149) | (1,131,531) |
| WC | (2,323,462) | (2,468,052) | (2,298,838) |
| Emp. | 178 | 156 | 165 |

DUNS 77-185-4353

## Syngenta Ltd

(**Subsidiary of:** Syngenta Ag)
30 Priestley Road, Guildford, Surrey GU2 7YH
**Tel:** 01483260000 **Fax:** 01483260001
**Web:** www3.syngenta.com
**Reg No:** 2710846 **VAT No:** 760346929
**Estd:** 1992 Private Limited Company
**Line of Business:** Manufacturers of agricultural chemicals
**Trading Style:** Syngenta Seeds Limited
**Issued Capital:** £85,000,000
**Directors:** Dr P A Botham, Dr A D Conn, A Johnson, Dr T Gray, J D Halliwell
**Co. Secretary:** Matthew Bayliss
**Responsibilities**
**Senior:** Ronald Hendrie *(Manager)*, Mark Peacock *(Manager)*
**Sales:** David Huggett *(Contract Manager)*
**Branches:** Syngenta Ltd, Po Box 30,Hexagon Tower, Delauneys Rd,Blackley, Manchester M46 9XJ
**US SIC:** 6711 **UK SIC:** 83962
**Auditors:** Ernst & Young LLP
**Bankers:** HSBC Bank plc (40-05-30)

| | 31-12-13 | 31-12-12 | 31-12-11 |
|---|---|---|---|
| TO | 457,000,000 | 426,000,000 | 397,000,000 |
| P/L | 115,000,000 | 87,000,000 | 87,000,000 |
| NW | 460,000,000 | 393,000,000 | 341,000,000 |
| WC | 172,000,000 | 140,000,000 | 97,000,000 |
| Emp. | 1,387 | 1,339 | 1,330 |

DUNS 29-011-1897 **Imp-Exp**

## Syngenta Seeds Ltd

(**Subsidiary of:** Syngenta Ag)
Market Stainton, Market Rasen, Lincolnshire LN8 5LJ
**Tel:** 01507343348
**Web:** www.syngenta.com
**Reg No:** 0345486 **VAT No:** 106795652
**Estd:** 1938 Private Limited Company
**Line of Business:** Agricultural service activities; landscape gardening
**Export Markets:** Western Europe
**Export Sales:** £46,000
**Issued Capital:** £3,521,869
**Directors:** A Johnson, N J Barkhouse, G Mills-Thomas
**Co. Secretary:** Matthew Bayliss
**Responsibilities**
**Senior:** Lynne Hannam *(Site Manager)*, Gary Oxley *(Manager)*
**Branches:** Syngenta Seeds Ltd, C P C 4, Capital Park, Fulbourn, Cambridge, Cambridgeshire CB21 5XE
**US SIC:** 0729 **UK SIC:** 01003
**Auditors:** Ernst & Young LLP
**Bankers:** HSBC Bank plc (40-31-24)

| | 31-12-13 | 31-12-12 | 31-12-11 |
|---|---|---|---|
| TO | 5,641,000 | 38,111,000 | 34,560,000 |
| P/L | 1,786,000 | 82,709,000 | 3,731,000 |
| NW | 86,575,000 | 78,451,000 | 13,406,000 |
| WC | 86,575,000 | 77,007,000 | 12,087,000 |
| Emp. | 85 | 89 | 92 |

DUNS 29-544-6611 **Imp-Exp**

## Synlatex Ltd

Liberty House, St Catherine Street, Gloucester, Gloucestershire GL1 2BX
**Tel:** 01452-565760
**Web:** www.slguk.com
**Reg No:** 1911296 **VAT No:** 421218007
**Estd:** 1985 Private Limited Company
**Line of Business:** Manufacturers of cosmetics
**Export Markets:** E U, Far East, U S A
**Export Sales:** £3,349,001
**Trading Style:** Sunlatex Lambournes Group Slg, Slg Beauty
**Issued Capital:** £284
**Principals:** Ms P A Topping *(Managing)*, G W Dunkley *(Marketing)*, M S Dunkley
**Co. Secretary:** Ms Patricia Topping
**Responsibilities**
**Senior:** Laurence Jones *(Network Engineer)*
**Engineering:** Laurence Jones *(Network Engineer)*
**US SIC:** 2844 **UK SIC:** 25820
**Auditors:** Pitt Godden & Taylor
**Bankers:** Lloyds TSB Bank plc (30-93-48)

| | 31-12-13 | 31-12-12 | 31-12-11 |
|---|---|---|---|
| TO | 17,232,472 | 13,855,466 | 12,012,068 |
| P/L | 2,847,512 | 1,785,586 | 1,438,847 |
| NW | 7,400,428 | 5,369,530 | 4,814,673 |
| WC | 5,829,488 | 3,770,756 | 3,488,317 |
| Emp. | 114 | 110 | 97 |

DUNS 76-983-6602 **Imp**

## Synopsys (Northern Europe) Ltd

(**Subsidiary of:** Synopsys Inc.)
100 Brook Drive, Reading, Berkshire RG2 6UJ
**Tel:** 01189313822
**Web:** www.synopsys.com
**Reg No:** 2642054 **VAT No:** 537505345
**Estd:** 1991 Private Limited Company
**Line of Business:** Computer software (development)
**Issued Capital:** £1,000
**Directors:** D R Power, C E Watchorn
**Co. Secretary:** Abogado Nominees Limited
**Responsibilities**
**Senior:** Brian Cabrera *(Manager)*
**US SIC:** 7379 **UK SIC:** 83940
**Auditors:** KPMG
**Bankers:** Barclays Bank Plc (20-71-03)

| | 01-11-14 | 02-11-13 | 03-11-12 |
|---|---|---|---|
| TO | 13,212,000 | 13,902,000 | 13,288,000 |
| P/L | 667,000 | 680,000 | 651,000 |
| NW | 2,020,000 | 2,085,000 | 2,000,000 |
| WC | 1,797,000 | 1,794,000 | 1,638,000 |
| Emp. | 96 | 92 | 89 |

DUNS 77-048-9136 **Exp**

## Synseal Extrusions Ltd

(**Subsidiary of:** Allerford Intermediate Newco Ltd)
Common Road, Sutton-In-Ashfield, Nottinghamshire NG17 6AD
**Tel:** 01623-443200
**Web:** www.synseal.co.uk
**Reg No:** 2668919 **VAT No:** 598465963
**Estd:** 1994 Private Limited Company
**Line of Business:** Plastic extruders
**Issued Capital:** £50,002
**Directors:** S Musgrave, T J Armatage, L Daveran, G Edwards, K J Bush, R Byron, D B Leng, S Brown
**Responsibilities**
**Senior:** Robert Byron *(Production Director)*
**Marketing:** Mark Schlotel *(Marketing Director)*
**IT:** Jase Newton *(Head of IT)*
**Operations:** Robert Byron *(Production Director)*
**Engineering:** Robert Byron *(Production Director)*
**US SIC:** 5084 **UK SIC:** 61490
**Auditors:** PricewaterhouseCoopers LLP

**Bankers:** National Westminster Bank Plc (60-12-01)

| | 31-03-14 | 31-03-13 | 31-03-12 |
|---|---|---|---|
| TO | 102,580,000 | 89,944,000 | 72,533,000 |
| P/L | 4,737,000 | 2,818,000 | 6,166,000 |
| NW | 35,859,000 | 30,997,000 | 54,324,000 |
| WC | 21,423,000 | 17,511,000 | 41,588,000 |
| Emp. | 778 | 729 | 498 |

DUNS 23-948-7007

## Syntec Projects Ltd

29 Warple Way, London W3 0RX
**Tel:** 02087407570
**Web:** www.syntec.uk.com
**Reg No:** 3938105 **VAT No:** 766613115
**Estd:** 2000 Private Limited Company
**Line of Business:** Shopfitting contractors
**Issued Capital:** £492
**Principals:** P Meagher *(Financial)*, D G Mac Gabhann, T D Bourke
**Co. Secretary:** Ronan Bourke
**US SIC:** 1796 **UK SIC:** 50400
**Auditors:** Lees-Buckley & Co CA

| | 30-06-13 | 30-06-12 | 30-06-11 |
|---|---|---|---|
| TA | 712,916 | 822,629 | 625,951 |
| NW | 142,851 | 140,307 | 84,439 |
| WC | 138,823 | 129,282 | 66,388 |

DUNS 45-889-6057

## Syntel Europe Ltd

Bolsover House, 5-6 Clipstone Street, London W1W 6BB
**Tel:** 020 7636 3587 **Fax:** 02076365975
**Web:** www.syntelinc.com
**Reg No:** 3227061 **Estd:** 1996 Private Limited Company
**Line of Business:** Computer support & services
**Issued Capital:** £100
**Directors:** A Godbole, D Moore, N Rakesh
**Co. Secretary:** Daniel Moore
**Responsibilities**
**Senior:** Amit Chatterjee *(President)*
**US SIC:** 7379 **UK SIC:** 83940
**Auditors:** KPMG LLP
**Bankers:** Lloyds TSB Bank plc (30-96-96)

| | 31-12-13 | 31-12-12 | 31-12-11 |
|---|---|---|---|
| TO | 16,701,099 | 10,914,785 | 12,500,240 |
| P/L | 731,984 | (740,210) | (491,783) |
| NW | 2,372,159 | 1,555,798 | 2,450,282 |
| WC | 2,212,754 | 1,668,970 | 2,314,208 |
| Emp. | 115 | 69 | 76 |

DUNS 21-833-7079 **Imp-Exp**

## Synthite Ltd

**(Subsidiary of:** Tennants Consolidated Ltd)
Alyn Works, Denbigh Road, Mold, Clwyd CH7 1BT
**Tel:** 01352-752521
**Web:** www.synthite.co.uk
**Reg No:** 0164640 **VAT No:** 276998869
**Estd:** 1920 Private Limited Company
**Line of Business:** Manufacture of other chemical products not elsewhere classified
**Export Markets:** Worldwide
**Export Sales:** £10,615,000
**Issued Capital:** £600,000
**Principals:** K G Jones *(Managing)*, S E Alexander, W P Alexander
**Co. Secretary:** David Kelso
**Responsibilities**
**Marketing:** Sana Niazi *(Sales & Marketing Manager)*
**Sales:** Sana Niazi *(Sales & Marketing Manager)*
**Operations:** Sana Niazi *(Sales & Marketing Manager)*
**Purchasing:** Sana Niazi *(Sales & Marketing Manager)*
**US SIC:** 2899 **UK SIC:** 25670
**Auditors:** Edwards
**Bankers:** Barclays Bank Plc (20-93-15)

| | 31-12-13 | 31-12-12 | 31-12-11 |
|---|---|---|---|
| TO | 69,356,000 | 65,034,000 | 62,809,000 |
| P/L | 4,416,000 | 4,510,000 | 3,979,000 |
| NW | 34,710,000 | 24,945,000 | 22,461,000 |
| WC | 19,116,000 | 17,820,000 | 14,953,000 |
| Emp. | 113 | 115 | 122 |

DUNS 21-098-1213 **Exp**

## Synthomer Plc

Central Road, Harlow, Essex CM20 2BH
**Tel:** 01279442791 **Fax:** 01279444025
**Web:** www.synthomer.com
**Reg No:** 0098381 **VAT No:** 213828767
**Estd:** 1933 Public Limited Company
**Line of Business:** Management activities of holding companies
**Issued Capital:** £33,988,077
**Directors:** The Hon A G Catto, C G Maclean, J Chen, H H Lee, D C Blackwood, B W Connolly, N A Johnson, J K Maiden
**Co. Secretary:** Richard Atkinson
**Responsibilities**
**Senior:** Lee Hian *(Non-Executive Director)*, Just Jansz *(Director)*, Calum MacLean *(Group Chief Executive Officer)*, Adrian Whitfield *(Chief Executive)*
**Marketing:** Adrian Whitfield *(Chief Executive)*
**Sales:** Adrian Whitfield *(Chief Executive)*
**IT:** Richard Ling *(Divisional IT Manager)*
**HR:** Suzanne Morgan *(Global HR Manager)*
**Facilities:** Adrian Whitfield *(Chief Executive)*
**Operations:** Andy Axford *(Vice President - Operational E)*
**Engineering:** Robin Harrison *(Global Innovation Director)*
**Branches:** Yule Catto & Co Plc,Roundwood Industrial Estate, Wakefield Road, Ossett, WF5 9BQ West Yorkshire
**US SIC:** 6711 **UK SIC:** 83962
**Auditors:** PricewaterhouseCoopers LLP
**Bankers:** HSBC Bank plc (40-23-10)
**Following financial data are in thousands**

| | 31-12-13 | 31-12-12 | 31-12-11 |
|---|---|---|---|
| TO | 992,700 | 1,111,800 | 1,116,862 |
| P/L | 59,100 | 62,300 | 39,439 |
| NW | (60,600) | (102,200) | (146,408) |
| WC | 43,000 | 51,200 | 54,946 |
| Emp. | 2,097 | 2,054 | 2,539 |

DUNS 34-944-3957

## Syscap Holdings Ltd

Wimbledon Bridge House, 1 Hartfield Road, London SW19 3RU
**Tel:** 02082541975
**Web:** www.syscap.com
**Reg No:** 5740449 **Estd:** 1993 Private Limited Company
**Line of Business:** Financial leasing
**Trading Style:** Syscap Holdings Limited
**Issued Capital:** £16,259
**Directors:** J Coombs, M J Henry, J R Allbrook, S M Dunne, P D White
**Co. Secretary:** Steven Dunne
**US SIC:** 6111 **UK SIC:** 81501
**Bankers:** The Royal Bank Of Scotland Plc (16-08-05)

| | 31-03-14 | 31-03-13 | 31-03-12 |
|---|---|---|---|
| TA | 36,841,000 | 42,343,000 | 46,182,000 |
| P/L | (1,701,000) | (1,402,000) | 12,823,000 |
| NW | 884,000 | 501,000 | (388,000) |
| WC | 770,000 | 3,983,000 | 2,671,000 |
| Emp. | 79 | 79 | 75 |

DUNS 34-973-4454

## Sysco Business Skills Academy Ltd

**(Subsidiary of:** Evolve Business Services Ltd)
Threlfall Building, Trueman Street, Liverpool, Merseyside L3 2BA
**Tel:** 0151-236-1748
**Web:** www.sysco.uk.com
**Reg No:** 5768964 **Estd:** 2006 Private Limited Company
**Line of Business:** Adult and other education not elsewhere classified
**Issued Capital:** £250,000
**Directors:** I Smith, P J Donaldson
**Co. Secretary:** Ms Veronica Forshaw
**US SIC:** 8249 **UK SIC:** 93300

| | 31-07-14 | 31-07-13 | 30-07-12 |
|---|---|---|---|
| TO | 3,011,784 | 2,603,906 | 4,262,119 |
| P/L | 204,292 | 130,988 | 123,625 |
| NW | 451,872 | 195,545 | 14,055 |
| WC | 369,222 | 356,496 | 176,397 |
| Emp. | 56 | 63 | 70 |

DUNS 23-276-4555 **Imp-Exp**

## Sysmex U K Ltd

**(Subsidiary of:** Sysmex Corporation)
Sysmex House Garamonde Drive, Milton Keynes, Buckinghamshire MK8 8DF
**Tel:** 08709029210 **Fax:** 08709029211
**Web:** www.sysmex.co.uk
**Reg No:** 2598523 **VAT No:** 563695992
**Estd:** 1991 Private Limited Company
**Line of Business:** Agents specialising in the sale of particular products or ranges of products not elsewhere classified
**Export Markets:** UNITED KINGDOM
**Export Sales:** £3,419,150
**Issued Capital:** £400,000
**Directors:** T Kubota, Dr J Schulze, N Pattinson, K L Howes
**Co. Secretary:** Robert Kaukis
**Responsibilities**
**Senior:** Philippa Pinn *(Manager)*
**Marketing:** Torsten Reinecke *(Marketing Director)*, Elly Stanley *(Market Analyst)*, Joanne Swales *(Marketing Specialist)*
**IT:** Lyn Renwick *(Director of Customer Support C)*
**US SIC:** 5199 **UK SIC:** 61900
**Auditors:** Deloitte & Touche LLP
**Bankers:** Barclays Bank Plc (20-57-40)

| | 31-03-14 | 31-03-13 | 31-03-12 |
|---|---|---|---|
| TO | 35,939,245 | 32,597,835 | 31,706,946 |
| P/L | 3,822,821 | 3,593,087 | 3,286,822 |
| NW | 16,185,674 | 13,347,638 | 10,488,359 |
| WC | 8,383,376 | 5,486,056 | 3,898,007 |
| Emp. | 110 | 102 | 93 |

DUNS 21-135-2227 **Imp**

## Systagenix Wound Management Ltd

**(Subsidiary of:** Acelity L.P. Inc.)
Airebank Mills, Skipton, North Yorkshire BD23 3RX
**Tel:** 01293842000 **Fax:** 08450896024
**Web:** www.systagenix.com
**Reg No:** 6682375 **Estd:** 2008 Private Limited Company
**Line of Business:** Other business activities not elsewhere classified
**Issued Capital:** £5,575,900
**Directors:** P W Huntley, J T Bibb, J P Panther
**Responsibilities**
**Senior:** Jonathan Warrick *(Director)*
**US SIC:** 7399 **UK SIC:** 83954
**Auditors:** PricewaterhouseCoopers LLP

| | 29-12-13 | 30-12-12 | 01-12-12 |
|---|---|---|---|
| TO | 82,265,000 | 69,080,000 | 72,383,000 |
| P/L | (589,000) | (6,083,000) | (15,340,000) |
| NW | (22,264,000) | (29,120,000) | (25,748,000) |
| WC | (24,348,000) | (31,720,000) | (29,711,000) |
| Emp. | 112 | 100 | 99 |

DUNS 21-135-2249

## Systagenix Wound Management Manufacturing Ltd

Airebank Mills, Gargrave, Skipton, North Yorkshire BD23 3RX
**Tel:** 01756749561 **Fax:** 01756748289
**Web:** www.systagenix.com
**Reg No:** 6682392 **Estd:** 2008 Private Limited Company
**Line of Business:** Medical practice activities
**Issued Capital:** £1,585,259
**Directors:** J P Panther, P W Huntley, J T Bibb
**Responsibilities**
**HR:** Carole Evans *(Human Resources Director)*
**Health & Safety:** Nicholas Voigt *(Health & Safety Manager)*
**Operations:** Nicholas Voigt *(Health & Safety Manager)*
**Engineering:** Brian Rayner *(Project Engineering Officer)*
**US SIC:** 8011, 2211
**UK SIC:** 95300, 43220
**Auditors:** PricewaterhouseCoopers LLP

| | 29-12-13 | 30-12-12 | 01-12-12 |
|---|---|---|---|
| TO | 45,025,000 | 39,986,000 | 38,740,000 |
| P/L | 2,854,000 | 2,460,000 | 2,062,000 |
| NW | 19,826,000 | 21,959,000 | 20,172,000 |
| WC | 3,923,000 | 6,746,000 | 4,281,000 |
| Emp. | 430 | 385 | 381 |

DUNS 23-792-0116

## Systech Group Ltd

Chapter House, Montague Close, London SE1 9DA
**Tel:** 02079407630 **Fax:** 02079407657
**Web:** www.systech-int.com
**Reg No:** 3784800 **Estd:** 1999 Private Limited Company
**Line of Business:** Management activities of holding companies
**Export Sales:** £20,626,865
**Issued Capital:** £100
**Directors:** M Woodward Smith, S F Jones
**Co. Secretary:** Simon Jones
**US SIC:** 6711 **UK SIC:** 83962
**Bankers:** National Westminster Bank Plc (50-42-28)

| | 31-03-14 | 31-03-13 | 31-03-12 |
|---|---|---|---|
| TO | 35,832,861 | 34,251,353 | 34,527,823 |
| P/L | 496,575 | 956,225 | 208,547 |
| NW | 789,776 | 3,453,589 | 3,484,013 |
| WC | 507,064 | 3,004,585 | 2,995,213 |
| Emp. | 159 | 196 | 199 |

DUNS 50-146-7955

## System 3 Ltd

Denton Hall, Farm Road, Manchester M34 2SY
**Tel:** 01613373000 **Fax:** 01613370222
**Web:** www.system3.ltd.uk
**Reg No:** 2324887 **VAT No:** 403347974
**Estd:** 1984 Private Limited Company
**Line of Business:** Representative office
**Issued Capital:** £400,000
**Managing Director:** A Brown
**Co. Secretary:** Michael Brown
**Responsibilities**
**Facilities:** Graham Murphy *(Maintenance Manager)*
**Engineering:** Graham Murphy *(Maintenance Manager)*
**US SIC:** 3229, 2421
**UK SIC:** 24791, 46101
**Auditors:** Booth Ainsworth
**Bankers:** Lloyds TSB Bank plc (30-16-79)

| | 31-12-13 | 31-12-12 | 31-12-11 |
|---|---|---|---|
| TO | 16,868,455 | 15,014,799 | 15,398,380 |
| P/L | 1,542,783 | 1,507,270 | 1,874,923 |
| NW | 8,246,235 | 6,645,070 | 5,519,329 |
| WC | 2,991,312 | 2,486,625 | 1,105,551 |
| Emp. | 183 | 180 | 206 |

DUNS 21-128-0670

## System Kitchens Ltd

**(Subsidiary of:** Pkl Intermediate Ltd)
Malvern View, Old Gloucester Road, Cheltenham, Gloucestershire GL51 0TG
**Tel:** 01242663000
**Web:** www.skl.co.uk
**Reg No:** 6627279 **Estd:** 2008 Private Limited Company
**Line of Business:** Miscellaneous Business Services
**Issued Capital:** £2
**Director:** C J Irving
**Co. Secretary:** Pkl Group (Uk) Ltd
**Responsibilities**
**Purchasing:** Lee Moore *(Purchasing Manager)*
**US SIC:** 7399 **UK SIC:** 83954

| | 30-06-14 | 30-06-13 | 30-06-12 |
|---|---|---|---|
| TA | 2 | 2 | 2 |
| NW | 2 | 2 | 2 |

DUNS 23-801-0768

## System Pipework Ltd

25 Hassock Lane North, Shipley, Heanor, Derbyshire DE75 7JB
**Tel:** 01773764080
**Reg No:** 3793695 **Estd:** 1999 Private Limited Company
**Line of Business:** Pipework contractors
**Issued Capital:** £100
**Director:** Ms P Atkin
**Co. Secretary:** William Atkin
**US SIC:** 1711 **UK SIC:** 50300

| | 31-03-14 | 31-03-13 | 31-03-12 |
|---|---|---|---|
| TA | 339,739 | 384,218 | 461,961 |
| NW | 333,516 | 379,910 | 441,262 |
| WC | 332,647 | 379,162 | 440,382 |

DUNS 21-776-3203

## System Training

Hargreaves House, Millshaw, Leeds, West Yorkshire LS11 8LZ
**Web:** www.hargreavestraining.com
**Estd:** 1992 Proprietorship
**Line of Business:** Training services
**Proprietor:** D Hopps
**US SIC:** 8299 **UK SIC:** 93300
**Employees:** 300

DUNS 73-739-2204

## Systemair Fans & Spares Ltd

**(Subsidiary of:** Systemair Ab)
72 Cheston Road, Birmingham, West Midlands B7 5EJ
**Tel:** 01213220200 **Fax:** 01213220311
**Web:** www.fansandspares.co.uk
**Reg No:** 4997065 **Estd:** 2004 Private Limited Company
**Line of Business:** Manufacture of non-domestic cooling and ventilation equipment
**Export Sales:** £100,094
**Trading Style:** Systemair Fans & Spares Ltd
**Issued Capital:** £1,000,000
**Directors:** G Engstrom, N A Rapley
**Co. Secretary:** Mudassar Ali
**Responsibilities**
**Senior:** Awais Jahandad *(Senior Accounts)*
**Finance:** Awais Jahandad *(Senior Accounts)*
**Marketing:** Paul Carberry *(Marketing Manager)*
**Admin:** Awais Jahandad *(Senior Accounts)*
**Branches:** Systemair Fans & Spares Ltd, 1 Chapel Avenue, Liverpool, Merseyside L9 2BZ
**US SIC:** 3585 **UK SIC:** 32841
**Bankers:** Svenska Handelsbanken Ab (publ) (40-51-62)

| | 30-04-14 | 30-04-13 | 30-04-12 |
|---|---|---|---|
| TO | 16,114,065 | 17,778,639 | 15,960,256 |
| P/L | 443,110 | 516,333 | 763,366 |
| NW | (222,392) | (502,545) | (1,352,856) |
| WC | 2,863,702 | 2,621,002 | 2,383,585 |
| Emp. | 83 | 89 | 69 |

DUNS 77-441-0724

## Systematic Logistics International Ltd

Old Ipswich Road, Ardleigh, Colchester, Essex CO7 7QL
**Tel:** 08453687000 **Fax:** 01206-231420
**Web:** www.systematic-uk.com
**Reg No:** 2950750 **Estd:** 1994 Private Limited Company
**Line of Business:** Freight transport by road not elsewhere classified
**Issued Capital:** £5,000
**Directors:** R Triolo, A Triolo
**Co. Secretary:** David Gullen
**Responsibilities**
**Senior:** Christopher Quinsee *(Manager)*
**US SIC:** 4213 **UK SIC:** 72300
**Auditors:** Whittle & Co
**Bankers:** HSBC Bank plc (40-18-51)

| | 31-08-14 | 31-08-13 | 31-08-12 |
|---|---|---|---|
| TA | 3,508,486 | 2,243,667 | 1,804,317 |
| NW | 488,366 | 409,437 | 255,698 |
| WC | (504,200) | (470,615) | (509,697) |

DUNS 21-149-0302
## Systematic Security Ltd
Allied Sanif House, 412 Greenford Road, Greenford, Middlesex UB6 9AH
**Tel:** 02085781935
**Web:** www.systematicsecurity.co.uk
**Reg No:** 6786680 **Estd:** 2009 Private Limited Company
**Line of Business:** Security activities
**Issued Capital:** £100
**Directors:** Mrs K Malik, A H Malik
**US SIC:** 7393 **UK SIC:** 83954

| | 28-02-14 | 28-02-13 | 29-02-12 |
|---|---|---|---|
| TA | 747,637 | 541,252 | 419,603 |
| NW | 124,696 | 75,212 | 71,520 |
| WC | 110,365 | 66,782 | 61,841 |

DUNS 49-316-7449
## Systems Adi Group Ltd
66 Melchett Road, Kings Norton, Birmingham, West Midlands B30 3HX
**Tel:** 0121 451 2255
**Web:** www.adiltd.co.uk
**Reg No:** 3124499 **Estd:** 1995 Private Limited Company
**Line of Business:** Management activities of holding companies
**Export Sales:** £7,674,050
**Issued Capital:** £200
**Director:** A Lusty
**Co. Secretary:** Mrs Tina Lusty
**Branches:** Systems Adi Group Ltd, Unit 1-3, Mayfield Road, Birmingham, West Midlands B30 2NS
**US SIC:** 6711 **UK SIC:** 83962
**Auditors:** Nicklin LLP

| | 31-12-13 | 31-12-12 | 31-12-11 |
|---|---|---|---|
| TO | 42,752,384 | 34,874,817 | 29,012,921 |
| P/L | 1,463,334 | 742,092 | 394,394 |
| NW | 5,656,165 | 5,162,114 | 4,913,117 |
| WC | 5,040,955 | 4,686,358 | 5,041,119 |
| Emp. | 354 | 266 | 250 |

DUNS 50-022-2328 Imp-Exp
## Systems Engineering & Assessment Ltd
**(Subsidiary of:** Cohort Plc)
17 Castle Corner, Frome, Somerset BA11 6TA
**Fax:** 01373851133
**Web:** www.sea.co.uk
**Reg No:** 2302168 **VAT No:** 501843965
**Estd:** 1988 Private Limited Company
**Line of Business:** Manufacture of aircraft and spacecraft
**Export Markets:** countries worldwide
**Export Sales:** £3,965,000
**Trading Style:** Sea
**Issued Capital:** £63,553
**Directors:** S J Hill, A S Thomis, S R Walther
**Co. Secretary:** Mrs Emily Davies
**Responsibilities**
**Senior:** Sara Mannix *(Manager)*
**Branches:** Systems Engineering & Assessment Ltd, 660 Bristol Business Park, Bristol, Avon BS16 1EJ
**US SIC:** 3721, 3799, 9711, 9221
**UK SIC:** 36400, 36502, 91300
**Auditors:** Baker Tilly UK Audit LLP
**Bankers:** National Westminster Bank Plc (60-02-05)

| | 30-04-14 | 30-04-13 | 30-04-12 |
|---|---|---|---|
| TO | 29,137,000 | 31,925,000 | 31,797,000 |
| P/L | 3,543,000 | 2,447,000 | 977,000 |
| NW | 15,391,000 | 12,461,000 | 9,911,000 |
| WC | 15,068,000 | 12,127,000 | 9,527,000 |
| Emp. | 210 | 213 | 217 |

DUNS 21-037-1909
## Systems for Learning
P O Box 184, Rotherwas Industrial Estate, Hereford, Herefordshire HR2 6WT
**Tel:** 01432-845143
**Web:** www.systems4learning.co.uk
**Proprietorship**
**Line of Business:** Wholesale of computers, computer peripheral equipment and software
**Proprietor:** I Peberdy
**Responsibilities**
**Senior:** Paul Shepherd *(Operations Manager)*
**Admin:** Maria Bullock *(Company Secratery)*
**US SIC:** 5081 **UK SIC:** 61490
**Employees:** 50

DUNS 21-150-4467
## Systems Labelling Express Ltd.
**(Subsidiary of:** Ryhall Ltd)
Unit 109 Tenth Avenue, Deeside Industrial Park, Deeside, Clwyd CH5 2UA
**Tel:** 01244-286300
**Web:** www.systemslabelling.com
**Reg No:** 6797731 **Estd:** 2009 Private Limited Company
**Line of Business:** Printers general
**Issued Capital:** £10
**Directors:** P ( Doran, D W Boyce
**Co. Secretary:** Desmond Boyce
**Responsibilities**
**Senior:** David Bouch *(Managing Director)*, Steven Pickford *(CEO)*
**US SIC:** 2794, 3554
**UK SIC:** 47545, 32754

| | 31-12-13 | 31-08-13 | 31-12-12 |
|---|---|---|---|
| TA | 10 | 10 | 10 |
| NW | 10 | 10 | 10 |

DUNS 50-191-2695
## Systems Technology (S.E.) Ltd
**(Subsidiary of:** Tallgrand Ltd)
Unit 41 Riverside Estate, Rochester, Kent ME2 4DP
**Tel:** 01634-291124 **Fax:** 01634-291125
**Web:** www.systemstechnology.co.uk
**Reg No:** 2330639 **VAT No:** 522674646
**Estd:** 1988 Private Limited Company
**Line of Business:** Wholesale of other office machinery and equipment
**Issued Capital:** £8,000
**Principals:** S J Gradus *(Chairman and Managing)*, Ms N Hildyard, J Gradus
**Co. Secretary:** Ms Zana Gradus
**Responsibilities**
**Senior:** Natasha Gradus *(Director Of Company)*
**US SIC:** 5081 **UK SIC:** 61490
**Auditors:** Baxter & Co
**Bankers:** National Westminster Bank Plc (60-60-08)

| | 30-06-14 | 30-06-13 | 30-06-12 |
|---|---|---|---|
| TO | 7,522,511 | 7,084,728 | N/A |
| P/L | 2,311,072 | 2,127,128 | N/A |
| NW | 3,764,972 | 3,220,470 | 2,348,146 |
| WC | 3,679,090 | 3,136,285 | 2,406,793 |
| Emp. | 46 | 46 | N/A |

DUNS 49-454-6716 Imp
## Systopia Consulting Ltd
Pixash Business Centre, Pixash Lane, Bristol, Avon BS31 1TP
**Tel:** 01179861611
**Web:** www.systopia.co.uk
**Reg No:** 3146555 **Estd:** 2011 Private Limited Company
**Line of Business:** Miscellaneous computer services
**Issued Capital:** £11,111
**Directors:** S Armstrong, C B Lyons
**Co. Secretary:** Leigh Thomas
**US SIC:** 7379, 7394
**UK SIC:** 83940, 84000
**Auditors:** Corrigan Associates Bristol LLP

| | 31-03-14 | 31-03-13 | 31-03-12 |
|---|---|---|---|
| TO | N/A | 2,035,159 | N/A |
| P/L | N/A | 307,354 | N/A |
| NW | 1,041,732 | 1,097,453 | 954,995 |
| WC | 996,054 | 1,066,771 | 908,573 |

DUNS 52-016-6018 Exp
## Systra Ltd
**(Subsidiary of:** Systra)
Fourth Floor Dukes Court, Woking, Surrey GU21 5BH
**Tel:** 01483-728051 **Fax:** 01483723899
**Web:** www.systra.co.uk
**Reg No:** 3383212 **Estd:** 1982 Private Limited Company
**Line of Business:** Business and management consultancy activities not elsewhere classified
**Export Markets:** REST OF WORLD
**Trading Style:** Systra
**Issued Capital:** £2,750,000
**Directors:** O J Dezorme, P Mercier, T O'Neill, B Schmitt, Ms S J Cambone
**Co. Secretary:** John Roberts
**Responsibilities**
**Senior:** Aidan Eaglestone *(Director - Business Consulting)*, Philippe Naudi *(Director)*, Pierre Odent *(Director)*
**Finance:** Mike Prager *(Financial Director)*
**Admin:** Maria Michael *(HR Assistant)*
**HR:** Maria Michael *(HR Assistant)*
**Health & Safety:** Linda Fuller *(Facilities Manager)*
**Facilities:** Dave Carter *(Deputy Divisional Director)*, Linda Fuller *(Facilities Manager)*
**Branches:** Systra Ltd, 78 St Vincent Street, Glasgow, Lanarkshire G2 5UB
**US SIC:** 7392 **UK SIC:** 83951
**Auditors:** PricewaterhouseCoopers

| | 31-12-13 | 31-12-12 | 31-12-11 |
|---|---|---|---|
| TO | 15,129,375 | 15,769,898 | 18,561,237 |
| P/L | 1,547,241 | 308,665 | (2,503,537) |
| NW | 2,975,827 | 2,454,553 | 1,921,959 |
| WC | 2,850,510 | 2,295,297 | 1,777,161 |
| Emp. | 157 | 158 | 204 |

DUNS 21-393-9173
## Sytner
Unit 1-7-8 Wolfe Close, Parkgate Industrial Estate, Knutsford, Cheshire WA16 8XJ
**Tel:** 01565654662
**Web:** www.gloryglobalsolutions.com
**Estd:** 2002 Proprietorship
**Line of Business:** Architectural woodwork
**Proprietor:** Ms L Orrell
**Responsibilities**
**Senior:** Greggor Dobbie *(Manager)*, Robert Sims *(Dealer Principal)*
**Sales:** Simon Hinsley *(After Sales Manager)*, Robert Sims *(Dealer Principal)*
**Operations:** Simon Hinsley *(After Sales Manager)*
**US SIC:** 8911 **UK SIC:** 83701
**Employees:** 100

DUNS 21-769-5577
## Sytner B M W
Bath Road, Maidenhead, Berkshire SL6 0BW
**Tel:** 01628680300
**Web:** www.sytnermaidenheadbmw.co.uk
**Estd:** 2001 Proprietorship
**Line of Business:** Sale of new motor vehicles
**Proprietor:** R Sims
**Responsibilities**
**Senior:** Paul Fruen *(Manager)*
**US SIC:** 5511 **UK SIC:** 65100
**Employees:** 60

DUNS 21-032-4777
## Sytner Bmw
575-647 London Road, High Wycombe, Buckinghamshire HP11 1EZ
**Tel:** 01494-455100
**Web:** www.sytnerhighwycombebmw.co.uk
**Proprietorship**
**Line of Business:** Sale of new motor vehicles
**Proprietor:** A Jordan
**Responsibilities**
**Senior:** Richard Berry *(Dealer Principal)*
**Marketing:** Liz Mayne *(Marketing Manager)*
**HR:** Victoria Clarke *(Human Resources Manager)*
**US SIC:** 5511 **UK SIC:** 65100
**Employees:** 150

DUNS 21-250-0098
## Sytner Bmw Ltd
128 Holyhead Road, Coventry, West Midlands CV5 8NA
**Web:** www.sytnercoventrybmw.co.uk
**Estd:** 1986
**Line of Business:** Car dealers (new & used)
**US SIC:** 5511 **UK SIC:** 65100
**Employees:** 70

DUNS 21-284-0558
## Sytner Cardiff Bmw
50 Penarth Road, Cardiff, South Glamorgan CF10 5RS
**Tel:** 02920550300
**Web:** www.stimacardiffbmw.co.uk
**Estd:** 2001 Proprietorship
**Line of Business:** Car dealers (new & used)
**Proprietor:** D Hall
**Responsibilities**
**Finance:** Becky Hale *(Accountant)*, Lee Perry *(Finance Administrator)*
**US SIC:** 5511 **UK SIC:** 65100
**Employees:** 80

DUNS 57-195-0930 Imp
## Sytner Group Ltd
**(Subsidiary of:** Penske Automotive Group Inc.)
2 Penman Way, Grove Park, Enderby, Leicester, Leicestershire LE19 1ST
**Tel:** 08454810148 **Fax:** 01162821010
**Web:** www.sytner.co.uk
**Reg No:** 2883766 **Estd:** 1993 Private Limited Company
**Line of Business:** Management activities of holding companies
**Trading Style:** Smart of Newcastle, Graypaul Ferrari Birmingham
**Issued Capital:** £2,724,020
**Principals:** L E Vaughan *(Managing)*, R S Penske, G E Nieuwenhuys, J R Mallett, D Edwards, R H Kurnick, J C Werner, G Page Morris
**Co. Secretary:** Adam Collinson
**Responsibilities**
**Senior:** Sue Sansome *(Training Director)*
**Admin:** Karl Matysik *(Network Administrator)*
**IT:** Peter Huxley *(Project Manager)*, Karl Matysik *(Network Administrator)*
**HR:** Melvin Rogers *(Head of Human Resources)*, Sue Sansome *(Training Director)*
**Health & Safety:** Alan Hollyhoake *(Health & Safety Manager)*
**Facilities:** Edward Lees *(Facilities Manager)*
**Branches:** Sytner Group Ltd, 33 Parker Dr, Leicester, Leicestershire LE4 0JP
**US SIC:** 6711, 5511
**UK SIC:** 83962, 65100
**Auditors:** KPMG Audit PLC
**Bankers:** National Westminster Bank Plc (60-80-09)

Following financial data are in thousands

| | 31-12-13 | 31-12-12 | 31-12-11 |
|---|---|---|---|
| TO | 3,220,886 | 2,967,035 | 2,659,497 |
| P/L | 64,660 | 54,609 | 49,153 |
| NW | 97,003 | 114,399 | 95,197 |
| WC | (105,199) | (64,545) | (76,205) |
| Emp. | 6,048 | 5,995 | 5,090 |

DUNS 21-606-4411
## Sytner Newport Mini & Bmw
Usk Way The Old Town Dock, Newport, Gwent NP20 2DS
**Tel:** 01633255322
**Web:** www.sytnernewportbmw.co.uk
**Estd:** 2007
**Line of Business:** Car dealers (new & used)
**Partners:** K Farrell, G Fowler
**US SIC:** 5511 **UK SIC:** 65100
**Employees:** 60

DUNS 21-584-1294
## Sytner Sunningdale
1 Lyndhurst Buildings, Lyndhurst Road, Ascot, Berkshire SL5 9ED
**Tel:** 01344637600
**Web:** www.sunningdalebmw.co.uk
**Estd:** 2011 Proprietorship
**Line of Business:** Car and commercial vehicle repairs
**Proprietor:** R Sims
**US SIC:** 7539 **UK SIC:** 67100
**Employees:** 50

DUNS 29-621-5866 Imp
## Szerelmey Ltd
**(Subsidiary of:** Tellisford Ltd)
369 Kennington Lane, London SE11 5QY
**Tel:** 020-7735-9995
**Web:** www.szerelmey.com
**Reg No:** 1948091 **VAT No:** 689645660
**Estd:** 1985 Private Limited Company
**Line of Business:** Stonemasons
**Issued Capital:** £500,100
**Directors:** A Buffa, D Moore, N J Maceachin
**Co. Secretary:** Paul Wisdom
**Responsibilities**
**Senior:** Andy Whiterod *(Manager)*
**Marketing:** Mark Chivers *(Marketing Director)*
**US SIC:** 1799, 1522
**UK SIC:** 50000, 50100
**Auditors:** The Trevor Jones Partnership LLP
**Bankers:** Barclays Bank Plc (20-82-94)

| | 31-12-13 | 31-12-12 | 31-12-11 |
|---|---|---|---|
| TO | 14,059,860 | 8,516,172 | 6,094,510 |
| P/L | 74,758 | 159,737 | 3,545 |
| NW | 911,324 | 847,518 | 727,086 |
| WC | 840,566 | 742,385 | 656,272 |
| Emp. | 49 | 57 | 55 |

# T

DUNS 21-579-5853
## T A Centre Barnet
Territorial Army Centre, St Albans Road, Barnet, Hertfordshire EN5 4JX
**Tel:** 02084491134
**Web:** www.army.com
**Estd:** 1938 Proprietorship
**Line of Business:** Armed forces
**Proprietor:** I Holt
**US SIC:** 9711
**UK SIC:** 50000, 50100
**Employees:** 108

DUNS 22-769-1987
## T A D Builders Ltd
Temple Works, Llanelli, Dyfed SA14 9SE
**Tel:** 01554-752884
**Web:** www.tadbuilders.co.uk
**Reg No:** 1436611 **VAT No:** 326990725
**Estd:** 1979 Private Limited Company
**Line of Business:** Building construction contractors
**Issued Capital:** £99
**Principals:** A L Jones *(Managing)*, Ms N M Jones, D V Jones, Ms M Jones
**Responsibilities**
**Senior:** Eileen Jones *(Manager)*
**US SIC:** 6552, 1541, 1522
**UK SIC:** 85000, 50100
**Bankers:** HSBC Bank plc (40-30-10)

| | 30-09-13 | 01-10-12 | 31-09-11 |
|---|---|---|---|
| TA | 4,158,846 | 3,264,871 | 3,037,522 |
| NW | 2,634,914 | 2,135,285 | 1,534,946 |
| WC | 1,541,658 | 1,281,372 | 801,941 |

**DUNS 21-213-0772**
## T A Gardner Dental Laboratory
2 Albertville Drive, Belfast BT14 7BX
**Tel:** 028-9035-1406
**Web:** www.tagdental.com
**Estd:** 1973 Proprietorship
**Line of Business:** Dental technicians
**Proprietor:** T A Gardner
**US SIC:** 8021 **UK SIC:** 95400
**Employees:** 49

**DUNS 28-832-2639**    *Imp*
## T A Savery & Co Ltd
(Subsidiary of: Brigam Ltd)
Grovelands, Coventry, West Midlands CV7 9NE
**Tel:** 01213804514
**Web:** www.savery.co.uk
**Reg No:** 0272170 **VAT No:** 110073045
**Estd:** 1933 Private Limited Company
**Line of Business:** Manufacture of pumps
**Export Sales:** £18,856,118
**Issued Capital:** £6,500
**Directors:** S Sahota, Ms L A Sahota
**Co. Secretary:** Ian Whiting
**Responsibilities**
**Senior:** Kulbir Kandhola *(Manager)*
**US SIC:** 3561 **UK SIC:** 32870
**Auditors:** Grant Thornton UK LLP
**Bankers:** National Westminster Bank Plc (60-02-35)

| | 30-06-14 | 30-06-13 | 30-06-12 |
|---|---|---|---|
| TO | 24,708,068 | 21,771,049 | 21,410,180 |
| P/L | 1,297,045 | 1,185,763 | 900,666 |
| NW | 7,128,479 | 6,058,211 | 4,912,578 |
| WC | 5,541,461 | 4,925,192 | 4,091,491 |
| Emp. | 235 | 211 | 186 |

**DUNS 22-926-3819**
## T & A Kernoghan (Holdings) Ltd
5 Blackwater Road, Newtownabbey, Co Antrim BT36 4TZ
**Tel:** 028-9084-2311
**Web:** www.t-agroup.com
**Reg No:** 0012993NI **Estd:** 1978 Private Limited Company
**Line of Business:** Residential building contractors
**Issued Capital:** £10,000
**Directors:** W A Kernoghan, Miss J Kernoghan, Mrs R Thompson, M Thompson
**Co. Secretary:** Martin Mcginn
**Responsibilities**
**Senior:** Gerald Maxwell *(Manager)*
**US SIC:** 1522, 6519
**UK SIC:** 50100, 85000
**Auditors:** PricewaterhouseCoopers LLP
**Bankers:** Ulster Bank Ltd (98-10-80)

| | 31-03-14 | 31-03-13 | 31-03-12 |
|---|---|---|---|
| TO | 25,516,609 | 26,675,930 | 35,917,335 |
| P/L | 145,970 | 115,602 | (4,609) |
| NW | 4,247,705 | 4,258,539 | 4,217,381 |
| WC | 2,180,816 | 2,189,967 | 2,129,458 |
| Emp. | 88 | 88 | 97 |

**DUNS 21-921-5720**    *Imp*
## T. & B. Containers Ltd
(Subsidiary of: Wrangle Box Holdings Ltd)
Brenton Villa, Wrangle Bank, Boston, Lincolnshire PE22 9DL
**Tel:** 01205-270200
**Web:** www.tbcontainers.com
**Reg No:** 1327043 **VAT No:** 288661507
**Estd:** 1977 Private Limited Company
**Line of Business:** Manufacturers of boxes and cartons
**Issued Capital:** £10,000
**Directors:** A J Dickinson, Ms D J Curtis, Mrs L A Dickinson, T J Curtis
**Co. Secretary:** Ms Brenda Dickinson
**US SIC:** 2651, 5199
**UK SIC:** 47253, 61900
**Auditors:** Duncan & Toplis
**Bankers:** Lloyds TSB Bank plc (30-91-04)

| | 30-09-13 | 30-09-12 | 30-09-11 |
|---|---|---|---|
| TO | 12,401,511 | 12,037,518 | 10,746,765 |
| P/L | 74,116 | 367,656 | 21,796 |
| NW | 4,707,992 | 4,644,810 | 4,484,141 |
| WC | 2,953,395 | 3,023,634 | 2,879,268 |
| Emp. | 66 | 61 | 63 |

**DUNS 28-958-6372**
## T & B (Contractors) Ltd
Riverside House, Place Farm, Wheathampstead, St Albans, Hertfordshire AL4 8SB
**Tel:** 01582833633 **Fax:** 01582-833899
**Web:** www.tandbcontractors.com
**Reg No:** 1667869 **VAT No:** 780011663
**Estd:** 1982 Private Limited Company
**Line of Business:** Builders
**Issued Capital:** £10,000
**Directors:** R W Wishart, M D Hickson, R Borras, N R Stephen, A Skilton, T L Swallow, K R Odell
**Co. Secretary:** Ms Carol Borras
**US SIC:** 1522 **UK SIC:** 50100

**Auditors:** Macintyre Hudson LLP
**Bankers:** The Royal Bank Of Scotland Plc (16-01-50)

| | 31-12-13 | 31-12-12 | 31-12-11 |
|---|---|---|---|
| TO | 36,892,083 | 30,909,967 | 29,720,699 |
| P/L | 563,325 | 201,416 | 256,213 |
| NW | 4,882,777 | 2,001,393 | 1,853,182 |
| WC | 4,139,739 | 1,356,552 | 1,291,971 |
| Emp. | 81 | 79 | 71 |

**DUNS 52-027-9936**
## T & C C Ltd
Minsthorpe Lane, South Elmsall, Pontefract, West Yorkshire WF9 2UJ
**Tel:** 01977657600 **Fax:** 01977657605
**Web:** www.minsthorpe.wakefield.sch.uk
**Reg No:** 3394512 **Estd:** 1999 Private Limited Company
**Line of Business:** Holding companies management activities
**Trading Style:** Minsthorpe Community College
**Issued Capital:** £100
**Directors:** R P Henshaw, Mrs B L Semper
**Co. Secretary:** Ms Gillian Earith
**US SIC:** 6711, 7392
**UK SIC:** 83962, 83951
**Auditors:** Child & Co

| | 30-09-13 | 30-09-12 | 30-09-11 |
|---|---|---|---|
| TA | 98,165 | 71,502 | 81,188 |
| NW | 65,161 | 57,497 | 53,936 |
| WC | 31,323 | 54,765 | 47,930 |

**DUNS 50-504-9536**
## T. & C. Site Services Ltd
Europa House, Garner Street, Stoke-On-Trent, Staffordshire ST4 7BE
**Web:** www.tcsiteservices.co.uk
**Reg No:** 2472574 **VAT No:** 435537935
**Estd:** 1986 Private Limited Company
**Line of Business:** Maintenance and repair of motor vehicles
**Export Sales:** £41,150
**Issued Capital:** £2
**Principals:** T J Adams *(Managing)*, N D Adams, T J Adams, M A Leedham
**Co. Secretary:** Mrs Christine Adams
**Branches:** T. & C. Site Services Ltd, Kings Cliffe Industrial Estate, Unit 12, Peterborough, Cambridgeshire PE8 6PB
**US SIC:** 7539, 5531
**UK SIC:** 67100, 65100
**Auditors:** Kevin J Burke
**Bankers:** HSBC Bank plc (40-34-13)

| | 31-05-14 | 31-05-13 | 31-05-12 |
|---|---|---|---|
| TO | 9,274,535 | 10,055,860 | 9,890,001 |
| P/L | (7,637) | 142,860 | 246,539 |
| NW | 1,735,539 | 1,743,331 | 1,630,561 |
| WC | 1,147,092 | 1,159,833 | 1,148,817 |
| Emp. | 55 | 54 | 54 |

**DUNS 21-676-7144**
## T & G Allan Holdings Ltd
Unit 5, Gateshead, Tyne and Wear NE11 0TX
**Web:** www.penshop.co.uk
**Reg No:** 7281343 **Estd:** 2010 Private Limited Company
**Line of Business:** Book retailers
**Issued Capital:** £160,292
**Directors:** J R Allan, A J Briggs, C P Mcclymont, Venture Stream Limited, Techvice Limited, A W Stephen, R B Allan, P H Turton
**Co. Secretary:** Mrs Margaret Stephen
**US SIC:** 5942 **UK SIC:** 65300
**Bankers:** National Westminster Bank Plc (60-15-08)

| | 28-09-13 | 29-09-12 | 01-09-11 |
|---|---|---|---|
| TO | 8,974,156 | 8,607,729 | 9,190,645 |
| P/L | 33,200 | 83,899 | (29,615) |
| NW | 1,610,609 | 1,674,423 | 1,600,736 |
| WC | 753,860 | 816,938 | 723,138 |
| Emp. | 152 | 150 | 169 |

**DUNS 28-846-9703**
## T. & G. Davies (Mumbles) Ltd
Gloucester Bakery, Gors Avenue, Cwmbwrla, Swansea, West Glamorgan SA1 6RH
**Tel:** 01792480213
**Reg No:** 0651728 **Estd:** 1960 Private Limited Company
**Line of Business:** Bakers shops
**Trading Style:** T. & G. Davies (Mumbles) Ltd
**Issued Capital:** £6,738
**Director:** A G James
**Co. Secretary:** Winifred Davies
**Responsibilities**
**Health & Safety:** Joanne James *(Health & Safety Officer)*
**Operations:** Joanne James *(Health & Safety Officer)*
**Branches:** T. & G. Davies (Mumbles) Ltd, Davies Of Mumbles Ltd, 520 Mumbles Road, Swansea, West Glamorgan SA3 4BU
**US SIC:** 5462 **UK SIC:** 64100
**Auditors:** K B Ferguson

**Bankers:** HSBC Bank plc (40-33-24)

| | 28-02-14 | 28-02-13 | 28-02-12 |
|---|---|---|---|
| TA | 433,278 | 472,146 | 436,790 |
| NW | 77,256 | 71,397 | 67,787 |
| WC | 18,060 | (39,476) | (42,020) |

**DUNS 22-511-0295**    *Imp-Exp*
## T & G Woodware Ltd
Old Mill Road, Portishead, Bristol, Avon BS20 7BX
**Tel:** 01275841841 **Fax:** 01275-841800
**Web:** www.tg-woodware.com
**Reg No:** 1226994 **VAT No:** 224267673
**Estd:** 1975 Private Limited Company
**Line of Business:** Kitchenware
**Export Markets:** Worldwide
**Issued Capital:** £37,500
**Principals:** P S Gardner *(Managing)*, Ms C E Stevens, Ms V E Saunders
**Co. Secretary:** Roger Adlam
**Responsibilities**
**Marketing:** Jenny Handley *(Marketing Manager)*, Gill Tovey *(Marketing Coordinator)*
**Sales:** Chris Mancini *(Sales Manager)*
**Operations:** Jenny Handley *(Marketing Manager)*
**US SIC:** 3551 **UK SIC:** 32441
**Auditors:** KPMG
**Bankers:** HSBC Bank plc (40-14-13)

| | 31-12-13 | 31-12-12 | 31-12-11 |
|---|---|---|---|
| TA | 2,395,982 | 2,112,987 | 2,328,802 |
| NW | 1,407,660 | 1,293,253 | 1,004,649 |
| WC | 1,318,878 | 1,272,723 | 983,711 |

**DUNS 39-689-0477**
## T. & N. Gilmartin (Contractors) Ltd
Mont-View House, Hangmans Lane, Cupar, Fife KY15 4PG
**Tel:** 01334-655512
**Web:** www.tngilmartin.co.uk
**Reg No:** 0105726SC **Estd:** 1987 Private Limited Company
**Line of Business:** Landscape contractors
**Issued Capital:** £1,004
**Principals:** T J Gilmartin *(Managing)*, Ms D M Mcelhinney
**Co. Secretary:** Ms Patricia Gilmartin
**Responsibilities**
**Senior:** Philip Mcelhinney *(Manager)*
**Purchasing:** Scott Mercer *(Purchasing Manager)*
**US SIC:** 0729, 1622
**UK SIC:** 01003, 50200
**Auditors:** Miller McIntyre & Gellatly CA
**Bankers:** Clydesdale Bank Plc (82-62-01)

| | 30-04-14 | 30-04-13 | 30-04-12 |
|---|---|---|---|
| TO | 6,047,227 | 5,307,091 | 5,686,223 |
| P/L | 665,436 | 745,976 | 489,807 |
| NW | 6,789,339 | 6,949,549 | 6,771,988 |
| WC | 3,392,922 | 4,866,322 | 4,983,279 |
| Emp. | 91 | 91 | 88 |

**DUNS 76-949-4113**
## T & P Fire Ltd
Mainline House, Roudham Park Industrial Estate, East Harling, Norwich, Norfolk NR16 2SN
**Tel:** 08450-770-079 **Fax:** 01953-718-200
**Web:** www.tpfire.co.uk
**Reg No:** 2476883 **VAT No:** 571526048
**Estd:** 1990 Private Limited Company
**Line of Business:** Installation of electrical wiring and fittings
**Trading Style:** Mainline House
**Issued Capital:** £17,333
**Directors:** M C Harris, C K James, T R Young, S J England
**Co. Secretary:** Brian Martin
**Responsibilities**
**Senior:** Steve Maggs *(Store Manager)*
**Branches:** T & P Fire Limited, Unit 6, Beauchamp Court, 10 Victors Way, Barnet, Hertfordshire EN5 5TZ
**US SIC:** 1731, 3629
**UK SIC:** 50300, 34350
**Auditors:** Haines Watts
**Bankers:** HSBC Bank plc (40-35-09)

| | 30-04-14 | 30-04-13 | 30-04-12 |
|---|---|---|---|
| TA | 1,691,999 | 1,222,894 | 1,174,325 |
| NW | 647,309 | 618,261 | 624,359 |
| WC | 365,114 | 467,465 | 492,904 |

**DUNS 29-822-2951**
## T & P Lead Roofing Ltd
5a Lampits Hill, Stanford-Le-Hope, Essex SS17 9AA
**Tel:** 01375676908
**Web:** www.tandpleadroofing.co.uk
**Reg No:** 2040422 **VAT No:** 451834155
**Estd:** 1986 Private Limited Company
**Line of Business:** Roofing contracting services
**Trading Style:** T & P Sheets Works
**Issued Capital:** £1,000
**Principals:** P L Hibbert *(Managing)*, T J Flaherty
**Co. Secretary:** Mrs Iris Hibbert

**Responsibilities**
**Senior:** Flaherty James *(Manager)*
**US SIC:** 1761 **UK SIC:** 50400
**Bankers:** Barclays Bank Plc (20-34-69)

| | 31-07-13 | 31-07-12 | 31-07-11 |
|---|---|---|---|
| TA | 845,050 | 1,379,319 | 1,098,241 |
| NW | 590,800 | 692,546 | 685,698 |
| WC | 468,053 | N/A | 560,850 |

**DUNS 73-667-5211**
## T & R Precision Engineering Ltd
Lowther Lane, Colne, Lancashire BB8 7JY
**Tel:** 01282862116
**Web:** www.trprecision.co.uk
**Reg No:** 4927024 **VAT No:** 823901638
**Estd:** 2003 Private Limited Company
**Line of Business:** Manufacture of tools
**Issued Capital:** £1,800
**Director:** T A Maddison
**Responsibilities**
**HR:** A Danson *(Buyer)*
**US SIC:** 7399 **UK SIC:** 83954

| | 31-08-13 | 31-08-12 | 31-08-11 |
|---|---|---|---|
| TO | 5,497,558 | N/A | N/A |
| P/L | 458,952 | N/A | N/A |
| NW | 939,874 | 780,808 | 390,937 |
| WC | 61,972 | 289,198 | 169,079 |
| Emp. | 61 | N/A | N/A |

**DUNS 29-569-9011**
## T. & S. (Holdings) Ltd
Unit 2 Central Trading Estate, Signal Way, Swindon, Wiltshire SN3 1PD
**Tel:** 01793613369
**Web:** www.allcap.co.uk
**Reg No:** 1931796 **Estd:** 1982 Private Limited Company
**Line of Business:** Manufacturers of bolts and fixings
**Issued Capital:** £49,992
**Principals:** P White *(Managing)*, Mrs C T Moore, Mrs A White
**Co. Secretary:** Peter White
**Responsibilities**
**Senior:** Clive Horne *(Manager)*, Mark Rodderick *(Manager)*
**US SIC:** 6711, 2599, 6552
**UK SIC:** 83962, 46720, 85000
**Auditors:** Monahans

| | 30-09-14 | 31-03-13 | 31-09-12 |
|---|---|---|---|
| TA | 932,205 | 806,640 | 892,766 |
| NW | 759,273 | 773,965 | 822,908 |
| WC | 42,281 | 42,973 | 77,916 |

**DUNS 21-580-9740**
## T B Lyttle & Sons
43 Lisnasure Road, Dromore, Co Down BT25 1JH
**VAT No:** 283077251 **Estd:** 1975 Partnership
**Line of Business:** Retail sale of electrical household appliances and radio and television goods
**Trading Style:** Lisnasure Interiors
**Partners:** N Lyttle, M Lyttle, A Lyttle, H Lyttle, J H Lyttle, Miss B Lyttle, D A Lyttle
**Branches:** T B Lyttle & Sons, 12A High Street, Craigavon, Co Armagh BT66 8AW
**US SIC:** 5732 **UK SIC:** 64800
**Bankers:** First Trust Bank (aib Group (uk) Plc) (93-81-14)
**Employees:** 70

**DUNS 28-908-0731**    *Imp*
## T. Baden Hardstaff Ltd
Hillside, Gotham Road, Kingston-On-Soar, Nottingham, Nottinghamshire NG11 0DF
**Tel:** 0115 983 2300
**Web:** www.hardstaffgroup.co.uk
**Reg No:** 1398234 **VAT No:** 309741552
**Estd:** 1978 Private Limited Company
**Line of Business:** Road haulage and transport services
**Trading Style:** Charnwood Truck Services
**Issued Capital:** £100,000
**Principals:** T L Fletcher *(Managing)*, N M Whittaker, M S Llewellyn
**Co. Secretary:** Charles Bryant
**Responsibilities**
**Senior:** Robert Ashby *(Director)*
**Finance:** Mark Lord *(Contracts Director)*
**HR:** Ian Sawyer *(Human Resources Manager)*
**US SIC:** 4789, 5511
**UK SIC:** 77002, 65100
**Auditors:** Deloitte LLP
**Bankers:** National Westminster Bank Plc (60-14-10)

| | 31-03-13 | 31-03-12 | 31-03-11 |
|---|---|---|---|
| TO | 24,398,683 | 22,340,608 | 21,734,124 |
| P/L | (561,919) | (1,297,875) | (749,422) |
| NW | 3,802,296 | 3,911,747 | 5,162,257 |
| WC | (1,670,765) | (2,477,336) | (1,523,094) |
| Emp. | 235 | 245 | 240 |

DUNS 22-658-3623
## T Balfe Construction Ltd
Richmond House, Low Fields, Grantham, Lincolnshire NG32 3JF
**Tel:** 01400-273700
**Web:** www.tbalfe.co.uk
**Reg No:** 1818688 **VAT No:** 116879440
**Estd:** 1949 Private Limited Company
**Line of Business:** Building construction contractors
**Trading Style:** T Balfe Construction Limited
**Issued Capital:** £100
**Principals:** D E Balfe *(Managing)*, S R Balfe, J E Boyle, S D Balfe
**Co. Secretary:** David Balfe
**Branches:** T Balfe Construction Ltd, Pump Hollow Lane, Forest Town, Mansfield, Nottinghamshire NG19 0AS
**US SIC:** 1522, 1541
**UK SIC:** 50100
**Auditors:** Wright Vigar Ltd
**Bankers:** Barclays Bank Plc (20-50-21)

| | 31-12-13 | 31-12-12 | 31-12-11 |
|---|---|---|---|
| TO | 10,975,055 | 8,472,615 | 13,698,503 |
| P/L | (360,803) | 270,307 | 177,512 |
| NW | 1,812,319 | 2,102,015 | 1,810,210 |
| WC | 2,293,755 | 2,481,343 | 1,155,412 |
| Emp. | 52 | 49 | 51 |

DUNS 21-728-5386 **Imp-Exp**
## T Bourne & Son Ltd
Harbour Road, Rye, East Sussex TN31 7TE
**Tel:** 01797228000 **Fax:** 01797228100
**Web:** www.bournes-uts.co.uk
**Reg No:** 0447169 **VAT No:** 201087708
**Estd:** 1947 Private Limited Company
**Line of Business:** Local hauliers & warehousers
**Trading Style:** Uts-Bournes
**Issued Capital:** £120
**Principals:** E J Bourne *(Managing)*, T R Bourne, W Bourne, L Bourne
**Co. Secretary:** Roy Bourne
**Responsibilities**
**Marketing:** Kirsty Parsons *(Marketing and Business Develop)*
**Sales:** Kirsty Parsons *(Marketing and Business Develop)*
**Branches:** T Bourne & Son Ltd, Draper Street, Tunbridge Wells, Kent TN4 0PG
**US SIC:** 4214, 4226
**UK SIC:** 72300, 77003
**Auditors:** Phipps & Co
**Bankers:** Lloyds TSB Bank plc (30-90-28)

| | 31-12-13 | 31-12-12 | 31-12-11 |
|---|---|---|---|
| TA | 3,828,216 | 2,744,171 | 2,825,980 |
| NW | 1,154,953 | 874,868 | 781,492 |
| WC | 570,382 | 48,845 | 49,385 |

DUNS 23-318-4118 **Imp**
## T Brewer & Co Ltd
Timber Mill Way, Gauden Road, London SW4 6LY
**Tel:** 020-7720-9494 **Fax:** 020-7622-0426
**Web:** www.tbrewer.co.uk
**Reg No:** 2683645 **VAT No:** 603154777
**Estd:** 1992 Private Limited Company
**Line of Business:** Agents involved in the sale of timber and building materials
**Issued Capital:** £18,000
**Principals:** N P Brewer *(Sales)*, K Fryer
**Co. Secretary:** Rodney Scoles
**Responsibilities**
**Health & Safety:** Gordon Beech *(Health & Safety Officer)*
**Branches:** T Brewer & Co Ltd, Old Station Yard, Springbank Road, London SE13 6SS
**US SIC:** 5072 **UK SIC:** 61500
**Auditors:** Cook & Partners Ltd
**Bankers:** Barclays Bank Plc (20-05-74)

| | 31-12-13 | 31-12-12 | 31-12-11 |
|---|---|---|---|
| TO | 10,574,255 | 9,070,546 | 8,592,372 |
| P/L | 668,870 | 213,952 | 280,829 |
| NW | 2,132,844 | 1,322,885 | 1,125,802 |
| WC | 609,562 | 266,629 | 103,136 |
| Emp. | 53 | 54 | 52 |

DUNS 21-723-5753
## T Brown Group Ltd
**(Subsidiary of:** T B G Holding C Ltd)
24 High Street, Ewell, Epsom, Surrey KT17 1SJ
**Tel:** 02087861200 **Fax:** 02083-939947
**Web:** www.tbrownheating.co.uk
**Reg No:** 1006630 **VAT No:** 209639741
**Estd:** 1971 Private Limited Company
**Line of Business:** Wholesale of hardware, plumbing and heating equipment and supplies
**Issued Capital:** £5,000
**Directors:** D J Williams, S T Brown
**Co. Secretary:** Jonathan Brown
**Responsibilities**
**Admin:** Sue Franklin *(Office Manager)*
**Health & Safety:** Sue Franklin *(Office Manager)*
**Operations:** Sue Franklin *(Office Manager)*
**Branches:** T Brown Group Ltd, 24 High Street, Epsom, Surrey KT17 1SJ
**US SIC:** 5074, 1711
**UK SIC:** 61300, 50300
**Auditors:** BDO LLP
**Bankers:** Barclays Bank Plc (20-29-90)

| | 30-04-14 | 30-04-13 | 30-04-12 |
|---|---|---|---|
| TO | 54,652,271 | 52,758,001 | 44,178,901 |
| P/L | 848,666 | 2,525,649 | 2,919,102 |
| NW | 6,412,391 | 6,266,386 | 8,529,703 |
| WC | 4,979,651 | 5,181,880 | 4,198,594 |
| Emp. | 541 | 486 | 392 |

DUNS 21-532-6351
## T C Brears
Fieldside, Scunthorpe, South Humberside DN17 4HH
**Web:** www.tcbrears.co.uk
**Estd:** 1968 Proprietorship
**Line of Business:** Straw merchants
**Proprietor:** J Brears
**US SIC:** 5159 **UK SIC:** 61100
**Employees:** 68

DUNS 22-138-4147
## T C Cars Ltd
Saxon House, Saxon Way, Birmingham, West Midlands B37 5AX
**Tel:** 01217704444
**Web:** www.tc-cars.co.uk
**Reg No:** 4157358 **VAT No:** 614396928
**Estd:** 1987 Private Limited Company
**Line of Business:** Taxis and private hire vehicles
**Trading Style:** T C Cars
**Issued Capital:** £100
**Director:** M P Smith
**US SIC:** 4121 **UK SIC:** 72200

| | 28-02-14 | 28-02-13 | 29-02-12 |
|---|---|---|---|
| TA | 1,229,983 | 1,072,530 | 1,093,622 |
| NW | 626,990 | 644,653 | 606,269 |
| WC | 239,389 | 160,982 | 108,786 |

DUNS 29-625-5854
## T C Communications Ltd
**(Subsidiary of:** Tc Communications Holdings Ltd)
Kings Ride, Ascot, Berkshire SL5 7JR
**Tel:** 01344-622280
**Web:** www.tccommunications.co.uk
**Reg No:** 1952030 **Estd:** 1985 Private Limited Company
**Line of Business:** Advertising agency services
**Issued Capital:** £60,000
**Directors:** A B Symmonds, T Leney
**Responsibilities**
**Senior:** Mathew Keane *(Manager)*, Anne Varney *(Manager)*
**US SIC:** 7319 **UK SIC:** 83800
**Auditors:** Civvals
**Bankers:** Lloyds TSB Bank plc (77-49-01)

| | 31-12-13 | 31-12-12 | 31-12-11 |
|---|---|---|---|
| TO | 4,624,059 | 4,697,238 | 5,821,011 |
| P/L | 352,868 | (697,030) | 352,983 |
| NW | 879,993 | 527,126 | 1,224,156 |
| WC | 801,337 | 437,031 | 1,109,149 |

DUNS 21-042-5390
## T C Harrison Ford
Horninglow Street, Burton-On-Trent, Staffordshire DE14 1NR
**Tel:** 01283524624
**Web:** www.tch.co.uk
**Estd:** 1936 Proprietorship
**Line of Business:** Car dealers (new & used)
**Proprietor:** N Baker
**Responsibilities**
**Senior:** Paul Grennall *(General Manager)*
**Finance:** Terry Earp *(Senior Financial Executive)*
**Sales:** Roman Czekalskyj *(Sales Manager)*
**Health & Safety:** William Clarke *(Service Manager)*
**Facilities:** Paul Grennall *(General Manager)*
**US SIC:** 5511 **UK SIC:** 65100
**Employees:** 80

DUNS 29-500-0756 **Imp**
## T. C. Harrison Group Ltd
Milford House, Mill Street, Bakewell, Derbyshire DE45 1HH
**Web:** www.tch.co.uk
**Reg No:** 1863311 **VAT No:** 172586736
**Estd:** 1984 Private Limited Company
**Line of Business:** Representative office
**Export Sales:** £2,490,000
**Trading Style:** Milford Motor Factors
**Issued Capital:** £1,448,724
**Directors:** T W Harrison, J E Harrison, J R Harrison
**Co. Secretary:** Anthony Coar
**Responsibilities**
**Marketing:** Joel Harrison *(Digital Marketing Development)*
**Branches:** T. C. Harrison Group Ltd, Repairs Only, 11A Lodge La, Newark, Nottinghamshire NG22 0NL
**US SIC:** 5511, 5082
**UK SIC:** 65100, 61490
**Auditors:** Barber Harrison & Platt
**Bankers:** The Royal Bank Of Scotland Plc (16-00-08)

| | 31-12-13 | 31-12-12 | 31-12-11 |
|---|---|---|---|
| TO | 224,581,000 | 215,035,000 | 216,812,000 |
| P/L | 2,643,000 | 2,341,000 | 2,147,000 |
| NW | 41,159,000 | 38,384,000 | 37,929,000 |
| WC | 1,215,000 | 1,070,000 | (1,883,000) |
| Emp. | 501 | 493 | 509 |

DUNS 73-375-8374
## T. C. Landscapes Ltd
**(Subsidiary of:** T.C.L. Holdings Ltd)
Covert Farm, Long Lane, Northampton, Northamptonshire NN6 8DU
**Tel:** 01604-821843
**Web:** www.tclandscapes.co.uk
**Reg No:** 4649316 **Estd:** 1983 Private Limited Company
**Line of Business:** Landscape contractors
**Issued Capital:** £100
**Directors:** S Abley, J C Highley, S J Cashmore
**US SIC:** 0729 **UK SIC:** 01003
**Auditors:** Cooper Parry LLP
**Bankers:** HSBC Bank plc (40-35-18)

| | 31-12-13 | 31-12-12 | 31-12-11 |
|---|---|---|---|
| TO | 14,158,374 | 13,009,486 | 10,900,892 |
| P/L | 653,954 | 595,905 | 229,760 |
| NW | 2,466,925 | 1,796,666 | 1,155,369 |
| WC | 1,893,211 | 1,528,006 | 1,201,644 |
| Emp. | 165 | 150 | 126 |

DUNS 21-743-6955
## T C Ltd
Po Box 130, Uxbridge, Middlesex UB8 2YS
**Tel:** 01895-252222
**Web:** www.tc.co.uk
**Reg No:** 1125377 **VAT No:** 223788055
**Estd:** 1970 Private Limited Company
**Line of Business:** Temperature monitoring equipment systems
**Issued Capital:** £130
**Principals:** R W Taylor *(Managing)*, Ms J M Taylor
**Co. Secretary:** Edmund Ross
**Responsibilities**
**Marketing:** Darren Shepherd *(Sales & Marketing Manager)*
**Sales:** Darren Shepherd *(Sales & Marketing Manager)*
**Health & Safety:** Darren Shepherd *(Sales & Marketing Manager)*
**US SIC:** 3643 **UK SIC:** 34203
**Auditors:** Arram Berlyn Gardner
**Bankers:** HSBC Bank plc (40-42-08)

| | 31-10-13 | 31-10-12 | 31-10-11 |
|---|---|---|---|
| TO | 16,098,114 | 15,284,115 | 14,099,107 |
| P/L | 1,432,918 | 1,343,402 | 912,782 |
| NW | 4,963,357 | 3,652,617 | 2,595,408 |
| WC | 3,987,262 | 2,755,816 | 1,933,900 |
| Emp. | 269 | 237 | 213 |

DUNS 21-753-6039
## T C P Solutions Plc
58a Waldeck Road, Strand On The Green, London W4 3NP
**Tel:** 02089960871
**Web:** www.tcpsolutions.com
**Reg No:** 7835216 **Estd:** 2011 Public Limited Company
**Line of Business:** Management activities of holding companies
**Export Sales:** £69,795,471
**Issued Capital:** £250,000
**Directors:** N J Chapman, M J Chapman, R Vermeulen, Mc Squared Management Limited
**Co. Secretary:** Waldeck Secretaries Limited
**US SIC:** 6711 **UK SIC:** 83962

| | 31-12-13 | 31-12-12 |
|---|---|---|
| TO | 74,735,373 | 72,612,455 |
| P/L | 548,722 | 497,079 |
| NW | 1,265,746 | 907,987 |
| WC | 1,193,490 | 392,419 |
| Emp. | 296 | 304 |

DUNS 22-281-6188
## T C R Uk Ltd
**(Subsidiary of:** Tcr Capvest Sa)
Enterprise House, Stansted, Essex CM24 1RY
**Tel:** 01279-661212 **Fax:** 01279-661213
**Web:** www.tcrgroup.com
**Reg No:** 4299549 **VAT No:** 783108525
**Estd:** 2004 Private Limited Company
**Line of Business:** Other supporting air transport activities
**Issued Capital:** £1,275,000
**Directors:** B Biebuyck, S Houlahan, M F Delvaux, D Meulebroek
**Co. Secretary:** Henri Sliepen
**Responsibilities**
**Senior:** Matthew Bourne *(General Manager)*
**Branches:** T C R Uk Ltd, London Gatwick Airport, Horley, Gatwick, West Sussex RH6 0EY
**US SIC:** 4582, 7394
**UK SIC:** 76400, 84000
**Auditors:** Woolford & Co
**Bankers:** HSBC Bank plc (40-44-15)

| | 30-06-14 | 30-06-13 | 30-06-12 |
|---|---|---|---|
| TO | 28,415,724 | 27,229,099 | 25,849,905 |
| P/L | 1,567,694 | 1,330,449 | 480,950 |
| NW | 4,113,600 | 5,766,067 | 4,659,218 |
| WC | (4,578,712) | (1,355,446) | (2,341,869) |
| Emp. | 163 | 129 | 116 |

DUNS 21-006-2139
## T Clarke Plc
45 Moorfields, London EC2Y 9AE
**Tel:** 02079977400
**Web:** www.tclarke.co.uk
**Reg No:** 0119351 **Estd:** 1911 Public Limited Company
**Line of Business:** Installation of electrical wiring and fittings
**Trading Style:** T Clarke Plc (Head Office)
**Issued Capital:** £4,140,167
**Directors:** A J Giddings, Ms B A Stewart, M Lawrence, I Mccusker, M Crowder, R D Henderson, D G Robson, M R Walton
**Co. Secretary:** Martin Walton
**Responsibilities**
**Senior:** Robin Aves *(Divisional Director)*, John Burrows *(Stores Manager)*, Iain Clenaghan *(Divisional Director)*
**IT:** Barrie Nightingale *(Technical Director)*
**HR:** Alan Crozier *(Human Resources Manager)*
**Facilities:** Danny Miller *(Facilities Manager)*
**Fleet:** John Burrows *(Stores Manager)*
**Branches:** T Clarke Plc, Fengate, Peterborough, Cambridgeshire PE1 5XB
**US SIC:** 1731, 1711
**UK SIC:** 50300
**Auditors:** PricewaterhouseCoopers LLP
**Bankers:** National Westminster Bank Plc (60-04-04)

| | 31-12-13 | 31-12-12 | 31-12-11 |
|---|---|---|---|
| TO | 217,100,000 | 193,834,000 | 183,805,000 |
| P/L | 1,700,000 | 1,197,000 | 4,900,000 |
| NW | 1,300,000 | 396,000 | 1,889,000 |
| WC | 4,700,000 | 4,239,000 | 3,752,000 |
| Emp. | 1,200 | 1,156 | 1,311 |

DUNS 23-077-2977
## T. Class Security Ltd
83 Victoria Street, London SW1H 0HW
**Tel:** 0203 585 5274 **Fax:** 0845 331 3261
**Web:** www.t-class.co.uk
**Reg No:** 3622392 **VAT No:** 731240575
**Estd:** 2012 Private Limited Company
**Line of Business:** Security activities
**Trading Style:** Bugner Bannon
**Issued Capital:** £400
**Directors:** K R Beasley, A J Bannon, J Bugner, P R Beasley, Miss K M Mansbridge
**Co. Secretary:** Miss Kelly Mansbridge
**Responsibilities**
**Senior:** Shelly Kelly *(Manager)*
**US SIC:** 7393 **UK SIC:** 83954

| | 31-08-13 | 31-08-12 | 31-08-11 |
|---|---|---|---|
| TA | 2,006,459 | 1,405,049 | 1,288,465 |
| NW | (33,333) | (111,024) | 475,196 |
| WC | (37,829) | (115,690) | 466,037 |

DUNS 37-782-4966
## T Cribb & Sons
3 Station Parade, Barking, Essex IG11 8ED
**Tel:** 02085942339
**Web:** www.tcribbandson.co
**Estd:** 1881 Partnership
**Line of Business:** Funeral directors
**Trading Style:** T Cribb and Sons Funeral Directors, T Cribb and Sons Carriage Masters, Tcs Exhumations T Cribb & Sons Ghana, The National Funeral Museum
**Partners:** S Cribb, G Harris, J Harris
**Responsibilities**
**Senior:** Roger Ferdinand *(Advertisement Manager)*, Vivien Huntley *(Manager)*
**Branches:** T Cribb & Sons, Middle Brook Farm, Murthering Lane, Romford, Essex RM4 1HL
**US SIC:** 7261 **UK SIC:** 98902
**Bankers:** Barclays Bank Plc (20-67-88)
**Employees:** 80

DUNS 34-611-7807
## T. Crossling & Co. Ltd
Po Box 5, Newcastle-Upon-Tyne, Tyne and Wear NE6 5TP
**Tel:** 0191 265 2821
**Web:** www.northerntools.co.uk
**Reg No:** 2749235 **Estd:** 1960 Private Limited Company
**Line of Business:** Plumbers merchants
**Trading Style:** Northern Tools & Accessories
**Issued Capital:** £39,034
**Principals:** R R Errington *(Managing)*, C P Errington *(Sales)*, Ms S M Errington, K C Clifford
**Co. Secretary:** Kevin Clifford
**Responsibilities**
**Senior:** Iain Crossman *(General Manager)*
**Branches:** T. Crossling & Co. Ltd, Crossling Ltd, Unit B4, Darlington, County Durham DL3 0XA
**US SIC:** 3546 **UK SIC:** 32852

**Auditors:** UNW LLP
**Bankers:** Lloyds TSB Bank plc (30-93-71)

| | 31-12-13 | 31-12-12 | 31-12-11 |
|---|---|---|---|
| TO | 54,279,000 | 53,256,000 | 60,759,000 |
| P/L | 2,897,000 | 2,019,000 | 3,119,000 |
| NW | 29,599,000 | 29,559,000 | 28,220,000 |
| WC | 24,041,000 | 23,627,000 | 22,236,000 |
| Emp. | 282 | 305 | 330 |

DUNS 21-619-8713 **Imp**
## T D Bridger Ltd
Avenue One, Letchworth, Hertfordshire SG6 2WP
**Tel:** 01462-636-465
**Web:** www.bridger.co.uk
**Reg No:** 0366193 **VAT No:** 196224057
**Estd:** 1927 Private Limited Company
**Line of Business:** Manufacturers of paper and cardboard
**Trading Style:** Bridger Packaging
**Issued Capital:** £2,003
**Principals:** L D Bridger *(Managing)*, Ms J E Bridger
**Co. Secretary:** Lawrence Bridger
**Responsibilities**
**Facilities:** Alan Keddy *(Maintenance Manager)*
**Engineering:** Alan Keddy *(Maintenance Manager)*
**Branches:** T D Bridger Ltd, Muddy Lane, Letchworth, Letchworth Garden City, Hertfordshire SG6 3TB
**US SIC:** 2631, 2752
**UK SIC:** 47017, 47544
**Bankers:** Barclays Bank Plc (20-32-29)

| | 31-03-14 | 31-03-13 | 31-03-12 |
|---|---|---|---|
| TA | 1,941,444 | 2,721,869 | 3,700,683 |
| NW | 1,525,147 | 2,093,296 | 2,102,064 |
| WC | 956,242 | 1,439,886 | 98,154 |

DUNS 64-084-5335 **Imp**
## T D C (Aberdeen) Ltd
Unit 5 Bankhead Avenue, Bucksburn, Aberdeen, Aberdeenshire AB21 9ET
**Tel:** 01224-710077 **Fax:** 01224-710088
**Web:** www.tdcaberdeen.co.uk
**Reg No:** 0181456SC **VAT No:** 703572355
**Estd:** 1998 Private Limited Company
**Line of Business:** Mechanical engineering general
**Issued Capital:** £75,042
**Directors:** N Milne, Ms H Milne
**Co. Secretary:** Clp Secretaries Limited
**US SIC:** 8911, 1731
**UK SIC:** 83701, 50300
**Auditors:** Barbara Cresswell

| | 31-03-14 | 31-03-13 | 31-03-12 |
|---|---|---|---|
| TO | 11,915,593 | 10,580,632 | 8,937,268 |
| P/L | 935,803 | 1,125,921 | 599,935 |
| NW | 4,316,359 | 3,598,614 | 2,668,341 |
| WC | 3,854,913 | 3,236,713 | 2,197,997 |
| Emp. | 138 | 119 | 98 |

DUNS 23-795-6714
## T D K Plastering Ltd
Unit 2 Arcadian Business Centre, Enfield Industrial Estate, Redditch, Worcestershire B97 6DE
**Tel:** 01527-595579 **Fax:** 01527-585063
**Web:** www.tdkplasteringltd.co.uk
**Reg No:** 3788408 **VAT No:** 738722608
**Estd:** 1999 Private Limited Company
**Line of Business:** Plastering
**Issued Capital:** £100
**Managing Director:** D Keane
**Co. Secretary:** Ms Angela Keane
**US SIC:** 1742 **UK SIC:** 50400

| | 30-06-14 | 30-06-13 | 30-06-12 |
|---|---|---|---|
| TO | N/A | N/A | 3,607,228 |
| P/L | N/A | N/A | 172,166 |
| NW | 667,549 | 151,801 | 46,966 |
| WC | 603,594 | 135,542 | 7,151 |

DUNS 21-823-9538
## T D Travel (Holdings) Ltd
(**Subsidiary of:** Cti Holdings Limited)
Brooke Court Handforth Dean, Wilmslow, Cheshire SK9 3ND
**Tel:** 0135523720
**Web:** www.tdtravelgroup.com
**Reg No:** 7951181 **Estd:** 2012 Private Limited Company
**Line of Business:** Management activities of holding companies
**Issued Capital:** £669,007
**Directors:** I P White, R B Porter, S R Harrison
**Co. Secretary:** Mrs Zoe Tibell
**Responsibilities**
**Senior:** Christopher Needham *(Director)*, Zo?vette Tibell *(Director)*
**US SIC:** 6711 **UK SIC:** 83962
**Auditors:** BDO LLP
**Bankers:** Lloyds TSB Bank plc (30-00-05)

| | 31-03-14 | 31-03-13 |
|---|---|---|
| TO | 54,340,721 | 44,989,448 |
| P/L | 251,853 | 277,719 |
| NW | 2,934,424 | 3,534,220 |
| WC | 2,328,186 | 3,212,820 |
| Emp. | 163 | 75 |

DUNS 23-776-1205
## T E S 2000 Ltd
Tes House, Heath Business Park Grange Way, Colchester, Essex CO2 8GU
**Tel:** 01206-799111
**Web:** www.tes2000.co.uk
**Reg No:** 3769392 **Estd:** 1999 Private Limited Company
**Line of Business:** Other business activities not elsewhere classified
**Issued Capital:** £2,485
**Directors:** M D Mclean, Ms Y Evans, T L Evans, G Desmond
**Responsibilities**
**Senior:** David Mawson *(Operations Director)*
**HR:** Lindsey Hayward *(Human Resources Manager)*, Martin Hyde *(Training Director)*
**Operations:** Debbie Briley *(Service Delivery Manager)*, Jack Howell *(PWAY Project Manager)*
**Branches:** T E S 2000 Ltd, Hydra Business Park, Nether La, Sheffield, South Yorkshire S35 9ZX
**US SIC:** 7399, 8999
**UK SIC:** 83954
**Auditors:** Lambert Chapman
**Bankers:** National Westminster Bank Plc (60-20-36)

| | 30-11-13 | 30-11-12 | 30-11-11 |
|---|---|---|---|
| TO | 17,198,359 | 9,784,689 | 7,452,946 |
| P/L | 274,009 | (186,707) | (212,011) |
| NW | 1,899,619 | 1,702,463 | 1,781,636 |
| WC | 1,621,231 | 1,546,172 | 1,714,514 |
| Emp. | 834 | 367 | 315 |

DUNS 73-902-5497
## The T F Bell Group Ltd
(**Subsidiary of:** Towergate Partnershipco Ltd)
Towergate House, Sittingbourne Road Eclipse Park, Maidstone, Kent ME14 3EN
**Tel:** 08448921700
**Web:** www.towergate.com
**Reg No:** 5156249 **Estd:** 2004 Private Limited Company
**Line of Business:** Business services
**Issued Capital:** £10,000
**Directors:** A D Lyons, S Egan
**Co. Secretary:** Ms Jennifer Owens
**Responsibilities**
**Senior:** Samuel Clark *(Manager)*
**US SIC:** 7399, 6399
**UK SIC:** 83954, 82001
**Auditors:** KPMG Audit PLC
**Bankers:** National Westminster Bank Plc (60-11-06)

| | 31-12-13 | 31-12-12 | 31-12-11 |
|---|---|---|---|
| TO | N/A | N/A | 2,123,619 |
| P/L | N/A | N/A | 8,177,979 |
| NW | 10,000 | 10,000 | 10,000 |
| Emp. | N/A | N/A | 40 |

DUNS 21-579-6174
## T F E Enterprise
The Depot, Old London Road, Penrith, Cumbria CA11 8GU
**Tel:** 01768212800
**Web:** www.amey.co.uk
**Estd:** 1997 Proprietorship
**Line of Business:** Building construction contractors
**Proprietor:** J Kemp
**US SIC:** 7392 **UK SIC:** 83951
**Employees:** 120

DUNS 21-150-1299
## T F S Buying Ltd
(**Subsidiary of:** Cartoon (Holdings) Ltd)
Churchill Point, Trafford Park Road, Lake Edge Green, Trafford Park, Manchester M17 1BL
**Tel:** 01618732118
**Reg No:** 6789840 **Estd:** 2009 Private Limited Company
**Line of Business:** Beauty products
**Issued Capital:** £2
**Directors:** V J Vadera, S J Vadera, J Holt
**US SIC:** 2844 **UK SIC:** 25820
**Bankers:** Yorkshire Bank Plc (05-00-01)

| | 31-03-14 | 31-03-13 | 31-03-12 |
|---|---|---|---|
| TO | 83,848,000 | 78,055,000 | 66,937,000 |
| P/L | 10,578,000 | 10,125,000 | 8,687,000 |
| NW | 30,039,000 | 21,880,000 | 14,154,000 |
| WC | 26,027,000 | 18,347,000 | 11,346,000 |
| Emp. | 832 | 763 | 678 |

DUNS 21-590-9409 **Imp**
## T F Woodside & Co Ltd
21-27 Main Street, Larne, Co Antrim BT40 1JQ
**Tel:** 028-2827-2378 **Fax:** 028-2827-9200
**Web:** www.tfwoodside.com
**Reg No:** 0008573NI **VAT No:** 253183079
**Estd:** 1972 Private Limited Company
**Line of Business:** Departmental stores
**Trading Style:** Woodsides
**Issued Capital:** £55
**Directors:** Ms H A Crothers, M F Mcconkey
**Co. Secretary:** Ms Hazel Crothers
**Branches:** T F Woodside & Co Ltd, 67-73 Church Street, Ballymena, Co Antrim BT43 6DD
**US SIC:** 5399 **UK SIC:** 65600
**Auditors:** W J Miscampbell & Co
**Bankers:** Northern Bank Ltd (95-03-51)

| | 31-01-14 | 31-01-13 | 31-01-12 |
|---|---|---|---|
| TO | 2,948,384 | 3,072,773 | 3,649,192 |
| P/L | 126,868 | 18,625 | (66,801) |
| NW | 2,233,133 | 2,176,442 | 3,253,590 |
| WC | (383,867) | (339,680) | (366,359) |
| Emp. | 48 | N/A | 59 |

DUNS 34-815-3201
## T French & Son Ltd
Stonebriggs Farm, Cronberry, Cumnock, Ayrshire KA18 3LP
**Tel:** 01290421609 **Fax:** 01290420900
**Reg No:** 0292873SC **Estd:** 2005 Private Limited Company
**Line of Business:** Other supporting land transport activities
**Issued Capital:** £100
**Directors:** Ms E French, Ms S A Graham, T French, T J French
**Co. Secretary:** Ms Elizabeth Mcmenemy
**US SIC:** 4789 **UK SIC:** 77002
**Bankers:** Bank Of Scotland (80-06-24)

| | 31-10-13 | 31-10-12 | 31-10-11 |
|---|---|---|---|
| TO | 14,304,560 | 15,145,382 | N/A |
| P/L | 529,452 | 1,044,671 | N/A |
| NW | 1,933,840 | 1,618,118 | 881,586 |
| WC | (412,350) | (618,285) | 199,846 |
| Emp. | 90 | 93 | N/A |

DUNS 21-705-3963
## T French & Sons
Stonebriggs, Cronberry, Cumnock, Ayrshire KA18 3LP
**Tel:** 01290425164
**Estd:** 1968 Partnership
**Line of Business:** Road haulage and transport services
**Principals:** T French *(Partner)*, T French *(Proprietor)*
**US SIC:** 1611 **UK SIC:** 50200
**Employees:** 120

DUNS 21-590-5679
## T G B Construction Services
P O Box 192, Epsom, Surrey KT18 6YT
**Tel:** 01372361100
**Estd:** 2011
**Line of Business:** Builders
**Proprietor:** T Baylif
**US SIC:** 1522 **UK SIC:** 50100
**Employees:** 300

DUNS 22-764-7013
## T G Builders Merchants Ltd
Wood Lane, Ellesmere, Shropshire SY12 0HY
**Web:** www.tggroup.co.uk
**Reg No:** 1402696 **Estd:** 1978 Private Limited Company
**Line of Business:** Agents involved in the sale of timber and building materials
**Issued Capital:** £10
**Directors:** J T Griffiths, K R Gardner, J M Griffiths
**Co. Secretary:** John Seaward
**Responsibilities**
**Finance:** Dee Jones *(Manager)*
**Branches:** T G Builders Merchants Ltd, Maesbury Road, Oswestry, Shropshire SY10 8NJ
**US SIC:** 5072 **UK SIC:** 61500
**Auditors:** Whittingham Riddell LLP
**Bankers:** Lloyds TSB Bank plc (30-93-03)

| | 31-03-14 | 31-03-13 | 31-03-12 |
|---|---|---|---|
| TO | 13,487,001 | 11,214,843 | 11,430,227 |
| P/L | 882,145 | 581,844 | 604,889 |
| NW | 9,263,775 | 8,722,810 | 8,275,767 |
| WC | 2,499,663 | 2,803,787 | 3,415,346 |
| Emp. | 69 | 67 | 64 |

DUNS 21-596-2193
## T G I Friday's
Kings Inch Road, Renfrew, Renfrewshire PA4 8XU
**Tel:** 03446920309
**Web:** www.tgifridays.co.uk
**Estd:** 2011 Proprietorship
**Line of Business:** Restaurant - thai
**Proprietor:** M Mclure
**Responsibilities**
**Senior:** Murray McLure *(Proprietor)*
**US SIC:** 5812 **UK SIC:** 66110
**Employees:** 70

DUNS 21-172-9467
## T G I Fridays
The Bentall Centre, Wood Street, Kingston-Upon-Thames, Surrey KT1 1TR
**Tel:** 08446920239
**Web:** www.tgifridays.co.uk
**Estd:** 2010 Proprietorship
**Line of Business:** Restaurant - american
**Proprietor:** J Dalton
**Responsibilities**
**Senior:** Trevor Reeves *(General Manager)*
**US SIC:** 5812 **UK SIC:** 66110
**Employees:** 100

DUNS 21-783-1453
## T G M
Office 8-15 Airways House, Aiw, London Stansted Airport, Stansted, Essex CM24 1RB
**Tel:** 01279681800
**Web:** www.arrivanet.com
**Estd:** 2011 Partnership
**Line of Business:** Other scheduled passenger land transport not elsewhere classified
**Partners:** C Johnson, T Gray
**Responsibilities**
**Senior:** Belinda Nicholls *(Service Delivery Manager)*
**US SIC:** 4119 **UK SIC:** 72200
**Employees:** 90

DUNS 23-038-5973 **Exp**
## T G Products Ltd
(**Subsidiary of:** United Technologies Corporation)
Chubb House, Sunbury-On-Thames, Middlesex TW16 7AR
**Tel:** 01616542222 **Fax:** 0800281035
**Web:** www.thomas-glover.co.uk
**Reg No:** 2774304 **Estd:** 1992 Private Limited Company
**Line of Business:** Manufacture of other fabricated metal products not elsewhere classified
**Export Markets:** Worldwide
**Export Sales:** £175,000
**Trading Style:** Glover Thomas & Co, Pyrene
**Issued Capital:** £41,000,000
**Directors:** A Brennan, Chubb Management Services Ltd, L Harvey, C A Forbes, S A Quillish
**Co. Secretary:** Robert Sloss
**Branches:** T G Products Ltd, Parkfield House Manchester Old Road, Manchester M24 4DY
**US SIC:** 3999 **UK SIC:** 49590
**Auditors:** PricewaterhouseCoopers
**Bankers:** Barclays Bank Plc (20-25-85)

| | 31-12-13 | 31-12-12 | 31-12-11 |
|---|---|---|---|
| TO | 15,493,000 | 16,849,000 | 16,166,000 |
| P/L | 1,810,000 | 1,426,000 | 542,000 |
| NW | 18,799,000 | 17,000,000 | 15,599,000 |
| WC | 18,734,000 | 16,913,000 | 15,568,000 |
| Emp. | 50 | 51 | 55 |

DUNS 21-409-2698
## T G S
Millbank House 171 185, Ewell Road, Surbiton, Surrey KT6 6AP
**Web:** www.tgs.com
**Estd:** 2010 Proprietorship
**Line of Business:** Geophysical consultants
**Partners:** P Gray, A Holt, Mrs L Stewart, J Small, P Anderson, N Burns
**US SIC:** 7397 **UK SIC:** 83702
**Employees:** 50

DUNS 22-542-0991
## T G S Coachworks
Woodpecker House, Balaclava Road, Fishponds, Bristol, Avon BS16 3LJ
**Tel:** 01179-659965
**Web:** www.tgs-group.com
**VAT No:** 302662392 **Estd:** 1975 Partnership
**Line of Business:** Manufacture of parts and accessories for motor vehicles and their engines
**Partners:** T G Smith, N Smith, Mrs H F Smith, J Smith, Mrs J M Smith, B M Smith, R H Smith
**Branches:** T G S Coachworks, Woodpecker House, Balaclava Road, Bristol, Avon BS16 3LJ
**US SIC:** 3714, 7699
**UK SIC:** 35300, 67303
**Bankers:** National Westminster Bank Plc (60-70-70)
**Employees:** 60

DUNS 21-581-2164
## T G W U
Bowling Back Lane, Bradford, West Yorkshire BD4 8SP
**Tel:** 01274307155
**Estd:** 2011 Proprietorship
**Line of Business:** Trade unions
**Proprietor:** T Falam
**US SIC:** 8611 **UK SIC:** 96312
**Employees:** 500

DUNS 21-822-6983

## T Gill & Son(Norwich) Ltd

(**Subsidiary of:** T Gill Holdings Ltd)
The Barn, Norwich, Norfolk NR9 5BZ
**Tel:** 01603-880812 **Fax:** 01603-881219
**Web:** www.gillbuilding.co.uk
**Reg No:** 0513973 **VAT No:** 571612255
**Estd:** 1952 Private Limited Company
**Line of Business:** Construction of commercial buildings
**Issued Capital:** £10,140
**Principals:** A T Gill *(Managing)*, D J Reeve, C F Gill, N L Gale
**Co. Secretary:** Mrs Margaret Gill
**US SIC:** 1541, 2421
**UK SIC:** 50100, 46101
**Auditors:** BDO Stoy Hayward
**Bankers:** National Westminster Bank Plc (01-06-28)

| | 31-12-13 | 31-12-12 | 31-12-11 |
|---|---|---|---|
| TA | 1,577,840 | 1,594,841 | 2,351,482 |
| NW | 448,803 | 409,681 | 742,733 |
| WC | 396,900 | 346,119 | 624,415 |

DUNS 22-151-1111

## T Gilmartin Ltd

102 Collingdon Street, Luton, Bedfordshire LU1 1RX
**Tel:** 01582726803 **Fax:** 01582721095
**Web:** www.gilmartins.co.uk
**Reg No:** 4169879 **VAT No:** 678897245
**Estd:** 2001 Private Limited Company
**Line of Business:** Property maintenance services
**Trading Style:** Gilmartins
**Issued Capital:** £1,000
**Directors:** D J Bradley, Mrs S L Gilmartin, T M Gilmartin, R Gilmartin
**Co. Secretary:** Sioban Gilmartin
**US SIC:** 1799 **UK SIC:** 50000
**Bankers:** National Westminster Bank Plc (60-12-42)

| | 31-03-14 | 31-03-13 | 31-03-12 |
|---|---|---|---|
| TA | 3,073,417 | 2,585,261 | 1,970,685 |
| NW | 1,564,771 | 1,155,958 | 1,124,990 |
| WC | 1,360,508 | 938,647 | 905,488 |

DUNS 22-901-5763

## T Graham & Son (Builders) Ltd

(**Subsidiary of:** Graham Group Holdings Ltd)
41a Henry Street, Langholm, Dumfriesshire DG13 0AR
**Web:** www.grahamgroupcos.com
**Reg No:** 0077382SC **VAT No:** 263434074
**Estd:** 1988 Private Limited Company
**Line of Business:** Building construction contractors
**Issued Capital:** £10,000
**Principals:** J H Muir *(Managing)*, M Shepherd, M L Bell, J Shepherd, W G Mitchell
**Co. Secretary:**
As Company Services Limited
**Branches:** T Graham & Son (Builders) Ltd, Unit 67D, Gilwilly Road, Penrith, Cumbria CA11 9BL
**US SIC:** 1522, 2421
**UK SIC:** 50100, 46101
**Auditors:** Welch & Co
**Bankers:** Bank Of Scotland (80-17-06)

| | 28-02-14 | 28-02-13 | 29-02-12 |
|---|---|---|---|
| TA | 542,384 | 527,710 | 374,656 |
| NW | 68,136 | 99,727 | 98,885 |
| WC | 565 | (46,763) | (64,480) |

DUNS 85-599-8378

## T. H. Baker Group Ltd

95 High Street, Brierley Hill, West Midlands DY5 3AU
**Tel:** 0138478368
**Web:** www.thbaker.co.uk
**Reg No:** 6217948 **Estd:** 2007 Private Limited Company
**Line of Business:** Management activities of holding companies
**Issued Capital:** £1,513,000
**Directors:** P J Higgs, A H Higgs, R Wylie, Mrs P J Higgs
**Co. Secretary:** Andrew Higgs
**US SIC:** 6711 **UK SIC:** 83962

| | 28-02-14 | 28-02-13 | 29-02-12 |
|---|---|---|---|
| TO | 31,141,029 | 25,966,182 | 23,519,724 |
| P/L | 2,668,034 | 1,364,294 | 2,203,988 |
| NW | 6,953,138 | 5,527,415 | 4,760,223 |
| WC | 4,767,715 | 3,352,837 | 2,309,759 |
| Emp. | 275 | 235 | 202 |

DUNS 21-611-3399

## T. H. White Holdings Ltd

Nursteed Road, Devizes, Wiltshire SN10 3EA
**Tel:** 01380-722381 **Fax:** 01380-729147
**Web:** www.thwhite.co.uk
**Reg No:** 0133886 **Estd:** 1914 Private Limited Company
**Line of Business:** Management activities of holding companies
**Trading Style:** White T H Insterlation, White T H
**Issued Capital:** £732,580
**Principals:** D B Scott *(Managing)*, M S Rigby, C G Scott, A D Scott, J E Lloyd
**Co. Secretary:** Peter Barker
**Responsibilities**
**Sales:** Michael Ardonlina *(Sales Manager)*
**HR:** Jacqui Kirby *(Human Resources Manager)*
**Operations:** Will Lanfear *(Service Manager)*
**Branches:** T. H. White Holdings Ltd, Eversley Rd, Reading, Berkshire RG2 9PJ
**US SIC:** 6711, 5083
**UK SIC:** 83962, 61490
**Auditors:** Ernst & Young
**Bankers:** Lloyds TSB Bank plc (30-92-13)

| | 31-12-13 | 31-12-12 | 31-12-11 |
|---|---|---|---|
| TO | 121,416,000 | 113,650,000 | 109,771,000 |
| P/L | 2,135,000 | 2,793,000 | 2,352,000 |
| NW | 21,224,000 | 20,745,000 | 19,774,000 |
| WC | 10,358,000 | 12,049,000 | 11,985,000 |
| Emp. | 513 | 501 | 492 |

DUNS 21-236-3931

## T. Hayselden Ltd

Huddersfield Road, Barnsley, South Yorkshire S75 1JA
**Web:** www.hayseldenvw.co.uk
**Reg No:** 1070329 **VAT No:** 181500883
**Estd:** 1972 Private Limited Company
**Line of Business:** Car dealers (new & used)
**Issued Capital:** £319,652
**Principals:** M R Hayselden *(Managing)*, M P Hayselden
**Co. Secretary:** Ms Gail Scott
**US SIC:** 5511 **UK SIC:** 65100
**Auditors:** Harris & Co
**Bankers:** HSBC Bank plc (40-45-29)

| | 31-12-13 | 31-12-12 | 31-12-11 |
|---|---|---|---|
| TO | 42,243,131 | 38,727,168 | 33,125,122 |
| P/L | 124,676 | 103,279 | 144,536 |
| NW | 2,294,363 | 1,026,867 | 1,701,814 |
| WC | (731,901) | (360,883) | 453,827 |
| Emp. | 133 | 129 | 135 |

DUNS 22-925-5971

## T Heatrick (Contracts) Ltd

297 Tandragee Road, Portadown, Craigavon, Co Armagh BT62 3RB
**Tel:** 028-3833-3681 **Fax:** 028-3835-0455
**Reg No:** 0019452NI **Estd:** 1971 Private Limited Company
**Line of Business:** Concrete products
**Trading Style:** Ty-Rock Products
**Issued Capital:** £30,000
**Directors:** C Heatrick, G Heatrick, R Heatrick
**Co. Secretary:** Thomas Heatrick
**Responsibilities**
**Senior:** Simon Davy *(Manager)*
**US SIC:** 3271 **UK SIC:** 24370
**Auditors:** Cavanagh Kelly
**Bankers:** First Trust Bank (aib Group (uk) Plc) (93-84-08)

| | 30-04-14 | 30-04-13 | 30-04-12 |
|---|---|---|---|
| TA | 4,010,871 | 3,357,767 | 3,182,657 |
| NW | 2,788,924 | 2,597,011 | 2,593,634 |
| WC | 2,191,253 | 2,037,566 | 1,881,142 |

DUNS 23-882-7252

## T I A (G B) Ltd

Unit C, Halesfield 14, Telford, Shropshire TF7 4QR
**Tel:** 0195-268-4168
**Web:** www.treadsetters.co.uk
**Reg No:** 3873873 **Estd:** 1999 Private Limited Company
**Line of Business:** Car accessories and parts
**Export Sales:** £34,183,652
**Trading Style:** Treadsetters
**Issued Capital:** £1,000,000
**Principals:** T Jones *(Financial)*, T M Davis, M Smith, P J Smith, Ms H Pei
**Co. Secretary:** Matthew Smith
**US SIC:** 5531 **UK SIC:** 65100
**Auditors:** Crowe Clark Whitehill LLP

| | 31-03-14 | 31-03-13 | 31-03-12 |
|---|---|---|---|
| TO | 87,759,419 | 75,987,600 | 72,630,032 |
| P/L | 157,347 | 120,794 | 1,944,830 |
| NW | 5,160,198 | 4,894,417 | 4,635,336 |
| WC | 1,843,048 | 3,582,908 | 4,028,055 |
| Emp. | 70 | 64 | 39 |

DUNS 51-993-5308 **Imp**

## T I Midwood & Co Ltd

Green Lane, Wardle, Nantwich, Cheshire CW5 6BJ
**Web:** www.timco.co.uk
**Reg No:** 3360713 **Estd:** 1997 Private Limited Company
**Line of Business:** Fasteners and fixings
**Issued Capital:** £100
**Directors:** Ms Y Messenger, S Rance
**Co. Secretary:** Simon Midwood
**Responsibilities**
**Sales:** Mary Havelin, Jonathon Jackson, Andy Moore *(Sales Representative)*
**US SIC:** 3452 **UK SIC:** 31371
**Auditors:** UHY Hacker Young
**Bankers:** National Westminster Bank Plc (60-40-08)

| | 31-12-13 | 31-12-12 | 31-12-11 |
|---|---|---|---|
| TO | 16,008,676 | 13,544,151 | 12,413,314 |
| P/L | 1,432,658 | 969,435 | 1,077,887 |
| NW | 8,133,611 | 7,208,032 | 6,595,615 |
| WC | 6,604,529 | 5,674,089 | 4,601,107 |
| Emp. | 58 | 49 | 45 |

DUNS 22-036-6897

## T J Brent Ltd

(**Subsidiary of:** Kier Group Plc)
Tempsford Hall, Sandy, Bedfordshire SG19 2BD
**Tel:** 01208-73038
**Web:** www.maygurney.co.uk
**Reg No:** 4039121 **Estd:** 1974 Private Limited Company
**Line of Business:** Construction of commercial buildings
**Trading Style:** May Guerney
**Issued Capital:** £98,650
**Directors:** D N Benson, H E Raven, H J Mursell
**Co. Secretary:** Matthew Armitage
**Responsibilities**
**Senior:** Robert Findlater *(Manager)*, Philip Prynne *(Manager)*, Kerry Stern *(Office Manager)*
**Branches:** T J Brent Ltd, Fishleigh Rock, Umberleigh, Devon EX37 9DX
**US SIC:** 1541 **UK SIC:** 50100
**Auditors:** Grant Thornton UK LLP

| | 31-03-13 | 31-03-12 | 31-03-11 |
|---|---|---|---|
| TA | 279,000 | 279,000 | 279,000 |
| NW | 279,000 | 279,000 | 279,000 |

DUNS 22-927-1846

## T J McGurran Ltd

(**Subsidiary of:** Tj Mc Gurran (Belfast) Ltd)
Errigle Inn, 312-320 Ormeau Road, Belfast BT7 2GE
**Tel:** 028-9064-1410 **Fax:** 028-9064-0772
**Web:** www.errigle.com
**Reg No:** 0006497NI **Estd:** 1935 Private Limited Company
**Line of Business:** Public house
**Trading Style:** Errigle Inn
**Issued Capital:** £100,000
**Directors:** Mrs E Mcgurran, P Mcgurran
**Co. Secretary:** Philip Mcgurran
**Responsibilities**
**Senior:** Phillip McGurran *(Proprietor)*
**US SIC:** 5813, 5812
**UK SIC:** 66200, 66110
**Auditors:** Baker Tilly Mooney Moore
**Bankers:** Northern Bank Ltd (95-01-06)

| | 31-03-14 | 31-03-13 | 31-03-12 |
|---|---|---|---|
| TA | 1,833,650 | 1,603,224 | 1,651,236 |
| NW | 984,070 | 896,514 | 996,056 |
| WC | 408,817 | 289,926 | 372,745 |

DUNS 21-809-0559

## T J Morris

Highbridge Retail Park, Waltham Abbey, Essex EN9 1BY
**Tel:** 01992719771
**Web:** www.homebargains.co.uk
**Estd:** 2012
**Line of Business:** Discount centres
**Responsibilities**
**Senior:** Yen Than *(Store Manager)*
**US SIC:** 5999 **UK SIC:** 65600
**Employees:** 50

DUNS 21-326-6646

## T. J. Morris Ltd

Axis Business Park, Portal Way, Off East Lancashire Road, Gilmos, Liverpool, Merseyside L11 0JA
**Tel:** 01515486101 **Fax:** 01515-302922
**Web:** www.homebargains.co.uk
**Reg No:** 1505036 **VAT No:** 320093700
**Estd:** 1980 Private Limited Company
**Line of Business:** Household stores
**Trading Style:** Homebargains
**Issued Capital:** £20,000
**Principals:** T J Morris *(Managing)*, J L Morris
**Co. Secretary:** Graeme Mcloughlin
**Responsibilities**
**Senior:** Jenny Mushrow *(Manager)*
**Health & Safety:** Tony Steed *(Health & Safety Officer)*
**Branches:** T. J. Morris Ltd, 9 Pepper Street, Nantwich, Cheshire CW5 5AB
**US SIC:** 5999 **UK SIC:** 65600
**Auditors:** Moore Stephens (North West) LLP
**Bankers:** National Westminster Bank Plc (60-15-38)

**Following financial data are in thousands**

| | 30-06-14 | 30-06-13 | 30-06-12 |
|---|---|---|---|
| TO | 1,277,324 | 1,058,399 | 914,821 |
| P/L | 124,760 | 110,856 | 84,193 |
| NW | 439,875 | 348,928 | 272,902 |
| WC | 100,414 | 132,485 | 94,236 |
| Emp. | 11,098 | 9,238 | 7,911 |

DUNS 21-215-1724 **Imp-Exp**

## T J Smith & Nephew Ltd

(**Subsidiary of:** Smith & Nephew Plc)
101 Hessle Road Graham Avenue, Hull, North Humberside HU4 7AW
**Tel:** 01482-225181 **Fax:** 01482222211
**Web:** www.smith-nephew.com
**Reg No:** 0093994 **Estd:** 1907 Private Limited Company
**Line of Business:** Manufacture of medical and surgical equipment and orthopaedic appliances
**Export Markets:** Worldwide
**Export Sales:** £255,955,000
**Trading Style:** Smith & Nephew Extruded Films, Smith & Nephew Healthcare
**Issued Capital:** £122,537
**Directors:** H T Waters, B S Sahota, I C Melling, Ms S M Swabey
**Co. Secretary:**
Smith & Nephew Nominee Services
**Responsibilities**
**Finance:** Peter Van Tiggledon *(Financial Director)*
**Facilities:** Jane Dixon *(Maintenance Coordinator)*
**US SIC:** 3841, 3079
**UK SIC:** 37201, 48360
**Auditors:** Ernst & Young LLP
**Bankers:** National Westminster Bank Plc (56-00-06)

| | 31-12-13 | 31-12-12 | 31-12-11 |
|---|---|---|---|
| TO | 443,618,000 | 394,036,000 | 378,902,000 |
| P/L | 53,902,000 | 64,129,000 | 53,944,000 |
| NW | 99,514,000 | 147,859,000 | 93,850,000 |
| WC | 75,166,000 | 93,788,000 | 53,503,000 |
| Emp. | 1,448 | 1,501 | 1,490 |

DUNS 57-832-1150

## T J Transport Ltd.

Charity Farm, Wickham Road, Fareham, Hampshire PO17 5BP
**Web:** www.tj-waste.co.uk
**Reg No:** 2889704 **Estd:** 1994 Private Limited Company
**Line of Business:** Freight transport by road not elsewhere classified
**Issued Capital:** £100,160
**Directors:** J D Gosling, J W Higgins, N Glazebrook, T J Higgins
**Co. Secretary:** Ms Lynne Higgins
**US SIC:** 4213 **UK SIC:** 72300
**Auditors:** Aspen Waite
**Bankers:** Barclays Bank Plc (20-94-74)

| | 31-12-13 | 31-12-12 | 31-12-11 |
|---|---|---|---|
| TO | 17,867,851 | 11,475,332 | 11,238,725 |
| P/L | 478,447 | (16,227) | (23,430) |
| NW | 1,726,376 | 1,326,500 | 1,371,317 |
| WC | (1,208,641) | (1,436,374) | (1,271,585) |
| Emp. | 126 | 102 | 104 |

DUNS 64-150-7363

## T Johnston Butchers

4 Main Street, Brightons, Falkirk, Stirlingshire FK2 0JT
**Tel:** 01324-717126
**Estd:** 1861 Partnership
**Line of Business:** Retail sale of meat and meat products
**Partners:** G Johnston, R Johnston
**Branches:** T Johnston Butchers, 7 Station Road, Dunfermline, Fife KY12 9QF
**US SIC:** 5423, 5147
**UK SIC:** 64100, 61700
**Bankers:** Clydesdale Bank Plc (82-63-12)
**Employees:** 47

DUNS 21-584-3979

## T K M Printing Solutions

6 Kingscroft, Welwyn Garden City, Hertfordshire AL7 2DL
**Estd:** 2011 Proprietorship
**Line of Business:** Lithographic printers
**Proprietor:** T Kearney
**US SIC:** 2752 **UK SIC:** 47544
**Employees:** 500

DUNS 21-268-6336

## T K Maxx

Paddington House, Town Centre, Basingstoke, Hampshire RG21 7LJ
**Tel:** 01256335812
**Web:** www.tkmaxx.com
**Estd:** 2012
**Line of Business:** Other retail sale in non-specialised stores
**Proprietor:** Mrs S Mcwicker
**Responsibilities**
**Senior:** S McWicker *(Proprietor)*, Sally Pang *(Manager)*
**Branches:** T K Maxx, Next Retail Ltdpark, Valentine Road, Lincoln, Lincolnshire LN6 7BH
**US SIC:** 5399 **UK SIC:** 65600
**Employees:** 53

DUNS 21-466-4083
## T L C Cares
Unit 2 Brunel Court, Brunel Road Gorse Lane Industrial Estate, Clacton-On-Sea, Essex CO15 4LU
**Tel:** 03331215901
**Web:** www.mihomecare.com
**Estd:** 1994 Partnership
**Line of Business:** Home care and help services
**Partners:** M Brown, Ms C Cornwall
**Responsibilities**
**Senior:** Natalie Mclellan *(Manager)*
**US SIC:** 8811 **UK SIC:** 99000
**Employees:** 80

DUNS 50-512-7191
## T L C (Southern) Ltd
Suite G Kings House, 68 Victoria Road, Burgess Hill, West Sussex RH15 9LH
**Fax:** 01293-614576
**Web:** www.tlc-direct.co.uk
**Reg No:** 2480571 **VAT No:** 550447258
**Estd:** 1990 Private Limited Company
**Line of Business:** Wholesale of other intermediate products
**Issued Capital:** £5,000
**Principals:** N Greenwood *(Managing)*, R D Macgregor, P C West, T J Carr
**Co. Secretary:** Nigel Greenwood
**Branches:** T L C (Southern) Ltd, Redlands, Unit A6, Coulsdon, Surrey CR5 2HT
**US SIC:** 5199 **UK SIC:** 61900
**Auditors:** Baker Tilly UK Audit LLP
**Bankers:** Barclays Bank Plc (20-12-75)

|       | 31-05-13   | 31-05-12   | 31-05-11   |
|-------|-----------|-----------|-----------|
| TO    | 52,337,367 | 48,890,859 | 42,795,535 |
| P/L   | 6,331,813  | 5,504,557  | 3,968,986  |
| NW    | 12,403,222 | 8,085,413  | 4,499,599  |
| WC    | 8,195,427  | 7,491,292  | 4,618,658  |
| Emp.  | 217        | 208        | 192        |

DUNS 50-451-7806
## T L Dallas Group Ltd
Dallas House, Cleckheaton Road, Bradford, West Yorkshire BD12 0HF
**Tel:** 01274-465500
**Web:** www.tldallas.com
**Reg No:** 2434450 **VAT No:** 556875195
**Estd:** 1921 Private Limited Company
**Line of Business:** Activities auxiliary to insurance and pension funding
**Issued Capital:** £124,119
**Principals:** J D Butterworth *(Managing)*, F C Penton, M P Martin, Mrs P E Staveley, G H Reid, R J Bottomley
**Co. Secretary:** Christopher Hudson
**Responsibilities**
**Senior:** Berric Usher *(Manager)*
**Branches:** T L Dallas Group Ltd, Haypark Business Centre, The Lodge Studio, Falkirk, Stirlingshire FK2 0NZ
**US SIC:** 6411 **UK SIC:** 83200
**Auditors:** Wbs
**Bankers:** Lloyds TSB Bank plc (30-91-12)

|      | 31-12-13   | 31-12-12   | 31-12-11   |
|------|-----------|-----------|-----------|
| TO   | 8,127,972  | 8,045,549  | 7,333,880  |
| P/L  | 1,210,194  | 1,334,831  | 1,030,510  |
| NW   | 3,615,677  | 2,945,512  | 2,467,077  |
| WC   | 2,618,319  | 2,031,863  | 1,784,300  |
| Emp. | 112        | 106        | 104        |

DUNS 23-536-2618
## T Lott Ltd
Unit 19, St Albans, Hertfordshire AL1 1XB
**Tel:** 01727-846850 **Fax:** 01727846355
**Web:** www.tlottltd.co.uk
**Reg No:** 3535034 **Estd:** 1998 Private Limited Company
**Line of Business:** Plastering
**Issued Capital:** £28
**Directors:** P Lott, T J Lott, Ms A Corbett
**Co. Secretary:** Ms Amanda Corbett
**Responsibilities**
**Health & Safety:** Spencer Baker *(Health & Safety Officer)*
**US SIC:** 1742 **UK SIC:** 50400
**Bankers:** HSBC Bank plc (40-12-27)

|     | 30-09-14  | 30-09-13  | 30-09-12  |
|-----|-----------|-----------|-----------|
| TA  | 3,101,960 | 2,432,395 | 2,865,803 |
| NW  | 886,898   | 551,037   | 446,893   |
| WC  | 938,437   | 662,164   | 618,518   |

DUNS 22-554-6324
## T M B Patterns
Unit 24 Brue Avenue, Bridgwater, Somerset TA6 5LT
**Web:** www.tmb-patterns.co.uk
**Estd:** 1977 Partnership
**Line of Business:** Industrial Machinery & Equipment Whlrs
**Partners:** M J Baker, T C Morley
**US SIC:** 5084 **UK SIC:** 61490
**Bankers:** Lloyds TSB Bank plc (30-98-45)
**Employees:** 70

DUNS 21-597-7041
## T M C Southern
Banks Place, Market Place, Dartford, Kent DA1 1EX
**Tel:** 01322293768
**Estd:** 2009 Proprietorship
**Line of Business:** Employment Agencies
**Proprietor:** Miss K Stewart
**US SIC:** 7361 **UK SIC:** 83954
**Employees:** 60

DUNS 29-491-0765
## T M Lewin (Shirtmakers) Ltd
**(Subsidiary of:** T.M. Lewin Group Ltd)
6-7 St Cross Street, London EC1N 8UA
**Tel:** 08453-891898
**Web:** www.tmlewin.co.uk
**Reg No:** 1854490 **VAT No:** 394935305
**Estd:** 1985 Private Limited Company
**Line of Business:** Other manufacturing not elsewhere classified
**Issued Capital:** £100
**Principals:** J S Francomb *(Managing)*, G Quinn
**Co. Secretary:** Robert Isaac
**US SIC:** 3999 **UK SIC:** 49590
**Auditors:** BDO LLP
**Bankers:** National Westminster Bank Plc (56-00-03)

|      | 01-03-14  | 02-03-13  | 03-03-12  |
|------|-----------|-----------|-----------|
| TA   | 1,505,988 | 1,505,988 | 1,505,988 |
| P/L  | N/A       | N/A       | 12        |
| NW   | 1,505,796 | 1,505,796 | 1,505,796 |
| WC   | 1,505,796 | 1,505,796 | 1,505,796 |

DUNS 73-630-3228
## T M S Support Solutions Ltd
Alpha Court, Swingbridge Road, Grantham, Lincolnshire NG31 7XT
**Tel:** 01476-583370
**Web:** www.tmsss.com
**Reg No:** 4890733 **Estd:** 1991 Private Limited Company
**Line of Business:** Other business activities not elsewhere classified
**Issued Capital:** £25,001
**Directors:** B R Cannon, T B Cannon, Mrs J K Cannon, Miss T Cannon
**Co. Secretary:** Mrs Michelle Allbones
**US SIC:** 7379 **UK SIC:** 83940
**Auditors:** Duncan & Toplis

|     | 31-07-14  | 31-07-13  | 31-07-12  |
|-----|-----------|-----------|-----------|
| TA  | 1,018,808 | 1,085,604 | 1,451,410 |
| NW  | 767,893   | 729,156   | 1,087,835 |
| WC  | 691,196   | 620,245   | 932,938   |

DUNS 22-114-3451
## T M T I Ltd
Corsley Heath, Corsley, Warminster, Wiltshire BA12 7PL
**Tel:** 0844-499-4744 **Fax:** 0844-499-4733
**Web:** www.tmti.net
**Reg No:** 4133536 **Estd:** 2000 Private Limited Company
**Line of Business:** Other computer related activities
**Export Sales:** £647,017
**Issued Capital:** £190,362
**Director:** C B Thomas
**Co. Secretary:** Neil Jones
**Branches:** T M T I Ltd, Corsley Heath, Warminster, Wiltshire BA12 7PL
**US SIC:** 7379 **UK SIC:** 83940
**Auditors:** Mazars

|      | 28-02-14  | 28-02-13  | 29-02-12  |
|------|-----------|-----------|-----------|
| TO   | 5,859,119 | 6,098,455 | 5,993,863 |
| P/L  | 1,842,934 | 1,371,617 | 1,209,507 |
| NW   | 438,932   | 972,556   | 1,615,940 |
| WC   | (218,185) | 125,266   | 737,537   |
| Emp. | 51        | 54        | 60        |

DUNS 21-565-7478
## T Mackenzie
27 Manchester Road, Rossendale, Lancashire BB4 5SL
**Tel:** 01706212518
**Estd:** 1984 Partnership
**Line of Business:** Medical practice
**Partner:** Dr P Rishton
**Responsibilities**
**Senior:** Elaine Bates *(Practice Manager)*
**US SIC:** 8011 **UK SIC:** 95300
**Employees:** 50

DUNS 21-227-0720
## T McConram
Tavanagh Avenue, Portadown, Craigavon, Co Armagh BT62 3BU
**Tel:** 028-38351497
**Web:** www.bannviewmedicalpractice.co.uk
**Estd:** 2010 Proprietorship
**Line of Business:** Doctors
**Proprietor:** Mrs A Todd
**Responsibilities**
**Senior:** Lynda Mcconaghy *(Practice Manager)*
**US SIC:** 8011 **UK SIC:** 95300
**Employees:** 128

DUNS 23-013-0416
## T. Met Ltd
84 Armagh Road, Dungannon, Co Tyrone BT71 7JA
**Tel:** 028-3754-9092 **Fax:** 02837436772
**Web:** www.t-met.co.uk
**Reg No:** 0036781NI **Estd:** 1999 Private Limited Company
**Line of Business:** Scrap metal dealers
**Issued Capital:** £1,140,047
**Directors:** C G Traynor, C O Traynor
**Co. Secretary:** Thomas Quinn
**Responsibilities**
**Senior:** Barry O'neill *(Manager)*
**US SIC:** 5093, 5051
**UK SIC:** 62200, 61200
**Auditors:** PricewaterhouseCoopers LLP
**Bankers:** The Bank Of Ireland (90-20-47)

|      | 31-12-13   | 31-12-12   | 31-12-11   |
|------|-----------|-----------|-----------|
| TO   | 24,717,790 | 35,449,782 | 42,846,844 |
| P/L  | 644,010    | 1,119,249  | 3,194,390  |
| NW   | 16,523,001 | 16,344,972 | 15,681,926 |
| WC   | 7,714,499  | 7,465,281  | 7,154,801  |
| Emp. | 56         | 66         | 66         |

DUNS 21-783-0486
## T N T
Mosley Road Central Park Estate, Manchester M17 1TT
**Tel:** 01618738888
**Web:** www.tnt.com
**Estd:** 2002 Proprietorship
**Line of Business:** Road haulage and transport services
**Proprietor:** D Hughes
**US SIC:** 4789 **UK SIC:** 77002
**Employees:** 446

DUNS 21-582-6917
## T N T Alton
Plot 3 Caker Stream Road, Alton, Hampshire GU34 2QA
**Tel:** 01420594300
**Web:** www.tnt.com
**Estd:** 2011 Proprietorship
**Line of Business:** Road haulage and transport services
**Proprietor:** J Hagley
**Responsibilities**
**Senior:** Bill McFetridge *(Manager)*
**US SIC:** 4789 **UK SIC:** 77002
**Employees:** 120

DUNS 21-582-7035
## T N T Basildon
Hovefields Avenue, Basildon, Essex SS13 1EB
**Tel:** 01268591100
**Web:** www.tnt.com
**Estd:** 2011 Proprietorship
**Line of Business:** Road haulage and transport services
**Proprietor:** Miss C Rose
**US SIC:** 4789 **UK SIC:** 77002
**Employees:** 400

DUNS 21-582-6956
## T N T Jersey
Tnt Co Ferryspeed Ci Ltd, Jersey, Channel Islands JE2 3NW
**Tel:** 01534871196
**Web:** www.tnt.com
**Estd:** 2011 Proprietorship
**Line of Business:** Road haulage and transport services
**Proprietor:** T Donnelly
**Responsibilities**
**Senior:** Richard Diegan *(General Manager)*
**US SIC:** 4789 **UK SIC:** 77002
**Employees:** 500

DUNS 21-777-5995
## T N T Special Services
Unit 134 Hartlebury Trading Estate, Hartlebury, Kidderminster, Worcestershire DY10 4JB
**Tel:** 01299250100
**Web:** www.tnt.com
**Estd:** 2002 Proprietorship
**Line of Business:** Goods delivery services
**Proprietor:** A Avery
**Responsibilities**
**Senior:** Rex Stenner *(Depot Manager)*
**US SIC:** 4213 **UK SIC:** 72300
**Employees:** 188

DUNS 21-582-7116
## T N T Teesside
Hangar 2, Darlington, County Durham DL2 1NJ
**Web:** www.tnt.com
**Estd:** 2000 Proprietorship
**Line of Business:** Road haulage and transport services

**Proprietor:** I Calder
**US SIC:** 4789 **UK SIC:** 77002
**Employees:** 100

DUNS 22-162-2538
## T N V Construction Ltd
1 Constable Gardens, Edgware, Middlesex HA8 5SF
**Tel:** 020-3114-9099
**Web:** www.tnvconstruction.com
**Reg No:** 4180810 **Estd:** 2001 Private Limited Company
**Line of Business:** Construction of commercial buildings
**Trading Style:** T R U Construction
**Issued Capital:** £10,000
**Director:** A V Patel
**Co. Secretary:** Mrs Vanisha Patel
**US SIC:** 1541 **UK SIC:** 50100
**Auditors:** Lubbock Fine

|     | 31-03-14  | 31-03-13  | 31-03-12  |
|-----|-----------|-----------|-----------|
| TA  | 2,598,594 | 2,169,268 | 2,490,229 |
| NW  | 273,064   | 221,479   | 205,577   |
| WC  | 202,300   | 177,850   | 164,010   |

DUNS 22-931-5890
## T O'Connell and Sons
2 New Street, Dungiven, Londonderry, Co Londonderry BT47 4LJ
**Tel:** 02877741370
**Web:** www.toconnells.com
**Estd:** 1967 Partnership
**Line of Business:** Groundwork contractors
**Partners:** T O'Connell, S O'Connell, G O'Connell
**Responsibilities**
**Senior:** Seamus O' Connell *(Partner)*, Gerard O' Connell *(Managing Director)*
**Branches:** T O'connell and Sons, 51 Glenshane Road, Londonderry, Co Londonderry BT47 3SF
**US SIC:** 1622 **UK SIC:** 50200
**Auditors:** T O'Connell And Sons
**Bankers:** Northern Bank Ltd (95-03-06)
**Employees:** 46
**Turnover:** £5,051,324

DUNS 21-777-9572
## T P C Solicitors
85 High Street, Manchester M4 1BD
**Tel:** 01618328867
**Web:** www.tpclaw.co.uk
**Estd:** 2011
**Line of Business:** Solicitors
**Proprietor:** R Hart
**Responsibilities**
**HR:** Lauren Lloyd *(HR Manager)*
**US SIC:** 8111 **UK SIC:** 83500
**Employees:** 50

DUNS 42-417-0517                                    Imp
## T P Engineering Ltd
Blythe Park Sandon Road, Stoke-On-Trent, Staffordshire ST11 9RD
**Tel:** 01782-399758
**Web:** www.tpcats.com
**Reg No:** 4404706 **Estd:** 2002 Private Limited Company
**Line of Business:** Manufacture of parts and accessories for motor vehicles and their engines
**Issued Capital:** £10,030
**Directors:** M A Flower, D Hall, P B Stubbs
**Co. Secretary:** Paul Stubbs
**US SIC:** 3714 **UK SIC:** 35300

|     | 30-04-14  | 30-04-13  | 30-04-12  |
|-----|-----------|-----------|-----------|
| TA  | 1,739,767 | 1,878,694 | 2,160,707 |
| NW  | 750,034   | 690,816   | 669,057   |
| WC  | 512,830   | 419,291   | 379,749   |

DUNS 36-480-0532
## T P Matrix Ltd
Tp House, Prince Of Wales Business Park, Vulcan Street, Oldham, Lancashire OL1 4ER
**Tel:** 01616264067
**Web:** www.tpmatrixprojectorrepairs.co.uk
**Reg No:** 3283023 **Estd:** 1996 Private Limited Company
**Line of Business:** Manufacture of electronic valves and tubes and other electronic components
**Issued Capital:** £1,050,100
**Directors:** J Marland, A Stott
**Co. Secretary:** Christopher Morris
**US SIC:** 3679 **UK SIC:** 34542

|     | 30-06-13  | 30-06-12  | 30-06-11  |
|-----|-----------|-----------|-----------|
| TA  | 1,299,406 | 1,477,682 | 1,423,919 |
| NW  | 1,059,246 | 1,095,455 | 1,063,196 |
| WC  | 255,152   | 294,700   | 217,908   |

DUNS 23-805-6584
## T P Niven
Woodhead, Palnackie, Castle Douglas, Kirkcudbrightshire DG7 1PG
**Web:** www.tpniven.co.uk
**VAT No:** 263328463 **Estd:** 1926 Partnership
**Line of Business:** Road haulage and transport services

**Partners:** J Niven (Jnr), J Niven (Jnr), J Niven, J Niven, T Niven
**Branches:** T P Niven, Arla Foods Plc, Lockerbie Creamery, Lockerbie, Dumfriesshire DG11 1LW
**US SIC:** 4789 **UK SIC:** 77002
**Bankers:** The Royal Bank Of Scotland Plc (83-17-24)
**Employees:** 68

DUNS 21-810-7669

## T P S Healthcare

42-46 Booth Drive, Park Farm Industrial Estate, Wellingborough, Northamptonshire NN8 6NL
**Tel:** 01933670430
**Web:** www.tpshealthcare.com
**Estd:** 2012
**Line of Business:** Other human health activities
**Responsibilities**
**Senior:** Catherine Mccallum (Manager), Harry Smelly (Manager)
**US SIC:** 8091 **UK SIC:** 95200
**Employees:** 100

DUNS 28-987-5015 **Imp**

## T. Print Ltd

Apparel House, Bristol Avenue, Bispham, Lancashire Fy2 0jf, Blackpool, Lancashire FY2 0JF
**Tel:** 01253359120 **Fax:** 01253-359130
**Web:** www.t-print.co.uk
**Reg No:** 1807261 **VAT No:** 340801241
**Estd:** 1980 Private Limited Company
**Line of Business:** Printing not elsewhere classified
**Issued Capital:** £200
**Managing Director:** A Bainbridge
**Co. Secretary:** Paul Bainbridge
**Responsibilities**
**Senior:** Darren Anderson (General Manager)
**Finance:** Kerry Andrews (Financial Controller)
**HR:** Darren Anderson (General Manager)
**Health & Safety:** Darren Anderson (General Manager)
**US SIC:** 2269, 2392
**UK SIC:** 43702, 45550
**Auditors:** Horne Brooke Shenton
**Bankers:** The Royal Bank Of Scotland Plc (16-13-29)

|    | 31-01-14 | 31-01-13 | 31-01-12 |
|----|----------|----------|----------|
| TA | 918,438 | 1,039,018 | 1,502,817 |
| NW | 400,116 | 510,435 | 550,231 |
| WC | 240,082 | 330,831 | 349,668 |

DUNS 45-808-9703

## T Q Training Management Services Ltd

Bragborough Farm, Welton Road Braunston, Daventry, Northamptonshire NN11 7JG
**Fax:** 01536-713913
**Web:** www.tqconsultancy.co.uk
**Reg No:** 3166956 **Estd:** 1996 Private Limited Company
**Line of Business:** Management activities of holding companies
**Issued Capital:** £100,000
**Principals:** Ms J Quarmby (Managing), K J Francis
**Co. Secretary:** Garry Quarmby
**Branches:** T Q Training Management Services Ltd, Nobottle, Northampton, Northamptonshire NN7 4HJ
**US SIC:** 6711, 8221
**UK SIC:** 83962, 93100
**Auditors:** Smith Hodge & Baxter

|    | 31-07-13 | 31-07-12 | 31-07-11 |
|----|----------|----------|----------|
| TA | 599,423 | 570,265 | 555,013 |
| NW | 102,526 | 112,154 | 102,479 |
| WC | 285,151 | 79,416 | 57,832 |

DUNS 21-811-1464

## T Q Twentyone

6 The Potteries, Wickham Road, Fareham, Hampshire PO16 7ET
**Tel:** 01329316409
**Web:** www.tqtwentyone.org
**Estd:** 2012
**Line of Business:** Home care service providers
**Responsibilities**
**Senior:** Phil Aubrey-Harris (Director Of Social Services)
**US SIC:** 8091 **UK SIC:** 95200
**Employees:** 1,100

DUNS 21-681-1273 **Imp**

## T. Quality Ltd

(Subsidiary of: Rethmann Se & Co. Kg)
Westmead Industrial Estate, Swindon, Wiltshire SN5 7YY
**Fax:** 01793512458
**Web:** www.tquality.co.uk
**Reg No:** 0437914 **VAT No:** 194611552
**Estd:** 1928 Private Limited Company

**Line of Business:** Frozen foods (wholesale)
**Export Sales:** £122,357
**Issued Capital:** £157,200
**Principals:** D A Ross (Commercial), R G Brooks, R J Mansfield, A R Smith, P A Morris
**Co. Secretary:** Eric Scott
**Responsibilities**
**Senior:** Laurent Henry (Operations Manager), Keith Jennison (Manager), Anthony Mulder (Manager)
**Admin:** Wendy Browning (Office Manager)
**IT:** Sam Drew (IT Manager), Nick Trumper (IT Manager)
**HR:** Wendy Browning (Office Manager)
**Operations:** Laurent Henry (Operations Manager)
**Branches:** T. Quality Ltd, Unit 9, Wyndham Court, Swansea, West Glamorgan SA6 8RB
**US SIC:** 5149, 5199
**UK SIC:** 61700, 61900
**Auditors:** Paylings
**Bankers:** National Westminster Bank Plc (60-21-40)

|      | 31-12-13 | 31-12-12 | 31-12-12 |
|------|----------|----------|----------|
| TO   | 70,025,247 | 55,226,858 | 68,473,061 |
| P/L  | 1,356,119 | 1,144,212 | 1,022,151 |
| NW   | 8,187,102 | 7,161,181 | 6,305,383 |
| WC   | 5,959,047 | 4,859,342 | 4,116,662 |
| Emp. | 215 | 217 | 214 |

DUNS 23-688-2408 **Imp**

## T R B Ltd

(Subsidiary of: Tokai Rika Co. Ltd.)
St Asaph Business Park Rhodfa Trb, St Asaph, Clwyd LL17 0JB
**Tel:** 01745-584000 **Fax:** 01745-584111
**Web:** www.trb-ltd.co.uk
**Reg No:** 3683198 **Estd:** 2000 Private Limited Company
**Line of Business:** Electronic equipment (assembly)
**Export Sales:** £17,822,204
**Issued Capital:** £3,500,000
**Directors:** K Hayashi, K Noguchi, T Hamamoto, N Goto
**Co. Secretary:** Naoki Oda
**Responsibilities**
**Senior:** Ikuzo Kojima (Manager), Annesley Wright (Manager), Roy Yamaguchi (Manager)
**US SIC:** 3643, 5531
**UK SIC:** 34203, 65100
**Auditors:** Deloitte & Touche LLP
**Bankers:** The Sanwa Bank, Ltd (40-51-28)

|      | 31-03-14 | 31-03-13 | 31-03-12 |
|------|----------|----------|----------|
| TO   | 27,812,553 | 18,724,103 | 22,369,568 |
| P/L  | 215,407 | (86,008) | 234,492 |
| NW   | 6,548,021 | 6,505,322 | 6,715,343 |
| WC   | 4,740,533 | 4,476,370 | 4,342,981 |
| Emp. | 135 | 126 | 131 |

DUNS 29-518-9005

## T R Bonnyman Son & Company Ltd

Bonnymans Willowburn Road, Beith, Ayrshire KA15 1LN
**Tel:** 01505504716
**Web:** www.bonnymans.co.uk
**Reg No:** 0091522SC **VAT No:** 428129060
**Estd:** 1985 Private Limited Company
**Line of Business:** Cleaning materials and equipment
**Issued Capital:** £95
**Principals:** S G Allam (Managing), H M Rogers, G Grant
**Co. Secretary:** Evelyn Allam
**Responsibilities**
**Finance:** Elaine Guffie (Accounts Manager)
**HR:** Sharon Adam (Office Manager)
**Purchasing:** Sharon Adam (Office Manager)
**US SIC:** 3357 **UK SIC:** 22470
**Auditors:** J. Bruce Andrew & Co

|    | 28-02-14 | 28-02-13 | 28-02-12 |
|----|----------|----------|----------|
| TA | 1,489,586 | 1,609,712 | 1,403,874 |
| NW | 346,484 | 231,147 | 287,071 |
| WC | 39,782 | (19,498) | 13,884 |

DUNS 21-601-8937 **Imp**

## T. R. Hayes Ltd

15-18 London Street, Bath, Avon BA1 5BX
**Tel:** 01225-465757 **Fax:** 01225-444849
**Web:** www.trhayes.co.uk
**Reg No:** 1103138 **VAT No:** 138304090
**Estd:** 1916 Private Limited Company
**Line of Business:** Furniture retail outlets
**Issued Capital:** £10,000
**Principals:** D R Hayes (Managing), Mrs M E Hayes (Financial), R J Hayes
**Co. Secretary:** Derek Hayes
**Branches:** T. R. Hayes Ltd, 34 Box Rd, Bath, Avon BA1 7QH
**US SIC:** 5719 **UK SIC:** 64700
**Auditors:** Pearson May

|    | 31-03-14 | 31-03-13 | 31-03-12 |
|----|----------|----------|----------|
| TA | 3,267,020 | 2,979,057 | 2,774,272 |
| NW | 1,991,568 | 1,875,616 | 1,759,821 |
| WC | 923,785 | 771,443 | 1,391,771 |

DUNS 42-476-4046

## T R J Holdings Ltd

Foundry Road, Ammanford, Dyfed SA18 2LS
**Tel:** 01269-591103 **Fax:** 01269-596207
**Web:** www.trichardjones.co.uk
**Reg No:** 4464050 **Estd:** 2002 Private Limited Company
**Line of Business:** Management activities of construction holding companies
**Issued Capital:** £378
**Directors:** D H Jones, D Jones, H Jones
**Co. Secretary:** Owain Jones
**US SIC:** 6711 **UK SIC:** 83962

|      | 31-07-13 | 31-07-12 | 31-07-11 |
|------|----------|----------|----------|
| TO   | 20,452,275 | 24,008,069 | 17,231,703 |
| P/L  | 511,513 | 191,544 | 101,561 |
| NW   | 5,853,407 | 5,365,010 | 5,967,716 |
| WC   | 4,699,052 | 4,127,080 | 4,042,009 |
| Emp. | 159 | 170 | 164 |

DUNS 21-117-4116

## T R N F Ltd

1st Floor Tudor House, 16 Cathedral Road, Cardiff, South Glamorgan CF11 9LJ
**Tel:** 02920196821
**Web:** www.nischr-crc.wales.nhs.uk
**Reg No:** 6572374 **Estd:** 2008 Private Limited Company
**Line of Business:** Research institutions and organisations
**Issued Capital:** £100
**Director:** J I Weerawardena
**Co. Secretary:** Ms Olivia Remond
**Responsibilities**
**Senior:** Lucy Seago (Operations Director)
**Admin:** Katheryn Cooke (Administrator)
**US SIC:** 7391 **UK SIC:** 94000

|    | 30-09-14 | 30-09-13 | 30-09-12 |
|----|----------|----------|----------|
| TA | 641,942 | 553,182 | 593,182 |
| NW | 17,007 | 100 | 100 |
| WC | (283,045) | (299,952) | (299,952) |

DUNS 23-934-3721 **Imp**

## T R T Ltd

(Subsidiary of: Chromalloy Uk Holdings Ltd)
3 Bramble Way, Clover Nook Industrial Park, Alfreton, Derbyshire DE55 4RH
**Tel:** 01773-524400
**Web:** www.trt-ltd.com
**Reg No:** 3924148 **Estd:** 2000 Private Limited Company
**Line of Business:** Manufacture of aircraft and spacecraft
**Export Sales:** £6,332,000
**Issued Capital:** £12,501
**Directors:** G W Davies, M R Bolton, W D Gee, P Howard
**Co. Secretary:** Mrs Karen Waldron
**US SIC:** 3721 **UK SIC:** 36400

|      | 31-12-13 | 31-12-12 | 31-12-11 |
|------|----------|----------|----------|
| TO   | 11,669,000 | 11,636,000 | 13,437,000 |
| P/L  | 2,939,000 | 2,834,000 | 4,343,000 |
| NW   | 6,536,000 | 6,283,000 | 6,640,000 |
| WC   | 5,250,000 | 4,821,000 | 5,098,000 |
| Emp. | 103 | 117 | 128 |

DUNS 23-968-9495 **Imp**

## T. Rowe Price International Ltd

(Subsidiary of: T. Rowe Price Group Inc.)
60 Queen Victoria Street, London EC4N 4TZ
**Tel:** 020-7651-8200 **Fax:** 020-7651-8480
**Web:** www.individual.troweprice.com
**Reg No:** 3957748 **Estd:** 2000 Private Limited Company
**Line of Business:** Investment companies and vehicles
**Directors:** E C Bernard, I D Kelson, C D Alderson, R C Higginbotham
**Co. Secretary:** David Oestreicher
**Responsibilities**
**Senior:** Emma Beal (Manager), Barbara Van Horn (Manager)
**US SIC:** 6211 **UK SIC:** 83100
**Auditors:** KPMG Audit PLC
**Employees:** 57

DUNS 50-190-2001

## T S Bloor & Sons Ltd

1-4 Old Station Close, Coalville, Leicestershire LE67 3FH
**Tel:** 01530-830920 **Fax:** 01530-830919
**Reg No:** 2329527 **Estd:** 1960 Private Limited Company
**Line of Business:** Animal by-product processing
**Issued Capital:** £100
**Directors:** B M Mcloughlin, C D Bloor
**Co. Secretary:** Mrs Rachel Bloor
**US SIC:** 2013 **UK SIC:** 41223
**Auditors:** Crowfoot & Co Ltd
**Bankers:** National Westminster Bank Plc (60-06-02)

|      | 31-12-13 | 31-12-12 | 31-12-11 |
|------|----------|----------|----------|
| TO   | 13,728,011 | 12,942,637 | 13,226,525 |
| P/L  | 504,693 | 855,686 | 954,213 |
| NW   | 6,134,381 | 5,713,769 | 5,258,188 |
| WC   | 4,079,328 | 3,765,379 | 3,250,060 |
| Emp. | 101 | 72 | 104 |

DUNS 29-538-9589 **Exp**

## T S Chemicals Ltd

Unit 3 Bentwood Road, Haslingden, Rossendale, Lancashire BB4 5HH
**Tel:** 01706-831423
**Web:** www.tschemicals.com
**Reg No:** 1905847 **VAT No:** 407201500
**Estd:** 1985 Private Limited Company
**Line of Business:** Manufacturers of chemicals
**Trading Style:** Ts Jeans Care
**Issued Capital:** £100,000
**Principals:** J D Pickard (Managing), M J Pickard, T Pickard
**Co. Secretary:** Mrs Christine Pickard
**Branches:** T S Chemicals Ltd, Unit 5 Bentwood Road, Haslingden, Haslingden, Rossendale, Lancashire BB4 5HH
**US SIC:** 2899 **UK SIC:** 25670
**Auditors:** PM&M Solutions for Business LLP
**Bankers:** National Westminster Bank Plc (60-20-11)

|    | 31-08-13 | 31-08-12 | 31-08-11 |
|----|----------|----------|----------|
| TA | 1,346,971 | 1,536,359 | 1,623,286 |
| NW | 563,199 | 696,088 | 890,579 |
| WC | 560,428 | 691,923 | 887,861 |

DUNS 39-928-7713 **Imp-Exp**

## T S E Europe Ltd

79 Fortess Road, London NW5 1AG
**Tel:** 020-3227-1046 **Fax:** 020-7263-4303
**Web:** www.tsecashmere.com
**Reg No:** 2242951 **VAT No:** 541631734
**Estd:** 1988 Private Limited Company
**Line of Business:** Manufacture of knitted and crocheted pullovers, cardigans and similar articles
**Export Markets:** Europe
**Trading Style:** T S E Europe Limited
**Issued Capital:** £5,841,000
**Directors:** Ms M Y Tang, E Murray
**Co. Secretary:** Mrs Diana Petre
**Responsibilities**
**IT:** John Oakland (Head of IT)
**US SIC:** 8999 **UK SIC:** 83954
**Auditors:** Levy Blair
**Bankers:** Standard Chartered Bank (60-91-04)

|    | 31-03-14 | 31-03-13 | 31-03-12 |
|----|----------|----------|----------|
| TA | 1,334,233 | 1,629,386 | 1,468,797 |
| NW | (8,861,195) | (8,686,988) | (7,495,929) |
| WC | (8,861,195) | (8,760,691) | (7,522,757) |

DUNS 34-688-8332

## T S S Group Plc

121 Canterbury Road, Croydon, Surrey CR0 3HH
**Tel:** 020-8683-1000 **Fax:** 02086831222
**Web:** www.thamesmotorgroup.co.uk
**Reg No:** 2776516 **Estd:** 1981 Public Limited Company
**Line of Business:** Management activities of holding companies
**Issued Capital:** £500,000
**Principals:** V Khanna (Managing), K P Khanna, Mrs A E Khanna, P W Featherstone, Ms N N Khanna
**Co. Secretary:** Kandasamy Jeyavarathan
**Responsibilities**
**IT:** I Illangovan (IT Manager)
**US SIC:** 6711, 5541
**UK SIC:** 83962, 65200
**Auditors:** Simpson Wreford & Partners
**Bankers:** Barclays Bank Plc (20-44-86)

|      | 31-12-13 | 31-12-12 | 31-12-11 |
|------|----------|----------|----------|
| TO   | 38,144,636 | 34,657,617 | 34,040,952 |
| P/L  | 971,129 | 793,026 | 705,948 |
| NW   | 6,746,442 | 6,243,525 | 5,877,916 |
| WC   | 2,281,531 | 791,746 | 683,177 |
| Emp. | 86 | 84 | 78 |

DUNS 23-633-9284

## T S (U K) Ltd

Unit 107 Stakehill Industrial Estate, Touchet Hall Road, Middleton, Manchester M24 2SJ
**Tel:** 0161-653-3888 **Fax:** 0161-654-4970
**Web:** www.ts-uk.co.uk
**Reg No:** 3630810 **Estd:** 1998 Private Limited Company
**Line of Business:** Manufacturers of plastic products
**Issued Capital:** £40,000
**Director:** S Tontarelli
**Co. Secretary:** Christian Tontarelli
**Responsibilities**
**Senior:** Darren Reynolds (Manager)
**US SIC:** 2821, 3079
**UK SIC:** 25140, 48360
**Auditors:** Thompson Gorton Jones
**Bankers:** Banca Monte Dei Paschi Di Siena Spa (40-51-68)

|      | 31-12-13 | 31-12-12 | 31-12-11 |
|------|----------|----------|----------|
| TO   | 14,278,589 | 14,175,481 | 13,561,798 |
| P/L  | 688,692 | 921,599 | (134,350) |
| NW   | 1,272,096 | 776,457 | 56,857 |
| WC   | (1,398,625) | (1,481,046) | (1,018,602) |
| Emp. | 78 | 74 | 67 |

**DUNS 38-786-0562**

## T Soanes & Son

Church Hill, Driffield, North Humberside
YO25 9UG
**Tel:** 01377-217243
**Web:** www.soanespoultry.co.uk
**Estd:** 1983 Proprietorship
**Line of Business:** Poultry farmers
**Proprietor:** C Soanes
**Responsibilities**
**Senior:** Nick Hudson (Operations Manager),
Melanie Jackson (Factory Manager),
Andrew Soanes (Manager)
**Operations:** Nick Hudson (Operations
Manager)
**Branches:** T Soanes & Son, Green Lane
Farm, Cadger Castle, Driffield, North
Humberside YO25 9LQ
**US SIC:** 0259, 2016
**UK SIC:** 01001, 41231
**Employees:** 50

**DUNS 22-706-1959**

## T-Systems Ltd

(**Subsidiary of:** Deutsche Telekom Ag)
Building 3 Ground Floor, Hatfield Business
Park, Hatfield, Hertfordshire AL10 9BW
**Tel:** 0207 121 3900
**Web:** www.t-systems.com
**Reg No:** 1668706 **Estd:** 1982 Private
Limited Company
**Line of Business:** Telecommunications
**Export Sales:** £38,955,000
**Issued Capital:** £550,001
**Directors:** C Malig, F S Hardt, N D Giebel
**Co. Secretary:** Jeevan D Silva
**Responsibilities**
**Senior:** Reinhard Clemens (Group Chief
Executive Officer), Samuel Kingston
(Manager), Peter Row (Manager)
**Branches:** T-Systems Ltd, Building
3,Ground Floor,Hatfield Business Park,
Hatfield, Hertfordshire AL10 9BW
**US SIC:** 4899, 7379
**UK SIC:** 79020, 83940
**Auditors:** PricewaterhouseCoopers LLP
**Bankers:** National Westminster Bank Plc
(60-14-55)

| | 31-12-13 | 31-12-12 | 31-12-11 |
|---|---|---|---|
| TO | 406,294,000 | 392,181,000 | 365,961,677 |
| P/L | 6,073,000 | (26,787,000) | (56,915,728) |
| NW | 14,729,000 | 9,545,000 | (2,939,437) |
| WC | (31,747,000) | 7,738,000 | 30,969,598 |
| Emp. | 835 | 933 | 1,055 |

**DUNS 29-405-8375**

## T-Systems Tmt Ltd

(**Subsidiary of:** Deutsche Telekom Ag)
Futura House, Bradbourne Drive, Milton
Keynes, Buckinghamshire MK7 8AZ
**Tel:** 08000364656 **Fax:** 0870-121-2751
**Web:** www.t-systems.co.uk
**Reg No:** 1371338 **VAT No:** 650706842
**Estd:** 1995 Private Limited Company
**Line of Business:** Computer software
(development)
**Issued Capital:** £500,000
**Director:** F S Hardt
**Co. Secretary:** Jeevan D'Silva
**Responsibilities**
**Sales:** Alan Hardiman (Sales Director)
**HR:** Sarah Sandbrook (HR Director)
**US SIC:** 7379 **UK SIC:** 83940
**Auditors:** PricewaterhouseCoopers LLP
**Bankers:** National Westminster Bank Plc
(60-14-55)

| | 31-12-13 | 31-12-12 | 31-12-11 |
|---|---|---|---|
| TA | 500,000 | 500,000 | 500,000 |
| NW | 500,000 | 500,000 | 500,000 |

**DUNS 21-584-3201**

## T T C LEAFLET2LETTERBOX Services

Ballards Road, 196 Ballards Road, 196
Ballards Road, Dagenham, Essex RM10 9AB
**Tel:** 08002289950
**Web:** www.ttcmarketingservices.co.uk
**Estd:** 2011
**Line of Business:** Marketing consultants
**Responsibilities**
**Senior:** Dom Caddle (Proprietor)
**US SIC:** 4311 **UK SIC:** 79010
**Employees:** 50

**DUNS 50-132-0022**    Imp-Exp

## T-T Pumps Ltd

Onneley Works, Newcastle Road, Woore,
Crewe, Cheshire CW3 9RU
**Tel:** 01630-647200
**Web:** www.ttpumps.com
**Reg No:** 2320012 **VAT No:** 318916832
**Estd:** 1959 Private Limited Company
**Line of Business:** Manufacturers of pump
devices
**Export Markets:** E U
**Issued Capital:** £50,000
**Principals:** R C Nash (Managing),
B W Nash, I E Hindley, H Peter

**Co. Secretary:** Stephen Thomas
**Responsibilities**
**Senior:** Sally Boulton (Purchasing Manager)
**Marketing:** Sheryl Birtles (Head of
Marketing), Bernard Hall (Marketing
Coordinator)
**Purchasing:** Sally Boulton (Purchasing
Manager)
**US SIC:** 3563, 3643
**UK SIC:** 32831, 34203
**Auditors:** BKR Haines Watts
**Bankers:** National Westminster Bank Plc
(01-01-38)

| | 30-11-13 | 30-11-12 | 30-11-11 |
|---|---|---|---|
| TO | 10,221,572 | 9,846,338 | 9,503,028 |
| P/L | 136,231 | 296,536 | 444,084 |
| NW | 1,690,629 | 1,564,055 | 1,410,234 |
| WC | 1,356,908 | 1,281,943 | 1,197,594 |
| Emp. | 84 | 81 | 80 |

**DUNS 64-714-1282**

## T Taylor

16 Taunton Road, Bridgwater, Somerset TA6
3LS
**Tel:** 01278720005
**Partnership**
**Line of Business:** Doctors
**Trading Style:** A Reed
**Partners:** Dr J Wrout, Dr T Taylor,
Dr J Wrout, Dr T Taylor
**US SIC:** 8011 **UK SIC:** 95300
**Employees:** 50

**DUNS 22-718-5170**    Exp

## T. Tazaki & Company Ltd

(**Subsidiary of:** Takara Holdings Inc.)
348a Regents Park Road, London N3 2LJ
**Tel:** 02083469273
**Reg No:** 1189428 **VAT No:** 241255883
**Estd:** 1972 Private Limited Company
**Line of Business:** Holding companies
management activities
**Export Markets:** Europe, Malaysia
**Export Sales:** £2,637,119
**Issued Capital:** £669,885
**Directors:** K Ito, H Kaneko
**Co. Secretary:** Hiroshi Kaneko
**Branches:** T. Tazaki & Company Ltd,
Fredericks Pl, London EC2R 8AB
**US SIC:** 6711, 7361
**UK SIC:** 83962, 83954
**Auditors:** Deloitte LLP

| | 31-12-13 | 31-12-12 | 31-12-11 |
|---|---|---|---|
| TO | 25,289,179 | 20,758,778 | 18,699,885 |
| P/L | 2,172,481 | 548,953 | 300,097 |
| NW | 2,918,790 | 1,189,015 | 858,095 |
| WC | 2,643,502 | 878,169 | 509,026 |
| Emp. | 70 | 79 | 76 |

**DUNS 28-963-6680**

## T V F (U K) Ltd

(**Subsidiary of:** Tristar Fire Corp)
59-63 Queens Road, High Wycombe,
Buckinghamshire HP13 6AH
**Tel:** 08000556872
**Web:** www.tvfltd.co.uk
**Reg No:** 1694263 **Estd:** 1982 Private
Limited Company
**Line of Business:** Other service activities
not elsewhere classified
**Issued Capital:** £60,000
**Directors:** E D Sebag, M Lunn
**Co. Secretary:** Richard Pollard
**US SIC:** 8999, 1731
**UK SIC:** 83954, 50300
**Auditors:** KPMG Audit PLC

| | 31-12-13 | 31-12-12 | 31-12-11 |
|---|---|---|---|
| TO | 8,606,868 | 8,707,636 | 8,413,779 |
| P/L | 1,383,761 | 1,316,654 | 1,162,243 |
| NW | 808,473 | 1,602,577 | 569,078 |
| WC | 753,817 | 1,552,108 | 414,559 |
| Emp. | 100 | 95 | 90 |

**DUNS 21-585-1616**

## T V Licensing Enquiries

100 Temple Street, Bristol, Avon BS98 1TL
**Tel:** 03007906135
**Web:** www.tvlicensing.co.uk
**Estd:** 2011 Proprietorship
**Line of Business:** Unknown
**Proprietor:** N Jeffries
**US SIC:** 9121 **UK SIC:** 91110
**Employees:** 200

**DUNS 21-585-1151**

## T V T

540 Chiswick High Road, London W4 5RG
**Web:** www.tvt.biz
**Estd:** 2011 Proprietorship
**Line of Business:** Video production
companies
**Proprietor:** K Thesiger
**Responsibilities**
**Senior:** Kim Thesiger (Director)
**US SIC:** 7819 **UK SIC:** 97111
**Employees:** 75

**DUNS 50-501-7517**

## T W Fabrications Ltd

Unit 8-10 Roughhey Place, Preston,
Lancashire PR2 5AR
**Tel:** 01772-704800 **Fax:** 01772-704926
**Web:** www.twfabrications.co.uk
**Reg No:** 2469777 **VAT No:** 322851767
**Estd:** 1977 Private Limited Company
**Line of Business:** Steel fabricators
**Issued Capital:** £1,000
**Principals:** M G Cross (Managing),
A J Cross
**Co. Secretary:** Ms Christine Cross
**US SIC:** 1622, 7699
**UK SIC:** 50200, 67303
**Auditors:** Alan Roberts
**Bankers:** HSBC Bank plc (40-37-25)

| | 31-12-13 | 31-12-12 | 31-12-11 |
|---|---|---|---|
| TA | 3,696,851 | 3,567,757 | 3,758,394 |
| NW | 1,603,513 | 1,435,061 | 1,283,055 |
| WC | 550,056 | 384,383 | 604,901 |

**DUNS 64-744-3910**

## T W Gaze & Son

10 Market Hill, Diss, Norfolk IP22 4WJ
**Web:** www.twgaze.co.uk
**Estd:** 1984 Partnership
**Line of Business:** Real estate agencies
**Partners:** P Nicholls, M Sarson, G Bowles,
A Smith
**Responsibilities**
**Senior:** James Baskerville (Rural Director),
James Bassam (Executive), Elizabeth Talbot
(Partner - Auctions)
**Finance:** Lesley Wilby (Accounts Assistant)
**Marketing:** Paul Head (Partnership
Manager)
**Sales:** Joyce Barnett (Commercial
Assistant), Oliver Chapman (Commercial
Director), Sally Pratt (Commercial Assistant)
**Admin:** Jacky Lond (Personal Assistant),
Angela Webster (Personal Assistant)
**Operations:** Rachael Hipperson (Rural
Director)
**US SIC:** 6531, 8911
**UK SIC:** 83400, 83701
**Employees:** 50

**DUNS 49-485-2106**    Imp-Exp

## T W Logistics Ltd

Silver St Ship Court, Gainsborough,
Lincolnshire DN21 2DW
**Tel:** 01427-614551
**Web:** www.twlogistics.co.uk
**Reg No:** 3150116 **Estd:** 1996 Private
Limited Company
**Line of Business:** Road haulage and
transport services
**Issued Capital:** £10,000
**Directors:** Ms V A Parker, M J Parker
**Co. Secretary:** Ms Patricia Sargent
**Responsibilities**
**Finance:** Joanne Daubney (Financial
Director)
**IT:** Steve Wain (Computer Manager)
**Facilities:** Jason Ledsham (General
Manager)
**Operations:** Steve Wain (Computer
Manager)
**Branches:** T W Logistics Ltd, Crosby
Grange, Ferry Road West, Scunthorpe,
South Humberside DN15 8UH
**US SIC:** 4789, 4213
**UK SIC:** 77002, 72300
**Auditors:** Malthouse & Co

| | 31-12-13 | 31-12-12 | 31-12-11 |
|---|---|---|---|
| TO | 5,216,962 | 5,315,428 | 5,624,463 |
| P/L | 178,067 | 106,283 | 172,733 |
| NW | 3,233,619 | 3,198,611 | 3,213,480 |
| WC | (229,465) | (148,316) | (105,416) |
| Emp. | 59 | 67 | 68 |

**DUNS 73-459-9157**

## T W M Solicitors Llp

65 Woodbridge Road, Guildford, Surrey GU1
4RD
**Tel:** 01483752700
**Web:** www.twmsolicitors.com
**Reg No:** 0304375OC **Estd:** 1870
**Line of Business:** Solicitors
**Trading Style:** T W M Attersolls
**Responsibilities**
**Senior:** Eileen Barry (Partner - Dispute
Resolution), Allison Crossman (Non-
designated Limited Liabili), Demelza Patricio
(Non-designated Limited Liabili), Guy
Perkins (Non-designated Limited Liabili),
Jonathan Potter (Non-designated Limited
Liabili), John Sandford Pike (Partner)
**HR:** Kathy Betts (Human Resources
Manager)
**Branches:** T W M Solicitors Llp, Broadoak
House, Horsham Road, Cranleigh, Surrey
GU6 8DJ
**US SIC:** 8111 **UK SIC:** 83500
**Bankers:** Lloyds TSB Bank plc (77-95-02)

| | 31-07-14 | 31-07-13 | 31-07-12 |
|---|---|---|---|
| TO | 13,101,890 | 10,608,961 | 10,747,636 |
| NW | 4,410,781 | N/A | N/A |
| WC | 4,365,428 | 2,446,186 | 2,231,505 |

**DUNS 76-551-6075**    Imp-Exp

## T W T Group Ltd

(**Subsidiary of:** Tradestock Ltd)
Poole Works, Wellington, Somerset TA21
9HW
**Tel:** 01823661717 **Fax:** 01823666543
**Web:** www.twtgroup.co.uk
**Reg No:** 2571799 **VAT No:** 568927283
**Estd:** 1987 Private Limited Company
**Line of Business:** Other manufacturing not
elsewhere classified
**Export Markets:** Europe and worldwide
**Issued Capital:** £549
**Directors:** D J Babington, K Nye
**Co. Secretary:** Sevgi Babington
**US SIC:** 3999, 5199
**UK SIC:** 49590, 61900
**Auditors:** Milsted Langdon
**Bankers:** Lloyds TSB Bank plc (30-98-45)

| | 31-12-12 | 31-12-11 |
|---|---|---|
| TA | 1,540,568 | 1,682,500 |
| NW | 1,072,820 | 979,393 |
| WC | 992,033 | 870,593 |

**DUNS 21-585-2816**

## T W White & Sons

Unit, 226-228 Cobham Road, Leatherhead,
Surrey KT22 9JQ
**Tel:** 01372387050
**Web:** www.twwhiteandsons.co.uk
**Estd:** 2011
**Line of Business:** Car accessories and parts
**Proprietor:** G Howland
**US SIC:** 5531 **UK SIC:** 65100
**Employees:** 50

**DUNS 21-201-4369**

## T Ward & Son Ltd

Unit 1 James Freel Close, Barrow-In-
Furness, Cumbria LA14 2NW
**Tel:** 01229811222
**Web:** www.wardgroup.co.uk
**Reg No:** 0222877 **Estd:** 1927 Private
Limited Company
**Line of Business:** Wholesale of other
household goods not elsewhere classified
**Trading Style:** Ward Group, Ward Glass,
Ward Contracting
**Issued Capital:** £104,551
**Directors:** L Wilson, R Barrow,
Mrs L R Redshaw, T Redshaw, I K Noble
**Co. Secretary:** Timothy Redshaw
**Responsibilities**
**Senior:** Simon Hulbert (Manager), Peter
Redshaw (Manager)
**US SIC:** 5199, 1711
**UK SIC:** 61900, 50300
**Auditors:** R F Miller & Co
**Bankers:** Barclays Bank Plc (20-04-68)

| | 31-12-13 | 31-12-12 | 31-12-11 |
|---|---|---|---|
| TO | N/A | N/A | 5,367,830 |
| P/L | N/A | N/A | 141,430 |
| NW | 527,034 | 575,304 | 1,157,177 |
| WC | 339,534 | 373,007 | 847,443 |

**DUNS 22-835-5368**    Imp-Exp

## T. Wilson & Sons (Farmers) Ltd

Maggotts Nook Farm, Maggotts Nook Road,
St Helens, Merseyside WA11 8PL
**Web:** www.twilsonandsons.co.uk
**Reg No:** 1311614 **VAT No:** 156863532
**Estd:** 1977 Private Limited Company
**Line of Business:** Fruit and vegetable
(producers)
**Export Markets:** France
**Issued Capital:** £200
**Director:** T Wilson
**Co. Secretary:** Mrs Caroline Wilson
**US SIC:** 0179, 0119
**UK SIC:** 01002, 01001
**Auditors:** Abrams Ashton LLP
**Bankers:** Lloyds TSB Bank plc (30-96-85)

| | 30-04-14 | 30-04-13 | 30-04-12 |
|---|---|---|---|
| TO | 15,872,360 | 13,211,586 | 11,645,054 |
| P/L | 185,940 | 306,460 | 449,957 |
| NW | 586,904 | 518,343 | 309,473 |
| WC | (1,108,737) | (1,110,324) | (1,265,318) |
| Emp. | 129 | 139 | 114 |

**DUNS 21-227-7945**

## T Y Enfys Care Home

Ty Enfys, Marle Close, Cardiff, South
Glamorgan CF23 7EP
**Tel:** 029-20548920
**Web:** www.hallmarkhealthcare.co.uk
**Proprietorship**
**Line of Business:** Nursing homes
**Proprietor:** Mrs L Accraman
**Responsibilities**
**Senior:** Fujjata Singh (Manager)
**US SIC:** 8051 **UK SIC:** 95100
**Employees:** 51

DUNS 21-579-6944
## T Y Olwen Hospice
Heol Maes Eglwys, Cwmrhydyceirw,
Swansea, West Glamorgan SA6 6NL
**Tel:** 01792703412
**Estd:** 1981 Partnership
**Line of Business:** Other human health
activities
**Partners:** Dr J Baker, Dr I Baker
**US SIC:** 8091 **UK SIC:** 95200
**Employees:** 65

DUNS 23-918-0396
## T2 Group Ltd
Melrose Hall, Cypress Drive, Cardiff, South
Glamorgan CF3 0EG
**Tel:** 02920799133 **Fax:** 029-2081-9515
**Web:** www.t2group.co.uk
**Reg No:** 3908267 **Estd:** 2000 Private
Limited Company
**Line of Business:** Management activities of
holding companies
**Issued Capital:** £1
**Directors:** R J Marr, R C Marr, D J Marr
**Co. Secretary:** Ms Christine Marr
**Responsibilities**
**HR:** Andrea Munroe (Human Resources
Manager)
**US SIC:** 6711 **UK SIC:** 83962

| | 31-07-13 | 31-07-12 | 31-07-11 |
|---|---|---|---|
| TA | 1,040,033 | 1,553,391 | 241,419 |
| NW | 809,821 | 225,510 | 57,347 |
| WC | 452,238 | 120,733 | (38,500) |

DUNS 21-232-0284
## Ta Centre
Boundary Lane, Manchester M15 6DH
**Tel:** 0161-2282185
**Estd:** 1995
**Line of Business:** Armed forces
**Proprietor:** Ms P Fosberg
**US SIC:** 9711 **UK SIC:** 83962
**Employees:** 200

DUNS 49-112-7858
## Ta Hotel Collection Ltd
Thorpeness, Leiston, Suffolk IP16 4NH
**Tel:** 01728-452176 **Fax:** 01728-453868
**Web:** www.thorpeness.co.uk
**Reg No:** 3098213 **VAT No:** 666032148
**Estd:** 1995 Private Limited Company
**Line of Business:** Other entertainment
activities not elsewhere classified
**Trading Style:** Thorpeness Hotel & Golf Club
**Issued Capital:** £2,346,513
**Directors:** T Rowan-Robinson,
Mrs L J Heald, G Tinnion, M G Heald,
Mrs J A Whybrow
**Co. Secretary:** Birketts Secretaries Limited
**Responsibilities**
**Finance:** Jill Page (Financial Manager)
**Marketing:** Suzanne Richardson (Marketing
Manager)
**IT:** Jenny Hill (IT Manager)
**HR:** Sandra Ralph (Personnel Coordinator)
**Health & Safety:** Sandra Ralph (Personnel
Coordinator)
**Branches:** Ta Hotel Collection Ltd, The
Parade, Aldeburgh, Aldeburgh, Suffolk IP15
5BU
**US SIC:** 7999 **UK SIC:** 97913
**Auditors:** Ensors

| | 31-03-14 | 31-03-13 | 31-03-12 |
|---|---|---|---|
| TO | 11,802,793 | 11,451,334 | 11,500,298 |
| P/L | 419,640 | 786,234 | 385,447 |
| NW | 3,064,426 | 2,774,613 | 2,341,419 |
| WC | (4,491,611) | (4,322,306) | (4,136,735) |
| Emp. | 335 | 324 | 340 |

DUNS 29-569-5811
## Tabfile Ltd
(**Subsidiary of:** Filing Acquisitions Ltd)
Railex Works, Crossens Way, Marine Drive,
Southport, Merseyside PR9 9LY
**Tel:** 01704226866 **Fax:** 01704-25814
**Web:** www.railex.co.uk
**Reg No:** 1931465 **Estd:** 1985 Private
Limited Company
**Line of Business:** Manufacture of paper
stationery
**Trading Style:** Railex
**Issued Capital:** £14,000
**Director:** R M Crane
**Branches:** Tabfile Ltd, Wilson Bldg, Curtain
Rd, London EC2A 3JX
**US SIC:** 2648 **UK SIC:** 47231
**Auditors:** McMillan & Co

| | 30-04-13 | 30-04-12 | 30-04-11 |
|---|---|---|---|
| TA | 14,000 | 25,688 | 44,637 |
| NW | 11,541 | 12,106 | (1,072) |
| WC | 11,541 | 12,106 | (1,578) |

DUNS 21-634-0373
## Tableau Software Uk Ltd
(**Subsidiary of:** Tableau Software Inc.)
Blue Fin Building, 110 Southwark Street,
London SE1 0SU
**Tel:** 02033104500
**Web:** www.tableausoftware.com
**Reg No:** 7118347 **Estd:** 2010 Private
Limited Company
**Line of Business:** Computer services
**Issued Capital:** £1
**Directors:** K M Conder, T E Walker, Jr.
**US SIC:** 7379 **UK SIC:** 83940
**Auditors:** Auria Audit LLP

| | 31-12-13 | 31-12-12 | 31-12-11 |
|---|---|---|---|
| TA | 3,171,559 | 851,001 | 520,005 |
| NW | 651,936 | 205,291 | 72,747 |
| WC | (126,233) | 128,573 | 55,183 |

DUNS 21-807-5554    Exp
## Tac Products Ltd
(**Subsidiary of:** Schneider Electric Sa)
Braywick House East, Maidenhead,
Berkshire SL6 1DN
**Tel:** 01628741050 **Fax:** 01628-741051
**Web:** www.tacproducts.com
**Reg No:** 0081433 **VAT No:** 669212422
**Estd:** 1904 Private Limited Company
**Line of Business:** Building construction
contractors
**Export Markets:** Europe, U S A, Asia,
Australia and Africa
**Trading Style:** Tac Uk
**Issued Capital:** £1,000,000
**Co. Secretary:** Garrie Naden
**Responsibilities**
**Senior:** Eddie Coxon (Vice President)
**IT:** Cris Trinder (Manager)
**Operations:** Ben Summers (Commissioning
Engineer)
**Branches:** Tac Products Ltd, Stanstead
House, Third Avenue, Stanstead Airport
North, Stansted, Essex CM24 1AE
**US SIC:** 1522 **UK SIC:** 50100
**Bankers:** National Westminster Bank Plc
(60-00-01)
**Employees:** 65

DUNS 23-552-4548
## Tac (Regional) Ltd
(**Subsidiary of:** Schneider Nordic Baltic A/S)
Smisby Road, Ashby-De-La-Zouch,
Leicestershire LE65 2UG
**Tel:** 01530417733 **Fax:** 01530-415436
**Web:** www.schneiderelectric.com
**Reg No:** 3550790 **Estd:** 1998 Private
Limited Company
**Line of Business:** Manufacturers of security
equipment suppliers and
**Trading Style:** Schneider-Electric
**Issued Capital:** £1,753,000
**Director:** G C Naden
**Responsibilities**
**Senior:** David Berardi (Manager), Eddie
Coxon (Manager), Jens Wikdesk (Manager)
**IT:** Sean Ellwell (IT Manager)
**US SIC:** 1541, 8911
**UK SIC:** 50100, 83701
**Auditors:** Mazars LLP
**Bankers:** Bank Of Scotland (12-17-50)

| | 31-12-13 | 31-12-12 | 31-12-11 |
|---|---|---|---|
| TA | 4,446,000 | 4,446,000 | 4,446,000 |
| NW | 3,227,000 | 3,227,000 | 3,227,000 |
| WC | 3,227,000 | 3,227,000 | 3,227,000 |

DUNS 77-097-1653    Exp
## Tachodisc Ltd
(**Subsidiary of:** Tachodisc Holdings Ltd)
19 Kingsland Grange Tatton Court,
Warrington, Cheshire WA1 4RR
**Tel:** 01925 820088 **Fax:** 01925 831300
**Web:** www.tachodisc.co.uk
**Reg No:** 2676818 **Estd:** 1992 Private
Limited Company
**Line of Business:** Manufacture of other
transport equipment not elsewhere classified
**Export Markets:** Italy; S Africa
**Issued Capital:** £2
**Directors:** M N Tollit, P R Jordan
**Co. Secretary:** Dennis Davies
**Responsibilities**
**Senior:** Karen Crispe (Manager), Ann
McDougall (Manager), Guy Reynolds
(Technical Director), Bruce Simpson
(Purchasing Manager), Paul Winterburn
(Site Manager)
**Marketing:** Karen Crispe (Manager)
**Sales:** Karen Crispe (Manager)
**IT:** Guy Reynolds (Technical Director), Paul
Winterburn (Site Manager)
**Facilities:** Paul Winterburn (Site Manager)
**Purchasing:** Bruce Simpson (Purchasing
Manager)
**Engineering:** Paul Winterburn (Site
Manager)
**Branches:** Tachodisc Ltd, 3 Greenfield Farm
Indstl Est, Congleton, Cheshire CW12 4TR
**US SIC:** 3799, 8299
**UK SIC:** 36502, 93300

**Bankers:** National Westminster Bank Plc
(53-61-38)

| | 31-12-13 | 31-12-12 | 31-12-11 |
|---|---|---|---|
| TA | 2,826,755 | 3,013,024 | 3,122,626 |
| NW | (2,919,705) | (2,502,463) | (1,185,475) |
| WC | 1,014,441 | 1,134,870 | 1,156,037 |

DUNS 23-230-3214
## Taff Housing Association Ltd
307-315 Cowbridge Road East, Cardiff,
South Glamorgan CF5 1JD
**Tel:** 02920259100
**Web:** www.taffhousing.co.uk
**Reg No:** 0021408IP **VAT No:** 869840565
**Estd:** 1975 Friendly Society
**Line of Business:** Housing associations
societies trusts & co-operatives
**Principals:** Ms M Hayes (Chairman),
J Ramsay (Chairman), S Dawson,
Ms P Davies, E Assuncao, R Perons,
B Oram, J Egan
**Co. Secretary:** Mark Hickson
**Responsibilities**
**Senior:** Elaine Ballard (Chief Executive),
Yvonene Bourne (Principal)
**Finance:** Rose Nyoni (Treasurer)
**Branches:** Taff Housing Association Ltd, 9
Clytha Park Road, Newport, Gwent NP20
4PB
**US SIC:** 6552 **UK SIC:** 85000
**Auditors:** Bevan & Buckland
**Bankers:** HSBC Bank plc (40-16-12)
**Employees:** 100
**Turnover:** £6,383,000

DUNS 34-515-9040
## Tafs Foods Ltd
590 Lea Bridge Road, London E10 7DN
**Tel:** 02089880654 **Fax:** 02085582050
**Reg No:** 2716126 **Estd:** 1992 Private
Limited Company
**Line of Business:** Restaurant - american
**Issued Capital:** £5,100
**Directors:** M A Chaudhry, F Tahir
**Co. Secretary:** Muhammed Tahir
**Responsibilities**
**HR:** Chada Ramish (Human Resources
Manager)
**Branches:** Tafs Foods Ltd, 3 Dalston Cross
Shopping Centre, London E8 2LX
**US SIC:** 5812 **UK SIC:** 66110
**Auditors:** Haslers
**Bankers:** Allied Irish Bank (gb) (23-84-86)

| | 30-11-13 | 30-11-12 | 30-11-11 |
|---|---|---|---|
| TO | 8,132,059 | 8,407,437 | 5,590,980 |
| P/L | 85,791 | 323,651 | 294,235 |
| NW | (181,463) | (533,843) | (839,050) |
| WC | (798,303) | (987,763) | (1,076,235) |
| Emp. | 159 | 143 | 160 |

DUNS 73-303-1160
## Tafs Garden Co. - Telford Ltd
Gower Street, Telford, Shropshire TF2 9BQ
**Tel:** 01952-620184 **Fax:** 01952617894
**Web:** www.tafs-garden.co.uk
**Reg No:** 4576938 **Estd:** 1976 Private
Limited Company
**Line of Business:** Garden centres
**Issued Capital:** £100
**Directors:** M D Prince, R J Batters
**Co. Secretary:** Mrs Karen Batters
**Responsibilities**
**Senior:** Gareth Master (Manager)
**US SIC:** 5999 **UK SIC:** 65600

| | 28-02-14 | 28-02-13 | 29-02-12 |
|---|---|---|---|
| TA | 577,222 | 460,802 | 431,076 |
| NW | 58,779 | (38,184) | (10,543) |
| WC | 58,571 | (58,230) | (12,961) |

DUNS 22-761-3460
## Tafs (Salop) Ltd
Gower Street, St Georges, Telford,
Shropshire TF2 9BQ
**Tel:** 01952617072 **Fax:** 01952-620379
**Web:** www.tafs-salop.ltd.uk
**Reg No:** 1274014 **VAT No:** 289451319
**Estd:** 1976 Private Limited Company
**Line of Business:** Saw milling and planing of
wood, impregnation of wood
**Trading Style:** Timber & Fencing Supplies
**Issued Capital:** £200
**Principals:** R J Batters (Managing),
M D Prince
**Co. Secretary:** Mrs Karen Batters
**Branches:** Tafs (Salop) Ltd, Unit 1F,
Centurion Park, Shrewsbury, Shropshire SY1
4EH
**US SIC:** 2421 **UK SIC:** 46101
**Auditors:** Dains
**Bankers:** Lloyds TSB Bank plc (30-18-55)

| | 31-08-13 | 31-08-12 | 31-08-11 |
|---|---|---|---|
| TA | 3,357,427 | 3,221,909 | 2,811,102 |
| NW | 524,087 | 658,609 | 449,361 |
| WC | 919,812 | 1,007,440 | 675,214 |

DUNS 23-645-5452    Imp
## Tag Aviation (Uk) Ltd
(**Subsidiary of:** Tag Aviation Holding Sa)
Farnborough Airport, Farnborough,
Hampshire GU14 6XA
**Tel:** 01252-377977
**Web:** www.tagaviation.com
**Reg No:** 3640741 **Estd:** 1998 Private
Limited Company
**Line of Business:** Airlines
**Issued Capital:** £500,000
**Principals:** G K Williamson (Managing),
C Spath, S Gillibrand, R Mcmullin
**Co. Secretary:** Ronald Hedges
**Responsibilities**
**Health & Safety:** Malcolm Rusby (safety
director)
**US SIC:** 4582 **UK SIC:** 76400
**Auditors:** Deloitte LLP
**Bankers:** Lloyds TSB Bank plc (30-12-18)

| | 31-12-13 | 31-12-12 | 31-12-11 |
|---|---|---|---|
| TO | 143,137,426 | 129,877,581 | 131,087,361 |
| P/L | 3,741 | (247,912) | 671,798 |
| NW | 1,410,414 | 1,422,197 | 1,675,816 |
| WC | 981,293 | 1,009,869 | 1,234,291 |
| Emp. | 165 | 145 | 148 |

DUNS 50-014-2864
## Tag Europe Ltd
(**Subsidiary of:** Deutsche Post Ag)
29 Clerkenwell Road, London EC1M 5TA
**Tel:** 020-7251-4571
**Web:** www.tagworldwide.com
**Reg No:** 2299109 **Estd:** 1971 Private
Limited Company
**Line of Business:** Photographic activities
not elsewhere classified
**Export Sales:** £46,944,190
**Trading Style:** Tag Europe Ltd
**Issued Capital:** £9,600
**Directors:** P D Zillig, S D Trood,
Ms A Lattimore, S J Faulkner
**Co. Secretary:**
Exel Secretarial Services Limite
**Responsibilities**
**Senior:** Angela Ford (President and Chief
Executive), Murray Stroud (Manager)
**HR:** Elisabeth Gill (Human Resources
Manager)
**US SIC:** 7333, 7395
**UK SIC:** 83953, 49300
**Auditors:** BDO Stoy Hayward LLP

| | 31-12-13 | 31-12-12 | 31-12-11 |
|---|---|---|---|
| TO | 112,656,901 | 90,508,592 | 80,760,186 |
| P/L | 2,020,453 | 3,049,940 | (6,870,292) |
| NW | 16,119,123 | 17,396,305 | 14,873,673 |
| WC | 9,877,301 | 12,513,791 | 9,093,060 |
| Emp. | 933 | 873 | 794 |

DUNS 64-098-8127
## Tag Farnborough (Holdings) Ltd
280 Farnborough Road, Farnborough,
Hampshire GU14 7NQ
**Tel:** 01252546105
**Web:** www.farnboroughabbey.org
**Reg No:** 3494464 **Estd:** 2004 Private
Limited Company
**Line of Business:** Book retailers
**Trading Style:** Tag Farnborough Airport
**Issued Capital:** £41,177,270
**Directors:** S Gillibrand, S H Young,
A B Subowo, R V Bradley, A Ojjeh,
J C Rosset, R Mcmullin, M A Ojjeh
**Co. Secretary:** Ronald Hedges
**Responsibilities**
**Finance:** Carol Knight (Bursar)
**US SIC:** 5942 **UK SIC:** 65300
**Auditors:** Deloitte & Touche

| | 31-12-13 | 31-12-12 | 31-12-11 |
|---|---|---|---|
| TO | 53,927,609 | 52,186,371 | 46,645,805 |
| P/L | 10,375,980 | 10,407,161 | 10,096,666 |
| NW | 71,781,593 | 63,880,736 | 56,173,488 |
| WC | (5,295,834) | (709,288) | (5,114,119) |
| Emp. | 133 | 136 | 131 |

DUNS 77-909-3439
## Tag Hotel Ltd
55 Farnborough Road, Farnborough,
Hampshire GU14 6EL
**Tel:** 01252555890 **Fax:** 08701112222
**Web:** www.aviatorbytag.com
**Reg No:** 5812669 **Estd:** 2006 Private
Limited Company
**Line of Business:** Hotels and motels without
restaurant
**Trading Style:** Aviator
**Issued Capital:** £100
**Directors:** J R Milne, S H Young, J C Rosset,
R V Bradley
**Co. Secretary:** Ronald Hedges
**Responsibilities**
**Senior:** Lorraine Evans (Acting General
Manager), Michael Helling (General
Manager)
**US SIC:** 7999, 5812
**UK SIC:** 97913, 66110

**Bankers:** Lloyds TSB Bank plc (30-12-18)

|      | 31-12-13 | 31-12-12 | 31-12-11 |
|------|----------|----------|----------|
| TO   | 7,671,047 | 8,499,549 | 7,329,449 |
| P/L  | 176,949 | 566,555 | (307,789) |
| NW   | (2,304,531) | (2,481,480) | (3,048,035) |
| WC   | (2,867,375) | 122,872 | (3,378,170) |
| Emp. | 128 | 150 | 136 |

DUNS 21-880-3974
## The Tager Centre
Nine Mile Ride, Crowthorne, Berkshire RG45 6BQ
**Web:** www.norwood.org.uk
**Estd:** 2012
**Line of Business:** Day and care centres
**Responsibilities**
**Senior:** Sue Ravey (Registered Home Manager)
**US SIC:** 8321  **UK SIC:** 96111
**Employees:** 63

DUNS 21-580-9314
## The Tagman Press
Layer Hall Farm, Church Road, Colchester, Essex CO2 0ET
**Tel:** 08456444186
**Web:** www.tagmanpress.com
**Estd:** 2011 Partnership
**Line of Business:** Publishers
**Trading Style:** The Tagman Press
**Partners:** J Wardley, Mrs J Wardley
**Responsibilities**
**Senior:** Anthony Grey (Owner), Sonja Haggett (General Manager)
**US SIC:** 2731  **UK SIC:** 47532
**Employees:** 65

DUNS 23-230-2505
## Taibach & Port Talbot Working Men's Club & Institute Ltd
Tir Caradoc, Port Talbot, West Glamorgan SA13 2UF
**Tel:** 01639883888  **Fax:** 01639-769944
**Reg No:** 0010351IP  **Estd:** 1921 Friendly Society
**Line of Business:** Clubs social and associations
**Principals:** T Jenkins (Chairman), B Davies, A Davies
**US SIC:** 8699  **UK SIC:** 96902
**Employees:** 124

DUNS 21-942-7651
## Taiko Foods Ltd
27-29 Brunel Road, London W3 7XR
**Tel:** 02087491515  **Fax:** 02087490550
**Web:** www.taikofoods.co.uk
**Reg No:** 8533529  **Estd:** 2013 Private Limited Company
**Line of Business:** Sushi manufacturer
**Issued Capital:** £2
**Director:** K Kurahara
**Co. Secretary:** Speafi Secretarial Limited
**Responsibilities**
**Senior:** Tushar Raval (Manager)
**US SIC:** 2099  **UK SIC:** 42399
**Auditors:** MHA MacIntyre Hudson

|      | 31-03-14 |
|------|----------|
| TO   | 4,758,616 |
| P/L  | 423,725 |
| NW   | 134,896 |
| WC   | 1,271,271 |
| Emp. | 165 |

DUNS 73-848-8613
## Tailored Recruitment Services Ltd
Units 4-5 Micklehead Business Vi, St Michaels Road, St Helens, Merseyside WA9 4YU
**Tel:** 08443350415  **Fax:** 01925-291847
**Web:** www.tailoredrecruitmentservices.co.uk
**Reg No:** 5103967  **Estd:** 2004 Private Limited Company
**Line of Business:** Labour recruitment and provision of personnel
**Issued Capital:** £1,000
**Director:** A O'Grady
**Co. Secretary:** Kevin Birch
**US SIC:** 7399  **UK SIC:** 83954
**Auditors:** Alexander Myerson & Co

|      | 31-12-13 | 31-12-12 | 31-12-11 |
|------|----------|----------|----------|
| TO   | 16,887,297 | 18,477,281 | 14,101,933 |
| P/L  | 120,343 | 354,804 | 587,084 |
| NW   | 43,960 | 44,792 | 199,464 |
| WC   | (311,074) | (67,196) | 62,239 |
| Emp. | 1,126 | 1,316 | 1,024 |

DUNS 21-136-9321
## Tait Walker Llp
Bulman House, Regent Centre, Newcastle-Upon-Tyne, Tyne and Wear NE3 3LS
**Tel:** 0191-285-0321  **Fax:** 0191 284 9117
**Web:** http://insolvency.taitwalker.co.uk
**Reg No:** 0340140OC  **Estd:** 1937 Private Limited Company
**Line of Business:** Accounting and auditing activities

**Responsibilities**
**Senior:** Kathryn Brunton (Manager), Elizabeth Crawley (Manager), Anne Moore (Manager)
**US SIC:** 7399  **UK SIC:** 83954

|      | 31-10-13 | 31-10-12 | 31-10-11 |
|------|----------|----------|----------|
| TA   | 3,218,330 | 2,815,294 | 2,932,280 |
| NW   | (865,612) | (865,612) | (865,612) |
| WC   | 851,674 | 422,437 | 651,295 |

DUNS 22-702-6994    Imp
## Taj International Hotels Ltd
(**Subsidiary of:** The Indian Hotels Company Limited)
51 Buckingham Gate, London SW1E 6BS
**Tel:** 02078346655
**Web:** www.51-buckinghamgate.com
**Reg No:** 1661824  **Estd:** 2000 Private Limited Company
**Line of Business:** Licensed restaurants
**Trading Style:** St. James Court Hotel, The Private Rooms
**Issued Capital:** £2
**Directors:** R H Parekh, A Pushkar
**Co. Secretary:** Chandrasekhar Nagarajan
**Responsibilities**
**Senior:** Raymond Bickson (Manager), Digvijay Singh (General Manager)
**Marketing:** Marta Warren (Marketing Manager)
**US SIC:** 5812  **UK SIC:** 66110
**Auditors:** PKF (UK) LLP
**Bankers:** National Westminster Bank Plc (56-00-17)

|      | 31-03-14 | 31-03-13 | 31-03-12 |
|------|----------|----------|----------|
| TO   | 7,599,320 | 7,524,081 | 7,514,906 |
| P/L  | 854,079 | 284,049 | 38,541 |
| NW   | 2,643,654 | 1,996,768 | 1,785,214 |
| WC   | 1,151,702 | 442,664 | 126,543 |
| Emp. | 87 | 95 | 97 |

DUNS 51-600-0986
## Take 2 Film Holdings Ltd
West Point Trading Estate, Alliance Road, London W3 0RA
**Tel:** 020-8992-2224
**Web:** www.take2films.co.uk
**Reg No:** 5880654  **Estd:** 2006 Private Limited Company
**Line of Business:** Management activities of holding companies
**Export Sales:** £924,146
**Issued Capital:** £263,069
**Directors:** M J Watson, I W Currie, G J Edridge, V J Smedley-Wild
**Co. Secretary:** Lyn Edridge
**US SIC:** 6711, 7394
**UK SIC:** 83962, 84000

|      | 28-02-14 | 28-02-13 | 29-02-12 |
|------|----------|----------|----------|
| TO   | 8,466,127 | 9,244,126 | 9,514,415 |
| P/L  | 470,482 | 661,322 | 839,115 |
| NW   | 5,883,229 | 5,399,795 | 4,699,015 |
| WC   | (4,098,041) | (3,090,987) | (3,416,925) |
| Emp. | 64 | 65 | 49 |

DUNS 22-074-1370
## Take A Break Warwickshire Ltd
Canterbury House Exhall Campus, Easter Way, Coventry, West Midlands CV7 9HP
**Tel:** 02476644909
**Web:** www.tabw.org.uk
**Reg No:** 4075624  **Estd:** 2000 Private Limited Company
**Line of Business:** Home care service providers
**Directors:** Mrs M Harding, Ms R B Pathan, R J Harris, Mrs L E Hines, Miss L M Swanborough
**Co. Secretary:** Kim Fathers
**US SIC:** 8091  **UK SIC:** 95200
**Auditors:** Harben Barker Ltd

|      | 31-03-14 | 31-03-13 | 31-03-12 |
|------|----------|----------|----------|
| TO   | 1,835,172 | 1,680,381 | 1,482,578 |
| P/L  | 226,249 | 152,910 | 163,139 |
| NW   | 663,988 | 437,739 | 284,829 |
| WC   | 659,049 | 431,761 | 279,357 |

DUNS 21-596-2369
## Take One Media
10 Eyre Street, Birmingham, West Midlands B18 7AA
**Tel:** 01216855000
**Web:** www.takeonemedia.co.uk
**Estd:** 2011
**Line of Business:** Distribution service providers
**Responsibilities**
**Senior:** Kelvyn Cooper (Administrator)
**US SIC:** 4311  **UK SIC:** 79010
**Employees:** 100

DUNS 22-016-0399
## Take One Media Ltd
(**Subsidiary of:** John Menzies Plc)
Orbital Park, Ashford, Kent TN24 0GA
**Tel:** 01233211411
**Web:** www.takeonemedia.co.uk
**Reg No:** 4018955  **Estd:** 2011 Private Limited Company

**Line of Business:** Distribution service providers
**Issued Capital:** £20,000
**Directors:** P R Mccourt, Ms P A Harris, D Johnston, F R Black, B P Tipping
**Co. Secretary:** John Geddes
**Responsibilities**
**Senior:** Chris Gibbon (Marketing Manager)
**Branches:** Take One Media Ltd, Unit C-D, Kingsmead, Folkestone, Kent CT19 5EU
**US SIC:** 4712, 8999
**UK SIC:** 77002, 83954

|      | 31-12-13 | 31-03-13 | 31-12-12 |
|------|----------|----------|----------|
| TO   | 3,285,642 | 3,784,190 | 3,677,869 |
| P/L  | 322,592 | 311,995 | 193,910 |
| NW   | 69,897 | (203,320) | (170,948) |
| WC   | (436,113) | (760,803) | (430,597) |
| Emp. | 81 | 78 | 85 |

DUNS 34-595-7187    Exp
## Take Two Interactive Software Europe Ltd
(**Subsidiary of:** Take-Two Interactive Software Inc.)
555 Kings Road, London SW6 2EB
**Tel:** 02073718800
**Web:** www.eggersmannlondon.com
**Reg No:** 2739756  **Estd:** 1992 Private Limited Company
**Line of Business:** Joinery installation
**Export Markets:** Worldwide
**Trading Style:** Take-Two
**Issued Capital:** £2,294,640
**Director:** J S Belcher
**Co. Secretary:** Daniel Emerson
**Responsibilities**
**Senior:** Veronica Felstead (Manager), Gary Singer (Manager)
**US SIC:** 7399  **UK SIC:** 83954
**Auditors:** PricewaterhouseCoopers LLP
**Bankers:** Barclays Bank Plc (20-19-90)

|      | 31-03-14 | 31-03-13 | 31-03-12 |
|------|----------|----------|----------|
| TO   | 20,362,000 | 17,545,000 | 14,892,000 |
| P/L  | 1,171,000 | 1,116,000 | 791,000 |
| NW   | 42,252,000 | 41,598,000 | 40,940,000 |
| WC   | 41,577,000 | 41,375,000 | 40,471,000 |
| Emp. | 126 | 120 | 112 |

DUNS 23-642-7006    Imp
## Takeda Development Centre Europe Ltd.
(**Subsidiary of:** Takeda Pharmaceutical Company Limited)
61 Aldwych, London WC2B 4AE
**Tel:** 02031168000  **Fax:** 08031168001
**Web:** www.takeda.com
**Reg No:** 3638034  **VAT No:** 726561428
**Estd:** 1995 Private Limited Company
**Line of Business:** Research and laboratory based activities
**Trading Style:** Takeda Global Research and Development
**Issued Capital:** £800,000
**Directors:** S A Breen, D Isaacs, Dr G G Ross, Mrs S Cheyne
**Co. Secretary:** Bryan Driscoll
**US SIC:** 7391  **UK SIC:** 94000
**Auditors:** Deloitte & Touche LLP
**Bankers:** Barclays Bank Plc (20-31-52)

|      | 31-03-14 | 31-03-13 | 31-03-12 |
|------|----------|----------|----------|
| TO   | 129,386,906 | 115,131,124 | 100,042,173 |
| P/L  | 5,335,919 | 5,538,516 | 4,408,238 |
| NW   | 5,795,252 | 5,811,601 | 4,879,888 |
| WC   | 2,937,270 | 3,315,909 | 2,275,157 |
| Emp. | 185 | 141 | 125 |

DUNS 51-995-6346
## Takeda U K Ltd
(**Subsidiary of:** Takeda Pharmaceutical Company Limited)
Building 3 Glory Park, Glory Park Avenue, Wooburn Green, High Wycombe, Buckinghamshire HP10 0DF
**Fax:** 01628-526615
**Web:** www.takeda.co.uk
**Reg No:** 3362860  **Estd:** 1997 Private Limited Company
**Line of Business:** Wholesale of pharmaceutical goods
**Issued Capital:** £86,300,100
**Directors:** T R Smith, Y Fukutomi
**Co. Secretary:** William Walker
**Responsibilities**
**Senior:** Kruti Popat (Business Intelligence Director)
**Finance:** Satoru Noguchi (Finance Director)
**US SIC:** 5122  **UK SIC:** 61800
**Auditors:** Arthur Andersen
**Bankers:** The Mitsubishi Trust & Banking Corporation (62-21-11)

|      | 31-03-14 | 31-03-13 | 31-03-12 |
|------|----------|----------|----------|
| TO   | 66,072,029 | 59,534,184 | 153,231,555 |
| P/L  | 2,823,162 | 2,410,229 | 5,135,062 |
| NW   | 59,712,531 | 58,267,878 | 51,547,868 |
| WC   | 61,777,007 | 55,484,038 | 51,408,429 |
| Emp. | 63 | 52 | 53 |

DUNS 23-240-2854
## Tal Group Ltd
Tal House Lissue Industrial Estate East, Lissue R, Lisburn, Co Antrim BT28 2RB
**Tel:** 028-9262-2345  **Fax:** 028-9262-0950
**Web:** www.taldistribution.com
**Reg No:** 0015011NI  **Estd:** 1981 Private Limited Company
**Line of Business:** Management activities of holding companies
**Trading Style:** Tal Distribution, Tal Civil Engineering
**Issued Capital:** £2
**Directors:** T J Hughes, D M Hughes
**US SIC:** 6711  **UK SIC:** 83962
**Bankers:** The Bank Of Ireland (90-21-94)

|      | 01-04-14 | 01-04-13 | 01-04-12 |
|------|----------|----------|----------|
| TO   | 20,943,394 | 17,134,550 | 13,609,849 |
| P/L  | 75,635 | 177,561 | 567,055 |
| NW   | 2,261,768 | 2,177,406 | 2,042,468 |
| WC   | 2,149,811 | 1,944,186 | 1,746,190 |
| Emp. | 49 | 49 | 48 |

DUNS 42-426-0078
## Talascend Holdings Ltd
16 Great Queen Street, Covent Garden, London WC2B 5AH
**Tel:** 02086001600  **Fax:** 02087412001
**Web:** www.talascend.com
**Reg No:** 4413598  **Estd:** 2002 Private Limited Company
**Line of Business:** Management activities of holding companies
**Export Sales:** £2,105,738
**Issued Capital:** £10,163,155
**Directors:** B P Sholk, R L Wood, Ms M A Wood
**US SIC:** 6711  **UK SIC:** 83962
**Auditors:** Deloitte & Touche LLP

|      | 31-12-13 | 31-12-12 | 31-12-11 |
|------|----------|----------|----------|
| TO   | 20,120,510 | 21,402,645 | 20,795,000 |
| P/L  | (375,895) | (84,172) | (782,000) |
| NW   | (2,861,203) | (2,581,567) | (2,503,000) |
| WC   | 836,079 | (2,596,435) | (2,535,000) |
| Emp. | 159 | 45 | 35 |

DUNS 50-436-8614
## Talbot Association Ltd
Kingston Halls, 344 Paisley Road, Glasgow, Lanarkshire G5 8RE
**Tel:** 01414180955
**Reg No:** 0120333SC  **Estd:** 1989 Private Company Limited By Guarantee
**Line of Business:** Hostels
**Directors:** J Mills, Mrs J Barr, Ms M Mitchell, J Mcgilly
**Co. Secretary:** Ms Margaret Stevenson
**Responsibilities**
**Senior:** Joseph Scott (Manager), Deborah Stephens (Manager)
**Facilities:** Debbie Glendinning (Project Manager)
**Branches:** Talbot Association Ltd, 892 Govan Road, Glasgow, Lanarkshire G51 3AF
**US SIC:** 8699, 6732
**UK SIC:** 96902, 83100
**Auditors:** Scott-Moncrieff

|      | 31-03-14 | 31-03-13 | 31-03-12 |
|------|----------|----------|----------|
| TO   | 5,024,703 | 4,741,547 | 4,337,134 |
| P/L  | 117,385 | 5,468 | 586 |
| NW   | 1,438,437 | 1,321,052 | 1,200,114 |
| WC   | 1,438,437 | 1,321,052 | 1,200,114 |
| Emp. | 159 | 163 | 150 |

DUNS 50-585-8415
## Talbot Design (Seale) Ltd
52 Victoria Road, Aldershot, Hampshire GU11 1SS
**Tel:** 01252-323323  **Fax:** 01252-323324
**Web:** www.talbot-design.com
**Reg No:** 2528515  **VAT No:** 572541735
**Estd:** 1978 Private Limited Company
**Line of Business:** Construction of domestic buildings
**Trading Style:** Talbot Construction
**Issued Capital:** £755,500
**Principals:** C J Talbot (Managing), G C Talbot
**Co. Secretary:** Stephen Hazelton
**Responsibilities**
**Marketing:** Vicky Baron (Marketing Manager)
**Purchasing:** Austin Patten (Contracts Director)
**Branches:** Talbot Design (Seale) Ltd, 52 Victoria Road, Aldershot, Hampshire GU11 1SS
**US SIC:** 1522  **UK SIC:** 50100
**Auditors:** Stewart & Co

|      | 31-03-14 | 31-03-13 | 31-03-12 |
|------|----------|----------|----------|
| TO   | 12,291,608 | 16,162,180 | 19,520,798 |
| P/L  | (11,514) | (254,950) | (346,942) |
| NW   | 355,216 | 442,558 | 1,445,088 |
| WC   | 296,478 | 379,884 | 1,359,873 |
| Emp. | 50 | 50 | 50 |

DUNS 21-588-6622
## Talbot Garden Products
Talbot Buildings, Newnham Bridge, Tenbury Wells, Worcestershire WR15 8JF
**Estd:** 2011 Proprietorship

**Line of Business:** Garden sheds
**Proprietor:** M Cox
**Responsibilities**
**HR:** Callum Talbot *(Purchaser)*
**US SIC:** 2499 **UK SIC:** 46500
**Employees:** 50

DUNS 28-942-3311
### Talbot Heath School Trust Ltd
Rothesay Road, Bournemouth, Dorset BH4 9NJ
**Tel:** 01202-761881
**Web:** www.talbotheath.org
**Reg No:** 1584957 **Estd:** 1981 Private Company Limited By Guarantee
**Line of Business:** Schools (independent)
**Directors:** Mrs J Richardson, D Whelan, Dr A Main, Mrs C M Norman, D A Townend, R K Peak, Mrs R S Small, Dr T M Battock
**Co. Secretary:** Mrs Jennifer Cameron
**Responsibilities**
**Senior:** Moray Day *(Manager)*, Sally Dennison *(Manager)*, Toby Granville *(Director)*, Angharad Holloway *(Headmistress)*, Diana Leadbetter *(Director)*, Christopher Rutledge *(Director)*, Gillian Slater *(Manager)*, Clodie Sutcliffe *(Director)*, Sandra Trapnell *(Manager)*
**IT:** Allan Maule *(Computer Manager)*
**HR:** Angharad Holloway *(Headmistress)*
**US SIC:** 8211 **UK SIC:** 93200
**Auditors:** Saffery Champness
**Bankers:** Lloyds TSB Bank plc (30-91-08)

| | 31-08-14 | 31-08-13 | 31-08-12 |
|---|---|---|---|
| TO | 5,398,038 | 5,014,495 | 4,771,921 |
| P/L | 182,568 | (6,133) | (170,160) |
| NW | 9,156,194 | 8,512,744 | 8,259,197 |
| WC | (606,691) | 118,815 | 324,875 |
| Emp. | 154 | 145 | 151 |

DUNS 21-579-5997
### Talbot Specialist School
Lees Hall Road, Sheffield, South Yorkshire S8 9JP
**Tel:** 01142507394
**Web:** www.talbot.sheffield.sch.uk
**Estd:** 1998 Proprietorship
**Line of Business:** General secondary education
**Proprietor:** Ms J Smith
**Responsibilities**
**Senior:** Jean Briggs *(Head Teacher)*
**US SIC:** 8211 **UK SIC:** 93200
**Employees:** 110

DUNS 77-930-7180
### Talbot Underwriting Services Ltd
(**Subsidiary of:** Validus Holdings Ltd.)
55 Gracechurch Street, London EC3V 0JP
**Tel:** 020-7550-3500 **Fax:** 020-7553-3555
**Reg No:** 3043304 **Estd:** 1995 Private Limited Company
**Line of Business:** Other business activities not elsewhere classified
**Trading Style:** Yauchtsure, Marinasure
**Issued Capital:** £1
**Directors:** P A Bilsby, N D Wachman, C N Atkin
**Co. Secretary:** Ms Jane Clouting
**US SIC:** 7399 **UK SIC:** 83954
**Auditors:** KPMG Audit Plc
**Bankers:** The Royal Bank Of Scotland Plc (15-00-00)

| | 31-12-13 | 31-12-12 | 31-12-11 |
|---|---|---|---|
| TO | 79,847,128 | 76,136,904 | 50,377,965 |
| P/L | 2,664,678 | 7,013,741 | (5,249,491) |
| NW | 18,538,694 | 11,061,578 | 1,527,508 |
| WC | 17,356,548 | 9,005,466 | (1,998,897) |
| Emp. | 335 | 313 | 297 |

DUNS 21-838-0778
### Talbots Law Ltd
63 Market Street, Stourbridge, West Midlands DY8 1AQ
**Tel:** 01216473970
**Web:** www.talbotslaw.co.uk
**Reg No:** 8058015 **Estd:** 2012 Private Limited Company
**Line of Business:** Solicitors
**Issued Capital:** £3
**Directors:** A E Wakeman, J Gwilliams, Mrs M E Mocklow, P W Hill, P M Adkins, Ms L M Jones, Ms G Macleod, M K Hodgson
**Responsibilities**
**Senior:** Martyn Morgan *(Director)*
**US SIC:** 8111 **UK SIC:** 83500

| | 31-12-13 | 30-04-13 |
|---|---|---|
| TO | 4,613,453 | N/A |
| P/L | 603,579 | N/A |
| NW | (4,834,327) | 3 |
| WC | 1,629,878 | N/A |
| Emp. | 156 | N/A |

DUNS 21-010-4165
### Talbott's Biomass Energy Systems Ltd
(**Subsidiary of:** Smith Brothers (Leicester) Ltd)
Unit 13, Walton Industrial Estate, Stone, Staffordshire ST15 0NN
**Tel:** 01785-213366
**Web:** www.talbotts.co.uk
**Reg No:** 6340312 **Estd:** 2005 Private Limited Company
**Line of Business:** Heating contractors
**Issued Capital:** £500
**Directors:** J T Wilkinson, Mrs A Fielding, M W Johnson, C J Smith
**Responsibilities**
**Senior:** Mark Grimes *(Financial Director)*
**Finance:** Mark Grimes *(Financial Director)*
**HR:** Mark Grimes *(Financial Director)*
**Health & Safety:** Mark Grimes *(Financial Director)*
**US SIC:** 3643, 1711
**UK SIC:** 34203, 50300

| | 31-01-14 | 31-01-13 | 31-01-12 |
|---|---|---|---|
| TA | 658,224 | 583,131 | 634,782 |
| NW | 24,693 | 48,751 | 33,788 |
| WC | (50,284) | (27,379) | (42,130) |

DUNS 73-412-7496
### Talent Recruitment Ltd
173 York Road, Hartlepool, Cleveland TS26 9EQ
**Tel:** 01642266167
**Web:** www.talent.co.uk
**Reg No:** 4686033 **Estd:** 1993 Private Limited Company
**Line of Business:** Labour recruitment and provision of personnel
**Issued Capital:** £1,000
**Directors:** Calder Holding B V, M Lekkerkerker
**Responsibilities**
**Senior:** Emma Lambert *(Finance Director)*
**Finance:** Emma Lambert *(Finance Director)*
**US SIC:** 7361 **UK SIC:** 83954
**Bankers:** Lloyds TSB Bank plc (30-16-91)

| | 31-12-13 | 31-12-12 | 31-12-11 |
|---|---|---|---|
| TO | 880,417 | 961,172 | 3,045,170 |
| P/L | 113,645 | 152,070 | 466,645 |
| NW | 735,977 | 680,246 | 808,833 |
| WC | 722,677 | 648,855 | 746,991 |

DUNS 21-162-6486 **Imp**
### Talisman Sinopec Energy Uk Ltd
(**Subsidiary of:** Talisman Energy Inc)
Talisman House, 163 Holburn Street, Aberdeen, Aberdeenshire AB10 6BZ
**Tel:** 01224 352 500
**Web:** www.talisman-sinopec.com
**Reg No:** 0825828 **VAT No:** 394805910
**Estd:** 2002 Private Limited Company
**Line of Business:** Oil companies
**Directors:** Y Zhang, P Warwick, R S Ramshaw, R R Rooney, J R Baillie
**Co. Secretary:** Miss Gemma Crawford
**Responsibilities**
**Senior:** Nick Walker *(Vice President)*
**Finance:** Aernout Vandergaag *(Financial Manager)*
**IT:** Shaun Porter *(IT Manager)*
**Purchasing:** Val Prosser *(Purchasing Manager)*
**Branches:** Talisman Sinopec Energy Uk Limited, Ithaca Energy (Uk) Ltd, Nigg Oil Terminal, Tain, Ross-Shire IV19 1QF
**US SIC:** 1389, 1311
**UK SIC:** 13000
**Auditors:** Ernst & Young LLP
**Employees:** 638
**Turnover:** £1,420,405,000

DUNS 34-897-5231
### Talk Direct (Leeds) Ltd
Suite 54, Annexe 3 Batley Business Technol, Batley, West Yorkshire WF17 6ER
**Tel:** 01924474906
**Reg No:** 5694978 **Estd:** 2006 Private Limited Company
**Line of Business:** Telecommunications
**Issued Capital:** £100
**Directors:** Z Patel, S Patel
**US SIC:** 4899 **UK SIC:** 79020
**Bankers:** Barclays Bank Plc (27-99-00)

| | 31-03-14 | 31-03-13 | 31-03-12 |
|---|---|---|---|
| TO | 19,466,122 | 14,937,245 | 8,376,151 |
| P/L | 2,557,815 | 243,311 | 1,255,566 |
| NW | 2,028,083 | 347,228 | 1,049,838 |
| WC | 2,639,561 | 643,957 | 868,670 |
| Emp. | 127 | 128 | 98 |

DUNS 21-109-0090
### Talk Matters
4 Arthur Street, Dunfermline, Fife KY12 0PR
**Web:** www.talkmatters.org
**Reg No:** 0338099SC **Estd:** 2008 Private Company Limited By Guarantee
**Line of Business:** Other human health activities

**Directors:** T P Bennison, S J Foxley, Mrs L White, D C Moore, E N Christie
**Co. Secretary:** Ms Shirley Iveson
**Responsibilities**
**Senior:** Susan Lloyd *(Trustee)*
**US SIC:** 8091 **UK SIC:** 95200
**Bankers:** The Royal Bank Of Scotland Plc (83-33-00)

| | 31-03-14 | 31-03-13 | 31-03-12 |
|---|---|---|---|
| TO | 92,334 | 83,318 | 122,379 |
| P/L | 2,134 | (33,232) | 10,019 |
| NW | 33,891 | 37,444 | 70,676 |
| WC | 33,009 | 36,292 | 68,941 |

DUNS 52-024-2801
### Talk Talk Mobile Phones Ltd
(**Subsidiary of:** Citrine Network Ltd)
1351 Yardley Wood Road, Shirley, Solihull, West Midlands B90 1JU
**Tel:** 01214300900
**Web:** www.o2.co.uk
**Reg No:** 3390782 **Estd:** 1997 Private Limited Company
**Line of Business:** Retail sale of mobile telephones
**Issued Capital:** £35,000
**Director:** S S Dhillon
**Co. Secretary:** Mrs Balvinder Dhillon
**Branches:** Talk Talk Mobile Phones Ltd, 591 Foleshill Road, Coventry, West Midlands CV6 5JR
**US SIC:** 5999 **UK SIC:** 65600
**Auditors:** Ormerod Rutter Ltd
**Bankers:** Barclays Bank Plc (20-12-05)

| | 31-03-14 | 31-03-13 | 31-03-12 |
|---|---|---|---|
| TO | 24,485,234 | 11,273,028 | N/A |
| P/L | 78,939 | 608,203 | N/A |
| NW | 1,210,995 | 1,182,705 | 882,697 |
| WC | 1,890,452 | 650,679 | 597,361 |
| Emp. | 166 | 86 | N/A |

DUNS 49-072-8458
### Talk Training Ltd
(**Subsidiary of:** Talk Training Solutions Ltd)
Unit 3, Charnwood Court, Parc Nantgarw Heol Billingsley, Cardiff, South Glamorgan CF15 7QZ
**Web:** www.talktraining.co.uk
**Reg No:** 3082724 **Estd:** 1996 Private Limited Company
**Line of Business:** Adult and other education not elsewhere classified
**Issued Capital:** £904
**Directors:** A Anthony, J R Hughes
**Co. Secretary:** Steven Evans
**Responsibilities**
**Marketing:** Tanya Parmee *(Sales & Marketing Manager)*
**Sales:** Tanya Parmee *(Sales & Marketing Manager)*
**HR:** Mandy Withers *(Human Resources Manager)*
**US SIC:** 8249, 8299
**UK SIC:** 93300
**Auditors:** LB Group
**Bankers:** Barclays Bank Plc (20-10-26)

| | 31-07-13 | 31-07-12 | 31-07-11 |
|---|---|---|---|
| TA | 1,062,596 | 1,048,338 | 1,131,572 |
| NW | 616,638 | 610,808 | 501,109 |
| WC | 570,895 | 562,320 | 455,509 |

DUNS 28-986-0793
### Talkback Productions Ltd
(**Subsidiary of:** Bertelsmann Se & Co. Kgaa)
1 Stephen Street, London W1T 1AL
**Tel:** 020-7861-8000 **Fax:** 020-7861-8001
**Web:** www.fremantlemedia.com
**Reg No:** 1801230 **Estd:** 1984 Private Limited Company
**Line of Business:** Video production companies
**Trading Style:** Fremantlemedia Uk
**Issued Capital:** £134
**Directors:** B R Veerasingham, Ms G E Ahluwalia
**Co. Secretary:** Ms Helen Farnaby
**Responsibilities**
**Senior:** Sarah Gater *(Chief Executive Officer)*, Sarah Tingay *(Manager)*
**US SIC:** 7819 **UK SIC:** 97111
**Bankers:** Coutts & Co (18-00-09)

| | 31-12-13 | 31-12-12 | 31-12-11 |
|---|---|---|---|
| TA | 134 | 134 | 134 |
| NW | 134 | 134 | 134 |

DUNS 23-948-2099
### Talkington Bates Ltd
Sanderum House, 38 Oakley Road, Chinnor, Oxfordshire OX39 4TW
**Tel:** 01844-211670
**Web:** www.talkingcontractcatering.co.uk
**Reg No:** 3937653 **Estd:** 2000 Private Limited Company
**Line of Business:** Catering
**Issued Capital:** £50,000
**Director:** Ms J A Talkington
**Co. Secretary:** Paul Bates

**US SIC:** 7399 **UK SIC:** 83954

| | 30-11-13 | 30-11-12 | 30-11-11 |
|---|---|---|---|
| TA | 1,365,670 | 1,449,231 | 1,283,972 |
| NW | 4,968 | (7,793) | 44,833 |
| WC | 4,968 | (7,793) | 34,835 |

DUNS 23-857-4870
### Talktalk Communications Ltd
(**Subsidiary of:** Talktalk Telecom Group Plc)
Stanford House, Garrett Field, Brichwood, Warrington, Cheshire WA3 7BH
**Tel:** 08453303456 **Fax:** 08453-305-265
**Web:** www.talktalkbusiness.co.uk
**Reg No:** 3849133 **VAT No:** 744032068
**Estd:** 1999 Private Limited Company
**Line of Business:** Telecom services
**Trading Style:** Talktalk Business
**Issued Capital:** £100,001,000
**Directors:** C Bligh, I W Torrens, G Steen, Ms D M Harding, G P Wilson
**Co. Secretary:** Timothy Morris
**US SIC:** 4899, 7399
**UK SIC:** 79020, 83954
**Auditors:** Deloitte LLP
**Following financial data are in thousands**

| | 31-03-14 | 31-03-13 | 31-03-12 |
|---|---|---|---|
| TO | 1,165,150 | 1,059,089 | 1,017,551 |
| P/L | (12,950) | (20,903) | (42,332) |
| NW | 55,772 | 68,038 | 73,314 |
| WC | (370,453) | (326,276) | (200,604) |

DUNS 21-112-3832
### Talktalk Group Ltd
(**Subsidiary of:** Talktalk Telecom Group Plc)
11 Evesham Street, London W11 4AR
**Tel:** 08001799653
**Web:** www.talktalk.co.uk
**Reg No:** 6534112 **Estd:** 2008 Private Limited Company
**Line of Business:** Telecom services
**Trading Style:** Talk Talk
**Issued Capital:** £214,171,947
**Directors:** I W Torrens, C W Dunstone
**Co. Secretary:** Timothy Morris
**Responsibilities**
**Senior:** Andrew Bradbury *(Senior Direct Marketing Manage)*
**US SIC:** 4899 **UK SIC:** 79020
**Auditors:** Deloitte LLP

| | 31-03-14 | 31-03-13 | 31-03-12 |
|---|---|---|---|
| TO | 36,159,000 | 68,746,000 | 57,740,000 |
| P/L | (3,242,000) | 109,729,000 | 6,637,000 |
| NW | 401,649,000 | 394,800,000 | 273,523,000 |
| WC | 181,000 | (4,308,000) | (145,583,000) |
| Emp. | 2,306 | 2,512 | 2,805 |

DUNS 52-568-6374 **Exp**
### Talktalk Telecom Holdings Ltd
(**Subsidiary of:** Talktalk Telecom Group Plc)
1 Portal Way, London W3 6RS
**Tel:** 08000497665 **Fax:** 020-8896-5005
**Web:** www.talktalkgroup.com
**Reg No:** 3253714 **Estd:** 1989 Private Limited Company
**Line of Business:** Telecom services
**Trading Style:** Car Phone Warehouse
**Issued Capital:** £914,108
**Director:** I W Torrens
**Co. Secretary:** Timothy Morris
**Responsibilities**
**Senior:** Charles Dunston *(Chief Executive)*
**Sales:** Ed Bembridge *(Salos Director)*
**Branches:** Talktalk Telecom Holdings Ltd, Unit B, Whiteknights Retail Centre, Shinfield Road, Reading, Berkshire RG2 8HA
**US SIC:** 4899, 5999
**UK SIC:** 79020, 65600
**Auditors:** Deloitte LLP
**Bankers:** HSBC Bank plc (40-00-00)
**Following financial data are in thousands**

| | 31-03-14 | 31-03-13 | 31-03-12 |
|---|---|---|---|
| TA | 1,007,598 | 1,000,142 | 991,000 |
| P/L | 14,297 | 3,992 | 158,000 |
| NW | 1,005,558 | 987,763 | 979,000 |
| WC | 759,710 | 745,413 | 741,000 |

DUNS 50-558-2841
### T.A.L.L. Security Print Ltd
(**Subsidiary of:** The Tall Group of Companies Ltd)
Unit 2 Pembroke Court, Runcorn, Cheshire WA7 1TJ
**Tel:** 01928579200 **Fax:** 01928-579294
**Web:** www.tallgroup.co.uk
**Reg No:** 2509525 **VAT No:** 534957317
**Estd:** 1990 Private Limited Company
**Line of Business:** Printers general
**Export Sales:** £652,507
**Issued Capital:** £280,000
**Principals:** P G Andrew *(Sales)*, B Carney, Mrs D Dowler, P D Long, M Ruda, B A Evison
**Co. Secretary:** William Lamb
**Responsibilities**
**Senior:** Eddie Langton *(Warehouse Manager)*
**Marketing:** David Pugsley *(Marketing Manager)*
**Sales:** Lee Howitt *(Commercial Director)*, David Pugsley *(Marketing Manager)*
**IT:** Wayne Carlisle *(IT Director)*

**Facilities:** Dave Knapper *(Engineering Manager)*, Eddie Langton *(Warehouse Manager)*
**Operations:** David Pugsley *(Marketing Manager)*
**Engineering:** Dave Knapper *(Engineering Manager)*
**US SIC:** 2752 **UK SIC:** 47544
**Auditors:** Arthur Andersen
**Bankers:** The Royal Bank Of Scotland Plc (16-00-01)

| | 31-12-13 | 31-12-12 | 31-12-11 |
|---|---|---|---|
| TO | 4,780,365 | 5,084,949 | 4,985,458 |
| P/L | (146,251) | (106,227) | (280,150) |
| NW | 1,678,265 | 1,800,283 | 1,904,102 |
| WC | 1,378,201 | 1,470,258 | 1,608,882 |
| Emp. | 78 | 79 | 83 |

DUNS 21-030-0152

### Tall Trees Hotel

Green Lane, Worsall Road, Kirklevington, Kirklevington, Yarm, Cleveland TS15 9PE
**Tel:** 01642786786
**Web:** www.talltrees.co.uk
**Estd:** 2002 Proprietorship
**Line of Business:** Hotels
**Proprietors:** N Kalid, J Magid, J Dean, V Ahmed
**Responsibilities**
**Senior:** Vena AHMED *(Purchasing Manager)*, Nina KALID *(Finance Manager)*, Javid MAGID *(Director)*, Sam Mekkaoui *(General Managor)*
**Finance:** Nina KALID *(Finance Manager)*
**Purchasing:** Vena AHMED *(Purchasing Manager)*
**US SIC:** 7011 **UK SIC:** 66500
**Employees:** 180

DUNS 21-686-1104 **Imp-Exp**

### Talley Group Ltd

Abbey Park Industrial Estate Premier Way, Romsey, Hampshire SO51 9DQ
**Tel:** 01794-503500 **Fax:** 01794-503555
**Web:** www.talleygroup.com
**Reg No:** 0520386 **VAT No:** 505374265
**Estd:** 1953 Private Limited Company
**Line of Business:** Manufacturers of medical equipment
**Export Markets:** Europe; U S A
**Export Sales:** £5,405,233
**Trading Style:** Talley Medical
**Issued Capital:** £25,000
**Directors:** J J Evans, K Mearns, M B Webb, C P Evans
**Co. Secretary:** Martin Webb
**Responsibilities**
**IT:** John Rammage *(Computer Manager)*
**Facilities:** Bill Summerton *(Maintenance Manager)*
**Branches:** Talley Group Ltd, 31 Station Road, Whitacre Heath, Birmingham, West Midlands B46 2JA
**US SIC:** 3841 **UK SIC:** 37201
**Auditors:** WMT
**Bankers:** National Westminster Bank Plc (60-08-46)

| | 31-10-13 | 31-10-12 | 31-10-11 |
|---|---|---|---|
| TO | 16,299,023 | 14,150,050 | 12,077,373 |
| P/L | 2,006,044 | 1,000,788 | 706,493 |
| NW | 5,315,396 | 4,233,827 | 3,835,674 |
| WC | 1,736,413 | 1,399,236 | 789,892 |
| Emp. | 172 | 160 | 162 |

DUNS 73-846-4804

### Tallington Lakes Leisure Park Ltd

Barholm Road, Tallington, Stamford, Lincolnshire PE9 4RJ
**Tel:** 01778347000 **Fax:** 01778-346213
**Web:** www.tallington.com
**Reg No:** 5101647 **Estd:** 1981 Private Limited Company
**Line of Business:** Stadiums and sports grounds
**Issued Capital:** £2
**Director:** N Morgan
**Co. Secretary:** Mrs Janet Jones
**US SIC:** 3949 **UK SIC:** 49420
**Auditors:** GreenStones Ltd

| | 31-12-13 | 31-12-12 | 31-12-11 |
|---|---|---|---|
| TA | 3,139,456 | 2,751,426 | 83,533 |
| NW | (219,565) | (87,811) | 2 |
| WC | (1,312,597) | (1,237,976) | 2 |

DUNS 73-444-8793

### Tallis Amos Group Ltd

(**Subsidiary of:** Tallis Property & Investments Ltd)
Clay Lane, Doncaster, South Yorkshire DN2 4RA
**Tel:** 01302322092
**Web:** www.christallis.co.uk
**Reg No:** 4697211 **VAT No:** 377274127
**Estd:** 1983 Private Limited Company
**Line of Business:** Suppliers of
**Export Sales:** £695,354
**Trading Style:** Tallis Amos Group
**Issued Capital:** £166
**Principals:** B J Tallis *(Managing)*, C Mcintyre, C J Tallis, C G Amos, A F Perkins, S C Amos
**Responsibilities**
**Senior:** Gillian Tallis *(Manager)*
**US SIC:** 3523 **UK SIC:** 32113
**Bankers:** Barclays Bank Plc (20-98-61)

| | 31-12-13 | 31-12-12 | 31-12-11 |
|---|---|---|---|
| TO | 46,040,427 | 38,632,604 | 18,101,304 |
| P/L | 915,028 | 723,289 | 208,730 |
| NW | 3,655,671 | 2,996,202 | 1,644,159 |
| WC | 2,285,706 | 1,579,515 | (174,343) |
| Emp. | 110 | 116 | 53 |

DUNS 22-762-8344 **Imp**

### Tallon International Ltd

(**Subsidiary of:** Zintello Merchants Ltd)
Unit 4, Coventry, West Midlands CV2 4QP
**Tel:** 024-7643-7000 **Fax:** 02476452946
**Web:** www.tallon.co.uk
**Reg No:** 1153586 **VAT No:** 307079759
**Estd:** 1973 Private Limited Company
**Line of Business:** Stationery suppliers
**Export Sales:** £734,729
**Issued Capital:** £5,000
**Directors:** E Quantrill, O R Gupwell, B Heath, J P Ellis
**Co. Secretary:** Ms Sheila Fisher
**Responsibilities**
**Senior:** Ronald Johnson *(Owner)*
**US SIC:** 5112 **UK SIC:** 61900
**Auditors:** Harrison Beale & Owen Ltd
**Bankers:** Bank Of Scotland (12-13-11)

| | 31-03-14 | 31-03-13 | 31-03-12 |
|---|---|---|---|
| TO | 13,612,933 | 13,163,380 | 12,567,958 |
| P/L | 549,370 | 573,527 | 606,657 |
| NW | 2,817,901 | 2,398,450 | 1,963,309 |
| WC | 2,583,152 | 2,223,179 | 2,039,603 |
| Emp. | 53 | 51 | 47 |

DUNS 21-776-2631

### Tally Ho Sports & Conference Centre

Tally House Training Centre, Pershore Road, Birmingham, West Midlands B5 7RN
**Tel:** 01216268228
**Web:** www.tallyhouk.com
**Estd:** 1994 Proprietorship
**Line of Business:** Conference centres and facilities
**Proprietor:** Ms L Smith
**US SIC:** 7011 **UK SIC:** 66500
**Employees:** 48

DUNS 21-731-7346 **Imp-Exp**

### Talon Engineering Ltd

(**Subsidiary of:** Talon Holdings Ltd)
44 Sea King Road, Lynx Trading Estate, Yeovil, Somerset BA20 2NZ
**Tel:** 01935-471508 **Fax:** 01935-431825
**Web:** www.talon-eng.co.uk
**Reg No:** 1213668 **VAT No:** 187533826
**Estd:** 1973 Private Limited Company
**Line of Business:** Other engineering activities
**Export Markets:** countries worldwide.
**Issued Capital:** £11,523
**Principals:** G Sartin *(Managing)*, Mrs V M Sartin, R Sartin
**Co. Secretary:** Mrs Karen Dawe
**Responsibilities**
**Sales:** Mike Mullett *(Sales Manager)*
**Health & Safety:** Alan Flooks *(Facilities Manager)*
**Facilities:** Alan Flooks *(Facilities Manager)*
**US SIC:** 8911 **UK SIC:** 83701
**Auditors:** Baker Tilly UK Audit LLP
**Bankers:** Barclays Bank Plc (20-99-40)

| | 31-03-14 | 31-03-13 | 31-03-12 |
|---|---|---|---|
| TA | 3,002,825 | 3,172,142 | 3,218,505 |
| NW | 1,632,325 | 1,734,307 | 1,569,445 |
| WC | 1,486,288 | 1,691,545 | 1,544,522 |

DUNS 22-177-9981

### Talos Securities Ltd

(**Subsidiary of:** Talos Holdings Ltd)
Boatmans House, 2 Selsdon Way, London E14 9LA
**Tel:** 02075174400 **Fax:** 02075132752
**Web:** www.selftrade.co.uk
**Reg No:** 4196325 **Estd:** 2001 Private Limited Company
**Line of Business:** Banks
**Issued Capital:** £5,216,300
**Directors:** A J Buffet, A Bataille, A Baumeister, J Reed, B M Grisoni, A J De Gaudemaris, P F Sommelet, P H Nunnerley
**Co. Secretary:** Mark Lloyd
**Responsibilities**
**Senior:** Marie Senecaut *(Director)*, Valentine Steadman *(Manager)*
**HR:** Rose Hodson *(Human Resources Administrator)*
**US SIC:** 6012, 6211
**UK SIC:** 81402, 83100

**Bankers:** National Westminster Bank Plc (60-00-01)

| | 31-12-13 | 31-12-12 | 31-12-11 |
|---|---|---|---|
| TA | 145,261,000 | 162,710,000 | 99,244,000 |
| P/L | (40,413,000) | 1,979,000 | 2,391,000 |
| NW | 15,578,000 | 16,701,000 | 15,265,000 |
| WC | 15,218,000 | 12,943,000 | 5,699,000 |
| Emp. | 116 | 105 | 104 |

DUNS 29-508-9528 **Imp-Exp**

### Tam International North Sea Ltd

(**Subsidiary of:** Tam International Inc.)
Unit A, Abbotswell Road, Aberdeen, Aberdeenshire AB12 3AB
**Tel:** 01224875105
**Web:** www.tamintl.com
**Reg No:** 1871303 **VAT No:** 415875042
**Estd:** 1984 Private Limited Company
**Line of Business:** Service activities incidental to oil and gas extraction excluding surveying
**Export Markets:** Europe, Middle East & U S A
**Export Sales:** £21,329,566
**Issued Capital:** £100
**Directors:** S R Scott, L B Sanford
**Co. Secretary:** Raeburn Christie Clark & Wallace
**Responsibilities**
**Finance:** Derek Thomson *(Financial Director)*
**Sales:** Ian Bayfield *(Senior Account Manager)*
**HR:** Hazel Murphy *(Human Resources Manager)*
**Health & Safety:** Bob Davies *(Health & Safety Officer)*
**US SIC:** 1389, 5251
**UK SIC:** 13000, 64800
**Auditors:** Deloitte & Touche
**Bankers:** The Royal Bank Of Scotland Plc (83-49-40)

| | 30-04-13 | 30-04-12 | 30-04-11 |
|---|---|---|---|
| TO | 23,599,164 | 16,402,508 | 16,453,444 |
| P/L | 5,241,364 | 2,892,407 | 1,820,465 |
| NW | 16,857,110 | 13,150,104 | 11,126,391 |
| WC | 12,619,731 | 9,034,200 | 6,775,276 |
| Emp. | 53 | 46 | 45 |

DUNS 21-736-1858

### Tamar Energy Ltd

Two London Bridge, London SE1 9RA
**Tel:** 02072557500
**Web:** www.tamar-energy.com
**Reg No:** 7703877 **Estd:** 2011 Private Limited Company
**Line of Business:** Construction of civil engineering constructions
**Issued Capital:** £460,926
**Directors:** N E Ferguson, M Shakil, S D Pitcher, A C Lovell, Lord J E Russell, R Kherati, W B Weil, Sir M C Peat
**Responsibilities**
**Senior:** Paul Crewe *(Director)*, William Heller *(Director)*, Dean Hislop *(Director)*, Benjamin Sautelle Smith *(Director)*
**Admin:** Sarah Ashford *(Office Manager)*
**US SIC:** 1622 **UK SIC:** 50200
**Auditors:** Wilkins Kennedy LLP

| | 31-03-14 | 31-03-13 | 31-03-12 |
|---|---|---|---|
| TO | 4,441,716 | 1,140,838 | N/A |
| P/L | (9,165,123) | (7,384,431) | (685,010) |
| NW | 51,658,742 | 16,213,351 | 12,629,966 |
| WC | 10,633,534 | 3,902,140 | 14,671,297 |
| Emp. | 77 | 50 | 3 |

DUNS 38-547-0851

### Tamaris Healthcare (England) Ltd

(**Subsidiary of:** Fshc (Guernsey) Holdings Ltd)
1st Floor Lingsield House, Mc Mullen Road, Darlington, County Durham DL1 1RW
**Tel:** 01325364586
**Web:** www.tancem.com
**Reg No:** 3328661 **Estd:** 1997 Private Limited Company
**Line of Business:** Other human health activities
**Issued Capital:** £2
**Directors:** Ms M C Royston, B R Taberner, I R Smith
**Co. Secretary:** Mrs Abigail Mattison
**Responsibilities**
**Senior:** Dominic Kay *(Director General)*
**Branches:** Tamaris Healthcare (England) Ltd, 52 Dyke Road Avenue, Brighton, East Sussex BN1 5LE
**US SIC:** 8091 **UK SIC:** 95200
**Auditors:** Ernst & Young
**Bankers:** Barclays Bank Plc (20-77-67)

| | 31-12-13 | 31-12-12 | 31-12-11 |
|---|---|---|---|
| TO | 49,550,000 | 49,838,000 | 48,898,000 |
| P/L | (196,000) | (1,947,000) | 663,000 |
| NW | 606,000 | 802,000 | 18,249,000 |
| WC | (4,584,000) | (5,467,000) | 12,028,000 |
| Emp. | 2,430 | 2,415 | 2,371 |

DUNS 21-751-2912

### Tamdown Group Ltd

(**Subsidiary of:** Garbol Ltd)
1 Tamdown Way, Braintree, Essex CM7 2QL
**Tel:** 01376320856 **Fax:** 01376-328969
**Web:** www.tamdown.com
**Reg No:** 1268060 **VAT No:** 299745092
**Estd:** 2000 Private Limited Company
**Line of Business:** Environmental consultants
**Trading Style:** Tamdown Group
**Issued Capital:** £100
**Principals:** M T Morris *(Managing)*, A Parton, M P Waine, M Weeks, J Crick, K J Breen, P D Holliday
**Co. Secretary:** Ms Dawn Hillman
**Branches:** Tamdown Group Ltd, Unit B5, Westacott Way, Maidenhead, Berkshire SL6 3RT
**US SIC:** 1541, 1611
**UK SIC:** 50100, 50200
**Auditors:** BDO Stoy Hayward LLP
**Bankers:** National Westminster Bank Plc (60-05-13)

| | 30-09-13 | 30-09-12 | 30-09-11 |
|---|---|---|---|
| TO | 82,655,785 | 60,534,408 | 68,025,010 |
| P/L | 4,609,409 | 2,235,684 | 2,828,121 |
| NW | 21,870,162 | 19,063,318 | 17,950,663 |
| WC | 18,642,378 | 16,781,262 | 15,077,761 |
| Emp. | 388 | 399 | 454 |

DUNS 54-864-0184

### Tameside & Glossop Community & Priority Services N H S Trust

Tameside General Hospital, Fountain Street, Ashton-Under-Lyne, Lancashire OL6 9RW
**Tel:** 0161-922-6000
**Web:** www.bureclinic.com
**Estd:** 1994
**Line of Business:** Healthcare companies
**Directors:** J R Davenport, M Roe
**Branches:** Tameside & Glossop Community & Priority Services N H S Trust, Guide Lane Clinic, Guide Lane, Manchester M34 5HY
**US SIC:** 8091 **UK SIC:** 95200
**Employees:** 1,900

DUNS 56-977-7485

### Tameside & Glossop Hospice Ltd

Willow Wood Hospice, Willow Wood Close, Ashton-Under-Lyne, Lancashire OL6 6SL
**Tel:** 0161-330-1100
**Web:** www.willowwood.info
**Reg No:** 2854091 **Estd:** 1993 Private Limited Company
**Line of Business:** Hospices
**Trading Style:** Willow Wood Hospice
**Directors:** M J Willescroft, P E Mccloskey, S Rogerson, J H Maltby, B Wild, P T Cowper, M Davies, Ms S Wilson
**Co. Secretary:** Peter Wood
**Responsibilities**
**Senior:** Alexander Barton *(Manager)*, Karen Houlston *(Manager)*, John Steward *(Manager)*
**Branches:** Tameside & Glossop Hospice Ltd, 122 Market St, Manchester M43 7AA
**US SIC:** 8091 **UK SIC:** 95200
**Auditors:** Scott Roberts Taylor
**Bankers:** National Westminster Bank Plc (01-00-39)

| | 30-04-14 | 30-04-13 | 30-04-12 |
|---|---|---|---|
| TO | 2,539,291 | 2,812,786 | 3,441,899 |
| P/L | (404,243) | 71,016 | 498,751 |
| NW | 5,914,994 | 6,239,977 | 6,101,947 |
| WC | (252,097) | (246,971) | (220,574) |
| Emp. | 85 | 61 | 62 |

DUNS 23-251-8543

### Tameside & Glossop Primary Care Trust

New Century House, Progress Way, Denton, Manchester M34 2GP
**Web:** www.tamesideandglossop.nhs.net
**Estd:** 2003
**Line of Business:** Primary care trust
**Trading Style:** Tameside & Glossop Pct
**Issued Capital:** £1
**Director:** M Ditchfield
**Branches:** Tameside & Glossop Primary Care Trust, 36 Queens Walk, Manchester M43 7AD
**US SIC:** 8062 **UK SIC:** 95100
**Employees:** 148

DUNS 34-826-2890

### Tameside College Services Ltd

(**Subsidiary of:** Tameside College)
Beaufort Road, Ashton-Under-Lyne, Lancashire OL6 6NX
**Tel:** 0161-908-6600
**Web:** www.tameside.ac.uk
**Reg No:** 2799735 **Estd:** 1993 Private Limited Company

**Line of Business:** Business and management consultancy activities not elsewhere classified
**Issued Capital:** £2
**Directors:** J A Lyne, P M Ryder
**US SIC:** 7392, 8249
**UK SIC:** 83951, 93300
**Bankers:** National Westminster Bank Plc (01-00-39)

| | 31-07-13 | 31-07-12 | 31-07-11 |
|---|---|---|---|
| TA | 2 | 2 | 2 |
| NW | 2 | 2 | 2 |

DUNS 23-701-0079
## Tameside Hospital Nhs Foundation Trust
Community Liaison Building, Fountain Street, Ashton-Under-Lyne, Lancashire OL6 9RP
**Tel:** 01613315173
**Web:** www.tameside.gov.uk
**VAT No:** 888880345 **Estd:** 1974
**Line of Business:** The dss
**Trading Style:** Tameside General Hospital
**Issued Capital:** £1
**Principals:** T Presswood *(Chairman)*, Ms K Brown *(Financial)*, A Griffiths, Mrs C Green, R Corless, Ms D Bates, T Ward, A Anderson
**Responsibilities**
**Senior:** Annette Clancy *(Team Manager)*, Philip Dylak *(Manager)*, Lorraine Scott *(Manager of Stores)*, Hilary Troop *(Senior Manager)*
**Facilities:** Mike Dean *(Associate Director of Faciliti)*
**Branches:** Tameside Hospital Nhs Foundation Trust, Crickets Lane Health Centre, Crickets Lane, Ashton-Under-Lyne, Lancashire OL6 6NG
**US SIC:** 8062, 9121
**UK SIC:** 95100, 91110
**Auditors:** KPMG LLP
**Bankers:** The Royal Bank Of Scotland Plc (16-00-02)

| | 31-03-14 | 31-03-13 | 31-03-12 |
|---|---|---|---|
| TO | 145,472,000 | 147,707,000 | 132,938,000 |
| P/L | 1,127,000 | (6,262,000) | (6,574,000) |
| NW | 39,749,000 | 35,652,000 | 51,038,000 |
| WC | (10,317,000) | (7,785,000) | (8,938,000) |
| Emp. | 2,457 | 2,312 | 2,317 |

DUNS 22-935-8999
## Tamlaght Private Nursing Home Ltd
34 Larne Road, Carrickfergus, Co Antrim BT38 7DY
**Tel:** 02893366194
**Web:** www.tamlaghtnursinghome.com
**Reg No:** 0020841NI **Estd:** 1987 Private Limited Company
**Line of Business:** Nursing homes
**Trading Style:** Tamlaght Private Nursing Home
**Issued Capital:** £2
**Director:** Miss L E Wheeler
**Responsibilities**
**Senior:** Ausgusta Anaele *(Home Manager)*
**HR:** Briege Kelly *(Matron)*
**Health & Safety:** Briege Kelly *(Matron)*
**Operations:** Briege Kelly *(Matron)*
**Purchasing:** Ausgusta Anaele *(Home Manager)*
**US SIC:** 8051 **UK SIC:** 95100
**Auditors:** Goldblatt McGuigan
**Bankers:** Ulster Bank Ltd (98-04-00)

| | 30-09-13 | 30-09-12 | 30-09-11 |
|---|---|---|---|
| TA | 753,228 | 1,564,712 | 1,229,809 |
| NW | 429,791 | 1,362,317 | 1,013,597 |
| WC | (179,451) | 749,275 | 380,361 |

DUNS 21-782-5088
## Tamlite Batch Sld
Pipers Road, Redditch, Worcestershire B98 0HU
**Web:** www.tamlite.co.uk
**Estd:** 1988 Partnership
**Line of Business:** Manufacturers of lighting equipment
**Partners:** D Vowles, P Vowles
**US SIC:** 3648 **UK SIC:** 34702
**Employees:** 50

DUNS 21-771-8103
## Tamlite Group
Unit 12, Stafford Park 12, Stafford Park, Telford, Shropshire TF3 3BJ
**Tel:** 01952292566
**Web:** www.tamlite.com
**Estd:** 1986 Proprietorship
**Line of Business:** Manufacturers and suppliers of chandeliers
**Proprietor:** M Northwood
**Responsibilities**
**Senior:** Martin Northwood *(Proprietor)*
**Admin:** Lisa Hay *(Administrator)*
**US SIC:** 3648 **UK SIC:** 34702
**Employees:** 50

DUNS 21-614-3963
## Tampopo
135 The Orient, Manchester M17 8EH
**Tel:** 01617478878
**Web:** www.tampopo.co.uk
**Estd:** 2011
**Line of Business:** Licensed restaurants
**Responsibilities**
**Senior:** Ben Cain *(General Manager)*
**US SIC:** 5812 **UK SIC:** 66110
**Employees:** 50

DUNS 45-810-7745
## Tampopo Ltd
1st Floor, Hq Building, Manchester M21 9EG
**Tel:** 01618322764
**Web:** www.tampopo.co.uk
**Reg No:** 3168752 **Estd:** 1997 Private Limited Company
**Line of Business:** Restaurant - american
**Trading Style:** Tampopo Ltd
**Issued Capital:** £139,312
**Directors:** A J Jayawickrema, N J Jeffrey, S Platts, T A Wates
**Co. Secretary:** David Fox
**Branches:** Tampopo Ltd, 140 Fulham Road, London SW10 9PY
**US SIC:** 5812 **UK SIC:** 66110
**Auditors:** Cowgill Holloway
**Bankers:** HSBC Bank plc (40-31-24)

| | 30-06-13 | 30-06-12 | 30-06-11 |
|---|---|---|---|
| TO | 7,074,604 | N/A | N/A |
| P/L | 1,627 | N/A | N/A |
| NW | 1,046,107 | 1,089,322 | 1,165,174 |
| WC | (667,168) | (885,636) | (702,642) |
| Emp. | 182 | N/A | N/A |

DUNS 23-560-2716
## Tamulst Care Ltd
(**Subsidiary of:** Fshc (Guernsey) Holdings Ltd)
Emerson Court, Alderley Road, Wilmslow, Cheshire SK9 1NX
**Tel:** 01223-224204
**Reg No:** 3558522 **Estd:** 1998 Private Limited Company
**Line of Business:** Other human health activities
**Issued Capital:** £2
**Directors:** B R Taberner, I R Smith, Ms M C Royston
**Co. Secretary:** Mrs Abigail Mattison
**US SIC:** 8091 **UK SIC:** 95200
**Auditors:** KPMG LLP

| | 31-12-13 | 31-12-12 | 31-12-11 |
|---|---|---|---|
| TO | 33,658,000 | 35,133,000 | 34,628,000 |
| P/L | 332,000 | 479,000 | 702,000 |
| NW | 2,749,000 | 2,417,000 | 14,938,000 |
| WC | (383,000) | (1,191,000) | 10,524,000 |
| Emp. | 1,675 | 1,722 | 1,691 |

DUNS 21-611-3126 **Imp-Exp**
## Tamura-Europe Ltd
Clarke Avenue, Calne, Wiltshire SN11 9BS
**Tel:** 01249812624 **Fax:** 01249816134
**Web:** www.tamura-europe.co.uk
**Reg No:** 0463530 **VAT No:** 501976645
**Estd:** 1949 Private Limited Company
**Line of Business:** Electronic engineers
**Export Markets:** E E C and U S A
**Export Sales:** £54,054,000
**Issued Capital:** £12,000,000
**Directors:** N Nanjo, M Asada, M Puliti, T Shinonuma
**Co. Secretary:** Jonathan Parker
**Responsibilities**
**HR:** Brian Ingleson *(Personnel Adviser)*
**Branches:** Tamura-Europe Ltd, 59 Deerdykes View, Glasgow, Lanarkshire G68 9HN
**US SIC:** 3621 **UK SIC:** 34201
**Auditors:** PricewaterhouseCoopers LLP
**Bankers:** The Bank Of Tokyo-Mitsubishi, Ltd (60-01-09)

| | 31-12-13 | 31-12-12 | 31-12-11 |
|---|---|---|---|
| TO | 61,539,000 | 42,906,000 | 43,950,000 |
| P/L | 653,000 | 1,466,000 | (3,808,000) |
| NW | (801,000) | (1,921,000) | 1,319,000 |
| WC | 1,729,000 | 1,381,000 | (293,000) |
| Emp. | 568 | 308 | 303 |

DUNS 23-261-2457
## Tamworth Borough Council
Marmion House, Lichfield Street, Tamworth, Staffordshire B79 7BZ
**Tel:** 01827709709
**Web:** www.direct.gov.uk
**Estd:** 2002
**Line of Business:** Local government
**Directors:** C Moore, R Wright, B Jenkins
**Responsibilities**
**Marketing:** Matthew Bowers *(Head of Strategic Planning and)*
**IT:** Nicki Burton *(IT Manager)*
**HR:** Zoe Blake *(Training Manager)*, Anica Goodwin *(Human Resources Manager)*
**Health & Safety:** Jonathan Topham *(Health and safety manager)*
**Branches:** Tamworth Borough Council, The Philip Dix Centre , Corpor, Tamworth, Staffordshire B79 7DN
**US SIC:** 9121 **UK SIC:** 91110
**Bankers:** The Co-Operative Bank Plc (08-92-46)
**Employees:** 570

DUNS 21-831-4110
## Tamworth Co-Operative Society Ltd
5 Colehill, Tamworth, Staffordshire B79 7HA
**Web:** www.co-operative.coop
**Reg No:** 0002582IP **VAT No:** 555077922
**Estd:** 1886 Friendly Society
**Line of Business:** Retail sale of alcoholic and other beverages
**Trading Style:** Co-Op Homemaker Homelectric
**Principals:** Ms A A Higginson *(Chairman)*, Ms D Trout, D Johnson, A M Poulten, R W Read, G W Johnson, A M King, A V King
**Responsibilities**
**Senior:** Julian Coles *(Chief Executive)*
**Finance:** Andy Richardson *(Financial Manager)*
**Marketing:** Adam Millward *(Marketing Manager)*
**Admin:** Sandra Bozward *(Office Manager)*
**IT:** Andy Richardson *(Financial Manager)*
**HR:** Julie Gasper *(Human Resources Manager)*
**Health & Safety:** Julie Gasper *(Human Resources Manager)*
**Branches:** Tamworth Co-Operative Society Ltd, 107 Amington Road, Tamworth, Staffordshire B77 3LN
**US SIC:** 5921, 5411, 5399
**UK SIC:** 64200, 64100, 65600
**Auditors:** Dains LLP
**Bankers:** The Co-Operative Bank Plc (08-90-08)

| | 26-01-13 | 21-01-12 | 22-01-11 |
|---|---|---|---|
| TO | 20,110,000 | 19,916,000 | 20,707,000 |
| P/L | 147,000 | 66,000 | (81,000) |
| NW | 12,326,000 | 13,997,000 | 14,652,000 |
| WC | 545,000 | 405,000 | 1,140,000 |
| Emp. | 329 | 350 | 364 |

DUNS 23-215-5770
## Tamworth College
Croft Street, Upper Gungate, Tamworth, Staffordshire B79 8AE
**Tel:** 01827310202
**Web:** www.tamworth.ac.uk
**Estd:** 2009
**Line of Business:** Colleges & universities
**Director:** C A Heard
**Responsibilities**
**IT:** Gary Booth *(IT Manager)*
**Branches:** Tamworth College, The Friary, Lichfield, Staffordshire WS13 6QG
**US SIC:** 8299 **UK SIC:** 93300
**Employees:** 1,300

DUNS 51-647-1802
## Tamworth Road Taxis
25a Aldergate, Tamworth, Staffordshire B79 7DX
**Tel:** 0182755595
**Web:** www.tamworth-taxis.co.uk
**Estd:** 1997 Proprietorship
**Line of Business:** Taxis and private hire vehicles
**Proprietor:** J Thompstone
**Responsibilities**
**Senior:** Claire Alton *(Proprietor)*
**US SIC:** 4121, 7512
**UK SIC:** 72200, 84801
**Employees:** 47

DUNS 21-907-1321 **Exp**
## Tamworth Steel Stockholders Ltd
Gagarin, Apollo, Lichfield Road Industrial Estate, Tamworth, Staffordshire B79 7TA
**Tel:** 0182761531 **Fax:** 01908560473
**Web:** www.tamworthsteel.co.uk
**Reg No:** 1109834 **VAT No:** 111704715
**Estd:** 1973 Private Limited Company
**Line of Business:** Steel stockholders
**Export Sales:** £175,631
**Issued Capital:** £1,000
**Principals:** J E Ratledge *(Managing)*, J W Ratledge
**Co. Secretary:** Mrs Lilian Ratledge
**Responsibilities**
**Senior:** Geoff Spring *(Warehouse Coordinator)*
**Sales:** Nick Bamford *(Commercial Manager)*
**Branches:** Tamworth Steel Stockholders Ltd, Mariner, Tamworth, Staffordshire B79 7UL
**US SIC:** 5051, 7399
**UK SIC:** 61200, 83954
**Auditors:** Michael Kay & Co Ltd

**Bankers:** National Westminster Bank Plc (60-21-50)

| | 31-03-14 | 31-03-13 | 31-03-12 |
|---|---|---|---|
| TO | 10,176,445 | 10,549,392 | 8,456,466 |
| P/L | 987,826 | 741,284 | 554,433 |
| NW | 5,740,280 | 4,975,544 | 4,402,336 |
| WC | 2,320,501 | 1,971,590 | 1,689,924 |
| Emp. | 89 | 90 | 67 |

DUNS 77-467-5342
## Tancia Ltd
(**Subsidiary of:** Tancia (Holdings) Ltd)
2-4 Mount Pleasant Road, Aldershot, Hampshire GU12 4NL
**Tel:** 01252400270 **Fax:** 01252334821
**Web:** www.pens.co.uk
**Reg No:** 2966120 **Estd:** 1994 Private Limited Company
**Line of Business:** Corporate promotional products
**Export Sales:** £268,276
**Issued Capital:** £579,292
**Directors:** N J Cleere, Ms A J Cleere
**Co. Secretary:** Anthony Cleere
**US SIC:** 7399 **UK SIC:** 83954
**Auditors:** Barnes Roffe

| | 31-05-13 | 31-05-12 | 31-05-11 |
|---|---|---|---|
| TO | 6,593,848 | N/A | N/A |
| P/L | 977,317 | N/A | N/A |
| NW | 2,715,215 | 2,079,808 | 1,775,050 |
| WC | 1,502,289 | 988,333 | 437,117 |
| Emp. | 133 | N/A | N/A |

DUNS 21-689-0434 **Imp-Exp**
## Tandem Group Plc
35 Tameside Drive, Castle Bromwich, Birmingham, West Midlands B35 7AG
**Web:** www.tandemgroup.co.uk
**Reg No:** 0616818 **Estd:** 1958 Public Limited Company
**Line of Business:** Management activities of holding companies
**Export Sales:** £2,406,000
**Trading Style:** Claud Butler, Falcon, Scorpion, Dawes; Barrosa; Dirty; Pot Black; Hedstrom and Kickmaster
**Issued Capital:** £1,503,370
**Principals:** M P Keene *(Financial)*, S Morris, A Q Bestwick, J C Shears, P Ratcliffe, S J Grant
**Co. Secretary:** James Shears
**Responsibilities**
**IT:** Steve Cannon *(IT Manager)*
**Branches:** Tandem Group Plc, 20 Turk St, Alton, Hampshire GU34 1AG
**US SIC:** 6711, 3949
**UK SIC:** 83962, 49420
**Auditors:** Grant Thornton UK LLP
**Bankers:** HSBC Bank plc (40-02-50)

| | 31-12-13 | 31-12-12 | 31-12-11 |
|---|---|---|---|
| TO | 28,347,000 | 28,952,000 | 29,042,000 |
| P/L | 16,000 | 830,000 | 820,000 |
| NW | 3,404,000 | 3,326,000 | 3,912,000 |
| WC | 3,195,000 | 4,768,000 | 4,535,000 |
| Emp. | 82 | 89 | 94 |

DUNS 22-055-9434
## T&K Gallagher Ltd
James Corbett Road, Salford, Lancashire M50 1DE
**Tel:** 0845 5000123 **Fax:** 0845 5000124
**Web:** www.gallagherltd.co.uk
**Reg No:** 4057938 **Estd:** 1993 Private Limited Company
**Line of Business:** Building of complete constructions or parts thereof; civil engineering
**Issued Capital:** £5,000
**Directors:** M P O'Sullivan, A R Tilbrook, T J Gallagher, S J Alderson, Mrs K A Duckworth, M V O'Connor
**Co. Secretary:** Michael O'Connor
**Responsibilities**
**IT:** Colin Surrey *(IT Manager)*
**US SIC:** 1541 **UK SIC:** 50100
**Auditors:** Haines Watts (Lancashire) LLP
**Bankers:** The Royal Bank Of Scotland Plc (16-28-16)

| | 31-03-14 | 31-03-13 | 31-03-12 |
|---|---|---|---|
| TO | 35,319,957 | 31,297,831 | 32,426,611 |
| P/L | 2,442,484 | 1,029,947 | 604,348 |
| NW | 2,602,366 | 1,673,208 | 1,161,799 |
| WC | 1,362,032 | 558,677 | 41,316 |
| Emp. | 169 | 152 | 145 |

DUNS 21-681-3638 **Imp**
## T&L Sugars Ltd
(**Subsidiary of:** Fanjul Corp.)
Thames Refinery, Factory Road, Silvertown, London E16 2EW
**Tel:** 02075401279 **Fax:** 02075-401-848
**Web:** www.tateandlylesugars.com
**Reg No:** 7318607 **VAT No:** 994463471
**Estd:** 1986 Private Limited Company
**Line of Business:** Sugar refining
**Trading Style:** Tate & Lyle Sugars
**Issued Capital:** £200
**Directors:** J Widmer, G Smith, I D Bacon, D Romain, A Tabernilla, R Sproull
**Co. Secretary:** Paul Stebbings
**US SIC:** 2062, 7392
**UK SIC:** 42000, 83951

**Auditors:** KPMG LLP

| | 29-09-13 | 30-09-12 | 25-09-11 |
|---|---|---|---|
| TO | 614,307,000 | 516,684,000 | 457,408,000 |
| P/L | 26,543,000 | 5,375,000 | (42,871,000) |
| NW | 65,396,000 | 43,144,000 | 46,026,000 |
| WC | 49,155,000 | 16,925,000 | 15,523,000 |
| Emp. | 506 | 502 | 542 |

DUNS 21-132-4522

## Tandom Metallurgical Group Ltd

Radnor Park Industrial Estate, Congleton, Cheshire CW12 4XE
**Web:** www.tandom.co.uk
**Reg No:** 6661279 **Estd:** 2008 Private Limited Company
**Line of Business:** Aluminium production
**Export Sales:** £21,891,805
**Issued Capital:** £286
**Directors:** T Muir, Dr R Chalabi, P M Dines
**Co. Secretary:** Andrew Lumsden
**Responsibilities**
**Senior:** Peter Nix *(Manager)*, Ruth Nix *(Manager)*, Thomas Pearce *(Manager)*
**US SIC:** 8999 **UK SIC:** 83954
**Auditors:** Bennett Verby LLP

| | 31-08-13 | 31-08-12 | 31-08-11 |
|---|---|---|---|
| TO | 58,210,971 | 44,037,495 | 36,287,030 |
| P/L | 1,942,605 | 1,304,000 | 2,004,275 |
| NW | 3,886,157 | 3,111,569 | 2,388,344 |
| WC | 1,141,558 | 1,344,258 | 1,610,302 |
| Emp. | 66 | 54 | 42 |

DUNS 22-548-1076

## Tandridge District Council

Station Road East, Oxted, Surrey RH8 0BT
**Web:** www.tandridge.gov.uk
**Estd:** 1974
**Line of Business:** The dss
**Directors:** K Dunbar, B W Farrell, P J Thomas, J Smith
**Responsibilities**
**Senior:** Keith Price *(Assistant Chief Executive Offi)*, Louise Round *(CEO, Managing Director)*
**Marketing:** Giuseppina Valenza *(Marketing Manager)*
**Sales:** Paul Newdick *(Head of Planning Policy)*
**Health & Safety:** Hilary New *(Community Safety Manager)*
**Facilities:** Jayne Godden-Miller *(Chief Housing Officer)*
**Operations:** Stephen Blount *(Project Control Manager)*
**Branches:** Tandridge District Council, Harestone Valley Road, Caterham, Surrey CR3 6HY
**US SIC:** 9121 **UK SIC:** 91110
**Bankers:** National Westminster Bank Plc (60-04-35)
**Employees:** 300

DUNS 21-595-5258

## Tanfast

6 St Leonards Road, Northampton, Northamptonshire NN4 8DP
**Estd:** 2002 Proprietorship
**Line of Business:** Hairdressers (unisex)
**Proprietor:** C Goodman
**Responsibilities**
**Senior:** Robert Gluth *(Manager)*, Hamish Prentice *(Manager)*
**US SIC:** 7231 **UK SIC:** 98200
**Employees:** 46

DUNS 23-979-2810

## Tangent Communications Plc

Threeways House, 40-44 Clipstone Street, London W1W 5DW
**Tel:** 020-7462-6100 **Fax:** 02075626111
**Web:** www.tangentuk.com
**Reg No:** 3967805 **Estd:** 2000 Public Limited Company
**Line of Business:** Holding companies management activities
**Export Sales:** £3,806,000
**Issued Capital:** £2,788,130
**Directors:** D A Steyn, K J Cameron, T B Green, M P Green, N E Kissack, N D Green
**Co. Secretary:** Kevin Cameron
**Responsibilities**
**Senior:** Tony Mason *(Production Director)*
**Sales:** Andy Davis *(Sales Director)*
**Purchasing:** Tony Mason *(Production Director)*
**Engineering:** Tony Mason *(Production Director)*
**US SIC:** 6711 **UK SIC:** 83962
**Auditors:** UHY Hacker Young
**Bankers:** HSBC Bank plc (40-05-30)

| | 28-02-14 | 28-02-13 | 29-02-12 |
|---|---|---|---|
| TO | 27,032,000 | 24,289,000 | 21,724,000 |
| P/L | 2,326,000 | 856,000 | 1,454,000 |
| NW | 6,176,000 | 5,178,000 | 4,109,000 |
| WC | 4,186,000 | 3,176,000 | 2,316,000 |
| Emp. | 276 | 274 | 249 |

DUNS 39-159-0635 **Exp**

## Tangent International Group Plc

11 Woodbrook Crescent, Billericay, Essex CM12 0EQ
**Fax:** 01277-633133
**Web:** www.tangent-international.com
**Reg No:** 2110920 **Estd:** 1987 Public Limited Company
**Line of Business:** Employment and recruitment companies and consultants
**Export Markets:** Europe
**Export Sales:** £30,724,688
**Issued Capital:** £1,040,350
**Principals:** W J Smallbone *(Chairman)*, G A Slyfield *(Managing)*, Mrs L Smallbone
**Co. Secretary:** Tkb Registrars Ltd
**Responsibilities**
**Marketing:** Sharon Cripps *(Administrator)*
**Admin:** Sharon Cripps *(Administrator)*
**Health & Safety:** Sharon Cripps *(Administrator)*
**Branches:** Tangent International Group Plc, Free Trade Wharf Suite 3, 350, The Highway, London E1W 3HU
**US SIC:** 6711 **UK SIC:** 83962
**Auditors:** Ernst & Young LLP
**Bankers:** Lloyds TSB Bank plc (30-97-13)

| | 31-03-14 | 31-03-13 | 31-03-12 |
|---|---|---|---|
| TO | 44,643,667 | 47,175,279 | 37,637,631 |
| P/L | 424,748 | 917,679 | 543,804 |
| NW | 3,578,424 | 3,643,306 | 3,321,303 |
| WC | 3,463,989 | 3,535,719 | 3,223,424 |
| Emp. | 64 | 67 | 54 |

DUNS 29-761-9652 **Imp**

## Tangerine Confectionery Ltd

(**Subsidiary of:** Taurus 3 Ltd)
Quality House, Vicarage Lane, Blackpool, Lancashire FY4 4NQ
**Tel:** 01253-761-201
**Web:** www.tangerineuk.net
**Reg No:** 2025064 **VAT No:** 529600742
**Estd:** 1986 Private Limited Company
**Line of Business:** Manufacture of sugar confectionery
**Export Sales:** £17,505,000
**Issued Capital:** £5,481,405
**Directors:** B Testard, R De Botton, S F Joseph, A D Roux, P L Sanders, J A Langan, A Hawley, L Y Assant
**Co. Secretary:** Clive Burnett
**Responsibilities**
**Senior:** Richard Brittle *(Manager)*, Eve Juhasz *(Director)*, David Prosser *(Manufacturing Director)*, Keiron Russell *(Director)*
**Sales:** Carolyn Roberts *(Office Manager)*
**Admin:** Carolyn Roberts *(Office Manager)*
**Operations:** Carolyn Roberts *(Office Manager)*
**Branches:** Tangerine Confectionery Ltd, Monkhill, Ferrybridge Road, Pontefract, West Yorkshire WF8 2JS
**US SIC:** 2065, 6711
**UK SIC:** 42142, 83962
**Auditors:** KPMG LLP
**Bankers:** Bank Of Scotland (80-20-00)

| | 31-12-13 | 31-12-12 | 31-12-11 |
|---|---|---|---|
| TO | 169,743,000 | 169,074,000 | 156,600,000 |
| P/L | 4,910,000 | 3,029,000 | 30,000 |
| NW | 17,085,000 | 13,081,000 | 10,068,000 |
| WC | 19,294,000 | 23,893,000 | 24,273,000 |
| Emp. | 1,554 | 1,577 | 1,282 |

DUNS 77-493-1992

## Tangerine Holdings Ltd

Docklands, Lytham St Annes, Lancashire FY8 5AQ
**Tel:** 01253667420
**Web:** www.tangerineholdings.co.uk
**Reg No:** 2976538 **Estd:** 1994 Private Limited Company
**Line of Business:** Holding companies management activities
**Export Sales:** £5,263,073
**Issued Capital:** £102,088
**Director:** Ms S Haythornthwaite
**Co. Secretary:** David Haythornthwaite
**US SIC:** 6711 **UK SIC:** 83962
**Auditors:** Haworth Moore

| | 30-06-13 | 30-06-12 | 30-06-11 |
|---|---|---|---|
| TO | 16,082,582 | 13,978,198 | 12,775,373 |
| P/L | 1,421,687 | 1,150,680 | 923,631 |
| NW | 3,432,082 | 2,274,129 | 1,553,222 |
| WC | 376,550 | (757,013) | (816,373) |
| Emp. | 136 | 123 | 114 |

DUNS 21-741-6511

## Tanglewood Care Homes Ltd

2 Endeavour Park, Wyberton, Boston, Lincolnshire PE21 7TQ
**Tel:** 01205358888
**Web:** www.tanglewoodcarehomes.co.uk
**Reg No:** 7745826 **Estd:** 2011 Private Limited Company
**Line of Business:** Management activities of holding companies
**Issued Capital:** £100
**Directors:** M Shelbourn, Mrs T A Shelbourn
**US SIC:** 6711 **UK SIC:** 83962
**Bankers:** National Westminster Bank Plc (60-13-15)

| | 31-01-14 | 31-01-13 | 31-01-12 |
|---|---|---|---|
| TO | 9,069,742 | 8,079,863 | 1,944,387 |
| P/L | 573,935 | 35,996 | 1,048,312 |
| NW | 12,435,701 | 7,386,269 | 7,846,243 |
| WC | (11,740,445) | 86,647 | 380,423 |
| Emp. | 488 | 496 | 467 |

DUNS 21-093-0389

## Tanglewood Nursing Home

36 Louth Road, Horncastle, Lincolnshire LN9 5EN
**Tel:** 01507527265
**Web:** www.housecarehealthcare.co.uk
**Estd:** 1988 Partnership
**Line of Business:** Nursing homes
**Partners:** Mrs T Shellbourne, M Shellbourne
**Responsibilities**
**Senior:** Emmail Shalborne *(CEO, Managing Director)*, Gillian Vernon *(Manager)*
**Branches:** Tanglewood Nursing Home, London Road, Boston, Lincolnshire PE21 7HB
**US SIC:** 8051 **UK SIC:** 95100
**Employees:** 50

DUNS 23-590-0321 **Imp**

## Tangmere Airfield Nurseries Ltd

(**Subsidiary of:** Basel Trust Corporation (Channel Islands) Ltd)
The Old Airfield, Tangmere, Chichester, West Sussex PO20 2GP
**Tel:** 01243-533696
**Web:** www.tangmere.co.uk
**Reg No:** 2263381 **VAT No:** 503818362
**Estd:** 1988 Private Limited Company
**Line of Business:** Growing of vegetables, horticultural specialities and nursery products
**Issued Capital:** £100,000
**Principals:** D Houweling *(Managing)*, D J Houweling
**Co. Secretary:** Robert Searle
**Responsibilities**
**Senior:** Keith Tiffany *(Finance Director)*
**Finance:** Keith Tiffany *(Finance Director)*
**US SIC:** 0161 **UK SIC:** 01001
**Auditors:** Spofforths LLP
**Bankers:** HSBC Bank plc (40-17-16)

| | 31-12-13 | 31-12-12 | 31-12-11 |
|---|---|---|---|
| TO | 32,441,801 | 33,396,000 | 33,090,000 |
| P/L | 573,851 | 2,019,000 | 518,000 |
| NW | 24,794,148 | 21,665,000 | 20,256,000 |
| WC | 8,107,579 | 7,202,000 | 5,533,000 |
| Emp. | 174 | 135 | 130 |

DUNS 22-027-2228

## Tango Security Ltd

Suite 453, 35, Frimley High Street, Camberley, Surrey GU16 7JQ
**Tel:** 01252650677
**Web:** www.tangosec.co.uk
**Reg No:** 4029814 **Estd:** 2000 Private Limited Company
**Line of Business:** Security and related activities
**Issued Capital:** £100
**Director:** M R Lockwood
**Co. Secretary:** Rodney Lockwood
**US SIC:** 7393 **UK SIC:** 83954
**Bankers:** Abbey National Treasury Services Plc (09-00-25)

| | 31-07-13 | 31-07-12 | 31-07-11 |
|---|---|---|---|
| TO | 452,712 | 402,623 | 308,192 |
| P/L | 7,241 | (17,793) | 978 |
| NW | (16,875) | (38,743) | (22,576) |
| WC | (19,317) | (41,999) | (26,918) |

DUNS 73-703-9300

## The Tank Museum Ltd

Bovington, Wareham, Dorset BH20 6JG
**Tel:** 01929405096
**Web:** www.tankmuseum.org
**Reg No:** 4962619 **Estd:** 2003 Private Company Limited By Guarantee
**Line of Business:** Operation of arts facilities
**Directors:** I M Wylie, D R Snow, M G Whitmore, M Gibb, Brigadier P D Hankinson, R S Wigley, R M Ogorkiewicz, J L Stace
**Co. Secretary:** Steven Dolan
**Responsibilities**
**Senior:** James Everard *(Director)*, Mike Hayton *(Workshop Manager)*, Jeremy Pope *(Director)*, Andrew Ridgway *(Director)*, Steven Rowbotham *(Director)*, Sarah Rutherford-Jones *(Director)*
**US SIC:** 8411 **UK SIC:** 97700
**Bankers:** Allied Irish Bank (gb) (23-83-95)

| | 31-12-13 | 31-12-12 | 31-12-11 |
|---|---|---|---|
| TO | 4,504,456 | 3,828,342 | 3,117,044 |
| P/L | 1,563,639 | 962,675 | (166,528) |
| NW | 18,890,439 | 17,156,668 | 16,083,352 |
| WC | 1,256,516 | 1,959,819 | 1,559,498 |
| Emp. | 61 | 54 | 55 |

DUNS 21-323-9908 **Imp-Exp**

## Tanks & Vessels Industries Ltd

Bankwood Lane Industrial Estate, Bankwood Lane, New Rossington, Doncaster, South Yorkshire DN11 0PS
**Tel:** 01302-867328 **Fax:** 01302-864990
**Web:** www.tanksandvessels.com
**Reg No:** 1307388 **VAT No:** 295297214
**Estd:** 1978 Private Limited Company
**Line of Business:** Manufacture of furnaces and furnace burners
**Export Markets:** Middle East; Far East; European Union (E U); Europe; Caribbean; Australasia; S America; Africa; U S A; Canada
**Trading Style:** Tanks & Vessels Industries
**Issued Capital:** £49,000
**Managing Director:** A D Morris
**Co. Secretary:** George Smith
**Branches:** Tanks & Vessels Industries Ltd, Bottle & Case Division, Bankwood La, New Rossington, Doncaster, South Yorkshire DN11 0PS
**US SIC:** 3999, 3551
**UK SIC:** 49590, 32441
**Auditors:** PricewaterhouseCoopers
**Bankers:** Yorkshire Bank Plc (05-04-14)

| | 30-04-14 | 30-04-13 | 30-04-12 |
|---|---|---|---|
| TA | 12,091,184 | 12,340,951 | 12,196,647 |
| NW | 7,442,726 | 7,417,107 | 7,660,737 |
| WC | 553,316 | 482,099 | 532,402 |

DUNS 42-449-3166 **Exp**

## Tann Uk Ltd

(**Subsidiary of:** Eurasia Invest Holding Ag)
Shaw Lane, Glossop, Derbyshire SK13 6EE
**Tel:** 01457-842600
**Web:** www.tanngroup.com
**Reg No:** 4436961 **Estd:** 2002 Private Limited Company
**Line of Business:** Paper merchants
**Export Sales:** £4,678,000
**Trading Style:** Tann Uk Limited
**Issued Capital:** £1,650,000
**Directors:** Ms C Trierenberg, G Gocek, T Interthal
**Co. Secretary:** Squire Sanders Secretarial Servi
**Responsibilities**
**Senior:** Lukas Jungreithmeir *(MD in austrian branch)*, Peter Rawlings *(Production Manager)*, Christian Trierenberg *(owner)*
**Health & Safety:** Paul Jenner *(Technical Manager)*
**Facilities:** Steve Cervi *(Maintenance Manager)*
**Operations:** Paul Jenner *(Technical Manager)*, Peter Rawlings *(Production Manager)*
**Engineering:** Steve Cervi *(Maintenance Manager)*, Peter Rawlings *(Production Manager)*
**US SIC:** 5199, 2752
**UK SIC:** 61900, 47544
**Auditors:** KPMG LLP

| | 31-12-13 | 31-12-12 | 31-12-11 |
|---|---|---|---|
| TO | 7,104,000 | 10,087,000 | 10,225,000 |
| P/L | 1,024,000 | 1,389,000 | 2,306,000 |
| NW | 3,530,000 | 4,673,000 | 4,916,000 |
| WC | 1,280,000 | 2,344,000 | 2,433,000 |
| Emp. | 59 | 61 | 61 |

DUNS 51-576-6819

## Tanner Automotive Ltd

277 Finchley Road, London NW3 6LT
**Tel:** 02035535604
**Web:** www.alandayvw.co.uk
**Reg No:** 5857937 **Estd:** 2006 Private Limited Company
**Line of Business:** Sale of new motor vehicles
**Issued Capital:** £200,000
**Director:** P J Tanner
**Co. Secretary:** Brian Searle
**US SIC:** 5511 **UK SIC:** 65100
**Bankers:** National Westminster Bank Plc (57-00-00)

| | 31-12-13 | 31-12-12 | 31-12-11 |
|---|---|---|---|
| TO | 70,771,261 | 68,496,142 | 62,104,617 |
| P/L | 664,159 | 78,279 | 159,697 |
| NW | 1,933,318 | 847,595 | 680,280 |
| WC | 1,257,132 | 210,222 | 1,169,819 |
| Emp. | 196 | 191 | 194 |

DUNS 21-827-2730 **Imp**

## Tanners (Shrewsbury) Ltd

26 Wyle Cop, Shrewsbury, Shropshire SY1 1XD
**Tel:** 01743-234500 **Fax:** 01743-234501
**Web:** www.tannerswines.co.uk
**Reg No:** 0111232 **Estd:** 1910 Private Limited Company
**Line of Business:** Wholesale of wine, beer, spirits and other alcoholic beverages
**Issued Capital:** £19,444
**Directors:** J J Tanner, Mrs K E Tanner, R J Morgan
**Co. Secretary:** Robert Morgan
**Branches:** Tanners (Shrewsbury) Ltd, 4 St. Peters Square, Hereford, Herefordshire HR1 2PG

**US SIC:** 5182, 5921, 6711
**UK SIC:** 61700, 64200, 83962
**Auditors:** Bentley Jennison
**Bankers:** Lloyds TSB Bank plc (30-97-62)

| | 31-05-14 | 31-05-13 | 31-05-12 |
|---|---|---|---|
| TO | 18,754,888 | 17,543,788 | 18,623,857 |
| P/L | 381,639 | (200,652) | 194,532 |
| NW | 3,811,703 | 3,563,019 | 3,176,939 |
| WC | 1,261,773 | 1,023,957 | 1,089,279 |
| Emp. | 101 | 97 | 101 |

DUNS 21-590-7502 Imp-Exp

## Tannoy Ltd

Ramoan Farm, Coatbridge Road, Coatbridge, Lanarkshire ML5 2PU
**Tel:** 01236-420199 **Fax:** 01236-428230
**Web:** www.tannoy.com
**Reg No:** 0498558 **Estd:** 1926 Private Limited Company
**Line of Business:** Manufacture of television and radio receivers, sound or video recording or reproducing apparatus and associated goods
**Export Markets:** Europe, North America, Middle East, Australasia, Far East
**Issued Capital:** £100
**Directors:** A M Sosna, C Berner Nielsen, H Lundum, A B Fauerskov
**Co. Secretary:** Anders Fisker
**Responsibilities**
**Senior:** Danny McGoogan *(Warehouse Supervisor)*
**Finance:** Lorraine Macdonald *(Payroll Manager)*
**Marketing:** Mark Flannagan *(Marketing Manager)*
**Sales:** Tim Lount *(Sales Manager)*
**IT:** Fraser Sanaghan *(IT Coordinator)*
**Facilities:** Clephane Frame *(Facilities Manager)*
**Branches:** Tannoy Ltd, Coronation Rd, Cressex Ind Est, Buckinghamshire High Wycombe
**US SIC:** 3651 **UK SIC:** 34541
**Auditors:** KPMG LLP
**Bankers:** Barclays Bank Plc (20-79-25)

| | 30-06-14 | 30-06-13 | 30-06-12 |
|---|---|---|---|
| TO | 20,674,000 | 19,693,000 | 16,872,000 |
| P/L | 779,000 | 466,000 | (1,710,000) |
| NW | 3,931,000 | 2,892,000 | 2,415,000 |
| WC | 4,055,000 | 3,846,000 | 3,310,000 |
| Emp. | 86 | 87 | 98 |

DUNS 22-258-2194

## Tant Laboratories Ltd

(**Subsidiary of:** Lenstec (Holdings) Ltd)
17 London Road Twyford Business Centre, Bishops Stortford, Hertfordshire CM23 3YT
**Tel:** 01279653785 **Fax:** 01279-713170
**Web:** www.tantlabs.com
**Reg No:** 4276285 **Estd:** 1901 Private Limited Company
**Line of Business:** Manufacturers of optical products
**Issued Capital:** £65,000
**Directors:** N Castle, M G Burroughs
**Co. Secretary:** Gerard Donovan
**Responsibilities**
**Senior:** Gez Donavan *(Manager)*
**US SIC:** 3861 **UK SIC:** 37330

| | 30-04-14 | 30-04-13 | 30-04-12 |
|---|---|---|---|
| TO | 7,063,661 | N/A | N/A |
| P/L | 504,817 | N/A | N/A |
| NW | 1,705,550 | 1,188,811 | 814,352 |
| WC | 1,044,168 | 689,891 | 386,505 |
| Emp. | 52 | N/A | N/A |

DUNS 21-893-7092 Imp

## Tanvic Group Ltd

96 Appleton Gate, Newark, Nottinghamshire NG24 1LS
**Tel:** 01636704166 **Fax:** 01636675221
**Web:** www.tanvicgroup.co.uk
**Reg No:** 0985614 **VAT No:** 117070991
**Estd:** 1970 Private Limited Company
**Line of Business:** Maintenance and repair of motor vehicles
**Trading Style:** Tanvic Spares, Tanvic Tyre & Service Centre, We Sell Tyres (Wholesale).
**Issued Capital:** £163,838
**Principals:** V Thompson *(Managing)*, A Zelos, K Bennett
**Co. Secretary:** Stephen Mccracken
**Branches:** Tanvic Group Ltd, 37 Derby Road, Loughborough, Leicestershire LE11 5AD
**US SIC:** 7539, 5531
**UK SIC:** 67100, 65100
**Auditors:** H.W. East Midlands Audit LLP
**Bankers:** Lloyds TSB Bank plc (77-16-01)

| | 31-12-13 | 31-12-12 | 31-12-11 |
|---|---|---|---|
| TO | 50,804,508 | 46,480,725 | 46,381,566 |
| P/L | 2,974,118 | 2,749,775 | 2,607,406 |
| NW | 18,243,900 | 16,346,150 | 14,450,551 |
| WC | 6,648,847 | 5,318,497 | 3,687,375 |
| Emp. | 248 | 249 | 249 |

DUNS 29-240-6410 Exp

## Tapestry Mm Ltd

(**Subsidiary of:** Ironfist Ltd)
51 52 Frith Street, London W1D 4SH
**Tel:** 020-7896-3000 **Fax:** 02078963339
**Web:** www.tapestrymm.com
**Reg No:** 1273835 **VAT No:** 234865054
**Estd:** 1972 Private Limited Company
**Line of Business:** Photographic processing
**Export Markets:** Europe
**Issued Capital:** £2,011,110
**Director:** Ms A M Green
**Co. Secretary:** Keith Green
**Responsibilities**
**Senior:** Jeff Keene *(Chairman)*, Kevin Mccormack *(Manager)*
**US SIC:** 8911 **UK SIC:** 83701
**Auditors:** HLB Av Audit PLC
**Bankers:** Lloyds TSB Bank plc (30-92-90)

| | 31-12-13 | 31-12-12 | 31-12-11 |
|---|---|---|---|
| TO | N/A | 5,956,256 | 6,912,594 |
| P/L | N/A | (18,352) | (275,560) |
| NW | 1,417,540 | 746,472 | 717,006 |
| WC | 1,182,686 | 460,709 | 340,414 |
| Emp. | N/A | 89 | 86 |

DUNS 28-856-6441

## Tapper & Son (Poole) Ltd

32 - 34 Parkstone Road, Poole, Dorset BH15 2QA
**Tel:** 01202-673164 **Fax:** 01202-661155
**Web:** www.tapperfuneralservice.co.uk
**Reg No.** 0014007 **Estd:** 1061 Private Limited Company
**Line of Business:** Funeral directors
**Trading Style:** Tapper Funeral Service
**Issued Capital:** £100
**Principals:** S J Tapper *(Managing)*, C J Tapper *(Financial)*, A Rice, Ms J A Tapper, P C Crutcher, P C Tapper
**Co. Secretary:** Steven Tapper
**Responsibilities**
**Senior:** Colin Hayley *(Manager)*, Julian Hayley *(Manager)*
**Admin:** Jan Wharmby *(Admin Manager)*
**Branches:** Tapper & Son (Poole) Ltd, 51-53 Old Milton Road, New Milton, Hampshire BH25 6DJ
**US SIC:** 7261 **UK SIC:** 98902
**Auditors:** Rothman Pantall & Co

| | 30-09-13 | 30-09-12 | 30-09-11 |
|---|---|---|---|
| TO | 6,005,808 | 5,341,624 | 5,144,876 |
| P/L | 1,017,472 | 1,026,804 | 1,116,112 |
| NW | 7,470,090 | 6,735,663 | 5,978,324 |
| WC | 190,445 | (20,557) | (357,271) |
| Emp. | 69 | 66 | 64 |

DUNS 37-782-4701

## Tapper Funeral Service

173 Lower Blandford Road, Broadstone, Dorset BH18 8DH
**Tel:** 01202-694449
**Web:** www.tapperfuneralservice.co.uk
**Estd:** 2002 Proprietorship
**Line of Business:** Funeral directors
**Proprietor:** C Tapper
**Responsibilities**
**HR:** Simon Spendlowe *(Health and Safety HR Director)*
**US SIC:** 7261 **UK SIC:** 98902
**Employees:** 60

DUNS 21-883-1527 Imp

## Tappex Thread Inserts Ltd

Masons Road, Stratford-Upon-Avon, Warwickshire CV37 9NT
**Fax:** 01789414194
**Web:** www.tappex.co.uk
**Reg No:** 0575166 **Estd:** 1956 Private Limited Company
**Line of Business:** Engineers (general)
**Export Sales:** £4,595,471
**Issued Capital:** £9,000
**Managing Director:** T J Barnsdale
**Co. Secretary:** Mrs Jennifer Bebbington
**US SIC:** 3452 **UK SIC:** 31371
**Auditors:** Grant Thornton UK LLP
**Bankers:** HSBC Bank plc (40-45-25)

| | 31-12-13 | 31-12-12 | 31-12-11 |
|---|---|---|---|
| TO | 6,977,817 | 6,426,379 | 6,672,827 |
| P/L | 455,293 | 382,256 | 809,456 |
| NW | 7,396,506 | 7,069,947 | 6,780,879 |
| WC | 6,229,337 | 5,905,111 | 5,708,506 |
| Emp. | 68 | 64 | 67 |

DUNS 21-881-6069

## Tappins Coaches Ltd

169 Greenham Busniess Park, Thatcham, Berkshire RG19 6HN
**Tel:** 01865772778
**Web:** www.tappins.co.uk
**Reg No:** 6065092 **Estd:** 2008 Private Limited Company
**Line of Business:** Coach and bus hire
**Issued Capital:** £1
**Directors:** S Weaver, Ms M Wadsworth
**Co. Secretary:** Ms Michelle Wadsworth
**US SIC:** 4119 **UK SIC:** 72200

| | 31-03-14 | 31-03-13 | 31-03-11 |
|---|---|---|---|
| TO | 3,385,475 | 3,127,971 | N/A |
| P/L | 152,779 | 1,030,365 | N/A |
| NW | 561,376 | 421,673 | (608,692) |
| WC | 418,454 | 419,913 | (147,100) |

DUNS 21-777-9967

## Tapton Park Innovation Centre

Tapton Park Innovation Centre, Chesterfield, Derbyshire S41 0TZ
**Tel:** 01246231234
**Web:** www.chesterfield.gov.uk
**Estd:** 1997 Proprietorship
**Line of Business:** Office rental
**Proprietor:** R Harvey
**Responsibilities**
**Senior:** Teri-Louise Horne *(CEO, Managing Director)*
**US SIC:** 7392 **UK SIC:** 83951
**Employees:** 131

DUNS 77-976-1498

## Taptonville House Ltd

Taptonville House, 1 Taptonville Road, Sheffield, South Yorkshire S10 5BQ
**Tel:** 08451227787 **Fax:** 01142-670200
**Web:** www.taptonvillehouse.com
**Reg No:** 5944622 **Estd:** 1996 Private Limited Company
**Line of Business:** Other human health activities
**Issued Capital:** £20
**Director:** Ms S Mallon
**Co. Secretary:** Nigel Mallon
**Responsibilities**
**Senior:** Angela Wraith *(Practice Manager)*
**US SIC:** 8091 **UK SIC:** 95200

| | 31-03-14 | 31-03-13 | 31-03-12 |
|---|---|---|---|
| TA | 1,274,477 | 1,050,107 | 858,455 |
| NW | 347,991 | 244,756 | 160,136 |
| WC | 147,371 | 63,931 | 53,697 |

DUNS 51-659-1760

## Taqa Bratani Ltd

Prospect Road, West Hill, Westhill, Aberdeenshire AB32 6FE
**Tel:** 01224275275
**Web:** www.taqa.ae
**Reg No:** 5975475 **Estd:** 2006 Private Limited Company
**Line of Business:** Other business activities not elsewhere classified
**Directors:** P D Jones, E D Lafehr
**Co. Secretary:** Carl Sheldon
**Branches:** Taqa Bratani Ltd, Prospect Road, Arnhall Business Park, Westhill, Aberdeenshire AB32 6FE
**US SIC:** 7399 **UK SIC:** 83954
**Auditors:** Ernst & Young LLP
**Employees:** 293
**Turnover:** £1,831,021,000

DUNS 29-584-3460

## Tara Developments Ltd

13a Parkhill Road, Burntwood, Staffordshire WS7 2ER
**Tel:** 01543670686
**Reg No:** 1946080 **Estd:** 1997 Private Limited Company
**Line of Business:** Management activities of holding companies
**Issued Capital:** £1,307,500
**Director:** N S Sweeney
**Co. Secretary:** Mrs Mary Sweeney
**Responsibilities**
**Senior:** Baljinder Gill *(Proprietor)*
**US SIC:** 6711 **UK SIC:** 83962
**Auditors:** PricewaterhouseCoopers LLP

| | 31-12-13 | 31-12-12 | 31-12-11 |
|---|---|---|---|
| TO | 53,399,384 | 41,535,698 | 30,257,471 |
| P/L | 3,638,382 | 2,188,856 | 1,444,064 |
| NW | 16,328,767 | 13,989,187 | 12,416,330 |
| WC | 14,681,314 | 11,998,412 | 11,363,203 |
| Emp. | 101 | 103 | 138 |

DUNS 21-147-7742

## Tarak Retail Ltd

(**Subsidiary of:** Shoar (Holdings) Ltd)
61 Hydepark Street, Glasgow, Lanarkshire G3 8BW
**Tel:** 01415691544
**Reg No:** 0352770SC **Estd:** 2008 Private Limited Company
**Line of Business:** Retail sale of clothing
**Issued Capital:** £10,000
**Directors:** K Akram, M T Ramzan, O Aziz, K Ramzan, S M Ramzan
**Co. Secretary:** Sheraz Ramzan
**US SIC:** 5699 **UK SIC:** 64500
**Bankers:** Lloyds TSB Bank plc (30-13-53)

| | 31-03-14 | 31-03-13 | 31-03-12 |
|---|---|---|---|
| TO | 14,325,931 | 10,053,179 | N/A |
| P/L | 1,065,910 | 878,575 | N/A |
| NW | 990,354 | 983,688 | 299,974 |
| WC | (332,567) | 1,624 | (166,846) |
| Emp. | 369 | 235 | N/A |

DUNS 23-623-2625

## Tardis Environmental Uk Ltd

(**Subsidiary of:** Tardis Environmental Uk (Holdings) Ltd)
74 Cannock Road, Willenhall, West Midlands WV12 5RZ
**Tel:** 01922402410 **Fax:** 01922402085
**Web:** www.tardishire.co.uk
**Reg No:** 2581818 **VAT No:** 559500922
**Estd:** 1991 Private Limited Company
**Line of Business:** Collection and treatment of other waste
**Trading Style:** Tardis
**Issued Capital:** £100
**Principals:** C Boydon *(Managing)*, A Boydon, Miss K Boydon, R Boydon, D Furlong
**Co. Secretary:** Mrs Jennifer Causer
**Branches:** Tardis Environmental Uk Ltd, Leighmore Enterprise Park, Fryers Road, Walsall, West Midlands WS2 7LZ
**US SIC:** 4953, 8999
**UK SIC:** 92110, 83954
**Auditors:** Crutchley & Associates
**Bankers:** Lloyds TSB Bank plc (30-99-63)

| | 28-02-14 | 28-02-13 | 29-02-12 |
|---|---|---|---|
| TO | 8,743,652 | 7,859,055 | 6,634,836 |
| P/L | 2,112,040 | 1,697,141 | 1,579,674 |
| NW | 3,505,562 | 1,889,196 | 4,606,578 |
| WC | 1,476,244 | (317,627) | 2,574,581 |
| Emp. | 69 | 74 | 60 |

DUNS 76-853-2525

## Targe Towing Ltd

Mountboy, Montrose, Angus DD10 9TN
**Tel:** 01674-820234
**Web:** www.targetowing.co.uk
**Reg No:** 0131733SC **VAT No:** 561716931
**Estd:** 1991 Private Limited Company
**Line of Business:** Towing services
**Issued Capital:** £100
**Principals:** T R Woolley *(Managing)*, N R Dorman, M K Cloodts
**Co. Secretary:** Ms Josephine Woolley
**Responsibilities**
**Senior:** Charles Manning *(Manager)*
**Branches:** Targe Towing Ltd, Berthing Masters Office, Albert Quay, Aberdeen, Aberdeenshire AB11 5QA
**US SIC:** 4789 **UK SIC:** 77002
**Auditors:** Murray Taylor & Co
**Bankers:** The Royal Bank Of Scotland Plc (83-25-16)

| | 31-10-14 | 31-10-13 | 30-10-12 |
|---|---|---|---|
| TO | N/A | 8,422,090 | N/A |
| P/L | N/A | 6,426,669 | N/A |
| NW | 13,367,046 | 11,990,023 | 7,015,625 |
| WC | 11,605,987 | 9,791,348 | 5,441,237 |

DUNS 49-148-3814 Imp

## Target Components Ltd

Unit 5 Pioneer Way, Pioneer Way, Castleford, West Yorkshire WF10 5QU
**Tel:** 01977-739300 **Fax:** 01977739301
**Web:** www.targetcomponents.co.uk
**Reg No:** 3113281 **VAT No:** 660103090
**Estd:** 1998 Private Limited Company
**Line of Business:** Manufacturers of electronic equipment and components
**Export Sales:** £873,135
**Issued Capital:** £200,000
**Principals:** P Cubbage *(Managing)*, Dr I D Prescott
**Co. Secretary:** Ms Susan Miller
**Responsibilities**
**Senior:** Daniel Pawson *(Computer Manager)*
**IT:** Daniel Pawson *(Computer Manager)*
**US SIC:** 3679 **UK SIC:** 34542
**Auditors:** Garbutt & Elliott LLP
**Bankers:** The Royal Bank Of Scotland Plc (16-34-80)

| | 31-03-14 | 31-03-13 | 31-03-12 |
|---|---|---|---|
| TO | 25,533,255 | 21,510,375 | 20,660,411 |
| P/L | 641,645 | 400,685 | 706,472 |
| NW | 2,592,955 | 2,105,669 | 1,800,338 |
| WC | 2,395,582 | 2,046,961 | 1,739,729 |
| Emp. | 56 | 53 | N/A |

DUNS 34-510-1992

## Target (Conservatories & Windows) Ltd

Queensville Interiors, Stone, Staffordshire ST15 0DJ
**Tel:** 01782398021
**Web:** www.targetwindows.co.uk
**Reg No:** 2715524 **Estd:** 1992 Private Limited Company
**Line of Business:** Double glazing installers
**Issued Capital:** £10,003
**Director:** A D Tune
**Co. Secretary:** Ms Nicola Basnett
**Branches:** Target (Conservatories & Windows) Ltd, 7 Ewell Rd, Grand Pde, Surbiton, Surrey KT6 7BE
**US SIC:** 1721, 1796
**UK SIC:** 50400
**Auditors:** Appletons

**Bankers:** National Westminster Bank Plc (51-61-02)

| | 30-06-13 | 30-06-12 | 30-06-11 |
|---|---|---|---|
| TA | 627,452 | 672,550 | 635,509 |
| NW | 157,124 | 177,104 | 188,279 |
| WC | 110,542 | 125,014 | 127,773 |

DUNS 23-984-3720 Imp

## Target Energy Group Ltd

(**Subsidiary of:** Maqsood Trading Co. (L.L.C.))
Badentoy Road, Badentoy Park Portlethen, Aberdeen, Aberdeenshire AB12 4YA
**Tel:** 01224783999
**Web:** www.target-energy.com
**Reg No:** 0206333SC **VAT No:** 751242555
**Estd:** 2000 Private Limited Company
**Line of Business:** Oil and gas exploration services
**Issued Capital:** £1,054,790
**Directors:** A N Al Mansoori, N A Al Alwai, H M Al Mansoori
**Co. Secretary:** Stronachs Secretaries Limited
**Responsibilities**
**Senior:** Steve Edghill *(Operations Manager)*
**Finance:** George McWilliam *(Finance Manager)*
**Sales:** Jose Patroni *(Senior Account Manager)*
**Operations:** Steve Edghill *(Operations Manager)*
**Engineering:** Ken Maitland *(Technical Manager)*
**US SIC:** 1389 **UK SIC:** 13000
**Auditors:** Deloitte & Touche LLP
**Bankers:** Bank Of Scotland (80-05-14)

| | 31-12-13 | 31-12-12 | 31-12-11 |
|---|---|---|---|
| TO | 15,876,511 | 14,160,425 | 7,559,578 |
| P/L | 2,018,582 | 2,071,210 | (2,048,761) |
| NW | 5,983,247 | 4,368,020 | 2,748,481 |
| WC | 2,832,367 | 985,563 | (527,770) |
| Emp. | 73 | 60 | 54 |

DUNS 23-927-5592

## Target Express Holdings Ltd

(**Subsidiary of:** Rentokil Initial Plc)
Woodlands Park Ashton Road, Newton-Le-Willows, Merseyside WA12 0HF
**Tel:** 01925570000
**Web:** www.city-link.com
**Reg No:** 3917510 **Estd:** 1982 Private Limited Company
**Line of Business:** Goods delivery services
**Trading Style:** City Link Limited
**Issued Capital:** £3,242,278
**Directors:** D P Fagan, J E Hauck
**Co. Secretary:** Ms Alexandra Laan
**Responsibilities**
**Senior:** Stuart Ingall-Tombs *(Director)*
**US SIC:** 4213 **UK SIC:** 72300
**Auditors:** KPMG LLP

| | 31-12-12 | 31-12-11 | 31-12-10 |
|---|---|---|---|
| TA | 98,267,000 | 98,267,000 | 98,267,000 |
| NW | 97,857,000 | 97,857,000 | 97,857,000 |
| WC | 97,857,000 | 97,857,000 | 97,857,000 |

DUNS 22-658-2872 Imp-Exp

## Target Furniture Ltd

(**Subsidiary of:** Target Furniture Group Ltd)
Studland Road, Northampton, Northamptonshire NN2 6PZ
**Tel:** 01604-792929
**Web:** www.targetfurniture.co.uk
**Reg No:** 1364954 **Estd:** 1978 Private Limited Company
**Line of Business:** Manufacture of other furniture
**Export Markets:** E U
**Issued Capital:** £50,000
**Directors:** R Darlow, P A Thomas
**Co. Secretary:** David Green
**Responsibilities**
**IT:** Chris Rimbault *(IT Manager)*
**Branches:** Target Furniture Ltd, Mobbs Miller House, Unit 1, Northampton, Northamptonshire NN1 5LP
**US SIC:** 3423 **UK SIC:** 31612
**Auditors:** Alan Heywood & Co
**Bankers:** National Westminster Bank Plc (56-00-60)

| | 31-12-13 | 31-12-12 | 31-12-11 |
|---|---|---|---|
| TO | 6,685,602 | N/A | 6,032,195 |
| P/L | 227,380 | N/A | 39,741 |
| NW | 1,407,258 | 1,254,123 | 1,533,127 |
| WC | 461,965 | 295,724 | 538,857 |
| Emp. | 81 | N/A | 79 |

DUNS 21-931-4168 Exp

## Target Group Ltd

(**Subsidiary of:** Target Topco Ltd)
Target House, Cowbridge Road East, Cardiff, South Glamorgan CF11 9AU
**Tel:** 08456506200
**Web:** www.targetgroup.net
**Reg No:** 1208137 **VAT No:** 329187730
**Estd:** 1975 Private Limited Company
**Line of Business:** Computer software (development)
**Export Sales:** £3,587,000
**Issued Capital:** £809,745
**Directors:** P M Byrne, W M Alley, R A Houghton, J R Snow, I D Larkin
**Co. Secretary:** Dafydd Bebb
**Responsibilities**
**Senior:** James Rudolf *(Manager)*, Mike Stephen *(Commercial Director)*
**Marketing:** Ann Beynon *(Administrator)*, Kirsten Tedder *(E-Business Strategist)*
**Admin:** Ann Beynon *(Administrator)*
**HR:** Rianna Williams *(Human Resources Director)*
**Branches:** Target Group Ltd, Iupert Street, Bristol, Avon BS1 2QJ
**US SIC:** 7379 **UK SIC:** 83940
**Auditors:** KPMG
**Bankers:** HSBC Bank plc (40-16-18)

| | 31-12-13 | 31-12-12 | 31-12-11 |
|---|---|---|---|
| TO | 34,655,000 | 30,797,000 | 23,978,000 |
| P/L | 817,000 | (13,521,000) | (1,642,000) |
| NW | 220,000 | (9,285,000) | 3,396,000 |
| WC | 8,935,000 | (11,631,000) | 329,000 |
| Emp. | 529 | 558 | 438 |

DUNS 34-799-6316

## Target Housing Ltd

Globe Business Centre, Penistone Road, Sheffield, South Yorkshire S6 3AE
**Tel:** 01142-815888
**Web:** www.targetshoffield.org.uk
**Reg No:** 2787689 **Estd:** 1993 Private Limited Company
**Line of Business:** Charities and charitable organisations
**Trading Style:** Target Housing Limited
**Directors:** Ms M R Oates, Ms M Dover, R Plews, Ms H Millington, J Hicks, M Ellaby, R H Plews
**Co. Secretary:** Shaun Needham
**Responsibilities**
**Senior:** Gillian Black *(Director)*, Jillian Corbett *(Project Manager)*, Margaret Hurley *(Manager)*, Timothy Mappin *(Manager)*, Eric Sainsbury *(Manager)*, Gino Toro *(Chief Executive Officer)*, Sylvia Unwin *(Manager)*
**US SIC:** 8321 **UK SIC:** 96111
**Auditors:** Hawsons
**Bankers:** National Westminster Bank Plc (56-00-09)

| | 31-03-14 | 31-03-13 | 31-03-12 |
|---|---|---|---|
| TO | 4,540,279 | 3,574,085 | 2,436,250 |
| P/L | 246,798 | 34,410 | 96,291 |
| NW | 1,163,907 | 917,109 | 882,699 |
| WC | 543,324 | 290,975 | 486,792 |
| Emp. | 66 | 59 | 53 |

DUNS 34-818-4230

## Target Servicing Ltd

(**Subsidiary of:** Target Topco Ltd)
Imperial Way, Coedkernew, Newport, Gwent NP10 8UH
**Tel:** 08456506200
**Web:** www.targetgroup.com
**Reg No:** 5618062 **Estd:** 2005 Private Limited Company
**Line of Business:** Other software consultancy and supply
**Issued Capital:** £4,000,000
**Directors:** P M Byrne, Mrs S J Colquhoun, J R Snow, S W Haggerty, W M Alley
**Co. Secretary:** Dafydd Bebb
**Responsibilities**
**Senior:** Paddy Byrne *(Chief Executive Officer)*
**US SIC:** 7379 **UK SIC:** 83940

| | 31-12-13 | 31-12-12 | 31-12-11 |
|---|---|---|---|
| TO | 20,620,000 | 19,415,125 | 14,648,384 |
| P/L | 776,000 | (6,507,765) | 371,261 |
| NW | 2,336,000 | 579,375 | 2,087,140 |
| WC | 1,290,000 | (1,552,279) | 99,000 |
| Emp. | 296 | 177 | 225 |

DUNS 22-646-2232

## Target Shopfitters Ltd

17-19 Towerfield Road, Southend-On-Sea, Essex SS3 9QL
**Tel:** 01702296321 **Fax:** 01702297072
**Web:** www.targetshopfitters.co.uk
**Reg No:** 1846887 **VAT No:** 420507103
**Estd:** 1984 Private Limited Company
**Line of Business:** Construction of commercial buildings
**Issued Capital:** £100
**Directors:** V R Chopping, N Reik
**Responsibilities**
**Senior:** Christopher Donald *(Manager)*, Paul Methley *(Manager)*
**US SIC:** 1541 **UK SIC:** 50100
**Auditors:** Segrave & Partners
**Bankers:** National Westminster Bank Plc (56-00-03)

| | 31-12-13 | 31-12-12 | 31-12-11 |
|---|---|---|---|
| TA | 1,092,736 | 1,438,856 | 1,730,397 |
| NW | 198,677 | 209,260 | 868,506 |
| WC | 112,045 | 23,408 | 606,569 |

DUNS 34-648-4041

## Targetfollow Estates Ltd

Riverside House, 11/12 Riverside Road, Norwich, Norfolk NR1 1SQ
**Tel:** 01603-767616
**Web:** www.targetfollow.com
**Reg No:** 2773528 **VAT No:** 651049062
**Estd:** 1992 Private Limited Company
**Line of Business:** Estate management services
**Issued Capital:** £110
**Directors:** C L Thoday, S Naghshineh
**Co. Secretary:** Ardeshir Naghshineh
**Responsibilities**
**Senior:** Nathan Dickinson *(Manager)*, Vanessa Fletcher *(Chairman)*, Tina Moore *(Senior Director)*, Ardeshir Neghohineh *(Manager)*
**US SIC:** 6531 **UK SIC:** 83400
**Auditors:** KPMG LLP
**Bankers:** The Royal Bank Of Scotland Plc (16-26-30)

| | 31-03-14 | 31-12-12 | 31-03-11 |
|---|---|---|---|
| TO | N/A | 2,582,909 | 6,146,801 |
| P/L | N/A | 22,148 | 174,505 |
| NW | (2,115,183) | (2,081,295) | (2,132,611) |
| WC | (2,440,423) | (2,413,106) | (2,563,296) |
| Emp. | N/A | 49 | 92 |

DUNS 22-719-5823 Imp-Exp

## Targus Europe Ltd

(**Subsidiary of:** Targus Group International Inc.)
527 Staines Road, Hounslow, Middlesex TW4 5DZ
**Tel:** 02088312000 **Fax:** 020-8607-7001
**Web:** www.targus.com
**Reg No:** 1743076 **VAT No:** 564278026
**Estd:** 1983 Private Limited Company
**Line of Business:** Manufacturers of pcs
**Export Markets:** European Union (E U)
**Export Sales:** £79,162,000
**Issued Capital:** £10,000
**Directors:** M Dunne, V C Streufert, M P Hoopis
**Responsibilities**
**Senior:** Elizabeth Blanchfield *(Manager)*
**Marketing:** Olli Frankish *(Marketing Director)*
**Operations:** Paula Luxford *(Operations Manager)*
**US SIC:** 3573, 3161
**UK SIC:** 33020, 44201
**Auditors:** Ernst & Young LLP
**Bankers:** Bank Of Scotland (12-01-03)

| | 30-09-13 | 30-09-12 | 30-09-11 |
|---|---|---|---|
| TO | 88,765,000 | 88,445,000 | 74,036,000 |
| P/L | 4,485,000 | 4,711,000 | 2,554,000 |
| NW | 7,121,000 | 12,818,000 | 12,504,000 |
| WC | 6,931,000 | 12,560,000 | 12,153,000 |
| Emp. | 69 | 105 | 69 |

DUNS 21-121-4336

## Tarka Housing Ltd

Tarka House, Clovelly Road Industrial Estate, Bideford, Devon EX39 3HN
**Tel:** 01237428080
**Web:** www.westwardhousing.org.uk
**Reg No:** 0030101IP **Estd:** 2009 Proprietorship
**Line of Business:** Housing associations societies trusts & co-operatives
**Proprietor:** Miss L Shaw
**Responsibilities**
**Senior:** Nigel Barnard *(Manager)*, Nicky Patt *(Personal Assistant)*
**Finance:** Tina Golland *(Finance Officer)*
**US SIC:** 8321 **UK SIC:** 96111
**Bankers:** National Westminster Bank Plc (55-70-01)

| | 31-03-12 | 31-03-11 | 31-03-10 |
|---|---|---|---|
| TO | 6,994,000 | 6,696,000 | 6,365,000 |
| P/L | 1,935,000 | (131,000) | (306,000) |
| NW | 6,132,000 | (2,474,000) | (2,309,000) |
| WC | (517,000) | (231,000) | (299,000) |
| Emp. | 80 | 67 | 66 |

DUNS 22-624-5108 Imp

## Tarkett Ltd

(**Subsidiary of:** Tarkett)
Dickley Lane, Lenham, Maidstone, Kent ME17 2QX
**Tel:** 01622-854000
**Web:** www.tarkett.co.uk
**Reg No:** 1277784 **VAT No:** 830575139
**Estd:** 1956 Private Limited Company
**Line of Business:** Manufacturers and wholesalers of floorcoverings
**Export Sales:** £3,437,000
**Trading Style:** Tarkett Sommer, Field Turf Tarkett
**Issued Capital:** £20,300,000
**Directors:** M Cangelosi, R J Teulings, J Crump
**Co. Secretary:** Christopher Holmes
**Responsibilities**
**Senior:** Dirk Jacobs *(Manager)*, David Jenner *(Director of Production)*
**Health & Safety:** Phil Welch *(Facilities Manager)*
**Facilities:** Phil Welch *(Facilities Manager)*
**Engineering:** Terry Guy *(Engineering Manager)*, David Jenner *(Director of Production)*
**US SIC:** 2279, 3079
**UK SIC:** 43852, 48360
**Auditors:** KPMG LLP
**Bankers:** Barclays Bank Plc (20-07-71)

| | 31-12-13 | 31-12-12 | 31-12-11 |
|---|---|---|---|
| TO | 48,599,000 | 48,201,000 | 47,988,000 |
| P/L | (428,000) | 870,000 | 523,000 |
| NW | 2,746,000 | 1,628,000 | 2,779,000 |
| WC | 3,746,000 | 3,657,000 | 3,125,000 |
| Emp. | 100 | 95 | 105 |

DUNS 49-419-5001

## Tarmac Central Ltd

(**Subsidiary of:** Lafarge Tarmac Holdings Ltd)
Tunstead House, Buxton, Derbyshire SK17 8TG
**Tel:** 08456007008
**Web:** www.tarmac.co.uk
**Reg No:** 3140503 **VAT No:** 532367943
**Estd:** 1995 Private Limited Company
**Line of Business:** Quarrying of stone
**Trading Style:** Tarmac North West
**Issued Capital:** £63,500,000
**Directors:** Lafarge Tarmac Directors (Uk) Li, G F Young, M J Choules, Mrs F P Penhallurick
**Co. Secretary:** Lafarge Tarmac Secretaries (Uk)
**Branches:** Tarmac Central Ltd, Kevin Quarry, Ramshorn, Stoke-On-Trent, Staffordshire ST10 3BX
**US SIC:** 3273, 1499
**UK SIC:** 24360, 23960
**Auditors:** Deloitte & Touche LLP
**Bankers:** Barclays Bank Plc (20-53-77)

| | 31-12-13 | 31-12-12 | 31-12-11 |
|---|---|---|---|
| TA | 114,110,000 | 109,825,000 | 104,876,000 |
| P/L | 4,285,000 | 4,949,000 | 5,204,000 |
| NW | 91,096,000 | 86,811,000 | 83,075,000 |
| WC | 91,096,000 | 86,811,000 | 83,075,000 |

DUNS 76-995-3761

## Tarmac Industrial Minerals Holdings Ltd

(**Subsidiary of:** Lafarge Tarmac Holdings Ltd)
Anglo American House, 20 Carlton House Terrace, London SW1Y 5AN
**Tel:** 02079688631 **Fax:** 02074308500
**Reg No:** 2649815 **Estd:** 1991 Private Limited Company
**Line of Business:** Holding companies management activities
**Trading Style:** Tarmac
**Issued Capital:** £28,570,002
**Directors:** M J Choules, G F Young, Mrs F P Penhallurick, Lafarge Tarmac Directors (Uk) Li
**Co. Secretary:** Lafarge Tarmac Secretaries (Uk)
**Branches:** Tarmac Industrial Minerals Holdings Ltd, Salisbury Rd, Ringwood, Hampshire BH24 1AS
**US SIC:** 6711, 1429
**UK SIC:** 83962, 23102
**Auditors:** Deloitte & Touche
**Bankers:** Barclays Bank Plc (20-00-00)

| | 31-12-13 | 31-12-12 | 31-12-11 |
|---|---|---|---|
| TA | 403,529,435 | 412,526,993 | 412,827,093 |
| P/L | 316 | 2,352 | 13,537 |
| NW | 290,005,382 | 290,005,066 | 290,305,166 |
| WC | 66,656,616 | 66,656,300 | 66,956,400 |

DUNS 49-425-9625 Exp

## Tarmac Northern Ltd

(**Subsidiary of:** Lafarge Tarmac Holdings Ltd)
Tarmac Wharf, Teesport, South Bank, Middlesbrough, Cleveland TS6 6UG
**Tel:** 01642454664 **Fax:** 01642430492
**Web:** www.tarmac.co.uk
**Reg No:** 3140596 **Estd:** 1955 Private Limited Company
**Line of Business:** Quarrying of stone
**Issued Capital:** £65,000,000
**Directors:** Lafarge Tarmac Directors (Uk) Li, M J Choules, Mrs F P Penhallurick
**Co. Secretary:** Lafarge Tarmac Secretaries (Uk)
**Responsibilities**
**Senior:** Aiden Rantler *(Manager)*
**Branches:** Tarmac Northern Ltd, Richardshaw La, Pudsey, West Yorkshire LS28 7NB
**US SIC:** 1429, 1499, 3275
**UK SIC:** 23102, 23960, 24370
**Auditors:** Deloitte & Touche LLP
**Bankers:** Barclays Bank Plc (20-33-51)

| | 31-12-13 | 31-12-12 | 31-12-11 |
|---|---|---|---|
| TA | 111,673,000 | 107,480,000 | 102,637,000 |
| P/L | 4,193,000 | 4,844,000 | 5,093,000 |
| NW | 91,572,000 | 87,379,000 | 83,722,000 |
| WC | 91,572,000 | 87,379,000 | 83,722,000 |

DUNS 21-807-2718
## Tarmac Southern Ltd
**(Subsidiary of:** Lafarge Tarmac Holdings Ltd)
Stancombe Lane, Bristol, Avon BS48 3QD
**Tel:** 01275-464441 **Fax:** 01793640080
**Web:** www.tarmac.co.uk
**Reg No:** 0415260 **Estd:** 1990 Private Limited Company
**Line of Business:** Asphalt & macadam supply
**Trading Style:** Tarmac
**Issued Capital:** £2,000
**Directors:** Lafarge Tarmac Directors (Uk) Li, Mrs F P Penhallurick
**Co. Secretary:** Lafarge Tarmac Secretaries (Uk)
**Responsibilities**
**Senior:** David Mcclleland *(Chief Executive Officer West)*, David Mclelland *(Manager)*, Johannes Serfontein *(Manager)*
**Branches:** Tarmac Southern Ltd, Bellhouse Pit, Warren Lane, Colchester, Essex CO3 0NN
**US SIC:** 7399 **UK SIC:** 83954
**Bankers:** Barclays Bank Plc (20-00-00)

| | 31-12-13 | 31-12-12 | 31-12-11 |
|---|---|---|---|
| TA | 126,000 | 126,000 | 126,000 |
| NW | 126,000 | 126,000 | 126,000 |

DUNS 39-808-1166
## Tarporley War Memorial Hospital Trust
14 Park Road, Tarporley, Cheshire CW6 0AP
**Tel:** 01829733559
**Web:** www.tarporleyhospital.fsnet.co.uk
**Reg No:** 2213003 **Estd:** 1987 Private Company Limited By Guarantee
**Line of Business:** Hospital activities
**Directors:** Mrs C E Lees Jones, C J Barlow, R W Elviss, M D Beaumont, Mrs G E Clough, P N Large, P C Okell, Mrs A W Smith
**Co. Secretary:** Anthony Gorman
**Responsibilities**
**Senior:** Alistair Campbell *(Manager)*, Neville Carr *(Director)*, John Cheshire *(Director)*, Roland Dawson *(Director)*, Sandra Dykes *(Director)*, Stanley Harrison *(Manager)*, Janet Heys *(Director)*, Dale Vimalchandran *(Director)*
**Facilities:** Kay Walker *(Facilities Manager)*
**US SIC:** 8062 **UK SIC:** 95100
**Auditors:** Craven Dalton Partnership
**Bankers:** National Westminster Bank Plc (55-61-31)

| | 31-03-14 | 31-03-13 | 31-03-12 |
|---|---|---|---|
| TO | 757,652 | 652,280 | 704,058 |
| P/L | (118,000) | (188,101) | (99,456) |
| NW | 2,601,083 | 2,605,256 | 2,621,082 |
| WC | (289,017) | (328,454) | (324,654) |
| Emp. | 40 | 46 | 49 |

DUNS 21-147-4568
## Tarsus Uk Holdings Ltd
**(Subsidiary of:** Tarsus Group Plc)
9th Floor Metro Building, 1 Butterwick, London W6 8DL
**Tel:** 02088462700
**Reg No:** 6774643 **Estd:** 2008 Private Limited Company
**Line of Business:** Management activities of other non-financial holding companies not elsewhere classified
**Issued Capital:** £100,001
**Directors:** D P O'Brien, J D Emslie
**Co. Secretary:** Simon Smith
**US SIC:** 6711 **UK SIC:** 83962

| | 31-12-13 | 31-12-12 | 31-12-11 |
|---|---|---|---|
| TA | 17,300,967 | 17,300,967 | 17,300,967 |
| NW | 17,300,001 | 17,300,001 | 17,300,001 |
| WC | (965) | (965) | N/A |

DUNS 21-120-4607
## Tarways Asphalte Co. Ltd
**(Subsidiary of:** Directscale Ltd)
Goodlass Road, Liverpool, Merseyside L24 9HJ
**Tel:** 0151-486-3287
**Web:** www.tarways.co.uk
**Reg No:** 1136219 **VAT No:** 165726445
**Estd:** 1973 Private Limited Company
**Line of Business:** Construction of motorways, roads, railways, airfields and sports facilities
**Issued Capital:** £5,000
**Principals:** D W Batterton *(Managing)*, D L Robinson, R W Lowe
**Co. Secretary:** Ms Tracey Batterton
**Branches:** Tarways Asphalte Co. Ltd, Turner Cr, Newcastle, Staffordshire ST5 7JZ
**US SIC:** 7399, 1611
**UK SIC:** 83954, 50200
**Auditors:** Horwath Langton Morland
**Bankers:** Barclays Bank Plc (20-51-01)

| | 31-12-13 | 31-12-12 | 31-12-11 |
|---|---|---|---|
| TO | 15,097,458 | 14,221,069 | 12,868,957 |
| P/L | 679,741 | 311,792 | 306,941 |
| NW | 1,792,392 | 1,693,128 | 1,614,237 |
| WC | 881,680 | 908,694 | 1,314,778 |
| Emp. | 63 | 60 | 54 |

DUNS 21-596-2449
## Tas Restaurant
33 The Cut, Lambeth, London SE1 8LF
**Tel:** 02079282111
**Web:** www.tasrestaurants.co.uk
**Estd:** 1998
**Line of Business:** Restaurant - turkish
**Proprietor:** S Guler
**Responsibilities**
**Senior:** Tunc Meral *(Branch Manager)*
**US SIC:** 5812 **UK SIC:** 66110
**Employees:** 49

DUNS 77-466-1557
## Tasca Tankers Ltd
Thornes Moor Road, Wakefield, West Yorkshire WF2 8PT
**Tel:** 01924-369007
**Web:** www.tascatankers.ltd.uk
**Reg No:** 2965713 **VAT No:** 656246521
**Estd:** 1994 Private Limited Company
**Line of Business:** Commercial vehicle servicing repairs parts & accessories
**Issued Capital:** £22,000
**Principals:** T P Mcdonnell *(Managing)*, A Stokes, A Bowering
**Co. Secretary:** Thomas Mcdonnell
**Responsibilities**
**Senior:** Graham Hardcastle *(customer services manager)*
**Marketing:** Vicki Wood *(operations manager)*
**IT:** Vicki Wood *(operations manager)*
**Operations:** Graham Hardcastle *(customer services manager)*, Vicki Wood *(operations manager)*
**US SIC:** 3799 **UK SIC:** 36502
**Auditors:** RSM Tenon Ltd
**Bankers:** Barclays Bank Plc (20-89-68)

| | 31-03-13 | 31-03-12 | 31-03-11 |
|---|---|---|---|
| TO | 6,186,958 | N/A | N/A |
| P/L | (38,904) | N/A | N/A |
| NW | 614,865 | 717,769 | 361,952 |
| WC | 311,996 | 426,156 | 209,630 |
| Emp. | 72 | N/A | N/A |

DUNS 51-601-3112
## Tascor Medical Services Ltd
**(Subsidiary of:** Capita Plc)
17 Rochester Row, London SW1P 1QT
**Tel:** 01895205000
**Reg No:** 5881801 **Estd:** 2006 Private Limited Company
**Line of Business:** Other human health activities
**Issued Capital:** £1
**Director:** O D Barry
**Co. Secretary:** Capita Group Secretary Limited
**US SIC:** 8091, 8011
**UK SIC:** 95200, 95300

| | 31-12-13 | 31-12-12 | 31-12-12 |
|---|---|---|---|
| TO | 10,146,515 | 6,883,828 | 7,060,235 |
| P/L | 924,127 | (418,175) | 1,469,812 |
| NW | 2,518,384 | 1,807,587 | 1,902,445 |
| WC | 2,557,384 | 3,313,124 | 1,902,445 |
| Emp. | 164 | 172 | 139 |

DUNS 22-524-0464 Imp
## Tasis the American School in England
**(Subsidiary of:** Tasis U K Ltd)
Coldharbour Lane, Thorpe, Egham, Surrey TW20 8TE
**Tel:** 01932 565 252 **Fax:** 01932 560 493
**Web:** www.england.tasis.com
**Reg No:** 1604308 **Estd:** 1976 Private Unlimited Company
**Line of Business:** Schools (independent)
**Trading Style:** Tasis England, Tasis
**Issued Capital:** £10,000
**Principals:** Ms L F Aeschlimann *(Managing)*, K J Hayes, Mrs R S Mcgrory, J S Wyper, P N Sourry, Mrs L N Smith, B H Dorman, F Gonzalez
**Co. Secretary:** David King
**Responsibilities**
**Senior:** William Fleming *(Manager)*, Per Troein *(Director)*
**IT:** John Arcay *(Head of IT)*
**HR:** Mary Ealey *(Human Resources Manager)*
**Health & Safety:** Mary Ealey *(Human Resources Manager)*
**Facilities:** Mary Ealey *(Human Resources Manager)*
**US SIC:** 8211 **UK SIC:** 93200
**Auditors:** Crowe Clark Whitehill LLP
**Bankers:** Lloyds TSB Bank plc (30-94-42)

| | 30-06-13 | 30-06-12 | 30-06-11 |
|---|---|---|---|
| TO | 19,894,244 | 18,996,118 | 17,607,260 |
| P/L | 480,637 | 467,097 | 410,160 |
| NW | 3,212,539 | 2,829,413 | 2,502,378 |
| WC | 2,470,730 | 2,110,882 | 2,201,263 |
| Emp. | 196 | 193 | 187 |

DUNS 45-806-9622 Imp
## Task Displays Ltd.
**(Subsidiary of:** Task Zero Four Ltd)
6 Uxbridge Road, Leicester, Leicestershire LE4 7ST
**Tel:** 01162663233
**Web:** www.taskdisplays.co.uk
**Reg No:** 3164947 **VAT No:** 765343320
**Estd:** 1996 Private Limited Company
**Line of Business:** Manufacture of other furniture
**Issued Capital:** £1,100
**Directors:** D Ashfield, M A Brown
**Co. Secretary:** Paul Johnson
**Responsibilities**
**Senior:** Glen Lafford-Smith *(Warehouse Manager)*, Christopher Torr *(Joint Managing Director)*
**Finance:** Christopher Torr *(Joint Managing Director)*
**HR:** Karen Comery *(Personnel Manager)*
**Engineering:** Christopher Torr *(Joint Managing Director)*
**US SIC:** 2517, 2599
**UK SIC:** 46714, 46720
**Auditors:** Macintyre Hudson
**Bankers:** National Westminster Bank Plc (56-00-55)

| | 31-03-14 | 31-03-13 | 31-03-12 |
|---|---|---|---|
| TO | 7,810,398 | 7,062,728 | 9,503,014 |
| P/L | 1,479,946 | 1,275,031 | 1,405,691 |
| NW | 2,484,094 | 2,179,709 | 1,301,869 |
| WC | 2,356,078 | 2,002,982 | 1,160,505 |
| Emp. | 68 | 70 | 68 |

DUNS 21-279-0133 Imp
## Taskers Plc
Unit B, Liverpool, Merseyside L9 7ES
**Tel:** 01515254844 **Fax:** 01518325499
**Web:** www.taskersonline.com
**Reg No:** 1267980 **VAT No:** 303539480
**Estd:** 1976 Private Limited Company
**Line of Business:** Representative office
**Issued Capital:** £50,000
**Principals:** J S Tasker *(Managing)*, Ms K L Tasker
**Co. Secretary:** Paul Schwartz
**Responsibilities**
**IT:** Aled Morgan *(IT Manager)*
**Branches:** Taskers Plc, Unit L2-L3, Long Lane, Liverpool, Merseyside L9 7ES
**US SIC:** 5251, 5719
**UK SIC:** 64800, 64700
**Auditors:** Alexander & Co
**Bankers:** HSBC Bank plc (40-31-24)

| | 28-02-14 | 28-02-13 | 29-02-12 |
|---|---|---|---|
| TO | 16,870,632 | 16,555,685 | 18,851,484 |
| P/L | 190,390 | 489,914 | (782,775) |
| NW | 5,077,271 | 4,934,271 | 4,611,505 |
| WC | 1,227,925 | 1,191,292 | 837,546 |
| Emp. | 224 | 229 | 239 |

DUNS 36-529-0592
## Taskmaster Resources Ltd
**(Subsidiary of:** Recruitmaster Ltd)
8 Leodis Court David Street, Leeds, West Yorkshire LS11 5JJ
**Tel:** 01132465995
**Web:** www.tmrec.com
**Reg No:** 3289148 **VAT No:** 684384301
**Estd:** 1996 Private Limited Company
**Line of Business:** Labour recruitment and provision of personnel
**Issued Capital:** £2,601,729
**Director:** A Godfrey
**Co. Secretary:** Andrew Skorupka
**Branches:** Taskmaster Resources Ltd, Third Floor Queens Chambers, 3 King St, Nottingham, Nottinghamshire NG1 2BH
**US SIC:** 7361 **UK SIC:** 83954
**Auditors:** Mazars LLP
**Bankers:** Barclays Bank Plc (20-45-14)

| | 31-12-13 | 31-12-12 | 31-12-11 |
|---|---|---|---|
| TO | 28,110,370 | 24,764,745 | 23,446,301 |
| P/L | 588,943 | 356,574 | 576,043 |
| NW | 3,529,228 | 3,318,151 | 3,217,235 |
| WC | 3,303,771 | 3,153,703 | 3,024,567 |
| Emp. | 1,841 | 1,707 | 1,613 |

DUNS 34-601-8906 Imp
## Tastetech Ltd
Wilverley Industrial Estate, Bristol, Avon BS4 5NL
**Tel:** 01179712719
**Web:** www.tastetech.com
**Reg No:** 2743403 **Estd:** 1992 Private Limited Company
**Line of Business:** Manufacturers and distribution of food colouring, flavouring & additives
**Issued Capital:** £367,500
**Directors:** O A Derome, Mrs J E Sinton
**Co. Secretary:** David James
**Responsibilities**
**Senior:** Elaine Jarvis *(Manager)*, Jason Ticktum *(Factory Manager)*
**Finance:** Joe Morris *(Accounts Manager)*
**Marketing:** Robert McCarthy *(Commercial Coordinator)*, Michelle Yates *(Product Manager)*
**Sales:** Robert McCarthy *(Commercial Coordinator)*
**Operations:** Jason Ticktum *(Factory Manager)*
**Engineering:** Gary Gray *(Technical Manager)*
**US SIC:** 2099 **UK SIC:** 42399
**Auditors:** HLB Kidsons
**Bankers:** HSBC Bank plc (40-14-06)

| | 30-09-13 | 30-09-12 | 30-09-11 |
|---|---|---|---|
| TA | 2,926,594 | 2,817,302 | 2,235,013 |
| NW | 2,066,805 | 1,716,571 | 1,168,142 |
| WC | 1,037,778 | 928,427 | 396,140 |

DUNS 77-165-4571
## Tasties of Chester Ltd
**(Subsidiary of:** Pk Food Concepts Ltd.)
Prince William Avenue, Sandycroft, Deeside, Clwyd CH5 2QZ
**Tel:** 01244-533888 **Fax:** 01244-533404
**Web:** www.tasties.co.uk
**Reg No:** 2707708 **Estd:** 2005 Private Limited Company
**Line of Business:** Manufacture of other food products not elsewhere classified
**Trading Style:** Tasties of Chester Ltd
**Issued Capital:** £50,000
**Directors:** P Kingsley-Bates, I M Rick
**Responsibilities**
**Senior:** Geraldine Roberts *(New Product Development Manage)*
**Engineering:** Neil Howarth *(Production Manager)*
**US SIC:** 2099 **UK SIC:** 42399
**Auditors:** Duncan Sheard Glass
**Bankers:** HSBC Bank plc (40-10-17)

| | 30-06-14 | 30-06-13 | 30-06-12 |
|---|---|---|---|
| TO | 9,338,283 | 6,206,763 | 6,120,940 |
| P/L | (380,930) | (31,406) | (262,094) |
| NW | (116,320) | 172,484 | 334,315 |
| WC | (1,029,976) | (631,043) | (409,894) |
| Emp. | 138 | 106 | 100 |

DUNS 77-923-4397
## Tasty Plc
115 Park Street, London W1K 7AP
**Tel:** 02076371166
**Web:** www.wildwoodrestaurants.co.uk
**Reg No:** 5826464 **Estd:** 2006 Public Limited Company
**Line of Business:** Licensed restaurants
**Issued Capital:** £4,792,795
**Directors:** A Kaye, D J Plant, S Kaye
**Co. Secretary:** Keith Lassman
**US SIC:** 5812 **UK SIC:** 66110
**Auditors:** BDO LLP
**Bankers:** Barclays Bank Plc (20-00-00)

| | 29-12-13 | 30-12-12 | 01-12-12 |
|---|---|---|---|
| TO | 23,192,000 | 19,315,000 | 14,565,000 |
| P/L | 1,742,000 | 1,552,000 | 1,066,000 |
| NW | 16,999,000 | 11,899,000 | 10,549,000 |
| WC | 461,000 | (2,029,000) | (90,000) |
| Emp. | 506 | 453 | 325 |

DUNS 21-701-4829 Imp
## Tata Chemicals Europe Holdings Ltd
**(Subsidiary of:** Tata Chemicals Limited)
Mond House Winnington, Northwich, Cheshire CW8 4DT
**Tel:** 01606724000
**Reg No:** 7462734 **Estd:** 2010 Private Limited Company
**Line of Business:** Management activities of production holding companies
**Issued Capital:** £10,000,000
**Directors:** M J Ashcroft, P K Ghose, M Ramakrishnan, E A Kshirsagar, J J Kerrigan
**Co. Secretary:** David Davies
**Responsibilities**
**Senior:** Delyle Bloomquist *(Director)*
**US SIC:** 6711 **UK SIC:** 83962

| | 31-03-14 | 31-03-13 | 31-03-12 |
|---|---|---|---|
| TO | 191,360,000 | 187,025,000 | 195,230,000 |
| P/L | (35,592,000) | (30,117,000) | 13,235,000 |
| NW | (90,842,000) | (59,870,000) | (24,662,000) |
| WC | 35,464,000 | 37,920,000 | 16,041,000 |
| Emp. | 555 | 586 | 586 |

DUNS 71-890-0173 Imp
## Tata Communications (Uk) Ltd
**(Subsidiary of:** Tata Communications Limited)
1st Floor, 20 Old Bailey, London EC4M 7AN
**Tel:** 02070-299-500 **Fax:** 02075-194-609
**Web:** www.tatacommunications.com
**Reg No:** 5272339 **Estd:** 2002 Private Limited Company
**Line of Business:** Business services
**Directors:** J R Freeman, Mrs N Sekuri, C Sassoulas
**Responsibilities**
**Senior:** Sanjay Baweja *(Cfo)*, Laurie Bowen *(Chief Executive)*, Laurence Mccormack *(Manager)*
**Finance:** Sanjay Baweja *(Cfo)*, Beatrice Davidson *(Sales development and account)*
**Sales:** Beatrice Davidson *(Sales development and account)*

**Branches:** Tata Communications (Uk) Limited, 2 Harbour Exchange Square, London E14 9GE
**US SIC:** 7399, 7379
**UK SIC:** 83954, 83940
**Auditors:** SPW (UK) LLP
**Employees:** 247
**Turnover:** £484,194,196

DUNS 23-843-5163
### Tata Global Beverages Group Ltd
325-327 Oldfield Lane North, Greenford, Middlesex UB6 0AZ
**Tel:** 02083384000
**Web:** www.tataglobalbeverages.com
**Reg No:** 3835716 **Estd:** 1999 Private Limited Company
**Line of Business:** Management activities of holding companies
**Export Sales:** £127,700,000
**Issued Capital:** £235,074,891
**Directors:** D D Pandole, K K Lakshmanan, H R Bhat, A K Misra
**Co. Secretary:** Miles Bailey
**US SIC:** 6711 **UK SIC:** 83962
**Auditors:** PricewaterhouseCoopers LLP

|      | 31-03-14 | 31-03-13 | 31-03-12 |
|------|----------|----------|----------|
| TO   | 257,300,000 | 276,000,000 | 261,000,000 |
| P/L  | 200,000 | 27,500,000 | 18,400,000 |
| NW   | 262,000,000 | 271,800,000 | 283,200,000 |
| WC   | 260,700,000 | 274,000,000 | 255,300,000 |
| Emp. | 1,051 | 1,277 | 946 |

DUNS 51-640-4485
### Tata Steel Europe Ltd
(Subsidiary of: Tata Steel Limited)
30 Millbank, London SW1P 4WY
**Tel:** 02079758382 **Fax:** 020 7717 4455
**Web:** www.tata-uk.com
**Reg No:** 5957565 **VAT No:** 238712260
**Estd:** 2012 Private Limited Company
**Line of Business:** Management activities of holding companies
**Trading Style:** Tata Steel, Tata, Tata Steel Tubes Europe
**Issued Capital:** £3,577,360,999
**Directors:** I Hussain, J H Schraven, N K Misra, K Chatterjee, T V Narendran, F P Royle, K U Kohler, A M Robb
**Co. Secretary:** Mrs Helen Matheson (Avontuur)
**Responsibilities**
**Senior:** Dinesh Mistry (Manager)
**US SIC:** 6711 **UK SIC:** 83962
**Auditors:** Deloitte LLP
**Following financial data are in thousands**

|      | 31-03-14 | 31-03-13 | 31-03-12 |
|------|----------|----------|----------|
| TO   | 8,556,000 | 8,706,000 | 10,111,000 |
| P/L  | (562,000) | (1,176,000) | (846,000) |
| NW   | (829,000) | (411,000) | 187,000 |
| WC   | (1,021,000) | (546,000) | 273,000 |
| Emp. | 31,400 | 32,600 | 33,900 |

DUNS 29-692-8120                                    Exp
### Tata Technologies Europe Ltd
(Subsidiary of: Tata Technologies Limited)
Citibase Bristol Business Park, 510 Bristol Busn Park, Coldharbour Lane, Bristol, Avon BS16 1EJ
**Fax:** 01582-878751
**Web:** www.tatatechnologies.co.uk
**Reg No:** 2016440 **VAT No:** 737479293
**Estd:** 1984 Private Limited Company
**Line of Business:** Hardware consultancy
**Export Markets:** E U, U S A  & Canada
**Export Sales:** £13,058,000
**Issued Capital:** £10,000
**Principals:** W K Harris (Managing), N J Sale, P P Kadle
**Co. Secretary:** Ovalsec Limited
**Responsibilities**
**Senior:** Patrick McGoldrick (Manager)
**Marketing:** Craig Mills (Sales & Marketing Manager)
**Sales:** Craig Mills (Sales & Marketing Manager)
**Branches:** Tata Technologies Europe Ltd, Caspian Rd, Atlantic St, Altrincham, Cheshire WA14 5HH
**US SIC:** 7379, 8911
**UK SIC:** 83940, 83701
**Auditors:** Deloitte LLP

|      | 31-03-14 | 31-03-13 | 31-03-12 |
|------|----------|----------|----------|
| TO   | 99,296,000 | 94,864,000 | 73,266,000 |
| P/L  | 7,358,000 | 10,132,000 | 6,139,000 |
| NW   | 23,966,000 | 17,836,000 | 9,696,000 |
| WC   | 23,483,000 | 17,236,000 | 9,151,000 |
| Emp. | 456 | 429 | 335 |

DUNS 21-028-9096                              Imp-Exp
### Tate & Lyle Plc
1 Kingsway, London WC2B 6AN
**Tel:** 02072-572-100 **Fax:** 020 7257 2200
**Web:** www.tateandlyle.com
**Reg No:** 0076535 **Estd:** 1903 Public Limited Company
**Line of Business:** Management activities of holding companies
**Export Sales:** £3,083,000,000

**Trading Style:** United Molasses
**Issued Capital:** £14,338,225
**Directors:** J Ahmed, Sir P O Gershon, Ms E P Airey, W H Camp, Ms V A Kamsky, A N Hampton, P A Forman, Dr A Puri
**Co. Secretary:** Ms Lucie Gilbert
**Responsibilities**
**Senior:** Anne Minto (Director)
**Branches:** Tate & Lyle Plc, Thames Refinery, Factory Road, London E16 2EW
**US SIC:** 6711, 2062
**UK SIC:** 83962, 42000
**Auditors:** PricewaterhouseCoopers LLP
**Bankers:** Lloyds TSB Bank plc (30-00-02)
**Following financial data are in thousands**

|      | 31-03-14 | 31-03-13 | 31-03-12 |
|------|----------|----------|----------|
| TO   | 3,147,000 | 3,256,000 | 3,088,000 |
| P/L  | 290,000 | 309,000 | 379,000 |
| NW   | 660,000 | 680,000 | 708,000 |
| WC   | 449,000 | 773,000 | 698,000 |
| Emp. | 4,467 | 4,382 | 4,562 |

DUNS 21-624-4772
### Tate Bros. Ltd
Avis Way, Newhaven, East Sussex BN9 0DH
**Tel:** 01698813495
**Web:** www.tatescars.co.uk
**Reg No:** 0515014 **VAT No:** 190223684
**Estd:** 1919 Private Limited Company
**Line of Business:** Other retail sale in specialised stores not elsewhere classified
**Trading Style:** Tates, Windsor Garden Buildings
**Issued Capital:** £18,550
**Principals:** J E Tate (Chairman), T I Meadows (Managing), J D Tate (Managing), Ms M J Tate
**Co. Secretary:** Nicholas Gentry
**Responsibilities**
**Senior:** Paul Homewood (Manager)
**Branches:** Tate Bros. Ltd, Trafalgar Road, Brighton, East Sussex BN41 1GU
**US SIC:** 5999, 7539
**UK SIC:** 65600, 67100
**Auditors:** Baker Tilly
**Bankers:** HSBC Bank plc (40-14-03)

|      | 31-12-13 | 31-12-12 | 31-12-11 |
|------|----------|----------|----------|
| TO   | 54,406,655 | 51,120,294 | 44,824,105 |
| P/L  | 1,655,873 | 1,280,819 | (548,106) |
| NW   | 25,289,650 | 24,078,834 | 23,246,497 |
| WC   | 9,904,399 | 8,494,302 | 7,574,048 |
| Emp. | 297 | 283 | 315 |

DUNS 39-811-0577                                    Exp
### Tate Business Group Ltd
Tate House, Dunstable, Bedfordshire LU5 4TT
**Tel:** 01582500200 **Fax:** 01582500205
**Web:** www.tatebg.com
**Reg No:** 2215481 **VAT No:** 490384138
**Estd:** 1988 Private Limited Company
**Line of Business:** Computer stationery
**Export Markets:** European Union (E U); Middle East
**Issued Capital:** £93,000
**Directors:** G J Tate, S Boardman, R H Beal, Mrs C A Tearle, M Murphy
**Co. Secretary:** Steven Du Plooy
**Responsibilities**
**Senior:** Claudine Tate (Manager)
**Operations:** Joanne Hakewill (Supply Chain Manager)
**Purchasing:** Joanne Hakewill (Supply Chain Manager), Joanne Zanna (Supply Chain Manager)
**US SIC:** 2752 **UK SIC:** 47544
**Auditors:** FKCA Ltd
**Bankers:** National Westminster Bank Plc (60-13-28)

|      | 31-07-14 | 31-07-13 | 31-07-12 |
|------|----------|----------|----------|
| TO   | 12,303,453 | 12,105,517 | 12,473,085 |
| P/L  | 170,797 | 222,465 | 150,597 |
| NW   | 1,073,520 | 1,001,742 | 925,704 |
| WC   | 521,933 | 322,919 | 218,248 |
| Emp. | 58 | 67 | 64 |

DUNS 45-816-2930
### Tate Enterprises Ltd
Millbank, London SW1P 4RG
**Tel:** 02078878869 **Fax:** 02078878007
**Web:** www.tate.org.uk
**Reg No:** 3173975 **Estd:** 1996 Private Limited Company
**Line of Business:** Other retail sale in specialised stores not elsewhere classified
**Issued Capital:** £2,495,320
**Directors:** Ms K Mogull, S Wingfield, C F Roxburgh, J W Schuijt, M Shah, C L Mayhew, Ms V Barnsley, G V Thomas
**Co. Secretary:** Ms Sarah Rogers
**Responsibilities**
**Senior:** Gabrielle Hase (Director), Leonardo Rosellini (Cafe Manager), Laura Wright (Director)
**Branches:** Tate Enterprises Ltd, 25 Sumner St, London SE1 9JZ
**US SIC:** 5999, 5812, 2731, 2741
**UK SIC:** 65600, 66110, 47532, 47541

**Auditors:** Grant Thornton

|      | 31-03-14 | 31-03-13 | 31-03-12 |
|------|----------|----------|----------|
| TO   | 27,075,187 | 29,520,450 | 27,801,523 |
| P/L  | 129,832 | (51,549) | (11,866) |
| NW   | 2,814,030 | 2,684,198 | 2,735,747 |
| WC   | 1,988,692 | 2,104,131 | 2,194,330 |
| Emp. | 475 | 495 | 498 |

DUNS 21-327-1299
### Tate Fuel Oils Ltd
Steelcroft Works, Gay Lane, Otley, West Yorkshire LS21 3BB
**Tel:** 01943467444 **Fax:** 01943464663
**Web:** www.tate-fuels.co.uk
**Reg No:** 1301975 **VAT No:** 301189982
**Estd:** 1972 Private Limited Company
**Line of Business:** Fuel and oil distributors
**Trading Style:** High Street Service Station, B H R Service Station, Rodley Service Station
**Issued Capital:** £5,002
**Principals:** G W Tate (Chairman and Managing), J K Ferguson, A G Tate, Ms J M Tate
**Branches:** Tate Fuel Oils Ltd, Skellbank, Ripon, North Yorkshire HG4 2PT
**US SIC:** 5052, 5999
**UK SIC:** 61200, 65600
**Auditors:** Mazars LLP
**Bankers:** National Westminster Bank Plc (54-21-20)

|      | 30-06-13 | 30-06-12 | 30-06-11 |
|------|----------|----------|----------|
| TO   | 87,026,644 | 76,237,045 | 80,977,275 |
| P/L  | 508,990 | 383,956 | 162,245 |
| NW   | 3,108,332 | 2,928,171 | 2,042,009 |
| WC   | 1,661,648 | 1,696,862 | 1,506,503 |
| Emp. | 80 | 54 | 48 |

DUNS 22-540-3195
### The Tate Gallery
20 John Islip Street, London SW1P 4JU
**Tel:** 02078878876
**Web:** www.tate.org.uk
**VAT No:** 240187582 **Estd:** 1897 Incorporate By Act Of Parliament
**Line of Business:** Art gallery.
**Trading Style:** Tate Britain
**Principals:** J Ashfield (Financial), Sir N Serota, A Bowness, R E Morphet, M G Compton, Dunluce, L A Parriz, M R Butlin
**Responsibilities**
**Senior:** Helen Alexander (Manager), R Alley (Principal), Brian Chadwick (Manager), Rachel Muckel (Store Manager), Amanda Pinto (Manager), Carol Propper (Manager), R Rattenbury (Principal), Laura Wright (Manager)
**Marketing:** Sarah Briggs (Marketing Manager), Bethany Bull (Assistant Communications Offic), Cecily Carbone (Press Officer), Elli Cartwright (Marketing Manager), Duncan Holden (Press Officer), Livia Ratcliffe (Marketing Manager)
**Sales:** Rebecca Williams (Director of Development)
**HR:** Colin Coombs (Training Manager), Cheryl Richardson (Head of Human Resources)
**Purchasing:** Richard Galliers (Estates Project Manager)
**Branches:** The Tate Gallery, Porthmear Beach, Beach Road, St. Ives, Cornwall TR26 1JY
**US SIC:** 8411 **UK SIC:** 97700
**Bankers:** Bank Of England (10-00-00)
**Employees:** 650

DUNS 21-746-8540
### Tate Liverpool
Albert Dock, Liverpool, Merseyside L3 4BB
**Tel:** 0151-702-7400
**Web:** www.tate.org.uk
**Estd:** 1997
**Line of Business:** Art gallery
**Director:** C Grueneberg
**Responsibilities**
**Senior:** Dawn Brady (Gallery Manager), Andrea Nixon (Executive Director)
**Marketing:** Jennifer Collingwood (Marketing Manager)
**IT:** Dawn Brady (Gallery Manager)
**Health & Safety:** Dawn Brady (Gallery Manager)
**Facilities:** Dawn Brady (Gallery Manager)
**US SIC:** 7911 **UK SIC:** 97913
**Employees:** 80

DUNS 29-198-0415
### Tate Members
Bankside, London SW1P 4RG
**Tel:** 02078878888 **Fax:** 020-7887-8755
**Web:** www.tate.org.uk
**Reg No:** 0600340 **Estd:** 1890 Private Company Limited By Guarantee
**Line of Business:** Activities of other membership organisations not elsewhere classified
**Trading Style:** Tate Online
**Directors:** Ms H Collins, Ms S Lee, Ms R Lloyd, N Scott, S C Wilson, C Chinaloy, A W Yates, Ms S Chakrabarti

**Co. Secretary:** Miss Monica Thomas
**Responsibilities**
**Senior:** David Adjaye (Director), Brian Chadwick (Director), Dominic Harris (Membership Director), Robert McCracken (Manager), Amanda Pinto (Director), Jonathan Snow (Director)
**US SIC:** 8699 **UK SIC:** 96902
**Auditors:** Grant Thornton UK LLP
**Bankers:** Coutts & Co (18-00-02)

|      | 31-03-14 | 31-03-13 | 31-03-12 |
|------|----------|----------|----------|
| TO   | 9,358,805 | 9,287,023 | 7,981,835 |
| P/L  | (1,573,734) | (432,522) | 2,982,476 |
| NW   | 3,393,656 | 4,967,390 | 5,399,912 |
| WC   | 3,393,656 | 4,967,390 | 5,399,912 |

DUNS 22-817-7333
### Tate of Leeds Ltd.
Balm Road, Leeds, West Yorkshire LS10 2RL
**Tel:** 01133852750 **Fax:** 01132-760407
**Web:** www.tateaccidentrepaircentre.co.uk
**Reg No:** 1693412 **VAT No:** 169082248
**Estd:** 1915 Private Limited Company
**Line of Business:** Car body repairers
**Trading Style:** Tate Cars
**Issued Capital:** £109,500
**Principals:** T P Tate (Chairman and Managing), R T Tate
**Co. Secretary:** Frances Tate
**US SIC:** 7539 **UK SIC:** 67100
**Auditors:** Armstrong Watson Audit Ltd
**Bankers:** Barclays Bank Plc (20-45-14)

|      | 31-12-13 | 31-12-12 | 31-12-11 |
|------|----------|----------|----------|
| TA   | 3,767,583 | 3,830,201 | 4,092,589 |
| P/L  | 22,777 | (220,286) | 423,763 |
| NW   | 2,360,078 | 2,309,701 | 2,597,337 |
| WC   | 1,167,346 | 1,222,569 | 1,483,855 |

DUNS 76-423-4787                                    Imp-Exp
### Tateossian Ltd
27 Conduit Street, London W1S 2XZ
**Tel:** 02074999924
**Web:** www.tateossian.com
**Reg No:** 2561039 **VAT No:** 562881319
**Estd:** 1990 Private Limited Company
**Line of Business:** Jewellery retailers
**Issued Capital:** £10,000
**Managing Director:** R Tateossian
**Co. Secretary:** Ms Ariel Thompson
**Responsibilities**
**Senior:** Eva Rockarova (Manager)
**Finance:** Christina Nicola (accounts manager), Yasmin Rahman (Head of Finance)
**HR:** Yasmin Rahman (Head of Finance)
**Health & Safety:** Yasmin Rahman (Head of Finance)
**Facilities:** Yasmin Rahman (Head of Finance)
**Branches:** Tateossian Ltd, 1 Royal Exchange, London EC3V 3DG
**US SIC:** 5944, 3961, 5094
**UK SIC:** 65400, 49103, 61900
**Auditors:** Greenback Alan
**Bankers:** Barclays Bank Plc (20-32-00)

|      | 31-12-13 | 31-12-12 | 31-12-11 |
|------|----------|----------|----------|
| TO   | 6,931,481 | 6,675,814 | N/A |
| P/L  | 283,959 | 201,644 | N/A |
| NW   | 1,509,572 | 1,433,639 | 1,437,970 |
| WC   | 1,187,878 | 1,156,464 | 1,046,868 |
| Emp. | 73 | 69 | N/A |

DUNS 54-852-7522
### Tates
Avis Way, Newhaven, East Sussex BN9 0DH
**Tel:** 01273512123
**Web:** www.paradisepark.co.uk
**Estd:** 1993 Proprietorship
**Line of Business:** Botanical and zoological gardens and nature reserve activities
**Trading Style:** Paradise Park
**Proprietor:** D Davies
**Responsibilities**
**Senior:** Gary Middleton (Facilities Manager)
**Finance:** Nick Gentry (Accountant)
**Marketing:** Karen Sexton (Advertising Manager)
**IT:** Graham Macton (Computer Manager)
**Health & Safety:** Gary Middleton (Facilities Manager)
**Facilities:** Gary Middleton (Facilities Manager)
**Operations:** Gary Middleton (Facilities Manager)
**US SIC:** 8421, 5999
**UK SIC:** 97700, 65600
**Employees:** 100

DUNS 22-521-2380
### Tates of Pyecombe Ltd
100 Old Shoreham Road, Brighton, East Sussex BN41 1TA
**Tel:** 01273857555 **Fax:** 01273857556
**Web:** www.wildlifegardening.co.uk
**Reg No:** 1376481 **Estd:** 1978 Private Limited Company
**Line of Business:** Sale of new motor vehicles

**Trading Style:** Tates Garden Buildings, Tates Garden World, Tates Leisure World
**Issued Capital:** £100
**Directors:** J D Tate, M J Gilbert, T I Meadows, B Sayers
**Co. Secretary:** Nicholas Gentry
**Responsibilities**
**Senior:** Stuart Laurie *(Sales Manager)*, Gary Middleton *(Manager)*
**Branches:** Tates Of Pyecombe Ltd, Brighton Rd, Horsham, West Sussex RH13 6QA
**US SIC:** 5511 **UK SIC:** 65100
**Auditors:** Baker Tilly

| | 31-12-13 | 31-12-12 | 31-12-11 |
|---|---|---|---|
| TO | 4,846,320 | 4,546,136 | 4,582,829 |
| P/L | 1,133,984 | 993,844 | 1,001,870 |
| NW | 7,640,749 | 6,788,977 | 6,058,945 |
| WC | 4,188,632 | 3,314,419 | 2,541,051 |
| Emp. | 80 | 78 | 79 |

DUNS 22-851-5920
## Tatham Miller Ltd
**(Subsidiary of:** Stemcor Holdings Ltd)
Shield Hall Works, Hardgate Road, Glasgow, Lanarkshire G51 4TB
**Tel:** 0141-445-6161 **Fax:** 01414456964
**Reg No:** 1546879 **Estd:** 1981 Private Limited Company
**Line of Business:** Metal merchants
**Trading Style:** Barclay and Mathieson
**Issued Capital:** £257,000
**Director:** N Watson
**Responsibilities**
**Senior:** Amanda Phillips *(Manager)*
**Branches:** Tatham Miller Ltd, Bangor Stn Yd, Caernarfon Rd, Bangor, Gwynedd LL57 2YB
**US SIC:** 5051 **UK SIC:** 61200
**Bankers:** HSBC Bank plc (40-46-35)

| | 31-12-13 | 31-12-12 | 31-12-11 |
|---|---|---|---|
| TA | 1,691,504 | 1,691,504 | 1,691,504 |
| NW | 1,691,504 | 1,691,504 | 1,691,504 |

DUNS 54-313-5859
## Tato Holdings Ltd
Bramling House, Bramling, Canterbury, Kent CT3 1NB
**Tel:** 01227721699 **Fax:** 01843229413
**Web:** www.tate.org.uk
**Reg No:** 3258156 **Estd:** 1976 Private Limited Company
**Line of Business:** Management activities of other non-financial holding companies not elsewhere classified
**Trading Style:** Thor
**Issued Capital:** £2,116,993
**Directors:** H J Schmidt, Ms J A Pujante Mitjavila, S Van De Vyver, T Muller, M L Jamieson, P Hahn, D A Hewitt
**Co. Secretary:** Simon Pearson
**US SIC:** 6711, 5161
**UK SIC:** 83962, 61200
**Auditors:** Mazars LLP

| | 31-12-13 | 31-12-12 | 31-12-11 |
|---|---|---|---|
| TO | 288,887,000 | 256,312,000 | 241,458,000 |
| P/L | 46,714,000 | 33,357,000 | 34,008,000 |
| NW | 314,020,000 | 270,569,000 | 252,138,000 |
| WC | 188,795,000 | 167,788,000 | 150,509,000 |
| Emp. | 1,130 | 1,060 | 1,024 |

DUNS 22-663-4764 **Imp-Exp**
## Tattersalls Ltd
Terrace House, 125 High Street, Newmarket, Suffolk CB8 9BT
**Tel:** 01638-665-931 **Fax:** 01638-660-850
**Web:** www.tattersalls.com
**Reg No:** 0791113 **Estd:** 1964 Private Limited Company
**Line of Business:** Livestock markets
**Export Markets:** Worldwide
**Export Sales:** £4,220,473
**Issued Capital:** £508,000
**Directors:** J R George, E C Mahony, P A Watt, G K Davies, P J Morrey, A I Russell Fifteenth Duke Of Bedfor
**Co. Secretary:** Paul Ryan
**Responsibilities**
**Senior:** E Mahonie *(Chairman)*
**Finance:** Philip Hilditch *(Sales Accounts Manager)*
**Marketing:** Rolline Kavanagh *(Marketing Executive)*, Alex Mommersteeg *(Marketing Executive)*, Jason Singh *(Marketing Manager)*
**Sales:** Philip Hilditch *(Sales Accounts Manager)*
**IT:** Frank Rowlands *(IT Manager)*
**US SIC:** 7399 **UK SIC:** 83954
**Auditors:** Deloitte LLP
**Bankers:** Lloyds TSB Bank plc (30-00-08)

| | 30-06-14 | 30-06-13 | 30-06-12 |
|---|---|---|---|
| TO | 23,332,105 | 20,105,392 | 18,496,530 |
| P/L | 6,591,804 | 4,944,163 | 3,924,288 |
| NW | 56,476,679 | 52,622,254 | 49,429,055 |
| WC | 17,318,360 | 17,848,864 | 17,139,482 |
| Emp. | 70 | 67 | 65 |

DUNS 21-623-2853
## The Taunton Academy
39 Cheddon Road, Taunton, Somerset TA2 7DB
**Tel:** 07947831273
**Web:** www.thetauntonacademy.com
**Reg No:** 7035873 **Estd:** 2009 Private Company Limited By Guarantee
**Line of Business:** General secondary education
**Directors:** D R Mcgregor, Mrs D L Smith, Mrs M C Cridge, Dr P Avery, J P Reed, M A Trusson, A Cross
**Co. Secretary:** Mrs Amanda Kotvics
**US SIC:** 8211 **UK SIC:** 93200

| | 31-08-14 | 31-08-13 | 31-08-12 |
|---|---|---|---|
| TO | 5,356,048 | 5,373,224 | 5,560,930 |
| P/L | (278,111) | (77,716) | 258,150 |
| NW | (1,246,847) | (638,736) | (496,020) |
| WC | 1,971 | 779,743 | 671,385 |
| Emp. | 93 | 102 | 112 |

DUNS 23-295-4990
## Taunton and Somerset Nhs Foundation Trust
Musgrove Park, Taunton, Somerset TA1 5DB
**Web:** www.tsft.nhs.uk
**VAT No:** 654945305 **Estd:** 1997
**Line of Business:** Provide NHS healthcare services.
**Trading Style:** Musgrove Park Hospital
**Issued Capital:** £1
**Principals:** Ms R Wyke *(Chairman)*, D Hobdey *(Financial)*, P Lewis *(Financial)*, D Allwright, J Cubbon, A Willis, A Barker, G Mccomas
**Responsibilities**
**Senior:** Cecil Blumgart *(Medical Director)*, Debbie Frankpitt *(Procurement Manager)*, Gill McComas *(Non-Executive Director)*, Peter Merson *(Non-Executive Director)*
**Facilities:** Simon Rigby *(Facilities Manager)*
**Purchasing:** Debbie Frankpitt *(Procurement Manager)*
**Branches:** Taunton and Somerset Nhs Foundation Trust, Bracken House, Crewkerne Road, Chard, Somerset TA20 1YA
**US SIC:** 9121, 8062
**UK SIC:** 91110, 95100
**Auditors:** PricewaterhouseCoopers LLP
**Bankers:** National Westminster Bank Plc (60-80-06)

| | 31-03-14 | 31-03-13 | 31-03-11 |
|---|---|---|---|
| TO | 225,243,000 | 225,701,000 | 217,100,000 |
| P/L | (17,478,000) | 471,000 | 1,096,000 |
| NW | 126,289,000 | 143,496,000 | 139,166,000 |
| WC | 4,114,000 | 24,586,000 | 18,731,000 |
| Emp. | 3,643 | 3,783 | 3,846 |

DUNS 23-690-9099
## Taunton School
Staplegrove Road, Taunton, Somerset TA2 6AD
**Tel:** 01823703110
**Web:** www.tauntonschoolevents.co.uk
**Estd:** 1848
**Line of Business:** Schools (independent)
**Directors:** M D Taylor, J Whiteley
**Responsibilities**
**Senior:** Ellie Humphrey *(Sports Club Manager)*
**Marketing:** Kathryn Howard *(General Manager)*
**Purchasing:** Kathryn Howard *(General Manager)*
**Branches:** Taunton International Study Centre, Taunton
**US SIC:** 7999 **UK SIC:** 97913
**Bankers:** National Westminster Bank Plc (60-80-06)
**Employees:** 160

DUNS 22-002-4819
## Taunton School Educational Charity
Taunton School, 206-216 Greenway Road, Taunton, Somerset TA2 6LJ
**Tel:** 01823703703
**Web:** www.tauntonschool.co.uk
**Reg No:** 4005803 **Estd:** 2000 Private Company Limited By Guarantee
**Line of Business:** Primary education
**Directors:** M R Hobbs, C N Arding, Mrs M P Trask, Sir D A Blackburn, Major General J M Hall, Mrs E M Waymouth, A M Saxton, C C Butters
**Co. Secretary:** David Taylor
**Responsibilities**
**Senior:** Charles Abram *(Manager)*, Michael Button *(Manager)*, Lee Glaser *(Head Teacher)*, Henry Keeling *(Director)*, Ruth Whitehead *(Director)*
**Finance:** Jimmy Beale *(Prep Head)*, Malcom Mackeith *(Finance Manager)*
**Marketing:** Kathryn Howard *(Marketing Manager)*
**IT:** Ben Moore *(IT Manager)*
**Branches:** Taunton School Educational Charity, Staplegrove Road, Taunton, Somerset TA2 6AD
**US SIC:** 8211 **UK SIC:** 93200
**Bankers:** HSBC Bank plc (40-44-04)

| | 31-07-14 | 31-07-13 | 31-07-12 |
|---|---|---|---|
| TO | 21,260,900 | 20,706,500 | 19,430,800 |
| P/L | 1,412,700 | 1,551,900 | 1,644,400 |
| NW | 14,116,600 | 12,697,100 | 10,905,900 |
| WC | (2,933,900) | (2,517,000) | (1,819,200) |
| Emp. | 355 | 333 | 334 |

DUNS 56-956-0626
## Taunton School Enterprises Ltd
Staplegrove Road, Taunton, Somerset TA2 6AD
**Tel:** 01823703703 **Fax:** 01823-348144
**Web:** www.tauntonschool.co.uk
**Reg No:** 2846335 **VAT No:** 634526932
**Estd:** 1993 Private Limited Company
**Line of Business:** Catering
**Trading Style:** Taunton School
**Issued Capital:** £100
**Director:** C C Butters
**Co. Secretary:** David Taylor
**US SIC:** 5812, 7999
**UK SIC:** 66110, 97913
**Auditors:** Crowe Clark Whitehill LLP
**Bankers:** HSBC Bank plc (40-44-04)

| | 31-07-14 | 31-07-13 | 31-07-12 |
|---|---|---|---|
| TO | 1,205,441 | 1,093,300 | 1,099,226 |
| NW | 578 | 578 | 578 |
| WC | (64,226) | (83,372) | (67,553) |

DUNS 50-696-6233
## Taurus Crafts
Old Park, Lydney, Gloucestershire GL15 6BU
**Tel:** 01594-844841
**Web:** www.tauruscrafts.co.uk
**Estd:** 1994 Proprietorship
**Line of Business:** Craft centres and retail outlets
**Proprietor:** Mrs W Baker
**Responsibilities**
**Senior:** Elizabeth Ball *(Manager)*
**Finance:** Andrea Stuckey *(Financial Manager)*
**Marketing:** Tom Haverley *(Sales & Marketing Manager)*
**Sales:** Tom Haverley *(Sales & Marketing Manager)*
**HR:** Elizabeth Ball *(Manager)*
**Health & Safety:** Elizabeth Ball *(Manager)*
**Operations:** Tom Haverley *(Sales & Marketing Manager)*
**US SIC:** 5999 **UK SIC:** 65600
**Employees:** 50

DUNS 22-264-0091
## Taurus Waste Recycling (Holdings) Ltd
Taurus House Lynchford Lane, Farnborough, Hampshire GU14 6JB
**Tel:** 01932-348480
**Web:** www.taurus-waste.com
**Reg No:** 4281987 **Estd:** 2001 Private Limited Company
**Line of Business:** Refuse systems
**Issued Capital:** £600,000
**Directors:** S T Watkins, S T Mills, P J Scarborough, R Bird, G R Bird
**Co. Secretary:** Ms Judy Scarborough
**US SIC:** 4953, 3341
**UK SIC:** 92110, 22470

| | 31-10-13 | 31-10-12 | 31-10-11 |
|---|---|---|---|
| TO | 7,034,853 | 7,155,571 | 9,204,349 |
| P/L | 140,489 | 16,042 | (650,601) |
| NW | 1,857,735 | 1,628,477 | 1,382,614 |
| WC | (1,094,634) | (1,372,349) | (1,571,380) |
| Emp. | 60 | 61 | 70 |

DUNS 21-182-4664
## The Tavern
Wigan Road Hunger Hill, Bolton, Lancashire BL3 4RH
**Tel:** 0120462861
**Web:** www.tavernfayre.net
**Estd:** 1985 Proprietorship
**Line of Business:** Public house
**Proprietor:** J Kelly
**US SIC:** 5813 **UK SIC:** 66200
**Employees:** 50

DUNS 42-393-8661
## Tavistock and Portman Nhs Foundation Trust
The Tavistock Centre, 120 Belsize Lane, London NW3 5BA
**Tel:** 020-7435-7111
**Web:** www.tavi-port.org
**Estd:** 1994
**Line of Business:** Public sector hospital activities, including nhs trusts
**Principals:** Ms A Greatley *(Chairman)*, S Young *(Financial)*, Ms T Klauber, Dr M Patrick, Ms J Moseley, M Bostock, A Kara, Ms E Satyamurti
**Responsibilities**
**Senior:** Judith Bell *(Manager)*, Danny Brent *(Executive)*, Louise Lyon *(Manager)*, Richard Strang *(Non-Executive Director)*
**Finance:** Carl Doherty *(Deputy Financial Director)*
**Marketing:** Britt Krause *(Editor and Reviews Editor)*, Janine Sternberg *(Editor)*
**Admin:** Samia Anfu *(Administrator)*, Carlo Cavalli *(Administrator)*, Paul Haviland *(Course Administrator)*, Debbie Lampon *(Course Administrator)*, Milvia Morra *(Course Administrator)*, Jessica Nwora *(Course Administrator)*, Sara Riley *(Course Administrator)*, Jas Sond *(Course Administrator)*
**Facilities:** Ashley Morse *(Estate Manager)*
**Purchasing:** Julian Swift *(Purchasing Manager)*
**Branches:** Tavistock and Portman Nhs Foundation Trust, 8 Fitzjohns Avenue, London NW3 5NA
**US SIC:** 8062 **UK SIC:** 95100
**Auditors:** KPMG LLP

| | 31-03-14 | 31-03-13 | 31-03-12 |
|---|---|---|---|
| TO | 40,367,000 | 36,163,000 | 14,163,000 |
| P/L | 1,104,000 | (737,000) | (1,077,000) |
| NW | 14,441,000 | 13,271,000 | 12,505,000 |
| WC | 525,000 | (666,000) | 48,000 |
| Emp. | 453 | 416 | 419 |

DUNS 21-580-7508
## Tavistock Centre for Couple Relationships
70 Warren Street, London W1T 5PB
**Tel:** 02073801975
**Web:** www.tccr.org.uk
**Estd:** 2007 Proprietorship
**Line of Business:** Counselling & advice services
**Proprietor:** Ms S Abse
**Responsibilities**
**Senior:** Badri Houshidar *(Administrator)*
**US SIC:** 8321 **UK SIC:** 96111
**Employees:** 50

DUNS 21-780-8066
## Tavistock General Hospital
Spring Hill, Tavistock, Devon PL19 8LD
**Tel:** 01822612233
**Web:** www.torbaycaretrust.nhs.uk
**Estd:** 2007 Partnership
**Line of Business:** Hospitals
**Partners:** S Collings, S Collins
**Responsibilities**
**Senior:** Mary Ballance *(CEO, Managing Director)*, Mary Barratt *(Matron)*
**US SIC:** 8062 **UK SIC:** 95100
**Employees:** 250

DUNS 64-255-4257
## Tavistock Hotel
Tavistock Square, London WC1H 9EU
**Tel:** 020-7636-8383
**Web:** www.bloomsburybowling.com
**Estd:** 1956 Proprietorship
**Line of Business:** Hotels
**Proprietor:** S Walduck
**Responsibilities**
**Senior:** Christine Farringdon *(Reservations Manager)*, Tom Walduck *(Joint Managing Director)*
**Marketing:** Christine Farringdon *(Reservations Manager)*
**US SIC:** 7011 **UK SIC:** 66500
**Employees:** 985

DUNS 28-887-3896
## Taw & Torridge Coaches Ltd
Grange Lane, Merton, Okehampton, Devon EX20 3ED
**Tel:** 01805-603400 **Fax:** 01805-603559
**Web:** www.tawandtorridge.co.uk
**Reg No:** 1247327 **Estd:** 1976 Private Limited Company
**Line of Business:** Other passenger land transport
**Trading Style:** Taw & Torridge Coaches Ltd
**Issued Capital:** £255
**Principals:** A G Hunt *(Managing)*, M A Hunt, Ms T A Laughton, C N Laughton
**Co. Secretary:** Ms Linda Hunt
**US SIC:** 4141 **UK SIC:** 72102
**Auditors:** Perrin & Co
**Bankers:** HSBC Bank plc (40-35-23)

| | 31-03-14 | 31-03-13 | 31-03-12 |
|---|---|---|---|
| TO | 3,514,661 | N/A | N/A |
| P/L | 209,523 | N/A | N/A |
| NW | 1,207,708 | 983,889 | 773,190 |
| WC | (497,441) | (407,123) | (388,001) |
| Emp. | 86 | N/A | N/A |

DUNS 21-705-0665
## Taw Garages Ltd
(Subsidiary of: Percy R Brend & Sons (Holdings) Ltd)
Victoria Road, Barnstaple, Devon EX32 8NP
Tel: 01271374173 Fax: 01271-346439
Web: www.taw-ford.co.uk
Reg No: 0923161 Estd: 1968 Private Limited Company
Line of Business: Car dealers (new & used)
Issued Capital: £30,000
Directors: M J Brend, J E Brend, P A Brend, R P Brend, J J Brend
Co. Secretary: Peter Brend
Responsibilities
Senior: Mark Brend (Manager), Adam Stone (Senior IT Executive)
Finance: Colin Hack (Senior Finance Administrator)
IT: Adam Stone (Senior IT Executive)
Branches: Taw Garages Ltd, Victoria Road, Barnstaple, Devon EX32 8NP
US SIC: 5511, 7539
UK SIC: 65100, 67100
Auditors: Bishop Fleming
Bankers: Lloyds TSB Bank plc (30-90-49)

|  | 31-03-14 | 31-03-13 | 31-03-12 |
|---|---|---|---|
| TO | 20,331,862 | 17,440,663 | 18,219,039 |
| P/L | 319,443 | 210,586 | (145,587) |
| NW | 2,471,149 | 2,216,808 | 2,051,311 |
| WC | 1,787,724 | 1,547,597 | 1,519,025 |
| Emp. | 61 | 60 | 66 |

DUNS 34-536-7911
## Tax Computer Systems Ltd
Centurion House, London Road, Staines, Middlesex TW18 4AX
Web: www.taxcomputersystems.com
Reg No: 5347048 Estd: 2005 Private Limited Company
Line of Business: Computer software (development)
Export Sales: £1,328,657
Issued Capital: £2,953
Director: Ms L Davies
Co. Secretary: Robert Davies
Responsibilities
Finance: Robert Ip (Financial Director)
Marketing: Jim Khan (Sales & Marketing Manager)
Sales: Jim Khan (Sales & Marketing Manager)
IT: Satpaul Mall (Computer Manager)
HR: Robert Ip (Financial Director)
US SIC: 7379 UK SIC: 83940
Bankers: Lloyds TSB Bank plc (77-88-88)

|  | 31-12-13 | 31-12-12 | 31-12-11 |
|---|---|---|---|
| TO | 12,867,056 | 12,325,000 | 12,572,699 |
| P/L | 7,105,524 | 6,620,228 | 4,300,064 |
| NW | 20,420,049 | 14,650,025 | 9,243,579 |
| WC | 20,352,261 | 14,622,982 | 9,202,437 |
| Emp. | 62 | 55 | 55 |

DUNS 21-776-8918
## The Taxi Centre
4 Bridge St Oswald Place, Leven, Fife KY8 4NW
Tel: 01333421111
Web: www.taxicentre.co.uk
Estd: 2011 Partnership
Line of Business: Taxis and private hire vehicles
Partners: K Wardhaugh, K Wordhaugh
Responsibilities
Senior: Murray Scott (Manager)
US SIC: 4121 UK SIC: 72200
Employees: 50

DUNS 42-335-4547
## Taxi-Link
136 Albion Street, Southwick, Brighton, East Sussex BN42 4DP
Tel: 01273410630
Web: www.taxilink595959.com
Estd: 2007 Partnership
Line of Business: Taxis and private hire vehicles
Trading Style: Taxi Link
Partners: S Forest, M Browning
Responsibilities
Senior: Derek Parr (Manager)
US SIC: 4121 UK SIC: 72200
Employees: 70

DUNS 77-744-6600
## Tay Restaurants Ltd
21-25 Reform Street, Dundee, Angus DD1 1SG
Tel: 01382200821
Web: www.mcdonalds.co.uk
Reg No: 0155550SC Estd: 1995 Private Limited Company
Line of Business: Solicitors
Trading Style: McDonalds
Issued Capital: £100
Director: Ms S Jeffrey
Co. Secretary: David Jeffrey
Branches: Tay Restaurants Ltd, Longtown Road, Dundee, Angus DD4 8JT

US SIC: 5812 UK SIC: 66110
Auditors: JLM

|  | 31-12-13 | 31-12-12 | 31-12-11 |
|---|---|---|---|
| TA | 751,460 | 772,859 | 848,412 |
| NW | 111,855 | 132,345 | 208,539 |
| WC | (263,753) | (71,690) | 37,732 |

DUNS 23-667-1129
## Tay Road Bridge Joint Board
Administration Office, Marine Parade, Dundee, Angus DD1 3JB
Tel: 01382-221881
Web: www.tayroadbridge.co.uk
Estd: 1966 Partnership
Line of Business: Other storage and warehousing not elsewhere classified
Partners: Fife Council, Angus Council, Dundee City Council
US SIC: 4226 UK SIC: 77003
Employees: 46

DUNS 54-842-2724
## Taybar Radio Taxis
St Leonards Warrior Square Station, Kings Road, St Leonards-On-Sea, East Sussex TN37 6HL
Tel: 01424-719719
Web: www.taybar719719.co.uk
Estd: 1983 Partnership
Line of Business: Taxis and private hire vehicles
Partners: A Smith, S Haitede
US SIC: 4121, 7512
UK SIC: 72200, 84801
Bankers: Lloyds TSB Bank plc (30-97-66)
Employees: 70

DUNS 21-620-2987
## Taybarns
Warrington Road, Wigan, Lancashire WN3 6XB
Tel: 01942493469
Web: www.taybarns.com
Estd: 2011 Proprietorship
Line of Business: Restaurants
Proprietor: Mrs H Littler
Responsibilities
Senior: Stewart Chambers (Manager)
US SIC: 5812 UK SIC: 66110
Employees: 50

DUNS 21-605-8175
## Taybarns Travel Inn
Talke Road, Red Street, Newcastle, Staffordshire ST5 7AH
Tel: 01782578900
Web: www.taybarns.com
Estd: 2001
Line of Business: Hotels and motels without restaurant
Partners: R Buchanan, C Wilde
US SIC: 7011 UK SIC: 66500
Employees: 55

DUNS 22-755-7782 Imp
## Tayburn Ltd
(Subsidiary of: Tayburn Holdings Ltd)
11-15 Kittle Yards, Edinburgh, Midlothian EH9 1PJ
Tel: 01316620662
Web: www.tayburn.co.uk
Reg No: 0067241SC VAT No: 327326857
Estd: 1979 Private Limited Company
Line of Business: Engineering design activities for industrial process and production
Issued Capital: £20,000
Principals: W D Davidson (Financial), S W Farrell, M N Stewart, R D Simpson, S Mitchell
Co. Secretary: Steven Clark
Responsibilities
Senior: Erick Davidson (Manager)
Marketing: Michael Salmon (Head of Digitial)
Sales: Jessica Wilson (Account Manager)
IT: Claire Williamson (Senior Artworker / Digital Pro)
Branches: Tayburn Ltd, Dobson House Regent Centre, Gosforth, Newcastle-Upon-Tyne, Tyne and Wear NE3 3PF
US SIC: 8911, 7999
UK SIC: 83701, 97913
Bankers: Bank Of Scotland (80-06-55)

|  | 31-03-14 | 31-03-13 | 31-03-12 |
|---|---|---|---|
| TA | 1,319,516 | 1,310,179 | 1,488,933 |
| NW | 661,463 | 650,201 | 643,211 |
| WC | 852,348 | 574,325 | 604,331 |

DUNS 39-745-8100
## Taycare Medical Ltd
(Subsidiary of: Taycare Holdings Ltd)
Unit 2, Leeds, West Yorkshire LS12 6LL
Tel: 01132311800 Fax: 01132-311805
Web: www.taycare.com
Reg No: 0204227 VAT No: 170105216
Estd: 1925 Private Limited Company

Line of Business: Manufacturers of surgical equipment
Issued Capital: £940
Directors: P N Taylor, B Taylor
Co. Secretary: Ben Taylor
Responsibilities
Senior: Mary Taylor (Manager)
US SIC: 3841, 5999
UK SIC: 37201, 65600
Auditors: Henton & Co LLP
Bankers: Barclays Bank Plc (20-48-42)

|  | 28-02-14 | 28-02-13 | 29-02-12 |
|---|---|---|---|
| TA | 1,363,825 | 2,159,169 | 1,909,885 |
| NW | 672,790 | 1,350,726 | 1,286,556 |
| WC | 416,560 | 1,121,688 | 1,073,346 |

DUNS 21-140-1750
## Taylor & Emmet Llp
57 Sheffield Road, Dronfield, South Yorkshire S18 2GF
Tel: 01142184000 Fax: 01246416195
Web: www.hallamediation.com
Reg No: 0340779OC Estd: 2009 Private Limited Company
Line of Business: Solicitors
Responsibilities
Senior: Michaela Heathcote (Non-designated Limited Liabili), Patricia Lennon (Partner), Anthony Long (Chief Executive), Jonatham Stittle (Non-designated Limited Liabili)
Health & Safety: Lee Stacey (Facilities Manager)
Facilities: Lee Stacey (Facilities Manager)
Purchasing: Lee Stacey (Facilities Manager)
US SIC: 8111 UK SIC: 83500
Bankers: National Westminster Bank Plc (56-00-09)

|  | 31-03-14 | 31-03-13 | 31-03-12 |
|---|---|---|---|
| TO | 9,408,357 | 8,490,871 | 8,110,725 |
| P/L | 1,883,103 | 1,868,951 | 1,712,245 |
| NW | 1,864,733 | 1,832,266 | 1,712,245 |
| WC | 2,703,461 | 2,527,292 | 2,562,735 |
| Emp. | 140 | 144 | 138 |

DUNS 77-609-2116
## Taylor & Fraser Ltd
(Subsidiary of: Barnaigh Group Ltd)
117 Abercorn Street, Paisley, Renfrewshire PA3 4DH
Tel: 01418-876151 Fax: 01418-890696
Web: www.taylor-and-fraser.co.uk
Reg No: 0155035SC VAT No: 652476719
Estd: 1994 Private Limited Company
Line of Business: Plumbing
Issued Capital: £100,000
Directors: G S Fingland, R E Vernon, J H Hamilton
Co. Secretary: Mrs Evelyn Kennedy
Responsibilities
Finance: Alan Fortune (Finance Director)
Branches: Taylor & Fraser Ltd, 25 Newtown, Cupar, Fife KY15 5LY
US SIC: 1711 UK SIC: 50300
Auditors: Ernst & Young LLP
Bankers: Lloyds Tsb Scotland Plc (87-34-01)

|  | 30-06-13 | 30-06-12 | 30-06-11 |
|---|---|---|---|
| TO | 17,785,572 | 17,885,941 | 20,387,599 |
| P/L | 558,464 | 630,643 | 832,524 |
| NW | 4,143,639 | 3,852,545 | 3,355,476 |
| WC | 3,824,241 | 3,652,824 | 3,166,425 |
| Emp. | 70 | 59 | 54 |

DUNS 22-866-1096
## Taylor Burgess Ltd
Norton Way, Moss Lane Industrial Estate, Sandbach, Cheshire CW11 3YT
Tel: 01270-767229 Fax: 01270-768703
Web: www.taylor-burgess.ltd.uk
Reg No: 1794941 VAT No: 374226061
Estd: 1977 Private Limited Company
Line of Business: Kitchen planners and installers
Issued Capital: £15,060
Chairman: J W Johnson
Co. Secretary: Mrs Elaine Swindell
Responsibilities
Senior: Michelle Barnes (Office Manager)
US SIC: 5199, 1751
UK SIC: 61900, 50400
Auditors: Barrowman Jackson Stephen
Bankers: National Westminster Bank Plc (55-61-31)

|  | 31-03-14 | 31-03-13 | 31-03-12 |
|---|---|---|---|
| TA | 244,792 | 233,395 | 255,019 |
| NW | 57,014 | 32,616 | 37,641 |
| WC | 31,669 | 562 | (1,912) |

DUNS 22-951-0342
## Taylor Clark Ltd
Fourth Floor South, 35 Portman Square, London W1H 6LR
Tel: 02074860100
Web: www.taylorclarke.co.uk
Reg No: 0340727 VAT No: 240092794
Estd: 1938 Private Limited Company
Line of Business: Activities of investment trusts
Export Sales: £14,747,000
Issued Capital: £934,711

Directors: A R Clark, R Bennison, R J Harvey
Co. Secretary: John Dippie
Responsibilities
IT: Anthony Cox (Computer Manager)
US SIC: 6733, 6711
UK SIC: 83100, 83962
Auditors: KPMG LLP
Bankers: Clydesdale Bank Plc (82-11-07)

|  | 31-03-14 | 31-03-13 | 31-03-12 |
|---|---|---|---|
| TO | 15,197,000 | 18,287,000 | 14,491,000 |
| P/L | 43,000 | (1,059,000) | (10,203,000) |
| NW | 157,015,000 | 156,288,000 | 151,700,000 |
| WC | 25,823,000 | 20,020,000 | 14,153,000 |
| Emp. | 216 | 215 | 215 |

DUNS 21-319-8666 Imp-Exp
## Taylor Engineering & Plastics Ltd
Molesworth Street, Rochdale, Lancashire OL16 2BD
Tel: 01706-714-700 Fax: 01706-714-707
Web: www.tep.co.uk
Reg No: 1316094 VAT No: 151442104
Estd: 1977 Private Limited Company
Line of Business: Manufacture of other plastic products
Export Sales: £3,592,581
Trading Style: Tep
Issued Capital: £192,500
Principals: R Taylor (Chairman and Managing), J G Newbold (Managing), J M Taylor, I B Taylor, J S Taylor
Co. Secretary: Alan Worth
Responsibilities
Facilities: Ion Greenwood (Maintenance Manager)
US SIC: 3079 UK SIC: 48360
Auditors: BDO LLP

|  | 30-09-13 | 30-09-12 | 30-09-11 |
|---|---|---|---|
| TO | 16,546,760 | 25,376,261 | 19,902,026 |
| P/L | 1,601,234 | 2,699,210 | 768,504 |
| NW | 12,462,097 | 11,730,901 | 9,687,367 |
| WC | 3,347,295 | 4,063,668 | 2,637,151 |
| Emp. | 196 | 205 | 178 |

DUNS 22-520-1805
## Taylor Gordon & Co. Ltd
95 London Road, Croydon, Surrey CR0 2RF
Tel: 02086810846 Fax: 02082535993
Web: www.planpersonnel.co.uk
Reg No: 0973693 VAT No: 190680845
Estd: 1970 Private Limited Company
Line of Business: Labour recruitment and provision of personnel
Trading Style: Plan Personnel
Issued Capital: £2,253
Principals: J G Gunn (Managing), J R Hutchings (Personnel), Ms J D Landymore
Co. Secretary: Ms June Landymore
Branches: Taylor Gordon & Co. Ltd, 85 Buckingham Palace Road, London SW1W 0QJ
US SIC: 7361 UK SIC: 83954
Auditors: Baker Tilly UK Audit LLP
Bankers: Lloyds TSB Bank plc (30-94-38)

|  | 30-03-14 | 31-03-13 | 01-03-12 |
|---|---|---|---|
| TO | 27,429,902 | 26,694,536 | 28,428,314 |
| P/L | 382,284 | 400,643 | 425,006 |
| NW | 5,292,415 | 5,214,652 | 4,912,491 |
| WC | 3,876,342 | 3,767,326 | 3,385,408 |
| Emp. | 135 | 135 | 141 |

DUNS 45-897-8194 Imp-Exp
## Taylor Hobson Ltd
(Subsidiary of: Ametek European Holdings Ltd)
Hackworth Industrial Park, Shildon, County Durham DL4 1LH
Web: www.taylor-hobson.com
Reg No: 3230332 VAT No: 670319639
Estd: 1933 Private Limited Company
Line of Business: Manufacture of electronic instruments and appliances for measuring, checking, testing, navigating and other purposes, except industrial process control equipment
Trading Style: Taylor Hobson Precision, Solatron Isa
Issued Capital: £5,150,000
Principals: B P Wilson (Managing), C T Howarth
Co. Secretary: David Coley
Responsibilities
Senior: Timothy Garner (Manufacturing Director), Phil Lockhart (General Manager), Darian Mauger (Warehouse Manager), Nigel Mcdonnell (Environmental Manager), John Molinelli (Manager)
Finance: Derrick Chilton (Financial Director)
Marketing: Nick Maddock (Marketing Manager)
Sales: Robert Brewer (Sales Manager), Kevin Grens (Sales Manager), Darian Mauger (Warehouse Manager), Rick Parnoff (Sales Director)
IT: Bob Bennett (Technical Director)
Operations: Timothy Garner (Manufacturing Director), Nigel Mcdonnell (Environmental Manager)

**Engineering:** Timothy Garner *(Manufacturing Director)*
**Branches:** Taylor Hobson Ltd, Unit 7, Hackworth Industrial Park, Shildon, County Durham DL4 1LH
**US SIC:** 3829, 3559
**UK SIC:** 37100, 32863
**Auditors:** Ernst & Young LLP
**Bankers:** National Westminster Bank Plc (56-00-55)

| | 31-12-13 | 31-12-12 | 31-12-11 |
|---|---|---|---|
| TO | 54,819,000 | 54,113,000 | 49,876,000 |
| P/L | 20,155,000 | 22,115,000 | 12,295,000 |
| NW | 30,724,000 | 25,826,000 | 31,791,000 |
| WC | 10,588,000 | 1,814,000 | 19,317,000 |
| Emp. | 236 | 233 | 220 |

DUNS 22-721-3113 **Exp**

## Taylor Kerr (Energy Products) Ltd

Disraeli House, 12 Aylesbury End, Beaconsfield, Buckinghamshire HP9 1LW
**Web:** www.teekaycouplings.com
**Reg No:** 1275915 **Estd:** 1976 Private Limited Company
**Line of Business:** Management activities of other non-financial holding companies not elsewhere classified
**Export Markets:** Worldwide
**Trading Style:** Teekay Couplings and Taylor Keer Couplings
**Issued Capital:** £10,000
**Director:** N J Taylor
**Co. Secretary:** Ian Webb
**US SIC:** 6711 **UK SIC:** 83902
**Auditors:** Rickaby & Co
**Bankers:** National Westminster Bank Plc (60-02-20)

| | 30-06-14 | 30-06-13 | 30-06-12 |
|---|---|---|---|
| TO | 7,424,130 | 7,966,560 | N/A |
| P/L | 347,784 | 376,429 | N/A |
| NW | 2,767,223 | 2,476,447 | 624,393 |
| WC | 2,376,814 | 2,106,535 | 240,614 |
| Emp. | 84 | 79 | N/A |

DUNS 23-662-6755

## Taylor Lane Timber Frame Ltd

Chapel Road, Rotherwas Industrial Estate, Hereford, Herefordshire HR2 6LD
**Tel:** 01432-271912
**Web:** www.taylor-lane.co.uk
**Reg No:** 3657606 **VAT No:** 359198506
**Estd:** 1982 Private Limited Company
**Line of Business:** Timber constructed buildings
**Issued Capital:** £136,658
**Managing Director:** B Lane
**Co. Secretary:** Colin Taylor
**Responsibilities**
**Senior:** Wayne Ricketts *(Business Development Manager)*, Collin Taylor *(Joint Managing Director)*
**Finance:** Collin Taylor *(Joint Managing Director)*
**Marketing:** Wayne Ricketts *(Business Development Manager)*, Collin Taylor *(Joint Managing Director)*
**Sales:** Wayne Ricketts *(Business Development Manager)*
**HR:** Collin Taylor *(Joint Managing Director)*
**Health & Safety:** Collin Taylor *(Joint Managing Director)*
**Facilities:** Collin Taylor *(Joint Managing Director)*
**US SIC:** 1541, 1799
**UK SIC:** 50100, 50000
**Auditors:** R.J. Francis & Co

| | 31-10-13 | 31-10-12 | 31-10-11 |
|---|---|---|---|
| TO | 8,447,420 | 8,624,170 | 12,036,884 |
| P/L | (135,945) | 91,408 | (180,198) |
| NW | 3,338,017 | 3,524,078 | 3,488,670 |
| WC | 1,335,942 | 1,540,876 | 1,484,330 |
| Emp. | 75 | 90 | 100 |

DUNS 21-818-9736

## Taylor Lindsey Ltd

98 Searby Road, Lincoln, Lincolnshire LN2 4BT
**Tel:** 01522512200
**Web:** www.taylorlindsey.co.uk
**Reg No:** 0519939 **VAT No:** 128931750
**Estd:** 1953 Private Limited Company
**Line of Business:** Property developers
**Issued Capital:** £4,835,744
**Principals:** J R Taylor *(Managing)*, R C Taylor
**Co. Secretary:** Mrs Shirley Taylor
**Responsibilities**
**Admin:** Sandra Williams *(Office Manager)*
**IT:** Sonya Turner *(Property Manager)*
**Branches:** Taylor Lindsey Ltd, Beech Rd, Brookfield, Branston, Lincoln, Lincolnshire LN4 1TF
**US SIC:** 6552, 1541, 1522
**UK SIC:** 85000, 50100
**Auditors:** Wright Vigar & Co
**Bankers:** HSBC Bank plc (40-28-20)

| | 31-07-13 | 31-07-12 | 31-07-11 |
|---|---|---|---|
| TA | 54,762,097 | 52,665,570 | 47,221,640 |
| NW | 46,220,990 | 44,033,946 | 40,061,453 |
| WC | 11,211,714 | 10,350,053 | 9,916,472 |

DUNS 22-105-8816

## Taylor Made Computer Solutions Ltd

Leroux House, Carnac Court, Cams Hall Estate, Fareham, Hampshire PO16 8UL
**Tel:** 01329-239900
**Web:** www.tmcs.co.uk
**Reg No:** 4125178 **VAT No:** 787869732
**Estd:** 2000 Private Limited Company
**Line of Business:** Miscellaneous computer services
**Issued Capital:** £9,143
**Principals:** N J Taylor *(Managing)*, I T Lockwood, T M Walker
**Co. Secretary:** Mrs Alison Taylor
**Responsibilities**
**Senior:** Simon Sparks *(Manager)*
**Marketing:** Charlie Loader *(Relations Manager)*, Michelle Rutland *(Product Manager)*
**Operations:** Matt Takhar *(Software Development Manager)*
**Engineering:** Simon Sparks *(Manager)*
**US SIC:** 7379, 7374
**UK SIC:** 83940
**Auditors:** BDO Stoy Hayward LLP
**Bankers:** Lloyds TSB Bank plc (30-93-17)

| | 30-11-13 | 30-11-12 | 30-11-11 |
|---|---|---|---|
| TO | 9,773,317 | 9,204,970 | 8,554,792 |
| P/L | 419,673 | 262,806 | 389,669 |
| NW | 333,886 | 250,798 | 271,646 |
| WC | (226,254) | (315,088) | (231,836) |
| Emp. | 106 | 110 | 101 |

DUNS 22-660-5012 **Imp**

## Taylor Made Joinery Interiors Ltd

Manor Wood, Ipswich Road, Ipswich, Suffolk IP7 7BH
**Tel:** 01449-740518
**Web:** www.tmjinteriors.com
**Reg No:** 1570434 **VAT No:** 360393950
**Estd:** 1981 Private Limited Company
**Line of Business:** Manufacturers of joinery
**Issued Capital:** £10,000
**Principals:** J G Taylor *(Managing)*, K J Hudson, M C Holmes, P J Coll, A P Catchpole
**Co. Secretary:** Roy Newman
**Responsibilities**
**Senior:** Peter Harkin *(Associate Director, Project Ma)*, Paul Merralls *(Site Manager)*, Roger Warren *(Site Manager)*
**Finance:** Brett Bayliss *(Finance Manager)*, Mark Campion *(Financial Manager)*, Josh Cole *(Trainee Financial Manager)*, Matt Rawlinson *(Financial Manager)*, Dave Robbins *(Senior Bid Manager)*, Declan Smith *(Trainee Financial Manager)*, Ollie Taylor *(Trainee Financial Manager)*
**Marketing:** Rakesh Gorasia *(Project Manager)*, Sarah Kerry *(Business Development Manager)*
**Sales:** Abigail Edwards *(Business Development Manager)*, Sarah Kerry *(Business Development Manager)*, Duane Kostrzewski *(Senior Commercial Manager)*
**IT:** John Everett *(Project Manager)*, Chris Gorham *(Project Manager)*, Steve Hider *(Project Manager)*
**HR:** Josh Cole *(Trainee Financial Manager)*, Declan Smith *(Trainee Financial Manager)*
**Health & Safety:** Teresa Keeble *(Health & Safety Manager)*
**Operations:** Richard Easey *(Production Manager)*, Mark Hazell *(Site Manager)*, Andy King *(Project Manager)*, Antony Pankhurst *(Site Manager)*, Nick Wager *(Site Manager)*
**Purchasing:** Laura Harman *(Procurement Manager)*
**Fleet:** Colin McWhinnie *(Site Manager)*
**Engineering:** Richard Danskin *(Design Development Manager)*, Dave Shiress *(Design Development manager)*, Kelvin Steel *(Design Development Manager)*
**US SIC:** 2431 **UK SIC:** 46300
**Auditors:** BDO LLP

| | 31-12-13 | 31-12-12 | 31-12-11 |
|---|---|---|---|
| TO | 16,055,977 | 18,878,718 | 14,360,433 |
| P/L | 269,429 | 963,092 | 502,258 |
| NW | 2,170,624 | 2,055,918 | 1,688,807 |
| WC | 867,397 | 1,118,980 | 782,411 |
| Emp. | 130 | 122 | 117 |

DUNS 34-929-4293 **Imp**

## Taylor Maxwell Group Ltd

3 Seaward Place, Glasgow, Lanarkshire G41 1HH
**Tel:** 01414180300 **Fax:** 01179706652
**Web:** www.taylor.maxwell.co.uk
**Reg No:** 5726000 **VAT No:** 433711375
**Estd:** 1999 Private Limited Company
**Line of Business:** Brick merchants
**Issued Capital:** £992,000
**Directors:** M A Rudge, A D Downes, A J Hammond, A E Kenny
**Co. Secretary:** Mark Phillips
**US SIC:** 5039 **UK SIC:** 61300
**Auditors:** PricewaterhouseCoopers LLP
**Bankers:** Lloyds TSB Bank plc (30-00-01)

| | 31-03-14 | 31-03-13 | 31-03-12 |
|---|---|---|---|
| TO | 140,558,602 | 109,536,125 | 118,339,017 |
| P/L | 1,830,244 | 444,457 | 1,468,463 |
| NW | 402,292 | (495,640) | (916,542) |
| WC | 2,814,985 | 4,013,242 | 4,467,458 |
| Emp. | 152 | 145 | 144 |

DUNS 23-450-0528

## Taylor Rowlands

8 High Street, Yarm, Cleveland TS15 9AE
**Web:** www.dcoates.co.uk
**Estd:** 1984 Partnership
**Line of Business:** Accounting and auditing activities
**Partners:** J H Madden, J B Taylor
**US SIC:** 8931, 7399
**UK SIC:** 83600, 83954
**Employees:** 51

DUNS 21-117-8878

## Taylor Shaw Ltd

**(Subsidiary of:** Waterfall Services Ltd)
Genesis Centre, Garrett Field, Birchwood, Warrington, Cheshire WA3 7BH
**Tel:** 01925-830577
**Web:** www.taylorshaw.com
**Reg No:** 6576188 **Estd:** 2008 Private Limited Company
**Line of Business:** Canteens and catering
**Issued Capital:** £1
**Directors:** V J Pearson, Mrs G Storey, J Lovett
**Co. Secretary:** James Lovett
**Responsibilities**
**HR:** Gary Palmer *(Human Resources Director)*
**Branches:** Taylor Shaw Ltd, 91-93 Stamford Hill, London N16 5TP
**US SIC:** 5812 **UK SIC:** 66110

| | 30-03-14 | 31-03-13 | 30-03-12 |
|---|---|---|---|
| TO | 31,337,895 | 26,755,982 | 25,516,919 |
| P/L | 1,842,097 | 575,589 | (13,008) |
| NW | 156,931 | (1,268,458) | (1,928,246) |
| WC | 363,763 | (995,495) | (1,662,790) |
| Emp. | 1,841 | 1,684 | 1,694 |

DUNS 73-313-1267

## Taylor Stanton & Co Ltd

61 Caroline Street, Birmingham, West Midlands B3 1UF
**Tel:** 0121-236-9837
**Web:** www.taylorstantonandcompany.com
**Reg No:** 4586886 **Estd:** 2002 Private Limited Company
**Line of Business:** Call centre activities
**Issued Capital:** £100
**Directors:** P Barrett, M Friel
**Co. Secretary:** Ms Loretta Hope
**Responsibilities**
**Senior:** Loretta Barrett *(Manager)*
**US SIC:** 7399 **UK SIC:** 83954

| | 30-11-13 | 30-11-12 | 30-11-11 |
|---|---|---|---|
| TA | 99,293 | 79,375 | 115,689 |
| NW | 3,735 | 106 | 301 |
| WC | 2,765 | (336) | (820) |

DUNS 21-154-2425

## Taylor Vinters Llp

Merlin Place, Milton Road, Cambridge, Cambridgeshire CB4 0DP
**Web:** www.taylorvinters.com
**Reg No:** 0343503OC **Estd:** 1893
**Line of Business:** Solicitors
**Responsibilities**
**Senior:** Christine Berry *(Non-designated Limited Liabili)*, Michaela Henson *(Non-designated Limited Liabili)*, Roger James *(Non-designated Limited Liabili)*, Rupert Melville-Ross *(Non-designated Limited Liabili)*, James Packer *(Non-designated Limited Liabili)*
**Marketing:** Alison Gamble *(Marketing & Brand Manager)*, Ingrid Koning *(Marketing Administrator)*
**HR:** Chrissie Easom *(Human Resources Manager)*
**US SIC:** 8111 **UK SIC:** 83500
**Bankers:** Lloyds TSB Bank plc (30-00-00)

| | 30-04-14 | 30-04-13 | 30-04-12 |
|---|---|---|---|
| TO | 15,615,397 | 16,337,180 | 16,106,696 |
| P/L | 103,990 | (23,637) | 122,743 |
| NW | 7,127,588 | N/A | N/A |
| WC | 6,242,015 | 2,945,262 | 3,293,426 |
| Emp. | 186 | 191 | 198 |

DUNS 21-000-6166

## Taylor Walton Llp

36-44 Alma Street, Luton, Bedfordshire LU1 2PL
**Tel:** 01582-731161
**Web:** www.taylorwalton.co.uk
**Reg No:** 0328698OC **Estd:** 2007 Private Limited Company
**Line of Business:** Solicitors
**Responsibilities**
**Senior:** Steven Griffiths *(Non-designated Limited Liabili)*, Ian Mcloone *(Non-designated Limited Liabili)*, Angela Thomas *(Non-designated Limited Liabili)*, Stuart Wickham *(Non-designated Limited Liabili)*
**US SIC:** 8111 **UK SIC:** 83500

| | 30-06-13 | 30-06-12 | 30-06-11 |
|---|---|---|---|
| TO | 7,979,122 | 8,057,060 | 7,660,334 |
| P/L | 146,802 | 331,465 | 153,906 |
| NW | 838,735 | N/A | N/A |
| WC | 1,691,482 | 1,900,406 | 1,775,529 |
| Emp. | 132 | 142 | 140 |

DUNS 51-639-5907

## Taylor Wessing Llp

5 New St Square, London EC4A 3TW
**Web:** www.taylorwessing.com
**Reg No:** 0322935OC **VAT No:** 524096748
**Estd:** 2002
**Line of Business:** Solicitors
**Responsibilities**
**Senior:** Omleen Ajimal *(Partner)*, Gilles Amsallem *(Non-designated Limited Liabili)*, Vinod Bange *(Partner)*, Mark Barron *(Partner)*, Malcolm Bates *(Non-designated Limited Liabili)*, William Belcher *(Non-designated Limited Liabili)*, Eva Bodenbach *(Partner)*, Mark Buzzoni *(Partner)*, Tom Cartwright *(Partner)*, Ann Casey *(Non-designated Limited Liabili)*, Laurence Cobb *(Partner)*, James Crabtree *(Partner)*, Nikol Davies *(Partner)*, Alistair Day *(Partner)*, David De Ferrars *(Non-designated Limited Liabili)*, France Delord *(Partner)*, Saleem Fazal *(Partner)*, Robert Fenner *(Non-designated Limited Liabili)*, Janka Gass *(Partner)*, Bob Gayford *(Partner)*, Shane Gleghorn *(Partner)*, Neil Hawley *(Associate)*, Nicholas Hazell *(Partner)*, Michael Helfgott *(Partner)*, Russell Holden *(Partner)*, Mustafa Hussain *(Partner)*, Rowena Kay *(Senior Associate)*, Peter Kempe *(Partner)*, Steven Kempster *(Partner)*, Roland Mallinson *(Partner)*, Adam Marks *(Partner)*, Anthony Menzies *(Partner)*, Tandeep Minhas *(Partner)*, Nick Moser *(Partner)*, Amanda Nelson *(Partner)*, Sean Nesbitt *(Partner)*, Howard Palmer *(Partner)*, Gemma Parker *(Senior Associate)*, Jason Rawkins *(Partner)*, Adam Rendle *(Senior Associate - Media and E)*, Daniel Rosenberg *(Partner)*, Jayne Schnider *(Partner)*, Sanjvee Shah *(Partner)*, Raman Sharma *(Partner)*, Tracey Sheehan *(Partner)*, Nigel Stoate *(Partner)*, Tim Stocks *(Partner)*, Christopher Turley *(Partner)*, Robert Vidal *(Partner)*, Edward Waldron *(Partner)*, Niki Walker *(Partner)*, Nick Warr *(Partner)*, Alistair Watson *(Partner)*, John Whitfield *(Partner)*, Richard Williamson *(Partner)*, Martin Yells *(Partner)*, Hamid Yunis *(Partner)*
**Finance:** Charlotte Beckett *(Financial Director)*, Talia Carman *(Associate Solicitor - Financia)*
**Marketing:** Chrissie Allanson *(Marketing Manager)*, Wendy Blakley *(Corporate Services Manager)*, Julie Crowhurst *(Webmaster)*, John Haresnape *(Head of Business Development)*, Polly Puddephat *(Head of Marketing and Communic)*
**Sales:** John Haresnape *(Head of Business Development)*, Sharon Philbey *(Head of Business Development)*
**Admin:** Rachel Baron *(Legal PA)*, Keith Binks *(Office Manager)*, Linda Blake *(Secretary)*, Amee Edwards *(Secretary)*, Rachel Fretwell *(Personal Assistant)*, Charlotte Gray *(Personal Assistant)*, Caroline Maughan *(Partner's Secretary)*, Hayley Monisse *(Personal Assistant)*, Annamaria Small *(Personal Assistant)*
**HR:** Naa Pinkcombe *(Training Manager)*, Caroline Rawes *(HR Director)*
**Health & Safety:** Keith Binks *(Office Manager)*
**Facilities:** Keith Binks *(Office Manager)*
**Operations:** Clare Singleton *(Chief Operating Officer)*
**US SIC:** 8111 **UK SIC:** 83500

| | 30-04-14 | 30-04-13 | 30-04-12 |
|---|---|---|---|
| TO | 109,872,000 | 101,683,000 | 97,412,000 |
| P/L | 33,800,000 | 29,393,000 | 30,268,000 |
| NW | 33,355,000 | 29,390,000 | 30,266,000 |
| WC | 45,896,000 | 38,970,000 | 37,410,000 |
| Emp. | 654 | 551 | 630 |

DUNS 21-031-8815

## Taylor Wimpey

1 Lumsdale Road, Stretford, Manchester M32 0UT
**Tel:** 0161-864-8900
**Web:** www.taylorwimpey.com
**Estd:** 2009 Proprietorship
**Line of Business:** Builders
**Proprietor:** B Pickthall
**US SIC:** 1522 **UK SIC:** 50100
**Employees:** 60

DUNS 21-029-0086

## Taylor Wimpey Plc

Gate House, Turnpike Road, High Wycombe, Buckinghamshire HP12 3NR
**Tel:** 01494558323 **Fax:** 020-7355-8196
**Web:** www.taylorwimpey.com
**Reg No:** 0296805 **Estd:** 1935 Public Limited Company
**Line of Business:** Management activities of holding companies
**Export Sales:** £24,100,000

**Issued Capital:** £288,074,167
**Directors:** P T Redfern, R D Mangold, M R Hussey, Baroness M A Ford, Ms K M Barker, K S Beeston, R O Rowley, M T Davies
**Co. Secretary:** James Jordan
**Responsibilities**
**Senior:** Anthony Reading (Non-Executive Director), Ingrid Skinner (Manager)
**Marketing:** Kevin Belshim (Marketing Director)
**Branches:** Taylor Wimpey Plc, Unit 4 Capital Court, Bittern Road, Sowton Industrial Estate, Exeter, Devon EX2 7FW
**US SIC:** 6711, 1522
**UK SIC:** 83962, 50100
**Auditors:** Deloitte LLP
**Bankers:** HSBC Bank plc (40-23-26)
**Following financial data are in thousands**

|     | 31-12-13 | 31-12-12 | 31-12-11 |
|-----|----------|----------|----------|
| TO  | 2,295,500 | 2,019,000 | 1,808,000 |
| P/L | 306,200  | 207,700  | 78,600   |
| NW  | 2,246,500 | 1,982,900 | 1,828,400 |
| WC  | 2,330,700 | 2,219,200 | 2,072,900 |
| Emp.| 3,700    | 3,527    | 3,866    |

DUNS 45-871-4698
### Taylor Woodrow Construction
(Subsidiary of: Vinci)
Norwest Holst Construction Ltd, Watford, Hertfordshire WD24 4WW
**Tel:** 01923478400 **Fax:** 01923-478401
**Web:** www.vinciconstruction.co.uk
**Reg No:** 3213873 **Estd:** 1921 Private Unlimited Company
**Line of Business:** Development and selling of real estate
**Issued Capital:** £25,028,000
**Directors:** B Dupety, A K Raikes, J P Gatward
**Co. Secretary:** Jean-Pierre Bonnet
**Branches:** Taylor Woodrow Construction, Unit 5 Tawe Bus Vill, Phoenix Way, Enterprise Pk, Llansamlet, Swansea, West Glamorgan SA7 9LA
**US SIC:** 6552, 1541
**UK SIC:** 85000, 50100
**Auditors:** KPMG LLP
**Bankers:** HSBC Bank plc (40-23-26)

|     | 31-12-13 | 31-12-12 | 31-12-11 |
|-----|----------|----------|----------|
| TO  | 95,795,000 | 129,488,000 | 222,569,000 |
| P/L | 15,237,000 | 15,733,000 | 19,411,000 |
| NW  | 74,505,000 | 59,279,000 | 46,866,000 |
| WC  | 75,829,000 | 55,106,000 | 43,419,000 |
| Emp.| 218      | 324      | 522      |

DUNS 21-209-9907
### Taylormade Timber Products Ltd
(Subsidiary of: Gt Timber Ltd)
Colliery Site, Sherburn Hill, Durham, County Durham DH6 1PS
**Tel:** 0191-372-0524
**Web:** www.taylormadetimber.co.uk
**Reg No:** 0584004 **Estd:** 1953 Private Limited Company
**Line of Business:** Activities of sawmills
**Issued Capital:** £22,600
**Directors:** Miss S C Wentworth, Miss J A Wentworth, D J Wentworth
**Co. Secretary:** Miss Suzanne Wentworth
**Responsibilities**
**Finance:** Ericia Wentworth (Finance Director)
**Marketing:** Andrea Wentworth (Operations Manager)
**Sales:** Andrea Wentworth (Operations Manager)
**HR:** Andrea Wentworth (Operations Manager)
**US SIC:** 2421 **UK SIC:** 46101
**Auditors:** Blueprint Audit Ltd
**Bankers:** Lloyds TSB Bank plc (30-92-52)

|     | 31-08-13 | 31-08-12 | 31-08-11 |
|-----|----------|----------|----------|
| TO  | 27,518,731 | 25,857,669 | 25,275,619 |
| P/L | 1,918,215 | 1,848,887 | 2,767,515 |
| NW  | 11,286,307 | 13,713,833 | 12,227,522 |
| WC  | 5,799,564 | 7,823,283 | 7,821,875 |
| Emp.| 142      | 139      | 137      |

DUNS 23-193-1411
### Taylor's Business Surveyors & Valuers Ltd
(Subsidiary of: T B S & V Ltd)
Unit 4, Basset Court, Northampton, Northamptonshire NN4 5EZ
**Tel:** 01604662950 **Fax:** 01604662959
**Web:** www.tbsv.co.uk
**Reg No:** 2999260 **Estd:** 2010 Private Limited Company
**Line of Business:** Other engineering activities
**Issued Capital:** £2
**Directors:** A Lait, R W Bower, D Hayton, C J Mitchell
**Branches:** Taylor's Business Surveyors & Valuers Ltd, 6 Castle Mound Way, Mitchell Court, Rugby, Warwickshire CV23 0UY
**US SIC:** 8911 **UK SIC:** 83701

|     | 31-03-14 | 31-03-13 | 31-03-12 |
|-----|----------|----------|----------|
| TA  | 2        | 2        | 2        |
| NW  | 2        | 2        | 2        |

DUNS 21-238-4937     **Imp-Exp**
### Taylor's Eye Witness Ltd
Eye Witness Works, Milton Street, Sheffield, South Yorkshire S3 7WJ
**Tel:** 01142726521
**Web:** www.taylors-eye-witness.co.uk
**Reg No:** 0218517 **Estd:** 1886 Private Limited Company
**Line of Business:** Manufacturers of cutlery
**Export Markets:** South Africa and Australia; U S A
**Export Sales:** £388,869
**Trading Style:** Taylors Eye Witness
**Issued Capital:** £16,465
**Principals:** C Inman (Managing), A H Fisher (Managing), P R Inman
**Co. Secretary:** Denyse Fisher
**US SIC:** 3421 **UK SIC:** 31621
**Auditors:** Holmes Widlake
**Bankers:** HSBC Bank plc (40-41-07)

|     | 31-01-14 | 31-01-13 | 31-01-12 |
|-----|----------|----------|----------|
| TO  | 7,323,398 | N/A      | N/A      |
| P/L | 1,193,730 | N/A      | N/A      |
| NW  | 2,511,585 | 1,422,225 | 1,135,543 |
| WC  | 1,579,964 | 1,285,017 | 991,308  |
| Emp.| 55       | N/A      | N/A      |

DUNS 21-103-0363
### Taylors Food Group Ltd
Moncur, Perth, Perthshire PH14 9QF
**Tel:** 01828-686688
**Reg No:** 0335705SC **Estd:** 2007 Private Limited Company
**Line of Business:** Processing and preserving of potatoes
**Issued Capital:** £5,000
**Director:** G C Taylor
**Co. Secretary:** Ms Wendy Taylor
**US SIC:** 2099 **UK SIC:** 42399

|     | 30-06-14 | 30-06-13 | 30-06-12 |
|-----|----------|----------|----------|
| TA  | 1,371,446 | 1,409,474 | 855,000  |
| NW  | 205,000  | 5,000    | 5,000    |
| WC  | (327,673)| (311,823)| 433,836  |

DUNS 23-667-0014
### Taylors Industrial Services
Hareness Circle, Altens Industrial Estate, Aberdeen, Aberdeenshire AB12 3LY
**Tel:** 01224-872972
**Web:** www.taylorsindustrial.co.uk
**VAT No:** 553248345 **Estd:** 1983 Partnership
**Line of Business:** Tanks repairing, cleaning and maintenance
**Partners:** K Taylor, A Taylor, Ms A Taylor
**US SIC:** 1799, 1622
**UK SIC:** 50000, 50200
**Bankers:** Bank Of Scotland (80-12-06)
**Employees:** 90

DUNS 21-693-9103
### Taylors of Grampound
Unit 2a Grampound Road Industrial Estate, Grampound Road, Truro, Cornwall TR2 4TB
**Tel:** 01726-884402
**Web:** www.taylorsofgrampound.co.uk
**Estd:** 2004 Proprietorship
**Line of Business:** Home care service providers
**Proprietor:** Mrs P Taylor
**Responsibilities**
**Senior:** Claire Taylor-Mchale (General Manager)
**US SIC:** 8091 **UK SIC:** 95200
**Employees:** 80

DUNS 21-925-2764
### Taylors Service Garages (Boston) Ltd
Chain Bridge, Sleaford Road, Boston, Lincolnshire PE21 7PQ
**Tel:** 01205-350000
**Web:** www.listers.co.uk
**Reg No:** 1167024 **VAT No:** 455515837
**Estd:** 1959 Private Limited Company
**Line of Business:** New & used motor vehicle dealers
**Trading Style:** Taylors Bmw, Listers Bmw Boston, Listers Mini Boston
**Issued Capital:** £750,500
**Directors:** N J Taylor, T C Taylor, Ms D J Taylor
**Co. Secretary:** David Ryan
**Branches:** Taylors Service Garages (Boston) Ltd, Berry Way, Skegness, Lincolnshire PE25 3QS
**US SIC:** 5511, 5521, 5531
**UK SIC:** 65100
**Auditors:** Duncan & Toplis
**Bankers:** HSBC Bank plc (40-12-30)

|     | 30-04-14 | 30-04-13 | 30-04-12 |
|-----|----------|----------|----------|
| TO  | 22,307,348 | 23,023,055 | 20,631,220 |
| P/L | 419,803  | 95,530   | (31,188) |
| NW  | 5,196,296 | 5,096,688 | 5,051,637 |
| WC  | 2,498,638 | 2,222,230 | 2,060,388 |
| Emp.| 84       | 89       | 93       |

DUNS 21-709-4910
### Taylors the Bakers 2011 Ltd
Taylor House Boodle Street, Ashton-Under-Lyne, Lancashire OL6 8NF
**Tel:** 01613394891
**Reg No:** 7500133 **Estd:** 2011 Private Limited Company
**Line of Business:** Retail sale of bread, cakes, flour confectionery and sugar confectionery
**Issued Capital:** £100
**Director:** S Taylor
**Co. Secretary:** Stanley Taylor
**US SIC:** 5462 **UK SIC:** 64100

|     | 31-01-14 | 31-01-13 | 31-01-12 |
|-----|----------|----------|----------|
| TO  | 7,352,409 | 7,083,705 | 6,687,769 |
| P/L | 245,892  | 243,453  | 127,313  |
| NW  | 82,406   | 56,467   | (17,708) |
| WC  | (223,734)| (154,073)| (191,634)|
| Emp.| 142      | 138      | 129      |

DUNS 21-846-2509
### Taylor's Timber Centre Ltd
330 Thornton Road, Bradford, West Yorkshire BD8 8LD
**Tel:** 01274484404
**Web:** www.taylortimber.co.uk
**Reg No:** 8119932 **Estd:** 1960 Private Limited Company
**Line of Business:** Timber merchants
**Issued Capital:** £200
**Directors:** Mrs J Taylor, C E Taylor
**Responsibilities**
**Senior:** Russell Tallant (Manager)
**Sales:** John Tallant (Sales Director)
**US SIC:** 5072 **UK SIC:** 61500

|     | 30-06-13 |
|-----|----------|
| TA  | 263,431  |
| NW  | 1,569    |
| WC  | 36,575   |

DUNS 73-782-3745     **Imp**
### Taylors Transport International Ltd
Nunn Brook Road, Sutton-In-Ashfield, Nottinghamshire NG17 2HU
**Tel:** 01623757900 **Fax:** 01623757175
**Web:** www.taylorsint.com
**Reg No:** 5039028 **VAT No:** 379244421
**Estd:** 2004 Private Limited Company
**Line of Business:** Cargo handling
**Issued Capital:** £100
**Director:** A Taylor
**Co. Secretary:** Ms Michaela Taylor
**US SIC:** 4712, 4213
**UK SIC:** 77002, 72300

|     | 31-03-14 | 31-03-13 | 31-03-12 |
|-----|----------|----------|----------|
| TA  | 1,639,475 | 1,336,876 | 1,188,844 |
| NW  | 689,726  | 547,004  | 428,977  |
| WC  | 683,776  | 534,541  | 426,471  |

DUNS 21-039-7343
### Taylorshaw Valves
St Thomas Road, Huddersfield, West Yorkshire HD1 3LG
**Tel:** 01484-484880
**Web:** www.taylorshaw.co.uk
**Estd:** 2007 Proprietorship
**Line of Business:** Manufacture of engines and turbines, except aircraft, vehicle and cycle engines
**Proprietor:** J Blackhall
**US SIC:** 3519 **UK SIC:** 32811
**Employees:** 55

DUNS 21-579-6054
### Taymer Nursing Home
Barton Road, Silsoe, Bedford, Bedfordshire MK45 4QP
**Tel:** 01525861833
**Web:** www.pressbeau.co.uk
**Estd:** 1990 Proprietorship
**Line of Business:** Nursing homes
**Proprietor:** S Saraogi
**Responsibilities**
**Senior:** Margaret Collins (Manager)
**US SIC:** 8051 **UK SIC:** 95100
**Employees:** 51

DUNS 21-699-1406
### Taymix Transport Ltd
(Subsidiary of: R & J Taymix Ltd)
Unit 1 Clump Farm Industrial Estate, Shaftesbury Lane, Blandford Forum, Dorset DT11 7TD
**Tel:** 01258452696
**Reg No:** 0630498 **VAT No:** 634448825
**Estd:** 1959 Private Limited Company
**Line of Business:** Other letting of own property
**Trading Style:** Taymix Ltd
**Issued Capital:** £222,000
**Managing Director:** C D Taylor
**Co. Secretary:** Mrs Claire Ridout
**US SIC:** 6519, 7394
**UK SIC:** 85000, 84000
**Auditors:** Mazars Neville Russell

**Bankers:** Barclays Bank Plc (20-75-01)

|     | 31-12-13 | 31-12-12 | 31-12-11 |
|-----|----------|----------|----------|
| TA  | 2,511,785 | 2,520,070 | 3,007,389 |
| NW  | 2,046,462 | 1,980,214 | 1,923,065 |
| WC  | 165,849  | 187,594  | 178,314  |

DUNS 33-970-9479
### Tayside Contracts
Soutar Street, Dundee, Angus DD3 8SS
**Tel:** 01382812721
**Web:** www.tayside-contracts.co.uk
**VAT No:** 664031947 **Estd:** 1982 Partnership
**Line of Business:** Caterers
**Trading Style:** Tayside Contracts
**Partners:** Dundee City Council, Perth & Kinross Council, Angus Council
**Responsibilities**
**Senior:** Iain Waddell (Manager)
**Finance:** Angus Milne (Head of Finance)
**HR:** Ron McCabe (Training Manager), Frank Reilly (Head of Personnel Services)
**Health & Safety:** Elaine Strachan (health & Safety Officer)
**Facilities:** Jane West (Facilities Manager)
**Branches:** Tayside Contracts, Glenearn Road, Perth, Perthshire PH2 0BD
**US SIC:** 5812, 7341, 7349
**UK SIC:** 66110, 92300
**Employees:** 200

DUNS 29-666-1846
### The Tayside Council on Alcohol
50 Constable St The Wishart Centre, Dundee, Angus DD4 6AD
**Tel:** 01382456012
**Reg No:** 0097522SC **Estd:** 1986 Private Limited Company
**Line of Business:** Social work activities without accommodation
**Directors:** Mrs S Ross, R M Rae, D Mitchell, Mrs C A Anderson, B Harkins, R Ross, Dr P M Rice, B Mutch
**Co. Secretary:** Robert Rae
**Responsibilities**
**Senior:** Muriel Anderson (Director), Frances Claridge (Manager)
**US SIC:** 8321 **UK SIC:** 96111
**Bankers:** The Royal Bank Of Scotland Plc (83-50-00)

|     | 31-03-14 | 31-03-13 | 31-03-12 |
|-----|----------|----------|----------|
| TO  | 1,060,270 | 924,246  | 825,448  |
| P/L | 15,559   | 71,321   | 82,945   |
| NW  | 528,110  | 512,551  | 441,230  |
| WC  | 443,780  | 430,011  | 354,947  |
| Emp.| 54       | 53       | 50       |

DUNS 42-487-3065     **Imp**
### Tayside Fire & Rescue
Fire And Rescue Headquarters, Blackness Road, Dundee, Angus DD1 5PA
**Tel:** 01382-322222 **Fax:** 01382-200791
**Web:** www.taysidefire.gov.uk
**Estd:** 1974 Incorporate By Act Of Parliament
**Line of Business:** Fire stations
**Director:** D S Marr
**Branches:** Tayside Fire & Rescue, Fire Station, Ponderlaw Street, Arbroath, Angus DD11 1EU
**US SIC:** 9224 **UK SIC:** 91400
**Employees:** 150

DUNS 23-282-3687
### Tayside Police
West Bell Street, Dundee, Angus DD1 9JU
**Tel:** 01382223200 **Fax:** 01382200449
**Web:** www.tayside.police.uk
**Estd:** 1975 Incorporate By Act Of Parliament
**Line of Business:** Public security, law and order activities
**Principals:** W Bald, D Cross, J Vine, Mrs M Docherty (Manager), I Macleod
**Responsibilities**
**Senior:** Steve House (Chief constable Police Scotlan)
**Branches:** Tayside Police, Barrack St, Perth, Perthshire PH1 5SF
**US SIC:** 9221 **UK SIC:** 91300
**Employees:** 1,000

DUNS 29-666-2604
### Tayside Public Transport Company Ltd
(Subsidiary of: National Express Group Plc)
44-48 East Dock Street, Dundee, Angus DD1 3JS
**Tel:** 01382-201121 **Fax:** 01382201997
**Web:** www.nxbus.co.uk
**Reg No:** 0097606SC **Estd:** 1986 Private Limited Company
**Line of Business:** Bus operators and stations
**Trading Style:** Travel Dundee, Travel Greyhound
**Issued Capital:** £1,700,000
**Directors:** Ms E P Turbyne, S Parker, T D Bonham, P T Coates, M D Hancock
**Co. Secretary:** Ms Dianne Robinson

**Responsibilities**
**Senior:** Barbara Lees *(Manager)*, Heather McDonald *(Chief Executive)*
**US SIC:** 4119 **UK SIC:** 72200
**Auditors:** Ernst & Young LLP
**Bankers:** The Royal Bank Of Scotland Plc (83-50-00)

| | 31-12-13 | 31-12-12 | 31-12-11 |
|---|---|---|---|
| TO | 16,159,000 | 15,992,000 | 15,879,000 |
| P/L | 1,308,000 | 1,357,000 | 1,234,000 |
| NW | 16,800,000 | 16,065,000 | 13,419,000 |
| WC | 5,004,000 | 5,735,000 | 4,755,000 |
| Emp. | 337 | 339 | 337 |

DUNS 23-528-6338

## Tayside Security Ltd

76a Camphill Road, Broughty Ferr, 76a Camphill Road, Broughty Ferry, Dundee, Angus DD5 2LX
**Tel:** 01382-730166 **Fax:** 01382730166
**Web:** www.taysidesecurity.co.uk
**Reg No:** 0183871SC **VAT No:** 271147571
**Estd:** 1998 Private Limited Company
**Line of Business:** Security activities
**Issued Capital:** £100,000
**Directors:** Ms E Cheape, D Cheape
**Co. Secretary:** Andrew Cheape
**US SIC:** 7393, 6411
**UK SIC:** 83954, 83200
**Auditors:** Walker Dunnett & Co
**Bankers:** Clydesdale Bank Plc (82-62-15)

| | 31-03-14 | 31-03-13 | 31-03-12 |
|---|---|---|---|
| TA | 344,075 | 239,518 | 249,227 |
| NW | 78,740 | 14,398 | 20,735 |
| WC | 65,460 | 1,674 | 7,527 |

DUNS 21-127-3981

## Tayto Group Ltd

**(Subsidiary of:** Manderley Food Group Ltd)
Princewood Road, Earlstrees Industrial Estate, Corby, Northamptonshire NN17 4AP
**Tel:** 01536204200
**Web:** www.tayto.com
**Reg No:** 6622104 **Estd:** 2007 Private Limited Company
**Line of Business:** Holding companies management activities
**Issued Capital:** £71,922,001
**Directors:** R L Hutchinson, Mrs A A Hutchinson Kane, P Allen
**Co. Secretary:** Stephen Hutchinson
**Responsibilities**
**Senior:** Bob Hartley *(Manager)*, Helen Jameson *(Personnel Manager)*, Martin Mcilhinney *(Operations Director)*, Simon Proctor *(General Manager)*
**Finance:** John Delanie *(Head of Finance)*
**HR:** Helen Jameson *(Personnel Manager)*
**Health & Safety:** Helen Jameson *(Personnel Manager)*
**Operations:** Helen Jameson *(Personnel Manager)*
**US SIC:** 6711, 2033
**UK SIC:** 83962, 41473
**Bankers:** Ulster Bank Ltd (98-00-00)

| | 29-06-13 | 30-06-12 | 31-06-11 |
|---|---|---|---|
| TO | 166,041,673 | 82,102,886 | 77,613,891 |
| P/L | 4,741,151 | (153,837) | (1,295,300) |
| NW | 39,830,496 | 36,222,037 | 51,001,861 |
| WC | 37,376,254 | 27,106,844 | (1,989,938) |
| Emp. | 1,380 | 1,345 | 244 |

DUNS 21-458-8568 Imp-Exp

## Tayto (N.I.) Ltd

**(Subsidiary of:** Manderley Food Group Ltd)
Tayto Castle, Craigavon, Co Armagh BT62 2AB
**Tel:** 028-3884-0249 **Fax:** 028-3884-0085
**Web:** www.tayto.com
**Reg No:** 0003670NI **VAT No:** 575490901
**Estd:** 1956 Private Limited Company
**Line of Business:** Manufacturers of food products
**Export Markets:** Republic of Ireland, Canada and U S A
**Trading Style:** G W Trading, C T O Holding, Real Crisps, Red Mill Snack
**Issued Capital:** £100,000
**Directors:** S T Hutchinson, P Allen, R L Hutchinson, Mrs A A Hutchinson-Kane
**Co. Secretary:** Raymond Hutchinson
**Responsibilities**
**Marketing:** Elly Hunter *(Sales & Marketing Manager)*
**Sales:** Elly Hunter *(Sales & Marketing Manager)*
**IT:** John McCann *(IT Executive)*
**HR:** Carolyn Beattie *(Human Resources Manager)*
**Operations:** Roberta Warnock *(Customer Services Manager)*
**Engineering:** Nigel Black *(Engineering Manager)*
**Branches:** Tayto (N.i.) Ltd, 6 Pit Hey Place, Skelmersdale, Lancashire WN8 9PS
**US SIC:** 2099 **UK SIC:** 42399
**Auditors:** PricewaterhouseCoopers LLP
**Bankers:** Ulster Bank Ltd (98-00-00)

| | 29-06-13 | 30-06-12 | 02-06-11 |
|---|---|---|---|
| TO | N/A | 20,845,793 | 18,313,215 |
| P/L | N/A | 227,356 | (591,458) |
| NW | 47,534,270 | 47,605,520 | 49,408,586 |
| WC | 47,534,270 | 47,605,520 | 42,731,183 |
| Emp. | N/A | 288 | 274 |

DUNS 21-160-5449 Imp-Exp

## Tazaki Foods Ltd

**(Subsidiary of:** Takara Holdings Inc.)
Unit 4, Delta Park Industrial Estate, Enfield, Middlesex EN3 7QJ
**Tel:** 02083443000
**Web:** www.tazakifoods.com
**Reg No:** 1380731 **VAT No:** 232006716
**Estd:** 1978 Private Limited Company
**Line of Business:** Importers of beer, wine and spirits
**Export Sales:** £2,637,119
**Issued Capital:** £357,000
**Directors:** H Kaneko, K Ito, H Omiya, C Furukawa
**Co. Secretary:** Hiroshi Kaneko
**US SIC:** 5149, 5411
**UK SIC:** 61700, 64100
**Auditors:** Richard Anthony & Co

| | 31-12-13 | 31-12-12 | 31-12-11 |
|---|---|---|---|
| TO | 25,289,179 | 20,758,778 | 17,042,689 |
| P/L | 2,172,231 | 779,937 | 90,490 |
| NW | 2,840,390 | 1,751,716 | 1,489,812 |
| WC | 2,565,102 | 1,440,870 | 1,140,742 |
| Emp. | 70 | 69 | 66 |

DUNS 34-637-3426

## Taziker Industrial Ltd

**(Subsidiary of:** Ti Industrial Group Ltd)
Unit 5-6 Lodge Bank, Crown Lane, Bolton, Lancashire BL6 5HY
**Fax:** 01204-695188
**Web:** www.tazikerindustrial.co.uk
**Reg No:** 2766990 **VAT No:** 560722063
**Estd:** 1992 Private Limited Company
**Line of Business:** Painting contractors
**Trading Style:** T I Protective Coatings
**Issued Capital:** £100
**Principals:** G P Moor *(Managing)*, M S Taziker, N T Taziker, J P Worrall, T Taziker
**Co. Secretary:** Mrs Beverley Moor
**Responsibilities**
**Senior:** Joan Taziker *(Manager)*
**Health & Safety:** Julie Taziker *(HSQE Manager)*
**US SIC:** 8911, 1799
**UK SIC:** 83701, 50000
**Auditors:** Rushtons
**Bankers:** Barclays Bank Plc (20-10-71)

| | 31-03-14 | 31-03-13 | 31-03-12 |
|---|---|---|---|
| TO | 42,538,223 | 35,051,094 | 16,534,216 |
| P/L | 8,507,455 | 7,898,003 | 3,410,337 |
| NW | 3,503,979 | 1,976,779 | 1,153,297 |
| WC | 2,617,823 | 986,132 | 168,156 |
| Emp. | 213 | 178 | 91 |

DUNS 53-620-0330 Exp

## Tba Textiles Ltd

**(Subsidiary of:** Ferotec Ltd)
Unit 3, Transpennine Trading Estate, Gorrells Way, Rochdale, Lancashire OL11 2PX
**Tel:** 01706-647-422
**Web:** www.tbatextiles.co.uk
**Reg No:** 3425139 **VAT No:** 707991893
**Estd:** 1997 Private Limited Company
**Line of Business:** Misc housefurnishing manufacturers
**Issued Capital:** £1
**Director:** B C Smith
**Co. Secretary:** Craig Smith
**Responsibilities**
**Senior:** Phillip Ingham *(General Manager)*
**Finance:** Duncan Morrison *(Financial Controller)*
**Marketing:** Viv Fisher *(Sales & Marketing Manager)*
**Sales:** Viv Fisher *(Sales & Marketing Manager)*
**Health & Safety:** Phillip Ingham *(General Manager)*
**Facilities:** Christine Oldroyd *(Facilities Manager)*
**Operations:** Phillip Ingham *(General Manager)*
**Purchasing:** Susan Holland *(Purchasing Coordinator)*
**Branches:** Tba Textiles Ltd, Unit 3 Trans Pennine Trading Estate, Gorrells Way, Rochdale, Lancashire OL11 2PX
**US SIC:** 2392, 2269, 2299
**UK SIC:** 45550, 43702, 43992
**Auditors:** Hawley & Co
**Bankers:** National Westminster Bank Plc (01-10-01)

| | 31-12-13 | 31-12-12 | 31-12-11 |
|---|---|---|---|
| TO | 7,724,228 | 7,728,389 | 8,693,998 |
| P/L | (120,711) | (10,870) | 247,422 |
| NW | 1,054,518 | 1,152,104 | 1,168,474 |
| WC | 887,768 | 1,076,950 | 919,105 |
| Emp. | 68 | 70 | 71 |

DUNS 73-538-6901 Imp

## Tbd (Owen Holland) Ltd

**(Subsidiary of:** T B Davies (Holdings) Ltd)
Waterton House, Waterton Industrial Estate, Bridgend, Mid Glamorgan CF31 3US
**Tel:** 01656-652-202
**Web:** www.tbduk.co.uk
**Reg No:** 4801056 **VAT No:** 821448834
**Estd:** 2003 Private Limited Company
**Line of Business:** Manufacturers and suppliers of aircrafts
**Export Sales:** £2,510,218
**Issued Capital:** £102,088
**Directors:** S C Meredith, R Kishor, P W Durigg, P L Summers, S G Williams
**Co. Secretary:** Ms Victoria Heycock
**US SIC:** 3721 **UK SIC:** 36400
**Auditors:** Watts Gregory LLP
**Bankers:** National Westminster Bank Plc (51-81-29)

| | 31-12-13 | 31-12-12 | 31-12-11 |
|---|---|---|---|
| TO | 6,008,743 | 4,418,852 | 4,405,845 |
| P/L | 32,537 | 33,584 | 226,275 |
| NW | 516,957 | 757,260 | 900,022 |
| WC | (456,180) | (54,517) | 44,462 |
| Emp. | 102 | 82 | 87 |

DUNS 23-503-6977

## T.B.E. (Motor Services) Ltd

35 Lawton Road, Alsager, Stoke-On-Trent, Staffordshire ST7 2AA
**Web:** www.tbecars.co.uk
**Reg No:** 1611795 **VAT No:** 319106772
**Estd:** 2002 Private Limited Company
**Line of Business:** Miscellaneous vehicle repair
**Issued Capital:** £82,500
**Director:** A Mantle
**Co. Secretary:** Ms Patricia Mantle
**Responsibilities**
**Senior:** Alan Mantele *(Managing Director)*
**Branches:** T.b.e. (Motor Services) Ltd, Congleton Road, Stoke-On-Trent, Staffordshire ST7 1LW
**US SIC:** 7539, 5531
**UK SIC:** 67100, 65100
**Auditors:** Murray
**Bankers:** Barclays Bank Plc (20-24-09)

| | 31-03-14 | 31-03-13 | 31-03-12 |
|---|---|---|---|
| TA | 2,605,556 | 2,670,640 | 2,615,144 |
| NW | 1,902,107 | 2,081,696 | 2,295,622 |
| WC | 1,342,633 | 1,513,174 | 1,692,770 |

DUNS 22-236-5905

## Tbg Digital Ltd

**(Subsidiary of:** Sprinklr Inc.)
Unit 100, Highgate Studios, 53-79 Highgate Road, London NW5 1TL
**Tel:** 020-7428-6650
**Web:** www.tbgdigital.com
**Reg No:** 4254616 **Estd:** 2001 Private Limited Company
**Line of Business:** Advertising
**Export Sales:** £31,403,000
**Issued Capital:** £13,000
**Directors:** S Mansell, D Freire
**Co. Secretary:** Diogo Freire
**Responsibilities**
**Senior:** Duncan Donald *(Manager)*, Ramola Mansell *(Manager)*, Charlotte Morris *(Office Manager)*, Bianca Ohannessian *(Office Manager)*
**US SIC:** 7311 **UK SIC:** 83800
**Auditors:** Sopher & Co

| | 31-12-13 | 31-12-12 | 31-12-11 |
|---|---|---|---|
| TO | 48,042,000 | 69,338,000 | 66,537,000 |
| P/L | 1,164,000 | 109,000 | 1,585,000 |
| NW | 2,135,000 | 1,508,000 | 1,940,000 |
| WC | 1,615,000 | 306,000 | 1,218,000 |
| Emp. | 93 | 98 | 65 |

DUNS 21-106-5756

## Tbo Services Ltd

**(Subsidiary of:** Tbo Holdings Ltd)
2nd Floor Marsland House, Marsland Road, Sale, Cheshire M33 3AQ
**Tel:** 0161 968 2042 **Fax:** 0161 973 9658
**Web:** http://insuranceoctopus.co.uk
**Reg No:** 6489013 **Estd:** 2008 Private Limited Company
**Line of Business:** Non-life insurance
**Trading Style:** The Insurance Octopus, The Business Octopus
**Issued Capital:** £100
**Directors:** M Winniczuk, K Norton
**Co. Secretary:** Mrs Hannah Norton
**Responsibilities**
**Marketing:** Matt Simpson *(Sales and Marketing Lead)*
**Sales:** Matt Simpson *(Sales and Marketing Lead)*
**US SIC:** 6399, 7399
**UK SIC:** 82001, 83954
**Auditors:** Mitten Clarke Ltd

| | 31-03-14 | 31-03-13 | 31-03-12 |
|---|---|---|---|
| TA | 3,509,062 | 1,045,132 | 1,145,821 |
| NW | 1,453,636 | 196,534 | 309,218 |
| WC | 1,999,918 | 172,234 | 291,890 |

DUNS 21-929-4139

## Tbs Building Supplies Ltd

**(Subsidiary of:** House of Goodness Ltd)
Hackwood Road, Daventry, Northamptonshire NN11 4ES
**Tel:** 01327-877378
**Web:** www.tbsmerchants.co.uk
**Reg No:** 1388913 **VAT No:** 294334346
**Estd:** 1978 Private Limited Company
**Line of Business:** Agents involved in the sale of timber and building materials
**Issued Capital:** £5,000
**Directors:** J A Thomason, S Bullock, E P Hunt, J Walsma, Ms H J Oldham, M J Farrant
**Co. Secretary:** Miss Hilary Oldham
**Branches:** Tbs Building Supplies Ltd, Old Greens Norton Road, Towcester, Northamptonshire NN12 8AX
**US SIC:** 5072 **UK SIC:** 61500
**Auditors:** PricewaterhouseCoopers
**Bankers:** Barclays Bank Plc (20-61-51)

| | 31-12-13 | 31-12-12 | 31-12-11 |
|---|---|---|---|
| TO | 8,651,238 | 8,620,616 | 8,095,866 |
| P/L | 249,409 | 225,672 | 320,422 |
| NW | 3,342,911 | 3,162,562 | 3,001,110 |
| WC | 610,354 | 203,703 | 115,382 |
| Emp. | 73 | 76 | 68 |

DUNS 50-481-9210 Exp

## Tbs Engineering Ltd

**(Subsidiary of:** Berkshire Hathaway Inc.)
Units 5-8, Gloucester Road Lansdown Trading Estate, Cheltenham, Gloucestershire GL51 8PW
**Fax:** 01242680909
**Web:** www.tbsengineering.co.uk
**Reg No:** 2455748 **VAT No:** 535832633
**Estd:** 1967 Private Limited Company
**Line of Business:** Manufacturers general
**Export Markets:** Europe
**Export Sales:** £25,526,318
**Issued Capital:** £1,229,002
**Principals:** L E Gardiner *(Managing)*, D J Longney, C Barge, T J Manenti
**Co. Secretary:** Ms Vivienne Empson
**Responsibilities**
**Senior:** Steve Minchin *(Works Manager)*
**Facilities:** Steve Minchin *(Works Manager)*
**Operations:** Steve Minchin *(Works Manager)*
**Purchasing:** Bill Stratton *(Purchasing Manager)*
**Engineering:** Steve Minchin *(Works Manager)*
**US SIC:** 3999 **UK SIC:** 49590
**Auditors:** Hazlewoods LLP
**Bankers:** Lloyds TSB Bank plc (30-12-18)

| | 31-12-13 | 31-12-12 | 31-12-11 |
|---|---|---|---|
| TO | 25,829,824 | 33,801,230 | 37,466,907 |
| P/L | 8,610,467 | 13,158,548 | 14,510,472 |
| NW | 8,908,233 | 9,848,989 | 3,756,089 |
| WC | 10,398,126 | 10,427,392 | 3,863,213 |
| Emp. | 119 | 133 | 133 |

DUNS 73-804-9548 Imp

## Tbs G.B. Telematic & Biomedical Services Ltd

**(Subsidiary of:** Ital Tbs Telematic & Biomedical Services Spa)
Central House, 8 Clifftown Road, Southend-On-Sea, Essex SS1 1AB
**Fax:** 01702-608729
**Web:** www.tbsgb.com
**Reg No:** 5061290 **Estd:** 2004 Private Limited Company
**Line of Business:** Other manufacturing not elsewhere classified
**Export Sales:** £453,290
**Issued Capital:** £500,000
**Directors:** N F Bosanquet, N Pangher, G Giusto, J D Sandham
**Co. Secretary:** Paolo Salotto
**Responsibilities**
**Senior:** Brian De Francesca *(Manager)*, Pietro Torrusio *(Manager)*
**US SIC:** 3999, 8091
**UK SIC:** 49590, 95200
**Auditors:** Ernst & Young LLP
**Bankers:** National Westminster Bank Plc (55-50-28)

| | 31-12-13 | 31-12-12 | 31-12-11 |
|---|---|---|---|
| TO | 18,972,503 | 16,286,826 | 14,267,075 |
| P/L | 2,341,864 | 2,354,152 | 2,500,181 |
| NW | 2,465,522 | 1,674,228 | 2,583,340 |
| WC | 716,501 | 178,377 | (931,430) |
| Emp. | 177 | 178 | 104 |

DUNS 21-826-7441

## T.Butler & Son(Sawston) Ltd

Common Lane, Sawston, Cambridge, Cambridgeshire CB22 3HW
**Tel:** 01223-832156
**Web:** www.tdptextiles.com
**Reg No:** 0555280 **Estd:** 1955 Private Limited Company
**Line of Business:** Builders
**Issued Capital:** £6,000
**Principals:** T A Butler *(Managing)*, Ms J A Briggs, B J Butler

**Co. Secretary:** Thomas Butler
**US SIC:** 1522, 1541, 1751
**UK SIC:** 50100, 50400
**Auditors:** Peters Elworthy & Moore
**Bankers:** Barclays Bank Plc (20-17-19)

|     | 30-09-13 | 30-09-12 | 30-09-11 |
|-----|----------|----------|----------|
| TO  | 5,305,003 | 4,734,902 | 5,738,244 |
| P/L | 104,502 | (83,787) | (171,655) |
| NW  | 959,729 | 867,811 | 937,234 |
| WC  | 813,038 | 682,543 | 719,428 |
| Emp.| 64 | 75 | 68 |

DUNS 22-702-5889      **Imp-Exp**

## Tbwa\London Ltd

**(Subsidiary of:** Omnicom Group Inc.)
Bryan House 76 80, Whitfield Street, London
W1T 4EZ
**Tel:** 020-7573-6666 **Fax:** 02075736728
**Web:** www.tbwa-london.com
**Reg No:** 1367372 **VAT No:** 656899461
**Estd:** 1979 Private Limited Company
**Line of Business:** Advertising
**Export Markets:** E U, U S A & Rest of world
**Export Sales:** £17,967,919
**Issued Capital:** £125,006
**Directors:** N V Baum, G J Smith, D J Streiff,
P A Souter
**Co. Secretary:** Mrs Sally Bray
**Responsibilities**
**Senior:** Robert Harwood-Matthews
(President), Mark Hunter (Manager)
**Health & Safety:** Penny Kemsley (Facilities
Manager)
**Facilities:** Penny Kemsley (Facilities
Manager)
**Branches:** Tbwa\london Ltd, 14 Charlotte
Square, Edinburgh, Midlothian EH2 4DJ
**US SIC:** 7311 **UK SIC:** 83800
**Auditors:** Arthur Andersen

|     | 31-12-13 | 31-12-12 | 31-12-11 |
|-----|----------|----------|----------|
| TO  | 34,939,457 | 27,620,000 | 24,890,000 |
| P/L | (735,398) | 1,503,000 | 1,743,000 |
| NW  | 9,956,389 | 6,757,000 | 4,873,000 |
| WC  | 8,405,963 | 5,981,000 | 4,522,000 |
| Emp.| 247 | 224 | 196 |

DUNS 23-838-6952

## T.C. Cornwell Ltd

15 High Street, Newcastle, Staffordshire ST5
1RB
**Web:** www.cornwell.co.uk
**Reg No:** 3830379 **Estd:** 1999 Private
Limited Company
**Line of Business:** Buying and selling of own
real estate
**Export Sales:** £9,744
**Issued Capital:** £15,000
**Principals:** J J Mitchell (Managing),
C H Mitchell
**Co. Secretary:** Charles Mitchell
**US SIC:** 6531, 6519
**UK SIC:** 83400, 85000
**Auditors:** Baker Tilly

|     | 31-03-14 | 31-03-13 | 31-03-12 |
|-----|----------|----------|----------|
| TO  | 10,274,557 | 10,514,563 | 11,308,547 |
| P/L | (41,216) | (28,977) | 18,432 |
| NW  | 2,185,235 | 2,123,069 | 2,107,228 |
| WC  | 213,315 | 468,382 | 335,858 |
| Emp.| 100 | 103 | 104 |

DUNS 76-497-6403

## Tc Facilities Management Ltd

Sapphire House, 74-76 Walton Street,
Tadworth, Surrey KT20 7RU
**Tel:** 01737-814016 **Fax:** 01737814019
**Web:** www.tc-contractors.co.uk
**Reg No:** 2567667 **VAT No:** 210663207
**Estd:** 1990 Private Limited Company
**Line of Business:** Cleaning contracting
commercial
**Trading Style:** T C Contractors
**Issued Capital:** £110
**Principals:** T G Cripps (Managing),
R Chappell, S J Cripps, P Kennedy Obe
**Co. Secretary:** Ms Jennifer Cripps
**Responsibilities**
**Marketing:** Kevin Meighan (Marketing
Manager)
**HR:** Rosemary Allen (Human Resources
Manager)
**Health & Safety:** Brian Mould (Facilities
Manager)
**Facilities:** Brian Mould (Facilities Manager)
**US SIC:** 7349 **UK SIC:** 92300
**Auditors:** PKF
**Bankers:** Barclays Bank Plc (20-05-75)

|     | 31-03-14 | 31-03-13 | 31-03-12 |
|-----|----------|----------|----------|
| TO  | 70,362,124 | 65,529,600 | 65,161,287 |
| P/L | 1,925,507 | 2,289,868 | 2,357,866 |
| NW  | 3,357,991 | 3,217,258 | 2,010,558 |
| WC  | 174,495 | (421,248) | (1,585,410) |
| Emp.| 5,222 | 4,985 | 4,640 |

DUNS 29-168-8760

## Tc Industries of Europe Ltd

**(Subsidiary of:** Tcr Corp.)
Skinningrove Works, Saltburn-By-The-Sea,
Cleveland TS13 4EE
**Tel:** 01287-642627
**Web:** www.tcindustries.com
**Reg No:** 1822054 **VAT No:** 409259149

---

**Estd:** 1984 Private Limited Company
**Line of Business:** Engineers (general)
**Export Sales:** £14,421,363
**Issued Capital:** £750,000
**Directors:** G A Berry Iv, T Z Hayward Jr
**Co. Secretary:** Ms Kathleen Martinez
**Responsibilities**
**Senior:** Richard Flounders (Works Manager)
**HR:** Anita Summerson (Human Resources
Manager)
**Facilities:** Richard Flounders (Works
Manager)
**Purchasing:** Richard Flounders (Works
Manager)
**Engineering:** Richard Flounders (Works
Manager)
**US SIC:** 8911, 3531
**UK SIC:** 83701, 32541
**Auditors:** M. Wasley Chapman & Co
**Bankers:** Barclays Bank Plc (20-56-74)

|     | 31-12-13 | 31-12-12 | 31-12-11 |
|-----|----------|----------|----------|
| TO  | 14,712,713 | 14,850,145 | 16,361,573 |
| P/L | 841,531 | 868,730 | 1,301,593 |
| NW  | 7,091,875 | 6,330,889 | 5,660,696 |
| WC  | 5,089,639 | 4,516,308 | 3,702,111 |
| Emp.| 77 | 80 | 85 |

DUNS 21-693-0411

## Tcct Retail Ltd

**(Subsidiary of:** Thomas Cook Group Plc)
Thomas Cook Business Park, Coningsby
Road, Peterborough, Cambridgeshire PE3
8SB
**Tel:** 08009160655
**Web:** www.thomascook.co.uk
**Reg No:** 7397858 **Estd:** 2010 Private
Limited Company
**Line of Business:** Travel agency activities
**Issued Capital:** £100
**Directors:**
Thomas Cook Group Management Ser,
P A Hemingway
**Co. Secretary:** Ms Shirley Bradley
**Responsibilities**
**Senior:** Carla Pettie (Manager), Joanna Wild
(Director)
**US SIC:** 4722 **UK SIC:** 77001
**Auditors:** PricewaterhouseCoopers LLP

|     | 30-09-13 | 30-09-12 | 30-09-11 |
|-----|----------|----------|----------|
| TO  | 341,775,000 | 299,697,000 | 286,764,000 |
| P/L | (25,869,000) | (20,344,000) | (162,432,000) |
| NW  | (429,845,000) | (369,569,000) | (244,238,000) |
| WC  | (432,295,000) | (483,421,000) | (345,112,000) |
| Emp.| 5,693 | 5,929 | 5,400 |

DUNS 21-225-0113

## Tcd Interior Solutions

30 Tinshill Mount, Leeds, West Yorkshire
LS16 7AX
**Tel:** 07947437779
**Web:** www.acominteriorsolutions.com
**Estd:** 1997 Proprietorship
**Line of Business:** Kitchen planners and
installers
**US SIC:** 1731 **UK SIC:** 50300
**Employees:** 50

DUNS 21-612-8959      **Imp-Exp**

## Tchibo Coffee International Ltd

**(Subsidiary of:** Maxingvest Ag)
Blenheim Road, Epsom, Surrey KT19 9AP
**Tel:** 01372729644 **Fax:** 01372748916
**Web:** www.tchibo-coffeeservice.co.uk
**Reg No:** 0761849 **Estd:** 1963 Private
Limited Company
**Line of Business:** Coffee and tea merchants
**Export Markets:** E U
**Issued Capital:** £44,821,364
**Directors:** P H Simpkins, P Chadderton
**Co. Secretary:** Mrs Kate Asamoa
**Responsibilities**
**Senior:** Luke Beresford-Ward (Marketing
Executive), Gunnar Steffek (Manager)
**Finance:** Ralph Baptista (Finance Director)
**Marketing:** Luke Beresford-Ward (Marketing
Executive)
**Sales:** Tina Hares (Sales Manager), Philippa
Kings (Operations Director)
**IT:** Philippa Kings (Operations Director)
**HR:** Lesley Lambert (Human Resources
Manager), Ian Stanley (Human Resources
Manager)
**Health & Safety:** Lesley Lambert (Human
Resources Manager), Ian Stanley (Human
Resources Manager)
**Facilities:** Colin Battrick (Purchasing
Manager)
**Purchasing:** Colin Battrick (Purchasing
Manager), Philippa Kings (Operations
Director)
**Branches:** Tchibo Coffee International Ltd,
6-8 London Rd, Bognor Regis, West Sussex
PO21 1AX
**US SIC:** 5149, 5084, 5199
**UK SIC:** 61700, 61490, 61900
**Auditors:** BDO Stoy Hayward LLP

---

**Bankers:** Barclays Bank Plc (20-77-67)

|     | 31-12-13 | 31-12-12 | 31-12-11 |
|-----|----------|----------|----------|
| TO  | 20,071,396 | 21,146,726 | 21,654,294 |
| P/L | 611,496 | 1,129,735 | 1,132,338 |
| NW  | 18,699,480 | 18,321,618 | 17,564,403 |
| WC  | 12,009,336 | 12,278,601 | 11,867,649 |
| Emp.| 130 | 139 | 130 |

DUNS 50-495-6202      **Imp-Exp**

## Tcl Manufacturing Ltd

Unit 1 Gateway Xiii Industrial Estate, Ferry
Lane, Rainham, Essex RM13 9JY
**Tel:** 01708-526-361
**Web:** www.perrinandrowe.co.uk
**Reg No:** 2463775 **VAT No:** 342279065
**Estd:** 1978 Private Limited Company
**Line of Business:** Manufacture of taps and
valves
**Export Markets:** Worldwide
**Export Sales:** £4,589,578
**Trading Style:** Perrin and Rowe
**Issued Capital:** £4,002,126
**Directors:** L Rohl, S C Cole
**Co. Secretary:** Ian Walker
**Responsibilities**
**Senior:** Frederick Kwok (Manager), Klaus
Rasmussen (Manager)
**Branches:** Tcl Manufacturing Ltd, 1
Buckwins Square, Basildon, Essex SS13 1BJ
**US SIC:** 3499 **UK SIC:** 31694
**Auditors:** BDO LLP
**Bankers:** The Royal Bank Of Scotland Plc
(16-00-35)

|     | 31-10-13 | 31-12-12 | 31-10-11 |
|-----|----------|----------|----------|
| TO  | 7,835,845 | 9,157,580 | 11,446,905 |
| P/L | (16,815) | (1,414,097) | (887,535) |
| NW  | 1,126,054 | 634,377 | 1,739,956 |
| WC  | 544,093 | (115,103) | 610,887 |
| Emp.| 141 | 147 | 161 |

DUNS 23-798-1910      **Imp**

## Tcl Packaging Ltd

**(Subsidiary of:** Goldstrom Ltd)
Unit C7, Hortonwood 10, Telford, Shropshire
TF1 7ES
**Tel:** 01952677374 **Fax:** 01952-670-473
**Web:** www.tcl-packaging.co.uk
**Reg No:** 3790889 **VAT No:** 738716306
**Estd:** 1999 Private Limited Company
**Line of Business:** Manufacture of printed
packaging materials.
**Export Sales:** £294,807
**Issued Capital:** £12,500
**Directors:** M Jarvstrom, M J Golding
**Co. Secretary:** Kevin Edwards
**Responsibilities**
**Senior:** Timothy Crow (Director & CEO)
**US SIC:** 2654, 3079
**UK SIC:** 47280, 48360
**Auditors:** Lancaster Haskins LLP
**Bankers:** Barclays Bank Plc (20-97-78)

|     | 30-09-14 | 30-09-13 | 30-09-12 |
|-----|----------|----------|----------|
| TO  | 10,433,530 | 9,665,919 | 8,780,113 |
| P/L | 432,753 | 513,668 | 449,487 |
| NW  | 2,137,787 | 1,743,970 | 1,264,320 |
| WC  | 528,301 | 883,142 | 410,127 |
| Emp.| 59 | 50 | 50 |

DUNS 21-708-8202      **Imp**

## T.Cox & Son Ltd

Hargreaves Business Park, Hargreaves
Road, Eastbourne, East Sussex BN23 6QW
**Reg No:** 0575753 **Estd:** 1896 Private
Limited Company
**Line of Business:** Management activities of
holding companies
**Issued Capital:** £28,094
**Chairman:** D G Piper
**Co. Secretary:** Michael Cleary
**Responsibilities**
**Admin:** Stephanie Arnold (Admin)
**US SIC:** 6711 **UK SIC:** 83962
**Auditors:** Watson Associates (Audit
Services) Ltd
**Bankers:** Barclays Bank Plc (20-27-91)

|     | 31-12-13 | 31-12-12 | 31-12-11 |
|-----|----------|----------|----------|
| TO  | 13,389,726 | 12,276,434 | 12,045,113 |
| P/L | 286,367 | 105,198 | 152,918 |
| NW  | 6,002,224 | 6,000,566 | 5,995,522 |
| WC  | 1,597,022 | 1,437,156 | 1,425,612 |
| Emp.| 131 | 139 | 156 |

DUNS 23-887-9311

## Tcp Managed Services Ltd

**(Subsidiary of:** T C P Solutions Plc)
58a Waldeck Road, London W4 3NP
**Tel:** 02085800800 **Fax:** 02089960871
**Web:** www.tcpsolutions.com
**Reg No:** 3878996 **Estd:** 1999 Private
Limited Company
**Line of Business:** Management of real
estate on a fee or contract basis
**Export Sales:** £4,258,456
**Issued Capital:** £1
**Directors:** M J Chapman, N J Chapman
**Co. Secretary:** Waldeck Secretaries Limited
**US SIC:** 7399 **UK SIC:** 83954

---

**Auditors:** Felton Pumphrey

|     | 31-12-13 | 31-12-12 | 30-12-12 |
|-----|----------|----------|----------|
| TO  | 8,389,043 | 4,132,497 | 9,821,878 |
| P/L | 71,574 | 35,936 | (150,716) |
| NW  | 144,706 | 56,027 | 24,447 |
| WC  | 249,101 | 155,913 | 124,423 |
| Emp.| 85 | 111 | 134 |

DUNS 28-916-5532      **Imp-Exp**

## Tcs John Huxley Europe Ltd

**(Subsidiary of:** Pata-Pata Ab)
Unit 9 Mulberry Business Centre,
Rotherhithe, London SE16 7LB
**Tel:** 01782-260-220
**Web:** www.tcsjohnhuxley.com
**Reg No:** 1449986 **VAT No:** 548028830
**Estd:** 1979 Private Limited Company
**Line of Business:** Activities of exhibition and
fair organisers
**Export Markets:** E U, U.S.A.
**Export Sales:** £8,461,586
**Issued Capital:** £1,000
**Directors:** T N Sjoberg, E Poulton
**Responsibilities**
**Senior:** David Heap (Manager)
**Marketing:** Tracy Cohen (Marketing
Manager)
**Branches:** Tcs John Huxley Europe Ltd,
Forge La, Stoke-On-Trent, Staffordshire ST1
5NP
**US SIC:** 7399, 5199
**UK SIC:** 83954, 61900
**Auditors:** Wingrave Yeats Partnership LLP
**Bankers:** Lloyds TSB Bank plc (30-93-80)

|     | 31-12-13 | 31-12-12 | 31-12-11 |
|-----|----------|----------|----------|
| TO  | 22,440,545 | 22,594,061 | 22,659,047 |
| P/L | 89,200 | 600,412 | 1,583,321 |
| NW  | 12,564,700 | 13,320,825 | 13,350,316 |
| WC  | 13,473,756 | 12,576,158 | 12,008,813 |
| Emp.| 165 | N/A | 139 |

DUNS 49-372-8216

## Tcs John Huxley Ltd

**(Subsidiary of:** Pata-Pata Ab)
9g Albert Embankment Salamanca Square,
London SE1 7SP
**Tel:** 02078400000 **Fax:** 020-8807-4261
**Web:** www.tcsjohnhuxley.com
**Reg No:** 3126419 **Estd:** 2012 Private
Limited Company
**Line of Business:** Manufacture of
professional and arcade games and toys
**Issued Capital:** £1,000
**Directors:** T N Sjoberg, E Poulton
**Responsibilities**
**Senior:** Ruth Andrews (Manager), David
Heap (Manager), Carl Knutson (Manager),
Michael Knutsson (Director)
**Admin:** Ruth Andrews (Manager)
**US SIC:** 7399 **UK SIC:** 83954

|     | 31-12-13 | 31-12-12 | 31-12-11 |
|-----|----------|----------|----------|
| TO  | 304,350 | 304,350 | N/A |
| P/L | 140,677 | 125,857 | N/A |
| NW  | 293,074 | 149,591 | (2,714) |
| WC  | (2,918,951) | (3,111,347) | (3,351,179) |

DUNS 29-571-7326

## Tcv Employment & Training Services Ltd

**(Subsidiary of:** Conservation Volunteers)
Sedum House, Mallard Way, Doncaster,
South Yorkshire DN4 8DB
**Tel:** 01302388888
**Web:** www.tcv.org.uk
**Reg No:** 1933576 **VAT No:** 404808172
**Estd:** 1985 Private Limited Company
**Line of Business:** Activities of private
training providers
**Issued Capital:** £2
**Directors:** Mrs O M Cochrane, P A Hirst,
N W Kerfoot, Mrs J Hopes
**Co. Secretary:** Ms Wendy Ellis
**Responsibilities**
**Senior:** Mark Gibson (Md)
**Branches:** Tcv Employment & Training
Services Ltd, 6 Manners View, Newport, Isle
Of Wight PO30 5FA
**US SIC:** 8999 **UK SIC:** 83954
**Auditors:** Grant Thornton UK LLP
**Bankers:** Yorkshire Bank Plc (05-04-14)

|     | 31-03-14 | 31-03-13 | 31-03-12 |
|-----|----------|----------|----------|
| TO  | 11,078,856 | 9,064,518 | 10,682,715 |
| P/L | 29,405 | (52,099) | N/A |
| NW  | 982,214 | 960,679 | 1,001,778 |
| WC  | 365,164 | 262,249 | 210,711 |
| Emp.| 239 | 254 | 212 |

DUNS 23-191-2049

## T.D. Bailey Investments Ltd

**(Subsidiary of:** Ganymede Care Ltd)
93 Knollys Road, London SW16 2JP
**Tel:** 02086776902 **Fax:** 020-8769-5959
**Web:** www.dulwichcarecentre.co.uk
**Reg No:** 2984237 **Estd:** 1994 Private
Limited Company
**Line of Business:** Residential care
establishments
**Trading Style:** Kingsdale Nursing Home
**Issued Capital:** £750,000
**Directors:** M Gash, S Dhandsa, Ms C Buse
**Co. Secretary:** John Caird

**Responsibilities**
**Senior:** Diana O'hare (*Centre Director*)
**US SIC:** 8321 **UK SIC:** 96111
**Auditors:** Haywood & Co
**Bankers:** National Westminster Bank Plc (60-11-17)

| | 29-03-14 | 30-03-13 | 31-03-12 |
|---|---|---|---|
| TO | 1,379,830 | 2,108,949 | 1,860,824 |
| P/L | (198,810) | (81,400) | 16,528 |
| NW | 4,272,676 | 4,471,487 | 5,807,703 |
| WC | (3,931,841) | (3,724,184) | (3,421,792) |
| Emp. | 68 | 93 | 89 |

DUNS 22-762-5167    Imp-Exp

## T.D. Cross Ltd

(**Subsidiary of:** Cross Holdings Ltd)
Shady Lane, Birmingham, West Midlands B44 9EU
**Tel:** 01213600155 **Fax:** 0121-325-1079
**Web:** www.crossmorse.com
**Reg No:** 1631813 **VAT No:** 661556231
**Estd:** 1982 Private Limited Company
**Line of Business:** Power transmission equipment
**Export Markets:** E U, Middle East
**Trading Style:** Cross & Morse
**Issued Capital:** £388,761
**Director:** M D Scudamore
**Co. Secretary:** David Shadbolt
**Responsibilities**
**Senior:** Charlie Till (*Works Manager*)
**Sales:** David Keatley (*Sales Manager*)
**Operations:** Charlie Till (*Works Manager*)
**Purchasing:** Patricia Pearson (*Purchasing Manager*)
**Engineering:** Charlie Till (*Works Manager*)
**US SIC:** 3568 **UK SIC:** 32613
**Auditors:** Rochesters Audit Services Ltd
**Bankers:** HSBC Bank plc (40-11-04)

| | 31-12-13 | 31-12-12 | 31-12-11 |
|---|---|---|---|
| TA | 3,272,030 | 3,224,226 | 3,111,203 |
| NW | 2,067,354 | 1,707,095 | 1,301,475 |
| WC | 1,352,280 | 1,053,260 | 782,987 |

DUNS 29-933-1454

## Td Direct Investing (Europe) Ltd

(**Subsidiary of:** Toronto-Dominion Bank The)
Exchange Court, Duncombe Street, Leeds, West Yorkshire LS1 4AX
**Fax:** 01133462501
**Web:** www.tddirectinvesting.ie
**Reg No:** 2101863 **Estd:** 1987 Private Limited Company
**Line of Business:** Financial intermediation not elsewhere classified
**Issued Capital:** £170,996,186
**Directors:** J M Wilson, M Singh, J B Eaton, B G Smith, D W Sutherland, P Masterson, J W Tracy, J G See
**Co. Secretary:** Mark Curle
**Responsibilities**
**Senior:** Philip Ireland (*Vice President*)
**Marketing:** Barbara Czyzowski (*Sales & Marketing Manager*)
**Sales:** Barbara Czyzowski (*Sales & Marketing Manager*)
**US SIC:** 6111, 7399
**UK SIC:** 81501, 83954
**Auditors:** Ernst & Young LLP
**Bankers:** National Westminster Bank Plc (01-05-31)

| | 31-10-13 | 31-10-12 | 31-10-11 |
|---|---|---|---|
| TA | 348,211,000 | 299,663,000 | 330,878,000 |
| P/L | (12,936,000) | (6,517,000) | 1,781,000 |
| NW | 34,168,000 | 45,247,000 | 51,147,000 |
| WC | 19,933,000 | 21,007,000 | 28,384,000 |
| Emp. | 562 | 569 | 611 |

DUNS 21-709-0687    Imp-Exp

## T.D. Williamson (U.K.) Ltd

(**Subsidiary of:** T. D. Williamson Inc.)
Faraday Road, Dorcan Way, Swindon, Wilts Sn3 5hf, Swindon, Wiltshire SN3 5HF
**Tel:** 01793-603600 **Fax:** 01793-603601
**Web:** www.tdwilliamson.com
**Reg No:** 0815090 **VAT No:** 195118354
**Estd:** 1964 Private Limited Company
**Line of Business:** Other manufacturing not elsewhere classified
**Export Markets:** W Europe, Middle East, E Europe, Africa
**Export Sales:** £6,318,069
**Issued Capital:** £2,584,869
**Directors:** Mrs P A Da Silva Mendonca, R M Pearce, Ms A Siebel, B A Thames, R Mcgrew
**Co. Secretary:** Paul Ackerman
**Branches:** Woksop
**US SIC:** 3999, 7399
**UK SIC:** 49590, 83954
**Auditors:** PricewaterhouseCoopers LLP
**Bankers:** Barclays Bank Plc (20-84-58)

| | 31-12-13 | 31-12-12 | 31-12-11 |
|---|---|---|---|
| TO | 6,842,953 | 10,189,070 | 9,158,330 |
| P/L | (29,755) | (1,625,101) | (1,829,886) |
| NW | (6,390,818) | (6,290,643) | (4,665,492) |
| WC | (9,080,498) | (8,929,626) | (6,547,894) |
| Emp. | 58 | 63 | 50 |

DUNS 21-602-1923

## Tdg (Uk) Ltd

(**Subsidiary of:** Dentressangle Intitiatives)
Euroterminal, Westinghouse Road, Manchester M17 1PY
**Tel:** 01675467447 **Fax:** 01618726084
**Web:** www.tdg.eu.com
**Reg No:** 0540403 **Estd:** 1954 Private Limited Company
**Line of Business:** Cargo handling
**Trading Style:** Norbert Dentressanglie
**Issued Capital:** £101,100,000
**Directors:** D S Myers, Ms L G Navid Lane, P Bataillard, Dr H F Montjotin, G De La Rochebrochard, P J Shaw, M Wilson
**Co. Secretary:** Ms Lyndsay Navid Lane
**Responsibilities**
**Senior:** Mike Brannigan (*Chief Executive Officer*), Michael Bridges (*Manager*)
**Branches:** Tdg (Uk) Ltd, Goodwood Road, Eastleigh, Hampshire SO50 4NT
**US SIC:** 4712 **UK SIC:** 77002
**Auditors:** KPMG LLP
**Bankers:** Barclays Bank Plc (20-00-00)

| | 31-12-13 | 31-12-12 | 31-12-11 |
|---|---|---|---|
| TO | N/A | 6,489,000 | 377,620,000 |
| P/L | 4,130,000 | 12,790,000 | 155,042,000 |
| NW | 131,915,000 | 153,989,000 | 363,657,000 |
| WC | 147,985,000 | 149,522,000 | 346,234,000 |
| Emp. | N/A | N/A | 3,649 |

DUNS 21-625-4581    Imp-Exp

## Tdk-Lambda Uk Ltd

(**Subsidiary of:** Tdk Corporation)
Kingsley Avenue, Ilfracombe, Devon EX34 8ES
**Tel:** 01271-856600 **Fax:** 01271867185
**Web:** www.uk.tdk-lambda.com
**Reg No:** 0634143 **VAT No:** 862788866
**Estd:** 1966 Private Limited Company
**Line of Business:** Representative office
**Export Markets:** Western Europe, South Africa, U S A, Australasia, Middle East, Japan, India, Canada
**Export Sales:** £26,262,000
**Trading Style:** Tdk Lambda
**Issued Capital:** £3,818,443
**Principals:** A Rawicz Szczerbo (*Managing*), A Dykes (*Financial*), W M Davies, P J Scotcher, T Ono, M Southam, G W Wilby
**Co. Secretary:** Oss Secretaries Limited
**Responsibilities**
**Senior:** Andrew Blackburn (*Manager*), Debbie Moss (*Purchasing Manager*), Stephen Tennison (*Manager*), Glenys Tennison (*Manager*)
**Marketing:** Hannah Owen (*Senior Marketing Executive*)
**IT:** Kevin Jarratt (*IT Technician*), Debbie Moss (*Purchasing Manager*)
**HR:** Lis Gillingham (*Human Resources Manager*), Jane Worley (*Training Officer*)
**Health & Safety:** Tony Puttick (*Health & Safety Officer*)
**Facilities:** Colin Knill (*Maintenance Manager*)
**Purchasing:** Debbie Moss (*Purchasing Manager*)
**Branches:** Ilfracombe
**US SIC:** 7399 **UK SIC:** 83954
**Auditors:** KPMG LLP
**Bankers:** Lloyds TSB Bank plc (30-00-02)

| | 31-03-14 | 31-03-13 | 31-03-12 |
|---|---|---|---|
| TO | 35,599,000 | 34,281,000 | 40,383,000 |
| P/L | 827,000 | 1,006,000 | 3,018,000 |
| NW | 12,667,000 | 12,401,000 | 12,743,000 |
| WC | 6,243,000 | 7,444,000 | 8,799,000 |
| Emp. | 310 | 301 | 300 |

DUNS 45-812-2637

## T.D.L. Analytical Ltd

(**Subsidiary of:** Sonic Healthcare Limited)
60 Whitfield Street, London W1T 4EU
**Tel:** 02073077409
**Web:** www.tdlpathology.com
**Reg No:** 3169980 **Estd:** 2012 Private Limited Company
**Line of Business:** Research and experimental development on natural sciences and engineering
**Issued Capital:** £100
**Directors:** D A Byrne, Dr R Prudo-Chlebosz, T G Amies, Dr C S Goldschmidt, C D Wilks
**Co. Secretary:** Paul Alexander
**US SIC:** 7391 **UK SIC:** 94000
**Auditors:** Bdo Stoy Hayward
**Bankers:** The Royal Bank Of Scotland Plc (15-00-00)

| | 30-06-13 | 30-06-12 | 30-06-11 |
|---|---|---|---|
| TO | 6,997,000 | 7,699,000 | 6,968,000 |
| P/L | 145,000 | 810,000 | 660,000 |
| NW | 3,604,000 | 3,473,000 | 2,658,000 |
| WC | 3,461,000 | 3,423,000 | 2,663,000 |
| Emp. | 46 | 45 | 48 |

DUNS 22-653-4246    Imp-Exp

## T.D.P. Textiles Ltd

Top House, Rawdon Road, Swadlincote, Derbyshire DE12 6DT
**Tel:** 01283550400
**Web:** www.tdptextiles.com
**Reg No:** 1633119 **VAT No:** 439413446
**Estd:** 1982 Private Limited Company
**Line of Business:** Manufacture of household textiles
**Export Markets:** Finland, U S A & Eire
**Export Sales:** £2,121,487
**Issued Capital:** £5,382
**Principals:** T J Dawson (*Managing*), T A Myerscough (*Financial*), N S Henfrey (*Marketing*), Ms A M Dawson, B C O'Connor
**Co. Secretary:** Tony Myerscough
**US SIC:** 2392 **UK SIC:** 45550
**Auditors:** PKF (UK) LLP
**Bankers:** National Westminster Bank Plc (60-60-06)

| | 31-01-14 | 31-01-13 | 31-01-12 |
|---|---|---|---|
| TO | 23,355,412 | 24,010,428 | 25,612,754 |
| P/L | 501,400 | 734,974 | 1,046,809 |
| NW | 9,202,001 | 8,827,059 | 8,784,180 |
| WC | 6,998,870 | 6,625,953 | 6,496,036 |
| Emp. | 112 | 110 | 104 |

DUNS 73-803-6289

## Tdx Group Ltd

(**Subsidiary of:** Equifax Inc.)
8 Fletcher Gate, Nottingham, Nottinghamshire NG1 5FS
**Tel:** 01159-531200
**Web:** www.tdxgroup.com
**Reg No:** 5059906 **Estd:** 2004 Private Limited Company
**Line of Business:** Debt advice centre
**Issued Capital:** £133
**Directors:** P Moore, L Hamilton
**Responsibilities**
**Senior:** Jyoti Cusion (*Manager*)
**US SIC:** 7392 **UK SIC:** 83951
**Auditors:** BDO LLP

| | 31-12-13 | 31-12-12 | 31-12-11 |
|---|---|---|---|
| TO | 46,197,000 | 41,136,088 | 33,157,050 |
| P/L | (4,245,000) | 6,209,252 | 3,040,239 |
| NW | 1,136,000 | 6,060,909 | 2,766,017 |
| WC | 4,311,000 | 8,623,184 | 2,356,074 |
| Emp. | 295 | 241 | 175 |

DUNS 73-736-9970

## Tdx Industry Solutions Ltd

(**Subsidiary of:** Equifax Inc.)
The Stables, Grange Lane, York, North Yorkshire YO23 3QZ
**Tel:** 08445430333
**Web:** www.sawfishsoftware.com
**Reg No:** 4994926 **Estd:** 2003 Private Limited Company
**Line of Business:** Computer software (development)
**Issued Capital:** £251,020
**Directors:** L Hamilton, P Moore
**Responsibilities**
**Senior:** Craig White (*Manager*)
**US SIC:** 7379 **UK SIC:** 83940
**Bankers:** Yorkshire Bank Plc (05-00-20)

| | 31-12-13 | 31-12-12 | 31-12-12 |
|---|---|---|---|
| TO | 1,699,000 | N/A | 1,169,542 |
| P/L | (4,155,000) | N/A | (500,217) |
| NW | (7,395,000) | (273,598) | (985,913) |
| WC | (7,668,000) | 4,051,352 | 1,830,196 |

DUNS 23-504-5239

## Tdy Holdings Ltd

Atlas House, Sheffield, South Yorkshire S4 7UY
**Tel:** 01142-720081
**Reg No:** 3503813 **Estd:** 1998 Private Limited Company
**Line of Business:** Holding companies management activities
**Trading Style:** Ati Allvac Ltd
**Issued Capital:** £36,557,261
**Directors:** E S Davis, P Decourcy
**Co. Secretary:** Gravitas Company Secretarial Ser
**Responsibilities**
**Senior:** Mick Sparks (*Manager*)
**US SIC:** 6711, 6111
**UK SIC:** 83962, 81501
**Auditors:** Ernst & Young LLP
**Bankers:** HSBC Bank plc (40-42-12)

| | 31-12-13 | 31-12-12 | 31-12-11 |
|---|---|---|---|
| TA | 149,122,000 | 159,123,000 | 133,328,000 |
| P/L | (5,237,000) | 24,468,000 | (3,205,000) |
| NW | 52,667,000 | 65,006,000 | 55,493,000 |
| WC | (17,916,000) | (5,577,000) | 2,065,000 |

DUNS 64-075-4839

## Teach First

4 More London Riverside, Lambeth, London SE1 2AU
**Tel:** 0844-880-1800 **Fax:** 01215804265
**Web:** www.teachfirst.org.uk
**Reg No:** 4478840 **Estd:** 2007 Private Company Limited By Guarantee
**Line of Business:** Charities and charitable organisations

**Directors:** Dr M Meaney, L Mccrimlisk, Sir D R Bell Kcb, Miss S N Alibhai, P J Drechsler, J R Owen, Lord A Adonis, Ms S L Shillingford
**Co. Secretary:** Mrs Gillian Budd
**Responsibilities**
**Senior:** Glenn Earle (*Director*), Darren Purnell (*Coordinator*)
**IT:** Sanja Bhagat (*IT Manager*)
**US SIC:** 8699, 8299
**UK SIC:** 96902, 93300
**Auditors:** Dixon Wilson
**Bankers:** Barclays Bank Plc (20-00-50)

| | 31-08-13 | 31-08-12 | 31-08-11 |
|---|---|---|---|
| TO | 25,292,395 | 21,449,788 | 16,613,201 |
| P/L | 2,071,946 | 2,454,482 | 1,292,877 |
| NW | 9,213,558 | 7,141,612 | 4,687,130 |
| WC | 9,996,754 | 7,681,112 | 4,964,712 |
| Emp. | 303 | 216 | 164 |

DUNS 23-678-4492

## Teacher Stern Selby

37-41 Bedford Row, London WC1R 4JH
**Tel:** 02072423191
**Web:** www.tsslaw.com
**Estd:** 1967 Partnership
**Line of Business:** Solicitors
**Partners:** P Berry, D Teacher, C Richman, S Stern, J Rabinowicz
**Responsibilities**
**Marketing:** Anna Pitt-Stanley (*Marketing Manager*)
**Admin:** Joanna Bartley (*Office Manager*)
**HR:** Joanna Bartley (*Office Manager*)
**Health & Safety:** Joanna Bartley (*Office Manager*)
**Facilities:** Joanna Bartley (*Office Manager*)
**US SIC:** 8111 **UK SIC:** 83500
**Bankers:** Lloyds TSB Bank plc (30-94-25)
**Employees:** 80

DUNS 71-921-1554

## Teacheractive Ltd

158 Edmund Street, Birmingham, West Midlands B3 2HB
**Tel:** 01212003224
**Web:** www.teacheractive.com
**Reg No:** 5302511 **Estd:** 2004 Private Limited Company
**Line of Business:** Labour recruitment and provision of personnel
**Issued Capital:** £100
**Director:** S Ryder
**Co. Secretary:** Jagjeet Uppal
**US SIC:** 7361 **UK SIC:** 83954
**Auditors:** Briants Chartered Accountants

| | 31-12-13 | 31-12-12 | 31-12-11 |
|---|---|---|---|
| TO | 10,994,437 | N/A | N/A |
| P/L | 1,095,820 | N/A | N/A |
| NW | 629,219 | 383,857 | 111,583 |
| WC | 619,850 | 379,524 | 102,183 |
| Emp. | 78 | N/A | N/A |

DUNS 21-562-0324

## Teachers Assurance

Tringham House, Wessex Fields, Bournemouth, Dorset BH7 7DT
**Tel:** 01202435050
**Web:** www.teachersassurance.co.uk
**Estd:** 1986
**Line of Business:** Stockbrokers
**Responsibilities**
**Senior:** Ian Blanchard (*Financial Director*), Janet Shenton (*Manager*)
**Finance:** Ian Blanchard (*Financial Director*)
**IT:** Ian Dave (*Computer Manager*)
**US SIC:** 7392, 6411
**UK SIC:** 83951, 83200
**Employees:** 125

DUNS 36-491-0567

## Teachers Provident Society Ltd

Tringham House, Wessex Fields, Bournemouth, Dorset BH7 7DT
**Tel:** 01202-435000
**Web:** www.teachersassurance.co.uk
**Reg No:** 0110009I **Estd:** 1877 Friendly Society
**Line of Business:** Stockbrokers
**Principals:** J Wallbridge (*Chairman*), D Furniss, Ms A Moran, L Eagles, R Edwards, Ms J Clarkson, G Morris
**Branches:** Teachers Provident Society Ltd, 20 Tramside Way, Carlisle, Cumbria CA1 2FH
**US SIC:** 6311 **UK SIC:** 82002
**Auditors:** Mazars LLP
**Bankers:** National Westminster Bank Plc (56-00-35)

| | 31-12-13 | 31-12-12 | 31-12-11 |
|---|---|---|---|
| TO | 23,517,000 | 26,694,000 | 40,104,000 |
| P/L | 3,733,000 | 2,495,000 | 1,484,000 |
| NW | 138,204,000 | 121,078,000 | 108,020,000 |
| WC | 323,614,000 | 50,793,000 | 41,283,000 |
| Emp. | 134 | 127 | 155 |

**DUNS 21-828-3049**

## Teaching Leaders

65 Kingsway, London WC2B 6TD
**Tel:** 02031160828
**Web:** www.teachingleaders.org.uk
**Reg No:** 7984030 **Estd:** 2012 Private
Company Limited By Guarantee
**Line of Business:** Schools
**Directors:** H J Monk, R K Hobby, M Sandall,
J R Owen, Baroness S Morgan,
Miss H Watkins
**Co. Secretary:** Thomas Ebbutt
**Responsibilities**
**Senior:** James Toop (Chief Executive
Officer)
**US SIC:** 8211, 7392
**UK SIC:** 93200, 83951
**Bankers:** Lloyds TSB Bank plc (30-92-45)

|     | 31-08-14 | 31-08-13 |
| --- | --- | --- |
| TO | 6,772,294 | 5,004,454 |
| P/L | 542,947 | 201,764 |
| NW | 1,814,338 | 1,271,391 |
| WC | 1,814,338 | 1,271,391 |
| Emp. | 68 | 49 |

**DUNS 45-887-7826**

## Teaching Personnel Ltd

(**Subsidiary of:** Arthur Bidco Ltd)
Personnel House, Welwyn Garden City,
Hertfordshire AL7 1GL
**Tel:** 01707386212 **Fax:** 01707386386
**Web:** www.teachingpersonnel.com
**Reg No:** 3225158 **Estd:** 1996 Private
Limited Company
**Line of Business:** Employment and
recruitment companies and consultants
**Issued Capital:** £100
**Directors:** J Bowman, Miss F J Crownshaw,
G Evans, Mrs C A Cheale, A R Lee
**Co. Secretary:** Jonathan Roback
**Responsibilities**
**Senior:** Caroline McCarthy (Manager)
**Finance:** F Anwar (Financial Manager)
**HR:** Tamasine Hickey (Human Resources
Manager)
**Health & Safety:** Bianca Carter (Facilities
Manager)
**Facilities:** Bianca Carter (Facilities
Manager)
**Branches:** Teaching Personnel Ltd, St.
James House, Vicar Lane, Sheffield, South
Yorkshire S1 2EX
**US SIC:** 7361 **UK SIC:** 83954
**Auditors:** KPMG LLP

|     | 30-11-13 | 30-11-12 | 30-11-11 |
| --- | --- | --- | --- |
| TO | 63,652,000 | 53,541,000 | 48,493,000 |
| P/L | 13,164,000 | 10,552,000 | 7,859,000 |
| NW | 43,629,000 | 34,053,000 | 26,563,000 |
| WC | 43,227,000 | 33,822,000 | 26,369,000 |
| Emp. | 224 | 194 | 199 |

**DUNS 21-671-2833**

## Teads Ltd

5th Floor East, London W1W 9QJ
**Web:** www.ebuzzing.co.uk
**Reg No:** 7239735 **Estd:** 2010 Private
Limited Company
**Line of Business:** Advertising, radio, tv and
other media
**Issued Capital:** £50,000
**Directors:** J A Arditi, B R Quesada
**Responsibilities**
**Senior:** Danielle Burnham (Office Manager)
**US SIC:** 7319, 7379
**UK SIC:** 83800, 83940
**Auditors:** Cooper Murray

|     | 31-12-13 | 31-12-12 | 31-12-11 |
| --- | --- | --- | --- |
| TA | 3,746,050 | 2,668,842 | 1,007,617 |
| NW | (411,119) | 18,975 | (174,178) |
| WC | 695,666 | 659,681 | 484,596 |

**DUNS 21-632-6363**                                             **Exp**

## Teagle Holdings Ltd

Tywarnhayle, Truro, Cornwall TR4 8HG
**Tel:** 01872560592
**Web:** www.teagle.co.uk
**Reg No:** 0378978 **VAT No:** 679603493
**Estd:** 1943 Private Limited Company
**Line of Business:** Manufacturers and
suppliers of industrial machinery
**Export Markets:** France, Scandinavia, U S
A, Canada, Australia, Japan
**Export Sales:** £4,268,672
**Trading Style:** Teagle Machinery
**Issued Capital:** £108,100
**Principals:** F Teagle (Chairman),
G Osborne, T J Teagle, R F Teagle
**Co. Secretary:** William Teagle
**Branches:** Teagle Holdings Ltd, Tuckingmill,
Cornwall Camborne
**US SIC:** 3559 **UK SIC:** 32863
**Auditors:** Robinson Reed Layton
**Bankers:** Barclays Bank Plc (20-87-94)

|     | 30-06-13 | 30-06-12 | 30-06-11 |
| --- | --- | --- | --- |
| TO | 12,557,270 | 12,402,438 | 11,791,433 |
| P/L | 1,330,006 | 1,471,775 | 1,345,366 |
| NW | 6,392,721 | 5,743,815 | 4,998,749 |
| WC | 4,054,850 | 3,546,538 | 2,867,211 |
| Emp. | 135 | 146 | 154 |

**DUNS 21-215-2367**

## Teal & Mackrill Ltd

Lockwood Street, Hull, North Humberside
HU2 0HN
**Tel:** 01482328053 **Fax:** 01482-219266
**Web:** www.teamac.co.uk
**Reg No:** 0126674 **VAT No:** 167679507
**Estd:** 1908 Private Limited Company
**Line of Business:** Paint varnish & lacquer
**Trading Style:** Coo-Var, Teamac
**Issued Capital:** £7,538
**Director:** Ms M J Mackrill
**Co. Secretary:** Stephen Moore
**Responsibilities**
**Senior:** Mike Bond (Warehouse Manager),
Benjamin Mackrill (Manager), Geoff Mackrill
(Manager)
**Sales:** Jack Bruce (Area Sales Manager),
Sharron Drayton (Sales Manager)
**Health & Safety:** Paul Ellwood (Quality
Manager)
**Operations:** Sharron Drayton (Sales
Manager), Paul Ellwood (Quality Manager)
**Purchasing:** Paul Ellwood (Quality
Manager)
**US SIC:** 2891 **UK SIC:** 25620
**Bankers:** HSBC Bank plc (40-25-20)

|     | 31-12-13 | 31-12-12 | 31-12-11 |
| --- | --- | --- | --- |
| TA | 2,368,226 | 1,994,238 | 1,937,156 |
| NW | 830,082 | 836,760 | 728,275 |
| WC | 475,411 | 551,862 | 440,380 |

**DUNS 21-750-3242**                                             **Imp**

## Teal Furniture Ltd

(**Subsidiary of:** Senator International Ltd)
Branch Road, Darwen, Lancashire BB3 0PR
**Tel:** 01254688210 **Fax:** 01494482519
**Web:** www.teal.co.uk
**Reg No:** 1331980 **Estd:** 1977 Private
Limited Company
**Line of Business:** Manufacturers of seats
**Issued Capital:** £25,000
**Director:** C G Mustoe
**Co. Secretary:** Robert Mustoe
**Responsibilities**
**Senior:** Paul Goodall (Manager)
**Finance:** Claire Johnson (Financial
Manager)
**Sales:** Mike Brewster (Sales Manager)
**IT:** Claire Johnson (Financial Manager)
**Facilities:** Claire Johnson (Financial
Manager)
**Branches:** Teal Furniture Ltd, Hillbottom
Road, High Wycombe, Buckinghamshire
HP12 4HJ
**US SIC:** 2599 **UK SIC:** 46720
**Auditors:** Grant Thornton
**Bankers:** Barclays Bank Plc (20-40-71)

|     | 31-12-13 | 31-12-12 | 31-12-11 |
| --- | --- | --- | --- |
| TO | N/A | N/A | 5,041,314 |
| P/L | N/A | N/A | (523,091) |
| NW | 25,000 | 25,000 | 3,474,296 |
| WC | N/A | N/A | 3,324,251 |
| Emp. | N/A | N/A | 42 |

**DUNS 76-953-7887**

## Team 17 Software Ltd

Longlands House, Wakefield Road, Ossett,
West Yorkshire WF5 9JS
**Web:** www.team17.com
**Reg No:** 2621976 **VAT No:** 590641630
**Estd:** 1991 Private Limited Company
**Line of Business:** Computer software
(development)
**Issued Capital:** £120
**Principals:** Miss D J Bestwick (Marketing),
J P Bray
**Co. Secretary:** Jonathan Bray
**Branches:** Team 17 Software Ltd, Longland
Ho Wakefield Rd, Ossett, West Yorkshire
WF5 9JS
**US SIC:** 7379 **UK SIC:** 83940
**Auditors:** Dutton Moore
**Bankers:** Yorkshire Bank Plc (05-09-64)

|     | 31-12-13 | 31-12-12 | 31-12-11 |
| --- | --- | --- | --- |
| TO | 6,558,611 | 4,830,997 | 5,657,359 |
| P/L | 3,139,534 | 1,507,369 | 2,141,683 |
| NW | 4,516,302 | 4,824,320 | 4,824,283 |
| WC | 4,390,665 | 4,706,877 | 3,796,379 |
| Emp. | 70 | 66 | 63 |

**DUNS 21-014-1897**

## Team Antistat Ltd

(**Subsidiary of:** Ant Group Ltd)
108 Claydon Business Park, Great
Blakenham, Ipswich, Suffolk IP6 0NL
**Tel:** 01473836200
**Web:** www.antistat.co.uk
**Reg No:** 6369172 **Estd:** 2007 Private
Limited Company
**Line of Business:** Other business activities
not elsewhere classified
**Issued Capital:** £1
**Director:** J A Hensley
**Co. Secretary:** Mrs Michele King
**US SIC:** 7399 **UK SIC:** 83954

|     | 30-09-13 | 30-09-12 | 30-09-11 |
| --- | --- | --- | --- |
| TA | 1 | 1 | 1 |
| NW | 1 | 1 | 1 |

**DUNS 29-869-5883**                                             **Imp-Exp**

## Team Consulting Ltd

(**Subsidiary of:** Team Medical Devices Ltd)
Abbey Barns, Duxford Road, Ickleton,
Ickleton, Saffron Walden, Essex CB10 1SX
**Tel:** 01799-532700 **Fax:** 01763848668
**Web:** www.team-consulting.com
**Reg No:** 2072719 **VAT No:** 432215101
**Estd:** 1986 Private Limited Company
**Line of Business:** Engineers (consulting)
**Export Markets:** U S A, Europe
**Issued Capital:** £12,386
**Principals:** J J Turner (Managing),
D J Flicos, A R Fry, C J Mathews
**Co. Secretary:** Dudley Dyer Bartlett
**US SIC:** 8911 **UK SIC:** 83701
**Auditors:** Lakin Rose
**Bankers:** Lloyds TSB Bank plc (30-91-56)

|     | 31-12-13 | 31-12-12 | 31-12-11 |
| --- | --- | --- | --- |
| TO | 7,771,094 | N/A | N/A |
| P/L | 871,306 | N/A | N/A |
| NW | 2,887,448 | 2,048,440 | 1,661,338 |
| WC | 2,580,685 | 1,741,989 | 1,379,388 |
| Emp. | 53 | N/A | N/A |

**DUNS 22-191-3507**

## Team Contract Services (Scotland) Ltd

Unit 6/8, The Anderston Centre, Glasgow,
Lanarkshire G2 7PH
**Tel:** 0141-204-4100
**Web:** www.teamtrainingservices.co.uk
**Reg No:** 0218786SC **Estd:** 2001 Private
Limited Company
**Line of Business:** Security activities
**Issued Capital:** £4,000
**Directors:** G Lloyd, Ms F J Mcmurdie
**Co. Secretary:** Michael Hankey
**Branches:** Team Contract Services
(Scotland) Ltd, 251 Blythswood Court,
Glasgow, Lanarkshire G2 7PH
**US SIC:** 6531 **UK SIC:** 83400
**Bankers:** HSBC Bank plc (40-22-47)

|     | 31-08-13 | 31-08-12 | 31-08-11 |
| --- | --- | --- | --- |
| TA | 341,008 | 398,430 | 424,024 |
| NW | 34,270 | 68,152 | 107,956 |
| WC | 5,829 | 33,558 | 69,730 |

**DUNS 29-546-0174**

## Team Dynamics International Ltd

Court Lodge Down, Hawkenbury Road, Bells
Yew Green, Tunbridge Wells, Kent TN3 9AP
**Web:** www.teamdynamics.co.uk
**Reg No:** 1912713 **Estd:** 1985 Private
Limited Company
**Line of Business:** Training providers
**Issued Capital:** £3
**Directors:** J C Wallace, B R Scales, A Patel
**Co. Secretary:** Charles De Garston
**Responsibilities**
**Senior:** Lisa De Garston (Team Leader)
**US SIC:** 8299 **UK SIC:** 93300
**Auditors:** Deeks Evans
**Bankers:** Barclays Bank Plc (20-14-33)

|     | 31-10-13 | 31-10-12 | 31-10-11 |
| --- | --- | --- | --- |
| TA | 78,530 | 90,337 | 141,665 |
| NW | 24,710 | (8,349) | 30,426 |
| WC | 25,811 | (17,785) | 23,202 |

**DUNS 22-122-9573**

## Team Fostering

6 Hedley Court, Orion Business Park, North
Shields, Tyne and Wear NE29 7ST
**Tel:** 01912576806
**Web:** www.teamfostering.co.uk
**Reg No:** 4141990 **VAT No:** 933158916
**Estd:** 2001 Private Company Limited By
Guarantee
**Line of Business:** Social work activities
without accommodation
**Trading Style:** Team Fostering
**Directors:** J B Payne, Dr J A Dibdin,
Ms R Holden, W Young,
Ms V M Davidson Boyd
**Co. Secretary:** Ms Hayley Payne
**Branches:** Team Fostering, Enterprise
House, Unit 2G, Darlington, County Durham
DL1 1GY
**US SIC:** 8321 **UK SIC:** 96111
**Auditors:** The Growth Partnership

|     | 31-03-14 | 31-03-13 | 31-03-12 |
| --- | --- | --- | --- |
| TO | 8,650,836 | 7,872,572 | 7,608,150 |
| P/L | 439,520 | 185,565 | 583,716 |
| NW | 3,150,713 | 2,807,212 | 2,661,590 |
| WC | 3,120,665 | 2,777,765 | 2,613,573 |
| Emp. | 61 | 67 | 69 |

**DUNS 22-191-9280**

## Team (Impression) Ltd

(**Subsidiary of:** Team (Impression) Holdings
Plc)
1 Lockwood Close, Leeds, West Yorkshire
LS11 5UU
**Tel:** 01132-724-800 **Fax:** 01132-724-801
**Web:** www.team-impression.com
**Reg No:** 4210104 **Estd:** 1901 Private
Limited Company

**Line of Business:** Printing not elsewhere
classified
**Export Sales:** £172,939
**Issued Capital:** £534,666
**Directors:** P J Crowson, S J Bucktrout,
J P Crowson
**Responsibilities**
**Admin:** Nichola Thornton (Manager)
**US SIC:** 2752, 2794
**UK SIC:** 47544, 47545
**Auditors:** Montpelier Audit Ltd
**Bankers:** Barclays Bank Plc (20-48-42)

|     | 31-05-14 | 31-05-13 | 31-05-12 |
| --- | --- | --- | --- |
| TO | 6,934,810 | 6,445,362 | 7,843,343 |
| P/L | 157,300 | 34,552 | (125,882) |
| NW | 1,446,695 | 1,441,256 | 1,473,450 |
| WC | (842,325) | (754,202) | (622,671) |
| Emp. | 80 | 81 | 97 |

**DUNS 21-168-6834**                                             **Imp**

## Team Precision Pipe Assemblies Ltd

Parc Hendre Industrial Estate, Ammanford,
Dyfed SA18 3SJ
**Tel:** 01269844100
**Web:** www.team-precision.co.uk
**Reg No:** 6936831 **Estd:** 2009 Private
Limited Company
**Line of Business:** Tube benders
**Export Sales:** £1,610,000
**Issued Capital:** £100,000
**Directors:** Dr N C Trilk, M P Urquhart
**Responsibilities**
**Senior:** Tony Salini (Manager)
**Finance:** Della Rossiter (Head of Finance)
**HR:** Della Rossiter (Head of Finance)
**Health & Safety:** Della Rossiter (Head of
Finance)
**Facilities:** Lee Rawlinson (Maintenance
Manager)
**US SIC:** 3542 **UK SIC:** 32212
**Bankers:** National Westminster Bank Plc
(01-06-57)

|     | 30-09-13 | 30-09-12 | 30-09-11 |
| --- | --- | --- | --- |
| TO | 6,709,000 | 7,001,000 | N/A |
| P/L | 14,000 | 69,000 | N/A |
| NW | 1,382,000 | 1,037,000 | 981,000 |
| WC | 1,135,000 | 1,022,000 | 930,000 |
| Emp. | 116 | 115 | N/A |

**DUNS 34-975-2654**

## Team Prevent Uk Ltd

(**Subsidiary of:** Berufsgenossenschaftlicher
Arbeitsmedizinischer Un)
Pury Hill Business Park, Alderton Road,
Towcester, Northamptonshire NN12 7LS
**Tel:** 01788559305
**Web:** www.teamprevent.co.uk
**Reg No:** 5770728 **Estd:** 2006 Private
Limited Company
**Line of Business:** Safety advisers and
technicians
**Issued Capital:** £405,630
**Directors:** Ms M Dummer, O R Hook,
B Siegemund
**US SIC:** 8091 **UK SIC:** 95200
**Auditors:** Haysom Silverton & Partners Ltd

|     | 31-12-13 | 31-12-12 | 31-12-11 |
| --- | --- | --- | --- |
| TA | 950,420 | 817,967 | 707,602 |
| NW | (925,838) | (992,143) | (1,527,109) |
| WC | 138,668 | 84,547 | (213,775) |

**DUNS 23-626-7399**

## Team Q Maintenance Ltd

(**Subsidiary of:** Turner & Co. (Glasgow) Ltd.)
Collier House, Mead Lane, Hertford,
Hertfordshire SG13 7AX
**Tel:** 01992 507320 **Fax:** 01992 503672
**Web:** www.teamq.co.uk
**Reg No:** 2642291 **VAT No:** 589785843
**Estd:** 1982 Private Limited Company
**Line of Business:** Other construction work
involving special trades
**Issued Capital:** £100
**Directors:** I Parrack, S J Faulkner,
A G Turner
**Co. Secretary:** Ian Parrack
**Responsibilities**
**Senior:** John Fullick (Manager)
**Branches:** Team Q Maintenance Ltd, 2A
Zephyr Ho, Calleva Pk, Reading, Berkshire
RG7 8JN
**US SIC:** 1799 **UK SIC:** 50000
**Auditors:** Davis Grant LLP
**Bankers:** National Westminster Bank Plc
(55-70-49)

|     | 28-03-14 | 29-03-13 | 30-03-12 |
| --- | --- | --- | --- |
| TO | 22,662,339 | 16,032,952 | 17,144,383 |
| P/L | (516,715) | (51,469) | 77,945 |
| NW | 875,509 | 1,279,297 | 1,608,199 |
| WC | 1,465,042 | 1,783,455 | 2,499,588 |
| Emp. | 244 | 196 | 192 |

DUNS 77-087-8486 Exp

## Team Relocations Ltd

(**Subsidiary of:** Zenic International Holdings Limited)
Unit 10 Drury Way, London NW10 0JN
**Tel:** 020-8784-0100 **Fax:** 020-8955-1400
**Web:** www.teamrelocations.com
**Reg No:** 2675059 **Estd:** 1992 Private Limited Company
**Line of Business:** Freight forwarders
**Export Sales:** £6,313,820
**Trading Style:** Team Allied
**Issued Capital:** £100
**Director:** Y Mehta
**Co. Secretary:** Timothy Romer
**Branches:** Team Relocations Ltd, Unit 9, Ascot Rd, Feltham, Middlesex TW14 8QH
**US SIC:** 4712, 4226, 7399
**UK SIC:** 77002, 77003, 83954
**Auditors:** Ernst & Young LLP
**Bankers:** Barclays Bank Plc (20-37-16)

| | 30-09-13 | 30-09-12 | 30-09-11 |
|---|---|---|---|
| TO | 28,557,575 | 31,302,459 | 30,978,164 |
| P/L | 3,723,167 | 4,078,244 | 3,807,669 |
| NW | 9,978,538 | 9,649,949 | 9,363,234 |
| WC | 7,529,671 | 7,237,141 | 6,312,962 |
| Emp. | 141 | 142 | 142 |

DUNS 23-031-3272

## Team Search

Crown House, Crown Street, Halifax, West Yorkshire HX1 1TT
**Tel:** 01422-360371
**Web:** www.teamsearchmr.co.uk
**Estd:** 1998 Partnership
**Line of Business:** Market research organisations
**Trading Style:** Researchers At Crown
**Partners:** C J Brooks, Mrs P Machin
**Responsibilities**
**Senior:** Robert Hogan *(Manager)*
**US SIC:** 7392, 7399
**UK SIC:** 83951, 83954
**Bankers:** Barclays Bank Plc (20-35-84)
**Employees:** 90

DUNS 21-405-2917

## Team Support Services Plc

Cadley Hill Industrial Estate, Ryder Close, Swadlincote, Derbyshire DE11 9EU
**Tel:** 01892839990
**Line of Business:** Home care service providers
**Responsibilities**
**Senior:** Derek Springett *(Manager)*
**Branches:** Team Support Services Plc, 18 Broadway, London E15 4QS
**US SIC:** 5051 **UK SIC:** 61200
**Employees:** 50

DUNS 67-211-7694

## Teampol Ltd

31 Keyes Avenue, Chatham, Kent ME4 5TH
**Tel:** 01634830220
**Web:** www.teampol.co.uk
**Reg No:** 6019865 **Estd:** 2008 Private Limited Company
**Line of Business:** Insulation installers
**Issued Capital:** £100
**Director:** T Talaska
**Co. Secretary:** Mrs Natalla Talaska
**US SIC:** 1742, 1799
**UK SIC:** 50400, 50000

| | 31-12-13 | 31-12-12 | 31-12-11 |
|---|---|---|---|
| TA | 205,496 | 299,055 | 241,727 |
| NW | 109,726 | 113,656 | 85,189 |
| WC | 84,065 | 103,454 | 117,437 |

DUNS 21-682-6720

## Teamsport Indoor Karting (London) Ltd

(**Subsidiary of:** Teamsport Holdings Ltd)
Unit C1 Endeavour Place 11 Coxbridge, Business Park, Alton Road, Farnham, Surrey GU10 5EH
**Tel:** 08449980000
**Web:** www.team-sports.co.uk
**Reg No:** 7328664 **Estd:** 2010 Private Limited Company
**Line of Business:** Other entertainment activities not elsewhere classified
**Issued Capital:** £100
**Directors:** Ms M P Delany, D Gaynor
**US SIC:** 7999 **UK SIC:** 97913

| | 30-06-13 | 30-06-12 | 30-06-11 |
|---|---|---|---|
| TA | 599,335 | 687,275 | 943,711 |
| NW | (40,513) | (164,195) | (261,442) |
| WC | (445,975) | (169,824) | (366,600) |

DUNS 21-394-9337

## Teamwork

68a Wide Bargate, Boston, Lincolnshire PE21 6RY
**Tel:** 01205359183
**Web:** www.webspawner.com
**Estd:** 1993
**Line of Business:** Employment and recruitment companies and consultants
**Proprietor:** Mrs S Epton
**Branches:** Teamwork, Hecton House, Friday Street, Maidstone, Kent ME17 3EA
**US SIC:** 7361 **UK SIC:** 83954
**Bankers:** Barclays Bank Plc (20-10-71)
**Employees:** 150

DUNS 22-952-6553 Imp

## Tearfund

100 Church Road, Teddington, Middlesex TW11 8QE
**Web:** www.tearfund.org
**Reg No:** 0994339 **VAT No:** 224533388
**Estd:** 1970 Private Company Limited By Guarantee
**Line of Business:** Charities and charitable organisations
**Directors:** D B Campanale, R M Camp, D Mahtani, Mrs S Heald, Ms J Mills, D A Todd, Mrs J C Ogilvy, J Shaw
**Co. Secretary:** Mrs Alison Hopkinson
**Responsibilities**
**Senior:** Ian Angell *(Manager)*, David Bainbridge *(International Director)*, Jennifer Baker *(Director)*, Henrietta Blyth *(Director for People and Organi)*, Paul Brigham *(Marketing Manager)*, Eddie Cole *(Facilities Manager)*, Tim Magowan *(Northern Ireland Director)*, Harold Mather *(Director)*, Mark Melluish *(Board Member)*, Craig Rowland *(Board Member)*, Sudarshan Sathianathan *(Head of Asia Region)*
**Marketing:** Paul Brigham *(Marketing Manager)*, David Deekin *(Senior Marketing Executive)*
**Sales:** Henrietta Blyth *(Director for People and Organi)*
**IT:** Gordon May *(Global Head of IT)*
**HR:** Zoe Hayes *(Youth Relationship Manager)*
**Health & Safety:** Eddie Cole *(Facilities Manager)*
**Facilities:** Eddie Cole *(Facilities Manager)*
**Operations:** Eddie Cole *(Facilities Manager)*
**Purchasing:** Eddie Cole *(Facilities Manager)*
**Branches:** Tearfund, 23 University St, Belfast, Belfast BT7 1FY
**US SIC:** 8321, 6732
**UK SIC:** 96111, 83100
**Auditors:** Deloitte & Touche
**Bankers:** The Co-Operative Bank Plc (08-90-61)

| | 31-03-14 | 31-03-13 | 31-03-12 |
|---|---|---|---|
| TO | 59,372,000 | 60,046,000 | 70,296,000 |
| P/L | (2,952,000) | (1,044,000) | 5,250,000 |
| NW | 24,611,000 | 27,563,000 | 28,607,000 |
| WC | 23,082,000 | 25,966,000 | 26,849,000 |
| Emp. | 1,139 | 1,307 | 1,439 |

DUNS 28-977-6270

## Teasdales Bakers (Holdings) Ltd

Unit 11 Frontier Works King Edward Road, Doncaster, South Yorkshire DN8 4HU
**Tel:** 01405-817202
**Reg No:** 1763677 **Estd:** 1986 Private Limited Company
**Line of Business:** Bakers shops
**Trading Style:** Atkinson's
**Issued Capital:** £10,000
**Principals:** J D Atkinson *(Managing)*, Miss S Atkinson, J T Atkinson
**Co. Secretary:** Ms Susan Atkinson
**Branches:** Teasdales Bakers (Holdings) Ltd, 31 Market Street, Scunthorpe, South Humberside DN15 9PS
**US SIC:** 5462 **UK SIC:** 64100
**Auditors:** Hewitt Card
**Bankers:** Yorkshire Bank Plc (05-09-54)

| | 31-03-14 | 31-03-13 | 31-03-12 |
|---|---|---|---|
| TA | 1,169,919 | 985,800 | 1,080,715 |
| NW | 878,140 | 888,189 | 896,680 |
| WC | 58,643 | 49,395 | 376,292 |

DUNS 22-078-2598

## Teatime Tasties Ltd

Unit 5 Old Fieldhouse Lane Industrial Es, Huddersfield, West Yorkshire HD2 1AG
**Tel:** 01484514331
**Reg No:** 4079701 **Estd:** 2000 Private Limited Company
**Line of Business:** Fast food delivery
**Issued Capital:** £28,400
**Directors:** P V Young, D L Brind, Miss P A Rice
**Co. Secretary:** Ms Patricia Rice
**Responsibilities**
**Senior:** Michael Musgrave *(Manager)*
**Health & Safety:** Michael Musgrave *(Manager)*
**Facilities:** Michael Musgrave *(Manager)*
**US SIC:** 5812 **UK SIC:** 66110
**Auditors:** Connelly & Co Ltd
**Bankers:** Barclays Bank Plc (20-59-42)

| | 27-04-14 | 30-04-13 | 31-04-12 |
|---|---|---|---|
| TO | 11,322,729 | 14,285,253 | 11,482,171 |
| P/L | 444,223 | 960,817 | 486,844 |
| NW | 1,802,262 | 1,450,831 | 922,732 |
| WC | 1,403,325 | 1,066,349 | 607,221 |
| Emp. | 58 | 58 | 60 |

DUNS 28-965-6761

## Tebway Ltd

56 Oswald Road, Scunthorpe, South Humberside DN15 7PQ
**Tel:** 01724-847844
**Web:** www.polypearl.co.uk
**Reg No:** 1703510 **Estd:** 1983 Private Limited Company
**Line of Business:** Insulation work activities
**Trading Style:** Polypearl
**Issued Capital:** £4,000
**Principals:** I R Tebb *(Managing)*, Ms H M Tebb, A G Tebb
**Co. Secretary:** Ms Denise Hickson
**Responsibilities**
**Senior:** Marie Robinson *(Finance Manager)*
**Branches:** Tebway Ltd, Ardon House, Unit 20, Nottingham, Nottinghamshire NG4 2HF
**US SIC:** 1742 **UK SIC:** 50400
**Auditors:** R N Store & Co
**Bankers:** Barclays Bank Plc (20-76-14)

| | 31-07-13 | 31-07-12 | 31-07-11 |
|---|---|---|---|
| TO | 22,579,749 | N/A | N/A |
| P/L | 6,047,904 | N/A | N/A |
| NW | 8,158,939 | 2,467,832 | 902,287 |
| WC | 7,063,602 | 2,111,404 | 561,998 |
| Emp. | 50 | N/A | N/A |

DUNS 21-633-3304

## Tec Group International (Worldwide) Ltd

(**Subsidiary of:** Compello Staffing Group Ltd)
00 Dothwell Street, Glasgow, Lanarkshire G2 6NL
**Tel:** 01412 705000 **Fax:** 01412 705555
**Web:** www.fpsg.co.uk
**Reg No:** 0370584SC **Estd:** 1998 Private Limited Company
**Line of Business:** Employment and recruitment companies and consultants
**Issued Capital:** £2
**Directors:** J Hailstone, Miss L Taylor
**Co. Secretary:** Robert Watson
**Responsibilities**
**Senior:** Andrew Spratt *(Manager)*
**US SIC:** 6711 **UK SIC:** 83962
**Bankers:** The Royal Bank Of Scotland Plc (16-12-53)

| | 31-05-13 | 31-05-12 | 31-05-11 |
|---|---|---|---|
| TA | 395 | 236 | 236 |
| NW | 2 | 2 | 2 |
| WC | (391) | (232) | (232) |

DUNS 21-708-4805 Imp-Exp

## Tecalemit Garage Equipment Co Ltd

(**Subsidiary of:** Bronze Golf Ltd)
Eagle Road, Plymouth, Devon PL7 5JY
**Tel:** 01752219111
**Web:** www.tecalemit.co.uk
**Reg No:** 1099738 **VAT No:** 723418156
**Estd:** 1973 Private Limited Company
**Line of Business:** Manufacture of other special purpose machinery not elsewhere classified
**Export Markets:** E U, Middle East, U.S.A., Africa, Australasia, Canada
**Export Sales:** £202,000
**Trading Style:** Tecalemit
**Issued Capital:** £500,000
**Principals:** J R Devonport *(Managing)*, E Zanini, P H Cledwyn, Dr C Ciseri
**Co. Secretary:** James Devonport
**Responsibilities**
**Admin:** Allison Stovel *(National Accounts Assistant)*
**IT:** Jim Brown *(Systems Administrator)*
**HR:** Nicci Walke *(Human Resources Manager)*
**Health & Safety:** Karen Shazell *(Health & Safety Officer)*
**US SIC:** 3559, 8911, 5084
**UK SIC:** 32863, 83701, 61490
**Auditors:** PricewaterhouseCoopers LLP
**Bankers:** Lloyds TSB Bank plc (30-96-68)

| | 31-12-13 | 31-12-12 | 31-12-11 |
|---|---|---|---|
| TO | 11,560,000 | 11,517,000 | 11,468,000 |
| P/L | 30,000 | 73,000 | 7,000 |
| NW | 3,146,000 | 3,283,000 | 3,621,000 |
| WC | 3,053,000 | 3,207,000 | 3,512,000 |
| Emp. | 107 | 108 | 116 |

DUNS 21-141-8532 Imp

## Tecan Ltd

Tecan Way, Granby Industrial Estate, Weymouth, Dorset DT4 9TU
**Tel:** 01305765432 **Fax:** 01305-780194
**Web:** www.tecan.co.uk
**Reg No:** 6736647 **Estd:** 1970 Private Limited Company
**Line of Business:** Metal finishing and polishing services
**Export Sales:** £2,439,912
**Issued Capital:** £1
**Directors:** S Aitken, Stork Prints Bv
**Responsibilities**
**Senior:** Gerard Banbierendonbk *(Manager)*
**Marketing:** Vikki Cosgrove *(Sales & Marketing Assistant)*, David Worsdell *(Marketing Manager)*
**Sales:** Vikki Cosgrove *(Sales & Marketing Assistant)*
**HR:** Kerry O'Leary *(HR Officer)*
**Health & Safety:** Joy Barber *(Analysis Manager)*
**Operations:** Joy Barber *(Analysis Manager)*, Jonathan Woolls *(Manufacturing Manager)*
**Engineering:** Matt Kelly *(Estimator)*
**US SIC:** 3499 **UK SIC:** 31694
**Bankers:** National Westminster Bank Plc (60-23-35)

| | 31-12-13 | 31-12-12 | 31-12-11 |
|---|---|---|---|
| TO | 8,158,640 | 8,090,053 | 7,567,099 |
| P/L | 1,907,909 | 1,740,574 | 1,504,875 |
| NW | 1,342,362 | 887,393 | 965,663 |
| WC | 972,131 | 1,042,211 | 1,066,537 |
| Emp. | 99 | 104 | 111 |

DUNS 29-630-5139 Imp

## Tecaz Ltd

Tecaz House, Norham Road, North Shields, Tyne and Wear NE29 7TN
**Fax:** 01912728113
**Web:** www.tecaz.co.uk
**Reg No:** 1956506 **Estd:** 1986 Private Limited Company
**Line of Business:** Bathroom planners and furnishers
**Issued Capital:** £2,000
**Principals:** S P Dawson *(Managing)*, P T Dawson *(Managing)*, K D Dawson *(Financial)*, Ms J Dawson, Ms S Dawson, Ms D Dawson
**Co. Secretary:** Stephen Dawson
**Responsibilities**
**Health & Safety:** Gary Gullon *(Health & Safety Officer)*
**Branches:** Tecaz Ltd, Portrack Lane, Stockton-On-Tees, Cleveland TS18 2HG
**US SIC:** 3263 **UK SIC:** 24893
**Auditors:** Joseph Miller & Co
**Bankers:** National Westminster Bank Plc (54-10-58)

| | 31-12-13 | 31-12-12 | 31-12-11 |
|---|---|---|---|
| TO | 8,402,745 | 8,413,741 | 7,514,640 |
| P/L | 252,704 | 258,122 | (31,203) |
| NW | 2,127,819 | 2,054,936 | 1,972,307 |
| WC | 1,980,785 | 1,916,883 | 1,857,698 |
| Emp. | 70 | 69 | 63 |

DUNS 22-628-1707

## Tech Data Ltd

(**Subsidiary of:** Tech Data Corporation)
2 Crockford Lane Redwood, Basingstoke, Hampshire RG24 8WQ
**Tel:** 01256788000 **Fax:** 0870 060 7998
**Web:** www.maverick.co.uk
**Reg No:** 1691472 **VAT No:** 385524235
**Estd:** 2007 Private Limited Company
**Line of Business:** Wholesalers and distributors of audio visual equipment
**Trading Style:** Tech Data, Azlan, Datech
**Issued Capital:** £6,000,000
**Principals:** A Gass *(Financial)*, H Tuffnail, P Hubbard, S Amsellem, D Watts
**Co. Secretary:** Ms Rachel Ollis
**Responsibilities**
**Senior:** Neil Brittain *(General Manager Profitability)*, Sid Stanley *(General Manager)*, Kevin Wragg *(General Manager of the Periphe)*
**Finance:** Alex Tucker *(Tax Manager)*
**Marketing:** Blanka Bimi *(Promethean Product Manager)*, Andy Dow *(Marketing Director)*, Mark Glasspool *(Consumer Electronics & Strateg)*
**Sales:** Katherine Bond *(Sales Executive)*, Phil Bowden-Smith *(IBM Software Business Manager)*, Anna-Marie Constantinou *(Volume Business Manager)*, Grant Keenan *(Business Development Manager)*, Tracy Kennedy *(Business Development Manager)*, Jacqui Price *(Sales Executive)*
**Admin:** Lorraine Crowther *(PA)*
**IT:** Paul Hewitt *(Application Specialist)*, Steve Leslie *(IT Manager)*, Barrie Mills *(Principle Technical Consultant)*, Chris Nagy *(Technical Consultant)*, Paul Nicholas *(Networking Manager)*
**Branches:** Tech Data Ltd, Harrier Parkway, Lutterworth, Leicestershire LE17 4XT
**US SIC:** 3662, 7379
**UK SIC:** 34430, 83940
**Auditors:** Ernst & Young LLP
**Bankers:** Citibank Na (18-50-08)
**Following financial data are in thousands**

| | 31-01-14 | 31-01-13 | 31-01-12 |
|---|---|---|---|
| TO | 1,527,641 | 1,539,583 | 1,431,018 |
| P/L | (19,110) | 9,207 | 13,834 |
| NW | 134,843 | 229,449 | 79,255 |
| WC | 94,432 | 126,534 | 77,513 |
| Emp. | 768 | 657 | 642 |

DUNS 21-606-5294

## Tech Music School

Effie Road, Fulham, London SW6 1EN
**Tel:** 02087493131
**Web:** www.drum-tech.co.uk
**Estd:** 2011 Partnership
**Line of Business:** Schools of music

**Partners:** D Sucliffe, D Suckling
**US SIC:** 8299, 8249
**UK SIC:** 93300
**Employees:** 50

DUNS 22-016-1355

## The Tech Partnership Ltd

1-2 Castle Lane, London SW1E 6DR
**Tel:** 020-7963-8920
**Web:** www.e-skills.com
**Reg No:** 4019051 **Estd:** 2004 Private Limited Company
**Line of Business:** Certification and accreditation bodies
**Trading Style:** E-Skills Uk
**Directors:** G Hart, D M Hudd, A J Green, P P Smith, J C David, Ms K P Price, D W Lister
**Co. Secretary:** Dean Cassar
**Responsibilities**
**Senior:** Brian McBride *(Manager)*, Sinclair Stockman *(Manager)*
**Marketing:** Collette Lux *(Head of Sales & Marketing)*
**Sales:** Collette Lux *(Head of Sales & Marketing)*
**US SIC:** 8621, 8249
**UK SIC:** 96311, 93300
**Auditors:** Rothman Pantall & Co
**Bankers:** Lloyds TSB Bank plc (30-12-05)

| | 31-03-14 | 31-03-13 | 31-03-12 |
|---|---|---|---|
| TO | 7,097,469 | 7,139,827 | 6,813,623 |
| P/L | 141,438 | 84,169 | 96,778 |
| NW | 2,050,297 | 1,934,991 | 1,857,268 |
| WC | 2,065,926 | 1,935,448 | 1,751,807 |
| Emp. | 56 | 55 | 46 |

DUNS 28-877-2379

## Techaid Facilities Ltd

Loudwater House London Road, High Wycombe, Buckinghamshire HP10 9TL
**Tel:** 01494525721
**Web:** www.dfconsult.co.uk
**Reg No:** 1127239 **Estd:** 1984 Private Limited Company
**Line of Business:** Development and selling of real estate
**Trading Style:** Design Facilities
**Issued Capital:** £10,100
**Principals:** B E Gardener *(Managing)*, M J Gardener
**Co. Secretary:** Brian Gardener
**Responsibilities**
**Senior:** Jim Fastmadge *(Branch Manager)*
**Finance:** John Szydlowski *(Accounts Manager)*
**Marketing:** Lynn Ruby *(Sales & Marketing Manager)*
**Sales:** Lynn Ruby *(Sales & Marketing Manager)*
**Branches:** Techaid Facilities Ltd, Adelaide House, Perth Avenue, Slough, Berkshire SL1 4XX
**US SIC:** 6552, 6519
**UK SIC:** 85000
**Auditors:** Barnes Roffe LLP
**Bankers:** Lloyds TSB Bank plc (30-94-28)

| | 30-11-13 | 30-11-12 | 30-11-11 |
|---|---|---|---|
| TO | 3,462,110 | 3,273,071 | 4,201,194 |
| P/L | 275,915 | 242,200 | 505,826 |
| NW | 14,795,219 | 19,814,407 | 20,352,520 |
| WC | (682,858) | (422,395) | 635,769 |
| Emp. | 64 | 53 | 59 |

DUNS 34-907-4828 **Imp**

## Techflow Flexibles Ltd

(**Subsidiary of:** Techflow Flexibles (Holdings) Ltd)
Bassington Drive, Cramlington, Northumberland NE23 8AS
**Tel:** 01670706210 **Fax:** 01670706211
**Web:** www.techflowflexibles.co.uk
**Reg No:** 5704584 **VAT No:** 901409265
**Estd:** 2006 Private Limited Company
**Line of Business:** Manufacture of other rubber products
**Trading Style:** Brazenlight Ltd.
**Issued Capital:** £1
**Directors:** J C Fitzpatrick, G O Clark, K B Beattie, B P Beattie
**Responsibilities**
**Senior:** Lily Beattie *(Manager)*, Brett Latimer *(Sales Director)*, Andy Thompson *(Engineering Manager)*
**Finance:** Phil McClintock *(Accounts Manager)*
**Sales:** Brett Latimer *(Sales Director)*
**Engineering:** Andy Nicol *(Technical Manager)*
**US SIC:** 3069 **UK SIC:** 48123
**Auditors:** UNW LLP

| | 31-08-13 | 31-08-12 | 31-08-11 |
|---|---|---|---|
| TO | 23,440,537 | 17,845,833 | 9,754,452 |
| P/L | 1,369,722 | 2,090,924 | 1,294,294 |
| NW | 5,214,969 | 3,828,263 | 2,195,826 |
| WC | 4,515,659 | 3,361,070 | 2,208,973 |
| Emp. | 58 | 33 | 28 |

DUNS 50-484-8326 **Imp**

## Techman Engineering Ltd

(**Subsidiary of:** Berndorf Industrieholding Ag)
Broombank Park, Chesterfield, Derbyshire S41 9RT
**Fax:** 01246453734
**Web:** www.techman-engineering.co.uk
**Reg No:** 2458616 **VAT No:** 543705842
**Estd:** 1990 Private Limited Company
**Line of Business:** Precision engineers
**Export Sales:** £5,409,783
**Issued Capital:** £100
**Directors:** A H Domjahn, S Oxspring, F Gritsch, G Grohmann
**Responsibilities**
**Senior:** Keith Rycroft *(Purchasing Manager)*
**Admin:** Becky Mullis *(Administrator)*
**IT:** Mark Rooker *(Operations Manager)*
**Operations:** Mark Rooker *(Operations Manager)*
**Purchasing:** Keith Rycroft *(Purchasing Manager)*
**Branches:** Techman Engineering Ltd, 15-17 Chester Street, Chesterfield, Derbyshire S40 1DW
**US SIC:** 8911 **UK SIC:** 83701
**Auditors:** Martin Bruno
**Bankers:** National Westminster Bank Plc (60-10-19)

| | 31-12-13 | 31-12-12 | 31-12-11 |
|---|---|---|---|
| TO | 20,201,954 | 17,021,466 | 10,598,394 |
| P/L | 2,508,684 | 1,865,727 | (132,990) |
| NW | 6,090,693 | 4,121,006 | 2,724,841 |
| WC | 6,334,768 | 6,541,548 | 2,634,366 |
| Emp. | 122 | 108 | 81 |

DUNS 71-922-5331

## Technetix Group Ltd

Communications House, Edward Way, Burgess Hill, West Sussex RH15 9TZ
**Fax:** 01444258555
**Web:** www.technetix.com
**Reg No:** 5303822 **VAT No:** 711498731
**Estd:** 2004 Private Limited Company
**Line of Business:** Telecommunication networks
**Export Sales:** £45,992,000
**Trading Style:** Technetix Inc, Technetix Networks
**Issued Capital:** £6,852
**Directors:** J H Brougham, P A Broadhurst, A J Kellett, D J Mcintyre
**Co. Secretary:** Andrew Kellett
**Responsibilities**
**Senior:** Andrew Chater *(chief financial officer)*
**Finance:** Andrew Chater *(chief financial officer)*
**US SIC:** 4899, 3679, 3662
**UK SIC:** 79020, 34542, 34430
**Auditors:** Ernst & Young LLP
**Bankers:** HSBC Bank plc (40-18-22)

| | 31-12-13 | 31-12-12 | 31-12-11 |
|---|---|---|---|
| TO | 61,641,000 | 57,314,000 | 65,185,000 |
| P/L | 1,456,000 | (3,446,000) | 4,534,000 |
| NW | (1,690,000) | (2,689,000) | 729,000 |
| WC | (540,000) | 305,000 | 5,623,000 |
| Emp. | 158 | 195 | 180 |

DUNS 21-631-3997

## Technical Consumer Products Ltd

(**Subsidiary of:** Tcp B.V.)
Unit 1 Exchange Court, Cottingham Road, Corby, Northamptonshire NN17 1TY
**Tel:** 01536201503 **Fax:** 01604 831674
**Web:** www.tcpi.eu
**Reg No:** 7098127 **Estd:** 2009 Private Limited Company
**Line of Business:** Manufacturers of lighting equipment
**Issued Capital:** £1
**Directors:** E Yan, T Luecke
**Responsibilities**
**Finance:** Stuart Castle *(Finance and IT Director)*
**Marketing:** Mark polloway *(Sales and Marketing Manager)*
**Sales:** Mark polloway *(Sales and Marketing Manager)*
**Operations:** Jessica Parker *(Operations Director)*
**US SIC:** 3648 **UK SIC:** 34702
**Auditors:** Smith Hodge & Baxter

| | 31-12-13 | 31-12-12 | 31-12-11 |
|---|---|---|---|
| TA | 14,564,193 | 686,607 | 366,814 |
| NW | (1,702,010) | 72,656 | (1,223,614) |
| WC | 10,244,429 | (41,285) | 247,203 |

DUNS 21-300-2405 **Imp-Exp**

## Technical Control Systems Ltd

(**Subsidiary of:** North Hill Ltd)
Control Works, Gelderd Road Treefield Industrial Estate, Leeds, West Yorkshire LS27 7JU
**Tel:** 01132-525977 **Fax:** 01132-380095
**Web:** www.tcspanels.co.uk
**Reg No:** 0950111 **VAT No:** 427439635
**Estd:** 1969 Private Limited Company
**Line of Business:** Manufacturers of control panels
**Export Markets:** Kuwait; Hong Kong; China
**Issued Capital:** £400,000
**Directors:** D Fletcher, N C Stewart, J M Somers, D A Jessup, N P Foster
**Co. Secretary:** Paul Mountain
**US SIC:** 3679 **UK SIC:** 34542
**Auditors:** PKF
**Bankers:** National Westminster Bank Plc (60-60-05)

| | 31-03-14 | 31-03-13 | 31-03-12 |
|---|---|---|---|
| TO | 6,785,001 | 6,957,789 | 6,844,089 |
| P/L | 338,308 | 341,219 | 43,709 |
| NW | 2,736,891 | 2,639,768 | 2,366,061 |
| WC | 1,586,666 | 1,515,421 | 1,385,691 |
| Emp. | 50 | N/A | 45 |

DUNS 22-803-6588 **Exp**

## Technical Cranes Ltd

Holmes Lock Works, Steel Street, Rotherham, South Yorkshire S61 1DF
**Tel:** 01709561861
**Web:** www.technicalcranes.co.uk
**Reg No:** 1552256 **VAT No:** 308593150
**Estd:** 1981 Private Limited Company
**Line of Business:** Manufacture of lifting and handling equipment
**Export Markets:** Worlwide
**Issued Capital:** £100
**Directors:** D Simpson, J Simpson
**Co. Secretary:** Ms Kathryn Simpson
**US SIC:** 3534, 1795
**UK SIC:** 32553, 50000
**Auditors:** Hawsons
**Bankers:** Yorkshire Bank Plc (05-08-38)

| | 31-03-14 | 31-03-13 | 31-03-12 |
|---|---|---|---|
| TA | 3,796,750 | 2,817,674 | 2,882,980 |
| NW | 1,093,149 | 993,007 | 938,204 |
| WC | (192,808) | (171,604) | (63,678) |

DUNS 28-961-7060 **Exp**

## Technical Demolition Services Ltd

17 Hamilton Square, Birkenhead, Merseyside CH41 6AX
**Tel:** 0151-666-1272
**Web:** www.technicaldemolitionservices.com
**Reg No:** 1684019 **VAT No:** 387129326
**Estd:** 1982 Private Limited Company
**Line of Business:** Asbestos products & removal
**Export Markets:** Worldwide
**Issued Capital:** £100
**Principals:** T G Taperell *(Managing)*, C Wilson, A A Taperell, Miss V M Evans, D S Lee, Miss J A Hitchen
**Co. Secretary:** Mrs Helen Taperell
**Responsibilities**
**Senior:** Marc Danson *(Asbestos Manager)*, Roy Lawlan *(Maintenance Manager)*
**Finance:** Susan Moran *(Financial Director)*
**IT:** Susan Moran *(Financial Director)*
**US SIC:** 1799 **UK SIC:** 50000
**Auditors:** Douglas Fairless Partnership
**Bankers:** The Royal Bank Of Scotland Plc (16-24-06)

| | 31-12-13 | 31-12-12 | 31-12-11 |
|---|---|---|---|
| TO | 6,851,575 | 8,070,760 | 8,469,305 |
| P/L | 352,131 | 4,156 | 385,355 |
| NW | 5,147,891 | 4,928,439 | 5,025,466 |
| WC | 1,558,488 | 1,374,538 | 1,233,499 |
| Emp. | 64 | 68 | 70 |

DUNS 64-098-6600

## Technical Retail Services Ltd

26-28 Napier Court, Glasgow, Lanarkshire G68 0LG
**Tel:** 01236786010 **Fax:** 01417-712484
**Web:** www.trsweb.co.uk
**Reg No:** 0182224SC **VAT No:** 703765340
**Estd:** 2011 Private Limited Company
**Line of Business:** General mechanical engineering
**Issued Capital:** £1,000
**Directors:** R Yule, S J Lees
**Co. Secretary:** Bruce Mcintosh
**US SIC:** 8911 **UK SIC:** 83701
**Auditors:** Portlands
**Bankers:** The Royal Bank Of Scotland Plc (83-22-27)

| | 31-03-14 | 31-03-13 | 31-03-12 |
|---|---|---|---|
| TA | 3,378,723 | 3,058,951 | 1,823,989 |
| NW | 2,008,107 | 1,616,333 | 513,142 |
| WC | 1,672,871 | 1,320,101 | 407,352 |

DUNS 22-852-5119 **Exp**

## Technical Service Consultants Ltd

(**Subsidiary of:** Cobco (266) Ltd)
Microbiology House, Heywood, Lancashire OL10 1NW
**Tel:** 01706 620600
**Web:** www.tscswabs.co.uk
**Reg No:** 1494701 **VAT No:** 354708836
**Estd:** 1981 Private Limited Company
**Line of Business:** Manufacturers of medical equipment
**Export Markets:** Worldwide.
**Issued Capital:** £4,000
**Directors:** M R Cooper, S P Trenchard, A Kinsella, Ms E W Cooper, J R Rainbow
**Co. Secretary:** Robert Broad
**Responsibilities**
**Finance:** Gail Campbell *(Financial Manager)*
**IT:** Gail Campbell *(Financial Manager)*
**Purchasing:** Gail Campbell *(Financial Manager)*
**Branches:** Technical Service Consultants Ltd, Unit 13, Greenacres Rd, Oldham, Lancashire OL4 1LE
**US SIC:** 3841 **UK SIC:** 37201
**Auditors:** RSM Tenon Audit Ltd
**Bankers:** Barclays Bank Plc (20-16-08)

| | 31-05-14 | 31-05-13 | 31-05-12 |
|---|---|---|---|
| TA | 3,120,875 | 2,943,661 | 2,808,678 |
| NW | 2,278,886 | 2,089,853 | 1,895,421 |
| WC | 1,506,343 | 1,314,174 | 1,048,377 |

DUNS 77-818-5868

## Technical Sign Co Ltd

Hille Business Centre 132 St Albans Road, Watford, Hertfordshire WD24 4AE
**Tel:** 01923811999 **Fax:** 01923-811998
**Web:** www.technicalsigns.co.uk
**Reg No:** 3028486 **VAT No:** 654037152
**Estd:** 1992 Private Limited Company
**Line of Business:** Other manufacturing not elsewhere classified
**Trading Style:** Technical Signs
**Issued Capital:** £999
**Managing Director:** I J Bigley
**Co. Secretary:** Eric Bigley
**US SIC:** 3999, 3079
**UK SIC:** 49590, 48360
**Bankers:** National Westminster Bank Plc (60-17-32)

| | 31-03-14 | 31-03-13 | 31-03-12 |
|---|---|---|---|
| TO | N/A | N/A | 5,806,142 |
| P/L | N/A | N/A | 1,104,932 |
| NW | 1,614,367 | 1,479,403 | 1,111,738 |
| WC | 1,287,049 | 1,179,143 | 818,624 |

DUNS 45-883-2391

## Technical Ventures Ltd.

7 Tavistock Drive, Glasgow, Lanarkshire G43 2SJ
**Tel:** 07768581144
**Web:** www.technicalventures.com
**Reg No:** 0166849SC **Estd:** 1995 Private Limited Company
**Line of Business:** Computer software (development)
**Issued Capital:** £2
**Director:** K C Grant
**Co. Secretary:** Ms Elisabeth Judd
**US SIC:** 7379, 5074
**UK SIC:** 83940, 61300
**Auditors:** French Duncan LLP
**Bankers:** The Royal Bank Of Scotland Plc (83-20-22)

| | 31-07-13 | 31-07-12 | 31-07-11 |
|---|---|---|---|
| TA | 79,552 | 80,079 | 78,094 |
| NW | 34,428 | 43,404 | 40,460 |
| WC | 21,263 | 31,591 | 24,708 |

DUNS 22-110-3679 **Imp**

## Technicolor Disc Services International Ltd

(**Subsidiary of:** Technicolor)
Building 1, 3rd Floor, London W4 5BE
**Tel:** 020-8100-1000 **Fax:** 020-8100-1001
**Web:** www.technicolornetworkservices.com
**Reg No:** 4129617 **Estd:** 2002 Private Limited Company
**Line of Business:** Other business activities not elsewhere classified
**Export Sales:** £62,442,000
**Issued Capital:** £89,324,735
**Directors:** R C Fossett, Mrs P A Dave, S M Hibbins
**Co. Secretary:** Ms Sophie Le Menaheze
**Responsibilities**
**Senior:** Philippe Andrau *(Manager)*
**US SIC:** 7399 **UK SIC:** 83954
**Auditors:** Deloitte LLP
**Bankers:** Citibank Na (08-60-71)

| | 31-12-13 | 31-12-12 | 31-12-11 |
|---|---|---|---|
| TO | 62,442,000 | 59,364,000 | 54,541,000 |
| P/L | 17,028,000 | 8,075,000 | (5,054,000) |
| NW | 103,400,000 | 90,079,000 | 82,602,000 |
| WC | 105,445,000 | 92,136,000 | 84,267,000 |
| Emp. | 47 | 47 | 50 |

DUNS 76-960-9090

## Technicolor Distribution Services Ltd

(**Subsidiary of:** Technicolor)
16 Great Queen Street, Covent Garden, London WC2B 5AH
**Web:** www.technicolor.com
**Reg No:** 2625233 **Estd:** 1991 Private Limited Company
**Line of Business:** Distribution service providers
**Issued Capital:** £2
**Director:** R C Fossett
**Co. Secretary:** Ms Sophie Le Menaheze

**Responsibilities**
**Senior:** Philippe Andrau (Manager), Robert Sweet (Manager)
**Finance:** Robert Sweet (Manager)
**Marketing:** Robert Sweet (Manager)
**US SIC:** 4712  **UK SIC:** 77002

|  | 31-12-13 | 31-12-12 | 31-12-11 |
|---|---|---|---|
| TA | 2 | 2 | 2 |
| NW | 2 | 2 | 2 |

DUNS 22-714-3054
## Technicon Design Ltd
Technicon House, 905 Capability Green, Luton, Bedfordshire LU1 3LU
**Web:** www.techniconims.com
**Reg No:** 1392917  **Estd:** 1978 Private Limited Company
**Line of Business:** Speciality design activities
**Export Sales:** £30,206,999
**Trading Style:** Technicon Design
**Issued Capital:** £50,001
**Directors:** M C Shall, D Shall, S Goldblum, Mrs L Goldblum
**US SIC:** 8911, 7361
**UK SIC:** 83701, 83954
**Auditors:** Guner Mustafa
**Bankers:** HSBC Bank plc (40-03-01)

|  | 31-12-13 | 31-12-12 | 31-12-11 |
|---|---|---|---|
| TO | 31,407,308 | 29,494,793 | 29,477,594 |
| P/L | 179,580 | 584,543 | 1,177,764 |
| NW | 740,891 | 734,369 | 554,374 |
| WC | (57,899) | 155,376 | 171,987 |
| Emp. | 286 | 263 | 235 |

DUNS 21-748-8022
## Technik Ltd
(Subsidiary of: Writtle Holdings Ltd)
Unit 4 Riverpark Industrial Estate, Berkhamsted, Hertfordshire HP4 1HL
**Tel:** 01442-871117  **Fax:** 01442870891
**Web:** www.technik.com
**Reg No:** 1278908  **VAT No:** 596256203
**Estd:** 1976 Private Limited Company
**Line of Business:** Printers general
**Issued Capital:** £150,200
**Directors:** A E Knight, R T Essex, A J Wright, K D Cain, G A Booker, G R Harris
**Co. Secretary:** Matthew Gilmore
**Responsibilities**
**Senior:** Anthony Hampson (Manager), Michael Huber (Manager), Leonard Stickland (Manager), Dianne Walker (Manager)
**Marketing:** Matthew Ringer (Head of Marketing Communicatio), Leonard Stickland (Manager)
**Sales:** Leonard Stickland (Manager)
**IT:** Leonard Stickland (Manager)
**HR:** Leonard Stickland (Manager)
**Operations:** Leonard Stickland (Manager)
**Purchasing:** Leonard Stickland (Manager)
**Branches:** Technik Ltd, Centre Of Excellence, Hope Park, Bradford, West Yorkshire BD5 8HH
**US SIC:** 2753  **UK SIC:** 47545
**Auditors:** Everett Collins & Loosley
**Bankers:** National Westminster Bank Plc (55-70-10)

|  | 31-12-13 | 31-12-12 | 31-12-11 |
|---|---|---|---|
| TO | 2,984,192 | N/A | 3,144,613 |
| P/L | (110,276) | N/A | (57,507) |
| NW | 2,093,680 | 2,215,425 | 2,528,585 |
| WC | 1,892,776 | 1,980,451 | 2,356,195 |
| Emp. | N/A | N/A | 47 |

DUNS 21-912-0581  **Exp**
## Technik Technology Ltd
(Subsidiary of: Syspal Capital Ltd)
Cockshutt Lane, Broseley, Shropshire TF12 5JA
**Web:** www.techniktechnology.co.uk
**Reg No:** 1228287  **Estd:** 2001 Private Limited Company
**Line of Business:** Manufacturers of veterinary equipment
**Export Markets:** Australia; U S A; Middle East; E Europe
**Issued Capital:** £9,999
**Directors:** C J Truman, A Roberjot
**Responsibilities**
**Senior:** Matthew Rees (Manager)
**US SIC:** 3841  **UK SIC:** 37201

|  | 31-03-14 | 31-03-13 | 31-03-12 |
|---|---|---|---|
| TA | 9,999 | 9,999 | 9,999 |
| NW | 9,999 | 9,999 | 9,999 |

DUNS 22-704-8394  **Exp**
## Technip Maritime Uk Ltd.
(Subsidiary of: Technip)
262 High Holborn, London WC1V 7NA
**Tel:** 020-7611-5555  **Fax:** 020-7611-5550
**Web:** www.genesisoilandgas.com
**Reg No:** 1177671  **Estd:** 1975 Private Limited Company
**Line of Business:** Management activities of holding companies
**Export Markets:** Norway, E U, Canada, Far East
**Issued Capital:** £15,630,000
**Directors:** D P Mcguire, W E Morrice
**Co. Secretary:** Peter Lunny

---

**US SIC:** 6711  **UK SIC:** 83962
**Auditors:** Ernst & Young LLP

|  | 31-12-13 | 31-12-12 | 31-12-11 |
|---|---|---|---|
| TA | 1,364,000 | 1,364,000 | 1,364,000 |
| NW | 219,000 | 219,000 | 219,000 |
| WC | 219,000 | 219,000 | 219,000 |

DUNS 29-498-1204
## Technip Offshore Wind Ltd
(Subsidiary of: Technip)
Elrick House, Peregrine Road, Westhill Business Park, Westhill, Aberdeenshire AB32 6JL
**Tel:** 01224-270501  **Fax:** 01224-270503
**Web:** www.technip.com
**Reg No:** 1861407  **Estd:** 1984 Private Limited Company
**Line of Business:** Other engineering activities
**Issued Capital:** £5,000
**Directors:** C Prou, W E Morrice, C J Armengol
**Co. Secretary:** Peter Lunny
**Responsibilities**
**Senior:** Elaine Benton (Manager), Ronald Cookson (Manager), Patrick Picard (Manager)
**US SIC:** 8911  **UK SIC:** 83701
**Auditors:** Summers Morgan
**Bankers:** HSBC Bank plc (40-46-09)

|  | 31-12-13 | 31-12-12 | 31-12-11 |
|---|---|---|---|
| TO | 42,351,000 | 43,806,000 | 48,615,000 |
| P/L | (27,097,000) | (3,848,000) | (1,025,000) |
| NW | (24,537,000) | (5,642,000) | (2,653,000) |
| WC | (45,008,000) | (25,325,000) | (922,000) |
| Emp. | 212 | 203 | 210 |

DUNS 29-008-2601  **Exp**
## Technip Uk Ltd
(Subsidiary of: Technip)
Enterprise Drive, Westhill Industrial Estate, Westhill, Aberdeenshire AB32 6TQ
**Tel:** 01224 271000  **Fax:** 01224 271271
**Web:** www.technip.com
**Reg No:** 0200086  **VAT No:** 415345471
**Estd:** 1924 Private Limited Company
**Line of Business:** Service activities incidental to oil and gas extraction excluding surveying
**Export Sales:** £282,630,000
**Issued Capital:** £16,002,050
**Directors:** W E Morrice, D P Mcguire, I G Stevenson, K Boe, C Armengol
**Co. Secretary:** Peter Lunny
**Responsibilities**
**Senior:** Keith McRitchie (Logistics Team Leader)
**Marketing:** Richard Gibson (Sales & Marketing Manager)
**Sales:** Richard Gibson (Sales & Marketing Manager)
**Operations:** John Cowling (Project Manager)
**Engineering:** Francois Letournel (Lead Operations Engineer), Mike O'Donnell (Senior Project Engineer)
**Branches:** Technip Uk Ltd, Genesis Gas & Oil, 1 St. Paul's Churchyard, London EC4M 8AP
**US SIC:** 1389, 8911
**UK SIC:** 13000, 83701
**Auditors:** PricewaterhouseCoopers LLP
**Bankers:** Bank Of Scotland (80-05-11)
Following financial data are in thousands

|  | 31-12-13 | 31-12-12 | 31-12-11 |
|---|---|---|---|
| TO | 1,067,983 | 1,042,049 | 932,222 |
| P/L | 188,240 | 83,140 | 106,667 |
| NW | 295,720 | 202,941 | 149,325 |
| WC | (139,054) | (59,979) | 28,163 |
| Emp. | 908 | 759 | 670 |

DUNS 50-393-6379  **Imp-Exp**
## Technip Umbilicals Ltd
(Subsidiary of: Technip)
Walker Riverside, Nelson Road, Walker, Newcastle-Upon-Tyne, Tyne and Wear NE6 3NL
**Tel:** 01912-950-303  **Fax:** 01912-950-842
**Web:** www.technip.com
**Reg No:** 2400155  **VAT No:** 654293032
**Estd:** 1989 Private Limited Company
**Line of Business:** Tube fittings
**Trading Style:** Technip Umbilical Systems (Tus)
**Issued Capital:** £5,000,000
**Directors:** K Boe, C Armengol, J L Rostaing, A P Marion
**Co. Secretary:** Peter Lunny
**Responsibilities**
**Senior:** Florence Jacqueline (Manager), Emma Maddison (Communications Manager), Aline Montel (Manager), Dave Shillito (Stores Controller)
**Finance:** Malcolm Poulton (Financial Controller)
**Sales:** Dave Stables (Sales Manager)
**HR:** Sarah Hogarth (Personnel Manager)
**Engineering:** Alan Deighton (Principal Engineer (Cables)), Ian Probyn (Principal Engineer)

---

**Branches:** TECHNIP UMBILICALS LTD: Cobalt Business Exchange and Conference Centre, Cobalt Park Way, Wallsend, Newcastle-upon-Tyne, NE28 9NZ, TYNE & WEAR.
**US SIC:** 4619, 3494
**UK SIC:** 72601, 32880
**Auditors:** PricewaterhouseCoopers LLP

|  | 31-12-13 | 31-12-12 | 31-12-11 |
|---|---|---|---|
| TO | 90,168,000 | 92,882,000 | 87,096,000 |
| P/L | 6,647,000 | 4,791,000 | 1,979,000 |
| NW | 19,982,000 | 14,815,000 | 11,140,000 |
| WC | (4,927,000) | 1,432,000 | (802,000) |
| Emp. | 497 | 485 | 393 |

DUNS 29-629-6320  **Exp**
## Techniquest
Stuart Street, Cardiff, South Glamorgan CF10 5BW
**Tel:** 02920475475
**Web:** www.techniquest.org
**Reg No:** 1955696  **VAT No:** 483874106
**Estd:** 1985 Private Company Limited By Guarantee
**Line of Business:** Science centres
**Export Markets:** Worldwide
**Directors:** S H Best, Ms H E Mcnabb, Dr V E Chambers, D W Jenkins, Professor R H Williams, Dr G L Guilford
**Co. Secretary:** Ms Tracey Marsh
**Responsibilities**
**Marketing:** Justine Wilcox (Marketing Manager)
**HR:** Angela Roostam (Human Resources Manager)
**Health & Safety:** Bernard Cuff (Health & Safety Officer)
**Facilities:** Bernard Cuff (Health & Safety Officer)
**Operations:** Dave Breen (Programmes Manager)
**US SIC:** 8299  **UK SIC:** 93300
**Auditors:** KPMG
**Bankers:** HSBC Bank plc (40-16-13)

|  | 31-03-14 | 31-03-13 | 31-03-12 |
|---|---|---|---|
| TO | 3,234,235 | 3,440,659 | 3,286,349 |
| P/L | 139,527 | 166,243 | 122,173 |
| NW | 1,589,843 | 1,450,315 | 1,284,072 |
| WC | 1,465,406 | 1,369,782 | 1,098,467 |
| Emp. | 131 | 134 | 133 |

DUNS 29-667-3585
## Techno Engineering Ltd
(Subsidiary of: Celtic Engineering Holdings Ltd)
Jenkins & Davies, Pembroke Dock, Dyfed SA72 6BS
**Tel:** 01646-685895
**Web:** www.technoengineering.com
**Reg No:** 1993520  **VAT No:** 431777149
**Estd:** 1986 Private Limited Company
**Line of Business:** Mechanical engineering general
**Trading Style:** Jenkins & Davies Mechanical Engineering
**Issued Capital:** £111,150
**Directors:** D Wright, M R Kiss
**Co. Secretary:** David Wright
**Responsibilities**
**Health & Safety:** Lance Rose (Health & Safety Officer)
**Operations:** Lance Rose (Health & Safety Officer)
**US SIC:** 3441, 1799
**UK SIC:** 32042, 50000
**Auditors:** PricewaterhouseCoopers LLP
**Bankers:** Bank Of Wales Plc (12-23-00)

|  | 31-01-14 | 31-01-13 | 31-01-12 |
|---|---|---|---|
| TO | 8,969,000 | 10,152,000 | 10,917,000 |
| P/L | 563,000 | 203,000 | 853,000 |
| NW | 5,224,000 | 4,784,000 | 5,250,000 |
| WC | 4,673,000 | 4,224,000 | 4,693,000 |
| Emp. | 113 | 136 | 146 |

DUNS 21-932-5610
## Techno Group Ltd
Unit 3a, Roman Way, Glebe Farm Industrial Estate, Glebe Farm Industrial E, Rugby, Warwickshire CV21 1DB
**Tel:** 01788560522
**Web:** www.techno-group.co.uk
**Reg No:** 1338534  **VAT No:** 307003512
**Estd:** 1978 Private Limited Company
**Line of Business:** Fabricated metal products
**Issued Capital:** £78
**Managing Director:** F J Moser
**Co. Secretary:** Michael Ronayne
**Responsibilities**
**Senior:** Kevin Kayne (Manager)
**US SIC:** 8911, 3542
**UK SIC:** 83701, 32212
**Auditors:** Meyer Williams
**Bankers:** Lloyds TSB Bank plc (30-96-64)

|  | 31-12-13 | 31-12-12 | 31-12-11 |
|---|---|---|---|
| TO | 4,672,518 | N/A | N/A |
| P/L | 882,931 | N/A | N/A |
| NW | 4,033,857 | 1,410,990 | 1,378,322 |
| WC | 2,728,407 | 824,624 | 684,282 |
| Emp. | 67 | N/A | N/A |

---

DUNS 23-301-0461
## Techno Tyrone Ltd
Termon Business Park, Quarry Road, Carrickmore, Omagh, Co Tyrone BT79 9AL
**Tel:** 02880761000
**Web:** www.milestonecentre.co.uk
**Reg No:** 0025913NI  **Estd:** 1991 Private Company Limited By Guarantee
**Line of Business:** Activities of business and employers organisations
**Trading Style:** The Milestone Centre
**Directors:** G M Keyes, A Mc Garrity, Ms S Rooney, J Hadden, Ms A Clement
**Co. Secretary:** James Maguire
**Responsibilities**
**Senior:** Kathleen Mcnally (General Manager)
**US SIC:** 8611, 6531
**UK SIC:** 96312, 83400
**Auditors:** D A Kelly & Co
**Bankers:** First Trust Bank  (aib Group (uk) Plc) (93-81-30)

|  | 31-12-13 | 31-12-12 | 31-12-11 |
|---|---|---|---|
| TO | 74,177 | 61,493 | N/A |
| P/L | (156) | (11,134) | N/A |
| NW | 240,306 | 1,477,571 | 251,596 |
| WC | 7,419 | (7,556) | (7,633) |

DUNS 23-056-8529
## Technocover Ltd.
(Subsidiary of: Ensor Holdings P L C)
Unit C, Henfaes Lane, Welshpool, Powys SY21 7BE
**Tel:** 01938555511
**Web:** www.technocover.co.uk
**Reg No:** 2845757  **VAT No:** 594412919
**Estd:** 1993 Private Limited Company
**Line of Business:** Security equipment installers
**Export Sales:** £343,214
**Trading Style:** Technocover
**Issued Capital:** £1,000,000
**Directors:** Ms H Duncan, C M Tisdale, M D Miles, J G Wittenbrink, A R Harrison, K A Harrison
**Co. Secretary:** Marcus Chadwick
**Responsibilities**
**Purchasing:** Pat Ellis (Purchasing Manager)
**US SIC:** 7393, 8911, 3441
**UK SIC:** 83954, 83701, 32042
**Auditors:** Turner Peachey
**Bankers:** Barclays Bank Plc (20-61-08)

|  | 31-03-14 | 31-03-13 | 29-03-12 |
|---|---|---|---|
| TO | 10,046,613 | 13,525,944 | 12,977,782 |
| P/L | 192,384 | 854,822 | (912,385) |
| NW | 1,432,165 | 1,275,588 | 607,373 |
| WC | 358,021 | 1,258,384 | (342,906) |
| Emp. | 144 | 148 | 142 |

DUNS 23-079-2202  **Imp**
## Technogym U.K. Ltd
Two The Boulevard, Bracknell, Berkshire RG12 1WP
**Tel:** 01344-300236  **Fax:** 01344-300238
**Web:** www.technogym.com
**Reg No:** 2782468  **VAT No:** 628385120
**Estd:** 1993 Private Limited Company
**Line of Business:** Other business activities not elsewhere classified
**Export Sales:** £473,395
**Issued Capital:** £100,000
**Principals:** A M Drew (Financial), S Zanelli, G Bonollo, K Briffa, Ms A Bianchi
**Co. Secretary:** Ms Michelle Kenny
**Responsibilities**
**Senior:** Riccardo Losappio (Manager), Anthony Majakas (Manager)
**US SIC:** 7399, 5122
**UK SIC:** 83954, 61800
**Auditors:** PricewaterhouseCoopers LLP
**Bankers:** Barclays Bank Plc (20-11-74)

|  | 31-12-13 | 31-12-12 | 31-12-11 |
|---|---|---|---|
| TO | 56,238,029 | 56,769,478 | 50,808,221 |
| P/L | 6,101,800 | 5,548,834 | 5,447,601 |
| NW | 6,017,589 | 5,873,847 | 7,234,497 |
| WC | 10,758,510 | 11,117,364 | 11,854,939 |
| Emp. | 99 | 96 | 94 |

DUNS 22-023-1422
## Technolog Holdings Ltd
(Subsidiary of: Roper Industries Inc.)
Ravensdore Road, Matlock, Derbyshire DE4 4FY
**Tel:** 01629823611
**Web:** www.technolog.com
**Reg No:** 4025830  **Estd:** 2000 Public Limited Company
**Line of Business:** Management activities of other non-financial holding companies not elsewhere classified
**Export Sales:** £4,126,000
**Issued Capital:** £2,533,526
**Directors:** N C Fearn, S J Drury, B James, P J Soni, D B Liner, J R Humphrey, J Bignall
**US SIC:** 6711  **UK SIC:** 83962

**Auditors:** PricewaterhouseCoopers LLP

| | 31-12-13 | 31-12-12 | 31-12-11 |
|---|---|---|---|
| TO | 31,180,000 | 31,495,000 | 45,278,000 |
| P/L | 8,588,000 | 7,479,000 | 11,564,000 |
| NW | 18,172,000 | 13,228,000 | 6,864,000 |
| WC | 23,916,000 | 19,407,000 | 13,581,000 |
| Emp. | 248 | 249 | 252 |

DUNS 21-388-3413      **Imp**

## Technology Teaching Systems

Unit 1 Park Lane Business Park, Park Lane, Kirkby-In-Ashfield, Sutton-In-Ashfield, Nottinghamshire NG17 9LE
**Tel:** 0800-318-686
**Web:** www.tts-group.co.uk
**Estd:** 2003 Proprietorship
**Line of Business:** Wholesale of other machinery for use in industry, trade and navigation
**Proprietor:** P Ellse
**US SIC:** 5199   **UK SIC:** 61900
**Employees:** 100

DUNS 21-117-9670

## Technopolis Group Ltd

3 Pavillion Buildings, Brighton, East Sussex BN1 1EE
**Web:** www.technopolis-group.com
**Reg No:** 6576728   **Estd:** 2008 Private Limited Company
**Line of Business:** Management and business consultants
**Issued Capital:** £88
**Directors:** P E Arnold, Ms P E Boekholt
**Responsibilities**
**Senior:** Tom Wolfenden (Group General Manager)
**US SIC:** 7391   **UK SIC:** 94000

| | 30-04-14 | 30-04-13 | 30-04-12 |
|---|---|---|---|
| TO | 10,806,888 | 8,893,374 | 9,445,643 |
| P/L | 910,360 | 366,116 | 395,953 |
| NW | 4,052,193 | 3,441,191 | 3,400,142 |
| WC | 4,036,149 | 3,351,400 | 3,252,298 |
| Emp. | 88 | 89 | 81 |

DUNS 23-102-2906

## Techrete (U.K.) Ltd

Station Road, Scawby, Brigg, South Humberside DN20 9EB
**Tel:** 01652659454
**Web:** www.techrete.co.uk
**Reg No:** 2396734   **VAT No:** 503561084
**Estd:** 1989 Private Limited Company
**Line of Business:** Construction of commercial buildings
**Issued Capital:** £100,000
**Directors:** T G Corkery, A Rice, M O'Dea, C O'Dea
**Co. Secretary:** John Conaghy
**Responsibilities**
**Senior:** Andy Lane (Plant Manager), Christopher O' Dea (Chairman)
**Sales:** Steve Mould (Sales Director)
**Facilities:** Andy Lane (Plant Manager)
**Operations:** Henry Clifford (Technical, Production Manager), Andy Lane (Plant Manager)
**Branches:** Techrete (U.k.) Ltd, Warren Court, Unit 1, Leicester, Leicestershire LE19 4SD
**US SIC:** 1541, 3499
**UK SIC:** 50100, 31694
**Auditors:** Grant Thornton
**Bankers:** Allied Irish Bank (gb) (23-83-94)

| | 31-07-13 | 31-07-12 | 31-07-11 |
|---|---|---|---|
| TO | 21,510,550 | 17,850,884 | 23,979,481 |
| P/L | 713,223 | 123,052 | 272,966 |
| NW | 4,338,343 | 3,826,300 | 3,738,827 |
| WC | 221,948 | (487,768) | (756,319) |
| Emp. | 113 | 106 | 127 |

DUNS 50-428-5537

## Techset Composition Ltd

(Subsidiary of: S.R. Nova Private Limited)
Chalke House, 3 Brunel Road, Salisbury, Wiltshire SP2 7PU
**Tel:** 01722332949
**Web:** www.techset.co.uk
**Reg No:** 2420700   **Estd:** 1989 Private Limited Company
**Line of Business:** Pre-press activities
**Issued Capital:** £100
**Directors:** W L Ruttledge, V Nagarkatti, R B Barwale, S Viswanathan, R K Jalan
**Co. Secretary:** Balwant Patel
**US SIC:** 7399, 7392
**UK SIC:** 83954, 83951
**Auditors:** Moore Stephens
**Bankers:** Lloyds TSB Bank plc (30-97-41)

| | 31-03-14 | 31-03-13 | 31-03-12 |
|---|---|---|---|
| TA | 836,674 | 826,755 | 724,633 |
| NW | 204,186 | 408,197 | 368,781 |
| WC | 173,075 | 376,232 | 337,768 |

DUNS 22-770-2685

## Techtest Ltd

Street Court, Leominster, Herefordshire HR6 9QA
**Tel:** 01568 708744
**Web:** www.hr-smith.com
**Reg No:** 1363570   **Estd:** 1978 Private Limited Company
**Line of Business:** Manufacture of electronic valves and tubes and other electronic components
**Trading Style:** H R Smith
**Issued Capital:** £880
**Principals:** R E Smith (Managing), Miss S F Smith
**Co. Secretary:** Miss Susan Smith
**Responsibilities**
**Senior:** Millicent Smith (Manager)
**Branches:** Techtest Ltd, Unit 416 Tarsmill Court, Hereford, Herefordshire HR2 6JZ
**US SIC:** 3679, 3662
**UK SIC:** 34542, 34430
**Auditors:** Davies Mayers Barnett LLP
**Bankers:** Lloyds TSB Bank plc (30-97-41)

| | 31-01-14 | 31-01-13 | 31-01-12 |
|---|---|---|---|
| TO | 14,375,119 | 12,518,228 | 11,549,868 |
| P/L | 3,093,989 | 2,666,353 | 2,874,910 |
| NW | 16,178,801 | 15,609,203 | 13,153,573 |
| WC | 15,274,348 | 14,936,527 | 12,800,442 |
| Emp. | 159 | 144 | 139 |

DUNS 34-982-0626

## Techtex Holdings Ltd

Unit 7 8 Rhodes Business Park, Silburn Way, Middleton, Manchester M24 4NE
**Tel:** 0161-643-3000
**Web:** www.techtex.co.uk
**Reg No:** 5777424   **Estd:** 2006 Private Limited Company
**Line of Business:** Management activities of holding companies
**Issued Capital:** £100
**Directors:** D J Beardsworth, B J Whitney
**Co. Secretary:** Stephen Oldfield
**US SIC:** 6711, 2392
**UK SIC:** 83962, 45550
**Auditors:** Pierce CA Ltd
**Bankers:** Lloyds TSB Bank plc (30-96-41)

| | 31-12-13 | 31-12-12 | 31-12-11 |
|---|---|---|---|
| TO | 14,511,947 | 14,012,202 | 14,776,406 |
| P/L | 1,208,819 | 1,105,624 | 977,649 |
| NW | 2,572,916 | 2,297,802 | 1,888,450 |
| WC | 800,316 | 721,465 | 721,980 |
| Emp. | 62 | 62 | 51 |

DUNS 76-905-6029

## Techtrek Ltd

59 Bispham Road, London NW10 7HB
**Tel:** 01732841307   **Fax:** 02089989292
**Web:** www.techtrekindia.com
**Reg No:** 2617426   **Estd:** 1991 Private Limited Company
**Line of Business:** Hardware consultancy
**Issued Capital:** £100,000
**Directors:** A Malhotra, A C Gale
**Co. Secretary:** Naresh Malhotra
**Branches:** Techtrek Ltd, Secure Foundations Ltd, The Nursery, Aylesford, Kent ME20 6PE
**US SIC:** 7379, 5122
**UK SIC:** 83940, 61800
**Bankers:** National Westminster Bank Plc (60-07-10)

| | 30-06-13 | 30-06-12 | 30-06-11 |
|---|---|---|---|
| TO | 8,764,908 | 1,917,382 | 1,849,253 |
| P/L | (223,188) | 112,279 | 70,149 |
| NW | (2,716,994) | 368,798 | 265,884 |
| WC | (6,061,148) | (354,573) | (498,536) |
| Emp. | 166 | N/A | N/A |

DUNS 50-510-8704      **Imp**

## Techtronic Industries (Uk) Ltd

(Subsidiary of: A & M Industries Sarl)
Medina House, Thames Industrial Estate, Fieldhouse Lane, Marlow, Buckinghamshire SL7 1TB
**Tel:** 01628894400   **Fax:** 01628 894 401
**Web:** www.ryobitools.co.uk
**Reg No:** 2478762   **VAT No:** 551396338
**Estd:** 1990 Private Limited Company
**Line of Business:** Manufacturers of tools
**Export Sales:** £2,316,289
**Trading Style:** Tti, Ryobi, Ryobi Technologies
**Issued Capital:** £4,000,000
**Directors:** M G Rafferty, K P Chau
**Responsibilities**
**Senior:** Jenny Hartley (Manager), Michael Rints (Manager)
**IT:** Peter Rimmer (IT Analyst)
**US SIC:** 3423, 5074
**UK SIC:** 31612, 61300
**Auditors:** Deloitte LLP
**Bankers:** The Bank Of Tokyo-Mitsubishi, Ltd (60-01-09)

| | 31-12-13 | 31-12-12 | 31-12-11 |
|---|---|---|---|
| TO | 32,659,308 | 33,874,621 | 33,658,728 |
| P/L | 2,188,239 | (9,418,372) | (10,436,300) |
| NW | (44,827,623) | (47,015,862) | (37,597,490) |
| WC | 2,523,333 | (6,516,344) | (1,709,403) |
| Emp. | 102 | 100 | 79 |

DUNS 76-887-1535      **Exp**

## Techwax Ltd

(Subsidiary of: Ashland Inc.)
Unit 4b, Whinbank Park, Whinbank Road, Newton Aycliffe, County Durham DL5 6AY
**Tel:** 01325-301301
**Web:** www.ashland.com
**Reg No:** 2614599   **Estd:** 1991 Private Limited Company
**Line of Business:** Manufacturers of chemicals
**Export Markets:** worldwide
**Trading Style:** I S P
**Issued Capital:** £30,000
**Director:** F J Jumelet
**Co. Secretary:** Ms Julie Charlton
**Responsibilities**
**Senior:** Christopher Higgs (Manager)
**US SIC:** 2899   **UK SIC:** 25670
**Auditors:** Mitchell Gordon Ltd
**Bankers:** National Westminster Bank Plc (51-61-33)

| | 30-09-13 | 30-09-12 | 30-09-11 |
|---|---|---|---|
| TO | 11,893,014 | 15,003,099 | 11,002,137 |
| P/L | 267,622 | 434,902 | 321,397 |
| NW | 1,874,311 | 1,636,439 | 1,235,332 |
| WC | 391,619 | 310,819 | (127,639) |
| Emp. | 66 | 65 | 64 |

DUNS 53-638-0454

## Teckno Developments Ltd

Waterside Road, Beverley, North Humberside HU17 0PP
**Tel:** 01482 882266   **Fax:** 01482 863869
**Web:** www.tecknodev.com
**Reg No:** 3442807   **Estd:** 1997 Private Limited Company
**Line of Business:** Manufacture of other articles of paper and paperboard not elsewhere classified
**Issued Capital:** £643,539
**Principals:** A Langley (Managing), T A Langley
**US SIC:** 2649, 1541
**UK SIC:** 47280, 50100
**Auditors:** Graybrowne Ltd
**Bankers:** HSBC Bank plc (40-25-16)

| | 31-12-13 | 31-12-12 | 31-12-11 |
|---|---|---|---|
| TA | 2,438,876 | 2,433,904 | 2,895,856 |
| NW | 1,120,808 | 1,016,613 | 1,066,499 |
| WC | 667,557 | 463,216 | 268,077 |

DUNS 21-720-1979

## Tecni-Form Ltd

Goldstone Lane, Hove, East Sussex BN3 7BU
**Tel:** 01273723591
**Web:** www.tecni-form.com
**Reg No:** 0975813   **VAT No:** 192962918
**Estd:** 1970 Private Limited Company
**Line of Business:** Manufacture of other plastic products
**Issued Capital:** £10,000
**Principals:** C L Fecher (Managing), P Thompson, H H Wassink, J R Ross, Mrs C L Fecher, D E Moore
**Co. Secretary:** Howard Shaw
**Branches:** Tecni-Form Ltd, 8 Mount Industrial Estate, Mount Road, Stone, Staffordshire ST15 8LL
**US SIC:** 2821   **UK SIC:** 25140
**Bankers:** HSBC Bank plc (40-25-03)

| | 30-06-13 | 30-06-12 | 30-06-11 |
|---|---|---|---|
| TA | 1,325,968 | 1,298,795 | 1,703,767 |
| NW | 588,452 | 499,737 | 269,284 |
| WC | 368,927 | 205,367 | (76,775) |

DUNS 21-119-3211      **Imp**

## Tecquipment Ltd

(Subsidiary of: Lester Point Holdings Ltd)
Bonsall Street, Long Eaton, Nottingham, Nottinghamshire NG10 2AN
**Tel:** 01159-722611   **Fax:** 01159731520
**Web:** www.tecquipment.com
**Reg No:** 6587107   **VAT No:** 935270523
**Estd:** 1973 Private Limited Company
**Line of Business:** Wholesale of other machinery for use in industry, trade and navigation
**Export Sales:** £7,106,581
**Issued Capital:** £1,000
**Director:** S R Woods
**Responsibilities**
**Senior:** Helen Milsom (Manager)
**Finance:** Nigel Wynn (Financial Director)
**HR:** Yasmin Parratt (Human Resources Manager)
**US SIC:** 5199   **UK SIC:** 61900

| | 31-07-13 | 31-07-12 | 31-07-11 |
|---|---|---|---|
| TO | 7,864,167 | 7,095,094 | 6,973,915 |
| P/L | 1,443,050 | 1,686,359 | 1,249,603 |
| NW | 2,525,658 | 2,573,708 | 3,126,342 |
| WC | 2,564,198 | 2,540,437 | 3,208,056 |
| Emp. | 84 | 74 | 68 |

DUNS 76-952-4398      **Imp-Exp**

## Tectrade Computers Ltd

River Court, Mill Lane, Godalming, Surrey GU7 1EZ
**Web:** www.tectrade.com
**Reg No:** 2589951   **Estd:** 1991 Private Limited Company
**Line of Business:** Data storage solutions
**Export Markets:** Europe and U.S.A.
**Export Sales:** £13,583,541
**Issued Capital:** £190,970
**Principals:** Ms S A Elkins (Managing), P C Elkins, Mrs P Hogan, P Cameron, Mrs R Fagioli, A G Fagioli
**Co. Secretary:** Kenneth Hogan
**Responsibilities**
**Senior:** Nicola Kippersluis (Manager), Michael Rickards (Manager), Andrew Slater (Sales Director)
**Marketing:** Andrew Slater (Sales Director)
**Sales:** Andrew Slater (Sales Director)
**Branches:** TECTRADE COMPUTERS LTD: Alexandra House, Lawnswood Business Park, Redvers Close, Leeds, LS16 6QY, WEST YORKSHIRE.
**US SIC:** 7374, 7392, 7379
**UK SIC:** 83940, 83951
**Auditors:** BDO LLP
**Bankers:** National Westminster Bank Plc (60-11-18)

| | 31-03-14 | 31-03-13 | 31-03-12 |
|---|---|---|---|
| TO | 37,365,928 | 28,194,798 | 29,162,581 |
| P/L | 2,147,535 | 650,070 | 1,005,090 |
| NW | 4,175,786 | 2,954,875 | 2,678,040 |
| WC | 4,220,060 | 3,129,899 | 3,037,736 |
| Emp. | 88 | 80 | 76 |

DUNS 52-026-9762      **Exp**

## Ted Baker Plc

6a St Pancras Way, London NW1 0TB
**Tel:** 02072554800   **Fax:** 02072554961
**Web:** www.tedbaker.com
**Reg No:** 3393836   **Estd:** 1997 Public Limited Company
**Line of Business:** Representative office
**Issued Capital:** £2,159,902
**Principals:** R S Kelvin (Chairman), R Stewart, D A Bernstein, A R Jennings, L D Page, Ms A H Sheinfield
**Co. Secretary:** Charles Anderson
**Responsibilities**
**Senior:** Robert Breare (Manager)
**HR:** Jennifer Gray (Head of Human Resources)
**Health & Safety:** Jennifer Gray (Head of Human Resources)
**Facilities:** Matt Ashby (Facilities Director)
**Engineering:** Donald Browne (Production Director)
**Branches:** Ted Baker Plc, Dome Building, 3-4 The Quadrant, Richmond, Surrey TW9 1BP
**US SIC:** 5611, 5699, 5661, 5961
**UK SIC:** 64500, 64600, 65600
**Auditors:** KPMG Audit PLC
**Bankers:** The Royal Bank Of Scotland Plc (15-10-00)

| | 25-01-14 | 26-01-13 | 28-01-12 |
|---|---|---|---|
| TO | 321,921,000 | 254,466,000 | 215,625,000 |
| P/L | 38,923,000 | 28,922,000 | 24,255,000 |
| NW | 105,984,000 | 97,910,000 | 84,217,000 |
| WC | 54,863,000 | 47,105,000 | 45,350,000 |
| Emp. | 2,377 | 2,185 | 1,979 |

DUNS 76-721-9140

## Teddies Nurseries Ltd

(Subsidiary of: Bain Capital Llc)
Forest House, 3-5 Horndean Road, Bracknell, Berkshire RG12 0XQ
**Tel:** 01344486565   **Fax:** 02088-926711
**Web:** www.teddiesnurseries.co.uk
**Reg No:** 2596369   **Estd:** 1991 Private Limited Company
**Line of Business:** Pre school education
**Issued Capital:** £12,533,332
**Directors:** S Dreier, Ms E Boland, D Lissy, Ms M A Tocio
**Co. Secretary:** Stephen Kramer
**Responsibilities**
**Senior:** Sue Rengozzi (Customer Accounts Manager), Nathan Sweetman (Nursery Manager)
**Marketing:** Emma Hargrave (Marketing Manager)
**IT:** Johnny McCarthy (Communications Manager)
**Branches:** Teddies Nurseries Ltd, 4 Whitton Road, Twickenham, Middlesex TW1 1BJ
**US SIC:** 8211   **UK SIC:** 93200
**Auditors:** KPMG Audit PLC
**Bankers:** Bank Of Scotland (80-07-48)

| | 31-12-13 | 31-12-12 | 31-12-11 |
|---|---|---|---|
| TO | N/A | N/A | 19,569,380 |
| P/L | 860,999 | N/A | 4,394,984 |
| NW | 13,470,972 | 12,609,973 | 12,609,973 |
| WC | N/A | 12,584,973 | 4,474,005 |
| Emp. | N/A | N/A | 611 |

DUNS 21-728-5519 **Imp-Exp**
## Teddington Controls Ltd
**(Subsidiary of:** Henderson Industries Ltd)
Daniels Lane, St Austell, Cornwall PL25 3HG
**Tel:** 0172-674400
**Web:** www.tedcon.com
**Reg No:** 0533304 **VAT No:** 383876304
**Estd:** 1928 Private Limited Company
**Line of Business:** Manufacture of taps and valves
**Export Markets:** European Union (E U)
**Trading Style:** Teddington Appliance & Controls Ltd
**Issued Capital:** £1,063,801
**Director:** J I Henderson
**Co. Secretary:** Graham Mitchell
**Responsibilities**
**Senior:** Terry Wyatt *(Manager)*
**US SIC:** 3494, 3679
**UK SIC:** 32880, 34542
**Auditors:** Rothman Pantall & Co
**Bankers:** Bank Of Scotland (12-01-03)

| | 30-09-13 | 30-09-12 | 30-09-11 |
|---|---|---|---|
| TA | 355 | 356 | 553 |
| NW | (37,021) | (37,021) | (37,021) |
| WC | (11,321) | (11,321) | (11,321) |

DUNS 73-415-4607 **Imp-Exp**
## Teddington Engineered Solutions Ltd
Unit 1 Heol Cropin, Dafen, Llanelli, Dyfed SA14 8QW
**Tel:** 01554 744 500 **Fax:** 01554 746 435
**Web:** www.tes.uk.com
**Reg No:** 4688666 **VAT No:** 811554942
**Estd:** 2003 Private Limited Company
**Line of Business:** Bellows makers
**Trading Style:** Teddington Engineered Solutions, Teddington
**Issued Capital:** £100,200
**Co. Secretary:** Paul Greenwood
**Responsibilities**
**Health & Safety:** Gary Stanley *(Health & Safety Officer)*
**US SIC:** 8911, 3069
**UK SIC:** 83701, 48123
**Auditors:** Bevan & Buckland
**Bankers:** Lloyds TSB Bank plc (30-95-14)

| | 30-08-13 | 31-08-12 | 26-08-11 |
|---|---|---|---|
| TA | 2,962,581 | 3,287,397 | 2,755,414 |
| NW | 1,802,848 | 1,459,147 | 1,332,154 |
| WC | 1,523,601 | 1,121,599 | 956,996 |

DUNS 21-098-0839
## Teddy Clark (Holdings) Ltd
Unit 2, Therm Road, Hull, North Humberside HU8 7BF
**Tel:** 01482620437
**Reg No:** 6422650 **Estd:** 2007 Private Limited Company
**Line of Business:** Gambling and betting activities
**Issued Capital:** £1,001
**Directors:** W E Clark, C E Clark
**US SIC:** 7999 **UK SIC:** 97913
**Bankers:** Bank Of Scotland (12-16-30)

| | 31-03-14 | 31-03-13 | 31-03-12 |
|---|---|---|---|
| TO | 7,325,301 | 5,903,774 | 5,963,668 |
| P/L | 1,496,052 | 620,625 | 480,722 |
| NW | 2,028,327 | 4,077,538 | 3,498,680 |
| WC | (4,943,105) | (1,371,354) | (1,735,007) |
| Emp. | 225 | 160 | 163 |

DUNS 21-780-7753
## Teds Treatment Education Drug Service
Engine House, Depot Road, Aberdare, Mid Glamorgan CF44 8DL
**Tel:** 01685880090
**Web:** www.teds.org.uk
**Estd:** 1997 Proprietorship
**Line of Business:** Drug counselling
**Proprietor:** Mrs J Harrington
**Responsibilities**
**Senior:** Jean Harrington *(Manager)*
**US SIC:** 8321 **UK SIC:** 96111
**Employees:** 55

DUNS 38-584-5029
## Teedown Ltd
Hurst Lodge, Bagshot Road, Ascot, Berkshire SL5 9JU
**Tel:** 01344-622154 **Fax:** 01344629047
**Web:** www.hurstlodge.co.uk
**Reg No:** 3339182 **Estd:** 1997 Private Limited Company
**Line of Business:** Adult education locations
**Issued Capital:** £510,002
**Director:** T B Smit
**Co. Secretary:** Ms Victoria Smit
**US SIC:** 8299 **UK SIC:** 93300
**Auditors:** Gorrie Whitson

| | 31-08-13 | 31-08-12 | 31-08-11 |
|---|---|---|---|
| TA | 942,101 | 955,392 | 973,652 |
| NW | 860,832 | 861,228 | 861,600 |
| WC | 53,873 | 67,176 | 85,064 |

DUNS 23-546-1907 **Imp**
## Teekay Shipping (Glasgow) Ltd
144 Elliot Street, Glasgow, Lanarkshire G3 8EX
**Tel:** 01412 229000
**Web:** www.teekay.com
**Reg No:** 0184787SC **Estd:** 1998 Private Limited Company
**Line of Business:** Shipping companies
**Issued Capital:** £2,173,688
**Principals:** J Adams *(Managing)*, A J Bensler
**Co. Secretary:** Maclay Murray & Spens Llp
**Responsibilities**
**IT:** Gary Queen *(IT Manager)*
**US SIC:** 4712 **UK SIC:** 77002
**Auditors:** Ernst & Young LLP
**Bankers:** Bank Of Scotland (80-54-01)

| | 31-12-13 | 31-12-12 | 31-12-11 |
|---|---|---|---|
| TO | 6,675,510 | 9,051,219 | 8,583,689 |
| P/L | (151,424) | (1,000,548) | 382,398 |
| NW | 2,007,237 | 2,040,777 | 2,641,947 |
| WC | 1,464,039 | 1,406,332 | 2,243,179 |
| Emp. | 64 | 84 | 93 |

DUNS 73-870-3466
## Teeming Ltd
Invision House Wilbury Way, Hitchin, Hertfordshire SG4 0TY
**Tel:** 020-7436-7890
**Web:** www.teeming.co.uk
**Reg No:** 5124898 **Estd:** 2004 Private Limited Company
**Line of Business:** Business and management consultancy activities not elsewhere classified
**Issued Capital:** £2
**Co. Secretary:** James Powell
**US SIC:** 7399 **UK SIC:** 83954

| | 31-05-14 | 31-05-13 | 31-05-12 |
|---|---|---|---|
| TA | 14,201 | 21,128 | 30,283 |
| NW | 50 | 2 | 2 |
| WC | 7,409 | 9,905 | 11,877 |

DUNS 51-982-8156
## Teenage Cancer Trust
93 Newman Street, London W1T 3EZ
**Fax:** 020-7612-0371
**Web:** www.teenagecancertrust.org
**Reg No:** 3350311 **Estd:** 1997 Private Limited Company
**Line of Business:** Other business activities not elsewhere classified
**Directors:** R B Rosenberg, J S Matlin, D A Hoare, S J Davies, A N Hughes, P Spanswick, A J Patten, R M Harris
**Co. Secretary:** Ms Siobhan Dunn
**US SIC:** 8091 **UK SIC:** 95200
**Auditors:** Buzzacott
**Bankers:** Barclays Bank Plc (20-05-75)

| | 30-06-13 | 30-06-12 | 30-06-11 |
|---|---|---|---|
| TO | 13,529,241 | 12,998,788 | 12,677,818 |
| P/L | (1,469,030) | (295,971) | 32,834 |
| NW | 7,211,026 | 8,680,056 | 8,976,027 |
| WC | 7,203,353 | 6,650,841 | 5,949,027 |
| Emp. | 115 | 105 | 103 |

DUNS 22-786-3768 **Imp-Exp**
## Teer Coatings Ltd
West Stone House, West Stone, Droitwich, Worcestershire WR9 9AS
**Tel:** 08702203910 **Fax:** 08702-203911
**Web:** www.teercoatings.co.uk
**Reg No:** 1643376 **VAT No:** 376145539
**Estd:** 1982 Private Limited Company
**Line of Business:** Manufacture of mastics and sealants
**Export Markets:** Worldwide
**Export Sales:** £2,916,925
**Issued Capital:** £1,000
**Directors:** G Hehenfelder, M Blaimschein, M Hofer
**Co. Secretary:** Mrs Beverly Parker
**Responsibilities**
**Senior:** Matthias Gattinger *(Director)*, Therese Mitterbauer *(Manager)*, Therese Niss *(Director)*, Dennis Teer *(Manager)*
**IT:** Stephane Poulat *(Computer Manager)*
**HR:** Angela Byrne *(Human Resources Manager)*
**Health & Safety:** Neda Thomas *(Health & Safety Officer)*
**US SIC:** 2891 **UK SIC:** 25620
**Auditors:** Worton Rock
**Bankers:** The Royal Bank Of Scotland Plc (16-22-26)

| | 31-01-14 | 31-01-13 | 31-01-12 |
|---|---|---|---|
| TO | 4,323,348 | 3,528,359 | 2,789,028 |
| P/L | 358,411 | (153,720) | (131,723) |
| NW | 2,741,986 | 2,435,540 | 2,524,802 |
| WC | 1,275,348 | 946,023 | 1,187,430 |
| Emp. | 54 | 56 | 58 |

DUNS 36-519-5465
## Tees Active Ltd
Redheugh House, Thornaby Place, Stockton-On-Tees, Cleveland TS17 6SG
**Tel:** 01642-528539
**Web:** www.teesactive.co.uk
**Reg No:** 0029699IP **Estd:** 2009 Proprietorship
**Line of Business:** Operation of other sports arenas and stadiums not elsewhere classified
**Proprietor:** J Pratt
**Responsibilities**
**Senior:** Steven Chaytor *(Manager)*
**US SIC:** 7399 **UK SIC:** 83954
**Employees:** 350

DUNS 21-312-8259 **Exp**
## Tees Components Ltd
**(Subsidiary of:** Jeave 2 Ltd)
North Skelton, Saltburn-By-The-Sea, Cleveland TS12 2AP
**Web:** www.teescomponents.co.uk
**Reg No:** 0775765 **VAT No:** 258446923
**Estd:** 1963 Private Limited Company
**Line of Business:** Manufacture of metal structures and parts of structures
**Export Markets:** Worldwide
**Export Sales:** £1,299,852
**Trading Style:** Tees Components Ltd
**Issued Capital:** £1,000
**Principals:** C L Wood *(Managing)*, Ms S L Lane
**Co. Secretary:** Mrs Jean Wood
**Responsibilities**
**Senior:** Cliff Muir *(Chief Estimator)*
**Finance:** Christine Thorpe *(Accounts Manager)*
**Sales:** Malcolm Douglas *(Chief Estimator)*
**IT:** Malcolm Douglas *(Chief Estimator)*
**Operations:** Steve Horner *(Production Coordinator)*
**Engineering:** Steve Horner *(Production Coordinator)*
**Branches:** Tees Components Ltd, Bolckow Street, Saltburn-By-The-Sea, Cleveland TS12 2AP
**US SIC:** 3441, 8911
**UK SIC:** 32042, 83701
**Auditors:** Keith Robinson & Co
**Bankers:** Barclays Bank Plc (20-00-30)

| | 31-12-13 | 31-12-12 | 31-12-11 |
|---|---|---|---|
| TO | 4,752,453 | 5,281,142 | 4,494,974 |
| P/L | 262,771 | 478,085 | 187,927 |
| NW | 3,509,191 | 3,237,086 | 2,891,556 |
| WC | 1,426,825 | 1,541,675 | 1,764,256 |
| Emp. | 66 | 66 | 65 |

DUNS 21-225-7726
## Tees East & North Yorkshire Ambulance Service
York Way, Hull, North Humberside HU10 6HD
**Tel:** 01482670800
**Estd:** 2000 Proprietorship
**Line of Business:** Local Passenger Transport,NEC
**Responsibilities**
**Senior:** David Whitting *(Ceo)*
**US SIC:** 4119 **UK SIC:** 72200
**Employees:** 77

DUNS 36-490-3588
## Tees Esk & Wear Valleys Nhs Trust
West Park Hospital, Darlington, County Durham DL2 2TS
**Tel:** 01642288288
**Web:** www.tewv.nhs.uk
**Estd:** 2006
**Line of Business:** Accommodation advice
**Principals:** Mrs J Turnbull *(Chairman)*, C Martin *(Financial)*, M Barkley, Mrs C Stanbury, Dr N Land, L Morgan
**Responsibilities**
**Senior:** Graham Neave *(Manager)*, Mike Newell *(Principal)*, Christine Stanbury *(Principal)*
**IT:** Pauline King *(Computer Operations Manager)*
**HR:** David Levy *(Human Resources Manager)*
**US SIC:** 8091 **UK SIC:** 95200
**Employees:** 5,500
**Turnover:** £167,182,000

DUNS 21-317-8635
## Tees Licensed Foyboatmens Association Ltd
Tinkerdale Road, Tees Port, Middlesbrough, Cleveland TS6 7UD
**Tel:** 01642-454494
**Web:** www.teesfoyboatmen.co.uk
**Reg No:** 0762777 **Estd:** 1963 Private Limited Company
**Line of Business:** Activities of other transport agencies
**Issued Capital:** £35

**Directors:** J Appleton, L R Scott, J Scott, G Allen, D Appleton, N Wells, W Farren
**Responsibilities**
**Senior:** Ryan Ludrecius *(Manager)*, Paul Spashett *(Manager)*, Neil Todd *(Sharholder)*
**US SIC:** 4712 **UK SIC:** 77002
**Auditors:** Stead Flintoff & Co
**Bankers:** Barclays Bank Plc (20-56-74)

| | 30-06-13 | 30-06-12 | 30-06-11 |
|---|---|---|---|
| TA | 918,728 | 799,557 | 847,558 |
| NW | 417,624 | 352,146 | 297,600 |
| WC | 360,408 | 285,691 | 223,499 |

DUNS 21-779-4335
## Tees Valley Joint Strategy Unit
Cavendish House, Stockton-On-Tees, Cleveland TS17 6QY
**Tel:** 01642524400
**Web:** www.teesvalleyunlimited.gov.uk
**Partnership**
**Line of Business:** Activities of business and employers organisations
**Proprietor:** S Catchpole
**US SIC:** 8611 **UK SIC:** 96312
**Employees:** 45

DUNS 21-138-8842
## Tees Valley Telecom Ltd
Unit 1 Stephenson Court, Skippers Lane Industrial Estate, Skippers Lane Industrial Estate, Middlesbrough, Cleveland TS6 6UT
**Web:** www.tvtuk.co.uk
**Reg No:** 6712504 **Estd:** 2008 Private Limited Company
**Line of Business:** Telecom equipment and systems
**Issued Capital:** £1
**Director:** D Hartshorn
**US SIC:** 4899 **UK SIC:** 79020
**Employees:** 153

DUNS 45-830-9432
## Tees Valley Training Ltd
Harvard Avenue, Stockton-On-Tees, Cleveland TS17 6FB
**Web:** www.teesvalleytraining.co.uk
**Reg No:** 3182501 **Estd:** 1996 Private Limited Company
**Line of Business:** Technical and industrial schools
**Issued Capital:** £1
**Directors:** P M Cook, M S White
**Co. Secretary:** Ms Fiona Sharp
**US SIC:** 8249 **UK SIC:** 93300

| | 31-07-13 | 31-07-12 | 31-07-11 |
|---|---|---|---|
| TA | 1 | 1 | 1 |
| NW | 1 | 1 | 1 |

DUNS 21-780-9726
## Tees Wear Valleys Nhs Foundation Trust
Cross Lane, Scarborough, North Yorkshire YO12 6DN
**Tel:** 01723384600
**Estd:** 1903 Partnership
**Line of Business:** Mental health centres
**Partners:** P Hyde, J Ballatt
**US SIC:** 8091 **UK SIC:** 95200
**Employees:** 200

DUNS 21-100-0224
## Teeside Probation Service
Centre North East 73-75 Albert Road, Middlesbrough, Cleveland TS1 2RU
**Tel:** 01642230533
**Web:** www.dtvprobation.org.uk
**Line of Business:** Security activities
**Trading Style:** National Probation Service Teeside
**Proprietor:** Mrs E Lumley
**Responsibilities**
**IT:** T. Bitty *(IT Manager)*
**Branches:** Teeside Probation Service, Fieldwork Unit, 38 Station Rd, Redcar, Cleveland TS10 1AG
**US SIC:** 9121 **UK SIC:** 91110
**Employees:** 350

DUNS 21-811-4571
## Teesside Cheshire Home
Marske Hall, Redcar Road, Marske-By-The-Sea, Redcar, Cleveland TS11 6AA
**Tel:** 01642482672
**Web:** www.leonardcheshiredisability.org
**Estd:** 1964
**Line of Business:** Nursing homes
**US SIC:** 8051 **UK SIC:** 95100
**Employees:** 80

DUNS 28-842-7396
## Teesside High School Ltd
The Avenue, Eaglescliffe, Stockton-On-Tees, Cleveland TS16 9AT
**Tel:** 01642782095
**Web:** www.teessidehigh.co.uk
**Reg No:** 0572205 **Estd:** 1969 Private Company Limited By Guarantee

**Line of Business:** Schools (independent)
**Directors:** C G Neave, Mrs A Greenwood, C A Atha, T G Watson, Ms J Beeton, D H Lister, C G Watson, R R Tindle
**Co. Secretary:** Miss Edith Vane
**Responsibilities**
**Senior:** Caroline Chapman *(Manager)*, Deborah Duncan *(Head Teacher)*, Stephen Merckx *(Manager)*, Thomas Packer *(Headmaster)*
**Finance:** Caroline Chapman *(Manager)*, Stephanie Robson *(Senior Finance Administrator)*
**Marketing:** Helen Mellor *(Head of Marketing)*
**IT:** Andy Brass *(IT Coordinator)*
**HR:** Thomas Packer *(Headmaster)*
**Health & Safety:** Peter Herbert *(Facilities Manager)*
**Facilities:** Peter Herbert *(Facilities Manager)*
**US SIC:** 8211 **UK SIC:** 93200
**Auditors:** Anderson Barrowcliff LLP
**Bankers:** Barclays Bank Plc (20-00-52)

| | 31-07-13 | 31-07-12 | 31-07-11 |
|---|---|---|---|
| TO | 4,005,516 | 3,889,948 | 3,715,206 |
| P/L | 22,514 | 57,236 | (7,435) |
| NW | 2,194,691 | 2,163,778 | 2,104,312 |
| WC | (59,383) | 67,325 | 148,867 |
| Emp. | 102 | 102 | 95 |

DUNS 22-827-7133
## Teesside Hospice Care Foundation
1 Northgate Road, Middlesbrough, Cleveland TS5 5NW
**Tel:** 01642811060 **Fax:** 01642-823034
**Web:** www.teessidehospice.org
**Reg No:** 1642201 **Estd:** 1982 Private Company Limited By Guarantee
**Line of Business:** Medical practice activities
**Principals:** W A Gould *(Chairman)*, P E Whitaker *(Financial)*, R M Jewell, J L Fysh, Ms S M Storey, Dr R A Parkin, N Packer, Dr M Craig
**Co. Secretary:** Mrs Erica Turner
**Responsibilities**
**Senior:** Brian Footitt *(Director)*, Ann O'Hanlon *(Director)*, William Pickersgill *(Director)*, Thomas Waites *(Director)*
**Finance:** Anjie Werdle *(Account Manager)*
**Marketing:** Debbie Coulson *(Marketing Manager)*, Jane O'Bryne *(Fundraising Manager)*, Ashleigh Watts *(Marketing Assistant)*
**Purchasing:** Tracy O'Donnell *(Purchasing Manager)*
**US SIC:** 8011 **UK SIC:** 95300
**Auditors:** Chipchase Manners & Co
**Bankers:** The Royal Bank Of Scotland Plc (16-25-24)

| | 31-03-14 | 31-03-13 | 31-03-12 |
|---|---|---|---|
| TO | 4,270,225 | 3,632,777 | 3,815,429 |
| P/L | 168,110 | (106,938) | 286,749 |
| NW | 4,832,512 | 4,596,920 | 4,629,408 |
| WC | 1,934,154 | 2,022,665 | 2,077,605 |
| Emp. | 90 | 120 | 124 |

DUNS 21-579-6106
## Teesside Magistrates Court
The Law Court, Victoria Square, Middlesbrough, Cleveland TS1 2AS
**Tel:** 01642240301
**Web:** www.gov.uk
**Estd:** 2011 Proprietorship
**Line of Business:** Courts
**Proprietor:** C Mose
**US SIC:** 9211 **UK SIC:** 91200
**Employees:** 125

DUNS 21-308-2274
## Teesside Transport Commercial Services Ltd
1a Bolckow Road, Middlesbrough, Cleveland TS6 7BN
**Tel:** 01642469552
**Web:** www.davidfoxtransport.co.uk
**Reg No:** 1029911 **VAT No:** 258104078
**Estd:** 1971 Private Limited Company
**Line of Business:** Road haulage and transport services
**Trading Style:** David Fox Transport
**Issued Capital:** £1,000
**Directors:** R A Fox, D B Fox
**Branches:** Teesside Transport Commercial Services Ltd, 11 Oldfield Lane, Leeds, West Yorkshire LS12 4DH
**US SIC:** 4789 **UK SIC:** 77002
**Auditors:** Anderson Barrowcliff LLP
**Bankers:** Barclays Bank Plc (20-56-74)

| | 31-10-13 | 31-10-12 | 31-10-11 |
|---|---|---|---|
| TA | 2,710,629 | 2,539,729 | 2,681,095 |
| NW | 1,160,491 | 1,018,419 | 1,007,825 |
| WC | 336,921 | 4,376 | (49,305) |

DUNS 21-664-1706
## Teesside University Trust for Academies (Freebrough Academy)
Linden Road, Saltburn-By-The-Sea, Cleveland TS12 2SJ
**Tel:** 01287-676-305
**Web:** www.freebroughacademy.org
**Reg No:** 7185357 **Estd:** 2010 Private Company Limited By Guarantee
**Line of Business:** Schools (independent)
**Trading Style:** Freebrough Academy
**Directors:** Ms C Parker, Mrs K L Pink, Mrs S L Mccallum, Mrs P Gunner, Ms P White, G A Groom, Mrs J A Burton, Mrs A Holmes
**Co. Secretary:** Gary Singh
**Responsibilities**
**Senior:** Jonathan Anthony *(Director)*, Andrea Back *(Governor)*, Lesley Conroy *(Director)*, Jonathan Easby *(Governor)*, Linda Halbert *(Director)*, Elizabeth Holey *(Director)*, Asma Shaffi *(Director)*
**US SIC:** 8211 **UK SIC:** 93200
**Auditors:** KPMG LLP
**Bankers:** National Westminster Bank Plc (54-41-34)

| | 31-08-14 | 31-08-13 | 31-08-12 |
|---|---|---|---|
| TO | 5,069,000 | 8,148,000 | 5,984,000 |
| P/L | (476,000) | 2,266,000 | (154,000) |
| NW | 14,825,000 | 15,296,000 | 13,172,000 |
| WC | 973,000 | 1,013,000 | 606,000 |
| Emp. | 106 | 109 | 108 |

DUNS 28-878-4002
## Tef Transport Ltd
Great Hill, Eastfield, Scarborough, North Yorkshire YO11 3TX
**Tel:** 01723581259
**Web:** www.teftransport.co.uk
**Reg No:** 1142954 **Estd:** 1973 Private Limited Company
**Line of Business:** Road haulage and transport services
**Issued Capital:** £60
**Directors:** D F Beckett, A Mclaughlin
**Co. Secretary:** Mrs Linda Mclaughlin
**US SIC:** 4789 **UK SIC:** 77002
**Auditors:** Moore Stephens
**Bankers:** Yorkshire Bank Plc (05-07-47)

| | 31-10-13 | 31-10-12 | 31-10-11 |
|---|---|---|---|
| TO | 5,312,115 | 5,553,648 | N/A |
| P/L | 165,281 | 288,388 | N/A |
| NW | 1,307,573 | 1,275,657 | 1,200,648 |
| WC | (1,027,437) | (801,299) | (555,782) |
| Emp. | 57 | 59 | N/A |

DUNS 21-309-4360 **Imp**
## Tefal U K Ltd
**(Subsidiary of:** Seb Sa)
Riverside House, Riverside Walk, Windsor, Berkshire SL4 1NA
**Tel:** 0845602454 **Fax:** 01753583938
**Web:** www.tefal.co.uk
**Reg No:** 1051980 **VAT No:** 175874223
**Estd:** 1972 Private Limited Company
**Line of Business:** Wholesale of other household goods not elsewhere classified
**Trading Style:** Groupe Seb Uk Ltd
**Issued Capital:** £900,000
**Directors:** A Chatfield, L P Gaudemard, Ms I L Jurus-Seijsener
**Co. Secretary:** Andrew Chatfield
**US SIC:** 5199 **UK SIC:** 61900

| | 31-12-13 | 31-12-12 | 31-12-11 |
|---|---|---|---|
| TA | 6,718,000 | 6,718,000 | 6,718 |
| NW | 6,718,000 | 6,718,000 | 6,718 |

DUNS 29-530-3754
## Tegrel Ltd
Tundry Way, Blaydon-On-Tyne, Tyne and Wear NE21 5TT
**Tel:** 01914990888 **Fax:** 019141 40660
**Web:** www.tegrel.co.uk
**Reg No:** 1897468 **VAT No:** 569201143
**Estd:** 1978 Private Limited Company
**Line of Business:** Fabricated metal products
**Issued Capital:** £7,355
**Directors:** R D Leech, K Pallett
**Co. Secretary:** Roy Leech
**US SIC:** 3469, 8911
**UK SIC:** 31200, 83701
**Bankers:** Barclays Bank Plc (20-59-97)

| | 31-03-14 | 31-03-13 | 31-03-12 |
|---|---|---|---|
| TA | 2,125,198 | 2,102,331 | 2,182,270 |
| NW | 1,237,989 | 1,110,349 | 1,207,192 |
| WC | 785,415 | 600,675 | 661,607 |

DUNS 21-710-5360
## Teifi Timber Products Ltd
Cross Road, Pencader, Dyfed SA39 9DY
**Tel:** 01559-395325
**Web:** www.tlthomas.co.uk
**Reg No:** 1157507 **Estd:** 1974 Private Limited Company
**Line of Business:** Saw milling and planing of wood, impregnation of wood
**Trading Style:** T L Thomas & Son
**Issued Capital:** £100
**Directors:** Mrs S E Thomas, J G Thomas, T B Thomas
**Co. Secretary:** Anwen Lloyd Thomas
**Responsibilities**
**Senior:** Margaret Lloyd-Thomas *(Partner)*, Anwen Thomas *(Manager)*
**US SIC:** 2421, 2449
**UK SIC:** 46101, 46402
**Auditors:** Griffith & Miles

| | 31-03-14 | 31-03-13 | 31-03-12 |
|---|---|---|---|
| TA | 1,872,765 | 1,905,776 | 1,827,891 |
| NW | 1,071,221 | 947,139 | 951,710 |
| WC | 408,818 | 218,365 | 288,535 |

DUNS 21-041-5065
## Teign Housing
Pimplar House, Collett Way, Newton Abbot, Devon TQ12 4PH
**Web:** www.teignhousing.co.uk
**Proprietorship**
**Line of Business:** Housing associations societies trusts & co-operatives
**Proprietor:** Ms J Reece
**US SIC:** 6552 **UK SIC:** 85000
**Employees:** 80

DUNS 73-345-3323
## Teign Housing.
Millwood House, Collett Way, Newton Abbot, Devon TQ12 4PH
**Web:** www.teignhousing.co.uk
**Reg No:** 4619035 **Estd:** 2002 Private Limited Company
**Line of Business:** Other letting of own property
**Directors:** Mrs A Henderson, A Munro, J O'Dwyer, M Hall, S J Purser, P J Clarke, Mrs A M Edwards-Jones, A Daniels
**Co. Secretary:** Ms Joanna Reece
**Responsibilities**
**Senior:** Jacqueline Butler *(Manager)*, Mike Hanrahan *(Chief Executive Officer)*, Sandra Heath *(Manager)*, Robert Rodliffe *(Manager)*, Alan Soper *(Director)*, Peter Wharf *(Manager)*
**Marketing:** Katie Godfrey *(Communications Assistant)*
**HR:** Paula Birbeck *(Human Resources Manager)*
**Operations:** Paula Birbeck *(Human Resources Manager)*
**Branches:** Teign Housing., Church View, Newhay Close, Dawlish, Devon EX7 9QS
**US SIC:** 6519 **UK SIC:** 85000
**Bankers:** Barclays Bank Plc (20-18-15)

| | 31-03-14 | 31-03-13 | 31-03-12 |
|---|---|---|---|
| TO | 17,300,114 | 16,885,144 | 16,389,462 |
| P/L | 3,304,617 | 3,515,662 | 3,611,432 |
| NW | 37,680,314 | 28,485,069 | 24,979,407 |
| WC | (16,276,070) | (16,651,486) | (14,710,282) |
| Emp. | 84 | 84 | 91 |

DUNS 21-159-2386
## Teign School
Chudleigh Road, Kingsteignton, Newton Abbot, Devon TQ12 3JG
**Tel:** 01626-366969
**Web:** www.teignacademy.co.uk
**Estd:** 1941 Proprietorship
**Line of Business:** Schools (foundation)
**Proprietor:** A Pritchard
**Responsibilities**
**Senior:** V Gain *(Head Teacher)*, Vyv Game *(Head Teacher)*, Mark Woodlock *(Head Teacher)*
**Finance:** Kingsley Matthews *(Senior Finance Administrator)*
**US SIC:** 8211 **UK SIC:** 93200
**Employees:** 180

DUNS 23-644-0475
## Teignbridge District Council
Forde House, Brunel Road, Newton Abbot, Devon TQ12 4XX
**Tel:** 01626-361101 **Fax:** 01626215538
**Web:** www.teignbridge.gov.uk
**Estd:** 1974 Incorporate By Act Of Parliament
**Line of Business:** Local government
**Principals:** P Stabb *(Financial)*, B T Jones
**Responsibilities**
**Senior:** Nicola Bulbeck *(Chief Executive Officer)*, Phil Shears *(Deputy Chief Executive)*, Lesley Tucker *(Head of Finance)*
**Finance:** Lesley Tucker *(Head of Finance)*
**Marketing:** Tim Borret *(Service Manager Communications)*, Nina Ghabaldan *(Marketing Officer)*
**IT:** Rob Daulby *(IT Executive)*, Julian Niles *(IT Manager)*
**HR:** Jo Florence *(Training Officer)*
**Operations:** Ben Hosford *(Environmental Manager)*
**Branches:** Teignbridge District Council, The Lawn, The Strand, Dawlish, Devon EX7 9PW
**US SIC:** 9121 **UK SIC:** 91110
**Bankers:** National Westminster Bank Plc (54-10-39)
**Employees:** 600

DUNS 39-957-1124
## Teikyo Services (U.K.) Ltd
Fulmer Grange, Framewood Road, Slough, Berkshire SL2 4QS
**Tel:** 01753-663711
**Web:** www.teikyo.co.uk
**Reg No:** 2262739 **Estd:** 1989 Private Limited Company
**Line of Business:** Other tourist or short-stay accommodation
**Issued Capital:** £50,000
**Directors:** M Sasayama, M Imaseki, J Murai, H Okinaga, Y Okinaga, E Okinaga, M Okada
**Co. Secretary:** Junichi Murai
**Responsibilities**
**Senior:** Yasuo Asada *(Director)*, Fuminori Masubuchi *(Director)*
**US SIC:** 7021, 6519
**UK SIC:** 66500, 85000
**Auditors:** M R Salvage & Co
**Bankers:** National Westminster Bank Plc (60-04-53)

| | 31-03-14 | 31-03-13 | 31-03-12 |
|---|---|---|---|
| TO | 95,026 | 115,251 | 114,929 |
| P/L | 6,052 | 10,651 | 8,864 |
| NW | (244,443) | (244,443) | (244,443) |
| WC | 30,798 | 30,798 | 30,798 |

DUNS 76-711-8854
## Tejay Sportswear Ltd
67 Grace Road, Leicester, Leicestershire LE2 8AD
**Tel:** 01162864104 **Fax:** 01162440193
**Web:** www.tejay.co.uk
**Reg No:** 2594647 **Estd:** 1991 Private Limited Company
**Line of Business:** Manufacturers of sports goods
**Issued Capital:** £100
**Principals:** T A Smith *(Managing)*, Mrs K L Smith
**Co. Secretary:** Mrs Kerry Smith
**US SIC:** 3949 **UK SIC:** 49420
**Auditors:** Ashgates (Leicester) Ltd

| | 31-05-14 | 31-05-13 | 31-05-12 |
|---|---|---|---|
| TA | 1,385,819 | 1,338,719 | 1,217,325 |
| NW | 684,214 | 648,969 | 566,638 |
| WC | 486,990 | 429,459 | 343,305 |

DUNS 21-912-8311 **Imp-Exp**
## Tekdata Interconnections Ltd
**(Subsidiary of:** Avnet Inc.)
Innovation House, Bellringer Road, Stoke-On-Trent, Staffordshire ST4 8GH
**Tel:** 01782254700 **Fax:** 01782254701
**Web:** www.tekdata-interconnect.com
**Reg No:** 0967924 **VAT No:** 279803712
**Estd:** 1969 Private Limited Company
**Line of Business:** Manufactures cable and wire equipment
**Export Markets:** E U; U.S.A.
**Export Sales:** £345,000
**Issued Capital:** £15,000
**Directors:** W R Crowell, P Bielefeld, C A Friel, M R Mccoy
**Co. Secretary:** Ms Anne Van Der Zwalmen
**Responsibilities**
**Senior:** Glenn Downing *(Manager)*, Ernest Edwards *(Manager)*
**Finance:** Glenn Downing *(Manager)*
**Operations:** Glenn Downing *(Manager)*
**US SIC:** 3357 **UK SIC:** 22470
**Auditors:** RSM Tenon Audit Ltd
**Bankers:** Barclays Bank Plc (20-36-43)

| | 28-06-14 | 29-06-13 | 01-06-12 |
|---|---|---|---|
| TO | 6,205,000 | 7,188,000 | 6,233,000 |
| P/L | 674,000 | 316,000 | 685,000 |
| NW | 3,023,000 | 2,387,000 | 2,571,000 |
| WC | 2,895,000 | 2,259,000 | 2,495,000 |
| Emp. | 80 | 80 | 90 |

DUNS 21-004-5695 **Imp**
## Tekmar Energy Ltd
**(Subsidiary of:** Elysian Capital Llp)
Unit 1 Park 2000, Millennium Way, Heighington Lane Business Park, Heighington Lane, Newton Aycliffe, County Durham DL5 6AR
**Tel:** 01325379520
**Web:** www.tekmar.co.uk
**Reg No:** 6294325 **Estd:** 2007 Private Limited Company
**Line of Business:** Industrial engineers
**Export Sales:** £9,574,000
**Issued Capital:** £46
**Directors:** Ms S Hurst, J Tweedlie, T H Sheldrake, J Ritchie-Bland, A Macdonald
**Responsibilities**
**Marketing:** Sean Donkin *(Marketing and Business Develop)*
**US SIC:** 8911 **UK SIC:** 83701
**Auditors:** KPMG LLP

| | 31-03-14 | 31-03-13 | 31-03-11 |
|---|---|---|---|
| TO | 11,318,000 | 20,859,000 | 11,547,000 |
| P/L | 882,000 | 4,386,000 | 1,555,000 |
| NW | 6,540,000 | 6,215,000 | 2,885,000 |
| WC | 5,321,000 | 4,851,000 | 1,826,000 |
| Emp. | 67 | 72 | 48 |

DUNS 73-702-4534

## Tekmet Ltd.

**(Subsidiary of:** Viama Ltd)
P I Castings Ltd, Altrincham, Cheshire WA14 5DS
**Tel:** 01619-285811
**Web:** www.tekmet.ca
**Reg No:** 4961159 **Estd:** 2003 Private Limited Company
**Line of Business:** Other manufacturing not elsewhere classified
**Issued Capital:** £50,000
**Directors:** I C Taylor, B Mills
**Co. Secretary:** Malcolm Robertson
**US SIC:** 3999 **UK SIC:** 49590

| | 04-05-14 | 28-04-13 | 29-05-12 |
|---|---|---|---|
| TO | N/A | 5,873,589 | 6,258,551 |
| P/L | N/A | (415,985) | 887,243 |
| NW | 300,006 | 849,092 | 1,548,358 |
| WC | 225,019 | 843,718 | 3,031,553 |
| Emp. | N/A | 106 | 102 |

DUNS 21-112-3928

## Tekne Holdings Ltd

Midland House 2 Poole Road, Bournemouth, Dorset BH2 5QY
**Tel:** 01202672121
**Reg No:** 6534192 **Estd:** 2008 Private Limited Company
**Line of Business:** Management activities of holding companies
**Issued Capital:** £9
**Directors:** M Noble, P Mansbridge
**Co. Secretary:** Edward Sevestre
**US SIC:** 6711 **UK SIC:** 83962

| | 30-09-13 | 30-09-12 | 30-09-11 |
|---|---|---|---|
| TO | 6,758,759 | 6,627,475 | 6,859,358 |
| P/L | 143,119 | 123,586 | 112,944 |
| NW | 116,462 | 91,630 | 86,934 |
| WC | (64,632) | (93,263) | (117,647) |
| Emp. | 75 | 74 | 72 |

DUNS 76-910-1957

## Teknek Ltd

**(Subsidiary of:** Illinois Tool Works Inc.)
Teknek House, River Drive, Inchinnan, Renfrew, Renfrewshire PA4 9RT
**Tel:** 01415 688100
**Web:** www.teknek.co.uk
**Reg No:** 0102874SC **VAT No:** 839039016
**Estd:** 1987 Private Limited Company
**Line of Business:** Industrial engineers
**Export Sales:** £10,740,393
**Issued Capital:** £2
**Directors:** E Ufland, G M Hudson, P M Deakin
**Co. Secretary:** Tm Company Services Limited
**Responsibilities**
**Senior:** Colin Mackillop *(Manager)*
**IT:** David Conkie *(IT Manager)*
**US SIC:** 3639, 3549
**UK SIC:** 34600, 32212
**Auditors:** Milne Craig
**Bankers:** Bank Of Scotland (80-16-53)

| | 31-12-13 | 31-12-12 | 31-12-11 |
|---|---|---|---|
| TO | 11,833,029 | 11,506,104 | 7,089,644 |
| P/L | 2,550,347 | 1,894,303 | 1,316,802 |
| NW | 4,974,877 | 3,012,507 | 1,586,921 |
| WC | 4,657,377 | 2,589,209 | 885,912 |
| Emp. | 66 | 66 | 73 |

DUNS 71-925-7714

## Teknor Apex Uk Holdings Ltd

**(Subsidiary of:** Teknor Apex Company)
Tat Bank Road, Oldbury, West Midlands B69 4NH
**Tel:** 01216652100
**Web:** www.teknorapex.com
**Reg No:** 5306929 **Estd:** 2004 Private Limited Company
**Line of Business:** Management activities of holding companies
**Export Sales:** £9,248,725
**Issued Capital:** £10
**Directors:** J D Fain, W J Murray, J E Morrison
**Co. Secretary:** James Morrison
**Responsibilities**
**Senior:** Mark Clayton *(Plant Director)*, Simon Hubbard *(Business Director)*
**Finance:** Lewis Flowerdew *(Financial Manager)*
**HR:** Alwyn Galloway *(Human Resources Administrator)*
**Facilities:** Alwyn Galloway *(Human Resources Administrator)*
**US SIC:** 6711 **UK SIC:** 83962

| | 31-07-13 | 31-07-12 | 31-07-11 |
|---|---|---|---|
| TO | 15,911,085 | 15,713,189 | 17,362,428 |
| P/L | (193,319) | (759,775) | 55,050 |
| NW | 7,895,062 | 8,076,998 | 7,987,910 |
| WC | 4,705,340 | 4,582,902 | 4,187,874 |
| Emp. | 52 | 54 | 52 |

DUNS 21-010-0921 **Imp-Exp**

## Tektura Plc

**(Subsidiary of:** Vep Fund I Holding Coöperatief W.A.)
103 Harbour Island, London E14 9GE
**Tel:** 02075363300 **Fax:** 020-7536-3322
**Web:** www.tektura.com
**Reg No:** 0786933 **VAT No:** 662729610
**Estd:** 1964 Public Limited Company
**Line of Business:** Telephone answering services
**Export Markets:** Europe; Worldwide
**Export Sales:** £1,270,386
**Issued Capital:** £88,000
**Directors:** A Dimaria, J Van Meer, Ms A Paterson, N J Hooper
**Co. Secretary:** William Balogun
**Branches:** Tektura Plc, Suite 1 03 Harbour Island, Harbour Exchange Squrae, London E14 9GE
**US SIC:** 5199, 5133
**UK SIC:** 61900, 61600
**Auditors:** H.W. Fisher & Co
**Bankers:** Lloyds TSB Bank plc (30-93-23)

| | 31-12-13 | 31-12-12 | 31-12-11 |
|---|---|---|---|
| TO | 8,909,270 | 9,006,744 | 8,177,898 |
| P/L | 1,089,229 | 945,273 | 731,033 |
| NW | 709,577 | 691,977 | 643,582 |
| WC | 597,911 | 666,203 | 602,110 |
| Emp. | 50 | 47 | 45 |

DUNS 22-950-4337

## Tekzone Sound & Vision Ltd

Old Court, Tyrrells Wood, Leatherhead, Surrey KT22 8QW
**Tel:** 01372-376789 **Fax:** 01312378562
**Web:** www.tekzonesound.co.uk
**Reg No:** 0330823 **VAT No:** 293783315
**Estd:** 1937 Private Limited Company
**Line of Business:** Retail sale of electrical household appliances and radio and television goods
**Issued Capital:** £208
**Directors:** Ms M D Russell-Vick, C Gardner, J R Gardner, Ms H M Gardner
**Co. Secretary:** Christopher Gardner
**Branches:** London
**US SIC:** 5732 **UK SIC:** 64800
**Auditors:** Honey Barrett
**Bankers:** National Westminster Bank Plc (60-02-49)

| | 31-03-14 | 31-03-13 | 31-03-12 |
|---|---|---|---|
| TO | 13,450,200 | 9,810,991 | 14,616,551 |
| P/L | 623,140 | 17,187 | 703,470 |
| NW | 2,399,540 | 2,234,260 | 2,447,662 |
| WC | 1,758,867 | 1,821,564 | 2,245,367 |
| Emp. | 75 | 57 | 64 |

DUNS 50-138-7260 **Imp-Exp**

## Teleadapt Ltd

5 Rhodes Way Watford, Watford, Hertfordshire WD24 4YW
**Web:** www.teleadapt.com
**Reg No:** 2324696 **VAT No:** 581949493
**Estd:** 1988 Private Limited Company
**Line of Business:** Wholesale of other electronic parts and equipment
**Export Sales:** £9,733,399
**Issued Capital:** £120,000
**Principals:** G R Brown *(Managing)*, Mrs S B Brown, C D Corby
**Co. Secretary:** Kevin O'Connell
**Responsibilities**
**Senior:** Steve Kong *(Regional Manager)*
**Finance:** Dheeraj Chadha *(Financial controller)*
**Marketing:** Althea Chan *(Marketing Manager)*, Cheryl McGinty *(Marketing Manager)*, Matthew Needham *(Marketing Manager)*
**IT:** Jawad Mirza *(Network Controller)*
**US SIC:** 5065 **UK SIC:** 61500
**Auditors:** BDO Stoy Hayward LLP
**Bankers:** Lloyds TSB Bank plc (30-94-08)

| | 31-03-14 | 31-03-13 | 31-03-12 |
|---|---|---|---|
| TO | 10,642,009 | 11,497,651 | 9,890,865 |
| P/L | 286,042 | 154,950 | 169,678 |
| NW | 791,413 | 577,994 | 391,827 |
| WC | 751,314 | 720,489 | 677,483 |
| Emp. | 61 | 60 | 63 |

DUNS 34-803-7677

## Telecity Group Plc

Reynolds House, 4 Archway, Manchester M15 5RL
**Tel:** 01612323240
**Web:** www.telecity.com
**Reg No:** 5603875 **Estd:** 2005 Public Limited Company
**Line of Business:** Management activities of holding companies
**Export Sales:** £181,649,000
**Issued Capital:** £405,294
**Directors:** Ms C I Arney, W T Hageman, S G Batey, J P O'Reilly, J L Hughes, Mrs N Cruickshank, M Carli
**Co. Secretary:** Anthony Hunter
**Responsibilities**
**Senior:** Mike Tobin *(Manager)*
**Branches:** Telecity Group Plc, 6-7 Harbour Exchange Square, London E14 9HE
**US SIC:** 6711 **UK SIC:** 83962
**Auditors:** PricewaterhouseCoopers LLP
**Bankers:** Barclays Bank Plc (20-00-00)

| | 31-12-13 | 31-12-12 | 31-12-11 |
|---|---|---|---|
| TO | 325,550,000 | 282,950,000 | 239,818,000 |
| P/L | 88,440,000 | 76,146,000 | 59,438,000 |
| NW | 230,165,000 | 205,929,000 | 162,267,000 |
| WC | (61,077,000) | (67,485,000) | (54,885,000) |
| Emp. | 691 | 612 | 527 |

DUNS 29-185-0725

## Telecitygroup International Ltd

**(Subsidiary of:** Telecity Group Plc)
Exchange Tower, 4th Floor, 2 Harbour Exchange Square, London E14 9GE
**Tel:** 020 7001 0000 **Fax:** 020 7001 0001
**Web:** www.telecityredbus.com
**Reg No:** 0153088 **Estd:** 1919 Private Limited Company
**Line of Business:** Management activities of holding companies
**Issued Capital:** £2,589,568
**Directors:** R Coupland, D Crowther, W T Hageman
**Co. Secretary:** Anthony Hunter
**Responsibilities**
**Senior:** Michael Tobin *(Manager)*
**Marketing:** James Tyler *(Marketing and Communications D)*
**US SIC:** 6711, 7372
**UK SIC:** 83962, 83940
**Auditors:** PricewaterhouseCoopers LLP
**Bankers:** Barclays Bank Plc (20-00-50)

| | 31-12-13 | 31-12-12 | 31-12-11 |
|---|---|---|---|
| TO | 9,036,000 | 9,451,000 | 7,842,000 |
| P/L | 14,350,000 | 11,042,000 | 18,952,000 |
| NW | 140,089,000 | 122,764,000 | 122,010,000 |
| WC | (36,085,000) | (14,794,000) | (13,536,000) |
| Emp. | 62 | 69 | 62 |

DUNS 54-375-3768

## Telecom Plus Plc

Network Hq, London NW9 6TD
**Web:** www.utilitywarehouse.co.uk
**Reg No:** 3263464 **Estd:** 1996 Public Limited Company
**Line of Business:** Telecommunications
**Issued Capital:** £3,519,726
**Directors:** C F Wigoder, M A Lawson, N J Schoenfeld, J D Schild, M J Pavia, A Lindsay
**Co. Secretary:** David Baxter
**Responsibilities**
**Finance:** Clifford Wetherall *(Technical Operations and Billi)*
**Marketing:** Justin Bozzino *(Marketing and Communications D)*
**IT:** Gary Kaufman *(IT Director)*
**HR:** Katy Ostro *(Director of Human Resources an)*
**Operations:** Wayne Coupland *(Executive Services Director)*, Clifford Wetherall *(Technical Operations and Billi)*
**US SIC:** 4899 **UK SIC:** 79020
**Auditors:** BDO LLP

| | 31-03-14 | 31-03-13 | 31-03-12 |
|---|---|---|---|
| TO | 658,760,000 | 601,505,000 | 471,458,000 |
| P/L | 36,630,000 | 34,631,000 | 30,743,000 |
| NW | (18,554,000) | 64,031,000 | 56,100,000 |
| WC | 38,589,000 | 26,604,000 | 21,653,000 |
| Emp. | 702 | 610 | 541 |

DUNS 56-986-9779

## Telecom Service Centres Ltd

**(Subsidiary of:** Charterhouse Capital Partners Llp)
Bute House, Rothesay, Bute PA20 0DY
**Tel:** 01700500500
**Web:** www.webhelp.com
**Reg No:** 0146564SC **VAT No:** 808921124
**Estd:** 1993 Private Limited Company
**Line of Business:** Telecommunications
**Trading Style:** Webhelp Uk
**Issued Capital:** £830,394
**Directors:** D Turner, F A Jousset
**Co. Secretary:** Dean Hartley
**Responsibilities**
**Senior:** Rohit Chanana *(Manager)*, Prabhjot Likhari *(Manager)*
**HR:** Harry Hogg *(Human Resource Director)*
**Branches:** Telecom Service Centres Ltd, 44-46 St. John Street, London EC1M 4DF
**US SIC:** 4899 **UK SIC:** 79020
**Auditors:** Grant Thornton UK LLP
**Bankers:** Clydesdale Bank Plc (82-20-00)

| | 31-12-13 | 31-03-13 | 31-12-12 |
|---|---|---|---|
| TO | 93,225,000 | 111,139,000 | 81,651,000 |
| P/L | 10,288,000 | 124,000 | 8,997,000 |
| NW | 32,937,000 | 24,964,000 | 24,930,000 |
| WC | 33,285,000 | 28,581,000 | 17,128,000 |
| Emp. | 5,980 | 5,462 | 3,881 |

DUNS 21-332-1326 **Exp**

## Teledyne C.M.L. Group Ltd

**(Subsidiary of:** Teledyne Technologies Inc)
Price Street, Birkenhead, Merseyside CH41 3PT
**Tel:** 0151-647-5531 **Fax:** 0151-650-0668
**Web:** www.cml-group.com
**Reg No:** 1564040 **Estd:** 1952 Private Limited Company
**Line of Business:** Engineers (general)
**Export Sales:** £549,174
**Trading Style:** Cml Precision Machining, Cml Treatments, Cml Composites
**Issued Capital:** £100,000
**Directors:** R Mehrabian, A Pichelli, H T Barnshaw
**Co. Secretary:** Harry Barnshaw
**Responsibilities**
**Finance:** David Haden *(Financial Director)*
**IT:** Jonathan Allport *(Computer Manager)*
**Branches:** Teledyne C.m.l. Group Ltd, Unit 5 Wheatland Business Park, Wheatland Lane, Wallasey, Merseyside CH44 7ER
**US SIC:** 3799, 3999
**UK SIC:** 36502, 49590
**Auditors:** Ernst & Young LLP
**Bankers:** Bank One Na (40-50-20)

| | 31-12-13 | 31-12-12 | 31-12-11 |
|---|---|---|---|
| TO | 5,909,625 | 6,472,582 | 7,813,886 |
| P/L | (2,063,050) | (1,548,605) | (990,759) |
| NW | 1 | 95,294 | 152,027 |
| WC | N/A | (1,975,502) | (2,246,884) |
| Emp. | 91 | 111 | 111 |

DUNS 22-815-5917 **Imp-Exp**

## Teledyne Defence Ltd

**(Subsidiary of:** Teledyne Technologies Inc)
Airedale House, Acorn Park Industrial Estate, Charlestow, Shipley, West Yorkshire BD17 7SW
**Tel:** 01274531602
**Web:** www.teledynedefence.co.uk
**Reg No:** 1659830 **Estd:** 1982 Private Limited Company
**Line of Business:** Manufacturers of electronic equipment and components
**Export Markets:** Europe, North America, Asia Pacific
**Export Sales:** £4,894,000
**Issued Capital:** £2,250,000
**Co. Secretary:** Henry Barnshaw
**Responsibilities**
**Senior:** Melanie Cibik *(Director)*, Keith Ferguson *(Manager)*, Russell Shaller *(Director)*, Ian Skiggs *(Sales & Marketing Director)*, Daron Winspear *(Operations Manager)*
**Marketing:** Ian Skiggs *(Sales & Marketing Director)*
**Sales:** Ian Skiggs *(Sales & Marketing Director)*
**HR:** Angela Stalker *(Human Resources Manager)*
**Health & Safety:** Mick Buck *(Health & Safety Officer)*
**Facilities:** Michael Edmondson *(Facilities Manager)*
**Operations:** Mick Buck *(Health & Safety Officer)*, Daron Winspear *(Operations Manager)*
**Engineering:** Richard Ginn *(Engineering Team Leader)*
**Branches:** Teledyne Defence Ltd, Heighton Lane Bus Park, Newton Aycliffe, County Durham DL5 6JW
**US SIC:** 3679, 3573
**UK SIC:** 34542, 33020
**Auditors:** Ernst & Young LLP
**Bankers:** Barclays Bank Plc (20-11-81)

| | 31-12-13 | 31-12-12 | 31-12-11 |
|---|---|---|---|
| TO | 38,027,000 | 14,038,000 | 13,394,000 |
| P/L | 7,656,000 | 849,000 | 437,000 |
| NW | 9,818,000 | 3,543,000 | 3,956,000 |
| WC | N/A | 2,052,000 | 2,666,000 |
| Emp. | 146 | 134 | 128 |

DUNS 23-872-3121 **Imp-Exp**

## Teledyne Ltd

**(Subsidiary of:** Teledyne Technologies Inc)
The Lodge, Harmondsworth Lane, West Drayton, Middlesex UB7 0LQ
**Tel:** 02087593455
**Web:** www.teledyne-controls.com
**Reg No:** 3863642 **VAT No:** 742907620
**Estd:** 1999 Private Limited Company
**Line of Business:** Manufacturers and distributors of electronic components
**Export Markets:** E C and worldwide
**Export Sales:** £28,443,257
**Trading Style:** Teledyne Cormon / Teledyne Microelectronics, Teledyne Oil & Gas / Teledyne Relays, Teledyne Reynolds, Teledyne Lecroy
**Issued Capital:** £3,532,100
**Directors:** Ms S L Main, R Mehrabian, D A Mather
**Co. Secretary:** Henry Barnshaw
**Responsibilities**
**Senior:** John Kuelbs *(Manager)*
**HR:** Lesley Wallace *(Personnel Manager)*
**Health & Safety:** Lesley Wallace *(Personnel Manager)*
**Facilities:** Lesley Wallace *(Personnel Manager)*
**Branches:** Teledyne Limited, The Teledyne Building, Vantage Point Business Village, Mitcheldean, Gloucestershire GL17 0DD
**US SIC:** 3679, 3661, 8999
**UK SIC:** 34542, 34410, 83954
**Auditors:** Ernst & Young LLP

**Bankers:** Bank Of Scotland (80-91-29)

| | 31-12-13 | 31-12-12 | 31-12-11 |
|---|---|---|---|
| TO | 44,218,621 | 32,113,876 | 31,035,088 |
| P/L | 6,489,898 | 14,991,981 | 6,622,534 |
| NW | 39,712,495 | 48,623,611 | 63,900,631 |
| WC | 7,796,784 | 5,767,088 | 8,032,380 |
| Emp. | 234 | 222 | 202 |

DUNS 21-931-5199 **Imp**

## Teledyne Tss Ltd

(**Subsidiary of:** Teledyne Technologies Inc)
1 Blackmoor Lane, Watford, Hertfordshire WD18 8GA
**Web:** www.teledyne-tss.com
**Reg No:** 1406067 **VAT No:** 336013884
**Estd:** 1978 Private Limited Company
**Line of Business:** Manufacture of electronic instruments and appliances for measuring, checking, testing, navigating and other purposes, except industrial process control equipment
**Export Sales:** £12,069,000
**Issued Capital:** £101,816
**Directors:** A Pichelli, Ms S L Main
**Co. Secretary:** Henry Barnsahw
**Responsibilities**
**Senior:** Brian Huntsman *(General Manager)*
**Finance:** Angela Suggate *(Financial Director)*
**Marketing:** Jo Creasy *(Marketing Manager)*
**Sales:** Martyn Grange *(Sales Manager)*
**Facilities:** Michael Coventry *(Operations Manager)*, Neale Cumming *(Production Manager)*
**Operations:** Michael Coventry *(Operations Manager)*
**Engineering:** Neale Cumming *(Production Manager)*, Harpal Khamba *(Engineering Manager)*
**Branches:** Teledyne Tss Ltd, The Technology Centre, Claymore Drive, Bridge Of Don, Aberdeen, Aberdeenshire AB23 8GD
**US SIC:** 3829, 7391
**UK SIC:** 37100, 94000
**Auditors:** Grant Thornton UK LLP
**Bankers:** Lloyds TSB Bank plc (30-96-35)

| | 31-12-13 | 31-12-12 | 31-12-11 |
|---|---|---|---|
| TO | 20,003,000 | 17,523,000 | 16,290,000 |
| P/L | 4,020,000 | 4,362,000 | 3,832,000 |
| NW | 14,402,000 | 10,889,000 | 11,716,000 |
| WC | 13,558,000 | 10,102,000 | 10,835,000 |
| Emp. | 78 | 73 | 75 |

DUNS 28-912-3879

## Telefocus Ltd

(**Subsidiary of:** Hertfordshire Ltd)
1 The Russell Centre, Bedford, Bedfordshire MK45 5BY
**Tel:** 01525-720000
**Web:** www.telefocus.co.uk
**Reg No:** 1426644 **Estd:** 1979 Private Limited Company
**Line of Business:** Call centre activities
**Issued Capital:** £2,370,000
**Directors:** N A Shuker, N D Taylor, A Claytor
**Co. Secretary:** John Daw
**Responsibilities**
**Senior:** Nicolas Tsoucalas *(Manager)*
**HR:** Thomas Dunckley *(Training Manager)*
**US SIC:** 7399 **UK SIC:** 83954
**Auditors:** Baker Tilly UK Audit LLP
**Bankers:** National Westminster Bank Plc (60-02-42)

| | 30-06-13 | 30-06-12 | 30-06-11 |
|---|---|---|---|
| TA | 189,924 | 412,422 | 498,899 |
| NW | (2,295,175) | (1,664,439) | (999,314) |
| WC | (475,719) | (267,458) | (53,309) |

DUNS 21-815-2109

## Telefonica Digital Ltd

(**Subsidiary of:** Telefonica Sa)
20 Air Street, London W1B 5AN
**Tel:** 01753 565550
**Web:** www.telefonica.com
**Reg No:** 7884976 **Estd:** 2011 Private Limited Company
**Line of Business:** Motion picture and video distribution
**Issued Capital:** £2
**Directors:** A Marti Ciruelos, S J Shurrock
**Co. Secretary:** O2 Secretaries Limited
**Responsibilities**
**Senior:** Vivek Dev *(Director)*
**US SIC:** 7829, 4899
**UK SIC:** 97112, 79020
**Auditors:** Ernst & Young LLP

| | 31-12-13 | 31-12-12 |
|---|---|---|
| TO | 40,882,000 | 26,550,000 |
| P/L | (81,686,000) | (60,582,000) |
| NW | (13,844,000) | 60,315,000 |
| WC | (22,668,000) | 48,114,000 |
| Emp. | 229 | 227 |

DUNS 28-973-3107

## Telefonica Uk Ltd

(**Subsidiary of:** Telefonica Sa)
260 Bath Road, Slough, Berkshire SL1 4DX
**Tel:** 01132722000
**Web:** www.corporateo2.co.uk
**Reg No:** 1743099 **VAT No:** 778603785
**Estd:** 2004 Private Limited Company
**Line of Business:** Mobile phone suppliers
**Trading Style:** O2
**Issued Capital:** £50,005,000
**Directors:** R J Harwood, R J Dunne, M Evans
**Co. Secretary:** O2 Secretaries Limited
**Responsibilities**
**Finance:** Pilar Lopez *(Financial Director)*
**Sales:** Mark Stanfield *(Sales Director)*
**IT:** Derek McManus *(IT Director)*
**Branches:** Telefonica Uk Ltd, Unit 2 Guild Square, Aberdeen, Aberdeenshire AB11 5RG
**US SIC:** 5999 **UK SIC:** 65600
**Auditors:** Ernst & Young LLP
**Bankers:** Barclays Bank Plc (20-10-53)
**Following financial data are in thousands**

| | 31-12-13 | 31-12-12 | 31-12-11 |
|---|---|---|---|
| TO | 5,535,000 | 5,609,000 | 5,968,000 |
| P/L | 609,000 | 489,000 | 794,000 |
| NW | 9,949,000 | 9,931,000 | 9,908,000 |
| WC | 4,377,000 | 3,759,000 | 3,359,000 |
| Emp. | 8,692 | 10,280 | 10,532 |

DUNS 22-705-7528 **Imp**

## Telegenic Ltd

(**Subsidiary of:** Telegenic Holdings Ltd)
4 Lancaster Road The Merlin Centre, High Wycombe, Buckinghamshire HP12 3QL
**Tel:** 01494-557400 **Fax:** 01494557410
**Web:** www.telegenic.co.uk
**Reg No:** 1551526 **Estd:** 1981 Private Limited Company
**Line of Business:** Television activities
**Issued Capital:** £100,000
**Principals:** D A Barber *(Managing)*, M D Spencer, T P James
**Co. Secretary:** Peter Bates
**Responsibilities**
**HR:** Lorraine Robinson *(Human Resources Manager)*
**US SIC:** 4833 **UK SIC:** 97411
**Auditors:** Martin Greene Ravden
**Bankers:** National Westminster Bank Plc (50-41-10)

| | 31-03-14 | 31-03-13 | 31-03-12 |
|---|---|---|---|
| TO | 20,078,058 | 21,134,644 | 18,570,654 |
| P/L | 211,307 | 164,820 | 568,027 |
| NW | 7,371,012 | 6,968,437 | 6,852,110 |
| WC | 3,517,285 | 318,352 | 1,032,879 |
| Emp. | 88 | 86 | 81 |

DUNS 21-326-3702

## Telegraph Books Direct

Unit 5-6, Ffrwdgrech Industrial Estate East, Brecon, Powys LD3 8LA
**Tel:** 01874612612
**Estd:** 1997 Partnership
**Line of Business:** Book retailers
**Partners:** D Williams, I Burgess, S Locke, A Gentilli
**US SIC:** 7372 **UK SIC:** 83940
**Employees:** 115

DUNS 34-863-1185

## Telehouse Holdings Ltd

(**Subsidiary of:** Kddi Corporation)
Telehouse, Coriander Avenue, London E14 2AA
**Tel:** 020-7512-0550 **Fax:** 020-7512-0033
**Web:** www.telehouse.net
**Reg No:** 2814979 **Estd:** 1993 Private Limited Company
**Line of Business:** Computer software (development)
**Export Sales:** £51,080,000
**Trading Style:** Telehouse Europe
**Issued Capital:** £87,742,223
**Directors:** M Watanabe, H Soshi
**Responsibilities**
**Senior:** Hirofumi Kaida *(Manager)*, Tokuji Mitsui *(Manager)*, Takeo Miura *(Manager)*
**Finance:** Paul Gazzard *(Head of Account Management)*
**IT:** Paul Kanabahita *(Senior Systems Manager)*
**HR:** Nicky Everett *(Human Resources Manager)*
**Purchasing:** Samantha Blanchard *(Purchasing Ledger Administrato)*
**US SIC:** 7379 **UK SIC:** 83940
**Auditors:** Saffery Champness
**Bankers:** Barclays Bank Plc (20-77-67)

| | 31-12-13 | 31-12-12 | 31-12-11 |
|---|---|---|---|
| TO | 128,718,000 | 122,464,000 | 89,968,000 |
| P/L | 47,289,000 | 37,578,000 | 27,374,000 |
| NW | 201,864,000 | 166,944,000 | 112,454,000 |
| WC | (44,486,000) | (32,559,000) | (28,755,000) |
| Emp. | 217 | 209 | 188 |

DUNS 76-936-6964

## Telelarm Care Holdings (U K) Ltd

(**Subsidiary of:** Watling Street Capital Partners Llp)
Latour House, Chertsey Boulevard, Hanworth Lane, Chertsey, Surrey KT16 9JX
**Fax:** 01932-577744
**Reg No:** 2506370 **Estd:** 1990 Private Limited Company
**Line of Business:** Management activities of other non-financial holding companies not elsewhere classified
**Issued Capital:** £3,270,493
**Directors:** S Parker, P L Stobart
**Co. Secretary:** Jonathan Furniss
**US SIC:** 6711, 3629
**UK SIC:** 83962, 34350
**Auditors:** KPMG LLP

| | 30-09-14 | 30-09-13 | 30-09-12 |
|---|---|---|---|
| TA | 4,272,000 | 4,690,000 | 4,021,000 |
| P/L | (195,000) | 279,000 | 192,000 |
| NW | 2,713,000 | 2,880,000 | 2,652,000 |
| WC | 2,113,000 | 2,280,000 | 2,052,000 |
| Emp. | 2 | N/A | N/A |

DUNS 21-115-5969

## The Telemarketing Co (Consumer) Ltd

26-27 Regency Square, Brighton, East Sussex BN1 2FH
**Tel:** 01273-765000
**Web:** www.ttmc.co.uk
**Reg No:** 6558382 **Estd:** 1990 Private Limited Company
**Line of Business:** Other business activities not elsewhere classified
**Issued Capital:** £1
**Directors:** P N Habba, D L Habba
**US SIC:** 7399 **UK SIC:** 83954

| | 30-04-14 | 30-04-13 | 30-04-12 |
|---|---|---|---|
| TA | 1 | 1 | 1 |
| NW | 1 | 1 | 1 |

DUNS 42-357-2796

## Telemetry Ltd

39th Floor, London EC2N 1HQ
**Tel:** 020-7148-7777
**Web:** www.telemetry.com
**Reg No:** 4344899 **Estd:** 2001 Private Limited Company
**Line of Business:** Other computer related activities
**Export Sales:** £11,138,588
**Issued Capital:** £1,000
**Directors:** B N Chesluk, R W Irwin
**Co. Secretary:** Anthony Rushton
**Responsibilities**
**Operations:** Victoria Agayants *(Operations Manager - Media)*
**US SIC:** 7379, 7319
**UK SIC:** 83940, 83800
**Auditors:** Blinkhorns

| | 31-12-13 | 31-12-12 | 31-12-12 |
|---|---|---|---|
| TO | 12,173,993 | 20,840,683 | 30,287,685 |
| P/L | 1,987,288 | 102,072 | (1,957,119) |
| NW | 4,641,798 | 1,609,529 | 135,588 |
| WC | 4,062,064 | 817,215 | (610,855) |
| Emp. | 67 | 69 | 59 |

DUNS 21-011-6406 **Imp-Exp**

## Telent Ltd

(**Subsidiary of:** Co-Investment No. 5 Lp Incorporated)
Point 3, Warwick, Warwickshire CV34 5AH
**Tel:** 019-2669-3000 **Fax:** 019-2669-3888
**Web:** www.telent.com
**Reg No:** 0067307 **Estd:** 1900 Private Limited Company
**Line of Business:** Employment and recruitment companies and consultants
**Issued Capital:** £56,376,532
**Directors:** F J Mckay, M E Plato, D G Naylor-Leyland, Ms H M Green
**Co. Secretary:** Craig Donaldson
**Responsibilities**
**HR:** Janice Meade *(Human Resources Director)*
**Health & Safety:** Donna Collins *(Health & Safety Administrator)*
**Branches:** Telent Ltd, Carr Lane, Chorley, Lancashire PR7 3JP
**US SIC:** 4899, 6711
**UK SIC:** 79020, 83962
**Auditors:** KPMG LLP
**Bankers:** HSBC Bank plc (40-04-09)

| | 31-03-14 | 31-03-13 | 31-03-12 |
|---|---|---|---|
| TO | 321,000,000 | 318,200,000 | 348,900,000 |
| P/L | 47,900,000 | 48,500,000 | 3,600,000 |
| NW | 411,900,000 | 454,200,000 | 334,300,000 |
| WC | (20,600,000) | 57,100,000 | 4,100,000 |
| Emp. | 1,465 | 1,476 | 1,883 |

DUNS 21-773-0508

## Teleperformance

Unit 16 Coalfield Way, Ashby-De-La-Zouch, Leicestershire LE65 1JT
**Tel:** 01530419500
**Web:** www.teleperformance.co.uk
**Estd:** 2011
**Line of Business:** Call centres
**Responsibilities**
**Senior:** Gale Bidder *(Director Head Of Services & Pu)*, Debbie Phillips *(Director Of Intragated Service)*, alister needer *(CEO)*
**IT:** Debbie Fagan *(IT Support)*
**US SIC:** 7399 **UK SIC:** 83954
**Employees:** 100

DUNS 22-030-0425

## Teleperformance Holdings Ltd

(**Subsidiary of:** Teleperformance)
Bond Street, Moon Street, Bristol, Avon BS1 3LG
**Tel:** 01214105000
**Web:** www.teleperformance.co.uk
**Reg No:** 4032641 **Estd:** 2000 Private Limited Company
**Line of Business:** Call centres
**Export Sales:** £7,521,000
**Issued Capital:** £4,696,211
**Directors:** A Niederer, O C Rigaudy
**Co. Secretary:** Andrew Ashton
**Responsibilities**
**Senior:** Dominic Dato *(Manager)*
**US SIC:** 4899, 6711
**UK SIC:** 79020, 83962
**Auditors:** KPMG LLP

| | 31-12-13 | 31-12-12 | 31-12-11 |
|---|---|---|---|
| TO | 162,668,000 | N/A | N/A |
| P/L | 7,654,000 | (2,115,000) | (931,000) |
| NW | 30,475,000 | 19,000 | 969,000 |
| WC | 21,052,000 | (4,630,000) | (4,410,000) |
| Emp. | 7,537 | 4 | N/A |

DUNS 29-857-0375 **Imp**

## Teleperformance Ltd

(**Subsidiary of:** Teleperformance)
Bond Street, Bristol, Avon BS1 3LG
**Tel:** 01179168000
**Web:** www.teleperformance.co.uk
**Reg No:** 2060289 **VAT No:** 763098018
**Estd:** 1987 Private Limited Company
**Line of Business:** Telecom services
**Trading Style:** Head Office
**Issued Capital:** £11,745
**Director:** A Niederer
**Co. Secretary:** Andrew Ashton
**Responsibilities**
**Senior:** Gail Bidder *(Head Of Service Deliveries)*
**IT:** Dave Bridgewater *(Solution Delivery Manager)*, Jamie Ormiston *(PC Systems Manager)*
**HR:** Rachael Doherty *(Human Resources Director)*, Lee Edwards *(HR Manager)*, Natalie Molina *(Human Resources Manager)*
**US SIC:** 7399, 7374
**UK SIC:** 83954, 83940
**Auditors:** KPMG LLP

| | 31-12-13 | 31-12-12 | 31-12-11 |
|---|---|---|---|
| TO | 154,962,000 | 147,447,000 | 70,056,000 |
| P/L | 7,350,000 | 10,630,000 | (731,000) |
| NW | 19,389,000 | 14,490,000 | 5,302,000 |
| WC | 21,099,000 | 754,000 | (3,669,000) |
| Emp. | 6,801 | 6,513 | 2,958 |

DUNS 23-586-3557 **Imp**

## Teleplan Colchester Ltd

(**Subsidiary of:** Ams Holding B.V.)
Cowdray Centre, Colchester, Essex CO1 1BX
**Tel:** 01206-785000 **Fax:** 01206-785222
**Web:** www.teleplan.com
**Reg No:** 3583995 **Estd:** 1998 Private Limited Company
**Line of Business:** Other software consultancy and supply
**Export Sales:** £336,000
**Issued Capital:** £20,000
**Directors:** P J Gingras, G Haug
**Co. Secretary:** Alexander Zilli
**Responsibilities**
**Senior:** Tony Lambert *(Manager)*
**IT:** Keith Tyler *(Computer Coordinator)*
**US SIC:** 7379 **UK SIC:** 83940
**Auditors:** Unknown
**Bankers:** HSBC Bank plc (40-02-17)

| | 31-12-13 | 31-12-12 | 31-12-11 |
|---|---|---|---|
| TO | 2,252,000 | 3,172,000 | 3,745,000 |
| P/L | (234,000) | 230,000 | (389,000) |
| NW | 789,000 | 1,019,000 | 789,000 |
| WC | 781,000 | 1,005,000 | 1,115,000 |
| Emp. | 37 | 52 | 59 |

DUNS 21-174-8487

## Telesens International Ltd

New Derwent House, 69-73 Theobalds Road, London WC1X 8TA
**Tel:** 02034328178 **Fax:** 020 3239 5988
**Web:** www.telesens.co.uk
**Reg No:** 6984385 **VAT No:** 981830889
**Estd:** 2009 Private Limited Company
**Line of Business:** Publishing of software
**Issued Capital:** £1
**Director:** E Rubin
**Co. Secretary:** Seymour Secretaries Limited
**US SIC:** 7372 **UK SIC:** 83940

| | 31-12-13 | 31-12-12 | 31-12-11 |
|---|---|---|---|
| TA | 371,649 | 633,205 | 186,978 |
| NW | 109,764 | 65,814 | 54,192 |
| WC | 17,329 | 64,288 | 52,666 |

DUNS 76-947-9320 **Exp**

## Telesoft Technologies Ltd

Observatory House, Stour Park, Blandford St Mary, Blandford Forum, Dorset DT11 9LQ
**Web:** www.telesoft-technologies.com
**Reg No:** 2344740 **VAT No:** 515865234

**Estd:** 1989 Private Limited Company
**Line of Business:** Telecom equipment and systems
**Export Sales:** £11,230,000
**Issued Capital:** £67
**Principals:** R H Downham *(Managing)*, Dr D J Price, J M Scott, Mrs J Gordon, M Downham, P S Lewis
**Co. Secretary:** Mrs Paula Martin
**Responsibilities**
**Senior:** Janet Freeman *(Manager)*
**Marketing:** Andrew Evripides *(Marketing Director)*
**Sales:** Andrew Evripides *(Marketing Director)*
**HR:** John Dallison *(Training & Quality Manager)*
**Operations:** Ray Hutton *(Product Manager)*, Steve Patton *(Product Manager)*
**Branches:** Telesoft Technologies Ltd, 86 Prince Of Wales Road, Dorchester, Dorset DT1 1PR
**US SIC:** 4899 **UK SIC:** 79020
**Auditors:** PricewaterhouseCoopers LLP
**Bankers:** HSBC Bank plc (40-19-21)

| | 30-09-13 | 30-09-12 | 30-09-11 |
|---|---|---|---|
| TO | 15,037,000 | 14,559,000 | 14,031,000 |
| P/L | 4,088,000 | 3,364,000 | 1,899,000 |
| NW | 10,620,000 | 8,713,000 | 8,019,000 |
| WC | 7,346,000 | 6,021,000 | 6,441,000 |
| Emp. | 96 | 87 | 95 |

DUNS 21-696-0186
## Telespazio Vega Uk Ltd
(**Subsidiary of:** Finmeccanica Spa)
350 Capability Green, Luton, Bedfordshire LU1 3LU
**Web:** www.telespazio-vega.com
**Reg No:** 7420777 **Estd:** 2010 Private Limited Company
**Line of Business:** Engineers (general)
**Issued Capital:** £14,400,048
**Directors:** A De Benedictis, P Young, P A Lacey, G Aridon, V Colella Albino
**Co. Secretary:** Patrick Lacey
**US SIC:** 8911 **UK SIC:** 83701
**Auditors:** PricewaterhouseCoopers LLP

| | 31-12-13 | 31-12-12 | 31-12-11 |
|---|---|---|---|
| TO | 14,852,000 | 18,814,000 | 21,140,000 |
| P/L | (105,000) | (1,197,000) | (403,000) |
| NW | 4,471,000 | 4,715,000 | 29,369,000 |
| WC | 2,799,000 | 2,951,000 | 4,229,000 |
| Emp. | 103 | 104 | 109 |

DUNS 23-242-8974
## Telestack Ltd
(**Subsidiary of:** Astec Industries Inc.)
Bankmore Way East, Omagh, Co Tyrone BT79 0NZ
**Tel:** 028 8225 1100 **Fax:** 028 8225 2211
**Web:** www.telestack.com
**Reg No:** 0040206NI **Estd:** 2001 Private Limited Company
**Line of Business:** Quarries
**Trading Style:** Telestack International
**Issued Capital:** £200,002
**Directors:** R Patek, A A Mccutcheon, D C Silvious, J Elliott, M Gribben
**Co. Secretary:** David Silvious
**Responsibilities**
**Senior:** Joseph Vig *(Director)*
**US SIC:** 8911, 3534
**UK SIC:** 83701, 32553
**Auditors:** Moore & Grimley

| | 28-02-14 | 28-02-13 | 29-02-12 |
|---|---|---|---|
| TO | 16,188,073 | 16,313,503 | 14,084,053 |
| P/L | 2,777,803 | 2,581,585 | 2,484,942 |
| NW | 5,857,461 | 4,884,056 | 3,276,012 |
| WC | 2,710,446 | 1,736,031 | 36,932 |
| Emp. | 94 | 84 | 70 |

DUNS 45-827-0873
## Teletech U K Ltd
(**Subsidiary of:** Teletech Holdings Inc.)
Arndale House, Manchester M4 3AQ
**Tel:** 0289 057 5000 **Fax:** 0289 057 5991
**Web:** www.teletech.com
**Reg No:** 3180171 **Estd:** 1996 Private Limited Company
**Line of Business:** Call centre activities
**Trading Style:** Teletech U K Ltd
**Issued Capital:** £2
**Directors:** P W Miller, Ms R M Paolillo
**Co. Secretary:** Ms Rose Sexton
**Branches:** Teletech U K Ltd, 225 Bath St, Glasgow, Lanarkshire G2 4GZ
**US SIC:** 8999 **UK SIC:** 83954
**Auditors:** PricewaterhouseCoopers LLP
**Bankers:** Bank Of America, Na (30-03-16)

| | 31-12-13 | 31-12-12 | 31-12-11 |
|---|---|---|---|
| TO | 10,442,355 | 11,304,406 | 17,723,222 |
| P/L | 718,860 | 1,002,620 | 1,539,814 |
| NW | (3,564,958) | (3,481,783) | (4,539,628) |
| WC | (3,801,276) | 7,404,130 | 8,456,613 |
| Emp. | 348 | 449 | 923 |

DUNS 73-913-8274
## Teleware Group Plc
Thirsk Industrial Park, York Road, Thirsk, North Yorkshire YO7 3BX
**Tel:** 01845526378
**Web:** www.teleware.com
**Reg No:** 5167266 **Estd:** 2004 Public Limited Company
**Line of Business:** Telecom consultants
**Export Sales:** £1,127,000
**Issued Capital:** £11,162,229
**Directors:** Mrs H K Aston, S R Haworth, G R Haworth, Mrs C Haworth
**Co. Secretary:** Ged Cooney
**US SIC:** 4899 **UK SIC:** 79020
**Bankers:** HSBC Bank plc (40-35-03)

| | 31-03-14 | 31-03-13 | 31-03-12 |
|---|---|---|---|
| TO | 10,432,000 | 9,496,374 | 7,012,548 |
| P/L | (455,000) | (92,606) | (1,133,366) |
| NW | (1,010,000) | (859,911) | (943,120) |
| WC | 461,000 | 623,808 | 338,066 |
| Emp. | 87 | 89 | 88 |

DUNS 23-636-9096
## Telewest Communications (Midlands & North West) Ltd
(**Subsidiary of:** The Depository Trust & Clearing Corporation)
160 Great Portland Street, London W1W 5QA
**Tel:** 08000520626
**Web:** www.virginmedia.com
**Reg No:** 2795350 **Estd:** 1993 Private Limited Company
**Line of Business:** Telecommunications
**Trading Style:** Virgin Media
**Issued Capital:** £138,618,048
**Directors:** M O Hifzi, R D Dunn
**Co. Secretary:** Ms Gillian James
**Branches:** Telewest Communications (Midlands & North West) Ltd, Cable House, 1 Waterside Drive, Langley, Langley, Slough, Berkshire SL3 6EY
**US SIC:** 4899, 7379
**UK SIC:** 79020, 83940
**Auditors:** Ernst & Young LLP

| | 31-12-13 | 31-12-12 | 31-12-11 |
|---|---|---|---|
| TO | 226,125,000 | 217,855,000 | 201,925,000 |
| P/L | 210,546,000 | (26,342,000) | (42,694,000) |
| NW | (42,646,000) | (253,192,000) | (226,850,000) |
| WC | (317,514,000) | (307,165,000) | (295,020,000) |

DUNS 49-003-0970
## Telewest Communications Networks Ltd
(**Subsidiary of:** The Depository Trust & Clearing Corporation)
Export House, Cawsey Way, Woking, Surrey GU21 6QX
**Tel:** 01483750900
**Web:** www.virginmedia.com
**Reg No:** 3071086 **Estd:** 1989 Private Limited Company
**Line of Business:** Other business activities not elsewhere classified
**Issued Capital:** £4,065,283,906
**Directors:** M O Hifzi, R D Dunn
**Co. Secretary:** Ms Gillian James
**Branches:** Telewest Communications Networks Ltd, Staverton Technology Park, Staverton, Cheltenham, Gloucestershire GL51 6TQ
**US SIC:** 7399, 4899
**UK SIC:** 83954, 79020
**Auditors:** Ernst & Young LLP
**Following financial data are in thousands**

| | 31-12-13 | 31-12-12 | 31-12-11 |
|---|---|---|---|
| TA | 9,589,900 | 7,529,775 | 7,301,912 |
| P/L | 3,150,301 | 240,573 | 268,045 |
| NW | 5,178,811 | 2,028,510 | 1,787,937 |
| WC | 330,729 | (19,430) | (252,339) |

DUNS 39-971-5119
## Telewest Communications (South Thames Estuary) Ltd
Telewest Communications Ltd, Gillingham, Kent ME8 0NZ
**Tel:** 01634301000 **Fax:** 01634-300199
**Web:** www.virginmedia.co.uk
**Reg No:** 2270763 **Estd:** 1988 Private Limited Company
**Line of Business:** Telecommunications
**Trading Style:** Telewest Broadband
**Issued Capital:** £2
**Directors:** M O Hifzi, R D Dunn
**Co. Secretary:** Ms Gillian James
**US SIC:** 4899, 7379
**UK SIC:** 79020, 83940
**Auditors:** Ernst & Young LLP

| | 31-12-13 | 31-12-12 | 31-12-11 |
|---|---|---|---|
| TA | 116,000 | 97,000 | 97,000 |
| P/L | (7,000) | (16,000) | 33,000 |
| NW | (2,834,000) | (2,827,000) | (2,811,000) |
| WC | (139,000) | (158,000) | (158,000) |

DUNS 39-972-0192
## Telewest Communications (South West) Ltd
(**Subsidiary of:** The Depository Trust & Clearing Corporation)
700 Waterside Drive, Aztec West, Almondsbury, Bristol, Avon BS32 4ST
**Tel:** 08009530180
**Web:** www.telewest.co.uk
**Reg No:** 2271287 **Estd:** 1988 Private Limited Company
**Line of Business:** Telecommunications
**Trading Style:** N T L Telewest
**Issued Capital:** £5,072,148
**Directors:** M O Hifzi, R D Dunn
**Co. Secretary:** Ms Gillian James
**Branches:** Telewest Communications (South West) Ltd, 700 Aztec West, Waterside Dr, Bristol, Avon BS32 4ST
**US SIC:** 4899, 7379
**UK SIC:** 79020, 83940
**Auditors:** Ernst & Young LLP
**Bankers:** Barclays Bank Plc (20-13-42)

| | 31-12-13 | 31-12-12 | 31-12-11 |
|---|---|---|---|
| TA | 6,741,000 | 6,101,000 | 5,649,000 |
| P/L | 689,000 | 232,000 | 266,000 |
| NW | 417,000 | (223,000) | (675,000) |
| WC | 23,000 | (659,000) | (1,153,000) |

DUNS 36-535-3689
## Telewest Ltd
(**Subsidiary of:** The Depository Trust & Clearing Corporation)
Media House, Berkley Way, Hook, Hampshire RG27 9UP
**Tel:** 012-5675-2000
**Web:** www.telewest.co.uk
**Reg No:** 3291383 **Estd:** 1996 Private Limited Company
**Line of Business:** Management activities of production holding companies
**Trading Style:** Virgin Media
**Issued Capital:** £7,732,635
**Directors:** R D Dunn, M O Hifzi
**Co. Secretary:** Ms Gillian James
**Responsibilities**
**Senior:** Caroline Withers *(Manager)*
**Branches:** Telewest Ltd, Beechcroft, Bakewell Road, Peterborough, Cambridgeshire PE2 6YS
**US SIC:** 7399, 6711
**UK SIC:** 83954, 83962
**Following financial data are in thousands**

| | 31-12-13 | 31-12-12 | 31-12-11 |
|---|---|---|---|
| TA | 1,613,843 | 925,874 | 896,569 |
| P/L | 687,968 | 29,305 | 387,626 |
| NW | 952,803 | 264,834 | 235,529 |
| WC | 8,780 | (17,233) | (46,538) |

DUNS 21-042-4777
## Telford and District Land Registry
Parkside Court, Hall Park Way, Telford, Shropshire TF3 4LR
**Tel:** 01952-290355
**Partnership**
**Line of Business:** General (overall) public service activities
**Partners:** Ms J Slaven, Ms J Slaven, Mrs J Hughes, Ms S Heaword
**Responsibilities**
**Health & Safety:** Beverley Doggett *(Facilities Manager)*
**Facilities:** Beverley Doggett *(Facilities Manager)*
**US SIC:** 9121 **UK SIC:** 91110
**Employees:** 150

DUNS 22-741-4190
## Telford & Wrekin Council
22 Rodney Road, Cheltenham, Gloucestershire GL50 1JJ
**Tel:** 01242267600
**Web:** www.wynne-jones.com
**Estd:** 1974
**Line of Business:** Patent agents
**Trading Style:** Hollinswood Primary School
**Directors:** S Wellings, J Coughlan, Ms C Davies, M Evans, Ms S Heely, M Frater
**Responsibilities**
**Sales:** Kate Callis *(Assistant Director Development)*, David Sidaway *(Director of Business Developme)*
**HR:** Kate Callis *(Assistant Director Development)*
**Branches:** Telford & Wrekin Council, Tan Bank, Larkin Way, Telford, Shropshire TF1 1LX
**US SIC:** 9121, 8211, 8091
**UK SIC:** 91110, 93200, 95200
**Bankers:** National Westminster Bank Plc (60-21-57)
**Employees:** 5,000

DUNS 22-087-0815
## Telford & Wrekin Services Ltd
(**Subsidiary of:** Fomento De Construcciones Y Contratas Sa)
Granville House, St Georges Road, Telford, Shropshire TF2 7RA
**Tel:** 01952567001 **Fax:** 01952-619985
**Web:** www.tandws.co.uk
**Reg No:** 4088472 **Estd:** 2000 Private Limited Company
**Line of Business:** Other engineering activities
**Issued Capital:** £10,000
**Directors:** P Taylor, A S Minchan, V F Orts-Llopis
**Co. Secretary:** Miss Carol Nunn
**Responsibilities**
**Senior:** Victoria Bunton *(Manager)*, Claire Favier Tilston *(Manager)*, Dave Hanley *(Head Of Mobility)*
**US SIC:** 8911, 3031, 4953
**UK SIC:** 83701, 48123, 92110
**Auditors:** Deloitte & Touche LLP
**Bankers:** Lloyds TSB Bank plc (30-13-66)

| | 31-12-13 | 31-12-12 | 31-12-11 |
|---|---|---|---|
| TO | 20,116,000 | 16,748,269 | 18,356,295 |
| P/L | 798,000 | 1,217,907 | 1,358,734 |
| NW | 3,798,000 | 4,981,400 | 3,949,865 |
| WC | 3,483,000 | 2,218,532 | 697,274 |
| Emp. | 252 | 264 | 287 |

DUNS 23-985-2452
## Telford College
Haybridge Road, Telford, Shropshire TF1 2NP
**Tel:** 01952642237
**Web:** www.tcat.ac.uk
**Estd:** 1930
**Line of Business:** Further education schools and colleges
**Principals:** H Wilson *(Chairman)*, D F Boynton
**Responsibilities**
**Marketing:** Alison Gray *(Marketing Manager)*
**IT:** Adrian Beckett *(IT Manager)*
**HR:** Mark Newbrook *(Training Manager)*
**Facilities:** Andy Wilkinson *(Head of Estates)*
**Operations:** Andy Wilkinson *(Head of Estates)*
**Purchasing:** Andy Wilkinson *(Head of Estates)*
**Engineering:** Dale Kynaston *(Engineer)*, Sue Trickett *(Program Manager)*
**US SIC:** 8221, 8249
**UK SIC:** 93100, 93300
**Bankers:** Barclays Bank Plc (20-85-46)
**Employees:** 250

DUNS 50-328-3327
## Telford Copper & Stainless Cylinders Ltd
(**Subsidiary of:** Telford Consumer Products Ltd)
Haybridge Road Industrial Estate, Hadley, Telford, Shropshire TF1 2FF
**Tel:** 01952 257961 **Fax:** 01952 253452
**Web:** www.telford-group.com
**Reg No:** 2353068 **Estd:** 1989 Private Limited Company
**Line of Business:** Wholesale of hardware, plumbing and heating equipment and supplies
**Issued Capital:** £161,000
**Principals:** N Leonard *(Managing)*, R J Wightwick *(Sales)*, D Leonard
**Co. Secretary:** Ms Diane Leonard
**Branches:** Telford Copper Cylinders Ltd, Atcham Industrial Estate, Shrewsbury, Shropshire SY4 4UG
**US SIC:** 5074, 1711
**UK SIC:** 61300, 50300
**Auditors:** Morris Cook
**Bankers:** Barclays Bank Plc (20-97-78)

| | 31-03-14 | 30-09-12 | 30-03-11 |
|---|---|---|---|
| TO | 16,662,921 | 9,834,388 | 11,126,805 |
| P/L | 55,140 | 101,562 | 77,797 |
| NW | 1,734,236 | 2,175,150 | 2,099,815 |
| WC | 1,604,070 | 1,945,206 | 1,809,063 |
| Emp. | 81 | 81 | 83 |

DUNS 64-118-3017
## Telford Homes Plc
Telford House, Queens Gate Britannia Road, Waltham Cross, Hertfordshire EN8 7TF
**Tel:** 01992-809800 **Fax:** 01992-809801
**Web:** www.telfordhomes.plc.uk
**Reg No:** 4118370 **Estd:** 2000 Public Limited Company
**Line of Business:** Property developers
**Issued Capital:** £5,000,000
**Directors:** J G Di Stefano, F E Nelson, R C Clarke, J H Furlong, D L Durant, M A Parker, D M Campbell, Mrs K Rogers
**Co. Secretary:** Richard Ellis
**Responsibilities**
**Senior:** Sheena Ellwood *(Sales & Marketing Director)*, Andrew Wiseman *(Chairman)*
**Marketing:** Sheena Ellwood *(Sales & Marketing Director)*

**Sales:** Sheena Ellwood *(Sales & Marketing Director)*
**HR:** Steve Nicoll *(Health & Safety Manager)*
**Health & Safety:** Steve Nicoll *(Health & Safety Manager)*
**Purchasing:** Darron Stump *(Purchasing Manager)*
**US SIC:** 6552  **UK SIC:** 85000
**Auditors:** PricewaterhouseCoopers LLP
**Bankers:** The Royal Bank Of Scotland Plc (16-15-19)

|      | 31-03-14    | 31-03-13    | 31-03-12    |
|------|-------------|-------------|-------------|
| TO   | 140,771,000 | 142,408,000 | 124,352,000 |
| P/L  | 19,230,000  | 9,037,000   | 3,045,000   |
| NW   | 105,392,000 | 72,729,000  | 66,203,000  |
| WC   | 103,435,000 | 71,596,000  | 65,670,000  |
| Emp. | 195         | 185         | 177         |

---

DUNS 21-581-1657

## Telford Vehicle Rentals

Upper Coalmoor Farm, Moreton Coppice, Telford, Shropshire TF4 2PX
**Tel:** 01952632851
**Web:** www.spholding.co.uk
**Estd:** 2011 Partnership
**Line of Business:** Vehicle rental (car)
**Partners:** Mrs S Deans, S Holding
**US SIC:** 7512  **UK SIC:** 84801
**Employees:** 80

---

DUNS 29-757-2521                                    Imp-Exp

## Telindus Ltd

*(Subsidiary of: Etat Belge)*
Centurion, Watchmoor Park, Camberley, Surrey GU15 3YL
**Tel:** 01276406100  **Fax:** 01276406101
**Web:** www.telindus.co.uk
**Reg No:** 2020395  **VAT No:** 823853029
**Estd:** 1987 Private Limited Company
**Line of Business:** Other computer related activities
**Export Markets:** Europe
**Export Sales:** £1,928,000
**Issued Capital:** £3,212,635
**Co. Secretary:** Edgard Van Den Bergh
**Responsibilities**
**Senior:** Patrick Van Der Perren *(Director)*
**Marketing:** Gordon Wardrop *(Head of Sales and Marketing)*
**Sales:** Gordon Wardrop *(Head of Sales and Marketing)*
**Operations:** Jenny O'Donoghue *(Head of Service Operations)*, John Tonner *(Head of Technical Operations)*
**Branches:** Telindus Ltd, Cheshire Suite, St James Ct Wilderspool Causeway, Warrington, Cheshire WA4 6PS
**US SIC:** 7379  **UK SIC:** 83940
**Auditors:** Deloitte LLP
**Bankers:** Fortis Bank London Bch (formerly Generale Bk) (40-52-62)

|      | 31-12-13    | 31-12-12    | 31-12-11   |
|------|-------------|-------------|------------|
| TO   | 53,815,000  | 61,558,000  | 61,366,000 |
| P/L  | (5,808,000) | (2,714,000) | (1,199,000)|
| NW   | (5,171,000) | 637,000     | 3,351,000  |
| WC   | (7,604,000) | (3,737,000) | (2,097,000)|
| Emp. | 174         | 177         | 185        |

---

DUNS 71-919-1483

## Telit Communications Plc

1 Furzeground Way, Uxbridge, Middlesex UB11 1BD
**Web:** www.telit.com
**Reg No:** 5300693  **Estd:** 2004 Public Limited Company
**Line of Business:** Telecommunications
**Trading Style:** Telit Communications
**Directors:** E Testa, O Cats, D Gilo, Y Fait, L Reger, R Zeevi
**Co. Secretary:** Michael Galai
**US SIC:** 4899  **UK SIC:** 79020
**Auditors:** KPMG Audit PLC
**Employees:** 474
**Turnover:** £243,224,000

---

DUNS 34-542-8218

## Telldeal Ltd

Sams Lane, West Bromwich, West Midlands B70 7EG
**Tel:** 01215-534845
**Reg No:** 5352987  **Estd:** 2005 Private Limited Company
**Line of Business:** Holding companies management activities
**Issued Capital:** £3,600
**Directors:** C D Smith, G F Smith, R Smith, M J Smith, Ms E L Cottam
**Co. Secretary:** James Smith
**US SIC:** 6711  **UK SIC:** 83962

|      | 30-06-13  | 30-06-12  | 30-06-11 |
|------|-----------|-----------|----------|
| TO   | 6,106,816 | N/A       | N/A      |
| P/L  | 148,111   | 256,204   | 312,751  |
| NW   | 3,660,865 | 3,634,959 | 3,529,727|
| WC   | (131,409) | 231,387   | 242,106  |
| Emp. | 63        | 65        | 63       |

---

DUNS 22-723-9373                                    Imp-Exp

## Tellermate Ltd

*(Subsidiary of: Cash Management Solutions Ltd)*
Leeway Industrial Estate, Newport, Gwent NP19 4SL
**Tel:** 01633270000
**Web:** www.tellermate.co.uk
**Reg No:** 1522341  **VAT No:** 370915351
**Estd:** 1981 Private Limited Company
**Line of Business:** Manufacture of electronic instruments and appliances for measuring, checking, testing, navigating and other purposes, except industrial process control equipment
**Export Markets:** Worldwide
**Export Sales:** £5,969,955
**Trading Style:** Tellermate
**Issued Capital:** £1
**Directors:** D W Lunn, D Hawks Iii, P J Rendell, G R Davies, M Laconti, J A Sopher
**Co. Secretary:** Gareth Davies
**Responsibilities**
**Senior:** Margaret Biss *(Manager)*, Edgar Biss *(Manager)*, Richard Dell Aquila *(Director)*
**IT:** Jay Cooke *(Network Security Manager)*
**Branches:** Tellermate Ltd, Leeway Industrial Estate, Newport, Gwent NP19 4SL
**US SIC:** 3829  **UK SIC:** 37100
**Auditors:** PKF (UK) LLP
**Bankers:** Barclays Bank Plc (20-60-58)

|      | 31-12-13  | 31-12-12  | 31-12-11  |
|------|-----------|-----------|-----------|
| TO   | 7,715,433 | 7,122,814 | 6,285,123 |
| P/L  | 1,543,004 | 1,251,150 | (278,354) |
| NW   | 2,480,247 | 1,288,348 | 1,589,070 |
| WC   | 2,641,180 | 1,400,061 | 1,700,104 |
| Emp. | 53        | 50        | 46        |

---

DUNS 50-393-4580

## Telling (Finishings) Ltd

Kestral House, Kestral Road, Mansfield, Nottinghamshire NG18 5FT
**Tel:** 01623-428181  **Fax:** 01623-428182
**Web:** www.tellingfinishings.co.uk
**Reg No:** 2399988  **VAT No:** 520821873
**Estd:** 1989 Private Limited Company
**Line of Business:** Plastering and related building services
**Issued Capital:** £100
**Managing Directors:** P A Telling, M A Telling
**Co. Secretary:** Ms Jane Hartshorne
**Responsibilities**
**Senior:** Neil Telling *(Manager)*
**US SIC:** 1742, 1752
**UK SIC:** 50400
**Auditors:** Grant Thornton UK LLP
**Bankers:** HSBC Bank plc (40-32-01)

|      | 31-10-13  | 31-10-12  | 31-10-11  |
|------|-----------|-----------|-----------|
| TO   | 6,265,968 | 9,115,134 | 8,648,298 |
| P/L  | 168,932   | (27,660)  | 22,336    |
| NW   | 1,110,444 | 1,095,530 | 1,149,064 |
| WC   | 960,466   | 937,390   | 977,637   |
| Emp. | 75        | 82        | 87        |

---

DUNS 23-265-3811                                    Imp-Exp

## T.E.L.S. Transeuropean Logistic Services Ltd

11 Rosemont Road, London NW3 6NG
**Tel:** 020-7431-3800  **Fax:** 02074333160
**Web:** www.eng.telsgroup.com
**Reg No:** 4303303  **Estd:** 2001 Private Limited Company
**Line of Business:** Transportation services.
**Export Markets:** EU,CIS
**Issued Capital:** £3
**Managing Director:** I Levin
**US SIC:** 4011, 4213
**UK SIC:** 71000, 72300
**Auditors:** Thomas Alexander & Co Ltd
**Bankers:** Barclays Bank Plc (20-00-00)

|      | 31-10-13   | 31-10-12   | 31-10-11   |
|------|------------|------------|------------|
| TO   | 35,886,600 | 32,753,715 | 27,909,652 |
| P/L  | 215,578    | 197,866    | 103,388    |
| NW   | 1,358,188  | 1,189,959  | 1,053,713  |
| WC   | 818,956    | 678,450    | 852,918    |
| Emp. | N/A        | 156        | 125        |

---

DUNS 34-734-1914

## Telsis Group Ltd

16-18 Barnes Wallis Road, Fareham, Hampshire PO15 5TT
**Fax:** 01489760076
**Web:** www.telsis.com
**Reg No:** 5536322  **Estd:** 2005 Private Limited Company
**Line of Business:** Management activities of holding companies
**Issued Capital:** £2,742,100
**Co. Secretary:** Richard Webb
**Responsibilities**
**Senior:** Jeffrey Wilson *(Manager)*
**US SIC:** 6711  **UK SIC:** 83962
**Auditors:** PricewaterhouseCoopers LLP

---

**Bankers:** Barclays Bank Plc (20-00-00)

|      | 31-12-12  | 31-12-11  | 31-12-10   |
|------|-----------|-----------|------------|
| TO   | 8,931,000 | 9,892,000 | 11,532,000 |
| P/L  | 185,000   | (1,294,000)| (2,120,000)|
| NW   | (1,685,000)| (2,142,000)| (1,039,000)|
| WC   | (3,781,000)| (3,629,000)| (3,466,000)|
| Emp. | 89        | 118       | 138        |

---

DUNS 23-838-9519

## Telstra Ltd

*(Subsidiary of: Telstra Corporation Limited)*
2nd Floor Blue Fin Building, London SE1 0TA
**Tel:** 01223920000  **Fax:** 02075378787
**Web:** www.telstraglobal.com
**Reg No:** 3830643  **Estd:** 1992 Private Limited Company
**Line of Business:** Telecom services
**Export Sales:** £1,191,000
**Issued Capital:** £600,000
**Director:** D J Rogerson
**Co. Secretary:** John Gould
**Responsibilities**
**Senior:** Murray Hankinson *(Senior Marketing Executive)*, Tom Homer *(Chief Executive Officer)*, Ming Hong *(Manager)*, Alexander Kelton *(Manager)*, Simon Vya *(CEO, Managing Director)*
**Marketing:** Murray Hankinson *(Senior Marketing Executive)*
**Branches:** Telstra Ltd, 1st Floor Platinum Building, Cambridge, Cambridgeshire CB4 0WS
**US SIC:** 4899  **UK SIC:** 79020
**Auditors:** Ernst & Young LLP
**Bankers:** Barclays Bank Plc (20-00-50)

|      | 30-06-13    | 30-06-12    | 30-06-11    |
|------|-------------|-------------|-------------|
| TO   | 67,959,000  | 69,149,000  | 80,371,000  |
| P/L  | (2,201,000) | (3,376,000) | (4,830,000) |
| NW   | 14,071,000  | 14,025,000  | 15,915,000  |
| WC   | (61,763,000)| (57,707,000)| (56,920,000)|
| Emp. | 143         | 145         | 160         |

---

DUNS 22-750-6268

## Telwey Ltd

43-45 Windsor Road, Penarth, South Glamorgan CF64 1JD
**Tel:** 02920703915  **Fax:** 029-2070-3119
**Reg No:** 1353515  **VAT No:** 315083974
**Estd:** 1978 Private Limited Company
**Line of Business:** Hardware and ironmongers merchants
**Trading Style:** Wasons
**Issued Capital:** £100
**Managing Director:** N G Osborne
**Co. Secretary:** Ms Marilyn Mumford
**Branches:** Telwey Ltd, Cogan Station Yd, Penarth, South Glamorgan CF64 0XX
**US SIC:** 5251  **UK SIC:** 64800
**Bankers:** Barclays Bank Plc (20-18-27)

|    | 31-03-14 | 31-03-13 | 31-03-12 |
|----|----------|----------|----------|
| TA | 309,381  | 318,357  | 335,534  |
| NW | 75,029   | 84,161   | 48,823   |
| WC | 102,657  | 126,284  | 92,845   |

---

DUNS 67-210-9480

## Temco Facility Services Ltd

6-7 Windsor Street, Uxbridge, Middlesex UB8 1AB
**Tel:** 01895-520370  **Fax:** 01895-549652
**Web:** www.temco-services.co.uk
**Reg No:** 6040907  **VAT No:** 761430352
**Estd:** 2011 Private Limited Company
**Line of Business:** Management of real estate on a fee or contract basis
**Trading Style:** Temco Services
**Issued Capital:** £1
**Directors:** Benoit Maerten Bvba, A T Philpot, H Thomassian
**Responsibilities**
**Senior:** Josef Genyn *(Manager)*
**US SIC:** 7399  **UK SIC:** 83954
**Auditors:** Kingston Smith LLP
**Bankers:** Kredietbank Nv (16-54-87)

|      | 30-09-13  | 30-09-12  | 30-09-11  |
|------|-----------|-----------|-----------|
| TO   | 4,305,255 | 4,112,571 | 3,854,327 |
| P/L  | 24,586    | 10,516    | 77,805    |
| NW   | 386,794   | 367,969   | 358,892   |
| WC   | 433,315   | 467,418   | 593,251   |

---

DUNS 29-646-4761                                    Exp

## Temenos Uk Ltd

*(Subsidiary of: Temenos Group Ag)*
5 Milbanke Court, Milbanke Way, Bracknell, Berkshire RG12 1RP
**Tel:** 02074233700  **Fax:** 01488-685-160
**Web:** www.temenos.com
**Reg No:** 1972767  **VAT No:** 437411660
**Estd:** 1985 Private Limited Company
**Line of Business:** Computer software (development)
**Export Markets:** USA, Europe and others
**Issued Capital:** £2,198,844
**Directors:** M N Gunning, D J Noctor
**Co. Secretary:** David Carruthers
**Responsibilities**
**Senior:** Graham Goble *(Manager)*, Constantine Pangalos *(Director)*
**Branches:** Temenos Uk Ltd, 2 Maylands Avenue, Peoplebuilding Estate, Hemel Hempstead, Hertfordshire HP2 4NW
**US SIC:** 7379  **UK SIC:** 83940

---

**Auditors:** PricewaterhouseCoopers LLP
**Bankers:** HSBC Bank plc (40-01-08)

|      | 31-12-13     | 31-12-12     | 31-12-11     |
|------|--------------|--------------|--------------|
| TO   | 25,626,000   | 26,425,000   | 32,765,000   |
| P/L  | 37,000       | (2,603,000)  | (6,153,000)  |
| NW   | (27,523,000) | (28,078,000) | (25,671,000) |
| WC   | (10,249,000) | (10,824,000) | (26,548,000) |
| Emp. | 307          | 291          | 330          |

---

DUNS 22-036-2094                                    Imp

## Temperley Ltd

*(Subsidiary of: Temperley Holdings Ltd)*
2-10 Colville Mews, London W11 2DA
**Tel:** 020-7229-7957
**Web:** www.temperleylondon.com
**Reg No:** 4038659  **VAT No:** 766134717
**Estd:** 2000 Private Limited Company
**Line of Business:** Other business activities not elsewhere classified
**Export Sales:** £5,311,470
**Trading Style:** Temperley London
**Issued Capital:** £165
**Directors:** C R Grimsdell, L Von Bennigsen, Ms A Temperley, N U Garde Due
**Responsibilities**
**Senior:** Ruth Coleman *(Manager)*, Kath Hayes *(Manager)*, Eric Koby *(Manager)*, Lars von Bennigsen *(Chief Executive Officer)*
**Finance:** Ruth Coleman *(Manager)*
**US SIC:** 7399, 5699, 5661
**UK SIC:** 83954, 64500, 64600
**Auditors:** Ivan Sopher & Co
**Bankers:** Barclays Bank Plc (20-35-93)

|      | 30-09-12   | 30-09-11  | 30-09-10  |
|------|------------|-----------|-----------|
| TO   | 10,209,562 | 7,034,359 | 8,504,267 |
| P/L  | (727,726)  | (1,272,528)| 395,355  |
| NW   | 1,581,357  | 2,309,083 | 4,791,663 |
| WC   | 411,289    | 1,452,864 | 3,629,282 |
| Emp. | 78         | 76        | 89        |

---

DUNS 73-352-9346

## Tempero Ltd

*(Subsidiary of: Dentsu Inc.)*
The Lightwell, 12-16 Laystall Street, London EC1R 0JH
**Tel:** 020-7278-3222
**Web:** www.tempero.co.uk
**Reg No:** 4626526  **Estd:** 2002 Private Limited Company
**Line of Business:** Advertising, radio, tv and other media
**Issued Capital:** £1,000
**Directors:** K Bilous, D Sparkes, Ms T De Groose, Ms C Price, Miss J Mcgarr
**Responsibilities**
**Senior:** Peter McGarr *(Manager)*
**Marketing:** Maxim Fernandez *(Community Manager)*, Frank Sheahan *(Community Manager)*, Kelda Wallis *(New Business Manager)*
**Sales:** Claire Dikecoglu *(Account Manager)*, Lucy McElhinney *(Account Director)*, Coral Summers *(Account Manager)*
**US SIC:** 7319, 7379
**UK SIC:** 83800, 83940
**Auditors:** MHA Macintyre Hudson

|    | 31-05-14  | 31-05-13  | 31-05-12  |
|----|-----------|-----------|-----------|
| TA | 1,861,782 | 1,601,834 | 1,761,034 |
| NW | 953,695   | 732,183   | 750,517   |
| WC | 890,829   | 711,811   | 717,243   |

---

DUNS 21-417-2049

## Tempest

6 Sedan Avenue, Omagh, Co Tyrone BT79 7AQ
**Tel:** 028-82256050
**Web:** www.totallytempest.com
**Estd:** 2003
**Line of Business:** Retail sale of other women's clothing
**Responsibilities**
**Senior:** Laura Gromley *(Deputy Manager)*, Debra Lewsley *(Store Manager)*, Deborah Mclearon *(Manager)*
**Finance:** Theresa Breen *(Senior Finance Administrator)*
**US SIC:** 5621  **UK SIC:** 64500
**Employees:** 50

---

DUNS 22-519-2780                                    Imp-Exp

## The Templar Co Ltd

*(Subsidiary of: Albert Bonnier Ab)*
10 North Street, Dorking, Surrey RH4 1DN
**Tel:** 01306876361
**Web:** www.templarco.co.uk
**Reg No:** 1549157  **VAT No:** 356719229
**Estd:** 1981 Private Limited Company
**Line of Business:** Publishing of books
**Export Markets:** U S A, Europe and Australasia.
**Export Sales:** £6,509,000
**Issued Capital:** £80,824
**Co. Secretary:** Richard Johnson
**Responsibilities**
**Senior:** Karen Ellison *(Production Director)*
**Marketing:** Ruth Huddleston *(Sales & Marketing Director)*
**Sales:** Ruth Huddleston *(Sales & Marketing Director)*

**IT:** Nigel Longuet (*IT Manager*), Amo Paak (*Computer Manager*)
**Engineering:** Karen Ellison (*Production Director*)
**Branches:** The Templar Co Ltd, 37 Floral St, London WC2E 9DJ
**US SIC:** 2731, 7399
**UK SIC:** 47532, 83954
**Auditors:** haysmacintyre
**Bankers:** Barclays Bank Plc (20-92-60)

|  | 31-12-13 | 31-12-12 | 31-12-11 |
|---|---|---|---|
| TO | 11,935,125 | 11,282,932 | 13,047,991 |
| P/L | 137,944 | 1,653 | 41,641 |
| NW | 2,066,965 | 2,085,662 | 2,197,247 |
| WC | 1,631,316 | 1,577,730 | 1,706,934 |
| Emp. | 47 | 48 | 45 |

DUNS 39-778-0529     Imp-Exp
## Temple Fields 534 Ltd
(**Subsidiary of:** Synthomer Plc)
Zinc Works Road, Hartlepool, Cleveland TS25 2DT
**Tel:** 01429863222 **Fax:** 01429-867567
**Web:** www.cemex.co.uk
**Reg No:** 2201740 **Estd:** 1973 Private Limited Company
**Line of Business:** Manufacture of other inorganic basic chemicals
**Export Markets:** Worldwide
**Issued Capital:** £1
**Director:** A D Burnett
**Co. Secretary:** Richard Atkinson
**US SIC:** 2819 **UK SIC:** 25110
**Auditors:** Deloitte LLP
**Bankers:** Barclays Bank Plc (20-00-00)

|  | 31-12-12 | 31-12-11 |
|---|---|---|
| TA | N/A | 7,727,000 |
| P/L | 95,000 | N/A |
| NW | N/A | 7,727,000 |

DUNS 89-669-8560
## Temple House Care Home Ltd
107 Mauchline Road, Mossblown, Ayr, Ayrshire KA6 5AR
**Tel:** 01292521350
**Web:** www.templehousenursinghome.co.uk
**Reg No:** 0172503SC **Estd:** 1991 Private Limited Company
**Line of Business:** Residential care establishments
**Issued Capital:** £100,000
**Directors:** R Hope, Ms E G Hope
**Co. Secretary:** Alistair Hope
**US SIC:** 8321, 8051
**UK SIC:** 96111, 95100
**Bankers:** The Royal Bank Of Scotland Plc (83-15-26)

|  | 31-07-14 | 31-07-13 | 31-07-12 |
|---|---|---|---|
| TA | 1,055,557 | 1,059,092 | 1,100,022 |
| NW | 878,181 | 877,135 | 824,367 |
| WC | (23,225) | (55,442) | (121,117) |

DUNS 21-590-2608
## Temple-Knightswood After Schoolcare
36 Knightscliffe Avenue, Glasgow, Lanarkshire G13 2TE
**Tel:** 01419593284
**Web:** www.knightswood-pri.glasgow.sch.uk
**Estd:** 2001
**Line of Business:** Schools (local authority)
**Proprietor:** Mrs J Mackie
**Responsibilities**
**Senior:** Ann Mcintosh (*Head Teacher*)
**US SIC:** 8211 **UK SIC:** 93200
**Employees:** 50

DUNS 50-379-4422
## Temple Lifts Ltd
(**Subsidiary of:** Temple Lifts Group 2010 Ltd)
Hayward House, London SE12 0DZ
**Tel:** 02088518900 **Fax:** 02088517756
**Web:** www.templelifts.ltd.uk
**Reg No:** 2388497 **VAT No:** 523715950
**Estd:** 1989 Private Limited Company
**Line of Business:** Lifts (maintenance and repair)
**Issued Capital:** £1,000
**Directors:** J M Phillips, B J Harden, S J Hamlin
**Co. Secretary:** Mark Kane
**Responsibilities**
**Finance:** David Barden (*Financial Controller*)
**Marketing:** Colin Pavitt (*Sales & Marketing Director*)
**Sales:** Colin Pavitt (*Sales & Marketing Director*)
**HR:** Gill Hamlin (*Human Resources Manager*)
**Health & Safety:** Gill Hamlin (*Human Resources Manager*)
**Operations:** Darren Fogg (*?Major Works Field Manager*), Colin Pavitt (*Sales & Marketing Director*)
**Branches:** Temple Lifts Ltd, Langstone Technology Park, Langstone Road, Havant, Hampshire PO9 1SA
**US SIC:** 3534 **UK SIC:** 32553

**Auditors:** Kingston Smith LLP
**Bankers:** HSBC Bank plc (40-02-07)

|  | 31-12-13 | 31-12-12 | 31-12-11 |
|---|---|---|---|
| TO | 14,107,158 | 13,262,530 | 10,111,567 |
| P/L | 190,091 | 466,744 | 294,170 |
| NW | 1,136,836 | 1,206,925 | 1,077,212 |
| WC | 1,079,389 | 1,160,247 | 1,040,287 |
| Emp. | 109 | 101 | 100 |

DUNS 22-010-6038
## Templegate Electrical Supplies Ltd
19 Blackberry Drive, Barry, South Glamorgan CF62 7JQ
**Tel:** 01446733021
**Web:** www.templegate-electrical.co.uk
**Reg No:** 4013699 **VAT No:** 753370434
**Estd:** 2000 Private Limited Company
**Line of Business:** Electrical wholesalers
**Issued Capital:** £1,000
**Principals:** G I Bailey (*Managing*), A J Rowsell, P Williams, C Sawyer
**Co. Secretary:** Nigel Firmin
**Responsibilities**
**Senior:** Gari Cooke (*Branch Manager*)
**US SIC:** 5074 **UK SIC:** 61300
**Auditors:** HW Chartered Accountants
**Bankers:** Bristol And West Plc (12-22-12)

|  | 31-12-13 | 31-12-12 | 31-12-11 |
|---|---|---|---|
| TO | 10,737,335 | 9,593,017 | 9,891,015 |
| P/L | 286,919 | 225,717 | 112,888 |
| NW | 1,488,188 | 1,447,171 | 1,245,962 |
| WC | 1,392,046 | 1,362,796 | 1,137,155 |
| Emp. | 49 | 45 | 46 |

DUNS 23-652-3887
## Templestock Ltd
Systems House, Central Business Park, Mackadown Lane, Birmingham, West Midlands B33 0JL
**Tel:** 01215085888
**Web:** www.templestock.co.uk
**Reg No:** 3647588 **VAT No:** 705341662
**Estd:** 2012 Private Limited Company
**Line of Business:** Furniture retail outlets
**Issued Capital:** £100
**Directors:** P E White, Ms T L White, Ms L G White, Ms J S White
**Co. Secretary:** Peter Talbot
**Branches:** Templestock Ltd, Unit 5B, Lionel Road South, Brentford, Middlesex TW8 9QR
**US SIC:** 2599 **UK SIC:** 46720
**Auditors:** Cotterell & Co

|  | 31-12-13 | 31-12-12 | 31-12-11 |
|---|---|---|---|
| TA | 361,094 | 500,343 | 860,791 |
| NW | 118,559 | 105,831 | 101,293 |
| WC | 118,559 | 105,831 | 101,293 |

DUNS 33-990-1779
## Templeton Hotel
882 Antrim Road, Ballyclare, Co Antrim BT39 0AH
**Tel:** 02894432984
**Web:** www.templetonhotel.com
**Estd:** 2012 Proprietorship
**Line of Business:** Hotels
**Proprietor:** S Mccombe
**Responsibilities**
**Senior:** Stephen McCombe (*Proprietor*), Alison Mccombe (*General Manager*), Ivan O'Neil (*Head Chef*)
**Finance:** Alison Mccombe (*General Manager*)
**IT:** Miles Carville (*IT Manager*)
**HR:** Claire Kerr (*Human Resources Manager*)
**Health & Safety:** Andrea Steel (*Health & Safety Officer*)
**Purchasing:** Veronica Andrews (*Purchasing Manager*)
**US SIC:** 7011, 5812, 6531
**UK SIC:** 66500, 66110, 83400
**Bankers:** The Bank Of Ireland (90-23-89)
**Employees:** 150

DUNS 21-713-0555
## Templetons Cleaning Ltd
Unit 24 The I O Trading Centre, 57a Croydon Road, Beddington, Croydon, Surrey CR0 4WQ
**Tel:** 02086808271
**Web:** www.templetonsltd.co.uk
**Reg No:** 7527399 **Estd:** 2011 Private Limited Company
**Line of Business:** Cleaning/maintenance svcs to buildings
**Issued Capital:** £2
**Directors:** Mrs M Templeton, F Templeton
**Co. Secretary:** Razvan Sabau
**US SIC:** 7349, 8999
**UK SIC:** 92300, 83954

|  | 30-04-14 | 28-02-13 | 29-04-12 |
|---|---|---|---|
| TA | 100 | 2 | 2 |
| NW | 100 | 2 | 2 |

DUNS 39-746-6129
## Templine Employment Agency Ltd
(**Subsidiary of:** Siamo Azzuri Ltd)
36-38 High Street, Birmingham, West Midlands B23 6RH
**Tel:** 01213848488
**Web:** www.templinerecruitment.co.uk
**Reg No:** 2186417 **Estd:** 1987 Private Limited Company
**Line of Business:** Labour recruitment and provision of personnel
**Issued Capital:** £100
**Directors:** L Robinson, A S Bucciero
**Co. Secretary:** Neil Himsworth
**Responsibilities**
**Senior:** Maria Hehir (*Branch Manager*), Christine Zhu (*Senior Manager Accountant*)
**Branches:** Templine Employment Agency Ltd, Imex House 40 Princess Street, Manchester M1 6DE
**US SIC:** 7361 **UK SIC:** 83954
**Auditors:** James Stanley & Co
**Bankers:** Lloyds TSB Bank plc (77-85-01)

|  | 31-12-13 | 31-12-12 | 31-12-11 |
|---|---|---|---|
| TO | 39,592,627 | 36,592,587 | 31,850,310 |
| P/L | 1,052,688 | 967,882 | 1,093,969 |
| NW | 3,237,634 | 2,562,633 | 2,001,389 |
| WC | 2,973,009 | 2,443,887 | 1,872,038 |
| Emp. | 2,684 | 2,468 | 2,180 |

DUNS 77-878-5063
## Tempo Graphic Design Ltd
(**Subsidiary of:** Chime Communications Plc)
First Floor Heather Court, 6 Maidstone Road, Sidcup, Kent DA14 5HH
**Tel:** 020-7231-5160
**Web:** www.tempo-uk.com
**Reg No:** 3037362 **VAT No:** 662957985
**Estd:** 1995 Private Limited Company
**Line of Business:** Graphic designers
**Issued Capital:** £1,000
**Director:** E P Leask
**Co. Secretary:** Robert Davison
**Responsibilities**
**Senior:** Andrew Akerman (*Manager*)
**US SIC:** 7399, 2752
**UK SIC:** 83954, 47544
**Auditors:** Baker Tilly
**Bankers:** Lloyds TSB Bank plc (30-96-73)

|  | 31-12-13 | 31-12-12 | 31-12-11 |
|---|---|---|---|
| TA | 34,000 | 34,000 | 34,000 |
| NW | 34,000 | 34,000 | 34,000 |

DUNS 21-140-0442
## Tempo Insulation Services Ltd
Princes Park, 2 Princes Drive, Colwyn Bay, Clwyd LL29 8PL
**Tel:** 08001522011 **Fax:** 08442097441
**Web:** www.tempoenergy.co.uk
**Reg No:** 6721354 **Estd:** 2008 Private Limited Company
**Line of Business:** Heating contractors
**Issued Capital:** £80
**Directors:** A N Dodds, J Gregory, M Bryant
**US SIC:** 1799, 1742
**UK SIC:** 50000, 50400

|  | 31-10-13 | 31-10-12 | 31-10-11 |
|---|---|---|---|
| TA | 2,025,669 | 959,469 | 236,726 |
| NW | 460,714 | 153,418 | 50,234 |
| WC | 377,250 | 139,288 | 32,646 |

DUNS 21-033-8593
## Temptations T2
2 Union Street, Plymouth, Devon PL1 2SR
**Tel:** 01752-604005
**Web:** www.temptationst3.co.uk
**Estd:** 2004 Proprietorship
**Line of Business:** Managed public houses and bars
**US SIC:** 5813 **UK SIC:** 66200
**Employees:** 65

DUNS 23-377-9586     Imp
## Tempur Uk Ltd
(**Subsidiary of:** Tempur Danish Holdings Aps)
Caxton Point, Printing House Lane, Hayes, Middlesex UB3 1AP
**Tel:** 02085897000 **Fax:** 020-8589-7001
**Web:** www.tempur.co.uk
**Reg No:** 2748033 **Estd:** 1999 Private Limited Company
**Line of Business:** Manufacture of mattresses
**Trading Style:** Tempur Uk Ltd
**Issued Capital:** £2,200,000
**Principals:** Mrs J M Stefanov (*Managing*), D Montgomery, D Williams
**Co. Secretary:** Mrs Paula Thomas
**Responsibilities**
**HR:** Pauline Tamplin (*HR Manager*)
**US SIC:** 2515, 7399
**UK SIC:** 46715, 83954
**Auditors:** Ernst & Young LLP

**Bankers:** HSBC Bank plc (40-22-30)

|  | 31-12-13 | 31-12-12 | 31-12-11 |
|---|---|---|---|
| TO | 31,844,000 | 31,445,000 | 27,702,000 |
| P/L | 1,629,000 | 1,008,000 | 1,985,000 |
| NW | 14,362,000 | 12,821,000 | 11,100,000 |
| WC | 13,139,000 | 11,587,000 | 9,957,000 |
| Emp. | 83 | 65 | 60 |

DUNS 22-907-8423     Imp-Exp
## Ten Alps Plc
Commonwealth House, London WC1A 1NU
**Tel:** 02073060300 **Fax:** 02078782483
**Web:** www.tenalps.com
**Reg No:** 0075133SC **VAT No:** 392602647
**Estd:** 1981 Public Limited Company
**Line of Business:** Advertising agency services
**Issued Capital:** £5,050,820
**Directors:** R F Geldof, P M Bertram, A B Walden, T J Hoare, M W Wood
**Co. Secretary:** Nitil Patel
**Responsibilities**
**Senior:** Denys Blakeway (*Chairman, Blakeway Productions*), Adrian Dunleavy (*Manager*), Roger Graef (*CEO, Films of Record*), Fiona Lawson-Baker (*Managing Director, Ten Alps As*), Derek Morren (*Manager*)
**Admin:** Moira McManus-Dixon (*Personal Assistant to CEO*)
**Operations:** Alison Lewis (*Production Manager*), Sarah Murch (*Executive Producer*)
**Engineering:** Alison Lewis (*Production Manager*)
**US SIC:** 7319, 7399
**UK SIC:** 83800, 83954
**Auditors:** Grant Thornton UK LLP
**Bankers:** Bank Of Scotland (12-26-06)

|  | 30-06-14 | 31-03-13 | 31-06-12 |
|---|---|---|---|
| TO | 29,454,000 | 27,641,000 | 43,519,000 |
| P/L | (2,556,000) | (8,002,000) | (3,912,000) |
| NW | (8,349,000) | (6,141,000) | (6,103,000) |
| WC | (581,000) | (342,000) | (901,000) |
| Emp. | 197 | 294 | 380 |

DUNS 50-002-4286     Imp-Exp
## Ten Cate Advanced Composites Ltd
(**Subsidiary of:** Hal Trust)
94 Station Road, Langley Mill, Nottingham, Nottinghamshire NG16 4BP
**Tel:** 01773-530899
**Web:** www.ambercomposites.co.uk
**Reg No:** 2271414 **Estd:** 1988 Private Limited Company
**Line of Business:** Plastics - engineering materials
**Export Markets:** Worldwide
**Export Sales:** £3,820,623
**Issued Capital:** £100
**Directors:** F J Meurs, L De Vries
**Co. Secretary:** Ian Pratt
**Responsibilities**
**Sales:** Jed Illsley (*Export Sales Manager*)
**Engineering:** Andy Spendiff (*Senior Sales Engineer*)
**US SIC:** 2873 **UK SIC:** 25130
**Auditors:** KPMG LLP
**Bankers:** The Royal Bank Of Scotland Plc (16-26-32)

|  | 31-12-13 | 31-12-12 | 31-12-11 |
|---|---|---|---|
| TO | 9,517,911 | 8,840,203 | 8,084,194 |
| P/L | 578,776 | 473,476 | 338,868 |
| NW | 3,119,136 | 2,936,486 | 2,558,483 |
| WC | 1,725,836 | 2,071,838 | 1,708,195 |
| Emp. | 56 | 54 | 54 |

DUNS 21-003-5771     Imp
## Ten Health & Fitness Ltd
Unit 7a 2 Exmoor Street, London W10 6BD
**Tel:** 02089699677
**Web:** www.tenpilates.com
**Reg No:** 6286799 **Estd:** 2007 Private Limited Company
**Line of Business:** Yoga
**Issued Capital:** £1,165
**Directors:** J G Rogers, Ms J Mathews
**Responsibilities**
**Senior:** Joanne Matthews (*Director*)
**Marketing:** Sandra Storgards (*Marketing Assistant*)
**Health & Safety:** Joanne Matthews (*Director*)
**US SIC:** 8091 **UK SIC:** 95200

|  | 31-12-13 | 31-12-12 | 31-12-11 |
|---|---|---|---|
| TA | 1,282,065 | 1,033,387 | 739,300 |
| NW | 482,118 | 368,529 | 222,843 |
| WC | (186,143) | 143,390 | (81,187) |

DUNS 73-415-4524
## Ten Lifestyle Management Ltd
(**Subsidiary of:** Ten Lifestyle Holdings Ltd)
30 Market Place, London W1W 8AP
**Tel:** 02074793412 **Fax:** 07000-102000
**Web:** www.tenlifestyle.com
**Reg No:** 4688658 **Estd:** 1999 Private Limited Company
**Line of Business:** Activities of travel agencies
**Export Sales:** £182,268

**Trading Style:** Ten U K, Ten Group
**Issued Capital:** £3,188
**Directors:** A M Long, Ms S L Hornbuckle, K Von Unger, M J Berry, B B Horner
**Co. Secretary:** Alexander Cheatle
**Responsibilities**
**Senior:** Joachim Jaeckle *(Manager)*
**US SIC:** 4722, 7399
**UK SIC:** 77001, 83954
**Auditors:** TWP Accounting LLP

| | 31-08-13 | 31-08-12 | 31-08-11 |
|---|---|---|---|
| TO | 18,226,831 | 18,737,015 | 20,113,600 |
| P/L | 66,480 | 396,998 | 451,599 |
| NW | 1,618,383 | (209,178) | (134,932) |
| WC | 1,416,569 | (531,916) | (292,647) |
| Emp. | 285 | 264 | 274 |

DUNS 42-379-3678
## Ten Sixty Six Housing Association Ltd
44 Wellington Square Wellington Centre, Hastings, East Sussex TN34 1PN
**Tel:** 01424439663 **Fax:** 01424728255
**Web:** www.hastingsphysiotherapy.co.uk
**Reg No:** 0028131IP **Estd:** 2012 Friendly Society
**Line of Business:** Physiotherapists
**Trading Style:** Hastings Lifeline, Hastings, 1066 Property Services
**Co. Secretary:** Keith Donaldson
**Responsibilities**
**Senior:** Matthew Herriott *(Practice Manager)*
**Branches:** Ten Sixty Six Housing Association Ltd, Bristol Road, St Leonards-On-Sea, St. Leonards-On-Sea, East Sussex TN38 9EN
**US SIC:** 6531 **UK SIC:** 83400
**Bankers:** Barclays Bank Plc (20-27-91)
**Employees:** 78
**Turnover:** £17,409,000

DUNS 21-582-8992
## Ten Square
Yorkshire House, 10 Donegall Square South, Belfast BT1 5JD
**Tel:** 028-9024-1001
**Web:** www.tensquare.co.uk
**Estd:** 2000 Partnership
**Line of Business:** Hotels
**Partners:** N Hill, P Hill
**Responsibilities**
**Senior:** Katie Hamilton *(General Manager)*
**US SIC:** 7011 **UK SIC:** 66500
**Employees:** 62

DUNS 21-029-1258 **Imp-Exp**
## Tenable Screw Co Ltd
16 Deer Park Road, London SW19 3UB
**Tel:** 020-8542-6225
**Web:** www.tenable.co.uk
**Reg No:** 0363073 **VAT No:** 216317585
**Estd:** 1934 Private Limited Company
**Line of Business:** Precision engineers
**Export Markets:** U S A; S Africa; European Union (E U); Canada; Denmark; Singapore
**Issued Capital:** £25,000
**Directors:** N M Schlaefli, S T Schlaefli
**Co. Secretary:** Simon Schlaefli
**Responsibilities**
**Senior:** Trevor Peacock *(Works Manager)*, Carol Rowe *(Administrator)*
**Health & Safety:** Trevor Peacock *(Works Manager)*
**Facilities:** Trevor Peacock *(Works Manager)*
**Engineering:** Trevor Peacock *(Works Manager)*
**Branches:** Tenable Screw Co Ltd, Tenable House, Torrington Avenue, Coventry, West Midlands CV4 9HN
**US SIC:** 8911, 3714
**UK SIC:** 83701, 35300
**Auditors:** Schonhut Carr & Co
**Bankers:** HSBC Bank plc (40-07-30)

| | 31-08-13 | 31-08-12 | 31-08-11 |
|---|---|---|---|
| TA | 8,007,654 | 8,070,714 | 7,984,153 |
| P/L | (138,228) | 146,263 | 150,571 |
| NW | 6,028,495 | 6,115,550 | 6,003,474 |
| WC | 2,795,440 | 3,440,650 | 3,171,861 |
| Emp. | 107 | 108 | 95 |

DUNS 21-775-7342
## Tenbury Community Hospital
Worcester Road, Burford, Tenbury Wells, Worcestershire WR15 8AP
**Tel:** 01584810643
**Estd:** 2011 Partnership
**Line of Business:** Hospitals
**Partner:** Mrs V Snape
**Responsibilities**
**Senior:** Jayne Brown *(Ward Manager)*
**US SIC:** 8062 **UK SIC:** 95100
**Employees:** 70

DUNS 21-783-3019
## Tenbury High School
Oldwood Road, Tenbury Wells, Worcestershire WR15 8XA
**Tel:** 01584811405
**Web:** www.tenburyhigh.worcs.sch.uk
**Estd:** 1953 Proprietorship
**Line of Business:** Other sporting activities not elsewhere classified
**Proprietor:** S Cooke
**Responsibilities**
**Senior:** Adrian Price *(Head Teacher)*
**US SIC:** 7999 **UK SIC:** 97913
**Employees:** 60

DUNS 21-782-5229
## Tenchley Manor
Ursula Square, Selsey, Chichester, West Sussex PO20 0HS
**Web:** www.cheerhealth.com
**Estd:** 1982 Partnership
**Line of Business:** Nursing homes
**Partners:** Mrs E Harmsworth, Miss A Bessey
**US SIC:** 8051 **UK SIC:** 95100
**Employees:** 54

DUNS 21-391-3664
## Tender Loving Care Agency
27 Great Oak Street, Llanidloes, Powys SY18 6BW
**Proprietorship**
**Line of Business:** Home care service providers
**Proprietor:** Mrs G Perks
**US SIC:** 8091 **UK SIC:** 95200
**Employees:** 100

DUNS 73-269-7482
## Tender Loving Carers Domiciliary Ltd
Unit 108-109, John Wilson Business Park, Harvey Drive, Chestfiel, Whitstable, Kent CT5 3QT
**Tel:** 01227-772515 **Fax:** 01227772527
**Web:** www.tenderlovingcarers.com
**Reg No:** 4543480 **Estd:** 2002 Private Limited Company
**Line of Business:** Home care service providers
**Issued Capital:** £100
**Principals:** Ms B E Grutzmacher *(Managing)*, K Grutzmacher, J Grutzmacher
**Co. Secretary:** Ms Brigitte Grutzmacher
**US SIC:** 8091, 8321
**UK SIC:** 95200, 96111

| | 30-09-13 | 30-09-12 | 30-09-11 |
|---|---|---|---|
| TA | 75,948 | 83,929 | 88,624 |
| NW | 11,047 | 58 | (4,786) |
| WC | 7,489 | (2,699) | (8,211) |

DUNS 23-988-7396
## Tender Sleep Beds Ltd
71 Kings Road, Tyseley, Birmingham, West Midlands B11 2AX
**Tel:** 0121-707-1221 **Fax:** 01217061300
**Web:** www.tendersleepbeds.co.uk
**Reg No:** 3977031 **Estd:** 2000 Private Limited Company
**Line of Business:** Manufacturers of household furnishings
**Issued Capital:** £100
**Managing Director:** C M Hussain
**Co. Secretary:** Zulfiqar Ali
**Responsibilities**
**Senior:** Kamran Kiyani *(Manager)*
**US SIC:** 2517 **UK SIC:** 46714
**Auditors:** MSGee

| | 31-08-13 | 31-08-12 | 31-08-11 |
|---|---|---|---|
| TA | 1,152,635 | 1,138,591 | 1,064,244 |
| NW | 503,713 | 509,276 | 482,238 |
| WC | 79,139 | 63,619 | 62,673 |

DUNS 50-147-6345 **Imp**
## Tendercare Nurseries Ltd
Southlands Road, Denham, Uxbridge, Middlesex UB9 4HD
**Tel:** 01895835544 **Fax:** 01895-835036
**Web:** www.tendercare.co.uk
**Reg No:** 2325757 **Estd:** 1988 Private Limited Company
**Line of Business:** Agricultural service activities; landscape gardening
**Issued Capital:** £100
**Managing Director:** A Halksworth
**Co. Secretary:** Mrs Angela Halksworth
**US SIC:** 0729, 5199
**UK SIC:** 01003, 61900
**Auditors:** Kingston Smith
**Bankers:** HSBC Bank plc (40-45-08)

| | 31-08-13 | 31-08-12 | 31-08-11 |
|---|---|---|---|
| TA | 1,178,888 | 1,290,299 | 1,230,957 |
| NW | 130,116 | 177,614 | 209,865 |
| WC | (115,477) | (206,994) | (122,579) |

DUNS 23-181-1857
## Tendring District Council
Town Hall, Clacton-On-Sea, Essex CO15 1SE
**Tel:** 01255686868
**Web:** www.tendringdc.gov.uk
**Estd:** 2010
**Line of Business:** Local government
**Trading Style:** Wix Parish Council
**Director:** J Hawkins
**Responsibilities**
**Senior:** Debianne Messenger *(Manager)*
**Finance:** Karen Neath *(Financial Director)*
**Admin:** Karen Neath *(Financial Director)*
**HR:** Stuart Brian *(Staff Development Manager)*
**Facilities:** Toni Wright *(Facilities Manager)*
**Branches:** Tendring District Council, 23 Pier Avenue, Clacton-On-Sea, Essex CO15 1FB
**US SIC:** 9121 **UK SIC:** 91110
**Employees:** 250

DUNS 21-161-9775
## Tendring Technology & Sixth Form College
150 Rochford Way, Frinton-On-Sea, Essex CO13 0AZ
**Tel:** 01255-672116
**Web:** www.ttc.uk.net
**Estd:** 1996 Proprietorship
**Line of Business:** Schools (local authority)
**Proprietor:** M Watson
**Responsibilities**
**Senior:** Mark Rowson *(Business Manager)*
**Marketing:** Gail Lewis *(Child Protection)*
**Health & Safety:** Stephen Hayes *(Estates Manager)*
**Facilities:** Stephen Hayes *(Estates Manager)*
**Operations:** Ruth Burden *(Quality Director)*, Michael Muldoon *(Quality control and evaluation)*
**Fleet:** Gavin Byford *(Logistics Director)*
**US SIC:** 8211 **UK SIC:** 93200
**Employees:** 300

DUNS 23-938-5177 **Imp**
## Teneo Ltd
**(Subsidiary of:** Teneo Group Ltd)
Unit 20, Reading, Berkshire RG7 4GB
**Tel:** 01189703900
**Web:** www.teneo.co.uk
**Reg No:** 3928202 **VAT No:** 732569813
**Estd:** 2000 Private Limited Company
**Line of Business:** Telecommunication networks
**Export Sales:** £5,919,660
**Issued Capital:** £245,000
**Directors:** M J Sollars, J S Hall, R Jones
**Co. Secretary:** Piers Carey
**Responsibilities**
**Senior:** Mathew Matthews *(Manager)*
**US SIC:** 7379, 7392
**UK SIC:** 83940, 83951
**Auditors:** Moore Stephens (South) LLP

| | 30-06-13 | 30-06-12 | 30-06-11 |
|---|---|---|---|
| TO | 20,275,603 | 14,470,057 | 11,872,595 |
| P/L | 1,010,789 | 1,016,687 | 646,947 |
| NW | 1,159,609 | 882,599 | 498,066 |
| WC | 1,139,620 | 933,440 | 298,342 |
| Emp. | 53 | 43 | 33 |

DUNS 23-919-1864
## Tenet Group Ltd
5 Lister Hill, Horsforth, Leeds, West Yorkshire LS18 5AZ
**Tel:** 01132-390011
**Web:** www.tenetgroup.co.uk
**Reg No:** 3909395 **Estd:** 2000 Private Limited Company
**Line of Business:** Financial intermediation not elsewhere classified
**Trading Style:** Tenet Business Solutions
**Issued Capital:** £24,731
**Directors:** D J Wild, A M Beswick, R D Smith, M J O'Brien, P Hilling, D G Jarrett, Mrs C J Bradley, A B Meeks
**Co. Secretary:** Richard Fletcher
**Responsibilities**
**Senior:** Geoffrey Clarkson *(Manager)*, Graeham Sampson *(Manager)*
**Marketing:** Emma Bull *(Relations Manager)*, Jonathan Hydes *(Marketing Manager)*
**US SIC:** 6111 **UK SIC:** 81501
**Auditors:** Deloitte LLP
**Bankers:** Barclays Bank Plc (20-48-42)

| | 30-09-14 | 30-09-13 | 30-09-12 |
|---|---|---|---|
| TA | 47,158,829 | 47,756,679 | 53,570,060 |
| P/L | 355,414 | 301,183 | (4,543,461) |
| NW | 16,682,970 | 15,944,068 | 16,784,631 |
| WC | 22,141,230 | 24,356,500 | 29,810,789 |
| Emp. | 261 | 247 | 247 |

DUNS 23-962-5338
## Tenetconnect Ltd
**(Subsidiary of:** Tenet Group Ltd)
5 Lister Hill, Horsforth, Leeds, West Yorkshire LS18 5AZ
**Tel:** 01132591717
**Web:** www.tenetgroup.co.uk
**Reg No:** 2654877 **VAT No:** 568504517
**Estd:** 1991 Private Limited Company
**Line of Business:** Financial intermediation not elsewhere classified
**Issued Capital:** £1,542,416
**Directors:** M J Greenwood, Mrs C J Bradley, Ms H M Turner, Mrs G M Davidson, Ms G E Harle, M J O'Brien
**Co. Secretary:** Richard Fletcher
**Responsibilities**
**Senior:** Geoffrey Clarkson *(Manager)*, Mark Youngman *(Manager)*
**US SIC:** 6111 **UK SIC:** 81501
**Auditors:** Arthur Andersen
**Bankers:** Barclays Bank Plc (20-48-42)

| | 30-09-13 | 30-09-12 | 30-09-11 |
|---|---|---|---|
| TA | 16,779,084 | 15,341,363 | 11,695,708 |
| P/L | 1,329,311 | (918,195) | 1,179,398 |
| NW | 4,608,148 | 3,284,741 | 3,991,820 |
| WC | 11,486,206 | 9,489,430 | 8,136,799 |
| Emp. | 82 | 74 | 71 |

DUNS 22-531-8104 **Imp**
## Tenkay Electronics Ltd
Marlborough Road, Lancing, West Sussex BN15 8TR
**Tel:** 01903-855455
**Web:** www.tenkay.co.uk
**Reg No:** 1925067 **Estd:** 1983 Private Limited Company
**Line of Business:** Assembling and wiring
**Issued Capital:** £447
**Director:** S J Dixon
**Co. Secretary:** Mrs Georgia Dixon
**Responsibilities**
**Admin:** Alison Gray *(Administration Manager)*
**IT:** Andy Penny *(IT Engineer)*, Maxine Sloate *(Computer Manager)*
**HR:** Alison Gray *(Administration Manager)*
**Purchasing:** Adam Buckley *(Purchasing Manager)*
**Branches:** Tenkay Electronics Ltd, 25 Clarendon Villas, Hove, East Sussex BN3 3RE
**US SIC:** 1731, 3679
**UK SIC:** 50300, 34542
**Bankers:** The Royal Bank Of Scotland Plc (16-14-24)

| | 31-12-13 | 31-12-12 | 31-12-11 |
|---|---|---|---|
| TA | 1,293,849 | 1,327,970 | 1,569,408 |
| NW | 638,568 | 731,183 | 730,614 |
| WC | 613,277 | 674,213 | 638,748 |

DUNS 89-677-2332
## Tenmat Ltd
**(Subsidiary of:** Diamorph Ab (Publ))
Ashburton Road West, Trafford Park, Manchester M17 1RU
**Tel:** 0161-872-2181
**Web:** www.tenmat.com
**Reg No:** 3342498 **Estd:** 1997 Private Limited Company
**Line of Business:** Chemicals & allied product wholesalers
**Export Sales:** £19,177,000
**Issued Capital:** £1
**Directors:** C E Lawrence, G Macleman, M A Hutchison, A P Moore, F A Svedberg
**Co. Secretary:** Frank Hopkins
**Responsibilities**
**Marketing:** Julian Greenhalgh *(Business Manager)*
**Facilities:** Chris Finerty *(Maintenance Manager)*
**Engineering:** Chris Finerty *(Maintenance Manager)*
**Branches:** Tenmat Ltd, 15 Woods Lane, Cradley Heath Factory Centre, Cradley Heath, West Midlands B64 7AE
**US SIC:** 5161, 3269, 3272, 3999
**UK SIC:** 61200, 24894, 24370, 49590
**Auditors:** KPMG LLP
**Bankers:** Barclays Bank Plc (20-55-34)

| | 31-12-13 | 31-12-12 | 30-12-11 |
|---|---|---|---|
| TO | 24,913,000 | 37,051,000 | 23,621,000 |
| P/L | 7,713,000 | 14,182,000 | 8,134,000 |
| NW | 17,305,000 | 9,267,000 | 8,135,000 |
| WC | 13,749,000 | 5,907,000 | 4,541,000 |
| Emp. | 201 | 204 | 195 |

DUNS 21-445-8168
## Tennant Transport Ltd
**(Subsidiary of:** Tennant Transport (Forth) Ltd)
Ayre Road, Hyndford Bridge, Lanark, Lanarkshire ML11 8SG
**Tel:** 01555-811211
**Web:** www.tennanttransport.co.uk
**Reg No:** 0055283SC **Estd:** 1900 Private Limited Company
**Line of Business:** Road haulage and transport services

**Issued Capital:** £93,500
**Directors:** I T Tennant, J Tennant
**Co. Secretary:** Graham Sorbie
**US SIC:** 4789 **UK SIC:** 77002
**Auditors:** Scott-Moncrieff
**Bankers:** The Royal Bank Of Scotland Plc (83-20-15)

| | 30-04-14 | 30-04-13 | 30-04-12 |
|---|---|---|---|
| TA | 3,473,178 | 2,576,419 | 2,421,912 |
| NW | 1,299,340 | 1,038,864 | 1,076,740 |
| WC | (102,274) | (72,610) | (73,318) |

DUNS 21-587-2615 Exp
## Tennant U K Cleaning Solutions Ltd
**(Subsidiary of:** Jpmorgan Chase & Co.)
Bankside, Falkirk, Stirlingshire FK2 7XE
**Tel:** 01324611666 **Fax:** 01324611886
**Web:** www.greenmachines.com
**Reg No:** 0042491SC **VAT No:** 804116373
**Estd:** 1965 Private Limited Company
**Line of Business:** Car kit assemblers
**Export Markets:** E U
**Issued Capital:** £32,221
**Directors:** Mrs K Stokes, N W Hayes, Y A Derycke, S W Winship, T Paulson
**Co. Secretary:** Ms Heidi Wilson
**Responsibilities**
**Senior:** Andrew Galashan *(Manager)*, Justin Hallquist *(Site Manager)*, Joost Verburg *(Manager)*
**Branches:** Tennant U K Cleaning Solutions Ltd, Bromley House, Unit 1, Kettering, Northamptonshire NN15 6JQ
**US SIC:** 3711 **UK SIC:** 35101
**Auditors:** KPMG LLP
**Bankers:** Bank Of Scotland (80-15-95)

| | 31-12-13 | 31-12-11 | 31-12-10 |
|---|---|---|---|
| TO | 21,483,427 | 23,759,935 | 23,067,498 |
| P/L | 1,502,088 | 1,370,460 | 1,095,240 |
| NW | 2,276,161 | 2,343,104 | 778,746 |
| WC | 2,028,661 | 4,426,751 | 5,279,740 |
| Emp. | 180 | 217 | 243 |

DUNS 21-097-8839 Exp
## Tennants Consolidated Ltd
12 Upper Belgrave Street, London SW1X 8BA
**Tel:** 020-7493-5451
**Web:** www.tennants.net
**Reg No:** 0250915 **VAT No:** 240507888
**Estd:** 1930 Private Limited Company
**Line of Business:** Management activities of holding companies
**Export Sales:** £206,965,000
**Issued Capital:** £4,608,270
**Directors:** K G Jones, S E Alexander, A C Gingell, M G Hughes, A F Mitchell, J H Cartwright, D J Alexander, P C Hancock
**Co. Secretary:** Nigel Collin
**US SIC:** 6711, 2819
**UK SIC:** 83962, 25110
**Auditors:** Grant Thornton UK LLP
**Bankers:** Bank Of Scotland (12-11-03)

| | 31-12-13 | 31-12-12 | 31-12-11 |
|---|---|---|---|
| TO | 400,522,000 | 394,080,000 | 409,208,000 |
| P/L | 19,413,000 | 21,697,000 | 18,900,000 |
| NW | 176,893,000 | 170,996,000 | 156,706,000 |
| WC | 130,902,000 | 124,344,000 | 113,335,000 |
| Emp. | 956 | 988 | 974 |

DUNS 51-625-2913
## Tennants Crust Bakery
13a Wood Lane, Hednesford, Cannock, Staffordshire WS12 1BW
**Estd:** 1976 Proprietorship
**Line of Business:** Bakers shops
**Proprietor:** P Tennant
**Branches:** Tennants Crust Bakery, 157 Hednesford Road, Cannock, Staffordshire WS12 3HN
**US SIC:** 5462 **UK SIC:** 64100
**Employees:** 60

DUNS 23-651-0660
## Tennants (Elgin) Ltd
Brumley Brae, Elgin, Morayshire IV30 5PP
**Tel:** 01343860244
**Web:** www.tennantselgin.com
**Reg No:** 0190066SC **Estd:** 1998 Private Limited Company
**Line of Business:** Wholesale of wood, construction materials and sanitary equipment
**Issued Capital:** £100,000
**Principals:** G B Tennant *(Managing)*, Ms P R Anderson, G J Tennant
**Co. Secretary:** Ms Sandra Tennant
**Responsibilities**
**Purchasing:** Ian Willcox *(Purchasing Manager)*
**Engineering:** Douglas Curry *(Technical, Production Manager)*
**US SIC:** 7399 **UK SIC:** 83954
**Bankers:** Clydesdale Bank Plc (82-63-07)

| | 31-03-14 | 30-11-12 | 30-03-11 |
|---|---|---|---|
| TA | 3,032,686 | 2,778,782 | 2,981,536 |
| NW | 2,214,319 | 2,008,077 | 2,085,115 |
| WC | 469,938 | 343,389 | 396,521 |

DUNS 21-229-8756
## Tennants (Lancashire) Ltd
**(Subsidiary of:** Tennants Consolidated Ltd)
Hazelbottom Road, Manchester M8 0GR
**Tel:** 01612054454 **Fax:** 01612034298
**Web:** www.tennantsdistribution.com
**Reg No:** 0246637 **VAT No:** 145088562
**Estd:** 1930 Private Limited Company
**Line of Business:** Chemicals distribution and wholesale
**Issued Capital:** £300,000
**Directors:** W P Alexander, A F Mitchell
**Co. Secretary:** Barry Price
**Responsibilities**
**Senior:** Sean Sloan *(Manager)*
**Branches:** Tennants (Lancashire) Ltd, Ryders Green Rd, West Bromwich, West Midlands B70 0AX
**US SIC:** 5161 **UK SIC:** 61200
**Bankers:** Bank Of Scotland (12-08-95)

| | 31-12-13 | 31-12-12 | 31-12-11 |
|---|---|---|---|
| TA | 347,000 | 347,000 | 347,000 |
| NW | 300,000 | 300,000 | 300,000 |
| WC | 255,000 | 255,000 | 255,000 |

DUNS 21-566-8773 Imp
## Tenneco-Walker(U.K.)Ltd
**(Subsidiary of:** Tenneco Inc.)
Unit 3 Tafarnaubach Industrial Estate, Tafarnaubach, Tredegar, Gwent NP22 3AA
**Tel:** 01495713816
**Reg No:** 0985395 **VAT No:** 174740650
**Estd:** 1965 Private Limited Company
**Line of Business:** Manufacture of parts and accessories for motor vehicles and their engines
**Export Sales:** £1,655,000
**Issued Capital:** £12,322,200
**Directors:** E Orta Cid, D I Richards
**Co. Secretary:** Lesley Vogt
**Responsibilities**
**HR:** Janice Andrews *(Human Resources Manager)*
**Branches:** Tenneco-Walker(U.k.)ltd, Unit 3, Tafarnaubach Industrial Estate, Tredegar, Gwent NP22 3AA
**US SIC:** 3714, 5531
**UK SIC:** 35300, 65100
**Auditors:** Deloitte & Touche LLP
**Bankers:** Barclays Bank Plc (20-15-70)

| | 31-12-13 | 31-12-12 | 31-12-11 |
|---|---|---|---|
| TO | 121,185,000 | 65,108,000 | 67,650,000 |
| P/L | (324,000) | (778,000) | (3,210,000) |
| NW | 11,985,000 | (30,263,000) | (30,584,000) |
| WC | 10,444,000 | (26,693,000) | (23,967,000) |
| Emp. | 269 | 248 | 234 |

DUNS 21-401-6222
## Tennent Caledonian Breweries Wholesale Ltd
**(Subsidiary of:** C & C Group Plc)
Crompton Way, North Newmoor Industrial Estate, Irvine, Ayrshire KA11 4HU
**Tel:** 01294203000
**Web:** www.wallacesexpress.com
**Reg No:** 0081527SC **VAT No:** 264551554
**Estd:** 1983 Private Limited Company
**Line of Business:** Wholesale of wine, beer, spirits and other alcoholic beverages
**Trading Style:** Wallaces Express, Wallaces, Wallaces Licence Premises, Wallaces Inn
**Issued Capital:** £513,158
**Directors:** A Daly, B J Calder, K E Barclay, C Cosh
**Co. Secretary:** C&C Management Services Ltd
**Responsibilities**
**Senior:** Ian Meikle *(Manager)*
**Finance:** Alan Deans *(Finance Controller)*
**IT:** Brian McBurney *(IT Executive)*
**Branches:** Tennent Caledonian Breweries Wholesale Ltd, 3 St. Marnock Place, Kilmarnock, Ayrshire KA1 1DU
**US SIC:** 5182 **UK SIC:** 61700
**Auditors:** Robert J Hart & Co
**Bankers:** Clydesdale Bank Plc (82-60-30)

| | 31-03-14 | 31-03-13 | 31-03-12 |
|---|---|---|---|
| TO | 91,708,820 | 82,606,688 | 82,739,964 |
| P/L | 2,137,443 | 3,870,795 | 4,154,175 |
| NW | 39,336,979 | 37,698,715 | 35,331,596 |
| WC | 36,123,476 | 34,655,522 | 32,074,465 |
| Emp. | 289 | 286 | 293 |

DUNS 55-075-7173
## Tennent Street Care Centre
1 Tennent Street, Belfast BT13 3GD
**Tel:** 028-9031-2318
**Web:** www.fshc.co.uk
**Estd:** 1994 Proprietorship
**Line of Business:** Residential care establishments
**Proprietor:** Mrs J Cairnes
**Responsibilities**
**Senior:** Jacquelyn Cairnes *(Manager)*
**US SIC:** 8321 **UK SIC:** 96111
**Employees:** 62

DUNS 23-540-7223
## Tennis Gb Ltd
**(Subsidiary of:** Lawn Tennis Association Ltd)
National Tennis Centre, 100 Priory Lane, London SW15 5JQ
**Tel:** 02084877100 **Fax:** 020-738175965
**Web:** www.gbtennisgirls.com
**Reg No:** 3539322 **Estd:** 1998 Private Limited Company
**Line of Business:** Publishing of journals and periodicals
**Trading Style:** The Lawn Tennis Association
**Issued Capital:** £100
**Directors:** T B Davies, Mrs C M Sabin, M S Downey
**Co. Secretary:** Mrs Pauline Preston
**US SIC:** 2721, 2752
**UK SIC:** 47522, 47544
**Auditors:** PricewaterhouseCoopers

| | 30-09-13 | 30-09-12 | 30-09-11 |
|---|---|---|---|
| TA | N/A | N/A | 19,509 |
| P/L | N/A | (125) | (1,413) |
| NW | (72,551) | (72,551) | (72,426) |
| WC | N/A | N/A | (72,426) |

DUNS 21-579-6144
## Tenovus Cancer Charity
9th Floor Gleider House, Ty Glas Road, Llanishen, Cardiff, South Glamorgan CF14 5BD
**Tel:** 08088081010
**Web:** www.tenovus.org.uk
**Estd.** 1900 Partnership
**Line of Business:** Charities and charitable organisations
**Partners:** D Clarke, Mrs J Jenkins, R Williams, B Williams, H Lloyd, Miss H Ross, M Cornish
**Responsibilities**
**Senior:** Claudia Mcvie *(Chief Executive Officer)*
**US SIC:** 8699 **UK SIC:** 96902
**Employees:** 60

DUNS 73-527-0568
## Tenpin Ltd
**(Subsidiary of:** Essenden Plc)
Aragon House, University Way, Cranfield Technology Park, Cranfield, Bedford, Bedfordshire MK43 0EQ
**Tel:** 08712210000
**Web:** www.tenpin.co.uk
**Reg No:** 4789703 **Estd:** 2009 Private Limited Company
**Line of Business:** Bowling centres
**Issued Capital:** £29,575,002
**Directors:** N A Basing, R J Darwin
**Co. Secretary:** Richard Darwin
**Responsibilities**
**Senior:** Kailayapillai Ranjan *(Non-Executive Director)*, Donna Walsh *(General Manager)*
**HR:** Donna Walsh *(General Manager)*
**Health & Safety:** Donna Walsh *(General Manager)*
**Facilities:** Donna Walsh *(General Manager)*
**Branches:** Tenpin Ltd, Aragon House, University Way, Cranfield Technology Park, Cranfield, Bedford, Bedfordshire MK43 0EQ
**US SIC:** 7999 **UK SIC:** 97913
**Auditors:** PricewaterhouseCoopers LLP

| | 29-12-13 | 30-12-12 | 01-12-12 |
|---|---|---|---|
| TO | 45,648,000 | 47,107,000 | 49,724,000 |
| P/L | 4,182,000 | 782,000 | 2,573,000 |
| NW | 18,660,000 | 14,376,000 | 14,275,000 |
| WC | 2,552,000 | 1,257,000 | (823,000) |
| Emp. | 868 | 973 | 1,045 |

DUNS 21-108-0968
## Tensar Environmental Systems Ltd
**(Subsidiary of:** Tensar International Corporation)
Unit 2-4 Cunningham Court, Blackburn, Lancashire BB1 2QX
**Tel:** 01514281157 **Fax:** 01254-266868
**Web:** www.tensar-international.com
**Reg No:** 6500714 **Estd:** 2008 Private Limited Company
**Line of Business:** Other business activities not elsewhere classified
**Trading Style:** Tensar International
**Issued Capital:** £1
**Directors:** D J Morris, D B Meltzer
**US SIC:** 7399 **UK SIC:** 83954
**Bankers:** Bank Of Scotland (12-01-03)

| | 31-12-13 | 31-12-12 | 31-12-11 |
|---|---|---|---|
| NW | (83,418) | (83,418) | (83,418) |

DUNS 21-274-5574 Imp-Exp
## Tensar International Ltd
**(Subsidiary of:** Tensar International Corporation)
Cunningham Court, Blackburn, Lancashire BB1 2QX
**Tel:** 01254-262-431 **Fax:** 01254266868
**Web:** www.tensar-international.com
**Reg No:** 0503172 **VAT No:** 174366252
**Estd:** 1973 Private Limited Company
**Line of Business:** Manufacturers of netting and netting product
**Export Markets:** W Europe, Middle East, Canada, S America, Africa, S & S E Asia, Australasia, Hungary, U S A
**Trading Style:** Tenstar
**Issued Capital:** £345,420
**Directors:** D J Morris, D B Meltzer
**Responsibilities**
**Senior:** Andy Battersby *(Warehouse Manager)*, Joe Cavanaugh *(Manager)*, Jennifer Kelly *(General Manager)*
**Health & Safety:** Joe Crane *(Plant Engineering Manager)*
**Facilities:** Andy Battersby *(Warehouse Manager)*, Ray Houghton *(Maintenance Controller)*
**Purchasing:** Ray Houghton *(Maintenance Controller)*
**Engineering:** Mike Horton *(Product and Technology Manager)*
**US SIC:** 2298, 6711, 7399
**UK SIC:** 43960, 83962, 83954
**Auditors:** Ernst & Young LLP
**Bankers:** Bank Of Scotland (80-20-00)

| | 31-12-13 | 31-12-12 | 31-12-11 |
|---|---|---|---|
| TO | 31,567,000 | 36,674,000 | 38,879,000 |
| P/L | 1,317,000 | 3,488,000 | 3,932,000 |
| NW | 53,474,000 | 52,351,000 | 49,743,000 |
| WC | 51,347,000 | 49,799,000 | 46,952,000 |
| Emp. | 59 | 61 | 61 |

DUNS 23-676-3442 Exp
## Tensor Plc
Halo, Weston House, Hail Weston, St Neots, Cambridgeshire PE19 5JY
**Tel:** 01480-215530
**Web:** www.tensor.co.uk
**Reg No:** 3670909 **Estd:** 1998 Public Limited Company
**Line of Business:** Cctv & video equipment
**Issued Capital:** £400,000
**Directors:** A D Smith, N V Smith
**Co. Secretary:** Ms Heather Smith
**Responsibilities**
**Marketing:** Graham Moorby *(IT Director)*
**IT:** Graham Moorby *(IT Director)*
**Operations:** Graham Moorby *(IT Director)*
**Engineering:** Phil Reeves *(Engineering Manager)*
**Branches:** Tensor Plc, Hale, Weston House, Hail Weston, St. Neots, Cambridgeshire PE19 5JY
**US SIC:** 3651, 3629
**UK SIC:** 34541, 34350
**Auditors:** FKCA Ltd
**Bankers:** Barclays Bank Plc (20-74-81)

| | 31-05-14 | 31-05-13 | 31-05-12 |
|---|---|---|---|
| TO | 2,043,076 | 1,870,447 | 2,294,058 |
| P/L | 292,229 | 127,473 | 167,552 |
| NW | 3,941,951 | 3,777,322 | 3,739,852 |
| WC | 1,711,962 | 1,549,801 | 4,076,197 |
| Emp. | 69 | 71 | 87 |

DUNS 39-970-0913 Imp-Exp
## Tentec Ltd
Plymouth House, Guns Lane, West Bromwich, West Midlands B70 9HS
**Tel:** 01215241990
**Web:** www.tentec.net
**Reg No:** 2269292 **VAT No:** 487120149
**Estd:** 1988 Private Limited Company
**Line of Business:** Engineering consultative and design activities
**Export Markets:** Worldwide
**Export Sales:** £7,271,377
**Issued Capital:** £1,549
**Directors:** J S Jonsson, A C Bongaerts, W R Wroblewski
**Co. Secretary:** Jon Jonsson
**Responsibilities**
**Senior:** Adrian Pegler *(CEO)*
**Finance:** Sharon Chambers *(Accountant)*
**Marketing:** Paul Egginton *(Marketing Manager)*
**HR:** Sharon Chambers *(Accountant)*, Jon Gibbs *(Quality Manager)*
**Health & Safety:** Jon Gibbs *(Quality Manager)*
**Operations:** Jon Gibbs *(Quality Manager)*
**Purchasing:** Jon Gibbs *(Quality Manager)*
**US SIC:** 3999 **UK SIC:** 49590
**Auditors:** Baldwins (Leamington) Ltd
**Bankers:** The Royal Bank Of Scotland Plc (16-33-31)

| | 31-12-13 | 31-12-12 | 31-12-11 |
|---|---|---|---|
| TO | 9,243,009 | 9,754,642 | 7,895,460 |
| P/L | 738,130 | 294,323 | 367,646 |
| NW | 2,084,848 | 1,637,309 | 1,396,983 |
| WC | 1,640,378 | 1,800,146 | 1,356,963 |
| Emp. | 62 | 58 | 54 |

DUNS 42-470-4182
## Tenterden Leisure Centre Trust
Recreation Ground Road, Tenterden, Kent TN30 6RA
**Tel:** 01580-765987
**Web:** www.tenterdenleisure.com
**Reg No:** 4457980 **Estd:** 1991 Private Company Limited By Guarantee
**Line of Business:** Leisure centres

**Directors:** Ms J Hutchinson, Mrs S J Ferguson, A J Buttler, M J Bennett, Mrs J West, P T Huckin, Lieutenant Colonel J A Rymer-Jones, Ms S Newick
**Co. Secretary:** Colin Mawston
**Responsibilities**
**Senior:** Christopher Cheesman *(Trustee)*, Donna Kavanagh *(General Manager)*, Craig King *(Contracts Manager)*, Neil Pillai *(Manager)*, Pauline Saunders *(Manager)*
**Finance:** Donna Kavanagh *(General Manager)*
**Marketing:** Donna Kavanagh *(General Manager)*
**Sales:** Donna Kavanagh *(General Manager)*
**HR:** Donna Kavanagh *(General Manager)*
**Health & Safety:** Donna Kavanagh *(General Manager)*
**Facilities:** Donna Kavanagh *(General Manager)*, Jason Still *(Facilities Manager)*
**Purchasing:** Matyas Varga *(Centre Manager)*
**US SIC:** 7999, 7996
**UK SIC:** 97913
**Bankers:** Cafcash Ltd (40-52-40)

| | 31-03-14 | 31-03-13 | 31-03-12 |
|---|---|---|---|
| TO | 1,215,749 | 1,139,088 | 1,018,118 |
| P/L | (5,437) | 2,507 | (9,535) |
| NW | 35,137 | 40,574 | 38,067 |
| WC | 35,137 | 35,513 | 20,862 |
| Emp. | 91 | 87 | 85 |

DUNS 23-539-5584

## Tenva Ts Holdings Ltd

(**Subsidiary of:** Avnet Inc.)
The Capital Building, Bracknell, Berkshire RG12 8FZ
**Web:** www.avnet.com
**Reg No:** 3538262 **Estd:** 1995 Private Limited Company
**Line of Business:** Computer software (development)
**Export Sales:** £27,269,000
**Issued Capital:** £20,000,002
**Directors:** Ms B Reimann, M R Mccoy, G A Watt
**Responsibilities**
**HR:** Margaret Duke *(Human Resources Manager)*
**Branches:** Tenva Ts Holdings Limited, 2 St. Crispin Way, Rossendale, Lancashire BB4 4PW
**US SIC:** 6711, 5065, 7372
**UK SIC:** 83962, 61500, 83940
**Auditors:** KPMG LLP

| | 29-06-13 | 29-06-12 | 02-06-11 |
|---|---|---|---|
| TO | 302,990,000 | 697,514,000 | 532,466,000 |
| P/L | (8,862,000) | 1,106,000 | 1,586,000 |
| NW | 12,162,000 | (8,008,000) | (7,140,000) |
| WC | N/A | (101,821,000) | (98,532,000) |
| Emp. | 328 | 648 | 725 |

DUNS 76-722-4470

## Teparay Precision Sheet Metal Ltd

1-5 Hainault Business Park Fowler Road, Ilford, Essex IG6 3UT
**Tel:** 02085-011222 **Fax:** 02085-011888
**Web:** www.tpsm.co.uk
**Reg No:** 2596921 **VAT No:** 594885077
**Estd:** 1986 Private Limited Company
**Line of Business:** General mechanical engineering
**Issued Capital:** £745
**Directors:** R D Belcher, R L North
**Co. Secretary:** Terence Belcher
**Responsibilities**
**Senior:** Zaffar Iqbal *(Manager)*
**HR:** Claire Gonzalez *(Human Resources Coordinator)*
**US SIC:** 7399 **UK SIC:** 83954
**Auditors:** Raffingers Stuart
**Bankers:** Barclays Bank Plc (20-44-22)

| | 31-12-13 | 31-12-12 | 31-12-11 |
|---|---|---|---|
| TO | N/A | N/A | 7,346,640 |
| P/L | N/A | N/A | 459,319 |
| NW | 1,085,045 | 1,170,338 | 1,042,443 |
| WC | 506,954 | 468,378 | 122,868 |

DUNS 77-097-5589

## Tequila Uk

239 Old Marylebone Road, London NW1 5QT
**Fax:** 020-7557-6111
**Web:** www.tequila-uk.com
**Reg No:** 2677234 **Estd:** 1993 Private Limited Company
**Line of Business:** Management and business consultants
**Trading Style:** Tequila London
**Issued Capital:** £2
**Directors:** S G Price, P Fothergill
**Co. Secretary:** Mrs Sally Bray
**US SIC:** 7392 **UK SIC:** 83951
**Bankers:** HSBC Bank plc (40-03-09)

| | 31-12-13 | 31-12-12 | 31-12-11 |
|---|---|---|---|
| TA | 861 | 861 | 861 |
| NW | 861 | 861 | 861 |

DUNS 84-698-3869

## Teradata (Uk) Ltd

(**Subsidiary of:** Teradata Bermuda Operation Holdings Ulc)
206-216 Marylebone Road, London NW1 6LY
**Tel:** 02075353602
**Web:** www.teradata.com
**Reg No:** 6239196 **Estd:** 2007 Private Limited Company
**Line of Business:** Computer services
**Issued Capital:** £3,375,002
**Directors:** C J Armitage, E A Hughes
**Co. Secretary:** Jonathan Steel
**US SIC:** 7379 **UK SIC:** 83940
**Auditors:** Blick Rothenberg LLP

| | 31-12-13 | 31-12-12 | 31-12-11 |
|---|---|---|---|
| TO | 66,290,000 | 62,922,000 | 64,105,000 |
| P/L | 1,243,000 | 106,000 | (1,042,000) |
| NW | 3,231,000 | 1,190,000 | (518,000) |
| WC | 3,336,000 | 1,229,000 | (210,000) |
| Emp. | 232 | 210 | 174 |

DUNS 77-950-5697

## Terasaki Electric (Europe) Ltd

(**Subsidiary of:** Terasaki Electric Co. Ltd.)
79-80 Beardmore Way, Clydebank, Dunbartonshire G81 4HT
**Tel:** 01419529246 **Fax:** 01419-529246
**Web:** www.terasaki.co.uk
**Reg No:** 0307759SC **VAT No:** 290369147
**Estd:** 2006 Private Limited Company
**Line of Business:** Manufacture of other electrical equipment not elsewhere classified
**Export Sales:** £19,369,788
**Trading Style:** Terasaki
**Issued Capital:** £999,000
**Directors:** T Craig, H Noguchi, Mrs G T Smith, M Suto, Y Nishimura
**Co. Secretary:** Vaughan Turner
**US SIC:** 3629, 5065
**UK SIC:** 34350, 61500
**Auditors:** Ernst & Young LLP
**Bankers:** Clydesdale Bank Plc (82-48-08)

| | 31-03-14 | 31-03-13 | 31-03-12 |
|---|---|---|---|
| TO | 25,507,296 | 22,127,558 | 22,885,146 |
| P/L | 1,332,501 | 771,596 | 1,047,929 |
| NW | 8,426,154 | 7,406,261 | 6,817,814 |
| WC | 8,020,278 | 7,018,727 | 6,362,908 |
| Emp. | 126 | 122 | 123 |

DUNS 23-584-4797 **Imp**

## Terberg D T S (U K) Ltd

Lowfields Way, Elland, West Yorkshire HX5 9HD
**Web:** www.terbergdts.co.uk
**Reg No:** 3582151 **Estd:** 2000 Private Limited Company
**Line of Business:** Commercial vehicle servicing repairs parts & accessories
**Issued Capital:** £100,000
**Directors:** A N Couper, G J Terberg
**Co. Secretary:** Nigel Chubb
**Responsibilities**
**HR:** Margaret Small *(Human Resources Manager)*
**US SIC:** 3713, 5084
**UK SIC:** 35201, 61490
**Auditors:** Fairhurst
**Bankers:** HSBC Bank plc (40-23-05)

| | 31-12-13 | 31-12-12 | 31-12-11 |
|---|---|---|---|
| TO | 28,090,648 | 33,075,921 | 23,524,240 |
| P/L | 2,882,734 | 2,385,359 | 1,121,871 |
| NW | 5,944,418 | 5,158,848 | 3,715,459 |
| WC | (310,002) | 1,952,991 | 1,504,241 |
| Emp. | 84 | 65 | 55 |

DUNS 52-037-9173 **Imp**

## Terberg Matec U K Ltd

Leacroft Road, Birchwood, Warrington, Cheshire WA3 6PJ
**Tel:** 01925283905
**Web:** www.terbergmatec.com
**Reg No:** 3404297 **VAT No:** 560878510
**Estd:** 1997 Private Limited Company
**Line of Business:** Refuse collection
**Issued Capital:** £100,000
**Principals:** T J Conlon *(Managing)*, G Terberg, W Marzano, R D Colby
**Co. Secretary:** Rodger Dekker
**Responsibilities**
**Sales:** Bob Doust *(Commercial Manager, Truck-Moun)*
**HR:** Michelle King *(Training Coordinator)*, Dawn Patel *(Training Coordinator)*
**Fleet:** Gary Fisher *(Transport Manager)*
**Branches:** Terberg Matec U K Ltd, Highgrounds Road, Worksop, Nottinghamshire S80 3AT
**US SIC:** 4953, 7539
**UK SIC:** 92110, 67100
**Auditors:** Fairhurst
**Bankers:** HSBC Bank plc (40-45-24)

| | 31-12-13 | 31-12-12 | 31-12-11 |
|---|---|---|---|
| TO | 31,741,896 | 29,173,843 | 22,453,580 |
| P/L | 1,538,645 | 1,273,481 | 1,493,228 |
| NW | 5,929,323 | 5,284,840 | 5,237,999 |
| WC | 4,840,824 | 4,286,757 | 4,038,276 |
| Emp. | 161 | 173 | 157 |

DUNS 23-583-2248 **Imp**

## Tercet Precision Ltd

(**Subsidiary of:** Tercet Holdings Ltd)
Millarston Industrial Estate, Paisley, Renfrewshire PA1 2XR
**Tel:** 01418874153
**Web:** www.tercet.co.uk
**Reg No:** 0186797SC **Estd:** 1998 Private Limited Company
**Line of Business:** Fabricators
**Issued Capital:** £164,746
**Managing Director:** A H Burns
**Responsibilities**
**Finance:** Valerie Docherty *(CFO)*, Paul Gibb *(Senior Finance Administrator)*
**HR:** Gerry Coyle *(Human Resources Manager)*
**Operations:** Audrey Burns *(Operations Director)*
**Engineering:** Raymond Bolland *(Manufacturing Engineer)*
**US SIC:** 8911 **UK SIC:** 83701
**Auditors:** McLay McAlister & McGibbon
**Bankers:** Bank Of Scotland (80-91-27)

| | 31-03-14 | 31-03-13 | 31-03-12 |
|---|---|---|---|
| TA | 3,002,043 | 3,051,430 | 3,168,990 |
| NW | 1,604,000 | 1,565,495 | 1,538,386 |
| WC | 805,816 | 725,790 | 870,154 |

DUNS 29-573-6334

## Terence O'Rourke Ltd

(**Subsidiary of:** Terence o'Rourke Holdings Ltd)
Everdene House, Deansleigh Road, Bournemouth, Dorset BH7 7DU
**Web:** www.torltd.co.uk
**Reg No:** 1935454 **VAT No:** 905095727
**Estd:** 1985 Private Limited Company
**Line of Business:** Town and city planning
**Issued Capital:** £160,962
**Directors:** D R Ellis, H B Morris, Ms J Mulliner, Ms C F Simpson, R W Burton, T L Hancock
**Co. Secretary:** Craig Hardman
**Responsibilities**
**Senior:** Amanda Balson *(Manager)*
**IT:** Sarah Beale *(Information and Communications)*, Stewart Mccutcheon *(IT Manager)*
**Branches:** Terence O'rourke Ltd, Everdene House, Deansleigh Road, Bournemouth, Dorset BH7 7DU
**US SIC:** 8911, 7399
**UK SIC:** 83701, 83954
**Auditors:** BDO Stoy Hayward LLP
**Bankers:** The Royal Bank Of Scotland Plc (16-14-16)

| | 31-03-14 | 31-03-13 | 31-03-12 |
|---|---|---|---|
| TO | 7,553,039 | 7,044,587 | 7,463,343 |
| P/L | 684,134 | 196,169 | 785,353 |
| NW | 1,332,165 | 1,972,625 | 1,828,506 |
| WC | 1,381,547 | 1,980,593 | 1,874,985 |
| Emp. | 72 | 86 | 89 |

DUNS 22-907-4109 **Imp-Exp**

## Terex Equipment Ltd

(**Subsidiary of:** Terex Corporation)
Newhouse Industrial Estate, Newhouse, Motherwell, Lanarkshire ML1 5RY
**Tel:** 01698-732121
**Web:** www.terex.co.uk
**Reg No:** 0086323SC **VAT No:** 603484652
**Estd:** 1984 Private Limited Company
**Line of Business:** Manufacturers and suppliers of industrial machinery
**Export Sales:** £119,281,000
**Trading Style:** Tdl Equipment
**Issued Capital:** £23,439,000
**Directors:** P Douglas, S D Villanueva, C Lockwood
**Co. Secretary:** Simon Villanueva
**Responsibilities**
**Senior:** Robert Isaman *(Manager)*, Phillip Widman *(Manager)*
**Sales:** John Rotherford *(Sales Director)*
**Health & Safety:** Gary Maine-Watts *(Health & Safety Officer)*
**Branches:** Terex Equipment Ltd - Tdl Equipment, Wentworth Way, Wentworth Industrial Park, Tankersley, S75 3DH South Yorkshire
**US SIC:** 3559, 5199
**UK SIC:** 32863, 61900
**Auditors:** PricewaterhouseCoopers LLP
**Bankers:** HSBC Bank plc (40-22-47)

| | 31-12-13 | 31-12-12 | 31-12-11 |
|---|---|---|---|
| TO | 126,850,000 | 207,694,000 | 194,688,000 |
| P/L | (1,632,000) | 7,794,000 | 1,409,000 |
| NW | 34,655,000 | 37,080,000 | 30,874,000 |
| WC | 25,273,000 | 29,676,000 | 23,551,000 |
| Emp. | 444 | 498 | 520 |

DUNS 21-456-7273 **Imp**

## Terex Gb Ltd

(**Subsidiary of:** Terex Corporation)
200 Coalisland Road, Dungannon, Co Tyrone BT71 4DR
**Tel:** 02887740701 **Fax:** 02887747231
**Web:** www.terex.co.uk
**Reg No:** 0006669NI **VAT No:** 253117487
**Estd:** 1966 Private Limited Company
**Line of Business:** Crushing plants
**Trading Style:** Powerscreen, Terex Uk Service Centre
**Issued Capital:** £240,000
**Directors:** R M De Feo, K P Bradley
**Co. Secretary:** Eric Cohen
**Responsibilities**
**Senior:** Damien Power *(General Manager)*
**IT:** Allan Patterson *(IT Manager)*
**Branches:** TEREX GB LIMITED: Mammoth Street, Coalville, LE67 3GN, LEICESTERSHIRE.
**US SIC:** 1795, 3559
**UK SIC:** 50000, 32863
**Auditors:** PricewaterhouseCoopers LLP
**Bankers:** The Bank Of Ireland (90-48-51)

| | 31-12-13 | 31-12-12 | 31-12-11 |
|---|---|---|---|
| TO | 282,202,000 | 286,973,000 | 308,366,000 |
| P/L | 42,464,000 | 36,947,000 | 36,000,000 |
| NW | 157,854,000 | 127,423,000 | 103,144,000 |
| WC | 170,090,000 | 139,621,000 | 113,517,000 |
| Emp. | 1,017 | 847 | 278 |

DUNS 21-809-4969 **Exp**

## Terex Pegson Ltd

(**Subsidiary of:** Terex Corporation)
Mammoth Street, Coalville, Leicestershire LE67 3GN
**Tel:** 01530-518600 **Fax:** 01530-518618
**Web:** www.terexpegson.com
**Reg No:** 0258409 **Estd:** 1931 Private Limited Company
**Line of Business:** Engineers (general)
**Export Markets:** European Union (E U); Africa
**Issued Capital:** £2,530,782
**Directors:** K P Bradley, R M Defeo
**Co. Secretary:** Eric Cohen
**Responsibilities**
**Senior:** Simon Croker *(Manager)*, Andrew Dakin *(Manager)*, Phillip Widman *(Manager)*
**Marketing:** J Sault *(Marketing Manager)*
**IT:** Lee Axten *(IS/IT Lead)*
**Purchasing:** E O'Connell *(Purchasing Manager)*
**US SIC:** 3559, 3532
**UK SIC:** 32863, 32510
**Auditors:** PricewaterhouseCoopers LLP
**Bankers:** HSBC Bank plc (40-22-47)

| | 31-12-13 | 31-12-12 | 31-12-11 |
|---|---|---|---|
| TO | 12,410,000 | 13,006,000 | 11,796,000 |
| P/L | 6,399,000 | 4,929,000 | 2,416,000 |
| NW | 101,349,000 | 96,575,000 | 92,932,000 |
| WC | 99,122,000 | 94,315,000 | 91,742,000 |
| Emp. | 72 | 54 | 49 |

DUNS 21-832-7583 **Imp-Exp**

## Terex United Kingdom Ltd

(**Subsidiary of:** Terex Corporation)
Central Boulevard, Prologis Park, Coventry, West Midlands CV6 4BX
**Tel:** 02476339459 **Fax:** 024-7633-9500
**Web:** www.terexce.com
**Reg No:** 0494347 **VAT No:** 272328070
**Estd:** 1937 Private Limited Company
**Line of Business:** Manufacture of pumps
**Export Markets:** E U, Africa, South & South East Asia, Australasia, U.S.A., Canada
**Issued Capital:** £618,300
**Directors:** R M Defeo, G W Ellis, K P Bradley
**Co. Secretary:** Eric Cohen
**Responsibilities**
**Senior:** Phillip Widman *(Manager)*
**Branches:** Terex United Kingdom Ltd, Central Boulevard, Coventry, West Midlands CV6 4BX
**US SIC:** 3561, 3532
**UK SIC:** 32870, 32510
**Auditors:** PricewaterhouseCoopers LLP
**Bankers:** HSBC Bank plc (40-22-47)

| | 31-12-13 | 31-12-12 | 31-12-11 |
|---|---|---|---|
| TO | 128,681,000 | 123,286,000 | 140,116,000 |
| P/L | (158,000) | 6,767,000 | (7,530,000) |
| NW | (23,129,000) | (23,013,000) | (30,023,000) |
| WC | (27,263,000) | (28,007,000) | (31,760,000) |
| Emp. | 448 | 463 | 363 |

DUNS 73-677-8395 **Exp**

## Terinex Ltd

(**Subsidiary of:** Clear Sky Catering Consumables Ltd)
Hammond Road, Elm Farm Industrial Estate, Bedford, Bedfordshire MK41 0ND
**Tel:** 01234-364411 **Fax:** 01234-271486
**Web:** www.terinex.co.uk
**Reg No:** 4937132 **Estd:** 2003 Private Limited Company
**Line of Business:** Other manufacturing not elsewhere classified
**Export Sales:** £5,268,392
**Issued Capital:** £100
**Directors:** P Garside, Ms A C Brewster, D Simpson, P Wightman
**Co. Secretary:** Paul Wightman
**Responsibilities**
**Senior:** Myles McCann *(Warehouse Manager)*, Paul Whiteman *(Chairman)*, Paul Wrightman *(Group Managing Director)*
**Finance:** Julian Littleton *(Finance Manager)*

**Marketing:** Mark Hallam *(Marketing Manager)*
**Sales:** Tracy Mowbray *(Key Account Manager)*, Thierry Soto *(Export Manager)*
**Admin:** Julia Day *(Office Manager)*, Jenny Pegg *(Office Manager)*
**Purchasing:** Frances Whitworth *(Purchasing & Supply Chain Mana)*
**Fleet:** Myles McCann *(Warehouse Manager)*
**US SIC:** 3999, 3334
**UK SIC:** 49590, 22451
**Auditors:** Wellers

| | 31-05-13 | 31-05-12 | 31-05-11 |
|---|---|---|---|
| TO | 10,280,192 | 11,809,174 | 10,365,876 |
| P/L | 1,093,175 | 1,519,760 | 1,475,941 |
| NW | 3,247,894 | 2,985,556 | 2,381,146 |
| WC | 2,675,823 | 2,521,308 | 2,026,184 |
| Emp. | 92 | 80 | 68 |

DUNS 21-605-4500
## Terminus
40 Liverpool Street, London EC2M 7QN
**Tel:** 02076187400
**Web:** www.andazdining.com
**Estd:** 1999
**Line of Business:** Restaurant - french
**Responsibilities**
**Senior:** Angnieszka Szewczyk *(Manager)*
**US SIC:** 5812 **UK SIC:** 66110
**Employees:** 99

DUNS 21-326-9074
## Termoncanice Primary School
Rathbrady Road, Limavady, Co Londonderry BT49 9BH
**Tel:** 028-7772-2885
**Web:** www.termoncanice.limavady.ni.sch.uk
**Estd:** 2002 Proprietorship
**Line of Business:** Schools (local authority)
**Proprietor:** J Coyle
**Responsibilities**
**Senior:** Christina Dohrtey *(Head Teacher)*
**US SIC:** 8211 **UK SIC:** 93200
**Employees:** 98

DUNS 21-318-3775
## Termrim Construction Ltd
(**Subsidiary of:** Patrick Construction Group Ltd)
1 Pellon Place, Bradley Business Park Dyson Wood Way, Huddersfield, West Yorkshire HD2 1GT
**Tel:** 01484-547525
**Web:** www.termrim.co.uk
**Reg No:** 1263512 **VAT No:** 378695873
**Estd:** 1976 Private Limited Company
**Line of Business:** Building construction contractors
**Trading Style:** Termrim Construction Ltd
**Issued Capital:** £10,000
**Directors:** S J Taylor, G C Bird
**Co. Secretary:** Ms Beverley Rockett
**Branches:** Termrim Construction Ltd, 28 Cliff Road, Leeds, West Yorkshire LS6 2ET
**US SIC:** 1522, 1541
**UK SIC:** 50100
**Auditors:** RSM Bentley Jennison
**Bankers:** National Westminster Bank Plc (53-61-07)

| | 31-12-13 | 31-12-12 | 31-12-11 |
|---|---|---|---|
| TO | 5,820,678 | 7,128,075 | 7,172,874 |
| P/L | 148,128 | 229,983 | 137,788 |
| NW | 4,303,361 | 4,311,280 | 5,154,605 |
| WC | 4,260,020 | 4,264,559 | 5,103,341 |
| Emp. | 51 | 71 | 76 |

DUNS 22-201-3638
## Terra Firma Capital Partners Ltd
(**Subsidiary of:** London 58 Limited)
2 More London Riverside, London SE1 2AP
**Tel:** 02070 159 500 **Fax:** 02070 159 501
**Web:** www.terrafirma.com
**Reg No:** 4219556 **Estd:** 1901 Private Limited Company
**Line of Business:** Investment consultants
**Issued Capital:** £5,401
**Directors:** Ms D J Pluck, T J Pryce, R N Barr
**Co. Secretary:** William Burnand
**Responsibilities**
**Senior:** Arjan Breure *(CEO / Managing Director)*, Damian Darragh *(Manager)*, Stefan Thiele *(Operations Manager)*, Steven Webber *(Financial Director)*, Julie Williamson *(Financial Director)*
**Facilities:** Lee Colvin *(Facilities Manager)*
**Operations:** Lorenzo Levi *(Operational Managing Director)*
**US SIC:** 6111 **UK SIC:** 81501
**Auditors:** Deloitte LLP

| | 31-03-14 | 31-03-13 | 31-03-12 |
|---|---|---|---|
| TA | 14,714,000 | 13,751,000 | 11,194,000 |
| P/L | 2,964,000 | 4,465,000 | 2,476,000 |
| NW | 3,335,000 | 4,081,000 | 3,818,000 |
| WC | 3,973,000 | 4,440,000 | 3,458,000 |
| Emp. | 85 | 91 | 84 |

DUNS 21-847-7485
## Terrapin Ltd
(**Subsidiary of:** Dale Acquisitions Ltd)
Bomnd Avenue, Bletchley, Bletchley, Milton Keynes, Buckinghamshire MK1 1JJ
**Web:** www.terrapin-ltd.co.uk
**Reg No:** 8131233 **Estd:** 1961 Private Limited Company
**Line of Business:** Development and selling of real estate
**Issued Capital:** £1,000
**Director:** S D Dale
**Responsibilities**
**Senior:** Warren Eyres *(Manager)*
**US SIC:** 6552 **UK SIC:** 85000

| | 31-07-13 |
|---|---|
| TA | 1,000 |
| NW | 1,000 |

DUNS 34-692-4731
## Terrapinn Ltd
(**Subsidiary of:** Terrapinn Limited)
Wren House, London EC1N 8EL
**Tel:** 02072421548 **Fax:** 02072421508
**Web:** www.terrapinn.com
**Reg No:** 2778638 **VAT No:** 625821051
**Estd:** 1987 Private Limited Company
**Line of Business:** Activities of conference organisers
**Export Sales:** £5,066,799
**Issued Capital:** £2
**Directors:** S D Willis, A Steel, A Ewer
**Co. Secretary:** Gregory Hitchen
**Responsibilities**
**Senior:** Jordan Hooper *(General Manager)*, Richard Ireland *(Chief Executive Officer - Asia)*, Kellie Jenkins *(General Manager)*, Nia Jones *(Operations Director)*, Issa Mauthoor *(General Manager)*, John Pozoglou *(Manager)*, Lisa Weiner *(Manager)*
**Finance:** Pregasen Francis *(Finance Manager)*, Osborne Marques *(Financial Controller)*
**Marketing:** Alina Fisher *(Marketing Manager)*, Sharon Roessen *(Chief Marketing Officer)*, Rebecca Sloan *(Marketing Director)*
**Sales:** Bladimir Estevez *(Director of Sales)*, Philip Kwok *(Business Development Manager)*, Kelly Lim *(Sales Manager)*, Layal Wehbe *(Sales Manager)*
**Admin:** Jackie Brightman *(Office Manager)*
**IT:** Paul Charters *(IT Manager)*
**Health & Safety:** Jackie Brightman *(Office Manager)*
**Facilities:** Jackie Brightman *(Office Manager)*
**US SIC:** 7999, 6531
**UK SIC:** 97913, 83400
**Auditors:** Ernst & Young LLP
**Bankers:** Lloyds TSB Bank plc (30-94-31)

| | 31-12-13 | 31-12-12 | 31-12-11 |
|---|---|---|---|
| TO | 8,805,583 | 11,174,613 | 14,535,161 |
| P/L | (12,772) | 442,893 | 803,247 |
| NW | (26,124) | 1,208,762 | 946,344 |
| WC | (109,160) | 1,106,131 | 781,209 |
| Emp. | 58 | 73 | 103 |

DUNS 23-364-1778
## Terraquest Group Ltd
(**Subsidiary of:** Mears Group Plc)
Burnt Tree Island, Tipton, West Midlands DY4 7UF
**Tel:** 01215202100
**Web:** www.terraquest.co.uk
**Reg No:** 2852722 **Estd:** 1993 Private Limited Company
**Line of Business:** Information services
**Issued Capital:** £50,000
**Directors:** B R Westran, Mears Group Plc
**Branches:** Terraquest Group Ltd, Manchester Business Park, 3000 Aviator Way, Manchester M22 5TG
**US SIC:** 6711, 7399
**UK SIC:** 83962, 83954
**Auditors:** Flint & Thompson

| | 31-12-13 | 31-12-12 | 31-12-11 |
|---|---|---|---|
| TA | 1,174 | 1,174 | 1,174 |
| NW | 1,174 | 1,174 | 1,174 |

DUNS 73-292-5818
## Terratruck Distribution Services Ltd
34-36 Gipsy Lane, Leicester, Leicestershire LE4 6TD
**Tel:** 01162662456 **Fax:** 01162-610304
**Web:** www.terratruck.co.uk
**Reg No:** 4566361 **Estd:** 2002 Private Limited Company
**Line of Business:** Renting of construction and civil engineering machinery and equipment
**Issued Capital:** £34,004
**Directors:** S J Heanaghan, C B Heath
**Co. Secretary:** Stephen Porter
**Branches:** Terratruck Distribution Services Ltd, 87-89 Portland Road, Nottingham, Nottinghamshire NG15 7SF
**US SIC:** 7394 **UK SIC:** 84000

**Bankers:** Barclays Bank Plc (20-49-08)

| | 31-12-13 | 31-12-12 | 31-12-11 |
|---|---|---|---|
| TA | 2,493,262 | 2,491,519 | 2,439,872 |
| NW | 757,887 | 588,987 | 933,770 |
| WC | 179,787 | (40,896) | 303,300 |

DUNS 28-980-7695 **Imp**
## The Terrence Higgins Trust
Acorn House 314-320, Gray's Inn Road, London WC1X 8DP
**Tel:** 020-7812-1600
**Web:** www.tht.org.uk
**Reg No:** 1778149 **Estd:** 1983 Private Company Limited By Guarantee
**Line of Business:** Other human health activities
**Directors:** P T Jenkins, G A Wills, A J Babajee, Mrs J S Morton, Ms C Minchington, R A Glick, Professor R F Miller, W G Roberts
**Co. Secretary:** Mrs Hannah Bodek
**Responsibilities**
**Senior:** Neil Beasley *(Trustee)*, Ben Bradshaw *(Trustee)*, Donald Branch *(Director, Service Development)*, Samuel De Silva *(Chair of Audit Committee)*, Paul Flowers *(Trustee)*, Victoria Gamble *(Centre Manager)*, Rosemary Gillespie *(Chief Executive Officer)*, Tom Greenwood *(Centre Manager)*, Karen Jochelson *(Triustee)*, Mike Marchant *(Trustee)*, Glen Mendes *(Senior Manager)*
**Finance:** Samuel De Silva *(Chair of Audit Committee)*, Sonya Trivedy *(Head of Fundraising)*
**Marketing:** Garry Brough *(Membership and Involvement Off)*, Dominic Edwardes *(Executive Director of Digital)*, Sonya Trivedy *(Head of Fundraising)*
**Sales:** Kerry Blair *(Executive Director of Sales an)*
**IT:** Dominic Edwardes *(Executive Director of Digital)*
**Health & Safety:** Cary James *(Head of Health Promotion)*
**Operations:** Adam Wilkinson *(Operations Manager)*
**Engineering:** Donald Branch *(Director, Service Development)*
**Branches:** The Terrence Higgins Trust, 29-30 Lower Essex Street, Birmingham, West Midlands B5 6SN
**US SIC:** 8091, 8321
**UK SIC:** 95200, 96111
**Auditors:** Buzzacott
**Bankers:** National Westminster Bank Plc (50-41-06)

| | 31-03-14 | 31-03-13 | 31-03-12 |
|---|---|---|---|
| TO | 19,646,000 | 20,107,000 | 20,343,000 |
| P/L | 258,000 | 332,000 | 995,000 |
| NW | 7,367,000 | 6,550,000 | 6,551,000 |
| WC | 1,571,000 | 1,585,000 | 1,342,000 |
| Emp. | 289 | 307 | 303 |

DUNS 21-605-5909
## Territorial Army
Glencryan Road, Cumbernauld, Glasgow, Lanarkshire G67 2UH
**Tel:** 01236721060
**Estd:** 1983
**Line of Business:** Defence activities
**Proprietor:** Captain D Somerville
**Responsibilities**
**Senior:** Dave Somerville *(Manager)*
**US SIC:** 8999 **UK SIC:** 83954
**Employees:** 63

DUNS 21-920-6984
## Terry & Thomas (Construction) Ltd
34 Redfern Road, Birmingham, West Midlands B11 2BH
**Tel:** 0121-707-7566 **Fax:** 0121-707-7566
**Web:** www.isl-wasteservices.co.uk
**Reg No:** 1227167 **Estd:** 1975 Private Limited Company
**Line of Business:** Road haulage and transport services
**Issued Capital:** £500
**Director:** A Grant
**Co. Secretary:** Ms Teresa Grant
**US SIC:** 5039 **UK SIC:** 61300
**Auditors:** Thursfield & Co
**Bankers:** Allied Irish Bank (gb) (23-83-93)

| | 31-10-13 | 31-10-12 | 31-10-11 |
|---|---|---|---|
| TA | 1,101,874 | 1,132,881 | 1,126,067 |
| NW | 546,403 | 461,963 | 417,103 |
| WC | 49,181 | (42,663) | (45,432) |

DUNS 29-824-6893 **Exp**
## Terry Farrell & Partners Ltd
(**Subsidiary of:** Terry Farrell Holdings Ltd)
7 Hatton Street, London NW8 8PL
**Tel:** 020-7258-3433 **Fax:** 020-7723-7059
**Web:** www.terryfarrell.co.uk
**Reg No:** 2042783 **Estd:** 1986 Private Limited Company
**Line of Business:** Architectural activities
**Export Sales:** £466,395
**Issued Capital:** £100,000

**Principals:** Sir T Farrell *(Chairman and Managing)*, M Stowell
**Co. Secretary:** Sir Terry Farrell
**Responsibilities**
**Senior:** Brian Chantler *(Finance Director)*, John Letherland *(Manager)*
**Finance:** Brian Chantler *(Finance Director)*
**Marketing:** Max Farrell *(Marketing Director)*
**US SIC:** 7399, 8911
**UK SIC:** 83954, 83701
**Auditors:** The Leaman Partnership LLP
**Bankers:** Barclays Bank Plc (20-36-47)

| | 31-03-14 | 31-03-13 | 31-03-12 |
|---|---|---|---|
| TO | 4,068,830 | 5,398,440 | 4,888,848 |
| P/L | 1,014,705 | 261,020 | (108,078) |
| NW | 1,025,177 | 478,482 | 395,153 |
| WC | 1,024,450 | 173,325 | 163,712 |
| Emp. | N/A | 58 | 54 |

DUNS 22-583-5545 **Imp-Exp**
## Terry Group Ltd
(**Subsidiary of:** Heat-Pumps & Engineering (Knutsford) Ltd)
Longridge Trading Estate, Knutsford, Cheshire WA16 8PR
**Tel:** 08453655366
**Web:** www.terrylifts.co.uk
**Reg No:** 1683339 **VAT No:** 370551073
**Estd:** 1948 Private Limited Company
**Line of Business:** Agents specialising in the sale of particular products or ranges of products not elsewhere classified
**Export Markets:** Worldwide
**Issued Capital:** £1,000
**Principals:** P Morrey *(Managing)*, G J Gnyp, K J Goodacre, Ms S V Maddox, J G Mcsweeney
**Co. Secretary:** Mrs Elizabeth Turnbull
**US SIC:** 5199, 3534
**UK SIC:** 61900, 32553
**Auditors:** Baker Tilly UK Audit LLP
**Bankers:** Barclays Bank Plc (20-55-34)

| | 31-03-14 | 31-03-13 | 31-03-12 |
|---|---|---|---|
| TO | 10,384,188 | 10,496,965 | 10,853,224 |
| P/L | 303,263 | 342,960 | 634,236 |
| NW | 961,195 | 975,589 | 963,702 |
| WC | 780,220 | 749,081 | 764,171 |
| Emp. | 89 | 88 | 89 |

DUNS 29-545-4409
## Tersus Consultancy Ltd
(**Subsidiary of:** Oakjet Ltd)
Unit C Prospect House, The Hyde, Brighton, East Sussex BN2 4JE
**Tel:** 01273621100
**Web:** www.tersusgroup.co.uk
**Reg No:** 1912115 **Estd:** 1985 Private Limited Company
**Line of Business:** Asbestos products & removal
**Issued Capital:** £54,450
**Directors:** Dr A Hamed, A D Peck
**Branches:** Tersus Consultancy Ltd, 12 Dunns Close, Nuneaton, Warwickshire CV11 4NF
**US SIC:** 1799, 8911
**UK SIC:** 50000, 83701
**Auditors:** Clemence Hoar Cummings
**Bankers:** National Westminster Bank Plc (60-18-01)

| | 31-03-14 | 31-03-13 | 31-03-12 |
|---|---|---|---|
| TO | N/A | N/A | 5,575,228 |
| P/L | N/A | N/A | 364,429 |
| NW | 2,564,816 | 2,459,958 | 2,361,878 |
| WC | 2,494,466 | 2,371,371 | 2,263,073 |

DUNS 23-364-9834
## Terumo Bct Ltd.
(**Subsidiary of:** Terumo Corporation)
Old Belfast Road, Millbrook, Larne, Co Antrim BT40 2SH
**Tel:** 028-2827-3631
**Web:** www.ivex.co.uk
**Reg No:** 0049717NI **Estd:** 2004 Private Limited Company
**Line of Business:** Manufacturers of pharmaceutical products
**Export Sales:** £23,149,747
**Trading Style:** Terumo Bct
**Issued Capital:** £2,575,000
**Directors:** S C Henderson, C Rinehardt
**Co. Secretary:** Stephen Brunt
**Responsibilities**
**Senior:** James McKelvey *(Manager)*
**Sales:** James McKelvey *(Manager)*
**IT:** Craig O' Flaherty *(Computer Manager)*
**Engineering:** Darren Mitchell *(Production Manager)*
**US SIC:** 2834, 5199
**UK SIC:** 25700, 61900
**Auditors:** KPMG
**Bankers:** The Bank Of Ireland (90-21-27)

| | 31-03-14 | 31-03-13 | 31-03-12 |
|---|---|---|---|
| TO | 27,226,136 | 22,685,525 | 26,554,777 |
| P/L | 2,012,208 | 1,921,713 | 1,944,050 |
| NW | 6,686,039 | 5,006,116 | 3,524,849 |
| WC | 9,804,724 | 1,474,877 | 660,682 |
| Emp. | 279 | 230 | 231 |

DUNS 29-754-1716 **Exp**
## Tes Global Ltd
(**Subsidiary of:** Tpg Capital Llp)
26 Red Lion Square, London WC1R 4HQ
**Tel:** 020-3194-3000 **Fax:** 02077823202
**Web:** www.tsleducation.com
**Reg No:** 2017289 **VAT No:** 550684731
**Estd:** 1986 Private Limited Company
**Line of Business:** Publishing of journals and periodicals
**Export Markets:** U S A; European Union (E U)
**Issued Capital:** £10,000
**Director:** Ms L Rogers
**Co. Secretary:** Matthew O'Sullivan
**Responsibilities**
**Marketing:** Somik Halder *(Digital Marketing Manager)*
**Sales:** Duncan Fairbrother *(Account Manager)*
**Branches:** Tes Global Ltd, Scott House, 10 South St. Andrew Street, Edinburgh, Midlothian EH2 2AZ
**US SIC:** 2721, 7379
**UK SIC:** 47522, 83940
**Auditors:** PricewaterhouseCoopers LLP
**Bankers:** HSBC Bank plc (40-03-05)

| | 31-08-13 | 31-08-12 | 31-08-11 |
|---|---|---|---|
| TO | 87,560,000 | 73,756,000 | 59,551,000 |
| P/L | 33,574,000 | 24,219,000 | 9,673,000 |
| NW | 45,461,000 | 12,750,000 | (11,358,000) |
| WC | 37,083,000 | 6,679,000 | (15,108,000) |
| Emp. | 281 | 268 | 251 |

DUNS 23-013-6439 **Imp**
## Tes (Ni) Ltd
Unit 16 Kilcronagh Business Park, Cookstown, Co Tyrone BT80 9HJ
**Fax:** 028-8676-9732
**Web:** www.tes-ni.com
**Reg No:** 0037020NI **VAT No:** 743694602
**Estd:** 1999 Private Limited Company
**Line of Business:** Manufacturers and wholesalers of electrical products
**Trading Style:** Tes
**Issued Capital:** £272,002
**Directors:** N J Mccracken, B G Taylor
**Co. Secretary:** Noel Mc Cracken
**Responsibilities**
**Senior:** Joan Laverty *(Office Manager)*
**Finance:** Sean Wylie *(Accountant)*
**Admin:** Joan Laverty *(Office Manager)*
**US SIC:** 3629, 3679
**UK SIC:** 34350, 34542
**Auditors:** ASM (M) Ltd
**Bankers:** Ulster Bank Ltd (98-04-50)

| | 30-09-13 | 30-09-12 | 30-09-11 |
|---|---|---|---|
| TO | 12,019,103 | 10,174,283 | 7,105,919 |
| P/L | 1,016,585 | 585,528 | 328,381 |
| NW | 2,044,663 | 1,407,676 | 1,307,113 |
| WC | 976,571 | 508,164 | 563,078 |
| Emp. | 143 | 129 | 62 |

DUNS 23-328-3365 **Imp-Exp**
## Tesab Engineering Ltd
(**Subsidiary of:** L C Holmqvist Ab)
Unit 9 Gortrush Industrial Estate, Omagh, Co Tyrone BT78 5EJ
**Tel:** 028-8225-2781
**Web:** www.tesab.com
**Reg No:** 0026214NI **VAT No:** 516885906
**Estd:** 1992 Private Limited Company
**Line of Business:** Engineers (general)
**Export Markets:** Worldwide
**Issued Capital:** £50,000
**Director:** L C Holmkvist
**Co. Secretary:** Donald Smyth
**Responsibilities**
**HR:** Rod Campbell *(Production Manager)*
**Health & Safety:** Rod Campbell *(Production Manager)*
**Facilities:** Rod Campbell *(Production Manager)*
**Engineering:** Rod Campbell *(Production Manager)*
**US SIC:** 8911, 3532
**UK SIC:** 83701, 32510
**Auditors:** PFS & Partners Ltd
**Bankers:** The Bank Of Ireland (90-50-02)

| | 30-04-14 | 30-04-13 | 30-04-12 |
|---|---|---|---|
| TO | 17,822,440 | 20,633,903 | 17,239,893 |
| P/L | 57,009 | (66,368) | 10,024 |
| NW | 4,754,711 | 4,720,164 | 4,792,024 |
| WC | 3,551,770 | 3,723,770 | 3,794,441 |
| Emp. | 53 | 58 | 46 |

DUNS 28-966-6117 **Imp-Exp**
## Tesam Distribution Ltd
Shrewsbury Avenue Woodston Business, Centre, Peterborough, Cambridgeshire PE2 7EF
**Tel:** 01733-367500 **Fax:** 01733236278
**Web:** www.tesam.biz
**Reg No:** 1708646 **Estd:** 1983 Private Limited Company
**Line of Business:** Distribution service providers
**Export Markets:** Countries Worldwide
**Issued Capital:** £195,133
**Directors:** S W Smith, A Welch Mbe, M Evans, R A Rotor
**Co. Secretary:** Ms Judy Drew
**US SIC:** 4712 **UK SIC:** 77002
**Auditors:** Gane Jackson Scott
**Bankers:** National Westminster Bank Plc (60-13-14)

| | 30-06-13 | 30-06-12 | 30-06-11 |
|---|---|---|---|
| TO | 14,079,623 | 12,463,668 | 13,197,486 |
| P/L | 381,584 | 1,031,835 | 1,287,406 |
| NW | 1,784,517 | 1,502,105 | 1,461,982 |
| WC | 750,859 | 245,525 | 511,923 |
| Emp. | 99 | 88 | 83 |

DUNS 21-685-4067 **Imp**
## Tesco Plc
New Tesco House, Delamare Road, Waltham Cross, Hertfordshire EN8 9SL
**Tel:** 08456-719-464 **Fax:** 01992-630-794
**Web:** www.tescoplc.com
**Reg No:** 0445790 **Estd:** 1992 Public Limited Company
**Line of Business:** Representative office
**Trading Style:** Tesco
**Issued Capital:** £403,978,703
**Directors:** Ms J A Tammenoms Bakker, Sir R J Broadbent, S J Chambers, A B Ohlsson, G R Bullock, A J Stewart, D J Lewis, K G Hanna
**Co. Secretary:** Paul Moore
**Responsibilities**
**Senior:** Olivia Garfield *(Director)*, Chris Griffith *(Manager)*, Deanna Oppenheimer *(Director)*
**Branches:** Tesco Plc, Hatfield Shopping Centre, 157 Creggan Rd, Londonderry, Co Londonderry BT48 0RX
**US SIC:** 5411 **UK SIC:** 64100
**Auditors:** PricewaterhouseCoopers LLP
**Bankers:** HSBC Bank plc (40-17-13)
**Following financial data are in thousands**

| | 22-02-14 | 23-02-13 | 25-02-12 |
|---|---|---|---|
| TO | 63,557,000 | 64,826,000 | 64,539,000 |
| P/L | 2,259,000 | 1,960,000 | 3,835,000 |
| NW | 10,920,000 | 12,281,000 | 13,157,000 |
| WC | (5,827,000) | (5,889,000) | (6,386,000) |
| Emp. | 510,444 | 537,784 | 519,671 |

DUNS 21-172-6270
## Tesco Underwriting Ltd
London Court, 39 London Road, Reigate, Surrey RH2 9AQ
**Tel:** 01737738000
**Web:** www.tescounderwriting.com
**Reg No:** 6967289 **Estd:** 2009 Private Limited Company
**Line of Business:** Non-life insurance
**Issued Capital:** £166,667,667
**Directors:** R C Townsend, R F Pierce, M N Urmston, M D Thomas, P D Bole, K D Bedlow, G R Carter, A J Clarke
**Co. Secretary:** Ms Rosemary Smith
**Responsibilities**
**Senior:** Stephen Grainge *(Director)*, Darren Mccauley *(Director)*
**US SIC:** 6399 **UK SIC:** 82001
**Auditors:** KPMG Audit PLC
**Bankers:** HSBC Bank plc (40-42-22)

| | 31-12-13 | 31-12-12 | 31-12-11 |
|---|---|---|---|
| TO | 480,500,000 | 617,600,000 | 393,200,000 |
| P/L | 14,800,000 | 28,900,000 | 9,200,000 |
| NW | 143,400,000 | 180,100,000 | 131,700,000 |
| WC | 171,400,000 | (26,100,000) | 81,200,000 |
| Emp. | 368 | 361 | 272 |

DUNS 45-848-8111 **Imp**
## Tesla Exploration International Ltd
(**Subsidiary of:** Tesla Exploration Ltd)
Unit 2, Nix's Hill, Alfreton, Derbyshire DE55 7GN
**Tel:** 01773838950 **Fax:** 01773836492
**Web:** www.teslaexploration.com
**Reg No:** 3195445 **Estd:** 1996 Private Limited Company
**Line of Business:** Service activities incidental to oil and gas extraction excluding surveying
**Export Sales:** £15,984,000
**Trading Style:** Imc Group
**Issued Capital:** £1,000
**Directors:** R R Habiak, S E Craven, C M Rees, D C Cooper, C K Latham
**Co. Secretary:** David Cooper
**Responsibilities**
**Senior:** David Elgie *(Manager)*, Randall Strandberg *(Manager)*, Diane Watson *(Manager)*
**Admin:** Pauline Marshall *(Operations Administrator)*
**US SIC:** 1389 **UK SIC:** 13000
**Auditors:** PricewaterhouseCoopers LLP

| | 31-12-13 | 31-12-12 | 31-12-11 |
|---|---|---|---|
| TO | 19,782,000 | 12,756,000 | 20,157,000 |
| P/L | (5,000) | (2,554,000) | 1,023,000 |
| NW | 2,161,000 | 2,736,000 | 4,846,000 |
| WC | (2,445,000) | (339,000) | 1,645,000 |
| Emp. | 115 | 105 | 103 |

DUNS 42-396-3466 **Imp**
## Tesla Motors Ltd
Kings Chase 107 123, King Street, Maidenhead, Berkshire SL6 1DP
**Tel:** 01628450600
**Web:** www.teslamotors.com
**Reg No:** 4384008 **Estd:** 2009 Private Limited Company
**Line of Business:** Manufacturers of cars
**Export Sales:** £6,186,279
**Issued Capital:** £100
**Directors:** D Ahuja, P Patel, M B Taylor
**Co. Secretary:** Michael Taylor
**Branches:** Tesla Motors Ltd, Wymondham Business Park Chestnut, Wymondham, Norfolk NR18 9SB
**US SIC:** 5511, 7539, 5531
**UK SIC:** 65100, 67100
**Auditors:** PricewaterhouseCoopers LLP
**Bankers:** National Westminster Bank Plc (54-21-06)

| | 31-12-13 | 31-12-12 | 31-12-11 |
|---|---|---|---|
| TO | 6,571,152 | 11,271,319 | 14,191,654 |
| P/L | 192,735 | (155,858) | (133,007) |
| NW | 1,860,267 | 925,123 | 1,160,029 |
| WC | 1,320,765 | 1,464,005 | 1,388,489 |
| Emp. | 61 | 61 | 92 |

DUNS 21-847-1085
## Tessella Holdings Ltd
26 The Quadrant, Abingdon Science Park, Abingdon, Oxfordshire OX14 3YS
**Web:** www.tessella.com
**Reg No:** 8126402 **Estd:** 2012 Private Limited Company
**Line of Business:** Other software consultancy and supply
**Export Sales:** £8,605,460
**Issued Capital:** £1,493,656
**Directors:** Dr S J Curl, A Gaby, N M Chown, K J Gell, M Kirwan, G V Blackburn, Mrs S A Elliott, J F Tilbury
**US SIC:** 7379 **UK SIC:** 83940

| | 31-03-14 | 31-03-13 |
|---|---|---|
| TO | 23,146,436 | 14,443,407 |
| P/L | 1,107,051 | 300,222 |
| NW | (6,614,735) | (7,820,099) |
| WC | 3,849,837 | 3,343,878 |
| Emp. | 245 | 237 |

DUNS 50-479-5279
## Tessera Credit Services Ltd
(**Subsidiary of:** Tessera Credit Group Llp)
Maitland House, Warrior Square, Southend-On-Sea, Essex SS1 2JS
**Tel:** 01702444777 **Fax:** 01702444781
**Web:** www.tessera.co.uk
**Reg No:** 2453485 **Estd:** 1989 Private Limited Company
**Line of Business:** Financial intermediation not elsewhere classified
**Issued Capital:** £2
**Directors:** J M Lyndon Smith, D M Ford, G F Berkley, T E Fearon, N Thompstone
**Responsibilities**
**Senior:** Susan Alabaster *(HR Director)*, Leigh Berkley *(Chief Executive)*
**HR:** Susan Alabaster *(HR Director)*
**US SIC:** 6111 **UK SIC:** 81501
**Auditors:** Arram Berlyn Gardner

| | 31-01-14 | 31-01-13 | 30-01-12 |
|---|---|---|---|
| TA | 1,036,590 | 1,877,386 | 3,214,426 |
| P/L | N/A | 117,412 | 135,155 |
| NW | 2 | 2 | 651,581 |
| WC | 2 | 2 | 592,198 |
| Emp. | N/A | 79 | 79 |

DUNS 34-841-7630
## Tessuti Ltd
(**Subsidiary of:** Pentland Group P L C)
43-45 Bridge Street Row East, Chester, Cheshire CH1 1NW
**Tel:** 01513462600
**Web:** www.tessuti.co.uk
**Reg No:** 5640916 **Estd:** 2005 Private Limited Company
**Line of Business:** Menswear retail
**Issued Capital:** £200
**Directors:** P A Cowgill, B M Small, D A Light
**Co. Secretary:** Andrew Batchelor
**Responsibilities**
**Senior:** Barry Bown *(Manager)*, Jane Brisley *(Manager)*
**US SIC:** 5699 **UK SIC:** 64500
**Auditors:** KPMG Audit PLC

| | 01-02-14 | 02-02-13 | 31-02-12 |
|---|---|---|---|
| TO | 15,134,000 | 4,513,000 | N/A |
| P/L | (1,361,000) | 18,000 | N/A |
| NW | (1,197,000) | 320,000 | 358,553 |
| WC | (3,081,000) | (843,000) | (71,140) |
| Emp. | 158 | 48 | N/A |

DUNS 34-965-4785 **Imp**
## Test Equipment Asset Management Ltd
Unit 1 Hailsham Drive Waverley, Industrial Estate, Harrow, Middlesex HA1 4TR
**Tel:** 02084200200
**Web:** www.microlease.com
**Reg No:** 5760974 **Estd:** 2006 Private Limited Company
**Line of Business:** Manufacture of electronic instruments and appliances for measuring, checking, testing, navigating and other purposes, except industrial process control equipment
**Export Sales:** £47,934,000
**Trading Style:** Microlease
**Issued Capital:** £162,542
**Directors:** Y Soulliard, W P Colley, P J Mccloskey, N Brown
**Co. Secretary:** Paul Smith
**Responsibilities**
**Marketing:** George Acris *(Marketing Director)*
**Operations:** Rob Gershon *(Chief Operating Officer)*, Paul Rawlins *(Product Manager)*
**US SIC:** 7399 **UK SIC:** 83954
**Auditors:** PricewaterhouseCoopers LLP
**Bankers:** The Royal Bank Of Scotland Plc (16-08-05)

| | 28-02-14 | 28-02-13 | 29-02-12 |
|---|---|---|---|
| TO | 83,213,000 | 84,339,000 | 60,424,000 |
| P/L | (682,000) | (260,000) | 4,578,000 |
| NW | (8,199,000) | (8,369,000) | (9,457,000) |
| WC | 7,438,000 | 3,866,000 | 6,703,000 |
| Emp. | 220 | 225 | 200 |

DUNS 21-008-6875
## The Test People Ltd
Albion Court 5 Albion Place, Leeds, West Yorkshire LS1 6JL
**Tel:** 02071007794
**Web:** www.thetestpeople.com
**Reg No:** 6326413 **Estd:** 2007 Private Limited Company
**Line of Business:** Hardware consultancy
**Issued Capital:** £8,900
**Directors:** C P Thompson, G Winter, A Slight, A W Gawthorp, C Jones
**Co. Secretary:** Stephen Bentley
**US SIC:** 7379 **UK SIC:** 83940

| | 31-03-14 | 31-03-13 | 31-03-12 |
|---|---|---|---|
| TA | 1,689,645 | 1,614,575 | 907,177 |
| NW | 788,712 | 675,875 | 374,918 |
| WC | 772,768 | 666,320 | 361,679 |

DUNS 22-544-2698 **Imp**
## Test Valley Borough Council
Beech Hurst, Weyhill Road, Andover, Hampshire SP10 3AJ
**Tel:** 01264-368000
**Web:** www.testvalley.gov.uk
**Estd:** 1974
**Line of Business:** Local government
**Principals:** P Giddings *(Financial)*, G Blythe, B Sully, D Lyon, M Orchard, J Pybus, M Gratton
**Responsibilities**
**Marketing:** Teresa Bradley *(Marketing Manager)*
**Sales:** Teresa Bradley *(Marketing Manager)*
**Admin:** Bekkie Bacon *(Client Services Account Manage)*
**IT:** Tony Borovich *(Network, Security Manager)*, Tony Fawcett *(Computer Manager)*
**HR:** Jessie Bell *(Human Resources Manager)*
**Health & Safety:** Pauline Thrush *(Health & Safety Officer)*
**Facilities:** Tom Weston *(Premises Manager)*
**Purchasing:** Bekkie Bacon *(Client Services Account Manage)*, David Gagen *(Purchasing Manager)*
**Fleet:** Konrad Firth *(Transport Manager)*
**Branches:** Test Valley Borough Council, Anton County Junior School, Barlows Lane, Andover, Hampshire SP10 2HA
**US SIC:** 9121 **UK SIC:** 91110
**Bankers:** Lloyds TSB Bank plc (30-90-21)
**Employees:** 500

DUNS 77-104-2306
## Testactive Ltd
(**Subsidiary of:** Embrace Realty (Central) Ltd)
Tyntyla Avenue, Ystrad, Pentre, Mid Glamorgan CF41 7SU
**Tel:** 01443433544
**Web:** www.embracegroup.co.uk
**Reg No:** 2681169 **Estd:** 1991 Private Limited Company
**Line of Business:** Residential care establishments
**Trading Style:** Rhondda Nursing Home
**Issued Capital:** £750
**Directors:** Ms P L Lee, D L Manson

**Responsibilities**
**Senior:** Jaqui Davenport *(Manager)*, Jacqueline Davenport *(Home Manager)*, Katharine Kandelaki *(Manager)*, Barbara Mkosi *(Manager)*
**Finance:** Hannah Clatworthy *(Administrator)*
**Admin:** Hannah Clatworthy *(Administrator)*
**HR:** Jacqueline Davenport *(Home Manager)*
**Health & Safety:** Jacqueline Davenport *(Home Manager)*
**Purchasing:** Hannah Clatworthy *(Administrator)*
**US SIC:** 8321, 6732
**UK SIC:** 96111, 83100
**Auditors:** Medina Lynch

| | 30-06-14 | 30-06-13 | 31-06-11 |
|---|---|---|---|
| TA | 908 | 908 | 908 |
| NW | 908 | 908 | 908 |

DUNS 29-314-1495 **Imp-Exp**
## Testbank Ship Repair Ltd
(**Subsidiary of:** Burgess Marine Ltd)
Western Avenue, Western Docks, Southampton, Hampshire SO15 0HH
**Tel:** 023-8078-7878
**Web:** www.burgessmarine.co.uk
**Reg No:** 1758534 **VAT No:** 665068516
**Estd:** 1983 Private Limited Company
**Line of Business:** Building and repairing of ships and boats
**Export Markets:** Worldwide
**Trading Style:** Burgess Marine Ltd
**Issued Capital:** £413,801
**Principals:** J Coltman *(Managing)*, D N Warren, B A Needle, A A Coyne, N J Warren
**Co. Secretary:** Adrian Coyne
**Responsibilities**
**Senior:** Adrian Farwell *(Warehouse Manager)*
**Finance:** Amanda Howells *(Accountant)*
**Engineering:** Martin Overington *(Electrical Manager)*
**Branches:** Testbank Ship Repair Ltd, Trafalgar Wharf, Unit 1B, Portsmouth, Hampshire PO6 4PX
**US SIC:** 3731, 4712
**UK SIC:** 36101, 77002
**Auditors:** Dove Marsh & Jones

| | 31-03-13 | 31-12-11 | 31-03-10 |
|---|---|---|---|
| TA | 2,581,061 | 2,810,223 | 2,479,082 |
| NW | 638,031 | 907,913 | 1,109,384 |
| WC | 514,072 | 818,077 | 1,016,784 |

DUNS 23-083-1542
## Testbourne Community School
Micheldever Road, Whitchurch, Hampshire RG28 7JF
**Tel:** 01256-892061
**Web:** www.testbourne.hants.sch.uk
**Line of Business:** General secondary education
**Director:** M England
**Responsibilities**
**Senior:** Ruth Beasley *(Head Teacher)*, Eric Dunlop *(Governor)*, Andrea Harman *(Governor)*, Penny Horner *(Chair of Governors)*, Theresa Inglis *(Governor)*, Jill Parry *(Governor)*, Melissa Paxton *(Governor)*, Jane Rolfe *(Governor)*, Sarah Romain *(Science Teacher)*, Clare Scheckter *(Governor)*
**Admin:** Sue Macwilliam *(Admissions Officer)*
**US SIC:** 8211 **UK SIC:** 93200
**Employees:** 100

DUNS 22-844-2729
## Testerworld Ltd
(**Subsidiary of:** Maymask (199) Ltd)
Regents Drive, Low Prudhoe Industrial Estate, Prudhoe, Northumberland NE42 6PX
**Tel:** 01661835755 **Fax:** 01661835010
**Web:** www.depharma.co.uk
**Reg No:** 2008846 **Estd:** 2008 Private Limited Company
**Line of Business:** Pharmaceutical suppliers and wholesalers
**Trading Style:** Scm Pharma
**Issued Capital:** £20,000
**Principals:** M Gulliford *(Managing)*, L King, D A Wilson
**Responsibilities**
**Senior:** Fiona Cruickshank *(Non-Executive Chairman)*, Dianne Sharp *(Manager)*
**Sales:** Mike Parry *(Business Development Manager)*
**IT:** Gideon Adams *(IT Director)*
**Purchasing:** Craig Daglish *(International Trade Adviser)*
**Branches:** Testerworld Ltd, D E Pharmaceuticals, Unit 7, Prudhoe, Northumberland NE42 6PX
**US SIC:** 5122 **UK SIC:** 61800
**Auditors:** Dodd & Co

**Bankers:** Bank Of Scotland (12-05-94)

| | 31-03-14 | 31-03-13 | 31-03-12 |
|---|---|---|---|
| TO | 102,219,000 | 85,722,000 | 77,221,000 |
| P/L | 4,168,000 | 2,741,000 | 2,537,000 |
| NW | 9,622,000 | 6,413,000 | 4,432,000 |
| WC | 9,141,000 | 8,368,000 | 6,216,000 |
| Emp. | 159 | 150 | 218 |

DUNS 23-930-4988
## Testhouse Ltd
8 Lanark Square, London E14 9RE
**Tel:** 02085555577 **Fax:** 02030697077
**Web:** www.testhouse.net
**Reg No:** 3920400 **Estd:** 2000 Private Limited Company
**Line of Business:** Other software consultancy and supply
**Issued Capital:** £1,010
**Principals:** S Sahadevan *(Managing)*, A Gopinath
**Responsibilities**
**Finance:** Saila Anandan *(Finance Director)*
**Marketing:** Melanie Ancheta *(Marketing Manager)*
**US SIC:** 7379 **UK SIC:** 83940
**Auditors:** Cytec Solutions Ltd

| | 31-03-14 | 31-03-13 | 31-03-12 |
|---|---|---|---|
| TO | 1,719,685 | N/A | N/A |
| P/L | 57,748 | N/A | N/A |
| NW | 398,355 | 518,048 | 445,558 |
| WC | 93,165 | 454,369 | 364,357 |

DUNS 23-481-7658 **Imp**
## Testlink Services Ltd
1 Factory Road, Poole, Dorset BH16 5SJ
**Tel:** 01202621100
**Web:** www.testlink.co.uk
**Reg No:** 2598460 **Estd:** 2011 Private Limited Company
**Line of Business:** Cash machines
**Export Sales:** £1,436,537
**Issued Capital:** £1,000
**Director:** N J Beer
**Co. Secretary:** Gregory Hughes
**Responsibilities**
**Senior:** Richard Bairstow *(IT Manager)*, Andrew Sandsome *(Customer Services Manager)*
**Finance:** Simon Yeomans *(Financial Controller)*
**Sales:** Rastislav Justh *(Business Development Manager)*
**US SIC:** 7379 **UK SIC:** 83940
**Auditors:** Harrisons
**Bankers:** National Westminster Bank Plc (52-10-20)

| | 31-05-13 | 31-05-12 | 31-05-11 |
|---|---|---|---|
| TO | 7,182,686 | 6,075,301 | 8,513,506 |
| P/L | 576,107 | 198,932 | 148,729 |
| NW | 725,728 | 632,919 | 814,607 |
| WC | 194,334 | 130,637 | 296,659 |
| Emp. | N/A | 89 | 91 |

DUNS 53-608-8438 **Imp**
## Testronic Laboratories Ltd
Lyon House, 160-166 Borough High Street, London SE1 1LB
**Tel:** 02070421700
**Web:** www.testroniclabs.com
**Reg No:** 3414065 **Estd:** 1998 Private Limited Company
**Line of Business:** Other computer related activities
**Export Sales:** £2,799,000
**Issued Capital:** £2
**Directors:** B P Morris, D M Wheatley
**Responsibilities**
**Senior:** Tristan Smith *(Manager)*
**US SIC:** 7379, 7819
**UK SIC:** 83940, 97111
**Auditors:** Mazars LLP
**Bankers:** HSBC Bank plc (40-41-30)

| | 31-12-12 | 31-12-11 | 31-12-10 |
|---|---|---|---|
| TO | 5,188,000 | 4,395,173 | 5,129,836 |
| P/L | (206,000) | (904,664) | (438,843) |
| NW | (3,024,000) | (2,817,950) | (1,913,286) |
| WC | (3,193,000) | (2,947,888) | (2,070,393) |
| Emp. | 103 | 97 | 103 |

DUNS 21-736-1762
## Testwood Sports College
Testwood Lane, Totton, Southampton, Southampton, Hampshire SO40 3ZW
**Tel:** 02380862146 **Fax:** 02380666514
**Web:** www.testwood.hants.sch.uk
**Reg No:** 7703800 **Estd:** 1946 Private Company Limited By Guarantee
**Line of Business:** General secondary education
**Directors:** G Pike, N Gilbert, A J Jerrett, K D Walsh, J L Lawrence, S Isaac, Mrs V L Ford, Mrs J Pitman
**Co. Secretary:** Mrs Jacqueline Barker
**Responsibilities**
**Senior:** Ian Appleton *(Head Teacher)*, Dawn Bushrod *(Director)*, A Chapsomidis *(Head Teacher)*, Hadleigh Garland *(Director)*, Heather Holmes *(Director)*, Pepita Monk *(Director)*

**US SIC:** 8211 **UK SIC:** 93200

| | 31-08-13 | 31-08-12 |
|---|---|---|
| TO | 4,614,662 | 16,828,030 |
| P/L | (281,894) | 11,975,663 |
| NW | 10,875,769 | 11,142,663 |
| WC | 432,866 | 482,055 |
| Emp. | 96 | 101 |

DUNS 21-596-2972
## Tetbury Audi
Tetbury Audi, Quercus Road, Tetbury, Gloucestershire GL8 8GX
**Tel:** 01666505155
**Web:** www.tetbury.audi.co.uk
**Estd:** 1963 Partnership
**Line of Business:** Car dealers (new & used)
**Partners:** J Ahl, S Lock, M Wheatley, C Mccormack
**Responsibilities**
**Senior:** Connor McCormack *(Partner)*, Gary Tombs *(Head Of Business)*
**US SIC:** 5511 **UK SIC:** 65100
**Employees:** 60

DUNS 21-626-2402 **Imp**
## Tetra Pak Ltd
(**Subsidiary of:** Tetra Laval Holdings B.V.)
The Foundation, Wrexham, Clwyd LL13 0UT
**Tel:** 01244688000 **Fax:** 01978834001
**Web:** www.tetrapak.com
**Reg No:** 0551434 **VAT No:** 800446468
**Estd:** 1950 Private Limited Company
**Line of Business:** Other wholesale
**Export Sales:** £3,128,000
**Issued Capital:** £450,000
**Directors:** F E Griemsmann, Mrs M Markovic, I T Chambers, S Fagerang
**Co. Secretary:** A G Secretarial Limited
**Responsibilities**
**Senior:** Stephen Fangarn *(Manager)*
**Branches:** Tetra Pak Ltd, 12 Langlands Ave, Kelvin South Business Park, Glasgow, Lanarkshire G75 0YG
**US SIC:** 5199, 7394
**UK SIC:** 61900, 84000
**Auditors:** Ernst & Young LLP
**Bankers:** Skandinaviska Enskilda Banken Ab (publ) (40-48-65)

| | 31-12-13 | 31-12-12 | 31-12-11 |
|---|---|---|---|
| TO | 83,444,000 | 84,407,000 | 106,733,000 |
| P/L | (5,824,000) | 3,259,000 | 3,693,000 |
| NW | 30,720,000 | 51,746,000 | 42,160,000 |
| WC | 32,581,000 | 44,726,000 | 42,651,000 |
| Emp. | 116 | 119 | 127 |

DUNS 29-471-2518 **Imp-Exp**
## Tetra Technologies U K Ltd
(**Subsidiary of:** Tetra Technologies Inc.)
Unit 1a, Airport Industrial Park, Howe Moss Drive, Aberdeen, Aberdeenshire AB21 0GL
**Tel:** 01224-773811
**Web:** www.tetratec.com
**Reg No:** 1774672 **VAT No:** 604918833
**Estd:** 1983 Private Limited Company
**Line of Business:** Oil and gas exploration services
**Export Markets:** Europe
**Issued Capital:** £10
**Directors:** R T Short Iii, S M Brightman
**Co. Secretary:** Ms O'Brien
**Responsibilities**
**Senior:** Maurice Boyle *(Manager)*, Brian Forgie *(Regional Manager)*, Philip Longorio *(Manager)*, Bass Wallace *(Manager)*
**Finance:** Akex Dellaquaglia *(Accountant)*
**Marketing:** Stacey Rezin *(Marketing Manager)*
**Health & Safety:** Steve Forsyth *(Health & Safety Officer)*
**US SIC:** 1389 **UK SIC:** 13000
**Auditors:** Ernst & Young LLP
**Bankers:** Clydesdale Bank Plc (82-62-22)

| | 31-12-13 | 31-12-12 | 31-12-11 |
|---|---|---|---|
| TO | 18,172,004 | 16,853,000 | 9,207,000 |
| P/L | 1,612,105 | 1,698,000 | (178,000) |
| NW | 4,824,463 | 3,629,000 | 2,293,000 |
| WC | 4,054,856 | 2,786,000 | 1,776,000 |
| Emp. | 55 | 47 | 40 |

DUNS 21-294-1520 **Imp-Exp**
## Tetrad Ltd
Hartford Mill, Swan Street, Preston, Lancashire PR1 5PQ
**Web:** www.tetrad.co.uk
**Reg No:** 0936239 **VAT No:** 604451373
**Estd:** 1968 Private Limited Company
**Line of Business:** Manufacture of other furniture
**Export Markets:** E U & others
**Export Sales:** £2,334,000
**Trading Style:** Contrast Upholstery, Flame Upholstery, Contract Division
**Issued Capital:** £78,138
**Directors:** C J Fletcher, A D Pickup, J R Cooper, P F Sherliker, Dr I A Borthwick
**Co. Secretary:** Mrs Carmel Lodge
**Responsibilities**
**Marketing:** Rachel Wilkinson *(Marketing)*
**Sales:** Nick Murphy *(Sales Director)*
**Branches:** Tetrad Ltd, Cobden Mill, Whalley Road, Clitheroe, Lancashire BB7 9DZ
**US SIC:** 2517 **UK SIC:** 46714
**Auditors:** KPMG LLP
**Bankers:** Yorkshire Bank Plc (05-06-74)

| | 27-04-14 | 26-04-13 | 29-04-12 |
|---|---|---|---|
| TO | 10,649,000 | 10,721,000 | 12,029,000 |
| P/L | (471,000) | (565,000) | (938,000) |
| NW | 1,506,000 | 2,019,000 | 2,389,000 |
| WC | (1,105,000) | (514,000) | (288,000) |
| Emp. | 187 | 208 | 271 |

DUNS 73-951-4896 **Imp-Exp**
## Tetrosyl Group Ltd
Bevis Green Works, Walmersley, Bury, Lancashire BL9 6RE
**Tel:** 0161-764-5981 **Fax:** 0161-797-5899
**Web:** www.tetrosyl.com
**Reg No:** 5204036 **Estd:** 1953 Private Limited Company
**Line of Business:** Management activities of holding companies
**Export Sales:** £36,203,000
**Trading Style:** Tetrosyl Group Limited
**Issued Capital:** £760
**Director:** P D Schofield
**Co. Secretary:** Stephen Brennan
**Responsibilities**
**Marketing:** Martyn Sharpe *(Marketing Manager)*, Ian Tench *(Marketing Manager)*
**Health & Safety:** Stewart Roberts *(Health & Safety Manager)*
**Facilities:** Stewart Roberts *(Health & Safety Manager)*
**Operations:** Robin Palmer *(Environmental Manager)*
**Purchasing:** John McCarthy *(Buyer)*
**US SIC:** 6711, 2891
**UK SIC:** 83962, 25620
**Auditors:** KPMG LLP

| | 31-12-13 | 31-12-12 | 31-12-11 |
|---|---|---|---|
| TO | 149,519,000 | 146,464,000 | 157,701,000 |
| P/L | (1,103,000) | 6,717,000 | 10,821,000 |
| NW | 60,376,000 | 59,360,000 | 56,379,000 |
| WC | 49,198,000 | 47,169,000 | 45,534,000 |
| Emp. | 1,232 | 1,172 | 1,246 |

DUNS 23-503-6340
## Tettenhall College (Incorporated)
Towers Lodge, Wood Road, Wolverhampton, West Midlands WV6 8QU
**Tel:** 01902-751119 **Fax:** 01902793000
**Web:** www.tettenhallcollege.co.uk
**Reg No:** 0141727 **Estd:** 1863 Private Limited Company
**Line of Business:** Schools (independent)
**Directors:** K Bruerton, J F Woolridge, Mrs D Margetts, Rev G Wynne, Mrs H Hawkins, Mrs S J Isbister, S C Maddox, G D Sower
**Co. Secretary:** Christopher Way
**Responsibilities**
**Senior:** Linda Cook *(Director)*, Peter Creed *(Manager)*, Catharine Hammond *(Director)*, Jill Parker *(Director)*
**US SIC:** 8211 **UK SIC:** 93200
**Auditors:** BDO Stoy Hayward
**Bankers:** Lloyds TSB Bank plc (30-99-83)

| | 31-08-13 | 31-08-12 | 31-08-11 |
|---|---|---|---|
| TO | 3,576,580 | 4,159,472 | 4,267,129 |
| P/L | (286,487) | 16,042 | (34,343) |
| NW | 2,988,024 | 3,258,325 | 3,236,858 |
| WC | (763,457) | (421,399) | (270,796) |
| Emp. | 92 | 99 | 102 |

DUNS 28-879-1155
## Tettix Turbo Ltd
Unit 6 Royal Way, Loughborough, Leicestershire LE11 5XR
**Tel:** 01509633300 **Fax:** 01509-628558
**Web:** www.ttauto.co.uk
**Reg No:** 1153016 **Estd:** 1973 Private Limited Company
**Line of Business:** Maintenance and repair of motor vehicles
**Trading Style:** T T Automotive
**Issued Capital:** £1,053
**Principals:** D E Friend *(Managing)*, Ms A D Esworthy, C Paxman, Mrs J M Hammond, Mrs J E Friend, R A Russell
**Co. Secretary:** Neil Hammond
**Responsibilities**
**Senior:** Barry Sinclair *(Manager)*
**IT:** Barry Coleman *(IT Manager)*
**US SIC:** 7539, 5531
**UK SIC:** 67100, 65100
**Auditors:** Thomas May & Co
**Bankers:** The Royal Bank Of Scotland Plc (16-24-23)

| | 31-12-13 | 31-12-12 | 31-12-11 |
|---|---|---|---|
| TO | 8,130,377 | N/A | N/A |
| P/L | 389,627 | N/A | N/A |
| NW | 906,127 | 853,687 | 825,917 |
| WC | 457,841 | 407,823 | 410,494 |
| Emp. | 48 | N/A | N/A |

DUNS 73-604-4830 **Imp-Exp**

## Tev Ltd

(**Subsidiary of:** Thermal Energy Ventures Ltd)
Armitage Road, Brighouse, West Yorkshire HD6 1UJ
**Tel:** 01484-405600
**Web:** www.tevlimited.com
**Reg No:** 4865581 **VAT No:** 827732413
**Estd:** 1970 Private Limited Company
**Line of Business:** Air conditioning equipment
**Issued Capital:** £1,225,001
**Directors:** J A Vigor, J W Lightfoot, A C Hammersley, C Chisman
**Co. Secretary:** Richard Dossett
**US SIC:** 3585 **UK SIC:** 32841
**Auditors:** PKF (UK) LLP
**Bankers:** The Royal Bank Of Scotland Plc (16-13-18)

| | 31-12-13 | 31-12-12 | 31-12-11 |
|---|---|---|---|
| TO | 5,419,718 | 5,772,010 | 5,581,769 |
| P/L | 15,566 | (69,141) | (244,345) |
| NW | 3,171,769 | 3,124,555 | 3,150,730 |
| WC | 3,187,058 | 3,177,507 | 3,224,626 |
| Emp. | 55 | 62 | 64 |

DUNS 21-207-8331 **Imp-Exp**

## Teva Uk Ltd

(**Subsidiary of:** Teva Pharmaceutical Industries Limited)
Ridings Point, Castleford, West Yorkshire WF10 5HX
**Tel:** 01977 628500
**Web:** www.tevauk.com
**Reg No:** 0302461 **Estd:** 1935 Private Limited Company
**Line of Business:** Manufacture of medicaments
**Export Sales:** £24,713,000
**Issued Capital:** £340,555
**Directors:** R G Daniell, J Beighton, M Schrewe, T Oreskovic
**Responsibilities**
**Marketing:** Kim Innes *(Sales & Marketing Manager)*
**Sales:** Isobel Diamond *(Business Development Director)*, Christian Griffin *(Head of Commercial Excellence)*, Kim Innes *(Sales & Marketing Manager)*, Petra Page *(Business Development Manager)*, Andrew Ridsdale *(Commercial Manager)*
**Purchasing:** Albert Hills *(Purchasing Manager)*, Ria Lawton *(Hospital Contracts Manager)*
**Branches:** Teva Uk Ltd, Brampton Road, Eastbourne, East Sussex BN22 9AG
**US SIC:** 2834 **UK SIC:** 25700
**Auditors:** PricewaterhouseCoopers LLP
**Bankers:** Lloyds TSB Bank plc (30-12-99)

| | 31-12-13 | 31-12-12 | 31-12-11 |
|---|---|---|---|
| TO | 383,491,000 | 354,880,000 | 381,405,000 |
| P/L | 7,998,000 | (3,337,000) | 1,556,000 |
| NW | (11,265,000) | (19,081,000) | (13,730,000) |
| WC | (580,000) | (15,965,000) | (8,074,000) |
| Emp. | 707 | 701 | 665 |

DUNS 29-509-0849 **Imp**

## Teversham Engineering Ltd

Hall Farm Church Road, Cambridge, Cambridgeshire CB1 9AP
**Tel:** 01223-293904
**Web:** www.tevershamengineering.co.uk
**Reg No:** 1872287 **VAT No:** 432147871
**Estd:** 1984 Private Limited Company
**Line of Business:** Powder coating specialists
**Issued Capital:** £5,000
**Managing Director:** A P Willis
**Co. Secretary:** Mrs Janet Willis
**Responsibilities**
**Senior:** David Teather *(General Manager)*
**US SIC:** 2891, 2851
**UK SIC:** 25620, 25510
**Bankers:** Barclays Bank Plc (20-17-19)

| | 31-12-13 | 31-12-12 | 31-12-11 |
|---|---|---|---|
| TA | 2,596,080 | 2,568,709 | 2,660,130 |
| NW | 2,220,626 | 2,036,438 | 1,792,689 |
| WC | 1,677,846 | 1,446,652 | 1,225,582 |

DUNS 22-646-6423

## Tevo Ltd

(**Subsidiary of:** Carl Bennet Ab)
Maddison House, High Wycombe, Buckinghamshire HP10 0PE
**Tel:** 01628-528034 **Fax:** 01628523292
**Web:** www.tevo.eu.com
**Reg No:** 1540940 **VAT No:** 342973342
**Estd:** 1981 Private Limited Company
**Line of Business:** Vehicle conversions
**Export Sales:** £55,861
**Issued Capital:** £90
**Director:** U R Mickelson
**Co. Secretary:** Mrs Rowan Revell
**Responsibilities**
**Sales:** Paul Railston *(Commercial Director)*
**US SIC:** 2599 **UK SIC:** 46720
**Auditors:** PricewaterhouseCoopers LLP
**Bankers:** Barclays Bank Plc (20-40-71)

| | 31-12-13 | 31-12-12 | 31-12-11 |
|---|---|---|---|
| TO | 9,185,542 | 8,304,992 | 8,993,466 |
| P/L | 600,171 | 741,361 | 692,638 |
| NW | 1,724,863 | 1,869,127 | 1,302,194 |
| WC | 1,391,829 | 1,528,658 | 1,195,375 |
| Emp. | 54 | 56 | 60 |

DUNS 22-950-8007 **Imp-Exp**

## Tew Engineering Ltd

(**Subsidiary of:** Tew Holdings (2012) Ltd)
6 The Midway, Nottingham, Nottinghamshire NG7 2TS
**Tel:** 01159-354354
**Web:** www.tew.co.uk
**Reg No:** 1134730 **Estd:** 1973 Private Limited Company
**Line of Business:** Manufacture of other special purpose machinery not elsewhere classified
**Export Markets:** Worldwide
**Export Sales:** £1,284,000
**Issued Capital:** £105,000
**Directors:** P D Jones, R I Crosby, Mrs S Roberts, T Hadfield, Dr M G Paradise
**Co. Secretary:** Simon Barnes
**Responsibilities**
**Senior:** Philip Chester *(Director)*, Ian Malson *(Warehouse Manager)*
**Facilities:** Ian Malson *(Warehouse Manager)*
**Branches:** Tew Engineering Ltd, The Midway Redfield Road, Nottingham, Nottinghamshire NG7 2UJ
**US SIC:** 3559 **UK SIC:** 32863
**Auditors:** RSM Tenon Audit Ltd
**Bankers:** National Westminster Bank Plc (60-80-09)

| | 30-04-14 | 30-04-13 | 30-04-12 |
|---|---|---|---|
| TO | 11,272,000 | 11,739,000 | 10,191,000 |
| P/L | 1,945,000 | 1,051,000 | 547,000 |
| NW | 6,215,000 | 4,475,000 | 3,374,000 |
| WC | 4,142,000 | 2,549,000 | 1,394,000 |
| Emp. | 85 | 85 | 84 |

DUNS 23-617-8398

## Tewin Bury Farm Hotel

B1000hertford Road, Tewin, Welwyn, Hertfordshire AL6 0JB
**Tel:** 01438841490
**Web:** www.tewinbury.co.uk
**Estd:** 1989 Partnership
**Line of Business:** Hotels
**Trading Style:** Tewin Bury Farm Hotel
**Partners:** D V Williams, Mrs A Williams
**Responsibilities**
**Senior:** Vaughan Williams *(Proprietor)*
**HR:** sarah whitman *(Human Resources Manager)*
**US SIC:** 7011 **UK SIC:** 66500
**Bankers:** Barclays Bank Plc (20-20-37)
**Employees:** 82

DUNS 73-568-2283

## Tewin Bury Farm Ltd

Tewin, Welwyn, Hertfordshire AL6 0JB
**Web:** www.tewinbury.co.uk
**Reg No:** 4829994 **Estd:** 2003 Private Limited Company
**Line of Business:** Hotels
**Issued Capital:** £4
**Directors:** D V Williams, I C Williams
**Responsibilities**
**Senior:** Salem Retibi *(Deputy General Manager)*, sarah whitman *(Human resources officer)*
**Finance:** Denise Welsh *(Accounts Manager)*
**HR:** Debbie Glinnon *(Human Resources Manager)*, sarah whitman *(Human resources officer)*
**US SIC:** 7011 **UK SIC:** 66500

| | 30-09-13 | 30-09-12 | 30-09-11 |
|---|---|---|---|
| TA | 2,598,374 | 2,108,276 | 2,144,537 |
| NW | 851,043 | 502,935 | 458,055 |
| WC | (357,151) | (453,173) | (389,409) |

DUNS 23-274-0399

## Tewkesbury Borough Council

Council Offices, Gloucester Road, Tewkesbury, Gloucestershire GL20 5TT
**Tel:** 01684-295010
**Web:** www.tewkesbury.gov.uk
**Estd:** 2002
**Line of Business:** Local government
**Principals:** P Anthill *(Financial)*, H M Davies, C J Shaw, G F Kent
**Responsibilities**
**Senior:** Michael Dawson *(Chief Executive)*, Rachel North *(Deputy CEO)*, Oliver Rider *(Executive)*, David Steels *(Manager)*
**Finance:** Simon Dix *(Director of Finance)*
**Marketing:** Anna Sanders *(Marketing Director)*
**IT:** Tina Nicholls *(IT Manager)*, G Quint *(IT Manager)*
**Health & Safety:** Kay Meddings *(Health & Safety Officer)*
**Facilities:** Val Garside *(Group Manager Environmental an)*, Andy Noble *(Property Manager)*
**Operations:** Nick Firkins *(Service Manager)*, Tina Nicholls *(IT Manager)*, Julie Wood *(Development Services Manager)*
**Fleet:** John Hinett *(Senior Planning Officer)*
**Branches:** Tewkesbury Borough Council, Spring Gardens, Tewkesbury, Gloucestershire GL20 5DN
**US SIC:** 6732, 7392, 4953
**UK SIC:** 83100, 83951, 92110
**Bankers:** National Westminster Bank Plc (60-05-16)
**Employees:** 300

DUNS 21-754-2458

## Tewkesbury School

Ashchurch Road, Tewkesbury, Gloucestershire GL20 8DF
**Tel:** 01684292152
**Web:** www.tewkesburyschool.org
**Reg No:** 7840060 **Estd:** 2011 Private Company Limited By Guarantee
**Line of Business:** General secondary education
**Directors:** J M Potter, S Hawkins, Mrs S Maizonnier, J A Thomas, E P Fair, P Evans, D J Chamberlain, Mrs F Castle
**Co. Secretary:** Mrs Julia Whybrow
**Responsibilities**
**Senior:** Clive Ainsworth *(Director)*, Anne Bartholomew *(Director)*, Alison Hek *(Director)*, Gareth Hill *(Director)*, Stephanie Kettell *(Director)*, Christine Leyfield *(Manager)*, Martin Mcleman *(Acting Head Teacher)*
**US SIC:** 8211 **UK SIC:** 93200
**Bankers:** HSBC Bank plc (40-00-00)

| | 31-08-14 | 31-08-13 | 31-08-12 |
|---|---|---|---|
| TO | 9,221,061 | 9,202,079 | 25,237,793 |
| P/L | 56,122 | 159,047 | 19,398,466 |
| NW | 16,926,745 | 17,575,630 | 17,675,466 |
| WC | 745,266 | 653,647 | 435,837 |
| Emp. | 149 | 155 | 231 |

DUNS 21-717-0745 **Exp**

## Tews Engineering Ltd

34 Lavant Street, Petersfield, Hampshire GU32 3EF
**Tel:** 01730-268531 **Fax:** 01730-262141
**Web:** www.tews.uk.com
**Reg No:** 0971412 **VAT No:** 503806078
**Estd:** 1910 Private Limited Company
**Line of Business:** Precision engineers
**Export Markets:** Europe, North America
**Export Sales:** £774,363
**Issued Capital:** £60,309
**Managing Director:** M J Hankin
**US SIC:** 8911, 3714
**UK SIC:** 83701, 35300
**Auditors:** Sheen Stickland
**Bankers:** National Westminster Bank Plc (60-16-26)

| | 31-03-13 | 31-03-12 | 31-03-11 |
|---|---|---|---|
| TO | 7,093,370 | 9,886,703 | 6,867,493 |
| P/L | 50,482 | 53,544 | 88,495 |
| NW | 1,797,316 | 1,831,566 | 1,845,398 |
| WC | 936,353 | 717,064 | 638,714 |
| Emp. | 117 | 134 | 102 |

DUNS 21-609-5984 **Imp-Exp**

## Tex Holdings Plc

Claydon Industrial Park, Ipswich, Suffolk IP6 0NL
**Web:** www.tex-holdings.co.uk
**Reg No:** 0405838 **Estd:** 1946 Public Limited Company
**Line of Business:** Management activities of holding companies
**Export Markets:** Europe, North America, Central & South America, Africa, Middle East, Asia Pacific, Australasia
**Export Sales:** £7,862,000
**Issued Capital:** £635,145
**Principals:** A R Burrows *(Chairman)*, D Redhead, C D Palmer-Tomkinson, C T Varley
**Co. Secretary:** Christopher Parker
**Responsibilities**
**Senior:** Matthew Cadbury *(Manager)*
**US SIC:** 6711, 3531
**UK SIC:** 83962, 32541
**Auditors:** Larking Gowen Ltd
**Bankers:** National Westminster Bank Plc (60-06-06)

| | 31-12-13 | 31-12-12 | 31-12-11 |
|---|---|---|---|
| TO | 38,379,000 | 38,997,000 | 36,829,000 |
| P/L | 744,000 | 1,109,000 | 1,541,000 |
| NW | 9,209,000 | 7,176,000 | 6,753,000 |
| WC | 6,500,000 | 7,042,000 | 5,193,000 |
| Emp. | 416 | 442 | 412 |

DUNS 21-602-4232 **Imp-Exp**

## Texas Instruments Ltd

(**Subsidiary of:** Texas Instruments Incorporated)
800 Pavilion Drive, Northampton, Northamptonshire NN4 7YL
**Tel:** 01604-663000
**Web:** www.ti.com
**Reg No:** 0574102 **Estd:** 1956 Private Limited Company
**Line of Business:** Manufacturers agents
**Export Markets:** E U, Far East, U.S.A. & other
**Export Sales:** £7,489,000
**Issued Capital:** £41,237
**Directors:** Dr K Weisel, A K Schwaiger, Dr G J Mccarthy
**Co. Secretary:** Ms Adrienne Mcglynn
**Responsibilities**
**Senior:** Michael Cowles *(Manager)*, Edgar Frank *(Manager)*, Karen Pharoah *(Manager)*, Anita Richardson *(Manager)*, Roger Winson *(Manager)*
**Finance:** Michael Cowles *(Manager)*
**HR:** Karen Lathaen *(Human Resources Director)*
**Health & Safety:** Anna Fildes *(Health & Safety Officer)*
**Facilities:** Dave Bazeley *(Facilities Manager)*
**US SIC:** 3679, 5065
**UK SIC:** 34542, 61500
**Auditors:** Ernst & Young LLP
**Bankers:** Barclays Bank Plc (20-05-74)

| | 31-12-13 | 31-12-12 | 31-12-11 |
|---|---|---|---|
| TO | 14,498,000 | 15,422,000 | 24,220,000 |
| P/L | 1,371,000 | 1,721,000 | 5,711,000 |
| NW | 30,380,000 | 28,373,000 | 26,574,000 |
| WC | 27,437,000 | 25,767,000 | 25,247,000 |
| Emp. | 66 | 75 | 104 |

DUNS 21-100-6523 **Imp-Exp**

## Texas Instruments (U.K.) Ltd

(**Subsidiary of:** Texas Instruments Incorporated)
Earnhill Road, Larkfield Industrial Estate, Greenock, Renfrewshire PA16 0EQ
**Tel:** 01475-633733 **Fax:** 01475638515
**Web:** www.ti.com
**Reg No:** 0957879 **VAT No:** 408447155
**Estd:** 1969 Private Limited Company
**Line of Business:** Manufacturers of control panels
**Export Markets:** France, Spain, Middle East, E U
**Directors:** A K Schwaiger, Ms A H Mcglynn, Dr K Weisel, Dr G J Mccarthy
**Co. Secretary:** Peter Tomlinson
**Branches:** Texas Instruments (U.k.) Ltd, Earnhill Road, Greenock, Renfrewshire PA16 0EQ
**US SIC:** 3679 **UK SIC:** 34542
**Auditors:** Ernst & Young LLP
**Bankers:** Bank Of America, Na (16-50-50)
**Employees:** 440
**Turnover:** £113,050,000

DUNS 76-852-1643 **Exp**

## Texcel Technology Plc

(**Subsidiary of:** Texcel (2011) Ltd)
Thames Road, Dartford, Kent DA1 4SB
**Tel:** 01322621700 **Fax:** 01322 557733
**Web:** www.texceltechnology.com
**Reg No:** 2607732 **VAT No:** 547872108
**Estd:** 1926 Public Limited Company
**Line of Business:** Manufacture of electronic valves and tubes and other electronic components
**Export Markets:** E U
**Export Sales:** £209,603
**Issued Capital:** £950,000
**Principals:** W H Bryce *(Managing)*, P J Shawyer *(Technical)*, A N Mcleod, G J Tilsed
**Co. Secretary:** Ms Sandra Suckling
**Responsibilities**
**Sales:** Paul Dickson *(Business Development Manager)*, Katherine Gooderson *(Sales Administrator)*
**Admin:** Katherine Gooderson *(Sales Administrator)*
**Operations:** Paul Beal *(Production Manager)*
**US SIC:** 3679, 3629, 3662
**UK SIC:** 34542, 34350, 34430
**Auditors:** Barnes Roffe LLP
**Bankers:** National Westminster Bank Plc (60-13-10)

| | 31-01-14 | 31-01-13 | 31-01-12 |
|---|---|---|---|
| TO | 7,800,330 | 7,541,180 | 7,455,574 |
| P/L | 472,610 | 467,064 | 35,972 |
| NW | 1,916,450 | 1,623,519 | 1,155,356 |
| WC | 1,808,649 | 1,661,155 | 1,361,488 |
| Emp. | 89 | 91 | 90 |

DUNS 23-386-1793

## Texon International Group Ltd

Skelton Industrial Estate, Skelton-In-Clevelandindustrial, Saltburn-By-The-Sea, Cleveland TS12 2LH
**Tel:** 01287-650551
**Web:** www.texon.com
**Reg No:** 5329617 **Estd:** 2005 Private Limited Company
**Line of Business:** Management activities of holding companies
**Export Sales:** £72,373,000
**Trading Style:** Texon Nonwoven Ltd
**Issued Capital:** £5,428,452
**Directors:** S Lamb, Dr A W Henfrey, G B Campbell, N C Allen, S R Smith
**Co. Secretary:** Robin Sims

**Responsibilities**
**Senior:** Gary Hollins *(Head Of Global Supply Chain)*
**US SIC:** 6711 **UK SIC:** 83962
**Auditors:** KPMG LLP

| | 31-12-13 | 31-12-12 | 31-12-11 |
|---|---|---|---|
| TO | 72,794,000 | 74,867,000 | 76,245,000 |
| P/L | 7,219,000 | 1,328,000 | 1,425,000 |
| NW | (21,151,000) | (27,306,000) | (28,250,000) |
| WC | 2,263,000 | 2,670,000 | 1,332,000 |
| Emp. | 274 | 320 | 422 |

DUNS 42-363-0532 Imp-Exp
## Texthelp Ltd.
David Sanders, Antrim, Co Antrim BT41 2RU
**Tel:** 02894-428105 **Fax:** 02894-428574
**Web:** www.texthelp.com
**Reg No:** 0031186NI **VAT No:** 516805252
**Estd:** 2008 Private Limited Company
**Line of Business:** Computer software sales
**Export Markets:** Worldwide
**Export Sales:** £4,829,609
**Issued Capital:** £249
**Directors:** A Bordon, M Mccusker, M Roche, M A Mckay
**Co. Secretary:** Seamus Scullion
**Responsibilities**
**HR:** Kerry Alderdice *(Human Resources Manager)*
**Health & Safety:** Jackie Prentice *(Health & Safety Officer)*
**US SIC:** 7379, 7399
**UK SIC:** 83940, 83954
**Bankers:** Northern Bank Ltd (95-02-02)

| | 30-09-13 | 30-09-12 | 30-09-11 |
|---|---|---|---|
| TO | 9,799,093 | 9,444,898 | 10,218,743 |
| P/L | 1,479,918 | 1,311,237 | 1,906,468 |
| NW | 5,798,820 | 4,345,683 | 3,000,238 |
| WC | 5,515,011 | 4,028,288 | 2,909,432 |
| Emp. | 103 | 105 | 102 |

DUNS 39-685-1966
## Textile Recycling for Aid & International Development
47 Wood Lane, London W12 7RZ
**Tel:** 02082010001
**Web:** www.recyclingforlondon.co.uk
**Reg No:** 2143753 **Estd:** 2011 Private Company Limited By Guarantee
**Line of Business:** Refuse collection
**Directors:** Miss M Mcdonald, S N Robertson, L Klouda, I Hagg, D Williams, A M Rutherford, N J Garrett
**Co. Secretary:** Ms Maria Chenoweth Casey
**Responsibilities**
**Senior:** Jamie Weinrich *(Marketing Director)*
**Marketing:** Jamie Weinrich *(Marketing Director)*
**Branches:** Textile Recycling For Aid & International Development, Unit 5, Victoria Road, London W3 6UU
**US SIC:** 4953, 5714
**UK SIC:** 92110, 64700
**Auditors:** H.W. Fisher & Co

| | 31-12-13 | 31-12-12 | 31-12-11 |
|---|---|---|---|
| TO | 4,959,479 | 4,589,652 | 4,283,519 |
| P/L | 531,545 | 386,634 | 488,046 |
| NW | 3,200,276 | 2,668,731 | 2,282,097 |
| WC | 2,517,064 | 2,012,972 | 1,806,439 |
| Emp. | 86 | 84 | 76 |

DUNS 51-980-4590
## Textron Acquisition Ltd
**(Subsidiary of:** Textron Inc.)
23 Bedford Row, London WC1R 4EB
**Web:** www.tempo.textron.com
**Reg No:** 3443385 **Estd:** 1997 Private Limited Company
**Line of Business:** Holding companies management activities
**Issued Capital:** £531,918,481
**Directors:** Ms A T Willaman, J H Bracken
**Co. Secretary:** Mrs Pauline Preston
**US SIC:** 6711 **UK SIC:** 83962
**Auditors:** Ernst & Young LLP

| | 28-12-13 | 29-12-12 | 31-12-11 |
|---|---|---|---|
| TA | 467,078,000 | 440,659,000 | 426,915,000 |
| P/L | 22,362,000 | 7,676,000 | (10,956,000) |
| NW | 164,776,000 | 142,394,000 | 134,718,000 |
| WC | (299,518,000) | (294,157,000) | (289,090,000) |

DUNS 77-107-5587
## Texturing Technology Ltd
Po Box 22, Port Talbot, West Glamorgan SA13 2YJ
**Tel:** 01639-872197 **Fax:** 01639872196
**Web:** www.texturingtechnology.net
**Reg No:** 2684488 **Estd:** 1992 Private Limited Company
**Line of Business:** Manufacture of metal structures and parts of structures
**Issued Capital:** £2,000,000
**Directors:** Ms S Court, J X Descamps, F P Royle, M J Wixey, P D Court, J Phillips, Ms L Deeming
**Co. Secretary:** Ms Sharone Gidwani
**Responsibilities**
**Senior:** Michael Court *(Manager)*, Allison Scandrett *(Manager)*
**US SIC:** 3441, 3325
**UK SIC:** 32042, 31110

**Auditors:** PricewaterhouseCoopers
**Bankers:** Barclays Bank Plc (20-84-41)

| | 30-03-14 | 30-03-13 | 31-03-12 |
|---|---|---|---|
| TO | 5,278,000 | 4,811,000 | 3,822,000 |
| P/L | 313,000 | 165,000 | (297,000) |
| NW | 4,760,000 | 4,531,000 | 4,381,000 |
| WC | 942,000 | 560,000 | 218,000 |
| Emp. | 70 | 60 | 66 |

DUNS 21-216-9569 Exp
## T.F. & J.H. Braime (Holdings) P.L.C.
Hunslet Road, Leeds, West Yorkshire LS10 1JZ
**Tel:** 01132457491 **Fax:** 01132-435021
**Web:** www.braimepressings.com
**Reg No:** 0488001 **Estd:** 1950 Public Limited Company
**Line of Business:** Metal pressworkers
**Issued Capital:** £540,000
**Principals:** O N Braime *(Chairman)*, P J Alcock, M L Mills, C O Braime, A Q Braime, A W Walker
**Co. Secretary:** Marcus Mills
**Responsibilities**
**Senior:** Edward Charlson *(Operations Director)*, Mark Sutcliffe *(Production Manager)*
**Sales:** Linzi Stockhill *(Sales Manager)*
**Facilities:** Edward Charlson *(Operations Director)*
**Operations:** Edward Charlson *(Operations Director)*, Linzi Stockhill *(Sales Manager)*
**Engineering:** Mark Sutcliffe *(Production Manager)*
**US SIC:** 6711, 3317
**UK SIC:** 83962, 22200
**Auditors:** BDO Stoy Hayward LLP
**Bankers:** National Westminster Bank Plc (60-60-05)

| | 31-12-13 | 31-12-12 | 31-12-11 |
|---|---|---|---|
| TO | 22,953,805 | 21,211,887 | 20,067,905 |
| P/L | 1,010,233 | 678,221 | 1,244,233 |
| NW | 6,668,639 | 6,199,278 | 5,940,987 |
| WC | 4,826,304 | 5,198,604 | 5,048,273 |
| Emp. | 125 | 118 | 115 |

DUNS 22-505-0012 Imp-Exp
## Tfc Ltd
**(Subsidiary of:** Tfc Europe Ltd)
Hale House, Ghyll Industrial Estate, Heathfield, East Sussex TN21 8AW
**Tel:** 01435-866-011 **Fax:** 01435-866-620
**Web:** www.tfcplc.com
**Reg No:** 0675195 **VAT No:** 351338568
**Estd:** 1960 Private Limited Company
**Line of Business:** Other wholesale
**Export Sales:** £6,300,065
**Issued Capital:** £150,850
**Principals:** E J Davis *(Financial)*, M Burgoyne, M H Clarke
**Co. Secretary:** Graham Smith
**Responsibilities**
**Senior:** Berndt Herhold *(Director)*, Andy Seymour *(Warehouse Manager)*
**Marketing:** Greg Templeman *(Business Manager)*
**IT:** Brian Goode *(Technical Director)*
**Facilities:** Andy Seymour *(Warehouse Manager)*
**Branches:** Tfc Ltd, Westside Centre, London Road, Stanway, Colchester, Essex CO3 8PH
**US SIC:** 5199 **UK SIC:** 61900
**Auditors:** Crowe Clark Whitehill LLP
**Bankers:** National Westminster Bank Plc (60-10-30)

| | 31-03-14 | 31-03-13 | 31-03-12 |
|---|---|---|---|
| TO | 19,454,261 | 18,053,499 | 13,422,884 |
| P/L | 2,131,500 | 1,769,809 | 1,547,970 |
| NW | 9,727,704 | 8,174,413 | 6,781,449 |
| WC | 8,730,513 | 7,246,192 | 5,961,541 |
| Emp. | 102 | 101 | 64 |

DUNS 39-991-7020
## T.F.G. Ltd
81 Whitfield Street, London W1T 4HF
**Tel:** 02072555100
**Web:** www.tfgworldwide.com
**Reg No:** 2280182 **Estd:** 1988 Private Limited Company
**Line of Business:** Marketing consultants
**Issued Capital:** £100
**Managing Director:** R S Fox
**Co. Secretary:** Mrs Phyllis Fox
**Responsibilities**
**Senior:** Adam Kirby *(Manager)*, John Pendelton *(Building Manager)*
**US SIC:** 7392, 8911
**UK SIC:** 83951, 83701
**Bankers:** National Westminster Bank Plc (60-06-23)

| | 31-07-13 | 31-07-12 | 31-07-11 |
|---|---|---|---|
| TA | 12,073 | 13,662 | 12,560 |
| NW | 179 | 701 | 138 |
| WC | (3,374) | (2,491) | (3,286) |

DUNS 23-037-9067
## Tfm Farm & Country Superstore Ltd
**(Subsidiary of:** Telford Farm Machinery Ltd)
Stableford, Bridgnorth, Shropshire WV15 5LS
**Tel:** 01746-784000
**Web:** www.tfmsuperstore.co.uk
**Reg No:** 3075855 **VAT No:** 661537334
**Estd:** 1995 Private Limited Company
**Line of Business:** Agricultural merchants
**Issued Capital:** £2
**Directors:** T G Littleford, Steketee Beheer B.V.
**Co. Secretary:** Richard Luckett
**Responsibilities**
**Senior:** Mark Dayus *(Manager)*, Mark Littleford *(Manager)*
**Marketing:** Mark Dayus *(Manager)*
**Sales:** Mark Littleford *(Manager)*
**HR:** Mark Dayus *(Manager)*
**Health & Safety:** Mark Dayus *(Manager)*
**Facilities:** Mark Dayus *(Manager)*
**US SIC:** 5159 **UK SIC:** 61100
**Auditors:** Deloitte & Touche

| | 31-12-13 | 31-12-12 | 31-12-11 |
|---|---|---|---|
| TO | 8,708,332 | 8,176,206 | 7,246,117 |
| P/L | 236,553 | 85,934 | (174,700) |
| NW | 1,173,952 | 1,005,733 | 945,679 |
| WC | 863,643 | 728,803 | 583,912 |
| Emp. | 59 | 58 | 60 |

DUNS 21-140-4247
## Tfs Stores Ltd
**(Subsidiary of:** Cartoon (Holdings) Ltd)
Unit 6 Churchill Point, Lake Edge Green, Trafford Park, Manchester M17 1BL
**Tel:** 01618487111
**Web:** www.thefragranceshop.co.uk
**Reg No:** 6789842 **Estd:** 2009 Private Limited Company
**Line of Business:** Representative office
**Issued Capital:** £2
**Directors:** V J Vadera, P King, S J Vadera
**Responsibilities**
**Senior:** Sanjay Bavera *(Manager)*
**US SIC:** 5999 **UK SIC:** 65600
**Bankers:** Yorkshire Bank Plc (05-05-73)

| | 31-03-14 | 31-03-13 | 31-03-12 |
|---|---|---|---|
| TO | 69,284,000 | 63,347,000 | 56,237,000 |
| P/L | 6,601,000 | 6,534,000 | 5,374,000 |
| NW | 18,926,000 | 13,831,000 | 8,942,000 |
| WC | 15,986,000 | 11,344,000 | 7,301,000 |
| Emp. | 747 | 694 | 638 |

DUNS 21-582-7403 Imp
## T.G. Baker (Sound) Ltd
173-175 Glasgow Road, Clydebank, Dunbartonshire G81 1LQ
**Tel:** 0141-941-3399 **Fax:** 0141-952-6003
**Web:** www.tgbaker.com
**Reg No:** 0053364SC **VAT No:** 261841071
**Estd:** 1973 Private Limited Company
**Line of Business:** Other retail sale in specialised stores not elsewhere classified
**Issued Capital:** £55,000
**Principals:** T G Baker *(Managing)*, I A Newport, J A Baker
**Co. Secretary:** Ms Myra Baker
**Responsibilities**
**Finance:** Alistair Cowan *(Office Manager & Accountant)*
**Admin:** Alistair Cowan *(Office Manager & Accountant)*
**Branches:** T.g. Baker (Sound) Ltd, Unit 9, Sedgley Park Trading Estate, Prestwich, Manchester M25 9WD
**US SIC:** 5999, 1799
**UK SIC:** 65600, 50000
**Bankers:** Bank Of Scotland (80-07-14)

| | 30-06-14 | 30-06-13 | 30-06-12 |
|---|---|---|---|
| TA | 1,966,949 | 2,465,327 | 2,197,541 |
| NW | 1,006,602 | 916,078 | 927,601 |
| WC | 931,449 | 912,810 | 981,844 |

DUNS 28-875-7768
## T.G. Holdcroft (Motors) Ltd
Leek Road, Stoke-On-Trent, Staffordshire ST1 6AT
**Tel:** 01782202330
**Web:** www.holdcroft.com
**Reg No:** 1107554 **Estd:** 1969 Private Limited Company
**Line of Business:** Car dealers (new & used)
**Trading Style:** Hyundai Motors Stoke
**Issued Capital:** £10
**Director:** T G Holdcroft
**Co. Secretary:** Terence Holdcroft
**Responsibilities**
**Senior:** Paula Holdcroft *(Director)*
**Branches:** T.g. Holdcroft (Motors) Ltd, Leek Road, Stoke-On-Trent, Staffordshire ST1 6AT
**US SIC:** 5511 **UK SIC:** 65100
**Auditors:** D P C

**Bankers:** Barclays Bank Plc (20-36-43)

| | 31-12-13 | 31-12-12 | 31-12-11 |
|---|---|---|---|
| TO | 32,941,239 | 27,812,105 | 33,573,874 |
| P/L | (105,707) | (102,478) | (119,488) |
| NW | 60,783 | 166,490 | 268,968 |
| WC | (536,546) | (536,200) | (815,169) |
| Emp. | 94 | 92 | 93 |

DUNS 21-710-7077
## T.G. Jeary Ltd
Romarsh Ltdindu, Clarke Avenue Porte, Calne, Wiltshire SN11 9BS
**Tel:** 01249-814700
**Web:** www.agricentre.net
**Reg No:** 0703064 **Estd:** 1961 Private Limited Company
**Line of Business:** Distribution service providers
**Trading Style:** Agricentre
**Issued Capital:** £13,975
**Directors:** Miss J H Jeary, P R Ashdown, N J Stead, Ms N C Ashdown, I R Jeary, Miss E Taylor, J T Brown, Ms T Tough
**Co. Secretary:** Paul Sealey
**Responsibilities**
**Senior:** Paul Antrobus *(Manager)*, Geoffrey Jeary *(Manager)*
**Branches:** T.g. Jeary Ltd, Long Lane, Newport, Isle Of Wight PO30 2NW
**US SIC:** 5159 **UK SIC:** 61100
**Auditors:** RSM Bentley Jennison
**Bankers:** Barclays Bank Plc (20-05-06)

| | 31-12-13 | 31-12-12 | 31-12-11 |
|---|---|---|---|
| TO | 15,381,022 | 15,291,597 | 13,640,976 |
| P/L | (157,711) | 217,432 | 218,025 |
| NW | 3,626,289 | 3,537,177 | 3,449,361 |
| WC | 2,235,542 | 2,327,320 | 2,220,311 |
| Emp. | 77 | 75 | 73 |

DUNS 21-018-6896
## T.G. Lynes Ltd.
115 Brancroft Way, Enfield, Middlesex EN3 7QE
**Tel:** 02082161900 **Fax:** 020-7278-1560
**Web:** www.tglynes.co.uk
**Reg No:** 0287486 **VAT No:** 232820979
**Estd:** 1916 Private Limited Company
**Line of Business:** Plumbing
**Issued Capital:** £116,401
**Principals:** M D Lynes *(Managing)*, D G Wheeler, Mrs L M Lynes
**Co. Secretary:** Derek Wheeler
**Responsibilities**
**Senior:** Andrew Lynes *(Manager)*, David Lynes *(Chief Executive)*, Stephen Lynes *(Manager)*, Robert Pratt *(Operations Director)*
**Marketing:** Bob Jarvis *(Business Development Manager)*
**Sales:** Tony Branton *(Sales Manager)*, Michael Brett *(Sales Manager)*, Owen Cover *(Sales Manager)*, Adam Ellwood *(Sales Manager)*, Tom Figura *(Sales Manager)*, Bob Jarvis *(Business Development Manager)*, Joe Kane *(Sales Director)*, Gerry Wood *(Sales Manager)*
**IT:** Robert Pratt *(Operations Director)*
**HR:** Lesley Davall *(Human Resources Manager)*
**Facilities:** Robert Pratt *(Operations Director)*
**Operations:** Robert Pratt *(Operations Director)*
**Engineering:** Paul Draper *(Plant Hire Manager)*
**Branches:** T.g. Lynes Ltd., 115 Brancroft Way, Enfield, Middlesex EN3 7QE
**US SIC:** 1711 **UK SIC:** 50300
**Auditors:** Price Bailey LLP
**Bankers:** Lloyds TSB Bank plc (30-00-09)

| | 30-06-14 | 30-06-13 | 30-06-12 |
|---|---|---|---|
| TO | 18,315,844 | 17,296,377 | 18,690,231 |
| P/L | 2,099,140 | 1,734,460 | 1,911,988 |
| NW | 9,696,095 | 8,605,934 | 8,731,126 |
| WC | 5,373,602 | 4,391,756 | 4,469,116 |
| Emp. | 56 | 55 | 55 |

DUNS 22-152-6085
## Tgc International Ltd
12 Stirling Park, Laker Road, Rochester, Kent ME1 3QR
**Fax:** 01634-687-037
**Web:** www.tgc.uk.com
**Reg No:** 4171318 **Estd:** 2001 Private Limited Company
**Line of Business:** Manufacture of electricity distribution and control apparatus
**Export Sales:** £104,643
**Trading Style:** The Generator Company
**Issued Capital:** £100
**Directors:** J N Stickings, Ms S M Allen
**Co. Secretary:** Jayson Stickings
**Branches:** Tgc International Ltd, 12 Laker Road, Stirling Park, Rochester, Kent ME1 3QR
**US SIC:** 3643, 7399
**UK SIC:** 34203, 83954
**Auditors:** Reeves & Co LLP

| | 31-03-14 | 31-03-13 | 31-03-12 |
|---|---|---|---|
| TO | 7,989,450 | 8,401,302 | 4,440,791 |
| P/L | 656,147 | 1,168,754 | (295,099) |
| NW | 2,509,823 | 2,106,523 | 1,325,074 |
| WC | (125,322) | (69,433) | (510,372) |
| Emp. | 39 | 48 | 34 |

**DUNS 21-826-0453**　　　　　　　　**Imp-Exp**
## T.Groocock & Co.(Rothwell) Ltd
Kettering Parkway, Kettering Venture Park, Kettering, Northamptonshire NN15 6WY
**Tel:** 01536534988
**Web:** www.padders.co.uk
**Reg No:** 0351563 **VAT No:** 119905359
**Estd:** 1939 Private Limited Company
**Line of Business:** Manufacture of footwear
**Export Markets:** Worldwide
**Export Sales:** £774,932
**Trading Style:** Padders
**Issued Capital:** £79,911
**Principals:** T E Groocock (Chairman and Managing), J R Bligh, S R Valentine, J I Groocock
**Co. Secretary:** Ms Jane Garner
**Responsibilities**
**Senior:** Kate Rowe (Manager)
**Branches:** T.groocock & Co.(Rothwell) Ltd, 79-81 Main St, Sedbergh, Cumbria LA10 5AB
**US SIC:** 3149 **UK SIC:** 45100
**Auditors:** Grant Thornton UK LLP
**Bankers:** National Westminster Bank Plc (53-61-33)

|     | 31-01-14 | 31-01-13 | 31-01-12 |
|-----|----------|----------|----------|
| TO  | 6,641,920 | 6,525,061 | 8,018,031 |
| P/L | (88,444) | (267,893) | 268,714 |
| NW  | 6,877,170 | 6,953,060 | 8,192,387 |
| WC  | 4,838,370 | 4,800,022 | 5,569,017 |
| Emp. | 39 | 47 | 49 |

**DUNS 34-935-2729**
## Tgs Geophysical Co (Uk) Ltd
(Subsidiary of: Tgs Nopec Geophysical Company Asa)
Standard House, Weyside Park, Catteshall Lane, Godalming, Surrey GU7 1XE
**Web:** www.tgs.com
**Reg No:** 5731700 **Estd:** 2006 Private Limited Company
**Line of Business:** Service activities incidental to oil and gas extraction excluding surveying
**Directors:** T L Pool, M A Bett, A Bhartia, K K Johansen, T Sutula
**Co. Secretary:** The Briars Group Ltd
**US SIC:** 1389, 7391
**UK SIC:** 13000, 94000
**Auditors:** PricewaterhouseCoopers LLP
**Employees:** 12
**Turnover:** £35,830,796

**DUNS 67-141-6308**
## Tgw Ltd
(Subsidiary of: Tgw-Future Privatstiftung)
Falcon Court, Off Rockingham Road, Market Harborough, Leicestershire LE16 7XY
**Tel:** 01858-468-855 **Fax:** 01858-419-613
**Web:** www.tgw-group.com
**Reg No:** 6000337 **Estd:** 2006 Private Limited Company
**Line of Business:** Manufacture of lifting and handling equipment
**Export Sales:** £9,168,272
**Trading Style:** Tgw Group
**Issued Capital:** £100,000
**Directors:** N Goudie, I M Powell, G Kirchmayr, D M Jenkinson, A J Smith
**Responsibilities**
**Senior:** Jamie Bunting (Project Manager)
**Sales:** Phillip Steeds (Sales Director)
**US SIC:** 3534 **UK SIC:** 32553
**Auditors:** Mark J Rees LLP

|     | 30-06-14 | 30-06-13 | 30-06-12 |
|-----|----------|----------|----------|
| TO  | 34,553,750 | 41,082,495 | 21,780,119 |
| P/L | 1,102,010 | 1,936,928 | 808,018 |
| NW  | 2,413,831 | 3,710,957 | 2,797,575 |
| WC  | 1,460,461 | 4,403,318 | 3,723,036 |
| Emp. | 117 | 88 | 67 |

**DUNS 21-229-8005**
## Thackley Green Specialist Care Centre
Lewin Road, Great Oakley, Corby, Northamptonshire NN18 8JS
**Tel:** 01536-462720
**Estd:** 2004
**Line of Business:** Residential care establishments
**Proprietor:** Mrs G Makanda
**Responsibilities**
**Senior:** Laura Wood (Manager)
**US SIC:** 8321 **UK SIC:** 96111
**Employees:** 70

**DUNS 21-102-7462**
## Thackray Williams Llp
Kings House 32-40, Widmore Road, Bromley, Kent BR1 1RY
**Tel:** 020-8290-0440 **Fax:** 020-8464-5282
**Web:** www.thackraywilliams.com
**Reg No:** 0333759OC **Estd:** 1986 Private Limited Company
**Line of Business:** Solicitors

**Responsibilities**
**Senior:** Linda Gabriel (Senior Partner), Kevin Gauntlett (Designated Limited Liability P)
**Finance:** Nicole Simon (Accountant)
**Sales:** Nicole Simon (Accountant)
**Admin:** Sharon Woods (Office Manager)
**IT:** Garry Ling (IT Manager)
**HR:** Sharon Woods (Office Manager)
**Health & Safety:** Sharon Woods (Office Manager)
**Facilities:** Sharon Woods (Office Manager)
**Purchasing:** Sharon Woods (Office Manager)
**US SIC:** 8111 **UK SIC:** 83500

|     | 31-03-14 | 31-03-13 | 31-03-12 |
|-----|----------|----------|----------|
| TO  | 7,501,893 | 7,018,919 | 7,201,828 |
| P/L | N/A | N/A | 2,327,349 |
| NW  | 30,000 | 15,000 | 3,146,021 |
| WC  | 2,115,557 | 2,223,033 | 2,570,174 |
| Emp. | 124 | 109 | 113 |

**DUNS 22-718-4249**
## Thai Airways International Public Co Ltd
(Subsidiary of: Thai Airways International Public Company Limited)
41 Albemarle Street, London W1S 4BF
**Tel:** 08445610911 **Fax:** 02074091463
**Web:** www.thaiairways.co.uk
**Reg No:** 0008418FC **Estd:** 2009 Foreign Company
**Line of Business:** Airlines
**Trading Style:** Thai Airways International
**Principals:** Air Chief Marshall G Pimantip (Chairman), E Kiriwat, A Thammano, P Chakkaphak, P Pakkasem, Professor S Chatusripitak, R Sriprasertsuk, Air Chief Marshall S Sodsatit
**Co. Secretary:** Chatrachai Bunya-Ananta
**Responsibilities**
**Senior:** Komain Bhatarabhirom (Director), Prachoom Chaisiri (Director), Mahidol Chantrangkurn (Vice Chairperson), Manoj Pompibul (Director)
**US SIC:** 4511 **UK SIC:** 75000

**DUNS 21-022-0286**
## Thain's Bakery
341 George Street, Aberdeen, Aberdeenshire AB25 1EE
**Tel:** 01224627101
**Web:** www.thains.com
**Estd:** 1968 Partnership
**Line of Business:** Bakers and confectioners supplies
**Partners:** A Thain, G Thain
**Responsibilities**
**Senior:** Graheme Thain (Managing Director)
**Branches:** Thain's Bakery, 227 Rosemount Pl, Aberdeen, Aberdeenshire AB25 2XS
**US SIC:** 5462 **UK SIC:** 64100
**Employees:** 50

**DUNS 76-836-9860**
## Thainstone House Hotel Ltd
(Subsidiary of: Lloyds Banking Group Plc)
Thainstone House Hotel Country Club, Inverurie, Aberdeenshire AB51 5NT
**Tel:** 01467-621643
**Web:** www.swallow-hotels.com
**Reg No:** 0131433SC **VAT No:** 384774603
**Estd:** 1991 Private Limited Company
**Line of Business:** Hotels
**Issued Capital:** £440,000
**Co. Secretary:** Robert Fraser
**Responsibilities**
**Senior:** Eric Baine (General Manager), Barry Clark (General Manager), Jurgen Krujit (General Manager), Robin Osmin (General Manager), Peter Sangster (General Manager), Dawn Wood (Financial Controller)
**Finance:** Dawn Wood (Financial Controller)
**IT:** Dawn Wood (Financial Controller)
**Health & Safety:** Graham Ritchie (Operations Manager)
**US SIC:** 7011, 6531
**UK SIC:** 66500, 83400
**Auditors:** KPMG Audit Plc
**Bankers:** Bank Of Scotland (80-08-41)

|     | 27-03-14 | 31-03-13 | 29-03-12 |
|-----|----------|----------|----------|
| TA  | 1,050,000 | 1,050,000 | 1,050,000 |
| NW  | 1,050,000 | 1,050,000 | 1,050,000 |

**DUNS 73-389-5010**
## Thairama Restaurants Ltd
Sydenham Road, Guildford, Surrey GU1 3RT
**Tel:** 01483503350 **Fax:** 01483503360
**Reg No:** 4662985 **Estd:** 2003 Private Limited Company
**Line of Business:** Restaurant - thai
**Trading Style:** Thaiterrace Restaurant
**Issued Capital:** £100,000
**Directors:** W Poonum, N Poonum
**Co. Secretary:** Wanjai Poonum
**Responsibilities**
**Senior:** Siva Khumehuen (CEO, Managing Director)

**US SIC:** 5812, 5813
**UK SIC:** 66110, 66200

|     | 30-04-14 | 30-04-13 | 30-04-12 |
|-----|----------|----------|----------|
| TA  | 792,216 | 728,116 | 680,374 |
| NW  | 175,960 | 80,486 | 103,160 |
| WC  | 200,302 | 96,486 | 61,509 |

**DUNS 21-042-2771**
## Thalassa Nursing Home
79 Western Way, Gosport, Hampshire PO12 2NF
**Tel:** 02392582382
**Estd:** 1974
**Line of Business:** Nursing homes
**Responsibilities**
**Senior:** Fiona Clemson (Manager)
**US SIC:** 8051 **UK SIC:** 95100
**Employees:** 55

**DUNS 22-643-2763**　　　　　　　　**Exp**
## Thales Communications Ltd
(Subsidiary of: Thales)
Newton Road, Crawley, West Sussex RH10 9TS
**Tel:** 01293446374
**Web:** www.thalesgroup.com
**Reg No:** 1272585 **Estd:** 1938 Private Limited Company
**Line of Business:** Management activities of holding companies
**Export Markets:** E U, U.S.A, Africa, Far East, Australia and other areas.
**Trading Style:** Thales Land & Join Systems
**Issued Capital:** £9,500,000
**Director:** P J Rowley
**Co. Secretary:** Michael Seabrook
**Branches:** Thales Communications Ltd, Manor Royal, Crawley, West Sussex RH10 9HA
**US SIC:** 7399 **UK SIC:** 83954
**Bankers:** HSBC Bank plc (40-02-50)

|     | 31-12-13 | 31-12-12 | 31-12-11 |
|-----|----------|----------|----------|
| TA  | 28,448,000 | 28,448,000 | 28,448,000 |
| NW  | 15,850,000 | 28,448,000 | 28,448,000 |
| WC  | 15,850,000 | N/A | N/A |

**DUNS 21-407-6192**　　　　　　　　**Imp-Exp**
## Thales Optronics Ltd
(Subsidiary of: Thales)
1 Linthouse Road, Glasgow, Lanarkshire G51 4BZ
**Tel:** 0141-440-4000
**Web:** www.thalesgroup.com
**Reg No:** 0008495SC **VAT No:** 198955680
**Estd:** 1994 Private Limited Company
**Line of Business:** Manufacturers of scientific machinery and instrument
**Export Markets:** E U, Australasia, North America, South America
**Issued Capital:** £31,663,000
**Directors:** S M Boulton, G M Blanguernon, Ms M E Broughton
**Co. Secretary:** Michael Seabrook
**Responsibilities**
**Senior:** Alexander Cresswell (Manager), Ewen Mccrorie (Financial Director)
**Finance:** Ewen Mccrorie (Financial Director)
**Marketing:** Julian Grinstead (Sub Contract Manager), Alan Steveson (Senior Marketing Manager)
**IT:** Carla Valentini (IT Manager)
**HR:** Jim Finlayson (Human Resources Manager)
**Health & Safety:** S MacAleese (Health & Safety Officer)
**Facilities:** George Greer (Facilities Manager)
**Operations:** William Gibb (Quality Manager), S MacAleese (Health & Safety Officer)
**Purchasing:** Simon Heggie (Purchasing Manager)
**Engineering:** Paul Packard (Engineering Manager)
**Branches:** Thales Optronics Ltd, Paceycombe Way, Dorchester, Dorset DT1 3SY
**US SIC:** 3829, 3832
**UK SIC:** 37100, 37320
**Auditors:** Mazars LLP

|     | 31-12-13 | 31-12-12 | 31-12-11 |
|-----|----------|----------|----------|
| TO  | 214,971,000 | 230,218,000 | 229,197,000 |
| P/L | (20,889,000) | 31,867,000 | 24,361,000 |
| NW  | 42,514,000 | 110,311,000 | 87,385,000 |
| WC  | N/A | 102,272,000 | 94,475,000 |
| Emp. | 698 | 679 | 716 |

**DUNS 49-385-3923**
## Thales Transport & Security Ltd
(Subsidiary of: Thales)
7 Fleet Place, London EC4M 7RD
**Tel:** 01189-086000
**Web:** www.thalesgroup.com
**Reg No:** 3132438 **Estd:** 1994 Private Limited Company
**Line of Business:** Management activities of holding companies
**Trading Style:** Security Solutions & Services
**Issued Capital:** £79,650,001

**Directors:** G J Marsh, K J Ford, Y Pathmanathan, P Maynard, M S Garrity, A J Welch, G J Cunningham, A D Mcphee
**Co. Secretary:** Michael Seabrook
**Responsibilities**
**Senior:** Shaun Jones (Director), Philip Wellstead (Director)
**Finance:** Ewen McCrorie (Vice President, Finance)
**Marketing:** Trevor Lampen (Strategy, Sales & Marketing Di)
**Sales:** Trevor Lampen (Strategy, Sales & Marketing Di)
**IT:** Edward Lowe (Vice President, Defence Missio)
**HR:** Kathy Jenkins (Vice President Human Resources)
**Health & Safety:** Nigel Webb (senior health & safety manager)
**Operations:** Justin Walker (Vice President, Services & Ope)
**Engineering:** Peter Hitchcock (Vice President, Avionics), Alvin Wilby (Vice President, Strategy & Tec)
**Branches:** Thales Transport & Security Ltd, Hudson House, Toft Green, York, North Yorkshire YO1 6JT
**US SIC:** 6711 **UK SIC:** 83962
**Auditors:** Mazars LLP
**Bankers:** Barclays Bank Plc (20-00-00)

|     | 31-12-13 | 31-12-12 | 31-12-11 |
|-----|----------|----------|----------|
| TO  | 115,803,000 | 107,411,000 | 78,635,000 |
| P/L | 20,730,000 | 1,982,000 | (20,988,000) |
| NW  | (42,329,000) | (6,264,000) | (12,843,000) |
| WC  | (35,808,000) | (57,263,000) | (61,674,000) |
| Emp. | 712 | 686 | 612 |

**DUNS 28-859-7297**
## Thales Uk Ltd
(Subsidiary of: Thales)
2 Dashwood Lang Road, The Bourne Business Park, Addlestone, Surrey KT15 2NX
**Fax:** 01932-824-948
**Web:** www.thalesgroup.com
**Reg No:** 0868273 **Estd:** 1893 Private Limited Company
**Line of Business:** Manufacture of electronic valves and tubes and other electronic components
**Issued Capital:** £481,937,600
**Directors:** P M Naybour, Ms K H Jenkins, G E Baruchel, Ms M E Broughton, P Gosling, A D Mcphee, W A Wilby, P J Rowley
**Co. Secretary:** Michael Seabrook
**Responsibilities**
**Senior:** Mark Hearn (Partner), Peter Hitchcock (Director), Edward Lowe (Director), Dean Mason (Director), Ewen Mccrorie (Director), Mark Rowson (General Manager), Bruno Vazzoler (Partner), Justin Walker (Director)
**Marketing:** Dean Mason (Director), John Warehand (Communications Manager)
**Sales:** Dean Mason (Director)
**Admin:** Jane Buckell (Personal Assistant)
**HR:** David Tournadre (Human Resources Manager)
**Engineering:** Steve Emery (Project Engineering Manager)
**Branches:** Thales Uk Ltd, Lyon Road, Walton-On-Thames, Surrey KT12 3PU
**US SIC:** 3679, 3662, 8911, 9711
**UK SIC:** 34542, 34430, 83701
**Auditors:** Mazars LLP
**Bankers:** National Westminster Bank Plc (50-00-00)

|     | 31-12-13 | 31-12-12 | 31-12-11 |
|-----|----------|----------|----------|
| TO  | 346,166,000 | 358,347,000 | 413,733,000 |
| P/L | 146,113,000 | (61,348,000) | (683,000) |
| NW  | 29,512,000 | 209,855,000 | 270,634,000 |
| WC  | 185,244,000 | (170,778,000) | (93,625,000) |
| Emp. | 1,664 | 1,954 | 1,896 |

**DUNS 21-719-4711**
## Thalest Ltd
(Subsidiary of: Larsen and Toubro Limited)
Endeavour House, Holloway Road, Heybridge, Maldon, Essex CM9 4ER
**Tel:** 01621862583 **Fax:** 01621862584
**Web:** www.servowatch.com
**Reg No:** 1201246 **VAT No:** 282777908
**Estd:** 1975 Private Limited Company
**Line of Business:** Marine engines and engineering
**Export Sales:** £2,412,400
**Issued Capital:** £233,656
**Directors:** S C Bhargava, M Goel, W Ross
**Responsibilities**
**Senior:** Colin Barrell (Manager), Brian Blackwell (Manager), Martyn Dickinson (Sales Manager)
**Sales:** Martyn Dickinson (Sales Manager)
**US SIC:** 8911, 5065
**UK SIC:** 83701, 61500
**Auditors:** Berke Fine Fussell Ltd
**Bankers:** HSBC Bank plc (40-28-11)

|     | 31-12-13 | 31-12-12 | 31-12-12 |
|-----|----------|----------|----------|
| TO  | 3,440,388 | 2,135,704 | 3,736,205 |
| P/L | (1,322,639) | (569,863) | (253,682) |
| NW  | (2,011,984) | (395,532) | 264,536 |
| WC  | (1,397,163) | (1,051,640) | (319,762) |

DUNS 21-607-4736
## Thame Leisure Centre
Oxford Road, Thame, Oxfordshire OX9 2BB
**Tel:** 01844215607
**Web:** www.sol-leisure.co.uk
**Estd:** 2011 Proprietorship
**Line of Business:** Other sporting activities not elsewhere classified
**Proprietor:** N Latham
**US SIC:** 8999 **UK SIC:** 83954
**Employees:** 100

DUNS 21-391-5621
## Thames Accord
Pondfield House, 100 Wantz Road, Dagenham, Essex RM10 8PP
**Tel:** 020-85927388
**Web:** www.lbbd.gov.uk
**Partnership**
**Line of Business:** Property maintenance services
**Trading Style:** Housing Repairs and Maintenance - Barking and Dagenham
**Partners:** S White, G Stygalls
**US SIC:** 1799 **UK SIC:** 50000
**Employees:** 296

DUNS 23-651-7186
## Thames Ambulance Service Ltd
Canvey Road, Canvey Island, Essex SS8 0PA
**Tel:** 01268511151 **Fax:** 01268660838
**Web:** www.thamesambulance.co.uk
**Reg No:** 3646929 **VAT No:** 809846883
**Estd:** 1996 Private Limited Company
**Line of Business:** Hospital activities
**Issued Capital:** £400
**Directors:** Mrs M J Serna, S Pellegri
**Responsibilities**
**Senior:** Michelle Dudbridge *(Manager)*, William Dudbridge *(Manager)*, Nancy Etherington *(Manager)*
**Finance:** Angela Gilbert *(Financial Manager)*
**HR:** Angela Gilbert *(Financial Manager)*
**US SIC:** 8062 **UK SIC:** 95100
**Bankers:** Barclays Bank Plc (20-70-93)

| | 31-03-14 | 31-03-13 | 31-03-12 |
|---|---|---|---|
| TO | 7,630,524 | N/A | 5,423,485 |
| P/L | 403,684 | N/A | 307,116 |
| NW | 936,729 | 1,028,953 | 586,129 |
| WC | 158,929 | 110,603 | (260,359) |
| Emp. | 210 | N/A | N/A |

DUNS 29-622-2102 **Imp-Exp**
## Thames & Hudson (Holdings) Ltd
(**Subsidiary of:** Dolphin (Bahamas) Limited)
Esavian House, 181a High Holborn, London WC1V 7QX
**Tel:** 020-7845-5000
**Web:** www.thamesandhudson.com
**Reg No:** 1948746 **Estd:** 1985 Private Limited Company
**Line of Business:** Book publishers
**Export Markets:** Worldwide
**Export Sales:** £16,301,000
**Issued Capital:** £2,700,000
**Principals:** T M Neurath *(Managing)*, Ms C Kaine, Ms J M Neurath, Mrs S A Reisz Neurath
**Co. Secretary:** Brian Meek
**US SIC:** 2731 **UK SIC:** 47532
**Auditors:** PricewaterhouseCoopers
**Bankers:** Barclays Bank Plc (20-78-98)

| | 31-12-13 | 31-12-12 | 31-12-11 |
|---|---|---|---|
| TO | 24,364,000 | 26,836,000 | 24,306,000 |
| P/L | 561,000 | 1,079,000 | 1,447,000 |
| NW | 24,962,000 | 26,274,000 | 23,156,000 |
| WC | 22,671,000 | 23,975,000 | 23,101,000 |
| Emp. | 162 | 166 | 164 |

DUNS 22-705-8146
## Thames Cleaning & Support Services Ltd
14 Hatherley Road, Sidcup, Kent DA14 4BG
**Tel:** 02083026633
**Web:** www.thamescleaning.co.uk
**Reg No:** 0940586 **VAT No:** 206267577
**Estd:** 1968 Private Limited Company
**Line of Business:** Cleaning activities not elsewhere classified
**Trading Style:** Thames Service Group
**Issued Capital:** £50,000
**Principals:** M Weller *(Managing)*, Ms J M Weller, A M Weller
**Co. Secretary:** Michael Weller
**Responsibilities**
**Operations:** Clive Saint *(Operations Director)*
**US SIC:** 7349 **UK SIC:** 92300
**Auditors:** Opass Billings Wilson & Honey
**Bankers:** Barclays Bank Plc (20-14-33)

| | 31-03-14 | 31-03-13 | 31-03-12 |
|---|---|---|---|
| TA | 961,842 | 1,039,814 | 1,035,616 |
| NW | 703,329 | 771,254 | 867,697 |
| WC | 55,522 | 123,109 | 233,879 |

DUNS 64-103-8880
## Thames Direct Ltd
Thames House, Arterial Road, Rayleigh, Essex SS6 7UQ
**Tel:** 01268-775555 **Fax:** 01268775556
**Web:** www.thamescardtechnology.com
**Reg No:** 3498657 **Estd:** 1998 Private Limited Company
**Line of Business:** Other manufacturing not elsewhere classified
**Trading Style:** Thames Direct Ltd
**Issued Capital:** £100
**Directors:** P G Underwood, D Watkins
**Co. Secretary:** Gary Short
**US SIC:** 3999 **UK SIC:** 49590
**Auditors:** Wilkins Kennedy
**Bankers:** National Westminster Bank Plc (60-05-13)

| | 30-11-13 | 30-11-12 | 30-11-11 |
|---|---|---|---|
| TA | 19,115 | 19,115 | 19,115 |
| NW | 19,115 | 19,115 | 19,115 |

DUNS 28-892-6728
## Thames Ditton Sports & Squash Club Ltd
St Nicholas Road, Thames Ditton, Surrey KT7 0PH
**Tel:** 020-8398-7108 **Fax:** 02083988275
**Web:** www.coletshealthclub.co.uk
**Reg No:** 1293948 **Estd:** 1977 Private Company Limited By Guarantee
**Line of Business:** Health clubs
**Trading Style:** Colets Health & Fitness Club
**Directors:** N J Carr, B A Michels, B M Roberts, L P Jopp, B D Moss, A A Holder, J M Dennis, P Mothersill
**Co. Secretary:** Bart Michels
**Responsibilities**
**Senior:** Raymond Burton *(Director)*, Kay Crawford *(Marketing Manager)*
**US SIC:** 7299 **UK SIC:** 98902
**Auditors:** Garner Bleasdale Chandler

| | 30-09-13 | 30-09-12 | 30-09-11 |
|---|---|---|---|
| TO | 3,396,503 | 3,300,683 | 3,091,586 |
| P/L | 281,326 | 223,795 | 188,947 |
| NW | 3,917,054 | 3,626,211 | 3,411,836 |
| WC | (933,045) | (1,271,298) | (1,406,468) |
| Emp. | 160 | 146 | 128 |

DUNS 71-936-1201
## Thames Hospice
Pine Lodge, Hatch Lane, Windsor, Berkshire SL4 3RW
**Tel:** 01753842121
**Web:** www.thameshospice.org.uk
**Reg No:** 5316964 **Estd:** 1986 Private Company Limited By Guarantee
**Line of Business:** Charities and charitable organisations
**Directors:** Mrs J M Ashworth, M L Jervis, C G Aitken, G R Kaminski-Cook, Dr R H Furness, S J Moore, K F Coppock, R Goss
**Co. Secretary:** Ms Ruth Bartholomew
**Responsibilities**
**Senior:** Jacqueline Clark *(Chief Executive Officer)*, Robert Dwyer *(Director)*, Margaret Neal *(Director)*
**Branches:** Thames Hospice, 69 Rockingham Road, Uxbridge, Middlesex UB8 2UA
**US SIC:** 8091 **UK SIC:** 95200
**Bankers:** Cafcash Ltd (40-52-40)

| | 31-03-14 | 31-03-13 | 31-03-12 |
|---|---|---|---|
| TO | 5,380,000 | 11,478,445 | 5,969,302 |
| P/L | (637,000) | 5,879,340 | 510,223 |
| NW | 17,446,000 | 17,887,593 | 11,464,476 |
| WC | 3,776,000 | 6,340,919 | 3,178,041 |
| Emp. | 107 | 97 | 98 |

DUNS 22-832-8928
## Thames Housing Association Ltd
Aura House, London SW12 8PQ
**Tel:** 020-8333-6000
**Web:** www.thames-housing.co.uk
**Reg No:** 0017809IP **Estd:** 1969 Friendly Society
**Line of Business:** Housing associations societies trusts & co-operatives
**Principals:** D G Reynolds *(Chairman)*, Ms D Hodson *(Chairman)*, D R Bogle *(Managing)*, A Marks, Ms D Hodson, Ms J Longstreth, A W Hill, J Castelberg
**Co. Secretary:** David Bogle
**Responsibilities**
**Senior:** Richard Bethell-Jones *(Designated Limited Liability P)*, Jean Lucas *(Designated Limited Liability P)*, Philippa Newsam *(Designated Limited Liability P)*
**US SIC:** 8321 **UK SIC:** 96111
**Auditors:** B D O Stoy Hayward
**Bankers:** National Westminster Bank Plc (60-01-34)
**Employees:** 63
**Turnover:** £12,165,000

DUNS 21-460-4683
## Thames Meditation Society
49 Dulverton Road, South Croydon, Surrey CR2 8PJ
**Estd:** 2010
**Line of Business:** Charities and charitable organisations
**Responsibilities**
**Senior:** Herat Kulara *(President)*
**US SIC:** 8699 **UK SIC:** 96902
**Employees:** 400

DUNS 21-579-6189
## Thames Reach
1a Daley Thompson Way, London SW8 3DA
**Tel:** 02077209505
**Web:** www.thamesreach.org.uk
**Estd:** 1995 Partnership
**Line of Business:** Housing associations societies trusts & co-operatives
**Partners:** M Robson, J Swain
**US SIC:** 8321 **UK SIC:** 96111
**Employees:** 100

DUNS 23-230-9419
## Thames Reach Housing Association Ltd
29 Peckham Road, London SE5 8UA
**Tel:** 02036176070
**Web:** www.thamesreach.org.uk
**Reg No:** 0024377IP **Estd:** 1984 Friendly Society
**Line of Business:** Charities and charitable organisations
**Principals:** K Olisa *(Chairman)*, R Stern, T Hitchcock
**Co. Secretary:** B Steele
**Responsibilities**
**Senior:** Sandra Barrett *(Area Manager)*, Ed Doherty *(Team Manager)*, Hannah Gaston *(Area Manager)*, Katy Porter *(Area Director)*
**Finance:** Christine Smith-Gillespie *(Finance Director)*
**Marketing:** Mike Nicholas *(Communications Manager)*
**Sales:** Martyn Robson *(Business Development Manager)*
**IT:** Garth Hicks *(IT Manager)*
**HR:** John Ames *(Training Manager)*
**Facilities:** Bill Tidnam *(Director of Housing)*
**Operations:** Catherine Parsons *(Operations Support Manager)*
**Branches:** Thames Reach Housing Association Ltd, Parker Ho, 144 Evelyn St, London SE8 5DD
**US SIC:** 8699 **UK SIC:** 96902
**Auditors:** Jordan Frank
**Employees:** 93

DUNS 21-196-4887
## Thames Rico Ltd
(**Subsidiary of:** Patron Scimitar Holding Sarl)
Greycaines House Greycaines Road, Watford, Hertfordshire WD2 4PS
**Tel:** 01923270793 **Fax:** 01923-230941
**Reg No:** 1027878 **Estd:** 1971 Private Limited Company
**Line of Business:** Other letting of own property
**Issued Capital:** £10,000
**Directors:** W B Bannister, T E Allan, T M Biggart
**Branches:** Thames Rico Ltd, Evesham Road, Tewkesbury, Gloucestershire GL20 8NE
**US SIC:** 6519, 5541
**UK SIC:** 85000, 65200
**Auditors:** Ernst & Young
**Bankers:** Bank Of Scotland (12-02-56)

| | 31-12-13 | 30-09-12 | 30-12-11 |
|---|---|---|---|
| TA | 81,154 | 81,154 | 81,154 |
| NW | 10,000 | 10,000 | 10,000 |
| WC | 10,000 | 10,000 | 10,000 |

DUNS 77-719-8771
## Thames Trains Ltd
(**Subsidiary of:** The Go-Ahead Group Plc)
Burnham Taxilsway, Station Road, Cippenham, Slough, Berkshire SL1 6JT
**Tel:** 08457484950
**Web:** www.firstgreatwestern.co.uk
**Reg No:** 3007943 **Estd:** 1996 Private Limited Company
**Line of Business:** Other transport via railways
**Trading Style:** First Great Western Link
**Issued Capital:** £4,250,000
**Directors:** D A Brown, K Down, Mrs W M Allan
**Co. Secretary:** Ms Carolyn Ferguson
**Branches:** Thames Trains Ltd, North Camp Railway Station, Lynchford Road, Aldershot, Hampshire GU12 5QA
**US SIC:** 4011 **UK SIC:** 71000
**Auditors:** Ernst & Young LLP

| | 29-06-13 | 30-06-12 | 02-06-11 |
|---|---|---|---|
| TA | 4,250,000 | 4,250,000 | 4,250,000 |
| NW | 4,250,000 | 4,250,000 | 4,250,000 |

DUNS 21-580-1894
## Thames Valley Fire Protection
59-63 Queens Road, High Wycombe, Buckinghamshire HP13 6AH
**Tel:** 01494769700
**Web:** www.tvfltd.co.uk
**Estd:** 1979 Proprietorship
**Line of Business:** Fire protection consultants and engineers
**Proprietor:** M Lunn
**US SIC:** 8911 **UK SIC:** 83701
**Employees:** 79

DUNS 23-113-6664
## Thames Valley Foods Ltd
(**Subsidiary of:** Stonegate Holdings Ltd)
Whites Farm, Chippenham, Wiltshire SN15 4JW
**Tel:** 01249730700 **Fax:** 01249732200
**Web:** www.stonegate.co.uk
**Reg No:** 2751833 **VAT No:** 199087506
**Estd:** 1992 Private Limited Company
**Line of Business:** Manufacture of other food products not elsewhere classified
**Issued Capital:** £6,093,046
**Directors:** J D Sheppard, R G Corbett
**Co. Secretary:** James Sheppard
**Responsibilities**
**IT:** Jason Gillam *(IT Manager)*
**Branches:** Thames Valley Foods Ltd, Bleach Farm, Hardwick Road, Starston, Harleston, Norfolk IP20 9PJ
**US SIC:** 2099 **UK SIC:** 42399
**Auditors:** Deloitte LLP
**Bankers:** Barclays Bank Plc (20-01-09)

| | 28-09-13 | 29-09-12 | 01-09-11 |
|---|---|---|---|
| TO | 27,609,851 | 24,311,704 | 20,717,180 |
| P/L | 503,879 | 378,147 | (3,578,878) |
| NW | 5,695,855 | 5,086,019 | 4,707,872 |
| WC | (17,199,858) | (16,960,373) | (8,151,593) |
| Emp. | 156 | 158 | 199 |

DUNS 21-101-3862
## Thames Valley Ford
Unit 1, Petersfield Avenue, Slough, Berkshire SL2 5EA
**Proprietorship**
**Line of Business:** Sale of motor vehicle parts and accessories
**US SIC:** 5531 **UK SIC:** 65100
**Employees:** 80

DUNS 22-505-4246
## Thames Valley Housing Association Ltd
Premier House, 52 London Road, Twickenham, Middlesex TW1 3RP
**Tel:** 020-8607-0607 **Fax:** 020-8607-9923
**Web:** www.tvha.co.uk
**Reg No:** 0017375IP **VAT No:** 342821373
**Estd:** 1966 Friendly Society
**Line of Business:** Housing associations societies trusts & co-operatives
**Principals:** P Williams *(Chairman)*, J Garrity *(Chairman)*, Ms J Devereux, D Azubike, D Smith, D Mayer, R Stanley, B Mehra
**Responsibilities**
**Senior:** Roland Beadle *(Principal)*, Laura Duhot *(Principal)*, Steven Henson *(Principal)*, Jayne Hilditch *(Corporate Services Director)*, Suki Kahlon *(Facilities Manager)*, Iain Long *(Principal)*, Jane Staveley *(Principal)*
**Finance:** Jack Stephen *(Financial Director)*
**Marketing:** Z Hanis *(Sales & Marketing Manager)*, Nick Lloyd *(New Business Project Manager)*, Alex Noonoo *(Marketing Manager)*, Mark Stuart *(Digital Communications Manager)*
**Sales:** Mark Allnutt *(Commercial Director)*, Chatinder Bal *(Land & New Business Manager)*, Guy Burnett *(Development Director)*, Z Hanis *(Sales & Marketing Manager)*
**IT:** Caroline Morgan *(Computer Manager)*, A Orbe *(IT Manager)*
**HR:** Jonathan Ling *(Head Of HR)*, Sarbjit Mann *(Assistant Human Resources Advi)*
**Branches:** Thames Valley Housing Association Ltd, Holtye Road, East Grinstead, West Sussex RH19 3DZ
**US SIC:** 8321 **UK SIC:** 96111
**Auditors:** BDO Stoy Hayward LLP
**Bankers:** Barclays Bank Plc (20-90-56)

| | 31-03-12 | 31-03-11 | 31-03-10 |
|---|---|---|---|
| TO | 84,583,000 | 72,960,000 | 74,166,000 |
| P/L | 17,637,000 | 11,244,000 | 10,753,000 |
| NW | 253,236,000 | 171,957,000 | 164,173,000 |
| WC | 61,343,000 | 75,592,000 | 59,670,000 |
| Emp. | 204 | 212 | 220 |

DUNS 23-293-5879
## Thames Valley Primary Care Agency
7-9 Cremyll Road, Reading, Berkshire RG1 8NQ
**Tel:** 01189-183333
**Web:** www.tvpca.nhs.uk
**Estd:** 1999
**Line of Business:** Health authorities
**Issued Capital:** £1
**General Manager:** Ms M Crawford
**Responsibilities**
**Senior:** Penny Thorpe *(Manager)*
**Branches:** Thames Valley Primary Care Agency, Russell Street Doctors Surgery, 79 Russell Street, Reading, Berkshire RG1 7XG
**US SIC:** 8062, 8091
**UK SIC:** 95100, 95200
**Employees:** 54

DUNS 42-342-1809
## Thames Valley University
Crescent Road, Reading, Berkshire RG1 5RQ
**Tel:** 01189675000
**Web:** www.tvu.ac.uk
**Line of Business:** Further education college with 5 sites
**Director:** F Mccrindle
**Branches:** Thames Valley University, Raymond Rd, Maidenhead, Berkshire SL6 6DF
**US SIC:** 8221 **UK SIC:** 93100
**Employees:** 500

DUNS 21-851-9364
## Thames View Infants
Thames View Infants, Bastable Avenue, Barking, Essex IG11 0LG
**Reg No:** 8163191 **Estd:** 2012 Private Company Limited By Guarantee
**Line of Business:** Primary education
**Directors:** Major J K Schultz, Ms S A Leitch, Mrs S J Rigglesford, Mrs S Choudhary, A Alim, Ms M F Rogers, Ms R V Clark, Ms D M Bonifacio
**US SIC:** 8211 **UK SIC:** 93200
**Bankers:** Lloyds TSB Bank plc (30-90-47)

| | 31-08-13 |
|---|---|
| TO | 5,231,000 |
| P/L | 3,022,000 |
| NW | 3,076,000 |
| WC | 78,000 |
| Emp. | 47 |

DUNS 21-778-8245
## Thames View Infants School
Bastable Avenue, Barking, Essex IG11 0LG
**Tel:** 02085946521
**Estd:** 2011 Proprietorship
**Line of Business:** General secondary education
**Proprietor:** P Jordan
**US SIC:** 8211 **UK SIC:** 93200
**Employees:** 70

DUNS 23-776-0434
## Thames Water Ltd
**(Subsidiary of:** Kemble Water Holdings Ltd)
13-14 Woodbridge Meadows, Guildford, Surrey GU1 1BA
**Tel:** 08459200800
**Web:** www.thameswater.co.uk
**Reg No:** 2366623 **Estd:** 1989 Private Limited Company
**Line of Business:** Collection, purification and distribution of water
**Issued Capital:** £355,770,743
**Directors:** R Greenleaf, Ms R Blomfield Smith, F Sheng, Ms C B Heijningen, M C Hill, L H Webb, L Webb, G Lambert
**Co. Secretary:** Ms Carolyn Campbell-Wales
**Responsibilities**
**Senior:** Luis Abraira *(Director)*, Perry Noble *(Director)*, Nghi Pham *(Director)*, Kevin Roseke *(Director)*
**HR:** Katherine Riley *(Human Resources Director)*
**Facilities:** Bob Collington *(Director of Operational Manage)*
**Engineering:** Bob Collington *(Director of Operational Manage)*
**Branches:** Thames Water Ltd, Unit 4B-C Horwich Business Pk, Chorley New Rd, Bolton, Lancashire BL6 5UE
**US SIC:** 4941 **UK SIC:** 17000
**Auditors:** KPMG Audit PLC
**Bankers:** National Westminster Bank Plc (60-00-01)
**Following financial data are in thousands**

| | 31-03-14 | 31-03-13 | 31-03-12 |
|---|---|---|---|
| TA | 2,339,500 | 3,943,700 | 3,812,200 |
| P/L | 196,700 | 150,200 | 231,300 |
| NW | 1,956,000 | 1,989,800 | 2,040,300 |
| WC | 1,936,500 | 1,969,900 | 1,934,400 |

DUNS 23-820-0323 **Imp**
## Thames Water Utilities Ltd
**(Subsidiary of:** Kemble Water Holdings Ltd)
Clearwater Court, Reading, Berkshire RG1 8DB
**Tel:** 02035774364
**Web:** www.thameswater.co.uk
**Reg No:** 2366661 **VAT No:** 537456915
**Estd:** 1989 Private Limited Company
**Line of Business:** Collection, purification and distribution of water
**Issued Capital:** £29,050,000
**Directors:** R Greenleaf, Ms R Blomfield Smith, S J Siddall, M W Baggs, G Lambert, D J Shah, Dame D M Hutton, M J Pavia
**Co. Secretary:** David Hughes
**Responsibilities**
**Senior:** Lorraine Baldry *(Director)*, Kristine Boudreau *(Kempton Nature Reserve Site Ma)*, Ian Buck *(General Manager)*, Ian Cain *(Managing Director Customer Ser)*, Bob Collington *(Managing Director Wholesale Wa)*, Christopher Deacon *(Director)*, Michael Gerrard *(Managing Director for the Tham)*, Joel Hanson *(Manager)*, Stan Kolenc *(Non-Executive Director)*, Perry Noble *(Director)*, Kevin Roseke *(Director)*, Antonio Santos *(Non-Executive Director)*, Yaping Shi *(Non-Executive Director)*, Steve Tuck *(Chairman)*
**Finance:** Andrew Beaumont *(Group Treasurer)*
**Marketing:** Nick Fincham *(Strategy and Regulation Direct)*
**Sales:** Bob Collington *(Managing Director Wholesale Wa)*
**HR:** Janet Burr *(Human Resources Director)*
**Operations:** Keith Gardner *(Area Operations Manager, South)*, Lawrence Gosden *(Capital Delivery Director)*, Catherine Hunt *(Senior Water Planner, Asset Ma)*, Radu Joltea *(Operations Liaison Engineer)*, Lee King *(Project Manager)*, Kevan Mossman *(Transformation Director)*, Suzanna Smart *(Executive)*, Phil Stride *(Head of London Tideway Tunnels)*
**Purchasing:** Ian Bolger *(Head of Supply Chain)*
**Engineering:** Nic Clay-Michael *(Water, networks and pipes Mana)*, Rupert Kruger *(Head of Innovation)*
**Branches:** Thames Water Utilities Ltd, Cumnor Rd, Oxford, Oxfordshire OX2 9NS
**US SIC:** 4941, 4952
**UK SIC:** 17000, 92120
**Auditors:** KPMG Audit PLC
**Bankers:** National Westminster Bank Plc (60-00-01)
**Following financial data are in thousands**

| | 31-03-14 | 31-03-13 | 31-03-12 |
|---|---|---|---|
| TO | 1,943,700 | 1,791,900 | 1,694,900 |
| P/L | 259,300 | 144,900 | 222,200 |
| NW | 1,392,000 | 1,233,700 | 1,400,600 |
| WC | 2,137,900 | 2,387,600 | 1,834,200 |
| Emp. | 4,682 | 4,681 | 4,551 |

DUNS 21-326-5867
## Thamesbridge College
Northumberland Avenue, Reading, Berkshire RG2 8DJ
**Tel:** 01189015415
**Estd:** 1997
**Line of Business:** Social work activities with accommodation
**US SIC:** 8321 **UK SIC:** 96111
**Employees:** 50

DUNS 54-853-1722
## Thamesdown Glass Recycling
Kingshill Recycling Centre, Cricklade, Calcutt, Swindon, Wiltshire SN6 6JR
**Tel:** 01793-751310
**Web:** www.thamesdownrecycling.co.uk
**VAT No:** 392076735 **Estd:** 1989 Proprietorship
**Line of Business:** Wholesale of waste and scrap
**Trading Style:** Richard Freeth
**Proprietor:** J Freeth
**US SIC:** 7399 **UK SIC:** 83954
**Employees:** 50

DUNS 22-549-6157
## Thamesdown Transport Ltd
Barnfield Road, Swindon, Wiltshire SN2 2DJ
**Tel:** 01793428400 **Fax:** 01793-428405
**Web:** www.thamesdown-transport.co.uk
**Reg No:** 1997617 **VAT No:** 448300561
**Estd:** 1986 Private Limited Company
**Line of Business:** Bus operators and stations
**Issued Capital:** £1,489,000
**Directors:** D A Hall, Ms M Howard, G H Frost, D J Heenan, C Connor, N D Martin, S R Allsopp, C Lovell
**Co. Secretary:** Clifford Connor
**Responsibilities**
**Marketing:** Derek Pemberton *(Senior Marketing Executive)*
**IT:** Damon Swatridge *(Systems Manager)*
**US SIC:** 4119 **UK SIC:** 72200
**Auditors:** Ernst & Young LLP
**Bankers:** Lloyds TSB Bank plc (30-98-41)

| | 31-03-14 | 31-03-13 | 31-03-12 |
|---|---|---|---|
| TO | 9,928,534 | 10,442,197 | 10,718,583 |
| P/L | (154,172) | 860,485 | (184,015) |
| NW | 4,710,866 | 4,664,452 | 4,311,072 |
| WC | (992,002) | (762,753) | (903,978) |
| Emp. | 226 | 241 | 247 |

DUNS 53-647-7979
## Thameside Fire Protection Co. Ltd
Cranes Farm Road, Basildon, Essex SS14 3JD
**Tel:** 01268597999 **Fax:** 01268597998
**Web:** www.thamesidefire.co.uk
**Reg No:** 3453185 **Estd:** 1985 Private Limited Company
**Line of Business:** Engineering related scientific and technical consulting activities
**Export Sales:** £55,792
**Issued Capital:** £1,000
**Directors:** N Cannon, G Burnall, J L Allen, J G Allen, D Petrovic, A J Belsey
**Co. Secretary:** Ms Susan Allen
**Responsibilities**
**IT:** Vence Whinston *(Computer Operations Manager)*
**US SIC:** 7399 **UK SIC:** 83954
**Auditors:** Bland Baker

| | 31-10-13 | 31-10-12 | 31-10-11 |
|---|---|---|---|
| TO | 8,963,840 | 9,121,376 | N/A |
| P/L | 305,579 | 133,723 | N/A |
| NW | 1,285,627 | 1,219,704 | 1,223,509 |
| WC | 908,099 | 876,106 | 900,853 |
| Emp. | 93 | 85 | N/A |

DUNS 21-579-6170
## Thameside Primary School
Harley Road, Caversham, Reading, Berkshire RG4 8DB
**Tel:** 01189375551
**Web:** www.thameside.reading.sch.uk
**Estd:** 1998 Proprietorship
**Line of Business:** Schools (local authority)
**Proprietor:** Mrs H Wallace
**US SIC:** 8211 **UK SIC:** 93200
**Employees:** 50

DUNS 39-806-0525
## Thamesport (London) Ltd
**(Subsidiary of:** Hutchison Whampoa Limited)
Isle Of Grain, Rochester, Kent ME3 0EP
**Fax:** 01634-270384
**Web:** www.londonthamesport.co.uk
**Reg No:** 2191687 **Estd:** 1987 Private Limited Company
**Line of Business:** Freight forwarders
**Issued Capital:** £2
**Directors:** Ms E Shih, S C Ip, C C Cheng
**Co. Secretary:** Simon Mullett
**Responsibilities**
**Senior:** James Tsien *(Manager)*
**US SIC:** 4712, 4226, 4789
**UK SIC:** 77002, 77003
**Auditors:** PricewaterhouseCoopers LLP
**Bankers:** Lloyds TSB Bank plc (30-00-02)

| | 31-12-13 | 31-12-12 | 31-12-11 |
|---|---|---|---|
| TO | 18,433,000 | 22,157,000 | 23,650,000 |
| P/L | 513,000 | 499,000 | 499,000 |
| NW | 1,282,000 | 146,000 | 282,000 |
| WC | 2,631,000 | 2,683,000 | 2,633,000 |
| Emp. | 228 | 248 | 281 |

DUNS 23-242-8826
## Thamesview Estate Agents Ltd
2 Green St Brooklands Terrace, Sunbury-On-Thames, Middlesex TW16 6RW
**Tel:** 02084873174
**Web:** www.thamesview.co.uk
**Reg No:** 4160511 **Estd:** 2001 Private Limited Company
**Line of Business:** Real estate agencies
**Issued Capital:** £1,173
**Directors:** A Kashyap, Ms E Merrison, A P Finneran, D A Fielding, A C Shepherd, J I Doble, R Merrison, Ms C A Millis
**Co. Secretary:** Ms Carol Doble
**Branches:** Thamesview Estate Agents Ltd, 20 Claremont Road, Surbiton, Surrey KT6 4QU
**US SIC:** 6531 **UK SIC:** 83400
**Auditors:** Menzies LLP

| | 30-09-13 | 30-09-12 | 30-09-11 |
|---|---|---|---|
| TO | 40,669,547 | 33,966,838 | 25,861,716 |
| P/L | 2,909,090 | 1,967,519 | 3,287,010 |
| NW | 7,226,237 | 5,189,789 | 3,539,401 |
| WC | 7,765,731 | 5,749,392 | 5,145,775 |
| Emp. | 550 | 476 | 428 |

DUNS 23-082-8332
## Thamesview School
Thong Lane, Gravesend, Kent DA12 4LF
**Tel:** 01474-566552
**Web:** www.thamesview.kent.sch.uk
**Line of Business:** General secondary education
**Director:** V Leese
**US SIC:** 8211 **UK SIC:** 93200
**Employees:** 109

DUNS 23-995-6618
## Thanet College of Further Education
Ramsgate Road, Broadstairs, Kent CT10 1PN
**Tel:** 01843-605040
**Web:** www.eastkent.ac.uk
**Estd:** 2006
**Line of Business:** Further education schools and colleges
**Trading Style:** East Kent College
**Principals:** D Leah *(Financial)*, G Burney
**Responsibilities**
**Senior:** Karen Evens *(Business Development)*, Penelope Kimber *(Head of Marketing and Communic)*, Graham Razey *(CEO, Managing Director)*
**Finance:** Karen Pilgrim *(Director of Finance)*
**Marketing:** Penelope Kimber *(Head of Marketing and Communic)*
**Sales:** Chris Legg *(Strategic Director of Finance)*
**Admin:** Tara Ashman *(Clerk)*
**Branches:** Thanet College Of Further Education, 6 Cecil Sq, Margate, Kent CT9 1BD
**US SIC:** 8221 **UK SIC:** 93100
**Bankers:** The Royal Bank Of Scotland Plc (15-10-00)
**Employees:** 350

DUNS 22-747-6017
## Thanet District Council
Po Box 9, Margate, Kent CT9 1XZ
**Tel:** 01843-577000
**Web:** www.thanet.gov.uk
**Incorporate By Act Of Parliament**
**Line of Business:** Local government
**Trading Style:** Thanet Crematorium, Royal Harbour & Ramsgate New Port, St Mildreds County Infant School
**Directors:** D Ralls, A Rush
**Responsibilities**
**Senior:** Sue Mcgonigal *(Chief Executive Officer)*, Geoff Musk *(Head of Property Services)*, Richard Samuel *(Chief Executive)*
**Finance:** Sarah Martin *(Finance Manager)*
**Admin:** Debra Jennings *(Administrative Assistant)*
**IT:** William Neech *(Company Services Manager)*
**HR:** Sarah Carroll *(Human Resources Manager)*
**Health & Safety:** Jessica Bailey *(Health and Safety Executive)*, Debbie Huckstep *(Lead Health and Safety Inspect)*
**Operations:** Mark Seed *(Director of Operations)*
**Purchasing:** Jane Hatcher *(Procurements Officer)*
**Fleet:** Jane Hatcher *(Procurements Officer)*
**Branches:** Thanet District Council, Victoria Parade, Broadstairs, Kent CT10 1QS
**US SIC:** 9121 **UK SIC:** 91110
**Bankers:** National Westminster Bank Plc (60-14-05)
**Employees:** 600

DUNS 73-417-0330
## Thanet Early Years Project
Mobile Building Newlands Cp School, Dumpton Lane, Ramsgate, Kent CT11 7AJ
**Tel:** 01843591200
**Web:** www.thanetearlyyears.org
**Reg No:** 4690236 **Estd:** 2003 Private Company Limited By Guarantee
**Line of Business:** Primary education
**Directors:** H C Kemp, Mrs I Tittensor, Mrs J E Bonner
**Co. Secretary:** Mrs Isabel Tittensor
**US SIC:** 8211 **UK SIC:** 93200
**Bankers:** Lloyds TSB Bank plc (77-62-01)

| | 31-07-14 | 31-07-13 | 31-07-12 |
|---|---|---|---|
| TO | 974,670 | 1,009,506 | 1,213,153 |
| P/L | 3,805 | 12,510 | 6,594 |
| NW | 514,942 | 511,137 | 498,627 |
| WC | 514,942 | 511,137 | 498,627 |
| Emp. | 48 | 49 | 50 |

DUNS 21-985-6551 **Imp**
## Thanet Earth Marketing Ltd
**(Subsidiary of:** Thanet Growers Eight Ltd)
Barrow Man Road, Birchington, Kent CT7 0AX
**Tel:** 01843844700
**Web:** www.thanetearth.com
**Reg No:** 6167025 **VAT No:** 937480105
**Estd:** 2011 Private Limited Company
**Line of Business:** Fruit and vegetable (producers)
**Issued Capital:** £100
**Directors:** C P Mack, A J De Gier, M Huckstep, W J Grootscholten, I A Craig, H J Lambriex, D A Kingsley
**Co. Secretary:** Michael Musk

**Responsibilities**
**Senior:** Robert Bal *(Director)*, Edwina Kilford *(Senior Administrator)*, Rebecca Turner *(Manager)*, Cornelis Van Der Kaaij *(Manager)*
**US SIC:** 0179 **UK SIC:** 01002
**Auditors:** BDO Stoy Hayward LLP
**Bankers:** Lloyds TSB Bank plc (30-14-37)

| | 25-04-14 | 26-04-13 | 27-04-12 |
|---|---|---|---|
| TO | 81,176,000 | 74,686,000 | 66,856,000 |
| P/L | 1,424,000 | 965,000 | 653,000 |
| NW | (1,641,000) | (2,766,000) | (3,484,000) |
| WC | (5,087,000) | (3,432,000) | (3,088,000) |
| Emp. | 159 | 149 | 123 |

DUNS 58-159-1526
## Thankq Ltd
(**Subsidiary of:** Ingleby (1863) Ltd)
Loughborough Technology Centre, Loughborough, Leicestershire LE11 3GE
**Tel:** 01509235544
**Web:** www.thankq.co.uk
**Reg No:** 2906581 **VAT No:** 616945615
**Estd:** 1994 Private Limited Company
**Line of Business:** Computer software (development)
**Issued Capital:** £106
**Director:** A J Brown
**Responsibilities**
**Senior:** Rose Farris *(Office Manager)*, Christopher Tossell *(Director)*
**Branches:** Thankq, Barrown 86-88 High St, Barro, Nairn, Nairnshire IV12 4BW
**US SIC:** 7070 **UK SIC:** 00940

| | 30-06-13 | 31-03-12 | 31-06-11 |
|---|---|---|---|
| TA | 116,685 | 1,217,570 | 828,189 |
| NW | 116,685 | 323,059 | 177,291 |
| WC | N/A | 235,354 | 80,634 |

DUNS 53-617-8262
## Tharsus Engineering Ltd
(**Subsidiary of:** Tharsus Group Ltd)
Birmayne House, Blyth, Northumberland NE24 5TF
**Tel:** 01670368000
**Web:** www.tharsus.co.uk
**Reg No:** 3422948 **Estd:** 1997 Private Limited Company
**Line of Business:** Manufacture of metal structures and parts of structures
**Issued Capital:** £200,000
**Directors:** B A Palmer, P A Sayer, R W Palmer, M J Hutchinson, D P Swan
**Co. Secretary:** Miss Michelle Donnan
**Responsibilities**
**Senior:** Graham Parkins *(Joint Managing Director)*
**IT:** Graham Parkins *(Joint Managing Director)*
**Engineering:** Graham Parkins *(Joint Managing Director)*
**Branches:** Tharsus Engineering Ltd, Unit 3, Rekendyke Industrial Estate, South Shields, Tyne and Wear NE33 5BZ
**US SIC:** 3441, 3499
**UK SIC:** 32042, 31694
**Auditors:** HLB Kidsons
**Bankers:** National Westminster Bank Plc (54-10-31)

| | 30-11-13 | 30-11-12 | 30-11-11 |
|---|---|---|---|
| TO | 4,060,634 | 5,120,030 | N/A |
| P/L | (153,767) | 22,547 | N/A |
| NW | 1,502,592 | 1,518,179 | 1,434,069 |
| WC | (171,173) | 485,140 | 191,901 |
| Emp. | 86 | 91 | N/A |

DUNS 21-041-9949
## Thatcham Park C of E School
Park Avenue, Thatcham, Berkshire RG18 4NP
**Tel:** 01635870950
**Web:** www.thatchampark.w-berks.sch.uk
**Estd:** 2005 Proprietorship
**Line of Business:** Schools (local authority)
**Proprietor:** Mrs M Cornwell
**Responsibilities**
**Senior:** Alison Webster *(Head Teacher)*
**US SIC:** 8211 **UK SIC:** 93200
**Employees:** 50

DUNS 54-835-0222
## The Thatched Barn Inn
14 Hobbs Hill, Croyde, Braunton, Devon EX33 1LZ
**Tel:** 01271-890349
**Web:** www.thethatchcroyde.com
**Estd:** 1984 Partnership
**Line of Business:** Managed public houses and bars
**Partners:** R Barouh, T Pickersgill
**US SIC:** 5813, 5812
**UK SIC:** 66200, 66110
**Employees:** 50

DUNS 22-506-1910 **Exp**
## Thatchers Cider Co Ltd
(**Subsidiary of:** Thatchers Holdings Ltd)
Myrtle Farm, Station Road, Winscombe, Avon BS25 5RA
**Web:** www.thatcherscider.co.uk
**Reg No:** 0550634 **VAT No:** 130704805
**Estd:** 1955 Private Limited Company
**Line of Business:** Manufacture of other fermented fruit beverages
**Export Markets:** New Zealand & Sweden
**Trading Style:** Thatchers
**Issued Capital:** £1,500,000
**Principals:** M Thatcher *(Managing)*, M Gazzard, B W Pocock, R G Thompson, C Milton, N Day
**Responsibilities**
**Health & Safety:** Paul Dockerty *(Quality Assurance Manager)*
**Operations:** Paul Dockerty *(Quality Assurance Manager)*
**Engineering:** Gary Delafield *(Production Manager)*
**US SIC:** 2082, 5182
**UK SIC:** 42702, 61700
**Auditors:** Brooking Ruse & Co
**Bankers:** Lloyds TSB Bank plc (30-91-84)

| | 31-08-14 | 31-08-13 | 31-08-12 |
|---|---|---|---|
| TO | 60,296,676 | 51,832,800 | 40,832,023 |
| P/L | 5,566,409 | 5,599,366 | 4,080,591 |
| NW | 9,121,102 | 7,974,573 | 5,823,150 |
| WC | 1,598,445 | 3,326,774 | 562,650 |
| Emp. | 119 | 100 | 88 |

DUNS 22-951-2082 **Exp**
## Thb Group Ltd
(**Subsidiary of:** Amwins Global Group Limited)
Bankside House, 107-112 Leadenhall Street, London EC3A 4AF
**Tel:** 02074-690100 **Fax:** 02076-219574
**Web:** www.thbgroup.com
**Reg No:** 1514749 **Estd:** 1974 Private Limited Company
**Line of Business:** Management activities of holding companies
**Export Markets:** Worldwide
**Trading Style:** Thb Clues, Thb Eggerlawson, Thb Northern, Thb Risk Solutions
**Issued Capital:** £3,947,355
**Directors:** R S Wilkinson, A J Preston, W H Cooper, Ms J Joslin, M S Decarlo, S M Purviance, F M Murphy
**Co. Secretary:** Christopher Sturgess
**Responsibilities**
**Senior:** Claire Carpenter *(Manager)*, Corinne Hepworth *(Manager)*, Nigel Moorhouse *(Manager)*
**Marketing:** Rachel Maidment *(Sales & Marketing Manager)*
**Sales:** Rachel Maidment *(Sales & Marketing Manager)*
**IT:** Shaun Williams *(Systems Manager)*
**HR:** Corrine Bennett *(Head of Human Resources)*
**Health & Safety:** Corrine Bennett *(Head of Human Resources)*
**Operations:** Rachel Maidment *(Sales & Marketing Manager)*
**US SIC:** 6711 **UK SIC:** 83962
**Auditors:** Mazars LLP
**Bankers:** Barclays Bank Plc (20-14-33)

| | 31-12-13 | 31-12-12 | 31-12-11 |
|---|---|---|---|
| TO | 49,399,000 | 48,994,000 | 55,673,000 |
| P/L | (8,447,000) | (412,000) | 2,000 |
| NW | 5,309,000 | 11,501,000 | (15,410,000) |
| WC | (3,544,000) | 6,887,000 | (3,065,000) |
| Emp. | 434 | 375 | 409 |

DUNS 21-614-1689
## T.H.Brickell & Son Ltd
(**Subsidiary of:** Brickell Holdings Ltd)
Longmead Industrial Estate, Shaftesbury, Dorset SP7 8PX
**Tel:** 01747-853034
**Web:** www.blackmore.co.uk
**Reg No:** 0366134 **VAT No:** 601202615
**Estd:** 1910 Private Limited Company
**Line of Business:** Printing not elsewhere classified
**Trading Style:** Blackmore
**Issued Capital:** £127,957
**Director:** P R Smith
**Co. Secretary:** Stuart Morris
**US SIC:** 2752 **UK SIC:** 47544
**Auditors:** Nexia Smith & Williamson
**Bankers:** Lloyds TSB Bank plc (30-90-92)

| | 30-06-13 | 30-06-12 | 30-06-11 |
|---|---|---|---|
| TO | 9,695,440 | 10,043,444 | 10,469,276 |
| P/L | 123,736 | (39,458) | (658,458) |
| NW | 269,892 | 153,353 | 365,471 |
| WC | (1,703,527) | (2,046,774) | (2,695,495) |
| Emp. | 102 | 112 | 122 |

DUNS 21-004-7312
## T.H.Bull & Sons Ltd
305 Liverpool Road, London N1 1NF
**Tel:** 020-7607-9448
**Reg No:** 0263015 **Estd:** 1932 Private Limited Company
**Line of Business:** Other tourist or short-stay accommodation
**Issued Capital:** £40,000
**Directors:** Ms M A Brazier, Ms I J Bull, Ms J Topping, M C Bull, G P Bull
**Co. Secretary:** Ms Dorothy Shaw
**Responsibilities**
**Senior:** Leonard Bull *(Manager)*
**US SIC:** 6531 **UK SIC:** 83400
**Auditors:** Hereward Philips

| | 31-12-13 | 31-12-12 | 31-12-11 |
|---|---|---|---|
| TA | 6,434,419 | 6,446,414 | 6,369,979 |
| NW | 6,204,534 | 6,244,090 | 6,212,398 |
| WC | 104,534 | 184,090 | 132,398 |

DUNS 21-917-3432 **Imp-Exp**
## T.H.Clements & Son Ltd
West End Road, Boston, Lincolnshire PE22 0EJ
**Tel:** 01205760456
**Web:** www.thclements.co.uk
**Reg No:** 0869514 **VAT No:** 127739938
**Estd:** 1966 Private Limited Company
**Line of Business:** Growing of vegetables, horticultural specialities and nursery products
**Export Markets:** France
**Export Sales:** £336,424
**Issued Capital:** £1,465
**Directors:** Ms K V Eley, C T Gedney, C A Clements, R J Mowbray
**Co. Secretary:** Simon Lingard
**Responsibilities**
**HR:** Rchel Gedney *(HR Manager)*
**Branches:** T.h.clements & Son Ltd, Illogan, Redruth, Cornwall TR16 4PU
**US SIC:** 0161 **UK SIC:** 01001
**Auditors:** Duncan & Toplis
**Bankers:** Barclays Bank Plc (20-11-13)

| | 05-04-14 | 05-04-13 | 05-04-12 |
|---|---|---|---|
| TO | 31,985,786 | 31,839,416 | 26,888,584 |
| P/L | 631,184 | 660,846 | 551,398 |
| NW | 10,084,872 | 9,596,420 | 9,090,604 |
| WC | 1,796,546 | 2,314,410 | 2,558,433 |
| Emp. | 208 | 169 | 124 |

DUNS 22-286-2679
## (the) Bread Roll Holding Co Ltd
Unit 2 Lyon Way, St Albans, Hertfordshire AL4 0LQ
**Tel:** 01727-818000
**Web:** www.breadroll.co.uk
**Reg No:** 4304197 **Estd:** 2002 Private Limited Company
**Line of Business:** Renting of other machinery and equipment not elsewhere classified
**Trading Style:** (The) Bread Roll Co Ltd
**Issued Capital:** £72,320
**Principals:** S E Ville *(Managing)*, D M Dutton
**Co. Secretary:** Mrs Sue Ville
**Branches:** (The) Bread Roll Holding Co Ltd, Unit W/17, Lenton Business Centre, Nottingham, Nottinghamshire NG7 2BY
**US SIC:** 7394 **UK SIC:** 84000
**Bankers:** National Westminster Bank Plc (60-18-01)

| | 26-01-14 | 27-01-13 | 22-01-12 |
|---|---|---|---|
| TA | 2,643,440 | 2,339,963 | 1,784,033 |
| NW | 2,066,363 | 1,700,679 | 1,626,730 |
| WC | 1,520,712 | 1,174,034 | 1,124,045 |

DUNS 21-303-1735
## T.H.E. Smart Corporation Ltd
12a Tower Street, Hartlepool, Cleveland TS24 7HD
**Tel:** 01429275890
**Web:** www.thesmartcorporation.co.uk
**Reg No:** 1281478 **VAT No:** 300961196
**Estd:** 1968 Private Limited Company
**Line of Business:** Retail sale of hardware, paints and glass
**Trading Style:** Bulman A Tools, Scorers
**Issued Capital:** £45,100
**Directors:** Ms S Colman, D Hornsey
**Co. Secretary:** Ms Melissa Howlett
**Responsibilities**
**Senior:** Sheila Coleman *(Director)*
**Branches:** T.h.e. Smart Corporation Ltd, 79 Newbottle Street, Houghton-Le-Spring, Tyne and Wear DH4 4AR
**US SIC:** 5251, 5732
**UK SIC:** 64800
**Auditors:** Straughans
**Bankers:** Yorkshire Bank Plc (05-09-75)

| | 31-03-14 | 31-03-13 | 31-03-12 |
|---|---|---|---|
| TO | N/A | 2,862,863 | 3,162,379 |
| P/L | N/A | (141,861) | (123,704) |
| NW | 1,351,897 | 2,820,750 | 2,932,112 |
| WC | 1,032,066 | 666,043 | 723,280 |
| Emp. | N/A | 60 | 68 |

DUNS 34-579-4429
## ThE7STARS Uk Ltd
13 David Mews, London W1U 6EQ
**Tel:** 02074367275
**Web:** www.the7stars.co.uk
**Reg No:** 5387218 **Estd:** 2005 Private Limited Company
**Line of Business:** Advertising
**Export Sales:** £11,572,930
**Issued Capital:** £17,160
**Directors:** G M Jones, Ms J E Biggam, M Jarvis
**US SIC:** 7311 **UK SIC:** 83800
**Bankers:** Barclays Bank Plc (20-71-74)

| | 31-03-14 | 31-03-13 | 31-03-12 |
|---|---|---|---|
| TO | 100,780,293 | 72,926,731 | 53,853,725 |
| P/L | 864,922 | 983,996 | 1,367,814 |
| NW | 1,273,378 | (183,443) | (1,234,342) |
| WC | 1,965,687 | 1,282,496 | 78,564 |
| Emp. | 67 | 46 | 35 |

DUNS 34-863-5400
## Theale Green Community School Trust Co Ltd
Church Street, Reading, Berkshire RG7 5DA
**Tel:** 01189302741
**Web:** www.thealegreen.w-berks.sch.uk
**Reg No:** 2815440 **Estd:** 1993 Private Company Limited By Guarantee
**Line of Business:** General secondary education
**Trading Style:** Theale Green School
**Directors:** J D Fishburn, P G Lowndes, T W Llewellyn
**Responsibilities**
**Senior:** Graham Bridgman *(Manager)*, David Bromfield *(Director)*, Jonathan Chiswick *(Manager)*
**US SIC:** 7999 **UK SIC:** 97913
**Auditors:** Edwin Smith
**Bankers:** Barclays Bank Plc (20-71-02)

| | 31-05-13 | 31-05-12 | 31-05-11 |
|---|---|---|---|
| TO | 5,222 | 14,291 | 14,634 |
| P/L | (44,919) | 3,788 | (5,154) |
| NW | 42,102 | 87,021 | 83,233 |
| WC | 42,102 | 87,021 | 83,233 |

DUNS 28-960-6758
## Theatre of Comedy Co Ltd
(**Subsidiary of:** Dlt Entertainment Ltd.)
210 Shaftesbury Avenue, London WC2H 8DP
**Tel:** 02073795399 **Fax:** 020-7836-8181
**Web:** www.thecomedytheatre.co.uk
**Reg No:** 1678553 **VAT No:** 605931350
**Estd:** 1982 Private Limited Company
**Line of Business:** Theatres & concert halls
**Trading Style:** Shaftesbury Theatre
**Issued Capital:** £578,124
**Directors:** J Cotugno, D L Taffner Jr
**Co. Secretary:** Robert Chester
**Responsibilities**
**Senior:** Donald Taffner *(Proprietor)*
**US SIC:** 7911 **UK SIC:** 97913
**Auditors:** Nyman Libson Paul
**Bankers:** National Westminster Bank Plc (60-40-04)

| | 31-12-13 | 31-12-12 | 31-12-11 |
|---|---|---|---|
| TO | 4,477,799 | 13,112,922 | 7,275,334 |
| P/L | (1,498,816) | 290,255 | 407,550 |
| NW | 9,710,475 | 13,491,036 | 13,271,614 |
| WC | (714,116) | 2,349,328 | 2,485,494 |
| Emp. | 52 | 80 | 71 |

DUNS 28-910-5967
## The Theatre Royal Bath Ltd
Saw Close, Bath, Avon BA1 1ET
**Tel:** 01225448844 **Fax:** 01225316297
**Web:** www.theatreroyal.org
**Reg No:** 1416448 **VAT No:** 600923378
**Estd:** 1979 Private Company Limited By Guarantee
**Line of Business:** Theatres & concert halls
**Trading Style:** Theatre Royal Bath
**Directors:** Mrs C L Walker, P B Heal, C J Fry, D J Eaton, G J Ingham, P J Addis, Mrs S M East, D H Hoare
**Co. Secretary:** Mrs Gabrielle Akbar
**Responsibilities**
**Senior:** Andrew Furse *(Director)*, Marcus Harvey *(Manager)*, Daniel Moar *(Theatre Director)*, Victoria Moffatt *(Director)*, John Monohan *(Director)*, Bel Mooney *(Manager)*, Leonard Pearcey *(Director)*
**Marketing:** Tom Baughan *(Development Director)*, Anna O'Callaghan *(Sales & Marketing Manager)*, Graeme Savage *(Marketing Officer)*
**Sales:** Anna O'Callaghan *(Sales & Marketing Manager)*
**Admin:** Nicky Palmer *(Administration Officer)*
**IT:** Joe Wright *(Technical Manager)*
**HR:** Eugene Hibbert *(General Manager)*
**Health & Safety:** Nicky Palmer *(Administration Officer)*
**Operations:** Anna O'Callaghan *(Sales & Marketing Manager)*
**US SIC:** 7911 **UK SIC:** 97913
**Auditors:** KPMG
**Bankers:** National Westminster Bank Plc (56-00-34)

| | 31-05-13 | 31-05-12 | 31-05-11 |
|---|---|---|---|
| TO | 14,983,134 | 13,177,136 | 11,266,442 |
| P/L | (2,825) | (382,296) | (1,741,911) |
| NW | 7,624,600 | 7,628,556 | 8,008,035 |
| WC | 2,656,869 | 2,558,116 | 2,819,382 |
| Emp. | 63 | 63 | 64 |

DUNS 29-186-3900

## Theatre Royal Haymarket Ltd

(**Subsidiary of:** Louis I.Michaels Ltd)
18 Suffolk Street, London SW1Y 4HT
**Tel:** 02079308890 **Fax:** 02073899696
**Web:** www.trh.co.uk
**Reg No:** 0242846 **VAT No:** 242570575
**Estd:** 1929 Private Limited Company
**Line of Business:** Theatrical presentation companies
**Issued Capital:** £30,000
**Directors:** A M Crook, N P Everett, R L Kennett, G H Brown
**Co. Secretary:** John Lawrie
**Responsibilities**
**Senior:** Enid Chanelle *(President and Director)*
**US SIC:** 7911 **UK SIC:** 97913
**Auditors:** Blueprint Audit Ltd
**Bankers:** The Royal Bank Of Scotland Plc (16-00-83)

| | 30-03-14 | 01-04-13 | 01-03-12 |
|---|---|---|---|
| TO | 3,734,750 | 4,244,697 | 4,113,366 |
| P/L | 364,400 | 576,024 | 1,533,568 |
| NW | 587,947 | 708,821 | 275,156 |
| WC | 284,272 | 400,804 | (37,203) |
| Emp. | 62 | 62 | 62 |

DUNS 28-867-8535

## Theatre Royal (Norwich) Trust Ltd

Theatre Street, Norwich, Norfolk NR2 1RL
**Tel:** 01603630000
**Web:** www.theatreroyalnorwich.co.uk
**Reg No:** 0997352 **VAT No:** 104742302
**Estd:** 1970 Private Company Limited By Guarantee
**Line of Business:** Other artistic and literary creation and interpretation
**Directors:** Ms M Jarrold, D Moore, C G Moscrip-Coubrough, M C Newey, R P Hall, Ms C E Crawley, T H Blofeld, W J Northam
**Co. Secretary:** Ms Tessa Haskey
**Responsibilities**
**Senior:** Erika Clegg *(Director)*, Frank Eliel *(Director)*, Steven Jaggard *(Director)*, Angela Robson *(Director)*, Han Yap *(Director)*
**Marketing:** Mark Hazell *(Sales & Marketing Director)*
**Sales:** Mark Hazell *(Sales & Marketing Director)*
**Admin:** Hanna MacQueen *(Administrator)*
**HR:** Jason Raper *(Training Manager)*
**Purchasing:** Hanna MacQueen *(Administrator)*
**Branches:** Theatre Royal (Norwich) Trust Ltd, 14 Chapelfield, Norwich, Norfolk NR13 3LY
**US SIC:** 8999, 7999
**UK SIC:** 83954, 97913
**Auditors:** Larking Gowen
**Bankers:** Lloyds TSB Bank plc (30-96-17)

| | 30-03-14 | 31-03-13 | 01-03-12 |
|---|---|---|---|
| TO | 13,157,837 | 13,360,208 | 12,058,192 |
| P/L | 314,043 | 62,472 | 143,505 |
| NW | 7,149,478 | 6,835,435 | 6,772,963 |
| WC | 537,046 | (17,138) | (428,894) |
| Emp. | 167 | 166 | 164 |

DUNS 22-557-7964 **Imp**

## Theatre Royal (Plymouth) Ltd

Royal Parade, Plymouth, Devon PL1 2TR
**Tel:** 01752668282 **Fax:** 01752252546
**Web:** www.theatreroyal.com
**Reg No:** 1560651 **Estd:** 1981 Private Company Limited By Guarantee
**Line of Business:** Theatres & concert halls
**Directors:** R L Tatam, Ms J Grace, P L Woods, N B Buckland, Mrs B L Lacey, F D Drake, P G Vosper, Sir M G Lickiss
**Co. Secretary:** Mrs Laura Edwards
**Responsibilities**
**Senior:** Nicola Cutts *(Manager)*, Glenn Jordan *(Manager)*, Jack Mellor *(Theatre Manager)*
**HR:** Jack Mellor *(Theatre Manager)*
**Facilities:** Kevin Faulkner *(Facilities Manager)*
**Operations:** Helen Costello *(Operations Director)*, Jack Mellor *(Theatre Manager)*
**Purchasing:** Jack Mellor *(Theatre Manager)*
**US SIC:** 7911, 7399
**UK SIC:** 97913, 83954
**Auditors:** KPMG LLP
**Bankers:** National Westminster Bank Plc (56-00-63)

| | 31-03-14 | 31-03-13 | 31-03-12 |
|---|---|---|---|
| TO | 22,789,000 | 18,474,000 | 17,689,000 |
| P/L | 6,047,000 | 699,000 | 854,000 |
| NW | 17,346,000 | 11,299,000 | 10,600,000 |
| WC | 2,141,000 | 2,641,000 | 2,728,000 |
| Emp. | 140 | 124 | 165 |

DUNS 21-582-5354

## Theatre Severn

Frankwell Quay, Shrewsbury, Shropshire SY3 8FT
**Tel:** 01743281281
**Web:** www.theatresevern.co.uk
**Estd:** 2003 Partnership
**Line of Business:** Theatres & concert halls
**Partners:** P Nicholson, D Jack
**US SIC:** 7911 **UK SIC:** 97913
**Employees:** 50

DUNS 34-750-3489

## Thebigword Group Plc

Ring Road, Leeds, West Yorkshire LS12 6AB
**Tel:** 08707488000
**Web:** www.thebigword.com
**Reg No:** 5551907 **Estd:** 2005 Public Limited Company
**Line of Business:** Translation activities
**Export Sales:** £9,245,000
**Issued Capital:** £112,970
**Directors:** Mrs D Cheesebrough, L J Gould, Ms B J Byrne, Mrs K Milner, J Gould, Ms M Gould, K Sendel, M L Toynton
**Co. Secretary:** Mrs Diane Cheesebrough
**Responsibilities**
**Senior:** William Vi *(Proprietor)*
**Finance:** Jeremy Earnshaw *(Financial Manager)*
**Health & Safety:** Howard Coney *(Health & Safety Officer)*
**US SIC:** 7339 **UK SIC:** 83954
**Auditors:** PricewaterhouseCoopers LLP
**Bankers:** Lloyds TSB Bank plc (30-00-05)

| | 31-05-13 | 31-05-12 | 31-05-11 |
|---|---|---|---|
| TO | 43,431,000 | 41,811,000 | 40,143,000 |
| P/L | (370,000) | 1,925,000 | 1,635,000 |
| NW | 2,873,000 | 3,132,000 | 2,784,000 |
| WC | 1,388,000 | 1,481,000 | 708,000 |
| Emp. | 436 | 434 | 444 |

DUNS 49-372-8273 **Imp**

## Theme Traders Ltd

(**Subsidiary of:** Crinklewood Holdings Ltd)
The Stadium, Oaklands Road, London NW2 6DL
**Tel:** 020-8452-8518 **Fax:** 020-8450-7322
**Web:** www.themetraders.com
**Reg No:** 3126426 **Estd:** 1995 Private Limited Company
**Line of Business:** Plant and tool hire
**Issued Capital:** £1,000
**Directors:** D Jamilly, M Godden
**Co. Secretary:** Mrs Kim Einhorn
**Responsibilities**
**Senior:** Kim Ihorne *(Manager)*
**Finance:** John O'Conner *(Accounts Manager)*, Rob Owusi *(Accounts Manager)*
**Branches:** Theme Traders Ltd, 22 Angle Park Terrace, Edinburgh, Midlothian EH11 2JX
**US SIC:** 7999, 8999
**UK SIC:** 97913, 83954
**Auditors:** Simmons Gainsford

| | 31-07-13 | 31-07-12 | 31-07-11 |
|---|---|---|---|
| TA | 927,299 | 1,281,984 | 933,673 |
| NW | 622,914 | 601,839 | 588,092 |
| WC | 577,928 | 557,186 | 534,067 |

DUNS 42-400-4760

## Thenue Housing Association Ltd

423 London Road, Glasgow, Lanarkshire G40 1AG
**Tel:** 01415503581
**Web:** www.thenuehousing.co.uk
**Reg No:** 0001933I **Estd:** 1978 Friendly Society
**Line of Business:** Housing associations societies trusts & co-operatives
**Directors:** Ms A More, J Anderson, T Duncan, Ms M Brailey, Ms A More, J Anderson, Ms M Brailey, T Duncan
**Co. Secretary:** Mrs Marian Jacobs
**Responsibilities**
**Finance:** Kevin Dunsmuir *(Income Maximisation Assistant)*, Douglas Hosie *(Finance Manager)*, Lorraine Salisbury *(Finance Officer)*, Willie Sinclair *(Financial Inclusion Officer)*
**Admin:** Carol Lingard *(Receptionist)*, Margaret Mclean *(Administration Assistant)*, Lorraine Morgan *(Administration Assistant)*
**Facilities:** Jim Barr *(Maintenance Officer)*, Marie Rafferty *(Property Services Manager)*, Beth Reilly *(Head of Property Services)*
**Branches:** Thenue Housing Association Limited, 49 Blaeloch Drive, Glasgow, Lanarkshire G45 9QJ
**US SIC:** 6531 **UK SIC:** 83400
**Auditors:** Alexander Sloan
**Bankers:** Clydesdale Bank Plc (82-20-00)
**Employees:** 70
**Turnover:** £9,427,949

DUNS 29-629-4754 **Imp-Exp**

## Theo Fennell Ltd

(**Subsidiary of:** Mirfield 1964 Plc)
169 Fulham Road, Chelsea, London SW3 6SP
**Fax:** 020-7591-5001
**Web:** www.theofennell.com
**Reg No:** 1955534 **Estd:** 1985 Private Limited Company
**Line of Business:** Jewellery retailers
**Export Sales:** £265,351
**Issued Capital:** £1,157,901
**Principals:** A T Fennell *(Managing)*, R A Shaheen, M D Jatania, A Salam
**Co. Secretary:** Daniel Steptoe
**Responsibilities**
**Senior:** Theo Fennell *(Acting Managing Director)*
**Finance:** Gavin Saunders *(Finance Director)*
**Branches:** Theo Fennell Ltd, Unit 4, Royal Exchange, London EC3V 3LQ
**US SIC:** 5944, 5094, 5961
**UK SIC:** 65400, 61900, 65600
**Auditors:** Grant Thornton UK LLP
**Bankers:** Clydesdale Bank Plc (82-04-03)

| | 31-01-14 | 31-03-13 | 31-01-12 |
|---|---|---|---|
| TO | 8,253,316 | 10,706,341 | 12,383,774 |
| P/L | (3,791,760) | (878,616) | (1,702,621) |
| NW | 3,597,293 | 5,078,009 | 5,934,639 |
| WC | 2,925,205 | 4,528,811 | 5,230,097 |
| Emp. | 57 | 55 | 60 |

DUNS 34-873-3937

## Theoco Accident Repair Centres Ltd

Knightsbridge House, Kingsbury Road, London NW9 8XG
**Tel:** 02082055524 **Fax:** 02082054523
**Web:** www.theoco.co.uk
**Reg No:** 5671590 **Estd:** 2006 Private Limited Company
**Line of Business:** Maintenance and repair of motor vehicles
**Issued Capital:** £100
**Director:** D J Theodossiades
**Co. Secretary:** Mrs Pamela Theodossiades
**Responsibilities**
**HR:** Pat Wallemsay *(Human Resources Manager)*
**Health & Safety:** Pat Wallemsay *(Human Resources Manager)*
**Facilities:** Pat Wallemsay *(Human Resources Manager)*
**US SIC:** 7539 **UK SIC:** 67100

| | 31-12-13 | 31-12-12 | 31-12-11 |
|---|---|---|---|
| TA | 1,430,744 | 1,248,286 | 1,271,904 |
| NW | 380,079 | 352,297 | 359,960 |
| WC | 418,405 | 376,195 | 357,455 |

DUNS 50-352-0926 **Exp**

## Theorem Clinical Research Ltd

3 Oakmere Close, Manchester M22 9SQ
**Tel:** 01249-444212 **Fax:** 01249-444189
**Web:** www.theoremclinical.com
**Reg No:** 2374122 **Estd:** 1989 Private Limited Company
**Line of Business:** Research institutions and organisations
**Export Markets:** Worldwide
**Issued Capital:** £1,749
**Directors:** J A Monteleone, J G Potthoff, A G Lambert
**Co. Secretary:** Andrew Lambert
**Responsibilities**
**Senior:** S Jevons *(Manager)*
**Branches:** Unit 15-16 King Charles Ho, Cavalier Ct, Bumpers Farm Indstl Est, Chippenham
**US SIC:** 7391 **UK SIC:** 94000
**Auditors:** Pearson May
**Bankers:** Barclays Bank Plc (20-84-58)

| | 31-12-13 | 31-12-12 | 31-12-11 |
|---|---|---|---|
| TA | 4,543,244 | 4,293,606 | 4,013,262 |
| NW | 4,145,548 | 3,967,680 | 3,674,490 |
| WC | 4,140,082 | 3,970,044 | 3,502,471 |

DUNS 34-765-1841

## Thera East Anglia

134 Edmund Street, Birmingham, West Midlands B3 2ES
**Web:** www.thera.co.uk
**Reg No:** 5566295 **Estd:** 2005 Private Company Limited By Guarantee
**Line of Business:** Other human health activities
**Directors:** M R Dearlove, Ms L H Weston, Ms J Garrigan, D A Parker, C C Blake, K M Horne, C J Rheinberg, S L Conway
**US SIC:** 8091, 8321
**UK SIC:** 95200, 96111
**Auditors:** Clement Keys LLP
**Bankers:** Barclays Bank Plc (20-84-17)

| | 31-03-14 | 31-03-13 | 31-03-12 |
|---|---|---|---|
| TO | 10,759,106 | 10,937,721 | 11,015,767 |
| WC | 511,010 | 158,323 | N/A |
| Emp. | 488 | 505 | 544 |

DUNS 34-532-6339

## Thera North

The West House Alpha Court, Swingbridge Road, Grantham, Lincolnshire NG31 7XT
**Tel:** 01476513930 **Fax:** 03003-031285
**Web:** www.thera.co.uk
**Reg No:** 5343088 **VAT No:** 874756963
**Estd:** 2005 Private Company Limited By Guarantee
**Line of Business:** Healthcare companies
**Trading Style:** Thera North
**Directors:** A A Chalmers, Ms J Garrigan, K P Griffin, J Staples, A Bright, Dr J D Hooper, D J Mcmullan
**Co. Secretary:** Simon Conway
**Responsibilities**
**Senior:** Gareth Jackson *(Manager)*, Lorraine O'Brien *(Manager)*
**US SIC:** 8321 **UK SIC:** 96111
**Auditors:** Clement Keys
**Bankers:** Barclays Bank Plc (20-84-13)

| | 31-03-14 | 31-03-13 | 31-03-12 |
|---|---|---|---|
| TO | 2,806,385 | 2,975,731 | 3,528,451 |
| P/L | (72,878) | (130,965) | 261,239 |
| NW | (328,702) | (255,824) | (124,859) |
| WC | (83,619) | 133,599 | 311,748 |

DUNS 23-595-9637

## Thera Trust

Alpha Court, Swingbridge Road, Grantham, Lincolnshire NG31 7XT
**Tel:** 01476562777 **Fax:** 01476562677
**Web:** www.thera.co.uk
**Reg No:** 3593418 **Estd:** 2005 Private Unlimited Company
**Line of Business:** Other human health activities
**Directors:** Mrs C E Mackness, B Young, Ms J Garrigan, W B Carter, M A Morgan, P M Jones, M J Smith, Ms K T Boyce-Dawson
**Co. Secretary:** Simon Conway
**Responsibilities**
**Senior:** Jeffrey Dandridge *(Manager)*, Lorraine O'Brien *(Manager)*
**Marketing:** Alison McBride *(Head of Development)*
**IT:** Janice Garrigan *(Computer Operations Manager)*
**Health & Safety:** Danny Wilson *(Health & Safety Officer)*
**Branches:** Thera Trust, Alpha Court, The West House, Grantham, Lincolnshire NG31 7XT
**US SIC:** 8091, 8321
**UK SIC:** 95200, 96111
**Auditors:** Clarkson Hyde
**Bankers:** National Westminster Bank Plc (56-00-61)

| | 31-03-14 | 31-03-13 | 31-03-12 |
|---|---|---|---|
| TO | 46,850,198 | 44,549,844 | 44,188,079 |
| P/L | 212,484 | 268,115 | 435,761 |
| NW | 4,802,548 | 5,590,403 | 5,697,852 |
| WC | (327,296) | 1,477,870 | 824,095 |
| Emp. | 2,312 | 2,251 | 2,352 |

DUNS 77-167-5535 **Exp**

## Theradex (Europe) Ltd

Unit 7 Pelham Place Pelham Court, Crawley, West Sussex RH11 9SH
**Tel:** 01293-510319
**Web:** www.theradex.com
**Reg No:** 2708052 **Estd:** 1992 Private Limited Company
**Line of Business:** Research and experimental development on natural sciences and engineering
**Trading Style:** Theradex (Europe) Ltd
**Issued Capital:** £100
**Directors:** Ms M J Valnoski, B D Anderson, J S Hannan, Ms M E Moores
**Co. Secretary:** John Hannan
**Responsibilities**
**Senior:** Jeff Adley *(Manager)*, Jeffery Adley *(Manager)*, Jess Adley *(Manager)*, Sean Hannan *(Manager)*, Robert Royds *(Manager)*
**Finance:** Jeff Adley *(Manager)*
**Admin:** Mariana Lee *(Administration Coordinator)*
**HR:** Mariana Lee *(Administration Coordinator)*
**Health & Safety:** Mariana Lee *(Administration Coordinator)*
**Facilities:** Mariana Lee *(Administration Coordinator)*
**Purchasing:** Mariana Lee *(Administration Coordinator)*
**US SIC:** 7391 **UK SIC:** 94000
**Auditors:** Wilkins Kennedy
**Bankers:** Barclays Bank Plc (20-23-97)

| | 30-06-14 | 30-06-13 | 30-06-12 |
|---|---|---|---|
| TA | 967,175 | 896,726 | 942,081 |
| NW | 443,903 | 673,933 | 701,693 |
| WC | 396,887 | 661,873 | 688,815 |

DUNS 21-227-4594

## Therakos

West Forest Gate, Wellington Road, Wokingham, Berkshire RG40 2AT
**Tel:** 01183150810
**Web:** www.therakos.co.uk
**Estd:** 1988 Proprietorship
**Line of Business:** Manufacture of basic pharmaceutical products
**US SIC:** 2834 **UK SIC:** 25700
**Employees:** 70

DUNS 73-711-8708 **Imp**

## Therco Ltd

1 Long Acre Close, Sheffield, South Yorkshire S20 3FR
**Fax:** 01142510564
**Web:** www.thercoheatexchangers.com
**Reg No:** 4970481 **Estd:** 2003 Private Limited Company
**Line of Business:** Engineers (general)
**Export Sales:** £1,264,691
**Issued Capital:** £94
**Directors:** J G Brooks, D M Toseland
**Co. Secretary:** Robert Sawtell
**US SIC:** 8911, 3441
**UK SIC:** 83701, 32042
**Auditors:** Smith Craven
**Bankers:** HSBC Bank plc (40-41-11)

| | 31-12-13 | 31-12-12 | 31-12-11 |
|---|---|---|---|
| TO | 9,071,923 | 7,013,484 | 7,731,271 |
| P/L | 311,311 | 548,810 | 121,663 |
| NW | 839,305 | 808,137 | 673,584 |
| WC | 185,395 | 432,521 | 233,013 |
| Emp. | 66 | 59 | 61 |

DUNS 23-502-1255 **Imp**

## Thermacore Europe Ltd

(**Subsidiary of:** Thermacore Inc.)
Unit 12 Rotary Parkway Wansbeck Business, Park, Ashington, Northumberland NE63 8QW
**Fax:** 01670-859539
**Web:** www.thermacore.co.uk
**Reg No:** 3501481 **Estd:** 1998 Private Limited Company
**Line of Business:** Heating contractors
**Issued Capital:** £201
**Principals:** J D Yates *(Managing)*, J E Toth, J E Rothenberger
**Co. Secretary:** James Yates
**Responsibilities**
**Senior:** Kevin Hetherington *(Warehouse Manager)*, Jim Robson *(Operations Director)*
**Marketing:** John Broadbent *(Sales & Marketing Manager)*
**Sales:** John Broadbent *(Sales & Marketing Manager)*
**HR:** Nicola Gleghorn *(Human Resources Officer)*
**Health & Safety:** Kevin Lynn *(Engineering Manager)*
**Facilities:** Kevin Lynn *(Engineering Manager)*
**Purchasing:** Kevin Hetherington *(Warehouse Manager)*
**Fleet:** Kevin Hetherington *(Warehouse Manager)*
**US SIC:** 8911, 3499
**UK SIC:** 83701, 31694
**Auditors:** Tait Walker LLP
**Bankers:** Barclays Bank Plc (20-59-42)

| | 31-12-13 | 31-12-12 | 31-12-11 |
|---|---|---|---|
| TO | N/A | 4,614,773 | 5,512,942 |
| P/L | N/A | 130,360 | 380,504 |
| NW | 1,667,561 | 1,733,787 | 1,706,885 |
| WC | 992,792 | 971,861 | 1,111,253 |
| Emp. | N/A | 58 | 61 |

DUNS 53-643-1638

## Thermae Development Co Ltd

(**Subsidiary of:** Ytl Corporation Berhad)
3 Royal Crescent, Bath, Avon BA1 2LR
**Tel:** 08448880844
**Web:** www.thermaebathspa.com
**Reg No:** 3448628 **Estd:** 2001 Private Limited Company
**Line of Business:** Other sporting activities not elsewhere classified
**Issued Capital:** £260,000
**Directors:** C F Skellett, S K Yeoh
**Co. Secretary:** Andrew Phillips
**US SIC:** 7999 **UK SIC:** 97913
**Auditors:** Moore Stephens

| | 31-12-13 | 31-12-12 | 31-12-11 |
|---|---|---|---|
| TO | 9,254,329 | 8,478,405 | 7,989,318 |
| P/L | 2,181,659 | 1,733,249 | 1,361,559 |
| NW | 4,094,374 | 2,471,168 | 1,161,861 |
| WC | (458,462) | (2,222,721) | (1,166,224) |
| Emp. | 171 | 159 | 163 |

DUNS 21-813-3965 **Imp-Exp**

## Thermaglow Ltd

Units 5-7 Boundary Road, Great Yarmouth, Norfolk NR31 0LY
**Tel:** 01493-440060 **Fax:** 01493604138
**Web:** www.thermaglow.co.uk
**Reg No:** 0588483 **VAT No:** 105919962
**Estd:** 1957 Private Limited Company
**Line of Business:** Heating appliances (spare parts)
**Export Markets:** Europe
**Issued Capital:** £6,500
**Principals:** T C Dodd *(Managing)*, Ms P T Dodd
**Co. Secretary:** Timothy Dodd
**Responsibilities**
**Facilities:** Colin Stephenson *(Engineering Manager)*
**Engineering:** Colin Stephenson *(Engineering Manager)*
**Branches:** Thermaglow Ltd, Unit 5-6-7 Boundary Road, Faraday Road, Great Yarmouth, Norfolk NR31 0LY
**US SIC:** 5074, 3357
**UK SIC:** 61300, 22470
**Auditors:** Farmiloes
**Bankers:** Barclays Bank Plc (20-99-21)

| | 31-03-14 | 31-03-13 | 31-03-12 |
|---|---|---|---|
| TA | 2,373,779 | 2,388,270 | 2,363,375 |
| NW | 577,538 | 539,974 | 537,959 |
| WC | 429,791 | 360,207 | 323,549 |

DUNS 39-933-9373 **Imp-Exp**

## Thermal Engineering Ltd

Orchard Road, Stoke-On-Trent, Staffordshire ST8 5GZ
**Tel:** 01763242067 **Fax:** 01763245959
**Web:** www.thermalengineering.co.uk
**Reg No:** 2212132 **VAT No:** 997314475
**Estd:** 1988 Private Limited Company
**Line of Business:** Aviation supplies
**Export Markets:** Europe
**Export Sales:** £4,233,943
**Issued Capital:** £50,000
**Directors:** D J Harding, A J Bodenham, M Rollins
**Co. Secretary:** Andrew Bodenham
**Responsibilities**
**Senior:** Maxwell Humber *(Manager)*
**Health & Safety:** Brian Lougher *(Quality, Health & Safety Manag)*
**Operations:** Avais Chaudhri *(Operations Director)*
**Engineering:** Miguel Calvo *(Engineering Director)*, Brian Lougher *(Quality, Health & Safety Manag)*
**US SIC:** 3721 **UK SIC:** 36400
**Auditors:** KPMG LLP

| | 31-12-13 | 31-12-12 | 31-12-11 |
|---|---|---|---|
| TO | 17,251,118 | 16,157,108 | 12,535,552 |
| P/L | 265,416 | 1,242,910 | (749,701) |
| NW | 1,584,514 | 1,383,682 | 140,772 |
| WC | (2,864,221) | (1,283,549) | (4,006,751) |
| Emp. | 246 | 222 | 207 |

DUNS 29-537-8350 **Imp-Exp**

## Thermal Fluid Systems Ltd

Lyons Road, Horsham, West Sussex RH13 0QS
**Tel:** 01403791535 **Fax:** 01983531888
**Web:** www.thermalfluidsystems.co.uk
**Reg No:** 1904870 **VAT No:** 446872906
**Estd:** 1986 Private Limited Company
**Line of Business:** Heating contractors
**Export Markets:** Worldwide
**Issued Capital:** £2,467
**Directors:** J Clery, B Johnson
**Co. Secretary:** Barry Johnson
**US SIC:** 3499, 7399
**UK SIC:** 31694, 83954
**Auditors:** John A. Tuffin & Co
**Bankers:** National Westminster Bank Plc (60-30-09)

| | 30-09-13 | 30-09-12 | 30-09-11 |
|---|---|---|---|
| TA | 153,563 | 182,282 | 145,124 |
| NW | 59,925 | 78,513 | 130,859 |
| WC | 56,351 | 73,748 | 124,505 |

DUNS 21-329-9811 **Imp**

## Thermal Hire Ltd

Unit 12 Pagefield Industrial Estate, Miry Lane, Wigan, Lancashire WN6 7LA
**Tel:** 01942-620062
**Web:** www.thermalhire.com
**Reg No:** 1174472 **VAT No:** 535049452
**Estd:** 1974 Private Limited Company
**Line of Business:** Heat treatment (metals)
**Trading Style:** Thermal Hire Ltd
**Issued Capital:** £3,160
**Principals:** J B Riley *(Managing)*, B D Riley
**Responsibilities**
**Senior:** Alan Deakin *(Warehouse Manager)*
**Branches:** Thermal Hire Ltd, Tees Bay Business Park, Brenda Road, Hartlepool, Cleveland TS25 2BU
**US SIC:** 3398 **UK SIC:** 31380
**Auditors:** PM&M
**Bankers:** National Westminster Bank Plc (60-13-20)

| | 31-10-13 | 31-10-12 | 31-10-11 |
|---|---|---|---|
| TO | 8,479,860 | 7,231,251 | 6,751,412 |
| P/L | 872,472 | 640,434 | 356,413 |
| NW | 4,284,838 | 3,729,543 | 3,364,793 |
| WC | 2,721,680 | 2,163,516 | 1,756,052 |
| Emp. | 84 | 70 | 76 |

DUNS 64-111-9409 **Imp**

## Thermal Resources Management Ltd

21 Sedling Road, Wear Industrial Estate, Washington, Tyne and Wear NE38 9BZ
**Tel:** 01914-168884
**Web:** www.temperature-house.com
**Reg No:** 4112049 **Estd:** 2000 Private Limited Company
**Line of Business:** Manufacture of electronic instruments and appliances for measuring, checking, testing, navigating and other purposes, except industrial process control equipment
**Trading Style:** Temperature House
**Issued Capital:** £504
**Directors:** M Liddell, K D Dooley
**Co. Secretary:** Kenneth Parker
**Responsibilities**
**Finance:** Gemma Souter *(Accounts Manager)*
**Branches:** Thermal Resources Management Ltd, 21 Sedling Road, Wear Industrial Estate, Washington, Tyne and Wear NE38 9BZ
**US SIC:** 3999 **UK SIC:** 49590
**Auditors:** Ribchesters
**Bankers:** Lloyds TSB Bank plc (30-92-79)

| | 30-11-13 | 30-11-12 | 30-11-11 |
|---|---|---|---|
| TA | 1,473,325 | 1,250,737 | 721,859 |
| NW | 327,841 | 164,008 | 128,336 |
| WC | 303,705 | 151,327 | 129,855 |

DUNS 34-617-1093 **Imp-Exp**

## Thermal Transfer Technology Ltd

(**Subsidiary of:** Three T Jersey Ltd)
Seaham Court, Hall Dene Way, Seaham, County Durham SR7 0PU
**Tel:** 0191-523-8002
**Web:** www.three-t.co.uk
**Reg No:** 2754482 **VAT No:** 569278485
**Estd:** 2002 Private Limited Company
**Line of Business:** Manufacturers of boilers
**Export Markets:** Europe; Scandinavia
**Export Sales:** £2,493,385
**Trading Style:** 3 T
**Issued Capital:** £1,215,308
**Directors:** S J Barnes, D Hill, A G Thomsen
**Co. Secretary:** Iain Pearson
**US SIC:** 3567 **UK SIC:** 32452
**Auditors:** Ernst & Young LLP
**Bankers:** Barclays Bank Plc (20-59-42)

| | 30-09-13 | 30-09-12 | 30-09-11 |
|---|---|---|---|
| TO | 8,007,554 | 7,657,391 | 8,396,182 |
| P/L | 442,919 | 394,439 | 489,200 |
| NW | 5,000,916 | 4,599,377 | 4,276,400 |
| WC | 3,492,700 | 3,213,251 | 2,894,942 |
| Emp. | 97 | 102 | 105 |

DUNS 29-135-9131

## Thermalite (U.K.) Ltd

(**Subsidiary of:** Merilux Sarl)
Thermalite House, Station Road, Coleshill, Birmingham, West Midlands B46 1HP
**Reg No:** 1667421 **Estd:** 1982 Private Limited Company
**Line of Business:** Business services
**Issued Capital:** £100
**Directors:** G A Ray, V J Holmes
**Co. Secretary:** Robert Harris
**Branches:** Ferry Rd, South Alloa, SK7 7LS, Stirling
**US SIC:** 7399 **UK SIC:** 83954
**Bankers:** Barclays Bank Plc (20-76-55)
**Employees:** 70

DUNS 21-701-6644

## Thermasys Cs Uk Holding Ltd

(**Subsidiary of:** Thermasys Group Holding Company)
Covrad Sir Henry Parkes Road, Canley, Coventry, West Midlands CV5 6BN
**Tel:** 02476675544
**Reg No:** 7464159 **Estd:** 2010 Private Limited Company
**Line of Business:** Management activities of holding companies
**Export Sales:** £9,828,032
**Issued Capital:** £2,210,829
**Director:** J Cordosi
**Co. Secretary:** Philip Cox
**US SIC:** 6711 **UK SIC:** 83962

| | 31-12-13 | 31-12-12 | 31-12-11 |
|---|---|---|---|
| TO | 32,585,726 | 38,109,980 | 41,312,554 |
| P/L | 560,049 | 734,550 | 2,298,532 |
| NW | (2,744,167) | (3,977,701) | (3,717,735) |
| WC | (184,013) | (1,200,513) | (2,224,525) |
| Emp. | 188 | 224 | 244 |

DUNS 52-034-4342

## Thermatic Maintenance Ltd

(**Subsidiary of:** Thermatic Ltd)
Unit 3, Salford, Lancashire M50 3UP
**Tel:** 01618 723724
**Web:** www.thermatic.co.uk
**Reg No:** 3400910 **VAT No:** 628930419
**Estd:** 1997 Private Limited Company
**Line of Business:** Plumbing
**Issued Capital:** £100,000
**Principals:** D Oakley *(Managing)*, S J Black, C R Tennent, D Oakley
**Co. Secretary:** Eric Wratten
**Branches:** Thermatic Maintenance Ltd, Park Lane House, 47 Broad Street, Glasgow, Lanarkshire G40 2QW
**US SIC:** 1711 **UK SIC:** 50300
**Auditors:** Edwards Veeder LLP
**Bankers:** The Royal Bank Of Scotland Plc (16-32-21)

| | 31-12-13 | 31-12-12 | 31-12-12 |
|---|---|---|---|
| TO | 14,580,427 | 9,677,211 | 15,894,642 |
| P/L | (428,018) | 234,015 | (2,345,837) |
| NW | (1,745,890) | (1,326,725) | (1,511,728) |
| WC | 133,759 | 226,786 | (1,085,622) |
| Emp. | 78 | 74 | 83 |

DUNS 22-534-4332 **Imp-Exp**

## Thermo Electron Ltd

(**Subsidiary of:** Thermo Fisher Scientific Inc.)
Solaar House, 19 Mercers Row, Cambridge, Cambridgeshire CB5 8BY
**Tel:** 01223347400 **Fax:** 01279 713329
**Web:** www.thermo.com
**Reg No:** 1735858 **VAT No:** 226362083
**Estd:** 2004 Private Limited Company
**Line of Business:** Business services
**Export Markets:** Europe and Worldwide
**Export Sales:** £20,115,000
**Trading Style:** Thermo Fisher Scientific, Fisher Bioservices
**Issued Capital:** £300,000
**Directors:** Ms L M Grant, K N Wheeler, Ms K R Wright
**Co. Secretary:**
Oakwood Corporate Secretary Limi
**Responsibilities**
**Senior:** Nicola Ward *(Manager)*
**Branches:** Thermo Electron Ltd, Unit 2A Altbarn Industrial Estate, Hawkins Road, Colchester, Essex CO2 8LG
**US SIC:** 7349 **UK SIC:** 92300
**Auditors:** PricewaterhouseCoopers LLP
**Bankers:** Barclays Bank Plc (20-00-00)

| | 31-12-13 | 31-12-12 | 31-12-11 |
|---|---|---|---|
| TO | 29,955,000 | 36,227,000 | 43,653,000 |
| P/L | 11,358,000 | 10,075,000 | 10,889,000 |
| NW | 62,286,000 | 48,019,000 | 37,532,000 |
| WC | 61,155,000 | 47,551,000 | 36,577,000 |
| Emp. | 163 | 227 | 252 |

DUNS 21-860-7703 **Imp**

## Thermo Electron Manufacturing Ltd

(**Subsidiary of:** Thermo Fisher Scientific Inc.)
Stafford House, 1 Boundary Way Boundary Park, Hemel Hempstead, Hertfordshire HP2 7GE
**Tel:** 01442233555
**Web:** www.thermo.com
**Reg No:** 0441506 **VAT No:** 827900029
**Estd:** 1947 Private Limited Company
**Line of Business:** Manufacture of electronic instruments and appliances for measuring, checking, testing, navigating and other purposes, except industrial process control equipment
**Export Sales:** £37,638,000
**Trading Style:** Thermo Fisher Scientific, Thermo Scientific
**Issued Capital:** £1,438,231
**Directors:** Ms L M Grant, K N Wheeler, Ms K R Wright
**Co. Secretary:**
Oakwood Corporate Secretary Limi
**Responsibilities**
**Senior:** Maurice Cornish *(CEO, Managing Director)*
**Branches:** Thermo Electron Manufacturing Ltd, 112 Chadwick Road, Runcorn, Cheshire WA7 1PW
**US SIC:** 3829, 3832
**UK SIC:** 37100, 37320
**Auditors:** PricewaterhouseCoopers LLP
**Bankers:** Barclays Bank Plc (20-00-00)

| | 31-12-13 | 31-12-12 | 31-12-11 |
|---|---|---|---|
| TO | 84,206,000 | 83,995,000 | 75,486,000 |
| P/L | 9,153,000 | 7,124,000 | 7,648,000 |
| NW | 55,925,000 | 47,861,000 | 40,866,000 |
| WC | 54,117,000 | 42,750,000 | 35,555,000 |
| Emp. | 343 | 333 | 295 |

DUNS 49-490-8387 **Exp**

## Thermo Fast U.K. Ltd

(**Subsidiary of:** Thermo Bioanalysis Ltd)
1 St Georges Court, Altrincham, Cheshire WA14 5TP
**Tel:** 01928534000
**Web:** www.thermofisher.com
**Reg No:** 3153083 **Estd:** 1996 Private Limited Company
**Line of Business:** Computer software (development)
**Trading Style:** Thermo Fisher Scientific, Lab Systems Affinity Sensors, Thermo Electron Corporation
**Issued Capital:** £2

**Directors:** Ms L M Grant, K N Wheeler, Ms K R Wright
**Co. Secretary:**
Oakwood Corporate Secretary Limi
**Responsibilities**
**Senior:** Nicola Ward *(Manager)*
**Branches:** 1 St George's Ct, Altrincham
**US SIC:** 7379, 3823
**UK SIC:** 83940, 37100
**Auditors:** PricewaterhouseCoopers LLP
**Bankers:** Barclays Bank Plc (20-00-00)

| | 31-12-13 | 31-12-12 | 31-12-11 |
|---|---|---|---|
| TA | 6,617,368 | 6,617,368 | 6,617,368 |
| NW | 6,617,368 | 6,617,368 | 6,617,368 |

DUNS 36-481-1752 **Imp**

## Thermo Onix Ltd

(**Subsidiary of:** Onix Systems Inc.)
Factory One, Road Three Ion Path, Winsford, Cheshire CW7 3GA
**Tel:** 01606548700
**Web:** www.thermoonix.com
**Reg No:** 3284171 **Estd:** 1996 Private Limited Company
**Line of Business:** Manufacture of electronic instruments and appliances for measuring, checking, testing, navigating and other purposes, except industrial process control equipment
**Export Sales:** £12,570,000
**Issued Capital:** £1
**Directors:** Ms K R Wright, K N Wheeler, Ms L M Grant
**Co. Secretary:**
Oakwood Corporate Secretary Limi
**Responsibilities**
**Senior:** Nicola Ward *(Manager)*
**US SIC:** 3829 **UK SIC:** 37100
**Auditors:** Saffery Champness
**Bankers:** Barclays Bank Plc (20-00-00)

| | 31-12-13 | 31-12-12 | 31-12-11 |
|---|---|---|---|
| TO | 14,790,000 | 14,386,000 | 16,428,000 |
| P/L | 3,047,000 | 2,426,000 | 5,149,000 |
| NW | 20,394,000 | 17,260,000 | 14,821,000 |
| WC | 26,961,000 | 23,845,000 | 21,333,000 |
| Emp. | 53 | 56 | 79 |

DUNS 76-717-1796 **Exp**

## Thermo Optek Ltd

(**Subsidiary of:** Thermo Fisher Scientific Inc.)
Po Box 207, Cambridge, Cambridgeshire CB5 8BZ
**Tel:** 01223-347400
**Web:** www.thermoscientific.com
**Reg No:** 2595732 **Estd:** 1991 Private Limited Company
**Line of Business:** Management activities of holding companies
**Export Markets:** E U, E Europe, Middle East, South America, North America
**Issued Capital:** £30,017,444
**Directors:** K N Wheeler, Ms L M Grant, Ms K R Wright
**Co. Secretary:**
Oakwood Corporate Secretary Limi
**Responsibilities**
**Senior:** Nicola Ward *(Manager)*
**US SIC:** 6711, 3829
**UK SIC:** 83962, 37100
**Auditors:** PricewaterhouseCoopers LLP
**Bankers:** Barclays Bank Plc (20-17-35)

| | 31-12-13 | 31-12-12 | 31-12-11 |
|---|---|---|---|
| TO | N/A | N/A | 88,000 |
| P/L | (191,000) | (251,000) | (53,000) |
| NW | 138,582,000 | 138,773,000 | 139,024,000 |
| WC | 979,000 | 1,170,000 | 1,381,000 |

DUNS 21-910-3512 **Imp-Exp**

## Thermo Shandon Ltd

(**Subsidiary of:** Thermo Fisher Scientific Inc.)
Tudor Road, Tudor Road, Manor Park, Runcorn, Cheshire WA7 1TA
**Tel:** 01928 534 000
**Web:** www.thermofisher.com
**Reg No:** 0330973 **Estd:** 2009 Private Limited Company
**Line of Business:** Science centres
**Export Markets:** E U, U S A & Rest of World
**Export Sales:** £51,525,000
**Trading Style:** Thermo Fisher Scientific
**Issued Capital:** £2,000,001
**Directors:** Ms L M Grant, Ms K R Wright, K N Wheeler
**Co. Secretary:**
Oakwood Corporate Secretary Limi
**US SIC:** 3829, 3841
**UK SIC:** 37100, 37201
**Auditors:** PricewaterhouseCoopers LLP
**Bankers:** Barclays Bank Plc (20-00-00)

| | 31-12-13 | 31-12-12 | 31-12-11 |
|---|---|---|---|
| TO | 55,621,000 | 56,314,000 | 54,008,000 |
| P/L | 16,263,000 | 19,679,000 | 18,851,000 |
| NW | 226,616,000 | 208,216,000 | 190,763,000 |
| WC | 108,838,000 | 92,328,000 | 72,648,000 |
| Emp. | 183 | 184 | 176 |

DUNS 73-905-8092

## Thermodynamix (Holdings) Ltd

(**Subsidiary of:** Tdx (Europe) Ltd)
3 Princes Park, Princesway North, Gateshead, Tyne and Wear NE11 0NF
**Tel:** 0191-440-7000 **Fax:** 01914407001
**Web:** www.tdx-tss.com
**Reg No:** 5159440 **Estd:** 2004 Private Limited Company
**Line of Business:** Manufacturers of tools
**Export Sales:** £3,033,084
**Trading Style:** Thermodynamix (Holdings) Limited
**Issued Capital:** £646,577
**Directors:** T J Marr, N Atkinson, M S Prinn
**Responsibilities**
**Senior:** Jeffrey Brunskill *(Manager)*, Harry Reed *(Manager)*, Gail Reed *(Manager)*
**Finance:** Gail Reed *(Manager)*
**US SIC:** 3423 **UK SIC:** 31612
**Bankers:** Yorkshire Bank Plc (05-06-23)

| | 31-12-13 | 31-12-12 | 31-12-11 |
|---|---|---|---|
| TO | 19,076,243 | 16,507,952 | 16,249,240 |
| P/L | 784,402 | 689,679 | 386,573 |
| NW | 1,625,895 | 995,810 | 488,513 |
| WC | (1,155,459) | (717,429) | (1,035,889) |
| Emp. | 95 | 78 | 81 |

DUNS 21-326-5565

## Thermofisher Scientific

Beacon Road, Stone, Staffordshire ST15 0SA
**Tel:** 01702303350
**Web:** www.electrothermal.co.uk
**Estd:** 2008
**Line of Business:** Manufacturers and suppliers of laboratory equipment
**Trading Style:** Electrothermal / Bibby Scientific
**Proprietor:** D Overfield
**US SIC:** 3357 **UK SIC:** 22470
**Employees:** 48

DUNS 22-651-0220 **Imp**

## Thermoform Ltd

Moor Farm Road, Ashbourne, Derbyshire DE6 1HD
**Tel:** 01335-343-757
**Web:** www.thermoform-limited.co.uk
**Reg No:** 1114149 **VAT No:** 127218876
**Estd:** 1973 Private Limited Company
**Line of Business:** Vacuum formed plastics
**Issued Capital:** £5,000
**Principals:** D C Perks *(Managing)*, Mrs N Banks-Siddons, M C Perks
**Co. Secretary:** Ms Natalie Banks
**Responsibilities**
**Senior:** Denis Fitzgerald *(General Manager)*
**Marketing:** Keith Woodworth *(Sales & Marketing Manager)*
**Sales:** Keith Woodworth *(Sales & Marketing Manager)*
**US SIC:** 3079, 2654
**UK SIC:** 48360, 47280
**Auditors:** Johnson Tidsall
**Bankers:** Lloyds TSB Bank plc (30-92-59)

| | 31-07-13 | 31-07-12 | 31-07-11 |
|---|---|---|---|
| TA | 4,092,064 | 3,361,726 | 3,420,127 |
| NW | 2,645,596 | 2,142,281 | 1,876,781 |
| WC | 2,222,205 | 1,733,636 | 1,463,155 |

DUNS 22-780-7187 **Imp-Exp**

## Thermoseal Group Ltd

Nexus Point, Birmingham, West Midlands B6 7AF
**Tel:** 0121-331-3950 **Fax:** 0121-331-3999
**Web:** www.thermosealgroup.com
**Reg No:** 1705619 **VAT No:** 377524622
**Estd:** 1983 Private Limited Company
**Line of Business:** Double glazing suppliers
**Export Markets:** Greece, Italy and France
**Issued Capital:** £10,760
**Principals:** G R Paterson *(Managing)*, M A Hickox
**Co. Secretary:** Gwain Paterson
**Responsibilities**
**Sales:** Norman Cameron *(Sales Manager)*
**Branches:** Thermoseal Group Ltd, Unit 12 Abbey Enterprise Park, Mill Road, Newtownabbey, Co Antrim BT36 7EE
**US SIC:** 1721 **UK SIC:** 50400
**Auditors:** McCranors Ltd
**Bankers:** Barclays Bank Plc (20-23-55)

| | 31-12-13 | 31-12-12 | 31-12-11 |
|---|---|---|---|
| TO | 21,523,319 | 20,131,834 | 20,644,202 |
| P/L | 1,462,814 | 1,314,933 | 2,159,477 |
| NW | 10,296,921 | 9,182,618 | 8,166,693 |
| WC | 8,017,010 | 7,398,932 | 7,040,263 |
| Emp. | 100 | 85 | 79 |

DUNS 28-986-2732

## Thesis Asset Management Plc

(**Subsidiary of:** Thomas Eggar Llp)
Exchange Building, St Johns Street, Chichester, West Sussex PO19 1UP
**Tel:** 01273728188 **Fax:** 01243-539094
**Web:** www.thesis-plc.com
**Reg No:** 1802101 **Estd:** 1984 Public Limited Company
**Line of Business:** Fund management activities
**Issued Capital:** £1,680,000
**Directors:** Mrs A H Gilbert, M J Lally, G S Dalton, G E Hedley Dent, S P Richards, Miss A Y King-Jones, A J Edwards, D W Tyerman
**Co. Secretary:** Michael Camps
**Responsibilities**
**Senior:** Stephen Mugford *(Director)*
**Marketing:** James Goward *(Marketing Manager)*
**Admin:** Sue Hoggarth *(Personal Assistant)*
**Health & Safety:** Rob Renshaw *(Health & Safety Officer)*
**Branches:** Thesis Asset Management Plc, 84 North Street, Guildford, Surrey GU1 4AU
**US SIC:** 7399 **UK SIC:** 83954
**Auditors:** Deloitte & Touche
**Bankers:** Barclays Bank Plc (20-20-62)

| | 30-04-14 | 30-04-13 | 30-04-12 |
|---|---|---|---|
| TO | 52,200,581 | 40,606,414 | 34,721,218 |
| P/L | 5,000,772 | 4,734,367 | 4,797,722 |
| NW | 5,202,009 | 4,340,832 | 4,041,116 |
| WC | 5,638,100 | 4,465,228 | 3,756,210 |
| Emp. | 86 | 78 | 68 |

DUNS 22-814-1560 **Imp-Exp**

## Thessco Ltd

(**Subsidiary of:** Solpro Manufacturing Ltd)
Royds Mills, Sheffield, South Yorkshire S4 7WB
**Tel:** 01142-720966
**Web:** www.thessco.co.uk
**Reg No:** 1819860 **Estd:** 1984 Private Limited Company
**Line of Business:** Recovery of precious metals
**Export Markets:** W Europe, Middle East, U S A, India, Scandinavia, Far East, Canada
**Issued Capital:** £50,000
**Principals:** P J Tear *(Managing)*, M Rathbone *(Financial)*, R P Cosgrove, J A Tear
**Co. Secretary:** John Dunn
**Responsibilities**
**Sales:** Graham Brough *(Sales Manager)*
**IT:** Peter Hooley *(Operations Manager)*
**HR:** Julia Crookes *(Human Resources Coordinator)*
**Operations:** Peter Hooley *(Operations Manager)*
**Purchasing:** Wendy Dickinson *(Purchasing Manager)*
**Engineering:** Sam Hayes *(Engineering Manager)*
**US SIC:** 3339 **UK SIC:** 22470
**Auditors:** Baker Tilly
**Bankers:** Barclays Bank Plc (20-76-89)

| | 31-12-13 | 31-12-12 | 31-12-11 |
|---|---|---|---|
| TO | 32,471,723 | 40,713,225 | 49,107,700 |
| P/L | 63,001 | 237,108 | 143,089 |
| NW | 7,146,928 | 7,083,368 | 6,908,048 |
| WC | 1,646,316 | 1,560,664 | 1,405,141 |
| Emp. | 107 | 102 | 99 |

DUNS 77-007-9986

## The Thetford Garden Centre Ltd

Kilverstone Road, Kilverstone, Thetford, Norfolk IP24 2RL
**Tel:** 01842763267
**Web:** www.thetfordgardencentre.co.uk
**Reg No:** 2658285 **VAT No:** 571311861
**Estd:** 1982 Private Limited Company
**Line of Business:** Other retail sale in specialised stores not elsewhere classified
**Issued Capital:** £90,000
**Principals:** Mrs J H Nixon *(Financial)*, Ms L Nixon
**Co. Secretary:** Paul Reeve
**Responsibilities**
**Senior:** Jeanette Jones *(Operations Manager)*
**Operations:** Jeanette Jones *(Operations Manager)*
**US SIC:** 5999 **UK SIC:** 65600
**Auditors:** Lovewell Blake
**Bankers:** Barclays Bank Plc (20-62-68)

| | 31-01-14 | 31-01-13 | 31-01-12 |
|---|---|---|---|
| TA | 2,356,284 | 2,129,166 | 2,163,062 |
| NW | 1,882,363 | 1,754,113 | 1,728,254 |
| WC | 387,418 | 347,774 | 537,393 |

DUNS 22-665-6544 **Exp**

## Thetford International Products Ltd

(**Subsidiary of:** Thetford International Compactors Ltd)
Rymer Point, Bury Road, Barnham, Thetford, Norfolk IP24 2PN
**Tel:** 01842-890500
**Web:** www.thetford-int.co.uk
**Reg No:** 1607721 **Estd:** 1982 Private Limited Company
**Line of Business:** Agents involved in the sale of machinery, industrial equipment, ships and aircraft
**Export Markets:** Scandinavia.
**Trading Style:** Thetford International
**Issued Capital:** £100
**Principals:** K R Ellis *(Managing)*, J R Ellis
**Co. Secretary:** Mrs Kathleen Ellis
**US SIC:** 5084, 3559
**UK SIC:** 61490, 32863
**Auditors:** Stacey & Partners
**Bankers:** Barclays Bank Plc (20-16-12)

| | 31-12-13 | 31-12-12 | 31-12-11 |
|---|---|---|---|
| TA | 207,237 | 319,860 | 408,908 |
| NW | 85,391 | 92,570 | 99,508 |
| WC | 85,391 | 92,570 | 99,508 |

DUNS 21-903-2729

## Thetford Ltd

Unit 6 Brookfields Way, Manvers, Rotherham, South Yorkshire S63 5DL
**Tel:** 01709766750 **Fax:** 01142753094
**Web:** www.thetford.eu
**Reg No:** 1001165 **VAT No:** 114632108
**Estd:** 1971 Private Limited Company
**Line of Business:** Manufacture of electric domestic appliances
**Issued Capital:** £200
**Directors:** B Anderson, P J Struijs, J H Fitzsimons, S P Cordeille
**Co. Secretary:**
Edwin Coe Secretaries Limited
**US SIC:** 3639, 6711
**UK SIC:** 34600, 83962
**Auditors:** Deloitte LLP
**Bankers:** Abn Amro Bank Nv (40-50-30)

| | 31-12-13 | 31-12-12 | 31-12-11 |
|---|---|---|---|
| TO | 21,634,676 | 22,381,326 | 25,766,582 |
| P/L | 256,407 | (613,287) | (173,550) |
| NW | 702,597 | 152,044 | 268,691 |
| WC | 2,064,324 | 2,015,912 | 2,537,918 |
| Emp. | 129 | 141 | 137 |

DUNS 21-879-7424

## The Thimble Guild

Thistle Mill, Station Road, Biggar, Lanarkshire ML12 6LP
**Tel:** 08445731650
**Web:** www.thescottishgourmet.com
**Estd:** 2012
**Line of Business:** Mail Order Houses
**US SIC:** 5961 **UK SIC:** 65600
**Employees:** 50

DUNS 73-299-8666

## Think Ltd

55 Degrees North, Newcastle-Upon-Tyne, Tyne and Wear NE1 6BF
**Tel:** 01912417000 **Fax:** 01912-417002
**Web:** www.think.eu
**Reg No:** 4573723 **Estd:** 2002 Private Limited Company
**Line of Business:** Web site design and development
**Export Sales:** £1,666,822
**Issued Capital:** £993
**Principals:** T A Nseir *(Managing)*, Ms M T Rainey, T M Hope
**Responsibilities**
**Senior:** Steven Johnston *(operations Director)*
**Marketing:** Steven Johnston *(operations Director)*
**Sales:** Steven Johnston *(operations Director)*
**IT:** Steven Askwith *(Lead Systems Administrator)*
**US SIC:** 7379 **UK SIC:** 83940
**Auditors:** UNW LLP
**Bankers:** Barclays Bank Plc (20-18-41)

| | 31-10-13 | 31-10-12 | 31-10-11 |
|---|---|---|---|
| TO | 8,036,947 | 10,184,671 | 12,674,718 |
| P/L | (415,983) | 1,548,230 | 1,451,181 |
| NW | 1,426,650 | 1,865,424 | 1,280,442 |
| WC | 2,208,558 | 2,083,178 | 445,241 |
| Emp. | 97 | 99 | N/A |

DUNS 22-289-0118

## Think Money Holdings Ltd

(**Subsidiary of:** Milan Swapco Ltd)
16 Carolina Way, Salford, Lancashire M50 2ZY
**Tel:** 08000747772
**Web:** www.thinkmoney.com
**Reg No:** 4306995 **Estd:** 2001 Private Limited Company
**Line of Business:** Business services
**Issued Capital:** £500,000

**Directors:** S A Stylianou, J G Warr
**Co. Secretary:** Simon Kay
**US SIC:** 6111 **UK SIC:** 81501

| | 31-01-14 | 31-01-13 | 31-01-12 |
|---|---|---|---|
| TA | 87,954,000 | 83,615,000 | 74,554,000 |
| P/L | 10,765,000 | 14,617,000 | 14,696,000 |
| NW | 42,590,000 | 33,683,000 | 30,933,000 |
| WC | 36,546,000 | 31,838,000 | 24,161,000 |
| Emp. | 814 | 970 | 930 |

DUNS 21-919-4969
## Think One Ltd
(**Subsidiary of:** Group 1 Automotive Inc.)
Chandlers, Victoria Road, Brighton, East Sussex BN41 1YH
**Tel:** 01252 490482
**Web:** www.thinkford.co.uk
**Reg No:** 8357141 **VAT No:** 675965766
**Estd:** 2013 Private Limited Company
**Line of Business:** Sale of new motor vehicles
**Trading Style:** Think Ford, Think Ford Farnborough, Think Ford Guildford, Think Ford Bracknell
**Issued Capital:** £1
**Directors:** E J Hesterberg, D M Burman, D J Mchenry, J Rickel
**Branches:** Think One Ltd - Think Ford Farnborough, Elles Road, Farnborough, GU14 7QW Hampshire
**US SIC:** 5521 **UK SIC:** 65100

| | 31-12-13 |
|---|---|
| TO | 127,145,960 |
| P/L | 138,398 |
| NW | 1,020,944 |
| WC | 2,068,940 |
| Emp. | 238 |

DUNS 53-613-1196 **Imp**
## Think Print (U K) Ltd
Cameron Court, Northwich, Cheshire CW8 4DU
**Tel:** 01606-784567 **Fax:** 01606-784777
**Web:** www.thinkprint.co.uk
**Reg No:** 3418318 **Estd:** 1997 Private Limited Company
**Line of Business:** Printing not elsewhere classified
**Issued Capital:** £100
**Directors:** I C Thomson, M Roberts
**Co. Secretary:** Ms Lisa Thomson
**Branches:** Think Print (U K) Ltd, 33 Station Rd, Northwich, Cheshire CW9 5LT
**US SIC:** 2752, 2753, 7399
**UK SIC:** 47544, 47545, 83954
**Auditors:** Anderson & Co

| | 31-12-13 | 31-12-12 | 31-12-11 |
|---|---|---|---|
| TO | 9,587,821 | 8,206,776 | 7,062,607 |
| P/L | 1,482,133 | 785,336 | 179,927 |
| NW | 959,043 | 961,043 | 963,180 |
| WC | 215,320 | 251,745 | 287,346 |
| Emp. | 49 | 48 | 45 |

DUNS 23-825-5785
## Think Publishing Ltd
Pall Mall Deposit, London W10 6BL
**Tel:** 02089623020 **Fax:** 02089628689
**Web:** www.thinkpublishing.co.uk
**Reg No:** 3817566 **Estd:** 1999 Private Limited Company
**Line of Business:** Publishing of books
**Issued Capital:** £50,000
**Directors:** Mrs P Arnold, I F Mcauliffe
**Co. Secretary:** Ms Matilda Boulter
**Responsibilities**
**Senior:** Tilly Boulter *(Manager)*
**US SIC:** 2731 **UK SIC:** 47532
**Auditors:** Benriches
**Bankers:** Barclays Bank Plc (20-17-19)

| | 31-12-13 | 31-12-12 | 31-12-11 |
|---|---|---|---|
| TO | 9,725,117 | N/A | N/A |
| P/L | 658,384 | N/A | N/A |
| NW | 1,114,282 | 1,017,313 | 677,741 |
| WC | 1,065,697 | 973,498 | 615,769 |
| Emp. | 52 | N/A | N/A |

DUNS 21-857-4458
## Think Renewable Energy Ltd
The Stables, Newby, Weeton, Leeds, West Yorkshire LS17 0EY
**Tel:** 01423 227 227
**Web:** www.thinkrenewableenergy.co.uk
**Reg No:** 8204882 **Estd:** 2012 Private Limited Company
**Line of Business:** Production of electricity
**Trading Style:** Think Renewable Energy Yorkshire, Think Renewable Energy Scotland, Think Renewable Energy London
**Issued Capital:** £1,000
**Directors:** P J Ogden, A M Barrett
**Branches:** Think Renewable Energy Ltd, 14 Murray Court, Hillhouse Industrial Estate, ML3 9BQ Hamilton
**US SIC:** 4911 **UK SIC:** 16101

| | 28-02-14 |
|---|---|
| TA | 1,071,294 |
| NW | (454,764) |
| WC | (644,547) |

DUNS 52-535-5368
## Thinktank Trust
Curzon Street, Birmingham, West Midlands B4 7XG
**Tel:** 01212022244 **Fax:** 0121-464-2054
**Web:** www.thinktank.ac
**Reg No:** 3239119 **Estd:** 1996 Private Limited Company
**Line of Business:** Museums & art galleries
**Issued Capital:** £2
**Directors:** L Clark, G L Allen, Viscountess P A Cobham, S R Freer
**Co. Secretary:** Mrs Judith Wilson
**Responsibilities**
**Senior:** Judith Petts *(Board Member)*, Kenny Webster *(General Manager)*
**Marketing:** Caroline Durbin *(PR Manager)*
**Branches:** Thinktank Trust, Curzon Street, Birmingham, West Midlands B4 7XG
**US SIC:** 8411 **UK SIC:** 97700
**Auditors:** HLB Kidsons
**Bankers:** HSBC Bank plc (40-11-18)

| | 31-03-14 | 31-03-13 | 31-03-12 |
|---|---|---|---|
| TO | 1,672,000 | 2,349,000 | 5,833,000 |
| P/L | (322,000) | 1,813,000 | 614,000 |
| NW | 3,233,000 | 3,668,000 | 1,855,000 |
| WC | 627,000 | 1,463,000 | 1,600,000 |
| Emp. | N/A | N/A | 108 |

DUNS 22-809-8224
## Thirsk Farmers Auction Mart Company Ltd
Blakey Lane, Thirsk, North Yorkshire YO7 3AB
**Tel:** 01845523165
**Web:** www.thirskmarket.com
**Reg No:** 0091818 **Estd:** 1909 Private Limited Company
**Line of Business:** Livestock markets
**Issued Capital:** £324,000
**Principals:** A Armstrong *(Financial)*, T S Kirby, T J Swiers, B Phillips, J I Woodhead
**Co. Secretary:** Michael Stephenson
**Responsibilities**
**Senior:** Thomas Bell *(Manager)*, Harry Woodhead *(Manager)*
**Branches:** Thirsk Farmers Auction Mart Company Ltd, 19 Market Pl, Thirsk, North Yorkshire YO7 1HD
**US SIC:** 0729, 5021
**UK SIC:** 01003, 61500
**Auditors:** The Barker Partnership
**Bankers:** Lloyds TSB Bank plc (77-71-68)

| | 30-06-14 | 30-06-13 | 30-06-12 |
|---|---|---|---|
| TO | 1,423,078 | 1,372,875 | 1,387,573 |
| P/L | (249,789) | (229,936) | (165,958) |
| NW | 3,170,416 | 3,382,975 | 3,645,681 |
| WC | (805,185) | (654,387) | (509,660) |
| Emp. | 59 | 61 | 64 |

DUNS 39-666-2520
## Thirteen Care & Support Ltd
The Exchange, Newcastle-Upon-Tyne, Tyne and Wear NE2 2JA
**Tel:** 0191-261-2228 **Fax:** 0191-261-2260
**Web:** www.norcare.co.uk
**Reg No:** 1810498 **Estd:** 1984 Private Company Limited By Guarantee
**Line of Business:** Charities and charitable organisations
**Trading Style:** Norcare
**Directors:** Mrs G Rollings, Ms H C Batey, D A Cheetham, J Scollen, Lieutenant General R V Brims, N S Ahmad, Mrs C Storrs, Mrs S M Bickerton
**Co. Secretary:** Ms Heather Ashton
**Responsibilities**
**Senior:** Judith Browne *(Director)*, Roderick Jones *(Chairman)*, Deirdre Pearson *(Financial Director)*, Veena Soni *(Manager)*
**Finance:** Esther Jayesimi *(Finance Director)*, Deirdre Pearson *(Financial Director)*
**HR:** Alison Haigh *(Human Resources Officer)*
**Health & Safety:** Alison Haigh *(Human Resources Officer)*
**Facilities:** Alison Haigh *(Human Resources Officer)*
**Branches:** Thirteen Care & Support Ltd, 8A Westgate Road, Graingerville North, Newcastle Upon Tyne, Tyne and Wear NE4 6UJ
**US SIC:** 8321 **UK SIC:** 96111
**Auditors:** H W
**Bankers:** Lloyds TSB Bank plc (30-19-54)

| | 31-03-14 | 31-03-13 | 31-03-12 |
|---|---|---|---|
| TO | 2,366,738 | 2,491,582 | 2,767,704 |
| P/L | 16,069 | 36,705 | (251,433) |
| NW | 1,646,584 | 1,630,515 | 1,593,810 |
| WC | 555,373 | 516,615 | 644,588 |
| Emp. | 46 | 50 | 65 |

DUNS 21-105-0957
## Thirteen Housing Group Ltd
2 Hudson Quay, Windward Way, Middlesbrough, Cleveland TS2 1QG
**Tel:** 01642-773-600 **Fax:** 01642-773-611
**Web:** www.fabrickgroup.co.uk
**Reg No:** 6477162 **Estd:** 2008 Private Company Limited By Guarantee
**Line of Business:** Estate agents
**Directors:** Mrs G V Rollings, Ms A C Thain, B J Dinsdale, Mrs S J Jeffrey, S Irwin, Mrs M Fay, Mrs J Clarke, M R Simpson
**Co. Secretary:** Mrs Barbara Ashton
**Responsibilities**
**Senior:** Andrew Lean *(Director)*, David Murtagh *(Director)*
**Branches:** Thirteen Housing Group Ltd, 33 Markby Green, Middlesbrough, Cleveland TS3 0QT
**US SIC:** 6531, 8321
**UK SIC:** 83400, 96111
**Auditors:** PricewaterhouseCoopers LLP

| | 31-03-14 | 31-03-13 | 31-03-12 |
|---|---|---|---|
| TO | 75,504,000 | 72,606,000 | 67,228,000 |
| P/L | 11,788,000 | 9,860,000 | 7,421,000 |
| NW | 307,918,000 | 278,030,000 | 248,302,000 |
| WC | 32,028,000 | 34,103,000 | 4,468,000 |
| Emp. | 882 | 655 | 628 |

DUNS 21-700-8066
## Thirty Nine Essex Street Llp
39 Essex Street, London WC2R 3AT
**Tel:** 02078321111
**Web:** www.39essex.com
**Reg No:** 0360005OC **Estd:** 2010
**Line of Business:** Solicitors
**Responsibilities**
**Senior:** Judith Ayling *(Non-designated Limited Liabili)*, Bruce Brodie *(Non-designated Limited Liabili)*, Charles Cory Wright Qc *(Non-designated Limited Liabili)*, John Denis Smith *(Non-designated Limited Liabili)*, Luke Diebelius *(Practice Manager)*, Sheraton Doyle *(Practice Manager)*, Gemma Goodwin *(Assistant Practice Manager)*, Steven Kovats Qc *(Non-designated Limited Liabili)*, Charles Manzoni Qc *(Non-designated Limited Liabili)*, Anna Markey *(Senior Receptionist)*, Colin Mccaul Qc *(Non-designated Limited Liabili)*, Niki Merison *(Assistant Practice Manager)*, Fenella Morris *(Non-designated Limited Liabili)*, Gordon Nardell Qc *(Non-designated Limited Liabili)*, Parishil Patel *(Non-designated Limited Liabili)*, Nigel Plemming *(Principal)*, Andrew Poyser *(Practice Manager)*, Adam Robb *(Non-designated Limited Liabili)*, Duncan Sinclair *(Non-designated Limited Liabili)*, Ben Sundborg *(Practice Manager)*, Justine Thornton *(Non-designated Limited Liabili)*, Richard Wald *(Barrister)*, Sean Wilken Qc *(Non-designated Limited Liabili)*, Christian Zwart *(Non-designated Limited Liabili)*
**Finance:** Gary Worsdell *(Finance Director)*
**Marketing:** Charlie Leppington *(Marketing Manager)*, Beth Williams *(Marketing Administrator)*
**Admin:** Lelia Di Domenico *(Legal Secretary)*
**IT:** Mark Brealey *(IT Support)*, Adam Critchell *(IT Support)*, Alex Herbet *(IT Manager)*
**HR:** Leonie Jamieson *(Facilities and Personnel Manag)*
**Facilities:** Leonie Jamieson *(Facilities and Personnel Manag)*
**US SIC:** 8111 **UK SIC:** 83500

| | 31-12-13 | 31-12-12 | 31-12-11 |
|---|---|---|---|
| TA | 825,004 | 535,040 | 602,496 |
| NW | (2,179,999) | (2,304,999) | (2,309,999) |
| WC | 819,999 | 155,000 | 180,000 |

DUNS 23-629-6682
## Thirty Three Group Ltd
40 Clerkenwell Close, London EC1R 0AW
**Tel:** 020-7336-4533 **Fax:** 020-7336-4545
**Web:** www.thirtythree.co.uk
**Reg No:** 3626724 **Estd:** 1998 Private Limited Company
**Line of Business:** Advertising
**Issued Capital:** £12,857
**Principals:** A J Young *(Managing)*, S Goold, G J Anderson, B T Forde, A J Bamford
**Co. Secretary:** Richard Clark
**US SIC:** 7311 **UK SIC:** 83800
**Auditors:** Grant Thornton UK LLP
**Bankers:** Bank Of Scotland (12-01-03)

| | 31-03-14 | 31-03-13 | 31-03-12 |
|---|---|---|---|
| TO | 17,680,894 | 17,342,510 | 26,116,075 |
| P/L | (237,186) | 99,454 | 982,917 |
| NW | 761,084 | 582,950 | 349,306 |
| WC | 550,539 | 375,203 | (8,514) |
| Emp. | 83 | 93 | 95 |

DUNS 85-615-2553
## This Is Global Ltd
(**Subsidiary of:** Global Radio Group Limited)
30 Leicester Square, London WC2H 7LA
**Tel:** 020 7766 6000
**Web:** www.thisisglobal.com
**Reg No:** 6251684 **Estd:** 1969 Private Limited Company
**Line of Business:** Management activities of holding companies
**Issued Capital:** £1
**Directors:** I L Hanson, C L Allen, W Harding, M D Connole, R F Park, M Gordon, Lord C L Allen, S G Miron
**Co. Secretary:** Clive Potterell
**US SIC:** 6711 **UK SIC:** 83962
**Auditors:** Deloitte LLP

| | 31-03-14 | 31-03-13 | 31-03-12 |
|---|---|---|---|
| TO | 223,645,000 | 219,516,000 | 209,448,000 |
| P/L | (38,446,000) | (29,290,000) | (27,723,000) |
| NW | (773,502,000) | (697,339,000) | (683,302,000) |
| WC | 46,481,000 | 29,997,000 | (11,387,000) |
| Emp. | 1,074 | 1,111 | 1,059 |

DUNS 50-638-7419
## Thistle Aberdeen Altens
Souter Head Road, Aberdeen, Aberdeenshire AB12 3LF
**Tel:** 08719711703
**Web:** www.thistle.com
**Estd:** 2004 Proprietorship
**Line of Business:** Hotels and motels without restaurant
**Responsibilities**
**Senior:** Simon Thatcher *(Proprietor)*
**US SIC:** 7011, 6531
**UK SIC:** 66500, 83400
**Employees:** 150

DUNS 21-229-4475
## Thistle Birmingham City
St Chads Queensway, Birmingham, West Midlands B4 6HY
**Tel:** 08713769005
**Web:** www.thistle.com
**Estd:** 1994
**Line of Business:** Hotels
**Proprietor:** Mrs T Win
**Responsibilities**
**Senior:** Lewis Diaz *(Food & Beverage Manager)*, Chris Falcus *(Hotel Manager)*
**Sales:** Elizabeth Mee *(Sales Coordinator)*
**US SIC:** 7011 **UK SIC:** 66500
**Employees:** 77

DUNS 28-821-5601
## Thistle Foundation
Niddrie Mains Road, Edinburgh, Midlothian EH16 4EA
**Tel:** 01316613366
**Web:** www.thistle.org.uk
**Reg No:** 0024409SC **Estd:** 1944 Private Company Limited By Guarantee
**Line of Business:** Social work activities with accommodation
**Directors:** I Williams, J D Dalrymple, Mrs D A Kong, Mrs G P Wilson, Ms D Paton, D R Giffin, Miss G Currie
**Co. Secretary:** John Campbell
**Responsibilities**
**Senior:** Diana Noel-Patton *(Chief Executive)*
**Branches:** Thistle Foundation, 25 High Mair, Renfrew, Renfrewshire PA4 0SE
**US SIC:** 8321 **UK SIC:** 96111
**Auditors:** Geoghegan & Co
**Bankers:** The Royal Bank Of Scotland Plc (83-06-08)

| | 31-03-14 | 31-03-13 | 31-03-12 |
|---|---|---|---|
| TO | 6,067,411 | 5,844,364 | 5,312,559 |
| P/L | (345,386) | 399,405 | (971,448) |
| NW | 9,208,611 | 9,501,062 | 8,887,066 |
| WC | 461,712 | 531,788 | 567,304 |
| Emp. | 313 | 284 | 280 |

DUNS 29-841-8559
## Thistle Healthcare Ltd
Scholars Gate East Kilbride, Glasgow, Lanarkshire G75 9JL
**Tel:** 01355-235508 **Fax:** 01355237043
**Web:** www.thistlehealthcare.co.uk
**Reg No:** 0100505SC **Estd:** 2012 Private Limited Company
**Line of Business:** Medical nursing home activities
**Issued Capital:** £16,564
**Principals:** D Fowdar *(Managing)*, Mrs R Ormshaw
**Co. Secretary:** Devanand Fowdar
**Responsibilities**
**Operations:** Eileen Welch *(Operations Director)*
**Branches:** Thistle Healthcare Ltd, 2 Tabernacle Street, Glasgow, Lanarkshire G72 8JN
**US SIC:** 7399 **UK SIC:** 83954
**Auditors:** PKF
**Bankers:** Bank Of Scotland (80-54-01)

| | 30-04-14 | 30-04-13 | 30-04-12 |
|---|---|---|---|
| TO | 14,634,934 | 14,368,754 | 13,810,921 |
| P/L | 784,766 | 1,250,957 | 780,287 |
| NW | 2,518,161 | 2,345,778 | 2,151,015 |
| WC | 1,038,322 | (589,752) | (433,070) |
| Emp. | 569 | 624 | 619 |

DUNS 21-783-6958
## Thistle Hotel
The Quay, Poole, Dorset BH15 1HD
**Tel:** 01202666800
**Web:** www.thistle.com
**Estd:** 1982 Partnership
**Line of Business:** Hotels
**Partners:** M Postlethwaite, M Postlethwaite
**Responsibilities**
**Senior:** Craig Findleton *(General Manager)*
**US SIC:** 7011 **UK SIC:** 66500
**Employees:** 230

DUNS 21-232-3887
## Thistle Hotel Euston
43 Cardington Street, London NW1 2LP
**Tel:** 08713769017
**Web:** www.thistle.com
**Estd:** 1972 Proprietorship
**Line of Business:** Hotels
**Proprietor:** M Moffatt
**Responsibilities**
**Senior:** Steve Caine *(General Manager)*, Premod Thomas *(Manager)*
**Finance:** Chris Kowal *(Financial Controller)*
**US SIC:** 7011 **UK SIC:** 66500
**Employees:** 150

DUNS 21-225-3919
## Thistle Hotel Inverness
Millburn Road, Inverness, Inverness-Shire IV2 3TR
**Tel:** 01463239666
**Web:** www.thistlehotels.com
**Estd:** 1975 Partnership
**Line of Business:** Hotels
**Partners:** Ms D Maclean, Ms S Mcgibbon, A Salter, Ms K Macleod, R Ball
**Responsibilities**
**Senior:** Dorothy MacLean *(Partner)*, Sarah McGibbon *(Partner)*
**US SIC:** 7011 **UK SIC:** 66500
**Employees:** 72

DUNS 21-225-6104
## Thistle Hotel Newcastle
Neville Street, Newcastle-Upon-Tyne, Tyne and Wear NE1 5DF
**Tel:** 08713769029
**Web:** www.thistle.com
**Estd:** 2014 Proprietorship
**Line of Business:** Hotels
**Proprietor:** D Roberts
**Responsibilities**
**Senior:** Stephen Devine *(General Manager)*
**Finance:** Scot Telford *(Accounts Officer)*
**Health & Safety:** Mike Beall *(Maintenance Porter)*
**Facilities:** Mike Beall *(Maintenance Porter)*
**US SIC:** 7011, 6531
**UK SIC:** 66500, 83400
**Employees:** 80

DUNS 42-342-4048
## Thistle Marble Arch Ltd
Thistle Marble Arch Hotel, 1-5 Br, Mayfair, London W1H 7EQ
**Tel:** 08713769027 **Fax:** 08703339216
**Web:** www.thistle.com
**Reg No:** 4330117 **Estd:** 2001 Private Limited Company
**Line of Business:** Hotels
**Issued Capital:** £1
**Directors:** N Gallagher, K M Ho, M B Denoma, M Ostridge
**Co. Secretary:** Seok Blackwell
**US SIC:** 7011 **UK SIC:** 66500

| | 30-06-13 | 30-06-12 | 03-06-11 |
|---|---|---|---|
| TO | 36,310,000 | 34,337,000 | 32,225,000 |
| P/L | 9,680,000 | 8,793,000 | 7,977,000 |
| NW | 149,400,000 | 137,423,000 | 126,924,000 |
| WC | (4,767,000) | (15,508,000) | (25,606,000) |
| Emp. | 180 | 170 | 190 |

DUNS 22-271-6693 Imp-Exp
## Thistle Seafoods Ltd
The Harbour, Harbour Street, Boddam, Peterhead, Aberdeenshire AB42 3AU
**Tel:** 01779478991
**Web:** www.thistleseafoods.com
**Reg No:** 0223362SC **Estd:** 1980 Private Limited Company
**Line of Business:** Fish merchants (wholesale)
**Export Markets:** Rest of Europe, Canada
**Export Sales:** £1,065,000
**Issued Capital:** £2,114,994
**Directors:** Ms P D Macdougal, Ms L E Scatterty, A J Scatterty, Ms E A Scatterty, R F Scatterty
**Co. Secretary:**
D.W. Company Services Limited
**Responsibilities**
**Senior:** Francis Clark *(Manager)*
**Finance:** Sandy Anderson *(Senior Finance Administrator)*
**US SIC:** 5146 **UK SIC:** 61700
**Auditors:** Deloitte LLP
**Bankers:** Bank Of Scotland (80-09-38)

| | 31-12-13 | 31-12-12 | 31-12-11 |
|---|---|---|---|
| TO | 67,557,000 | 56,191,000 | 54,218,760 |
| P/L | 1,428,000 | 1,071,000 | 979,433 |
| NW | 9,437,000 | 9,599,000 | 10,024,383 |
| WC | 8,209,000 | 4,452,000 | 7,688,811 |
| Emp. | 315 | 247 | 240 |

DUNS 23-505-2847
## Thistle Timber & Building Supplies Ltd
20 The Wisp, Edinburgh, Midlothian EH16 4SQ
**Tel:** 01316694125 **Fax:** 0131-669-8774
**Web:** www.thistletimbersupplies.co.uk
**Reg No:** 0182761SC **Estd:** 1998 Private Limited Company
**Line of Business:** Wholesale of wood, construction materials and sanitary equipment
**Issued Capital:** £51
**Director:** D J Allen
**Co. Secretary:** Ms Ann Allen
**Responsibilities**
**Senior:** Steven Maule *(Manager)*
**US SIC:** 5039 **UK SIC:** 61300
**Auditors:** Springfords

| | 31-12-13 | 31-12-12 | 31-12-11 |
|---|---|---|---|
| TA | 2,390,196 | 2,211,155 | 2,161,450 |
| NW | 964,362 | 787,664 | 662,362 |
| WC | 689,683 | 534,852 | 377,727 |

DUNS 22-702-0773
## T.H.March & Co.Ltd
10-12 Ely Place, London EC1N 6RY
**Web:** www.thmarch.co.uk
**Reg No:** 0116175 **Estd:** 1887 Private Limited Company
**Line of Business:** Insurance brokers
**Export Sales:** £53,000
**Trading Style:** T H March Insurance Broker
**Issued Capital:** £402,000
**Principals:** M J Ferraro *(Chairman)*, M R Smith, N R Mcfarlane
**Co. Secretary:** David Alcock
**Responsibilities**
**HR:** Joannae Morgan *(HR Manager)*
**Branches:** T.h.march & Co.ltd, T H March & Co Ltd, Hare Park House, Yelverton, Devon PL20 7LS
**US SIC:** 6411 **UK SIC:** 83200
**Auditors:** PricewaterhouseCoopers LLP

| | 31-03-14 | 31-03-13 | 31-03-12 |
|---|---|---|---|
| TO | 7,813,000 | 7,619,000 | 7,492,000 |
| P/L | 366,000 | 287,000 | 461,000 |
| NW | 1,379,000 | 1,285,000 | (201,000) |
| WC | 2,320,000 | 2,212,000 | 2,071,000 |
| Emp. | 94 | 94 | 89 |

DUNS 21-240-0105 Imp-Exp
## Thomas A. Ashton Ltd
Cortonwood Drive, Brampton, Barnsley, South Yorkshire S73 0UF
**Tel:** 01226273700
**Web:** www.ashton-groups.co.uk
**Reg No:** 0560837 **Estd:** 1866 Private Limited Company
**Line of Business:** Management activities of holding companies
**Issued Capital:** £4,768
**Chairman and Managing Director:** T A Wills
**Co. Secretary:** Ms Jane Burley
**Branches:** Thomas A. Ashton Ltd, 68B High St, Milton Keynes, Buckinghamshire MK11 1AQ
**US SIC:** 6711, 5199
**UK SIC:** 83962, 61900
**Auditors:** Hawsons
**Bankers:** National Westminster Bank Plc (56-00-09)

| | 31-12-13 | 31-12-12 | 31-12-11 |
|---|---|---|---|
| TA | 1,219,535 | 1,276,538 | 1,322,938 |
| NW | 524,300 | 598,318 | 698,129 |
| WC | 284,617 | 362,483 | 460,623 |

DUNS 37-873-1475
## Thomas & Adamson International Ltd
10 Wemyss Place, Edinburgh, Midlothian EH3 6DL
**Tel:** 0131-225-4072 **Fax:** 0131-225-5514
**Web:** www.thomasandadamson.com
**Reg No:** 0171733SC **Estd:** 1997 Private Limited Company
**Line of Business:** Architectural activities
**Trading Style:** Thomas and Adamson
**Issued Capital:** £1,000
**Directors:** Ms N Kravchuk, A Wallace, L D Banks, M W Reid, B Donaldson, D Young, C W Narrowmore
**Co. Secretary:** John Miller
**Responsibilities**
**Senior:** Alaistair Wallace *(Senior Partner)*
**US SIC:** 8911 **UK SIC:** 83701
**Auditors:** Thomson Cooper & Co
**Bankers:** Bank Of Scotland (80-11-00)

| | 31-01-14 | 31-01-13 | 31-01-12 |
|---|---|---|---|
| TA | 475,848 | 279,533 | 248,092 |
| NW | (41,990) | (254,630) | (266,943) |
| WC | (53,147) | (263,401) | (280,199) |

DUNS 21-166-4987
## Thomas Aveling School
Arethusa Road, Rochester, Kent ME1 2UW
**Tel:** 01634813121
**Web:** www.thomasaveling.co.uk
**Estd:** 1990
**Line of Business:** Schools (local authority)
**Director:** Mrs C Christopher
**Responsibilities**
**Senior:** Andrew Minchin *(Deputy Head Teacher)*, Paul Wintle *(Project Manager)*
**US SIC:** 8211 **UK SIC:** 93200
**Employees:** 100

DUNS 21-258-3058 Imp-Exp
## Thomas B. Ramsden & Co. (Bradford) Ltd
**(Subsidiary of:** Thomas Ramsden (Holdings) Ltd)
Gordon Mills, Netherfield Road, Guiseley, Leeds, West Yorkshire LS20 9PD
**Web:** www.tbramsden.co.uk
**Reg No:** 0658571 **Estd:** 1960 Private Limited Company
**Line of Business:** Manufacture of household textiles
**Export Markets:** Worldwide
**Export Sales:** £575,711
**Issued Capital:** £900
**Principals:** T B Ramsden *(Managing)*, Mrs A M Mohr, R A Ramsden, P Mongomery, T P Ramsden
**Co. Secretary:** Mrs Amanda Mohr
**Branches:** Thomas B. Ramsden & Co. (Bradford) Ltd, Greenroyd Mill, High St, Sutton In Craven, Keighley, West Yorkshire BD20 7NG
**US SIC:** 2392 **UK SIC:** 45550
**Auditors:** Kirk Newsholme
**Bankers:** Barclays Bank Plc (20-89-68)

| | 30-04-14 | 30-04-13 | 30-04-12 |
|---|---|---|---|
| TO | 6,844,746 | 7,424,792 | 7,019,793 |
| P/L | 293,458 | 261,769 | 164,005 |
| NW | 2,265,637 | 1,758,179 | 1,950,110 |
| WC | 5,457,823 | 5,219,671 | 4,980,252 |
| Emp. | 78 | 79 | 72 |

DUNS 64-244-6785
## Thomas Bakeries
8 Wattstown Business Park, Newbridge Road, Coleraine, Co Londonderry BT52 1BS
**Tel:** 02870353512
**Web:** www.thomasthebaker.co.uk
**Estd:** 2012 Partnership
**Line of Business:** Bakers shops
**Partners:** Mrs L Thomas, D I Thomas
**Responsibilities**
**Senior:** Edward Kowalski *(Proprietor)*
**Branches:** Thomas Bakeries, 72 Cavendish Street, Barrow-In-Furness, Cumbria LA14 1PZ
**US SIC:** 5462 **UK SIC:** 64100
**Employees:** 48

DUNS 21-795-4315
## Thomas Bewick School
Linhope Road, Newcastle-Upon-Tyne, Tyne and Wear NE5 2LW
**Tel:** 01912296020
**Web:** www.thomasbewick.newcastle.sch.uk
**Estd:** 2011
**Line of Business:** Primary education
**Responsibilities**
**Senior:** Diane Scott *(Head Teacher)*
**US SIC:** 8999 **UK SIC:** 83954
**Employees:** 80

DUNS 21-590-3844
## Thomas Birkhead & Son
Yew Tree Mills, Holmbridge, Huddersfield, West Yorkshire HD9 2NN
**Tel:** 01484691510
**Estd:** 2011
**Line of Business:** Manufacturers of textiles
**Responsibilities**
**Senior:** Trevor Hynd *(Manager)*
**US SIC:** 2392 **UK SIC:** 45550
**Employees:** 50

DUNS 21-237-9739
## Thomas Black.Ltd
**(Subsidiary of:** Ogden Properties Ltd)
Boston Hall, High Street, Boston Spa, Wetherby, West Yorkshire LS23 6AD
**Tel:** 01937-541234 **Fax:** 0113-254-1472
**Web:** www.ogdengroup.co.uk
**Reg No:** 0233901 **Estd:** 1890 Private Limited Company
**Line of Business:** Buying and selling of own real estate
**Issued Capital:** £30,000
**Principals:** F N Colvin *(Financial)*, Sir R Ogden Cbe Lld, J C Garnett, W Marchant
**Branches:** Goldthorpe Yorkshire
**US SIC:** 6531, 6519
**UK SIC:** 83400, 85000
**Auditors:** Clough & Co
**Bankers:** National Westminster Bank Plc (50-00-00)

| | 31-12-13 | 31-12-12 | 31-12-11 |
|---|---|---|---|
| TA | 286,531 | 282,923 | 230,308 |
| NW | (29,652) | (27,878) | 8,027 |
| WC | (313,972) | (304,822) | (219,746) |

DUNS 22-788-7841 Imp
## Thomas Blunt Partnership
New Road, Kidderminster, Worcestershire DY10 1AL
**Tel:** 01562-744022
**Web:** www.kidderminsterfootwear.com
**Estd:** 2002 Partnership
**Line of Business:** Footwear wholesalers
**Trading Style:** Kidderminster Footwear
**Partners:** R H Blunt, Ms V Borne, R Blunt, T A Blunt, Ms L Hickerton, M R Blunt, Ms J Drysdale
**Responsibilities**
**Health & Safety:** Max Willey *(Health & Safety Officer)*
**Branches:** Thomas Blunt Partnership, Rooley Lane, Bradford, West Yorkshire BD4 7SA
**US SIC:** 5136, 5661
**UK SIC:** 61600, 64600
**Bankers:** HSBC Bank plc (40-26-08)
**Employees:** 560

DUNS 21-213-5214 Imp-Exp
## Thomas Broadbent & Sons Ltd
Queen Street South, Huddersfield, West Yorkshire HD1 3DU
**Fax:** 01484-516142
**Web:** www.broadbent.co.uk
**Reg No:** 0043017 **Estd:** 1895 Private Limited Company
**Line of Business:** Manufacture of insulated wire and cable
**Export Sales:** £20,469,410
**Issued Capital:** £364,185
**Principals:** N H Couch *(Chairman)*, S A Broadbent *(Managing)*, J Wright, A J Dean, I Livesey, Dr G C Grimwood
**Co. Secretary:** John Knapp
**Responsibilities**
**Senior:** Martin Standring *(Factory Manager)*
**Operations:** Alan Ainsworth *(Engineering Manager)*
**Engineering:** Alan Ainsworth *(Engineering Manager)*
**US SIC:** 3357 **UK SIC:** 22470
**Auditors:** KPMG LLP
**Bankers:** HSBC Bank plc (40-25-10)

| | 30-09-13 | 30-09-12 | 30-09-11 |
|---|---|---|---|
| TO | 25,958,479 | 27,645,009 | 21,295,642 |
| P/L | 1,376,970 | 1,450,365 | 796,816 |
| NW | 4,745,133 | 4,125,559 | 2,830,652 |
| WC | 3,425,325 | 2,319,097 | 1,014,946 |
| Emp. | 183 | 164 | 148 |

DUNS 21-617-5372
## Thomas Brooker & Sons Ltd
Unit 4 Bilton Road, Hitchin, Hertfordshire SG4 0SB
**Tel:** 01462450333
**Web:** www.easidrive.com
**Reg No:** 0101749 **VAT No:** 196229238
**Estd:** 1876 Private Limited Company
**Line of Business:** Builders merchants
**Issued Capital:** £101,036
**Principals:** T P Brooker *(Financial)*, D J Brooker *(Sales)*, P R Brooker *(Personnel)*, D W Brooker
**Co. Secretary:** Thomas Brooker
**Responsibilities**
**Senior:** Alison Brooker *(Manager)*, Liam Dunn *(Operations Manager)*
**Finance:** Alison Brooker *(Manager)*
**Admin:** Lisa Cooke *(Office Manager)*
**HR:** Sandra Baddell *(Human Resources Manager)*
**Health & Safety:** Sandra Baddell *(Human Resources Manager)*
**Branches:** Thomas Brooker & Sons Ltd, Cadwell Sidings, Arlesey Rd, Hitchin, Hertfordshire SG5 3UA
**US SIC:** 5072, 5732
**UK SIC:** 61500, 64800
**Auditors:** WKH
**Bankers:** National Westminster Bank Plc (60-11-10)

| | 30-09-13 | 30-09-12 | 30-09-11 |
|---|---|---|---|
| TO | 4,230,486 | 4,393,661 | 4,464,610 |
| P/L | 99,417 | 93,716 | 11,268 |
| NW | 7,079,180 | 7,026,936 | 7,026,899 |
| WC | 1,565,821 | 1,575,899 | 1,532,671 |
| Emp. | 73 | 75 | 45 |

DUNS 28-900-1570
## Thomas C. Adams (Home & Business Finance) Ltd
44 Lower Bridge Street, Chester, Cheshire CH1 1RS
**Tel:** 01244-340340
**Web:** www.thomascadamsltd.com
**Reg No:** 1342081 **Estd:** 1977 Private Limited Company
**Line of Business:** Estate agents
**Issued Capital:** £1,000
**Managing Director:** N Wilson
**Responsibilities**
**Health & Safety:** Jane Howarth *(Health & Safety Officer)*

**Branches:** Thomas C. Adams (Home & Business Finance) Ltd, 50 Chester Rd West, Shotton, Deeside, Clwyd CH5 1BY
**US SIC:** 6531 **UK SIC:** 83400
**Auditors:** Conways
**Bankers:** National Westminster Bank Plc (60-40-08)

| | 31-12-13 | 31-12-12 | 31-12-11 |
|---|---|---|---|
| TA | 43,762 | 43,325 | 41,881 |
| NW | (262,378) | (265,815) | (263,767) |
| WC | (262,574) | (266,077) | (264,116) |

DUNS 21-209-0823
## Thomas Chadwick & Sons Ltd
Eastfield Mills, Sands Lane, Dewsbury, West Yorkshire WF12 8EH
**Tel:** 01924-465023
**Web:** www.standardwool.co.uk
**Reg No:** 0181094 **Estd:** 1904 Private Limited Company
**Line of Business:** Hair and wool brokers
**Issued Capital:** £40,000
**Director:** P T Hughes
**US SIC:** 5159 **UK SIC:** 61100

| | 31-03-14 | 31-03-13 | 31-03-12 |
|---|---|---|---|
| TA | 40,000 | 40,000 | 40,000 |
| NW | 40,000 | 40,000 | 40,000 |

DUNS 23-300-1572
## Thomas Contracting Ltd
(**Subsidiary of:** Thomas Holdings (North West) Ltd)
Penllwyn Farm, Llyn Helyg, Lloc, Holywell, Clwyd CH8 8SB
**Tel:** 01352-721216
**Web:** www.thomasplanthire.co.uk
**Reg No:** 4496458 **Estd:** 2002 Private Limited Company
**Line of Business:** Engineering machine services
**Issued Capital:** £1
**Director:** W Lloyd Thomas
**Co. Secretary:** Ms Sarah Thomas
**Responsibilities**
**Senior:** Wyn Thomas *(Manager)*
**US SIC:** 7394, 1795, 1799
**UK SIC:** 84000, 50000
**Auditors:** John Davies & Co

| | 31-05-14 | 31-05-13 | 31-05-12 |
|---|---|---|---|
| TO | 13,093,453 | 11,427,547 | 8,543,361 |
| P/L | 241,808 | 686,582 | 1,206,061 |
| NW | 728,504 | 2,848,282 | 2,539,461 |
| WC | 728,504 | 2,848,282 | (252,752) |
| Emp. | 77 | 68 | 50 |

DUNS 42-351-4053
## Thomas Cook Aircraft Engineering Ltd
(**Subsidiary of:** Thomas Cook Group Plc)
Hangar 1 Western Maintenance Are, Manchester Airport, Manchester M90 5FL
**Tel:** 0161-498-4400 **Fax:** 0161-498-4417
**Web:** www.thomascook.com
**Reg No:** 4339114 **Estd:** 2001 Private Limited Company
**Line of Business:** Manufacture of aircraft and spacecraft
**Export Sales:** £13,374,000
**Issued Capital:** £1,000
**Directors:** J K Schildt, C Debus, J M Boler, Thomas Cook Group Management Ser
**Co. Secretary:** Ms Emma Langford
**Responsibilities**
**Senior:** Cor Vrieswijk *(Chief Operating Officer)*
**Health & Safety:** Christopher Goulston *(Health And Safety Manager)*
**Facilities:** Andy Lilly *(Facilities Manager)*
**Operations:** Cor Vrieswijk *(Chief Operating Officer)*
**US SIC:** 7399 **UK SIC:** 83954
**Auditors:** PricewaterhouseCoopers LLP

| | 30-09-13 | 30-09-12 | 30-09-11 |
|---|---|---|---|
| TO | 39,599,000 | 35,986,000 | 37,125,000 |
| P/L | 265,000 | (567,000) | (7,058,000) |
| NW | (5,503,000) | (5,156,000) | (4,589,000) |
| WC | (9,349,000) | (9,502,000) | (9,211,000) |
| Emp. | 441 | 24 | 50 |

DUNS 21-905-9008
## Thomas Cook Group Plc
3rd Floor South Building, London EC1A 4HD
**Tel:** 02075576400 **Fax:** 02075576401
**Web:** www.thomascookgroup.com
**Reg No:** 6091951 **Estd:** 2007 Public Limited Company
**Line of Business:** Management activities of holding companies
**Export Sales:** £6,059,000,000
**Trading Style:** Thomas Cook Publishing
**Issued Capital:** £90,502,476
**Directors:** Ms D E Airey, W G Tucker, Dr P Fankhauser, H Klein, M J Healy, Ms A Aris, Ms M Verluyten, C G Symon
**Co. Secretary:** Derek Woodward
**Responsibilities**
**Senior:** Emre Berkin *(Director)*, Roger Burnell *(Non-Executive Director)*, Peter Constanti *(Chief Executive Officer, Group)*, Thomas Doering *(Chief Executive Officer, East)*, Peter Fankhasuer *(Chief Executive Officer)*, Michael Friisdahl *(Chief Executive, North America)*, Bo Lerenius *(Non-Executive Director)*, François Meysman *(Director)*, Ralf Teckentrup *(Chief Executive Officer, Airli)*, Sam Weihagen *(Deputy Chief Executive Officer)*
**Marketing:** Linda Booth *(Head of Retail Marketing)*, Jenny Peters *(Group Head of Communications)*, John Straw *(Head of Digital)*
**HR:** Sandra Campopiano *(Chief People Officer)*, Tim Cheal *(Training Manager)*
**Health & Safety:** Hazel Corocran *(Cabin Safety Officer)*
**Operations:** Ludger Heuberg *(Chief Executive Officer, Group)*
**Fleet:** Linton Foat *(Flight Operations, Safety & Qu)*
**Branches:** Thomas Cook Group Plc, 9 High Street, Canterbury, Kent CT1 2JH
**US SIC:** 6711 **UK SIC:** 83962
**Auditors:** PricewaterhouseCoopers LLP
**Following financial data are in thousands**

| | 30-09-14 | 30-09-13 | 30-09-12 |
|---|---|---|---|
| TO | 8,588,000 | 9,314,500 | 9,491,200 |
| P/L | (114,000) | (158,100) | (485,300) |
| NW | (2,626,000) | (2,645,200) | (2,752,400) |
| WC | (2,065,000) | (1,701,600) | (2,015,900) |
| Emp. | 22,672 | 26,448 | 33,593 |

DUNS 21-733-8714
## Thomas Cook Retail Ltd
(**Subsidiary of:** Thomas Cook Group Plc)
Unit 15-30, The Thomas Cook Business Park, Coningsby Road, Peterborough, Cambridgeshire PE3 8SB
**Tel:** 08443357564 **Fax:** 0161 941 3890
**Web:** www.thomascook.com
**Reg No:** 0102630 **Estd:** 2002 Private Limited Company
**Line of Business:** Activities of travel agencies
**Trading Style:** Thomas Cook Sports, Thomas Cook, Thomas Cook, Thomas Cook Tv
**Issued Capital:** £455,000,000
**Directors:**
Thomas Cook Group Management Ser, P A Hemingway
**Co. Secretary:** Ms Shirley Bradley
**Responsibilities**
**Senior:** Natasha Emms *(Branch Manager)*, Manny Fontenla-Nova *(Chief Executive Officer)*
**Branches:** Thomas Cook Retail Ltd, 104 Upper Level, White Rose Shopping Centre, Leeds, West Yorkshire LS11 8LU
**US SIC:** 4722 **UK SIC:** 77001
**Auditors:** PricewaterhouseCoopers LLP

| | 30-09-13 | 30-09-12 | 30-09-11 |
|---|---|---|---|
| TO | 1,929,000 | 259,471,000 | 176,259,000 |
| P/L | (43,879,000) | (35,273,000) | (31,357,000) |
| NW | 72,407,000 | 163,785,000 | 179,740,000 |
| WC | (88,060,000) | (43,628,000) | 168,057,000 |
| Emp. | 880 | 530 | 646 |

DUNS 21-922-5265
## Thomas Cook Scheduled Tour Operations Ltd
(**Subsidiary of:** Thomas Cook Group Plc)
The Thomas Cook Business Park, Coningsby Road, Peterborough, Cambridgeshire PE3 8SB
**Tel:** 08443357563
**Web:** www.thomascook.com
**Reg No:** 0960252 **VAT No:** 239384142
**Estd:** 1969 Private Limited Company
**Line of Business:** Travel agency activities
**Issued Capital:** £100,000
**Directors:** P A Hemingway, Thomas Cook Group Management Ser, Ms S Bradley
**US SIC:** 4722 **UK SIC:** 77001
**Auditors:** PricewaterhouseCoopers LLP

| | 30-09-13 | 30-09-12 | 30-09-11 |
|---|---|---|---|
| TO | 130,414,000 | 145,815,000 | 168,246,000 |
| P/L | (3,991,000) | (1,727,000) | (9,789,000) |
| NW | (36,104,000) | (33,236,000) | (22,011,000) |
| WC | (36,061,000) | (33,095,000) | (30,903,000) |
| Emp. | 159 | 197 | 248 |

DUNS 21-039-1445
## The Thomas Coram C of E School
Swing Gate Lane, Berkhamsted, Hertfordshire HP4 2RP
**Tel:** 01442-866757
**Web:** www.thomascoram.herts.sch.uk
**Estd:** 1989 Partnership
**Line of Business:** Schools (local authority)
**Partner:** E Delasalle
**Responsibilities**
**Senior:** Eduard Delasalle *(Head Teacher)*
**US SIC:** 8211 **UK SIC:** 93200
**Employees:** 50

DUNS 22-951-0391 Exp
## Thomas Cradley Holdings Ltd
Gorsey Lane, Widnes, Cheshire WA8 0GG
**Tel:** 01514202020 **Fax:** 01514203010
**Web:** www.suttonsgroup.com
**Reg No:** 1334869 **Estd:** 1977 Private Limited Company
**Line of Business:** Management activities of holding companies
**Export Markets:** Worldwide
**Export Sales:** £71,559,505
**Issued Capital:** £30,000
**Principals:** A M Sutton *(Chairman)*, A J Palmer, T R Stockley, Mrs C M Kerry, T N Broadhurst, J Sutton, K Broom
**Co. Secretary:** Christopher Orger
**US SIC:** 6711, 4213
**UK SIC:** 83962, 72300
**Auditors:** Jackson Stephen
**Bankers:** HSBC Bank plc (40-29-08)

| | 30-04-14 | 30-04-13 | 30-04-12 |
|---|---|---|---|
| TO | 156,955,028 | 154,656,360 | 148,545,875 |
| P/L | 9,811,500 | 7,458,027 | 7,225,004 |
| NW | 54,588,345 | 49,116,329 | 44,432,606 |
| WC | 7,268,898 | 8,504,069 | 8,056,985 |
| Emp. | 775 | 776 | 738 |

DUNS 73-835-3726
## The Thomas Deacon Academy
Queens Gardens, Peterborough, Cambridgeshire PE1 2UW
**Tel:** 01733426060
**Web:** www.thomasdeaconacademy.com
**Reg No:** 5090788 **Estd:** 2004 Private Company Limited By Guarantee
**Line of Business:** General secondary education
**Directors:** J Peach, Miss L S Faulkner, Mrs K R Bretten, J D Lewis, R J Wade, M J Gross, P A Clegg, Mrs J A Taylor
**Co. Secretary:** David Brooks
**Responsibilities**
**Senior:** Donna Augustine *(Director)*, Ian Clarkson *(Director)*, Miles Delap *(Director)*, Alan McMurdo *(Manager)*, Christopher Woolhouse *(Director)*
**US SIC:** 8211 **UK SIC:** 93200
**Auditors:** Peters, Elworthy & Moore
**Bankers:** HSBC Bank plc (40-03-22)

| | 31-08-14 | 31-08-13 | 31-08-12 |
|---|---|---|---|
| TO | 17,184,000 | 15,567,000 | 14,723,000 |
| P/L | 1,293,000 | (823,000) | (1,740,000) |
| NW | 40,147,000 | 39,538,000 | 40,036,000 |
| WC | 2,161,000 | 1,613,000 | 1,056,000 |
| Emp. | 288 | 296 | 320 |

DUNS 21-811-8776 Exp
## Thomas Dudley Group Ltd
Dauntless Works, P O Box 28, Birmingham New Road, Dudley, West Midlands DY1 4SN
**Fax:** 0121-557-5345
**Web:** www.thomasdudleygroup.co.uk
**Reg No:** 0732459 **Estd:** 1920 Private Limited Company
**Line of Business:** Manufacture of builders ware of plastic
**Export Sales:** £1,167,135
**Issued Capital:** £318,852
**Principals:** H J Dudley *(Chairman)*, M J Dudley *(Managing)*
**Co. Secretary:** Harold Dudley
**US SIC:** 3079, 3321, 6711
**UK SIC:** 48360, 31110, 83962
**Auditors:** Clement Keys
**Bankers:** Barclays Bank Plc (20-93-15)

| | 31-07-14 | 31-07-13 | 31-07-12 |
|---|---|---|---|
| TO | 31,772,452 | 29,637,569 | 29,026,574 |
| P/L | 4,447,618 | 2,911,674 | 3,578,954 |
| NW | 38,220,731 | 35,480,422 | 31,082,651 |
| WC | 25,286,732 | 22,099,786 | 19,930,479 |
| Emp. | 347 | 345 | 322 |

DUNS 22-977-0680
## Thomas Eggar
The Corn Exchange, Baffins Lane, Chichester, West Sussex PO19 1GE
**Tel:** 01243-786111
**Web:** www.thomaseggar.com
**VAT No:** 209582159 **Estd:** 2007 Partnership
**Line of Business:** Solicitors
**Trading Style:** Thomas Eggar
**Partners:** C J Bell, M Crooks, J Stappleton
**Responsibilities**
**Senior:** Victoria Brackett *(Managing Partner)*
**IT:** Neil Renfrew *(Computer Manager)*
**Branches:** Thomas Eggar, 76 Shoe Lane, London EC4A 3JB
**US SIC:** 8111 **UK SIC:** 83500
**Bankers:** National Westminster Bank Plc (60-30-06)
**Employees:** 101

DUNS 21-605-2735
## Thomas Eggar Llp
Brunel House, 21 Brunswick Place, Southampton, Hampshire SO15 2AQ
**Tel:** 02380831100
**Web:** www.thomaseggar.com
**Estd:** 2011 Proprietorship
**Line of Business:** Solicitors
**Proprietor:** Mrs E Smith
**Responsibilities**
**Senior:** Leon Arnold *(Partner)*, Matthew Bridger *(Associate)*, Hannah Clipston *(Partner)*, Steven Eldred *(Partner)*, David Fanchi *(Partner)*, Charles Frank *(Senior Associate)*, Philip Gray *(Senior Associate)*, Kylie Morsley *(Associate)*, Richard Purcell *(Partner)*, Biddy Walker *(Partner)*
**Admin:** Jessica Morgan *(Claims Administrator)*
**US SIC:** 8111 **UK SIC:** 83500
**Employees:** 50

DUNS 21-230-4722
## Thomas Eggar Solicitors
Newbury House 20 Kings Road West, Newbury, Berkshire RG14 5XR
**Tel:** 01635-571000
**Web:** www.thomaseggar.com
**Estd:** 2004 Partnership
**Line of Business:** Solicitors
**Partners:** J Chadwick, Ms R Philpott
**Responsibilities**
**Senior:** Claire Hamilton-Russell *(Partner and Family Mediator)*, Richard Hornsby *(Partner)*, Daisy Hutchinson *(Associate and Family Mediator)*
**US SIC:** 8111 **UK SIC:** 83500
**Employees:** 63

DUNS 22-952-6777 Imp-Exp
## Thomas Fattorini (Holdings) Ltd
Regent Street, Birmingham, West Midlands B1 3HQ
**Web:** www.fattorini.co.uk
**Reg No:** 0154245 **VAT No:** 343412878
**Estd:** 1827 Private Limited Company
**Line of Business:** Management activities of other non-financial holding companies not elsewhere classified
**Export Markets:** Worldwide
**Export Sales:** £1,242,284
**Issued Capital:** £47,000
**Principals:** G T Fattorini *(Managing)*, S T Fattorini, T H Fattorini, T R Fattorini, A H Fattorini
**Branches:** Thomas Fattorini (Holdings) Ltd, 150 Minories, London EC3N 1LS
**US SIC:** 6711 **UK SIC:** 83962
**Auditors:** Robertshaw & Myers
**Bankers:** Barclays Bank Plc (20-78-42)

| | 31-12-13 | 31-12-12 | 31-12-11 |
|---|---|---|---|
| TO | 5,621,193 | 7,805,538 | 10,205,200 |
| P/L | 86,226 | 993,107 | 1,207,715 |
| NW | 5,741,575 | 5,774,893 | 5,239,991 |
| WC | 4,138,358 | 4,219,057 | 4,060,242 |
| Emp. | 126 | 129 | 132 |

DUNS 21-207-4116
## Thomas Fawcett & Sons Ltd
Eastfield Lane, Castleford, West Yorkshire WF10 4LE
**Tel:** 01977-552490
**Web:** www.fawcett-maltsters.co.uk
**Reg No:** 0153755 **VAT No:** 181482066
**Estd:** 1919 Private Limited Company
**Line of Business:** Manufacture of malt
**Issued Capital:** £70,000
**Directors:** F T Jordan, Mrs J M Pratt, J A Fawcett, Ms L S Fawcett, I Hall, Mrs S H Fawcett
**Co. Secretary:** Miss Joanne Tonks
**Responsibilities**
**Senior:** Denis Gallivan *(Manager)*
**Finance:** David Mortimer *(Manager)*
**IT:** David Mortimer *(Manager)*
**Health & Safety:** Jim Taylor *(General Manager)*
**Operations:** David Mortimer *(Manager)*
**US SIC:** 2083 **UK SIC:** 42702
**Auditors:** PKF
**Bankers:** Barclays Bank Plc (20-89-68)

| | 30-09-14 | 30-09-13 | 30-09-12 |
|---|---|---|---|
| TO | 12,764,420 | 11,421,452 | 11,266,644 |
| P/L | 1,163,951 | 933,494 | 1,050,781 |
| NW | 7,169,134 | 6,576,643 | 6,014,628 |
| WC | 1,785,095 | 2,069,460 | 1,623,697 |
| Emp. | 66 | 64 | 66 |

DUNS 21-780-6503
## Thomas Fortune Work Centre
195a & 195d Drumry Road East, Glasgow, Lanarkshire G15 8NS
**Tel:** 01419444383
**Web:** www.enableglasgow.org.uk
**Estd:** 2001 Proprietorship
**Line of Business:** Charities and charitable organisations
**Proprietor:** C Menabney
**Responsibilities**
**Senior:** Anne Ainsworth *(Manager)*
**US SIC:** 8299 **UK SIC:** 93300
**Employees:** 72

DUNS 73-918-6307

## Thomas Franks Ltd

Bloxham Grove Farm, Banbury, Oxfordshire OX15 4LL
**Tel:** 01608738070 **Fax:** 01608-737941
**Web:** www.thomasfranks.co.uk
**Reg No:** 5171922 **VAT No:** 844505528
**Estd:** 2005 Private Limited Company
**Line of Business:** Caterers
**Issued Capital:** £85,714
**Directors:** Ms L Wilson, F J Bothwell, Ms E C Bothwell, J A Brown
**Co. Secretary:** Miss Lorraine Wilson
**Responsibilities**
**Senior:** Simon Cule *(Director of Purchasing)*
**Marketing:** Jamie Burrell *(Creative Director)*
**HR:** Vicky Freeman *(HR Manager)*, Jenny Teesdale *(HR Manager)*
**Operations:** Aidan Ross *(Operations Manager)*
**Purchasing:** Simon Cule *(Director of Purchasing)*
**US SIC:** 5812 **UK SIC:** 66110
**Auditors:** Michael J. Emery & Co Ltd

| | 30-09-13 | 30-09-12 | 30-09-11 |
|---|---|---|---|
| TO | 15,864,120 | 12,125,968 | 9,130,361 |
| P/L | 548,148 | 409,347 | 300,816 |
| NW | 665,314 | 439,984 | 123,080 |
| WC | 562,046 | 345,950 | 66,290 |
| Emp. | 548 | 455 | 372 |

DUNS 36-522-0446

## Thomas Gabrielle Nursing Home

Victoria Street, Cwmbran, Gwent NP44 3JP
**Tel:** 01633-868241
**Web:** www.virgocarehomes.com
**Estd:** 2001 Proprietorship
**Line of Business:** Medical nursing home activities
**Proprietor:** T Gabrielle
**US SIC:** 8051 **UK SIC:** 95100
**Employees:** 50

DUNS 21-012-2206 **Imp-Exp**

## Thomas Goode & Co. Ltd

(**Subsidiary of:** Breezy Holdings Limited)
19 South Audley Street, London W1K 2BN
**Tel:** 02074992823
**Web:** www.thomasgoode.com
**Reg No:** 0151415 **VAT No:** 238475634
**Estd:** 1867 Private Limited Company
**Line of Business:** Other retail sale in non-specialised stores
**Export Markets:** Rest of World
**Trading Style:** Goode Thomas & Co
**Issued Capital:** £824,000
**Directors:** K Verjee, M Verjee
**Co. Secretary:** Ms Jacqueline Fendick
**Responsibilities**
**Senior:** Jim Gill *(General Manager)*, Claire Guest *(Manager)*
**US SIC:** 5719 **UK SIC:** 64700
**Auditors:** Price Bailey LLP

| | 31-03-14 | 31-03-13 | 31-03-12 |
|---|---|---|---|
| TA | 20,499,294 | 18,247,266 | 24,350,138 |
| NW | 1,304,016 | 868,409 | 719,767 |
| WC | 5,434,899 | 8,134,810 | 3,008,863 |

DUNS 21-207-1526 **Imp**

## Thomas Graham & Sons (Iron & Steel) Ltd

Northgate, White Lund Industrial Estate, Morecambe, Lancashire LA3 3AZ
**Tel:** 0152469112 **Fax:** 01228547313
**Web:** www.thomas-graham.co.uk
**Reg No:** 0656879 **VAT No:** 288237913
**Estd:** 1960 Private Limited Company
**Line of Business:** Agents specialising in the sale of particular products or ranges of products not elsewhere classified
**Trading Style:** Graham Thomas & Sons
**Issued Capital:** £253,751
**Principals:** I D Smith *(Managing)*, R D Smith *(Managing)*, G M Smith, C G Styth, Ms A J Ward, M C Davidson, R M Smith, P S Barnes
**Co. Secretary:** Ms Patricia Smith
**Responsibilities**
**Marketing:** Sue Barnes *(Human Resources Manager)*
**HR:** Sue Barnes *(Human Resources Manager)*
**Health & Safety:** Sue Barnes *(Human Resources Manager)*
**Facilities:** Mike Milbourn *(Facilities Manager)*
**Branches:** Thomas Graham & Sons (Iron & Steel) Ltd, Unit 9, Bridge End Industrial Estate, Egremont, Cumbria CA22 2RD
**US SIC:** 5199, 5074
**UK SIC:** 61900, 61300
**Auditors:** Armstrong Watson

**Bankers:** HSBC Bank plc (40-16-22)

| | 31-05-14 | 31-05-13 | 31-05-12 |
|---|---|---|---|
| TO | 28,916,002 | 26,327,582 | 23,855,993 |
| P/L | 1,922,770 | 1,347,584 | 1,264,457 |
| NW | 13,395,300 | 11,942,759 | 11,195,485 |
| WC | 4,384,527 | 9,267,268 | 8,129,378 |
| Emp. | 140 | 137 | 126 |

DUNS 23-813-5474 **Imp**

## Thomas Gunn Navigation Services Ltd

(**Subsidiary of:** Global Navigation Solutions Holdings Ltd)
Amec Group Ltd, Aberdeen, Aberdeenshire AB11 5AN
**Tel:** 01224-595045
**Web:** www.thomasgunn.com
**Reg No:** 0198034SC **Estd:** 1999 Private Limited Company
**Line of Business:** Agents specialising in the sale of particular products or ranges of products not elsewhere classified
**Issued Capital:** £100
**Directors:** M L Cauter, P R Stanley
**Co. Secretary:** Michael Cauter
**Responsibilities**
**Senior:** Linda Gunn *(Manager)*, Thomas Gunn *(Manager)*, Gareth Kirkwood *(Director)*
**Finance:** Linda Gunn *(Manager)*
**US SIC:** 5199, 8999
**UK SIC:** 61900, 83954
**Auditors:** Johnston Carmichael LLP
**Bankers:** Lloyds TSB Bank plc (30-00-02)

| | 31-12-13 | 31-07-12 | 31-12-11 |
|---|---|---|---|
| TO | 32,006,718 | 24,801,225 | 23,941,988 |
| P/L | 721,529 | 2,495,775 | 2,259,030 |
| NW | 2,187,485 | 2,600,591 | 2,795,509 |
| WC | 1,500,887 | 1,128,652 | 1,340,655 |
| Emp. | 69 | 78 | 69 |

DUNS 28-884-8773

## Thomas H. Collison Ltd

17-19 Station Road, Ashford, Middlesex TW15 2UP
**Tel:** 01784258432 **Fax:** 01784-249124
**Web:** www.thcollison.co.uk
**Reg No:** 1221194 **Estd:** 1975 Private Limited Company
**Line of Business:** Opticians dispensing
**Issued Capital:** £64,500
**Director:** B T Collison
**Co. Secretary:** Ms Eileen Collison
**Branches:** Thomas H. Collison Ltd, 15 Court Yard, London SE9 5PR
**US SIC:** 8091 **UK SIC:** 95200
**Auditors:** H G Field & Co
**Bankers:** Barclays Bank Plc (20-97-58)

| | 30-09-13 | 30-09-12 | 30-09-11 |
|---|---|---|---|
| TO | 3,961,929 | 3,835,679 | 3,906,590 |
| P/L | 872,570 | 593,597 | 590,219 |
| NW | 10,418,834 | 10,184,689 | 9,994,755 |
| WC | 3,115,459 | 3,380,166 | 3,192,512 |
| Emp. | 64 | 66 | 68 |

DUNS 77-921-7913

## Thomas Hardie Truck & Bus Ltd

Newstet Road, Knowsley Industrial Park, Liverpool, Merseyside L33 7TJ
**Tel:** 01515493000
**Web:** www.thardie.co.uk
**Reg No:** 5824873 **Estd:** 2006 Private Limited Company
**Line of Business:** Management activities of holding companies
**Trading Style:** Thomas Hardie Commercials Liverpool
**Issued Capital:** £624
**Director:** M O Woosnam
**Co. Secretary:** Stephen Kenyon
**US SIC:** 6711 **UK SIC:** 83962
**Bankers:** The Royal Bank Of Scotland Plc (16-24-06)

| | 31-12-13 | 31-12-12 | 31-12-11 |
|---|---|---|---|
| TO | 78,402,127 | 65,591,766 | 74,158,742 |
| P/L | 934,049 | 561,275 | 492,035 |
| NW | 2,223,682 | 2,361,025 | 2,130,406 |
| WC | (2,208,334) | (891,658) | 366,305 |
| Emp. | 304 | 303 | 316 |

DUNS 23-694-5692

## Thomas Hardy Kendal Ltd

(**Subsidiary of:** Thomas Hardy Holdings Ltd)
Bold Lane, Warrington, Cheshire WA5 4TH
**Tel:** 01925220022 **Fax:** 01539-730915
**Web:** www.thomashardybrewery.co.uk
**Reg No:** 3689339 **Estd:** 1999 Private Limited Company
**Line of Business:** Bottlers
**Issued Capital:** £100
**Directors:** J C Ward, Ms M R Ward, N M Voss, P M Armstrong
**Responsibilities**
**Finance:** Andrew Zubel *(Financial Controller & IT Coor)*
**Branches:** Beezon Road, Kendal, Cumbria LA9 6BS
**US SIC:** 2086, 2085
**UK SIC:** 42831, 42402
**Auditors:** Deloitte & Touche LLP

**Bankers:** Bank Of Scotland (12-05-77)

| | 30-09-13 | 30-09-12 | 30-09-11 |
|---|---|---|---|
| TO | 12,510,000 | 15,453,000 | 17,793,000 |
| P/L | 1,818,000 | 2,131,000 | 2,849,000 |
| NW | 5,951,000 | 5,544,000 | 4,924,000 |
| WC | 3,389,000 | 3,102,000 | 2,736,000 |
| Emp. | 85 | 102 | 98 |

DUNS 50-570-1003

## Thomas International Uk Ltd

(**Subsidiary of:** Raymond Reed Executive Services Ltd)
Harris House, 17 West Street, Marlow, Buckinghamshire SL7 2LS
**Tel:** 01628475366
**Web:** www.thomasinternational.net
**Reg No:** 2518079 **VAT No:** 538025454
**Estd:** 1981 Private Limited Company
**Line of Business:** Management and business consultants
**Issued Capital:** £636,600
**Principals:** R Reed *(Chairman)*, S Isaacs *(Financial)*, M Reed, R A Cornwell, P Farrow
**Co. Secretary:** Stephen Isaacs
**Responsibilities**
**Senior:** Sally Wells *(Manager)*
**Branches:** Thomas International Uk Ltd, Park Ho, Mill St, East Malling, West Malling, Kent ME19 6BU
**US SIC:** 7392 **UK SIC:** 83951
**Auditors:** Barnes Roffe LLP
**Bankers:** National Westminster Bank Plc (60-14-12)

| | 31-12-13 | 31-12-12 | 31-12-11 |
|---|---|---|---|
| TO | 7,313,866 | 6,474,492 | 6,409,824 |
| P/L | 415,667 | 311,090 | 555,125 |
| NW | 1,586,315 | 1,185,583 | 926,013 |
| WC | 1,500,850 | 1,152,125 | 901,210 |

DUNS 23-614-9642

## Thomas Johnstone (Holdings) Ltd

Cartside Avenue, Inchinnan, Renfrew, Renfrewshire PA4 9RU
**Tel:** 01418127000 **Fax:** 0141-812-7001
**Web:** www.thomasjohnstoneltd.com
**Reg No:** 0188367SC **Estd:** 1998 Private Limited Company
**Line of Business:** Shopfitting contractors
**Issued Capital:** £353,168
**Directors:** W Hynes, T Green, G T Kelly, G A Alexander, D S Haddow, J W Mckerrow, R Young, D Yorke
**Co. Secretary:** Colin Buttar
**US SIC:** 6711 **UK SIC:** 83962
**Auditors:** Deloitte & Touche
**Bankers:** Bank Of Scotland (80-91-27)

| | 31-12-13 | 31-12-12 | 31-12-11 |
|---|---|---|---|
| TO | 36,242,512 | 37,585,248 | 35,923,994 |
| P/L | 649,187 | 487,767 | 4,589 |
| NW | 4,049,498 | 3,613,339 | 3,306,581 |
| WC | 747,840 | 795,187 | 554,265 |
| Emp. | 180 | 188 | 166 |

DUNS 21-328-4628

## Thomas Knight Nursing Home

Beaconsfield Street, Blyth, Northumberland NE24 2DP
**Estd:** 1989 Proprietorship
**Line of Business:** Nursing homes
**Proprietor:** S Gill
**Responsibilities**
**Senior:** Lee Lancaster *(Home Manager)*, Brenda Nicholson *(Home Manager)*
**US SIC:** 8051 **UK SIC:** 95100
**Employees:** 55

DUNS 21-722-2023

## Thomas Knyvett College

Stanwell Road, Ashford, Middlesex TW15 3DU
**Tel:** 01784243824 **Fax:** 01784240050
**Web:** www.howard-of-effingham.surrey.sch.uk
**Reg No:** 7597306 **Estd:** 2011 Private Company Limited By Guarantee
**Line of Business:** General secondary education
**Trading Style:** The Howard Partnership
**Directors:** Ms R J Barnfield, Ms S M Smith, Ms T B Crombie
**Co. Secretary:** Mrs Joanne Moore
**Responsibilities**
**Senior:** Nicola Aboud *(Head Teacher)*, David Blissett *(Governors)*, John Murdock *(Chair of Governors)*
**Finance:** V Bruggert *(Finance Manager)*
**US SIC:** 8211 **UK SIC:** 93200
**Bankers:** HSBC Bank plc (40-08-42)

| | 31-08-14 | 31-08-13 | 31-08-12 |
|---|---|---|---|
| TO | 605,506 | 5,208,311 | 12,755,724 |
| P/L | (9,806,850) | 1,384,351 | 8,485,499 |
| NW | N/A | 9,815,850 | 8,415,499 |
| WC | N/A | 572,942 | 419,134 |
| Emp. | 65 | 74 | 62 |

DUNS 21-934-1013 **Imp**

## Thomas Lloyd Mail Order Ltd

(**Subsidiary of:** Thomas Lloyd Home Furnishers Ltd)
Abergorki Industrial Estate, Treorchy, Mid Glamorgan CF42 6DL
**Tel:** 01443771333
**Web:** www.thomaslloyd.com
**Reg No:** 1438380 **Estd:** 1979 Private Limited Company
**Line of Business:** Furniture for home and office
**Issued Capital:** £25,000
**Principals:** D J Tomlins *(Managing)*, T G Ridgwell, C E Ridgwell
**Co. Secretary:** Barrie John
**Responsibilities**
**Senior:** Phillip Harris *(Manager)*
**Facilities:** Alan Huggleston *(Production manager)*
**US SIC:** 2599 **UK SIC:** 46720
**Auditors:** Clyne & Co
**Bankers:** Barclays Bank Plc (20-68-76)

| | 30-04-14 | 30-04-13 | 30-04-12 |
|---|---|---|---|
| TA | 1,530,354 | 1,582,632 | 1,410,379 |
| NW | 916,718 | 962,071 | 844,237 |
| WC | 558,801 | 545,700 | 382,292 |

DUNS 42-414-8070

## Thomas Maxwell & Sons Ltd

53 Largy Road, Belfast BT29 4RW
**Tel:** 02894422814 **Fax:** 028-9442-2815
**Web:** www.maxwellfreight.com
**Reg No:** 0014292NI **Estd:** 1991 Private Limited Company
**Line of Business:** Road haulage and transport services
**Trading Style:** Maxwell Freight Services, Antrim Bathroom Centre
**Issued Capital:** £7,777
**Directors:** T A Maxwell, T W Maxwell
**Co. Secretary:** Ms Deborah Maxwell
**Branches:** Antrim Bathroom Centre, Unit 4, Castle Walk, Castle Centre, Antrim, Antrim
**US SIC:** 4789 **UK SIC:** 77002
**Auditors:** G Brennan & Co
**Bankers:** Northern Bank Ltd (95-03-95)

| | 31-07-14 | 31-07-13 | 31-07-12 |
|---|---|---|---|
| TO | 6,378,109 | 6,361,545 | 6,591,753 |
| P/L | 149,525 | 165,003 | 89,560 |
| NW | 2,786,715 | 2,839,514 | 2,876,885 |
| WC | (168,683) | (229,068) | (328,635) |
| Emp. | 52 | 64 | 67 |

DUNS 21-573-4294

## Thomas May & Co

Regent House, 80 Regent Road, Leicester, Leicestershire LE1 7NH
**Tel:** 01162471234
**Web:** www.grant-thornton.co.uk
**VAT No:** 114950482 **Estd:** 1900 Partnership
**Line of Business:** Financial services
**Partners:** D N Radford, J A Calow, K Bethia, B S Carrusthers, K Gladders, S E Marshall, K N Woodthorpe
**Responsibilities**
**Senior:** Chris Frostwick *(Partner)*
**US SIC:** 8931 **UK SIC:** 83600
**Bankers:** Lloyds TSB Bank plc (30-94-97)
**Employees:** 50

DUNS 23-238-8558

## Thomas McConaghy & Sons Ltd

81 William Street, Craigavon, Co Armagh BT66 6JB
**Tel:** 02838325711
**Web:** www.theashburnhotel.com
**Reg No:** 0010866NI **Estd:** 1975 Private Limited Company
**Line of Business:** Hotels
**Trading Style:** Ashburn Hotel, Ashburn Hotel
**Issued Capital:** £100,000
**Directors:** J F Mcconaghy, C J Mcconaghy, A Mcconaghy, T Mcconaghy
**Co. Secretary:** James Mcconaghy
**Responsibilities**
**Purchasing:** Shaun Mcconaghy *(Purchasing Manager)*
**Branches:** Thomas Mcconaghy & Sons Ltd, 46 William Street, Craigavon, Co Armagh BT66 6JB
**US SIC:** 7011, 5813
**UK SIC:** 66500, 66200
**Auditors:** Henry Murray & Co
**Bankers:** Northern Bank Ltd (95-03-71)

| | 30-09-13 | 30-09-12 | 30-09-11 |
|---|---|---|---|
| TO | 4,577,623 | 4,689,588 | 4,660,917 |
| P/L | 148,021 | 291,788 | 121,383 |
| NW | 3,463,731 | 3,569,857 | 3,422,939 |
| WC | 775,083 | 657,592 | 300,839 |
| Emp. | 125 | 118 | 138 |

DUNS 21-402-8201

## Thomas McLean & Sons Ltd

144 Cumbernauld Road, Muirhead, Glasgow, Lanarkshire G69 9DX
**Tel:** 01417792712
**Reg No:** 0022725SC **VAT No:** 259961703

**Estd:** 1944 Private Limited Company
**Line of Business:** Chemists dispensing
**Issued Capital:** £100,006
**Director:** R Mclean
**Responsibilities**
**Senior:** Monica Farrelly (Manager)
**Branches:** Thomas Mclean & Sons Ltd, Copelands Chemist, 100-102 Stonelaw Road, Glasgow, Lanarkshire G73 3ED
**US SIC:** 5912 **UK SIC:** 64300
**Auditors:** Sinclair Wood & Co
**Bankers:** The Royal Bank Of Scotland Plc (83-17-31)

| | 30-09-13 | 30-09-12 | 30-09-11 |
|---|---|---|---|
| TA | 1,809,088 | 2,026,823 | 2,278,735 |
| NW | 329,908 | 341,596 | 350,992 |
| WC | 538,971 | 521,575 | 642,713 |

DUNS 21-323-8538

## Thomas Milburn (Property) Ltd

Beech Road, St Bees, Cumbria CA27 0ET
**Tel:** 01946-822777
**Web:** www.seacote.com
**Reg No:** 1185519 **VAT No:** 288139520
**Estd:** 1974 Private Limited Company
**Line of Business:** Holiday caravan site operators
**Trading Style:** Seacote Hotel & Holiday Parks
**Issued Capital:** £300
**Chairman and Managing Director:** T Milburn
**Co. Secretary:** Richard Milburn
**Branches:** Seacote Hotel, St Bees, Cumbria CA28
**US SIC:** 7033, 6531
**UK SIC:** 66701, 83400
**Auditors:** Armstrong Watson
**Bankers:** National Westminster Bank Plc (01-09-54)

| | 31-03-14 | 31-03-13 | 31-03-12 |
|---|---|---|---|
| TO | 3,154,466 | 3,737,501 | 3,079,773 |
| P/L | 852,560 | 1,168,561 | 633,370 |
| NW | 11,929,380 | 11,252,016 | 10,280,285 |
| WC | 1,604,463 | 1,272,454 | 756,867 |
| Emp. | 56 | 51 | 53 |

DUNS 29-531-0734    Imp

## Thomas Miller & Co. Ltd

(**Subsidiary of:** Thomas Miller Holdings Ltd.)
Thomas Miller & Co Ltd, London EC3M 4ST
**Tel:** 02073380150 **Fax:** 020-7338-0151
**Web:** www.thomasmiller.com
**Reg No:** 1898192 **Estd:** 1985 Private Limited Company
**Line of Business:** Business and management consultancy activities not elsewhere classified
**Issued Capital:** £500,000
**Principals:** B M Kesterton (Financial), R M Grainger, A K Mactavish, K P Halpenny, B C O'Sullivan, K D Sweet, J E Anderson, A Salim
**Co. Secretary:** Kieran Halpenny
**Responsibilities**
**Senior:** Gregory Fleming (Director), Jonathan Goldthorpe (Director), Michael Jarrett (Director), Simon Main (Director)
**Facilities:** Alan Chaston (Facilities Manager)
**Purchasing:** Alan Chaston (Facilities Manager)
**US SIC:** 7392 **UK SIC:** 83951
**Auditors:** Deloitte LLP
**Bankers:** HSBC Bank plc (40-04-12)

| | 31-12-13 | 31-12-12 | 31-12-11 |
|---|---|---|---|
| TO | 81,356,000 | 71,870,000 | 65,486,000 |
| P/L | 10,784,000 | 5,374,000 | 4,661,000 |
| NW | (15,844,000) | (26,724,000) | (24,775,000) |
| WC | 5,314,000 | (2,731,000) | (5,231,000) |
| Emp. | 402 | 381 | 385 |

DUNS 21-723-2178

## Thomas Mills High School

Saxtead Road, Framlingham, Woodbridge, Suffolk IP13 9HE
**Tel:** 01728723493
**Web:** www.thomasmills.suffolk.sch.uk
**Reg No:** 7605059 **Estd:** 1966 Private Company Limited By Guarantee
**Line of Business:** General secondary education
**Directors:** Ms S J Preston, D W Stewart, Ms B N Howard, M G Wright, J D Hibberd, P J Hurst, Ms S E Thorne, Miss T Hill
**Responsibilities**
**Senior:** Genevieve Christie (Director), Rebecca Cresdee (Director), Richard Hanley (Director), Bruce Hinton (Director), Colin Hirst (Head Teacher), Stephen Lovett (Director), Andrew Maskery (Director), Penelope Miller-Williams (Director), Mark Mugliston (Director), Minnie Riley (Director), Robert Snell (Director)
**US SIC:** 8211 **UK SIC:** 93200
**Bankers:** Barclays Bank Plc (20-83-50)

| | 31-08-14 | 31-08-13 | 31-08-12 |
|---|---|---|---|
| TO | 6,196,647 | 6,595,703 | 15,565,769 |
| P/L | (95,630) | 201,958 | 8,226,573 |
| NW | 7,949,901 | 8,357,531 | 8,121,573 |
| WC | 671,082 | 637,956 | 260,511 |
| Emp. | 100 | 105 | 105 |

DUNS 22-183-9165

## Thomas Murray Ratings Ltd

77-85 Fulham Palace Road, Hammersmith, London W6 8JC
**Tel:** 02086002300
**Reg No:** 4202273 **Estd:** 2001 Private Limited Company
**Line of Business:** Activities auxiliary to insurance and pension funding
**Export Sales:** £1,793,334
**Trading Style:** Thomas Murray Network Management Ltd
**Issued Capital:** £8
**Directors:** S R Thomas, R C Fishwick
**Co. Secretary:** Peter Sturdy
**US SIC:** 6411 **UK SIC:** 83200

| | 31-03-14 | 31-03-13 | 31-03-12 |
|---|---|---|---|
| TO | 2,637,256 | 418,703 | 460,686 |
| P/L | (377,245) | (305,236) | (28,495) |
| NW | (1,502,014) | 33,647 | 338,876 |
| WC | 68,974 | 25,800 | 338,876 |

DUNS 22-756-6304

## Thomas of York Ltd

The Bakers Yard, Sawmill Lane, Helmsley, York, North Yorkshire YO62 5DQ
**Tel:** 01439770870
**Web:** www.thomasthebaker.co.uk
**Reg No:** 0752911 **VAT No:** 332328580
**Estd:** 1981 Private Limited Company
**Line of Business:** Retail sale of bread, cakes, flour confectionery and sugar confectionery
**Trading Style:** Thomas the Baker
**Issued Capital:** £100
**Principals:** J Thomas (Chairman and Managing), Mrs N Bale, G J Thomas, S P Thomas, S Simpson
**Co. Secretary:** Ms Valerie Thomas
**Responsibilities**
**Senior:** Nicola Ridley (Manager)
**Branches:** Thomas Of York Ltd, 153A Tang Hall Lane, York, North Yorkshire YO10 3SD
**US SIC:** 7399, 5462
**UK SIC:** 83954, 64100
**Auditors:** Townends
**Bankers:** Barclays Bank Plc (20-99-56)

| | 31-12-13 | 31-12-12 | 31-12-11 |
|---|---|---|---|
| TO | 12,272,449 | 11,721,524 | 11,684,516 |
| P/L | 9,545 | (40,250) | (215,501) |
| NW | 5,105,808 | 5,123,651 | 5,191,972 |
| WC | 97,927 | 241,988 | 362,257 |
| Emp. | 368 | 376 | 406 |

DUNS 34-733-5213

## Thomas Panels & Profiles Ltd

(**Subsidiary of:** Panels & Profiles Ltd)
Southern Avenue, Leominster, Herefordshire HR6 0QF
**Tel:** 01568-610-000
**Web:** www.panelsandprofiles.co.uk
**Reg No:** 5535688 **VAT No:** 135764456
**Estd:** 2005 Private Limited Company
**Line of Business:** Agents involved in the sale of timber and building materials
**Issued Capital:** £1,000
**Directors:** G R Thomas, R E Thomas
**Co. Secretary:** Ms Patricia Thomas
**US SIC:** 5072, 1761
**UK SIC:** 61500, 50400
**Auditors:** Chris Duckett Ltd

| | 31-12-13 | 31-12-12 | 31-12-11 |
|---|---|---|---|
| TO | 14,872,830 | 12,347,903 | 11,338,655 |
| P/L | 762,585 | 1,162,255 | 946,893 |
| NW | 3,291,280 | 2,681,819 | 1,818,966 |
| WC | 2,995,680 | 2,132,678 | 1,269,083 |
| Emp. | 60 | 51 | 42 |

DUNS 29-669-5257    Imp-Exp

## Thomas Pink Ltd

(**Subsidiary of:** Lvmh Moet Hennessy Louis Vuitton)
1 Palmerston Way Court Palmerston, Battersea, London SW8 4AJ
**Tel:** 020-7498-2202 **Fax:** 02074984286
**Web:** www.thomaspink.com
**Reg No:** 1995666 **VAT No:** 627348917
**Estd:** 1986 Private Limited Company
**Line of Business:** Manufacture of other wearing apparel and accessories not elsewhere classified
**Export Sales:** £5,557,000
**Issued Capital:** £120,000
**Principals:** J C Heilbron (Financial), A J Merriman
**Co. Secretary:** Andrew Merriman
**Responsibilities**
**Senior:** Melanie Traub (Manager)
**Marketing:** Alex Field (Marketing Director)
**IT:** Guy Allen (IT Manager)
**Health & Safety:** Wendy Aldridge (Property Manager)
**Facilities:** Wendy Aldridge (Property Manager)
**Branches:** Thomas Pink Ltd, 24 Cullum Street, London EC3M 7JJ
**US SIC:** 2389, 5961
**UK SIC:** 45393, 65600
**Auditors:** Deloitte LLP

**Bankers:** National Westminster Bank Plc (60-04-04)

| | 31-12-13 | 31-12-12 | 31-12-11 |
|---|---|---|---|
| TO | 34,444,000 | 34,837,000 | 33,870,000 |
| P/L | 722,000 | 1,904,000 | 1,584,000 |
| NW | 14,080,000 | 12,202,000 | 10,416,000 |
| WC | 9,667,000 | 8,191,000 | 6,178,000 |
| Emp. | 309 | 319 | 335 |

DUNS 53-606-4678    Imp

## Thomas Plant (Birmingham) Ltd

Plumb Bob House, Valepits Road, Birmingham, West Midlands B33 0TD
**Fax:** 0121-604-2222
**Web:** www.kitchencraft.co.uk
**Reg No:** 3411690 **Estd:** 1997 Private Limited Company
**Line of Business:** Activities of other transport agencies
**Export Sales:** £6,445,221
**Trading Style:** Kitchen Craft
**Issued Capital:** £698,334
**Directors:** D T Siegel, R Shiftan, P W Bushell, A C Perry, J G Siegel, A J Plant, R T Plant
**Co. Secretary:** Anthony Perry
**Responsibilities**
**Marketing:** Claire Budgen (Marketing Manager)
**Admin:** Noreen Sweeney (Office Manager)
**US SIC:** 4712 **UK SIC:** 77002
**Auditors:** BDO LLP
**Bankers:** Lloyds TSB Bank plc (30-92-99)

| | 31-12-13 | 27-05-13 | 27-12-12 |
|---|---|---|---|
| TO | 26,836,825 | 42,827,000 | 38,566,000 |
| P/L | 3,814,502 | 1,751,000 | 3,880,000 |
| NW | 17,273,897 | 14,593,000 | 13,615,000 |
| WC | 15,995,216 | 14,184,000 | 14,528,000 |
| Emp. | 139 | 135 | 126 |

DUNS 21-780-4497

## Thomas Pocklington Trust

100 Chatham Road, Birmingham, West Midlands B31 2JW
**Tel:** 01214764161
**Web:** www.pocklington-trust.org.uk
**Estd:** 1972 Partnership
**Line of Business:** Activities of households as employers of domestic staff
**Partners:** S Craven, Mrs M Jukes
**Responsibilities**
**Senior:** Claire Ravenhall (Care Manager)
**US SIC:** 8811 **UK SIC:** 99000
**Employees:** 62

DUNS 34-549-2875

## Thomas Pocklington Trust Ltd

The Gift Of Thomas Pocklington, London W4 4JQ
**Tel:** 020-8995-0880
**Web:** www.pocklington-trust.org.uk
**Reg No:** 5359336 **Estd:** 2005 Private Company Limited By Guarantee
**Line of Business:** Social work activities
**Directors:** Mrs J S Pearce, Dr J D Lewis, C J Mairs, Mrs M C Heathcote, R S Powell, M J Williamson, A B Chapman
**Co. Secretary:** Peter Corbett
**Responsibilities**
**Senior:** Ronald Bramley (Manager)
**US SIC:** 7399 **UK SIC:** 83954
**Auditors:** Nexia Smith & Williamson
**Bankers:** The Co-Operative Bank Plc (08-01-00)

| | 31-03-14 | 31-03-13 | 31-03-12 |
|---|---|---|---|
| TO | 8,495,000 | 9,539,000 | 9,360,000 |
| P/L | (1,562,000) | (103,000) | 574,000 |
| NW | 157,558,000 | 118,444,000 | 106,284,000 |
| WC | (1,138,000) | (1,176,000) | 62,000 |
| Emp. | 152 | 201 | 196 |

DUNS 21-880-7063

## Thomas Ridley & Son Ltd

(**Subsidiary of:** Ridley Godfrey (Holdings) Ltd)
Unit 10 Rougham Industrial Estat, Rougham, Bury St Edmunds, Suffolk IP30 9ND
**Tel:** 01359270536
**Web:** www.thomasridley.co.uk
**Reg No:** 0148692 **VAT No:** 102350826
**Estd:** 1917 Private Limited Company
**Line of Business:** Cash and carry wholesalers
**Issued Capital:** £45,667
**Principals:** H E Godfrey (Managing), J A Godfrey, Mrs R C Summers, I M Snelling, Mrs J P Godfrey
**Co. Secretary:** Hugh Godfrey
**Responsibilities**
**Senior:** Ash Snowdon (Brand Marketing Manager)
**Finance:** Mike Dube (finance manager)
**Branches:** Bury St. Edmumds
**US SIC:** 5921, 5149
**UK SIC:** 64200, 61700
**Auditors:** Whiting & Partners

**Bankers:** Barclays Bank Plc (20-44-51)

| | 28-12-13 | 31-12-12 | 28-12-11 |
|---|---|---|---|
| TO | 39,569,403 | 36,476,084 | 32,503,826 |
| P/L | 1,637,700 | 1,643,603 | 683,325 |
| NW | 9,126,737 | 7,882,628 | 6,634,128 |
| WC | 4,534,948 | 4,154,100 | 3,286,565 |
| Emp. | 166 | 159 | 150 |

DUNS 23-225-7519

## Thomas Rotherham College

Moorgate, Rotherham, South Yorkshire S60 2BE
**Tel:** 01709300600
**Web:** www.thomroth.ac.uk
**Estd:** 1993 Incorporate By Act Of Parliament
**Line of Business:** Post-graduate level higher education
**Director:** G Peplar
**Responsibilities**
**Finance:** Sarah Lapping (Credit Controller)
**Admin:** Julie Lynskey (Registrar)
**IT:** Kevin Eaton (Computer Operations Manager), Maxine Marsden (Non-PC Systems Manager)
**Purchasing:** Sarah Lapping (Credit Controller)
**US SIC:** 8221 **UK SIC:** 93100
**Employees:** 250

DUNS 73-743-9815

## Thomas Sabo (Uk) Ltd

Part Ground Floor Battersea Studios 2, 82 Silverthorne Road, London SW8 3AG
**Fax:** 02077209726
**Web:** www.thomassabo.com
**Reg No:** 5001738 **Estd:** 2003 Private Limited Company
**Line of Business:** Wholesale of jewellery
**Issued Capital:** £500,000
**Directors:** Dr H Winzer, G Binder
**Co. Secretary:** James Parker
**Responsibilities**
**Senior:** C Bourn (Proprietor), Jon Crossick (Manager), Thomas Sabo (Manager)
**Branches:** Thomas Sabo Uk Ltd, K5, Brigstowe Street, Bristol, Avon BS1 3BH
**US SIC:** 5094, 5944
**UK SIC:** 61900, 65400
**Auditors:** William Evans & Partners

| | 30-06-13 | 30-06-12 | 30-06-11 |
|---|---|---|---|
| TO | 24,591,086 | 25,936,815 | 23,563,774 |
| P/L | 3,020,344 | 5,302,807 | 4,986,214 |
| NW | 6,134,256 | 3,894,991 | 3,770,599 |
| WC | 2,635,576 | 436,745 | 417,769 |
| Emp. | 258 | 244 | 208 |

DUNS 73-353-2316    Imp

## Thomas Sanderson Ltd

(**Subsidiary of:** Hunter Douglas N.V.)
Tileasy House, Waterberry Drive, Waterlooville, Hampshire PO7 7UW
**Tel:** 02392232600 **Fax:** 023-9223-2700
**Web:** www.thomassanderson.co.uk
**Reg No:** 4626841 **Estd:** 1991 Private Limited Company
**Line of Business:** Other manufacturing not elsewhere classified
**Export Sales:** £326,000
**Issued Capital:** £1,000
**Directors:** N J Campkin, A Kuiper
**Co. Secretary:** James Curley
**Responsibilities**
**HR:** Laura Johnston (Human Resources Manager)
**Health & Safety:** Roy Harris (Health & Safety Officer)
**Facilities:** Roy Harris (Health & Safety Officer)
**US SIC:** 3999 **UK SIC:** 49590
**Auditors:** Ernst & Young LLP
**Bankers:** Lloyds TSB Bank plc (30-00-02)

| | 31-12-13 | 31-12-12 | 31-12-11 |
|---|---|---|---|
| TO | 33,854,000 | 35,815,000 | 38,218,000 |
| P/L | (7,960,000) | 1,215,000 | 2,917,000 |
| NW | (2,630,000) | 5,504,000 | 4,293,000 |
| WC | (6,209,000) | 1,911,000 | 543,000 |
| Emp. | 275 | 277 | 281 |

DUNS 21-805-4880

## Thomas Savery Pumps Ltd

(**Subsidiary of:** Brigam Ltd)
Grovelands, Longford Road, Exhall, Coventry, West Midlands CV7 9NE
**Tel:** 02476645555
**Web:** www.oleo.co.uk
**Reg No:** 0113048 **Estd:** 1910 Private Limited Company
**Line of Business:** Manufacturers general
**Trading Style:** Thomas Savery Pumps Ltd
**Issued Capital:** £5,631
**Directors:** Ms L A Sahota, S Sahota
**Co. Secretary:** Ian Whiting
**US SIC:** 6711, 3563
**UK SIC:** 83962, 32831
**Auditors:** Kendall Wadley
**Bankers:** National Westminster Bank Plc (60-02-35)

| | 30-06-14 | 30-06-13 | 30-06-12 |
|---|---|---|---|
| TA | 11,492 | 1,723,845 | 1,723,845 |
| NW | 11,492 | 11,492 | 11,492 |
| WC | N/A | 4,992 | 4,992 |

DUNS 21-274-4692
## Thomas Sherriff & Company Ltd
Implement Road, West Barns, Dunbar, East Lothian EH42 1UN
**Tel:** 01368-862736
**Web:** www.thomassherriff.co.uk
**Reg No:** 0906135 **VAT No:** 176771133
**Estd:** 1967 Private Limited Company
**Line of Business:** Agricultural engineers
**Issued Capital:** £5,393
**Principals:** J Winter *(Managing)*, J H Greenwood *(Financial)*, S C Forsyth, C Weatherhead, R Lyall
**Responsibilities**
**Senior:** Helen Welsh *(Office Manager)*
**Admin:** Helen Welsh *(Office Manager)*
**Branches:** Thomas Sherriff & Company Ltd, 162 Galashiels Road, Galashiels, Selkirkshire TD1 2RA
**US SIC:** 3523 **UK SIC:** 32113
**Auditors:** Greaves West & Ayre
**Bankers:** Barclays Bank Plc (20-29-23)

| | 31-01-14 | 31-01-13 | 31-01-12 |
|---|---|---|---|
| TO | 20,416,551 | 22,843,982 | 24,416,842 |
| P/L | 402,766 | 504,456 | 518,630 |
| NW | 5,396,115 | 5,098,631 | 4,704,943 |
| WC | 4,146,986 | 3,977,669 | 3,600,041 |
| Emp. | 74 | 72 | 72 |

DUNS 37-876-9335
## Thomas Sinden Ltd
137-145 Church Road, Romford, Essex RM3 0JA
**Tel:** 01708-335350 **Fax:** 01708-335351
**Web:** www.thomas-sinden.co.uk
**Reg No:** 3308698 **VAT No:** 690931709
**Estd:** 1991 Private Limited Company
**Line of Business:** Development and selling of real estate
**Issued Capital:** £20,000
**Directors:** G Sinden, D F Thomas
**Co. Secretary:** Jonathan Taylor
**Responsibilities**
**Senior:** Steve McMahon *(Regional Manager)*
**IT:** Dave White *(IT Manager)*
**Branches:** THOMAS SINDEN LTD: Africa House, 64-78 Kingsway, WC2B 6AH, LONDON.
**US SIC:** 6552, 1541
**UK SIC:** 85000, 50100
**Auditors:** Fisher Michael

| | 31-03-14 | 31-03-13 | 31-03-12 |
|---|---|---|---|
| TO | 21,807,953 | 21,247,030 | 20,248,198 |
| P/L | 435,625 | 339,761 | 401,915 |
| NW | 2,526,452 | 2,435,571 | 2,373,415 |
| WC | 2,400,095 | 2,267,176 | 2,184,071 |
| Emp. | 92 | 91 | 96 |

DUNS 21-805-7909
## Thomas Startin Junr. Ltd
**(Subsidiary of:** Freeman Junior Ltd)
Far Moor Lane Coventry Highway, Redditch, Worcestershire B98 0SD
**Tel:** 01527883800 **Fax:** 0121-327-4699
**Reg No:** 0300464 **Estd:** 1840 Private Limited Company
**Line of Business:** Sale of new motor vehicles
**Issued Capital:** £200,000
**Principals:** G P Freeman *(Sales)*, C J Barrett, M A Geobey
**Co. Secretary:** Ms Elizabeth Freeman
**US SIC:** 5511 **UK SIC:** 65100
**Auditors:** Moore Stephens
**Bankers:** HSBC Bank plc (40-11-02)

| | 31-12-13 | 31-12-12 | 31-12-11 |
|---|---|---|---|
| TO | 35,078,207 | 26,620,820 | 21,851,365 |
| P/L | 587,718 | 653,905 | 835,722 |
| NW | 949,048 | 763,896 | 164,788 |
| WC | 887,796 | 707,321 | 60,014 |
| Emp. | 67 | 66 | 59 |

DUNS 21-208-2770 Imp-Exp
## Thomas Swan & Co.Ltd
Rotary Way, Consett, County Durham DH8 7ND
**Web:** www.thomas-swan.co.uk
**Reg No:** 0210794 **VAT No:** 532607168
**Estd:** 1926 Private Limited Company
**Line of Business:** Manufacturers of chemicals
**Export Sales:** £18,185,801
**Issued Capital:** £38,000
**Principals:** T M Swan *(Managing)*, H M Swan, D P Gresham, I G Bonas, E A Richardson
**Co. Secretary:** David Cavet
**Responsibilities**
**Sales:** Andy Goodwin *(Commercial Director - Advanced)*, Tom Porter *(Commercial Director)*, Jamie Rutherford *(Business Manager)*
**HR:** Phil Rutter *(Production Manager)*
**Health & Safety:** Steve Raisbeck *(Quality, Health and Safety and)*
**Operations:** Phil Rutter *(Production Manager)*
**Engineering:** Phil Rutter *(Production Manager)*
**Branches:** Thomas Swan & Co.ltd, Pegasus Way, Rushden, Northamptonshire NN10 6ER
**US SIC:** 2899, 2819
**UK SIC:** 25670, 25110
**Auditors:** KPMG LLP
**Bankers:** HSBC Bank plc (40-34-18)

| | 31-03-14 | 31-03-13 | 31-03-12 |
|---|---|---|---|
| TO | 25,350,393 | 25,079,721 | 27,085,951 |
| P/L | 225,070 | 796,711 | 3,413,288 |
| NW | 14,102,829 | 13,940,458 | 13,929,634 |
| WC | 6,930,156 | 7,355,014 | 7,973,921 |
| Emp. | 165 | 159 | 148 |

DUNS 23-318-4225 Imp-Exp
## Thomas Tucker Ltd
**(Subsidiary of:** Teampartner Ltd)
Coach Crescent, Shireoaks, Worksop, Nottinghamshire S81 8AD
**Tel:** 01909-506622
**Web:** www.candy-pop.co.uk
**Reg No:** 2690618 **VAT No:** 580984303
**Estd:** 1992 Private Limited Company
**Line of Business:** Confectioners (retail)
**Export Markets:** Netherlands
**Export Sales:** £178,532
**Issued Capital:** £145,100
**Director:** D S Gregg
**Co. Secretary:** Simon Stanham
**Branches:** Thomas Tucker Ltd, Aurillac Court, Unit 3, Retford, Nottinghamshire DN22 7PX
**US SIC:** 5462 **UK SIC:** 64100
**Auditors:** Darbys Ltd
**Bankers:** National Westminster Bank Plc (60-24-30)

| | 31-12-13 | 31-12-12 | 31-12-11 |
|---|---|---|---|
| TO | 9,044,320 | 7,606,101 | 7,780,585 |
| P/L | 241,944 | 201,953 | 206,691 |
| NW | 1,303,342 | 1,083,981 | 958,248 |
| WC | 8,909 | (343,587) | (485,110) |
| Emp. | 50 | 43 | 42 |

DUNS 21-449-3967 Imp-Exp
## Thomas Tunnock Ltd
34 Old Mill Road, Uddingston, Glasgow, Lanarkshire G71 7HH
**Tel:** 01698-813551
**Web:** www.tunnock.co.uk
**Reg No:** 0028747SC **VAT No:** 259569992
**Estd:** 1952 Private Limited Company
**Line of Business:** Manufacturers of biscuits
**Export Markets:** U S A, Canada, Middle East, Far East, W Europe
**Export Sales:** £9,093,412
**Issued Capital:** £176,500
**Principals:** A B Tunnock *(Chairman and Managing)*, Mrs K M Loudon, Ms E A Tunnock, R F Loudon, Miss F E Gow
**Co. Secretary:** Bruce Reidford
**Responsibilities**
**Senior:** B Redford *(Manager)*
**Marketing:** Fergus Loudon *(Sales & Marketing Manager)*
**Sales:** Fergus Loudon *(Sales & Marketing Manager)*
**Health & Safety:** Brendan Braidwood *(Health & Safety Coordinator)*
**Facilities:** Keith Rodmell *(Maintenance Manager)*
**Branches:** Thomas Tunnock Ltd, Bilton Hse, Uxbridge Rd, London W5 2TZ
**US SIC:** 2052 **UK SIC:** 41970
**Auditors:** Grant Thornton UK LLP
**Bankers:** Bank Of Scotland (80-09-93)

| | 28-02-14 | 28-02-13 | 29-02-12 |
|---|---|---|---|
| TO | 47,846,156 | 42,249,396 | 37,865,426 |
| P/L | 6,484,870 | 6,062,380 | 3,835,346 |
| NW | 38,379,390 | 34,398,586 | 29,828,267 |
| WC | 20,059,491 | 16,881,473 | 14,783,746 |
| Emp. | 489 | 514 | 517 |

DUNS 21-587-6922
## Thomas Vale Bilston
10 Union Street, Bilston, West Midlands WV14 0QT
**Tel:** 01902497334
**Web:** www.thomasvale.com
**Estd:** 2011
**Line of Business:** Building construction contractors
**US SIC:** 1522 **UK SIC:** 50100
**Employees:** 50

DUNS 77-120-8642
## Thomas Vale Group Ltd
**(Subsidiary of:** Amelia Investments (1869) Ltd)
Lombard House, Worcester Road, Stourport-On-Severn, Worcestershire DY13 9BZ
**Fax:** 01299822880
**Web:** www.thomasvale.com
**Reg No:** 2693391 **Estd:** 1992 Private Limited Company
**Line of Business:** Construction of domestic buildings
**Trading Style:** Thomas Vale Construction
**Issued Capital:** £450,051
**Directors:** B P Moyne, O Montfort, M Sow, O Racine, P D Jouy
**Co. Secretary:** Ms Carole Ditty
**Responsibilities**
**Senior:** Gary Mail *(Group Construction Director)*
**Branches:** Thomas Vale Group Ltd, Shottery Brook Office Park, Unit 16, Stratford-Upon-Avon, Warwickshire CV37 9NR
**US SIC:** 1522 **UK SIC:** 50100
**Auditors:** Mazars LLP
**Bankers:** National Westminster Bank Plc (56-00-69)

| | 31-12-13 | 31-12-12 | 31-12-12 |
|---|---|---|---|
| TO | 147,688,431 | 151,033,737 | 231,476,898 |
| P/L | (3,787,365) | (1,881,422) | 2,004,099 |
| NW | 17,812,389 | 22,366,621 | 25,071,487 |
| WC | 17,170,986 | 21,732,477 | 22,536,995 |
| Emp. | 443 | 598 | 684 |

DUNS 21-603-4132 Imp-Exp
## Thomas Ware Properties Ltd
**(Subsidiary of:** Thomas Ware & Sons Ltd)
Clift House Tannery, Coronation Road, Southville, Bristol, Avon BS3 1RN
**Tel:** 01179-664021
**Web:** www.thomasware.co.uk
**Reg No:** 0589764 **VAT No:** 229861043
**Estd:** 1916 Private Limited Company
**Line of Business:** Tanning and dressing of leather
**Export Markets:** Worldwide
**Issued Capital:** £50,000
**Directors:** A D Brearley, A D Brearley
**US SIC:** 3111, 5153
**UK SIC:** 44101, 61100
**Auditors:** Grant Thornton
**Bankers:** HSBC Bank plc (40-14-13)
**Employees:** 50

DUNS 42-354-4621
## Thomas Westcott Financial Management Ltd
26-28 Southernhay East, Exeter, Devon EX1 1NS
**Tel:** 01392-288555
**Web:** www.thomaswestcott.co.uk
**Reg No:** 4342122 **Estd:** 2001 Private Limited Company
**Line of Business:** Activities auxiliary to financial intermediation not elsewhere classified
**Directors:** I C Andrews, C J Hill, D H Simpson, M T Portman, Mrs S E Godefroy, S J Carrington, S R Smith, N Smy
**Co. Secretary:** Richard Thomas
**Responsibilities**
**Senior:** Steve Creswell *(Director)*, Judith Flood *(Partner)*, Roger Gillard *(Partner)*, Michael Marsh *(Director)*, Mark Ohlsen *(Director)*, Jonathan Poyner *(Manager)*, Mark Tibbert *(Director)*, Sabine Tuckett *(Associate Partner)*, Sarah Watts *(Partner)*
**Admin:** Jan Pringle *(Administration Manager)*
**IT:** Colin Masters *(Computer Manager)*
**HR:** Judith Flood *(Partner)*, Tracey Tyerman *(Training Manager)*
**Health & Safety:** Tracey Tyerman *(Training Manager)*
**Facilities:** Jan Pringle *(Administration Manager)*
**US SIC:** 6111, 7392
**UK SIC:** 81501, 83951

| | 30-04-14 | 30-04-13 | 30-04-12 |
|---|---|---|---|
| TA | 175,974 | 185,116 | 625,701 |
| NW | 107,893 | 130,425 | 417,399 |
| WC | 105,602 | 129,650 | 416,897 |

DUNS 21-205-9562 Imp
## Thomas Wright/Thorite Group Ltd
Thorite House, Laisterdyke, Bradford, West Yorkshire BD4 8BZ
**Tel:** 01274-663471
**Web:** www.thorite.co.uk
**Reg No:** 0177707 **VAT No:** 179305837
**Estd:** 1921 Private Limited Company
**Line of Business:** Plumbers
**Issued Capital:** £38,490
**Directors:** R Gowler, A Donkersley
**Co. Secretary:** Stephen Wright
**Responsibilities**
**Finance:** Ian Gurmin *(Financial Controller)*
**Branches:** Thomas Wright/Thorite Group Ltd, Unit 10 Whittingtons Court, Wheatley Hall Road, Doncaster, South Yorkshire DN2 4PE
**US SIC:** 3563, 7699
**UK SIC:** 32831, 67303
**Auditors:** Naylor Wintersgill
**Bankers:** National Westminster Bank Plc (56-00-36)

| | 31-03-14 | 31-03-13 | 31-03-12 |
|---|---|---|---|
| TO | 13,853,793 | 12,045,897 | 11,721,284 |
| P/L | 398,797 | 316,912 | 289,568 |
| NW | 1,707,883 | 1,418,550 | 1,140,255 |
| WC | 540,602 | 247,648 | (8,232) |
| Emp. | 104 | 99 | 101 |

DUNS 21-935-5256
## Thomasons Holdings Ltd
86 Epsom Road, Guildford, Surrey GU1 2BX
**Reg No:** 8478706 **Estd:** 2013 Private Limited Company
**Line of Business:** Building construction management
**Export Sales:** £175,758
**Issued Capital:** £2
**Directors:** P D Jarvis, R J Barnes, N Russell, D E Manion, S E Mcsorley, F J Robb
**US SIC:** 1622 **UK SIC:** 50200
**Bankers:** Barclays Bank Plc (20-35-35)

| | 31-03-14 |
|---|---|
| TO | 3,538,749 |
| P/L | 204,044 |
| NW | (734,718) |
| WC | 792,828 |
| Emp. | 76 |

DUNS 21-015-1753
## Thomasons Ltd
**(Subsidiary of:** Thomasons Holdings Ltd)
86 Epsom Road, Guildford, Surrey GU1 2DH
**Tel:** 08000837101
**Web:** www.thomasons.co.uk
**Reg No:** 6376815 **Estd:** 2007 Private Limited Company
**Line of Business:** Engineers (structural)
**Export Sales:** £175,758
**Issued Capital:** £266,661
**Directors:** P D Jarvis, F J Robb, R J Barnes, D E Manion, S E Mcsorley, N Russell
**Responsibilities**
**Senior:** Robert Hackman *(Manager)*, Arthur Park *(Manager)*, Christopher Shorter *(Manager)*
**US SIC:** 8911 **UK SIC:** 83701
**Bankers:** Barclays Bank Plc (20-35-35)

| | 31-03-14 | 31-03-13 | 31-03-12 |
|---|---|---|---|
| TO | 4,900,568 | 5,033,222 | 5,575,117 |
| P/L | 343,725 | 235,138 | 474,096 |
| NW | 242,671 | 20,410 | (671,909) |
| WC | 674,727 | 903,878 | 1,022,989 |
| Emp. | 68 | 86 | 86 |

DUNS 64-255-8100
## Thomas's London Day School
Monmouth Court, Southampton Road, Ringwood, Hampshire BH24 1HE
**Tel:** 01425481500
**Web:** www.thomas-s.co.uk
**Estd:** 1992 Partnership
**Line of Business:** Schools (independent)
**Partners:** Ms J Thomas, D Thomas
**Responsibilities**
**Senior:** Debbie Appleby *(Finance Director)*, Carol Clare *(Manager)*
**Finance:** Debbie Appleby *(Finance Director)*
**Branches:** Thomas's London Day School, 14 Ranelagh Grove, London SW1W 8PD
**US SIC:** 8211 **UK SIC:** 93200
**Employees:** 80

DUNS 42-439-0763 Imp
## Thompson Aero Seating Ltd
50 Seagoe Industrial Area, Portadown, Craigavon, Co Armagh BT63 5QE
**Tel:** 028-3833-4000 **Fax:** 075-2567-0974
**Web:** www.thompsonaeroseating.com
**Reg No:** 0032654NI **VAT No:** 726507042
**Estd:** 1997 Private Limited Company
**Line of Business:** Aviation supplies
**Issued Capital:** £442,007
**Directors:** G Montgomery, A Taylor, C Adamson, Ms J E Rusk, Ms N J Rusk, S Rusk
**Co. Secretary:** Annagate
**US SIC:** 3721 **UK SIC:** 36400
**Auditors:** Jackson Andrews

| | 31-03-14 | 31-03-13 | 31-03-12 |
|---|---|---|---|
| TO | 26,935,404 | 20,763,663 | 10,421,531 |
| P/L | 6,111,690 | 4,554,807 | 2,831,790 |
| NW | 10,944,773 | 5,989,183 | 2,536,878 |
| WC | 9,800,768 | 5,761,012 | 2,347,303 |
| Emp. | 119 | 79 | N/A |

DUNS 28-831-4776 Imp-Exp
## Thompson & Capper Ltd
**(Subsidiary of:** Dcc Plc)
9-12 Hardwick Road, Runcorn, Cheshire WA7 1PH
**Tel:** 01928-573734 **Fax:** 01928-580694
**Web:** www.thompsonandcapper.com
**Reg No:** 0235815 **VAT No:** 153327187
**Estd:** 1798 Private Limited Company
**Line of Business:** Manufacturers of pharmaceutical products
**Export Markets:** Worldwide
**Export Sales:** £14,206,404
**Issued Capital:** £8,200,000
**Principals:** R L Witheridge *(Managing)*, M R Dyal, J Downey, C Costigan, R Mcevoy, S C O'Connor
**Co. Secretary:** Ms Karen Leay
**Responsibilities**
**Sales:** Sarah Tittle *(Sales Manager)*
**Engineering:** Kevin Fairhurst *(Production Manager)*
**US SIC:** 2834, 5122

**UK SIC:** 25700, 61800
**Auditors:** PricewaterhouseCoopers
**Bankers:** Barclays Bank Plc (20-13-42)

| | 31-03-14 | 31-03-13 | 31-03-12 |
|---|---|---|---|
| TO | 26,643,927 | 23,990,276 | 22,942,294 |
| P/L | 4,525,186 | 3,389,576 | 2,730,990 |
| NW | 18,202,861 | 14,319,889 | 12,200,576 |
| WC | 7,261,565 | 10,047,239 | 10,755,472 |
| Emp. | 171 | 158 | 144 |

DUNS 42-403-4192
## Thompson & Morgan Group Holdings Ltd
Thompson & Morgan, Group Holdings Limited, Ipswich, Suffolk IP8 3BU
**Tel:** 08445731818
**Reg No:** 4391063 **Estd:** 2002 Private Limited Company
**Line of Business:** Management activities of holding companies
**Export Sales:** £2,619,000
**Issued Capital:** £539,359
**Directors:** E W Boss, P Jacobs, J H May, P Hansord, B R Magrath
**Co. Secretary:** Keith Lewis
**US SIC:** 6711 **UK SIC:** 83962

| | 30-06-13 | 30-06-12 | 30-06-11 |
|---|---|---|---|
| TO | 32,322,000 | 41,489,000 | 42,859,000 |
| P/L | (4,071,000) | 818,000 | 878,000 |
| NW | 1,585,000 | 4,735,000 | 3,238,000 |
| WC | (1,818,000) | 1,885,000 | 926,000 |
| Emp. | 336 | 309 | 312 |

DUNS 23-232-2487
## Thompson Automobiles Ltd
(**Subsidiary of:** Eirsise Ltd)
250 Donegall Road, Belfast BT12 5NE
**Tel:** 028-9031-6866
**Reg No:** 0028930NI **Estd:** 1996 Private Limited Company
**Line of Business:** Other retail sale in non-specialised stores
**Trading Style:** Thompson's Donegall Rd
**Issued Capital:** £2
**Directors:** J G Mcmillan, G Wall
**Co. Secretary:** Gavan Wall
**US SIC:** 5399, 5999
**UK SIC:** 65600
**Auditors:** Wilkinson Hegarty
**Bankers:** First Trust Bank (aib Group (uk) Plc) (93-80-92)

| | 30-04-14 | 30-04-13 | 30-04-12 |
|---|---|---|---|
| TA | 1,494,977 | 1,539,098 | 1,537,787 |
| NW | 104,530 | 191,757 | 61,916 |
| WC | 142,724 | 182,373 | 119,891 |

DUNS 21-725-4556
## Thompson Bros. (Esher) Ltd
Garson Farm, Winterdown Road, Esher, Surrey KT10 8LS
**Tel:** 01372460181
**Web:** www.garsons.co.uk
**Reg No:** 0549258 **VAT No:** 448886485
**Estd:** 1955 Private Limited Company
**Line of Business:** Growing of other fruit, nuts and spice crops; growing of other beverage crops
**Trading Style:** Garsons, Garsons Garden Centre
**Issued Capital:** £30,000
**Principals:** D M Richardson *(Chairman)*, I L Richardson, Mrs C P James, B Thompson, P R Thompson, A P Richardson
**Responsibilities**
**Senior:** Sally Tunley *(Manager)*
**IT:** Chris Tourell *(Information Technology Manager)*
**HR:** Lucy Taylor *(Personnel Manager)*
**Branches:** Thompson Bros. (Esher) Ltd, Fontley Road, Fareham, Hampshire PO15 6QX
**US SIC:** 0179, 5431
**UK SIC:** 01002, 64100
**Auditors:** Alliotts
**Bankers:** National Westminster Bank Plc (60-08-04)

| | 30-03-14 | 31-03-13 | 01-03-12 |
|---|---|---|---|
| TO | 12,521,827 | 11,227,085 | 12,654,929 |
| P/L | 353,188 | 76,811 | 669,539 |
| NW | 8,401,381 | 8,250,865 | 8,311,054 |
| WC | 1,908,313 | 2,300,587 | 2,388,957 |
| Emp. | 97 | 102 | 106 |

DUNS 21-201-8329
## Thompson Commercials Ltd
(**Subsidiary of:** Thompson Commercials Group Ltd)
Salvesen Way Brighton St Industrial, Estate, Hull, North Humberside HU3 4UQ
**Tel:** 01482322331
**Web:** www.thompsoncommercials.com
**Reg No:** 0532879 **VAT No:** 167552835
**Estd:** 1954 Private Limited Company
**Line of Business:** Van and truck dealers
**Trading Style:** Thompson Commercials
**Issued Capital:** £308,000
**Directors:** G T Harper, S D Bruce
**Co. Secretary:** Paul Simpson
**Responsibilities**
**Senior:** Paul Collingwood *(Manager)*
**Branches:** Thompson Commercials Ltd, Nuffield Rd, Cowpen Lane Indstl Est, Billingham, Cleveland TS23 4DA
**US SIC:** 5511 **UK SIC:** 65100
**Auditors:** Smailes Goldie
**Bankers:** Barclays Bank Plc (20-43-47)

| | 31-12-13 | 31-12-12 | 31-12-11 |
|---|---|---|---|
| TO | 43,228,493 | 33,320,500 | 34,363,913 |
| P/L | 1,188,825 | 400,139 | 372,999 |
| NW | 1,874,589 | 1,127,353 | 853,206 |
| WC | 786,275 | (244,175) | (425,438) |
| Emp. | 140 | 138 | 137 |

DUNS 49-716-4335
## Thompson Gorton Jones
Bridge House Yeargate Industrial, Heap Bridge, Bury, Lancashire BL9 7HT
**Tel:** 01614478383
**Web:** www.tjca.co.uk
**Estd:** 1959 Partnership
**Line of Business:** Financial advisers (independent)
**Trading Style:** Stanmore Financial Services
**Partners:** P Boddis, K Jones, J Stone, J Gorton, P Carling, J Gorton, D Emery
**Branches:** Thompson Gorton Jones, Stanmore House, 64-68 Blackburn Street, Manchester M26 2JS
**US SIC:** 8931 **UK SIC:** 83600
**Employees:** 55

DUNS 22-018-6527
## Thompson Motor Co (Preston) Ltd
Riversway Motor Park Nelson Way, Preston, Lancashire PR2 2JZ
**Fax:** 01234-359827
**Web:** www.audinorthwest.com
**Reg No:** 4021476 **Estd:** 2000 Private Limited Company
**Line of Business:** Car dealers (used)
**Issued Capital:** £100,000
**Directors:** A V Stoyle, D J Bland, S Thompson
**Co. Secretary:** Mrs Sarah Jones
**US SIC:** 5521, 7539
**UK SIC:** 65100, 67100
**Auditors:** ASE Audit LLP

| | 31-12-13 | 31-12-12 | 31-12-11 |
|---|---|---|---|
| TO | 138,128,609 | 112,531,074 | 100,503,700 |
| P/L | 2,389,122 | 1,254,962 | 836,061 |
| NW | 4,765,081 | 3,609,056 | 3,329,605 |
| WC | 3,258,430 | 1,502,866 | 1,258,515 |
| Emp. | 226 | 192 | 203 |

DUNS 77-104-3239
## Thompson Smith & Puxon (Secretarial Services) Ltd
4 North Hill, Colchester, Essex CO1 1EB
**Tel:** 01206-574431 **Fax:** 01206-563174
**Web:** www.tsplegal.com
**Reg No:** 2681266 **Estd:** 1992 Private Limited Company
**Line of Business:** Solicitors
**Issued Capital:** £2
**Director:** M G Wilson
**Co. Secretary:** Mrs Mary Fedeyko
**Responsibilities**
**Senior:** Nicola Crisell *(Business Development)*
**Branches:** Thompson Smith & Puxon (Secretarial Services) Ltd, 95 Church Rd, Colchester, Essex CO5 0AB
**US SIC:** 8111 **UK SIC:** 83500

| | 31-12-13 | 31-12-12 | 31-12-11 |
|---|---|---|---|
| TA | 2 | 2 | 2 |
| NW | 2 | 2 | 2 |

DUNS 34-806-7174 **Imp-Exp**
## Thompson Valves Ltd
(**Subsidiary of:** Imi Plc)
17 Balena Close, Poole, Dorset BH17 7EF
**Tel:** 01202-697521 **Fax:** 01202-605385
**Web:** www.thompson-valves.co.uk
**Reg No:** 2791464 **VAT No:** 619537027
**Estd:** 1993 Private Limited Company
**Line of Business:** Manufacture of taps and valves
**Export Markets:** Germany; Far East; France; U S A; Canada; Middle East
**Export Sales:** £15,315,000
**Trading Style:** Thompson Valve
**Issued Capital:** £1,000,000
**Directors:** O Starovic, C W Prince
**Co. Secretary:** John Rawlings
**Responsibilities**
**Senior:** Paul Cleaver *(Manager)*, Ognjen Starcovic *(Managing Director)*, David Whitfield *(Manager)*
**Sales:** Mike Loder *(Business Improvement Manager)*
**Health & Safety:** Bob Hartwell *(Health & Safety Officer)*
**Facilities:** Robert Conroy *(Maintenance Coordinator)*
**Branches:** Thompson Valves Ltd, Westward Road, Witton, Birmingham, West Midlands B44 8LR
**US SIC:** 3494, 3519
**UK SIC:** 32880, 32811

**Auditors:** Ernst & Young LLP
**Bankers:** Barclays Bank Plc (20-00-00)

| | 31-12-13 | 31-12-12 | 31-12-11 |
|---|---|---|---|
| TO | 21,283,000 | 19,004,000 | 15,292,000 |
| P/L | 5,036,000 | 4,319,000 | 2,192,000 |
| NW | 5,296,000 | 4,564,000 | 4,760,000 |
| WC | 4,606,000 | 4,051,000 | 4,928,000 |
| Emp. | 162 | 153 | 135 |

DUNS 21-770-1140
## Thompsons
Berkeley House, 285 Bath Street, Glasgow, Lanarkshire G2 4HQ
**Tel:** 01412218840
**Web:** www.thompsons-scotland.co.uk
**Estd:** 1980 Proprietorship
**Line of Business:** Solicitors
**Proprietor:** Mrs H Bell
**Responsibilities**
**Senior:** Jacqueline Donnelly *(Manager)*
**US SIC:** 8111 **UK SIC:** 83500
**Employees:** 50

DUNS 28-985-3152
## Thompsons Nursery Ltd
Perry Street, Chislehurst, Kent BR7 6HA
**Tel:** 07971226864
**Web:** www.thompsons-plants.co.uk
**Reg No:** 1797815 **VAT No:** 332957933
**Estd:** 1975 Private Limited Company
**Line of Business:** Growing of cereals and other crops not elsewhere classified
**Trading Style:** Motspur Park Nursery; Thompsons Plant & Garden Centre, Woodlands Nursery, Greentiles Nursery, Longlands Nursery
**Issued Capital:** £320,100
**Principals:** J Thompson *(Financial)*, P Thompson, M Bramley
**Co. Secretary:** Mrs Ursula Thompson
**Responsibilities**
**Senior:** Celia Eade *(Proprietor)*
**Branches:** Thompsons Nursery Ltd, Stone Street, Canterbury, Kent CT4 5PW
**US SIC:** 0119 **UK SIC:** 01001
**Auditors:** Audit Assure
**Bankers:** National Westminster Bank Plc (60-04-27)

| | 30-06-13 | 31-12-11 | 31-06-10 |
|---|---|---|---|
| TO | 5,994,993 | 4,598,969 | 4,699,424 |
| P/L | 15,648 | 181,493 | 110,034 |
| NW | 4,073,474 | 3,533,075 | 3,400,572 |
| WC | 96,305 | 763,190 | 616,206 |
| Emp. | 109 | 126 | 129 |

DUNS 21-315-1145 **Exp**
## Thompsons of Prudhoe Holding Ltd.
Princess Waythompsonsofprudhoe, Prudhoe, Northumberland NE42 6PL
**Tel:** 01661-832422 **Fax:** 01661833687
**Web:** www.thompsonsofprudhoe.com
**Reg No:** 0579506 **VAT No:** 176863224
**Estd:** 1957 Private Limited Company
**Line of Business:** Management activities of other non-financial holding companies not elsewhere classified
**Export Markets:** Europe
**Trading Style:** Waythompsonsofpridhoe
**Issued Capital:** £1,500
**Principals:** J Thompson *(Managing)*, J Thompson, Ms H M Hillary
**Co. Secretary:** John Thompson
**US SIC:** 7399 **UK SIC:** 83954
**Auditors:** Deloitte & Touche
**Bankers:** Barclays Bank Plc (20-59-42)

| | 31-03-14 | 31-03-13 | 31-03-12 |
|---|---|---|---|
| TO | 27,408,916 | 23,442,629 | 25,005,517 |
| P/L | 871,306 | 359,576 | 625,670 |
| NW | 9,409,417 | 10,298,833 | 10,236,863 |
| WC | 2,331,355 | 2,375,531 | 2,371,352 |
| Emp. | 254 | 246 | 253 |

DUNS 21-680-9101
## Thompsons Solicitors Llp
Congress House, 23-28 Great Russell Street, London WC1B 3LW
**Web:** www.thompsons.law.co.uk
**Reg No:** 0356468OC **Estd:** 1996 Limited Partnership
**Line of Business:** Solicitors
**Trading Style:** Thompsons Solicitors
**Responsibilities**
**Senior:** Erica Allen *(Marketing Executive)*, Richard Arthur *(Non-designated Limited Liabili)*, Julie Blackburn *(Non-designated Limited Liabili)*, Michelle Cronin *(Non-designated Limited Liabili)*, Judith Gledhill *(Non-designated Limited Liabili)*, Reuben Greenwood *(Non-designated Limited Liabili)*, Vineeta Kaura *(Non-designated Limited Liabili)*, James Mcfall *(Non-designated Limited Liabili)*, Peter Mulhern *(Non-designated Limited Liabili)*, Henrietta Phillips *(Non-designated Limited Liabili)*
**Marketing:** Erica Allen *(Marketing Executive)*
**US SIC:** 8111 **UK SIC:** 83500

**Auditors:** Deloitte LLP

| | 30-04-14 | 30-04-13 | 30-04-12 |
|---|---|---|---|
| TO | 81,588,000 | 84,231,000 | 82,311,000 |
| P/L | 18,633,000 | 10,804,000 | 12,616,000 |
| NW | 21,966,000 | 16,956,000 | 10,099,000 |
| WC | 42,020,000 | 38,987,000 | 41,121,000 |
| Emp. | 949 | 1,045 | 1,142 |

DUNS 22-516-9473 **Imp**
## Thompsons (U K) Ltd
Rutland Works, Vulcan Way, Croydon, Surrey CR9 0DE
**Tel:** 01689-843016 **Fax:** 01689-841574
**Web:** www.thompsonsuk.com
**Reg No:** 1101154 **VAT No:** 344894128
**Estd:** 1973 Private Limited Company
**Line of Business:** Manufacturers of vans and trucks
**Issued Capital:** £52,500
**Directors:** B Mullaney, Mrs M E Burton, S K Shields, S L Burton
**Co. Secretary:** Patrick Thomas
**Responsibilities**
**Senior:** Allan Burton *(Manager)*
**Finance:** Trevor Russell *(Financial Manager)*
**Sales:** Angie Bevan *(Internal Sales & Support)*, Andrew Gunn *(Business Development Manager)*
**IT:** Trevor Russell *(Financial Manager)*
**HR:** Trevor Russell *(Financial Manager)*
**Health & Safety:** Victor Butcher *(Health & Safety Officer)*
**Operations:** Nathan Ewins *(Service Manager)*, Neil Griffin *(Design Engineer)*, Trevor Russell *(Financial Manager)*
**Engineering:** Neil Griffin *(Design Engineer)*, Gary West *(Service Manager)*
**US SIC:** 3711 **UK SIC:** 35101
**Auditors:** O'Neill Foley
**Bankers:** Barclays Bank Plc (20-24-61)

| | 30-09-13 | 30-09-12 | 30-09-11 |
|---|---|---|---|
| TO | 16,044,802 | 16,986,873 | 11,308,346 |
| P/L | 242,571 | 290,523 | 112,202 |
| NW | 2,753,456 | 2,361,786 | 1,900,722 |
| WC | 1,489,724 | 1,241,051 | 635,322 |
| Emp. | 111 | 113 | 99 |

DUNS 64-074-3873
## Thomson Ecology Ltd
Compass House, 60 Priestley Road, Guildford, Surrey GU2 7AG
**Tel:** 01483-466000 **Fax:** 01943-467472
**Web:** www.thomsonecology.com
**Reg No:** 4477751 **Estd:** 2008 Private Limited Company
**Line of Business:** Environmental consultants
**Issued Capital:** £10,001
**Directors:** R W Arnold, Ms N E Thomson, M I Rennie
**Responsibilities**
**Senior:** Mike Harris *(Associate Director)*, Steve Steve *(Executive)*
**Marketing:** Caroline Mackay *(Marketing Manager)*
**US SIC:** 8911 **UK SIC:** 83701

| | 31-10-13 | 31-10-12 | 31-10-11 |
|---|---|---|---|
| TA | 2,072,694 | 2,756,278 | 2,223,943 |
| NW | 1,215,201 | 1,385,191 | 1,256,373 |
| WC | 1,405,417 | 1,292,290 | 604,420 |

DUNS 23-871-8816
## Thomson Financial (Holdings) Ltd
(**Subsidiary of:** The Thomson Organisation (No. 10))
Aldgate House, 33 Aldgate High Street, London EC3N 1DL
**Tel:** 02073697000
**Reg No:** 3863253 **Estd:** 1999 Private Limited Company
**Line of Business:** Miscellaneous activities auxiliary to financial intermediation not elsewhere classified
**Issued Capital:** £63,883,002
**Directors:** P Thorn, S N Corbin
**Co. Secretary:** Ms Susan Jenner
**US SIC:** 6111 **UK SIC:** 81501
**Auditors:** PricewaterhouseCoopers LLP

| | 31-12-13 | 31-12-12 | 31-12-11 |
|---|---|---|---|
| TA | 69,928,000 | 69,928,000 | 69,928,000 |
| NW | 69,928,000 | 69,928,000 | 69,928,000 |

DUNS 21-317-9641 **Exp**
## Thomson Ltd
Monk Fryston Park, Betteras Hill Road, Hillam, Leeds, West Yorkshire LS25 5PF
**Web:** www.thomson-group.co.uk
**Reg No:** 1161276 **Estd:** 1974 Private Limited Company
**Line of Business:** Engineers (general)
**Issued Capital:** £5,000
**Principals:** R A Thomson *(Managing)*, Ms E C Thomson-Kaiser, S Pickard, J G Scott
**Co. Secretary:** Trevor Giles
**Branches:** Thomson Ltd, Unit 214 St 7, Thorp Arch Trad Est, Wetherby, West Yorkshire LS23 7BJ
**US SIC:** 8911, 7399
**UK SIC:** 83701, 83954

Auditors: Kirk Newsholme
Bankers: HSBC Bank plc (40-27-29)

|  | 30-11-13 | 30-11-12 | 30-11-11 |
|---|---|---|---|
| TO | 8,538,887 | 10,199,155 | 7,553,250 |
| P/L | 502,477 | 1,249,799 | 692,530 |
| NW | 3,527,475 | 3,486,640 | 2,533,389 |
| WC | 3,207,779 | 3,215,426 | 2,296,042 |
| Emp. | 56 | 54 | 58 |

DUNS 34-843-4275　　　　　　　　　　Exp
### Thomson Pettie Group Ltd
Whiteshaw Works, Carluke, Lanarkshire ML8 5EJ
Fax: 01555770455
Web: www.thomsonpettie.com
Reg No: 0143710SC　VAT No: 624017573
Estd: 1993 Private Limited Company
Line of Business: Steel fabricators
Export Markets: Holland
Export Sales: £176,186
Issued Capital: £204,619
Principals: T M Thomson (Managing), W J Baxter, Ms A M Thomson
Co. Secretary: James Borrows
US SIC: 1622　UK SIC: 50200
Auditors: Martin Aitken & Co
Bankers: Bank Of Scotland (80-07-48)

|  | 31-03-14 | 31-03-13 | 31-03-12 |
|---|---|---|---|
| TO | 7,251,482 | 10,819,673 | 10,903,465 |
| P/L | 272,895 | 493,076 | 397,905 |
| NW | 1,847,055 | 1,971,418 | 1,826,488 |
| WC | 467,738 | (55,852) | 148,205 |
| Emp. | 224 | 219 | 212 |

DUNS 22-727-2184　　　　　　　　　　Exp
### Thomson Reuters (Professional) Uk Ltd
(Subsidiary of: The Thomson Organisation (No. 10))
19 Hatfields, London SE1 8DJ
Tel: 02072021200 Fax: 02072021211
Web: http://uk.practicallaw.com
Reg No: 1679046　Estd: 2011 Private Limited Company
Line of Business: Miscellaneous business services
Export Markets: E U
Export Sales: £269,048,000
Trading Style: Thomson Reuters
Issued Capital: £129,000,148
Directors: I G Drane, Ms H E Campbell, M B Keen, C Sanderson, S P Hartman, D M Mitchley, J Beak, Ms I Fraser
Co. Secretary: Ms Susan Jenner
Responsibilities
Senior: Christine Are (Office Manager)
Marketing: Peggy Westlotorn (Marketing Manager)
IT: Niels Montanana (IT Director)
Operations: Amanda Milsom (?VP Integration & Business Ope)
US SIC: 7399, 7374, 2731
UK SIC: 83954, 83940, 47532
Auditors: PricewaterhouseCoopers LLP
Bankers: National Westminster Bank Plc (56-00-27)

|  | 31-12-13 | 31-12-12 | 31-12-11 |
|---|---|---|---|
| TO | 418,679,000 | 357,514,000 | 263,960,000 |
| P/L | (79,191,000) | (144,876,000) | (25,364,000) |
| NW | (21,780,000) | (70,619,000) | (81,755,000) |
| WC | (225,251,000) | (217,253,000) | (239,554,000) |
| Emp. | 1,922 | 1,950 | 1,748 |

DUNS 29-486-3865
### Thomson Reuters (Summit 1) Uk Ltd
(Subsidiary of: The Thomson Organisation (No. 10))
3 Tonbridge Chambers, Pembury Road, Tonbridge, Kent TN9 2HZ
Tel: 01732500901
Web: www.thomsonreuters.com
Reg No: 1849601　Estd: 2012 Private Limited Company
Line of Business: Financial management
Issued Capital: £100
Directors: P Thorn, S N Corbin
Co. Secretary: Ms Susan Jenner
US SIC: 7392　UK SIC: 83951
Auditors: PricewaterhouseCoopers
Bankers: Barclays Bank Plc (20-71-64)

|  | 31-12-13 | 31-12-12 | 31-12-11 |
|---|---|---|---|
| NW | (1,253,241) | (1,253,241) | (1,253,241) |

DUNS 77-088-0953
### Thomson: Hayes Retail Display Ltd
51-54 Highcliffe Road, Leicester, Leicestershire LE5 1TY
Tel: 01162-464033
Web: www.thomsonhayes.com
Reg No: 2675335　Estd: 1992 Private Limited Company
Line of Business: Manufacturers of shop fittings
Issued Capital: £4,000
Director: F J Hayes
Co. Secretary: Christopher Thomson

Responsibilities
Finance: Prash Shah (Financial Manager)
IT: Prash Shah (Financial Manager)
US SIC: 2599　UK SIC: 46720
Auditors: Moore Stephens

|  | 31-03-14 | 31-03-13 | 31-03-12 |
|---|---|---|---|
| TA | 726,350 | 563,573 | 950,479 |
| NW | 168,901 | (45,206) | 108,815 |
| WC | 148,708 | (66,457) | 84,814 |

DUNS 21-394-9577
### Thorite - Blackburn
Unit 1 Forrest Street, Blackburn, Lancashire BB1 3BB
Tel: 01254-679922
Proprietorship
Line of Business: Pneumatic systems and equipment
Proprietor: S Wright
US SIC: 3563　UK SIC: 32831
Employees: 100

DUNS 73-826-0012　　　　　　　　　　Imp
### Thorlabs Ltd
(Subsidiary of: Thorlabs Inc.)
1 St Thomas Place, Ely, Cambridgeshire CB7 4EX
Tel: 01353-654440 Fax: 01353654444
Web: www.thorlabs.com
Reg No: 5081788　VAT No: 834506826
Estd: 2004 Private Limited Company
Line of Business: Fibre optics
Issued Capital: £1
Director: A Cable
Co. Secretary: Dr Keith Dhese
Responsibilities
Marketing: Julia Hudson (Marketing Manager)
US SIC: 3861, 3629, 5199
UK SIC: 37330, 34350, 61900
Bankers: HSBC Bank plc (40-46-03)

|  | 31-12-13 | 31-12-12 | 31-12-11 |
|---|---|---|---|
| TO | 26,575,514 | 23,900,576 | 22,594,140 |
| P/L | 4,302,681 | 4,157,897 | 4,009,701 |
| NW | 6,240,905 | 7,914,006 | 9,744,078 |
| WC | 4,752,219 | 6,822,124 | 9,105,959 |
| Emp. | 131 | 127 | 121 |

DUNS 50-547-1037
### Thorley Taverns Ltd
58-60 Gladstone Road, Broadstairs, Kent CT10 2TA
Tel: 01843602010
Web: www.thorleytaverns.co.uk
Reg No: 2501551　VAT No: 236162576
Estd: 1990 Private Limited Company
Line of Business: Bars
Issued Capital: £100,000
Principals: F G Thorley (Managing), Ms L D Thorley, P Thorley, Ms A S Thorley
Co. Secretary: Ms Ruth Goldfinch
Branches: Thorley Taverns Ltd, 50 Marine Terrace, Margate, Kent CT9 1XJ
US SIC: 7399, 5812
UK SIC: 83954, 66110
Auditors: Lakin Clark Ltd
Bankers: National Westminster Bank Plc (60-09-10)

|  | 30-06-14 | 30-06-13 | 30-06-12 |
|---|---|---|---|
| TO | 11,533,463 | 11,511,218 | 12,341,415 |
| P/L | 409,911 | 108,919 | (522,901) |
| NW | 12,004,980 | 10,983,415 | 10,908,088 |
| WC | (292,007) | 45,278 | 38,046 |
| Emp. | 384 | 407 | 418 |

DUNS 50-502-7748
### Thorn Baker Ltd
4th Floor, Nottingham, Nottinghamshire NG1 6DQ
Tel: 01159-472005 Fax: 01623656929
Web: www.thornbaker.co.uk
Reg No: 2470455　VAT No: 772086027
Estd: 2001 Private Limited Company
Line of Business: Labour recruitment and provision of personnel
Issued Capital: £33
Directors: M Page, Mrs K E Robinson, M Dann, P Jackman
Co. Secretary: John Robinson
Responsibilities
Finance: Cassandra Thompson (Health & Safety Officer)
Health & Safety: Cassandra Thompson (Health & Safety Officer)
Engineering: Gregg Marrett (Midlands Regional Manager, Con)
Branches: Thorn Baker Ltd, The Hub, 40 Friar Lane, Nottingham, Nottinghamshire NG1 6DQ
US SIC: 7361　UK SIC: 83954
Auditors: Cooper Parry Group Ltd
Bankers: National Westminster Bank Plc (60-80-09)

|  | 30-04-14 | 30-04-13 | 30-04-12 |
|---|---|---|---|
| TO | 21,040,562 | 19,529,566 | 19,975,888 |
| P/L | 130,939 | 188,599 | 190,530 |
| NW | 961,598 | 880,539 | 744,440 |
| WC | 830,444 | 743,960 | 611,567 |
| Emp. | 1,078 | 1,023 | 1,081 |

DUNS 21-331-5682
### Thorn Security Ltd
(Subsidiary of: Tyco International Finance Sa)
Dunhams Lane, Letchworth Garden City, Letchworth, Hertfordshire SG6 1BE
Tel: 01613326333 Fax: 01614-554245
Web: www.thorne-security.com
Reg No: 0728246　VAT No: 754530140
Estd: 1962 Private Limited Company
Line of Business: Measuring instruments and appliances
Export Sales: £13,350,000
Trading Style: Tyco Safety Products
Issued Capital: £15,000,000
Directors: C R Weston, J M Herzog, A Bowie
Co. Secretary: Anton Alphonsus
Responsibilities
Senior: David Stonehouse (Operations Director)
Branches: Thorn Security Ltd, Brymers Ave, Portland, Dorset DT5 1JS
US SIC: 3829　UK SIC: 37100
Auditors: Deloitte LLP
Bankers: Barclays Bank Plc (20-53-30)

|  | 27-09-13 | 28-09-12 | 30-09-11 |
|---|---|---|---|
| TO | 72,379,000 | 68,380,000 | 66,302,000 |
| P/L | (4,634,000) | (3,442,000) | (5,571,000) |
| NW | 15,032,000 | 20,561,000 | 24,143,000 |
| WC | 13,611,000 | 19,014,000 | 22,711,000 |
| Emp. | 191 | 186 | 195 |

DUNS 23-626-9739　　　　　　　　　　Imp
### Thornbridge Sawmills Ltd
Thornbridge Yard, Laurieston Road, Grangemouth, Stirlingshire FK3 8XX
Tel: 01324620620
Web: www.scania.co.uk
Reg No: 0188920SC　Estd: 2011 Private Limited Company
Line of Business: Saw milling and planing of wood, impregnation of wood
Issued Capital: £81,819
Directors: A B Muirhead, J I Kerr
Co. Secretary: Derek Easton
Branches: Thornbridge Sawmills Ltd, Unit 17, Braidhurst Industrial Estate, Motherwell, Lanarkshire ML1 3ST
US SIC: 2421, 2431, 5072, 5039
UK SIC: 46101, 46300, 61500, 61300
Auditors: Grant Thornton UK LLP
Bankers: Clydesdale Bank Plc (82-63-12)

|  | 31-12-13 | 31-12-12 | 31-12-11 |
|---|---|---|---|
| TO | 27,765,325 | 27,018,224 | 25,624,755 |
| P/L | 331,514 | 132,985 | 111,241 |
| NW | 3,181,611 | 3,011,045 | 2,991,933 |
| WC | (414,794) | (511,822) | (425,876) |
| Emp. | 125 | 125 | 130 |

DUNS 21-054-7837
### Thornbury Castle
Thornbury Castle, Castle Street, Bristol, Avon BS35 1HH
Tel: 01454-281182
Web: www.thornburycastle.co.uk
Estd: 2010 Proprietorship
Line of Business: Hotels
Proprietor: D Robertson
Responsibilities
Senior: Brian Jarvis (General Manager)
Finance: Brian Jarvis (General Manager)
Marketing: Brian Jarvis (General Manager)
Sales: Brian Jarvis (General Manager)
IT: Brian Jarvis (General Manager)
HR: Brian Jarvis (General Manager)
Health & Safety: Marco Mellace (Restaurant Manager)
Facilities: Brian Jarvis (General Manager)
Operations: Brian Jarvis (General Manager)
Purchasing: Brian Jarvis (General Manager)
US SIC: 7011　UK SIC: 66500
Employees: 50

DUNS 36-798-4648
### Thornbury Golf Centre
Bristol Road, Thornbury, Bristol, Avon BS35 3XL
Tel: 01454-281144
Web: www.thornburygc.co.uk
Estd: 1992 Proprietorship
Line of Business: Golf clubs
Proprietor: K Pickett
Responsibilities
Senior: Melanie Drake (Manager), Graham Marshall (General Manager)
US SIC: 7999, 6531
UK SIC: 97913, 83400
Employees: 50

DUNS 23-630-4080
### Thorncliffe Building Supplies Ltd
Unit 1, Ewloe Barn Industrial Estate, Mold Road, Mold, Clwyd CH7 6LG
Tel: 01745570670 Fax: 01244551004
Web: www.thorncliffebs.co.uk
Reg No: 3627393　Estd: 1998 Private Limited Company
Line of Business: Builders merchants
Issued Capital: £1,000
Principals: T J Harper (Managing), J P Monks, Ms D J Harper, P T Pierce
Co. Secretary: Jonathan Newman
Responsibilities
Senior: Adam Harper (Manager)
US SIC: 5072, 5251
UK SIC: 61500, 64800
Auditors: Harold Smith

|  | 31-12-13 | 31-12-12 | 31-12-11 |
|---|---|---|---|
| TO | 14,928,899 | 13,125,076 | 12,057,872 |
| P/L | 819,210 | 593,652 | 476,671 |
| NW | 1,281,060 | 972,634 | 622,853 |
| WC | (452,370) | (543,714) | (755,835) |
| Emp. | 121 | 112 | 105 |

DUNS 21-510-5714
### Thorncliffe Grange
2 Windmill Lane, Denton, Manchester M34 3RN
Tel: 01613200740
Web: www.thorncliffegrange.co.uk
Estd: 1990 Partnership
Line of Business: Medical nursing home activities
Partner: R Parker
Responsibilities
Senior: Sarah Hitchcock (General Manager)
US SIC: 8051, 6732
UK SIC: 95100, 83100
Employees: 56

DUNS 21-717-7128
### Thornden School
Winchester Road, Chandler's Ford, Eastleigh, Hampshire SO53 2DW
Tel: 02380269722
Web: www.thornden.hants.sch.uk
Reg No: 7562918　Estd: 2011 Private Company Limited By Guarantee
Line of Business: General secondary education
Directors: Ms P Roberts, P N Sampson, Dr V M Radford, Dr R Sykes, Dr A J Innes, Ms L Fogleman-Peaston, P Gedikoglu, Ms T Beven
Co. Secretary: Ms Petra Isaacs
Responsibilities
Senior: Aiman Alzetani (Director), Jacqueline Beckingham (Director), Richard Boden (Director), Elizabeth Challand (Director), Simone Holley (Director), Melanie Jeffery (Director), Kathleen Mccallum (Director), Timothy Ricketts (Director)
US SIC: 8211　UK SIC: 93200

|  | 31-08-14 | 31-08-13 | 31-08-12 |
|---|---|---|---|
| TO | 7,608,196 | 7,746,725 | 28,080,762 |
| P/L | (1,160,984) | (797,334) | 17,284,528 |
| NW | 14,977,210 | 16,202,194 | 16,968,528 |
| WC | 891,265 | 1,036,877 | 936,671 |
| Emp. | 137 | 157 | 160 |

DUNS 76-959-7915
### Thorndene Ltd
Canterbury Road, Swingfield, Dover, Kent CT15 7HZ
Tel: 01303892244
Web: www.thorndene.com
Reg No: 2624175　Estd: 1991 Private Limited Company
Line of Business: Social work activities with accommodation
Issued Capital: £757,000
Directors: Ms H Jedwab, Mrs W R Mills, R G Andersen, Dr J M Ribchester
Co. Secretary: John Leingang
Responsibilities
Senior: Debby Brown (Manager)
US SIC: 8321　UK SIC: 96111
Auditors: Diana H Ibbetson

|  | 31-03-14 | 31-03-13 | 31-03-12 |
|---|---|---|---|
| TA | 1,517,668 | 1,551,823 | 1,572,350 |
| NW | 1,195,683 | 1,207,653 | 1,233,648 |
| WC | (26,021) | (13,002) | (31,331) |

DUNS 21-553-1075
### Thorndon Park Golf Club
Ingrave, Brentwood, Essex CM13 3RH
Tel: 01277810345
Web: www.thorndonparkgolfclub.com
Estd: 1920 Partnership
Line of Business: Golf clubs
Partners: C Gillies, G Thomas, K Gunby, Ms C Gillies, M Pepper, Mrs M Pierce
US SIC: 7999　UK SIC: 97913
Employees: 46

DUNS 29-772-6952
## Thorne Poultry Ltd
(**Subsidiary of:** Stichting Administratiekantoor Sbt)
Coulman Street, Doncaster, South Yorkshire DN8 5JT
**Tel:** 01405-746200
**Web:** www.thornespoultrycentre.co.uk
**Reg No:** 2035669 **Estd:** 1986 Private Limited Company
**Line of Business:** Production of meat and poultry meat products
**Issued Capital:** £1,570,000
**Director:** L B Abbitt
**Co. Secretary:** Tmf Corporate Administration Ser
**Responsibilities**
**Senior:** Barry Hopkinson *(Works Manager)*
**Finance:** Lawrence Stead *(Accountant)*
**Purchasing:** Barry Hopkinson *(Works Manager)*
**US SIC:** 2013 **UK SIC:** 41223
**Auditors:** BDO LLP
**Bankers:** Bank Of Scotland (80-73-30)

| | 31-12-13 | 31-12-12 | 31-12-11 |
|---|---|---|---|
| TA | 13,328,000 | 13,364,000 | 12,662,000 |
| P/L | 294,000 | 372,000 | N/A |
| NW | 13,328,000 | 13,034,000 | 12,662,000 |
| WC | N/A | 13,034,000 | N/A |

DUNS 73-672-8440
## Thorneycroft Solicitors Ltd
(**Subsidiary of:** Harts 1101 Ltd)
Bridge Street, Mills Bridge Street, Macclesfield, Cheshire SK11 6QA
**Tel:** 01625460236 **Fax:** 01625506601
**Web:** www.thorneycrofts.co.uk
**Reg No:** 4932249 **Estd:** 1997 Private Limited Company
**Line of Business:** Solicitors
**Issued Capital:** £1
**Directors:** Ms R L Stow, M J Coghlan, M D Belfield, R P Thorneycroft
**Co. Secretary:** Ms Judith Copley
**Responsibilities**
**Admin:** Lianne Simpson *(Personal Assistant)*
**IT:** Peter Reeves *(IT Manager)*
**Branches:** Thorneycroft Solicitors Ltd, 16A The Square London Road, Crewe, Cheshire CW4 7AB
**US SIC:** 7399 **UK SIC:** 83954

| | 31-10-13 | 31-10-12 | 31-10-11 |
|---|---|---|---|
| TO | 12,126,486 | 13,143,494 | 11,482,623 |
| P/L | 37,730 | 1,404,468 | 223,393 |
| NW | (1,843,686) | (1,788,216) | (2,570,247) |
| WC | (1,845,625) | (884,774) | (630,454) |
| Emp. | 134 | 125 | 119 |

DUNS 21-200-8838
## Thorngate Almshouse Trust
Clare House, Melrose Gardens, Gosport, Hampshire PO12 3BZ
**Tel:** 02392534999
**Web:** www.thorngate.org.uk
**Estd:** 1981
**Line of Business:** Sheltered housing accommodation
**Responsibilities**
**Senior:** Stella Crampton *(Housing Manager)*, Doug Scorey *(Clerk to the Trustees)*
**Finance:** Doug Scorey *(Clerk to the Trustees)*
**Health & Safety:** Doug Scorey *(Clerk to the Trustees)*
**Facilities:** Alan Hounsham *(Technical Officer)*
**Branches:** Thorngate Almshouse Trust, Melrose Gardens, Gosport, Hampshire PO12 3BE
**US SIC:** 8321 **UK SIC:** 96111
**Auditors:** Menzies LLP

| | 31-03-12 | 31-03-11 | 31-03-10 |
|---|---|---|---|
| TO | 1,503,325 | 1,422,926 | 1,235,051 |
| P/L | 113,090 | 30,696 | (10,850) |
| NW | 1,412,395 | 1,314,125 | 1,286,729 |
| WC | 91,194 | 6,219 | (80,112) |
| Emp. | 72 | 65 | 65 |

DUNS 23-644-2166
## Thornhill College
121 Culmore Road, Londonderry, Co Londonderry BT48 8JF
**Tel:** 02871351233
**Web:** www.thornhillministries.co.uk
**Estd:** 2001
**Line of Business:** Religious organisations and places of worship
**Proprietor:** P Mcnulty
**Responsibilities**
**Senior:** Marguerite Hamilton *(Principal)*, Perpetua McNulty *(Proprietor)*
**Finance:** Brandon Mclaughlan *(Senior Finance Administrator)*
**IT:** Wendy Baxter *(IT Executive)*
**US SIC:** 8661 **UK SIC:** 96600
**Employees:** 4

DUNS 50-348-5534 **Imp-Exp**
## Thornhill Heat Exchangers Ltd
Long Royd, Grimethorpe, Barnsley, South Yorkshire S72 7PT
**Tel:** 01226-710000
**Web:** www.thornhill-ltd.co.uk
**Reg No:** 2370591 **VAT No:** 779756157
**Estd:** 1989 Private Limited Company
**Line of Business:** Manufacturers of heat exchangers
**Export Markets:** U S A
**Export Sales:** £2,001,355
**Issued Capital:** £81,350
**Principals:** M H Thornhill *(Managing)*, Ms G M Bredin, Ms E Thornhill, Miss E Thornhill
**Co. Secretary:** Ms Catherine Thornhill
**Responsibilities**
**HR:** Robert Holman *(Commercial Manager)*
**Health & Safety:** Robert Holman *(Commercial Manager)*
**Facilities:** Jim Sharpe *(Maintenance Manager)*
**Operations:** Robert Holman *(Commercial Manager)*
**US SIC:** 3567, 3069
**UK SIC:** 32452, 48123
**Auditors:** Grant Thornton UK LLP
**Bankers:** National Westminster Bank Plc (51-61-35)

| | 31-12-13 | 31-12-12 | 31-12-11 |
|---|---|---|---|
| TO | 7,439,983 | 7,273,771 | 7,563,899 |
| P/L | 467,808 | 355,219 | 457,359 |
| NW | 2,133,390 | 1,950,871 | 2,010,548 |
| WC | 1,335,112 | 1,038,847 | 1,156,442 |
| Emp. | 111 | 122 | 121 |

DUNS 21-783-6445
## Thornleigh Salesian College
Sharples Park, Bolton, Lancashire BL1 6PQ
**Web:** www.thornleigh.bolton.sch.uk
**Estd:** 2002 Proprietorship
**Line of Business:** Schools (foundation)
**Proprietor:** Mrs A Burrowes
**US SIC:** 8211 **UK SIC:** 93200
**Employees:** 130

DUNS 77-087-3586
## Thornley Groves Ltd
(**Subsidiary of:** Thornley Groves Estate Agents Ltd)
16-18 Lloyd Street, Altrincham, Cheshire WA14 2DE
**Tel:** 0161-941-4111 **Fax:** 0161-941-4091
**Web:** www.thornleygroves.co.uk
**Reg No:** 2674298 **Estd:** 1991 Private Limited Company
**Line of Business:** Representative office
**Issued Capital:** £76
**Directors:** J Watkins, S M Pender, B E Robertson, M S Thornley Groves, R Hamilton
**Co. Secretary:** Michael Groves
**Branches:** Thornley Groves Ltd, 33 King Street, Knutsford, Cheshire WA16 6DW
**US SIC:** 6531 **UK SIC:** 83400
**Auditors:** John Sheppard & Co
**Bankers:** Barclays Bank Plc (20-01-96)

| | 31-12-13 | 31-12-12 | 31-12-11 |
|---|---|---|---|
| TO | 4,317,283 | N/A | N/A |
| P/L | 839,480 | N/A | N/A |
| NW | 321,658 | 780,578 | 961,747 |
| WC | (23,702) | (151,511) | (253,973) |
| Emp. | 88 | N/A | N/A |

DUNS 28-895-4399
## Thornley Leisure (Sales) Ltd
William Sutcliffe Suite, Raymond Court Princes Drive, Colwyn Bay, Clwyd LL29 8HT
**Tel:** 01492532300
**Web:** www.thornleyleisure.co.uk
**Reg No:** 1314194 **Estd:** 1977 Private Limited Company
**Line of Business:** Camping sites, including caravan sites
**Issued Capital:** £2,400
**Principals:** D M Thornley *(Managing)*, D E Thornley, Miss E V Richards
**Co. Secretary:** Andrew Mailer
**Branches:** Thornley Leisure (Sales) Ltd, Beach Road, Llanddulas, Abergele, Clwyd LL22 8HB
**US SIC:** 7033 **UK SIC:** 66701
**Auditors:** Pritchett & Co

| | 31-10-13 | 31-10-12 | 31-10-11 |
|---|---|---|---|
| TA | 2,628,455 | 2,396,601 | 2,302,998 |
| NW | 1,586,059 | 1,395,498 | 1,146,809 |
| WC | 16,006 | (188,749) | (321,673) |

DUNS 21-219-1886 **Exp**
## Thornton & Ross Ltd
(**Subsidiary of:** Stada Arzneimittel Ag)
Linthwaite Laboratories, Manchester Road, Linthwaite, Huddersfield, West Yorkshire HD7 5QH
**Tel:** 01484-842-217 **Fax:** 01484-847-301
**Web:** www.thorntonandross.co.uk
**Reg No:** 0185947 **VAT No:** 183463549
**Estd:** 1922 Private Limited Company
**Line of Business:** Manufacture of cleaning and polishing preparations
**Export Sales:** £9,226,466
**Issued Capital:** £31,554
**Directors:** D George, L M Slegers, D George, N G Edwards
**Co. Secretary:** Ms Janet Alpin
**Responsibilities**
**Senior:** Mark Carlisle *(IT Manager)*, Patrick Dunn *(Warehouse Supervisor)*
**Marketing:** Bryan Close *(Product Development Manager)*, Caroline Wheeler *(Marketing Manager)*
**IT:** Mark Carlisle *(IT Manager)*, Richard Stratford *(IT Manager)*
**HR:** Nicola Shewring *(Personnel Manager)*
**Health & Safety:** Helen Rutherford *(Health & Safety Officer)*
**Facilities:** Mark Boucherat *(Chief Engineer)*
**Engineering:** Mark Boucherat *(Chief Engineer)*
**US SIC:** 2842, 2834
**UK SIC:** 25990, 25700
**Auditors:** Wheawill & Sudworth Ltd
**Bankers:** Barclays Bank Plc (20-43-04)

| | 31-12-13 | 31-03-13 | 01-12-12 |
|---|---|---|---|
| TO | 50,162,476 | 65,178,298 | 59,069,335 |
| P/L | 9,911,806 | 12,997,493 | 6,679,489 |
| NW | 40,979,388 | 55,821,426 | 45,023,784 |
| WC | 24,874,127 | 45,042,359 | 35,835,553 |
| Emp. | 469 | 457 | 455 |

DUNS 54-373-7803
## Thornton Burns Recruitment Ltd
210-212 Manchester Road Northwich, Northwich, Cheshire CW9 7NN
**Tel:** 01483488500
**Web:** www.tbruk.co.uk
**Reg No:** 3261790 **Estd:** 1996 Private Limited Company
**Line of Business:** Employment and recruitment companies and consultants
**Issued Capital:** £2
**Co. Secretary:** John Mitchell
**US SIC:** 7361 **UK SIC:** 83954
**Auditors:** B A Hulme FCCA

| | 28-06-14 | 28-06-13 | 28-06-12 |
|---|---|---|---|
| TA | 2 | 2 | 181,984 |
| NW | 2 | 2 | (16,265) |
| WC | N/A | N/A | (24,919) |

DUNS 42-367-1288
## Thornton Grammer School
Leaventhorpe Lane, Thornton, Bradford, West Yorkshire BD13 3BH
**Tel:** 01274881082
**Web:** www.tgsonline.co.uk
**Estd:** 1999
**Line of Business:** Schools (local authority)
**Director:** J Mcguiness
**Responsibilities**
**Senior:** Karen Kingston *(Assistant Head Teacher)*, Chris Sampson *(Head Teacher)*
**IT:** Dylan Bullock *(IT Manager)*
**US SIC:** 8211 **UK SIC:** 93200
**Employees:** 200

DUNS 39-703-5312
## Thornton Hall Hotel Ltd
(**Subsidiary of:** Thompson (Holdings) Ltd)
Neston Road Thornton Hough, Wirral, Thornton Hough, Wirral, Merseyside CH63 1JF
**Tel:** 0151-336-3938 **Fax:** 0151-336-7864
**Web:** www.thorntonhallhotel.com
**Reg No:** 2156621 **VAT No:** 625088634
**Estd:** 1987 Private Limited Company
**Line of Business:** Physical well-being activities
**Issued Capital:** £2
**Principals:** A L Thompson *(Managing)*, P L Webster, Mrs N Thompson
**Co. Secretary:** Andrew Thompson
**Responsibilities**
**Marketing:** Wendy Lucas *(Sales & Marketing Manager)*, Jenny Tasker *(Sales & Marketing Manager)*
**Sales:** Wendy Lucas *(Sales & Marketing Manager)*, Jenny Tasker *(Sales & Marketing Manager)*
**HR:** Geoff Dale *(General Manager)*
**Health & Safety:** Geoff Dale *(General Manager)*
**Facilities:** Geoff Dale *(General Manager)*
**Purchasing:** Geoff Dale *(General Manager)*
**US SIC:** 7299, 8999
**UK SIC:** 98902, 83954
**Auditors:** Blease Lloyd & Co
**Bankers:** Barclays Bank Plc (20-20-44)

| | 30-09-13 | 30-09-12 | 30-09-11 |
|---|---|---|---|
| TO | 3,599,953 | 3,557,097 | 3,350,810 |
| P/L | 5,586 | 37,727 | 28,384 |
| NW | 682,954 | 659,258 | 643,430 |
| WC | (1,104,560) | (1,243,023) | (1,248,371) |
| Emp. | 143 | 138 | 141 |

DUNS 23-137-3994
## Thornton Heath Cleaners
100 High Street, Thornton Heath, Surrey CR7 8LF
**Tel:** 020-8689-5300
**Web:** www.fusion-lifestyle.com
**Estd:** 2005 Proprietorship
**Line of Business:** Leisure centres
**Proprietor:** M Bell
**Responsibilities**
**Senior:** Dan Roger *(Manager)*
**US SIC:** 7999 **UK SIC:** 97913
**Employees:** 60

DUNS 23-834-4931
## Thornton Hill Residential Home
Church Road, Thornton In Craven, Skipton, North Yorkshire BD23 3TN
**Tel:** 01282842023
**VAT No:** 325417767 **Estd:** 1979 Proprietorship
**Line of Business:** Non-charitable social work activities with accommodation
**Principals:** R Bovensiepen, R Bovensiepen *(Proprietor)*
**Responsibilities**
**Senior:** Joanne Hickey *(Manager)*, Dianne Pattison *(Home Manager)*
**US SIC:** 8321, 6732
**UK SIC:** 96111, 83100
**Bankers:** Yorkshire Bank Plc (05-09-09)
**Employees:** 65

DUNS 21-771-6134
## Thornton House
Whimbrel Drive, Thornton-Cleveleys, Lancashire FY5 2LR
**Tel:** 01253825845
**Estd:** 1979 Proprietorship
**Line of Business:** Social work activities with accommodation
**Proprietor:** Mrs S Chippendale
**US SIC:** 8321 **UK SIC:** 96111
**Employees:** 60

DUNS 34-856-1304
## Thorntons Budgens Ltd
21-23 The Broadway, Hornsey, London N8 8DU
**Tel:** 02083409636
**Web:** www.thorntonsbudgens.com
**Reg No:** 5654837 **Estd:** 2005 Private Limited Company
**Line of Business:** Retail sale in non-specialised stores (excluding ctns) not holding an alcohol licence with food, beverages or tobacco predominating
**Issued Capital:** £10,000
**Director:** A J Thornton
**Co. Secretary:** Mrs Sivashanthy Premachandralal
**US SIC:** 5411, 5993
**UK SIC:** 64100, 64200

| | 30-09-13 | 30-09-12 | 30-09-11 |
|---|---|---|---|
| TO | 13,553,981 | 15,854,639 | 15,650,727 |
| P/L | 392,628 | 158,066 | 68,115 |
| NW | (236,314) | (1,680,312) | (1,762,644) |
| WC | 115,491 | (518,058) | (313,459) |
| Emp. | 164 | 191 | 187 |

DUNS 73-882-2910
## Thorntons Law Llp
Whitehall House, 33 Yeaman Shore, Dundee, Angus DD1 4BJ
**Web:** www.thorntons-law.co.uk
**Reg No:** 0300381SO **Estd:** 2004
**Line of Business:** Solicitors
**Responsibilities**
**Senior:** Elizabeth Barr *(Designated Limited Liability P)*, George Dunlop *(Designated Limited Liability P)*, Malcolm Farquhar *(Designated Limited Liability P)*, Anne Mckeown *(Designated Limited Liability P)*, Scott Milne *(Designated Limited Liability P)*, Michael Royden *(Non-designated Limited Liabili)*
**US SIC:** 8111 **UK SIC:** 83500
**Auditors:** Henderson Loggie
**Bankers:** The Royal Bank Of Scotland Plc (83-50-00)

| | 31-05-14 | 31-05-13 | 31-05-12 |
|---|---|---|---|
| TO | 16,277,661 | 14,382,439 | 13,199,201 |
| P/L | 3,982,584 | N/A | N/A |
| NW | 2,345,860 | N/A | N/A |
| WC | 5,654,656 | 4,938,766 | 3,545,296 |
| Emp. | 247 | 245 | 236 |

DUNS 21-239-7947 **Imp-Exp**
## Thorntons Plc
Thornton Park, Somercotes, Alfreton, Derbyshire DE55 4XJ
**Tel:** 08450757565 **Fax:** 01773540842
**Web:** www.thorntons.co.uk
**Reg No:** 0174706 **VAT No:** 172841360
**Estd:** 1921 Public Limited Company
**Line of Business:** Manufacture of cocoa and chocolate confectionery
**Issued Capital:** £6,836,552

**Directors:** J D Hart, M P George, B Bloomer, M D Killick, Ms D J Houghton, P N Wilkinson
**Co. Secretary:** Mark Henson
**Responsibilities**
**Marketing:** Eve Roberts *(Customer Marketing Manager)*
**Sales:** Lysanne McCallion *(Retail Director)*
**HR:** Emily Campbell *(Training Manager)*
**Operations:** Paul Mullard *(Hygiene Coordinator)*
**Branches:** Thorntons Plc, Centre Management Office, Queensgate Centre, Peterborough, Cambridgeshire PE1 1NT
**US SIC:** 2066, 5462
**UK SIC:** 42141, 64100
**Auditors:** PricewaterhouseCoopers LLP
**Bankers:** HSBC Bank plc (40-10-07)

| | 28-06-14 | 29-06-13 | 30-06-12 |
|---|---|---|---|
| TO | 222,437,000 | 221,052,000 | 217,144,000 |
| P/L | 5,968,000 | 5,170,000 | (2,214,000) |
| NW | 16,579,000 | 14,886,000 | 10,016,000 |
| WC | 3,230,000 | (666,000) | (3,238,000) |
| Emp. | 3,872 | 3,819 | 3,778 |

DUNS 23-214-7835
## Thorntons W S
11 Albert Square, Meadowside, Dundee, Angus DD1 1DD
**Web:** www.beatthebanks.co.uk
**Estd:** 2012 Partnership
**Line of Business:** Legal services
**Partner:** G Mcnicholls
**Responsibilities**
**Senior:** Graham McNicholls *(Partner)*, Clara Orozco *(Proprietor)*
**Branches:** Thorntons W S, Anatalia Restaurant, 3 Whitehall Crescent, Dundee, Angus DD1 4AR
**US SIC:** 8111, 6531
**UK SIC:** 83500, 83400
**Employees:** 100

DUNS 76-911-1709
## Thorntoun Ltd
(**Subsidiary of:** Thorntoun (2008) Ltd)
Crosshouse, Crosshouse, Kilmarnock, Ayrshire KA2 0BH
**Tel:** 01563-572626
**Web:** www.thorntoun.co.uk
**Reg No:** 0129587SC **Estd:** 1991 Private Limited Company
**Line of Business:** Medical nursing home activities
**Trading Style:** Thorntoun Estate Nursing Home
**Issued Capital:** £8,000
**Directors:** R B Johnstone, Ms A M Johnstone, W M Johnstone
**Co. Secretary:** David Brown
**Responsibilities**
**Senior:** Rhona Gibson *(Home Manager)*, Angela Wiyper *(Manager)*
**Marketing:** Rhona Gibson *(Home Manager)*
**Facilities:** Rhona Gibson *(Home Manager)*
**US SIC:** 8051, 8321
**UK SIC:** 95100, 96111
**Auditors:** William Duncan & Co
**Bankers:** Bank Of Scotland (80-12-39)

| | 31-03-14 | 31-03-13 | 31-03-12 |
|---|---|---|---|
| TO | 3,760,891 | 3,866,606 | 3,821,620 |
| P/L | 648,845 | 798,200 | 850,123 |
| NW | 4,093,535 | 3,746,801 | 3,303,929 |
| WC | 2,668,515 | 2,546,589 | 2,355,930 |
| Emp. | 185 | 193 | 192 |

DUNS 21-781-2517
## Thorntree Mews
17 Arnot Hill, Falkirk, Stirlingshire FK1 5RZ
**Tel:** 01324441347
**Web:** www.countrywidecarehomes.co.uk
**Estd:** 1990 Proprietorship
**Line of Business:** Nursing homes
**Proprietor:** Mrs M Meason
**US SIC:** 8051 **UK SIC:** 95100
**Employees:** 54

DUNS 39-692-3294
## Thorogood Associates Ltd
Building E Ealing Studios, Ealing Green, London W5 5EP
**Web:** www.thorogood.com
**Reg No:** 2149616 **VAT No:** 479552302
**Estd:** 1987 Private Limited Company
**Line of Business:** Secretarial and translation activities
**Export Sales:** £3,984,048
**Issued Capital:** £40,363
**Principals:** M J Kightley *(Managing)*, T R Jones *(Managing)*, P W Nicol, P Balacky, Ms P J Honigsberger
**Co. Secretary:** Ms Siobhan Boyer
**Responsibilities**
**Senior:** Ita Harris *(Manager)*, Libby Kemp *(Facilities Manager)*
**Marketing:** Harprett Nandhra *(Marketing Manager)*
**IT:** Evelyn Heyes *(General Manager)*
**HR:** Ita Harris *(Manager)*
**Health & Safety:** Ita Harris *(Manager)*
**Facilities:** Libby Kemp *(Facilities Manager)*
**Branches:** Thorogood Associates Ltd, Dralda Ho, 24-28 Crendon St, High Wycombe, Buckinghamshire HP13 6LS
**US SIC:** 7399 **UK SIC:** 83954
**Auditors:** Grant Thornton
**Bankers:** HSBC Bank plc (40-24-17)

| | 30-09-13 | 30-09-12 | 30-09-11 |
|---|---|---|---|
| TO | 10,035,385 | 8,417,610 | 7,098,424 |
| P/L | 1,389,114 | 815,199 | 711,933 |
| NW | 2,760,561 | 2,266,177 | 1,602,210 |
| WC | 2,406,977 | 1,943,346 | 1,356,186 |
| Emp. | 123 | 104 | N/A |

DUNS 21-699-9273
## Thorokleen Trading Ltd
(**Subsidiary of:** Thorokleen Holdings Ltd)
84 Papyrus Road, Peterborough, Cambridgeshire PE4 5BH
**Tel:** 01733325500 **Fax:** 01733325511
**Web:** www.thorokleen.co.uk
**Reg No:** 7450688 **Estd:** 1988 Private Limited Company
**Line of Business:** Washing and dry cleaning of textile and fur products
**Issued Capital:** £889
**Directors:** P A Dalliday, Mrs A C Cresswell, R W Stone, R L Cresswell
**US SIC:** 7219 **UK SIC:** 98110

| | 31-03-14 | 31-03-13 | 31-03-12 |
|---|---|---|---|
| TA | 400,526 | 337,436 | 325,524 |
| NW | 220,754 | 161,823 | 106,431 |
| WC | 191,229 | 131,908 | 73,801 |

DUNS 23-378-6537
## Thorp Precast Ltd
Valley Sawmills, Apedale Road, Newcastle, Staffordshire ST5 6BN
**Tel:** 01782561155
**Web:** www.thorpprecast.co.uk
**Reg No:** 5219420 **Estd:** 2004 Private Limited Company
**Line of Business:** Die casting equipment and services
**Issued Capital:** £100,000
**Directors:** P Willett, C Jones, H R Thorp
**Co. Secretary:** Graham Shaw
**Branches:** Thorp Precast Ltd, Chynance, Woodlane Close, Falmouth, Cornwall TR11 4QU
**US SIC:** 3559, 3273
**UK SIC:** 32863, 24360
**Auditors:** HWCA Ltd

| | 31-12-13 | 31-12-12 | 31-12-11 |
|---|---|---|---|
| TO | 11,034,577 | 6,664,799 | N/A |
| P/L | 926,244 | 387,124 | N/A |
| NW | 2,643,824 | 2,348,292 | 2,157,503 |
| WC | 2,023,673 | 1,859,045 | 1,480,085 |
| Emp. | 56 | 51 | N/A |

DUNS 42-367-5255
## The Thorpe Bay School
School House, Southchurch Boulevard, Southend-On-Sea, Essex SS2 4XA
**Tel:** 01702616145
**Estd:** 1980
**Line of Business:** Clubs social and associations
**US SIC:** 8211 **UK SIC:** 93200
**Employees:** 100

DUNS 76-946-3068
## Thorpe Hall School Trust
Wakering Road, Southend-On-Sea, Essex SS1 3RD
**Tel:** 01702582340
**Reg No:** 2187958 **Estd:** 1987 Private Limited Company
**Line of Business:** General secondary education
**Directors:** Ms C J Graves, J R Gorridge, M Reddan, D W Sills, Ms L L Andrews, Ms S J Goldsworthy, M J Miller, M I Brudenell
**US SIC:** 8211 **UK SIC:** 93200
**Auditors:** Porter Gee & Co
**Bankers:** Barclays Bank Plc (20-19-95)

| | 31-08-13 | 31-08-12 | 31-08-11 |
|---|---|---|---|
| TO | 2,571,281 | 2,524,149 | 2,552,952 |
| P/L | 97,907 | 82,324 | 203,304 |
| NW | 3,135,659 | 3,037,752 | 2,955,428 |
| WC | 2,499,020 | 2,413,330 | 2,565,846 |
| Emp. | 52 | 49 | 61 |

DUNS 29-585-2024
## Thorpe House School Trust
Thorpe House School Oval Way, Gerrards Cross, Buckinghamshire SL9 8PZ
**Tel:** 01753-882474
**Web:** www.thorpehouse.co.uk
**Reg No:** 1946972 **Estd:** 1923 Private Limited Company
**Line of Business:** Schools (independent)
**Trading Style:** Thorpe House School
**Directors:** Ms G E Stanning, R G Marris, R J Coward, C D Gorner, Mrs D J Raven, P J Millins, G P Mccarthy, Mrs M A Frost
**Co. Secretary:** Matthew Watts
**Responsibilities**
**Senior:** Hendrick Botha *(Director)*, James Curtis *(Manager)*, Roy Macmillan *(Director)*, Amanda Myers *(Director)*, David Stanning *(Director)*, Caroline Witty *(Director)*
**US SIC:** 8249 **UK SIC:** 93300
**Auditors:** G R Skinner
**Bankers:** Barclays Bank Plc (20-74-09)

| | 31-07-13 | 31-07-12 | 31-07-11 |
|---|---|---|---|
| TO | 3,222,857 | 2,573,871 | 2,501,070 |
| P/L | 47,280 | 136,359 | 158,133 |
| NW | 1,190,998 | 1,110,264 | 1,751,952 |
| WC | 279,874 | 342,963 | 255,625 |
| Emp. | 77 | 59 | 53 |

DUNS 52-017-9375
## Thorpe Molloy Recruitment Ltd
38 Albyn Place, Aberdeen, Aberdeenshire AB10 1YN
**Web:** www.thorpemolloy.com
**Reg No:** 0176282SC **Estd:** 1997 Private Limited Company
**Line of Business:** Employment and recruitment companies and consultants
**Trading Style:** Thorpe Molloy Recruitment Ltd
**Issued Capital:** £704
**Directors:** Ms A J Mcculloch, Ms J Thorpe
**Co. Secretary:** Ms Karen Molloy
**Responsibilities**
**Senior:** Jacqueline Christie *(Marketing Manager)*
**Branches:** Thorpe Molloy Recruitment Ltd, 3 Queens Terrace, Aberdeen, Aberdeenshire AB10 1XL
**US SIC:** 7361 **UK SIC:** 83954
**Auditors:** Anderson Anderson & Brown

| | 30-09-13 | 30-09-12 | 30-09-11 |
|---|---|---|---|
| TA | 2,853,192 | 2,683,336 | 2,822,070 |
| NW | 830,370 | 1,038,900 | 899,093 |
| WC | 611,074 | 804,013 | 668,801 |

DUNS 34-550-9314
## Thorpe Wood Management Co Ltd
Thorpe Wood Police Station, Thorpe Wood, Peterborough, Cambridgeshire PE3 6SD
**Reg No:** 5360928 **Estd:** 2005 Private Company Limited By Guarantee
**Line of Business:** Management of real estate on a fee or contract basis
**Director:** W French
**Co. Secretary:** Ms Sara Fowler
**US SIC:** 6531 **UK SIC:** 83400

| | 31-12-13 | 31-12-12 | 31-12-11 |
|---|---|---|---|
| TA | 11,984 | 10,826 | 8,390 |
| NW | 5,783 | 4,366 | 5,133 |
| WC | 5,651 | 4,190 | 4,898 |

DUNS 28-858-2265 **Exp**
## Thos. Bentley & Son Ltd
Po Box 305, Listerhills Road, Leeds, West Yorkshire LS18 5PU
**Tel:** 01132050900 **Fax:** 01332050901
**Web:** www.stephensongroupuk.com
**Reg No:** 0841624 **Estd:** 1965 Private Limited Company
**Line of Business:** Estate agents
**Export Markets:** U S A, E U, Middle East, Far East
**Export Sales:** £15,229,703
**Trading Style:** Stevenson Group
**Issued Capital:** £100,000
**Principals:** T R Bentley *(Managing)*, T J Bentley
**US SIC:** 6519, 2834
**UK SIC:** 85000, 25700
**Auditors:** Firth Parish
**Bankers:** HSBC Bank plc (40-13-15)

| | 30-09-13 | 30-09-12 | 30-09-11 |
|---|---|---|---|
| TO | 20,088,470 | 19,415,218 | 18,465,220 |
| P/L | 310,530 | 227,120 | 316,057 |
| NW | 738,236 | 892,914 | 1,121,661 |
| WC | 1,424,729 | 1,364,826 | 1,304,425 |
| Emp. | 74 | 75 | 72 |

DUNS 34-712-8774 **Exp**
## Thos. C. Wild Ltd
Vulcan Works, Tinsley Park Road, Sheffield, South Yorkshire S9 5DP
**Tel:** 01142-442471
**Web:** www.tc-wild.co.uk
**Reg No:** 5516830 **Estd:** 1958 Private Limited Company
**Line of Business:** Forging, pressing, stamping and roll forming of metal; powder metallurgy
**Export Sales:** £898,000
**Issued Capital:** £68,400
**Directors:** M R Justice, M Howson, J Hancock, Ms I Y Hancock, G J Lewis
**Co. Secretary:** Mrs Irene Hancock
**Responsibilities**
**HR:** Steve Walkinshaw *(Project Manager)*
**Health & Safety:** Steve Walkinshaw *(Project Manager)*
**US SIC:** 3469 **UK SIC:** 31200
**Bankers:** Bank Of Scotland (12-18-68)

| | 31-08-14 | 31-08-13 | 31-08-12 |
|---|---|---|---|
| TO | 9,131,000 | 10,131,000 | 10,631,000 |
| P/L | 240,000 | 724,000 | 917,000 |
| NW | 3,136,000 | 2,967,000 | 2,077,000 |
| WC | 658,000 | 569,000 | (250,000) |
| Emp. | 63 | 58 | 56 |

DUNS 73-697-0190 **Imp-Exp**
## Thos. Storey Fabrications Ltd
(**Subsidiary of:** Hallco 1431 Ltd)
Stainburn Road, Manchester M11 2EB
**Web:** www.thos-storey.co.uk
**Reg No:** 4955870 **Estd:** 2003 Private Limited Company
**Line of Business:** Manufacture of metal structures and parts of structures
**Export Sales:** £580,869
**Issued Capital:** £500,002
**Directors:** M R Walton, J Huggins, Mrs J Lynch, A J Ramsdale
**Co. Secretary:** Frederick Ellis
**US SIC:** 3441 **UK SIC:** 32042
**Auditors:** Hurst & Co Accountants LLP

| | 31-12-13 | 31-12-12 | 31-12-11 |
|---|---|---|---|
| TO | 11,551,515 | 12,288,581 | 16,316,928 |
| P/L | 211,950 | (260,106) | 155,904 |
| NW | 1,544,248 | 1,341,299 | 1,522,055 |
| WC | 30,544 | (341,847) | (383,002) |
| Emp. | 122 | 136 | 181 |

DUNS 22-090-1784 **Imp**
## Thoughtworks Ltd
(**Subsidiary of:** Thoughtworks Inc.)
168/176 High Holborn, London WC1V 7AA
**Web:** www.thoughtworks.com
**Reg No:** 4091535 **Estd:** 2001 Private Limited Company
**Line of Business:** Computer software (development)
**Export Sales:** £274,284
**Issued Capital:** £2
**Directors:** Ms R Parsons, X Guo, C Dill, G De Gregorio, N R Singham
**Co. Secretary:** Jonas Feschuk
**Responsibilities**
**Marketing:** Catherine Casale *(Marketing Manager)*
**Operations:** Kirsty Day *(Operations Consultant)*
**US SIC:** 7379 **UK SIC:** 83940
**Auditors:** Grant Thornton UK LLP
**Bankers:** Abn Amro Bank Nv (40-50-30)

| | 31-12-13 | 31-12-12 | 31-12-11 |
|---|---|---|---|
| TO | 40,171,913 | 37,268,938 | 29,528,154 |
| P/L | 5,724,305 | 4,182,180 | 396,283 |
| NW | 17,926,158 | 13,163,944 | 9,679,490 |
| WC | 17,634,726 | 12,899,859 | 9,550,326 |
| Emp. | 225 | 210 | 177 |

DUNS 38-567-1409
## T.H.P.A. Group Services Ltd
(**Subsidiary of:** Brookfield Asset Management Inc)
17-27 Queens Square, Middlesbrough, Cleveland TS2 1AH
**Tel:** 01642-877007 **Fax:** 01642-877056
**Reg No:** 3336386 **Estd:** 1990 Private Limited Company
**Line of Business:** Business services
**Issued Capital:** £2
**Director:** D J Robinson
**Co. Secretary:** Dermot Russell
**US SIC:** 7399 **UK SIC:** 83954
**Auditors:** Arthur Andersen

| | 31-12-13 | 31-12-12 | 31-12-11 |
|---|---|---|---|
| TO | 6,973,000 | 6,697,000 | 5,047,000 |
| Emp. | 205 | 206 | 164 |

DUNS 23-706-5870
## Threadneedle Investment Services Ltd
(**Subsidiary of:** Ameriprise Financial Inc.)
St Mary Axe House, 60 St Mary Axe, London EC3A 8JQ
**Tel:** 020-7621-9100
**Web:** www.threadneedle.co.uk
**Reg No:** 3701768 **Estd:** 1999 Private Limited Company
**Line of Business:** Financial intermediation not elsewhere classified
**Issued Capital:** £17,020,001
**Directors:** N J Ring, T N Gillbanks, C D Fleming, D A Jordison, Mrs A L Roughead
**Co. Secretary:** Alan Kaye
**Responsibilities**
**Senior:** Philip Reed *(Manager)*
**Branches:** Threadneedle Investment Services Ltd, Signal Point, Po Box 1457, Swindon, Wiltshire SN1 1FE
**US SIC:** 6111, 6211
**UK SIC:** 81501, 83100
**Auditors:** Ernst & Young LLP

| | 31-12-13 | 31-12-12 | 31-12-11 |
|---|---|---|---|
| TA | 498,103,000 | 320,116,000 | 324,614,000 |
| P/L | 60,363,000 | 37,655,000 | 25,910,000 |
| NW | 110,561,000 | 91,553,000 | 90,420,000 |
| WC | 110,423,000 | 91,602,000 | 90,953,000 |
| Emp. | 103 | 82 | 70 |

**DUNS 29-219-9635**
## Threadneedle Pensions Ltd
(**Subsidiary of:** Ameriprise Financial Inc.)
St Mary Axe House, 60 St Mary Axe, London EC3A 8JQ
**Tel:** 02074645000 **Fax:** 020-7626-1266
**Web:** www.threadneedle.com
**Reg No:** 0984167 **Estd:** 1970 Private Limited Company
**Line of Business:** Life insurance
**Issued Capital:** £11,300,000
**Directors:** D A Jordison, M A Burgess, C D Fleming, T N Gillbanks
**Co. Secretary:** Alan Kaye
**Responsibilities**
**Senior:** Crispin Henderson (Manager)
**Admin:** Crispin Henderson (Manager)
**US SIC:** 6311, 6371
**UK SIC:** 82002
**Auditors:** PricewaterhouseCoopers LLP

|     | 31-12-13 | 31-12-12 | 31-12-11 |
| --- | --- | --- | --- |
| TO | 286,560,000 | 165,667,000 | 190,673,000 |
| P/L | 7,665,000 | 8,013,000 | 5,953,000 |
| NW | 24,176,000 | 18,295,000 | 40,199,000 |
| WC | 3,451,000 | (1,714,000) | (368,000) |

**DUNS 21-329-8846**
## Threadneedle Property Unit Trust C/O Workman Llp
Minton Place, Station Road, Swindon, Wiltshire SN1 1DA
**Tel:** 01793645111
**Web:** www.workman.co.uk
**Estd:** 2013
**Line of Business:** Building consultants and advisors
**US SIC:** 6531 **UK SIC:** 83400
**Employees:** 64

**DUNS 39-480-3811**
## Three A's Pertemps Training Ltd
(**Subsidiary of:** Employment Services Holdings Pty Limited)
School Walk, Nuneaton, Warwickshire CV11 4PJ
**Tel:** 024-7637-0979
**Reg No:** 2132768 **Estd:** 1981 Private Limited Company
**Line of Business:** Activities of private training providers
**Trading Style:** Pertemps People Development Group
**Issued Capital:** £1,000
**Directors:** S A King, G R Edwards
**Co. Secretary:** A G Secretarial Limited
**Branches:** Three A's Pertemps Training Ltd, Milton Ho, 7 High St, Fareham, Hampshire PO16 7AN
**US SIC:** 7399 **UK SIC:** 83954
**Auditors:** Andersons KBS Ltd
**Bankers:** HSBC Bank plc (40-35-20)

|     | 30-06-13 | 30-06-12 | 30-06-11 |
| --- | --- | --- | --- |
| TO | 7,881,973 | 5,769,410 | 8,488,236 |
| P/L | 377,041 | 155,435 | 1,386,268 |
| NW | 3,098,843 | 2,405,942 | 1,139,187 |
| WC | 3,004,924 | 2,358,838 | 1,071,235 |
| Emp. | 166 | 162 | 136 |

**DUNS 21-780-5640**
## Three Cliffs
Cefn Bryn, Uplands, Swansea, West Glamorgan SA4 3ET
**Tel:** 01792371500
**Web:** www.threecliffscare.co.uk
**Estd:** 1995 Proprietorship
**Line of Business:** Residential care establishments
**Proprietor:** T Wattson
**Responsibilities**
**Senior:** Marion Reading (Manager)
**US SIC:** 8321 **UK SIC:** 96111
**Employees:** 50

**DUNS 22-754-4939**
## Three Cross (Imports) Ltd
6 Old Barn Farm Road, Wimborne, Dorset BH21 6SP
**Tel:** 01202-824531 **Fax:** 01202823056
**Web:** www.3xmotorcycles.com
**Reg No:** 1611379 **Estd:** 1982 Private Limited Company
**Line of Business:** Retail sale of sports goods, games and toys, stamps and coins
**Issued Capital:** £100
**Principals:** K L Davies (Managing), R L Davies
**US SIC:** 5941 **UK SIC:** 65400
**Auditors:** Wise & Co

|     | 31-12-13 | 31-12-12 | 31-12-11 |
| --- | --- | --- | --- |
| TA | 100 | 100 | 100 |
| NW | 100 | 100 | 100 |

**DUNS 34-641-4808**
## Three C's Support
110-114 Norman Road, London SE10 9QJ
**Tel:** 020-8269-4340
**Web:** www.threecs.co.uk
**Reg No:** 2768427 **Estd:** 1992 Private Limited Company
**Line of Business:** Disability services
**Trading Style:** Three C''s Support
**Directors:** R Coe, Ms D A Smith, P Craven, A Meyer, K I Wilson, J Collins, Miss R K Hill, Mrs A Everson
**Co. Secretary:** Stuart Ryland
**Responsibilities**
**Senior:** Brian Akintokun (Director), Trevor Branch (Manager)
**Admin:** Karen Melck (Office Manager)
**US SIC:** 8321 **UK SIC:** 96111
**Auditors:** Sayer Vincent
**Bankers:** Barclays Bank Plc (20-49-81)

|     | 31-03-14 | 31-03-13 | 31-03-12 |
| --- | --- | --- | --- |
| TO | 4,438,383 | 4,289,967 | 3,920,383 |
| P/L | (96,024) | (162,371) | (155,022) |
| NW | 2,284,546 | 2,282,995 | 2,251,827 |
| WC | 1,040,080 | 890,626 | 1,077,914 |
| Emp. | 122 | 126 | 120 |

**DUNS 29-646-7582**
## Three Elms Residential Home Ltd
(**Subsidiary of:** Wisteria Investments Ltd)
Three Elms, Station Road, Warrington, Cheshire WA5 2UG
**Tel:** 01925723274
**Web:** www.minstercaregroup.co.uk
**Reg No:** 1973070 **Estd:** 1985 Private Limited Company
**Line of Business:** Rest and retirement homes
**Trading Style:** Three Elms Residential Home
**Issued Capital:** £100
**Directors:** M S Patel, S S Patel
**Co. Secretary:** John Alflatt
**Responsibilities**
**Senior:** Linda Briscoe (CEO, Managing Director)
**US SIC:** 8321 **UK SIC:** 96111
**Auditors:** Moore Stephe

|     | 31-03-14 | 31-03-13 | 31-03-12 |
| --- | --- | --- | --- |
| TA | 2,632,982 | 2,632,982 | 2,632,982 |
| NW | 2,632,982 | 2,632,982 | 2,632,982 |

**DUNS 76-972-4998**
## Three Oceans Fish Co Ltd
Ocean House, Witty Street, Hull, North Humberside HU3 4TT
**Tel:** 01482-306000 **Fax:** 01482-306001
**Web:** www.3oceans.co.uk
**Reg No:** 2633844 **VAT No:** 598802094
**Estd:** 1992 Private Limited Company
**Line of Business:** Processing and preserving of fish and fish products
**Issued Capital:** £57,500
**Principals:** T D Rose (Managing), M H Jones, J S Dale, G D Druce, M Holmes
**Co. Secretary:** Mark Holmes
**Branches:** Hull
**US SIC:** 2092 **UK SIC:** 41501
**Auditors:** Dutton Moore
**Bankers:** National Westminster Bank Plc (60-21-40)

|     | 31-03-14 | 31-03-13 | 31-03-12 |
| --- | --- | --- | --- |
| TO | 20,169,785 | 19,457,526 | 23,532,775 |
| P/L | 476,304 | 665,531 | 793,575 |
| NW | 3,929,675 | 3,801,942 | 3,484,204 |
| WC | 4,067,134 | 3,939,103 | 2,610,079 |
| Emp. | 58 | 58 | 59 |

**DUNS 21-118-8693**
## Three Rivers District Council
Three Rivers House, Rickmansworth, Hertfordshire WD3 1RL
**Web:** www.threerivers.gov.uk
**Estd:** 2002
**Line of Business:** Local government
**Trading Style:** Watersmeet
**Principals:** R Clements (Chairman), Ms A Shaw
**Responsibilities**
**Senior:** Mike Colbert (communications manager), kemal butt (health and safety officer)
**Marketing:** Kevin Snow (Commercial Manager)
**IT:** Avni Patel (IT Manager)
**HR:** Terry Baldwin (Head of Human Resources)
**Operations:** Fred Alnutt (Elections Manager), Claire May (Principal Planning Officer)
**Purchasing:** Derek Hatcher (Procurement Officer)
**Branches:** Three Rivers District Council, Grove Crescent, Rickmansworth, Hertfordshire WD3 3JU
**US SIC:** 7011 **UK SIC:** 66500
**Employees:** 250

**DUNS 21-553-1364**
## Three Rivers Golf & Country Club
Stow Road, Purleigh, Chelmsford, Essex CM3 6RR
**Tel:** 01621828631
**Web:** www.stockbrook.com
**Estd:** 1973 Proprietorship
**Line of Business:** Other sporting activities not elsewhere classified
**Proprietor:** T Ceachey
**Responsibilities**
**Senior:** Fernando Teixeira (General Manager), F Teizeria (General Manager)
**Finance:** Lisa Stanislaus (Financial Manager)
**Marketing:** Jane Peachey (Marketing Director)
**IT:** Fernando Teixeira (General Manager)
**Health & Safety:** Fernando Teixeira (General Manager)
**Facilities:** Fernando Teixeira (General Manager)
**Purchasing:** Fernando Teixeira (General Manager)
**US SIC:** 7999 **UK SIC:** 97913
**Employees:** 50

**DUNS 23-042-4298**
## Three Shires Hospital
The Avenue, Cliftonville, Northampton, Northamptonshire NN1 5DR
**Tel:** 01604620311
**Web:** www.bmihealthcare.co.uk
**VAT No:** 729501630 **Estd:** 1982 Proprietorship
**Line of Business:** Hospitals
**Proprietor:** P Mcpartaln
**Responsibilities**
**Senior:** Dominics Bath (Proprietor), John Evanjelista (Manager), Jenny Masson (Director of Nursing)
**Finance:** Mollie Graham (Office Manager), Robert Henson (Financial Director), Sarah Martin (Finance Director)
**Marketing:** Jackie Brinicombe (Press Officer), L Dodwell (Sales & Marketing Manager)
**Sales:** L Dodwell (Sales & Marketing Manager)
**Admin:** Mollie Graham (Office Manager)
**IT:** Carolyn Hammond (Computer Manager)
**HR:** Shirley Adams (Human Resources Manager), Jenny Masson (Director of Nursing)
**Health & Safety:** Shirley Adams (Human Resources Manager)
**US SIC:** 8062 **UK SIC:** 95100
**Employees:** 200

**DUNS 21-033-4865**
## The Three Sisters
139 Cowgate, Edinburgh, Midlothian EH1 1JS
**Tel:** 0131-622-6801
**Web:** www.festival-inns.co.uk
**Estd:** 2004 Proprietorship
**Line of Business:** Hotels
**Proprietor:** J Podkowa
**US SIC:** 7011 **UK SIC:** 66500
**Employees:** 50

**DUNS 21-615-7533**
## Three Sisters
139 Cowgate, Edinburgh, Midlothian EH1 1JS
**Tel:** 01316226802
**Web:** www.thethreesistersbar.co.uk
**Estd:** 2011
**Line of Business:** Public house
**Responsibilities**
**Senior:** Donal Hurrell (General Manager)
**US SIC:** 5813 **UK SIC:** 66200
**Employees:** 50

**DUNS 21-593-8882**
## Three Swans Surgery
Rollestone Street, Salisbury, Wiltshire SP1 1DX
**Tel:** 01722333161
**Web:** www.3swanssurgery.nhs.uk
**Estd:** 2011 Partnership
**Line of Business:** Doctors
**Partners:** Mrs T Wakeman, Mrs T Wakeman
**Responsibilities**
**Senior:** DEBORAH VYAS (Doctor)
**US SIC:** 8011 **UK SIC:** 95300
**Employees:** 1

**DUNS 21-034-2776**
## Three Valleys Housing
Three Valleys House, Bramley Road, Long Eaton, Nottingham, Nottinghamshire NG10 3SX
**Tel:** 08003898083
**Web:** www.threevalleyshousing.com
**Estd:** 2012
**Line of Business:** Housing associations societies trusts & co-operatives
**Responsibilities**
**Senior:** Sue Coulson (Manager), Chris Rollins (Head Of Customer Contact)
**US SIC:** 8321 **UK SIC:** 96111
**Employees:** 50

**DUNS 76-971-6622**
## Threen House (Medicare) Ltd
29 Mattock Lane, London W5 5BH
**Tel:** 020-8840-2646 **Fax:** 0208-840-0611
**Reg No:** 2632994 **Estd:** 1991 Private Limited Company
**Line of Business:** Nursing homes
**Issued Capital:** £100
**Director:** P J Hannon
**Co. Secretary:** Alan Hannon
**Responsibilities**
**Finance:** Mohammed Lakha (Financial Director)
**IT:** Mohammed Lakha (Financial Director)
**US SIC:** 8051 **UK SIC:** 95100
**Auditors:** Michael Evans & Co

|     | 31-12-13 | 31-12-12 | 31-12-11 |
| --- | --- | --- | --- |
| TA | 2,373,072 | 2,009,436 | 2,380,041 |
| NW | 1,947,817 | 1,999,623 | 1,862,509 |
| WC | (615,990) | (553,613) | (614,116) |

**DUNS 73-426-0180**
## Threeways Holdings Ltd
Faenol Avenue, Abergele, Clwyd LL22 7HT
**Tel:** 01745822072
**Reg No:** 4699124 **Estd:** 2003 Private Limited Company
**Line of Business:** Management activities of holding companies
**Issued Capital:** £1,300,002
**Director:** J L Cunnah
**Co. Secretary:** Stavros Williams
**US SIC:** 6711 **UK SIC:** 83962

|     | 30-11-13 | 30-11-12 | 30-11-11 |
| --- | --- | --- | --- |
| TO | 23,577,659 | 22,253,405 | 18,517,412 |
| P/L | 426,386 | 345,047 | 273,251 |
| NW | 2,115,810 | 1,943,602 | 1,822,988 |
| WC | (315,167) | (500,679) | (493,803) |
| Emp. | 51 | 49 | 49 |

**DUNS 21-319-9826**
## Threeways Nursing Home
40 Beacon Road, Seaford, East Sussex BN25 2LT
**Web:** www.threewaysnh.co.uk
**Estd:** 2002 Partnership
**Line of Business:** Nursing homes
**Partners:** Mrs B Clarke, B Clarke, Mrs C Mills
**Branches:** Threeways Nursing Home, 95 Carlisle Road, Eastbourne, East Sussex BN20 7TB
**US SIC:** 8051 **UK SIC:** 95100
**Employees:** 117

**DUNS 49-727-1031**
## Thrifty Car Rental
Estate Road 7, South Humberside Industrial Esta, Grimsby, South Humberside DN31 2TP
**Web:** http://home2.btconnect.com
**Estd:** 1988
**Line of Business:** Vehicle rental (car)
**Proprietor:** M Godfrey
**Branches:** Thrifty Car Rental, Ipswich Road, Cardiff, South Glamorgan CF23 9AQ
**US SIC:** 7512 **UK SIC:** 84801
**Employees:** 250

**DUNS 21-296-2518**      Exp
## The Thrislington Engineering Co Ltd
Durham Way South, Aycliffe Industrial Estate, Newton Aycliffe, County Durham DL5 6SW
**Tel:** 01325301333
**Reg No:** 0425105 **VAT No:** 675372116
**Estd:** 1946 Private Limited Company
**Line of Business:** Partition manufacturers, wholesalers and installers
**Export Markets:** Middle East, E U, E Europe, Africa, U S A, Far East, Australia, New Zealand
**Issued Capital:** £4,384
**Director:** D A Beecroft
**Co. Secretary:** Peter Beecroft
**US SIC:** 2542, 2541
**UK SIC:** 31694, 46720
**Auditors:** Chipchase Nelson
**Bankers:** HSBC Bank plc (40-19-03)
**Employees:** 22
**Turnover:** £6,228,255

DUNS 21-122-0209
## Thrive Homes Ltd
Building 3, Hatters Lane, Watford, Hertfordshire WD18 8YG
**Tel:** 01923-693800
**Web:** www.thrivehomes.org.uk
**Reg No:** 0030398IP **VAT No:** 926633707
**Estd:** 2008
**Line of Business:** Housing associations societies trusts & co-operatives
**Responsibilities**
**Senior:** Elspeth Mackenzie *(Chief Executive)*
**US SIC:** 8699 **UK SIC:** 96902
**Auditors:** Mazars LLP
**Bankers:** Barclays Bank Plc (20-00-00)

| | 31-03-12 | 31-03-11 | 31-03-10 |
|---|---|---|---|
| TO | 19,288,000 | 18,357,000 | 18,113,000 |
| P/L | 3,531,000 | 5,068,000 | 5,936,000 |
| NW | 18,797,000 | 16,166,000 | 9,545,000 |
| WC | 3,655,000 | 2,333,000 | (2,317,000) |
| Emp. | 103 | 102 | 99 |

DUNS 77-499-6987
## Through Transport Mutual Services (U K) Ltd
International House, London EC3M 4ST
**Web:** www.ttclub.com
**Reg No:** 2979794 **Estd:** 1982 Private Limited Company
**Line of Business:** Insurance services
**Trading Style:** T T Group, Transport Mutual
**Issued Capital:** £5,000
**Directors:** C E Fenton, E S Chowdhury, B K Wood
**Co. Secretary:** Kieran Halpenny
**US SIC:** 6411 **UK SIC:** 83200
**Auditors:** Deloitte & Touche LLP
**Bankers:** HSBC Bank plc (40-04-12)

| | 31-12-13 | 31-12-12 | 31-12-11 |
|---|---|---|---|
| TO | 19,945,501 | 21,522,805 | 19,629,780 |
| P/L | 154,451 | 696,849 | 793,480 |
| NW | 1,045,953 | 2,927,408 | 2,401,268 |
| WC | 1,045,953 | 2,927,408 | 2,401,268 |

DUNS 22-285-0658 Imp
## Thunderhead Ltd
4th Floor Ingeni Building, London W1F 0DJ
**Tel:** 02074945000 **Fax:** 02074945001
**Web:** www.thunderhead.com
**Reg No:** 4303041 **VAT No:** 758193690
**Estd:** 2001 Private Limited Company
**Line of Business:** Representative office
**Issued Capital:** £1,000,000
**Directors:** P A Milton, Mrs J A Lumsden, G R Manchester
**Co. Secretary:** Paul Milton
**Responsibilities**
**Senior:** Laura Dear *(HR Assistant)*, Julie Holland *(Non Executive Director)*, Neal Keene *(Chairman)*, Lisa O' Reilly *(Vice President)*
**Finance:** Bill Youngberg *(Director, Financial Services)*
**Sales:** Celine Collins *(Business Development Executive)*, Rodney Frye *(Vice President, Sales)*
**IT:** Ray Gerber *(CTO)*
**Operations:** Chris Manton-Jones *(COO)*, Marc Plant *(SVP Global Service Operations)*
**Engineering:** Dean Heckman *(Senior Solution Architect)*
**US SIC:** 7399, 7379
**UK SIC:** 83954, 83940
**Auditors:** Deloitte LLP
**Bankers:** Allied Irish Bank (gb) (23-83-97)

| | 31-12-12 | 31-12-11 | 31-12-10 |
|---|---|---|---|
| TO | 39,811,052 | 35,732,508 | 25,669,441 |
| P/L | (1,275,299) | 3,792,838 | 5,086,325 |
| NW | 8,596,020 | 12,237,771 | 8,671,619 |
| WC | 8,258,939 | 12,254,165 | 9,465,706 |
| Emp. | 237 | 188 | 128 |

DUNS 21-773-8800
## Thundersley Primary School
Hart Road, Benfleet, Essex SS7 3PT
**Tel:** 01268793251
**Web:** www.thundersleyprimary.co.uk
**Estd:** 1981 Proprietorship
**Line of Business:** Schools (local authority)
**Proprietor:** S Mckay
**Responsibilities**
**Senior:** Emma Dawson *(Head Teacher)*
**US SIC:** 8211 **UK SIC:** 93200
**Employees:** 73

DUNS 50-451-7145 Imp-Exp
## Thurlby Thandar Instruments Ltd
**(Subsidiary of:** Aim-Tti Holdings Ltd)
2 Glebe Road, Huntingdon, Cambridgeshire PE29 7DR
**Tel:** 01480-412451 **Fax:** 01480-450409
**Web:** www.ttitest.com
**Reg No:** 2434384 **VAT No:** 330333800
**Estd:** 1999 Private Limited Company
**Line of Business:** Manufacturers of industrial instrumentation
**Export Markets:** E U, U S A, Canada, Far East
**Export Sales:** £2,706,102
**Trading Style:** T T I
**Issued Capital:** £838
**Principals:** J T Nichols *(Chairman)*, C T Wilding *(Technical)*, K I Pauley, M R Edwards
**Co. Secretary:** Derek Holley
**Responsibilities**
**Senior:** John Cornwell *(Manager)*
**Finance:** Mary Eborall *(Financial Controller)*
**HR:** Val Stacey *(Human Resources Coordinator)*
**Facilities:** Les Raven *(Maintenance Manager)*
**Purchasing:** Michael Gaadt *(Purchasing Manager)*
**US SIC:** 3823, 3679
**UK SIC:** 37100, 34542
**Auditors:** RSM Robson Rhodes LLP
**Bankers:** Lloyds TSB Bank plc (77-05-18)

| | 31-12-13 | 31-12-12 | 31-12-11 |
|---|---|---|---|
| TO | 9,868,623 | 11,292,262 | 10,628,836 |
| P/L | 1,010,531 | 1,272,320 | 1,117,200 |
| NW | 4,236,759 | 4,280,233 | 4,115,845 |
| WC | 3,551,807 | 3,584,272 | 3,445,850 |
| Emp. | 101 | 106 | 100 |

DUNS 21-714-6653
## Thurlestone Estates Ltd
Hope Beach House, Kingsbridge, Devon TQ7 3HP
**Tel:** 01548-560382 **Fax:** 01548461069
**Web:** www.thurlestone.co.uk
**Reg No:** 0271793 **VAT No:** 141828668
**Estd:** 1937 Private Limited Company
**Line of Business:** Hotels
**Trading Style:** Thurlestone Hotel
**Issued Capital:** £10,449
**Principals:** D W Grose *(Managing)*, Ms J George *(Managing)*, G R Grose *(Managing)*, M D Grose, S E Grose, R Cotton Obe Fih, Mrs L C Harrison, C M Clapp
**Co. Secretary:** Peter Wyatt
**Responsibilities**
**Admin:** Teresa Hamilton *(Office Manager)*
**Facilities:** Roland Johns *(Facilities Manager)*
**Purchasing:** Piers Rogers *(Purchasing Manager)*
**US SIC:** 7011 **UK SIC:** 66500
**Auditors:** PricewaterhouseCoopers
**Bankers:** Barclays Bank Plc (20-68-10)

| | 31-10-13 | 31-10-12 | 31-10-11 |
|---|---|---|---|
| TO | 5,774,493 | 5,565,940 | 5,964,904 |
| P/L | 700,228 | 654,121 | 621,025 |
| NW | 8,424,674 | 11,322,898 | 10,872,886 |
| WC | (1,047,587) | (1,615,426) | (790,061) |
| Emp. | 115 | 95 | 103 |

DUNS 28-881-7604
## Thurlow Educational Trust
70 Thurlow Park Road, London SE21 8HZ
**Tel:** 020-8670-5865 **Fax:** 020-8761-9159
**Web:** www.rosemeadprepschool.org.uk
**Reg No:** 1186165 **Estd:** 1974 Private Company Limited By Guarantee
**Line of Business:** General secondary education
**Trading Style:** Rosemead Preparatory School
**Directors:** Ms F M Pearson, S Thorogood, B I Ellis, Ms A E Crane, K A Volz, A A Clark, C G Broadbent, T Shimazaki
**Co. Secretary:** Raymond Sawyer
**Responsibilities**
**Senior:** Arthur Bray *(Headmaster)*, Sheldon Clair *(Manager)*, Moyra Horseman *(Manager)*, Lindsey Mallors *(Board of Directors)*, Michael Mittelman *(Manager)*, Alexandra Proctor Wood *(Director)*, Susan Sawyer *(Board of Directors)*, Oliver Wyncoll *(Board of Directors)*
**US SIC:** 8211 **UK SIC:** 93200
**Auditors:** Landau Baker & Co
**Bankers:** Barclays Bank Plc (20-94-67)

| | 31-08-14 | 31-08-13 | 31-08-12 |
|---|---|---|---|
| TO | 3,786,575 | 3,506,437 | 3,191,656 |
| P/L | 509,775 | 429,610 | 343,637 |
| NW | 3,013,796 | 2,454,021 | 1,908,927 |
| WC | (208,689) | (419,556) | (241,904) |
| Emp. | 56 | 51 | 50 |

DUNS 34-708-8887
## Thurlow Nunn (Jv) Ltd
**(Subsidiary of:** George Thurlow & Sons (Holdings) Ltd)
Wisbech Road, Littleport, Littleport, Ely, Cambridgeshire CB6 1RA
**Tel:** 01353863038 **Fax:** 01353864070
**Web:** www.tnsgroup.co.uk
**Reg No:** 5513039 **Estd:** 2004 Private Limited Company
**Line of Business:** Plant dealers
**Trading Style:** Thurlow Nunn (Jv) Ltd
**Issued Capital:** £1,700,000
**Directors:** J R Thurlow, Motors Directors Limited, Motors Secretaries Limited, S N Grylls, S Bottomley, G B Osborn
**Co. Secretary:** Philip Addinall
**US SIC:** 5084, 5521, 7539, 5531
**UK SIC:** 61490, 65100, 67100

| | 31-12-13 | 31-12-12 | 31-12-11 |
|---|---|---|---|
| TO | 83,378,000 | 74,447,000 | 58,811,000 |
| P/L | 951,000 | 525,000 | 460,000 |
| NW | 3,925,000 | 3,209,000 | 2,882,000 |
| WC | 2,814,000 | 2,829,000 | 2,542,000 |
| Emp. | 262 | 272 | 238 |

DUNS 21-129-6108
## Thurrock Borough Council
Civic Offices, New Road, Grays, Essex RM17 6SL
**Web:** www.thurrock.gov.uk
**Estd:** 2013
**Line of Business:** Housing advice
**Trading Style:** Compass Children's Centre, Purfleet Community Forum
**Principals:** K Barnes *(Chairman)*, D Luck, P Woodrow
**Responsibilities**
**Senior:** Barbara Brownley *(Head Of Housing)*
**Finance:** Noel Moloney *(Corporate Head of Services)*
**Marketing:** Andy Lever *(Marketing Media Coordinator)*
**IT:** Steve Abbott *(Head of IT)*
**HR:** Susan Moretta *(Human Resources Manager)*
**Health & Safety:** Gavin Dennett *(Health & Safety Officer)*
**Facilities:** Elaine Field *(Facilities Manager)*
**Operations:** Bill Newman *(Head of Environmental)*
**Branches:** Thurrock Borough Council, 38 St. Cedds Court, Crammavill Street, Grays, Essex RM16 2BA
**US SIC:** 9121 **UK SIC:** 91110
**Employees:** 2,000

DUNS 23-789-9096
## Thurrock Community Leisure Ltd
Blackshots Lane, Grays, Essex RM16 2JU
**Web:** www.impulseleisure.co.uk
**Reg No:** 3782811 **Estd:** 1999 Private Limited Company
**Line of Business:** Operation of sports arenas and stadiums
**Directors:** B J Grayston, C D Seamark, Ms L Miller, Mrs J Muggeridge, W A Warner, D R Stanton, T Ojetola, A W Fish
**Co. Secretary:** Jonathan Tatchell
**Responsibilities**
**Senior:** Holly Barton *(Life guard)*, Geoffrey Bifield *(Manager)*
**Health & Safety:** Holly Barton *(Life guard)*
**Branches:** Thurrock Community Leisure Ltd, Springhouse Road, Stanford-Le-Hope, Essex SS17 7NB
**US SIC:** 7941, 7999
**UK SIC:** 97911, 97913
**Bankers:** National Westminster Bank Plc (60-09-11)

| | 31-03-14 | 31-03-13 | 31-03-12 |
|---|---|---|---|
| TO | 5,223,413 | 5,157,167 | 5,218,001 |
| P/L | (21,110) | (37,311) | 388,268 |
| NW | 744,985 | 689,095 | 668,406 |
| WC | 928,529 | 860,122 | 1,072,348 |
| Emp. | 130 | 128 | N/A |

DUNS 21-524-4539
## The Thurrock Hotel
Ship Lane, Purfleet, Essex RM19 1YN
**Tel:** 01708860222
**Web:** www.thurrockhotel.co.uk
**Estd:** 2010 Proprietorship
**Line of Business:** Hotels
**Proprietor:** H South
**Responsibilities**
**Senior:** Trisha Bishop *(Food & Beverage Manager)*, Daniel Mack *(Operations Manager)*
**Marketing:** Tara Bishop *(Marketing Manager)*
**Sales:** Mel Myers *(Sales Manager)*
**Purchasing:** Govind Hirani *(Purchasing Manager)*
**US SIC:** 7011 **UK SIC:** 66500
**Employees:** 50

DUNS 29-628-3435
## Thursdays (Holdings) Ltd
**(Subsidiary of:** Sentinel Capital Partners Llc)
6 Bedford Street, London WC2E 9HZ
**Tel:** 08446920229
**Web:** www.tgifridays.co.uk
**Reg No:** 1954346 **Estd:** 2002 Private Limited Company
**Line of Business:** Restaurant - american
**Issued Capital:** £2
**Directors:** S A Greener, Ms K M Forrester
**Responsibilities**
**Senior:** Liegh Dolby *(General Manager)*, Kathryn Kotel *(Manager)*, Elaine Ryan *(Manager)*
**US SIC:** 5812 **UK SIC:** 66110
**Auditors:** Deloitte LLP

| | 29-12-13 | 31-12-12 | 25-12-11 |
|---|---|---|---|
| TO | 161,783,000 | 147,703,000 | 123,924,000 |
| P/L | 8,795,000 | 7,456,000 | 7,376,000 |
| NW | 28,757,000 | 21,116,000 | 14,804,000 |
| WC | (6,517,000) | (11,071,000) | (12,084,000) |
| Emp. | 2,540 | 2,319 | 2,073 |

DUNS 67-227-1202
## Thursdays (Uk) Ltd
**(Subsidiary of:** Sentinel Capital Partners Llc)
253-254 Capability Green, Luton, Bedfordshire LU1 3LU
**Tel:** 08448469944
**Web:** www.tgifridays.co.uk
**Reg No:** 6034603 **Estd:** 2006 Private Limited Company
**Line of Business:** Licensed restaurants
**Issued Capital:** £1
**Directors:** Ms K Forrester, S A Greener
**Responsibilities**
**Senior:** Kathryn Kotel *(Manager)*
**US SIC:** 5812 **UK SIC:** 66110
**Auditors:** Deloitte LLP

| | 29-12-13 | 31-12-12 | 25-12-11 |
|---|---|---|---|
| TO | 161,783,000 | 147,703,000 | 123,924,000 |
| P/L | 11,788,000 | 10,893,000 | 10,979,000 |
| NW | 26,550,000 | 17,675,000 | 10,127,000 |
| WC | (8,044,000) | (15,803,000) | (20,112,000) |
| Emp. | 2,540 | 2,319 | 2,073 |

DUNS 21-076-0210
## Thursfields Llp
14 Church Street, Kidderminster, Worcestershire DY10 2AH
**Web:** www.thursfields.com
**Reg No:** 0355657OC **Estd:** 2010
**Line of Business:** Legal Services
**US SIC:** 8111 **UK SIC:** 83500

| | 30-04-13 | 30-04-12 | 30-04-11 |
|---|---|---|---|
| TA | 2,422,739 | 2,424,241 | 2,186,472 |
| WC | 357,227 | 326,665 | (329,655) |

DUNS 28-896-6716
## Thursford Enterprises Ltd
**(Subsidiary of:** The Thursford Collection)
The Street, Thursford, Fakenham, Norfolk NR21 0AS
**Tel:** 01328-878477
**Web:** www.thursford.com
**Reg No:** 1321878 **Estd:** 1977 Private Limited Company
**Line of Business:** Museums
**Issued Capital:** £300,000
**Directors:** J G Purling, Mrs A Preston, A N Wells, C N Long, J R Cushing
**Co. Secretary:** Ms Geraldine Rye
**US SIC:** 8411 **UK SIC:** 97700
**Auditors:** Price Bailey

| | 31-12-13 | 31-12-12 | 31-12-11 |
|---|---|---|---|
| TO | 4,463,105 | N/A | 4,215,826 |
| NW | 300,000 | 300,000 | 100 |
| WC | (483,213) | (607,168) | (1,006,627) |

DUNS 21-306-7986 Imp-Exp
## Thurston Group Ltd
**(Subsidiary of:** Thurston Holdings Ltd)
Quarry Hill Industrial Estate, Hawking Croft Road, Wakefield, West Yorkshire WF4 6AJ
**Tel:** 01924-265461 **Fax:** 01924-280246
**Web:** www.thurstongroup.co.uk
**Reg No:** 0998540 **VAT No:** 734018947
**Estd:** 1970 Private Limited Company
**Line of Business:** Manufacturers of containers
**Export Markets:** Western Europe
**Trading Style:** Thurston Group Ltd?, Thurston Building Systems
**Issued Capital:** £51,000
**Principals:** J L Petch *(Managing)*, E Mould *(Financial)*, G B Thurston *(Sales)*
**Co. Secretary:** David Harvey
**Branches:** Thurston Group Ltd, 251 Whitehall Rd, Leeds, West Yorkshire LS12 6ER
**US SIC:** 3999, 3443
**UK SIC:** 49590, 32051
**Auditors:** Grant Thornton UK LLP
**Bankers:** Barclays Bank Plc (20-37-13)

| | 31-10-13 | 31-10-12 | 31-10-11 |
|---|---|---|---|
| TO | 21,232,670 | 29,034,353 | 18,623,566 |
| P/L | 458,875 | 108,986 | 20,712 |
| NW | 3,569,896 | 3,194,158 | 3,099,955 |
| WC | 3,312,802 | 2,971,803 | 2,701,846 |
| Emp. | 209 | 229 | 183 |

DUNS 21-816-8763 Imp-Exp
## Thwaites Ltd
Welsh Road Works Cubbington, Leamington Spa, Warwickshire CV32 7UB
**Tel:** 01926422471
**Web:** www.thwaitesdumpers.co.uk
**Reg No:** 0387579 **VAT No:** 272334078
**Estd:** 1940 Private Limited Company
**Line of Business:** Agricultural machinery sales service and repair
**Export Markets:** Worldwide
**Issued Capital:** £11,520

**Principals:** The Lord M Dulverton (*Chairman and Managing*), I C Brown (*Sales*), The Honourable R I Wills, A E Earles
**Co. Secretary:** Steven Trotman
**Responsibilities**
**Finance:** Trevor Round (*Financial Controller*)
**HR:** Trevor Round (*Financial Controller*)
**US SIC:** 3534 **UK SIC:** 32553
**Auditors:** Saffery Champness
**Bankers:** HSBC Bank plc (40-27-06)

|     | 31-08-13 | 31-08-12 | 31-08-11 |
|-----|----------|----------|----------|
| TO  | 35,552,000 | 35,755,000 | 33,451,000 |
| P/L | 4,149,000 | 3,678,000 | 3,572,000 |
| NW  | 18,375,000 | 17,215,000 | 16,187,000 |
| WC  | 16,236,000 | 15,490,000 | 14,573,000 |
| Emp. | 154 | 160 | 145 |

---

**DUNS 58-112-3817**    **Imp**
## Thyson Technology Ltd
(**Subsidiary of:** Thyson Technology Holdings Ltd)
2 Burnell Road, Ellesmere Port, Cheshire CH65 5EX
**Tel:** 01513555594 **Fax:** 01513557961
**Web:** www.thyson.com
**Reg No:** 2905789 **VAT No:** 643602358
**Estd:** 1994 Private Limited Company
**Line of Business:** Manufacture of electronic industrial process control equipment
**Issued Capital:** £78
**Directors:** I Camp, D M Barrowclough
**Co. Secretary:** Roger Brown
**US SIC:** 3823, 8911
**UK SIC:** 37100, 83701
**Bankers:** National Westminster Bank Plc (01-09-17)

|     | 31-03-14 | 31-03-13 | 31-03-12 |
|-----|----------|----------|----------|
| TO  | 9,924,000 | N/A | N/A |
| P/L | 1,322,000 | N/A | N/A |
| NW  | 2,861,000 | 1,970,118 | 1,560,973 |
| WC  | 2,520,000 | 1,711,867 | 2,236,929 |
| Emp. | 49 | N/A | N/A |

---

**DUNS 28-849-0774**    **Imp**
## Thyssenkrupp Elevator Uk Ltd
(**Subsidiary of:** Thyssenkrupp Ag)
2nd Floor The Lookout, Nottingham, Nottinghamshire NG7 2UL
**Tel:** 01159868213 **Fax:** 01159-861549
**Web:** www.thyssenkrupp.com
**Reg No:** 0688790 **VAT No:** 772726995
**Estd:** 1961 Private Limited Company
**Line of Business:** Manufacture of other transport equipment not elsewhere classified
**Issued Capital:** £2,300,000
**Directors:** K P Taylor, Dr W Nehring, G Burits
**Responsibilities**
**Senior:** Alexander Kocherscheidt (*Director CFO*), R Mcglory (*Manager*)
**IT:** Terry Watson (*Application Support Manager*)
**HR:** Rod Graham (*Personnel Manager*)
**Health & Safety:** Jennifer Ward (*Health & Safety Officer*)
**Branches:** Thyssenkrupp Elevator Uk Ltd, Prysmain House, Dew Lane, Eastleigh, Hampshire SO50 9PX
**US SIC:** 7699 **UK SIC:** 67303
**Auditors:** KPMG LLP

|     | 30-09-13 | 30-09-12 | 30-09-11 |
|-----|----------|----------|----------|
| TO  | 54,363,000 | 56,784,000 | 56,408,000 |
| P/L | (1,560,000) | (3,729,000) | (5,336,000) |
| NW  | 4,890,000 | 5,883,000 | 4,305,000 |
| WC  | 3,972,000 | 5,605,000 | 4,847,000 |
| Emp. | 499 | 582 | 620 |

---

**DUNS 76-247-6489**
## Thyssenkrupp Encasa Ltd
(**Subsidiary of:** Thyssenkrupp Ag)
Unit 3 Eagle Court, Preston Farm Business Park, Stockton-On-Tees, Cleveland TS18 3TB
**Tel:** 01642704850 **Fax:** 01642-766590
**Web:** www.tkencasa.co.uk
**Reg No:** 2541007 **VAT No:** 546965985
**Estd:** 1989 Private Limited Company
**Line of Business:** Lifts (maintenance and repair)
**Export Sales:** £4,481
**Trading Style:** Thyssenkrupp Encasa Limited
**Issued Capital:** £6,666
**Directors:** M A Carneiro, M Whetton
**Responsibilities**
**Senior:** Diane Ingham (*Manager*)
**Branches:** Thyssenkrupp Encasa Ltd, Avonlea Road, Sale, Cheshire M33 4HY
**US SIC:** 3534, 5084
**UK SIC:** 32553, 61490
**Auditors:** KPMG LLP
**Bankers:** Yorkshire Bank Plc (05-06-01)

|     | 30-09-13 | 30-09-12 | 30-09-11 |
|-----|----------|----------|----------|
| TO  | 9,127,217 | 10,101,890 | 9,120,906 |
| P/L | 5,039 | (810,225) | (733,508) |
| NW  | 179,288 | (508,229) | 437,496 |
| WC  | 241,380 | (112,251) | 167,223 |
| Emp. | 77 | 80 | 82 |

---

**DUNS 21-029-4211**    **Imp-Exp**
## Thyssenkrupp Materials (Uk) Ltd
(**Subsidiary of:** Thyssenkrupp Ag)
Coxs Lane, Cradley Heath, West Midlands B64 5QU
**Tel:** 01384-563-100 **Fax:** 01384-563-199
**Web:** www.thyssenkruppmaterials.co.uk
**Reg No:** 0645702 **VAT No:** 695967844
**Estd:** 1959 Private Limited Company
**Line of Business:** Aluminium stockholders
**Export Sales:** £12,634,000
**Trading Style:** Vetchberry Steels, Metalfast, Alserco
**Issued Capital:** £12,032,469
**Directors:** T R Sargeant, Mrs I I Henne
**Co. Secretary:** William Street
**Responsibilities**
**Senior:** Jürgen Funke (*Director*), Joachim Limberg (*Manager*), Steve Murray (*Head of Operations*), Claude Weber (*Manager*)
**Finance:** Bob Baggaley (*Head of Sales & Marketing*)
**Marketing:** Bob Baggaley (*Head of Sales & Marketing*)
**Sales:** Bob Baggaley (*Head of Sales & Marketing*)
**IT:** Jamie Spittle (*IT Manager*)
**Health & Safety:** Bob Platten (*Quality Manager*)
**Facilities:** Steve Murray (*Head of Operations*)
**Operations:** Bob Baggaley (*Head of Sales & Marketing*), Bob Platten (*Quality Manager*)
**Purchasing:** Phil Ralph (*Purchasing Manager*)
**Fleet:** Steve Murray (*Head of Operations*)
**Branches:** Thyssenkrupp Materials (Uk) Ltd, 331 Charles Street, Glasgow, Lanarkshire G21 2RD
**US SIC:** 5051, 5161
**UK SIC:** 61200
**Auditors:** PricewaterhouseCoopers LLP
**Bankers:** The Royal Bank Of Scotland Plc (16-00-83)

|     | 30-09-13 | 30-09-12 | 30-09-11 |
|-----|----------|----------|----------|
| TO  | 160,758,000 | 151,220,000 | 153,339,000 |
| P/L | 1,855,000 | 2,035,000 | 2,643,000 |
| NW  | 56,590,000 | 26,689,000 | 26,883,000 |
| WC  | 42,873,000 | 16,150,000 | 15,852,000 |
| Emp. | 410 | 381 | 357 |

---

**DUNS 50-511-5360**    **Imp-Exp**
## Thyssenkrupp Woodhead Ltd
(**Subsidiary of:** Thyssenkrupp Ag)
177 Kirkstall Road, Leeds, West Yorkshire LS4 2AQ
**Tel:** 01132-441202
**Web:** www.thyssenkrupp.com
**Reg No:** 2479379 **VAT No:** 545440550
**Estd:** 1990 Private Limited Company
**Line of Business:** Manufacturers of springs
**Export Markets:** E U
**Export Sales:** £9,723,000
**Trading Style:** Thyssenkrupp Bilstein Woodhead Ltd
**Issued Capital:** £7,610,000
**Director:** J A Sandground
**Co. Secretary:** Peter Bearfield
**Responsibilities**
**Senior:** Norman Charlton (*Despatch Manager*)
**IT:** Glynn Taylor (*IT Manager*)
**Health & Safety:** Lionel Theobald (*Facilities Manager*)
**Facilities:** Lionel Theobald (*Facilities Manager*)
**Purchasing:** Norman Charlton (*Despatch Manager*)
**Branches:** Sheffield
**US SIC:** 3452 **UK SIC:** 31371
**Auditors:** PricewaterhouseCoopers LLP
**Bankers:** National Westminster Bank Plc (60-60-05)

|     | 30-09-13 | 30-09-12 | 30-09-11 |
|-----|----------|----------|----------|
| TO  | 21,590,000 | 23,530,000 | 25,510,000 |
| P/L | 3,596,000 | 2,706,000 | 3,629,000 |
| NW  | 12,815,000 | 11,864,000 | 13,212,000 |
| WC  | 6,551,000 | 4,569,000 | 6,817,000 |
| Emp. | 99 | 102 | 102 |

---

**DUNS 22-096-6274**
## Ti Automotive Ltd
(**Subsidiary of:** Ti Fluid Systems Ltd)
46-50 Kingsgate, Cascade Way, Oxford Business Park South, Oxford, Oxfordshire OX4 2SU
**Tel:** 01865-871820
**Web:** www.tiautomotive.com
**Reg No:** 4097913 **VAT No:** 773657783
**Estd:** 2000 Private Limited Company
**Line of Business:** Other engineering activities
**Issued Capital:** £13,000,000
**Directors:** T J Knutson, T D Edwards, W L Kozyra
**Co. Secretary:** David Ludlow

---

**Responsibilities**
**Senior:** Timothy Guerriero (*General Counsel and Company So*), Ronald Hampel (*Manager*), Ken Langone (*Manager*)
**US SIC:** 8911, 5531
**UK SIC:** 83701, 65100
**Auditors:** PricewaterhouseCoopers LLP
Following financial data are In thousands

|     | 31-12-13 | 31-12-12 | 31-12-11 |
|-----|----------|----------|----------|
| TO  | 2,192,587 | 1,985,628 | 1,810,988 |
| P/L | 173,817 | 127,433 | 117,795 |
| NW  | 18,218 | 68,090 | 304,875 |
| WC  | 269,616 | 213,750 | 242,710 |
| Emp. | 20,010 | 22,115 | 17,360 |

---

**DUNS 76-998-4014**
## Ti Callenberg Uk Ltd
(**Subsidiary of:** Wilh. Wilhelmsen Holding Asa)
2 Buchanan Gate, Stepps, Glasgow, Lanarkshire G33 6FB
**Web:** www.ti-marinecontracting.no
**Reg No:** 0134398SC **VAT No:** 596910202
**Estd:** 1991 Private Limited Company
**Line of Business:** Other building installation
**Export Sales:** £608,174
**Trading Style:** Ticon Insulation Limited
**Issued Capital:** £1,000
**Directors:** J P Traaholt, T Stark, T Flo, P J Bannerman
**Co. Secretary:** David Stark
**Responsibilities**
**Senior:** Rolf Andresen (*Manager*), Tor Oiseth (*Manager*), Anstein Sorensen (*Manager*)
**Branches:** TI Callenberg Uk Ltd, B A E Systems Ltd, Michaelson Rd, Barrow-In-Furness, Cumbria LA14 1AF
**US SIC:** 1796, 1742
**UK SIC:** 50400
**Auditors:** McLay McAlister & McGibbon
**Bankers:** The Royal Bank Of Scotland Plc (83-21-16)

|     | 31-12-13 | 31-12-12 | 31-12-11 |
|-----|----------|----------|----------|
| TO  | 19,014,606 | 16,442,034 | 11,658,678 |
| P/L | 2,132,914 | 1,836,347 | 1,168,814 |
| NW  | 2,504,305 | 4,889,872 | 3,488,888 |
| WC  | 2,105,521 | 4,442,598 | 3,026,713 |
| Emp. | 149 | 138 | 102 |

---

**DUNS 34-776-3919**    **Exp**
## Tibard Holdings Ltd
Tibard House, Globe Lane Industrial Estate, Broadway, Dukinfield, Cheshire SK16 4UU
**Tel:** 01613-421000 **Fax:** 01613-432016
**Web:** www.tibard.co.uk
**Reg No:** 5577238 **Estd:** 2005 Private Limited Company
**Line of Business:** Management activities of holding companies
**Export Sales:** £164,017
**Issued Capital:** £101
**Directors:** Mrs C D Shacklady, R C Shonfeld, I D Mitchell, M D Shonfeld, J C Shonfeld
**Co. Secretary:** Mrs Susan Shonfeld
**Responsibilities**
**Senior:** Stephen Shore (*Warehouse Manager*)
**US SIC:** 6711 **UK SIC:** 83962
**Auditors:** Hurst & Co Accountants LLP
**Bankers:** National Westminster Bank Plc (60-08-31)

|     | 31-08-13 | 31-08-12 | 31-08-11 |
|-----|----------|----------|----------|
| TO  | 8,348,551 | 8,769,087 | 7,969,378 |
| P/L | 278,324 | 265,648 | 112,208 |
| NW  | (1,626,004) | (1,797,444) | (1,997,957) |
| WC  | (1,281,250) | (1,288,267) | (1,382,305) |
| Emp. | 85 | 79 | 71 |

---

**DUNS 34-733-9124**    **Imp**
## The Tibbetts Group Ltd
Unit 1h-1j Vantage Business Park, Bloxham Road, Banbury, Oxfordshire OX16 9UX
**Tel:** 01295-257010
**Web:** www.tibbettsgroup.co.uk
**Reg No:** 5536038 **Estd:** 2005 Private Limited Company
**Line of Business:** Other business activities not elsewhere classified
**Export Sales:** £23,473,325
**Issued Capital:** £100
**Directors:** S Wilkinson, Ms P A Tibbetts, J P Tibbetts, H J Tibbetts
**US SIC:** 7399 **UK SIC:** 83954

|     | 30-04-14 | 30-04-13 | 30-04-12 |
|-----|----------|----------|----------|
| TO  | 32,230,296 | 23,981,623 | 25,365,002 |
| P/L | 4,425,104 | 3,487,798 | 3,441,741 |
| NW  | 6,389,561 | 5,832,976 | 4,184,631 |
| WC  | 5,547,671 | 4,526,024 | 3,119,987 |
| Emp. | 70 | 49 | 48 |

---

**DUNS 23-884-9058**    **Imp-Exp**
## Tibco Software Ltd
(**Subsidiary of:** Tibco Software Inc.)
Braywick Gate, Braywick Road, Maidenhead, Berkshire SL6 1DA
**Tel:** 0162-878-6800 **Fax:** 0162-878-6877
**Web:** www.tibco.com
**Reg No:** 3875990 **Estd:** 1999 Private Limited Company

---

**Line of Business:** Computer software (development)
**Trading Style:** Tibco
**Issued Capital:** £3
**Directors:** A E Kolar, Ms N Janson-Ebeling
**Co. Secretary:** William Hughes
**Responsibilities**
**Senior:** Todd Bradley (*President*), Tom Lafferty (*Executive Vice President*), Vivek Ranadive (*Chief Executive Officer*)
**Finance:** Jim Johnson (*Chief Finance Officer*), Bennett Smith (*Finance Director*)
**Marketing:** Lori Wright (*Chief Marketing Officer*)
**Sales:** Mark Rattley (*Sales Manager*)
**IT:** Sam Ismail (*IT Manager*)
**Operations:** Murray Rode (*Chief Operations Officer*)
**Branches:** Tibco Software Ltd, City Gate East, Tollhouse Hill, Nottingham, Nottinghamshire NG1 5FS
**US SIC:** 7379 **UK SIC:** 83940
**Auditors:** PricewaterhouseCoopers LLP
**Bankers:** The Royal Bank Of Scotland Plc (15-10-00)

|     | 30-11-13 | 30-11-12 | 30-11-11 |
|-----|----------|----------|----------|
| TA  | 100,915,000 | 127,694,000 | 122,450,000 |
| P/L | 18,210,000 | 7,632,000 | 6,845,000 |
| NW  | 91,151,000 | 84,966,000 | 81,134,000 |
| WC  | 90,983,000 | 84,973,000 | 81,560,000 |
| Emp. | 315 | 310 | 242 |

---

**DUNS 67-234-8836**    **Imp**
## Tibra Trading Europe Ltd
(**Subsidiary of:** Tibra Capital Pty Limited)
5 Aldermanbury Square, London EC2V 7HR
**Tel:** 02076000643
**Web:** www.tibracareers.com
**Reg No:** 6061713 **Estd:** 2007 Private Limited Company
**Line of Business:** Other business activities not elsewhere classified
**Issued Capital:** £8,100,000
**Directors:** C T Norwood, H Hesse, T J Berry
**Co. Secretary:** Timothy Knipe
**US SIC:** 7399 **UK SIC:** 83954

|     | 30-06-13 | 30-06-12 | 30-06-11 |
|-----|----------|----------|----------|
| TO  | 18,343,000 | 21,636,000 | 16,508,000 |
| P/L | 3,957,000 | 5,653,000 | 857,000 |
| NW  | 34,272,000 | 31,808,000 | 30,767,000 |
| WC  | 30,445,000 | 27,604,000 | 25,872,000 |
| Emp. | N/A | 57 | 81 |

---

**DUNS 51-996-6506**
## Tican (Chilled) Ltd
(**Subsidiary of:** Andelsselskabet Tican A.M.B.A.)
Stockton Close, Walsall, West Midlands WS2 8LH
**Tel:** 01420560000 **Fax:** 01922644990
**Web:** www.ticanchilled.co.uk
**Reg No:** 4003353 **Estd:** 2010 Private Limited Company
**Line of Business:** Meat wholesalers
**Issued Capital:** £100,000
**Directors:** A Jones, S R Halliday, J Wilkie
**Co. Secretary:** Matthew Mcgeough
**Responsibilities**
**Senior:** James Dugdale (*Watrehouse Manager*)
**US SIC:** 5147 **UK SIC:** 61700
**Bankers:** Den Danske Bank Aktieselskab (30-12-81)

|     | 29-09-13 | 30-09-12 | 02-09-11 |
|-----|----------|----------|----------|
| TO  | 56,055,000 | 53,284,000 | 46,969,000 |
| P/L | 1,350,000 | 1,000,000 | 745,000 |
| NW  | 5,121,000 | 3,869,000 | 2,873,000 |
| WC  | 5,052,000 | 3,605,000 | 2,559,000 |
| Emp. | 74 | 69 | 67 |

---

**DUNS 77-497-6716**
## Ticco Foods Ltd
(**Subsidiary of:** Ticco Foods Holdings Ltd)
Unit B2y, Slough, Berkshire SL3 0BQ
**Tel:** 01753-685444 **Fax:** 01753-689813
**Web:** www.ticco.co.uk
**Reg No:** 2978769 **Estd:** 1994 Private Limited Company
**Line of Business:** Bakers and confectioners supplies
**Trading Style:** Ticco Foods Limited
**Issued Capital:** £103
**Director:** J K Sanghera
**Co. Secretary:** Paolo Solari
**Responsibilities**
**Senior:** Paul Lelew (*Manager*), Huguette Tanner (*Managing Director PA*)
**Admin:** Mia Hutchings (*Personal Assistant to CEO*)
**US SIC:** 5145, 5812, 5149
**UK SIC:** 61700, 66110
**Auditors:** The McCay Partnership

|     | 31-12-13 | 31-10-12 | 31-12-11 |
|-----|----------|----------|----------|
| TO  | 10,961,014 | 10,044,726 | 9,000,596 |
| P/L | 292,246 | 289,923 | 391,723 |
| NW  | 239,405 | 134,761 | 67,311 |
| WC  | 860,328 | (454,876) | (61,998) |
| Emp. | 56 | 63 | 25 |

**DUNS 22-554-7322**

## Tice & Son Ltd
Wimborne Road, Wimborne, Dorset BH21 1NW
**Web:** www.tice.co.uk
**Reg No:** 0659950 **Estd:** 1960 Private Limited Company
**Line of Business:** Maintenance and repair of motor vehicles
**Trading Style:** Tice & Sons
**Issued Capital:** £250,000
**Principals:** G M Tice (Managing), M J Tice, Ms M J Tice
**Co. Secretary:** Geoffrey Tice
**Branches:** Tice & Son Ltd, Blandford Heights, Blandford Forum, Dorset DT11 7TH
**US SIC:** 7539, 5411
**UK SIC:** 67100, 64100
**Auditors:** Saffery Champness
**Bankers:** Barclays Bank Plc (20-68-79)

|    | 31-12-13 | 31-12-12 | 31-12-11 |
|----|----------|----------|----------|
| TA | 899,319 | 798,203 | 641,187 |
| NW | 627,865 | 607,313 | 472,647 |
| WC | 444,230 | 416,931 | 238,237 |

**DUNS 21-600-0954**

## Ticket Line
21-31 Oldham Street, Manchester M1 1JG
**Tel:** 08719781271
**Web:** www.ticketline.co.uk
**Estd:** 1998 Partnership
**Line of Business:** Other entertainment activities
**Partners:** C Mableson, P Betesh
**US SIC:** 8999 **UK SIC:** 83954
**Employees:** 100

**DUNS 28-972-4718**

## Ticketgrange Ltd
36-42 Lumley Road, Skegness, Lincolnshire PE25 3NG
**Tel:** 01754763312
**Reg No:** 1738825 **Estd:** 1983 Private Limited Company
**Line of Business:** Gambling and betting activities
**Issued Capital:** £300
**Director:** R Harris
**Co. Secretary:** John Harris
**US SIC:** 7999 **UK SIC:** 97913
**Auditors:** Romon Lee Jacobs
**Bankers:** Barclays Bank Plc (20-52-78)

|    | 31-03-14 | 31-03-13 | 31-03-12 |
|----|----------|----------|----------|
| TO | 3,728,308 | 3,092,212 | N/A |
| P/L | 1,454,257 | 692,559 | N/A |
| NW | 9,237,504 | 8,116,573 | 7,605,784 |
| WC | 348,883 | (855,222) | (1,616,073) |
| Emp. | 64 | 59 | N/A |

**DUNS 56-976-3865**

## The Ticketline Network Ltd
Thorp Road, Manchester M40 5BJ
**Tel:** 01618321111
**Web:** www.ticketline.co.uk
**Reg No:** 2853184 **Estd:** 2011 Private Limited Company
**Line of Business:** Other entertainment activities
**Issued Capital:** £100
**Principals:** P A Betesh (Managing), C Mableson, Mrs S E Betesh, Mrs T A Betesh
**Co. Secretary:** Mrs Linda Betesh
**Branches:** The Ticketline Network Ltd, Po Box 4061, Manchester M60 1YT
**US SIC:** 8999 **UK SIC:** 83954
**Auditors:** Addis & Co
**Bankers:** The Royal Bank Of Scotland Plc (16-10-80)

|    | 31-03-14 | 31-03-13 | 31-03-12 |
|----|----------|----------|----------|
| TO | 3,519,946 | 3,595,894 | 3,524,857 |
| P/L | 759,307 | 563,870 | 551,062 |
| NW | 3,740,479 | 3,415,851 | 3,185,374 |
| WC | 3,585,172 | 3,210,989 | 2,916,528 |
| Emp. | 5 | 63 | 73 |

**DUNS 22-759-5568**     Exp

## Ticketmaster Systems Ltd
(**Subsidiary of:** Live Nation Entertainment Inc.)
4 Pentonville Road, London N1 9HF
**Tel:** 02079804395
**Web:** www.ticketmaster.co.uk
**Reg No:** 1433187 **Estd:** 1991 Private Limited Company
**Line of Business:** Representative office
**Export Markets:** Worldwide
**Export Sales:** £496,998
**Trading Style:** Ticket Master
**Issued Capital:** £20,000
**Directors:** Ms S H Emeny, C J Edmonds, M J Yovich, A J Parsons
**Co. Secretary:** David Hamilton
**Responsibilities**
**Senior:** Terry Barnes (Chairman), Simon Presswell (Manager)
**Admin:** Tracey Thornhill (Administration Manager)
**IT:** Dave Hulse (Senior Programmer)

**Facilities:** Tracey Thornhill (Administration Manager)
**Branches:** London
**US SIC:** 7399, 7379
**UK SIC:** 83954, 83940
**Auditors:** Ernst & Young LLP
**Bankers:** Barclays Bank Plc (20-36-43)

|    | 31-12-13 | 31-12-12 | 31-12-11 |
|----|----------|----------|----------|
| TO | 9,704,321 | 6,997,431 | 6,694,698 |
| P/L | 837,326 | 361,142 | 1,258,998 |
| NW | 7,268,946 | 6,409,642 | 6,032,510 |
| WC | 6,916,667 | 5,898,480 | 5,732,944 |
| Emp. | 69 | 56 | 51 |

**DUNS 77-012-8551**

## Ticketmaster U K Ltd
(**Subsidiary of:** Live Nation Entertainment Inc.)
4 Pentonville Road, London N1 9HF
**Tel:** 02073444000
**Web:** www.ticketmaster.co.uk
**Reg No:** 2662632 **Estd:** 1980 Private Limited Company
**Line of Business:** Retail sale via mail order house
**Issued Capital:** £1,900,001
**Directors:** A J Parsons, M J Yovich, C J Edmonds, Ms S H Emeny
**Co. Secretary:** David Hamilton
**Responsibilities**
**Senior:** Helen Wear (Operations Director)
**Sales:** Sian Snelling (Sales Director)
**IT:** Elizabeth Jerrard (IT Project Manager), Connon Macrae (Senior Director, Systems Opera), Paul Nye (Field IT Executive), Rob Thornley (IT Manager)
**Operations:** Dale Ballentine (Manager, Technical Ticketing O), Helen Wear (Operations Director)
**Branches:** Ticketmaster U K Ltd, 20 Donegall Place, Belfast, Belfast BT1 5BA
**US SIC:** 5961, 7379
**UK SIC:** 65600, 83940
**Auditors:** Ernst & Young LLP
**Bankers:** Barclays Bank Plc (20-82-94)

|    | 31-12-13 | 31-12-12 | 31-12-11 |
|----|----------|----------|----------|
| TO | 76,090,000 | 96,489,000 | 82,683,000 |
| P/L | 6,917,000 | 17,977,000 | 16,946,000 |
| NW | 73,482,000 | 68,808,000 | 53,833,000 |
| WC | 56,061,000 | 54,683,000 | 40,784,000 |
| Emp. | 598 | 635 | 530 |

**DUNS 21-281-1749**

## Tickhill Engineering Co Ltd
Cow House Lane, Doncaster, South Yorkshire DN3 3ED
**Tel:** 01302831911
**Web:** www.haith.co.uk
**Reg No:** 0809228 **Estd:** 1964 Private Limited Company
**Line of Business:** Agricultural and farm contractors
**Issued Capital:** £122,000
**Managing Director:** G G Haith
**Co. Secretary:** Mrs Jennifer Brindley
**Responsibilities**
**Senior:** Carol Patrick (Manager)
**IT:** Carol Patrick (Manager)
**Branches:** Tickhill Engineering Co Ltd, 133 Sunderland Street, Doncaster, South Yorkshire DN11 9ES
**US SIC:** 0729, 4952
**UK SIC:** 01003, 92120
**Auditors:** Warrens
**Bankers:** Barclays Bank Plc (20-26-55)

|    | 31-12-13 | 31-12-12 | 31-12-11 |
|----|----------|----------|----------|
| TO | 9,555,565 | 9,806,141 | 11,698,910 |
| P/L | 853,783 | 1,041,231 | 1,706,045 |
| NW | 6,444,616 | 5,558,090 | 4,620,462 |
| WC | 4,408,925 | 3,764,163 | 2,848,432 |
| Emp. | 58 | 57 | 56 |

**DUNS 28-922-7118**

## Tickton Grange Ltd
Main Street, Beverley, North Humberside HU17 9SH
**Tel:** 01964-543666
**Web:** www.ticktongrange.co.uk
**Reg No:** 1483689 **VAT No:** 347729814
**Estd:** 1980 Private Limited Company
**Line of Business:** Hotels
**Trading Style:** Tickton Grange Hotel
**Issued Capital:** £200
**Principals:** P R Whymant (Managing), Ms M A Whymant (Financial), Ms H E Whymant, Ms D L Whymant
**Co. Secretary:** Miss Helen Whymant
**US SIC:** 7011 **UK SIC:** 66500
**Auditors:** PKF

|    | 30-09-13 | 30-09-12 | 30-09-11 |
|----|----------|----------|----------|
| TO | 1,189,902 | 1,272,749 | 1,324,520 |
| P/L | (134,704) | (15,955) | (3,614) |
| NW | 23,103 | 139,003 | 159,541 |
| WC | (167,442) | (117,380) | (119,200) |

**DUNS 34-816-6802**

## The Tidy Britain Group
Elizabeth House, Pottery Road, Wigan, Lancashire WN3 4EX
**Tel:** 01942824620 **Fax:** 01942-824778
**Web:** www.keepbritaintidy.org
**Reg No:** 2796148 **VAT No:** 534982908
**Estd:** 1993 Private Company Limited By Guarantee
**Line of Business:** Social work activities without accommodation
**Trading Style:** Encams
**Director:** P M Barton
**Co. Secretary:** Philip Barton
**Responsibilities**
**Marketing:** Simone Spray (Business Development Director), Andy Walker (Campaigns and Communications D)
**Operations:** Richard McIlwain (Operations Director)
**Branches:** The Tidy Britain Group, Chandos Ho, 26 North St, Brighton, East Sussex BN1 1EB
**US SIC:** 8321, 6732
**UK SIC:** 96111, 83100
**Auditors:** H L B Kidsons
**Bankers:** National Westminster Bank Plc (01-05-14)
**Employees:** 60

**DUNS 23-728-1493**     Exp

## Tie Rack Retail Group Ltd
(**Subsidiary of:** Trakice Ltd)
Capital Interchange, Brentford, Middlesex TW8 0EX
**Tel:** 02082-302-300
**Web:** www.tie-rack.co.uk
**Reg No:** 3722742 **Estd:** 1999 Private Limited Company
**Line of Business:** Management activities of holding companies
**Export Markets:** Worldwide
**Export Sales:** £20,732,000
**Trading Style:** Tie Rack
**Issued Capital:** £1,500,074
**Director:** S Curtis
**Co. Secretary:** Rjp Secretaries Ltd
**Responsibilities**
**Senior:** Jacopo Fratini (Manager), Julian Hunt (Manager), Cesare Peretti (Manager)
**Branches:** Tie Rack Retail Group Ltd, 152A The Harlequin, Watford, Hertfordshire WD17 2TL
**US SIC:** 6711 **UK SIC:** 83962
**Auditors:** Deloitte LLP

|    | 31-01-14 | 31-01-13 | 31-01-12 |
|----|----------|----------|----------|
| TO | 51,485,000 | 52,624,000 | 63,055,000 |
| P/L | 56,977,000 | (15,982,000) | (6,813,000) |
| NW | (769,000) | (57,915,000) | (41,654,000) |
| WC | (970,000) | (59,748,000) | (3,443,000) |
| Emp. | 627 | 707 | 799 |

**DUNS 23-713-4478**

## Tier 1 Asset Management Ltd
59 Stanley Road, Manchester M45 8GZ
**Tel:** 01617771000 **Fax:** 01617771087
**Web:** www.tier1.com
**Reg No:** 3708416 **Estd:** 1999 Private Limited Company
**Line of Business:** Computer stationery
**Issued Capital:** £80
**Directors:** J D Rose, J A Basso
**Co. Secretary:** Mark Sullivan
**Responsibilities**
**Senior:** Anthony Stansfield (IT Manager)
**IT:** Anthony Stansfield (IT Manager)
**US SIC:** 7379 **UK SIC:** 83940
**Auditors:** Edwards Veeder
**Bankers:** National Westminster Bank Plc (01-10-01)

|    | 31-03-14 | 31-03-13 | 31-03-12 |
|----|----------|----------|----------|
| TA | 3,013,832 | 2,544,535 | 3,007,325 |
| NW | 734,155 | 751,622 | 713,941 |
| WC | 598,315 | 691,095 | 187,822 |

**DUNS 21-096-8192**     Imp

## Tiffany & Co. Ltd
(**Subsidiary of:** Tiffany & Co.)
25 Old Bond Street, London W1S 4QB
**Tel:** 02074994577
**Web:** www.tiffany.co.uk
**Reg No:** 6412897 **Estd:** 1986 Private Limited Company
**Line of Business:** Manufacture of jewellery and related articles not elsewhere classified
**Export Sales:** £9,639,529
**Trading Style:** Tiffany & Co.
**Issued Capital:** £2
**Directors:** L M Harlan, F P Cumenal, Ms F Rollet, R Nicoletti
**Co. Secretary:** Reed Smith Corporate Services Li
**Responsibilities**
**Senior:** Patrick Dorsey (Manager), Melvyn Kirtley (Manager), Robert Silsbury (Director Of Uk And Europe)
**Sales:** Melvyn Kirtley (Manager)
**HR:** Verity Hill (Human Resources Manager)

**Health & Safety:** Danny Cox (Facilities Manager)
**Facilities:** Danny Cox (Facilities Manager)
**Branches:** Tiffany & Co. Ltd, Heathrow Airport T3 (Airside), Hounslow TW6 1QG Heathrow Airport
**US SIC:** 3911 **UK SIC:** 49101
**Auditors:** PricewaterhouseCoopers LLP

|    | 31-01-14 | 31-01-13 | 31-01-12 |
|----|----------|----------|----------|
| TO | 134,117,945 | 125,499,941 | 129,066,606 |
| P/L | 9,708,512 | 8,999,049 | 12,465,100 |
| NW | 54,199,478 | 59,826,267 | 50,807,777 |
| WC | 48,890,558 | 52,196,418 | 41,712,851 |
| Emp. | 278 | 336 | 309 |

**DUNS 23-647-9361**     Exp

## Tiger Aspect Productions Ltd
(**Subsidiary of:** Endemol Group Ltd)
4th Floor Shepherd?s Building Central, London W14 0EE
**Tel:** 020-7434-6700 **Fax:** 02082224700
**Web:** www.tigeraspect.co.uk
**Reg No:** 3643117 **Estd:** 1998 Private Limited Company
**Line of Business:** Television activities
**Export Sales:** £802,220
**Issued Capital:** £100
**Directors:** Ms S A Clarke-Jervoise, R R Johnston, L J Church
**Co. Secretary:** John Parsons
**Responsibilities**
**Senior:** Sophie Clarke-Jervios (Manager), Andrew Zein (Manager), Carmi Zlotnik (Manager)
**Finance:** Julie Berry (Financial Reporting Manager), C Dungey (Financial Director), Kevin Khan (Financial Director)
**Marketing:** Clare Israel (Brand Manager), Iain McCallum (Head of Press)
**Admin:** Sarah Bichard (Personal Assistant)
**IT:** Owen Orton (Computer Manager)
**HR:** Darren Fahy (Facilities Manager), Maria Keaveney (Human Resources Manager)
**Health & Safety:** Darren Fahy (Facilities Manager)
**Facilities:** Darren Fahy (Facilities Manager)
**Operations:** Phillipa Catt (Head of Production), Claudia Lloyd (Head of Animation (Children's)), Nicky Poulton (Production Manager), Colm Reilly (Commercial Production Manager), Frith Tiplady (Head of Production)
**Engineering:** Phillipa Catt (Head of Production), Nicky Poulton (Production Manager)
**US SIC:** 4833 **UK SIC:** 97411
**Auditors:** Deloitte LLP
**Bankers:** Adam & Company Plc (83-91-35)

|    | 31-12-13 | 31-12-12 | 31-12-11 |
|----|----------|----------|----------|
| TO | 50,704,052 | 44,110,987 | 37,995,068 |
| P/L | 2,991,549 | 2,941,145 | 3,737,287 |
| NW | 7,488,149 | 4,549,403 | 1,661,505 |
| WC | 7,618,103 | 5,762,038 | 4,405,153 |
| Emp. | 59 | 68 | 69 |

**DUNS 42-371-8464**

## Tiger Resourcing Solutions Ltd
55 Calverley Road, Tunbridge Wells, Kent TN1 2TU
**Tel:** 01892704136 **Fax:** 01892750990
**Web:** www.tiger-it.com
**Reg No:** 4359482 **Estd:** 2002 Private Limited Company
**Line of Business:** Employment and recruitment companies and consultants
**Issued Capital:** £2
**Director:** P R Clifford
**Co. Secretary:** Guy Woods
**Branches:** Tiger Resourcing Solutions Ltd, 36 Mount Pleasant Road, Tunbridge Wells, Kent TN1 1RB
**US SIC:** 7361 **UK SIC:** 83954
**Bankers:** National Westminster Bank Plc (55-70-13)

|    | 31-12-13 | 31-12-12 | 31-12-11 |
|----|----------|----------|----------|
| TA | 488,826 | 321,712 | 358,837 |
| NW | 161,220 | 204,427 | 195,731 |
| WC | 159,742 | 202,370 | 109,482 |

**DUNS 34-632-4580**

## Tiger Retail Ltd
21-22 High Chelmer, Chelmsford, Essex CM1 1XL
**Tel:** 02088347527
**Web:** www.tigerstores.co.uk
**Reg No:** 5438600 **Estd:** 2005 Private Limited Company
**Line of Business:** Other retail sale in non-specialised stores
**Issued Capital:** £100,000
**Director:** C Mariager
**Co. Secretary:** Philip Bier
**Responsibilities**
**Senior:** Sarah Ruddick (Branch Manager)
**Branches:** Tiger Retail Ltd, 14-16 Chelsea House, Town Centre, Basingstoke, Hampshire RG21 7JR
**US SIC:** 5399 **UK SIC:** 65600

**Auditors:** Civvals

| | 31-12-13 | 31-12-12 | 31-12-11 |
|---|---|---|---|
| TO | 21,318,758 | 14,695,498 | N/A |
| P/L | 2,477,303 | 1,522,830 | N/A |
| NW | 3,786,676 | 1,992,681 | 1,101,800 |
| WC | 1,513,851 | 911,629 | 618,532 |
| Emp. | 267 | 169 | N/A |

DUNS 73-489-7932

## Tiger Software Ltd

77-79 Christchurch Road, Ringwood, Hampshire BH24 1DH
**Tel:** 01425-891000
**Web:** www.tigercomms.com
**Reg No:** 4753235 **Estd:** 2003 Private Limited Company
**Line of Business:** Telecommunications
**Trading Style:** Tiger Communications
**Issued Capital:** £1
**Directors:** S R Mccallum, B P Hoadley
**Co. Secretary:** Simon Udell
**Responsibilities**
**Senior:** Nicola Sutton *(General Manager)*
**US SIC:** 4899 **UK SIC:** 79020

| | 31-05-14 | 31-05-13 | 31-05-12 |
|---|---|---|---|
| TA | 1 | 1 | 1 |
| NW | 1 | 1 | 1 |

DUNS 21-106-8064

## Tiger Taxis

20 Holland Street, Hurstead, Rochdale, Lancashire OL16 2SD
**Tel:** 01706641115
**Estd:** 1985 Proprietorship
**Line of Business:** Taxis
**Proprietor:** J Hussain
**US SIC:** 4121 **UK SIC:** 72200
**Bankers:** Barclays Bank Plc (20-72-67)
**Employees:** 83

DUNS 21-576-5202

## Tiger Tiger

16 High Street, Croydon, Surrey CR0 1GT
**Tel:** 020-8662-4949
**Web:** www.tigertiger-newcastle.co.uk
**Estd:** 2002 Proprietorship
**Line of Business:** Public house
**Proprietor:** B Beattie
**US SIC:** 5813, 5812
**UK SIC:** 66200, 66110
**Employees:** 50

DUNS 21-721-1721 **Exp**

## Tiger Tim Products Ltd

(**Subsidiary of:** Shoo 570 Ltd)
Rhosesmor Industrial Estate, Mold, Clwyd CH7 6PZ
**Tel:** 01352-780861 **Fax:** 01352-781294
**Web:** www.tigertimproducts.co.uk
**Reg No:** 1393841 **VAT No:** 863157318
**Estd:** 1978 Private Limited Company
**Line of Business:** Barbecue & grilling equipment and accessories
**Export Markets:** Worldwide
**Issued Capital:** £301,611
**Directors:** J J Kamps, N R Popham
**Co. Secretary:** Ms Patricia Thomas
**Responsibilities**
**Senior:** Edward Birkett *(Warehouse Manager)*
**Finance:** Trisha Thomas *(Financial Director)*
**HR:** Debbie Morton *(Personnel Manager)*, Debbie Poul *(Personnel Manager)*
**Facilities:** Edward Birkett *(Warehouse Manager)*
**Operations:** Amanda Graves *(Purchasing Manager)*, Sheila Keidel *(Purchasing Manager)*
**Purchasing:** Sheila Keidel *(Purchasing Manager)*
**US SIC:** 2899 **UK SIC:** 25670
**Auditors:** Grant Thornton UK LLP
**Bankers:** Barclays Bank Plc (20-25-69)

| | 31-03-14 | 31-03-13 | 31-03-12 |
|---|---|---|---|
| TO | 28,073,000 | 25,676,000 | 22,306,000 |
| P/L | 2,489,000 | 2,027,000 | 748,000 |
| NW | 8,441,000 | 7,240,000 | 5,641,000 |
| WC | 6,948,000 | 6,458,000 | 4,298,000 |
| Emp. | 110 | 108 | 103 |

DUNS 21-422-2076

## Tigerlily Edinburgh

125 George Street, Edinburgh, Midlothian EH2 4JN
**Tel:** 0131-2255005
**Web:** www.tigerlilyedinburgh.co.uk
**Estd:** 2010 Proprietorship
**Line of Business:** Managed public houses and bars
**Proprietor:** D Hall
**Responsibilities**
**Senior:** Stephen Mackenzie *(General Manager)*
**Finance:** Antonia Jackson *(Financial Manager)*
**US SIC:** 5813 **UK SIC:** 66200
**Employees:** 60

DUNS 22-513-5391 **Imp-Exp**

## Tigers Global Logistics Ltd

(**Subsidiary of:** La Poste)
Unit 4, Ashford, Middlesex TW15 1BL
**Tel:** 01784-266400
**Web:** www.kamino.com
**Reg No:** 1651122 **VAT No:** 226127878
**Estd:** 1982 Private Limited Company
**Line of Business:** Activities of other transport agencies
**Export Markets:** Worldwide
**Export Sales:** £3,088,814
**Issued Capital:** £58,016
**Directors:** Tigers Uk Holding Limited, D J Riordan
**Co. Secretary:** Clive Baker
**Responsibilities**
**Senior:** Daniel Crowley *(Ceo)*
**Branches:** Tigers Global Logistics Ltd, Unit A3, Stuart Road, Altrincham, Cheshire WA14 5GJ
**US SIC:** 4712 **UK SIC:** 77002
**Auditors:** UHY Hacker Young LLP
**Bankers:** HSBC Bank plc (40-18-22)

| | 31-12-13 | 31-12-12 | 31-12-11 |
|---|---|---|---|
| TO | 10,167,085 | 24,780,287 | 22,602,331 |
| P/L | (740,786) | (212,245) | (52,114) |
| NW | 199,880 | 985,884 | 1,162,966 |
| WC | 368,337 | 1,172,142 | 1,404,296 |
| Emp. | 50 | 53 | N/A |

DUNS 21-776-1843

## Tigers Nursery

Henwick Court, Turnpike Road, Thatcham, Berkshire RG18 3QY
**Tel:** 01635528857
**Web:** www.tigersdaynurseries.co.uk
**Estd:** 2011 Proprietorship
**Line of Business:** Primary education
**Proprietor:** Mrs J Tubb
**US SIC:** 8211 **UK SIC:** 93200
**Employees:** 50

DUNS 42-332-5740

## Tigers Sport & Education Trust

The Circle, Anlaby Road, Hull, North Humberside HU3 6HU
**Tel:** 01482358371 **Fax:** 01482-304760
**Web:** www.tigerstrust.co.uk
**Reg No:** 4320313 **Estd:** 2001 Private Limited Company
**Line of Business:** Operation of other sports arenas and stadiums not elsewhere classified
**Directors:** R Krzywicki, S M Royce, Professor R W Walker, T S Boanas, M D Wild
**Co. Secretary:**
Taylored Business Secretaries Li
**Responsibilities**
**Senior:** John Brignall *(Manager)*, Paul Duffen *(Manager)*
**US SIC:** 7999 **UK SIC:** 97913

| | 31-07-13 | 31-07-12 | 31-07-11 |
|---|---|---|---|
| TO | 707,976 | 704,935 | 575,560 |
| P/L | (56,874) | 30,617 | (20,726) |
| NW | 136,343 | 193,217 | 162,600 |
| WC | 128,921 | 176,891 | 143,132 |
| Emp. | 51 | 59 | 43 |

DUNS 52-523-7103

## Tigi International Ltd

(**Subsidiary of:** Unilever Plc)
Unilever House, Springfield Drive, Leatherhead, Surrey KT22 7GR
**Tel:** 08448440944
**Web:** www.tigi.co.uk
**Reg No:** 3231415 **Estd:** 1996 Private Limited Company
**Line of Business:** Hairdressing and other beauty treatment
**Export Sales:** £23,209,280
**Issued Capital:** £2,300,000
**Directors:** A C Wilkins, P J Cheadle, T Monaghan
**Co. Secretary:** Mrs Amarjit Conway
**US SIC:** 7231 **UK SIC:** 98200
**Auditors:** PricewaterhouseCoopers LLP

| | 31-12-13 | 31-12-12 | 31-12-11 |
|---|---|---|---|
| TO | 40,906,485 | 42,126,336 | 45,873,359 |
| P/L | (2,253,657) | (5,213,303) | (5,760,947) |
| NW | 5,097,306 | 6,609,994 | 11,039,838 |
| WC | (6,174,741) | (1,332,709) | 2,112,082 |
| Emp. | 163 | 195 | 201 |

DUNS 57-746-5362

## Tikit Ltd

(**Subsidiary of:** Bt Group Plc)
12 Gough Square, London EC4A 3DW
**Tel:** 020-7400-3737
**Web:** www.tikit.com
**Reg No:** 2885516 **Estd:** 1994 Private Limited Company
**Line of Business:** Other computer related activities
**Export Sales:** £3,807,000
**Trading Style:** Bt
**Issued Capital:** £957
**Directors:** C G Lees, J A Ford, D Morris, R P Gray, Ms K Ainley, D Hoffman, S J Hill
**Co. Secretary:**
Newgate Street Secretaries Limit
**Responsibilities**
**Senior:** Simon Elven *(Director of Managed Services)*, Emmanuel Potvin *(Manager)*, Timothy Springham *(Chief Executive Officer)*, Kathryn Stewart *(Manager)*
**Marketing:** Kirsty Moore *(Marketing Manager)*, Denise Prior *(Senior Marketing Manager)*, Darren Stewart *(Digital Marketing Executive)*
**Sales:** Ben Read *(Managed Services Account Manag)*
**Admin:** Michelle Curtis *(Office Manager)*, Sara North *(Office Manager)*
**IT:** Simon Elven *(Director of Managed Services)*, Meena Patel *(CRM Project Coordinator)*, Franklyn Whittick *(Product Support Manager)*
**HR:** Alison Sproat *(Training Manager)*
**Health & Safety:** Michelle Curtis *(Office Manager)*, Sara North *(Office Manager)*
**Facilities:** Michelle Curtis *(Office Manager)*, Sara North *(Office Manager)*
**Operations:** Nathan Lusher *(Product Development Manager)*
**Purchasing:** Michelle Curtis *(Office Manager)*, Sara North *(Office Manager)*
**US SIC:** 7379 **UK SIC:** 83940
**Auditors:** Grant Thornton
**Bankers:** National Westminster Bank Plc (60-05-11)

| | 31-03-14 | 31-12-12 | 31-03-11 |
|---|---|---|---|
| TO | 20,285,000 | 20,312,000 | 18,680,000 |
| P/L | 2,075,000 | 3,012,000 | 2,527,000 |
| NW | 12,176,000 | 10,505,000 | 8,783,000 |
| WC | 11,962,000 | 10,283,000 | 8,533,000 |
| Emp. | 126 | 131 | 129 |

DUNS 22-815-6428

## Til-Ex Ltd

(**Subsidiary of:** Richard Elliott (Holdings) Ltd)
Healey Road, Ossett, West Yorkshire WF5 8LN
**Tel:** 01924-265331 **Fax:** 01924-262654
**Web:** www.til-ex.com
**Reg No:** 1834276 **VAT No:** 399334308
**Estd:** 1984 Private Limited Company
**Line of Business:** Road surfacers
**Issued Capital:** £100
**Director:** R Elliott
**Co. Secretary:** Mrs Vicki Elliott
**US SIC:** 1611 **UK SIC:** 50200
**Auditors:** Montpelier Audit Ltd
**Bankers:** Yorkshire Bank Plc (05-06-56)

| | 30-09-13 | 30-09-12 | 30-09-11 |
|---|---|---|---|
| TA | 3,489,617 | 3,001,167 | 3,364,318 |
| NW | 1,841,890 | 1,862,017 | 1,745,242 |
| WC | 1,229,966 | 1,157,326 | 998,794 |

DUNS 22-290-1899

## Tile Giant Ltd

(**Subsidiary of:** Travis Perkins Plc)
Anchor Works, Stoke-On-Trent, Staffordshire ST3 5XX
**Tel:** 01782597740 **Fax:** 01782-597744
**Web:** www.tilegiant.co.uk
**Reg No:** 4308218 **VAT No:** 408556737
**Estd:** 2002 Private Limited Company
**Line of Business:** Retail sale of furniture, lighting equipment and household articles not elsewhere classified
**Issued Capital:** £10,694,322
**Directors:** R D Proctor, N Bell, J P Carter, A D Buffin, M R Meech, A D Morrison, Ms C Kavanagh
**Co. Secretary:**
Tpg Management Services Limited
**Responsibilities**
**Senior:** Jason Weaver *(Store Manager)*
**Branches:** Tile Giant Ltd, Enterprise Trade Centre, Roman Farm Road, Bristol, Avon BS4 1UN
**US SIC:** 5719 **UK SIC:** 64700
**Auditors:** Hurst & Co Accountants LLP

| | 31-12-13 | 31-12-12 | 31-12-11 |
|---|---|---|---|
| TO | 42,148,000 | 40,383,000 | 36,257,000 |
| P/L | 956,000 | 1,019,000 | 358,000 |
| NW | 5,472,000 | 3,983,000 | 2,635,000 |
| WC | 2,065,000 | 196,000 | 351,000 |
| Emp. | 429 | 422 | 404 |

DUNS 21-096-4930

## Tileco Group (2007) Ltd

(**Subsidiary of:** Tileco (2012) Topco Ltd)
Unit 3 Molesey Business Centre, Central Avenue, West Molesey, Surrey KT8 2QZ
**Fax:** 02084819501
**Reg No:** 6410432 **Estd:** 2001 Private Limited Company
**Line of Business:** Management activities of holding companies
**Export Sales:** £397,382
**Issued Capital:** £40,045
**Directors:** E H Castenskiold, J M Newey
**US SIC:** 6711 **UK SIC:** 83962

**Bankers:** Lloyds TSB Bank plc (30-14-37)

| | 31-12-13 | 31-12-12 | 31-12-11 |
|---|---|---|---|
| TO | 23,608,909 | 20,430,343 | 18,426,131 |
| P/L | 188,384 | 693,639 | 531,276 |
| NW | (2,160,544) | (2,746,324) | (3,406,591) |
| WC | (2,218,538) | (1,872,564) | 968,398 |
| Emp. | 114 | 110 | 100 |

DUNS 21-723-1752 **Imp**

## Tileflair Ltd

(**Subsidiary of:** Tileflair Group Ltd)
Unit 2, Cribbs Causeway Centre, Cribbs Causeway Highwood Lane, Bristol, Avon BS10 7TT
**Tel:** 01179598888
**Web:** www.tileflair.co.uk
**Reg No:** 1051487 **VAT No:** 885438869
**Estd:** 1972 Private Limited Company
**Line of Business:** Representative office
**Export Sales:** £63,195
**Trading Style:** Tile Market, Kdp Tiles
**Issued Capital:** £60,000
**Principals:** P J Broadhurst *(Chairman and Managing)*, M T Johnson, D A Brown, K J Nichols
**Co. Secretary:** Mrs Lesley Broadhurst
**Branches:** Tileflair Ltd, 90 Bristol Road, Gloucester, Gloucestershire GL1 5SQ
**US SIC:** 5719, 5999
**UK SIC:** 64700, 65600
**Auditors:** Houghton Stone
**Bankers:** National Westminster Bank Plc (60-03-26)

| | 31-12-13 | 31-12-12 | 31-12-11 |
|---|---|---|---|
| TO | 10,173,684 | 9,740,783 | 7,785,237 |
| P/L | 496,205 | 374,529 | 334,529 |
| NW | 5,812,009 | 5,515,528 | 5,364,900 |
| WC | 3,893,235 | 3,732,287 | 3,587,979 |
| Emp. | 76 | 76 | 66 |

DUNS 52-553-5712 **Exp**

## Tilhill Forestry Ltd

(**Subsidiary of:** Upm-Kymmene Oyj)
Kings Park House, Stirling, Stirlingshire FK7 9NS
**Tel:** 01786-435000
**Web:** www.upm-tilhill.com
**Reg No:** 3242286 **Estd:** 1996 Private Limited Company
**Line of Business:** Forestry advisers
**Export Sales:** £8,564,000
**Trading Style:** Upm Tillhill
**Issued Capital:** £5,000,001
**Directors:** P R Whitfield, G M Mcrobbie
**Co. Secretary:** Andrew Hudson
**Branches:** Tilhill Forestry Ltd, Bank House, 40 High Street, Jedburgh, Roxburghshire TD8 6DQ
**US SIC:** 0851 **UK SIC:** 02000
**Auditors:** PricewaterhouseCoopers LLP
**Bankers:** Unibank A/s (40-48-78)

| | 31-12-13 | 31-12-12 | 31-12-11 |
|---|---|---|---|
| TO | 113,752,000 | 123,916,000 | 140,411,000 |
| P/L | 1,053,000 | (277,000) | 1,732,000 |
| NW | 8,846,000 | 8,060,000 | 9,035,000 |
| WC | 3,634,000 | 2,383,000 | 3,169,000 |
| Emp. | 192 | 279 | 452 |

DUNS 21-229-9267 **Imp**

## Till & Whitehead Ltd

Bradley House, 66 Barrington Road, Altrincham, Cheshire WA14 1HY
**Tel:** 01132-490641
**Web:** www.tillwite.com
**Reg No:** 0046963 **Estd:** 1876 Private Limited Company
**Line of Business:** Wholesale of hardware, plumbing and heating equipment and supplies
**Issued Capital:** £125,000
**Principals:** S F Napper *(Managing)*, S D Padmore *(Managing)*, G Turner
**Co. Secretary:** Stuart Padmore
**Branches:** Till & Whitehead Ltd, 9 Alexandra Court, James Street, York, North Yorkshire YO10 3DP
**US SIC:** 5074, 5084
**UK SIC:** 61300, 61490
**Auditors:** Beever & Struthers
**Bankers:** HSBC Bank plc (40-43-20)

| | 31-03-14 | 31-03-13 | 31-03-12 |
|---|---|---|---|
| TO | N/A | N/A | 6,502,074 |
| P/L | N/A | N/A | (59,861) |
| NW | 136,332 | 189,470 | 242,617 |
| WC | (439,378) | (624,117) | (459,918) |
| Emp. | N/A | N/A | 47 |

DUNS 23-890-8409

## The Till Roll Co. Ltd

28 Chapelgate, Retford, Nottinghamshire DN22 6PJ
**Tel:** 08456021436 **Fax:** 01777709847
**Web:** www.thetillrollcoltd.co.uk
**Reg No:** 3881772 **Estd:** 1999 Private Limited Company
**Line of Business:** Cash register and epos equipment
**Issued Capital:** £100
**Director:** M R Watson
**Co. Secretary:** Ms Karen Watson
**US SIC:** 3579, 5199, 5081

**UK SIC:** 33010, 61900, 61490
**Bankers:** National Westminster Bank Plc (60-17-28)

| | 31-12-13 | 31-12-12 | 31-12-11 |
|---|---|---|---|
| TA | 1,023,588 | 1,133,194 | 1,322,071 |
| NW | 49,542 | 245,669 | 426,574 |
| WC | (239,179) | (47,428) | 135,257 |

DUNS 29-862-2465
## Tillery Valley Foods Ltd
(**Subsidiary of:** Sodexo)
Unit 2-3, Cwmtillery Industrial Estate, Abertillery, Gwent NP13 1LZ
**Tel:** 01495-211555
**Web:** www.tilleryvalley.com
**Reg No:** 2065462 **VAT No:** 402322514
**Estd:** 1984 Private Limited Company
**Line of Business:** Manufacture of other food products not elsewhere classified
**Trading Style:** Tillery Valley Foods Ltd
**Issued Capital:** £1,635,100
**Directors:** W S Scrivens, S A Carter, Sodexo Corporate Services (No.1), Mrs L C Mawdsley
**Co. Secretary:** Gareth John
**Responsibilities**
**IT:** Cath Lillow *(Technical Director)*
**HR:** Rebecca Gwilliam *(Human Resources Manager)*
**Operations:** David Kavanagh *(Operational Services Director)*
**Purchasing:** Denis Farrell *(Purchasing Director)*
**US SIC:** 2099 **UK SIC:** 42399
**Auditors:** KPMG LLP
**Bankers:** Barclays Bank Plc (20-60-58)

| | 31-08-14 | 31-08-13 | 31-08-12 |
|---|---|---|---|
| TO | 29,870,000 | 28,876,000 | 28,493,000 |
| P/L | (559,000) | (245,000) | 1,271,000 |
| NW | 8,163,000 | 8,217,000 | 9,472,000 |
| WC | 860,000 | 580,000 | 1,530,000 |
| Emp. | 364 | 350 | 348 |

DUNS 21-449-2605
## Tillicoultry Quarries Ltd
Tulliallan, Alloa, Clackmannanshire FK10 4DT
**Tel:** 01259730481
**Web:** www.tillicoultryquarries.com
**Reg No:** 0016360SC **VAT No:** 261250394
**Estd:** 2012 Private Limited Company
**Line of Business:** Quarries
**Issued Capital:** £812
**Principals:** I W Menzies *(Managing)*, W J Menzies
**Co. Secretary:** David Menzies
**Responsibilities**
**Sales:** Joe Hadnum *(Sales Manager)*
**Branches:** Tillicoultry Quarries Ltd, Lochead Quarry, Dunfermline, Fife KY12 0RX
**US SIC:** 1499, 3272
**UK SIC:** 23960, 24370
**Auditors:** Scott-Moncrieff
**Bankers:** Clydesdale Bank Plc (82-65-33)

| | 31-03-14 | 31-03-13 | 31-03-12 |
|---|---|---|---|
| TO | 44,948,751 | 43,834,052 | 42,508,938 |
| P/L | 1,253,070 | 2,667,417 | 8,004,453 |
| NW | 27,926,614 | 30,281,801 | 28,409,814 |
| WC | 7,873,416 | 16,607,073 | 14,859,818 |
| Emp. | 113 | 88 | 80 |

DUNS 76-312-5028 **Imp**
## Tillomed Laboratories Ltd
(**Subsidiary of:** Tillomed Holdings Ltd)
3 Howard Road Industrial Estate, Eaton Socon, St Neots, Cambridgeshire PE19 8ET
**Tel:** 01480-402400
**Web:** www.tillomed.co.uk
**Reg No:** 2544103 **VAT No:** 563645523
**Estd:** 1990 Private Limited Company
**Line of Business:** Pharmaceutical suppliers and wholesalers
**Export Sales:** £48,651
**Issued Capital:** £1,000
**Directors:** S S Mehta, S R Mehta, V Thapar, M M Ginai
**Co. Secretary:** Ian Walter
**Responsibilities**
**Senior:** Musharraff Ginai *(Manager)*
**IT:** Fawad Khokhar *(IT Support Manager)*
**HR:** Jeannette Culpin *(Human Resources Manager)*
**Health & Safety:** Jeff Wysocki *(Facilities Manager)*
**Facilities:** Jeff Wysocki *(Facilities Manager)*
**Operations:** Stewart Humphreys *(Warehouse coordinator)*, John Millett *(Operations Manager)*
**US SIC:** 5122 **UK SIC:** 61800
**Auditors:** PricewaterhouseCoopers LLP
**Bankers:** Barclays Bank Plc (20-92-54)

| | 31-03-14 | 31-03-13 | 31-03-12 |
|---|---|---|---|
| TO | 12,725,098 | 11,311,195 | 13,267,545 |
| P/L | 603,485 | (81,443) | 391,995 |
| NW | 6,340,089 | 5,911,842 | 6,013,429 |
| WC | 3,977,823 | 3,630,138 | 3,755,826 |
| Emp. | 54 | 68 | 74 |

DUNS 34-750-6003
## Tilly Bailey & Irvine Llp
York Chambers, York Road, Hartlepool, Cleveland TS26 9DP
**Web:** www.tbilaw.co.uk
**Reg No:** 0315000OC **Estd:** 1905
**Line of Business:** Solicitors
**Principals:** M A Levinson, J R Ellwood, J B Hall, J Walters, M H Ellis, R N Taylor, Mrs A Leith, Tbi (Corporate Partners) Limited
**Responsibilities**
**Senior:** Helen Dexter *(Non-designated Limited Liabili)*, Kirstey Maloney *(Non-designated Limited Liabili)*, Carolyn Tilly *(Non-designated Limited Liabili)*
**Branches:** Tilly Bailey & Irvine Llp, 8 Newgate, Barnard Castle, County Durham DL12 8NG
**US SIC:** 8111 **UK SIC:** 83500

| | 31-03-14 | 31-03-13 | 31-03-12 |
|---|---|---|---|
| TO | 7,733,606 | 8,946,474 | 7,064,303 |
| P/L | 1,878,796 | 3,375,256 | 4,000 |
| NW | 2,100,992 | 3,667,521 | 292,265 |
| WC | 1,913,723 | 3,406,853 | 636,729 |
| Emp. | 134 | 137 | 138 |

DUNS 29-686-9894
## Tilney Investment Management
(**Subsidiary of:** Deutsche Bank Ag)
Royal Liver Building, Liverpool, Merseyside L3 1NY
**Tel:** 03330143108 **Fax:** 0151-236-1252
**Web:** www.tilney.co.uk
**Reg No:** 2010520 **VAT No:** 618708522
**Estd:** 1836 Private Unlimited Company
**Line of Business:** Security broking and related activities
**Issued Capital:** £2,430,319
**Directors:** J D Norbury, P Lindop Hall, D W Reid
**Co. Secretary:** Frederick Calitz
**Branches:** Tilney Investment Management, Murivance House, Murivance, Shrewsbury, Shropshire SY1 1JW
**US SIC:** 6211 **UK SIC:** 83100
**Auditors:** KPMG Audit PLC
**Bankers:** The Royal Bank Of Scotland Plc (16-24-06)

| | 31-12-13 | 31-12-12 | 31-12-11 |
|---|---|---|---|
| TO | 45,040,000 | 42,281,000 | 50,168,000 |
| P/L | (13,578,000) | (9,501,000) | (8,931,000) |
| NW | 15,531,000 | 18,589,000 | 11,015,000 |
| WC | 32,883,000 | 32,189,000 | 24,732,000 |
| Emp. | 141 | 167 | 140 |

DUNS 28-871-2334
## Tilsa Yarns Ltd
(**Subsidiary of:** Sirdar Holdings Ltd)
Flanshaw Lane, Wakefield, West Yorkshire WF2 9ND
**Tel:** 01924375742
**Web:** www.tilsatec.com
**Reg No:** 1044853 **Estd:** 1972 Private Limited Company
**Line of Business:** Protective clothing and workwear
**Issued Capital:** £2
**Director:** R P Morris
**Co. Secretary:** Ian Stead
**US SIC:** 2389 **UK SIC:** 45393

| | 30-06-13 | 30-06-12 | 30-06-11 |
|---|---|---|---|
| TA | 2 | 2 | 2 |
| NW | 2 | 2 | 2 |

DUNS 21-880-5271
## Timberdine Nursing & Rehabilitation Units
Timberdine Close Bath, Worcester, Worcestershire WR5 2DD
**Tel:** 01905361840
**Estd:** 2012
**Line of Business:** Clinics private
**Responsibilities**
**Senior:** Ann Barry *(Manager)*, Gill Pratt *(Manager)*
**US SIC:** 8051 **UK SIC:** 95100
**Employees:** 60

DUNS 73-946-5792
## Timberland Idc Ltd.
77-79 Farringdon Road, Slough, Berkshire SL3 6PJ
**Tel:** 020-3077-0900
**Web:** www.timberlandonline.co.uk
**Reg No:** 5199227 **Estd:** 2004 Private Limited Company
**Line of Business:** Clothing wholesale and suppliers
**Trading Style:** Timberland Uk Limited
**Issued Capital:** £100
**Directors:** P J Emmerson, B H Mcneill, K H Salzburger, C A Holtz
**US SIC:** 5136, 5661
**UK SIC:** 61600, 64600
**Auditors:** Deloitte & Touche LLP

| | 31-12-13 | 31-12-12 | 31-12-11 |
|---|---|---|---|
| TO | 5,467,000 | 5,608,000 | 4,737,000 |
| P/L | 393,000 | 358,000 | 317,000 |
| NW | 1,882,000 | 1,626,000 | 1,354,000 |
| WC | 1,440,000 | 1,180,000 | 759,000 |
| Emp. | 74 | 57 | 48 |

DUNS 29-820-4314 **Imp-Exp**
## Timberland (Uk) Ltd
(**Subsidiary of:** V.F. Corporation)
Wexham Springs, Framewood Road, Wexham, Slough, Berkshire SL3 6PJ
**Tel:** 01753497000 **Fax:** 01753497001
**Web:** www.timberlandonline.co.uk
**Reg No:** 2038598 **VAT No:** 635778987
**Estd:** 1986 Private Limited Company
**Line of Business:** Wholesale of clothing and footwear
**Trading Style:** Timberland
**Issued Capital:** £4,737,799
**Directors:** B H Mcneill, J D Crimmins Iii, P J Emmerson, C A Holtz, K H Salzburger
**Co. Secretary:** Tmf Corporate Administration Ser
**Responsibilities**
**Senior:** Richard O' Rourke *(Manager)*, Carol Wallace *(Office Manager)*
**Marketing:** Danny Chinnery *(IT Manager)*
**Admin:** Carol Wallace *(Office Manager)*
**IT:** Danny Chinnery *(IT Manager)*
**Facilities:** Carol Wallace *(Office Manager)*
**Operations:** Danny Chinnery *(IT Manager)*
**Branches:** Timberland (Uk) Limited, 72 New Bond St, London W1S 1RR
**US SIC:** 5136, 5661
**UK SIC:** 61600, 64600
**Auditors:** PricewaterhouseCoopers LLP
**Bankers:** Barclays Bank Plc (20-00-00)

| | 31-12-13 | 31-12-12 | 31-12-11 |
|---|---|---|---|
| TO | 18,665,000 | 71,167,000 | 74,546,000 |
| P/L | 23,956,000 | 2,741,000 | 2,428,000 |
| NW | 34,134,000 | 10,627,000 | 8,568,000 |
| WC | 34,134,000 | 9,077,000 | 6,813,000 |
| Emp. | 139 | 384 | 387 |

DUNS 45-897-8434
## Timberwise (U K) Ltd
(**Subsidiary of:** Timberwise Holdings Ltd)
1 Drake Mews, Gadbrook Park, Rudheath, Northwich, Cheshire CW9 7XF
**Tel:** 01606339070
**Web:** www.timberwise.co.uk
**Reg No:** 3230356 **VAT No:** 677339196
**Estd:** 2004 Private Limited Company
**Line of Business:** Damp and dry rot preservation services
**Issued Capital:** £100,000
**Principals:** M J Edwards *(Managing)*, N Hartley, J R Allan, C J Edwards
**Co. Secretary:** Timothy Riley
**Branches:** Timberwise (U K) Ltd, Coombe Works, Coombe, Oborne, Sherborne, Dorset DT9 4AU
**US SIC:** 1799 **UK SIC:** 50000
**Auditors:** Kay Johnson Gee
**Bankers:** National Westminster Bank Plc (01-10-01)

| | 31-12-13 | 31-12-12 | 31-12-11 |
|---|---|---|---|
| TA | 2,101,863 | 1,743,208 | 1,501,300 |
| NW | 557,199 | 506,927 | 492,808 |
| WC | 452,681 | 403,481 | 396,633 |

DUNS 21-103-7720
## Timbmet Holdings Ltd
Kemp House, Cumnor Hill, Cumnor, Oxford, Oxfordshire OX2 9PH
**Tel:** 01865860361
**Reg No:** 6466786 **Estd:** 2008 Private Limited Company
**Line of Business:** Wholesale of wood, construction materials and sanitary equipment
**Export Sales:** £2,442,000
**Issued Capital:** £32,725
**Directors:** S L Fineman, J P Cole, Dr E F Kemp
**US SIC:** 5039 **UK SIC:** 61300
**Bankers:** Barclays Bank Plc (20-65-18)

| | 31-03-14 | 31-03-13 | 31-03-12 |
|---|---|---|---|
| TO | 75,797,000 | 76,442,000 | 85,822,000 |
| P/L | 437,000 | (4,639,000) | (8,915,000) |
| NW | 4,984,000 | 4,417,000 | 10,263,000 |
| WC | 3,264,000 | 3,123,000 | 9,025,000 |
| Emp. | 282 | 293 | 310 |

DUNS 77-738-2060 **Imp**
## Timbmet Ltd
(**Subsidiary of:** Timbmet Holdings Ltd)
Kemp House, Chawley Park, Cumnor Hill, Oxford, Oxfordshire OX2 9PH
**Tel:** 01865860350
**Web:** www.timbmet.com
**Reg No:** 3009353 **Estd:** 1995 Private Limited Company
**Line of Business:** Wholesale of wood, construction materials and sanitary equipment
**Export Sales:** £2,424,840
**Issued Capital:** £100,000
**Directors:** S L Fineman, P E Rivers, S D O'Sullivan, C R Thewlis, N M Cox
**Co. Secretary:** Clive Thewlis
**Responsibilities**
**Senior:** Marko Bjelic *(Marketing Assistant)*, Phil Trueman *(Logistics Manager)*
**Marketing:** Marko Bjelic *(Marketing Assistant)*
**Health & Safety:** Pete Feakes *(Quality Manager)*
**Fleet:** Phil Trueman *(Logistics Manager)*
**Branches:** Timbmet Ltd, Launton Rd, Bicester, Oxfordshire OX26 4JT
**US SIC:** 5039 **UK SIC:** 61300
**Auditors:** PricewaterhouseCoopers LLP
**Bankers:** Barclays Bank Plc (20-65-18)

| | 31-03-14 | 31-03-13 | 31-03-12 |
|---|---|---|---|
| TO | 75,532,504 | 74,974,163 | 81,863,841 |
| P/L | 53,676 | (2,885,383) | (8,265,728) |
| NW | 8,387,017 | 8,348,778 | 11,319,847 |
| WC | 4,985,410 | (8,655,274) | 7,292,627 |
| Emp. | 278 | 285 | 301 |

DUNS 22-565-4565 **Imp**
## Time 24 Ltd
(**Subsidiary of:** Time 24 Holdings Ltd)
69 Victoria Road, Burgess Hill, West Sussex RH15 9TR
**Tel:** 01444257655 **Fax:** 01444-259-000
**Web:** www.time24.com
**Reg No:** 2165350 **VAT No:** 475794685
**Estd:** 1987 Private Limited Company
**Line of Business:** Manufacturers cable and wire equipment
**Trading Style:** Time 24
**Issued Capital:** £1,086,100
**Managing Directors:** M E Willifer, D A Shore
**Co. Secretary:** Mark Willifer
**Responsibilities**
**HR:** Mark Gillam *(Production Manager)*, Anamarie Spicer *(Human Resources Manager)*
**Health & Safety:** Mark Gillam *(Production Manager)*
**Facilities:** Mark Gillam *(Production Manager)*
**Operations:** Mark Gillam *(Production Manager)*
**Engineering:** Mark Gillam *(Production Manager)*
**Branches:** Time 24 Limited, Endland Industrial Estate, Parcel Terrace, Derby, Derbyshire DE1 1LY
**US SIC:** 3357 **UK SIC:** 22470
**Auditors:** Wilkins Kennedy LLP
**Bankers:** National Westminster Bank Plc (60-10-26)

| | 30-06-13 | 30-06-12 | 30-06-11 |
|---|---|---|---|
| TO | 8,315,150 | 4,438,689 | 5,930,391 |
| P/L | 515,733 | 94,048 | 1,314,294 |
| NW | 1,687,465 | 1,187,210 | 1,001,118 |
| WC | 1,518,678 | 1,029,893 | 817,045 |
| Emp. | N/A | 142 | 76 |

DUNS 21-051-2679 **Imp-Exp**
## Time Inc. (Uk) Ltd
(**Subsidiary of:** Time Warner Inc.)
Blue Fin Building, 110 Southwark Street, London SE1 0SU
**Tel:** 020-3148-5000
**Web:** www.timeincuk.com
**Reg No:** 0053626 **Estd:** 1897 Private Limited Company
**Line of Business:** Publishing of journals and periodicals
**Export Sales:** £31,397,000
**Trading Style:** Southbank Publishing Group, Connect Publications 1, T X Publications, Music & Sport Group
**Issued Capital:** £2,580,500
**Directors:** P R Williams, Ms J A Newcombe, S J May, S Hirst, J J Bairstow, M A Rich, Ms F A Dent, Ms L Swarbrick
**Co. Secretary:** Ms Lauren Klein
**Responsibilities**
**Senior:** Andrea Davies *(Director)*
**IT:** Sue Anderson *(Projects Manager)*, Andrew Wildey *(?IT Services Manager)*
**HR:** Katie Golden *(Learning Coordinator)*, Dee Mair *(Human Resources Director)*
**Facilities:** Tony Floyde *(Facilities Manager)*
**Branches:** Time Inc. (Uk) Ltd, Cudham Tithe Barn, Berrys Hill, Westerham, Kent TN16 3AG
**US SIC:** 2721 **UK SIC:** 47522
**Auditors:** Ernst & Young LLP
**Bankers:** National Westminster Bank Plc (60-00-01)

| | 31-12-13 | 31-12-12 | 31-12-11 |
|---|---|---|---|
| TO | 292,701,000 | 314,803,000 | 331,243,000 |
| P/L | 21,514,000 | 11,412,000 | 45,490,000 |
| NW | 218,699,000 | 211,930,000 | 208,550,000 |
| WC | 142,734,000 | 141,029,000 | 109,975,000 |
| Emp. | 1,676 | 1,760 | 1,755 |

DUNS 77-495-3251

## Time Out New York Ltd

(**Subsidiary of:** Tony (Bermuda) Limited)
4th Floor, 125 Shaftesbury Avenue, London WC2H 8AD
**Tel:** 020-7813-3000
**Web:** www.timeout.com
**Reg No:** 2977606 **Estd:** 1969 Private Limited Company
**Line of Business:** Publishing of journals and periodicals
**Issued Capital:** £8,917,662
**Directors:** T Arthur, A F Collins, M J White, P A Dubens
**US SIC:** 2721 **UK SIC:** 47522
**Bankers:** Lloyds TSB Bank plc (30-12-18)

| | 31-12-13 | 31-12-12 | 31-12-11 |
|---|---|---|---|
| TO | 10,718,884 | 10,538,785 | 7,454,107 |
| P/L | (6,623,534) | (4,949,491) | (4,629,037) |
| NW | (5,790,375) | (7,700,815) | (6,033,538) |
| WC | (452,807) | (1,629,059) | (1,173,743) |
| Emp. | 106 | 105 | 100 |

DUNS 39-030-2099 **Imp-Exp**

## Time Systems (U K) Ltd

Systems House, Wavendon, Milton Keynes, Buckinghamshire MK17 8AA
**Tel:** 01908-281000 **Fax:** 01908-281291
**Web:** www.timesystemsuk.com
**Reg No:** 2110018 **VAT No:** 461069259
**Estd:** 1987 Private Limited Company
**Line of Business:** Manufacture of watches and clocks
**Trading Style:** Time Cards (U K)
**Issued Capital:** £3,000
**Director:** Miss R C Coppeletti
**Co. Secretary:** Miss Samantha Whiteside
**Responsibilities**
**Senior:** Jeanette Thompson *(Manager)*
**Finance:** Jeanette Thompson *(Manager)*
**Branches:** Time Systems (U K) Ltd, Ladywood Road, Birmingham, West Midlands B16 8SZ
**US SIC:** 3873, 3629
**UK SIC:** 37400, 34350
**Auditors:** M J Emery & Co
**Bankers:** Barclays Bank Plc (20-57-40)

| | 31-03-14 | 31-03-13 | 31-03-12 |
|---|---|---|---|
| TA | 998,002 | 1,003,441 | 955,123 |
| NW | 738,407 | 752,901 | 664,397 |
| WC | 405,576 | 419,477 | 284,698 |

DUNS 49-180-9521

## Time Warner Holdings Ltd

(**Subsidiary of:** Time Warner Inc.)
44 Great Marlborough Street, London W1F 7JL
**Reg No:** 3115253 **Estd:** 1995 Private Limited Company
**Line of Business:** Management activities of holding companies
**Issued Capital:** £994,155,621
**Directors:** P J Hosemann, Ms J M Stewart
**Co. Secretary:** Ms Bronwen Jones
**US SIC:** 6711, 6794
**UK SIC:** 83962, 83100
**Auditors:** Ernst & Young LLP
**Bankers:** Barclays Bank Plc (20-36-47)

**Following financial data are in thousands**

| | 31-12-13 | 31-12-12 | 31-12-11 |
|---|---|---|---|
| TO | 1,430,802 | 1,463,098 | 1,552,783 |
| P/L | 33,019 | (180,233) | (41,413) |
| NW | (116,379) | (185,007) | (208,530) |
| WC | (346,706) | (421,016) | 87,998 |
| Emp. | 4,703 | 4,700 | 3,694 |

DUNS 21-229-0003

## Timebridge Youth & Community Centre

Fieldway, New Addington, Croydon, Surrey CR0 9AZ
**Tel:** 01689842992
**Estd:** 2002 Proprietorship
**Line of Business:** Community centres
**Proprietor:** Mrs S Rivers
**Responsibilities**
**Senior:** Terry Gillam *(Manager)*
**US SIC:** 8699 **UK SIC:** 96902
**Employees:** 78

DUNS 21-211-8210 **Exp**

## Timeform Ltd

Timeform House, Northgate, Halifax, West Yorkshire HX1 1XF
**Tel:** 01422330330 **Fax:** 01422398017
**Web:** www.timeform.com
**Reg No:** 0477913 **VAT No:** 183740747
**Estd:** 1950 Private Limited Company
**Line of Business:** Publishing of books
**Export Markets:** France; Italy; New Zealand; Republic of Ireland; U S A
**Trading Style:** Timeform
**Issued Capital:** £5,000
**Directors:** N Townsend, R Ozcan, P Rushton, K Packman
**Co. Secretary:** Recep Ozcan

**Responsibilities**
**Senior:** Stephen Burn *(Manager)*, Ian Chuter *(Director)*, Martin Cruddace *(Manager)*, Mathias Entenmann *(Manager)*, Darrell Neave *(Maintenance Manager)*
**Facilities:** Darrell Neave *(Maintenance Manager)*
**Engineering:** Darrell Neave *(Maintenance Manager)*
**US SIC:** 2731 **UK SIC:** 47532
**Auditors:** Spenser Wilson & Co
**Bankers:** National Westminster Bank Plc (60-09-27)

| | 30-04-14 | 30-04-13 | 30-04-12 |
|---|---|---|---|
| TO | 3,485,489 | 3,161,150 | 3,207,497 |
| P/L | (209,912) | (450,151) | (64,696) |
| NW | (203,049) | 6,863 | 457,014 |
| WC | (875,528) | (666,052) | (270,696) |

DUNS 21-108-2451

## Timeline (Ph) Ltd

Precision House, Ring Road, Leeds, West Yorkshire LS14 1NH
**Tel:** 01132-650000
**Reg No:** 6501965 **Estd:** 1900 Private Limited Company
**Line of Business:** Taxis and private hire vehicles
**Issued Capital:** £2
**Co. Secretary:** Mohammad Fayaz
**Responsibilities**
**Senior:** Faisal Sjad *(Proprietor)*
**US SIC:** 4121, 7512
**UK SIC:** 72200, 84801

| | 31-03-14 | 31-03-13 | 31-03-12 |
|---|---|---|---|
| TA | 41,710 | 50,807 | 46,862 |
| NW | 441 | 19,475 | 20,497 |
| WC | (2,595) | 17,847 | 17,855 |

DUNS 52-307-1017 **Imp**

## Timeline Television Ltd

(**Subsidiary of:** Timeline Television Group Ltd)
Ealing Studios, Ealing Green, London W5 5EP
**Tel:** 08450944445
**Web:** www.timeline.tv
**Reg No:** 6019292 **Estd:** 2006 Private Limited Company
**Line of Business:** Broadcasting services
**Issued Capital:** £1,000
**Director:** R M Sewell
**Co. Secretary:** Daniel Mcdonnell
**Branches:** Timeline Television Ltd T/A Timeline Tv Stratford, Icity, International Broadcast Centre, E20 3BS London
**US SIC:** 4833 **UK SIC:** 97411
**Auditors:** Alliotts

| | 31-12-13 | 31-12-12 | 31-12-11 |
|---|---|---|---|
| TO | 15,132,389 | N/A | N/A |
| P/L | 308,904 | N/A | N/A |
| NW | 1,269,826 | 1,110,773 | 945,670 |
| WC | (464,256) | (383,289) | (154,793) |
| Emp. | 75 | N/A | N/A |

DUNS 50-147-1932 **Exp**

## Timeplan Education Group Ltd

20-21 Arcadia Avenue, London N3 2JU
**Tel:** 02083718030
**Web:** www.timeplan.com
**Reg No:** 2325304 **VAT No:** 553871324
**Estd:** 1989 Private Limited Company
**Line of Business:** Labour recruitment and provision of personnel
**Issued Capital:** £66,666
**Principals:** Ms T E Seabourne *(Managing)*, I Penman, Miss I Penman
**Co. Secretary:** Ms Teresa Seabourne
**Responsibilities**
**Senior:** Tish Seabourne *(Manager)*
**Branches:** Timeplan Education Group Ltd, 25 Kingston Road, London SW19 1JX
**US SIC:** 7361, 8299
**UK SIC:** 83954, 93300
**Auditors:** HB Accountants

| | 31-08-13 | 31-08-12 | 31-08-11 |
|---|---|---|---|
| TO | 15,794,708 | 13,617,391 | 13,550,751 |
| P/L | 1,027,776 | 636,854 | 775,250 |
| NW | 1,958,984 | 1,242,882 | 3,758,139 |
| WC | 1,250,709 | 201,700 | 2,464,138 |
| Emp. | 662 | 596 | 579 |

DUNS 22-062-3263

## Timerest Ltd

(**Subsidiary of:** Levant Restaurants Group Ltd)
76 Wigmore St Jason Court, London W1U 2SJ
**Tel:** 02072241111 **Fax:** 0207 486 0586
**Web:** www.levant.co.uk
**Reg No:** 4064058 **Estd:** 1999 Private Limited Company
**Line of Business:** Canteens and catering
**Trading Style:** Lavant
**Issued Capital:** £900
**Director:** A Kitous
**Co. Secretary:** Ais Secretarial Services Limited

**Responsibilities**
**Senior:** Madjid Kitous *(Manager)*, Tony Kitous *(Owner)*, Giuseppe Riviezzo *(General Manager)*
**Branches:** Timerest Ltd, Oceana, 76 Wigmore Street, London W1U 2SH
**US SIC:** 5812 **UK SIC:** 66110
**Auditors:** UHY Hacker Young

| | 31-12-13 | 31-12-12 | 31-12-11 |
|---|---|---|---|
| TA | 2,411,933 | 2,385,085 | 2,134,885 |
| NW | 1,292,946 | 1,042,590 | 837,969 |
| WC | 755,900 | 242,506 | (59,623) |

DUNS 21-779-1275

## Times Bedding

Unit 1 Warneford Avenue, Ossett, West Yorkshire WF5 9NJ
**Tel:** 01924270988
**Estd:** 2005 Proprietorship
**Line of Business:** Manufacturers of beds and mattresses
**Proprietor:** I Hussain
**US SIC:** 2515 **UK SIC:** 46715
**Employees:** 50

DUNS 21-036-0293

## Times Newspapers Ltd

(**Subsidiary of:** News Corporation)
1 Virginia Walk, London SW2 2BX
**Tel:** 02076806833 **Fax:** 02077825112
**Web:** www.niadsdirect.com
**Reg No:** 0894646 **Estd:** 1965 Private Limited Company
**Line of Business:** Newspapers publishing
**Trading Style:** Times Newspapers Limited
**Issued Capital:** £1,000,000
**Directors:** M C Gill, M W Darcey, C C Longcroft, M P Ivens, J Witherow
**Responsibilities**
**Senior:** James Mcpherson *(Manager)*, Susan Panuccio *(Manager)*, Carla Stone *(Manager)*
**Marketing:** Robbie Millen *(?Literary Editor)*
**Branches:** Times Newspapers Limited, Times House, 10 Pennington Street, London E1W 2BB
**US SIC:** 2711 **UK SIC:** 47512
**Auditors:** Ernst & Young LLP
**Bankers:** HSBC Bank plc (40-03-05)

| | 29-06-14 | 30-06-13 | 01-06-12 |
|---|---|---|---|
| TO | 346,985,000 | 347,992,000 | 360,637,000 |
| P/L | (935,000) | (24,444,000) | (28,731,000) |
| NW | (503,690,000) | (502,833,000) | (478,607,000) |
| WC | (460,234,000) | (459,373,000) | (435,146,000) |
| Emp. | 454 | 473 | 513 |

DUNS 21-207-3753 **Imp-Exp**

## Timet Uk Ltd

(**Subsidiary of:** Timet Bermuda Limited)
1 Plant, Holford Drive, Perry Barr, Birmingham, West Midlands B42 2TU
**Tel:** 0121-356-1155
**Web:** www.timet.com
**Reg No:** 0530589 **Estd:** 1954 Private Limited Company
**Line of Business:** Fabricated metal products
**Export Sales:** £105,824,000
**Issued Capital:** £29,000,002
**Directors:** T L Gibbons, R P Becker, S G Hackett, Mrs S R Hagel, Ms R A Beyer, S C Blackmore, R S Pattee
**Co. Secretary:** Kamran Munir
**Responsibilities**
**Senior:** Ian Hodges *(Manager)*, Bobby O'Brien *(Manager)*
**Branches:** Timet Uk Ltd, St. Illtyds Church, The Parish Hall, Swansea, West Glamorgan SA5 4BT
**US SIC:** 3441 **UK SIC:** 32042
**Auditors:** PricewaterhouseCoopers LLP
**Bankers:** Lloyds TSB Bank plc (30-00-03)

| | 30-03-14 | 31-12-12 | 31-03-11 |
|---|---|---|---|
| TO | 271,171,000 | 208,261,000 | 185,554,000 |
| P/L | 18,638,000 | 18,453,000 | 31,567,000 |
| NW | 123,391,000 | 105,465,000 | 109,681,000 |
| WC | 109,982,000 | 112,984,000 | 107,892,000 |
| Emp. | 710 | 748 | 670 |

DUNS 22-527-8274

## Timeweave Washosp Ltd

(**Subsidiary of:** Mayfair Capital Investments Uk Ltd)
Torex Hospitality Solutions Ltd, Unit 1, Guildford, Surrey GU1 4JY
**Tel:** 01483407700
**Reg No:** 1662440 **VAT No:** 384112859
**Estd:** 1982 Private Limited Company
**Line of Business:** Computer software (development)
**Directors:** D C Craven, R A Robson
**US SIC:** 7379 **UK SIC:** 83940
**Auditors:** The Carley Partnership
**Bankers:** Lloyds TSB Bank plc (30-98-77)

| | 31-12-13 |
|---|---|
| TA | 5,000 |
| NW | 5,000 |

DUNS 39-684-7683

## Timewell Properties Ltd

Mill House, Market Road Burgh Road, Great Yarmouth, Norfolk NR31 9ED
**Web:** www.zaks.uk.com
**Reg No:** 0747225 **Estd:** 1979 Private Limited Company
**Line of Business:** Camping sites, including caravan sites
**Trading Style:** Blue Sky Leisure
**Issued Capital:** £359,100
**Principals:** Mrs E M Timewell *(Chairman)*, P R Timewell *(Managing)*, D J Bye, Miss K F Smith, M C Timewell
**Co. Secretary:** Mrs Edna Timewell
**Branches:** Timewell Properties Ltd, Sandy Hill Lane, Holt, Norfolk NR25 7HW
**US SIC:** 7399, 7033
**UK SIC:** 83954, 66701
**Auditors:** Lovewell Blake
**Bankers:** National Westminster Bank Plc (60-15-31)

| | 31-03-14 | 31-03-13 | 31-03-12 |
|---|---|---|---|
| TO | 10,430,015 | 10,096,383 | 9,093,553 |
| P/L | 629,739 | 67,281 | 269,020 |
| NW | 2,488,846 | 2,051,551 | 2,030,364 |
| WC | (5,497,584) | (7,426,364) | (5,573,850) |
| Emp. | 212 | 222 | 218 |

DUNS 21-696-8931

## Timico Technology Group Ltd

Beaconhill Park Cafferata Way, Newark, Nottinghamshire NG24 2TN
**Tel:** 08700949600
**Web:** www.timicotecnnologygroup.co.uk
**Reg No:** 7427648 **Estd:** 2010 Private Limited Company
**Line of Business:** Internet service providers
**Export Sales:** £335,000
**Issued Capital:** £7,752,333
**Directors:** H W Pepper, J V Radford, T P Radford, B L Marnham, Lord P G Daresbury, N J Garrett, C J Tombs
**Co. Secretary:** Jonathan Radford
**US SIC:** 4899 **UK SIC:** 79020
**Auditors:** Deloitte LLP
**Bankers:** Girobank Plc (72-00-00)

| | 31-12-13 | 31-12-12 | 31-12-11 |
|---|---|---|---|
| TO | 42,526,000 | 38,484,000 | 31,543,000 |
| P/L | 866,000 | (134,000) | 1,264,000 |
| NW | (1,484,000) | (4,835,000) | (3,163,000) |
| WC | (4,885,000) | (3,903,000) | 12,000 |
| Emp. | 267 | 222 | 183 |

DUNS 51-993-0924 **Imp**

## Timken Ils Ltd

(**Subsidiary of:** The Timken Company)
85a St Modwen Road, Plymouth, Devon PL6 8LH
**Tel:** 01752676000 **Fax:** 01752-676001
**Web:** www.interlubesystems.co.uk
**Reg No:** 3999847 **Estd:** 2000 Private Limited Company
**Line of Business:** Lubrication equipment
**Export Sales:** £3,118,000
**Issued Capital:** £54,561
**Directors:** J T Mihaila, K A Roellgen, C A Coughlin
**Co. Secretary:** Michael Williams
**Responsibilities**
**Senior:** Leslie Ashford *(Manager)*
**Facilities:** Bradley Platt *(Senior Production Manager)*
**Operations:** Steven Bettey *(Operations Manager)*, Bradley Platt *(Senior Production Manager)*
**US SIC:** 3559 **UK SIC:** 32863
**Auditors:** Ernst & Young LLP
**Bankers:** Bank Of Scotland (12-13-55)

| | 31-12-13 | 31-03-13 | 31-12-12 |
|---|---|---|---|
| TO | 4,449,000 | 8,328,000 | 8,474,000 |
| P/L | 2,795,000 | 531,000 | 1,004,000 |
| NW | 3,133,000 | 2,580,000 | 1,774,000 |
| WC | 1,991,000 | 1,989,000 | 1,332,000 |
| Emp. | 74 | 96 | 87 |

DUNS 52-025-6413 **Imp**

## Timken Uk Ltd

(**Subsidiary of:** The Timken Company)
P O Box 667, Upper Villiers Street, Wolverhampton, West Midlands WV2 4UH
**Tel:** 01902-719300 **Fax:** 01902-771448
**Web:** www.timken.com
**Reg No:** 3392504 **Estd:** 1997 Private Limited Company
**Line of Business:** Manufacturers of bearings
**Trading Style:** Garrad Hassan & Partners Ltd
**Issued Capital:** £3,500,004
**Directors:** A Roellgen, J T Mihaila
**Co. Secretary:** Michael Williams
**Responsibilities**
**Senior:** Mathew Happach *(Manager)*, Sharron Hartshorne *(Supply Chain Manager)*, James Menning *(Vice President)*, Andrew Millerchip *(Plant Manager)*
**Health & Safety:** Lee Evans *(Health & Safety Manager)*
**Operations:** Claire Payne *(Quality and Engineering Manage)*

**Engineering:** Lee Evans *(Health & Safety Manager)*
**Branches:** Timken Uk Ltd, Churchill House, 29 Mill Hill Road, Pontefract, West Yorkshire WF8 4HY
**US SIC:** 3568 **UK SIC:** 32613
**Auditors:** Ernst & Young LLP
**Bankers:** HSBC Bank plc (40-02-50)

| | 31-12-13 | 31-12-12 | 31-12-11 |
|---|---|---|---|
| TO | 21,610,214 | 23,597,674 | 22,411,565 |
| P/L | 4,306,647 | 4,666,169 | 1,077,838 |
| NW | (1,570,926) | (12,982,573) | (23,898,785) |
| WC | (1,238,990) | (1,608,686) | 2,097,984 |
| Emp. | 176 | 177 | 188 |

DUNS 73-665-1857

## Timothy James Consulting Ltd

(**Subsidiary of:** Tjc Professional Ltd)
Vintry House, London
**Tel:** 01179-459000
**Web:** www.timothyjamesconsulting.com
**Reg No:** 4924795 **Estd:** 2003 Private Limited Company
**Line of Business:** Employment and recruitment companies and consultants
**Export Sales:** £1,961,320
**Issued Capital:** £1,000
**Directors:** D Stuart-Smith, T N Ramus, D Jalan, A J Fletcher
**Co. Secretary:** Graham Dolan
**Responsibilities**
**Senior:** Andrew Backhouse *(Contracts Director)*, Kerry Demitriou *(Chief Executive Officer)*, James Khan *(Partner)*, Iain O'Dair *(Operations Director)*, Sarah Wilton *(Manager)*
**Finance:** Iain O'Dair *(Operations Director)*
**Operations:** Iain O'Dair *(Operations Director)*
**US SIC:** 7361 **UK SIC:** 83954

| | 31-10-13 | 31-10-12 | 31-10-11 |
|---|---|---|---|
| TO | 20,902,524 | 20,054,648 | 17,318,412 |
| P/L | 305,317 | 827,868 | 708,840 |
| NW | 1,004,319 | 759,669 | 148,647 |
| WC | 1,269,457 | 688,890 | 53,489 |
| Emp. | 52 | 66 | 57 |

DUNS 21-216-0493

## Timothy Taylor & Co. Ltd

Knowle Spring Brewery, Queens Road, Keighley, West Yorkshire BD21 1AW
**Tel:** 01535-603139
**Web:** www.timothytaylor.co.uk
**Reg No:** 0243794 **VAT No:** 179885779
**Estd:** 1858 Private Limited Company
**Line of Business:** Brewers
**Issued Capital:** £163,764
**Principals:** C J Dent *(Managing)*, T W Dewey, M L Bramley, J R Gamble, P W Eells, T Clarke, Mrs D M Dent
**Co. Secretary:** Stephen Drinkwater
**Responsibilities**
**Senior:** Nigel Bankes *(Manager)*, Angela Edward *(Manager)*
**Health & Safety:** Andrew Leman *(second brewer)*
**Branches:** Timothy Taylor & Co. Ltd, Lawkholme Lane, Keighley, West Yorkshire BD21 3LB
**US SIC:** 2082 **UK SIC:** 42702
**Auditors:** Stirk Lambert & Co
**Bankers:** Barclays Bank Plc (20-45-14)

| | 30-09-13 | 30-09-12 | 30-09-11 |
|---|---|---|---|
| TO | 21,876,538 | 22,149,688 | 22,055,255 |
| P/L | 1,224,673 | 2,116,878 | 2,735,519 |
| NW | 26,991,612 | 27,378,430 | 26,905,375 |
| WC | 6,816,867 | 4,395,965 | 2,658,599 |
| Emp. | 183 | 215 | 188 |

DUNS 23-803-9655

## Timpson Group Plc

(**Subsidiary of:** Offerhappy Ltd)
Timpson House, Claverton Road, Roundthorn Industrial Estate, Wyt, Manchester M23 9TT
**Web:** www.timpson.co.uk
**Reg No:** 2339274 **Estd:** 1989 Public Limited Company
**Line of Business:** Management activities of holding companies
**Issued Capital:** £1,553,682
**Principals:** W J Timpson *(Chairman and Managing)*, S P Robertson, J Timpson, R Lane Smith
**Co. Secretary:** Paresh Majithia
**Responsibilities**
**Purchasing:** Sally Eve *(Head of Buying)*
**Branches:** Timpson Group Plc, 20A High Street, Walton-On-Thames, Surrey KT12 1DA
**US SIC:** 6711, 7251
**UK SIC:** 83962, 67200
**Auditors:** Deloitte LLP
**Bankers:** National Westminster Bank Plc (01-10-01)

| | 28-09-13 | 29-09-12 | 01-09-11 |
|---|---|---|---|
| TO | 144,597,000 | 136,494,000 | 131,976,000 |
| P/L | 14,533,000 | 10,148,000 | 12,836,000 |
| NW | 42,024,000 | 39,103,000 | 34,991,000 |
| WC | 5,649,000 | 6,393,000 | 4,962,000 |
| Emp. | 2,648 | 2,508 | 2,488 |

DUNS 28-987-0990

## Tims Dairy Ltd

Mopes Farmhouse, Denham Lane, Chalfont St Peter, Gerrards Cross, Buckinghamshire SL9 0QH
**Tel:** 01753888380
**Web:** www.timsdairy.co.uk
**Reg No:** 1805834 **Estd:** 2002 Private Limited Company
**Line of Business:** Dairies
**Issued Capital:** £36,000
**Principals:** C Timotheou *(Managing)*, P Timotheou
**Co. Secretary:** Christodoulos Timotheou
**Responsibilities**
**Senior:** Panayiotis Timotheou *(Customer Fulfilment Manager)*, Tony Timotheou *(Production Manager)*
**Branches:** Tims Dairy Ltd, Mopes Farm, Denham Lane, Gerrards Cross, Buckinghamshire SL9 0QH
**US SIC:** 2023 **UK SIC:** 41303
**Auditors:** A L G

| | 30-04-14 | 30-04-13 | 30-04-12 |
|---|---|---|---|
| TO | 9,209,262 | 7,597,134 | N/A |
| P/L | 720,137 | 669,328 | N/A |
| NW | 2,003,854 | 1,725,202 | 1,497,560 |
| WC | 804,913 | 654,757 | 453,977 |
| Emp. | 62 | 56 | N/A |

DUNS 39-872-3734 **Imp-Exp**

## Timstar Laboratory Suppliers Ltd

Unit 12 Ion Pass, Road 3, Winsford Industrial Estate, Winsford, Cheshire CW7 3BX
**Tel:** 01270-250459 **Fax:** 01270250601
**Web:** www.timstar.co.uk
**Reg No:** 2223843 **VAT No:** 158916428
**Estd:** 1988 Private Limited Company
**Line of Business:** Wholesale of pharmaceutical goods
**Export Markets:** Middle East
**Export Sales:** £615,000
**Issued Capital:** £10,000
**Directors:** Ms L J Cross, R Conway, Ms A M Wall, S Holdeman, Ms L M Macdonald, J V James, P Wall, R Fisk
**Co. Secretary:** Hs Secretarial Limited
**Responsibilities**
**Senior:** Jonathan Hickey *(Director)*, Simon Leggett *(Manager)*
**Sales:** Jonathan Hickey *(Director)*
**US SIC:** 5122, 5161
**UK SIC:** 61800, 61200
**Auditors:** Cooper Taylor
**Bankers:** The Royal Bank Of Scotland Plc (16-26-14)

| | 31-12-13 | 31-12-12 | 31-12-11 |
|---|---|---|---|
| TO | 8,032,000 | 7,401,000 | 6,516,000 |
| P/L | 223,000 | 402,000 | 398,000 |
| NW | 1,193,000 | 1,069,000 | 756,000 |
| WC | 814,000 | 915,000 | 582,000 |
| Emp. | 61 | 64 | 61 |

DUNS 28-873-9667 **Exp**

## Tincknell Fuels Ltd

(**Subsidiary of:** Tincknell Fuels (Holdings) Ltd)
Cathedral View Offices, Wookey Hole Road, Wells, Somerset BA5 2BT
**Tel:** 01749673661
**Web:** www.tincknells.com
**Reg No:** 1081952 **Estd:** 1972 Private Limited Company
**Line of Business:** Oil companies
**Issued Capital:** £10,000
**Directors:** Ms J M Tincknell, R F Ormond, Ms D J Tincknell, R J Tincknell
**Co. Secretary:** Philip Tincknell
**Responsibilities**
**Senior:** David Sexton *(General Manager)*, Phillip Tincknell *(Managing Director)*
**Finance:** Phillip Tincknell *(Managing Director)*
**IT:** Simon Blaymires *(IT Manager)*
**HR:** David Sexton *(General Manager)*, Shirley Tincknell *(Human Resources Manager)*
**Facilities:** Phillip Tincknell *(Managing Director)*
**Operations:** David Sexton *(General Manager)*
**Purchasing:** David Sexton *(General Manager)*
**Branches:** Tincknell Fuels Ltd, Royal Edward Dock, Bristol, Avon BS11 9BT
**US SIC:** 2999 **UK SIC:** 11150
**Auditors:** Gordon Wood, Scott & Partners
**Bankers:** Lloyds TSB Bank plc (30-99-29)

| | 30-04-14 | 30-04-13 | 30-04-12 |
|---|---|---|---|
| TO | 35,640,736 | 50,503,241 | 85,212,630 |
| P/L | 613,190 | 1,594,360 | (1,447,727) |
| NW | 3,756,929 | 3,462,720 | 2,292,035 |
| WC | 3,100,578 | 2,396,057 | 79,732 |
| Emp. | 84 | 106 | 132 |

DUNS 22-505-1002

## Tindle Newspapers Ltd

(**Subsidiary of:** Tindle Press Holdings Ltd)
The Old Court House, Union Road, Farnham, Surrey GU9 7PT
**Tel:** 01252735667 **Fax:** 01252-734007
**Web:** www.tindlenews.co.uk
**Reg No:** 0798870 **Estd:** 1964 Private Limited Company
**Line of Business:** Newspapers publishing
**Export Sales:** £330,281
**Issued Capital:** £18,002
**Principals:** Sir R S Tindle *(Chairman and Managing)*, O C Tindle, Mrs K L Fyfield, Mrs W D Craig
**Co. Secretary:** Lady Beryl Tindle
**Responsibilities**
**Senior:** Brian Doel *(Manager)*
**Branches:** Tindle Newspapers Ltd, Webbs House, The Tindle Suite, Liskeard, Cornwall PL14 6AH
**US SIC:** 2711 **UK SIC:** 47512
**Auditors:** Grant Thornton UK LLP
**Bankers:** Lloyds TSB Bank plc (30-93-74)

| | 31-03-13 | 31-03-12 | 31-03-11 |
|---|---|---|---|
| TO | 34,283,673 | 36,112,709 | 38,554,695 |
| P/L | 1,386,656 | 2,062,002 | 1,289,991 |
| NW | 27,177,966 | 26,327,678 | 26,508,160 |
| WC | 22,743,244 | 19,674,027 | 19,462,110 |
| Emp. | 725 | 761 | 788 |

DUNS 39-160-0426

## Tingdene Developments Ltd

(**Subsidiary of:** Tingdene (Mj) Ltd)
Bradfield Road, Finedon Road Industrial Estate, Wellingborough, Northamptonshire NN8 4HB
**Tel:** 01933230130 **Fax:** 01933230113
**Web:** www.tingdene-parks.net
**Reg No:** 2111947 **Estd:** 1987 Private Limited Company
**Line of Business:** Other letting of own property
**Issued Capital:** £1,450
**Principals:** M C Gibbard *(Managing)*, I C Collier, J M Pearson
**Co. Secretary:** Charles Liebscher
**Branches:** Tingdene Developments Ltd, Caddington Park, Skimpot Lane, Skimpot, Luton, Bedfordshire LU1 4AY
**US SIC:** 6519, 6552
**UK SIC:** 85000
**Auditors:** Grant Thornton
**Bankers:** Yorkshire Bank Plc (05-06-33)

| | 31-12-13 | 31-12-12 | 31-12-11 |
|---|---|---|---|
| TA | 6,185,494 | 6,185,494 | 6,185,494 |
| NW | 2,810,513 | 2,810,513 | 2,810,513 |
| WC | 4,911,002 | 1,591,465 | 1,591,465 |

DUNS 34-628-3513

## Tingdene (Mj) Ltd

45-49 Bradfield Road, Finedon Road Industrial Estate, Wellingborough, Northamptonshire NN8 4HB
**Tel:** 01933-230111
**Web:** www.tingdene.net
**Reg No:** 5434628 **Estd:** 2005 Private Limited Company
**Line of Business:** Other letting of own property
**Issued Capital:** £2,008,000
**Directors:** M C Gibbard, I C Collier, J M Pearson
**Co. Secretary:** Charles Liebscher
**Responsibilities**
**Senior:** James Gibbard *(Manager)*
**US SIC:** 6519 **UK SIC:** 85000
**Bankers:** National Westminster Bank Plc (55-81-42)

| | 31-12-13 | 31-12-12 | 31-12-11 |
|---|---|---|---|
| TO | 21,665,356 | 18,287,672 | 18,972,502 |
| P/L | 3,441,304 | 2,686,946 | 1,865,826 |
| NW | 12,172,414 | 9,736,421 | 7,098,375 |
| WC | (888,039) | (2,291,876) | (3,310,183) |
| Emp. | 135 | 130 | 121 |

DUNS 21-726-0793

## Tingham Grange Ltd

Old Mill Works, Gelligroes, Pontllanfraith, Blackwood, Gwent NP12 2HY
**Tel:** 01495-227331
**Web:** http://gryphonn.co.uk
**Reg No:** 1069558 **Estd:** 1972 Private Limited Company
**Line of Business:** Manufacture of concrete products for construction purposes
**Trading Style:** Gryphonn Concrete Products
**Issued Capital:** £4,700
**Principals:** A Gilson *(Managing)*, D M Gilson, A W Gilson, H Gilson, D R Gilson
**Co. Secretary:** Roger Gilson
**Responsibilities**
**Finance:** Dickie Dimic *(Finance Director)*
**US SIC:** 3999 **UK SIC:** 49590
**Auditors:** Shepherd & Co

**Bankers:** Barclays Bank Plc (20-60-58)

| | 31-10-13 | 31-10-12 | 31-10-11 |
|---|---|---|---|
| TO | 4,911,488 | 4,528,802 | 4,581,104 |
| P/L | 29,276 | (62,536) | 26,504 |
| NW | 2,521,751 | 2,502,861 | 2,520,996 |
| WC | 675,124 | 789,441 | 943,215 |
| Emp. | 66 | 61 | 60 |

DUNS 21-728-3685

## Tinglobal Holdings Ltd

(**Subsidiary of:** Asvida Uk Ltd)
Bankside Park 15 Love Lane, Cirencester, Gloucestershire GL7 1YG
**Tel:** 02088319339
**Web:** www.tinglobal.com
**Reg No:** 7644383 **Estd:** 2011 Private Limited Company
**Line of Business:** Other business activities not elsewhere classified
**Issued Capital:** £147,333
**Directors:** T S Murphy, P S Hodson, C F Tong, D J Gutteridge, K G Ya, K K Wong, M G Jordan
**Co. Secretary:** Pinsent Masons Secretarial Limit
**Responsibilities**
**Senior:** Chee Wong *(Director)*
**US SIC:** 7399 **UK SIC:** 83954
**Bankers:** HSBC Bank plc (40-00-00)

| | 31-12-13 | 31-05-13 | 31-12-12 |
|---|---|---|---|
| TO | 9,915,000 | 19,016,857 | 18,359,984 |
| P/L | 209,000 | (161,977) | (384,522) |
| NW | (5,938,000) | (6,082,353) | (6,655,308) |
| WC | 1,106,000 | 1,881,762 | (1,249,617) |
| Emp. | 88 | 79 | 83 |

DUNS 23-840-7188 **Imp**

## Tinopolis Ltd

(**Subsidiary of:** Dmwsl 660 Ltd)
20 Park Street, Llanelli, Dyfed SA15 3YE
**Tel:** 01554-880880 **Fax:** 01554-880881
**Web:** www.tinopolis.com
**Reg No:** 3832383 **Estd:** 1999 Private Limited Company
**Line of Business:** Television activities
**Issued Capital:** £2,063,984
**Directors:** Ms J Roberts, J E Willis, O G Jones, A Mair, W A Rees, J Foulser
**Co. Secretary:** Ms Jennifer Roberts
**Responsibilities**
**Senior:** Glynog Davies *(Programming Director)*, Jeffrey Foulster *(Director)*, Ron Jones *(Chairman)*
**Finance:** Catrin Bowen *(Senior Finance Administrator)*, Catrin Curry *(Senior Finance Administrator)*
**Admin:** Janette Jones *(Office Manager)*
**IT:** Paul Bowen *(Computer Manager)*
**Facilities:** Peter Harston *(Chief Engineer)*
**Operations:** Janette Jones *(Office Manager)*, Mike Reynolds *(Studio Floor Manager)*
**Purchasing:** Janette Jones *(Office Manager)*
**Engineering:** Orig Jones *(Technical and IT Director)*
**US SIC:** 4833 **UK SIC:** 97411
**Auditors:** KPMG Audit PLC

| | 30-09-13 | 30-09-12 | 30-09-11 |
|---|---|---|---|
| TO | 101,812,000 | 73,792,000 | 69,102,000 |
| P/L | 7,078,000 | 8,425,000 | 5,551,000 |
| NW | (17,065,000) | 6,933,000 | 2,531,000 |
| WC | (20,758,000) | 2,952,000 | (1,291,000) |
| Emp. | 488 | 347 | 364 |

DUNS 63-461-8367

## Tinsdill Solicitors

Hays House, 25 Albion Street, Stoke-On-Trent, Staffordshire ST1 1QF
**Tel:** 01782-262031
**Web:** www.tinsdills.co.uk
**Estd:** 2001 Partnership
**Line of Business:** Solicitors
**Partners:** F G Botham, P R Rhodes
**Responsibilities**
**Senior:** Tim Cogan *(Partner)*
**Marketing:** Karen Pieters *(Marketing Director)*
**Branches:** Tinsdill Solicitors, Hays House, 25 Albion Street, Stoke-On-Trent, Staffordshire ST1 1QF
**US SIC:** 8111 **UK SIC:** 83500
**Employees:** 58

DUNS 39-415-4678 **Exp**

## Tinsley Bridge (Holdings) Ltd

335 Shepcote Lane, Sheffield, South Yorkshire S9 1TG
**Web:** www.tinsleybridge.co.uk
**Reg No:** 2122308 **VAT No:** 457844017
**Estd:** 1987 Private Limited Company
**Line of Business:** Management activities of production holding companies
**Export Markets:** E U, Worldwide
**Export Sales:** £9,593,583
**Issued Capital:** £125,632
**Principals:** M C Webber *(Marketing)*, B S Cunliffe, D Owens, D I Campbell, K Charlesworth, M Shield
**Co. Secretary:** Barry Cunliffe

**Responsibilities**
**Senior:** Paul Dunleavy *(Warehouse Manager)*
**Marketing:** Claire Campbell *(IT Manager)*
**IT:** Claire Campbell *(IT Manager)*
**Operations:** Claire Campbell *(IT Manager)*
**US SIC:** 6711 **UK SIC:** 83962
**Auditors:** Grant Thornton UK LLP
**Bankers:** The Royal Bank Of Scotland Plc (16-26-32)

| | 30-09-14 | 30-09-13 | 30-09-12 |
|---|---|---|---|
| TO | 14,633,523 | 15,690,251 | 16,841,878 |
| P/L | (295,936) | 452,347 | 1,122,100 |
| NW | 10,990,921 | 10,688,414 | 10,532,818 |
| WC | 4,315,093 | 5,592,828 | 5,344,106 |
| Emp. | 180 | 174 | 174 |

DUNS 21-627-7863 Imp-Exp
## The Tintometer Ltd
**(Subsidiary of:** Tintometer Gesellschaft Mit Beschränkter Haftung)
Solar Way, Solstice Park, Amesbury, Salisbury, Wiltshire SP4 7SZ
**Tel:** 01980664800 **Fax:** 01902625412
**Web:** www.lovibondcolour.com
**Reg No:** 0045024 **VAT No:** 188854010
**Estd:** 1885 Private Limited Company
**Line of Business:** Manufacture of other inorganic basic chemicals
**Export Markets:** Worldwide
**Export Sales:** £9,253,140
**Trading Style:** Tintometer, Lovibond
**Issued Capital:** £8,750
**Directors:** M Reid, R E Lambourne, C A Counsell, Mrs M C Voss, C P Voss
**Co. Secretary:** Graham Belbin
**Responsibilities**
**Senior:** Manfred Nowak *(Manager)*, Len Tryhorn *(Works Manager)*
**IT:** Nick Pitman *(Senior IT Executive)*
**HR:** Lynda Toomer *(Human Resources Manager)*, Len Tryhorn *(Works Manager)*
**Health & Safety:** Len Tryhorn *(Works Manager)*
**Facilities:** Eva Snowdon *(Purchasing Manager)*
**Operations:** Len Tryhorn *(Works Manager)*
**Purchasing:** Eva Snowdon *(Purchasing Manager)*, Len Tryhorn *(Works Manager)*
**Engineering:** Len Tryhorn *(Works Manager)*
**Branches:** The Tintometer Ltd, Palmers Way, Unit 1, Wadebridge, Cornwall PL27 6HB
**US SIC:** 2819, 3823, 3999
**UK SIC:** 25110, 37100, 49590
**Auditors:** Nexia Smith & Williamson
**Bankers:** Lloyds TSB Bank plc (30-97-41)

| | 31-12-13 | 31-12-12 | 31-12-11 |
|---|---|---|---|
| TO | 12,861,769 | 9,122,657 | 7,748,369 |
| P/L | 2,895,334 | 1,124,522 | 629,623 |
| NW | 4,421,177 | 1,496,856 | 1,775,040 |
| WC | 4,316,816 | 2,694,487 | 1,805,951 |
| Emp. | 95 | 92 | 91 |

DUNS 23-529-4761
## Tio Ltd
**(Subsidiary of:** Russell Burgess Ltd)
13 Greshop Road, Greshop Industrial Estate, Forres, Morayshire IV36 2GU
**Web:** www.tio.co.uk
**Reg No:** 0183910SC **Estd:** 1998 Private Limited Company
**Line of Business:** Wholesalers of fruit and vegetable
**Trading Style:** This Is Organics
**Issued Capital:** £100,000
**Directors:** D W Burgess, P Jones
**US SIC:** 5148, 0161, 5146
**UK SIC:** 61700, 01001
**Auditors:** Johnston Carmichael LLP
**Bankers:** The Royal Bank Of Scotland Plc (83-23-10)

| | 31-05-14 | 31-05-13 | 31-05-12 |
|---|---|---|---|
| TO | 8,453,936 | 8,570,226 | 8,539,820 |
| P/L | 331,673 | 271,760 | (51,527) |
| NW | 2,361,773 | 2,128,360 | 1,977,195 |
| WC | (103,399) | 171,861 | (763,564) |
| Emp. | 49 | 55 | 67 |

DUNS 45-809-5668 Imp-Exp
## Tioga Ltd
St Thomas House, Mansfield Road, Derby, Derbyshire DE1 3TN
**Tel:** 01332-360884 **Fax:** 01332-360885
**Web:** www.tioga.co.uk
**Reg No:** 3167564 **VAT No:** 683947479
**Estd:** 1996 Private Limited Company
**Line of Business:** Manufacturers of printed circuits
**Export Markets:** Worldwide
**Export Sales:** £573,649
**Trading Style:** Q C E, Quality Component Europe
**Issued Capital:** £251,250
**Principals:** W Adams *(Managing)*, R B Hoyle, J A Mumby, J A Hislop
**Co. Secretary:** Mrs Helen Higginbotham
**Responsibilities**
**IT:** Ian Wingfield *(Computer Manager)*
**Facilities:** Lloyd Bruce *(Production Manager)*
**Purchasing:** Karl Belmar *(Strategic Materials Manager)*, Matt Button *(Purchasing Manager)*, Debbie Garon *(Purchasing Manager)*
**Engineering:** Lloyd Bruce *(Production Manager)*
**Branches:** Tioga Ltd, 1st Floor, 20 Grove Pl, Bedford, Bedfordshire MK40 3JJ
**US SIC:** 3643, 5065
**UK SIC:** 34203, 61500
**Auditors:** Cooper Parry LLP
**Bankers:** National Westminster Bank Plc (60-80-09)

| | 31-03-14 | 31-03-13 | 31-03-12 |
|---|---|---|---|
| TO | 6,349,473 | 8,544,961 | 9,024,670 |
| P/L | 128,019 | 678,791 | 1,205,319 |
| NW | 1,911,527 | 1,688,432 | 1,109,190 |
| WC | 512,070 | 330,551 | 38,442 |
| Emp. | 62 | 78 | 71 |

DUNS 21-090-1377
## Tioxide Europe Ltd
**(Subsidiary of:** Huntsman (Holdings) Uk)
Tees Road, Hartlepool, Cleveland TS25 2DD
**Tel:** 01642376600
**Web:** www.huntsman.com
**Reg No:** 0832447 **VAT No:** 257529139
**Estd:** 1964 Private Limited Company
**Line of Business:** Manufacture of dyes and pigments
**Trading Style:** Huntsman Pigments, Huntsman Polyurethanes, Huntsman Advanced Materials, Huntsman Petro Chemicals
**Issued Capital:** £297,456,996
**Directors:** D Emerson, K Esplin, T G Fisher, M C Dixon
**Co. Secretary:** Richard Phillipson
**Responsibilities**
**Senior:** Wilton Beattie *(Manager)*
**Branches:** Tioxide Europe Ltd, Pyewipe, Grimsby, South Humberside DN31 2SW
**US SIC:** 2816 **UK SIC:** 25160
**Auditors:** Deloitte LLP
**Bankers:** The Chase Manhattan Bank (60-91-41)

| | 31-12-13 | 31-12-12 | 31-12-11 |
|---|---|---|---|
| TO | 275,995,000 | 430,477,000 | 360,994,000 |
| P/L | (4,139,000) | 111,437,000 | 74,293,000 |
| NW | 290,866,000 | 319,169,000 | 207,791,000 |
| WC | 210,209,000 | 232,039,000 | 136,078,000 |
| Emp. | 502 | 492 | 497 |

DUNS 21-152-8617 Exp
## Tioxide Group Services Ltd
**(Subsidiary of:** Huntsman (Holdings) Uk)
Haverton Hill Road, Billingham, Cleveland TS23 1PS
**Tel:** 01642370300
**Web:** www.huntsman.com
**Reg No:** 0995450 **Estd:** 1990 Private Limited Company
**Line of Business:** Chemicals and allied products
**Trading Style:** Huntsman Tioxide
**Issued Capital:** £25,000,000
**Principals:** M C Dixon *(Financial)*, D Emerson, T G Fisher, R J Phillipson
**Co. Secretary:** Richard Phillipson
**Responsibilities**
**Senior:** Michael Maughan *(Manager)*
**Sales:** David Foulger *(Sales Manager)*
**HR:** Ian Bellerby *(Training Officer)*
**Operations:** George Best *(Environmental Support Manager)*
**Branches:** Tioxide Group Services Ltd, Haverton Hill Road, Billingham, Cleveland TS23 1PS
**US SIC:** 2899 **UK SIC:** 25670
**Bankers:** Lloyds TSB Bank plc (30-00-02)

| | 31-12-13 | 31-12-12 |
|---|---|---|
| TA | 1 | 1 |
| NW | 1 | 1 |

DUNS 29-680-6052
## T.I.P. Europe Ltd
**(Subsidiary of:** General Electric Company)
Carrington Works, Isherwood Road, Carrington, Manchester M31 4QZ
**Tel:** 01617776789 **Fax:** 0161-905-5740
**Web:** www.tip.ge.com
**Reg No:** 2004028 **VAT No:** 449472516
**Estd:** 1986 Private Limited Company
**Line of Business:** Leasing companies
**Trading Style:** T I P Trailer Rentals
**Issued Capital:** £36,523,293
**Directors:** D T Clark, N C Smith
**Co. Secretary:** Oakwood Corporate Secretary Limi
**Responsibilities**
**Senior:** Anthony Goulden *(Branch Manager)*
**Branches:** T.i.p. Europe Ltd, Uxbridge Rd, Mill End, Rickmansworth, Hertfordshire WD3 8XA
**US SIC:** 7513 **UK SIC:** 84802
**Auditors:** KPMG Audit PLC

| | 30-06-13 | 31-12-11 | 31-06-10 |
|---|---|---|---|
| TO | 67,978,000 | 46,742,000 | 46,465,000 |
| P/L | 416,000 | 480,000 | (5,737,000) |
| NW | 58,859,000 | 98,634,000 | 101,916,000 |
| WC | 3,692,000 | 24,547,000 | 15,945,000 |
| Emp. | 202 | 193 | 206 |

DUNS 21-619-7140
## Tipek Security Services
Manchester Road, Walmersley, Bury, Lancashire BL9 5NB
**Tel:** 01706282310
**Web:** www.tipek.co.uk
**Estd:** 2006 Partnership
**Line of Business:** manned guarding services
**US SIC:** 7393 **UK SIC:** 83954
**Employees:** 70

DUNS 50-359-1349 Imp-Exp
## Tipografic Ltd
Unit 6 Morpeth Wharf, Twelve Quays, Birkenhead, Merseyside CH41 1LF
**Tel:** 01516474898 **Fax:** 01516-660212
**Web:** www.tipografic.co.uk
**Reg No:** 2376227 **VAT No:** 482956892
**Estd:** 1989 Private Limited Company
**Line of Business:** Printing not elsewhere classified
**Export Markets:** Europe
**Issued Capital:** £22,650
**Principals:** J R Cornell *(Managing)*, S J Cole *(Sales)*, Mrs V A Cornell, Mrs J R Cole, Miss K A Cornell
**Co. Secretary:** Mrs Lesley Price
**US SIC:** 2752, 2651
**UK SIC:** 47544, 47253
**Auditors:** Duncan Sheard Glass
**Bankers:** Lloyds TSB Bank plc (30-15-52)

| | 31-10-13 | 31-10-12 | 31-10-11 |
|---|---|---|---|
| TO | 14,776,195 | 13,758,536 | 13,104,938 |
| P/L | 1,073,764 | 1,039,041 | 872,124 |
| NW | 2,762,641 | 2,445,540 | 1,748,675 |
| WC | 1,035,221 | 636,401 | 102,603 |
| Emp. | 88 | 84 | 85 |

DUNS 21-226-6575
## Tippethill Hospital
Hurst Cottage, Armadale Road, Bathgate, West Lothian EH47 0ET
**Tel:** 01501-745917
**Estd:** 2000 Proprietorship
**Line of Business:** Hospitals
**Proprietor:** Mrs A Sneddon
**US SIC:** 8051 **UK SIC:** 95100
**Employees:** 58

DUNS 23-877-7002
## Tipton & Coseley Building Society Charitable Foundation
70 Owen Street, Tipton, West Midlands DY4 8HG
**Tel:** 0121 557 2551
**Web:** www.thetipton.co.uk
**Reg No:** 3869002 **Estd:** 1999 Private Unlimited Company
**Line of Business:** Building societies
**Directors:** R C Savage, Mrs S J Schofield, S Downing, R Hazel, Miss S Sandbrook
**Co. Secretary:** John Miller
**Branches:** Tipton & Coseley Building Society Charitable Foundation, 6 Bull Ring, Dudley, West Midlands DY3 1RX
**US SIC:** 7399 **UK SIC:** 83954
**Auditors:** Higgs & Sons

| | 31-05-14 | 31-05-13 | 31-05-12 |
|---|---|---|---|
| TO | N/A | 10,378 | 10,439 |
| P/L | N/A | (111) | (4,014) |
| NW | 2,749 | 271 | 382 |
| WC | 2,749 | 271 | 382 |

DUNS 73-937-1623 Imp
## Tis Hydraulics Ltd
Kirkhill Place, Aberdeen, Aberdeenshire AB21 0GU
**Tel:** 01224-775277
**Web:** www.tis-hydraulics.com
**Reg No:** 0151682SC **VAT No:** 605279443
**Estd:** 1994 Private Limited Company
**Line of Business:** Hydraulic equipment & accessories - sales & service
**Trading Style:** T I S
**Issued Capital:** £200
**Principals:** N R Forrest *(Managing)*, N Forrest
**Co. Secretary:** Burnett & Reid Llp
**Responsibilities**
**Finance:** Elaine Dunbar *(Senior Account Administrator)*
**US SIC:** 3999 **UK SIC:** 49590
**Auditors:** Anderson Anderson & Brown
**Bankers:** Bank Of Scotland (80-06-60)

| | 30-06-13 | 30-06-12 | 30-06-11 |
|---|---|---|---|
| TA | 5,081,180 | 4,476,718 | 3,715,825 |
| NW | 4,181,878 | 3,536,798 | 2,842,099 |
| WC | 4,151,092 | 3,500,418 | 2,815,282 |

DUNS 23-794-1559
## T.I.S.Cumbria Ltd
Isabella Road, Workington, Cumbria CA14 2JS
**Tel:** 0190065752
**Web:** www.tiscumbrialtd.com
**Reg No:** 3786942 **Estd:** 1999 Private Limited Company
**Line of Business:** Steel fabricators
**Issued Capital:** £2
**Directors:** P Edmondson, J W Bragg, W A O'Pray, Ms A O'Pray
**Co. Secretary:** Ms Margaret Nicholson
**US SIC:** 5084, 1622
**UK SIC:** 61490, 50200
**Bankers:** National Westminster Bank Plc (55-81-37)

| | 30-06-13 | 30-06-12 | 30-06-11 |
|---|---|---|---|
| TA | 2,968,915 | 1,569,969 | 1,358,034 |
| NW | 1,430,509 | 854,912 | 670,432 |
| WC | 213,241 | 429,659 | 480,351 |

DUNS 23-558-6570
## Tishman Speyer Properties U K Ltd
**(Subsidiary of:** Tishman Speyer Properties L.P.)
6th Floor, London WC2B 4AE
**Tel:** 020-7333-2400 **Fax:** 020-7333-2500
**Web:** www.tishmanspeyer.com
**Reg No:** 3556917 **VAT No:** 718953009
**Estd:** 1998 Private Limited Company
**Line of Business:** Property investment company
**Export Sales:** £38,964,033
**Trading Style:** Tishman Speyer
**Issued Capital:** £17,873,436
**Directors:** R S Orr, Ms K G Farley, B E Penaud, J I Speyer, R Speyer, M Spies, G R Hatzmann
**Co. Secretary:** Michael Spies
**Responsibilities**
**Senior:** Eric Adler *(Manager)*, Paul Galiano *(Senior Managing Director)*, Dan Nicholson *(Manager)*, Toby Phelps *(Manager)*, Julian Stocks *(Manager)*
**HR:** Alison Beaton *(Head of Human Resources)*
**Health & Safety:** Ian Lydon *(Property Manager)*
**Facilities:** Ian Lydon *(Property Manager)*
**US SIC:** 6552, 6531
**UK SIC:** 85000, 83400
**Auditors:** Ernst & Young LLP
**Bankers:** Barclays Bank Plc (20-71-74)

| | 31-12-13 | 31-12-12 | 31-12-11 |
|---|---|---|---|
| TO | 44,292,206 | 40,153,857 | 40,386,756 |
| P/L | 4,535,379 | 3,992,008 | 4,574,261 |
| NW | 15,947,656 | 13,660,466 | 25,265,389 |
| WC | 14,725,469 | 12,183,316 | 23,601,236 |
| Emp. | 161 | 146 | 136 |

DUNS 77-902-1240
## Tissue Regenix Ltd
**(Subsidiary of:** Tissue Regenix Group Plc)
The Biocentre Innovation Way, Heslington, York, North Yorkshire YO10 5NY
**Tel:** 01904567609 **Fax:** 01904380517
**Web:** www.tissueregenix.com
**Reg No:** 5807272 **Estd:** 2006 Private Limited Company
**Line of Business:** Research and laboratory based activities
**Issued Capital:** £110
**Directors:** A R Odell, I D Jefferson, A J Miller, J A Samuel, Ip2ipo Services Limited
**Co. Secretary:** Ian Jefferson
**Responsibilities**
**Operations:** Bill McCarthy *(Quality Manager & Microbiologi)*
**US SIC:** 7391 **UK SIC:** 94000
**Auditors:** Baker Tilly UK Audit LLP

| | 31-01-14 | 31-01-13 | 31-01-12 |
|---|---|---|---|
| TO | 6,000 | 49,000 | 109,000 |
| P/L | (2,500,000) | (3,461,000) | (2,085,000) |
| NW | (6,780,000) | (4,605,000) | (1,618,000) |
| WC | (7,235,000) | (4,843,000) | (1,775,000) |
| Emp. | 46 | 34 | 25 |

DUNS 23-966-4217
## Titan Automotive Ltd
Unit 3, Harley Industrial Park, Paxton H, St Neots, Cambridgeshire PE19 6TA
**Tel:** 01480471668 **Fax:** 01480-485668
**Reg No:** 3955291 **Estd:** 2000 Private Limited Company
**Line of Business:** manufacturers of racing car parts
**Issued Capital:** £2
**Managing Director:** L R Timms
**Co. Secretary:** Mrs Diana Thomas
**US SIC:** 3559 **UK SIC:** 32863

| | 30-09-13 | 30-09-12 | 30-09-11 |
|---|---|---|---|
| TA | 11,129 | 11,129 | 11,129 |
| NW | 11,129 | 11,129 | 11,129 |

DUNS 52-031-9278 Imp
## Titan Elevators Ltd
Innovation House, Cray Road, Sidcup, Kent DA14 5DP
**Fax:** 0208 303 0022
**Web:** www.titanelevators.co.uk
**Reg No:** 3398412 **Estd:** 1997 Private Limited Company
**Line of Business:** Lifts (maintenance and repair)
**Issued Capital:** £10,000

**Directors:** J Flynn, M Rutter, D A Warr, Ms J E Warr, S K Collcutt
**Co. Secretary:** Matthew Dykes
**US SIC:** 3534, 7399
**UK SIC:** 32553, 83954
**Auditors:** Haslers

|  | 31-03-14 | 31-03-13 | 31-03-12 |
|---|---|---|---|
| TO | 8,432,370 | 7,061,613 | N/A |
| P/L | 304,586 | 127,069 | N/A |
| NW | 1,053,062 | 824,610 | 731,922 |
| WC | 647,588 | 338,147 | 547,090 |
| Emp. | 74 | 71 | N/A |

DUNS 34-898-2257   Imp
## Titan Entertainment Group Ltd
Ross House, 144 Southwark Street, London SE1 0UP
**Tel:** 02076200200
**Web:** http://titanbooks.com
**Reg No:** 2829144 **VAT No:** 629608318
**Estd:** 1993 Private Limited Company
**Line of Business:** Management activities of holding companies
**Export Sales:** £11,094,247
**Issued Capital:** £1,204
**Managing Director:** N A Landau
**Co. Secretary:** Dr Vivian Cheung
**US SIC:** 6711, 5942
**UK SIC:** 83962, 65300
**Auditors:** Leigh Saxton Green
**Bankers:** Barclays Bank Plc (20-03-53)

|  | 31-12-13 | 31-12-12 | 31-12-11 |
|---|---|---|---|
| TO | 35,134,668 | 28,215,788 | 26,417,185 |
| P/L | 1,517,392 | 950,512 | 321,986 |
| NW | 8,872,085 | 7,838,651 | 7,240,569 |
| WC | 2,736,389 | 2,838,768 | 2,246,242 |
| Emp. | 243 | 230 | 224 |

DUNS 77-755-5368   Imp-Exp
## Titan Europe Ltd
(**Subsidiary of:** Titan International Inc.)
Bridge Road, Cookley, Kidderminster, Worcestershire DY10 3SD
**Tel:** 01562-850561 **Fax:** 01562851554
**Web:** www.titaneurope.com
**Reg No:** 3018340 **Estd:** 1995 Private Limited Company
**Line of Business:** Management activities of holding companies
**Export Markets:** Worldwide
**Trading Style:** Titan Steel Wheels
**Issued Capital:** £35,129,195
**Directors:** M Troyanovich, Ms M C La Manna, P Reitz
**Co. Secretary:** Gary Chesterton
**Responsibilities**
**Senior:** Mike Akers (Chief Executive Officer), John Akers (Chief Executive), Erwin Billig (Manager), Maria Manna (Manager), Vincent Wicks (Manager)
**Sales:** Lindsey Akers (European Sales Manager)
**IT:** Stuart Bethell (Network Manager)
**US SIC:** 6711 **UK SIC:** 83962
**Auditors:** PricewaterhouseCoopers LLP
**Bankers:** The Royal Bank Of Scotland Plc (16-13-18)

|  | 31-12-13 | 31-12-12 | 31-12-11 |
|---|---|---|---|
| TO | 354,367,000 | 451,898,000 | 492,521,000 |
| P/L | (21,898,000) | (14,026,000) | 21,644,000 |
| NW | 124,741,000 | 76,520,000 | 107,756,000 |
| WC | 98,067,000 | 17,285,000 | 60,302,000 |
| Emp. | 2,453 | 2,666 | 2,669 |

DUNS 21-705-3651   Imp-Exp
## Titan Ladders Holdings Ltd
Mendip Road, Yatton, Bristol, Avon BS49 4ET
**Tel:** 01934-832161 **Fax:** 01934-876180
**Web:** www.titanladders.co.uk
**Reg No:** 0881103 **VAT No:** 130499278
**Estd:** 1933 Private Limited Company
**Line of Business:** Manufacture of other fabricated metal products not elsewhere classified
**Issued Capital:** £4,000
**Principals:** R D Starke (Managing), G S Starke
**Co. Secretary:** Bruce Candy
**Responsibilities**
**HR:** Sue Bennett (Manager)
**Facilities:** Paul Routley (Works Manager)
**Purchasing:** Paul Routley (Works Manager)
**US SIC:** 3499 **UK SIC:** 31694
**Auditors:** Bruce N Simmonds & Associates
**Bankers:** National Westminster Bank Plc (56-00-05)

|  | 31-12-13 | 31-12-12 | 31-12-11 |
|---|---|---|---|
| TO | 3,889,472 | 4,373,658 | 5,240,818 |
| P/L | 327,553 | (213,562) | 12,376 |
| NW | 3,690,454 | 3,518,752 | 3,732,314 |
| WC | 1,967,515 | 1,928,995 | 2,063,173 |
| Emp. | 48 | 50 | 54 |

DUNS 22-660-5319
## Titan Motorsport & Automotive Engineering Ltd
Unit 3, St Neots, Cambridgeshire PE19 6TA
**Tel:** 01480-474402
**Web:** www.titan.uk.net
**Reg No:** 1213297 **VAT No:** 214798738

---

**Estd:** 2010 Private Limited Company
**Line of Business:** Car accessories and parts
**Issued Capital:** £1,000
**Managing Director:** L R Timms
**Co. Secretary:** Mrs Diana Thomas
**Responsibilities**
**Marketing:** Zoe Timbrell (Marketing Manager)
**US SIC:** 3714 **UK SIC:** 35300
**Bankers:** Barclays Bank Plc (20-74-81)

|  | 30-09-13 | 30-09-12 | 30-09-11 |
|---|---|---|---|
| TA | 2,508,720 | 2,283,883 | 2,007,248 |
| NW | 1,338,034 | 1,144,338 | 1,042,786 |
| WC | 843,893 | 630,183 | 664,874 |

DUNS 73-333-0091
## Titan Security Services Ltd
18 Friar Lane, Nottingham, Nottinghamshire NG1 6DQ
**Tel:** 01159-507797
**Web:** www.titan-security.co.uk
**Reg No:** 4606824 **Estd:** 2002 Private Limited Company
**Line of Business:** Security activities
**Issued Capital:** £1
**Director:** T Yousaf
**US SIC:** 7393 **UK SIC:** 83954

|  | 31-12-13 | 31-12-12 | 31-12-11 |
|---|---|---|---|
| TA | 87,054 | 89,048 | 50,235 |
| NW | 66,777 | 71,303 | 47,676 |
| WC | 56,623 | 58,334 | 33,989 |

DUNS 21-069-0666
## Titan Transport Ltd
(**Subsidiary of:** Acromas Holdings Ltd)
Crossoak Lane, Southfords, Redhill, Redhill, Surrey RH1 5EX
**Tel:** 01293450849
**Web:** www.titandrivers.co.uk
**Reg No:** 6372780 **Estd:** 2007 Private Limited Company
**Line of Business:** Activities of travel organisers
**Issued Capital:** £1
**Directors:** A J Strong, A C Donald
**Co. Secretary:** Ms Victoria Haynes
**US SIC:** 4722 **UK SIC:** 77001

|  | 31-01-14 | 31-01-13 | 31-01-12 |
|---|---|---|---|
| TO | 64,458,000 | 56,649,000 | 52,293,000 |
| P/L | 10,048,000 | 10,979,000 | 10,973,000 |
| NW | N/A | 133,000 | 135,000 |
| WC | (1,577,000) | (2,131,000) | (731,000) |
| Emp. | 78 | 81 | 88 |

DUNS 21-624-9977
## Titan Travel Ltd
(**Subsidiary of:** Acromas Holdings Ltd)
Hitours House, Redhill, Surrey RH1 5EX
**Tel:** 01293450460
**Web:** www.titantravel.co.uk
**Reg No:** 7049375 **Estd:** 2009 Private Limited Company
**Line of Business:** Tour operators
**Trading Style:** Titian Travel
**Issued Capital:** £1
**Director:** A J Strong
**Co. Secretary:** Ms Victoria Haynes
**Responsibilities**
**Marketing:** Joanna Morfield (Online Marketing Manager), Dan Whitehouse (Marketing Director)
**Sales:** Jackie Willis (Commercial Director)
**Branches:** Titan Travel Ltd, Glenhaven Drive, Unit 1, Staines, Middlesex TW19 6AF
**US SIC:** 7999 **UK SIC:** 97913

|  | 31-01-14 | 31-01-13 | 31-01-12 |
|---|---|---|---|
| TA | 1 | 1 | 1 |
| NW | 1 | 1 | 1 |

DUNS 67-137-1669
## Titchfield Group Ltd
Sopers Road, Cuffley, Potters Bar, Hertfordshire EN6 4RY
**Tel:** 01707874777
**Web:** www.titchfieldgroup.com
**Reg No:** 5995931 **Estd:** 2006 Private Limited Company
**Line of Business:** Other building completion
**Issued Capital:** £100,000
**Director:** N E Brunt
**Co. Secretary:** Ms Carol Brunt
**Responsibilities**
**Senior:** Keith Perry (Manager)
**US SIC:** 1799, 1751
**UK SIC:** 50000, 50400

|  | 30-06-13 | 30-06-12 | 30-06-11 |
|---|---|---|---|
| TA | 1,222,124 | 1,222,124 | 1,222,124 |
| NW | 63,685 | 63,685 | 63,685 |

DUNS 21-815-5836   Exp
## Titchmarsh & Goodwin
Back Hamlet, Ipswich, Suffolk IP3 8AL
**Tel:** 01473-252158
**Web:** www.titchmarsh-goodwin.co.uk
**Reg No:** 0840316 **VAT No:** 102803322
**Estd:** 1920 Private Unlimited Company
**Line of Business:** Manufacture of other furniture
**Export Markets:** Europe

---

**Trading Style:** Witenshaw Sawmills
**Issued Capital:** £50,000
**Director:** A Kabelev
**Responsibilities**
**Senior:** David Bullard (Works Manager), Jamie Cooper (Manager)
**Facilities:** David Bullard (Works Manager)
**Engineering:** David Bullard (Works Manager)
**Branches:** Titchmarsh & Goodwin, Mow Hill, Ipswich, Suffolk IP6 9EH
**US SIC:** 2517 **UK SIC:** 46714
**Bankers:** HSBC Bank plc (40-25-31)
**Employees:** 50

DUNS 21-241-1391   Exp
## Tithebarn Ltd
(**Subsidiary of:** Lloyds Banking Group Plc)
Road Five, Winsford, Cheshire CW7 3PG
**Tel:** 01606595000 **Fax:** 01606-595045
**Web:** www.tithebarn.co.uk
**Reg No:** 0300375 **VAT No:** 164240192
**Estd:** 1935 Private Limited Company
**Line of Business:** Animal feed and pet foods
**Export Markets:** E U, worldwide
**Export Sales:** £15,726,785
**Issued Capital:** £2,709
**Directors:** J Sample, J B Mahan
**Co. Secretary:** John Melling
**Responsibilities**
**Senior:** Steve Warner (Warehouse Manager)
**Finance:** Sue Ashley (Financial Manager)
**US SIC:** 2047 **UK SIC:** 42221
**Auditors:** Macfarlane & Co
**Bankers:** National Westminster Bank Plc (60-15-29)

|  | 31-07-14 | 31-07-13 | 31-07-12 |
|---|---|---|---|
| TO | 27,544,770 | 23,394,180 | 20,951,958 |
| P/L | 4,182,313 | 3,020,802 | 2,043,079 |
| NW | 11,462,651 | 8,517,185 | 6,759,732 |
| WC | 8,170,923 | 5,719,799 | 3,951,691 |
| Emp. | 168 | 167 | 151 |

DUNS 28-986-3987
## Tithegrove Ltd
Marshgate House, Marshgate, Swindon, Wiltshire SN1 2PA
**Tel:** 01793-509600 **Fax:** 01793509629
**Web:** www.tithegrove.com
**Reg No:** 1802721 **Estd:** 1984 Private Limited Company
**Line of Business:** Building construction management
**Issued Capital:** £1,250
**Principals:** P H Walton (Managing), S R Rayson, C R Waddell, D Bell, G J Tucker, D Torchia
**Responsibilities**
**Health & Safety:** Bob Acock (Health & Safety Officer)
**US SIC:** 1622, 1799
**UK SIC:** 50200, 50000
**Auditors:** Dennis & Turnbull
**Bankers:** Lloyds TSB Bank plc (30-98-41)

|  | 31-03-14 | 31-03-13 | 31-03-12 |
|---|---|---|---|
| TO | 43,737,843 | 42,769,098 | 30,717,690 |
| P/L | 2,116,762 | 1,419,966 | 874,919 |
| NW | 3,975,683 | 2,667,127 | 1,931,236 |
| WC | 3,220,612 | 2,003,730 | 1,427,109 |
| Emp. | 270 | 248 | 192 |

DUNS 23-876-5676
## Titian Software Ltd
(**Subsidiary of:** Titian Software Holdings Ltd)
2 Newhams Road, London SE1 3UZ
**Tel:** 020-7367-6869
**Web:** www.titian.co.uk
**Reg No:** 3867924 **VAT No:** 740970527
**Estd:** 1999 Private Limited Company
**Line of Business:** Other computer related activities
**Export Sales:** £6,112,159
**Issued Capital:** £2
**Director:** E C Wilson
**US SIC:** 7379 **UK SIC:** 83940
**Auditors:** Berg Kaprow Lewis LLP
**Bankers:** Lloyds TSB Bank plc (30-13-55)

|  | 31-03-14 | 31-03-13 | 31-03-12 |
|---|---|---|---|
| TO | 8,596,567 | N/A | N/A |
| P/L | 2,594,040 | N/A | N/A |
| NW | 2,431,358 | 1,521,274 | 383,556 |
| WC | 2,583,970 | 1,631,541 | 499,985 |
| Emp. | 59 | N/A | N/A |

DUNS 23-908-7450
## Titleworth Employee Trustees Ltd
(**Subsidiary of:** Titleworth Holdings Ltd)
Titleworth House, Alexandra Place, Guildford, Surrey GU1 3QH
**Tel:** 01483790070 **Fax:** 01483575185
**Web:** www.titleworth.com
**Reg No:** 3899276 **Estd:** 1999 Private Limited Company
**Line of Business:** Other business activities not elsewhere classified
**Issued Capital:** £1
**Co. Secretary:** Julien Payne

---

**Responsibilities**
**HR:** Shirley Wise (Human Resources Manager)
**Branches:** Titleworth Employee Trustees Ltd, 12 Katharine St, Croydon, Surrey CR0 1NX
**US SIC:** 7399 **UK SIC:** 83954
**Auditors:** Baker Tilly

|  | 31-12-13 | 31-12-12 | 31-12-11 |
|---|---|---|---|
| TA | 1 | 1 | 1 |
| NW | 1 | 1 | 1 |

DUNS 51-608-5136
## Titleworth Holdings Ltd
Titleworth House, Alexandra Place, Guildford, Surrey GU1 3QH
**Tel:** 01483790070 **Fax:** 01483575185
**Web:** www.titleworth.com
**Reg No:** 5888881 **Estd:** 2006 Private Limited Company
**Line of Business:** Management activities of other non-financial holding companies not elsewhere classified
**Issued Capital:** £1
**Directors:** J G Payne, M J Spencer, D A Coombs
**Responsibilities**
**Admin:** Kelly Newell (Office Manager)
**US SIC:** 7399, 8321
**UK SIC:** 83954, 96111
**Bankers:** Royal Bank Of Canada Europe Ltd (60-92-82)

|  | 31-12-13 | 31-12-12 | 31-12-11 |
|---|---|---|---|
| TO | 7,419,650 | 7,632,029 | 7,179,000 |
| P/L | 628,961 | 713,757 | 607,000 |
| NW | 1,570,862 | 1,201,284 | 749,000 |
| WC | 275,009 | 331,960 | 51,000 |
| Emp. | 267 | 220 | 195 |

DUNS 22-637-6960   Imp-Exp
## Titon Holdings Plc
International House, Peartree Road, Stanway, Colchester, Essex CO3 0JL
**Tel:** 01206713800 **Fax:** 01206-543126
**Web:** www.titon.com
**Reg No:** 1604952 **VAT No:** 368615325
**Estd:** 1972 Public Limited Company
**Line of Business:** Management activities of other non-financial holding companies not elsewhere classified
**Export Sales:** £7,475,000
**Trading Style:** Titon Hardware
**Issued Capital:** £1,055,565
**Principals:** J N Anderson (Chairman), K A Ritchie, T N Anderson, C S Jarvis, N C Howlett
**Co. Secretary:** David Ruffell
**US SIC:** 6711, 3079
**UK SIC:** 83962, 48360
**Auditors:** BDO LLP
**Bankers:** Barclays Bank Plc (20-97-40)

|  | 30-09-14 | 30-09-13 | 30-09-12 |
|---|---|---|---|
| TO | 19,256,000 | 15,740,000 | 14,548,000 |
| P/L | 1,333,000 | 505,000 | (984,000) |
| NW | 9,335,000 | 8,503,000 | 8,292,000 |
| WC | 6,323,000 | 5,304,000 | 5,101,000 |
| Emp. | 189 | 170 | 177 |

DUNS 21-776-9354
## Tiverton & District Hospital
Kennedy Way, Tiverton, Devon EX16 6NT
**Estd:** 2011 Partnership
**Line of Business:** Hospitals
**Partners:** S Hudson, L Hickman
**Responsibilities**
**Senior:** Ian Parsonage (Manager)
**US SIC:** 8062 **UK SIC:** 95100
**Employees:** 500

DUNS 21-776-9768
## Tividale Hall Primary School
213 Regent Road, Tividale, Oldbury, West Midlands B69 1RZ
**Tel:** 01384256500
**Web:** www.raylane.co.uk
**Estd:** 1972 Proprietorship
**Line of Business:** Chemists dispensing
**Proprietor:** Mrs P Willetts
**Responsibilities**
**Senior:** Dinesh Patel (Proprietor), C Waterworth (Deputy Head Teacher), D Waterworth (Deputy Head Teacher)
**Finance:** Nicola Kyte (Senior Finance Administrator)
**US SIC:** 8211 **UK SIC:** 93200
**Employees:** 60

DUNS 23-320-8458
## Tiwana Supersave
14 Highview Street, Dudley, West Midlands DY2 7JR
**Tel:** 01384252573
**Web:** www.unisys.com
**Estd:** 1988 Proprietorship
**Line of Business:** Retailers of beer, wine and spirits
**Proprietor:** B Singh
**Responsibilities**
**Senior:** Balvir Singh (Proprietor)
**US SIC:** 5921, 5411

**UK SIC:** 64200, 64100
**Bankers:** National Westminster Bank Plc (01-09-31)
**Employees:** 3,500

DUNS 21-739-2821
## Tizir Ltd
Portland House, Bressenden Place, London SE1 2AQ
**Tel:** 0208 433 6741
**Web:** www.tizir.co.uk
**Reg No:** 7727671 **Estd:** 2011 Private Limited Company
**Line of Business:** Mining of non-ferrous metal ores, except uranium and thorium ores
**Directors:** M C Ackland, N J Limb, L Egeland, A R Tissidre, W L Sharp, P G Vecten
**Co. Secretary:** Norose Company Secretarial Servi
**US SIC:** 1099 **UK SIC:** 21000
**Auditors:** Constantin
**Employees:** 938
**Turnover:** £215,131,000

DUNS 23-718-2907    Imp
## T.J. Crump Oakwrights Ltd
The Lakes, Swainshill, Hereford, Herefordshire HR4 7PU
**Tel:** 01432353353
**Web:** www.oakwrights.co.uk
**Reg No:** 3713116 **Estd:** 1999 Private Limited Company
**Line of Business:** Construction of civil engineering constructions
**Issued Capital:** £200
**Managing Director:** T J Crump
**Co. Secretary:** Ms Belinda Ryder
**Responsibilities**
**Senior:** Charles Price (Manager)
**IT:** Roland Horwood (Head of IT)
**US SIC:** 1622, 1751
**UK SIC:** 50200, 50400
**Auditors:** Knipe Whiting Heath

| | 31-12-13 | 31-12-12 | 31-12-11 |
|---|---|---|---|
| TA | 2,151,562 | 2,185,646 | 2,334,785 |
| NW | 1,166,240 | 1,093,590 | 1,325,619 |
| WC | 585,749 | 509,752 | 680,720 |

DUNS 21-632-0085
## T.J.Evers Ltd
(**Subsidiary of:** Trevester Ltd)
New Road, Tiptree, Colchester, Essex CO5 0HQ
**Tel:** 01621-815787 **Fax:** 01621-818085
**Web:** www.tjevers.co.uk
**Reg No:** 0383513 **VAT No:** 102263328
**Estd:** 1943 Private Limited Company
**Line of Business:** Building construction contractors
**Issued Capital:** £14,411
**Directors:** A M Evers, S Ewers, K P Howell, K P Browning, M J Denney
**Co. Secretary:** Ms Marie Paveley
**Responsibilities**
**Senior:** Robert Gladwin (Manager)
**Facilities:** Dave Harrison (Facilities Manager)
**Branches:** T.j.evers Ltd, 56A York Way, Thetford, Norfolk IP24 1EJ
**US SIC:** 1522 **UK SIC:** 50100
**Auditors:** Scrutton Bland
**Bankers:** Barclays Bank Plc (20-97-40)

| | 31-10-13 | 31-10-12 | 31-10-11 |
|---|---|---|---|
| TO | 14,274,023 | 15,438,102 | 12,946,449 |
| P/L | 226,285 | 239,217 | 184,215 |
| NW | 2,399,538 | 2,816,346 | 2,631,009 |
| WC | 874,823 | 1,364,644 | 1,240,970 |
| Emp. | 105 | 108 | 102 |

DUNS 28-966-7594
## T.J.Lowery (Developments) Ltd
(**Subsidiary of:** T. J. Lowery Group Holdings Ltd)
Riverside View, Basing Road, Old Basing, Basingstoke, Hampshire RG24 7AL
**Tel:** 01256-465601
**Reg No:** 1709373 **Estd:** 1983 Private Limited Company
**Line of Business:** Development and selling of real estate
**Issued Capital:** £100
**Director:** T J Lowery
**Co. Secretary:** Mrs Glenys Lowery
**US SIC:** 6552 **UK SIC:** 85000
**Auditors:** Harris Walters

| | 30-04-14 | 30-04-13 | 30-04-12 |
|---|---|---|---|
| NW | (8,570) | (8,570) | (8,570) |

DUNS 21-241-5699    Exp
## T.J.Thomson & Son Ltd
Millfield Works, Grangefield Road, Stockton-On-Tees, Cleveland TS18 4AE
**Tel:** 01642-672551 **Fax:** 01642-672556
**Web:** www.tjthomson.co.uk
**Reg No:** 0638347 **Estd:** 1871 Private Limited Company
**Line of Business:** Scrap metal dealers
**Export Markets:** E U & other countries.
**Export Sales:** £6,409,967
**Issued Capital:** £182,500
**Principals:** J B Turner (Chairman and Managing), R J Turner, D B Turner
**Co. Secretary:** Mrs Margaret Turner
**Responsibilities**
**Finance:** Richard Winterschladen (Financial Accountant)
**IT:** Richard Winterschladen (Financial Accountant)
**HR:** Richard Winterschladen (Financial Accountant)
**Branches:** T.j.thomson & Son Ltd, Jarrow Rd, South Shields, Tyne and Wear NE34 9PS
**US SIC:** 3341 **UK SIC:** 22470
**Auditors:** Anderson Barrowcliff
**Bankers:** National Westminster Bank Plc (54-10-04)

| | 31-03-14 | 31-03-13 | 31-03-12 |
|---|---|---|---|
| TO | 16,594,760 | 23,322,877 | 30,854,013 |
| P/L | (840,099) | 624,883 | 836,816 |
| NW | 7,731,988 | 8,585,328 | 8,111,437 |
| WC | 6,926,285 | 7,544,667 | 7,051,276 |
| Emp. | 55 | 54 | 51 |

DUNS 21-717-6971
## Tjw Contract Solutions Ltd
1st Floor Haleworth House, Tite Hill, Egham, Surrey TW20 0LR
**Tel:** 08452410280
**Web:** www.tjwcontracts.co.uk
**Reg No:** 7562791 **Estd:** 2011 Private Limited Company
**Line of Business:** Other business activities not elsewhere classified
**Issued Capital:** £1
**Directors:** K G Williams, D E Underwood, Mrs T Williams
**US SIC:** 7399 **UK SIC:** 83954

| | 31-12-13 | 31-12-12 | 31-12-11 |
|---|---|---|---|
| TO | 15,479,482 | 16,354,145 | 12,434,413 |
| P/L | 117,036 | 44,708 | (29,582) |
| NW | (42,828) | (87,652) | (126,248) |
| WC | (55,993) | (106,257) | (103,843) |
| Emp. | 359 | 358 | 389 |

DUNS 49-101-3975
## Tjx Uk
(**Subsidiary of:** The Tjx Companies Inc)
50 Clarendon Road, Watford, Hertfordshire WD17 1TX
**Tel:** 01923473000 **Fax:** 01923-473500
**Web:** www.homesense.com
**Reg No:** 3094828 **VAT No:** 662563524
**Estd:** 1995 Private Unlimited Company
**Line of Business:** Representative office
**Trading Style:** Homesense, Tk Maxx
**Issued Capital:** £74,223,263
**Directors:** S L Goldenberg, Ms M B Reynolds, D L Averill, M C Macmillan
**Co. Secretary:** Ms Alicia Kelly
**Responsibilities**
**Senior:** Alfred Appel (Manager), Jeffrey Naylor (Manager), P Sweetenham (President)
**Facilities:** Patrick Turnbull (Property Development Director)
**Branches:** Tjx Uk, The Cross Keys Shopping Centre, 22 Queen Street, Salisbury, Wiltshire SP1 1EY
**US SIC:** 5511, 5719
**UK SIC:** 65100, 64700
**Auditors:** PricewaterhouseCoopers LLP
**Bankers:** National Westminster Bank Plc (50-00-00)
**Following financial data are in thousands**

| | 01-02-14 | 02-02-13 | 28-02-12 |
|---|---|---|---|
| TO | 1,995,000 | 1,814,600 | 1,353,600 |
| P/L | 91,500 | 80,500 | 35,400 |
| NW | 501,700 | 437,400 | 370,600 |
| WC | 261,000 | 207,300 | 158,300 |
| Emp. | 15,659 | 14,421 | 14,239 |

DUNS 50-132-0774    Imp
## T.K. Components Ltd
Unit 3 Cranberry Drive, Denton, Manchester M34 3UL
**Fax:** 01613363638
**Web:** www.tkcomponents.co.uk
**Reg No:** 2320087 **VAT No:** 508354255
**Estd:** 1989 Private Limited Company
**Line of Business:** Manufacture of other kitchen furniture
**Export Sales:** £68,066
**Issued Capital:** £900
**Principals:** T W Kelly (Managing), Ms H Kelly (Financial), C B Hazelhurst
**Co. Secretary:** Paul Arrowsmith
**Responsibilities**
**Senior:** Norman Yates (Sales Director)
**Sales:** Norman Yates (Sales Director)
**US SIC:** 2599, 5039
**UK SIC:** 46720, 61300
**Auditors:** Moss & Williamson

**Bankers:** The Royal Bank Of Scotland Plc (16-30-15)

| | 30-09-13 | 30-09-12 | 30-09-11 |
|---|---|---|---|
| TO | 13,680,574 | 13,080,165 | 13,375,101 |
| P/L | 2,092,414 | 1,750,596 | 2,187,649 |
| NW | 3,355,768 | 6,659,750 | 5,327,187 |
| WC | 2,419,626 | 5,757,015 | 4,477,117 |
| Emp. | 93 | 87 | 84 |

DUNS 21-790-9479
## Tk Maxx
Southside Shopping Centre, London SW18 4TQ
**Tel:** 02088750739
**Web:** www.tkmaxx.com
**Estd:** 2011
**Line of Business:** Departmental stores
**US SIC:** 5399 **UK SIC:** 65600
**Employees:** 60

DUNS 73-910-0852
## Tk One Ltd
91 Gower Street, London WC1E 6AB
**Tel:** 02076099632 **Fax:** 020-7343-6667
**Web:** www.tkone.co.uk
**Reg No:** 5163610 **Estd:** 2004 Private Limited Company
**Line of Business:** Film production services and studios
**Issued Capital:** £100
**Director:** A F Penn
**Co. Secretary:** David Yeo
**US SIC:** 7819, 4833
**UK SIC:** 97111, 97411
**Auditors:** Edwards

| | 30-06-13 | 30-06-12 | 30-06-11 |
|---|---|---|---|
| TA | 307,365 | 296,544 | 125,656 |
| NW | 35,182 | (66,805) | 18,083 |
| WC | (102,886) | (227,837) | 2,472 |

DUNS 73-598-2709
## Tkg Ltd
(**Subsidiary of:** Tkg Holdings Ltd)
75-77 Lydden Grove, London SW18 4LY
**Tel:** 02088754900 **Fax:** 020-8875-4905
**Web:** www.thekeengroup.co.uk
**Reg No:** 4859512 **Estd:** 2003 Private Limited Company
**Line of Business:** Taxis
**Trading Style:** The Keen Group
**Issued Capital:** £100
**Directors:** B S Rehal, J Novakova, K M Keen
**Co. Secretary:** Ian Ferguson
**Responsibilities**
**Senior:** Caren Voad (Manager)
**US SIC:** 4121, 4311
**UK SIC:** 72200, 79010

| | 31-10-13 | 31-10-12 | 31-10-11 |
|---|---|---|---|
| TA | 1,060,483 | 1,319,166 | 1,808,819 |
| NW | (93,023) | (246,009) | (710,397) |
| WC | (307,702) | (528,617) | (977,078) |

DUNS 42-433-1572
## T.K.L. Demolition Services Ltd
(**Subsidiary of:** Tkl Earthworks Ltd)
The Foundry, Rotherham, South Yorkshire S63 7DX
**Tel:** 01709-870900
**Web:** www.thetklgroup.co.uk
**Reg No:** 4420805 **Estd:** 2002 Private Limited Company
**Line of Business:** Demolition and wrecking of buildings; earth moving
**Issued Capital:** £2
**Directors:** M T Lynskey, G A Morley
**US SIC:** 1795 **UK SIC:** 50000
**Auditors:** Warrens
**Employees:** 150

DUNS 73-713-7521
## T.L. Care Ltd
(**Subsidiary of:** Synova Capital Llp)
31 Highfield Road, Middlesbrough, Cleveland TS4 2PE
**Tel:** 01223248202
**Web:** www.hillcare.net
**Reg No:** 2915956 **Estd:** 2010 Private Limited Company
**Line of Business:** Nursing homes
**Trading Style:** The Gables
**Issued Capital:** £500
**Directors:** J Hill, Mrs W J Waddicor
**Co. Secretary:** Ian Mitchell
**Responsibilities**
**Senior:** Jaqueline Pallister (Home Manager), Carol Singleton (home manager)
**Branches:** T.l. Care Ltd, Queens Meadow Care Home, 327 Stockton Road, Hartlepool, Cleveland TS25 5DF
**US SIC:** 8051 **UK SIC:** 95100
**Auditors:** Gilchrist Tash
**Bankers:** The Co-Operative Bank Plc (08-90-01)

| | 31-03-14 | 31-10-12 | 31-03-11 |
|---|---|---|---|
| TO | 7,300,817 | 4,205,491 | 3,751,579 |
| P/L | 836,293 | 291,110 | 572,860 |
| NW | 10,211,104 | 2,696,042 | 2,692,619 |
| WC | (198,017) | (593,417) | 33,950 |
| Emp. | 228 | 198 | 182 |

DUNS 22-954-0257
## T.L. Darby (Holdings) Ltd
Brigade House, New Street, Burton-On-Trent, Staffordshire DE14 3QW
**Tel:** 01283-531331 **Fax:** 01283-534929
**Web:** www.tldarby.volkswagen.co.uk
**Reg No:** 1157303 **Estd:** 1974 Private Limited Company
**Line of Business:** Management activities of holding companies
**Trading Style:** T.L. Darby (Holdings) Limited
**Issued Capital:** £36,484
**Principals:** T L Darby (Managing), J M Peach, Ms L M Darby, R L Darby
**Co. Secretary:** David Tagg
**US SIC:** 6711, 5511
**UK SIC:** 83962, 65100
**Auditors:** D A Owen & Co
**Bankers:** Lloyds TSB Bank plc (30-91-47)

| | 31-12-13 | 31-12-12 | 31-12-11 |
|---|---|---|---|
| TO | 21,706,345 | 19,360,279 | 19,227,091 |
| P/L | 294,523 | 296,545 | 51,253 |
| NW | 3,536,571 | 3,303,748 | 3,098,717 |
| WC | 1,091,877 | 866,677 | 664,923 |
| Emp. | 79 | 77 | 59 |

DUNS 23-575-0150
## Tla Distribution Ltd
(**Subsidiary of:** Tla Electrical Holdings Ltd)
Unit 16 High Hazles Road, Cotgrave, Nottingham, Nottinghamshire NG12 3GZ
**Tel:** 01159-893999 **Fax:** 01159-894999
**Web:** www.tlauk.net
**Reg No:** 3572974 **Estd:** 1998 Private Limited Company
**Line of Business:** Electrical wholesalers
**Issued Capital:** £200
**Managing Director:** T Leverton
**Co. Secretary:** Dean Curtis
**Responsibilities**
**Finance:** Elaine Tomlinson (Financial Controller)
**Branches:** Tla Distribution Ltd, Unit 4 Brindley Close, Stafford, Staffordshire ST16 3SU
**US SIC:** 5074 **UK SIC:** 61300
**Auditors:** Hewitt Card
**Bankers:** Barclays Bank Plc (20-55-62)

| | 31-08-13 | 31-08-12 | 31-08-11 |
|---|---|---|---|
| TO | 10,814,868 | 10,467,186 | N/A |
| P/L | 604,703 | 756,947 | N/A |
| NW | 1,559,501 | 1,401,602 | 1,014,385 |
| WC | 1,388,146 | 1,378,965 | 1,018,406 |
| Emp. | 47 | 43 | N/A |

DUNS 45-847-0416
## Tlc Care Homes Ltd
Mount Hill, Halstead, Essex CO9 1LR
**Tel:** 01787-479491
**Web:** www.tlccarehomes.co.uk
**Reg No:** 3193730 **Estd:** 1996 Private Limited Company
**Line of Business:** Social work activities with accommodation
**Issued Capital:** £1,000
**Principals:** G S Harms (Managing), R G Charles, Mrs S Harms
**Co. Secretary:** Mrs Maureen Charles
**US SIC:** 7399 **UK SIC:** 83954
**Auditors:** Edmund Carr
**Bankers:** National Westminster Bank Plc (60-09-29)

| | 31-03-14 | 31-03-13 | 31-03-12 |
|---|---|---|---|
| TO | 6,591,620 | 6,444,723 | 6,724,182 |
| P/L | 807,249 | 774,690 | 469,039 |
| NW | 1,230,147 | 1,045,140 | 812,009 |
| WC | (1,629,758) | (717,366) | (839,335) |
| Emp. | 263 | 243 | 274 |

DUNS 77-126-0296
## Tlc Care Services
St Leonards, 11 Ambleside Road, London NW10 3UH
**Tel:** 02070172839
**Web:** www.cardelicious.com
**Reg No:** 2698380 **Estd:** 1991 Private Limited Company
**Line of Business:** Social work activities without accommodation
**Directors:** Ms S Campbell, K Rubie, Ms J A Andrews, R A Chapman, R Garcia
**Co. Secretary:** Simon Passman
**Responsibilities**
**IT:** Barry-Lee Jenner (IT Manager)
**Branches:** Tlc Care Services, Lefevre Walk, London E3 2RL
**US SIC:** 7399, 7299
**UK SIC:** 83954, 98902
**Auditors:** Streets Audit LLP
**Bankers:** Barclays Bank Plc (20-46-57)

| | 31-03-14 | 31-03-13 | 31-03-12 |
|---|---|---|---|
| TO | 4,489,867 | 3,766,006 | 3,134,106 |
| P/L | (25,492) | 97,134 | (64,565) |
| NW | 564,530 | 590,022 | 492,888 |
| WC | 511,224 | 584,102 | 474,906 |
| Emp. | 240 | 206 | 179 |

DUNS 23-724-6397
## Tlc Group Ltd
36 Railway Approach, Harrow, Middlesex HA3 5AA
**Web:** www.tlc-group.net
**Reg No:** 3719278 **Estd:** 1999 Private Limited Company
**Line of Business:** Management activities of wholesale holding companies
**Issued Capital:** £100
**Directors:** Mrs S Popat, G Puri, Mrs A J Jackson, P Popat
**Co. Secretary:** Gagan Puri
**Responsibilities**
**Senior:** Jennifer Acres *(Manager)*
**Finance:** Roselyn Hawkes *(Finance Director)*
**US SIC:** 7399 **UK SIC:** 83954
**Auditors:** H W Fisher & Co
**Bankers:** National Westminster Bank Plc (60-18-11)

| | 30-04-14 | 30-04-13 | 30-04-12 |
|---|---|---|---|
| TO | 21,103,949 | 19,465,863 | 18,310,142 |
| P/L | 3,456,589 | 1,554,956 | 2,266,851 |
| NW | 51,655,717 | 49,142,878 | 44,724,027 |
| WC | 5,257,394 | 1,187,160 | 2,841,524 |
| Emp. | 586 | 543 | 492 |

DUNS 53-611-0935
## Tlc Marketing Group Ltd
17a-19 Harcourt Street, London W1H 4HF
**Tel:** 02077256000 **Fax:** 020-7725-6300
**Web:** www.tlcmarketing.com
**Reg No:** 3416307 **Estd:** 1997 Private Limited Company
**Line of Business:** Advertising activities not elsewhere classified
**Export Sales:** £22,914,480
**Issued Capital:** £110
**Principals:** N E True *(Managing)*, A J Johnson *(Sales)*
**Co. Secretary:** Phill Markham
**Responsibilities**
**Senior:** Lauren Harmer *(Office Manager)*
**Branches:** Tlc Marketing Group Ltd, Suite 401, 63 Bloom St, Manchester M1 3LR
**US SIC:** 7319 **UK SIC:** 83800
**Auditors:** UHY Hacker Young

| | 31-12-13 | 31-12-12 | 31-12-11 |
|---|---|---|---|
| TO | 25,745,148 | 23,116,533 | 19,850,215 |
| P/L | 714,459 | 1,409,712 | 184,007 |
| NW | 2,282,309 | 1,881,266 | 1,300,594 |
| WC | 1,495,344 | 1,216,908 | 572,806 |
| Emp. | 248 | 224 | 250 |

DUNS 21-804-6829
## Tlg Ltd
(**Subsidiary of:** Zumtobel Group Ag)
Macbeth Street, London W6 9JJ
**Tel:** 02033930969 **Fax:** 020-8905-1283
**Web:** www.tlg.org.uk
**Reg No:** 0680313 **Estd:** 1961 Private Limited Company
**Line of Business:** Charities and charitable organisations
**Issued Capital:** £20,500
**Directors:** P M Coggins, Ms C T Thomson
**Co. Secretary:**
St John'S Square Secretaries Lim
**Responsibilities**
**Senior:** Deborah Barnett *(Head Teacher)*, Hannah Rowland *(Head Teacher)*
**US SIC:** 3648 **UK SIC:** 34702
**Bankers:** National Westminster Bank Plc (60-30-06)

| | 30-04-14 | 30-04-13 | 30-04-12 |
|---|---|---|---|
| NW | (301,839) | (301,839) | (301,839) |

DUNS 36-514-4687
## Tlh Leisure Resort
Belgrave Road, Torquay, Devon TQ2 5HL
**Tel:** 01803400500
**Web:** www.tlh.co.uk
**Estd:** 1992 Proprietorship
**Line of Business:** Hotels
**Proprietor:** Ms L Murrall
**Responsibilities**
**Senior:** David Klein *(Manager)*, Lawrence Morall *(CEO, Managing Director)*
**Marketing:** Julia Browne *(Marketing manager)*
**Admin:** Sue Hine *(Reservations Administrator)*
**IT:** John Shepard *(Senior IT Director)*
**HR:** Gary Brenton *(Human Resources Manager)*, Mary-Ann Fudge *(Training Manager)*, Mia Stalstedt *(Personnel Manager)*
**Operations:** Denis Hockridge *(Team Leader Decorator)*, Vicky Johnston *(Operations Administrator)*
**Engineering:** Keith Brueton *(Hotel Maintenance)*, Russell Herdman *(Technical Manager)*, Ian Murrell *(Maintenance Manager)*, Paul Zaple *(Hotel Maintenance)*
**US SIC:** 7011 **UK SIC:** 66500
**Employees:** 244

DUNS 73-928-1603
## Tlt Llp
One Redcliff Street, Bristol, Avon BS1 6TP
**Web:** www.tltsolicitors.com
**Reg No:** 0308658OC **Estd:** 2004
**Line of Business:** Solicitors
**Trading Style:** Tlt Solicitors
**Responsibilities**
**Senior:** Paul Butterworth *(Partner)*, Sasha Butterworth *(Designated Limited Liability P)*, Gavin Dowell *(Partner)*, Katherine Evans *(Designated Limited Liability P)*, Neil Franklin *(Partner)*, Simon Goss *(Designated Limited Liability P)*, Kerry Gwyther *(Designated Limited Liability P)*, Richard Hayllar *(Partner)*, William Hull *(Designated Limited Liability P)*, Charles Jervis *(Designated Limited Liability P)*, Peter Kimpton *(Partner)*, Julian Mant *(Designated Limited Liability P)*, David Pester *(Managing Partner)*, David Smithen *(Non-designated Limited Liabili)*, Graham Walters *(Designated Limited Liability P)*
**Branches:** Tlt Llp, 1 Redcliff Street, Bristol, Avon BS1 6TP
**US SIC:** 8111 **UK SIC:** 83500
**Auditors:** Deloitte & Touche LLP

| | 30-04-14 | 30-04-13 | 30-04-12 |
|---|---|---|---|
| TO | 58,238,000 | 49,049,000 | 43,435,000 |
| P/L | 452,000 | 129,000 | N/A |
| NW | (138,000) | (181,000) | N/A |
| WC | 16,119,000 | 13,029,000 | 7,595,000 |
| Emp. | 832 | 779 | 655 |

DUNS 28-839-5080
## T.M. Engineers (Midlands) Ltd
(**Subsidiary of:** T.M. Property Ltd)
Oak Works, Oak Lane, Brierley Hill, West Midlands DY6 7JW
**Fax:** 01384-296019
**Web:** www.tmengineers.co.uk
**Reg No:** 0507062 **VAT No:** 277278025
**Estd:** 1948 Private Limited Company
**Line of Business:** Manufacture of metal structures and parts of structures
**Issued Capital:** £3,069
**Directors:** R M Holland, Mrs P A Holland
**Co. Secretary:** Ms Phillipa Holland
**Responsibilities**
**Senior:** Trevor Ball *(Materials Manager)*, James Holland *(Manager)*
**Facilities:** Trevor Ball *(Materials Manager)*
**Purchasing:** Trevor Ball *(Materials Manager)*
**US SIC:** 3441, 3423
**UK SIC:** 32042, 31612
**Auditors:** Lancaster & Co
**Bankers:** National Westminster Bank Plc (56-00-69)

| | 31-03-14 | 31-03-13 | 31-03-12 |
|---|---|---|---|
| TA | 2,355,734 | 2,770,474 | 2,347,188 |
| NW | 942,751 | 843,864 | 596,318 |
| WC | 900,701 | 478,797 | 339,944 |

DUNS 71-896-0052
## Tm Group (Uk) Ltd
1200 Delta Business Park, Welton Road, Swindon, Wiltshire SN5 7XZ
**Tel:** 08442499200
**Web:** www.tmgroup.co.uk
**Reg No:** 5278187 **Estd:** 2004 Private Limited Company
**Line of Business:** Other business activities not elsewhere classified
**Issued Capital:** £96,187
**Directors:** I D Crabb, P L Creffield, B E Harris, P E Albone, R S Shipperley
**Co. Secretary:** Trevor Brown
**US SIC:** 7399, 8111
**UK SIC:** 83954, 83500

| | 31-12-13 | 31-12-12 | 31-12-11 |
|---|---|---|---|
| TO | 49,475,000 | 41,583,000 | 32,812,000 |
| P/L | 2,164,000 | 1,920,000 | 1,135,000 |
| NW | 1,335,000 | 1,913,000 | 2,622,000 |
| WC | 948,000 | 1,648,000 | 2,390,000 |
| Emp. | 93 | 76 | 64 |

DUNS 22-509-9662
## T.M. Hotels (Heathrow) Ltd
Colnbrook By Pass, Harmondsworth, West Drayton, Middlesex UB7 0HJ
**Tel:** 02087592424 **Fax:** 020-8759-2091
**Web:** www.sheraton.com
**Reg No:** 1518773 **VAT No:** 225701978
**Estd:** 1964 Private Limited Company
**Line of Business:** Hotels
**Trading Style:** Sheraton Heathrow Hotel
**Issued Capital:** £1,000
**Directors:** S A Mussallam, I Musallam
**Co. Secretary:** Mohamed Mouilah
**Responsibilities**
**Senior:** Andrew Huxsted *(General Manager)*, Sheikh Mussallam *(Manager)*
**HR:** N Tibbles *(Personnel Manager)*
**Branches:** T.m. Hotels (Heathrow) Ltd, Colnbrook By Pass, West Drayton, Middlesex UB7 0HJ
**US SIC:** 7011 **UK SIC:** 66500
**Auditors:** Ernst & Young LLP

**Bankers:** National Westminster Bank Plc (60-10-43)

| | 31-12-13 | 31-12-12 | 31-12-11 |
|---|---|---|---|
| TO | 11,160,000 | 10,572,000 | 11,275,000 |
| P/L | (761,000) | 565,000 | 1,810,000 |
| NW | 34,630,000 | 35,500,000 | 35,662,000 |
| WC | 4,350,000 | 3,833,000 | 8,737,000 |
| Emp. | 121 | 118 | 122 |

DUNS 34-890-8356
## T.M. Lewin Group Ltd
6-7 St Cross Street, London EC1N 8UA
**Fax:** 02079294891
**Web:** www.tmlewin.co.uk
**Reg No:** 5688521 **Estd:** 1938 Private Limited Company
**Line of Business:** Clothing retailers
**Issued Capital:** £802,000
**Directors:** G Quinn, M Trotman, L A Campbell, K R Nesbitt, J S Francomb, A V Mossman
**Co. Secretary:** Robert Isaac
**US SIC:** 7399, 2329
**UK SIC:** 83954, 45350
**Auditors:** BDO LLP

| | 01-03-14 | 02-03-13 | 03-03-12 |
|---|---|---|---|
| TO | 106,780,000 | 106,724,000 | 106,478,000 |
| P/L | 636,000 | (1,409,000) | 1,295,000 |
| NW | (14,882,000) | (15,892,000) | (15,606,000) |
| WC | (24,171,000) | 2,150,000 | (5,800,000) |
| Emp. | 922 | 937 | 960 |

DUNS 23-524-5433
## Tm Steels Ltd
Sheepbridge Works, Dunston Road, Chesterfield, Derbyshire S41 9QD
**Tel:** 01246-268312 **Fax:** 01246-268313
**Web:** www.tmsteels.co.uk
**Reg No:** 3523526 **VAT No:** 706261457
**Estd:** 1998 Private Limited Company
**Line of Business:** Wholesale of metals and ores
**Issued Capital:** £2,750
**Directors:** R M Hemingway, R Greaves, A E Tasker, P Mahmood
**Co. Secretary:** Barry Tucker
**Responsibilities**
**Facilities:** Joanne Jarvis *(Quality Manager)*
**US SIC:** 7399 **UK SIC:** 83954
**Auditors:** Hebblethwaites

| | 30-09-13 | 30-09-12 | 30-09-11 |
|---|---|---|---|
| TO | 12,039,994 | 11,651,032 | 10,314,279 |
| P/L | 670,719 | 528,019 | 514,884 |
| NW | 2,905,243 | 2,641,408 | 2,296,183 |
| WC | 2,708,715 | 2,437,487 | 2,100,440 |
| Emp. | 64 | 60 | 53 |

DUNS 21-010-2276
## Tm Telford Dairy Ltd
Donnington Wood Business Park, Granville Road, Donnington Wood, Telford, Shropshire TF2 7GJ
**Tel:** 01952620500 **Fax:** 08704-289483
**Web:** www.nomdairy.co.uk
**Reg No:** 6338801 **VAT No:** 920008084
**Estd:** 2007 Private Limited Company
**Line of Business:** Wholesale of dairy produce
**Export Sales:** £1,381,000
**Issued Capital:** £27,820,000
**Directors:** A Mcinnes, R K Kers, L Greenbury, P F Clancy
**Responsibilities**
**Senior:** Feb Jones *(Manager)*, Christoph Wenisch *(Manager)*
**US SIC:** 5143 **UK SIC:** 61700
**Auditors:** KPMG LLP
**Bankers:** Barclays Bank Plc (20-07-71)

| | 31-12-13 | 31-12-12 | 31-12-11 |
|---|---|---|---|
| TO | 40,140,000 | 42,575,000 | 47,769,000 |
| P/L | (21,842,000) | (10,683,000) | (11,734,000) |
| NW | 17,942,000 | 10,497,000 | 17,019,000 |
| WC | (5,050,000) | (15,078,000) | (8,901,000) |
| Emp. | 165 | 155 | 172 |

DUNS 22-196-8642
## Tmac Wireless Solutions Ltd
13 St Matthews Street, Ipswich, Suffolk IP1 3EL
**Tel:** 01473-400002 **Fax:** 01473400003
**Web:** www.nexusuk.com
**Reg No:** 4215008 **Estd:** 2001 Private Limited Company
**Line of Business:** Telecommunications
**Trading Style:** Nexus Telecommunications Limited
**Issued Capital:** £90
**Directors:** Miss J F Southgate, C W Everitt
**Branches:** Tmac Wireless Solutions Ltd, 16 Fonnereau Rd, Ipswich, Suffolk IP1 3JP
**US SIC:** 4899 **UK SIC:** 79020
**Bankers:** Barclays Bank Plc (20-44-51)

| | 31-03-14 | 31-03-13 | 31-03-12 |
|---|---|---|---|
| TA | 113,285 | 99,161 | 90,130 |
| NW | (37,458) | (61,280) | (149,446) |
| WC | (39,182) | (63,047) | (150,546) |

DUNS 21-159-6212 **Imp**
## Tmat Ltd
Park Road, Chesterfield, Derbyshire S42 5UY
**Tel:** 01246-850828
**Web:** www.tmatuk.com
**Reg No:** 6867435 **VAT No:** 948954458
**Estd:** 2009 Private Limited Company
**Line of Business:** Other construction work involving special trades
**Export Sales:** £5,478,809
**Issued Capital:** £295,000
**Directors:** J M Lippitt, D Mccoy, J Blachford
**Responsibilities**
**Senior:** Andrew Ramsbottom *(Manager)*
**US SIC:** 1799, 3079
**UK SIC:** 50000, 48360
**Auditors:** RSM Tenon Audit Ltd
**Bankers:** HSBC Bank plc (40-47-11)

| | 31-12-13 | 31-12-12 | 31-12-11 |
|---|---|---|---|
| TO | 10,282,903 | 9,663,359 | 9,348,075 |
| P/L | (215,574) | 164,063 | 134,385 |
| NW | 28,443 | 297,188 | 28,577 |
| WC | (558,401) | (215,758) | (148,527) |
| Emp. | 118 | 121 | 113 |

DUNS 23-293-8881 **Imp**
## Tmc Dairies (N.I.) Ltd
(**Subsidiary of:** Town of Monaghan Co-Operative Agricultural & Dairy)
47 Berryhill Road, Artigarvan, Strabane, Co Tyrone BT82 0HN
**Tel:** 02871382275 **Fax:** 028-7138-2059
**Web:** www.tmcdairiesni.co.uk
**Reg No:** 0043248NI **Estd:** 2002 Private Limited Company
**Line of Business:** Dairies
**Issued Capital:** £2
**Directors:** H Maguire, V Gilhawley
**Co. Secretary:** Vincent Gilhawley
**Responsibilities**
**Senior:** Tommy Thompson *(Manager)*
**US SIC:** 0241, 2043
**UK SIC:** 01001, 42398
**Auditors:** Duignan Carthy O'Neill

| | 31-12-13 | 31-12-12 | 31-12-11 |
|---|---|---|---|
| TO | 136,369,648 | 131,545,787 | 155,263,313 |
| P/L | 3,068,354 | (5,436,607) | 2,280,842 |
| NW | (12,738,625) | (15,806,979) | (10,370,372) |
| WC | 1,896,373 | (1,345,244) | 4,253,489 |
| Emp. | 49 | 48 | 48 |

DUNS 42-342-5219 **Imp**
## Tmd Friction Uk Ltd
(**Subsidiary of:** Nisshinbo Holdings Inc.)
Hunsworth Lane, Cleckheaton, West Yorkshire BD19 4EJ
**Tel:** 01274-854000 **Fax:** 01274-854001
**Web:** www.tmdfriction.com
**Reg No:** 4330235 **Estd:** 1985 Private Limited Company
**Line of Business:** Manufacturers of brakes and clutches
**Export Sales:** £45,408,000
**Issued Capital:** £64,191,000
**Directors:** Mrs D Pugh, Dr. R Milczarek, S Firbank, M S Scott
**Co. Secretary:** Malcolm Hartland
**Responsibilities**
**Senior:** Margaret Senior *(Executive Officer)*, Rob Sweetnam *(Manager)*
**Marketing:** D Baine *(Marketing Manager)*
**IT:** Helena Nuttall *(Group IT Manager)*
**HR:** Anne Gardener *(HR Manager)*
**Branches:** Tmd Friction Uk Ltd, Oakesway, Hartlepool, Cleveland TS24 0RE
**US SIC:** 3568 **UK SIC:** 32613
**Auditors:** PricewaterhouseCoopers LLP
**Bankers:** HSBC Bank plc (40-17-27)

| | 31-12-13 | 31-12-12 | 31-12-11 |
|---|---|---|---|
| TO | 78,547,000 | 74,054,000 | 78,075,000 |
| P/L | 9,569,000 | 6,953,000 | 3,858,000 |
| NW | 68,349,000 | 58,038,000 | 52,727,000 |
| WC | 69,677,000 | 59,688,000 | 52,344,000 |
| Emp. | 535 | 537 | 515 |

DUNS 34-625-2351
## Tmd Holdings Ltd
Unit 3, Swallowfield Way, Hayes, Middlesex UB3 1DQ
**Tel:** 02085735555
**Reg No:** 5431613 **Estd:** 2005 Private Limited Company
**Line of Business:** Management activities of holding companies
**Export Sales:** £17,517,000
**Issued Capital:** £47,500
**Directors:** V H Smith, P J Butcher
**US SIC:** 6711 **UK SIC:** 83962

| | 31-03-14 | 31-03-13 | 31-03-12 |
|---|---|---|---|
| TO | 21,559,000 | 30,223,000 | 30,062,000 |
| P/L | (3,027,000) | 4,418,000 | 4,673,000 |
| NW | 15,882,000 | 18,653,000 | 15,780,000 |
| WC | 14,623,000 | 17,794,000 | 15,016,000 |
| Emp. | 207 | 219 | 203 |

DUNS 23-563-6748
## Tmf Management (Uk) Ltd
(**Subsidiary of:** Tmf Orange Holding B.V.)
400 Capability Green, Luton, Bedfordshire LU1 3AE
**Tel:** 01582439200
**Web:** www.tmf-group.com
**Reg No:** 3561975 **Estd:** 1998 Private Limited Company
**Line of Business:** Management activities of holding companies
**Issued Capital:** £13,334
**Directors:** R N Arthur, M C Adams, V Cheshire
**Co. Secretary:**
Joint Secretarial Services Limit
**Responsibilities**
**Senior:** Diana Austin *(Manager)*, Kerry Webbe *(Facilities Manager)*
**US SIC:** 6711 **UK SIC:** 83962
**Auditors:** PricewaterhouseCoopers LLP
**Bankers:** HSBC Bank plc (40-01-04)

| | 31-12-13 | 31-12-12 | 31-12-11 |
|---|---|---|---|
| TO | 5,246,653 | 4,983,974 | 4,454,765 |
| P/L | 1,672,310 | 1,615,680 | 24,028 |
| NW | 4,428,414 | 2,836,753 | 951,647 |
| WC | 4,042,284 | 2,490,805 | 1,008,842 |
| Emp. | 59 | 58 | 66 |

DUNS 73-297-1697 Imp-Exp
## Tmi Foods Ltd
(**Subsidiary of:** Dawn Farm Foods Ltd)
Lodge Way, Lodge Farm Industrial Estate, Northampton, Northamptonshire NN5 7US
**Tel:** 01604-583421
**Web:** www.tmifoods.co.uk
**Reg No:** 4571020 **Estd:** 1980 Private Limited Company
**Line of Business:** Manufacturers of food products
**Issued Capital:** £30,189
**Directors:** J Queally, P Queally, L Murrin, M Queally, A R Smith
**Co. Secretary:**
Arrow Secretarial Services Limit
**Responsibilities**
**Senior:** Declan Kennedy *(Manager)*, Nigel Richmond *(Manager)*
**US SIC:** 2099, 7399
**UK SIC:** 42399, 83954
**Auditors:** Ernst & Young

| | 31-12-13 | 31-12-12 | 31-12-11 |
|---|---|---|---|
| TO | 34,611,537 | 27,077,911 | N/A |
| P/L | 405,189 | (439,572) | (628,591) |
| NW | 5,082,605 | 4,734,098 | 5,331,820 |
| WC | 1,486,226 | 359,472 | 375,479 |
| Emp. | 176 | 176 | 173 |

DUNS 34-849-0710
## Tmp (Holdings) Ltd
265 Tottenham Court Road, London W1T 7RQ
**Tel:** 02072689239 **Fax:** 020 7265 9201
**Web:** www.tmpw.co.uk
**Reg No:** 5648042 **VAT No:** 872904502
**Estd:** 1965 Private Limited Company
**Line of Business:** Marketing consultants
**Trading Style:** Tmp Worldwide
**Issued Capital:** £314,375
**Directors:** Miss E Jewer, J M Porter, A P Wilkinson, W D Eccles, S J Cooney
**Co. Secretary:** Stephen Cooney
**Responsibilities**
**Health & Safety:** Sarah Mccormack *(office manager)*
**Facilities:** Sarah Mccormack *(office manager)*
**US SIC:** 7392, 7361
**UK SIC:** 83951, 83954
**Auditors:** Ernst & Young LLP
**Bankers:** Lloyds TSB Bank plc (30-00-02)

| | 31-12-13 | 31-12-12 | 31-12-11 |
|---|---|---|---|
| TO | 69,902,974 | 68,931,182 | 66,920,524 |
| P/L | 2,679,045 | (1,286,215) | (2,046,672) |
| NW | (8,555,992) | (14,692,622) | (17,715,216) |
| WC | (2,520,190) | (5,767,272) | (6,638,298) |
| Emp. | 363 | 289 | 295 |

DUNS 34-895-5233
## Tms Ltd
Trinity Marina Coventry Road, Hinckley, Leicestershire LE10 0NF
**Tel:** 01455-632478
**Web:** www.tmsmotorgroup.co.uk
**Reg No:** 5693106 **VAT No:** 881669084
**Estd:** 2006 Private Limited Company
**Line of Business:** New & used motor vehicle dealers
**Issued Capital:** £245,775
**Directors:** R E Ingram, L J Hallows, A N Petrie, D W Kerr
**Co. Secretary:** Derek Kerr
**Responsibilities**
**Senior:** Roderick Taylor *(Manager)*
**Branches:** Tms Ltd, Hinckley C Of E Infant School, Station Road, Hinckley, Leicestershire LE10 1AW
**US SIC:** 5511, 5521, 7539, 5531
**UK SIC:** 65100, 67100

| | 31-12-13 | 31-12-12 | 31-12-11 |
|---|---|---|---|
| TO | 17,723,484 | 16,068,109 | 16,279,776 |
| P/L | 80,006 | 86,396 | 35,874 |
| NW | 451,653 | 392,271 | 323,262 |
| WC | 12,572 | 31,557 | 16,492 |
| Emp. | 55 | 55 | 50 |

DUNS 52-559-5468
## Tms Motor Spares Ltd.
Downies Wynd, Annan, Dumfriesshire DG12 6EE
**Web:** www.tmsmotorspares.co.uk
**Reg No:** 0168087SC **Estd:** 1996 Private Limited Company
**Line of Business:** Car accessories and parts
**Issued Capital:** £1,191,756
**Directors:** N Bunting, G W Harkness, J A Martin, J S Martin, H C Martin
**Co. Secretary:** James Knox
**Responsibilities**
**Senior:** Diane Lamb *(Manager)*
**Branches:** Tms Motor Spares Ltd., 10 Wilson Place, Glasgow, Lanarkshire G74 4QD
**US SIC:** 5531 **UK SIC:** 65100
**Auditors:** Graham Dent & Co

| | 31-10-13 | 31-10-12 | 31-10-11 |
|---|---|---|---|
| TO | 22,669,155 | 22,526,219 | 20,857,084 |
| P/L | 1,014,336 | 1,374,381 | 1,339,799 |
| NW | 2,850,192 | 3,017,398 | 2,948,407 |
| WC | 1,324,516 | 1,552,041 | 1,521,094 |
| Emp. | 314 | 296 | 280 |

DUNS 22-045-3448
## Tmwi Ltd
(**Subsidiary of:** Tmw Group Ltd)
81 Kings Road, London SW3 4NX
**Tel:** 02073494000
**Web:** www.tmw.co.uk
**Reg No:** 4047669 **Estd:** 2001 Private Limited Company
**Line of Business:** Advertising
**Issued Capital:** £50,000
**Managing Director:** C H Phillips
**US SIC:** 7311 **UK SIC:** 83800
**Auditors:** McCranors Ltd

| | 31-03-14 | 31-03-13 | 31-03-12 |
|---|---|---|---|
| TA | 3,139,422 | 3,153,469 | 2,533,301 |
| NW | 629,141 | 428,383 | 757,021 |
| WC | 705,992 | 411,580 | 746,514 |

DUNS 77-048-5217 Imp-Exp
## T.N.A. Europe Ltd
(**Subsidiary of:** Tna Australia Pty Limited)
166 Clapgate Lane, Birmingham, West Midlands B32 3DE
**Tel:** 0121-628-8900
**Web:** www.tnasolutions.com
**Reg No:** 2668491 **Estd:** 1991 Private Limited Company
**Line of Business:** Packaging equipment
**Issued Capital:** £1,000
**Principals:** A A Taylor *(Managing)*, Mrs N J Taylor
**Co. Secretary:** Mrs Jessica Boulton
**Responsibilities**
**Senior:** Tim Moulsdale *(Manager)*
**Finance:** Kevin Guest *(Financial Controller)*
**Marketing:** Isabel Regalado *(Marketing Coordinator)*
**US SIC:** 3551 **UK SIC:** 32441
**Auditors:** Trevor Jones & Co
**Bankers:** Barclays Bank Plc (20-07-82)

| | 30-06-13 | 30-06-12 | 30-06-11 |
|---|---|---|---|
| TO | 20,840,671 | 18,141,247 | 7,086,649 |
| P/L | 139,884 | 309,791 | (336,462) |
| NW | 1,946,743 | 1,768,329 | 1,505,616 |
| WC | 3,533,574 | 1,622,287 | 1,460,161 |
| Emp. | 62 | 72 | 53 |

DUNS 23-901-1484
## Tnei Services Ltd
(**Subsidiary of:** Petrofac Ltd)
Milburn House, Newcastle-Upon-Tyne, Tyne and Wear NE1 1LE
**Tel:** 01912-111400 **Fax:** 01912-111432
**Web:** www.tnei.co.uk
**Reg No:** 3891836 **Estd:** 1999 Private Limited Company
**Line of Business:** Engineering related scientific and technical consulting activities
**Export Sales:** £424,900
**Issued Capital:** £100
**Directors:** R G Smith, M D Barnes
**Co. Secretary:** Robert Smith
**Responsibilities**
**Senior:** Andy Edgar *(Manager)*, Charlotte Higgins *(Principal consultant)*
**US SIC:** 7399 **UK SIC:** 83954
**Auditors:** Ernst & Young LLP
**Bankers:** Lloyds TSB Bank plc (30-90-87)

| | 31-12-13 | 31-12-12 | 31-12-11 |
|---|---|---|---|
| TO | 4,667,458 | 4,602,446 | 4,989,169 |
| P/L | 196,963 | 181,877 | 701,118 |
| NW | 1,897,466 | 1,747,515 | 1,605,091 |
| WC | 1,754,978 | 1,539,446 | 1,401,764 |
| Emp. | 51 | 58 | 52 |

DUNS 21-626-6394
## Tnk (2009) Ltd
77 Marylebone High Street, London W1U 5JX
**Fax:** 02072242562
**Web:** www.thenaturalkitchen.com
**Reg No:** 7061987 **Estd:** 2009 Private Limited Company
**Line of Business:** Organic food production and supply
**Issued Capital:** £1,000
**Directors:** J Green, E Bernerd, R P Burrow, H S Hungin, J S Cameron
**Co. Secretary:** John Cameron
**US SIC:** 5812 **UK SIC:** 66110

| | 31-12-13 | 31-12-12 | 31-12-11 |
|---|---|---|---|
| TO | 5,317,327 | N/A | N/A |
| P/L | 29,421 | N/A | N/A |
| NW | (1,199,477) | (1,121,057) | (1,071,255) |
| WC | (650,215) | (430,694) | (561,069) |
| Emp. | 102 | N/A | N/A |

DUNS 21-829-1755 Imp
## T.N.Robinson Ltd
94-98 Daw Bank, Stockport, Cheshire SK3 0EH
**Tel:** 01614809678 **Fax:** 01614773074
**Web:** www.tnr.co.uk
**Reg No:** 0354544 **VAT No:** 473507931
**Estd:** 1923 Private Limited Company
**Line of Business:** Wholesale of other electronic parts and equipment
**Issued Capital:** £270,000
**Principals:** M R Drake *(Managing)*, Ms J E Drake, Ms M C Anderson, S M Thwaite, C J Drake, A P Drake, Ms P M Yates
**Co. Secretary:** Ian Gregory
**Branches:** T.n.robinson Ltd, Westbury Street, Hyde, Cheshire SK14 4QP
**US SIC:** 5065 **UK SIC:** 61500
**Auditors:** PKF (UK) LLP
**Bankers:** National Westminster Bank Plc (01-08-38)

| | 31-03-14 | 31-03-13 | 31-03-12 |
|---|---|---|---|
| TO | 12,134,951 | 12,528,267 | 13,184,238 |
| P/L | (56,315) | 4,661 | (304,743) |
| NW | 2,632,537 | 2,671,860 | 2,682,452 |
| WC | 1,107,983 | 1,248,557 | 1,411,364 |
| Emp. | 93 | 96 | 99 |

DUNS 73-549-4721
## T(N)S Catering Management Ltd
51 Parade, Leamington Spa, Warwickshire CV32 4BA
**Tel:** 01926-335444
**Web:** www.tnscatering.co.uk
**Reg No:** 4811572 **Estd:** 2003 Private Limited Company
**Line of Business:** Caterers
**Issued Capital:** £80,000
**Directors:** T M Smith, P Tyas
**Co. Secretary:** Ms Sandra Smith
**US SIC:** 5812, 7349
**UK SIC:** 66110, 92300

| | 31-12-13 | 31-12-12 | 31-12-11 |
|---|---|---|---|
| TO | 11,318,363 | 10,680,475 | 9,296,988 |
| P/L | 773,971 | 763,788 | 680,942 |
| NW | 326,184 | 317,738 | 278,181 |
| WC | 277,759 | 261,890 | 191,156 |
| Emp. | 400 | 411 | 391 |

DUNS 29-874-5803
## Tns Research Ltd
(**Subsidiary of:** Wpp Plc)
Wah Kwong House, 10 Albert Embankment, London SE1 7SP
**Tel:** 02077818040 **Fax:** 020-7820-4709
**Web:** www.twitternetworksolutions.co.uk
**Reg No:** 2077760 **Estd:** 1973 Private Limited Company
**Line of Business:** Holding company for group of market research consultants
**Issued Capital:** £100,000
**Directors:** D R Burgess, R Bowtell
**Co. Secretary:**
Wpp Group (Nominees) Limited
**US SIC:** 6711, 7392
**UK SIC:** 83962, 83951
**Auditors:** Deloitte LLP
**Bankers:** Barclays Bank Plc (20-69-17)

| | 31-12-13 | 31-12-12 | 31-12-11 |
|---|---|---|---|
| TA | 2,260,000 | 2,042,000 | 415,000 |
| P/L | 216,000 | 1,625,000 | 824,000 |
| NW | 2,246,000 | 2,030,000 | 405,000 |
| WC | 2,078,000 | 1,862,000 | 237,000 |

DUNS 23-039-9040 Imp
## Tns Uk Ltd
(**Subsidiary of:** Wpp Plc)
6 More London Place, London SE1 2QY
**Tel:** 02076565000 **Fax:** 02089-671-458
**Web:** www.tnsglobal.com
**Reg No:** 3073845 **Estd:** 1980 Private Limited Company
**Line of Business:** Market research and public opinion polling
**Export Sales:** £49,534,000
**Trading Style:** Digitab / Tns Uk, Kantar Healthcare, Kantar Worldpanel, Europanel
**Issued Capital:** £33,416,101
**Directors:** T R Kidd, D R Burgess, Ms M F Duffy, C W Welle, I C Dunkley, C P Sweetland
**Co. Secretary:**
Wpp Group (Nominees) Limited
**Responsibilities**
**Senior:** Neil Bayne *(Manager)*, Andrew Chappin *(Manager)*, Andrew Czarnowski *(Manager)*, Paul Delaney *(Manager)*
**Branches:** Tns Uk Ltd, ExtradigitaL,1st Floor, 6-8 Bonhill Street, London EC2A 4BX
**US SIC:** 7392 **UK SIC:** 83951
**Auditors:** Deloitte LLP
**Bankers:** Nationwide Building Society (07-00-20)

| | 31-12-13 | 31-12-12 | 31-12-11 |
|---|---|---|---|
| TO | 194,140,000 | 194,309,000 | 191,246,000 |
| P/L | 18,379,000 | 11,502,000 | (670,000) |
| NW | 30,201,000 | 19,110,000 | 15,027,000 |
| WC | 17,691,000 | 7,954,000 | (1,583,000) |
| Emp. | 1,757 | 1,460 | 1,498 |

DUNS 21-363-2639
## Tnt Express
176 Camford Way, Luton, Bedfordshire LU3 3AN
**Tel:** 01582561000
**Web:** www.tnt.co.uk
**Proprietorship**
**Line of Business:** Goods delivery services
**Proprietor:** M Palmer
**Responsibilities**
**Senior:** Kevin Ashton *(General Manager)*, Nina Chapman *(Operations Manager)*
**IT:** Nina Chapman *(Operations Manager)*
**HR:** Nina Chapman *(Operations Manager)*, Steve Clerkin *(Transport Manager)*
**Purchasing:** Nina Chapman *(Operations Manager)*
**Fleet:** Steve Clerkin *(Transport Manager)*
**US SIC:** 4213 **UK SIC:** 72300
**Employees:** 148

DUNS 21-795-2330
## Tnt Special Services
Peterfield Road, Kingstown Industrial Estate, Carlisle, Cumbria CA3 0EY
**Tel:** 01228590484
**Estd:** 2011
**Line of Business:** Renting of passenger air transport equipment
**Responsibilities**
**Senior:** Craig Mattinson *(Manager)*
**US SIC:** 7394 **UK SIC:** 84000
**Employees:** 78

DUNS 28-951-1057 Imp-Exp
## Tnt Uk Ltd
(**Subsidiary of:** Tnt Express N.V.)
Tnt Express House, Holly Lane, Atherstone, Warwickshire CV9 2RY
**Tel:** 01827-303-030 **Fax:** 01827-301-301
**Web:** www.tnt.com
**Reg No:** 1628530 **Estd:** 1982 Private Limited Company
**Line of Business:** Goods delivery services
**Trading Style:** Tnt Document Services
**Issued Capital:** £25,000,000
**Directors:** Mrs M Culver, D J Vines, Mrs S E Barnes, S R Harper, J C Downing, S D Stobie
**Co. Secretary:** Justin Clarke
**Responsibilities**
**Senior:** Mary O'Rourke *(Manager)*
**Sales:** Neil Pierssene *(Commercial Manager)*
**Facilities:** Sharon Johnson *(Facilities Manager)*
**Purchasing:** Joy Horne *(Contracts Manager)*, Joanne Mcdowall *(Purchasing Director)*
**Branches:** Tnt Uk Ltd, Unit 4, Mills Road, Aylesford, Kent ME20 7NA
**US SIC:** 4213, 4511
**UK SIC:** 72300, 75000
**Auditors:** PricewaterhouseCoopers LLP
**Bankers:** Barclays Bank Plc (20-55-34)

| | 31-12-13 | 31-12-12 | 31-12-11 |
|---|---|---|---|
| TO | 742,880,000 | 782,865,000 | 791,107,000 |
| P/L | (6,413,000) | 13,843,000 | 3,490,000 |
| NW | 178,082,000 | 209,243,000 | 199,554,000 |
| WC | 54,209,000 | 51,509,000 | 33,491,000 |
| Emp. | 9,484 | 10,242 | 10,227 |

DUNS 23-561-6112
## Toa Taxis (North Ayrshire) Ltd
A P L Centre, Stevenston Industrial Estate, Stevenston, Ayrshire KA20 3LR
**Tel:** 01294-465000
**Reg No:** 0185578SC **Estd:** 1998 Private Limited Company
**Line of Business:** Taxis and private hire vehicles
**Issued Capital:** £24
**Directors:** J Mckerrell, J F Mcdowall, D Rourke, Ms I D Agnew
**Co. Secretary:** Stephen Mcnamee

**US SIC:** 4121 **UK SIC:** 72200
**Auditors:** John Kerr & Co
**Bankers:** Clydesdale Bank Plc (82-67-32)

| | 31-05-14 | 31-05-13 | 31-05-12 |
|---|---|---|---|
| TA | 85,077 | 81,809 | 74,551 |
| NW | 48,287 | 33,124 | 21,565 |
| WC | 20,189 | 142 | (5,985) |

DUNS 21-754-9709
## Tobar Worldwide Ltd
Yare House 62-64 Thorpe Road, Norwich, Norfolk NR1 1RY
**Tel:** 08445734299
**Reg No:** 7845633 **Estd:** 2011 Private Limited Company
**Line of Business:** Management activities of holding companies
**Export Sales:** £2,346,674
**Issued Capital:** £1,885
**Directors:** G J Heddle, D J Mordecai, T J Norris, O S Melliss, G Loveday
**Co. Secretary:** David Mordecai
**US SIC:** 6711 **UK SIC:** 83962

| | 31-12-13 | 29-12-12 |
|---|---|---|
| TO | 22,650,050 | 20,445,956 |
| P/L | (664,081) | (208,497) |
| NW | (3,583,622) | (3,391,609) |
| WC | 2,679,347 | 3,711,505 |
| Emp. | 292 | 213 |

DUNS 23-249-7651 Exp
## Tobermore Concrete Products Ltd
2 Lisnamuck Road, Tobermore, Obermore County, Magherafelt, Co Londonderry BT45 5QF
**Tel:** 02879642411 **Fax:** 02879-644145
**Web:** www.tobermore.co.uk
**Reg No:** 0011280NI **VAT No:** 252377753
**Estd:** 1947 Private Limited Company
**Line of Business:** Manufacture of other articles of concrete, plaster and cement
**Export Markets:** Republic of Ireland
**Issued Capital:** £510,750
**Directors:** D G Henderson, W T Kirkpatrick
**Co. Secretary:** William Kirkpatrick
**Responsibilities**
**Senior:** Claire Conway *(Sales Marketing Executive)*, Paul McKeever *(Warehouse Manager)*, Robert Paul *(Works Manager)*
**Marketing:** Claire Conway *(Sales Marketing Executive)*
**Sales:** Claire Conway *(Sales Marketing Executive)*
**Health & Safety:** Robert Paul *(Works Manager)*
**Facilities:** Trevor Smyth *(Maintenance Manager)*
**Engineering:** Trevor Smyth *(Maintenance Manager)*
**Branches:** Tobermore Concrete Products Ltd, 18 Hill View Gardens, Halifax, West Yorkshire HX3 7BT
**US SIC:** 3272 **UK SIC:** 24370
**Auditors:** BDO Northern Ireland
**Bankers:** The Bank Of Ireland (90-49-82)

| | 30-04-14 | 30-04-13 | 30-04-12 |
|---|---|---|---|
| TO | 22,745,087 | 19,739,069 | 21,913,013 |
| P/L | 3,002,505 | 1,022,387 | 2,065,904 |
| NW | 45,385,754 | 43,127,906 | 42,344,524 |
| WC | 6,432,788 | 11,066,040 | 8,356,596 |
| Emp. | 150 | 135 | 154 |

DUNS 21-391-1875
## The Toby Carvery
Brighouse Road, Huddersfield, West Yorkshire HD2 2LB
**Tel:** 01422374360
**Web:** www.toby-carvery.co.uk
**Estd:** 2009 Proprietorship
**Line of Business:** Licensed restaurants
**Proprietor:** Ms H Willis
**US SIC:** 5813 **UK SIC:** 66200
**Employees:** 50

DUNS 21-326-5876
## Toby Carvery
Willerby Village, Hull, North Humberside HU10 6NT
**Tel:** 01482651518
**Web:** www.innkeeperslodge.com
**Estd:** 2012
**Line of Business:** Public house
**US SIC:** 5813 **UK SIC:** 66200
**Employees:** 49

DUNS 21-802-9912
## Toby Carvery Basildon
Unit 5 Festival Leisure Park Festival, Way, Basildon, Essex SS14 3WB
**Web:** www.tobycarvery.co.uk
**Estd:** 2011
**Line of Business:** Restaurant - pub food
**Responsibilities**
**Senior:** Dave Sloan *(Manager)*
**US SIC:** 5813 **UK SIC:** 66200
**Employees:** 50

DUNS 21-592-9671
## Toby Carvery Fleets Bridge
Fleets Corner, Wimborne Road, Poole, Dorset BH15 3EH
**Tel:** 01202673607
**Web:** www.toby-carvery.co.uk
**Estd:** 1986 Proprietorship
**Line of Business:** Restaurants
**Proprietor:** O Bennett
**Responsibilities**
**Senior:** Jan Truter *(General Manager)*
**US SIC:** 5812 **UK SIC:** 66110
**Employees:** 49

DUNS 28-861-2286
## Tockington Manor School Ltd
Washingpool Hill Road, Tockington, Bristol, Avon BS32 4NY
**Tel:** 01454613229
**Web:** www.tockingtonmanorschool.com
**Reg No:** 0894685 **Estd:** 1966 Private Limited Company
**Line of Business:** Schools (independent)
**Directors:** A R Turrell, A R Blackwell, G A Sheppard, R S Caul, Dr P N Hutchinson, P E Smith, M V Grocott, Ms H M Holloway
**Co. Secretary:** Michael Gupwell
**Responsibilities**
**Senior:** Philippa Leggate *(Director)*, Anthony Spratling *(Manager)*, Stephen Symonds *(Head Teacher)*, Julian Wheldon *(Director)*
**US SIC:** 8211 **UK SIC:** 93200
**Auditors:** Gardiner Hunter & Catt
**Bankers:** National Westminster Bank Plc (55-61-38)

| | 31-08-13 | 31-08-12 | 31-08-11 |
|---|---|---|---|
| TO | 1,847,749 | 1,787,191 | 1,824,014 |
| P/L | (60,715) | (184,653) | (194,812) |
| NW | 399,722 | 153,124 | 337,777 |
| WC | (230,427) | (184,957) | (567,128) |
| Emp. | 48 | 83 | 83 |

DUNS 57-022-7033 Imp-Exp
## Tocris Cookson Ltd
**(Subsidiary of:** Bio-Techne Corporation)
Tocris House, Io Center, Moorend Farm Avenue, Bristol, Avon BS11 0QL
**Fax:** 01179-163344
**Web:** www.customsynthesis.co.uk
**Reg No:** 2869577 **VAT No:** 415514476
**Estd:** 1994 Private Limited Company
**Line of Business:** Manufacture of other chemical products not elsewhere classified
**Export Markets:** E U and, Japan, U.S.A.
**Export Sales:** £5,318,000
**Trading Style:** Tocris Bioscience
**Issued Capital:** £30,616
**Directors:** Dr D A Peters, F Mortari, C R Kummeth, Ms K Backes
**Co. Secretary:** Ms Ruth Bright
**Responsibilities**
**Senior:** Laurence Ede *(Manager)*, Greg Melsen *(Manager)*
**US SIC:** 2899 **UK SIC:** 25670
**Auditors:** KPMG LLP
**Bankers:** HSBC Bank plc (40-17-32)

| | 30-06-13 | 30-06-12 | 30-06-11 |
|---|---|---|---|
| TO | 8,859,000 | 10,751,000 | 6,091,000 |
| P/L | 3,584,000 | 6,240,000 | 4,409,000 |
| NW | 17,264,000 | 14,572,000 | 9,876,000 |
| WC | 16,584,000 | 13,922,000 | 9,249,000 |
| Emp. | 52 | 47 | 51 |

DUNS 21-155-1032 Imp
## Todd & Duncan Ltd
**(Subsidiary of:** Ningxia Zhongyin Cashmere Co. Ltd.)
Lochleven Mills, Kinross, Kinross-Shire KY13 8DH
**Tel:** 01577-863521 **Fax:** 01577-864533
**Web:** www.todd-duncan.com
**Reg No:** 0355840SC **Estd:** 1955 Private Limited Company
**Line of Business:** Manufacture of household textiles
**Export Sales:** £16,190,000
**Trading Style:** Cashmere At Loch Leven
**Issued Capital:** £6,500,000
**Directors:** S Ma, F Ma, I M Cormack, J M Almeida, B M Cameron
**Co. Secretary:** Iain Cormack
**Responsibilities**
**Finance:** Graham Ferrier *(Finance Director)*
**Admin:** Scott Belfour *(Systems Administrator)*, H Devany *(Personnel Administrator)*
**HR:** R Binch *(Personnel Director)*
**Operations:** Eric Phipps *(Production Director)*
**US SIC:** 2392 **UK SIC:** 45550
**Auditors:** Deloitte LLP
**Bankers:** Barclays Bank Plc (20-00-50)

| | 31-12-12 | 31-12-11 | 31-12-10 |
|---|---|---|---|
| TO | 25,231,000 | 24,176,000 | 22,436,000 |
| P/L | (265,000) | 402,000 | 1,689,000 |
| NW | 12,028,000 | 12,244,000 | 7,450,000 |
| WC | 7,012,000 | 7,272,000 | 2,688,000 |
| Emp. | 206 | 202 | 188 |

DUNS 29-583-2216 Imp
## Todd Doors Ltd
**(Subsidiary of:** The Todd Group Ltd)
Unit 6 Northolt Industrial Estate, Belvue Road, Northolt, Middlesex UB5 5HP
**Tel:** 02088452493
**Web:** www.todd-doors.co.uk
**Reg No:** 1945019 **VAT No:** 863602818
**Estd:** 1985 Private Limited Company
**Line of Business:** Representative office
**Issued Capital:** £100
**Director:** M C Todd
**Co. Secretary:** Ms Virginia Todd
**Responsibilities**
**Senior:** Mike Cunningham *(Support Services Manager)*
**US SIC:** 1751, 5039
**UK SIC:** 50400, 61300
**Bankers:** Barclays Bank Plc (20-27-48)

| | 31-12-13 | 31-12-12 | 30-12-11 |
|---|---|---|---|
| TO | 9,763,574 | 11,299,924 | N/A |
| P/L | 153,699 | 672,384 | N/A |
| NW | 869,024 | 990,585 | 484,665 |
| WC | 511,029 | 697,444 | 111,064 |
| Emp. | 58 | 50 | N/A |

DUNS 21-774-6372
## Todmorden High School
Ewood Lane, Todmorden, Lancashire OL14 7DG
**Web:** www.todhigh.co.uk
**Estd:** 1974 Proprietorship
**Line of Business:** Schools (local authority)
**Proprietor:** Miss H Plaice
**Responsibilities**
**Senior:** Andrew Whitaker *(Head Teacher)*
**US SIC:** 8211 **UK SIC:** 93200
**Employees:** 110

DUNS 21-606-4478
## Todmorden Sports Centre
Ewood Lane, Todmorden, Lancashire OL14 7DF
**Tel:** 01706839090
**Web:** www.calderdale.gov.uk
**Estd:** 2011
**Line of Business:** Operation of other sports arenas and stadiums not elsewhere classified
**Responsibilities**
**Senior:** Nick Hartley *(Senior Manager)*
**US SIC:** 7999 **UK SIC:** 97913
**Employees:** 50

DUNS 23-890-7815 Imp
## Tod's Uk Ltd
**(Subsidiary of:** Di.Vi. Finanziaria Di Diego Della Valle & Co. Srl)
The Prow 4th Floor, 1 Wylder Road, London W1B 5AP
**Tel:** 020-7499-0155 **Fax:** 020-7493-0155
**Web:** www.todsgroup.com
**Reg No:** 3881713 **Estd:** 2005 Private Limited Company
**Line of Business:** Representative office
**Issued Capital:** £350,000
**Directors:** E Macellari, H W Wallage
**Co. Secretary:** Bibi Ally
**US SIC:** 7399 **UK SIC:** 83954
**Auditors:** Deloitte LLP
**Bankers:** HSBC Bank plc (40-05-01)

| | 31-12-13 | 31-12-12 | 31-12-11 |
|---|---|---|---|
| TO | 20,658,889 | 19,085,410 | 15,117,909 |
| P/L | 3,622,205 | 4,183,279 | 3,240,648 |
| NW | 8,079,599 | 10,557,370 | 7,411,938 |
| WC | 7,251,849 | 9,452,236 | 6,102,194 |
| Emp. | 52 | 55 | 52 |

DUNS 21-008-5566
## Tog 24 Ltd
Spen Vale, Mills Station Lane, Heckmondwike, West Yorkshire WF16 0NQ
**Tel:** 01924409311
**Web:** www.tog24.com
**Reg No:** 6325417 **Estd:** 2007 Private Limited Company
**Line of Business:** Retail sale of clothing
**Export Sales:** £1,076,448
**Issued Capital:** £11,096
**Directors:** I Ward, C J Ward, M J Ward, M D Wood
**Co. Secretary:** Brian Ward
**Responsibilities**
**Senior:** Dawn Armitage *(Manager)*
**Branches:** Tog 24 Ltd, 89 Church Street, Whitby, North Yorkshire YO22 4BH
**US SIC:** 5699 **UK SIC:** 64500

| | 29-06-14 | 30-06-13 | 01-06-12 |
|---|---|---|---|
| TO | 19,165,879 | 18,636,966 | 16,099,872 |
| P/L | 205,950 | 183,499 | 32,131 |
| NW | 5,818,934 | 5,670,056 | 5,578,217 |
| WC | 4,901,055 | 4,741,342 | 4,732,197 |
| Emp. | 299 | 279 | 275 |

DUNS 29-537-0951
## Togel Contractors Ltd
1-3 Hexthorpe Road, Doncaster, South Yorkshire DN4 0AD
**Tel:** 01302-342579 **Fax:** 01302-349131
**Web:** www.togel.co.uk
**Reg No:** 1904087 **Estd:** 1985 Private Limited Company
**Line of Business:** Building construction contractors
**Issued Capital:** £17,447
**Principals:** G Gargett *(Managing)*, T A Scott, P Leggott, R Leggott
**Co. Secretary:** Tony Richardson
**Responsibilities**
**Senior:** Walter Crapper *(Manager)*, Ron Gray *(Joinery Shop Manager)*
**Marketing:** Walter Crapper *(Manager)*
**Branches:** Togel Contractors Ltd, 1-3 Hexthorpe Rd, Doncaster, South Yorkshire DN4 0AD
**US SIC:** 1522 **UK SIC:** 50100
**Auditors:** Brodericks
**Bankers:** Barclays Bank Plc (20-26-55)

| | 30-09-14 | 30-09-13 | 30-09-12 |
|---|---|---|---|
| TO | 14,493,845 | 13,802,401 | 10,572,593 |
| P/L | 254,805 | 82,735 | (208,486) |
| NW | 448,614 | 292,837 | 256,470 |
| WC | 306,474 | 157,730 | 70,155 |
| Emp. | 109 | 97 | 111 |

DUNS 29-014-7859
## Together for Mental Wellbeing
12 Old Street, London EC1V 9BE
**Tel:** 020 7780 7300 **Fax:** 020 7780 7301
**Web:** www.together-uk.org
**Reg No:** 0463505 **Estd:** 1879 Private Company Limited By Guarantee
**Line of Business:** Charities and charitable organisations
**Directors:** Ms E Ward, Ms S D Turner, Ms H A Davies, A Larmie, Ms A Majekodunmi, Mrs S F Young, Ms B Lawton, Miss L Goodwin
**Co. Secretary:** Ms Anne Oates
**Responsibilities**
**Senior:** Paul Farrimond *(Director)*, Mark Hardcastle *(Director)*, Ashley Hook *(Director)*, Susan Murray *(Director)*, Zaidee O'Dell *(Director)*, William Obomanu *(Manager)*, Sau Reynolds *(Director)*, Anneke Westra *(Manager)*
**HR:** Norma Clayton *(Human Resources Manager)*
**Health & Safety:** Norma Clayton *(Human Resources Manager)*
**Branches:** Together For Mental Wellbeing, 10 Norfolk Road, Sheffield, South Yorkshire S2 2SX
**US SIC:** 8321 **UK SIC:** 96111
**Auditors:** haysmacintyre
**Bankers:** National Westminster Bank Plc (60-30-03)

| | 31-03-14 | 31-03-13 | 31-03-12 |
|---|---|---|---|
| TO | 18,465,818 | 18,225,749 | 19,600,829 |
| P/L | (57,447) | (479,449) | 604,073 |
| NW | 8,857,101 | 9,029,259 | 9,574,976 |
| WC | 3,120,622 | 1,247,657 | 1,902,917 |
| Emp. | 577 | 619 | 644 |

DUNS 34-900-3884
## Together Housing Group Ltd
Bull Green House, Bull Green, Halifax, West Yorkshire HX1 2EB
**Tel:** 01422-284500
**Web:** www.togetherhousing.co.uk
**Reg No:** 5697708 **Estd:** 2006 Private Company Limited By Guarantee
**Line of Business:** Other letting of own property
**Trading Style:** Penine Housing
**Directors:** P Caffrey, Ms H M Massie, Mrs I Heaney, J Kitchen, G H Butler, D A Wild, Mrs H Lockwood, M I Harrison
**Co. Secretary:** Ian Clark
**Responsibilities**
**Senior:** Jonathan Bemrose *(Director)*, Christopher Cotton *(Manager)*, Tom Miskell *(Chief Executive)*
**US SIC:** 6519 **UK SIC:** 85000
**Auditors:** Grant Thornton UK LLP
**Bankers:** National Westminster Bank Plc (60-09-27)

| | 31-03-14 | 31-03-13 | 31-03-12 |
|---|---|---|---|
| TO | 184,454,000 | 148,779,000 | 152,508,000 |
| P/L | 22,119,000 | 6,971,000 | 15,493,000 |
| NW | 97,748,000 | 52,139,000 | 49,903,000 |
| WC | 113,362,000 | 20,418,000 | 13,117,000 |
| Emp. | 1,237 | 1,190 | 1,185 |

DUNS 29-344-5052
## Together Trust
Schools Hill, Cheadle, Cheshire SK8 1JE
**Web:** www.togethertrust.org.uk
**Reg No:** 0301722 **VAT No:** 611400506
**Estd:** 1870 Private Company Limited By Guarantee
**Line of Business:** Business and management consultancy activities not elsewhere classified

**Principals:** B E Chesworth *(Chairman)*, Dr V Owen-Smith, R J Stevenson, J T Bowden, H J Rylands, S C Lees-Jones, Mrs W Coomer, G H Gaddum
**Co. Secretary:** Mark Lee
**Responsibilities**
**Senior:** Ralph Ellerton *(Director)*, Janet Heath *(Director)*, Irene Hegarty *(Director)*, Roger Horne *(Director)*, Julie Isted *(Partner)*, Rosemary Pike *(Director)*
**Finance:** Helena Brailsford *(Fundraising Manager)*
**Admin:** Dee Jones *(Administration Manager)*
**Branches:** Together Trust, Walkden Road, Manchester M28 7FG
**US SIC:** 7392, 8321
**UK SIC:** 83951, 96111
**Auditors:** Mazars LLP
**Bankers:** The Royal Bank Of Scotland Plc (16-71-38)

| | 31-03-14 | 31-03-13 | 31-03-12 |
|---|---|---|---|
| TO | 21,995,803 | 20,623,652 | 21,894,041 |
| P/L | 323,450 | 738,567 | 1,126,263 |
| NW | 18,654,652 | 17,996,842 | 17,172,078 |
| WC | 3,778,840 | 4,579,695 | 4,364,071 |
| Emp. | 546 | 519 | 538 |

DUNS 28-989-1715 **Imp**

## Toiletry Sales Ltd

**(Subsidiary of:** Toiletry Sales Group Ltd)
Crigglestone Industrial Estate, High Street, Crigglestone, Wakefield, West Yorkshire WF4 3HT
**Tel:** 01924-250017
**Web:** www.toiletrysales.com
**Reg No:** 1813823 **VAT No:** 361612278
**Estd:** 1984 Private Limited Company
**Line of Business:** Toilet articles
**Export Sales:** £1,703,899
**Trading Style:** Toiletry Sales Limited
**Issued Capital:** £100,000
**Principals:** D L Barraclough *(Managing)*, R J Walker, K Randall, M F Davies
**Co. Secretary:** David Milnes
**Responsibilities**
**Senior:** Greg Noble *(Director Operations)*
**US SIC:** 5122 **UK SIC:** 61800
**Auditors:** Binder Hamlyn
**Bankers:** Lloyds TSB Bank plc (77-19-01)

| | 31-12-13 | 30-06-12 | 30-12-11 |
|---|---|---|---|
| TO | 39,849,895 | 27,740,967 | 26,079,875 |
| P/L | 2,911,304 | 1,929,372 | 1,480,209 |
| NW | 9,717,277 | 7,484,959 | 5,683,584 |
| WC | 6,568,034 | 4,858,209 | 4,252,817 |
| Emp. | 61 | 55 | 50 |

DUNS 21-443-5547 **Imp-Exp**

## Tokheim U K Ltd

**(Subsidiary of:** Motion Equity Partners Llp)
Unit 3, Dundee, Angus DD5 3RT
**Tel:** 01382-598000 **Fax:** 01382-598001
**Web:** www.tokheim.com
**Reg No:** 0058090SC **VAT No:** 271793729
**Estd:** 1975 Private Limited Company
**Line of Business:** Manufacturers and suppliers of petrol pumps
**Export Markets:** Western Europe, North America, Africa, S America, U S A
**Export Sales:** £59,247,000
**Issued Capital:** £12,780,000
**Directors:** B Du Fayet De La Tour, L Nguyen
**Co. Secretary:** William Scobie
**Responsibilities**
**Senior:** Patrick Berthon *(Manager)*, Thierry Dervieux *(Manager)*
**HR:** Lorna Dickson *(Training Manager)*
**Health & Safety:** Lorna Dickson *(Training Manager)*
**Operations:** Steven Boyd *(Production Manager)*
**Purchasing:** Gordon Hume *(Purchasing Manager)*
**Engineering:** Steven Boyd *(Production Manager)*
**Branches:** Tokheim U K Ltd, 4 Cliveden Office Village, Lancaster Rd, Cressex Indstl Est, High Wycombe, Buckinghamshire HP12 3YZ
**US SIC:** 3563, 3549
**UK SIC:** 32831, 32212
**Auditors:** Ernst & Young LLP
**Bankers:** Clydesdale Bank Plc (82-68-31)

| | 30-04-14 | 30-04-13 | 30-04-12 |
|---|---|---|---|
| TO | 72,729,000 | 75,611,000 | 81,851,000 |
| P/L | (3,744,000) | (2,219,000) | 3,465,000 |
| NW | 6,138,000 | 13,063,000 | 17,284,000 |
| WC | 1,464,000 | 9,217,000 | 6,589,000 |
| Emp. | 458 | 453 | 483 |

DUNS 77-436-4962

## Tokio Marine Kiln Group Ltd

**(Subsidiary of:** Tokio Marine Holdings Inc.)
Furness House, 106 Fenchurch Street, London EC3M 5NR
**Tel:** 020-7886-9000
**Web:** www.belmarine.com
**Reg No:** 2949032 **Estd:** 1994 Private Limited Company
**Line of Business:** Management activities of holding companies
**Trading Style:** Kiln Syndicate
**Issued Capital:** £1,000,000
**Directors:** I Brimecome, C A Franks, K Fujii, C Kojima, R C Lewis, S Ruoff, M Yoda, Y Otsuka
**Co. Secretary:** Ms Fiona Molloy
**Responsibilities**
**Senior:** Robert Chase *(Manager)*, James Dover *(Director)*, Paul Hewitt *(Director)*
**US SIC:** 6711 **UK SIC:** 83962
**Auditors:** PricewaterhouseCoopers LLP

| | 31-12-13 | 31-12-12 | 31-12-11 |
|---|---|---|---|
| TO | 510,417,000 | 514,941,000 | 462,110,000 |
| P/L | 63,081,000 | 46,577,000 | (9,499,000) |
| NW | 281,556,000 | 224,766,000 | 206,129,000 |
| WC | 188,465,000 | (101,751,000) | 96,775,000 |
| Emp. | 363 | 370 | 386 |

DUNS 22-711-4493

## Tokio Marine Kiln Insurance Ltd

**(Subsidiary of:** Tokio Marine Holdings Inc.)
Allianz House, 60 Gracechurch Street, London EC3V 0HR
**Tel:** 02072-838-844
**Web:** www.tokiomarine.eu
**Reg No:** 0989421AC **Estd:** 1970
**Line of Business:** Underwriters of commercial property, casualty and marine insurance.
**Trading Style:** Tokio Marine Capital Research, Tokio Marine Asset Managment
**Issued Capital:** £35,000,000
**Directors:** I I Hara, R J Bucknall, Y Otsuka, Ms D Garland, C A Franks, M Camps, C Kojima
**Co. Secretary:** Mrs Fiona Molloy
**Responsibilities**
**Senior:** G?rd Lancner *(Director)*
**Branches:** Tokio Marine Kiln Insurance Limited, Saxon Ho, Friary St, Derby, Derbyshire DE1 1NL
**US SIC:** 6411, 6399, 6331
**UK SIC:** 83200, 82001, 82002
**Auditors:** Ernst & Young LLP
**Bankers:** The Bank Of Tokyo-Mitsubishi, Ltd (60-01-09)

| | 31-12-13 | 31-12-12 | 31-12-11 |
|---|---|---|---|
| TO | 128,678,000 | 126,942,180 | 119,439,188 |
| P/L | 9,779,000 | 22,316,868 | 6,516,889 |
| NW | 136,948,000 | 139,307,509 | 127,833,611 |
| WC | 27,169,000 | 30,066,421 | 37,496,112 |
| Emp. | 297 | 323 | 305 |

DUNS 76-381-2500

## Tokio Millennium Re (Uk) Ltd

Tokio Marine Kiln Syndicate 1880, London EC3M 5NR
**Tel:** 0207-397-4000 **Fax:** 02074807451
**Web:** www.tokiomillennium.com
**Reg No:** 2553288 **Estd:** 1990 Private Limited Company
**Line of Business:** Non-life re-insurance
**Issued Capital:** £125,000,000
**Directors:** S Ruoff, D J Finch, M Yoda, C Von Bechtolsheim, T Sumi
**Co. Secretary:** Elliot Dunseath
**Responsibilities**
**Senior:** Tatsuhiko Hoshina *(Manager)*, Kazuya Kojima *(Manager)*
**US SIC:** 6399 **UK SIC:** 82001
**Auditors:** PricewaterhouseCoopers LLP
**Bankers:** The Dai-Ichi Kangyo Bank, Ltd. (40-50-69)

| | 31-12-13 | 31-12-12 | 31-12-11 |
|---|---|---|---|
| TO | 91,167,000 | 82,367,000 | 102,600,000 |
| P/L | 11,075,000 | 9,450,000 | 10,570,000 |
| NW | 197,473,000 | 190,308,000 | 187,614,000 |
| WC | 70,946,000 | 79,304,000 | 65,511,000 |
| Emp. | 81 | 78 | 72 |

DUNS 73-746-7324 **Imp**

## Tokyo Electron Europe Ltd

**(Subsidiary of:** Tokyo Electron Limited)
Pioneer Building, Crawley, West Sussex RH10 9QL
**Web:** www.tel.com
**Reg No:** 2923252 **Estd:** 1994 Private Limited Company
**Line of Business:** Manufacturers of semiconductors
**Export Sales:** £194,108,000
**Issued Capital:** £11,550,000
**Directors:** T Nagakubo, D C Brough, H Ito, T Tsuneishi
**Co. Secretary:** Christopher Kelly
**Responsibilities**
**Senior:** Kiyoshi Sato *(Manager)*, Hiroshi Takenaka *(Manager)*, Chiaki Yamaguchi *(Manager)*
**IT:** Byron Trent *(IT Specialist)*
**Health & Safety:** Colin Brough *(Health & Safety Officer)*
**Operations:** Colin Brough *(Health & Safety Officer)*
**US SIC:** 3999, 5084
**UK SIC:** 49590, 61490
**Auditors:** KPMG LLP

| | 31-03-14 | 31-03-13 | 31-03-12 |
|---|---|---|---|
| TO | 197,622,000 | 292,947,000 | 377,451,000 |
| P/L | 9,443,000 | 33,740,000 | 54,170,000 |
| NW | 93,074,000 | 89,729,000 | 88,371,000 |
| WC | 96,836,000 | 99,819,000 | 97,838,000 |
| Emp. | 374 | 332 | 308 |

DUNS 21-103-1892

## Tokyo Group Ltd

17 Westgate Road, Newcastle-Upon-Tyne, Tyne and Wear NE1 1SE
**Tel:** 0191-232-1122
**Web:** www.tokyonewcastle.com
**Reg No:** 6462216 **Estd:** 2008 Private Limited Company
**Line of Business:** Managed public houses and bars
**Issued Capital:** £100
**Director:** A M Mellor
**Responsibilities**
**Senior:** Robert Cameron *(Operation Director)*
**US SIC:** 5813 **UK SIC:** 66200
**Auditors:** Kay Johnson Gee

| | 31-12-13 | 31-12-12 | 31-12-11 |
|---|---|---|---|
| TO | 5,156,825 | 6,203,410 | 6,626,651 |
| P/L | (962,018) | 784,925 | 1,073,434 |
| NW | (914,875) | 994,261 | 641,627 |
| WC | (1,094,944) | (1,194,360) | (1,153,069) |
| Emp. | 163 | 168 | 170 |

DUNS 23-012-0177

## Tolent Plc

Ravensworth House, 5th Avenue Business Park, Team Valley Trading Estate, Gateshead, Tyne and Wear NE11 0HF
**Tel:** 0191-487-0505 **Fax:** 0191-487-2990
**Web:** www.tolent.co.uk
**Reg No:** 3819314 **Estd:** 1999 Public Limited Company
**Line of Business:** Burglar alarm systems
**Trading Style:** Tolent Corparation
**Issued Capital:** £1,283,263
**Directors:** J G Wood, M R Speakman, Dr A W Ospelt, T Phillipson, P K Hems
**Co. Secretary:** Andrew Clark
**Responsibilities**
**Senior:** John Gibbon Wood *(Chief Executive Officer)*
**US SIC:** 6711 **UK SIC:** 83962
**Auditors:** Grant Thornton UK LLP

| | 31-12-13 | 31-12-12 | 31-12-11 |
|---|---|---|---|
| TO | 97,198,000 | 109,782,000 | 105,043,000 |
| P/L | (4,577,000) | (187,000) | (2,813,000) |
| NW | 5,066,000 | 9,469,000 | 9,285,000 |
| WC | 3,648,000 | 3,161,000 | 2,783,000 |
| Emp. | 405 | 405 | 434 |

DUNS 73-752-8034

## Toll Global Forwarding Group (Uk) Ltd

**(Subsidiary of:** Toll Holdings Limited)
Unit 7 Building 311, World Freight Terminal, Manchester Airport, Manchester M90 5TE
**Web:** www.tollglobalforwarding.com
**Reg No:** 2924145 **VAT No:** 830965417
**Estd:** 1994 Private Limited Company
**Line of Business:** Management activities of holding companies
**Issued Capital:** £6,100,000
**Directors:** J D Eyre, S Buckerfield, J F Irving, P W Coutts
**Responsibilities**
**Senior:** Hugh Cushing *(Manager)*, Mark Wardman *(Manager)*
**US SIC:** 6711, 4712
**UK SIC:** 83962, 77002
**Auditors:** Brebners
**Bankers:** Citibank Na (18-50-08)

| | 30-06-13 | 30-06-12 | 30-06-11 |
|---|---|---|---|
| TO | 89,728,000 | 42,097,000 | N/A |
| P/L | (5,546,000) | (6,433,000) | N/A |
| NW | 1,591,000 | 2,533,000 | 2,467,571 |
| WC | 7,287,000 | 2,065,000 | (490,382) |
| Emp. | 267 | 71 | N/A |

DUNS 23-677-9252

## Toller Beattie

Devonshire House, Riverside Road, Pottington Business Park, Barnstaple, Devon EX31 1QN
**Tel:** 01271-341000
**Web:** www.tollerbeattie.co.uk
**Partnership**
**Line of Business:** Solicitors
**Partners:** M T Fudge, A Gordon-Lee, R H Beattie, D Baker
**Responsibilities**
**Senior:** Robert Beattie *(Designated Limited Liability P)*, David Eastman *(Non-designated Limited Liabili)*, Alan Gordon-Lee *(Consultant)*, Robert Gross *(Non-designated Limited Liabili)*, Michael Kingman *(Designated Limited Liability P)*, Gillian Lindquist Jones *(Designated Limited Liability P)*, Mark Roome *(Partner)*, Maria Rowan *(Practice Manager)*
**Finance:** Mandie Dockery *(Accounts Assistant)*, Cathy Edwards *(Accounts Clerk)*, Tim Hook *(Criminal Lawyer)*
**Sales:** Cathy Edwards *(Accounts Clerk)*
**Admin:** Hannah Beck *(Secretary)*, Anne Dudley *(Receptionist)*, Liz Rigden *(Secretary)*
**Branches:** Toller Beattie, 14 Caen St, Braunton, Devon EX33 1AA
**US SIC:** 8111 **UK SIC:** 83500
**Employees:** 50

DUNS 21-006-7580

## Tollers Llp

2 Castilian Street, Northampton, Northamptonshire NN1 1JX
**Tel:** 01604-258558
**Web:** www.tollers.co.uk
**Reg No:** 0329775OC **Estd:** 1900 Private Limited Company
**Line of Business:** Solicitors
**Responsibilities**
**Senior:** Maureen Addison *(Partner)*, Katie Herrod *(Partner)*, Tristan Holdom *(Partner)*, Ingemar Hunnings *(Equity Partner)*, Thomas Hunnings *(Designated Limited Liability P)*
**Finance:** Nicola Dodman *(Senior Wills Trusts & Estates)*, Sophie Malik *(Costs Assistant)*, Katie-Rose Tyrrell *(Credit Controller)*
**Admin:** Jayne Barber *(Personal Assistant)*, Hannah Chambers *(Office Assistant)*, Sarah Finlayson *(Human Resources Administrator)*, Marcella Jeffers-Nicholls *(Receptionist)*, Bev Kellett *(Personal Assistant)*, Milly Kwolek *(Personal Assistant)*, Kath Maile *(Personal Assistant)*, Cheryl Minshull *(Personal Assistant)*, Helen Riddle *(Personal Assistant)*, Tracey Whittemore *(Personal Assistant)*
**IT:** Helen Brewer *(IT Trainer)*, Billy Long *(Assistant IT Support Technicia)*, Mark May *(Head of IT)*
**HR:** Helen Brewer *(IT Trainer)*, Sarah Finlayson *(Human Resources Administrator)*
**US SIC:** 8111 **UK SIC:** 83500

| | 31-03-14 | 31-03-13 | 31-03-12 |
|---|---|---|---|
| TO | 8,911,201 | 8,619,708 | 8,449,999 |
| NW | 1,256,591 | 881,059 | 887,346 |
| WC | 847,846 | 816,393 | 633,920 |
| Emp. | 150 | 139 | 148 |

DUNS 21-775-5667

## Tollesby Hall Nursing Home

1 Slip Inn Bank, Ladgate Lane, Hemlington, Middlesbrough, Cleveland TS8 9EJ
**Web:** www.hc-one.co.uk
**Estd:** 2002 Proprietorship
**Line of Business:** Nursing homes
**Proprietor:** Mrs M Hodgetts
**Responsibilities**
**Senior:** Julia Laverick *(Manager)*
**US SIC:** 8051 **UK SIC:** 95100
**Employees:** 85

DUNS 54-875-1940

## Tollgate Hotel

18 Camp Road, Gerrards Cross, Buckinghamshire SL9 7PE
**Tel:** 01753890073
**Web:** www.tollgate.co.uk
**Partnership**
**Line of Business:** Hotel
**Partners:** Mrs S Allan, R Allan
**Branches:** Tollgate Hotel, Watling Street, Gravesend, Kent DA13 9RA
**US SIC:** 7011 **UK SIC:** 66500
**Employees:** 50

DUNS 28-911-4332

## Tollgate Hotel & Leisure Ltd

Ripon Road, Stoke-On-Trent, Staffordshire ST3 3BS
**Tel:** 01782-313029 **Fax:** 01782593959
**Web:** www.tollgate.co.uk
**Reg No:** 1421312 **Estd:** 1979 Private Limited Company
**Line of Business:** Hotels
**Issued Capital:** £1,002
**Principals:** G W Oldfield *(Managing)*, A Oldfield
**Co. Secretary:** Mrs Gwendoline Oldfield
**US SIC:** 7011, 7999, 7399
**UK SIC:** 66500, 97913, 83954
**Auditors:** Barringtons
**Bankers:** Barclays Bank Plc (20-59-23)

| | 30-09-13 | 30-09-12 | 30-09-11 |
|---|---|---|---|
| TA | 1,735,606 | 1,761,818 | 1,648,989 |
| NW | 1,018,034 | 1,043,236 | 1,046,073 |
| WC | (321,867) | (239,227) | (243,025) |

DUNS 21-933-9314 **Imp-Exp**

## Tollgate Products Ltd

**(Subsidiary of:** Tollgate Products Holdings Ltd)
Helsop, Telford, Shropshire TF7 4NX
**Tel:** 01952520130 **Fax:** 01952520131
**Web:** www.tollgateproducts.co.uk
**Reg No:** 1461701 **VAT No:** 326558541
**Estd:** 1970 Private Limited Company
**Line of Business:** Engineers (general)
**Export Markets:** Hong Kong, Turkey, U S A, Portugal, France, Taiwan
**Issued Capital:** £10,000

**Principals:** E A Sneade *(Managing)*, B H Ashley *(Sales)*, J P Sneade, I C Sturdy
**Co. Secretary:** Edward Sneade
**Responsibilities**
**Senior:** Andrea Couta *(Network, Security Manager)*
**IT:** Andrea Couta *(Network, Security Manager)*
**US SIC:** 8911 **UK SIC:** 83701
**Auditors:** Barron & Barron
**Bankers:** Barclays Bank Plc (20-85-46)

| | 31-10-13 | 31-10-12 | 31-10-11 |
|---|---|---|---|
| TA | 949,615 | 1,039,473 | 1,188,814 |
| NW | 252,667 | 399,689 | 605,703 |
| WC | 242,764 | 452,196 | 614,168 |

DUNS 45-804-8691 **Imp-Exp**

## Tolsa Uk Ltd

**(Subsidiary of:** Tolsa Sociedad Anonima)
Second Avenue, Flixborough Industrial Estate, Flixborou, Scunthorpe, South Humberside DN15 8SD
**Tel:** 01724280155 **Fax:** 01777-700344
**Web:** www.tolsa.com
**Reg No:** 3162812 **VAT No:** 927298877
**Estd:** 1996 Private Limited Company
**Line of Business:** Manufacture of other non-metallic mineral products not elsewhere classified
**Export Markets:** E U
**Export Sales:** £4,542,000
**Issued Capital:** £2,200,000
**Directors:** S D Pattison, Tolsa, Sa
**Co. Secretary:** David Simpson
**Responsibilities**
**Finance:** Anne Caudwell *(Financial Controller)*
**IT:** Guy Vickery *(IT Controller)*
**Branches:** Tolsa Uk Ltd, Middlesbrough Works, Cargo Fleet Road, Middlesbrough, Cleveland TS3 6AF
**US SIC:** 3299 **UK SIC:** 24504
**Auditors:** Mazars LLP
**Bankers:** National Westminster Bank Plc (60-24-30)

| | 31-12-13 | 31-12-12 | 31-12-11 |
|---|---|---|---|
| TO | 36,077,000 | 35,067,000 | 34,702,000 |
| P/L | 2,158,000 | 2,283,000 | 2,330,000 |
| NW | 5,836,000 | 5,430,000 | 3,770,000 |
| WC | 3,495,000 | 3,168,000 | 1,201,000 |
| Emp. | 61 | 69 | 68 |

DUNS 23-967-3143

## Toluna Uk Ltd

**(Subsidiary of:** Itwp Acquisitions Ltd)
Ealing Cross Uxbridge Road, London W5 5TH
**Tel:** 02088321700
**Reg No:** 3956201 **Estd:** 2000 Private Limited Company
**Line of Business:** Market research and public opinion polling
**Issued Capital:** £246
**Director:** R P Bernstein
**Co. Secretary:** Frederic Petit
**US SIC:** 7392 **UK SIC:** 83951

| | 31-12-13 | 31-12-12 | 31-12-11 |
|---|---|---|---|
| TO | 21,254,613 | 19,960,511 | 17,801,334 |
| P/L | 2,225,225 | 1,722,095 | 2,244,248 |
| NW | 10,047,047 | 8,104,037 | 6,533,902 |
| WC | 9,781,853 | 7,772,585 | 6,442,412 |
| Emp. | 70 | 71 | 74 |

DUNS 29-634-2462

## Tom Blackwell (Contractors & Plant Hire) Ltd

White Ash Green, Halstead, Essex CO9 1PD
**Web:** www.tomblackwell.co.uk
**Reg No:** 1960319 **VAT No:** 434852639
**Estd:** 1985 Private Limited Company
**Line of Business:** Plant hire and leasing
**Issued Capital:** £100
**Managing Director:** A E Blackwell
**Co. Secretary:** Ms Anne Blackwell
**Responsibilities**
**Senior:** Tom Blackwell *(Manager)*
**Finance:** Tom Blackwell *(Manager)*
**Marketing:** Tom Blackwell *(Manager)*
**US SIC:** 7394 **UK SIC:** 84000
**Auditors:** Elliot Woolfe & Rose
**Bankers:** Barclays Bank Plc (20-19-95)

| | 31-12-13 | 31-12-12 | 31-12-11 |
|---|---|---|---|
| TO | 7,095,266 | N/A | N/A |
| P/L | 554,589 | N/A | N/A |
| NW | 2,018,063 | 1,663,733 | 1,451,526 |
| WC | 776,271 | 775,113 | 515,077 |
| Emp. | 49 | N/A | N/A |

DUNS 28-899-2647 **Imp**

## Tom Chambers Ltd

A W Nielsen Road, Goole, North Humberside DN14 6UE
**Tel:** 01405-766856
**Web:** www.tomchambers.co.uk
**Reg No:** 1336802 **Estd:** 1997 Private Limited Company
**Line of Business:** Activities of business and employers organisations
**Issued Capital:** £100
**Principals:** R J Medley *(Managing)*, Ms V C Medley
**Co. Secretary:** Stephen Medley
**US SIC:** 3999, 5021
**UK SIC:** 49590, 61500
**Auditors:** John Lawson Wild & Co
**Bankers:** Barclays Bank Plc (20-48-42)

| | 31-07-13 | 31-07-12 | 31-07-11 |
|---|---|---|---|
| TO | 8,762,120 | 8,050,776 | 8,431,698 |
| P/L | (23,798) | (75,160) | 198,743 |
| NW | 954,613 | 1,187,750 | 1,261,083 |
| WC | 303,188 | 355,199 | 301,619 |
| Emp. | 70 | 75 | 82 |

DUNS 21-208-9148

## Tom Chandley Ltd

Unit 20, Alpha Court, Windmill Lane Industrial Estate, Manchester M34 3RB
**Tel:** 01613365444 **Fax:** 0161-335-0972
**Web:** www.chandleyovens.co.uk
**Reg No:** 0387243 **VAT No:** 157144762
**Estd:** 1944 Private Limited Company
**Line of Business:** Manufacturers and suppliers of bakery equipment
**Export Sales:** £569,132
**Issued Capital:** £4,350
**Principals:** E Dyson *(Managing)*, M R Dyson
**Co. Secretary:** Carl Fenton
**Responsibilities**
**Senior:** Brian Watmough *(Production Installation Manage)*
**Health & Safety:** Jill Roberts *(Health & Safety Officer)*
**Operations:** Brian Watmough *(Production Installation Manage)*
**Engineering:** Brian Watmough *(Production Installation Manage)*
**US SIC:** 3551 **UK SIC:** 32441
**Auditors:** Royce Peeling Green
**Bankers:** Barclays Bank Plc (20-82-14)

| | 31-05-14 | 31-05-13 | 31-05-12 |
|---|---|---|---|
| TO | 5,928,027 | 5,763,285 | 7,573,175 |
| P/L | 444,165 | 347,441 | 855,879 |
| NW | 2,201,106 | 2,257,212 | 2,043,602 |
| WC | 1,778,436 | 1,784,532 | 1,554,718 |
| Emp. | 92 | 95 | 102 |

DUNS 77-107-9175

## Tom Cobleigh (Inns) Ltd

**(Subsidiary of:** Spirit Pub Company Plc)
The Spirit Group, 107 Station Street, Burton-On-Trent, Staffordshire DE14 1BX
**Tel:** 01623627122 **Fax:** 01604-745001
**Reg No:** 2684842 **Estd:** 1992 Private Limited Company
**Line of Business:** Real estate agents & managers
**Issued Capital:** £100
**Directors:** J R Langford, D A Kelly, P J Gallagher, Ms L J Bell
**Co. Secretary:** Ms Claire Stewart
**Branches:** Tom Cobleigh (Inns) Ltd, 68-74 Carlton Road, Worksop, Nottinghamshire S80 1PH
**US SIC:** 6531 **UK SIC:** 83400

| | 23-08-14 | 17-08-13 | 18-08-12 |
|---|---|---|---|
| TA | 2,430,000 | 2,430,000 | 2,430,000 |
| NW | 2,430,000 | 2,430,000 | 2,430,000 |

DUNS 21-569-0272 **Imp-Exp**

## Tom Hannah (Agencies) Ltd

Walkinshaw Works, Walkinshaw Street, Johnstone, Renfrewshire PA5 8AB
**Tel:** 01505-321131 **Fax:** 01505-329281
**Web:** www.hannahssweets.co.uk
**Reg No:** 0023799SC **Estd:** 1946 Private Limited Company
**Line of Business:** Manufacturers of confectionery
**Export Markets:** Worldwide
**Export Sales:** £271,992
**Trading Style:** Hannah's of Johnstone
**Issued Capital:** £1,650
**Principals:** T C Munro *(Managing)*, Ms C M Munro *(Managing)*, K D Munro
**Co. Secretary:** Ms Carole Munro
**US SIC:** 2065, 5149
**UK SIC:** 42142, 61700
**Auditors:** Henderson & Co
**Bankers:** Bank Of Scotland (80-91-27)

| | 31-01-14 | 31-01-13 | 31-01-12 |
|---|---|---|---|
| TO | 10,162,934 | 9,730,245 | 9,908,210 |
| P/L | 259,798 | 231,387 | (22,200) |
| NW | 2,427,262 | 2,370,965 | 2,354,114 |
| WC | 1,200,924 | 1,179,120 | 1,183,577 |
| Emp. | 47 | 50 | 53 |

DUNS 49-002-1953 **Imp**

## Tom James Uk Ltd

**(Subsidiary of:** Tom James Company)
11 Old Jewry, London EC2R 8DU
**Tel:** 01612375823
**Web:** www.tomjameseurope.com
**Reg No:** 3070154 **Estd:** 1995 Private Limited Company
**Line of Business:** Tailors
**Issued Capital:** £100
**Directors:** J P Williams, W L Salyer
**Co. Secretary:** Mrs Joanna Colby
**Responsibilities**
**Senior:** Paul Copp *(Manager)*
**Branches:** Tom James Uk Ltd, 15-17 Christopher Street, London EC2A 2BS
**US SIC:** 5963 **UK SIC:** 65600
**Auditors:** Michael Simon & Co

| | 31-12-13 | 31-12-12 | 31-12-11 |
|---|---|---|---|
| TA | 1,504,945 | 1,755,860 | 1,354,333 |
| NW | (1,336,500) | (784,053) | (890,422) |
| WC | (1,493,232) | (972,167) | (1,080,982) |

DUNS 21-288-0181 **Imp-Exp**

## Tom Martin & Company Ltd

**(Subsidiary of:** Tom Martin Metal Holdings 2011 Ltd)
123 Walton Summit Centre Seedlee Road, Preston, Lancashire PR5 8AE
**Tel:** 01772-626-828
**Web:** www.tom-martin.co.uk
**Reg No:** 0990667 **VAT No:** 764531032
**Estd:** 1970 Private Limited Company
**Line of Business:** Scrap metal dealers
**Export Markets:** Worldwide
**Export Sales:** £25,963,293
**Issued Capital:** £400,000
**Directors:** G E Brettle, A Slater, C Mcneil
**Co. Secretary:** Sean Hallinan
**Branches:** Tom Martin & Company Ltd, Mosley Rd, Trafford Pk, Manchester M17 1PG
**US SIC:** 5093 **UK SIC:** 62200
**Auditors:** RSM Tenon Audit Ltd
**Bankers:** Lloyds TSB Bank plc (30-93-66)

| | 31-12-13 | 31-12-12 | 31-12-11 |
|---|---|---|---|
| TO | 44,392,971 | 48,944,587 | 53,812,311 |
| P/L | 2,783,315 | 3,008,372 | 3,528,341 |
| NW | 12,779,658 | 10,794,077 | 8,822,380 |
| WC | 11,371,661 | 9,318,890 | 7,254,657 |
| Emp. | 67 | 68 | 62 |

DUNS 21-319-1265 **Imp-Exp**

## Tom Parker Ltd

Marsh Lane Mill, Preston, Lancashire PR1 1HY
**Tel:** 01772255100 **Fax:** 01772563475
**Web:** www.tom-parker.co.uk
**Reg No:** 1068402 **VAT No:** 154677048
**Estd:** 1972 Private Limited Company
**Line of Business:** Hydraulic equipment & accessories - sales & service
**Export Markets:** India, Sweden, Germany, Switzerland, Republic of Ireland, W Europe
**Export Sales:** £309,441
**Issued Capital:** £6,221
**Principals:** T Parker *(Managing)*, R A Parker *(Sales)*, M T Parker *(Technical)*
**Co. Secretary:** Timothy Parker
**Branches:** Tom Parker Ltd, Tom Parker Ltd, Parker House, Basingstoke, Hampshire RG21 7QB
**US SIC:** 3999, 5084
**UK SIC:** 49590, 61490
**Auditors:** RST Audits Ltd
**Bankers:** Yorkshire Bank Plc (05-06-74)

| | 30-04-14 | 30-04-13 | 30-04-12 |
|---|---|---|---|
| TO | 9,043,086 | 8,374,104 | 9,270,636 |
| P/L | 731,039 | 892,651 | 307,861 |
| NW | 3,760,043 | 3,772,062 | 3,050,336 |
| WC | 2,882,771 | 2,846,499 | 2,466,027 |
| Emp. | 65 | 65 | 60 |

DUNS 21-655-8154

## T.O.M. Vehicle Rental Ltd

Ninian Road, Brownsburn Industrial Estate, Airdrie, Lanarkshire ML6 9SE
**Tel:** 01236749889
**Web:** www.unitedrentalsystem.co.uk
**Reg No:** 0371327SC **Estd:** 2010 Private Limited Company
**Line of Business:** Car, van and truck leasing and contract hire
**Export Sales:** £174,000
**Issued Capital:** £1,176,100
**Directors:** J G Rafferty, D Rutherford, H Stewart, R W Stewart, G J Grier, M Grier, J W Rafferty
**US SIC:** 7512 **UK SIC:** 84801
**Auditors:** Johnston Carmichael

| | 31-03-14 | 31-03-13 | 31-03-12 |
|---|---|---|---|
| TO | 98,455,000 | 62,339,000 | 38,422,000 |
| P/L | 1,632,000 | 1,301,000 | 2,005,000 |
| NW | 8,772,000 | 7,618,000 | 6,845,000 |
| WC | (22,806,000) | (15,980,000) | (12,907,000) |
| Emp. | 374 | 357 | 255 |

DUNS 28-883-1316

## Tom White Waste Ltd

Stonebrook Way, Blackburn Road Industrial Estate, Coventry, West Midlands CV6 6LN
**Tel:** 024-7666-2525
**Web:** www.tomwhitewaste.co.uk
**Reg No:** 1201361 **VAT No:** 273664045
**Estd:** 1975 Private Limited Company
**Line of Business:** Waste disposal
**Issued Capital:** £100
**Directors:** I R White, P T White
**Co. Secretary:** Ian White
**Responsibilities**
**Senior:** Tom White *(CEO, Managing Director)*
**Branches:** Tom White Waste Ltd, Newhall Green, Coventry, West Midlands CV7 8DW
**US SIC:** 4953 **UK SIC:** 92110
**Auditors:** BDO Stoy Hayward
**Bankers:** Allied Irish Bank (gb) (23-83-99)

| | 31-03-14 | 31-03-13 | 31-03-12 |
|---|---|---|---|
| TO | 7,446,024 | 6,426,153 | 6,098,169 |
| P/L | 164,068 | 211,637 | 192,381 |
| NW | 2,778,487 | 2,652,668 | 2,487,896 |
| WC | (789,768) | (950,961) | (844,583) |
| Emp. | 75 | 74 | 73 |

DUNS 22-914-4555 **Imp-Exp**

## The Tomatin Distillery Company Ltd

**(Subsidiary of:** Takara Holdings Inc.)
Tomatin Road, Inverness, Inverness-Shire IV2 4UA
**Tel:** 01463248144 **Fax:** 01808511373
**Web:** www.tomatin.com
**Reg No:** 0095810SC **VAT No:** 664095519
**Estd:** 2008 Private Limited Company
**Line of Business:** Distilleries
**Export Markets:** Germany, France, Belgium, Netherlands, Spain, Portugal & U S A
**Issued Capital:** £3,297,244
**Directors:** R W Anderson, T Kakimoto, Y Ogasawara, H Yamada, K Ito, S Bremner, D Nakao, H Omiya
**Co. Secretary:** Ms Catherine Davis
**Responsibilities**
**Senior:** Hiroyuki Ito *(Director)*
**Branches:** The Tomatin Distillery Company Ltd,, Strathclyde Homes Stadium, Castle Rd, Dumbarton, Dunbartonshire G82 1JJ
**US SIC:** 2085 **UK SIC:** 42402
**Auditors:** Deloitte LLP
**Bankers:** The Royal Bank Of Scotland Plc (83-23-10)

| | 31-12-13 | 31-12-12 | 31-12-11 |
|---|---|---|---|
| TO | 15,140,326 | 14,319,120 | 13,362,190 |
| P/L | 1,557,235 | 1,113,959 | 1,371,758 |
| NW | 22,467,750 | 21,287,030 | 19,730,411 |
| WC | 29,202,301 | 28,146,907 | 27,424,131 |
| Emp. | 48 | 53 | 48 |

DUNS 23-898-7460

## Tombola Ltd

Wylam Wharf, Low Street, Sunderland, Tyne and Wear SR1 2JR
**Tel:** 08002988873 **Fax:** 0191-564-2266
**Web:** www.tombola.co.uk
**Reg No:** 3889481 **Estd:** 1999 Private Limited Company
**Line of Business:** Online gaming
**Issued Capital:** £100
**Directors:** M A Cronin, J E Cronin, R A Cronin, P J Cronin
**Co. Secretary:** Alison Cronin
**US SIC:** 7999 **UK SIC:** 97913
**Auditors:** Robson Laidler LLP

| | 30-04-14 | 30-04-13 | 30-04-12 |
|---|---|---|---|
| TO | 44,215,728 | 39,800,664 | 32,661,329 |
| P/L | 12,215,895 | 9,079,864 | 7,548,442 |
| NW | 31,125,629 | 28,638,972 | 21,727,143 |
| WC | 30,524,620 | 28,011,562 | 21,517,305 |
| Emp. | 243 | 220 | 168 |

DUNS 49-387-9209

## Tomburn Ltd

Gunstore Road, Portsmouth, Hampshire PO3 5HL
**Tel:** 023-9269-2020
**Web:** www.tomburn.co.uk
**Reg No:** 3134975 **VAT No:** 673884680
**Estd:** 1995 Private Limited Company
**Line of Business:** Powder coating specialists
**Export Sales:** £962,790
**Trading Style:** L B L Finishers, L B L Finishers and Birmingham Powder Coatings
**Issued Capital:** £5,083
**Principals:** D H Hepburn *(Managing)*, J C Tomlinson
**Co. Secretary:** John Tomlinson
**Responsibilities**
**Marketing:** Simon Rowles *(Sales & Marketing Manager)*
**Sales:** Simon Rowles *(Sales & Marketing Manager)*
**Facilities:** Martin Gawthorpe *(Maintenance Officer)*
**Purchasing:** Des Hill *(Purchasing Manager)*
**Branches:** Tomburn Ltd, Clonmel Road, Birmingham, West Midlands B30 2BU
**US SIC:** 2891, 3398
**UK SIC:** 25620, 31380
**Auditors:** KPMG

| | 30-03-14 | 31-03-13 | 25-03-12 |
|---|---|---|---|
| TO | 5,566,035 | 5,800,035 | N/A |
| P/L | 247,972 | 445,027 | N/A |
| NW | 1,789,624 | 1,684,962 | 1,124,467 |
| WC | (30,410) | (191,562) | (407,277) |
| Emp. | 104 | 104 | N/A |

DUNS 21-313-5650

## Tomlinson Longstaff Ltd

Chapel Street, West Auckland, Bishop Auckland, County Durham DL14 9HP
**Tel:** 01388833836
**Web:** www.tomlinsonlongstaff.co.uk
**Reg No:** 1206464 **Estd:** 1975 Private Limited Company
**Line of Business:** Installation of electrical wiring and fittings

**Issued Capital:** £6,050
**Principals:** A J Kirkup (Managing), Miss A J Reid, Mrs A C Kirkup
**Co. Secretary:** Ms Jill O Hare
**Responsibilities**
**Purchasing:** Jeremy Foster (Contracts Manager)
**US SIC:** 1731 **UK SIC:** 50300
**Auditors:** Allen Sykes Ltd
**Bankers:** HSBC Bank plc (40-12-01)

|    | 31-05-14 | 31-05-13 | 31-05-12 |
|----|----------|----------|----------|
| TA | 423,505  | 366,734  | 365,292  |
| NW | 217,072  | 213,083  | 173,587  |
| WC | 138,563  | 151,316  | 107,338  |

DUNS 23-892-0198    Imp

## Tomlinson's Dairies Ltd
Penypalmant Farm, Old Road, Minera, Wrexham, Clwyd LL11 3YR
**Tel:** 01978-758833
**Web:** www.welovemilk.co.uk
**Reg No:** 3882919 **Estd:** 1999 Private Limited Company
**Line of Business:** Dairies
**Issued Capital:** £100
**Managing Director:** P N Tomlinson
**Co. Secretary:** John Tomlinson
**US SIC:** 0241, 2023
**UK SIC:** 01001, 41303

|     | 31-03-14    | 31-03-13    | 31-03-12   |
|-----|-------------|-------------|------------|
| TO  | 38,207,073  | 16,130,885  | 11,729,516 |
| P/L | 1,165,135   | (301,882)   | 167,432    |
| NW  | 6,692,199   | 5,979,621   | 5,918,008  |
| WC  | (1,502,738) | (2,626,167) | (401,526)  |
| Emp.| 123         | 88          | 62         |

DUNS 29-865-0078    Imp-Exp

## Tomoe Valve Ltd
(**Subsidiary of:** Tomoe Valve Co. Ltd.)
Clearwater Road, Queensway Meadows Industrial Estate, Newport, Gwent NP19 4ST
**Tel:** 01633 274707 **Fax:** 01633292600
**Web:** www.tomoe.co.uk
**Reg No:** 2068216 **VAT No:** 433397639
**Estd:** 1987 Private Limited Company
**Line of Business:** Manufacture of other fabricated metal products not elsewhere classified
**Export Markets:** Germany, Italy, France & Saudi Arabia
**Export Sales:** £4,125,000
**Issued Capital:** £1,000,001
**Directors:** A Yamamoto, T Mihara, T Yamamoto, H Kawase, J Sakakibara
**Co. Secretary:** Ms Denise Road
**US SIC:** 3494 **UK SIC:** 32880
**Auditors:** PricewaterhouseCoopers LLP
**Bankers:** The Bank Of Tokyo-Mitsubishi, Ltd (60-01-09)

|     | 31-12-13  | 31-12-12  | 31-12-11    |
|-----|-----------|-----------|-------------|
| TO  | 5,755,000 | 7,519,000 | 6,305,000   |
| P/L | 2,000     | 1,000     | (759,000)   |
| NW  | 2,321,000 | 2,317,000 | (7,269,000) |
| WC  | 1,694,000 | 1,788,000 | (817,000)   |
| Emp.| 54        | 53        | 53          |

DUNS 54-828-7408

## Tomorrows People Trust
Altitude Business Park, The Drift, Nacton Road, Ipswich, Suffolk IP3 9QN
**Tel:** 01473725757
**Web:** www.tomorrows-people.org.uk
**Estd:** 2007
**Line of Business:** Charities and charitable organisations
**Trading Style:** Getting London Working
**Partners:** Ms P Vaz, Ms J Calvert Lee, Ms E Gibson Bolton, G Bush, D Stewart, Ms C Glenn
**Responsibilities**
**Senior:** Maurice Biriotti (Manager), Jane Calvert-Lee (Director), Elaine Gibson-bolton (Director), Theresa Pollard (Lead Local Operations Manager), Debbi Scott (Chief Executive), Stelio Stefanou (Manager)
**Finance:** Nick Warran-Smith (Financial Director)
**Branches:** Tomorrows People Trust, 109 Uxbridge Rd, London W5 5TL
**US SIC:** 8699, 7361
**UK SIC:** 96902, 83954
**Employees:** 175

DUNS 73-760-1968

## Tomorrow's People Trust Ltd
York Road, Eastbourne, East Sussex BN21 4ST
**Tel:** 01323418164
**Web:** www.tomorrows-people.co.uk
**Reg No:** 5017566 **Estd:** 1983 Private Company Limited By Guarantee
**Line of Business:** Other business activities not elsewhere classified
**Directors:** A Dakin, Dr N E Watson-Druee, Mrs S M Van Dijk, Ms K B Bolsover, Miss M S Lai, Ms E M Gibson-Bolton, J Tizzard
**Co. Secretary:** Charles Shaw

**Responsibilities**
**Senior:** Kaye Crittell (Manager), Arthur Mapletoft (Manager), Ronald Naylor (Manager), Theresa Pollard (Regional Manager), Sylvia Tidy (Manager)
**Marketing:** Abi Levitt (Marketing & Communications Dir)
**Operations:** Simon Branscomb (Chief Operating Officer)
**US SIC:** 7399 **UK SIC:** 83954
**Bankers:** National Westminster Bank Plc (60-10-15)

|     | 31-03-14  | 31-03-13  | 31-03-12  |
|-----|-----------|-----------|-----------|
| TO  | 9,000,085 | 7,025,122 | 6,841,192 |
| P/L | 1,158,372 | (378,405) | 23,127    |
| NW  | 5,525,255 | 4,366,179 | 4,744,584 |
| WC  | 5,098,959 | 3,926,558 | 4,304,277 |
| Emp.| 180       | 162       | 136       |

DUNS 21-558-0237

## Tompkins & May Partnership
Derby House, 73-77 East Street, Epsom, Surrey KT17 1BP
**Web:** www.tompkinsmay.com
**VAT No:** 933083826 **Estd:** 1869 Partnership
**Line of Business:** Traditional cleaning activities
**Trading Style:** Altius
**Partners:** J May, Mrs C May, D May
**Branches:** Tompkins & May Partnership, Suite 27 & 28 Space Ho, Space Business Park Abbey Road, London NW10 7SU
**US SIC:** 7349, 1522, 1541
**UK SIC:** 92300, 50100
**Bankers:** HSBC Bank plc (40-06-21)
**Employees:** 100

DUNS 21-391-3749

## Tom's Kitchen
27 Cale Street, London SW3 3QP
**Tel:** 020-73490202
**Web:** www.tomskitchen.co.uk
**Estd:** 2009 Proprietorship
**Line of Business:** Restaurant - english
**Proprietor:** T Aikens
**US SIC:** 5812 **UK SIC:** 66110
**Employees:** 50

DUNS 21-140-2361

## Tom's Kitchen Ltd
(**Subsidiary of:** London Doors Restaurant Group Ltd)
11 Westferry Circus, London E14 4HD
**Tel:** 02030111555
**Web:** www.tomskitchen.co.uk
**Reg No:** 6722850 **Estd:** 2008 Private Limited Company
**Line of Business:** Licensed restaurants
**Issued Capital:** £1
**Director:** L Veziroglu
**Responsibilities**
**Senior:** Levent Buyukurgur (Manager)
**US SIC:** 5812 **UK SIC:** 66110

|    | 31-12-13  | 31-12-12  | 31-12-11 |
|----|-----------|-----------|----------|
| TA | 1,421,039 | 1,113,570 | 920,696  |
| NW | 476,760   | 342,399   | 256,616  |
| WC | 322,471   | 172,200   | 70,150   |

DUNS 64-084-3256

## Tomsetts Distribution Ltd
North Quay Road, Newhaven, East Sussex BN9 0AB
**Tel:** 01273513347
**Web:** www.tomsetts.co.uk
**Reg No:** 3479530 **Estd:** 1967 Private Limited Company
**Line of Business:** Road haulage and transport services
**Issued Capital:** £194,000
**Director:** S Tucknott
**Co. Secretary:** Raymond Tucknott
**US SIC:** 4789, 7399
**UK SIC:** 77002, 83954
**Auditors:** BDO Stoy Hayward

|     | 31-03-14  | 31-03-13  | 31-03-12 |
|-----|-----------|-----------|----------|
| TO  | 4,809,793 | 3,890,683 | 3,855,818 |
| P/L | 104,140   | (34,568)  | (35,950) |
| NW  | 694,059   | 624,765   | 654,437  |
| WC  | 336,434   | 292,235   | 320,990  |

DUNS 22-602-3059    Imp-Exp

## Tomy Uk Co Ltd
(**Subsidiary of:** Tomy Company Ltd.)
Hembury House, Pynes Hill, Rydon Lane, Exeter, Devon EX2 5AZ
**Tel:** 01392 281900
**Web:** www.tomy.com
**Reg No:** 1634124 **VAT No:** 365793312
**Estd:** 1982 Private Limited Company
**Line of Business:** Manufacturers of games, toys and sporting products
**Export Markets:** E U
**Trading Style:** Tomy Uk, Tomy
**Issued Capital:** £272
**Director:** G Kilrea
**Co. Secretary:** Damien Weight
**Responsibilities**
**Senior:** Damian Waite (Manager), Clive Wooster (Marketing Director)

**Marketing:** Clive Wooster (Marketing Director)
**Sales:** Clive Wooster (Marketing Director)
**IT:** Stuart Kahn (IT Manager)
**Purchasing:** Sue Samuel (Purchasing Manager)
**US SIC:** 3949 **UK SIC:** 49420
**Auditors:** KPMG LLP
**Bankers:** HSBC Bank plc (40-20-30)

|     | 31-03-14    | 31-03-13    | 31-03-12   |
|-----|-------------|-------------|------------|
| TO  | 69,100,000  | 66,525,000  | 39,935,000 |
| P/L | (593,000)   | (3,231,000) | 4,955,000  |
| NW  | 1,070,000   | 4,608,000   | 8,184,000  |
| WC  | 657,000     | 4,293,000   | 8,352,000  |
| Emp.| 90          | 102         | 58         |

DUNS 21-125-5617

## Tonbridge & Malling Borough Council
Gibson Building, Gibson Drive, West Malling, Kent ME19 4LZ
**Tel:** 01732844522 **Fax:** 01732842170
**Web:** www.tmbc.gov.uk
**Estd:** 1974 Incorporate By Act Of Parliament
**Line of Business:** Local government
**Directors:** D Hughes, D Milner
**Responsibilities**
**Senior:** Julie Beilby (Chief Executive), Cliff Cochrane (General Manager), John Dicker (Executive), Delia Gordon (Training Officer), Mark Raymond (Marketing & Regeneration Manag), Adrian Stanfield (Director of Central Services a), Charlie Steel (Personnel & Customer Services)
**Finance:** Sharon Shelton (Financial Director)
**Marketing:** Mark Raymond (Marketing & Regeneration Manag)
**IT:** Darren Everden (IT Manager), Viv London (?Technical Support Manager)
**HR:** Delia Gordon (Training Officer), Charlie Steel (Personnel & Customer Services)
**Health & Safety:** Bill Parkinson (Health & Safety Officer)
**Facilities:** John Deknop (Facilities Manager), Jane Smither (Housing Officer)
**Operations:** Charlie Steel (Personnel & Customer Services)
**Fleet:** Steve Humphrey (Director, Planning and Transpo)
**Branches:** Tonbridge & Malling Borough Council, Tonbridge Castle, Castle Street, Tonbridge, Kent TN9 1BG
**US SIC:** 9121 **UK SIC:** 91110
**Bankers:** National Westminster Bank Plc (55-81-07)
**Employees:** 400

DUNS 21-700-5684

## Tonbridge Grammar School
Deakin Leas, Tonbridge, Kent TN9 2JR
**Tel:** 01732365125
**Web:** www.tgs.kent.sch.uk
**Reg No:** 7455728 **Estd:** 1989 Private Company Limited By Guarantee
**Line of Business:** Schools (foundation)
**Directors:** R J Hubble, A B Wessels, Mrs J E Wheeler, M R Joyner, Mrs A C Senior, Ms N Hoban, Mrs S J Dyson, Ms P Bullen
**Co. Secretary:** Mrs Alison Hook
**Responsibilities**
**Senior:** Wendy Balcombe (Manager), Rowan Connell (Director), Philip Da Silva (Manager), Anna Firth (Director), Melanie Gailey (Director), Steven Holdcroft (Director), Geraldine Hughes (Director), Rosemary Joyce (Director), Benjamin Pennells (Director), Stephen Seagrove (Director), Suzette Thorpe (Director)
**US SIC:** 8211 **UK SIC:** 93200
**Bankers:** Lloyds TSB Bank plc (30-16-87)

|     | 31-08-14  | 31-08-13  | 31-08-12  |
|-----|-----------|-----------|-----------|
| TO  | 6,692,000 | 5,896,000 | 6,212,000 |
| P/L | 678,000   | 182,000   | 272,000   |
| NW  | 9,558,000 | 8,954,000 | 8,786,000 |
| WC  | 1,846,000 | 1,254,000 | 906,000   |
| Emp.| 91        | 101       | 103       |

DUNS 73-524-3664

## Tonbridge School
High Street, Tonbridge, Kent TN9 1JP
**Web:** www.tonbridge-school.co.uk
**Reg No:** 4787097 **VAT No:** 821944919
**Estd:** 2003 Private Company Limited By Guarantee
**Line of Business:** General secondary education
**Directors:** M F Dobbs, C A Stuart Clark, D P Devitt, Mrs K M Wheadon, C J Rudge, A H Mayer, R N Nottidge, Professor S E Stallebrass
**Co. Secretary:** Anthony Moore
**Responsibilities**
**Senior:** Johnny Aisher (Director), David Coldman (Board member), Christopher Emms (Director), Tracy Luke (Board member), Samantha Price (Director), Sara Tozzi (Board member), Marie Wallace (Business Development Manager), Cathy Wilkin (Manager), Simon Woolton (Director)

**Finance:** Champa Dissanayake (Accountant), Jane Fentiman (Financial Controller), Alison Hale (Accounts Administrator), Becky Pettite (Accounts), Vicki Rushton (Assistant Financial Controller)
**Sales:** Marie Wallace (Business Development Manager)
**Admin:** Wendy Bardwell (Fee Administrator), Sue Streeter (PA of the Bursar)
**HR:** Silvia Iskrova (Catering Personnel Officer)
**Purchasing:** Janice Waltham (Purchase Administrator)
**Engineering:** Tom Millis (Technician officer), Jonathan Waight (Senior Technician)
**US SIC:** 8211 **UK SIC:** 93200
**Auditors:** Saffery Champness
**Bankers:** Lloyds TSB Bank plc (30-25-36)

|     | 30-06-13   | 30-06-12   | 30-06-11   |
|-----|------------|------------|------------|
| TO  | 24,703,251 | 23,932,009 | 22,427,927 |
| P/L | 2,016,871  | 2,347,601  | 1,582,109  |
| NW  | 18,049,502 | 15,837,148 | 13,538,230 |
| WC  | 3,965,182  | 2,815,065  | 2,411,652  |
| Emp.| 390        | 404        | 407        |

DUNS 51-576-6561

## Tone Leisure Group Ltd
The Deane House, Belvedere Road, Taunton, Somerset TA1 1HE
**Tel:** 01823356311
**Web:** www.toneleisure.co.uk
**Reg No:** 5857912 **Estd:** 2006 Private Company Limited By Guarantee
**Line of Business:** Operation of sports arenas and stadiums
**Directors:** Ms K L Arnold, J H Coates, Miss A Priscott, R A Crisp, Ms J Dickinson
**Co. Secretary:** Miss Ann Powell
**US SIC:** 7941, 8999
**UK SIC:** 97911, 83954

|     | 31-03-14  | 31-03-13  | 31-03-12  |
|-----|-----------|-----------|-----------|
| TO  | 7,296,488 | 7,433,060 | 7,589,124 |
| P/L | (315,563) | (223,847) | 65,202    |
| NW  | 1,057,766 | 1,055,329 | 1,015,176 |
| WC  | 104,643   | 78,789    | 218,501   |
| Emp.| 503       | 497       | 501       |

DUNS 23-758-4656

## Tone Scaffolding Services Ltd
(**Subsidiary of:** Tone Group Ltd)
Sky House 87-91 Beddington Lane, Croydon, Surrey CR0 4TD
**Tel:** 02086-843771 **Fax:** 02086843772
**Web:** www.tonescaffolding.co.uk
**Reg No:** 3752249 **VAT No:** 664154925
**Estd:** 1995 Private Limited Company
**Line of Business:** Renting of scaffold
**Issued Capital:** £75,000
**Managing Director:** A S Needham
**Co. Secretary:** Madhu Ahluwalia
**US SIC:** 1799 **UK SIC:** 50000
**Auditors:** Carter Backer Winter
**Bankers:** Barclays Bank Plc (20-84-17)

|     | 31-12-13   | 31-12-12   | 30-12-11  |
|-----|------------|------------|-----------|
| TO  | 11,809,152 | 11,235,548 | 8,251,367 |
| P/L | 31,675     | 600,509    | 145,240   |
| NW  | 1,584,731  | 1,553,135  | 1,154,241 |
| WC  | 228,435    | 128,155    | 203,576   |
| Emp.| 155        | 123        | 100       |

DUNS 42-359-4860

## Toner's Supermarkets
26-28 High Street, Draperstown, Magherafelt, Co Londonderry BT45 7AA
**Tel:** 02879628999
**Web:** www.tonersstores.co.uk
**Reg No:** 0030720NI **VAT No:** 516609446
**Estd:** 1988 Private Limited Company
**Line of Business:** Retail sale in non-specialised stores (excluding ctns) not holding an alcohol licence with food, beverages or tobacco predominating
**Trading Style:** Castledawson Centra, Magherafelt Centra
**Issued Capital:** £2
**Directors:** Ms M H Toner, P Toner
**Co. Secretary:** Ms Mary Toner
**Responsibilities**
**Senior:** Anne Mclaughlin (Human Resources Manager)
**HR:** Anne Mclaughlin (Human Resources Manager)
**Branches:** Toner's Supermarkets, 19 Main Street, Magherafelt, Co Londonderry BT45 8AA
**US SIC:** 5411 **UK SIC:** 64100
**Auditors:** ASM Horwath
**Bankers:** The Bank Of Ireland (90-48-43)
**Employees:** 267

DUNS 29-631-0261    Imp-Exp

## Tong Engineering Ltd
Ashby Road, Spilsby, Lincolnshire PE23 5DW
**Tel:** 01790752771
**Web:** www.tongpeal.co.uk
**Reg No:** 1957036 **VAT No:** 128490754
**Estd:** 1947 Private Limited Company
**Line of Business:** Manufacture of other agricultural and forestry machinery

**Export Markets:** Worldwide
**Export Sales:** £3,394,756
**Issued Capital:** £157,500
**Principals:** C E Tong (Managing), E C Tong
**Co. Secretary:** Douglas Mcarthur
**Responsibilities**
**Senior:** Ian Evison (Spares Manager), David Hook (Works Manager), Kenneth Tong (Manager)
**IT:** David Hook (Works Manager)
**HR:** David Hook (Works Manager)
**Health & Safety:** Brian Laud (Engineering Manager)
**Engineering:** Brian Laud (Engineering Manager)
**US SIC:** 3523  **UK SIC:** 32113
**Auditors:** PKF
**Bankers:** The Royal Bank Of Scotland Plc (16-34-80)

|  | 31-01-14 | 31-01-13 | 31-01-12 |
|---|---|---|---|
| TO | 12,228,941 | 11,095,794 | 11,122,577 |
| P/L | 638,261 | 212,170 | 80,402 |
| NW | 2,652,751 | 2,161,558 | 1,853,028 |
| WC | 1,753,681 | 1,527,536 | 1,391,639 |
| Emp. | 142 | 143 | 147 |

DUNS 21-110-4216
## Toni & Guy
Eastgate Court, 195-205 High Street, Guildford, Surrey GU1 3EH
**Tel:** 01483-304215
**Web:** www.toniandguy.com
**Estd:** 1989 Proprietorship
**Line of Business:** Hairdressers (unisex)
**Proprietor:** T E Avory
**US SIC:** 7231  **UK SIC:** 98200
**Employees:** 85

DUNS 64-230-7342
## Toni and Guy Chelmsford
225-226 Moulsham Street, Chelmsford, Essex CM2 0LR
**Tel:** 01245-256460
**Web:** www.toniandguy.com
**Estd:** 1996 Proprietorship
**Line of Business:** Hairdressers (unisex)
**Proprietor:** S Braithwaite
**Responsibilities**
**Senior:** Mark Guerrini (Manager)
**US SIC:** 7231  **UK SIC:** 98200
**Employees:** 48

DUNS 21-627-3109
## Toni & Guy International Ltd
58-60 Stamford Street, London SE1 9LX
**Tel:** 02079219101
**Web:** www.toniandguy.com
**Reg No:** 7067159  **Estd:** 2009 Private Limited Company
**Line of Business:** Hairdressing and other beauty treatment
**Export Sales:** £10,616,000
**Issued Capital:** £311
**Directors:** G T Mascolo, Mrs S M Mascolo-Tarbuck
**Co. Secretary:** Rupert Berrow
**US SIC:** 8999  **UK SIC:** 83954

|  | 31-08-12 | 31-08-11 | 31-08-10 |
|---|---|---|---|
| TO | 68,250,000 | 62,417,000 | N/A |
| P/L | (4,123,000) | (2,126,000) | N/A |
| NW | 19,072,000 | 18,875,000 | 17,941,000 |
| WC | 2,354,000 | 4,071,000 | 4,865,000 |
| Emp. | 1,536 | 1,443 | N/A |

DUNS 37-766-3026
## Toni & Guy Salon
8a Church Street, High Wycombe, Buckinghamshire HP11 2DE
**Web:** www.toniandguy.com
**Estd:** 2002 Proprietorship
**Line of Business:** Hairdressers (unisex)
**Proprietor:** A Owen
**Responsibilities**
**Senior:** Becky Sharp (Proprietor)
**US SIC:** 7231  **UK SIC:** 98200
**Employees:** 50

DUNS 55-063-6336
## Toni Godber
60 Cornwall Road, Harrogate, North Yorkshire HG1 2NE
**Web:** www.waldernheath.co.uk
**Estd:** 1967 Proprietorship
**Line of Business:** Individual & Family Social Services
**Proprietor:** Mrs T Godber
**US SIC:** 8321  **UK SIC:** 96111
**Employees:** 50

DUNS 73-258-9861
## Tonna Care Services Ltd
49 Beacontree Plaza, Gillette Way, Reading, Berkshire RG2 0BS
**Tel:** 01189-759222
**Web:** www.tonnacareservices.com
**Reg No:** 4532773  **Estd:** 2002 Private Limited Company

**Line of Business:** Home care and help services
**Issued Capital:** £2
**Director:** C G Tonna
**Co. Secretary:** Kyla Tonna
**Responsibilities**
**Senior:** Brian Bignell (Manager)
**US SIC:** 8811  **UK SIC:** 99000

|  | 01-03-14 | 01-03-13 | 01-03-12 |
|---|---|---|---|
| TO | 1,219,157 | 931,324 | 639,330 |
| P/L | 260,441 | 154,335 | 83,262 |
| NW | 183,721 | 85,731 | 28,153 |
| WC | 182,287 | 83,819 | 27,021 |

DUNS 21-579-6622
## Tonna Hospitial
Tonna Uchaf, Tonna, Neath, West Glamorgan SA11 3LX
**Tel:** 01639862862
**Estd:** 2011 Proprietorship
**Line of Business:** Hospitals
**Proprietor:** Ms P Thomas
**Responsibilities**
**Senior:** Karen Francis (Team Leader)
**US SIC:** 8062  **UK SIC:** 95100
**Employees:** 50

DUNS 45-800-5931
## Tonstate Group Ltd
3 Park Place, London SW1A 1LP
**Tel:** 020-7493-5357
**Web:** www.tonstate.co.uk
**Reg No:** 3162082  **Estd:** 1996 Private Limited Company
**Line of Business:** Development and selling of real estate
**Issued Capital:** £180,001
**Principals:** Dr E Wojakovski (Managing), Mrs R E Robertson, A Matyas, N A Smith, Mrs R Matyas
**Co. Secretary:** Dr Edward Wojakovski
**US SIC:** 6552  **UK SIC:** 85000
**Auditors:** H W Fisher & Co
**Bankers:** The Royal Bank Of Scotland Plc (16-00-30)

|  | 31-03-14 | 31-03-13 | 31-03-12 |
|---|---|---|---|
| TO | 9,043,299 | 8,731,410 | 7,806,261 |
| P/L | 3,204,593 | 1,639,451 | 1,727,304 |
| NW | 32,842,214 | 32,550,876 | 37,307,970 |
| WC | 12,502,430 | 3,602,444 | 7,188,675 |
| Emp. | 42 | 49 | 38 |

DUNS 22-928-6927
## The Tontine Rooms Holding Company Ltd
56 Scotch Street, Armagh, Co Armagh BT61 7DQ
**Tel:** 02837522639
**Web:** www.ulstergazette.co.uk
**Reg No:** 0012192NI  **Estd:** 1843 Private Limited Company
**Line of Business:** Newspapers publishing
**Issued Capital:** £6,684
**Directors:** J D Taylor, E R Curran, Rt Hon J D Taylor, W R Todd
**Co. Secretary:** Thomas Mcfeeters
**Responsibilities**
**IT:** Andrew Mussen (IT Manager)
**Branches:** The Tontine Rooms Holding Company Ltd, 36 The Square, Ballyclare, Co Antrim BT39 9BB
**US SIC:** 2711  **UK SIC:** 47512
**Auditors:** Michael Hunter & Co
**Bankers:** Northern Bank Ltd (95-02-06)

|  | 31-12-13 | 31-12-12 | 31-12-11 |
|---|---|---|---|
| TA | 34,367,144 | 34,151,009 | 34,144,428 |
| NW | 439,884 | 10,143 | (105,787) |
| WC | (20,151,913) | (5,141,222) | (4,418,201) |

DUNS 21-582-0507                                            Exp
## Tony Beal Ltd
(Subsidiary of: The Beal Group Ltd)
18 Station Road, Baillieston, Glasgow, Lanarkshire G69 7UF
**Web:** www.tonybeal.com
**Reg No:** 0067541SC  **VAT No:** 328624646
**Estd:** 1979 Private Limited Company
**Line of Business:** Manufacturers of tarpaulins
**Export Markets:** Portugal; India
**Issued Capital:** £20,000
**Director:** D J Beal
**Responsibilities**
**Finance:** Victoria Beal (Finance Director)
**Sales:** Emma Russell (Account Manager), Gerry Sinclair (Sales Manager)
**Branches:** Tony Beal Ltd, 1 Brierley Street, Ashton On Ribble, Preston, Lancashire PR2 2AU
**US SIC:** 2392, 5199
**UK SIC:** 45550, 61900
**Auditors:** PricewaterhouseCoopers LLP
**Bankers:** Clydesdale Bank Plc (82-64-04)

|  | 30-04-14 | 30-04-13 | 30-04-12 |
|---|---|---|---|
| TA | 4,134,517 | 4,219,700 | 3,960,505 |
| NW | 3,038,731 | 2,987,284 | 2,854,734 |
| WC | 1,915,998 | 1,843,330 | 1,698,024 |

DUNS 67-228-7596
## Tony Chapman Electronics Ltd
5 Robin Hood Lane, Sutton, Surrey SM1 2SW
**Tel:** 01992578231  **Fax:** 01355242198
**Web:** www.tceltd.co.uk
**Reg No:** 6055684  **Estd:** 2007 Private Limited Company
**Line of Business:** Agents specialising in the sale of particular products or ranges of products not elsewhere classified
**Issued Capital:** £200
**Directors:** S M Bali, I A Croxford
**Responsibilities**
**Senior:** Mark Campson (General Manager)
**US SIC:** 5199  **UK SIC:** 61900

|  | 31-12-13 | 31-12-12 | 31-12-11 |
|---|---|---|---|
| TA | 362,441 | 138,566 | 165,839 |
| NW | 3,392 | 2,687 | 2,131 |
| WC | (6,598) | (10,636) | (6,306) |

DUNS 22-123-0340
## Tony Fresko Ltd
Warren Farm, White Lane, Ash Green, Aldershot, Hampshire GU12 6HW
**Tel:** 01252-315528
**Web:** www.tonyfresko.com
**Reg No:** 4142068  **Estd:** 1973 Private Limited Company
**Line of Business:** Ice cream parlours
**Issued Capital:** £2
**Director:** J Sawyer
**Co. Secretary:** Ms Barbara Kinge
**US SIC:** 5812  **UK SIC:** 66110

|  | 31-01-14 | 31-01-13 | 31-01-12 |
|---|---|---|---|
| TA | 409,389 | 341,873 | 353,207 |
| NW | 255,149 | 164,346 | 143,919 |
| WC | 165,425 | 71,531 | (27,182) |

DUNS 34-849-4670                                            Exp
## Tony Gee & Partners Llp
140 High Street, Esher, Surrey KT10 9QJ
**Tel:** 01372461600
**Web:** www.tonygee.com
**Reg No:** 0316614OC  **Estd:** 1974
**Line of Business:** Civil engineers
**Export Sales:** £4,611,923
**Responsibilities**
**Senior:** Iain Fletcher (Non-designated Limited Liabili), Alasdair Fowler (Non-designated Limited Liabili), Nicholas Southward (Non-designated Limited Liabili), Robert Spackman (Partner)
**Finance:** Richard Tsoukala (Financial Controller)
**Marketing:** Robert Spackman (Partner)
**Admin:** Jay Taylor (Office Manager)
**IT:** Robert Spackman (Partner)
**HR:** Robert Spackman (Partner)
**Health & Safety:** Robert Spackman (Partner)
**Facilities:** Robert Spackman (Partner)
**Operations:** Jay Taylor (Office Manager)
**US SIC:** 8911  **UK SIC:** 83701

|  | 31-12-13 | 31-12-12 | 31-12-11 |
|---|---|---|---|
| TO | 22,985,630 | 17,601,615 | 17,169,062 |
| P/L | 78,295 | 567,066 | (126,086) |
| NW | 7,820,155 | 8,042,496 | 7,686,849 |
| WC | 8,664,412 | 6,739,766 | 6,874,552 |
| Emp. | 184 | 158 | 172 |

DUNS 77-045-6069
## Tony Page Ltd
Unit 6, Chapman Park Industrial Estate, 378 High Road, London NW10 2DY
**Tel:** 02088304000
**Web:** www.tonypage.com
**Reg No:** 2668376  **Estd:** 1991 Private Limited Company
**Line of Business:** Corporate entertainment and hospitality
**Issued Capital:** £83,433
**Directors:** M A Bentley, D Gould
**Co. Secretary:** Anthony Page
**Branches:** Tony Page Ltd, Chapman Park Industrial Estate, Unit 6, London NW10 2DY
**US SIC:** 7999, 5812
**UK SIC:** 97913, 66110
**Auditors:** Hacker Young
**Bankers:** The Royal Bank Of Scotland Plc (16-00-83)

|  | 31-12-13 | 31-12-12 | 31-12-11 |
|---|---|---|---|
| TA | 1,543,626 | 2,134,829 | 1,835,503 |
| NW | 171,997 | 257,957 | 164,274 |
| WC | (310,635) | (169,907) | (234,350) |

DUNS 73-468-5659
## Tony Roma Uk Ltd
Phoenix Court, 42 Hawkins Road, Colchester, Essex CO2 8LA
**Tel:** 01206225173
**Web:** www.tonyromas.co.uk
**Reg No:** 4732573  **Estd:** 2003 Private Limited Company
**Line of Business:** Representative office
**Issued Capital:** £2
**Director:** P A Sakal
**Responsibilities**
**Senior:** Rob Reber (Operations Director)

**US SIC:** 7399  **UK SIC:** 83954

|  | 30-09-13 | 30-09-12 | 30-09-11 |
|---|---|---|---|
| TA | 2 | 2 | 2 |
| NW | 2 | 2 | 2 |
| WC | 2 | N/A | N/A |

DUNS 21-233-3633
## Tony Romas Restaurant
Unit 10 Xscape, Kings Inch Road, Renfrew, Renfrewshire PA4 8XQ
**Tel:** 0141-8868630
**Web:** www.tonyromas.co.uk
**Proprietorship**
**Line of Business:** Restaurant - american
**Proprietor:** G Buchanan
**Responsibilities**
**Senior:** Hakan Ozegemen (Manager), Julian Xheka (General Manager)
**US SIC:** 5812  **UK SIC:** 66110
**Employees:** 77

DUNS 21-579-6666
## Tonypandy Community College
Llewellyn Street, Tonypandy, Mid Glamorgan CF40 1HQ
**Tel:** 01443436171
**Web:** www.tonypandycollege.co.uk
**Estd:** 1989 Partnership
**Line of Business:** Schools (local authority)
**Partners:** S Parry, Mrs H O'Sullivan
**US SIC:** 8211  **UK SIC:** 93200
**Employees:** 66

DUNS 50-639-0512
## Tooks Chambers
81 Farringdon Street, London EC4A 4BL
**Tel:** 02078427575
**Web:** www.tooks.co.uk
**Estd:** 1984 Proprietorship
**Line of Business:** Barristers at law
**Proprietor:** M Mansfield
**Responsibilities**
**Senior:** Peggy Ekeledo (Board Member), Kieran Mccool (Executive), Alistair Roberts (Executive)
**Finance:** Lee Wakeling (Financial Director)
**Admin:** Sandra Joseph (Personnel & Administration), Lennox Lees (Office Services Assistant)
**HR:** Sandra Joseph (Personnel & Administration)
**US SIC:** 8111  **UK SIC:** 83500
**Employees:** 80

DUNS 29-642-5374                                            Imp-Exp
## The Tool Connection Ltd
Kineton Road, Southam, Warwickshire CV47 0DR
**Tel:** 01926815000  **Fax:** 01926-815888
**Web:** www.toolconnection.co.uk
**Reg No:** 1968900  **Estd:** 1976 Private Limited Company
**Line of Business:** Tool suppliers
**Export Markets:** E C countries
**Issued Capital:** £21,000
**Principals:** M T Smith (Managing), B Allen, E G Altham
**Co. Secretary:** Ms Paulette Brisker
**Responsibilities**
**Senior:** Grant Arthur (Warehouse Manager)
**Marketing:** Wendy Braybrook (Marketing Manager)
**Facilities:** Grant Arthur (Warehouse Manager)
**US SIC:** 5084  **UK SIC:** 61490
**Auditors:** Williams, Anderson & Dudley
**Bankers:** Barclays Bank Plc (20-48-08)

|  | 31-12-13 | 31-12-12 | 31-12-11 |
|---|---|---|---|
| TO | 14,721,158 | 13,251,629 | 13,104,571 |
| P/L | 1,685,219 | 1,128,055 | 1,759,695 |
| NW | 12,781,753 | 11,397,313 | 10,448,496 |
| WC | 7,994,574 | 6,740,706 | 6,301,106 |
| Emp. | 118 | 122 | 111 |

DUNS 22-180-5547                                            Imp
## Tool-Temp Ltd
3 Everitt Close, Denington Industrial Estate, Wellingborough, Northamptonshire NN8 2QE
**Tel:** 01933442623  **Fax:** 01908-513309
**Web:** www.tool-temp.net
**Reg No:** 4198945  **VAT No:** 776068690
**Estd:** 2001 Private Limited Company
**Line of Business:** Manufacturers of refrigeration equipment
**Issued Capital:** £71,500
**Directors:** J A Bailey, C A Robb, J Radcliffe
**Co. Secretary:** Charles Robb
**US SIC:** 3585  **UK SIC:** 32841
**Auditors:** Cowgill, Holloway & Co
**Bankers:** National Westminster Bank Plc (60-14-55)

|  | 30-04-14 | 30-04-13 | 30-04-12 |
|---|---|---|---|
| TA | 1,293,462 | 1,387,005 | 1,438,581 |
| NW | 455,573 | 425,653 | 387,982 |
| WC | 123,066 | 112,529 | 105,122 |

DUNS 50-131-4330
## Tooles Transport Ltd
Rushock Trading Estate, Droitwich, Worcestershire WR9 0NR
**Tel:** 01299254545
**Web:** www.toolestransport.co.uk
**Reg No:** 2220700 **Estd:** 1988 Private Limited Company
**Line of Business:** Road haulage and transport services
**Issued Capital:** £100
**Managing Director:** J R Toole
**Co. Secretary:** Mrs Judith Toole
**US SIC:** 4789 **UK SIC:** 77002
**Auditors:** Paul Alton

| | 31-08-13 | 31-08-12 | 31-08-11 |
|---|---|---|---|
| TO | 7,823,945 | 8,318,673 | 6,731,100 |
| P/L | 52,199 | 120,905 | (8,747) |
| NW | 1,808,457 | 1,792,432 | 1,721,701 |
| WC | 1,073,589 | 1,095,355 | 1,142,473 |
| Emp. | 95 | 92 | 89 |

DUNS 21-881-4408 **Imp-Exp**
## Tooling & Developments Ltd
Waterside Road, Leicester, Leicestershire LE5 1TL
**Tel:** 01162461400
**Web:** www.pmagroup.co.uk
**Reg No:** 0731834 **Estd:** 1962 Private Limited Company
**Line of Business:** Manufacture of parts and accessories for motor vehicles and their engines
**Export Markets:** Australia, Middle East
**Export Sales:** £117,917
**Trading Style:** P M A Radiators, P M A Sandalloy, Fraser Products, P M A Group
**Issued Capital:** £2,667
**Principals:** P I Westwood *(Managing)*, Ms M Westwood, M Westwood
**Co. Secretary:** Ms Margaret Westwood
**Responsibilities**
**Health & Safety:** Alan Guinan *(Health & Safety Officer)*
**Branches:** Tooling & Developments Ltd, 1 St James Indstl Est, Westhampnett Rd, Chichester, West Sussex PO19 7JU
**US SIC:** 3714, 5531
**UK SIC:** 35300, 65100
**Auditors:** Grant Thornton

| | 31-08-14 | 31-08-13 | 31-08-12 |
|---|---|---|---|
| TO | 5,302,821 | 5,768,939 | 5,907,886 |
| P/L | (152,242) | (44,528) | 10,251 |
| NW | 3,002,943 | 3,155,185 | 3,239,301 |
| WC | 2,127,563 | 2,255,673 | 2,329,760 |
| Emp. | 95 | 96 | 94 |

DUNS 42-384-5390
## Toolstation Ltd
(**Subsidiary of:** Travis Perkins Plc)
Express Park, Bristol Road. Bridgewater, Somerset, Bridgwater, Somerset TA6 4RN
**Tel:** 0808 1007211 **Fax:** 0808 1007210
**Web:** www.toolstation.com
**Reg No:** 4372131 **Estd:** 2002 Private Limited Company
**Line of Business:** Retail sale of hardware, paints and glass
**Issued Capital:** £2,300,100
**Directors:** N T Carroll, A C Keates, Mrs L J Lynch, C D Higgins, A D Buffin, D J Cox, J F Clapperton, N Bell
**Co. Secretary:** Tpg Management Services Limited
**Responsibilities**
**Senior:** Helen Squires *(Director)*
**Branches:** Toolstation Ltd, Watercombe Park, Lynx West Trading Estate, Yeovil, Somerset BA20 2HL
**US SIC:** 5251, 5732
**UK SIC:** 64800
**Auditors:** KPMG LLP

| | 31-12-13 | 31-12-12 | 31-12-11 |
|---|---|---|---|
| TO | 163,759,000 | 135,254,000 | 103,925,000 |
| P/L | 9,488,000 | 4,690,000 | (2,215,000) |
| NW | (12,385,000) | (19,426,000) | (29,004,000) |
| WC | 7,653,000 | 5,301,000 | 790,000 |
| Emp. | 1,646 | 1,462 | 1,137 |

DUNS 22-263-1470 **Imp**
## Toolstream Ltd
(**Subsidiary of:** Group Silverline Ltd)
Boundary Way, Lufton Trading Estate, Lufton, Yeovil, Somerset BA22 8HZ
**Tel:** 01935382222
**Web:** www.toolstream.com
**Reg No:** 4281144 **VAT No:** 785402124
**Estd:** 2001 Private Limited Company
**Line of Business:** Manufacturers and suppliers of powertools
**Export Sales:** £3,525,932
**Issued Capital:** £1,000
**Directors:** R A O'Donnell, A V Jane, M A Byrne, D J Morris
**Responsibilities**
**Marketing:** Ruth Mapstone *(Head of Marketing)*
**US SIC:** 3546 **UK SIC:** 32852
**Auditors:** Dixon Walsh
**Bankers:** National Westminster Bank Plc (60-24-37)

| | 31-07-13 | 31-07-12 | 31-07-11 |
|---|---|---|---|
| TO | 31,179,615 | 28,211,694 | 23,092,148 |
| P/L | 3,518,200 | 2,272,396 | 1,652,322 |
| NW | 8,082,112 | 5,339,008 | 4,722,133 |
| WC | 7,218,882 | 4,663,885 | 4,039,104 |
| Emp. | 137 | 137 | 125 |

DUNS 21-584-9487
## Toomey Motor Group
Rochford Business Park, Cherry Orchard Way, Rochford, Essex SS4 1GP
**Web:** www.toomey.uk.com
**Estd:** 2011 Proprietorship
**Line of Business:** Car dealers (new & used)
**Proprietor:** A Spurge
**Responsibilities**
**Senior:** Daniel Sycamore *(Sales Manager)*
**US SIC:** 5511 **UK SIC:** 65100
**Employees:** 70

DUNS 21-909-2038
## Toons Carpet & Furniture Centre Ltd
Burton Road, Castle Gresley, Swadlincote, Derbyshire DE11 9HQ
**Tel:** 01283-214729
**Web:** www.toonsfurnishers.co.uk
**Reg No:** 1111146 **VAT No:** 127250394
**Estd:** 1969 Private Limited Company
**Line of Business:** Retail sale of furniture, lighting equipment and household articles not elsewhere classified
**Issued Capital:** £5,000
**Principals:** Mrs J M Toon *(Managing)*, Miss B J Field, Miss M K Toon
**Responsibilities**
**Senior:** Belinda Toon *(Manager)*
**Branches:** Toons Carpet & Furniture Centre Ltd, Derby Road, Uttoxeter, Staffordshire ST14 8EE
**US SIC:** 5713, 5719
**UK SIC:** 64700
**Auditors:** Bates Weston
**Bankers:** National Westminster Bank Plc (52-10-35)

| | 03-08-13 | 03-08-12 | 03-08-11 |
|---|---|---|---|
| TA | 1,328,322 | 1,568,738 | 1,582,861 |
| NW | 571,391 | 678,975 | 736,854 |
| WC | 415,647 | 541,948 | 637,702 |

DUNS 23-731-8733
## Top Banana Communication Ltd
The Studio, Broome, Stourbridge, West Midlands DY9 0HA
**Tel:** 01562700404
**Web:** www.top-b.com
**Reg No:** 3726387 **VAT No:** 705555538
**Estd:** 1980 Private Limited Company
**Line of Business:** Video production companies
**Issued Capital:** £2
**Director:** N J Terry
**Co. Secretary:** Richard Bridge
**Responsibilities**
**Senior:** Jacqueline Clement *(Manager)*
**US SIC:** 7819 **UK SIC:** 97111
**Auditors:** Folkes Worton LLP
**Bankers:** National Westminster Bank Plc (60-20-48)

| | 31-03-14 | 31-03-13 | 31-03-12 |
|---|---|---|---|
| TA | 2,239,212 | 1,482,842 | 1,420,691 |
| NW | 987,119 | 497,710 | 623,625 |
| WC | 888,701 | 416,245 | 521,930 |

DUNS 22-103-8594
## Top Banana Team Ltd
Units K1-K2 The Courtyard, Jenson Avenue, Commerce Park, Frome, Somerset BA11 2FG
**Tel:** 01373 469220
**Web:** www.tbtltd.com
**Reg No:** 4123188 **VAT No:** 763094618
**Estd:** 2013 Private Limited Company
**Line of Business:** Other entertainment activities not elsewhere classified
**Trading Style:** Tbt
**Issued Capital:** £100
**Principals:** P W Saunders *(Managing)*, Mrs D J Craven Smith, A E Craven Smith
**Co. Secretary:** Mrs Belinda Saunders
**US SIC:** 7999 **UK SIC:** 97913
**Auditors:** Pinnacle
**Bankers:** Lloyds TSB Bank plc (30-98-75)

| | 31-12-13 | 31-12-12 | 31-12-12 |
|---|---|---|---|
| TA | 2,013,896 | 1,396,279 | 1,129,138 |
| NW | 825,558 | 726,755 | 539,889 |
| WC | 758,186 | 689,881 | 485,452 |

DUNS 21-718-5943
## Top Cars (Minicab) Ltd
734 Lordship Lane, London N22 5JP
**Tel:** 02088880111
**Web:** www.topcarslondon.com
**Reg No:** 7569671 **Estd:** 2011 Private Limited Company
**Line of Business:** Taxis and private hire vehicles
**Issued Capital:** £100
**Director:** S Balci
**Responsibilities**
**Senior:** Sarah David *(Manager)*, Memili Koc *(Manager)*
**US SIC:** 4121 **UK SIC:** 72200

| | 31-03-12 |
|---|---|
| TA | 60,484 |
| NW | (18,547) |
| WC | (55,106) |

DUNS 21-579-5736
## Top Golf
Moated Farm Drive, Addlestone, Surrey KT15 2DW
**Tel:** 01932858551
**Web:** www.topgolf.com
**Estd:** 1998 Proprietorship
**Line of Business:** Golf practice ranges
**Proprietor:** Miss H Lloys
**US SIC:** 7299 **UK SIC:** 98902
**Employees:** 50

DUNS 22-012-8966
## Top Notch Contractors Ltd
Unit 4 Durranhill Industrial Estate, Brunel Way, Durranhill Industrial Estate, Carlisle, Cumbria CA1 3NQ
**Tel:** 01228524117
**Web:** www.topnotchcontractors.co.uk
**Reg No:** 4015903 **Estd:** 2000 Private Limited Company
**Line of Business:** Building construction contractors
**Issued Capital:** £100
**Principals:** P P Rheinbach *(Managing)*, A B Halford
**Co. Secretary:** Ms Alyson Rheinbach
**US SIC:** 1522 **UK SIC:** 50100
**Auditors:** Saint & Co

| | 31-08-13 | 31-08-12 | 31-08-11 |
|---|---|---|---|
| TA | 3,296,249 | 3,314,879 | 3,316,829 |
| NW | 946,726 | 929,933 | 1,231,869 |
| WC | 694,483 | 912,116 | 1,020,255 |

DUNS 29-573-2127
## Top Oil Products Ltd
(**Subsidiary of:** Hoo Hing Holdings Ltd)
Unit 1 Dorma Trading Park, Staffa Road, London E10 7QX
**Tel:** 020-8988-6228 **Fax:** 020-8548-3650
**Web:** www.hoohing.com
**Reg No:** 1934994 **Estd:** 2003 Private Limited Company
**Line of Business:** Other wholesale
**Issued Capital:** £10,000
**Principals:** K Poon *(Managing)*, T F Poon
**Co. Secretary:** Ken Poon
**Responsibilities**
**Senior:** Eric Tung *(Manager)*
**US SIC:** 5411 **UK SIC:** 64100

| | 30-06-13 | 30-06-12 | 30-06-11 |
|---|---|---|---|
| TA | 10,000 | 10,000 | 10,000 |
| NW | 10,000 | 10,000 | 10,000 |

DUNS 21-825-2401 **Exp**
## Top Right Group Ltd
(**Subsidiary of:** The Scott Trust Ltd)
The Prow 1, London W1B 5AP
**Tel:** 02075165000 **Fax:** 01733-562636
**Web:** www.emap.com
**Reg No:** 0435820 **Estd:** 1947 Private Limited Company
**Line of Business:** Management activities of holding companies
**Export Markets:** U K; France; Germany; Rest of Europe; U.S.A & Worldwide
**Export Sales:** £117,300,000
**Trading Style:** Top Right Group
**Issued Capital:** £276,191,524
**Directors:** D A Painter, Ms A J Gradden
**Co. Secretary:** Ms Shanny Looi
**Responsibilities**
**Senior:** Darren Peacock *(Facilities Manager)*
**Marketing:** Kim Slaney *(Marketing Director-Brand)*
**Sales:** Richard Hewes *(Account Manager)*
**IT:** Alice Lewthwaite *(Operations and Technology Dire)*
**Health & Safety:** Darren Peacock *(Facilities Manager)*
**Facilities:** Darren Peacock *(Facilities Manager)*
**Purchasing:** Darren Peacock *(Facilities Manager)*
**Branches:** Top Right Group Ltd, Bushfield House, Orton Centre, Peterborough, Cambridgeshire PE2 5RQ
**US SIC:** 6711 **UK SIC:** 83962
**Auditors:** KPMG LLP
**Bankers:** Barclays Bank Plc (20-67-37)

| | 31-12-13 | 31-12-12 | 31-12-11 |
|---|---|---|---|
| TO | 271,400,000 | 251,700,000 | 249,400,000 |
| P/L | 2,600,000 | 186,200,000 | 52,400,000 |
| NW | 31,600,000 | 71,500,000 | (88,300,000) |
| WC | 197,100,000 | 304,900,000 | 168,400,000 |
| Emp. | 1,674 | 1,517 | 1,461 |

DUNS 21-233-4156
## Top Sante
Endeavour House, 189 Shaftesbury Avenue, London WC2H 8JG
**Tel:** 02072955000
**Web:** www.bauermedia.co.uk
**Proprietorship**
**Line of Business:** Newspapers publishing
**Proprietor:** Mrs S Parsons
**Responsibilities**
**Senior:** Olivia Saponaro *(Facilities Manager)*, Jane Truker *(Manager)*
**US SIC:** 2711 **UK SIC:** 47512
**Employees:** 128

DUNS 50-111-2155
## Top Shop/Top Man Ltd
(**Subsidiary of:** Taveta Ltd)
Unit 1 New Change, London EC4M 9AD
**Tel:** 02072480180
**Web:** www.topman.com
**Reg No:** 2317752 **Estd:** 2011 Private Limited Company
**Line of Business:** Fashion shops
**Export Sales:** £121,167,000
**Issued Capital:** £2
**Directors:** I M Grabiner, D Shepherd, P E Budge, J Sokoloff, Sir P N Green, C B Harris, Ms S Forey, J Halper
**Co. Secretary:** Adam Goldman
**Responsibilities**
**Senior:** Mary Homer *(Director)*
**Branches:** Top Shop/Top Man Ltd, The Corner, 1 Newport Road, Middlesbrough, Cleveland TS1 1LF
**US SIC:** 5611, 5621
**UK SIC:** 64500
**Auditors:** PricewaterhouseCoopers LLP

| | 31-08-13 | 27-08-11 | 28-08-10 |
|---|---|---|---|
| TO | 984,037,000 | 763,000 | 733,000 |
| P/L | 154,237,000 | 763,000 | 733,000 |
| NW | (395,929,000) | 3,389,000 | 2,833,000 |
| WC | 93,485,000 | N/A | N/A |
| Emp. | 9,194 | N/A | N/A |

DUNS 77-583-2157
## Top Tubes Ltd
Steetley Industrial Estate, Bilston, West Midlands WV14 9EE
**Fax:** 01902-674110
**Web:** www.toptubes.co.uk
**Reg No:** 3000662 **Estd:** 1994 Private Limited Company
**Line of Business:** Other business activities not elsewhere classified
**Export Sales:** £1,158,885
**Issued Capital:** £700
**Managing Director:** A J Bradley
**Co. Secretary:** Matthew Bradley
**Responsibilities**
**Marketing:** Craig Gibbs *(Sales & Marketing Manager)*
**Sales:** Craig Gibbs *(Sales & Marketing Manager)*
**US SIC:** 7399 **UK SIC:** 83954
**Auditors:** Edwards Pearson & White (Audit) Ltd
**Bankers:** Barclays Bank Plc (20-27-17)

| | 31-03-14 | 31-03-13 | 31-03-12 |
|---|---|---|---|
| TO | 31,223,706 | 26,679,699 | 28,446,213 |
| P/L | 1,272,234 | 425,776 | 128,510 |
| NW | 3,493,982 | 2,484,021 | 2,060,328 |
| WC | 1,589,949 | 1,094,062 | 400,446 |
| Emp. | 104 | 96 | 97 |

DUNS 21-037-8654
## Top Wok Take Away
61 High Street, Metheringham, Lincoln, Lincolnshire LN4 3DZ
**Tel:** 01526322188
**Estd:** 2002 Proprietorship
**Line of Business:** Chinese take away
**US SIC:** 5812 **UK SIC:** 66110
**Employees:** 88

DUNS 34-525-3939
## Topcashback Ltd
(**Subsidiary of:** Top Online Partners Group Ltd)
Lion Buildings 8 Market Place, Uttoxeter, Staffordshire ST14 8HP
**Tel:** 01889 562562
**Web:** www.topcashback.co.uk
**Reg No:** 5336020 **Estd:** 2005 Private Limited Company
**Line of Business:** Database activities
**Trading Style:** Talk Cashback
**Issued Capital:** £3
**Director:** O M Ragg
**Co. Secretary:** Michael Tomkins
**US SIC:** 7374 **UK SIC:** 83940
**Bankers:** The Co-Operative Bank Plc (08-01-00)

| | 31-01-14 | 31-01-13 | 31-01-12 |
|---|---|---|---|
| TO | 37,522,500 | 30,839,725 | 21,185,788 |
| P/L | 1,131,289 | 787,713 | 589,309 |
| NW | 895,329 | 1,312,258 | 1,006,777 |
| WC | 789,462 | 1,256,927 | 977,340 |
| Emp. | 77 | 44 | 30 |

DUNS 22-629-1904 **Imp-Exp**

### Topcon (Great Britain) Ltd

(**Subsidiary of:** Topcon Corporation)
Kennet Side, Newbury, Berkshire RG14 5PX
**Tel:** 01635-551120 **Fax:** 01635-551170
**Web:** www.global.topcon.com
**Reg No:** 1522615 **VAT No:** 347148349
**Estd:** 1980 Private Limited Company
**Line of Business:** Other treatment of petroleum products (excluding petrochemicals manufacture)
**Export Markets:** European Union (E U); Worldwide
**Issued Capital:** £2,500,000
**Directors:** E C Franken, A F Yorke, N Smit, J P Paetz
**Co. Secretary:** Christopher Pratley
**Responsibilities**
**Senior:** Ewout Korpershoek *(Manager)*, Toshio Ushiyama *(Manager)*
**Branches:** Topcon (Great Britain) Ltd, Unit 2 Lodge Works, Bury St. Edmunds, Suffolk IP31 3HA
**US SIC:** 7399, 7394
**UK SIC:** 83954, 84000
**Auditors:** Ernst & Young LLP
**Bankers:** HSBC Bank plc (40-23-18)

| | 31-03-14 | 31-03-13 | 31-03-12 |
|---|---|---|---|
| TO | 23,475,407 | 18,959,447 | 21,224,625 |
| P/L | 710,386 | 324,044 | 61,795 |
| NW | 4,481,708 | 3,361,112 | 3,037,068 |
| WC | 12,671,002 | 8,361,298 | 7,048,616 |
| Emp. | 78 | 74 | 80 |

DUNS 23-729-9669

### Topgolf Ltd

(**Subsidiary of:** Topgolf International Inc.)
Abridge Road, Chigwell, Essex IG7 6BX
**Tel:** 02085002644
**Web:** www.topgolf.com
**Reg No:** 3724493 **Estd:** 2004 Private Limited Company
**Line of Business:** Other entertainment activities not elsewhere classified
**Issued Capital:** £3,257,920
**Directors:** W B Davenport, D R Gooder, K A May
**Co. Secretary:** Kieren Mildwaters
**Responsibilities**
**Senior:** Neil Allen *(Manager)*, Robbie Edmondson *(General Manager)*, Conrad Simon *(General Manager)*, Lee Verallas *(General Manager)*
**Branches:** Topgolf Ltd, Topgolf Surrey, Moated Farm Drive, Surrey KT15 2DW Addlestone
**US SIC:** 7999 **UK SIC:** 97913
**Auditors:** Grant Thornton UK LLP
**Bankers:** HSBC Bank plc (40-10-02)

| | 31-12-13 | 31-12-12 | 31-12-11 |
|---|---|---|---|
| TO | 10,068,859 | 8,406,722 | 6,912,082 |
| P/L | 1,070,881 | (1,014,967) | (588,991) |
| NW | 2,797,353 | 1,726,472 | 2,741,439 |
| WC | (3,407,047) | (5,008,398) | (3,954,298) |
| Emp. | 268 | 298 | 221 |

DUNS 49-395-0570 **Exp**

### Topgrade Sportswear Ltd

(**Subsidiary of:** Pentland Group P L C)
22 Leacroft Road, Birchwood, Warrington, Cheshire WA3 6PJ
**Tel:** 01925-848300 **Fax:** 01925848301
**Web:** www.topgradesportswear.com
**Reg No:** 3139070 **VAT No:** 787440102
**Estd:** 2002 Private Limited Company
**Line of Business:** Sportswear wholesalers
**Export Markets:** Ireland
**Issued Capital:** £1,000
**Directors:** I S Simpson, P A Cowgill, B M Small, P R Simpson
**Co. Secretary:** Oakwood Corporate Secretary Limi
**Responsibilities**
**Senior:** Jane Brisley *(Manager)*
**Marketing:** Liz McNamara *(Marketing Manager)*
**Branches:** Topgrade Sportswear Ltd, 22 Leacroft Road, Warrington, Cheshire WA3 6PJ
**US SIC:** 5941, 5699
**UK SIC:** 65400, 64500
**Auditors:** KPMG Audit PLC
**Bankers:** National Westminster Bank Plc (01-09-02)

| | 01-02-14 | 02-02-13 | 28-02-12 |
|---|---|---|---|
| TO | 31,997,000 | 32,733,000 | 31,424,000 |
| P/L | (1,007,000) | (259,000) | (531,000) |
| NW | 55,000 | 850,000 | 1,065,000 |
| WC | (1,324,000) | (650,000) | (453,000) |
| Emp. | 139 | 139 | 131 |

DUNS 45-865-0157

### Topmarx Ltd

Culverlands, Winchester Road, Southampton, Hampshire SO32 2JF
**Tel:** 01329-834400
**Web:** www.topmarx.co.uk
**Reg No:** 3207600 **Estd:** 1996 Private Limited Company
**Line of Business:** Builders
**Issued Capital:** £1,000
**Directors:** M A Fuller, M R Newman, Ms T D Newman, B D Haines
**Branches:** Topmarx Ltd, Palmers Brook Farm, Park Road, Wootton Bridge, Ryde, Isle Of Wight PO33 4NS
**US SIC:** 1522 **UK SIC:** 50100

| | 31-12-13 | 31-12-12 | 31-12-11 |
|---|---|---|---|
| TO | 6,498,276 | 8,572,471 | 10,454,561 |
| P/L | (21,701) | (341,367) | 298,391 |
| NW | 1,180,173 | 1,201,874 | 1,506,450 |
| WC | 1,069,696 | 1,063,334 | 1,331,123 |
| Emp. | 81 | 104 | 113 |

DUNS 23-361-5496

### Toppesfield Ltd

Unit 12 Hillview Business Park, Tinkers Lane, Hadleigh, Ipswich, Suffolk IP7 5NG
**Tel:** 01473-829129
**Web:** www.toppesfield.com
**Reg No:** 5054176 **Estd:** 2004 Private Limited Company
**Line of Business:** Construction of roads
**Issued Capital:** £110
**Directors:** M A Salmon, N J Burman, M J Pryor, C J Germeney, D J Last
**Co. Secretary:** Mrs Gale Pryor
**US SIC:** 1611 **UK SIC:** 50200

| | 31-05-14 | 31-05-13 | 31-05-12 |
|---|---|---|---|
| TO | 39,095,463 | 19,882,724 | 24,059,355 |
| P/L | 2,856,860 | 1,770,245 | 1,422,586 |
| NW | 2,289,327 | 1,009,955 | 619,874 |
| WC | 147,854 | (523,893) | (534,361) |
| Emp. | 71 | 46 | 41 |

DUNS 23-613-8913 **Exp**

### Topps Europe Holdings Ltd

(**Subsidiary of:** Joe Tornante-Mdp Holding Llc)
18 Vincent Avenue, Crownhill, Milton Keynes, Buckinghamshire MK8 0AW
**Tel:** 01908-800100
**Web:** www.toppsdirect.com
**Reg No:** 2331336 **Estd:** 1989 Private Limited Company
**Line of Business:** Printing not elsewhere classified
**Export Markets:** Italy, Netherlands, Spain, France, Far East, South Amercia, Australia
**Export Sales:** £398,143
**Trading Style:** Merlin Collections
**Issued Capital:** £180,357
**Managing Director:** C J Rodman
**Co. Secretary:** William Hillier
**Responsibilities**
**Marketing:** Rod Pearson *(Marketing Director)*
**US SIC:** 2752 **UK SIC:** 47544
**Auditors:** BDO LLP
**Bankers:** Bank Of Scotland (80-11-00)

| | 28-12-13 | 29-12-12 | 31-12-11 |
|---|---|---|---|
| TO | 17,336,348 | 16,520,024 | 15,607,415 |
| P/L | (77,263) | 2,107,234 | 7,118,238 |
| NW | 3,507,274 | 3,584,537 | 3,456,574 |
| WC | 3,480,784 | 3,558,047 | 3,430,084 |

DUNS 77-086-1466 **Exp**

### Topps Europe Ltd

(**Subsidiary of:** Joe Tornante-Mdp Holding Llc)
18 Vincent Avenue, Crownhill, Milton Keynes, Buckinghamshire MK8 0AW
**Tel:** 08701203630 **Fax:** 01908444200
**Web:** www.topps.co.uk
**Reg No:** 2673753 **VAT No:** 608693513
**Estd:** 1991 Private Limited Company
**Line of Business:** Publishing of books
**Export Sales:** £32,273,752
**Trading Style:** Merlin Publishing, Merlin Collections
**Issued Capital:** £2
**Director:** C J Rodman
**Co. Secretary:** William Hillier
**Responsibilities**
**Senior:** S Silverstein *(Chairman)*
**HR:** Toni Rampello *(Personnel Manager)*
**Purchasing:** Sharon Sheriton *(Purchasing Coordinator)*
**Branches:** Topps Europe Ltd, 18 Vincent Avenue, Milton Keynes, Buckinghamshire MK8 0AW
**US SIC:** 2731 **UK SIC:** 47532
**Auditors:** Deloitte & Touche LLP
**Bankers:** Bank Of Scotland (80-11-00)

| | 28-12-13 | 29-12-12 | 31-12-11 |
|---|---|---|---|
| TO | 45,095,033 | 47,718,945 | 51,515,834 |
| P/L | (64,672) | 698,641 | 3,158,188 |
| NW | 4,376,087 | 4,440,759 | 5,740,182 |
| WC | 2,905,610 | 3,697,833 | 5,278,573 |
| Emp. | 50 | 46 | 47 |

DUNS 45-871-3856

### Topps Tiles Plc

Thorpe Park, Leicester, Leicestershire LE19 1SU
**Tel:** 01162-828-000 **Fax:** 01162-828-100
**Web:** www.toppstiles.co.uk
**Reg No:** 3213782 **VAT No:** 453154268
**Estd:** 1996 Public Limited Company
**Line of Business:** Supply of tile, wood flooring and associated accessories for trade and retail
**Trading Style:** Topps Tiles
**Issued Capital:** £6,390,418
**Directors:** A J King, Rt Hon J M Jack, A White, R Parker, M T Williams, Ms C Tiney
**Co. Secretary:** Stuart Davey
**Responsibilities**
**Senior:** Michael Ban-Sittert *(Store Manager)*, Scott Williams *(Area Manager)*
**Sales:** Christina Partakides *(Account Manager)*
**IT:** Nigel Hickman *(IT Director)*
**Branches:** Topps Tiles Plc, Unit E Ashley Retail Park, Lugsdale Road, Widnes, Cheshire WA8 7YT
**US SIC:** 5039, 5961, 5713
**UK SIC:** 61300, 65600, 64700
**Auditors:** Deloitte LLP
**Bankers:** HSBC Bank plc (40-16-15)

| | 27-09-14 | 28-09-13 | 29-09-12 |
|---|---|---|---|
| TO | 195,237,000 | 177,849,000 | 177,693,000 |
| P/L | 16,691,000 | 10,601,000 | 12,493,000 |
| NW | 598,000 | (10,429,000) | (17,593,000) |
| WC | 11,189,000 | 11,673,000 | 14,716,000 |
| Emp. | 1,794 | 1,720 | 1,654 |

DUNS 23-591-5472 **Imp**

### Topps Tiles Quest Trustee Ltd

(**Subsidiary of:** Topps Tiles Plc)
Stanley Green Business Park Oak Green, Cheadle, Cheshire SK8 6QL
**Tel:** 01614862400 **Fax:** 01614862500
**Web:** www.toppstiles.co.uk
**Reg No:** 3589294 **Estd:** 1975 Private Limited Company
**Line of Business:** Retail sale of furniture, lighting equipment and household articles not elsewhere classified
**Trading Style:** Multi Tile
**Issued Capital:** £100
**Director:** Ms J Burgess
**Co. Secretary:** Stuart Davey
**Responsibilities**
**Senior:** Christopher Moores *(Manager)*
**Branches:** Topps Tiles Quest Trustee Ltd, Topps Tiles, 111-117 Teignmouth Road, Torquay, Devon TQ1 4HA
**US SIC:** 5719 **UK SIC:** 64700
**Auditors:** Arthur Andersen
**Bankers:** HSBC Bank plc (40-16-15)

| | 28-09-13 | 29-09-12 | 01-09-11 |
|---|---|---|---|
| NW | (29) | (29) | (29) |

DUNS 73-518-3258

### Topps Tiles (Uk) Ltd

(**Subsidiary of:** Topps Tiles Plc)
Tower Road, South Lowestoft Industrial Estate, Lowestoft, Suffolk NR33 7NG
**Tel:** 01502539528
**Web:** www.toppstiles.co.uk
**Reg No:** 4781209 **Estd:** 2003 Private Limited Company
**Line of Business:** Tile wholesalers and suppliers
**Issued Capital:** £5,485,316
**Directors:** M T Williams, R Parker, Rt Hon J M Jack
**Co. Secretary:** Stuart Davey
**Responsibilities**
**Senior:** Darren Connor *(Manager)*
**Branches:** Topps Tiles (Uk) Ltd, Derby Road, Long Eaton, Nottingham, Nottinghamshire NG10 4QB
**US SIC:** 5039, 3253
**UK SIC:** 61300, 24891
**Auditors:** Deloitte LLP
**Bankers:** HSBC Bank plc (40-16-15)

| | 28-09-13 | 29-09-12 | 01-09-11 |
|---|---|---|---|
| TO | 175,177,000 | 170,136,000 | 162,901,000 |
| P/L | (4,309,000) | 720,000 | 4,054,000 |
| NW | (86,635,000) | (90,788,000) | (98,599,000) |
| WC | (39,297,000) | (40,715,000) | (44,311,000) |
| Emp. | 1,394 | 1,282 | 1,248 |

DUNS 73-353-1722

### Topsource Global Solutions Ltd

4th Floor Marlborough House, 10 Earlham Street, London WC2H 9LN
**Tel:** 0845-129-4993 **Fax:** 02070991118
**Web:** www.topsource.co.uk
**Reg No:** 4626779 **Estd:** 2003 Private Limited Company
**Line of Business:** Data processing
**Export Sales:** £281,579
**Issued Capital:** £1
**Directors:** M Santhanam, S Bane, R Lynch
**Co. Secretary:** William Hastings
**US SIC:** 7374 **UK SIC:** 83940
**Bankers:** Bank Of Scotland (12-09-49)

| | 31-03-14 | 31-03-13 | 31-03-12 |
|---|---|---|---|
| TO | 3,392,524 | 3,610,576 | N/A |
| P/L | 65,549 | 269,142 | N/A |
| NW | (307,725) | (234,630) | 121,613 |
| WC | 6,443 | 100,527 | (401,708) |

DUNS 22-099-8665

### Toquin Sa Ltd

Unit 3 Knight House, Lenthall Road, Loughton, Essex IG10 3UD
**Tel:** 02084180457
**Web:** www.toquinsa.co.uk
**Reg No:** 4101176 **Estd:** 2010 Private Limited Company
**Line of Business:** Employment and recruitment companies and consultants
**Issued Capital:** £100
**Director:** Q B Seger
**Co. Secretary:** Christian Scheepers
**Responsibilities**
**Senior:** Angela Markides *(Branch Manager)*, Tony Skippers *(Manager)*
**US SIC:** 7361 **UK SIC:** 83954

| | 30-11-13 | 30-11-12 | 30-11-11 |
|---|---|---|---|
| TA | 463,214 | 467,535 | 403,947 |
| NW | 53,722 | 85,576 | 177,278 |
| WC | 133,439 | 340,942 | 299,659 |

DUNS 21-720-5123

### Tor Bridge Academy Trust

Tor Bridge High, Miller Way, Plymouth, Devon PL6 8UN
**Tel:** 01752702024
**Reg No:** 7584372 **Estd:** 2011 Private Company Limited By Guarantee
**Line of Business:** General secondary education
**Directors:** B Embry, M A Loveman, C P Huitson, Mrs S J Wills, Mrs S W Cox, Ms D E Dunstan, J P Byatt, P J Elliott
**Co. Secretary:** Mrs Ann Anstis
**Responsibilities**
**Senior:** Beryl Badger *(Director)*
**US SIC:** 8211 **UK SIC:** 93200

| | 31-08-14 | 31-08-13 | 31-08-12 |
|---|---|---|---|
| TO | 7,583,000 | 7,818,000 | 32,496,000 |
| P/L | (807,000) | (561,000) | 31,377,000 |
| NW | 29,168,000 | 29,781,000 | 30,417,000 |
| WC | 1,077,000 | 998,000 | 682,000 |
| Emp. | 148 | 150 | 145 |

DUNS 21-592-9346

### Tor Bridge High

Miller Way, Plymouth, Devon PL6 8UN
**Tel:** 01752207907
**Web:** www.torbridge.net
**Estd:** 1978 Proprietorship
**Line of Business:** Schools (foundation)
**Partners:** G Browne, P Spur
**Responsibilities**
**Senior:** Liz Dunstan *(Principal)*
**US SIC:** 8211 **UK SIC:** 93200
**Employees:** 250

DUNS 64-100-3871 **Imp-Exp**

### Tor Coatings Ltd

(**Subsidiary of:** Rpm International Inc.)
Shadon Way, Chester-Le-Street, County Durham DH3 2RE
**Tel:** 01914-106611
**Web:** www.tor-coatings.com
**Reg No:** 4503854 **VAT No:** 894868542
**Estd:** 2002 Private Limited Company
**Line of Business:** Wholesale of wood, construction materials and sanitary equipment
**Issued Capital:** £6,020,000
**Directors:** E W Moore, T E Reed, E W Moore, C Carter, R A Rice
**Responsibilities**
**Senior:** Nick Bowman *(Warehouse Manager)*, Collin Carter *(Managing Director)*, William Whiting *(Manager)*
**Engineering:** Ian Mccormack *(Technical Manager)*
**US SIC:** 5039 **UK SIC:** 61300
**Auditors:** Ernst & Young LLP
**Bankers:** Bank Of America, Na (16-50-50)

| | 31-05-14 | 31-05-13 | 31-05-12 |
|---|---|---|---|
| TO | 32,448,616 | 25,998,352 | 28,125,480 |
| P/L | 4,379,738 | (8,072,839) | 4,003,654 |
| NW | 11,756,696 | 18,245,051 | 27,169,459 |
| WC | 6,928,655 | 13,664,633 | 9,155,703 |
| Emp. | 192 | 180 | 177 |

DUNS 50-347-8968

### Toray Industries Inc.

(**Subsidiary of:** Toray Industries Inc.)
7 Old Park Lane, London W1K 1QR
**Tel:** 02076637700
**Reg No:** 0014886FC **Estd:** 1989 Foreign Company
**Line of Business:** Wholesale of other machinery for use in industry, trade and navigation
**Principals:** T Hosono *(Managing)*, T Ohzeki *(Managing)*, K Fukuchi, Y Sugimoto, M Yoshinaga, N Onozawa, T Sano, K Ito
**Responsibilities**
**Senior:** Junichi Fujikawa *(Director)*, Kazushi Hashimoto *(Director)*, Masayoshi Kamiura *(Director)*, Shinichi Koizumi *(Director)*, Kazuhiro Maruyama *(Director)*, Satoru Masuzaki *(Director)*, Osamu Nakatani

**(Director),** Akihiro Nikkaku *(Director),* Hideyasu Okawara *(Director),* Norihiko Saitou *(Director),* Sadayuki Sakakibara *(Director),* Akikazu Shimomura *(Director),* Eizo Tanaka *(Director),* Chiaki Tanaka *(Director),* Akira Uchida *(Director)*
**US SIC:** 5084 **UK SIC:** 61490

DUNS 23-610-1606      Imp-Exp
## Toray Textiles Europe Ltd
**(Subsidiary of:** Toray Industries Inc.)
Crown Farm Way, Forest Town, Mansfield, Nottinghamshire NG19 0FT
**Tel:** 01623-415000
**Web:** www.ttel.co.uk
**Reg No:** 2340979 **VAT No:** 746131348
**Estd:** 1989 Private Limited Company
**Line of Business:** Misc housefurnishing manufacturers
**Export Markets:** Europe; Scandinavia; E Europe; European Union (E U)
**Export Sales:** £7,227,795
**Trading Style:** Toray Textiles Europe Ltd
**Issued Capital:** £103,120,000
**Directors:** A Karasawa, M Nakase, R J Stephens
**Co. Secretary:** Richard Stephens
**Responsibilities**
**Senior:** Mick Skinner *(Warehouse Manager)*
**Engineering:** Matt Nicholson *(Production Manager)*
**Branches:** Toray Textiles Europe Ltd, Wharf Mill, Dunkinfield Road, Hyde, Cheshire SK14 4R3
**US SIC:** 2392, 2269, 2299
**UK SIC:** 45550, 43702, 43992
**Auditors:** Ernst & Young LLP
**Bankers:** Barclays Bank Plc (20-63-25)

| | 31-03-14 | 31-03-13 | 31-03-12 |
|---|---|---|---|
| TO | 14,266,775 | 13,339,004 | 14,768,407 |
| P/L | (130,743) | (677,371) | (619,195) |
| NW | 10,372,236 | 10,426,066 | 11,103,437 |
| WC | (1,334,048) | (1,528,252) | (1,398,600) |
| Emp. | 155 | 155 | 162 |

DUNS 23-271-5529
## Torbay and Southern Devon Health and Care Nhs Trust
Bay House, Nicholson Road, Torquay, Devon TQ2 7TD
**Tel:** 01803210500
**Web:** www.tsdhc.nhs.uk
**Estd:** 2005
**Line of Business:** Activities of households as employers of domestic staff
**Trading Style:** Torby Southern Devon
**Issued Capital:** £1
**Principals:** Ms J Dent *(Chairman),* S Wallwork *(Financial),* A Farnsworth, Ms D Stark, Ms S Matso, Ms C Schneider, J Welch, Ms M Holmes
**Responsibilities**
**Senior:** Jon Andrewes *(Non Executive Member),* John Brockwell *(Non Executive Member),* Mandy Fullmore *(CEO),* Mandy Seymour *(Chief Executive Officer)*
**Branches:** Torbay and Southern Devon Health and Care Nhs Trust, Hookhills Road, Paignton, Devon TQ4 7SH
**US SIC:** 8811, 8011
**UK SIC:** 99000, 95300
**Employees:** 100

DUNS 22-747-1133
## Torbay Council
Town Hall, Castle Circus, Torquay, Devon TQ1 3DR
**Tel:** 01803-201201
**Web:** www.torbay.gov.uk
**Estd:** 2010
**Line of Business:** Local government
**Trading Style:** Torbay Council, Torbay Tourist Board, Torbay Industrial Services
**Director:** Ms E Raikes
**Responsibilities**
**Senior:** Caroline Dimond *(Director of Public Health),* Sally Farley *(General Manager),* Tara Fowler *(Manager),* Gareth Fudge *(Manager),* Steve Parrock *(Chief Executive Officer),* Jo Penhaligon *(Youth Service Development Work),* Simon Wallace *(Manager)*
**Finance:** Steve Bowden *(Finance Manager),* Paul Looby *(Financial Director)*
**Marketing:** Anna Gilroy *(Head of Marketing),* Michelle Pierce *(Communications Manager)*
**HR:** Anne-Marie Bond *(Head of Human Resources),* Annabelle Knowles *(Learning and Standards Manager),* Lucinda Wills *(Workforce Development and Lear)*
**Health & Safety:** Colin Dejongh *(Health & Safety Officer)*
**Facilities:** Stuart Left *(Facilities Manager)*
**Operations:** Steve Hurley *(Town Services Manager)*
**Purchasing:** Josie Medforth *(Procurement Officer),* Joanna Pascoe *(Procurement Officer)*
**Engineering:** Kevin Michell *(Technical Engineer)*

**Branches:** Torbay Council, Babbacombe C Of E Primary School, Quinta Road, Torquay, Devon TQ1 3RN
**US SIC:** 9121, 7392
**UK SIC:** 91110, 83951
**Bankers:** National Westminster Bank Plc (55-70-01)
**Employees:** 1,550

DUNS 21-614-6005
## Torbay Hotel
Torbay Road, Torquay, Devon TQ2 5EY
**Tel:** 01803295218
**Web:** www.shearings.co.uk
**Estd:** 1991 Proprietorship
**Line of Business:** Hotels and motels without restaurant
**Proprietor:** S Murray
**Responsibilities**
**Senior:** Aneta Edge *(General Manager)*
**US SIC:** 7011 **UK SIC:** 66500
**Employees:** 70

DUNS 29-821-9734
## Torcare Ltd
**(Subsidiary of:** Torcare (Holdings) Ltd)
Vicarage Road, Torpoint, Cornwall PL11 2BW
**Tel:** 01752814469 **Fax:** 01752-816323
**Web:** www.torcare.co.uk
**Reg No:** 2040079 **Estd:** 1986 Private Limited Company
**Line of Business:** Non-charitable social work activities with accommodation
**Issued Capital:** £4
**Directors:** T Fourniss, B Fourniss, Ms M E Fourniss
**Co. Secretary:** Paul Fourniss
**Responsibilities**
**HR:** Ann Newcombe *(Human Resources Coordinator)*
**Health & Safety:** Patricia Knell *(Health & Safety Officer)*
**US SIC:** 8321 **UK SIC:** 96111
**Auditors:** Francis Clark

| | 30-09-13 | 30-09-12 | 30-09-11 |
|---|---|---|---|
| TO | 2,770,328 | 2,705,432 | N/A |
| P/L | 400,306 | 295,916 | N/A |
| NW | 1,728,838 | 1,459,760 | 1,304,147 |
| WC | 827,938 | 615,053 | 534,254 |
| Emp. | 152 | 156 | N/A |

DUNS 21-727-2188
## Torch Academy Gateway Trust
Toot Hill School The Banks, Bingham, Nottingham, Nottinghamshire, Nottingham, Nottinghamshire NG13 8BL
**Tel:** 01949863044
**Web:** www.torchacademy.co.uk
**Reg No:** 7635510 **Estd:** 2011 Private Company Limited By Guarantee
**Line of Business:** General secondary education
**Directors:** Ms S Macdougall, K S Ghattaora, J Tomasevic, K Gray, J N Mills, Ms J White, D A Hooker, A J Woods
**Co. Secretary:** Mrs Susanna Edyvean
**Responsibilities**
**Senior:** Richard Flewitt *(Director),* June Ibbotson *(Director),* Ashfaq Rahman *(Director)*
**US SIC:** 8211 **UK SIC:** 93200
**Bankers:** The Royal Bank Of Scotland Plc (16-26-32)

| | 31-08-14 | 31-08-13 | 31-08-12 |
|---|---|---|---|
| TO | 19,831,000 | 22,885,000 | 22,895,000 |
| P/L | 4,561,000 | 8,049,000 | 13,053,000 |
| NW | 24,308,000 | 20,395,000 | 12,661,000 |
| WC | 2,341,000 | 1,215,000 | 131,000 |
| Emp. | 288 | 255 | 156 |

DUNS 42-441-6290
## Torestin Care Home Ltd
Tiers Cross, Haverfordwest, Dyfed SA62 3DB
**Tel:** 01437-891373
**Reg No:** 4429323 **Estd:** 2002 Private Limited Company
**Line of Business:** Nursing homes
**Issued Capital:** £100,001
**Director:** G T Williams
**Co. Secretary:** David Davies
**US SIC:** 8051 **UK SIC:** 95100
**Auditors:** D.M.B. Davies Ltd

| | 31-03-14 | 31-03-13 | 31-03-12 |
|---|---|---|---|
| TA | 1,316,605 | 1,467,024 | 1,280,096 |
| NW | 297,952 | 308,937 | 61,313 |
| WC | (112,885) | (563,693) | (826,549) |

DUNS 21-810-1035
## Torex
Innovation House, Pynes Hill, Exeter, Devon EX2 5TU
**Web:** www.micros.com
**Estd:** 2012
**Line of Business:** Photocopier suppliers
**Trading Style:** Torex

**Responsibilities**
**Senior:** Mark Lavallin *(Manager),* Frank Ward *(Senior Vice President)*
**US SIC:** 3579 **UK SIC:** 33010
**Employees:** 60

DUNS 21-001-8822
## Torex Retail Holdings Ltd
**(Subsidiary of:** Oracle Corporation)
The Xn Centre, Houghton Hall Park, Houghton Regis, Dunstable, Bedfordshire LU5 5YG
**Tel:** 01582869600 **Fax:** 01582-869601
**Web:** www.micros.com
**Reg No:** 6273940 **Estd:** 2007 Private Limited Company
**Line of Business:** Other computer related activities
**Export Sales:** £3,097,000
**Issued Capital:** £50,071,082
**Directors:** D J Hudson, Oracle Corporation Nominees Limi, K Niroomand, S P Rowley
**Responsibilities**
**Facilities:** Sheila Kaur *(Facilities Manager)*
**Operations:** Sheila Kaur *(Facilities Manager)*
**Purchasing:** Sharon Baddeley *(Purchasing Coordinator)*
**Branches:** Torex Retail Holdings Ltd, Crompton House, Barrs Fold Road, Bolton, Lancashire BL5 3XP
**US SIC:** 7379, 7372
**UK SIC:** 83940
**Auditors:** PricewaterhouseCoopers LLP
**Bankers:** The Royal Bank Of Scotland Plc (16-29-25)

| | 30-06-13 | 30-06-12 | 30-06-11 |
|---|---|---|---|
| TO | 48,822,000 | 58,052,000 | 135,545,000 |
| P/L | (7,343,000) | (10,091,000) | (8,043,000) |
| NW | (9,366,000) | (9,345,000) | (46,279,000) |
| WC | 3,527,000 | 22,983,000 | 4,345,000 |
| Emp. | 543 | 548 | 1,160 |

DUNS 39-719-7435
## Torex Retail Solutions (Uk) Ltd
**(Subsidiary of:** Oracle Corporation)
Manor Farm Courtyard, Main Street, Frolesworth, Lutterworth, Leicestershire LE17 5EE
**Web:** www.torex.com
**Reg No:** 2168644 **Estd:** 1983 Private Limited Company
**Line of Business:** Computer software sales
**Issued Capital:** £1
**Directors:**
Oracle Corporation Nominees Limi, D J Hudson
**Responsibilities**
**Senior:** Mark Hollister *(Chief Operating Officer),* Charlotte Przezwanski *(General Manager),* Richard Quarmby *(Manager),* Cynthia Russo *(Director),* Stephen Walder *(Director),* Frank Ward *(Director)*
**Operations:** Mark Hollister *(Chief Operating Officer)*
**Branches:** Torex Retail Solutions (Uk) Ltd, 4th Floor Beaumont House, Southam Road, Banbury, Oxfordshire OX16 1RH
**US SIC:** 7379 **UK SIC:** 83940
**Auditors:** Grant Thornton UK LLP
**Bankers:** Lloyds TSB Bank plc (30-96-35)

| | 30-06-11 |
|---|---|
| TA | 1 |
| NW | 1 |

DUNS 23-781-6319
## Torfaen County Borough Council
Civic Centre, Pontypool, Gwent NP4 6YB
**Tel:** 01495-762-200
**Web:** www.torfaen.gov.uk
**Estd:** 1969
**Line of Business:** Local government
**Trading Style:** Ty George Lansbury Care Home, Garndiffaith Millenium Hall, Communities First
**Principals:** P Nash *(Financial),* Dr C Grace
**Responsibilities**
**Senior:** Adrian Huckin *(Director Community Housing),* Denise Langman *(Manager),* Terri Relph *(Manager),* Amy Taylor *(Senior Manager)*
**HR:** Graeme Russell *(Head of Pensions and Employee)*
**Operations:** Linda King *(Customer Service Manager)*
**Engineering:** Lesa Tuckwell *(Officer)*
**Branches:** Torfaen County Borough Council, Parkside, Old Cwmbran, Cwmbran, Gwent NP44 3LW
**US SIC:** 9121 **UK SIC:** 91110
**Bankers:** The Co-Operative Bank Plc (08-90-07)
**Employees:** 6,500

DUNS 21-500-3653
## Torfaen Salvage
Polo Grounds, New Inn, Pontypool, Gwent NP4 0TW
**Tel:** 01495752259
**Estd:** 2008 Proprietorship
**Line of Business:** Reclamation centres
**Proprietor:** J Mathews
**Responsibilities**
**Senior:** Jabez Matthews *(Managing Director)*
**US SIC:** 5093, 5039
**UK SIC:** 62200, 61300
**Employees:** 59

DUNS 73-295-2887
## Torin Sifan Ltd
**(Subsidiary of:** Volution Group Plc)
Greenbridge, Swindon, Wiltshire SN3 3JB
**Tel:** 01793-524291
**Web:** www.torin-sifan.com
**Reg No:** 4569050 **Estd:** 2002 Private Limited Company
**Line of Business:** Manufacture of other electrical equipment not elsewhere classified
**Export Sales:** £9,771,000
**Issued Capital:** £5,000,000
**Directors:** R George, I Dew
**Branches:** Torin Sifan Ltd, Drakes Way, Swindon, Wiltshire SN3 3JB
**US SIC:** 3629 **UK SIC:** 34350
**Auditors:** Ernst & Young LLP

| | 31-07-14 | 31-07-13 | 31-07-12 |
|---|---|---|---|
| TO | 20,590,000 | 20,942,000 | 19,771,000 |
| P/L | 3,003,000 | 3,613,000 | 2,618,000 |
| NW | 21,855,000 | 19,152,000 | 16,067,000 |
| WC | 18,964,000 | 16,822,000 | 13,885,000 |
| Emp. | 218 | 202 | 215 |

DUNS 28-941-0920
## Tormage Ltd
West Hanningfield Road, Great Baddow, Chelmsford, Essex CM2 8HR
**Tel:** 01245-476444 **Fax:** 01245-478393
**Web:** www.reflectionsspa.co.uk
**Reg No:** 1579250 **Estd:** 1981 Private Limited Company
**Line of Business:** Hotels and motels without restaurant
**Trading Style:** Pontlands Park, Ivy Hill Hotel, Furze Hill Bar & Brasserie, Reflections Spa
**Issued Capital:** £100
**Managing Director:** J J Bartella
**Co. Secretary:** Mrs Julia Kilham
**US SIC:** 7011, 5812
**UK SIC:** 66500, 66110
**Auditors:** Clay Ratnage Strevens & Hills

| | 31-12-13 | 31-12-12 | 31-12-11 |
|---|---|---|---|
| TO | 1,960,038 | 1,739,456 | 1,585,586 |
| P/L | 112,645 | (49,729) | 8,612 |
| NW | 2,381,901 | 2,665,095 | 2,734,648 |
| WC | (576,345) | (256,303) | (442,040) |
| Emp. | 86 | 83 | 72 |

DUNS 21-019-0179      Imp
## Tormax United Kingdom Ltd
**(Subsidiary of:** Landert Motoren Ag)
42-50 Hersham Road, Walton-On-Thames, Surrey KT12 1RZ
**Tel:** 08444124707 **Fax:** 08713157150
**Web:** www.tormax.co.uk
**Reg No:** 0447952 **VAT No:** 494522134
**Estd:** 1948 Private Limited Company
**Line of Business:** Manufacturers of industrial doors
**Issued Capital:** £699,552
**Directors:** S J Roberts, Dr P Heiniger, W Schwyter
**Co. Secretary:** David Snook
**Responsibilities**
**Senior:** Sonke Bandixen *(Manager),* Elizabeth Parsons *(Manager)*
**Branches:** Tormax United Kingdom Ltd, 21 Norman Street, Elland, West Yorkshire HX5 9BS
**US SIC:** 2431, 3823
**UK SIC:** 46300, 37100
**Auditors:** Chantrey Vellacott DFK LLP
**Bankers:** National Westminster Bank Plc (60-40-04)

| | 31-12-13 | 31-12-12 | 31-12-11 |
|---|---|---|---|
| TO | 4,345,653 | 3,999,547 | 4,268,572 |
| P/L | (69,414) | (191,581) | (30,596) |
| NW | (435,155) | (365,194) | (171,366) |
| WC | (481,929) | (416,556) | (189,125) |
| Emp. | 52 | 53 | 54 |

DUNS 28-838-5420
## Tormead Ltd
Cranley Road, Guildford, Surrey GU1 2JD
**Web:** www.tormeadschool.org.uk
**Reg No:** 0485947 **Estd:** 1950 Private Company Limited By Guarantee
**Line of Business:** Primary education
**Trading Style:** Tormead School
**Directors:** Mrs R Harris, R J Jewkes, Dr J E Page, Mrs J M Wicks, W T Gillen, D M Williams, Doctor C M Kissin, Professor G M Nicholls
**Co. Secretary:** Michael O Donovan

**Responsibilities**
**Senior:** Rowan Edbrooke *(Director)*, Christine Foord *(Headmistress)*, Deborah Forbes *(Manager)*, Colston Herbert *(Director)*, Sue Marks *(Headmistress)*, Peter O Keefe *(Director)*, Nicole Rockliff *(Manager)*, Anna Spender *(Director)*
**Marketing:** Lucy Apsey *(Marketing Manager)*, Cherry Scott *(Marketing Registrar)*
**Admin:** Lesley Hiscutt *(Office Manager)*
**US SIC:** 8211 **UK SIC:** 93200
**Auditors:** HLB Kidsons
**Bankers:** Lloyds TSB Bank plc (30-93-74)

| | 31-08-13 | 31-08-12 | 31-08-11 |
|---|---|---|---|
| TO | 8,980,694 | 8,900,894 | 8,477,785 |
| P/L | 1,034,796 | 958,651 | 848,923 |
| NW | 9,536,723 | 8,501,927 | 7,543,276 |
| WC | 355,261 | 1,299,762 | 1,023,247 |
| Emp. | 128 | 127 | 122 |

DUNS 29-337-0078
## Tornado Wire Ltd
(**Subsidiary of:** Tornado Group Ltd)
Muthill Road, Crieff, Perthshire PH7 4HQ
**Web:** www.tornadowire.co.uk
**Reg No:** 0064920SC **VAT No:** 864447203
**Estd:** 2002 Private Limited Company
**Line of Business:** Fence and gate suppliers
**Trading Style:** Tornado Wire Ltd
**Issued Capital:** £105,300
**Directors:** J Miller, Mrs L J Hall, S Mckay, P W Harris
**Co. Secretary:** Kenneth Campbell
**Responsibilities**
**Sales:** Malcolm Blackford *(Sales director)*, Morgan Webley *(Sales Manager)*
**Branches:** Tornado Wire Ltd, 20 Lindisfarne Road, Durham, County Durham DH1 5YQ
**US SIC:** 5072, 5074
**UK SIC:** 61500, 61300
**Auditors:** Smith Cooper
**Bankers:** The Royal Bank Of Scotland Plc (83-17-15)

| | 31-12-13 | 31-12-12 | 31-12-11 |
|---|---|---|---|
| TO | 14,257,795 | 13,575,127 | 14,530,183 |
| P/L | 1,064,762 | 681,936 | 1,286,645 |
| NW | 4,118,665 | 3,749,778 | 3,425,136 |
| WC | 2,785,829 | 2,654,191 | 2,778,315 |
| Emp. | 71 | 75 | 73 |

DUNS 21-024-1345
## Toronto Dominion Holdings (U.K.) Ltd
(**Subsidiary of:** Toronto-Dominion Bank The)
60 Threadneedle Street, London EC2R 8AP
**Tel:** 02079200272
**Web:** www.tdsecurities.com
**Reg No:** 1455450 **Estd:** 1979 Private Limited Company
**Line of Business:** Management activities of holding companies
**Directors:** B G Smith, D S Cerovic, J N Stewart
**Co. Secretary:** Andrew Jeffrey
**US SIC:** 6711, 6111
**UK SIC:** 83962, 81501
**Auditors:** Ernst & Young LLP
**Employees:** 300

DUNS 23-023-0588
## Torotrak Plc
1 Aston Way, Moss Side, Preston, Lancashire PR26 7UX
**Tel:** 01772900900
**Web:** www.torotrak.com
**Reg No:** 3580465 **Estd:** 1998 Public Limited Company
**Line of Business:** Design engineers
**Trading Style:** Torotrak Development
**Issued Capital:** £17,671,349
**Directors:** J J Hilton, J R Deering, Dr N F Barter, J P Weston, R Q Vevers, J A Mclaren
**Co. Secretary:** Rawdon Vevers
**Responsibilities**
**Senior:** Dick Elsy *(Chief Executive)*
**Finance:** Phillip Ainscough *(Financial Controller)*, Rex Vevers *(Finance Director)*, Carol astin *(Financial Controller)*
**Marketing:** Marco Foley *(Press and Media Manager)*
**Admin:** Samantha Marsh *(Executive Assistant)*
**IT:** Jason Frankes *(IT Manager)*, Glyn Merga *(IT Manager)*
**HR:** Phillip Ainscough *(Financial Controller)*
**Health & Safety:** Graham Riding *(Operations Manager)*
**Facilities:** Graham Riding *(Operations Manager)*
**Purchasing:** Graham Riding *(Operations Manager)*
**US SIC:** 6711 **UK SIC:** 83962
**Auditors:** PricewaterhouseCoopers LLP

**Bankers:** Barclays Bank Plc (20-00-00)

| | 31-03-14 | 31-03-13 | 31-03-12 |
|---|---|---|---|
| TO | 3,520,000 | 7,479,000 | 4,294,000 |
| P/L | (4,733,000) | (391,000) | (1,919,000) |
| NW | 10,622,000 | 11,669,000 | 8,771,000 |
| WC | 10,981,000 | 7,414,000 | 7,560,000 |
| Emp. | 76 | 39 | 40 |

DUNS 37-847-9323
## Torpedo Factory Group Ltd
The Old Torpedo Factory, St Leonards Road, London NW10 6ST
**Tel:** 02085371000 **Fax:** 02085371011
**Web:** www.torpedofactory.co.uk
**Reg No:** 3298917 **Estd:** 1997 Private Limited Company
**Line of Business:** Management activities of holding companies
**Export Sales:** £54,529
**Trading Style:** Phenomenon Limited
**Issued Capital:** £140,289
**Principals:** N Clark *(Managing)*, F W Jenner, Dr K G Mccullagh, J D Papworth, M C Gower, A R Osman
**Co. Secretary:** Freddie Jenner
**Responsibilities**
**Finance:** Chris Slaney *(Senior Account Manager)*
**Admin:** Karen Hughes *(Office Manager)*
**Operations:** Seth Beighton *(Operations Manager)*, Andrew Grady *(Project Coordinator)*, Daniel Marlow *(Project Manager)*
**Fleet:** Peter Bush *(Logistics Manager)*
**US SIC:** 6711 **UK SIC:** 83962
**Auditors:** Wheelers
**Bankers:** Barclays Bank Plc (20-65-18)

| | 31-12-13 | 31-12-12 | 31-12-11 |
|---|---|---|---|
| TO | 4,069,351 | 3,846,299 | 4,632,148 |
| P/L | 291,398 | 121,894 | (174,153) |
| NW | 449,822 | 133,223 | (102,917) |
| WC | (283,194) | (576,738) | (788,321) |
| Emp. | N/A | 44 | 60 |

DUNS 73-631-9091
## Torpedo Marketing Ltd
(**Subsidiary of:** Torpedo Group Ltd)
The Long Barn Worton Park, Cassington, Witney, Oxfordshire OX29 4SX
**Tel:** 01865-733710 **Fax:** 01865733711
**Web:** www.torpedogroup.com
**Reg No:** 4892196 **Estd:** 2003 Private Limited Company
**Line of Business:** Speciality design activities
**Issued Capital:** £1
**Director:** Ms T Lewis
**Co. Secretary:** Iain Lewis
**US SIC:** 7399 **UK SIC:** 83954

| | 31-12-13 | 31-12-12 | 31-12-11 |
|---|---|---|---|
| TA | 1 | 1 | 1 |
| NW | 1 | 1 | 1 |

DUNS 34-747-9164
## Torpoint Ltd
Commercial House, 1 Foundry Terrace, Cleckheaton, West Yorkshire BD19 3JZ
**Tel:** 01274-872622 **Fax:** 01274-851973
**Web:** www.torpoint.ltd.uk
**Reg No:** 2783356 **VAT No:** 567024050
**Estd:** 1993 Private Limited Company
**Line of Business:** Building construction contractors
**Trading Style:** Torpoint Ltd
**Issued Capital:** £1,000
**Directors:** R L Metcalfe, G Cox
**Co. Secretary:** Robin Gravestock
**Responsibilities**
**Admin:** Gillian Calverly *(Office Coordinator)*
**US SIC:** 1522 **UK SIC:** 50100
**Auditors:** Harrison & Co
**Bankers:** Yorkshire Bank Plc (05-03-73)

| | 28-02-14 | 28-02-13 | 29-02-12 |
|---|---|---|---|
| TA | 2,952,741 | 1,930,111 | 1,818,023 |
| NW | 1,239,152 | 1,231,995 | 1,164,968 |
| WC | 785,229 | 677,722 | 509,730 |

DUNS 21-207-9953
## Torpoint Nursing
Antony, Torpoint, Cornwall PL11 3AQ
**Tel:** 01752812384
**Web:** www.torcare.com
**Estd:** 2002 Proprietorship
**Line of Business:** Residential care establishments
**Proprietor:** P B Fourniss
**US SIC:** 8321 **UK SIC:** 96111
**Employees:** 80

DUNS 21-692-6359
## Torquay Boys' Grammar School
Torquay Boys' Grammar School, Shiphay Manor, Torquay, Devon TQ2 7EL
**Tel:** 01803615501
**Web:** www.tbgs.co.uk
**Reg No:** 7394671 **Estd:** 2010 Private Company Limited By Guarantee
**Line of Business:** General secondary education

**Directors:** B W Wills-Pope, R M Lidbetter, Mrs C Weston, Mrs A C Derbyshire, Mrs L M Critchlow, M E Penfold, V Flower
**Co. Secretary:** Andrew Medhurst
**US SIC:** 8211 **UK SIC:** 93200
**Bankers:** HSBC Bank plc (40-44-22)

| | 31-08-14 | 31-08-13 | 31-08-12 |
|---|---|---|---|
| TO | 12,152,000 | 36,454,000 | 6,310,000 |
| P/L | (970,000) | 23,867,000 | 32,000 |
| NW | 37,982,000 | 39,320,000 | 16,163,000 |
| WC | 1,065,000 | 1,104,000 | 129,000 |
| Emp. | 248 | 233 | 119 |

DUNS 21-708-7919
## Torquay Girls' Grammar School
30 Shiphay Lane, Torquay, Devon TQ2 7DY
**Tel:** 01803613215
**Web:** www.tggsacademy.org
**Reg No:** 7494620 **Estd:** 2011 Private Company Limited By Guarantee
**Line of Business:** Schools (local authority)
**Directors:** Dr A Tyler, Ms J Neal, Mrs L S White, A E Pengelly, Mrs A White, Mrs S J Wright, B S Mcphail, R G Webber
**Co. Secretary:** Mrs Sharon Wallwork
**Responsibilities**
**Senior:** Alan Furniss *(Director)*, Penny Rogers *(Director)*
**US SIC:** 8211 **UK SIC:** 93200
**Bankers:** Lloyds TSB Bank plc (30-98-67)

| | 31-08-14 | 31-08-13 | 31-08-12 |
|---|---|---|---|
| TO | 4,856,016 | 4,638,564 | 6,209,537 |
| P/L | (172,346) | 64,775 | 1,625,793 |
| NW | 11,328,407 | 11,565,753 | 11,585,978 |
| WC | 510,869 | 403,826 | 2,126,888 |
| Emp. | 96 | 142 | 138 |

DUNS 22-557-2684
## Torquay Leisure Hotels Ltd
22-44 Belgrave Road, Torquay, Devon TQ2 5HS
**Tel:** 01803400100 **Fax:** 01803400110
**Web:** www.tlh.co.uk
**Reg No:** 0430051 **VAT No:** 585889556
**Estd:** 1947 Private Limited Company
**Line of Business:** Hotels
**Trading Style:** Toorak Hotel, Victoria Hotel, Derwent Hotel, Carlton Hotel
**Issued Capital:** £36,258
**Principals:** L Murrell *(Chairman and Managing)*, Mrs C P Raymond, D Murrell, Mrs J M Murrell
**Co. Secretary:** Ms Karen Murrell
**Responsibilities**
**Senior:** Jason Garside *(General Manager)*, Peter Raven *(Group Operations Manager)*
**US SIC:** 7011 **UK SIC:** 66500
**Auditors:** Bishop Fleming
**Bankers:** Barclays Bank Plc (20-60-88)

| | 30-04-14 | 30-04-13 | 30-04-12 |
|---|---|---|---|
| TO | 11,550,223 | 11,048,126 | 11,156,804 |
| P/L | 514,279 | 202,245 | 386,020 |
| NW | 5,466,101 | 5,142,469 | 5,051,804 |
| WC | (3,458,436) | (9,561,138) | (3,353,455) |
| Emp. | 406 | 400 | 409 |

DUNS 76-429-4575
## The Torquay Palace Ltd
Babbacombe Road, Torquay, Devon TQ1 3TG
**Tel:** 01803-200200
**Web:** www.palacetorquay.co.uk
**Reg No:** 2561399 **Estd:** 1980 Private Limited Company
**Line of Business:** Hotels
**Trading Style:** The Palace Hotel
**Issued Capital:** £3,170,750
**Principals:** P D Uphill *(Managing)*, V T Duker, M H Singer
**Co. Secretary:** Graham Forward
**Responsibilities**
**Senior:** Mark Beedell *(Manager)*
**Finance:** Helen Shears *(Financial Director)*
**Marketing:** Clare Bushby *(Sales & Marketing Manager)*
**Sales:** Clare Bushby *(Sales & Marketing Manager)*
**Facilities:** Gary Ayres *(Operations Manager)*
**Purchasing:** Helen Shears *(Financial Director)*
**US SIC:** 7011, 7999
**UK SIC:** 66500, 97913
**Auditors:** Bishop Fleming
**Bankers:** Barclays Bank Plc (20-06-05)

| | 31-12-13 | 31-12-12 | 31-12-11 |
|---|---|---|---|
| TO | 3,001,675 | 3,060,452 | 2,736,625 |
| P/L | (30,603) | 37,396 | (51,799) |
| NW | 4,531,178 | 4,622,797 | 4,646,417 |
| WC | (586,434) | (483,724) | (439,045) |
| Emp. | 76 | 81 | 100 |

DUNS 76-960-7615
## Torque Logistics Ltd
Wortley Moor Road, Leeds, West Yorkshire LS12 4JH
**Tel:** 01132-636444 **Fax:** 01132-310374
**Web:** www.torque.eu
**Reg No:** 2625079 **Estd:** 1991 Private Limited Company
**Line of Business:** Storage and warehousing

**Trading Style:** Elite Group
**Issued Capital:** £51,000
**Principals:** E P Darcy *(Financial)*, T S Howarth, S P Firth
**Co. Secretary:** Eamonn Darcy
**Responsibilities**
**Operations:** Craig Hemingway *(Projects Manager)*
**Fleet:** Paul Boland *(Head of Freight)*, Paul Linyard *(Assistant Group Transport Mana)*
**Branches:** Torque Logistics Ltd, Unit 3, Galleymead Road, Slough, Berkshire SL3 0EN
**US SIC:** 4226, 4469, 4582
**UK SIC:** 77003, 76300, 76400
**Auditors:** Deloitte LLP
**Bankers:** National Westminster Bank Plc (60-14-34)

| | 30-04-14 | 30-04-13 | 30-04-12 |
|---|---|---|---|
| TO | 51,710,000 | 53,165,000 | 49,752,000 |
| P/L | 1,439,000 | 746,000 | 1,227,000 |
| NW | 19,699,000 | 18,700,000 | 18,258,000 |
| WC | 6,547,000 | 5,403,000 | 5,320,000 |
| Emp. | 693 | 599 | 607 |

DUNS 22-766-9116 **Imp-Exp**
## Torquemeters Ltd
West Haddon Road, Ravensthorpe, Northampton, Northamptonshire NN6 8ET
**Web:** www.torquemeters.com
**Reg No:** 0492122 **VAT No:** 119897420
**Estd:** 1951 Private Limited Company
**Line of Business:** Manufacturers of testing apparatus
**Export Markets:** Worldwide
**Export Sales:** £7,393,103
**Issued Capital:** £8,925
**Principals:** J D Van Millingen *(Managing)*, P G Johnson, A C Delves, B A Van Millingen
**Co. Secretary:** Ms Moira Bennett
**Responsibilities**
**Senior:** Jas Milingen *(Manager)*, Martin Yeates *(Quality Manager)*
**Health & Safety:** Martin Aldwinckle *(Quality Manager)*
**US SIC:** 3811 **UK SIC:** 37100
**Auditors:** Macintyre Hudson
**Bankers:** The Royal Bank Of Scotland Plc (15-10-00)

| | 31-03-14 | 31-03-13 | 31-03-12 |
|---|---|---|---|
| TO | 7,801,849 | N/A | N/A |
| P/L | 208,934 | N/A | N/A |
| NW | 3,613,047 | 3,394,314 | 3,093,207 |
| WC | 2,856,751 | 2,664,316 | 2,368,477 |
| Emp. | 52 | N/A | N/A |

DUNS 77-909-7729
## Torr Home
The Drive, Plymouth, Devon PL3 5SY
**Web:** www.torrhome.org.uk
**Reg No:** 5812992 **Estd:** 2005 Private Company Limited By Guarantee
**Line of Business:** Residential care establishments
**Directors:** J Roberts, Mrs E Bosworth, N G Major, Ms S E Stidever
**Co. Secretary:** John Roberts
**Responsibilities**
**Senior:** Elizabeth Carter *(Manager)*, Richard Persson *(Manager)*
**US SIC:** 8321 **UK SIC:** 96111

| | 31-12-13 | 31-12-12 | 31-12-11 |
|---|---|---|---|
| TO | 2,127,477 | 1,703,261 | 1,523,817 |
| P/L | 122,102 | 37,380 | 194,518 |
| NW | 4,454,718 | 4,179,093 | 4,062,288 |
| WC | (15,840) | (74,050) | (669,632) |
| Emp. | 84 | 96 | 59 |

DUNS 23-644-3081
## Torridge District Council
Riverbank House, Bideford, Devon EX39 2QG
**Web:** www.torridge.gov.uk
**Estd:** 1974
**Line of Business:** Local government
**Directors:** Miss G Bowering, J M Wyatt, Mrs J M Wallace, D A Pinney, D White, R K Brasington
**Responsibilities**
**Senior:** Nicola Bulbeck *(Chief Executive)*, Andy Fenge *(Executive)*, Sean Kearney *(Economic Regeneration Officer)*, Jenny Wallace *(Head of Paid Services)*
**Finance:** Jenny Wallace *(Head of Paid Services)*
**Marketing:** Jenny Wallace *(Head of Paid Services)*
**IT:** Roger Bonaparte *(ICT Manager)*
**Facilities:** Andrew Waite *(Head of Property)*
**Operations:** Adrian Blight *(Senior Caretaker)*, Andy Champion *(Building Surveyor)*, Ricky Mccormack *(Production and Operations Mana)*, Vanessa Saunders *(Special Projects Manager)*
**Purchasing:** Doug Jenkin *(Purchasing Manager)*, Gill Tallamy *(Procurement Officer)*
**Engineering:** Tara Sanders *(Engineer)*
**Branches:** Torridge District Council, Kingsley Rd, Bideford, Devon EX39 2QQ
**US SIC:** 9121 **UK SIC:** 91110
**Employees:** 230

DUNS 21-781-9623
## Torridon Infants School
Torridon Road Library, Torridon Road, London SE6 1RQ
**Tel:** 02086985822
**Web:** www.torridoninfants.lewisham.sch.uk
**Estd:** 1948 Proprietorship
**Line of Business:** Schools (local authority)
**Proprietor:** Miss L Pearson
**US SIC:** 8211 **UK SIC:** 93200
**Employees:** 50

DUNS 21-780-1579
## Torridon Junior School
Hazelbank Road, London SE6 1TG
**Tel:** 02086972762
**Web:** www.torridonj.lewisham.sch.uk
**Estd:** 1904 Proprietorship
**Line of Business:** General secondary education
**Proprietor:** Mrs M Mcpherson
**Responsibilities**
**Senior:** Mary McPherson *(Proprietor)*
**US SIC:** 8211 **UK SIC:** 93200
**Employees:** 52

DUNS 21-585-0847
## Torrwood Care Centre
Gilbert Scott Road, Wells, Somerset BA5 3FB
**Tel:** 01749675533
**Estd:** 2011
**Line of Business:** Residential care establishments
**US SIC:** 8321 **UK SIC:** 96111
**Employees:** 90

DUNS 22-289-3674
## Torry Harris Business Solutions (Europe) Ltd
(**Subsidiary of:** Torry Harris Business Solution Private Limited)
4 North Court, Woodlands The Courtyard, Bristol, Avon BS32 4NQ
**Tel:** 01454617762
**Web:** www.thbs.com
**Reg No:** 4307378 **Estd:** 2001 Private Limited Company
**Line of Business:** Computer services
**Issued Capital:** £1
**Director:** G S Boggaram Nagaraj
**Responsibilities**
**Senior:** Sujay Gupta *(Manager)*
**US SIC:** 7379 **UK SIC:** 83940

| | 31-12-13 | 31-12-12 | 31-12-11 |
|---|---|---|---|
| TO | 13,814,246 | 11,825,522 | 16,072,625 |
| P/L | 725,248 | 612,537 | 465,049 |
| NW | 1,934,262 | 1,381,760 | 921,979 |
| WC | 1,928,803 | 1,374,369 | 915,992 |
| Emp. | 112 | 177 | 189 |

DUNS 50-639-1494
## Torry Nursing Home
36 Balnagask Road, Aberdeen, Aberdeenshire AB11 8HR
**Tel:** 01224-890600
**Web:** www.renaissance-care.co.uk
**Estd:** 2000
**Line of Business:** Non-charitable social work activities with accommodation
**Partners:** Mrs K Macleod, Mrs K Macloud
**Responsibilities**
**Senior:** Heather Harold *(Manager)*, Cath Mcleod *(Manager)*
**US SIC:** 8321 **UK SIC:** 96111
**Employees:** 100

DUNS 21-824-7344 **Exp**
## Torton Bodies Ltd
Pilot Works, Holyhead Road, Telford, Shropshire TF2 6BB
**Tel:** 01952-612648
**Web:** www.torton.com
**Reg No:** 0683438 **VAT No:** 160590769
**Estd:** 1961 Private Limited Company
**Line of Business:** Activities of exhibition and fair organisers
**Export Markets:** E U & Russia
**Issued Capital:** £27,000
**Principals:** C T Andrews *(Sales)*, Ms J S Andrews
**Co. Secretary:** Miss Claire Andrews
**Responsibilities**
**Finance:** Steve Gosnell *(Finance Director)*
**Sales:** Jason Kilroy *(Sales Manager)*
**IT:** Ron Brothwood *(Drawing Office Manager)*
**Operations:** Ron Brothwood *(Drawing Office Manager)*
**Purchasing:** Celia Jenkins *(Buyer)*
**Fleet:** Julie Bunce *(Transport Coordinator)*
**Engineering:** Ron Brothwood *(Drawing Office Manager)*, Andrew Sudlow *(Technical Manager)*
**Branches:** Telford
**US SIC:** 7399, 7394, 3711
**UK SIC:** 83954, 84000, 35101
**Auditors:** Garratts Wolverhampton Ltd
**Bankers:** Lloyds TSB Bank plc (30-10-12)

| | 31-12-13 | 31-12-12 | 31-12-11 |
|---|---|---|---|
| TA | 3,281,518 | 2,466,103 | 2,658,449 |
| NW | 1,624,188 | 1,338,443 | 1,133,256 |
| WC | 612,553 | 224,324 | 120,884 |

DUNS 21-097-0028
## Torus Insurance Marketing Ltd
5th Floor 88 Leadenhall Street, London EC3A 3BP
**Tel:** 02032068000
**Reg No:** 6414328 **Estd:** 2007 Private Limited Company
**Line of Business:** Non-life insurance
**Directors:** T J Wilkes, T Fillingham
**Co. Secretary:** Ms Siobhan Hextall
**US SIC:** 6399 **UK SIC:** 82001
**Employees:** 122
**Turnover:** £102,677,000

DUNS 23-767-7880
## Torus Measurement Systems Ltd
(**Subsidiary of:** Torus Technology Group Ltd)
Nedge Hill 1, Nedge Hill Campus, Telford, Shropshire TF3 3AJ
**Web:** www.torus-group.com
**Reg No:** 3761292 **Estd:** 1999 Private Limited Company
**Line of Business:** Manufacture of electronic instruments and appliances for measuring, checking, testing, navigating and other purposes, except industrial process control equipment
**Export Sales:** £4,933,142
**Issued Capital:** £1,390
**Directors:** Ms V L Robinson, M J Parry, L A Robinson
**Co. Secretary:** Martin Golden
**US SIC:** 3829 **UK SIC:** 37100
**Auditors:** Mazars
**Bankers:** HSBC Bank plc (40-42-11)

| | 30-06-14 | 30-06-13 | 30-06-12 |
|---|---|---|---|
| TO | 7,008,573 | 9,164,030 | 7,186,725 |
| P/L | 307,458 | 2,100,749 | 1,028,233 |
| NW | 2,534,989 | 6,895,457 | 5,299,994 |
| WC | 3,167,498 | 6,175,935 | 4,683,985 |
| Emp. | 64 | 59 | 54 |

DUNS 22-056-5555
## Torwood House School Ltd
(**Subsidiary of:** S C J M Holdings Ltd)
27-29 Durdham Park, Bristol, Avon BS6 6XE
**Tel:** 01179735620 **Fax:** 01179-735620
**Web:** www.torwoodhouseschool.co.uk
**Reg No:** 4058527 **Estd:** 1996 Private Limited Company
**Line of Business:** Schools (independent)
**Issued Capital:** £2
**Managing Director:** Miss S J Packer
**Co. Secretary:** Ms Emily Ward
**Responsibilities**
**Senior:** Dionne Seagrove *(Head Teacher)*, Emily Spring *(Manager)*
**HR:** Dionne Seagrove *(Head Teacher)*
**US SIC:** 8211 **UK SIC:** 93200
**Auditors:** Waddingtons

| | 31-08-13 | 31-08-12 | 31-08-11 |
|---|---|---|---|
| TA | 916,921 | 751,434 | 752,864 |
| NW | 386,180 | 207,906 | 445,528 |
| WC | 295,628 | 118,401 | 240,897 |

DUNS 23-729-2359 **Imp-Exp**
## Toshiba Carrier Uk Ltd.
(**Subsidiary of:** United Technologies Corporation)
United Technologies House, Leatherhead, Surrey KT22 9UT
**Tel:** 01372220240 **Fax:** 01372220241
**Web:** www.toshiba-aircon.co.uk
**Reg No:** 3723803 **VAT No:** 724617927
**Estd:** 1999 Private Limited Company
**Line of Business:** Plumbing
**Export Markets:** Worldwide
**Trading Style:** Carrier Air Conditioning, Toshiba Air Conditioning
**Issued Capital:** £17,600,000
**Directors:** H Tsuru, T Wazawa, Y Saito, J Hendrickx, R H Jones, D C Da Costa, A Brennan
**Co. Secretary:** Ms Agnes D'Cruz
**Responsibilities**
**Senior:** David Appel *(Manager)*, Christian Blanc *(Manager)*, Agnes D' Cruz *(Manager)*, Yuriko Matsumoto *(Manager)*, Gboyega Obafemi *(Manager)*
**IT:** John Buckingham *(IT Director)*
**HR:** Debra Whitefoot *(HR Manager)*
**Facilities:** Paul Oakley *(Facilities Manager)*
**Branches:** Toshiba Carrier Uk Ltd., United Technologies House, Guildford Road, Fetcham, Leatherhead, Surrey KT22 9UT
**US SIC:** 1711, 5084
**UK SIC:** 50300, 61490
**Auditors:** PricewaterhouseCoopers LLP
**Bankers:** HSBC Bank plc (40-36-22)

| | 30-11-13 | 30-11-12 | 30-11-11 |
|---|---|---|---|
| TO | 68,061,000 | 73,069,000 | 75,899,000 |
| P/L | 3,258,000 | 4,220,000 | 3,187,000 |
| NW | (2,942,000) | (3,492,000) | (6,328,000) |
| WC | (11,918,000) | (13,651,000) | (16,661,000) |
| Emp. | 256 | 259 | 259 |

DUNS 21-197-1288 **Imp-Exp**
## Toshiba Information Systems (Uk) Ltd
(**Subsidiary of:** Toshiba Corporation)
Weybridge Business Park, Addlestone, Surrey KT15 2UL
**Tel:** 01932-841600 **Fax:** 08702383776
**Web:** www.toshiba.co.uk
**Reg No:** 0918861 **VAT No:** 217915555
**Estd:** 1967 Private Limited Company
**Line of Business:** Wholesale of computers, computer peripheral equipment and software
**Export Sales:** £57,543,705
**Issued Capital:** £30,300,000
**Directors:** K Kakudo, D H Jaume
**Co. Secretary:** Patrick Whelan
**Responsibilities**
**Senior:** Andy Bass *(Manager)*, Robert Rawlings *(Warehouse Manager)*
**Finance:** tom cunliffe *(Financial Director)*
**Marketing:** Rupert Stanley *(Marketing Manager)*
**Health & Safety:** Richard Brand *(Facilities Manager)*
**Facilities:** Richard Brand *(Facilities Manager)*
**Branches:** Toshiba Information Systems (Uk) Ltd, Unit B, Windmill Road West, Sunbury-On-Thames, Middlesex TW16 7HE
**US SIC:** 5081, 5065, 5199
**UK SIC:** 61490, 61500, 61900
**Auditors:** Ernst & Young LLP
**Bankers:** Barclays Bank Plc (20-68-10)

| | 31-03-14 | 31-03-13 | 31-03-12 |
|---|---|---|---|
| TO | 381,440,520 | 512,366,925 | 511,216,530 |
| P/L | 7,023,931 | 8,427,194 | 11,221,663 |
| NW | 35,491,843 | 32,340,123 | 14,165,828 |
| WC | 57,823,998 | 55,367,803 | 46,396,365 |
| Emp. | 233 | 242 | 254 |

DUNS 21-721-5979 **Imp-Exp**
## Toshiba Medical Systems Ltd
(**Subsidiary of:** Toshiba Corporation)
Gatwick Road, Crawley, West Sussex RH10 9AX
**Tel:** 01293-653-700
**Web:** www.toshiba-medical.co.uk
**Reg No:** 0983579 **VAT No:** 218138866
**Estd:** 1970 Private Limited Company
**Line of Business:** Retail sale of medical and orthopaedic goods not elsewhere classified
**Issued Capital:** £2,130,000
**Directors:** H Tachikawa, H Sato, J M Hitchman
**Co. Secretary:** Hiroyuki Tachikawa
**Responsibilities**
**IT:** Matt Aylen *(IT Manager)*
**HR:** Caroline Tomlinson *(Human Resources Manager)*
**Branches:** Toshiba Medical Systems Ltd, Hillside House, Laurelhill Business Park, Stirling, Stirlingshire FK7 9JQ
**US SIC:** 5999 **UK SIC:** 65600
**Auditors:** Ernst & Young LLP
**Bankers:** Barclays Bank Plc (20-92-60)

| | 31-03-14 | 31-03-13 | 31-03-12 |
|---|---|---|---|
| TO | 57,656,000 | 48,470,000 | 51,467,000 |
| P/L | 1,315,000 | 906,000 | 1,593,000 |
| NW | 4,685,000 | 5,413,000 | 6,961,000 |
| WC | 8,212,000 | 5,087,000 | 7,140,000 |
| Emp. | 125 | 124 | 122 |

DUNS 21-117-3959
## Toshiba Medical Visualization Systems Europe Ltd
(**Subsidiary of:** Toshiba Corporation)
Bonnington Bond, 2 Anderson Place, Edinburgh, Midlothian EH6 5NP
**Tel:** 0131-472-4792
**Web:** www.tmvse.com
**Reg No:** 0341779SC **Estd:** 2008 Private Limited Company
**Line of Business:** Research and experimental development on natural sciences and engineering
**Export Sales:** £13,493,000
**Issued Capital:** £101
**Directors:** Dr K G Sutherland, H Tachikawa, Y Sakamitsu, H Kura
**Co. Secretary:** Fredric Friedberg
**Responsibilities**
**Senior:** Callum Cunningham *(Senior Vice President)*, Chikao Kamijima *(Manager)*, Keiji Tanaka *(Manager)*, Satoshi Tsunakawa *(Manager)*
**HR:** Jannine Anderson *(Human Resources Manager)*
**Health & Safety:** Jannine Anderson *(Human Resources Manager)*
**US SIC:** 8091 **UK SIC:** 95200
**Auditors:** Ernst & Young LLP
**Bankers:** The Royal Bank Of Scotland Plc (16-00-01)

| | 31-03-14 | 31-03-13 | 31-03-12 |
|---|---|---|---|
| TO | 13,723,000 | 14,230,000 | 13,611,000 |
| P/L | 2,452,000 | 3,621,000 | 1,872,000 |
| NW | 8,665,000 | 6,276,000 | 1,263,000 |
| WC | 7,760,000 | 5,319,000 | 407,000 |
| Emp. | 117 | 114 | 104 |

DUNS 76-905-1616
## Toshiba Research Europe Ltd
(**Subsidiary of:** Toshiba Corporation)
32 Queen Square, Bristol, Avon BS1 4ND
**Tel:** 01179060700
**Web:** www.toshiba.eu
**Reg No:** 2519556 **VAT No:** 572986977
**Estd:** 1991 Private Limited Company
**Line of Business:** Research and laboratory based activities
**Issued Capital:** £1,032,000
**Directors:** Dr S Saito, S Baba, Professor R Cipolla, Professor I J Craddock, N Hashimoto, Dr N Nishida, Dr H Asai
**Co. Secretary:** Yukio Inoue
**Responsibilities**
**Senior:** Junichi Ishikawa *(Manager)*, Mutsumu Serizawa *(Research & Development)*, Akira Sudo *(Manager)*, Shuichi Uchikoga *(Chief Executive)*
**Admin:** Carol Meldrun *(Administrator)*
**Operations:** Mutsumu Serizawa *(Research & Development)*
**Engineering:** Saraansh Dave *(Research Engineer)*, Sedat Gorumus *(Principal R&D Engineer)*
**US SIC:** 7391 **UK SIC:** 94000
**Auditors:** Arthur Andersen

| | 31-03-14 | 31-03-13 | 31-03-12 |
|---|---|---|---|
| TO | 10,982,548 | 10,363,266 | 10,060,762 |
| P/L | 215,048 | 352,536 | 218,975 |
| NW | 2,146,163 | 2,156,122 | 2,480,228 |
| WC | 2,355,923 | 2,142,857 | 2,749,967 |
| Emp. | 80 | 77 | 75 |

DUNS 22-105-4419 **Imp**
## Toshiba Tec U.K. Imaging Systems Ltd
(**Subsidiary of:** Toshiba Corporation)
Abbey Cloisters, Abbey Green, Chertsey, Surrey KT16 8RB
**Tel:** 08432244944 **Fax:** 0843 3512024
**Web:** www.imaging.toshiba.co.uk
**Reg No:** 4124726 **Estd:** 2001 Private Limited Company
**Line of Business:** Manufacture of other electrical equipment not elsewhere classified
**Issued Capital:** £21,717,000
**Directors:** K Kawaguchi, Y Nozawa, T Yanaga, A N Sheppard
**Co. Secretary:** Martin Langridge
**Responsibilities**
**Senior:** Steve Hewson *(Marketing Director)*, Toshifumi Matsumoto *(Manager)*
**Marketing:** Steve Hewson *(Marketing Director)*
**Branches:** Toshiba Tec U.k. Imaging Systems Ltd, 7 Mark Road, The Progression Centre, Hemel Hempstead, Hertfordshire HP2 7DW
**US SIC:** 3629, 7699
**UK SIC:** 34350, 67303
**Auditors:** KPMG LLP

| | 31-03-14 | 31-03-13 | 31-03-12 |
|---|---|---|---|
| TO | 50,466,000 | 48,624,000 | 47,361,000 |
| P/L | 2,083,000 | 1,520,000 | 1,267,000 |
| NW | 12,525,000 | 9,677,000 | 6,884,000 |
| WC | 14,821,000 | 8,997,000 | 7,008,000 |
| Emp. | 262 | 264 | 268 |

DUNS 50-541-9267 **Imp**
## T.O.T. Shirts Ltd
Unit 13a, Banksia Road, London N18 3BF
**Web:** www.totshirts.co.uk
**Reg No:** 2496239 **VAT No:** 439945109
**Estd:** 1985 Private Limited Company
**Line of Business:** Screen printers
**Issued Capital:** £100
**Principals:** P T Joyce *(Managing)*, D N Smith
**Co. Secretary:** Ms Elizabeth Joyce
**Responsibilities**
**Marketing:** Pauline Whiskin *(Sales & Marketing Manager)*
**Sales:** Pauline Whiskin *(Sales & Marketing Manager)*
**IT:** M Stoughton *(IT Manager)*
**US SIC:** 2752 **UK SIC:** 47544

| | 31-01-14 | 31-01-13 | 31-01-12 |
|---|---|---|---|
| TA | 1,682,543 | 2,021,286 | 1,505,942 |
| NW | 1,180,240 | 1,132,896 | 789,389 |
| WC | 1,070,437 | 975,946 | 621,207 |

DUNS 77-261-9383
## Total Access (Uk) Ltd
(**Subsidiary of:** Arco Ltd)
Unit 5b, Raleigh Hall Industrial Estate, Stafford, Staffordshire ST21 6JL
**Tel:** 01785-850333 **Fax:** 01785850339
**Web:** www.totalaccess.co.uk
**Reg No:** 2712780 **Estd:** 1992 Private Limited Company

**Line of Business:** Other business activities not elsewhere classified
**Issued Capital:** £1,000
**Directors:** Ms C J Reynolds, N Jowsey, T G Martin, B J Lawrie, G B Haughton, D Evison
**Co. Secretary:** Jonathan Barrett
**Responsibilities**
**Senior:** Andrew Dack (Manager), Catherine Needham (Manager)
**US SIC:** 7399 **UK SIC:** 83954
**Auditors:** Dean Statham LLP

|    | 31-12-13 | 31-12-12 | 31-12-11 |
|----|----------|----------|----------|
| TA | 2,631,040 | 2,434,242 | 2,683,240 |
| NW | 1,137,303 | 1,129,426 | 1,123,616 |
| WC | 815,008 | 810,312 | 830,574 |

DUNS 34-640-5645    **Imp**
## Total Aircraft Product Support (Holdings) Ltd
Westley House, Jenner Road, Crawley, West Sussex RH10 9GA
**Tel:** 01293516651 **Fax:** 01293522759
**Web:** www.aerotron.co.uk
**Reg No:** 5446411 **Estd:** 2005 Private Limited Company
**Line of Business:** Airlines
**Export Sales:** £54,561,079
**Trading Style:** Aerotron
**Issued Capital:** £333
**Directors:** R J Wilson, G W Mashlan, M P Westley, N A Westley, K Goodall, A M Westley
**Co. Secretary:** Mrs Jacqueline Westley
**US SIC:** 4511 **UK SIC:** 75000

|      | 31-12-13 | 31-12-12 | 31-12-11 |
|------|----------|----------|----------|
| TO   | 68,789,661 | 60,263,280 | 59,773,570 |
| P/L  | 6,704,947 | 7,018,198 | 4,685,885 |
| NW   | 19,164,639 | 15,237,862 | 10,666,505 |
| WC   | 5,260,608 | 5,643,357 | 3,179,424 |
| Emp. | 55 | 47 | 44 |

DUNS 42-466-4766    **Imp**
## Total Care & Support Ltd
Unit 28, Time Technology Park, Blackburn Road, Burnley, Lancashire BB12 7TW
**Tel:** 01282 214000
**Web:** www.totalcaresupport.com
**Reg No:** 4454150 **Estd:** 2002 Private Limited Company
**Line of Business:** Other business activities not elsewhere classified
**Issued Capital:** £1
**Director:** P A Walker
**Co. Secretary:** Elite Logo Company Limited
**US SIC:** 7399 **UK SIC:** 83954
**Auditors:** PM&M Solutions for Business LLP

|    | 30-06-13 | 30-06-12 | 30-06-11 |
|----|----------|----------|----------|
| TA | 2,328,210 | 1,108,138 | 1,520,055 |
| NW | 798,082 | 725,909 | 138,639 |
| WC | 798,082 | 725,909 | 138,639 |

DUNS 73-699-3689    **Imp**
## Total Computer Networks Ltd
1 Brooklands Court, Kettering, Northamptonshire NN15 6FD
**Tel:** 08456470000 **Fax:** 01604-780227
**Web:** http://totalcomputers.co.uk
**Reg No:** 4958126 **Estd:** 2003 Private Limited Company
**Line of Business:** Wholesale of computers, computer peripheral equipment and software
**Export Sales:** £3,174,045
**Issued Capital:** £200
**Director:** A D Groom
**Co. Secretary:** Paul Jones
**US SIC:** 5081, 7379
**UK SIC:** 61490, 83940
**Auditors:** Grant Thornton UK LLP

|      | 31-12-13 | 31-12-12 | 31-12-11 |
|------|----------|----------|----------|
| TO   | 30,653,103 | 20,278,389 | 16,596,003 |
| P/L  | 1,040,581 | 528,960 | 729,823 |
| NW   | 842,890 | 664,774 | 599,945 |
| WC   | 679,271 | 496,730 | 456,707 |
| Emp. | 50 | 34 | N/A |

DUNS 21-611-4517
## Total Dental Care
64 Pencester Road, Dover, Kent CT16 1BW
**Web:** www.totaldentalcare.co.uk
**Estd:** 2002 Partnership
**Line of Business:** Dental practice activities
**Partners:** A Zybutz, P Gavin, M Zybutz
**Responsibilities**
**Senior:** Emma Collins (Practice Manager), PAUL GAVIN (Partner), MICHAEL ZYBUTZ (Partner), ANTHONY ZYBUTZ (Partner)
**Branches:** TOTAL DENTAL CARE: 92 Sandgate Road, Folkestone, CT20 2BE, KENT.
**US SIC:** 8021 **UK SIC:** 95400
**Employees:** 54

DUNS 21-091-0048    **Imp**
## Total E&P Uk Ltd
(**Subsidiary of:** Total Sa)
Crawpeel Road, Altens Industrial Estate, Aberdeen, Aberdeenshire AB12 3FG
**Tel:** 01224297000 **Fax:** 01224-298999
**Web:** www.totalgraduate.com
**Reg No:** 0811900 **VAT No:** 384540637
**Estd:** 1964 Private Limited Company
**Line of Business:** Service activities incidental to oil and gas extraction excluding surveying
**Issued Capital:** £2,500,000
**Directors:** P P De Martin De Vivies, P H Bousquet, A Pouthas
**Co. Secretary:** Andrew Powell
**Responsibilities**
**Senior:** Alastair Deer (Warehouse Manager), Philippe Guys (Director)
**Finance:** Jean Fournier (Financial Manager)
**Marketing:** Brian O'Neill (Sales & Marketing Manager)
**Sales:** Brian O'Neill (Sales & Marketing Manager)
**HR:** Rachel Tong (Training Manager)
**Health & Safety:** Ray Riddoch (Health & Safety Officer)
**Facilities:** Jacques Leroy (Maintenance Manager)
**Operations:** Ray Riddoch (Health & Safety Officer)
**Engineering:** Rod Cuthill (Head of Production), Alain Marchal (Engineering Manager)
**Branches:** Total E&p Uk Ltd, St. Fergus, Peterhead, Aberdeenshire AB42 3EP
**US SIC:** 1389 **UK SIC:** 13000
**Auditors:** Ernst & Young LLP
**Bankers:** HSBC Bank plc (40-01-13)
Following financial data are in thousands

|      | 31-12-13 | 31-12-12 | 31-12-11 |
|------|----------|----------|----------|
| TO   | 1,460,536 | 1,313,704 | 1,548,789 |
| P/L  | 474,126 | 532,676 | 629,335 |
| NW   | 88,549 | 33,492 | 299,221 |
| WC   | 71,620 | 1,328 | 168,463 |
| Emp. | 672 | 657 | 625 |

DUNS 23-278-3170
## Total Electrical Services Ltd
14 Tynwald Street, Douglas, Isle of Man IM1 1BG
**Tel:** 01624-664112
**Reg No:** 0097038M **VAT No:** 001823524
**Estd:** 1999 Private Limited Company
**Line of Business:** Installation of electrical wiring and fittings
**Directors:** J Towle, G Kelly
**Co. Secretary:** Miss Janine Towle
**US SIC:** 1731 **UK SIC:** 50300
**Employees:** 46

DUNS 49-141-0098    **Imp-Exp**
## Total Engine Support Ltd
(**Subsidiary of:** Tes Holdings Ltd)
Aviation House, Brocastle Avenue, Waterton Industrial Estate, Bridgend, Mid Glamorgan CF31 3XR
**Tel:** 01656 765200 **Fax:** 01656667987
**Web:** www.tes-uk.com
**Reg No:** 3110892 **VAT No:** 800552079
**Estd:** 1995 Private Limited Company
**Line of Business:** Aviation consultants
**Export Markets:** Europe; U S A
**Export Sales:** £3,775,000
**Issued Capital:** £10,000
**Directors:** K S Gibson, N W Louden
**Co. Secretary:** Mathew Burris
**US SIC:** 4582, 4712
**UK SIC:** 76400, 77002
**Auditors:** PricewaterhouseCoopers LLP
**Bankers:** Barclays Bank Plc (20-18-15)

|      | 31-12-13 | 31-12-12 | 31-12-11 |
|------|----------|----------|----------|
| TO   | 3,817,000 | 4,462,000 | 3,585,000 |
| P/L  | 962,000 | 673,000 | 669,000 |
| NW   | 2,937,000 | 2,299,000 | 1,934,000 |
| WC   | 8,243,000 | 7,475,000 | 10,424,000 |
| Emp. | 132 | 120 | 100 |

DUNS 34-649-8731
## Total Exotics Ltd
(**Subsidiary of:** Total Produce Plc)
Enterprise Way, Pinchbeck, Spalding, Lincolnshire PE11 3YR
**Tel:** 01775-716-800 **Fax:** 01775-716-808
**Web:** www.totalproduce.com
**Reg No:** 5455409 **VAT No:** 896567842
**Estd:** 2005 Private Limited Company
**Line of Business:** Food import and exporters and agents
**Issued Capital:** £1
**Directors:** A R Allmond, S Mulvenna, M C Owen, D L Punter
**Co. Secretary:** Mark Owen
**Responsibilities**
**Senior:** Ian Ball (Operations & Supply Chain Dire), Nigel West (Manager)
**US SIC:** 5149 **UK SIC:** 61700
**Auditors:** KPMG LLP

**Bankers:** National Westminster Bank Plc (56-00-05)

|    | 31-12-13 | 31-12-12 |
|----|----------|----------|
| TA | 1 | 1 |
| NW | 1 | 1 |

DUNS 56-994-1040    **Imp-Exp**
## Total Fabrications Ltd
(**Subsidiary of:** Total Solutions Holdings Ltd)
Unit 3/4 Kingston Industrial Estate, Birmingham, West Midlands B9 4EN
**Tel:** 0121-772-5234 **Fax:** 0121-772-5231
**Web:** www.trussing.com
**Reg No:** 2859297 **VAT No:** 650349935
**Estd:** 1995 Private Limited Company
**Line of Business:** Manufacture of metal structures and parts of structures
**Export Markets:** Far East, Singapore, China, Hong Kong and Europe
**Trading Style:** Total Solutions
**Issued Capital:** £1,000
**Directors:** W I Goh, C P Cronin, I R Hall, M H Thomas, Ms K L Cronin
**Co. Secretary:** Denis Willis
**Responsibilities**
**Health & Safety:** Chris Higgs (Health & Safety Officer)
**Facilities:** Brendon Cusack (Production Manager)
**US SIC:** 3441 **UK SIC:** 32042
**Auditors:** Heaver & Co
**Bankers:** Lloyds TSB Bank plc (30-00-06)

|    | 30-06-13 | 30-06-12 | 30-06-11 |
|----|----------|----------|----------|
| TA | 879,023 | 1,098,614 | 1,065,579 |
| NW | 167,308 | 243,247 | 181,036 |
| WC | 272,043 | 372,829 | 334,705 |

DUNS 21-683-4855
## Total Fitness Health Clubs Ltd
(**Subsidiary of:** Total Fitness Hc Holdings Ltd)
Wilmslow Way, Wilmslow, Cheshire SK9 3PE
**Tel:** 01614402615
**Web:** www.totalfitness.co.uk
**Reg No:** 7334974 **Estd:** 2010 Private Limited Company
**Line of Business:** Other sporting activities not elsewhere classified
**Issued Capital:** £1
**Directors:** R F Millman, A P Mellor, B J Davidson, W J Ley
**Responsibilities**
**Senior:** Richard Milmer (Joint Chairman)
**Finance:** Worrick Lee (Financial Director)
**IT:** Dean Rooney (Senior It Executive)
**HR:** Russel Teale (Hr)
**US SIC:** 7999 **UK SIC:** 97913
**Bankers:** Barclays Bank Plc (20-10-71)

|      | 31-12-13 | 31-12-12 | 31-12-11 |
|------|----------|----------|----------|
| TO   | 29,649,000 | 29,709,000 | 46,393,000 |
| P/L  | 1,688,000 | (157,000) | (4,693,000) |
| NW   | (10,682,000) | (14,481,000) | (15,475,000) |
| WC   | (20,722,000) | (23,895,000) | (25,001,000) |
| Emp. | 572 | 609 | 722 |

DUNS 21-809-3907
## Total Foodservice Solutions
Ribble Valley Enterprise Park, North Road, Barrow, Clitheroe, Lancashire BB7 9QZ
**Tel:** 01254828340
**Web:** www.totalfoodservice.co.uk
**Estd:** 2012
**Line of Business:** Catering food and drink suppliers
**Proprietor:** S Howarth
**US SIC:** 5149 **UK SIC:** 61700
**Employees:** 100

DUNS 73-804-8490
## Total Foodservice Solutions Ltd
Green Lea Mills, Huddersfield, West Yorkshire HD5 9XX
**Tel:** 01484558500 **Fax:** 08703669502
**Web:** www.totalfoodservice.com
**Reg No:** 5061181 **Estd:** 2004 Private Limited Company
**Line of Business:** Catering food and drink suppliers
**Issued Capital:** £64,583
**Directors:** R G Howarth, Mrs M E Moriarty Eames, S G Howarth, P Nowell, Mrs S J Howarth
**US SIC:** 5149 **UK SIC:** 61700
**Auditors:** Wheawill & Sudworth
**Bankers:** Barclays Bank Plc (20-43-04)

|      | 30-04-14 | 30-04-13 | 30-04-12 |
|------|----------|----------|----------|
| TO   | 16,767,838 | 16,197,688 | 14,936,009 |
| P/L  | 895,498 | 513,937 | 297,424 |
| NW   | 4,612,303 | 4,007,846 | 3,726,410 |
| WC   | 1,714,316 | 1,603,897 | 1,152,400 |
| Emp. | 114 | 118 | 113 |

DUNS 39-730-0294    **Imp**
## Total Gas & Power Ltd
(**Subsidiary of:** Total Sa)
10 Upper Bank Street, London E14 5BF
**Tel:** 020-7718-6000 **Fax:** 08705275213
**Web:** www.totalgp.com
**Reg No:** 2172239 **Estd:** 1987 Private Limited Company
**Line of Business:** Manufacture of gas
**Export Sales:** £9,102,833,000
**Trading Style:** Total Gp
**Issued Capital:** £145,800,000
**Directors:** P C Chauvain, F Agnes, J P Mateille, Y L Darricarrere, J G Shead, P R Lautard, D A Cranfield, G M Broggi
**Co. Secretary:** David Faragher
**Responsibilities**
**Senior:** Bernadette Baudier (Manager)
**Branches:** Total Gas & Power Ltd, Bridge Gate, 55-57 High Street, Redhill, Surrey RH1 1RX
**US SIC:** 4925, 4911, 4932
**UK SIC:** 25670, 16101, 16200
**Auditors:** Ernst & Young LLP
**Bankers:** HSBC Bank plc (40-06-02)
Following financial data are in thousands

|      | 31-12-13 | 31-12-12 | 31-12-11 |
|------|----------|----------|----------|
| TO   | 15,509,788 | 16,620,084 | 14,845,783 |
| P/L  | 218,519 | 260,200 | 165,655 |
| NW   | 1,181,187 | 1,097,664 | 970,101 |
| WC   | 1,184,029 | 1,099,860 | 967,471 |
| Emp. | 541 | 518 | 469 |

DUNS 23-825-1987
## Total Glass Ltd
(**Subsidiary of:** Total Glass Holdings Ltd)
The Total Complex, Overbrook Lane, Knowsley, Prescot, Merseyside L34 9FB
**Tel:** 01515492339 **Fax:** 01515460022
**Web:** www.totalglass.com
**Reg No:** 2465267 **Estd:** 2007 Private Limited Company
**Line of Business:** Manufacture of other builders ware of plastic
**Issued Capital:** £43,002
**Principals:** F O Deary (Managing), J Wetherall (Financial)
**Co. Secretary:** Mrs Georgina Deary
**US SIC:** 3334 **UK SIC:** 22451
**Auditors:** ERC Accountants & Business Advisers Ltd
**Bankers:** National Westminster Bank Plc (60-12-25)

|      | 31-01-14 | 31-01-13 | 31-01-12 |
|------|----------|----------|----------|
| TO   | 20,345,123 | 19,627,964 | 18,495,995 |
| P/L  | 1,007,977 | 1,116,616 | 873,472 |
| NW   | 2,924,265 | 2,238,907 | 1,745,208 |
| WC   | 1,604,516 | 1,020,696 | 512,846 |
| Emp. | 181 | 168 | 148 |

DUNS 21-820-5656    **Imp**
## Total Integrated Solutions Ltd
Hamilton Way, Oakham Business Park, Mansfield, Nottinghamshire NG18 5BU
**Tel:** 01623425800 **Fax:** 01623-650767
**Web:** www.tis.co.uk
**Reg No:** 0490674 **VAT No:** 117202710
**Estd:** 1947 Private Limited Company
**Line of Business:** Manufacturers of electronic equipment and components
**Trading Style:** Tis, Tis Systems
**Issued Capital:** £103,000
**Principals:** E W Cook (Managing), J J Twigg, C Lewis, P Cook
**Co. Secretary:** Ernest Cook
**Responsibilities**
**Senior:** Karl Hayman (Factory Manager)
**Finance:** Mark Wiggington (Project Manager - Key Accounts)
**Operations:** Roger Hands (Project Manager - Large Projec), Karl Hayman (Factory Manager), Terry Lazarri (Project Manager - Large Projec), Clive Pearce (Project Manager), Mark Wiggington (Project Manager - Key Accounts)
**Engineering:** Nick Cook (Engineering Manager), Dale Gregory (Technical Manager), Karl Hayman (Factory Manager), Morn Marwaha (Technical Manager - South Regi)
**US SIC:** 3679, 7393
**UK SIC:** 34542, 83954
**Auditors:** Smith Cooper LLP
**Bankers:** Lloyds TSB Bank plc (30-95-43)

|      | 31-12-13 | 31-12-12 | 31-12-11 |
|------|----------|----------|----------|
| TO   | 10,733,243 | 9,503,916 | 13,776,027 |
| P/L  | 440,136 | (1,043,998) | 82,358 |
| NW   | 1,640,327 | 1,028,920 | 2,036,261 |
| WC   | 464,379 | 936 | 1,059,535 |
| Emp. | 129 | 128 | 121 |

DUNS 23-038-6187
## Total Laminate Systems Ltd
East Dorset Trade Park Nimrod Way, Wimborne, Dorset BH21 7SH
**Tel:** 01202 877 600 **Fax:** 01202 861 638
**Web:** www.total-laminate.co.uk
**Reg No:** 2793768 **Estd:** 1973 Private Limited Company
**Line of Business:** Ancillary activities related to printing

**Issued Capital:** £2
**Directors:** C D Nunn, K A Lloyd
**Co. Secretary:** Ms Jacqueline Andrews
**Responsibilities**
**Senior:** Christopher Haycock *(Joint Managing Director)*
**HR:** Mandy Yates *(Human Resources Manager)*
**Engineering:** Kenny Woodhead *(Production Manager)*
**Branches:** TOTAL LAMINATE SYSTEMS LTD, Unit 4, Thame Forty, Jane Morbey Road, Thame, Oxon OX9 3RR,
**US SIC:** 3999, 1799
**UK SIC:** 49590, 50000
**Auditors:** Thomas Westcott
**Bankers:** HSBC Bank plc (40-46-11)

| | 31-03-14 | 31-03-13 | 31-03-12 |
|---|---|---|---|
| TO | 8,822,265 | 9,840,193 | 14,135,819 |
| P/L | 82,198 | (27,810) | 477,803 |
| NW | 2,058,894 | 1,991,597 | 2,020,699 |
| WC | 1,767,020 | 1,617,677 | 1,777,522 |
| Emp. | 82 | 91 | 95 |

DUNS 21-893-4503
## Total Lindsey Oil Refinery Ltd
**(Subsidiary of:** Total Sa)
Eastfield Road, Immingham, South Humberside DN40 3LW
**Tel:** 01469563300 **Fax:** 01469563766
**Web:** www.uk.total.com
**Reg No:** 0564599 **VAT No:** 127781060
**Estd:** 1956 Private Limited Company
**Line of Business:** Mineral oil refining
**Export Sales:** £839,335,000
**Issued Capital:** £5,650,000
**Directors:** J Beuckelaers, O J Alexandre, E B Stobseth-Brown
**Co. Secretary:** Ms Georgina Crowhurst
**Responsibilities**
**Senior:** Andrew Lashbrook *(Supply Officer)*, Fabien Mornand *(Director)*, Tom Schockaert *(Director)*
**Finance:** Steve Odlin *(Manager)*
**IT:** Fred Marsden *(IT Manager)*
**Purchasing:** Andrew Lashbrook *(Supply Officer)*
**US SIC:** 2911, 5171, 5052
**UK SIC:** 14010, 61200
**Auditors:** KPMG LLP
**Bankers:** HSBC Bank plc (40-22-24)
**Following financial data are in thousands**

| | 31-12-13 | 31-12-12 | 31-12-11 |
|---|---|---|---|
| TO | 3,748,422 | 16,348 | 44,845 |
| P/L | (88,460) | N/A | 9,316 |
| NW | 107,467 | 7,436 | (8,240) |
| WC | 23,103 | N/A | N/A |
| Emp. | 524 | 268 | 552 |

DUNS 23-992-9644
## Total Media Group Ltd
125 Kensington High Street, London W8 5SF
**Tel:** 020-7937-3793 **Fax:** 02079377015
**Web:** www.totalmedia.co.uk
**Reg No:** 3981236 **Estd:** 1982 Private Limited Company
**Line of Business:** Advertising agency services
**Export Sales:** £9,495,646
**Issued Capital:** £50,196
**Directors:** T J Laranjo, M J Drake, M G Sell, W H Rowe, D D'Mello, G L Sellers, Mrs C Saturnino, L R Brown
**Responsibilities**
**Senior:** James Cowing *(General Manager)*, Daniel D' Mello *(Director)*, Thu-Mai Oram *(International Director)*, Thu-Mai Sage *(International Director)*, Andy Travis *(Company Director)*
**Finance:** Daniel D' Mello *(Director)*, Rebecca Kuczer *(Finance Manager)*, Catherine Vaughan-Williams *(Credit Control Manager)*
**Marketing:** Madeleine Ware *(Marketing Manager)*
**IT:** Ged O'Loughlin *(IT Manager)*
**Operations:** Jacqui Purdy *(Operations Director)*
**Purchasing:** Pedro Martins *(Director - Media Planning & Bu)*
**Branches:** Total Media Group Ltd, 68 Oakfield Road, Bristol, Avon BS8 2BG
**US SIC:** 7319 **UK SIC:** 83800

| | 31-12-13 | 31-12-12 | 31-12-11 |
|---|---|---|---|
| TO | 59,004,278 | 53,405,876 | 59,979,713 |
| P/L | 1,199,353 | 524,677 | 257,066 |
| NW | 2,247,385 | 1,875,322 | 1,811,821 |
| WC | 2,087,091 | 1,644,024 | 1,560,501 |
| Emp. | 101 | 93 | 87 |

DUNS 21-158-2252
## Total Medication Management Services Ltd
**(Subsidiary of:** Hamsard 3149 Ltd)
Unit 3, Ardane Park, Phoenix Avenue, Pontefract, West Yorkshire WF7 6EP
**Tel:** 08452234494
**Web:** www.biodoseservices.co.uk
**Reg No:** 6856641 **Estd:** 2009 Private Limited Company
**Line of Business:** Drug stores outlets
**Issued Capital:** £12,459
**Directors:** I J Pearce, A J Scaife, M J Such
**US SIC:** 5912 **UK SIC:** 64300
**Bankers:** Barclays Bank Plc (20-00-00)

| | 31-01-14 | 31-01-13 | 31-01-12 |
|---|---|---|---|
| TO | 3,388,872 | 4,643,656 | 3,372,307 |
| P/L | (3,539,391) | (2,875,032) | (2,483,894) |
| NW | (8,835,404) | (5,870,088) | (3,591,694) |
| WC | (8,781,220) | (6,376,373) | (4,368,165) |
| Emp. | 73 | 110 | 71 |

DUNS 21-956-9915
## Total Orthodontics Ltd
16-18 Worthing Road, Horsham, West Sussex RH12 1SL
**Tel:** 01403-754545 **Fax:** 01403274743
**Web:** www.totalorthodontics.co.uk
**Reg No:** 6138535 **Estd:** 2007 Private Limited Company
**Line of Business:** Dentists
**Trading Style:** Total Orthodontics
**Issued Capital:** £101,830
**Directors:** Miss S L Cox-Horton, M Root, K R Ferguson, J P Costello, Dr G R Harris, K J Harvey, Dr R M Jones, R D George
**Co. Secretary:** David Morrison
**Responsibilities**
**Senior:** Lucy Craig *(Manager)*, Peter Doe *(Manager)*
**Marketing:** Alice Clarke *(Marketing Manager)*
**US SIC:** 8021 **UK SIC:** 95400

| | 30-04-14 | 30-04-13 | 30-04-12 |
|---|---|---|---|
| TO | 7,798,335 | 7,287,289 | 7,000,656 |
| P/L | 1,514,639 | 920,145 | 622,450 |
| NW | (486,398) | (721,075) | (1,465,530) |
| WC | (784,916) | (858,465) | (1,505,871) |
| Emp. | 94 | 96 | 86 |

DUNS 21-096-2801
## Total People Employee Benefit Trustee Ltd
Group House King Street, Middlewich, Cheshire CW10 9LZ
**Tel:** 01606-734000
**Web:** www.totalpeople.co.uk
**Reg No:** 6408721 **Estd:** 2007 Private Limited Company
**Line of Business:** Training services
**Issued Capital:** £100
**Director:** D Watts
**Co. Secretary:** Nigel Hartley
**US SIC:** 8299 **UK SIC:** 93300

| | 31-07-13 | 31-07-12 | 31-07-11 |
|---|---|---|---|
| TA | 2 | 2 | 2 |
| NW | 2 | 2 | 2 |

DUNS 21-913-0940
## Total Plastics Centers Ltd
Lower Road Trading Estate, Ledbury, Herefordshire HR8 2DJ
**Tel:** 01531633589
**Web:** www.davant.co.uk
**Reg No:** 6100967 **Estd:** 2007 Private Limited Company
**Line of Business:** Plumbers merchants
**Issued Capital:** £1,000
**Director:** D R Merrick
**Co. Secretary:** Ms Katherine Lewis
**Responsibilities**
**Senior:** Andy Burrows *(General Manager)*
**US SIC:** 5074 **UK SIC:** 61300

| | 28-02-14 | 28-02-13 | 29-02-12 |
|---|---|---|---|
| TA | 1,000 | 1,000 | 1,000 |
| NW | 1,000 | 1,000 | 1,000 |

DUNS 22-235-5369 **Imp**
## Total Polyfilm Ltd
**(Subsidiary of:** Total Polyfilm Group Ltd)
95 Seedlee Road, Walton Summit Centre, Bamber Bridge, Preston, Lancashire PR5 8AE
**Fax:** 01772 314276
**Web:** www.totalpolyfilm.com
**Reg No:** 4253528 **VAT No:** 776974653
**Estd:** 2001 Private Limited Company
**Line of Business:** Manufacture of plastic packing goods
**Export Sales:** £11,549,000
**Issued Capital:** £52,429,109
**Directors:** A L Murdoch, D W Dean, D M Dawson
**Co. Secretary:** Trevor Pilling
**Responsibilities**
**Engineering:** Adrian Power *(Production Manager)*
**Branches:** Total Polyfilm Ltd, Carterton Industrial Estate, Carterton, Oxfordshire OX18 3EZ
**US SIC:** 3079, 2752
**UK SIC:** 48360, 47544
**Auditors:** MacIntyre Hudson LLP
**Bankers:** Barclays Bank Plc (20-07-71)

| | 30-09-13 | 30-09-12 | 30-09-11 |
|---|---|---|---|
| TO | 50,715,000 | 54,689,000 | 53,638,000 |
| P/L | (657,000) | 467,000 | (413,000) |
| NW | 13,433,000 | 14,090,000 | 13,623,000 |
| WC | 10,811,000 | 11,431,000 | 10,867,000 |
| Emp. | 233 | 232 | 230 |

DUNS 21-584-4693
## Total Produce Gateshead
21-24 N E Fruit Market, Gateshead, Tyne and Wear NE11 0RE
**Tel:** 01914879441
**Web:** www.totalproduce.com
**Estd:** 2011 Proprietorship
**Line of Business:** Wholesalers of fruit and vegetable
**Proprietor:** M Pritchard
**US SIC:** 5148 **UK SIC:** 61700
**Employees:** 75

DUNS 51-636-0091
## Total Produce Ltd
**(Subsidiary of:** Total Produce Plc)
Enterprise Way, Spalding, Lincolnshire PE11 3YR
**Tel:** 01775 717660 **Fax:** 01775 717676
**Web:** www.totalproduce.com
**Reg No:** 5953208 **VAT No:** 896567842
**Estd:** 2006 Private Limited Company
**Line of Business:** Wholesale of fruit and vegetables
**Trading Style:** Total Stone Fruit, Total Import, Total Produce Food Service
**Issued Capital:** £108
**Directors:** Ms J F Devine, S M Webster, A R Allmond, D L Punter, M C Owen, S Mulvenna
**Co. Secretary:** Mark Owen
**Responsibilities**
**Senior:** Roger Alling *(Finance Director)*, Graham Broomhall *(Director)*
**Finance:** Roger Alling *(Finance Director)*
**Branches:** Total Produce Ltd, Wholesale Fruit & Flower Market, C16-C21, Nottingham, Nottinghamshire NG2 3JJ
**US SIC:** 5148 **UK SIC:** 61700
**Auditors:** KPMG LLP

| | 31-12-13 | 31-12-12 | 31-12-11 |
|---|---|---|---|
| TO | 82,439,000 | 78,565,000 | 78,466,000 |
| P/L | 1,467,000 | 1,345,000 | 1,199,000 |
| NW | 16,412,000 | 9,323,000 | 9,007,000 |
| WC | (397,000) | (330,000) | (1,783,000) |
| Emp. | 336 | 330 | 310 |

DUNS 23-607-6647
## Total Reinstatement Services Ltd
Po Box 21038, Stirling, Stirlingshire FK8 1XJ
**Tel:** 08452726999
**Web:** www.reinstatement.co.uk
**Reg No:** 0188039SC **VAT No:** 717159331
**Estd:** 1998 Private Limited Company
**Line of Business:** Other construction work involving special trades
**Issued Capital:** £2
**Director:** B C Gillies
**Co. Secretary:** Ms Karen Gillies
**US SIC:** 1799 **UK SIC:** 50000
**Auditors:** Harley Hepburn
**Bankers:** Bank Of Scotland (80-16-84)

| | 31-08-14 | 31-08-13 | 31-08-12 |
|---|---|---|---|
| TA | 2,070,943 | 1,648,398 | 2,192,034 |
| NW | 1,403,241 | 1,122,410 | 1,411,853 |
| WC | 1,233,482 | 986,025 | 1,260,077 |

DUNS 34-877-5222
## Total Support Services Ltd
Unit 20, Io Centre, Croydon, Surrey CR0 4QE
**Tel:** 02086804927 **Fax:** 02086889954
**Web:** www.tss-uk.com
**Reg No:** 2821660 **VAT No:** 627233549
**Estd:** 1993 Private Limited Company
**Line of Business:** Traditional cleaning activities
**Issued Capital:** £25,000
**Directors:** D Gostt, Ms S M Hadjidakis
**Responsibilities**
**Senior:** Katrina Gostt *(Manager)*, Anthony Hadjidakis *(Manager)*
**US SIC:** 7349, 7399
**UK SIC:** 92300, 83954
**Auditors:** Baxter & Co
**Bankers:** Lloyds TSB Bank plc (30-00-00)

| | 30-06-13 | 30-06-12 | 30-06-11 |
|---|---|---|---|
| TO | 13,963,860 | 11,977,447 | 10,183,231 |
| P/L | 479,510 | 258,105 | 203,224 |
| NW | 1,648,834 | 1,307,419 | 1,165,457 |
| WC | 1,359,183 | 991,807 | 898,779 |
| Emp. | 1,597 | 1,228 | 1,203 |

DUNS 22-608-3079
## Total Systems (Western) Ltd
**(Subsidiary of:** Total Systems Plc)
392-394 City Road, London EC1V 2QA
**Web:** www.totalsystems.co.uk
**Reg No:** 1487458 **Estd:** 1970 Private Limited Company
**Line of Business:** Other software consultancy and supply
**Trading Style:** Total Systems
**Issued Capital:** £1,000
**Managing Director:** T P Bourne
**Co. Secretary:** Granville Harris
**Responsibilities**
**Senior:** Arthur Weber *(Technical Director)*
**Operations:** Arthur Weber *(Technical Director)*
**US SIC:** 7379 **UK SIC:** 83940
**Bankers:** Lloyds TSB Bank plc (30-94-57)

| | 31-03-14 | 31-03-13 | 31-03-12 |
|---|---|---|---|
| NW | (35,510) | (35,510) | (35,510) |

DUNS 21-029-5929 **Imp-Exp**
## Total Uk Ltd
**(Subsidiary of:** Total Sa)
One Euston Square, 40 Melton Street, London NW1 2FD
**Tel:** 02073398000 **Fax:** 02073398033
**Web:** www.total.co.uk
**Reg No:** 0553535 **VAT No:** 232648173
**Estd:** 1997 Private Limited Company
**Line of Business:** Other treatment of petroleum products (excluding petrochemicals manufacture)
**Export Sales:** £755,000,000
**Issued Capital:** £43,000,000
**Directors:** D M Guyot, R J Laden, B Luc, Ms M Rodriguez Bartolome
**Co. Secretary:** Mrs Aminta Hall
**Responsibilities**
**Senior:** Didier Harel *(Manager)*
**Finance:** Eric Bozec *(Financial Director)*
**HR:** Leonne Newell *(Training Manager)*
**Health & Safety:** James Coull *(Health & Safety Officer)*
**Branches:** Total Uk Ltd, 1 Mill Hatch, Edinburgh Way, Harlow, Essex CM20 2DG
**US SIC:** 2999, 5171, 5052, 6711
**UK SIC:** 11150, 61200, 83962
**Auditors:** KPMG LLP
**Bankers:** HSBC Bank plc (40-06-02)
**Following financial data are in thousands**

| | 31-12-13 | 31-12-12 | 31-12-11 |
|---|---|---|---|
| TO | 2,264,000 | 5,828,000 | 6,108,000 |
| P/L | 70,000 | (79,000) | (21,000) |
| NW | 75,000 | 9,000 | (110,000) |
| WC | 67,000 | 100,000 | 247,000 |
| Emp. | 763 | 837 | 2,910 |

DUNS 39-803-2722 **Imp**
## Total Worldfresh Ltd
**(Subsidiary of:** Total Produce Plc)
19th Floor Tolworth Tower, Surbiton, Surrey KT6 7EL
**Tel:** 020-839-01133 **Fax:** 020-8390-9100
**Web:** www.totalworldfresh.com
**Reg No:** 2208873 **VAT No:** 896567842
**Estd:** 1987 Private Limited Company
**Line of Business:** Wholesale of fruit and vegetables
**Trading Style:** The Summer Fruit Co., Worldfresh, Total Cherry
**Issued Capital:** £4,270
**Directors:** M C Owen, S Mulvenna, A R Allmond, D L Punter
**Co. Secretary:** Mark Owen
**Responsibilities**
**Senior:** Graham Broomhall *(Director)*
**Branches:** Total Worldfresh Ltd, Tolworth Tower, Ewell Road, Surbiton, Surrey KT6 7EL
**US SIC:** 5148 **UK SIC:** 61700
**Auditors:** KPMG LLP
**Bankers:** National Westminster Bank Plc (56-00-05)

| | 31-12-13 | 31-12-12 | 31-12-11 |
|---|---|---|---|
| TO | 122,913,000 | 126,192,000 | 138,083,000 |
| P/L | 2,072,000 | 1,360,000 | 1,309,000 |
| NW | 3,875,000 | 5,035,000 | 4,194,000 |
| WC | 1,454,000 | 2,540,000 | 1,755,000 |
| Emp. | 167 | 150 | 161 |

DUNS 29-551-0002
## Totalglaze Windows Ltd
Unit M, Enterprise Road, Westwood Industrial Estate, Margate, Kent CT9 4JA
**Tel:** 01843-297555
**Web:** www.totalglaze.com
**Reg No:** 1917819 **Estd:** 1985 Private Limited Company
**Line of Business:** Double glazing installers
**Issued Capital:** £100
**Principals:** S Wrightson *(Managing)*, Mrs M E Wrightson *(Financial)*
**Responsibilities**
**Sales:** Stephen Letchford *(Senior Sales Executive)*
**US SIC:** 1721 **UK SIC:** 50400
**Auditors:** McCabe Ford Williams
**Bankers:** Lloyds TSB Bank plc (30-95-45)

| | 30-06-14 | 30-06-13 | 30-06-12 |
|---|---|---|---|
| TA | 866,153 | 924,187 | 921,191 |
| NW | 458,102 | 433,019 | 462,223 |
| WC | 169,057 | 146,059 | 167,452 |

DUNS 21-737-3477
## Totalis Solutions Ltd
Grove Street East, Belfast BT5 5GH
**Tel:** 02890454544
**Web:** www.totalissolutions.co.uk
**Reg No:** 0608299NI **Estd:** 2011 Private Limited Company
**Line of Business:** Management of real estate on a fee or contract basis
**Issued Capital:** £1

**Directors:** P G Woods, Mrs L Given, T R Fyfe
**US SIC:** 6531 **UK SIC:** 83400

| | 31-07-13 | 31-07-12 |
|---|---|---|
| TO | 6,929,119 | 6,947,439 |
| P/L | 1,096,839 | 904,916 |
| NW | 1,467,216 | 635,322 |
| WC | 1,349,447 | 681,511 |
| Emp. | 119 | N/A |

DUNS 21-758-6633
## Totaljobs Group Ltd
(**Subsidiary of:** Friede Springer Gmbh & Co. Kg)
Holden House, London W1T 1JU
**Tel:** 02077699200 **Fax:** 02075724201
**Web:** www.totaljobs.com
**Reg No:** 4269861 **Estd:** 2001 Private Limited Company
**Line of Business:** Employment and recruitment companies and consultants
**Issued Capital:** £1,000
**Directors:** M M Little, T Otte, R W Baumann, P P Wehrmann
**Responsibilities**
**Marketing:** Elin Ballsten *(Marketing Executive - Sales Co)*, Helen Guyver *(Marketing Manager)*, Jonathan Hedger *(Head of e-Commerce)*, Caterina Masso *(Senior Marketing Manager)*, Hannah Searle *(Senior Marketing Manager)*, Steve Warnham *(Marketing Executive - Sales Co)*
**Sales:** Elin Ballsten *(Marketing Executive - Sales Co)*, Kate Kavanagh *(Sales Manager)*, Steve Warnham *(Marketing Executive - Sales Co)*
**IT:** Nigel Sterndale *(Chief Information Officer)*, Edward Vassie *(Chief Information Officer)*
**HR:** Thomas Pink *(Human Resources Director)*
**US SIC:** 7361 **UK SIC:** 83954
**Auditors:** Ernst & Young LLP

| | 31-12-13 | 31-12-12 | 31-12-11 |
|---|---|---|---|
| TO | 48,418,502 | 45,522,445 | 41,077,186 |
| P/L | 8,848,008 | 7,250,475 | 6,075,235 |
| NW | 4,012,430 | (2,406,140) | (7,247,222) |
| WC | 260,222 | (6,337,314) | 4,542,133 |
| Emp. | 368 | 341 | 327 |

DUNS 77-928-1281
## Totally Inbound Ltd
(**Subsidiary of:** The Totally Group Holdings Ltd)
Ttg House, Flag Business Exchange, Vicarage Farm Road, Peterborough, Cambridgeshire PE1 5TP
**Tel:** 08451177000
**Web:** www.totally247.co.uk
**Reg No:** 5830907 **Estd:** 2006 Private Limited Company
**Line of Business:** Non-charitable social work activities without accommodation
**Issued Capital:** £100
**Directors:** Ms H Adams, D A Lazarus
**US SIC:** 8321 **UK SIC:** 96111

| | 31-12-13 | 31-12-12 | 31-12-11 |
|---|---|---|---|
| TA | 620,274 | 492,107 | 473,582 |
| NW | 54,964 | 51,791 | 529 |
| WC | 39,794 | 21,002 | (48,541) |

DUNS 21-848-9952
## Totally Wicked Ltd
Totally Wicked, Stancliffe Street, Blackburn, Lancashire BB2 2QR
**Tel:** 08456029661
**Web:** www.totallywicked-eliquid.com
**Reg No:** 8140744 **Estd:** 2012 Private Limited Company
**Line of Business:** Management activities of holding companies
**Export Sales:** £1,649,927
**Issued Capital:** £58,800
**Directors:** F B Cropper, B G Williamson, S J Mercer, R M Ingham
**US SIC:** 6711 **UK SIC:** 83962
**Bankers:** HSBC Bank plc (40-12-04)

| | 31-03-14 | 31-03-13 |
|---|---|---|
| TO | 22,624,959 | 15,728,237 |
| P/L | 7,747,117 | 5,191,680 |
| NW | 12,185,686 | 6,933,878 |
| WC | 6,037,898 | 4,156,430 |
| Emp. | 93 | 58 |

DUNS 73-258-6446 **Imp-Exp**
## Totalpost Services Plc
Total Postweigh International Ltd, Alston, Cumbria CA9 3TR
**Tel:** 01434381182 **Fax:** 08454900361
**Web:** www.postway.com
**Reg No:** 4532416 **VAT No:** 801483259
**Estd:** 2002 Public Limited Company
**Line of Business:** Mailing process machines and equipment
**Export Sales:** £1,045,613
**Issued Capital:** £50,002
**Principals:** D Hymers *(Managing)*, J W Leach, W J Wright, B P Qualey
**Co. Secretary:** Bruce Lenton
**Branches:** Totalpost Services Plc, Pure Ho, 64-66 Westwick St, Norwich, Norfolk NR2 4SZ
**US SIC:** 3579, 3829
**UK SIC:** 33010, 37100
**Auditors:** Christian Douglass LLP
**Bankers:** HSBC Bank plc (40-18-10)

| | 31-12-13 | 31-12-12 | 31-12-11 |
|---|---|---|---|
| TO | 4,046,980 | 3,007,190 | 2,172,505 |
| P/L | 55,647 | 240,386 | 136,696 |
| NW | 587,543 | 620,638 | 427,765 |
| WC | 278,716 | 418,049 | 393,945 |
| Emp. | 46 | 33 | 24 |

DUNS 23-714-1846
## Totalstay Ltd
(**Subsidiary of:** Totalstay Holdings Ltd)
8 Holmes Road, Kentish Town, London NW5 3AB
**Tel:** 02088-294-275 **Fax:** 08700-112-293
**Web:** www.totalstay.com
**Reg No:** 3709151 **Estd:** 1999 Private Limited Company
**Line of Business:** Tourist information offices
**Trading Style:** The Hotel Shop, Exclusively Hotels, Hotel Pronto
**Issued Capital:** £100,100
**Directors:** P Clements, N J Berger
**Responsibilities**
**Senior:** Tanya Clements *(Manager)*
**US SIC:** 7999, 7011
**UK SIC:** 97913, 66500
**Auditors:** Harris & Trotter LLP
**Bankers:** The Royal Bank Of Scotland Plc (16-08-05)

| | 31-12-13 | 31-01-13 | 31-12-12 |
|---|---|---|---|
| TO | 25,641,354 | 21,355,116 | 21,011,067 |
| P/L | 4,394,813 | 2,387,562 | 2,957,754 |
| NW | 4,960,650 | 4,750,216 | 2,961,975 |
| WC | 4,109,312 | 4,411,724 | 2,659,384 |
| Emp. | 190 | 164 | 70 |

DUNS 21-158-0725
## Tote Bookmakers Ltd
(**Subsidiary of:** Betfred Group Ltd)
Douglas House, Green Street, Wigan, Lancashire WN3 4DQ
**Tel:** 01925285000 **Fax:** 01942820040
**Web:** www.betfredcorporate.com
**Reg No:** 0852040 **Estd:** 1965 Private Limited Company
**Line of Business:** Gambling and betting activities
**Trading Style:** T/A Betfred Corporate
**Issued Capital:** £50,000
**Directors:** J K Haddock, F Done
**Co. Secretary:** Michael Hamilton
**Branches:** Tote Bookmakers Ltd, 115 Crankhall La, Wednesbury, West Midlands WS10 0EF
**US SIC:** 7999 **UK SIC:** 97913
**Auditors:** Ernst & Young LLP
**Bankers:** Lloyds TSB Bank plc (30-00-02)
**Following financial data are in thousands**

| | 31-03-13 | 25-03-12 | 31-03-11 |
|---|---|---|---|
| TO | 124,061 | 2,357,716 | 2,256,753 |
| P/L | 6,419 | (10,135) | 11,009 |
| NW | 33,642 | 15,428 | 9,453 |
| WC | 19,449 | (818) | (10,510) |
| Emp. | 1,910 | 1,900 | 1,939 |

DUNS 23-636-7462
## Totemic Ltd
(**Subsidiary of:** Totemic (2014) Holdings Ltd)
Kempton House, Dysart Road, Grantham, Lincolnshire NG31 7LE
**Tel:** 01476-539200 **Fax:** 01476839202
**Web:** www.totemic.co.uk
**Reg No:** 2789854 **VAT No:** 613746346
**Estd:** 1993 Private Limited Company
**Line of Business:** Other business activities not elsewhere classified
**Trading Style:** Payplan
**Issued Capital:** £39,000
**Directors:** Ms S Rann, J Fairhurst, D Jackman, Mrs R E Duffey, D M Chick, Mrs M A Stewart, A Taylor, M J Modder-Fitch
**Co. Secretary:** Mrs Halina Briggs
**Responsibilities**
**Senior:** Alice Olsson *(Director)*, Louise Payne *(Manager)*
**Sales:** Tony Marshall *(Sales Director)*
**IT:** Craig Fretwell *(IT Manager)*
**HR:** Jane Clack *(Training Coordinator)*
**US SIC:** 7399 **UK SIC:** 83954
**Auditors:** Mumby Heppenstall
**Bankers:** Barclays Bank Plc (20-50-21)

| | 31-12-13 | 31-12-12 | 31-12-11 |
|---|---|---|---|
| TO | 36,401,955 | 43,079,761 | 33,717,570 |
| P/L | 1,983,016 | 3,200,554 | 748,032 |
| NW | 4,459,659 | 9,050,505 | 6,605,906 |
| WC | 1,562,132 | 5,798,033 | 5,448,725 |
| Emp. | 914 | 903 | 960 |

DUNS 22-710-1771 **Imp**
## Totes Isotoner (U K) Ltd
(**Subsidiary of:** Indra Holdings Corp)
Eastman House, Radford Cresent, Billericay, Essex CM12 0DN
**Tel:** 01277-630277 **Fax:** 01277-630276
**Web:** www.totesuk.com
**Reg No:** 1530567 **VAT No:** 344788811
**Estd:** 1981 Private Limited Company
**Line of Business:** Fashion accessories
**Issued Capital:** £100,000
**Principals:** M Bate *(Managing)*, K Bowden, D Gernert
**Co. Secretary:** Karl Bowden
**Responsibilities**
**Senior:** Graham Elvidge *(Senior Finance Administrator)*
**Finance:** Graham Elvidge *(Senior Finance Administrator)*
**US SIC:** 5621 **UK SIC:** 64500
**Auditors:** PricewaterhouseCoopers
**Bankers:** Bankboston, Na (60-01-62)

| | 31-07-13 | 31-07-12 | 31-07-11 |
|---|---|---|---|
| TO | 15,596,000 | 13,965,000 | 11,767,000 |
| P/L | 629,000 | 511,000 | 308,000 |
| NW | 4,303,000 | 3,762,000 | 5,149,000 |
| WC | 3,652,000 | 2,297,000 | 2,289,000 |
| Emp. | 87 | 85 | 78 |

DUNS 73-783-6093
## Totfc Ltd
Unit 2a, Hownsgill Industrial Park, Knitsley Lane, Consett, County Durham DH8 7NU
**Tel:** 01207-585380 **Fax:** 01207-582915
**Web:** www.lookwhatwefound.co.uk
**Reg No:** 5040327 **Estd:** 2006 Private Limited Company
**Line of Business:** Manufacturers of food products
**Export Sales:** £41,009
**Issued Capital:** £4,964,595
**Directors:** S J Gray, W Reichenberger, D G Allison
**Co. Secretary:** Muckle Secretary Limited
**US SIC:** 2099 **UK SIC:** 42399
**Auditors:** Ryecroft Glenton
**Bankers:** Barclays Bank Plc (20-59-42)

| | 31-03-14 | 31-03-13 | 31-03-12 |
|---|---|---|---|
| TO | 7,793,596 | 9,042,046 | 8,786,648 |
| P/L | (2,540,367) | (1,361,417) | (2,974,774) |
| NW | 1,025,870 | (1,641,983) | (270,004) |
| WC | (594,725) | (3,306,112) | (477,581) |
| Emp. | 107 | 110 | 110 |

DUNS 21-606-4165
## Totnes Pavilion & Swimming Pool
Borough Park Road, Totnes, Devon TQ9 5XW
**Tel:** 01803862992
**Web:** www.toneleisure.com
**Estd:** 2011 Partnership
**Line of Business:** Leisure centres
**Partner:** K Teague
**US SIC:** 7999 **UK SIC:** 97913
**Employees:** 50

DUNS 21-160-4228
## Tottenham Hotspur Football & Athletic Co. Ltd
(**Subsidiary of:** Tottenham Hotspur Ltd)
748 High Road, London N17 0AP
**Tel:** 0283655056
**Web:** www.tottenhamhotspur.com
**Reg No:** 0057186 **Estd:** 1983 Private Limited Company
**Line of Business:** Operation of sports arenas and stadiums
**Trading Style:** Tottenham Hotspur Football Club
**Issued Capital:** £53,812
**Directors:** D P Levy, Ms D Cullen
**Co. Secretary:** Matthew Collecott
**Branches:** Tottenham Hotspur Football & Athletic Co. Ltd, Travelodge Hotels Ltd, 1-3 Park Lane, London E15 2JG
**US SIC:** 7941 **UK SIC:** 97911
**Auditors:** Deloitte & Touche
**Bankers:** HSBC Bank plc (40-05-20)

| | 30-06-13 | 30-06-12 | 30-06-11 |
|---|---|---|---|
| TO | 132,455,000 | 131,751,000 | 149,207,000 |
| P/L | (5,451,000) | (10,081,000) | (9,944,000) |
| NW | (53,562,000) | (29,375,000) | (67,829,000) |
| WC | (29,859,000) | (22,508,000) | (50,181,000) |
| Emp. | 306 | 281 | 261 |

DUNS 22-734-5485 **Imp-Exp**
## Tottenham Hotspur Ltd
Bill Nicholson Way, London N17 0AP
**Tel:** 02083655000
**Web:** www.tottenhamhotspur.com
**Reg No:** 1706358 **Estd:** 2012 Private Limited Company
**Line of Business:** Educational training
**Issued Capital:** £10,693,027
**Directors:** Mrs D Cullen, R A Robson, D P Levy, K V Watts, Sir K E Mills
**Co. Secretary:** Matthew Collecott
**Responsibilities**
**Senior:** David Lyall *(Centre Manager)*
**Marketing:** Jon Claxton *(Marketing Director)*
**Sales:** Aidan Mullally *(Business Development Manager)*
**IT:** Alex Haddow *(IT Manager)*
**HR:** Ann Vetere *(Personnel Manager)*
**Facilities:** Jon Babbs *(Stadium Manager)*
**Operations:** Andy Rogers *(Football Development Manager I)*
**Purchasing:** Denise Burgher *(Property Department Administra)*
**US SIC:** 8299, 5961
**UK SIC:** 93300, 65600
**Auditors:** Deloitte LLP
**Bankers:** Lloyds TSB Bank plc (30-00-00)

| | 30-06-13 | 30-06-12 | 30-06-11 |
|---|---|---|---|
| TO | 147,392,000 | 144,156,000 | 163,486,000 |
| P/L | 3,682,000 | (7,304,000) | 402,000 |
| NW | 7,287,000 | 20,905,000 | (17,687,000) |
| WC | (92,319,000) | (87,724,000) | (78,439,000) |
| Emp. | 368 | 341 | 315 |

DUNS 21-777-2903
## Tottington Primary School
Moorside Road, Tottington, Bury, Lancashire BL8 3HR
**Tel:** 01204886169
**Web:** www.tottingtonprimaryschool.org.uk
**Estd:** 1975 Proprietorship
**Line of Business:** Schools (local authority)
**Proprietor:** M Pinder
**US SIC:** 8211 **UK SIC:** 93200
**Employees:** 50

DUNS 55-067-3990
## Tottington Private Nursery School
The Old Police House, Kirklees Street, Tottington, Bury, Lancashire BL8 3NJ
**Tel:** 01204488416
**Web:** www.mulberrybush-nursery.co.uk
**Estd:** 1990 Partnership
**Line of Business:** Nursery schools
**Partners:** Mrs S Robinson, J Robinson
**US SIC:** 8211 **UK SIC:** 93200
**Bankers:** Barclays Bank Plc (20-16-08)
**Employees:** 48

DUNS 23-223-9905
## Totton College
Water Lane, Totton, Southampton, Hampshire SO40 3ZX
**Tel:** 02380874874
**Web:** www.totton.ac.uk
**Line of Business:** Colleges (higher education)
**Director:** M Bramwell
**Responsibilities**
**Senior:** Tony Malcolm *(Estates Manager)*
**Admin:** Kirsty Hayes *(Office Manager)*, Sheila Webb *(Office Manager)*
**HR:** Louise Fowle *(Head of Personnel)*
**Health & Safety:** Tony Malcolm *(Estates Manager)*
**Facilities:** Tony Malcolm *(Estates Manager)*
**Operations:** Kirsty Hayes *(Office Manager)*, Sheila Webb *(Office Manager)*
**Purchasing:** Kirsty Hayes *(Office Manager)*, Sheila Webb *(Office Manager)*
**Branches:** Totton College, Wade Park Farm, Salisbury Road, Romsey, Hampshire SO51 6AG
**US SIC:** 8221 **UK SIC:** 93100
**Employees:** 400

DUNS 42-468-5936 **Imp**
## Touch Bionics Plc
3 Ashwood Court, Oakbank Park Way, Livingston, West Lothian EH53 0TH
**Fax:** 01506439698
**Web:** www.touchbionics.com
**Reg No:** 0232512SC **VAT No:** 828488873
**Estd:** 2002 Public Limited Company
**Line of Business:** Manufacture of medical and surgical equipment and orthopaedic appliances
**Export Sales:** £11,938,638
**Issued Capital:** £30,090
**Directors:** Dr J Brown, Archangel Directors Limited, C S Mcgill, I H Stevens, Mrs J A Mcgregor, J A Grant
**Co. Secretary:** Mrs Jill Mcgregor
**US SIC:** 3841 **UK SIC:** 37201
**Auditors:** Ernst & Young LLP
**Bankers:** Bank Of Scotland (80-08-80)

| | 31-12-13 | 31-12-12 | 31-12-11 |
|---|---|---|---|
| TO | 12,307,874 | 10,018,774 | 8,567,990 |
| P/L | (93,684) | (969,485) | (2,570,422) |
| NW | 753,157 | 838,348 | 412,840 |
| WC | 1,295,485 | 1,316,873 | 1,255,913 |
| Emp. | 102 | 92 | 79 |

DUNS 57-746-6253
## Touch Local Ltd
(**Subsidiary of:** Web.Com Group Inc.)
Frontiers Group Ltd, London SE1 7TP
**Tel:** 020-7840-4300 **Fax:** 020-7840-4301
**Web:** www.touchlocal.com
**Reg No:** 2885607 **VAT No:** 896112114
**Estd:** 1995 Private Limited Company
**Line of Business:** Directory enquiries services
**Issued Capital:** £15,847
**Directors:** K M Carney, M P Mcclure, D L Brown
**Responsibilities**
**Senior:** Gary Dannatt *(Manager)*, Mark Livingstone *(Manager)*

**US SIC:** 7399 **UK SIC:** 83954
**Auditors:** KPMG LLP
**Bankers:** HSBC Bank plc (40-02-50)

| | 31-12-13 | 31-12-12 | 31-12-11 |
|---|---|---|---|
| TO | 5,061,000 | 6,534,000 | 8,972,000 |
| P/L | 510,000 | 1,222,000 | (627,000) |
| NW | (5,128,000) | (5,645,000) | (6,859,000) |
| WC | (2,989,000) | (3,411,000) | (5,414,000) |
| Emp. | 89 | 91 | 214 |

DUNS 73-467-0396 Imp-Exp
## Touchstar Technologies Ltd
(**Subsidiary of:** Belgravium Technologies P L C)
7 Commerce Way, Manchester M17 1HW
**Tel:** 0161-874-5050 **Fax:** 0161-874-5088
**Web:** www.fuel-logistics-it.com
**Reg No:** 4731086 **Estd:** 1986 Private Limited Company
**Line of Business:** Manufacturers of pcs
**Export Sales:** £2,308,000
**Issued Capital:** £100,000
**Directors:** C F Phillips, J P Kembery, M W Hardy
**Co. Secretary:** Michael Unwin
**Responsibilities**
**Purchasing:** Warren Shipman *(Purchasing Manager)*
**US SIC:** 3573, 7379
**UK SIC:** 33020, 83940
**Auditors:** Barlow Andrews
**Bankers:** Barclays Bank Plc (20-30-47)

| | 31-12-13 | 31-12-12 | 31-12-11 |
|---|---|---|---|
| TO | 7,522,000 | 6,448,000 | 8,330,000 |
| P/L | (312,000) | 596,000 | 1,017,000 |
| NW | 1,778,000 | 2,260,000 | 3,340,000 |
| WC | 2,368,000 | 3,073,000 | 4,009,000 |
| Emp. | 68 | 44 | 43 |

DUNS 50-706-8658
## Touchstone
Touchstone House, 2-4 Middleton Crescent, Leeds, West Yorkshire LS11 6JU
**Tel:** 01132-718277
**Web:** www.touchstonesupport.org.uk
**Estd:** 1991
**Line of Business:** Charities and charitable organisations
**Director:** J Murori
**Responsibilities**
**Senior:** David Jorysz *(Manager)*, Abdur Khan *(Manager)*, Sylvia Landells *(Manager)*, Edward Long *(Financial Director)*, Virginia Minogue *(Manager)*, Ramindar Singh *(Manager)*, Maria Trainer *(Manager)*
**Finance:** Edward Long *(Financial Director)*
**Marketing:** Edward Long *(Financial Director)*
**IT:** Edward Long *(Financial Director)*
**HR:** Kathryn Hart *(Human Resources Manager)*
**Facilities:** Edward Long *(Financial Director)*
**Purchasing:** Edward Long *(Financial Director)*
**US SIC:** 8699 **UK SIC:** 96902
**Employees:** 75

DUNS 23-538-5080
## Touchstone Group Plc
3rd Floor, 1 Triton Square, London NW1 3DX
**Web:** www.touchstone.co.uk
**Reg No:** 3537238 **VAT No:** 730671840
**Estd:** 1982 Public Limited Company
**Line of Business:** Other computer related activities
**Issued Capital:** £1,260,557
**Directors:** D R Thompson, K G Birch, C Butler
**Co. Secretary:** David Birch
**Responsibilities**
**Marketing:** Julien Davies *(Digital Campaign Manager)*, Natalie Edwards *(Marketing Director)*
**Sales:** Andes Loukianos *(Business Development Director)*
**Branches:** Touchstone Group Plc, Winchcombe House, Winchcombe Street, Cheltenham, Gloucestershire GL52 2NA
**US SIC:** 7379 **UK SIC:** 83940
**Auditors:** Baker Tilly UK Audit LLP
**Bankers:** National Westminster Bank Plc (60-04-24)

| | 31-03-14 | 31-03-13 | 31-03-12 |
|---|---|---|---|
| TO | 17,665,000 | 17,567,000 | 18,928,000 |
| P/L | 381,000 | 189,000 | 1,506,000 |
| NW | 2,396,000 | 5,008,000 | 6,034,000 |
| WC | 2,272,000 | 4,863,000 | 5,948,000 |
| Emp. | 127 | 120 | 128 |

DUNS 23-259-6155
## Touchstone Housing Association Ltd
Po Box 160, Coventry, West Midlands CV3 4HZ
**Tel:** 02476507100
**Web:** www.touchstone.org.uk
**Reg No:** 0017393IP **VAT No:** 584913800
**Estd:** 1966 Friendly Society
**Line of Business:** Property developers
**Trading Style:** Midland Heart
**Directors:** A Mottram, Mrs B Matthews, B Gray, R Thompson, Mrs H Atherton, M Ellis, W R Powell, S Loraine
**Responsibilities**
**Senior:** G Kellet *(Principal)*
**Marketing:** Ranjit Kang *(Marketing Manager)*
**US SIC:** 8699 **UK SIC:** 96902
**Auditors:** Kidsons Impey
**Bankers:** Barclays Bank Plc (20-97-78)
**Employees:** 237
**Turnover:** £35,587,000

DUNS 56-957-0948
## Touchstone Learning & Skills Ltd
(**Subsidiary of:** Babcock Education & Training Holdings Llp)
65 Scarisbrick New Road, Southport, Merseyside PR8 6LF
**Tel:** 01704502222 **Fax:** 01704-564030
**Reg No:** 2847388 **Estd:** 1993 Private Limited Company
**Line of Business:** Training services
**Trading Style:** Touchstone Group
**Issued Capital:** £2
**Directors:** F Martinelli, G D Leeming
**Co. Secretary:** Babcock Corporate Secretaries Li
**Branches:** Touchstone Learning & Skills Ltd, London House Pickford Street, Aldershot, Hampshire GU11 1TY
**US SIC:** 8299, 8249
**UK SIC:** 93300
**Auditors:** Tenon Audit Ltd
**Bankers:** National Westminster Bank Plc (01-06-45)

| | 31-03-14 | 31-03-13 | 31-03-12 |
|---|---|---|---|
| TA | 11,000 | 11,000 | 11,000 |
| P/L | N/A | N/A | (5,000) |

DUNS 21-580-0483
## Tough Construction Ltd
(**Subsidiary of:** Tough Civil Engineering Ltd)
60 Munro Place, Glasgow, Lanarkshire G13 2UW
**Tel:** 01419548015 **Fax:** 0141-950-1360
**Web:** www.tough-construction.com
**Reg No:** 0055889SC **VAT No:** 262190573
**Estd:** 1974 Private Limited Company
**Line of Business:** Civil engineers
**Issued Capital:** £5,000
**Directors:** R D Leishman, K Mackenzie
**Co. Secretary:** George Duncan
**Responsibilities**
**Senior:** Hugh Connor *(CEO, Managing Director)*, Ian Lumsden *(Manager)*
**US SIC:** 8911 **UK SIC:** 83701
**Auditors:** Bowers
**Bankers:** Clydesdale Bank Plc (82-69-02)

| | 31-07-13 | 31-07-12 | 31-07-12 |
|---|---|---|---|
| TO | 23,248,819 | 10,065,149 | 14,889,039 |
| P/L | (126,912) | 284,898 | (551,318) |
| NW | 4,558,897 | 4,663,776 | 4,422,244 |
| WC | 3,732,843 | 3,918,291 | 3,600,681 |
| Emp. | 215 | 182 | 138 |

DUNS 45-846-5283 Imp
## Toughglaze (U K) Ltd
Chandos Park Industrial Estate, London NW10 6NF
**Tel:** 020-8838-4400
**Web:** www.toughglaze.com
**Reg No:** 3193221 **Estd:** 1996 Private Limited Company
**Line of Business:** Glass (safety)
**Issued Capital:** £59,100
**Directors:** B K Varsani, A K Varsani
**Co. Secretary:** Vipul Vora
**Responsibilities**
**Sales:** Terry Woodfine *(Sales Director and IT Manager)*
**US SIC:** 3231 **UK SIC:** 24791
**Auditors:** The MAP Partnership
**Bankers:** National Westminster Bank Plc (60-12-17)

| | 31-05-13 | 31-05-12 | 31-05-11 |
|---|---|---|---|
| TO | 13,081,137 | 12,974,301 | 11,997,738 |
| P/L | 2,181,142 | 1,617,361 | 610,104 |
| NW | 743,506 | 1,340,237 | 162,678 |
| WC | (1,313,390) | (188,224) | (1,117,248) |
| Emp. | 111 | 106 | 111 |

DUNS 21-777-6134
## Toughrack
1 East Poultry Avenue, London EC1A 9PT
**Tel:** 02033278189
**Web:** www.toughrack.co.uk
**Estd:** 2011 Proprietorship
**Line of Business:** Computer systems and software (sales)
**Proprietor:** C Gilfoy
**Responsibilities**
**Senior:** Adam Froud *(Commercial Director)*
**US SIC:** 2599 **UK SIC:** 46720
**Employees:** 200

DUNS 51-618-2156
## Toureen Group Ltd
25 Cecil Road, Harrow, Middlesex HA3 5QY
**Web:** www.toureenmangan.co.uk
**Reg No:** 5898339 **Estd:** 2006 Private Limited Company
**Line of Business:** Holding and management company services.
**Issued Capital:** £1,020
**Directors:** D Nolan, D Nolan, N M Gibson
**Co. Secretary:** David Parker
**US SIC:** 6711, 7399
**UK SIC:** 83962, 83954
**Auditors:** Riordan O'Sullivan & Co
**Bankers:** Allied Irish Bank (gb) (23-84-81)

| | 31-07-13 | 31-07-12 | 31-07-11 |
|---|---|---|---|
| TO | 46,432,881 | 37,701,704 | 39,894,449 |
| P/L | 1,845,843 | 1,096,163 | 677,021 |
| NW | 3,585,045 | 2,805,679 | 2,086,008 |
| WC | 63,415 | 106,052 | 155,910 |
| Emp. | 114 | 101 | 104 |

DUNS 22-730-1256
## Tourmajor Ltd
(**Subsidiary of:** Thomas Cook Group Plc)
54 Kirkgate, Bradford, West Yorkshire BD1 1QT
**Tel:** 08443357104 **Fax:** 01274387773
**Web:** www.thomascook.com
**Reg No:** 1450464 **VAT No:** 340088380
**Estd:** 1979 Private Limited Company
**Line of Business:** Tourist information offices
**Trading Style:** Club 18-30 Sunset, Neilson Thomas Cook, J M C, Holiday Essentials
**Issued Capital:** £21,352,998
**Directors:** P A Hemingway, Thomas Cook Group Management Ser
**Co. Secretary:** Ms Shirley Bradley
**Responsibilities**
**Senior:** Manny Fontella Nueva *(CEO, Managing Director)*, Simon Speding *(Manager)*
**Branches:** Tourmajor Ltd, Main Terminal, London International Airport, Luton, Bedfordshire LU2 9LU
**US SIC:** 7999 **UK SIC:** 97913
**Bankers:** Banco Bilbao-Vizcaya (23-59-11)

| | 30-09-13 | 30-09-12 | 30-09-11 |
|---|---|---|---|
| TA | 343,533,000 | 346,338,000 | 346,338,000 |
| P/L | (3,810,000) | N/A | N/A |
| NW | 307,068,000 | 310,878,000 | 310,878,000 |
| WC | 249,881,000 | 250,540,000 | 250,540,000 |

DUNS 73-778-1752 Imp
## Tourvest Duty Free (U K) Ltd
(**Subsidiary of:** Tourism Investment Corporation Ltd)
Suite 6f Gatwick House, Peeks Brook Lane, Horley, Surrey RH6 9ST
**Tel:** 01293772711 **Fax:** 01293773018
**Web:** www.tourvest.co.za
**Reg No:** 5034988 **Estd:** 2004 Private Limited Company
**Line of Business:** Airline related services
**Issued Capital:** £1,250,000
**Directors:** Ms M Delaney, C Jones, Mrs M J Van Der Schyff
**Co. Secretary:** Ms Margaret Delaney
**Responsibilities**
**Senior:** Paul Els *(Manager)*, Selwyn Grimsley *(CEO)*, Patrick Knibbs *(Sec)*, Adrian Stratter *(General Manager)*, John Von Gottberg *(Manager)*
**US SIC:** 5963 **UK SIC:** 65600
**Auditors:** Deloitte LLP
**Bankers:** Barclays Bank Plc (20-03-80)

| | 31-08-13 | 31-08-12 | 31-08-11 |
|---|---|---|---|
| TO | 55,287,848 | 45,987,363 | 16,269,345 |
| P/L | 162,214 | (988,009) | 140,477 |
| NW | 800,474 | 703,611 | 1,752,251 |
| WC | 4,154,135 | 1,963,729 | 841,442 |
| Emp. | 46 | 36 | 21 |

DUNS 34-605-7680
## The Towel Rail Ltd
Crimple Court Hornbeam Business Park, Harrogate, North Yorkshire HG2 8QT
**Tel:** 01429234911 **Fax:** 01423815536
**Web:** www.towelradiator.co.uk
**Reg No:** 2747149 **VAT No:** 567022742
**Estd:** 1992 Private Limited Company
**Line of Business:** Linen retail
**Trading Style:** The Yorkshire Linen Co
**Issued Capital:** £1,000
**Principals:** R L Leventhal *(Managing)*, Ms L Shreeve *(Financial)*, Ms K Leventhal, S J Worrall
**Co. Secretary:** Ross Leventhal
**Branches:** The Towel Rail Ltd, 3 Washington Centre, The Galleries, Washington, Tyne and Wear NE38 7SA
**US SIC:** 5714, 5699
**UK SIC:** 64700, 64500
**Auditors:** Tony Teale & Co
**Bankers:** Lloyds TSB Bank plc (30-93-91)

| | 31-03-14 | 31-03-13 | 31-03-12 |
|---|---|---|---|
| TO | 12,881,596 | 13,298,253 | N/A |
| P/L | 601,983 | 465,128 | 594,699 |
| NW | 4,653,330 | 4,195,201 | 3,731,757 |
| WC | 3,664,039 | 3,206,614 | 2,986,821 |
| Emp. | 256 | 274 | 266 |

DUNS 42-331-9172
## Towens of Weston Ltd
(**Subsidiary of:** Twinmile Ltd)
Twrc Warne Road, Weston-Super-Mare, Avon BS23 3YD
**Tel:** 01934613598
**Web:** www.towens.co.uk
**Reg No:** 4319664 **VAT No:** 130544113
**Estd:** 2001 Private Limited Company
**Line of Business:** Waste disposal
**Issued Capital:** £901
**Directors:** S M Telling, A F Towens, N A Towens, J A Telling
**Co. Secretary:** Graham Carrington
**US SIC:** 4953 **UK SIC:** 92110
**Auditors:** Lawes & Co UK Ltd

| | 30-09-13 | 30-09-12 | 30-09-11 |
|---|---|---|---|
| TA | 1,104,335 | 904,751 | 667,592 |
| NW | 491,392 | 321,632 | 253,053 |
| WC | 414,066 | 237,783 | 182,699 |

DUNS 22-250-4560
## Tower & Access Hire Ltd
Bridgelands Farm, Cowlinge, Newmarket, Suffolk CB8 9HN
**Tel:** 01638-500666 **Fax:** 01638-500077
**Web:** www.towerandaccess.co.uk
**Reg No:** 4268429 **VAT No:** 777027606
**Estd:** 2004 Private Limited Company
**Line of Business:** Scaffolds and work platform erectors
**Issued Capital:** £10,000
**Director:** G Jarman
**Co. Secretary:** Ms Phillippa Jarman
**Responsibilities**
**Senior:** Glynn Jarman *(Proprietor)*
**US SIC:** 7394 **UK SIC:** 84000
**Bankers:** Lloyds TSB Bank plc (30-91-49)

| | 31-10-13 | 31-10-12 | 31-10-11 |
|---|---|---|---|
| TA | 765,287 | 959,474 | 879,767 |
| NW | 370,831 | 387,642 | 387,168 |
| WC | 187,671 | 190,253 | 195,129 |

DUNS 23-703-4702
## Tower Bakery Ltd
Shore Road, Perth, Perthshire PH2 8BH
**Tel:** 01738563333
**Web:** www.towerbakery.co.uk
**Reg No:** 0192714SC **Estd:** 1981 Private Limited Company
**Line of Business:** Bakers and confectioners supplies
**Issued Capital:** £2
**Director:** A Mckinnon
**Co. Secretary:** Ms Angela Mckinnon
**Responsibilities**
**Senior:** Angela McKinnien *(Partner)*
**Marketing:** Angela McKinnien *(Partner)*
**Sales:** Angela McKinnien *(Partner)*
**HR:** Angela McKinnien *(Partner)*
**Health & Safety:** Juliette Lane *(Quality Manager)*
**Purchasing:** Angela McKinnien *(Partner)*
**Branches:** Tower Bakery Ltd, Main Street, Perth, Perthshire PH2 9PL
**US SIC:** 5462 **UK SIC:** 64100

| | 31-10-13 | 31-10-12 | 31-10-11 |
|---|---|---|---|
| TA | 45,808 | 55,242 | 20,132 |
| NW | 45,347 | 45,014 | 15,728 |
| WC | 45,347 | 45,014 | 15,728 |

DUNS 53-614-7127
## Tower Business Communications Ltd
(**Subsidiary of:** Tower Publishing Ltd)
40 Compton Street, London EC1V 0BD
**Tel:** 02070140330 **Fax:** 02070140301
**Web:** www.theneweconomy.com
**Reg No:** 3419925 **Estd:** 1997 Private Limited Company
**Line of Business:** Newspapers publishing
**Trading Style:** Estates Review, The New Economy
**Issued Capital:** £100
**Director:** H J Angel
**US SIC:** 2711 **UK SIC:** 47512
**Auditors:** Chris Syrimis & Co
**Bankers:** Barclays Bank Plc (20-03-80)

| | 31-08-13 | 31-08-12 | 31-08-11 |
|---|---|---|---|
| TA | 2,068,659 | 1,840,200 | 2,010,505 |
| NW | 1,030,110 | 927,545 | 925,864 |
| WC | 912,793 | 820,496 | 845,909 |

DUNS 33-948-1459
## Tower Cleaning Services
Burcott Grange, Soulbury Road, Burcott, Leighton Buzzard, Bedfordshire LU7 0JU
**Tel:** 01296-681497
**Web:** www.towercleaning.biz
**Estd:** 1976 Partnership
**Line of Business:** Cleaning contracting commercial
**Partners:** M Foot, Mrs S Foot
**US SIC:** 7349 **UK SIC:** 92300
**Bankers:** Lloyds TSB Bank plc (30-92-77)
**Employees:** 90

DUNS 34-936-2728
## Tower Crane Asset Management Holdings Ltd
Unit 3 Airfield Industrial Estat, Shipdham, Thetford, Norfolk IP25 7SD
**Tel:** 01362-821048 **Fax:** 01362821233
**Web:** www.falconcranes.co.uk
**Reg No:** 5732617 **Estd:** 2006 Private Limited Company
**Line of Business:** Crane sales, service and hire
**Export Sales:** £223,263
**Issued Capital:** £225,000
**Directors:** Mrs B I Brown, S Paxman, I Gray, P Gale, D C Genge
**Co. Secretary:** Barabra Brown
**US SIC:** 7394 **UK SIC:** 84000

| | 31-12-13 | 31-12-12 | 31-12-11 |
|---|---|---|---|
| TO | 21,224,151 | 13,465,062 | 9,186,566 |
| P/L | 1,208,329 | 493,745 | 116,788 |
| NW | 1,433,143 | 401,871 | (557,257) |
| WC | (3,158,862) | (3,212,529) | (4,059,994) |
| Emp. | 210 | 178 | 111 |

DUNS 34-606-5709
## Tower Group Services Ltd
15 Osidge Lane, London N14 5JD
**Tel:** 02083613636 **Fax:** 020-8368-4626
**Web:** www.towergroup.com
**Reg No:** 2747940 **VAT No:** 625793904
**Estd:** 1992 Private Limited Company
**Line of Business:** Cleaning activities not elsewhere classified
**Issued Capital:** £100,000
**Director:** C S Economou
**Responsibilities**
**Senior:** Panayiota Economou (Manager), Sandra Winborn (Manager)
**Finance:** Panayiota Economou (Manager)
**Admin:** Sandra Winborn (Manager)
**US SIC:** 7349 **UK SIC:** 92300
**Auditors:** Moore Stephens

| | 31-03-14 | 31-03-13 | 31-03-12 |
|---|---|---|---|
| TA | 211,183 | 186,372 | 207,423 |
| NW | 26,031 | 19,548 | 40,635 |
| WC | 26,031 | 19,223 | 39,150 |

DUNS 23-131-5144
## Tower Hamlets
Town Hall, 5 Clove Crescent, London E14 2BG
**Web:** www.towerhamlets.gov.uk
**Line of Business:** Local government
**Director:** E Kelly
**Responsibilities**
**Admin:** Jasmine Sargeant (Office Manager)
**Health & Safety:** Steve Crawley (Health & Safety Director)
**Operations:** Steve Crawley (Health & Safety Director)
**Branches:** Tower Hamlets, The Larches, Grove Hill, Stansted, Essex CM24 8SR
**US SIC:** 9121 **UK SIC:** 91110
**Employees:** 3,000

DUNS 23-226-7567
## Tower Hamlets College
112 Poplar High Street, London E14 0AF
**Tel:** 02075107510
**Web:** www.tower.ac.uk
**Estd:** 1990
**Line of Business:** Further education schools and colleges
**Director:** Mrs A Zeri
**Responsibilities**
**Senior:** Gerry Mcdonald (Principal)
**Branches:** Tower Hamlets College, Arbour Square, London E1 0PT
**US SIC:** 8221 **UK SIC:** 93100
**Bankers:** National Westminster Bank Plc (51-50-03)
**Employees:** 600

DUNS 23-597-6292
## Tower Hamlets Community Housing Ltd
285 Commercial Road, Whitechapel, London E1 2PS
**Tel:** 02077803070
**Web:** www.thch.org
**Reg No:** 3595080 **Estd:** 1998 Private Limited Company
**Line of Business:** Other letting of own property
**Directors:** M Ali, G Gibbs, C E Moran, Ms L Ingham, K Beech, R Kloss, R G Booth, S Madewell
**Co. Secretary:** Michael Tyrrell
**Responsibilities**
**Senior:** Helal Abbas (Board Member), Kabir Ahmed (Board Member), Mosabbir Ali (Board Member), Anne Ambrose (Vice Chair), Christina Chesterman (Board Member), Giancario Gibbs (Board Member), Dionne Harrison (Board Member), Sirajul Islam (Board Member), John Lau (Board Member), Michael Meir (Board Member), Helal Uddin (Board Member)

**Finance:** Esther Kamaray (Financial Officer), David Mathers (Management Accountant), Vinod Sabharwal (Financial Controller)
**Admin:** Pav Sehmby (Pa to CEO/ Finance Director)
**Facilities:** Peter Exton (Director of Assets)
**Branches:** Tower Hamlets Community Housing Ltd, 54 Bigland Street, London E1 2ND
**US SIC:** 6519 **UK SIC:** 85000
**Auditors:** Smith & Williamson
**Bankers:** The Co-Operative Bank Plc (08-02-28)

| | 31-03-14 | 31-03-13 | 31-03-12 |
|---|---|---|---|
| TO | 25,965,000 | 35,147,000 | 15,490,000 |
| P/L | 6,523,000 | 5,923,000 | (687,000) |
| NW | 22,168,000 | 15,345,000 | 10,104,000 |
| WC | 2,255,000 | 2,964,000 | 3,395,000 |
| Emp. | 102 | 101 | 102 |

DUNS 21-584-1533
## Tower Hamlets London Borough Councils
Mulberry Place, 5 Clove Crescent, London E14 2BG
**Tel:** 02073645012
**Web:** www.towerhamlets.gov.uk
**Estd:** 2011
**Line of Business:** General (overall) public service activities
**Responsibilities**
**Senior:** Kevin Collins (Chief Executive), Stephen Halsey (Manager)
**US SIC:** 9121 **UK SIC:** 91110
**Employees:** 600

DUNS 39-969-6012
## The Tower Hotel (London) Ltd
2 The Calls, Leeds, West Yorkshire LS2 7JU
**Tel:** 01132439111 **Fax:** 0870-333-9299
**Web:** www.guoman.com
**Reg No:** 0466069 **Estd:** 2002 Private Limited Company
**Line of Business:** Hotels
**Issued Capital:** £80,000
**Directors:** K M Ho, M Ostridge, N Gallagher, M B Denoma
**Co. Secretary:** Ms Fiona Keddie
**Responsibilities**
**Senior:** Jocelyn Ng (Manager)
**US SIC:** 7011 **UK SIC:** 66500
**Auditors:** PricewaterhouseCoopers

| | 30-06-13 | 30-06-12 | 03-06-11 |
|---|---|---|---|
| TO | 35,990,000 | 34,408,000 | 35,773,000 |
| P/L | 3,387,000 | 1,658,000 | 2,816,000 |
| NW | 152,042,000 | 147,373,000 | 145,005,000 |
| WC | (66,096,000) | (70,510,000) | (73,648,000) |
| Emp. | 212 | 213 | 244 |

DUNS 21-765-2877
## Tower House Medical Centre
Nailsea Family Practice Tower House, Medical Centre, Nailsea, Bristol, Avon BS48 2XX
**Tel:** 01275866777
**Web:** www.towerhouse.nhs.uk
**Estd:** 2011
**Line of Business:** Doctors
**Responsibilities**
**Senior:** Edward Mann (General Practitioner)
**US SIC:** 8011 **UK SIC:** 95300
**Employees:** 50

DUNS 38-578-1455
## The Tower Project
45-55 White Horse Road, Stepney, London E1 0ND
**Tel:** 02077909085 **Fax:** 020-7791-3085
**Web:** www.towerproject.org.uk
**Reg No:** 3338883 **Estd:** 1993 Private Limited Company
**Line of Business:** Non-charitable social work activities with accommodation
**Trading Style:** Tower Project Job Enterprise Training
**Directors:** D R Barnett, Mrs A O David Ogundele, Mrs G Tenen, Ms J Mason, Mrs P J Mason, K Kotecha, W J Mason
**Co. Secretary:** David Barnett
**Responsibilities**
**Senior:** Gerald O'shaughnessy (Manager)
**Finance:** Kuddus Miah (Financial Officer)
**HR:** Cathy Cocklin (Human Resources Manager)
**Facilities:** Frank Smithers (Caretaker)
**US SIC:** 8321 **UK SIC:** 96111
**Auditors:** Ramon Lee & Partners
**Bankers:** Lloyds TSB Bank plc (77-95-10)

| | 31-03-14 | 31-03-13 | 31-03-12 |
|---|---|---|---|
| TO | 2,995,936 | 2,824,736 | 2,772,957 |
| P/L | (108,527) | (3,607) | (16,927) |
| NW | 1,206,902 | 1,315,429 | 1,319,036 |
| WC | 660,591 | 724,792 | 934,385 |
| Emp. | 177 | 171 | 173 |

DUNS 21-607-2652
## Tower Radio Ltd
**(Subsidiary of:** Tower Radio (Basildon) Ltd)
41-43 High Street, Canvey Island, Essex SS8 7RD
**Tel:** 01268682211 **Fax:** 01268471003
**Web:** www.towerdirect.co.uk
**Reg No:** 0657998 **VAT No:** 250482869
**Estd:** 1927 Private Limited Company
**Line of Business:** Electrical products (sales)
**Issued Capital:** £46,661
**Principals:** B P Litman (Managing), Ms S Litman-Lanceron, Ms M Litman
**Co. Secretary:** Bernard Litman
**Branches:** Tower Radio Ltd, 62 High St, Grays, Essex RM17 6NA
**US SIC:** 5732, 7999
**UK SIC:** 64800, 97913
**Auditors:** Wilkins Kennedy
**Bankers:** Barclays Bank Plc (20-70-93)

| | 30-04-14 | 30-04-13 | 30-04-12 |
|---|---|---|---|
| TO | N/A | N/A | 7,251,538 |
| P/L | N/A | N/A | (17,011) |
| NW | 172,890 | 154,946 | 458,545 |
| WC | 38,973 | 30,476 | 324,100 |
| Emp. | N/A | N/A | 45 |

DUNS 51-714-7955
## The Tower Restaurant
352 Castlehill, Royal Mile, Edinburgh, Midlothian EH1 2NF
**Tel:** 0131-225-5613
**Estd:** 1979 Proprietorship
**Line of Business:** Restaurants
**Proprietor:** J Thomson
**US SIC:** 5812, 5813
**UK SIC:** 66110, 66200
**Employees:** 105

DUNS 23-562-8752
## The Tower Restaurant Ltd
352 Castlehill, Edinburgh, Midlothian EH1 2NF
**Tel:** 01312250976 **Fax:** 0131-220-4392
**Web:** www.tower-restaurant.com
**Reg No:** 0185656SC **Estd:** 1980 Private Limited Company
**Line of Business:** Restaurants
**Issued Capital:** £100
**Director:** J Thomson
**Co. Secretary:** Jacquie Sutherland
**US SIC:** 5812 **UK SIC:** 66110
**Auditors:** Tenon Ltd

| | 31-05-14 | 31-05-13 | 31-05-12 |
|---|---|---|---|
| TA | 100 | 100 | 100 |
| NW | 100 | 100 | 100 |

DUNS 23-082-9678
## Tower Road Primary School
Ashlawn Drive, Boston, Lincolnshire PE21 9PX
**Tel:** 01205365922
**Web:** www.towerroadacademy.co.uk
**Estd:** 1983
**Line of Business:** Schools (foundation)
**Directors:** D G Loyd, D G Loyd
**US SIC:** 8211 **UK SIC:** 93200
**Employees:** 70

DUNS 21-196-7500
## Tower Steel (Holdings) Ltd
Unit 1 Mayflower Close, Chandler's Ford, Eastleigh, Hampshire SO53 4AR
**Tel:** 02380260266 **Fax:** 02076605093
**Reg No:** 1041209 **Estd:** 1972 Private Limited Company
**Line of Business:** Management activities of holding companies
**Issued Capital:** £465
**Director:** T E Noakes
**Co. Secretary:** Mrs Susan Noakes
**US SIC:** 6711, 5051
**UK SIC:** 83962, 61200
**Auditors:** Alliott Bullimore, Canterbury Ho, Sydenham Rd, Croydon Surrey CR9 2DG.
**Bankers:** Clydesdale Bank Plc (82-12-08)

| | 31-12-13 | 31-12-12 | 31-12-11 |
|---|---|---|---|
| TA | 91,477 | 91,477 | 91,477 |
| P/L | N/A | 5,000 | 10,000 |
| NW | 89,343 | 89,343 | 89,343 |
| WC | 21,581 | 21,581 | 21,581 |

DUNS 21-872-0307
## Tower Transit Operations Ltd
**(Subsidiary of:** Tower Transit Group Ltd)
19 Eastbourne Terrace, London W2 6LG
**Tel:** 02072297131
**Reg No:** 8314506 **Estd:** 2012 Private Limited Company
**Line of Business:** Other scheduled passenger land transport not elsewhere classified
**Issued Capital:** £1
**Directors:** N E Smith, A D Leishman, P R Cox
**Co. Secretary:** Paul Cox

**US SIC:** 4119 **UK SIC:** 72200

| | 31-03-14 | | |
|---|---|---|---|
| TO | 74,936,216 | | |
| P/L | 751,852 | | |
| NW | (1,670,626) | | |
| WC | (18,241,109) | | |
| Emp. | 1,588 | | |

DUNS 64-090-2974
## Towergate Financial (East) Ltd
**(Subsidiary of:** Towergate Partnershipco Ltd)
Unit 2 Castlebridge Office Village, Castle Marina Road, Nottingham, Nottinghamshire NG7 1TN
**Tel:** 08701432100
**Web:** www.towergate.co.uk
**Reg No:** 4493781 **Estd:** 2003 Private Limited Company
**Line of Business:** Financial services
**Issued Capital:** £1,794,341
**Director:** S Egan
**Co. Secretary:** Ms Jennifer Owens
**Responsibilities**
**Senior:** Ian Darby (Manager), Charlotte Liley (Head Of Operations), Ian Patrick (Manager)
**Branches:** Towergate Financial (East) Ltd, 3 Temple Park, Uxbridge, Middlesex UB8 3HQ
**US SIC:** 6111 **UK SIC:** 81501
**Auditors:** Ward Mackenzie

| | 31-12-13 | 31-12-12 | 31-12-11 |
|---|---|---|---|
| TA | 4,900,705 | 4,335,125 | 3,432,560 |
| P/L | (433,169) | 46,646 | 283,696 |
| NW | 854,803 | 1,193,821 | 987,794 |
| WC | 1,030,989 | 1,302,976 | 1,072,790 |
| Emp. | 91 | 82 | 60 |

DUNS 50-002-0755
## Towergate Financial (West) Ltd
**(Subsidiary of:** Towergate Partnershipco Ltd)
Pegasus Court, Tachbrook Park, Warwick, Warwickshire CV34 6LW
**Tel:** 01926439499 **Fax:** 01926439440
**Web:** www.towergatefinancialservice.co.uk
**Reg No:** 2292688 **Estd:** 1988 Private Limited Company
**Line of Business:** Financial intermediation not elsewhere classified
**Trading Style:** John Charcol
**Issued Capital:** £810,000
**Director:** S Egan
**Co. Secretary:** Ms Jennifer Owens
**Responsibilities**
**Senior:** Gillian Cotter (Manager), Garry Guest (Manager)
**US SIC:** 6111, 6311
**UK SIC:** 81501, 82002
**Auditors:** KPMG Audit PLC
**Bankers:** Barclays Bank Plc (20-48-08)

| | 31-12-13 | 31-12-12 | 31-12-11 |
|---|---|---|---|
| TA | 8,913,419 | 7,250,342 | 6,247,690 |
| P/L | 1,521,605 | 1,351,861 | 1,238,928 |
| NW | 3,910,872 | 2,653,597 | 1,393,182 |
| WC | 3,654,986 | 2,241,970 | 1,014,119 |
| Emp. | 92 | 91 | 93 |

DUNS 21-703-2636
## Towergate Insurance Ltd
**(Subsidiary of:** Towergate Partnershipco Ltd)
Eclipse Park, Sittingbourne Road, Maidstone, Kent ME14 3EN
**Tel:** 01179452940
**Web:** www.towergate.co.uk
**Reg No:** 7476462 **Estd:** 2005 Private Limited Company
**Line of Business:** Financial intermediation not elsewhere classified
**Issued Capital:** £1,406,098,502
**Directors:** A D Lyons, S Egan
**Co. Secretary:** Ms Jennifer Owens
**Responsibilities**
**Senior:** Samuel Clark (Manager), Nick Hatch (Manager), Mark Hodges (CCO)
**US SIC:** 6111 **UK SIC:** 81501
**Auditors:** KPMG Audit PLC
Following financial data are in thousands

| | 31-12-13 | 31-12-12 | 31-12-11 |
|---|---|---|---|
| TA | 1,811,305 | 1,915,079 | 1,745,817 |
| P/L | (29,259) | (15,866) | 469 |
| NW | 1,476,560 | 1,500,027 | 1,393,606 |
| WC | (57,852) | (53,999) | (16,704) |
| Emp. | 207 | 226 | 192 |

DUNS 21-703-4418
## Towergate Partnershipco Ltd
Tower Gate House, Eclipse Park Sittingbourne Road, Maidstone, Kent ME14 3EN
**Tel:** 08448921500
**Reg No:** 7477841 **Estd:** 2010 Private Limited Company
**Line of Business:** Activities auxiliary to insurance and pension funding
**Issued Capital:** £33,040,383
**Directors:** Dr T Robson-Capps, A C Homer, N Rose, P W Moore, S Egan, A Lyons, H W Battcock, P G Cullum
**Co. Secretary:** Ms Jennifer Owens
**US SIC:** 6411, 6711

**UK SIC:** 83200, 83962
**Auditors:** KPMG Audit PLC

| | 31-12-13 | 31-12-12 | 31-12-11 |
|---|---|---|---|
| TO | 444,568,000 | 439,055,000 | 419,804,000 |
| P/L | (40,958,000) | (6,107,000) | (77,457,000) |
| NW | (1,123,630,000) | (1,044,224,000) | (939,807,000) |
| WC | 171,000 | 41,052,000 | 45,142,000 |
| Emp. | 5,408 | 5,334 | 5,155 |

DUNS 21-043-5679
### Towergate Risk Solutions
81-83 Broadway, Didcot, Oxfordshire OX11 8AJ
**Tel:** 0844-736-8326
**Web:** www.towergaterisksolutions.co.uk
**Proprietorship**
**Line of Business:** Insurance services
**Proprietor:** Miss L Payne
**US SIC:** 6411 **UK SIC:** 83200
**Employees:** 50

DUNS 21-284-8267
### Towergate Riskline
Downsview House 141-143, Station Road East, Oxted, Surrey RH8 0QE
**Tel:** 08448921384
**Web:** www.towergateinsurance.co.uk
**Proprietorship**
**Line of Business:** Insurance services
**Proprietor:** D King
**Responsibilities**
**Senior:** Martin Spackman (Manager)
**US SIC:** 6411, 7399
**UK SIC:** 83200, 83954
**Employees:** 150

DUNS 22-041-3814
### Towergate Underwriting Group Ltd
(Subsidiary of: Towergate Partnershipco Ltd)
Kempton House, Blackbrook Park Avenue, Taunton, Somerset TA1 2PX
**Tel:** 01823625500
**Web:** www.towergate.co.uk
**Reg No:** 4043759 **Estd:** 1995 Private Limited Company
**Line of Business:** Miscellaneous insurance carriers
**Trading Style:** Towergate Risk Solutions, Towergate Patrick, Towergate Professional Indemnity, Footman James
**Issued Capital:** £502,610,346
**Directors:** S Egan, P G Cullum, A C Homer
**Co. Secretary:** Ms Jennifer Owens
**Responsibilities**
**Senior:** Nick Hatch (Regional Managing Director), Matthew Newstead (Trading Director)
**US SIC:** 6399, 6411
**UK SIC:** 82001, 83200
**Auditors:** KPMG Audit PLC

| | 31-12-13 | 31-12-12 | 31-12-11 |
|---|---|---|---|
| TO | 227,269,230 | 220,980,594 | 213,160,200 |
| P/L | 9,910,319 | 24,801,784 | 17,102,008 |
| NW | 177,126,760 | 143,576,642 | 112,940,765 |
| WC | 160,649,059 | 121,759,318 | 92,052,576 |
| Emp. | 3,021 | 2,970 | 2,910 |

DUNS 23-082-8423
### The Towers Convent School
The Towers, Henfield Road, Upper Beeding, Steyning, West Sussex BN44 3TF
**Tel:** 01903-812185
**Web:** www.towers.w-sussex.sch.uk
**Estd:** 1960
**Line of Business:** Schools (independent)
**Director:** M Andrew
**Responsibilities**
**Marketing:** Sherie Knight (School Secretary)
**Admin:** Sherie Knight (School Secretary)
**IT:** Luke Baker (IT Technician), Jason Relf (IT Network Manager & Transport)
**HR:** Sherie Knight (School Secretary)
**Operations:** Sherie Knight (School Secretary)
**Purchasing:** Sherie Knight (School Secretary)
**Fleet:** Jason Relf (IT Network Manager & Transport)
**US SIC:** 8211 **UK SIC:** 93200
**Employees:** 70

DUNS 73-288-9204
### Towers Perrin Europe Ltd
(Subsidiary of: Towers Watson & Co.)
71 High Holborn, London WC1V 6TP
**Tel:** 02071702000 **Fax:** 02071702222
**Web:** www.towerswatson.com
**Reg No:** 4562676 **Estd:** 2002 Private Limited Company
**Line of Business:** Management activities of holding companies
**Trading Style:** Towers Watson Ltd
**Issued Capital:** £22,523,351
**Directors:** V J Raimondo, Ms T A Rhodes, P G Morris
**Co. Secretary:** David Loveridge

**Responsibilities**
**Senior:** Marco Boschetti (Manager), Lee Bressler (Senior Counsel), Norman Buchanan (Manager), Lucie Spurr (Manager)
**Marketing:** Thomas Clayton (Communications and Change Mana)
**HR:** Simone Hay (Human Resources Manager)
**US SIC:** 6711 **UK SIC:** 83962

| | 30-06-14 | 30-06-13 | 30-06-12 |
|---|---|---|---|
| TA | 126,484,000 | 123,237,000 | 120,246,000 |
| P/L | 4,887,000 | 2,885,000 | 93,403,000 |
| NW | 125,749,000 | 120,803,000 | 118,588,000 |
| WC | 125,749,000 | 119,532,000 | 117,317,000 |

DUNS 64-072-4647                                Exp
### Towers Thompson Holdings Ltd
Turnford Place, Great Cambridge Road, Turnford, Broxbourne, Hertfordshire EN10 6NH
**Tel:** 01992-456456
**Web:** www.towers-thompson.co.uk
**Reg No:** 3467913 **Estd:** 1997 Private Limited Company
**Line of Business:** Meat wholesalers
**Export Markets:** Europe, worlwide
**Export Sales:** £38,692,000
**Issued Capital:** £139,500
**Principals:** T G Goddard (Financial), P Dolan
**US SIC:** 5147 **UK SIC:** 61700
**Auditors:** KPMG LLP
**Bankers:** Barclays Bank Plc (20-31-52)

| | 31-12-13 | 31-12-12 | 31-12-11 |
|---|---|---|---|
| TO | 110,582,000 | 139,370,000 | 207,383,000 |
| P/L | 510,000 | (2,470,000) | (926,000) |
| NW | 5,551,000 | 5,504,000 | 8,316,000 |
| WC | 3,886,000 | 3,729,000 | 5,618,000 |
| Emp. | 157 | 168 | 179 |

DUNS 34-571-5432                                Imp-Exp
### Towers Watson Ltd
(Subsidiary of: Watson Wyatt European Investment Lp)
Watson House, London Road, Reigate, Surrey RH2 9PQ
**Tel:** 01737241144 **Fax:** 01737241496
**Web:** www.towerswatson.com
**Reg No:** 5379716 **VAT No:** 862462222
**Estd:** 1878 Private Limited Company
**Line of Business:** Activities auxiliary to insurance and pension funding
**Export Sales:** £29,335,000
**Trading Style:** Watson Wyatt
**Issued Capital:** £120,101
**Directors:** V J Raimondo, P G Morris, Ms T A Rhodes
**Co. Secretary:** David Loveridge
**Responsibilities**
**Finance:** Sophie Oxtoby (Head of Finance)
**Marketing:** Simon Bleach (Marketing Manager)
**Sales:** Clive Witherington (Business Development Director)
**IT:** Steven Hollands (Head of IT)
**HR:** Naomi Sutcliffe (Human Resources Manager)
**Branches:** Towers Watson Ltd, 2 Lochrin Square, Edinburgh, Midlothian EH3 9QA
**US SIC:** 7399 **UK SIC:** 83954
**Auditors:** Deloitte LLP

| | 30-06-14 | 30-06-13 | 30-06-12 |
|---|---|---|---|
| TO | 398,069,000 | 420,119,000 | 368,253,000 |
| P/L | 53,062,000 | 7,997,000 | 46,672,000 |
| NW | 162,995,000 | 108,290,000 | 215,657,000 |
| WC | 91,104,000 | (40,906,000) | 40,026,000 |
| Emp. | 2,878 | 3,059 | 2,597 |

DUNS 89-637-3917
### Towers Watson Software Ltd
(Subsidiary of: Watson Wyatt European Investment Lp)
Maddison House, 226 High Street, Croydon, Surrey CR9 1DF
**Tel:** 08007879258
**Web:** www.emb.co.uk
**Reg No:** 3318544 **Estd:** 1995 Private Limited Company
**Line of Business:** Publishing of software
**Export Sales:** £28,712,720
**Issued Capital:** £300
**Directors:** V J Raimondo, P G Morris
**Co. Secretary:** David Loveridge
**Responsibilities**
**Senior:** Andrew English (Manager)
**US SIC:** 7372 **UK SIC:** 83940
**Auditors:** Mazars Neville Russell

| | 30-06-13 | 30-06-12 | 30-06-11 |
|---|---|---|---|
| TO | 36,811,180 | 30,864,777 | 9,506,306 |
| P/L | 3,185,658 | 2,307,877 | 7,898,401 |
| NW | 8,004,728 | 4,839,636 | 3,279,060 |
| WC | 7,954,727 | 4,789,635 | 3,229,059 |
| Emp. | N/A | N/A | 2 |

DUNS 21-779-5862
### Towerview Primary School
100 Towerview Crescent, Bangor, Co Down BT19 6AZ
**Tel:** 02891270480
**Web:** www.towerviewps.co.uk
**Estd:** 2011
**Line of Business:** General secondary education
**US SIC:** 8211 **UK SIC:** 93200
**Employees:** 55

DUNS 21-601-9856
### Towler
Market Place, Easingwold, York, North Yorkshire YO61 3AD
**Tel:** 01347821733
**Estd:** 2005 Proprietorship
**Line of Business:** Newsagents
**Proprietor:** P Rushton
**Responsibilities**
**Senior:** Joseph Rushton (Manager), Susan Rushton (Manager)
**US SIC:** 5942 **UK SIC:** 65300
**Employees:** 50

DUNS 50-524-5555
### Town & Country Cleaners Ltd
St Andrews House, Station Road East, Canterbury, Kent CT1 2BJ
**Tel:** 01227-453878
**Web:** www.townandcountrycleaners.co.uk
**Reg No:** 2482612 **VAT No:** 530816463
**Estd:** 1990 Private Limited Company
**Line of Business:** Cleaning contracting commercial
**Trading Style:** Town & Country Cleaners Ltd, A J's Cleaning, Easiclean
**Issued Capital:** £10,000
**Principals:** D J Rushton (Managing), Ms E A Harrison
**Co. Secretary:** Ms Kay Carter
**Responsibilities**
**Admin:** Holly Archer (Administrator)
**Branches:** Town & Country Cleaners Ltd, St. Andrews House, Station Road East, Canterbury, Kent CT1 2BJ
**US SIC:** 7349 **UK SIC:** 92300
**Auditors:** Aggarwal & Co Ltd
**Bankers:** The Royal Bank Of Scotland Plc (16-15-20)

| | 31-07-14 | 31-07-13 | 31-07-12 |
|---|---|---|---|
| TA | 1,116,351 | 952,168 | 894,153 |
| NW | 320,059 | 288,264 | 251,846 |
| WC | 210,610 | 169,869 | 164,624 |

DUNS 77-446-3707
### Town & Country Glazing Ltd
(Subsidiary of: Fine Glass Buildings Ltd)
Whissonsett Road, Dereham, Norfolk NR20 5DJ
**Tel:** 01328700565
**Reg No:** 2955456 **Estd:** 1994 Private Limited Company
**Line of Business:** Other manufacturing not elsewhere classified
**Issued Capital:** £2
**Directors:** K Tuck, N M Jones
**Co. Secretary:** Arthur Lake
**US SIC:** 3999 **UK SIC:** 49590
**Auditors:** BDO Stoy Hayward
**Bankers:** Barclays Bank Plc (20-30-81)

| | 31-03-14 | 31-03-13 | 31-03-12 |
|---|---|---|---|
| TA | 2 | 2 | 2 |
| NW | 2 | 2 | 2 |

DUNS 21-558-2542
### Town and Country Housing Group
Monson House, Monson Way, Tunbridge Wells, Kent TN1 1LQ
**Web:** www.tchg.org.uk
**Reg No:** 0030167IP **Estd:** 2007
**Line of Business:** Housing associations societies trusts & co-operatives
**Principals:** N Cox (Chairman), Ms K Vowles, H Williams, P Healey, Ms S Robinson, P Cooke, Ms C Pointer, Ms J Molloy
**Responsibilities**
**Senior:** Denise Claxton (Senior HR Business Partner), Matt Hammond (Manager), Bob Heapy (Chief Executive), Wasim Khan (Board Member), Jenine Langrish (Board Member), Charles Leigh-Dugmore (Board Member), Duncan Onyango (Manager), Alan Riddell (Board Member), Jonathan Rosser (Managing Director, Director), Virginia Spence (Manager)
**Finance:** Petros Christen (Senior Finance Administrator), Mike Hyams (Assistant Director of Finance), Robin Tebbutt (Finance Director)
**Marketing:** Alexine Bullett (PR Manager), Colin Lissenden (Development Director), Christine Mumcuoglu (Business Services Director)
**Sales:** Jo Wrigley (Head of Business Improvement T)

**IT:** Tom Odoki-Olam (Head of Information and Commun)
**HR:** Denise Claxton (Senior HR Business Partner), Yvonne Jones (HR Director)
**Operations:** Richard Brothers (Programme Manager), Keith Cane (Regional Operations Manager), Darren Donoghue (Regional Operations Manager), Shawn Scott (Assistant Director Operations)
**Purchasing:** Kevin Thorne (Head of Contracts & Compliance)
**US SIC:** 8321 **UK SIC:** 96111
**Auditors:** Grant Thornton UK LLP

| | 31-03-12 | 31-03-11 | 31-03-10 |
|---|---|---|---|
| TO | 46,798,000 | 44,525,000 | 39,058,000 |
| P/L | 5,362,000 | 2,989,000 | 2,555,000 |
| NW | 262,343,000 | 233,731,000 | 233,359,000 |
| WC | 3,553,000 | 2,324,000 | 3,427,000 |
| Emp. | 143 | 151 | 145 |

DUNS 28-962-2748
### Town & Country Inns Plc
39 Summer Row, Birmingham, West Midlands B3 1JJ
**Tel:** 01217104222 **Fax:** 01212121144
**Web:** www.mechu.com
**Reg No:** 1686912 **VAT No:** 443529840
**Estd:** 1987 Public Limited Company
**Line of Business:** Managed public houses and bars
**Trading Style:** Apres Bars, Mechu
**Issued Capital:** £50,000
**Principals:** K R Williams (Managing), M A Jones
**Co. Secretary:** Nigel Owen
**Branches:** Town & Country Inns Plc, 45 Summer Row, Trowbridge, Wiltshire BA14 8QU
**US SIC:** 5813 **UK SIC:** 66200
**Auditors:** Harben Barker Ltd
**Bankers:** Barclays Bank Plc (20-07-71)

| | 31-05-14 | 31-05-13 | 31-05-12 |
|---|---|---|---|
| TO | 7,641,395 | 7,491,290 | 7,014,037 |
| P/L | (3,496,586) | (115,486) | (681,887) |
| NW | 2,363,472 | 6,109,235 | 6,483,038 |
| WC | (1,771,197) | (1,396,603) | (734,374) |
| Emp. | 200 | 228 | 204 |

DUNS 21-581-7245
### Town & Country Motor Guard
St Vincent House, 1 Cutler Street, Ipswich, Suffolk IP1 1LL
**Tel:** 01473221221
**Web:** www.wnsa.com
**Estd:** 2011 Proprietorship
**Line of Business:** Miscellaneous Vehicle Repair
**Proprietor:** E Harrell
**US SIC:** 7539 **UK SIC:** 67100
**Employees:** 160

DUNS 22-771-2114
### Town & County Leisure Ltd
Unit 6 Longacre Trading Estate, Birmingham, West Midlands B7 5JD
**Tel:** 0121-327-6984
**Web:** www.townandcountry.co.uk
**Reg No:** 1403950 **Estd:** 1978 Private Limited Company
**Line of Business:** Other service activities not elsewhere classified
**Issued Capital:** £200
**Principals:** P Langham (Managing), D W Duncan, J Langham, N Langham
**Co. Secretary:** Nick Langham
**US SIC:** 8999 **UK SIC:** 83954
**Auditors:** Harben Barker
**Bankers:** Lloyds TSB Bank plc (30-93-54)

| | 31-12-13 | 31-12-12 | 31-12-11 |
|---|---|---|---|
| TO | 6,272,910 | 4,926,995 | N/A |
| P/L | 797,233 | 863,857 | N/A |
| NW | 2,809,425 | 2,392,799 | 1,864,535 |
| WC | 960,676 | 513,708 | 452,368 |
| Emp. | 64 | 55 | N/A |

DUNS 21-313-2228
### Town Centre Securities Plc
Town Centre House, Merrion Centr, Woodhouse, Leeds, West Yorkshire LS2 8LY
**Tel:** 01132221234
**Web:** www.tcs-plc.co.uk
**Reg No:** 0623364 **VAT No:** 170156192
**Estd:** 1959 Public Limited Company
**Line of Business:** Property owners
**Issued Capital:** £13,290,487
**Principals:** E M Ziff (Managing), M A Ziff, R A Lewis, R A Lewis, D S Syers, E M Ziff, R H Bigley, H T Stanton
**Co. Secretary:** Ms Ann Mcgookin
**Responsibilities**
**Senior:** David Donkin (Associate Director)
**Finance:** Dan Riley (Financial Controller)
**Branches:** Town Centre Securities Plc, Chisholm House, 9 Queens Square, Corby, Northamptonshire NN17 1PD
**US SIC:** 6519 **UK SIC:** 85000
**Auditors:** PricewaterhouseCoopers LLP

**Bankers:** Lloyds TSB Bank plc (30-00-05)

| | 30-06-14 | 30-06-13 | 30-06-12 |
|---|---|---|---|
| TO | 18,954,000 | 18,548,000 | 22,011,000 |
| P/L | 27,434,000 | 3,563,000 | (4,129,000) |
| NW | 163,871,000 | 141,903,000 | 143,658,000 |
| WC | (1,814,000) | (10,721,000) | (5,434,000) |
| Emp. | 92 | 91 | 92 |

DUNS 28-863-9461

## Town Close House Educational Trust Ltd

14 Ipswich Road, Norwich, Norfolk NR2 2LR
**Web:** www.townclose.com
**Reg No:** 0940118 **Estd:** 1932 Private Limited Company
**Line of Business:** General secondary education
**Trading Style:** Town Close Preparatory School
**Directors:** Dr S M Carroll, D J Bolton, Ms S Jack, Mrs S Waddington, Ms C R Costello, A J Fish, P Taylor, P C Easter
**Co. Secretary:** Mrs Benita Ogg
**Responsibilities**
**Senior:** Nigel Back *(Warehouse Manager)*, Philip Couzens *(Manager)*, Alec Kingham *(Director)*, Nicola Ovenden *(Director)*
**IT:** Stuart Coulthart *(Head of IT)*, Chris Shone *(IT Manager)*
**HR:** Janine Stackwood *(Human Resources Manager)*
**US SIC:** 8211 **UK SIC:** 93200
**Auditors:** Grant Thornton
**Bankers:** Barclays Bank Plc (20-62-53)

| | 31-07-13 | 31-07-12 | 31-07-11 |
|---|---|---|---|
| TO | 4,631,446 | 4,416,930 | 4,266,270 |
| P/L | 372,455 | 221,793 | 283,932 |
| NW | 4,227,615 | 3,855,160 | 3,633,367 |
| WC | 584,257 | 206,811 | 85,336 |
| Emp. | 131 | 121 | 130 |

DUNS 21-811-1084

## Town Head Offices Rmbc

Fashion Corner, 57-59 Drake Street, Rochdale, Lancashire OL16 1XL
**Tel:** 01706925353
**Web:** www.rochdale.gov.uk
**Estd:** 2012
**Line of Business:** Social work activities without accommodation
**Trading Style:** Children Social Care Fashion Corner
**Responsibilities**
**Senior:** Michael Croff *(Service Manager)*
**US SIC:** 8321 **UK SIC:** 96111
**Employees:** 54

DUNS 73-774-0931

## Town House Restaurants Ltd

Auchinstarry Marina, Kilsyth, Glasgow, Lanarkshire G65 9SG
**Tel:** 01236829200
**Web:** www.boathousekilsyth.com
**Reg No:** 0262733SC **Estd:** 2008 Private Limited Company
**Line of Business:** Restaurants
**Issued Capital:** £360,000
**Directors:** Mrs J Binnie, Dr K R Deuchar, M J Binnie
**Co. Secretary:** Dr Robert Deuchar
**Responsibilities**
**Senior:** Iain Meiklejohn *(Manager)*
**US SIC:** 5812 **UK SIC:** 66110

| | 28-02-14 | 28-02-13 | 29-02-12 |
|---|---|---|---|
| TA | 2,060,905 | 2,111,754 | 2,221,349 |
| NW | 238,631 | 156,973 | 144,570 |
| WC | (385,439) | (398,925) | (432,801) |

DUNS 22-608-5678 **Imp-Exp**

## Town Mills Craft Centre Ltd

**(Subsidiary of:** Rosegarden Ltd)
Pottery Road, Bovey Tracey, Newton Abbot, Devon TQ13 9DS
**Web:** www.houseofmarbles.com
**Reg No:** 1063371 **VAT No:** 320748571
**Estd:** 1972 Private Limited Company
**Line of Business:** Other retail sale in specialised stores not elsewhere classified
**Export Markets:** E U, U S A
**Trading Style:** House of Marbles, Team Valley Glass
**Issued Capital:** £400,000
**Principals:** W R Bavin *(Managing)*, Miss S Campbell
**Co. Secretary:** Ms Teresa Bavin
**Responsibilities**
**Senior:** Ian Benmore *(Warehouse Manager)*
**Finance:** Wendy McCollum *(Financial Director)*
**HR:** Wendy McCollum *(Financial Director)*
**Facilities:** Eric Samler *(Maintenance Manager)*
**Purchasing:** Mark Povey *(Purchasing Manager)*
**Engineering:** Eric Samler *(Maintenance Manager)*
**US SIC:** 5199 **UK SIC:** 61900
**Auditors:** Butterworth Jones & Co

**Bankers:** HSBC Bank plc (40-34-31)

| | 31-12-13 | 31-12-12 | 31-12-11 |
|---|---|---|---|
| TA | 5,698,971 | 4,260,699 | 3,771,853 |
| NW | 2,482,997 | 2,000,528 | 1,870,000 |
| WC | 1,262,240 | 1,032,240 | 990,736 |

DUNS 64-269-4517

## Townends Estate Agents

240 Blythe Road, London W14 0HJ
**Tel:** 020-7602-5666
**Web:** www.townends.co.uk
**Estd:** 1996
**Line of Business:** Estate agents
**Proprietor:** M Connel
**Responsibilities**
**Senior:** Anton Neil *(Lettings Manager)*, Natalie Passore *(Manager)*
**Branches:** Townends Estate Agents, 4 Commercial Way, Woking, Surrey GU21 6ET
**US SIC:** 6531 **UK SIC:** 83400
**Employees:** 300

DUNS 76-998-7660

## Townends (Lettings & Management) Ltd

45 Baker Street, Weybridge, Surrey KT13 8AE
**Tel:** 01932858333 **Fax:** 01932-843089
**Web:** www.townends.co.uk
**Reg No:** 2653200 **Estd:** 1991 Private Limited Company
**Line of Business:** Real estate agencies
**Issued Capital:** £100
**Directors:** S Kavanagh, Mrs C F Kavanagh
**Co. Secretary:** Ryan Mathews
**Branches:** Townends (Lettings & Management) Ltd, 179 High Street, Egham, Surrey TW20 9EJ
**US SIC:** 6531 **UK SIC:** 83400
**Auditors:** Warrener Stewart

| | 31-12-13 | 31-12-12 | 31-12-11 |
|---|---|---|---|
| TO | 7,381,380 | 7,177,315 | 7,016,393 |
| P/L | 2,225,080 | 2,142,590 | 2,324,161 |
| NW | 1,841,563 | 6,012,015 | 5,704,233 |
| WC | 1,793,081 | 5,955,868 | 5,701,595 |
| Emp. | 104 | 99 | 91 |

DUNS 45-814-1066

## Townends (Twickenham) Ltd

**(Subsidiary of:** Badger Group (Holdings) Ltd)
25 London Road, Twickenham, Middlesex TW1 3SX
**Tel:** 020-8891-6371 **Fax:** 020-8744-2956
**Web:** www.townends.co.uk
**Reg No:** 3171781 **Estd:** 1996 Private Limited Company
**Line of Business:** Estate agents
**Issued Capital:** £100
**Directors:** R J Gray, A A Addinall, J D Stevens, S Kavanagh
**Co. Secretary:** Ryan Mathews
**Responsibilities**
**Senior:** Shamis Cavenough *(Manager)*, Steve Prior *(Manager)*
**Branches:** Townends (Twickenham) Ltd, 154 Station Road, Addlestone, Surrey KT15 2BD
**US SIC:** 6531 **UK SIC:** 83400
**Auditors:** Warrener Stewart

| | 31-12-13 | 31-12-12 | 31-12-11 |
|---|---|---|---|
| TO | N/A | 170,343 | 529,291 |
| P/L | N/A | 84,012 | 127,274 |
| NW | 4,112 | 231,112 | 154,010 |
| WC | 4,112 | 231,112 | 143,552 |

DUNS 21-781-2306

## Townley Grammar

Townley Road, Bexleyheath, Kent DA6 7AB
**Tel:** 02083048311
**Web:** www.townleygrammar.org.uk
**Estd:** 2011 Proprietorship
**Line of Business:** Schools (local authority)
**Proprietor:** D Deehan
**Responsibilities**
**Senior:** Davement Deehan *(Head Teacher)*
**IT:** James Ayres *(IT Manager)*
**US SIC:** 8211 **UK SIC:** 93200
**Employees:** 120

DUNS 23-517-3291

## Townscape International Ltd

**(Subsidiary of:** Townscape Products Ltd)
Fulwood Road South, Sutton-In-Ashfield, Nottinghamshire NG17 2JZ
**Tel:** 01623-513355 **Fax:** 01623440267
**Web:** www.townscape24.com
**Reg No:** 1901448 **Estd:** 1985 Private Limited Company
**Line of Business:** Other manufacturing not elsewhere classified
**Issued Capital:** £100
**Directors:** Ms Y Davies, G Davies
**US SIC:** 3999 **UK SIC:** 49590
**Auditors:** BKR Haines Watts

| | 31-03-14 | 31-03-13 | 31-03-12 |
|---|---|---|---|
| TA | 100 | 100 | 100 |
| NW | 100 | 100 | 100 |

DUNS 73-510-0914

## Towry Holdings Ltd

**(Subsidiary of:** Coleherne Holdings Lp)
Towry House, Western Road, Bracknell, Berkshire RG12 1TL
**Web:** www.towrylaw.com
**Reg No:** 4773122 **Estd:** 2003 Private Limited Company
**Line of Business:** Financial intermediation not elsewhere classified
**Trading Style:** Towry
**Issued Capital:** £111,887
**Directors:** L G Elson, R A Sandler, P V Wright, D A Knottenbelt, R A Devey, E G Unwin, Ms S A James
**Co. Secretary:** Mrs Jacqueline Gregory
**Responsibilities**
**Finance:** Tony Cant *(Head of Financial Strategy)*, Andy Cowan *(Head of Wealth Advice)*
**Marketing:** Jill Pinington *(Head of Marketing)*
**Sales:** Zulfikar Ali *(Specialist in Business Tranfor)*, Mark Formby *(Business Transformation Adviso)*
**IT:** Adam Nielsen *(IT Manager)*
**Operations:** David Percy *(Chief Operating Officer)*
**US SIC:** 6111, 6211
**UK SIC:** 81501, 83100
**Bankers:** The Royal Bank Of Scotland Plc (15-00-00)

| | 31-12-13 | 31-12-12 | 31-12-11 |
|---|---|---|---|
| TA | 96,304,000 | 96,962,000 | 74,479,000 |
| P/L | 9,815,000 | 9,393,000 | 8,254,000 |
| NW | (1,585,000) | (1,550,000) | (10,592,000) |
| WC | 17,427,000 | 27,553,000 | 3,698,000 |
| Emp. | 685 | 688 | 773 |

DUNS 21-325-9641 **Imp-Exp**

## Towsure Products Ltd

Rutland Way, Sheffield, South Yorkshire S3 8DG
**Tel:** 01142503000 **Fax:** 01142-503001
**Web:** www.towsure.com
**Reg No:** 1285236 **VAT No:** 174299530
**Estd:** 1974 Private Limited Company
**Line of Business:** Camping equipment suppliers
**Export Markets:** Worldwide
**Issued Capital:** £6
**Principals:** S Hogg *(Managing)*, A S Hogg
**Co. Secretary:** Stuart Hogg
**Responsibilities**
**Senior:** Natasha Willars *(Manager)*
**Branches:** Towsure Products Ltd, 151-183 Holme Lane, Sheffield, South Yorkshire S6 4JR
**US SIC:** 7539, 5999
**UK SIC:** 67100, 65600
**Auditors:** Thomas Coombs & Son
**Bankers:** The Royal Bank Of Scotland Plc (16-00-08)

| | 31-07-13 | 31-01-12 | 31-07-11 |
|---|---|---|---|
| TO | 14,826,812 | 11,768,377 | 14,115,982 |
| P/L | (1,290,597) | (1,113,283) | 278,062 |
| NW | 425,904 | 1,662,623 | 2,703,692 |
| WC | (514,921) | (1,167,580) | (569,193) |
| Emp. | 115 | 138 | 156 |

DUNS 21-029-6398 **Imp-Exp**

## Toye & Company Plc

19-21 Great Queen Street, London WC2B 5BE
**Tel:** 020-7242-0471 **Fax:** 020-7831-8692
**Web:** www.toye.co.uk
**Reg No:** 0198641 **Estd:** 1835 Public Limited Company
**Line of Business:** Management activities of holding companies
**Export Markets:** Europe, Africa, Australasia, Far East, North America and Rest of the World
**Export Sales:** £1,607,942
**Issued Capital:** £562,000
**Principals:** B E Toye *(Chairman and Managing)*, R W Ewards, R J Luck
**Co. Secretary:** Neil Haynes
**Responsibilities**
**Senior:** David Rowe-Beddoe Of Kilgetty *(Manager)*, Fiona Toye *(Manager)*, Nicholas Wills *(Non-Executive Director)*
**Branches:** Toye & Company Plc, Po Box 1077, Bedworth, Warwickshire CV12 8ZD
**US SIC:** 6711, 3499
**UK SIC:** 83962, 31694
**Auditors:** PKF (UK) LLP
**Bankers:** Barclays Bank Plc (20-10-53)

| | 31-12-13 | 31-12-12 | 31-12-11 |
|---|---|---|---|
| TO | 6,466,927 | 8,936,996 | 7,981,006 |
| P/L | 942,078 | 453,872 | (439,391) |
| NW | 2,619,960 | 1,677,882 | 1,224,010 |
| WC | 1,681,776 | 460,943 | 148,890 |
| Emp. | 133 | 134 | 139 |

DUNS 22-776-0170 **Exp**

## Toye Kenning & Spencer (Birmingham) Ltd

**(Subsidiary of:** Toye & Company Plc)
77 Warstone Lane, Birmingham, West Midlands B18 6NL
**Tel:** 01212622950 **Fax:** 0121-236-7217
**Web:** www.toye.com
**Reg No:** 0692479 **Estd:** 1961 Private Limited Company
**Line of Business:** Manufacturers of badges
**Export Markets:** Worldwide
**Trading Style:** Toye Group
**Issued Capital:** £66,485
**Chairman:** B E Toye
**Co. Secretary:** Neil Haynes
**Responsibilities**
**Senior:** Dot Burke *(Stores Manager)*
**Marketing:** Declan McHale *(Marketing Manager)*
**US SIC:** 2389 **UK SIC:** 45393
**Auditors:** PKF (UK) LLP
**Bankers:** Barclays Bank Plc (20-10-53)

| | 31-12-13 | 31-12-12 | 31-12-11 |
|---|---|---|---|
| TA | 66,485 | 66,485 | 66,485 |
| NW | 66,485 | 66,485 | 66,485 |

DUNS 21-719-7767

## Toynbee Hall Trading Ltd

28 Commercial Street, London E1 6LS
**Tel:** 02072476943
**Web:** www.toynbeehall.org.uk
**Reg No:** 7578738 **Estd:** 2011 Private Limited Company
**Line of Business:** Charities and charitable organisations
**Issued Capital:** £1
**Directors:** R B Allan, C N Triggs, C Ferguson, G Fisher
**US SIC:** 8321 **UK SIC:** 96111

| | 31-03-14 | 31-03-13 | 31-03-12 |
|---|---|---|---|
| TO | 334,383 | 193,928 | 11,931 |
| NW | 1 | 1 | 1 |
| WC | 1 | 1 | 1 |

DUNS 23-753-2705 **Imp-Exp**

## Toyoda Gosei Uk Ltd.

**(Subsidiary of:** Toyoda Gosei Co. Ltd.)
Centurion Business Park, Rotherham, South Yorkshire S60 1FB
**Tel:** 01709323150 **Fax:** 01709-323151
**Web:** www.toyoda-gosei.com
**Reg No:** 3747120 **Estd:** 1999 Private Limited Company
**Line of Business:** Manufacturers of automotive components
**Export Sales:** £6,417,000
**Issued Capital:** £31,000,000
**Directors:** D Kobayashi, A Suzuki, A Sumida, Y Hirayama
**Co. Secretary:** Gareth Thraves
**Responsibilities**
**Senior:** Yukio Kawakita *(Manager)*, Yoshimasa Kondo *(Manager)*, George Nakata *(Manager)*, Akira Nakata *(Manager)*
**US SIC:** 3714, 3079
**UK SIC:** 35300, 48360
**Auditors:** Deloitte LLP
**Bankers:** Barclays Bank Plc (20-76-89)

| | 31-03-14 | 31-03-13 | 31-03-12 |
|---|---|---|---|
| TO | 38,552,000 | 44,586,000 | 29,258,000 |
| P/L | (10,407,000) | (8,470,000) | (11,716,000) |
| NW | 9,432,000 | 10,564,000 | 9,031,000 |
| WC | (42,829,000) | (34,026,000) | (36,602,000) |
| Emp. | 570 | 668 | 614 |

DUNS 50-019-3867

## Toyota Financial Services (U K) Plc

**(Subsidiary of:** Toyota Motor Corporation)
Great Burgh, Epsom, Surrey KT18 5UZ
**Tel:** 01737-365400
**Web:** www.toyota.co.uk
**Reg No:** 2299961 **VAT No:** 524671153
**Estd:** 1988 Public Limited Company
**Line of Business:** Other credit granting not elsewhere classified
**Trading Style:** Toyota & Lexus Financial Services
**Issued Capital:** £99,200,000
**Directors:** J Yamada, M S Fonseca, M Harrison, D F Gillies, H Watanabe, Y Tomihara, Y Hiramine
**Co. Secretary:** Sukhraj Jouhal
**US SIC:** 6111 **UK SIC:** 81501
**Auditors:** PricewaterhouseCoopers LLP
**Following financial data are in thousands**

| | 31-03-14 | 31-03-13 | 31-03-12 |
|---|---|---|---|
| TA | 3,674,378 | 3,243,568 | 2,938,867 |
| P/L | 83,097 | 76,888 | 73,956 |
| NW | 301,127 | 279,945 | 281,179 |
| WC | 2,018,596 | 1,629,303 | 1,558,988 |
| Emp. | 361 | 358 | 346 |

DUNS 21-308-6499
## Toyota Industrial Equipment (Northern) Ltd
(**Subsidiary of:** Toyota Industries Corporation)
Pioneer Way, Castleford, West Yorkshire WF10 5QG
**Tel:** 01977717171 **Fax:** 01977-712001
**Web:** www.tony.mirai.co.uk
**Reg No:** 0996957 **Estd:** 1971 Private Limited Company
**Line of Business:** Wholesale of other machinery for use in industry, trade and navigation
**Trading Style:** Toyota Material Handling
**Issued Capital:** £2,043,000
**Directors:** A Wallis, L G Spencer
**Co. Secretary:** Liam Spencer
**Responsibilities**
**Senior:** Mike Mathias *(Manager)*
**US SIC:** 5084, 7394
**UK SIC:** 61490, 84000
**Auditors:** PricewaterhouseCoopers LLP
**Bankers:** Lloyds TSB Bank plc (30-00-02)

| | 31-03-14 | 31-03-13 | 31-03-12 |
|---|---|---|---|
| TA | 185,000 | 185,000 | 185,000 |
| NW | 185,000 | 185,000 | 185,000 |

DUNS 21-628-9694 Imp
## Toyota Material Handling Uk Ltd
(**Subsidiary of:** Toyota Industries Corporation)
705-707 Stirling Road, Slough, Berkshire SL1 4SY
**Tel:** 08708501400 **Fax:** 0870696095
**Web:** www.toyota-forklifts.co.uk
**Reg No:** 0699993 **VAT No:** 370269452
**Estd:** 1961 Private Limited Company
**Line of Business:** Agents involved in the sale of machinery, industrial equipment, ships and aircraft
**Issued Capital:** £7,250,000
**Directors:** M J Mathias, L G Spencer
**Co. Secretary:** Liam Spencer
**Responsibilities**
**IT:** Andy Cooksley *(Computer Manager)*
**Branches:** Toyota Material Handling Uk Ltd, Unit 42, Eldon Way, Tonbridge, Kent TN12 6BE
**US SIC:** 5084, 7394
**UK SIC:** 61490, 84000
**Auditors:** PricewaterhouseCoopers LLP
**Bankers:** Barclays Bank Plc (20-00-00)

| | 31-03-14 | 31-03-13 | 31-03-12 |
|---|---|---|---|
| TO | 194,825,000 | 171,000,000 | 167,831,000 |
| P/L | 13,540,000 | 10,520,000 | 12,380,000 |
| NW | 39,432,000 | 32,446,000 | 38,102,000 |
| WC | 27,396,000 | 19,351,000 | 22,108,000 |
| Emp. | 840 | 850 | 857 |

DUNS 50-327-6321
## Toyota Motor Manufacturing (Uk) Ltd
(**Subsidiary of:** Toyota Motor Corporation)
Burnaston, Derby, Derbyshire DE1 9TA
**Tel:** 01332282121
**Web:** www.toyotauk.com
**Reg No:** 2352348 **VAT No:** 558339213
**Estd:** 1989 Private Limited Company
**Line of Business:** Manufacture of motor vehicles
**Issued Capital:** £300,000,000
**Directors:** T C Freeman, J Crosbie, E Takeichi, T Gonno, T Numa, S Teramoto, Dr. A J Walker
**Co. Secretary:** Dr. Anthony Walker
**Responsibilities**
**Senior:** Dave Chapman *(Facilities Manager)*
**IT:** Tim Roast *(IT Manager)*
**HR:** Joe McGrath *(Training Manager)*
**Health & Safety:** Gavin Armstrong *(Health & Safety Manager)*
**Facilities:** Dave Chapman *(Facilities Manager)*
**Operations:** Dave Chapman *(Facilities Manager)*, Christie Cooke *(Purchasing Manager)*, Marvin Cooke *(Production Manager)*
**Purchasing:** Christie Cooke *(Purchasing Manager)*
**Engineering:** Marvin Cooke *(Production Manager)*
**Branches:** Toyota Motor Manufacturing (Uk) Ltd, Burnaston, Derby, Derbyshire DE1 9TA
**US SIC:** 3711 **UK SIC:** 35101
**Auditors:** PricewaterhouseCoopers LLP
**Bankers:** Barclays Bank Plc (20-25-85)
**Following financial data are in thousands**

| | 31-03-14 | 31-03-13 | 31-03-12 |
|---|---|---|---|
| TO | 2,378,751 | 1,587,850 | 1,782,021 |
| P/L | (87,931) | (169,492) | (68,776) |
| NW | (506,811) | (412,996) | (206,409) |
| WC | (602,632) | (583,018) | (394,169) |
| Emp. | 4,564 | 4,805 | 3,056 |

DUNS 29-097-0003
## Toyota Tsusho Automobile North London Ltd
(**Subsidiary of:** Toyota Tsusho Corporation)
The Hyde, Edgware Road, London NW9 6BH
**Tel:** 020-8203-1888
**Web:** www.toyotatsushouk.com
**Reg No:** 1462441 **VAT No:** 581685994
**Estd:** 1979 Public Limited Company
**Line of Business:** Sale of new motor vehicles
**Trading Style:** Jemca Toyota
**Issued Capital:** £1,100,000
**Directors:** D T Collis, S G Boxall, M Ito, S Kimura, H Niwa
**Co. Secretary:** Gary Brown
**Responsibilities**
**Senior:** Kazuyuki Muto *(Manager)*, Yukio Ogawa *(Manager)*
**US SIC:** 5511, 5521, 7539, 5531
**UK SIC:** 65100, 67100
**Auditors:** Smith & Williamson
**Bankers:** The Royal Bank Of Scotland Plc (16-01-50)

| | 31-03-14 | 31-03-13 | 31-03-12 |
|---|---|---|---|
| TO | 125,852,281 | 98,621,765 | 60,970,582 |
| P/L | 658,180 | 497,814 | (107,424) |
| NW | 4,924,611 | 4,186,429 | 4,035,282 |
| WC | 2,517,259 | 1,415,724 | 1,615,468 |
| Emp. | 235 | 195 | 134 |

DUNS 77-053-6332
## Toyota Tsusho U.K. Ltd
(**Subsidiary of:** Toyota Tsusho Corporation)
Unit 2 Pond End, Derby, Derbyshire DE74 2UB
**Tel:** 01332696930 **Fax:** 01332-696917
**Web:** www.toyota-tsusho-uk.com
**Reg No:** 2669193 **Estd:** 1992 Private Limited Company
**Line of Business:** Car importers
**Trading Style:** Toyota Tsusho Uk
**Issued Capital:** £18,000,000
**Directors:** H Takamizu, S Tada, Y Shirai, E Tani, M Asano, T Suzuki
**Co. Secretary:** Michael Deann-Valentine
**Responsibilities**
**Senior:** Marvin Cooke *(Deputy Manager Director)*, Junichi Tone *(Manager)*
**Branches:** Toyota Tsusho U.k. Ltd, 5th Floor. Saxon House, Heritage Gate. Friary Street, Derby, Derbyshire DE1 1NL
**US SIC:** 5511, 5531, 5084
**UK SIC:** 65100, 61490
**Auditors:** PricewaterhouseCoopers LLP
**Bankers:** Barclays Bank Plc (20-00-00)

| | 31-03-14 | 31-03-13 | 31-03-12 |
|---|---|---|---|
| TO | 213,962,000 | 184,354,000 | 194,776,000 |
| P/L | 4,159,000 | (1,341,000) | 2,377,000 |
| NW | 37,900,000 | 35,103,000 | 37,022,000 |
| WC | 22,912,000 | 5,579,000 | 19,877,000 |
| Emp. | 308 | 252 | 206 |

DUNS 21-114-3706 Imp
## Toyota(G.B.) Plc
(**Subsidiary of:** Toyota Motor Corporation)
Great Burgh, Burgh Heath, Epsom, Surrey KT18 5UX
**Tel:** 01737363633
**Web:** www.toyota.co.uk
**Reg No:** 0916634 **Estd:** 1967 Public Limited Company
**Line of Business:** Manufacture of motor vehicles
**Export Sales:** £20,144,000
**Issued Capital:** £2,600,002
**Directors:** M Nohara, M Harrison, T Gonno, Ms D Schillaci, K H Schlicht
**Co. Secretary:** Harry Jones
**Responsibilities**
**Senior:** David Hilbert *(General Manager, Vehicle Marke)*, Didier Leroy *(President & CEO)*, Jason Stanley *(General Manager, Marketing Com)*
**Marketing:** Lance Bates *(Operations Manager)*, Alain Uyttenhoven *(Vice-President Product plannin)*
**Sales:** Richard Balshaw *(Sales & After Sales Director)*
**IT:** Ian Gadsby *(Head of IT)*, Giles Vandepol *(Senior IT Executive)*, Caroline Vaughan *(IT Systems Administrator)*
**Facilities:** Clive Webster *(Facilities Manager)*
**Branches:** Toyota(G.b.) Plc, Lexus Hatfield, 172 Great North Road, Hatfield, Hertfordshire AL9 5JN
**US SIC:** 3711 **UK SIC:** 35101
**Auditors:** PricewaterhouseCoopers LLP
**Bankers:** HSBC Bank plc (40-02-50)
**Following financial data are in thousands**

| | 31-03-14 | 31-03-13 | 31-03-12 |
|---|---|---|---|
| TO | 1,682,702 | 1,528,326 | 1,362,817 |
| P/L | 6,636 | 3,790 | (34,789) |
| NW | 1,396 | 12,688 | 3,062 |
| WC | (11,885) | (10,488) | (12,474) |
| Emp. | 296 | 306 | 307 |

DUNS 28-991-9532
## Toys R Us Holdings Ltd
(**Subsidiary of:** Toys "R" Us Inc.)
Geoffrey House, Vanwall Road, Maidenhead, Berkshire SL6 4UB
**Tel:** 01628414141
**Web:** www.toysrus.co.uk
**Reg No:** 1826057 **Estd:** 1984 Private Limited Company
**Line of Business:** Management activities of holding companies
**Trading Style:** Toys 'R' Us
**Issued Capital:** £285,480
**Principals:** F C Muzika *(Financial)*, R S Zarra, R Mclaughlan
**Co. Secretary:** Mitre Secretaries Limited
**Branches:** Toys "R" Us Holdings Ltd, Parkwest Retail Interchange Park, Unit 6, Bedford, Bedfordshire MK42 7AP
**US SIC:** 6711 **UK SIC:** 83962
**Auditors:** Ernst & Young LLP

| | 01-02-14 | 02-02-13 | 28-02-12 |
|---|---|---|---|
| TO | 428,035,000 | 460,857,000 | 476,314,000 |
| P/L | 4,553,000 | 5,979,000 | 11,435,000 |
| NW | 385,542,000 | 197,253,000 | 192,730,000 |
| WC | 497,012,000 | (467,754,000) | (61,086,000) |
| Emp. | 3,167 | 3,299 | 3,931 |

DUNS 85-623-3184
## Tozers Llp
Broadwalk House, Southernhay West, Exeter, Devon EX1 1UA
**Tel:** 01392-207020
**Web:** www.tozers.co.uk
**Reg No:** 0327569OC **Estd:** 2007
**Line of Business:** Solicitors
**Responsibilities**
**Senior:** Tracey Bridgwater *(Non-designated Limited Liabili)*, Stephen Burtchaell *(Non-designated Limited Liabili)*, Nicholas Conner *(Non-designated Limited Liabili)*, Timothy Dyde *(Designated Limited Liability P)*, Clair Hemming *(Non-designated Limited Liabili)*, Tracy Lambert *(Designated Limited Liability P)*, James Orpin *(Non-designated Limited Liabili)*, Grainne Staunton *(Non-designated Limited Liabili)*, Richard Thorneycroft *(Designated Limited Liability P)*
**Admin:** Lorraine Foster *(Office Manager)*
**US SIC:** 8111 **UK SIC:** 83500

| | 30-06-13 | 30-06-12 | 30-06-11 |
|---|---|---|---|
| TO | 6,018,884 | 6,288,552 | 6,019,610 |
| P/L | 1,683,537 | 2,111,331 | 1,725,380 |
| NW | 1,683,537 | 2,111,331 | 1,725,380 |
| WC | 2,811,855 | 3,199,973 | 2,843,929 |
| Emp. | 112 | 110 | 111 |

DUNS 34-794-6985
## Tp Bennett Llp
One America Street, London SE1 0NE
**Tel:** 02072082000
**Web:** www.tpbennett.com
**Reg No:** 0315685OC **VAT No:** 867891750
**Estd:** 1920
**Line of Business:** Architects
**Export Sales:** £3,077,443
**Responsibilities**
**Senior:** Polly Barker *(Non-designated Limited Liabili)*, Robert Beacock *(Non-designated Limited Liabili)*, Vivien Fowler *(Board Member)*, Ruth Goddard *(Manager)*, Farrol Goldblatt *(Manager)*, Nenad Manasijevic *(Non-designated Limited Liabili)*, Martin Miesowicz *(Non-designated Limited Liabili)*, Gary Pemberton *(Non-designated Limited Liabili)*, Jeffrey Wall *(Non-designated Limited Liabili)*, Stephen Yates *(Non-designated Limited Liabili)*
**Marketing:** James Hollis *(?Marketing & New Business Exec)*
**US SIC:** 8911, 7399
**UK SIC:** 83701, 83954
**Auditors:** Grant Thornton UK LLP
**Bankers:** National Westminster Bank Plc (60-40-04)

| | 31-03-14 | 31-03-13 | 31-03-12 |
|---|---|---|---|
| TO | 19,251,660 | 15,798,028 | 14,746,119 |
| P/L | 7,543,895 | 3,397,500 | 3,045,598 |
| NW | 4,841,868 | 3,450,234 | 3,074,692 |
| WC | 5,916,571 | 4,695,671 | 4,649,260 |
| Emp. | 205 | 176 | 165 |

DUNS 21-224-7678
## Tp Connolly
21h Mountjoy Road, Omagh, Co Tyrone BT79 7BA
**Tel:** 08444773503
**Estd:** 2003 Proprietorship
**Line of Business:** Doctors
**Proprietor:** Mrs M Slane
**Responsibilities**
**Senior:** Rhonda Mckinney *(Practice Manager)*
**US SIC:** 8011 **UK SIC:** 95300
**Employees:** 137

DUNS 21-914-0902 Imp
## T.P. Hopwell (Holdings) Ltd
Glaisdale Drive East, Nottingham, Nottinghamshire NG8 4LU
**Tel:** 01159-291101 **Fax:** 01159-290432
**Web:** www.hopwells.com
**Reg No:** 1285847 **Estd:** 1976 Private Limited Company
**Line of Business:** Management activities of other non-financial holding companies not elsewhere classified
**Issued Capital:** £100,000
**Principals:** T C Hopwell *(Managing)*, Ms L Hopwell
**Co. Secretary:** David Plester
**US SIC:** 8999, 5149
**UK SIC:** 83954, 61700
**Auditors:** Clayton & Brewill
**Bankers:** National Westminster Bank Plc (54-21-07)

| | 27-12-13 | 28-12-12 | 30-12-11 |
|---|---|---|---|
| TO | 63,533,003 | 58,600,330 | 52,482,048 |
| P/L | 1,467,746 | 1,250,314 | 1,499,741 |
| NW | 5,274,351 | 4,663,631 | 4,377,323 |
| WC | 8,158,414 | 7,205,478 | 6,691,069 |
| Emp. | 260 | 257 | 253 |

DUNS 22-049-7924
## Tpg Disableaids Ltd
10 Plough Lane, Hereford, Herefordshire HR4 0ED
**Tel:** 01432-351666 **Fax:** 01432-351777
**Web:** www.tpg-disableaids.co.uk
**Reg No:** 4051923 **VAT No:** 412833180
**Estd:** 1984 Private Limited Company
**Line of Business:** Manufacture of invalid carriages
**Issued Capital:** £101,000
**Principals:** Ms P A Gibbs *(Managing)*, A J Gibbs, T N Gibbs
**Co. Secretary:** Ms Amanda Harrold
**Responsibilities**
**IT:** Steve Maynard *(IT Assistant)*
**US SIC:** 3799, 8699
**UK SIC:** 36502, 96902

| | 31-10-14 | 31-10-13 | 31-10-12 |
|---|---|---|---|
| TA | 2,316,086 | 2,152,134 | 1,949,469 |
| NW | 1,685,263 | 1,515,934 | 1,330,771 |
| WC | 1,551,804 | 1,414,729 | 1,213,377 |

DUNS 23-933-6642
## Tpp Net Ltd
Abbey House 7 Manor Road Coventry, Coventry, West Midlands CV1 2FW
**Tel:** 01926834500
**Web:** www.tppnet.com
**Reg No:** 3923473 **Estd:** 2000 Private Limited Company
**Line of Business:** Business and management consultancy activities not elsewhere classified
**Issued Capital:** £100
**Director:** C Gregory
**Co. Secretary:** Paul Smith
**Responsibilities**
**Senior:** Ryan Smith *(Proprietor)*
**US SIC:** 7392 **UK SIC:** 83951
**Bankers:** National Westminster Bank Plc (53-61-31)

| | 31-03-14 | 31-03-13 | 31-03-12 |
|---|---|---|---|
| TA | 123,968 | 129,492 | 143,071 |
| NW | 58,860 | 23,917 | 8,227 |
| WC | (35,024) | (69,767) | (75,017) |

DUNS 34-587-6825 Imp
## T.P.R. Ltd
Europa Way, Wisbech, Cambridgeshire PE13 2TZ
**Tel:** 01162-733633
**Web:** www.cressall.com
**Reg No:** 2731823 **VAT No:** 576704610
**Estd:** 1992 Private Limited Company
**Line of Business:** Car accessories and parts
**Export Sales:** £6,805,224
**Trading Style:** Cressall Resistors Ltd
**Issued Capital:** £439,205
**Directors:** M Fornari, D R Atkins
**Co. Secretary:** Peter Duncan
**US SIC:** 3629 **UK SIC:** 34350
**Auditors:** Streets Audit LLP
**Bankers:** Barclays Bank Plc (20-67-37)

| | 31-12-13 | 31-12-12 | 31-12-11 |
|---|---|---|---|
| TO | 11,885,856 | 12,671,129 | 10,830,969 |
| P/L | 1,373,015 | 1,145,067 | 1,654,452 |
| NW | 4,629,484 | 3,787,963 | 3,937,781 |
| WC | 4,062,126 | 3,228,070 | 3,443,484 |
| Emp. | 97 | 106 | 92 |

DUNS 76-573-2482 Exp
## Tps Consult Ltd
(**Subsidiary of:** Carillion Plc)
Centre Tower, Whitgift Centre, Croydon, Surrey CR9 0AU
**Tel:** 02082-564000
**Web:** www.tpsconsult.co.uk
**Reg No:** 2574820 **VAT No:** 661548523
**Estd:** 1991 Private Limited Company
**Line of Business:** Other engineering activities
**Export Markets:** Worldwide

**Issued Capital:** £58,368,002
**Directors:** A Hayward, F Huidobro, R J Howson, J V Dye, A Green, R J Adam, Dr P Forsyth
**Co. Secretary:** Timothy George
**Responsibilities**
**Senior:** David Fettes *(Manager)*, Steven Foskett *(Manager)*, Roger Yenn *(Manager)*
**Finance:** John Pell *(Financial Director)*
**Admin:** Martin Hillman *(Office Manager)*
**HR:** Kiernan Soughton *(Personnel Director)*
**Health & Safety:** Kiernan Soughton *(Personnel Director)*
**Purchasing:** Martin Hillman *(Office Manager)*
**Branches:** Tps Consult Ltd, 74 Commercial Street, Edinburgh, Midlothian EH6 6LX
**US SIC:** 8911 **UK SIC:** 83701
**Auditors:** KPMG Audit PLC
**Bankers:** HSBC Bank plc (40-47-11)

| | 31-12-13 | 31-12-12 | 31-12-11 |
|---|---|---|---|
| TO | 19,541,000 | 21,982,000 | 24,773,000 |
| P/L | (3,703,000) | (1,421,000) | 710,000 |
| NW | (2,103,000) | 1,246,000 | 2,461,000 |
| WC | (2,178,000) | 1,171,000 | 2,461,000 |
| Emp. | 251 | 282 | 306 |

DUNS 21-574-2198 **Imp-Exp**
## Tps Weldtech Ltd
Loreny Industrial Estate, Ayr Road, Kilmarnock, Ayrshire KA1 5LE
**Tel:** 01563529435
**Web:** www.tpsweldtech.com
**Reg No:** 0053928SC **VAT No:** 263648244
**Estd:** 1973 Private Limited Company
**Line of Business:** Plant and tool hire
**Export Markets:** Worldwide
**Trading Style:** Tps
**Issued Capital:** £150,000
**Principals:** T Palmer *(Chairman and Managing)*, K M Palmer
**Co. Secretary:** Mrs Margaret Palmer
**Branches:** Tps Weldtech Ltd, 108 Highfields Road, Bilston, West Midlands WV14 0LD
**US SIC:** 3629, 7394
**UK SIC:** 34350, 84000
**Auditors:** John Kerr & Co
**Bankers:** Clydesdale Bank Plc (82-60-30)

| | 31-12-13 | 31-12-12 | 31-12-11 |
|---|---|---|---|
| TA | 4,554,995 | 4,641,299 | 5,430,236 |
| NW | 3,648,696 | 3,494,498 | 3,424,748 |
| WC | 2,393,207 | 1,756,866 | 2,016,096 |

DUNS 23-966-2393
## Tpse Ltd
(**Subsidiary of:** A.S. Watson (Europe) Holdings B.V.)
Cypress House The Gateway Centre, Coronation Road Cressex Business Park, High Wycombe, Buckinghamshire HP12 3SU
**Tel:** 08456011950
**Web:** www.theperfumeshop.com
**Reg No:** 3955154 **Estd:** 2000 Private Limited Company
**Line of Business:** Other retail sale in non-specialised stores
**Trading Style:** The Perfume Shop
**Issued Capital:** £1
**Directors:** Ms G G Smith, Dr A J Heaton
**Co. Secretary:** Ms Edith Shih
**US SIC:** 5399 **UK SIC:** 65600
**Auditors:** PricewaterhouseCoopers

| | 28-12-13 | 29-12-12 | 31-12-11 |
|---|---|---|---|
| TA | 1 | 1 | 1 |
| NW | 1 | 1 | 1 |

DUNS 21-824-3251 **Exp**
## Tq Education and Training Ltd
(**Subsidiary of:** Pearson Plc)
Bangrave Road South, Corby, Northamptonshire NN17 1NN
**Tel:** 01536 351 300
**Web:** www.tq.com
**Reg No:** 0604934 **VAT No:** 295395411
**Estd:** 1958 Private Limited Company
**Line of Business:** Technical and vocational secondary education
**Export Markets:** Worldwide
**Export Sales:** £1,807,000
**Trading Style:** Pearson Academy of Vocational Training
**Issued Capital:** £594,350
**Directors:** J A Carroll, C H Samler, Ms T L Minick-Scokalo, C K Scobie, M J Leader
**Co. Secretary:** Stephen Jones
**Responsibilities**
**Senior:** Vicky Keyworph *(CEO, Managing Director)*, Helen Milsom *(Commercial Manager)*
**HR:** Graham Coe *(Director of Human Resources)*
**Engineering:** Bruce Cantrill *(Director of TQ Technical and V)*
**US SIC:** 8249 **UK SIC:** 93300
**Auditors:** PricewaterhouseCoopers LLP

**Bankers:** Barclays Bank Plc (20-07-71)

| | 31-12-13 | 31-12-12 | 31-12-11 |
|---|---|---|---|
| TO | 16,013,000 | 13,870,000 | 14,338,000 |
| P/L | 380,000 | 3,595,000 | 4,740,000 |
| NW | 12,792,000 | 12,528,000 | 11,525,000 |
| WC | 14,895,000 | 15,008,000 | 12,492,000 |
| Emp. | 179 | 151 | 130 |

DUNS 21-702-7136
## T'quila Ltd.
(**Subsidiary of:** Agave Consultants Limited)
1 Lindsey Street, Suite D, 2nd Floor, London EC1A 9HP
**Tel:** 02034291300
**Reg No:** 7472296 **Estd:** 2010 Private Limited Company
**Line of Business:** Hardware consultancy
**Issued Capital:** £1,000
**Directors:** J P Turner, M Wakelin
**Co. Secretary:** Joseph O'Neill
**US SIC:** 7379 **UK SIC:** 83940
**Auditors:** Jeffreys Henry LLP

| | 30-04-14 | 30-04-13 | 31-04-11 |
|---|---|---|---|
| TO | 10,148,645 | 7,603,185 | N/A |
| P/L | (340,971) | (1,941,770) | N/A |
| NW | (259,378) | (568,407) | (826,390) |
| WC | (332,391) | (636,874) | (128,628) |
| Emp. | 91 | 58 | N/A |

DUNS 21-717-2964 **Imp**
## T.R. Fastenings Ltd
(**Subsidiary of:** Trifast Plc)
Avenue West, Skyline 120, Great Notley, Braintree, Essex CM77 7AA
**Fax:** 01825747368
**Web:** www.trfastenings.com
**Reg No:** 1103675 **VAT No:** 390068451
**Estd:** 1973 Private Limited Company
**Line of Business:** Manufacture of fasteners, screw machine products, chains and springs
**Export Sales:** £13,653,000
**Issued Capital:** £10,200
**Principals:** G P Budd *(Managing)*, D Fisk, Ms A S Johnson, S A Meiklem, Ms G C Roberts, M M Diamond, J C Barker
**Co. Secretary:** Mark Belton
**Responsibilities**
**Senior:** Keith Gibb *(Manager)*
**Branches:** T.r. Fastenings Ltd, Unit N, Broadway, Salford, Lancashire M50 2UE
**US SIC:** 3452 **UK SIC:** 31371
**Auditors:** KPMG Audit PLC
**Bankers:** HSBC Bank plc (40-09-25)

| | 31-03-14 | 31-03-13 | 31-03-12 |
|---|---|---|---|
| TO | 60,974,000 | 55,579,000 | 55,747,000 |
| P/L | 4,152,000 | 3,038,000 | 2,310,000 |
| NW | 8,372,000 | 6,564,000 | 4,800,000 |
| WC | 8,969,000 | 7,377,000 | 6,437,000 |
| Emp. | 366 | 372 | 380 |

DUNS 42-454-2764 **Imp**
## Trac Group Ltd
(**Subsidiary of:** Chromalloy Uk Holdings Ltd)
9a Marshfield Employment Park, Middlewich Road, Crewe, Cheshire CW2 8UY
**Tel:** 01270500275
**Web:** http://trac-group.com
**Reg No:** 4441988 **Estd:** 2002 Private Limited Company
**Line of Business:** Management activities of holding companies
**Export Sales:** £20,759,186
**Issued Capital:** £2,819
**Directors:** S R Lowson, T Russett, R Kothari, M R Bolton
**Branches:** Trac Group Ltd, Unit 9A, Marshfield Bank, Crewe, Cheshire CW2 8UY
**US SIC:** 6711 **UK SIC:** 83962
**Bankers:** HSBC Bank plc (40-42-11)

| | 30-06-13 | 30-06-12 | 30-06-11 |
|---|---|---|---|
| TO | 49,443,808 | 38,921,880 | 31,248,466 |
| P/L | 5,051,317 | 2,273,271 | 850,834 |
| NW | 13,979,835 | 9,766,391 | 7,521,180 |
| WC | 5,850,771 | 3,824,072 | 3,662,763 |
| Emp. | 362 | 311 | 284 |

DUNS 23-723-9616
## Trac International Ltd
Unit 12 Howe Moss Drive, Aberdeen, Aberdeenshire AB21 0GL
**Tel:** 01224725800 **Fax:** 01224725801
**Web:** www.tracinternational.com
**Reg No:** 0193766SC **Estd:** 1999 Private Limited Company
**Line of Business:** Other business activities not elsewhere classified
**Export Sales:** £12,319,285
**Issued Capital:** £50,000
**Directors:** K D Hawthorn, R Watt, K R Stephen
**Co. Secretary:** Kevin Stephen
**Responsibilities**
**Senior:** Paul Stephen *(Ops Director)*
**Branches:** Trac International Ltd, 5 Sandpiper Way, 5 Sandpiper Way, Bellshill, Lanarkshire ML4 3NG
**US SIC:** 7399, 8911
**UK SIC:** 83954, 83701

**Auditors:** Williamson & Dunn

| | 31-03-14 | 31-03-13 | 31-03-12 |
|---|---|---|---|
| TO | 46,483,714 | 35,372,851 | 35,206,809 |
| P/L | 2,503,440 | 4,080,151 | 5,923,880 |
| NW | 10,426,796 | 10,200,538 | 9,179,756 |
| WC | 10,783,580 | 9,893,863 | 9,004,478 |
| Emp. | 430 | 336 | 286 |

DUNS 22-455-2484
## Trace Basement Systems
Unit 7 Graphite Way, Hadfield, Glossop, Derbyshire SK13 1QH
**Tel:** 08003899040
**Web:** www.tracebasementsystems.co.uk
**Proprietorship**
**Line of Business:** Asbestos products & removal
**US SIC:** 1799 **UK SIC:** 50000
**Employees:** 50

DUNS 21-028-7911
## Trace Elliot
Great Folds Road, Oakley Hay, Corby, Northamptonshire NN18 9ET
**Tel:** 01536424740
**Web:** www.trace-elliot.co.uk
**Proprietorship**
**Line of Business:** Repair not elsewhere classified
**US SIC:** 7699 **UK SIC:** 67303
**Employees:** 70

DUNS 50-379-7524 **Exp**
## Trace Group Ltd
(**Subsidiary of:** Tulip Holdings Ltd)
224-232 St John Street, London EC1V 4QR
**Tel:** 02078251000
**Web:** www.tracegroup.com
**Reg No:** 2388822 **VAT No:** 564426532
**Estd:** 1989 Private Limited Company
**Line of Business:** Computer software (development)
**Export Markets:** U S, Europe & Other
**Export Sales:** £1,100,939
**Issued Capital:** £728,735
**Principals:** C A Clarke *(Managing)*, R J Wolfe *(Managing)*, J C Mancell Smith, M F Flynn, A Bell, J Murphy
**Co. Secretary:** Peter Stolerman
**Responsibilities**
**Sales:** Nicholas Tonge *(Sales Director)*
**HR:** Peter Solomon *(Human Resources Director)*
**Facilities:** Bill Grice *(Maintenance Manager)*
**US SIC:** 6711, 7372
**UK SIC:** 83962, 83940
**Auditors:** Baker Tilly
**Bankers:** National Westminster Bank Plc (60-00-04)

| | 31-05-14 | 31-05-13 | 31-05-12 |
|---|---|---|---|
| TO | 14,437,690 | 13,237,304 | 12,759,818 |
| P/L | 1,674,310 | 1,109,672 | 936,268 |
| NW | 19,072,559 | 16,890,977 | 15,318,591 |
| WC | (537,109) | (1,139,634) | (1,748,921) |
| Emp. | 144 | 138 | 138 |

DUNS 49-084-3364
## Trace One (Uk) Ltd
(**Subsidiary of:** Siparex Ingenierie Et Finance Sigefi)
Verulam Point, St Albans, Hertfordshire AL1 5HE
**Tel:** 01727797400
**Web:** www.traceone.com
**Reg No:** 3088831 **VAT No:** 640179842
**Estd:** 1995 Private Limited Company
**Line of Business:** Other software consultancy and supply
**Issued Capital:** £189,760
**Directors:** P Kaser, J Malavoy, P Allman
**Co. Secretary:** Paul Allman
**Responsibilities**
**Senior:** Marc Bonnamour *(COO)*
**Finance:** Kanny Kananathan *(Financial Director)*
**US SIC:** 7379 **UK SIC:** 83940
**Auditors:** KPMG LLP
**Bankers:** HSBC Bank plc (40-40-01)

| | 31-12-13 | 31-12-12 | 31-12-11 |
|---|---|---|---|
| TO | N/A | 2,041,509 | 1,373,694 |
| P/L | N/A | (1,028,767) | 3,675,089 |
| NW | 4,977,149 | (480,797) | 547,970 |
| WC | N/A | (601,454) | 391,327 |

DUNS 21-772-9837
## Traceadebt.Com
Vilcol House, 97 Ewell Road, Surbiton, Surrey KT6 6AH
**Web:** www.traceadebt.com
**Estd:** 1991 Proprietorship
**Line of Business:** Credit reporting and collection agency activities
**Proprietor:** J Gordon Johnson
**US SIC:** 7321 **UK SIC:** 83954
**Employees:** 50

DUNS 54-384-2777
## Tracemotion Ltd
(**Subsidiary of:** Iheartmedia Inc.)
33 Golden Square, London W1F 9JT
**Tel:** 02074782271 **Fax:** 020-7287-9149
**Reg No:** 3269252 **Estd:** 1996 Private Limited Company
**Line of Business:** Management activities of holding companies
**Issued Capital:** £288,000
**Directors:** J M Cochrane, N J Andrews
**Co. Secretary:** Nick Andrews
**US SIC:** 6711 **UK SIC:** 83962

| | 31-12-13 | 31-12-12 | 31-12-11 |
|---|---|---|---|
| TA | 1,475,252 | 1,475,252 | 1,475,252 |
| NW | 1,475,252 | 1,475,252 | 1,475,252 |

DUNS 64-093-0686
## Tracerco Ltd
(**Subsidiary of:** Johnson Matthey Plc)
Pavillion 11, Belasis Hall Technology Park, Billingham, Cleveland TS23 4EA
**Tel:** 01642-375500
**Web:** www.tracerco.com
**Reg No:** 4496566 **Estd:** 2002 Private Limited Company
**Line of Business:** Manufacture of electronic valves and tubes and other electronic components
**Export Sales:** £24,078,000
**Trading Style:** Tracerco
**Issued Capital:** £40,000,002
**Directors:** A C Hurst, G P Otterman, D G Jones, S Slattery, M Pemberton, S P Robinson
**Co. Secretary:** Simon Farrant
**Branches:** Tracerco Ltd, Po Box 6, Billingham, Cleveland TS23 1LD
**US SIC:** 7399 **UK SIC:** 83954
**Auditors:** KPMG Audit PLC

| | 31-03-14 | 31-03-13 | 31-03-12 |
|---|---|---|---|
| TO | 37,796,000 | 35,035,000 | 30,619,000 |
| P/L | (3,000) | 570,000 | 1,665,000 |
| NW | 23,627,000 | 23,087,000 | 22,314,000 |
| WC | 9,031,000 | 18,079,000 | 17,793,000 |
| Emp. | 201 | 161 | 147 |

DUNS 23-835-2582
## Tracesmart Ltd
(**Subsidiary of:** Tracesmart Group Ltd)
Global Reach, Dunleavy Drive, Cardiff, South Glamorgan CF11 0SN
**Fax:** 02920376276
**Web:** www.tracesmart.co.uk
**Reg No:** 3827062 **VAT No:** 736830813
**Estd:** 1999 Private Limited Company
**Line of Business:** Data information services
**Issued Capital:** £100
**Directors:** R Trainor, S Walker, T Brown, D A Curtis, P D Weathersby
**Co. Secretary:** Re Secretaries Limited
**Responsibilities**
**Marketing:** Lindsey Tudor *(Admin Manager)*
**Admin:** Lindsey Tudor *(Admin Manager)*
**US SIC:** 7399, 7374
**UK SIC:** 83954, 83940
**Auditors:** Advantage Accountancy & Advisory LLP

| | 31-12-13 | 31-12-12 | 31-12-11 |
|---|---|---|---|
| TA | 3,975,678 | 3,001,487 | 2,720,937 |
| NW | 1,074,064 | 362,707 | 345,827 |
| WC | 744,537 | 105,374 | 302,663 |

DUNS 23-123-0702 **Imp**
## Tracey Brothers Ltd
Drumlyon House, Drumlyon, Enniskillen, Co Fermanagh BT74 5TB
**Tel:** 028-6632-3471 **Fax:** 028-6632-3843
**Web:** www.traceybros.com
**Reg No:** 0035032NI **Estd:** 1998 Private Limited Company
**Line of Business:** Construction of commercial buildings
**Issued Capital:** £500,000
**Directors:** R E Tracey, R T Tracey, G J Tracey
**Co. Secretary:** Patricia Mcbrien
**Responsibilities**
**Health & Safety:** Martina McCabe *(Health & Safety Officer)*
**US SIC:** 1541, 1622
**UK SIC:** 50100, 50200
**Auditors:** BDO Stoy Hayward
**Bankers:** First Trust Bank (aib Group (uk) Plc) (93-80-76)

| | 31-03-14 | 31-03-13 | 31-03-12 |
|---|---|---|---|
| TO | 17,498,330 | 13,900,264 | 15,863,105 |
| P/L | (222,752) | 1,007,069 | 1,571,139 |
| NW | 9,663,841 | 9,910,846 | 9,266,178 |
| WC | 7,655,359 | 8,369,959 | 7,961,160 |
| Emp. | 53 | 53 | 53 |

DUNS 22-752-8395
## Tracey Concrete Ltd
Old Rossorry Road, Enniskillen, Co Fermanagh BT74 7LF
**Tel:** 028-6632-6437 **Fax:** 028-6632-4908
**Web:** www.traceyconcrete.com
**Reg No:** 0013514NI **Estd:** 1979 Private Limited Company

**Line of Business:** Manufacture of ready-mixed concrete
**Trading Style:** Tracey Concrete Ltd
**Issued Capital:** £25,500
**Directors:** P T Tracey, R E Tracey, R T Tracey
**Co. Secretary:** Mrs Patricia Mcbrien
**Responsibilities**
**Senior:** Kierin Mc Hugh *(General Manager)*, Ken McTaggart *(General Manager)*
**Admin:** Margaret Conlon *(Office Manager)*
**IT:** Margaret Conlon *(Office Manager)*
**HR:** Margaret Conlon *(Office Manager)*, Francis Kearns *(Factory Manager)*
**Health & Safety:** Margaret Conlon *(Office Manager)*
**Facilities:** Ken McTaggart *(General Manager)*
**Operations:** Ken McTaggart *(General Manager)*
**Purchasing:** Ken McTaggart *(General Manager)*
**Engineering:** Ken McTaggart *(General Manager)*
**US SIC:** 3273, 7397
**UK SIC:** 24360, 83702
**Auditors:** BDO Stoy Hayward
**Bankers:** First Trust Bank (aib Group (uk) Plc) (93-80-76)

| | 31-03-14 | 31-03-13 | 31-03-12 |
|---|---|---|---|
| TO | 6,310,016 | 5,414,039 | 7,400,607 |
| P/L | 597,726 | 572,114 | 1,233,639 |
| NW | 11,139,211 | 10,820,989 | 10,439,328 |
| WC | 8,683,805 | 8,223,100 | 7,573,161 |
| Emp. | 54 | 51 | 54 |

DUNS 21-738-2198
## Track & Build Ltd
**(Subsidiary of:** Kmj Investments Ltd)
1d North Crescent, London E16 4TG
**Tel:** 02074764707
**Web:** www.trackandbuild.co.uk
**Reg No:** 7719498 **Estd:** 2011 Private Limited Company
**Line of Business:** Construction of domestic buildings
**Issued Capital:** £1
**Directors:** A L Maye, J Kelly
**Co. Secretary:** Alan Maye
**Responsibilities**
**Senior:** Nick Arkel *(Operations Director)*
**US SIC:** 1522 **UK SIC:** 50100

| | 31-07-13 | 31-07-12 |
|---|---|---|
| TA | 129,601 | 233,920 |
| NW | (10,250) | (19,313) |
| WC | (12,093) | (20,746) |

DUNS 76-971-4478
## Tracker Network (U K) Ltd
**(Subsidiary of:** Lysanda Ltd)
Otter House, 5 High Street Cowley Business Park, Uxbridge, Middlesex UB8 2AD
**Tel:** 01895234567 **Fax:** 01895-234117
**Web:** www.thankstotracker.com
**Reg No:** 2632771 **Estd:** 1993 Private Limited Company
**Line of Business:** Car security
**Issued Capital:** £7,906,500
**Directors:** H S Wolley, D J Wilson, Ms C De Boucaud, M A Hesketh
**Co. Secretary:** Hugh Wolley
**Responsibilities**
**Senior:** Stephen Doran *(Manager)*
**Branches:** Tracker Network (U K) Ltd, Units 1-2 Craufurd Business Park, Silverdale Road, Hayes, Middlesex UB3 3BN
**US SIC:** 5531, 7379
**UK SIC:** 65100, 83940
**Auditors:** Deloitte LLP
**Bankers:** Barclays Bank Plc (20-89-16)

| | 31-12-13 | 31-12-12 | 31-12-11 |
|---|---|---|---|
| TO | 18,251,000 | 18,069,000 | 19,046,000 |
| P/L | (3,125,000) | (3,894,000) | 27,000 |
| NW | (1,018,000) | 6,566,000 | 12,994,000 |
| WC | 1,091,000 | 7,724,000 | 13,972,000 |

DUNS 21-114-8757
## Trackwork Group Ltd
Sandall Lane, Doncaster, South Yorkshire DN3 1WZ
**Tel:** 01302888666
**Web:** www.trackwork.co.uk
**Reg No:** 6552957 **Estd:** 2008 Private Limited Company
**Line of Business:** Other construction work involving special trades
**Issued Capital:** £7,319
**Director:** M J Waind
**Co. Secretary:** Mark Waind
**Responsibilities**
**Operations:** Richard Thew *(Project Planner)*
**US SIC:** 1799 **UK SIC:** 50000

| | 30-09-13 | 30-09-12 | 30-09-11 |
|---|---|---|---|
| TO | 44,803,000 | 38,246,000 | 30,914,000 |
| P/L | 1,803,000 | 2,464,000 | 2,799,000 |
| NW | 19,088,000 | 17,742,000 | 15,853,000 |
| WC | 6,701,000 | 6,697,000 | 2,004,000 |
| Emp. | 402 | 362 | 291 |

DUNS 34-652-6739
## Tracscare 2006 Ltd
**(Subsidiary of:** Sundhet Holding Sa)
11 Staple Inn, London WC1V 7QH
**Tel:** 01792763896
**Web:** www.tracscare.co.uk
**Reg No:** 5458148 **Estd:** 2005 Private Limited Company
**Line of Business:** Healthcare companies
**Issued Capital:** £2
**Directors:** Ms C Conway, C D Cameron, Ms S G Hullin, R P Constable
**Co. Secretary:** Mh Secretaries Limited
**US SIC:** 8091 **UK SIC:** 95200

| | 31-03-14 | 31-03-13 | 31-03-12 |
|---|---|---|---|
| TO | 4,740,283 | 5,029,828 | 4,954,704 |
| P/L | 349,852 | 499,252 | 448,415 |
| NW | (6,005) | (1,476,381) | (3,096,157) |
| WC | 2,902,946 | 2,032,446 | 808,477 |
| Emp. | 177 | 180 | 192 |

DUNS 22-231-8557
## Tracscare 2007 Ltd
**(Subsidiary of:** Sundhet Holding Sa)
Staple Court, London WC1V 7QH
**Tel:** 029-2055-3444
**Web:** www.tracscare.co.uk
**Reg No:** 4249850 **Estd:** 2001 Private Limited Company
**Line of Business:** Other business activities not elsewhere classified
**Issued Capital:** £100
**Directors:** Ms C Conway, C D Cameron, R P Constable, Ms S G Hullin
**Co. Secretary:** Mh Secretaries Limited
**Responsibilities**
**Senior:** Valerie Owen *(Manager)*
**Finance:** Valerie Owen *(Manager)*
**US SIC:** 7399, 8321
**UK SIC:** 83954, 96111
**Bankers:** Lloyds TSB Bank plc (30-16-95)

| | 31-03-14 | 31-03-13 | 31-03-12 |
|---|---|---|---|
| TO | 3,000,426 | 2,579,754 | 2,395,007 |
| P/L | 1,282,997 | 1,048,289 | 959,382 |
| NW | 6,474,104 | 5,453,811 | 4,567,035 |
| WC | 5,461,901 | 4,201,517 | 3,289,429 |
| Emp. | 84 | 77 | 79 |

DUNS 73-745-6561
## Tracscare Group Ltd
**(Subsidiary of:** Sundhet Holding Sa)
11 Staple Inn, London WC1V 7QH
**Tel:** 03332407770
**Reg No:** 5003339 **Estd:** 2003 Private Limited Company
**Line of Business:** Other human health activities
**Issued Capital:** £1,146
**Directors:** C D Cameron, R P Constable, A E Smith, Ms C Conway, Ms S G Hullin
**Co. Secretary:** Mh Secretaries Limited
**US SIC:** 8091 **UK SIC:** 95200
**Auditors:** PricewaterhouseCoopers LLP

| | 31-03-14 | 31-03-13 | 31-03-12 |
|---|---|---|---|
| TO | 19,197,654 | 18,637,945 | 18,377,580 |
| P/L | 1,556,632 | 1,818,862 | 2,016,829 |
| NW | (8,593,838) | (11,756,934) | (13,901,287) |
| WC | (653,809) | (1,514,837) | (892,465) |
| Emp. | 667 | 655 | 629 |

DUNS 73-761-7840
## Tracsis Plc
Leeds Innovation Centre, 103 Clarendon Road, Leeds, West Yorkshire LS2 9DF
**Web:** www.tracsis.com
**Reg No:** 5019106 **Estd:** 2004 Public Limited Company
**Line of Business:** Publishing of software
**Export Sales:** £2,105,000
**Issued Capital:** £99,459
**Directors:** C Cole, C S Winward, M J Cawthra, J C Mcarthur, C S Lippell, J G Nelson
**Co. Secretary:** Maxwell Cawthra
**US SIC:** 7372, 7379
**UK SIC:** 83940
**Auditors:** KPMG Audit PLC
**Bankers:** HSBC Bank plc (40-27-15)

| | 31-07-14 | 31-07-13 | 31-07-12 |
|---|---|---|---|
| TO | 22,357,000 | 10,831,000 | 8,668,000 |
| P/L | 4,201,000 | 2,590,000 | 3,014,000 |
| NW | 7,125,000 | 7,142,000 | 6,187,000 |
| WC | 6,957,000 | 6,820,000 | 6,426,000 |
| Emp. | 295 | 138 | 65 |

DUNS 21-055-2983
## Tracy Park Golf and Country Club
Bath Road, Wick, Bristol, Avon BS30 5RN
**Tel:** 0117-937-1800
**Web:** www.tracypark.co.uk
**VAT No:** 936736391 **Estd:** 2010 Partnership
**Line of Business:** Manufacture of sports goods
**Partners:** Mrs A Knipe, I Knipe
**US SIC:** 3949 **UK SIC:** 49420
**Employees:** 50

DUNS 64-096-1124 **Imp-Exp**
## Trad Hire & Sales Ltd
**(Subsidiary of:** Altrad Investment Authority)
Cromwell Road, Bredbury, Stockport, Cheshire SK6 2RF
**Tel:** 01614304666 **Fax:** 01614304777
**Web:** www.trad.com
**Reg No:** 3491083 **VAT No:** 707540937
**Estd:** 2002 Private Limited Company
**Line of Business:** Renting of scaffold
**Export Markets:** Republic Of Ireland & Gibraltar
**Export Sales:** £627,997
**Issued Capital:** £606,538
**Directors:** M Ackers, I M Garcia, R K Neilson, A Ollivier, D Moore, H F Smith, J Paterson, Dr M Altrad
**Co. Secretary:** Alan Skeats
**Responsibilities**
**Senior:** Kevin Kenyon *(Manager)*
**Finance:** Alex Skeats *(Financial Director)*
**Purchasing:** John Ackers *(Buyer)*
**US SIC:** 7394 **UK SIC:** 84000
**Auditors:** Haslers
**Bankers:** Allied Irish Bank (gb) (23-85-81)

| | 30-11-13 | 30-11-12 | 30-11-11 |
|---|---|---|---|
| TO | 35,238,678 | 22,591,967 | 20,800,267 |
| P/L | 3,865,498 | 1,646,887 | 1,603,295 |
| NW | 12,004,602 | 8,876,322 | 7,854,812 |
| WC | (5,469,885) | (3,850,092) | (4,534,126) |
| Emp. | 165 | 101 | 100 |

DUNS 39-885-1733
## Trad Safety Systems Ltd
**(Subsidiary of:** Altrad Investment Authority)
Cromwell Road, Bredbury, Stockport, Cheshire SK6 2RF
**Tel:** 01614-943660 **Fax:** 01614-304888
**Web:** www.tradsafetydeck.co.uk
**Reg No:** 2225350 **VAT No:** 494248221
**Estd:** 2005 Private Limited Company
**Line of Business:** Other construction work involving special trades
**Issued Capital:** £50,425
**Principals:** D Moore *(Managing)*, H F Smith *(Managing)*, R K Neilson, A Ollivier, M Ackers, I M Garcia, J M Gorman, Dr M Altrad
**Co. Secretary:** Alan Skeats
**Branches:** Trad Safety Systems Ltd, Cross Green Way, Leeds, West Yorkshire LS9 0SE
**US SIC:** 1799, 7399
**UK SIC:** 50000, 83954
**Auditors:** Haslers
**Bankers:** Lloyds TSB Bank plc (30-95-74)

| | 30-11-13 | 30-11-12 | 30-11-11 |
|---|---|---|---|
| TA | 4,351,890 | 3,189,087 | 3,566,655 |
| NW | 192,266 | (115,804) | (219,889) |
| WC | (2,076,959) | (1,793,245) | (2,034,544) |

DUNS 22-715-3467
## Trad Scaffolding Co.Ltd
**(Subsidiary of:** Altrad Investment Authority)
Imperial Street, London E3 3ED
**Tel:** 02089801155 **Fax:** 02089813019
**Web:** www.trad.co.uk
**Reg No:** 1031385 **VAT No:** 236194950
**Estd:** 1977 Private Limited Company
**Line of Business:** Other construction work involving special trades
**Issued Capital:** £111,110
**Principals:** H F Smith *(Chairman)*, D Moore *(Managing)*, C H Smith, R K Neilson, Dr M Altrad, P Mcshane, A Ollivier, A D Mileham
**Co. Secretary:** Alan Skeats
**US SIC:** 1799 **UK SIC:** 50000
**Auditors:** Haslers
**Bankers:** Lloyds TSB Bank plc (30-95-74)

| | 30-11-13 | 30-11-12 | 30-11-11 |
|---|---|---|---|
| TO | 15,252,018 | 12,347,254 | 13,651,727 |
| P/L | (836,934) | (335,978) | 603,292 |
| NW | 10,232,664 | 9,750,735 | 9,751,291 |
| WC | 3,678,171 | 7,523,838 | 7,351,578 |
| Emp. | 216 | 154 | 143 |

DUNS 34-685-3943 **Imp**
## Trade Business Ltd
Units 13 & 15 Hartlebury Trading Estate, Kidderminster, Worcestershire DY10 4JB
**Tel:** 01299251100 **Fax:** 01299251131
**Web:** www.wyvern-furniture.co.uk
**Reg No:** 5490057 **Estd:** 2005 Private Limited Company
**Line of Business:** Manufacturers of upholstered chairs and seats
**Trading Style:** Wyvern Furniture, Wyvern Furniture
**Issued Capital:** £25,000
**Directors:** K Grainger, R P Thatcher, L J Hughes
**Co. Secretary:** Keith Willies
**US SIC:** 2599 **UK SIC:** 46720
**Auditors:** RSM Tenon Audit Ltd

| | 31-12-13 | 31-12-12 | 31-12-11 |
|---|---|---|---|
| TO | 12,358,281 | 12,778,265 | 14,274,427 |
| P/L | 531,348 | 499,550 | 455,743 |
| NW | 772,022 | 633,411 | 528,901 |
| WC | 788,028 | 640,613 | 515,477 |
| Emp. | 153 | 146 | 162 |

DUNS 22-520-0062
## Trade Direct Insurance Services Ltd
**(Subsidiary of:** Kelliher Insurance Group Ltd)
Trade Direct House Ockford Mill, Ockford Road, Godalming, Surrey GU7 1RH
**Tel:** 01483-521650 **Fax:** 01483521652
**Web:** www.tradedirectinsurance.co.uk
**Reg No:** 1580129 **Estd:** 1981 Private Limited Company
**Line of Business:** Insurance brokers
**Issued Capital:** £31,200
**Directors:** M J Coulbert, Ms J E Guyett, C J Calder, R N Donegan, Mrs I F Coggan, R Rees
**Co. Secretary:** Stephen Cox
**Responsibilities**
**Senior:** Richard French *(Manager)*, Richard Woolford *(Manager)*, damian kissane *(group cEO)*
**US SIC:** 6411 **UK SIC:** 83200
**Auditors:** BDO LLP
**Bankers:** Bank Of Scotland (80-20-22)

| | 31-12-13 | 31-12-12 | 31-12-11 |
|---|---|---|---|
| TO | 5,057,793 | 4,845,037 | 4,850,479 |
| P/L | 2,048,829 | 1,986,958 | 1,696,375 |
| NW | 1,242,154 | 814,771 | 622,371 |
| WC | 1,027,004 | 636,478 | 452,598 |
| Emp. | 47 | 45 | 45 |

DUNS 21-558-0504
## Trade Distribution Ltd
Distribution Centre, Douglas, Douglas, Isle of Man IM2 1QG
**Tel:** 01624699477 **Fax:** 01624-699588
**Web:** www.tdl.co.im
**Reg No:** 0100757M **Estd:** 2000 Private Limited Company
**Line of Business:** Freight forwarders
**Responsibilities**
**Senior:** Steve Pickett *(Manager)*, Alison Pickett *(Compliance Director)*
**Branches:** Trade Distribution Limited, Unit 1-3, Paxton Place, Skelmersdale, Lancashire WN8 9QH
**US SIC:** 4213 **UK SIC:** 72300
**Employees:** 250

DUNS 21-041-4518
## Trade It
7-9 Emery Road, Bristol, Avon BS4 5PF
**Tel:** 01179720800
**Web:** www.tradeit.co.uk
**Estd:** 1991 Proprietorship
**Line of Business:** Newspapers publishing
**Proprietor:** Mrs M Ackerman
**US SIC:** 2711 **UK SIC:** 47512
**Employees:** 67

DUNS 22-702-5756 **Exp**
## Trade Mark Owners Association Ltd
Sea Containers House, 20 Upper Ground, London SE1 9ZB
**Tel:** 02079252515 **Fax:** 020-7902-7111
**Reg No:** 0023558 **VAT No:** 243840762
**Estd:** 1886 Private Limited Company
**Line of Business:** Architectural services
**Export Markets:** Worldwide
**Trading Style:** T M O A
**Directors:** A C Smith, P N Matthews
**Co. Secretary:** Michael Stannard
**US SIC:** 8911 **UK SIC:** 83701
**Auditors:** Chantrey Vellacott DFK
**Bankers:** HSBC Bank plc (40-05-20)

| | 31-12-13 | 31-12-12 | 31-12-11 |
|---|---|---|---|
| TA | 225,000 | 1,300,008 | 1,300,008 |
| P/L | (1,075,008) | N/A | N/A |
| NW | 225,000 | 1,300,008 | 1,300,008 |

DUNS 76-446-2263
## Trade Master Property Services Ltd
Trade Master House, Birmingham, West Midlands B21 9NB
**Tel:** 01215514444
**Web:** www.trademaster.co.uk
**Reg No:** 2563595 **Estd:** 1990 Private Limited Company
**Line of Business:** Building of complete constructions or parts thereof; civil engineering
**Issued Capital:** £610
**Directors:** A J Broughton-Taylor, Ms L A Broughton-Taylor
**Co. Secretary:** Mrs Bernadette Broughton-Taylor
**US SIC:** 1541 **UK SIC:** 50100
**Auditors:** Hardeman Smith & Power

| | 28-02-14 | 28-02-13 | 29-02-12 |
|---|---|---|---|
| TA | 203,120 | 152,724 | 107,891 |
| NW | 35,968 | 36,618 | 34,089 |
| WC | 27,277 | 26,197 | 30,875 |

DUNS 22-753-3528 **Imp-Exp**
## Trade Mouldings Ltd
Cookstown Business Park, Sandholes Road, Cookstown, Co Tyrone BT80 9AR
**Tel:** 028-8676-2993 **Fax:** 028-8676-5684
**Web:** www.trademouldings.com
**Reg No:** 0015596NI **VAT No:** 349645223
**Estd:** 1982 Private Limited Company
**Line of Business:** Plastic injection moulding
**Export Markets:** Republic of Ireland
**Trading Style:** Trade Mouldings Ltd
**Issued Capital:** £100,000
**Directors:** Miss S M Macoscar, A Mcoscar, R K Macoscar
**Co. Secretary:** Conor Mcoscar
**Responsibilities**
**Senior:** Damian Connelly *(Senior Marketing Executive)*, Conor Macoscar *(Managing Director)*
**Finance:** Joy Cavanagh *(Senior IT Executive)*, Conor Macoscar *(Managing Director)*
**Marketing:** Damian Connelly *(Senior Marketing Executive)*
**Sales:** Damian Connelly *(Senior Marketing Executive)*
**Admin:** Jean Kempton *(Office Manager)*
**IT:** Joy Cavanagh *(Senior IT Executive)*
**HR:** Jean Kempton *(Office Manager)*
**Health & Safety:** Terry Campbell *(Health & Safety Officer)*
**Branches:** Trade Mouldings Ltd, Unit 3, Kingsway, Rochdale, Lancashire OL16 5DB
**US SIC:** 3079, 5039
**UK SIC:** 48360, 61300
**Auditors:** Mckinley & Co
**Bankers:** Ulster Bank Ltd (98-04-50)

| | 31-03-14 | 31-03-13 | 31-03-12 |
|---|---|---|---|
| TA | 11,126,258 | 9,655,477 | 8,655,022 |
| P/L | 1,245,150 | 1,480,309 | 1,290,613 |
| NW | 8,338,741 | 7,588,696 | 6,451,509 |
| WC | 4,968,972 | 5,516,772 | 3,955,250 |

DUNS 21-773-0127
## Trade Refuse Collection
Mansfield D C Depot, Maunside, Green Line Industrial Estate, Mansfield, Nottinghamshire NG18 5GU
**Tel:** 01623463092
**Web:** www.mansfield.gov.uk
**Estd:** 2011 Proprietorship
**Line of Business:** Fumigation services
**Proprietor:** Mrs D Wilcox
**Responsibilities**
**Senior:** Kevan Poyntz *(Manager)*
**US SIC:** 4953 **UK SIC:** 92110
**Employees:** 100

DUNS 22-016-3906 **Imp**
## Trade Solutions (Scotland) Ltd
East Gormack, Blairgowrie, Perthshire PH10 6TA
**Web:** www.trade-solutions.co.uk
**Reg No:** 0208389SC **Estd:** 2000 Private Limited Company
**Line of Business:** Wholesale of fruit and vegetables
**Issued Capital:** £718
**Directors:** Ms H F Morrison, O G Thomson
**Co. Secretary:** Michael Thomson
**US SIC:** 5148, 7399
**UK SIC:** 61700, 83954
**Bankers:** The Royal Bank Of Scotland Plc (83-16-33)

| | 30-04-14 | 30-04-13 | 30-04-12 |
|---|---|---|---|
| TA | 1,137,447 | 911,199 | 970,277 |
| NW | 567,726 | 424,029 | 355,022 |
| WC | 331,151 | 229,685 | 201,754 |

DUNS 21-579-6750
## Trade Waste Collection Service
Condercum Road, Newcastle-Upon-Tyne, Tyne and Wear NE4 8XN
**Tel:** 01912651414
**Estd:** 2002 Proprietorship
**Line of Business:** Skip hire
**Proprietor:** T Gribbins
**US SIC:** 7394 **UK SIC:** 84000
**Employees:** 87

DUNS 34-745-8101
## Trade Windows (Derby) Ltd
(**Subsidiary of:** Frame Fast (U K) Ltd)
Navigation Retail Park, Derby, Derbyshire DE24 8WA
**Web:** www.tradewindows.com
**Reg No:** 2782897 **Estd:** 1993 Private Limited Company
**Line of Business:** Other retail sale in specialised stores not elsewhere classified
**Issued Capital:** £200
**Director:** J Brocklehurst
**Co. Secretary:** George Lorraine
**Branches:** Trade Windows (Derby) Ltd, 109A King St, Derby, Derbyshire DE1 3EE
**US SIC:** 5999 **UK SIC:** 65600
**Auditors:** Cooper Parry
**Bankers:** The Royal Bank Of Scotland Plc (16-18-18)

| | 31-12-13 | 31-12-12 | 31-12-11 |
|---|---|---|---|
| TA | 354,868 | 765,895 | 724,651 |
| NW | 12,954 | 443,189 | 266,341 |
| WC | 33,212 | 432,683 | 278,127 |

DUNS 23-882-8458
## Tradebe Environmental Services Ltd
(**Subsidiary of:** Grupo Tradebe Medio Ambiente Sociedad Limitada)
Atlas House Third Avenue, Globe Park, Marlow, Buckinghamshire SL7 1EY
**Tel:** 01244-520122
**Web:** www.willacyoil.com
**Reg No:** 3873993 **Estd:** 1999 Private Limited Company
**Line of Business:** Management activities of other non-financial holding companies not elsewhere classified
**Export Sales:** £15,347,000
**Issued Capital:** £14,321,768
**Directors:** V C Creixell De Villalonga, Tradebe Management Sl, J S Mcgown
**Co. Secretary:** Jordi Creixell
**Responsibilities**
**Senior:** Alejandro Gazulla Planellas *(Manager)*, Victor Villalonga *(Director)*
**US SIC:** 6711 **UK SIC:** 83962
**Auditors:** Mazars LLP

| | 31-12-13 | 31-12-12 | 31-12-11 |
|---|---|---|---|
| TO | 81,675,000 | 73,421,000 | 60,854,000 |
| P/L | (2,946,000) | 483,000 | (700,000) |
| NW | 35,631,000 | 28,078,000 | 28,582,000 |
| WC | 3,734,000 | 4,946,000 | 8,938,000 |
| Emp. | 583 | 539 | 330 |

DUNS 34-782-5291
## Tradebe Fawley Ltd
(**Subsidiary of:** Grupo Tradebe Medio Ambiente Sociedad Limitada)
C/O Willacy Oil Services Ltd, Whittle Close, Engineer Park, Deeside, Clwyd CH5 2QE
**Tel:** 01244530489
**Reg No:** 2786680 **Estd:** 1993 Private Limited Company
**Line of Business:** Collection and treatment of other waste
**Export Sales:** £1,999,000
**Issued Capital:** £2
**Directors:** J S Mcgown, Tradebe Management Sl, V C Creixell De Villalonga
**Co. Secretary:** Jordi Creixell Sureda
**Branches:** Tradebe Fawley Ltd, Charleston Road, Hardley Heights, S04 53NX South Hampshire
**US SIC:** 4953 **UK SIC:** 92110
**Auditors:** Mazars LLP

| | 31-12-13 | 31-12-12 | 31-12-11 |
|---|---|---|---|
| TO | 16,479,000 | 14,173,000 | 28,303,000 |
| P/L | 841,000 | 249,000 | (17,000) |
| NW | 19,618,000 | 19,069,000 | 18,629,000 |
| WC | 2,275,000 | 1,587,000 | (427,000) |
| Emp. | N/A | N/A | 67 |

DUNS 21-734-1727
## Tradebe Fawley Midco Ltd
(**Subsidiary of:** Grupo Tradebe Medio Ambiente Sociedad Limitada)
Charleston Road, Hardley, Southampton, Hampshire SO45 3NX
**Tel:** 02380-883-000 **Fax:** 02380-883-010
**Web:** www.tradebe.co.uk
**Reg No:** 7688319 **Estd:** 2011 Private Limited Company
**Line of Business:** Collection and treatment of other waste
**Issued Capital:** £1
**Directors:** V C Creixell De Villalonga, Tradebe Management Sl, J S Mcgown
**Co. Secretary:** Jordi Creixell Sureda
**US SIC:** 4953 **UK SIC:** 92110

| | 31-12-13 | 31-12-12 |
|---|---|---|
| TA | 23,793,000 | 23,793,000 |

DUNS 23-891-5842
## Tradebe Healthcare National Ltd
(**Subsidiary of:** Grupo Tradebe Medio Ambiente Sociedad Limitada)
Edmonton Power Station, Advent Way, London N18 3AG
**Tel:** 08452300091
**Web:** www.polkacrest.co.uk
**Reg No:** 3882534 **Estd:** 1999 Private Limited Company
**Line of Business:** Collection and treatment of other waste
**Issued Capital:** £16,444,873
**Directors:** V Creixell De Villalonga, J S Mcgown, Tradebe Management Sl
**Co. Secretary:** Jordi Creixell Sureda
**Branches:** Tradebe Healthcare National Ltd, North Orbital Road, Watford, Hertfordshire WD25 7PR
**US SIC:** 4953, 8999
**UK SIC:** 92110, 83954
**Auditors:** PKF (UK) LLP

| | 31-12-13 | 31-12-12 | 31-12-11 |
|---|---|---|---|
| TO | 18,332,000 | 11,047,000 | 7,350,000 |
| P/L | (6,059,000) | (1,340,000) | (8,228,000) |
| NW | 2,239,000 | (2,033,000) | 208,000 |
| WC | (5,363,000) | (10,492,000) | (13,463,000) |
| Emp. | 129 | 112 | 53 |

DUNS 23-317-9501
## Tradebe Management Ltd
(**Subsidiary of:** Grupo Tradebe Medio Ambiente Sociedad Limitada)
Hendon Dock, Sunderland, Tyne and Wear SR1 2ES
**Tel:** 01909519406
**Web:** www.tradebe.com
**Reg No:** 4372081 **Estd:** 2002 Private Limited Company
**Line of Business:** Collection and treatment of other waste
**Trading Style:** Advanced Waste Solutions
**Issued Capital:** £2,920,002
**Directors:** J S Mcgown, V C Creixell De Villalonga, Tradebe Management Sl, J Creixell
**Responsibilities**
**Senior:** Mark Olpin *(joint director)*, Victor Sureda *(Director)*
**IT:** Mike Barlow *(IT Manager)*
**Branches:** Tradebe Management Ltd, Charleston Road, Southampton, Hampshire SO45 3NX
**US SIC:** 3031 **UK SIC:** 48123
**Auditors:** Mazars LLP

| | 31-12-13 | 31-12-12 | 31-12-11 |
|---|---|---|---|
| TO | 8,424,000 | 5,731,000 | 3,241,000 |
| P/L | (441,000) | 485,000 | (2,114,000) |
| NW | (112,000) | 962,000 | 359,000 |
| WC | (3,455,000) | (2,494,000) | (6,723,000) |
| Emp. | 96 | 26 | 23 |

DUNS 23-899-7956
## Tradebe Solvent Recycling Ltd
(**Subsidiary of:** Grupo Tradebe Medio Ambiente Sociedad Limitada)
Customer Services Centre, Morecambe, Lancashire LA3 3JW
**Tel:** 01524853053
**Web:** www.srm-ltd.com
**Reg No:** 3890526 **Estd:** 2000 Private Limited Company
**Line of Business:** Collection and treatment of other waste
**Export Sales:** £11,555,000
**Trading Style:** S R M
**Issued Capital:** £10,000,000
**Principals:** J S Mcgown *(Managing)*, Tradebe Management Sl, V C Creixell De Villalonga
**Co. Secretary:** Jordi Sureda
**Responsibilities**
**Senior:** Tony Feather *(Transport)*, Victor Villalonga *(Director)*, Antony Walmsley *(Manager)*
**Branches:** Tradebe Solvent Recycling Ltd, Middleton Road, Morecambe, Lancashire LA3 3JW
**US SIC:** 4953 **UK SIC:** 92110
**Auditors:** Ernst & Young LLP

| | 31-12-13 | 31-12-12 | 31-12-11 |
|---|---|---|---|
| TO | 39,806,000 | 38,726,000 | 39,793,000 |
| P/L | 751,000 | (869,000) | 2,065,000 |
| NW | 13,838,000 | 13,364,000 | 13,752,000 |
| WC | 347,000 | 1,230,000 | 3,379,000 |
| Emp. | N/A | N/A | 287 |

DUNS 23-932-1594
## Tradedoubler Ltd
(**Subsidiary of:** Tradedoubler Ab)
24th Floor Portland House, Bressenden Place, London SW1E 5BH
**Tel:** 020-7798-5800
**Web:** www.tradedoubler.com
**Reg No:** 3921985 **Estd:** 2000 Private Limited Company
**Line of Business:** Marketing consultants
**Export Sales:** £24,991,504
**Issued Capital:** £48,867,308
**Director:** M K Stadelmeyer
**Co. Secretary:** Goodwille Limited
**Responsibilities**
**Senior:** Karly Holmes *(Office Manager)*, Nils Ljungl f *(Director)*
**Marketing:** Els de Witte *(Marketing Manager)*
**Admin:** Sam McCalister *(Office Manager)*
**IT:** Ben Manning *(Head of Technical Services)*
**HR:** Louise Brunhoj *(Human Resources Manager)*
**Branches:** Tradedoubler Ltd, 15B Abingdon Road, London W8 6AH
**US SIC:** 7392, 7399
**UK SIC:** 83951, 83954
**Auditors:** Ernst & Young LLP
**Bankers:** Skandinaviska Enskilda Banken Ab (publ) (40-48-65)

| | 31-12-13 | 31-12-12 | 31-12-11 |
|---|---|---|---|
| TO | 49,002,949 | 57,021,654 | 66,548,910 |
| P/L | 1,092,730 | 1,639,519 | (38,708,531) |
| NW | 2,388,265 | 1,609,904 | 407,745 |
| WC | 2,214,038 | 1,328,955 | 244,121 |
| Emp. | 149 | 118 | 102 |

DUNS 77-027-5154
## Tradelink Direct Ltd
(**Subsidiary of:** L.H. Group Ltd)
Unit 4 4-14 Marwick Road, March, Cambridgeshire PE15 8PH
**Tel:** 01354657650 **Fax:** 01354-657440
**Web:** www.tradelinkdirect.co.uk
**Reg No:** 2665823 **VAT No:** 599500404
**Estd:** 1992 Private Limited Company
**Line of Business:** Manufacturers of joinery
**Issued Capital:** £6,000
**Principals:** A C Morley *(Managing)*, M Tarran Jones, J W Moody
**Co. Secretary:** Simon Richards
**Responsibilities**
**Senior:** Justin Smalley *(Stores Supervisor)*
**HR:** David Horsfall *(Human Resources Manager)*
**Operations:** Justin Smalley *(Stores Supervisor)*
**Purchasing:** Justin Smalley *(Stores Supervisor)*
**US SIC:** 2431, 3442
**UK SIC:** 46300, 31420
**Auditors:** Knights Lowe
**Bankers:** National Westminster Bank Plc (53-81-42)

| | 28-03-14 | 29-03-13 | 01-03-12 |
|---|---|---|---|
| TO | 13,959,800 | 12,551,889 | 14,126,835 |
| P/L | 885,039 | 441,412 | 933,386 |
| NW | 6,253,480 | 5,568,903 | 6,339,850 |
| WC | 5,670,784 | 4,989,308 | 5,739,072 |
| Emp. | 149 | 150 | 147 |

DUNS 50-345-3946 **Imp-Exp**
## Tradelink Wood Products Ltd
Tradelink House, London W10 4LG
**Tel:** 020-7460-7788
**Web:** www.tradelink-group.com
**Reg No:** 2365523 **VAT No:** 532410000
**Estd:** 1989 Private Limited Company
**Line of Business:** Agents involved in the sale of timber and building materials
**Export Markets:** E U, Africa, U S A, Philipines, Thailand, Korea
**Principals:** H P Schey *(Managing)*, C B Schey, M Grome, J A Lew, P K Gates, H L Stonefield, H M Da Silva Cristo
**Co. Secretary:** Noel Wright
**Responsibilities**
**IT:** Patrick Oppler *(IT Manager)*
**US SIC:** 5072 **UK SIC:** 61500
**Auditors:** Lewis Golden & Co
**Bankers:** National Westminster Bank Plc (50-00-00)
**Employees:** 313
**Turnover:** £73,680,973

DUNS 22-712-0854 **Imp**
## Trades Union Congress
Congress House, Great Russell Street, London WC1B 3LS
**Tel:** 02076364030
**Web:** www.tuc.org.uk
**VAT No:** 524176065 **Estd:** 2005
**Line of Business:** Trade unions
**Directors:** M Jones, J Scott, B Barber
**Responsibilities**
**Senior:** Sean Bamford *(Manager)*, Karen Bartram *(General Manager)*, David Hemington *(Head, Management Services and)*, Francis O' Grady *(General Secretary)*, Alhaji Oyetunji *(Chairman)*
**Finance:** Bandula Kothalawala *(International Officer)*
**Marketing:** Liz Chinchen *(Senior media officer)*, Craig Hawkins *(Web Development Executive)*, Tim Lezard *(Media Officer)*, Taj Mohammed *(Race Relations Committee Execu)*, Rachel Noble *(Spokesperson)*, Francis O' Grady *(General Secretary)*, Nigel Stanley *(Head, Campaigns and Communicat)*, Wilf Sullivan *(Race Relations Committee Execu)*
**Sales:** Owen Tudor *(Sales Manager)*
**Admin:** Francis O' Grady *(General Secretary)*
**IT:** Joe Mendes *(Senior IT Executive)*, Tanya Warlock *(Local Migration Project Worker)*
**HR:** Harry Cunningham *(Training Director)*, Jenny Dixon *(Human Resources Manager)*, Martin Hegarty *(Training Director)*, Sarah Veale *(Head of the Equality and Emplo)*
**Health & Safety:** Tom Mellish *(Policy Officer)*
**Operations:** Jay Stewart *(Head Chef)*
**Branches:** Trades Union Congress, 4th Floor John Smith House 145, Glasgow, Lanarkshire G2 4RZ
**US SIC:** 8699 **UK SIC:** 96902
**Auditors:** Hard Dowdy
**Bankers:** Unity Trust Bank Plc (08-60-01)
**Employees:** 200
**Turnover:** £51,452,000

DUNS 23-387-6429
## Tradestone Software Inc
(**Subsidiary of:** Tradestone Software Inc.)
Sienna Court, The Broadway, Maidenhead, Berkshire SL6 1NJ
**Web:** www.tradestonesoftware.com
**Reg No:** 0025604FC **Estd:** 2004 Foreign Company
**Line of Business:** Computer consumables suppliers
**Co. Secretary:** Jacob Zakarian
**Responsibilities**
**Senior:** Frederick Grein *(Director)*
**US SIC:** 5081 **UK SIC:** 61490

DUNS 21-587-8397
## Tradeteam Dhl
2 Bonehurst Road, Salfords, Redhill, Surrey RH1 5EH
**Tel:** 01293787400
**Estd:** 2011 Proprietorship
**Line of Business:** Drinks - delivered
**Proprietor:** R Rose
**US SIC:** 5921 **UK SIC:** 64200
**Employees:** 200

DUNS 49-066-5544
## Tradeteam Ltd
(**Subsidiary of:** Deutsche Post Ag)
Hams Hall Distribution Park Eddison Road, Birmingham, West Midlands B46 1TT
**Tel:** 01675-468500 **Fax:** 01675-467541
**Web:** www.tradeteam.com
**Reg No:** 3078367 **Estd:** 1995 Private Limited Company
**Line of Business:** Distribution service providers
**Issued Capital:** £1,455
**Directors:** T J Slater, N I Bowie, J E Gill, S M Stacey
**Co. Secretary:** Mrs Jane Li
**Responsibilities**
**Senior:** Matt Crampton *(Manager)*, Gavin Murdoch *(Manager)*
**HR:** Carol Peckham *(Human Resources Director)*
**Health & Safety:** Jayne Poston *(Health & Safety Officer)*
**Branches:** Tradeteam Ltd, Unit 3, Maryport Road, Workington, Cumbria CA14 1NH
**US SIC:** 7399, 4213, 4226
**UK SIC:** 83954, 72300, 77003
**Auditors:** PricewaterhouseCoopers LLP
**Bankers:** HSBC Bank plc (40-00-00)

| | 31-12-13 | 31-12-12 | 31-12-11 |
|---|---|---|---|
| TO | 141,536,000 | 144,582,000 | 160,346,000 |
| P/L | 33,617,000 | 10,433,000 | 11,121,000 |
| NW | 46,110,000 | 21,711,000 | 21,414,000 |
| WC | 27,350,000 | 232,000 | (60,000) |
| Emp. | 1,757 | 1,862 | 2,065 |

DUNS 53-601-8377 **Imp**
## Tradetrue Ltd
Building 15d Bilton Industrial Estate, Humber Avenue, Coventry, West Midlands CV3 1JL
**Tel:** 02476459500
**Web:** www.couriersupport.co.uk
**Reg No:** 3407032 **Estd:** 1997 Private Limited Company
**Line of Business:** Couriers
**Issued Capital:** £100
**Director:** D A Wilson
**Co. Secretary:** Ms Beverley Haw
**US SIC:** 4213 **UK SIC:** 72300

| | 30-09-13 | 30-09-12 | 30-09-11 |
|---|---|---|---|
| TA | 696,748 | 548,192 | 499,205 |
| NW | 157,132 | 78,739 | 79,115 |
| WC | 150,725 | 71,073 | 78,104 |

DUNS 23-922-7536 **Imp**
## Tradeweb Europe Ltd
(**Subsidiary of:** Thomson Company Inc The)
99 Gresham Street, London EC2V 7NG
**Fax:** 020-7776-3201
**Web:** www.tradeweb.com
**Reg No:** 3912826 **Estd:** 1900 Private Limited Company
**Line of Business:** Activities auxiliary to financial intermediation not elsewhere classified
**Issued Capital:** £800,000
**Directors:** Ms C Maliphant, E Bruni, S J Maisey, A T Bernard, A C Rutter
**Co. Secretary:** Stephen Hall
**Responsibilities**
**Senior:** Lee Olesky *(Chief Executive Officer)*, Jesper Olsen *(Manager)*
**Finance:** Claire Hembley *(Financial Director)*
**HR:** Reccoc Cornwell *(Human Resources Manager)*
**US SIC:** 6111 **UK SIC:** 81501
**Auditors:** PricewaterhouseCoopers LLP

| | 31-12-13 | 31-12-12 | 31-12-11 |
|---|---|---|---|
| TA | 41,848,000 | 37,564,000 | 39,319,000 |
| P/L | 19,071,000 | 15,330,000 | 14,182,000 |
| NW | 24,446,000 | 20,198,000 | 22,595,000 |
| WC | 22,694,000 | 18,700,000 | 21,137,000 |
| Emp. | 136 | 134 | 131 |

DUNS 64-105-5439
## Tradewind Recruitment Ltd
(**Subsidiary of:** Abaco Recruitment Ltd)
Castlewood House 77 91, New Oxford Street, London WC1A 1DG
**Tel:** 08458801271
**Web:** www.twrecruitment.com
**Reg No:** 4105705 **Estd:** 2000 Private Limited Company
**Line of Business:** Employment and recruitment companies and consultants
**Issued Capital:** £100
**Directors:** M R Kaye, Ms K Lynch, Ms T Mclennan
**Co. Secretary:** Michael Kaye
**Responsibilities**
**Senior:** Jeremy Waters *(Chief Executive Officer)*
**US SIC:** 7361 **UK SIC:** 83954
**Auditors:** Birch Sergeant

| | 31-08-13 | 31-08-12 | 31-08-11 |
|---|---|---|---|
| TO | 18,748,552 | 15,658,290 | 15,540,014 |
| P/L | 1,318,337 | 668,964 | 217,615 |
| NW | 741,515 | 542,679 | 409,314 |
| WC | 701,965 | 473,929 | 287,189 |
| Emp. | 160 | 98 | 219 |

DUNS 23-292-5870
## Tradewise Insurance Services Ltd
(**Subsidiary of:** Tradewise Group of Companies Ltd)
Link House, 292-308 Southbury Road, Enfield, Middlesex EN1 1TS
**Tel:** 02083504020 **Fax:** 08707002299
**Web:** www.tradewiseinsurance.com
**Reg No:** 4446259 **Estd:** 2002 Private Limited Company
**Line of Business:** Insurance companies and agents
**Issued Capital:** £100,000
**Directors:** W M Bradshaw, M R Tyler, J F Humphreys, B W Martin, D J Ratledge, A C Middleton, P Bates
**Co. Secretary:** Ms Annette Tyler
**Responsibilities**
**Health & Safety:** Kerry Russell *(Facilities Manager)*
**Facilities:** Kerry Russell *(Facilities Manager)*
**US SIC:** 6411 **UK SIC:** 83200
**Bankers:** Barclays Bank Plc (20-73-26)

| | 31-12-13 | 31-12-12 | 31-12-11 |
|---|---|---|---|
| TO | 19,709,521 | 19,582,424 | 16,245,739 |
| P/L | 1,059,215 | 1,528,415 | 964,931 |
| NW | 449,606 | 442,107 | 298,736 |
| WC | (1,831,976) | (1,587,501) | (1,029,801) |
| Emp. | 151 | 148 | 111 |

DUNS 77-511-3608
## Tradex Insurance Co Ltd
(**Subsidiary of:** Tradex Insurance Holdings Ltd)
Victory House, 7 Selsdon Way, London E14 9GL
**Tel:** 02070019200 **Fax:** 020-7068-7730
**Web:** www.tradex.com
**Reg No:** 2983873 **Estd:** 1994 Private Limited Company
**Line of Business:** Non-life insurance
**Trading Style:** Tradex
**Issued Capital:** £7,930,770
**Principals:** R W Clegg *(Managing)*, S R Braine, P Blake-Turner, S C Endean, J M Clark, Ms D A Austin, R E Still, Mrs S A Bellamy
**Co. Secretary:** Steven Moore
**Responsibilities**
**Senior:** Charles Reilly *(Director)*
**HR:** Christine Howell *(Human Resources Director)*
**Health & Safety:** Deborah Hall *(Facilities Manager)*
**Facilities:** Deborah Hall *(Facilities Manager)*
**Purchasing:** Deborah Hall *(Facilities Manager)*
**Branches:** Tradex Insurance Co Ltd, 128-129 Minories, London EC3N 1NT
**US SIC:** 6411 **UK SIC:** 83200
**Auditors:** CLB Littlejohn Frazer
**Bankers:** Lloyds TSB Bank plc (30-13-54)

| | 31-12-13 | 31-12-12 | 31-12-11 |
|---|---|---|---|
| TO | 31,013,000 | 30,557,000 | 28,534,000 |
| P/L | (5,620,000) | 40,000 | 6,081,000 |
| NW | 16,565,000 | 20,490,000 | 19,921,000 |
| WC | 35,773,000 | 50,646,000 | 40,865,000 |
| Emp. | 255 | 246 | 239 |

DUNS 23-215-6419
## The Trading Co Ltd
Prince Consort House, Albert Embankment, London SE1 7TJ
**Tel:** 02088759944
**Web:** www.phoenix-trading.co.uk
**Reg No:** 4060777 **Estd:** 2000 Private Limited Company
**Line of Business:** Other publishing
**Issued Capital:** £96
**Directors:** C Bruce, Ms R J Bradley
**Co. Secretary:** Ms Sheila Shaw
**US SIC:** 2741 **UK SIC:** 47541
**Auditors:** Owadally & King
**Bankers:** Lloyds TSB Bank plc (77-93-00)

| | 31-12-13 | 31-12-12 | 31-12-11 |
|---|---|---|---|
| TO | 9,299,809 | 11,103,579 | 12,425,445 |
| P/L | (116,653) | (205,869) | (11,924) |
| NW | 754,597 | 864,111 | 1,053,572 |
| WC | 769,817 | 683,444 | 358,830 |
| Emp. | 96 | 113 | 123 |

DUNS 71-876-8307
## Trading Standards South East Ltd
Consort House, Queensway, Redhill, Surrey RH1 1YB
**Tel:** 01372371700
**Web:** www.surreycc.gov.uk
**Reg No:** 5259365 **Estd:** 2004 Private Company Limited By Guarantee
**Line of Business:** General (overall) public service activities
**Directors:** D R Cross, Mrs J C Edsell, P Lipscomb, R N Strawson, P J Dart, S J Ruddy, I K Treacher, J Crosbie
**Co. Secretary:** Mrs Gaynor Jackson
**Responsibilities**
**Senior:** Lucy Corrie *(Director)*, Susan Crawley *(Director)*, Virginia De Haan *(Director)*, Amanda Gregory *(Director)*, Jody Kerman *(Director)*, John Peerless-Mountford *(Director)*, Joanne Player *(Director)*, Steve Ruddy *(Community Protection Manager)*, Richard Sargeant *(Director)*, Julie Woodhouse *(Director)*, Rosemary Zambra *(Director)*
**US SIC:** 9121 **UK SIC:** 91110

| | 31-03-14 | 31-03-13 | 31-03-12 |
|---|---|---|---|
| TA | 1,724,606 | 1,179,942 | 1,596,632 |
| NW | 40,036 | 32,263 | 28,050 |
| WC | 40,036 | 32,263 | 28,050 |

DUNS 22-713-3642
## Tradition Financial Services Ltd.
(**Subsidiary of:** Viel Et Cie Finances)
Beaufort House, 15 St Botolph Street, London EC3A 7QX
**Tel:** 02074549422 **Fax:** 020-7454-9421
**Web:** www.tfsbrokers.com
**Reg No:** 1046064 **Estd:** 1972 Private Limited Company
**Line of Business:** Financial intermediation not elsewhere classified
**Trading Style:** Tradition
**Issued Capital:** £250,000
**Directors:** F Brisebois, S C Tully, M S Leibowitz, S Vjestica, H P De Carmoy, D C Marcus, C M Baillet, M G Mccaig
**Co. Secretary:** Peter Weston
**Responsibilities**
**Senior:** William Wostyn *(Director)*
**US SIC:** 6111 **UK SIC:** 81501
**Auditors:** Ernst & Young LLP
**Bankers:** National Westminster Bank Plc (56-00-18)

| | 31-12-13 | 31-12-12 | 31-12-11 |
|---|---|---|---|
| TA | 22,440,000 | 26,081,000 | 20,508,000 |
| P/L | 1,800,000 | 5,911,000 | 7,703,000 |
| NW | 16,131,000 | 15,092,000 | 10,520,000 |
| WC | 14,444,000 | 15,399,000 | 11,022,000 |
| Emp. | 98 | 96 | 85 |

DUNS 23-416-1847
## Tradition Property Services Ltd
26 Aberdour Street, London SE1 4SG
**Tel:** 020-7231-5888
**Web:** www.traditionproperty.co.uk
**Reg No:** 5565929 **VAT No:** 865018128
**Estd:** 1985 Private Limited Company
**Line of Business:** Cleaning contracting commercial
**Issued Capital:** £10,000
**Director:** A Regan
**Co. Secretary:** Ms Jacqueline Fulton
**US SIC:** 7349 **UK SIC:** 92300

| | 30-09-13 | 30-09-12 | 30-09-11 |
|---|---|---|---|
| TA | 132,410 | 155,013 | 227,630 |
| NW | 37,147 | 77,695 | 143,924 |
| WC | 24,619 | 61,464 | 129,431 |

DUNS 22-703-8627 **Imp**
## Tradition (U K) Ltd
(**Subsidiary of:** Viel Et Cie Finances)
Beaufort House, 15 St Botolph Street, London EC3A 7QX
**Tel:** 02071981500 **Fax:** 0207260444
**Web:** www.tradition.com
**Reg No:** 0937647 **Estd:** 1972 Private Limited Company
**Line of Business:** Financial services
**Issued Capital:** £15,050,000
**Directors:** S A Umpelby, H P De Carmoy, F Brisebois, S Vjestica, D C Marcus, M J Anderson, S C Tully, M G Mccaig
**Co. Secretary:** Peter Weston
**Responsibilities**
**Senior:** Bruce Collins *(Manager)*, Richard Fels *(Executive)*, Stefan Green *(Manager)*, Philip Regan *(Manager)*, William Wostyn *(Director)*
**Finance:** Mark Graham-Hagg *(Financial Director)*, Mark Hagg *(Finance Director)*, Paul Horrmann *(Broker)*
**Marketing:** Regina Malzburg *(Sales & Marketing Manager)*
**Sales:** Will Aston-Reese *(Vice President for Money-Marke)*, Regina Malzburg *(Sales & Marketing Manager)*
**IT:** Alex Krovina *(Chief Technology Officer)*
**Health & Safety:** Mark Heneke *(Facilities Manager)*
**Facilities:** Mark Heneke *(Facilities Manager)*
**Branches:** Tradition (U K) Ltd, 109-117 Middlesex Street, London E1 7JF
**US SIC:** 6111, 6211
**UK SIC:** 81501, 83100
**Auditors:** Ernst & Young LLP
**Bankers:** National Westminster Bank Plc (56-00-18)

| | 31-12-13 | 31-12-12 | 31-12-11 |
|---|---|---|---|
| TA | 57,120,000 | 58,057,000 | 61,339,000 |
| P/L | 3,523,000 | 1,407,000 | 814,000 |
| NW | 26,883,000 | 24,664,000 | 24,448,000 |
| WC | 29,887,000 | 27,661,000 | 27,445,000 |
| Emp. | 251 | 280 | 309 |

DUNS 22-018-3433
## Traditional Norfolk Poultry Ltd
(**Subsidiary of:** Traditional Norfolk Properties Ltd)
Grange Farm, Hargham Road, Attleborough, Norfolk NR17 1DS
**Tel:** 01953-498434
**Web:** www.tnpltd.com
**Reg No:** 4021155 **Estd:** 1990 Private Limited Company
**Line of Business:** Wholesale of meat and meat products
**Issued Capital:** £50
**Director:** D Garner
**Co. Secretary:** Mark Gorton
**US SIC:** 5147, 2013
**UK SIC:** 61700, 41223
**Auditors:** CG Lee Ltd
**Bankers:** National Westminster Bank Plc (60-15-31)

| | 30-06-14 | 30-06-13 | 30-06-12 |
|---|---|---|---|
| TO | 20,979,700 | 18,004,340 | 14,372,245 |
| P/L | 933,687 | 38,430 | 692,615 |
| NW | 1,591,621 | 1,228,171 | 1,292,974 |
| WC | (400,942) | (380,524) | (244,980) |
| Emp. | 150 | 137 | 108 |

DUNS 22-690-1205 **Imp**
## Traditional Products Ltd
Little Fernhill Works, Oswestry, Shropshire SY10 7AL
**Tel:** 01691670567
**Web:** www.traditional-products.co.uk
**Reg No:** 1834211 **VAT No:** 418914242
**Estd:** 1984 Private Limited Company
**Line of Business:** Manufacture of builders carpentry and joinery
**Issued Capital:** £200
**Managing Director:** J Watson
**Co. Secretary:** Mrs Margaret Watson
**Branches:** Traditional Products Ltd, 270 Bilston Road, Wolverhampton, West Midlands WV2 2HU
**US SIC:** 2431 **UK SIC:** 46300
**Auditors:** Garner Pugh & Sinclair
**Bankers:** Lloyds TSB Bank plc (30-96-33)

| | 31-08-13 | 31-08-12 | 31-08-11 |
|---|---|---|---|
| TO | 4,390,293 | N/A | N/A |
| P/L | 82,666 | N/A | N/A |
| NW | 1,683,177 | 1,638,751 | 1,534,170 |
| WC | (151,455) | (87,153) | 310,654 |
| Emp. | 57 | N/A | N/A |

DUNS 42-440-2381
## Traditional Weatherwear Ltd
(**Subsidiary of:** Yagi Tsusho Limited)
10a Greens Road, Cumbernauld, Glasgow, Lanarkshire G67 2TW
**Tel:** 01236723338 **Fax:** 01236723924
**Web:** www.mackintosh.com
**Reg No:** 4427917 **Estd:** 1974 Private Limited Company
**Line of Business:** Waterproof garment and clothing
**Issued Capital:** £1
**Director:** W B Ross
**Co. Secretary:** William Burnett
**Responsibilities**
**Senior:** Daniel Dunko *(Manager)*, Atsushi Naemura *(Manager)*, Kent Nomura *(Manager)*
**US SIC:** 2328 **UK SIC:** 45340

| | 31-03-14 | 31-03-13 | 31-03-12 |
|---|---|---|---|
| TA | 1 | 1 | 1 |
| NW | 1 | 1 | 1 |

DUNS 28-928-4374
## Trafalgar Retail Travel Ltd
(**Subsidiary of:** The Travel Corporation Limited)
15 Grosvenor Place, London SW1X 7HH
**Tel:** 02072357090 **Fax:** 02078738614
**Web:** www.trafalgar.com
**Reg No:** 1514392 **Estd:** 1980 Private Limited Company

**Line of Business:** Retail sale of leather goods
**Trading Style:** Trafalgar Tours
**Issued Capital:** £469,000
**Directors:** Mrs A Chapman, D I Howie
**Co. Secretary:** Derek Howie
**Responsibilities**
**Senior:** Kevin Bunney (Finance Director), Brett Tolman (Proprietor)
**Finance:** Kevin Bunney (Finance Director)
**US SIC:** 7399  **UK SIC:** 83954
**Auditors:** KPMG LLP
**Bankers:** Lloyds TSB Bank plc (30-98-97)

|      | 31-12-13     | 31-12-12     | 31-12-11     |
|------|-------------|-------------|-------------|
| TO   | 20,901,100  | 18,992,286  | 18,510,834  |
| P/L  | 1,093,233   | 1,405,517   | 1,376,300   |
| NW   | 2,390,986   | 1,636,433   | 5,851,531   |
| WC   | (2,149,061) | (2,750,569) | 1,012,520   |
| Emp. | 304         | 288         | 278         |

DUNS 21-709-9007

## Traffic Management Services (Retford) Ltd

Hallcroft Industrial Estate, Aurillac Way, Retford, Nottinghamshire DN22 7PX
**Tel:** 01777705053
**Web:** www.traffic.org.uk
**Reg No:** 7503263  **Estd:** 1991 Private Limited Company
**Line of Business:** Activities of other transport agencies
**Issued Capital:** £1,000
**Directors:** C R Hewgill, Mrs S E Hewgill
**Responsibilities**
**Senior:** Lauren Hewgill (General Manager), Danny Jameson (General Manager)
**US SIC:** 4712  **UK SIC:** 77002

|    | 31-03-14 | 31-03-13 | 31-03-12 |
|----|----------|----------|----------|
| TA | 921,613  | 686,201  | 488,301  |
| NW | 495,002  | 285,448  | 110,514  |
| WC | 121,472  | 98,903   | 48,991   |

DUNS 21-580-8678

## Traffic Wales

M4 Junction 32, Pendwyallt Road, Cardiff, South Glamorgan CF14 7EF
**Tel:** 03001231213
**Estd:** 2011 Proprietorship
**Line of Business:** Manufacture of other electrical equipment not elsewhere classified
**Proprietor:** D Rees
**US SIC:** 7399  **UK SIC:** 83954
**Employees:** 50

DUNS 50-002-1019                    Imp-Exp

## Trafficmaster Ltd

(Subsidiary of: Danaher China Finance Ltd)
Martell House, Milton Keynes, Buckinghamshire MK4 0TR
**Tel:** 01234759000 **Fax:** 01234759317
**Web:** www.trafficmaster.co.uk
**Reg No:** 2292714 **VAT No:** 539970495
**Estd:** 1988 Private Limited Company
**Line of Business:** Renting of other machinery and equipment not elsewhere classified
**Export Markets:** overseas markets
**Trading Style:** Trafficmaster
**Issued Capital:** £625
**Directors:** S Berman, M D Schwarz, K G Ward
**Co. Secretary:** Radomir Lalovic
**Responsibilities**
**Senior:** Tony Eales (Chief Executive)
**Sales:** Andy Morrison (Sales Director)
**IT:** Derek Arnold (Systems Manager), Tony Eales (Chief Executive)
**HR:** kim mccormick (Facilities Manager)
**Facilities:** kim mccormick (Facilities Manager)
**Operations:** Craig Blount (Traffic Services Director), Tony Eales (Chief Executive)
**Fleet:** kim mccormick (Facilities Manager)
**Branches:** Trafficmaster Ltd, Glazeley House, Rockingham Drive, Linford Wood, Milton Keynes, Buckinghamshire MK14 6PD
**US SIC:** 7399, 3829
**UK SIC:** 83954, 37100
**Auditors:** KPMG LLP
**Bankers:** Barclays Bank Plc (20-39-07)

|      | 31-12-13   | 31-12-12   | 31-12-11   |
|------|-----------|-----------|-----------|
| TO   | 23,899,000 | 22,713,000 | 20,639,000 |
| P/L  | 20,892,000 | 21,254,000 | 1,017,000  |
| NW   | 2,915,000  | 31,752,000 | 30,325,000 |
| WC   | 4,727,000  | 28,602,000 | 26,755,000 |
| Emp. | 169        | 168        | 172        |

DUNS 22-288-2602

## Trafford Cars Ltd

Unit 4 Manway Business Park, Canal Road, Timperley, Altrincham, Cheshire WA14 1TD
**Tel:** 01619281111 **Fax:** 0161-962-6262
**Web:** www.traffordcars.co.uk
**Reg No:** 4306241  **Estd:** 2001 Private Limited Company
**Line of Business:** Taxi operation
**Issued Capital:** £100
**Director:** R L Tandy
**Co. Secretary:** Neil Tandy
**US SIC:** 4121  **UK SIC:** 72200

**Auditors:** National Private Hire Accountancy Services

|    | 31-10-13  | 31-10-12  | 31-10-11 |
|----|-----------|-----------|----------|
| TA | 1,073,789 | 1,021,795 | 724,992  |
| NW | 556,893   | 473,299   | 633,764  |
| WC | 263,594   | 199,257   | 375,101  |

DUNS 23-635-8412

## Trafford College

Manchester Music Base, Manchester M1 1EX
**Web:** www.trafford.ac.uk
**VAT No:** 603547948  **Estd:** 1930
**Line of Business:** Colleges (higher education)
**Principals:** J Funnell (Financial), W Grady
**Responsibilities**
**Senior:** Jacquie Hewitt (Head Of Music)
**Admin:** Janet Gathercole (Principal Secretary)
**Branches:** Trafford College, Moss Road, Manchester M32 0AZ
**US SIC:** 8221  **UK SIC:** 93100
**Employees:** 1,000

DUNS 23-274-6920

## Trafford General Hospital

Moorside Road, Urmston, Manchester M41 5SL
**Tel:** 0161-748-4022
**Web:** www.trafford.nhs.uk
**Estd:** 2002
**Line of Business:** Hospitals
**Trading Style:** Trafford General Hospital
**Issued Capital:** £1
**Principals:** N Cook (Financial), R Calvert, Dr I Nathan, B Frankal, J Sless, Ms M Olsen, Dr S Musgrave
**Responsibilities**
**Senior:** Liz Clarke (Manager), Tad Kondratowicz (Chairman), Shirley Smith (Manager), Beth Weston (Manager)
**Finance:** Margaret Pratt (Financial Director)
**Sales:** Pauline Jones (Senior Sales Executive)
**Facilities:** Tristram Reynolds (Facilities Manager)
**Branches:** Trafford General Hospital, Market Street, Altrincham, Cheshire WA14 1PE
**US SIC:** 8062, 9121
**UK SIC:** 95100, 91110
**Employees:** 2,000

DUNS 23-900-3155

## Trafford Health Authority

Trafford General Hospital, Moorside Road, Urmston, Manchester M41 5SL
**Web:** www.traffordhealthcentre.nhs.uk
**Estd:** 2012
**Line of Business:** Doctors
**Director:** D Caine
**Branches:** Trafford Health Authority, 68 Barrington Rd, Altrincham, Cheshire WA14 1JB
**US SIC:** 8062, 9121
**UK SIC:** 95100, 91110
**Employees:** 223

DUNS 73-569-4064

## Trafford Housing Trust Ltd

126-150 Sale Point, Washway Road, Sale, Cheshire M33 6AG
**Tel:** 03007777777 **Fax:** 0161-968-0143
**Web:** www.traffordhousingtrust.co.uk
**Reg No:** 4831118  **Estd:** 2003 Private Company Limited By Guarantee
**Line of Business:** Other letting of own property
**Directors:** J T Lamb, Ms A Bolton, G F Lucas, J Verbickas, Ms C Baker, A I Findlay, S B Anstee, Ms J Bennett
**Co. Secretary:** Ms Christine Little
**Responsibilities**
**Senior:** Ian Belnavis (Board Member), Barbara Macpherson (Manager)
**Finance:** Larry Gold (Managing Director of Finance &)
**Branches:** Trafford Housing Trust Ltd, Unit U65-66, Stretford Mall Chester Road, Manchester M32 9BD
**US SIC:** 6519  **UK SIC:** 85000
**Bankers:** Barclays Bank Plc (20-87-43)

|      | 31-03-14     | 31-03-13     | 31-03-12     |
|------|-------------|-------------|-------------|
| TO   | 44,614,000  | 40,715,000  | 38,885,000  |
| P/L  | 7,296,000   | 5,351,000   | 5,971,000   |
| NW   | 39,192,000  | 31,196,000  | 28,648,000  |
| WC   | (16,059,000)| (10,061,000)| (27,974,000)|
| Emp. | 361         | 346         | 359         |

DUNS 21-121-9399

## Trafford Metropolitan Borough Council

Trafford Town Hall, Talbot Road, Stretford, Manchester M32 0YT
**Tel:** 01619122000
**Web:** www.trafford.gov.uk
**Estd:** 1974 Incorporate By Act Of Parliament
**Line of Business:** General (overall) public service activities

**Directors:** R Armstrong, P Warrington, W A Lewis, M S Havenhand, D Morrisey, C J Radley
**Responsibilities**
**Senior:** Joanne Boyle (General Manager), Ken Larkin (Manager)
**Finance:** David Muggeridge (Finance Manager)
**Marketing:** Karen Galvin (Press Officer)
**IT:** Eddie Czok (Computer Operations Manager)
**Health & Safety:** Josh Arnold (Health & Safety Officer)
**Operations:** Gary Devine (Production and Operations Mana)
**Fleet:** Colin Maycroft (Transport Manager)
**Branches:** Trafford Metropolitan Borough Council, 8 Orchard Court, Baker Street, Altrincham, Cheshire WA15 7XH
**US SIC:** 9121  **UK SIC:** 91110
**Bankers:** Barclays Bank Plc (20-01-96)
**Employees:** 200

DUNS 36-517-5673

## Trafford Pct

2nd Floor Oakland House Talbot Road, Manchester M16 0PQ
**Tel:** 0161-873-9500
**Web:** www.traffordccg.nhs.uk
**Estd:** 2006
**Line of Business:** Hospitals
**Trading Style:** Nhs Trafford
**Principals:** P Connellan (Managing), Mrs A Akinola
**Responsibilities**
**Senior:** Nigel Guest (Chief Clinical Officer), Gina Lawrence (Chief Operating Officer), Kath Sutton (Chair), Graham Wallis (Manager)
**IT:** Mike Axon (IT Manager)
**Health & Safety:** Debbie Harrison (health & wellbeing manager)
**Branches:** Trafford Pct, Selby Road, Manchester M32 9PL
**US SIC:** 9121, 8062
**UK SIC:** 91110, 95100
**Employees:** 690

DUNS 34-740-2752

## The Trafford Trading Co Ltd

(Subsidiary of: The National Communities Resource Centre Ltd)
Trafford Hall, Chester, Cheshire CH2 4JP
**Tel:** 01244303259
**Web:** www.traffordhall.org.uk
**Reg No:** 2781694  **Estd:** 1993 Private Limited Company
**Line of Business:** Hotels
**Issued Capital:** £2
**Directors:** Ms M J White, G P Smith, Ms S R Wyatt
**Co. Secretary:** Professor Anne Power
**US SIC:** 7011, 8249
**UK SIC:** 66500, 93300
**Auditors:** Haslam Tunstall

|      | 31-03-14  | 31-03-13  | 31-03-12  |
|------|-----------|-----------|-----------|
| TO   | 891,350   | 1,031,391 | 1,064,623 |
| P/L  | (24,764)  | (59,960)  | (40,843)  |
| NW   | (178,028) | (153,266) | (93,305)  |
| WC   | (60,478)  | (107,067) | (4,721)   |

DUNS 34-593-8278                    Imp-Exp

## Trafigura Ltd

(Subsidiary of: Farringford N.V.)
Portman House, 2 Portman Street, London W1H 6EB
**Tel:** 02070091500 **Fax:** 020 7170 7800
**Web:** www.trafigura.com
**Reg No:** 2737924  **VAT No:** 606168253
**Estd:** 1993 Private Limited Company
**Line of Business:** Security broking and related activities
**Directors:** N J Konialidis, M K Davies, C Smallbone
**Responsibilities**
**Senior:** Claude Dauphin (Manager)
**Admin:** Michael Callaghan (Office Manager)
**Facilities:** Jeremy Message (Facilities Manager)
**US SIC:** 7399  **UK SIC:** 83954
**Auditors:** Bright Grahame Murray
**Employees:** 130
**Turnover:** £72,512,000

DUNS 21-748-3098

## Trago Mills (Falmouth) Ltd

Arwenack Street, Falmouth, Cornwall TR11 3LG
**Tel:** 01326-315738 **Fax:** 01326-315738
**Web:** www.trago.co.uk
**Reg No:** 1283363  **VAT No:** 133085688
**Estd:** 1976 Private Limited Company
**Line of Business:** Departmental stores
**Trading Style:** Trago Mills
**Issued Capital:** £1,000
**Directors:** G P Lord, C B Robertson, B A Pinhay

**Responsibilities**
**Senior:** Malcolm Sandbach (Manager), Geoffrey Witcher (Manager)
**Sales:** Stanley Max (Sales Executive)
**Health & Safety:** Len Ellmer (Health & Safety Officer)
**Operations:** Peter Cray (Security Officer)
**Engineering:** George Watts (Manager)
**US SIC:** 5399  **UK SIC:** 65600
**Auditors:** Francis Clark
**Bankers:** HSBC Bank plc (40-28-22)

|      | 31-12-13   | 31-12-12   | 31-12-11   |
|------|-----------|-----------|-----------|
| TO   | 8,317,987  | 8,570,854  | 8,692,478  |
| P/L  | 173,509    | 374,707    | 389,745    |
| NW   | 12,068,686 | 11,936,088 | 11,657,173 |
| WC   | 10,961,964 | 10,793,124 | 10,543,063 |
| Emp. | 105        | 104        | 103        |

DUNS 21-735-8936                    Imp

## Trago Mills Ltd

(Subsidiary of: Charles Robertson (Holdings) Limited)
Twowatersfoot, Liskeard, Plymouth, Cornwall Pl14 6hy, Liskeard, Cornwall PL14 6HY
**Tel:** 01579348877
**Web:** www.trago.co.uk
**Reg No:** 0629619  **Estd:** 1959 Private Limited Company
**Line of Business:** Other retail sale in non-specialised stores
**Trading Style:** Trago Mills
**Issued Capital:** £1,000
**Principals:** C B Robertson (Chairman), G P Lord, B A Pinhay, Mrs K J Weber
**Responsibilities**
**Senior:** Malcolm Sandbach (Group Managing Director)
**Finance:** Geoff Witcher (Financial Director)
**Sales:** Malcolm Sandbach (Group Managing Director)
**IT:** Ken Pallister (IT Manager), Mick Parker (Head of IT)
**HR:** Malcolm Sandbach (Group Managing Director)
**Facilities:** George Watts (Maintenance Manager)
**US SIC:** 5399  **UK SIC:** 65600
**Auditors:** Francis Clark
**Bankers:** HSBC Bank plc (40-28-22)

|      | 31-12-13   | 31-12-12   | 31-12-11   |
|------|-----------|-----------|-----------|
| TO   | 29,379,559 | 30,780,685 | 31,476,833 |
| P/L  | 1,446,879  | 719,005    | 418,282    |
| NW   | 28,230,238 | 30,552,525 | 30,097,029 |
| WC   | 2,423,240  | 1,061,489  | 765,503    |
| Emp. | 399        | 384        | 385        |

DUNS 21-725-7161

## Trago Mills (South Devon) Ltd

(Subsidiary of: Charles Robertson (Holdings) Limited)
Trago Mills, Newton Abbot, Devon TQ12 6JD
**Tel:** 01626-821111 **Fax:** 01626-821111
**Web:** www.trago.co.uk
**Reg No:** 0902430  **Estd:** 1967 Private Limited Company
**Line of Business:** Other retail sale in non-specialised stores
**Issued Capital:** £1,000
**Principals:** C B Robertson (Chairman), G P Lord, Mrs K J Weber, B A Pinhay
**Responsibilities**
**Senior:** Malcolm Sandbach (Manager), Geoffrey Witcher (Manager)
**HR:** Maria Marks (Deputy Store Manager)
**Facilities:** Brian Walters (Maintenance Manager)
**US SIC:** 5399  **UK SIC:** 65600
**Auditors:** Francis Clark
**Bankers:** HSBC Bank plc (40-28-22)

|      | 31-12-13   | 31-12-12   | 31-12-11   |
|------|-----------|-----------|-----------|
| TO   | 44,805,232 | 46,186,081 | 44,558,427 |
| P/L  | 1,341,296  | 1,343,883  | 1,861,625  |
| NW   | 41,463,023 | 41,506,625 | 41,253,872 |
| WC   | 15,442,106 | 15,435,572 | 15,996,291 |
| Emp. | 462        | 410        | 410        |

DUNS 67-214-4565

## Tragus Group Ltd

(Subsidiary of: Yoa Holdco Ltd)
163 Eversholt Street, London NW1 1BU
**Tel:** 020-7121-3200
**Web:** www.tragusgroup.com
**Reg No:** 6022528  **Estd:** 2006 Private Limited Company
**Line of Business:** Licensed restaurants
**Issued Capital:** £11,013,250
**Directors:** S Richards, T J Doubleday
**Responsibilities**
**Senior:** Joseph Baratta (Non-Executive Director), John Derkach (Ceo), Martin Ehrfeld (Non-Executive Director), Giles Thorley (Chairman)
**Facilities:** Phil Derbyshire (Property Director)
**US SIC:** 5812  **UK SIC:** 66110
**Auditors:** PricewaterhouseCoopers LLP

|      | 02-06-13     | 27-05-12     | 29-06-11     |
|------|-------------|-------------|-------------|
| TO   | 294,815,000 | 286,270,000 | 277,428,000 |
| P/L  | (36,122,000)| (18,374,000)| (14,351,000)|
| NW   | (267,800,000)| (264,659,000)| (274,892,000)|
| WC   | (21,095,000)| (16,768,000)| 7,609,000   |
| Emp. | 7,275       | 7,256       | 7,127       |

DUNS 22-800-4651 **Imp**

## Traidcraft Plc

Kingsway, Gateshead, Tyne and Wear NE11 0NE
**Tel:** 01914910591
**Web:** www.traidcraft.co.uk
**Reg No:** 1333367 **VAT No:** 302616596
**Estd:** 1977 Public Limited Company
**Line of Business:** Retail sale via mail order house
**Export Sales:** £644,000
**Trading Style:** Traidecraft
**Issued Capital:** £489,163
**Directors:** B Gidoomal, Mrs E A Cotton, Mrs J E Borden, A J Biggs, Mrs M M Sentamu, Ms S E Hughes, D H Neale, M Edmundson
**Co. Secretary:** Simon Grant
**Responsibilities**
**Senior:** Tessa Bees *(Director)*, David Bowman *(Non-Executive Director)*, Lawrence Bush *(Sales & Marketing Director)*, Justin Byworth *(Manager)*, Neeti Malhothra *(Country Director)*, Carolyn Ord *(Warehouse Manager)*, Joseph Osman *(Director)*, Liz Taylor *(Member)*
**Marketing:** Lawrence Bush *(Sales & Marketing Director)*, Jayne Peebles *(Media & Resources Officer)*
**Sales:** Lawrence Bush *(Sales & Marketing Director)*, Charlotte Timson *(Director of International Deve)*
**IT:** Lesley Heeley *(IT Manager)*, Maveen Pereira *(Head of Programmes)*
**Health & Safety:** Carolyn Ord *(Warehouse Manager)*
**Facilities:** Carolyn Ord *(Warehouse Manager)*
**Operations:** Rob Donnelly *(Head of Africa Programmes)*, Joseph Osman *(Director)*, Mags Vaughan *(Operations Director)*
**Purchasing:** Alistair Leadbetter *(Supplier Support Coordinator)*
**Branches:** Traidcraft Plc, 2 College St, Gloucester, Gloucestershire GL1 2NE
**US SIC:** 5199, 5961
**UK SIC:** 61900, 65600
**Auditors:** Baker Tilly UK Audit LLP
**Bankers:** HSBC Bank plc (40-34-21)

| | 31-03-14 | 31-03-13 | 31-03-12 |
|---|---|---|---|
| TO | 12,299,000 | 12,689,000 | 13,224,000 |
| P/L | (90,000) | (306,000) | (333,000) |
| NW | 4,467,000 | 4,250,000 | 4,397,000 |
| WC | 3,275,000 | 3,444,000 | 3,792,000 |
| Emp. | 99 | 104 | 116 |

DUNS 42-355-6468

## Trailfinders Group Ltd

42-50 Earls Court Road, London W8 6FT
**Web:** www.trailfinders.com
**Reg No:** 4343319 **Estd:** 2001 Private Limited Company
**Line of Business:** Travel clinics
**Export Sales:** £68,911,000
**Trading Style:** Trailfinders Group Ltd
**Issued Capital:** £100,000
**Directors:** A Russell, E R Lee, M D Gooley
**Co. Secretary:** Mark Bannister
**Branches:** Trailfinders Group Ltd, 105-106 St. Aldates, Oxford, Oxfordshire OX1 1BU
**US SIC:** 4722 **UK SIC:** 77001
**Auditors:** Elman Wall Ltd
**Bankers:** Barclays Bank Plc (20-00-00)

| | 28-02-14 | 28-02-13 | 29-02-12 |
|---|---|---|---|
| TO | 636,399,000 | 600,213,000 | 599,208,000 |
| P/L | 26,689,000 | 18,386,000 | 19,039,000 |
| NW | 199,263,000 | 185,220,000 | 170,540,000 |
| WC | 121,105,000 | 121,072,000 | 113,751,000 |
| Emp. | 1,019 | 1,017 | 1,060 |

DUNS 21-197-2450

## Trailfinders Ltd

(**Subsidiary of:** Trailfinders Group Ltd)
48 Earls Court Road, London W8 6FT
**Tel:** 02079383939
**Web:** www.trailfinders.com
**Reg No:** 1004502 **VAT No:** 241705388
**Estd:** 2001 Private Limited Company
**Line of Business:** Activities of travel agencies
**Issued Capital:** £94,080
**Principals:** M D Gooley *(Managing)*, A Russell *(Managing)*, T M Kelly, Mrs N Davies, M C Raymond, S R Gadd, J D Nye, R Mchardy
**Co. Secretary:** Mark Bannister
**Responsibilities**
**Senior:** Nick Anderton *(General Manager)*, Louise Breton *(Director)*, Gareth Dyer *(Director)*, Fiona Gooley *(Director)*, Tristan Gooley *(Director)*, Jim Jouett *(General Manager)*, Nigel Orlans *(Director)*
**IT:** Gordon Hearm *(Network, Security Manager)*
**HR:** Marcus Atkins *(Human Resources Director)*
**Branches:** Trailfinders Ltd, Trailfinders, 58 Deansgate, Manchester M3 2FF
**US SIC:** 4722 **UK SIC:** 77001
**Auditors:** Elman Wall Ltd
**Bankers:** Barclays Bank Plc (20-06-05)

| | 28-02-14 | 28-02-13 | 29-02-12 |
|---|---|---|---|
| TO | 566,231,000 | 530,548,000 | 513,797,000 |
| P/L | 30,007,000 | 19,338,000 | 21,555,000 |
| NW | 185,685,000 | 164,486,000 | 149,457,000 |
| WC | 99,165,000 | 97,824,000 | 89,742,000 |
| Emp. | 864 | 855 | 880 |

DUNS 50-365-7421

## Training 2000 Ltd

Harwood Street, Blackburn, Lancashire BB1 3BD
**Tel:** 01254546590 **Fax:** 01254-54424
**Web:** www.training2000.co.uk
**Reg No:** 2380675 **VAT No:** 174865426
**Estd:** 1967 Private Company Limited By Guarantee
**Line of Business:** Adult and other education not elsewhere classified
**Directors:** T J Webber, O J Mccann, S Rumbelow, S J Gray, S Collier, A Bryce
**Co. Secretary:** Mrs Kathryn Walkden
**Responsibilities**
**Senior:** Joanne Sherrington *(Financial Director)*, Cathy Walkden *(Personal Assistant)*
**Finance:** Joanne Sherrington *(Financial Director)*
**HR:** Nigel Rowlands *(Human Resources Manager)*
**Branches:** Training 2000 Ltd, Hurstdale House, Hurst Lane, Rossendale, Lancashire BB4 7SH
**US SIC:** 8210 **UK SIC:** 03300
**Auditors:** Waterworths
**Bankers:** National Westminster Bank Plc (01-00-85)

| | 31-07-13 | 31-07-12 | 31-07-11 |
|---|---|---|---|
| TO | 12,115,407 | 12,166,537 | 12,716,383 |
| P/L | (402,845) | 23,966 | (530,558) |
| NW | 6,643,568 | 6,328,197 | 7,588,179 |
| WC | 271,241 | 373,099 | 288,693 |
| Emp. | 288 | 264 | 291 |

DUNS 21-121-8574

## Training and Development Agency for Schools

City Tower, Manchester M1 4BE
**Tel:** 08456000991
**Web:** www.tda.gov.uk
**Estd:** 1994
**Line of Business:** Colleges (higher education)
**Trading Style:** T D A
**Principals:** H Hagos *(Financial)*, M Berger-North *(Marketing)*, Ms L Francis, Ms L Chapman, Ms L Hedden, Ms A Walsh, S Baker, A Bowling
**Responsibilities**
**Senior:** John Carr *(Director)*, Graham Holley *(Chief Executive Officer)*, Howard Kennedy *(Director)*, Jill Staley *(Director)*, Mike Watkins *(Director)*
**Operations:** Kate Straker *(Director Operations)*
**US SIC:** 8221, 8299
**UK SIC:** 93100, 93300
**Employees:** 300

DUNS 49-723-0821

## Training & Enterprise Northamptonshire Chamber of Commerce

Opus House, Anglia Way, Moulton Park Industrial Estate, Northampton, Northamptonshire NN3 6JA
**Tel:** 01604-490490
**Web:** www.northants-chamber.co.uk
**Estd:** 1917
**Line of Business:** Chambers of commerce
**Director:** M Wylie
**US SIC:** 9121, 8249, 7339, 8299
**UK SIC:** 91110, 93300, 83954
**Employees:** 130

DUNS 34-922-0512

## The Training Bureau Ltd

15 Warwick St Waterloo Place, Leamington Spa, Warwickshire CV32 5LA
**Tel:** 01926340992
**Web:** www.trainingbureau.co.uk
**Reg No:** 5718917 **Estd:** 2006 Private Limited Company
**Line of Business:** Other business activities not elsewhere classified
**Issued Capital:** £100
**Director:** Ms G B Dunster
**Co. Secretary:** John Dunster
**Responsibilities**
**Sales:** Anne Marshall *(Sales Manager)*
**US SIC:** 7399 **UK SIC:** 83954

| | 31-03-14 | 31-03-13 | 31-03-12 |
|---|---|---|---|
| TA | 100 | 100 | 100 |
| NW | 100 | 100 | 100 |

DUNS 29-638-4142

## Training for Bradford Ltd

39-41 Chapel Street, Bradford, West Yorkshire BD1 5BY
**Tel:** 01274-728316
**Web:** www.citytraining.org
**Reg No:** 1964653 **Estd:** 1885 Private Company Limited By Guarantee
**Line of Business:** Adult and other education not elsewhere classified
**Trading Style:** City Training Services
**Directors:** R M Hinchliffe, D Hambleton, A W Welsh
**Co. Secretary:** Alan Mangham
**Responsibilities**
**Senior:** Douglas Stott *(Manager)*, Michele Sutton *(Chief Executive)*
**Branches:** Training For Bradford Ltd, Enterprise Ho, 12 St Pauls St, Leeds, West Yorkshire LS1 2LE
**US SIC:** 8249 **UK SIC:** 93300
**Auditors:** PricewaterhouseCoopers

| | 31-07-13 | 31-07-12 | 31-07-11 |
|---|---|---|---|
| TO | 4,227,666 | 3,100,056 | 2,601,486 |
| P/L | 353,885 | 157,608 | 176,977 |
| NW | 3,458,393 | 3,119,695 | 2,967,368 |
| WC | 2,522,377 | 2,038,730 | 2,272,137 |
| Emp. | 53 | 49 | 47 |

DUNS 23-204-0204

## Training Regeneration Education Employment Sustainability Services Ltd

London Road, Hook, Hampshire RG27 9DJ
**Tel:** 01256762402 **Fax:** 01256762402
**Web:** www.thetreesgroup.org.uk
**Reg No:** 0025811IP **Estd:** 1966 Friendly Society
**Line of Business:** Newsagents
**Trading Style:** Trees
**Principals:** Ms K Burkhill *(Chairman)*, S Makwana, D Betterley, I Reid, Ms M Bell, Ms E Leadeatt, E Bayat, Ms P Sykes
**Co. Secretary:** Michael Howells
**Responsibilities**
**Senior:** Brian Hayes *(Manager)*, Aldrey Woolerton *(Director)*
**US SIC:** 6732 **UK SIC:** 83100
**Auditors:** Mazars
**Employees:** 108
**Turnover:** £8,653,737

DUNS 21-042-9803

## Training Shared Services Centre

Castleton Street, Bolton, Lancashire BL2 2JW
**Tel:** 01204338375
**Web:** www.bolton.gov.uk
**Estd:** 1990 Proprietorship
**Line of Business:** Training centres
**Proprietor:** Mrs C Hyams
**Responsibilities**
**Senior:** Beverley Lee *(Facilities Manager)*
**US SIC:** 8299 **UK SIC:** 93300
**Employees:** 300

DUNS 21-584-7437

## The Trainline Bookings & Enquiries

Covent Garden, London WC2H 7EG
**Tel:** 08712441545
**Estd:** 2011
**Line of Business:** Other entertainment activities
**US SIC:** 8999 **UK SIC:** 83954
**Employees:** 60

DUNS 23-854-9484 **Imp**

## Trainline.Com Ltd

(**Subsidiary of:** Trainline Investments Holdings Ltd)
The Matrix, London EC3N 1AH
**Tel:** 02031282000 **Fax:** 020-7484-4570
**Web:** www.thetrainline.com
**Reg No:** 3846791 **VAT No:** 791726106
**Estd:** 1997 Private Limited Company
**Line of Business:** Other computer related activities
**Issued Capital:** £35,882,028
**Directors:** B M Pearson, Ms C Gilmartin, J M Mitchell
**Co. Secretary:** Neil Murrin
**US SIC:** 4789 **UK SIC:** 77002
**Auditors:** KPMG LLP

| | 01-03-14 | 02-03-13 | 03-03-12 |
|---|---|---|---|
| TO | 107,437,000 | 106,005,000 | 105,524,000 |
| P/L | 38,271,000 | 42,272,000 | 38,465,000 |
| NW | 35,761,000 | 131,167,000 | 91,680,000 |
| WC | 20,446,000 | 111,160,000 | 70,987,000 |
| Emp. | 301 | 312 | 278 |

DUNS 21-169-7018

## Trak (Global Solutions) Ltd

The East Wing The Quadrangle, Crewe Hall, Crewe, Cheshire CW1 6UY
**Tel:** 01270501212
**Web:** www.trakglobal.co.uk
**Reg No:** 6944694 **Estd:** 2009 Private Limited Company
**Line of Business:** Telecommunications
**Issued Capital:** £1,391
**Directors:** K Mahmoudzadeh, A W Cottrill, N C Corrie, P D Gomes, P Finch
**US SIC:** 4899 **UK SIC:** 79020

| | 30-06-13 | 30-06-12 | 30-06-11 |
|---|---|---|---|
| TA | 1,755,583 | 1,506,944 | 1,012,610 |
| NW | 226,305 | (506,375) | (459,695) |
| WC | 561,311 | 210,353 | 54,075 |

DUNS 29-570-4449 **Imp-Exp**

## Trak Microwave Ltd

(**Subsidiary of:** Smiths Group Plc)
29 Dunsinane Avenue, Dunsinane Industrial Estate, Dundee, Angus DD2 3QF
**Tel:** 01382427200 **Fax:** 01382-833599
**Web:** www.trakeurope.com
**Reg No:** 0094479SC **VAT No:** 400768863
**Estd:** 1985 Private Limited Company
**Line of Business:** General mechanical engineering
**Export Markets:** E E C and other countries worldwide
**Export Sales:** £8,982,000
**Trading Style:** Trak Europe
**Issued Capital:** £2,897,934
**Directors:** G D Robertson, A A Mcneill
**Co. Secretary:** Ms Carla Campbell
**Responsibilities**
**Senior:** Tom Doak *(Production Manager)*, Ralph Phillips *(Manager)*
**Health & Safety:** Margaret Dobson *(Quality Manager)*
**Facilities:** Mike Dolan *(Facilities Manager)*
**Operations:** Margaret Dobson *(Quality Manager)*
**Purchasing:** Gerry Cavanagh *(Purchasing Manager)*
**Engineering:** Tom Doak *(Production Manager)*
**US SIC:** 8911 **UK SIC:** 83701
**Auditors:** PricewaterhouseCoopers LLP
**Bankers:** Clydesdale Bank Plc (82-44-04)

| | 31-07-13 | 31-07-12 | 31-07-11 |
|---|---|---|---|
| TO | 12,380,000 | 9,285,000 | 6,882,000 |
| P/L | 589,000 | 964,000 | 408,000 |
| NW | 8,778,000 | 8,202,000 | 7,487,000 |
| WC | 8,159,000 | 7,556,000 | 6,725,000 |
| Emp. | 50 | 50 | 47 |

DUNS 49-084-3943 **Imp**

## Traka Ltd

(**Subsidiary of:** Assa Abloy Ab)
30 Stilebrook Road, Olney, Buckinghamshire MK46 5EA
**Tel:** 01234-712345
**Web:** www.traka.com
**Reg No:** 3088893 **VAT No:** 670531155
**Estd:** 1995 Private Limited Company
**Line of Business:** Investment consultants
**Export Sales:** £4,741,523
**Issued Capital:** £62,500
**Directors:** N A Vann, J B Kent, A D Talbot-Cooper, D Winner, J A Sasse
**Co. Secretary:** Graham Penter
**Responsibilities**
**Senior:** Godfrey Anderson *(MHE Manager)*, Alan Fleary *(Relations Manager)*, Alexander Stern *(Manager)*
**Marketing:** Gemma Brennansmith *(Marketing Manager)*, Alan Fleary *(Relations Manager)*, Brenda Taylor *(Sales & Marketing Director)*
**Sales:** Godfrey Anderson *(MHE Manager)*, Alan Fleary *(Relations Manager)*, Brenda Taylor *(Sales & Marketing Director)*
**US SIC:** 3629 **UK SIC:** 34350
**Auditors:** PricewaterhouseCoopers LLP
**Bankers:** National Westminster Bank Plc (01-00-04)

| | 31-12-13 | 31-12-12 | 31-12-11 |
|---|---|---|---|
| TO | 13,647,117 | 12,531,380 | 10,130,704 |
| P/L | 2,318,223 | 232,505 | 1,047,167 |
| NW | 7,493,181 | 5,777,470 | 3,921,251 |
| WC | 6,780,181 | 5,644,708 | 2,852,455 |
| Emp. | 107 | 87 | 93 |

DUNS 21-948-0378

## Trakside Systems Ltd

(**Subsidiary of:** Spark Holdings Limited)
Unit A, Faraday Court, Crawley, West Sussex RH10 9PU
**Tel:** 08456 040336 **Fax:** 01293 537739
**Web:** www.tracksideintelligence.com
**Reg No:** 6129812 **VAT No:** 904313756
**Estd:** 2007 Private Limited Company
**Line of Business:** Other business activities not elsewhere classified
**Issued Capital:** £105
**Directors:** D J Webber, A Pierce
**Co. Secretary:** Bilal Zein
**US SIC:** 7399 **UK SIC:** 83954

**Auditors:** Haines Watts Kent LLP
**Bankers:** National Westminster Bank Plc
(60-24-31)

|    | 31-12-13 | 31-12-12 | 31-12-11 |
|----|----------|----------|----------|
| TA | 105      | 79,040   | 113,098  |
| NW | 105      | 79,040   | 113,098  |

DUNS 22-622-5811

## Tramar D & M Ltd
Biddlesden Road, Westbury, Brackley,
Northamptonshire NN13 5JL
**Tel:** 01280840692 **Fax:** 01280-840693
**Web:** www.sugarich.co.uk
**Reg No:** 1189427 **VAT No:** 209263963
**Estd:** 1959 Private Limited Company
**Line of Business:** Animal feed and pet foods
**Issued Capital:** £322
**Director:** D Evans
**Responsibilities**
**Senior:** Alex Keogh (Manager)
**Admin:** Jill Collings (Administrator)
**US SIC:** 2047, 5153
**UK SIC:** 42221, 61100
**Auditors:** Parry Kirkby Blackwell & Co
**Bankers:** National Westminster Bank Plc
(60-15-07)

|     | 30-04-13 | 30-04-12 |
|-----|----------|----------|
| TA  | 50       | 1,072    |
| P/L | (1,022)  | (823,214)|
| NW  | 50       | 1,072    |

DUNS 73-650-1490                              Imp-Exp

## Trane (U K) Ltd
(**Subsidiary of:** Ingersoll-Rand European
Holding Company B.V.)
Harrow House, Bessemer Road,
Basingstoke, Hampshire RG21 3NB
**Tel:** 08457165162 **Fax:** 01256-306001
**Web:** www.trane.com
**Reg No:** 4910068 **Estd:** 1981 Private
Limited Company
**Line of Business:** Air conditioning
equipment
**Issued Capital:** £1,500,000
**Directors:** S J Davies, R J Flinn
**Co. Secretary:** Mrs Katrina Smith
**Responsibilities**
**Senior:** George Carmona (Manager), Ross
Giles (Marketing Manager), Claire Meaden
(Personal Assistant)
**Finance:** David Hampsey (Finance Director)
**Branches:** Trane (U K) Ltd, Marsh Lane,
Solihull, West Midlands B92 0AJ
**US SIC:** 3585, 1711
**UK SIC:** 32841, 50300
**Auditors:** PricewaterhouseCoopers
**Bankers:** Lloyds TSB Bank plc (30-12-18)

|     | 31-12-13  | 31-12-12  | 31-12-11  |
|-----|-----------|-----------|-----------|
| TO  | 27,683,096| 30,827,714| 31,319,390|
| P/L | 740,273   | 747,737   | 319,709   |
| NW  | 5,280,197 | 4,534,193 | 3,763,518 |
| WC  | 3,681,187 | 4,191,643 | 3,614,069 |
| Emp.| 160       | 166       | 174       |

DUNS 28-829-6650

## Tranmere Rovers Football Club Ltd
Prenton Park, Prenton Road West,
Birkenhead, Merseyside CH42 9PY
**Tel:** 03330144452
**Web:** www.tranmererovers.co.uk
**Reg No:** 0118587 **Estd:** 1898 Private
Limited Company
**Line of Business:** Sports clubs
**Issued Capital:** £250,000
**Principals:** P R Johnson (Chairman),
M Palios, M Horton, Mrs N C Palios
**Co. Secretary:** Richard Hughes
**Responsibilities**
**Senior:** Lorraine Rogers (CEO, Managing
Director)
**Finance:** Julie McDonald (Accounts
Manager)
**IT:** Tony Coombes (IT Manager)
**Facilities:** Andy Quayle (Head Groundsman)
**Branches:** Tranmere Rovers Football Club
Ltd, Prenton Park, Prenton Road West,
Birkenhead, Merseyside CH42 9PY
**US SIC:** 7999 **UK SIC:** 97913
**Auditors:** Duncan Sheard Glass
**Bankers:** Allied Irish Bank (gb) (23-84-03)

|     | 30-06-13   | 30-06-12   | 30-06-11   |
|-----|------------|------------|------------|
| TO  | 3,539,462  | 3,348,697  | 3,462,776  |
| P/L | (422,277)  | 207,323    | (197,428)  |
| NW  | (4,146,722)| (3,666,547)| (3,828,472)|
| WC  | (2,957,398)| (2,601,918)| (2,844,235)|
| Emp.| 115        | 109        | 108        |

DUNS 77-490-8776

## Trans - Continental Group Ltd
Transcon House, Eastway, Fulwood,
Preston, Lancashire PR2 9WS
**Tel:** 01772708930
**Web:** www.transcon.co.uk
**Reg No:** 2974568 **VAT No:** 638910616
**Estd:** 1994 Private Limited Company
**Line of Business:** Other retail sale in
specialised stores not elsewhere classified
**Export Sales:** £140,371
**Trading Style:** Snow Time

**Issued Capital:** £106
**Directors:** H Withers, M Withers,
J P Marshall
**Co. Secretary:** Ms Rosemary Withers
**Responsibilities**
**Finance:** Paul Papworth (Financial Director)
**Health & Safety:** Bernie Smith (Warehouse
Manager)
**US SIC:** 5199 **UK SIC:** 61900
**Auditors:** KPMG LLP
**Bankers:** HSBC Bank plc (40-40-07)

|     | 31-12-13   | 31-12-12   | 31-12-11   |
|-----|------------|------------|------------|
| TO  | 13,601,124 | 10,636,820 | 15,807,102 |
| P/L | 136,293    | (49,257)   | 355,444    |
| NW  | 2,956,786  | 2,810,243  | 2,812,273  |
| WC  | 1,581,326  | 1,285,096  | 1,527,691  |
| Emp.| 47         | 58         | 74         |

DUNS 29-032-1256                                  Exp

## Trans Global Ltd
Birchwood, Dartford Road, Dartford, Kent
DA4 9HX
**Tel:** 08453376400 **Fax:** 08453376501
**Web:** www.transglobalgroup.com
**Reg No:** 0786387 **Estd:** 1963 Private
Limited Company
**Line of Business:** Management activities of
holding companies
**Export Markets:** India, Belgium, singapore,
Italy, France, Holland, Kazakhstan, USA
**Issued Capital:** £1,337,400
**Directors:** R A Knight, D Khaitan, S Saha,
B J Ruck, S R Dasgupta, S Knight,
P K Khaitan, K L Jones
**Co. Secretary:** Dilsher Sen
**Responsibilities**
**Senior:** Lee Bolsover (Manager), Jayne
Wilkinson (Manager)
**IT:** David Carpenter (IT Manager)
**US SIC:** 6711, 4712
**UK SIC:** 83962, 77002
**Auditors:** Moore Stephens LLP
**Bankers:** National Westminster Bank Plc
(50-00-00)

|     | 31-12-13   | 31-12-12    | 31-12-11    |
|-----|------------|-------------|-------------|
| TO  | 128,096,000| 116,558,000 | 97,453,000  |
| P/L | 797,000    | 618,000     | 320,000     |
| NW  | 519,000    | (645,000)   | (1,719,000) |
| WC  | (119,000)  | (1,033,000) | (1,733,000) |
| Emp.| 224        | 218         | 207         |

DUNS 29-541-9451

## Trans-It (Weston-Super-Mare) Ltd
(**Subsidiary of:** Fedex Corporation)
Unit 27 Lynx Crescent, Weston-Super-Mare,
Avon BS24 9DJ
**Tel:** 01934421200 **Fax:** 08450510280
**Web:** www.fedex.com
**Reg No:** 1908791 **Estd:** 2001 Private
Limited Company
**Line of Business:** Couriers
**Trading Style:** Fedex Uk
**Issued Capital:** £80,000
**Directors:** J E Hawkins, L T Hoyle, R J Staes
**Co. Secretary:** James Hawkins
**Responsibilities**
**Senior:** Leigh Morris (Manager)
**US SIC:** 4213 **UK SIC:** 72300
**Auditors:** T P Lewis & Partners
**Bankers:** Barclays Bank Plc (20-94-74)

|    | 31-03-13  | 31-03-12 | 31-03-11  |
|----|-----------|----------|-----------|
| TA | 1,043,212 | 940,657  | 1,710,516 |
| NW | 166,957   | 150,556  | 140,225   |
| WC | 180,329   | 292,401  | 282,593   |

DUNS 21-198-1493                              Imp-Exp

## Trans Oceanic Meat Co. Ltd
Oceanic House, 45 Sidcup Hill, Sidcup, Kent
DA14 6HJ
**Tel:** 02083-022-544 **Fax:** 02083-090-249
**Web:** www.transoceanic.co.uk
**Reg No:** 1079703 **VAT No:** 243871355
**Estd:** 1987 Private Limited Company
**Line of Business:** Meat wholesalers
**Export Markets:** France; Germany; Spain;
Italy; S Africa; Netherlands; Mauritius
**Export Sales:** £11,393,143
**Issued Capital:** £100,000
**Principals:** G Houghton (Managing),
S Tyndall
**Co. Secretary:** Peter Walk
**Responsibilities**
**Finance:** Paul Goldsmith (Accounts
Manager)
**Sales:** David Croft (Trader), Paul Goldsmith
(Accounts Manager)
**US SIC:** 5147 **UK SIC:** 61700
**Auditors:** Fisher Phillips
**Bankers:** Coutts & Co (18-00-01)

|     | 31-10-13   | 31-10-12   | 31-10-11   |
|-----|------------|------------|------------|
| TO  | 61,962,574 | 62,329,258 | 63,649,739 |
| P/L | 382,603    | 296,473    | 400,725    |
| NW  | 11,962,585 | 11,731,566 | 11,449,507 |
| WC  | 10,554,519 | 9,778,826  | 9,549,348  |
| Emp.| N/A        | 63         | 65         |

DUNS 64-082-8468                                  Imp

## Trans-Tronic Ltd
Whitting Valley Road, Old Whittington,
Chesterfield, Derbyshire S41 9EY
**Web:** www.trans-tronic.co.uk
**Reg No:** 4486313 **VAT No:** 804709730
**Estd:** 1978 Private Limited Company
**Line of Business:** Manufacturers of electric
transformers
**Issued Capital:** £1
**Director:** D P Goater
**Responsibilities**
**Sales:** Beverley Carpenter (Sales Manager),
Tom Parr (Sales Manager), Malgorzata
Rusin (Sales Manager)
**Engineering:** Daniel Tarrant (Design
Engineering Manager)
**US SIC:** 3621 **UK SIC:** 34201

|    | 31-12-13 | 31-12-12 | 31-12-11 |
|----|----------|----------|----------|
| TA | 935,669  | 770,799  | 677,149  |
| NW | 355,622  | 210,320  | 40,006   |
| WC | 301,308  | 181,939  | 69,578   |

DUNS 77-442-9161

## Transaction Network Services (U K) Ltd
(**Subsidiary of:** Trident Private Holdings I
Llc)
5 Europa View, Sheffield, South Yorkshire S9
1XH
**Tel:** 01142920200
**Web:** www.tnsi.com
**Reg No:** 2952557 **VAT No:** 648955577
**Estd:** 1994 Private Limited Company
**Line of Business:** Telecommunications
**Export Sales:** £2,683,239
**Issued Capital:** £130,002
**Directors:** S J Kershaw, M J Collins,
M Q Keegan, H H Graham Jr
**Co. Secretary:** Simon Kershaw
**Responsibilities**
**Senior:** Fintan Byrne (Director), Raymond
Low (Manager)
**Marketing:** Joanne Moorwood (Marketing
Manager)
**Admin:** Gaby Phelan (Secretary)
**IT:** Pete Elliot (Support Services Manager)
**Health & Safety:** Pete Elliot (Support
Services Manager)
**Operations:** Pete Elliot (Support Services
Manager), Ciaran Jones (Vice President
Operations)
**Purchasing:** Hariet Ross (Purchasing
Manager)
**Branches:** Transaction Network Services (U
K) Ltd, Orion House, Bessemer Road,
Welwyn Garden City, Hertfordshire AL7 1HH
**US SIC:** 7379 **UK SIC:** 83940
**Auditors:** Ernst & Young LLP
**Bankers:** Arbuthnot Latham And Co Ltd
(30-13-93)

|     | 31-12-13   | 31-12-12   | 31-12-11   |
|-----|------------|------------|------------|
| TO  | 44,822,872 | 44,609,406 | 42,726,717 |
| P/L | 5,768,227  | 5,414,923  | 3,837,945  |
| NW  | 26,049,115 | 22,644,482 | 19,102,693 |
| WC  | 20,119,086 | 16,349,884 | 11,966,741 |
| Emp.| 214        | 225        | 220        |

DUNS 21-606-8923

## Transactis
Atlantic Pavilion, Albert Dock, Liverpool,
Merseyside L3 4AE
**Tel:** 01512037100
**Web:** www.transactis.co.uk
**Estd:** 2011 Proprietorship
**Line of Business:** Database development
services
**Proprietor:** D Steele
**Responsibilities**
**Senior:** Barbara Kenney (Senior Customer
Services Execu)
**IT:** Jason Brooks (Senior IT Executive),
James Gallacher (Senior IT Executive)
**US SIC:** 7374 **UK SIC:** 83940
**Employees:** 120

DUNS 21-580-2204

## Transactor Global Solutions
Transactor House Leylands Business Park,
Nobs Crook, Colden Common, Winchester,
Hampshire SO21 1TH
**Tel:** 02380603800
**Web:** www.transactorgsl.com
**Estd:** 2011 Proprietorship
**Line of Business:** Other software
consultancy and supply
**Proprietor:** R Vincent
**US SIC:** 7379 **UK SIC:** 83940
**Employees:** 50

DUNS 23-313-8762

## Transactor Global Solutions Ltd
35 Walton Road, Stocton Heath, Warrington,
Cheshire WA4 6NW
**Tel:** 0123638100 **Fax:** 08700668585
**Web:** www.transactorgsl.com
**Reg No:** 4655396 **Estd:** 2003 Private
Limited Company
**Line of Business:** Other computer related
activities
**Issued Capital:** £350,096
**Directors:** P Williams, S C Young,
R J Vincent
**Co. Secretary:** Mrs Patricia Sharrock
**US SIC:** 7379 **UK SIC:** 83940
**Bankers:** HSBC Bank plc (40-42-18)

|    | 31-03-13  | 31-03-12  | 31-03-11  |
|----|-----------|-----------|-----------|
| TA | 3,254,661 | 2,648,733 | 2,465,841 |
| NW | 531,224   | 388,270   | 243,642   |
| WC | 437,761   | 303,339   | 197,160   |

DUNS 21-927-9627                              Imp-Exp

## Transam Trucking Ltd
7 Trinity Street, Bungay, Suffolk NR35 1EH
**Tel:** 01986-894545 **Fax:** 01986-894166
**Reg No:** 1305163 **VAT No:** 304766951
**Estd:** 1977 Private Limited Company
**Line of Business:** Road haulage and
transport services
**Issued Capital:** £64,030
**Managing Director:** A M Guterres
**Co. Secretary:** Ms Sandra Flatt
**Responsibilities**
**Senior:** Mark Guterres (Manager)
**US SIC:** 4789 **UK SIC:** 77002
**Auditors:** Scrutton Bland
**Bankers:** National Westminster Bank Plc
(50-30-20)

|     | 31-12-13   | 31-12-12  | 31-12-11    |
|-----|------------|-----------|-------------|
| TO  | 18,696,602 | 16,092,562| 14,985,652  |
| P/L | 1,421,963  | 3,173,099 | 1,013,384   |
| NW  | 3,997,814  | 3,157,514 | 1,312,084   |
| WC  | 42,137     | (150,688) | (1,731,996) |
| Emp.| 146        | 121       | 121         |

DUNS 28-820-6634                                  Imp

## Transatlantic Reinsurance Co
(**Subsidiary of:** Alleghany Corporation)
55 Mark Lane, London EC3R 7NE
**Tel:** 020-7204-8600
**Web:** www.transre.com
**Reg No:** 0010151FC **Estd:** 2010 Foreign
Company
**Line of Business:** Insurance companies and
agents
**Principals:** J H Spence, K W Brandt,
C K Dalrymple, R Jeffrey Iii (Proprietor)
**Co. Secretary:** Ms Amy Cinquegrana
**Responsibilities**
**Senior:** Paul Bonny (Manager)
**US SIC:** 6311 **UK SIC:** 82002

DUNS 29-648-7614                              Imp-Exp

## Transcal Ltd
(**Subsidiary of:** Transcal Holdings Ltd)
14-15 Portbury Grove, Bristol, Avon BS11
9TL
**Tel:** 01275374777 **Fax:** 01506 442 333
**Web:** www.transcal.co.uk
**Reg No:** 0096703SC **VAT No:** 446418246
**Estd:** 1986 Private Limited Company
**Line of Business:** Manufacturers of
automotive components
**Export Markets:** Worldwide
**Export Sales:** £1,812,124
**Issued Capital:** £60,008
**Principals:** R B Aitken (Managing), C S Sin,
D Mactaggart, S T Harvey, J C Thomson,
Ms D A Farnworth
**Co. Secretary:** Ms Donna Aitken
**Responsibilities**
**Senior:** Mike Barry (Manager)
**Branches:** Transcal Ltd, 88 Haymarket Ter,
Edinburgh, Midlothian EH12 5LQ
**US SIC:** 3714, 3111
**UK SIC:** 35300, 44101
**Auditors:** Stewart, Sheddan & Co
**Bankers:** Clydesdale Bank Plc (82-62-26)

|     | 31-03-13  | 31-03-12  | 31-03-11  |
|-----|-----------|-----------|-----------|
| TO  | 6,738,955 | 8,372,609 | 8,081,214 |
| P/L | 861,367   | 870,220   | 376,894   |
| NW  | 2,652,473 | 1,984,180 | 1,334,860 |
| WC  | 2,561,430 | 1,883,159 | 1,387,776 |
| Emp.| 66        | 67        | 60        |

DUNS 73-818-1259

## Transcast (Scotland) Ltd.
74 Glencraig Street, Airdrie, Lanarkshire ML6
9AS
**Tel:** 01236-754500 **Fax:** 01236-754995
**Web:** www.transcast.org.uk
**Reg No:** 0264935SC **Estd:** 1997 Private
Limited Company
**Line of Business:** Plastering and related
building services
**Trading Style:** Irs Scotland
**Issued Capital:** £2
**Co. Secretary:** Anthony Collum

**Responsibilities**
**Senior:** Brendan Collum *(company Director)*
**US SIC:** 1742, 1799
**UK SIC:** 50400, 50000
**Auditors:** Benson Wood & Co

| | 31-03-14 | 31-03-13 | 31-03-12 |
|---|---|---|---|
| TA | 2 | 2 | 2 |
| NW | 2 | 2 | 2 |

DUNS 23-448-2131
### Transcom Worldwide (Uk) Ltd
Limewood House, Limewood Way, Seacroft, Leeds, West Yorkshire LS14 1AB
**Tel:** 08453304800 **Fax:** 01727-840234
**Web:** www.transcom.com
**Reg No:** 2785250 **VAT No:** 640008878
**Estd:** 1993 Private Limited Company
**Line of Business:** Activities auxiliary to financial intermediation not elsewhere classified
**Issued Capital:** £44,403
**Directors:** K Dodd, R Boggio
**Co. Secretary:** Miss Cheryl Hutchinson
**Responsibilities**
**Senior:** Michael Purvis *(Manager)*
**US SIC:** 6111 **UK SIC:** 81501
**Auditors:** Ernst & Young LLP
**Bankers:** National Westminster Bank Plc (60-10-10)

| | 31-12-13 | 31-12-12 | 31-12-11 |
|---|---|---|---|
| TA | 11,024,265 | 8,857,920 | 3,308,080 |
| P/L | (260,298) | (573,660) | (1,005,326) |
| NW | 154,888 | 415,247 | 188,907 |
| WC | 99,630 | 308,096 | 133,077 |
| Emp. | 101 | 110 | 60 |

DUNS 22-722-7998
### Transcribe Copier Systems Ltd
**(Subsidiary of:** Asl Technology Holdings Ltd.)
Franks Hall, Dartford, Kent DA4 9JJ
**Fax:** 01322-420401
**Web:** www.thamesgroup.com
**Reg No:** 1744901 **Estd:** 1983 Private Limited Company
**Line of Business:** Wholesale of other office machinery and equipment
**Issued Capital:** £10,000
**Managing Director:** T R Rampling
**Co. Secretary:** Ms Kerry Maglennon
**US SIC:** 5081, 7399
**UK SIC:** 61490, 83954
**Auditors:** Wilkins Kennedy
**Bankers:** Barclays Bank Plc (20-24-61)
**Turnover:** £8,380,847

DUNS 21-122-7430
### Transcribe U K Ltd
High Peacockbank, Kilmarnock, Ayrshire KA3 5JG
**Tel:** 01560-486652
**Web:** www.transcribe-uk.com
**Reg No:** 0341090SC **Estd:** 2008 Private Limited Company
**Line of Business:** Secretarial and translation activities
**Issued Capital:** £1
**Director:** B Galloway
**Co. Secretary:** Mrs Ada Galloway
**Branches:** Transcribe U K Ltd, 16 Meadowbank Avenue, Stafford, Staffordshire ST18 0HE
**US SIC:** 7399 **UK SIC:** 83954
**Auditors:** T.B. Dunn & Co

| | 31-03-14 | 31-03-13 | 31-03-12 |
|---|---|---|---|
| TA | 21,425 | 13,443 | 7,713 |
| NW | (2,205) | (3,391) | 1,223 |
| WC | (389) | (2,851) | 1,317 |

DUNS 76-843-1827
### Transdev Blazefield Ltd
**(Subsidiary of:** Transdev Group)
Prospect Road, Harrogate, North Yorkshire HG2 7PB
**Tel:** 01423-884020
**Web:** www.transdevplc.co.uk
**Reg No:** 2605399 **VAT No:** 557237818
**Estd:** 1991 Private Limited Company
**Line of Business:** Other scheduled passenger land transport not elsewhere classified
**Issued Capital:** £50,000
**Directors:** G D Irvine, M J Gilbert, N Stevens, R G Revill, P I Brogden
**Co. Secretary:** James Wallace
**Responsibilities**
**Senior:** Nigel Eggleton *(Manager)*, Michael Mullins *(Manager)*
**Branches:** Transdev Blazefield Ltd, Manner Sutton Street, Blackburn, Lancashire BB1 5DT
**US SIC:** 4119, 4142
**UK SIC:** 72200, 72102
**Auditors:** Mazars LLP
**Bankers:** National Westminster Bank Plc (50-00-00)

| | 21-12-13 | 22-12-12 | 24-12-11 |
|---|---|---|---|
| TO | 53,249,000 | 54,700,000 | 52,710,000 |
| P/L | 149,000 | 1,380,000 | 3,182,000 |
| NW | (3,488,000) | (2,230,000) | (1,337,000) |
| WC | (4,956,000) | (5,930,000) | (6,972,000) |
| Emp. | 1,100 | 1,156 | 1,171 |

DUNS 52-570-8376
### Transfer 2000 Ltd
191 Vale Road, Tonbridge, Kent TN9 1ST
**Tel:** 08450602000 **Fax:** 01732-771222
**Web:** www.transfer2000.co.uk
**Reg No:** 3254431 **Estd:** 1996 Private Limited Company
**Line of Business:** Freight transport by road not elsewhere classified
**Issued Capital:** £2
**Director:** A M Whittaker
**Co. Secretary:** Mrs Laura Hayes
**Responsibilities**
**Senior:** Tim Deniz *(Manager)*
**US SIC:** 4213, 4311
**UK SIC:** 72300, 79010
**Auditors:** Gibbons & Mannington

| | 31-03-14 | 31-03-13 | 31-03-12 |
|---|---|---|---|
| TA | 1,006,471 | 859,921 | 813,354 |
| NW | 773,653 | 662,861 | 617,007 |
| WC | 667,425 | 583,691 | 566,819 |

DUNS 29-663-1765
### Transform Community Development
Unit 1 22 Kilspindie Road, Dundee, Angus DD2 3JP
**Tel:** 01382828553 **Fax:** 01382206508
**Web:** www.transformcd.org
**Reg No:** 0097367SC **Estd:** 1975 Private Company Limited By Guarantee
**Line of Business:** Other human health activities
**Directors:** T D Smith, J Mcallion, A W Macqueen, I J Warnock, J F Pickett, I M Macrae, S L Ball, R Gabriel
**Co. Secretary:** Simon Laidlaw
**Branches:** Transform Community Development, 2 Sugarhouse Wynd, Dundee, Angus DD1 2SH
**US SIC:** 8091 **UK SIC:** 95200
**Auditors:** Henderson Loggie
**Bankers:** The Royal Bank Of Scotland Plc (83-50-00)

| | 31-03-14 | 31-03-13 | 31-03-12 |
|---|---|---|---|
| TO | 1,760,163 | 1,853,082 | 1,808,400 |
| P/L | (31,238) | (15,157) | (13,055) |
| NW | 1,491,288 | 1,368,024 | 1,221,431 |
| WC | 135,646 | 349,910 | 339,122 |
| Emp. | 70 | 82 | 79 |

DUNS 45-894-3776 **Imp**
### Transform Medical Group (C S) Ltd
**(Subsidiary of:** Transform Holdings Ltd)
192 Altrincham Road, Manchester M22 4RZ
**Tel:** 01614952400 **Fax:** 0161-495-2401
**Web:** www.transforminglives.co.uk
**Reg No:** 3228476 **Estd:** 1996 Private Limited Company
**Line of Business:** Holding companies management activities
**Issued Capital:** £100
**Director:** T Spronk
**Co. Secretary:** Jeremy Rouch
**Responsibilities**
**Senior:** Patricia Dunion *(Chief Operation Officer)*, Anne Winterbottom *(Clinic Manager)*
**Facilities:** Alan Holt *(Maintenance Manager)*
**Branches:** Transform Medical Group (C S) Ltd, Transform Medical Group, Nightingale House, London SW6 3JH
**US SIC:** 8091 **UK SIC:** 95200
**Auditors:** Ernst & Young LLP
**Bankers:** The Royal Bank Of Scotland Plc (16-00-01)

| | 30-09-12 | 30-09-11 | 30-09-10 |
|---|---|---|---|
| TO | 39,605,000 | 36,557,000 | 36,265,000 |
| P/L | (1,017,000) | (698,000) | 504,000 |
| NW | 7,606,000 | 8,426,000 | 8,778,000 |
| WC | 1,475,000 | 990,000 | 170,000 |
| Emp. | 355 | 329 | 317 |

DUNS 51-637-4514 **Exp**
### Transformers & Rectifiers (Holdings) Ltd
15-16 Woodbridge Meadows, Guildford, Surrey GU1 1BJ
**Web:** www.transformers.co.uk
**Reg No:** 5954594 **Estd:** 2006 Private Limited Company
**Line of Business:** Manufacture of electric motors, generators and transformers
**Export Sales:** £807,415
**Issued Capital:** £1,000,000
**Directors:** Mrs A Cowley, Ms K Clarke
**Co. Secretary:** Ms Karen Clarke
**Responsibilities**
**Senior:** Paul Glasscock *(Marketing Manager)*, Clifford Kent *(Health & Safety Manager)*
**Marketing:** Paul Glasscock *(Marketing Manager)*
**Sales:** Paul Glasscock *(Marketing Manager)*
**Health & Safety:** Clifford Kent *(Health & Safety Manager)*
**Facilities:** Clifford Kent *(Health & Safety Manager)*
**Engineering:** Clifford Kent *(Health & Safety Manager)*
**US SIC:** 3621, 3829
**UK SIC:** 34201, 37100
**Bankers:** National Westminster Bank Plc (60-06-03)

| | 31-12-13 | 31-12-12 | 31-12-11 |
|---|---|---|---|
| TO | 8,868,960 | 8,495,462 | 7,932,081 |
| P/L | 587,811 | 1,929,400 | 1,436,273 |
| NW | 4,025,525 | 4,492,201 | 3,040,962 |
| WC | 4,025,384 | 4,433,647 | 2,956,719 |
| Emp. | 80 | 83 | 82 |

DUNS 21-839-7245
### Transforming Education in Norfolk
City College Norwich, Ipswich Road, Norwich, Norfolk NR2 2LJ
**Tel:** 01603773302
**Web:** www.tengroup.org.uk
**Reg No:** 8070464 **Estd:** 2012 Private Company Limited By Guarantee
**Line of Business:** General secondary education
**Directors:** R G Palmer, J A Fry, Professor D J Richardson, Ms S E Guest, C Maw, Ms B J Falkus
**Co. Secretary:** David Hall
**US SIC:** 8211, 8249, 8221
**UK SIC:** 93200, 93300, 93100
**Bankers:** Lloyds TSB Bank plc (30-96-17)

| | 31-08-13 |
|---|---|
| TO | 52,604,000 |
| P/L | 3,773,000 |
| NW | 13,011,000 |
| WC | 3,326,000 |
| Emp. | 1,013 |

DUNS 29-878-8217 **Imp-Exp**
### Transhock Distribution Ltd
Unit 1 Arden Road Industrial Estate, Birmingham, West Midlands B8 1DL
**Tel:** 0121-322-4200 **Fax:** 0121-327-6239
**Web:** www.online.mamsoft.co.uk
**Reg No:** 2081871 **VAT No:** 461995802
**Estd:** 1986 Private Limited Company
**Line of Business:** Mechanical engineering general
**Export Markets:** Andorra
**Trading Style:** Transhock Distribution Ltd
**Issued Capital:** £50,000
**Managing Director:** D Neale
**Co. Secretary:** David Davies
**Responsibilities**
**Marketing:** Mitchell Costello *(Marketing Manager)*
**US SIC:** 8911 **UK SIC:** 83701
**Bankers:** Lloyds TSB Bank plc (30-97-76)

| | 31-03-14 | 31-03-13 | 31-03-12 |
|---|---|---|---|
| TA | 1,942,305 | 2,157,292 | 3,065,210 |
| NW | 200,435 | 222,575 | 345,068 |
| WC | 350,411 | 402,423 | 229,870 |

DUNS 39-754-4941
### Transis Ltd
Stracathro Service Area, Brechin, Angus DD9 7PX
**Tel:** 01674840236
**Web:** www.shell.com
**Reg No:** 0107672SC **Estd:** 1987 Private Limited Company
**Line of Business:** Growing of crops combined with farming of animals (mixed farming)
**Trading Style:** Stracathro Service Station
**Issued Capital:** £10,000
**Directors:** W A Melville - Smith, Ms P J Melville-Evans
**Co. Secretary:** Ms Margaret Reid
**Responsibilities**
**Senior:** Gail Reid *(Manager)*
**Branches:** Transis Ltd, Chester Rd, Buckley, Clwyd CH7 3AJ
**US SIC:** 0291, 5541
**UK SIC:** 01001, 65200
**Auditors:** Condie & Co
**Bankers:** Clydesdale Bank Plc (82-66-06)

| | 31-03-14 | 31-03-13 | 31-03-12 |
|---|---|---|---|
| TA | 1,788,884 | 1,880,741 | 1,873,954 |
| NW | 260,657 | 306,528 | 374,627 |
| WC | (976,023) | (953,772) | (783,153) |

DUNS 34-561-9055
### Transition Extreme Sports Ltd
418 Great Western Road, Aberdeen, Aberdeenshire AB10 6NQ
**Tel:** 01224-626279
**Web:** www.transition-extreme.com
**Reg No:** 0280405SC **Estd:** 2005 Private Company Limited By Guarantee
**Line of Business:** Operation of sports arenas and stadiums
**Directors:** Ms K L Marshall, Ms J S Morrison, T D Smith, G M Paterson, D Mcewing, D P Briggs, G J Gerrard
**Co. Secretary:** Pinsent Masons Secretarial Limit
**Responsibilities**
**Senior:** Louise Ferguson *(Director)*, Rebecca Williams *(Facilities Manager)*
**US SIC:** 7941 **UK SIC:** 97911

| | 31-03-14 | 31-03-13 | 31-03-12 |
|---|---|---|---|
| TO | 842,309 | 798,990 | 958,139 |
| P/L | 7,338 | 663 | 216,476 |
| NW | 1,936,779 | 1,929,441 | 1,928,778 |
| WC | (233,959) | (229,778) | (213,825) |
| Emp. | 51 | 51 | 46 |

DUNS 23-881-2569
### Transitional Care Ltd
Park House, 8 Lombard Road Wimbledon, London SW19 3TZ
**Tel:** 020-8543-7878
**Web:** www.tces.org.uk
**Reg No:** 3872464 **Estd:** 1999 Private Limited Company
**Line of Business:** Other business activities not elsewhere classified
**Trading Style:** Tc Education Services, Transitional Care Education Services, North West London Independent Special School
**Issued Capital:** £50,000
**Director:** T Keaney
**Co. Secretary:** Richard Barron
**Responsibilities**
**Senior:** Christina Buckingham-Hack *(commercial director)*, Paula Ellens *(Manager)*, Leslie Fish *(Office Manager)*
**Marketing:** Christina Buckingham-Hack *(commercial director)*
**Admin:** Leslie Fish *(Office Manager)*
**Branches:** Transitional Care Ltd, 463 Southbank Ho, Black Prince Rd, London SE1 7SJ
**US SIC:** 7399 **UK SIC:** 83954
**Auditors:** Ward Williams

| | 31-08-13 | 31-08-12 | 31-08-11 |
|---|---|---|---|
| TO | 8,615,233 | N/A | N/A |
| P/L | 406,971 | N/A | N/A |
| NW | 840,007 | 764,965 | 599,620 |
| WC | (401,770) | (577,890) | (213,827) |
| Emp. | 98 | N/A | N/A |

DUNS 22-070-5821
### Transitive Ltd
**(Subsidiary of:** International Business Machines Corporation)
Maybrook House, 40 Blackfriars Street, Manchester M3 2EG
**Tel:** 01618362300
**Web:** www.transitiveltdmanchester.com
**Reg No:** 4072099 **Estd:** 2000 Private Limited Company
**Line of Business:** Other adult and other education not elsewhere classified
**Managing Director:** H P Nash
**Co. Secretary:** Alison Sullivan
**US SIC:** 8299 **UK SIC:** 93300
**Auditors:** Ernst & Young LLP
**Employees:** 76

DUNS 22-096-2208
### Translating & Interpreting Service
124 St Marys, Barking, Essex IG11 7TF
**Tel:** 020-8591-0050
**Web:** www.tisonline.org.uk
**Reg No:** 4097487 **Estd:** 2000 Private Unlimited Company
**Line of Business:** Secretarial and translation activities
**Directors:** S Milambo, Ms S Ashraf, K Landoure, M Quadri
**Responsibilities**
**Senior:** Sheila Delaney *(Manager)*, Nirmal Gill *(Manager)*, Kolado Landoure *(Director)*, Rukhsana Sohail *(General Manager)*, Verona Tucker *(Manager)*
**US SIC:** 7339, 9121, 8249, 8999
**UK SIC:** 83954, 91110, 93300
**Bankers:** Unity Trust Bank Plc (08-60-01)

| | 31-03-14 | 31-03-13 | 31-03-12 |
|---|---|---|---|
| TO | 197,962 | 327,789 | 348,052 |
| P/L | (30,585) | 15,342 | (19,728) |
| NW | 89,932 | 120,517 | 105,175 |
| WC | 88,901 | 119,143 | 103,344 |
| Emp. | 86 | 79 | 74 |

DUNS 21-881-2709 **Imp-Exp**
### Translift Bendi Ltd
**(Subsidiary of:** Articulated Lift Trucks Ltd)
Unit 22, Redditch, Worcestershire B98 0RB
**Tel:** 01527-527411 **Fax:** 01527-510177
**Web:** www.bendi.co.uk
**Reg No:** 0833384 **VAT No:** 670314164
**Estd:** 1964 Private Limited Company
**Line of Business:** Fork lift trucks
**Export Markets:** Worldwide.
**Export Sales:** £2,581,548
**Trading Style:** Bendi
**Issued Capital:** £500
**Principals:** S M Brown *(Managing)*, P D Overfield, P E Berrow

**Co. Secretary:** Mrs Jacqueline Kirby
**US SIC:** 3534, 5083
**UK SIC:** 32553, 61490
**Auditors:** Burman & Co
**Bankers:** Barclays Bank Plc (20-71-45)

| | 31-03-14 | 31-03-13 | 31-03-12 |
|---|---|---|---|
| TO | 19,748,203 | 21,934,454 | 17,305,220 |
| P/L | 327,234 | 461,450 | 526,730 |
| NW | 5,231,403 | 4,931,689 | 4,508,250 |
| WC | 4,723,009 | 4,740,201 | 4,355,804 |
| Emp. | 114 | 112 | 97 |

DUNS 21-039-3469
## Translink
Europa Business Centre, 10 Glengall Street, Belfast BT12 5AH
**Tel:** 028-9033-7004
**Web:** www.translink.co.uk
**Line of Business:** Other supporting land transport activities
**Responsibilities**
**HR:** Gordon Milligan *(Hr Director)*
**US SIC:** 4789 **UK SIC:** 77002
**Employees:** 4,000

DUNS 23-946-9146
## Translogistic Ltd
2nd Floor, Highview House, 165-167 Station Road, Edgware, Middlesex HA8 7JU
**Tel:** 01279655666 **Fax:** 01279-658865
**Web:** www.associated-taxis.com
**Reg No:** 3936360 **Estd:** 2000 Private Limited Company
**Line of Business:** Taxis and private hire vehicles
**Trading Style:** Associated Taxis
**Issued Capital:** £50,000
**Director:** C Knaggs
**Co. Secretary:** Christopher Knaggs
**US SIC:** 4121 **UK SIC:** 72200
**Auditors:** Martin Tiano & Co

| | 31-03-14 | 31-03-13 | 31-03-12 |
|---|---|---|---|
| TA | 173,346 | 145,678 | 144,443 |
| NW | 801 | (44,969) | (85,778) |
| WC | (26,842) | (78,289) | (112,432) |

DUNS 23-977-0576
## Translution (Uk) Ltd.
Unit 5 Brunswick Way Brunswick, Industrial Park, London N11 1JL
**Tel:** 02083620300
**Web:** www.decleor.co.uk
**Reg No:** 3965634 **Estd:** 2000 Private Limited Company
**Line of Business:** Manufacture of perfumes and toilet preparations
**Issued Capital:** £4,000
**Directors:** Mrs M Hills, C Ioannou, J A Hills
**Co. Secretary:** Mrs Susan Ioannou
**Responsibilities**
**Senior:** Tony Sykes *(Finance Director)*
**Finance:** Tony Sykes *(Finance Director)*
**US SIC:** 8999, 4311
**UK SIC:** 83954, 79010
**Auditors:** Mobile Accountants
**Bankers:** National Westminster Bank Plc (60-07-38)

| | 30-04-13 | 30-04-12 | 30-04-11 |
|---|---|---|---|
| TO | 4,765,781 | N/A | 2,228,813 |
| P/L | 962,746 | N/A | 101,812 |
| NW | 451,103 | 908,420 | (19,084) |
| WC | 340,073 | 47,744 | (41,489) |

DUNS 50-585-8456 **Imp-Exp**
## Transmec U K Ltd
**(Subsidiary of:** Transmec International Sa)
726 London Road, Grays, Essex RM20 3NL
**Tel:** 01708-682300
**Web:** www.transmecgroup.it
**Reg No:** 2528519 **VAT No:** 541404872
**Estd:** 1990 Private Limited Company
**Line of Business:** Freight forwarders
**Export Markets:** European Union (E U)
**Issued Capital:** £100,000
**Director:** D Montecchi
**Co. Secretary:** Mohammad Imran
**Responsibilities**
**Senior:** Adrian Hallett *(Warehouse Manager)*, Adrian Nicholls *(Manager)*, fabio bizzi *(Warehouse Manager)*
**Facilities:** Adrian Hallett *(Warehouse Manager)*
**Branches:** Transmec U K Ltd, Woodroyd Industrial Estate, Dealburn Road, Low Moor, Bradford, West Yorkshire BD12 0RG
**US SIC:** 4712, 4226
**UK SIC:** 77002, 77003
**Auditors:** Lipson & Co Ltd
**Bankers:** National Westminster Bank Plc (60-20-24)

| | 31-12-13 | 31-12-12 | 31-12-11 |
|---|---|---|---|
| TO | 24,106,441 | 24,918,145 | 24,298,185 |
| P/L | 50,425 | 909,525 | 761,086 |
| NW | 4,146,282 | 5,350,543 | 4,426,431 |
| WC | 5,293,793 | 6,860,995 | 4,258,143 |
| Emp. | 130 | 129 | 125 |

DUNS 22-541-0638 **Imp-Exp**
## Transmission Developments Co (Gb) Ltd
Unit 26 Dawkins Road, Poole, Dorset BH15 4HF
**Tel:** 01202-675555
**Web:** www.transdev.co.uk
**Reg No:** 1888295 **Estd:** 1962 Private Limited Company
**Line of Business:** Power transmission services
**Export Markets:** West Europe, U.S.A. & Australasia
**Issued Capital:** £480,000
**Principals:** I J Osborne *(Managing)*, C J Cowler
**Co. Secretary:** Ms Carole Osborne
**Responsibilities**
**Senior:** Dean Dennett *(Despatch Manager)*, Alec Temple *(Manager)*
**HR:** Kerry Pope *(Quality Assurance Manager)*
**Health & Safety:** Kerry Pope *(Quality Assurance Manager)*
**Facilities:** Kerry Pope *(Quality Assurance Manager)*
**Operations:** Kerry Pope *(Quality Assurance Manager)*
**Branches:** Transmission Developments Co (Gb) Ltd, Kennington Rd, Poole, Dorset BH17 0GF
**US SIC:** 3560 **UK SIC:** 32613
**Auditors:** John A. Hyde & Co

| | 31-03-14 | 31-03-13 | 31-03-12 |
|---|---|---|---|
| TO | 7,366,105 | 7,133,186 | 7,386,586 |
| P/L | 893,715 | 417,826 | 650,289 |
| NW | 6,604,313 | 6,096,110 | 5,955,871 |
| WC | 5,463,704 | 4,878,506 | 5,269,177 |
| Emp. | 85 | 84 | 80 |

DUNS 76-815-9725
## Transocean Drilling U.K. Ltd
**(Subsidiary of:** Transocean Ltd.)
Deepwater House, Aberdeen, Aberdeenshire AB15 8PU
**Tel:** 01224944000 **Fax:** 01224654401
**Web:** www.deepwater.com
**Reg No:** 0131375SC **VAT No:** 663730921
**Estd:** 2001 Private Limited Company
**Line of Business:** Test drilling and boring
**Trading Style:** Deepwater
**Directors:** Miss M A Clare, I Paterson, A P Rose
**Co. Secretary:** Burness Paull Llp
**Responsibilities**
**Senior:** Mike Scott *(Procurement & Purchasing Manag)*
**Health & Safety:** Bill Cairns *(Global Director of HSE Field S)*, Neil Clyne *(Health Safety Environment and)*
**Operations:** Mark Milne *(Operations Manager)*
**Purchasing:** Mike Scott *(Procurement & Purchasing Manag)*
**Branches:** Transocean Drilling U.k. Ltd, Langlands House, Huntly Street, Aberdeen, Aberdeenshire AB10 1SH
**US SIC:** 1381 **UK SIC:** 13000
**Auditors:** Ernst & Young LLP
**Bankers:** Bank Of Scotland (80-06-60)
**Employees:** 130
**Turnover:** £964,761,000

DUNS 22-176-7200
## Transperfect Translations Ltd
**(Subsidiary of:** Coöperatief Transperfect U.A.)
45 Moorfields, London EC2Y 9AE
**Tel:** 02073988200 **Fax:** 020-7398-8202
**Web:** www.transperfect.com
**Reg No:** 4195126 **Estd:** 2001 Private Limited Company
**Line of Business:** Translation activities
**Export Sales:** £2,295,430
**Issued Capital:** £100
**Directors:** Ms E Elting, P Shawe
**Co. Secretary:** Roy Trujillo
**Responsibilities**
**Senior:** Angela O'Sullivan *(President)*
**Branches:** Transperfect Translations Ltd, 46 Aldgate High Street, London EC3N 1AL
**US SIC:** 7339, 8299
**UK SIC:** 83954, 93300
**Auditors:** Frank Hirth & Co LLP
**Bankers:** HSBC Bank plc (40-01-08)

| | 31-12-13 | 31-12-12 | 31-12-11 |
|---|---|---|---|
| TO | 14,935,163 | 11,038,636 | 9,899,622 |
| P/L | 1,334,953 | 1,135,343 | 1,293,232 |
| NW | 5,851,554 | 4,831,971 | 3,991,150 |
| WC | 5,556,346 | 4,568,112 | 3,948,665 |
| Emp. | 154 | 139 | 116 |

DUNS 23-807-6371 **Imp**
## Transpiration Ltd
Unit 5, Queenford Farm, Wallingford, Oxfordshire OX10 7PH
**Tel:** 01865-340002
**Web:** www.transpiration-ventures.eu
**Reg No:** 3800040 **Estd:** 1999 Private Limited Company

**Line of Business:** Disability services
**Issued Capital:** £270
**Director:** Ms D Wright
**Responsibilities**
**Senior:** Garry Goodband *(Operations Manager)*, Marion Saville *(Manager)*, Mark Southgate *(Manager)*
**US SIC:** 4141 **UK SIC:** 72102
**Auditors:** Martin & Fahy

| | 31-08-13 | 31-08-12 | 31-08-11 |
|---|---|---|---|
| TO | N/A | 356,363 | N/A |
| P/L | N/A | 35,793 | N/A |
| NW | 73,657 | 39,291 | 52,372 |
| WC | 19,482 | 3,813 | 11,566 |

DUNS 23-294-6251
## Transport for Greater Manchester
2 Piccadilly Place, Manchester M1 3BG
**Tel:** 01612441000 **Fax:** 01612283291
**Web:** www.tfgm.com
**VAT No:** 146594245 **Estd:** 2011 Incorporate By Act Of Parliament
**Line of Business:** Transportation consultants
**Trading Style:** G M P T E
**Principals:** G S Inskip *(Financial)*, M C Renshaw, U Bramwell, T H Tristram, C Higton, C J Mulligan, D Lennox, K A Howcroft
**Responsibilities**
**Senior:** C Ainscow *(Non-Executive Director)*, K Giles *(Non-Executive Director)*, John Lamont *(Ceo)*
**Branches:** Transport For Greater Manchester, 2 Piccadilly Place, Manchester M1 3BG
**US SIC:** 9121, 7399, 7392
**UK SIC:** 91110, 83954, 83951
**Bankers:** The Co-Operative Bank Plc (08-90-00)
**Employees:** 500

DUNS 23-292-7041
## Transport for London
**(Subsidiary of:** Greater London Authority)
55 Broadway, London SW1H 0BD
**Tel:** 03432220000
**Web:** www.tfl.gov.uk
**Estd:** 1984
**Line of Business:** Rail transport services.
**Trading Style:** T F L
**Issued Capital:** £1
**Principals:** B Johnson *(Chairman)*, P Anderson *(Financial)*, Ms E Lindholm, K Williams, Ms J Hunt, C Belcher, B Oddy, S Wright
**Co. Secretary:** Tony West
**Responsibilities**
**Senior:** Christopher Garnett *(Vice Chairperson)*, Dame Grey-Thompson *(Principal)*, Mike Hodgkinson *(Principal)*, Kulveer Ranger *(Principal)*
**Branches:** Transport For London, 4th Floor, Zone Y4, North Greenwich, London SE10 0ES
**US SIC:** 9121, 4011
**UK SIC:** 91110, 71000
**Auditors:** KPMG LLP
**Bankers:** HSBC Bank plc (40-07-13)
**Following financial data are in thousands**

| | 31-03-14 | 31-03-13 | 31-03-12 |
|---|---|---|---|
| TO | 4,789,600 | 4,495,500 | 4,180,900 |
| P/L | 2,936,600 | 3,105,200 | 2,274,500 |
| NW | 22,051,800 | 18,507,100 | 15,999,500 |
| WC | 2,178,100 | 849,600 | (1,122,700) |
| Emp. | 28,359 | 28,020 | 27,494 |

DUNS 64-080-6980
## Transport Planning Associates Ltd
**(Subsidiary of:** Red Amber Green (Holdings) Ltd)
Mercury House, 1 Broadwater Road, Welwyn Garden City, Hertfordshire AL7 3BQ
**Fax:** 01603-660668
**Web:** www.transportplanningassociates.co.uk
**Reg No:** 3476060 **Estd:** 1997 Private Limited Company
**Line of Business:** Engineering related scientific and technical consulting activities
**Issued Capital:** £255
**Directors:** D A Knight, C M Rawlinson, S A Wanchoo, P N Evans, R T Lyons, I E Cameron, N P Hanks, J S Clarke
**Co. Secretary:** Miss Julia Justice
**Branches:** Transport Planning Associates Ltd, Fourth Floor, 25 King Street, Bristol, Avon BS1 4PB
**US SIC:** 8911 **UK SIC:** 83701
**Auditors:** Larking Gowen

| | 31-03-14 | 31-03-13 | 31-03-12 |
|---|---|---|---|
| TA | 3,232,455 | 2,702,593 | 2,731,817 |
| NW | 898,124 | 691,576 | 816,224 |
| WC | 812,093 | 621,037 | 730,033 |

DUNS 23-659-4594
## Transport Salaried Staff's Association
Walkden House, London NW1 2EJ
**Tel:** 02073872101
**Web:** www.tssa.org.uk
**Estd:** 1897
**Line of Business:** Trade unions
**Principals:** D A Horton *(President)*, R A Rosser
**Responsibilities**
**Senior:** Manuel Cortes *(General Secretary)*
**Branches:** Transport Salaried Staff's Association, Bar La, York, North Yorkshire YO1 6JU
**US SIC:** 8631 **UK SIC:** 96313
**Employees:** 55
**Turnover:** £3,729,031

DUNS 23-924-7690 **Imp**
## Transport Trading Ltd
**(Subsidiary of:** Greater London Authority)
Windsor House, 42-50 Victoria Street, London SW1H 0TL
**Web:** www.tfl.gov.uk
**Reg No:** 3914810 **Estd:** 2000 Private Limited Company
**Line of Business:** Urban and suburban passenger transportation by underground, metro and similar systems
**Trading Style:** Transport for London
**Issued Capital:** £1,120,000,000
**Directors:** S D Allen, M W Brown, L A Daniels, Sir P G Hendy
**Co. Secretary:** Howard Carter
**US SIC:** 4011, 4131
**UK SIC:** 71000, 72102
**Auditors:** KPMG LLP
**Following financial data are in thousands**

| | 31-03-14 | 31-03-13 | 31-03-12 |
|---|---|---|---|
| TO | 4,439,300 | 4,137,700 | 3,841,000 |
| P/L | (113,500) | 100,500 | (419,300) |
| NW | 17,433,900 | 14,971,500 | 13,597,300 |
| WC | (1,195,800) | (1,310,200) | (963,900) |
| Emp. | 21,186 | 21,419 | 22,178 |

DUNS 34-607-0522
## Transportation Infrastructure Group Ltd
Automation House, Warrington, Cheshire WA3 2AP
**Tel:** 01942-685555 **Fax:** 01942685518
**Web:** www.atgairports.com
**Reg No:** 5413992 **Estd:** 2005 Private Limited Company
**Line of Business:** Management activities of holding companies
**Export Sales:** £3,779,607
**Issued Capital:** £154
**Director:** G M Mcguinness
**Co. Secretary:** Miss Sandra Baxter
**US SIC:** 6711 **UK SIC:** 83962
**Bankers:** National Westminster Bank Plc (60-24-02)

| | 30-04-14 | 30-04-13 | 30-04-12 |
|---|---|---|---|
| TO | 14,689,622 | 14,685,075 | 17,360,139 |
| P/L | 981,863 | 757,883 | 482,508 |
| NW | 1,810,632 | 1,531,594 | 1,105,415 |
| WC | 1,305,344 | 1,214,301 | 1,036,387 |
| Emp. | 100 | 95 | 94 |

DUNS 51-980-6272
## Transputec Ltd
19 Heather Park Drive, Wembley, Middlesex HA0 1SS
**Tel:** 02085841400 **Fax:** 020-8584-1322
**Web:** www.transputec.com
**Reg No:** 3443568 **Estd:** 1977 Private Limited Company
**Line of Business:** Data processing
**Export Sales:** £992,256
**Issued Capital:** £10
**Directors:** A Seghal, S Sehgal, M K Turumella, A K Vedi, M N Nightingale
**Co. Secretary:** Anil Sehgal
**US SIC:** 7374 **UK SIC:** 83940
**Auditors:** MHA MacIntyre Hudson

| | 31-03-14 | 30-11-12 | 30-03-11 |
|---|---|---|---|
| TO | 18,944,299 | 16,191,256 | 12,039,347 |
| P/L | 255,888 | 310,530 | 372,599 |
| NW | 3,375,169 | 3,204,791 | 2,980,876 |
| WC | 3,131,324 | 3,142,530 | 2,915,489 |
| Emp. | 60 | 70 | 66 |

DUNS 76-719-6173
## Transworld Couriers Ltd
**(Subsidiary of:** Transworld Global Logistics Ltd)
Unit 3 Bricklayers Arms, London SE1 5SR
**Tel:** 020-7231-3131
**Web:** www.web.twc.uk.com
**Reg No:** 2596027 **VAT No:** 523460960
**Estd:** 1975 Private Limited Company
**Line of Business:** Activities of other transport agencies
**Issued Capital:** £55,000
**Directors:** A M Hussain, S M Hussain
**Co. Secretary:** Imran Hussain

**Responsibilities**
**Senior:** Natasha Ryan *(Hr Manager)*
**US SIC:** 4712, 4311
**UK SIC:** 77002, 79010
**Auditors:** Carter Backer Winter LLP
**Bankers:** HSBC bank plc (40-04-09)

| | 31-03-14 | 31-03-13 | 31-03-12 |
|---|---|---|---|
| TO | 12,706,311 | 7,539,132 | 6,854,202 |
| P/L | 403,582 | 116,602 | 377,431 |
| NW | 1,500,368 | 1,155,344 | 1,013,644 |
| WC | 976,610 | 1,018,982 | 891,482 |
| Emp. | 120 | 81 | 70 |

DUNS 21-629-7887 **Imp**
## Trant Engineering Ltd
**(Subsidiary of:** Trant Holding Company Limited)
Rushington House, Southampton, Hampshire SO40 9LT
**Tel:** 023-8066-5544
**Web:** www.trant.co.uk
**Reg No:** 0769274 **VAT No:** 411686167
**Estd:** 1963 Private Limited Company
**Line of Business:** Civil engineers
**Export Sales:** £8,964,045
**Issued Capital:** £30,000
**Principals:** P M Trant *(Chairman)*, T Trant *(Managing)*, S Trant, K H Wallace, P N Trant, M W Reed, S M Jordan, M W Swallow
**Co. Secretary:** Robin Horgan
**Responsibilities**
**Senior:** John Patten *(Systems Director)*, Fran Ravizza *(Contract Director, Power UKAE)*, Andy Rickard *(Manager)*, Gerry Somers *(Contract Director, Constructio)*, James Trant *(Director)*
**Admin:** Nikki Pullen *(Secretary)*
**IT:** John Patten *(Systems Director)*, Ryan Tranc *(IT Manager)*
**HR:** James Trant *(Director)*
**Operations:** Tim Bullen *(Process Manager)*, Fran Ravizza *(Contract Director, Power UKAE)*, Derek Sherlock *(Site Manager)*, Gerry Somers *(Contract Director, Constructio)*
**Engineering:** Wayne Broadbent *(Mechanical Design Manager)*, David Rich *(Electrical Engineering Manager)*
**Branches:** Trant Engineering Limited, Site Office Tank Farm Area, Magazine Lane, Marchwood, Southampton, Hampshire SO40 4UX
**US SIC:** 8911, 1629, 1622
**UK SIC:** 83701, 50000, 50200
**Auditors:** RSM Tenon Audit Ltd
**Bankers:** National Westminster Bank Plc (55-50-21)

| | 31-12-13 | 31-12-12 | 31-12-11 |
|---|---|---|---|
| TO | 79,419,193 | 67,324,479 | 77,988,344 |
| P/L | 596,436 | 853,713 | 1,419,972 |
| NW | 5,265,396 | 5,532,280 | 5,383,851 |
| WC | 4,633,015 | 5,806,381 | 6,752,914 |
| Emp. | 538 | 503 | 568 |

DUNS 22-141-9406 **Imp**
## Trapeze Group (Uk) Ltd
**(Subsidiary of:** Trapeze Group Europe Holding A/S)
The Mill, Staverton, Trowbridge, Wiltshire BA14 6PH
**Tel:** 08445616771
**Web:** www.trapezegroup.co.uk
**Reg No:** 4160790 **Estd:** 2000 Private Limited Company
**Line of Business:** Other software consultancy and supply
**Export Sales:** £594,305
**Issued Capital:** £3,675,000
**Directors:** Ms J Mcpherson, Clair Clarke, Dr C P Bell
**Co. Secretary:** Robert Clay
**Responsibilities**
**Finance:** Carrie Marks *(Financial Controller)*
**Marketing:** Damian Bown *(Director of Sales & Marketing)*, Mike Cartmel *(Digital Marketing Executive)*, Mike Killa *(Business Group Manager - ITS)*, Darren Turpin *(Marketing Manager)*
**Sales:** Alistair Aitken *(Sales Director)*, Damian Bown *(Director of Sales & Marketing)*, Larry Breen *(Business Development Director)*
**IT:** James Blannin *(Head of IT)*
**Health & Safety:** Keith Illingworth *(Health & Safety Officer)*
**Purchasing:** Brian Heath *(Purchasing Manager)*
**US SIC:** 7379 **UK SIC:** 83940
**Auditors:** RSM Bentley Jennison
**Bankers:** HSBC Bank plc (40-17-25)

| | 31-12-13 | 31-12-12 | 31-12-11 |
|---|---|---|---|
| TO | 15,520,445 | 14,130,121 | 15,768,353 |
| P/L | 250,613 | (762,923) | 389,727 |
| NW | (774,580) | (1,326,958) | (1,006,312) |
| WC | (571,502) | (1,288,117) | (1,989,842) |
| Emp. | 149 | 146 | 155 |

DUNS 21-171-7580 **Imp**
## Trapeze Its U.K. Ltd
**(Subsidiary of:** Trapeze Its Luxembourg Sarl)
The Mill, Staverton, Trowbridge, Wiltshire BA14 6PH
**Tel:** 08443352898
**Web:** www.trapezegroup.co.uk
**Reg No:** 6960657 **Estd:** 2009 Private Limited Company
**Line of Business:** Other software consultancy and supply
**Export Sales:** £2,894,871
**Issued Capital:** £1,000
**Directors:** R Clay, P Schneck, M Lohrer
**Co. Secretary:** Robert Clay
**Branches:** Trapeze Its U.k. Ltd, 1 High Street, Bridge View, Birmingham, West Midlands B46 1BE
**US SIC:** 7379 **UK SIC:** 83940
**Auditors:** RSM Tenon Audit Ltd

| | 31-12-13 | 31-12-12 | 31-12-11 |
|---|---|---|---|
| TO | 2,960,027 | 3,572,976 | 4,264,345 |
| P/L | 154,209 | 267,719 | 208,253 |
| NW | 652,498 | 496,369 | 269,422 |
| WC | 651,515 | 492,528 | 249,878 |
| Emp. | 46 | 43 | 25 |

DUNS 28-929-5602 **Imp**
## Traplet Publications Ltd
Traplet House, 1 Pendragon Close, Malvern, Worcestershire WR14 1GA
**Tel:** 01684588500 **Fax:** 01684594586
**Web:** www.traplet.com
**Reg No:** 1520372 **Estd:** 1980 Private Limited Company
**Line of Business:** Publishing of newspapers
**Issued Capital:** £100
**Principals:** A H Stephenson *(Managing)*, Mrs T Caleia Ferreira, T A Stephenson
**Co. Secretary:** Thomas Stephenson
**Responsibilities**
**Senior:** Pat Howard *(Warehouse Manager)*, Tony van Geffen *(Executive)*
**Finance:** Trudy Ferreira *(Financial Director)*
**Marketing:** Rebecca Hughes *(Editor)*, Mike Nott *(Editor)*, Helen Pallen *(Marketing Manager)*, Michelle Powell *(Editor)*
**Sales:** Vivienne Hill *(Sales Executive)*
**HR:** Jane Simmons *(HR Manager)*
**Fleet:** Pat Howard *(Warehouse Manager)*
**Branches:** Traplet Publications Ltd, 249 Worcester Road, Malvern, Worcestershire WR14 1SY
**US SIC:** 2711, 3652
**UK SIC:** 47512, 34520
**Auditors:** John Yelland & Co
**Bankers:** HSBC Bank plc (40-11-20)

| | 31-03-14 | 31-03-13 | 31-03-12 |
|---|---|---|---|
| TA | 1,864,001 | 1,896,304 | 1,894,885 |
| NW | 571,178 | 587,497 | 533,279 |
| WC | 41,109 | 62,380 | 17,759 |

DUNS 28-984-1702 **Exp**
## Trathens Travel Services Ltd
Walkham Park Burrington Way, Plymouth, Devon PL5 3LS
**Tel:** 01752790565
**Web:** www.parksofhamilton.co.uk
**Reg No:** 1792858 **Estd:** 1984 Private Limited Company
**Line of Business:** Other passenger land transport
**Export Markets:** W Europe
**Trading Style:** Parks of Hamliton Coach Hirers Limited
**Issued Capital:** £100,000
**Directors:** R W Park, A S Bryce, I B Mackay, D I Park, W Cumming
**Co. Secretary:** Gerard Donnachie
**Branches:** Trathens Travel Services Ltd, Royle Road, Rochdale, Lancashire OL11 3ET
**US SIC:** 4141, 4722
**UK SIC:** 72102, 77001
**Auditors:** Thomas Barrie & Co LLP
**Bankers:** Lloyds TSB Bank plc (30-96-68)
**Employees:** 120

DUNS 22-654-8105 **Imp**
## Tratos (Uk) Ltd
**(Subsidiary of:** Alma Srl)
1 Park Road Holmewood Industrial Park, Chesterfield, Derbyshire S42 6ER
**Tel:** 01246-858000
**Web:** www.tratos.co.uk
**Reg No:** 1524815 **VAT No:** 308575838
**Estd:** 1980 Private Limited Company
**Line of Business:** Other wholesale
**Issued Capital:** £100
**Directors:** A Bragagni, Dr M Bragagni, Dr E B Capaccini, J S Light, G Bragagni, N Ancell
**Co. Secretary:** Kevin Martin
**US SIC:** 5199 **UK SIC:** 61900
**Auditors:** Hewitt Card Ltd

**Bankers:** National Westminster Bank Plc (60-17-05)

| | 31-12-13 | 31-12-12 | 31-12-11 |
|---|---|---|---|
| TO | 19,677,032 | 22,214,902 | 23,682,513 |
| P/L | 292,869 | 97,459 | 294,636 |
| NW | 3,709,617 | 1,259,702 | 1,211,214 |
| WC | 2,496,809 | 2,684,333 | (742,566) |
| Emp. | 59 | 89 | 90 |

DUNS 51-704-9417
## Trattoria Bardigiana
5 Bernard Street, London WC1N 1LJ
**Tel:** 020-7837-8744
**Estd:** 1975 Partnership
**Line of Business:** Restaurant - italian
**Partners:** B Sidoli, G Sidoli, S Sidoli
**Responsibilities**
**Senior:** Sergio Sidoli *(Proprietor)*
**US SIC:** 5812 **UK SIC:** 66110
**Employees:** 50

DUNS 23-732-7809
## Trattoria Guidi Ltd
122-126 Deedes Street, Airdrie, Lanarkshire ML6 9AF
**Tel:** 01236-755321
**Web:** www.trattoriaguidi.com
**Reg No:** 0194109SC **Estd:** 1999 Private Limited Company
**Line of Business:** Restaurant - italian
**Issued Capital:** £2
**Directors:** Ms E Guidi, C Guidi
**Co. Secretary:** Alison Lynn
**US SIC:** 5812 **UK SIC:** 66110
**Bankers:** Clydesdale Bank Plc (82-60-18)

| | 31-03-14 | 31-03-13 | 31-03-12 |
|---|---|---|---|
| TA | 288,687 | 284,716 | 175,318 |
| NW | 38,503 | 14,500 | (46,102) |
| WC | (25,728) | (61,536) | (128,189) |

DUNS 28-898-8181
## Travail Employment Group Ltd
24 Southgate Street, Gloucester, Gloucestershire GL1 2DP
**Tel:** 01452415676
**Web:** www.travail.co.uk
**Reg No:** 1334361 **Estd:** 1977 Private Limited Company
**Line of Business:** Management activities of holding companies
**Trading Style:** Travail Employment
**Issued Capital:** £6,998
**Principals:** B J Bliss *(Chairman)*, A P Wyer *(Chairman and Managing)*, N Elford *(Managing)*, R E Flory, K Green
**Co. Secretary:** Ms Joanne Mullan
**Responsibilities**
**Senior:** Nick Rees-Elford *(Manager)*, Sue Thurgood *(Branch Manager)*
**Marketing:** Nick Rees-Elford *(Manager)*
**Branches:** Travail Employment Group Ltd, Unit D3, The Raylor Centre, James S, York, North Yorkshire YO10 3DW
**US SIC:** 6711, 7361
**UK SIC:** 83962, 83954
**Auditors:** Hazlewoods LLP
**Bankers:** HSBC Bank plc (40-22-09)

| | 31-12-13 | 31-12-12 | 31-12-11 |
|---|---|---|---|
| TO | 9,651,729 | 10,654,030 | 13,266,435 |
| P/L | 200,660 | 395,384 | 1,005,924 |
| NW | 1,369,294 | 1,369,294 | 1,369,294 |
| WC | 764,049 | 713,366 | 709,510 |
| Emp. | 54 | 58 | 61 |

DUNS 39-817-0803 **Exp**
## Travco International Ltd
Travco House, 92-94 Paul Street, London EC2A 4UX
**Tel:** 020-7739-3333 **Fax:** 020-7739-2233
**Web:** www.travco.co.uk
**Reg No:** 2216088 **VAT No:** 511101820
**Estd:** 1988 Private Limited Company
**Line of Business:** Activities of travel organisers
**Issued Capital:** £804
**Principals:** M S Allan *(Managing)*, J R Feilder
**Co. Secretary:** Roy Allan
**Responsibilities**
**Marketing:** Kevin Pooler *(Sales & Marketing Manager)*
**Sales:** Kevin Pooler *(Sales & Marketing Manager)*
**IT:** Rehan Shaikh *(Computer Manager)*
**HR:** Denise Careswell *(Human Resources Manager)*
**US SIC:** 4722, 7999
**UK SIC:** 77001, 97913
**Auditors:** Charterhouse (Accountants) LLP
**Bankers:** Barclays Bank Plc (20-74-63)

| | 28-02-14 | 28-02-13 | 29-02-12 |
|---|---|---|---|
| TA | 18,758,468 | 14,563,476 | 11,162,746 |
| NW | 17,394,600 | 13,229,700 | 9,716,358 |
| WC | (530,688) | (443,796) | (507,821) |

DUNS 39-947-6084 **Imp**
## Travel Buff Ltd
**(Subsidiary of:** Daunt Books Ltd)
83 Marylebone High Street, London W1U 4QW
**Tel:** 020-7224-2295
**Web:** www.dauntbooks.co.uk
**Reg No:** 2253675 **Estd:** 1990 Private Limited Company
**Line of Business:** Retail sale of books, newspapers and stationery
**Trading Style:** Daunt Books
**Issued Capital:** £240,100
**Director:** A J Daunt
**Co. Secretary:** Brett Wolstencroft
**US SIC:** 5942 **UK SIC:** 65300
**Auditors:** Sproull & Co
**Bankers:** Clydesdale Bank Plc (82-04-03)

| | 31-12-13 | 31-12-12 | 31-12-11 |
|---|---|---|---|
| TO | 7,877,358 | 8,029,818 | N/A |
| P/L | 688,557 | 763,446 | N/A |
| NW | 2,579,381 | 2,401,698 | 2,113,961 |
| WC | 2,085,315 | 1,832,269 | 1,448,280 |
| Emp. | 47 | 38 | N/A |

DUNS 73-512-6224
## Travel Claims Services Ltd
**(Subsidiary of:** Fundacion Mapfre)
Maitland House, Warrior Square, Southend-On-Sea, Essex SS1 2JY
**Tel:** 08448886464
**Web:** www.travelclaimsservices.com
**Reg No:** 4775583 **Estd:** 2003 Private Limited Company
**Line of Business:** Activities auxiliary to insurance and pension funding
**Issued Capital:** £100
**Directors:** N Antimissaris, P Alvert Sanz
**Co. Secretary:** Quayseco Ltd
**US SIC:** 7399 **UK SIC:** 83954

| | 31-12-13 | 31-12-12 | 31-12-11 |
|---|---|---|---|
| TO | 2,753,935 | 2,564,021 | 1,614,069 |
| P/L | 212,867 | 497,877 | 89,359 |
| NW | 779,894 | 616,707 | 245,956 |
| WC | 1,154,298 | 544,190 | 228,859 |
| Emp. | 106 | 83 | 55 |

DUNS 21-156-6500
## The Travel Company Ltd
**(Subsidiary of:** Bcd Holdings N.V.)
30 Eastbourne Terrace, London W2 6LA
**Tel:** 020-7262-5040 **Fax:** 020-7724-9883
**Web:** www.bcdtravel.co.uk
**Reg No:** 0422800 **VAT No:** 341287465
**Estd:** 1946 Private Limited Company
**Line of Business:** Activities of travel agencies
**Trading Style:** Bcd Travel, The Chapel Co.
**Issued Capital:** £250,000
**Principals:** M J Walley *(Managing)*, Ms M Lawley
**Co. Secretary:** Miss Laura Everitt
**Responsibilities**
**Senior:** Anna Ekkesies *(Manager)*, Clive Gathercole *(Financial Director)*, Robyn Robins *(General Manager)*
**Finance:** Clive Gathercole *(Financial Director)*
**Admin:** Jeannette Sutherland *(Personal Secretary)*
**Branches:** The Travel Company Limited, The Edge, Ground Floor Office, Salford, Lancashire M3 5NA
**US SIC:** 4722 **UK SIC:** 77001
**Auditors:** Deloitte LLP
**Bankers:** Barclays Bank Plc (20-06-75)

| | 31-12-13 | 31-12-12 | 31-12-11 |
|---|---|---|---|
| TO | 31,722,019 | 31,709,320 | 28,384,934 |
| P/L | 4,387,790 | 3,851,340 | 1,970,504 |
| NW | 13,203,450 | 11,978,837 | 10,742,362 |
| WC | 14,121,556 | 10,962,126 | 8,882,936 |
| Emp. | 564 | 579 | 536 |

DUNS 34-697-8013
## Travel Counsellors Group Ltd
Travel House, Churchgate, Bolton, Lancashire BL1 1TH
**Tel:** 01204536000
**Web:** www.travelcounsellors.co.uk
**Reg No:** 5502127 **Estd:** 2005 Private Limited Company
**Line of Business:** Travel agency activities
**Export Sales:** £20,404,545
**Issued Capital:** £144,725
**Directors:** Ms K Hughes, Miss A Speakman, S Byrne, Ms K Morris, M P Hingley
**Responsibilities**
**Senior:** Derek Lorton *(Financial Director)*, Paul Speakman *(Group IT Director)*
**Finance:** Derek Lorton *(Financial Director)*
**Marketing:** Victoria Fox *(Public Relations Manager)*, Aimee Loughney *(PR Executive)*, Victoria Mcclung *(Public Relations Executive)*, Carolyn Parish *(Public Relations Executive)*, Andie Walton *(Global Head of Marketing)*
**IT:** Paul Speakman *(Group IT Director)*
**US SIC:** 4722 **UK SIC:** 77001
**Auditors:** Nexia Smith & Williamson LLP

**Bankers:** Girobank Plc (72-00-03)

| | 31-10-13 | 31-10-12 | 31-10-11 |
|---|---|---|---|
| TO | 115,191,956 | 96,138,417 | 85,747,759 |
| P/L | 5,423,015 | 3,848,580 | 3,403,236 |
| NW | 6,245,933 | 2,852,126 | 9,243 |
| WC | 3,165,750 | 236,358 | (2,303,951) |
| Emp. | 226 | 234 | 229 |

DUNS 21-783-8922

## Travel Lodge
21 Tyn-Y-Parc Road, Cardiff, South Glamorgan CF14 6BH
**Tel:** 08715591811
**Web:** www.travelodge.co.uk
**Estd:** 2011 Proprietorship
**Line of Business:** Hotels and motels without restaurant
**Proprietor:** J Curtis
**US SIC:** 7011 **UK SIC:** 66500
**Employees:** 53

DUNS 29-655-5865

## Travel Management Group Plc
Worldfarer House, Leamington Spa, Warwickshire CV32 5AA
**Tel:** 01926-313112
**Web:** www.tmguk.com
**Reg No:** 1981934 **Estd:** 1998 Public Limited Company
**Line of Business:** Travel agency activities
**Issued Capital:** £100,000
**Principals:** I P Dunwoody (Managing), Miss S Dunwoody, P J Dick, Ms M A Dunwoody, I P Currington, D C Moore, G Dunwoody, J Smith
**Co. Secretary:** Stephen Mclurgh
**Responsibilities**
**Senior:** Michael Scholefield (Manager)
**Branches:** Travel Management Group Plc, Dormer Place, Leamington Spa, Warwickshire CV32 5AA
**US SIC:** 4722 **UK SIC:** 77001
**Auditors:** Prime Rafterys Ltd
**Bankers:** National Westminster Bank Plc (53-61-41)

| | 28-02-14 | 28-02-13 | 29-02-12 |
|---|---|---|---|
| TO | 29,614,631 | 27,743,340 | 27,521,252 |
| P/L | 341,196 | 118,087 | 237,421 |
| NW | 1,923,313 | 1,762,602 | 1,740,419 |
| WC | 1,185,202 | 1,025,190 | 971,021 |
| Emp. | 61 | 61 | 61 |

DUNS 21-034-7383

## Travel Managment Group
Worldfarer House 9 11, Dormer Place, Leamington Spa, Warwickshire CV32 5AA
**Web:** www.matchdays.com
**Proprietorship**
**Line of Business:** Travel agents
**Proprietor:** E Dumwoody
**Responsibilities**
**Finance:** Stephen McLurgh (Financial Director)
**Health & Safety:** Elaine Kennedy (Health & Safety Officer)
**US SIC:** 4722 **UK SIC:** 77001
**Employees:** 50

DUNS 39-791-1173

## Travel Merryhill Ltd
(Subsidiary of: National Express Group Plc)
Unit 35, Building 35, Second Avenue, Brierley Hill, West Midlands DY6 7UH
**Tel:** 01384555500
**Web:** www.merryhillprivatehire.co.uk
**Reg No:** 2203309 **Estd:** 1987 Private Limited Company
**Line of Business:** Bus line operators
**Issued Capital:** £100,000
**Directors:** P T Coates, M D Hancock
**Co. Secretary:** Ms Dianne Robinson
**Responsibilities**
**Senior:** Barbara Lees (Manager)
**US SIC:** 4111 **UK SIC:** 72102
**Auditors:** Ernst & Young
**Bankers:** Lloyds TSB Bank plc (30-91-22)

| | 31-12-13 | 31-12-12 | 31-12-11 |
|---|---|---|---|
| NW | (738,000) | (738,000) | (738,000) |

DUNS 42-350-5069

## Travel Nation Ltd
Level 7 New England House, New England Street, Brighton, East Sussex BN1 4GH
**Tel:** 01273320580
**Web:** www.travelnation.co.uk
**Reg No:** 4338219 **Estd:** 2001 Private Limited Company
**Line of Business:** Travel agency activities
**Issued Capital:** £50,000
**Director:** H G Wrath
**Co. Secretary:** Ms Karen Brewer
**US SIC:** 4722 **UK SIC:** 77001
**Auditors:** Elman Wall Ltd

| | 31-12-13 | 31-12-12 | 31-12-11 |
|---|---|---|---|
| TO | 12,001,527 | N/A | N/A |
| P/L | 76,876 | N/A | N/A |
| NW | 430,047 | 395,081 | 445,984 |
| WC | 377,759 | 340,665 | 420,248 |
| Emp. | 46 | N/A | N/A |

DUNS 23-380-5204

## Travel Republic Ltd
(Subsidiary of: Arabian Adventures)
Clarendon House, Kingston-Upon-Thames, Surrey KT2 6NH
**Tel:** 020 8974 7200 **Fax:** 02089747228
**Web:** www.travelrepublic.co.uk
**Reg No:** 4853546 **Estd:** 2003 Private Limited Company
**Line of Business:** Travel agency activities
**Issued Capital:** £41,238
**Directors:** N R Chinery, I D Simmonds, A H Parkar, I Andrew, A M Gill, Ms A Pollard
**Responsibilities**
**Senior:** Paul Furner (Manager), Kane Pirie (Manager)
**Marketing:** Elliott Pritchard (Chief Marketing Officer)
**US SIC:** 4722 **UK SIC:** 77001
**Auditors:** PKF (UK) LLP

| | 31-03-14 | 31-03-13 | 31-03-12 |
|---|---|---|---|
| TO | 67,531,790 | 58,975,956 | 48,233,595 |
| P/L | 13,708,175 | 12,527,831 | 10,377,208 |
| NW | 33,897,421 | 23,272,990 | 13,634,545 |
| WC | 33,310,391 | 22,571,970 | 13,152,340 |
| Emp. | 350 | 267 | 231 |

DUNS 21-167-4146

## Travel Weekly Group Ltd
3rd Floor, Terminal House, 52 Grosvenor Gardens, London SW1W 0AU
**Tel:** 02078814800
**Web:** www.aspiretravelclub.com
**Reg No:** 6927031 **Estd:** 2009 Private Limited Company
**Line of Business:** Publishers
**Trading Style:** Travel Weekly
**Issued Capital:** £3,154
**Directors:** C Morrison, D P Horton, C G Jacobs, M P East, I Findlay
**Co. Secretary:** Stuart Benson
**US SIC:** 2731, 2741, 7311
**UK SIC:** 47532, 47541, 83800

| | 31-12-13 | 31-12-12 | 31-12-11 |
|---|---|---|---|
| TA | 2,744,356 | 3,189,866 | 3,337,071 |
| NW | (1,152,490) | (1,367,785) | (1,619,331) |
| WC | (1,199,784) | (1,126,527) | (929,027) |

DUNS 21-916-0371

## Travel West Midlands Ltd
(Subsidiary of: National Express Group Plc)
51 Bordesley Green, Birmingham, West Midlands B9 4BZ
**Tel:** 01212547200 **Fax:** 01212547277
**Web:** www.travelwm.co.uk
**Reg No:** 0775806 **Estd:** 1991 Private Limited Company
**Line of Business:** Bus operators and stations
**Issued Capital:** £3,000
**Directors:** P T Coates, M D Hancock
**Co. Secretary:** Ms Dianne Robinson
**Branches:** Travel West Midlands Ltd, 51 Bordesley Green, Birmingham, West Midlands B9 4BZ
**US SIC:** 4119 **UK SIC:** 72200
**Bankers:** HSBC Bank plc (40-11-18)

| | 31-12-13 | 31-12-12 | 31-12-11 |
|---|---|---|---|
| TA | 3,000 | 3,000 | 3,000 |
| NW | 3,000 | 3,000 | 3,000 |

DUNS 34-636-6300     **Imp**

## Travel Zoo Europe Ltd
(Subsidiary of: Travelzoo Inc.)
Shaftesbury House, 151 Shaftesbury Avenue, London WC2H 8AL
**Fax:** 020-7203-2001
**Web:** www.travelzoo.co.uk
**Reg No:** 5442657 **Estd:** 2005 Private Limited Company
**Line of Business:** Solicitors
**Export Sales:** £9,830,938
**Issued Capital:** £1
**Directors:** S J Dunk, R Singer
**Co. Secretary:** Jafor Choudhury
**Responsibilities**
**Senior:** Pedro Hume-Rodriguez (Manager)
**US SIC:** 8111 **UK SIC:** 83500
**Auditors:** KPMG LLP

| | 31-12-13 | 31-12-12 | 31-12-11 |
|---|---|---|---|
| TO | 29,970,459 | 26,907,075 | 25,043,254 |
| P/L | 4,898,063 | 4,327,473 | 2,971,727 |
| NW | 11,052,857 | 6,587,257 | 2,133,159 |
| WC | 10,208,681 | 5,916,167 | 1,949,761 |
| Emp. | 160 | 156 | 127 |

DUNS 34-648-3340

## Travelco Ltd
East House 109 South Worple Way, London SW14 8TN
**Fax:** 020-7371-4222
**Web:** www.traveltis.co.uk
**Reg No:** 2773456 **Estd:** 1992 Private Limited Company
**Line of Business:** Travel agency activities
**Trading Style:** T I S
**Issued Capital:** £98,100
**Managing Director:** N R Smithson
**Co. Secretary:** Nigel Smithson

**Branches:** Travelco Ltd, 10 Barb Mews, London W6 7PA
**US SIC:** 4722 **UK SIC:** 77001
**Auditors:** White Hart Associates
**Bankers:** Lloyds TSB Bank plc (30-97-44)

| | 31-03-14 | 31-03-13 | 31-03-12 |
|---|---|---|---|
| TA | 939,462 | 772,121 | 624,526 |
| NW | (62,621) | (88,879) | (92,306) |
| WC | 269,866 | 173,970 | 177,936 |

DUNS 22-704-1068

## Travelers Insurance Company Ltd
(Subsidiary of: The Travelers Companies Inc)
61-63 London Road, Redhill, Surrey RH1 1NA
**Tel:** 01737 787787 **Fax:** 01737 787172
**Web:** www.travelers.co.uk
**Reg No:** 1034343 **Estd:** 1970 Private Limited Company
**Line of Business:** Insurance companies and agents
**Issued Capital:** £203,822,115
**Directors:** G J Mckean, S M Genden, S G Eccles, A G Coughlan, Sir J G Carter, M J Gent, K T Purvis, P H Eddy
**Co. Secretary:** John Abramson
**Responsibilities**
**Senior:** Gregory Conway (Non-Executive Director), Gary Dibb (Director), Martin Dyer (Assistant General Manager, App)
**Marketing:** Karen Bigwood (Marketing Manager)
**Admin:** Derek Maloney (Facilities Manager)
**HR:** Sarah Houston (General Manager Human Resource), Ben Redshaw (Assistant Vice President Human)
**Facilities:** Derek Maloney (Facilities Manager)
**Purchasing:** Derek Maloney (Facilities Manager)
**Branches:** Travelers Insurance Company Ltd, Exchequer Court: 11 ST9 Mary Axe, London EC1A 5AG
**US SIC:** 6399 **UK SIC:** 82001
**Auditors:** KPMG LLP

| | 31-12-13 | 31-12-12 | 31-12-11 |
|---|---|---|---|
| TO | 216,520,000 | 221,061,000 | 233,823,000 |
| P/L | (86,010,000) | 6,756,000 | 44,122,000 |
| NW | 489,353,000 | 558,918,000 | 554,176,000 |
| WC | 43,768,000 | 47,631,000 | 15,469,000 |

DUNS 21-771-3160

## Travelex
Thorpe Wood, Peterborough, Cambridgeshire PE3 6HN
**Tel:** 08453652929
**Estd:** 2011
**Line of Business:** Nursery schools
**US SIC:** 8211 **UK SIC:** 93200
**Employees:** 1,000

DUNS 34-546-5376     **Imp**

## Travelex Holdings Ltd
65 Kingsway, London WC2B 6TD
**Tel:** 02074004000 **Fax:** 02027372620
**Web:** www.travelex-corporate.com
**Reg No:** 5356574 **Estd:** 2005 Private Limited Company
**Line of Business:** Management activities of other non-financial holding companies not elsewhere classified
**Issued Capital:** £61,576,533
**Directors:** G C Laws, Lord J Stevens, P J Jackson, M D Ball
**Co. Secretary:** Sylvain Pignet
**Responsibilities**
**Senior:** Hafiz Chagani (Director), James Ruane (Non-Executive Director)
**Marketing:** Sean Cornwell (Chief Digital Officer), Rachael Douglas (CRM and Content Manager)
**Admin:** Amy Choi (Personal Assistant), Rebecca Stadward (Personal Assistant to Products)
**US SIC:** 7399 **UK SIC:** 83954
**Auditors:** PricewaterhouseCoopers LLP

| | 31-12-13 | 31-12-12 | 31-12-11 |
|---|---|---|---|
| TO | 639,600,000 | 570,900,000 | 554,800,000 |
| P/L | (181,700,000) | (122,600,000) | 159,400,000 |
| NW | (1,290,900,000) | (897,800,000) | (750,500,000) |
| WC | (74,600,000) | 116,100,000 | 48,200,000 |
| Emp. | 7,717 | 6,536 | 7,022 |

DUNS 21-706-3624

## Travelex Uk Ltd
(Subsidiary of: Travelex Holdings Ltd)
65 Kingsway, London WC2B 6TD
**Web:** www.travelex.co.uk
**Reg No:** 1985596 **Estd:** 1986 Private Limited Company
**Line of Business:** Other service activities not elsewhere classified
**Issued Capital:** £200,000
**Directors:** M Madden, A Wagerman, G Williams, D Norman
**Co. Secretary:** Sylvain Pignet
**US SIC:** 8999 **UK SIC:** 83954

**Auditors:** PricewaterhouseCoopers LLP

| | 31-12-13 | 31-12-12 | 31-12-11 |
|---|---|---|---|
| TO | 105,827,000 | 106,366,000 | 99,369,000 |
| P/L | 1,916,000 | 9,596,000 | 11,756,000 |
| NW | 12,903,000 | 11,448,000 | 19,272,000 |
| WC | 8,706,000 | 7,784,000 | 17,376,000 |
| Emp. | 770 | 838 | 806 |

DUNS 21-623-5120     **Imp**

## Travelfast Ltd
Unit 11 Grange Road Industrial Estate, Grange Road, Batley, West Yorkshire WF17 6LN
**Tel:** 01924477778
**Web:** www.samplingint.co.uk
**Reg No:** 7037429 **Estd:** 2002 Private Limited Company
**Line of Business:** Manufacturers of textiles
**Trading Style:** Sampling International
**Issued Capital:** £1,000
**Directors:** J Windsor, I P Jennings, S D Hubbard
**Co. Secretary:** Ian Jennings
**US SIC:** 2392 **UK SIC:** 45550

| | 31-12-13 | 31-12-12 | 31-12-11 |
|---|---|---|---|
| TA | 1,716,007 | 1,447,642 | 1,208,050 |
| NW | 270,151 | 239,214 | 241,463 |
| WC | (194,681) | (177,432) | (152,990) |

DUNS 73-926-7222

## Traveljigsaw Ltd
(Subsidiary of: The Priceline Group Inc)
Floors 9-12 Sunlight House, Manchester M3 3JZ
**Tel:** 01618366707 **Fax:** 01618366724
**Web:** www.traveljigsawgroup.com
**Reg No:** 5179829 **VAT No:** 855349007
**Estd:** 2005 Private Limited Company
**Line of Business:** Taxi operation
**Export Sales:** £425,498,000
**Trading Style:** Carhire 3000, Rentalcars.Com
**Issued Capital:** £100
**Directors:** Ms N L Wills, G D Wills, I Brown, L Marlor, J N Barnes
**Co. Secretary:** Adam Ryan
**US SIC:** 7399 **UK SIC:** 83954
**Auditors:** Deloitte LLP
**Bankers:** HSBC Bank plc (40-25-33)

| | 31-12-13 | 31-12-12 | 31-12-11 |
|---|---|---|---|
| TO | 544,115,000 | 372,771,000 | 261,150,000 |
| P/L | 48,744,000 | 34,209,000 | 18,130,000 |
| NW | 17,451,000 | 48,856,000 | 21,286,000 |
| WC | 8,713,000 | 41,622,000 | 16,840,000 |
| Emp. | 784 | 606 | 429 |

DUNS 22-527-2392

## The Travellers' Club
106 Pall Mall, London SW1Y 5EP
**Tel:** 020-7930-8688
**Web:** www.thetravellersclub.org.uk
**Estd:** 1819
**Line of Business:** Clubs social and associations
**Trading Style:** Private Gentleman's Club
**Principals:** T L Bramall (Chairman), M S Allcock
**Responsibilities**
**Senior:** David Broadhead (Club Secretary)
**Finance:** Morag Luff (Financial Controller)
**Marketing:** David Broadhead (Club Secretary)
**Sales:** David Broadhead (Club Secretary)
**IT:** Conrad Winter (House Manager)
**HR:** Conrad Winter (House Manager)
**Health & Safety:** Conrad Winter (House Manager)
**Facilities:** Conrad Winter (House Manager)
**Operations:** David Broadhead (Club Secretary)
**US SIC:** 5813 **UK SIC:** 66200
**Bankers:** The Royal Bank Of Scotland Plc (16-01-23)
**Employees:** 55

DUNS 22-629-7968     **Imp-Exp**

## Travelport International Ltd
(Subsidiary of: The Blackstone Group L P)
Axis Park, Hurricane Way, Slough, Berkshire SL3 8AG
**Tel:** 01753288000 **Fax:** 01753-288001
**Web:** www.travelport.com
**Reg No:** 1254977 **VAT No:** 290536746
**Estd:** 1976 Private Limited Company
**Line of Business:** Computer software (development)
**Export Markets:** E U
**Export Sales:** £124,225,000
**Trading Style:** Galileo U K
**Issued Capital:** £440,000
**Directors:** J R Clarke, D M Dillard-Iii, T J Hampton
**Co. Secretary:** Mrs Helen Wenman
**Responsibilities**
**Senior:** Philip Emery (Financial Director), Maria Marchant (Manager), Mark Meehan (Managing Director, Africa)
**Finance:** Philip Emery (Financial Director)

**Branches:** Travelport International Ltd, Grove Park, Waltham Road, White Waltham, Maidenhead, Berkshire SL6 3LB
**US SIC:** 7379 **UK SIC:** 83940
**Auditors:** Deloitte LLP
**Bankers:** Barclays Bank Plc (20-00-00)

| | 31-12-13 | 31-12-12 | 31-12-11 |
|---|---|---|---|
| TO | 127,255,000 | 129,353,000 | 140,604,000 |
| P/L | 5,899,000 | 6,822,000 | 5,196,000 |
| NW | 22,211,000 | 18,544,000 | 11,693,000 |
| WC | 17,723,000 | 15,899,000 | 9,419,000 |
| Emp. | 548 | 525 | 527 |

DUNS 23-598-0047

## Travelsmith Investments Ltd

Travelsmith Ltd, Southminster, Essex CM0 8AA
**Tel:** 01621784666 **Fax:** 01621-785001
**Web:** www.flyguernsey.com
**Reg No:** 3595394 **Estd:** 1998 Private Limited Company
**Line of Business:** Travel agency activities
**Issued Capital:** £374,798
**Directors:** R P Smith, J D Smith
**Co. Secretary:** Ms Kathryn Smith
**US SIC:** 6711 **UK SIC:** 83962
**Auditors:** Bird Luckin
**Bankers:** Barclays Bank Plc (20-19-95)

| | 31-10-13 | 31-10-12 | 31-10-11 |
|---|---|---|---|
| TO | 6,340,806 | 6,873,732 | 7,527,685 |
| P/L | 24,855 | (316,337) | (542,951) |
| NW | 2,914,082 | 3,056,236 | 3,298,196 |
| WC | 276,684 | 389,493 | 669,511 |
| Emp. | 62 | 66 | 78 |

DUNS 21-118-4186

## Travers Smith Llp

10 Snow Hill, London EC1A 2AL
**Web:** www.traverssmith.com
**Reg No:** 0336962OC **Estd:** 2008
**Line of Business:** Solicitors
**Responsibilities**
**Senior:** Charles Bischoff *(Partner - Banking)*, Lucinda Cawood *(Manager)*, Helen Croke *(Partner - Private Equity, Merg)*, Peter Esam *(Designated Limited Liability P)*, Tim Gilbert *(Partner - Head of Employment)*, Anthony Judge *(Non-designated Limited Liabili)*, Sian Keall *(Non-designated Limited Liabili)*, Stephen Paget-Brown *(Non-designated Limited Liabili)*, Tom Purton *(Partner)*, Daniel Reavill *(Non-designated Limited Liabili)*, James Renahan *(Manager)*, Toby Robinson *(Non-designated Limited Liabili)*, Kathleen Russ *(Non-designated Limited Liabili)*, Philip Sanderson *(Manager)*, Nigel Seay *(Non-designated Limited Liabili)*, Aaron Stocks *(Partner)*, Rick Stratton *(Partner)*, Adrian West *(Manager)*
**Finance:** Charles Bischoff *(Partner - Banking)*
**Marketing:** Lesley O'Leary *(Marketing Manager)*
**Admin:** Michelle Clegg *(Secretary)*
**IT:** Ann Cant *(IT Manager)*
**US SIC:** 8111 **UK SIC:** 83500
**Auditors:** Deloitte LLP

| | 30-06-13 | 30-06-12 | 30-06-11 |
|---|---|---|---|
| TO | 87,287,000 | 83,739,000 | 70,860,000 |
| P/L | 41,000,000 | 36,899,000 | 29,471,000 |
| NW | 12,300,000 | 11,070,000 | 8,841,000 |
| WC | 42,041,000 | 36,990,000 | 35,704,000 |
| Emp. | 415 | 384 | 365 |

DUNS 21-688-0153 **Imp**

## Travis Perkins Plc

Lodge Way House, Lodge Way, Northampton, Northamptonshire NN5 7UG
**Tel:** 01604752424 **Fax:** 01604758718
**Web:** www.travisperkinsplc.com
**Reg No:** 0824821 **VAT No:** 408556737
**Estd:** 1797 Public Limited Company
**Line of Business:** Wholesale of wood, construction materials and sanitary equipment
**Trading Style:** Travis Perkins Trading Co, Archer D W, Keyline Roofing Centre, Travis Perkins
**Issued Capital:** £24,421,943
**Directors:** J P Carter, C C Rogers, P T Redfern, J T Rogers, R M Walker, A D Buffin, Ms M R Anderson, Mrs C L Mcconville
**Co. Secretary:** Miss Deborah Grimason
**Responsibilities**
**Senior:** Arthur Davidson *(Divisional Chief Executive Off)*, Gary Dobson *(Branch Manager)*
**Marketing:** Rachel Booton *(Marketing Assistant)*, Emma Churchill *(?Group Corporate Communication)*, Vikki Lomas *(Head of Corporate Communicatio)*, Gary Phillips *(Communications Manager)*
**Health & Safety:** Mike O'Hara *(Health & Safety Officer)*
**Operations:** Jim Mckenna *(Head of Group Security)*
**Fleet:** Graham Bellman *(Director of Fleet - Services)*
**Branches:** Travis Perkins Plc, 61-79 Norwood High Street, London SE27 9JS
**US SIC:** 5039 **UK SIC:** 61300
**Auditors:** Deloitte LLP
**Bankers:** National Westminster Bank Plc (60-60-08)

Following financial data are in thousands

| | 31-12-13 | 31-12-12 | 31-12-11 |
|---|---|---|---|
| TO | 5,148,700 | 4,844,900 | 4,779,100 |
| P/L | 312,600 | 313,300 | 269,600 |
| NW | 291,500 | 75,800 | 12,700 |
| WC | 243,300 | (115,300) | 132,700 |
| Emp. | 21,937 | 21,887 | 21,423 |

DUNS 21-617-9952

## Travis Perkins Trading Co Ltd

(**Subsidiary of:** Travis Perkins Plc)
32 St Peters Road, Huntingdon, Cambridgeshire PE29 7DA
**Tel:** 0148052358
**Web:** www.travisperkins.co.uk
**Reg No:** 0733503 **VAT No:** 408556737
**Estd:** 1797 Private Limited Company
**Line of Business:** Agents involved in the sale of timber and building materials
**Trading Style:** Travis Perkins Builders Merchants
**Issued Capital:** £49,155,645
**Directors:** A D Buffin, Ms C Kavanagh, D P Saunderson, R D Proctor, J P Carter, P Gransden, N Bell, D Kelman
**Co. Secretary:** Tpg Management Services Limited
**Responsibilities**
**Senior:** Daniel Beresford *(General Manager)*, Mark Nottingham *(Director)*
**Branches:** Travis Perkins Trading Co Ltd, Sandilands Road, Tywyn, Gwynedd LL36 9AP
**US SIC:** 5072 **UK SIC:** 61500
**Auditors:** Deloitte LLP
**Bankers:** HSBC Bank plc (40-35-04)

Following financial data are in thousands

| | 31-12-13 | 31-12-12 | 31-12-11 |
|---|---|---|---|
| TO | 1,947,392 | 1,755,318 | 1,682,611 |
| P/L | 129,959 | 100,606 | 122,046 |
| NW | 610,978 | 619,828 | 597,296 |
| WC | 512,425 | 536,067 | 518,818 |
| Emp. | 7,633 | 7,617 | 7,221 |

DUNS 23-560-7723 **Imp**

## Trawlpac Seafoods Ltd

Craigshaw Place, West Tullos Industrial Estate, Aberdeen, Aberdeenshire AB12 3AH
**Tel:** 01224-871093
**Web:** www.trawlpacseafoods.co.uk
**Reg No:** 0185563SC **Estd:** 1998 Private Limited Company
**Line of Business:** Fish merchants (wholesale)
**Issued Capital:** £288,500
**Managing Director:** Ms L Cross
**Co. Secretary:** Scott Chapman
**Responsibilities**
**Senior:** Andrew Crockford *(Manager)*
**US SIC:** 5146 **UK SIC:** 61700
**Auditors:** Anderson Anderson & Brown

| | 30-06-13 | 30-06-12 | 30-06-11 |
|---|---|---|---|
| TO | 4,999,242 | 6,403,517 | 6,093,791 |
| P/L | (161,595) | (96,067) | (46,610) |
| NW | 389,336 | 394,093 | 665,382 |
| WC | 973,018 | 1,039,520 | 1,390,797 |
| Emp. | 67 | 74 | 81 |

DUNS 21-788-7513 **Imp**

## Trax Windsport Centre

Clifton Drive North, Lytham St Annes, Lancashire FY8 2PP
**Tel:** 01253789116
**Web:** www.traxwindsportcentre.co.uk
**Estd:** 2009 Proprietorship
**Line of Business:** Training centres
**Proprietor:** E Sloane
**Responsibilities**
**Senior:** Stuart Dollman *(Manager)*
**US SIC:** 8299 **UK SIC:** 93300
**Employees:** 100

DUNS 21-782-9132

## Traxx Tyres

Maxx House, Western Road, Bracknell, Berkshire RG12 1QP
**Tel:** 01344398900
**Web:** www.traxxtyres.co.uk
**Estd:** 2012 Proprietorship
**Line of Business:** Sale of motor vehicle parts and accessories
**Proprietor:** Miss K Manners
**Responsibilities**
**Senior:** Charlie Ker *(Manager)*
**US SIC:** 5531 **UK SIC:** 65100
**Employees:** 50

DUNS 21-693-7456 **Imp**

## Traxx Tyres Ltd

Maxx House Western Road, Bracknell, Berkshire RG12 1QP
**Tel:** 01494461826
**Web:** www.traxxtyres.co.uk
**Reg No:** 7403215 **Estd:** 2010 Private Limited Company
**Line of Business:** Sale of motor vehicle parts and accessories
**Issued Capital:** £2,000,800
**Directors:** C W Hathorn, S L White, I W Allpress, V M James, S J Salisbury, B N Doouss, S T Chirnside, G P Spencer
**US SIC:** 5531 **UK SIC:** 65100

| | 31-03-14 | 31-03-13 | 31-03-12 |
|---|---|---|---|
| TO | 17,688,371 | 15,951,087 | 17,050,522 |
| P/L | (330,093) | (1,459,937) | (4,371,835) |
| NW | (3,345,218) | (3,134,130) | (2,293,299) |
| WC | 7,082,006 | 6,929,181 | 7,395,008 |
| Emp. | 52 | 53 | 67 |

DUNS 23-216-9953 **Imp-Exp**

## Traynors Ltd

86 Armagh Road, Dungannon, Co Tyrone BT71 7JA
**Tel:** 028-3889-1242 **Fax:** 028-3889-1611
**Web:** www.traynors.co.uk
**Reg No:** 0026457NI **Estd:** 1975 Private Limited Company
**Line of Business:** Car breakers
**Export Markets:** Republic of Ireland
**Issued Capital:** £2
**Directors:** D M Mc Colgan, P A Traynor, Mrs J M Traynor
**Co. Secretary:** Ms Agnes Gray
**Branches:** Traynors Ltd, 9 Trench Road, Newtownabbey, Co Antrim BT36 4TY
**US SIC:** 5093 **UK SIC:** 62200
**Auditors:** PricewaterhouseCoopers
**Bankers:** The Bank Of Ireland (90-20-47)

| | 31-12-13 | 31-12-12 | 31-12-11 |
|---|---|---|---|
| TO | 7,043,355 | 7,112,175 | 7,033,213 |
| P/L | 959,384 | 562,767 | 201,966 |
| NW | 4,798,276 | 3,878,101 | 3,466,692 |
| WC | 887,078 | 108,381 | (208,761) |
| Emp. | 64 | 65 | 66 |

DUNS 34-641-9294 **Imp**

## Trayport Ltd

(**Subsidiary of:** Gfi Tp Holdings Pte. Ltd.)
7th Floor, London EC2A 2AP
**Web:** www.trayport.com
**Reg No:** 2769279 **VAT No:** 626207947
**Estd:** 2013 Private Limited Company
**Line of Business:** Computer software (development)
**Export Sales:** £26,792,519
**Issued Capital:** £120
**Principals:** E Piggott *(Financial)*, C J Heffron, R D Levi, K L Heffron, P K Naik
**Co. Secretary:** Nigel Brahams
**Responsibilities**
**Senior:** Paul Constantinou *(Regional Managing Director)*, Combie Cryan *(Head Of Client Relations)*, Carl Daucher *(Head Of Global Commodities)*
**IT:** Oliver Rooney *(Computer Manager)*
**US SIC:** 7379 **UK SIC:** 83940
**Auditors:** Nexia Audit Ltd
**Bankers:** Barclays Bank Plc (20-14-33)

| | 31-12-13 | 31-12-12 | 31-12-11 |
|---|---|---|---|
| TO | 43,106,833 | 39,594,553 | 32,367,897 |
| P/L | 19,346,953 | 16,304,395 | 12,938,281 |
| NW | 10,157,909 | 5,766,044 | 6,908,941 |
| WC | 4,738,634 | 4,803,399 | 5,859,118 |
| Emp. | 167 | 166 | 165 |

DUNS 21-811-4418

## The Treacle Mine

Hailsham Road, Town Centre, Polegate, East Sussex BN26 6QL
**Tel:** 01323489520
**Web:** www.tabletable.co.uk
**Estd:** 2012
**Line of Business:** Public house
**Responsibilities**
**Senior:** Lisa Deboick *(General Manager)*
**US SIC:** 5813 **UK SIC:** 66200
**Employees:** 50

DUNS 21-819-7416

## Treasure & Son Ltd

Temeside, Ludlow, Shropshire SY8 1JW
**Tel:** 01584-872161
**Web:** www.treasureandson.co.uk
**Reg No:** 0828005 **VAT No:** 133852571
**Estd:** 1964 Private Limited Company
**Line of Business:** Building and timber preservation services
**Issued Capital:** £80
**Principals:** S M Treasure *(Managing)*, N E Hill, G A Robertson
**Co. Secretary:** Paul Daniels
**Responsibilities**
**Admin:** L Sankey *(Administrator)*
**Purchasing:** L Sankey *(Administrator)*
**US SIC:** 2421, 1541
**UK SIC:** 46101, 50100
**Auditors:** A F R Benson FCA
**Bankers:** National Westminster Bank Plc (53-81-18)

| | 31-12-13 | 31-12-12 | 31-12-11 |
|---|---|---|---|
| TA | 1,878,404 | 2,031,481 | 2,188,812 |
| NW | 972,410 | 1,284,735 | 1,249,044 |
| WC | 870,870 | 801,966 | 749,984 |

DUNS 21-481-4555

## The Treasure Chest

Fore Street, Beer, Seaton, Devon EX12 3JQ
**Estd:** 2002 Proprietorship
**Line of Business:** Book retailers
**Proprietor:** H Hall
**US SIC:** 5942, 5999
**UK SIC:** 65300, 65600
**Employees:** 47

DUNS 50-007-7805

## Treasure Homes Ltd

Abbots Leigh Manor Manor Road Abbots, Leigh, Bristol, Avon BS8 3RP
**Tel:** 01275-374669 **Fax:** 01275379825
**Web:** www.treasure-homes.co.uk
**Reg No:** 2297384 **Estd:** 1989 Private Limited Company
**Line of Business:** Social work activities with accommodation
**Issued Capital:** £250,100
**Co. Secretary:** David Gillespie
**Branches:** Treasure Homes Ltd, 125 Long Ashton Road, Bristol, Avon BS41 9JE
**US SIC:** 8321, 6732
**UK SIC:** 96111, 83100
**Auditors:** Hazlewoods

| | 30-11-13 | 30-11-12 | 30-11-11 |
|---|---|---|---|
| TO | 4,735,375 | 4,517,604 | 4,127,654 |
| P/L | 1,565,823 | 1,381,641 | (1,550,555) |
| NW | 5,720,028 | 4,509,130 | 3,472,908 |
| WC | 2,701,422 | 1,384,243 | 276,901 |
| Emp. | 155 | 151 | 158 |

DUNS 21-813-1233

## Treasure Transport Services Ltd

Triangle Park, Occupation Lane, Gonerby Moor, Grantham, Lincolnshire NG32 2BP
**Tel:** 01476594263
**Web:** www.treasuretransport.co.uk
**Reg No:** 0540875 **Estd:** 1954 Private Limited Company
**Line of Business:** Other supporting land transport activities
**Issued Capital:** £105,151
**Director:** G Greenhalgh
**Co. Secretary:** Peter Greenhalgh
**Responsibilities**
**Engineering:** Rui Castro-Vieira *(Technical and Production Manag)*
**US SIC:** 4789, 1611
**UK SIC:** 77002, 50200
**Auditors:** Nicholsons
**Bankers:** Lloyds TSB Bank plc (30-93-58)

| | 31-12-13 | 31-12-12 | 31-12-11 |
|---|---|---|---|
| TO | 6,253,979 | N/A | N/A |
| P/L | 381,861 | N/A | N/A |
| NW | 2,620,791 | 2,317,953 | 2,274,149 |
| WC | 387,375 | 256,918 | 286,181 |
| Emp. | 56 | N/A | N/A |

DUNS 21-558-0680

## The Treasury Solicitor's Department

One Kemble Street, London WC2B 4TS
**Tel:** 020-7210-3000
**Web:** www.tsol.gov.uk
**Estd:** 1651
**Line of Business:** Legal services
**Trading Style:** Treasury Solicitor's Department
**Responsibilities**
**Finance:** Caroline Harold *(Deputy Director Commercial and)*, Tim Hurdle *(Financial Director)*
**IT:** Peter Batt *(IT Manager)*
**Branches:** The Treasury Solicitor's Department, One Kemble Street, London WC2B 4TS
**US SIC:** 9121 **UK SIC:** 91110
**Auditors:** Comptroller & Auditor General
**Employees:** 850

DUNS 29-855-8750 **Imp**

## Treasury Wine Estates Emea Ltd

(**Subsidiary of:** Sabmiller Australia Beverage Holdings Llp)
Regal House, 70 London Road, Twickenham, Middlesex TW1 3QS
**Tel:** 02088438411 **Fax:** 020-8843-8401
**Web:** www.tweglobal.com
**Reg No:** 2059191 **Estd:** 1993 Private Limited Company
**Line of Business:** Wholesalers of beer and spirits
**Issued Capital:** £102,995,028
**Directors:** D W Townsend, Mrs M E Brampton
**Responsibilities**
**Senior:** Damien Jackman *(Manager)*, Derek Nicol *(Manager)*
**Finance:** Stuart Pickles *(Finance Director)*, Richard Renwick *(Financial Director)*
**US SIC:** 5182, 7399
**UK SIC:** 61700, 83954
**Auditors:** PricewaterhouseCoopers LLP

| | 30-06-13 | 30-06-12 | 30-06-11 |
|---|---|---|---|
| TO | 132,206,000 | 128,660,000 | 156,618,000 |
| P/L | 6,689,000 | 5,204,000 | 4,217,000 |
| NW | 90,486,000 | 85,379,000 | 81,241,000 |
| WC | 155,837,000 | 125,170,000 | 118,521,000 |
| Emp. | 113 | 132 | 148 |

DUNS 34-631-2408
## Trebah Enterprises Ltd
Trebah, Falmouth, Cornwall TR11 5JZ
**Tel:** 01326-252200
**Web:** www.trebah-garden.co.uk
**Reg No:** 2764907 **Estd:** 1992 Private
Limited Company
**Line of Business:** Other retail sale in non-specialised stores
**Issued Capital:** £2
**Directors:** Ms L M Nottingham,
R F Townsend, Ms G F Pipkin, T Hubbard,
H S Bradshaw, A B Vyvyan, J K Miln,
R Dudley Cooke
**Co. Secretary:** Nigel Burnett
**Responsibilities**
**Senior:** Carolyn Brodie (Director), Jay
Mcdonnagh (Manager), Susan Nathan
(Director), Charles Richardson (Director)
**IT:** Chris Hibbert (Head of IT)
**US SIC:** 5399, 5999
**UK SIC:** 65600
**Auditors:** Ward Ohly
**Bankers:** Barclays Bank Plc (20-87-94)

|    | 31-01-14 | 31-01-13 | 31-01-12 |
|----|----------|----------|----------|
| TA | 113,837 | 143,831 | 146,795 |
| NW | 21,513 | 36,303 | 37,872 |
| WC | 2,651 | 502 | (2,178) |

DUNS 34-626-6281
## Treble-Twenty Cars & Couriers Ltd
(**Subsidiary of:** Treble Twenty Holdings Ltd)
Unit 3 St James Road, Brentwood, Essex
CM14 4LF
**Tel:** 01277-202020
**Web:** www.202020.co.uk
**Reg No:** 2760439 **Estd:** 1992 Private
Limited Company
**Line of Business:** Taxi operation
**Issued Capital:** £2,600
**Director:** S Smith
**Co. Secretary:** Graham Dinning
**US SIC:** 4121, 4712
**UK SIC:** 72200, 77002
**Auditors:** Portman Partnership Ltd

|    | 30-09-13 | 30-09-12 | 30-09-11 |
|----|----------|----------|----------|
| TA | 371,650 | 417,710 | 478,801 |
| NW | 23,302 | 24,238 | 9,479 |
| WC | (50,926) | (121,446) | (163,504) |

DUNS 21-224-5320
## Tredegar Police Station
Tredegar Police Station, Spencer Square,
Tredegar, Gwent NP22 3YD
**Tel:** 01495-723162
**Proprietorship**
**Line of Business:** Police forces
**Proprietor:** Mrs L Smith
**US SIC:** 9221 **UK SIC:** 91300
**Employees:** 100

DUNS 23-541-0359     Imp-Exp
## Tree of Life U K Ltd
(**Subsidiary of:** Brands of Distinction Ltd)
Coaldale Road, Lymedale Business Park,
Newcastle, Staffordshire ST5 9QX
**Tel:** 01782567100 **Fax:** 01782-567199
**Web:** www.treeoflife.co.uk
**Reg No:** 3539683 **Estd:** 1998 Private
Limited Company
**Line of Business:** Health food retailers
**Export Markets:** Worldwide
**Export Sales:** £5,833,000
**Issued Capital:** £128,980
**Directors:** S M Cuthbertson, J W Weaver
**Co. Secretary:** Sean Linehan
**Responsibilities**
**Finance:** Joannes Heemskerk (Director and
Company Secretary)
**US SIC:** 5499 **UK SIC:** 64100
**Auditors:** BDO LLP
**Bankers:** The Royal Bank Of Scotland Plc
(16-13-18)

|      | 31-03-14 | 31-03-13 | 31-03-12 |
|------|----------|----------|----------|
| TO | 36,296,000 | 33,595,000 | 43,485,000 |
| P/L | 796,000 | 379,000 | (93,000) |
| NW | 6,870,000 | 6,311,000 | 6,058,000 |
| WC | 5,106,000 | 4,735,000 | 4,502,000 |
| Emp. | 118 | 124 | 138 |

DUNS 21-209-7229
## Tree Tops
Ryndleside, Scarborough, North Yorkshire
YO12 6AD
**Tel:** 01723372729
**Web:** www.treetops-newbury.co.uk
**Estd:** 1988 Partnership
**Line of Business:** Medical nursing home
activities
**Partners:** Ms C West, T Compton
**Responsibilities**
**Senior:** Chris Pomphrett (Deputy Manager),
Susan Woodcock (Manager)
**US SIC:** 8051 **UK SIC:** 95100
**Bankers:** The Royal Bank Of Scotland Plc
(16-31-14)
**Employees:** 48

DUNS 21-574-6574
## Tree Tops Residential Home
23-25 Station Road, Epping, Essex CM16
4HH
**Tel:** 01992-573322
**Web:** www.treetopsepping.webs.com
**Estd:** 1989 Proprietorship
**Line of Business:** Rest and retirement
homes
**Proprietor:** A Pabani
**Responsibilities**
**Senior:** Hayley Dawkins (Home Manager),
Akbar Pabani (Proprietor), Sultan Pabani
(Manager)
**US SIC:** 8321 **UK SIC:** 96111
**Employees:** 62

DUNS 21-583-3213
## Treelands
Westerhill Road, Oldham, Lancashire OL8
2QH
**Tel:** 01616267173
**Web:** www.handsale.co.uk
**Estd:** 2011 Proprietorship
**Line of Business:** Residential care
establishments
**Proprietor:** Mrs L White
**Responsibilities**
**Senior:** June Harvey (Home Manager)
**US SIC:** 8321 **UK SIC:** 96111
**Employees:** 63

DUNS 52-002-4258
## Trees Park (East Ham) Ltd
(**Subsidiary of:** Lansbury Limited)
211-219 High Street South, London E6 3PD
**Tel:** 020-8548-8686
**Reg No:** 3369515 **Estd:** 1997 Private
Limited Company
**Line of Business:** Non-charitable social
work activities with accommodation
**Issued Capital:** £1,000
**Director:** P S Sodhi
**Co. Secretary:** Tony Yoe
**Responsibilities**
**Senior:** Rajesh Doshi (Manager), Banu
Mulloor (Office Manager)
**US SIC:** 8321 **UK SIC:** 96111
**Bankers:** The Bank Of Ireland (30-14-58)

|      | 31-12-13 | 31-12-12 | 31-12-11 |
|------|----------|----------|----------|
| TA | 12,146,115 | 11,411,223 | 10,441,627 |
| NW | 1,724,180 | 2,052,710 | 2,344,042 |
| WC | (61,029) | 805,917 | 1,699,957 |

DUNS 29-322-6486
## Treetops Hospice Trust
Derby Road, Risley, Derby, Derbyshire DE72
3SS
**Tel:** 01159399339
**Web:** www.treetops.org.uk
**Reg No:** 1801708 **Estd:** 1984 Private
Limited Company
**Line of Business:** Hospices
**Directors:** Dr H Godridge, A L Wardle,
Miss S Ansley, R W Jones, Dr S J Miller,
Ms K Ashcroft, S Beeley, Mrs J D Heath
**Co. Secretary:** Richard Thomas
**Responsibilities**
**Senior:** George Cameron (Chief Executive),
John Dornan (Director), Alan Perkins
(Director), Kate Shaw (Manager)
**Branches:** Treetops Hospice Trust, 83 Bath
St, Ilkeston, Derbyshire DE7 8AP
**US SIC:** 8091 **UK SIC:** 95200
**Auditors:** Johnson Murkett & Hurst
**Bankers:** Alliance & Leicester Plc (72-50-00)

|      | 31-03-14 | 31-03-13 | 31-03-12 |
|------|----------|----------|----------|
| TO | 3,064,311 | 2,413,102 | 2,091,033 |
| P/L | 351,613 | 49,833 | 1,544 |
| NW | 3,046,691 | 2,695,078 | 2,645,245 |
| WC | 1,105,133 | 1,040,521 | 972,673 |
| Emp. | 71 | 61 | 56 |

DUNS 76-950-9118
## Treetops Nurseries Ltd
(**Subsidiary of:** Electra Private Equity Plc)
1 St James Court, Friar Gate, Derby,
Derbyshire DE1 1BT
**Tel:** 01332223553
**Web:** www.treetopsnurseries.co.uk
**Reg No:** 2537480 **Estd:** 1990 Private
Limited Company
**Line of Business:** Representative office
**Issued Capital:** £80,001
**Directors:** C E Eggleston, Ms C E Wilson
**Co. Secretary:** Ms Clare Wilson
**Responsibilities**
**Senior:** Isabel Garbey (Director of
Childcare), Alan Proto (Manager)
**Branches:** Treetops Nurseries Ltd, 28 Grove
Road, Leeds, West Yorkshire LS6 4EE
**US SIC:** 7399, 6531
**UK SIC:** 83954, 83400

**Bankers:** The Royal Bank Of Scotland Plc
(16-26-32)

|      | 30-09-13 | 30-09-12 | 30-09-11 |
|------|----------|----------|----------|
| TO | 14,909,971 | 14,009,625 | 8,890,124 |
| P/L | 1,328,940 | 1,119,243 | (694,105) |
| NW | 9,914,104 | 8,886,347 | 10,364,435 |
| WC | (1,430,442) | (262,064) | (6,639,029) |
| Emp. | 811 | 762 | 482 |

DUNS 28-897-0700
## Treeway Fencing Ltd
Cannock Wood Industrial Estate, Unit 9
Cannock Wood Street, Cannock,
Staffordshire WS12 0PL
**Tel:** 01543-425893 **Fax:** 01543-423654
**Web:** www.treeway.co.uk
**Reg No:** 1324257 **VAT No:** 316447070
**Estd:** 1977 Private Limited Company
**Line of Business:** Manufacture of builders
carpentry and joinery
**Trading Style:** Treeway Fencing Ltd
**Issued Capital:** £10,000
**Principals:** K N Greenaway (Managing),
K D Greenaway, T D Greenaway
**Co. Secretary:** Timothy Greenaway
**Responsibilities**
**Senior:** Ann Greenaway (Manager)
**IT:** Mahendra Bhatia (Works Engineer)
**Health & Safety:** Mahendra Bhatia (Works
Engineer)
**Facilities:** Mahendra Bhatia (Works
Engineer)
**Engineering:** Mahendra Bhatia (Works
Engineer)
**US SIC:** 2431 **UK SIC:** 46300
**Auditors:** Crompton, Ward & Co
**Bankers:** Allied Irish Bank (gb) (23-85-85)

|      | 31-03-14 | 31-03-13 | 31-03-12 |
|------|----------|----------|----------|
| TA | 1,884,808 | 1,607,407 | 1,749,442 |
| NW | 567,174 | 441,718 | 449,614 |
| WC | 295,395 | 139,540 | 143,143 |

DUNS 76-722-1658     Imp
## Treforest Textiles Ltd
(**Subsidiary of:** Treforest Textiles Holdings
Ltd)
Factory E6, Treforest Industrial Estate,
Pontypridd, Mid Glamorgan CF37 5ST
**Tel:** 01443842286
**Web:** www.fabricworld.uk.com
**Reg No:** 2596634 **VAT No:** 588058202
**Estd:** 1991 Private Limited Company
**Line of Business:** Manufacturers of textiles
**Issued Capital:** £34,201
**Director:** N P Harris
**Co. Secretary:** Glynn Hotchkiss
**Responsibilities**
**IT:** Glyn Hoskiss (IT Manager)
**Branches:** Treforest Textiles Ltd, St
Georges Hall, Lower Union Lane, Torquay,
Devon TQ2 5PN
**US SIC:** 2392 **UK SIC:** 45550
**Auditors:** PricewaterhouseCoopers LLP

|      | 31-12-13 | 31-12-12 | 31-12-11 |
|------|----------|----------|----------|
| TA | 1,024,233 | 928,854 | 1,132,354 |
| NW | 443,456 | 472,396 | 534,693 |
| WC | 568,069 | 594,683 | 615,754 |

DUNS 21-209-7245
## Trefula House Nursing Home
St Day Road, Trefula, Redruth, Cornwall
TR16 5ET
**Web:** www.trecaregroup.co.uk
**Estd:** 1986 Proprietorship
**Line of Business:** Nursing homes
**Proprietor:** B Craig
**Responsibilities**
**Senior:** Dee Ward (Manager), Denise Ward
(Manager)
**Health & Safety:** Malcolm Hawkins
(Maintenance Engineer)
**Facilities:** Malcolm Hawkins (Maintenance
Engineer)
**US SIC:** 8051 **UK SIC:** 95100
**Employees:** 56

DUNS 77-090-9778
## Tregenna Castle Hotel Ltd
(**Subsidiary of:** M. & P. Food Products Ltd)
Treganna Castle Estate, St Ives, St Ives,
Cornwall TR26 2DE
**Tel:** 01736795254
**Web:** www.tregenna-castle.co.uk
**Reg No:** 2675532 **Estd:** 1992 Private
Limited Company
**Line of Business:** Hotels
**Issued Capital:** £100
**Director:** J H Mason
**Co. Secretary:** Ms Amanda Mason
**Responsibilities**
**Senior:** Sheila Barker (General Manager)
**Admin:** Sheila Barker (General Manager)
**Branches:** Tregenna Castle Hotel Ltd, Care
Of Tregenna Castle Hotel, St Ives, St. Ives,
Cornwall TR26 2DE
**US SIC:** 7011 **UK SIC:** 66500
**Auditors:** Weheatherer Bailey Bragg

**Bankers:** Lloyds TSB Bank plc (30-00-03)

|      | 31-10-13 | 31-10-12 | 31-10-11 |
|------|----------|----------|----------|
| TO | 4,602,950 | 4,697,380 | 4,288,664 |
| P/L | 209,358 | 387,625 | 348,259 |
| NW | 9,385,408 | 8,736,428 | 8,354,319 |
| WC | 2,896,828 | (1,412,924) | (1,257,653) |
| Emp. | 144 | 150 | 134 |

DUNS 21-810-7913
## Treherne Care & Consultancy
Tremora, Barmouth, Gwynedd LL42 1AJ
**Tel:** 01341280824
**Web:** www.trehernecaregroup.com
**Estd:** 2003
**Line of Business:** Home care service
providers
**Responsibilities**
**Senior:** Diane Royce (Manager)
**HR:** Dawn Axworthy (Human Resources
Manager)
**US SIC:** 8091 **UK SIC:** 95200
**Employees:** 120

DUNS 23-848-3973
## Treherne Care & Consultancy Ltd
Garthangharad, Penmaenpool, Dolgellau,
Gwynedd LL40 1YF
**Tel:** 01341421925 **Fax:** 01341-282017
**Web:** www.trehernecaregroup.com
**Reg No:** 3840377 **Estd:** 2001 Private
Limited Company
**Line of Business:** Home care service
providers
**Issued Capital:** £1,133
**Director:** Mrs D J Royce
**Co. Secretary:** Ms Lesley Hughes
**Responsibilities**
**Senior:** Patty Morris (Head Of Care), Mark
Pigden (Manager), Roy Treherne (Manager)
**US SIC:** 8091 **UK SIC:** 95200
**Auditors:** Derek Draper
**Bankers:** Barclays Bank Plc (20-51-23)

|      | 30-09-13 | 30-09-12 | 30-09-11 |
|------|----------|----------|----------|
| TO | 3,650,601 | 3,756,019 | 3,840,315 |
| P/L | 288,395 | 454,397 | 614,744 |
| NW | 3,373,630 | 3,357,577 | 3,015,451 |
| WC | 887,562 | 899,377 | 576,011 |
| Emp. | 115 | 119 | 113 |

DUNS 50-331-2316     Imp
## Trek Bicycle Corporation Ltd
(**Subsidiary of:** Trek Bicycle Corporation)
Elder Gate, Milton Keynes, Buckinghamshire
MK9 1EN
**Tel:** 01908671122
**Web:** www.trekbikes.com
**Reg No:** 2355933 **VAT No:** 476107541
**Estd:** 1989 Private Limited Company
**Line of Business:** Other business activities
not elsewhere classified
**Export Sales:** £5,297,346
**Issued Capital:** £799,327
**Directors:** C R Brown, J Burke
**Co. Secretary:** Robert Burns
**Responsibilities**
**Senior:** Neil Fitton (Branch Manager),
Joseph Siefkes (Director)
**US SIC:** 7399 **UK SIC:** 83954
**Auditors:** Deloitte & Touche
**Bankers:** Barclays Bank Plc (20-57-40)

|      | 31-12-13 | 31-12-12 | 31-12-11 |
|------|----------|----------|----------|
| TO | 39,123,479 | 33,850,161 | 30,779,816 |
| P/L | 2,980,927 | 2,703,316 | 1,446,252 |
| NW | 12,002,170 | 11,267,998 | 10,248,699 |
| WC | 10,977,015 | 10,128,467 | 9,014,889 |
| Emp. | 64 | 68 | 50 |

DUNS 29-820-3498     Imp-Exp
## Trek Diagnostic Systems Ltd
(**Subsidiary of:** Trek Holding Co Ltd)
Imberhorne Lane, East Grinstead, West
Sussex RH19 1QX
**Tel:** 01342318777
**Web:** www.thermofisher.com
**Reg No:** 2038515 **Estd:** 1986 Private
Limited Company
**Line of Business:** Manufacture of medical
and surgical equipment and orthopaedic
appliances
**Export Markets:** Worldwide
**Export Sales:** £7,995,000
**Trading Style:** Thermo Fisher Scientific
**Issued Capital:** £7,765,000
**Directors:** K N Wheeler, Ms K R Wright,
Ms L M Grant
**Co. Secretary:**
Oakwood Corporate Secretary Limi
**Responsibilities**
**Senior:** Trevor Field (Manager), Pamela
Gornall (Manager), James Whelan
(Manager)
**US SIC:** 3841 **UK SIC:** 37201
**Auditors:** Ernst & Young LLP
**Bankers:** HSBC Bank plc (40-18-22)

|      | 31-12-13 | 31-12-12 | 31-12-11 |
|------|----------|----------|----------|
| TO | 8,497,000 | 7,340,000 | 6,844,000 |
| P/L | 421,000 | 753,000 | (313,000) |
| NW | 7,324,000 | 6,732,000 | 6,182,000 |
| WC | 2,920,000 | 1,900,000 | 999,000 |
| Emp. | 55 | 55 | 59 |

DUNS 21-590-8970

## Trek Highway Services

Unit 4a, Greens Road, Dereham, Norfolk NR20 3TG
**Tel:** 01362652953
**Web:** www.trekserv.co.uk
**Estd:** 2011 Proprietorship
**Line of Business:** Manufacture of other electrical equipment not elsewhere classified
**Proprietor:** S Halsey
**US SIC:** 7399 **UK SIC:** 83954
**Employees:** 120

DUNS 21-771-9778

## Trelai Primary School

Bishopston Road, Cardiff, South Glamorgan CF5 5DY
**Tel:** 02920402814
**Estd:** 2003 Proprietorship
**Line of Business:** Schools (local authority)
**Proprietor:** Mrs L Leckie
**Responsibilities**
**Senior:** Lesley Leckie *(Head Teacher)*
**US SIC:** 8211 **UK SIC:** 93200
**Employees:** 50

DUNS 23-082-9306

## Treliske Preparatory School

Treliske Lane, Truro, Cornwall TR1 3QN
**Web:** www.truroschool.com
**Estd:** 1950
**Line of Business:** Schools (independent)
**Trading Style:** Truro School Prep
**Directors:** R L Hollins, R Burdell
**Responsibilities**
**Senior:** Matthew Lovett *(Head Teacher)*
**Finance:** Sue McIntosh *(Domestic Bursar)*
**HR:** Sue McIntosh *(Domestic Bursar)*
**Health & Safety:** Sue McIntosh *(Domestic Bursar)*
**US SIC:** 8211 **UK SIC:** 93200
**Employees:** 50

DUNS 21-581-1087

## Trelissick Gallery

Trelissick Garden, Feock, Truro, Cornwall TR3 6QL
**Tel:** 01872861039
**Web:** www.trelissickgallery.co.uk
**Estd:** 2011 Proprietorship
**Line of Business:** Art gallery
**Proprietor:** G Elworthy
**Responsibilities**
**Senior:** Gareth Lay *(Property Manager)*
**US SIC:** 7911 **UK SIC:** 97913
**Employees:** 50

DUNS 21-324-5996 **Imp-Exp**

## Trelleborg Offshore Uk Ltd

(**Subsidiary of:** Crp 1998 Ltd)
Stanley Way, Stanley Industrial Estate, Skelmersdale, Lancashire WN8 8EA
**Tel:** 01695-712000 **Fax:** 01695-712111
**Web:** www.trelleborg.com
**Reg No:** 1369166 **VAT No:** 876325203
**Estd:** 1973 Private Limited Company
**Line of Business:** Service activities incidental to oil and gas extraction excluding surveying
**Export Sales:** £49,046,000
**Trading Style:** Trelleborg Offshore Uk Ltd
**Issued Capital:** £41,590
**Directors:** T H Eriksen, C F Meuller, A M Burgess, L E Olsson
**Co. Secretary:** Ian Elcock
**Responsibilities**
**Senior:** Chris Kelsall *(Purchasing Manager)*
**IT:** David Harmer *(MIS Manager)*
**HR:** andy wood *(human resources officer)*
**Health & Safety:** Robbie Craig *(Health & Safety Officer)*
**Facilities:** Paul Leggett *(Maintenance Manager)*
**Purchasing:** Chris Kelsall *(Purchasing Manager)*
**US SIC:** 1389 **UK SIC:** 13000
**Auditors:** PricewaterhouseCoopers LLP
**Bankers:** Barclays Bank Plc (20-96-37)

| | 31-12-13 | 31-12-12 | 31-12-11 |
|---|---|---|---|
| TO | 77,157,000 | 60,340,000 | 50,240,000 |
| P/L | 7,536,000 | 4,924,000 | (7,358,000) |
| NW | 53,124,000 | 47,008,000 | 43,017,000 |
| WC | 42,133,000 | 39,016,000 | 38,117,000 |
| Emp. | 368 | 310 | 365 |

DUNS 21-028-3263 **Imp-Exp**

## Tremco Illbruck Coatings Ltd

(**Subsidiary of:** Rpm International Inc.)
Coupland Road, Hindley Green, Wigan, Lancashire WN2 4HT
**Tel:** 01942258011 **Fax:** 01942521923
**Web:** www.illbruck.co.uk
**Reg No:** 0251311 **VAT No:** 227001610
**Estd:** 1930 Private Limited Company
**Line of Business:** Miscellaneous manufacturing industries
**Export Sales:** £15,413,552
**Issued Capital:** £300,000
**Directors:** J Gordon, E W Moore, B J Altena, R H Eisenhut, R A Rice
**Responsibilities**
**Health & Safety:** Mark Baxter *(Health & Safety Officer)*
**US SIC:** 3999, 2899
**UK SIC:** 49590, 25670
**Auditors:** Ernst & Young LLP
**Bankers:** HSBC Bank plc (40-42-09)

| | 31-05-14 | 31-05-13 | 31-05-12 |
|---|---|---|---|
| TO | 26,554,771 | 23,633,920 | 20,379,169 |
| P/L | 24,586,007 | (2,589,655) | 2,177,282 |
| NW | 61,849,866 | 37,042,321 | 37,753,985 |
| WC | (6,834,626) | (29,481,694) | (25,326,906) |
| Emp. | 76 | 80 | 81 |

DUNS 34-836-4746

## Tremco Illbruck Ltd

(**Subsidiary of:** Rpm International Inc.)
Coupland Road, Wigan, Lancashire WN2 4HT
**Tel:** 01942251400 **Fax:** 01942 251410
**Web:** www.tremco-illbruck.co.uk
**Reg No:** 2802593 **Estd:** 1988 Private Limited Company
**Line of Business:** Adhesive & sealant manufacturers
**Export Sales:** £831,421
**Issued Capital:** £600,000
**Directors:** J Altena, R M Hill, R H Eisenhut
**Responsibilities**
**IT:** Simon Quinn *(Pc Manager)*
**HR:** Debbie Mullerworth *(Human Resources Manager)*
**Branches:** Tremco Illbruck Ltd, 3A Walton Road, Pattinson North, Washington, Tyne and Wear NE38 8QA
**US SIC:** 2891, 5161
**UK SIC:** 25620, 61200
**Auditors:** Ernst & Young LLP
**Bankers:** National Westminster Bank Plc (54-10-31)

| | 31-05-14 | 31-05-13 | 31-05-12 |
|---|---|---|---|
| TO | 24,440,502 | 20,935,004 | 22,247,627 |
| P/L | 553,859 | (890,274) | 1,849,210 |
| NW | 1,198,925 | 1,225,116 | 1,715,993 |
| WC | 1,241,303 | 1,266,057 | 1,791,756 |
| Emp. | 68 | 58 | 60 |

DUNS 85-616-0890

## Tremorfa Group Ltd

Cypress House, Pascal Close, St Mellons, Cardiff, South Glamorgan CF3 0LW
**Tel:** 02920330000
**Web:** www.tremorfa.com
**Reg No:** 6209568 **Estd:** 2007 Private Limited Company
**Line of Business:** Management of real estate on a fee or contract basis
**Issued Capital:** £100,000
**Directors:** Ms A Roberts, P R Hopkins
**Co. Secretary:** Mark Hosken
**US SIC:** 6531 **UK SIC:** 83400
**Auditors:** Graham Paul Ltd

| | 30-04-14 | 30-04-13 | 30-04-12 |
|---|---|---|---|
| TO | 10,076,339 | 9,066,872 | 9,506,936 |
| P/L | 714,414 | 629,221 | 862,257 |
| NW | 1,680,470 | 1,380,565 | 1,149,297 |
| WC | 1,428,710 | 1,149,548 | 943,729 |
| Emp. | 107 | 111 | 118 |

DUNS 21-744-6616 **Imp-Exp**

## Trend Machinery & Cutting Tools Ltd

Unit 6 St Albans Road Odhams Trading, Estate, Watford, Hertfordshire WD24 7TR
**Tel:** 01923-249911 **Fax:** 01923-236879
**Web:** www.trend-uk.com
**Reg No:** 1338493 **Estd:** 1977 Private Limited Company
**Line of Business:** Woodturning activities
**Export Markets:** Iceland, Malta & U.S.A.
**Export Sales:** £1,680,688
**Trading Style:** Trend Cutting Tools
**Issued Capital:** £8,000
**Directors:** Ms A Kelly, M P Tideswell, Ms S F Phillips, N Mcmillan, S J Phillips
**Co. Secretary:** Jeffrey Willcocks
**Responsibilities**
**Senior:** Jess Willcocks *(Manager)*, Jeffrey Willcox *(CEO, Managing Director)*
**HR:** John Tigg *(Human Resources Manager)*
**Health & Safety:** John Tigg *(Human Resources Manager)*
**Facilities:** John Tigg *(Human Resources Manager)*
**US SIC:** 2431, 5084
**UK SIC:** 46300, 61490
**Auditors:** Geo Little Sebire & Co

| | 31-12-13 | 31-12-12 | 31-12-11 |
|---|---|---|---|
| TO | 13,541,171 | 12,528,499 | 11,947,859 |
| P/L | 319,808 | 452,638 | 244,955 |
| NW | 2,637,867 | 2,613,365 | 2,417,936 |
| WC | 2,312,509 | 2,324,962 | 2,376,790 |
| Emp. | 67 | 63 | 63 |

DUNS 21-912-6091 **Imp-Exp**

## Trend Marine Products Ltd

(**Subsidiary of:** Taylor Made Group Holdings Inc.)
Sutton Road, Catfield, Catfield, Great Yarmouth, Norfolk NR29 5BG
**Tel:** 01692581307 **Fax:** 01692582550
**Web:** www.trendmarine.com
**Reg No:** 1173006 **VAT No:** 107299953
**Estd:** 1973 Private Limited Company
**Line of Business:** Manufacture of other electrical equipment not elsewhere classified
**Export Markets:** U S A, Taiwan, Turkey, Netherlands, Canada, Germany, Australia, Egypt
**Issued Capital:** £102,500
**Directors:** J Taylor, J W Taylor, J A Jobbins, D F Flint
**Co. Secretary:** Robert Khalife
**Responsibilities**
**Senior:** Frank Buckley *(Manager)*
**Branches:** Trend Marine Products Ltd, The Maltings, Norwich, Norfolk NR12 9LL
**US SIC:** 7399, 8911
**UK SIC:** 83954, 83701
**Auditors:** PricewaterhouseCoopers LLP
**Bankers:** National Westminster Bank Plc (60-15-31)

| | 30-09-13 | 30-09-12 | 30-09-11 |
|---|---|---|---|
| TO | 12,750,657 | 13,552,862 | 12,800,139 |
| P/L | 690,202 | 1,139,131 | 941,256 |
| NW | 7,950,503 | 7,392,539 | 6,492,327 |
| WC | 6,694,167 | 5,905,095 | 4,877,071 |
| Emp. | 190 | 188 | 186 |

DUNS 29-682-4659 **Imp**

## Trendaset Ltd

(**Subsidiary of:** Mulmar Group Limited)
152 Great North Road, Hatfield, Hertfordshire AL9 5JN
**Tel:** 01707286920 **Fax:** 02082075795
**Web:** www.mulmar.com
**Reg No:** 2005998 **Estd:** 1991 Private Limited Company
**Line of Business:** Other retail sale in non-specialised stores
**Export Sales:** £193,282
**Trading Style:** Mulmar U K
**Issued Capital:** £106,059
**Principals:** A Luggeri *(Managing)*, E Frangiamore
**Co. Secretary:** Michael Canning
**US SIC:** 5399 **UK SIC:** 65600
**Auditors:** Parker Lloyd
**Bankers:** Barclays Bank Plc (20-20-37)

| | 30-06-13 | 30-06-12 | 30-06-11 |
|---|---|---|---|
| TO | 8,053,559 | N/A | N/A |
| P/L | 158,290 | N/A | N/A |
| NW | 256,842 | 361,944 | 363,478 |
| WC | (34,855) | 69,456 | 67,342 |
| Emp. | 81 | N/A | N/A |

DUNS 76-792-1679

## Trendleway Cleaners Ltd

Globe House, Manchester M15 4AL
**Tel:** 0161-226-6313 **Fax:** 0161-227-9747
**Web:** www.faheygroup.co.uk
**Reg No:** 2599573 **Estd:** 1977 Private Limited Company
**Line of Business:** Traditional cleaning activities
**Issued Capital:** £2
**Principals:** A P Fahey *(Managing)*, S J Fahey
**Responsibilities**
**Senior:** Margaret Fahey *(Manager)*
**US SIC:** 8999 **UK SIC:** 83954
**Auditors:** Edwards Veeder
**Bankers:** Barclays Bank Plc (20-54-58)

| | 31-03-14 | 31-03-13 | 31-03-12 |
|---|---|---|---|
| TA | 687,551 | 641,187 | 541,469 |
| NW | 309,677 | 303,675 | 301,434 |
| WC | 278,977 | 267,550 | 263,084 |

DUNS 21-319-1323 **Imp-Exp**

## Trendmost Ltd

(**Subsidiary of:** A.C.S. Textiles Ltd)
49 Mere Lane, Rochdale, Lancashire OL11 3TD
**Tel:** 01706-657321 **Fax:** 01706-861813
**Web:** www.trendmost.com
**Reg No:** 1205953 **Estd:** 1975 Private Limited Company
**Line of Business:** Manufacturers of soft furnishings
**Export Markets:** Eire; Norway; Sweden; Belgium; Singapore
**Issued Capital:** £900
**Principals:** C Taylor *(Managing)*, S J Taylor
**Co. Secretary:** Ms Stephanie Taylor
**Responsibilities**
**Finance:** Margaret Rosbottom *(Accounts Manager)*
**US SIC:** 2392 **UK SIC:** 45550
**Auditors:** Tenon Ltd

**Bankers:** Singer & Friedlander Ltd (60-01-56)

| | 30-04-14 | 30-04-13 | 30-04-12 |
|---|---|---|---|
| TO | N/A | 7,471,258 | 7,089,453 |
| P/L | N/A | 425,703 | 414,886 |
| NW | 1,309,285 | 1,534,569 | 1,609,203 |
| WC | 1,086,806 | 1,299,845 | 1,371,814 |
| Emp. | N/A | 44 | 46 |

DUNS 21-615-8411

## Trent Bridge

2 Radcliffe Road, West Bridgford, Nottingham, Nottinghamshire NG2 6AA
**Tel:** 01159822786
**Web:** www.jdwetherspoon.co.uk
**Estd:** 2011
**Line of Business:** Public house
**US SIC:** 5813, 1751, 6531, 1711
**UK SIC:** 66200, 50400, 83400, 50300
**Employees:** 50

DUNS 28-828-7766

## Trent College Ltd

Derby Road, Nottingham, Nottinghamshire NG10 4AD
**Tel:** 01158-494949 **Fax:** 01158-494997
**Web:** www.trentcollege.net
**Reg No:** 0032983 **Estd:** 1868 Private Limited Company
**Line of Business:** Colleges (higher education)
**Issued Capital:** £19,000
**Directors:** Dr R Field, C D Swallow, Professor A J Avery, Miss I Ellis, Ms R E Rowley, M E Ronan, I F Bowness, M Doleman
**Co. Secretary:** Stephen Burnham
**Responsibilities**
**Senior:** Stephen Anelay *(Director)*, Sandra Betts *(Catering Manager)*, Gill Dixon *(Headmistress)*, Diane Farmer *(Director)*, Louise Gray *(Director)*, Gillian Hinks *(Director)*, Paul Macildowie *(Director)*, Bill Penty *(Head Teacher)*, Rebecca Singleton *(Director)*
**Marketing:** Nicola Callow *(Marketing Manager)*
**US SIC:** 8211 **UK SIC:** 93200
**Auditors:** KPMG
**Bankers:** The Royal Bank Of Scotland Plc (16-24-21)

| | 31-08-13 | 31-07-12 | 31-08-11 |
|---|---|---|---|
| TO | 16,868,000 | 14,519,000 | 13,660,000 |
| P/L | (849,000) | (497,000) | (600,000) |
| NW | 30,983,000 | 32,848,000 | 33,340,000 |
| WC | (2,079,000) | (785,000) | (552,000) |
| Emp. | 372 | 366 | 348 |

DUNS 21-615-8351

## Trent Fm Arena Nottingham

Bolero Square Lace Market, Nottingham, Nottinghamshire NG1 1LA
**Tel:** 08433733000
**Web:** www.capitalfmarena.com
**Estd:** 2011 Proprietorship
**Line of Business:** Operation of arts facilities
**Proprietor:** Ms K Bor
**US SIC:** 7911 **UK SIC:** 97913
**Employees:** 125

DUNS 21-811-4833

## The Trent Motor Traction Company Ltd

(**Subsidiary of:** Wellglade Holdings Ltd)
Mansfield Road, Heanor, Derbyshire DE75 7BG
**Tel:** 01773-712265
**Web:** www.trentbarton.co.uk
**Reg No:** 0131912 **VAT No:** 439377121
**Estd:** 1913 Private Limited Company
**Line of Business:** Bus operators and stations
**Trading Style:** Trent Barton, Trent Buses
**Issued Capital:** £1,500,000
**Principals:** B R King *(Managing)*, R I Morgan, J Counsell
**Co. Secretary:** Graham Sutton
**Branches:** The Trent Motor Traction Company Ltd, The Old Bus Station, Morledge, Derby, Derbyshire DE1 2AY
**US SIC:** 4119, 4142
**UK SIC:** 72200, 72102
**Auditors:** Deloitte & Touche LLP
**Bankers:** HSBC Bank plc (40-19-15)

| | 31-12-13 | 31-12-12 | 31-12-11 |
|---|---|---|---|
| TO | 30,133,000 | 30,018,000 | 32,553,000 |
| P/L | 2,337,000 | 805,000 | 2,562,000 |
| NW | 15,207,000 | 19,306,000 | 17,705,000 |
| WC | 7,599,000 | 9,203,000 | 11,665,000 |
| Emp. | 749 | 759 | 820 |

DUNS 34-588-1353 **Imp**

## Trent Shopfitters Ltd

Gateway House, Beechdale Road, Nottingham, Nottinghamshire NG8 3EZ
**Tel:** 01159-425151
**Web:** www.trentshopfitters.co.uk
**Reg No:** 2732256 **VAT No:** 568181416
**Estd:** 1990 Private Limited Company
**Line of Business:** Shopfitting contractors

**Trading Style:** Set Out Services
**Issued Capital:** £1,000
**Principals:** P A Peacock *(Managing)*, K Laats, A T Guy
**Co. Secretary:** Mrs Marie Mullan
**Responsibilities**
**Senior:** Duncan Coy *(Contracts Manager)*
**Facilities:** Duncan Coy *(Contracts Manager)*
**US SIC:** 1796 **UK SIC:** 50400
**Auditors:** Roger Spencar & Co
**Bankers:** Yorkshire Bank Plc (05-06-40)

| | 30-11-13 | 30-11-12 | 30-11-11 |
|---|---|---|---|
| TA | 1,907,900 | 2,206,313 | 1,874,103 |
| NW | 706,040 | 855,973 | 816,237 |
| WC | 192,213 | 399,168 | 415,614 |

DUNS 42-381-8681
## Trentham Leisure Ltd.
(**Subsidiary of:** St. Modwen Properties Plc)
Trentham Gardens, Stone Road, Stoke-On-Trent, Staffordshire ST4 8JG
**Tel:** 01782646644 **Fax:** 01782644303
**Web:** www.bluediamond.gg
**Reg No:** 3246990 **VAT No:** 687899924
**Estd:** 2005 Private Limited Company
**Line of Business:** Other retail sale in specialised stores not elsewhere classified
**Trading Style:** Trentham Gardens
**Issued Capital:** £100,000
**Directors:** W A Oliver, M W Herbert
**Co. Secretary:** Michael Dunn
**Responsibilities**
**Senior:** Mark Loeptien *(Manager)*, Debbie Mabbutt *(Manager)*
**US SIC:** 5999 **UK SIC:** 65600
**Auditors:** Ernst & Young LLP
**Bankers:** Barclays Bank Plc (20-36-43)

| | 30-11-13 | 30-11-12 | 30-11-11 |
|---|---|---|---|
| TO | 4,116,362 | 3,905,655 | 3,900,869 |
| P/L | 407,960 | 305,109 | 505,948 |
| NW | (4,470,175) | (5,208,709) | (5,078,401) |
| WC | (19,364,612) | (19,663,230) | (19,891,803) |
| Emp. | N/A | 42 | 37 |

DUNS 71-940-0355
## Trenton Box Co Ltd
3 Marston Road, St Neots, Cambridgeshire PE19 2HF
**Tel:** 01480473693
**Web:** www.trentonbox.co.uk
**Reg No:** 5320737 **Estd:** 1951 Private Limited Company
**Line of Business:** Manufacturers of boxes and cartons
**Issued Capital:** £1
**Directors:** G Gibson, E R Douglas, Ms Y B Wood
**Co. Secretary:** Mrs Sheila Douglas
**US SIC:** 2651, 2752
**UK SIC:** 47253, 47544

| | 28-02-14 | 28-02-13 | 29-02-12 |
|---|---|---|---|
| TO | 6,508,142 | 7,324,264 | 7,299,737 |
| P/L | (397,642) | 195,954 | 274,879 |
| NW | 216,800 | 540,403 | 392,370 |
| WC | (859,363) | (546,048) | (468,509) |
| Emp. | 69 | 70 | 66 |

DUNS 21-600-6546
## Trenton Renault
45-52 Witham, Hull, North Humberside HU9 1BS
**Tel:** 01482222515
**Web:** www.trentonhull.co.uk
**Estd:** 1895 Partnership
**Line of Business:** Car dealers (used)
**Partners:** Mrs S Roberts, J Rix, T Rix, K Taylor, D Wilson, Ms S Rix, P Hasnip
**Responsibilities**
**Senior:** Peter Staveley *(Dealer Principal)*
**US SIC:** 5521 **UK SIC:** 65100
**Employees:** 319

DUNS 21-657-0407
## Trentpack Ltd
10, Stadium Business Court, Millenni, Derby, Derbyshire DE24 8HP
**Tel:** 01159822622
**Web:** www.trentpack.com
**Reg No:** 7136725 **Estd:** 2010 Private Limited Company
**Line of Business:** Packaging activities
**Issued Capital:** £1
**Directors:** L A Shaw, Mrs L J Shaw
**Co. Secretary:** Mrs Linda Shaw
**US SIC:** 8911 **UK SIC:** 83701

| | 31-12-13 | 31-12-12 | 31-12-11 |
|---|---|---|---|
| TA | 187,898 | 137,441 | 147,250 |
| NW | 28,036 | 21,144 | 11,633 |
| WC | 57,249 | 50,979 | 37,136 |

DUNS 21-781-6471
## Trentside Clinic
Stafford Road, Stone, Staffordshire ST15 0TT
**Estd:** 1990 Proprietorship
**Line of Business:** Nhs clinics
**Proprietor:** Ms J Browne
**US SIC:** 8062 **UK SIC:** 95100
**Employees:** 50

DUNS 55-079-9951
## Treorchy Rugby Football Club
Regent Street, Treorchy, Mid Glamorgan CF42 6PN
**Tel:** 01443432874
**Estd:** 1957
**Line of Business:** Misc Amusement & Recreation Services
**Chairman:** B James
**US SIC:** 7999 **UK SIC:** 97913
**Employees:** 70

DUNS 50-566-5745 **Imp**
## Trepko (Uk) Ltd
(**Subsidiary of:** H.C.Holding. Investeringsaktieselskab)
Marshall Way, Heapham Road Industrial Estate, Gainsborough, Lincolnshire DN21 1GD
**Tel:** 01427-612244
**Web:** www.trepko.co.uk
**Reg No:** 2514342 **VAT No:** 555493122
**Estd:** 1990 Private Limited Company
**Line of Business:** Manufacture of machinery for food, beverage and tobacco processing
**Export Sales:** £4,029,121
**Issued Capital:** £750,000
**Directors:** J O Knudsen, A A Newman-Carter, J B Hansen, H C Hansen
**Co. Secretary:** Gary Rains
**Responsibilities**
**Senior:** Trevor Gilliot *(Warehouse Manager)*, John Morfin *(Manager)*, Chris Morfin *(Sales Director)*
**Finance:** Samantha Shipley *(Human Resources Coordinator)*
**Sales:** Chris Morfin *(Sales Director)*
**IT:** Chris duehurst *(IT Manager)*
**HR:** Samantha Shipley *(Human Resources Coordinator)*
**US SIC:** 3551 **UK SIC:** 32441
**Auditors:** Marriott Gibbs
**Bankers:** National Westminster Bank Plc (52-41-46)

| | 31-12-13 | 31-12-12 | 31-12-11 |
|---|---|---|---|
| TO | 8,254,249 | N/A | N/A |
| P/L | 829,204 | N/A | N/A |
| NW | 2,681,863 | 2,240,622 | 1,455,111 |
| WC | 2,378,858 | 1,932,511 | 1,116,095 |
| Emp. | 50 | N/A | N/A |

DUNS 21-126-3530
## Trescal Ltd
(**Subsidiary of:** 3i Group Plc)
Blackbushe Business Park Saxony Way, Yateley, Hampshire GU46 6GT
**Tel:** 01252 533 300 **Fax:** 01252 533 333
**Web:** www.trescal.co.uk
**Reg No:** 6614164 **Estd:** 2008 Private Limited Company
**Line of Business:** Calibration equipment services
**Export Sales:** £5,355,022
**Issued Capital:** £5,000
**Directors:** O Delrieu, J A Evans, R B Hastie, G Caroit, D C Chauveinc, J Gelbert Maury
**Branches:** Trescal Ltd, Unit 3 Bredbury Park Way Park Gate Close, Stockport, Cheshire SK6 2SL
**US SIC:** 3811 **UK SIC:** 37100
**Auditors:** Constantin

| | 31-12-13 | 31-12-12 | 31-12-11 |
|---|---|---|---|
| TO | 32,156,696 | 28,911,623 | 17,058,947 |
| P/L | (984,176) | (1,715,590) | (818,048) |
| NW | (16,172,681) | (6,264,260) | (5,495,360) |
| WC | 2,111,946 | 83,640 | (466,926) |
| Emp. | 394 | 390 | 360 |

DUNS 21-600-7214
## Treshold West of Scotland
7 Glenview, Larkhall, Lanarkshire ML9 1DA
**Estd:** 1993 Proprietorship
**Line of Business:** Home care and help services
**Proprietor:** Mrs B Galbraith
**Responsibilities**
**Senior:** Sandra Rorrison *(Team Leader)*
**US SIC:** 8699 **UK SIC:** 96902
**Employees:** 86

DUNS 21-148-2140
## Trethowans Llp
London Road, Salisbury, Wiltshire SP1 3HP
**Tel:** 01722-412512
**Web:** www.trethowans.com
**Reg No:** 0342356OC **Estd:** 1994 Private Limited Company
**Line of Business:** Solicitors
**Responsibilities**
**Senior:** Jeremy Burns *(Partner)*, Clare Carter *(Non-designated Limited Liabili)*, Michael Catchbole *(Partner)*, Neil Elliott *(Partner)*, Kelvin Farmaner *(Non-designated Limited Liabili)*, Nicholas Gent *(Non-designated Limited Liabili)*, Gavin Lane *(Non-designated Limited Liabili)*, Jon Loney *(Non-designated Limited Liabili)*, Paul Longman *(Non-designated Limited Liabili)*, Catherine Macrae *(Manager)*, Caroline Matthews *(Non-designated Limited Liabili)*, Paul Mildred *(Partner)*, Michael Ricketts *(Manager)*, Jennifer Rogerson *(Non-designated Limited Liabili)*, Kimberley Singleton *(Non-designated Limited Liabili)*, Timothy Spender *(Partner)*, Marcus Thorpe *(Non-designated Limited Liabili)*, Robert Wassall *(Non-designated Limited Liabili)*
**Finance:** Andy Duckworth *(Financial Director)*
**Marketing:** Clare Fanner *(Marketing Director)*
**IT:** Andy Duckworth *(Financial Director)*
**Facilities:** Julie Cummings *(Facilities Manager)*
**Purchasing:** Julie Cummings *(Facilities Manager)*
**US SIC:** 8111 **UK SIC:** 83500

| | 31-03-14 | 31-03-13 | 31-03-12 |
|---|---|---|---|
| TA | 6,987,416 | 6,243,523 | 5,459,769 |
| WC | 5,638,980 | 4,640,294 | 3,882,393 |
| Emp. | 120 | 115 | 110 |

DUNS 77-461-3517
## Trethowans Services Ltd
(**Subsidiary of:** Trethowans Llp)
Director Generals House, 15 Rockstone Place, Southampton, Hampshire SO15 2EP
**Tel:** 02380321000 **Fax:** 02380321001
**Web:** www.trethowans.com
**Reg No:** 2963123 **Estd:** 2001 Private Limited Company
**Line of Business:** Solicitors
**Issued Capital:** £2
**Directors:** M W Watson, S J Rhodes
**Responsibilities**
**Senior:** Michael Biddle *(Partner)*, Nick Gent *(Partner)*, Gavin Lane *(Partner - Personal Injury Team)*, Jon Loney *(Partner)*, Paul Longman *(Partner & Head of Commercial P)*, Catherine MacRae *(Partner)*, Caroline Matthews *(Partner & Head of Licensing)*, Jennifer Rogerson *(Partner)*, Robert Wassall *(Partner and Head of Social Hou)*
**Finance:** Melanie Traynor *(Debt Recovery Assistant)*
**Sales:** Paul Longman *(Partner & Head of Commercial P)*
**Admin:** Amy Brooks *(Legal Secretary)*, Amy Clatworthy *(Office Administrator-Operation)*, Amy Gregory *(Legal Secretary)*
**HR:** Sarah Barfoot *(HR Assistant)*, Kate Ellis *(HR Officer)*
**Facilities:** Julie Cummings *(Facilities Manager)*, Robert Wassall *(Partner and Head of Social Hou)*
**Branches:** Trethowans Services Ltd, 3 Salisbury St, Salisbury, Wiltshire SP4 7AW
**US SIC:** 8111, 7399, 8999
**UK SIC:** 83500, 83954
**Auditors:** Fletcher & Partners

| | 31-03-14 | 31-03-13 | 31-03-12 |
|---|---|---|---|
| TA | 2 | 2 | 2 |
| NW | 2 | 2 | 2 |

DUNS 77-101-8546
## Trevelgue Leisure Ltd
(**Subsidiary of:** Aquiline Capital Partners Llc)
Trevelgue, Newquay, Newquay, Cornwall TR8 4AS
**Tel:** 01637851851
**Web:** www.trevelgue.co.uk
**Reg No:** 2678853 **Estd:** 1992 Private Limited Company
**Line of Business:** Holiday centres and holiday villages
**Trading Style:** Edgcumbe Hotel
**Issued Capital:** £100
**Director:** A S Christopheros
**Co. Secretary:** Andrew Black
**Responsibilities**
**Senior:** Mike Finnegan *(Manager)*, Charlotte Nutman *(Reception Manager)*
**Branches:** Trevelgue Leisure Ltd, Porth, Newquay, Cornwall TR8 4AS
**US SIC:** 7021 **UK SIC:** 66500
**Auditors:** Ernst & Young
**Bankers:** National Westminster Bank Plc (54-10-38)

| | 30-11-13 | 30-11-12 | 29-11-12 |
|---|---|---|---|
| TO | 2,683,416 | 2,978,089 | 3,525,091 |
| P/L | (544,200) | (332,349) | (363,000) |
| NW | 605,111 | 1,017,311 | 1,300,660 |
| WC | (1,302,223) | (979,358) | (728,173) |
| Emp. | 65 | 87 | 78 |

DUNS 28-922-1319 **Imp**
## Trevellyan Developments Ltd
Greenhills Estate Office, Greenhills Estate Tilford Road, Farnham, Surrey GU10 2DZ
**Reg No:** 1480424 **Estd:** 1980 Private Limited Company
**Line of Business:** Development and selling of real estate
**Issued Capital:** £125,100
**Principals:** L J Trevellyan *(Managing)*, L D Trevellyan, Mrs A H Trevellyan
**Co. Secretary:** Lance Trevellyan
**US SIC:** 6552, 6711, 6531
**UK SIC:** 85000, 83962, 83400
**Auditors:** JVR Jerrom LLP

**Bankers:** National Westminster Bank Plc (60-08-15)

| | 31-07-13 | 31-07-12 | 31-07-11 |
|---|---|---|---|
| TO | 42,235,707 | 38,563,433 | 32,956,307 |
| P/L | 1,745,916 | 1,644,487 | 1,511,323 |
| NW | 37,137,727 | 31,722,055 | 27,734,838 |
| WC | 1,497,103 | 1,774,277 | 1,830,795 |
| Emp. | 100 | 98 | 97 |

DUNS 21-778-8098
## Trevelyan College
Elvet Hill Road, Durham, County Durham DH1 3LN
**Web:** www.trevelyancollege.co.uk
**Estd:** 2002 Proprietorship
**Line of Business:** Further education schools and colleges
**Proprietor:** Mrs J Miller
**Responsibilities**
**Senior:** Martyn Evans *(Principal)*
**US SIC:** 8221 **UK SIC:** 93100
**Employees:** 50

DUNS 23-567-8760
## Trevelyan Hall Ltd
(**Subsidiary of:** Minhoco 20 Ltd)
15 St James Street, Newcastle-Upon-Tyne, Tyne and Wear NE1 4NF
**Tel:** 0191-230-0200 **Fax:** 0191-223-5205
**Web:** www.trevelyan.com
**Reg No:** 1281153 **VAT No:** 499961854
**Estd:** 1976 Private Limited Company
**Line of Business:** Cleaning activities not elsewhere classified
**Trading Style:** Litterboss
**Issued Capital:** £100,000
**Directors:** P Mcmorris, Ms N L Tucker, J A Johnson, R F Johnson
**Co. Secretary:** James Johnson
**US SIC:** 7349 **UK SIC:** 92300
**Auditors:** McCowie & Co
**Bankers:** Lloyds TSB Bank plc (30-91-50)

| | 31-03-14 | 31-03-13 | 31-03-12 |
|---|---|---|---|
| TO | 11,176,569 | 13,938,206 | 10,029,084 |
| P/L | 2,153,310 | 366,676 | 1,986,475 |
| NW | 6,874,863 | 5,217,206 | 4,926,529 |
| WC | 6,664,365 | 4,978,014 | 4,801,496 |
| Emp. | 275 | 257 | 284 |

DUNS 21-773-9694
## Trevelyan Middle School
Wood Close, Windsor, Berkshire SL4 3LL
**Web:** www.trevelyan.org.uk
**Estd:** 1945 Partnership
**Line of Business:** Schools (local authority)
**Partners:** J Griffith, T Woods
**US SIC:** 8211 **UK SIC:** 93200
**Employees:** 50

DUNS 21-224-5024
## Treverne
72 Melvill Road, Falmouth, Cornwall TR11 4DD
**Tel:** 01326-312833
**Web:** www.cornwallcare.org
**Estd:** 1991
**Line of Business:** Nursing homes
**Partners:** Mrs S Colston, Mrs A Rowe, Mrs A Rowe
**Responsibilities**
**Senior:** Penny Green *(Manager)*
**US SIC:** 8051 **UK SIC:** 95100
**Employees:** 60

DUNS 50-451-4381 **Imp-Exp**
## Treves Uk Ltd
(**Subsidiary of:** Financiere Severt)
Farnham Lane, Farnham, Knaresborough, North Yorkshire HG5 9JR
**Tel:** 01423-798800
**Web:** www.treves.fr
**Reg No:** 2434099 **VAT No:** 540861843
**Estd:** 1989 Private Limited Company
**Line of Business:** Manufacturers of car accessories
**Export Sales:** £1,154,217
**Issued Capital:** £450,000
**Directors:** A S Abreu, B Treves, G Treves
**Co. Secretary:** Mh Secretaries Limited
**Responsibilities**
**IT:** Mark Fawcett *(IT Manager)*
**Purchasing:** Romain Briand *(Purchasing Manager)*
**Branches:** Treves Uk Ltd, 28 Hepworth Road, Coventry, West Midlands CV3 2XJ
**US SIC:** 3714 **UK SIC:** 35300
**Auditors:** Mazars LLP

| | 31-12-13 | 31-12-12 | 31-12-11 |
|---|---|---|---|
| TO | 34,715,506 | 38,714,263 | 33,649,063 |
| P/L | (718,563) | 473,125 | 1,762,300 |
| NW | 5,945,688 | 6,161,601 | 6,510,440 |
| WC | 1,699,603 | 3,056,955 | 4,294,153 |
| Emp. | 176 | 172 | 115 |

**DUNS 21-714-0944**

## Trevithick Learning Academy

Mount Pleasant Road, Camborne, Cornwall TR14 7RH
**Tel:** 01209713460
**Web:** www.trevithick.cornwall.sch.uk
**Reg No:** 7535379 **Estd:** 2011 Private Company Limited By Guarantee
**Line of Business:** General secondary education
**Directors:** Ms A O'Neill, A Honeybone, A J Mercer, Ms A O'Neill, A J Mercer, P J Robinson, Ms K R Horner, I Raggett
**Responsibilities**
**Senior:** Georgina French (Director), Martin Kennedy (Director), Sean Powers (Director), Kaye Troth (Director)
**US SIC:** 8211 **UK SIC:** 93200
**Bankers:** Lloyds TSB Bank plc (30-12-21)

|      | 31-08-14 | 31-08-13 | 31-08-12 |
|------|----------|----------|----------|
| TO   | 1,941,000 | 2,047,000 | 1,461,000 |
| P/L  | 161,000 | 416,000 | 11,000 |
| NW   | 4,944,000 | 5,047,000 | 4,623,000 |
| WC   | 395,000 | 163,000 | 179,000 |
| Emp. | 51 | 49 | 44 |

**DUNS 22-673-9654**

## Trevor Benton Construction Ltd

(**Subsidiary of:** Trevor Benton Group Ltd)
10-12 St Thomas Place, Ely, Cambridgeshire CB7 4EX
**Tel:** 01353663807
**Web:** www.trevorbentongroup.co.uk
**Reg No:** 1859265 **Estd:** 1987 Private Limited Company
**Line of Business:** Plumbers
**Issued Capital:** £66,000
**Principals:** T J Benton (Managing), A T Benton
**Responsibilities**
**Senior:** Jane Benton (Manager)
**US SIC:** 1711, 7349
**UK SIC:** 50300, 92300
**Auditors:** Ashgates Corporate Services Ltd
**Bankers:** Barclays Bank Plc (20-29-68)

|    | 30-06-13 | 30-06-12 | 30-06-11 |
|----|----------|----------|----------|
| TA | 1,860,212 | 1,711,061 | 1,795,015 |
| NW | 241,098 | 257,787 | 255,671 |
| WC | 231,359 | 242,873 | 243,671 |

**DUNS 22-856-0462**

## Trevor Bolton Engineering Services Ltd

(**Subsidiary of:** Kervin Ltd)
George Street West, Blackburn, Lancashire BB2 1PQ
**Tel:** 01254-663934 **Fax:** 01254-691313
**Web:** www.precisionsheetmetal.co.uk
**Reg No:** 1509153 **VAT No:** 326043585
**Estd:** 1980 Private Limited Company
**Line of Business:** Manufacture of other fabricated metal products not elsewhere classified
**Trading Style:** Trevor Bolton Engineering Services Ltd
**Issued Capital:** £100
**Director:** M Bolton
**US SIC:** 3499 **UK SIC:** 31694
**Auditors:** Pierce
**Bankers:** National Westminster Bank Plc (01-00-85)

|    | 31-05-14 | 31-05-13 | 31-05-12 |
|----|----------|----------|----------|
| TA | 3,840,189 | 3,418,777 | 2,553,453 |
| NW | 590,820 | 697,951 | 615,134 |
| WC | 155,701 | 279,238 | 256,726 |

**DUNS 29-659-1613** Exp

## Trevor Sorbie International Plc

Old Station Approach, Randalls Road, Leatherhead, Surrey KT22 7TE
**Tel:** 01372375435
**Web:** www.trevorsorbie.com
**Reg No:** 1985359 **Estd:** 1986 Public Limited Company
**Line of Business:** Hairdressers supplies
**Export Markets:** U S A, Sweden, Norway, Canada
**Export Sales:** £400,799
**Issued Capital:** £180,000
**Principals:** T Sorbie (Managing), G S Peet
**Co. Secretary:** Ms Jane Henry
**Branches:** Trevor Sorbie International Plc, 27 Floral Street, London WC2E 9DP
**US SIC:** 5199, 7399
**UK SIC:** 61900, 83954
**Auditors:** Sobell Rhodes
**Bankers:** Barclays Bank Plc (20-77-67)

|      | 31-03-14 | 31-03-13 | 31-03-12 |
|------|----------|----------|----------|
| TO   | 5,725,705 | 5,849,929 | 5,651,216 |
| P/L  | 6,288 | (146,772) | (334,035) |
| NW   | 1,222,039 | 1,241,926 | 1,373,441 |
| WC   | 513,770 | 458,192 | 471,026 |
| Emp. | 123 | 127 | 125 |

**DUNS 23-815-5295**

## Trevornick Camping Park

Holywell Bay, Holywell Bay, Newquay, Cornwall TR8 5PW
**Tel:** 01637-830531
**Web:** www.trevornick.co.uk
**Estd:** 1965 Partnership
**Line of Business:** Camping site operators
**Partners:** Ms J Hartley, R Hartley, R Hartley, Ms C Hartley
**Responsibilities**
**IT:** Clare Reynolds (Reservations Manager)
**Operations:** Clare Reynolds (Reservations Manager)
**US SIC:** 5813, 7399
**UK SIC:** 66200, 83954
**Bankers:** Lloyds TSB Bank plc (30-96-03)
**Employees:** 50

**DUNS 28-831-2473**

## Trevose Ltd

Constantine Bay, Padstow, Cornwall PL28 8JB
**Tel:** 01841520208 **Fax:** 01841-521057
**Web:** www.trevose-gc.co.uk
**Reg No:** 0222839 **Estd:** 2011 Private Limited Company
**Line of Business:** Other sporting activities not elsewhere classified
**Trading Style:** Trevose Golf Club
**Issued Capital:** £46,740
**Directors:** C P Gammon, A J Gammon, W P Harriman, Ms C E Gammon, D Layton
**Co. Secretary:** Nicholas Gammon
**Responsibilities**
**Senior:** Jo Stuttaford (Proprietor)
**US SIC:** 7999, 7011
**UK SIC:** 97913, 66500
**Auditors:** Robinson Reed Layton
**Bankers:** Lloyds TSB Bank plc (30-98-98)

|      | 03-04-14 | 04-04-13 | 29-04-12 |
|------|----------|----------|----------|
| TO   | 2,938,647 | 3,024,484 | 2,906,551 |
| P/L  | (103,555) | (156,515) | (45,196) |
| NW   | 3,796,884 | 3,916,797 | 4,077,540 |
| WC   | (1,019,752) | (1,135,472) | (848,233) |
| Emp. | 67 | 70 | 79 |

**DUNS 76-852-8614**

## Trg Recruitment Services Ltd

Westerfield Business Centre, Ipswich, Suffolk IP6 9AB
**Tel:** 01473288018
**Web:** www.thetrggroup.co.uk
**Reg No:** 2608410 **VAT No:** 577692186
**Estd:** 1991 Private Limited Company
**Line of Business:** Legal services
**Trading Style:** The Trg Group
**Issued Capital:** £100
**Chairman:** T R Gilbert
**Co. Secretary:** Maretta Gilbert
**Branches:** Trg Recruitment Services Ltd, Ridgefield Ho, 14 John Dalton St, Manchester M2 6JR
**US SIC:** 7361, 7392
**UK SIC:** 83954, 83951
**Bankers:** Barclays Bank Plc (20-60-38)

|    | 31-08-13 | 31-08-12 | 31-08-11 |
|----|----------|----------|----------|
| TA | 358,218 | 451,302 | 412,784 |
| NW | 161,547 | 200,076 | 199,612 |
| WC | 160,983 | 199,228 | 198,849 |

**DUNS 21-136-7919**

## Trgom Ltd

Rawdon Road, Moira, Swadlincote, Derbyshire DE12 6DA
**Tel:** 01283229069
**Reg No:** 6696901 **Estd:** 2008 Private Limited Company
**Line of Business:** Holding companies management activities
**Export Sales:** £4,513,000
**Issued Capital:** £33,336
**Director:** A W Brealey
**Co. Secretary:** Malcolm Watkins
**US SIC:** 6711 **UK SIC:** 83962
**Auditors:** PricewaterhouseCoopers LLP

|      | 31-12-13 | 31-12-12 | 31-12-11 |
|------|----------|----------|----------|
| TO   | 19,291,000 | 22,335,000 | 24,779,000 |
| P/L  | 75,000 | 589,000 | 989,000 |
| NW   | 4,758,000 | 4,645,000 | 4,187,000 |
| WC   | 1,524,000 | 1,385,000 | 1,480,000 |
| Emp. | 200 | 220 | 235 |

**DUNS 21-918-1575** Imp

## Tri-Pack Plastics Ltd

Estate Road 1, Grimsby, South Humberside DN31 2TB
**Tel:** 01472-355038 **Fax:** 01472-266930
**Web:** www.tri-pack.co.uk
**Reg No:** 1146130 **VAT No:** 129475349
**Estd:** 1973 Private Limited Company
**Line of Business:** Manufacturers of boxes and cartons
**Trading Style:** Tri-Pack
**Issued Capital:** £7,847
**Principals:** S W Clarke (Managing), J Oddgeirsson
**Co. Secretary:** Mrs Wendy Thompson

**Responsibilities**
**Senior:** Peter Whittle (Manager)
**Finance:** Simon Drewery (Account Manager/ IT)
**Facilities:** Steve Merritt (Engineering Manager)
**Engineering:** Steve Merritt (Engineering Manager)
**US SIC:** 2651, 3079
**UK SIC:** 47253, 48360
**Auditors:** Pelham
**Bankers:** HSBC Bank plc (40-30-26)

|    | 30-09-13 | 30-09-12 | 30-09-11 |
|----|----------|----------|----------|
| TA | 3,500,909 | 3,153,141 | 3,197,643 |
| NW | 1,774,738 | 1,677,077 | 1,426,633 |
| WC | 662,504 | 553,809 | 274,061 |

**DUNS 76-269-5807** Imp-Exp

## Tri-Star Packaging Supplies Ltd

Unit 4, Enfield, Middlesex EN3 7NL
**Tel:** 02084439100 **Fax:** 020-8443-9118
**Web:** www.tri-star.co.uk
**Reg No:** 2542502 **Estd:** 2012 Private Limited Company
**Line of Business:** Food packers
**Export Markets:** Europe; Far East
**Issued Capital:** £1,002
**Principals:** K B Curran (Managing), K B Prosser
**Co. Secretary:** Kevin Curran
**Responsibilities**
**Sales:** Lee Richards (Sales Manager)
**US SIC:** 3551 **UK SIC:** 32441
**Auditors:** Brindley Goldstein Ltd
**Bankers:** Barclays Bank Plc (20-29-77)

|      | 31-12-13 | 31-12-12 | 31-12-11 |
|------|----------|----------|----------|
| TO   | 23,587,638 | 21,442,267 | 19,466,671 |
| P/L  | 1,008,164 | 926,154 | 948,870 |
| NW   | 2,503,027 | 2,043,692 | 1,571,142 |
| WC   | 2,073,354 | 1,687,989 | 1,310,332 |
| Emp. | 130 | 120 | 103 |

**DUNS 39-996-9443** Exp

## Triad Group Plc

Weyside Park, Godalming, Surrey GU7 1XE
**Web:** www.triadgroup.plc.uk
**Reg No:** 2285049 **VAT No:** 492999762
**Estd:** 1988 Public Limited Company
**Line of Business:** Computer software (development)
**Export Markets:** E U
**Issued Capital:** £151,496
**Principals:** J C Rigg (Chairman), N E Burrows, A M Fulton, S M Sanderson
**Co. Secretary:** Nicholas Burrows
**Responsibilities**
**Senior:** Ian Haynes (Manager)
**Marketing:** Tim Eckes (Principal Consultant)
**HR:** Nick Waite (Human Resources Manager)
**US SIC:** 7379 **UK SIC:** 83940
**Auditors:** BDO LLP
**Bankers:** Bank Of Scotland (12-01-03)

|      | 31-03-14 | 31-03-13 | 31-03-12 |
|------|----------|----------|----------|
| TO   | 19,702,000 | 18,880,000 | 19,447,000 |
| P/L  | 11,000 | 28,000 | (76,000) |
| NW   | 327,000 | 191,000 | 98,000 |
| WC   | 839,000 | 830,000 | 1,017,000 |
| Emp. | 57 | 65 | 66 |

**DUNS 23-584-7279**

## Triage Central Ltd

(**Subsidiary of:** Dynamus Group Ltd)
Unit 22h, Stirling, Stirlingshire FK7 7QQ
**Tel:** 01786-451513
**Web:** www.triagecentral.co.uk
**Reg No:** 0186908SC **Estd:** 1997 Private Limited Company
**Line of Business:** Employment and recruitment companies and consultants
**Issued Capital:** £20,000
**Principals:** Ms K Carnegie (Managing), Ms G Kennedy, Mrs L K Henderson, L A Entwistle, D J Cowie, Ms J M Dewar, Ms S J Sanderson, Miss A Smith
**Co. Secretary:** Brian Donaldson
**Responsibilities**
**Senior:** Elaine Mcmahon (Centre Manager)
**Finance:** Marion McLachlan (Office Manager)
**Admin:** Margaret Hunter (Office Manager), Marion McLachlan (Office Manager)
**IT:** Lynn McAllister (Systems Manager)
**Facilities:** John McBride (Commercial Manager)
**Operations:** Margaret Hunter (Office Manager)
**Branches:** Triage Central Ltd, Carron House, Carron Way, Glasgow, Lanarkshire G67 1ER
**US SIC:** 7361 **UK SIC:** 83954
**Auditors:** Tindell, Grant & Co

|      | 31-03-14 | 31-03-13 | 31-03-12 |
|------|----------|----------|----------|
| TO   | 12,326,052 | 9,603,941 | 7,962,630 |
| P/L  | 3,221,610 | 964,942 | 836,481 |
| NW   | 1,567,594 | 1,070,145 | 941,205 |
| WC   | 1,334,870 | 702,269 | 722,190 |
| Emp. | 237 | 220 | 219 |

**DUNS 53-654-5205** Imp

## Triage Services Ltd

(**Subsidiary of:** Triage Holdings Ltd)
1st Floor, Stevenage, Hertfordshire SG1 2EF
**Tel:** 01438213000 **Fax:** 01438313748
**Web:** www.triage-services.com
**Reg No:** 3459830 **VAT No:** 700335586
**Estd:** 2002 Private Limited Company
**Line of Business:** Cash register and epos equipment
**Export Sales:** £1,308,000
**Issued Capital:** £500,000
**Directors:** S Ralph, M J Norris
**Co. Secretary:** Steven Ralph
**Responsibilities**
**Senior:** Vince Hann (Manager), Gary Moinet (Manager), Fay Simmons (Human Resources Manager)
**Finance:** Nicola Eversley (Finance Controller)
**IT:** Louis Kotze (Information Technology And Ser)
**HR:** Fay Simmons (Human Resources Manager)
**Operations:** Claire Bolton (Operations Support Manager)
**Branches:** Triage Services Ltd, 7 South Gyle Crescent, Edinburgh, Midlothian EH12 9EB
**US SIC:** 7379 **UK SIC:** 83940
**Auditors:** PricewaterhouseCoopers LLP
**Bankers:** The Royal Bank Of Scotland Plc (15-20-25)

|      | 31-12-13 | 31-12-12 | 31-12-11 |
|------|----------|----------|----------|
| TO   | 8,488,000 | 8,961,000 | 8,797,000 |
| P/L  | (4,000) | 308,000 | 716,000 |
| NW   | 3,365,000 | 3,288,000 | 3,033,000 |
| WC   | 3,607,000 | 3,557,000 | 3,204,000 |
| Emp. | 146 | 141 | 137 |

**DUNS 76-951-4647**

## Triangle Estate & Petroleum Ltd

Merrick Road, Southall, Middlesex UB2 4AU
**Tel:** 02088439436 **Fax:** 02088439436
**Web:** www.firstgreatwestern.co.uk
**Reg No:** 2556827 **Estd:** 1990 Private Limited Company
**Line of Business:** Petrol service stations
**Trading Style:** Triangle Southall
**Issued Capital:** £1
**Directors:** P W Featherstone, S B Chicksand
**US SIC:** 6711, 5541
**UK SIC:** 83962, 65200
**Bankers:** The Royal Bank Of Scotland Plc (15-10-00)

|    | 31-03-14 | 31-03-13 | 31-03-12 |
|----|----------|----------|----------|
| TA | 96 | 96 | 96 |
| NW | 96 | 96 | 96 |

**DUNS 42-455-9433**

## Triangle Housing Association

60 Eastermeade Gardens, Ballymoney, Co Antrim BT53 6BD
**Tel:** 028-2766-6880 **Fax:** 028-2766-2994
**Web:** www.trianglehousing.org.uk
**Reg No:** 0000193IP **Estd:** 1977 Friendly Society
**Line of Business:** Housing associations societies trusts & co-operatives
**Principals:** Ms S Dwyer (Chairman), Ms K Mackenzie, Ms M Nesbitt, Ms O Boyle, Ms L Dougherty, Ms A Watters, Ms J Kerr, Ms B Conway
**Responsibilities**
**Senior:** Betty Christie (Partner), Hilary Hamill (Designated Limited Liability P), Avril Watson (Manager)
**Branches:** Triangle Housing Association, 7 Tower Court, 9 Warden Street, Ballymena, Co Antrim BT43 7DT
**US SIC:** 8321 **UK SIC:** 96111
**Auditors:** Crawford Sedgewick & Co
**Bankers:** Northern Bank Ltd (95-02-77)
**Employees:** 98

**DUNS 54-374-9741**

## Triangle Lift Services Ltd

8 Windmill Road Windmill Business Park, Clevedon, Avon BS21 6SR
**Tel:** 01275-344050 **Fax:** 01275344051
**Web:** www.trianglelifts.co.uk
**Reg No:** 3262929 **Estd:** 1983 Private Limited Company
**Line of Business:** Manufacture of lifting and handling equipment
**Issued Capital:** £100
**Directors:** C R Mills, Ms A M Mills, R S Hooper
**Co. Secretary:** Ms Sandra Hooper
**US SIC:** 3534 **UK SIC:** 32553
**Auditors:** Alanbrookes Ltd

|    | 30-11-13 | 30-11-12 | 30-11-11 |
|----|----------|----------|----------|
| TA | 1,965,523 | 1,608,835 | 1,805,212 |
| NW | 928,600 | 864,923 | 787,844 |
| WC | 751,097 | 694,731 | 641,866 |

DUNS 21-215-2664
## Triangle Motor Co. Ltd
Newport Road, Brough, North Humberside HU15 2NZ
**Tel:** 01430-425038 **Fax:** 01482227780
**Reg No:** 0435273 **Estd:** 1963 Private Limited Company
**Line of Business:** Retail sale of automotive fuel
**Issued Capital:** £8,292
**Principals:** J N Hardy *(Financial)*, Mrs J M Hardy, Ms A L Wright, Mrs A C Bogg
**Co. Secretary:** Alan Moore
**Branches:** Triangle Motor Co. Ltd, South Orbital Trading Park, Unit 1, Hull, North Humberside HU9 1NJ
**US SIC:** 5541, 5531
**UK SIC:** 65200, 65100
**Auditors:** Duton Moore
**Bankers:** National Westminster Bank Plc (56-00-06)

| | 28-02-14 | 28-02-13 | 29-02-12 |
|---|---|---|---|
| TO | 15,031,459 | 14,851,273 | 15,103,532 |
| P/L | 121,478 | 32,841 | 51,394 |
| NW | 5,618,115 | 5,697,556 | 5,754,485 |
| WC | 1,962,169 | 2,228,819 | 2,452,059 |
| Emp. | 63 | 58 | 54 |

DUNS 21-324-8214 Exp
## Triangle Wholefoods Collective Ltd
Unit G15, Lacy Way, Elland, West Yorkshire HX5 9DB
**Tel:** 01422313840
**Web:** www.suma.coop
**Reg No:** 0021975IP **VAT No:** 313417003
**Estd:** 1975 Friendly Society
**Line of Business:** Frozen foods (wholesale)
**Export Markets:** Europe, Rest of the World
**Export Sales:** £3,541,939
**Trading Style:** Suma, Suma Wholefoods
**Directors:** J Hayhurst, D Weaver, G Hewitt, M Pinnell, M Stocks, Ms R Owens, Ms M Li, D Rebout
**Co. Secretary:** G Findley
**Responsibilities**
**Senior:** Alex Stappard *(Sales & Marketing Coordinator)*
**Marketing:** Alex Stappard *(Sales & Marketing Coordinator)*
**Sales:** Alex Stappard *(Sales & Marketing Coordinator)*
**US SIC:** 5149 **UK SIC:** 61700
**Auditors:** PM & M Solutions for Business LLP
**Bankers:** National Westminster Bank Plc (60-60-05)

| | 29-09-13 | 30-09-12 | 30-09-11 |
|---|---|---|---|
| TO | 33,771,838 | 29,987,636 | 27,850,562 |
| P/L | 290,731 | 239,584 | 216,036 |
| NW | 2,901,101 | 2,674,555 | 2,682,385 |
| WC | 2,123,181 | 2,342,589 | 2,119,413 |
| Emp. | 168 | 161 | 153 |

DUNS 22-275-9107
## Triangular Care Services Ltd
Main House, 29-31 Main Road, Wellingborough, Northamptonshire NN8 2UB
**Tel:** 01933272497
**Reg No:** 4293789 **Estd:** 2001 Private Limited Company
**Line of Business:** Home care service providers
**Issued Capital:** £6
**Director:** Mrs J Rutter
**Co. Secretary:** George Spikesley
**US SIC:** 8091 **UK SIC:** 95200
**Auditors:** Cottons Accountants LLP

| | 31-05-14 | 31-05-13 | 31-05-12 |
|---|---|---|---|
| TA | 182,269 | 177,604 | 192,974 |
| NW | 141,718 | 133,244 | 141,507 |
| WC | 138,555 | 128,971 | 139,941 |

DUNS 39-809-3112 Imp-Exp
## Triax U K Ltd
**(Subsidiary of:** Nielsen & Nielsen Holding A/S)
Unit 14, Treorchy, Mid Glamorgan CF42 6DL
**Tel:** 01443-778908
**Web:** www.triax.co.uk
**Reg No:** 2213714 **VAT No:** 492045252
**Estd:** 1988 Private Limited Company
**Line of Business:** Manufacturers general
**Export Markets:** Denmark; U S A
**Export Sales:** £997,005
**Issued Capital:** £1,000
**Directors:** C Omann, G Vaughan
**Co. Secretary:** Kevin Laken
**Responsibilities**
**Senior:** Jorgen Nederby *(Manager)*
**US SIC:** 7394, 4582
**UK SIC:** 84000, 76400
**Auditors:** Meadows & Co
**Bankers:** Den Danske Bank Aktieselskab (30-12-81)

| | 30-04-14 | 30-04-13 | 30-04-12 |
|---|---|---|---|
| TO | 10,626,330 | 10,759,085 | 12,593,470 |
| P/L | 1,131,239 | 1,176,289 | 1,845,070 |
| NW | 1,866,176 | 2,750,805 | 3,038,925 |
| WC | 1,373,354 | 2,235,246 | 2,658,129 |
| Emp. | 49 | 43 | 47 |

DUNS 21-605-3784
## Tribal Group
Unit 6 Hesslewood Office Park, Ferriby Road, Hessle, North Humberside HU13 0PD
**Tel:** 01482647220
**Web:** www.tribalgroup.com
**Estd:** 2011 Proprietorship
**Line of Business:** Computer software (development)
**Proprietor:** Mrs M Simpson
**US SIC:** 7379 **UK SIC:** 83940
**Employees:** 60

DUNS 22-109-5768
## Tribal Group Plc
Kings Orchard, Bristol, Avon BS2 0HQ
**Tel:** 08451236001
**Web:** www.tribalgroup.co.uk
**Reg No:** 4128850 **Estd:** 2000 Public Limited Company
**Line of Business:** Education services
**Export Sales:** £32,776,000
**Issued Capital:** £4,684,799
**Directors:** S D Breach, D J Egan, J Ormerod, Lady K C Innes Ker, Dr K M Evans, R J Crewe
**Co. Secretary:** Robert Ewin
**Responsibilities**
**Sales:** Steve Hope *(Software Sales Director)*
**HR:** Virginia Rothwell *(Group Human Resources Director)*
**Branches:** Tribal Group Plc, Suite 2, Saturn Centre, Greenbank Technology Park Challenge Way, Blackburn, Lancashire BB1 5QB
**US SIC:** 8299 **UK SIC:** 93300
**Auditors:** Deloitte LLP
**Bankers:** Bank Of Scotland (80-07-48)

| | 31-12-13 | 31-12-12 | 31-12-11 |
|---|---|---|---|
| TO | 125,485,000 | 115,395,000 | 108,231,000 |
| P/L | 13,497,000 | 9,973,000 | 3,740,000 |
| NW | (27,154,000) | (26,868,000) | (32,384,000) |
| WC | (19,193,000) | (12,832,000) | (11,962,000) |
| Emp. | 1,415 | 1,395 | 1,456 |

DUNS 22-183-3291
## Tribourne Catering Services Ltd
48c Middle Hillgate, Stockport, Cheshire SK1 3DL
**Tel:** 0161-477-6780 **Fax:** 01614771357
**Web:** www.tribourne.co.uk
**Reg No:** 4201668 **Estd:** 2001 Private Limited Company
**Line of Business:** Licensed restaurants
**Issued Capital:** £100
**Director:** Ms B Hopkins
**Co. Secretary:** Stephen Kelly
**Responsibilities**
**Finance:** Mike Bateman *(Financial Director)*
**US SIC:** 5812, 7399
**UK SIC:** 66110, 83954
**Auditors:** Harold Sharp

| | 31-10-14 | 31-10-13 | 31-10-12 |
|---|---|---|---|
| TA | 402,032 | 247,276 | 413,629 |
| NW | (125,104) | (182,768) | (50,281) |
| WC | (161,306) | (242,138) | (120,714) |

DUNS 21-414-0017
## The Tribunals Service
Victory House, London WC2B 6EX
**Tel:** 020-72738641
**Web:** www.employmenttribunals.co.uk
**Proprietorship**
**Line of Business:** Central government
**Principals:** B Ayling *(Chairman)*, S Gillspie *(Financial)*, K Sadler, S Mcnally, P Handcock
**Responsibilities**
**Senior:** Nicole Leen *(Office Manager)*, Shaun McNally *(Director)*
**US SIC:** 9211 **UK SIC:** 91200
**Employees:** 50

DUNS 73-933-8903
## Tricon Services Ltd
**(Subsidiary of:** Mjf Holdings Ltd)
Silkwood Court, Ossett, West Yorkshire WF5 9TP
**Tel:** 01924-237450 **Fax:** 01924237451
**Web:** www.triconservices.co.uk
**Reg No:** 2940505 **VAT No:** 642764133
**Estd:** 2012 Private Limited Company
**Line of Business:** Electrical contractors and electricians
**Trading Style:** Tricon Services Ltd
**Issued Capital:** £92,783
**Managing Director:** M J Firth
**Co. Secretary:** Steven Raikes
**Responsibilities**
**Finance:** David Vautrey *(finance Manager)*
**Branches:** Tricon Services Ltd, Fieldhouse Industrial Estate, Fieldhouse Road, Rochdale, Lancashire OL12 0AA
**US SIC:** 1731, 1711
**UK SIC:** 50300
**Auditors:** Henton & Co

**Bankers:** National Westminster Bank Plc (55-70-23)

| | 30-06-13 | 30-06-12 | 30-06-11 |
|---|---|---|---|
| TA | 1,828,758 | 1,918,898 | 2,036,328 |
| NW | 682,941 | 614,726 | 847,190 |
| WC | 581,216 | 505,471 | 739,075 |

DUNS 23-518-3907
## Tricrest Homes Ltd
2 Burringham Road, Scunthorpe, South Humberside DN17 2BB
**Tel:** 01724-856963 **Fax:** 01724857989
**Web:** www.tricresthomes.com
**Reg No:** 3517455 **Estd:** 1999 Private Limited Company
**Line of Business:** Nursing homes
**Trading Style:** Sycamore Lodge Management
**Issued Capital:** £403
**Directors:** B Marjara, S L Marjara, S Marjara
**Co. Secretary:** Apr Secretaries Ltd
**US SIC:** 8051 **UK SIC:** 95100

| | 30-04-14 | 30-04-13 | 30-04-12 |
|---|---|---|---|
| TA | 1,474,482 | 1,276,816 | 1,335,134 |
| NW | 277,265 | 241,966 | 135,387 |
| WC | 267,837 | 267,763 | 183,712 |

DUNS 23-619-7633
## Trident Building Consultancy Ltd
10 King William Street, London EC4N 7TW
**Tel:** 020-7280-8181 **Fax:** 02072426838
**Web:** www.tridentbc.com
**Reg No:** 3616946 **Estd:** 1998 Private Limited Company
**Line of Business:** Technical testing and analysis
**Issued Capital:** £270
**Directors:** R N Watts, S Rutherford, M J Tracey, D M Roe, K Richards, A M Walker, T V Dowd, M Clare
**Co. Secretary:** M & R Secretarial Services Limit
**Responsibilities**
**Senior:** Carl Dawson *(Director)*, Craig Keogh *(Director)*, Craig Mcguire *(Director)*, Owen Pottle *(Director)*, Scott Young *(Director)*
**US SIC:** 7397, 8911
**UK SIC:** 83702, 83701
**Auditors:** AEL Partners LLP
**Bankers:** The Royal Bank Of Scotland Plc (16-75-75)

| | 31-03-14 | 31-03-13 | 31-03-12 |
|---|---|---|---|
| TA | 1,779,761 | 1,146,634 | 1,115,941 |
| NW | 597,432 | 458,200 | 617,266 |
| WC | 543,633 | 415,324 | 545,695 |

DUNS 29-763-9171 Imp-Exp
## Trident Foams Ltd
B K B House, Station Road Goyt Valley Industrial, Estate, High Peak, Derbyshire SK23 7SN
**Web:** www.tridentfoams.co.uk
**Reg No:** 2026997 **Estd:** 1986 Private Limited Company
**Line of Business:** Manufacture of other plastic products
**Export Markets:** Worldwide
**Issued Capital:** £466,200
**Director:** C F Kenyon
**Co. Secretary:** Charles Kenyon
**Responsibilities**
**IT:** Malcolm Longmate *(Accountant)*
**Facilities:** Andy Kendall *(Chief Maintenance Engineer)*
**US SIC:** 3079 **UK SIC:** 48360
**Auditors:** Parker Gradwell & Co
**Bankers:** National Westminster Bank Plc (01-10-01)

| | 31-03-14 | 31-03-13 | 31-03-12 |
|---|---|---|---|
| TA | 2,876,190 | 2,711,447 | 2,880,159 |
| NW | 2,043,291 | 1,962,252 | 2,034,904 |
| WC | 931,652 | 860,265 | 969,648 |

DUNS 21-727-2046
## Trident Garages Ltd
Guildford Road, Ottershaw, Chertsey, Surrey KT16 0NZ
**Tel:** 01932-874411
**Web:** www.shell.co.uk
**Reg No:** 0764299 **VAT No:** 211420040
**Estd:** 1963 Private Limited Company
**Line of Business:** Retail sale of automotive fuel
**Trading Style:** Trident Honda
**Issued Capital:** £211,200
**Principals:** R M Roberts *(Managing)*, J Roberts, S N Henderson
**Co. Secretary:** Christopher Roberts
**Responsibilities**
**Senior:** Terry Stickland *(General Services Manager)*
**Health & Safety:** Terry Stickland *(General Services Manager)*
**Facilities:** Terry Stickland *(General Services Manager)*
**Branches:** Trident Garages Ltd, Portsmouth Road, Thames Ditton, Surrey KT7 0EQ
**US SIC:** 5541, 5521, 7539

**UK SIC:** 65200, 65100, 67100
**Auditors:** The Dyer Partnership
**Bankers:** Barclays Bank Plc (20-35-35)

| | 31-12-13 | 31-12-12 | 31-12-11 |
|---|---|---|---|
| TO | 26,512,280 | 26,379,136 | 24,955,346 |
| P/L | 73,965 | 82,819 | (129,376) |
| NW | 3,862,016 | 3,803,664 | 3,712,169 |
| WC | (744,935) | (122,228) | (625,513) |
| Emp. | 96 | 97 | 102 |

DUNS 23-261-3463
## Trident Housing Association Ltd
239 Holliday Street, Birmingham, West Midlands B1 1SJ
**Fax:** 0121-643-0260
**Web:** www.trident-ha.org.uk
**Reg No:** 0017133IP **VAT No:** 487183802
**Estd:** 1965 Friendly Society
**Line of Business:** Housing associations societies trusts & co-operatives
**Issued Capital:** £2
**Principals:** F Slater *(Chairman)*, M Mclean, L Graham, N Jones, C Harte, D Hart, G King, L Bodart
**Co. Secretary:** P Roden
**Responsibilities**
**Senior:** V Brittin *(Director)*, Rebecca Fownes *(Communication Manager)*, J Hargrave *(Director)*
**Finance:** Noel Grace *(Financial Director)*
**IT:** Edward Reed *(Computer Manager)*
**Purchasing:** Noel Grace *(Financial Director)*
**Branches:** Trident Housing Association Ltd, 87 Stirling Rd, Birmingham, West Midlands B16 9BD
**US SIC:** 8321 **UK SIC:** 96111
**Auditors:** Mazars Neville Russell

| | 31-03-12 | 31-03-11 | 31-03-10 |
|---|---|---|---|
| TO | 29,619,000 | 27,735,000 | 23,414,000 |
| P/L | 1,683,000 | 1,342,000 | 971,000 |
| NW | 12,434,000 | 10,924,000 | 9,176,000 |
| WC | 3,016,000 | 1,001,000 | (478,000) |
| Emp. | 645 | 570 | 470 |

DUNS 21-699-0853 Imp
## Tridonic Uk Ltd
**(Subsidiary of:** Zumtobel Group Ag)
Unit 7, Lindenwood, Crockford Lane, Basingstoke, Hampshire RG24 8LB
**Tel:** 01256-374300 **Fax:** 01256-374200
**Web:** www.tridonic.com
**Reg No:** 0887600 **Estd:** 1966 Private Limited Company
**Line of Business:** Manufacture of lighting equipment and electric lamps
**Issued Capital:** £8,789,000
**Directors:** R C Strode, D B Barnby
**Co. Secretary:** Nigel Dew
**Responsibilities**
**Senior:** Gavin Brydon *(Manager)*, David Hawes *(Manager)*, Rudiger Kofahl *(Manager (Austria))*, Peter Novak *(Manager)*
**Facilities:** Gavin Brydon *(Manager)*
**Branches:** Tridonic Uk Ltd, Butchers Race, Greenlane Industr, Spennymoor, County Durham DL16 6JE
**US SIC:** 3648, 5065
**UK SIC:** 34702, 61500
**Auditors:** KPMG LLP
**Bankers:** Barclays Bank Plc (20-05-00)

| | 30-04-13 | 30-04-12 | 30-04-11 |
|---|---|---|---|
| TO | 62,714,524 | 65,919,838 | 73,778,693 |
| P/L | 1,483,534 | 1,703,352 | 3,541,709 |
| NW | 11,332,347 | 11,401,658 | 12,731,416 |
| WC | 6,864,329 | 6,743,088 | 7,675,701 |
| Emp. | 168 | 174 | 158 |

DUNS 21-312-2740
## Triesse Ltd
**(Subsidiary of:** Triesse Group Ltd)
Lancaster Close Sherburn Enterprise Park, Sherburn In Elmet, Leeds, West Yorkshire LS25 6NS
**Tel:** 01977-687600 **Fax:** 01977-687601
**Web:** www.triesseltd.co.uk
**Reg No:** 1196158 **VAT No:** 184568523
**Estd:** 1975 Private Limited Company
**Line of Business:** Wooden goods other than furniture
**Export Sales:** £30,730
**Issued Capital:** £10,000
**Directors:** S D Holdsworth, J D Nield, G Mccardle, D J Colman, M J Meyer
**Responsibilities**
**Senior:** Rachel Stoker *(Manager)*
**US SIC:** 2499, 5039
**UK SIC:** 46500, 61300
**Auditors:** Clough & Co LLP
**Bankers:** Barclays Bank Plc (20-48-42)

| | 31-03-14 | 31-03-13 | 31-03-12 |
|---|---|---|---|
| TO | 14,165,594 | 13,093,091 | 12,421,832 |
| P/L | 930,551 | 638,829 | 611,215 |
| NW | 3,917,384 | 3,210,586 | 2,771,304 |
| WC | 3,483,440 | 2,784,166 | 2,473,615 |
| Emp. | 63 | 63 | 62 |

DUNS 29-555-4216 **Exp**

## Trifast Plc

Trifast House, Bolton Close, Uckfield, East Sussex TN22 1QW

**Tel:** 01825747366 **Fax:** 01825747368

**Web:** www.trifast.com

**Reg No:** 1919797 **VAT No:** 390068451

**Estd:** 1994 Public Limited Company

**Line of Business:** Manufacturers of bolts and fixings

**Export Sales:** £66,538,000

**Trading Style:** Tr, Tr Fastenings

**Issued Capital:** £5,343,385

**Principals:** M M Diamond *(Chairman and Managing)*, G P Budd *(Marketing)*, S Mac Meekin, J P Shearman, Mrs G C Roberts, M Belton, N S Chapman, J C Barker

**Co. Secretary:** Mark Belton

**Responsibilities**

**Senior:** Daniel Baldock *(Manager)*, Jim Barker *(Chief Executive Officer)*, Jerry Howe *(Manager)*, Steve Meiklem *(General Manager, TR Northern R)*

**Marketing:** Abi Burnett *(Marketing Manager)*

**HR:** Louise Hobden *(Human Resources Assistant)*, Helen Toole *(HR Advisor)*

**Branches:** Trifast Plc, T R Fastenings Ltd, Trifast House, Uckfield, East Sussex TN22 1QW

**US SIC:** 3452 **UK SIC:** 31371

**Auditors:** KPMG Audit PLC

**Bankers:** HSBC Bank plc (40-09-25)

| | 31-03-14 | 31-03-13 | 31-03-12 |
|---|---|---|---|
| TO | 129,775,000 | 121,544,000 | 112,510,000 |
| P/L | 8,874,000 | 6,442,000 | 4,759,000 |
| NW | 44,708,000 | 42,056,000 | 35,619,000 |
| WC | 35,871,000 | 33,755,000 | 28,478,000 |
| Emp. | 1,038 | 1,027 | 907 |

DUNS 21-704-0316

## Triffitt Trailers U.K. Ltd

Unit C16-C18 Junction 7 Business Park, Blackburn Road, Accrington, Lancashire BB5 5JW

**Tel:** 01759372459

**Web:** www.triffitttrailers.co.uk

**Reg No:** 7482377 **Estd:** 2002 Private Limited Company

**Line of Business:** Manufacture of trailers and semi-trailers

**Issued Capital:** £100

**Directors:** J Harrison, C H Mckelvey, S Chapman

**US SIC:** 3715 **UK SIC:** 35220

| | 30-11-13 | 30-11-12 | 30-11-11 |
|---|---|---|---|
| TA | 1 | 100 | 100 |
| NW | 1 | 100 | 100 |

DUNS 22-668-4694 **Imp-Exp**

## Trifibre Ltd

(**Subsidiary of:** Trifibre Group Ltd)

17 Boston Road, Leicester, Leicestershire LE4 1AW

**Fax:** 01473811873

**Web:** www.trifibre.co.uk

**Reg No:** 1890698 **VAT No:** 395523231

**Estd:** 1985 Private Limited Company

**Line of Business:** Manufacturers of cases

**Export Markets:** Europe

**Issued Capital:** £40,723

**Principals:** N N Cox *(Financial)*, C D Cox, Mrs L H Cox, M Champaneria, M K Truman

**Co. Secretary:** Ms Lucia Cox

**Responsibilities**

**Senior:** John Burley *(Manager)*

**Sales:** Sophie Roberts *(Sales Manager)*

**Branches:** Trifibre Ltd, 14 The Studio Oldbury Business, Oldbury Business Pk,Oldbury Rd, Cwmbran, Gwent NP44 3JU

**US SIC:** 3999, 3079

**UK SIC:** 49590, 48360

**Auditors:** Mark J. Rees Chartered Accountants

**Bankers:** National Westminster Bank Plc (60-60-06)

| | 31-03-14 | 31-03-13 | 31-03-12 |
|---|---|---|---|
| TA | 2,612,070 | 2,273,538 | 2,061,552 |
| NW | 541,222 | 477,123 | 468,107 |
| WC | 119,111 | 84,359 | 73,938 |

DUNS 21-677-0857

## Triggerdown Ltd

Denton Holme Sawmills, Denton Street, Carlisle, Cumbria CA2 5EQ

**Tel:** 01933-223301

**Reg No:** 7284161 **Estd:** 2010 Private Limited Company

**Line of Business:** Business services

**Issued Capital:** £50,000

**Directors:** M Barker, V Woods

**Co. Secretary:** Ms Christine Barker

**US SIC:** 7399 **UK SIC:** 83954

| | 31-12-13 | 31-12-12 | 31-12-11 |
|---|---|---|---|
| TO | 9,083,967 | 8,495,180 | 7,917,394 |
| P/L | 213,775 | 138,345 | 55,718 |
| NW | 886,491 | 826,729 | 815,213 |
| WC | 642,733 | 602,171 | 763,686 |
| Emp. | 57 | 57 | 54 |

DUNS 50-597-0806

## Trilam Technology Ltd

7 Shaftesbury Avenue, Bedford, Bedfordshire MK40 3SA

**Tel:** 01234-881471

**Reg No:** 2535669 **Estd:** 1990 Private Limited Company

**Line of Business:** Management and business consultants

**Issued Capital:** £200

**Directors:** C Buxton, A Christensen

**Co. Secretary:** Ms Karen Christensen

**US SIC:** 7392 **UK SIC:** 83951

**Auditors:** Lithgow Perkins LLP

| | 31-12-13 | 31-12-12 | 31-12-11 |
|---|---|---|---|
| TA | 48,390 | 80,487 | 111,997 |
| NW | 6,727 | 12,239 | 51,547 |
| WC | 6,079 | 10,714 | 49,302 |

DUNS 21-658-6194 **Imp**

## Trilanco Ltd

Bracewell Avenue, Poulton Le Fylde Industrial Esta, Poulton Industrial Estate, Poulton-Le-Fylde, Lancashire FY6 8JF

**Tel:** 01253-891697

**Web:** www.trilanco.com

**Reg No:** 7148679 **Estd:** 1979 Private Limited Company

**Line of Business:** Agents specialising in the sale of particular products or ranges of products not elsewhere classified

**Export Sales:** £431,890

**Issued Capital:** £1,021

**Directors:** D Balmer, M Balmer, Ms J W Holmes, Ms L Balmer

**US SIC:** 0741, 5199

**UK SIC:** 95601, 61900

**Auditors:** Barbara M. Thompson

**Bankers:** HSBC Bank plc (40-37-20)

| | 30-04-14 | 30-04-13 | 30-04-12 |
|---|---|---|---|
| TO | 50,917,289 | 44,094,027 | 31,746,479 |
| P/L | 1,143,751 | 1,195,943 | 898,250 |
| NW | 2,162,569 | 834,576 | (119,229) |
| WC | 1,895,662 | 543,414 | (422,268) |
| Emp. | 87 | 67 | 50 |

DUNS 21-113-1974

## Triland Metals Ltd

(**Subsidiary of:** Mitsubishi Corporation)

Mid City Place, 71 High Holborn, London WC1V 6BA

**Tel:** 02070615500 **Fax:** 02070615623

**Web:** www.triland.com

**Reg No:** 1011637 **VAT No:** 244154187

**Estd:** 1971 Private Limited Company

**Line of Business:** Financial intermediation not elsewhere classified

**Trading Style:** Triland Metals Ltd

**Issued Capital:** £15,000,000

**Directors:** K Ishikawa, T Nambu, Y Nasu, M J Pratt, N Tsubonuma, T A Wilkinson, H Hayashi, J A Wilson

**Co. Secretary:** Guy Usher

**Responsibilities**

**Senior:** Daiju Mita *(Director)*, Hideki Nakagawa *(Chairman)*, Herwig Schmidt *(Sales & Marketing Manager)*, Keiichi Shiobara *(Director)*

**Marketing:** Herwig Schmidt *(Sales & Marketing Manager)*

**Sales:** Herwig Schmidt *(Sales & Marketing Manager)*

**US SIC:** 6111 **UK SIC:** 81501

**Auditors:** Deloitte & Touche LLP

**Bankers:** HSBC Bank plc (40-00-04)

| | 31-03-14 | 31-03-13 | 31-03-12 |
|---|---|---|---|
| TA | 702,568,591 | 705,370,384 | 536,585,856 |
| P/L | 8,939,751 | 39,155,814 | 8,438,529 |
| NW | 45,950,398 | 71,067,376 | 61,027,293 |
| WC | 101,840,371 | 139,692,685 | 126,100,034 |
| Emp. | 61 | 57 | 56 |

DUNS 64-092-2472

## Trillium Holdings Ltd

(**Subsidiary of:** London Wall Outsourcing Investments Ltd)

Bastion House, 140 London Wall, London EC2Y 5DN

**Fax:** 02077965501

**Web:** www.telerealtrillium.com

**Reg No:** 3487308 **Estd:** 1944 Private Limited Company

**Line of Business:** Management of real estate on a fee or contract basis

**Issued Capital:** £25,000,000

**Directors:** W Persky, A Dakin, G H Edwards, R C Gurnhill

**Co. Secretary:** Aaron Burns

**Responsibilities**

**Senior:** David Godden *(Manager)*

**Branches:** Trillium Holdings Ltd, Bastion House, 140 London Wall, London EC2Y 5DN

**US SIC:** 6531 **UK SIC:** 83400

**Auditors:** PricewaterhouseCoopers LLP

| | 31-03-14 | 31-03-13 | 31-03-12 |
|---|---|---|---|
| TO | 676,468,000 | 710,909,000 | 687,395,000 |
| P/L | 113,964,000 | 111,621,000 | 91,297,000 |
| NW | 190,049,000 | 227,172,000 | 284,799,000 |
| WC | (86,045,000) | 45,031,000 | 3,721,000 |
| Emp. | 784 | 790 | 662 |

DUNS 23-567-2412 **Imp**

## Trilogy Communications Holdings Ltd

Unit 26 Focus 303 Business Centre, Focus Way, Andover, Hampshire SP10 5NY

**Tel:** 01264-384000

**Web:** www.trilogycomms.com

**Reg No:** 3565367 **Estd:** 1998 Private Limited Company

**Line of Business:** Television activities

**Export Sales:** £3,033,405

**Trading Style:** Trilogy Communications Ltd

**Issued Capital:** £69,800

**Directors:** B C Hewitt, R W Hartman, M D Peck, I R Henderson

**Responsibilities**

**Marketing:** Andy Covey *(Marketing Manager)*

**IT:** Joe Ellis *(IT Manager)*

**US SIC:** 4833, 4899

**UK SIC:** 97411, 79020

**Auditors:** Fiander Tovell LLP

**Bankers:** Bank Of Scotland (12-09-61)

| | 28-02-14 | 28-02-13 | 29-02-12 |
|---|---|---|---|
| TO | 4,005,145 | 4,948,089 | 8,555,316 |
| P/L | (1,352,360) | (1,450,795) | 449,289 |
| NW | (4,049,684) | (2,798,688) | (1,406,026) |
| WC | 770,195 | 789,749 | 2,261,625 |
| Emp. | 41 | 48 | 55 |

DUNS 52-037-3655 **Imp**

## Trimark Europe Ltd

(**Subsidiary of:** Trimark Corporation)

Unit B Cedar Court, Bardon Hill, Coalville, Leicestershire LE67 1TU

**Tel:** 01530-512460

**Web:** www.trimarkeu.com

**Reg No:** 3403771 **Estd:** 1997 Private Limited Company

**Line of Business:** Manufacturers of automotive components

**Export Sales:** £5,826,660

**Issued Capital:** £3,125,000

**Directors:** J B Grace, S Perkins, R L Marzolf, K D Dolbear, C P Webb, Ms K K Knowlton

**Co. Secretary:** Christopher Webb

**Responsibilities**

**Senior:** Patricia Knowlton *(Manager)*

**Sales:** Gregory Tebb *(Sales Director)*

**US SIC:** 3714, 3423

**UK SIC:** 35300, 31612

**Auditors:** Ernst & Young LLP

**Bankers:** Barclays Bank Plc (20-63-66)

| | 31-12-13 | 31-12-12 | 31-12-11 |
|---|---|---|---|
| TO | 7,693,883 | 7,739,601 | 8,085,394 |
| P/L | 257,036 | 138,625 | 1,168 |
| NW | 1,420,408 | 1,198,030 | 1,060,857 |
| WC | 1,335,953 | 2,080,295 | 1,787,079 |
| Emp. | 56 | 59 | 59 |

DUNS 22-068-2558 **Imp**

## Trimble Uk Ltd

(**Subsidiary of:** Trimble Navigation Limited Inc)

1 Bath Street, 48 Felaw Street, Ipswich, Suffolk IP2 8SD

**Tel:** 01473696300 **Fax:** 01473696444

**Web:** www.trimble.com

**Reg No:** 4069823 **Estd:** 2000 Private Limited Company

**Line of Business:** Electrical products (sales)

**Issued Capital:** £76,413

**Directors:** J H Heelas, S Berglund, B Fosburgh

**Co. Secretary:** James Kirkland

**Responsibilities**

**Senior:** Nancy Peterson *(Manager)*

**Finance:** Vicky Nixon *(Finance assistant)*

**Marketing:** Caroline Pennington *(PR & Analyst Relations Manager)*, Tabitha Taylor-Higginson *(Director of Marketing Communic)*

**Health & Safety:** Anna Solanke *(General Manager)*

**Facilities:** Anna Solanke *(General Manager)*

**US SIC:** 5732, 5081

**UK SIC:** 64800, 61490

**Auditors:** KPMG LLP

**Bankers:** HSBC Bank plc (40-16-08)

| | 31-12-13 | 31-12-12 | 31-12-11 |
|---|---|---|---|
| TO | 12,913,000 | 13,392,000 | 10,956,000 |
| P/L | 575,000 | 527,000 | (781,000) |
| NW | 1,611,000 | 1,313,000 | 316,000 |
| WC | (289,000) | 3,345,000 | 8,651,000 |
| Emp. | 119 | 120 | 122 |

DUNS 21-682-3534 **Imp-Exp**

## Trimline Ltd

Trimline House, Paget Street, Southampton, Hampshire SO14 5GN

**Tel:** 023-8033-4242 **Fax:** 023-8033-4235

**Web:** www.trimline.co.uk

**Reg No:** 0837766 **VAT No:** 188645707

**Estd:** 1965 Private Limited Company

**Line of Business:** Boat furnishings

**Export Markets:** Worldwide

**Trading Style:** Trimline Furnishing

**Issued Capital:** £5,200

**Principals:** G S Oliver *(Managing)*, M N Oliver

**Co. Secretary:** Steven Penfound

**Responsibilities**

**Senior:** Clive Hawkins *(Transport Manager)*, Naomi Hazell *(partner)*

**Finance:** Naomi Hazell *(partner)*, Lynn Holdsworth *(Accounts Manager)*

**Marketing:** James Bonner *(Trainee Project Surveyor)*, Ally Grant *(Receptionist)*, Alan Mattingly *(Project Surveyor)*

**Sales:** James Bonner *(Trainee Project Surveyor)*, Alan Mattingly *(Project Surveyor)*, Kristin Thompson *(VP Business Development North)*, Ashley Yates *(Contracts Coordinator)*

**Admin:** Leanne Hackett *(Administration Manager)*, Georgina Holdsworth *(PA)*

**IT:** Doug Munford *(Head of IT)*

**HR:** Wendy Wood *(Operations Director)*

**Facilities:** Kenny Carter *(Production Manager)*

**Operations:** Tom Bishop *(Joiner)*, Ian Broomfield *(Joinery Manager)*, Ash Bundy *(Joiner)*, Kenny Carter *(Production Manager)*, Ian Collins *(Workshop Foreman)*, Steve Darnton *(Transport & Warehouse Operativ)*, Mike Denton *(Project Planner)*, Lisa Frackiewicz *(CAD Operator)*, Tim Gallagher *(Contract Manager)*, Clive Gardiner *(OMD Manager)*, Karen Harmer *(Soft Furnishings Team)*, Malcolm Lee *(Wood Machinist)*, John McStay *(Upholsterer)*, Peter O'Riordan *(CAD Draughtsman)*, Trevor Patten *(CAD Manager)*, Gareth Preston *(Operations Maintenance Departm)*, Jo Raven *(Contract Manager)*, Andy Smith *(Joiner)*, Pete Witcher *(Wood Machinist)*, Wendy Wood *(Operations Director)*

**Purchasing:** Lawrence Bradley *(Purchasing Administrator)*

**Fleet:** Clive Hawkins *(Transport Manager)*

**Engineering:** Kenny Carter *(Production Manager)*

**US SIC:** 3732, 7399

**UK SIC:** 36102, 83954

**Auditors:** BDO LLP

**Bankers:** Lloyds TSB Bank plc (30-97-58)

| | 30-09-13 | 30-09-12 | 30-09-11 |
|---|---|---|---|
| TO | 18,518,701 | 18,586,746 | 7,993,785 |
| P/L | 1,861,665 | 303,263 | 102,719 |
| NW | 2,561,528 | 1,439,352 | 1,413,898 |
| WC | 2,315,261 | 1,246,879 | 1,287,894 |
| Emp. | 82 | 77 | 61 |

DUNS 23-874-4952 **Imp**

## Trimmings by Design Ltd

Gresham Road, Derby, Derbyshire DE24 8AW

**Fax:** 01332-292977

**Web:** www.trimmingsbydesign.co.uk

**Reg No:** 3865853 **Estd:** 1999 Private Limited Company

**Line of Business:** Manufacture of household textiles

**Issued Capital:** £100,000

**Directors:** D G Chapman, G M Redfern, G A Fowler

**Co. Secretary:** Richard Corkett

**US SIC:** 2298 **UK SIC:** 43960

| | 31-12-13 | 31-12-12 | 31-12-11 |
|---|---|---|---|
| TA | 2,409,749 | 2,335,678 | 2,166,345 |
| NW | 1,103,891 | 959,095 | 866,638 |
| WC | 1,835,549 | 1,697,745 | 1,628,080 |

DUNS 21-586-5422

## Trinity C of E Secondary School

Trinity School, Taunton Road, London SE12 8PD

**Tel:** 02088523191

**Web:** www.trinitylewisham.org

**Estd:** 2002 Proprietorship

**Line of Business:** Schools (local authority)

**Proprietor:** R Pear

**US SIC:** 8211 **UK SIC:** 93200

**Employees:** 86

DUNS 22-005-6381

## Trinity Care Services Ltd

1445 London Road, London SW16 4AQ

**Tel:** 020-8764-3240

**Web:** www.trinitycares.co.uk

**Reg No:** 4008858 **Estd:** 1999 Private Limited Company

**Line of Business:** Social work activities without accommodation

**Issued Capital:** £50

**Director:** Ms J Albert

**Co. Secretary:** Ms Margaret Iriogbe

**US SIC:** 8999 **UK SIC:** 83954

| | 31-07-13 | 31-07-12 | 31-07-11 |
|---|---|---|---|
| TA | 18,015 | 15,843 | 14,635 |
| NW | 7,586 | 5,216 | 6,594 |
| WC | 7,272 | 4,744 | 5,964 |

DUNS 21-038-0526

## Trinity Catholic School

Beechdale Road, Nottingham, Nottinghamshire NG8 3EZ

**Tel:** 01159-296251

**Web:** www.trinity.nottingham.sch.uk

**Estd:** 1987

**Line of Business:** General secondary education
**US SIC:** 8211 **UK SIC:** 93200
**Employees:** 120

DUNS 21-749-9842
## Trinity Church of England High School
Cambridge Street, Manchester M15 6HP
**Tel:** 0161-226-2272
**Web:** www.trinityhigh.com
**Estd:** 2011
**Line of Business:** Schools (local authority)
**Director:** D Ainsworth
**Responsibilities**
**Senior:** David (The Bishop Of Manchester) *(Manager)*, Ian Artus *(Manager)*, Rupert Caesar *(Manager)*, Admos Chimhowu *(Manager)*, Rogers Govender (In His Capacity As Dea *(Manager)*, Diane Gray-Stephenson *(Manager)*, Pamela Lord *(Manager)*, Nigel Mcculloch (In His Corporate Capa *(Manager)*, Olwen Mcnamara *(Manager)*, Ann Meadowcroft *(Manager)*, Bernice Sherwin *(Manager)*, Eunice Stennett *(Manager)*, Patricia Travis *(Manager)*, Simon Worsley *(Manager)*
**US SIC:** 8211 **UK SIC:** 93200
**Employees:** 150

DUNS 36-489-0710
## Trinity College
Atlas House, Cambridge Place, Cambridge, Cambridgeshire CB2 1NS
**Web:** www.trin.cam.ac.uk
**Estd:** 1865
**Line of Business:** University
**Director:** Dr J Fairbrother
**Responsibilities**
**HR:** Georgina Salmon *(Personnel Coordinator)*
**Facilities:** Will Duckworth *(Facilities Manager)*
**US SIC:** 8221 **UK SIC:** 93100
**Auditors:** PricewaterhouseCoopers LLP

| | 30-06-13 | 30-06-12 | 30-06-11 |
|---|---|---|---|
| TO | 60,234,000 | 60,142,000 | 58,081,000 |
| P/L | 15,205,000 | 14,287,000 | 11,867,000 |
| NW | 926,174,000 | 832,733,000 | 838,257,000 |
| WC | 29,138,000 | 16,108,000 | 17,866,000 |
| Emp. | 491 | 503 | 477 |

DUNS 42-366-1743
## Trinity College
College Road, Carmarthen, Dyfed SA31 3EP
**Tel:** 01267-676767
**Web:** www.trinity-cm.ac.uk
**Estd:** 1848
**Line of Business:** Colleges (higher education)
**Director:** D Jones-Davies
**Responsibilities**
**Senior:** Eleri Beynon *(Marketing Manager)*
**Finance:** Gwyndaf Tobias *(Finance Vice Chancellor)*
**Marketing:** Eleri Beynon *(Marketing Manager)*
**HR:** Annette Gravell *(Human Resources Manager)*
**US SIC:** 8221 **UK SIC:** 93100
**Auditors:** Mazars LLP
**Bankers:** HSBC Bank plc (40-16-23)
**Employees:** 300
**Turnover:** £10,538,283

DUNS 28-872-0501
## Trinity College (Bristol) Ltd
Stoke Hill, Bristol, Avon BS9 1JP
**Tel:** 01179-682803
**Web:** www.trinity-bris.ac.uk
**Reg No:** 1056656 **Estd:** 1972 Private Limited Company
**Line of Business:** Adult and other education not elsewhere classified
**Directors:** C J Trickey, D J Mills, A C Miles, B Shepherd, Dr M Clark, Reverend S P Hollinghurst, C S Cleverly, Mrs J M Jones
**Co. Secretary:** Andrew Lucas
**Responsibilities**
**Senior:** John Dunnett *(Director)*, Emma Ineson *(Principle)*, George Kovoor *(Principal)*
**Finance:** Erica Hogg *(Chartered Accountant)*
**US SIC:** 8249 **UK SIC:** 93300
**Auditors:** Elliott Bunker
**Bankers:** Lloyds TSB Bank plc (30-99-38)

| | 31-08-13 | 31-08-12 | 31-08-11 |
|---|---|---|---|
| TO | 1,335,395 | 1,416,409 | 2,044,594 |
| P/L | 45,279 | (159,621) | (117,983) |
| NW | 775,470 | 728,048 | 909,569 |
| WC | (328,412) | (390,158) | (181,588) |
| Emp. | 46 | 46 | 45 |

DUNS 77-106-1132 Exp
## Trinity College London
Blue Fin Building, 110 Southwark Street, London SE1 0TA
**Web:** www.trinitycollege.co.uk
**Reg No:** 2683033 **Estd:** 1992 Private Company Limited By Guarantee
**Line of Business:** Other adult and other education not elsewhere classified
**Export Sales:** £20,115,000
**Trading Style:** Trinity College London Examination Board
**Directors:** Ms S D Eastburn, M J Butcher, Dr G M Copland, Sir J K Stuart, Ms L J Sibley, M E Saunders, A E Britten, M Esplen
**Co. Secretary:** Mrs Fiona Butcher
**Responsibilities**
**Senior:** Euan Geddes *(Manager)*, Michael Hildesley *(Director)*, Sarah Kent *(Chief Executive)*, Janette Mckay *(Director)*, James Mullan *(Director)*, Norton York *(Manager)*
**US SIC:** 8299 **UK SIC:** 93300
**Auditors:** KPMG LLP
**Bankers:** National Westminster Bank Plc (50-41-06)

| | 31-03-14 | 31-03-13 | 31-03-12 |
|---|---|---|---|
| TO | 32,535,000 | 30,564,000 | 28,266,000 |
| P/L | 308,000 | 806,000 | 1,003,000 |
| NW | 4,532,000 | 4,524,000 | 4,059,000 |
| WC | (127,000) | 336,000 | (379,000) |
| Emp. | 155 | 151 | 129 |

DUNS 37-870-7111 Imp
## Trinity Fire & Security Systems Ltd
**(Subsidiary of:** Trinity Ten Limited)
Little Bridge Business Park, Exeter, Devon EX5 1AU
**Tel:** 01392-874455
**Web:** www.trinityprotection.co.uk
**Reg No:** 3304503 **Estd:** 1997 Private Limited Company
**Line of Business:** Security and related activities
**Issued Capital:** £107,480
**Directors:** A R Cotton, S R Corbett, R Holliday
**Co. Secretary:** Paul Clayton
**Responsibilities**
**IT:** Paul Solari *(IT Manager)*
**HR:** Steve Spill *(Health & Safety Manager)*
**Health & Safety:** Steve Spill *(Health & Safety Manager)*
**Branches:** Trinity Fire & Security Systems Ltd, Brambles Enterprise Centre, Waterberry Drive, Waterlooville, Hampshire PO7 7TH
**US SIC:** 8911, 7399
**UK SIC:** 83701, 83954
**Auditors:** Francis Clark
**Bankers:** HSBC Bank plc (40-20-30)

| | 30-06-14 | 30-06-13 | 30-06-12 |
|---|---|---|---|
| TO | 21,755,548 | 19,172,589 | 19,015,816 |
| P/L | 224,177 | 137,341 | 72,906 |
| NW | 971,339 | 796,720 | 685,539 |
| WC | 755,910 | 617,404 | 526,079 |
| Emp. | 215 | 189 | 180 |

DUNS 36-513-5453
## Trinity Hall
Trinity Hall, Cambridge, Cambridgeshire CB2 1TJ
**Web:** www.trinhall.cam.ac.uk
**Estd:** 1993
**Line of Business:** University
**Directors:** Prof C Austin, Prof M Daunton, Dr J Bradley, Dr T Tokieda, Dr V Kumar, Dr N Bampos, P F Davis, Dr P Hutchinson
**Responsibilities**
**Senior:** Martin Ellwood *(Principal)*, Jerome Jarrett *(Principal)*, Angus Johnston *(Principal)*, Tom Korner *(Principal)*, Christopher Padfield *(Principal)*, Kylie Richardson *(Principal)*, David Runciman *(Principal)*
**US SIC:** 8221 **UK SIC:** 93100
**Auditors:** Peters Elworthy & Moore

| | 30-06-13 | 30-06-12 | 30-06-11 |
|---|---|---|---|
| TO | 11,553,229 | 11,053,591 | 10,148,580 |
| P/L | 1,153,328 | 40,499 | (796,258) |
| NW | 205,439,367 | 190,045,115 | 210,745,452 |
| WC | 5,036,317 | 4,711,296 | 3,015,356 |
| Emp. | 199 | 195 | 175 |

DUNS 77-086-2258
## Trinity Hospice
30 Clapham Common North Side, Clapham, London SW4 0RN
**Tel:** 02077871000
**Web:** www.trinityhospice.org.uk
**Reg No:** 2673845 **Estd:** 1991 Private Company Limited By Guarantee
**Line of Business:** Other business activities not elsewhere classified
**Directors:** Ms T K Howard, J H Thellusson, D W Clarson, Ms G Walters, Ms J Robertson, Mrs K M Jackson, D M Wyatt, Dr T E Ladbrooke
**Co. Secretary:** David Coggins
**Responsibilities**
**Senior:** Lynne Ager *(Director)*, Paul Aylieff *(Manager)*, Peter Gluckman *(Director)*, Stefan Karas *(Stores Manager)*, Johanna Kitson *(Manager)*, Mark Mildred *(Manager)*, Dallas Pounds *(Chief Executive Officer)*, Adian Williams *(Director)*
**Marketing:** Sally Bateson *(Director of Fundraising and Co)*, Anna MacLeod *(Head of Press and PR)*
**Sales:** Stefan Karas *(Stores Manager)*
**IT:** Jason Coleman *(Senior IT Executive)*
**HR:** Mark Barling *(Human Resources Manager)*, Sue Boreham *(Human Resources Manager)*, Julie Parry *(Human Resources Manager)*
**US SIC:** 7399 **UK SIC:** 83954
**Auditors:** Saffery Champnes
**Bankers:** C Hoare & Co (15-99-00)

| | 31-03-14 | 31-03-13 | 31-03-12 |
|---|---|---|---|
| TO | 10,802,632 | 10,320,154 | 10,036,301 |
| P/L | 58,174 | 177,628 | 596,816 |
| NW | 17,182,219 | 16,959,652 | 16,488,659 |
| WC | 2,991,584 | 2,628,725 | 2,463,740 |
| Emp. | 189 | 186 | 169 |

DUNS 29-429-9425
## Trinity Hospice & Palliative Care Services Ltd
Low Moor Road, Bispham, Blackpool, Lancashire FY2 0BG
**Tel:** 01253368881
**Web:** www.trinityhospice.co.uk
**Reg No:** 1537498 **Estd:** 1981 Private Company Limited By Guarantee
**Line of Business:** Charities and charitable organisations
**Directors:** W A Holmes, C J Beverley, K A Hunter, Dr M C Wren-Hilton, P Jackson, Miss K Burn, T Inman, N A Law
**Co. Secretary:** Mrs Helena Lavin
**Responsibilities**
**Senior:** Richard Debicki *(Trustee)*, David Euston *(Chief Executive)*, Helen Grenier *(Director)*, Mansel Jones *(Director)*, Maureen Mcdermott *(Director)*
**US SIC:** 8699, 8011
**UK SIC:** 96902, 95300
**Auditors:** Rushtons
**Bankers:** HSBC Bank plc (40-12-13)

| | 31-03-14 | 31-03-13 | 31-03-12 |
|---|---|---|---|
| TO | 9,376,493 | 7,038,664 | 6,440,819 |
| P/L | 2,287,423 | 113,280 | (418,892) |
| NW | 19,624,648 | 16,849,755 | 15,752,634 |
| WC | 4,158,139 | 2,535,391 | 2,390,356 |
| Emp. | 129 | 145 | 148 |

DUNS 23-989-8422
## Trinity House
Trinity House, Trinity Square, London EC3N 4DH
**Tel:** 02074816900
**Web:** www.trinityhouse.co.uk
**Estd:** 1986
**Line of Business:** Function room for hire
**Principals:** P B Rowe *(Chairman)*, K W Clark *(Financial)*, M G Wannell, Captain N Macturner, Captain P H King, D I Brewer, M Rawlinson, W A Thomson
**Responsibilities**
**Senior:** Graham Hockley *(General Manager)*, Ian Mcnaught *(Chief Executive Officer)*
**Sales:** Lynn Pomares *(Commercial Administrator)*, Nina Wright *(Commercial Manager)*
**Admin:** Lynn Pomares *(Commercial Administrator)*
**HR:** Lizzie Firmin *(Human Resources Manager)*
**Health & Safety:** Russell Dunham *(Insurance Claims Coordinator)*
**Branches:** Trinity House, Light House House, Orkney, Orkney KW17 2BG
**US SIC:** 7011 **UK SIC:** 66500
**Bankers:** Bank Of England (10-00-00)
**Employees:** 250

DUNS 50-485-1593 Imp
## Trinity International Services Ltd
11 Bon Accord Square, Aberdeen, Aberdeenshire AB11 6DJ
**Tel:** 01224-211755
**Web:** www.trinity-int.com
**Reg No:** 0122366SC **VAT No:** 552877312
**Estd:** 1990 Private Limited Company
**Line of Business:** Caterers
**Export Sales:** £4,660,287
**Issued Capital:** £11,745
**Principals:** Captain S C Macbride *(Managing)*, D C Burgess, Mrs S H Macbride, C D Macbride
**Co. Secretary:** Mrs Sarah Pettigrew
**Responsibilities**
**Finance:** Anne Sengster *(Financial Director)*
**HR:** Lynn Rankin *(Personnel Manager)*
**Operations:** Shona Cartney *(HSEQ Controller)*, Kurt Gjertsen *(Operations Manager)*
**US SIC:** 5812, 7011
**UK SIC:** 66110, 66500
**Auditors:** Graeme D McKay
**Bankers:** The Royal Bank Of Scotland Plc (83-49-40)

| | 31-08-13 | 31-08-12 | 31-08-11 |
|---|---|---|---|
| TO | 8,441,295 | 12,534,956 | 8,945,285 |
| P/L | 747,091 | 1,530,580 | 602,951 |
| NW | 4,446,916 | 4,044,440 | 2,906,788 |
| WC | 4,182,537 | 3,531,325 | 2,246,961 |
| Emp. | 49 | 49 | 14 |

DUNS 28-828-9143
## Trinity Laban Conservatoire of Music & Dance Ltd
King Charles Court, Old Royal Naval College, King William Walk, London SE10 9JF
**Tel:** 02083054444 **Fax:** 020-8305-9444
**Web:** www.trinitylaban.ac.uk
**Reg No:** 0051090 **Estd:** 1897 Private Company Limited By Guarantee
**Line of Business:** Universities, colleges, prof. schools
**Directors:** S D Jackson, Ms H L Lindley-Milton, Ms E K Wedmore, R A Brown, Ms H E Oliver, M J Kettle, A Bowne, H Klier
**Co. Secretary:** Jonathan Peel
**Responsibilities**
**Senior:** Esther Cavett *(Board Member)*, Joanna Embling *(Director)*, David Lipsey *(Director)*, Nirmala Rao *(Director)*, Vimmi Singh *(Director)*
**Marketing:** Jamie Harber *(Performance Marketing Manager)*
**IT:** Yvonne Connell *(IT Manager)*
**Branches:** Trinity Laban Conservatoire Of Music & Dance Ltd, 4 Blandford St, London W1U 4BA
**US SIC:** 8221, 8249
**UK SIC:** 93100, 93300
**Auditors:** RSM Robson Rhodes
**Bankers:** Allied Irish Bank (gb) (23-83-97)

| | 31-07-13 | 31-07-12 | 31-07-11 |
|---|---|---|---|
| TO | 22,220,648 | 22,736,927 | 20,531,107 |
| P/L | 1,177,212 | 1,126,229 | 413,760 |
| NW | 30,054,762 | 27,755,625 | 28,863,870 |
| WC | (2,615,177) | (3,685,911) | (2,632,303) |
| Emp. | 252 | 252 | 268 |

DUNS 29-537-7352
## Trinity Mirror Digital Recruitment Ltd
**(Subsidiary of:** Trinity Mirror Plc)
One Canada Square, London E14 5AP
**Tel:** 02073485010 **Fax:** 0870-202-0131
**Web:** www.tmdr.com
**Reg No:** 1904765 **VAT No:** 442541764
**Estd:** 1995 Private Limited Company
**Line of Business:** Employment and recruitment companies and consultants
**Trading Style:** Fish4jobs
**Issued Capital:** £304,615
**Directors:** S R Fox, V L Vaghela, T M Directors Limited
**Co. Secretary:** T M Secretaries Limited
**Responsibilities**
**Finance:** Warren Dale *(Finance Director)*
**Marketing:** Sarah El Doori *(Group Marketing Director)*
**Sales:** Dan Richards *(Sales Director)*
**HR:** Lesley Somerville *(HR Director)*
**US SIC:** 7319, 7311, 7361, 7399
**UK SIC:** 83800, 83954
**Auditors:** Deloitte & Touche LLP
**Bankers:** Barclays Bank Plc (20-46-73)

| | 29-12-13 | 30-12-12 | 01-12-12 |
|---|---|---|---|
| TO | 8,083,000 | 10,468,072 | 8,151,407 |
| P/L | (1,450,000) | 3,060 | 1,530,984 |
| NW | (3,527,000) | (2,361,489) | (2,401,828) |
| WC | (3,070,000) | (2,297,186) | (2,844,599) |
| Emp. | 79 | 138 | 89 |

DUNS 21-814-5928
## Trinity Mirror Midlands Ltd
**(Subsidiary of:** Trinity Mirror Plc)
Floor 6 Unit 601 Fort Dunlop, Fort Parkway, Birmingham, West Midlands B24 9FF
**Tel:** 01212345000 **Fax:** 0121-234-5190
**Web:** www.birminghammail.net
**Reg No:** 0211184 **VAT No:** 114390692
**Estd:** 1994 Private Limited Company
**Line of Business:** Newspapers publishing
**Trading Style:** The Birmingham Post & Mail, Coventry Evening Telegragh, Midland Weekly Media
**Issued Capital:** £651,683
**Directors:** T M Directors Limited, V L Vaghela, S R Fox
**Co. Secretary:** T M Secretaries Limited
**Responsibilities**
**Senior:** Dave Brookes *(Editor)*, Sam Fox *(Ceo)*, Dean Matthieson *(Warehouse Manager)*
**Marketing:** Emma McKinney *(Editor)*, Enda Mullen *(Reporter)*
**Facilities:** Ian Randle *(Facilities Manager)*
**Fleet:** Dean Matthieson *(Warehouse Manager)*
**US SIC:** 2711 **UK SIC:** 47512
**Auditors:** Deloitte LLP

**Bankers:** HSBC Bank plc (40-24-19)

|  | 29-12-13 | 30-12-12 | 01-12-12 |
|---|---|---|---|
| TO | 34,916,000 | 39,089,000 | 45,357,000 |
| P/L | 1,558,000 | 1,653,000 | (835,000) |
| NW | 52,397,000 | 51,325,000 | 50,145,000 |
| WC | (178,459,000) | (181,537,000) | (184,998,000) |
| Emp. | 277 | 315 | 497 |

---

DUNS 21-220-9829    Imp

## Trinity Mirror Plc

One Canada Square, Canary Wharf, London E14 5AP
**Tel:** 02075103000
**Web:** www.trinitymirror.com
**Reg No:** 0082548 **VAT No:** 440356767
**Estd:** 1904 Public Limited Company
**Line of Business:** Management activities of holding companies
**Issued Capital:** £25,769,052
**Directors:** Ms H C Stevenson, Dr D T Kelly, D J Grigson, D T Smith, L D Ginsberg, V L Vaghela, S R Fox, Ms J E Lighting
**Co. Secretary:** Jeremy Rhodes
**Responsibilities**
**Senior:** Simon Edgley (*Manager*)
**Marketing:** Harry Carter (*Press Officer*)
**Sales:** Arthur Locke (*Business Development Manager*), Kirsty Mckenzie (*Senior Account Manager*)
**IT:** Sara Kalber (*IT Manager*), Simon Picken (*IT Infrastructure Provisioning*)
**Branches:** Trinity Mirror Plc, 5 Craigton House, Redcar, Cleveland TS10 1DL
**US SIC:** 6711, 2711
**UK SIC:** 83962, 47512
**Auditors:** Deloitte LLP
**Bankers:** The Royal Bank Of Scotland Plc (16-24-06)

|  | 29-12-13 | 30-12-12 | 01-12-12 |
|---|---|---|---|
| TO | 663,800,000 | 706,500,000 | 746,600,000 |
| P/L | (160,800,000) | 18,900,000 | 74,400,000 |
| NW | (111,400,000) | (273,700,000) | (300,300,000) |
| WC | (26,000,000) | (43,600,000) | (69,700,000) |
| Emp. | 5,033 | 5,392 | 6,242 |

---

DUNS 29-652-9787

## Trinity Mirror Printing Ltd

(**Subsidiary of:** Trinity Mirror Plc)
St Albans Road, Watford, Hertfordshire WD24 7RG
**Tel:** 01923230455 **Fax:** 01923-249861
**Web:** www.mirror.co.uk
**Reg No:** 1979335 **VAT No:** 440356767
**Estd:** 1986 Private Limited Company
**Line of Business:** Newspaper publishers & printers
**Issued Capital:** £70,050,000
**Directors:** V L Vaghela, S R Fox, T M Directors Limited
**Co. Secretary:** T M Secretaries Limited
**Responsibilities**
**Senior:** Colin Brookes (*Manager*)
**Health & Safety:** Ian Mcwhinnie (*Health & Safety Officer*)
**Engineering:** Paul Dominic (*Production Manager*)
**US SIC:** 2711, 6711
**UK SIC:** 47512, 83962
**Auditors:** Deloitte & Touche LLP
**Bankers:** National Westminster Bank Plc (60-00-01)

|  | 29-12-13 | 30-12-12 | 01-12-12 |
|---|---|---|---|
| TO | 119,253,000 | 141,460,000 | 165,459,000 |
| P/L | 334,000 | 333,000 | 6,538,000 |
| NW | (79,971,000) | (81,927,000) | (83,162,000) |
| WC | (409,381,000) | (408,760,000) | (425,229,000) |

---

DUNS 21-657-0536

## Trinity Public Sector

130 College Road, Harrow, Middlesex HA1 1BQ
**Tel:** 02088613434
**Estd:** 2000 Partnership
**Line of Business:** Employment service
**Partners:** K Ryan, T Vaughan
**US SIC:** 7361 **UK SIC:** 83954
**Employees:** 50

---

DUNS 21-749-8976

## Trinity Restaurant

4 The Polygon, Clapham, London SW4 0JG
**Tel:** 020-7622-1199
**Web:** www.trinityrestaurant.co.uk
**Estd:** 2004 Partnership
**Line of Business:** Restaurant - english
**Partners:** A Byatt, A Jones
**Responsibilities**
**Senior:** Leah Kirkland (*General Manager*)
**Marketing:** Ursula Ferreira (*Guest Relations Manager*)
**US SIC:** 5812 **UK SIC:** 66110
**Employees:** 47

---

DUNS 21-773-3519

## Trinity Road County Primary School

Trinity Road, Chelmsford, Essex CM2 6HS
**Tel:** 01245354517
**Web:** www.trinityroad.essex.sch.uk
**Estd:** 1905 Partnership
**Line of Business:** Schools (local authority)
**Partners:** Mrs M Staley, Mrs M Staley
**Responsibilities**
**Senior:** Nicola Soane (*Head Teacher*)
**US SIC:** 8211 **UK SIC:** 93200
**Employees:** 50

---

DUNS 34-573-8884

## Trinity School (Carlisle) Ltd

Strand Road, Carlisle, Cumbria CA1 1JB
**Tel:** 01228516051
**Web:** www.trinity.cumbria.sch.uk
**Reg No:** 2723747 **Estd:** 1992 Private Limited Company
**Line of Business:** General secondary education
**Directors:** T S Leach, Mrs D Libby, A Mottershead, D B Armstrong
**Responsibilities**
**Senior:** Peter Temple (*Governor*)
**US SIC:** 8211 **UK SIC:** 93200

|  | 05-04-14 | 05-04-13 | 05-04-12 |
|---|---|---|---|
| TO | 10,354 | 8,544 | 12,560 |
| P/L | 3,756 | (147,344) | 10,806 |
| NW | 227,816 | 224,075 | 353,890 |
| WC | 22,853 | 19,014 | 157,307 |

---

DUNS 21-803-0399

## Trinity St David Students Union

College Street, Lampeter, Dyfed SA48 7ED
**Tel:** 01570422619
**Web:** www.tsdsu.co.uk
**Estd:** 2011
**Line of Business:** Trade unions
**Responsibilities**
**Senior:** Scott Farmer (*Acting Chief Executive Officer*), Nicky Mcginley (*Acting Chief Executive Officer*)
**US SIC:** 8221 **UK SIC:** 93100
**Employees:** 100

---

DUNS 21-241-1276

## Trinity Weekly Newspapers Ltd

(**Subsidiary of:** Trinity Mirror Plc)
26-32 Tulketh Street, Southport, Merseyside PR8 1BT
**Tel:** 01704-536655
**Web:** www.southportvisitor.co.uk
**Reg No:** 0013297 **Estd:** 1996 Private Limited Company
**Line of Business:** Newspapers publishing
**Trading Style:** Southport Visitor
**Issued Capital:** £40,000
**Directors:** V L Vaghela, S R Fox, T M Directors Limited
**Co. Secretary:** T M Secretaries Limited
**Branches:** Liverpool, Ormskirk
**US SIC:** 2711 **UK SIC:** 47512
**Auditors:** Deloitte & Touche
**Bankers:** The Royal Bank Of Scotland Plc (16-24-06)

|  | 29-12-13 | 30-12-12 | 01-12-12 |
|---|---|---|---|
| TA | 1,152,000 | 1,152,000 | 1,215,000 |
| NW | 1,152,000 | 1,152,000 | 1,152,000 |
| WC | N/A | N/A | 1,152,000 |

---

DUNS 23-559-0077

## Trinity Youth Association

Oval Community Centre, The Oval, Bedlington, Northumberland NE22 5HU
**Tel:** 01670-531843
**Web:** www.trinityyouth.org.uk
**Reg No:** 3557279 **Estd:** 1989 Private Unlimited Company
**Line of Business:** Technical and vocational secondary education
**Trading Style:** Trinity Youth Association
**Directors:** Ms K Lawson, L Daley, D M Watson, Ms T A Mcleod, Mrs J Masters
**Co. Secretary:** Robert Poxon
**Responsibilities**
**Senior:** Sheelagh Goodwin (*Manager*), Marion Stewart (*Manager*), Paul Vurlan (*Manager*)
**Branches:** Trinity Youth Association, Valley Road, Whitley Bay, Tyne and Wear NE25 0LN
**US SIC:** 8249, 7999, 8321, 8999
**UK SIC:** 93300, 97913, 96111, 83954

|  | 31-12-13 | 31-12-12 | 31-12-11 |
|---|---|---|---|
| TO | N/A | N/A | 589,443 |
| P/L | N/A | N/A | (44,489) |
| NW | 68,721 | 63,260 | 60,629 |
| WC | 68,657 | 63,182 | 60,537 |

---

DUNS 36-531-5188

## Triodos Bank Nv

(**Subsidiary of:** Stichting Administratiekantoor Aandelen Triodos Ba)
Brunel House The Promenade, Clifton Down, Bristol, Avon BS8 3NN
**Tel:** 01179739339
**Web:** www.triodos.co.uk
**Reg No:** 0018646FC **Estd:** 1995 Foreign Company
**Line of Business:** Banks and financial institutions
**Directors:** P H Aeby, P Blom, A A Bekman, P Blom, W E Scherpenhuysen Rom, W M De Brauw, F E Matthijsen Gerst, P Mackay
**Responsibilities**
**Senior:** Jeltje Banga (*Director*), Kit Beazley (*Finance Director*), Pauline Kruseman (*Director*), Charles Midleton (*Manager*), Jacob Vis (*Director*), Lyden Walker (*Manager*), Willem de Brauw (*Director*)
**Finance:** Kit Beazley (*Finance Director*), Dan Hird (*Finance Director*)
**Marketing:** Peter Borgers (*Relations Manager*), Louise Rengozzi (*Marketing Coordinator*)
**US SIC:** 8999 **UK SIC:** 83954

---

DUNS 23-619-4895

## Trios Property Ltd

(**Subsidiary of:** Triosgroup Plc)
224-232 High Street, Erdington, Birmingham, West Midlands B23 6SJ
**Tel:** 08453005969 **Fax:** 01213285758
**Web:** www.services-mgs.com
**Reg No:** 3616663 **VAT No:** 860219635
**Estd:** 1963 Private Limited Company
**Line of Business:** Other building completion
**Issued Capital:** £1,133,397
**Principals:** B E Swayne (*Managing*), Ms S Harris, R H Hall, D A Borthwick, R S Purewal, R P Marriott
**Co. Secretary:** Bruce Swayne
**Responsibilities**
**Senior:** Jenny Parsons (*Manager*)
**Finance:** Anthony Grout (*Finance Director*)
**Branches:** Trios Property Ltd, 20 Meadowsweet Avenue, Bristol, Avon BS34 7AL
**US SIC:** 1799 **UK SIC:** 50000
**Auditors:** Garratts Wolverhampton Ltd
**Bankers:** Barclays Bank Plc (20-07-71)

|  | 31-03-14 | 31-03-13 | 31-03-12 |
|---|---|---|---|
| TO | 27,222,000 | 27,371,000 | 22,013,000 |
| P/L | 1,447,000 | 662,000 | 496,000 |
| NW | 3,199,000 | 2,779,000 | 2,777,000 |
| WC | 3,541,000 | 2,839,000 | 3,695,000 |
| Emp. | 294 | 312 | 294 |

---

DUNS 22-142-7417

## Tripack Solutions Ltd

(**Subsidiary of:** Scott Group Investments Ltd)
Block 3, Bothwell Park Industrial Estate, Glasgow, Lanarkshire G71 6NZ
**Tel:** 01698801340 **Fax:** 01698-712801
**Web:** www.pallet.co.uk
**Reg No:** 0215872SC **Estd:** 1901 Private Limited Company
**Line of Business:** Manufacturers of cases
**Trading Style:** Graham Douglas Tripack
**Issued Capital:** £30,000
**Directors:** S Alexander, Mrs T J Trotter, A Gibson
**Co. Secretary:** Norman Scott
**Responsibilities**
**Senior:** Douglas McAllister (*General Manager*)
**HR:** Douglas McAllister (*General Manager*)
**Facilities:** Douglas McAllister (*General Manager*)
**US SIC:** 3999, 2653
**UK SIC:** 49590, 47251
**Bankers:** The Royal Bank Of Scotland Plc (83-21-42)

|  | 31-12-13 | 31-12-12 | 31-12-11 |
|---|---|---|---|
| TA | 30,000 | 30,000 | 30,000 |
| NW | 30,000 | 30,000 | 30,000 |

---

DUNS 34-812-9284    Imp

## Tripadvisor Ltd

(**Subsidiary of:** Tripadvisor Uk2 Lp)
7 Soho Square, London W1D 3QQ
**Tel:** 02033203277
**Web:** www.tripadvisor.co.uk
**Reg No:** 5612751 **Estd:** 2005 Private Limited Company
**Line of Business:** Travel advisory services.
**Directors:** F J Erskine, Ms J Bradley, S Kalvert, S Kaufer, M E Charron
**Co. Secretary:** Kemp Little Llp
**Responsibilities**
**Sales:** Martin Verdon-Roe (*Head of Sales - Europe*)
**US SIC:** 4722 **UK SIC:** 77001
**Auditors:** Ernst & Young LLP
**Employees:** 248
**Turnover:** £362,994,564

---

DUNS 52-006-9634

## Triple A Express Ltd

11a Uxbridge Road, Marlborough Parade, Uxbridge, Middlesex UB10 0LR
**Tel:** 01895272727
**Web:** www.skyexpresscars.net
**Reg No:** 3373896 **Estd:** 1997 Private Limited Company
**Line of Business:** Taxi operation
**Issued Capital:** £1
**Director:** G R Jassi
**Co. Secretary:** Mrs Kanta Jassi
**Branches:** Triple A Express Ltd, East Avenue, Hayes, Middlesex UB3 2HW
**US SIC:** 4121 **UK SIC:** 72200
**Auditors:** Johal & Company

|  | 30-04-14 | 30-04-13 | 31-04-12 |
|---|---|---|---|
| TA | 450,319 | 483,853 | 299,866 |
| NW | 298,029 | 267,973 | 227,470 |
| WC | (14,365) | 119,029 | 65,289 |

---

DUNS 73-259-9415

## Triplearc Uk Ltd

(**Subsidiary of:** Pittsburgh Apartment Rental Guide)
Dorcan Three Hundred, Murdock Road Dorcan, Swindon, Wiltshire SN3 5HY
**Tel:** 08448001050
**Web:** www.triplearc.com
**Reg No:** 4533729 **Estd:** 2001 Private Limited Company
**Line of Business:** Other business activities not elsewhere classified
**Trading Style:** Office to Office
**Issued Capital:** £100
**Directors:** R R Baldrey, A P Gale
**US SIC:** 7399 **UK SIC:** 83954
**Auditors:** KPMG
**Bankers:** HSBC Bank plc (40-14-13)

|  | 31-12-11 |
|---|---|
| TA | 45,099 |
| NW | 45,099 |

---

DUNS 39-974-9399    Imp-Exp

## Tripp Ltd

(**Subsidiary of:** Sandrini Investments Limited)
2-5 St John's Square, London EC1M 4DE
**Tel:** 020-7014-5800 **Fax:** 020-7014-5858
**Web:** www.tripp.co.uk
**Reg No:** 2271587 **VAT No:** 506795522
**Estd:** 1988 Private Limited Company
**Line of Business:** Other retail sale in specialised stores not elsewhere classified
**Export Markets:** Spain, France
**Export Sales:** £2,752,000
**Trading Style:** Tripp
**Issued Capital:** £2,604,375
**Directors:** S L Glasgow, Ms D M Dedross, J W Mcdiarmid
**Co. Secretary:** Aidan Creedon
**Responsibilities**
**HR:** Julia Howgego (*Human Resources Manager*)
**Health & Safety:** Julia Howgego (*Human Resources Manager*)
**Branches:** Tripp Ltd, Care Of Debenhams, 1-11 Sidwell Street, Exeter, Devon EX4 6NW
**US SIC:** 5399, 5948, 5961
**UK SIC:** 65600, 64600
**Auditors:** Ernst & Young LLP
**Bankers:** Bank Of Scotland (80-11-80)

|  | 25-01-14 | 26-01-13 | 28-01-12 |
|---|---|---|---|
| TO | 34,695,000 | 31,561,000 | 29,892,000 |
| P/L | 2,762,000 | 2,805,000 | 2,375,000 |
| NW | 3,024,000 | 941,000 | (1,148,000) |
| WC | 4,273,000 | 2,257,000 | 100,000 |
| Emp. | 337 | 361 | 348 |

---

DUNS 21-014-1796    Imp

## Triscan Systems Ltd

Unit 4 Petre Court Petre Road, Clayton Le Moors, Accrington, Lancashire BB5 5HY
**Tel:** 08452253102 **Fax:** 01254680381
**Web:** www.triscansystems.com
**Reg No:** 6369088 **Estd:** 2007 Private Limited Company
**Line of Business:** Fuel saving and economy devices
**Issued Capital:** £8,333
**Directors:** D J Lamont, Ms A L Whittaker, J E Black
**Co. Secretary:**
Morton Fraser Secretaries Limite
**Responsibilities**
**Marketing:** Simon Connelly (*Sales & Marketing Director*)
**Sales:** Simon Connelly (*Sales & Marketing Director*)
**US SIC:** 7399, 7379
**UK SIC:** 83954, 83940
**Auditors:** Springfords LLP

|  | 31-08-14 | 31-08-13 | 31-08-12 |
|---|---|---|---|
| TA | 2,932,810 | 2,546,716 | 1,830,729 |
| NW | 826,412 | 447,302 | 16,028 |
| WC | 1,160,553 | 1,346,082 | 946,172 |

DUNS 73-697-0398
## Trisoft Ltd
3 Canalside, Canal Street, Nottingham, Nottinghamshire NG1 7ET
**Tel:** 01158-223-456 **Fax:** 01158-223-433
**Web:** www.trisoft.co.uk
**Reg No:** 4955894 **VAT No:** 829224914
**Estd:** 2004 Private Limited Company
**Line of Business:** Hardware consultancy
**Issued Capital:** £300,000
**Directors:** W J Smith, N Hyder, N P Rogers
**Co. Secretary:** Nigel Rogers
**Responsibilities**
**Senior:** Roger Lloyd *(Manager)*, Philip Moakes *(Manager)*
**Branches:** Trisoft Ltd, Unit 2, Bakewell Road, Peterborough, Cambridgeshire PE2 6XS
**US SIC:** 7379 **UK SIC:** 83940
**Auditors:** Clayton & Brewill

| | 31-12-13 | 31-12-12 | 31-12-11 |
|---|---|---|---|
| TA | 5,526,384 | 5,600,969 | 5,029,245 |
| NW | 773,147 | 612,272 | 580,680 |
| WC | (3,446,164) | (613,396) | (367,990) |

DUNS 39-963-3932
## Tristar Cars Ltd
**(Subsidiary of:** Project Tristar Ltd)
Unit 1-2, Horton Road, West Drayton, Middlesex UB7 8BQ
**Tel:** 01895432000
**Web:** www.tristarworldwide.com
**Reg No:** 2263554 **VAT No:** 528537034
**Estd:** 1988 Private Limited Company
**Line of Business:** Chauffeur driven car hire
**Export Sales:** £6,274,000
**Trading Style:** Tristar World Wide Chauffeur
**Issued Capital:** £338,543
**Directors:** A R Withers Green, D P De Beer
**Co. Secretary:** Andrew Hohne
**Responsibilities**
**Admin:** Rosie Jeszke *(Office Manager)*
**HR:** Karen Cul *(Human Resources Officer)*
**Health & Safety:** Karen Cul *(Human Resources Officer)*
**Branches:** Tristar Cars Ltd, Frodsham Business Centre, Bridge Lane, Frodsham, Cheshire WA6 7FZ
**US SIC:** 4141 **UK SIC:** 72102
**Auditors:** BDO Stoy Hayward LLP
**Bankers:** Lloyds TSB Bank plc (30-94-38)

| | 31-05-13 | 31-05-12 | 31-05-11 |
|---|---|---|---|
| TO | 33,715,000 | 33,184,000 | 32,432,000 |
| P/L | 2,555,000 | 2,380,000 | 1,218,000 |
| NW | 11,852,000 | 10,082,000 | 8,364,000 |
| WC | 10,914,000 | 9,635,000 | 8,458,000 |
| Emp. | 501 | 634 | 617 |

DUNS 42-386-0688
## Tristar Homes Ltd
Council Offices, Town Centre, Billingham, Cleveland TS23 2LW
**Tel:** 03001111000 **Fax:** 01642526614
**Web:** www.tristarhomes.co.uk
**Reg No:** 4373638 **Estd:** 2002 Private Company Limited By Guarantee
**Line of Business:** Management of real estate on a fee or contract basis
**Directors:** T Large, P Thomas, M R Simpson, Mrs A E Clark, G Rudd, D W Pickard, N Stephenson, Ms M Bendelow
**Co. Secretary:** Ms Linda Minns
**Responsibilities**
**Senior:** Robert Gibson *(Director)*, Adele Mcclaren *(Supervisor)*, Denise Ross *(Director)*
**Finance:** Heather Hall *(Finance Manager)*
**Marketing:** Debbie Robertson *(Relations Manager)*
**Branches:** Tristar Homes Ltd, Inskip Walk, 18 Hardwick, Stockton-On-Tees, Cleveland TS19 8EF
**US SIC:** 6531 **UK SIC:** 83400
**Bankers:** National Westminster Bank Plc (55-61-00)

| | 31-03-14 | 31-03-13 | 31-03-12 |
|---|---|---|---|
| TO | 42,741,000 | 40,939,000 | 36,997,000 |
| P/L | (2,574,000) | (4,419,000) | 6,882,000 |
| NW | 119,078,000 | 121,017,000 | 114,832,000 |
| WC | 165,361,000 | 188,075,000 | 214,703,000 |
| Emp. | 307 | 284 | 313 |

DUNS 73-464-1090 Imp
## Tristel Plc
Lynx Business Park, Fordham Road, Snailwell, Newmarket, Suffolk CB8 7NY
**Tel:** 01638721500
**Web:** www.tristel.com
**Reg No:** 4728199 **Estd:** 2003 Public Limited Company
**Line of Business:** Manufacture of medical and surgical equipment and orthopaedic appliances
**Export Sales:** £4,531,000
**Issued Capital:** £399,847
**Directors:** P M Barnes, F A Soler, Ms E A Dixon, P C Swinney
**Co. Secretary:** Ms Elizabeth Dixon
**US SIC:** 3841 **UK SIC:** 37201
**Auditors:** Grant Thornton UK LLP

| | 30-06-14 | 30-06-13 | 30-06-12 |
|---|---|---|---|
| TO | 13,470,000 | 10,558,000 | 10,939,000 |
| P/L | 1,823,000 | (1,750,000) | 578,000 |
| NW | 5,934,000 | 4,732,000 | 4,824,000 |
| WC | 4,624,000 | 3,231,000 | 3,486,000 |
| Emp. | 98 | 92 | 96 |

DUNS 34-629-6143
## Tritech Group Ltd
**(Subsidiary of:** Universal Ferro & Allied Chemicals Limited)
Bridge North Road, Wrexham Industrial Estate, Wrexham, Clwyd LL13 9PS
**Tel:** 01978661111
**Web:** www.tritechgroup.co.uk
**Reg No:** 5435846 **Estd:** 2005 Private Limited Company
**Line of Business:** Manufacture of other fabricated metal products not elsewhere classified
**Export Sales:** £3,344,000
**Issued Capital:** £5,764,076
**Directors:** R Gosrani, S E Goodfellow, R Ramanathan, A F Neterwala, S J Goodier, A R White, I J Walker, F D Neterwala
**Co. Secretary:** Martin Parry
**Responsibilities**
**Marketing:** Thomas Middleton *(Marketing Manager)*
**US SIC:** 3499 **UK SIC:** 31694
**Auditors:** Ernst & Young LLP
**Bankers:** Barclays Bank Plc (20-06-05)

| | 31-03-14 | 31-03-13 | 01-03-12 |
|---|---|---|---|
| TO | 27,313,000 | 22,168,000 | 18,945,000 |
| P/L | 2,643,000 | 1,986,000 | 1,640,000 |
| NW | 9,880,000 | 7,828,000 | 6,105,000 |
| WC | 8,065,000 | 6,378,000 | 4,721,000 |
| Emp. | 381 | 320 | 288 |

DUNS 28-827-6470 Imp-Exp
## Tritech International Ltd
**(Subsidiary of:** Moog Inc.)
Westhill Business Park Peregrine Road, Westhill, Aberdeenshire AB32 6JL
**Tel:** 01224744111 **Fax:** 01224741771
**Web:** www.tritech.co.uk
**Reg No:** 0085501SC **VAT No:** 384888679
**Estd:** 1981 Private Limited Company
**Line of Business:** Marine engines and engineering
**Export Markets:** Singapore; Norway; U S A; Netherlands; France
**Export Sales:** £11,670,223
**Issued Capital:** £25,200
**Directors:** D J Norman, M J Glister, Ms J Mccloy, D Bradley, L J Ball, S Mclay
**Co. Secretary:** Christopher Head
**Responsibilities**
**Senior:** Brian Bullock *(Manager)*, Marcus Cardew *(Manager)*, Allan Stamper *(Manager)*
**Sales:** Chris MacFarlane *(Sales Engineer)*
**US SIC:** 3559 **UK SIC:** 32863
**Auditors:** Deloitte LLP
**Bankers:** Bank Of Scotland (80-05-14)

| | 28-09-13 | 31-03-12 | 02-09-11 |
|---|---|---|---|
| TO | 21,091,004 | 12,308,706 | 9,494,966 |
| P/L | 3,855,237 | 2,326,907 | 1,603,759 |
| NW | 6,378,724 | 4,343,635 | 4,061,345 |
| WC | 4,584,839 | 6,118,077 | 5,965,335 |
| Emp. | 98 | 93 | 84 |

DUNS 29-380-5339 Exp
## Tritech Precision Products (Barnstaple) Ltd
**(Subsidiary of:** Universal Ferro & Allied Chemicals Limited)
Unit 8, Barnstaple, Devon EX32 8PA
**Tel:** 01271376521
**Web:** www.tritech-precision-products.co.uk
**Reg No:** 1089958 **Estd:** 1985 Private Limited Company
**Line of Business:** Casting of light metals
**Export Markets:** France, Germany, Sweden, North America, China, Australia
**Export Sales:** £14,000
**Issued Capital:** £50,000
**Directors:** S J Goodier, N S Fugre, R Gosrani, F D Neterwala, R Ramanathan, S E Goodfellow, A R White, I J Walker
**Co. Secretary:** Martin Parry
**Responsibilities**
**Engineering:** Robin Saxby *(Technical Director)*
**US SIC:** 3361 **UK SIC:** 31120
**Auditors:** Mitten Clarke Ltd
**Bankers:** Barclays Bank Plc (20-90-08)

| | 31-03-14 | 31-03-13 | 01-03-12 |
|---|---|---|---|
| TO | 5,080,000 | 4,344,000 | 3,720,000 |
| P/L | 686,000 | 353,000 | 448,000 |
| NW | 3,024,000 | 2,451,000 | 2,255,000 |
| WC | 2,587,000 | 2,120,000 | 2,015,000 |
| Emp. | 65 | 54 | 43 |

DUNS 50-370-2953 Imp-Exp
## Triten International Ltd
**(Subsidiary of:** Til Corporation Ltd)
Shawfield Road, Barnsley, South Yorkshire S71 3HS
**Web:** www.tritenapg.com
**Reg No:** 2385191 **Estd:** 1989 Private Limited Company
**Line of Business:** Representative office
**Export Markets:** Worldwide
**Trading Style:** Trimay Engineering
**Issued Capital:** £1,867,917
**Director:** P J Leonard
**Co. Secretary:** Nicholas Bush
**Responsibilities**
**Senior:** John Arnoldy *(Chairman)*
**Purchasing:** Andy Smith *(Logistics Manager)*
**Fleet:** Andy Smith *(Logistics Manager)*
**US SIC:** 3398, 8911, 3499
**UK SIC:** 31380, 83701, 31694
**Auditors:** Ernst & Young LLP
**Bankers:** National Westminster Bank Plc (54-21-34)

| | 30-04-14 | 30-04-13 | 30-04-12 |
|---|---|---|---|
| TO | 7,612,738 | 7,168,013 | 6,023,277 |
| P/L | 684,957 | 631,611 | 303,639 |
| NW | 3,708,413 | 3,168,120 | 2,682,597 |
| WC | 3,210,386 | 2,817,536 | 1,442,479 |
| Emp. | 82 | 72 | 63 |

DUNS 73-381-9697
## Triton Global Ltd
80 Mosley Street, Peter Square, Manchester M2 3FX
**Tel:** 0870-839-0800
**Reg No:** 4655428 **Estd:** 2003 Private Limited Company
**Line of Business:** Insurance services
**Export Sales:** £2,320,377
**Issued Capital:** £145
**Directors:** A L Macleod, C P Hatfield, M N Robin, J H Coleman, J A Ford, J D Simon, D Stoica, N Sully
**US SIC:** 6411, 8111
**UK SIC:** 83200, 83500
**Bankers:** Svenska Handelsbanken Ab (publ) (40-51-62)

| | 01-08-13 | 30-04-12 | 30-08-11 |
|---|---|---|---|
| TO | 12,119,443 | 8,460,245 | 7,960,262 |
| P/L | (397,178) | (249,380) | 330,966 |
| NW | (1,351,492) | (734,749) | (600,476) |
| WC | 2,136,874 | (675,665) | (385,203) |
| Emp. | 138 | 123 | 116 |

DUNS 29-372-1957
## Triton Industry Ltd
**(Subsidiary of:** Norcros Plc)
Shepperton Business Park, Caldwell Road, Nuneaton, Warwickshire CV11 4NR
**Tel:** 02476344441 **Fax:** 024-7634-9828
**Web:** www.tritonshowers.co.uk
**Reg No:** 0957610 **Estd:** 1969 Private Limited Company
**Line of Business:** Manufacture of other fabricated metal products not elsewhere classified
**Trading Style:** Triton Showers
**Issued Capital:** £7,453,002
**Directors:** M G Vaughan, R H Collins
**Co. Secretary:** Mathew Vaughan
**Responsibilities**
**Senior:** Lorna Fellows *(Company Director)*, Chris Whitell *(Manager)*
**HR:** Sheila Ridgway *(Hr Manager)*
**US SIC:** 3499 **UK SIC:** 31694
**Auditors:** PricewaterhouseCoopers

| | 31-03-14 | 31-03-13 | 31-03-12 |
|---|---|---|---|
| TA | 7,453,000 | 7,453,000 | 7,453,000 |
| NW | 7,453,000 | 7,453,000 | 7,453,000 |

DUNS 23-178-0599
## The Triton Inn
Ellerker Road, Brantingham, Brough, North Humberside HU15 1QE
**Tel:** 01482-667261
**Web:** www.thetritoninn.com
**Estd:** 1999 Proprietorship
**Line of Business:** Restaurant - pub food
**Proprietor:** S Rennison
**Responsibilities**
**Senior:** Paul Rusling *(Proprietor)*
**US SIC:** 5812, 5813
**UK SIC:** 66110, 66200
**Employees:** 71

DUNS 28-976-0910 Imp
## Triumph Actuation Systems - Uk Ltd
**(Subsidiary of:** Triumph Aerospace Systems Group - Uk Ltd)
Unit 9/10, Catheralls Industrial Estate, Mold, Clwyd CH7 3PS
**Tel:** 01244550022
**Web:** www.triumphgroup.com
**Reg No:** 1756863 **VAT No:** 453662343
**Estd:** 1983 Private Limited Company
**Line of Business:** Other business activities not elsewhere classified
**Export Sales:** £1,044,906
**Trading Style:** Triumph Actuation Systems - Uk & Iom
**Issued Capital:** £25,000
**Directors:** M D Kornblatt, J Frisby, M Mcdonald
**Co. Secretary:** John Wright 11
**Responsibilities**
**Senior:** Richard Ill *(Manager)*, Gary Parkes *(Joint Managing Director)*
**Health & Safety:** Gary Parkes *(Joint Managing Director)*
**Facilities:** Gary Parkes *(Joint Managing Director)*
**Purchasing:** Nick Cropper *(Purchasing Manager)*
**Engineering:** J Foulkes *(Manufacturing Manager)*
**US SIC:** 7399, 3679, 3721
**UK SIC:** 83954, 34542, 36400
**Auditors:** Ernst & Young LLP
**Bankers:** Lloyds TSB Bank plc (30-12-96)

| | 31-03-13 | 31-03-12 | 31-03-11 |
|---|---|---|---|
| TO | 6,693,161 | 8,032,835 | 9,286,907 |
| P/L | (859,869) | 162,724 | 1,395,152 |
| NW | 3,481,443 | 4,364,268 | 4,159,300 |
| WC | 2,714,484 | 3,509,094 | 3,754,829 |
| Emp. | 48 | 53 | 51 |

DUNS 21-721-4846 Imp
## Triumph Furniture Ltd
Triumph Works, The Willows, Merthyr Tydfil, Mid Glamorgan CF48 1YH
**Tel:** 01685384041 **Fax:** 01685352202
**Web:** www.triumph-tbs.com
**Reg No:** 7591856 **Estd:** 1941 Private Limited Company
**Line of Business:** Office furniture and equipment suppliers
**Export Sales:** £880,417
**Issued Capital:** £50,000
**Directors:** Mrs E R Jackson, A C Jackson
**Responsibilities**
**Senior:** Helen Coggan *(Customer Services Director)*, Simon Harwood *(Manager)*
**US SIC:** 2599 **UK SIC:** 46720
**Auditors:** Willis Jones
**Bankers:** Abbey National Plc (09-03-95)

| | 01-06-14 | 03-06-13 | 03-06-12 |
|---|---|---|---|
| TO | 15,796,780 | N/A | N/A |
| P/L | 205,740 | (29,617) | 107,475 |
| NW | 468,145 | 307,037 | 136,080 |
| WC | 853,040 | 1,071,094 | 392,400 |
| Emp. | 225 | 213 | 198 |

DUNS 21-631-3346 Imp-Exp
## Triumph International Ltd
**(Subsidiary of:** Triumph International Spiesshofer & Braun Kommandi)
Arkwright Road, Swindon, Wiltshire SN25 5BE
**Tel:** 01793-722200
**Web:** www.triumph.com
**Reg No:** 0536483 **Estd:** 1954 Private Limited Company
**Line of Business:** Lingerie retail
**Export Sales:** £2,194,000
**Issued Capital:** £3,500,000
**Directors:** C Flock, N Hewitt, Ms C A Burns, Ms S A Hamilton
**Co. Secretary:** Neville Hewitt
**Responsibilities**
**Senior:** Tina Day *(Manager)*, Lassi Haikola *(Manager)*
**Admin:** Glen Newman *(?IT Technical Administrator)*
**IT:** Glen Newman *(?IT Technical Administrator)*
**Branches:** Triumph International Ltd, 40 Pingle Drive, Bicester, Oxfordshire OX26 6WD
**US SIC:** 5621 **UK SIC:** 64500
**Auditors:** PricewaterhouseCoopers LLP
**Bankers:** Barclays Bank Plc (20-84-58)

| | 31-12-13 | 31-12-12 | 31-12-11 |
|---|---|---|---|
| TO | 35,198,000 | 34,648,000 | 45,274,000 |
| P/L | 1,175,000 | 860,000 | (2,722,000) |
| NW | (1,824,000) | (5,481,000) | (3,930,000) |
| WC | 849,000 | 1,150,000 | 3,156,000 |
| Emp. | 162 | 152 | 169 |

DUNS 29-463-8564 Imp
## Triumph Motorcycles Ltd
**(Subsidiary of:** Bloor Investments Ltd)
Jacknell Road, Hinckley, Leicestershire LE10 3BS
**Tel:** 01708752111 **Fax:** 01455-453-005
**Web:** www.jacklilley.com
**Reg No:** 1735844 **VAT No:** 439493610
**Estd:** 1983 Private Limited Company
**Line of Business:** Manufacture of motorcycles
**Export Sales:** £281,446,000
**Trading Style:** Triumph
**Issued Capital:** £35,000,000
**Principals:** J S Bloor *(Managing)*, S J Sargent, G G Clarke, J L Eastham, P J Graves, P A Stroud, N S Bloor, Lord D M Jones
**Co. Secretary:** Dinesh Mehta

**Branches:** Triumph Motorcycles Limited, Normandy Way, Hinckley, Leicestershire LE10 2NN
**US SIC:** 5571 **UK SIC:** 65100
**Auditors:** Ernst & Young LLP
**Bankers:** National Westminster Bank Plc (60-80-09)

| | 30-06-13 | 30-06-12 | 30-06-11 |
|---|---|---|---|
| TO | 333,702,000 | 316,760,000 | 297,452,000 |
| P/L | (12,792,000) | 2,659,000 | 4,580,000 |
| NW | 34,894,000 | 44,320,000 | 42,298,000 |
| WC | 29,558,000 | 28,535,000 | 30,946,000 |
| Emp. | 490 | 478 | 478 |

DUNS 21-613-4700 **Imp-Exp**

## Triumph Structures - Farnborough Ltd

21 Invincible Road Industrial Estate, Farnborough, Hampshire GU14 7QU
**Tel:** 01252304000
**Web:** www.primusint.com
**Reg No:** 0706645 **VAT No:** 211743302
**Estd:** 1961 Private Limited Company
**Line of Business:** Manufacturers and suppliers of aircrafts
**Export Markets:** W Europe, U S A, Canada
**Export Sales:** £26,408,785
**Issued Capital:** £74,074
**Directors:** J D Frisby, J Mcrae, M Thomas, J B Wright Ii
**Responsibilities**
**Senior:** Douglas Fletcher *(Manager)*, Paul Jerrem *(Manager)*
**Branches:** Farnborough
**US SIC:** 3721 **UK SIC:** 36400
**Auditors:** Ernst & Young LLP
**Bankers:** National Westminster Bank Plc (60-02-49)

| | 31-03-13 | 01-04-12 | 31-03-10 |
|---|---|---|---|
| TO | 37,963,968 | 31,400,613 | 22,635,392 |
| P/L | 7,232,637 | (10,795,665) | (2,023,986) |
| NW | 6,058,374 | 569,714 | 7,156,450 |
| WC | 11,018,942 | 9,944,599 | 3,077,141 |
| Emp. | 387 | 303 | 240 |

DUNS 49-427-6199

## Trl Ltd

(**Subsidiary of:** Transport Research Foundation)
Crowthorne House, Nine Mile Ride, Wokingham, Berkshire RG40 3GA
**Web:** www.trl.co.uk
**Reg No:** 3142272 **VAT No:** 664625321
**Estd:** 1995 Private Limited Company
**Line of Business:** Research institutions and organisations
**Trading Style:** Transport Research Laboratory
**Issued Capital:** £2
**Directors:** R Wallis, T W Andrews
**Co. Secretary:** Peter Millard
**Responsibilities**
**Senior:** Bob Collis *(Director, Infrastructure)*, Iain York *(General Manager)*
**IT:** Sally Cotter *(Principal Project Manager)*, Gavin Jackman *(Software Director)*, Iwan Parry *(Program Manager)*
**HR:** Andi Flint *(Head of Human Factors and Simu)*, Nick Reed *(HR Director)*
**Operations:** Iain Rillie *(Head of Operations-Safety & Ri)*
**Fleet:** Robert Lyndfell *(Transport Manager)*
**Engineering:** Michael Mchale *(Engineer)*, Vijay Ramdas *(Senior Technical Manager)*
**Branches:** Trl Ltd, Sighthill Campus, 9 Sighthill Court, Edinburgh, Midlothian EH11 4BN
**US SIC:** 4712, 7399
**UK SIC:** 77002, 83954
**Auditors:** Ernst & Young LLP
**Bankers:** National Westminster Bank Plc (60-19-28)

| | 30-06-14 | 31-03-13 | 31-06-12 |
|---|---|---|---|
| TO | 39,493,000 | 30,431,000 | 29,633,000 |
| P/L | 2,065,000 | 1,513,000 | 796,000 |
| NW | 317,000 | (18,389,000) | (16,736,000) |
| WC | 6,956,000 | (2,800,000) | (2,111,000) |
| Emp. | 330 | 325 | 328 |

DUNS 28-965-9690 **Imp-Exp**

## Trl Technology Ltd

(**Subsidiary of:** L-3 Communications Holdings Inc.)
Unit 11 Shannon Way, Tewkesbury, Gloucestershire GL28 8ND
**Tel:** 01684278700
**Web:** www.trltech.co.uk
**Reg No:** 1705039 **VAT No:** 487927969
**Estd:** 1983 Private Limited Company
**Line of Business:** Other engineering activities
**Export Sales:** £12,191,000
**Trading Style:** L-3 Trl Technology
**Issued Capital:** £605,911
**Directors:** R Cook, J Chapman, D Y Azmon
**Co. Secretary:** Peter Dann
**Responsibilities**
**Senior:** Mark Hutchings *(Manager)*
**IT:** Adrian Head *(Head of Computers)*
**Facilities:** Mark Boughton *(Facilities Manager)*
**US SIC:** 8911, 7379
**UK SIC:** 83701, 83940
**Auditors:** PricewaterhouseCoopers LLP
**Bankers:** Barclays Bank Plc (20-74-05)

| | 31-12-13 | 31-12-12 | 31-12-11 |
|---|---|---|---|
| TO | 79,761,000 | 59,056,000 | 57,526,000 |
| P/L | 15,776,000 | 12,456,000 | 9,569,000 |
| NW | 23,080,000 | 23,611,000 | 16,611,000 |
| WC | 19,773,000 | 21,287,000 | 21,037,000 |
| Emp. | 338 | 375 | 410 |

DUNS 22-238-2991 **Imp**

## Trm Packaging Ltd

Red Cat Lane, Burscough, Ormskirk, Lancashire L40 0SY
**Tel:** 01704892811 **Fax:** 01704-895546
**Web:** www.trmpack.co.uk
**Reg No:** 4256359 **Estd:** 2001 Private Limited Company
**Line of Business:** Manufacturers of boxes and cartons
**Issued Capital:** £234,000
**Directors:** M J Enright, M L Introna, B E Sutcliffe, T R Maund, M Giles
**Co. Secretary:** Matthew Enright
**US SIC:** 2651, 2752
**UK SIC:** 47253, 47544
**Auditors:** Baker Tilly
**Bankers:** National Westminster Bank Plc (01-10-01)

| | 31-08-14 | 31-08-13 | 31-08-12 |
|---|---|---|---|
| TO | 39,271,000 | 37,100,000 | 37,970,000 |
| P/L | 3,110,000 | 3,960,000 | 3,283,000 |
| NW | 9,583,000 | 7,950,000 | 5,169,000 |
| WC | (766,000) | (558,000) | (1,307,000) |
| Emp. | 245 | 243 | 242 |

DUNS 76-711-4648

## T.R.M. Tisch Ltd

(**Subsidiary of:** Talisker Ltd)
67 Kingsway, London WC2B 6TD
**Tel:** 02072427469 **Fax:** 02072427493
**Web:** www.belgo-restaurants.co.uk
**Reg No:** 2594188 **VAT No:** 523413383
**Estd:** 1992 Private Limited Company
**Line of Business:** Licensed restaurants
**Trading Style:** Belgo Noord
**Issued Capital:** £69,665
**Directors:** T J Doubleday, S Richards
**Responsibilities**
**Senior:** Mohan Mansigani *(Manager)*, Thomas Moravec *(General Manager)*
**US SIC:** 5812 **UK SIC:** 66110
**Auditors:** BDO Stoy Hayward LLP
**Bankers:** Barclays Bank Plc (20-00-50)

| | 02-06-13 | 27-05-12 | 29-06-11 |
|---|---|---|---|
| TO | 7,152,811 | 7,270,857 | 7,487,781 |
| P/L | 443,296 | (142,004) | 652,447 |
| NW | 4,395,033 | 3,925,053 | 3,959,802 |
| WC | 2,714,300 | 2,330,856 | 1,997,696 |
| Emp. | 159 | 170 | 183 |

DUNS 36-516-3617

## Trmg Ltd

Winchester Court, 1 Fiddlebridge Lane Forum Place, Hatfield, Hertfordshire AL10 0RN
**Tel:** 01707273999
**Web:** www.trmg.co.uk
**Reg No:** 3285694 **Estd:** 1990 Private Limited Company
**Line of Business:** Other publishing
**Export Sales:** £1,873,887
**Trading Style:** The Really Motoring Group
**Issued Capital:** £4,000
**Directors:** Ms J M Fellows, J A Fellows, Ms A J Stevens
**Co. Secretary:** Andrew Stevens
**US SIC:** 2741 **UK SIC:** 47541
**Auditors:** Ashleys (Hitchin) Ltd

| | 31-12-13 | 31-12-12 | 31-12-11 |
|---|---|---|---|
| TO | 6,246,293 | 7,317,578 | 7,156,370 |
| P/L | 400,326 | 104,465 | 326,399 |
| NW | 335,510 | 221,110 | 237,900 |
| WC | 302,116 | 162,144 | 159,222 |
| Emp. | 89 | 84 | 77 |

DUNS 50-337-7350 **Exp**

## Tro Group Ltd

(**Subsidiary of:** Omnicom Group Inc.)
11 Penfold Drive, Wymondham, Norfolk NR18 0WZ
**Tel:** 01603785700
**Web:** www.tro-group.com
**Reg No:** 2361809 **Estd:** 1996 Private Limited Company
**Line of Business:** Marketing consultants
**Export Markets:** European Union (E U)
**Issued Capital:** £100
**Directors:** P D Trueman, J W Klingender, P M Wyrley-Birch, K O'Loughlin, T W Preece
**Co. Secretary:** Mrs Sally Bray
**Responsibilities**
**Senior:** Thomas Gentle *(Manager)*, Robert Harber *(Manager)*
**Marketing:** Sarah Mayo *(Brands Manager)*
**IT:** Steve Howlett *(IT Manager)*
**HR:** Thomas Gentle *(Manager)*
**Operations:** Dougie Martin *(Operations Manager)*
**Branches:** Tro Group Ltd, 9-11 Penfold Drive, Wymondham, Norfolk NR18 0WZ
**US SIC:** 7392, 7399
**UK SIC:** 83951, 83954
**Auditors:** KPMG Audit PLC
**Bankers:** Barclays Bank Plc (20-62-53)

| | 31-12-13 | 31-12-12 | 31-12-11 |
|---|---|---|---|
| TO | 10,472,769 | 9,741,676 | 11,588,790 |
| P/L | 2,070,021 | 2,123,370 | 3,573,285 |
| NW | 3,042,972 | 2,284,143 | 2,553,694 |
| WC | 2,812,620 | 2,116,934 | 2,295,462 |
| Emp. | 211 | 193 | 200 |

DUNS 34-785-2944

## Trod Ltd

Unit 1-2, Tay Road Frankley Industrial Park, Birmingham, West Midlands B45 0LD
**Tel:** 0121-457-7233
**Web:** www.buyforlessonline.co.uk
**Reg No:** 5585871 **Estd:** 2005 Private Limited Company
**Line of Business:** Retail sale of sports goods, games and toys, stamps and coins
**Export Sales:** £8,196,774
**Issued Capital:** £1
**Director:** D W Aston
**Responsibilities**
**Senior:** Ian Briant *(Manager)*
**US SIC:** 5941 **UK SIC:** 65400
**Auditors:** Briants Chartered Accountants

| | 31-03-14 | 31-03-13 | 31-03-11 |
|---|---|---|---|
| TO | 18,094,688 | 24,388,457 | N/A |
| P/L | 122,454 | (634,197) | N/A |
| NW | 128,492 | 25,052 | 581,212 |
| WC | (1,820,480) | (1,081,155) | 508,639 |
| Emp. | 125 | 119 | N/A |

DUNS 76-320-9855 **Imp-Exp**

## Trodat (Uk) Ltd

(**Subsidiary of:** Trodat Trotec Holding Gmbh)
144 Neilston Road, Paisley, Renfrewshire PA2 6QH
**Tel:** 01418846441 **Fax:** 01418847819
**Web:** www.trodat.co.uk
**Reg No:** 0127743SC **Estd:** 1990 Private Limited Company
**Line of Business:** Manufacturers and suppliers of rubber stamps
**Export Markets:** E U, Worlwide
**Trading Style:** Funstamps, Dormy Custom Products
**Issued Capital:** £5,629,483
**Directors:** I P Bradbeer, R Rier, M Peduzzi, P Hofmann, M Prinz
**Responsibilities**
**Senior:** Eddie Guthrie *(Manager)*
**Marketing:** Jill Langley *(Marketing Manager)*
**Branches:** Trodat (Uk) Ltd, Battersea Rd, Stockport, Cheshire SK4 3EN
**US SIC:** 3069, 3953
**UK SIC:** 48123, 49541
**Auditors:** Hurst & Co
**Bankers:** Bank Of Scotland (80-54-01)

| | 31-12-13 | 31-12-12 | 31-12-11 |
|---|---|---|---|
| TO | 6,149,768 | 5,662,268 | 5,907,521 |
| P/L | 122,921 | 257,671 | 644,059 |
| NW | 1,155,986 | 1,224,803 | (762,594) |
| WC | 1,314,103 | 1,568,983 | 1,064,189 |
| Emp. | 63 | 60 | 59 |

DUNS 21-589-1573 **Imp**

## Trojan Crates Ltd

90-98 Sinclair Road, Aberdeen, Aberdeenshire AB11 9PP
**Web:** www.trojancrates.co.uk
**Reg No:** 0069827SC **VAT No:** 297250827
**Estd:** 1979 Private Limited Company
**Line of Business:** Manufacture of wooden containers
**Issued Capital:** £3,000
**Principals:** A E Paterson *(Managing)*, C Middleton, R G Paterson, I D Morrice, K Morrison, C Sim
**Co. Secretary:**
Stronachs Secretaries Limited
**Responsibilities**
**Senior:** Agnes Paterson *(Manager)*
**US SIC:** 3999 **UK SIC:** 49590
**Auditors:** Hall Morrice Partners
**Bankers:** The Royal Bank Of Scotland Plc (83-26-16)

| | 31-05-14 | 31-05-13 | 31-05-12 |
|---|---|---|---|
| TA | 2,900,151 | 2,436,705 | 2,307,403 |
| NW | 1,953,958 | 1,656,047 | 1,472,824 |
| WC | 1,544,727 | 1,372,351 | 1,250,064 |

DUNS 22-106-6256 **Imp**

## Trojan Electronics Ltd

Unit 10-11, Swansea, West Glamorgan SA4 9WG
**Tel:** 01792-892221 **Fax:** 01792-891119
**Web:** www.trojanelectronics.co.uk
**Reg No:** 4125912 **Estd:** 2000 Private Limited Company
**Line of Business:** Electronic equipment (assembly)
**Export Sales:** £142,899
**Issued Capital:** £30,833
**Directors:** C J Murphy, M C Jones, D O'Keeffe, J J Morgan, M E Rash
**Co. Secretary:** Malcolm Rash
**US SIC:** 3643, 5961, 7629
**UK SIC:** 34203, 65600, 67301
**Auditors:** Cross & Bowen
**Bankers:** HSBC Bank plc (40-35-04)

| | 31-03-14 | 31-03-13 | 31-03-12 |
|---|---|---|---|
| TO | 9,651,090 | 8,773,341 | 7,830,076 |
| P/L | 572,679 | 107,335 | 75,591 |
| NW | 616,107 | 297,305 | 339,879 |
| WC | 347,996 | 22,533 | 82,283 |

DUNS 37-991-7123 **Imp**

## Trojan Manufacturing Group Ltd

Fryers Road, Walsall, West Midlands WS2 7LZ
**Tel:** 01922-713933 **Fax:** 01922713890
**Web:** www.trojan-hardware.com
**Reg No:** 3293512 **Estd:** 1996 Private Limited Company
**Line of Business:** Management activities of holding companies
**Issued Capital:** £40,000
**Principals:** T J Dolman *(Managing)*, A Chadwick
**Responsibilities**
**Senior:** Terence Moore *(Manager)*
**US SIC:** 6711, 3423
**UK SIC:** 83962, 31612
**Auditors:** Daw White Murrall
**Bankers:** National Westminster Bank Plc (55-70-46)

| | 30-04-14 | 30-04-13 | 30-04-12 |
|---|---|---|---|
| TA | 1,979,992 | 3,070,526 | 3,057,401 |
| NW | 209,719 | 1,594,708 | 1,310,668 |
| WC | (690,982) | 896,277 | 688,862 |

DUNS 29-669-6792 **Exp**

## Trojan Plastics Ltd

Ramsden Mills, Britannia Road, Huddersfield, West Yorkshire HD3 4QG
**Tel:** 01484648181 **Fax:** 01484-657098
**Web:** www.trojanplastics.co.uk
**Reg No:** 1995822 **VAT No:** 525809631
**Estd:** 1973 Private Limited Company
**Line of Business:** Manufacture of taps and valves
**Export Markets:** Germany, Netherlands, Italy, Austria, Spain, Portugal, Middle East, Scandinavia, Singapore, Malaysia, Japan, South Korea, Indonesia
**Trading Style:** Trojan Plastics Limited
**Issued Capital:** £100
**Principals:** J M Mosley *(Managing)*, A P Mosley, D J Mosley
**Co. Secretary:** Adam Mosley
**Responsibilities**
**Senior:** Ernest Hatton *(Manager)*
**Finance:** Daniel Hirst *(Accounts Manager)*
**Marketing:** Ernest Hatton *(Manager)*
**Sales:** Ernest Hatton *(Manager)*
**IT:** Daniel Hirst *(Accounts Manager)*
**HR:** Ernest Hatton *(Manager)*
**Health & Safety:** Barry Gerry *(Production Manager)*
**Facilities:** Ernest Hatton *(Manager)*
**Purchasing:** Barry Gerry *(Production Manager)*
**Engineering:** Barry Gerry *(Production Manager)*
**US SIC:** 3494, 3261
**UK SIC:** 32880, 24892
**Auditors:** Connelly & Co Ltd
**Bankers:** Barclays Bank Plc (20-43-04)

| | 30-04-14 | 30-04-13 | 30-04-12 |
|---|---|---|---|
| TO | 19,167,943 | 16,378,503 | 16,889,100 |
| P/L | 535,626 | 349,075 | 196,459 |
| NW | 4,108,498 | 3,572,872 | 3,315,817 |
| WC | 5,305,020 | 5,618,004 | 5,442,526 |
| Emp. | 125 | 107 | 108 |

DUNS 21-890-7293 **Imp-Exp**

## Trolex Ltd

(**Subsidiary of:** Trolex Group Ltd)
Newby Road Industrial Estate, Newby Road, Hazel Grove, Stockport, Cheshire SK7 5DY
**Tel:** 0161-483-1435
**Web:** www.trolex.com
**Reg No:** 0644260 **VAT No:** 157441854
**Estd:** 1959 Private Limited Company
**Line of Business:** Manufacturers of electronic equipment and components
**Export Markets:** Worldwide
**Issued Capital:** £61,739
**Principals:** J Pierce-Jones *(Managing)*, G D Christopher, G Pierce-Jones, L Pierce-Jones, P R Brian
**Co. Secretary:** Gary Christopher
**Responsibilities**
**Senior:** Andy Dawson *(Works Manager)*
**Health & Safety:** Ian Burroughs *(Quality Manager)*
**Facilities:** Andy Dawson *(Works Manager)*
**US SIC:** 3679 **UK SIC:** 34542
**Auditors:** BKR Hainess Watts

**Bankers:** National Westminster Bank Plc
(01-08-38)

|     | 31-12-13 | 31-12-12 | 31-12-11 |
|-----|----------|----------|----------|
| TO  | 7,554,543 | 10,519,313 | 9,075,971 |
| P/L | (749,209) | 880,143 | 629,797 |
| NW  | 3,799,851 | 4,396,190 | 3,615,793 |
| WC  | 1,389,910 | 2,120,047 | 1,504,991 |
| Emp. | 77 | 65 | 53 |

DUNS 28-826-2892

## Tron Theatre Ltd

63 Trongate, Glasgow, Lanarkshire G1 5HB
**Tel:** 01415524267
**Web:** www.tron.co.uk
**Reg No:** 0077475SC **Estd:** 1982 Private
Company Limited By Guarantee
**Line of Business:** Operation of arts facilities
**Trading Style:** Tron Theatre
**Directors:** Miss J L Macsween, M R Leese,
K Miller, Ms J K Austin, Mrs A A Junner,
Ms D Mcdougall, Ms N S Walls,
Miss S Nanjiani
**Co. Secretary:** Stewart Coulter
**Responsibilities**
**Senior:** Louise Beattie (Manager), Brian
McLaren (Manager)
**Marketing:** Lindsay Mitchell (Press and
Marketing Manager)
**Admin:** Craig Ferguson (Administrative
Assistant), Lisa Keenan (Education and
Outreach Manager)
**Facilities:** Billy Humes (Property
Supervisor)
**Operations:** Deborah McArthur (Drama
Officer)
**Engineering:** Karen Bryce (Technical
Manager), Barry McCall (Head of Sound)
**US SIC:** 7911 **UK SIC:** 97913
**Auditors:** James Stewart Thom
**Bankers:** Clydesdale Bank Plc (82-64-31)

|     | 31-03-14 | 31-03-13 | 31-03-12 |
|-----|----------|----------|----------|
| TA  | 531,447 | 460,249 | 559,128 |
| NW  | 322,217 | 321,743 | 319,763 |
| WC  | 185,372 | 186,141 | 158,438 |

DUNS 22-852-0029

## The Trophy & Rosette Award Co. Ltd

(**Subsidiary of:** Rosettes Direct (Holdings)
Ltd)
York Street, Accrington, Lancashire BB5
3NU
**Tel:** 01254397880 **Fax:** 01254-394839
**Web:** www.award-ifa.co.uk
**Reg No:** 1553234 **Estd:** 1980 Private
Limited Company
**Line of Business:** Horticultural supplies
**Trading Style:** T R A
**Issued Capital:** £24,000
**Principals:** D L Wallace (Managing),
S R Freegard
**Co. Secretary:** David Wallace
**US SIC:** 5083, 3911
**UK SIC:** 61490, 49101
**Auditors:** Kidsons Impey
**Bankers:** National Westminster Bank Plc
(01-07-29)

|     | 31-12-13 | 31-12-12 | 31-12-11 |
|-----|----------|----------|----------|
| TA  | 566,477 | 595,864 | 572,880 |
| NW  | 407,225 | 396,488 | 374,708 |
| WC  | 360,936 | 336,307 | 306,962 |

DUNS 45-834-0411                                          Imp

## Tropical Blinds Ltd

Unit 5-6 Five Arches Business Centre,
Maidstone Road, Sidcup, Kent DA14 5AE
**Fax:** 020-8269-6401
**Web:** www.tropicalblinds.com
**Reg No:** 3184810 **Estd:** 1996 Private
Limited Company
**Line of Business:** Manufacturers and
retailers of curtains
**Issued Capital:** £320,000
**Director:** Ms S S Fells
**Co. Secretary:** Martin Fells
**Responsibilities**
**Senior:** Kirstie Gibbons (Manager)
**Marketing:** Vicky Gayle (Marketing
Manager)
**Sales:** Amy Williams (Sales Manager)
**IT:** Vicky Bowler (Computer Manager)
**HR:** Ann Bowler (Human Resources
Manager)
**Facilities:** Bob Collington (Engineering
Manager)
**Engineering:** Bob Collington (Engineering
Manager)
**US SIC:** 2392, 3999
**UK SIC:** 45550, 49590
**Auditors:** McBrides
**Bankers:** National Westminster Bank Plc
(60-01-21)

|     | 30-04-14 | 30-04-13 | 30-04-12 |
|-----|----------|----------|----------|
| TA  | 2,305,296 | 2,255,972 | 2,337,066 |
| NW  | 137,144 | 355,188 | 511,132 |
| WC  | (90,617) | (101,097) | (52,754) |

DUNS 21-151-2792                                          Imp

## Tropical Marine Centre Ltd

(**Subsidiary of:** Tropical Marine Centre
(2012) Ltd)
Pexton Road, Driffield, North Humberside
YO25 9DJ
**Tel:** 01377200888
**Web:** www.gardenhealth.com
**Reg No:** 6804160 **Estd:** 2009 Private
Limited Company
**Line of Business:** Fish farming
**Export Sales:** £4,390,000
**Trading Style:** Westland Horticulture
**Issued Capital:** £2,424,563
**Directors:** D J Black, P D West
**Co. Secretary:** Ms Amanda Taylor
**Responsibilities**
**Senior:** Barry Humble (Financial Manager)
**Finance:** Barry Humble (Financial Manager)
**Marketing:** Rachael Dickinson (Marketing
Manager)
**Health & Safety:** Hayley Stone (Health &
Safety Officer)
**Facilities:** Peter Suggitt (Engineering
Manager)
**Branches:** Tropical Marine Centre Ltd,
Kelleythorpe Industrial Estate, Driffield, North
Humberside YO25 9DJ
**US SIC:** 0921, 2047
**UK SIC:** 03002, 42221
**Auditors:** KPMG LLP

|     | 31-03-14 | 31-03-13 | 07-03-12 |
|-----|----------|----------|----------|
| TO  | 16,499,000 | 16,147,000 | 57,460,000 |
| P/L | 429,000 | 262,000 | 8,929,000 |
| NW  | 2,274,000 | 4,709,000 | 4,469,000 |
| WC  | 2,314,000 | 4,744,000 | 3,382,000 |
| Emp. | 90 | 90 | 208 |

DUNS 34-618-7979

## Tropical Sky Ltd

(**Subsidiary of:** Vivid Skies Ltd)
Kings House, First Floor North, 13/21
Cantelupe Road, East Grinstead, West
Sussex RH19 3BE
**Tel:** 08443329369 **Fax:** 01342322391
**Web:** www.tropicalsky.co.uk
**Reg No:** 5425418 **Estd:** 2005 Private
Limited Company
**Line of Business:** Tour operators
**Issued Capital:** £70,000
**Directors:** Mrs J Collins, D A Hennessy
**Co. Secretary:** Michael Collins
**Responsibilities**
**Senior:** Gail Bolton (General Manager)
**US SIC:** 7999 **UK SIC:** 97913
**Bankers:** Barclays Bank Plc (20-23-97)

|     | 31-10-13 | 31-10-12 | 31-10-11 |
|-----|----------|----------|----------|
| TO  | 30,102,701 | 27,135,897 | 25,568,081 |
| P/L | 323,242 | 281,368 | 154,589 |
| NW  | 975,065 | 733,268 | 511,066 |
| WC  | 1,026,391 | 1,032,917 | 848,668 |
| Emp. | 75 | 62 | 56 |

DUNS 21-386-4988                                          Imp

## Tropicana Health & Fitness

Minworth Industrial Park, Sutton Coldfield,
West Midlands B76 1AH
**Tel:** 0121-351-3110
**Web:** www.tropicanaprofessional.com
**Estd:** 2004 Proprietorship
**Line of Business:** Health food retailers
**Proprietor:** G Hill
**US SIC:** 5499 **UK SIC:** 64100
**Employees:** 50

DUNS 64-082-5113

## Tropicana Health & Fitness Ltd

53 Lichfield Road, Sutton Coldfield, West
Midlands B76 1AH
**Tel:** 0845-345-0916 **Fax:** 08453450917
**Web:** www.tropicanafitness.com
**Reg No:** 3477706 **Estd:** 1997 Private
Limited Company
**Line of Business:** Agents specialising in the
sale of particular products or ranges of
products not elsewhere classified
**Issued Capital:** £55,552
**Directors:** Mrs A Howkins, Ms S Ford,
Ms M A Mcinerney, S D Ford
**Responsibilities**
**Senior:** Yvonne Hill (Finance Director and
Company S)
**Finance:** Yvonne Hill (Finance Director and
Company S)
**US SIC:** 5199, 7999
**UK SIC:** 61900, 97913
**Auditors:** Thomas & Young
**Bankers:** HSBC Bank plc (40-42-12)

|     | 31-07-13 | 31-07-12 | 31-07-11 |
|-----|----------|----------|----------|
| TO  | 18,890,531 | 18,240,155 | 15,361,565 |
| P/L | 1,270,658 | 1,147,819 | 720,430 |
| NW  | 1,523,377 | 2,215,466 | 1,856,933 |
| WC  | 1,707,721 | 1,638,515 | 1,513,627 |
| Emp. | 52 | 45 | 42 |

DUNS 42-434-8576

## Tros Gynnal Plant

12 North Road, Cardiff, South Glamorgan
CF10 3DY
**Tel:** 02920396974
**Web:** www.trosgynnal.org.uk
**Reg No:** 4422485 **Estd:** 2002 Private
Company Limited By Guarantee
**Line of Business:** Charities and charitable
organisations
**Directors:** Mrs D J French, A M Price,
R Hibbs, Dr R Young, B D Jenkins,
Ms D S Daniel, Ms E J Marshman,
Miss P A Newman
**Co. Secretary:** Ms Jacqueline Murphy
**Responsibilities**
**Senior:** Christine Walby (Director)
**Branches:** Tros Gynnal Plant, 12 North
Road, Cardiff, South Glamorgan CF10 3DY
**US SIC:** 6732 **UK SIC:** 83100
**Auditors:** Hodge Bakshi
**Bankers:** Unity Trust Bank Plc (08-60-01)

|     | 31-03-14 | 31-03-13 | 31-03-12 |
|-----|----------|----------|----------|
| TO  | 2,031,695 | 1,530,942 | 1,602,275 |
| P/L | 60,366 | (41,017) | 54,225 |
| NW  | 714,676 | 654,310 | 695,327 |
| WC  | 546,587 | 481,213 | 520,715 |
| Emp. | 72 | 60 | 64 |

DUNS 21-781-2102

## Trosnant Junior School

Stockheath Lane, Havant, Hampshire PO9
3BD
**Web:** www.trosnantschools.co.uk
**Estd:** 1996 Proprietorship
**Line of Business:** Schools (foundation)
**Proprietor:** B Harwood
**Responsibilities**
**Senior:** Jim Hartley (Executive Head
Teacher), Ian Waine (Executive Head
Teacher)
**US SIC:** 8211 **UK SIC:** 93200
**Employees:** 50

DUNS 50-523-4096                                          Imp

## Trotters (Childrenswear & Accessories) Ltd

3 Gorst Road, North Acton, London NW10
6LA
**Tel:** 02073715773
**Web:** www.trotters.co.uk
**Reg No:** 2481498 **VAT No:** 497637287
**Estd:** 1990 Private Limited Company
**Line of Business:** Retail sale of clothing
**Trading Style:** Trotters Children's Wear
**Issued Capital:** £50,000
**Managing Director:** Ms S Mirman
**Co. Secretary:** Richard Ross
**Responsibilities**
**Senior:** Lara Austin-Brock (Office Manager),
Alison Lakey (Human Resources Manager)
**Admin:** Lara Austin-Brock (Office Manager)
**HR:** Alison Lakey (Human Resources
Manager)
**Operations:** Alison Lakey (Human
Resources Manager)
**Branches:** Trotters (Childrenswear &
Accessories) Ltd, 127 Kensington High
Street, London W8 5SF
**US SIC:** 5699, 5661
**UK SIC:** 64500, 64600
**Auditors:** A.S. Zanettos & Co Ltd
**Bankers:** Lloyds TSB Bank plc (30-00-09)

|     | 30-06-14 | 30-06-13 | 30-06-12 |
|-----|----------|----------|----------|
| TO  | 9,794,221 | 8,686,339 | N/A |
| P/L | 520,248 | 439,184 | N/A |
| NW  | 1,722,379 | 1,538,857 | 1,083,836 |
| WC  | 1,092,250 | 834,439 | 821,798 |
| Emp. | 242 | 196 | N/A |

DUNS 22-817-1625

## Trotters Family Bakers

Broad Road Industrial Estate, Broad Road,
North Sunderland, Seahouses,
Northumberland NE68 7UP
**Web:** www.trottersfamilybakers.co.uk
**VAT No:** 176657128 **Estd:** 1974 Partnership
**Line of Business:** Bakers shops
**Partners:** Mrs S E Trotter, H Trotter,
G Trotter
**Responsibilities**
**Finance:** Robert Turnbull (Accountant)
**IT:** Robert Turnbull (Accountant)
**Branches:** Trotters Family Bakers, 55
Bondgate Within, Alnwick, Northumberland
NE66 1HZ
**US SIC:** 5462 **UK SIC:** 64100
**Bankers:** Barclays Bank Plc (20-58-17)
**Employees:** 70

DUNS 22-047-4493

## The Troubadour Club Ltd

(**Subsidiary of:** The Troubadour Cafe Ltd)
263-267 Old Brompton Road Earl's Court,
London SW5 9JA
**Tel:** 020-7370-1434
**Web:** www.troubadour.co.uk
**Reg No:** 4049679 **Estd:** 2000 Private
Limited Company

**Line of Business:** Restaurants
**Trading Style:** The Troubadour Cafe
**Issued Capital:** £2
**Director:** S Thornhill
**Co. Secretary:** Ms Susan Thornhill
**US SIC:** 5812 **UK SIC:** 66110
**Bankers:** C Hoare & Co (15-99-00)

|     | 31-08-12 | 31-08-11 |
|-----|----------|----------|
| TA  | 1,815 | 6,620 |
| NW  | (59,510) | (59,510) |

DUNS 29-551-1166

## Troughton McAslan Ltd

(**Subsidiary of:** Caledonia Ltd)
7-9 William Road, London NW1 3ER
**Tel:** 02077272663 **Fax:** 020-7221-8835
**Reg No:** 1917945 **Estd:** 1985 Private
Limited Company
**Line of Business:** Architectural activities
**Issued Capital:** £10,000
**Managing Director:** J R Mcaslan
**Co. Secretary:** Mrs Natasha Manzaroli
**Responsibilities**
**Senior:** Tony Skipper (Manager)
**US SIC:** 8911 **UK SIC:** 83701
**Auditors:** Beavis Walker

|     | 31-10-13 | 31-10-12 | 31-10-11 |
|-----|----------|----------|----------|
| TA  | 10,000 | 10,000 | 10,000 |
| NW  | 10,000 | 10,000 | 10,000 |

DUNS 34-592-2249

## Troup Bywaters & Anders Ltd

183 Eversholt Street, London NW1 1BU
**Tel:** 02075 041400
**Web:** www.tbanda.com
**Reg No:** 2736372 **Estd:** 1991 Private
Limited Company
**Line of Business:** Engineering related
scientific and technical consulting activities
**Issued Capital:** £2
**Directors:** P J Anderson, N Weller
**Co. Secretary:** Clive Healey
**Branches:** Troup Bywaters & Anders Ltd, 83
Eversholt Street, NW1 1BU London
**US SIC:** 8911 **UK SIC:** 83701

|     | 31-12-13 | 31-12-12 | 31-12-11 |
|-----|----------|----------|----------|
| TA  | 2 | 2 | 2 |
| NW  | 2 | 2 | 2 |

DUNS 23-539-3761

## Trousdale Ltd

Wildmere Road, Banbury, Oxfordshire OX16
3JU
**Tel:** 01295251000
**Web:** www.touchoxford.com
**Reg No:** 3538074 **Estd:** 1998 Private
Limited Company
**Line of Business:** Manufacture of bread;
manufacture of fresh pastry goods and cakes
**Issued Capital:** £160,000
**Directors:** C A Redkey, T A Mcrae,
D W Tremblay, J M Sykes
**Co. Secretary:** Thomas Mcrae
**Responsibilities**
**Senior:** Diana Haines (Manager), Seamus
Kane (Manager), Steve Packer (General
Manager), Mike Saracen (General Manager)
**US SIC:** 2051 **UK SIC:** 41960
**Auditors:** Pannell Kerr Forster
**Bankers:** HSBC Bank plc (40-35-04)

|     | 26-04-14 | 27-04-13 | 28-04-12 |
|-----|----------|----------|----------|
| TO  | 20,158,221 | 18,429,423 | 15,865,118 |
| P/L | 1,059,085 | (837,298) | 652,834 |
| NW  | 2,420,356 | 1,617,008 | 2,272,997 |
| WC  | (2,033,034) | (3,097,716) | (2,633,219) |
| Emp. | 78 | 78 | 73 |

DUNS 50-026-7240

## Trout Hotels (Cumbria) Ltd

7-11 Earsdon Road, Whitley Bay, Tyne and
Wear NE25 9SX
**Tel:** 01912528740
**Web:** www.trouthotel.co.uk
**Reg No:** 2304994 **Estd:** 1988 Private
Limited Company
**Line of Business:** Hotels
**Issued Capital:** £150,000
**Principals:** N J Mills (Managing), G Lurie
**Co. Secretary:** Philip Upton
**US SIC:** 7011 **UK SIC:** 66500
**Auditors:** PricewaterhouseCoopers LLP

|     | 27-07-14 | 28-07-13 | 29-07-12 |
|-----|----------|----------|----------|
| TO  | 2,984,855 | 2,765,976 | 2,398,571 |
| P/L | 382,927 | 370,673 | 325,098 |
| NW  | 2,997,334 | 2,843,510 | 2,546,145 |
| WC  | (354,775) | (354,312) | (409,837) |
| Emp. | 52 | 52 | 49 |

DUNS 21-771-5410

## Troutbeck

Crossbeck Road, Ilkley, West Yorkshire
LS29 9JP
**Tel:** 01943602755
**Web:** www.maria-mallaband.co.uk
**Estd:** 1994 Proprietorship
**Line of Business:** Nursing homes
**Proprietor:** Mrs E Harris
**Responsibilities**
**Senior:** Carole Glew (Operations Manager)

**Operations:** Vicky Craddock *(Operations Director)*
**US SIC:** 8051 **UK SIC:** 95100
**Employees:** 80

DUNS 21-689-6365 **Imp-Exp**
## Trouw (U K) Ltd
(**Subsidiary of:** Nutreco N.V.)
Wincham, Northwich, Cheshire CW9 6DF
**Tel:** 01606561000 **Fax:** 0160641963
**Web:** www.trouwnutrition.co.uk
**Reg No:** 0291738 **VAT No:** 616170266
**Estd:** 1934 Private Limited Company
**Line of Business:** Animal feed and pet foods
**Export Markets:** France, Scandinavia, Netherlands
**Export Sales:** £24,897,000
**Trading Style:** Trouw Nutrition, Trouw Aquaculture, Skretting
**Issued Capital:** £5,404,136
**Directors:** J M Williamson, Miss L Ross, H De Wildt, S Stevenson, Mrs K Smith, Miss A Maddock
**Co. Secretary:** Mrs Janine Bolton
**Branches:** Trouw (U K) Ltd, Blacksness Pier, Shetland, Shetland ZE1 0TQ
**US SIC:** 0921, 2834
**UK SIC:** 03002, 25700
**Auditors:** KPMG LLP
**Bankers:** The Royal Bank Of Scotland Plc (16-22-27)

| | 31-12-13 | 31-12-12 | 31-12-11 |
|---|---|---|---|
| TO | 108,583,000 | 100,601,000 | 119,127,000 |
| P/L | 2,938,000 | (536,000) | 883,000 |
| NW | 29,970,000 | 26,550,000 | 29,429,000 |
| WC | 23,973,000 | 22,637,000 | 23,751,000 |
| Emp. | 134 | 143 | 146 |

DUNS 50-588-7562
## Trowbridge Office Cleaning Services Ltd
76 North Street, Bristol, Avon BS3 1HJ
**Tel:** 01179-635260 **Fax:** 01179-660373
**Web:** www.trowbridgeofficecleaning.co.uk
**Reg No:** 2531412 **Estd:** 1988 Private Limited Company
**Line of Business:** Cleaning contracting commercial
**Issued Capital:** £101
**Principals:** C J Belcher *(Managing)*, A J Belcher
**Co. Secretary:** Mrs Judith Belcher
**US SIC:** 7349 **UK SIC:** 92300
**Auditors:** Blomfield & Co
**Bankers:** Lloyds TSB Bank plc (30-98-75)

| | 30-09-14 | 30-09-13 | 30-09-12 |
|---|---|---|---|
| TA | 502,552 | 520,967 | 463,288 |
| NW | 272,139 | 275,330 | 363,183 |
| WC | 236,686 | 238,399 | 324,280 |

DUNS 21-126-0313
## Trowers & Hamlins Llp
3 Bunhill Row, London EC1Y 8YZ
**Tel:** 020 7423 8000
**Web:** www.trowers.com
**Reg No:** 0337852OC **Estd:** 1995
**Line of Business:** Solicitors
**Principals:** P R Clarke, Ms H J Randall, M J Pattinson, C J Morrish, I D Graham, R M Hildebrand, Ms S Bailey, D Mosey
**Responsibilities**
**Senior:** Julien Allen *(Non-designated Limited Liabili)*, Adrian Carter *(Designated Limited Liability P)*, Jennifer Gubbins *(Designated Limited Liability P)*, Katherine Saunders *(Non-designated Limited Liabili)*, Georgina Savill *(Non-designated Limited Liabili)*, Jennifer Shaw *(Non-designated Limited Liabili)*, Andrew Sneddon *(Non-designated Limited Liabili)*, Amanda Stubbs *(Non-designated Limited Liabili)*, Tania Tandon *(Non-designated Limited Liabili)*, Alan Tate *(Non-designated Limited Liabili)*, Neil Waller *(Non-designated Limited Liabili)*, Janet Winrow *(Non-designated Limited Liabili)*
**Marketing:** Naomi Moss *(Marketing Manager)*
**IT:** Bob Greenwood *(Computer Manager)*
**US SIC:** 8111 **UK SIC:** 83500
**Auditors:** Crowe Clark Whitehill LLP

| | 31-03-14 | 31-03-13 | 31-03-12 |
|---|---|---|---|
| TO | 77,176,000 | 78,231,000 | 81,168,000 |
| P/L | 22,696,000 | 16,398,000 | 26,496,000 |
| NW | 2,282,000 | 3,048,000 | 9,665,000 |
| WC | 21,576,000 | 20,703,000 | 33,035,000 |
| Emp. | 604 | 628 | 595 |

DUNS 21-612-6839 **Imp-Exp**
## Trox Uk Ltd
(**Subsidiary of:** Trox Gmbh)
Caxton Way, Thetford, Norfolk IP24 3SQ
**Tel:** 01842851200
**Web:** www.troxuk.co.uk
**Reg No:** 0713650 **VAT No:** 102455708
**Estd:** 1962 Private Limited Company
**Line of Business:** Manufacture of non-domestic cooling and ventilation equipment
**Export Markets:** Far East, Middle East, S & S E Asia
**Export Sales:** £2,480,000
**Issued Capital:** £9,053,750
**Directors:** H G Lambourn, R D Fawkner, M H Bauer, N Addison, D Muller, Ms S P Ranson, T O Jagdt
**Co. Secretary:** Ms Suzanne Ranson
**Responsibilities**
**Senior:** Ludger Bokmann *(Manager)*, Raymond Calver *(Despatch Manager)*, Heinz Trox *(Chairman)*
**Sales:** Amanda Sayers *(Commercial Director)*, Janice Tabb *(Sales Coordinator)*
**Admin:** Lee Daniels *(Computer Manager)*, Lorraine Toone *(Office Manager)*
**IT:** Lee Daniels *(Computer Manager)*
**HR:** Lorraine Toone *(Office Manager)*
**Operations:** Lorraine Toone *(Office Manager)*
**Engineering:** Martyn Mills *(Senior Design Engineer)*
**Branches:** Trox Uk Ltd, Caxton Way, Thetford, Norfolk IP24 3SQ
**US SIC:** 3585 **UK SIC:** 32841
**Auditors:** PricewaterhouseCoopers LLP
**Bankers:** HSBC Bank plc (40-44-42)

| | 31-12-13 | 31-12-12 | 31-12-11 |
|---|---|---|---|
| TO | 13,494,000 | 17,609,000 | 15,290,000 |
| P/L | (2,442,000) | (1,126,000) | (5,168,000) |
| NW | 3,435,000 | 3,877,000 | 2,849,000 |
| WC | (1,090,000) | (1,047,000) | (2,060,000) |
| Emp. | 143 | 171 | 187 |

DUNS 23-350-5481
## Troy Management Services (Manchester Palace) Ltd
(**Subsidiary of:** Sof-9 Rome Investments Lux Sarl)
Fountains Bent, Darley Road, Bristwith, Harrogate, North Yorkshire HG3 2PN
**Tel:** 01423771150
**Reg No:** 4977164 **Estd:** 2003 Private Limited Company
**Line of Business:** Hotels
**Issued Capital:** £462,001
**Directors:** A Troy, Ms G S Hunter, J A Burrell, Mrs G J Gallagher
**US SIC:** 7011 **UK SIC:** 66500
**Auditors:** Deloitte LLP
**Bankers:** The Royal Bank Of Scotland Plc (16-08-05)

| | 31-12-13 | 31-12-12 | 31-12-11 |
|---|---|---|---|
| TO | 10,164,000 | 9,355,000 | 9,311,000 |
| P/L | (447,000) | (728,000) | (732,000) |
| NW | 3,283,000 | 3,730,000 | 4,458,000 |
| WC | 1,986,000 | 2,579,000 | 3,187,000 |
| Emp. | 218 | 221 | 205 |

DUNS 22-770-4368 **Imp-Exp**
## Trp Sealing Systems Ltd
Unit 24 Netherwood Road, Hereford, Herefordshire HR2 6JU
**Tel:** 01432-279366
**Web:** www.trpsealing.com
**Reg No:** 1588087 **Estd:** 1981 Private Limited Company
**Line of Business:** Manufacturers of gaskets
**Export Markets:** European Union (E U)
**Export Sales:** £23,325,848
**Issued Capital:** £5,000
**Principals:** S J Children *(Managing)*, Ms R A Tobey, Mrs S M Mason
**Co. Secretary:** Ms Rosemary Children
**Responsibilities**
**Finance:** Mike Greenhill *(Financial Manager)*
**US SIC:** 5531 **UK SIC:** 65100
**Auditors:** Young & Co
**Bankers:** National Westminster Bank Plc (53-50-41)

| | 30-04-13 | 30-04-12 | 30-04-11 |
|---|---|---|---|
| TO | 23,956,936 | 23,195,322 | 21,211,253 |
| P/L | 1,010,644 | 900,322 | 1,102,390 |
| NW | 4,576,846 | 3,991,964 | 3,588,333 |
| WC | 1,747,101 | 1,288,736 | 940,164 |
| Emp. | 322 | 329 | 320 |

DUNS 50-394-3706
## Trs Investments Ltd
(**Subsidiary of:** Trs Investments (Holdings) Ltd)
3 Martin Court, Southbridge Way, Southall, Middlesex UB2 4QW
**Tel:** 02085713252 **Fax:** 020-8574-5254
**Web:** www.trs.co.uk
**Reg No:** 2400888 **Estd:** 1989 Private Limited Company
**Line of Business:** Development and selling of real estate
**Issued Capital:** £1,000
**Principals:** F T Suterwalla *(Managing)*, I T Suterwalla, M T Suterwalla, S T Suterwalla
**Co. Secretary:** Hatim Suterwalla
**US SIC:** 6552 **UK SIC:** 85000
**Auditors:** Mehta & Tengra
**Bankers:** National Westminster Bank Plc (60-12-18)

| | 31-12-13 | 31-12-12 | 31-12-11 |
|---|---|---|---|
| TO | 145,380 | 37,825 | N/A |
| P/L | 148,508 | (795,179) | (615,346) |
| NW | (817,505) | (1,279,078) | (482,751) |
| WC | (317,076) | (421,322) | (374,495) |

DUNS 39-028-6854 **Imp-Exp**
## Trs Wholesale Co. Ltd
(**Subsidiary of:** Trs Group (Uk) Ltd)
2 Southbridge Way, Southall, Middlesex UB2 4BY
**Tel:** 02088 435400 **Fax:** 02085 741716
**Web:** www.trs.co.uk
**Reg No:** 2108436 **VAT No:** 109779728
**Estd:** 1968 Private Limited Company
**Line of Business:** Cash and carry wholesalers
**Export Markets:** U S A; Europe, Scandinavia, Switzerland
**Issued Capital:** £100,000
**Principals:** F T Suterwalla *(Managing)*, S T Suterwalla *(Financial)*, I T Suterwalla, M T Suterwalla
**Co. Secretary:** Hatim Suterwalla
**US SIC:** 5149 **UK SIC:** 61700
**Auditors:** Mehta & Tengra
**Bankers:** National Westminster Bank Plc (60-12-18)

| | 31-12-13 | 31-12-12 | 31-12-11 |
|---|---|---|---|
| TO | 39,063,146 | 39,692,777 | 41,692,237 |
| P/L | 2,858,648 | 3,766,318 | 3,717,550 |
| NW | 15,702,324 | 15,514,773 | 15,999,013 |
| WC | 13,330,857 | 13,152,693 | 13,920,105 |
| Emp. | 107 | 108 | 102 |

DUNS 77-167-7184
## Tru (Transitional Rehabilitation Unit) Ltd
Margaret House, 342 Haydock Lane, St Helens, Merseyside WA11 9UY
**Tel:** 01942-707000 **Fax:** 01942-707030
**Web:** www.trurehab.com
**Reg No:** 2708234 **Estd:** 1992 Private Limited Company
**Line of Business:** Medical practice activities
**Issued Capital:** £100
**Principals:** Dr H Jackson *(Managing)*, A Kenyon, Mrs G Barker
**Co. Secretary:** Ms Gillian Barker
**Responsibilities**
**HR:** Peter Melling *(Human Resources Manager)*
**Health & Safety:** Ian France *(Health & Safety Officer)*
**Facilities:** Ian France *(Health & Safety Officer)*
**Branches:** Tru (Transitional Rehabilitation Unit) Ltd, Lyme House, Grange Road, St. Helens, Merseyside WA11 0XF
**US SIC:** 8011, 8091
**UK SIC:** 95300, 95200
**Auditors:** The Walker Begley Partnership
**Bankers:** The Co-Operative Bank Plc (08-90-00)

| | 30-06-13 | 30-06-12 | 30-06-11 |
|---|---|---|---|
| TO | 9,251,849 | 9,116,593 | 8,030,288 |
| P/L | 293,080 | 726,006 | 298,483 |
| NW | 662,556 | 891,926 | 808,325 |
| WC | (142,610) | (1,257,057) | (713,222) |
| Emp. | 280 | 328 | 303 |

DUNS 29-502-4368
## Truck & Trailer Components Ltd
(**Subsidiary of:** Unipart Group of Companies Ltd)
Unipart House, Garsington Road, Cowley, Oxford, Oxfordshire OX4 2PG
**Tel:** 08442642363 **Fax:** 0800361677
**Web:** www.ttcparts.com
**Reg No:** 1865675 **Estd:** 1984 Private Limited Company
**Line of Business:** Motor factors
**Issued Capital:** £2
**Directors:** A J Mourgue, Mrs A J Wyner, P M Dessain
**Co. Secretary:** Michael Rimmer
**Responsibilities**
**Senior:** Michael Hopper *(Manager)*, Darren Miller *(Manager)*, Tony Sackett *(Manager)*
**Branches:** Ttc Preston, 187 Walton Summit, Bradkirk Place, Bamber Bridge, PR5 8AJ Preston
**US SIC:** 7539 **UK SIC:** 67100

| | 31-12-13 | 31-12-12 | 31-12-11 |
|---|---|---|---|
| TA | 2 | 2 | 2 |
| NW | 2 | 2 | 2 |

DUNS 21-824-9662 **Imp-Exp**
## Truck-Lite Co. Ltd
(**Subsidiary of:** Penske Corporation)
Waterfall Lane Trading Estate, Cradley Heath, West Midlands B64 6QB
**Tel:** 01215617000 **Fax:** 01215617072
**Web:** www.truck-lite.eu.com
**Reg No:** 0460489 **VAT No:** 276848307
**Estd:** 1948 Private Limited Company
**Line of Business:** Commercial vehicle accessories
**Export Markets:** European Union (E U); U S A
**Export Sales:** £43,099,000
**Issued Capital:** £675,902
**Directors:** B M Kupchella, T C Walker, A Rylance
**Co. Secretary:** Mark Speed
**Responsibilities**
**Operations:** N Dodtaietsky *(Design Manager)*
**US SIC:** 5531 **UK SIC:** 65100
**Auditors:** Deloitte & Touche LLP
**Bankers:** The Royal Bank Of Scotland Plc (16-34-31)

| | 31-12-13 | 31-12-12 | 31-12-11 |
|---|---|---|---|
| TO | 56,242,000 | 54,325,000 | 61,057,000 |
| P/L | 474,000 | (780,000) | (1,625,000) |
| NW | (12,605,000) | (15,639,000) | (14,691,000) |
| WC | 15,489,000 | 9,386,000 | 10,566,000 |
| Emp. | 512 | 499 | 489 |

DUNS 21-612-7175 **Imp-Exp**
## Truck-Lite Europe Ltd
(**Subsidiary of:** Penske Corporation)
Barrows Road, Harlow, Essex CM19 5FA
**Tel:** 01279-406406 **Fax:** 01279-406407
**Web:** www.truck-lite.eu.com
**Reg No:** 0195431 **VAT No:** 246186941
**Estd:** 1924 Private Limited Company
**Line of Business:** Commercial vehicle accessories
**Export Markets:** E U, worldwide
**Export Sales:** £21,281,000
**Trading Style:** Rubbolite Lamps, S L
**Issued Capital:** £1,207,500
**Directors:** A Rylance, B M Kupchella
**Co. Secretary:** Mark Speed
**Responsibilities**
**Senior:** Mark Cording *(Senior Marketing Manager)*, Mike Elsworth *(Supplier Support Manager)*, Scott Fink *(Manager)*, Tom McClure *(Area Manager)*, Stephan Pfingsten *(Manager)*
**Marketing:** Paul Lucchi *(Marketing Manager)*
**Sales:** Paul Lucchi *(Marketing Manager)*
**IT:** Paul Beavis *(IT Manager)*
**HR:** Jenny O' Gelspy *(HR Officer)*
**Branches:** Truck-Lite Europe Ltd, International House, Horsecroft Road, Harlow, Essex CM19 5SU
**US SIC:** 5531 **UK SIC:** 65100
**Auditors:** Deloitte LLP
**Bankers:** Bank Of Scotland (12-20-10)

| | 31-12-13 | 31-12-12 | 31-12-11 |
|---|---|---|---|
| TO | 33,800,000 | 31,689,000 | 35,668,000 |
| P/L | 288,000 | (1,202,000) | 402,000 |
| NW | 8,851,000 | 6,143,000 | 7,800,000 |
| WC | 9,342,000 | 4,724,000 | 5,079,000 |
| Emp. | 328 | 294 | 310 |

DUNS 21-580-3533
## Truckeast
Stewarts Road, Finedon Road Industrial Estate, Wellingborough, Northamptonshire NN8 4RJ
**Tel:** 01933303303
**Web:** www.truckeast.co.uk
**Estd:** 2002 Partnership
**Line of Business:** Maintenance and repair of motor vehicles
**Partners:** J Armstrong, J Biggin
**US SIC:** 7539 **UK SIC:** 67100
**Employees:** 80

DUNS 34-646-2955
## Truckeast Ltd
(**Subsidiary of:** Dci Group Ltd)
Po Box 191, Stowmarket, Suffolk IP14 1WW
**Tel:** 01449-613553 **Fax:** 01449614951
**Web:** www.truckeast.co.uk
**Reg No:** 2771432 **VAT No:** 571496613
**Estd:** 1992 Private Limited Company
**Line of Business:** Commercial vehicle servicing repairs parts & accessories
**Trading Style:** Truckeast
**Issued Capital:** £317,000
**Directors:** D S Hall, J A Biggin
**Co. Secretary:** Simon Hobson
**Responsibilities**
**IT:** Martyn Griggs *(IT Manager)*
**Branches:** Truckeast Ltd, Hamlin Way, King's Lynn, Norfolk PE30 4NG
**US SIC:** 5511 **UK SIC:** 65100
**Auditors:** Mazars LLP
**Bankers:** National Westminster Bank Plc (60-20-49)

| | 31-12-13 | 31-12-12 | 31-12-11 |
|---|---|---|---|
| TO | 98,054,709 | 63,318,864 | 55,518,489 |
| P/L | 2,188,799 | 1,982,891 | 2,046,047 |
| NW | 6,154,907 | 4,842,147 | 4,047,138 |
| WC | 3,466,062 | 2,208,159 | 1,642,824 |
| Emp. | 276 | 263 | 272 |

DUNS 23-926-8530
## Trucklog Ltd
(**Subsidiary of:** Davis Derby Holdings Ltd)
Chequers Lane, Derby, Derbyshire DE21 6AW
**Tel:** 01332-227500
**Web:** www.davisderby.com
**Reg No:** 3916853 **Estd:** 2000 Private Limited Company
**Line of Business:** Manufacture of other electrical equipment not elsewhere classified
**Trading Style:** Davis Derby

**Issued Capital:** £1
**Director:** G Beetles
**Co. Secretary:** Andrew Cooper
**Responsibilities**
**Marketing:** Jayne Kennedy (Marketing Assistant)
**Operations:** Steve Gratton (Operations Manager)
**US SIC:** 3629 **UK SIC:** 34350

| | 31-12-13 | 31-12-12 | 31-12-11 |
|---|---|---|---|
| TA | 1 | 1 | 1 |
| NW | 1 | 1 | 1 |

DUNS 37-892-7305
## Truckmasters Hire Ltd
(Subsidiary of: Willoughby (30) Ltd)
Boston Road, Wainfleet St Mary, Skegness, Lincolnshire PE24 4HA
**Tel:** 01754-880481
**Web:** www.truckmasters.co.uk
**Reg No:** 3311814 **Estd:** 1997 Private Limited Company
**Line of Business:** Renting of other land transport equipment
**Issued Capital:** £2
**Director:** G Elsam
**Co. Secretary:** John Aiken
**Responsibilities**
**Senior:** John-Paul Aitken (IT)
**Finance:** John-Paul Aitken (IT)
**Sales:** Ian Shelley (Senior Sales Executive)
**IT:** John-Paul Aitken (IT)
**US SIC:** 7513 **UK SIC:** 84802
**Auditors:** Neville Russell
**Bankers:** The Royal Bank Of Scotland Plc (16-26-32)

| | 31-12-13 | 31-12-12 | 31-12-11 |
|---|---|---|---|
| TA | 2,463,842 | 2,617,912 | 2,144,018 |
| NW | 1,112,848 | 1,059,767 | 1,005,285 |
| WC | (241,288) | (454,703) | (415,333) |

DUNS 51-992-7003
## Tructyre Fleet Management Ltd
(Subsidiary of: Tfm Holdings Ltd)
Goodwood House, Goodwood Road, Eastleigh, Hampshire SO50 4NT
**Tel:** 03301007707
**Web:** www.tructyre.co.uk
**Reg No:** 3999449 **Estd:** 2000 Private Limited Company
**Line of Business:** Fleet management
**Issued Capital:** £100
**Director:** G W Sherwood
**Co. Secretary:** Keith Cooper
**Branches:** Tructyre Fleet Management Ltd, 7 Cabot Lane, Poole, Dorset BH17 7BX
**US SIC:** 7399 **UK SIC:** 83954
**Bankers:** National Westminster Bank Plc (51-81-41)

| | 31-12-13 | 31-05-13 | 31-12-12 |
|---|---|---|---|
| TO | 15,417,951 | 14,685,791 | 13,909,844 |
| P/L | 150,258 | 326,884 | 346,709 |
| NW | 2,265,090 | 2,112,483 | 1,872,369 |
| WC | 1,080,603 | 1,566,166 | 1,350,362 |
| Emp. | 138 | 79 | 80 |

DUNS 37-890-2357
## True Design Ltd
Ruddington Manor, Nottingham, Nottinghamshire NG11 6HD
**Tel:** 01159-844200
**Web:** www.jupiterdesign.co.uk
**Reg No:** 3310200 **Estd:** 1997 Private Limited Company
**Line of Business:** Advertising related services
**Issued Capital:** £112
**Director:** Ms K J Mayled
**Co. Secretary:** Ms Glenys Blacknell
**Responsibilities**
**Finance:** Mark Bairstow (Financial Director)
**Health & Safety:** Sherryl Johnson (Health & Safety Officer)
**US SIC:** 8911, 2752
**UK SIC:** 83701, 47544
**Auditors:** Streeter West & Co
**Bankers:** Barclays Bank Plc (20-63-25)

| | 31-03-14 | 31-03-13 | 31-03-12 |
|---|---|---|---|
| TA | 2,013,771 | 1,557,531 | 1,850,356 |
| NW | 1,333,021 | 1,064,019 | 919,875 |
| WC | 1,212,248 | 945,966 | 844,477 |

DUNS 57-021-9006
## True Gas Ltd
Phoenix House, Desborough Park Road, High Wycombe, Buckinghamshire HP12 3BQ
**Tel:** 01494835835
**Web:** www.truegas.co.uk
**Reg No:** 2868765 **Estd:** 1993 Private Limited Company
**Line of Business:** Gas suppliers
**Issued Capital:** £100
**Director:** M G Holland
**Co. Secretary:** Jean Witte
**Responsibilities**
**Sales:** Danny Williams (Sales Manager)
**Admin:** Allan Bedford (Administrator)
**IT:** Leon Mulder (IT Manager)

**HR:** Allan Bedford (Administrator)
**Health & Safety:** Allan Bedford (Administrator)
**Purchasing:** Allan Bedford (Administrator)
**Branches:** True Gas Ltd, 11 Edison House, Fullerton Rd, Glenrothes, Fife KY7 5QR
**US SIC:** 5199 **UK SIC:** 61900
**Auditors:** Pinkney Keith Gibbs
**Bankers:** HSBC Bank plc (40-24-38)

| | 30-09-13 | 30-09-12 | 30-09-11 |
|---|---|---|---|
| TA | 308,208 | 319,733 | 291,731 |
| NW | (484,965) | (441,597) | (382,225) |
| WC | (558,648) | (457,213) | (434,343) |

DUNS 42-442-5382
## True North Productions Ltd
Marshall Mills, Marshall Street, Leeds, West Yorkshire LS11 9YJ
**Tel:** 01133945460 **Fax:** 01133945495
**Web:** www.truenorth.tv
**Reg No:** 4430230 **Estd:** 2002 Private Limited Company
**Line of Business:** Film production services and studios
**Issued Capital:** £300
**Directors:** M Allen, A Sheldon
**Co. Secretary:** Jessica Fowle
**Responsibilities**
**Senior:** Glyn Middleton (creative director)
**US SIC:** 7819 **UK SIC:** 97111

| | 31-03-14 | 31-03-13 | 31-03-12 |
|---|---|---|---|
| TO | 9,433,595 | N/A | N/A |
| P/L | 915,963 | N/A | N/A |
| NW | 718,122 | 276,369 | 122,658 |
| WC | 147,005 | (172,583) | (264,508) |
| Emp. | 58 | N/A | N/A |

DUNS 21-860-2106
## True Telecom Ltd
Ground Floor, Lakeview West, Galleon Boulevard, Dartford, Kent DA2 6QE
**Tel:** 08008404060
**Web:** www.truetelecom.com
**Reg No:** 8225783 **Estd:** 2012 Private Limited Company
**Line of Business:** Telecom services
**Director:** S J Griffiths
**Responsibilities**
**Operations:** Craig Christiaens (Operations Manager)
**US SIC:** 4899 **UK SIC:** 79020

| | 30-09-13 |
|---|---|
| TA | 99,422 |
| NW | (562,895) |
| WC | (563,990) |

DUNS 22-510-5907    Imp-Exp
## Trueform Engineering Ltd
(Subsidiary of: Trueform Engineering Holdings Ltd)
Unit 12 Pasadena Trading Estate, Hayes, Middlesex UB3 3NQ
**Tel:** 02085 614959
**Web:** www.trueform.co.uk
**Reg No:** 1324196 **VAT No:** 224864652
**Estd:** 1972 Private Limited Company
**Line of Business:** Manufacture of other fabricated metal products not elsewhere classified
**Export Markets:** U S A; Germany
**Export Sales:** £368,552
**Issued Capital:** £26,593
**Directors:** J Morley, C Mallaby
**Co. Secretary:** Ms Maxine Fuller
**Responsibilities**
**Senior:** George Kofteros (Manager)
**Finance:** Maxine Bailey (Financial Controller)
**HR:** Hayley Russell (Human Resources Manager)
**Branches:** Trueform Engineering Ltd, Trading Estate, Unit 4, Hayes, Middlesex UB3 3NQ
**US SIC:** 3499, 4712
**UK SIC:** 31694, 77002
**Auditors:** RSM Tenon Audit Ltd
**Bankers:** HSBC Bank plc (40-45-08)

| | 31-12-13 | 31-12-12 | 31-12-11 |
|---|---|---|---|
| TO | 15,317,193 | 21,836,762 | 18,675,089 |
| P/L | (467,785) | (635,163) | (687,515) |
| NW | 496,231 | 1,021,536 | 1,737,404 |
| WC | 482,729 | 1,066,295 | 1,008,017 |
| Emp. | 151 | 174 | 176 |

DUNS 76-498-1049
## Truereason Ltd
Losvoe Close Foxbrigeway, Normanton, West Yorkshire WF6 1TN
**Tel:** 01924220511 **Fax:** 01924-220512
**Reg No:** 2568121 **Estd:** 1990 Private Limited Company
**Line of Business:** Licensed clubs
**Issued Capital:** £10,000
**Director:** C Edwards
**Co. Secretary:** Lawrence Edwards
**Branches:** Truereason Ltd, 14 Cheapside, Bradford, West Yorkshire BD1 4HU
**US SIC:** 5813 **UK SIC:** 66200

**Auditors:** Clough & Co LLP

| | 31-03-14 | 31-03-13 | 31-03-12 |
|---|---|---|---|
| TA | 530,985 | 1,490,209 | 1,586,263 |
| NW | (1,394,247) | (995,829) | (1,074,893) |
| WC | (1,305,682) | (1,715,779) | (2,017,636) |

DUNS 50-565-2107
## Trufab Ltd
Fishwick Street, Rochdale, Lancashire OL16 5NA
**Web:** www.trufab.co.uk
**Reg No:** 2512966 **Estd:** 1990 Private Limited Company
**Line of Business:** Sheet metal fabricators
**Issued Capital:** £100
**Managing Director:** M Hickford
**Co. Secretary:** Neil Hickford
**US SIC:** 3469, 1799
**UK SIC:** 31200, 50000
**Auditors:** Cleworth Beardsley
**Bankers:** Barclays Bank Plc (20-72-67)

| | 31-05-13 | 31-05-12 | 31-05-11 |
|---|---|---|---|
| TO | 7,272,580 | 7,777,385 | N/A |
| P/L | 137,382 | 470,049 | N/A |
| NW | 1,205,637 | 1,206,562 | 1,024,319 |
| WC | 649,807 | 613,487 | 477,137 |
| Emp. | 115 | 115 | N/A |

DUNS 34-696-5622    Imp-Exp
## Truflo Air Movement Ltd
Station Street, Tipton, West Midlands DY4 8UG
**Tel:** 0121-557-4101
**Web:** www.truflo-airmovement.com
**Reg No:** 5500950 **VAT No:** 866258487
**Estd:** 2005 Private Limited Company
**Line of Business:** Fabricated metal products
**Export Sales:** £6,486,000
**Issued Capital:** £5,758,578
**Directors:** I G Wharton, H Sumpter
**Co. Secretary:** Wolodymyr Pelenski
**Responsibilities**
**Senior:** Theodore Laufik (Manager), John Lutsi (Manager), Alfred Stanley (Manager), Karen Tuleta (Manager)
**HR:** Sarah Bourne (Human Resources Manager)
**US SIC:** 3441, 3714
**UK SIC:** 32042, 35300
**Bankers:** The Royal Bank Of Scotland Plc (16-34-31)

| | 30-09-13 | 30-09-12 | 30-09-11 |
|---|---|---|---|
| TO | 8,340,000 | 11,871,000 | 11,378,000 |
| P/L | 659,000 | 897,000 | 432,000 |
| NW | 873,000 | 169,000 | (2,252,000) |
| WC | 2,087,000 | 2,173,000 | 801,000 |
| Emp. | 74 | 86 | 68 |

DUNS 21-625-4825
## Truframe Glass Solutions Ltd
(Subsidiary of: Truframe Holdings Ltd)
Unit 3klm Saxby Road Industrial Estate, Hudson Road, Melton Mowbray, Leicestershire LE13 1BS
**Tel:** 01664410140 **Fax:** 01664410141
**Web:** www.truframe.co.uk
**Reg No:** 7053033 **Estd:** 2008 Private Limited Company
**Line of Business:** Manufacturers and suppliers of pvc based products
**Issued Capital:** £2
**Director:** D P Firmager
**US SIC:** 3079 **UK SIC:** 48360

| | 31-03-14 | 31-03-13 | 31-03-12 |
|---|---|---|---|
| TA | 2 | 2 | 2 |
| NW | 2 | 2 | 2 |

DUNS 28-972-8891
## Trulife Ltd
(Subsidiary of: Trulife Group Ltd)
Unit 41 Meadowcourt, Amos Road, Sheffield, South Yorkshire S9 1BX
**Tel:** 0800581596 **Fax:** 01142610074
**Web:** www.trulife.com
**Reg No:** 1740905 **Estd:** 1983 Private Limited Company
**Line of Business:** Manufacture of medical and surgical equipment and orthopaedic appliances
**Export Sales:** £1,709,988
**Issued Capital:** £200
**Directors:** A Cooke, N J Murphy, J J Collier
**Responsibilities**
**Senior:** Kay Purnell (Uk General Manager)
**Sales:** Dean Maxwell (Purchasing Manager)
**Purchasing:** Dean Maxwell (Purchasing Manager)
**US SIC:** 3841 **UK SIC:** 37201
**Auditors:** KPMG
**Bankers:** The Bank Of Ireland (30-14-58)

| | 31-12-13 | 31-12-12 | 31-12-11 |
|---|---|---|---|
| TO | 15,178,501 | 16,248,211 | 16,387,411 |
| P/L | 180,737 | 337,840 | (173,421) |
| NW | 2,858,748 | 2,648,273 | 2,331,731 |
| WC | 1,263,360 | 889,664 | 427,298 |
| Emp. | 165 | 180 | 197 |

DUNS 21-633-7255    Imp
## Trumeter Technologies Ltd
Trumeter House, Bury, Lancashire BL9 5BT
**Tel:** 01617054318 **Fax:** 01617-249-455
**Web:** www.trumeter.com
**Reg No:** 7115948 **Estd:** 2010 Private Limited Company
**Line of Business:** Manufacture of electronic valves and tubes and other electronic components
**Export Sales:** £5,585,484
**Issued Capital:** £100,000
**Directors:** J P Carr, J C Smith
**Co. Secretary:** Daniel Weidenbaum
**Responsibilities**
**Senior:** Peter Weidenbaum (Managing Director, Director)
**HR:** Yvonne Massey (Hr/ Health And Safety)
**Health & Safety:** Yvonne Massey (Hr/ Health And Safety)
**US SIC:** 3679, 3823
**UK SIC:** 34542, 37100
**Auditors:** Saffery Champness

| | 31-12-13 | 31-12-12 | 31-12-11 |
|---|---|---|---|
| TO | 10,843,364 | 7,473,223 | 8,273,082 |
| P/L | 1,399,941 | (108,730) | 394,032 |
| NW | 1,765,509 | 736,985 | 780,954 |
| WC | 1,343,037 | 698,703 | 916,370 |
| Emp. | 181 | 253 | 165 |

DUNS 34-799-0082
## Trump International Golf Club Scotland Ltd
Saltire Court, 20 Castle Terrace, Edinburgh, Midlothian EH1 2EN
**Tel:** 01358743300
**Web:** www.trumpgolfscotland.com
**Reg No:** 0292100SC **Estd:** 2005 Private Limited Company
**Line of Business:** Other business activities not elsewhere classified
**Issued Capital:** £1,000
**Directors:** A Weisselberg, I Trump, D Trump Jr, D J Trump, E Trump
**Co. Secretary:** George Sorial
**Responsibilities**
**Senior:** Sarah Mallone (Evp)
**US SIC:** 7399 **UK SIC:** 83954

| | 31-12-13 | 31-12-12 | 31-12-11 |
|---|---|---|---|
| TO | 2,274,009 | N/A | N/A |
| P/L | (1,822,577) | N/A | N/A |
| NW | (7,480,639) | (5,658,062) | (3,908,419) |
| WC | (209,086) | (1,164,762) | 106,634 |
| Emp. | 66 | N/A | N/A |

DUNS 21-725-8011    Imp
## Trumpf Ltd
(Subsidiary of: Trumpf Gmbh + Co. Kg)
Airport Executive Park, Luton, Bedfordshire LU2 9NL
**Tel:** 01582725335 **Fax:** 01582-399250
**Web:** www.uk.trumpf.com
**Reg No:** 1160907 **VAT No:** 198420635
**Estd:** 1974 Private Limited Company
**Line of Business:** Abattoir machinery and equipment
**Issued Capital:** £4,500,000
**Directors:** S Simpson, G W Ruebling, S A Binns, L Moakes
**Co. Secretary:** Simon Binns
**Responsibilities**
**Senior:** Hartmut Pannen (Manager), Carol Vyse (Sales Manager)
**Marketing:** Dave Foulkes (General Manager)
**Sales:** Dave Foulkes (General Manager)
**Health & Safety:** Alan Gower (Health & Safety Officer)
**US SIC:** 3559 **UK SIC:** 32863
**Auditors:** KPMG LLP
**Bankers:** Lloyds TSB Bank plc (30-95-28)

| | 30-06-14 | 30-06-13 | 30-06-12 |
|---|---|---|---|
| TO | 45,764,735 | 38,682,663 | 43,234,336 |
| P/L | 757,852 | (641,529) | 650,303 |
| NW | 3,519,713 | 2,607,088 | 3,248,617 |
| WC | 3,158,975 | 2,107,612 | 2,878,785 |
| Emp. | 88 | 91 | 86 |

DUNS 29-640-4320    Imp-Exp
## Trupart Ltd
(Subsidiary of: Inhoco 2082 Ltd)
Decoy Bank, Doncaster, South Yorkshire DN4 5JD
**Tel:** 01302344919
**Web:** www.trupart.co.uk
**Reg No:** 1966822 **VAT No:** 656282615
**Estd:** 1986 Private Limited Company
**Line of Business:** Sale of motor vehicle parts and accessories
**Export Markets:** E U
**Issued Capital:** £100
**Managing Director:** I Biddle
**Co. Secretary:** Mrs Karen Bramhall
**Responsibilities**
**Senior:** Dean Learoyd (Sales Director), Keith Tomlinson (Warehouse Manager)
**Finance:** Jane Farrell (Financial Manager)
**Sales:** Dean Learoyd (Sales Director)
**Health & Safety:** Keith Tomlinson (Warehouse Manager)

**Purchasing:** Les Hardwick *(Purchasing Manager)*
**US SIC:** 5531 **UK SIC:** 65100
**Auditors:** Grant Thornton
**Bankers:** Barclays Bank Plc (20-26-55)

| | 31-12-13 | 31-12-12 | 31-12-11 |
|---|---|---|---|
| TO | 10,225,763 | 10,016,819 | 9,468,366 |
| P/L | 341,477 | 570,189 | 569,285 |
| NW | 2,341,008 | 2,250,340 | 2,045,773 |
| WC | 1,718,363 | 1,651,056 | 1,474,026 |
| Emp. | 60 | 54 | 49 |

DUNS 22-168-5881 Imp
## Truphone Ltd
Johnson Smirke Building, London EC3N 4HJ
**Tel:** 020 3002 6565
**Web:** www.truphone.com
**Reg No:** 4187081 **VAT No:** 851527819
**Estd:** 2001 Private Limited Company
**Line of Business:** Misc communication services
**Export Sales:** £3,989,000
**Trading Style:** Tru
**Issued Capital:** £833
**Directors:** N C ,Orland, J P Fletcher, N A Burkey, S J Robertson, E W Plattfaut, J P Tagg, A P De Cort, G E Robinson
**Co. Secretary:** Gregory Mappledoram
**Responsibilities**
**Senior:** Nicholas Orland *(Director)*
**Marketing:** Melissa Lehrer *(Head of B2 to B2 Marketing)*
**US SIC:** 4899, 7379
**UK SIC:** 79020, 83940
**Auditors:** PricewaterhouseCoopers LLP

| | 31-12-13 | 31-12-12 | 31-12-11 |
|---|---|---|---|
| TO | 8,043,000 | 9,800,000 | 10,137,000 |
| P/L | (91,373,000) | (35,075,000) | (30,051,000) |
| NW | 25,814,000 | 14,235,000 | 9,553,000 |
| WC | 4,690,000 | (359,000) | 8,311,000 |
| Emp. | 547 | 315 | 252 |

DUNS 21-031-1790
## Truro & Penwith College
Truro College - College Road, Truro, Cornwall TR1 3XX
**Tel:** 01872-267000
**Web:** www.truro-penwith.ac.uk
**VAT No:** 711776436 **Estd:** 2013
**Line of Business:** Further education schools and colleges
**Proprietor:** Miss K Woolven
**Responsibilities**
**Senior:** Jonathan Burnett *(Principal)*, Michelle Treen *(Manager)*
**US SIC:** 8221 **UK SIC:** 93100
**Employees:** 1,535

DUNS 29-886-5932
## Truscotts (Launceston) Ltd
Unit 3, Launceston, Cornwall PL15 8EX
**Tel:** 01566-772277
**Web:** www.dealer.peugeot.co.uk
**Reg No:** 2089600 **Estd:** 1975 Private Limited Company
**Line of Business:** Car dealers (new & used)
**Issued Capital:** £50,000
**Directors:** D S Carr, A J Barrett, Mrs B V Carr, J C Glanville
**Co. Secretary:** Paul Mitchell
**Responsibilities**
**Finance:** Victoria Harrison *(Accounts Coordinator)*
**Branches:** Newport Industrial Estate, Launceston, Cornwall PL15 8EX
**US SIC:** 5511, 5521
**UK SIC:** 65100
**Auditors:** Messrs Kitchen & Brown
**Bankers:** Lloyds TSB Bank plc (30-94-07)

| | 31-12-13 | 31-12-12 | 31-12-11 |
|---|---|---|---|
| TO | 29,970,000 | 28,893,000 | 28,743,000 |
| P/L | 225,000 | 160,000 | 155,000 |
| NW | 1,417,000 | 1,222,000 | 1,077,000 |
| WC | (982,000) | (1,128,000) | (1,285,000) |
| Emp. | 79 | 86 | 86 |

DUNS 34-748-5463
## Trust Group Uk Ltd
Millennium House, Audnam, Stourbridge, West Midlands DY8 4AH
**Tel:** 01384397600
**Web:** www.trustgroupuk.com
**Reg No:** 5550119 **Estd:** 2005 Private Limited Company
**Line of Business:** Sale of new motor vehicles
**Trading Style:** Stourbridge Volkswagen, Trust Autopark
**Issued Capital:** £199,540
**Director:** A J Hockedy
**Co. Secretary:** Nigel White
**Branches:** Trust Group Uk Ltd, Washford Drive, Park Farm Industrial Estate, Redditch, Worcestershire B98 0HX
**US SIC:** 5511, 5521, 7539, 5531
**UK SIC:** 65100, 67100
**Auditors:** ASE Audit LLP

**Bankers:** National Westminster Bank Plc (60-14-55)

| | 31-12-13 | 31-12-12 | 31-12-11 |
|---|---|---|---|
| TO | 61,133,772 | 53,978,511 | 41,047,976 |
| P/L | 961,767 | 458,094 | 167,275 |
| NW | 1,781,624 | 1,409,218 | 922,687 |
| WC | 660,505 | 169,735 | 133,450 |
| Emp. | 213 | 193 | 141 |

DUNS 22-755-9929
## Trust Housing Association Ltd
12 New Mart Road, Edinburgh, Midlothian EH14 1RL
**Tel:** 01314-441200
**Web:** www.trustha.org.uk
**Reg No:** 0001778T **Estd:** 1973 Friendly Society
**Line of Business:** Housing associations societies trusts & co-operatives
**Principals:** Rev J Stevenson *(Chairman)*, Dr D L Smith, W Lochead, A Duncan, Rev R Tuton, J B Forrest, C Grant, I D Baillie
**Co. Secretary:** Roger Trueman
**Responsibilities**
**Senior:** Alex Bennie *(Director)*, Cathy Canbell *(Director)*, Walter Clarkson *(Sub Committee Convener)*, Edward Davidson *(Board Member)*, Lilias Dunlop *(Sub Committee Convener)*, Alison Flynn *(Board Member)*, Doreen Inskip *(Board Member)*, Bob McDougall *(Chief Executive Officer)*, David McIndoe *(Director of Asset Management)*, Robert Mcculloch *(Director)*, Inez Paisley *(Director)*, Heather Pearson *(Vice Chair)*, J Rev *(Director)*, Pam Russell *(Chairman)*
**Marketing:** Stacey Williamson *(Marketing and Communication Di)*
**Branches:** Trust Housing Association Ltd, Glencloy Road, Isle Of Arran, Brodick, Isle Of Arran KA27 8DA
**US SIC:** 8699 **UK SIC:** 96902
**Auditors:** Findley & Co
**Bankers:** The Royal Bank Of Scotland Plc (83-00-81)
**Employees:** 297
**Turnover:** £17,519,000

DUNS 50-532-9748
## Trust Inheritance Ltd
Crown House, 1 Stafford Place, Weston-Super-Mare, Avon BS23 2QZ
**Tel:** 01934-422991
**Web:** www.trustinheritance.com
**Reg No:** 2490912 **Estd:** 1990 Private Limited Company
**Line of Business:** Other legal activities not elsewhere classified
**Issued Capital:** £250,000
**Directors:** S Jenkins, A M Cardus Hall, Miss K Simmonds, Mrs J Jenkins, A R Spencer
**Co. Secretary:** Mrs Karen Channon
**Responsibilities**
**Senior:** Dale Summers *(IT Director)*
**IT:** Dale Summers *(IT Director)*
**US SIC:** 7399 **UK SIC:** 83954
**Auditors:** T P Lewis & Partners
**Bankers:** National Westminster Bank Plc (60-23-32)

| | 30-04-14 | 30-04-13 | 30-04-12 |
|---|---|---|---|
| TA | 1,076,738 | 1,077,851 | 1,098,989 |
| NW | 473,508 | 494,209 | 381,498 |
| WC | 32,925 | 15,836 | (119,159) |

DUNS 77-741-2354
## Trust Inns Ltd
**(Subsidiary of:** Dollagh Ltd)
Blenheim House, Ackhurst Business Park, Foxhole Road, Chorley, Lancashire PR7 1NY
**Tel:** 01257238800 **Fax:** 01257-238801
**Web:** www.trustinns.co.uk
**Reg No:** 3011034 **Estd:** 1995 Private Limited Company
**Line of Business:** Managed public houses and bars
**Issued Capital:** £2,753,936
**Directors:** Ms L D'Arcy, J C Kay, Miss K Revitt
**Co. Secretary:** Ms Anne Kelleher
**Responsibilities**
**Senior:** Marianne Rose *(Marketing Manager)*
**Marketing:** Marianne Rose *(Marketing Manager)*
**Health & Safety:** Peter Hemmings *(Acquisitions Director)*
**Facilities:** Peter Hemmings *(Acquisitions Director)*
**Purchasing:** Peter Hemmings *(Acquisitions Director)*
**Branches:** Trust Inns Ltd, Dalton Road, Barrow-In-Furness, Cumbria LA14 2EX
**US SIC:** 5813 **UK SIC:** 66200
**Auditors:** KPMG LLP

| | 31-03-14 | 31-03-13 | 31-03-12 |
|---|---|---|---|
| TO | 49,371,000 | 52,447,000 | 43,248,000 |
| P/L | 3,002,000 | 2,261,000 | 2,118,000 |
| NW | 90,580,000 | 88,365,000 | 90,058,000 |
| WC | (12,071,000) | (139,667,000) | (6,776,000) |
| Emp. | 112 | 130 | 170 |

DUNS 21-250-9336
## Trust Insurance Group
Lynchwood House, Peterborough Business Park, Lynch Wood, Peterborough, Cambridgeshire PE2 6GG
**Tel:** 08701600645
**Web:** www.rsagroup.com
**Estd:** 1992
**Line of Business:** Insurance services
**Responsibilities**
**Senior:** Adrian Adam *(Manager)*
**US SIC:** 6311 **UK SIC:** 82002
**Employees:** 800

DUNS 21-780-3367
## Trust National & City Cars
Unit M - N Curzon Street, Burton-On-Trent, Staffordshire DE14 2DH
**Estd:** 2011
**Line of Business:** Taxis
**Responsibilities**
**Senior:** Sahid Bashir *(Manager)*
**US SIC:** 4121 **UK SIC:** 72200
**Employees:** 48

DUNS 21-557-7051
## The Trust of St Benedict's Abbey Ealing
St Benedicts School, London W5 2ES
**Web:** www.stbenedictsealing.org.uk
**Estd:** 1947
**Line of Business:** Trustee company
**Principals:** Rt Revd M Shipperlee *(Chairman)*, T Stapleford, A Hughes, A Bevan, V Cooper, Rt Revd F Rossiter, T Gorham
**US SIC:** 6732 **UK SIC:** 83100
**Auditors:** Buzzacott LLP
**Employees:** 248
**Turnover:** £11,281,281

DUNS 22-760-4121 Exp
## Trust Pet Products Ltd
**(Subsidiary of:** Trustmede Holdings Ltd)
Hiron Way, Budbrooke Industrial Estate, Warwick, Warwickshire CV34 5WP
**Tel:** 01926498880
**Web:** www.trustpet.co.uk
**Reg No:** 1185795 **Estd:** 1973 Private Limited Company
**Line of Business:** Other retail sale in specialised stores not elsewhere classified
**Export Markets:** E U and Eastern Europe
**Issued Capital:** £41,000
**Principals:** T A Colegate *(Chairman)*, R J Higgs *(Managing)*
**Co. Secretary:** Trevor Colegate
**US SIC:** 5999, 5499
**UK SIC:** 65600, 64100
**Auditors:** Ollis & Co
**Bankers:** The Royal Bank Of Scotland Plc (16-23-15)

| | 31-10-13 | 31-10-12 | 31-10-11 |
|---|---|---|---|
| TO | 14,578,394 | 17,920,371 | N/A |
| P/L | 79,893 | 394,516 | N/A |
| NW | 2,577,240 | 2,527,929 | 2,233,776 |
| WC | 2,511,429 | 2,461,569 | 2,164,874 |
| Emp. | 56 | 63 | N/A |

DUNS 28-889-7218
## Trust Thamesmead Ltd
19a Joyce Dawson Way, London SE28 8RA
**Tel:** 020-8320-4470
**Web:** www.trust-thamesmead.co.uk
**Reg No:** 1267728 **Estd:** 1976 Private Company Limited By Guarantee
**Line of Business:** Community networks
**Directors:** K W Miller, V Grimes, M Cleaver, Mrs L Portis, S Burns, R Elliott
**Co. Secretary:** Ms Sarah Cameron
**Responsibilities**
**Senior:** David Leaf *(Independent Non-Executive Dire)*, Joel Ogundayo *(Manager)*, Keeley Savill *(Independent Non-Executive Dire)*, Janice Ward-Wilson *(Vice Chair - Independent)*, Helen Webb *(Manager)*
**HR:** Frances Jones *(Head of Staff)*
**Branches:** Trust Thamesmead Ltd, Kingsley Court, Flat 11, London SE28 8AA
**US SIC:** 8699, 7392, 8321
**UK SIC:** 96902, 83951, 96111
**Auditors:** McBrides
**Bankers:** National Westminster Bank Plc (60-02-12)

| | 31-03-14 | 31-03-13 | 31-03-12 |
|---|---|---|---|
| TO | 3,149,296 | 3,612,247 | 6,006,351 |
| P/L | 1,206,315 | 711,692 | 3,556,824 |
| NW | 54,962,251 | 53,755,936 | 57,688,244 |
| WC | 1,079,768 | 1,660,327 | 2,846,260 |
| Emp. | 69 | 50 | 41 |

DUNS 21-007-1715
## Trustcare International Ltd.
Millbank House Millbank Lane, Cumnock, Ayrshire KA18 1AB
**Tel:** 01290429000
**Web:** www.trustcareinternational.org.uk
**Reg No:** 0327856SC **Estd:** 2007 Private Limited Company
**Line of Business:** Security and related activities
**Issued Capital:** £50,002
**Directors:** J Mccreath, J G Mccreath, R Barr
**US SIC:** 7393 **UK SIC:** 83954

| | 31-07-13 | 31-07-12 | 31-07-11 |
|---|---|---|---|
| TA | 164,499 | 157,738 | 142,205 |
| NW | (55,191) | 52,900 | (66,421) |
| WC | (7,513) | 11,785 | N/A |

DUNS 39-762-6003
## The Trustee of Wykeham House School Trust
17-19 East Street, Fareham, Hampshire PO16 0BW
**Tel:** 01329282356
**Web:** www.wykehamhouse.com
**Reg No:** 2199674 **Estd:** 1995 Private Limited Company
**Line of Business:** Primary education
**Directors:** W Pitt, P M Bryant, Mrs B Gudgeon, Mrs C A Freemantle, D F Luckett, D J Arthur, Ms H A Tyler, G Zaki
**Co. Secretary:** David Bryant
**Responsibilities**
**Senior:** Sally Davenport *(Director)*, James Fullarton *(Director)*, Sara Heaysman *(Director)*, Simon Hocquard *(Director)*
**IT:** Philip Gago *(IT Manager)*
**US SIC:** 8211 **UK SIC:** 93200
**Employees:** 55

DUNS 21-761-6369
## The Trustees of the British Museum
Great Russell Street, London WC1B 3DG
**Tel:** 02073-238000
**Web:** www.thebritishmuseum.ac.uk
**VAT No:** 710521585 **Estd:** 1753
**Line of Business:** Museums & art galleries
**Director:** N Macgregor
**Responsibilities**
**Senior:** Neil MacGregor *(Director)*
**US SIC:** 7911 **UK SIC:** 97913
**Employees:** 1,000

DUNS 22-711-2414 Imp
## Trustees of the London Clinic Ltd
Devonshire Place, Harley Street, London W1G 6BW
**Tel:** 020-7935-4444 **Fax:** 020-7486-3782
**Web:** www.thelondonclinic.co.uk
**Reg No:** 0307579 **Estd:** 2007 Private Company Limited By Guarantee
**Line of Business:** Hospitals
**Trading Style:** The London Clinic
**Directors:** M J Chande, I H Leslie Melville, Ms A C Cavendish Duchess Of Devonshire, C R Balfour, Professor R C Williamson, Lady H M Otton, R S Ponsonby
**Co. Secretary:** Ms Fiona Morrison
**Responsibilities**
**Marketing:** Karen Bullivant *(Sales & Marketing Director)*
**Sales:** Karen Bullivant *(Sales & Marketing Director)*
**Health & Safety:** Peter Delaney *(Clinical Government Manager)*
**Operations:** Peter Delaney *(Clinical Government Manager)*
**Purchasing:** M Simms *(Purchasing Manager)*
**Branches:** Trustees of The London Clinic Ltd, The London Clinic Finance Payments, Po Box 20275, London NW1 4WS
**US SIC:** 8062 **UK SIC:** 95100
**Auditors:** Deloitte LLP
**Bankers:** National Westminster Bank Plc (56-00-03)

| | 31-12-13 | 31-12-12 | 31-12-11 |
|---|---|---|---|
| TO | 136,654,000 | 131,173,000 | 124,428,000 |
| P/L | 9,886,000 | 12,672,000 | 17,331,000 |
| NW | 175,716,000 | 160,072,000 | 155,787,000 |
| WC | 15,508,000 | (14,282,000) | 24,087,000 |
| Emp. | 1,042 | 1,045 | 981 |

DUNS 73-766-2440
## Trusting Hands Ltd
**(Subsidiary of:** Helen Vowles Ltd)
Anchor House, Ebbw Vale, Gwent NP23 6UQ
**Tel:** 01495301777
**Reg No:** 5023487 **Estd:** 2008 Private Limited Company
**Line of Business:** Home care and help services
**Issued Capital:** £100
**Director:** Ms S B Lewis
**Co. Secretary:** Mrs Helen Vowles

**US SIC:** 8811 **UK SIC:** 99000

| | 31-05-14 | 31-05-13 | 31-05-12 |
|---|---|---|---|
| TA | 181,817 | 176,773 | 147,004 |
| NW | 91,541 | 46,209 | 20,966 |
| WC | 86,246 | 43,064 | 19,686 |

DUNS 34-873-6252

## Trustmarque Group Ltd

(**Subsidiary of:** Project Lennon (Topco) Ltd)
Unit 3, Alpha Court, Monks Cross Drive, York, North Yorkshire YO32 9WN
**Tel:** 08452101500
**Web:** www.trustmarque.com
**Reg No:** 5671829 **Estd:** 2006 Private Limited Company
**Line of Business:** Management activities of holding companies
**Issued Capital:** £479,693
**Directors:** M J Trainer, N M Simpson, J C Woolley, D J Joyce
**Co. Secretary:** Peter Mills
**US SIC:** 6711, 7379
**UK SIC:** 83962, 83940
**Auditors:** Grant Thornton UK LLP
**Bankers:** The Royal Bank Of Scotland Plc (16-23-37)

| | 31-12-13 | 31-08-12 | 31-12-11 |
|---|---|---|---|
| TO | N/A | 131,305,104 | 115,323,642 |
| P/L | (1,724,228) | 1,040,195 | 2,605,153 |
| NW | (13,500,469) | (23,678,474) | (25,638,542) |
| WC | (40,750,469) | (5,699,732) | (5,996,902) |
| Emp. | 3 | 169 | 134 |

DUNS 39-742-8608

## Trustmarque Solutions Ltd

(**Subsidiary of:** Ardvarna Investment Capital Ltd)
Trustmarque House Unit 3, Alpha Court, Monks Cross Drive, Huntin, York, North Yorkshire YO32 9WN
**Tel:** 08701210321 **Fax:** 08452101525
**Web:** www.trustmarquesolutions.com
**Reg No:** 2183240 **VAT No:** 500606303
**Estd:** 1987 Private Limited Company
**Line of Business:** Computer software sales
**Export Sales:** £2,016,660
**Trading Style:** Trustmarque Solutions
**Issued Capital:** £50,000
**Directors:** J C Woolley, D J Joyce, M J Trainer
**Co. Secretary:** Peter Mills
**Responsibilities**
**Senior:** Kevin Trinkwon *(Manager)*
**Admin:** Heather Dawkins *(Office Administrator)*
**IT:** Gavin Pipes *(Computer Manager)*
**HR:** Liz Reynolds *(Human Resources Director)*
**Health & Safety:** Heather Dawkins *(Office Administrator)*
**Facilities:** Heather Dawkins *(Office Administrator)*
**US SIC:** 7379 **UK SIC:** 83940
**Auditors:** Grant Thornton UK LLP
**Bankers:** Bank Of Scotland (12-09-49)

| | 31-12-13 | 31-08-12 | 31-12-11 |
|---|---|---|---|
| TO | 157,002,997 | 131,305,104 | 115,323,642 |
| P/L | 2,658,127 | 5,037,796 | 4,646,444 |
| NW | 22,390,313 | 22,007,954 | 19,685,950 |
| WC | 19,481,287 | 21,073,479 | 19,076,365 |
| Emp. | 179 | 169 | 134 |

DUNS 21-228-3892

## Trustplus

280 Watford Road, Harrow, Middlesex HA1 3TZ
**Web:** www.trustplus.co.uk
**Estd:** 1993
**Line of Business:** Public sector hospital activities, including nhs trusts
**Proprietor:** Mrs R Lal
**Responsibilities**
**Senior:** A O'Neil *(General Manager)*
**US SIC:** 8062 **UK SIC:** 95100
**Employees:** 61

DUNS 49-140-0396

## Trustseal Ltd

(**Subsidiary of:** Trustseal Holdings Ltd)
10 Southfield Lane Industrial Estate, Worksop, Nottinghamshire S80 4NW
**Tel:** 01909-722662 **Fax:** 01909-720228
**Web:** www.trustseal.co.uk
**Reg No:** 3109968 **VAT No:** 657720222
**Estd:** 1995 Private Limited Company
**Line of Business:** Road surfacers
**Issued Capital:** £1,000
**Directors:** G J Redhead, J S Wragg
**Co. Secretary:** Christopher Booth
**Responsibilities**
**Health & Safety:** Rob Horne *(Health & Safety Officer)*
**US SIC:** 1611 **UK SIC:** 50200
**Auditors:** Groucott Moor Ltd
**Bankers:** National Westminster Bank Plc (60-24-30)

| | 31-10-13 | 31-10-12 | 31-10-11 |
|---|---|---|---|
| TA | 4,734,382 | 4,961,020 | 4,751,738 |
| NW | 2,499,188 | 2,332,986 | 2,074,843 |
| WC | 935,011 | 652,327 | 358,619 |

DUNS 73-852-6552

## Trustwave Ltd

(**Subsidiary of:** Trustwave Corporation)
8 Lincolns Inn Fields, London WC2A 3BP
**Tel:** 08454569611 **Fax:** 0845-456-9612
**Web:** www.trustwave.com
**Reg No:** 5107724 **VAT No:** 839852478
**Estd:** 2004 Private Limited Company
**Line of Business:** Other computer related activities
**Export Sales:** £6,834,931
**Issued Capital:** £100
**Directors:** R J Mccullen, M R Butler, Miss A R Lewis
**Co. Secretary:** F&L Cosec Limited
**US SIC:** 7379 **UK SIC:** 83940
**Auditors:** Wilson Wright & Co
**Bankers:** HSBC Bank plc (40-33-14)

| | 31-12-13 | 31-12-12 | 31-12-11 |
|---|---|---|---|
| TO | 15,114,775 | 12,665,849 | 11,112,627 |
| P/L | 567,007 | 253,472 | 286,018 |
| NW | (408,813) | (912,664) | (1,066,560) |
| WC | 214,049 | (1,330,944) | 1,537,931 |
| Emp. | 73 | 55 | 51 |

DUNS 21-656-5313 **Imp**

## Trutex Ltd

(**Subsidiary of:** Trutex Investments Ltd)
Jubilee Mill, Taylor Street, Clitheroe, Lancashire BB7 1NL
**Tel:** 01200 421200 **Fax:** 01200 421209
**Web:** www.trutex.com
**Reg No:** 7132787 **Estd:** 1995 Private Limited Company
**Line of Business:** Children and babywear retail
**Export Sales:** £537,000
**Issued Capital:** £164
**Directors:** A J Ducker, M J Easter, D B Manning, Ms H Walker, M D Hargreaves, T Hallas
**Co. Secretary:** Martin Hargreaves
**Responsibilities**
**Senior:** Kelly Cottier *(Sales And Marketing Assistant)*
**Marketing:** Kelly Cottier *(Sales And Marketing Assistant)*
**Sales:** Kelly Cottier *(Sales And Marketing Assistant)*
**IT:** Rob Mullins *(Computer Operations Manager)*
**Branches:** Trutex Ltd, Unit 13, 4 Billacombe Road, Plymouth, Devon PL9 7HT
**US SIC:** 5641 **UK SIC:** 64500
**Auditors:** Ernst & Young LLP
**Bankers:** HSBC Bank plc (40-05-26)

| | 29-12-13 | 31-12-12 | 31-12-11 |
|---|---|---|---|
| TO | 21,005,000 | 21,291,000 | 19,535,000 |
| P/L | 44,000 | 539,000 | (222,000) |
| NW | (2,478,000) | (2,636,000) | (3,290,000) |
| WC | (420,000) | 245,000 | 729,000 |
| Emp. | 108 | 111 | 104 |

DUNS 21-913-5639 **Imp**

## Trw Ltd

(**Subsidiary of:** Trw Automotive Holdings Corp.)
Technical Centre Stratford Road, Solihull, West Midlands B90 4GW
**Web:** www.trwaftermarket.com
**Reg No:** 0872948 **Estd:** 1905 Private Limited Company
**Line of Business:** Manufacture of electrical equipment for engines and vehicles not elsewhere classified
**Export Sales:** £190,450,000
**Trading Style:** Trw-Automotive Electronics, Trw-Automotive, Trw-Aftermarket Operations, Trw-Conekt
**Issued Capital:** £652
**Directors:** F Chittka, P R Rapin, R Lechner, M D Gwozdz, M C Furber, M J Way, S M Batterbee
**Co. Secretary:** Ms Jane Pegg
**Branches:** Trw Ltd, 543 Ipswich Rd, Slough, Berkshire SL1 4EG
**US SIC:** 3629, 3714
**UK SIC:** 34350, 35300
**Auditors:** Ernst & Young LLP
**Bankers:** Barclays Bank Plc (20-59-23)

| | 31-12-13 | 31-12-12 | 31-12-11 |
|---|---|---|---|
| TO | 296,781,000 | 274,764,000 | 295,109,000 |
| P/L | 29,645,000 | 24,582,000 | 17,615,000 |
| NW | 92,727,000 | 93,448,000 | 89,398,000 |
| WC | 59,806,000 | 67,947,000 | 70,429,000 |
| Emp. | 1,826 | 1,787 | 1,680 |

DUNS 21-613-4809 **Imp**

## Trw Systems Ltd

(**Subsidiary of:** Trw Automotive Holdings Corp.)
Mercantile Road, Rainton Bridge Industrial Estate, Houghton-Le-Spring, Tyne and Wear DH4 5PH
**Tel:** 01915-123-700
**Web:** www.trw.com
**Reg No:** 0352824 **VAT No:** 109432094
**Estd:** 1939 Private Limited Company
**Line of Business:** Manufacture of parts and accessories for motor vehicles and their engines
**Export Sales:** £147,115,000
**Trading Style:** Trw Automotive
**Issued Capital:** £200,050,000
**Directors:** S M Batterbee, P R Rapin, M J Way, M C Furber, M D Gwozdz, R Lechner
**Co. Secretary:** Ms Jane Pegg
**Responsibilities**
**Senior:** Steve Lunn *(Chief Executive)*
**Finance:** Paul Willson *(Financial Manager)*
**Marketing:** Jon Sellars *(Marketing Manager)*
**Sales:** Mike Southwell *(Business Manager)*
**HR:** Julia Braithwaite *(Human Resources Manager)*
**Operations:** Alan Allsopp *(Purchasing Manager)*
**Purchasing:** Alan Allsopp *(Purchasing Manager)*
**Fleet:** Alan Allsopp *(Purchasing Manager)*
**Branches:** Trw Systems Ltd, Resolven, Neath, West Glamorgan SA11 4HN
**US SIC:** 3714, 3629, 7397
**UK SIC:** 35300, 34350, 83702
**Auditors:** Ernst & Young LLP
**Bankers:** Barclays Bank Plc (20-00-00)

| | 31-12-13 | 31-12-12 | 31-12-11 |
|---|---|---|---|
| TO | 154,053,000 | 161,578,000 | 176,600,000 |
| P/L | (6,109,000) | (2,179,000) | 1,189,000 |
| NW | 65,176,000 | 68,995,000 | 71,079,000 |
| WC | 27,455,000 | 48,643,000 | 53,691,000 |
| Emp. | 742 | 770 | 864 |

DUNS 76-851-2923

## Try Homes Ltd

(**Subsidiary of:** Galliford Try Plc)
Linden House, Guards Avenue, Caterham, Surrey CR3 5XL
**Tel:** 01883-334400 **Fax:** 01883331169
**Web:** www.lindenhomes.co.uk
**Reg No:** 2606856 **Estd:** 1991 Private Limited Company
**Line of Business:** Property developers
**Trading Style:** Linden Homes
**Issued Capital:** £1,267,209
**Directors:** G P Fitzgerald, K A Corbett
**Co. Secretary:** Galliford Try Secretariat Servic
**Responsibilities**
**Senior:** Darren Maddox *(Manager)*
**Finance:** Colin Rogers *(Financial Director)*
**Sales:** Claire Yates *(Sales Manager)*
**IT:** Declan O'Reilly *(IT Manager)*
**Health & Safety:** Michelle Bromley *(Health & Safety Officer)*
**Facilities:** Claire Yates *(Sales Manager)*
**US SIC:** 1541, 1522
**UK SIC:** 50100
**Auditors:** Deloitte & Touche LLP
**Bankers:** Bank Of Scotland (80-11-00)

| | 30-06-13 | 30-06-12 | 30-06-11 |
|---|---|---|---|
| TA | 27,714,000 | 27,714,000 | 30,279,000 |
| P/L | N/A | (2,565,000) | N/A |
| NW | 27,414,000 | 27,414,000 | 29,979,000 |
| WC | 16,419,000 | 12,877,000 | 12,877,000 |

DUNS 77-961-0294

## Tryzens Ltd

(**Subsidiary of:** Scottish Equity Partners Llp)
5th Floor, London EC2A 1RS
**Tel:** 020-7264-5900 **Fax:** 020-7264-5901
**Web:** www.tryzens.com
**Reg No:** 3064392 **Estd:** 1995 Private Limited Company
**Line of Business:** Web site design and development
**Issued Capital:** £2
**Directors:** A P Davison, E G Unwin, I G Stephens, A M Burton
**Responsibilities**
**Senior:** Euan Hendry *(Manager)*
**Finance:** Euan Hendry *(Manager)*
**Operations:** Ken Konsein *(Operations Director)*
**US SIC:** 7379, 7374
**UK SIC:** 83940
**Auditors:** Grant Thornton UK LLP
**Bankers:** National Westminster Bank Plc (60-15-33)

| | 31-03-14 | 31-03-13 | 31-03-12 |
|---|---|---|---|
| TO | 13,684,000 | 9,441,000 | 10,017,437 |
| P/L | (4,537,000) | 382,000 | 804,942 |
| NW | (3,997,000) | 1,118,000 | 823,007 |
| WC | (4,313,000) | 789,000 | 756,818 |
| Emp. | 114 | 119 | 62 |

DUNS 54-374-2613

## T.S. Booker & Son (Manufacturing) Ltd

(**Subsidiary of:** Readco 187 Ltd)
Fox Lane, Wakefield, West Yorkshire WF1 2AJ
**Fax:** 01924-290964
**Web:** www.tsbooker.co.uk
**Reg No:** 3262258 **VAT No:** 722002988
**Estd:** 1963 Private Limited Company
**Line of Business:** School equipment
**Issued Capital:** £1,000
**Director:** K J Steel
**Co. Secretary:** Samuel Steel
**Responsibilities**
**Senior:** Stuart Olney *(Manager)*
**Sales:** Adrian Wyles *(Senior Sales Executive)*
**US SIC:** 5199 **UK SIC:** 61900
**Auditors:** Paylings
**Bankers:** HSBC Bank plc (40-45-11)

| | 31-12-13 | 31-12-12 | 31-12-11 |
|---|---|---|---|
| TA | 1,558,237 | 1,501,479 | 1,894,942 |
| NW | 561,438 | 521,343 | 556,343 |
| WC | 441,950 | 406,827 | 496,392 |

DUNS 22-928-1282 **Imp-Exp**

## T.S. Foods Ltd

40 Mary Street, Castlewellan, Co Down BT31 9DU
**Tel:** 02843778227 **Fax:** 028-4377-1498
**Web:** www.tsfoods.co.uk
**Reg No:** 0014115NI **Estd:** 1980 Private Limited Company
**Line of Business:** Manufacturers of food products
**Export Markets:** Republic of Ireland
**Issued Capital:** £250,000
**Directors:** Ms A Steele, D A Steele, Ms J M Molloy, A Steele
**Co. Secretary:** Ms Ann Steele
**Responsibilities**
**Senior:** Brian Steele *(Manager)*
**Finance:** Patrick O'Hare *(Accountant)*
**US SIC:** 2099 **UK SIC:** 42399
**Auditors:** Jones Peters
**Bankers:** First Trust Bank (aib Group (uk) Plc) (93-80-33)

| | 31-05-13 | 31-05-12 | 31-05-11 |
|---|---|---|---|
| TA | 3,353,613 | 3,252,346 | 3,222,824 |
| NW | 2,495,966 | 2,269,147 | 2,082,729 |
| WC | 1,444,476 | 1,215,554 | 1,033,648 |

DUNS 23-725-7188 **Imp**

## Ts Tech Uk Ltd

(**Subsidiary of:** Ts Tech Co. Ltd.)
Blackworth Industrial Estate, Swindon, Wiltshire SN6 7NA
**Tel:** 01793767030
**Web:** www.tstech.co.jp
**Reg No:** 3720346 **Estd:** 1999 Private Limited Company
**Line of Business:** Manufacturers of car interiors
**Issued Capital:** £12,000,000
**Directors:** D Stone, Y Yui, T Naoi
**Co. Secretary:** Tmf Corporate Administration Ser
**Responsibilities**
**Senior:** Malcom Corcoran *(Manager)*, Tsuyoshi Sakakura *(Manager)*, Naoi Takeshi *(Manager)*, Arai Takuo *(Manager)*
**IT:** Phil Hazel *(IT Manager)*
**Health & Safety:** Kelly Huntbach *(Health & Safety Officer)*
**Operations:** Kelly Huntbach *(Health & Safety Officer)*
**US SIC:** 3714 **UK SIC:** 35300
**Auditors:** Deloitte LLP
**Bankers:** The Sanwa Bank, Ltd (40-51-28)

| | 31-12-13 | 31-12-12 | 31-12-11 |
|---|---|---|---|
| TO | 128,571,026 | 151,556,185 | 95,373,800 |
| P/L | 7,276,026 | 8,758,459 | (3,336,992) |
| NW | 26,191,412 | 19,813,508 | 12,832,379 |
| WC | 12,173,119 | 7,034,942 | (521,503) |
| Emp. | 578 | 597 | 484 |

DUNS 22-298-0356

## Ts&P Ltd

3 Lonsdale Gardens, Tunbridge Wells, Kent TN1 1NX
**Web:** www.ts-p.co.uk
**Reg No:** 4315932 **Estd:** 2001 Private Limited Company
**Line of Business:** Solicitors
**Issued Capital:** £1
**Director:** W M Partridge
**Co. Secretary:** Roland Millar
**Responsibilities**
**Senior:** Brian Bacon *(Partner - Private Client)*, Ray Beard *(Partner)*, Miranda Best *(Marketing Manager)*, James Cahan *(Associate)*, Jonathan Clement *(Partner)*, Sue Currie *(Legal Executive Senior Associa)*, Erin Denness *(Associate)*, Sarah Easton *(Senior Associate)*, Richard Ellard *(Partner)*, Eddie Fardell *(Partner)*, Patricia Fearnley *(Partner)*, Nick Gabay *(Partner)*, Susanna Gilmartin *(Partner)*, Stuart Goodbody *(Partner)*, Gilbert Green *(Partner)*, Alastair Harvey *(Partner)*, Ruth Harwood *(Partner)*, Nick Hobden *(Partner)*, Sarah Keily *(Senior Associate)*, Joel Kelly *(Senior Associate)*, Kirstie Law *(Partner)*, Sue Lister *(Senior Associate)*, Fiona Mills *(Partner)*, Desmond O'Donnell *(Senior Associate)*, Dominique Parker *(Associate)*, Jeremy Passmore *(Partner)*, Mark Politz *(Partner)*, Joanna Pratt *(Partner)*, Mary Rimmer *(Associate)*, Mark Steggles *(Senior Associate)*, Rebecca Swain *(Partner)*, Martin Terrell *(Partner)*, Helen Waite *(Senior Associate)*, Felicity Warran-Smith *(Partner)*, Heather West *(Associate)*, Josephine Willoughby *(Partner)*
**Finance:** Kristina Mathieson *(Personal Tax Manager)*

**Marketing:** Miranda Best (*Marketing Manager*), Alexa Twort (*Marketing Executive*)
**Admin:** Tess Harris (*Legal Secretary*)
**US SIC:** 8111 **UK SIC:** 83500

| | 30-11-14 | 30-11-13 | 30-11-12 |
|---|---|---|---|
| TA | 1 | 1 | 1 |
| NW | 1 | 1 | 1 |

**DUNS 29-006-8980**

## Tsb Bank Plc

(**Subsidiary of:** Lloyds Banking Group Plc)
Henry Duncan House, 118-124 George Street, Edinburgh, Midlothian EH2 4LH
**Tel:** 0131-225-4555 **Fax:** 0131-220-0240
**Web:** www.lloydsbank.com
**Reg No:** 0095237SC **Estd:** 1985 Public Limited Company
**Line of Business:** Banks and financial institutions
**Trading Style:** Tsb Bank Plc
**Issued Capital:** £76,349,991
**Directors:** Dame S J Dawson, W M Samuel, Doctor N M Bryson, S W Sinclair, D S Pope, P J Augar, M A Fisher, Mrs A B Kinney
**Co. Secretary:** Ms Susan Crichton
**Responsibilities**
**Senior:** Paul Pester (*Director*), Godfrey Robson (*Director*)
**Marketing:** Charlotte Sjoberg (*Head of Media Relations and Ev*), Lisa Stephenson (*Business Development Manager*)
**Sales:** Lisa Stephenson (*Business Development Manager*)
**HR:** Stephen McDonald (*Head of Human Resources*)
**Health & Safety:** Eleanor Dykes (*Facilities Manager*)
**Facilities:** Eleanor Dykes (*Facilities Manager*)
**Operations:** Stephen McDonald (*Head of Human Resources*)
**Purchasing:** Lisa Stephenson (*Business Development Manager*)
**Branches:** Tsb Bank Plc, 3rd Floor, 193 Bath Street, Glasgow, Lanarkshire G2 4HU
**US SIC:** 6012 **UK SIC:** 81402
**Auditors:** PricewaterhouseCoopers LLP
**Bankers:** Bank Of England (10-00-00)
Following financial data are in thousands

| | 31-12-13 | 31-12-12 | 31-12-11 |
|---|---|---|---|
| TA | 24,954,400 | 14,763,000 | 16,078,100 |
| P/L | 74,500 | 109,800 | 134,400 |
| NW | 1,295,200 | 751,300 | 668,000 |
| WC | 1,172,600 | 691,800 | 6,176,700 |
| Emp. | 4,721 | 1,352 | 1,475 |

**DUNS 52-527-0500**

## T.S.B. (Developments) Ltd

The Cumsey, Lye Green Clav, Claverdon, Warwick, Warwickshire CV35 8LR
**Tel:** 01926843111
**Web:** www.ardencote.com
**Reg No:** 3232897 **Estd:** 1996 Private Limited Company
**Line of Business:** Hotels
**Trading Style:** The Ardencote Manor Hotel
**Issued Capital:** £4,339,050
**Directors:** D Huckerby, I G Huckerby
**Co. Secretary:** Ms Dawn Sale
**US SIC:** 7011 **UK SIC:** 66500
**Auditors:** Target Consulting Ltd
**Bankers:** Barclays Bank Plc (20-71-45)

| | 31-08-13 | 31-08-12 | 31-08-11 |
|---|---|---|---|
| TO | 4,883,436 | N/A | N/A |
| P/L | 249,112 | N/A | N/A |
| NW | 8,398,733 | 8,148,985 | 7,834,495 |
| WC | (743,460) | (157,663) | (330,737) |
| Emp. | 130 | N/A | N/A |

**DUNS 73-519-3687**

## Tsc Engineering Ltd

Shipley Wharfe, Wharf Street, Shipley, West Yorkshire BD17 7DW
**Tel:** 01274531862
**Web:** www.tscoffshore.com
**Reg No:** 4782202 **Estd:** 2003 Private Limited Company
**Line of Business:** Industrial engineers
**Issued Capital:** £1
**Directors:** B Jiang, M Zhang, M L Chung
**Responsibilities**
**Senior:** Sudhir Kochhar (*General Manager*), Nigel Proctor (*Engineering Manager*)
**HR:** Nigel Proctor (*Engineering Manager*)
**Facilities:** Nigel Proctor (*Engineering Manager*)
**Operations:** Nigel Proctor (*Engineering Manager*)
**Engineering:** Nigel Proctor (*Engineering Manager*)
**US SIC:** 8911 **UK SIC:** 83701

| | 31-12-13 | 31-12-12 | 31-12-11 |
|---|---|---|---|
| TO | 14,145,087 | 11,129,539 | 11,672,253 |
| P/L | 704,513 | 1,804,562 | 2,238,927 |
| NW | 8,349,060 | 7,644,547 | 5,839,985 |
| WC | 8,331,816 | 7,609,308 | 5,934,048 |
| Emp. | 51 | 50 | 53 |

**DUNS 50-545-1302** *Imp*

## Tsc Foods Ltd

(**Subsidiary of:** Dickens 2014 Ltd)
Unit 3-4 Arkwright Way, Scunthorpe, South Humberside DN16 1AL
**Tel:** 01724-272900 **Fax:** 01724-272901
**Web:** www.tscfoods.com
**Reg No:** 2499642 **VAT No:** 555719121
**Estd:** 1991 Private Limited Company
**Line of Business:** Production of meat and poultry meat products
**Trading Style:** Tsc Foods Limited
**Issued Capital:** £3,240,000
**Directors:** G M Blake, D Marshall, L L Whiteley, M Wood
**Co. Secretary:** David Marshall
**Responsibilities**
**Senior:** David Bondi (*Director*), Jonothan Skofic (*Manager*), Dave Westhead (*Warehouse Manager*)
**Marketing:** Mark Allibone (*Commercial Director*)
**Sales:** Mark Allibone (*Commercial Director*)
**US SIC:** 2013, 2033
**UK SIC:** 41223, 41473
**Auditors:** Ernst & Young LLP
**Bankers:** Barclays Bank Plc (20-43-47)

| | 21-12-13 | 22-12-12 | 24-12-11 |
|---|---|---|---|
| TO | 45,241,000 | 44,217,000 | 42,674,000 |
| P/L | 4,241,000 | 3,439,000 | 3,323,000 |
| NW | 18,709,000 | 15,245,000 | 12,480,000 |
| WC | 12,409,000 | 9,101,000 | 6,534,000 |
| Emp. | 399 | 375 | 364 |

**DUNS 22-252-4964**

## Tsf Retail Solutions Ltd

(**Subsidiary of:** Muckle Llp)
2 Cook Way, North West Industrial Estate, Peterlee, County Durham SR8 2HY
**Tel:** 01915691400 **Fax:** 01915691401
**Web:** www.tsf.uk.co
**Reg No:** 4270505 **Estd:** 2001 Private Limited Company
**Line of Business:** Joinery installation
**Issued Capital:** £200
**Director:** D Craggs
**Co. Secretary:** John Newman
**Responsibilities**
**Senior:** Patrick Brown (*MD*)
**Finance:** Patrick Brown (*MD*)
**IT:** Natalie McClelland (*IT Manager*)
**US SIC:** 1751, 1799
**UK SIC:** 50400, 50000
**Auditors:** Baker Tilly UK Audit LLP
**Bankers:** Barclays Bank Plc (20-33-51)

| | 30-09-13 | 30-09-12 | 30-09-11 |
|---|---|---|---|
| TO | 14,783,190 | 13,829,642 | 18,554,644 |
| P/L | 238,787 | (53,949) | 185,719 |
| NW | 2,176,768 | 1,962,564 | 2,047,263 |
| WC | 1,890,158 | 1,758,570 | 1,777,348 |
| Emp. | 87 | 90 | 101 |

**DUNS 23-918-4919**

## T.S.G. Building Services Plc

Tsghse Cranbourne Industrial Estate, Cranbourne Road, Potters Bar, Hertfordshire EN6 3JN
**Tel:** 01707800361 **Fax:** 01707-800-678
**Web:** www.tsgplc.co.uk
**Reg No:** 3908728 **VAT No:** 974980167
**Estd:** 1977 Public Limited Company
**Line of Business:** Plumbing
**Trading Style:** Tsg Mechanical Services, Tsg Construction Services, Tsg Gas Services
**Issued Capital:** £60,000
**Directors:** Mrs C A Thrussell, B P Thrussell, S J Gwynn, A J Thrussell, B L Rees, J P Holloway
**Co. Secretary:** Robert Glendinning
**Responsibilities**
**Senior:** Paul Brigden (*Manager*), Roderick Thrussell (*CEO, Managing Director*)
**Finance:** Paul Brigden (*Manager*)
**IT:** Mark Terenzio (*Head of IT*)
**Fleet:** Paul Brigden (*Manager*)
**US SIC:** 1711, 8911
**UK SIC:** 50300, 83701
**Auditors:** Newton & Garner Ltd

| | 30-04-14 | 30-04-13 | 30-04-12 |
|---|---|---|---|
| TO | 27,802,596 | 28,358,089 | 24,776,127 |
| P/L | 810,790 | 408,620 | 117,161 |
| NW | 2,120,853 | 1,755,013 | 1,661,464 |
| WC | 1,263,157 | 1,185,405 | 1,144,503 |
| Emp. | 185 | 161 | 159 |

**DUNS 73-332-6156**

## Tsk Workplace Ltd

(**Subsidiary of:** The Tsk Group Ltd)
130 Metroplex Business Park, Broadway, Salford, Lancashire M50 2UW
**Web:** www.tskgroup.co.uk
**Reg No:** 4606484 **Estd:** 2002 Private Limited Company
**Line of Business:** Furniture designers
**Trading Style:** Tsk Group Private Limited Company
**Issued Capital:** £1
**Director:** A Burns
**Co. Secretary:** Iain Holden
**US SIC:** 7399 **UK SIC:** 83954

**Auditors:** Moore & Smalley LLP
**Bankers:** The Royal Bank Of Scotland Plc (16-28-33)

| | 31-07-13 | 31-01-13 | 31-07-11 |
|---|---|---|---|
| TA | 1 | 1 | 1 |
| NW | 1 | 1 | 1 |

**DUNS 22-911-0804**

## T.S.L. Contractors Ltd.

Craignure, Ulva Ferry, Isle of Mull
**Tel:** 01680812475 **Fax:** 01680-812393
**Web:** www.tslcontractors.co.uk
**Reg No:** 0067094SC **VAT No:** 293455042
**Estd:** 1979 Private Limited Company
**Line of Business:** Residential building contractors
**Issued Capital:** £21,800
**Managing Director:** A D Knight
**Responsibilities**
**Finance:** Fiona Shannon (*Manager*)
**Branches:** T.s.l. Contractors Ltd., 6 Mcleod Buildings, Lochavullin Road, Oban, Argyll PA34 4PL
**US SIC:** 1522, 1541, 4213
**UK SIC:** 50100, 72300
**Auditors:** Johnston Carmichael
**Bankers:** The Royal Bank Of Scotland Plc (83-26-04)

| | 31-07-13 | 31-07-12 | 31-07-11 |
|---|---|---|---|
| TO | 9,091,513 | 7,463,174 | 6,706,353 |
| P/L | 690,241 | 491,151 | 309,220 |
| NW | 2,752,599 | 2,359,042 | 1,983,954 |
| WC | 875,770 | 1,113,932 | 776,081 |
| Emp | 63 | 66 | 71 |

**DUNS 64-088-9775**

## Tsl Projects Ltd

(**Subsidiary of:** Tonroe Group Ltd)
24-26 Chapel Street, Marlow, Buckinghamshire SL7 1DD
**Tel:** 08453 307311
**Web:** www.tslprojects.com
**Reg No:** 4492402 **Estd:** 2002 Private Limited Company
**Line of Business:** Specialised building trade contractors
**Issued Capital:** £100
**Director:** M A Mcdonnell
**Co. Secretary:** Ms Jacqueline Wild
**Responsibilities**
**Senior:** Mark Rowland (*Manager*)
**Health & Safety:** Jason Wigglesworth (*health & safety Manager*)
**US SIC:** 1799, 1796
**UK SIC:** 50000, 50400
**Auditors:** Cube Partners Ltd
**Bankers:** National Westminster Bank Plc (56-00-60)

| | 30-06-14 | 30-06-13 | 30-06-12 |
|---|---|---|---|
| TO | 33,603,138 | 28,189,059 | 19,356,831 |
| P/L | 738,976 | 686,350 | 731,525 |
| NW | 1,354,516 | 1,011,611 | 853,917 |
| WC | 1,033,077 | 757,205 | 654,377 |
| Emp. | 82 | 56 | 30 |

**DUNS 22-815-2906** *Exp*

## Tsl Vanguard Ltd

Bell Hill Wood Lane Rothwell, Leeds, West Yorkshire LS26 6PS
**Tel:** 01132887435 **Fax:** 01132820210
**Web:** www.tslvanguard.co.uk
**Reg No:** 1667871 **Estd:** 2010 Private Limited Company
**Line of Business:** Road haulage and transport services
**Export Markets:** Europe, Scandinavia
**Trading Style:** T S L Vanguard
**Issued Capital:** £25,000
**Principals:** A G Liversidge (*Managing*), J H Liversidge, I Liverside
**Co. Secretary:** Mrs Patricia Liversidge
**Responsibilities**
**Senior:** Ian Liversidge (*Managing Director*)
**US SIC:** 4789 **UK SIC:** 77002
**Auditors:** Fullertons
**Bankers:** National Westminster Bank Plc (60-60-05)

| | 31-03-14 | 31-03-13 | 31-03-12 |
|---|---|---|---|
| TA | 1,301,594 | 945,437 | 838,142 |
| NW | 243,463 | 146,786 | 85,910 |
| WC | (143,734) | 15,524 | (4,870) |

**DUNS 73-358-0935**

## Tsquared Group Ltd

Optimus Building, 2 Robroyston Oval, Glasgow, Lanarkshire G33 1AP
**Web:** www.tsquared.co.uk
**Reg No:** 0242071SC **Estd:** 2003 Private Limited Company
**Line of Business:** Management activities of holding companies
**Issued Capital:** £10,000
**Directors:** R A Dinwoodie, D E Nicol, A Simpson
**Co. Secretary:** Graham Malcolm
**US SIC:** 6711 **UK SIC:** 83962

**Bankers:** Bank Of Scotland (80-06-64)

| | 31-03-14 | 31-03-13 | 31-03-12 |
|---|---|---|---|
| TO | 14,591,224 | 15,968,558 | 13,092,433 |
| P/L | 2,931,643 | 2,550,420 | 2,117,077 |
| NW | 3,425,276 | 4,169,538 | 2,322,996 |
| WC | 3,622,339 | 4,360,045 | 2,530,568 |
| Emp. | 84 | 76 | 67 |

**DUNS 21-745-2010** *Imp-Exp*

## T.S.R.Plastics Ltd

37 Finedon Station Road, Wellingborough, Northamptonshire NN9 5NX
**Tel:** 01536-722333
**Web:** www.tsrplastics.co.uk
**Reg No:** 0977014 **VAT No:** 208451283
**Estd:** 1970 Private Limited Company
**Line of Business:** Manufacture of other plastic products
**Trading Style:** T.S.R.Plastics Limited
**Issued Capital:** £249,840
**Principals:** H J Tai (*Chairman*), C D Tai (*Managing*), J P Tai, Ms N Tai
**Co. Secretary:** Carlo Tai
**Responsibilities**
**Senior:** Mariuccia Tai (*Manager*), Greg Trebski (*Warehouse Manager*)
**Marketing:** Tony Mew (*Sales & Marketing Manager*)
**Sales:** Ian Brookes (*Sales Director*), Tony Mew (*Sales & Marketing Manager*)
**Facilities:** Barry Watts (*Facilities Manager*)
**Engineering:** Barry Watts (*Facilities Manager*)
**US SIC:** 7399 **UK SIC:** 83954
**Auditors:** H L B Vantis Audit PLC

| | 31-03-14 | 31-03-13 | 31-03-12 |
|---|---|---|---|
| TA | 1,910,346 | 2,136,623 | 3,028,237 |
| NW | 1,121,059 | 1,556,649 | 2,307,755 |
| WC | 478,498 | 753,936 | 1,372,090 |

**DUNS 50-439-0105**

## T.S.S. (Total Security Services) Ltd

Security House, 485 Hale End Road, London E4 9PT
**Tel:** 020-8523-5533 **Fax:** 020-8527-0739
**Web:** www.tss-guarding.co.uk
**Reg No:** 2426982 **VAT No:** 544381640
**Estd:** 1989 Private Limited Company
**Line of Business:** Security and related activities
**Issued Capital:** £490
**Directors:** R L Gardezi, J Caplin, D Dossett
**Co. Secretary:** Declan Dossett
**Responsibilities**
**Senior:** Ricky Gardezi (*Manager*)
**US SIC:** 7393 **UK SIC:** 83954
**Auditors:** J K Shah
**Bankers:** National Westminster Bank Plc (56-00-27)

| | 31-10-13 | 31-10-12 | 31-10-11 |
|---|---|---|---|
| TO | 63,474,052 | 55,501,361 | 52,675,631 |
| P/L | 4,592,591 | 3,944,058 | 4,268,249 |
| NW | 15,849,076 | 12,314,381 | 10,926,040 |
| WC | 13,084,746 | 9,982,836 | 8,561,947 |
| Emp. | 3,509 | 3,202 | 3,049 |

**DUNS 21-915-3921** *Imp*

## Tsubakimoto U K Ltd

(**Subsidiary of:** Tsubakimoto Chain Co.)
Osier Drive Sherwood Park, Nottingham, Nottinghamshire NG15 0DX
**Tel:** 01623-688700
**Web:** www.tsubaki.co.uk
**Reg No:** 1201947 **VAT No:** 115723783
**Estd:** 1975 Private Limited Company
**Line of Business:** Manufacturers of chains
**Export Sales:** £15,638,900
**Issued Capital:** £550,000
**Principals:** B R Mellink (*Managing*), F Rosmolen
**Co. Secretary:** Philip Shaw
**Responsibilities**
**Senior:** Bart Mellink (*Manager*)
**Marketing:** Bob Young (*Marketing Manager*)
**US SIC:** 3568 **UK SIC:** 32613
**Auditors:** Deloitte LLP
**Bankers:** National Westminster Bank Plc (60-02-41)

| | 31-03-14 | 31-03-13 | 31-03-12 |
|---|---|---|---|
| TO | 21,796,622 | 20,101,113 | 19,570,670 |
| P/L | 1,324,971 | 855,418 | 1,085,100 |
| NW | 10,560,809 | 9,851,894 | 9,608,354 |
| WC | 6,794,202 | 7,445,685 | 7,132,576 |
| Emp. | 67 | 64 | 62 |

**DUNS 77-979-2543**

## Tsys Managed Services Emea Ltd

(**Subsidiary of:** Total System Services Inc.)
Burystead Court, 120 Caldecotte Lake Drive, Caldecotte, Milton Keynes, Buckinghamshire MK7 8LE
**Tel:** 01908681573
**Web:** www.tsys.com
**Reg No:** 5947723 **Estd:** 2006 Private Limited Company
**Line of Business:** Financial intermediation not elsewhere classified
**Issued Capital:** £100,000

**Directors:** A C Foster, D Figgat, D Jones, A S Briggs, Ms K C Knutson, A S Garton, D L Chew, J Patel
**Co. Secretary:** Citco Management (Uk) Limited
**US SIC:** 6111, 7379
**UK SIC:** 81501, 83940
**Auditors:** KPMG LLP

| | 31-12-13 | 31-12-12 | 31-12-11 |
|---|---|---|---|
| TA | 10,892,000 | 10,549,000 | 10,283,000 |
| P/L | 5,832,000 | (790,000) | 1,739,000 |
| NW | 8,269,000 | 2,649,000 | 5,674,000 |
| WC | 4,953,000 | 4,527,000 | 3,719,000 |
| Emp. | 635 | 660 | 548 |

DUNS 23-245-7841
## Tsys Total Systems Services Europe
Fulford Moor House, York, North Yorkshire YO10 4EY
**Tel:** 01904562000
**Web:** www.tsyseuropecareers.com
**Estd:** 2001
**Line of Business:** Data processing
**Responsibilities**
**Senior:** Kelly Knutson *(CEO, Managing Director)*
**Admin:** Julie Harper *(PA)*
**IT:** Keith Herrison *(Senior IT Executive)*, Johnathan Hill *(Computer Operations Manager)*
**Operations:** Johnathan Hill *(Computer Operations Manager)*
**US SIC:** 7374 **UK SIC:** 83940
**Employees:** 200

DUNS 42-428-6271
## Tt Assembly Systems (Uk) Ltd
(**Subsidiary of:** Toyota Tsusho Corporation)
Unit 9a Willow Farm Business Park, Castle Donnington, Castle Donington, Derby, Derbyshire DE74 2UD
**Tel:** 01332-814082 **Fax:** 01332-814083
**Web:** www.ttas-uk.com
**Reg No:** 4416133 **Estd:** 2002 Private Limited Company
**Line of Business:** Manufacture of parts and accessories for motor vehicles and their engines
**Issued Capital:** £2,500,000
**Directors:** M Okada, S Tada, H Funeno, M J Storey
**Co. Secretary:** Michael Deann-Valentine
**Responsibilities**
**Senior:** Hiroki Nakayama *(Manager)*, Junichi Tone *(Manager)*
**US SIC:** 3714 **UK SIC:** 35300

| | 31-03-14 | 31-03-13 | 31-03-12 |
|---|---|---|---|
| TO | 17,381,215 | 10,131,553 | 5,403,765 |
| P/L | (138,274) | (5,259,292) | 319,997 |
| NW | 3,284,825 | 3,380,588 | 7,341,725 |
| WC | 1,793,184 | (13,896,638) | 1,447,997 |
| Emp. | 127 | 83 | 39 |

DUNS 21-899-3954 Imp-Exp
## Tt Electronics Integrated Manufacturing Services Ltd
(**Subsidiary of:** Tt Electronics Plc)
Tregwilym Industrial Estate, Newport, Gwent NP10 9YA
**Tel:** 01633892345 **Fax:** 01633895755
**Web:** www.ttelectronics.com
**Reg No:** 0896672 **VAT No:** 555969874
**Estd:** 1985 Private Limited Company
**Line of Business:** Electronic equipment (assembly)
**Export Markets:** U S A; Republic of Ireland; Israel
**Export Sales:** £5,643,000
**Issued Capital:** £1,000,000
**Directors:** M Hoad, S D Dasani, S J Mather, R W Moseley
**Co. Secretary:** Lynton Boardman
**Responsibilities**
**Senior:** Bob Hannah *(Operations Director)*
**HR:** Denise Machon *(Human Resources Manager)*
**Health & Safety:** Allan Brooks *(Facilities Manager)*
**Facilities:** Allan Brooks *(Facilities Manager)*
**Branches:** Tt Electronics Integrated Manufacturing Services Limited, Tregwilym Industrial Estate, Newport, Gwent NP10 9YA
**US SIC:** 3643 **UK SIC:** 34203
**Auditors:** KPMG Audit PLC
**Bankers:** HSBC Bank plc (40-34-18)

| | 31-12-13 | 31-12-12 | 31-12-11 |
|---|---|---|---|
| TO | 60,465,000 | 33,969,000 | 32,250,000 |
| P/L | 604,000 | 137,000 | 1,160,000 |
| NW | 2,947,000 | 2,343,000 | 2,462,000 |
| WC | 10,431,000 | 9,610,000 | 9,029,000 |
| Emp. | 383 | 268 | 240 |

DUNS 21-239-8689 Exp
## Tt Electronics Plc
Clive House, 12-18 Queens Road, Weybridge, Surrey KT13 9XB
**Tel:** 01932-825-300
**Web:** www.abinterconnect.co.uk
**Reg No:** 0087249 **Estd:** 1906 Public Limited Company
**Line of Business:** Management activities of holding companies
**Export Markets:** Rest of Europe, North America, Rest of the World
**Export Sales:** £428,100,000
**Issued Capital:** £39,538,243
**Directors:** M Hoad, J C Shakeshaft, S M Watson, J R Tyson, S A King, S Dasani, M J Baunton
**Co. Secretary:** Lynton Boardman
**Branches:** Tt Electronics Plc, Durham Rd North, Chester Le Street, County Durham DH3 1LE
**US SIC:** 6711, 5065
**UK SIC:** 83962, 61500
**Auditors:** KPMG Audit PLC
**Bankers:** HSBC Bank plc (40-46-22)

| | 31-12-13 | 31-12-12 | 31-12-11 |
|---|---|---|---|
| TO | 532,200,000 | 476,900,000 | 591,300,000 |
| P/L | 18,300,000 | 23,400,000 | 31,800,000 |
| NW | 119,300,000 | 110,700,000 | 110,300,000 |
| WC | 80,600,000 | 68,400,000 | 92,400,000 |
| Emp. | 5,674 | 5,464 | 6,215 |

DUNS 23-980-6180
## T.T. Express (Oldham) Ltd
Woodstock Distribution Centre, Meek Street, Royton, Oldham, Lancashire OL2 6HL
**Tel:** 08456783334 **Fax:** 08456 783335
**Web:** www.ttexpress.co.uk
**Reg No:** 3969120 **VAT No:** 151038110
**Estd:** 2000 Private Limited Company
**Line of Business:** Other supporting land transport activities
**Issued Capital:** £100
**Directors:** C R Green, D W Taylor
**Co. Secretary:** Mrs Pamela Taylor
**Responsibilities**
**Senior:** Doru Costache *(Operations Manager)*
**US SIC:** 4789, 4226
**UK SIC:** 77002, 77003
**Auditors:** Wrigley Partington
**Bankers:** Yorkshire Bank Plc (05-07-37)

| | 30-03-14 | 31-03-13 | 31-03-12 |
|---|---|---|---|
| TO | 6,235,977 | 6,339,075 | 5,406,232 |
| P/L | 45,557 | 19,882 | 161,345 |
| NW | 626,267 | 599,659 | 589,317 |
| WC | 515,175 | 412,942 | 275,221 |
| Emp. | 75 | 85 | 104 |

DUNS 21-104-8659
## Tt International (London) Ltd
Moor House Level 13, 120 London Wall, London EC2Y 5ET
**Tel:** 02075091000
**Reg No:** 6475385 **Estd:** 2008 Private Limited Company
**Line of Business:** Other business activities not elsewhere classified
**Issued Capital:** £200,000
**Directors:** F Goasguen, J G Ip, A J Moorhouse, S A Allison
**Co. Secretary:** Ms Linda Somuah
**US SIC:** 7399 **UK SIC:** 83954
**Bankers:** Hsbc Investment Bank Plc (40-04-42)

| | 30-06-13 | 30-06-12 | 30-06-11 |
|---|---|---|---|
| TO | 584,929 | 533,887 | 623,313 |
| P/L | 36,406 | 34,685 | 37,956 |
| NW | 332,307 | 302,486 | 274,611 |
| WC | 332,307 | 302,486 | 274,611 |

DUNS 21-011-3158
## Tt2 Ltd
(**Subsidiary of:** Tt2 (Holdings) Ltd)
Tyne Tunnels, Wallsend, Tyne and Wear NE28 0PD
**Tel:** 01912624451
**Web:** www.tt2.co.uk
**Reg No:** 6346957 **Estd:** 2007 Private Limited Company
**Line of Business:** Other supporting land transport activities
**Issued Capital:** £50,000
**Directors:** M C Wayment, M A Donn, T N Jackson, R J Newton, C A Paradis, A L Tennant
**Co. Secretary:** Ms Rachel Turnbull
**US SIC:** 4789 **UK SIC:** 77002

| | 31-03-14 | 31-03-13 | 31-03-12 |
|---|---|---|---|
| TO | 21,016,480 | 231,051,056 | 6,713,780 |
| P/L | 1,703,307 | 8,474,457 | 2,210,205 |
| NW | 3,270,767 | 1,754,160 | (6,091,548) |
| WC | 37,000,013 | 31,718,941 | 196,867,778 |
| Emp. | 56 | 55 | 58 |

DUNS 21-014-5695
## Tta (2007) Ltd.
Albion House, High Street, Woking, Surrey GU21 6BD
**Tel:** 08456008308
**Web:** www.mod.uk
**Reg No:** 6372120 **Estd:** 2007 Private Limited Company
**Line of Business:** Holding companies management activities
**Issued Capital:** £154,002
**Directors:** G I Lewis, N R Seaman, S J Clark, S J Hargreaves, J N Stones, T L Carpenter
**Co. Secretary:** Mark Storey
**US SIC:** 6711 **UK SIC:** 83962
**Bankers:** Barclays Bank Plc (20-00-30)

| | 30-06-14 | 30-06-13 | 30-06-12 |
|---|---|---|---|
| TO | 5,236,390 | 4,962,296 | 4,759,262 |
| P/L | (544,738) | (234,692) | (1,034,264) |
| NW | (12,591,961) | (12,541,756) | (12,722,633) |
| WC | 771,908 | (554,332) | 353,250 |
| Emp. | 67 | 62 | 52 |

DUNS 77-112-2520
## Ttap Group Ltd
St Margarets Way Stukeley Meadows, Industrial Estate, Huntingdon, Cambridgeshire PE29 6EB
**Tel:** 01480-412345
**Web:** www.ttapgroup.com
**Reg No:** 2689126 **VAT No:** 576628790
**Estd:** 1992 Private Limited Company
**Line of Business:** Manufacture of other plastic products
**Trading Style:** Ttap Group Ltd
**Issued Capital:** £28,000
**Directors:** P A Leach, M Tyson, D I Leach
**Co. Secretary:** Ms Deborah Munn
**US SIC:** 3079 **UK SIC:** 48360
**Auditors:** Baker Tilly
**Bankers:** Lloyds TSB Bank plc (30-94-47)

| | 30-04-13 | 30-04-12 | 30-04-11 |
|---|---|---|---|
| TO | 4,900,528 | 5,022,119 | 4,794,364 |
| P/L | 138,552 | 72,829 | 68,093 |
| NW | (78,319) | (171,907) | (250,104) |
| WC | (1,239,424) | (1,219,672) | (1,061,816) |

DUNS 50-335-8004
## The Tte Technical Training Group
Edison House, Middlesbrough Road East, Middlesbrough, Cleveland TS6 6TZ
**Tel:** 01642-462266
**Web:** www.tte.co.uk
**Reg No:** 2360140 **VAT No:** 789385357
**Estd:** 2001 Private Company Limited By Guarantee
**Line of Business:** Training services
**Trading Style:** The Tte Technical Training Group
**Directors:** A Moore, G B Jones, K Mutimer, P J Lennon
**Co. Secretary:** Mrs Andrea Preston
**Branches:** The Tte Technical Training Group, Wilton Training Centre, Po Box 36, Middlesbrough, Cleveland TS6 8YX
**US SIC:** 8249 **UK SIC:** 93300
**Auditors:** PricewaterhouseCoopers
**Bankers:** HSBC Bank plc (40-33-01)

| | 31-08-13 | 31-08-12 | 31-08-11 |
|---|---|---|---|
| TO | 7,925,706 | 7,754,098 | 8,588,859 |
| P/L | (852,179) | (1,090,457) | (2,822,370) |
| NW | 995,280 | (701,055) | (507,507) |
| WC | 1,089,025 | 402,394 | (809,086) |
| Emp. | 101 | 94 | 136 |

DUNS 50-509-7279
## Tte Training Ltd
New Horizons House, New Bridge Road, Ellesmere Port, Cheshire CH65 4LT
**Tel:** 01513-576100
**Web:** www.tteltd.co.uk
**Reg No:** 2477635 **Estd:** 1990 Private Company Limited By Guarantee
**Line of Business:** Sub-degree level higher education
**Trading Style:** New Horizons
**Directors:** Dr J E Przeworski, Ms S Stacey, S G Wilson, N P Smith, M J Jessop
**Co. Secretary:** Ms Shirley Stacey
**US SIC:** 8221, 8249
**UK SIC:** 93100, 93300
**Auditors:** Baker Tilly

| | 31-08-13 | 31-08-12 | 31-08-11 |
|---|---|---|---|
| TA | 2,483,419 | 2,572,164 | 2,848,757 |
| NW | 1,342,553 | 1,343,204 | 1,367,896 |
| WC | (25,829) | (106,949) | (122,922) |

DUNS 21-136-2585
## Tti (Europe) Ltd
6 Olympus Court, Olympus Avenue, Tachbrook Park, Warwick, Warwickshire CV34 6RZ
**Tel:** 01926425250
**Reg No:** 6691266 **Estd:** 2008 Private Limited Company
**Line of Business:** Other business activities not elsewhere classified
**Export Sales:** £9,704,000
**Issued Capital:** £2,001,000
**Director:** D J Kennedy
**Co. Secretary:** Ms Lori Blaker
**Branches:** Tti (Europe) Ltd, 5G Langley Business Center, Station Road, Langley, Slough, Berkshire SL3 8DS
**US SIC:** 7399 **UK SIC:** 83954

| | 31-12-13 | 31-12-12 | 31-12-11 |
|---|---|---|---|
| TO | 9,704,000 | 10,226,000 | 2,151,299 |
| P/L | 230,000 | 646,000 | 216,760 |
| NW | 2,277,000 | 2,138,000 | 231,125 |
| WC | 2,143,000 | 1,932,000 | 213,015 |
| Emp. | 99 | 91 | N/A |

DUNS 21-117-2002 Imp-Exp
## Tti Group Ltd
(**Subsidiary of:** Aalberts Industries N.V.)
39-43 Bilton Way, Luton, Bedfordshire LU1 1UU
**Tel:** 01582488344 **Fax:** 01582488394
**Web:** www.ttigroup.org.uk
**Reg No:** 0884462 **VAT No:** 419026859
**Estd:** 1966 Private Limited Company
**Line of Business:** Treatment and coating of metals
**Export Markets:** Worldwide
**Export Sales:** £607,000
**Trading Style:** Acorn Surface Technology, Nitriding Services
**Issued Capital:** £30,000
**Directors:** A N Borg, O Jaeger
**Co. Secretary:** Mrs Denise Coughlan
**Responsibilities**
**Senior:** Denise Osborn *(Financial Controller)*
**Finance:** Denise Osborn *(Financial Controller)*
**Operations:** Pawel Danielewicz *(Operations Manager)*
**Branches:** Tti Group Ltd, 5-7 Bickford Road, Birmingham, West Midlands B6 7EE
**US SIC:** 3398 **UK SIC:** 31380
**Auditors:** PricewaterhouseCoopers LLP
**Bankers:** HSBC Bank plc (40-03-27)

| | 31-12-13 | 31-12-12 | 31-12-11 |
|---|---|---|---|
| TO | 17,896,000 | 17,181,000 | 16,072,000 |
| P/L | 1,316,000 | 1,285,000 | 484,000 |
| NW | (2,702,000) | (2,775,000) | (2,975,000) |
| WC | (5,461,000) | (5,640,000) | (6,547,000) |
| Emp. | 206 | 203 | 201 |

DUNS 39-887-3992 Exp
## Ttp Group Plc
Melbourn Science Park, Cambridge Road-Melbourn, Royston, Hertfordshire SG8 6HQ
**Tel:** 01763-262626 **Fax:** 01763261582
**Web:** www.ttpgroup.com
**Reg No:** 2170755 **Estd:** 1987 Public Limited Company
**Line of Business:** Business and management consultancy activities not elsewhere classified
**Export Markets:** U S A, Japan, South Korea, Australia, Germany, Switzerland, France, Belgium
**Export Sales:** £26,198,000
**Issued Capital:** £2,363,274
**Directors:** Dr C D Wall, P J Taylor, Dr G Avison, Dr J C Fox
**Co. Secretary:** Keith Haddow
**Responsibilities**
**Senior:** Martin Orrell *(General Manager)*
**US SIC:** 7392, 7391
**UK SIC:** 83951, 94000
**Auditors:** Ernst & Young
**Bankers:** Lloyds TSB Bank plc (30-25-04)

| | 31-03-14 | 31-03-13 | 31-03-12 |
|---|---|---|---|
| TO | 43,700,000 | 38,950,000 | 39,000,000 |
| P/L | 1,753,000 | 757,000 | 2,670,000 |
| NW | 49,617,000 | 45,660,000 | 46,639,000 |
| WC | 26,030,000 | 28,735,000 | 29,149,000 |
| Emp. | 317 | 312 | 315 |

DUNS 77-912-5603
## Ttr Pt Ltd
First Floor Waterloo House, Fleets Corner, Wat, Poole, Dorset BH17 0HL
**Tel:** 02381611011
**Web:** www.thetrainingroom.com
**Reg No:** 5815801 **Estd:** 2006 Private Limited Company
**Line of Business:** Technical and vocational secondary education
**Issued Capital:** £11
**Director:** J R Davies
**US SIC:** 8249 **UK SIC:** 93300
**Bankers:** Lloyds TSB Bank plc (30-00-00)

| | 31-05-13 | 31-05-12 | 31-05-11 |
|---|---|---|---|
| TO | 8,592,269 | N/A | N/A |
| P/L | 1,307,585 | N/A | N/A |
| NW | 1,922,512 | 1,521,565 | 53,985 |
| WC | 2,399,099 | 1,893,522 | 788,138 |
| Emp. | 114 | N/A | N/A |

DUNS 21-740-8418 Imp
## T.T.S. Truck Tyre Specialists Ltd
(**Subsidiary of:** Warne Properties Ltd)
Warne Road, Weston-Super-Mare, Avon BS23 3UU
**Tel:** 01934-622626
**Web:** www.trucktyrespecialists.co.uk
**Reg No:** 1379569 **VAT No:** 302750985

**Estd:** 1974 Private Limited Company
**Line of Business:** Tyre dealers
**Trading Style:** T T S Truck Tyre Specialists
**Issued Capital:** £7,199
**Principals:** R Collins *(Managing)*, Ms A V Binning, D Moody, D J Collins, G F Simpson, Ms A V Binning
**Co. Secretary:** Philip Binning
**US SIC:** 5531 **UK SIC:** 65100
**Auditors:** Evans & Partners
**Bankers:** HSBC Bank plc (40-47-46)

| | 31-12-13 | 31-12-12 | 31-12-11 |
|---|---|---|---|
| TA | 2,118,874 | 2,116,807 | 1,900,806 |
| NW | 265,428 | 159,551 | 147,406 |
| WC | (55,606) | (134,848) | (123,828) |

DUNS 22-707-5918 **Imp**

## Ttt Moneycorp Ltd

(**Subsidiary of:** Bridgepoint Advisers Group Ltd)
2 Sloane Street, London SW1X 9LA
**Tel:** 02078237700 **Fax:** 02072354335
**Web:** www.moneycorp.com
**Reg No:** 0738837 **VAT No:** 897393454
**Estd:** 1962 Private Limited Company
**Line of Business:** Bureau de change
**Trading Style:** Ttt Foreign Exchange Corporation, The Money Corporation, Moneycorp (Commercial Foreign Exchange)
**Issued Capital:** £350,000
**Directors:** N A Heslop, R P Moores, S N Green, P R Lever, N J Haslehurst, M Horgan
**Responsibilities**
**Senior:** Michael England *(Non-Executive Director)*
**Finance:** Malcolm Weinberg *(Financial Director)*
**HR:** Andrea Barton *(Personnel Manager)*
**Health & Safety:** Thomas Kadri *(Health & Safety Officer)*
**Facilities:** Ian Silverstone *(Facilities Manager)*
**Branches:** Ttt Moneycorp Ltd, 369A Oxford St, London W1C 2JW
**US SIC:** 6111 **UK SIC:** 81501
**Auditors:** PricewaterhouseCoopers LLP
**Bankers:** HSBC Bank plc (40-05-01)
**Following financial data are in thousands**

| | 31-12-13 | 31-12-12 | 31-12-11 |
|---|---|---|---|
| TA | 1,799,797 | 1,247,256 | 335,589 |
| P/L | 9,980 | 4,703 | 1,036 |
| NW | 27,505 | 18,469 | 23,574 |
| WC | 22,474 | 12,623 | 19,347 |
| Emp. | 696 | 526 | 587 |

DUNS 21-452-2807 **Imp-Exp**

## Tube Developments Ltd

Queenzieburn Industrial Estate, Glasgow, Lanarkshire G65 9BN
**Tel:** 01236823551 **Fax:** 01236-825660
**Web:** www.tubedev.com
**Reg No:** 0042597SC **VAT No:** 260635667
**Estd:** 1965 Private Limited Company
**Line of Business:** Wholesale of metals and ores
**Export Markets:** Europe, America, Asia & Africa, Australia
**Issued Capital:** £10,000
**Principals:** J F Fraser *(Chairman)*, I F Fraser *(Managing)*, A D Chalmers, G Fraser, S D Fraser, Ms F M Mcluckie, Ms T M Fraser-Hartman, G D Brown
**Co. Secretary:** Douglas Kay
**Responsibilities**
**Senior:** Theresa Fraser *(Manager)*
**Marketing:** John Robbie *(Marketing Manager)*
**Admin:** Gail Ure *(Human Resources Manager)*
**HR:** Gail Ure *(Human Resources Manager)*
**Facilities:** Patrick Friel *(Works Manager)*
**US SIC:** 3999 **UK SIC:** 49590
**Auditors:** Henderson Loggie
**Bankers:** Bank Of Scotland (80-54-01)

| | 30-09-13 | 30-09-12 | 30-09-11 |
|---|---|---|---|
| TO | 30,345,142 | 35,156,424 | 26,540,709 |
| P/L | 1,488,806 | 3,736,009 | 2,580,333 |
| NW | 27,307,779 | 26,199,178 | 23,518,834 |
| WC | 24,624,491 | 23,388,373 | 20,528,408 |
| Emp. | 63 | 62 | 62 |

DUNS 23-933-6162

## Tube Lines Ltd

15 Westferry Circus, London E14 4HD
**Tel:** 0845 660 5466
**Web:** www.tubelines.com
**Reg No:** 3923425 **Estd:** 2000 Private Limited Company
**Line of Business:** Road haulage and transport services
**Issued Capital:** £4,500,001
**Directors:** M W Brown, Ms J Collis, D G Waboso, A Pollins, Ms S A Atkins
**Co. Secretary:** Howard Carter
**Responsibilities**
**Senior:** P Forsdick *(Manager)*
**Operations:** Stuart Harvey *(Director of Projects)*
**Engineering:** Peter Slaney *(Engineering Manager (Safety &)*
**Branches:** Tube Lines Ltd, Tubelines Distribution Services Ltd, 130 Bollo Lane, London W3 8BZ
**US SIC:** 4789 **UK SIC:** 77002
**Auditors:** Unknown

| | 31-03-14 | 31-03-13 | 31-03-12 |
|---|---|---|---|
| TO | 597,800,000 | 649,800,000 | 585,100,000 |
| P/L | (17,200,000) | 33,900,000 | 18,200,000 |
| NW | 45,300,000 | 43,100,000 | 49,200,000 |
| WC | 56,400,000 | 80,300,000 | 65,500,000 |
| Emp. | 1,826 | 2,394 | 2,206 |

DUNS 21-879-3871

## Tubelines

Stratford Market Traincare Centre, London E15 2SP
**Estd:** 2012
**Line of Business:** Local & Suburban Transport Operators
**US SIC:** 4111 **UK SIC:** 72102
**Employees:** 100

DUNS 54-897-7859

## Tubervilles

118 High Street, Uxbridge, Middlesex UB8 1JT
**Web:** www.turbervilles.co.uk
**Estd:** 1997 Partnership
**Line of Business:** Solicitors
**Partner:** R Hallam
**Responsibilities**
**Senior:** Sess Sigre *(Senior Partner)*
**Finance:** Sess Sigre *(Senior Partner)*
**Marketing:** Sess Sigre *(Senior Partner)*
**HR:** Norma Yeo *(Human Resources Manager)*
**Health & Safety:** Peter Moynihan *(Practice Manager)*
**Facilities:** Peter Moynihan *(Practice Manager)*
**Purchasing:** Peter Moynihan *(Practice Manager)*
**Branches:** Tubervilles, 27 Peterborough Rd, Harrow, Middlesex HA1 2AU
**US SIC:** 8111 **UK SIC:** 83500
**Employees:** 50

DUNS 73-263-4618

## Tubex Ltd

(**Subsidiary of:** Fiberweb Ltd)
12-14 Aberaman Park, Aberdare, Mid Glamorgan CF44 6DA
**Tel:** 01621874201 **Fax:** 01621874299
**Web:** www.tubex.com
**Reg No:** 4537236 **Estd:** 2002 Private Limited Company
**Line of Business:** Manufacture of other plastic products
**Issued Capital:** £223,820
**Director:** D Norman
**Co. Secretary:** Intertrust (Uk) Limited
**Responsibilities**
**Senior:** Anthony O'carroll *(Manager)*
**Facilities:** Darren Ralph *(Maintenance Manager)*
**Branches:** Tubex Ltd, 5 Westgarth Avenue, Edinburgh, Midlothian EH13 0BB
**US SIC:** 3079 **UK SIC:** 48360
**Auditors:** PricewaterhouseCoopers LLP
**Bankers:** HSBC Bank plc (40-16-13)

| | 28-12-13 | 31-12-12 | 31-12-11 |
|---|---|---|---|
| TO | N/A | N/A | 8,129,000 |
| P/L | N/A | N/A | 128,000 |
| NW | 1,520,000 | 1,520,000 | 1,540,000 |
| WC | N/A | N/A | 1,063,000 |
| Emp. | N/A | N/A | 79 |

DUNS 21-566-3440

## Tuckers 24 Hour Criminal Lawyers

63-65 Mosley Street, Manchester M2 3HZ
**Web:** www.tuckerssolicitors.com
**Estd:** 1978 Partnership
**Line of Business:** Solicitors
**Partner:** F Sinclair
**US SIC:** 8111 **UK SIC:** 83500
**Employees:** 75

DUNS 63-454-4316

## Tuckers Solicitors

39 Warren Street, Euston, London W1T 6AF
**Web:** www.tuckerssolicitors.com
**VAT No:** 403564279 **Estd:** 1978 Partnership
**Line of Business:** Solicitors
**Partners:** B M Tucker, F M Sinclair
**Responsibilities**
**Senior:** Jules Carey *(Partner)*, Sehra Desai *(Partner)*, Paul Hurd *(Senior IT Executive)*
**IT:** Paul Hurd *(Senior IT Executive)*
**Branches:** Tuckers Solicitors, 7 St. John Street, Manchester M3 4DN
**US SIC:** 8111 **UK SIC:** 83500
**Employees:** 91

DUNS 21-139-5626 **Imp**

## Tudor Capital Europe Llp

10 New Burlington Street, London W1S 3BE
**Tel:** 02087864005
**Web:** www.tudorfunds.com
**Reg No:** 0340673OC **Estd:** 2008 Private Limited Company
**Line of Business:** Financial services
**Responsibilities**
**Senior:** Andrew Bound *(Non-designated Limited Liabili)*, Gavin Boyle *(Non-designated Limited Liabili)*, William Holt *(Non-designated Limited Liabili)*, Robin Howes *(Non-designated Limited Liabili)*, Toby Lodge *(Non-designated Limited Liabili)*, Aardarsh Malde *(Non-designated Limited Liabili)*, Alister Mitchell *(Non-designated Limited Liabili)*, Simon Silverston *(Non-designated Limited Liabili)*, Nigel Whittaker *(Non-designated Limited Liabili)*
**US SIC:** 7399 **UK SIC:** 83954
**Employees:** 94
**Turnover:** £251,645,309

DUNS 34-819-3442

## Tudor Capital (U.K.) Ltd

Yew Tree Bottom Road, Epsom, Surrey KT18 5XT
**Tel:** 02087863900
**Web:** www.tudorfunds.com
**Reg No:** 2796275 **Estd:** 1993 Private Limited Company
**Line of Business:** Financial intermediation not elsewhere classified
**Directors:** C J Greene, J R Torell
**Co. Secretary:** Andrew Paul
**US SIC:** 6111 **UK SIC:** 81501
**Auditors:** Ernst & Young LLP
**Employees:** 60

DUNS 49-081-2872

## Tudor Contract Cleaners Ltd

5 James Nasmyth Way, Eccles, Manchester M30 0SF
**Tel:** 0161-789-3550
**Web:** http://tudorcc.com
**Reg No:** 3087189 **Estd:** 1995 Private Limited Company
**Line of Business:** Cleaning contracting commercial
**Issued Capital:** £100
**Director:** A T Camilleri
**Responsibilities**
**Senior:** Ann Christie *(Human Resources Manager)*
**Marketing:** Paula Camilleri *(Sales & Marketing Manager)*
**Sales:** Paula Camilleri *(Sales & Marketing Manager)*
**HR:** Ann Christie *(Human Resources Manager)*
**Facilities:** Sue Norman *(Operations Manager)*
**US SIC:** 7349 **UK SIC:** 92300
**Bankers:** The Royal Bank Of Scotland Plc (16-71-38)

| | 31-12-13 | 31-12-12 | 31-12-11 |
|---|---|---|---|
| TA | 1,649,707 | 1,392,118 | 1,479,762 |
| NW | 905,802 | 571,360 | 570,051 |
| WC | 709,609 | 335,833 | 381,766 |

DUNS 21-167-0650

## Tudor Grange Academy Worcester Trust

Bilford Road, Worcester, Worcestershire WR3 8HN
**Tel:** 01905454627 **Fax:** 01905756517
**Web:** www.tgaw.org.uk
**Reg No:** 6924496 **Estd:** 1997 Private Company Limited By Guarantee
**Line of Business:** Schools (foundation)
**Directors:** Prof J M Winterbottom, R W Edwards, A J Newman, Dr W P Rock, W J George
**Responsibilities**
**Admin:** Dot Green *(PA to Head)*
**US SIC:** 8211 **UK SIC:** 93200

| | 31-08-14 | 31-08-13 | 31-08-12 |
|---|---|---|---|
| TO | 5,675,302 | 19,473,896 | 6,271,569 |
| P/L | (575,630) | 9,447,772 | 488,874 |
| NW | 13,473,074 | 14,232,704 | 4,718,932 |
| WC | (41,493) | (179,980) | (34,246) |
| Emp. | 140 | 143 | 132 |

DUNS 77-540-0146

## Tudor Hall School

Wykham Lane, Banbury, Oxfordshire OX16 9UR
**Tel:** 01295263434
**Web:** www.tudorhallschool.com
**Reg No:** 2995266 **Estd:** 1994 Private Company Limited By Guarantee
**Line of Business:** Schools (independent)
**Trading Style:** Tudor Hall School
**Directors:** Mrs R J Hayes, Ms L A Mayne, Ms C P Duncombe, S J Biggart, Miss H Holden-Brown, Mrs A V Harley, J Gloag, Mrs K Fidgeon
**Co. Secretary:** Ms Helen Jackson
**Responsibilities**
**Senior:** Charles Dodson *(Manager)*, Barry Gamble *(Director)*, Mary Kinnear *(Director)*, Sarah Maxted *(Director)*, Sarah North *(Manager)*, Benedetta Polk *(Manager)*, Peter Whittle *(Manager)*
**Marketing:** Polly Skye *(Website Manager)*
**IT:** Nigel Watson *(Computer Manager)*
**HR:** Linda Tubb *(Human Resources Manager)*
**US SIC:** 8211 **UK SIC:** 93200
**Auditors:** Auditor's Name (Illigible)
**Bankers:** The Royal Bank Of Scotland Plc (15-80-00)

| | 31-08-14 | 31-08-13 | 31-08-12 |
|---|---|---|---|
| TO | 10,925,289 | 10,428,810 | 9,477,222 |
| P/L | 387,062 | 907,371 | 462,818 |
| NW | 13,647,114 | 13,078,398 | 12,110,610 |
| WC | (482,910) | 127,492 | (329,402) |
| Emp. | 224 | 220 | 212 |

DUNS 21-400-1104

## Tudor House

4 Birdhurst Road, South Croydon, Surrey CR2 7EA
**Tel:** 020-8410-3399
**Web:** www.tudorhouse.com
**Estd:** 1999 Partnership
**Line of Business:** Nursing homes
**Partners:** M Amin, P Amin, V Patel
**US SIC:** 8051 **UK SIC:** 95100
**Employees:** 48

DUNS 29-650-2388

## Tudor Roof Tile Co. Ltd

Dengemarsh Road, Lydd, Romney Marsh, Kent TN29 9JH
**Web:** www.tudorrooftiles.co.uk
**Reg No:** 1976344 **Estd:** 1986 Private Limited Company
**Line of Business:** Manufacture of ceramic tiles and flags
**Issued Capital:** £463,005
**Principals:** J M Harris *(Chairman)*, B H Luckhurst *(Financial)*, P J Lythgoe
**Co. Secretary:** Paul Lythgoe
**Responsibilities**
**Senior:** Pauline Willis *(Manager)*
**US SIC:** 3253 **UK SIC:** 24891
**Auditors:** Gibbons & Mannington
**Bankers:** National Westminster Bank Plc (60-19-02)

| | 31-03-14 | 31-03-13 | 31-03-12 |
|---|---|---|---|
| TA | 2,110,328 | 2,115,843 | 2,181,384 |
| NW | 1,430,507 | 1,439,963 | 1,436,008 |
| WC | 502,185 | 535,677 | 567,557 |

DUNS 73-976-5852

## Tudor Williams (Holdings) Ltd

53 High Street, New Malden, Surrey KT3 4BU
**Tel:** 020-8942-2277
**Web:** www.tudorwilliams.co.uk
**Reg No:** 5227377 **Estd:** 2004 Private Limited Company
**Line of Business:** Beds and bedding
**Issued Capital:** £254,000
**Director:** T K Williams
**Co. Secretary:** John Morris
**US SIC:** 2392 **UK SIC:** 45550
**Auditors:** Haines Watts

| | 02-02-14 | 26-01-13 | 28-02-12 |
|---|---|---|---|
| TO | 8,172,049 | 7,411,485 | 7,399,610 |
| P/L | 218,064 | 204,152 | 233,271 |
| NW | 6,499,868 | 6,199,928 | 6,008,771 |
| WC | 281,704 | 400,314 | 517,103 |
| Emp. | 154 | 149 | 155 |

DUNS 77-106-6537

## Tudorborne Ltd

9 Coal Pit Lane, Atherton, Manchester M46 0RY
**Tel:** 08452177150
**Web:** www.neary.co.uk
**Reg No:** 2683590 **VAT No:** 603409081
**Estd:** 1992 Private Limited Company
**Line of Business:** Building services
**Trading Style:** Neary Construction
**Issued Capital:** £48,308
**Managing Director:** M Neary
**Co. Secretary:** Nigel Hooper
**Branches:** Tudorborne Ltd, Robertson St, Glasgow, Lanarkshire G78 1QW
**US SIC:** 1522 **UK SIC:** 50100
**Auditors:** HW Chartered Accountants
**Bankers:** The Royal Bank Of Scotland Plc (16-33-30)

| | 31-03-14 | 31-03-13 | 31-03-12 |
|---|---|---|---|
| TO | 11,561,772 | 10,426,705 | 14,057,944 |
| P/L | (589,812) | (21,522) | 450,337 |
| NW | 3,189,347 | 3,648,817 | 3,653,956 |
| WC | 1,287,903 | 1,673,422 | 1,906,543 |
| Emp. | 114 | 140 | 174 |

DUNS 73-774-0758

## Tuffin Ferraby Taylor Llp

65 Woodbridge Road, Guildford, Surrey GU1 4RD
**Tel:** 02034797777
**Web:** www.tftconsultants.com
**Reg No:** 0306766OC **VAT No:** 833044063

**Estd:** 1973
**Line of Business:** Building consultants and advisors
**Export Sales:** £101,187
**Responsibilities**
**Senior:** Alistair Allison *(Non-designated Limited Liabili)*, James Bent *(Non-designated Limited Liabili)*, Hugo Bradley *(Non-designated Limited Liabili)*, Malcolm Flegg *(Manager)*, Neil Gilbert *(Non-designated Limited Liabili)*, Christine Keates Lewis *(Non-designated Limited Liabili)*, Seth Love Jones *(Non-designated Limited Liabili)*, Alan Pemberton *(Designated Limited Liability P)*, Paul Raymont *(Designated Limited Liability P)*, Paul Spaven *(Designated Limited Liability P)*, David Tuffin *(Manager)*
**US SIC:** 8911, 6531
**UK SIC:** 83701, 83400
**Auditors:** Baker Tilly UK Audit LLP

| | 31-03-14 | 31-03-13 | 31-03-12 |
|---|---|---|---|
| TO | 10,118,705 | 8,881,910 | 8,599,728 |
| P/L | 1,450,982 | 1,018,845 | 695,680 |
| NW | 1,450,982 | 1,018,845 | N/A |
| WC | 2,400,889 | 1,701,295 | 1,359,406 |
| Emp. | 78 | 78 | 84 |

DUNS 21-239-8416 **Imp-Exp**
## Tuffnells Parcels Express Ltd
(**Subsidiary of:** The Big Green Parcel Holding Co Ltd)
Shepcote House, Shepcote Lane, Sheffield, South Yorkshire S9 1UW
**Tel:** 01142561111 **Fax:** 01142-560-459
**Web:** www.tuffnells.co.uk
**Reg No:** 0319964 **VAT No:** 173317863
**Estd:** 1914 Private Limited Company
**Line of Business:** Freight transport by road not elsewhere classified
**Issued Capital:** £1,091,800
**Directors:** L J Dunn, N J Gresham, M R Cashmore, I P Brewer, J M Bunting
**Co. Secretary:** Stuart Marriner
**Responsibilities**
**Marketing:** David Tippett *(Marketing Manager)*
**Health & Safety:** Dave Gibbs *(Health & Safety Officer)*
**Operations:** Dave Gibbs *(Health & Safety Officer)*
**Branches:** Tuffnells Parcels Express Ltd, Caswell Road, Brackmills Industrial Estate, Northampton, Northamptonshire NN4 7PW
**US SIC:** 4213 **UK SIC:** 72300
**Auditors:** Deloitte & Touche LLP
**Bankers:** Bank Of Scotland (12-08-83)

| | 31-12-13 | 31-12-12 | 31-12-11 |
|---|---|---|---|
| TO | 127,801,000 | 114,647,000 | 109,329,000 |
| P/L | 10,423,000 | 9,877,000 | 8,703,000 |
| NW | 11,458,000 | 11,466,000 | 11,074,000 |
| WC | (1,827,000) | (1,468,000) | 2,313,000 |
| Emp. | 2,029 | 1,897 | 1,880 |

DUNS 71-878-8164 **Imp-Exp**
## Tufnol Composites Ltd
Wellhead Lane, Birmingham, West Midlands B42 2TB
**Tel:** 01213569351
**Web:** www.tufnol.com
**Reg No:** 5261357 **Estd:** 2011 Private Limited Company
**Line of Business:** Chemicals & allied product wholesalers
**Trading Style:** Countrose Bearings
**Issued Capital:** £90,000
**Principals:** R Thomason *(Managing)*, P L Jackson
**Co. Secretary:** Roy Thomason
**Responsibilities**
**Purchasing:** Diane Somerfield *(Purchasing Manager)*
**Engineering:** Dave Bedington *(Production Manager)*
**US SIC:** 5161, 8911, 3568, 3534
**UK SIC:** 61200, 83701, 32613, 32553
**Auditors:** CK Audit

| | 31-10-13 | 31-10-12 | 31-10-11 |
|---|---|---|---|
| TA | 2,384,519 | 2,511,968 | 2,483,661 |
| NW | 347,960 | 242,641 | 149,456 |
| WC | 404,408 | 226,364 | 137,006 |

DUNS 64-094-9327 **Exp**
## Tui Northern Europe Ltd
(**Subsidiary of:** Tui Ag)
Wigmore House, Wigmore Place, Wigmore Lane, Luton, Bedfordshire LU2 9TN
**Tel:** 024-7628-2828
**Web:** www.thonson.co.uk
**Reg No:** 3490138 **Estd:** 1998 Public Limited Company
**Line of Business:** Printers general
**Export Markets:** E U; worldwide
**Issued Capital:** £250,458,515
**Directors:** C G Mckinlay, N Evans
**Co. Secretary:** Joyce Walter
**US SIC:** 6711 **UK SIC:** 83962
**Auditors:** PricewaterhouseCoopers LLP

**Following financial data are in thousands**

| | 30-09-13 | 30-09-12 | 30-09-11 |
|---|---|---|---|
| TA | 528,000 | 1,179,000 | 2,728,000 |
| P/L | 42,000 | (16,000) | (518,000) |
| NW | 37,000 | 7,000 | 32,000 |
| WC | 3,000 | (52,000) | (26,000) |

DUNS 21-888-6765
## Tui Travel Ltd
(**Subsidiary of:** Tui Ag)
Tui Travel House, Crawley Business Quarter, Fleming Way, Crawley, West Sussex RH10 9QL
**Web:** www.tuitravelplc.com
**Reg No:** 6072876 **VAT No:** 233368762
**Estd:** 1965 Private Limited Company
**Line of Business:** Management activities of holding companies
**Export Sales:** £9,967,000,000
**Trading Style:** Tui Uk
**Issued Capital:** £111,801,067
**Directors:** W H Waggott, Ms J Walter, Dr J Lundgren
**Co. Secretary:** Ms Joyce Walter
**Responsibilities**
**Senior:** David Burling *(Managing Director TUI UK & Ire)*
**Marketing:** Tim Williamson *(Senior Marketing Executive)*
**IT:** Russell Barrett *(PC Manager)*, Mittu Sridhara *(Chief Information Officer)*, Neil Swanson *(Head of Web Sales, Operations)*
**HR:** Bill Logan *(Human Resources Manager)*, Jacky Simmonds *(Group HR Director)*
**Facilities:** Joan VilÓ *(Managing Director, Accommodati)*
**US SIC:** 6711, 4722
**UK SIC:** 83962, 77001
**Auditors:** PricewaterhouseCoopers LLP

**Following financial data are in thousands**

| | 30-09-14 | 30-09-13 | 30-09-12 |
|---|---|---|---|
| TO | 14,619,000 | 15,051,000 | 14,460,000 |
| P/L | 362,000 | 181,000 | 201,000 |
| NW | (2,700,000) | (2,934,000) | (2,917,000) |
| WC | (2,560,000) | (2,618,000) | (2,737,000) |
| Emp. | 57,389 | 55,406 | 54,090 |

DUNS 29-417-0345
## Tui Uk Retail Ltd
(**Subsidiary of:** Tui Ag)
3rd Floor, Redstone House, Crowngate, Harlow, Essex CM20 1NL
**Tel:** 01237425666
**Web:** www.latedeals.co.uk
**Reg No:** 1456086 **Estd:** 1979 Private Limited Company
**Line of Business:** Activities of travel agencies
**Issued Capital:** £88,000,000
**Directors:** I J Strachan, F M Ellacott, C G Mckinlay, Dr J Lundgren
**Co. Secretary:** Mrs Joyce Walter
**Branches:** Tui Uk Retail Ltd, Within Asda Store, Acle New Rd, Great Yarmouth, Norfolk NR30 1SF
**US SIC:** 4722 **UK SIC:** 77001
**Auditors:** KPMG Audit PLC
**Bankers:** Fortis Bank London Bch (formerly Generale Bk) (60-93-89)

| | 30-09-13 | 30-09-12 | 30-09-11 |
|---|---|---|---|
| TO | 206,661,000 | 197,258,000 | 207,427,000 |
| P/L | (5,330,000) | (28,694,000) | (87,445,000) |
| NW | (111,185,000) | (107,967,000) | (91,319,000) |
| WC | (124,752,000) | (75,209,000) | (156,003,000) |
| Emp. | 5,110 | 5,360 | 5,738 |

DUNS 21-818-7185 **Exp**
## Tuke & Bell Ltd
Patent Drive, Wednesbury, West Midlands WS10 7XD
**Tel:** 01215067330
**Web:** www.tukeandbell.co.uk
**Reg No:** 0125585 **VAT No:** 580384235
**Estd:** 2007 Private Limited Company
**Line of Business:** Water and sewage engineers
**Export Markets:** Middle East, Far East
**Issued Capital:** £56,010
**Managing Director:** R G Lewis
**Co. Secretary:** Richard Lewis
**Responsibilities**
**Senior:** Richard Wainwright *(Warehouse Manager)*
**Sales:** Derek Jessop *(Service Manager)*
**Branches:** Tuke & Bell Ltd, Galaxy Point, Patent Drive, Moorcroft Park, Wednesbury, West Midlands WS10 7XD
**US SIC:** 4952 **UK SIC:** 92120
**Auditors:** Cotterell & Co
**Bankers:** HSBC Bank plc (40-28-18)

| | 31-12-13 | 31-12-12 | 31-12-11 |
|---|---|---|---|
| TO | 6,152,825 | N/A | 2,922,700 |
| P/L | 54,605 | N/A | 14,595 |
| NW | 1,027,073 | 905,872 | 928,678 |
| WC | 259,348 | 214,205 | 274,110 |
| Emp. | 96 | N/A | N/A |

DUNS 22-017-2451
## Tulchan Communications Group Ltd
(**Subsidiary of:** Milton House Investments Ltd)
85 Fleet Street, London EC4Y 1AE
**Tel:** 02074271550
**Web:** www.tulchangroup.com
**Reg No:** 4020139 **Estd:** 2000 Private Limited Company
**Line of Business:** Public relations activities
**Issued Capital:** £968
**Directors:** A W Grant, H R Mackenzie, Ms H Tuppen, R H Sutton, D M Shriver
**Co. Secretary:** Mrs Ruth Royston
**Responsibilities**
**Senior:** D Thakar *(Manager)*
**US SIC:** 7399 **UK SIC:** 83954
**Auditors:** BDO Stoy Hayward LLP
**Bankers:** C Hoare & Co (15-99-00)

| | 31-03-14 | 31-03-13 | 31-03-12 |
|---|---|---|---|
| TA | 1,412,661 | 2,347,797 | 2,856,765 |
| P/L | N/A | N/A | 179,522 |
| NW | 1,054,876 | 2,172,611 | 2,632,355 |
| WC | 956,070 | 763,690 | 1,208,560 |

DUNS 22-038-0948
## Tulchan Ltd
(**Subsidiary of:** Milton House Investments Ltd)
85 Fleet Street, London EC4Y 1AE
**Tel:** 020-7353-4200
**Web:** www.tulchangroup.com
**Reg No:** 4040517 **Estd:** 2002 Private Limited Company
**Line of Business:** Business services
**Trading Style:** Tulchan Communications Llp
**Issued Capital:** £1
**Director:** A W Grant
**Co. Secretary:** Ms Ruth Royston
**Responsibilities**
**Admin:** Kirsty Amos *(Account Administrator)*
**US SIC:** 7399 **UK SIC:** 83954

| | 31-03-14 | 31-03-13 | 31-03-12 |
|---|---|---|---|
| TA | 1 | 1 | 1 |
| NW | 1 | 1 | 1 |

DUNS 22-955-7558 **Imp-Exp**
## Tulip International (U K) Ltd
Riverview Road, Wirral, Merseyside CH62 3RL
**Tel:** 01513 434444 **Fax:** 01513 434433
**Web:** www.tulipint.com
**Reg No:** 1330427 **Estd:** 1977 Private Limited Company
**Line of Business:** Management activities of holding companies
**Export Markets:** E U
**Trading Style:** Tulip
**Issued Capital:** £13,240,000
**Directors:** E Bredholt, P J Andersen, K Johannesen, S C Gilliland, F N Enevoldsen, C Thomas
**Co. Secretary:** Herluf Jensen
**Responsibilities**
**Senior:** Asger Krogsgaard *(Manager)*, Niels Mikkelsen *(Manager)*, Steven Murrells *(Manager)*
**Finance:** Lorna Crail *(Senior Finance Administrator)*
**Admin:** Lorna Crail *(Senior Finance Administrator)*
**HR:** Sarah Emes Young *(Human Resources Manager)*
**Branches:** Tulip International (U K) Ltd, 12 The Broadway, Norwood Court, Amersham, Buckinghamshire HP7 0HW
**US SIC:** 6711, 2013
**UK SIC:** 83962, 41223
**Auditors:** Deloitte LLP
**Bankers:** Barclays Bank Plc (20-85-93)

| | 29-09-13 | 30-09-12 | 02-09-11 |
|---|---|---|---|
| TA | 238,050,000 | 238,050,000 | 114,050,000 |
| P/L | N/A | 130,000,000 | 17,000,000 |
| NW | 189,711,000 | 189,711,000 | 65,711,000 |

DUNS 21-831-4888
## Tulip Ltd
(**Subsidiary of:** Tulip International (U K) Ltd)
Seton House, Warwick Technology Park, Gallows Hill, Warwick, Warwickshire CV34 6DA
**Tel:** 01926-475680
**Web:** www.tulipltd.co.uk
**Reg No:** 0608077 **VAT No:** 390583825
**Estd:** 1958 Private Limited Company
**Line of Business:** Production of meat products
**Export Sales:** £33,865,000
**Issued Capital:** £7,540,000
**Directors:** K Johannesen, P J Andersen, C Thomas, E Bredholt, F N Enevoldsen, S C Gilliland
**Co. Secretary:** Herluf Jensen
**Responsibilities**
**Operations:** Tom Begg *(Operations Director)*
**Branches:** Tulip Ltd, The Holmes", Selby, North Yorkshire YO8 3EL
**US SIC:** 2013 **UK SIC:** 41223
**Auditors:** Deloitte LLP
**Bankers:** Unibank A/s (40-48-78)

**Following financial data are in thousands**

| | 29-09-13 | 30-09-12 | 02-09-11 |
|---|---|---|---|
| TO | 1,156,017 | 1,118,060 | 1,106,055 |
| P/L | 21,782 | 25,975 | 33,841 |
| NW | 164,334 | 148,204 | 142,776 |
| WC | 196,443 | 61,331 | 197,780 |
| Emp. | 6,518 | 6,603 | 6,516 |

DUNS 77-902-4368 **Exp**
## Tullett Prebon Plc
155 Bishopsgate, London EC2M 3TQ
**Tel:** 02072007000 **Fax:** 0207 200 7176
**Web:** www.tullettprebon.com
**Reg No:** 5807599 **Estd:** 1985 Public Limited Company
**Line of Business:** Financial intermediation not elsewhere classified
**Trading Style:** Tullett Prebon
**Issued Capital:** £54,434,926
**Directors:** J P Phizackerley, S J Pull, Ms A A Knight, R H Robson, R K Perkin, P R Mainwaring, D P Shalders
**Co. Secretary:** Ms Tiffany Brill
**Responsibilities**
**Senior:** Richard Kilsby *(Non-Executive Director)*
**US SIC:** 6111 **UK SIC:** 81501
**Auditors:** Deloitte LLP

**Following financial data are in thousands**

| | 31-12-13 | 31-12-12 | 31-12-11 |
|---|---|---|---|
| TA | 6,492,300 | 6,565,600 | 6,116,900 |
| P/L | 84,400 | (33,500) | 119,200 |
| NW | 98,900 | 69,400 | 57,500 |
| WC | 260,700 | 266,500 | 251,200 |
| Emp. | 2,603 | 2,645 | 2,550 |

DUNS 73-713-1284 **Imp-Exp**
## Tullis Russell Group Ltd
Markinch, Glenrothes, Fife KY7 6PB
**Tel:** 01592-753311
**Web:** www.tullisrussell.com
**Reg No:** 0150075SC **VAT No:** 652002877
**Estd:** 1994 Private Limited Company
**Line of Business:** Manufacture of paper and paperboard
**Export Markets:** Worldwide
**Export Sales:** £117,403,000
**Trading Style:** Tullis Russell Paper Makers
**Issued Capital:** £4,352,364
**Principals:** C A Parr *(Managing)*, F A Bowden, B M Jackson, M R Arrowsmith
**Co. Secretary:** Geoffrey Miller
**Responsibilities**
**Senior:** Tim Bowdler *(Board Member)*
**Marketing:** Derek Guthrie *(Marketing Services Manager)*, Charlotte Payce-Drury *(Marketing Manager)*, Amanda Treend *(Marketing Manager)*
**Sales:** Nick Shepherd *(Sales Director)*
**HR:** Helen Brady *(HR Manager)*, Linda Brailsford *(HR Manager)*
**Health & Safety:** Ken McDougall *(Safety, Health & Environmental)*
**Engineering:** Scott Birrell *(Building Services Coordinator)*
**Branches:** Tullis Russell Group Ltd, Church Street, Macclesfield, Cheshire SK10 5QF
**US SIC:** 2631 **UK SIC:** 47017
**Auditors:** PricewaterhouseCoopers LLP
**Bankers:** The Royal Bank Of Scotland Plc (83-17-23)

| | 31-03-14 | 31-03-13 | 31-03-12 |
|---|---|---|---|
| TO | 158,585,000 | 159,492,000 | 165,950,000 |
| P/L | (2,980,000) | (3,259,000) | (4,018,000) |
| NW | 33,189,000 | 34,838,000 | 36,406,000 |
| WC | 9,209,000 | 8,426,000 | 9,277,000 |
| Emp. | 692 | 738 | 744 |

DUNS 45-870-7155
## Tulloch Homes Group Ltd
Stoneyfield Business Park, Inverness, Inverness-Shire IV2 7PA
**Tel:** 01463229300 **Fax:** 01463-701401
**Web:** www.tulloch-homes.com
**Reg No:** 0166347SC **Estd:** 1996 Private Limited Company
**Line of Business:** Construction of domestic buildings
**Trading Style:** Tulloch
**Issued Capital:** £80,000,826
**Directors:** A J Grant, T E Allison, G C More, G G Fraser
**US SIC:** 1522, 1541
**UK SIC:** 50100
**Auditors:** Johnston Carmichael
**Bankers:** Clydesdale Bank Plc (82-65-18)

| | 30-06-13 | 30-06-12 | 31-06-10 |
|---|---|---|---|
| TO | 44,950,000 | 69,455,000 | 53,702,000 |
| P/L | 964,000 | (66,349,000) | (9,137,000) |
| NW | 16,905,000 | 16,306,000 | 28,125,000 |
| WC | 10,868,000 | 86,942,000 | 153,925,000 |
| Emp. | 168 | 159 | 171 |

DUNS 34-876-5223
## Tulloch Recruitment (Aberdeen) Ltd
508 Union Street, Aberdeen, Aberdeenshire AB10 1TT
**Tel:** 01224625097 **Fax:** 01224-625109
**Web:** www.tullochrecruitment.co.uk
**Reg No:** 0144511SC **Estd:** 1993 Private Limited Company
**Line of Business:** Employment and recruitment companies and consultants
**Export Sales:** £142,593
**Issued Capital:** £1,000
**Principals:** T M Allan *(Managing)*, Ms C Donaldson
**Co. Secretary:** Stronachs Secretaries Limited
**US SIC:** 7361 **UK SIC:** 83954
**Auditors:** Bain Henry Reid
**Bankers:** The Royal Bank Of Scotland Plc (83-23-10)

| | 31-08-13 | 31-08-12 | 31-08-11 |
|---|---|---|---|
| TO | 30,649,171 | 24,974,641 | 20,183,990 |
| P/L | 3,459,614 | 2,312,634 | 1,889,439 |
| NW | 3,586,230 | 3,368,867 | 1,836,141 |
| WC | 2,797,822 | 2,710,821 | 1,968,721 |
| Emp. | 455 | 470 | 434 |

DUNS 23-929-3439 **Imp**
## Tullow Oil Plc
Building 9, Chiswick Park, 566 Chiswick High Road, Chiswick, London W4 5XT
**Tel:** 02032499000 **Fax:** 02032498801
**Web:** www.tullowoil.com
**Reg No:** 3919249 **Estd:** 2000 Public Limited Company
**Line of Business:** Service activities incidental to oil and gas extraction excluding surveying
**Trading Style:** Tullow Oil
**Directors:** I Springett, A J Heavey, J R Wilson, Ms A Grant, Ms A Drinkwater, M C Daly, K T Agyare, A M Mccoss
**Co. Secretary:** Alan Martin
**Responsibilities**
**Senior:** Pete Dickerson *(Head of Corporate Planning and)*, Steve Lucas *(Non-Executive Director)*, Paul McDade *(Chief Operating Officer)*, Tim O' Hanlon *(Vice President)*, Pat Padayachee *(Board Member)*, Franco Uliana *(General Manager)*
**Finance:** Julian Tedder *(Group Financial Director)*
**Marketing:** George Cazemove *(Head of Media Relations)*, Sharan Dhami *(Investor Relations Assistant)*
**Sales:** Caroline Herbert *(Sales Executive)*
**Admin:** Tako Koning *(Advisor)*, Joanne Spearing *(Office Manager)*
**HR:** Georgina Baines *(Human Resources Manager)*, Aleksandra Griffin *(Recruiter)*
**Health & Safety:** Graham Brunton *(Group Environment, Health & Sa)*, Marie Early *(Health & Safety Advisor)*
**Operations:** John Balmer *(EHS Operations Manager)*, Michelle Duckworth *(Shipping Operations Manager)*, Paul McDade *(Chief Operating Officer)*, Martyn Morris *(Group Production and Developme)*, Godfrey Ojambo *(Field Operations Supervisor)*, Roger Swaine *(Head of Projects)*, Rowland Wright *(EHS Operations Manager)*
**Fleet:** Bill McHugh *(Logistics Manager)*
**Engineering:** Klisthenis Dimitriadis *(Chief Well Engineer)*, Gert-Jan Smulders *(Technical Director)*, Simon Sparke *(Engineer)*, Andries Steyn *(Engineer)*
**US SIC:** 1389 **UK SIC:** 13000
**Auditors:** Deloitte LLP
**Bankers:** Barclays Bank Plc (20-00-34)
**Employees:** 1,679
**Turnover:** £2,646,900,000

DUNS 29-545-4474
## Tully De'ath Ltd
Sheridan House Hartfield Road, Forest Row, East Sussex RH18 5EA
**Web:** www.tullydeath.com
**Reg No:** 1912122 **Estd:** 1990 Private Limited Company
**Line of Business:** Engineers (consulting)
**Issued Capital:** £10,000
**Principals:** R C De'Ath *(Managing)*, D L Hughes
**Co. Secretary:** Stephen White
**Branches:** Tully De'ath Ltd, The Uckfield Mill, Mill La, Uckfield, East Sussex TN22 5AA
**US SIC:** 8911, 8999
**UK SIC:** 83701, 83954
**Auditors:** Creaseys
**Bankers:** National Westminster Bank Plc (60-07-17)

| | 30-04-14 | 30-04-13 | 30-04-12 |
|---|---|---|---|
| TA | 522,417 | 511,582 | 378,633 |
| NW | 152,003 | 151,276 | 128,265 |
| WC | 82,298 | 68,466 | 69,428 |

DUNS 22-936-3817
## Tullyglass House Hotel
178 Galgorm Road, Ballymena, Co Antrim BT42 1HJ
**Tel:** 028-2565-2639
**Web:** www.tullyglass.com
**Estd:** 1966 Proprietorship
**Line of Business:** Hotels
**Proprietor:** C Mcconville
**Responsibilities**
**Senior:** Christopher McConville *(Proprietor)*, Agustine Mcconville *(Proprietor)*
**Purchasing:** Pauline Santos *(Purchasing Manager)*
**US SIC:** 7011 **UK SIC:** 66500
**Bankers:** Northern Bank Ltd (95-02-31)
**Employees:** 100

DUNS 23-557-4282
## Tunbridge Wells Borough Council
Town Hall, Mount Pleasant Road, Tunbridge Wells, Kent TN1 1RS
**Tel:** 01892-526121
**Web:** www.tunbridgewells.gov.uk
**VAT No:** 210900911 **Estd:** 1974 Incorporate By Act Of Parliament
**Line of Business:** Local government
**Directors:** R Stone, M Harris, G Levett
**Responsibilities**
**Marketing:** Louisa Luxford *(Head of Communications)*
**HR:** Lois Howell *(Head of Personnel)*
**Operations:** Garry Stevenson *(Head of Environmental)*
**Engineering:** David Bonninga *(Technical Officer)*
**Branches:** Tunbridge Wells Borough Council, The Old Fish Market, The Pantiles, Tunbridge Wells, Kent TN2 5TN
**US SIC:** 9121 **UK SIC:** 91110
**Bankers:** National Westminster Bank Plc (55-70-13)
**Employees:** 400

DUNS 21-005-3889
## Tunbridge Wells Care Centre Ltd
**(Subsidiary of:** Canford Healthcare Ltd)
Russell House, Oxford Road, Bournemouth, Dorset BH8 8EX
**Tel:** 01202545967
**Web:** www.tunbridgewells-carecentre.co.uk
**Reg No:** 6300724 **Estd:** 2007 Private Limited Company
**Line of Business:** Other business activities not elsewhere classified
**Issued Capital:** £2
**Directors:** B P Cooney, B M Lambert
**Co. Secretary:** Lester Aldridge Company Secretar
**US SIC:** 7399 **UK SIC:** 83954

| | 31-05-14 | 31-05-13 | 31-05-12 |
|---|---|---|---|
| TO | 3,665,722 | 3,167,441 | 2,291,241 |
| P/L | 429,828 | 196,120 | (7,689) |
| NW | (212,252) | (591,432) | (756,982) |
| WC | 3,222,328 | 3,107,351 | 3,171,287 |
| Emp. | 96 | 97 | 69 |

DUNS 22-636-6037
## Tunbridge Wells Equitable Friendly Society Ltd
Brockbourne House, Tunbridge Wells, Kent TN4 8GN
**Fax:** 01892533710
**Web:** www.travelodge.co.uk
**Reg No:** 0000190IP **Estd:** 2013 Friendly Society
**Line of Business:** Hotels
**Trading Style:** The Children's Mutual
**Directors:** N Kirkland, O Johnson, R Spragg, A Brown, M Bolton, K Percy, G Mcausland
**Co. Secretary:** S Allford
**Responsibilities**
**Senior:** S Allard *(Manager)*, Graeme McAusland *(Chief Operating Officer)*, Ewa Stecki *(Manager)*
**Facilities:** Graeme McAusland *(Chief Operating Officer)*
**US SIC:** 7011 **UK SIC:** 66500
**Auditors:** Deloitte & Touche
**Employees:** 15

DUNS 50-320-0677
## Tunbridge Wells Independent Hospital Ltd
**(Subsidiary of:** Spire Healthcare Holdings 1)
Tunbridge Wells Hospital, Fordcombe Road, Tunbridge Wells, Kent TN3 0RD
**Tel:** 08006121345
**Web:** www.clickhearing.com
**Reg No:** 2345011 **Estd:** 1989 Private Limited Company
**Line of Business:** Hearing aid suppliers
**Issued Capital:** £2
**Directors:** R Roger, S Gordon
**Co. Secretary:** Daniel Toner
**Responsibilities**
**Senior:** Phil Belton *(Estates Manager)*
**Marketing:** Hannah Browning *(Business Development Manager)*
**HR:** Sian Edwards *(Human Resources Manager)*
**Health & Safety:** Phil Belton *(Estates Manager)*
**Facilities:** Phil Belton *(Estates Manager)*
**Purchasing:** Barbara Cooper *(Supplies Coordinator)*
**US SIC:** 8062 **UK SIC:** 95100
**Bankers:** National Westminster Bank Plc (55-70-13)

| | 31-12-13 | 31-12-12 | 31-12-11 |
|---|---|---|---|
| TA | 769,608 | 769,608 | 769,608 |
| NW | 769,608 | 769,608 | 769,608 |

DUNS 21-582-1436
## Tunbridge Wells Mazda
Longfield Road, Tunbridge Wells, Kent TN2 3EY
**Web:** www.motorparks.co.uk
**Estd:** 2011 Proprietorship
**Line of Business:** Car dealers (new & used)
**Proprietor:** P Hutchinson
**Responsibilities**
**Senior:** Mark Tandy *(General Manager)*, Neil Wiseman *(Dealer Principal)*
**US SIC:** 5511 **UK SIC:** 65100
**Employees:** 50

DUNS 34-534-0199 **Imp**
## Tungate Holdings Ltd
Brook House Industrial Estate, Brook House Way, Cheadle, Stoke-On-Trent, Staffordshire ST10 1SR
**Tel:** 01538755755
**Web:** www.tungate.co.uk
**Reg No:** 5344425 **Estd:** 2005 Private Limited Company
**Line of Business:** Management activities of holding companies
**Export Sales:** £887,116
**Issued Capital:** £82,500
**Directors:** K P Paszek, R J Tungate, G R Wright
**Co. Secretary:** Philip Elks
**Responsibilities**
**Senior:** Gareth Partlet *(Sales Manager)*
**Sales:** Gareth Partlet *(Sales Manager)*
**US SIC:** 6711 **UK SIC:** 83962

| | 31-12-13 | 31-12-12 | 31-12-11 |
|---|---|---|---|
| TO | 14,785,262 | 14,040,007 | 12,106,399 |
| P/L | 2,286,880 | 1,807,197 | 1,426,793 |
| NW | 7,845,991 | 6,454,480 | 5,089,219 |
| WC | 6,465,515 | 5,122,608 | 3,613,058 |
| Emp. | 72 | 65 | 62 |

DUNS 21-821-7068
## Tungsten Corporation Plc
Vestry House Laurence Pountney Hill, London EC4R 0EH
**Tel:** 020-3435-5680
**Web:** www.tungstencorporationplc.com
**Reg No:** 7934335 **Estd:** 2012 Public Limited Company
**Line of Business:** Financial intermediation not elsewhere classified
**Export Sales:** £4,386,000
**Directors:** P A Kiernan, L P Jopp, R Hirwitz, D F Truell, P Ashdown, A Hoevenaars, E G Truell
**Co. Secretary:** Mrs Georgina Behrens
**US SIC:** 6111 **UK SIC:** 81501
**Auditors:** PricewaterhouseCoopers LLP

| | 30-04-14 | 30-04-13 |
|---|---|---|
| TA | 188,594,000 | 4,901,712 |
| P/L | (11,140,000) | (9,925,456) |
| NW | 56,889,000 | 4,724,545 |
| WC | 58,090,000 | 4,504,173 |
| Emp. | 235 | 5 |

DUNS 23-969-2309
## Tungsten Network Ltd
**(Subsidiary of:** Tungsten Corporation Plc)
Melbourne House, 44-46 Aldwych, London WC2B 4LL
**Tel:** 08701657410 **Fax:** 020-7240-2696
**Web:** www.ob10.com
**Reg No:** 3958038 **VAT No:** 754922608
**Estd:** 2001 Private Limited Company
**Line of Business:** Data storage solutions
**Issued Capital:** £33,013
**Directors:** E G Truell, L P Jopp
**Co. Secretary:** Patrick Clark
**Responsibilities**
**Senior:** Jeffrey Belkin *(Director)*, Fiona Leahy *(Proprietor)*
**US SIC:** 7374 **UK SIC:** 83940
**Auditors:** PricewaterhouseCoopers LLP
**Bankers:** HSBC Bank plc (40-05-20)

| | 30-04-14 | 30-04-13 | 30-04-12 |
|---|---|---|---|
| TO | 11,254,487 | 17,631,471 | 16,282,668 |
| P/L | (3,688,832) | (3,665,107) | (2,955,634) |
| NW | 8,929,692 | (7,355,559) | (4,263,420) |
| WC | (2,160,284) | (7,779,824) | (4,547,810) |
| Emp. | 87 | 215 | 200 |

DUNS 34-581-1905
## Tunnelcraft Ltd
Highbury House, 516 High Road, Ilford, Essex IG3 8EG
**Tel:** 020-8597-1102
**Web:** www.tunnelcraft.co.uk
**Reg No:** 2728757 **Estd:** 1992 Private Limited Company
**Line of Business:** Civil engineers
**Issued Capital:** £710
**Directors:** C P Hicks, J J Riordan
**Co. Secretary:** John Riordan
**US SIC:** 8911 **UK SIC:** 83701
**Auditors:** Raffingers Stuart

| | 31-10-13 | 31-10-12 | 31-10-11 |
|---|---|---|---|
| TO | 22,986,349 | N/A | N/A |
| P/L | 61,170 | N/A | N/A |
| NW | 407,602 | 361,858 | 317,015 |
| WC | 363,506 | 322,221 | 302,540 |
| Emp. | 154 | N/A | N/A |

DUNS 21-107-4361
## Tunstall Healthcare Group Ltd
**(Subsidiary of:** Watling Street Capital Partners Llp)
Whitley Lodge, Doncaster Road, Whitley, Goole, North Humberside DN14 0HR
**Tel:** 01977661234
**Web:** www.tunstall.co.uk
**Reg No:** 6495696 **Estd:** 1957 Private Limited Company
**Line of Business:** Life saving appliances
**Export Sales:** £153,797,000
**Issued Capital:** £07,630
**Directors:** R P Moores, G Prestia, P L Stobart, S Parker, M M Miller, T E James
**Co. Secretary:** Jonathan Furniss
**Responsibilities**
**Senior:** Jason Cicero *(Finance Director)*, Kevin Dyson *(Manager)*
**Finance:** Jason Cicero *(Finance Director)*
**US SIC:** 3841 **UK SIC:** 37201

| | 30-09-14 | 30-09-13 | 30-09-12 |
|---|---|---|---|
| TO | 215,241,000 | 220,980,000 | 182,050,000 |
| P/L | (171,075,000) | (123,387,000) | (87,666,000) |
| NW | (1,034,181,000) | (919,252,000) | (787,259,000) |
| WC | 67,193,000 | (29,966,000) | (25,013,000) |
| Emp. | 2,950 | 2,912 | 1,891 |

DUNS 21-710-8711
## Tunstall International Ltd
**(Subsidiary of:** Watling Street Capital Partners Llp)
Whitley Lodge, Whitley Bridge, Goole, North Humberside DN14 0HR
**Tel:** 01977782004
**Reg No:** 1076005 **Estd:** 1972 Private Limited Company
**Line of Business:** The Notes to the accounts for the period ending 30.09.2014 state that the subject acts as an agent for Tunstall Healthcare (UK) Ltd.
**Issued Capital:** £1,000
**Directors:** S Parker, S A Arnold, P L Stobart
**Co. Secretary:** Jonathan Furniss
**US SIC:** 3699 **UK SIC:** 34542
**Bankers:** HSBC Bank plc (40-46-04)

| | 30-09-14 | 30-09-13 | 30-09-07 |
|---|---|---|---|
| TA | 12,037 | 12,037 | 12,037 |
| NW | 12,037 | 12,037 | 12,037 |
| WC | 12,037 | 12,037 | N/A |
| Emp. | 500 | 500 | N/A |

DUNS 23-231-9988
## Tuntum Housing Association Ltd
90 Beech Avenue, New Basford, Nottingham, Nottinghamshire NG7 7LW
**Fax:** 01159166067
**Web:** www.tuntum.co.uk
**Reg No:** 0026310IP **Estd:** 1988 Friendly Society
**Line of Business:** Housing associations societies trusts & co-operatives
**Trading Style:** Tuntum Housing Association Ltd
**Principals:** S Riley *(Chairman)*, M Jones-Bowen, T Browne, P Williams, R Richardson, K Alick, R Taylor, H Joshua
**Co. Secretary:** E Campbell
**Responsibilities**
**Senior:** Katherine Bush *(Chief Executive Officer)*, L Gilzean *(Director)*, O Harvey *(Director)*, L Pennycooke *(Director)*, Richard Renwick *(CEO)*
**Finance:** Dawn Morley *(Finance Assistant)*, Martin Ramsdale *(Finance Manager)*
**Marketing:** Symone Darby *(Relations Manager)*, Cherelle Dyce *(Relations Manager)*
**HR:** Lynsey Baum *(Human Resources Assistant)*
**Facilities:** Tahir Mahmood *(Maintenance Officer)*, Delores Price *(Head of Supported Housing)*, Jo Wilby *(Head of Housing)*
**Branches:** Tuntum Housing Association Ltd, Old Vicarage, Scotholme Avenue, Nottingham, Nottinghamshire NG7 6FB
**US SIC:** 8321 **UK SIC:** 96111
**Auditors:** Rogers, Spencer & Co

**Bankers:** The Co-Operative Bank Plc (08-90-74)

| | 31-03-12 | 31-03-11 | 31-03-10 |
|---|---|---|---|
| TO | 6,347,087 | 6,305,246 | 6,174,448 |
| P/L | 949,575 | 655,340 | 401,239 |
| NW | 4,750,299 | 4,303,294 | 3,647,956 |
| WC | (1,034,851) | (1,130,012) | (452,425) |
| Emp. | 66 | 90 | 60 |

DUNS 22-037-6904

## Turbine Surface Technologies Ltd

Unit 13a, Little Oak Drive, Nottingham, Nottinghamshire NG15 0DR
**Tel:** 01623720040
**Reg No:** 4040105 **Estd:** 2000 Private Limited Company
**Line of Business:** Manufacture of mastics and sealants
**Issued Capital:** £4,400,200
**Directors:** P C Gowtage, C Luzzatto, G W Davies, Dr A Partridge, P Howard
**Co. Secretary:** Mrs Karen Waldron
**Responsibilities**
**Senior:** Wies Sissons *(Business Administrator)*
**US SIC:** 2891 **UK SIC:** 25620
**Auditors:** KPMG LLP

| | 31-12-13 | 31-12-12 | 31-12-11 |
|---|---|---|---|
| TO | 47,769,000 | 38,870,000 | 34,620,000 |
| P/L | 6,572,000 | 5,431,000 | 6,801,000 |
| NW | 14,749,000 | 13,085,000 | 14,261,000 |
| WC | 5,363,000 | 6,543,000 | 7,639,000 |
| Emp. | 320 | 271 | 227 |

DUNS 34-653-0256 **Imp**

## Turbo Power Systems Ltd

**(Subsidiary of:** Caixa De Previdência Dos Funcionários Do Banco Do)
1 Queens Park, Queensway North, Gateshead, Tyne and Wear NE11 0QD
**Tel:** 01914829200 **Fax:** 01914829201
**Web:** www.turbopowersystems.com
**Reg No:** 2774899 **Estd:** 1986 Private Limited Company
**Line of Business:** Manufacture of electric motors, generators and transformers
**Export Sales:** £16,103,198
**Issued Capital:** £15,061,222
**Directors:** A Aigner, F Senhora, R J Piper
**Co. Secretary:** Charles Rendell
**Responsibilities**
**Senior:** Colin Besant *(General Manager)*, Terry Burke *(It Manager)*, Doug Glossop *(Manager)*, Justin Hall *(Manager)*, Hassan Mansir *(Chief Technical Officer)*, Carlos Neves *(Chief Executive Officer)*, Patrick Sinnott *(Manager)*, Ian Waring *(Manager)*
**Finance:** Harsha Raghavan *(Senior Manager - Commercial an)*
**Marketing:** Hassan Mansir *(Chief Technical Officer)*
**Sales:** Hassan Mansir *(Chief Technical Officer)*, Brian McFall *(Product Support Business Manag)*, Harsha Raghavan *(Senior Manager - Commercial an)*
**IT:** Terry Burke *(It Manager)*
**Engineering:** Tomas Hornik *(Senior Control Engineer)*, Ian McDonald *(Systems Chief Engineer)*
**US SIC:** 3621 **UK SIC:** 34201
**Auditors:** KPMG LLP

| | 31-12-13 | 31-12-12 | 31-12-11 |
|---|---|---|---|
| TO | 18,956,281 | 15,664,428 | 13,311,852 |
| P/L | (2,621,334) | (4,910,814) | (4,676,697) |
| NW | (69,651,908) | (67,045,445) | (72,916,576) |
| WC | 4,542,928 | (9,631,667) | (21,411,940) |
| Emp. | 164 | 187 | 148 |

DUNS 73-504-4245 **Imp-Exp**

## Turbo Systems Ltd

1 Gillett Street, Hull, North Humberside HU3 4JA
**Tel:** 01482325651 **Fax:** 01482211434
**Web:** www.turbo-systems.com
**Reg No:** 4767575 **Estd:** 1979 Private Limited Company
**Line of Business:** Engineers (general)
**Issued Capital:** £1,125
**Director:** A R Lang
**Co. Secretary:** Vaughan Davies
**Responsibilities**
**Senior:** Maureen Guest *(Manager)*
**Finance:** Trevor Medd *(Finance Manager)*
**Marketing:** Mike Moss *(Sales & Marketing Manager)*
**Sales:** Charles Guest *(Sales Director)*, Mike Moss *(Sales & Marketing Manager)*
**US SIC:** 3551 **UK SIC:** 32441

| | 31-03-14 | 31-03-13 | 31-03-12 |
|---|---|---|---|
| TA | 2,110,927 | 1,982,556 | 1,820,756 |
| NW | 279,439 | 251,164 | (153,326) |
| WC | 125,726 | 201,062 | (123,350) |

DUNS 21-717-6619 **Imp-Exp**

## Turbomeca Uk Ltd

**(Subsidiary of:** Safran)
Concorde Way, Fareham, Hampshire PO15 5RL
**Tel:** 01489563931 **Fax:** 01489564653
**Web:** www.turbomicro.co.uk
**Reg No:** 1148466 **VAT No:** 108482374
**Estd:** 1973 Private Limited Company
**Line of Business:** Manufacture of aircraft and spacecraft
**Export Markets:** European Union (E U); U S A
**Export Sales:** £29,380,000
**Issued Capital:** £500,000
**Directors:** F Saudo, F C Fouriangue
**Co. Secretary:** Michael Risdon
**Responsibilities**
**Senior:** Christian Hamel *(Manager)*, Alan McCahon *(Facilities Manager)*
**IT:** Jayne Glover *(IT Manager)*
**Facilities:** Alan McCahon *(Facilities Manager)*
**Purchasing:** Alan McCahon *(Facilities Manager)*
**Engineering:** Hiram Pargeter *(Engineering Services Manager)*
**US SIC:** 3721 **UK SIC:** 36400
**Auditors:** Ernst & Young
**Bankers:** HSBC Bank plc (40-35-18)

| | 31-12-13 | 31-12-12 | 31-12-11 |
|---|---|---|---|
| TO | 87,402,000 | 62,261,000 | 68,897,000 |
| P/L | 4,193,000 | 1,202,000 | 3,409,000 |
| NW | 6,639,000 | 14,207,000 | 15,458,000 |
| WC | 1,384,000 | 9,401,000 | 10,463,000 |
| Emp. | 192 | 178 | 176 |

DUNS 21-684-2303

## Turcan Connell Asset Management Ltd

Princes Exchange, 1 Earl Grey Street, Edinburgh, Midlothian EH3 9EE
**Tel:** 01312288111
**Web:** www.turcanconnell.com
**Reg No:** 0383455SC **Estd:** 2010 Private Limited Company
**Line of Business:** Solicitors
**Issued Capital:** £1,825,668
**Directors:** A R Montgomery, H R Bathgate, E D Murray, I R Clark, R D Fulton, Mrs L M Knox, S A Mackintosh, R C Turcan
**Co. Secretary:** Turcan Connell Company Secretari
**Responsibilities**
**Senior:** Douglas Connell *(Director)*
**US SIC:** 7399 **UK SIC:** 83954

| | 31-03-14 | 31-03-13 | 31-03-12 |
|---|---|---|---|
| TO | 7,046,864 | 6,139,486 | N/A |
| P/L | 413,373 | 556,655 | (3,064) |
| NW | 2,161,438 | 2,005,802 | 1,596,939 |
| WC | 543,084 | 385,266 | (3,061) |
| Emp. | 56 | 64 | N/A |

DUNS 21-231-5681

## Turfcote Nursing Home

Turfcote Nursing & Residential, Helmshore Road, Rossendale, Lancashire BB4 4DP
**Tel:** 01706-229735
**Web:** www.turfcotecarehome.co.uk
**Estd:** 1987 Proprietorship
**Line of Business:** Nursing homes
**Proprietor:** Mrs E Irwin
**Responsibilities**
**Senior:** Elizabeth Irwin *(Home Manager)*
**HR:** Elizabeth Irwin *(Home Manager)*
**Health & Safety:** Elizabeth Irwin *(Home Manager)*
**Facilities:** Sudhakara Balappa *(Handy Manager)*
**US SIC:** 8051 **UK SIC:** 95100
**Employees:** 54

DUNS 76-985-1288

## Turkish Bank (U K) Ltd

84-86 Borough High Street, London SE1 1LN
**Tel:** 020-7403-5656
**Web:** www.turkishbank.co.uk
**Reg No:** 2643004 **Estd:** 1991 Private Limited Company
**Line of Business:** Banks and financial institutions
**Issued Capital:** £12,000,000
**Directors:** D I Stewart, D Blackmore, R W Long, M Arig, M A Rahmioglu, I H Bortecene, P E Ryan
**Co. Secretary:** Jonathan Kent
**Responsibilities**
**Senior:** Resat Bilgin *(General Manager)*
**HR:** Seniz Angay Bayindir *(Human Resources Officer)*
**Branches:** Turkish Bank (U K) Ltd, 121 Kingsland High Street, London E8 2PB
**US SIC:** 6012 **UK SIC:** 81402
**Auditors:** Deloitte & Touche LLP
**Bankers:** HSBC Bank plc (40-02-38)

| | 31-12-13 | 31-12-12 | 31-12-11 |
|---|---|---|---|
| TA | 132,041,000 | 117,829,000 | 123,181,000 |
| P/L | 746,000 | 540,000 | 59,000 |
| NW | 22,084,000 | 21,450,000 | 21,027,000 |
| WC | 15,068,000 | 8,711,000 | 13,559,000 |
| Emp. | 80 | 80 | 75 |

DUNS 23-860-1954

## Turkish Cypriot Community Association

266-268 High Street, Waltham Cross, Hertfordshire EN8 7EA
**Tel:** 01992700055
**Reg No:** 3851759 **Estd:** 1999 Private Company Limited By Guarantee
**Line of Business:** Social work activities without accommodation
**Directors:** Dr M Mehmet-Yesil, O T Ibrahim
**Co. Secretary:** Dr Mek Mehmet-Yesil
**Responsibilities**
**Senior:** Duran Husnu *(Manager)*
**US SIC:** 8321 **UK SIC:** 96111
**Bankers:** The Co-Operative Bank Plc (08-92-28)

| | 31-03-14 | 31-03-13 | 31-03-12 |
|---|---|---|---|
| TO | 1,216,686 | 1,170,911 | 1,106,490 |
| P/L | 77,656 | 171,781 | 62,561 |
| NW | 584,779 | 507,123 | 335,342 |
| WC | 387,293 | 293,320 | 104,327 |
| Emp. | 47 | 46 | 49 |

DUNS 21-388-0760

## Turkish Delight

10 High Street, Congleton, Cheshire CW12 1BL
**Tel:** 01260-299064
**Estd:** 2002
**Line of Business:** Take away meal outlets
**Responsibilities**
**Senior:** Ali Demer *(Manager)*
**US SIC:** 5812 **UK SIC:** 66110
**Employees:** 64

DUNS 23-638-2024

## Turkish Embassy

43 Belgrave Square, London SW1X 8PA
**Tel:** 02073930202
**Web:** www.turkisheconomy.org.uk
**Estd:** 1800
**Line of Business:** Embassies
**Directors:** C Onhon, K Hakganir
**Responsibilities**
**Senior:** Ahmet Cevikoz *(Chairman)*
**Branches:** 29 Bedford Sq, London WC1B 3ED
**US SIC:** 9121 **UK SIC:** 91110
**Employees:** 78

DUNS 39-930-9855

## Turley Associates Ltd

1 New York Street, Manchester M1 4HD
**Tel:** 01612337676 **Fax:** 01612337677
**Web:** www.turley.co.uk
**Reg No:** 2235387 **Estd:** 1988 Private Limited Company
**Line of Business:** Planning consultants
**Issued Capital:** £100,000
**Directors:** M J Best, R M Lucas, R J Peters, Mrs E A Peace, M A Lowndes, G Forster, J N Isbister, P G Deehan
**Co. Secretary:** Paul Deehan
**Responsibilities**
**Senior:** David Trimingham *(Director)*
**Admin:** Joanne Whalley *(Receptionist)*
**Branches:** Turley Associates Ltd, 2 Palatine Road, Manchester M20 3JA
**US SIC:** 8911 **UK SIC:** 83701
**Auditors:** Mckellen & Co
**Bankers:** The Royal Bank Of Scotland Plc (16-00-01)

| | 31-05-13 | 31-05-12 | 31-05-11 |
|---|---|---|---|
| TO | 16,253,895 | 15,840,838 | 14,240,860 |
| P/L | 469,352 | 930,986 | 241,163 |
| NW | 7,472,401 | 7,213,201 | 6,617,637 |
| WC | 8,827,746 | 8,260,346 | 7,559,199 |
| Emp. | 174 | 166 | 153 |

DUNS 21-585-0321

## Turn Furlong Specialist Care Centre

Turn Furlong, Northampton, Northamptonshire NN2 8BZ
**Tel:** 01604850800
**Web:** www.shawhealthcare.co.uk
**Estd:** 2011 Proprietorship
**Line of Business:** Charities and charitable organisations
**Proprietor:** Miss S Spires
**US SIC:** 8062 **UK SIC:** 95100
**Employees:** 80

DUNS 49-373-0972 **Imp-Exp**

## Turnaround Publisher Services Ltd

Unit 3, Olympia Industrial Estate, Coburg Road, London N22 6TZ
**Tel:** 020-8829-3000 **Fax:** 020-8881-5088
**Web:** www.turnaround-uk.com
**Reg No:** 3126700 **Estd:** 1995 Private Limited Company
**Line of Business:** Book publishers
**Export Sales:** £1,032,792
**Issued Capital:** £81
**Principals:** N A Godber *(Managing)*, A Webb, Ms S Gregg
**Co. Secretary:** Ms Claire Thompson
**Responsibilities**
**Senior:** Barry Conway *(Warehouse Manager)*
**Sales:** Jim Crawley *(Field Sales Manager)*
**US SIC:** 2731 **UK SIC:** 47532
**Auditors:** Sayer Vincent
**Bankers:** National Westminster Bank Plc (60-04-24)

| | 31-03-13 | 31-03-12 | 31-03-11 |
|---|---|---|---|
| TO | 15,687,640 | 15,840,358 | 14,528,679 |
| P/L | 240,486 | 337,206 | 196,038 |
| NW | 1,437,936 | 1,264,350 | 1,036,079 |
| WC | 1,385,487 | 1,189,355 | 956,078 |
| Emp. | 58 | 57 | 53 |

DUNS 22-953-8442 **Exp**

## Turnbull & Asser Ltd

71-72 Jermyn Street, London SW1Y 6PF
**Fax:** 02078083010
**Web:** www.turnbullandasser.co.uk
**Reg No:** 1066321 **Estd:** 1885 Private Limited Company
**Line of Business:** Manufacturers of shirts
**Export Markets:** U S A; Italy
**Export Sales:** £4,447,000
**Issued Capital:** £2,450,000
**Principals:** A Fayed *(Chairman)*, N C Clifford, N C Blow, D I Foster, S J Quin, J A Fayed, S C Mccoy
**Co. Secretary:** David Foster
**Responsibilities**
**Senior:** Evelyn Mulligan *(Manager)*
**Marketing:** Charles O'Reilly *(Marketing Manager)*
**Admin:** Cleo Holmess *(Office Manager)*
**Branches:** Turnbull & Asser Ltd, Unit 28-30, Sabre Close, Gloucester, Gloucestershire GL2 4NZ
**US SIC:** 2389, 5136, 5699
**UK SIC:** 45393, 61600, 64500
**Auditors:** PricewaterhouseCoopers
**Bankers:** HSBC Bank plc (40-05-01)

| | 01-02-14 | 02-02-13 | 28-02-12 |
|---|---|---|---|
| TO | 9,736,000 | 9,394,000 | 10,249,000 |
| P/L | (259,000) | 449,000 | 1,179,000 |
| NW | 7,121,000 | 7,295,000 | 6,971,000 |
| WC | 4,374,000 | 4,190,000 | 3,775,000 |
| Emp. | 150 | 148 | 148 |

DUNS 21-827-4645

## Turnbull & Co Ltd

**(Subsidiary of:** Hopkins Group Ltd)
95 Southgate, Sleaford, Lincolnshire NG34 7RQ
**Tel:** 01529303025 **Fax:** 01529303026
**Web:** www.turnbull24-7.co.uk
**Reg No:** 0536685 **Estd:** 1954 Private Limited Company
**Line of Business:** Agents involved in the sale of timber and building materials
**Trading Style:** Builders Merchants
**Issued Capital:** £15,100
**Principals:** G J Hopkins *(Managing)*, C E Hopkins *(Commercial)*, M P Hopkins, S J Vickers
**Co. Secretary:** Terence Hopkins
**Responsibilities**
**Senior:** Nigel Donner *(Yard Manager)*
**Admin:** Trudy Barnes *(Office Manager)*
**IT:** Adrian Hopkins *(Head of IT)*
**HR:** Tara Oates *(Personnel Manager)*
**Branches:** Turnbull & Co Ltd, Unit 7, Woodbridge Road, Sleaford, Lincolnshire NG34 7EW
**US SIC:** 5072, 5021, 5074
**UK SIC:** 61500, 61300
**Auditors:** Streets
**Bankers:** Lloyds TSB Bank plc (30-97-70)

| | 31-12-13 | 31-12-12 | 31-12-11 |
|---|---|---|---|
| TO | 19,046,492 | 17,417,006 | 17,906,066 |
| P/L | 420,238 | 222,189 | 346,244 |
| NW | 3,094,363 | 2,976,193 | 2,893,608 |
| WC | 1,362,619 | 1,401,110 | 1,540,290 |
| Emp. | 110 | 104 | 97 |

DUNS 21-443-1504

## Turner & Co. (Glasgow) Ltd.

65 Craigton Road, Glasgow, Lanarkshire G51 3EQ
**Tel:** 01414-400-666 **Fax:** 01414-454-123
**Web:** www.turner.co.uk
**Reg No:** 0027900SC **VAT No:** 343371372
**Estd:** 1950 Private Limited Company
**Line of Business:** Management activities of holding companies
**Export Sales:** £30,619,000
**Issued Capital:** £83,774
**Principals:** W S Sharp *(Financial)*, I Parrack, A G Turner, G B Knox, A G Turner
**Co. Secretary:** Ian Parrack
**Responsibilities**
**Senior:** Richard Fee *(Manager)*
**Sales:** Sandra Marchment *(Head of Commercial Operations)*, Tom Mckellar *(Commercial Director)*, Brodie Shepherd *(Business Development Manager)*
**IT:** Leslie Barclay *(IT Manager)*, Lynne Rafferty *(Head of ISIT)*

**Operations:** Sandra Marchment *(Head of Commercial Operations)*, Bill McNeil *(Operations Manager)*
**Branches:** Turner & Co. (Glasgow) Ltd., First Floor, Park Ho, 22 Park St, Croydon, Surrey CR0 1YE
**US SIC:** 6711 **UK SIC:** 83962
**Auditors:** Ernst & Young LLP
**Bankers:** The Royal Bank Of Scotland Plc (83-41-00)

| | 28-03-14 | 29-03-13 | 30-03-12 |
|---|---|---|---|
| TO | 325,748,000 | 262,514,000 | 270,207,000 |
| P/L | 17,528,000 | 16,109,000 | 14,483,000 |
| NW | 134,141,000 | 131,386,000 | 123,600,000 |
| WC | 56,940,000 | 67,133,000 | 67,831,000 |
| Emp. | 2,142 | 1,889 | 2,059 |

DUNS 23-375-8275

## Turner & Debenham Solicitors

48 Watling Street, Radlett, Hertfordshire WD7 7NN
**Tel:** 01923857171
**Web:** www.dolegal.co.uk
**Estd:** 1800 Partnership
**Line of Business:** Solicitors
**Partners:** C Debenham, G D Elgood, O Britton
**Responsibilities**
**Senior:** Ruth Boulton *(Partner)*, Brigid Brennan *(Partner)*, Kate Carroll *(Partner)*, Denis Keegan *(Partner)*
**Branches:** Turner & Debenham Solicitors, Debenhams Ottaway, Ivy House, St. Albans, Hertfordshire AL1 3EW
**US SIC:** 8111 **UK SIC:** 83500
**Employees:** 80

DUNS 34-588-0249 **Imp**

## Turner & Price Ltd

Wiltshire Road, Dairycoates Industrial Estate, Hull, North Humberside HU4 6PD
**Tel:** 01482577100 **Fax:** 01482-577190
**Web:** www.turnerprice.com
**Reg No:** 2732141 **VAT No:** 598964353
**Estd:** 1992 Private Limited Company
**Line of Business:** Catering food and drink suppliers
**Export Sales:** £11,135,201
**Issued Capital:** £457,260
**Principals:** D P Gould *(Managing)*, C G Andrews, J R Gould, T C Harrison, R J Brown, R D Gould, J P Owen
**Co. Secretary:** Paul Brittain
**Responsibilities**
**IT:** Mark Kitchen *(Computer Manager)*
**HR:** Fiona Gibson *(Personnel Manager)*
**US SIC:** 5149 **UK SIC:** 61700
**Auditors:** Sowerby & Rushforth

| | 31-03-14 | 31-03-13 | 31-03-12 |
|---|---|---|---|
| TO | 46,295,261 | 38,526,373 | 33,939,951 |
| P/L | 2,110,261 | 1,404,816 | 718,021 |
| NW | 4,388,938 | 3,187,857 | 2,472,580 |
| WC | 2,068,407 | 1,049,424 | 315,188 |
| Emp. | 181 | 162 | 150 |

DUNS 21-104-0032

## Turner & Townsend Plc

61 Fountain Street, Belfast BT1 5EB
**Tel:** 02890334750
**Web:** www.turnerandtownsend.com
**Reg No:** 6468643 **Estd:** 2008 Public Limited Company
**Line of Business:** Business and management consultancy activities not elsewhere classified
**Export Sales:** £174,025,000
**Issued Capital:** £70,156
**Directors:** G C Horsfield, T N Harrison, V P Clancy, T G Wray, J C White
**Co. Secretary:** Martin Lathom-Sharp
**Responsibilities**
**Senior:** Freddie Luke *(Manager)*
**Branches:** Turner & Townsend Plc, 7 Savoy Court, London WC2R 0JP
**US SIC:** 7392 **UK SIC:** 83951

| | 30-04-14 | 30-04-13 | 30-04-12 |
|---|---|---|---|
| TO | 322,201,000 | 286,303,000 | 244,347,000 |
| P/L | 33,303,000 | 29,739,000 | 23,005,000 |
| NW | 29,498,000 | 22,084,000 | 12,231,000 |
| WC | 34,169,000 | 31,301,000 | 27,394,000 |
| Emp. | 3,430 | 2,991 | 2,484 |

DUNS 21-229-9838 **Imp-Exp**

## Turner Bianca Plc

Bell Mill, Claremont Street, Oldham, Lancashire OL8 3EJ
**Tel:** 0161-627-0045 **Fax:** 01616-270660
**Web:** www.turner-bianca.co.uk
**Reg No:** 0473824 **VAT No:** 150197775
**Estd:** 1949 Public Limited Company
**Line of Business:** Textile merchants
**Trading Style:** Turner Bianca Group, Turner Bianca, Turner Uk, Bianca
**Issued Capital:** £1,177,000
**Principals:** J E Turner *(Chairman)*, R M Bullbrook *(Managing)*, M K Walmsley *(Financial)*, D Bullbrook, J W Young, K Rutherford, P J Fitzpatrick, Ms J R Bloomfield
**Co. Secretary:** Mrs Barbara Morrison
**Responsibilities**
**Senior:** Leonard Pashley *(Director)*, Michael Travis *(Manager)*
**HR:** Liz Rich *(Human Resources Manager)*
**Branches:** Turner Bianca Plc, 2-4 Midland Street, Manchester M12 6LB
**US SIC:** 5133 **UK SIC:** 61600
**Auditors:** Beever & Struthers
**Bankers:** HSBC Bank plc (40-37-27)

| | 31-03-14 | 31-03-13 | 31-03-12 |
|---|---|---|---|
| TO | 92,357,756 | 87,753,206 | 86,307,598 |
| P/L | 1,878,578 | 1,460,624 | 234,728 |
| NW | 25,726,168 | 24,702,509 | 23,641,891 |
| WC | 22,454,361 | 21,225,494 | 20,717,014 |
| Emp. | 260 | 255 | 296 |

DUNS 29-566-0161 **Exp**

## Turner Broadcasting System Europe Ltd

**(Subsidiary of:** Time Warner Inc.)
16 Great Marlborough Street, London W1F 7HS
**Tel:** 020 7693 1000
**Web:** www.turner.com
**Reg No:** 1927955 **VAT No:** 440514387
**Estd:** 1986 Private Limited Company
**Line of Business:** Television activities
**Export Markets:** Europe, Africa, Middle East, South East Asia, U S A
**Export Sales:** £191,044,634
**Issued Capital:** £151,038,206
**Directors:** A Van Der Wal, Mrs E C Browne, G Stock
**Co. Secretary:** Ms Eleanor Browne
**Responsibilities**
**Senior:** Patrick English *(European Facilities Director)*, Susan Kelsall *(Director, Programming, Present)*
**Operations:** Stewart Curtis *(Programme Manager, Technology)*, Patrick English *(European Facilities Director)*, Chris McIntyre *(Intl Sales Operations Manager)*
**Branches:** Turner Broadcasting System Europe Ltd, C N N House, 16 Great Marlborough Street, London W1F 7HS
**US SIC:** 4833, 7829, 7374
**UK SIC:** 97411, 97112, 83940
**Auditors:** Ernst & Young LLP
**Bankers:** HSBC Bank plc (40-07-07)

| | 31-12-13 | 31-12-12 | 31-12-11 |
|---|---|---|---|
| TO | 255,714,609 | 267,470,697 | 289,946,623 |
| P/L | 9,258,461 | 1,719,989 | (2,744,437) |
| NW | 95,112,811 | 80,048,673 | 91,796,308 |
| WC | 66,037,482 | 41,843,677 | 40,645,065 |
| Emp. | 496 | 568 | 562 |

DUNS 21-147-1558 **Imp**

## Turner Contemporary

The Rendezvous, Margate, Kent CT9 1HG
**Tel:** 01843233000
**Web:** www.turnercontemporary.org
**Reg No:** 6772337 **Estd:** 2008 Private Company Limited By Guarantee
**Line of Business:** Art galleries and dealers
**Directors:** M A Wickham, Ms S N Woodward, J Wilmot, N G Webster, Ms T F Dillon, C R Stevens, F Fitzgibbon, J P Kampfner
**Co. Secretary:** Ms Victoria Pomery
**Responsibilities**
**Senior:** Laura Ford *(Director)*, Sarah Hohler *(Director)*, Angela Hunter *(Director)*, Roland Keating *(Director)*, Evelyn Stern *(Director)*
**US SIC:** 7911 **UK SIC:** 97913
**Bankers:** Barclays Bank Plc (20-17-92)

| | 31-03-14 | 31-03-13 | 31-03-12 |
|---|---|---|---|
| TO | 2,777,830 | 4,112,983 | 2,506,834 |
| P/L | 248,609 | 1,144,322 | (58,493) |
| NW | 1,733,032 | 1,446,673 | 302,351 |
| WC | 953,870 | 1,383,958 | 239,691 |
| Emp. | 87 | 81 | 34 |

DUNS 28-903-0348

## Turner Development Ltd

Mill House, Kings Coughton, Alcester, Warwickshire B49 5QG
**Tel:** 01789-762180
**Reg No:** 1361393 **Estd:** 1978 Private Limited Company
**Line of Business:** Management activities of holding companies
**Export Sales:** £4,353,401
**Issued Capital:** £33,750
**Principals:** A L Turner *(Chairman)*, J A Turner, Ms R H Rodd, Ms C A Pages
**Co. Secretary:** Mrs Cheryl Turner-Pages
**US SIC:** 6711 **UK SIC:** 83962
**Auditors:** Charles Lovell & Co

| | 30-06-13 | 30-06-12 | 30-06-11 |
|---|---|---|---|
| TO | 7,136,723 | 6,684,041 | 6,031,584 |
| P/L | 269,772 | 321,079 | 154,861 |
| NW | 4,669,911 | 4,350,229 | 4,109,624 |
| WC | 1,681,286 | 1,627,592 | 1,545,934 |
| Emp. | 61 | 65 | 61 |

DUNS 22-212-7156

## Turner Estate Solutions Ltd

**(Subsidiary of:** Turner & Co. (Glasgow) Ltd.)
Forthview House, Inverkeithing, Fife KY11 2BL
**Tel:** 01383-648619 **Fax:** 01383-648024
**Web:** www.turnerfm.co.uk
**Reg No:** 0220014SC **Estd:** 1912 Private Limited Company
**Line of Business:** Other construction work involving special trades
**Issued Capital:** £10,000
**Directors:** J W Laverty, T D Mackellar, G B Knox, I Parrack, A J Mitchinson
**Co. Secretary:** Ian Parrack
**Responsibilities**
**Senior:** Jennifer Nisbet *(Administrator)*
**Marketing:** Jennifer Nisbet *(Administrator)*
**IT:** Lynne Rafferty *(Computer Manager)*
**HR:** Jon Dodds *(Training Officer)*
**Health & Safety:** Karen Primrose *(Health & Safety Manager)*
**Purchasing:** Jennifer Nisbet *(Administrator)*
**Branches:** Turner Estate Solutions Ltd, Building 112, Cameron Barracks, Inverness, Inverness-Shire IV2 3XE
**US SIC:** 1541, 8911
**UK SIC:** 50100, 83701
**Auditors:** KPMG LLP

| | 28-03-14 | 29-03-13 | 31-03-12 |
|---|---|---|---|
| TO | 94,084,000 | 77,576,000 | 82,668,000 |
| P/L | 6,518,000 | 5,084,000 | 3,905,000 |
| NW | 2,897,000 | 1,887,000 | 2,074,000 |
| WC | 2,897,000 | 1,887,000 | 1,504,000 |
| Emp. | 221 | 311 | 209 |

DUNS 55-063-5437

## The Turner Home

Dingle Lane, Liverpool, Merseyside L8 9RN
**Estd:** 1993
**Line of Business:** Nursing home
**Chairman:** T I Tod
**US SIC:** 7231 **UK SIC:** 98200
**Employees:** 60

DUNS 21-226-2407

## Turner Memorial Hospital

Turner Street, Keith, Banffshire AB55 5DJ
**Tel:** 01542-882526
**Web:** www.keiths.grampian.scot.nhs.uk
**Estd:** 2002 Partnership
**Line of Business:** Hospitals
**Partners:** Mrs U Miller, Mrs A Kreft
**US SIC:** 8062 **UK SIC:** 95100
**Employees:** 50

DUNS 49-120-5423 **Imp-Exp**

## Turner Powertrain Systems Ltd

**(Subsidiary of:** Caterpillar Inc.)
Assembly Plant, Wolverhampton, West Midlands WV6 0QT
**Tel:** 01902779200 **Fax:** 01902836900
**Web:** www.turner-powertrain.co.uk
**Reg No:** 3100164 **VAT No:** 661022770
**Estd:** 1900 Private Limited Company
**Line of Business:** Manufacture of other transport equipment not elsewhere classified
**Export Markets:** U S A, France, Italy, Turkey, Brazil
**Export Sales:** £41,003,000
**Trading Style:** Turner Powertrain Systems Ltd
**Issued Capital:** £12,040,002
**Directors:** M D Cleaver, N J Burroughs, N G Murphy, A J Goldspink
**Co. Secretary:** Mrs Janette Nicholls
**Responsibilities**
**Senior:** Bonnie Setch *(Manager)*, Mark Stansforth *(Logistics Manager)*
**Finance:** Hazel Jones *(Head of Finance)*, Jesus Sandovil *(Financial Director)*
**Marketing:** Sean Perfetti *(Marketing Manager)*
**IT:** Paul Gosney *(Computer Operations Manager)*, Tim McMorran *(IT Manager)*
**HR:** Joretha Augostine *(Human Resources Manager)*
**Fleet:** Mark Stansforth *(Logistics Manager)*
**US SIC:** 3799, 3714
**UK SIC:** 36502, 35300
**Auditors:** PricewaterhouseCoopers LLP
**Bankers:** Lloyds TSB Bank plc (30-00-02)

| | 31-12-13 | 31-12-12 | 31-12-11 |
|---|---|---|---|
| TO | 55,780,000 | 55,094,000 | 66,643,000 |
| P/L | (5,665,000) | (12,196,000) | (4,378,000) |
| NW | 2,312,000 | 2,627,000 | 4,355,000 |
| WC | 2,378,000 | 2,181,000 | 2,065,000 |
| Emp. | 263 | 246 | 206 |

DUNS 38-781-8685

## Turners

1 Poole Road, Bournemouth, Dorset BH2 5QQ
**Web:** www.turners-solicitors.co.uk
**Estd:** 1982 Partnership
**Line of Business:** Caravan parks
**Partners:** M Shutler, D Blackmore, M Shutler, Mrs M Russell, Ms S Hobby, R Tombs, Ms S Carmichael
**Branches:** Turners, 18 High Street, Poole, Dorset BH15 1BP
**US SIC:** 8111 **UK SIC:** 83500
**Employees:** 50

DUNS 22-527-0263 **Exp**

## Turners Coachways (Bristol) Ltd

59 Days Road, St Philips, Bristol, Avon BS2 0QS
**Tel:** 01179-559086
**Web:** www.turnerscoachways.co.uk
**Reg No:** 1369495 **VAT No:** 358021566
**Estd:** 1978 Private Limited Company
**Line of Business:** Coach and bus hire
**Trading Style:** Turners
**Issued Capital:** £1,000
**Principals:** A J Turner *(Managing)*, Ms C J Turner
**Co. Secretary:** Paul Burt
**Responsibilities**
**Senior:** Olive Turner *(Manager)*
**US SIC:** 4119 **UK SIC:** 72200
**Auditors:** Deloitte & Touche
**Bankers:** Lloyds TSB Bank plc (30-94-80)

| | 31-03-14 | 31-03-13 | 31-03-12 |
|---|---|---|---|
| TA | 3,037,550 | 3,018,814 | 3,029,352 |
| NW | 2,435,874 | 2,459,736 | 2,366,822 |
| WC | 391,811 | 594,862 | 559,379 |

DUNS 04-004-5001

## Turners (East Anglia) Ltd

Turner Motor Group Tayfen Road, Bury St Edmunds, Suffolk IP33 1TB
**Tel:** 01284724999
**Reg No:** 5440722 **Estd:** 2005 Private Limited Company
**Line of Business:** Holding companies management activities
**Issued Capital:** £5,004
**Directors:** Mrs P E Turner, G P Turner
**Co. Secretary:** Ian Turner
**US SIC:** 6711 **UK SIC:** 83962

| | 31-12-13 | 31-12-12 | 30-12-11 |
|---|---|---|---|
| TO | 22,337,833 | 50,075,595 | 18,846,291 |
| P/L | 342,852 | 733,676 | 37,487 |
| NW | 1,942,169 | 1,647,621 | 100,221 |
| WC | (720,320) | (1,182,862) | (1,512,016) |
| Emp. | 58 | 94 | 72 |

DUNS 21-815-8161

## Turners (Soham) Holdings Ltd

Fordham Road, Newmarket, Suffolk CB8 7NR
**Tel:** 01638720335
**Web:** www.turners-distribution.com
**Reg No:** 7889555 **Estd:** 2011 Private Limited Company
**Line of Business:** Freight transport by road not elsewhere classified
**Issued Capital:** £62,660
**Directors:** Ms W M Day, P E Day
**US SIC:** 4213, 4226
**UK SIC:** 72300, 77003

| | 28-12-13 | 29-12-12 |
|---|---|---|
| TO | 253,225,000 | 235,785,000 |
| P/L | 23,327,000 | 23,508,000 |
| NW | 181,368,000 | 162,344,000 |
| WC | 54,596,000 | 51,304,000 |
| Emp. | 2,426 | 2,355 |

DUNS 21-159-3673

## Turney Grant Maintained School

Turney Road, London SE21 8LX
**Tel:** 020-8670-7220
**Web:** www.turneyschool.co.uk
**Estd:** 2003 Proprietorship
**Line of Business:** Schools (special)
**Proprietor:** Mrs L Adams
**Responsibilities**
**Senior:** Linda Adams *(Executive Head Teacher)*
**Finance:** Susan Manning *(Finance Director)*
**IT:** Bela Handa *(Senior IT Executive)*
**US SIC:** 8299 **UK SIC:** 93300
**Employees:** 50

DUNS 77-741-1638

## Turney Landscapes Ltd

Park Farm, Milton Keynes, Buckinghamshire MK17 8AS
**Tel:** 01908281127
**Web:** www.turneylandscapes.co.uk
**Reg No:** 3010954 **Estd:** 1985 Private Limited Company
**Line of Business:** Landscape contractors
**Issued Capital:** £24,000
**Principals:** S N Turney *(Managing)*, A W Turney, D F Turney, R Cox
**Co. Secretary:** Stephen Turney
**Branches:** Turney Landscapes Ltd, 57 Newton Road, Rushden, Northamptonshire NN10 0HF
**US SIC:** 0729 **UK SIC:** 01003

**Auditors:** Keens Shay Keens

| | 30-04-14 | 30-04-13 | 30-04-12 |
|---|---|---|---|
| TA | 1,996,599 | 1,724,278 | 1,931,305 |
| NW | 709,026 | 667,102 | 660,642 |
| WC | 27,806 | 69,920 | 3,273 |

DUNS 21-289-0289

## Turney Wylde (Construction) Ltd

(Subsidiary of: Twcl (Northern) Holdings Ltd)
Tyne View Terrace, Wallsend, Tyne and Wear NE28 6SG
**Tel:** 0191-295-8600 **Fax:** 01912958601
**Web:** www.turneywylde.co.uk
**Reg No:** 0924584 **Estd:** 1967 Private Limited Company
**Line of Business:** Building construction contractors
**Issued Capital:** £2,000
**Directors:** K Parkin, I Cuthbertson
**Responsibilities**
**Senior:** Lesley Wylde (Manager), David Wylde (Manager)
**Branches:** Turney-Wylde (Construction) Ltd, Tyne View Terr, Wallsend, Tyne and Wear NE28 6SG
**US SIC:** 1522 **UK SIC:** 50100
**Auditors:** Bell Tindle Williamson
**Bankers:** Lloyds TSB Bank plc (30-91-94)

| | 31-12-13 | 31-12-12 | 31-12-11 |
|---|---|---|---|
| TO | 5,742,341 | 5,386,471 | 10,065,774 |
| P/L | 132,807 | 139,953 | 129,842 |
| NW | 443,579 | 421,772 | 315,170 |
| WC | 153,453 | 107,620 | (21,307) |
| Emp. | N/A | 46 | 77 |

DUNS 21-162-0724

## Turnham Primary School

Turnham Road, London SE4 2HH
**Tel:** 020-7639-0440
**Web:** www.turnham.lewisham.sch.uk
**Estd:** 1930
**Line of Business:** Creches
**Director:** Miss D Dance
**US SIC:** 8211 **UK SIC:** 93200
**Employees:** 50

DUNS 28-855-3415

## Turning Point

21 Mansell Street, London E1 8AA
**Tel:** 020-7481-7600 **Fax:** 020-7481-7620
**Web:** www.turning-point.co.uk
**Reg No:** 0793558 **Estd:** 1964 Private Company Limited By Guarantee
**Line of Business:** Manufacture of fasteners, screw machine products, chains and springs
**Directors:** D Hoare, C Parker, A D James, P W Picknett, Mrs S A Wood, Dr A I Prideaux, Mrs J B Williams, C S Bailey
**Co. Secretary:** Lord Victor Adebowale
**Responsibilities**
**Senior:** Angela Lennox (Board Member), Fiona Ritchie (Director of Learning Disabilit)
**Branches:** Turning Point, Westcliffe House, Flat 3, Rochdale, Lancashire OL12 9UZ
**US SIC:** 7399, 6732, 8321
**UK SIC:** 83954, 83100, 96111
**Auditors:** Mazars
**Bankers:** The Royal Bank Of Scotland Plc (16-00-53)

| | 31-03-14 | 31-03-13 | 31-03-12 |
|---|---|---|---|
| TO | 93,522,000 | 80,195,000 | 79,351,000 |
| P/L | 239,000 | (50,000) | 302,000 |
| NW | 6,057,000 | 5,818,000 | 5,868,000 |
| WC | 2,380,000 | 620,000 | 834,000 |
| Emp. | 2,575 | 2,347 | 2,084 |

DUNS 21-232-0148

## The Turning Point Scotland

4c Citadel Place, Ayr, Ayrshire KA7 1JN
**Tel:** 01292-886589
**Web:** www.turningpointscotland.com
**Estd:** 2007 Proprietorship
**Line of Business:** Disability services
**Proprietor:** Mrs E Manderson
**Responsibilities**
**Senior:** Julieanne Mcghee (Service Manager)
**Admin:** June Macfarlane (Administrator)
**US SIC:** 8321 **UK SIC:** 96111
**Employees:** 50

DUNS 23-744-8001

## Turning Point Scotland

54 Govan Road, Glasgow, Lanarkshire G51 1JL
**Tel:** 01414278200
**Web:** www.turningpointscotland.com
**Reg No:** 0194639SC **Estd:** 1996 Private Company Limited By Guarantee
**Line of Business:** Sheltered housing accommodation
**Directors:** E C Mcintyre, T A Cameron, Mrs D Mcelroy, Dr B A Langa-Ferreira, Mrs S Fazal, Ms J C Pike, B O'Suilleabhain, C Findlay
**Co. Secretary:** Tc Young Llp

---

**Responsibilities**
**Senior:** Martin Cawley (Manager), Paula Gilder (Manager), Brian Macdonald (Manager), Robert Macintosh (Director), Colin Rae (Manager), Michelle Ronald (IT Manager), Vinaykant Ruparella (Manager), Alyn Smith (Director), Katherine Wainwright (Human Resources Director)
**Marketing:** Marisa Mahood (Communications Manager)
**IT:** Michelle Ronald (IT Manager)
**Branches:** Turning Point Scotland, Unit 9, 7 Kyle Road, Irvine, Ayrshire KA12 8JF
**US SIC:** 8321 **UK SIC:** 96111
**Auditors:** BDO Stoy Hayward

| | 31-03-14 | 31-03-13 | 31-03-12 |
|---|---|---|---|
| TO | 26,169,786 | 25,344,529 | 25,456,531 |
| P/L | 114,186 | 536,262 | 772,864 |
| NW | 10,916,904 | 10,802,718 | 10,812,465 |
| WC | 5,668,085 | 5,734,988 | 5,301,075 |
| Emp. | 1,210 | 1,099 | 1,055 |

DUNS 28-927-0001     Imp

## Turnspeed Precision Engineering Co Ltd

3 Boundary Way, Lufton Trading Estate, Lufton, Yeovil, Somerset BA22 8HZ
**Tel:** 01935-424347
**Web:** www.turnspeed.co.uk
**Reg No:** 1506978 **VAT No:** 323727270
**Estd:** 1968 Private Limited Company
**Line of Business:** Precision engineers
**Trading Style:** Turnspeed Precision Engineering Co Ltd
**Issued Capital:** £4,500
**Managing Director:** R J Davies
**Co. Secretary:** Jamie Davies
**Responsibilities**
**Admin:** Jenny Dobson (Administration Assistant)
**US SIC:** 8911 **UK SIC:** 83701
**Auditors:** Ivan Rendall & Co
**Bankers:** HSBC Bank plc (40-47-28)

| | 31-07-13 | 31-07-12 | 31-07-11 |
|---|---|---|---|
| TO | 6,034,102 | 6,101,622 | 6,070,129 |
| P/L | (129,963) | (258,954) | 563,026 |
| NW | 4,779,181 | 4,825,040 | 4,907,949 |
| WC | (302,145) | (99,597) | 623,901 |
| Emp. | 54 | 58 | 51 |

DUNS 28-898-3158     Imp

## Turpin Distribution Services Ltd

(Subsidiary of: Eurospan Ltd)
Stratton Business Park Pegasus Drive, Biggleswade, Bedfordshire SG18 8TQ
**Fax:** 01767-601640
**Web:** www.turpin-distribution.com
**Reg No:** 1331778 **Estd:** 1977 Private Limited Company
**Line of Business:** Miscellaneous transportation services
**Issued Capital:** £151,000
**Directors:** N Castle, Mrs J Barnes, Ms L Summers, M A Geelan
**Co. Secretary:** Richard Stroud
**Responsibilities**
**Senior:** Anita Monaghan (Senior Client Manager), Phil Rushton (Senior Client Manager), Laurna Summers (Managing Director)
**US SIC:** 4789, 4226
**UK SIC:** 77002, 77003
**Auditors:** UHY George Hay
**Bankers:** Coutts & Co (18-00-02)

| | 31-12-13 | 31-12-12 | 31-12-11 |
|---|---|---|---|
| TO | 5,602,905 | 5,704,094 | 5,997,246 |
| P/L | 972,581 | 1,184,880 | 1,247,982 |
| NW | 2,466,475 | 2,554,651 | 2,701,625 |
| WC | 2,606,546 | 2,677,993 | 2,770,454 |
| Emp. | 73 | 76 | 84 |

DUNS 21-291-1325

## Turret Motor Co Ltd

Clarkehouse Road, Sheffield, South Yorkshire S10 2LJ
**Tel:** 01142682361
**Reg No:** 0929618 **VAT No:** 173010900
**Estd:** 1970 Private Limited Company
**Line of Business:** Car dealers (used)
**Issued Capital:** £2
**Principals:** P Womack (Chairman), A D Womack
**Co. Secretary:** Mrs Anne Womack
**US SIC:** 5521 **UK SIC:** 65100
**Auditors:** J S Bethell & Co
**Bankers:** Lloyds TSB Bank plc (30-97-51)

| | 30-04-14 | 30-04-13 | 30-04-12 |
|---|---|---|---|
| TA | 13,578 | 13,579 | 18,465 |
| P/L | N/A | N/A | (1,681) |
| NW | 635 | 634 | 4,920 |
| WC | (9,365) | (9,366) | (5,080) |

DUNS 42-313-6175

## Turtle Transport

8 Cashel Road, Broughshane, Ballymena, Co Antrim BT42 4PL
**Tel:** 02825861454
**Estd:** 2002 Partnership
**Line of Business:** Road haulage and transport services

---

**Partners:** C Turtle, R Turtle
**US SIC:** 4789 **UK SIC:** 77002
**Bankers:** First Trust Bank (aib Group (uk) Plc) (93-80-17)
**Employees:** 54

DUNS 77-895-4052

## Tuscan Connects Ltd

(Subsidiary of: Bull)
Beevor Court 1 Pontefract Road, Barnsley, South Yorkshire S71 1HG
**Tel:** 01226773289 **Fax:** 01226773299
**Web:** www.bull.co.uk
**Reg No:** 5799215 **VAT No:** 680951904
**Estd:** 2006 Private Limited Company
**Line of Business:** Other business activities not elsewhere classified
**Issued Capital:** £1,000
**Directors:** P Guimard, J M Sagajllo Batterberry
**Co. Secretary:** Tmf Corporate Administration Ser
**Responsibilities**
**Finance:** Emily Durdey (Senior Finance Administrator)
**Admin:** Emily Durdey (Senior Finance Administrator)
**IT:** Phil Reed (Operations Manager)
**HR:** Erica Greaves (HR Manager)
**Operations:** Phil Reed (Operations Manager)
**US SIC:** 7399 **UK SIC:** 83954
**Auditors:** Deloitte LLP
**Bankers:** Barclays Bank Plc (20-25-29)

| | 31-12-13 | 31-12-12 | 31-12-11 |
|---|---|---|---|
| TO | 9,247,951 | 9,773,411 | 9,717,518 |
| P/L | 386,512 | 416,404 | 383,455 |
| NW | 1,659,561 | 1,386,655 | 1,074,352 |
| WC | (352,735) | (860,424) | (1,086,837) |
| Emp. | 104 | 103 | 108 |

DUNS 23-873-3138

## Tuskerdirect Ltd

(Subsidiary of: Filia As)
3 George Street, Watford, Hertfordshire WD18 0YH
**Tel:** 08719955500 **Fax:** 08719955501
**Web:** www.tuskerdirect.com
**Reg No:** 3864648 **Estd:** 1999 Private Limited Company
**Line of Business:** Maintenance and repair of motor vehicles
**Issued Capital:** £780,443
**Directors:** Sir T E Chinn, S English, J A Lerner, D Hosking, M C Sinclair, I Carmichael, R P Toms
**Co. Secretary:** David Brockwell
**Responsibilities**
**Senior:** Matthew Rumbles (General Manager)
**US SIC:** 7539 **UK SIC:** 67100
**Auditors:** KPMG LLP

| | 31-12-13 | 31-12-12 | 31-12-11 |
|---|---|---|---|
| TO | 60,367,175 | 46,601,820 | 37,395,162 |
| P/L | 1,432,064 | 1,058,198 | 419,060 |
| NW | 4,633,406 | 3,585,316 | 1,854,103 |
| WC | 4,985,197 | 4,389,839 | 2,604,347 |
| Emp. | 75 | 54 | 40 |

DUNS 21-173-8137

## Tustain Motors Ltd

(Subsidiary of: J B Tustain Motors Holdings Ltd)
13 Freeman Way, North Seaton Industrial Estate, Ashington, Northumberland NE63 0YB
**Tel:** 01670813191
**Reg No:** 6976428 **Estd:** 2009 Private Limited Company
**Line of Business:** Sale of new motor vehicles
**Issued Capital:** £625,000
**Directors:** Motors Secretaries Limited, J B Tustain, D Storey, Motors Directors Limited, B W Baxter
**Co. Secretary:** David Storey
**US SIC:** 5511 **UK SIC:** 65100

| | 31-12-13 | 31-12-12 | 31-12-11 |
|---|---|---|---|
| TO | 29,379,114 | 22,937,155 | 19,774,176 |
| P/L | 446,920 | 152,422 | (30,547) |
| NW | 631,703 | 252,869 | 60,291 |
| WC | 849,126 | 1,094,191 | 1,066,076 |
| Emp. | 76 | 64 | 61 |

DUNS 21-726-5099     Imp-Exp

## Tuthill U.K. Ltd

(Subsidiary of: Tuthill Corporation)
Birkdale Close, Manners Industrial Estate, Ilkeston, Derbyshire DE7 8YA
**Tel:** 01159325226
**Web:** www.tuthill.com
**Reg No:** 0912417 **VAT No:** 190937339
**Estd:** 1897 Private Limited Company
**Line of Business:** Manufacture of pumps
**Export Markets:** E U
**Export Sales:** £3,789,000
**Trading Style:** Tuthill Controls, Tuthill Pump Group
**Issued Capital:** £250,000
**Directors:** J Lavingia, A Belmonte, T Carmazzi

---

**Co. Secretary:** Lemans
**Branches:** Tuthill U.k. Ltd, Berkdale Close, Manner Industrial Estate, Ilkeston, Derbyshire DE7 8YA
**US SIC:** 3561, 5065
**UK SIC:** 32870, 61500
**Auditors:** Grant Thornton UK LLP
**Bankers:** Barclays Bank Plc (20-27-91)

| | 31-12-13 | 31-12-12 | 31-12-11 |
|---|---|---|---|
| TO | 6,463,000 | 6,433,000 | 7,263,000 |
| P/L | (33,000) | 353,000 | 940,000 |
| NW | 5,844,000 | 5,828,000 | 5,501,000 |
| WC | 5,210,000 | 4,691,000 | 4,773,000 |
| Emp. | N/A | 45 | 43 |

DUNS 29-454-5496

## Tuttons Brasserie Ltd

(Subsidiary of: Cg Restaurants Holdings Ltd)
60 Doughty Street, London WC1N 2JT
**Tel:** 02078363375 **Fax:** 0171-379-9979
**Web:** www.tuttons.com
**Reg No:** 1683447 **Estd:** 1982 Private Limited Company
**Line of Business:** Licensed restaurants
**Issued Capital:** £123,463
**Directors:** D R Coffer, D A Coffer
**Co. Secretary:** Miss Jacqueline Wright
**Responsibilities**
**Senior:** Pedro Nunes (General Manager), Racquel Olicavera (Manager)
**US SIC:** 5812, 7000
**UK SIC:** 66110, 97913
**Auditors:** Goldblatts
**Bankers:** Barclays Bank Plc (20-65-82)

| | 31-12-13 | 31-12-12 | 31-12-11 |
|---|---|---|---|
| TO | 6,306,735 | 3,805,881 | 5,384,000 |
| P/L | 192,552 | (1,213,134) | 65,000 |
| NW | 4,735,368 | 4,542,816 | 2,386,000 |
| WC | (35,544) | (86,300) | 1,982,000 |
| Emp. | 88 | 75 | 83 |

DUNS 22-130-0291

## Tuv Sud Ltd

(Subsidiary of: Tüv Süd E.V.)
Scottish Enterprise Technology Park, Glasgow, Lanarkshire G75 0QF
**Tel:** 01355-220222
**Web:** www.tuvnel.com
**Reg No:** 0215164SC **Estd:** 2001 Private Limited Company
**Line of Business:** Engineers (consulting)
**Export Sales:** £12,478,000
**Issued Capital:** £500,000
**Directors:** P M Crystal, M Valente, H Schneider
**Co. Secretary:** William Mcknight
**Responsibilities**
**Senior:** David Herriot (Facilities Manager)
**Marketing:** Phil Mark (Sales and Marketing Director)
**Sales:** Phil Mark (Sales and Marketing Director)
**Facilities:** David Herriot (Facilities Manager)
**US SIC:** 8911, 1389
**UK SIC:** 83701, 13000
**Auditors:** Ernst & Young LLP
**Bankers:** National Westminster Bank Plc (52-41-32)

| | 31-12-13 | 31-12-12 | 31-12-11 |
|---|---|---|---|
| TO | 53,129,000 | 29,571,000 | 13,686,000 |
| P/L | 3,872,000 | 2,513,000 | 1,298,000 |
| NW | (12,832,000) | (15,377,000) | (9,440,000) |
| WC | 5,851,000 | 5,089,000 | 1,628,000 |
| Emp. | 508 | 304 | 167 |

DUNS 22-587-9493     Imp-Exp

## Tv One Ltd

(Subsidiary of: Barcom (Uk) Holdings Ltd)
Continental Approach, Margate, Kent CT9 4JG
**Web:** www.tvone.com
**Reg No:** 1973948 **VAT No:** 445178047
**Estd:** 1985 Private Limited Company
**Line of Business:** Computer software (development)
**Export Markets:** Germany; U S A; Sweden; Europe; Australia; Worldwide
**Export Sales:** £6,925,750
**Issued Capital:** £105
**Directors:** A C Hall, R L Bready, K W Donnelly, S E Mattingly
**Co. Secretary:** Kevin Donnelly
**Responsibilities**
**Finance:** L Mallery Collins (Financial Manager)
**HR:** Amanda Holges (Head Human Resources)
**Operations:** Dana Weaver (Product Manager)
**Branches:** Vine Farm, Marshborough, Sandwich
**US SIC:** 7379, 3573
**UK SIC:** 83940, 33020
**Auditors:** Spain Brothers & Co
**Bankers:** Barclays Bank Plc (20-17-92)

| | 31-12-13 | 31-12-12 | 31-12-11 |
|---|---|---|---|
| TO | 7,610,714 | 6,853,092 | N/A |
| P/L | (259,849) | 580,519 | N/A |
| NW | 2,972,440 | 3,947,046 | 3,481,896 |
| WC | 2,105,576 | 2,972,006 | 2,684,037 |
| Emp. | 68 | 47 | N/A |

DUNS 23-982-4766 Exp
## Tvedt Group Ltd
Silvertree, Coxbridge Business Park, Farnham, Surrey GU10 5EH
**Web:** www.tvedt.co.uk
**Reg No:** 2340495 **VAT No:** 572516242
**Estd:** 1987 Private Limited Company
**Line of Business:** Management activities of holding companies
**Export Markets:** Worldwide
**Export Sales:** £520,906
**Issued Capital:** £105,100
**Chairman and Managing Director:** G Tvedt
**Co. Secretary:** Mackee Management Services Limit
**Responsibilities**
**Finance:** G MacKee *(Financial Director)*
**Marketing:** J Veitch *(Sales & Marketing Manager)*
**Sales:** J Veitch *(Sales & Marketing Manager)*
**Engineering:** C Crookes *(Production Manager)*
**US SIC:** 6711, 7399
**UK SIC:** 83962, 83954
**Auditors:** Wise & Co
**Bankers:** National Westminster Bank Plc (60-01-08)

| | 31-12-13 | 31-12-12 | 31-12-11 |
|---|---|---|---|
| TO | 12,577,078 | 14,089,554 | 13,163,110 |
| P/L | 209,222 | 377,307 | (526,751) |
| NW | 5,713,823 | 5,667,227 | 5,374,520 |
| WC | 2,621,974 | 2,742,133 | 2,427,591 |
| Emp. | 70 | 54 | 59 |

DUNS 21-179-7918
## Tvm Fashion Lab Ltd
Icon Business Centre, Lake View Drive, Nottingham, Nottinghamshire NG15 0DT
**Tel:** 020 7706 6357
**Web:** www.fashion-lab.co.uk
**Reg No:** 7022432 **Estd:** 2009 Private Limited Company
**Line of Business:** Wholesale of clothing not elsewhere classified
**Export Sales:** £2,274,000
**Issued Capital:** £20
**Directors:** D P Famulak, R K Smits
**Co. Secretary:** Ms Alice Wishart
**US SIC:** 5199, 2328
**UK SIC:** 61900, 45340
**Auditors:** PricewaterhouseCoopers LLP

| | 31-12-13 | 31-12-12 | 31-12-11 |
|---|---|---|---|
| TO | 34,548,000 | 30,194,000 | N/A |
| P/L | 3,012,000 | 2,474,000 | N/A |
| NW | 128,000 | 1,058,000 | 252,218 |
| WC | 13,000 | 1,004,000 | 206,187 |
| Emp. | 65 | 51 | N/A |

DUNS 21-177-3868
## Tvs Logistics Investment Uk Ltd
**(Subsidiary of:** T.V. Sundram Iyengar & Sons Limited)
Logistics House Buckshaw Avenue, Chorley, Lancashire PR6 7AJ
**Tel:** 01257270456
**Web:** www.multipart-parts.com
**Reg No:** 7003943 **Estd:** 2009 Private Limited Company
**Line of Business:** Management activities of other non-financial holding companies not elsewhere classified
**Export Sales:** £22,649,000
**Issued Capital:** £7,601,000
**Directors:** R Sargunaraj, P J Roberts, D Ramachandran, A Jayaraman
**Co. Secretary:** Paul Roberts
**US SIC:** 6711 **UK SIC:** 83962
**Auditors:** KPMG LLP
**Bankers:** State Bank Of India (60-01-59)

| | 31-03-14 | 31-03-13 | 31-03-12 |
|---|---|---|---|
| TO | 165,669,000 | 110,905,000 | 68,458,000 |
| P/L | 3,771,000 | 3,492,000 | 1,268,000 |
| NW | 6,777,000 | 4,575,000 | 7,130,000 |
| WC | 14,568,000 | 14,363,000 | (621,000) |
| Emp. | 919 | 441 | 267 |

DUNS 23-078-1502
## Tvs Supply Chain Solutions Ltd
**(Subsidiary of:** T.V. Sundram Iyengar & Sons Limited)
Logistics House, Buckshaw Avenue, Chorley, Lancashire PR6 7AJ
**Tel:** 01257-265-531 **Fax:** 01257232872
**Web:** www.tvsscs.com
**Reg No:** 2748952 **VAT No:** 927288293
**Estd:** 1993 Private Limited Company
**Line of Business:** Freight services
**Export Sales:** £6,976,000
**Trading Style:** Tvs Supply Chain Solutions
**Issued Capital:** £2
**Directors:** A Jones, R Sargunaraj, D Ramachandran
**Co. Secretary:** Paul Roberts
**Responsibilities**
**Senior:** Siobhan Campbell *(Marketing Manager)*, Richard Slee *(Manager)*
**Marketing:** Siobhan Campbell *(Marketing Manager)*
**Sales:** Brian Hewer *(Defence Business Development &)*, Martin Warrington *(Business Development Director)*
**IT:** Keith Dewhurst *(Senior IT manager)*
**Facilities:** Ian Bushrod *(Maintenance Manager)*
**Operations:** Brendan Leach *(Operations and Business Soluti)*
**Branches:** Tvs Supply Chain Solutions Ltd, Multipart, Logistics Ho, Eldon Way Indstl Est, Crick, Northampton, Northamptonshire NN6 7SL
**US SIC:** 5531, 4226
**UK SIC:** 65100, 77003
**Auditors:** KPMG LLP
**Bankers:** Barclays Bank Plc (20-13-42)

| | 31-03-14 | 31-03-13 | 31-03-12 |
|---|---|---|---|
| TO | 92,987,000 | 82,119,000 | 66,326,000 |
| P/L | 670,000 | 1,939,000 | 1,100,000 |
| NW | 26,200,000 | 26,020,000 | 24,525,000 |
| WC | 17,552,000 | 17,400,000 | 16,753,000 |
| Emp. | 302 | 296 | 246 |

DUNS 21-686-7911 Imp-Exp
## Tw Metals Ltd
**(Subsidiary of:** o'Neal Industries Inc)
Unit 43, Southampton, Hampshire SO16 0AF
**Tel:** 023 8073 9333 **Fax:** 023 8073 9601
**Web:** www.twmetals.com
**Reg No:** 0961098 **VAT No:** 188284616
**Estd:** 1963 Private Limited Company
**Line of Business:** Steel stockholders
**Export Markets:** E U, The Middle East, North America, Africa
**Export Sales:** £77,982,000
**Issued Capital:** £290,168
**Directors:** H Craft O'Neal, Ms G L Thomas, J H Elrod Iii
**Co. Secretary:** Michael Rowland
**Responsibilities**
**Senior:** Louise Brown *(Accountant)*, Henry Craft O' Neal *(Director)*, Mary Valenta *(Chief Executive)*
**Finance:** Louise Brown *(Accountant)*
**US SIC:** 5051 **UK SIC:** 61200
**Auditors:** PricewaterhouseCoopers LLP
**Bankers:** Lloyds TSB Bank plc (30-97-80)

| | 31-12-13 | 31-12-12 | 31-12-11 |
|---|---|---|---|
| TO | 106,910,000 | 62,641,000 | 57,473,000 |
| P/L | 4,171,000 | 3,557,000 | 4,607,000 |
| NW | 27,295,000 | 24,099,000 | 21,307,000 |
| WC | 26,356,000 | 22,762,000 | 21,449,000 |
| Emp. | 220 | 175 | 159 |

DUNS 21-746-2845
## T.W. White & Sons (Holdings) Ltd
242 Lower Road, Leatherhead, Surrey KT23 4DE
**Tel:** 01483426424 **Fax:** 01483-426018
**Web:** www.twwhiteandsons.co.uk
**Reg No:** 1280477 **VAT No:** 296067034
**Estd:** 1962 Private Limited Company
**Line of Business:** Activities of other membership organisations not elsewhere classified
**Trading Style:** Guildford Masda
**Issued Capital:** £7,500
**Principals:** T W White *(Chairman)*, N P White *(Managing)*
**Co. Secretary:** Miss Kirsty White
**Branches:** T.w. White & Sons (Holdings) Ltd, 19 Wintersells Road, West Byfleet, Surrey KT14 7LF
**US SIC:** 6711, 7539
**UK SIC:** 83962, 67100
**Auditors:** Baker Tilly
**Bankers:** Lloyds TSB Bank plc (30-93-49)

| | 30-04-14 | 30-04-13 | 30-04-12 |
|---|---|---|---|
| TO | 29,901,091 | 25,690,114 | 21,828,768 |
| P/L | 129,716 | 207,241 | (553,615) |
| NW | 2,456,746 | 2,168,401 | 1,965,044 |
| WC | (580,080) | (185,035) | (347,439) |
| Emp. | 89 | 93 | 94 |

DUNS 21-729-9551
## T.W. White & Sons Ltd
**(Subsidiary of:** T.W. White & Sons (Holdings) Ltd)
242 Lower Road, Bookham, Leatherhead, Surrey KT23 4DE
**Tel:** 01372452701
**Web:** www.twwhiteandsons.co.uk
**Reg No:** 0997024 **VAT No:** 209592841
**Estd:** 1970 Private Limited Company
**Line of Business:** New & used motor vehicle dealers
**Issued Capital:** £66,000
**Principals:** T W White *(Chairman)*, N P White *(Managing)*
**Co. Secretary:** Miss Kirsty White
**Branches:** T.w. White & Sons Ltd, 7 Wintersells Road, West Byfleet, Surrey KT14 7LF
**US SIC:** 5511, 5521, 7539, 5531
**UK SIC:** 65100, 67100
**Auditors:** Baker Tilly
**Bankers:** Lloyds TSB Bank plc (30-93-49)

| | 30-04-14 | 30-04-13 | 30-04-12 |
|---|---|---|---|
| TO | 29,901,091 | 25,690,114 | 21,828,768 |
| P/L | 129,716 | 207,241 | (553,615) |
| NW | 1,584,047 | 1,295,702 | 1,092,345 |
| WC | (580,082) | (185,037) | (347,441) |
| Emp. | 89 | 93 | 94 |

DUNS 42-330-1717
## Tweed Enterprises Ltd
Unit 8 Greencroft Industrial Estate, Stanley, County Durham DH9 7XP
**Tel:** 01207-529901 **Fax:** 01207529902
**Web:** www.tweed-enterprises.co.uk
**Reg No:** 4317943 **Estd:** 2001 Private Limited Company
**Line of Business:** Activities of other transport agencies
**Issued Capital:** £49,600
**Director:** Mrs B Welch
**Co. Secretary:** Ms Helen Harsh
**Responsibilities**
**Senior:** Dave Welch *(Manager)*
**US SIC:** 5199 **UK SIC:** 61900

| | 31-03-14 | 31-03-13 | 31-03-12 |
|---|---|---|---|
| TA | 206,317 | 135,418 | 173,012 |
| NW | 83,833 | 24,315 | 101,279 |
| WC | 94,613 | 29,422 | 87,649 |

DUNS 21-784-2840
## Tweeddale Primary School
Tweeddale Road, Carshalton, Surrey SM5 1SW
**Tel:** 02086445665
**Web:** www.tweeddaleprimary.sutton.sch.uk
**Estd:** 1998 Proprietorship
**Line of Business:** Schools (local authority)
**Proprietor:** Mrs M Smith
**Responsibilities**
**Senior:** Michael Lovett *(Head Teacher)*
**US SIC:** 8211 **UK SIC:** 93200
**Employees:** 60

DUNS 56-940-5780
## Tweedmill Factory Shopping Ltd
**(Subsidiary of:** Ddfi Ltd)
Llannerch Park, St Asaph, Clwyd LL17 0UY
**Tel:** 01745-730072
**Web:** www.tweedmill.co.uk
**Reg No:** 2840101 **Estd:** 1993 Private Limited Company
**Line of Business:** Other retail sale in non-specialised stores
**Issued Capital:** £666
**Directors:** R J Booth, Ms L G Johns, J C Salisbury
**Co. Secretary:** Russell Booth
**US SIC:** 5399, 5699, 5812
**UK SIC:** 65600, 64500, 66110
**Auditors:** Royce Peeling Green

| | 28-02-14 | 28-02-13 | 29-02-12 |
|---|---|---|---|
| TO | 2,193,831 | 2,212,081 | 2,230,781 |
| P/L | 59,144 | 114,227 | (17,390) |
| NW | 3,229,603 | 3,446,107 | 3,371,925 |
| WC | (2,424,046) | (775,577) | (574,860) |
| Emp. | 74 | 73 | 72 |

DUNS 21-929-4272
## Tweendykes School
Tweendykes School, Midmere Learning Village, Midmer, Hull, North Humberside HU7 4PW
**Tel:** 01482826508
**Reg No:** 8432506 **Estd:** 2013 Private Company Limited By Guarantee
**Line of Business:** Adult and other education not elsewhere classified
**Directors:** M Pinchbeck, J R Barnes, G A Gibbons, D R Ellis, Mrs E C Clark, M Bateman, Ms K E Goncalves, Ms K A Oliver
**Co. Secretary:** Ms Julie Clark
**Responsibilities**
**Senior:** Patricia Baggaley *(Director)*, Lesley Kemp *(Director)*
**US SIC:** 8299 **UK SIC:** 93300
**Bankers:** Barclays Bank Plc (20-43-47)

| | 31-08-13 |
|---|---|
| TA | 597,872 |
| P/L | (1,304,140) |
| NW | (1,151,140) |
| WC | 177,883 |
| Emp. | 61 |

DUNS 21-409-6488
## Twelves Company
2 Providence Road, West Drayton, Middlesex UB7 8HJ
**Tel:** 01895-445757
**Estd:** 2010 Proprietorship
**Line of Business:** Community networks
**Proprietor:** M Evans
**Responsibilities**
**Senior:** Mandy Pidgeon *(Manager)*, Barry Weir *(Partner)*
**US SIC:** 8699 **UK SIC:** 96902
**Employees:** 80

DUNS 28-841-6126 Exp
## Twentieth Century-Fox Film Co (Export) Ltd
**(Subsidiary of:** Twentieth Century-Fox Film Company Ltd)
31-32 Soho Square, London W1D 3AP
**Tel:** 02074377766
**Reg No:** 0550516 **Estd:** 1955 Private Limited Company
**Line of Business:** Motion picture and video distribution
**Export Sales:** £5,836,834
**Trading Style:** Twentieth Century Fox Film Co Ltd
**Issued Capital:** £2
**Directors:** M Doodan, Ms S A Atkin, P L Higginson
**Co. Secretary:** Bsp Secretarial Limited
**Responsibilities**
**Senior:** Ian Collins *(Finance Director)*
**Finance:** Ian Collins *(Finance Director)*
**US SIC:** 7829 **UK SIC:** 97112
**Auditors:** Arthur Andersen

| | 30-06-14 | 30-06-13 | 30-06-12 |
|---|---|---|---|
| TO | 5,836,834 | 8,217,603 | 5,754,161 |
| P/L | 265,562 | 719,785 | 1,135,385 |
| NW | 4,115,179 | 4,031,500 | 3,537,646 |
| WC | 4,115,179 | 4,031,496 | 3,537,642 |

DUNS 29-445-8922 Exp
## Twentieth Century Fox Home Entertainment Ltd
**(Subsidiary of:** Twenty-First Century Fox Inc.)
31-32 Soho Square, London W1D 3AP
**Tel:** 02077538686 **Fax:** 020-7434-2170
**Web:** www.fox.co.uk
**Reg No:** 1633880 **Estd:** 1982 Private Limited Company
**Line of Business:** Motion picture and video distribution
**Export Sales:** £4,289,000
**Issued Capital:** £100
**Directors:** M J Dunn, R S Price, K R Feldman
**Co. Secretary:** Ms Radhika Radhakrishnan
**Responsibilities**
**Senior:** Radhika krishnan *(Manager)*
**US SIC:** 7829 **UK SIC:** 97112
**Auditors:** Ernst & Young LLP
**Bankers:** Lloyds TSB Bank plc (30-92-82)

| | 31-05-14 | 31-05-13 | 31-05-12 |
|---|---|---|---|
| TO | 112,024,000 | 155,010,000 | 137,395,000 |
| P/L | 3,068,000 | 4,298,000 | 3,488,000 |
| NW | 12,668,000 | 10,334,000 | 37,652,000 |
| WC | 12,666,000 | 10,330,000 | 37,148,000 |
| Emp. | 89 | 88 | 87 |

DUNS 22-082-0000
## Twenty Four Seven Recruitment Services Ltd
Oakwood House, Ash Road South Wrexham Industrial Estate, Wrexham, Clwyd LL13 9UG
**Tel:** 01978-664195 **Fax:** 01978-661065
**Web:** www.24-7recruitment.net
**Reg No:** 4083397 **Estd:** 2006 Private Limited Company
**Line of Business:** Employment and recruitment companies and consultants
**Issued Capital:** £34
**Directors:** C J Webley, J C Williams
**Responsibilities**
**Senior:** Gary Cottom *(Financial Director)*, Emma Fisher *(Manager)*, Marlene Willetts *(Manager)*, Fred Willetts *(Manager)*, Sam Wood *(Manager)*
**Branches:** Twenty Four Seven Recruitment Services Ltd, Nursling Industrial Estate, Canberra Road, Nursling, Southampton, Hampshire SO16 0WB
**US SIC:** 7361 **UK SIC:** 83954
**Auditors:** Guy Walmsley & Co
**Bankers:** HSBC Bank plc (40-29-08)

| | 31-03-14 | 31-03-13 | 31-03-12 |
|---|---|---|---|
| TO | 93,651,991 | 75,027,469 | 55,346,943 |
| P/L | 67,414 | 70,702 | 72,833 |
| NW | 111,848 | (241,780) | (183,876) |
| WC | (543,330) | (884,187) | (747,628) |
| Emp. | 3,016 | 3,601 | 2,999 |

DUNS 29-294-4774 Imp-Exp
## Twenty Ten Properties Ltd
Salter Road, Eastfield, Scarborough, North Yorkshire YO11 3UP
**Tel:** 01723-584091
**Web:** www.duraweld.co.uk
**Reg No:** 1647624 **Estd:** 1984 Private Limited Company
**Line of Business:** Other letting of own property
**Export Markets:** Ireland
**Issued Capital:** £11,000
**Principals:** R M Senior *(Chairman)*, Mrs H Yeung, Miss P Senior, Miss S Senior, Mrs K Robinson, Mrs J Senior
**Responsibilities**
**Senior:** Lee Embleton *(Warehouse Officer)*, Hannah Senior *(Manager)*
**Sales:** Hannah Senior *(Manager)*
**Admin:** Terry Cooke *(Design Manager)*

**HR:** Terry Cooke *(Design Manager)*
**Health & Safety:** Hannah Senior *(Manager)*
**Operations:** Terry Cooke *(Design Manager)*
**Engineering:** Jamie Swan *(Production Manager)*
**Branches:** Twenty Ten Properties Ltd, 3 Walkers Way, Peterborough, Cambridgeshire PE3 9AX
**US SIC:** 6519, 3079
**UK SIC:** 85000, 48360
**Auditors:** Moore Stephens
**Bankers:** National Westminster Bank Plc (54-41-24)

| | 30-06-14 | 30-06-13 | 30-06-12 |
|---|---|---|---|
| TA | 1,814,980 | 2,035,897 | 1,999,982 |
| NW | 1,705,351 | 1,965,390 | 1,958,585 |
| WC | 351,143 | 661,840 | 858,505 |

DUNS 45-825-3960

## Twentysix Ltd

**(Subsidiary of:** Msq Partners Group Ltd)
183 Eversholt Street, London NW1 1BU
**Tel:** 0207 909 0470
**Web:** www.twentysixdigital.com
**Reg No:** 3178478 **Estd:** 1996 Private Limited Company
**Line of Business:** Sale or leasing activities of advertising space or time
**Export Sales:** £2,200,000
**Issued Capital:** £100
**Directors:** D Yardley, Ms G Dudleston, P D Reid
**Co. Secretary:** Ashish Shah
**US SIC:** 7319 **UK SIC:** 83800
**Auditors:** Grant Thornton UK LLP
**Bankers:** Halifax Plc (11-07-42)

| | 28-02-14 | 28-02-13 | 29-02-12 |
|---|---|---|---|
| TO | 8,774,000 | 6,831,000 | 5,697,000 |
| P/L | 798,000 | 525,000 | 612,000 |
| NW | 1,703,000 | 898,000 | 467,000 |
| WC | 1,591,000 | 720,000 | 1,003,000 |
| Emp. | 109 | 99 | 90 |

DUNS 29-520-3715 **Imp-Exp**

## Twg Services Ltd

**(Subsidiary of:** The Warranty Group Inc)
2 Floor, Aspen Building, Vantage Point Business Village, Mitcheldean, Gloucestershire GL17 0AF
**Tel:** 01594863000 **Fax:** 08448-718271
**Web:** www.uk.thewarrantygroup.com
**Reg No:** 1883565 **VAT No:** 896118291
**Estd:** 1985 Private Limited Company
**Line of Business:** Insurance agents, brokers & services
**Export Markets:** E U
**Export Sales:** £4,560,000
**Trading Style:** Twg Services
**Issued Capital:** £10,300,000
**Directors:** D I Vickers, J M Kelly, R C Powell, Miss E J Owen
**Co. Secretary:** David Owen
**Responsibilities**
**Senior:** Desmond Miller *(Manager)*
**US SIC:** 6411, 7399
**UK SIC:** 83200, 83954
**Auditors:** Ernst & Young LLP
**Bankers:** National Westminster Bank Plc (60-30-06)

| | 31-12-13 | 31-12-12 | 31-12-11 |
|---|---|---|---|
| TO | 26,537,000 | 26,401,000 | 23,788,000 |
| P/L | (1,794,000) | 1,460,000 | (1,589,000) |
| NW | 3,301,000 | 3,794,000 | 735,000 |
| WC | 7,597,000 | 8,013,000 | 1,790,000 |
| Emp. | 434 | 405 | 404 |

DUNS 23-630-2519

## Twichen Musters & Kelly

County Chambers, 25-27 Weston Road, Southend-On-Sea, Essex SS1 1BB
**Tel:** 01702339222
**Web:** www.tmksols.co.uk
**Partnership**
**Line of Business:** Solicitors.
**Partners:** P Kelly, J K Twichen, P Musters
**Branches:** Twichen Musters & Kelly, Suite 15, Eastgate Business Centre, Southernhay, Basildon, Essex SS14 1EB
**US SIC:** 8111 **UK SIC:** 83500
**Employees:** 60

DUNS 21-624-3063 **Exp**

## Twickenham Plating Group Ltd

**(Subsidiary of:** Twickenham Plating Ltd)
12-13 Balena Close, Poole, Dorset BH17 7DB
**Tel:** 01202-692416
**Web:** www.twickenham.co.uk
**Reg No:** 0436536 **Estd:** 1939 Private Limited Company
**Line of Business:** Metal finishing and polishing services
**Export Markets:** Germany, Malaysia and Manilla.
**Issued Capital:** £8,092
**Principals:** J W Hill *(Chairman)*, R S Dearing *(Financial)*, J J Hill, D J Hill
**Responsibilities**
**IT:** Melvin Hector *(Technical Manager)*
**HR:** Justine Le Marinel *(Support Manager)*
**Operations:** Justine Le Marinel *(Support Manager)*
**Purchasing:** Justine Le Marinel *(Support Manager)*
**US SIC:** 3499, 3398
**UK SIC:** 31694, 31380
**Auditors:** Carter Backer Winter LLP
**Bankers:** HSBC Bank plc (40-22-26)

| | 31-12-13 | 31-12-12 | 31-12-11 |
|---|---|---|---|
| TA | 2,547,161 | 2,357,795 | 2,098,301 |
| NW | 2,165,797 | 1,890,407 | 1,539,561 |
| WC | 1,980,704 | 1,687,379 | 1,339,701 |

DUNS 23-869-9743

## Twickenham Plating Trustees Ltd

**(Subsidiary of:** Twickenham Plating Ltd)
7-9 Edwin Road, Twickenham, Middlesex TW1 4JJ
**Tel:** 02087449389
**Web:** www.twickenham.co.uk
**Reg No:** 3861385 **Estd:** 1999 Private Limited Company
**Line of Business:** Treatment and coating of metals
**Issued Capital:** £100
**Directors:** J J Hill, D J Hill, J W Hill
**Co. Secretary:** Robert Dearing
**US SIC:** 3398 **UK SIC:** 31380

| | 31-12-13 | 31-12-12 | 31-12-11 |
|---|---|---|---|
| TA | 99 | 99 | 99 |
| NW | 99 | 99 | 99 |

DUNS 21-710-7814

## Twickler Industries Ltd

Pressurefab House Baird Avenue, Dryburgh Industrial Estate, Dundee, Angus DD2 3TN
**Tel:** 01382642223
**Reg No:** 0392520SC **Estd:** 2011 Private Limited Company
**Line of Business:** Management activities of holding companies
**Issued Capital:** £100
**Director:** H Twickler
**US SIC:** 6711 **UK SIC:** 83962
**Bankers:** Bank Of Scotland (80-73-31)

| | 31-01-14 | 31-01-13 | 31-01-12 |
|---|---|---|---|
| TO | 5,335,366 | 5,688,744 | 2,547,519 |
| P/L | 918,475 | 991,624 | 473,690 |
| NW | 1,654,543 | 1,120,196 | 398,309 |
| WC | 885,630 | 794,313 | 169,544 |

DUNS 21-632-9300 **Imp-Exp**

## Twiflex Ltd

**(Subsidiary of:** Altra Industrial Motion Corp.)
Briar Road, Twickenham, Middlesex TW2 5AQ
**Tel:** 020-8894-1161 **Fax:** 020-8894-6056
**Web:** www.twiflex.com
**Reg No:** 0404531 **VAT No:** 422481375
**Estd:** 1946 Private Limited Company
**Line of Business:** Manufacturers of brakes and clutches
**Export Markets:** E U; S Africa; U.S.A.
**Export Sales:** £14,018,000
**Issued Capital:** £100
**Directors:** C R Christenson, C Storch
**Co. Secretary:** Richard Laws
**Responsibilities**
**Senior:** Richard Playford *(Financial Director)*
**Finance:** Richard Playford *(Financial Director)*
**IT:** Richard Playford *(Financial Director)*
**US SIC:** 3568 **UK SIC:** 32613
**Auditors:** BDO LLP
**Bankers:** Barclays Bank Plc (20-00-00)

| | 31-12-13 | 31-12-12 | 31-12-11 |
|---|---|---|---|
| TO | 16,350,000 | 15,642,000 | 13,954,000 |
| P/L | 5,022,000 | 4,455,000 | 2,928,000 |
| NW | 6,946,000 | 3,067,000 | 6,300,000 |
| WC | 5,855,000 | 1,978,000 | 7,612,000 |
| Emp. | 70 | 71 | 68 |

DUNS 34-601-8935

## Twilight Years Ltd

114 Rawlinson Street, Barrow-In-Furness, Cumbria LA14 2DG
**Tel:** 01229-835200
**Web:** www.twilighthomecare.co.uk
**Reg No:** 5409029 **Estd:** 2007 Private Limited Company
**Line of Business:** Activities of households as employers of domestic staff
**Issued Capital:** £100
**Director:** Ms M E Geldart
**Co. Secretary:** Michael Keay
**US SIC:** 8811 **UK SIC:** 99000
**Bankers:** Barclays Bank Plc (20-26-20)

| | 31-03-14 | 31-03-13 | 31-03-12 |
|---|---|---|---|
| TA | 768,250 | 613,550 | 695,720 |
| NW | 502,282 | 528,845 | 549,394 |
| WC | 501,116 | 526,811 | 545,275 |

DUNS 21-208-3211

## Twin Oaks Nursing Home

1 Hudson Way, Norwich, Norfolk NR5 9NJ
**Tel:** 01603743195
**Web:** www.twinoaksnursinghome.co.uk
**Estd:** 1995 Proprietorship
**Line of Business:** Nursing homes
**Proprietor:** Mrs R J Francis
**Responsibilities**
**Senior:** Susan Nolan *(Financial Director)*, Richard Nolan *(Administrator)*
**Finance:** Susan Nolan *(Financial Director)*
**Marketing:** Richard Nolan *(Administrator)*
**Admin:** Richard Nolan *(Administrator)*
**IT:** Richard Nolan *(Administrator)*
**HR:** Susan Nolan *(Financial Director)*, Richard Nolan *(Administrator)*
**Health & Safety:** Richard Nolan *(Administrator)*
**Facilities:** Richard Nolan *(Administrator)*
**Operations:** Susan Nolan *(Financial Director)*
**Purchasing:** Susan Nolan *(Financial Director)*
**Branches:** Twin Oaks Nursing Home, 12 Candlers Lane, Harleston, Norfolk IP20 9JA
**US SIC:** 8051 **UK SIC:** 95100
**Bankers:** Barclays Bank Plc (20-92-08)
**Employees:** 70

DUNS 49-249-8175

## Twin Training International Ltd

Tower House, London SE13 5JX
**Tel:** 02082971132
**Web:** www.twinuk.com
**Reg No:** 3118260 **VAT No:** 892215026
**Estd:** 1995 Private Limited Company
**Line of Business:** Sub-degree level higher education
**Trading Style:** Twin Group
**Issued Capital:** £100
**Director:** Ms C M Fox
**Co. Secretary:** Ms Jacqueline Fox
**Responsibilities**
**Senior:** Joanne Sayer *(Manager)*
**US SIC:** 8221 **UK SIC:** 93100
**Auditors:** Arram Berlyn Gardner
**Bankers:** HSBC Bank plc (40-04-15)

| | 31-12-13 | 31-12-12 | 31-12-11 |
|---|---|---|---|
| TO | 12,783,628 | 14,618,254 | 11,465,013 |
| P/L | 13,469 | 65,564 | (339,995) |
| NW | (850,483) | (616,607) | (580,345) |
| WC | 36,627 | (938,045) | (647,261) |
| Emp. | 79 | 172 | 136 |

DUNS 21-597-8658

## Twin Valley Homes

Prospect House, Wharf Street, Blackburn, Lancashire BB1 1JD
**Tel:** 03005555560
**Web:** www.twinvalleyhomes.com
**Estd:** 2001
**Line of Business:** Other human health activities
**Responsibilities**
**Sales:** Glen Finch *(Head of Regeneration)*
**US SIC:** 8091 **UK SIC:** 95200
**Employees:** 300

DUNS 50-483-4425 **Exp**

## Twinfix Ltd

201 Cavendish Place, Warrington, Cheshire WA3 6WU
**Tel:** 01925811311
**Web:** www.twinfix.co.uk
**Reg No:** 2457221 **VAT No:** 528347530
**Estd:** 1990 Private Limited Company
**Line of Business:** Roofing materials and related products
**Export Markets:** Europe; Scandinavia; Middle East
**Trading Style:** Twinfix
**Issued Capital:** £10,000
**Directors:** M R Fleet, S Western, Mrs V Evans, D A Smith, Mrs S G Kench, P Greenfield
**Responsibilities**
**Senior:** Susan Judd *(Manager)*, Graham Kench *(Manager)*
**US SIC:** 3271, 5039
**UK SIC:** 24370, 61300
**Auditors:** Styles & Co Accountants Ltd
**Bankers:** Barclays Bank Plc (20-24-09)

| | 31-12-13 | 31-12-12 | 31-12-11 |
|---|---|---|---|
| TA | 1,265,372 | 1,460,574 | 1,422,636 |
| NW | 337,150 | 319,779 | 340,429 |
| WC | 207,199 | 191,271 | 191,796 |

DUNS 21-580-2297

## Twinglobe

481 Lea Bridge Road, London E10 7EB
**Tel:** 02085589579
**Web:** www.twinglobe.com
**Estd:** 2004 Partnership
**Line of Business:** Social work activities with accommodation
**Partners:** Ms J Burton, Mrs R Gummer
**Responsibilities**
**Senior:** Wendy Pike *(Home Manager)*, Jade Shea *(Manager)*
**US SIC:** 8321 **UK SIC:** 96111
**Employees:** 100

DUNS 21-691-2345 **Imp**

## Twinmar Ltd

12-14 Maxted Road, Hemel Hempstead, Hertfordshire HP2 7DX
**Tel:** 01442-241431
**Web:** www.soletrader.co.uk
**Reg No:** 0763926 **Estd:** 1963 Private Limited Company
**Line of Business:** Representative office
**Trading Style:** Sole Trader, Soled Out
**Issued Capital:** £3
**Principals:** S Bordon *(Chairman)*, M Bordon
**Co. Secretary:** Mrs Lilly Bordon
**Responsibilities**
**Marketing:** Emma Powell *(Marketing Manager)*
**HR:** Helen Tout *(Personnel Manager)*
**Purchasing:** Derrick Hoyle *(Buyer)*
**Branches:** Twinmar Ltd, 129B North End, Croydon, Surrey CR0 1TL
**US SIC:** 5661 **UK SIC:** 64600
**Auditors:** Landau Morley LLP
**Bankers:** Lloyds TSB Bank plc (30-00-08)

| | 29-06-13 | 30-06-12 | 25-06-11 |
|---|---|---|---|
| TO | 37,031,787 | 34,542,044 | 33,465,273 |
| P/L | 1,258,779 | 1,031,123 | 1,725,593 |
| NW | 22,400,941 | 21,981,998 | 21,751,535 |
| WC | 22,387,633 | 22,174,238 | 21,950,106 |
| Emp. | 306 | 295 | 288 |

DUNS 23-510-9332

## Twintec Ltd

**(Subsidiary of:** Twintec International Sa)
1 Valley Drive Prospect Park, Rugby, Warwickshire CV21 1TF
**Tel:** 01788-567722
**Web:** www.twintec.co.uk
**Reg No:** 3510165 **Estd:** 2008 Private Limited Company
**Line of Business:** Agents involved in the sale of timber and building materials
**Export Sales:** £3,834,538
**Issued Capital:** £1,052,693
**Directors:** B Lazzari, J Lazzari, B Perpete, B O Gendebien, A L Cantarella
**Co. Secretary:** Gordon Wilson
**Responsibilities**
**Finance:** Mark Ezzat *(Managing Accountant)*, Lynn Griffiths *(Accounts Administrator)*
**Operations:** Alan Dobbins *(Operations Manager)*, Janet Higgs *(Production Administrator)*, Rory Lancaster *(Operations Manager)*
**Fleet:** Andy Wakeford *(Transport and Logistic Manager)*
**US SIC:** 5072, 1799
**UK SIC:** 61500, 50000
**Auditors:** WPA Audit Ltd
**Bankers:** National Westminster Bank Plc (54-41-00)

| | 31-12-13 | 31-12-12 | 31-12-11 |
|---|---|---|---|
| TO | 15,104,055 | 23,596,514 | 18,332,923 |
| P/L | (931,495) | (490,264) | (392,627) |
| NW | 1,383,071 | 2,141,048 | 1,109,672 |
| WC | 1,014,080 | 1,933,832 | 1,643,403 |
| Emp. | 55 | 68 | 73 |

DUNS 23-972-5224

## Twma Group Ltd

Broadfold House, Aberdeen, Aberdeenshire AB23 8EE
**Tel:** 01224-222520 **Fax:** 01224222589
**Web:** www.twma.co.uk
**Reg No:** 0205718SC **Estd:** 2000 Private Limited Company
**Line of Business:** Environmental consultants
**Export Sales:** £20,630,476
**Trading Style:** Total Waste Management Alliance
**Issued Capital:** £4,091,275
**Directors:** M W Press, R L Garrick, R A Willings
**Co. Secretary:** Douglas Garrick
**Responsibilities**
**Senior:** David Garrick *(Manager)*, Alister Kirkness *(Manager)*
**US SIC:** 6711, 4953
**UK SIC:** 83962, 92110
**Auditors:** Anderson Anderson & Brown LLP
**Bankers:** The Royal Bank Of Scotland Plc (83-15-31)

| | 31-12-13 | 31-12-12 | 31-12-11 |
|---|---|---|---|
| TO | 35,487,937 | 30,008,420 | 36,533,883 |
| P/L | (2,750,989) | (870,109) | 5,424,743 |
| NW | 3,218,437 | 5,300,649 | 6,167,199 |
| WC | (4,290,764) | (748,423) | 2,599,821 |
| Emp. | 333 | 311 | 288 |

DUNS 22-811-5929

## Two Castles Housing Association Ltd

3 Paternoster Row, Carlisle, Cumbria CA3 8TT
**Web:** www.twocastles.org.uk
**Reg No:** 0017663IP **Estd:** 1985 Friendly Society
**Line of Business:** Housing associations societies trusts & co-operatives

**Directors:** E J Slee, L Stobbs, M Young, D Thompson, M Mcintyre, T W Swan, A Toal, E Gray
**Responsibilities**
**Senior:** Fraser Clark *(Manager)*, Dorothy Dalton *(Manager)*, Stephanie Murphy *(Chief Executive)*, Hedley Whitehead *(Director)*
**Facilities:** Dave Armstrong *(Housing Services Director)*
**US SIC:** 8321 **UK SIC:** 96111
**Auditors:** Beever & Struthers
**Bankers:** Barclays Bank Plc (20-18-47)

| | 31-03-12 | 31-03-11 | 31-03-10 |
|---|---|---|---|
| TO | 12,372,000 | 12,296,000 | 11,853,000 |
| P/L | 1,606,000 | 1,125,000 | 1,547,000 |
| NW | 24,327,000 | 24,710,000 | 23,407,000 |
| WC | 276,000 | 2,335,000 | 5,241,000 |
| Emp. | 94 | 95 | 87 |

DUNS 21-781-1572
## Two Gates Primary School
Tamworth Road, Tamworth, Staffordshire B77 1EN
**Tel:** 01827475051
**Web:** www.twogates.staffs.sch.uk
**Estd:** 1981 Partnership
**Line of Business:** Schools (local authority)
**Partners:** Mrs L Cook, Mrs A Jones
**Responsibilities**
**Senior:** Nesta Llewelyn-Cook *(Head Teacher)*
**IT:** Sue Watts *(IT Manager)*
**US SIC:** 8211 **UK SIC:** 93200
**Employees:** 40

DUNS 53-642-4716
## T.W.O. Holdings Ltd.
Hovefields Lodge, 2 Hovefields Avenue, Basildon, Essex SS13 1EB
**Web:** www.two-services.com
**Reg No:** 3447971 **Estd:** 1997 Private Limited Company
**Line of Business:** Environmental consultants
**Issued Capital:** £100
**Directors:** A F Osborn, Ms S A Osborn
**Co. Secretary:** Jon Osborn
**Responsibilities**
**Senior:** Barry Osborn *(Manager)*
**US SIC:** 5812, 3542
**UK SIC:** 66110, 32212

| | 31-10-13 | 31-10-12 | 31-10-11 |
|---|---|---|---|
| TA | 200 | 200 | 200 |
| NW | 100 | 100 | 100 |

DUNS 21-780-8019
## Two Rivers High School
Silver Link Road, Tamworth, Staffordshire B77 2HJ
**Tel:** 01827475690
**Web:** www.tworiversschool.net
**Estd:** 2005 Proprietorship
**Line of Business:** Schools (special)
**Proprietor:** Mrs V Vernon
**Responsibilities**
**Senior:** Tony Dooley *(Head Teacher)*
**US SIC:** 8299 **UK SIC:** 93300
**Employees:** 50

DUNS 22-245-7306
## Two Rivers Housing
Rivers Meet Cleeve Mill Lane, Gloucestershire, Newent, Gloucestershire GL18 1DS
**Tel:** 08003160897 **Fax:** 01594546164
**Web:** www.tworiverhousing.org.uk
**Reg No:** 4263691 **Estd:** 2003 Private Limited Company
**Line of Business:** Other letting of own property
**Directors:** V J O'Brien, Ms G C Robins, D L Powell, C A Birch, Mrs S A Renwick, J Bloxsom, A J Blundell, C S Lumsden
**Co. Secretary:** Garry King
**Responsibilities**
**Senior:** Ann Christian *(Board Member)*
**Branches:** Two Rivers Housing, Rowandean Sheltered Housing, Cinderford, Gloucestershire GL14 2XP
**US SIC:** 6519 **UK SIC:** 85000

| | 31-03-14 | 31-03-13 | 31-03-12 |
|---|---|---|---|
| TO | 19,396,000 | 17,784,000 | 16,629,000 |
| P/L | 4,790,000 | 5,286,000 | 1,870,000 |
| NW | 26,052,000 | 21,549,000 | 16,729,000 |
| WC | (26,121,000) | (17,206,000) | (929,000) |
| Emp. | 120 | 125 | 123 |

DUNS 21-453-3932
## Two Saints
35 Waterside Gardens, Fareham, Hampshire PO16 8SD
**Tel:** 01329-234600
**Web:** www.twosaints.org.uk
**Estd:** 2003
**Line of Business:** Hostels
**Principals:** J O Bullock *(Chairman)*, S Taylor, Mrs M Smuland, Ms N L Xavier, A Quall, J Randall, T Jack, Ms R Sammons
**Responsibilities**
**Senior:** Louise Barnden *(Chief Executive)*, Steve Benson *(Chief Executive)*, M McKenzie *(Designated Limited Liability P)*
**Finance:** Annette Lewis-Gow *(Financial Director)*
**Branches:** Two Saints, Duke Of Edinburgh House, Cumberland Street, Portsmouth, Hampshire PO1 3JU
**US SIC:** 7021 **UK SIC:** 66500
**Auditors:** Nexia Smith & Williamson

| | 31-03-14 | 31-03-12 | 31-03-11 |
|---|---|---|---|
| TO | 9,544,000 | 9,943,490 | 10,185,302 |
| P/L | 432,000 | 216,738 | 230,504 |
| NW | 4,324,000 | 3,558,814 | 3,537,389 |
| WC | 2,990,000 | 2,275,175 | 1,922,105 |
| Emp. | 170 | 228 | 244 |

DUNS 50-326-4517
## Twofour Broadcast Ltd
**(Subsidiary of:** Lloyds Banking Group Plc)
Two Four Studios, Plymouth, Devon PL6 7RG
**Tel:** 01752-727400 **Fax:** 01752727450
**Web:** www.twofourbroadcast.com
**Reg No:** 2351132 **VAT No:** 462972813
**Estd:** 1989 Private Limited Company
**Line of Business:** Television activities
**Issued Capital:** £100,000
**Directors:** A Mackenzie, A J Hughes, Ms S Ward, D Adamson, Ms M Leach
**Co. Secretary:** Timothy Jackman
**Responsibilities**
**Senior:** Charles Wace *(CEO)*
**Branches:** Twofour Broadcast Ltd, 6-7 St Cross St, London EC1N 8UA
**US SIC:** 4833, 7999
**UK SIC:** 97411, 97913
**Auditors:** PricewaterhouseCoopers LLP
**Bankers:** Barclays Bank Plc (20-68-10)

| | 31-12-13 | 31-12-12 | 31-12-11 |
|---|---|---|---|
| TO | 35,749,000 | 30,193,000 | 17,423,000 |
| P/L | 634,000 | 1,925,000 | 640,000 |
| NW | 3,744,000 | 950,000 | 820,000 |
| WC | 3,207,000 | 383,000 | 503,000 |
| Emp. | 169 | 135 | 92 |

DUNS 21-276-0797 **Imp**
## T.W.Parker(Paper) Ltd
Unit 52-54, Farriers Way, Bootle, Merseyside L30 4XL
**Tel:** 01515-237308
**Web:** www.twparker.net
**Reg No:** 0496399 **VAT No:** 164197646
**Estd:** 1951 Private Limited Company
**Line of Business:** Labels finishing and supply
**Issued Capital:** £5,000
**Principals:** T C Parker *(Managing)*, T Parker, P M Hood, E Roche
**Co. Secretary:** Timothy Parker
**Responsibilities**
**HR:** Sue Flaherty *(Personnel Manager)*
**Health & Safety:** Sue Flaherty *(Personnel Manager)*
**Facilities:** Eddie Jenkins *(Engineering Manager)*
**Engineering:** Eddie Jenkins *(Engineering Manager)*
**US SIC:** 2752 **UK SIC:** 47544
**Bankers:** National Westminster Bank Plc (60-13-19)

| | 31-12-13 | 31-12-12 | 31-12-11 |
|---|---|---|---|
| TO | 6,502,768 | 7,247,249 | N/A |
| P/L | 126,362 | 492,329 | N/A |
| NW | 1,489,789 | 1,468,816 | 1,117,845 |
| WC | (12,693) | 321,049 | 202,974 |
| Emp. | 51 | 53 | N/A |

DUNS 73-606-0989
## Twt Logistics Ltd
14 Sycamore Close, Hengoed, Mid Glamorgan CF82 7RJ
**Tel:** 01443-815020 **Fax:** 01443-815030
**Web:** www.twt-logistics.com
**Reg No:** 2914472 **Estd:** 1994 Private Limited Company
**Line of Business:** Freight transport by road not elsewhere classified
**Issued Capital:** £2,011,567
**Directors:** T T Taylor, G S Marr
**Co. Secretary:** Ms Margaret Lewis
**Responsibilities**
**Senior:** Dave Murphy *(Transport Manager)*
**Admin:** Dave Murphy *(Transport Manager)*
**Facilities:** Dave Murphy *(Transport Manager)*
**Operations:** Moira Thomas *(Customer Services Manager)*
**Purchasing:** Claire Davies *(Purchasing Manager)*
**Fleet:** Dave Murphy *(Transport Manager)*
**US SIC:** 4213 **UK SIC:** 72300
**Auditors:** Willis Jones
**Bankers:** Barclays Bank Plc (20-18-15)

| | 31-03-14 | 31-03-13 | 31-03-12 |
|---|---|---|---|
| TO | 11,113,580 | 11,776,517 | 11,839,674 |
| P/L | 260,340 | 53,441 | 87,649 |
| NW | 2,226,542 | 2,228,894 | 2,196,603 |
| WC | (752,219) | (822,824) | (829,747) |
| Emp. | 126 | 141 | 133 |

DUNS 77-894-7556
## Twycross House School Ltd
1 Main Road, Twycross, Atherstone, Warwickshire CV9 3PL
**Tel:** 01827-880651
**Web:** www.twycrosshouseschool.org.uk
**Reg No:** 3041021 **Estd:** 1995 Private Limited Company
**Line of Business:** Schools (independent)
**Issued Capital:** £1,600
**Directors:** Ms R T Assinder, S D Assinder
**Co. Secretary:** Ms Honor Kirkpatrick
**US SIC:** 8211 **UK SIC:** 93200
**Auditors:** Philip Barnes & Co
**Bankers:** The Royal Bank Of Scotland Plc (16-14-70)

| | 31-08-13 | 31-08-12 | 31-08-11 |
|---|---|---|---|
| TA | 3,691,178 | 3,199,935 | 2,642,936 |
| NW | 2,463,880 | 2,211,784 | 1,856,847 |
| WC | (227,536) | (673,747) | (180,613) |

DUNS 28-872-3620
## Twycross Zoo - East Midland Zoological Society Ltd
Burton Road, Twycross, Atherstone, Warwickshire CV9 3PX
**Tel:** 08444741777 **Fax:** 08444741888
**Web:** www.twycrosszoo.org
**Reg No:** 1060956 **VAT No:** 544900057
**Estd:** 1963 Private Company Limited By Guarantee
**Line of Business:** Botanical and zoological gardens and nature reserve activities
**Directors:** J P Helas, Dr M Hughes, M J Hesketh, D J Keep, A G Greenwood, Dr D J Chivers, M Brewer
**Responsibilities**
**Senior:** Lorraine Ariano *(Marketing Assistant)*, Sharon Redrobe *(Chief Executive Officer)*
**US SIC:** 8421, 8999
**UK SIC:** 97700, 83954
**Auditors:** HLB Kidsons
**Bankers:** HSBC Bank plc (40-43-28)

| | 31-12-13 | 31-12-12 | 31-12-11 |
|---|---|---|---|
| TO | 8,641,847 | 8,059,610 | 8,206,436 |
| P/L | 291,053 | (110,433) | (775,458) |
| NW | 18,385,591 | 18,094,538 | 18,121,095 |
| WC | (1,112,757) | (2,093,252) | (1,945,196) |
| Emp. | 151 | 178 | 178 |

DUNS 21-714-0615 **Imp-Exp**
## Twyford Bathrooms
**(Subsidiary of:** Sanitec Uk Ltd)
Lawton Road, Alsager, Stoke-On-Trent, Staffordshire ST7 2DF
**Tel:** 01270-879777 **Fax:** 01270-873864
**Web:** www.twyfordbathrooms.com
**Reg No:** 0546129 **Estd:** 1955 Private Limited Company
**Line of Business:** Bathroom fixtures and fittings
**Export Sales:** £8,434,000
**Trading Style:** Doulton Bathrooms, Alstone
**Issued Capital:** £13,524,907
**Directors:** B W Hudson, G Nilsson, J Sillanpaa
**Co. Secretary:** Bbm Secretaries Limited
**Responsibilities**
**Finance:** Stephanie Kenway *(Financial Manager)*
**HR:** Helen Berwick *(Training Coordinator)*
**Branches:** Twyford Bathrooms, Lawton Road, Stoke-On-Trent, Staffordshire ST7 2DF
**US SIC:** 3499, 5074
**UK SIC:** 31694, 61300
**Auditors:** KPMG LLP

| | 31-12-13 | 31-12-12 | 31-12-11 |
|---|---|---|---|
| TO | 49,486,000 | 51,639,000 | 58,840,000 |
| P/L | 7,019,000 | 8,251,000 | 5,509,000 |
| NW | 41,534,000 | 37,527,000 | 24,967,000 |
| WC | 35,142,000 | 28,856,000 | 24,694,000 |
| Emp. | 151 | 162 | 266 |

DUNS 28-842-0177
## Twyford School
High Street, Twyford, Winchester, Hampshire SO21 1NW
**Tel:** 01962714622
**Web:** www.twyfordschool.com
**Reg No:** 0558147 **Estd:** 1955 Private Limited Company
**Line of Business:** Primary education
**Directors:** Ms J Gandee, Mrs C E Chaplin-Rogers, S P Kelly, C B Howman, S C Henderson, A J Thould, Mrs J N Naismith, Dr J E Hodgins
**Responsibilities**
**Senior:** Fiona Dunger *(Director)*, Patrick Herring *(Director)*, Mark Wills *(Director)*
**US SIC:** 8211 **UK SIC:** 93200
**Auditors:** Blueprint Audit Ltd
**Bankers:** Barclays Bank Plc (20-96-98)

| | 31-08-13 | 31-08-12 | 31-08-11 |
|---|---|---|---|
| TO | 6,330,522 | 5,461,209 | 5,418,945 |
| P/L | 1,084,153 | 283,827 | 51,578 |
| NW | 7,066,556 | 5,982,403 | 5,698,576 |
| WC | 524,927 | 262,494 | 16,749 |
| Emp. | 135 | 133 | 102 |

DUNS 23-231-9624
## Twynham Housing Association Ltd
2nd Floor, Dolphin House, Wick Lane, Christchurch, Dorset BH23 1HX
**Tel:** 01202460460 **Fax:** 01202-479303
**Web:** www.twynham-housing.co.uk
**Reg No:** 0026769IP **Estd:** 2009 Friendly Society
**Line of Business:** Housing associations societies trusts & co-operatives
**Trading Style:** Twynham Housing
**Principals:** Ms I Rawson *(Chairman)*, M Hudson, M Cone, N Alvis, Ms S Holloway, J Pond, Ms J Evans, E Wood
**Responsibilities**
**Senior:** Marion Franks *(Manager)*, John Lofts *(Director)*, Clive Rusden *(Director)*, Kathleen Symes *(Director)*
**US SIC:** 6531, 6732
**UK SIC:** 83400, 83100
**Auditors:** Deloitte & Touche
**Bankers:** Lloyds TSB Bank plc (30-92-02)
**Employees:** 87

DUNS 21-717-9877
## Twynham Learning
Sopers Lane, Christchurch, Dorset BH23 1JF
**Tel:** 01202486237
**Web:** www.twynham.dorset.sch.uk
**Reg No:** 7565088 **Estd:** 2011 Private Company Limited By Guarantee
**Line of Business:** Schools (local authority)
**Directors:** J R Sephton, M A Turvey, Ms D K Place, A P Lilley, J Burton, S M Dossett, J E England, M T Herrity
**Co. Secretary:** Mrs Heather Watson
**Responsibilities**
**Senior:** Erin Berry-Hicks *(Director)*, Jessica Broomfield *(Director)*, Steven Connolly *(Director)*, Douglas Croucher *(Director)*, Alison Curtis *(Director)*, Terence Fish *(Director)*, Kim Hazeldine *(Director)*, Laura Lamble *(Director)*, Debra Martin *(Director)*, Yasmin Maybank *(Director)*, Susan Verstage *(Director)*
**US SIC:** 8211 **UK SIC:** 93200

| | 31-08-13 | 31-08-12 |
|---|---|---|
| TO | 9,450,000 | 29,530,000 |
| P/L | 418,000 | 17,364,000 |
| NW | 16,145,000 | 15,776,000 |
| WC | 1,179,000 | 763,000 |
| Emp. | 184 | 175 |

DUNS 76-964-3560 **Exp**
## Tx Group Europe Ltd.
**(Subsidiary of:** Timex Group B.V.)
2 Sovereign Court, South Portway Close, Northampton, Northamptonshire NN3 8RH
**Tel:** 01604-678940 **Fax:** 01604 678950
**Web:** www.tx-europe.com
**Reg No:** 2629025 **VAT No:** 503089665
**Estd:** 1991 Private Limited Company
**Line of Business:** Wholesale of jewellery
**Export Markets:** Norway, Denmark, Holland, Germany & Hong Kong
**Export Sales:** £1,060,000
**Trading Style:** Sequel Uk
**Issued Capital:** £500,000
**Directors:** S Leonardi, A L Stone-Wigg, G J Crilly-Mckean, Mrs V A Uttridge, C D Arsenault
**Co. Secretary:** Robert Barberi
**Responsibilities**
**Senior:** Daniel Dodane *(President)*, Bill Leonard *(Manager)*
**Branches:** Tx Group Europe Ltd., Southerton House Boundary Business Court 92-94, Church Road, Mitcham, Surrey CR4 3TD
**US SIC:** 5094 **UK SIC:** 61900
**Auditors:** KPMG LLP
**Bankers:** The Royal Bank Of Scotland Plc (16-26-27)

| | 31-12-13 | 31-12-12 | 31-12-11 |
|---|---|---|---|
| TO | 15,131,000 | 16,181,000 | 18,136,000 |
| P/L | (2,007,000) | (1,464,000) | (763,000) |
| NW | (1,983,000) | 44,000 | 1,578,000 |
| WC | (1,587,000) | 317,000 | 1,739,000 |
| Emp. | 76 | 86 | 87 |

DUNS 34-749-3517
## Txm Recruit Ltd
Walnut House, Blackhill Drive, Wolverton Mill, Milton Keynes, Buckinghamshire MK12 5TS
**Tel:** 08452263454 **Fax:** 08452263453
**Web:** www.txmrecruit.co.uk
**Reg No:** 5550878 **Estd:** 2005 Private Limited Company
**Line of Business:** Labour recruitment and provision of personnel
**Export Sales:** £7,667,049
**Trading Style:** Txm Recruit
**Issued Capital:** £129
**Directors:** A Midgley, G L Hanrahan, L J Seward, G C Eccles, J N Poulton, K Gallimore, J J Bettell

**Responsibilities**
**Senior:** Brian Chatfield *(Manager)*, Alan Leach *(Manager)*, Anthony Sprigg *(Director)*
**US SIC:** 7361 **UK SIC:** 83954
**Auditors:** MacIntyre Hudson LLP

| | 31-12-13 | 31-12-12 | 31-12-11 |
|---|---|---|---|
| TO | 29,928,300 | 37,451,309 | 41,263,094 |
| P/L | (1,538,745) | 715,116 | 1,472,130 |
| NW | 1,045,524 | 2,190,444 | 1,808,126 |
| WC | 1,202,592 | 1,801,153 | 1,692,254 |
| Emp. | 112 | 114 | 149 |

DUNS 23-408-6499
## Txo Systems Ltd
Unit 3 Severn Cross Distribution Park, Newhouse Farm Industrial Estate, Chepstow, Gwent NP16 6UP
**Tel:** 01291 623 813 **Fax:** 01291 626 166
**Web:** www.txo-systems.com
**Reg No:** 5479601 **VAT No:** 840431165
**Estd:** 2005 Private Limited Company
**Line of Business:** Telecommunications
**Issued Capital:** £20,000
**Directors:** A J Ockenden, Mrs A Pritchard, C L Coakley, Mrs R Ockenden
**US SIC:** 4899 **UK SIC:** 79020
**Auditors:** UHY Hacker Young
**Bankers:** The Royal Bank Of Scotland Plc (16-26-24)

| | 30-06-13 | 30-06-12 | 30-06-11 |
|---|---|---|---|
| TO | 18,808,155 | 11,588,997 | 8,839,344 |
| P/L | 3,587,721 | 1,459,044 | 1,277,888 |
| NW | 4,529,763 | 1,741,299 | 1,441,799 |
| WC | 4,274,469 | 1,484,855 | 1,267,825 |
| Emp. | 92 | 64 | 31 |

DUNS 22-212-2637
## Txt E-Solutions Ltd
*(Subsidiary of:* Txt E Solutions Spa*)*
11 Glenthome Road, Hammersmith, London W6 0LH
**Fax:** 020-7324-7509
**Web:** www.txtgroup.com
**Reg No:** 4230389 **Estd:** 2001 Private Limited Company
**Line of Business:** Other software consultancy and supply
**Export Sales:** £2,550,434
**Issued Capital:** £2,000,000
**Directors:** A Cencini, P Matarazzo, M Guida
**US SIC:** 7379 **UK SIC:** 83940

| | 31-12-13 | 31-12-12 | 31-12-11 |
|---|---|---|---|
| TO | 6,599,400 | 5,078,250 | N/A |
| P/L | (146,646) | 997,860 | N/A |
| NW | (121,211) | (844,032) | 746,063 |
| WC | (148,511) | (1,053,758) | 741,753 |
| Emp. | 52 | 26 | N/A |

DUNS 21-208-3237
## Ty Ceirios Nursing Home
Pontnewynydd, Pontnewynydd, Pontypool, Gwent NP4 6TJ
**Tel:** 01495-752358
**Estd:** 1988 Partnership
**Line of Business:** Nursing homes
**Partners:** P E Perry, Mrs E Williams, Mrs S Perry
**US SIC:** 8051 **UK SIC:** 95100
**Employees:** 70

DUNS 21-208-3245
## Ty Gwyn Private Nursing Home
21-23 Stanwell Road, Penarth, South Glamorgan CF64 2EZ
**Tel:** 029-2070-3600
**Web:** www.mha.org.uk
**Estd:** 1973 Partnership
**Line of Business:** Convalescent homes
**Partners:** Ms D Boland, Mrs A Boland, M Boland
**Responsibilities**
**Admin:** Anna Notley *(Administrator)*
**US SIC:** 8091 **UK SIC:** 95200
**Bankers:** Barclays Bank Plc (20-18-27)
**Employees:** 60

DUNS 49-064-0018
## Ty Hafan
St Hilary Court, Copthorne Way, Cardiff, South Glamorgan CF5 6ES
**Tel:** 02920672060 **Fax:** 01446739994
**Web:** www.tyhafan.org
**Reg No:** 3077406 **Estd:** 2004 Private Company Limited By Guarantee
**Line of Business:** Medical nursing home activities
**Directors:** Mrs R M Clarke, M J Davies, C Pearse, Dr T D Jenkins, Mrs I Davies, Dr T J Morris, Ms K Palmer, Mrs C Williams
**Co. Secretary:** Christopher James
**Responsibilities**
**Senior:** Rosie Clarke *(Administrator)*, David Farnsworth *(Trustee)*, Raymond Hurcombe *(Chief Executive)*, Elizabeth Read *(Manager)*, Maria Timon Samra *(Director)*
**Branches:** Ty Hafan, 15A Gwent Shopping Centre, Tredegar, Gwent NP22 3EJ
**US SIC:** 8051, 8091
**UK SIC:** 95100, 95200
**Auditors:** Resting Davis & Partners

**Bankers:** Cafcash Ltd (40-52-40)

| | 31-03-14 | 31-03-13 | 31-03-12 |
|---|---|---|---|
| TO | 8,305,159 | 8,085,216 | 7,198,588 |
| P/L | (61,147) | 542,990 | (109,401) |
| NW | 15,288,927 | 14,920,871 | 13,459,463 |
| WC | (123,475) | 90,655 | (249,407) |
| Emp. | 177 | 171 | 168 |

DUNS 21-229-1714
## Ty Hafan the Childrens Hospice in Wales
Hayes Road, Sully, Penarth, South Glamorgan CF64 5XX
**Tel:** 02920532200
**Web:** www.tyhafan.org
**Estd:** 1999
**Line of Business:** Hospices
**Proprietor:** Mrs J Saunders
**US SIC:** 8091, 6732
**UK SIC:** 95200, 83100
**Employees:** 70

DUNS 21-213-1242
## Ty Mair Nursing Home
12 Pen Y Gaer Cottages, Llanelli, Dyfed SA14 8AG
**Tel:** 01554-754711
**Estd:** 1987 Proprietorship
**Line of Business:** Medical nursing home activities
**Partner:** P Michael
**Responsibilities**
**Senior:** Eve Hughes *(Home Manager)*, Charlotte Michael *(Manager)*
**US SIC:** 8051 **UK SIC:** 95100
**Employees:** 62

DUNS 29-171-5175
## Ty Mawr Ltd
Station Road, Caehopkin, Abercrave, Swansea, West Glamorgan SA9 1TP
**Tel:** 01639730687
**Reg No:** 1832321 **Estd:** 1984 Private Limited Company
**Line of Business:** Nursing homes
**Trading Style:** Ty-Mawr Nursing Home
**Issued Capital:** £100
**Managing Director:** W M Davies
**Responsibilities**
**Senior:** Eirlys Adrian *(Manager)*
**US SIC:** 8051 **UK SIC:** 95100

| | 31-12-13 | 31-12-12 | 31-12-11 |
|---|---|---|---|
| TA | 2,757,397 | 2,675,863 | 2,685,952 |
| NW | 1,587,628 | 1,608,966 | 1,582,116 |
| WC | (433,849) | (324,972) | (308,433) |

DUNS 77-153-2702
## Ty Nant Ltd
*(Subsidiary of:* Biscaldi Luigi Import Export Srl*)*
Bethania, Llanon, Dyfed SY23 5LS
**Tel:** 01974272111
**Reg No:** 2706802 **Estd:** 1992 Private Limited Company
**Line of Business:** Manufacture of mineral waters and soft drinks
**Issued Capital:** £2
**Director:** P Biscaldi
**Co. Secretary:** Alan Davies
**US SIC:** 2086 **UK SIC:** 42831

| | 30-04-14 | 30-04-13 | 30-04-12 |
|---|---|---|---|
| TA | 2 | 2 | 2 |
| NW | 2 | 2 | 2 |

DUNS 21-516-2129
## Ty-Nant Nursing Home
Cymmer, Port Talbot, West Glamorgan SA13 3NR
**Tel:** 01639-851852
**Web:** www.tynanthome.co.uk
**Estd:** 1987 Partnership
**Line of Business:** Nursing homes
**Partners:** Mrs T Ahmed, R Ahmed
**Responsibilities**
**Senior:** Riaz Ahmad *(Proprietor)*, Ann Summers *(Home Manager)*
**Finance:** Niclas Ball *(Senior Finance Administrator)*
**US SIC:** 8051 **UK SIC:** 95100
**Employees:** 100

DUNS 21-070-7521
## Ty Porth Care Home
Cemetery Road, Porth, Mid Glamorgan CF39 0BH
**Tel:** 01443-680011
**Web:** www.embracegroup.co.uk
**Estd:** 2004
**Line of Business:** Medical nursing home activities
**Proprietor:** Mrs E Clews
**US SIC:** 8051, 6732
**UK SIC:** 95100, 83100
**Employees:** 100

DUNS 21-213-1267
## Ty Ross Private Nursing Home
Ninian Street, Treherbert, Treorchy, Mid Glamorgan CF42 5RD
**Tel:** 01443-778305
**Estd:** 1994 Partnership
**Line of Business:** Residential care establishments
**Partners:** Mrs T Elsdon, D George
**Responsibilities**
**Senior:** Marilyn Peters *(Area Manager)*, Sue Warren *(Home Manager)*
**US SIC:** 8321 **UK SIC:** 96111
**Employees:** 52

DUNS 21-788-5686
## Ty Sign
Elm Drive, Risca, Newport, Gwent NP11 6HJ
**Tel:** 01633612813
**Web:** www.tysign.caerphilly.sch.uk
**Estd:** 1968 Proprietorship
**Line of Business:** Restaurants
**Proprietor:** A Hussain
**Responsibilities**
**Senior:** Alison Dacey *(Head Teacher)*
**US SIC:** 5812 **UK SIC:** 66110
**Employees:** 88

DUNS 76-414-7393        Imp-Exp
## Tyco Building Services Products (Uk) Ltd
*(Subsidiary of:* Tyco International Finance Sa*)*
Tyco Building Services Products Ltd, Manchester M17 1QS
**Tel:** 0161-875-0400 **Fax:** 0161-875-0509
**Web:** www.tyco-fsbp.com
**Reg No:** 2559027 **VAT No:** 555102764
**Estd:** 1990 Private Limited Company
**Line of Business:** Other wholesale
**Export Markets:** Republic of Ireland; S Africa
**Export Sales:** £22,328,000
**Trading Style:** Tyco Building Services
**Issued Capital:** £501,000
**Directors:** J J Schumer, A Bowie, L Swennenhuis
**Co. Secretary:** Anton Alphonsus
**Responsibilities**
**Senior:** Simon Giles *(Manager)*, Daniel Sawyer *(Financial Director)*, Jo Vause *(Marketing Manager)*
**Finance:** Daniel Sawyer *(Financial Director)*
**Facilities:** Mel Tynne *(Facilities Coordinator)*
**Branches:** Tyco Building Services Products (Uk) Ltd, Pump Lane, Hayes, Middlesex UB3 3NB
**US SIC:** 5199 **UK SIC:** 61900
**Auditors:** Deloitte & Touche LLP
**Bankers:** National Westminster Bank Plc (01-08-38)

| | 27-09-13 | 28-09-12 | 30-09-11 |
|---|---|---|---|
| TO | 35,927,000 | 34,283,000 | 15,159,000 |
| P/L | 1,226,000 | 1,438,000 | (71,000) |
| NW | 721,000 | 5,073,000 | 3,642,000 |
| WC | 7,887,000 | 5,569,000 | 4,151,000 |
| Emp. | 72 | 76 | 57 |

DUNS 21-005-5259
## Tyco Electronics Uk Holdings Ltd
*(Subsidiary of:* Te Connectivity Ltd.*)*
Company Secretariat, Faraday Road, Dorcan, Swindon, Wiltshire SN3 5HH
**Tel:** 01793-572-432
**Web:** www.te.com
**Reg No:** 6301775 **Estd:** 1955 Private Limited Company
**Line of Business:** Management activities of holding companies
**Issued Capital:** £366,179,518
**Directors:** S C Cooper, H G Barksdale, J D Pegler, Ms S A Hicks, A R Fulford
**Responsibilities**
**Senior:** Mark Sawyer *(Sales Director)*
**Finance:** Terry Wilkinson *(Financial Director)*
**Sales:** Mark Sawyer *(Sales Director)*
**US SIC:** 6711 **UK SIC:** 83962
**Auditors:** Deloitte LLP

| | 30-09-13 | 30-09-12 | 30-09-11 |
|---|---|---|---|
| TA | 632,710,000 | 427,800,000 | 400,982,000 |
| P/L | 924,000 | (1,063,000) | 4,701,000 |
| NW | 202,168,000 | 201,244,000 | 202,307,000 |
| WC | (143,112,000) | (144,422,000) | (143,459,000) |

DUNS 21-630-3594        Imp-Exp
## Tyco Electronics Uk Ltd
*(Subsidiary of:* Te Connectivity Ltd.*)*
Faraday Road, Swindon, Wiltshire SN3 5HH
**Tel:** 01793528171 **Fax:** 01793572516
**Web:** www.te.com
**Reg No:** 0550926 **Estd:** 1955 Private Limited Company
**Line of Business:** Other engineering activities
**Export Sales:** £130,395,000
**Trading Style:** Te Connectivity
**Issued Capital:** £338,786,340

**Directors:** H G Barksdale, T M Gatt, J D Pegler, S C Cooper, A R Fulford, Ms S A Hicks
**Responsibilities**
**Senior:** Stuart Allan *(Human Resources Director)*, Martin Cimini *(Business Development Director)*, Andrew Donachie *(Director of Operations)*, Tom Lynch *(CEO)*, Peter Sirs *(Sales Director)*, Terry Wilkinson *(Financial Director)*
**Finance:** Terry Wilkinson *(Financial Director)*
**Sales:** Martin Cimini *(Business Development Director)*, Ralf Hagedorrt *(Area Sales Manager)*, Peter Sirs *(Sales Director)*, Barry Stunt *(Senior Sales Executive)*, Paul Vince *(Area Sales Manager)*
**IT:** Paula Penny *(IT Manager)*, Maureen Squires *(IT Manager)*
**HR:** Stuart Allan *(Human Resources Director)*, Helen Haresign *(Training Manager)*, Jane McInerney *(Human Resources Manager)*
**Health & Safety:** Bryan Neaves *(Health & Safety Officer)*
**Facilities:** Chris Ockwell *(Facilities Manager)*
**Operations:** Bill Arbogast *(Project Manager)*, Tony Hyde *(Operations Manager)*, Sheru Khan *(QU Consultant)*, John Sandwell *(Global Product Manager)*, John Spindler *(Director of Product Management)*
**Engineering:** Alvin Bowyer *(Production Manager)*, Ben Kane *(Head Of Global Engineering)*, Damian Kirtland *(Engineering/Maintenance Manage)*
**Branches:** Tyco Electronics Uk Ltd, Site A, Edison Road, Dorcan, Swindon, Wiltshire SN3 5JA
**US SIC:** 8911 **UK SIC:** 83701
**Auditors:** Deloitte LLP
**Bankers:** Barclays Bank Plc (20-00-00)

| | 30-09-13 | 30-09-12 | 30-09-11 |
|---|---|---|---|
| TO | 192,115,000 | 221,745,000 | 232,403,000 |
| P/L | 17,593,000 | 28,315,000 | 22,247,000 |
| NW | 262,224,000 | 255,164,000 | 263,707,000 |
| WC | 239,787,000 | 145,466,000 | 124,832,000 |
| Emp. | 1,501 | 1,548 | 1,512 |

DUNS 21-780-8855
## Tyco Fire & Integrated Solution
Altec Centre, Minto Drive, Altens Industrial Estate, Aberdeen, Aberdeenshire AB12 3LW
**Tel:** 01224295191
**Web:** www.tycofis.com
**Estd:** 2011 Partnership
**Line of Business:** Firefighting equipment
**Partners:** B Adams, R Miller
**Responsibilities**
**Finance:** James Earn *(Finance Director)*
**US SIC:** 8911 **UK SIC:** 83701
**Employees:** 150

DUNS 29-173-7849        Imp-Exp
## Tyco Fire Products Manufacturing Ltd
*(Subsidiary of:* Tyco International Finance Sa*)*
A3-A5 Stockport Trading Estate, Yew Street, Stockport, Cheshire SK4 2JW
**Web:** www.tycofireproducts.co.uk
**Reg No:** 1841522 **VAT No:** 431540878
**Estd:** 1984 Private Limited Company
**Line of Business:** Firefighting equipment
**Export Markets:** Europe, Asia, Australia
**Export Sales:** £32,685,000
**Trading Style:** Jw Singer
**Issued Capital:** £2
**Directors:** D Morris, M Turco, A Bowie, M J Macmichael, M Denning, D C Linay
**Co. Secretary:** Anton Alphonsus
**Responsibilities**
**Senior:** Steve Quigley *(Warehouse Supervisor)*
**HR:** Michelle Atkinson *(Human Resources Director)*
**Health & Safety:** David Langdon *(Health & Safety Manager)*
**Facilities:** David Langdon *(Health & Safety Manager)*
**Purchasing:** Richard Treasure *(Purchasing Manager)*
**Branches:** Tyco Fire Products Manufacturing Ltd, Downing Street, Smethwick, West Midlands B66 2JL
**US SIC:** 3559 **UK SIC:** 32863
**Auditors:** Deloitte LLP
**Bankers:** National Westminster Bank Plc (01-10-01)

| | 27-09-13 | 28-09-12 | 30-09-11 |
|---|---|---|---|
| TO | 33,735,000 | 29,617,000 | 27,438,000 |
| P/L | 3,929,000 | 3,338,000 | 1,344,000 |
| NW | 56,849,000 | 52,889,000 | 48,786,000 |
| WC | 57,219,000 | 53,138,000 | 52,295,000 |
| Emp. | 159 | 175 | 188 |

DUNS 21-933-4034
## Tycroes Group Ltd
(**Subsidiary of:** Tycroes Holdings Ltd)
Unit 28 Heol Stanllyd, Cross Hands, Llanelli, Dyfed SA14 6RB
**Tel:** 01269-842255 **Fax:** 01269-845243
**Web:** www.tycroesgroup.co.uk
**Reg No:** 1194839 **VAT No:** 558105149
**Estd:** 1993 Private Limited Company
**Line of Business:** Building construction contractors
**Issued Capital:** £322,500
**Director:** R Williams
**Co. Secretary:** Richard Williams
**Responsibilities**
**HR:** Caroline Willavoys *(Human Resources Manager)*
**US SIC:** 1522 **UK SIC:** 50100
**Auditors:** PricewaterhouseCoopers LLP
**Bankers:** Lloyds TSB Bank plc (30-95-14)

| | 31-03-14 | 31-03-13 | 31-03-12 |
|---|---|---|---|
| TO | N/A | N/A | 4,832,082 |
| P/L | N/A | N/A | 196,241 |
| NW | 600,621 | 431,211 | 379,344 |
| WC | 495,051 | 316,796 | 278,798 |
| Emp. | N/A | N/A | 41 |

DUNS 76-946-7226
## Tyddyn Mon
Brynrefail, Dulas, Gwynedd LL70 9PJ
**Tel:** 01248-410580
**Web:** www.tyddynmon.co.uk
**Reg No:** 2228346 **Estd:** 1988 Private Limited Company
**Line of Business:** Other human health activities
**Directors:** O D Williams, Mrs T A Davies, H E Williams, J G Webster, Ms C M Mackay, J L Pritchard, Ms E M Clarke, A T Lewis
**Co. Secretary:** Stephen Mcenhill
**Responsibilities**
**Senior:** Doris Jones *(Manager)*
**Finance:** Damien McGuire *(Treasurer)*
**Branches:** Tyddyn Mon, 17 Water Street, Menai Bridge, Gwynedd LL59 5DD
**US SIC:** 8091 **UK SIC:** 95200
**Auditors:** I G Jones & Co
**Bankers:** Barclays Bank Plc (20-35-47)

| | 31-03-14 | 31-03-13 | 31-03-12 |
|---|---|---|---|
| TO | 1,547,936 | 1,595,734 | 1,590,835 |
| P/L | 125,281 | 146,593 | 95,200 |
| NW | 1,492,679 | 1,367,398 | 1,220,805 |
| WC | 867,945 | 740,771 | 622,885 |
| Emp. | 52 | 52 | 53 |

DUNS 37-763-7699
## Tyddyn Morthwyl Campsite
Tyddyn Morthwyl, Rhoslan, Criccieth, Gwynedd LL52 0NF
**Web:** www.trianglewood.co.uk
**Estd:** 1979 Proprietorship
**Line of Business:** Camping site operators
**Proprietor:** Mrs M S Trumper
**Responsibilities**
**Senior:** Jg Trumper *(Proprietor)*
**US SIC:** 7033 **UK SIC:** 66701
**Employees:** 58

DUNS 50-504-6680
## Tydfil Training Consortium Ltd
114 High Street, Merthyr Tydfil, Mid Glamorgan CF47 8AP
**Tel:** 01685-371747
**Web:** www.tydfil.com
**Reg No:** 2472331 **Estd:** 1990 Private Limited Company
**Line of Business:** Training services
**Directors:** T P Collins, D J Robbins, A Bush, P Brill, R O Wilding, C Parker, M Howell, Mrs S Hamer
**Co. Secretary:** Paul Gray
**Branches:** Tydfil Training Consortium Ltd, 20-21 Gelliwastad Road, Pontypridd, Mid Glamorgan CF37 2BW
**US SIC:** 8299 **UK SIC:** 93300
**Auditors:** Martin Howell & Co
**Bankers:** Barclays Bank Plc (20-56-56)

| | 31-08-13 | 31-08-12 | 31-08-11 |
|---|---|---|---|
| TO | 1,875,624 | 1,834,210 | 3,051,782 |
| P/L | 100,419 | (160,525) | (17,381) |
| NW | 1,172,508 | 1,072,089 | 1,232,614 |
| WC | 688,521 | 598,471 | 714,120 |
| Emp. | 56 | 55 | 83 |

DUNS 21-585-1222
## Tyeirin Care Home
Parceiren, Porth, Mid Glamorgan CF39 8EE
**Tel:** 01443675010
**Web:** www.fshc.co.uk
**Estd:** 2011 Proprietorship
**Line of Business:** Residential care establishments
**Proprietor:** Mrs J Smith
**Responsibilities**
**Senior:** Judith Nicholas *(Manager)*
**US SIC:** 8321 **UK SIC:** 96111
**Employees:** 100

DUNS 23-981-2779
## Tyne & Wear Passenger Transport Executive
Nexus House, 33 St James Boulevard, Newcastle-Upon-Tyne, Tyne and Wear NE1 4AX
**Tel:** 01912020747 **Fax:** 0191-203-3180
**Web:** www.nexus.org.uk
**Estd:** 1969 Incorporate By Act Of Parliament
**Line of Business:** Other transport via railways
**Trading Style:** Nexus
**Principals:** G Cook, T Mccrady, D Johnson, R Smith
**Co. Secretary:** Geoffrey Brindle
**Responsibilities**
**Senior:** Terence McCrady *(Non-Executive Director)*, Colin Whittle *(Manager)*
**Branches:** Tyne & Wear Passenger Transport Executive, Regent Centre Statio, Great North Rd, Newcastle-Upon-Tyne, Tyne and Wear NE3 3JN
**US SIC:** 4011, 4469, 4722
**UK SIC:** 71000, 76300, 77001
**Bankers:** HSBC Bank plc (40-34-18)
**Employees:** 961

DUNS 21-226-5199
## Tyne & Wear Service Hq
Headquarters, Nissan Way, Sunderland, Tyne and Wear SR5 3QY
**Tel:** 0191-4441500
**Web:** www.twfire.org
**Proprietorship**
**Line of Business:** Fire stations
**Proprietor:** I Bathgate
**Responsibilities**
**Senior:** Thomas Capeling *(Chief Fire Officer)*
**Marketing:** Ian Allsop *(Head of Marketing)*, Michelle Atkinson *(Marketing Manager)*
**Sales:** Joy Brindle *(Assistant Chief Officer (Strat)*, Nina Griffiths *(Area Manager, Strategic Planni)*
**HR:** John Baines *(Chief HR Officer)*, Alan Robson *(HR Manager)*
**Health & Safety:** Thomas Capeling *(Chief Fire Officer)*, Chris Lowther *(Assistant Chief Officer, Commu)*
**US SIC:** 9224 **UK SIC:** 91400
**Employees:** 200

DUNS 76-491-1947
## Tyne Logistics Co Ltd
Tyne Dock, South Shields, Tyne and Wear NE33 5SP
**Tel:** 01914275000
**Web:** www.portoftyne.co.uk
**Reg No:** 2566501 **Estd:** 1990 Private Limited Company
**Line of Business:** Animal transportation services
**Issued Capital:** £40,000
**Principals:** I Gibson *(Managing)*, Dr J M Hudson, A N Moffat
**Co. Secretary:** Muckle Secretary Limited
**US SIC:** 4712, 4226
**UK SIC:** 77002, 77003
**Auditors:** Arthur Anderson

| | 31-12-13 | 31-12-12 | 31-12-11 |
|---|---|---|---|
| TO | 5,593,000 | 6,233,000 | 6,863,000 |
| P/L | 562,000 | 1,112,000 | 1,217,000 |
| NW | 5,844,000 | 5,376,000 | 4,518,000 |
| WC | 526,000 | 3,838,000 | 3,498,000 |
| Emp. | 59 | 57 | 58 |

DUNS 22-805-7949
## Tyne Tees Packaging Ltd
Grindon Way, Aycliffe Business Park, Newton Aycliffe, County Durham DL5 6DQ
**Tel:** 01325-311114 **Fax:** 01325-311301
**Web:** www.tyneteespackaging.co.uk
**Reg No:** 1646511 **VAT No:** 360708167
**Estd:** 1982 Private Limited Company
**Line of Business:** Packaging activities
**Issued Capital:** £901
**Principals:** G V Wiper *(Managing)*, Ms C L Armstrong
**Co. Secretary:** Ms Lucy Wiper
**Responsibilities**
**Senior:** Eric Williams *(Transport Manager)*
**Finance:** Lucy Donald *(Commercial Director)*
**Marketing:** Lucy Donald *(Commercial Director)*
**Sales:** Lucy Donald *(Commercial Director)*
**HR:** Lucy Donald *(Commercial Director)*
**Health & Safety:** Eric Williams *(Transport Manager)*
**Facilities:** Eric Williams *(Transport Manager)*
**Operations:** Eric Williams *(Transport Manager)*
**Purchasing:** Lucy Donald *(Commercial Director)*
**Fleet:** Eric Williams *(Transport Manager)*
**Engineering:** Joanne Bellingham *(Production Manager)*
**US SIC:** 7399 **UK SIC:** 83954
**Auditors:** Mitchell Gordon
**Bankers:** HSBC Bank plc (40-34-32)

| | 31-10-13 | 31-10-12 | 31-10-11 |
|---|---|---|---|
| TO | 7,016,403 | 6,838,969 | N/A |
| P/L | 210,184 | 475,434 | N/A |
| NW | 758,658 | 704,053 | 1,527,414 |
| WC | (865,428) | (799,796) | (936,676) |
| Emp. | 47 | 44 | N/A |

DUNS 76-716-8743
## Tynemace Ltd
23 High Street, Doncaster, South Yorkshire DN1 1DW
**Tel:** 01302812099
**Reg No:** 2595415 **Estd:** 1992 Private Limited Company
**Line of Business:** Financial intermediation not elsewhere classified
**Trading Style:** Doncaster Pawnbrokers
**Issued Capital:** £100
**Directors:** Ms P Batish, R K Batish
**Co. Secretary:** Ms Penny Batish
**Branches:** Tynemace Ltd, 3 Station Rd, Terminus Pde, Leeds, West Yorkshire LS15 7JZ
**US SIC:** 6111 **UK SIC:** 81501
**Auditors:** Whitehead & Aldrich

| | 31-03-14 | 31-03-13 | 31-03-12 |
|---|---|---|---|
| TA | 417,067 | 462,522 | 486,698 |
| NW | 411,773 | 446,545 | 152,932 |
| WC | 411,773 | 446,545 | 152,916 |

DUNS 22-656-0191
## Tynemill Ltd
Queens Bridge Road, Nottingham, Nottinghamshire NG2 1NB
**Tel:** 01159851615
**Web:** www.tynemill.co.uk
**Reg No:** 1211426 **VAT No:** 555462333
**Estd:** 1977 Private Limited Company
**Line of Business:** Manufacture of beer
**Issued Capital:** £143,670
**Directors:** C F Wilde, P R Brettell, G D Newton, G N Kelso, A W Eastwood, P J Wilde, Ms V L Saxby
**Co. Secretary:** Neil Kellett
**Branches:** Tynemill Ltd, 203 Siddals Road, Derby, Derbyshire DE1 2QE
**US SIC:** 2082, 5813
**UK SIC:** 42702, 66200
**Auditors:** Shorts
**Bankers:** Barclays Bank Plc (20-50-21)

| | 31-03-14 | 31-03-13 | 31-03-12 |
|---|---|---|---|
| TO | 7,916,554 | 7,833,924 | 8,097,592 |
| P/L | (398,828) | 75,512 | 314,655 |
| NW | 4,250,432 | 4,604,929 | 5,959,097 |
| WC | 111,801 | 126,614 | 107,198 |
| Emp. | 158 | 118 | 157 |

DUNS 51-563-3832
## Tynemouth College
Hawkeys Lane, North Shields, Tyne and Wear NE29 9BZ
**Tel:** 01912196603
**Web:** www.tynemet.ac.uk
**Estd:** 2012
**Line of Business:** College of further and higher education.
**Directors:** R C Bailey, Mrs A Crozier
**Responsibilities**
**Senior:** Jill Common *(Manager)*
**Branches:** Tynemouth College, Hawkeys Lane, North Shields, Tyne and Wear NE29 9BZ
**US SIC:** 8221 **UK SIC:** 93100
**Employees:** 100

DUNS 21-777-6358
## Tyneside Audi
Silverlink, Wallsend, Tyne and Wear NE28 9ND
**Tel:** 01912260100
**Web:** www.drivebenfield.com
**Estd:** 2011
**Line of Business:** Car dealers (new & used)
**US SIC:** 5511 **UK SIC:** 65100
**Employees:** 48

DUNS 21-211-0209 **Imp-Exp**
## Tyneside Safety Glass Co Ltd
(**Subsidiary of:** Suntex Safety Glass Industries Ltd)
Kingsway North, Team Valley Trading Estate, Gateshead, Tyne and Wear NE11 0JX
**Tel:** 01914875064 **Fax:** 01914870358
**Web:** www.tynesidesafetyglass.co.uk
**Reg No:** 0359744 **VAT No:** 176254353
**Estd:** 1940 Private Limited Company
**Line of Business:** Glass (safety)
**Export Markets:** Europe
**Export Sales:** £4,323,404
**Issued Capital:** £3,328
**Directors:** C M Hannant, R S Torns
**Co. Secretary:** Richard Torns
**Responsibilities**
**Senior:** Michael Matson *(Manager)*
**Finance:** Trevor Storey *(Financial Director)*
**Branches:** Tyneside Safety Glass Co Ltd, Kingsway North, Gateshead, Tyne and Wear NE11 0JX
**US SIC:** 3231 **UK SIC:** 24791
**Auditors:** BDO Stoy Hayward LLP
**Bankers:** Lloyds TSB Bank plc (30-99-64)

| | 30-04-14 | 30-04-13 | 30-04-12 |
|---|---|---|---|
| TO | 12,716,125 | 12,843,730 | 13,865,155 |
| P/L | 50,509 | 468,133 | 930,598 |
| NW | 2,517,660 | 2,396,745 | 1,786,846 |
| WC | 1,163,453 | 681,583 | 530,118 |
| Emp. | 188 | 193 | 177 |

DUNS 23-959-1592
## The Tyneside Society of Model & Experimental Engineers Ltd
12 Mitchell Drive, Ashington, Northumberland NE63 9JT
**Tel:** 01670816072
**Web:** www.tsmee.co.uk
**Reg No:** 3948278 **Estd:** 2000 Private Limited Company
**Line of Business:** Activities of professional organisations
**Directors:** I Spencer, J A Stephenson
**Co. Secretary:** Mrs Linda Nicholls
**US SIC:** 3999, 7999
**UK SIC:** 49590, 97913

| | 31-03-14 | 31-03-13 | 31-03-12 |
|---|---|---|---|
| TA | 40,086 | 34,310 | 30,764 |
| NW | 33,343 | 34,310 | 30,764 |
| WC | 10,718 | N/A | N/A |

DUNS 28-957-7744 **Imp**
## Tynetec Ltd
(**Subsidiary of:** Legrand (U K) Ltd)
Unit 10, Blyth, Northumberland NE24 5TF
**Tel:** 01670-352371 **Fax:** 01670-362807
**Web:** www.tynetec.co.uk
**Reg No:** 1663928 **VAT No:** 436259930
**Estd:** 1979 Private Limited Company
**Line of Business:** Electronic engineers
**Export Sales:** £249,367
**Trading Style:** Aid Call
**Issued Capital:** £57,906
**Directors:** A D Burel, Legrand Uk Limited, A J Greig
**Co. Secretary:** Philip Middlemast
**Responsibilities**
**Finance:** Stan Harrison *(Financial Director)*
**Sales:** Stuart Carroll *(Sales Manager)*, Lisa Daughtrey *(Corporate/Export Sales Manager)*, Wendy Kendall *(Head of Sales)*, Aaron Longstaff *(Business Development Manager)*, Kieran Mccausland *(Business Development Manager)*, Scott Robinson *(Sales Manager)*
**IT:** Scott Robinson *(Sales Manager)*
**Operations:** Ian Case *(Manufacturing Manager)*, Scott Robinson *(Sales Manager)*
**Engineering:** Mark Shepherd *(Technical Manager)*
**US SIC:** 8911 **UK SIC:** 83701
**Auditors:** Tait Walker LLP
**Bankers:** Lloyds TSB Bank plc (30-95-76)

| | 31-12-13 | 30-06-13 | 30-12-12 |
|---|---|---|---|
| TO | 6,538,537 | 12,816,094 | 13,782,830 |
| P/L | 1,105,303 | 1,914,286 | 1,909,462 |
| NW | 7,563,415 | 6,625,483 | 5,053,268 |
| WC | N/A | 4,658,908 | 3,085,819 |
| Emp. | 113 | 109 | 103 |

DUNS 23-352-3229
## Tyntec Ltd
11-12 Hope Street, Douglas, Douglas, Isle of Man IM1 1AQ
**Tel:** 01624667735
**Web:** www.tyntec.com
**Reg No:** 0107081M **VAT No:** 002172634
**Estd:** 2002 Private Limited Company
**Line of Business:** Facsimile machines
**Directors:** D Parnell, M Kowalzik
**Responsibilities**
**Senior:** Kochem Dose *(Ceo)*
**US SIC:** 4899 **UK SIC:** 79020

| | 31-03-13 | 31-03-12 | 31-03-08 |
|---|---|---|---|
| TO | 19,934,072 | 17,650,345 | 9,785,622 |
| P/L | (1,157,149) | (3,175,290) | 2,955,523 |
| NW | (14,410,464) | (13,104,677) | 5,441,739 |
| WC | 4,060,297 | 5,128,538 | 5,436,439 |

DUNS 34-772-5579 **Imp**
## Typhoo Tea Ltd
Pasture Road, Moreton, Wirral, Merseyside CH46 8XF
**Tel:** 01515224000 **Fax:** 01515-224020
**Web:** www.typhoo.com
**Reg No:** 5573418 **VAT No:** 867262300
**Estd:** 1903 Private Limited Company
**Line of Business:** Tea processing
**Issued Capital:** £31,510,005
**Directors:** M Mcbrien, A Ghosh, Ms M Tapal, A K Bhargava, P Paul, T Vyner Cbe, Hon Frcp, K Paul, R Agarwal
**Co. Secretary:** Somnath Saha
**Responsibilities**
**Senior:** Keith Packer *(Chief Executive)*
**Marketing:** Jeremy Coles *(Marketing Director)*
**Sales:** Keith Packer *(Chief Executive)*
**IT:** Darren Tam *(IT Manager)*

**Purchasing:** Alan Hargreaves (Purchasing Manager)
**US SIC:** 2099 **UK SIC:** 42399
**Auditors:** Grant Thornton UK LLP
**Bankers:** Barclays Bank Plc (20-36-47)

| | 31-03-14 | 31-03-13 | 31-03-12 |
|---|---|---|---|
| TO | 70,660,000 | 67,724,000 | 67,773,000 |
| P/L | 988,000 | (661,000) | (2,163,000) |
| NW | (59,780,000) | (60,768,000) | (60,132,000) |
| WC | (28,553,000) | (23,776,000) | (19,822,000) |
| Emp. | 253 | 260 | 277 |

DUNS 54-427-4046
## Typhoon Holdings Ltd
Limerick Road, Redcar, Cleveland TS10 5JU
**Web:** www.typhoon-int.co.uk
**Reg No:** 3273550 **Estd:** 1996 Private Limited Company
**Line of Business:** Management activities of holding companies
**Export Sales:** £3,024,805
**Issued Capital:** £940,000
**Directors:** D J Baxter, Lady C M Bibby, Sir M J Bibby, P J Bibby, G J Mccutcheon, D T Lonsdale
**US SIC:** 6711, 3949
**UK SIC:** 83962, 49420
**Auditors:** Westmore Brennand

| | 31-10-13 | 31-10-12 | 31-10-11 |
|---|---|---|---|
| TO | 8,175,148 | 7,443,876 | 8,457,807 |
| P/L | 184,981 | (35,450) | (50,964) |
| NW | 1,192,768 | 1,005,939 | 992,400 |
| WC | 3,671,503 | 4,235,711 | 3,792,188 |
| Emp. | 91 | 81 | 87 |

DUNS 50-460-5627 Exp
## Typocolor Ltd
(Subsidiary of: J & A Group Ltd)
Unit 5 Prospect Place, Skelmersdale, Lancashire WN8 9QD
**Tel:** 01695-720551 **Fax:** 01695729056
**Web:** www.typocolor.com
**Reg No:** 2443090 **VAT No:** 535038851
**Estd:** 1989 Private Limited Company
**Line of Business:** Colour analysts
**Export Markets:** E U, Middle East
**Issued Capital:** £100
**Director:** A J Holcroft
**Co. Secretary:** Jonathan Hare
**Responsibilities**
**HR:** Jayne Prior (Human Resources Manager)
**US SIC:** 7231 **UK SIC:** 98200
**Auditors:** Ernst & Young
**Bankers:** National Westminster Bank Plc (60-19-49)

| | 31-12-13 | 31-12-12 | 31-12-11 |
|---|---|---|---|
| TA | 1,900,165 | 1,488,109 | 923,653 |
| NW | 268,637 | 274,146 | 54,857 |
| WC | 201,392 | 186,605 | 174,143 |

DUNS 21-207-3290 Imp-Exp
## Tyre Services Great Britain Ltd
(Subsidiary of: Goodyear Dunlop Tyres Uk Ltd)
Tyre Fort, 94-98 Wingfoot Way, Erdington, Birmingham, West Midlands B24 9HY
**Fax:** 01905-731203
**Web:** www.dunloptyres.co.uk
**Reg No:** 0480259 **Estd:** 1950 Private Limited Company
**Line of Business:** Tyre dealers
**Export Markets:** Worldwide
**Trading Style:** Goodyear Dunlop, H I Q
**Issued Capital:** £16,531
**Directors:** E Fric, M A Lins
**Co. Secretary:** Dale Mochan
**Responsibilities**
**Senior:** Michael McNulty (Manager)
**Finance:** Michael McNulty (Manager)
**Branches:** Tyre Services Great Britain Ltd, Unit 5 100 Brook St, Dundee, Angus DD1 5BP
**US SIC:** 5531 **UK SIC:** 65100
**Bankers:** Barclays Bank Plc (20-97-78)

| | 31-12-13 | 31-12-12 | 31-12-11 |
|---|---|---|---|
| TA | 107,934 | 107,934 | 107,934 |
| NW | 107,934 | 107,934 | 107,934 |
| WC | 107,934 | 107,934 | N/A |
| Emp. | 1,100 | 1,100 | N/A |

DUNS 56-977-8426 Imp
## Tyre Spot Ltd
Unit 4a, Sandy Lane, Newcastle-Upon-Tyne, Tyne and Wear NE3 5HE
**Tel:** 01912170066 **Fax:** 0191-236-2567
**Web:** www.tyrespot.co.uk
**Reg No:** 2854187 **Estd:** 1997 Private Limited Company
**Line of Business:** Sale of motor vehicle parts and accessories
**Issued Capital:** £100,000
**Directors:** J T Shaw, J W Shaw
**Co. Secretary:** Mrs Pauline Shaw
**Branches:** Tyre Spot Ltd, Newbottle Street, Houghton Le Spring, Tyne and Wear DH4 4AS
**US SIC:** 5531 **UK SIC:** 65100

**Auditors:** Kenneth Easby LLP

| | 31-03-14 | 31-03-13 | 31-03-12 |
|---|---|---|---|
| TO | 18,651,064 | 18,498,924 | 18,907,628 |
| P/L | 559,615 | 571,944 | 698,651 |
| NW | 3,710,766 | 3,267,535 | 2,824,470 |
| WC | 933,317 | 773,630 | 395,761 |
| Emp. | 105 | 103 | 102 |

DUNS 22-850-1227
## Tyrer Tours Ltd
16 Lomeshaye Industrial Estate Kirby, Road, Nelson, Lancashire BB9 6RS
**Tel:** 01282619141
**Web:** www.holmeswoodcoaches.com
**Reg No:** 1458953 **VAT No:** 343424574
**Estd:** 1979 Private Limited Company
**Line of Business:** Other scheduled passenger land transport not elsewhere classified
**Issued Capital:** £5,000
**Principals:** R Tyrer (Managing), H P Tyrer
**Co. Secretary:** Howard Tyrer
**Responsibilities**
**Finance:** Lorraine Tyrer (Manager)
**Health & Safety:** Janice Bolton (Health & Safety Officer)
**Facilities:** James Holloway (Maintenance Manager)
**Operations:** Lorraine Tyrer (Manager)
**US SIC:** 4119 **UK SIC:** 72200
**Auditors:** Cassons
**Bankers:** Barclays Bank Plc (20-15-70)

| | 31-03-14 | 31-03-13 | 31-03-12 |
|---|---|---|---|
| TA | 1,197,390 | 1,441,044 | 2,117,975 |
| NW | 748,490 | 768,086 | 1,016,469 |
| WC | (30,227) | (93,499) | (286,570) |

DUNS 22-800-0055
## Tyrespot
Drum Road, Chester-Le-Street, County Durham DH3 2AF
**Web:** www.tyrespot.co.uk
**Estd:** 1978 Partnership
**Line of Business:** Tyre dealers
**Partners:** J T Shaw, Mrs P Shaw
**Branches:** Tyrespot, 29 Second Avenue, Team Valley Trading Estate, Gateshead, Tyne and Wear NE11 0ND
**US SIC:** 5531 **UK SIC:** 65100
**Bankers:** Barclays Bank Plc (20-80-47)
**Employees:** 88

DUNS 22-858-4777
## Tyrewise
Hornhouse Lane, Knowsley Industrial Park, Liverpool, Merseyside L33 7YQ
**Tel:** 01515472301
**Web:** www.tyrewise.co.uk
**VAT No:** 325341778 **Estd:** 1982 Partnership
**Line of Business:** Sale of motor vehicle parts and accessories
**Partners:** W J Watts, B W Lindsay
**Responsibilities**
**Senior:** Chris Lyndsay (Manager)
**US SIC:** 5531 **UK SIC:** 65100
**Bankers:** HSBC Bank plc (40-29-08)
**Employees:** 48

DUNS 21-155-9158 Imp
## Tyrolit Ltd
(Subsidiary of: D. Swarovski Kg)
Eldon Close, Northampton, Northamptonshire NN6 7UD
**Tel:** 01788823738
**Web:** www.tyrolit.co.uk
**Reg No:** 1190584 **Estd:** 1974 Private Limited Company
**Line of Business:** Wholesale suppliers of abrasive products
**Export Sales:** £548,000
**Issued Capital:** £100,000
**Principals:** J E Willis (Managing), K H Mader, C J Koidl, A Landl
**Co. Secretary:** Paul Stephenson
**Responsibilities**
**Marketing:** Kevin Bailey (Marketing Manager), Lisa Lancaster (Marketing Manager)
**Admin:** Debbie Sitford (Administrator)
**Branches:** Tyrolit Ltd, Unit C2 Windsor Place, Faraday Road, Crawley, West Sussex RH10 9TF
**US SIC:** 5039, 7399
**UK SIC:** 61300, 83954
**Auditors:** PricewaterhouseCoopers LLP
**Bankers:** Barclays Bank Plc (20-36-47)

| | 31-12-13 | 31-12-12 | 31-12-11 |
|---|---|---|---|
| TO | 15,431,000 | 15,467,951 | 15,508,923 |
| P/L | 272,000 | 24,921 | 569,983 |
| NW | 1,481,000 | 1,482,450 | 1,889,808 |
| WC | 612,000 | 483,735 | 965,028 |
| Emp. | 51 | 49 | 49 |

DUNS 23-719-9120 Exp
## Tyrone Fabrication Ltd
(Subsidiary of: Redcherry Investments Ltd)
87 Goland Road, Ballygawley, Dungannon, Co Tyrone BT70 2LA
**Tel:** 028-8556-7200 **Fax:** 028-8556-7089
**Web:** www.tyronefabrication.co.uk
**Reg No:** 0027091NI **Estd:** 1992 Private Limited Company
**Line of Business:** Steel fabricators
**Export Markets:** E U & New Zealand
**Issued Capital:** £200,002
**Directors:** Ms M T Mcdermott, B Mcdermott
**Co. Secretary:** Brendan Mcdermott
**Responsibilities**
**Operations:** Martin O' Hagan (Maintenance Manager)
**Purchasing:** John McMahon (Electrical Purchasing Manager)
**US SIC:** 2517, 3325
**UK SIC:** 46714, 31110
**Auditors:** Cavanagh Kelly
**Bankers:** First Trust Bank (aib Group (uk) Plc) (93-81-30)

| | 31-12-13 | 31-12-12 | 31-12-11 |
|---|---|---|---|
| TO | 5,712,319 | 5,895,126 | 4,799,684 |
| P/L | 337,396 | 275,484 | 179,005 |
| NW | 3,580,031 | 3,250,149 | 3,026,941 |
| WC | 1,295,640 | 989,600 | 987,404 |
| Emp. | 78 | 59 | 63 |

DUNS 42-351-9342
## Tyrrells Potato Crisps Ltd
(Subsidiary of: Crisps Topco Ltd)
Tyrrells Court, Stretford, Leominster, Herefordshire HR6 9DQ
**Tel:** 01568720244
**Web:** www.tyrrellspotatochips.co.uk
**Reg No:** 4339626 **Estd:** 1994 Private Limited Company
**Line of Business:** Manufacturers of food products
**Export Sales:** £8,793,000
**Trading Style:** Tyrrells Potato Crisps Ltd
**Issued Capital:** £1,875
**Director:** D R Milner
**Co. Secretary:** Ms Joanne Jones
**Responsibilities**
**Senior:** William Chase (Manager), Sharon Gardner (Manager), Oliver Wyncoll (Manager)
**Marketing:** Julie Davis (Marketing Manager)
**IT:** Mike Pledge (IT Manager)
**US SIC:** 2099 **UK SIC:** 42399
**Auditors:** BDO Stoy Hayward LLP

| | 28-03-14 | 29-03-13 | 30-03-12 |
|---|---|---|---|
| TO | 40,344,000 | 34,175,000 | 27,886,000 |
| P/L | 3,912,000 | 5,265,000 | 6,544,000 |
| NW | 26,855,000 | 23,133,000 | 19,020,000 |
| WC | 24,684,000 | 17,434,000 | 17,189,000 |
| Emp. | 149 | 150 | 138 |

DUNS 22-238-4088
## Tyser & Co. Ltd
(Subsidiary of: Hawkes Bay Holdings Ltd)
15 St Botolph Street, London EC3A 7EE
**Tel:** 02030378111 **Fax:** 02073974852
**Web:** www.tysers.com
**Reg No:** 4256470 **Estd:** 1901 Private Unlimited Company
**Line of Business:** Financial advisers (independent)
**Export Sales:** £32,744,000
**Issued Capital:** £101,772
**Directors:** G J Andrews, C J Elliott, Mrs K A Cross, P C Haynes, C M Spratt, I M Witt, T P Newbery, J J Macey
**Co. Secretary:** Mark James
**US SIC:** 6411 **UK SIC:** 83200
**Auditors:** Deloitte LLP

| | 31-12-13 | 31-12-12 | 31-12-11 |
|---|---|---|---|
| TO | 38,700,000 | 37,585,000 | 36,066,000 |
| P/L | 6,412,000 | 6,622,000 | 6,495,000 |
| NW | 5,356,000 | 5,880,000 | 4,330,000 |
| WC | 5,342,000 | 5,866,000 | 4,316,000 |

DUNS 22-722-0308
## Tyser Group Services Ltd
(Subsidiary of: Hawkes Bay Holdings Ltd)
Bowford House, 15 St Botolphs, London EC3A 7EE
**Tel:** 02030378000 **Fax:** 020-7621-9042
**Web:** www.tysers.com
**Reg No:** 1224375 **Estd:** 1975 Private Limited Company
**Line of Business:** Management activities of holding companies
**Issued Capital:** £1,351
**Directors:** I M Witt, D B Green, E C Slade, M S Takhtar, M James, Mrs S Panesar, Mrs K A Cross, G J Andrews
**Co. Secretary:** Mark James
**US SIC:** 6711, 6411
**UK SIC:** 83962, 83200
**Auditors:** Arthur Andersen

**Bankers:** HSBC Bank plc (40-04-12)

| | 31-12-13 | 31-12-12 | 31-12-11 |
|---|---|---|---|
| TO | 21,586,000 | 29,542,000 | 26,615,000 |
| P/L | 1,893,000 | 382,000 | (1,648,000) |
| NW | (5,777,000) | (6,220,000) | (5,228,000) |
| WC | (3,061,000) | (3,862,000) | (3,843,000) |
| Emp. | 172 | 199 | 204 |

DUNS 21-326-0615
## Tyson H. Burridge Ltd
Old Coach Works, Distington, Workington, Cumbria CA14 5XJ
**Fax:** 01946-830777
**Web:** www.tysonhburridge.co.uk
**Reg No:** 1301344 **VAT No:** 288147228
**Estd:** 1962 Private Limited Company
**Line of Business:** Other supporting land transport activities
**Issued Capital:** £50,000
**Principals:** T H Burridge (Managing), N A Robinson, D R Burridge, Ms H M Agnew, Ms A Burridge, A T Burridge
**Co. Secretary:** Mrs Helen Agnew
**Responsibilities**
**Senior:** J Buridge (Manager)
**US SIC:** 4789 **UK SIC:** 77002
**Auditors:** J F W Robinson & Co
**Bankers:** National Westminster Bank Plc (01-02-17)

| | 31-03-14 | 31-03-13 | 31-03-12 |
|---|---|---|---|
| TO | 7,027,943 | 6,719,919 | 6,430,695 |
| P/L | 411,154 | 203,195 | 335,012 |
| NW | 6,404,763 | 5,196,403 | 5,090,185 |
| WC | 3,398,997 | 3,104,505 | 3,128,203 |
| Emp. | 66 | 64 | 64 |

DUNS 21-781-8029
## Tyssen Krupp Services
Lode Lane, Solihull, West Midlands B92 8NW
**Tel:** 01217003446
**Estd:** 2011 Proprietorship
**Line of Business:** Cleaning contracting commercial
**Proprietor:** O Tighe
**US SIC:** 7349 **UK SIC:** 92300
**Employees:** 250

DUNS 42-433-7749
## Tytherington Ltd
(Subsidiary of: Club Co Holdings Ltd)
The Old Hall, Dorchester Way, Macclesfield, Cheshire SK10 2LQ
**Tel:** 01625-506000 **Fax:** 01625-506040
**Web:** www.theclubcompany.com
**Reg No:** 0904206 **VAT No:** 616167445
**Estd:** 1986 Private Limited Company
**Line of Business:** Sports clubs
**Trading Style:** The Tytherington Club, Tytherington Golf & Country Club
**Issued Capital:** £1,000
**Director:** T Delsol
**Co. Secretary:** Martin Hemmings
**Responsibilities**
**Senior:** Charlotte Bainbridge (Duty Manager)
**US SIC:** 7999 **UK SIC:** 97913
**Bankers:** Barclays Bank Plc (20-82-14)
**Employees:** 1,000

DUNS 73-664-0223
## Tywyn Kid's Club
Channel View, Port Talbot, West Glamorgan SA12 6JF
**Tel:** 07727137258
**Web:** www.tywynprimaryschool.ik.org
**Reg No:** 4923602 **Estd:** 2003 Private Company Limited By Guarantee
**Line of Business:** Primary education
**Directors:** Mrs G Needs, R H Phillips, Ms M O'Kane, M Aplin
**US SIC:** 8211 **UK SIC:** 93200

| | 31-08-13 | 31-08-12 | 31-08-11 |
|---|---|---|---|
| TO | 15,281 | 29,216 | 22,344 |
| P/L | (3,552) | N/A | 2,642 |
| NW | 5,646 | 7,177 | 7,177 |

# U

DUNS 22-846-1620
## U C B Home Loans Corporation Ltd
(Subsidiary of: Nationwide Building Society)
36 Sutton Court Road, Sutton, Surrey SM1 4TE
**Tel:** 02084014000
**Web:** www.ucbhomeloans.com
**Reg No:** 1063539 **Estd:** 1972 Private Limited Company
**Line of Business:** Investment consultants
**Trading Style:** Ucbhl
**Issued Capital:** £45,100,000
**Directors:** H Jordan, C S Rhodes, A B Matson, I Laing, R S Napier

**Co. Secretary:** Jason Lindsey
**Responsibilities**
**Senior:** Andrew Mcqueen (*Manager*), Mark Rennison (*Manager*), Matthew Wyles (*Manager*)
**Finance:** Philip Vinall (*Finance Director*)
**US SIC:** 6111 **UK SIC:** 81501
**Auditors:** PricewaterhouseCoopers LLP
**Bankers:** Lloyds TSB Bank plc (30-92-45)
Following financial data are in thousands

|     | 31-03-14 | 31-03-13 | 31-03-12 |
|-----|----------|----------|----------|
| TA  | 3,941,059 | 4,497,490 | 5,002,498 |
| P/L | 71,810 | 43,054 | 55,858 |
| NW  | 313,821 | 258,588 | 250,903 |
| WC  | (3,450,457) | (4,005,718) | (4,225,124) |

DUNS 21-878-7623
## U C L the Department of Political Science
29-30 Tavistock Square, London WC1H 9QU
**Tel:** 02076794999
**Web:** www.ucl.ac.uk
**Estd:** 2012
**Line of Business:** University
**Responsibilities**
**Senior:** David Coen (*Manager*)
**US SIC:** 8221 **UK SIC:** 93100
**Employees:** 50

DUNS 23-183-9007
## U C L Union
Institute Of Archaeology, London WC1H 0PY
**Tel:** 02076797495
**Web:** www.ucl.ac.uk
**Estd:** 1094
**Line of Business:** First-degree level higher education
**Trading Style:** University College London
**Responsibilities**
**Senior:** Ben McMechan (*Designated Limited Liability P*)
**Admin:** Fiona McClean (*Receptionist*)
**IT:** Ash Rennie (*IT Manager*)
**Health & Safety:** Sandra Bond (*Facilities Manager*)
**Facilities:** Sandra Bond (*Facilities Manager*), George Davies (*Building Officer*)
**US SIC:** 7399 **UK SIC:** 83954
**Bankers:** Barclays Bank Plc (20-05-75)
**Employees:** 100

DUNS 21-589-9443
## U C U
Carlow Street, London NW1 7LH
**Tel:** 02077562500
**Web:** www.ucu.org.uk
**Estd:** 2011
**Line of Business:** Activities of business and employers organisations
**Responsibilities**
**Admin:** Sally Hunt (*General Secretary*)
**US SIC:** 8611 **UK SIC:** 96312
**Employees:** 120

DUNS 45-833-2608
## U-Drive Ltd
48-56 Old Wareham Road, Poole, Dorset BH12 4QR
**Web:** www.u-drive.co.uk
**Reg No:** 3183986 **Estd:** 1996 Private Limited Company
**Line of Business:** Car, van and truck leasing and contract hire
**Trading Style:** U-Drive Ltd
**Issued Capital:** £25,000
**Director:** D A Hamblin
**Co. Secretary:** Mrs Gillian Hamblin
**Responsibilities**
**Admin:** Bill Langtree (*Office Manager*)
**Branches:** U-Drive Ltd, 9 Malmesbury Road, Southampton, Hampshire SO15 5FT
**US SIC:** 7512 **UK SIC:** 84801
**Auditors:** Moore Stephens (South) LLP

|     | 31-12-13 | 31-12-12 | 31-12-11 |
|-----|----------|----------|----------|
| TO  | 9,847,648 | 9,248,084 | 8,423,961 |
| P/L | 409,267 | (156,935) | 224,168 |
| NW  | 3,706,410 | 3,573,003 | 3,568,279 |
| WC  | (2,649,738) | (3,876,643) | (3,180,495) |
| Emp. | 142 | 132 | 121 |

DUNS 22-714-8566 **Imp-Exp**
## U K Atomic Energy Authority
Culham Science Centre, Abingdon, Oxfordshire OX14 3DB
**Tel:** 01235463000 **Fax:** 01235 432916
**Web:** www.ccfe.ac.uk
**VAT No:** 570101391 **Estd:** 1954 Incorporate By Act Of Parliament
**Line of Business:** Research and laboratory based activities
**Export Markets:** Worldwide
**Trading Style:** U K A E A Nuclear Services, U K A E A, Culham Centre for Fusion Energy
**Principals:** Ms K Eaton (*Chairman*), D Shah
**Branches:** U K Atomic Energy Authority, D N P D E, Thurso, Caithness KW14 7TZ
**US SIC:** 9121 **UK SIC:** 91110
**Bankers:** Barclays Bank Plc (20-00-00)
**Employees:** 1,000

DUNS 21-098-4826
## U K Commission for Employment & Skills
Adwick Park, Manvers, Rotherham, South Yorkshire S63 5NB
**Tel:** 01709 774800 **Fax:** 01709 774801
**Web:** www.ukces.gov.uk
**Reg No:** 6425800 **Estd:** 2007 Private Company Limited By Guarantee
**Line of Business:** Central government
**Trading Style:** Ukces, Investors in People International
**Directors:** Mrs F M Kendrick, S M Johnson, T G Peyton-Jones, Ms F L O'Grady, Ms B Spicer, P J Mckelvie, D A Mccormick, W D Butler-Adams
**Co. Secretary:** Ms Lesley Giles
**Responsibilities**
**Senior:** Deirdre Hughes (*Commissioner*), William Mcginnis (*Director*), Julie Pepper (*Business Services Manager*), David Prentis (*Director*), Nigel Whitehead (*Director*)
**Branches:** Uk Commission For Employment and Skills, 6 Austin Boulevard, Quay West Riverside Business Village, SR5 2AL Sunderland
**US SIC:** 9121 **UK SIC:** 91110
**Auditors:** Comptroller & Auditor General

|     | 31-03-14 | 31-03-13 | 31-03-12 |
|-----|----------|----------|----------|
| TO  | 422,000 | 255,000 | 517,714 |
| P/L | (61,604,000) | (62,104,000) | (62,975,667) |
| NW  | (7,229,000) | (5,865,000) | (4,614,470) |
| WC  | (7,468,000) | (6,252,000) | (5,016,649) |
| Emp. | 105 | 104 | 101 |

DUNS 22-101-3725 **imp**
## U K Distributors (Footwear) Ltd
Marlow House, Leicester, Leicestershire LE8 8UD
**Tel:** 01162403232 **Fax:** 01162-402762
**Web:** www.ukdistributors.co.uk
**Reg No:** 4120969 **Estd:** 1925 Private Limited Company
**Line of Business:** Footwear wholesalers
**Export Sales:** £1,188,397
**Issued Capital:** £361,213
**Directors:** G W Marlow, J P Marlow, C Brown
**Co. Secretary:** Derek Marlow
**Responsibilities**
**Marketing:** Mike Barton (*Sales & Marketing Director*)
**Sales:** Mike Barton (*Sales & Marketing Director*), Frank Brennan (*Account Manager*), Don Brenner (*Account Manager*), Ernie Dickinson (*Account Manager*), Andy Hayes (*Account Manager*), Stuart Hildersley (*Account Manager*), Chris Skehill (*Account Manager*)
**IT:** David Fincham (*Computer Manager*)
**Operations:** Mike Barton (*Sales & Marketing Director*)
**US SIC:** 5136 **UK SIC:** 61600
**Auditors:** Newby Castleman

|     | 30-04-14 | 30-04-13 | 30-04-12 |
|-----|----------|----------|----------|
| TO  | 16,410,796 | 16,062,389 | 14,881,097 |
| P/L | 810,447 | 762,395 | 800,624 |
| NW  | 16,653,608 | 16,032,369 | 15,464,831 |
| WC  | 14,457,162 | 13,819,491 | 13,223,614 |
| Emp. | 69 | 68 | 64 |

DUNS 21-916-4595
## U K Fire Doors Ltd
Pinfold Lane, Mold, Clwyd CH7 6NZ
**Tel:** 01244551360
**Web:** www.firedoors.co.uk
**Reg No:** 8335821 **Estd:** 2012 Private Limited Company
**Line of Business:** Manufacture of builders carpentry and joinery
**Issued Capital:** £100
**Directors:** Directorc01 Limited, T D Askew, Mrs D L Askew, Directorc02 Limited
**US SIC:** 2431 **UK SIC:** 46300

|     | 30-09-13 |
|-----|----------|
| TA  | 1,900,497 |
| NW  | 121,844 |
| WC  | 163,332 |

DUNS 77-948-0219
## U K Point of Sale Ltd
(**Subsidiary of:** Uk Point of Sale Group Ltd)
Unit A, Horsfield Way, Stockport, Cheshire SK6 2TD
**Tel:** 08451308091 **Fax:** 01614314411
**Web:** www.ukpos.com
**Reg No:** 3054353 **Estd:** 1995 Private Limited Company
**Line of Business:** Display equipment and fixtures
**Trading Style:** Uk Point of Sale Group Limited
**Issued Capital:** £100
**Directors:** W M Leslie, J S Leslie
**Co. Secretary:** Mrs Debra Jamieson
**US SIC:** 7399, 5199
**UK SIC:** 83954, 61900

|     | 31-05-13 | 31-05-12 | 31-05-11 |
|-----|----------|----------|----------|
| TA  | 100 | 100 | 100 |
| NW  | 100 | 100 | 100 |

DUNS 21-635-2006
## U K Property Rectifiers Ltd
Redberry House, Gargrave Road, Broughton, Skipton, North Yorkshire BD23 3AQ
**Tel:** 01423790145
**Web:** www.property-rectifiers.co.uk
**Reg No:** 7120787 **Estd:** 2010 Private Limited Company
**Line of Business:** Other building completion
**Issued Capital:** £20,004
**Director:** J Totty
**US SIC:** 1799 **UK SIC:** 50000

|     | 31-03-14 | 31-03-13 | 31-03-12 |
|-----|----------|----------|----------|
| TA  | 118,294 | 133,696 | 130,007 |
| NW  | 108,817 | 121,969 | 113,914 |
| WC  | 105,536 | 94,704 | 77,174 |

DUNS 50-327-3302
## U K Shuttle Ltd
(**Subsidiary of:** Z5 Enterprises Ltd)
Unit D Europa Industrial Estate, Radway Road, Swindon, Wiltshire SN3 4ND
**Tel:** 01793832668 **Fax:** 01793-825084
**Web:** www.ukshuttle.co.uk
**Reg No:** 2352038 **VAT No:** 535554634
**Estd:** 2005 Private Limited Company
**Line of Business:** Goods delivery services
**Issued Capital:** £10,000
**Director:** S Ziaullah
**Responsibilities**
**Senior:** Mervyn Gibbs (*Facilities Manager*), Bryan Rose (*Manager*)
**Finance:** Bryan Rose (*Manager*)
**IT:** Bryan Rose (*Manager*)
**Health & Safety:** Mervyn Gibbs (*Facilities Manager*)
**Facilities:** Mervyn Gibbs (*Facilities Manager*)
**Branches:** U K Shuttle Ltd, Unit 20-20A, Okus Trading Estate, Swindon, Wiltshire SN1 2PG
**US SIC:** 4213, 4226
**UK SIC:** 72300, 77003
**Auditors:** Bentley Jennison
**Bankers:** National Westminster Bank Plc (60-21-40)

|     | 31-08-13 | 31-08-12 | 31-08-11 |
|-----|----------|----------|----------|
| TA  | 826,624 | 809,603 | 880,733 |
| NW  | 68,538 | 71,159 | 51,171 |
| WC  | (92,550) | (111,989) | (163,010) |

DUNS 77-958-8966
## U Lock-It Ltd
60-64 Chapel Street, Wincham, Northwich, Cheshire CW9 6DA
**Tel:** 08450264615
**Web:** www.rojac-uk.co.uk
**Reg No:** 5927877 **Estd:** 2006 Private Limited Company
**Line of Business:** Road haulage and transport services
**Issued Capital:** £100
**Directors:** S J Roberts, M J Roberts, W T Shipsides
**Co. Secretary:** Julian Jackson
**Responsibilities**
**Senior:** Tim Stoke (*Manager*)
**US SIC:** 6519 **UK SIC:** 85000

|     | 30-09-13 | 30-09-12 | 30-09-11 |
|-----|----------|----------|----------|
| TA  | 705,553 | 437,818 | 372,611 |
| NW  | 176,822 | 103,784 | 64,099 |
| WC  | (51,231) | (35,862) | 990 |

DUNS 50-039-2576
## U P V C Distributors Ltd
(**Subsidiary of:** Burles Group Plc)
Imperial Building, Bridge Street, Newport, Gwent NP11 4SB
**Tel:** 01495248030 **Fax:** 01495-247990
**Web:** www.nationalplastics.co.uk
**Reg No:** 2310163 **Estd:** 1989 Private Limited Company
**Line of Business:** Other wholesale
**Trading Style:** National Plastics
**Issued Capital:** £10,000
**Principals:** D A Burles (*Managing*), J K Lewis, P G Brough, G P Foster
**Co. Secretary:** Ms Heidi Sachs
**Branches:** U P V C Distributors Ltd, Maritme Yd, Maritime Indstl Est, Pontypridd, Mid Glamorgan CF37 1NY
**US SIC:** 5161 **UK SIC:** 61200
**Auditors:** Owens Thomas
**Bankers:** Barclays Bank Plc (20-10-26)

|     | 31-12-13 | 31-12-12 | 31-12-11 |
|-----|----------|----------|----------|
| TO  | 15,662,710 | 13,614,284 | 12,386,736 |
| P/L | 417,838 | 210,581 | 138,264 |
| NW  | 1,010,204 | 682,944 | 548,826 |
| WC  | 719,645 | 389,383 | 323,338 |
| Emp. | 98 | 95 | 92 |

DUNS 21-833-0983 **Imp-Exp**
## U-Pol Ltd
(**Subsidiary of:** Graphite Capital Management Llp)
1-3 Totteridge Lane, Whetstone, London N20 0EY
**Tel:** 020-8492-5900
**Web:** www.u-pol.com
**Reg No:** 0464919 **VAT No:** 232449670
**Estd:** 1949 Private Limited Company
**Line of Business:** Manufacturers of chemicals
**Export Markets:** Worldwide
**Export Sales:** £35,694,000
**Trading Style:** U-Pol
**Issued Capital:** £15,000
**Directors:** P J May, M Coombes
**Responsibilities**
**Finance:** Andrew Ayres (*Financial Director*), Kate Moules (*Accountant*)
**Branches:** U-Pol Ltd, Denington Road, Wellingborough, Northamptonshire NN8 2QP
**US SIC:** 2899 **UK SIC:** 25670
**Auditors:** KPMG LLP
**Bankers:** HSBC Bank plc (40-07-37)

|     | 31-12-13 | 31-12-12 | 31-12-11 |
|-----|----------|----------|----------|
| TO  | 52,759,000 | 51,663,000 | 49,736,000 |
| P/L | 14,150,000 | 11,175,000 | 10,183,000 |
| NW  | 93,645,000 | 82,974,000 | 73,405,000 |
| WC  | 89,963,000 | 79,100,000 | 69,758,000 |
| Emp. | 237 | 236 | 227 |

DUNS 22-168-6848
## U2013 Ltd
The Hive, Camrose Avenue, Edgware, Middlesex HA8 6AG
**Tel:** 02083813800
**Web:** www.barnetfc.com
**Reg No:** 4187180 **Estd:** 2001 Private Limited Company
**Line of Business:** Sports clubs
**Issued Capital:** £300,000
**Director:** A A Kleanthous
**Co. Secretary:** Andrew Adie
**US SIC:** 7999 **UK SIC:** 97913

|     | 30-06-13 | 30-06-12 | 30-06-11 |
|-----|----------|----------|----------|
| TO  | 3,303,790 | 3,481,071 | 3,078,617 |
| P/L | 352,111 | 172,060 | 69,614 |
| NW  | 1,021,036 | 791,421 | 764,359 |
| WC  | (3,802,381) | (2,795,330) | (1,516,531) |
| Emp. | 242 | 152 | 145 |

DUNS 21-168-8219
## Uae Exchange Uk Ltd
(**Subsidiary of:** Uae Exchange Centre Llc)
14-15 Carlisle Street, London W1D 3BS
**Tel:** 02089037884 **Fax:** 02074949543
**Web:** www.uaeexchange.com
**Reg No:** 6937891 **Estd:** 2003 Private Limited Company
**Line of Business:** Financial intermediation not elsewhere classified
**Issued Capital:** £7,500,000
**Directors:** Dr B R Shetty, B R Shetty, M Shetty
**Responsibilities**
**Senior:** Marwan Humaid Al Mazrouei (*Manager*)
**Branches:** Uae Exchange Uk Ltd, 276 Soho Road, Birmingham, West Midlands B21 9LZ
**US SIC:** 6111 **UK SIC:** 81501
**Auditors:** Ernst & Young LLP
**Bankers:** HSBC Bank plc (40-02-33)

|     | 31-12-13 | 31-12-12 | 31-12-11 |
|-----|----------|----------|----------|
| TA  | 11,102,481 | 12,591,830 | 12,603,469 |
| P/L | (975,342) | (697,477) | 10,459 |
| NW  | 5,299,829 | 6,261,888 | 6,959,365 |
| WC  | (9,890) | 654,789 | 1,661,640 |
| Emp. | 84 | 86 | 67 |

DUNS 23-748-9682 **Imp-Exp**
## Ubh International Ltd
(**Subsidiary of:** Baxi Partnership Ltd)
Orrell Lane, Ormskirk, Lancashire L40 0SL
**Tel:** 01704 898 500
**Web:** www.ubh.co.uk
**Reg No:** 3742928 **Estd:** 1970 Private Limited Company
**Line of Business:** Manufacturers and suppliers of tanks and cisterns
**Issued Capital:** £883,839
**Directors:** F Williams, P R Johnson, J Isherwood, P T Harding, M Himbury, D T Doyle, K Bragg, A Mcgonagle
**Co. Secretary:** Malcolm Lynch
**Responsibilities**
**Senior:** Alan Hodgkinson (*Manager*)
**Marketing:** Tom Harding (*Sales and Marketing Director*)
**Sales:** Alex Edwards (*Senior Sales Engineer*), Tom Harding (*Sales and Marketing Director*)
**Health & Safety:** Mike Horne (*Health & Safety Officer*)
**Facilities:** Graham Gaskell (*Facilities Manager*)
**US SIC:** 3443, 5074
**UK SIC:** 32051, 61300
**Auditors:** Moore & Smalley LLP

**Bankers:** HSBC Bank plc (40-40-39)

| | 30-09-13 | 30-09-12 | 30-09-11 |
|---|---|---|---|
| TO | 9,116,767 | 12,307,147 | 9,875,021 |
| P/L | 723,408 | 1,215,464 | 1,846,162 |
| NW | 6,180,164 | 5,894,933 | 5,264,704 |
| WC | 3,483,765 | 5,767,074 | 5,138,133 |
| Emp. | 76 | 76 | 68 |

DUNS 21-752-1734
## Ubico Ltd
Central Depot, Swindon Road, Cheltenham, Gloucestershire GL51 9JZ
**Tel:** 03003 009000
**Web:** www.ubico.co.uk
**Reg No:** 7824292 **Estd:** 2011 Private Limited Company
**Line of Business:** Environmental consultants
**Issued Capital:** £2
**Directors:** R K Bell, R Young, M A North, F M Wilson
**US SIC:** 4953 **UK SIC:** 92110
**Bankers:** Lloyds TSB Bank plc (30-91-87)

| | 31-03-14 | 31-03-13 |
|---|---|---|
| TO | 12,014,831 | 9,853,778 |
| P/L | 14,903 | 25,097 |
| NW | (181,998) | (446,901) |
| WC | 125,420 | (4,482) |
| Emp. | 257 | 190 |

DUNS 22-081-5455
## Ubique Systems U K Ltd
(**Subsidiary of:** Ubique Consultancy Private Limited)
Suite 13 Beaufort Court, Admirals Way, London E14 9XL
**Tel:** 020-7987-8811 **Fax:** 02079875379
**Web:** www.ubiquesystems.co.uk
**Reg No:** 4082982 **Estd:** 2000 Private Limited Company
**Line of Business:** Other software consultancy and supply
**Issued Capital:** £400,000
**Directors:** D R Barik, N S Vaidya, S Bhowmik
**Co. Secretary:** Ranajit Banerjee
**Responsibilities**
**Senior:** Somen Chatterjee *(Manager)*, Debjani Das *(Manager)*, Ishan Pattnaik *(Manager)*, Chirag Tailor *(Manager)*
**US SIC:** 7379 **UK SIC:** 83940
**Auditors:** NP & US Accountants

| | 31-03-14 | 31-03-13 | 31-03-12 |
|---|---|---|---|
| TO | 8,920,939 | N/A | N/A |
| P/L | 157,771 | N/A | N/A |
| NW | 706,775 | 606,658 | 515,945 |
| WC | 643,250 | 543,572 | 449,508 |
| Emp. | 68 | N/A | N/A |

DUNS 39-969-5220
## Ubiquitous Chip Ltd.
8-12 Ashton Lane, Glasgow, Lanarkshire G12 8SJ
**Tel:** 01413345007 **Fax:** 0141-337-1302
**Web:** www.theubiquitouschipwebsite.com
**Reg No:** 0111803SC **Estd:** 1988 Private Limited Company
**Line of Business:** Licensed restaurants
**Issued Capital:** £1,054,540
**Directors:** Ms C S Wright, C Clydesdale
**Co. Secretary:** Ms Carol Wright
**Responsibilities**
**Senior:** Ronald Clydesdale *(Manager)*
**US SIC:** 5812, 5813
**UK SIC:** 66110, 66200
**Auditors:** Gilchrist & Co
**Bankers:** The Royal Bank Of Scotland Plc (83-07-06)

| | 31-03-14 | 31-03-13 | 31-03-12 |
|---|---|---|---|
| TA | 2,920,682 | 2,893,618 | 2,900,902 |
| NW | 1,339,053 | 1,278,175 | 1,153,886 |
| WC | 1,134,128 | 783,532 | 668,667 |

DUNS 34-566-6135
## Ubiquity Software Corporation Ltd
(**Subsidiary of:** Avaya Holdings Corp.)
Building, 3 The Eastern Business Park, Cardiff, South Glamorgan CF3 5EA
**Tel:** 02920817500 **Fax:** 029-2081-7501
**Web:** www.thrupoint.com
**Reg No:** 2719723 **Estd:** 1992 Private Limited Company
**Line of Business:** Hardware consultancy
**Issued Capital:** £204,454,301
**Directors:** L Hastings, K A Loidi
**Co. Secretary:** Lee Hastings
**Responsibilities**
**Senior:** Sarah Paul *(Project Manager)*, Nancy Scott *(Manager)*
**US SIC:** 7379, 7391
**UK SIC:** 83940, 94000
**Auditors:** PricewaterhouseCoopers LLP
**Bankers:** Citibank Na (08-60-71)

| | 30-09-13 | 30-09-12 | 30-09-11 |
|---|---|---|---|
| TA | 2,258,000 | 2,411,000 | 2,338,000 |
| P/L | (2,503,000) | (937,000) | (380,000) |
| NW | (28,326,000) | (25,823,000) | (24,886,000) |
| WC | (28,326,000) | (25,823,000) | (24,587,000) |

DUNS 53-639-0370 Imp
## Ubiqus Uk Ltd
(**Subsidiary of:** Ubiqus)
Clifford's Inn, Fetter Lane, London EC4A 1LD
**Tel:** 02072690370
**Web:** www.ubiqus.co.uk
**Reg No:** 3444614 **VAT No:** 701997814
**Estd:** 1997 Private Limited Company
**Line of Business:** Secretarial and translation activities
**Export Sales:** £484,822
**Trading Style:** Ubiqus Uk Ltd
**Issued Capital:** £1,000
**Director:** V Nguyen
**Co. Secretary:** Laurent Decaudaveine
**US SIC:** 7339 **UK SIC:** 83954
**Auditors:** Lucentum Ltd

| | 31-12-13 | 31-12-12 | 31-12-11 |
|---|---|---|---|
| TO | 6,728,366 | 6,690,314 | 6,921,587 |
| P/L | 1,196,192 | 1,158,628 | 1,141,368 |
| NW | 1,081,737 | 965,316 | 915,981 |
| WC | 766,418 | 670,369 | 608,215 |
| Emp. | 119 | 98 | 80 |

DUNS 34-789-1868
## Ubisense Group Plc
St Andrews House, 90 St Andrews Road, Newmarket, Suffolk
**Tel:** 01223-535170
**Web:** www.ubisense.net
**Reg No:** 5589712 **Estd:** 2005 Public Limited Company
**Line of Business:** Management activities of holding companies
**Export Sales:** £26,463,000
**Issued Capital:** £436,139
**Directors:** I E Kershaw, Professor A Hopper, P G Harverson, R T Green, R G Parker, P R Taylor, R D Sansom
**Co. Secretary:** Robert Parker
**US SIC:** 6711 **UK SIC:** 83962
**Auditors:** Grant Thornton LLP
**Bankers:** HSBC Bank plc (40-16-07)

| | 31-12-13 | 31-12-12 | 31-12-11 |
|---|---|---|---|
| TO | 27,002,000 | 24,292,000 | 23,785,000 |
| P/L | (1,719,000) | (728,000) | 141,000 |
| NW | 2,732,000 | 8,602,000 | 9,562,000 |
| WC | 8,594,000 | 8,634,000 | 9,905,000 |
| Emp. | 239 | 184 | 138 |

DUNS 22-902-5200 Imp-Exp
## UbL1002 Ltd
(**Subsidiary of:** Uniform Brands Ltd)
Hareness Circle, Altens Industrial Estate, Aberdeen, Aberdeenshire AB12 3LY
**Tel:** 01224894000 **Fax:** 01224-878789
**Web:** www.wenaasusa.com
**Reg No:** 0062062SC **VAT No:** 296561321
**Estd:** 1988 Private Limited Company
**Line of Business:** Workwear hire
**Export Markets:** E U
**Trading Style:** Fronter
**Issued Capital:** £211,200
**Director:** N P Teagle
**Responsibilities**
**Senior:** Grattan Boylan *(Chief Executive Officer)*, Rich Cowie *(Warehouse Manager)*, Michael Haverty *(Manager)*
**Finance:** Gordan Miller *(Financial Controller)*
**Sales:** Stephen Poultney *(Sales Director)*
**Branches:** UBL1002 Ltd, Kwintet House, Syke Side Drive, Altham, Accrington, Lancashire BB5 5YE
**US SIC:** 2389, 5136
**UK SIC:** 45393, 61600
**Auditors:** KPMG LLP
**Bankers:** Unibank A/s (40-48-78)

| | 31-12-13 | 31-12-12 | 31-12-11 |
|---|---|---|---|
| TO | N/A | N/A | 13,098,000 |
| P/L | N/A | N/A | (1,779,000) |
| NW | 3,370,000 | 3,370,000 | 3,370,000 |
| WC | N/A | N/A | 1,839,000 |
| Emp. | N/A | N/A | 66 |

DUNS 21-558-1790
## Ubm Plc
Ludgate House, 245 Blackfriars Road, London SE1 9UY
**Tel:** 020-7921-5000
**Web:** www.ubm.com
**Reg No:** 0100460J **Estd:** 2008 Private Limited Company
**Line of Business:** Newspapers publishing
**Export Sales:** £710,300,000
**Trading Style:** U B M
**Principals:** J Botts *(Chairman)*, R Gray *(Financial)*, D Levin, J Newcomb, T Neill, P Kar, Ms K Thomson, A Gillespie
**Responsibilities**
**Senior:** Helen Alexander *(Chairman)*, Corrin Kaye *(Interim Group Director of Peop)*, Anne Siddell *(Manager)*
**Finance:** Chris Light *(Group Financial Controller)*, Neil Mepham *(Head of Mergers & Acquisitions)*, Emma Morgan *(Group Financial Reporting Mana)*, Peter Wrankmore *(Head of Treasury)*
**Marketing:** Peter Bancroft *(Director of Communications)*, Kimberley Flloyd *(Events Coordinator)*, Ruth Galpine *(Group Marketing Manager)*, Anna Knight *(Group Marketing Manager - Tran)*, Julie Mann *(Events Advisor)*, Paula Millburn *(Events Director)*, Emilie Oliveira *(Marketing Manager)*, Jason Rampersaud *(Event Manager)*, Rebecca Slater *(Marketing Executive)*
**Admin:** Cathy Oates *(Administrator)*
**IT:** Jeremy Pettitt *(Project Director - Group Opera)*, Richard Piercy *(Group Chief Information Office)*
**HR:** Sally Shankland *(Group HR Director)*
**Operations:** Luke Bilton *(Head of Content)*, Andrew Crow *(Group Operations Director)*, Imke Lessmann *(Projects Analyst)*
**US SIC:** 7392, 7399
**UK SIC:** 83951, 83954
**Auditors:** Ernst & Young LLP

| | 31-12-13 | 31-12-11 | 31-12-10 |
|---|---|---|---|
| TO | 793,900,000 | 972,300,000 | 889,200,000 |
| P/L | 109,500,000 | 102,000,000 | 115,500,000 |
| NW | (672,400,000) | (865,800,000) | (824,500,000) |
| WC | (141,200,000) | (201,100,000) | (193,900,000) |
| Emp. | 5,012 | 6,565 | 6,141 |

DUNS 21-002-1432
## Ubm (Uk) Ltd
(**Subsidiary of:** Maypond Ltd)
322 High Holborn, London WC1V 7PB
**Tel:** 02073215000
**Web:** www.markssattin.co.uk
**Reg No:** 0370721 **Estd:** 1996 Private Limited Company
**Line of Business:** Employment and recruitment companies and consultants
**Trading Style:** Ttg Digital, United Business Media, Ubm Conferences
**Issued Capital:** £4,369,738
**Directors:** R J Kerr, Ms C Corbett, B B Grover, Unm Investments Limited, C Adrian, S Foster
**Co. Secretary:** Crosswall Nominees Limited
**Responsibilities**
**Senior:** Dave Way *(Manager)*
**Branches:** Ubm (Uk) Ltd, Riverbank House, Angel Lane, Tonbridge, Kent TN9 1SE
**US SIC:** 7399, 7374
**UK SIC:** 83954, 83940
**Auditors:** Ernst & Young LLP

| | 31-12-13 | 31-12-12 | 31-12-11 |
|---|---|---|---|
| TO | 74,812,000 | 86,763,000 | 101,210,000 |
| P/L | (21,984,000) | (11,648,000) | (36,203,000) |
| NW | 75,082,000 | 77,822,000 | 70,076,000 |
| WC | 19,820,000 | 18,332,000 | 9,998,000 |
| Emp. | 666 | 756 | 765 |

DUNS 21-070-6601
## Ubs Ag Jersey
24 Union Street, St Helier, Jersey, Channel Islands JE4 8UJ
**Tel:** 01534-701-000
**Web:** www.ubs.com
**Estd:** 1998
**Line of Business:** Banks
**Responsibilities**
**Senior:** Tom Hill *(CEO)*, Helene Narcy *(Senior Finance Administrator)*
**Finance:** Helene Narcy *(Senior Finance Administrator)*
**IT:** Louis Lai *(Senior IT Executive)*
**US SIC:** 6012, 6732
**UK SIC:** 81402, 83100
**Employees:** 200

DUNS 39-945-4305
## Ubs Global Asset Management Holding Ltd
(**Subsidiary of:** Ubs Ag)
Triton Court, 14 Finsbury Square, London EC2A 1PD
**Fax:** 020-7929-0487
**Reg No:** 2251850 **Estd:** 1989 Private Limited Company
**Line of Business:** Management activities of holding companies
**Issued Capital:** £151,380,168
**Directors:** E J Bennett, Ms R Beechey, I F Barnes, Ms R Beechey
**US SIC:** 6711 **UK SIC:** 83962
**Auditors:** Ernst & Young LLP
**Bankers:** HSBC Bank plc (40-05-30)

| | 31-12-13 | 31-12-12 | 31-12-11 |
|---|---|---|---|
| TO | 120,615,000 | 115,350,000 | 129,674,000 |
| P/L | N/A | (1,678,000) | N/A |
| NW | 139,838,000 | 140,300,000 | 138,265,000 |
| WC | (29,777,000) | (29,388,000) | (39,714,000) |
| Emp. | 377 | 386 | 407 |

DUNS 23-529-5164
## Ubs Global Asset Management Holding (No.2) Ltd
(**Subsidiary of:** Ubs Ag)
Triton Court, 2 Worship Street, London EC2A 2AH
**Tel:** 01512275818
**Web:** www.ubs.com
**Reg No:** 3528371 **Estd:** 1998 Private Limited Company
**Line of Business:** Other business activities not elsewhere classified
**Issued Capital:** £17,100
**Directors:** I F Barnes, E J Bennett, Ms R Beechey, Ms R Beechey
**US SIC:** 7399 **UK SIC:** 83954
**Auditors:** Ernst & Young LLP

| | 31-12-13 | 31-12-12 | 31-12-11 |
|---|---|---|---|
| TO | 137,496,000 | 135,552,000 | 121,150,000 |
| P/L | 17,771,000 | 21,642,000 | (9,979,000) |
| NW | 134,878,000 | 120,403,000 | 99,238,000 |
| WC | 137,992,000 | 123,649,000 | 101,296,000 |
| Emp. | 377 | 386 | 407 |

DUNS 29-112-8106
## Ubs Global Asset Management (Uk) Ltd
(**Subsidiary of:** Ubs Ag)
21 Lombard Street, London EC3V 9AH
**Tel:** 020-7901-5000 **Fax:** 02079290487
**Web:** www.ubs.com
**Reg No:** 1546400 **Estd:** 1981 Private Limited Company
**Line of Business:** Security broking and related activities
**Issued Capital:** £125,000,000
**Directors:** A J Davies, E J Bennett, Ms R Beechey, I F Barnes, Ms R Beechey
**Responsibilities**
**Senior:** Trevor Hunt *(Manager)*, John Nestor *(Manager)*
**Operations:** Zahid Anwar *(Surveillance Manager)*
**US SIC:** 6211 **UK SIC:** 83100
**Auditors:** Ernst & Young LLP
**Bankers:** HSBC Bank plc (40-05-30)

| | 31-12-13 | 31-12-12 | 31-12-11 |
|---|---|---|---|
| TA | 118,135,000 | 92,383,000 | 83,837,000 |
| P/L | 17,029,000 | 20,280,000 | (11,536,000) |
| NW | 80,530,000 | 66,050,000 | 49,319,000 |
| WC | 80,291,000 | 65,811,000 | 49,058,000 |

DUNS 73-679-4467 Imp
## Ubt (Eu) Ltd
(**Subsidiary of:** The Grace Trading Group Ltd)
Tarbolton Road, Bogend, Symington, Kilmarnock, Ayrshire KA1 5PJ
**Tel:** 03307-000-800 **Fax:** 02476-306-800
**Web:** www.providoregifts.co.uk
**Reg No:** 4938684 **VAT No:** 821900261
**Estd:** 2003 Private Limited Company
**Line of Business:** Mail order houses
**Export Sales:** £4,448,240
**Trading Style:** Providore, Montrose Collection, Escape Calendars, Arte Chocolate
**Issued Capital:** £200
**Directors:** R Paterson, G B Gates, J E Lynes, R J Freeman
**Co. Secretary:** Martin Tydeman
**US SIC:** 5961, 5999
**UK SIC:** 65600
**Auditors:** Baker Tilly UK Audit LLP

| | 30-06-14 | 30-06-13 | 30-06-12 |
|---|---|---|---|
| TO | 71,371,754 | 57,784,582 | 59,122,507 |
| NW | 202 | 202 | 200 |
| WC | (2,034,582) | (1,938,675) | (2,054,411) |
| Emp. | 96 | 98 | 85 |

DUNS 34-593-1489 Imp
## Ucas Media Ltd
Rosehill, New Barr Lane, Cheltenham, Gloucestershire GL52 3LZ
**Tel:** 03303330230
**Web:** www.ucas.com
**Reg No:** 2737300 **Estd:** 1992 Private Limited Company
**Line of Business:** Business and management consultancy activities not elsewhere classified
**Issued Capital:** £2
**Directors:** T M Grote, P Robinson, Ms K A Bell, L D Mitchell, J A Phillips, Mrs M E Curnock Cook, Professor T D Salt
**Co. Secretary:** Mrs Helen Cornish
**US SIC:** 7392, 2752
**UK SIC:** 83951, 47544
**Auditors:** Smith & Williamson Solomon Hare Audit LLP
**Bankers:** Lloyds TSB Bank plc (30-95-72)

| | 31-07-13 | 31-07-12 | 31-07-11 |
|---|---|---|---|
| TO | 12,217,450 | 10,547,302 | 9,645,656 |
| P/L | (752,486) | (15,797) | (90,049) |
| NW | (2,076,133) | (15,374) | (45,070) |
| WC | (2,458,077) | (1,452,290) | (1,599,220) |
| Emp. | 55 | 64 | 54 |

DUNS 21-317-7975 **Imp-Exp**

### Ucb Pharma Ltd

**(Subsidiary of:** Ucb Nv)
216 Bath Road, Slough, Berkshire SL1 4EE
**Web:** www.ucbpharma.co.uk
**Reg No:** 0209905 **VAT No:** 449451037
**Estd:** 1925 Private Limited Company
**Line of Business:** Manufacture of basic pharmaceutical products
**Export Markets:** Africa; U S A; Asia; Australasia; E U
**Export Sales:** £39,174,000
**Trading Style:** Ucb Celltech
**Issued Capital:** £125
**Directors:** S C Price, Mrs H V Blanco, B K Iversen, Y Khatri, M N Khoso Baluch, Miss A R Fargher, S Arnold, J Moreau
**Co. Secretary:** Mark Hardy
**US SIC:** 2834 **UK SIC:** 25700
**Auditors:** PricewaterhouseCoopers LLP
**Bankers:** National Westminster Bank Plc (50-00-00)

| | 31-12-13 | 31-12-12 | 31-12-11 |
|---|---|---|---|
| TO | 124,690,000 | 126,021,000 | 149,646,000 |
| P/L | 28,097,000 | 28,988,000 | 5,911,000 |
| NW | 130,341,000 | 92,657,000 | 64,342,000 |
| WC | 131,267,000 | 94,228,000 | 66,032,000 |
| Emp. | 133 | 136 | 141 |

DUNS 39-706-5665 **Imp**

### Ucc Coffee Uk Ltd

**(Subsidiary of:** Ucc Coffee Uk Holdings Ltd)
2 Bradbourne Drive, Tilbrook, Tilbrook, Milton Keynes, Buckinghamshire MK7 8AT
**Tel:** 01908-275520 **Fax:** 01908648444
**Web:** www.unitedcoffeeuk.com
**Reg No:** 2159182 **Estd:** 1987 Private Limited Company
**Line of Business:** Coffee machine suppliers
**Export Sales:** £2,166,033
**Trading Style:** United Coffee
**Issued Capital:** £1,031
**Directors:** P D Cooke, P Harkjaer, A Jessup, Drie Mollen Holding B V, S Ueshima, M R Swift, Mrs E Higginson, Miss L Turrell
**Co. Secretary:** Anthony Jessup
**US SIC:** 3551 **UK SIC:** 32441
**Auditors:** KPMG LLP
**Bankers:** The Royal Bank Of Scotland Plc (16-24-30)

| | 31-12-13 | 31-12-12 | 31-12-11 |
|---|---|---|---|
| TO | 79,064,265 | 48,319,036 | 48,820,851 |
| P/L | 6,441,906 | 1,930,119 | 6,659,455 |
| NW | 22,668,600 | 14,354,574 | 11,952,726 |
| WC | 21,110,831 | 12,331,740 | 9,935,654 |
| Emp. | 386 | 257 | 218 |

DUNS 21-832-6638

### Ucc Europe Ltd

**(Subsidiary of:** Ucc Holdings Co. Ltd.)
Craven House, 40-44 Uxbridge Road, London W5 2BS
**Tel:** 020-8799-4370
**Web:** www.ucc-europe.co.uk
**Reg No:** 8016911 **Estd:** 2012 Private Limited Company
**Line of Business:** Production of coffee and coffee substitutes
**Export Sales:** £268,130,000
**Directors:** M Ueshima, G Ueshima, S Ueshima, Y Shimura, T Sato
**Co. Secretary:** Tmf Corporate Administration Ser
**US SIC:** 2095 **UK SIC:** 42391
**Auditors:** Ernst & Young LLP

| | 31-12-13 | 31-12-12 |
|---|---|---|
| TO | 342,405,000 | 205,780,000 |
| P/L | (15,192,000) | 734,000 |
| NW | (103,440,000) | (116,332,000) |
| WC | 26,530,000 | 27,920,000 |
| Emp. | 1,150 | 1,069 |

DUNS 73-643-6812 **Imp**

### Ucd (Southwell) Ltd

**(Subsidiary of:** Ucd (Developments) Ltd)
Crew Lane, Southwell, Nottinghamshire NG25 0TX
**Tel:** 01636-815500
**Web:** www.ucd.co.uk
**Reg No:** 4903727 **VAT No:** 842855015
**Estd:** 2004 Private Limited Company
**Line of Business:** Shopfitting contractors
**Export Sales:** £143,639
**Issued Capital:** £100
**Directors:** S C Saunders, D Scates, D Tinley, N P Marshall
**Co. Secretary:** David Rice
**US SIC:** 1796, 4226
**UK SIC:** 50400, 77003
**Auditors:** UHY Hacker Young LLP

| | 31-12-13 | 31-12-12 | 31-12-11 |
|---|---|---|---|
| TO | 8,071,421 | 6,600,510 | 7,702,135 |
| P/L | 491,891 | 208,499 | 8,015 |
| NW | 1,413,619 | 1,314,976 | 1,226,658 |
| WC | 1,347,901 | 1,233,908 | 1,139,298 |
| Emp. | 57 | 56 | 56 |

DUNS 22-110-8686

### Uch Logistics Ltd

Skylink House, Stanwell Moor Road, Staines, Middlesex TW19 6AB
**Tel:** 01784-242824 **Fax:** 01784-245222
**Web:** www.uchlogistics.co.uk
**Reg No:** 4130090 **VAT No:** 776420711
**Estd:** 2001 Private Limited Company
**Line of Business:** Activities of other transport agencies
**Issued Capital:** £100
**Directors:** V Bhardwaj, S K Bhardwaj, V Bhardwaj
**US SIC:** 4712 **UK SIC:** 77002
**Auditors:** R.E. Gordon & Co

| | 30-04-14 | 30-04-13 | 30-04-12 |
|---|---|---|---|
| TO | 12,638,581 | 10,206,038 | 8,847,088 |
| P/L | 461,946 | 645,363 | 392,392 |
| NW | 3,541,543 | 3,193,757 | 2,725,299 |
| WC | 2,884,608 | 2,794,674 | 2,326,893 |
| Emp. | 116 | 74 | 64 |

DUNS 21-234-0826

### Uckg Help Centre

First Floor The Mall, George Street, Luton, Bedfordshire LU1 2LJ
**Tel:** 01582486777
**Web:** www.uckg.org
**Line of Business:** Counselling & advice services
**Proprietor:** C Barcelos
**Responsibilities**
**Senior:** Fabian Moares *(Pastor)*
**US SIC:** 8699 **UK SIC:** 96902
**Employees:** 100

DUNS 34-690-8825

### Ucl Business Plc

**(Subsidiary of:** University College London)
The Network Building, 97 Tottenham Court Road, London W1T 4TP
**Tel:** 02076799000
**Web:** www.uclb.com
**Reg No:** 2776963 **Estd:** 1993 Public Limited Company
**Line of Business:** Research institutions and organisations
**Issued Capital:** £8,412,502
**Directors:** P Reeve, C A Tarhan, Professor S Caddick, Dr G M Samuels, Sir I G Mcallister, Professor A C Finkelstein, D M Dutton, D E Hunter
**Co. Secretary:** Mrs Hilary Rothera
**US SIC:** 7391 **UK SIC:** 94000
**Auditors:** Deloitte & Touche
**Bankers:** National Westminster Bank Plc (56-00-31)

| | 31-07-14 | 31-07-13 | 31-07-12 |
|---|---|---|---|
| TO | 5,415,455 | 8,302,497 | 8,177,087 |
| P/L | 1,497,730 | 245,735 | 287,142 |
| NW | 8,310,634 | 6,812,904 | 6,471,169 |
| WC | 2,516,514 | 1,396,366 | 2,966,230 |
| Emp. | 45 | 55 | 46 |

DUNS 21-120-8179

### Uclh Nhs Foundation Trust

Pathology Divisional Office, 5th Floor Central, 250 Euston Road, London NW1 2PG
**Web:** www.uclh.nhs.uk
**Line of Business:** General medical and surgical hospital services.
**Trading Style:** Unverisity Collage Londan Hospital
**US SIC:** 8062 **UK SIC:** 95100
**Employees:** 368

DUNS 64-069-7640

### U.C.O.S. Holdings Ltd

Meadow Court, Dukesway, Gateshead, Tyne and Wear NE11 0PZ
**Tel:** 01914875541
**Reg No:** 4473115 **Estd:** 2002 Private Limited Company
**Line of Business:** Management activities of holding companies
**Issued Capital:** £5
**Directors:** J Watson, M A Bryce, J Ellis, M D Nelson, W M Colby
**Co. Secretary:** Paul Dawson
**US SIC:** 6711 **UK SIC:** 83962
**Bankers:** Barclays Bank Plc (20-33-51)

| | 30-06-13 | 30-06-12 | 30-06-11 |
|---|---|---|---|
| TO | 12,845,853 | 11,841,013 | 11,374,313 |
| P/L | 2,932,444 | 2,632,352 | 2,246,282 |
| NW | 4,211,522 | 3,723,468 | 2,852,474 |
| WC | 3,781,079 | 3,501,421 | 2,725,349 |
| Emp. | 88 | 84 | 84 |

DUNS 22-240-1700

### Ucs Systems Ltd

**(Subsidiary of:** Universal Computer Systems Inc.)
4 Lichfield Street, Wolverhampton, West Midlands WV1 1DG
**Tel:** 01902428688 **Fax:** 01902428670
**Web:** www.ucs.co.uk
**Reg No:** 4258232 **Estd:** 1995 Private Limited Company

**Line of Business:** Holding companies management activities
**Export Sales:** £68,637,000
**Issued Capital:** £1,500,003
**Directors:** T W Jones, C M Cooper, N T Barras, D S Agan, R M Nalley, R D Burnett, R Brockman
**Co. Secretary:** Craig Moss
**Responsibilities**
**Senior:** Alex Sharifi *(Manager)*
**Finance:** Diana Sharifi *(Finance Director)*
**US SIC:** 6711 **UK SIC:** 83962
**Auditors:** RSM Tenon Audit Ltd
**Bankers:** National Westminster Bank Plc (60-01-35)

| | 31-12-13 | 31-12-12 | 31-12-11 |
|---|---|---|---|
| TO | 85,947,000 | 84,077,000 | 86,296,000 |
| P/L | 16,093,000 | 9,714,000 | 12,783,000 |
| NW | 15,400,000 | (48,000) | (5,914,000) |
| WC | 17,213,000 | 5,508,000 | 23,007,000 |
| Emp. | 695 | 682 | 707 |

DUNS 21-162-0864

### Uffculme School

Uffculme School, Uffculme, Cullompton, Devon EX15 3AG
**Tel:** 01884-840458
**Web:** www.uffculmeschool.net
**Estd:** 2002
**Line of Business:** General secondary education
**Chairman:** F Rosamond
**Responsibilities**
**Senior:** Lorraine Heath *(Head Teacher)*
**Finance:** Tony Aspden *(Business Manager)*
**Marketing:** Tony Aspden *(Business Manager)*
**Health & Safety:** Tony Aspden *(Business Manager)*
**Facilities:** Tony Aspden *(Business Manager)*
**US SIC:** 8211 **UK SIC:** 93200
**Employees:** 150

DUNS 23-663-3504

### Ufi Charitable Trust

U F I Ltd, 1 Young Street, Sheffield, South Yorkshire S1 4UP
**Tel:** 02030867974
**Web:** www.ufi.com
**Reg No:** 3658378 **Estd:** 1998 Private Limited Company
**Line of Business:** Adult and other education not elsewhere classified
**Trading Style:** Learn Direct
**Directors:** R G Barnes, T Wilson, Ms G L Pope, D S Frost, B J Davies, R W Harrison, Baroness S V Brinton
**Co. Secretary:** Haysmacintyre Company Secretarie
**Branches:** Ufi Charitable Trust, 72-74 Middle St, Yeovil, Somerset BA20 1LU
**US SIC:** 8249, 8299
**UK SIC:** 93300
**Auditors:** PricewaterhouseCoopers LLP
**Bankers:** Barclays Bank Plc (20-59-42)

| | 31-12-13 | 31-12-12 | 31-12-11 |
|---|---|---|---|
| TO | 1,223,000 | 496,000 | 155,845,000 |
| P/L | 439,000 | (9,000) | 1,980,000 |
| NW | 53,307,000 | 51,067,000 | 20,841,000 |
| WC | 1,254,000 | 953,000 | 15,019,000 |
| Emp. | N/A | N/A | 506 |

DUNS 57-828-6635 **Imp**

### Ufp (Uk) Ltd

**(Subsidiary of:** Ufp International)
Enterprise House, Roydsdale Way, Euroway Trading Estate, Bradford, West Yorkshire BD4 6SE
**Tel:** 01274-651800
**Web:** www.ufpuk.com
**Reg No:** 2886891 **Estd:** 1981 Private Limited Company
**Line of Business:** Computer consumables suppliers
**Trading Style:** @clowgroup.Co.Uk
**Issued Capital:** £527,778
**Directors:** C Zarka, S Arshad
**Co. Secretary:** Nicholas Stokes
**Responsibilities**
**Sales:** Rick Thaper *(Sales Director)*
**HR:** Mayo Arshad *(Human Resources Manager)*
**Health & Safety:** Mayo Arshad *(Human Resources Manager)*
**US SIC:** 7379 **UK SIC:** 83940
**Auditors:** Grant Thornton UK LLP
**Bankers:** National Westminster Bank Plc (56-00-36)

| | 31-12-13 | 31-12-12 | 31-12-11 |
|---|---|---|---|
| TO | 135,790,212 | 114,287,053 | 123,558,976 |
| P/L | 3,588,316 | 1,493,245 | 1,750,999 |
| NW | 17,797,404 | 15,924,107 | 15,267,432 |
| WC | 14,580,232 | 13,011,509 | 12,657,488 |
| Emp. | 93 | 99 | 110 |

DUNS 21-000-5747

### Ugam International Ltd

**(Subsidiary of:** Ugam Solutions Private Limited)
9th Floor, London SE1 7NX
**Tel:** 020-7803-1480
**Web:** www.ugaminteractive.com
**Reg No:** 6263644 **Estd:** 2007 Private Limited Company
**Line of Business:** Market research organisations
**Trading Style:** Ugam International Limited
**Issued Capital:** £825,000
**Directors:** S P Mirani, J Mold, R G Nair
**Co. Secretary:** Jackie Mold
**Responsibilities**
**Senior:** Simon Glanville *(Manager)*, Jacqueline Mold *(Managing Director)*
**Admin:** Lavinia Macneilage *(Office Manager)*
**Operations:** Felix Rios *(Operation Manager)*
**US SIC:** 7392, 7399
**UK SIC:** 83951, 83954
**Auditors:** Chamberlains UK LLP

| | 31-03-14 | 31-03-13 | 31-03-12 |
|---|---|---|---|
| TA | 412,595 | 1,091,701 | 999,683 |
| NW | (741,372) | (596,028) | (445,217) |
| WC | (18,389) | 132,235 | 290,085 |

DUNS 21-617-5878

### Ugg

1108 Westfield White City, Ariel Way, London W12 7GF
**Tel:** 02087408116
**Web:** www.uggaustralia.com
**Estd:** 2011
**Line of Business:** Retail sale of leather goods
**Responsibilities**
**Senior:** Mark Treleven *(Manager)*
**US SIC:** 5948 **UK SIC:** 64600
**Employees:** 75

DUNS 21-030-0448 **Imp-Exp**

### Ugo Foods Group Ltd

1 Hertsmere Park, Borehamwood, Hertfordshire WD6 1GT
**Tel:** 020-8207-0100
**Web:** www.ugogroup.co.uk
**Reg No:** 0344808 **VAT No:** 544329346
**Estd:** 1929 Private Limited Company
**Line of Business:** Manufacturers of food products
**Export Markets:** Scandinavia
**Issued Capital:** £16,073
**Principals:** P L Ugo *(Managing)*, D M Scott, B P Klug, H Anand, L A Moss
**Co. Secretary:** Craig Waldron
**Responsibilities**
**Sales:** Stacey Dawkins *(Sales Office & Customer Servic)*, Liz Howard *(New Product Development Manage)*
**Facilities:** Sav Savva *(Maintenance Engineer)*
**Engineering:** Sav Savva *(Maintenance Engineer)*
**Branches:** Ugo Foods Group Ltd, 196-200 York Way, London N7 9AX
**US SIC:** 2099 **UK SIC:** 42399
**Auditors:** Arram Berlyn Gardner

| | 30-04-14 | 30-04-13 | 30-04-12 |
|---|---|---|---|
| TO | 14,929,485 | 13,614,071 | 12,704,613 |
| P/L | 65,073 | 363,523 | 507,363 |
| NW | 879,619 | 2,091,568 | 1,863,142 |
| WC | (552,584) | (354,658) | (191,467) |
| Emp. | 138 | 120 | 105 |

DUNS 85-608-4496

### Uhy Hacker Young Llp

Quadrant House, London E1W 1YW
**Tel:** 020-7216-4600 **Fax:** 02077672600
**Web:** www.uhy-uk.com
**Reg No:** 0327384OC **Estd:** 1924 Private Limited Company
**Line of Business:** Accounting and auditing activities
**Responsibilities**
**Senior:** Andreas Abdronikou *(Non-designated Limited Liabili)*, Matthew Anderson *(Partner)*, Subarna Banerjee *(Non-designated Limited Liabili)*, Robert Bursey *(Owner)*, Christine Dilworth *(Manager)*, Jack Easton *(Non-designated Limited Liabili)*, Mark Giddens *(Tax Investigations / Enquiries)*, Derek Levy *(Non-designated Limited Liabili)*, Richard Lloyd-Warne *(Corporation Tax Compliance Off)*, Elizabeth Searby *(Non-designated Limited Liabili)*, Howard Spencer *(Non-designated Limited Liabili)*, Guy Swarbreck *(Partner)*, Vinodkumar Vadgama *(Non-designated Limited Liabili)*, David Voskou *(Director - Turnaround and Reco)*, Jonathan Warsop *(Non-designated Limited Liabili)*
**Finance:** Mark Giddens *(Tax Investigations / Enquiries)*, Cathy Hand *(Tax Manager)*, Richard Lloyd-Warne *(Corporation Tax Compliance Off)*, Christopher Lowry *(Chartered Accountant)*, Elizabeth Mitchell *(Chartered Accountant)*, Simon Newark

*(Head of VAT Department)*, Steve Patten *(Financial Controller)*, Bob Savic *(Tax Advisor)*, Vinodkumar Vadgama *(Non-designated Limited Liabili)*, Manohar Varsani *(Senior Tax Advisor)*, Andrew Waterman *(Manager in Business Advisory a)*
**Marketing:** Zowie Paradine *(Marketing Manager)*
**HR:** Louise Tennant *(Human Resources Manager)*
**Operations:** Zowie Paradine *(Marketing Manager)*
**Engineering:** Jack Easton *(Non-designated Limited Liabili)*
**US SIC:** 8931 **UK SIC:** 83600

| | 30-04-14 | 30-04-13 | 30-04-12 |
|---|---|---|---|
| TO | 19,311,595 | 18,485,528 | 19,996,647 |
| P/L | 131,341 | 95,019 | 110,484 |
| NW | 4,208,682 | 10,545 | (21,280) |
| WC | 6,170,917 | 6,629,074 | 7,204,738 |
| Emp. | 229 | 234 | 218 |

DUNS 52-033-9599
### Uia (Call Centres) Ltd
(**Subsidiary of:** U I A (Insurance) Ltd)
Kings Court, London Road, Stevenage, Hertfordshire SG1 2TP
**Reg No:** 3400457 **Estd:** 1997 Private Limited Company
**Line of Business:** Call centres
**Issued Capital:** £125,000
**Directors:** M A Hayes, I R Cracknell
**Co. Secretary:** Benjamin Terrett
**US SIC:** 7399, 6399
**UK SIC:** 83954, 82001
**Auditors:** Mazars LLP

| | 31-12-13 | 31-12-12 | 31-12-11 |
|---|---|---|---|
| TO | 1,568,000 | 1,561,000 | 1,621,000 |
| P/L | (1,000) | (1,000) | (6,000) |
| NW | 8,000 | 9,000 | 11,000 |
| WC | 8,000 | 7,000 | 2,000 |
| Emp. | 52 | 57 | 64 |

DUNS 50-512-7829
### Uib Holdings (Uk) Ltd
Mansell Court, 69 Mansell Street, London E1 8AN
**Tel:** 020-7488-0551
**Web:** www.uibgroup.com
**Reg No:** 2480634 **Estd:** 1990 Private Limited Company
**Line of Business:** Financial intermediation not elsewhere classified
**Issued Capital:** £522,283
**Principals:** B S Kabban *(Managing)*, R J Sharp, K M Anderson, G J Kabban, A J Dilley, P A Tuite-Dalton, M G Kabban
**Co. Secretary:** Paul Sinfield
**Responsibilities**
**Senior:** Michael Lack *(Manager)*
**US SIC:** 6111 **UK SIC:** 81501
**Auditors:** Mazars
**Bankers:** The Royal Bank Of Scotland Plc (15-19-99)

| | 31-12-13 | 31-12-12 | 31-12-11 |
|---|---|---|---|
| TA | 30,735,212 | 32,092,111 | 30,526,252 |
| P/L | 4,119,105 | 4,740,800 | 202,806 |
| NW | 17,908,783 | 16,779,481 | 15,885,531 |
| WC | 21,149,412 | 19,701,761 | 21,270,785 |
| Emp. | 386 | 356 | 364 |

DUNS 73-573-8549
### Uk Access Solutions Ltd
Uk Access Solutions Ltd, 1 Bilport Lane, Wednesbury, West Midlands WS10 0NT
**Tel:** 0121-500-5055 **Fax:** 01215-255873
**Web:** www.ukaccesssolutions.co.uk
**Reg No:** 4835444 **Estd:** 2003 Private Limited Company
**Line of Business:** Other construction work involving special trades
**Issued Capital:** £355
**Directors:** J Cottrell, J Freeman
**Co. Secretary:** Robert Jones
**Branches:** Uk Access Solutions Ltd, Lyncastle Road, Barleycastle Lane, Appleton, Warrington, Cheshire WA4 4SN
**US SIC:** 1799, 7394
**UK SIC:** 50000, 84000
**Auditors:** Lewis Smith & Co

| | 30-09-13 | 30-09-12 | 30-09-11 |
|---|---|---|---|
| TO | 3,430,394 | 3,535,268 | 4,322,607 |
| P/L | 128,896 | 124,373 | (168,757) |
| NW | 1,797,092 | 1,735,282 | 1,619,486 |
| WC | (821,801) | (400,948) | (505,876) |
| Emp. | 83 | 109 | 108 |

DUNS 21-231-5046
### Uk Aea Pensions Administration Office
Brimms House, Forss Business & Technology Park, Forss, Thurso, Caithness KW14 7UZ
**Estd:** 2002 Proprietorship
**Line of Business:** Pension companies
**Proprietor:** Miss Y Mcarthey
**US SIC:** 6371 **UK SIC:** 82002
**Employees:** 65

DUNS 23-590-5416 **Imp**
### Uk Affymetrix Ltd
(**Subsidiary of:** Affymetrix Inc.)
Mercury Park, Wycombe Lane, High Wycombe, Buckinghamshire HP10 0HH
**Tel:** 01628-552500
**Web:** www.affymetrix.com
**Reg No:** 3588144 **Estd:** 1998 Private Limited Company
**Line of Business:** Other business activities not elsewhere classified
**Trading Style:** Uk Affymetrix Ltd
**Directors:** R J Palmer, G H Wood
**Co. Secretary:** Abogado Nominees Limited
**Responsibilities**
**Senior:** Timothy Barabe *(Manager)*, John Batty *(Manager)*, Helen Belcher *(Manager)*, David Coorey *(Vice President Commercial Oper)*, Emma Shipstone *(Marketing Director)*, John Turk *(Manager)*
**Marketing:** Emma Shipstone *(Marketing Director)*
**Sales:** David Coorey *(Vice President Commercial Oper)*, Deepak Singh *(Sales Director)*, Helen Whelan *(Northern Europe Sales Manager)*
**HR:** Denise Brittaine *(Human Resources Manager)*, Kayti Foster *(Human Resources Generalist)*
**US SIC:** 7399 **UK SIC:** 83954
**Auditors:** Ernst & Young LLP
**Bankers:** Barclays Bank Plc (20-71-03)
**Employees:** 64
**Turnover:** £73,972,739

DUNS 76-962-8223
### Uk & International Press Ltd
Abinger House, Church Street, Dorking, Surrey RH4 1DF
**Tel:** 01306743744 **Fax:** 01306-742525
**Web:** www.ukipme.com
**Reg No:** 2627492 **Estd:** 1991 Private Limited Company
**Line of Business:** Publishers
**Trading Style:** Uk & International Press, Post Expo 2003
**Issued Capital:** £2
**Managing Director:** A D Robinson
**Co. Secretary:** Robert Kirke
**US SIC:** 2731 **UK SIC:** 47532

| | 30-11-13 | 30-11-12 | 30-11-11 |
|---|---|---|---|
| TA | 2 | 2 | 2 |
| NW | 2 | 2 | 2 |

DUNS 21-592-8814
### Uk Assitance Accident Repair Cemtre
Ripley Drive, Normanton Industrial Estate, Normanton, West Yorkshire WF6 1TZ
**Tel:** 01924856757
**Estd:** 2011 Partnership
**Line of Business:** Car body repairers
**Partners:** C Lewis, R Barnett, D Grimshaw
**US SIC:** 7539 **UK SIC:** 67100
**Employees:** 150

DUNS 73-720-5323 **Imp**
### Uk Biobank Ltd
Units 1 & 2 Spectrum Way, Adswood, Stockport, Cheshire SK3 0SA
**Tel:** 01614755360
**Web:** www.ukbiobank.ac.uk
**Reg No:** 4978912 **Estd:** 2003 Private Limited Company
**Line of Business:** Charities and charitable organisations
**Directors:** Dr P J Vallance, J E Tross, Ms S A Baines, R S Buckle, A P Haines, Ms G Kiff, Professor A Hattersley, Sir M Rawlins
**Co. Secretary:** Jonathan Sellors
**Responsibilities**
**Senior:** William Ollier *(Director)*, Tim Peakman *(Manager)*, Ian Viney *(Director)*
**US SIC:** 8091 **UK SIC:** 95200
**Bankers:** The Co-Operative Bank Plc (08-90-00)

| | 30-09-13 | 30-09-12 | 30-09-11 |
|---|---|---|---|
| TO | 21,785,291 | 4,908,651 | 6,101,158 |
| P/L | 6,052,264 | (474,732) | 1,943,169 |
| NW | 15,811,573 | 9,759,309 | 10,243,899 |
| WC | 5,059,360 | 766,870 | 807,200 |
| Emp. | 66 | 35 | 32 |

DUNS 21-222-5308
### Uk Border Agency
Lunar House, 40 Wellesley Road, Croydon, Surrey CR9 2BY
**Web:** www.homeoffice.gov.uk
**Estd:** 2008
**Line of Business:** Local government
**Principals:** R Whiteman, D Green, N Herbert
**Co. Secretary:** Ms Lynne Featherstone
**Branches:** Uk Border Agency, Drumkeen House, 1 Drumkeen Complex, Belfast BT8 6TB Upper Galwally
**US SIC:** 9121 **UK SIC:** 91110
**Employees:** 25,000

DUNS 21-810-7591
### Uk Border Agency
Custom House, View Point Road, Felixstowe, Suffolk IP11 3RF
**Tel:** 01394303270
**Web:** www.ukborderagency.co.uk
**Estd:** 2012
**Line of Business:** Child Day Care Services
**Responsibilities**
**Senior:** Joanne Webster *(Manager)*
**US SIC:** 8351 **UK SIC:** 96111
**Employees:** 300

DUNS 73-449-2734 **Imp**
### Uk Broadband Ltd
(**Subsidiary of:** Pccw Limited)
3rd Floor International House, 7 High Street Ealing, London W5 5DB
**Tel:** 08433624888 **Fax:** 020-8622-3244
**Web:** www.ukbroadband.com
**Reg No:** 4713634 **Estd:** 2003 Private Limited Company
**Line of Business:** Telecom services
**Issued Capital:** £1
**Directors:** N J Williams, Sir D R Ford
**Co. Secretary:** Jordan Cosec Limited
**US SIC:** 4899 **UK SIC:** 79020
**Auditors:** PricewaterhouseCoopers LLP

| | 31-12-13 | 31-12-12 | 31-12-11 |
|---|---|---|---|
| TO | 2,016,825 | 4,339,881 | 80,372 |
| P/L | (10,354,708) | (7,541,156) | (13,507,143) |
| NW | (172,652,823) | (157,427,439) | (151,070,760) |
| WC | (198,798,879) | (177,886,100) | (171,812,766) |
| Emp. | 63 | 55 | 58 |

DUNS 71-906-5760
### Uk Business Advisors Ltd
4 The Old School Close, Tideswell, Buxton, Derbyshire SK17 8NG
**Tel:** 08704202756 **Fax:** 07092808482
**Web:** www.ukba.co.uk
**Reg No:** 5288512 **Estd:** 2004 Private Limited Company
**Line of Business:** Management and business consultants
**Issued Capital:** £1
**Directors:** D Shenkin, C R Ball, G W Steward, B E Dash
**Co. Secretary:** Philip Stanyer
**US SIC:** 7392 **UK SIC:** 83951

| | 31-03-14 | 31-03-13 | 31-03-12 |
|---|---|---|---|
| TA | 4,346 | 2,962 | 8,098 |
| NW | (2,015) | 2,384 | 2,572 |
| WC | (2,015) | 2,384 | 2,572 |

DUNS 21-128-4189
### Uk Case Management Ltd
Providence Court, Low Crankley, Easingwold, York, North Yorkshire YO61 3NY
**Tel:** 01347824447 **Fax:** 01347822275
**Web:** www.ukcasemanagement.co.uk
**Reg No:** 6630044 **Estd:** 2008 Private Limited Company
**Line of Business:** Healthcare companies
**Issued Capital:** £100
**Directors:** R C Barnes, Mrs S J Cassidy
**Responsibilities**
**Senior:** Paul Marks *(Operations Manager)*, Janet Penny *(Registered Manager)*
**US SIC:** 8091 **UK SIC:** 95200
**Bankers:** HSBC Bank plc (40-16-27)

| | 30-06-14 | 30-06-13 | 30-06-12 |
|---|---|---|---|
| TA | 208,840 | 318,237 | 231,858 |
| NW | 26,143 | 68,889 | 91,330 |
| WC | 62,601 | 111,635 | 45,070 |

DUNS 34-880-5305
### Uk Construction Recruitment Ltd
The Old Airfield, Moreton Valence, Gloucester, Gloucestershire GL2 7NG
**Tel:** 01452726200
**Web:** www.carillion.com
**Reg No:** 5678561 **Estd:** 2006 Private Limited Company
**Line of Business:** Civil engineers
**Issued Capital:** £10
**Director:** B A Mcgurk
**Co. Secretary:** Eamonn Mcgurk
**US SIC:** 8911 **UK SIC:** 83701

| | 30-06-13 | 30-06-12 | 30-06-11 |
|---|---|---|---|
| TA | 10 | 10 | 10 |
| NW | 10 | 10 | 10 |

DUNS 34-531-4707 **Imp**
### U.K. Dies Group Ltd
15 Birchall Street, Birmingham, West Midlands B12 0RP
**Tel:** 0121-773-5770
**Web:** www.ukdiesgroup.com
**Reg No:** 5341953 **Estd:** 1996 Private Limited Company
**Line of Business:** Manufacture of tools
**Issued Capital:** £657,401
**Directors:** N Chall, P Chall, Mrs J Kaur, Mrs H Kaur, M Singh
**Co. Secretary:** Mrs Hardeep Kaur

**Responsibilities**
**Senior:** John Silk *(Manager)*
**Finance:** Sonia Colton *(Finance Director)*
**US SIC:** 3423 **UK SIC:** 31612

| | 31-03-14 | 31-03-13 | 31-03-12 |
|---|---|---|---|
| TO | 3,279,578 | 3,415,039 | 3,248,403 |
| P/L | (4,522,260) | 417,238 | 455,174 |
| NW | 172,896 | 4,675,356 | 4,226,338 |
| WC | 264,864 | 196,021 | 184,078 |
| Emp. | 59 | 59 | 56 |

DUNS 22-714-4656 **Exp**
### Uk Export Finance
1 Horse Guards Road, London SW1A 2HQ
**Tel:** 020-7512-7000 **Fax:** 020-7512-7649
**Web:** www.ukexportfinance.gov.uk
**Estd:** 1919 Incorporate By Act Of Parliament
**Line of Business:** Other credit granting not elsewhere classified
**Trading Style:** Ecgd
**Principals:** R Healey *(Financial)*, V Lunn-Rockliffe, V Brown
**Responsibilities**
**Finance:** Nigel Addison-Smith *(Financial Director)*
**Health & Safety:** Ian Dykstra *(Service Manager)*
**Purchasing:** Ian Dykstra *(Service Manager)*
**Branches:** Uk Export Finance, Crown Building, 4th Floor, Credit Information Dept, Cardiff, South Glamorgan CF10 3NQ
**US SIC:** 9121 **UK SIC:** 91110
**Employees:** 200

DUNS 39-807-2116
### Uk Fuels Ltd
(**Subsidiary of:** Radius Payment Solutions Ltd)
Eurocard Centre Herald Park, Herald Drive, Crewe, Cheshire CW1 6EG
**Tel:** 01270500400
**Web:** www.ukfuels.co.uk
**Reg No:** 2212080 **VAT No:** 473523053
**Estd:** 1990 Private Limited Company
**Line of Business:** Wholesale of other fuels and related products
**Export Sales:** £797,544
**Issued Capital:** £64,143
**Directors:** R A Sciortino, W S Holmes
**Responsibilities**
**Admin:** Karen Brady *(Office Manager)*
**Health & Safety:** Adam Thopliss *(Health & Safety Officer)*
**Facilities:** Karen Brady *(Office Manager)*
**US SIC:** 5052 **UK SIC:** 61200
**Auditors:** Baker Tilly UK Audit LLP
**Bankers:** Barclays Bank Plc (20-53-77)

| | 31-03-14 | 31-03-13 | 31-03-12 |
|---|---|---|---|
| TO | 937,094,381 | 761,272,343 | 754,235,744 |
| P/L | 17,133,324 | 3,883,304 | 1,770,176 |
| NW | 33,797,597 | 5,576,654 | 3,526,786 |
| WC | (3,977,339) | 4,912,753 | 2,882,735 |
| Emp. | 327 | 153 | 138 |

DUNS 29-353-5563
### Uk Funerals Ltd
(**Subsidiary of:** Dignity Plc)
4 King Edwards Court, King Edwards Square, Sutton Coldfield, West Midlands B73 6AP
**Tel:** 08007310651 **Fax:** 01386-49137
**Reg No:** 0591096 **VAT No:** 473831040
**Estd:** 1957 Private Limited Company
**Line of Business:** Funeral services
**Issued Capital:** £2,000
**Directors:** S L Whittern, M K Mccollum
**Co. Secretary:** Richard Portman
**Branches:** Uk Funerals Ltd, Howard Jenkins Funeral Services, 6 Smithdown Road, Liverpool, Merseyside L7 4JG
**US SIC:** 7261 **UK SIC:** 98902
**Auditors:** K P M G Peat Marwick
**Bankers:** National Westminster Bank Plc (60-02-35)

| | 27-12-13 | 28-12-12 | 30-12-11 |
|---|---|---|---|
| NW | (2,049,647) | (2,049,647) | (2,049,647) |

DUNS 73-292-6345
### Uk Future Inns Ltd
Hemingway Road, Cardiff, South Glamorgan CF10 4AU
**Tel:** 02920487111 **Fax:** 029-2043-2796
**Web:** www.a10sm.com
**Reg No:** 4566419 **Estd:** 2003 Private Limited Company
**Line of Business:** Hotels
**Issued Capital:** £1
**Directors:** Ms M J Brett, D G Brett
**Co. Secretary:** Graham Stockman
**US SIC:** 7011 **UK SIC:** 66500
**Auditors:** Solomon Hare Audit LLP
**Bankers:** Allied Irish Bank (gb) (23-84-80)

| | 31-12-13 | 31-12-12 | 31-12-11 |
|---|---|---|---|
| TA | 1,046,808 | 996,835 | 974,268 |
| NW | 1 | 1 | 1 |
| WC | (999) | (999) | (999) |

DUNS 21-175-4526
## Uk General Insurance Group Ltd
(**Subsidiary of:** Uk General Insurance Holdings Limited)
Cast House, Gibraltar Island Road, Old Mill Business Park, Leeds, West Yorkshire LS10 1RJ
**Tel:** 01132729000
**Reg No:** 6989180 **Estd:** 2009 Private Limited Company
**Line of Business:** Non-life re-insurance
**Issued Capital:** £11,786,711
**Directors:** R M Gill, M P Smith, P J Hubbard, Mrs K A Beales, P R Carter
**Co. Secretary:** Jeffrey Orton
**US SIC:** 6399 **UK SIC:** 82001
**Auditors:** PricewaterhouseCoopers LLP
**Bankers:** Barclays Bank Plc (20-00-00)

| | 31-03-14 | 31-03-13 | 31-03-12 |
|---|---|---|---|
| TO | 24,551,231 | 22,780,984 | 23,562,109 |
| P/L | 1,711,352 | (1,697,677) | 483,302 |
| NW | (26,397,016) | (30,286,788) | (25,940,854) |
| WC | (7,363,860) | (10,272,434) | (6,472,890) |
| Emp. | 264 | 253 | 247 |

DUNS 21-839-4696
## Uk Green Investment Bank Plc
Atria One Level 7, 144 Morrison Street, Edinburgh, Edinburgh, Midlothian EH3 8EX
**Tel:** 03301232167
**Web:** www.greeninvestmentbank.com
**Reg No:** 0424067SC **Estd:** 2012 Public Limited Company
**Line of Business:** Banks and financial institutions
**Trading Style:** Green Investment Bank
**Issued Capital:** £145,850,000
**Directors:** T S Murley, D T Nish, J E King, Ms I N Sharp, F I Maroudas, Lord R H Smith Of Kelvin, Ms T M Tennant, P R Knott
**Co. Secretary:** Euan Mcvicar
**Responsibilities**
**Senior:** Shaun Kingsbury *(Director)*, Anthony Odgers *(Director)*, Anthony Poulter *(Director)*
**US SIC:** 6012 **UK SIC:** 81402
**Auditors:** The Comptroller & Auditor General

| | 31-03-14 | 31-03-13 |
|---|---|---|
| TA | 420,231,000 | 153,014,000 |
| P/L | (5,746,000) | (6,212,000) |
| NW | 302,664,000 | 145,362,000 |
| WC | (74,871,000) | 27,805,000 |
| Emp. | 86 | 23 |

DUNS 21-582-4569
## Uk Greetings
Mercury House, 15 Princewood Road, Earlstrees Industrial Estate, Corby, Northamptonshire NN17 4AY
**Tel:** 01536409940
**Web:** www.ukgreetings.co.uk
**Estd:** 2011 Proprietorship
**Line of Business:** Distribution service providers
**Proprietor:** B Atkins
**Responsibilities**
**Senior:** Barry Aktins *(Manager)*
**US SIC:** 2731 **UK SIC:** 47532
**Employees:** 50

DUNS 64-085-5730 **Imp-Exp**
## Uk Greetings Ltd
(**Subsidiary of:** Century Intermediate Holding Company)
High Street, Cobham, Surrey KT11 3DJ
**Tel:** 01924465200
**Web:** www.ukgreetings.co.uk
**Reg No:** 3480710 **VAT No:** 168966988
**Estd:** 1997 Private Limited Company
**Line of Business:** Manufacture of other articles of paper and paperboard not elsewhere classified
**Export Sales:** £9,187,000
**Issued Capital:** £4
**Directors:** G L Rowley, Z D Weiss
**Co. Secretary:** Kevin Vaux
**Responsibilities**
**Marketing:** Keith Auty *(Marketing Director)*, James Conn *(Sales & Marketing Director)*, Ceri Stirland *(Marketing Director)*
**Sales:** James Conn *(Sales & Marketing Director)*
**Operations:** Tommy Olesinski *(Operations Manager)*
**Branches:** Uk Greetings Ltd, Roundwood Industrial Estate, Ossett, West Yorkshire WF5 9SQ
**US SIC:** 2649, 2741
**UK SIC:** 47280, 47541
**Auditors:** Ernst & Young LLP
**Bankers:** Barclays Bank Plc (20-00-00)

| | 28-02-14 | 28-02-13 | 29-02-12 |
|---|---|---|---|
| TO | 159,763,000 | 158,923,000 | 155,403,000 |
| P/L | 22,892,000 | (1,138,000) | 9,143,000 |
| NW | 57,366,000 | 59,369,000 | 57,795,000 |
| WC | 38,565,000 | 53,314,000 | 51,447,000 |
| Emp. | 3,691 | 3,821 | 3,569 |

DUNS 71-933-5155
## Uk Healthcare Group Ltd
Seabrook House Topsham Road, Exeter, Devon EX2 7DR
**Tel:** 01392873995
**Reg No:** 5314436 **Estd:** 2004 Private Limited Company
**Line of Business:** Other human health activities
**Issued Capital:** £1
**Directors:** Ms R C Callow, Ms S A O'Neill
**US SIC:** 8091 **UK SIC:** 95200

| | 31-07-13 | 31-07-12 | 31-07-11 |
|---|---|---|---|
| TA | 516,840 | 390,103 | 252,676 |
| NW | 492,662 | 386,103 | 248,676 |
| WC | 492,660 | 386,101 | 248,674 |

DUNS 29-325-5352
## The Uk Holiday Group Ltd
The Old Bakery, Norwich, Norfolk NR1 3PL
**Tel:** 01603886700 **Fax:** 01603886702
**Web:** www.theukholidaygroup.com
**Reg No:** 1815672 **VAT No:** 394307733
**Estd:** 1984 Private Limited Company
**Line of Business:** Tour operators
**Trading Style:** Grand Ash Hotel Study U K, Go Places Travel, Grand U K Holidays
**Issued Capital:** £50,000
**Directors:** P W Bennett, H A Burke, N P Fletcher
**Co. Secretary:** David Arnold
**Responsibilities**
**Sales:** David Lote *(Sales Development Manager)*
**Admin:** Nicola Copus *(Office Manager)*
**HR:** Nicola Copus *(Office Manager)*
**Health & Safety:** Nicola Copus *(Office Manager)*
**Branches:** The Uk Holiday Group Ltd, Station Road, Kendal, Cumbria LA9 6BT
**US SIC:** 7999, 4722
**UK SIC:** 97913, 77001
**Auditors:** BDO Stoy Hayward
**Bankers:** Bank Of Scotland (12-09-25)

| | 31-10-13 | 31-10-12 | 31-10-11 |
|---|---|---|---|
| TO | 18,273,682 | 17,351,537 | 18,111,866 |
| P/L | 1,115,819 | 1,076,406 | 1,051,429 |
| NW | 4,370,955 | 3,315,834 | 2,541,600 |
| WC | (1,691,649) | (1,760,212) | (1,574,036) |
| Emp. | 293 | 283 | 272 |

DUNS 22-600-6583 **Imp-Exp**
## The U.K. Lift Company Ltd
(**Subsidiary of:** Kone Oyj)
1 Millfield House, Woodshots Meadow, Watford, Hertfordshire WD18 8YX
**Tel:** 01923656200 **Fax:** 01923-221231
**Web:** www.uk-lift.co.uk
**Reg No:** 1397101 **Estd:** 1978 Private Limited Company
**Line of Business:** Miscellaneous electrical repair shops
**Export Markets:** European Union (E U)
**Issued Capital:** £200
**Directors:** Kone Public Limited Company, G K Loty
**Co. Secretary:** Simon White
**Responsibilities**
**Senior:** Rachel Loaring *(Manager)*
**Branches:** The U.k. Lift Company Ltd, Westminster Works, Unit 1A, Watford, Hertfordshire WD24 7UB
**US SIC:** 1731 **UK SIC:** 50300
**Auditors:** PricewaterhouseCoopers LLP
**Bankers:** Barclays Bank Plc (20-91-79)

| | 31-12-13 | 31-12-12 | 31-12-11 |
|---|---|---|---|
| TA | 8,616,526 | 8,616,526 | 8,616,526 |
| NW | 8,616,526 | 8,616,526 | 8,616,526 |

DUNS 23-078-0140
## Uk Mail Group Plc
Express House, 832-833 Yeovil Road, Slough, Berkshire SL1 4JG
**Tel:** 01753-706-070 **Fax:** 01753-706-071
**Web:** www.ukmail.com
**Reg No:** 2800218 **Estd:** 1993 Public Limited Company
**Line of Business:** Management activities of holding companies
**Issued Capital:** £5,473,298
**Principals:** P Kane *(Chairman)*, W Spencer, M A Findlay, C G Buswell, C E Moore, Mrs J J Burley
**Co. Secretary:** Steven Glew
**Branches:** Uk Mail Group Plc, 71 St. James Mill Road, Northampton, Northamptonshire NN5 5JP
**US SIC:** 6711, 4213
**UK SIC:** 83962, 72300
**Auditors:** PricewaterhouseCoopers LLP
**Bankers:** The Royal Bank Of Scotland Plc (15-10-00)

| | 31-03-14 | 31-03-13 | 31-03-12 |
|---|---|---|---|
| TO | 508,500,000 | 475,400,000 | 429,000,000 |
| P/L | 22,800,000 | 17,800,000 | 12,900,000 |
| NW | 54,800,000 | 50,000,000 | 47,600,000 |
| WC | 13,600,000 | 17,500,000 | 16,400,000 |
| Emp. | 2,756 | 2,649 | 2,587 |

DUNS 34-800-6722 **Imp**
## Uk Mission Enterprise Ltd
22 Melton Street, London NW1 2BW
**Tel:** 08717041000
**Reg No:** 5600850 **Estd:** 2005 Private Limited Company
**Line of Business:** Employment service
**Issued Capital:** £250,000
**Directors:** M S Al Marzooqi, A Noorani, A M Shakeri
**Co. Secretary:** Sanjay Pathak
**Responsibilities**
**HR:** Sue Aslet *(Human Resources Manager)*
**US SIC:** 7361 **UK SIC:** 83954
**Auditors:** Grant Thornton UK LLP

| | 31-12-13 | 31-12-12 | 31-12-11 |
|---|---|---|---|
| TA | 5,197,834 | 3,214,489 | 3,254,371 |
| NW | 1,177,822 | 1,082,765 | 987,087 |
| WC | 1,126,419 | 1,007,719 | 951,727 |

DUNS 39-698-5350 **Imp-Exp**
## Uk-Nsi Co. Ltd
(**Subsidiary of:** Nippon Seiki Co. Ltd.)
Merse Road, Moons Moat North Industrial Estate, Redditch, Worcestershire B98 9HL
**Tel:** 01527-585-055 **Fax:** 01527-585-025
**Web:** www.uk-nsi.co.uk
**Reg No:** 2141243 **VAT No:** 462254066
**Estd:** 1987 Private Limited Company
**Line of Business:** Manufacturers of vehicle components
**Export Markets:** Europe
**Export Sales:** £25,508,984
**Issued Capital:** £12,761,500
**Directors:** T Nakamura, M Sato
**Co. Secretary:** Roger Graham
**Responsibilities**
**Senior:** Linda Stanley *(Purchasing Manager)*
**HR:** Ken Wilkes *(Training Coordinator)*
**Health & Safety:** Ken Wilkes *(Training Coordinator)*
**Facilities:** Richard Coutts *(Facilities Manager)*
**Operations:** Ken Wilkes *(Training Coordinator)*
**Purchasing:** Linda Stanley *(Purchasing Manager)*
**US SIC:** 3714 **UK SIC:** 35300
**Auditors:** BDO LLP
**Bankers:** The Bank Of Tokyo-Mitsubishi, Ltd (60-01-09)

| | 31-03-14 | 31-03-13 | 31-03-12 |
|---|---|---|---|
| TO | 62,449,473 | 55,269,618 | 49,326,987 |
| P/L | 2,967,814 | (796,744) | (941,591) |
| NW | 12,588,170 | 10,277,062 | 11,038,983 |
| WC | 7,286,925 | 4,046,092 | 6,317,858 |
| Emp. | 321 | 289 | 262 |

DUNS 22-723-8367
## The Uk Oil & Gas Industry Association Ltd
Portland House, Bressenden Place, London SW1E 5BH
**Tel:** 020-7802-2400
**Web:** www.oilandgasuk.co.uk
**Reg No:** 1119804 **VAT No:** 241421995
**Estd:** 1973 Private Company Limited By Guarantee
**Line of Business:** Crude petroleum & natural gas extraction
**Trading Style:** Oil & Gas Uk
**Directors:** G G Ballard, N Kirkbride, P A Kirk, A W Kennedy, T W Garlick, J A Edens, T N Savage, Mrs S T Elston
**Co. Secretary:** Graham Elgie
**Responsibilities**
**Senior:** Glen Cayley *(Director)*, Eric Du Plessis D'Argentre *(Director)*, Louca Farajallah *(Director)*, Philippe Guys *(Director)*, Thomas Hares *(Director)*, Marcus Samuel *(Director)*
**Branches:** The Uk Oil & Gas Industry Association, 9 Albyn Terrace, Aberdeen, Aberdeenshire AB10 1YP
**US SIC:** 1311, 8621
**UK SIC:** 13000, 96311
**Auditors:** haysmacintyre
**Bankers:** Barclays Bank Plc (20-65-82)

| | 31-12-13 | 31-12-12 | 31-12-11 |
|---|---|---|---|
| TO | 16,715,410 | 15,328,028 | 17,517,812 |
| P/L | 780,770 | 638,819 | 684,845 |
| NW | 3,940,240 | 3,362,196 | 3,213,952 |
| WC | 2,387,695 | 2,383,026 | 2,285,264 |
| Emp. | 70 | 61 | 52 |

DUNS 29-491-3116 **Imp**
## U.K. Packaging Supplies Ltd
100 Brantwood Road, London N17 0XY
**Tel:** 020-8801-8144 **Fax:** 020-8365-0847
**Web:** www.ukplc.co.uk
**Reg No:** 1854737 **VAT No:** 406481561
**Estd:** 1984 Private Limited Company
**Line of Business:** Manufacturers of packaging materials
**Issued Capital:** £100,000
**Principals:** A G Dark *(Managing)*, Ms T M Sullivan *(Financial)*, Ms D T Dark
**Co. Secretary:** Anthony Dark
**Responsibilities**
**Senior:** Julia Bickell *(Sales Manager)*
**Sales:** Julia Bickell *(Sales Manager)*
**Admin:** Maria Hammil *(Office Manager)*
**Health & Safety:** Maria Hammil *(Office Manager)*
**Purchasing:** P Bowdon *(Purchasing Manager)*
**Branches:** U.k. Packaging Supplies Ltd, 120 Frederick St, Luton, Bedfordshire LU2 7QU
**US SIC:** 2654 **UK SIC:** 47280
**Auditors:** Chegwidden & Co
**Bankers:** National Westminster Bank Plc (60-23-08)

| | 31-10-13 | 31-10-12 | 31-10-11 |
|---|---|---|---|
| TO | 21,125,093 | 19,469,497 | 18,818,834 |
| P/L | 680,619 | 418,238 | 395,204 |
| NW | 3,689,337 | 3,674,151 | 3,659,904 |
| WC | 133,173 | 289,810 | 625,390 |
| Emp. | 92 | 70 | 65 |

DUNS 29-573-2267
## Uk Payments Administration Ltd
2 Thomas More Square, London E1W 1YN
**Tel:** 02032178259
**Web:** www.ukpayments.org.uk
**Reg No:** 1935025 **VAT No:** 397229118
**Estd:** 2013 Private Limited Company
**Line of Business:** Activities auxiliary to financial intermediation not elsewhere classified
**Trading Style:** Uk Payments
**Issued Capital:** £29
**Directors:** Ms K J Milton, A Slough, G Hocking, Mrs J A Crawford, R J Saunders
**Co. Secretary:** St James Secretaries Limited
**Responsibilities**
**Senior:** Jason Kempton *(Executive)*, Chris Starr *(Executive)*
**Finance:** Richard Mabbott *(Director Special Project - Fas)*
**Marketing:** Michelle Whiteman *(Press Officer)*
**Admin:** Kathy Ryan *(Standards Administrator)*
**US SIC:** 7399 **UK SIC:** 83954
**Auditors:** Barnes Roffe LLP
**Bankers:** National Westminster Bank Plc (60-08-23)

| | 31-12-13 | 31-12-12 | 31-12-11 |
|---|---|---|---|
| TO | 27,262,371 | 22,364,274 | 21,149,175 |
| P/L | 23,655 | 52,107 | 28,480 |
| NW | 29 | 29 | 29 |
| WC | (1,791,432) | (2,211,349) | (2,409,840) |
| Emp. | 215 | 176 | 163 |

DUNS 22-108-7195
## Uk Piers Ltd
Grand Parade, Skegness, Lincolnshire PE25 2UE
**Tel:** 01754-767376 **Fax:** 01754-766939
**Web:** www.skegnesspier.co.uk
**Reg No:** 4128020 **Estd:** 2000 Private Limited Company
**Line of Business:** Places of interest
**Issued Capital:** £100,000
**Director:** C J Paine
**Co. Secretary:** Mrs Carolyn Wilkinson
**Responsibilities**
**Marketing:** Amanda Hewitt *(Marketing Manager)*
**Branches:** Uk Piers Ltd, Vine Road, Skegness, Lincolnshire PE25 3DB
**US SIC:** 8411, 7999
**UK SIC:** 97700, 97913

| | 31-12-13 | 31-12-12 | 31-12-11 |
|---|---|---|---|
| TO | 2,575,000 | 2,585,000 | 2,701,000 |
| P/L | 18,000 | 305,000 | 43,000 |
| NW | 2,460,000 | 2,553,000 | 2,687,000 |
| WC | 166,000 | 223,000 | (127,000) |
| Emp. | 60 | 61 | 57 |

DUNS 23-936-1897
## Uk Platforms Ltd
(**Subsidiary of:** Exponent Private Equity Partners Gp Ii Lp)
Unit 3, The Recovery Centre, Wakefield Road, Barnsley, South Yorkshire S71 1NU
**Tel:** 01226786677
**Web:** www.ukplatforms.co.uk
**Reg No:** 3925935 **Estd:** 2000 Private Limited Company
**Line of Business:** Access equipment
**Trading Style:** Uk Platforms Limited
**Issued Capital:** £4,000,000
**Directors:** J B Gill, J C Davies, S N Trowbridge
**Co. Secretary:** Patrick Hartrey
**Responsibilities**
**Senior:** Brett Harley *(Operations Director)*, Andy Moulds *(Manager)*, Alexandre Saubot *(Manager)*, David Simmonite *(Sales Director)*
**Sales:** David Simmonite *(Sales Director)*
**Branches:** Uk Platforms Limited, The Recovery Centre, Unit 3, Barnsley, South Yorkshire S71 1NU
**US SIC:** 7394 **UK SIC:** 84000
**Auditors:** PricewaterhouseCoopers LLP

**Bankers:** Fortis Bank London Bch (formerly Generale Bk) (40-52-62)

| | 31-12-13 | 31-12-12 | 31-12-11 |
|---|---|---|---|
| TO | 21,069,000 | 18,412,000 | 17,764,000 |
| P/L | (807,000) | (634,000) | (1,843,000) |
| NW | (4,374,000) | (18,347,000) | (17,713,000) |
| WC | (21,534,000) | (23,427,000) | (25,098,000) |
| Emp. | 105 | 109 | 105 |

DUNS 21-677-9197

## Uk Power Networks Holdings Ltd

237 Southwark Bridge Road, London SE1 6NP
**Tel:** 0845-6014516
**Web:** www.ukpowernetworksservices.co.uk
**Reg No:** 7290590 **Estd:** 2010 Private Limited Company
**Line of Business:** Production of electricity
**Issued Capital:** £610,000,000
**Directors:** Ms W W Tong-Barnes, Ms M F Ngan, D N Macrae, C C Tsai, L S Chan, H S Chong, H L Kam, A J Hunter
**Co. Secretary:** Christopher Baker
**Responsibilities**
**Senior:** Kee Chan *(Director)*
**US SIC:** 4911 **UK SIC:** 16101
**Auditors:** Deloitte LLP
**Following financial data are in thousands**

| | 31-12-13 | 31-12-12 | 31-12-11 |
|---|---|---|---|
| TO | 1,607,600 | 1,480,400 | 1,354,600 |
| P/L | 649,000 | 527,200 | 361,400 |
| NW | 369,200 | 4,100 | (337,000) |
| WC | (285,000) | (126,100) | (371,100) |
| Emp. | 5,607 | 5,234 | 5,532 |

DUNS 45-884-2614

## Uk Power Networks Services Powerlink Ltd

(**Subsidiary of:** Uk Power Networks Holdings Ltd)
Newington House, London SE1 6NP
**Tel:** 08007838838 **Fax:** 020 7561 6142
**Web:** www.ukpowernetworks.co.uk
**Reg No:** 3221818 **Estd:** 1998 Private Limited Company
**Line of Business:** Electricity companies
**Issued Capital:** £10,000,000
**Directors:** S D Trotter, D H Sussams, D J Dawson, T J Gregory, P A Clarke, Ms L Gladwell, B R Walker, D P Mitchell
**Co. Secretary:** Nicholas Zentner
**Branches:** Uk Power Networks Services Powerlink Ltd, 49-51 Southwark Bridge Road, London SE1 9HH
**US SIC:** 4911 **UK SIC:** 16101
**Auditors:** KPMG Audit PLC

| | 31-12-13 | 31-12-12 | 31-12-11 |
|---|---|---|---|
| TO | 33,063,000 | 52,434,000 | 61,247,000 |
| P/L | 13,689,000 | 70,321,000 | 3,158,000 |
| NW | 3,260,000 | 54,508,000 | 13,358,000 |
| WC | 4,594,000 | 56,045,000 | 15,688,000 |
| Emp. | 172 | 253 | 247 |

DUNS 23-617-0304

## Uk Power Networks Services (South East) Ltd

(**Subsidiary of:** Uk Power Networks Holdings Ltd)
1 Forest Gate, Crawley, West Sussex RH11 9PT
**Tel:** 08000969636
**Web:** www.edfenergy.com
**Reg No:** 2366867 **VAT No:** 587723395
**Estd:** 1948 Private Limited Company
**Line of Business:** Production of electricity
**Trading Style:** Seeboard Energy
**Issued Capital:** £125,846,852
**Directors:** L S Chan, A J Hunter, B Scarsella
**Co. Secretary:** Christopher Baker
**Branches:** Uk Power Networks Services (South East) Ltd, Po Box 4, Po Box 4, Morecambe, Lancashire LA3 2XQ
**US SIC:** 4911, 1731
**UK SIC:** 16101, 50300
**Auditors:** Deloitte LLP
**Bankers:** HSBC Bank plc (40-47-22)

| | 31-12-13 | 31-12-12 | 31-12-11 |
|---|---|---|---|
| TO | 2,300,000 | 3,000,000 | 2,600,000 |
| P/L | 31,300,000 | 3,200,000 | (1,600,000) |
| NW | 244,000,000 | 245,000,000 | 244,200,000 |
| WC | (687,000,000) | (686,500,000) | (688,000,000) |

DUNS 21-732-1270

## Uk Safety Management Ltd

Unit 5 Temple Point, Bullerthorpe Lane, Leeds, West Yorkshire LS15 9JL
**Tel:** 08448004180
**Web:** www.uksafetymanagement.co.uk
**Reg No:** 7672780 **Estd:** 2011 Private Limited Company
**Line of Business:** Electrical testing services
**Issued Capital:** £100
**US SIC:** 1731 **UK SIC:** 50300
**Auditors:** B.M. Howarth Ltd

| | 30-06-14 | 30-06-13 | 30-06-12 |
|---|---|---|---|
| TO | 7,508,882 | N/A | N/A |
| P/L | 419,718 | N/A | N/A |
| NW | 3,296 | (201,478) | (386,547) |
| WC | (174,017) | (341,941) | (509,767) |
| Emp. | 184 | N/A | N/A |

DUNS 76-903-2376

## Uk Sailing Academy

Arctic Road, Cowes, Isle of Wight PO31 7PQ
**Tel:** 01983-294941 **Fax:** 01983-295938
**Web:** www.uksa.org
**Reg No:** 2251024 **Estd:** 1988 Private Company Limited By Guarantee
**Line of Business:** Other sporting activities not elsewhere classified
**Directors:** D J Lister, S J Chipperfield, W M Garnett, R L Palmer, Mrs D K Haig-Thomas, Ms C M Suckling, M J Kerrison
**Co. Secretary:** Mrs Erica Howard
**Responsibilities**
**Senior:** John Ely *(Chief Executive)*
**Marketing:** Sally-Anne Bowerman *(Marketing Director)*, Mimah Cullen *(Marketing Director)*
**Sales:** Chris Mannion *(Head of Sales)*
**HR:** Ben Willows *(Director, Operations)*
**Health & Safety:** Gareth Ely *(Head of Maintenance)*
**Facilities:** Gareth Ely *(Head of Maintenance)*
**US SIC:** 7999 **UK SIC:** 97913
**Auditors:** Hopper Williams & Bell
**Bankers:** National Westminster Bank Plc (52-30-04)

| | 31-01-14 | 31-01-13 | 31-01-12 |
|---|---|---|---|
| TO | 5,373,000 | 5,651,000 | 5,256,208 |
| P/L | (299,000) | 47,000 | 83,827 |
| NW | 4,384,000 | 4,683,000 | 4,636,512 |
| WC | 603,000 | 374,000 | 459,984 |
| Emp. | 132 | 139 | 151 |

DUNS 21-009-2291 **Imp**

## Uk Shared Business Services Ltd

North Star House, North Star Avenue, Swindon, Wiltshire SN2 1FF
**Tel:** 01793867000
**Web:** www.uksbs.co.uk
**Reg No:** 6330639 **VAT No:** 618367325
**Estd:** 2007 Private Limited Company
**Line of Business:** Research institutions and organisations
**Trading Style:** Uk Sbs
**Issued Capital:** £62,016,366
**Directors:** Dr L Thompson, Mrs C B Bernstein, N H Winterton, Miss J M Brigham, E P Lester, Baroness I T Fritchie, Dr C L Grace, Ms E A Mcmahon
**Co. Secretary:** Miss Merinda Wilson
**Responsibilities**
**Senior:** Jonathan Preece *(Manager)*
**Facilities:** Martin Richards *(Facilities Manager)*
**US SIC:** 7391 **UK SIC:** 94000
**Auditors:** Comptroller & Auditor General
**Bankers:** Lloyds TSB Bank plc (30-98-41)

| | 31-03-14 | 31-03-13 | 31-03-12 |
|---|---|---|---|
| TO | 57,331,000 | 55,238,000 | 44,653,000 |
| P/L | (9,062,000) | (11,934,000) | (7,882,000) |
| NW | (570,000) | 6,633,000 | 7,871,000 |
| WC | 836,000 | 6,746,000 | 6,947,000 |
| Emp. | 867 | 750 | 638 |

DUNS 73-353-4320 **Imp**

## Uk Snacks Ltd

Unit 2-3, Golden Business Park, Orient Way, London E10 7FE
**Tel:** 020-8988-0806
**Web:** www.nageena.net
**Reg No:** 4627046 **Estd:** 2003 Private Limited Company
**Line of Business:** Manufacturers of food products
**Issued Capital:** £300,000
**Directors:** G A Nazir, S Ahmed
**Co. Secretary:** Shamim Akhtar
**Responsibilities**
**IT:** Aaron Cyrus *(IT Manager)*
**Health & Safety:** Ayub Ahmed *(Production Manager)*
**Facilities:** Rashmi Lathigra *(Facilities Manager)*
**Engineering:** Ayub Ahmed *(Production Manager)*
**US SIC:** 2099, 2043
**UK SIC:** 42399, 42398
**Bankers:** Allied Irish Bank (gb) (23-84-81)

| | 31-03-13 | 31-03-12 | 31-03-11 |
|---|---|---|---|
| TO | 15,068,402 | 13,077,596 | 9,844,580 |
| P/L | 224,676 | 176,569 | 144,312 |
| NW | 1,779,812 | 1,598,097 | 1,680,949 |
| WC | 1,199,117 | 900,147 | 821,195 |
| Emp. | 63 | 52 | 52 |

DUNS 21-034-2000

## Uk Steel Stockholders

Overend Road, Unit 8 Congreaves Trading Estate, Cradley Heath, West Midlands B64 7DD
**Tel:** 01384-565822
**Web:** www.uk-steel.co.uk
**Partnership**
**Line of Business:** Aluminium stockholders
**Trading Style:** Uk Steel Stockholders

**Partners:** N Firth, A Walcup, T Buckle
**US SIC:** 5051 **UK SIC:** 61200
**Employees:** 50

DUNS 23-321-5206

## Uk Tissue Ltd

(**Subsidiary of:** Calchas Sa)
Heysham Business Park, Middleton, Morecambe, Lancashire LA3 3PP
**Tel:** 01524850066
**Web:** www.tissue.co.uk
**Reg No:** 4695313 **Estd:** 2003 Private Limited Company
**Line of Business:** Manufacture speciality tissue paper head office with 2 sites
**Issued Capital:** £1,000
**Directors:** F Boschi, S Mulcahy
**Co. Secretary:** Gary Walker
**Responsibilities**
**Sales:** Stafford Woods *(Sales Manager)*
**IT:** Jason Curl *(IT Manager)*
**Engineering:** Gary Willis *(Production Manager)*
**US SIC:** 2631 **UK SIC:** 47017

| | 31-12-13 | 31-12-12 | 31-12-11 |
|---|---|---|---|
| TA | 1,000 | 1,000 | 1,000 |
| NW | 1,000 | 1,000 | 1,000 |

DUNS 34-718-9149

## Uk Wholesale Direct Ltd

4th Floor Meadow Mill, Water Street, Stockport, Cheshire SK1 2BU
**Web:** www.uk-wholesale.co.uk
**Reg No:** 5522535 **VAT No:** 974619281
**Estd:** 2005 Private Limited Company
**Line of Business:** Telecommunications
**Issued Capital:** £1
**Director:** Miss V Knight
**US SIC:** 4899 **UK SIC:** 79020

| | 31-07-13 | 31-07-12 | 31-07-11 |
|---|---|---|---|
| TA | 110,471 | 65,075 | 19,989 |
| NW | 63,321 | 27,541 | 4,156 |
| WC | 61,098 | 26,271 | 3,300 |

DUNS 22-249-5348

## Uk Woods Flakt Holdings Ltd

(**Subsidiary of:** Stromboli Investissements Sas)
Axial Way, Axial Way, Colchester, Essex CO4 5ZD
**Tel:** 01206544122
**Web:** www.flaktwoods.com
**Reg No:** 4267528 **Estd:** 2001 Private Limited Company
**Line of Business:** Ventilation systems
**Trading Style:** Flakt Woods
**Issued Capital:** £2,079,256
**Director:** R D Osborn
**Co. Secretary:** Stephen Mirrington
**Responsibilities**
**Senior:** Ellen Hurdel *(Manager)*
**US SIC:** 6711 **UK SIC:** 83962

| | 31-12-13 | 31-12-12 | 31-12-11 |
|---|---|---|---|
| TA | 12,029,000 | 11,493,000 | 11,382,000 |
| P/L | 98,000 | 1,025,000 | 97,000 |
| NW | 2,381,000 | 2,306,000 | 2,187,000 |
| WC | 2,381,000 | 2,306,000 | 2,187,000 |

DUNS 76-894-2849

## Ukais Ltd

(**Subsidiary of:** Ageas Nv)
Prospect House, Gordon Banks Drive, Trentham Lakes North, Stoke-On-Trent, Staffordshire ST4 4TW
**Tel:** 01782793900
**Web:** www.eas.com
**Reg No:** 2613429 **VAT No:** 542798019
**Estd:** 1991 Private Limited Company
**Line of Business:** Insurance brokers
**Trading Style:** Eas Insurance Solutions
**Issued Capital:** £50,000
**Directors:** A S Watson, G F Ball, F K Dyson, A E Middle, J R Furse, N J Lemans, M Cliff
**Co. Secretary:** Ms Rosemary Smith
**Responsibilities**
**Sales:** Carl Bromley *(Sales Manager)*
**Purchasing:** Alyson Washington *(Buyer)*
**Branches:** Ukais Ltd, 28 Gt Moor St, Bolton, Lancashire BL1 1NJ
**US SIC:** 6411 **UK SIC:** 83200
**Auditors:** KPMG Audit PLC
**Bankers:** HSBC Bank plc (40-34-27)

| | 31-12-13 | 31-12-12 | 31-12-11 |
|---|---|---|---|
| TO | 25,372,000 | 24,722,000 | 23,396,000 |
| P/L | 2,110,000 | 3,182,000 | 2,565,000 |
| NW | 1,110,000 | 2,764,000 | 2,220,000 |
| WC | 3,602,000 | 1,291,000 | 303,000 |
| Emp. | 454 | 469 | 479 |

DUNS 21-999-3062

## Ukb Networks Ltd

3rd Floor International House, 7 High Street, London W5 5DB
**Tel:** 02030067801
**Reg No:** 8966182 **Estd:** 2014 Private Limited Company
**Line of Business:** Telecommunications
**Directors:** N J Williams, A A Arena

**Co. Secretary:** Jordan Cosec Limited
**US SIC:** 4899 **UK SIC:** 79020
**Employees:** 70

DUNS 21-780-1926

## Ukcleaning

Broad Quay House, Broad Quay, Bristol, Avon BS1 4DJ
**Tel:** 01179758675
**Web:** www.ukcleaning.co.uk
**Estd:** 2011 Proprietorship
**Line of Business:** Hygiene and cleaning services
**Proprietor:** J Warrack
**Responsibilities**
**Senior:** J W *(Manager)*
**US SIC:** 7349 **UK SIC:** 92300
**Employees:** 50

DUNS 23-761-5278

## Ukd Groundworks & Civil Engineering Ltd

Nash House, 12 London Road, Hemel Hempstead, Hertfordshire HP3 9SR
**Fax:** 01442-232464
**Reg No:** 3755161 **Estd:** 1999 Private Limited Company
**Line of Business:** Other engineering activities
**Trading Style:** Ukd Groundworks & Civil Engineering Ltd
**Issued Capital:** £2
**Director:** M J Bosher
**Co. Secretary:** Ms Emma Carter
**Responsibilities**
**Senior:** clare llewellyn *(purchasing manager)*
**Health & Safety:** Mike Thorneycroft *(health & safety officer)*
**Purchasing:** clare llewellyn *(purchasing manager)*
**US SIC:** 8911, 1622, 1611
**UK SIC:** 83701, 50200

| | 30-04-14 | 30-04-13 | 30-04-12 |
|---|---|---|---|
| TO | 20,155,059 | 20,061,233 | 20,196,776 |
| P/L | 131,623 | 100,751 | 59,612 |
| NW | 1,098,040 | 993,018 | 915,225 |
| WC | 864,548 | 801,627 | 702,581 |
| Emp. | 75 | 70 | 88 |

DUNS 73-406-2628

## Ukdn Waterflow Ltd

(**Subsidiary of:** Ukdn Waterflow Group Ltd)
Unit 4 Bridgeside, Bredbury, Stockport, Cheshire SK6 4QT
**Tel:** 01617637222
**Web:** www.ukdnwaterflow.co.uk
**Reg No:** 4679632 **Estd:** 2004 Private Limited Company
**Line of Business:** Drainage contractors
**Issued Capital:** £85,714
**Directors:** N Harris, S F Shine, N M Powell, G Shannon, K C Mouatt, W B Hunter
**Responsibilities**
**Senior:** Tony Killgannon *(Manager)*, Stuart Pace *(Manager)*
**US SIC:** 4952 **UK SIC:** 92120
**Auditors:** BDO LLP
**Bankers:** HSBC Bank plc (40-28-36)

| | 31-12-13 | 31-12-12 | 31-12-11 |
|---|---|---|---|
| TO | 18,488,000 | 20,585,974 | 24,634,026 |
| P/L | (2,030,000) | (29,815) | 3,854,252 |
| NW | 29,000 | 1,715,674 | 1,416,459 |
| WC | (713,000) | 1,213,438 | 2,946,716 |
| Emp. | 328 | 335 | 354 |

DUNS 21-722-5358 **Exp**

## Ukdn Waterflow Technical Services Ltd

(**Subsidiary of:** Ukdn Waterflow Group Ltd)
12 David Road, Colnbrook, Slough, Berkshire SL3 0DG
**Tel:** 01753-810999 **Fax:** 01753-681442
**Web:** www.waterflow.co.uk
**Reg No:** 0858432 **VAT No:** 844282324
**Estd:** 2010 Private Limited Company
**Line of Business:** Sanitation, remediation and similar activities
**Issued Capital:** £991,000
**Directors:** G Shannon, S F Shine, K C Mouatt, N Harris
**US SIC:** 4952, 1711
**UK SIC:** 92120, 50300
**Auditors:** Harris & Trotter LLP
**Bankers:** National Westminster Bank Plc (60-22-40)

| | 31-12-13 | 31-12-12 | 31-12-11 |
|---|---|---|---|
| TO | 29,909,000 | 24,432,831 | 24,367,195 |
| P/L | 2,250,000 | 1,582,142 | 948,438 |
| NW | 11,245,000 | 8,905,222 | 7,573,105 |
| WC | 9,274,000 | 6,868,280 | 5,642,803 |
| Emp. | 205 | 176 | 168 |

DUNS 21-002-2173

## Ukf Stainless Holdings Ltd

12 Buntsford Park Road, Bromsgrove, Worcestershire B60 3DX
**Tel:** 01527578686
**Web:** www.ukfstainless.co.uk
**Reg No:** 6276285 **Estd:** 2007 Private Limited Company
**Line of Business:** Management activities of other non-financial holding companies not elsewhere classified
**Export Sales:** £855,155
**Issued Capital:** £102
**Director:** P Morris
**Co. Secretary:** Simon Greenhill
**US SIC:** 6711 **UK SIC:** 83962

| | 30-09-14 | 30-09-13 | 30-09-12 |
|---|---|---|---|
| TO | 13,602,239 | 11,646,646 | 10,910,269 |
| P/L | 887,231 | 325,154 | 517,420 |
| NW | 1,867,215 | 1,218,222 | 1,289,579 |
| WC | 634,069 | (890) | 140,755 |
| Emp. | 44 | 46 | 44 |

DUNS 22-039-0020

## Ukfast Ltd

1 Archway Birley Fields, Manchester M15 5QJ
**Tel:** 08454584545 **Fax:** 08704584545
**Web:** www.ukfast.co.uk
**Reg No:** 4041421 **Estd:** 2010 Private Limited Company
**Line of Business:** Internet service providers
**Issued Capital:** £2
**Director:** L N Jones
**Co. Secretary:** Ms Gail Jones
**US SIC:** 7379 **UK SIC:** 83940

| | 31-12-13 | 31-12-12 | 31-12-11 |
|---|---|---|---|
| TA | 2 | 2 | 2 |
| NW | 2 | 2 | 2 |
| WC | N/A | N/A | 2 |
| Emp. | N/A | N/A | 100 |

DUNS 23-853-7570 **Imp**

## Ukfast.Net Ltd

Birley Fields, Manchester M15 5QJ
**Tel:** 08445763900 **Fax:** 0870 458 4545
**Web:** www.ukfast.co.uk
**Reg No:** 3845616 **Estd:** 2010 Private Limited Company
**Line of Business:** Data processing
**Issued Capital:** £2
**Directors:** J D Ryland, D J Taylor, L N Jones, N Lathwood, J Bowers
**Co. Secretary:** Ms Gail Jones
**US SIC:** 7374 **UK SIC:** 83940
**Auditors:** Ernst & Young LLP
**Bankers:** National Westminster Bank Plc (01-02-02)

| | 31-12-13 | 31-12-12 | 31-12-11 |
|---|---|---|---|
| TO | 23,424,573 | 19,869,984 | 16,018,747 |
| P/L | 4,925,865 | 5,334,579 | 3,354,769 |
| NW | 9,609,504 | 5,708,696 | 3,886,993 |
| WC | (3,103,747) | (1,437,170) | (246,781) |
| Emp. | 170 | 147 | 118 |

DUNS 52-022-2951

## Ukn Group Ltd

300 Crockford Lane Cedarwood, Basingstoke, Hampshire RG24 8WD
**Tel:** 08456 436060 **Fax:** 01189881201
**Web:** www.ukngroup.com
**Reg No:** 3388748 **Estd:** 1997 Private Limited Company
**Line of Business:** Computer support & services
**Issued Capital:** £52,787
**Directors:** Mrs M O'Malley, M D Watson, C P Telfer, M Eaton
**Co. Secretary:** Mrs Margarita O'Malley
**US SIC:** 7379 **UK SIC:** 83940

| | 31-05-14 | 31-05-13 | 31-05-12 |
|---|---|---|---|
| TA | 2,143,624 | 2,513,899 | 2,669,941 |
| NW | 1,051,676 | 1,157,437 | 1,250,722 |
| WC | 931,021 | 1,011,390 | 1,092,314 |

DUNS 23-936-3117

## Ukos Plc

Unit 7-8, Enterprise Way, Hemel Hempstead, Hertfordshire HP2 7YJ
**Tel:** 01442288300 **Fax:** 01442-288399
**Web:** www.ukosplc.com
**Reg No:** 3926059 **Estd:** 2000 Public Limited Company
**Line of Business:** Wholesale of other household goods not elsewhere classified
**Issued Capital:** £724,500
**Directors:** O C Andrew, P Ratcliffe, A A Stannard, I M Haywood, P J Gowing, D Johnson
**Responsibilities**
**Senior:** Terry Coulson *(Manager)*, Roy Cowan *(Chief Executive Officer)*
**Purchasing:** Terry Coulson *(Manager)*
**US SIC:** 5199, 5942
**UK SIC:** 61900, 65300
**Auditors:** Hillier Hopkins
**Bankers:** Barclays Bank Plc (20-72-17)

| | 31-12-13 | 31-12-12 | 31-12-11 |
|---|---|---|---|
| TO | 9,520,393 | 9,405,306 | 9,812,544 |
| P/L | (97,926) | 30,186 | 143,042 |
| NW | 302,180 | 108,415 | 68,180 |
| WC | 206,961 | 19,791 | (609) |
| Emp. | 72 | 69 | 69 |

DUNS 34-578-3096

## Ukrd Group Ltd

Carn Brea Studios, Barncoose Industrial Estate, Redruth, Cornwall TR15 3XX
**Tel:** 01209310435
**Web:** www.ukrd.com
**Reg No:** 2725453 **Estd:** 1992 Private Limited Company
**Line of Business:** Television and radio station operators
**Issued Capital:** £3,240,996
**Directors:** G H Aaronson, A R Preece, W J Rogers, A D Everett, Lord J P St-Levan, T Smallwood, J K Hepburn
**Co. Secretary:** Andrew Preece
**Responsibilities**
**Senior:** James Aubyn *(Manager)*, Roger Humm *(Manager)*, Kirsty Petty *(Finance Manager)*
**Branches:** Ukrd Group Ltd, Unit 3 Brunel Mall, London Rd, Stroud, Gloucestershire GL5 2BP
**US SIC:** 4833 **UK SIC:** 97411
**Auditors:** Ernst & Young LLP
**Bankers:** National Westminster Bank Plc (60-09-21)

| | 30-09-13 | 30-09-12 | 30-09-11 |
|---|---|---|---|
| TO | 17,173,175 | 16,850,961 | 15,888,658 |
| P/L | (523,607) | 493,044 | 740,095 |
| NW | 1,956,517 | 2,107,419 | 1,798,613 |
| WC | (365,308) | (56,874) | (259,958) |
| Emp. | 283 | 265 | 250 |

DUNS 34-778-8254

## Ukrt Group Ltd

Coolair House, Globe Lane, Dukinfield, Cheshire SK16 4UJ
**Tel:** 08702416697
**Web:** www.ukfmgroup.com
**Reg No:** 5579570 **Estd:** 2005 Private Limited Company
**Line of Business:** Management activities of holding companies
**Issued Capital:** £9,600
**Directors:** D Abernethy, A Smith, J Gay
**Co. Secretary:** Darren Abernethy
**US SIC:** 6711 **UK SIC:** 83962

| | 31-12-13 | 31-12-12 | 31-12-11 |
|---|---|---|---|
| TO | 6,770,891 | 10,570,360 | N/A |
| P/L | (401,809) | 496,871 | N/A |
| NW | 3,013,701 | 3,307,296 | 879,318 |
| WC | 2,807,656 | 3,004,855 | (205,891) |
| Emp. | 80 | 118 | N/A |

DUNS 49-497-3332 **Imp**

## Ul International (Uk) Ltd

**(Subsidiary of:** Whm Holdings Llc)
Wonersh House, The Guildway, Old Portsmouth Road, Artington, Guildford, Surrey GU3 1LR
**Tel:** 01483-302130 **Fax:** 01483-302230
**Web:** www.uk.ul.com
**Reg No:** 3159495 **Estd:** 1996 Private Limited Company
**Line of Business:** Activities auxiliary to insurance and pension funding
**Export Sales:** £6,620,713
**Trading Style:** Underwriters Laboratories
**Issued Capital:** £100
**Directors:** S Jesudas, M A Saltzman, G Schjotz
**Co. Secretary:** Columbus Gangemi
**Responsibilities**
**Senior:** Sylvia Gaff *(Office Administrator)*, Stephen Wenc *(Manager)*
**Admin:** Sylvia Gaff *(Office Administrator)*
**Branches:** Ul International (Uk) Ltd, Wonersh House The Guildway, Old Portsmouth Road, Artington, Artington, Guildford, Surrey GU3 1LR
**US SIC:** 6411 **UK SIC:** 83200
**Auditors:** Unknown
**Bankers:** Lloyds TSB Bank plc (30-00-08)

| | 31-12-13 | 31-12-12 | 31-12-11 |
|---|---|---|---|
| TO | 6,620,713 | 6,812,928 | 15,214,401 |
| P/L | 650,633 | 488,780 | (1,326,489) |
| NW | 2,309,020 | 1,473,010 | (7,127,937) |
| WC | 2,639,809 | 1,660,637 | 2,277,076 |
| Emp. | 73 | 72 | 172 |

DUNS 39-233-1856 **Imp-Exp**

## Ul Vs Ltd

**(Subsidiary of:** Whm Holdings Llc)
Pavilion A, Ashwood Way Ashwood Park, Basingstoke, Hampshire RG23 8BG
**Tel:** 01256312000 **Fax:** 01256851192
**Web:** www.ul.com
**Reg No:** 2117901 **VAT No:** 479433802
**Estd:** 1987 Private Limited Company
**Line of Business:** Technical testing and analysis
**Export Markets:** Worldwide
**Export Sales:** £11,160,665
**Trading Style:** R F I
**Issued Capital:** £74,937
**Principals:** S A Kirk *(Managing)*, M A Saltzman, S Jesudas, B Watson
**Co. Secretary:** Stephen Kirk
**Responsibilities**
**Finance:** Joanne Rose *(Financial Manager)*
**Sales:** Grant Taylor *(Senior Sales Executive)*
**US SIC:** 7397, 7391, 7392
**UK SIC:** 83702, 94000, 83951
**Auditors:** KPMG LLP
**Bankers:** HSBC Bank plc (40-09-18)

| | 31-12-13 | 31-12-12 | 31-12-11 |
|---|---|---|---|
| TO | 13,603,376 | 11,416,077 | 8,370,733 |
| P/L | (1,225,124) | (1,681,873) | (253,559) |
| NW | (1,128,931) | 96,193 | 1,778,066 |
| WC | (28,300) | (313,043) | 475,025 |
| Emp. | 150 | 117 | 97 |

DUNS 21-163-7249

## Ulidia Integrated College

112 Victoria Road, Carrickfergus, Co Antrim BT38 7JL
**Web:** www.ulidiacollege.com
**Estd:** 2001
**Line of Business:** Schools (local authority)
**Chairman:** E Martin
**US SIC:** 8211 **UK SIC:** 93200
**Employees:** 100

DUNS 52-023-4378

## Ullesthorpe Court Hotel & Golf Club Ltd

Sovereign House, 12 Warwick Street, Coventry, West Midlands CV5 6ET
**Tel:** 01455209023
**Web:** www.bw-ullesthorpecourt.co.uk
**Reg No:** 3389927 **Estd:** 1997 Private Limited Company
**Line of Business:** Hotels
**Issued Capital:** £207,053
**Directors:** T J Woolley, P Burgess
**Co. Secretary:** Gary Woolley
**US SIC:** 7011 **UK SIC:** 66500

| | 31-08-13 | 31-08-12 | 31-08-11 |
|---|---|---|---|
| TO | 3,017,143 | 2,891,319 | 2,874,607 |
| P/L | 53,703 | 57,641 | (473,078) |
| NW | 543,293 | 436,616 | 373,538 |
| WC | (778,289) | (938,897) | (884,605) |
| Emp. | 107 | 108 | 116 |

DUNS 21-035-4320 **Imp**

## Uln ( U K ) Ltd

**(Subsidiary of:** Stichting Administratiekantoor Esf)
Brook Lane, Westbury, Wiltshire BA13 4HA
**Tel:** 01373866150
**Web:** www.dreamcheese.co.uk
**Reg No:** 0596550 **VAT No:** 232703689
**Estd:** 1958 Private Limited Company
**Line of Business:** Dairy produce merchants
**Issued Capital:** £2,490,817
**Directors:** P Ragnet, A M Bongrain, S J Sixou
**Co. Secretary:** Philippe Marie
**Responsibilities**
**Senior:** Rene Briquette *(General Manager)*, Dominique Huth *(General Manager)*, Jean Larmande *(Manager)*, John Starling *(Manager)*
**Finance:** Stephen Bouchayer *(Financial Director)*
**Marketing:** Rene Briquette *(General Manager)*
**Sales:** Rene Briquette *(General Manager)*
**IT:** Geoff Ifill *(Computer Manager)*
**Facilities:** Rene Briquette *(General Manager)*
**Operations:** Dennis Winfield *(Production Manager)*
**Purchasing:** James Toomey *(Buyer)*
**US SIC:** 2021, 5199
**UK SIC:** 41302, 61900
**Auditors:** KPMG LLP
**Bankers:** HSBC Bank plc (40-44-33)

| | 31-12-13 | 31-12-12 | 31-12-11 |
|---|---|---|---|
| TO | 51,246,000 | 49,797,000 | 55,310,000 |
| P/L | 462,000 | 253,000 | (429,000) |
| NW | 4,875,000 | 4,814,000 | 4,955,000 |
| WC | 2,989,000 | 3,285,000 | 3,517,000 |
| Emp. | 100 | 100 | 106 |

DUNS 22-285-3405

## Ulookubook Ltd

Tyne House, 26 Side, Newcastle-Upon-Tyne, Tyne and Wear NE1 3JA
**Tel:** 01912446160 **Fax:** 01912 485051
**Web:** www.holidaydiscountcentre.co.uk
**Reg No:** 4303324 **Estd:** 2001 Private Limited Company
**Line of Business:** Travel agency activities
**Trading Style:** Travel Bubble
**Issued Capital:** £219,000
**Director:** Ms S Winter
**Co. Secretary:** Stephen Campion
**US SIC:** 4722 **UK SIC:** 77001
**Auditors:** A. Nichol & Co

| | 31-10-13 | 31-10-12 | 31-10-11 |
|---|---|---|---|
| TA | 590,304 | 721,492 | 1,527,596 |
| NW | 56,849 | 59,808 | 61,136 |
| WC | 199,455 | 122,715 | (59,568) |

DUNS 23-634-6628 **Imp**

## Ulrich Attachments Ltd

Unit 9b Triangle Business Park, Quilters Way, Stoke Mandeville, Aylesbury, Buckinghamshire HP22 5BL
**Tel:** 01296-616780 **Fax:** 01296-614903
**Web:** www.ulrich.co.uk
**Reg No:** 3631564 **VAT No:** 717916904
**Estd:** 2006 Private Limited Company
**Line of Business:** Manufacturers of plant machinery
**Export Sales:** £460,652
**Issued Capital:** £100,300
**Managing Director:** J M Hopkinson
**Co. Secretary:** Martin Webb
**US SIC:** 3531, 5082
**UK SIC:** 32541, 61490
**Bankers:** National Westminster Bank Plc (60-10-10)

| | 30-09-13 | 30-09-12 | 30-09-11 |
|---|---|---|---|
| TO | 6,675,704 | 6,931,662 | N/A |
| P/L | 444,380 | 517,162 | N/A |
| NW | 1,294,033 | 865,287 | 1,292,000 |
| WC | 1,151,342 | 694,950 | 968,227 |
| Emp. | 81 | 84 | N/A |

DUNS 21-583-1785 **Exp**

## Ulstein (U.K.) Ltd

**(Subsidiary of:** Rolls-Royce Holdings Plc)
Taxi Way, Dunfermline, Fife KY11 9JT
**Tel:** 01383-823188 **Fax:** 01383-824038
**Web:** www.rolls-royce.com
**Reg No:** 0056372SC **VAT No:** 345886022
**Estd:** 2002 Private Limited Company
**Line of Business:** Marine engines and engineering
**Trading Style:** Rolls-Royce
**Issued Capital:** £3,755,048
**Directors:** Mrs D J Goma, Rolls-Royce Directorate Limited
**Co. Secretary:** Rolls-Royce Secretariat Limited
**Responsibilities**
**Senior:** Tom Archibald *(Warehouse Manager)*
**Sales:** Peter Bonallo *(Proposals and Sales Manager)*
**Health & Safety:** Brian Kinniburgh *(Health & Safety Officer)*
**Operations:** Bill McDiarmid *(Naval Architect)*
**Engineering:** Ewan Bell *(Senior Design Engineer)*, Bill McDiarmid *(Naval Architect)*
**US SIC:** 3731, 3823, 8911
**UK SIC:** 36101, 37100, 83701
**Bankers:** Bank Of Scotland (80-19-93)

| | 31-12-11 |
|---|---|
| P/L | (22,000) |
| Emp. | 2 |

DUNS 22-935-8635

## Ulster American Folk Park

2 Mellon Road, Castletown, Omagh, Co Tyrone BT78 5QU
**Tel:** 028-8224-3292
**Web:** www.folkpark.com
**Estd:** 1967
**Line of Business:** Museums
**Co. Secretary:** Peter Kelly
**Branches:** Ulster American Folk Park, 4 The Mount, Belfast, Belfast BT5 4NA
**US SIC:** 8411 **UK SIC:** 97700
**Bankers:** Northern Bank Ltd (95-04-07)
**Employees:** 75

DUNS 21-455-8645

## Ulster Bank Ltd

**(Subsidiary of:** Hm Treasury)
11-16 Donegall Square East, Belfast BT1 5UB
**Tel:** 02890244112 **Fax:** 02890275507
**Web:** www.ulsterbank.com
**Reg No:** 0000733R **Estd:** 1867 Private Limited Company
**Line of Business:** Banks
**Issued Capital:** £1,208,440,000
**Directors:** R M Gallagher, C G Mills, C M Mccarthy, S Dorgan, Dr P M Nolan, T G Bowen, S J Murphy, I W Webb
**Co. Secretary:** Ms Mary Mullen
**Responsibilities**
**Senior:** Bobbie Bergin *(Director of Communications/Cor)*, Robert Boyd *(Branch Manager)*, Jim Brown *(Chief Executive)*, Noel Clarke *(Regional Director)*, Neil Cooke *(Area Director NI)*, Caroline Costello *(Branch Manager)*, Mark Crimmins *(Senior Manager At Business Cen)*, Stephen Cruise *(Manager)*, Steve Dalton *(Senior Manager)*, Dermot Gath *(Area Manager)*, Eileen Gleeson *(Non-Executive Director)*, Nigel Hamilton *(Non-Executive Director)*, Iain Hogan *(General Manager)*, Tom Leahy *(?Regional Director South)*, Gervaise McAteer *(Associate Director)*, Seamus McGuckin *(Senior Manager)*, Mary O'Neill *(Partner)*, Dolores Roche *(Area Manager)*, Nora Shanahan *(Manager)*, Nicky Sheary *(Manager)*, Orna Stokes *(Manager)*, Kathleen Traynor *(Branch Manager)*

**Finance:** Simon Barry *(Chief Economist)*, Shauna Burns *(Finance Manager)*, Jason Campbell *(Associate Director, Corporate)*, Jean Conroy *(Business Manager)*, Eddie Cullen *(Head of Corporate and Institut)*, Pauline Devlin *(Business Executive)*, Kenton Hilman *(?Director Corporate & Institut)*, Ken Kennedy *(Finance Manager)*, Ken Murnaghan *(Regional Director Corporate Co)*, Gordon Myers *(Financial Planning Manager)*, Patrick Passmore *(Capital Markets Manager)*, John Turkington *(Director, Corporate Banking)*
**Marketing:** Bobbie Bergin *(Director of Communications/Cor)*, Orla Bird *(Head of Media Relations & Publ)*, Niall Caldwell *(Media Relations Consultant)*, Sarah Dempsey *(Relations Manager)*, Samantha Gregan *(Communications Manager)*, Joe Heneghan *(Head of Product Management)*, Andrew McLaughlin *(Director of Communications)*, Debbie Mccaughey *(Senior Employee Communications)*, Goretti Priestly *(Marketing Manager)*, Terry Robb *(Head of Business)*, Henry Roberts *(Relationship Manager, South Mi)*
**Sales:** Bernie Canavan *(Business Manager)*, Bob Clements *(Sales Director)*, Paul Erskine *(Commercial Manager)*, Philip Hill *(Business Development Manager)*, Ryan Mawhinney *(Business Manager)*, John McGrane *(Head of Product and Service Sa)*, Ciara McGrath *(Account Manager)*, Tina Minogue *(Commercial Manager)*, Fergus O' Neill *(Account Manager)*, Eoin Ryan *(Commercial Manager)*
**Admin:** Margaret Robinson *(PA to Brian Alan)*
**IT:** Frank O' Dwyer *(Information Security)*
**HR:** Steve Daniels *(Human Resources Director)*, Therese Killeen *(Senior Training Consultant)*, Fiona Steen *(Network Support Manager)*
**Operations:** Angela Maguire *(Product Manager)*, Philip McClurg *(Production and Operations Mana)*, John McGrane *(Head of Product and Service Sa)*
**Purchasing:** James Cleary *(Group Purchasing Manager)*
**Branches:** Ulster Bank Ltd, 75 Main Street, Bangor, Co Down BT20 5AF
**US SIC:** 6012 **UK SIC:** 81402
**Auditors:** Deloitte & Toche
**Following financial data are in thousands**

| | 31-12-13 | 31-12-12 | 31-12-11 |
|---|---|---|---|
| TA | 40,010,000 | 44,695,000 | 48,945,000 |
| P/L | (4,374,000) | (2,091,000) | (3,072,000) |
| NW | 3,443,000 | 6,894,000 | 6,301,000 |
| WC | 5,144,000 | 8,080,000 | 5,993,000 |
| Emp. | 5,377 | 5,590 | 5,752 |

DUNS 21-458-5663 **Imp-Exp**

## Ulster Carpet Mills (Holdings) Ltd

Castleisland Factory, Craigavon, Co Armagh BT62 1EE
**Tel:** 028-3833-4433 **Fax:** 028-3833-3142
**Web:** www.ulstercarpets.com
**Reg No:** 0001207NI **Estd:** 1938 Private Limited Company
**Line of Business:** Manufacture of carpets and rugs
**Export Markets:** Worldwide
**Trading Style:** Ul
**Issued Capital:** £1
**Directors:** J K Jensen, Mrs M A Montgomery, R J Wilson, N D Coburn, E B Wilson, J E Wilson
**Co. Secretary:** David Acheson
**Responsibilities**
**IT:** Angela McAleer *(IT Manager)*
**Purchasing:** Raymond McKeown *(Procurement Manager)*
**Branches:** Ulster Carpet Mills (Holdings) Ltd, 322 King Street, London W6 0RR
**US SIC:** 2279 **UK SIC:** 43852
**Auditors:** Ernst & Young LLP
**Bankers:** Northern Bank Ltd (95-04-11)

| | 31-03-14 | 31-03-13 | 31-03-12 |
|---|---|---|---|
| TO | 61,363,687 | 54,048,404 | 55,411,577 |
| P/L | 6,532,428 | 7,552,078 | 4,985,231 |
| NW | 38,017,362 | 33,988,826 | 30,550,580 |
| WC | 27,601,461 | 24,129,820 | 21,541,855 |
| Emp. | 520 | 517 | 505 |

DUNS 21-229-6269

## Ulster Community & Hospital Trust

Upper Newtownards Road, Dundonald, Belfast BT16 1RH
**Tel:** 02890484511
**Web:** www.setrust.hscni.net
**Estd:** 2002
**Line of Business:** Hospitals
**Branches:** Ulster Community & Hospital Trust, Bangor Hospital Undah Trust, Castle Street, Bangor, Co Down BT20 4TA
**US SIC:** 9121 **UK SIC:** 91110
**Employees:** 54

DUNS 22-930-6295

## Ulster Independent Clinic Ltd

245 Stranmillis Road, Belfast BT9 5JH
**Tel:** 028-9066-1212 **Fax:** 02803817041
**Web:** www.uic.org.uk
**Reg No:** 0012066NI **Estd:** 1977 Private Company Limited By Guarantee
**Line of Business:** Hospitals
**Directors:** Mrs A Beckett, Doctor M D Crone, W R Wilson, J R Gillvray, C F Russell, T M Diamond, Dr K Fitzpatrick, R M Slater
**Co. Secretary:** Ms Nicola Mcgregor
**Responsibilities**
**Senior:** James Aiken *(Director)*
**Admin:** Wendy Caulfield *(PA)*
**IT:** Gary Heasley *(ITAdministrator)*, David Mc Cartney *(IT Manager)*, Kyle Tableton *(IT Manager)*
**HR:** Shona Dawson *(Human Resources Manager)*
**US SIC:** 8062 **UK SIC:** 95100
**Auditors:** Fitch Campbell
**Bankers:** Northern Bank Ltd (95-01-32)

| | 30-04-14 | 30-04-13 | 30-04-12 |
|---|---|---|---|
| TO | 23,798,770 | 24,141,206 | 24,035,826 |
| P/L | 1,249,530 | 1,604,357 | 1,974,030 |
| NW | 32,819,884 | 28,408,553 | 27,494,196 |
| WC | 13,400,724 | 11,305,851 | 9,853,578 |
| Emp. | 336 | 333 | 338 |

DUNS 22-937-7239

## The Ulster Orchestra Society Ltd

Ulster Hall, 30 Bedford Street, Belfast BT2 7FF
**Tel:** 02890239900 **Fax:** 02890260483
**Web:** www.ulsterorchestra.com
**Reg No:** 0014222NI **Estd:** 1980 Private Company Limited By Guarantee
**Line of Business:** Arts the
**Directors:** A A Doherty, L D Morrison, M P Mcsorley, P T Davies, V A Hewitt, D F Desmond, G J Spence, Dr F Keeling
**Co. Secretary:** Mrs Barbara Mckinley
**Responsibilities**
**Senior:** George Bain *(Director)*, Sheila Davidson *(Director)*, Piers Hellawell *(Director)*, Auveen Sands *(Head of Finance and Operations)*, Rosa Solinas *(Chief Executive)*
**Finance:** Seamus Conway *(Finance Officer)*, Yvonne McKnight *(Finance Assistant)*, Auveen Sands *(Head of Finance and Operations)*
**Marketing:** Veronica Morris *(Head of External Relations)*, Lou Purdy *(External Relations Coordinator)*
**US SIC:** 7922 **UK SIC:** 97412
**Auditors:** PricewaterhouseCoopers LLP
**Bankers:** The Bank Of Ireland (90-02-95)

| | 31-03-14 | 31-03-13 | 31-03-12 |
|---|---|---|---|
| TO | 3,729,268 | 4,114,254 | 4,153,366 |
| P/L | (565,603) | 201,674 | 274,430 |
| NW | 510,188 | 1,075,791 | 874,117 |
| WC | 482,831 | 1,056,107 | 836,884 |
| Emp. | 78 | 79 | 75 |

DUNS 22-925-5237

## Ulster Stores Ltd

**(Subsidiary of:** Nevco (Ni) Ltd)
Strand House, Loughanhill Busine, Coleraine, Co Londonderry BT52 2NR
**Tel:** 02870344444 **Fax:** 028-7032-5399
**Web:** www.adegruchy.com
**Reg No:** 0008394NI **Estd:** 1971 Private Limited Company
**Line of Business:** Other retail sale in non-specialised stores
**Trading Style:** Factwhite House Ulster Stores, Moores of Colraine, Captain Cooks Homestores
**Issued Capital:** £205,000
**Directors:** R J Reid, N K Moore, Ms G F Moore-Wilson
**Co. Secretary:** Neville Moore
**Branches:** Ulster Stores Ltd, De Gruchy, King St & New St, Jersey JE4 8NN St Helier
**US SIC:** 5399 **UK SIC:** 65600
**Auditors:** BDO Northern Ireland
**Bankers:** The Bank Of Ireland (90-23-97)

| | 31-01-14 | 31-01-13 | 31-01-12 |
|---|---|---|---|
| TO | 13,240,944 | 12,517,579 | 13,182,512 |
| P/L | 30,416 | 5,745 | 13,317 |
| NW | 2,730,744 | 2,752,290 | 2,793,372 |
| WC | 608,354 | 724,794 | 843,855 |
| Emp. | 187 | 198 | 209 |

DUNS 22-925-3752 **Imp**

## Ulster Supported Employment Ltd

182-188 Cambrai Street, Belfast BT13 3JH
**Tel:** 02890356600 **Fax:** 028-9035-6611
**Web:** www.usel.co.uk
**Reg No:** 0005192NI **VAT No:** 252979717
**Estd:** 1962 Private Company Limited By Guarantee
**Line of Business:** Beds and bedding
**Trading Style:** Usel
**Directors:** T Hinds, A Bennett, J E Perry, D Mackay, Dr G Adams, Mrs J E Kelly
**Co. Secretary:** David Macedo
**Responsibilities**
**Senior:** Sam Humphries *(Chief Executive)*, Brenda Maitland *(Manager)*, Eileen McMahon *(Production Manager)*, Brian Mcmurray *(Manager)*
**Marketing:** Katherine Redpath *(Marketing Officer)*
**HR:** Linda Laird *(Human Resources Manager)*
**Purchasing:** Brendan O'Kane *(Purchasing Manager)*
**Engineering:** Eileen McMahon *(Production Manager)*
**Branches:** Ulster Supported Employment Ltd, 75 Strand Road, Londonderry, Co Londonderry BT48 7BW
**US SIC:** 7361, 9121
**UK SIC:** 83954, 91110
**Auditors:** PricewaterhouseCoopers LLP
**Bankers:** Northern Bank Ltd (95-01-45)

| | 31-03-14 | 31-03-13 | 31-03-12 |
|---|---|---|---|
| TO | 6,756,072 | 6,876,625 | 6,998,266 |
| P/L | (776,423) | (643,569) | (849,838) |
| NW | (509,816) | (1,252,001) | (1,071,335) |
| WC | 412,972 | 339,734 | 393,631 |
| Emp. | 524 | 570 | 592 |

DUNS 21-560-2350 **Imp**

## Ulsterbus Ltd

3 Milewater Road, Belfast BT3 9BG
**Tel:** 02890666630 **Fax:** 02870325419
**Web:** www.translink.co.uk
**Reg No:** 0006725NI **Estd:** 1966 Private Limited Company
**Line of Business:** Bus operators and stations
**Trading Style:** Ulsterbus Tours, Translink
**Issued Capital:** £10,273,000
**Directors:** J Trethowen, B Mitchell, F A Hewitt, J Brown, P A Oneill, A Depledge, Ms A Coffey, D E Strahan
**Co. Secretary:** John Irvine
**Responsibilities**
**Senior:** Ciaran Doherty *(Manager)*
**IT:** A McWilliams *(Chief Clerk)*, Allan McWilliams *(Chief Clerk)*, Samuel Thompson *(IT Manager)*, John Woollams *(IT Development Manager)*
**Branches:** Ulsterbus Ltd, 96 Newry Street, Banbridge, Co Down BT32 3HE
**US SIC:** 4119 **UK SIC:** 72200
**Auditors:** Deloitte LLP
**Bankers:** The Bank Of Ireland (90-21-27)

| | 30-03-14 | 31-03-13 | 25-03-12 |
|---|---|---|---|
| TO | 97,767,000 | 100,260,000 | 93,667,000 |
| P/L | (3,416,000) | 7,940,000 | 3,078,000 |
| NW | 98,108,000 | (7,084,000) | 96,077,000 |
| WC | 25,477,000 | 17,274,000 | 14,754,000 |
| Emp. | 2,266 | 2,264 | 2,226 |

DUNS 50-573-4145 **Imp**

## Ultima Business Solutions Ltd.

448a Basingstoke Road, Reading, Berkshire RG2 0RX
**Tel:** 01189-027500 **Fax:** 01189-027400
**Web:** www.ultimabusiness.com
**Reg No:** 2521249 **VAT No:** 569722792
**Estd:** 1990 Private Limited Company
**Line of Business:** Other software consultancy and supply
**Export Sales:** £2,489,584
**Issued Capital:** £100,000
**Directors:** Mrs R J Bourne, M S Mcneill, R J Shuff
**Co. Secretary:** Mrs Jennifer Hall
**Responsibilities**
**HR:** A Shuff *(Human Resources Manager)*
**Health & Safety:** R Gosnell *(Facilities Manager)*
**Facilities:** R Gosnell *(Facilities Manager)*
**Purchasing:** G Esslemont *(Purchasing Manager)*
**US SIC:** 7379 **UK SIC:** 83940
**Auditors:** Horwath Clark Whitehill LLP
**Bankers:** The Bank Of Ireland (30-11-54)

| | 31-03-14 | 31-03-13 | 31-03-12 |
|---|---|---|---|
| TO | 73,898,375 | 75,920,892 | 67,055,242 |
| P/L | 2,002,818 | 1,755,981 | 1,524,482 |
| NW | 3,170,490 | 2,732,972 | 2,523,553 |
| WC | 2,171,718 | 2,267,283 | 1,958,713 |
| Emp. | 279 | 264 | 251 |

DUNS 29-554-5370

## Ultima Furniture Systems Ltd

**(Subsidiary of:** Silkstone Finance Ltd)
26 Lidgate Crescent, Langthwaite Grange Industrial Estate, Pontefract, West Yorkshire WF9 3NR
**Tel:** 01977-608608 **Fax:** 01977-608888
**Web:** www.ultimafurniture.co.uk
**Reg No:** 1918871 **VAT No:** 436502956
**Estd:** 1985 Private Limited Company
**Line of Business:** Manufacturers of kitchen furniture
**Issued Capital:** £50,100
**Managing Director:** A W Ellis
**Co. Secretary:** Ms Clare Ellis
**US SIC:** 2599, 2517
**UK SIC:** 46720, 46714

**Auditors:** Lishman Sidwell Campbell & Price
**Bankers:** Yorkshire Bank Plc (05-04-69)

| | 31-01-14 | 31-01-13 | 31-01-12 |
|---|---|---|---|
| TO | 18,363,415 | 14,347,264 | 11,838,774 |
| P/L | 1,937,447 | 1,750,345 | 1,263,270 |
| NW | 6,114,790 | 5,015,357 | 3,958,819 |
| WC | (996,452) | (834,582) | (1,064,359) |
| Emp. | 140 | 115 | 69 |

DUNS 42-362-9612

## Ultimate Finance Group Ltd

First Floor, Unit 1, Westpoint Court, Great Park Road, Bristol, Avon BS32 4PS
**Tel:** 08452513030
**Web:** www.ultimatefinance.net
**Reg No:** 4350565 **Estd:** 2013 Private Limited Company
**Line of Business:** Factoring
**Issued Capital:** £2,862,953
**Directors:** J H Coombes, R Mcdowell, D J Blain, J D Brooke, M Cooper, J D Cranston
**Co. Secretary:** David Blain
**Branches:** Ultimate Finance Group P L C, 7A Mere Green Road, Sutton Coldfield, West Midlands B75 5BL
**US SIC:** 6111 **UK SIC:** 81501
**Auditors:** Deloitte LLP
**Bankers:** Bank Of Scotland (12-08-95)

| | 31-12-13 | 30-06-12 | 30-12-11 |
|---|---|---|---|
| TA | 15,390,000 | 40,313,000 | 42,118,000 |
| P/L | (156,000) | 1,190,000 | 718,000 |
| NW | 9,647,000 | 2,078,000 | 392,000 |
| WC | 2,900,000 | 4,129,000 | 2,786,000 |
| Emp. | N/A | 86 | 74 |

DUNS 21-128-7293

## Ultimate Law Ltd

1 Ashley Road, Altrincham, Cheshire WA14 2DT
**Tel:** 01617102030
**Web:** www.ultimatelawltd.com
**Reg No:** 6632455 **Estd:** 2008 Private Limited Company
**Line of Business:** Solicitors
**Issued Capital:** £100
**Directors:** Ms D R Lipszyc, B P Abrahams
**Co. Secretary:** Anthony Sultan
**US SIC:** 8111 **UK SIC:** 83500

| | 30-06-13 | 30-06-12 | 30-06-11 |
|---|---|---|---|
| TA | 457,811 | 372,917 | 174,508 |
| NW | 108,053 | 125,839 | 7,495 |
| WC | 94,743 | 115,591 | 3,185 |

DUNS 22-660-0047 **Imp-Exp**

## Ultimate Packaging Ltd

Pegasus Way, Grimsby, South Humberside DN37 9TS
**Web:** www.ultimate-packaging.co.uk
**Reg No:** 1625575 **VAT No:** 360083479
**Estd:** 1982 Private Limited Company
**Line of Business:** Manufacture of other containers
**Export Markets:** E U; worldwide
**Export Sales:** £1,809,630
**Issued Capital:** £15,075
**Principals:** N Tonge *(Managing)*, J P Hodson *(Financial)*, J R Mccarthy, C M Tonge
**Co. Secretary:** Michael Tonge
**Branches:** Ultimate Packaging Ltd, Telephone House, Wentworth Street, Peterborough, Cambridgeshire PE1 1BA
**US SIC:** 2654, 2752, 5199
**UK SIC:** 47280, 47544, 61900
**Auditors:** Baker Tilly UK Audit LLP
**Bankers:** Barclays Bank Plc (20-76-14)

| | 28-02-14 | 28-02-13 | 29-02-12 |
|---|---|---|---|
| TO | 43,053,637 | 39,024,310 | 36,833,592 |
| P/L | 1,165,833 | 766,316 | 2,028,659 |
| NW | 9,861,017 | 9,341,308 | 9,193,276 |
| WC | 2,221,299 | 1,542,164 | 3,141,438 |
| Emp. | 268 | 261 | 235 |

DUNS 23-849-4640

## Ultimate Security Services Ltd

Unit 4, Saxon House, Warley St Upminster Trading Park, Upminster, Essex RM14 3PJ
**Tel:** 01708-227100 **Fax:** 01708-250140
**Web:** www.ultimatesecurity.co.uk
**Reg No:** 3841431 **Estd:** 1999 Private Limited Company
**Line of Business:** Security and related activities
**Issued Capital:** £900
**Directors:** Mrs E R Bright, M D Edwards
**Co. Secretary:** Stephen Hall
**Responsibilities**
**Finance:** Michelle Curtis *(Finance Director)*
**HR:** Taryn Garwood *(Human Resources Manager)*
**Health & Safety:** Taryn Garwood *(Human Resources Manager)*
**Branches:** Ultimate Security Services Ltd, Upminster Trad Pk, Warley St, Upminster, Essex RM14 3PJ
**US SIC:** 7393 **UK SIC:** 83954

**Auditors:** Robertson Milroy Ltd

| | 31-12-13 | 31-12-12 | 31-12-11 |
|---|---|---|---|
| TO | 48,482,192 | 39,370,391 | 34,183,965 |
| P/L | 2,314,144 | 1,722,969 | 1,453,152 |
| NW | 1,715,143 | 1,285,540 | 834,700 |
| WC | 1,540,649 | 1,083,658 | 628,038 |
| Emp. | 1,446 | 1,200 | 1,050 |

DUNS 73-475-6724

## Ultimate Travel Holdings Ltd

C O Stein Richards & Co, 10 London Mews, London W2 1HY
**Reg No:** 4739538 **Estd:** 2003 Private Limited Company
**Line of Business:** Management activities of holding companies
**Issued Capital:** £400,000
**Directors:** R J Paterson, C H Delevingne, D R Thompson, M C Thompson, N R Van Gruisen, Mrs I P Van Gruisen
**Co. Secretary:** Ms Caroline Bence-Trower
**US SIC:** 6711 **UK SIC:** 83962

| | 30-06-14 | 30-06-13 | 30-06-12 |
|---|---|---|---|
| TO | 17,476,629 | 17,942,242 | 13,389,286 |
| P/L | 1,009,831 | 908,566 | 510,056 |
| NW | 3,005,941 | 2,151,059 | 1,609,789 |
| WC | 1,208,333 | 306,228 | 433,862 |
| Emp. | 51 | 54 | 51 |

DUNS 23-718-7166 **Imp-Exp**

## Ultra Building Products Ltd

Deerpark Industrial Estate, Omagh, Co Tyrone BT78 4EX
**Tel:** 028-8166-1316 **Fax:** 028-8166-1815
**Web:** www.ultrabuilding.com
**Reg No:** 0019194NI **Estd:** 1981 Private Limited Company
**Line of Business:** Agents involved in the sale of timber and building materials
**Export Markets:** Republic of Ireland
**Trading Style:** Ultra Building Products, Ultra Galvanisers
**Issued Capital:** £9,001
**Directors:** P J Lynch, A Mc Guigan
**Co. Secretary:** Sean Mc Guigan
**US SIC:** 5072, 5963, 5039
**UK SIC:** 61500, 65600, 61300
**Auditors:** S. O'Neill & Co Ltd
**Bankers:** Northern Bank Ltd (95-04-01)

| | 30-04-14 | 30-04-13 | 30-04-12 |
|---|---|---|---|
| TO | 6,314,080 | 5,712,073 | 5,720,817 |
| P/L | 745,454 | 594,253 | 370,034 |
| NW | 6,313,360 | 5,945,612 | 5,596,009 |
| WC | 4,860,323 | 4,448,520 | 3,951,296 |
| Emp. | 79 | 67 | 62 |

DUNS 37-782-7282

## Ultra Clean Cleaning Services

33a High Street, Cheshunt, Waltham Cross, Hertfordshire EN8 0BS
**Tel:** 01992633184
**Web:** www.cleandustrial.co.uk
**Estd:** 1985 Partnership
**Line of Business:** Cleaning contracting commercial
**Partners:** Mrs C Crump, Mrs C Neal
**US SIC:** 7349 **UK SIC:** 92300
**Employees:** 100

DUNS 34-908-4822

## Ultra Electronics Holdings Plc

417 Bridport Road, Greenford, Middlesex UB6 8UE
**Tel:** 020-8813-4321 **Fax:** 020-8813-4322
**Web:** www.ultra-electronics.com
**Reg No:** 2830397 **VAT No:** 645074342
**Estd:** 1993 Public Limited Company
**Line of Business:** Management activities of holding companies
**Export Sales:** £501,504,000
**Trading Style:** Ultra Electronics
**Issued Capital:** £3,479,169
**Principals:** D Caster *(Managing)*, J R Hirst, M Anderson, M T Broadhurst, Ms M E Waldner, C S Bailey, R Sharma, Sir R Walmsley
**Co. Secretary:** Ms Sharon Harris
**Responsibilities**
**Senior:** Carlos Santiago *(President, Sonar and Undersea)*
**Engineering:** Phil Heredge *(Head Of Engineering)*
**Branches:** Ultra Electronics Holdings Plc, Fallow Pk, Rugeley Rd, Hednesford, Cannock, Staffordshire WS12 0QP
**US SIC:** 6711 **UK SIC:** 83962
**Auditors:** Deloitte LLP
**Bankers:** The Royal Bank Of Scotland Plc (16-04-00)

| | 31-12-13 | 31-12-12 | 31-12-11 |
|---|---|---|---|
| TO | 745,154,000 | 760,826,000 | 731,733,000 |
| P/L | 49,281,000 | 82,806,000 | 91,179,000 |
| NW | (57,063,000) | (117,458,000) | (133,704,000) |
| WC | 28,226,000 | (20,313,000) | (60,585,000) |
| Emp. | 4,274 | 4,430 | 4,206 |

DUNS 23-055-0436 **Imp**

## Ultra Electronics Ltd

(**Subsidiary of:** Ultra Electronics Holdings Plc)
417 Bridport Road, Greenford, Middlesex UB6 8UA
**Tel:** 020-8813-4321 **Fax:** 020-8813-4322
**Web:** www.ultra-electrics.com
**Reg No:** 2830644 **VAT No:** 645074342
**Estd:** 1993 Private Limited Company
**Line of Business:** Electrical engineers
**Export Sales:** £142,864,000
**Trading Style:** Ultra Electronics Precision Air & Land Systems (Pals), Ultra Electronics Airport Systems Ultra Electronics Controls, Ultra Electronics Pmes Ultra Electronics Precision Air Systems, Ultra Electronics Electrics
**Issued Capital:** £2
**Directors:** K Thomson, R Sharma, Ms M E Waldner, C N Gane, M Anderson, G D Stacey
**Co. Secretary:** Ms Sharon Harris
**Responsibilities**
**Senior:** Cherise Trumper *(Office Manager)*
**Branches:** Ultra Electronics Limited, 417 Bridport Road, Greenford, Middlesex UB6 8UE
**US SIC:** 3999, 8911
**UK SIC:** 49590, 83701
**Auditors:** Deloitte LLP

| | 31-12-13 | 31-12-12 | 31-12-11 |
|---|---|---|---|
| TO | 372,741,000 | 347,510,000 | 379,493,000 |
| P/L | 65,565,000 | 63,815,000 | 59,060,000 |
| NW | 20,070,000 | 30,656,000 | 25,529,000 |
| WC | 1,295,000 | 15,971,000 | 36,760,000 |
| Emp. | 2,257 | 2,033 | 2,138 |

DUNS 22-857-0024 **Imp-Exp**

## Ultra Finishing Ltd

(**Subsidiary of:** Ultra Finishing Group Ltd)
Heasandford Trading Estate, Burnley, Lancashire BB10 2BE
**Tel:** 01282-436934 **Fax:** 01282-428915
**Web:** www.homeofultra.com
**Reg No:** 1869659 **VAT No:** 375156538
**Estd:** 1984 Private Limited Company
**Line of Business:** Metal finishing and polishing services
**Export Sales:** £1,267,374
**Issued Capital:** £18,100
**Principals:** S Heys *(Managing)*, A Wood, M Duggleby, D I Cullen
**Responsibilities**
**Senior:** John Durkin *(Warehouse Manager)*, Keith Heys *(Director)*, Colm Lalor *(Director)*, Linda Lamprecht *(Director)*
**Finance:** Alex Cramm *(Financial Director)*, Linda Lamprecht *(Director)*
**Marketing:** Ian Grymer *(Sales & Marketing Director)*
**Sales:** Ian Grymer *(Sales & Marketing Director)*
**HR:** Ian Grymer *(Sales & Marketing Director)*, Eileen Irwin *(Personnel Manager)*
**Branches:** Ultra Finishing Ltd, Widow Hill Road, Burnley, Lancashire BB10 2TJ
**US SIC:** 3494, 3261
**UK SIC:** 32880, 24892
**Auditors:** Cassons
**Bankers:** National Westminster Bank Plc (01-01-35)

| | 31-12-13 | 31-12-12 | 31-12-11 |
|---|---|---|---|
| TO | 46,688,531 | 32,763,874 | 36,192,880 |
| P/L | 1,151,834 | 1,342,430 | 457,834 |
| NW | 18,828,597 | 18,058,610 | 15,770,448 |
| WC | 7,734,937 | 7,931,165 | 9,695,906 |
| Emp. | 139 | 121 | 116 |

DUNS 51-997-4229

## Ultra Tough Ltd

(**Subsidiary of:** Ultra Tough Holding Ltd)
Unit 1-2 Travellers Lane, North Mymms, Hatfield, Hertfordshire AL9 7HF
**Tel:** 01707 269 000
**Web:** www.ultratough.co.uk
**Reg No:** 4101990 **Estd:** 2008 Private Limited Company
**Line of Business:** Manufacturers of glass
**Issued Capital:** £480,000
**Directors:** N V Nakrani, N L Makani, S Patel, D J Modha, J Patel, M D Patel, M Bhagat, K Barlow
**Co. Secretary:** Bipin Patel
**US SIC:** 3231 **UK SIC:** 24791
**Auditors:** Haines Watts
**Bankers:** National Westminster Bank Plc (60-07-25)

| | 31-03-14 | 31-03-13 | 31-03-12 |
|---|---|---|---|
| TO | 8,451,903 | 8,677,732 | 8,953,068 |
| P/L | 111,613 | 312,536 | 736,559 |
| NW | 2,680,962 | 2,689,683 | 2,630,747 |
| WC | 2,159,212 | 1,849,287 | 1,663,303 |
| Emp. | 92 | 93 | 83 |

DUNS 22-702-9733 **Imp-Exp**

## Ultrachem Ltd

Euro House, London N20 9UL
**Tel:** 02084468263
**Web:** www.ultrachem.co.uk
**Reg No:** 1588903 **VAT No:** 245980337
**Estd:** 1981 Private Limited Company
**Line of Business:** Manufacturers of chemicals
**Export Markets:** U.S.A., Far East, Europe, Asia
**Export Sales:** £5,808,286
**Issued Capital:** £100,000
**Principals:** A J Brinton *(Managing)*, Ms J A Brinton, A A Brinton, Ms L L Brinton, S Brinton
**Co. Secretary:** Mrs Susan Brinton
**Branches:** Ultrachem Ltd, 8 Astley Lane Industrial Estate, Astley Way, Leeds, West Yorkshire LS26 8XT
**US SIC:** 2899 **UK SIC:** 25670
**Auditors:** PricewaterhouseCoopers LLP
**Bankers:** Barclays Bank Plc (20-95-61)

| | 31-03-13 | 31-03-12 | 31-03-11 |
|---|---|---|---|
| TO | 14,620,262 | 17,738,823 | 23,828,000 |
| P/L | (30,370) | (220,937) | (891,000) |
| NW | 2,310,931 | 2,304,605 | 2,786,000 |
| WC | 2,050,812 | 1,897,332 | 2,121,000 |
| Emp. | 77 | 87 | 114 |

DUNS 28-978-0884 **Imp-Exp**

## Ultraframe (U K) Ltd

(**Subsidiary of:** Latium Plastics Enterprises Ltd)
Salthill Road, Clitheroe, Lancashire BB7 1PE
**Tel:** 01200-443311
**Web:** www.ultraframe-conservatories.co.uk
**Reg No:** 1765701 **VAT No:** 375191341
**Estd:** 1983 Private Limited Company
**Line of Business:** Conservatories
**Export Markets:** Worldwide
**Export Sales:** £620,000
**Issued Capital:** £55,555
**Directors:** A J Crowe, D J Challinor, A W Thomson, J Slade, J Martoccia
**Responsibilities**
**Senior:** Lee Calvert *(General Manager)*, Iain Thomson *(Manager)*
**Marketing:** Mark Hanson *(Marketing Manager)*
**Branches:** Ultraframe (U K) Ltd, Chittening Indstl Est, Avonmouth Docks Est, Bristol, Avon BS11 0YA
**US SIC:** 3441, 2421
**UK SIC:** 32042, 46101
**Auditors:** KPMG Audit LLP
**Bankers:** National Westminster Bank Plc (01-00-85)

| | 01-11-13 | 02-11-12 | 28-11-11 |
|---|---|---|---|
| TO | 29,385,000 | 26,287,000 | 26,901,000 |
| P/L | 2,610,000 | 1,414,000 | 1,487,000 |
| NW | 15,402,000 | 13,179,000 | 11,393,000 |
| WC | 6,538,000 | 3,842,000 | 7,366,000 |
| Emp. | 248 | 228 | 257 |

DUNS 21-754-3313 **Imp-Exp**

## Ultravision International Ltd

(**Subsidiary of:** Contact Lens Precision Laboratories Ltd)
Commerce Way, Leighton Buzzard, Bedfordshire LU7 4RW
**Tel:** 01525-381112
**Web:** www.ultravision.co.uk
**Reg No:** 1408851 **VAT No:** 322550981
**Estd:** 1979 Private Limited Company
**Line of Business:** Manufacturers of optical products
**Issued Capital:** £450,000
**Director:** J K Lomas
**Co. Secretary:** John Clamp
**US SIC:** 3861 **UK SIC:** 37330
**Auditors:** Ernst & Young
**Bankers:** Barclays Bank Plc (20-57-40)

| | 30-09-13 | 30-09-12 | 30-09-11 |
|---|---|---|---|
| TA | 2,910,218 | 3,179,124 | 3,175,150 |
| NW | 1,740,418 | 2,048,506 | 2,061,618 |
| WC | 560,787 | 2,764,231 | 2,754,335 |

DUNS 42-409-6308

## Ulyett Landscapes Ltd

(**Subsidiary of:** Mwb Associates Ltd)
Burma Road, Mansfield, Nottinghamshire NG21 0RT
**Tel:** 01623-793834
**Web:** www.ulyettlandscapes.com
**Reg No:** 4397287 **Estd:** 1967 Private Limited Company
**Line of Business:** Landscape contractors
**Issued Capital:** £100
**Director:** M W Burton
**Co. Secretary:** Mrs Katrina Burton
**Responsibilities**
**Senior:** Philip Rosillo *(Manager)*
**Operations:** Nick Bradley *(?Senior Achitect manager)*, Kevin Plastow *(Grounds Maintenance Manager)*, Neil Todd *(Operations Manager)*
**US SIC:** 0729 **UK SIC:** 01003
**Bankers:** Lloyds TSB Bank plc (30-95-43)

| | 31-03-14 | 31-03-13 | 31-03-12 |
|---|---|---|---|
| TA | 997,461 | 1,059,563 | 1,190,474 |
| NW | 515,237 | 603,567 | 648,670 |
| WC | 321,813 | 441,936 | 490,782 |

DUNS 21-172-9288

## Umbrella-Company Ltd

Baron Court, Manchester Road, Wilmslow, Cheshire SK9 1BQ
**Tel:** 08001216513
**Web:** www.umbrellacompany.tv
**Reg No:** 6969639 **Estd:** 2009 Private Limited Company
**Line of Business:** Financial services
**Issued Capital:** £6
**Directors:** Mrs S L Kilmartin, J Biddle, S C Davis, M D Grady, Mrs S Holmes, P Langham, S B Pearson, A J Kilmartin
**Responsibilities**
**Senior:** Sarah Grady *(Director)*
**US SIC:** 8931 **UK SIC:** 83600

| | 31-12-13 | 31-12-12 | 31-12-11 |
|---|---|---|---|
| TO | 57,679,087 | 50,913,126 | N/A |
| P/L | 61,122 | 138,027 | N/A |
| NW | (2,120,569) | (2,546,342) | 3 |
| WC | (2,210,996) | (2,648,161) | N/A |
| Emp. | 1,657 | N/A | N/A |

DUNS 21-700-6173

## Umbrella Paraplus Ltd

(**Subsidiary of:** Brookfield Rose Ltd)
Booths Park 1, Chelford Road, Knutsford, Cheshire WA16 8GS
**Tel:** 08448460444
**Web:** www.umbrellaparaplus.co.uk
**Reg No:** 7455993 **Estd:** 2010 Private Limited Company
**Line of Business:** Labour recruitment and provision of personnel
**Issued Capital:** £100
**Directors:** S Webb, M W Sanders, P Mcdonald
**Co. Secretary:** James Hulsken
**US SIC:** 7361 **UK SIC:** 83954

| | 31-12-13 | 31-12-12 | 31-12-11 |
|---|---|---|---|
| TO | 18,105,260 | N/A | N/A |
| P/L | (386,977) | N/A | N/A |
| NW | (1,851,249) | (1,464,151) | (756,834) |
| WC | (2,140,299) | (1,474,688) | (771,202) |
| Emp. | 4,431 | N/A | N/A |

DUNS 23-598-9071

## Umbrella Risk Management (Uk) Ltd

(**Subsidiary of:** Umbrella Holdings Ltd)
2 The Barn, Aylesbury, Buckinghamshire HP18 9NA
**Tel:** 01844202045
**Web:** www.team-umbrella.co.uk
**Reg No:** 3596287 **Estd:** 1998 Private Limited Company
**Line of Business:** Marketing consultants
**Issued Capital:** £1
**Directors:** N J Carter, Mrs E Johnson
**Co. Secretary:** Nigel Ashdown
**Responsibilities**
**Senior:** Brendan Fraser-Smith *(Business Development Director)*
**Sales:** Brendan Fraser-Smith *(Business Development Director)*
**Operations:** Zoe Curnow *(Project Manager)*, Kelly Hinds *(Project Management)*
**US SIC:** 7392 **UK SIC:** 83951

| | 31-03-14 | 31-03-13 | 31-03-12 |
|---|---|---|---|
| TA | 196,588 | 203,043 | 315,122 |
| NW | 32,974 | 20,582 | 163,322 |
| WC | 32,974 | 20,582 | 163,322 |

DUNS 85-622-5292

## Ume Diagnostics Ltd

(**Subsidiary of:** Ume Group Llp)
27 Harley Street, London W1G 9QP
**Tel:** 02072990500
**Web:** www.umegroup.com
**Reg No:** 6258724 **Estd:** 2007 Private Limited Company
**Line of Business:** Clinics private
**Issued Capital:** £25,000,000
**Directors:** S M El Seif, Ms K A Miller, P S Thompson
**US SIC:** 6711 **UK SIC:** 83962
**Auditors:** Deloitte LLP

| | 31-12-13 | 31-12-12 | 31-12-11 |
|---|---|---|---|
| TO | 8,532,119 | 10,685,535 | 12,444,493 |
| P/L | (5,761,497) | (13,272,476) | (3,832,126) |
| NW | (29,377,034) | (24,210,745) | (19,451,035) |
| WC | (4,857,154) | (7,351,931) | (26,884,859) |
| Emp. | 63 | 82 | 87 |

DUNS 73-471-5167

## Ummah Foods Ltd

P O Box 1858, Ilford, Essex IG5 0WD
**Tel:** 020-8252-6004 **Fax:** 020-8550-7793
**Web:** www.ummahfoods.com
**Reg No:** 4735516 **Estd:** 2003 Private Limited Company
**Line of Business:** Manufacture of cocoa and chocolate confectionery
**Issued Capital:** £2
**Director:** K Sharif
**Co. Secretary:** Mohammed Sharif
**Responsibilities**
**Finance:** Zaibunisa Sharif *(Finance Director)*
**US SIC:** 2066, 5145

**UK SIC:** 42141, 61700

| | 31-03-14 | 31-03-13 | 31-03-12 |
|---|---|---|---|
| TO | 3,073 | 19,530 | N/A |
| P/L | (67) | 15,135 | N/A |
| NW | (229) | (162) | (6,467) |
| WC | (516) | (521) | (6,915) |

DUNS 23-243-4709
## Unanimis Consulting Ltd
(**Subsidiary of:** Atlas Services Belgium Sa)
100 New Oxford Street, London WC1A 1HB
**Tel:** 02070162300 **Fax:** 02070162301
**Web:** www.switchconcepts.com
**Reg No:** 4167171 **Estd:** 2001 Private Limited Company
**Line of Business:** Internet services
**Export Sales:** £881,288
**Issued Capital:** £103
**Directors:** Mrs J D Spector, J E Spector, T R Barnett
**Co. Secretary:** Julian Spector
**Responsibilities**
**Senior:** Mathieu Chauchat *(Manager)*, Dominic Collins *(Manager)*, Sophia Rodrigues *(Office Manager)*, Luc Tran-Thang *(Manager)*, Christine Walser-Sacau *(Manager)*
**Sales:** Dan Ginns *(Sales Director)*
**Admin:** Sophia Rodrigues *(Office Manager)*
**US SIC:** 7379, 7399
**UK SIC:** 83940, 83954
**Auditors:** Buzzacott LLP
**Bankers:** Barclays Bank Plc (20-03-80)

| | 31-12-13 | 31-12-12 | 31-12-11 |
|---|---|---|---|
| TO | 8,545,833 | 12,978,211 | 20,076,506 |
| P/L | (4,921,130) | (1,755,776) | (1,533,838) |
| NW | (11,078,087) | (7,181,169) | (5,900,408) |
| WC | (2,461,945) | (1,793) | 1,095,051 |
| Emp. | 47 | 74 | 89 |

DUNS 53-623-2184 **Imp-Exp**
## Unatrac Ltd
188 Bath Road, Slough, Berkshire SL1 3GA
**Tel:** 01753695555 **Fax:** 01753-695569
**Web:** www.unatrac.com
**Reg No:** 3428184 **VAT No:** 669452885
**Estd:** 1997 Private Limited Company
**Line of Business:** Representative office
**Export Sales:** £184,967,000
**Issued Capital:** £600,000
**Directors:** Y M Mansour, O E Bakary, S D Woodfield, M Y Mansour, G J Robinson
**Co. Secretary:** Abogado Nominees Limited
**Responsibilities**
**Senior:** Yaseen Mansour *(Manager)*
**HR:** J Ruse *(Head of Human Resources)*, Jane Ruth *(Human Resources Manager)*
**US SIC:** 5084 **UK SIC:** 61490
**Auditors:** Deloitte LLP
**Bankers:** Barclays Bank Plc (20-78-58)

| | 31-12-13 | 31-12-12 | 31-12-11 |
|---|---|---|---|
| TO | 184,967,000 | 228,943,000 | 215,730,000 |
| P/L | 3,900,000 | 8,069,000 | 7,893,000 |
| NW | 14,825,000 | 21,843,000 | 15,788,000 |
| WC | 13,207,000 | 21,088,000 | 15,505,000 |
| Emp. | 147 | 116 | 86 |

DUNS 21-602-9892 **Imp-Exp**
## Unbar Rothon Ltd
2 Radford Crescent, Billericay, Essex CM12 0DR
**Tel:** 01277632211 **Fax:** 01277-630151
**Web:** www.unbarrothon.co.uk
**Reg No:** 0173381 **VAT No:** 250352103
**Estd:** 1951 Private Limited Company
**Line of Business:** Herb growers
**Export Markets:** Worldwide
**Export Sales:** £545,000
**Trading Style:** Unbar Rothon Limited
**Issued Capital:** £1,000,000
**Principals:** W L Rothon *(Managing)*, M L Rothon, R M Rothon, Ms C A Rothon, P L Rothon
**Co. Secretary:** Ms Carol Rothon
**Responsibilities**
**Senior:** Peter Rothon *(Development Director)*
**Finance:** David Freeman *(Accountant)*
**IT:** Peter Rothon *(Development Director)*
**Facilities:** Peter Rothon *(Development Director)*
**Operations:** Peter Rothon *(Development Director)*
**Purchasing:** Peter Rothon *(Development Director)*
**Engineering:** Peter Rothon *(Development Director)*
**US SIC:** 2099 **UK SIC:** 42399
**Auditors:** Rowland Hall
**Bankers:** Barclays Bank Plc (20-12-21)

| | 28-02-14 | 28-02-13 | 29-02-12 |
|---|---|---|---|
| TO | 4,991,212 | 4,994,966 | 4,990,550 |
| P/L | 443,088 | 356,475 | 210,830 |
| NW | 5,350,443 | 4,987,796 | 4,695,660 |
| WC | 3,343,361 | 2,943,591 | 2,731,994 |
| Emp. | 62 | 65 | 71 |

DUNS 21-304-1624
## Uncle Henry's Farm Shop
The Grange, Grayingham, Gainsborough, Lincolnshire DN21 4JD
**Tel:** 01652640308
**Web:** www.unclehenrys.co.uk
**Estd:** 2009 Proprietorship
**Line of Business:** Other retail sale of food, beverages and tobacco in specialised stores
**Proprietor:** Miss F Bowen
**Responsibilities**
**Senior:** Emma Green *(Marketing Manager)*
**Marketing:** Simon Catchpole *(Marketing Manager)*, Emma Green *(Marketing Manager)*, Fran Sykes *(Marketing Manager)*
**US SIC:** 5499 **UK SIC:** 64100
**Employees:** 80

DUNS 21-004-2471
## Underground Vision (Uk) Ltd
Allan Morris Yard Factory Road, Sandycroft, Deeside, Clwyd CH5 2QJ
**Tel:** 01244-539952 **Fax:** 01244817966
**Web:** www.draintv.co.uk
**Reg No:** 6291834 **VAT No:** 909192707
**Estd:** 2007 Private Limited Company
**Line of Business:** Collection and treatment of sewage
**Issued Capital:** £1,000
**Directors:** C Kluiters, L C Van Der Valk
**Responsibilities**
**Senior:** Brad Commins *(Manager)*, Anthony Foden *(Manager)*
**Branches:** Underground Vision Uk Ltd, Unit 3, Tonge Bridge Way, Bolton, Lancashire BL2 6BD
**US SIC:** 4952 **UK SIC:** 92120
**Auditors:** Noel Popplewell & Co
**Bankers:** HSBC Bank plc (40-41-29)

| | 31-12-13 | 30-09-12 | 30-12-11 |
|---|---|---|---|
| TO | 7,623,424 | 5,486,630 | 2,278,596 |
| P/L | 1,868,296 | 1,623,631 | 447,431 |
| NW | 1,332,719 | 1,614,273 | 539,770 |
| WC | 153,193 | 896,724 | 12,919 |
| Emp. | 78 | N/A | N/A |

DUNS 52-014-4460
## Underley Educational Services
Kirkby Lonsdale, Carnforth, Lancashire LA6 2DZ
**Fax:** 01524279129
**Web:** www.acorncare.co.uk
**Reg No:** 3381128 **Estd:** 1997 Private Unlimited Company
**Line of Business:** Primary education
**Trading Style:** Underley Garden School
**Issued Capital:** £2
**Directors:** J E Janet, Dr N A Macdonald
**Co. Secretary:** Mrs Helen Lecky
**Responsibilities**
**Senior:** Mark Croghan *(Manager)*, John Gilfillan *(Principal)*, William Napier-Fenning *(Manager)*
**HR:** John Gilfillan *(Principal)*
**US SIC:** 8299, 8211
**UK SIC:** 93300, 93200

| | 31-08-13 | 31-08-12 |
|---|---|---|
| TA | 8,713,423 | 8,188,139 |
| P/L | (940,247) | (1,078,689) |
| NW | 1,403,367 | 2,141,099 |
| WC | (2,817,036) | (2,251,618) |

DUNS 22-504-5830
## Underpin & Makegood (Contracting) Ltd
(**Subsidiary of:** U&M Group Ltd)
Franklin House, Crown Road, Enfield, Middlesex EN1 1FE
**Tel:** 02088054000 **Fax:** 020-8805-4222
**Web:** www.underpin.com
**Reg No:** 1323310 **VAT No:** 589693556
**Estd:** 1977 Private Limited Company
**Line of Business:** Construction of domestic buildings
**Issued Capital:** £1,602
**Principals:** D R Gakhar *(Managing)*, H D Maddox, G Scard
**Co. Secretary:** John Playfair Associates
**Responsibilities**
**Senior:** Mike Forni *(Piling Director)*
**Admin:** Sharon Tindale *(Office Manager)*
**Purchasing:** Michelle Callaghan *(Materials Buyer)*, Ali Shah *(Contracts Manager)*
**Engineering:** Mike Forni *(Piling Director)*
**Branches:** Underpin & Makegood (Contracting) Ltd, 37 Millmarsh Lane, Enfield, Middlesex EN3 7UY
**US SIC:** 1522 **UK SIC:** 50100
**Auditors:** Gane Jackson Scott LLP
**Bankers:** HSBC Bank plc (40-20-23)

| | 28-02-14 | 28-02-13 | 28-02-12 |
|---|---|---|---|
| TA | 2,499,271 | 2,147,618 | 2,038,644 |
| NW | 1,301,111 | 1,097,804 | 1,033,077 |
| WC | 1,208,952 | 1,151,619 | 1,162,931 |

DUNS 73-853-5835
## The Underwater Centre (Fort William) Ltd
Marine Walk, Carmichael Way, Fort William, Inverness-Shire PH33 6FF
**Tel:** 01397703786
**Web:** www.theunderwatercentre.com
**Reg No:** 0266805SC **Estd:** 2004 Private Limited Company
**Line of Business:** Engineers (general)
**Trading Style:** The Underwater Centre (Fort William) Ltd
**Issued Capital:** £1,000
**Directors:** C Williams, F D Finlayson, Ms L H Finlayson
**Co. Secretary:** John Reed
**Responsibilities**
**Sales:** Lorna Macpherson *(Sales Manager)*
**US SIC:** 8299 **UK SIC:** 93300
**Auditors:** R.A. Clement Associates

| | 31-12-13 | 31-12-12 | 31-12-11 |
|---|---|---|---|
| TO | 5,506,160 | 4,330,847 | 3,132,159 |
| P/L | 882,564 | 645,337 | (210,371) |
| NW | 2,091,857 | 1,287,048 | 795,984 |
| WC | (300,921) | (624,023) | (878,101) |
| Emp. | 56 | 48 | 49 |

DUNS 73-297-5953
## Underwood Meat (Holdings) Ltd
Unit 15-17, Ashley Industrial Estate, Rawmarsh Road, Rotherham, South Yorkshire S60 1RU
**Tel:** 01709-789100 **Fax:** 01709368653
**Web:** www.underwoodmeat.co.uk
**Reg No:** 4571476 **Estd:** 2002 Private Limited Company
**Line of Business:** Management activities of holding companies
**Trading Style:** Underwood Meat Company
**Issued Capital:** £83,334
**Directors:** J D Heeley, R Mather, T M Bennett, K A Jones
**Co. Secretary:** Mrs Cora Bennett
**Responsibilities**
**Senior:** Graham Pointon *(Manager)*
**Marketing:** Katherine Abdy *(Marketing Manager)*
**IT:** Laura Dodd *(Technical manager)*
**US SIC:** 6711, 5147
**UK SIC:** 83962, 61700
**Auditors:** Barber Harrison & Platt

| | 31-10-13 | 31-10-12 | 31-10-11 |
|---|---|---|---|
| TO | 35,366,136 | 39,092,447 | 37,522,085 |
| P/L | 1,014,845 | 599,555 | (136,888) |
| NW | 1,921,421 | 1,629,387 | 1,294,720 |
| WC | 603,252 | 632,933 | 329,718 |
| Emp. | 165 | 163 | 151 |

DUNS 22-631-7451
## Underwoods Garage (Tiptree) Ltd
5 Church Road, Tiptree, Colchester, Essex CO5 0LG
**Tel:** 01621817781 **Fax:** 01621-817748
**Web:** www.ford.co.uk
**Reg No:** 1590739 **VAT No:** 368530827
**Estd:** 1981 Private Limited Company
**Line of Business:** Sale of new motor vehicles
**Trading Style:** Underwoods of Colchester
**Issued Capital:** £150
**Principals:** G Wiggins *(Managing)*, Mrs C A O'Keeffe *(Financial)*
**Co. Secretary:** Gerald Wiggins
**Branches:** Underwoods Garage (Tiptree) Ltd, 2 Auto Way, Colchester, Essex CO4 9HS
**US SIC:** 5511, 5521, 7539, 5531
**UK SIC:** 65100, 67100
**Auditors:** Lambert Chapman
**Bankers:** HSBC Bank plc (40-18-51)

| | 31-12-13 | 31-12-12 | 31-12-11 |
|---|---|---|---|
| TO | 73,363,197 | 71,327,662 | 71,155,388 |
| P/L | 280,843 | 204,033 | 298,129 |
| NW | 5,510,712 | 5,299,830 | 5,177,735 |
| WC | 1,360,784 | 1,831,927 | 1,699,203 |
| Emp. | 197 | 199 | 197 |

DUNS 39-873-1208
## Underwoods Group Ltd
Unit 6 Brunswick Industrial Park, Brunswick Way, London N11 1JL
**Tel:** 02083620226
**Web:** www.uep.uk.com
**Reg No:** 2224604 **VAT No:** 505799810
**Estd:** 1955 Private Limited Company
**Line of Business:** Engineers (general)
**Issued Capital:** £494,188
**Directors:** L H Smith, D A Hill
**Co. Secretary:** Stephen Kneebone
**Responsibilities**
**Senior:** Jamie Murdoch *(Senior Sales Manager)*
**Sales:** Jamie Murdoch *(Senior Sales Manager)*
**Branches:** Underwoods Group Ltd, Stirling House, 7 St Johns Road, Hedge End, Southampton, Hampshire SO30 4AA
**US SIC:** 8911 **UK SIC:** 83701
**Auditors:** Deloitte & Touche
**Bankers:** Barclays Bank Plc (20-95-61)

| | 30-04-14 | 30-04-13 | 30-04-12 |
|---|---|---|---|
| TO | 29,266,119 | 26,687,482 | 24,119,505 |
| P/L | 904,835 | 686,810 | 501,159 |
| NW | 2,713,855 | 2,005,646 | 1,494,541 |
| WC | 2,507,060 | 1,823,720 | 1,270,727 |
| Emp. | 95 | 88 | 90 |

DUNS 23-659-5950
## The Underwriter Insurance Co Ltd
(**Subsidiary of:** Ship (2006) Ltd)
117 Fenchurch Street, London EC3M 5DY
**Tel:** 020-7220-8888 **Fax:** 02076237477
**Web:** www.theunderwriter.com
**Reg No:** 3654581 **Estd:** 1999 Private Limited Company
**Line of Business:** Non-life insurance
**Issued Capital:** £76,200,000
**Directors:** Mrs D J Gately, Ms S L Rogers, A G Hines, G P Nash, R Katzenberg
**Co. Secretary:** Ms Shirley Rogers
**US SIC:** 6399 **UK SIC:** 82001
**Auditors:** Ernst & Young LLP
**Bankers:** HSBC Bank plc (40-06-37)

| | 31-12-13 | 31-12-12 | 31-12-11 |
|---|---|---|---|
| TO | N/A | 177,000 | N/A |
| P/L | 1,983,000 | 1,527,000 | (706,000) |
| NW | 10,108,000 | 8,125,000 | 6,598,000 |
| WC | (4,098,000) | (2,764,000) | (4,579,000) |
| Emp. | N/A | 5 | N/A |

DUNS 42-358-8573 **Imp**
## Uneek Clothing Co Ltd
Unit 1, Wellesley Court, Apsley Way, London NW2 7HF
**Tel:** 08458718711
**Web:** www.uneekclothing.com
**Reg No:** 3172736 **Estd:** 2008 Private Limited Company
**Line of Business:** Manufacture of workwear
**Export Sales:** £1,947,228
**Issued Capital:** £100
**Director:** R A Khan
**Co. Secretary:** Nasser Khan
**Responsibilities**
**Senior:** Nasser Razakahn *(Proprietor)*
**US SIC:** 2328 **UK SIC:** 45340
**Auditors:** Martin - Heller

| | 31-03-14 | 31-03-13 | 31-03-12 |
|---|---|---|---|
| TO | 31,615,751 | 30,554,017 | 30,008,924 |
| P/L | 4,344,518 | 2,721,088 | 2,320,500 |
| NW | 14,086,245 | 11,030,488 | 9,125,335 |
| WC | 12,788,309 | 9,737,268 | 8,377,344 |
| Emp. | 79 | 75 | 75 |

DUNS 21-370-4980
## Unepwcmc
219 Huntingdon Road, Cambridge, Cambridgeshire CB3 0DL
**Tel:** 01223-277314
**Web:** www.unep-wcmc.org
**Proprietorship**
**Line of Business:** Defence activities
**Proprietor:** K Zahedi
**Responsibilities**
**Finance:** Lynn Kisielowski *(Financial Controller)*
**HR:** Jean Ward *(Human Resources Manager)*
**Facilities:** Stuart Douglas-Whitehead *(Facilities Manager)*
**US SIC:** 9711 **UK SIC:** 45340
**Employees:** 60

DUNS 21-088-0787 **Imp-Exp**
## Ungerer Ltd
(**Subsidiary of:** Ungerer Industries Inc.)
Sealand Road, Chester, Cheshire CH1 4LP
**Tel:** 01244-371711
**Web:** www.ungererandcompany.com
**Reg No:** 0629190 **VAT No:** 421990943
**Estd:** 1959 Private Limited Company
**Line of Business:** Pharmaceutical goods wholesalers
**Export Markets:** E U
**Export Sales:** £24,215,000
**Issued Capital:** £5,000
**Principals:** J G Percy *(Managing)*, K G Voorhees Jr, K G Voorhees Iii
**Co. Secretary:** John Percy
**Responsibilities**
**Marketing:** Gaynor Roberts *(Marketing Manager)*
**Health & Safety:** Adrian Gledhill *(Health & Safety Officer)*
**Facilities:** Peter Willetts *(Production Manager)*
**Engineering:** Peter Willetts *(Production Manager)*
**US SIC:** 5122, 2844, 2899
**UK SIC:** 61800, 25820, 25670
**Auditors:** Ernst & Young
**Bankers:** Barclays Bank Plc (20-20-46)

| | 31-10-13 | 31-10-12 | 31-10-11 |
|---|---|---|---|
| TO | 31,088,000 | 34,627,000 | 26,258,000 |
| P/L | 3,154,000 | 1,899,000 | 1,040,000 |
| NW | 8,958,000 | 6,556,000 | 5,155,000 |
| WC | 5,324,000 | 5,230,000 | 3,877,000 |
| Emp. | 100 | 95 | 93 |

DUNS 28-965-2117
## Uni-Build (Wiltshire) Ltd
Rivermead Drive, Rivermead Industrial Estate, Westlea, Swindon, Wiltshire SN5 7EX
**Tel:** 01793614747 **Fax:** 01793-693544
**Web:** www.uni-mill.com
**Reg No:** 1701550 **Estd:** 1983 Private Limited Company
**Line of Business:** Management activities of holding companies
**Export Sales:** £1,582,278
**Issued Capital:** £1,880
**Principals:** A D Rayner *(Managing)*, P R Hill, Ms N J Ogle, S V Hill
**US SIC:** 6711 **UK SIC:** 83962
**Auditors:** Derrick Newman & Co
**Bankers:** Lloyds TSB Bank plc (30-13-35)

| | 30-09-13 | 30-09-12 | 30-09-11 |
|---|---|---|---|
| TO | 5,962,758 | 7,756,590 | 7,680,199 |
| P/L | 1,517,326 | 2,399,610 | 2,825,242 |
| NW | 9,983,581 | 10,806,092 | 10,975,099 |
| WC | 7,796,477 | 8,993,147 | 9,366,945 |
| Emp. | 59 | 64 | 64 |

DUNS 21-232-7219
## Uni Lever
Carrow Works, Bracondale, Norwich, Norfolk NR1 2DD
**Tel:** 01603692095
**Web:** www.unilever.com
**Estd:** 2005 Proprietorship
**Line of Business:** Manufacturers of food products
**Proprietor:** D Smith
**Responsibilities**
**Senior:** Duncan Stickler *(Factory Director)*
**Finance:** Nathan Drake *(Financial Manager)*, Helen Winandy *(Financial Manager)*
**HR:** Carole Andrews *(Human Resources Manager)*
**Facilities:** Duncan Stickler *(Factory Director)*
**Engineering:** Jon Skinner *(Project Engineer)*
**US SIC:** 2099 **UK SIC:** 42399
**Employees:** 200

DUNS 21-041-6304
## Uni of Cambridge
Pembroke Street, Cambridge, Cambridgeshire CB2 3RA
**Proprietorship**
**Line of Business:** Manufacture of workwear
**US SIC:** 7399, 8221
**UK SIC:** 83954, 93100
**Employees:** 114

DUNS 21-580-1424 **Exp**
## Uni-Trunk Ltd
**(Subsidiary of:** Uni-Trunk Holdings Ltd)
Blaris Industrial Estate, Lisburn, Co Antrim BT27 5QB
**Tel:** 02892-625-100 **Fax:** 02892625102
**Web:** www.unitrunk.co.uk
**Reg No:** 0005095NI **Estd:** 1961 Private Limited Company
**Line of Business:** Manufacture of insulated wire and cable
**Export Markets:** Republic Of Ireland
**Issued Capital:** £144,138
**Directors:** Mrs H Morrow, M Morrow, M Morrow
**Co. Secretary:** Michael Clarke
**Responsibilities**
**Senior:** John Cullum *(Depot Manager)*, Neil Houston *(Stores Manager)*, David Marrow *(General Manager)*
**Marketing:** Ivan Major *(Sales & Marketing Manager)*, Graeme Milligan *(Marketing Manager)*
**Sales:** Ivan Major *(Sales & Marketing Manager)*
**IT:** Nicky Hopkins *(IT Manager)*
**HR:** Jess Heather *(HR Manager)*, Heather Jess *(Human Resources Manager)*
**Facilities:** Neil Houston *(Stores Manager)*
**Operations:** Neil Houston *(Stores Manager)*
**Purchasing:** David Marrow *(General Manager)*
**Engineering:** David Marrow *(General Manager)*
**Branches:** Uni-Trunk Ltd, Titan 2 Coxwell Avenue, Wolverhampton Science Park, Wolverhampton, West Midlands WV10 9RT
**US SIC:** 3357, 3629
**UK SIC:** 22470, 34350
**Auditors:** Cunningham, Wilkinson, Maxwell & Co Ltd
**Bankers:** Northern Bank Ltd (95-03-61)

| | 31-12-13 | 31-12-12 | 31-12-11 |
|---|---|---|---|
| TO | 20,620,107 | 23,604,679 | 22,195,459 |
| P/L | 673,836 | 1,365,405 | 2,424,739 |
| NW | 5,961,230 | 5,993,707 | 5,499,674 |
| WC | 5,543,831 | 5,443,888 | 4,477,821 |
| Emp. | 107 | 108 | 105 |

DUNS 53-628-9705
## Unibet (London) Ltd
**(Subsidiary of:** Ugp Limited)
Wimbledon Bridge House, 1 Hartfield Road, London SW19 3RU
**Tel:** 02085458021
**Web:** www.unibet.com
**Reg No:** 3433883 **Estd:** 1997 Private Limited Company
**Line of Business:** Gambling and betting activities
**Issued Capital:** £17,007
**Director:** M A Stetz
**Responsibilities**
**Senior:** Peter Nylander *(Chief Executive)*
**Marketing:** Peter Nylander *(Chief Executive)*
**US SIC:** 7999 **UK SIC:** 97913
**Auditors:** PricewaterhouseCoopers LLP

| | 31-12-13 | 31-12-12 | 31-12-11 |
|---|---|---|---|
| TO | 62,862,000 | 82,460,000 | 73,742,000 |
| P/L | 5,135,000 | 2,427,000 | 2,683,000 |
| NW | 14,875,000 | 10,653,000 | 8,470,000 |
| WC | 14,384,000 | 10,144,000 | 7,821,000 |
| Emp. | 215 | 190 | 167 |

DUNS 73-299-4194
## Uniblue Ltd
Unit 3 Sawley Street, Skipton, North Yorkshire BD23 1SX
**Tel:** 01756790079 **Fax:** 08443-350582
**Web:** www.eventmedic.co.uk
**Reg No:** 4573265 **Estd:** 2002 Private Limited Company
**Line of Business:** Ambulance and medical transportation services
**Trading Style:** Event Medical Services, Ems Ambulance
**Issued Capital:** £999
**Directors:** A Howsen, M J Morgan
**Co. Secretary:** Nawaz Mohammed
**US SIC:** 8091, 8011
**UK SIC:** 95200, 95300
**Auditors:** Clough & Co LLP

| | 31-12-13 | 31-12-12 | 31-12-11 |
|---|---|---|---|
| TA | 752,054 | 774,174 | 509,257 |
| NW | 307,269 | 305,454 | 73,352 |
| WC | (6,360) | 17,680 | (47,994) |

DUNS 21-724-6586 **Imp**
## Unicarriers Uk Ltd
Jane Morbey Road, Thame, Oxfordshire OX9 3RR
**Tel:** 01844-215501
**Web:** www.atlet.co.uk
**Reg No:** 0958167 **VAT No:** 195192634
**Estd:** 1969 Private Limited Company
**Line of Business:** Manufacture of lifting and handling equipment
**Issued Capital:** £1,500,000
**Principals:** M A Gibb *(Managing)*, J W Hesse, K Ikeda
**Co. Secretary:** Mark Gibb
**Responsibilities**
**Senior:** John Dunham *(Parts Manager)*, Paul Forster *(Joint Managing Director)*
**Marketing:** Paul Forster *(Joint Managing Director)*, Lindsay Pocock *(Marketing and Pr)*
**Sales:** Paul Forster *(Joint Managing Director)*, Louise Lewis *(Sales)*
**IT:** Mar Puentes *(IT Manager)*
**HR:** Mandy Greig *(HR Manager)*
**Purchasing:** Paul Forster *(Joint Managing Director)*
**Fleet:** Aidan Coles *(Fleet Manager)*
**US SIC:** 3534 **UK SIC:** 32553
**Auditors:** Deloitte LLP
**Bankers:** Skandinaviska Enskilda Banken Ab (publ) (40-48-65)

| | 31-03-14 | 31-03-13 | 31-03-11 |
|---|---|---|---|
| TO | 36,198,253 | 44,122,721 | 31,189,900 |
| P/L | 4,388,283 | 2,342,887 | 1,468,773 |
| NW | 9,189,415 | 7,776,159 | 8,002,084 |
| WC | 5,430,445 | 3,949,288 | 3,926,040 |
| Emp. | 178 | 167 | 166 |

DUNS 21-409-0576
## Unicom
Aquis House, 12 Greek Street, Leeds, West Yorkshire LS1 5RU
**Tel:** 01132445200
**Web:** www.switchingon.com
**Estd:** 2010 Proprietorship
**Line of Business:** Telecom services
**Proprietor:** S Palmer
**Responsibilities**
**Senior:** Jordan Moss *(Branch Manager)*, Dave Tibbert *(Sales Director)*
**Sales:** Dave Tibbert *(Sales Director)*
**US SIC:** 4899 **UK SIC:** 79020
**Employees:** 60

DUNS 23-038-8571 **Imp-Exp**
## Unicorn Containers Ltd
**(Subsidiary of:** Fhs Group Ltd)
5 Ferguson Drive, Knockmore Hill Industrial Park, Lisburn, Co Antrim BT28 2EX
**Tel:** 02892640827 **Fax:** 02892640830
**Web:** www.unicorn-selfserve.com
**Reg No:** 0029839NI **VAT No:** 663104167
**Estd:** 1995 Private Limited Company
**Line of Business:** Manufacture of other fabricated metal products not elsewhere classified
**Issued Capital:** £2
**Directors:** R J Pannell, S E Greeves
**Co. Secretary:** Stephen Greeves
**US SIC:** 3499, 3534
**UK SIC:** 31694, 32553
**Auditors:** Grant Thornton U K LLP
**Bankers:** Ulster Bank Ltd (98-00-17)

| | 30-09-14 | 30-09-13 | 30-09-12 |
|---|---|---|---|
| TA | 1,785,383 | 2,411,324 | 3,017,271 |
| NW | 1,202,076 | 1,277,411 | 1,398,189 |
| WC | 938,504 | 1,057,650 | 1,159,684 |

DUNS 42-314-0615
## Unicorn Grocery Ltd
89 Albany Road, Manchester M21 0BN
**Tel:** 0161-861-0010
**Web:** www.unicorn-grocery.co.uk
**Reg No:** 0028242IP **Estd:** 1995 Friendly Society
**Line of Business:** Grocers
**Principals:** D White *(Chairman)*, A York, G Dines
**Responsibilities**
**Senior:** Dan Weston *(Manager)*
**Operations:** Leah De Quattro *(Production and Operations Mana)*
**US SIC:** 5411, 5499, 2834
**UK SIC:** 64100, 25700
**Employees:** 50

DUNS 21-030-0752 **Exp**
## Unicorn Products Ltd
Crockham Park, Edenbridge, Kent TN8 6UP
**Tel:** 01159853500 **Fax:** 01732-782801
**Web:** www.unicorngroup.com
**Reg No:** 0370646 **VAT No:** 217815462
**Estd:** 2005 Private Limited Company
**Line of Business:** Manufacturers of sportswear
**Export Markets:** U S A, E E C.
**Issued Capital:** £24,586
**Principals:** S R Lowy *(Chairman and Managing)*, E R Lowy *(Managing)*, D A Broughton, R F Lowy, P G Wright
**Co. Secretary:** William Stone
**Branches:** Unicorn Products Ltd, Crockham Park, South Barn, Edenbridge, Kent TN8 6UP
**US SIC:** 3949, 2329
**UK SIC:** 49420, 45350
**Auditors:** Rawlinson & Hunter
**Bankers:** National Westminster Bank Plc (60-50-01)

| | 31-12-13 | 31-12-12 | 31-12-11 |
|---|---|---|---|
| TO | 11,902,458 | 11,529,295 | 13,519,677 |
| P/L | (183,404) | (439,051) | (230,127) |
| NW | 3,472,222 | 3,770,714 | 4,980,561 |
| WC | 3,002,403 | 2,569,286 | 3,168,503 |
| Emp. | 64 | 68 | 70 |

DUNS 21-581-0611
## Unicorn Training
Warnford Court, 29 Throgmorton Street, London EC2N 2AT
**Tel:** 02030360382
**Web:** www.unitrain.com
**Estd:** 2011 Proprietorship
**Line of Business:** Activities of private training providers
**Proprietor:** N Mcwilliams
**Responsibilities**
**Senior:** Claire Johnson *(Manager)*
**US SIC:** 8299 **UK SIC:** 93300
**Employees:** 50

DUNS 34-596-4449
## Unicorn Training Group Ltd
99 Holdenhurst Road, Bournemouth, Dorset BH8 8DY
**Tel:** 01202306050
**Web:** www.unicorntraining.com
**Reg No:** 2740509 **Estd:** 1992 Private Limited Company
**Line of Business:** Other software consultancy and supply
**Issued Capital:** £5,505
**Principals:** P I Phillips *(Managing)*, P D Unsworth *(Financial)*, Mrs H P Watts, M D Jones, H R Green, N Mcwilliams, Ms J Kennedy, K Pringle
**Co. Secretary:** Stuart Sawyer
**Responsibilities**
**Senior:** Henry Phillips *(Director)*
**US SIC:** 7379, 8249
**UK SIC:** 83940, 93300
**Auditors:** Schofields

**Bankers:** Lloyds TSB Bank plc (30-98-91)

| | 30-04-14 | 30-04-13 | 30-04-12 |
|---|---|---|---|
| TO | 4,847,939 | 4,548,025 | 4,199,816 |
| P/L | 409,870 | 370,112 | 253,628 |
| NW | 668,604 | 360,635 | 126,037 |
| WC | 594,136 | 355,276 | 64,088 |
| Emp. | 79 | 65 | N/A |

DUNS 21-458-5721
## Unidare Environmental Ltd
**(Subsidiary of:** Glen Dimplex)
Unidare Works, Seagoe Church Road, Portadown, Craigavon, Co Armagh BT63 5HU
**Tel:** 02838333131
**Web:** www.unidareenvironmental.co.uk
**Reg No:** 0003928NI **Estd:** 1957 Private Limited Company
**Line of Business:** Manufacture of other electrical equipment not elsewhere classified
**Trading Style:** Seagoe Technology
**Issued Capital:** £300,000
**Directors:** S O'Driscoll, M L Naughton, J S Gault
**Co. Secretary:** Ms Vanessa King
**Responsibilities**
**Senior:** Sean O'driscoll *(Director)*, Lochlann Quinn *(Manager)*
**Branches:** Unidare Environmental, Peakdale Rd, Glossop, Derbyshire SK13 6XE
**US SIC:** 3629 **UK SIC:** 34350
**Auditors:** KPMG
**Bankers:** Ulster Bank Ltd (98-12-90)

| | 31-03-14 | 31-03-13 | 31-03-12 |
|---|---|---|---|
| TA | 4,441,000 | 4,441,000 | 4,441,000 |
| NW | 4,441,000 | 4,441,000 | 4,441,000 |

DUNS 29-676-1109 **Imp-Exp**
## Uniexpress Ltd
Olympic Freight Terminal, Bennett Street, Manchester M12 5AP
**Tel:** 0161-272-8880 **Fax:** 0161-272-8890
**Web:** www.uniexpress.co.uk
**Reg No:** 2002472 **VAT No:** 431640873
**Estd:** 1986 Private Limited Company
**Line of Business:** Cargo handling
**Export Markets:** Worldwide
**Issued Capital:** £25,000
**Directors:** M J Burrows, C M Fitzpatrick
**Co. Secretary:** Barry Burrows
**Responsibilities**
**Senior:** Susie Burrows *(Manager)*
**Sales:** Una Gooch *(Export Sales)*
**Operations:** Catherine Grace *(Export Operations)*
**Branches:** Uniexpress Ltd, Headway Business Centre, Unit 1, Bradford, West Yorkshire BD4 9SW
**US SIC:** 4712 **UK SIC:** 77002
**Auditors:** Beever & Struthers
**Bankers:** The Co-Operative Bank Plc (08-90-24)

| | 30-06-13 | 30-06-12 | 30-06-11 |
|---|---|---|---|
| TO | 21,124,668 | 25,455,311 | 25,266,072 |
| P/L | 531,737 | 759,873 | 694,381 |
| NW | 3,257,211 | 3,165,795 | 2,795,877 |
| WC | 2,936,832 | 2,850,273 | 2,458,746 |
| Emp. | 53 | 48 | 42 |

DUNS 21-169-7691
## Uniform Brands Trading Ltd
**(Subsidiary of:** Uniform Brands Ltd)
303-307 Oak Drive, Hartlebury Trading Estate, Hartlebury, Kidderminster, Worcestershire DY10 4JB
**Tel:** 08442259640 **Fax:** 01332 226940
**Web:** www.vacuum-reflex.com
**Reg No:** 6945143 **VAT No:** 973408696
**Estd:** 2009 Private Limited Company
**Line of Business:** Wholesale of clothing and footwear
**Export Sales:** £340,113
**Trading Style:** Monarch Textiles, Allen & Douglas Corporatewear, Wensum Corporatewear, Rainbow Corporatewear
**Issued Capital:** £11,121,072
**Director:** N P Teagle
**Responsibilities**
**Senior:** Julian Budd *(Manager)*
**Finance:** Jonathan Peto *(Financial Director)*
**IT:** Jonathan Peto *(Financial Director)*
**US SIC:** 5136, 5611, 7394
**UK SIC:** 61600, 64500, 84000
**Auditors:** Deloitte LLP
**Bankers:** National Westminster Bank Plc (56-00-14)

| | 31-05-13 | 31-05-12 | 31-05-11 |
|---|---|---|---|
| TO | 11,868,071 | 11,792,142 | 12,234,356 |
| P/L | (253,990) | (1,210,203) | (16,898) |
| NW | 6,675,400 | 1,008,319 | 2,218,522 |
| WC | 6,428,731 | 757,862 | 2,117,819 |
| Emp. | 76 | 85 | 148 |

**DUNS 29-653-4183**　　　　　　　**Exp**

## Unifrax Emission Control Europe Ltd

(Subsidiary of: Unifrax Ltd)
Unit 34, Holywell, Clwyd CH8 7HJ
**Tel:** 01352714555
**Web:** www.saffil.com
**Reg No:** 1978805　**VAT No:** 439771903
**Estd:** 1986 Private Limited Company
**Line of Business:** Temperature monitoring equipment systems
**Export Markets:** E E C countries; U S A
**Export Sales:** £20,560,908
**Issued Capital:** £1,515
**Directors:** J C Dandolph Iv, Dr M W Briscoe, S ' Martins, F B Von Arx
**Responsibilities**
**Senior:** Renier Liebenberg (Site Manager), Ben Moore (Manager)
**Finance:** David Bushell (Accountant)
**Health & Safety:** Renier Liebenberg (Site Manager)
**Facilities:** Renier Liebenberg (Site Manager)
**Purchasing:** David Bushell (Accountant)
**Engineering:** Renier Liebenberg (Site Manager)
**US SIC:** 3643, 3263
**UK SIC:** 34203, 24893
**Auditors:** Ernst & Young LLP
**Bankers:** Barclays Bank Plc (20-20-46)

|  | 31-12-13 | 31-12-12 | 31-12-11 |
|---|---|---|---|
| TO | 20,809,366 | 16,507,533 | 4,230,004 |
| P/L | (469,240) | (871,265) | (25,608) |
| NW | (4,010,237) | (3,775,773) | (2,876,988) |
| WC | (8,239,512) | (5,354,749) | (3,537,013) |
| Emp. | 107 | 80 | 80 |

**DUNS 22-003-8587**　　　　　　　**Imp**

## Unifrax Ltd

Mill Lane, Rainford, St Helens, Merseyside WA11 8LP
**Tel:** 01744887600　**Fax:** 01744-889916
**Web:** www.unifrax.com
**Reg No:** 4007148　**Estd:** 2000 Private Limited Company
**Line of Business:** Cladding and insulation materials
**Export Sales:** £16,146,000
**Issued Capital:** £15,828,069
**Directors:** E D Yardley, J C Dandolph Iv, K P Woodcock, V Chambon
**Co. Secretary:** John Tupman
**Responsibilities**
**Sales:** Trevor Bailey (Sales Director)
**Health & Safety:** Philip Wilde (Health & Safety Officer)
**Engineering:** Steve Rendell (Production Manager)
**US SIC:** 3079　**UK SIC:** 48360
**Auditors:** Ernst & Young LLP
**Bankers:** National Westminster Bank Plc (60-70-08)

|  | 31-12-13 | 31-12-12 | 31-12-11 |
|---|---|---|---|
| TO | 21,218,000 | 20,424,000 | 24,369,000 |
| P/L | 10,036,000 | 1,987,000 | 3,151,000 |
| NW | 41,914,000 | 32,656,000 | 29,942,000 |
| WC | 25,417,000 | 17,203,000 | 15,774,000 |
| Emp. | 114 | 111 | 105 |

**DUNS 51-623-7133**　　　　　　　**Imp**

## Unify Enterprise Communications Ltd

(Subsidiary of: Unify Holdings B.V.)
Brickhill Street, Milton Keynes, Buckinghamshire MK15 0DJ
**Tel:** 01908817215
**Web:** www.unify.com
**Reg No:** 5903714　**Estd:** 1860 Private Limited Company
**Line of Business:** Telecommunication networks
**Issued Capital:** £2
**Directors:** T J Connell, S E Radcliffe
**Co. Secretary:** Ms Judith Bird
**Responsibilities**
**Senior:** Eve Middleton (Manager)
**Branches:** Siemens Enterprise Communications Ltd, 10 Foster Lane, EC2V 6HH London
**US SIC:** 4899　**UK SIC:** 79020
**Auditors:** Deloitte LLP

|  | 30-09-13 | 30-09-12 | 30-09-11 |
|---|---|---|---|
| TO | 116,140,000 | 137,078,000 | 157,753,000 |
| P/L | 2,758,000 | 3,933,000 | 4,160,000 |
| NW | 4,666,000 | 2,696,000 | 16,614,000 |
| WC | (5,033,000) | (7,991,000) | 5,547,000 |
| Emp. | 764 | 867 | 939 |

**DUNS 21-615-2660**

## Unigate Dairies Ltd

(Subsidiary of: Dairy Crest Group Plc)
14-40 Victoria Road, Aldershot, Hampshire GU11 1TH
**Tel:** 01252366966　**Fax:** 01252-310937
**Reg No:** 0367806　**Estd:** 1930 Private Limited Company
**Line of Business:** Liquid milk and cream production
**Trading Style:** Dairy Crest Group Plc
**Issued Capital:** £131,645,401

**Directors:** R P Miller, T A Atherton
**Co. Secretary:** Mrs Isobel Hinton
**Responsibilities**
**Senior:** Andrew Money (Manager)
**Branches:** Unigate Dairies Ltd, 42 Morfa Rd, Swansea, West Glamorgan SA1 2EN
**US SIC:** 2026　**UK SIC:** 41301
**Auditors:** Ernst & Young LLP
**Bankers:** Barclays Bank Plc (20-61-82)

|  | 31-03-14 | 31-03-13 | 31-03-12 |
|---|---|---|---|
| TA | 138,100,000 | 138,100,000 | 138,100,000 |
| NW | 137,100,000 | 137,100,000 | 137,100,000 |
| WC | 137,100,000 | 137,100,000 | 137,100,000 |

**DUNS 28-823-6458**　　　　　　　**Imp-Exp**

## Unika Color Products Ltd

(Subsidiary of: Unika Group Ltd)
Unika Color Products, Newcastle-Upon-Tyne, Tyne and Wear NE27 0QF
**Tel:** 0191-259-0033
**Web:** www.unika.co.uk
**Reg No:** 0056325SC　**VAT No:** 556491808
**Estd:** 1990 Private Limited Company
**Line of Business:** Kitchenware
**Export Markets:** Worldwide
**Issued Capital:** £292,500
**Principals:** P Rogers (Managing), M F Wrightson, Mrs S Wrightson
**Co. Secretary:** Lee Etherington
**Responsibilities**
**Marketing:** Louise Scott (Sales & Marketing Manager)
**Sales:** Louise Scott (Sales & Marketing Manager)
**Health & Safety:** Bill Dunn (Health & Safety Manager)
**US SIC:** 5199　**UK SIC:** 61900
**Auditors:** KPMG LLP
**Bankers:** Clydesdale Bank Plc (82-62-26)

|  | 31-12-13 | 31-12-12 | 31-12-11 |
|---|---|---|---|
| TA | 12,736,120 | 11,244,573 | 9,848,176 |
| NW | 10,783,844 | 9,362,311 | 8,112,945 |
| WC | 9,949,723 | 8,478,954 | 7,257,173 |

**DUNS 64-115-7110**

## Unilabs Ltd

(Subsidiary of: Cidra Sarl)
Evelyn House, London W1W 6YF
**Tel:** 020-7299-4490
**Web:** www.unilabs.co.uk
**Reg No:** 4115820　**VAT No:** 911209856
**Estd:** 2000 Private Limited Company
**Line of Business:** Other human health activities
**Export Sales:** £376,006
**Trading Style:** Ipoct Ihs
**Issued Capital:** £274,996
**Directors:** J W Lamers, P Delborn, Dr A P Gallimore
**Co. Secretary:** Andrew Coutts
**Responsibilities**
**Senior:** Andrew Lunt (Manager)
**Marketing:** Carolyn Wood (Marketing Manager)
**IT:** Jason Biggs (IT Director)
**Branches:** Unilabs Ltd, Nesfield House, Ground Floor, Skipton, North Yorkshire BD23 3AN
**US SIC:** 8091　**UK SIC:** 95200
**Auditors:** Ernst & Young LLP
**Bankers:** Unibank A/s (40-48-78)

|  | 31-12-13 | 31-12-12 | 31-12-11 |
|---|---|---|---|
| TO | 9,985,676 | 9,391,057 | 8,661,392 |
| P/L | 1,046,736 | 707,815 | 49,658 |
| NW | 5,406,387 | 4,573,327 | 4,023,135 |
| WC | 5,126,082 | 4,350,666 | 3,631,439 |
| Emp. | 51 | 54 | 54 |

**DUNS 28-898-2648**

## Unilathe Ltd

Ford Green Business Park, Ford Green Road Smallthorne, Stoke-On-Trent, Staffordshire ST6 1NG
**Tel:** 01782532000
**Web:** www.unilathe.co.uk
**Reg No:** 1331504　**VAT No:** 280741362
**Estd:** 1977 Private Limited Company
**Line of Business:** Engineers (general)
**Trading Style:** Lysbor
**Issued Capital:** £100
**Principals:** E Sims (Managing), M Oakley, Ms J Sims, A J Sims, J G Martin
**Co. Secretary:** Mrs Emma White
**Responsibilities**
**IT:** Tony Bailey (Technical Manager)
**Purchasing:** Gavin Richardson (Purchasing Manager)
**Engineering:** Tony Bailey (Technical Manager)
**US SIC:** 8911　**UK SIC:** 83701
**Auditors:** Walletts
**Bankers:** Barclays Bank Plc (20-36-43)

|  | 31-12-13 | 31-12-12 | 31-12-11 |
|---|---|---|---|
| TO | 6,729,593 | 7,998,389 | 8,233,076 |
| P/L | (191,302) | 398,242 | 807,585 |
| NW | 2,395,233 | 2,323,316 | 2,154,257 |
| WC | 634,511 | 675,751 | 474,338 |
| Emp. | 106 | 122 | 111 |

**DUNS 21-030-0901**

## Unilever Plc

100 Victoria Embankment, London EC4Y 0DY
**Tel:** 020 7822 5252　**Fax:** 020 7822 5951
**Web:** www.unilever.com
**Reg No:** 0041424　**VAT No:** 243359756
**Estd:** 1894 Public Limited Company
**Line of Business:** Management activities of holding companies
**Trading Style:** Unilever Uk, Unilever Europe I T
**Issued Capital:** £40,860,420
**Directors:** Sir M Rifkind, Ms L M Cha, K J Storm, Dr B E Grote, F Sijbesma, L O Fresco, R J Huet, N M Treschow
**Co. Secretary:** Ms Tonia Lovell
**Responsibilities**
**Senior:** Glaister Anderson (Manager), Genevieve Berger (Chief Research and Development), Sunil Bharti Mittal (Manager), Wim Dik (Non-Executive Director), Ann Fudge (Director), Sue Garrard (Senior Vice President Global C), Jonathan Hague (VP Open Innovation), Kees Kruythoff (President, North America), Mary Ma (Director), Sunil Mittal (Non-Executive Director), Gavin Neath (Senior Vice President Sustaina), Hixonia Nyasulu (Non-Executive Director), John Odada (Manager), Miguel Pestana (Vice President), Michael Polk (President, Americas), Paulus Polman (Chief Executive), Kees Storm (Non-Executive Director), Michael Treschow (Chairman), Jan Zijderveld (President - Europe), Jeroen van der Veer (Non-Executive Director)
**Finance:** Charles Nichols (Group Controller)
**Marketing:** Laura Collister (Government Relations Manager), Adam Fisher (Senior Corporate Media Relatio), Trevor Gorin (Global Media Relations Directo), Jonathan Hague (VP Open Innovation), Nivia Liba (Product Development Manager), Clare Logan (Brand Manager - Surf & Persil), Andriana Matsangou (Global Press Office Coordinato), Paul Quinlan (Open Innovation Director)
**Admin:** Suzanne Batley (PA to VP Sustainability)
**IT:** Willem Eelman (Chief Information Officer)
**HR:** Douglas Baillie (Chief HR Officer), Helen Wyatt (SVP HR Europe)
**Operations:** Clive Curzon (Global Manufacturing Technolog), George Garland (Assistant Manufacturing Manage), Greg Gillaspy (Manufacturing Technology Manag), Kevin Joinson (Group Manufacturing Process an)
**Engineering:** Alyn Hine (Category Technology Engineerin), Daniel Musto (Engineering Manager), Dave Penrith (Engineering and Technology Dir)
**Branches:** Unilever Plc, Colworth House, Bedford, Bedfordshire MK44 1YY
**US SIC:** 6711, 5149
**UK SIC:** 83962, 61700
**Auditors:** PricewaterhouseCoopers LLP
**Bankers:** HSBC Bank plc (40-05-30)
Following financial data are in thousands

|  | 31-12-13 | 31-12-12 | 31-12-11 |
|---|---|---|---|
| TO | 43,408,045 | 41,603,234 | 40,426,290 |
| P/L | 6,201,274 | 5,417,240 | 5,433,150 |
| NW | (5,718,351) | (5,316,725) | (6,629,400) |
| WC | (4,585,141) | (2,973,281) | (3,165,060) |
| Emp. | 174,000 | 172,000 | 169,000 |

**DUNS 21-042-1524**

## Unilever Uk Ice Cream

Phoenix Factory, Barnwood, Gloucester, Gloucestershire GL4 3BW
**Tel:** 01452392000
**Web:** www.unilever.com
**Line of Business:** Manufacture of ice cream
**Responsibilities**
**Senior:** Juergen Ansorge (General Manager)
**Finance:** Simon Rodger (Commercial Manager), Areeb Syed (Commercial Manager)
**US SIC:** 2024　**UK SIC:** 42130
**Employees:** 450

**DUNS 21-017-7945**　　　　　　　**Imp**

## Unilever Uk Ltd

(Subsidiary of: Unilever Plc)
3 St James Road, Kingston-Upon-Thames, Surrey KT1 2BA
**Tel:** 0208-439-6100　**Fax:** 0208-541-8488
**Web:** www.unilever.com
**Reg No:** 0334527　**VAT No:** 727040458
**Estd:** 1872 Private Limited Company
**Line of Business:** Soap & other detergent manufacturers
**Export Sales:** £13,899,000
**Issued Capital:** £444,668,297
**Directors:** P D Logan, G D Pitkethly, Ms S Newbitt, Ms T S Rogers, T J Munden
**Co. Secretary:** Richard Hazell
**Responsibilities**
**Senior:** G Fulford (Logistics Director)
**Finance:** Jean-Marc Huet (Chief Financial Officer)

**HR:** Douglas Baillie (Chief HR Officer)
**Fleet:** G Fulford (Logistics Director)
**Branches:** Unilever Uk Ltd, Unilever Bestfoods Uk, Trafford Park Road, Manchester M17 1NH
**US SIC:** 2841　**UK SIC:** 25810
**Auditors:** PricewaterhouseCoopers LLP
**Bankers:** National Westminster Bank Plc (60-13-19)
Following financial data are in thousands

|  | 31-12-13 | 31-12-12 | 31-12-11 |
|---|---|---|---|
| TO | 2,109,024 | 2,005,751 | 1,828,642 |
| P/L | 75,747 | 100,464 | 112,900 |
| NW | 785,698 | 640,827 | 653,079 |
| WC | 263,103 | (251,613) | 43,117 |
| Emp. | 4,067 | 4,340 | 4,310 |

**DUNS 23-719-5540**　　　　　　　**Imp-Exp**

## Unilin Distribution Ltd

(Subsidiary of: Mohawk Global Investments Sarl)
Unit 5 Rampart Road Greenbank Industrial, Estate, Newry, Co Down BT34 2QU
**Tel:** 02830250477　**Fax:** 02830-250223
**Web:** www.quick-step.co.uk
**Reg No:** 0025830NI　**Estd:** 2011 Private Limited Company
**Line of Business:** Distribution service providers
**Export Markets:** Republic of Ireland
**Issued Capital:** £492
**Directors:** F H Boykin, Ms B Goetz, B P Thiers, N Mcmanus, P F De Cock, N Mcmanus, P Bourguignon
**Co. Secretary:** Bernard Thiers
**Responsibilities**
**Senior:** Nigel Mcmannus (Managing Director)
**IT:** Daniel Robinson (IT Manager)
**Branches:** Unilin Distribution Ltd, Unit 4, The Furrows, Stretford, Manchester M32 0SZ
**US SIC:** 4712, 5199
**UK SIC:** 77002, 61900
**Auditors:** BDO Northern Ireland
**Bankers:** The Bank Of Ireland (90-23-38)

|  | 31-12-13 | 31-12-12 | 31-12-11 |
|---|---|---|---|
| TO | 41,228,509 | 40,053,604 | 41,276,241 |
| P/L | 2,085,846 | (428,452) | 22,026 |
| NW | 8,225,209 | 3,023,151 | 3,460,580 |
| WC | 8,848,589 | 5,082,299 | 5,681,838 |
| Emp. | 67 | 65 | 64 |

**DUNS 36-528-8237**

## Unimush Ireland Ltd

Edenaveys Industrial Estate, Armagh, Co Armagh BT60 1NF
**Tel:** 02837517120
**Web:** www.unimushireland.com
**Reg No:** 0059580NI　**Estd:** 2006 Private Limited Company
**Line of Business:** Other business activities not elsewhere classified
**Issued Capital:** £2
**Directors:** P Curry, S Cassidy
**Co. Secretary:** Seamus Cassidy
**US SIC:** 7399　**UK SIC:** 83954
**Bankers:** The Bank Of Ireland (90-22-90)

|  | 31-10-13 | 31-10-12 | 31-10-11 |
|---|---|---|---|
| TO | 9,440,795 | N/A | N/A |
| P/L | 347,753 | N/A | N/A |
| NW | 566,730 | 261,568 | (213,172) |
| WC | (433,102) | (822,947) | (593,711) |
| Emp. | 61 | N/A | N/A |

**DUNS 42-318-7384**

## Uninterruptible Power Supplies Ltd

Bacchus House, Reading, Berkshire RG7 8EN
**Tel:** 01189815151　**Fax:** 01256 386701
**Web:** www.upspower.co.uk
**Reg No:** 3150129　**VAT No:** 876321411
**Estd:** 1996 Private Limited Company
**Line of Business:** Other business activities not elsewhere classified
**Issued Capital:** £48,000
**Directors:** J M Robinson Iv, S Heling, D Renton
**Co. Secretary:** James Robinson Iv
**Responsibilities**
**Senior:** Alex Emms (Field Service Manager), Richard Fotsch (Manager), Natalie-ann Kohler (Manager)
**IT:** Justin Lucas (Technical Support Manager)
**Health & Safety:** Justin Lucas (Technical Support Manager)
**Facilities:** John Bladon (Operations Director)
**Purchasing:** Stuart Insch (Contracts Manager)
**US SIC:** 7399　**UK SIC:** 83954
**Auditors:** Deloitte LLP
**Bankers:** HSBC Bank plc (40-11-06)

|  | 31-12-13 | 30-12-12 | 31-12-11 |
|---|---|---|---|
| TO | 16,708,450 | 18,880,169 | 17,946,937 |
| P/L | 3,443,675 | 3,913,373 | 3,684,571 |
| NW | 7,214,054 | 8,906,768 | 10,109,373 |
| WC | 2,198,014 | 3,737,199 | 9,224,601 |
| Emp. | 74 | 71 | 68 |

DUNS 49-108-3952
## The Union Advertising Agency Ltd
Union House, 18 Inverleith Terrace, Edinburgh, Midlothian EH3 5NS
**Tel:** 01316256000 **Fax:** 0131-625-6025
**Web:** www.union.co.uk
**Reg No:** 0160047SC **VAT No:** 671004863
**Estd:** 2010 Private Limited Company
**Line of Business:** Advertising agency services
**Issued Capital:** £39,000
**Principals:** I H Mcateer *(Managing)*, M Hart, K G Hardie, A C Lindsay
**Co. Secretary:** Mark Reid
**Responsibilities**
**Finance:** Joyce Lehany *(Financial Controller)*
**HR:** Beverley Hart *(Training Manager)*
**Health & Safety:** Joyce Lehany *(Financial Controller)*
**Purchasing:** Beverley Hart *(Training Manager)*
**US SIC:** 7311 **UK SIC:** 83800
**Auditors:** Springfords
**Bankers:** Bank Of Scotland (80-31-20)

| | 31-12-13 | 31-12-12 | 31-12-11 |
|---|---|---|---|
| TA | 1,309,131 | 744,243 | 1,036,431 |
| NW | 158,879 | 146,142 | 174,253 |
| WC | 103,760 | 97,957 | 132,853 |

DUNS 76-552-6975
## Union Bancaire Privee Ubp Sa
(**Subsidiary of:** Cbi Holding Sa)
26 St James's Square, London SW1Y 4JH
**Tel:** 02073691350
**Web:** www.ubp.ch
**Reg No:** 0015816FC **Estd:** 1991 Foreign Company
**Line of Business:** Banks
**Principals:** E De Picciotto *(Chairman)*, E Ruehli, P Blum, S Goldstein, Ms S Emile, M Brunschwig, M Benbassat, M Monaco
**Co. Secretary:** Michel De Buren
**Responsibilities**
**Senior:** Lynda Cox *(Human Resources Manager)*, Emile Saadia *(Director)*, G Thoman *(Director)*, M de Dicciotto *(Chief Executive)*, Edgar de Picciotto *(Chairperson)*
**Finance:** D Peytcheva *(Finance Manager)*
**Branches:** 40 Esplanade, St Helier, Jersey
**US SIC:** 6012 **UK SIC:** 81402

DUNS 73-387-7026
## Union Bank Uk Plc
(**Subsidiary of:** Union Bank of Nigeria Plc)
14-18 Copthall Avenue, London EC2R 7BN
**Tel:** 02079 206 100
**Web:** www.unionbankuk.com
**Reg No:** 4661188 **Estd:** 1983 Public Limited Company
**Line of Business:** Banks and financial institutions
**Directors:** Dr K A Ali, A C Emuwa, M X Biglia, G C Laws, D J Forster, K S Kasongo
**Co. Secretary:** David Keene
**Responsibilities**
**Senior:** Mobolanle Ajomale *(Manager)*, Martin Obaro *(Manager)*, Nathaniel Ogbe *(Manager)*, Mohammed Yahaya *(Manager)*
**US SIC:** 6012, 6111
**UK SIC:** 81402, 81501
**Auditors:** KPMG Audit PLC
**Employees:** 50
**Turnover:** £12,802,000

DUNS 21-280-3613 **Imp-Exp**
## Union Electric Steel Uk Ltd
(**Subsidiary of:** Ampco-Pittsburgh Corporation)
Po Box 21, Gateshead, Tyne and Wear NE8 3DX
**Tel:** 01914-025200 **Fax:** 01914-778821
**Web:** www.unionesuk.co.uk
**Reg No:** 0162966 **VAT No:** 172384850
**Estd:** 1920 Private Limited Company
**Line of Business:** Manufacturers of stainless steel
**Trading Style:** The Davy Roll Company
**Issued Capital:** £60,000
**Principals:** S A Bell *(Managing)*, C Hersey *(Financial)*, J Stanik, R G Carothers
**Co. Secretary:** Mrs Rose Hoover
**Responsibilities**
**Senior:** David Attle *(IT Manager)*
**IT:** David Attle *(IT Manager)*
**HR:** Dominic Gillspie *(HR Manager)*
**Operations:** David Attle *(IT Manager)*
**US SIC:** 3325 **UK SIC:** 31110
**Auditors:** Deloitte LLP
**Bankers:** Barclays Bank Plc (20-00-00)

| | 31-12-13 | 31-12-12 | 31-12-11 |
|---|---|---|---|
| TO | 35,459,000 | 38,832,000 | 51,777,000 |
| P/L | 2,015,000 | 221,000 | 2,327,000 |
| NW | 27,032,000 | 23,994,000 | 25,512,000 |
| WC | 14,153,000 | 14,167,000 | 11,661,000 |
| Emp. | 269 | 272 | 299 |

DUNS 28-852-0992
## Union Estates (Manchester) Ltd
(**Subsidiary of:** Csc Construction Ltd)
Stanley House, 15 Ladybridge Road, Cheadle Hulme, Cheadle, Cheshire SK8 5BL
**Tel:** 01614869321 **Fax:** 01614884399
**Reg No:** 0739039 **Estd:** 1962 Private Limited Company
**Line of Business:** Buying and selling of own real estate
**Issued Capital:** £100
**Managing Directors:** R E Couzens, E Shottin
**Co. Secretary:** Eric Shottin
**US SIC:** 6531 **UK SIC:** 83400

| | 05-04-14 | 05-04-13 | 05-04-12 |
|---|---|---|---|
| TA | 250,000 | 250,000 | 250,000 |
| NW | 61,412 | 61,412 | 61,412 |

DUNS 50-455-4742
## Union Europeenne (U K) Ltd
(**Subsidiary of:** Credit Industriel Et Commercial)
Veritas House, 125 Finsbury Pavement, London EC2A 1HX
**Tel:** 020-7454-5400 **Fax:** 020-7588-6038
**Reg No:** 2436956 **Estd:** 1989 Private Limited Company
**Line of Business:** Other letting of own property
**Trading Style:** Cic - Credit Industrial and Commercial
**Issued Capital:** £2
**Director:** P D Hards-Nicholls
**Co. Secretary:** Paul Mais
**US SIC:** 6519, 6531
**UK SIC:** 85000, 83400
**Bankers:** National Westminster Bank Plc (60-00-01)

| | 31-12-13 | 31-12-12 | 31-12-11 |
|---|---|---|---|
| TA | 2 | 2 | 2 |
| NW | 2 | 2 | 2 |

DUNS 23-037-3821 **Imp**
## Union Four Electronics Ltd
5 Colmworth Business Park Marlborough, Road, St Neots, Cambridgeshire PE19 8YP
**Tel:** 01480-222480
**Web:** www.u4electronics.co.uk
**Reg No:** 3061290 **VAT No:** 563381730
**Estd:** 1995 Private Limited Company
**Line of Business:** Manufacturers of electronic equipment and components
**Issued Capital:** £100
**Directors:** D N Patel, M A Fox
**Co. Secretary:** Ms Angela Fox
**US SIC:** 3679 **UK SIC:** 34542
**Auditors:** N S Amin & Co
**Bankers:** Barclays Bank Plc (20-74-81)

| | 31-05-13 | 31-05-12 | 31-05-11 |
|---|---|---|---|
| TA | 3,096,274 | 2,904,531 | 2,659,902 |
| NW | 1,937,571 | 1,335,774 | 793,060 |
| WC | 1,230,743 | 616,028 | 17,481 |

DUNS 21-207-6587
## Union Health
Howgate, Bradford, West Yorkshire BD10 9RD
**Tel:** 01274350278
**Web:** www.countrywidecarehomes.co.uk
**Estd:** 1990 Proprietorship
**Line of Business:** Nursing homes
**Proprietor:** P Pearce
**Responsibilities**
**Senior:** Shelley Lobley *(General Manager)*
**Finance:** Shelley Lobley *(General Manager)*
**HR:** Shelley Lobley *(General Manager)*
**Health & Safety:** Shelley Lobley *(General Manager)*
**US SIC:** 8051 **UK SIC:** 95100
**Employees:** 60

DUNS 23-886-5526
## Union Income Benefit Holdings Ltd
(**Subsidiary of:** Embignell Ltd)
Linton House, 39/51 Highgate Road, London NW5 1RT
**Tel:** 02032274819 **Fax:** 0845 026 1102
**Web:** www.uibuk.com
**Reg No:** 3877610 **Estd:** 1999 Private Limited Company
**Line of Business:** Management activities of other non-financial holding companies not elsewhere classified
**Trading Style:** Uib, Uibuk
**Issued Capital:** £545,744
**Directors:** D L Harrison, Ms S A Mountford, Ms S C Jacobs, Lord L Sawyer, A Cheema, S Chaudhuri, A Cheema, R P Isaacs
**Co. Secretary:** Ms Fiona Echalier
**US SIC:** 7399, 6399
**UK SIC:** 83954, 82001
**Auditors:** Simmons Gainsford LLP

**Bankers:** Bank Of Scotland (12-11-03)

| | 30-09-13 | 30-09-12 | 30-09-11 |
|---|---|---|---|
| TO | 6,929,258 | 6,998,262 | 6,690,877 |
| P/L | 2,556,108 | 2,515,219 | 2,410,351 |
| NW | 5,040,613 | 4,527,056 | 4,666,343 |
| WC | 5,140,955 | 4,600,763 | 4,624,986 |
| Emp. | 122 | 122 | 104 |

DUNS 23-518-6368
## The Union Jack Club
Sandell Street, London SE1 8UJ
**Tel:** 02079026062 **Fax:** 020-7620-0565
**Web:** www.royalscotsclub.com
**Reg No:** 0080683 **Estd:** 1998 Private Company Limited By Guarantee
**Line of Business:** Hotels
**Directors:** H G Tilley, I C Mackay-Dick, W A Cowpe, R J Turpin, J J Brown, N G Ashford, P E Davidson, Air Commodore M A Barnes
**Co. Secretary:** Ms Renata Washington
**Responsibilities**
**Senior:** Colin Adams *(Director)*, David Albert *(Director)*, Simon Atkins *(Director)*, Elizabeth Dymock *(Director)*, Rachel Garside *(Director)*, Fabian Malbon Kbe *(Director)*, Susanne Swan *(Director)*
**Admin:** Sarah Jukes *(Office Manager)*
**US SIC:** 7011 **UK SIC:** 66500
**Auditors:** haysmacintyre
**Bankers:** Coutts & Co (18-00-93)

| | 31-12-13 | 31-12-12 | 31-12-11 |
|---|---|---|---|
| TO | 7,395,973 | 6,846,092 | 6,591,869 |
| P/L | 727,495 | 376,448 | 181,740 |
| NW | 7,638,641 | 6,809,231 | 6,290,486 |
| WC | 571,762 | 694,314 | 346,791 |
| Emp. | 153 | 156 | 125 |

DUNS 21-175-9241
## Union of Brunel Students
Cleveland Road, Uxbridge, Middlesex UB8 3PH
**Tel:** 01895462200
**Web:** www.brunelstudents.com
**Estd:** 1966
**Line of Business:** First-degree level higher education
**Trading Style:** Ubs
**Principals:** J Patel *(President)*, J Brasher-Jones, P Thompson, D James, Ms B Nzeadi, W Buettner, Ms J Gyateng, S Ahmed
**Responsibilities**
**Senior:** Samuel Kasumu *(Vice President)*, Craig Lithgow *(Ceo)*, Opeyemi Makinde *(Vice President)*, Brendan McGerty *(Principal)*, Danny O'Sullivan *(General Manager)*, Raju Patel *(Vice President)*
**US SIC:** 8221 **UK SIC:** 93100
**Employees:** 50

DUNS 23-697-5314
## Union of Shop Distributive & Allied Workers
188 Wilmslow Road, Manchester M14 6LJ
**Web:** www.usdaw.org.uk
**Estd:** 1930 Proprietorship
**Line of Business:** Trade unions
**Principals:** Ms M Carey *(President)*, J Youd, J Hannett
**Responsibilities**
**IT:** Trevor Parker *(IT Operations Manager)*
**Health & Safety:** Doug Russell *(Health & Safety Officer)*
**Branches:** Union Of Shop Distributive & Allied Workers, 1 Salway Pl, London E15 1NN
**US SIC:** 8631 **UK SIC:** 96313
**Auditors:** KPMG LLP
**Bankers:** Unity Trust Bank Plc (08-60-01)
**Employees:** 350
**Turnover:** £31,553,000

DUNS 77-936-2503
## Union Papertech Ltd
(**Subsidiary of:** Upt (Holdings) Ltd)
Simpson Clough Mill, Ashworth Road, Heywood, Lancashire OL10 4BE
**Tel:** 01706364121 **Fax:** 01706624944
**Web:** www.purico.co.uk
**Reg No:** 5838827 **VAT No:** 882822106
**Estd:** 2006 Private Limited Company
**Line of Business:** Manufacture of paper and paperboard
**Export Sales:** £21,484,935
**Issued Capital:** £250,000
**Directors:** A Puri, R Mochor, A J Hume, S Todd
**Co. Secretary:** M M Secretariat Limited
**Responsibilities**
**Senior:** Alister Hume *(Manager)*
**US SIC:** 2631 **UK SIC:** 47017
**Auditors:** PKF (UK) LLP
**Bankers:** National Westminster Bank Plc (60-80-09)

| | 31-12-13 | 31-12-12 | 31-12-11 |
|---|---|---|---|
| TO | 25,156,097 | 24,593,260 | 25,310,650 |
| P/L | 2,012,249 | 2,012,757 | 2,083,343 |
| NW | 4,547,823 | 3,758,885 | 2,989,572 |
| WC | 2,260,081 | 1,622,926 | 1,507,040 |
| Emp. | 113 | 111 | 109 |

DUNS 21-369-7545
## Union Plaza
1 Union Wynd, Aberdeen, Aberdeenshire AB10 1SL
**Tel:** 01224561251
**Proprietorship**
**Line of Business:** Serviced office facilities
**Proprietor:** B Polson
**US SIC:** 7399 **UK SIC:** 83954
**Employees:** 800

DUNS 22-075-0173
## Union Square Software Ltd
7 The Triangle, Nottingham, Nottinghamshire NG2 1AE
**Tel:** 01159-850055 **Fax:** 01159852115
**Web:** www.unionsquaresoftware.com
**Reg No:** 4076500 **Estd:** 2000 Private Limited Company
**Line of Business:** Computer software sales
**Issued Capital:** £100
**Directors:** T W Setchfield, W H Yandell, R D Vincent
**Co. Secretary:** Peter Wakefield
**Responsibilities**
**Senior:** Tina Chamberlain *(Office Manager)*
**Admin:** Tina Chamberlain *(Office Manager)*
**Operations:** Aidan Boustred *(Production and Operations Mana)*
**US SIC:** 7379 **UK SIC:** 83940
**Auditors:** Cobb Burgin & Co
**Bankers:** Lloyds TSB Bank plc (30-15-04)

| | 28-02-14 | 28-02-13 | 29-02-12 |
|---|---|---|---|
| TO | 5,838,000 | 4,831,000 | [illegible] |
| P/L | 1,327,000 | 1,033,000 | 736,353 |
| NW | 1,616,000 | 1,183,000 | 690,045 |
| WC | 577,000 | 7,000 | 171,587 |
| Emp. | 75 | 64 | 53 |

DUNS 49-087-1001
## Union Street Technologies Ltd
37 Sheen Road, Richmond, Surrey TW9 1AJ
**Tel:** 020-8614-9090
**Web:** www.unionstreet.uk.com
**Reg No:** 3089574 **Estd:** 2001 Private Limited Company
**Line of Business:** Telecommunications
**Issued Capital:** £100
**Directors:** A G Cook, S Cresswell, A Kazaca, R Bristow
**Co. Secretary:** Ms Sara Cook
**Responsibilities**
**Senior:** Paula Wright *(Manager)*
**Operations:** Paula Wright *(Manager)*
**US SIC:** 4899, 7379
**UK SIC:** 79020, 83940
**Auditors:** Perrys

| | 31-12-13 | 31-12-12 | 31-12-11 |
|---|---|---|---|
| TO | 3,853,846 | N/A | N/A |
| P/L | 689,301 | N/A | N/A |
| NW | 2,334,904 | 1,740,623 | 1,074,901 |
| WC | 484,880 | 635,030 | 934,712 |
| Emp. | 64 | N/A | N/A |

DUNS 23-103-5304
## Unionamerica Holdings Ltd
(**Subsidiary of:** Royston Run-Off Ltd)
27 Camperdown Street, London E1 8DS
**Tel:** 07971494870 **Fax:** 020-7617-5970
**Reg No:** 2822469 **Estd:** 1993 Private Limited Company
**Line of Business:** Management activities of holding companies
**Directors:** C P Thomas, A J Turner, D R Reid
**Co. Secretary:** Ms Siobhan Hextall
**US SIC:** 6711 **UK SIC:** 83962
**Auditors:** KPMG Audit PLC
**Employees:** 51

DUNS 29-492-8890
## Unionburger Ltd
(**Subsidiary of:** Bakers (Morriston) Ltd)
Suite 1 Vivian Court, Phoenix Way, Swansea Enterprise Park, Swansea, West Glamorgan SA7 9FG
**Tel:** 01792311060 **Fax:** 01792-311061
**Web:** www.wimpy.uk.com
**Reg No:** 1856258 **Estd:** 1984 Private Limited Company
**Line of Business:** Agricultural shows
**Trading Style:** Wimpy, Burger King
**Issued Capital:** £250,000
**Directors:** C I Baker, Ms T K Jenkins
**Co. Secretary:** Ms Teresa Jenkins
**Responsibilities**
**Senior:** Gordon Baker *(Manager)*
**Branches:** Unionburger Ltd, 12-14 St. John Street, Cardiff, South Glamorgan CF10 1GL
**US SIC:** 7399 **UK SIC:** 83954
**Auditors:** PricewaterhouseCoopers
**Bankers:** Barclays Bank Plc (20-84-41)

| | 30-03-14 | 31-03-13 | 25-03-12 |
|---|---|---|---|
| TO | 10,712,606 | 10,634,072 | 9,841,619 |
| P/L | 896,157 | (230,162) | 130,477 |
| NW | 371,371 | (313,375) | (18,364) |
| WC | 367,523 | 178,126 | 47,435 |
| Emp. | 212 | 206 | 181 |

DUNS 21-412-2733

### Unionlearn T U C

Congress House, 23-28 Great Russell Street, London WC1B 3LS
**Tel:** 02070796920
**Web:** www.unionlearn.org.uk
**Estd:** 2000 Partnership
**Line of Business:** Adult education locations
**Partners:** T Wilson, Dr A Lent, G Fawcett, Ms J Segars, A Young, Ms K Carberry
**US SIC:** 8299 **UK SIC:** 93300
**Employees:** 160

DUNS 39-159-9636

### Unipage Ltd

(**Subsidiary of:** Giftsign Ltd)
101-114 Holloway Head, Birmingham, West Midlands B1 1QP
**Tel:** 0121-631-3202
**Web:** www.unipage.com.au
**Reg No:** 2111867 **Estd:** 1987 Private Limited Company
**Line of Business:** Telecommunication networks
**Trading Style:** Intercity Mobile
**Issued Capital:** £100
**Director:** A R Jackson
**Co. Secretary:** Mrs Annette Jackson
**Responsibilities**
**Senior:** richard burke *(finance director)*
**Finance:** richard burke *(finance director)*
**HR:** nicki windridge *(h&R director)*
**US SIC:** 4899 **UK SIC:** 79020
**Auditors:** RSM Bentley Jennison

| | 31-12-13 | 31-12-12 | 31-12-11 |
|---|---|---|---|
| TA | 9,898 | 12,828 | 394,917 |
| NW | (485) | 2,298 | 3,664 |
| WC | (485) | 2,298 | 3,664 |

DUNS 64-101-3289 **Imp**

### Unipart Eberspacher Exhaust Systems Ltd

Beresford Avenue, Coventry, West Midlands CV6 5LZ
**Tel:** 024-7663-8663 **Fax:** 02476666901
**Web:** www.uees.co.uk
**Reg No:** 3496115 **VAT No:** 695683569
**Estd:** 1989 Private Limited Company
**Line of Business:** Manufacturers and wholesalers of exhaust sytems
**Export Sales:** £5,561,000
**Trading Style:** Unipart Group
**Issued Capital:** £2,800,000
**Principals:** Mrs C Burke *(Managing)*, A P Davis *(Financial)*, B S Jackson, J J Healey
**Co. Secretary:** Michael Rimmer
**Responsibilities**
**Senior:** Alexander Ade *(Director)*, Heinrich Baumann *(President)*, Uwe Brinkmann *(Director)*, Mortiz Gerig *(Manager)*, Detlef Pitan *(Director)*, Thomas Wunsche *(Manager)*
**Marketing:** Paul McClean *(Commercial Manager)*
**Sales:** Paul McClean *(Commercial Manager)*
**Health & Safety:** Glen Wakelin *(Health & Safety Officer)*
**Operations:** Malcolm Conduit *(Development Manager)*
**US SIC:** 3714 **UK SIC:** 35300
**Auditors:** Ernst & Young LLP

| | 31-12-13 | 31-12-12 | 31-12-11 |
|---|---|---|---|
| TO | 53,026,000 | 67,910,000 | 68,777,000 |
| P/L | 735,000 | 969,000 | 1,553,000 |
| NW | 9,265,000 | 7,591,000 | 7,055,000 |
| WC | 3,959,000 | 3,287,000 | 5,312,000 |
| Emp. | 323 | 325 | 278 |

DUNS 29-668-8880

### Unipart Group of Companies Ltd

Unipart House, Garsington Road, Cowley, Oxford, Oxfordshire OX4 2PG
**Tel:** 01865-778966 **Fax:** 01865-383763
**Web:** www.unipartlogistics.com
**Reg No:** 1994997 **Estd:** 1987 Private Limited Company
**Line of Business:** Management activities of holding companies
**Export Sales:** £363,100,000
**Issued Capital:** £407,931
**Principals:** A J Mourgue *(Financial)*, J M Neill, F W Burns, Dr B S Jackson, J D Clayton
**Co. Secretary:** Michael Rimmer
**Responsibilities**
**Senior:** Raymond Leung *(Manager)*, Michael Varnom *(Manager)*
**Branches:** Unipart Group Of Companies Ltd, Parkwood House, Charter Avenue, Coventry, West Midlands CV4 8DA
**US SIC:** 6711 **UK SIC:** 83962
**Auditors:** PricewaterhouseCoopers LLP
**Bankers:** Barclays Bank Plc (20-65-18)
**Following financial data are in thousands**

| | 31-12-13 | 31-12-12 | 31-12-11 |
|---|---|---|---|
| TO | 924,100 | 905,900 | 1,063,500 |
| P/L | (14,800) | 5,500 | (19,500) |
| NW | (203,600) | (107,800) | (59,100) |
| WC | 59,700 | 70,000 | 68,900 |
| Emp. | 6,931 | 7,521 | 8,533 |

DUNS 21-881-7211 **Imp-Exp**

### Unipart International Holdings Ltd

(**Subsidiary of:** Unipart Group of Companies Ltd)
Unit 9 11, Estate Industrial Estate, Bullsbrook Road, Hayes, Middlesex UB4 0JZ
**Fax:** 01865790372
**Web:** www.serckservicesmotorsport.co.uk
**Reg No:** 0592360 **Estd:** 1923 Private Limited Company
**Line of Business:** Management activities of holding companies
**Export Markets:** Middle East, U S A, Holland
**Trading Style:** Serck Intertruck, Serck Services, International Radiators
**Issued Capital:** £5,724,150
**Directors:** J Chitty, A J Mourgue, M J Stringer, J M Neill, P M Dessain
**Co. Secretary:** Michael Rimmer
**Responsibilities**
**Senior:** Ken Stansfield *(Manager)*
**Branches:** Unipart International Holdings Ltd, 30-31 Stewartfield Indstl Est, Off Newhaven Rd, Edinburgh, Midlothian EH6 4JY
**US SIC:** 6711, 3714
**UK SIC:** 83962, 35300
**Auditors:** PricewaterhouseCoopers LLP
**Bankers:** Lloyds TSB Bank plc (30-00-06)

| | 31-12-13 | 31-12-12 | 31-12-11 |
|---|---|---|---|
| TA | 19,015,000 | 34,026,000 | 31,627,000 |
| P/L | 8,507,000 | 11,905,000 | 61,000 |
| NW | 11,397,000 | 22,492,000 | 10,226,000 |
| WC | 1,068,000 | 5,138,000 | (7,128,000) |

DUNS 77-887-9999

### Unipart Rail Ltd

(**Subsidiary of:** Unipart Group of Companies Ltd)
Firstpoint, Balby Carr Bank, Doncaster, South Yorkshire DN4 5JQ
**Tel:** 01302731400
**Web:** www.unipartrail.com
**Reg No:** 3038418 **VAT No:** 900543758
**Estd:** 1995 Private Limited Company
**Line of Business:** Railway wagons and stock
**Export Sales:** £5,469,000
**Issued Capital:** £40,010,000
**Principals:** A J Mourgue *(Financial)*, G M Jackson, J M Neill, J D Clayton, G J Tillier, T G Johnstone, P M Dessain
**Co. Secretary:** Michael Rimmer
**Responsibilities**
**Marketing:** Dave Tilmount *(Head Of Marketing)*
**Sales:** Julien Baxter *(Head of Sales)*, Kevin Orton *(Head of Business Development)*
**IT:** Mike Boyle *(IT Director)*, Mark Field *(Software, Applications Manager)*, Shaun Roper *(IT Manager)*
**Fleet:** Nick Lamb *(Fleet Product Engineer)*
**Branches:** Unipart Rail Ltd, Wennington Road, Southport, Merseyside PR9 7TN
**US SIC:** 3743, 3559
**UK SIC:** 36201, 32863
**Auditors:** PricewaterhouseCoopers LLP
**Bankers:** The Royal Bank Of Scotland Plc (16-04-00)

| | 31-12-13 | 31-12-12 | 31-12-11 |
|---|---|---|---|
| TO | 195,630,000 | 181,750,000 | 175,752,000 |
| P/L | 8,621,000 | 6,820,000 | 8,172,000 |
| NW | 54,057,000 | 57,128,000 | 59,327,000 |
| WC | 56,576,000 | 58,547,000 | 57,132,000 |
| Emp. | 825 | 812 | 828 |

DUNS 21-228-5730

### Unipart Ugc

Unit 5220, Lutterworth, Leicestershire LE17 4XQ
**Tel:** 01455-557495
**Proprietorship**
**Line of Business:** Cinemas
**US SIC:** 7832 **UK SIC:** 97113
**Employees:** 190

DUNS 49-394-6453 **Imp**

### Unipec U.K. Co. Ltd

(**Subsidiary of:** China Petrochemical Corporation)
74 Shepherds Bush Green, London W12 8QE
**Tel:** 02088118588 **Fax:** 02076169889
**Web:** www.unipec.co.uk
**Reg No:** 3138679 **Estd:** 1995 Private Limited Company
**Line of Business:** Oil companies
**Directors:** B Chen, G Chen
**Co. Secretary:** Manxu Ma
**Responsibilities**
**Senior:** Jianfeng Gao *(Manager)*

**US SIC:** 2999, 5171
**UK SIC:** 11150, 61200
**Auditors:** KPMG LLP
**Employees:** 18
**Turnover:** £664,498,000

DUNS 22-575-1627 **Imp-Exp**

### Unipres U K Ltd

(**Subsidiary of:** Unipres Corporation)
Cherry Blossom Way, Sunderland, Tyne and Wear SR5 3NT
**Tel:** 01914-182000 **Fax:** 0191-418-2131
**Web:** www.unipres.co.uk
**Reg No:** 2163867 **VAT No:** 495932495
**Estd:** 1989 Private Limited Company
**Line of Business:** Engineers (general)
**Export Markets:** Spain
**Export Sales:** £432,000
**Issued Capital:** £12,000,000
**Directors:** S Izumi, M Yoshizawa, G Graham, J Cruddace, M Masuda, S Asahi
**Co. Secretary:** Graham Baines
**Responsibilities**
**Senior:** Kazunori Masuda *(Manager)*, Satoru Nito *(Manager)*
**US SIC:** 8911, 3499
**UK SIC:** 83701, 31694
**Auditors:** Deloitte LLP
**Bankers:** Bank Of Scotland (12-21-37)

| | 31-12-13 | 31-12-12 | 31-12-11 |
|---|---|---|---|
| TO | 171,850,000 | 182,979,000 | 173,589,000 |
| P/L | 16,964,000 | 17,955,000 | 17,760,000 |
| NW | 68,002,000 | 55,922,000 | 45,227,000 |
| WC | 2,534,000 | 19,912,000 | 21,201,000 |
| Emp. | 944 | 970 | 919 |

DUNS 73-583-5428 **Imp**

### Uniqlo Europe Ltd

(**Subsidiary of:** Fast Retailing Co. Ltd.)
311 Oxford Street, London W1C 2HP
**Tel:** 02072908090
**Web:** www.uniqlo.com
**Reg No:** 4845064 **Estd:** 2003 Private Limited Company
**Line of Business:** Representative office
**Issued Capital:** £4,000,000
**Directors:** T Kuwahara, I J Vliegen, Dr B Hauptkorn, T Yanai, N Domae
**Co. Secretary:** Takao Kuwahara
**Responsibilities**
**Senior:** Simon Coble *(Chief Executive Officer)*
**Facilities:** Gary Belcher *(Maintenance Manager)*
**Branches:** Uniqlo Europe Ltd, 93-97 Clarence Street, Kingston Upon Thames, Surrey KT1 1QY
**US SIC:** 5611, 5661
**UK SIC:** 64500, 64600
**Auditors:** Ernst & Young LLP

| | 31-08-13 | 31-08-12 | 31-08-11 |
|---|---|---|---|
| TO | 74,047,031 | 63,019,451 | 63,064,945 |
| P/L | (2,001,026) | (4,594,844) | (9,734,605) |
| NW | (19,895,054) | (17,894,028) | (13,299,184) |
| WC | (10,637,384) | (2,128,715) | (24,679,508) |
| Emp. | 562 | 532 | 562 |

DUNS 23-975-5254

### Unique Care Providers

29 St Johns Road, Huddersfield, West Yorkshire HD1 5DX
**Tel:** 01484223003
**Web:** www.unique-care.co.uk
**Reg No:** 3964167 **Estd:** 1999 Private Company Limited By Guarantee
**Line of Business:** Home care service providers
**Directors:** A Cox, A Sam, Mrs S V Mitchell
**Co. Secretary:** Mrs Gloria Green
**Responsibilities**
**Senior:** Harold Horsfall *(Manager)*, Fred Iyekekpolor *(Director)*, Jacque Machon *(Manager)*, Jacque Mcmohan *(Manager)*, Diane Ryan *(Manager)*
**US SIC:** 8091 **UK SIC:** 95200
**Bankers:** National Westminster Bank Plc (53-61-07)

| | 31-03-14 | 31-03-13 | 31-03-12 |
|---|---|---|---|
| TO | 756,331 | 653,870 | 583,163 |
| P/L | 34,887 | 23,173 | 43,033 |
| NW | 247,813 | 212,926 | 189,753 |
| WC | 243,990 | 208,724 | 184,500 |
| Emp. | 65 | 61 | 59 |

DUNS 67-244-8388

### Unique Care Solutions Ltd

Champfleurie Mews, Linlithgow, West Lothian EH49 6ND
**Tel:** 01506834078
**Web:** www.ucs-care.com
**Reg No:** 0319558SC **Estd:** 2007 Private Limited Company
**Line of Business:** Other human health activities
**Issued Capital:** £1,100
**Director:** M A Beaumont
**Co. Secretary:** Mrs Jacqueline Pestana

**US SIC:** 8091 **UK SIC:** 95200

| | 31-03-13 | 31-03-12 | 31-03-11 |
|---|---|---|---|
| TA | 322,446 | 247,496 | 166,935 |
| NW | 8,668 | 2,205 | 1,386 |
| WC | (3,256) | (26,591) | (8,664) |

DUNS 23-946-0731

### Unique Catering & Management Services Ltd

Plestowes Barn, Hareway Lane, Warwick, Warwickshire CV35 8DD
**Tel:** 01926-620011 **Fax:** 01926-620033
**Web:** www.uniquecatering.co.uk
**Reg No:** 3935606 **Estd:** 2000 Private Limited Company
**Line of Business:** Caterers
**Trading Style:** Unique Catering & Management Services Ltd
**Issued Capital:** £1,000
**Co. Secretary:** David Needham
**US SIC:** 5812 **UK SIC:** 66110
**Auditors:** The Ollis Partnership Ltd

| | 30-04-14 | 30-04-13 | 30-04-12 |
|---|---|---|---|
| TO | 8,723,902 | 9,515,609 | 10,067,009 |
| P/L | 352,940 | 444,124 | 627,551 |
| NW | 574,358 | 709,454 | 603,798 |
| WC | 462,793 | 613,338 | 504,030 |
| Emp. | 269 | 296 | 332 |

DUNS 22-119-1104

### Unique Digital Marketing Ltd

(**Subsidiary of:** Syzygy Ag)
The Johnson Building, 77 Hatton Garden, London EC1N 8JS
**Tel:** 02032064100 **Fax:** 02073541235
**Web:** www.unique-digital.co.uk
**Reg No:** 4138160 **Estd:** 2001 Private Limited Company
**Line of Business:** Advertising
**Export Sales:** £2,467,081
**Trading Style:** The Syzygy Group
**Issued Capital:** £800
**Directors:** A P Stevens, Mrs C Barber, J P Briscoe
**Co. Secretary:** Erwin Greiner
**Responsibilities**
**Senior:** Phil Stelter *(Manager)*
**Marketing:** Katrin Schreyer *(Public & Investor Relations Di)*
**US SIC:** 7311 **UK SIC:** 83800
**Auditors:** KPSR LLP
**Bankers:** National Westminster Bank Plc (56-00-27)

| | 31-12-13 | 31-12-12 | 31-12-11 |
|---|---|---|---|
| TO | 20,361,674 | 14,664,491 | 12,587,008 |
| P/L | 783,861 | 703,720 | 605,426 |
| NW | 2,122,096 | 1,530,426 | 1,510,210 |
| WC | 2,101,817 | 1,513,487 | 1,492,752 |
| Emp. | 50 | 43 | 30 |

DUNS 23-598-4643

### Unique Employment Services Ltd

5 Castle Street, Luton, Bedfordshire LU1 3AA
**Web:** www.unique-employment.co.uk
**Reg No:** 3595874 **VAT No:** 716012771
**Estd:** 1998 Private Limited Company
**Line of Business:** Labour recruitment and provision of personnel
**Issued Capital:** £201
**Directors:** P A Hughes, Ms M L Gustard, Ms C Mcelligott
**Co. Secretary:** Ms Angela Hughes
**Branches:** Unique Employment Services Ltd, 5 Castle Street, Luton, Bedfordshire LU1 3AA
**US SIC:** 7361 **UK SIC:** 83954
**Auditors:** Wallace & Co
**Bankers:** Barclays Bank Plc (20-53-30)

| | 31-07-14 | 31-07-13 | 31-07-12 |
|---|---|---|---|
| TO | 10,431,792 | 8,744,324 | 7,648,925 |
| P/L | 301,319 | 296,780 | 272,185 |
| NW | 346,597 | 295,627 | 235,291 |
| WC | 326,839 | 282,509 | 221,906 |
| Emp. | 25 | 489 | 645 |

DUNS 73-367-9372

### Unique Nursing Services Ltd

South Court, Sharston Road, Manchester M22 4BB
**Tel:** 01619982132 **Fax:** 01619988560
**Web:** www.uniquenursing.co.uk
**Reg No:** 4641418 **Estd:** 2001 Private Limited Company
**Line of Business:** Nursing agencies
**Issued Capital:** £100
**Director:** Miss F M Lusack
**Co. Secretary:** Hyacinth Lusack
**Responsibilities**
**Senior:** Cynthia Lusack *(Manager)*
**US SIC:** 8091 **UK SIC:** 95200
**Bankers:** The Royal Bank Of Scotland Plc (16-15-33)

| | 31-01-14 | 31-01-13 | 31-01-12 |
|---|---|---|---|
| TO | N/A | 505,788 | 528,840 |
| P/L | N/A | 7,635 | 36,975 |
| NW | 163,440 | 204,966 | 218,967 |
| WC | (4,011) | 35,346 | 46,250 |

DUNS 22-200-7986
## Unique Personnel (U.K.) Ltd
256 Brixton Hill, London SW2 1HF
**Tel:** 02086717665 **Fax:** 02085527070
**Web:** www.uniquepersonneluk.com
**Reg No:** 4218958 **Estd:** 2010 Private Limited Company
**Line of Business:** Employment agencies
**Issued Capital:** £10
**Directors:** H M Aghoghoubia, Ms G E Aghoghovbia
**Co. Secretary:** Jeffrey Aghoghovbia
**Responsibilities**
**Senior:** Elizabeth Oghenedaro *(Manager)*, Mote Oyonwo *(Manager)*
**US SIC:** 7361, 8091
**UK SIC:** 83954, 95200
**Auditors:** SOA & Associates
**Bankers:** HSBC Bank plc (40-01-22)

| | 30-04-14 | 30-04-13 | 30-04-12 |
|---|---|---|---|
| TO | N/A | 3,998,658 | N/A |
| P/L | N/A | 300,250 | N/A |
| NW | 569,835 | 539,409 | 393,657 |
| WC | 557,756 | 536,276 | 419,588 |

DUNS 23-738-7860
## Unique Pubs Ltd
(**Subsidiary of:** Enterprise Inns Plc)
3 Monkspath Hall Road, Shirley, Solihull, West Midlands B90 4SJ
**Tel:** 02084444224
**Reg No:** 3733077 **Estd:** 1999 Private Limited Company
**Line of Business:** Management activities of other non-financial holding companies not elsewhere classified
**Trading Style:** Lord Kelvin
**Directors:** N R Smith, W S Townsend
**Co. Secretary:** Ms Loretta Togher
**Branches:** Unique Pubs Ltd, Main Street, Wadworth, Doncaster, South Yorkshire DN11 9AY
**US SIC:** 6711, 5813
**UK SIC:** 83962, 66200
**Auditors:** PricewaterhouseCoopers

| | 30-09-13 | 30-09-12 | 30-09-11 |
|---|---|---|---|
| TA | 392,812,000 | 392,732,000 | 391,354,000 |
| P/L | 65,000,000 | 65,000,000 | 65,000,000 |
| NW | 12,500,000 | 14,979,000 | 14,918,000 |
| WC | (145,326,000) | (142,847,000) | (142,908,000) |

DUNS 21-919-4310
## Unique Seafood Holdings Ltd
Unit 35.6 And 35.7 Cobalt, White Hart Avenue, London SE28 0GU
**Tel:** 02032474858
**Reg No:** 8356599 **Estd:** 2013 Private Limited Company
**Line of Business:** Management activities of other non-financial holding companies not elsewhere classified
**Issued Capital:** £1
**Directors:** Ms I M Sperre, H Nissen, O Nielsen, K Sperre
**US SIC:** 6711 **UK SIC:** 83962
**Auditors:** F W Berringer & Co

| | 31-12-13 |
|---|---|
| TO | 24,077,413 |
| P/L | 197,992 |
| NW | 796,280 |
| WC | 255,992 |
| Emp. | 64 |

DUNS 76-870-7176
## Unique Television Ltd
(**Subsidiary of:** Uctal Ltd)
100 Talbot Road, Old Trafford, Manchester M16 0PG
**Tel:** 01618762588
**Web:** www.uniqueconveyancing.co.uk
**Reg No:** 2614264 **Estd:** 1991 Private Limited Company
**Line of Business:** Conveyancing services
**Issued Capital:** £2
**Directors:** M I Davis, P H Pascoe
**Co. Secretary:** Ms Joy Daglish
**Responsibilities**
**Senior:** Vijay Amarnani
**US SIC:** 4833 **UK SIC:** 97411
**Auditors:** Grant Thornton UK LLP
**Bankers:** Bank Of Scotland (12-01-59)

| | 31-10-13 | 31-10-12 | 31-10-11 |
|---|---|---|---|
| TA | 868,892 | 808,985 | 3,881,674 |
| NW | (336,176) | (513,442) | (876,246) |
| WC | 854,109 | 746,629 | 3,435,274 |

DUNS 73-803-8152
## Unique Window Systems Ltd
161 Parker Drive, Leicester, Leicestershire LE4 0JP
**Tel:** 01162-364656 **Fax:** 01162364237
**Web:** www.uniquewindowsystems.com
**Reg No:** 5060094 **VAT No:** 857592279
**Estd:** 2004 Private Limited Company
**Line of Business:** Door and window furniture
**Issued Capital:** £1,000
**Directors:** J W Raven, A J Patel
**Co. Secretary:** Sunil Patel

**Responsibilities**
**Purchasing:** Manish Rathad *(Purchasing Manager)*
**Engineering:** Steve Birkin *(Production Manager)*
**US SIC:** 3442 **UK SIC:** 31420
**Auditors:** PKF (UK) LLP
**Bankers:** The Royal Bank Of Scotland Plc (16-23-21)

| | 30-04-14 | 30-04-13 | 30-04-12 |
|---|---|---|---|
| TO | 9,679,629 | 6,941,701 | 7,874,991 |
| P/L | 542,229 | (145,126) | 70,215 |
| NW | 758,408 | 337,043 | 449,083 |
| WC | 550,316 | 348,486 | 335,269 |
| Emp. | 85 | 78 | 76 |

DUNS 22-195-8072
## Uniqwin (U K) Ltd
Integrity House Unit 8 Centre 21, Warrington, Cheshire WA1 4AW
**Tel:** 01925286100
**Web:** www.uniqwin.co.uk
**Reg No:** 4213762 **VAT No:** 703975032
**Estd:** 2001 Private Limited Company
**Line of Business:** Cctv & video equipment
**Issued Capital:** £400
**Principals:** C Unwin *(Managing)*, S Unwin, G T Higgins
**Co. Secretary:** Jean Unwin
**US SIC:** 7393, 7349
**UK SIC:** 83954, 92300
**Bankers:** National Westminster Bank Plc (01-09-17)

| | 31-03-14 | 31-03-13 | 31-03-12 |
|---|---|---|---|
| TA | 569,178 | 704,051 | 617,300 |
| NW | 273,193 | 228,268 | 192,592 |
| WC | 222,275 | 171,572 | 129,092 |

DUNS 23-371-6021 **Imp**
## Unisant (Holdings) Ltd
Unisant Trading Estate, Powke Lane, Cradley Heath, West Midlands B64 5PY
**Tel:** 01215-612157
**Reg No:** 5155194 **Estd:** 2004 Private Limited Company
**Line of Business:** Holding companies management activities
**Issued Capital:** £280,771
**Director:** D J Cooling
**Co. Secretary:** Stephen Young
**US SIC:** 6711 **UK SIC:** 83962
**Auditors:** RSM Bentley Jennison

| | 31-07-13 | 31-07-12 | 31-07-11 |
|---|---|---|---|
| TO | 4,742,976 | 4,111,749 | 2,903,027 |
| P/L | 67,102 | (364,363) | (783,779) |
| NW | 6,191,891 | 6,122,604 | 6,486,967 |
| WC | 4,865,043 | 4,783,119 | 5,186,795 |
| Emp. | 61 | 58 | 63 |

DUNS 39-909-7823
## Uniserve Holdings Ltd
London Mega Terminal, Thurrock Park Way, Tilbury, Essex RM18 7HD
**Tel:** 01375-856060
**Web:** www.uniservegroup.co.uk
**Reg No:** 2234562 **Estd:** 1988 Private Limited Company
**Line of Business:** Management activities of holding companies
**Issued Capital:** £100,000
**Directors:** P Stone, S W Ireland, I R Liddell
**Co. Secretary:** Barry Tuck
**Responsibilities**
**Senior:** Grant Liddell *(Manager)*, Anthony Viles *(Manager)*
**Branches:** Uniserve Holdings Ltd, Unit 2D, Hockney Road Industrial Estate, Bradford, West Yorkshire BD8 9HQ
**US SIC:** 6711 **UK SIC:** 83962
**Auditors:** Elliott, Mortlock, Busby & Co
**Bankers:** Barclays Bank Plc (20-34-69)

| | 31-03-14 | 31-03-13 | 31-03-12 |
|---|---|---|---|
| TO | 151,553,000 | 154,538,000 | 120,383,114 |
| P/L | 5,631,000 | 5,221,000 | 6,496,719 |
| NW | 59,736,000 | 56,080,000 | 52,229,411 |
| WC | 34,304,000 | 34,248,000 | 32,735,690 |
| Emp. | 312 | 243 | 243 |

DUNS 21-771-7964
## Unison Birmingham Branch
The Mclaren Building, 46 The Priory Queensway, Birmingham, West Midlands B4 7LR
**Tel:** 01212003331
**Web:** www.unison.co.uk
**Estd:** 2011 Proprietorship
**Line of Business:** Trade unions
**Proprietor:** G Horn
**Responsibilities**
**Senior:** Mark Rose *(Branch Secretary)*
**US SIC:** 8631 **UK SIC:** 96313
**Employees:** 50

DUNS 22-811-4575 **Imp-Exp**
## Unison Ltd
Faroe House, Thornburgh Road, Cayton Low Road, Eastfield, Scarborough, North Yorkshire YO11 3UY
**Web:** www.unisonltd.com
**Reg No:** 1105991 **VAT No:** 168496414
**Estd:** 1993 Private Limited Company

**Line of Business:** Misc special industry machinery mfrs
**Export Markets:** U.S.A. (35%), Europe (15%)
**Trading Style:** Unison
**Issued Capital:** £107,143
**Principals:** T J Pickering *(Managing)*, P J Wilkinson, A B Pickering, J Kidger
**Co. Secretary:** Julian Kidger
**US SIC:** 3559, 8911, 7391
**UK SIC:** 32863, 83701, 94000
**Auditors:** PKF (UK) LLP
**Bankers:** HSBC Bank plc (40-40-22)

| | 30-09-13 | 30-09-12 | 30-09-11 |
|---|---|---|---|
| TA | 2,980,683 | 2,470,018 | 1,415,971 |
| NW | 200,735 | 44,871 | (105,375) |
| WC | (430,547) | 16,820 | (71,600) |

DUNS 21-879-7474
## Unison Office
23 Tipperlinn Road, Edinburgh, Midlothian EH10 5HF
**Estd:** 2012
**Line of Business:** Trade unions
**Responsibilities**
**Senior:** Michael Mcgahey *(Branch Secretary)*
**US SIC:** 8631 **UK SIC:** 96313
**Employees:** 2,000

DUNS 21-117-2978 **Imp-Exp**
## Unistrut Ltd
(**Subsidiary of:** Allied Luxembourg Sarl)
Unit 18, Bedford, Bedfordshire MK41 0LU
**Tel:** 02085610200 **Fax:** 02085618487
**Web:** www.unistrut.co.uk
**Reg No:** 1050870 **VAT No:** 491179327
**Estd:** 1972 Private Limited Company
**Line of Business:** Fasteners and fixings
**Export Markets:** Europe, Middle East, Africa, Hong-Kong
**Export Sales:** £8,896,000
**Issued Capital:** £1,320,000
**Directors:** J A Mallak, G E Uren, J P Williamson, P G Merrick, C E Jones
**Co. Secretary:** Ms Eileen Tierney
**Responsibilities**
**Senior:** Gordon Browning *(Manager)*, Eric Cartelet *(Manager)*, Robert Cocks *(Manager)*
**Finance:** Kathryn Woods *(Finance Director)*
**Branches:** Unistrut Ltd, Pump Lane, Hayes, Middlesex UB3 3NB
**US SIC:** 3452, 3469, 8911
**UK SIC:** 31371, 31200, 83701
**Auditors:** Deloitte & Touche LLP
**Bankers:** Barclays Bank Plc (20-05-74)

| | 27-09-13 | 28-09-12 | 30-09-11 |
|---|---|---|---|
| TO | 21,333,000 | 22,600,000 | 22,704,000 |
| P/L | (1,801,000) | (682,000) | 419,000 |
| NW | 8,056,000 | 9,425,000 | 9,986,000 |
| WC | 7,009,000 | 9,644,000 | 10,326,000 |
| Emp. | 97 | 100 | 97 |

DUNS 39-809-6180
## Unisurge International Ltd
Unit 1 Formula Drive, Newmarket, Suffolk CB8 0BF
**Tel:** 08455213111 **Fax:** 01223499401
**Web:** www.unisurge.com
**Reg No:** 2214024 **VAT No:** 049747269
**Estd:** 1988 Private Limited Company
**Line of Business:** Medical equipment leasing and rental
**Export Sales:** £1,983,000
**Issued Capital:** £5,000,000
**Directors:** A Farboud, M C Moon, A Farboud, Ms R H Farboud, J Farboud, T F Turner
**Co. Secretary:** Azizeh Farboud
**US SIC:** 7394, 5122
**UK SIC:** 84000, 61800
**Auditors:** Deloitte LLP

| | 31-12-13 | 31-12-12 | 31-12-11 |
|---|---|---|---|
| TO | 20,432,000 | 17,259,000 | 14,560,000 |
| P/L | 1,348,000 | 588,000 | 396,000 |
| NW | 8,248,000 | 7,134,000 | 5,302,000 |
| WC | 3,633,000 | 2,822,000 | 2,544,000 |
| Emp. | 179 | 147 | 135 |

DUNS 23-361-6155 **Imp**
## Unisurge Ltd
Farboud Innovation Park, Formula Drive, Newmarket, Suffolk CB8 0BF
**Tel:** 01223499400 **Fax:** 01223499401
**Web:** www.unisurge.com
**Reg No:** 5060206 **Estd:** 2004 Private Limited Company
**Line of Business:** Manufacturers of instruments for medical purposes
**Issued Capital:** £2
**Director:** A Farboud
**Co. Secretary:** Azizeh Farboud
**Responsibilities**
**Finance:** Mathew Moon *(Senior Finance Administrator)*
**Sales:** Terrance Turner *(Senior Sales Executive)*
**IT:** Bahram Farboud *(Senior IT Executive)*

**HR:** Houri Farboub *(Human Resources Manager)*
**US SIC:** 3841 **UK SIC:** 37201

| | 31-03-14 | 31-03-13 | 31-03-12 |
|---|---|---|---|
| TA | 2 | 2 | 2 |
| NW | 2 | 2 | 2 |

DUNS 21-055-2808
## Unisys Group Services Ltd
(**Subsidiary of:** Unisys Nederland Holding B.V.)
Gazette House, 28 Bakers Road, Uxbridge, Middlesex UB8 1RG
**Tel:** 01895451000 **Fax:** 01895451090
**Web:** www.unisys.com
**Reg No:** 0377778 **Estd:** 1942 Private Limited Company
**Line of Business:** Management activities of holding companies
**Issued Capital:** £199,118,100
**Directors:** M Piercy, F P Mallia
**Responsibilities**
**Senior:** Lynne Baker *(Office Manager)*, Simon Edgley *(Manager)*
**Marketing:** Simon Edgley *(Manager)*
**Sales:** Simon Edgley *(Manager)*
**Admin:** Lynne Baker *(Office Manager)*
**Health & Safety:** Lynne Baker *(Office Manager)*
**Facilities:** Lynne Baker *(Office Manager)*
**Branches:** Unisys Group Services Ltd, Unisys House, 20 Barrington Road, Altrincham, Cheshire WA14 1HB
**US SIC:** 6711 **UK SIC:** 83962
**Auditors:** Ernst & Young LLP
**Bankers:** HSBC Bank plc (40-06-02)

| | 31-12-13 | 31-12-12 | 31-12-11 |
|---|---|---|---|
| P/L | (3,591,000) | (2,237,000) | (3,251,000) |
| NW | (101,182,000) | (97,591,000) | (94,549,000) |

DUNS 21-618-0794 **Exp**
## Unisys Ltd
(**Subsidiary of:** Unisys Nederland Holding B.V.)
Hertford House, Hertford Place, Maple Cross, Rickmansworth, Hertfordshire WD3 9AB
**Tel:** 01895237137
**Web:** www.unisys.com
**Reg No:** 0103709 **Estd:** 1909 Private Limited Company
**Line of Business:** Other software consultancy and supply
**Export Markets:** Europe; U S A; Middle East
**Issued Capital:** £280,412,684
**Directors:** M Piercy, F P Mallia, M Walker, N P Fraser, M R Godfrey
**Co. Secretary:** Gwyn Reeves
**Responsibilities**
**Senior:** Tony O'Connor *(Procurement Director)*
**Purchasing:** Tony O'Connor *(Procurement Director)*
**Branches:** Unisys Ltd, Nationwide House, Pipers Way, Swindon, Wiltshire SN3 1TA
**US SIC:** 7379 **UK SIC:** 83940
**Auditors:** KPMG LLP
**Bankers:** HSBC Bank plc (40-06-02)

| | 31-12-13 | 31-12-12 | 31-12-11 |
|---|---|---|---|
| TO | 153,390,000 | 197,314,000 | 154,091,000 |
| P/L | 29,345,000 | 40,815,000 | 18,611,000 |
| NW | 96,711,000 | 55,717,000 | 42,109,000 |
| WC | 234,881,000 | 232,671,000 | 211,167,000 |
| Emp. | 684 | 701 | 726 |

DUNS 37-971-2243
## Unit 9 Ltd
1st Floor The Lux Building, 2-4 Hoxton Square, London N1 6NU
**Tel:** 02076133330 **Fax:** 02070333299
**Web:** www.unit9.com
**Reg No:** 3279060 **Estd:** 1996 Private Limited Company
**Line of Business:** Computer software (development)
**Issued Capital:** £6,000
**Directors:** D Y Buckley, Dr N Caderni, Mrs V Culatti, P Frescobaldi, G A Boisselet
**Co. Secretary:** Tommaso Sacchi
**Responsibilities**
**Senior:** Susan Mccrystal *(Office Manager)*
**Marketing:** Susan Mccrystal *(Office Manager)*
**Admin:** Susan Mccrystal *(Office Manager)*
**Health & Safety:** Susan Mccrystal *(Office Manager)*
**Facilities:** Susan Mccrystal *(Office Manager)*
**Purchasing:** Susan Mccrystal *(Office Manager)*
**US SIC:** 7372, 7379
**UK SIC:** 83940
**Bankers:** Barclays Bank Plc (20-00-00)

| | 31-12-13 | 31-12-12 | 31-12-11 |
|---|---|---|---|
| TA | 1,769,634 | 1,509,341 | 1,686,764 |
| NW | 669,738 | 746,969 | 474,991 |
| WC | 498,754 | 580,516 | 309,745 |

## DUNS 64-246-6353
### Unit Clean
23 Badby Road West, Daventry, Northamptonshire NN11 4HJ
**Estd:** 1985 Partnership
**Line of Business:** Contract cleaning services, carpet cleaners, painting and decorating, landscape gardening and maintenance, paper goods and ladies hygiene service provider.
**Partners:** Mrs M Unit, S Unit, K Unit
**US SIC:** 7217, 1721, 0782
**UK SIC:** 98120, 50400, 01003
**Employees:** 100

## DUNS 21-770-9675
### Unit Engineers & Constructor
Lancaster Approach, North Killingholme, Immingham, South Humberside DN40 3JZ
**Tel:** 01469540478
**Web:** www.unitbirwelco.com
**Estd:** 2010 Proprietorship
**Line of Business:** Engineers (general)
**Proprietor:** D Mcintyre
**Responsibilities**
**Senior:** Dave McIntyre (Proprietor)
**US SIC:** 8911 **UK SIC:** 83701
**Employees:** 50

## DUNS 73-292-0454
### Unit Engineers & Constructors Ltd
Warrior Way, Pembroke Dock, Dyfed SA72 6UB
**Tel:** 01646-623980 **Fax:** 01646-623989
**Web:** www.unitbirwelco.com
**Reg No:** 4565799 **VAT No:** 801311984
**Estd:** 2002 Private Limited Company
**Line of Business:** Manufacture of metal structures and parts of structures
**Export Sales:** £1,523,074
**Trading Style:** Unit Engineers & Constructors Ltd
**Issued Capital:** £372,870
**Directors:** W F Ledwood, M W Oliver, L Jenkins
**Co. Secretary:** Leighton Jenkins
**US SIC:** 8911, 3443, 1796
**UK SIC:** 83701, 32051, 50400
**Auditors:** Haines Watts Wales LLP
**Bankers:** Lloyds TSB Bank plc (30-16-20)

| | 31-12-13 | 25-12-12 | 25-12-11 |
|---|---|---|---|
| TO | 26,486,835 | 28,120,859 | 18,728,931 |
| P/L | 112,976 | 11,608 | (693,959) |
| NW | 734,081 | 237,209 | (68,817) |
| WC | 257,970 | 339,541 | 480,235 |
| Emp. | 199 | 199 | 219 |

## DUNS 22-867-1046    Imp
### Unit Pallets Ltd
(**Subsidiary of:** James Jones & Sons Ltd)
Bank Street, Golborne, Warrington, Cheshire WA3 3RN
**Web:** www.unit-pallets.co.uk
**Reg No:** 1725860 **VAT No:** 437595415
**Estd:** 1970 Private Limited Company
**Line of Business:** Packing crate and pallet suppliers
**Issued Capital:** £2,551,000
**Principals:** M G March (Managing), I A Pirie, T A Bruce Jones, W G Covey, R T Stevenson
**Co. Secretary:** Michael March
**Responsibilities**
**Senior:** Gil Covey (Manager), Lawrence Johnston (Human Resources Manager)
**Finance:** Gil Covey (Manager)
**Marketing:** Michael Collopy (Sales & Marketing Manager)
**Sales:** Michael Collopy (Sales & Marketing Manager)
**IT:** Alan Lowe-Jones (Computer Operations Manager)
**HR:** Lawrence Johnston (Human Resources Manager)
**Health & Safety:** Lawrence Johnston (Human Resources Manager)
**Facilities:** Lawrence Johnston (Human Resources Manager)
**Operations:** Michael Collopy (Sales & Marketing Manager), Lawrence Johnston (Human Resources Manager), Zahir Rayani (Quality Manager)
**Engineering:** Lawrence Johnston (Human Resources Manager)
**US SIC:** 2449 **UK SIC:** 46402
**Auditors:** Deloitte & Touche
**Bankers:** The Royal Bank Of Scotland Plc (83-27-08)

| | 31-12-13 | 31-12-12 | 31-12-11 |
|---|---|---|---|
| TO | 14,561,450 | 16,004,306 | 15,573,498 |
| P/L | 179,880 | 339,723 | 65,520 |
| NW | 3,453,661 | 3,316,905 | 3,059,021 |
| WC | 4,365,889 | 4,029,708 | 3,581,280 |
| Emp. | 120 | 129 | 140 |

## DUNS 51-584-2867
### Unit Two Security Ltd
(**Subsidiary of:** Security Guarding Services Ltd)
17 Hareleeshill Road, Larkhall, Lanarkshire ML9 2EX
**Tel:** 01698881855
**Web:** www.unitgroup.co.uk
**Reg No:** 0304933SC **Estd:** 2006 Private Limited Company
**Line of Business:** Security services
**Issued Capital:** £100
**Director:** C A Wiltshire
**Co. Secretary:** Guy Dungworth
**US SIC:** 7393 **UK SIC:** 83954

| | 31-07-13 | 31-07-12 | 31-07-11 |
|---|---|---|---|
| TA | 1 | 100 | 100 |
| NW | 1 | 100 | 100 |

## DUNS 22-531-4921    Exp
### UnIT4 Business Software Ltd
(**Subsidiary of:** Unit4 N.V.)
St Georges Hall, Easton-In-Gordano, Easton-In-Gordano, Bristol, Avon BS20 0PX
**Tel:** 01275377200
**Web:** www.unit4software.co.uk
**Reg No:** 1737985 **VAT No:** 358179027
**Estd:** 1983 Private Limited Company
**Line of Business:** Hardware consultancy
**Export Sales:** £3,675,000
**Issued Capital:** £51,565,227
**Directors:** Mrs H F Sutton, D G Harwood, Mrs C J Bishop, G Leitao, P Vogel
**Co. Secretary:** Mrs Claire Bishop
**Responsibilities**
**Senior:** Anwen Robinson (Ceo / Managing Director Uk and), Arie van Marion (Manager)
**HR:** Jennie Cox (Human Resources Manager)
**Health & Safety:** Edwina Moore (Facilities Manager)
**Facilities:** Edwina Moore (Facilities Manager)
**US SIC:** 7379 **UK SIC:** 83940
**Auditors:** Ernst & Young LLP
**Bankers:** Lloyds TSB Bank plc (30-97-41)

| | 31-12-13 | 31-12-12 | 31-12-11 |
|---|---|---|---|
| TO | 67,829,000 | 62,816,000 | 62,610,000 |
| P/L | 68,915,000 | 6,526,000 | 15,574,000 |
| NW | 100,389,000 | 52,128,000 | 77,572,000 |
| WC | 10,709,000 | (27,881,000) | 2,953,000 |
| Emp. | 563 | 564 | 569 |

## DUNS 21-011-5755
### Unite Amicus Section Pension Trustee Ltd
Hayes Courtrkeley Street, West Common Road, Keston, Kent BR2 7AU
**Tel:** 02076112500
**Reg No:** 6349044 **Estd:** 2007 Private Company Limited By Guarantee
**Line of Business:** Credit unions
**Directors:** P Canavan, B Freake, P S Harwood, Ms A F Tolmie, D S Patterson, R N Fletcher Obe, A G Woodhouse, T Mitchell
**Co. Secretary:** Alexander Ryan
**Responsibilities**
**Senior:** Dorothy Fogg (Director), Ken MacIntyre (Pensions Manager)
**US SIC:** 8631 **UK SIC:** 96313
**Employees:** 1,000

## DUNS 50-396-2060
### Unite Integrated Solutions Plc
(**Subsidiary of:** Unite Group Plc)
The Core, 40 St Thomas Street, Bristol, Avon BS1 6JX
**Tel:** 01173-027000 **Fax:** 01179078101
**Web:** www.unite-students.com
**Reg No:** 2402714 **VAT No:** 609436532
**Estd:** 1989 Public Limited Company
**Line of Business:** Other letting of own property
**Issued Capital:** £50,000
**Directors:** M C Allan, R S Smith, J J Lister, R C Simpson, N Richards, S R Grant
**Co. Secretary:** Christopher Szpojnarowicz
**Responsibilities**
**Admin:** Helen Alton (Office Manager)
**Branches:** Unite Integrated Solutions Plc, 2 Acton Sq, Salford, Lancashire M5 4NY
**US SIC:** 6519 **UK SIC:** 85000
**Auditors:** KPMG Audit Plc
**Bankers:** Lloyds TSB Bank plc (30-90-54)

| | 31-12-13 | 31-12-12 | 31-12-11 |
|---|---|---|---|
| TO | 111,710,000 | 90,954,000 | 133,382,000 |
| P/L | 2,553,000 | 3,740,000 | 2,080,000 |
| NW | 33,667,000 | 30,620,000 | 26,727,000 |
| WC | 27,991,000 | 25,842,000 | 20,968,000 |
| Emp. | 890 | 895 | 752 |

## DUNS 23-602-6618
### Unite London (Two) Ltd
(**Subsidiary of:** Unite London Ltd)
The Core, 40 St Thomas Street, Bristol, Avon BS1 6JX
**Tel:** 02088085445
**Web:** www.unite-students.com
**Reg No:** 3600001 **Estd:** 1998 Private Limited Company
**Line of Business:** Other letting of own property
**Issued Capital:** £2
**Director:** M C Allan
**Co. Secretary:** Christopher Szpojnarowicz
**US SIC:** 6519 **UK SIC:** 85000

| | 31-12-13 | 31-12-12 | 31-12-11 |
|---|---|---|---|
| TA | 17,570,954 | 17,570,954 | 17,570,954 |
| NW | (1,011,745) | (1,011,745) | (1,011,745) |
| WC | (1,011,745) | (1,011,745) | (1,011,745) |

## DUNS 21-557-7046    Imp
### Unite the Union
Unite House, 128 Theobalds Road, London WC1X 8TN
**Tel:** 08001216556
**Web:** www.tgwu.org.uk
**Estd:** 2000
**Line of Business:** Trade unions
**Directors:** D Simpson, Ms G Cartmail, J Dromey, Ms L Bayliss, D Collins, A Woodley, P Talbot, T Burke
**Responsibilities**
**Senior:** Jennie Bremner (Director), Jim D'avila (Senior Officer)
**Branches:** Unite The Union, 2A Wentworth House, Vernon Gate, Derby, Derbyshire DE1 1UR
**US SIC:** 8631 **UK SIC:** 96313
**Auditors:** H W Fisher & Co
**Employees:** 1,464
**Turnover:** £102,341,000

## DUNS 76-996-7845
### Unitech Industries Ltd
Unitech, Prospect Road, Burntwood, Staffordshire WS7 0AL
**Tel:** 01543-675800
**Web:** www.unitech.uk.com
**Reg No:** 2651228 **Estd:** 1991 Private Limited Company
**Line of Business:** Other letting of own property
**Export Sales:** £1,390,619
**Trading Style:** Unitech Industries Ltd
**Issued Capital:** £100,000
**Directors:** A M Imlah, Ms M Imlah
**Co. Secretary:** Mark Street
**Responsibilities**
**Senior:** Nick Imlah (Manager), Tom Prendergast (Factory Manager)
**Facilities:** Tom Prendergast (Factory Manager)
**Operations:** Tom Prendergast (Factory Manager)
**Engineering:** Wayne Regan (Factory Manager)
**Branches:** Unitech Industries Ltd, 2 Murraysgate Indstl Est, Bathgate, West Lothian EH47 0LE
**US SIC:** 6519 **UK SIC:** 85000
**Auditors:** Malcolm Willcox & Co
**Bankers:** National Westminster Bank Plc (60-02-35)

| | 31-12-13 | 31-12-12 | 31-12-11 |
|---|---|---|---|
| TO | 36,919,731 | 27,738,454 | 29,132,115 |
| P/L | 1,192,868 | (100,986) | 1,170,180 |
| NW | 3,328,581 | 2,683,513 | 2,989,835 |
| WC | (227,619) | (218,911) | 314,159 |
| Emp. | 395 | 387 | 304 |

## DUNS 34-821-1269    Imp
### United Agri Products Ltd
(**Subsidiary of:** Origin Enterprises Plc)
Crossways Distribution Centre, Alconbury Hill, Alconbury Weston, Huntingdon, Cambridgeshire PE28 4JH
**Fax:** 08456073322
**Web:** www.agrii.co.uk
**Reg No:** 2798041 **VAT No:** 599066288
**Estd:** 1993 Private Limited Company
**Line of Business:** Chemicals distribution and wholesale
**Trading Style:** U A P
**Issued Capital:** £10,397,366
**Directors:** Ms I Hurley, C S Matthews, D P Giblin, R A Hughes, R P Priestley, D S Downie
**Responsibilities**
**Senior:** Tony Brennan (Manager), Stephen Derbyshire (Manager)
**Marketing:** Steve Masters (Products Manager)
**IT:** John Kuczora (IT Applications Manager)
**HR:** Wendy Edwards (Human Resources Manager)
**Branches:** United Agri Products Ltd, Robsheugh Farm, Robsheugh, Newcastle Upon Tyne, Tyne and Wear NE20 0JQ
**US SIC:** 5161 **UK SIC:** 61200
**Auditors:** Grant Thornton UK LLP

**Bankers:** Barclays Bank Plc (27-99-00)

| | 31-07-13 | 31-07-12 | 31-07-11 |
|---|---|---|---|
| TO | 124,285,000 | 129,143,000 | 116,499,000 |
| P/L | 4,942,000 | 10,472,000 | 4,559,000 |
| NW | 37,744,000 | 35,165,000 | 26,927,000 |
| WC | 35,913,000 | 32,476,000 | 24,314,000 |
| Emp. | 272 | 283 | 275 |

## DUNS 29-542-1242    Imp
### United Airlines Inc
(**Subsidiary of:** United Continental Holdings Inc.)
Administration Offices, Beulah Court, Horley, Surrey RH6 7HP
**Tel:** 08450264882 **Fax:** 01614368646
**Web:** www.coair.com
**Reg No:** 0012875FC **Estd:** 1994 Foreign Company
**Line of Business:** Airlines
**Principals:** F A Lorenzo (Chairman), R H Shuyler (Financial), J Smisek, C R Pohlad, J W Wilson, R L Sakowitz, J L Mckenney, M P Foret
**Co. Secretary:** Richard Shuyler
**Responsibilities**
**Senior:** R Bacoxs (Manager), Jose Carral (Director), James Compton (Director), Harold Hook (Director), James McKenney (Director), Peer Mcdonald (Director), Richard Schroeter (Vice President), Bob Schumacher (Manager)
**Finance:** Andrea Claydon (Financial Director)
**Sales:** Bob Schumacher (Manager)
**IT:** Mark Irving (IT Manager)
**HR:** Maxine Hamilton (Training Manager), Bob Schumacher (Manager)
**Facilities:** Bob Schumacher (Manager)
**Branches:** Room No 610, North Roof Office Block, Gatwick Airport.
**US SIC:** 4511 **UK SIC:** 75000

## DUNS 22-184-6962
### United Anodisers Ltd
(**Subsidiary of:** Emc Properties Ltd)
Field Mills, Red Doles Lane, Huddersfield, West Yorkshire HD2 1YG
**Tel:** 01484533142 **Fax:** 01484-435175
**Web:** www.hmfltd.co.uk
**Reg No:** 4203034 **Estd:** 2001 Private Limited Company
**Line of Business:** Metal finishing and polishing services
**Issued Capital:** £1,234,708
**Directors:** P M Watts, J P Clarke, R I Nelson
**Co. Secretary:** Robert Nelson
**Responsibilities**
**HR:** Karen Nurse (Accounts Officer)
**Branches:** United Anodisers Ltd, Wallingford Road, Uxbridge, Middlesex UB8 2SR
**US SIC:** 3398 **UK SIC:** 31380
**Auditors:** BDO LLP
**Bankers:** Bank Of Scotland (12-08-83)

| | 31-12-13 | 31-12-12 | 31-12-11 |
|---|---|---|---|
| TO | 9,803,917 | 9,574,833 | 6,558,904 |
| P/L | 2,099,764 | 1,057,885 | 742,676 |
| NW | 1,694,212 | 514,353 | 443,722 |
| WC | 1,378,414 | 284,360 | 288,447 |
| Emp. | 125 | 109 | 105 |

## DUNS 67-143-7734
### United Auctions Ltd
Stirling Agricultural Centre, Stirling, Stirlingshire FK9 4RN
**Tel:** 01786473055
**Web:** www.uagroup.co.uk
**Reg No:** 0312196SC **Estd:** 2006 Private Limited Company
**Line of Business:** Auctioneers and valuers
**Issued Capital:** £16,350
**Directors:** W R Tough, H D Leggat
**Co. Secretary:** Neil Mclean
**US SIC:** 0729 **UK SIC:** 01003
**Bankers:** Bank Of Scotland (80-91-28)

| | 31-12-13 | 31-12-12 | 31-12-11 |
|---|---|---|---|
| TO | 20,885,699 | 18,739,780 | 16,845,811 |
| P/L | 1,671,504 | 1,456,007 | 1,529,833 |
| NW | 9,964,268 | 8,688,536 | 7,628,957 |
| WC | 2,898,993 | 2,567,879 | 3,460,432 |
| Emp. | 50 | 46 | 45 |

## DUNS 39-965-0555
### United Bible Societies Association
Stonehill Green, Westlea, Swindon, Wiltshire SN5 7PJ
**Tel:** 01189-500200
**Web:** www.unitedbiblesocieties.org
**Reg No:** 2264875 **Estd:** 1988 Private Company Limited By Guarantee
**Line of Business:** Religious organisations and places of worship
**Directors:** E Ghartey, A Lamuel, R J Sandy, Dr J Henner, Dr J A Buehner, R Zimmer, M K Kotila, R Briggs
**Co. Secretary:** Mrs Calister Munjeri

## Responsibilities

**Senior:** Claude Auger (Manager), Grace Ho (Unclassified), Charles Jansz (Manager), Gerrit Kritzinger (Chief Executive), Michael Perreau (Manager), Simon Strachan (Manager), Ranutinojo Supardan (Manager)
**Operations:** Ines Galliani (Senior Manager)
**US SIC:** 8661 **UK SIC:** 96600
**Auditors:** Deloitte LLP
**Bankers:** National Westminster Bank Plc (60-17-21)
**Employees:** 163
**Turnover:** £47,174,000

DUNS 50-554-5707

## United Biscuits (Uk) Ltd

(Subsidiary of: United Biscuits Luxco Sca)
Hayes Park, Hayes End Road, Hayes, Middlesex UB4 8EE
**Tel:** 020 8234 5000
**Web:** www.unitedbiscuits.co.uk
**Reg No:** 2506007 **VAT No:** 225476656
**Estd:** 1999 Private Limited Company
**Line of Business:** Manufacturers of biscuits
**Export Sales:** £152,400,000
**Issued Capital:** £10,000,000
**Directors:** Ms H J Mccarthy, M R Glenn, J P Van Der Eems, R W Brown, S A Rose
**Co. Secretary:** Mark Oldham
**Responsibilities**
**Senior:** Susan Furst (Manager)
**Branches:** United Biscuits (Uk) Ltd, Chesterton Road, Rotherham, South Yorkshire S66 1TD
**US SIC:** 2052 **UK SIC:** 41970
**Auditors:** Ernst & Young LLP
**Bankers:** The Royal Bank Of Scotland Plc (15-10-00)
**Following financial data are in thousands**

|  | 28-12-13 | 29-12-12 | 31-12-11 |
|---|---|---|---|
| TO | 907,000 | 1,127,200 | 1,119,500 |
| P/L | 546,300 | 174,500 | 156,600 |
| NW | 1,196,300 | 648,800 | 572,000 |
| WC | 1,008,500 | 678,800 | 569,500 |
| Emp. | 4,405 | 5,869 | 6,039 |

DUNS 21-229-8911

## United Bristol Healthcare Nhs Trust

Hareclive Road, Bristol, Avon BS13 0JP
**Tel:** 01173015200
**Web:** www.bristolswpct.nhs.uk
**Line of Business:** Hospital activities
**Responsibilities**
**Senior:** Marilyn Evans (CEO, Managing Director)
**US SIC:** 8062 **UK SIC:** 95100
**Employees:** 48

DUNS 39-344-4666

## United Carlton Office Systems Ltd

(Subsidiary of: U.C.O.S. Holdings Ltd)
Meadow Court, Meadow Court, Gateshead, Tyne and Wear NE11 0PZ
**Tel:** 01914222700 **Fax:** 01914 825603
**Web:** www.united-carlton.co.uk
**Reg No:** 2118025 **VAT No:** 455067444
**Estd:** 1987 Private Limited Company
**Line of Business:** Printing not elsewhere classified
**Issued Capital:** £16,443
**Principals:** J Watson (Managing), W M Colby, M D Nelson, M A Bryce, J Ellis
**Co. Secretary:** Paul Dawson
**US SIC:** 2752 **UK SIC:** 47544
**Auditors:** Deloitte LLP
**Bankers:** Barclays Bank Plc (20-33-51)

|  | 30-06-13 | 30-06-12 | 30-06-11 |
|---|---|---|---|
| TO | 12,417,083 | 11,774,231 | 11,262,850 |
| P/L | 1,036,720 | 1,193,704 | 1,195,245 |
| NW | 4,651,914 | 3,870,546 | 2,988,246 |
| WC | 4,091,015 | 3,557,483 | 2,727,358 |
| Emp. | 65 | 64 | 64 |

DUNS 71-920-1878 — Imp

## United Carpets Group Plc

Moorhead House, Moorhead Way, Off Bawtry Road, Bramley, Rotherham, South Yorkshire S66 1YY
**Tel:** 01709-732666 **Fax:** 01709732667
**Web:** www.unitedcarpetsandbeds.net
**Reg No:** 5301665 **Estd:** 2004 Public Limited Company
**Line of Business:** Retail sale of floor coverings
**Issued Capital:** £4,070,000
**Directors:** P A Cowgill, K S Piggott, Ms D Grayson, P R Eyre
**Co. Secretary:** Ian Bowness
**US SIC:** 7399 **UK SIC:** 83954
**Auditors:** RSM Tenon Audit Ltd
**Bankers:** National Westminster Bank Plc (60-13-15)

|  | 31-03-14 | 31-03-13 | 05-03-12 |
|---|---|---|---|
| TO | 21,059,000 | 11,302,000 | N/A |
| P/L | 937,000 | 250,000 | (715,000) |
| NW | 2,958,000 | 1,826,000 | 1,669,000 |
| WC | 2,471,000 | 1,680,000 | 1,374,000 |
| Emp. | 113 | 128 | 164 |

DUNS 21-260-6623

## United Cars

Glenwood Business Centre, 25 Glenwood Place, Glasgow, Lanarkshire G45 9UH
**Tel:** 01416343514
**Estd:** 1996 Partnership
**Line of Business:** Taxicab operators
**Partners:** Ms B Thomson, P Smith
**US SIC:** 4121 **UK SIC:** 72200
**Employees:** 120

DUNS 21-819-3324 — Imp-Exp

## United Cast Bar (Uk) Ltd

(Subsidiary of: The National Industries Group)
Spital Lane, Chesterfield, Derbyshire S41 0EX
**Tel:** 01246-201194 **Fax:** 01246-236684
**Web:** www.unitedcastbar.com
**Reg No:** 0050918 **VAT No:** 114536492
**Estd:** 1897 Private Limited Company
**Line of Business:** Manufacture of basic iron and steel and of ferro-alloys
**Export Markets:** E U
**Export Sales:** £24,459,098
**Issued Capital:** £8,000,000
**Directors:** A B Rottach, P R Moore, J Brand, A M Rodger, Y M Mohsen
**Responsibilities**
**Senior:** Thomas Blum (Manager), Martin Knytl (Executive), Luca Scotto (Executive), Alfredo Tresoldi (Executive)
**Finance:** Chris Trinder (Group Financial Director)
**Marketing:** Fatima Lee (Relations Manager)
**Sales:** Mercedes Minguez (Sales Administrator), Nieves Plou (Sales Administrator), Gabriele Rajacic (Sales Manager), David Topham (Sales and Planning Coordinator)
**IT:** Chris Trinder (Group Financial Director)
**US SIC:** 3325 **UK SIC:** 31110
**Auditors:** KPMG
**Bankers:** HSBC Bank plc (40-11-04)

|  | 30-11-13 | 30-11-12 | 30-11-11 |
|---|---|---|---|
| TO | 27,311,650 | 25,484,954 | 29,935,197 |
| P/L | 2,041,202 | 1,048,855 | 3,741,809 |
| NW | 16,471,688 | 14,375,322 | 13,271,303 |
| WC | 6,615,606 | 6,900,883 | 9,345,125 |
| Emp. | 107 | 104 | 103 |

DUNS 50-331-3009

## United Central Bakeries Ltd

(Subsidiary of: Finsbury Food Group Plc)
43 Inchmuir Road, Bathgate, West Lothian EH48 2EP
**Tel:** 01506-633622 **Fax:** 01506-631266
**Web:** www.geniusglutenfree.com
**Reg No:** 0116630SC **VAT No:** 553562536
**Estd:** 1989 Private Limited Company
**Line of Business:** Bakers and confectioners supplies
**Export Sales:** £1,348,000
**Trading Style:** Genius Foods
**Issued Capital:** £111,692
**Directors:** Ms R Cuschieri, Ms S H Morse
**Co. Secretary:** Hbjg Secretarial Limited
**Responsibilities**
**Senior:** Liam McHugh (Manager)
**IT:** Derek Thomson (Project Manager)
**Branches:** United Central Bakeries Ltd, 303 Auchinairn Road, Bishopbriggs, Glasgow, Lanarkshire G64 1JJ
**US SIC:** 2051 **UK SIC:** 41960
**Auditors:** Deloitte LLP
**Bankers:** Bank Of Scotland (80-08-80)

|  | 29-06-13 | 30-06-12 | 02-06-11 |
|---|---|---|---|
| TO | 25,577,000 | 19,813,000 | 18,319,000 |
| P/L | 1,366,000 | 875,000 | 1,457,000 |
| NW | 3,074,000 | 6,986,000 | 6,479,000 |
| WC | 3,099,000 | 1,570,000 | 1,653,000 |
| Emp. | 242 | 178 | 208 |

DUNS 23-259-9100 — Imp

## United Christian Broadcasters Ltd

Hanchurch Lane Centre, Hanchurch, Stoke-On-Trent, Staffordshire ST4 8RY
**Tel:** 01782642000
**Web:** www.ucb.co.uk
**Reg No:** 2182533 **Estd:** 1987 Private Company Limited By Guarantee
**Line of Business:** Radio and television production services
**Trading Style:** U C B
**Directors:** A W Welford, Reverend D A Stacey, A K Scotland, E D Edwards, R Hay
**Co. Secretary:** Richard Willoughby
**Responsibilities**
**Senior:** Neil Elliott (Director-Broadcasting)
**IT:** Ian De'Soyza (IT Manager), Jeremy Sherlock (IT Manager)
**Health & Safety:** Deborah Roughton (Health and Safety Manager)
**Branches:** United Christian Broadcasters Ltd, P O Box 650, Belfast, Belfast BT1 2AP
**US SIC:** 4833 **UK SIC:** 97411
**Auditors:** Afford Astbury Bond

**Bankers:** HSBC Bank plc (40-23-07)

|  | 31-12-13 | 31-12-12 | 31-12-11 |
|---|---|---|---|
| TO | 8,845,707 | 8,836,937 | 9,243,624 |
| P/L | 55,751 | 330,278 | (345,011) |
| NW | 2,273,382 | 2,217,631 | 1,887,353 |
| WC | 377,517 | 374,668 | 260,827 |
| Emp. | 102 | 103 | 109 |

DUNS 29-341-0825

## United Church Schools Foundation Ltd

Fairline House, Peterborough, Cambridgeshire PE8 4HN
**Tel:** 01832864444 **Fax:** 01832-734760
**Web:** www.ult.org.uk
**Reg No:** 0018582 **VAT No:** 576756093
**Estd:** 1883 Private Limited Company
**Line of Business:** Other letting of own property
**Trading Style:** United Learning
**Issued Capital:** £64,935
**Directors:** Mrs A Crowe, M D George, M J Litchfield, N R Robson, M J Graydon, Dr S R Critchley, Sir A A Greener, J G Irwin
**Co. Secretary:** Stephen Whiffen
**Responsibilities**
**Senior:** Jen Allan (Deputy Director ? Academies)
**Marketing:** Jonathan Allen (Marketing Director)
**US SIC:** 6519 **UK SIC:** 85000
**Auditors:** Grant Thornton UK LLP
**Bankers:** National Westminster Bank Plc (53-61-33)

|  | 31-08-13 | 31-08-12 | 31-08-11 |
|---|---|---|---|
| TO | 322,727,000 | 302,614,000 | 325,687,000 |
| P/L | 47,647,000 | 51,489,000 | 85,722,000 |
| NW | 548,442,000 | 497,083,000 | 455,980,000 |
| WC | 12,176,000 | 24,806,000 | 18,583,000 |
| Emp. | 6,276 | 5,756 | 5,369 |

DUNS 50-397-3471 — Exp

## United Closures & Plastics Ltd

(Subsidiary of: Global Closure Systems Uk Ltd)
1 Steuart Road, Stirling, Stirlingshire FK9 4JG
**Tel:** 01786-833613 **Fax:** 01786-834233
**Web:** www.ucpltd.com
**Reg No:** 0119026SC **Estd:** 1989 Public Limited Company
**Line of Business:** Manufacturers of packaging materials
**Export Markets:** U S A, Europe, Asia, Africa, Worldwide
**Export Sales:** £26,625,000
**Trading Style:** U C P
**Issued Capital:** £3,509,000
**Directors:** D C Richardson, C G Voegeli, L Meyerowitz
**Co. Secretary:** Matthew Harrison
**Responsibilities**
**Facilities:** Peter MacLeod (Engineering Manager)
**Engineering:** Peter MacLeod (Engineering Manager)
**Branches:** United Closures & Plastics Ltd, U C P Plc Zeller Plastik, Salhouse Road, Norwich, Norfolk NR7 9AL
**US SIC:** 2654, 3411
**UK SIC:** 47280, 31641
**Auditors:** PricewaterhouseCoopers LLP
**Bankers:** National Westminster Bank Plc (50-00-00)

|  | 31-12-13 | 31-12-12 | 31-12-11 |
|---|---|---|---|
| TO | 97,859,000 | 90,961,000 | 92,808,000 |
| P/L | 7,034,000 | 4,969,000 | 5,764,000 |
| NW | 23,440,000 | 22,015,000 | 17,231,000 |
| WC | 1,136,000 | 2,004,000 | (2,087,000) |
| Emp. | 542 | 539 | 512 |

DUNS 23-986-8557 — Imp

## United Dairy Farmers Ltd

Dale Farm House, Belfast BT3 9LS
**Tel:** 02890372237
**Web:** www.utdni.co.uk
**Reg No:** 0000350IP **Estd:** 1995 Friendly Society
**Line of Business:** Dairy farmers
**Principals:** J R Hamilton (Chairman), J A Walker, O R Gault, R Harpur, R J Kelso, F Ledwidge, J Warden, W Morton
**Co. Secretary:** S Agnew
**Responsibilities**
**Senior:** D Adair (Principal), David Dobbin (Chief Executive Officer), David Mcneill (Director), Billy Morton (Director)
**IT:** Sean McLaughlin (IT Manager)
**US SIC:** 0241 **UK SIC:** 01001
**Auditors:** Ernst & Young LLP
**Bankers:** First Trust Bank (aib Group (uk) Plc) (93-83-19)
**Employees:** 817
**Turnover:** £269,273,000

DUNS 50-568-7236 — Imp

## United Fillings Ltd

27 Vine Street, Billingborough, Sleaford, Lincolnshire NG34 0QE
**Tel:** 01529-240207
**Web:** www.unitedfillings.co.uk
**Reg No:** 2516423 **VAT No:** 568007337
**Estd:** 1990 Private Limited Company
**Line of Business:** Representative office
**Export Sales:** £45,229
**Issued Capital:** £44,118
**Principals:** N W Prue (Managing), P D Herszaft
**Co. Secretary:** Nigel Prue
**Responsibilities**
**Senior:** Nigel Crewe (Manager), Linda Prue (Human Resources Manager), Lloyd Walker (Transport Manager)
**Finance:** Sylvia Banks (Financial Controller)
**HR:** Linda Prue (Human Resources Manager)
**Health & Safety:** Linda Prue (Human Resources Manager)
**Facilities:** Linda Prue (Human Resources Manager)
**Fleet:** Lloyd Walker (Transport Manager)
**Branches:** United Fillings Ltd, Goodwin Mills, Bridge Street, Nottingham, Nottinghamshire NG10 4QT
**US SIC:** 2392 **UK SIC:** 45550
**Auditors:** PKF
**Bankers:** National Westminster Bank Plc (51-81-08)

|  | 31-07-13 | 31-07-12 | 31-07-11 |
|---|---|---|---|
| TO | 8,102,028 | 7,667,212 | 8,256,994 |
| P/L | 259,575 | 223,534 | 117,669 |
| NW | 4,729,747 | 4,482,717 | 4,265,767 |
| WC | 4,095,787 | 3,838,846 | 3,661,088 |
| Emp. | 128 | 133 | 134 |

DUNS 23-079-5999 — Imp

## United Fish Industries (U K) Ltd

(Subsidiary of: United Fish Industries)
Gilbey Road, Grimsby, South Humberside DN31 2SL
**Tel:** 01472263333 **Fax:** 01472-263444
**Web:** www.iaws.ie
**Reg No:** 2746845 **Estd:** 1993 Private Limited Company
**Line of Business:** Agricultural services
**Export Sales:** £2,016,000
**Issued Capital:** £50
**Directors:** M Mcellone, A Hoddevik
**Co. Secretary:** Michael Mcellone
**Responsibilities**
**Senior:** Michael Haryskowian (General Manager), Stephanie Snowden (Office Manager)
**Branches:** United Fish Industries (U K) Ltd, 8 Reclaimed Ground, Fraserburgh, Aberdeenshire AB43 9TD
**US SIC:** 2047, 5149
**UK SIC:** 42221, 61700
**Auditors:** PricewaterhouseCoopers
**Bankers:** National Westminster Bank Plc (60-30-22)

|  | 31-12-13 | 31-12-12 | 31-12-11 |
|---|---|---|---|
| TO | 37,798,000 | 33,450,000 | 32,324,000 |
| P/L | 4,119,000 | 3,708,000 | 3,625,000 |
| NW | 10,841,000 | 10,528,000 | 9,718,000 |
| WC | 43,000 | 1,469,000 | 3,763,000 |
| Emp. | 58 | 59 | 60 |

DUNS 21-588-2119 — Imp-Exp

## United Fish Products Ltd

(Subsidiary of: United Fish Industries)
Greenwell Place, East Tullos Industrial Estate, Aberdeen, Aberdeenshire AB12 3AY
**Tel:** 01224-854444
**Web:** www.ufp.co.uk
**Reg No:** 0074108SC **VAT No:** 945621709
**Estd:** 1981 Private Limited Company
**Line of Business:** Animal feed and pet foods
**Trading Style:** United Fish Industries Uk Ltd
**Issued Capital:** £422,000
**Directors:** A Hoddevik, M Mcellone
**Co. Secretary:** Michael Mcellone
**Responsibilities**
**Senior:** Marshall Harper (Production Manager), Michael Macellone (Financial Controller), Tom Tynan (Manager)
**Finance:** Michael Macellone (Financial Controller), Michael Rafferty (Financial Director), Tom Tynan (Manager)
**Facilities:** Marshall Harper (Production Manager)
**Engineering:** Marshall Harper (Production Manager)
**US SIC:** 2047, 2048
**UK SIC:** 42221, 42210
**Bankers:** National Westminster Bank Plc (60-30-22)
**Employees:** 55

DUNS 77-121-0135
## United Fork Trucks (1992) Ltd
St Helens House, St Helens Way, Thetford, Norfolk IP24 1HG
**Tel:** 01842754841
**Web:** www.unitedforktrucks.co.uk
**Reg No:** 2693495 **VAT No:** 571361743
**Estd:** 1992 Private Limited Company
**Line of Business:** Renting of other land transport equipment
**Trading Style:** United Fork Trucks 1992
**Issued Capital:** £837
**Principals:** C J Compson *(Financial)*, M R Underwood
**Co. Secretary:** Paul Nichol
**Responsibilities**
**Senior:** Jason Hole *(Stores Manager)*
**IT:** Freda Glanville *(IT Manager)*
**Facilities:** Rod Forder *(Maintenance Manager)*
**Branches:** United Fork Trucks (1992) Ltd, Northern Court Vernon Road, Nottingham, Nottinghamshire NG6 0BJ
**US SIC:** 7513 **UK SIC:** 84802
**Auditors:** Stacey & Partners
**Bankers:** National Westminster Bank Plc (60-04-16)

| | 30-04-14 | 30-04-13 | 30-04-12 |
|---|---|---|---|
| TO | 6,513,906 | 5,521,337 | 6,286,601 |
| P/L | (60,693) | (110,584) | 82,501 |
| NW | 1,335,872 | 1,378,340 | 1,449,801 |
| WC | (87,327) | 27,965 | 149,742 |
| Emp. | 92 | 90 | 92 |

DUNS 34-971-1254
## United Health Group Ltd
The Old Coach House, Gainsborough Road, Lincoln, Lincolnshire LN1 2JJ
**Tel:** 01522-560951
**Reg No:** 5766627 **Estd:** 2006 Private Limited Company
**Line of Business:** Construction of commercial buildings
**Trading Style:** United Health Group Ltd
**Issued Capital:** £900
**Directors:** C R Jackson, P J Pearson, I R Pullan, Mrs M T Cheriton-Metcalfe
**Co. Secretary:** Michael Brown
**US SIC:** 1541, 8091
**UK SIC:** 50100, 95200
**Bankers:** National Westminster Bank Plc (56-00-29)

| | 31-01-14 | 31-01-13 | 31-01-12 |
|---|---|---|---|
| TO | 13,022,813 | 10,824,517 | 9,079,638 |
| P/L | 1,091,263 | 572,289 | (366,374) |
| NW | 7,283,323 | 2,163,038 | 1,769,136 |
| WC | (8,966) | (3,248,824) | (3,468,010) |
| Emp. | 505 | 459 | 454 |

DUNS 71-934-4538
## United Holdings Uk Ltd.
246 Flemington Street, Glasgow, Lanarkshire G21 4BY
**Tel:** 0141-557-2255
**Reg No:** 0277568SC **Estd:** 2004 Private Limited Company
**Line of Business:** Non-specialised wholesale of food, beverages and tobacco
**Issued Capital:** £5,500
**Directors:** M Ramzan, N Ramzan
**Co. Secretary:** Kamran Javed
**US SIC:** 5149 **UK SIC:** 61700
**Auditors:** KKMJ (UK) LLP
**Bankers:** Clydesdale Bank Plc (82-20-00)

| | 31-12-13 | 31-12-12 | 31-12-11 |
|---|---|---|---|
| TO | 128,350,531 | 131,524,536 | 125,159,690 |
| P/L | 938,836 | 1,618,469 | 1,437,373 |
| NW | 9,197,960 | 8,711,546 | 7,676,307 |
| WC | 478,893 | (367,697) | (1,158,983) |
| Emp. | 144 | 146 | 146 |

DUNS 85-611-4038
## United Home Services Ltd
**(Subsidiary of:** Uls Technology Plc)
The Old Grammar School, Thame, Oxfordshire OX9 3AJ
**Tel:** 01844-265385 **Fax:** 01844265371
**Web:** www.econveyancer.com
**Reg No:** 6204972 **Estd:** 2007 Private Limited Company
**Line of Business:** Real estate agencies
**Trading Style:** Ehips Limited
**Issued Capital:** £100
**Directors:** N J Ainger, B D Thompson, N P Hoath
**Co. Secretary:** Andrew Weston
**US SIC:** 6531 **UK SIC:** 83400

| | 31-03-14 | 31-03-13 | 31-03-12 |
|---|---|---|---|
| TO | 90,494 | 25,901 | 85,338 |
| P/L | (107,590) | (14,967) | 3,284 |
| NW | (218,992) | (142,911) | (96,435) |
| WC | (219,152) | (143,465) | (97,759) |

DUNS 77-547-7888
## United House Group Ltd
**(Subsidiary of:** United House Group Holdings Ltd)
United House, Goldsel Road, Swanley, Kent BR8 8EX
**Tel:** 01322665522
**Web:** www.unitedhouse.net
**Reg No:** 2998303 **Estd:** 1994 Private Limited Company
**Line of Business:** Management activities of holding companies
**Issued Capital:** £1,828,000
**Directors:** T N Wood, I G Burnett, S W Laird, J W Adams
**Responsibilities**
**Senior:** Keith Allington *(Manager)*, Sharon Carter *(Executive)*, Stephen Halbert *(Non Executive Chairman)*, Vicki Haynes *(Manager)*, Andrew Mickleburgh *(Managing Director, United Hous)*, Nick Stonley *(Managing Director, United Hous)*, Martyn Vitty *(Director)*
**Marketing:** Antony Crovella *(Sales and Marketing Director)*
**Sales:** Antony Crovella *(Sales and Marketing Director)*
**Admin:** Susan Briggs *(Legal Secretary)*, Debbie Chapman *(Managing Director PA)*, Damon Potter *(IT Administrator)*, Trudy Rowland *(Managing Director PA)*
**IT:** Damon Potter *(IT Administrator)*
**Engineering:** John Coveney *(Head of Design and Technical M)*, Bill Kelso *(Design Manager)*
**Branches:** United House Group Ltd, Markenfield Villa, Markenfield Road, Guildford, Surrey GU1 4PF
**US SIC:** 6711 **UK SIC:** 83962
**Auditors:** KPMG LLP
**Bankers:** HSBC Bank plc (40-15-05)

| | 31-12-13 | 31-12-12 | 31-12-11 |
|---|---|---|---|
| TO | N/A | 181,118,000 | 222,897,000 |
| P/L | 16,812,000 | 21,385,000 | 14,786,000 |
| NW | 20,081,000 | 61,592,000 | 44,149,000 |
| WC | 18,252,000 | 49,004,000 | 37,646,000 |
| Emp. | 3 | 324 | 374 |

DUNS 23-954-0565
## United Iff Ltd
**(Subsidiary of:** Interbulk Group Plc)
4 Beacon Way, Hull, North Humberside HU3 4AE
**Tel:** 01482223428
**Reg No:** 3943342 **Estd:** 2000 Private Limited Company
**Line of Business:** Distribution service providers
**Trading Style:** Interbult Group
**Issued Capital:** £1
**Directors:** S T Cunningham, L F Kullberg
**US SIC:** 4213 **UK SIC:** 72300

| | 30-09-13 | 30-09-12 | 30-09-11 |
|---|---|---|---|
| TA | 1 | 1 | 1 |
| NW | 1 | 1 | 1 |

DUNS 21-036-8996
## United International College
Language House, 76-78 Mortimer Street, London W1W 7SA
**Tel:** 02070793333
**Web:** www.uiclondon.com
**Estd:** 2006 Proprietorship
**Line of Business:** Language schools
**Proprietor:** N Opton
**Responsibilities**
**Senior:** Claire Woollam *(Principal)*
**US SIC:** 8249 **UK SIC:** 93300
**Employees:** 50

DUNS 22-727-1541 **Imp-Exp**
## United International Pictures
**(Subsidiary of:** United International Pictures B.V.)
Building 5, Oakleigh Road South North London, Business Park, London N11 1GN
**Tel:** 02031842500
**Web:** www.uip.com
**Reg No:** 1683912 **VAT No:** 386151736
**Estd:** 1982 Private Unlimited Company
**Line of Business:** Film distributors
**Trading Style:** U I P
**Issued Capital:** £100,000
**Directors:** Miss E Por, I F H International Film Holding, United International Pictures B
**Co. Secretary:** Miss Hayley Coleman
**Responsibilities**
**Senior:** John Holgan *(Manager)*
**Marketing:** Claire Backhouse *(Marketing Manager)*
**Facilities:** Mark Furmston *(Facilities Manager)*
**Branches:** United International Pictures, 12 Golden Square, London W1F 9JD
**US SIC:** 7829 **UK SIC:** 97112
**Auditors:** PricewaterhouseCoopers
**Bankers:** National Westminster Bank Plc (60-50-06)
**Employees:** 280

DUNS 50-964-4068
## United Jewish Israel Appeal
37 Kentish Town Road, London NW1 8NX
**Tel:** 02074246400 **Fax:** 02074246401
**Web:** www.ujia.org
**Reg No:** 3295115 **Estd:** 1996 Private Company Limited By Guarantee
**Line of Business:** Social work activities
**Trading Style:** The United Jewish Israel Appeal
**Directors:** J S Morris, W S Benjamin, W A Persky, J M Isaacs, K J Black, J L Burchell, Mrs K Harris, S M Levy
**Co. Secretary:** Maurice Stone
**Responsibilities**
**Senior:** Mick Davis *(Chairman)*, Alexander Dwek *(Director)*, David Goldberg *(Communications Director)*, Geoffrey Ognall *(Director)*, Michael Wegier *(Chief Executive)*
**Finance:** Eyal Samuel *(Financial Director)*
**Marketing:** Zac Gazit *(Director of MG Development, He)*, David Goldberg *(Communications Director)*, Debbie Joseph *(Marketing Manager)*
**Admin:** Etty Gafan *(Administration Coordinator)*
**HR:** Cyndy Bloom *(Human Resources Manager)*, Emma Collins *(Human Resources Manager)*, Nicky Goldman *(Human Resources Manager)*
**Health & Safety:** Valentina Rapuano *(Facilities Coordinator)*
**Facilities:** Valentina Rapuano *(Facilities Coordinator)*
**Branches:** United Jewish Israel Appeal, Balfour House, 399 Street Lane, Leeds, West Yorkshire LS17 6HQ
**US SIC:** 8999 **UK SIC:** 83954
**Auditors:** Horwath Clark Whitehill
**Bankers:** Barclays Bank Plc (20-00-50)

| | 30-09-13 | 30-09-12 | 30-09-11 |
|---|---|---|---|
| TO | 10,180,000 | 10,275,000 | 12,437,000 |
| P/L | (481,000) | (2,875,000) | (1,504,000) |
| NW | 9,588,000 | 10,069,000 | 12,944,000 |
| WC | 9,340,000 | 9,774,000 | 12,648,000 |
| Emp. | 56 | 58 | 81 |

DUNS 73-935-9396
## United Kenning Rental Group Ltd
**(Subsidiary of:** Sixt Se)
Durrant House, Chesterfield, Derbyshire S41 7SJ
**Tel:** 01246282000 **Fax:** 01246-506118
**Web:** www.urg.co.uk
**Reg No:** 2942541 **Estd:** 1991 Private Limited Company
**Line of Business:** Renting of automobiles
**Trading Style:** United Kenning Group
**Issued Capital:** £1,298,306
**Directors:** D K Paetsch, I W Lawrence, Miss W - Fung, Dr J Z Putlitz
**Co. Secretary:** Ian Lawrence
**Responsibilities**
**Senior:** Karen Blow *(Rental Services Manager)*
**Branches:** United Kenning Rental Group Ltd, Durrant House, 47 Holywell Street, Chesterfield, Derbyshire S41 7SJ
**US SIC:** 7512 **UK SIC:** 84801
**Auditors:** Deloitte LLP
**Bankers:** Barclays Bank Plc (20-07-71)

| | 31-12-13 | 31-12-12 | 31-12-11 |
|---|---|---|---|
| TO | 64,337,000 | 54,127,000 | 46,139,000 |
| P/L | 10,015,000 | 5,765,000 | 7,511,000 |
| NW | 47,125,000 | 37,738,000 | 31,240,000 |
| WC | (50,856,000) | (44,482,000) | (26,200,000) |
| Emp. | 352 | 307 | 256 |

DUNS 49-050-5294 **Exp**
## United Kingdom Accreditation Service
Accreditation House, 21-47 High Street, Feltham, Middlesex TW13 4UN
**Tel:** 020-8917-8400
**Web:** www.ukas.com
**Reg No:** 3076190 **Estd:** 1995 Private Company Limited By Guarantee
**Line of Business:** Calibration equipment services
**Export Sales:** £2,630,309
**Directors:** P Stennett, Ms S Leather, Sir P R Judge, Professor M R Mainelli, Sir D K Nichol, Mrs G Alsop, J R Lindsay
**Co. Secretary:** Mrs Georgia Alsop
**Responsibilities**
**Senior:** Richard Crookes *(Manager)*, John Hurll *(Assessment Manager)*, Sylvia Paice *(Office Manager)*, Jeff Ruddle *(Board Member)*
**Marketing:** Malcolm Hynd *(External Affairs Manager)*, Jon Murthy *(Communications Manager)*
**Admin:** Sylvia Paice *(Office Manager)*
**IT:** Tony Vernel *(Business Information Manager)*
**HR:** Debbie Bartlett *(Personnel Manager)*
**Health & Safety:** Sylvia Paice *(Office Manager)*
**Facilities:** Sylvia Paice *(Office Manager)*
**Operations:** Rob Bettinson *(Accreditation Manager)*, Lal Ilan *(Accreditation Manager)*, Jon Murthy *(Communications Manager)*
**Purchasing:** Sylvia Paice *(Office Manager)*
**Engineering:** Kevin Belson *(Technical Manager)*
**Branches:** United Kingdom Accreditation Service, Queens Rd, Teddington, Middlesex TW11 0LW
**US SIC:** 8621 **UK SIC:** 96311
**Auditors:** Oury Clark
**Bankers:** HSBC Bank plc (40-07-13)

| | 31-03-14 | 31-03-13 | 31-03-12 |
|---|---|---|---|
| TO | 23,453,166 | 21,838,165 | 19,345,257 |
| P/L | 1,235,473 | 1,881,801 | 884,399 |
| NW | 3,038,487 | 1,153,777 | 182,112 |
| WC | 5,229,488 | 4,496,804 | 3,271,013 |
| Emp. | 206 | 178 | 178 |

DUNS 21-175-7007 **Imp**
## United Kingdom Anti-Doping Ltd
1a Cockspur Street, London SW1Y 5BG
**Tel:** 02078423450 **Fax:** 020 7766 7351
**Web:** www.ukad.org.uk
**Reg No:** 6990867 **Estd:** 2009 Private Company Limited By Guarantee
**Line of Business:** Manufacture of trailers and semi-trailers
**Directors:** Professor J Brewer, A J Sellers, D R Kenworthy, Ms J B Shardlow, P G Carling, Dr. J J Turner, M T Brace
**US SIC:** 7399, 9121, 7999
**UK SIC:** 83954, 91110, 97913
**Auditors:** Comptroller & Auditor General

| | 31-03-14 | 31-03-13 | 31-03-12 |
|---|---|---|---|
| TO | 1,421,000 | 1,322,000 | 955,000 |
| P/L | (6,257,000) | (6,591,000) | (6,588,000) |
| NW | (408,000) | (220,000) | (283,000) |
| WC | 12,000 | (25,000) | (23,000) |
| Emp. | 47 | 46 | 48 |

DUNS 21-596-6038
## United Kingdom Border Agency
North Terminal, London Gatwick Airport, Horley, Surrey RH6 0PJ
**Tel:** 01293507075
**Web:** www.ukba.homeoffice.gov.uk
**Estd:** 2011
**Line of Business:** Immigration advice & services
**Responsibilities**
**Senior:** Dean Oughton *(Assistant Director)*
**US SIC:** 9121 **UK SIC:** 91110
**Employees:** 300

DUNS 23-668-1297
## The United Kingdom Committee for Unicef
Unicef House, London EC1V 0DU
**Tel:** 02074902388 **Fax:** 02072501733
**Web:** www.unicef.org.uk
**Reg No:** 3663181 **Estd:** 2012 Private Company Limited By Guarantee
**Line of Business:** Charities and charitable organisations
**Trading Style:** Unicef Uk
**Directors:** Sir A G Redmond, R G Isherwood, Baroness D E Massey, Baroness S V Brinton, Professor M J Renfrew, R L Scott, Professor M Woodhead, G M Badman
**Co. Secretary:** David Bull
**Responsibilities**
**Senior:** Margaret Cund *(Director)*, Ilse Howling *(Director)*, Anne Jenkin *(Director)*, Surinder Sharma *(Director)*
**Finance:** William Cottle *(Financial Director)*
**Marketing:** Joe English *(Media Officer)*, Liz Jones *(Media Officer)*, Alice Klein *(Senior Media Manager)*, Debbie Stokes *(Head of Marketing)*, Helen Wylie *(Media Manager)*
**Admin:** Amanda Bourne *(Office Manager)*
**IT:** Phil Durbin *(Head of IT)*, Bonny Turner *(Database Support Officer)*
**HR:** Helen Griffin *(Head of Personnel)*
**Health & Safety:** Amanda Bourne *(Office Manager)*
**Facilities:** Amanda Bourne *(Office Manager)*
**Branches:** The United Kingdom Committee For Unicef, Unit 1 Industrial Estate, Rignals Lane, Chelmsford, Essex CM2 8TU
**US SIC:** 8249, 8091, 8321
**UK SIC:** 93300, 95200, 96111
**Auditors:** Sayer Vincent
**Bankers:** HSBC Bank plc (40-06-02)

| | 31-12-13 | 31-12-12 | 31-12-11 |
|---|---|---|---|
| TO | 79,120,000 | 62,326,000 | 95,013,000 |
| P/L | 804,000 | 903,000 | 116,000 |
| NW | 4,615,000 | 3,811,000 | 2,908,000 |
| WC | 3,391,000 | 2,334,000 | 1,071,000 |
| Emp. | 216 | 203 | 200 |

DUNS 76-837-2559

## The United Kingdom Science Park Association

Garden Cottage, Chesterford Research Park, Little Chesterford, Saffron Walden, Essex CB10 1XL
**Web:** www.ukspa.org.uk
**Reg No:** 2601480 **Estd:** 1991 Private Limited Company
**Line of Business:** Activities of business and employers organisations
**Directors:** P J Bonnett, J Chaffer, Mrs T L Smith, G A Walker, Mrs S A Forsyth, Ms C Johns, Dr D J Hardman, M R Watley
**Co. Secretary:** George Walker
**Responsibilities**
**Senior:** David Gillham *(Manager)*, David Lupson *(Manager)*, Caroline Mairs *(Director)*, Malcolm Parry *(Manager)*
**US SIC:** 8611 **UK SIC:** 96312
**Bankers:** HSBC Bank plc (40-11-36)

| | 31-03-14 | 31-03-13 | 31-03-12 |
|---|---|---|---|
| TA | 242,898 | 226,091 | 181,003 |
| NW | 92,629 | 71,322 | 63,995 |
| WC | 88,611 | 69,371 | 61,892 |

DUNS 42-452-1461

## United Learning Trust

Nene Valley Business Park, Oundle, Peterborough, Cambridgeshire PE8 4HN
**Tel:** 01832-735105 **Fax:** 01832-734760
**Web:** www.ucstrust.org.uk
**Reg No:** 4439859 **Estd:** 2002 Private Company Limited By Guarantee
**Line of Business:** General secondary education
**Trading Style:** Barnsley Academy, Carter Community School
**Directors:** N R Robson, Sir A A Greener, Dame Y Bevan, Mrs A Crowe, J A Coles, D B Robinson, M D George, M J Graydon
**Co. Secretary:** Stephen Whiffen
**Branches:** United Learning Trust, Blandford Close, Poole, Dorset BH15 4BQ
**US SIC:** 8211, 8299
**UK SIC:** 93200, 93300
**Auditors:** Grant Thornton UK LLP
**Bankers:** Barclays Bank Plc (20-00-00)

| | 31-08-13 | 31-08-12 | 31-08-11 |
|---|---|---|---|
| TO | 201,143,000 | 184,048,000 | 129,495,000 |
| P/L | 49,910,000 | 47,093,000 | (6,285,000) |
| NW | 381,742,000 | 328,830,000 | 289,606,000 |
| WC | 17,675,000 | 21,737,000 | 19,265,000 |
| Emp. | 3,495 | 3,113 | 2,365 |

DUNS 23-770-5207

## United Marine Aggregates Ltd

(**Subsidiary of:** Lafarge Tarmac Holdings Ltd)
Uma House, Shopwyke Road, Chichester, West Sussex PO20 2AD
**Tel:** 01243-817200
**Web:** www.uma.co.uk
**Reg No:** 2336081 **Estd:** 1989 Private Limited Company
**Line of Business:** Other wholesale
**Trading Style:** Tarmac Limited
**Issued Capital:** £100
**Directors:** Lafarge Tarmac Directors (Uk) Li, Mrs F P Penhallurick
**Co. Secretary:** Lafarge Tarmac Secretaries (Uk)
**Branches:** United Marine Aggregates Ltd, Marine Pde, Southampton, Hampshire SO14 5JF
**US SIC:** 5199 **UK SIC:** 61900
**Auditors:** Deloitte & Touche
**Bankers:** National Westminster Bank Plc (56-00-61)

| | 31-12-13 | 31-12-12 | 31-12-11 |
|---|---|---|---|
| TA | 7,489,000 | 7,489,000 | 7,489,000 |
| NW | 49,000 | 49,000 | 49,000 |
| WC | (1,951,000) | (1,951,000) | (1,951,000) |
| Emp. | N/A | N/A | 3 |

DUNS 21-671-5299

## United Minicab Services Ltd

363 Cambridge Heath Road, London E2 9RA
**Tel:** 02077293355
**Web:** www.unitedminicab.co.uk
**Reg No:** 7241500 **Estd:** 2010 Private Limited Company
**Line of Business:** Taxis and private hire vehicles
**Issued Capital:** £1
**Director:** A H Choudhury
**Co. Secretary:** Anisul Choudhury
**US SIC:** 4121 **UK SIC:** 72200

| | 31-05-13 | 31-05-12 | 31-05-11 |
|---|---|---|---|
| TA | 990 | 466 | 1,391 |
| NW | (1,889) | (1,744) | 167 |
| WC | (1,889) | (1,744) | 167 |

DUNS 23-569-7703

## United Molasses Purchasing Ltd

(**Subsidiary of:** W & R Barnett Ltd)
48 Gracechurch Street, London EC3V 0EJ
**Tel:** 02072839244 **Fax:** 020-7480-6611
**Web:** www.umgroup.com
**Reg No:** 1531255 **Estd:** 1980 Private Limited Company
**Line of Business:** Wholesale of grain, seeds and animal feeds
**Trading Style:** United Molasses Group Limited
**Issued Capital:** £101
**Directors:** W B Barnett, B N Mcdonnell, C F Roberts
**Co. Secretary:** Geoffrey Jordan
**Responsibilities**
**Senior:** Trevor Wiggins *(Credit Manager)*
**Finance:** Trevor Wiggins *(Credit Manager)*
**Branches:** United Molasses Purchasing Ltd, Royal Portbury Dock, Bristol, Avon BS20 7XW
**US SIC:** 5153 **UK SIC:** 61100

| | 31-07-13 | 31-07-12 | 31-07-11 |
|---|---|---|---|
| TA | 131 | 131 | 17,481 |
| NW | 131 | 131 | 17,481 |

DUNS 22-127-8331

## United National Bank Ltd

(**Subsidiary of:** United Bank Ltd)
2 Brook Street, London W1S 1BQ
**Tel:** 02072908000
**Web:** www.unbankltd.com
**Reg No:** 4146820 **Estd:** 2001 Private Limited Company
**Line of Business:** Banks and financial institutions
**Issued Capital:** £30,000,004
**Directors:** M Kamal, W Husain, S A Ashraf, M M Khan, M Aslam, R B Wilton
**Co. Secretary:** Brian Firth
**Responsibilities**
**Senior:** Rayomond Kotwal *(Director)*
**Finance:** Santanu Kapas *(Credit Administrator)*, Nejib Rahman *(Head of Commercial and Retail)*
**Sales:** Nejib Rahman *(Head of Commercial and Retail)*
**HR:** Jas Bolla *(Head of Human Resources)*
**Branches:** United National Bank Ltd, 35-36 Lowndes Square, London SW1X 9JN
**US SIC:** 6012 **UK SIC:** 81402
**Auditors:** BDO LLP

| | 31-12-13 | 31-12-12 | 31-12-11 |
|---|---|---|---|
| TA | 379,478,094 | 394,147,771 | 209,012,920 |
| P/L | 6,220,521 | 1,340,848 | 74,745 |
| NW | 45,286,705 | 48,783,146 | 44,965,697 |
| WC | 25,837,655 | 26,709,054 | 20,593,295 |
| Emp. | 84 | 80 | 78 |

DUNS 77-945-8652

## United Optical Industries Ltd

(**Subsidiary of:** Seckloe 270 Ltd)
583 Moseley Road, Birmingham, West Midlands B12 9BL
**Fax:** 01214-499993
**Web:** www.godeolali.co.uk
**Reg No:** 3052147 **Estd:** 1995 Private Limited Company
**Line of Business:** Restaurant - indian
**Trading Style:** Birmingham Optical
**Issued Capital:** £2,787,418
**Directors:** N Townsend, C Tyler
**US SIC:** 6711 **UK SIC:** 83962
**Auditors:** Ernst & Young LLP
**Bankers:** Barclays Bank Plc (20-55-34)

| | 31-10-13 | 31-10-12 | 31-10-11 |
|---|---|---|---|
| TA | 5,600,000 | 5,600,000 | 5,600,000 |
| NW | (4,194,000) | (4,194,000) | (4,194,000) |
| WC | (4,194,000) | (4,194,000) | (4,194,000) |

DUNS 22-087-8305

## United Pallet Network (Uk) Ltd

(**Subsidiary of:** March (Holdings) Ltd)
Asfordby Business Park, Melton Mowbray, Leicestershire LE14 3JL
**Tel:** 08702413482 **Fax:** 0870-241-3483
**Web:** www.u-p-n.co.uk
**Reg No:** 4089198 **Estd:** 2001 Private Limited Company
**Line of Business:** Distribution service providers
**Issued Capital:** £1,854
**Directors:** Ms L Urwin, N Chappelow, D H Clarkson, A Spencer, G P Boldy, M B Chapman, D J Brown, A J Lowe
**Responsibilities**
**Finance:** Geoffrey Allard *(Finance Director)*
**Marketing:** Cathy Whittall *(Marketing Manager)*
**US SIC:** 4213 **UK SIC:** 72300
**Bankers:** HSBC Bank plc (40-46-03)

| | 31-03-14 | 31-03-13 | 31-03-12 |
|---|---|---|---|
| TO | 5,871,712 | N/A | N/A |
| P/L | 1,406,600 | N/A | N/A |
| NW | 2,692,636 | 2,092,711 | 1,590,201 |
| WC | 2,492,677 | 1,901,729 | 1,420,105 |
| Emp. | 71 | N/A | N/A |

DUNS 34-952-0903

## United Pallets (Scotland) Ltd

Buchanan Business Park, Cumbernauld Road, Stepps, Glasgow, Lanarkshire G33 6HZ
**Tel:** 01417798250
**Web:** www.unitedpallets.co.uk
**Reg No:** 0299210SC **Estd:** 2006 Private Limited Company
**Line of Business:** Other scheduled air transport
**Issued Capital:** £2
**Director:** A B Booth
**Co. Secretary:** Ms Teresa Mckeown
**US SIC:** 4511 **UK SIC:** 75000

| | 31-03-14 | 31-03-13 | 31-03-12 |
|---|---|---|---|
| TA | 1,357,248 | 916,957 | 729,419 |
| NW | 58,456 | 126,225 | 65,444 |
| WC | (82,996) | 19,251 | (122,405) |

DUNS 28-829-8649

## The United Reformed Church Trust

Church House, London WC1H 9RT
**Tel:** 020-7916-2020
**Web:** www.urc.org.uk
**Reg No:** 0135934 **Estd:** 1914 Private Company Limited By Guarantee
**Line of Business:** Activities of religious organisations
**Trading Style:** U.R.C., United Reformed Church
**Directors:** M Hopkins, Mrs M M Thompson, R G Gray, J Proctor, Rev M J Davies, N M Mackenzie, A C Forsyth, P M Pay
**Co. Secretary:** Ms Sandi Hallam-Jones
**Responsibilities**
**Senior:** Andrew Atkinson *(Director)*, Jane Baird *(Director)*, Claudette Binns *(Manager)*, James Breslin *(Manager)*, David Grosch-Miller *(Director)*, Gwen Morrison *(Director)*, Charles Pearce *(Manager)*, Roberta Rominger *(General Secretary)*, Isobel Simmons *(Manager)*, Andrew Summers *(Director)*, Brian Woodhall *(Manager)*
**Finance:** Andrew Grimwade *(Financial Accountant)*
**Marketing:** Martin Hazell *(Director of Communications)*, Gill Nichol *(Interim Director of Communicat)*
**Branches:** The United Reformed Church Trust, 6 Honeypot Lane, Basildon, Essex SS14 2JZ
**US SIC:** 8661 **UK SIC:** 96600
**Auditors:** PricewaterhouseCoopers LLP
**Bankers:** HSBC Bank plc (40-03-28)

| | 31-12-13 | 31-12-12 | 31-12-11 |
|---|---|---|---|
| TO | 27,286,000 | 29,954,000 | 27,133,000 |
| P/L | 2,628,000 | 3,816,000 | 736,000 |
| NW | 50,308,000 | 42,892,000 | 44,393,000 |
| WC | 7,567,000 | 8,933,000 | 6,536,000 |
| Emp. | N/A | 617 | 649 |

DUNS 28-877-7147

## United Response

Vantage House, 1 Weir Road, Wimbledon, London SW19 8UX
**Fax:** 020-8780-9538
**Web:** www.unitedresponse.org.uk
**Reg No:** 1133776 **Estd:** 1973 Private Company Limited By Guarantee
**Line of Business:** Charities and charitable organisations
**Directors:** Ms S Jagelman, B D Aird, W J Churchill, D C Aitman, M E Rumbold, Ms S B Hannington, Ms K M Clifford, P Shah
**Co. Secretary:** Ms Clare Million
**Responsibilities**
**Senior:** Ian Mcleish *(Director)*
**Marketing:** Diane Lightfoot *(Head of Fundraising)*
**Operations:** Diane Lightfoot *(Head of Fundraising)*
**Branches:** United Response, Armstrong Street, Gateshead, Tyne and Wear NE8 4YW
**US SIC:** 8321, 6732
**UK SIC:** 96111, 83100
**Auditors:** Kingston Smith LLP
**Bankers:** Lloyds TSB Bank plc (30-95-74)

| | 31-03-14 | 31-03-13 | 31-03-12 |
|---|---|---|---|
| TO | 76,992,000 | 76,776,000 | 69,124,000 |
| P/L | 208,000 | 3,345,000 | 4,010,000 |
| NW | 26,766,000 | 26,380,000 | 22,645,000 |
| WC | 13,607,000 | 12,889,000 | 11,451,000 |
| Emp. | 3,368 | 3,313 | 3,007 |

DUNS 21-696-3851

## United Steels Holding Co Ltd

Gibbons Industrial Park, Dudley Road, Brierley Hill, West Midlands DY6 8XF
**Tel:** 01384401166
**Web:** www.unitedsteels.com
**Reg No:** 7423677 **VAT No:** 632198342
**Estd:** 2010 Private Limited Company
**Line of Business:** Other letting of own property
**Issued Capital:** £1,001
**Directors:** G J Cashmore, Mrs M T Cashmore, J C Cashmore, Mrs K Tiltman, G Dudley, R G Cashmore

**US SIC:** 6519 **UK SIC:** 85000
**Auditors:** Price Pearson

| | 31-12-13 | 31-12-12 | 31-12-11 |
|---|---|---|---|
| TO | 41,040,669 | 49,751,233 | 48,759,109 |
| P/L | (3,058,288) | (702,674) | 593,216 |
| NW | 2,140,938 | 3,957,526 | 4,446,315 |
| WC | (6,263,333) | (5,918,508) | (3,998,252) |
| Emp. | 225 | 192 | 180 |

DUNS 23-674-4470

## United Synagogue

305 Ballards Lane, London N12 8GB
**Tel:** 020-8343-8989
**Web:** www.theus.org.uk
**Estd:** 1990
**Line of Business:** Building services
**Principals:** P Sheldon *(President)*, E D Levy
**Responsibilities**
**Senior:** Stephen Fenton *(Manager)*, Simon Hochhauser *(Manager)*, steven Sheldon *(President)*
**Admin:** Jackey Stanley *(Executive Assistant)*
**IT:** M Shear *(Senior It Executive)*
**Branches:** United Synagogue, Cecil Park, Pinner, Middlesex HA5 5HJ
**US SIC:** 8661, 6732
**UK SIC:** 96600, 83100
**Auditors:** Crowe Clark Shitehill LLP

| | 31-12-12 | 31-12-11 | 31-12-10 |
|---|---|---|---|
| TO | 33,308,000 | 31,818,000 | 30,905,000 |
| P/L | 2,692,000 | 2,477,000 | 101,000 |
| NW | 75,198,000 | 72,231,000 | 69,913,000 |
| WC | 7,433,000 | 7,024,000 | 3,983,000 |
| Emp. | 623 | 645 | 603 |

DUNS 22-114-1901

## United Taxis (Contracts) Ltd

35 Gladstone Street, Darlington, County Durham DL3 6JU
**Tel:** 01325-381999
**Web:** www.united-taxis.co.uk
**Reg No:** 4133377 **Estd:** 2000 Private Limited Company
**Line of Business:** Taxis
**Issued Capital:** £10,300
**Director:** M Wilson
**Co. Secretary:** Ms Christine Wilson
**US SIC:** 4121 **UK SIC:** 72200

| | 31-03-14 | 31-03-13 | 31-03-12 |
|---|---|---|---|
| TA | 260,445 | 305,499 | 161,624 |
| NW | 61,123 | 63,841 | 58,606 |
| WC | (29,150) | (13,042) | (31,087) |

DUNS 50-319-6677

## United Utilities International Ltd

(**Subsidiary of:** United Utilities Group Plc)
Dawson House, Liverpool Road, Great Sankey, Warrington, Cheshire WA5 3LW
**Tel:** 08457462200
**Web:** www.unitedutilities.com
**Reg No:** 2344587 **VAT No:** 483797387
**Estd:** 1989 Private Limited Company
**Line of Business:** Collection, purification and distribution of water
**Trading Style:** United Utilities
**Issued Capital:** £77,000,504
**Directors:** J A Hodgkin, S R Gardiner, M A Gee, Uu Secretariat Limited, S R Fraser
**Co. Secretary:** Uu Secretariat Limited
**Branches:** United Utilities International Ltd, Chorley Road, Wigan, Lancashire WN1 2XP
**US SIC:** 4941, 6711
**UK SIC:** 17000, 83962
**Auditors:** Deloitte & Touche LLP

| | 31-03-14 | 31-03-13 | 31-03-12 |
|---|---|---|---|
| TO | 973,000 | 1,063,000 | 1,144,000 |
| P/L | 6,743,000 | 16,094,000 | 1,480,000 |
| NW | 29,411,000 | 24,670,000 | 8,071,000 |
| WC | 22,658,000 | 19,206,000 | (71,066,000) |
| Emp. | 5 | N/A | 2 |

DUNS 23-776-0277

## United Utilities P L C

(**Subsidiary of:** United Utilities Group Plc)
Haweswater House, Lingley Mere Business Park, Lingley Green Avenue Great, Sankey, Warrington, Cheshire WA5 3LP
**Tel:** 01925-237-000 **Fax:** 01925-237-073
**Web:** www.unitedutilities.com
**Reg No:** 2366616 **Estd:** 1989 Public Limited Company
**Line of Business:** Management activities of holding companies
**Issued Capital:** £881,787,479
**Directors:** P A Aspin, J R Houlden, S R Fraser, S L Mogford
**Co. Secretary:** Simon Gardiner
**Branches:** United Utilities P L C, Comtech Business Park, Unit 1, Bolton, Lancashire BL5 3QY
**US SIC:** 6711, 4953
**UK SIC:** 83962, 92110
**Auditors:** Deloitte LLP

**Bankers:** National Westminster Bank Plc (01-09-17)
**Following financial data are in thousands**

| | 31-03-14 | 31-03-13 | 31-03-12 |
|---|---|---|---|
| TO | 1,704,500 | 1,636,000 | 1,564,900 |
| P/L | 570,000 | 337,200 | 315,300 |
| NW | 4,075,700 | 3,672,500 | 3,717,700 |
| WC | 1,496,700 | 1,435,400 | 1,741,800 |
| Emp. | 5,329 | 5,301 | 5,096 |

DUNS 76-907-9278
## United Welsh Housing Association Ltd
Y Borth, 13 Beddau Way, Caerphilly, Mid Glamorgan CF83 2AX
**Tel:** 02920-858100 **Fax:** 029-2085-8110
**Web:** www.unitedwelsh.com
**Reg No:** 0266239IP **Estd:** 1989 Private Limited Company
**Line of Business:** Housing associations societies trusts & co-operatives
**Principals:** L Raglan *(President)*, P Liang *(Chairman)*, D Lock, M Bugler, R Dafydd, Ms M Jones, D Curtis, I Gilbert
**Co. Secretary:** Anthony Wittaker
**Responsibilities**
**Senior:** Michelle Collins *(General Manager)*, Paddy Doyle *(Designated Limited Liability P)*, Mark Howcroft *(Designated Limited Liability P)*, Judith Lewis *(Designated Limited Liability P)*
**Finance:** Amy Barrett *(Head of Finance)*, Gareth Hexter *(Finance Director)*, Kellie Jones *(Finance Assistant)*
**Marketing:** Greg England *(Marketing and Communications M)*, Dionne Jayne *(Marketing Assistant)*, Libby Tucker *(Marketing and Communications A)*
**Admin:** Lesley Bevan *(Administrator)*, Sarah Jameson *(Secretary to Director of Devel)*, Jane Love *(Personal Assistant)*, Claire Phillips *(Administrator)*
**HR:** Donna Howells *(Head of Human Resources)*
**Facilities:** Lynda Sagona *(Director of Housing and Commun)*
**Engineering:** Helen Galsworthy *(Development Surveyor)*
**US SIC:** 8321 **UK SIC:** 96111
**Auditors:** KPMG LLP
**Bankers:** Lloyds TSB Bank plc (30-92-07)
**Employees:** 119
**Turnover:** £18,088,000

DUNS 23-082-9637
## United Westminster Schools Foundation
Alexandra House, 55a Catherine Place, London SW1E 6DY
**Tel:** 02078283055
**Web:** www.uws-gch.co.uk
**Estd:** 1999
**Line of Business:** Social work activities
**Principals:** E W Andrewes *(Chairman)*, R Blackwell, J O Nesbitt, Ms M Litt, J A Hall, C J Perrin, J J Love, P A Dunt
**Responsibilities**
**Senior:** C Marnham *(Vice Chairperson)*
**Admin:** S Muncaster *(Secretary)*
**Branches:** United Westminster Schools Foundation, Chart Road, Maidstone, Kent ME17 3RF
**US SIC:** 7399, 8299
**UK SIC:** 83954, 93300
**Auditors:** Buzzacott LLP
**Employees:** 348
**Turnover:** £19,742,000

DUNS 22-296-6678
## United Wholesale (Scotland) Ltd
110 Easter Queenslie Road, Glasgow, Lanarkshire G33 4UL
**Tel:** 0141-781-6600 **Fax:** 01417715618
**Web:** www.uniteduk.co.uk
**Reg No:** 0224822SC **Estd:** 2001 Private Limited Company
**Line of Business:** Wholesalers of beer and spirits
**Export Sales:** £489,247
**Issued Capital:** £13,555
**Directors:** M Sarwar, M G Saxton, A Sarwar
**Co. Secretary:** Razvan Syyed
**Branches:** United Wholesale (Scotland) Ltd, 164 Maxwell Road, Glasgow, Lanarkshire G41 1SS
**US SIC:** 5182, 5194
**UK SIC:** 61700
**Auditors:** PKF (UK) LLP
**Bankers:** Habib Bank Ag Zurich (60-91-96)

| | 31-12-13 | 31-12-12 | 31-12-11 |
|---|---|---|---|
| TO | 211,999,990 | 202,486,616 | 184,217,157 |
| P/L | 2,081,316 | 2,060,326 | 1,683,902 |
| NW | 10,224,377 | 8,852,472 | 7,499,927 |
| WC | 6,118,358 | 1,171,711 | 961,990 |
| Emp. | 193 | 196 | 187 |

DUNS 73-738-8459
## Unitedhealth Uk Ltd
**(Subsidiary of:** Unitedhealth Group Incorporated)
20 Grenfell Road, Maidenhead, Berkshire SL6 1EH
**Tel:** 02071-210-560 **Fax:** 02071-210-561
**Web:** www.scriptswitch.com
**Reg No:** 4996678 **Estd:** 2007 Private Limited Company
**Line of Business:** Business and management consultancy activities not elsewhere classified
**Issued Capital:** £51,633,948
**Directors:** P K Malhotra, A J Weir, N D Anderson
**Co. Secretary:** Ms Brigid Spicola
**Responsibilities**
**Senior:** Angela Woodward *(PA Chief Executive)*
**Branches:** Unitedhealth Uk Ltd, 3 Sheldon Square, London W2 6HY
**US SIC:** 7392 **UK SIC:** 83951
**Auditors:** Mazars LLP
**Bankers:** National Westminster Bank Plc (57-00-00)

| | 31-12-13 | 31-12-12 | 31-12-11 |
|---|---|---|---|
| TO | 5,216,756 | 4,273,102 | 5,829,457 |
| P/L | (8,234,419) | (8,247,146) | (8,435,690) |
| NW | (1,405,713) | 3,223,804 | (21,129,276) |
| WC | (2,123,710) | 2,493,712 | (21,942,861) |
| Emp. | 62 | 56 | 67 |

DUNS 23-513-9545 **Exp**
## Unitex Uk. Ltd
**(Subsidiary of:** Comitex Holding N.V.)
Marling Mills, Nelson Street, Leek, Staffordshire ST13 6BB
**Tel:** 01538-384108 **Fax:** 01538-387350
**Web:** www.marling.co.uk
**Reg No:** 3513150 **Estd:** 1971 Private Limited Company
**Line of Business:** Manufacture of narrow fabrics
**Issued Capital:** £2,875,028
**Director:** A Clemmet
**Co. Secretary:** Lloyd Repetto
**Responsibilities**
**Senior:** Michael Muston *(Manager)*, Alan Starkey *(Commercial Manager)*
**IT:** Kevin Holroyd *(Technical Manager)*
**HR:** Eileen Keates *(Personnel Manager)*
**Health & Safety:** Eileen Keates *(Personnel Manager)*
**Operations:** Kevin Holroyd *(Technical Manager)*
**Purchasing:** Angela Lancaster *(Purchasing Manager)*
**US SIC:** 2241 **UK SIC:** 43982
**Auditors:** KPMG
**Bankers:** Ing Bank Nv (16-53-88)

| | 31-12-13 | 31-12-12 | 31-12-11 |
|---|---|---|---|
| TO | 7,771,212 | 10,380,152 | 8,841,988 |
| P/L | (698,062) | (891,171) | (641,472) |
| NW | (3,132,486) | (2,434,424) | (1,543,253) |
| WC | 2,583,502 | 2,657,820 | 3,068,298 |
| Emp. | 88 | 100 | 105 |

DUNS 22-511-0436
## Unitrans Ltd
**(Subsidiary of:** Steinhoff International Holdings Ltd)
Astron Centre, Unit 2, Bracknell, Berkshire RG12 1QP
**Tel:** 02087447100 **Fax:** 02087-44710
**Web:** www.unitrans.eu.com
**Reg No:** 1372780 **VAT No:** 530385561
**Estd:** 1978 Private Limited Company
**Line of Business:** Freight transport by road not elsewhere classified
**Issued Capital:** £199,531
**Directors:** S B Campbell, P J Dieperink
**Co. Secretary:** John Robins
**Branches:** Unitrans Ltd, 73 Mercers Drive, Milton Keynes, Buckinghamshire MK13 7HJ
**US SIC:** 4213 **UK SIC:** 72300
**Auditors:** BDO Stoy Hayward LLP
**Bankers:** Barclays Bank Plc (20-38-83)

| | 29-06-13 | 30-06-12 | 30-06-11 |
|---|---|---|---|
| TO | 31,355,962 | 8,868,294 | 10,066,232 |
| P/L | 587,772 | 851,402 | 661,640 |
| NW | 1,813,198 | 1,383,550 | 509,224 |
| WC | 1,655,717 | 3,152,680 | 2,224,242 |
| Emp. | 445 | 109 | 101 |

DUNS 21-624-6779
## Unitrust Protection Services Holdings Ltd
Unitrust House, Heather Park Drive, London
**Web:** www.unitrust.co.uk
**Reg No:** 7046832 **Estd:** 2009 Private Limited Company
**Line of Business:** Security activities
**Issued Capital:** £211
**Directors:** R N Griffin, P R Griffin, I Yexley
**Co. Secretary:** Ms Lisa Griffin

**US SIC:** 7393 **UK SIC:** 83954

| | 31-03-14 | 31-03-13 | 31-03-12 |
|---|---|---|---|
| TO | 5,597,864 | 5,077,655 | 5,490,831 |
| P/L | 216,989 | 191,793 | 255,486 |
| NW | 1,187,682 | 1,219,701 | 1,259,826 |
| WC | 901,240 | 927,450 | 946,998 |
| Emp. | 149 | 133 | 133 |

DUNS 21-682-1118
## Unitum Ltd
Unitum House 1 The Chase, John Tate Road, Hertford, Hertfordshire SG13 7NN
**Tel:** 02031953700
**Web:** www.unitum.co.uk
**Reg No:** 7324383 **Estd:** 2010 Private Limited Company
**Line of Business:** Management activities of other non-financial holding companies not elsewhere classified
**Issued Capital:** £11,000
**Directors:** T J Cumberland, P L Benson, A Little, C M Howell
**US SIC:** 6711 **UK SIC:** 83962
**Bankers:** HSBC Bank plc (40-12-03)

| | 05-04-14 | 05-04-13 | 05-04-12 |
|---|---|---|---|
| TO | 65,153,000 | 67,710,000 | 59,767,000 |
| P/L | 623,000 | 1,086,000 | 450,000 |
| NW | (2,223,000) | (2,442,000) | (2,794,000) |
| WC | (2,483,000) | (2,683,000) | (2,996,000) |
| Emp. | 1,519 | 1,571 | 1,640 |

DUNS 21-739-0152
## Unity Autofactors Ltd
24 High Road, Byfleet, West Byfleet, Surrey KT14 7QG
**Tel:** 01932340100
**Web:** www.unityautofactors.co.uk
**Reg No:** 0600571 **VAT No:** 413641088
**Estd:** 1954 Private Limited Company
**Line of Business:** Car accessories and parts
**Trading Style:** Unity Autofactors, Unity Motor Spares & Accessories
**Issued Capital:** £14,938
**Principals:** K R Newman-Bale *(Chairman and Managing)*, G Newman-Bale
**Co. Secretary:** Neil Newman Bale
**US SIC:** 5531 **UK SIC:** 65100
**Auditors:** HPCA Ltd
**Bankers:** Lloyds TSB Bank plc (30-99-80)

| | 30-04-14 | 30-04-13 | 30-04-12 |
|---|---|---|---|
| TO | 4,940,247 | 4,728,836 | 4,549,519 |
| P/L | 276,367 | 279,055 | 443,338 |
| NW | 3,537,672 | 3,403,090 | 3,248,361 |
| WC | 1,950,108 | 1,824,524 | 1,661,173 |
| Emp. | 75 | 66 | 62 |

DUNS 21-694-2742
## Unity Automotive Group Ltd
459 Earlston Road, Leicester, Leicestershire LE2 8TB
**Tel:** 01162831052
**Web:** www.unityautomotive.co.uk
**Reg No:** 7407301 **Estd:** 2010 Private Limited Company
**Line of Business:** Management activities of holding companies
**Issued Capital:** £2,000
**Directors:** P Hunt, J Mathers
**US SIC:** 6711 **UK SIC:** 83962

| | 30-04-14 | 30-04-13 | 30-04-12 |
|---|---|---|---|
| TO | 23,903,595 | 16,490,174 | N/A |
| P/L | 306,716 | 31,280 | N/A |
| NW | 668,075 | 522,377 | 264,039 |
| WC | 347,901 | 260,901 | N/A |
| Emp. | 50 | 42 | N/A |

DUNS 28-983-5860
## The Unity Centre Ltd
The Unity Centre, 85 Bole Hill Road, Sheffield, South Yorkshire S6 5DD
**Web:** www.sheffieldchildcare.co.uk
**Reg No:** 1790507 **Estd:** 1984 Private Company Limited By Guarantee
**Line of Business:** Schools
**Director:** R Oxley
**Co. Secretary:** James Mann
**Responsibilities**
**Senior:** Tony Bevis *(Executive Director)*
**US SIC:** 8211, 8321, 7999, 8999
**UK SIC:** 93200, 96111, 97913, 83954
**Auditors:** Hawsons
**Bankers:** HSBC Bank plc (40-41-07)

| | 31-03-14 | 31-03-13 | 31-03-12 |
|---|---|---|---|
| TO | 801,497 | 641,592 | 704,536 |
| P/L | 85,216 | (62,752) | 32,079 |
| NW | 384,383 | 299,167 | 361,919 |
| WC | 198,324 | 98,176 | 144,739 |
| Emp. | 55 | 48 | 48 |

DUNS 21-046-6855
## Unity Chartered Accountants
Po Box 117, Fulwood, Preston, Lancashire PR2 5TE
**Tel:** 01772216000
**Web:** www.bakertilly.co.uk
**Estd:** 2009 Partnership
**Line of Business:** Accounting activities
**Trading Style:** Tenon
**Proprietor:** P Donnelly
**US SIC:** 8931 **UK SIC:** 83600
**Employees:** 90

DUNS 42-369-3717
## Unity City Academy Trust
Ormesby Road, Middlesbrough, Cleveland TS3 8RE
**Tel:** 01642-326262
**Web:** www.unityacademy.org.uk
**Reg No:** 4357009 **Estd:** 2012 Private Company Limited By Guarantee
**Line of Business:** General secondary education
**Directors:** D Triggs, H G Leighton, Ms S M Hare, I T Comfort, Ms B G Kirby, Reverend A Gaunt, Ms J R Lewis, Mrs D Clapham
**Co. Secretary:** Christopher Crowther
**Responsibilities**
**Senior:** John Catron *(Manager)*, Patricia Towey *(Manager)*
**HR:** Emma Donaldson *(Training Manager)*
**US SIC:** 8211, 8249
**UK SIC:** 93200, 93300
**Bankers:** Barclays Bank Plc (20-00-77)

| | 31-08-13 | 31-08-12 | 31-08-11 |
|---|---|---|---|
| TO | 6,231,000 | 6,793,000 | 6,721,000 |
| P/L | (52,000) | 318,000 | (197,000) |
| NW | 23,339,000 | 22,973,000 | 23,428,000 |
| WC | 868,000 | 336,000 | 404,000 |
| Emp. | 132 | 144 | 145 |

DUNS 21-782-0220
## Unity College
Warbreck Hill Road, Blackpool, Lancashire FY2 0TS
**Tel:** 01253355493
**Web:** www.beacon-hill-blackpool.sch.uk
**Estd:** 1992 Proprietorship
**Line of Business:** Schools (foundation)
**Proprietor:** Mrs B Lund
**Responsibilities**
**Senior:** Christopher Lickiss *(Principal)*
**US SIC:** 8211 **UK SIC:** 93200
**Employees:** 61

DUNS 50-444-1056
## Unity Enterprise
7 Harmony Row, Glasgow, Lanarkshire G51 3BB
**Tel:** 01414450166 **Fax:** 0141-559-5529
**Web:** www.unity-enterprise.com
**Reg No:** 0120777SC **Estd:** 1989 Private Company Limited By Guarantee
**Line of Business:** Social work activities
**Trading Style:** Traveloptions by Unity Enterprise
**Directors:** Ms A Nicol, Mrs C Adams, D S Gray, I E Fraser, M Ross (Mbe), J M Mooney, Rev L Ireland, Reverend P M Fletcher
**Co. Secretary:** William Wallace
**Responsibilities**
**Senior:** Donna Bell *(Manager)*, Thomas Moyes *(Director)*, Mattew Smith *(Director)*
**Branches:** Unity Enterprise, 12 Commercial Road, Glasgow, Lanarkshire G5 0PQ
**US SIC:** 7399 **UK SIC:** 83954
**Auditors:** Hay & Co
**Bankers:** Clydesdale Bank Plc (82-46-06)

| | 31-03-14 | 31-03-13 | 31-03-12 |
|---|---|---|---|
| TO | 2,410,000 | 2,493,000 | 2,436,000 |
| P/L | 21,000 | 31,000 | 50,000 |
| NW | 503,000 | 482,000 | 451,000 |
| WC | 394,000 | 355,000 | 291,000 |
| Emp. | 101 | 108 | 100 |

DUNS 76-398-9217
## Unity Homes Ltd
1 Murray Street, Salford, Lancashire M7 2DX
**Tel:** 0161-792-6674
**Web:** www.unityhomes.co.uk
**Reg No:** 2556536 **Estd:** 1990 Private Limited Company
**Line of Business:** Nursing homes
**Trading Style:** The Willows Nursing Home
**Issued Capital:** £100
**Director:** Ms S Sandher
**Co. Secretary:** Manjit Sandher
**US SIC:** 8051 **UK SIC:** 95100
**Auditors:** Gupta & Co
**Bankers:** Girobank Plc (72-00-00)

| | 31-03-14 | 31-03-13 | 31-03-12 |
|---|---|---|---|
| TA | 13,076,976 | 11,256,095 | 10,009,489 |
| NW | 6,328,001 | 6,107,664 | 5,989,624 |
| WC | 200,983 | 454,704 | 535,114 |

DUNS 21-150-7757
## Unity in Care Ltd
99 Alexandra Road The Pavilion, Farnborough, Hampshire GU14 6BN
**Tel:** 01252-544423
**Web:** www.unityincareltd.co.uk
**Reg No:** 6800250 **VAT No:** 974767262
**Estd:** 2012 Private Limited Company
**Line of Business:** Nutritionists
**Issued Capital:** £1
**Director:** Ms B L Garrett
**Co. Secretary:** Miss Sian Garrett
**US SIC:** 8091, 6732
**UK SIC:** 95200, 83100

**Bankers:** Barclays Bank Plc (20-61-82)

|     | 31-03-13 | 31-03-12 | 31-03-11 |
|-----|----------|----------|----------|
| TO  | N/A      | 473,952  | 357,656  |
| P/L | N/A      | 27,796   | (58,753) |
| NW  | 34,910   | (18,536) | (46,332) |
| WC  | 34,910   | (18,536) | (46,332) |

DUNS 21-169-0432

## Unity Is Consulting Ltd
5 Jupiter House, Calleva Park, Aldermaston, Reading, Berkshire RG7 8NN
**Tel:** 01173310789
**Web:** www.jisc.ac.uk
**Reg No:** 6939652 **Estd:** 2012 Private Limited Company
**Line of Business:** Hardware consultancy
**Issued Capital:** £110
**Director:** D Beartup
**Co. Secretary:** Mrs Jean Beartup
**US SIC:** 8299 **UK SIC:** 93300

|     | 31-03-14 | 31-03-13 | 31-03-12 |
|-----|----------|----------|----------|
| TA  | 69,470   | 29,370   | 40,235   |
| NW  | 46,249   | 18,516   | 22,800   |
| WC  | 45,078   | 18,515   | 22,532   |

DUNS 22-626-1709     **Exp**

## Unity Media Plc
Becket House, Vestry Road, Sevenoaks, Kent TN14 6EJ
**Tel:** 01732-748000 **Fax:** 01732-748001
**Web:** www.unity-media.com
**Reg No:** 1529036 **VAT No:** 347373636
**Estd:** 1980 Public Limited Company
**Line of Business:** Publishers
**Export Markets:** Worldwide
**Export Sales:** £13,490
**Issued Capital:** £50,000
**Principals:** D Taylor (Chairman and Managing), Mrs J Taylor
**Co. Secretary:** Ms Helen Lawson
**Responsibilities**
**Finance:** Claire Brown (Assistant Finance Manager)
**Marketing:** Jo Claydon-Smith (Trade link AD Manager), Andy Dunn (Sales & Marketing Director), Sarah Halls (Advertising Manager), Bob Harper (Editor), Sarah Norwood (Group Advertising Manager)
**Sales:** Jo Claydon-Smith (Trade link AD Manager), Andy Dunn (Sales & Marketing Director)
**US SIC:** 2731, 2741
**UK SIC:** 47532, 47541
**Auditors:** Baker Tilly
**Bankers:** Lloyds TSB Bank plc (30-91-60)

|     | 30-06-14 | 30-06-13 | 30-06-12 |
|-----|----------|----------|----------|
| TO  | 3,936,960| 4,684,153| 5,252,694|
| P/L | 38,224   | (38,300) | 116,225  |
| NW  | 573,647  | 548,813  | 605,292  |
| WC  | 500,949  | 459,293  | 468,459  |
| Emp.| 55       | 67       | 72       |

DUNS 21-781-4421

## Unity Partnership
Henshaw House, Cheapside, Oldham, Lancashire OL1 1NY
**Tel:** 01617705678
**Web:** www.unitypartnership.com
**Estd:** 2011
**Line of Business:** Call centres
**Responsibilities**
**Senior:** Emma Alexander (Manager), Andrew Kendall (Manager), Karen Mckenna (Manager)
**US SIC:** 7399 **UK SIC:** 83954
**Employees:** 100

DUNS 22-715-6247     **Exp**

## Unity (Services) Ltd
(**Subsidiary of:** T N C Ltd)
Portland House, Cheltenham, Gloucestershire GL52 2LG
**Tel:** 01242529424 **Fax:** 01242222834
**Web:** www.transnationalgroup.co.uk
**Reg No:** 1639615 **Estd:** 1982 Private Limited Company
**Line of Business:** Debt collection agencies
**Trading Style:** A1 Credit Reference Bureau
**Issued Capital:** £100
**Managing Director:** P Buckland
**Co. Secretary:** Ms Lorraine Buckland
**Branches:** Unity (Services) Ltd, Portland House, 4 Albion Street, Cheltenham, Gloucestershire GL52 2LG
**US SIC:** 7321 **UK SIC:** 83954
**Auditors:** Kingscott Dix & Co
**Bankers:** National Westminster Bank Plc (60-40-02)

|     | 30-04-14  | 30-04-13  | 30-04-12  |
|-----|-----------|-----------|-----------|
| TA  | 1,364,333 | 1,511,395 | 1,673,987 |
| NW  | 975,374   | 927,456   | 951,146   |
| WC  | (78,779)  | (120,960) | (131,802) |

DUNS 28-967-4657

## Unity Trust Bank Plc
Rail Station, Galton Bridge, Smethwick, West Midlands B66 1HU
**Tel:** 01216342040 **Fax:** 08451130003
**Web:** www.unity.co.uk
**Reg No:** 1713124 **Estd:** 1983 Public Limited Company
**Line of Business:** Banks
**Issued Capital:** £16,679,452
**Directors:** W Hayes, J P Kelly, E V Sabisky, S R Tasker, R A Chamberlain, I D Morrison, P T Noon, A Kearns
**Co. Secretary:** Miss Katherine Eldridge
**Responsibilities**
**Senior:** Michael Osborne (Financial Director), David Prentis (Director), Kevin Turmore (Manager), Allan Wylie (Director)
**Finance:** Michael Osborne (Financial Director)
**IT:** Tom Anderson (Computer Manager)
**Health & Safety:** Michael Osborne (Financial Director)
**Branches:** Unity Trust Bank Plc, Po Box 98, Whitley Bay, Tyne and Wear NE25 9WQ
**US SIC:** 6012 **UK SIC:** 81402
**Auditors:** KPMG Audit PLC
**Bankers:** Unity Trust Bank Plc (08-60-01)

|     | 31-12-13  | 31-12-12  | 31-12-11  |
|-----|-----------|-----------|-----------|
| TA  | 717,487,000| 664,045,000| 606,809,000|
| P/L | 2,319,000 | 398,000   | 3,294,000 |
| NW  | 46,006,000| 44,531,000| 44,788,000|
| WC  | 45,981,000| 44,359,000| 44,516,000|
| Emp.| 88        | 84        | 83        |

DUNS 21-592-5113

## Univar Food Ingredients
Bramley Road, Bletchley, Milton Keynes, Buckinghamshire MK1 1PT
**Tel:** 01908362200
**Web:** www.univareurope.com
**Estd:** 1978
**Line of Business:** Chemicals distribution and wholesale
**Partners:** P Harvey, C Jeusse, Miss D Rothwell
**US SIC:** 5161 **UK SIC:** 61200
**Employees:** 50

DUNS 21-717-5546

## Univar Specialty Consumables Ltd
(**Subsidiary of:** Ellis & Everard (U K Holdings) Ltd)
Usc House, Vanguard, Tame Park, Wilnecote, Tamworth, Staffordshire B77 5DY
**Tel:** 01827 255 200
**Web:** www.univarsc.com
**Reg No:** 0994213 **Estd:** 2006 Private Limited Company
**Line of Business:** Activities of other transport agencies
**Export Sales:** £1,172,000
**Issued Capital:** £4,615,010
**Directors:** W T Hill, S N Landsman
**Co. Secretary:** Pinsent Masons Secretarial Limit
**Responsibilities**
**Senior:** Sabine Duyfjes (Director)
**US SIC:** 4712 **UK SIC:** 77002
**Auditors:** Ernst & Young LLP
**Bankers:** Barclays Bank Plc (20-47-34)

|     | 31-12-13  | 31-12-12  | 31-12-11  |
|-----|-----------|-----------|-----------|
| TO  | 25,650,000| 24,722,000| 26,269,000|
| P/L | 950,000   | 537,000   | 36,000    |
| NW  | 7,666,000 | 6,605,000 | 5,965,000 |
| WC  | 7,581,000 | 6,461,000 | 5,957,000 |
| Emp.| 76        | 83        | 90        |

DUNS 50-414-7067     **Imp**

## Univeg Katope Uk Ltd
(**Subsidiary of:** Fieldlink Nv)
Stephensons Avenue, Spalding, Lincolnshire PE11 3SW
**Tel:** 01775711565 **Fax:** 01775711571
**Web:** www.univeguk.co.uk
**Reg No:** 2411719 **VAT No:** 514054875
**Estd:** 1989 Private Limited Company
**Line of Business:** Wholesale of fruit and vegetables
**Issued Capital:** £1,054
**Directors:** M D Harpham, F J Kint, P K Gain, H V Deprez, A A Forrester
**Co. Secretary:** Richard Baker
**US SIC:** 5148 **UK SIC:** 61700
**Auditors:** Ernst & Young LLP
**Bankers:** National Westminster Bank Plc (55-50-36)

|     | 31-12-13  | 31-12-12  | 31-12-11  |
|-----|-----------|-----------|-----------|
| TO  | 76,659,902| 79,485,050| 79,169,129|
| P/L | 724,803   | 663,454   | 373,335   |
| NW  | 3,939,562 | 3,436,567 | 2,971,291 |
| WC  | 137,894   | (184,473) | (614,079) |
| Emp.| 213       | 212       | 204       |

DUNS 49-486-6924

## Universal Arches Ltd
(**Subsidiary of:** Universal Arches (Holdings) Ltd)
103 Peasley Cross Lane, St Helens, Merseyside WA9 3AL
**Tel:** 01744-612844 **Fax:** 01744-694250
**Web:** www.universalarches.com
**Reg No:** 3151585 **Estd:** 1996 Private Limited Company
**Line of Business:** Polythene sheeting supplies
**Issued Capital:** £100
**Directors:** G K Day, L S Day
**Co. Secretary:** Mrs Anita Day
**US SIC:** 3079 **UK SIC:** 48360
**Auditors:** Styles & Co
**Bankers:** National Westminster Bank Plc (60-70-08)

|     | 31-12-14  | 31-12-13  | 31-12-12  |
|-----|-----------|-----------|-----------|
| TA  | 1,338,549 | 653,377   | 495,970   |
| NW  | 495,494   | 423,505   | 329,557   |
| WC  | 323,774   | 383,757   | 282,324   |

DUNS 23-191-3203     **Imp**

## Universal Automotive Ltd
Greenhill Industrial Estate, Kidderminster, Worcestershire DY10 2RN
**Tel:** 01562512502 **Fax:** 01562743466
**Web:** www.bremboshop.co.uk
**Reg No:** 2981923 **Estd:** 1994 Private Limited Company
**Line of Business:** Car accessories and parts
**Trading Style:** Universal Automotive
**Issued Capital:** £104
**Co. Secretary:** Nicholas Davies
**Branches:** Universal Automotive Ltd, Davis Ho, Lodge Causeway Trading Est, Bristol, Avon BS16 3JB
**US SIC:** 5531 **UK SIC:** 65100
**Auditors:** Cognitor Ltd

|     | 31-12-13  | 31-12-12  | 31-12-11  |
|-----|-----------|-----------|-----------|
| TO  | 9,153,075 | 9,627,395 | 10,211,730|
| P/L | 189,254   | 174,346   | 242,662   |
| NW  | 858,701   | 821,821   | 798,352   |
| WC  | 834,053   | 800,379   | 760,401   |
| Emp.| 55        | 63        | 62        |

DUNS 50-542-1933

## Universal A.V. Services Ltd
Guy Street, Bradford, West Yorkshire BD4 7BB
**Tel:** 01274307763
**Web:** www.uniav.com
**Reg No:** 2496514 **VAT No:** 556942016
**Estd:** 1990 Private Limited Company
**Line of Business:** Hire and rental of television goods
**Issued Capital:** £400
**Principals:** C A Harris (Managing), J P Eden, Ms K E Waine, N A Fitzpatrick
**Responsibilities**
**Senior:** Clive Meggison (General Manager)
**Sales:** Phil Beattie (Sales Manager)
**Branches:** Universal A.v. Services Ltd, 10 Spread Eagle St, Accrington, Lancashire BB5 4NB
**US SIC:** 7394, 1731
**UK SIC:** 84000, 50300
**Auditors:** Clough & Co LLP
**Bankers:** Yorkshire Bank Plc (05-01-06)

|     | 31-12-13  | 31-12-12  | 31-12-11  |
|-----|-----------|-----------|-----------|
| TO  | 13,657,069| 8,661,511 | 10,102,931|
| P/L | 377,087   | 156,951   | 479,585   |
| NW  | 3,325,128 | 3,347,183 | 3,415,996 |
| WC  | 2,248,021 | 2,590,136 | 2,521,297 |
| Emp.| 87        | 63        | 68        |

DUNS 28-986-6337     **Imp**

## Universal Aviation (U K) Ltd
Building 130, London Stansted Airport, Stansted, Essex CM24 1QH
**Tel:** 01279-680349 **Fax:** 01279680372
**Web:** www.universalaviation.aero
**Reg No:** 1803815 **Estd:** 1984 Private Limited Company
**Line of Business:** Aircraft - services for
**Export Sales:** £13,739,636
**Trading Style:** Universal Weather & Aviation U K
**Issued Capital:** £100
**Directors:** J A Howells, F Ahmed, S A Raftery
**Co. Secretary:** Michael Weberpal
**Responsibilities**
**Senior:** Jason Hayward (General Manager)
**Finance:** Leigh Stockbridge (Financial Manager)
**HR:** Sue Kirkwood (Human Resources Coordinator), Simon Wade (Health & Safety Manager)
**Health & Safety:** Simon Wade (Health & Safety Manager)
**US SIC:** 4582 **UK SIC:** 76400
**Auditors:** PricewaterhouseCoopers LLP

**Bankers:** Barclays Bank Plc (20-36-98)

|     | 30-06-13  | 30-06-12  | 30-06-11  |
|-----|-----------|-----------|-----------|
| TO  | 13,739,636| 12,609,990| 12,544,542|
| P/L | 1,391,013 | 1,165,682 | 1,535,818 |
| NW  | 7,122,400 | 6,075,608 | 5,210,584 |
| WC  | 6,253,328 | 5,532,345 | 5,654,468 |
| Emp.| 55        | 54        | 49        |

DUNS 21-097-2982

## Universal Beverages Ltd
(**Subsidiary of:** L'Arche Green N.V.)
Robertsons Business Park, Little Marcle Road, Ledbury, Herefordshire HR8 2JT
**Tel:** 01531633200
**Web:** www.universalbeverages.co.uk
**Reg No:** 6416610 **Estd:** 2007 Private Limited Company
**Line of Business:** Brewers
**Issued Capital:** £100
**Directors:** G A Colquhoun, J P Van Der Burg, D M Forde
**US SIC:** 2082 **UK SIC:** 42702
**Auditors:** KPMG LLP

|     | 31-12-13    | 31-12-12    | 31-12-11    |
|-----|-------------|-------------|-------------|
| TO  | 22,916,000  | 18,030,000  | 19,892,000  |
| P/L | (9,851,000) | (8,634,000) | (48,269,000)|
| NW  | (78,270,000)| (77,125,000)| (69,877,000)|
| WC  | 9,972,000   | (845,000)   | 3,977,000   |
| Emp.| 137         | 151         | 169         |

DUNS 42-429-6663     **Imp**

## Universal Church of the Kingdom of God
Rainbow Theatre, 232-238 Seven Sisters Road, Finsbury Par, London N4 3NX
**Tel:** 020-7686-6000
**Web:** www.uckg.org
**Reg No:** 1043985RC **Estd:** 2002
**Line of Business:** Places of worship
**Trading Style:** U C K G, Uckg Helpcentre
**Director:** F E Eghobaen
**Responsibilities**
**Senior:** Victor Akutu (Chief Executive), Audrey Medeiros (Chief Executive)
**Branches:** Universal Church Of The Kingdom Of God, 386-388 Brixton Road, London SW9 7AW
**US SIC:** 8661 **UK SIC:** 96600
**Auditors:** Baker Tilly UK Audit LLP
**Bankers:** Barclays Bank Plc (20-00-00)
**Employees:** 60
**Turnover:** £10,936,909

DUNS 57-852-5230

## Universal Commercial Guarding Ltd
326 City Road, London EC1V 2AA
**Tel:** 020-7837-3535 **Fax:** 020-7837-9793
**Web:** www.universal-security.co.uk
**Reg No:** 2899949 **VAT No:** 645020374
**Estd:** 1994 Private Limited Company
**Line of Business:** Security and related activities
**Trading Style:** Universal Security
**Issued Capital:** £1,200
**Principals:** P G Baldwin (Managing), A P Baldwin
**Responsibilities**
**Senior:** Rob Platais (Chief Executive Officer)
**Branches:** Universal Commercial Guarding Ltd, 326 City Road, London EC1V 2AA
**US SIC:** 7393 **UK SIC:** 83954
**Auditors:** Grant Thornton UK LLP

|     | 28-09-13  | 29-09-12  | 30-09-11  |
|-----|-----------|-----------|-----------|
| TO  | 6,211,613 | 6,675,504 | 7,039,151 |
| P/L | (92,582)  | 27,101    | 77,533    |
| NW  | (387,591) | (295,009) | (338,538) |
| WC  | (383,702) | (283,413) | (283,488) |
| Emp.| 225       | 232       | 229       |

DUNS 22-701-3612     **Exp**

## Universal Commercial Relocation (Holdings) Ltd
Unit 1c Lyon Way, Greenford, Middlesex UB6 0BN
**Tel:** 02085751133
**Web:** www.ucr.uk.com
**Reg No:** 1401352 **VAT No:** 242741182
**Estd:** 1978 Private Limited Company
**Line of Business:** Furniture removal activities
**Export Markets:** France; Germany; Worldwide
**Issued Capital:** £300
**Principals:** W Murray (Managing), Mrs M Murray, Mrs S K Cole
**US SIC:** 4214 **UK SIC:** 72300
**Auditors:** GKP Ltd
**Bankers:** Allied Irish Bank (gb) (23-85-83)

|     | 31-01-14  | 31-01-13  | 31-01-12  |
|-----|-----------|-----------|-----------|
| TA  | 3,017,629 | 3,116,364 | 3,097,014 |
| NW  | 951,348   | 1,027,979 | 1,096,133 |
| WC  | (168,707) | (64,334)  | 17,365    |

DUNS 73-919-4962     **Imp**
## Universal Components Uk Ltd
(Subsidiary of: Tvs Europe Distribution Ltd)
8 Stevenson Way, Sheffield, South Yorkshire
S9 3WZ
**Tel:** 01142611188
**Web:** www.ucukltd.com
**Reg No:** 5172752 **VAT No:** 845259211
**Estd:** 2004 Private Limited Company
**Line of Business:** Manufacturers of van and
truck components
**Trading Style:** Universal Components Uk
**Issued Capital:** £50,000
**Directors:** S Subramanian, P J Roberts,
S R Gopalan, D Kernahan
**Co. Secretary:** Paul Roberts
**Responsibilities**
**Senior:** Andrew Cattell *(Marketing
Manager)*, Mark Mellish *(Manager)*
**Marketing:** Dean Arnold *(Marketing
Manager)*, Andrew Cattell *(Marketing
Manager)*, Mark Mellish *(Manager)*
**Sales:** Mark Mellish *(Manager)*
**IT:** Andrew Cattell *(Marketing Manager)*
**Purchasing:** S Ashall *(Purchasing Manager)*
**Branches:** Universal Components Uk Ltd,
Unit 5, Guinness Road, Manchester M17
1SB
**US SIC:** 3714 **UK SIC:** 35300
**Auditors:** Baker Tilly UK Audit LLP
**Bankers:** Yorkshire Bank Plc (05-08-03)

| | 31-03-14 | 31-03-13 | 31-03-12 |
|---|---|---|---|
| TO | 24,832,000 | 21,474,000 | 5,057,000 |
| P/L | 1,860,000 | 1,635,000 | 411,000 |
| NW | 4,916,000 | 4,347,000 | 2,957,000 |
| WC | 5,243,000 | 4,622,000 | 3,280,000 |
| Emp. | 118 | 102 | 95 |

DUNS 33-934-8104
## Universal Computers
9 Storforth Lane Trading Estate, Hasland,
Chesterfield, Derbyshire S41 0QD
**Tel:** 01708606133
**VAT No:** 598525092 **Estd:** 1996
Proprietorship
**Line of Business:** Joinery and carpentry
**Proprietor:** Ms R Bromley
**Branches:** Universal Group, Wheatbridge
Retail Pk, Off Chatsworth Rd, Chesterfield,
Derbyshire S40 2AB
**US SIC:** 2431, 5732
**UK SIC:** 46300, 64800
**Employees:** 60

DUNS 22-213-2164
## Universal Design Studio Ltd
37-42 Charlotte Road, London EC2A 3PG
**Tel:** 020-7033-3881
**Web:** www.universaldesignstudio.com
**Reg No:** 4231346 **Estd:** 2001 Private
Limited Company
**Line of Business:** Interior designers
**Issued Capital:** £100
**Directors:** J Osgerby, E S Barber,
Doctor A I Smith
**Responsibilities**
**Senior:** Jason Holley *(Manager)*
**US SIC:** 1799 **UK SIC:** 50000

| | 31-03-14 | 31-03-13 | 31-03-12 |
|---|---|---|---|
| TA | 1,104,135 | 1,182,782 | 952,873 |
| NW | 430,507 | 398,192 | 417,281 |
| WC | 370,610 | 679,545 | 379,110 |

DUNS 49-096-5753     **Imp**
## Universal Flexible Packaging Ltd
(Subsidiary of: Universal Developments Ltd)
61 Lunsford Road, Leicester, Leicestershire
LE5 0HJ
**Tel:** 0116 276 9992
**Web:** www.uniflex.co.uk
**Reg No:** 3092987 **VAT No:** 620035008
**Estd:** 1993 Private Limited Company
**Line of Business:** Manufacturers of
packaging materials
**Trading Style:** Ufp
**Issued Capital:** £1,000
**Directors:** U S Durrani, J P Harrison
**Co. Secretary:** Mubushar Durrani
**Responsibilities**
**Senior:** Anjum Durrani *(Manager)*, Pinku
Durrani *(Manager)*
**US SIC:** 2654, 4712
**UK SIC:** 47280, 77002
**Auditors:** Mark J. Rees LLP
**Bankers:** The Royal Bank Of Scotland Plc
(16-23-20)

| | 31-12-13 | 31-12-12 | 31-12-11 |
|---|---|---|---|
| TO | 14,491,333 | 10,422,930 | 10,537,159 |
| P/L | 694,322 | 272,189 | 224,701 |
| NW | 1,626,827 | 1,346,164 | 1,175,555 |
| WC | 161,563 | 110,984 | 14,787 |
| Emp. | 124 | 118 | 96 |

DUNS 73-678-2470     **Imp**
## Universal Hose Ltd
Unit 24 Gas House Road Castle View,
Business Centre, Rochester, Kent ME1 1PB
**Tel:** 01634832211
**Web:** www.hydraquip.co.uk
**Reg No:** 4937556 **VAT No:** 830633744
**Estd:** 2010 Private Limited Company
**Line of Business:** Manufacture of plastic
plates, sheets, tubes and profiles
**Trading Style:** Hydraquip Hose & Hydraulics
**Issued Capital:** £1,000
**Directors:** D M Macbain, F C Ennis
**Co. Secretary:** Nigel Wray
**Responsibilities**
**Senior:** Tim Fulton *(Engineering Manager)*,
Paul Reardon *(Branch manager)*
**US SIC:** 3999, 3069, 5084
**UK SIC:** 49590, 48123, 61490
**Auditors:** Foot & Ellis-Smith Ltd

| | 31-12-13 | 31-12-12 | 31-12-11 |
|---|---|---|---|
| TO | 10,009,315 | 8,233,713 | 7,501,048 |
| P/L | 543,121 | 362,580 | 453,484 |
| NW | 1,664,090 | 1,285,246 | 1,120,991 |
| WC | 1,267,028 | 918,451 | 787,632 |
| Emp. | 118 | 93 | 85 |

DUNS 21-138-2335
## Universal Media Studios International Ltd
(Subsidiary of: Universal Studios Ltd)
1 Central St Giles, St Giles High Street,
London WC2H 8NU
**Tel:** 02036185971
**Web:** www.uninetworks.tv
**Reg No:** 6707440 **Estd:** 2008 Private
Limited Company
**Line of Business:** Television activities
**Export Sales:** £19,195,000
**Issued Capital:** £1
**Directors:** M Edelstein, Ms J F Moreton,
Ms S F Cooper
**Co. Secretary:** Alison Mansfield
**US SIC:** 4833, 6711
**UK SIC:** 97411, 83962

| | 31-12-13 | 31-12-12 | 31-12-11 |
|---|---|---|---|
| TO | 35,396,000 | 14,238,000 | 8,045,000 |
| P/L | (8,406,000) | (3,853,000) | (4,401,000) |
| NW | (19,216,000) | (10,813,000) | (6,958,000) |
| WC | (20,846,000) | (12,423,000) | (8,613,000) |
| Emp. | 57 | 46 | 35 |

DUNS 21-723-9300     **Imp**
## Universal Music Operations Ltd
(Subsidiary of: Vivendi)
364-366 Kensington High Street, London
W14 8NS
**Tel:** 02074715000
**Web:** www.umusic.co.uk
**Reg No:** 0950138 **Estd:** 1969 Private
Limited Company
**Line of Business:** Operation of arts facilities
**Export Sales:** £94,608,000
**Trading Style:** Umo, Universal Music
**Issued Capital:** £17,045
**Directors:** D R Sharpe, R M Constant,
D S Joseph, A M Barker, M J Swatton,
S G Miron, K T Brown
**Co. Secretary:** Mrs Abolanle Abioye
**Branches:** Universal Music Operations Ltd,
Chippengen Drive, Milton Keynes,
Buckinghamshire MK10 0AT
**US SIC:** 7911 **UK SIC:** 97913
**Auditors:** Ernst & Young LLP
**Bankers:** HSBC Bank plc (40-05-30)

| | 31-12-13 | 31-12-12 | 31-12-11 |
|---|---|---|---|
| TO | 314,366,000 | 328,800,000 | 322,387,000 |
| P/L | (21,539,000) | (15,864,000) | (20,378,000) |
| NW | 145,646,000 | 166,619,000 | 173,153,000 |
| WC | 293,450,000 | 310,338,000 | 318,904,000 |

DUNS 28-862-1444     **Imp-Exp**
## Universal Music Publishing Mgb Ltd
(Subsidiary of: Vivendi)
20 Fulham Broadway, London SW6 1AH
**Tel:** 02078355200
**Web:** www.universalmusicpublishing.com
**Reg No:** 0910829 **Estd:** 1967 Private
Limited Company
**Line of Business:** Other publishing
**Export Markets:** Worldwide
**Export Sales:** £17,178,000
**Issued Capital:** £2,001
**Directors:** P E Connolly, R J Morris,
Ms J G Alway
**Co. Secretary:** Mrs Abolanle Abioye
**Branches:** Universal Music Publishing Mgb
Ltd, A17 Brookfield Business Centre, 333
Crumlin Rd, Belfast, Belfast BT14 7EA
**US SIC:** 2741, 3652
**UK SIC:** 47541, 34520
**Auditors:** KPMG LLP
**Bankers:** Barclays Bank Plc (20-00-00)

| | 31-12-13 | 31-12-12 | 31-12-11 |
|---|---|---|---|
| TO | 26,686,000 | 27,294,000 | 25,902,000 |
| P/L | 4,230,000 | 4,243,000 | 2,911,000 |
| NW | 94,665,000 | 95,900,000 | 91,017,000 |
| WC | 91,844,000 | 93,079,000 | 88,196,000 |

DUNS 73-686-9590     **Exp**
## Universal Pictures International Ltd
(Subsidiary of: Universal Studios Ltd)
Central St Giles, 1 St Giles High Street,
London WC2H 8AR
**Tel:** 02070796000 **Fax:** 020-7079-6500
**Web:** www.universalpicturesinternational.com
**Reg No:** 4946051 **Estd:** 2003 Private
Limited Company
**Line of Business:** Motion picture and video
distribution
**Issued Capital:** £1
**Directors:** D Bullock, J J Beesley, D C Clark
**Co. Secretary:** Alison Mansfield
**Responsibilities**
**Marketing:** Gareth Lowrie *(Senior Marketing
Manager)*
**US SIC:** 7829, 6711
**UK SIC:** 97112, 83962
**Auditors:** KPMG LLP

| | 31-12-13 | 31-12-12 | 31-12-11 |
|---|---|---|---|
| TO | 77,699,000 | 86,859,000 | 80,881,000 |
| P/L | 3,036,000 | 3,267,000 | 3,921,000 |
| NW | 9,911,000 | 6,708,000 | 4,200,000 |
| WC | 8,873,000 | 5,136,000 | 2,402,000 |
| Emp. | 80 | 78 | 72 |

DUNS 21-324-1342     **Imp-Exp**
## Universal Products (Lytham) Manufacturing Ltd
(Subsidiary of: Fairfield Universal Holdings
Ltd)
Bradshaw Lane, Preston, Lancashire PR4
3JA
**Tel:** 01772685777 **Fax:** 01772-685888
**Web:** www.universal-laboratories.co.uk
**Reg No:** 1262458 **VAT No:** 156590348
**Estd:** 1976 Private Limited Company
**Line of Business:** Manufacturers of
pharmaceutical products
**Export Sales:** £1,471,492
**Issued Capital:** £400,000
**Directors:** C Costigan, S C O'Connor,
D R Stroud, Mrs J Senior, R Mcevoy,
T P O'Connor
**Co. Secretary:** Giles Harrison
**Responsibilities**
**Senior:** David Hilton *(Manager)*, Andy
McKenna *(Warehouse Controller)*, Jane
Peters *(Manager)*
**Facilities:** Charlie Richardson *(Engineering
Manager)*
**Operations:** Andy McKenna *(Warehouse
Controller)*
**Engineering:** Charlie Richardson
*(Engineering Manager)*, Ian de Havilland
*(Production Director)*
**US SIC:** 2834 **UK SIC:** 25700
**Auditors:** Ashworth Treasure Ltd
**Bankers:** National Westminster Bank Plc
(01-67-14)

| | 31-03-14 | 31-10-13 | 31-03-12 |
|---|---|---|---|
| TO | 14,835,309 | 33,049,390 | 31,965,875 |
| P/L | (4,980) | 1,669,174 | 1,172,349 |
| NW | 5,162,290 | 5,330,762 | 3,949,697 |
| WC | 3,690,299 | 4,183,405 | 3,043,523 |
| Emp. | 254 | 243 | 238 |

DUNS 42-343-6786
## Universal Recruitment Solutions Ltd
30 Parkstone Road, Poole, Dorset BH15
2PG
**Web:** www.universalrecruitment.com.au
**Reg No:** 4331413 **Estd:** 2001 Private
Limited Company
**Line of Business:** Labour recruitment and
provision of personnel
**Trading Style:** Team Recruitment Solutions
**Issued Capital:** £146,206
**Directors:** J C Gault, Mrs J Kegie
**Co. Secretary:** Clive Wood
**US SIC:** 7361 **UK SIC:** 83954
**Bankers:** Lloyds TSB Bank plc (77-50-36)

| | 31-01-14 | 31-01-13 | 31-01-12 |
|---|---|---|---|
| TO | 12,607,791 | 11,299,863 | 11,702,652 |
| P/L | 351,304 | 367,638 | 489,351 |
| NW | 195,045 | 188,681 | 226,547 |
| WC | 183,336 | 132,899 | 140,965 |
| Emp. | 627 | 569 | 531 |

DUNS 89-637-1028
## Universal Steels & Aluminium Group Ltd
7 Lostock Industrial Estate, Cranfield Road,
Bolton, Lancashire BL6 4SB
**Tel:** 01204-669356
**Web:** www.usanda.co.uk
**Reg No:** 3318279 **Estd:** 1997 Private
Limited Company
**Line of Business:** Secretarial and translation
activities
**Issued Capital:** £50,000
**Directors:** E W Kwiatkowski, G W Frances,
H Z Kwiatkowski, C Scott, R Corrigan,
A Chadwick
**Co. Secretary:** Antoni Kwiatkowski
**US SIC:** 7339 **UK SIC:** 83954

**Auditors:** John Kerr & Co

| | 31-03-14 | 31-03-13 | 31-03-12 |
|---|---|---|---|
| TO | N/A | 8,767,699 | 9,203,485 |
| P/L | 636,627 | 117,562 | 94,729 |
| NW | 1,299,281 | 1,587,809 | 1,485,035 |
| WC | 360,131 | 666,462 | 307,712 |

DUNS 67-245-3180
## Universal Telecom 5G Ltd
Phoenix House, Desborough Park Road,
High Wycombe, Buckinghamshire HP12 3BQ
**Tel:** 01494-833833
**Web:** www.5gcomms.com
**Reg No:** 6182956 **Estd:** 2007 Private
Limited Company
**Line of Business:** Telecom services
**Issued Capital:** £1,000
**Director:** M G Holland
**Co. Secretary:** Jean Witte
**Responsibilities**
**Sales:** Graham Gerred *(Sales Manager)*
**IT:** Andre Mellet *(IT Director)*
**HR:** Simon Wade *(HR Director)*, Rhiannon
Waters *(Recruitment Manager)*
**Operations:** Melissa Holland *(Operations
Manager)*
**Purchasing:** Susan Simpson *(Purchasing
Manager)*
**US SIC:** 4899 **UK SIC:** 79020

| | 30-09-14 | 30-09-13 | 30-09-12 |
|---|---|---|---|
| TA | 1,000 | 1,000 | 1,000 |
| NW | 1,000 | 1,000 | 1,000 |

DUNS 29-820-8505     **Imp**
## Universal Tool & Production Co Ltd
280-282 West Street, Fareham, Hampshire
PO16 0HT
**Tel:** 01329-232795 **Fax:** 01329823223
**Reg No:** 2003935 **VAT No:** 446779106
**Estd:** 1952 Private Limited Company
**Line of Business:** Precision engineers
**Issued Capital:** £10,000
**Principals:** G C Papworth *(Chairman)*,
D E Ferris, Ms L J Edge, M E Leonard,
E C Papworth
**Co. Secretary:** Mrs Sybil Papworth
**US SIC:** 8911, 3799
**UK SIC:** 83701, 36502
**Auditors:** Arthur Daniels & Co
**Bankers:** Barclays Bank Plc (20-69-34)

| | 31-03-14 | 31-03-13 | 31-03-12 |
|---|---|---|---|
| TO | 7,380,543 | N/A | N/A |
| P/L | 306,000 | N/A | N/A |
| NW | 1,651,179 | 1,416,233 | 1,199,863 |
| WC | 777,445 | 845,059 | 438,772 |

DUNS 21-030-2659     **Imp**
## The Universal Tyre Co (Deptford) Ltd
Unit 8-9, Green Street Green Road Orbital
One, Dartford, Kent DA1 1QG
**Tel:** 01322-421980
**Web:** www.universal-tyres.co.uk
**Reg No:** 0278970 **Estd:** 1923 Private
Limited Company
**Line of Business:** Tyre dealers
**Trading Style:** Universal Tyres & Auto
Centre
**Issued Capital:** £45,110
**Directors:** S P Wright, M J Abbott,
J D Wright, A A Wright, Ms S J Wright
**Responsibilities**
**Senior:** Timothy Elster *(Manager)*, Sally
Musgrave *(Manager)*
**Branches:** The Universal Tyre Co (Deptford)
Ltd, 108 Selsdon Road, South Croydon,
Surrey CR2 6PG
**US SIC:** 7539, 5531
**UK SIC:** 67100, 65100
**Auditors:** Target
**Bankers:** Barclays Bank Plc (20-77-67)

| | 31-12-13 | 31-12-12 | 31-12-11 |
|---|---|---|---|
| TO | 25,176,315 | 22,224,339 | 25,562,197 |
| P/L | 512,967 | 274,299 | 395,562 |
| NW | 7,966,005 | 7,427,254 | 7,162,217 |
| WC | 523,071 | 291,986 | 210,455 |
| Emp. | 124 | 122 | 125 |

DUNS 64-821-0078
## Universal Tyres
5 Chatsworth Terrace, Harrogate, North
Yorkshire HG1 5HT
**Tel:** 01423500688
**Web:** www.harrogatetyres.co.uk
**Estd:** 1994 Proprietorship
**Line of Business:** Tyre dealers
**Proprietor:** G Coolican
**Responsibilities**
**Senior:** Graham Coolican *(Partner)*
**US SIC:** 5531 **UK SIC:** 65100
**Employees:** 100

DUNS 23-672-9070

## Universal Utilities Ltd

**(Subsidiary of:** Vitruvian Partners Llp)
Universal House, 1 Sharston Road, Manchester M22 4RX
**Tel:** 01619464440 **Fax:** 01619464445
**Web:** www.switchingon.com
**Reg No:** 3667643 **Estd:** 1998 Private Limited Company
**Line of Business:** Telecom services
**Trading Style:** Unicom
**Issued Capital:** £50,000
**Directors:** C J Earle, P Nowosad, Ms J Palmer, P Doherty
**Co. Secretary:** Miss Emma Shaw
**Responsibilities**
**Senior:** David Siddall *(Manager)*
**Branches:** Universal Utilities Ltd, Tootal House 19 21 Spring Garden, Manchester M2 1FB
**US SIC:** 4899 **UK SIC:** 79020
**Auditors:** PricewaterhouseCoopers LLP
**Bankers:** HSBC Bank plc (40-31-24)

| | 30-04-14 | 30-04-13 | 30-04-12 |
|---|---|---|---|
| TO | 59,263,000 | 60,015,000 | 55,656,000 |
| P/L | 22,479,000 | 20,223,000 | 18,404,000 |
| NW | 48,098,000 | 30,751,000 | 15,365,000 |
| WC | 44,622,000 | 27,953,000 | 14,238,000 |
| Emp. | 619 | 501 | 495 |

DUNS 21-155-7293 **Exp**

## Universal/Island Music Ltd

**(Subsidiary of:** Vivendi)
20 Fulham Broadway, London SW6 1AH
**Tel:** 02078355300 **Fax:** 020-8748-1998
**Web:** www.unippm.co.uk
**Reg No:** 0761597 **Estd:** 2010 Private Limited Company
**Line of Business:** Sound recording studios
**Export Markets:** Overseas
**Export Sales:** £2,773,000
**Issued Capital:** £200
**Directors:** R J Morris, P E Connolly
**Co. Secretary:** Mrs Abolanle Abioye
**Responsibilities**
**Senior:** Farah Hasan *(Head Of International Sales An)*, Simon Mortimer *(Head Of International Producti)*
**Marketing:** Farah Hasan *(Head Of International Sales An)*
**Sales:** Farah Hasan *(Head Of International Sales An)*
**US SIC:** 2741 **UK SIC:** 47541
**Auditors:** Ernst & Young LLP

| | 31-12-13 | 31-12-12 | 31-12-11 |
|---|---|---|---|
| TO | 3,770,000 | 3,940,000 | 4,069,000 |
| P/L | 1,386,000 | 1,502,000 | 1,534,000 |
| NW | 25,546,000 | 24,482,000 | 23,348,000 |
| WC | 25,658,000 | 24,724,000 | 23,590,000 |

DUNS 76-980-9591 **Exp**

## Universe Group Plc

Southampton International Park, Southampton, Hampshire SO18 2RX
**Web:** www.universe-group.co.uk
**Reg No:** 2639726 **Estd:** 1991 Public Limited Company
**Line of Business:** Management activities of holding companies
**Export Markets:** North America & Rest of the world including Europe
**Export Sales:** £3,640,000
**Issued Capital:** £2,115,306
**Directors:** R J Smeeton, R J Goddard, M D Coster, J M Lewis
**Co. Secretary:** Robert Smeeton
**Responsibilities**
**Senior:** Stephen Mcleod *(Chief Executive Officer)*
**Health & Safety:** Andy Wakely *(Facilities Manager)*
**Facilities:** Andy Wakely *(Facilities Manager)*
**US SIC:** 6711 **UK SIC:** 83962
**Auditors:** BDO LLP
**Bankers:** Barclays Bank Plc (20-05-75)

| | 31-12-13 | 31-12-12 | 31-12-11 |
|---|---|---|---|
| TO | 15,874,000 | 11,851,000 | 12,082,000 |
| P/L | 1,200,000 | 1,012,000 | (1,067,000) |
| NW | 468,000 | 1,953,000 | 7,000 |
| WC | 152,000 | 983,000 | (556,000) |
| Emp. | 174 | 170 | 163 |

DUNS 29-688-9611 **Exp**

## Universe Media Group Ltd

**(Subsidiary of:** Daisyyellow Ltd)
Alberton House, St Marys Parsonage, Manchester M3 2WJ
**Tel:** 01612141200 **Fax:** 0161-488-1701
**Web:** www.thecatholicuniverse.com
**Reg No:** 2012469 **VAT No:** 440445279
**Estd:** 2012 Private Limited Company
**Line of Business:** Publishers
**Export Markets:** Eire
**Export Sales:** £55,366
**Trading Style:** Diocesan Newspapers, Church Building Magazine, The Universe Newspaper
**Issued Capital:** £15,910
**Directors:** J Kelly, Ms M D Concannon, C W Leach, N T Condon
**Branches:** Universe Media Group Ltd, Unit 2 Sovereign Enterprise Park, King William Street, Salford, Lancashire M50 3UP
**US SIC:** 2731, 2721
**UK SIC:** 47532, 47522
**Auditors:** Pannell Kerr Forster
**Bankers:** Allied Irish Bank (gb) (23-83-98)

| | 31-12-13 | 31-12-12 | 31-12-11 |
|---|---|---|---|
| TO | 2,306,922 | 2,414,787 | 2,692,348 |
| P/L | 51,061 | (196,891) | (206,278) |
| NW | (641,697) | (739,562) | (589,493) |
| WC | (382,191) | (548,518) | (551,992) |

DUNS 56-940-2720

## The Universities & Colleges Admissions Service

Rose Hill, New Barn Lane, Cheltenham, Gloucestershire GL52 3LZ
**Tel:** 08714680468
**Web:** www.ucas.com
**Reg No:** 2839815 **VAT No:** 618230657
**Estd:** 1992 Private Company Limited By Guarantee
**Line of Business:** Business and management consultancy activities not elsewhere classified
**Trading Style:** U C A S
**Directors:** Professor C B Riordan, T M Grote Obe, Dr D J Ashton, Professor J P Beer, G P Pennell, Professor D N Fleming, I D Diamond, S M Smith
**Co. Secretary:** Mrs Helen Cornish
**Responsibilities**
**Senior:** Jennie Bullock *(Manager)*, Wendy Trainor *(Manager)*
**Marketing:** Charlotte Knowles *(Senior Marketing Channel Manag)*
**Admin:** Paul Sisterson *(Admissions Manager)*
**IT:** James Munson *(Interim Director of IT)*
**Health & Safety:** Caroline Hawkins *(Health & Safety Coordinator)*
**Facilities:** Dean Griffiths *(Facilities Manager)*
**Operations:** Fatuma Mahad *(Director of Corporate Services)*
**Branches:** The Universities & Colleges Admissions Service, 12 The Links, St. Andrews, Fife KY16 9JB
**US SIC:** 7392 **UK SIC:** 83951
**Auditors:** Wenn Townsend
**Bankers:** Lloyds TSB Bank plc (30-95-72)

| | 31-07-13 | 31-07-12 | 31-07-11 |
|---|---|---|---|
| TO | 35,998,862 | 34,371,011 | 33,341,385 |
| P/L | (13,231) | 183,393 | 2,887,196 |
| NW | 24,755,103 | 16,068,166 | 23,160,812 |
| WC | 15,275,909 | 19,063,772 | 19,660,537 |
| Emp. | 406 | 425 | 404 |

DUNS 29-189-6827

## Universities & Colleges Christian Fellowship

Blue Boar House, 5 Blue Boar Street, Oxford, Oxfordshire OX1 4EE
**Web:** www.uccf.org.uk
**Reg No:** 0387932 **Estd:** 2011 Private Company Limited By Guarantee
**Line of Business:** Religious organisations and places of worship
**Trading Style:** U C C F
**Directors:** Rev G C Lewis, Dr C J Willmott, Dr J Mckenzie, G C Lewis, P W Loose, Dr M A Bonnington, H Williams, R E Borgonon
**Co. Secretary:** Timothy Edwards
**Responsibilities**
**Senior:** John Lenton *(Director)*
**US SIC:** 8661 **UK SIC:** 96600
**Auditors:** Deloitte & Touche
**Bankers:** HSBC Bank plc (40-28-08)

| | 30-04-14 | 30-04-13 | 30-04-12 |
|---|---|---|---|
| TO | 4,607,957 | 4,338,704 | 4,996,041 |
| P/L | 313,989 | 148,636 | 862,320 |
| NW | 3,962,904 | 3,644,666 | 3,455,051 |
| WC | 922,012 | 491,886 | 285,595 |
| Emp. | 116 | 102 | 107 |

DUNS 22-857-8084

## Universities Superannuation Scheme Ltd

Royal Liver Building, Pier Head, Liverpool, Merseyside L3 1PY
**Tel:** 01512274711 **Fax:** 0151-236-3173
**Web:** www.usshq.co.uk
**Reg No:** 1167127 **Estd:** 2013 Private Company Limited By Guarantee
**Line of Business:** Pension companies
**Directors:** Ms K English, G M Breakwell, J W Trythall, Professor D S Eastwood, D C Mcdonnell, Dr K J Carter, I R Maybury, Dr A M Roger
**Co. Secretary:** Ian Sherlock
**Responsibilities**
**Senior:** John Callister *(Manager)*, Joseph Devlin *(Director)*, Michael Merton *(Director)*, Michael Poisson *(Director)*
**Finance:** Elizabeth Fernando *(Head of Equity)*
**Branches:** Universities Superannuation Scheme Ltd, 1336 Greenford Road, Greenford, Middlesex UB6 0HL
**US SIC:** 6371 **UK SIC:** 82002
**Auditors:** Grant Thornton UK LLP
**Bankers:** Barclays Bank Plc (20-51-01)

| | 31-03-14 | 31-03-13 | 31-03-12 |
|---|---|---|---|
| TO | 83,403,000 | 72,682,000 | N/A |
| P/L | N/A | N/A | (69,628,000) |
| WC | (1,899,000) | (711,000) | (2,115,000) |
| Emp. | 348 | 334 | 296 |

DUNS 21-605-7226

## University & College Union

25-31 Tavistock Place, London WC1H 9UT
**Tel:** 02076709700
**Estd:** 1915
**Line of Business:** Misc Schools & Educational Services
**Proprietor:** Ms B Newman
**US SIC:** 8299 **UK SIC:** 93300
**Employees:** 49

DUNS 73-822-6443

## University Campus Suffolk Ltd

Waterfront Building, 19-21 Neptune Quay, Ipswich, Suffolk IP4 1QJ
**Tel:** 01473338000
**Web:** www.eehub.co.uk
**Reg No:** 5078498 **Estd:** 2011 Private Company Limited By Guarantee
**Line of Business:** Training services
**Directors:** Ms D A Cadman, Professor W Pope, Professor P E Cavenagh, Professor E D Acton, P Winter, Doctor N Savvas, Mrs C A Edey, D S Edwards
**Co. Secretary:** Timothy Greenacre
**Responsibilities**
**Senior:** Mohamed Abdel-Maguid *(Director)*, Benjamin Adofo *(Director)*, Fiona Hotston Moore *(Director)*, Simon Mead *(Manager)*, Owen Morris *(Director)*, Mark Pendlington *(Director)*, Brian Summers *(Director)*
**Marketing:** Kate Bourne *(Marketing Officer)*
**US SIC:** 8221 **UK SIC:** 93100
**Auditors:** PricewaterhouseCoopers LLP
**Bankers:** Barclays Bank Plc (20-44-51)

| | 31-07-14 | 31-07-13 | 31-07-12 |
|---|---|---|---|
| TO | 37,459,000 | 37,987,000 | 38,782,000 |
| P/L | (729,000) | 921,000 | 1,822,000 |
| NW | 47,395,000 | 51,106,000 | 52,106,000 |
| WC | 6,496,000 | 6,316,000 | 5,506,000 |
| Emp. | 424 | 430 | 412 |

DUNS 51-595-0327

## University Centre

Granta Place, Cambridge, Cambridgeshire CB2 1RU
**Web:** www.unicen.cam.ac.uk
**Estd:** 1971 Proprietorship
**Line of Business:** Conference centres and facilities
**Proprietor:** T Walston
**US SIC:** 6531 **UK SIC:** 83400
**Employees:** 67

DUNS 21-775-2784

## University Centre of Hastings

Priory Square, Priory Street, Hastings, East Sussex TN34 1EA
**Tel:** 08456020607
**Web:** www.brighton.ac.uk
**Estd:** 2003 Proprietorship
**Line of Business:** University
**Proprietor:** Mrs M Wallis
**Responsibilities**
**Senior:** Paul Frost *(Campus Director)*
**US SIC:** 8221 **UK SIC:** 93100
**Employees:** 70

DUNS 21-753-5678

## University Centre Oldham

Cromwell Street, Oldham, Lancashire OL1 1BB
**Tel:** 0161-213-5000
**Web:** www.hud.ac.uk
**Partnership**
**Line of Business:** Sub-degree level higher education
**Partners:** W Winterbottom, Ms D Bridge
**US SIC:** 8221 **UK SIC:** 93100
**Employees:** 50

DUNS 22-817-5642

## University College

The Castle, Palace Green, Durham, County Durham DH1 3RW
**Web:** www.dur.ac.uk
**Estd:** 1999
**Line of Business:** University
**Director:** Castmell
**Responsibilities**
**Senior:** Michelle Crawford *(Bursar)*
**US SIC:** 8221 **UK SIC:** 93100
**Bankers:** Barclays Bank Plc (20-27-41)
**Employees:** 60

DUNS 23-065-7421

## University College Birmingham

Summer Row, Birmingham, West Midlands B3 1JB
**Tel:** 01216-041-000
**Web:** www.ucb.ac.uk
**VAT No:** 580577808 **Estd:** 1950 Private Company Limited By Guarantee
**Line of Business:** Restaurant - pub food
**Responsibilities**
**Senior:** Don Hacker *(Manager)*
**Marketing:** Vicki Bull *(Marketing Administrator)*, Eileen Pryer *(Marketing Manager)*
**Admin:** Stuart Petrie *(IT Administrator)*
**IT:** Stuart Petrie *(IT Administrator)*
**HR:** Phil Godwin *(Human Resources Manager)*
**Operations:** Eileen Pryer *(Marketing Manager)*
**Branches:** University College Birmingham, Heartlands Day Nursery, Francis Street, Birmingham, West Midlands B7 4JX
**US SIC:** 8221 **UK SIC:** 93100
**Bankers:** National Westminster Bank Plc (60-02-35)
**Employees:** 510

DUNS 22-541-0919 **Imp**

## University College London

Gower Street, London WC1E 6BT
**Tel:** 020 7679 2000
**Web:** www.ucl.ac.uk
**Reg No:** 0000631RC **VAT No:** 524371168
**Estd:** 1826 Incorporate By Act Of Parliament
**Line of Business:** University
**Trading Style:** Ucl, Ucl Energy Institute, Wellcome Trust Centre for Neuroimaging
**Principals:** J Foster *(Financial)*, Ms M Gallyer, Dr D H Roberts, H M Priestley
**Responsibilities**
**Senior:** John Ashburner *(Executive)*, Paul Ayris *(Planning Manager)*, Supneet Bajwa *(Executive)*, Suzanne Beeke *(Manager)*, Johan Berglund *(Board Member)*, John Braime *(Voluntary Services Coordinator)*, Martin Callanan *(Manager)*, Olga Ciccarelli *(Executive)*, Furio Cora *(Executive)*, Jana Dankovicova *(Senior Manager)*, Joseph Devlin *(Executive)*, Devis Di Tommaso *(Executive)*, Ray Dolan *(Executive)*, Nikolaos Donos *(Director of Research Strategy)*, Elizabeth Dow *(Coordinator)*, Daniel Feltham *(Chairman)*, Helen Fielding *(Board Member)*, Jacques Gianino *(Executive)*, Malcolm Grant *(Provost)*, Sarah Guise *(Senior Manager)*, Paul Hayden *(General Manager)*, Ian Hepburn *(Member)*, Graeme Hogarth *(Executive)*, Katherine Holt *(Executive)*, Masud Husain *(Deputy Director)*, Elizabeth Isaacs *(Member)*, Lily Islam *(Board Member)*, Rolf Jager *(Executive)*, Christine Johnston *(Senior Manager)*, Vjaceslavs Karolis *(Executive)*, Bernard Khoo *(Manager)*, Marianne Knight *(Deputy Director)*, David Macmanus *(Executive)*, Katherine Majid *(Executive)*, Mark Maslin *(Manager)*, Federica Mazzara *(Executive)*, Nick Mcnally *(Divisional Manager)*, Claire Morley *(Manager)*, Philippa Robins *(Head of Acquisitions and Catal)*, Stuart Rosen *(Executive)*, Martin Rossor *(Executive)*, Elena Rusconi *(Board Member)*, Gopinathan Sankar *(Executive)*, Eugene Schuster *(Executive)*, Tom Sheppard *(Executive)*, David Spratt *(Executive)*, Elizabeth Tan *(Vice President)*, Derek Thomas *(Chairman)*, Juergen Thurow *(Chairman)*, Elina Tripoliti *(Member)*, Paul Upchurch *(Chairman)*, Lidunka Vocadlo *(Executive)*, Patrice Ware *(Senior Manager)*, Scott Woodley *(Executive)*, Augusto Zani *(Executive)*
**Finance:** Celine Ahmed *(Financial Administrator)*, Jen Amery *(Financial Assistant)*, Sydonnie Hyman *(Website Editor)*, Patrick Molloy *(Finance Manager)*, Laura Mulcahy *(Finance Officer)*, Veena Sharma *(Financial Director)*, Anouchka Sterling *(Senior Finance Administrator)*, Trevor Willock *(Management Accountant)*
**Marketing:** Heather Beasley *(Admissions and Marketing Manag)*, Clare Bowerman *(Head of Communications)*, Ajay Chauhan *(Webmaster, Computer Support)*, Chris Donlan *(Department, Human Communicatio)*, Katie Grocott *(Graduate Marketing Manager)*, Cassie Harley *(Events Assistant)*, Melissa Lamptey *(Multimedia and Web Assistant)*, Patricia Newby *(Communications Officerf)*, Fiona Newman *(Clinic Coordinator, Department)*, Mark Pickerill *(International Liaison and Recr)*, Siobhan Pippa *(Marketing and Communications M)*, Mark Sudbury *(Director of Communications & M)*, Wendy Tester *(Events & Marketing Manager)*, Karen Widdowson *(Senior Manager)*

**Admin:** Sheema Ahmed *(ELSA Administrator)*, Sasha Aleksi *(Programme Administrator, Polit)*, Vinetta Archer-Dyer *(Personal Assistant)*, Martha Barsella *(HR Reception Manager)*, Sophie Bennett *(PhD Programme Administrator)*, Molly Bennett *(Administrator)*, David Blundred *(Administrative Assistant)*, Nick Cameron *(Administrator)*, Josephine Carr *(Administrator)*, Ben Chatterley *(Programme Administrator, Langu)*, Vince Clark *(Senior Teaching and Learning A)*, Catherine Conroy *(Administrator)*, Sonja Curtis *(Administrator)*, Marianne Dang *(Admissions Officer)*, Serife Dervish *(Administrator)*, Joe Fitzsimons *(Economics & Business Programme)*, Robert Heller *(Assistant Teaching Administrat)*, Pia Horbacki *(Teaching Administrator)*, Mary-Lou Jabore *(Admissions Administrator)*, Shauna Kearny *(Personal Assistant)*, Suse Keay *(Administrator)*, Alison Lambert *(Office Manager)*, Rochelle Libson *(PA and Team Secretary)*, Judy Okello *(Administrator)*, Sue Parkes *(Personal Assistant)*, Charlotte Pearce *(Administrator)*, Colin Penman *(Records Manager)*, Louise Price *(Administrator)*, Susie Rizvi *(Programme Administrator, Histo)*, Caroline Selai *(Administrator)*, Anouchka Sterling *(Senior Finance Administrator)*, Sahara Sultana *(Admissions Assistant)*, Deepa Visavadia *(Departmental Administrator)*, Cerine Yudin *(Administrator)*
**IT:** Sergei Chebankov *(Information Technology Manager)*, Peter Dayan *(Director of the Gatsby Computa)*, Mike Dunderdale *(IT Manager)*, Yusah Hamuth *(Information Technology Manager)*, Chris Knell *(Computer Manager)*, Dave Ladd *(Computing Officer/Waste Office)*, Jason Orchard *(Assistant Manager - Security S)*, Ian Patmore *(IT Technician)*, Bhavesh Varsani *(IT Manager)*
**HR:** Nishant Aggarwal *(HR Officer)*, Titi Ayinla *(Executive Assistant, HR)*, Martha Barsella *(HR Reception Manager)*, Charlotte Croffie *(Head of Organisational Develop)*, Fiona Daffern *(Head of Employment Policy Deve)*, Gail Davies *(Lecturer)*, Cristina Gardini *(Human Resources Manager)*, Geoff Lang *(Director, Head of HR Policy an)*, Joanna Lindsay *(HR Manager)*, Nik Maniatis *(Lecturer)*, Nick Mann *(Learning Resources Coordinator)*, Sian Minett *(Human Resources)*, Charles Oboh *(Director HR Consultancy)*, Mark Pickerill *(International Liaison and Recr)*, Claire Rowlinson *(Human Resources Consultant)*, Andres Ruiz-Linares *(Professor)*, Anne Skinner *(Human Resource Manager)*, Dallas Swallow *(Professor)*, Julie Wake *(Senior Human Officer)*, Nigel Waugh *(HR Director)*, Celine West *(Training Director)*
**Health & Safety:** Paul Stirk *(Safety Officer)*
**Facilities:** Henriette Bruun *(Research and Development Manag)*, Jacob Sweiry *(Research and Development Manag)*
**Operations:** Rex Knight *(Vice-Provost (Operations))*, Martin Moyle *(Digital Curation Manager and S)*, Andy Saffery *(Deputy Registrar Operations an)*, Pascale Searle *(Production and Operations Mana)*, Bob Sheil *(Programme Director)*
**Purchasing:** John Feraday *(Head of Purchasing)*
**Fleet:** Tristan Smith *(Lecturer of Energy and Transpo)*
**Engineering:** Marco Federighi *(Engineer)*, Clare Gryce *(Head of Research Computing & F)*, Joe Nolan *(Senior Manager)*, Nigel Titchener-Hooker *(Director, Engineering)*, Helena Titheridge *(Senior Lecturer of Civil, Envi)*, Andrew Todd-Pokropek *(Director, Engineering)*
**Branches:** University College London, Development Planning Unit, 9-11 Endsleigh Gardens, London WC1H 0ED
**US SIC:** 8221, 8091
**UK SIC:** 93100, 95200
**Auditors:** Deloitte LLP
**Bankers:** National Westminster Bank Plc (56-00-31)

| | 31-07-12 | 31-07-09 | 31-07-08 |
|---|---|---|---|
| TO | 868,735,000 | 713,736,000 | 29,874,000 |
| P/L | 23,804,000 | 11,167,000 | 510,000 |
| NW | 750,485,000 | 599,130,000 | 66,208,000 |
| WC | 67,489,000 | 30,940,000 | 2,160,000 |
| Emp. | 10,097 | N/A | 362 |

DUNS 54-864-0911

## University College London Hospitals Nhs Foundation Trust

235 Euston Road, London NW1 2BU
**Tel:** 08451555000
**Web:** www.uclh.nhs.uk
**Line of Business:** Public sector hospital activities, including nhs trusts
**Trading Style:** Hospital for Tropical Diseases / Macmillan Cancer Centre, National Hospital for Neurology&Neurosurgery /The Heart Hospit, Royal National Throat Nose&Ear Hospital / Eastman Dental Clini, The Royal London Hospital for Integrated Medicine
**Issued Capital:** £1
**Principals:** Sir P Dixon *(Chairman)*, R Alexander *(Financial)*, Sir R Naylor, Sir J Tooke, R Murley, N Monck, J Ramsey, Ms S Atkinson
**Responsibilities**
**Admin:** Jocelyn Laws *(Trust Administrator)*
**Operations:** Tony Mundy *(Corporate Medical Director)*
**Branches:** University College London Hospitals Nhs Foundation Trust, Ormond Ho, 27 Boswell St, London WC1N 3JZ
**US SIC:** 8062, 8091
**UK SIC:** 95100, 95200
**Auditors:** Deloitte LLP

| | 31-03-14 | 31-03-13 | 31-03-12 |
|---|---|---|---|
| TO | 912,630,000 | 842,992,000 | 596,609,000 |
| P/L | 16,070,000 | 5,341,000 | (16,144,000) |
| NW | 418,165,000 | 393,492,000 | 400,749,000 |
| WC | 89,540,000 | 91,183,000 | 58,417,000 |
| Emp. | 8,075 | 7,617 | 6,906 |

DUNS 21-333-1387

## The University College of St Mark & St John

Derriford Road, Plymouth, Devon PL6 8BH
**Tel:** 01752636700
**Web:** www.marjon.ac.uk
**Estd:** 1993
**Line of Business:** University
**Proprietor:** Professor M Noble
**Responsibilities**
**Senior:** Cara Aitchison *(Vice Chancellor)*
**Finance:** Karen Cook *(Manager)*
**Marketing:** Todd Pressman *(Marketing Manager)*
**IT:** David Riggs *(Computer Manager)*
**HR:** Lucy Pengelly *(Human Resources Manager)*
**Health & Safety:** Chris Rodham *(Health & Safety Officer)*
**US SIC:** 8221 **UK SIC:** 93100
**Employees:** 500
**Turnover:** £19,959,000

DUNS 21-324-9084

## University College Oxford

High Street, Oxford, Oxfordshire OX1 4BH
**Web:** www.univ.ox.ac.uk
**Line of Business:** Colleges (higher education)
**Trading Style:** University College, Uiv
**Director:** Lord F R Butler
**Responsibilities**
**Finance:** Peter Boreham *(Assistant Accountant)*, Tim Croft *(Accountant)*
**IT:** Richard Pye *(Senior IT Executive)*
**Branches:** University College Oxford, Annexe, 25 Staverton Rd, Oxford, Oxfordshire OX2 6XL
**US SIC:** 8221 **UK SIC:** 93100
**Employees:** 250

DUNS 23-082-9272

## University College School

Frognal, London NW3 6XH
**Tel:** 020-7435-2215
**Web:** www.ucs.org.uk
**Estd:** 1843
**Line of Business:** Schools (independent)
**Directors:** K Durham, C Clark
**Responsibilities**
**Finance:** Jerry Witts *(Bursar)*
**Marketing:** Jerry Witts *(Bursar)*
**Sales:** Paul Eggleton *(Enterprise Director)*
**IT:** Prad Samtani *(Technical Services Manager)*
**Health & Safety:** Jerry Witts *(Bursar)*
**Operations:** Keith Mainstone *(Operations Manager)*
**Purchasing:** Jerry Witts *(Bursar)*
**US SIC:** 8211 **UK SIC:** 93200
**Employees:** 200

DUNS 39-687-7870

## University Diagnostics Ltd

**(Subsidiary of:** Lgc Science Group Ltd)
L G C Building, Queens Road, Teddington, Middlesex TW11 0NJ
**Tel:** 02089438400
**Web:** www.lgc.co.uk
**Reg No:** 2146022 **VAT No:** 494801522
**Estd:** 1987 Private Limited Company
**Line of Business:** D n a profiling and genetic testing
**Trading Style:** Lgc
**Issued Capital:** £130,850
**Directors:** T M Robinson, S L Parsons
**Co. Secretary:** Keith Donald
**Responsibilities**
**Senior:** Lord Stevens *(Non-Executive Director)*
**US SIC:** 7399 **UK SIC:** 83954
**Auditors:** Ernst & Young LLP
**Bankers:** National Westminster Bank Plc (56-00-31)

| | 31-03-14 | 31-03-13 | 31-03-12 |
|---|---|---|---|
| TA | 596,010 | 596,010 | 596,010 |
| NW | 596,010 | 596,010 | 596,010 |

DUNS 23-999-2878 **Imp**

## University for the Creative Arts

Falkner Road, Farnham, Surrey GU9 7DS
**Tel:** 01252722441
**Web:** www.ucreative.ac.uk
**Estd:** 1989
**Line of Business:** Schools and colleges (art)
**Principals:** L Grossman *(Chairman)*, D Malhotra, A Jones, H Rich, J Whitehouse, D Hunter, Ms P Tambling, Ms B Brudsdon
**Responsibilities**
**Senior:** Wes Anderson *(Manager)*, Orest Baranyk *(President)*, Annmarie Borucki *(Manager)*, Martin Bouette *(Entrepreneurship Manager)*, Neil Breeden *(Manager)*, Jacqui Burke *(Vice Chairman)*, David Chalkley *(Manager)*, Iwanna Gorchynsky *(Member)*, Felicity Harvest *(Director)*, Christine Kapteijn *(Galleries Manager & Curator)*, Karen Millen *(Executive)*, Mike Osborn *(Manager)*, Julie Ross *(Executive)*, Carol Sheppard *(Executive)*, Marion Wilks *(University Secretary)*, Adele Wordsworth *(Executive)*, Guo Xiaoyan *(Manager)*
**Marketing:** Gemma Andrews *(Marketing Director)*, Vicky Downie *(UK Marketing Officer)*, Holly Hardy *(Marketing Director)*, Matthew Horton *(Head of Development)*, Coleen Myers *(Marketing Director)*, Jane Sales *(Marketing Director)*
**Admin:** Gill Cain *(Course Administrator)*, Katie Hamilton-Boxall *(Research Office Manager)*
**IT:** Marinella Vowles *(IT Project Manager)*
**HR:** Livy Leung *(Training Director)*, Michael Poraj-Wilczynski *(Director, Study, Design)*
**Operations:** Sheelagh Wright *(Project Director)*
**Engineering:** Valentina Elizabeth *(Executive)*, Mike Rymer *(Technical Engineer)*
**Branches:** University For The Creative Arts, Fort Pitt, Rochester, Kent ME1 1DZ
**US SIC:** 8221, 7333
**UK SIC:** 93100, 83953
**Auditors:** KPMG LLP
**Bankers:** Lloyds TSB Bank plc (30-91-60)
**Employees:** 300
**Turnover:** £57,681,000

DUNS 54-864-0556

## University Hospital Birmingham Nhs Foundation Trust

Queen Elizabeth Hospital, Metchley Park Road, Birmingham, West Midlands B15 2TQ
**Tel:** 01216272000
**Web:** www.uhb.nhs.uk
**Line of Business:** Public sector hospital activities, including nhs trusts
**Trading Style:** Queen Elizabeth Hospital, Selly Oak Hospital (Acute)
**Issued Capital:** £1
**Principals:** Sir A Bore *(Chairman)*, M Sexton *(Financial)*, T Jones, Ms J Moore, K Bolger, G Bains, D Bailey, D Ritchie
**Responsibilities**
**Senior:** Paul Brettle *(Manager)*, Anne Cope *(Associate Director of Pharmacy)*, Stewart Dobson *(Non-Executive Director)*, Louise Hill *(Centre Manager)*, Debbie Humphries *(Centre Manager)*, Nicola Parrott *(Business Manager, Cancer Resea)*, Clare Robinson *(Non-Executive Director)*, Dave Rosser *(Medical Director)*, Professor Sheppard *(Non Executive Member)*, Viv Tsesmelis *(Manager)*
**Marketing:** Fiona Alexander *(Director, Communications)*
**Admin:** Lorraine Bateman *(Personal Assistant)*, David Burbridge *(Administration Manager)*
**IT:** Rachel Brazier *(Project Manager)*, Mohandeep Randhawa *(Technical Infrastructure Manag)*
**HR:** Mike Clapham *(Training Director)*, Carol Rawlings *(Associate Director of Patient)*
**Operations:** Morag Jackson *(Project Director)*
**Branches:** University Hospital Birmingham Nhs Foundation Trust, 32-34 Melchett Rd, Kings Norton, Birmingham, West Midlands B30 3HS
**US SIC:** 8062 **UK SIC:** 95100
**Auditors:** KPMG LLP

| | 31-03-14 | 31-03-13 | 31-03-12 |
|---|---|---|---|
| TO | 691,896,000 | 640,031,000 | 469,081,000 |
| P/L | 29,043,000 | (6,200,000) | (33,632,000) |
| NW | (30,999,000) | (68,283,000) | (60,860,000) |
| WC | (10,388,000) | (5,108,000) | 85,000 |
| Emp. | 7,777 | 7,300 | 6,902 |

DUNS 50-422-3348

## University Hospital Day Nursery Ltd

**(Subsidiary of:** Uhdn Holdings Ltd)
Queens Medical Centre, Derby Road, Nottingham, Nottinghamshire NG7 2UH
**Tel:** 01159-420978 **Fax:** 01159-423332
**Reg No:** 2414617 **Estd:** 1989 Private Limited Company
**Line of Business:** Nursery schools
**Issued Capital:** £100
**Directors:** J F Hawkes, Mrs W S Hawkes
**Co. Secretary:** John Hawkes
**US SIC:** 8211 **UK SIC:** 93200
**Auditors:** Deloitte & Touche
**Bankers:** National Westminster Bank Plc (54-21-47)

| | 30-09-14 | 30-09-13 | 30-09-12 |
|---|---|---|---|
| TA | 614,370 | 604,951 | 536,321 |
| NW | 534,086 | 516,994 | 457,555 |
| WC | 506,767 | 491,680 | 428,041 |

DUNS 21-615-1152

## University Hospital of Hartlepool

Holdforth Road, Town Centre, Middlesbrough, Cleveland TS24 9AH
**Tel:** 01429266654
**Web:** www.nth.nhs.uk
**Estd:** 2011
**Line of Business:** Hospitals
**US SIC:** 8091 **UK SIC:** 95200
**Employees:** 4,000

DUNS 54-867-6469

## University Hospital of South Manchester Nhs Foundation Trust

Wythenshawe Hospital, Southmoor Road, Manchester M23 9LT
**Web:** www.uhsm.nhs.uk
**Estd:** 1994
**Line of Business:** Hospitals
**Trading Style:** Wythenshawe Hospital
**Issued Capital:** £1
**Principals:** Ms F Goodey Cbe Dl *(Chairman)*, J Silverwood Cfcipd *(Personnel)*, J Hartley, R Barlow, C Griffiths, Ms L E Clinton, G J Boulnois Bsc, Phd, P Smyth
**Responsibilities**
**Senior:** Graham Boulnois BSc PhD *(Non-Executive Director)*, Felicity Goodey CBE DL *(Chairperson)*, Andrea Roberts *(Nursery Manager)*
**Finance:** Nora Heery BSSc *(Financial Director)*
**HR:** John Silverwood CFCIPD *(Human Resources Director)*
**Purchasing:** Jackie Cottrell *(Head of Purchasing)*
**Branches:** University Hospital Of South Manchester Nhs Foundation Trust, Nell La, Manchester M20 2LR
**US SIC:** 8062 **UK SIC:** 95100
**Auditors:** Grant Thornton UK LLP

| | 31-03-14 | 31-03-13 | 31-03-12 |
|---|---|---|---|
| TO | 346,298,000 | 323,554,000 | 313,147,000 |
| P/L | (2,039,000) | 2,601,000 | (679,000) |
| NW | 116,383,000 | 84,148,000 | 85,710,000 |
| WC | (8,561,000) | (7,665,000) | (2,417,000) |
| Emp. | 5,446 | 5,212 | 5,061 |

DUNS 42-400-8746 **Imp**

## University Hospital of Wales Healthcare N H S Trust

University Hospital Of Wales Healthcare, Nhs Trust, Heath Park, Cardiff, South Glamorgan CF14 4XW
**Web:** www.wales.nhs.uk
**Estd:** 1994
**Line of Business:** Hospitals
**Principals:** D Morgan *(Chairman)*, Mrs W Hewitt-Sayer *(Personnel)*, A Stewart
**Branches:** University Hospital Of Wales Healthcare N H S Trust, Heath Park, Cardiff, South Glamorgan CF14 4XN
**US SIC:** 8062, 8091
**UK SIC:** 95100, 95200
**Employees:** 13,500

DUNS 23-263-5008 **Imp**

## University Hospital Southampton Nhs Foundation Trust

Tremona Road, Southampton, Hampshire SO16 6YD
**Tel:** 023-8077-7222
**Web:** www.uhs.nhs.uk
**VAT No:** 654942706 **Estd:** 1992
**Line of Business:** Hospitals
**Trading Style:** South West Cancer Intelligence Service, Southampton General Hospital
**Issued Capital:** £1

**Principals:** J Trewby, Cb Freng *(Chairman)*, A Matthews *(Financial)*, Ms J Hayward, M Hackett, P Williams, K Bamber, Ms L Samuels, P Bradshaw
**Responsibilities**
**Senior:** Judy Gillow *(Manager)*, Nick Marsden *(Non Executive Member)*, Caspar Ridley *(Manager)*, John Trewby, CB FREng *(Manager)*
**Admin:** Karen Belward *(Out Patients Co-orindinator)*
**HR:** Becci Essex *(Human Resources Manager)*
**Branches:** University Hospital Southampton Nhs Foundation Trust, 34-36 Waverley Road, Southsea, Hampshire PO5 2PW
**US SIC:** 8062 **UK SIC:** 95100
**Auditors:** KPMG LLP

| | 31-03-14 | 31-03-13 | 31-03-12 |
|---|---|---|---|
| TO | 346,298,000 | 581,027,000 | 221,231,000 |
| P/L | (2,039,000) | 751,000 | (2,007,000) |
| NW | 116,383,000 | 239,587,000 | 236,900,000 |
| WC | (8,561,000) | (3,134,000) | (5,853,000) |
| Emp. | 5,446 | 7,862 | 7,699 |

DUNS 54-864-0614

## University Hospitals Bristol Nhs Foundation Trust

Marlborough Street, Bristol, Avon BS1 3NU
**Tel:** 01179-230000
**Web:** www.uhbristol.nhs.uk
**Estd:** 1991 Incorporate By Act Of Parliament
**Line of Business:** Nhs clinics
**Trading Style:** United Bristol Hospitals, Bristol Royal Hospital for Children
**Issued Capital:** £1
**Directors:** G R Nix, P Durie, L Sherwood, Mrs M Maisey, I Stone, H Harrisson, Professor B Pickering, R B Pearson
**Responsibilities**
**Senior:** Mary Barnes *(Manager)*, Vivian Cox *(Director)*, Mairead Dent *(Manager)*, Steve Falk *(Chairman)*, Pat Fields *(Manager)*, Lisa Gardner *(Non-Executive Director)*, Rosemary Greenwood *(Executive)*, Selby Knox *(Non-Executive Director)*, Robert McKinlay *(Director)*, Patricia Mclarnon *(Manager)*, Louise Quincy *(General Manager)*, John Roylence *(Director)*, Hazel Taylor *(Executive)*, Charles Wakeley *(Manager)*, Tim Whittlestone *(Executive)*, James Wisheart *(Director)*, Emma Woollett *(Non-Executive Director)*, Robert Woolley *(Chief Executive Officer)*
**Finance:** Dean Bodill *(?Head of Financial Management)*, Paul Mapson *(Director of Finance & Informat)*
**Marketing:** Hannah Allen *(Assistant Press Officer)*, Kate Hanlon *(Communications Manager)*, Barry McCarthy *(Communications Officer)*, Stephanie Phillips *(Communications Manager)*, Marcella Pinto *(Web Communications Assistant)*, Fiona Reid *(Head of Communications)*
**Sales:** Deborah Lee *(Director of Strategic Developm)*
**Admin:** Lynn Dawson *(Oncology Secretary)*, Paul Mapson *(Director of Finance & Informat)*, Michelle Parfitt-Thomas *(Business Administration Manage)*
**IT:** Dave Oatway *(Network, Security Manager)*
**HR:** Steve Aumayer *(Human Resources Director)*, Claire Buchanan *(Acting Director of Human Resou)*, Sue Donaldson *(Director of Workforce and Orga)*, Maria Fox *(Membership Manager)*, Alex Nestor *(Head of Human Resources)*, Claudette Young *(Medical Human Resources Adviso)*
**Operations:** Sara Betteridge *(Production and Operations Mana)*, Jake Harley *(Production and Operations Mana)*, Moya Hinton *(Production and Operations Mana)*, Yvonne Quinn *(Project Director)*, Tony Ranzetta *(Chief Operating Officer)*, James Rimmer *(Chief Operating Officer)*, Katharine Wale *(Project Executive)*, Ross Walker *(Manager)*, Lisa Wheatley *(Project Manager)*
**Engineering:** Lindsay Ball *(Technical Engineer)*
**Branches:** University Hospitals Bristol Nhs Foundation Trust, Southwell Street, Bristol, Avon BS2 8EG
**US SIC:** 8062 **UK SIC:** 95100
**Auditors:** PricewaterhouseCoopers LLP

| | 31-03-14 | 31-03-13 | 31-03-12 |
|---|---|---|---|
| TO | 554,406,000 | 413,709,000 | 398,411,000 |
| P/L | (5,875,000) | 4,684,000 | 8,985,000 |
| NW | 317,132,000 | 318,821,000 | 317,806,000 |
| WC | 15,522,000 | 5,078,000 | 12,544,000 |
| Emp. | 7,434 | 7,278 | 7,412 |

DUNS 54-864-0259

## University Hospitals Coventry & Warwickshire N H S Trust

Clifford Bridge Road, Coventry, West Midlands CV2 2DX
**Tel:** 02476 964000
**Web:** www.uhcw.nhs.uk
**Estd:** 1992
**Line of Business:** Hospitals
**Issued Capital:** £1
**Principals:** B Stoten *(Chairman)*, A Hardy *(Financial)*, M Newbolt, N Elliott, Ms L Thiebe, M Lee, H Shaw, Ms H Scholefield
**Responsibilities**
**Senior:** John Amplhett *(Director of Planning)*, Yvonne Carter *(Non-Executive Director)*, Alice Casey *(Principal)*, Paul Crofton *(Principal)*, Lynne Elam *(Manager)*, David Eltringham *(Chief Operating Officer)*, Pat Hoffman *(Manager)*
**HR:** Ian Crich *(Human Resources Director)*
**Branches:** University Hospitals Coventry & Warwickshire N H S Trust, Morton Gdns, Lwr Hill Morton Rd, Rugby, Warwickshire CV21 3AQ
**US SIC:** 6732 **UK SIC:** 83100
**Bankers:** Bank Of England (10-00-00)
**Employees:** 8,000

DUNS 21-769-6063 Imp

## University Hospitals of Leicester Nhs Trust

Leicester Royal Infirmary, Infirmary Square, Leicester, Leicestershire LE1 5WW
**Tel:** 03003031573
**Web:** www.eastmidlandscongenitalheart.nhs.uk
**Estd:** 2011 Proprietorship
**Line of Business:** Hospitals
**Proprietor:** D Brown
**US SIC:** 8062 **UK SIC:** 95100
**Employees:** 11,000

DUNS 54-864-3931

## University Hospitals of Leicester Nhs Trust

Level 3, Balmoral Building, Leicester Royal Infirmary, Infirmary Square, Leicester, Leicestershire LE1 5WW
**Web:** www.leicestershospitals.nhs.uk
**Estd:** 1905
**Line of Business:** Health services
**Trading Style:** Glenfield Hospital, Leicester General Hospital, Leicester Royal Infirmary
**Directors:** S Ward, A Tierney, R Pinsent, M Hindle, M Wightman, J Aird, M Lowe-Lauri, D Rowbotham
**Responsibilities**
**Health & Safety:** Jolyon Folkett *(Senior Health & Safety Manager)*
**Facilities:** Tracey Beechey *(Estates Manager)*
**Branches:** University Hospitals Of Leicester Nhs Trust, Glenfield Hospital Nhs Trust, Groby Road, Leicester, Leicestershire LE3 9QP
**US SIC:** 8062, 7397
**UK SIC:** 95100, 83702
**Employees:** 1,600

DUNS 23-194-8469

## University Hospitals of Morecambe Bay Nhs Foundation Trust

Westmorland General Hospital, Burton Road, Kendal, Cumbria LA9 7RG
**Tel:** 01539732288
**Web:** www.uhmb.nhs.uk
**Estd:** 2010
**Line of Business:** Public sector hospital activities, including nhs trusts
**Issued Capital:** £1
**Principals:** A Cummins *(Financial)*, Ms J Daniel, Ms A Garden
**Branches:** University Hospitals Of Morecambe Bay Nhs Foundation Trust, Royal Lancaster Infirmary, Ashton Road, Lancaster, Lancashire LA1 4RP
**US SIC:** 8062 **UK SIC:** 95100
**Auditors:** Grant Thornton UK LLP

| | 31-03-14 | 31-03-13 | 31-03-12 |
|---|---|---|---|
| TO | 270,558,000 | 261,961,000 | 222,720,000 |
| P/L | (18,809,000) | (23,221,000) | (15,898,000) |
| NW | 128,823,000 | 124,831,000 | 142,837,000 |
| WC | (7,144,000) | (8,911,000) | 6,774,000 |
| Emp. | 4,435 | 4,334 | 4,137 |

DUNS 23-293-5531

## University Hospitals of North Midlands Nhs Trust

Royal Stoke University Hospital, Newcastle Road, Stoke-On-Trent, Staffordshire ST4 6QG
**Web:** www.uhns.nhs.uk
**Estd:** 1993
**Line of Business:** Hospitals
**Issued Capital:** £1
**Principals:** J Macdonald *(Chairman)*, C Adcock *(Financial)*, M Hackett, Ms E Rix
**Responsibilities**
**Senior:** Julia Bridgewater *(CEO, Managing Director)*, Margot Johnson *(Human Resources Manager)*, John MacDonald *(Chairperson)*
**IT:** Load Walker *(Senior IT Executive)*
**HR:** Margot Johnson *(Human Resources Manager)*
**Branches:** University Hospitals Of North Midlands Nhs Trust, University Hospital Of North Staffordshire, Hartshill Road, Stoke-On-Trent, Staffordshire ST4 7PA
**US SIC:** 8062 **UK SIC:** 95100
**Auditors:** Grant Thornton UK LLP

| | 31-03-14 | 31-03-13 | 31-03-12 |
|---|---|---|---|
| TO | 419,065,000 | 395,680,000 | 369,819,000 |
| P/L | (20,099,000) | (52,027,000) | (120,635,000) |
| NW | 37,557,000 | 17,101,000 | 73,251,000 |
| WC | (2,303,000) | (14,057,000) | 3,278,000 |
| Emp. | 6,855 | 6,813 | 6,457 |

DUNS 21-165-3923

## University in Shropshire

Shropshire Campus, Priorslee, Telford, Shropshire TF2 9NT
**Estd:** 1992
**Line of Business:** Universities and business schools
**Trading Style:** The University in Shropshire
**Director:** B Conway
**US SIC:** 8221 **UK SIC:** 93100
**Employees:** 150

DUNS 21-040-3383

## University of Aberdeen

Zoology Building, Tillydrone Avenue, Aberdeen, Aberdeenshire AB24 2TZ
**Web:** www.abdn.ac.uk
**Estd:** 2005 Incorporate By Act Of Parliament
**Line of Business:** University
**Directors:** A Arthur, Dr P Edwards, Ms J Craw, I Diamond, S Logan, B Pack, N Webster
**Responsibilities**
**Senior:** Elizabeth Baggs *(Head Of School)*
**US SIC:** 8221 **UK SIC:** 93100
**Auditors:** KPMF LLP
**Employees:** 1
**Turnover:** £225,386,000

DUNS 21-238-1045 Imp

## University of Aberdeen

King's College, Aberdeen, Aberdeenshire AB24 3FX
**Web:** www.abdn.ac.uk
**VAT No:** 267329044 **Estd:** 1946
**Line of Business:** University
**Director:** Dr A Alexander
**Responsibilities**
**Senior:** Angus Donaldson *(Estates Manager)*, Dragan Jovcic *(Chair in Engineering)*
**Marketing:** Lorraine Manders *(Marketing Director)*, Rachel Sanderson *(Marketing Director)*
**HR:** Caroline Inglis *(Human Resources Director)*
**Health & Safety:** Nigel Corby *(Security Manager)*
**Facilities:** Angus Donaldson *(Estates Manager)*
**Operations:** Nigel Corby *(Security Manager)*, Lorraine Manders *(Marketing Director)*
**Purchasing:** Gary McKinnon *(Head of Procurement)*
**Engineering:** Dragan Jovcic *(Chair in Engineering)*
**Branches:** University Of Aberdeen, George Street, Cromarty, Ross-Shire IV11 8YJ
**US SIC:** 8221 **UK SIC:** 93100
**Auditors:** KPMG LLP
**Employees:** 3,348
**Turnover:** £221,026,000

DUNS 21-039-8341 Imp

## University of Abertay Dundee

Kydd Building, 40 Bell Street, Dundee, Angus DD1 1HG
**Tel:** 01382308000
**Web:** www.abertay.ac.uk
**Estd:** 2013
**Line of Business:** Florists
**Responsibilities**
**Senior:** Campbell Bruce *(Marketing Manager)*
**Marketing:** Kirsty Cameron *(Communications Officer)*, Kevin Coe *(Director of Communications)*
**HR:** Jaime Boath *(Senior HR Officer)*, Carolyn Boland *(Senior HR Officer)*, Eilidh Fraser *(Human Resources Director)*, Jayne Kirby *(HR Assistant)*, Judith Lindsay *(HR Officer)*, Diane Norris *(Senior HR Officer)*, Alison Ross *(Senior HR Officer)*
**Health & Safety:** Jed Burke *(Health & Safety Manager)*
**US SIC:** 8221 **UK SIC:** 93100
**Auditors:** PricewaterhouseCoopers LLP
**Employees:** 1
**Turnover:** £36,252,000

DUNS 42-440-0661

## University of Bath

Claverton Down, Bath, Avon BA2 7AY
**Tel:** 01225388388
**Web:** www.bath.ac.uk
**Reg No:** 0000644RC **Estd:** 1966 Incorporate By Act Of Parliament
**Line of Business:** First-degree level higher education
**Trading Style:** University of Bath-Finance Department
**Principals:** D Henderson, R Mawditt, V Vandelinde
**Responsibilities**
**Senior:** Alex Jeffries *(Board Member)*, Geraldine Jones *(Executive)*, Iryna Withington *(Senior Manager)*
**Finance:** Diane Aderyn *(Director of Finance & Commerci)*, Richard Fairchild *(Lecturer)*
**Marketing:** Lachmi Bose *(Journal of Transport Economics)*, Katrina James, Vicky Just *(Press Officer)*, Tim Kaner, Stephen Rangecroft *(Director of Marketing & Extern)*, Carolyn Strong *(Marketing Director)*, Tom Trentham *(Web Developer)*, Angela Webley *(Marketing Manager)*
**Admin:** Catherine Aubin *(IMML and Exchanges Administrat)*, Margaret Birdsall *(Administrator)*, Ruth Burdett *(Administrator)*, Anny Colgan *(Admissions Officer)*, Kay Elliott *(Director, Administration)*, Lahra Hall *(ITE Administrator, Admissions)*, Diana Hamilton *(Staff Development Administrato)*, Ann-Marie Hartland *(Director, Administration)*, Sarah Mcinnes *(Personal Assistant)*, JulianAmy Phillips *(Admissions Secretary. Departme)*, Marie Pullen *(Administrator)*, Cynthia Spencer *(Administrator)*
**IT:** Joanna Bryson *(Reader of Computer Science)*, Zhimin Wang *(Software Engineering Analyst)*
**HR:** Bronagh Barrett *(HR Administrator)*, Sue Briault *(Careers Advisor)*, Sam Burgess *(HR Manager)*, Ian Cheetham *(Human Resources Director)*, Diana Hamilton *(Staff Development Administrato)*, Nicholas Kinnie *(Professor in Human Resource Ma)*, Jodie Knight *(Human Resources Manager)*, Emma Nash *(Staff Development Assistant)*
**Health & Safety:** Paul Maggs *(Health & Safety Advisor)*
**Operations:** Simon Hillier *(AV Support Manager)*
**Engineering:** Ewan Basterfield *(Senior Technician (Research))*, Craig Carter *(Electrical Assistant)*, Barry Crittenden *(Professor of Chemical Engineer)*, Jos Darling *(Senior Lecturer -Mechanical En)*, Tim Mays *(Head of Chemical Engineering)*, Stuart Meadwell *(Engineer)*, Tony Miles *(Head of Department of Mechanic)*, April Su *(Technical Engineer)*
**Branches:** University Of Bath, The Avenue, Bath, Avon BA2 7AY
**US SIC:** 8221 **UK SIC:** 93100
**Auditors:** KPMG LLP

| | 31-07-14 | 31-07-13 | 31-07-12 |
|---|---|---|---|
| TO | 222,773,000 | 208,139,000 | 196,648,000 |
| P/L | 17,199,000 | 16,257,000 | 10,572,000 |
| NW | 474,545,000 | 191,954,000 | 170,313,000 |
| WC | 87,282,000 | 51,601,000 | 67,678,000 |
| Emp. | 2,572 | 2,443 | 2,365 |

DUNS 23-225-6065 Imp

## University of Bedfordshire

University Square, Luton, Bedfordshire LU1 3JU
**Tel:** 01234400400
**Web:** www.beds.ac.uk
**VAT No:** 600498850 **Estd:** 1993
**Line of Business:** University
**Principals:** A Bentley *(Chairman)*, D Barrett, J Shea, Ms T Aldrich, C Brohier, Ms J Milns, J Sentinella, L Ebdon
**Responsibilities**
**Senior:** Graham Blake *(Facilities Director)*, Alan Bullimore *(General Manager)*, Kathryn Gray *(General Manager)*, Yasmin Jetha *(Vice Chairperson)*, Roisin Kendall *(General Manager)*
**Finance:** Donald Harley *(Financial Director)*
**Marketing:** Kevin Cunningham *(Communications Officer)*, Paddy Day *(Communications Assistant)*, Nick Hamilton-Brain *(Communications Assistant)*, Patricia Murchie *(Marketing Director)*, Nicolae Pavel *(?International Marketing Manag)*, Mima Rybanska *(Marketing Officer)*, Nick Sheppard *(Head of Communications)*, Simon Wesson *(Communications Assistant)*, June Wilson *(Systems & Mitigation Officer)*
**Sales:** Barbara Billington *(Business Support Coordinator)*, Sarah Waller *(Arts and Business Development)*
**Admin:** Carol Dawes-Binns *(Personal Assistant)*, Kathi Parker *(Administrator, Law, Accounting)*, Christie Roman *(Administrator)*, Debby Wakeham *(Disability Advice Team Adminis)*

IT: Marc Conrad (Senior Lecturer, Computer Scie), A Freimanis (IT Director), Wei Huang (Senior Lecturer, Computing), Carsten Maple (Pro Vice Chancellor (Research)), Andrea Thorogood (UBV Community Projects Manager)
HR: Cathy Abu (Human Resources Manager)
Health & Safety: Caroline Cousins (Health & Safety Officer), Gillian Malins (Student Advisor - Health and W)
Facilities: Graham Blake (Facilities Director)
Branches: University Of Bedfordshire, Stoneygate Road, Luton, Bedfordshire LU4 9TJ
US SIC: 8221  UK SIC: 93100
Auditors: KPMG LLP
Employees: 1,000
Turnover: £113,349,000

---

DUNS 22-784-2325    **Imp**
## University of Birmingham
Edgbaston Park Road, Birmingham, West Midlands B15 2TT
Tel: 0121 414 3344
Web: www.birmingham.ac.uk
Reg No: 0000645RC VAT No: 729856187
Estd: 1900 Incorporate By Act Of Parliament
Line of Business: University
Issued Capital: £2
Principals: Mrs G Ball (Financial), Professor M Sterling, W J Glover
Responsibilities
Senior: Gordon Allt (Manager), Mohammed Ansar (Executive), Ian Boomer (Manager), Victoria Burns (Executive), Justine Carolan (Executive), Caroline Chapain (Board Member), Mark Chesterman (Director of Post Qualifying Pr), M. Church (Board Member), Hayden Cohen (Executive), Lee Costin (Manager), Nick Crowson (Board Member), Natalie Elderfield (General Manager), Bess Evans (General Manager), Nicola Fenwick (Senior Manager), Carol Fowler (Executive), Janet Fuery (Executive), Monica Guise (General Manager), Luke Gunn (General Manager), Tim Haughton (Manager), Ronald Jubb (Manager), Paulette King (Executive), Carole Lambeth (Production and Operations Mana), Lynne Long (Executive), Philip Lumley (Board Member), Christine Mccarthy (Executive), Nandy Millan (Senior Manager), Emilio Porfiri (Executive), Claire Potter (General Manager), Joshua Rappoport (Manager), Kiran Rashid (Executive), Karim Raza (General Manager), Rob Rowlands (Board Member), Sian Sankey (Board Member), Chris Skelcher (Partner), Julie Tonks (Team Leader), John Winer (Executive), Cai Xiaoming (Doctor)
Finance: Gillian Ball (financial director), Erica Conway (Deputy Director of Finance), Julie Cope (Financial Analyst), Mike Dean (Accountant), Stuart Underhill (Accounting Assistant), Valerie Woolford (PA to Director of Finance)
Marketing: Jenny Ameghino (Media Relations Manager), Carla Amos (Head of Marketing), Catherine Byerley (International Media Relations), Martha Campos (Marketing Officer), Katie Connolly (Digital Marketing & Comms Mana), Claire Doggett (Marketing Director), Ken Jakeman (Operational Manager), Nathan Johnson (Web Project Development Office), Bryoney Johnson (Internal Communications Office), Jo Kite (Head of Communications and Mar), Ann Kite (Marketing Manager), Chris Mabey (Professor of Management), Andrew Pressey (Head of Marketing), Sean Rath (Community Action Officer), Steve Rea (Webmaster), Elizabeth Warner-Davies (Head of Library Customer Suppo)
Sales: Andy Mountain (Business Engagement Partner)
Admin: Wendy Banner (Social Work Administrative Man), Geraldine Biggerton (Administrator), Ann Bolstridge (Administrator), Parveen Chahal (Course Administrator), Alexia Chrysostomou (Admin Assistant), Sally Cliff (Personal Assistant), Janet Elwell (Administrator), Geraldine Geraldine Dora (Research Administrator), Susie Gilbert (Policy Programme Administrator), Jill Green (Administrator), Helen Harris (Administration), Yvonne Henderson (Administrator), Joanna Hine (Research Programme Administrat), Noreen Hynes (Administration & Bookings Offi), Christine Jennings (Administrative Assistant), Marian Jordan (Network Administrator), Sara Kinahan (Administrator), Catherine McNicholl (Administrator), Kieran Mcgovern (Administrator), Katie Mellor (Administrator), Yvonne O'Byrne (Head of Quality and Admin), Angela Oakley (Administrator), Andrea Potter (Administrator), Smriti Prinja (Administration & Bookings Offi), Donna Purkiss (Administrator), Caroline Rance (Administrator), Javed Rehman

(Accommodation Officer), Jasvinder Sihre (Administrator), Sarah Stimpson (Secretary), Carolyn Sweet (Secretary), Elizabeth Warner-Davies (Head of Library Customer Suppo), Hanna Wride (Teaching Programmes Administra)
IT: Mark Assinder (Head of Information Technology), Heather Behan (Head of IT Project Office), Laura Coult (Cultural Programming Coordinat), David Deighton (Chief Enterprise Architect), Andy Ferguson (Service Desk Manager), Marian Jordan (Network Administrator), Lin MacKenzie (Programmes Manager), John Turnbull (Head of Networks)
HR: Sharon Buckley (Medical Education Developer), Adrian Buckley (Assistant Director of HR (Stra), Stefan Buzar (Lecturer), Leigh Casey (Assistant Director of HR (Peop), Vanessa Chesterton (Admissions & Recruitment Assis), Jean Harris (HR Advisor), Jennifer Lapworth (Executive Officer HR), Hope Nightingale (HR Administrator), Caroline Radnor (Adult Cycle Trainor), Declan Vaughan (Assistant Director of HR), Helen Webb (?Executive Officer- HR)
Facilities: Clive Jeynes (Facilities Manager), Andrew Trevis-Smith (Manager)
Operations: Suki Basra (Executive), Sheriden Bevan (?Project Officer), Chris Boshell (Head of Student Systems), Margaret Donnison (Project Manager), Lisa Fuller (Project Development Coordinato), Loretta Gibson (Operations Manager), Adrian Scriven (Sports Club Development Office), Andrew Trevis-Smith (Manager)
Purchasing: Pauline Harrison (Procurement Manager), Susanna Ting (Assistant Procurement Advisor)
Fleet: Andrew Quinn (Lecturer - Aerodynamics of Tra), Mark Stirling (Lecturer- Aerodynamics of trai)
Engineering: Ann Ankcorn (Technical Engineer), Greg Denton (Engineer), Richard Greswell (Executive), Mandy Handley (Chemical Engineering), Shrikant Jondhale (Technical Support), Aruna Mistry (Teacher), Andy Moss (Technical Engineer), Andrzej Pacek (Professor of Multiphase System), James Peart (Head of Technical Services), Rashid Ravat (Technical Engineer), Christopher Stark (Technician), Andrew Tanner (Executive), Zhibing Zhang (Professor - Chemical Engineeri)
Branches: University Of Birmingham, Edgbaston, Birmingham, West Midlands B15 2TT
US SIC: 8221  UK SIC: 93100
Auditors: KPMG LLP
Bankers: Lloyds TSB Bank plc (30-19-14)
Employees: 6,089
Turnover: £462,373,000

---

DUNS 67-229-6373
## The University of Bolton Enterprises Co Ltd
Deane Road, Bolton, Lancashire BL3 5AB
Tel: 01204903903 Fax: 01204-399074
Web: www.bolton.ac.uk
Reg No: 6056588 Estd: 2007 Private Limited Company
Line of Business: Other business activities not elsewhere classified
Issued Capital: £1
Director: A Unsworth
US SIC: 7399  UK SIC: 83954

| | 31-07-13 | 31-07-12 | 31-07-11 |
|---|---|---|---|
| TA | 1 | 1 | 1 |
| NW | 1 | 1 | 1 |

---

DUNS 22-964-0750    **Imp**
## University of Bradford
Richmond Road, Bradford, West Yorkshire BD7 1DP
Tel: 01274234485 Fax: 01274232323
Web: www.bradford.ac.uk
Reg No: 0000647RC VAT No: 686548968
Estd: 1965 Incorporate By Act Of Parliament
Line of Business: University
Principals: G Hope-Terry (Financial), B Lockwood, D Hull, N Andrews
Responsibilities
Senior: Shirley Congdon (Pro Vice Chancellor), Stephen Garrity (Head of Hydrogeological), Brian Winn (Deputy Vice Chancellor)
Operations: Stephen Garrity (Head of Hydrogeological)
Branches: University Of Bradford, Trinity Green Campus, Easby Road, Bradford, West Yorkshire BD7 1JG
US SIC: 8221  UK SIC: 93100
Auditors: KPMG LLP
Bankers: National Westminster Bank Plc (56-00-36)
Employees: 250
Turnover: £123,102,000

---

DUNS 22-832-1451    **Imp**
## University of Brighton
Mithras House, Lewes Road, Brighton, East Sussex BN2 4AT
Tel: 01273600900
Web: www.brighton.ac.uk
VAT No: 620658352 Estd: 2011
Line of Business: Education services
Directors: Professor D J Watson, D E House
Responsibilities
Senior: Bruce Brown (Manager), Sarah Hare (Manager), Susan Mchugh (Manager), John Mogg (Manager), Tim Simpson (Manager)
Finance: Susan Mchugh (Manager)
Marketing: Elizabeth Sanz (Head of Marketing)
Health & Safety: Alan Cowen (Health & Safety Officer)
Facilities: Mike Clark (Director of Estates)
Branches: University Of Brighton, Paddock Field, University Of Brighton, Falmer, Brighton, East Sussex BN1 9SF
US SIC: 8221  UK SIC: 93100
Auditors: KPMG LLP
Bankers: Barclays Bank Plc (20-12-75)
Employees: 500
Turnover: £154,283,000

---

DUNS 21-880-0032
## University of Brighton School of Health Professions
49 Darley Road, Eastbourne, East Sussex BN20 7UR
Tel: 01273643772
Web: www.brighton.ac.uk
Estd: 2012
Line of Business: University
Responsibilities
Senior: Lynne Caladine (Head Of School)
US SIC: 8221  UK SIC: 93100
Employees: 80

---

DUNS 22-505-1309    **Imp**
## The University of Bristol
Senate House, Tyndall Avenue, Bristol, Avon BS8 1TH
Tel: 0117 928 9000 Fax: 01179250900
Web: www.bristol.ac.uk
Reg No: 0000648RC Estd: 1876 Incorporate By Act Of Parliament
Line of Business: University
Trading Style: Alspac (Children of the 90s), The Institute of Advanced Studies, School of Chemistry, The Medical School
Principals: J Kingman, Sir J Kingman, J Morse, I Crawford, M Parry, I Crawford, Sir J Morse, M Parry
Responsibilities
Senior: Andrew Nield (Financial Director)
Finance: Andrew Nield (Financial Director)
Branches: The University Of Bristol, Langford House, Bristol, Avon BS40 5DU
US SIC: 8221  UK SIC: 93100
Auditors: PricewaterhouseCoopers LLP
Bankers: National Westminster Bank Plc (56-00-05)
Employees: 5,000
Turnover: £385,300,000

---

DUNS 21-584-6617
## University of Bristol Biochemistry
University Walk, Bristol, Avon BS8 1TD
Tel: 01173312167
Web: www.bristol.ac.uk
Estd: 2011
Line of Business: University
Responsibilities
Senior: Leo Brady (Head Professor)
US SIC: 8221  UK SIC: 93100
Employees: 160

---

DUNS 42-440-0034    **Imp**
## The University of Buckingham
Yeomanry House, Hunter Street, Buckingham, Buckinghamshire MK18 1EG
Tel: 01280820220
Web: www.buckingham.ac.uk
Reg No: 0000730RC Estd: 1976
Line of Business: Higher education
Directors: R Tomkinson, Sir M Jacomb
Responsibilities
Senior: Lucy Hodges (Director, Communications)
US SIC: 8221  UK SIC: 93100
Employees: 200

---

DUNS 22-655-2610
## University of Cambridge
The Old School, Trinity Lane, Cambridge, Cambridgeshire CB2 1TN
Web: www.ch.cam.ac.uk
Estd: 2012 Incorporate By Act Of Parliament
Line of Business: University

Principals: A Reid (Financial), Ms P Stevens, Ms L Gladden, Sir L Borysiewicz
Co. Secretary: Dr Jonathan Nicholls
Responsibilities
Senior: Michael Bienias (Manager), Dan Frenkel (Head Of Department)
Finance: Andy Clarke (Head of Support Services)
Marketing: Jaq Saggers (Marketing Director)
Facilities: Michael Bienias (Manager)
Operations: Fehmi Cirak (Engineer)
Engineering: Bill Byrne (Professor of Information Engin)
Branches: University Of Cambridge, Hills Road, Cambridge, Cambridgeshire CB2 0SP
US SIC: 8221  UK SIC: 93100
Auditors: PricewaterhouseCoopers LLP
Bankers: Barclays Bank Plc (20-17-19)
Employees: 8,000
Turnover: £1,251,000,000

---

DUNS 21-038-8209
## University of Cambridge Judge Business School
University Of Cambridge, Trumpington Street, Cambridge, Cambridgeshire CB2 1QA
Web: www.jbs.cam.ac.uk
Estd: 2012
Line of Business: Schools - business
Responsibilities
Senior: Martin Kernan (Facilities Manager)
US SIC: 8221, 8249
UK SIC: 93100, 93300
Employees: 200

---

DUNS 21-033-8159
## University of Cambridge Pure Maths
Wilberforce Road, Cambridge, Cambridgeshire CB3 0WA
Web: www.damtp.cam.ac.uk
Estd: 2002 Proprietorship
Line of Business: University
Proprietor: Miss A Mobbs
US SIC: 8221  UK SIC: 93100
Employees: 76

---

DUNS 23-145-8647
## University of Cardiff School of Engineering
Queen St Queens Arcade, Cardiff, South Glamorgan CF10 2BY
Tel: 029-2087-4070
Web: www.engin.cf.ac.uk
Estd: 1883
Line of Business: University
Principals: Rt Hon N G Kinnock (President), W H John, V Kane, Sir R Lloyd Jones, Sir D Walker, K S Hopkins, S S Harries
Responsibilities
Senior: Phil Bowen (Head Of School)
Branches: University Of Cardiff School Of Engineering, Senghennydd Court, Salisbury Road, Cardiff, South Glamorgan CF24 4DS
US SIC: 8221  UK SIC: 93100
Employees: 3,000

---

DUNS 23-981-3694
## University of Central Lancashire Hec
Fylde Road, Preston, Lancashire PR1 2XQ
Tel: 01772-201-201
Web: www.uclan.ac.uk
VAT No: 677379376 Estd: 1882 Incorporate By Act Of Parliament
Line of Business: First-degree level higher education
Trading Style: Uclan, Media Innovation Studio
Directors: Ms M M Ayers, F Edwin, P L Jackson, J A Heaslip, B Hill, D E Eaves, C E Birch, N K Scott
Responsibilities
Senior: Brian Booth (Principal), Margaret Chadwick (Principal), Josephine Farrington (Principal), Philip Holifield (Principal), Francis Kennedy (Principal), John McGrath (Principal), Malcolm McVicar (Vice Chancellor), Kenneth Ridings (Principal)
Marketing: Alex Wale (Marketing Manager)
Health & Safety: Christine Edwards (Safety, Health and Environment)
Engineering: Susie Thorpe (Technician)
Branches: University Of Central Lancashire Hec, 24 Fylde Road, Preston, Lancashire PR1 7BQ
US SIC: 8221  UK SIC: 93100
Auditors: KPMG LLP
Bankers: HSBC Bank plc (40-37-25)

| | 31-07-12 | 31-07-11 | 31-07-10 |
|---|---|---|---|
| TO | 198,700,000 | 206,735,000 | 199,018,000 |
| P/L | 14,598,000 | 6,012,000 | 2,582,000 |
| NW | 226,144,000 | 226,683,000 | 193,252,000 |
| WC | 54,000,000 | 48,149,000 | 42,635,000 |
| Emp. | 2,356 | 2,466 | 2,540 |

DUNS 21-725-6946
## University of Central Lancashire Students' Union
Fylde Road, Preston, Lancashire PR1 7BY
**Tel:** 01772894354
**Web:** www.uclansu.co.uk
**Reg No:** 7623917 **Estd:** 2011 Private Company Limited By Guarantee
**Line of Business:** Retail sale in non-specialised stores with food, beverages or tobacco predominating
**Directors:** Miss M L Dixon, Miss J E Ellis, M Murphy, Mrs E J Riley, S D Seymour, Miss L D Haigh, Miss J H Linsel, L A Macneall
**Co. Secretary:** Peter Shilton Godwin
**Responsibilities**
**Senior:** Lucy Linsel (Director)
**US SIC:** 5411, 5813, 7361, 7392
**UK SIC:** 64100, 66200, 83954, 83951

| | 31-07-13 | 31-07-12 |
|---|---|---|
| TO | 4,782,501 | 4,923,485 |
| P/L | (132,516) | 106,289 |
| NW | 47,834 | 180,350 |
| WC | 191,141 | 391,916 |
| Emp. | 203 | 224 |

DUNS 23-286-7150
## University of Chester
Parkgate Road, Chester, Cheshire CH1 4BJ
**Tel:** 01244511000
**Web:** www.chester.ac.uk
**Estd:** 1839
**Line of Business:** University
**Directors:** Rev E V Binks, T Wheeler
**Responsibilities**
**Senior:** Jared Allen (Manager)
**Marketing:** Lynette Bailey (Director of Marketing), Andrew Muncey (IT Tutor), Shai Vure (Marketing Assistant)
**Admin:** Lucy Clough (Clerical Assistant), Kirsty Taylor (Administrative Assistant)
**IT:** Andy Davies (Lecturer, Web, Digital, IT)
**Branches:** University Of Chester, Warrington Campus, Crab Lane, Warrington, Cheshire WA2 0DB
**US SIC:** 8221 **UK SIC:** 93100
**Employees:** 650
**Turnover:** £56,582,000

DUNS 21-144-5841 *Imp*
## The University of Chichester
Bishop Otter Campus, College Lane, Chichester, West Sussex PO19 6PE
**Tel:** 01243816000
**Web:** www.chi.ac.uk
**Reg No:** 4740553 **Estd:** 2003 Incorporate By Act Of Parliament
**Line of Business:** First-degree level higher education
**Directors:** R Martin, P M Hollins, Professor C Behagg, Mrs K Vagg, M C Sowerby, Ms J L Hope, Dr A Naylor, T Hancock
**Co. Secretary:** Mrs Ann Holder
**Responsibilities**
**Senior:** Stephen Bowman (Director), Helen Bray (Director), Anthony Cane (Director), Jill Cook (Director), Richard Fortin (Manager), Joy Gilliver (Director), Nicola Nageon De Lestang (Director), Fiona Price (Director), John Stapleton (Director), Marilyn Surgeon (Director), Alex Twitchen (Director)
**Branches:** The University Of Chichester, Bognor Regis Campus, Upper Bognor Road, Bognor Regis, West Sussex PO21 1HR
**US SIC:** 8221 **UK SIC:** 93100
**Auditors:** BDO Stoy Hayward LLP
**Bankers:** National Westminster Bank Plc (60-03-08)

| | 31-07-14 | 31-07-13 | 31-07-12 |
|---|---|---|---|
| TO | 47,046,000 | 45,493,000 | 41,080,000 |
| P/L | 1,207,000 | 2,001,000 | 2,379,000 |
| NW | 52,143,000 | 54,687,000 | 50,060,000 |
| WC | 4,607,000 | 4,614,000 | 6,759,000 |
| Emp. | 526 | 517 | 488 |

DUNS 23-707-5460
## The University of Cumbria
Bowerham Road, Lancaster, Lancashire LA1 3JD
**Tel:** 01524590800
**Web:** www.cumbria.ac.uk
**VAT No:** 156670057 **Estd:** 1964
**Line of Business:** First-degree level higher education
**Director:** C Carr
**Responsibilities**
**Senior:** Julia Briggs (Manager)
**Admin:** Sue Alderson (IT Service Administrator)
**IT:** Sue Alderson (IT Service Administrator)
**HR:** Karen Chubb (Staff Development Officer)
**Purchasing:** Claire Gray (Purchasing Officer)
**Branches:** The University Of Cumbria, 18 Spencer St, Carlisle, Cumbria CA1 1BG
**US SIC:** 8221 **UK SIC:** 93100

**Bankers:** National Westminster Bank Plc (01-54-90)
**Employees:** 3,000
**Turnover:** £56,973,000

DUNS 67-225-7110
## The University of Cumbria
Fusehill Street, Carlisle, Cumbria CA1 2HH
**Tel:** 01228-616234
**Web:** www.cumbria.ac.uk
**Reg No:** 6033238 **Estd:** 2006 Private Company Limited By Guarantee
**Line of Business:** First-degree level higher education
**Directors:** G A Donnelly, Doctor S J Curl, I Johnson, A N Fraser, Mrs S E Southern, W H Sang, J W Newcome, S D Allen
**Co. Secretary:** Neil Harris
**Responsibilities**
**Senior:** Emma Bales (Director), Euan Cartwright (Director), Linda Challis (Director), Hilary Crowe (Director), Claire Hensman (Director), Stuart Hyde (Director), Roger Liddle (Board Member), Keith Snell (Director), Jill Stannard (Director), Peter Strike (Vice chancellor), Daniel Tomlinson (Director)
**Finance:** Kate McLaughlin-Flynn (Finance Director)
**Marketing:** Helen Fleming (Marketing Manager)
**US SIC:** 8221 **UK SIC:** 93100

| | 31-07-13 | 31-07-12 | 31-07-11 |
|---|---|---|---|
| TO | 73,566,000 | 78,156,000 | 86,250,000 |
| P/L | 4,205,000 | 7,597,000 | 6,566,000 |
| NW | 29,431,000 | 25,068,000 | 25,766,000 |
| WC | 10,588,000 | 2,858,000 | 1,874,000 |
| Emp. | 986 | 1,001 | 1,129 |

DUNS 21-592-5128
## University of Cumbria
Newton Rigg, Penrith, Cumbria CA11 0AH
**Tel:** 01768893400
**Web:** www.newtonrigg.ac.uk
**Estd:** 2011 Proprietorship
**Line of Business:** Further education schools and colleges
**Proprietor:** Mrs D Lishman
**Responsibilities**
**Senior:** Wes Johnson (Principal)
**US SIC:** 8221 **UK SIC:** 93100
**Employees:** 200

DUNS 23-982-2901 *Imp*
## University of Dundee
Nethergate, Dundee, Angus DD1 4DG
**Tel:** 01382383000
**Web:** www.dundee.ac.uk
**Reg No:** 0000649RC **Estd:** 1969
**Line of Business:** University
**Principals:** R S Walker (Financial), Sir A Langlands, Dr D Duncan
**Responsibilities**
**Senior:** Louise Aird (Procurement Officer), Peter Downes (Principal)
**Sales:** Julie Brady (Business Development Manager f), Fiona Mitchell (College Research Business Deve), Linda O'Neill (International Business Develop), Sahar Sabetnia (College Research Business Deve), Robbie Sharpe (College Research Business Deve), Duncan Simpson (College Research Business Deve), Michelle Swain (College Research Business Deve)
**IT:** Tom Mortimer (IT Director), Mark Whitehorn (Chair of Analytics)
**Health & Safety:** Ian Scragg (Head of Safety Services)
**Purchasing:** Louise Aird (Procurement Officer), Euan Banyard (Contracts Manager), Pauline Cheung (Contracts Manager), Martin Wilkie (Contracts Manager)
**Branches:** University Of Dundee, St Mary Place, Dundee, Angus DD1 5RB
**US SIC:** 8221 **UK SIC:** 93100
**Auditors:** Grant Thornton UK LLP
**Bankers:** The Royal Bank Of Scotland Plc (83-50-00)
**Employees:** 2,901
**Turnover:** £219,090,000

DUNS 21-030-1683
## University of Dundee Exhibitions Department
13 Perth Road, Dundee, Angus DD1 4HT
**Tel:** 01382385330
**Web:** www.exhibitions.dundee.ac.uk
**Estd:** 2005
**Line of Business:** Art gallery
**Partners:** Professor P Gregor, Mrs J Hughes
**Responsibilities**
**Senior:** Sophia Hao (Curator), Laura Simpson (Manager)
**US SIC:** 7911, 7999
**UK SIC:** 97913
**Employees:** 110

DUNS 23-642-7159 *Imp*
## University of Durham
The Palatine Centre, Durham University, Stockton Road, Durham, County Durham DH1 3LE
**Fax:** 01913-349-264
**Web:** www.dunelm.org.uk
**Reg No:** 0000650RC **VAT No:** 178075242
**Estd:** 1832 Incorporate By Act Of Parliament
**Line of Business:** First-degree level higher education
**Trading Style:** Durham University
**Principals:** Prof K Calman, Miss P Lubacz, Dr J Hogan
**Responsibilities**
**Marketing:** Claire Roper-Browning (Development Manager)
**HR:** Claire Curran (Director Of Hr)
**Branches:** University Of Durham, Palace Green, Durham, County Durham DH1 3RN
**US SIC:** 8221 **UK SIC:** 93100
**Auditors:** KPMG Audit PLC
**Bankers:** Barclays Bank Plc (20-27-41)
**Employees:** 3,460
**Turnover:** £248,920,000

DUNS 42-440-0075
## University of East Anglia
Norwich Research Park, Earlham Road, Norwich, Norfolk NR4 7TJ
**Tel:** 01603-456161
**Web:** www.uea.ac.uk
**Reg No:** 0000651RC **Estd:** 1963 Incorporate By Act Of Parliament
**Line of Business:** University
**Director:** Prof D Eastwood
**Responsibilities**
**Senior:** Stathis Banakas (Director Research), Christopher Bigsby (Professor), Marian Brandon (Reader in Social Work Director), John Charmley (Director of East Anglian Studi), Alan Coddington (Retirement Committee Represent), Sara Connolly (Reader in Personnel Economics), Kate Conway (Manager), Sue Cox (Board Member), Simona Florescu (Manager), Laura Glibbery (Manager), Marisa Goulden (Board Member), Matt Hume (Executive), Michelle Jones (Senior Manager), Peter Langdon (General Manager), Catherine Locke (Executive), Roy Love (Executive), Adrian Matthews (Executive), Maggie Mcarthur (Lecturer), Robbie Meehan (General Manager), Maria O' Connell (Manager), Iain Reeman (IT Manager), Claudina Richards (Senior Manager), Raymond Scott (Assistant Director Strategy, P), Thomas Sikor (Board Member), Anne-Marie Triggs (Executive), Katharine Trott (Executive), Sally Ward (General Manager), Liz Westaway (Executive)
**Finance:** Sarah Allen (Lecturer - Accounting), Lisa Blenkinsop (International Officer), Stephen Donaldson (Financial Director), Tracey Hearn (International Officer), Helen Latham (Finance Manager), Nilufar Rashidova (Senior International Officer)
**Marketing:** Haya Al-Dajani (Lecturer in Enterprenureship a), Simon Dunford (Assistant Head of Communicatio), Kate Franklin (Marketing Manager, Research an), Angela Hook (Marketing and Recruitment Mana), Robin Keith (Head of Web & Development), Laura Paul (Marketing and Communications A)
**Sales:** Nick Goodwin (Business Development Manager), Julie Schofield (Business Development Manager)
**Admin:** Louise Addison (Administrative Assistant), James Alborough (Office Manager), Shawn Alexander (Administrator), Sue Armes (Senior Administrative Assistan), Dawn Corby (Administrator), Sarah Cox (Administrator), Lynne Crossland (Administrator), Lucie Dack (Personal Assistant), Helen Dodgson (Senior Administrative Assistan), Sonia Fagan (Administrator), Carole Filer (Senior Administrative Assistan), Sue Fincham (Administrative Assistant), Lori Gilbert (Administrative Assistant), Bridget Gillies (Archives Assistant), Tracy Hempsall (Administrative Assistant), Kate Hesketh (Course Administrator, Academic), Janet Higgs (Clerical Assistant), Katherine Humphries (Administrative Assistant), Lynne James (Specialist Pharmacy Administra), Sue King (Administrator), Kaye Mackay (Secretary), Tracey Oak (Office Manager), John Pullinger (Secretary), Jason Rust (Administrator), Nicola Skivington (Admin Assistant), Debbie Slaughter (Administrator), Eve Slaymaker (Secretary), Timothy Southon (Administrator), Brian Summers (Registrar & Secretary), Gilly Totton (Administrative Assistant), Laura Vincent (Project Secretary), Liz Williams (Administrative Assistant), Julie Winner (Administrative Assistant)

**IT:** Dudley Beckles (Head of Information Technology), Dominic Belisario (Head of Desktop Services and C), Joanne Champeney (SIS Application Support Adviso), Jonathan Colam-French (Information Technology Directo), Leo Earl (Systems Developer HPC), Matthew Ladd (IT Systems Administrator), Keith Porter (Information Technology Manager), Iain Reeman (IT Manager), Jude Smith (Teacher), Simon Youngs (Web Developer)
**HR:** Sarah Elsegood (HUM Faculty Librarian), Santha Forder (Human Resources Manager), Natasha Garforth (Human Resources Assistant), Julie Goodridge (Human Resources Manager), Angela Hook (Marketing and Recruitment Mana), Steve Oldfield (Staff Development Officer), Cecile Piper (Personnel Director), Andrea Rippon (Research Staff Training and De), Kirsty Webb (Senior Human Resources Adviser)
**Health & Safety:** Paul Donson (Head of Safety Services)
**Facilities:** Roger Bond (Estates Director), Sarah Freeman (Research Associate and Educati)
**Operations:** Allison Carroll (Electronic Services Manager), Gurpreet Gill (Operations Manager)
**Fleet:** Javier Delgado-Esteban (Transport and Logistics Manage)
**Engineering:** Phillip Highfield (IT Support Technician), Andy Mee (Learning Technologist), Richard Rodda (IT Support Technician), Mitchell Wright (IT Support Technician (FMH))
**Branches:** University Of East Anglia, Landbeach Road, Cambridge, Cambridgeshire CB24 6DB
**US SIC:** 8221 **UK SIC:** 93100
**Auditors:** PricewaterhouseCoopers LLP
**Employees:** 2,647
**Turnover:** £185,068,000

DUNS 23-996-9033
## University of East London
Romford Road, London E15 4LZ
**Tel:** 020-8223-3000
**Web:** www.uel.ac.uk
**Estd:** 1975
**Line of Business:** Colleges & universities
**Directors:** Professor F Gould, D Fowlie, A Ingle
**Responsibilities**
**HR:** Mike Moore (Human Resources Director)
**Purchasing:** Chris Philpott (Purchasing Manager)
**Branches:** University Of East London, Hainault Rd, Romford, Essex RM6 5RX
**US SIC:** 9121, 8221
**UK SIC:** 91110, 93100
**Auditors:** Deloitte & Touche LLP
**Employees:** 1,500
**Turnover:** £159,676,000

DUNS 22-904-4300 *Imp*
## University of Edinburgh
Old College, South Bridge, Edinburgh, Midlothian EH8 9YL
**Tel:** 01316-501-000
**Web:** www.ed.ac.uk
**VAT No:** 592950700 **Estd:** 2013
**Line of Business:** University
**Trading Style:** The University of Edinburgh
**Principals:** G Sutherland (Financial), T O'Shea
**Responsibilities**
**Senior:** David Donaldson (Manager), Rong Flynn (Executive), Linda Gardner (Executive), Irene Gordon (Executive), Timothy O'Shea (Principal), Rowena Stewart (Executive)
**Finance:** Hrh Duke Of Edinburgh (Chancellor), Terry Fox (Assistant Director of Finance), Phil McNaull (Director of Finance), Nigel Paul (Director Corporate Services), Elizabeth Welch (Assistant Director of Finance)
**Marketing:** Anna Borthwick (Press and Public Relations Off), Eleanor Cowie (Press and Public Relations Off), Kathryn Dunlop (Public Relations Officer), Catriona Kelly (Press and Public Relations Off), Ronald Kerr (Press and Public Relations Man), Ranald Leask (Press and Public Relations Off), Jen Middleton (Press and Public Relations Off), Ianthe Sutherland (Library Software Developer), Dominic Tate (Communications Manager)
**Sales:** Lorraine Kerr (Commercial Relations Executive)
**Admin:** Nancy Baxter (Secretary), Michelle Gunn (PA to the Director of Library), Tess Hanna (PA to Director of Finance), Claire Maguire (Secretary), Helen Murphie (Business Administrator), Ianthe Sutherland (Library Software Developer)

**IT:** Chris Adie *(Deputy IT Director)*, Pam Clouston *(Information Systems Manager)*, Barry Croucher *(Head of Help Services)*, Nicola Edwards *(IT Senior Helpdesk Assistant)*, Patrick Spooner *(Research Systems Designer)*, Colin Watt *(Information Systems Manager)*
**HR:** Sarah Adam *(Head of HR)*, Mary Allison *(HR Advisor)*, Robbie Manson *(HR & Development Coordinator)*
**Purchasing:** Elize Rowan *(Acquisitions and Metadata Serv)*
**Engineering:** Gregory Payne *(Engineer)*, Steven Pilkington *(Engineering Student)*
**Branches:** University Of Edinburgh, 18 Buccleuch Place, Edinburgh, Midlothian EH8 9LN
**US SIC:** 8221 **UK SIC:** 93100
**Auditors:** KPMG LLP
**Bankers:** Bank Of Scotland (80-02-34)
**Employees:** 7,255
**Turnover:** £650,829,000

DUNS 42-440-0117 **Imp**
## University of Essex
Wivenhoe Park, Colchester, Essex CO4 3SQ
**Tel:** 01206 873 333 **Fax:** 01206873598
**Web:** www.essex.ac.uk
**Reg No:** 0000652RC **Estd:** 2002 Incorporate By Act Of Parliament
**Line of Business:** Printers general
**Trading Style:** Business and Management Training, E B S, Essex Business and Human Rights
**Principals:** L Nolan *(President)*, I Crewe, J P Gorringe, F Woodburn
**Responsibilities**
**Senior:** Maxwell Roberts *(Board Member)*
**Finance:** Lisa Jack *(Lecturer)*, Prem Sikka *(Professor)*, Dean Strohm *(Finance Manager)*
**Marketing:** Lucy Brown *(Marketing Officer)*, Kate Clayton *(Communications Manager)*, Sarah Nicholls *(Marketing Officer)*
**Sales:** Michelle Baker *(Business Development Administr)*, Reeves Watson *(Commercial Development Manager)*
**Admin:** Karen Bush *(Administrative Officer)*, Clare Chatfield *(Administrative Officer)*, Kate Cook *(Beckwith)*, Michelle Hall *(Graduate Administrator)*, Janice Pittis *(Director, Research and Entepri)*, Jacqui Taylor-Roberts *(Secretary)*, Jane Thorp *(Administrator)*, Sarah Wiblin *(Administrator)*
**IT:** Khaled Abdala *(Teacher)*, Kirstie Cochrane *(Research and Enterprise Manage)*
**HR:** Marilyn Shanks *(Social and Welfare Liaison Off)*
**Operations:** Ian Dudley *(Project Support Officer)*
**Engineering:** Daniel Chan *(Technician)*, Sarah Mucklow *(Technician)*
**Branches:** University Of Essex, Hatfields, Rectory Lane, Loughton, Essex IG10 3RY
**US SIC:** 8221 **UK SIC:** 93100
**Auditors:** Deloitte LLP
**Employees:** 1,785
**Turnover:** £138,960,000

DUNS 23-649-9703
## University of Essex Students Union
Wivenhoe Park, Colchester, Essex CO4 3SQ
**Tel:** 01206863211
**Web:** www.essexstudent.com
**VAT No:** 103967666 **Estd:** 2009
**Line of Business:** Trade unions
**Principals:** Ms T Oldham *(President)*, D Michael, P Harris, N Berg *(General Manager)*
**Responsibilities**
**Senior:** Craig Stephens *(General Manager)*
**Branches:** Wivenhoe Park, Colchester, Essex CO4 3SQ
**US SIC:** 8631 **UK SIC:** 96313
**Bankers:** Lloyds TSB Bank plc (30-92-16)
**Employees:** 200

DUNS 21-132-0981 **Imp**
## University of Exeter
Northcote House, The Queens Drive, Exeter, Devon EX4 4QJ
**Tel:** 01392661000
**Web:** www.exeter.ac.uk
**Reg No:** 0000653RC **VAT No:** 142047795
**Estd:** 1955 Incorporate By Act Of Parliament
**Line of Business:** First-degree level higher education
**Directors:** D J Allen, S Smith, J C Lindley
**Responsibilities**
**Marketing:** Amanda Brook *(Marketing Director)*
**HR:** Tash Khan-Davis *(Head of Training)*
**Operations:** Adrian Watson *(Operations Manager - Environme)*
**Branches:** University Of Exeter, Tremough Campus, Penryn, Cornwall TR10 9EZ
**US SIC:** 8221 **UK SIC:** 93100
**Auditors:** KPMG LLP
**Bankers:** National Westminster Bank Plc (60-08-06)

| | 31-07-12 | 31-07-11 | 31-07-10 |
|---|---|---|---|
| TO | 257,005,000 | 246,170,000 | 227,214,000 |
| P/L | 5,019,000 | 10,536,000 | 5,824,000 |
| NW | 490,707,000 | 472,891,000 | 398,339,000 |
| WC | 12,688,000 | 10,883,000 | 27,981,000 |
| Emp. | 386 | 3,091 | 2,938 |

DUNS 21-668-3572
## University of Exeter Students' Guild
Devonshire House, Stocker Road, Exeter, Devon EX4 4PZ
**Tel:** 01392 723528
**Web:** www.exeterguild.org
**Reg No:** 7217324 **Estd:** 1959 Private Company Limited By Guarantee
**Line of Business:** Activities of other membership organisations not elsewhere classified
**Directors:** Ms D L Watson, Mrs H Pam, J S Hammond, G G Gerald, N S Rahmel, H G Care, S Bedlow, K Eales
**Co. Secretary:** Ms Tracy Costello
**Responsibilities**
**Senior:** Matthew Bate *(Director)*, Anna Collin *(Director)*, Rachael Gillies *(Director)*, Katherine Hawkins *(Director)*, Ben Street *(Director)*
**US SIC:** 8699 **UK SIC:** 96902
**Auditors:** KPMG LLP
**Bankers:** National Westminster Bank Plc (60-08-06)

| | 31-07-13 | 31-07-12 | 31-07-11 |
|---|---|---|---|
| TO | 4,972,577 | 4,586,118 | 3,204,855 |
| P/L | 344,517 | 154,099 | 224,378 |
| NW | 1,197,646 | 853,129 | 556,430 |
| WC | 481,155 | 344,682 | 111,232 |
| Emp. | 76 | 68 | 67 |

DUNS 21-121-1211
## University of Glamorgan Union
Forest Grove, Treforest, Pontypridd, Mid Glamorgan CF37 1UF
**Tel:** 01443483500
**Web:** www.uswsu.com
**Estd:** 1970
**Line of Business:** University
**Principals:** D Davies *(President)*, Ms H Thomas *(Financial)*, C Parnham, Ms A Gore, S Nicklin, Ms J Kellner, P Shelley *(General Manager)*, Ms R Jones *(Manager)*
**Responsibilities**
**Senior:** Michael Borley *(Commercial Manager)*, Sian Taylor *(Chief Executive)*
**Sales:** Michael Borley *(Commercial Manager)*
**Admin:** Raymond Joyce *(Secretary)*
**Health & Safety:** Michael Borley *(Commercial Manager)*
**Purchasing:** Michael Borley *(Commercial Manager)*
**US SIC:** 8699 **UK SIC:** 96902
**Employees:** 59

DUNS 22-907-6096 **Imp**
## The University of Glasgow
University Avenue, Glasgow, Lanarkshire G12 8QQ
**Tel:** 01413303993
**Web:** www.gla.ac.uk
**Estd:** 1998
**Line of Business:** University
**Principals:** M Yuille *(Financial)*, F J Neil, Sir W K Fraser, Sir A K Cairncross, Sir R Smith
**Co. Secretary:** Robert Ewen
**Responsibilities**
**Senior:** James Conroy *(Dean)*, Marion Fisher *(Personal Assistant)*, Anton Muscatelli *(Principal)*
**IT:** Colin Cooper *(Network Manager)*, Philip Donnelly *(Computer Manager)*
**Branches:** The University Of Glasgow, 65 Hillhead Street, Glasgow, Lanarkshire G12 8QF
**US SIC:** 8221 **UK SIC:** 93100
**Auditors:** Ernst & Young LLP
**Bankers:** Bank Of Scotland (80-11-80)
**Employees:** 4,986
**Turnover:** £439,471,000

DUNS 23-308-3596
## University of Gloucestershire
Pittville Campus, Cheltenham, Gloucestershire GL52 3JG
**Tel:** 01242714940 **Fax:** 01242714949
**Web:** www.glos.ac.uk
**Incorporate By Act Of Parliament**
**Line of Business:** University
**Director:** Mrs J Harper
**Responsibilities**
**Senior:** Karen Morgan *(Manager)*
**Branches:** University Of Gloucestershire, Oxstalls Campus, Oxstalls Lane, Gloucester, Gloucestershire GL2 9HW
**US SIC:** 8221 **UK SIC:** 93100
**Auditors:** Grant Thornton UK LLP
**Employees:** 983
**Turnover:** £71,789,000

DUNS 67-215-4259 **Imp**
## University of Gloucestershire
The Park, Cheltenham, Gloucestershire GL50 2RH
**Tel:** 08448010001 **Fax:** 01242-715062
**Web:** www.glos.ac.uk
**Reg No:** 6023243 **Estd:** 2012 Private Company Limited By Guarantee
**Line of Business:** First-degree level higher education
**Directors:** S A Marston, Dr F T Harsent, Miss A C Noble, Sir G P Scott, Professor F M Chambers, R Patel, P D Bungard, M M Burgess
**Co. Secretary:** Mrs Julie Thackray
**Responsibilities**
**Senior:** Paul Hartley *(Vice Chancellor)*, Beverley Hodson *(Director)*, Allen Mawby *(Director)*, Karen Morgan *(Director)*, Michael Perham *(Director)*, Angus Taylor *(Director)*, Stephen Treble *(Director)*
**Finance:** Camille Stallard *(Financial Director)*
**Marketing:** Robin Livesey *(Web Development Manager)*
**IT:** Stuart McQuaid *(ICT Customer Services Manager)*
**HR:** Claire Hetherington *(Head of Personnel)*, Anna Lansley *(HR Administrator)*, Sue Wassell *(HR Business Partner)*
**Health & Safety:** Martin Foster *(Health & Safety Officer)*
**Facilities:** Nigel Wichall *(Director of Estates)*
**US SIC:** 8221 **UK SIC:** 93100
**Auditors:** Grant Thornton UK LLP
**Bankers:** The Royal Bank Of Scotland Plc (16-16-13)

| | 31-07-14 | 31-07-13 | 31-07-12 |
|---|---|---|---|
| TO | 70,925,000 | 69,249,000 | 70,817,000 |
| P/L | 2,448,000 | 3,988,000 | 6,961,000 |
| NW | 48,933,000 | 57,734,000 | 14,387,000 |
| WC | 6,117,000 | 5,221,000 | 3,965,000 |
| Emp. | 841 | 830 | 843 |

DUNS 28-867-0953
## University of Greenwich
King Charles Court, King William Walk Old Royal Naval, College, London SE10 9JF
**Fax:** 02083008000
**Web:** www.gre.ac.uk
**Reg No:** 0986729 **Estd:** 1890 Private Company Limited By Guarantee
**Line of Business:** First-degree level higher education
**Directors:** Professor D J Maguire, A R Brooks, Ms E S Passey, Ms D Khanna, S Howlett, Professor P Maras, Ms M L Hay, J C Barnes
**Co. Secretary:** Ms Louise Nadal
**Responsibilities**
**Senior:** Alan Albert *(Director)*, Tessa Blackstone *(Vice Chancellor)*, Ian Cakebread *(Support Services Manager)*, Alexander Coutroubis *(Director)*, Stephen Davie *(Director)*, Lee Devlin *(Director)*, Nicholas Eastwell *(Director)*, Christopher Hallas *(Director of Student Affairs)*, Wilson Leech *(Director)*, Helen Wyatt *(Director)*
**Finance:** Julia Mundy *(Lecturer)*
**Marketing:** Alev Adil *(Head of the Department of Comm)*, Philip Chambers *(Director of Development & Comm)*, Caron Jones *(Head of Public Relations)*, Trudi Knight *(Web Development Executive)*
**Admin:** Caroline Chapman *(Administrator)*, Ian Deakin *(Administration Officer)*, Christine Moses *(Database and System Administra)*
**IT:** Christine Moses *(Database and System Administra)*
**HR:** Patrick Ainley *(Professor of Training & Educat)*, Russell Brockett *(Head of Personnel)*, Frances Hewison *(Human Resources Director)*, Steve Wallis *(Director of Recruitment)*, Helen Wyatt *(Director)*
**Facilities:** Peter Fotheringham *(Director of Estates)*
**Operations:** Melanie Thorley *(Project Coordinator)*, Li Zhou *(Reader in Operations Managemen)*
**Purchasing:** Vincent John *(Procurement)*
**Branches:** University Of Greenwich, 30 Park Row, London SE10 9LS
**US SIC:** 8221 **UK SIC:** 93100
**Auditors:** Grant Thornton UK LLP
**Bankers:** Barclays Bank Plc (20-98-57)

| | 31-07-14 | 31-07-13 | 31-07-12 |
|---|---|---|---|
| TO | 191,928,000 | 187,627,000 | 187,830,000 |
| P/L | 13,059,000 | 10,442,000 | 3,783,000 |
| NW | 75,229,000 | 75,804,000 | 46,072,000 |
| WC | 26,277,000 | 52,873,000 | 60,374,000 |
| Emp. | 2,166 | 2,208 | 2,338 |

DUNS 21-775-6206
## University of Greenwich Avery Hill Students Union
Southwood Site Avery Hill Campus, Avery Hill Road, London SE9 2UG
**Web:** www.gre.ac.uk
**Estd:** 2011 Proprietorship
**Line of Business:** Trade unions
**Proprietor:** Ms J Greenfield
**US SIC:** 8221 **UK SIC:** 93100
**Employees:** 100

DUNS 22-595-1821
## University of Greenwich Students Union
Old Woolwich Public Baths Bathwa, London SE18 6QX
**Web:** www.greenwich.ac.uk
**Line of Business:** Committee managed organisations
**Principals:** V Choudhary *(President)*, Ms K Adomako, Ms S Appleton, Ms J Chan, K Kemsley, C Jones *(General Manager)*, K Songu *(Manager)*, D Lenton *(Manager)*
**Responsibilities**
**Senior:** Rachel Rogers *(Manager)*
**US SIC:** 8699 **UK SIC:** 96902
**Bankers:** Lloyds TSB Bank plc (30-99-88)
**Employees:** 50

DUNS 23-140-0714
## University of Hertfordshire
College Lane, Hatfield, Hertfordshire AL10 9AB
**Tel:** 01707284444
**Web:** www.herts.ac.uk
**Estd:** 1951 Incorporate By Act Of Parliament
**Line of Business:** Doctors
**Principals:** A Moffat *(Financial)*, Q Mckellar Cbe
**Co. Secretary:** Ms Sue Grant
**Responsibilities**
**Senior:** James Ridout *(Doctor)*
**HR:** Naomi Holloway *(Director of Human Resources)*
**Purchasing:** Rita Roberts *(Buyer)*
**US SIC:** 8221 **UK SIC:** 93100
**Auditors:** Grant Thornton UK LLP
**Bankers:** Barclays Bank Plc (20-74-09)

| | 31-07-13 | 31-07-12 | 31-07-11 |
|---|---|---|---|
| TO | 236,275,000 | 232,836,000 | 230,834,000 |
| P/L | 12,351,000 | 17,642,000 | 10,203,000 |
| NW | 249,996,000 | 166,345,000 | 161,262,000 |
| WC | 52,084,000 | 8,696,000 | (607,000) |
| Emp. | 2,406 | 2,358 | 2,329 |

DUNS 21-736-1873
## University of Hertfordshire Students' Union
College Lane, Hatfield, Hertfordshire AL10 9AB
**Tel:** 01707286175
**Web:** www.uhsu.co.uk
**Reg No:** 7703890 **Estd:** 2011 Private Company Limited By Guarantee
**Line of Business:** Activities of other membership organisations not elsewhere classified
**Directors:** G Singh, Miss S E Rock, Miss I Colafrancesco, R O Farooq, J Amos, K M Whiteford
**Co. Secretary:** Mrs Christine Dixon
**US SIC:** 8699 **UK SIC:** 96902
**Bankers:** Barclays Bank Plc (20-92-54)

| | 31-07-13 | 31-07-12 |
|---|---|---|
| TO | 13,928,138 | 11,645,965 |
| P/L | 42,991 | 111,479 |
| NW | 451,990 | 408,999 |
| WC | 330,661 | 148,785 |
| Emp. | 262 | 332 |

DUNS 22-809-9479
## The University of Huddersfield
Queensgate, Huddersfield, West Yorkshire HD1 3DH
**Tel:** 01484422288 **Fax:** 01484472385
**Web:** www.hud.ac.uk
**VAT No:** 516310190 **Estd:** 1970 Incorporate By Act Of Parliament
**Line of Business:** Limousine hire
**Trading Style:** The University Chaplaincy Centre, Schools Liaison Office
**Principals:** B Ward *(President)*, P A Smelt *(Financial)*, Professor F Arthur, Professor J R Tarrant, Rev D A Kirkby, Ms J V Carter, G W Downs
**Responsibilities**
**Senior:** Julie McClelland *(Human Resources Dirertor)*
**Sales:** Andrew Mandebura *(Director of International Deve)*
**Admin:** Sue White *(Computer and Library Services)*
**IT:** Alec Jackson *(Senior Voice Network Officer)*, Sue White *(Computer and Library Services)*
**HR:** Julie McClelland *(Human Resources Dirertor)*

**Health & Safety:** Michelle Muxworthy (Health & Safety Officer)
**Engineering:** Steve Donnelly (Head of Engineering and Techno)
**Branches:** The University Of Huddersfield, Lockside, Queensgate, Huddersfield, West Yorkshire HD1 3DH
**US SIC:** 8221 **UK SIC:** 93100
**Auditors:** KPMG LLP
**Bankers:** Lloyds TSB Bank plc (30-94-43)
**Employees:** 2,000
**Turnover:** £134,055,000

DUNS 22-845-1522     **Imp**
## University of Hull
Cottingham Road, Hull, North Humberside HU6 7RX
**Tel:** 01482464900
**Web:** www.hull.ac.uk
**Reg No:** 0000654RC **Estd:** 1927 Incorporate By Act Of Parliament
**Line of Business:** Business and commerce centres
**Trading Style:** Hull International Fisheries Institute (Hifi), Hull University Union Continental Cafe, Hull University
**Directors:** B Irvin, Prof D Dilks, W North, F Mattison
**Responsibilities**
**Sales:** Liz Johnson (Business Development Manager)
**IT:** Jane Eaman (Secretary, Department, Compute)
**Branches:** University Of Hull, 13 Salmon Gr, Hull, North Humberside HU6 7SX
**US SIC:** 8221, 7391
**UK SIC:** 93100, 94000

| | 31-07-14 | 31-07-10 | 31-07-07 |
|---|---|---|---|
| TO | 180,433,000 | 168,344,000 | 127,372,000 |
| P/L | 9,714,000 | 14,850,000 | 10,755,000 |
| NW | 119,337,000 | 92,768,000 | 64,455,000 |
| WC | 1,064,000 | 8,346,000 | (8,775,000) |
| Emp. | 2,080 | N/A | 2,500 |

DUNS 42-440-0646
## University of Keele
Keele Road, Newcastle, Staffordshire ST5 5AL
**Tel:** 01782732000 **Fax:** 017826584234
**Web:** www.keele.ac.uk
**Reg No:** 0000655RC **Estd:** 2010 Incorporate By Act Of Parliament
**Line of Business:** Higher education
**Responsibilities**
**Senior:** Aeurin Evans (Head Of Physics)
**Marketing:** John Mc Carthy (Director of Marketing & Commun)
**IT:** Graham Rogerson (Head of School of Mathematics)
**HR:** Claire Appleby (Director HR and Student Servic)
**Facilities:** Philip Butters (Director of Estates & Developm)
**Branches:** University Of Keele, Student Union Building, Newcastle, Staffordshire ST5 5BJ
**US SIC:** 8221 **UK SIC:** 93100
**Auditors:** KPMG LLP
**Bankers:** National Westminster Bank Plc (54-10-27)

| | 31-07-13 | 31-07-12 | 31-07-11 |
|---|---|---|---|
| TO | 120,859,000 | 119,215,000 | 115,415,000 |
| P/L | 5,345,000 | 4,893,000 | 3,544,000 |
| NW | 80,507,000 | 74,797,000 | 73,092,000 |
| WC | (16,562,000) | (29,080,000) | (26,205,000) |
| Emp. | 1,984 | 1,943 | 1,938 |

DUNS 42-440-0455     **Imp**
## University of Kent
The Registry, Canterbury, Kent CT2 7NZ
**Tel:** 01227-764000
**Web:** www.kent.ac.uk
**Reg No:** 0000656RC **VAT No:** 202060535
**Estd:** 1981
**Line of Business:** University
**Trading Style:** Durrell Trust for Conservation Biology, The Univertity of Kent At Canterbury, Ukc Hospitality
**Responsibilities**
**Finance:** A Dunning (Treasurer)
**Marketing:** Karen Baxter (Press Assistant), Martin Herrema (Press Officer)
**Admin:** Catherine Butler (Secretary), N McHard (Secretary), Maddy Withers (Secretary to Director of Human)
**IT:** John Sotillo (Director of Information Servic), Michael Wilcox (?Assistant Director of IT Deve)
**HR:** Mark Gilman (Senior Lecturer - Industrial R), Cindy Vallance (Head of Organisational Develop)
**Purchasing:** Jill Andrews (Purchasing Coordinator), Don Bowman (Procurement Manager)
**Branches:** University Of Kent, Tonbridge Library, 1 Avebury Avenue, Tonbridge, Kent TN9 1TG
**US SIC:** 8221 **UK SIC:** 93100
**Auditors:** Grant Thornton UK LLP
**Employees:** 1,985
**Turnover:** £173,027,000

DUNS 21-821-6462
## The University of Law Ltd
(Subsidiary of: L-J Finco Ltd)
Braboeuf Manor, Portsmouth Road, Guildford, Surrey GU3 1HA
**Tel:** 0800289997
**Web:** www.law.ac.uk
**Reg No:** 7933838 **Estd:** 1876 Private Limited Company
**Line of Business:** Post-graduate level higher education
**Issued Capital:** £1
**Directors:** Ms C A Nollent, Ms E Catchpole, J C Latham, D I Johnston, T G Boucher, A C Dabbous, Mrs L A Macdonagh, W A Stokhuyzen
**Co. Secretary:** David Hooper
**Responsibilities**
**Senior:** Philip Ely (Principal), Jillian Gale (Manager), Alan Humphreys (Manager), Denise Kingsmill (Principal), Peter Morley-Jacob (Principal)
**Marketing:** Ann-Marie Barker (Insight Manager)
**US SIC:** 8221 **UK SIC:** 93100

| | 31-07-13 |
|---|---|
| TO | 53,322,000 |
| P/L | (7,720,000) |
| NW | (103,098,000) |
| WC | (174,800,000) |
| Emp. | 656 |

DUNS 22-972-0834     **Imp**
## The University of Leeds
Woodhouse Lane, Leeds, West Yorkshire LS2 9JT
**Tel:** 01133432342
**Web:** www.bayfieldsopticians.com
**Reg No:** 0000658RC **VAT No:** 613451470
**Estd:** 1991 Incorporate By Act Of Parliament
**Line of Business:** Agricultural services
**Principals:** Ms J Madeley (Financial), M Hollmes (Marketing), M Knight (Personnel), R Sladdin, Prof M Atack, Prof S Scott, Mrs L Pollard, Prof V Jones
**Co. Secretary:** Roger Gair
**Responsibilities**
**Senior:** Tamsin Barrow (Executive), Royston Bayfield (Manager), Gregory Brachacki (Disability Coordinator Manager), Lord Bragg (Principal), Juliet Brown (Centre Manager), Debbie Burns (Senior Manager), Joanna Cannon (Senior Manager), Zoe Dillon (Board Member), Valerie Dupont (Supervisor), Joanne Homer (Board Member), Sarah Houlding (Board Member), Sheenagh Hull (Senior Manager), Robin Lane (General Manager), Jessica Lewis (Manager), Stephen Marsden (Chairman), Amanda May (International Applications Pro), Josie Mellor (Board Member), Jane Saunders (Senior Manager), Joanne Tipper (Executive), Debbie Westmoreland (Manager)
**Finance:** Naomi Armstrong (Finance Officer), Sophie Bower (?Financial Reporting Manager), Heather Cocker (Finance Manager), Kirsty Dillingham (Finance Manager), Ann Kenney (Finance Manager), Colleen Palmer (Finance Manager), Julie Reeves (Faculty Finance Manager), Shabbir Suleman (Finance Manager)
**Marketing:** Rachel Barson (Media Relations Team Leader), Ben Broadbent (Web Development Executive), Chris Bunting (Senior Press Officer), Gareth Dant (Press Officer), Guy Dixon (Senior Press Officer), Tessa Grant (Alumni Relations and Website E), Matt Hamnett (Marketing Advisor), Karen Innis (Head of Marketing), Hannah Love (Head of Digital Communications), Robert Picton (Faculty Marketing Manager), Sarah Reed (Press Officer), Katie Sandwell (Media Relations Assistant), Stephen Scales (Marketing Manager), Sue Underwood (Head of Communications Product), Anna Wellard (Alumni Relations Manager)
**Sales:** Matt Hamnett (Marketing Advisor)
**Admin:** Colin Avison (Administrator), Manjula Bakhetia (Faculty Finance, Clerk), Debra Baldwin (Administrative Support Officer), Sheila Booth (Admissions Coordinator), Glenys Bowles (Secretary), Michael Byde (Administrative Officer), Susan Carden (Personal Assistant to the Fina), Rosie Corbin (Executive Assistant to the Dea), Sue Davis (Administrator), Louise Gill (Administrator), Alison Gledhill (Receptionist), Emma Graham (School Administrator (HR)), Christine Holdstock (Teaching and Administrative Of), Christina Kiriakidou (Administrator), Amanda May (International Applications Pro), Andrew Shearing (Programme Administrator), Jeanne Shuttleworth (Postgraduate Admissions), Harriet Timmis (Administrative Assistant), Elaine Warden (Administrative Support Officer)
**IT:** Nancy Davies (Learning Technologies Officer), Hannah Love (Head of Digital Communications)

**HR:** Lisa Courtney (HR Business Officer), Annabelle Cross (Senior Careers Consultant), Barry Ewart (Training Director), Liz Felgate (HR Officer), Nichola Goodyear (HR Information Officer), Emma Graham (School Administrator (HR)), Penny Hatton (Staff Development Director), Caroline Langham (HR Services Manager), Matthew Lawrence (HR Information Officer), Kelly Lewis (Human Resources), Martin Mcareavey (Director, Learning and Teachin), Linda Mortimer Pine (Director of Human Resources), Michelle Nettleton (Human Resources Manager)
**Health & Safety:** Alan Wheeler (Health and Safety Manager)
**Facilities:** Dominic Emery (Facilities Officer), Jackie Goodall (Director, Facilities)
**Operations:** Maria Pervaiz (Production and Operations Mana), Sarah Simpson (LIME Business Manager), Tamsin Treasure-Jones (ALPS Mobile Technologies Proje)
**Fleet:** Greg Marsden (Senior Lecturer, Transport Pol)
**Engineering:** Simon Antony (Senior Lecturer, Chemical Engi), Mohammed Asaf (Technician), Narinder Gahir (Research Technician), Jerry Lee (Technical Services Manager), Tomasz Liskiewicz (Lecturer in Engineering), Tony May (Emeritus Professor in Transpor)
**Branches:** The University Of Leeds, York Campus, Lord Mayors Walk, York, North Yorkshire YO31 7EX
**US SIC:** 8221 **UK SIC:** 93100
**Auditors:** Deloitte & Touche LLP
**Bankers:** Barclays Bank Plc (20-48-46)
**Employees:** 7,700
**Turnover:** £543,002,000

DUNS 22-674-2724     **Imp**
## University of Leicester
University Road, Leicester, Leicestershire LE1 7RH
**Tel:** 01162856493
**Web:** www.le.ac.uk
**Reg No:** 0000659RC **VAT No:** 115121526
**Estd:** 1919 Incorporate By Act Of Parliament
**Line of Business:** Charities and charitable organisations
**Principals:** A Porter (President), R H Bettles (Chairman), Professor C Fyfe, Sir P Williams, K Julian, Professor M Thompson, Prof R Burgess, Professor I Posthlethwaite
**Responsibilities**
**Senior:** P Ash (Designated Limited Liability P), M Bodenham (Designated Limited Liability P), D Brunning (Designated Limited Liability P), P Cottingham (Designated Limited Liability P), Paul Goffin (Director of Estates), F Hussain (Designated Limited Liability P), A Linsell (Designated Limited Liability P)
**Admin:** Ian Saker (Office Manager)
**IT:** Mary Visser (Computer Centre Director)
**HR:** Alan Reynolds (Human Resources Director)
**Health & Safety:** Dave Widdowson (Safety Director)
**Facilities:** Paul Goffin (Director of Estates)
**Operations:** Gail Atkinson (Facilities Officer)
**Branches:** University Of Leicester, University Road, Leicester, Leicestershire LE1 7RH
**US SIC:** 8221 **UK SIC:** 93100
**Auditors:** Deloitte LLP
**Bankers:** HSBC Bank plc (40-28-06)
**Employees:** 3,111
**Turnover:** £255,715,000

DUNS 21-679-5482
## University of Leicester Students Union
University Road, Leicester, Leicestershire LE1 7RH
**Reg No:** 7303101 **Estd:** 2010 Private Company Limited By Guarantee
**Line of Business:** Activities of other membership organisations not elsewhere classified
**Directors:** K J Julian, J N Appleyard, M Rubin, S Kelly-Walsh, H J Hunt, Mrs V Nguhi, Y Nikolov
**Co. Secretary:** Trevor Page
**US SIC:** 7399 **UK SIC:** 83954
**Bankers:** National Westminster Bank Plc (56-00-55)

| | 31-07-13 | 31-07-12 | 31-07-11 |
|---|---|---|---|
| TO | 4,809,270 | 5,235,167 | 4,788,684 |
| P/L | 171,913 | (147,099) | 189,145 |
| NW | 881,191 | 604,186 | 610,691 |
| WC | 1,125,684 | 775,177 | 620,738 |
| Emp. | 186 | 170 | 192 |

DUNS 22-845-0896     **Imp**
## University of Lincoln
Brayford Pool, Lincoln, Lincolnshire LN6 7TS
**Tel:** 01522-882000
**Web:** www.lincoln.ac.uk
**VAT No:** 599033800 **Estd:** 1996 Incorporate By Act Of Parliament
**Line of Business:** Doctors

**Trading Style:** University of Lincoln
**Directors:** R King, S Bell, C Smith, A Pollard, K Pardere, F A Flear, J Wilson, D F Mcgowan
**Responsibilities**
**Senior:** Jayne Billam (Human Resources Manager), Alan Blackham (Facilities Manager), K Bridge (Principal), D McGowan (Principal), J McNeil (Principal), D Shelgrove (Principal), Mary Stuart (Vice Chancellor)
**Finance:** Catherine Connell (Senior Finance Manager), Catherine Hamblett (Senior Finance Manager), Debra Harry (Finance Controller)
**Marketing:** Catrin Rodda (Deputy Director of Communicati), Elly Sample (Director of Communications, De)
**Sales:** Jim Shutt (Business Development Director)
**IT:** Drew Cook (Director of ICT), Mike Donnerstag (Data Manager)
**HR:** Jayne Billam (Human Resources Manager), Sharon Keeton (HR Operational Services Manage)
**Facilities:** Alan Blackham (Facilities Manager)
**Engineering:** Julian Bartrup (Technical Manager), Ciara Casey (Technical Manager)
**Branches:** University Of Lincoln, University Of Lincoln, Campus Way, Lincoln, Lincolnshire LN6 7TS
**US SIC:** 8221 **UK SIC:** 93100
**Auditors:** Grant Thornton UK LLP
**Bankers:** HSBC Bank plc (40-25-20)
**Employees:** 1,121
**Turnover:** £87,239,000

DUNS 22-864-5628
## University of Liverpool
Po Box 147, Liverpool, Merseyside L69 3BX
**Web:** www.liv.ac.uk
**Reg No:** 0000660RC **VAT No:** 673598875
**Estd:** 1881 Incorporate By Act Of Parliament
**Line of Business:** University
**Principals:** M G Yuille (Financial), R Eastwood (Financial), Sir H Newby, Professor J D Bone, Professor K Everest, Professor J Crampton, Professor J Crampton, Professor C Gaskell
**Responsibilities**
**Senior:** Graham Dockray (Principal)
**Marketing:** Janet McDermott (Press Officer)
**Health & Safety:** Chris Bowes (Safety Officer)
**Branches:** University Of Liverpool, Morton House, North Mossley Hill Road, Liverpool, Merseyside L18 8DW
**US SIC:** 8221 **UK SIC:** 93100
**Auditors:** PricewaterhouseCoopers LLP
**Bankers:** Barclays Bank Plc (20-51-01)
**Employees:** 4,640
**Turnover:** £339,686,000

DUNS 22-723-7930     **Imp**
## University of London
Senate House, Malet Street, London WC1E 7HU
**Tel:** 02078628000
**Web:** www.london.ac.uk
**Reg No:** 0000661RC **Estd:** 2002 Incorporate By Act Of Parliament
**Line of Business:** University
**Directors:** Professor G J Zellick, S R Lhd, P Holwell, T Royal
**Responsibilities**
**Senior:** Anne Mckeown (Associate Director)
**Finance:** Simon Cruickshank (Deputy Director of Finance), Paulo Rodrigues-Alves (Finance Manager)
**Marketing:** Gabrielle Grant (Communications and Events Coor), Emma Harradine (Digital Marketing Manager), Binda Rai (Head of Communications and Ext)
**Admin:** Alison Hajlambi (Personal Assistant), Gabrielle Lawson (Administration)
**IT:** Lourdes Agapito (Lecturer, Engineering and Comp), Steve Knibbs (IT Manager)
**HR:** Susan Small (Human Resources Manager)
**Health & Safety:** Susan Small (Human Resources Manager)
**Facilities:** Martin Burchett (Estates Director)
**Branches:** University of London, Queen Mary University, Mile End Rd, London E1 4NS
**US SIC:** 8221 **UK SIC:** 93100
**Auditors:** Deloitte LLP
**Bankers:** National Westminster Bank Plc (60-80-07)
**Employees:** 300
**Turnover:** £157,045,000

DUNS 73-450-5642
## University of Manchester
Oxford Road, Manchester M13 9PL
**Tel:** 0161 306 6000
**Web:** www.manchester.ac.uk
**Reg No:** 4714889 **VAT No:** 849738956
**Estd:** 2003 Private Company Limited By Guarantee
**Line of Business:** College

**Director:** S W Spinks
**Co. Secretary:** Ms Joanne Rodger
**Branches:** University Of Manchester, 150 Deansgate, Manchester M3 3EH
**US SIC:** 8221 **UK SIC:** 93100

|  | 31-07-13 |
| --- | --- |
| TO | 826,970,000 |
| P/L | 38,409,000 |
| NW | 824,353,000 |
| WC | 262,207,000 |
| Emp. | 9,178 |

DUNS 21-743-4996
## University of Manchester Students' Union
Oxford Road, Manchester M13 9PR
**Tel:** 01612752930

**Web:** www.uni-vision.co.uk
**Reg No:** 7759820 **Estd:** 2011 Private Company Limited By Guarantee
**Line of Business:** Activities of other membership organisations not elsewhere classified
**Directors:** S K Williamson, Miss E M Mclaughlin, Miss R Dammers, Ms F G Muscatelli, Miss H E Hill-Payne, Ms E Cameron, J A Smith, Ms C Cook
**Co. Secretary:** Ben Ward
**Responsibilities**
**Senior:** Haroon Ahmed (Manager), Beverly Craig (Manager), Chris Jenkinson (Manager), Sohaib Khan (Manager), Asim Khan (Manager), Dominic Koole (Manager), Jessica Lishak (Director), Shabnam Mahmood (Manager), Tessy Maritim (Director), Conor Mcgurran (Director), Jeffery Meddemmen (Manager), Harriet Pugh (Director), Aleksei Schneider (Manager), Kavit Shah (Director), Thomas Skinner (Manager), Jan Sowa (Director), Lamia Zafrani (Manager)
**US SIC:** 8699 **UK SIC:** 96902
**Bankers:** The Co-Operative Bank Plc (08-60-20)

|  | 31-07-13 |
| --- | --- |
| TO | 5,169,224 |
| P/L | (1,614,309) |
| NW | 5,589,535 |
| WC | 367,356 |
| Emp. | 70 |

DUNS 23-700-9568    **Imp**
## The University of Northampton
St George's Avenue, Northampton, Northamptonshire NN2 6JD
**Web:** www.northampton.ac.uk
**Estd:** 1995 Incorporate By Act Of Parliament
**Line of Business:** University
**Principals:** R Aveling (Financial), Ms A Tate
**Responsibilities**
**Senior:** Janet Baines (Manager), Sue Donnelly (General Manager), Derrick Harris (Estates Manager), Vivien Houghton (Manager), Sarah Neill (Manager), Wendy Nikolaidis (Manager), Nick Petford (Vice Chancellor), Karen Stobart (General Manager)
**Finance:** Terry Neville (Financial Director), Jeremy Weeks (Chief Accountant)
**Marketing:** Nina Antell (Marketing Officer), Wray Irwin (Spokesperson), Verity Law (Marketing Officer), Kate Pascoe (Senior Lecturer in Marketing), Alan Seymour (Senior Lecturer, Marketing & E), Laura Wood (Health Administration)
**Sales:** Laura Wood (Health Administration)
**Admin:** Judith Allibone (Director, Academic Office), Lucie Armstrong (Administrator), Michelle Gabriel (Administrator), Debbie Mattock (Administrator), Miggie Pickton (Research Support Librarian), Beth Underwood (Administration & Project Suppo)
**IT:** Kevin Hardisty (Senior Technical Information S), Stuart Hodgson (IT Director), Scott Turner (Senior Lecturer, Computing), Beth Underwood (Administration & Project Suppo)
**HR:** Carrie Birnie (Human Resources Manager), Yvonne Nicholls (Human Resources Manager)
**Operations:** Ian Hardwick (Operations Manager), Matthew Waite (Head of Projects)
**Purchasing:** Carol Barrett (Procurement)
**Engineering:** Jonathan Adams (Head of Engineering & Technolo)
**Branches:** The University Of Northampton, Avenue Campus, St. Georges Avenue, Northampton, Northamptonshire NN2 6JD
**US SIC:** 8221 **UK SIC:** 93100
**Auditors:** Grant Thornton UK LLP
**Employees:** 3,000
**Turnover:** £89,111,000

DUNS 21-327-4884    **Imp**
## University of Notre Dame
1-4 Suffolk Street, London SW1Y 4HG
**Tel:** 02074847800
**Web:** www.international.nd.edu
**Estd:** 1998
**Line of Business:** Post-graduate level higher education

**Responsibilities**
**Senior:** Eschenbach Warren (Manager)
**Facilities:** Steve Whitnall (Facilities Manager)
**US SIC:** 8221 **UK SIC:** 93100
**Employees:** 55

DUNS 21-138-9598
## University of Nottingham
The Trent Building, University Park, Nottingham, Nottinghamshire NG7 2RD
**Web:** www.nottingham.ac.uk
**Reg No:** 0000664RC **VAT No:** 690391225
**Estd:** 1900 Incorporate By Act Of Parliament
**Line of Business:** University
**Principals:** R Haylock (President), D J Atkin, D Beeby, D Allen, S Russell, J Mills, K Hamill, Sir C Campbell
**Responsibilities**
**Senior:** David Greenaway (Vice Chancellor), Patrick Hopkins (Principal), Ellie McWilliam (Student Union President), Hannah White (Principal)
**Marketing:** Anthony Tunley (Head Of Communications)
**Branches:** University Of Nottingham, North St, Boston, Lincolnshire PE21 9BX
**US SIC:** 8221 **UK SIC:** 93100
**Auditors:** Deloitte LLP
**Bankers:** National Westminster Bank Plc (60-15-49)
**Employees:** 80
**Turnover:** £510,600,000

DUNS 21-669-9661
## The University of Nottingham Students' Union
University Park, Nottingham, Nottinghamshire NG7 2RD
**Web:** www.nottingham.ac.uk
**Reg No:** 7229624 **Estd:** 2010 Private Company Limited By Guarantee
**Line of Business:** Activities of business and employers organisations
**Directors:** Miss C Averill, Miss K Madhani, A Graham, Mrs C A Harvey, H Copson, N Ratcliffe, S J Spalding
**Co. Secretary:** Mrs Maria Brown
**US SIC:** 8611 **UK SIC:** 96312
**Bankers:** National Westminster Bank Plc (60-15-49)

|  | 31-07-13 | 31-07-12 | 31-07-11 |
| --- | --- | --- | --- |
| TO | 8,655,266 | 9,219,675 | 8,419,994 |
| P/L | (63,606) | (160,808) | (2,294) |
| NW | 1,568,309 | 1,561,945 | 1,747,337 |
| WC | 388,754 | 396,157 | 485,243 |
| Emp. | 180 | 168 | 179 |

DUNS 22-669-4883    **Imp**
## University of Oxford
University Offices, Wellington Square, Oxford, Oxfordshire OX1 2JD
**Web:** www.admin.ox.ac.uk
**VAT No:** 195275334 **Estd:** 1973
**Line of Business:** University
**Trading Style:** Oxford University Press
**Principals:** G Kerr (Financial), P A Hamilton
**Responsibilities**
**Senior:** B Duddy (Manager), Christopher Patton (Chancellor)
**Finance:** Dieter Helm (Official Fellow in Economics)
**Admin:** Lydia Berry (PA to Director Computing Syste)
**HR:** Julian Duxfield (Director of Human Resources)
**Engineering:** Malcolm McCulloch (Lecturer - Engineering Science)
**Branches:** University Of Oxford, 106 High Street, Oxford, Oxfordshire OX1 4BW
**US SIC:** 8221, 6732, 2731, 7391, 8091
**UK SIC:** 93100, 83100, 47532, 94000, 95200
**Auditors:** Deloitte & Touche LLP
**Employees:** 1,000
**Turnover:** £919,600,000

DUNS 23-801-1076    **Imp**
## University of Plymouth
Drake Circus, Plymouth, Devon PL4 8AA
**Tel:** 01752600600
**Web:** www.plymouth.ac.uk
**Estd:** 1992
**Line of Business:** University
**Principals:** R Clarke, Professor J Bull, A Wright
**Responsibilities**
**Senior:** Gina Connelly (Manager), Alexander Harris (President), Christopher Leversha (Principal), Andrea Roberts (Manager), Aaron Taylor (Vice President)
**Marketing:** Karen Mason (Head of Media and Communicatio), Andrew Merrington (Senior Press and PR Officer)
**Sales:** Adam Corney (Marine Commercial Director), Nicola Griffin (Conference Manager)
**IT:** Robert Bray (Computer Operations Manager), Nick Sharratt (T&IS Business Partner, Strateg)
**Facilities:** Martin Berkien (Facilities Director)

**Branches:** University Of Plymouth, Art & Education, Earl Richards Road North, Exeter, Devon EX2 6AS
**US SIC:** 8221 **UK SIC:** 93100
**Auditors:** PricewaterhouseCoopers LLP
**Bankers:** HSBC Bank plc (40-36-22)
**Employees:** 3,000
**Turnover:** £208,748,000

DUNS 23-973-0161    **Imp**
## University of Portsmouth
University House, Winston Churchill Avenue, Portsmouth, Hampshire PO1 2UP
**Tel:** 023-9284-8484 **Fax:** 02392843082
**Web:** www.port.ac.uk
**VAT No:** 504005214
**Incorporate By Act Of Parliament**
**Line of Business:** First-degree level higher education
**Principals:** M J Ace (Financial), Professor J A Craven, C T Monk, Ms A M Glasner
**Co. Secretary:** Dr Michael Bateman
**Responsibilities**
**Senior:** Chris Beaman (Manager), Ron Darville (Manager), Sarah Duckering (General Manager), Christine Giles (Executive), Ken Glanfield (Executive), Dariusz Gorecki (Senior Manager), Steve Hand (Manager), Imogen Jeffery (Manager), Brett Martinson (Manager), John Mcgeehan (Executive), Katie Mumford (Executive), Mike Nash (Head of Department), John Naysmith (Executive), James Ost (Executive), Vicky Purrington (Manager), Joe Ross (Senior Manager), Heather Sherwood (Manager), Mikhail Shevtsov (Executive), Catherine Teeling (Senior Manager), John Tsibouklis (Head of Division)
**Finance:** Allisson Cory (Course Assistant), Cheryl Johnson (Finance Officer), Sheree Mallinder (Senior Finance Officer), Barry Murphy (Senior Lecturer - Economics &), Louise Pulley (Finance Officer), Sonia Reeves (Senior Finance Officer), Richard Trafford (Principal Lecturer), Debbie Wilkins (Finance Manager), Emma Woollard (Financial Director)
**Marketing:** Paul Ankers (Human Resource and Marketing M), Jane Attwood (Corporate Communications Offic), Claire Brookes (Head of Marketing), Jill Brown (Principal Lecturer (Subject Gr), Anne Burrill (Deputy Director of Marketing a), Alison Cameron (Senior Lecturer in Marketing), Alison Coote (Press and PR Officer), Alice Crowe (Marketing Campaigns Officer), Roger Dace (Senior Lecturer - Marketing &), Teresa Dale (Market Research Manager), Kate Daniell (Senior Press and PR Officer), Lisa Egan (Press Officer), Ray Gilby (Web and New Media Production O), Ceri Gorman (Marketing Campaigns Officer), Lucy Higgins (Public Relations Assistant), Tracy Hunt (Corporate Communications Manag), Maricar Jagger (Public Relations Officer), Alexandra Jones (Marketing Campaigns Officer), Marcella Kirb (Marketing Administration Manag), Paul Krycler (eMarketing Coordinator), Lauren McPeak (Marketing Campaigns Manager), James Mellor (Web and New Media Manager), Alison Pople (Senior Lecturer in Marketing), Jennie Rawling (Press and PR Officer), Peter Reader (Director of Marketing and Comm)
**Sales:** Roger Dace (Senior Lecturer - Marketing &)
**Admin:** Shirley Begg (Administrator), Karen Betts (Administrator), Erika Cartland (Senior Registry Officer), Kim Collins (Senior Course Administrator), Lauren Cummings (Course Administrator), Sarah Eaton (Course Administrator), Maria Hare (Project Administrator), Melissa Howells (Education Administrator), Anne Hunt (Course Administrator), Rebecca Isaia (Secretary), Melanie Lang (Administrator), Kirsty Mitchell (Course Administrator), Debbie Newman (Administrative Assistant), Brenda Newman (Quality Assurance & Curriculum), Ann Patey (Senior Lecturer/Course Leader), Peta Tattersall (Faculty Registrar), Ann Treagus (Administrator), Laura Ward (Administrator), Barbara Wells (Course Administrator)
**IT:** Stuart Graves (Service Delivery Manager)
**HR:** Paul Ankers (Human Resource and Marketing M), Peter Brook (Personnel Director), Stephen Pilbeam (Director - Organisation Studie), Katie Prior (Training Director)
**Operations:** Denise Callender, Karen Nixon (Production and Operations Mana)
**Purchasing:** Douglas Fenton (Purchasing Manager)

**Engineering:** Martin Devonshire (Senior Technician), Avril Druce (Senior Technician), Valene Ferrigan (Senior Technician), Christine Hughes (Technician), David Maund (Senior Technician), Alex Mellor (Technician), Niru Nahar (Senior Technician), Vanessa Peters (Technical Manager), Clifford Phillips (Senior Technical), Maureen Sims (Senior Technician), Anna Swiderska (Senior Technician)
**Branches:** University Of Portsmouth, Learner Support, The Belmont Bldg, Belmont St, Southsea, Hampshire PO5 1NA
**US SIC:** 8221 **UK SIC:** 93100
**Auditors:** Mazars LLP
**Bankers:** Barclays Bank Plc (20-69-34)
**Employees:** 2,201
**Turnover:** £169,494,000

DUNS 22-643-4843    **Imp**
## University of Reading
Po Box 217, Reading, Berkshire RG6 6AH
**Tel:** 01189875123
**Web:** www.reading.ac.uk
**Reg No:** 0000665RC **Estd:** 1926 Incorporate By Act Of Parliament
**Line of Business:** University
**Principals:** T G Ford (President), Professor R G Marshall, The Right Hon L Carrington, Dr G P Botting
**Responsibilities**
**Senior:** Gordon Marshall (Vice Chancellor), Susan Matos (Knowledge Transfer Centre Mana)
**Finance:** Martha Brookes (Contracts Manager)
**Marketing:** Carey Singleton (College Liaison Director)
**Sales:** Richard Messer (Chief Strategy Officer), Frances Young (Business Development & Recruit)
**HR:** Frances Young (Business Development & Recruit)
**Operations:** Carey Singleton (College Liaison Director)
**Purchasing:** Lisa Jeffries (Purchasing Officer)
**Branches:** University Of Reading, St. Andrews Hall, Redlands Road, Reading, Berkshire RG1 5EY
**US SIC:** 8221 **UK SIC:** 93100
**Auditors:** KPMG LLP
**Bankers:** National Westminster Bank Plc (60-17-21)
**Employees:** 3,061
**Turnover:** £221,821,000

DUNS 22-863-2840    **Imp**
## The University of Salford
43 The Crescent, Salford, Lancashire M5 4WT
**Tel:** 01612955000
**Web:** www.i-pol.org
**Reg No:** 0000666RC **Estd:** 1968 Incorporate By Act Of Parliament
**Line of Business:** First-degree level higher education
**Directors:** S R Bosworth, Ms H R Princess, Prof J Husband, G Bent, M Goldsmith, D W Hill, J Spencer, E Parker
**Responsibilities**
**Senior:** Edward Wickham (Principal), Ernest Wilde (Principal)
**Branches:** The University Of Salford, Maxwell Bldg, Salford, Lancashire M5 4WT
**US SIC:** 8221 **UK SIC:** 93100
**Auditors:** Grant Thornton UK LLP

|  | 31-07-12 | 31-07-11 | 31-07-10 |
| --- | --- | --- | --- |
| TO | 184,722,000 | 187,396,000 | 189,638,000 |
| P/L | (12,243,000) | (818,000) | 2,360,000 |
| NW | 92,964,000 | 136,172,000 | 73,007,000 |
| WC | 6,790,000 | 13,565,000 | 18,796,000 |
| Emp. | 2,311 | 2,440 | 2,432 |

DUNS 22-814-7328    **Imp**
## The University of Sheffield
Western Bank, Sheffield, South Yorkshire S10 2TN
**Tel:** 0114 2222 000
**Web:** www.sheffield.ac.uk
**Reg No:** 0000667RC **Estd:** 1905 Incorporate By Act Of Parliament
**Line of Business:** Locksmiths
**Trading Style:** Department of Psychology, Faculty of Engineering
**Principals:** R Rabone (Financial), J S Padley, Sir P Middleton, Dr D E Fletcher, Professor K Burnett, A M Staniforth
**Responsibilities**
**Senior:** Christina Abson (Executive), Lee Adams (Deputy Chief Executive Officer), Sally Ann (Executive), Natalie Billau (Executive), Kathryn Conway (Senior Manager), Roland Givans (Partner), Suzanne Hubbard (Senior Manager), Bob Johnston (Archaeology Department Executi), Richard Leegood (Executive), George Nicholson (Head of Composition and Direct), Dave Rodgers (Manager), Christine Sexton (Operations Director), Gail Street (Executive), Glyn Thomas (Executive), Kath Wainwright (Executive)

**Marketing:** Kathy Aston (Press Officer), Sean Barton (Media Relations Assistant), Lindsey Bird (Relations Manager), Shemina Davis (Media Relations Manager), Clare Parkin (Media Relations Officer), Hannah Postles (Media Relations Officer), Amy Pullan (Media Relations Officer)
**Admin:** Maria Baldam (Administrative Officer (Infras), James Clay (Clerical Assistant), Andrea Hewett (Administrator), Sue Kirk (Administrator), Liz Kitchin (Clerical Assistant), Jackie Mcshane (Personal Assistant), Laura Richards (Office Administrator), Ailsa Shanks (Administrator)
**IT:** Razia Ali (ICT Support Coordinator), Stuart Barkworth (IT Coordinator), Daniel Courtney (IT Centres Supervisor), Mike Greenwood (Data Network Manager), Ed Hartley (ICT Support Analyst), Christine Sexton (Operations Director), Errol Sweetland (IT Support Manager), Mark Wainwright (Information Technology Officer)
**HR:** Sharron Crapper (HR Adviser), Teresa Ellis (HR Manager), Susannah Hall (Human Resources Assistant), Cheryl Oliver (Special Projects/Central Resou), Rose Valerio (Human Resources Manager)
**Facilities:** Ralph Negrine (Head of Department and Profess), Christine Sexton (Operations Director)
**Operations:** Valerie Cotter (Faculty Director of Operations), Terry Croft (Director of Operations), Neil Hopkinson (Head of Department - Centre fo), Julie Scholes (Project Executive), Richard Yates (Head of Security)
**Engineering:** Yvonne Beach (Engineering Manager), Russell Hand (Professor of Glass Science & E), Ian Lyne (Technical Manager), Nicola Reilly (Program Manager), David Revill (Technical Engineer), Jiabin Wang (Professor of Electrical Engine), David Wengraf (Technical Engineer), Ian Wraith (Senior Technician)
**Branches:** The University Of Sheffield, Beech Hill Road, Sheffield, South Yorkshire S10 2RX
**US SIC:** 8221 **UK SIC:** 93100
**Auditors:** KPMG LLP
**Bankers:** Lloyds TSB Bank plc (30-97-51)
**Employees:** 5,533
**Turnover:** £430,000,000

---

DUNS 23-283-5652
### University of South Wales
Pontypridd, Pontypridd, Mid Glamorgan CF37 1DL
**Tel:** 01633432432
**Web:** www.newport.ac.uk
**Estd:** 1900 Incorporate By Act Of Parliament
**Line of Business:** University.
**Principals:** P Andrews (Chairman), Ms P Lydon
**Responsibilities**
**Marketing:** Mike Hill (Director of Commercial & Exter)
**Sales:** Mike Hill (Director of Commercial & Exter)
**Branches:** University Of South Wales, Treforest, Pontypridd, Mid Glamorgan CF37 1DL
**US SIC:** 8221, 6531
**UK SIC:** 93100, 83400
**Auditors:** PricewaterhouseCooper LLp
**Bankers:** National Westminster Bank Plc (56-00-59)
**Employees:** 684
**Turnover:** £49,693,000

---

DUNS 22-559-5503　　Imp
### University of Southampton
University Road, Southampton, Hampshire SO17 1BJ
**Tel:** 02380593121
**Web:** www.southampton.ac.uk
**Reg No:** 0000668RC **VAT No:** 568630414
**Estd:** 2014 Incorporate By Act Of Parliament
**Line of Business:** Computer services
**Principals:** M Ace (Financial), S Higman, A Walker, Prof C Thomas, Prof A Wheeler, Prof P Nelson
**Responsibilities**
**Senior:** Janis Baird (Executive), Lisa Blenkinsop (Manager), G. Coleman (Executive), Mark Cranshaw (Deputy Director (Development), Louise Dubras (Senior Manager), Nick Jennings (Chairman), Don Nutbeam (Vice Chancellor), Fabrizio Renna (Board Member), Sarah Rule (Executive), Jayanta Sahu (Board Member), Neville Stanton (Chairman), Bill Warburton (Executive), Francis Wenban-Smith (Chairman), Rebecca Young (Manager)
**Finance:** Maria Ceron Cervantes (Finance Officer), Aimee Ellis (Finance Officer), Sue Granshaw (School Accountant), Joanne Payne (Service Group Accountant), Niki Price (Bid Manager), James Sturgess (Faculty Finance Manager), Chris Tollerfield (Finance Manager), Richard Trowbridge (Faculty Finance Manager)

---

**Marketing:** Richard Milton (Senior Marketing Manager), Ewa Placzek-Neves (Marketing Officer), Ines Teresa-Palacio (Head of Strategic Marketing)
**Sales:** Jeremy Howells (Dean of Faculty of Business &), Laura Luff (Senior Development Manager), Nikki Matthews (Faculty of Business & Law Mana), Katherine de Retuerto (Senior Development Manager)
**Admin:** Nicky Baverstock (Academic Administrator), Betty Draper (Administrator), Sarah Dunlop (Administrator), Victoria Hayter (Administrator), Mary Hudson (Information Librarian), Tina Johnson (Administrator), Carolyn Wallis (Administrator), Jacobo Weinstock (Admissions Tutor), Fiona Wright (PA to COO), Sonia Zakrzewski (Admissions Tutor)
**IT:** Sarah Howes (Associate Director - Analytics), Daniel Keyworth (Reporting and Data Analytics M), Robert Standish (Technical Manager)
**Operations:** Thom Bull (Head of Faculty Operations), Sarah Denson (Senior Manager), Zoe Heathcote (Head of Faculty Operations for), Kirsty McLean (Faculty Executive Operations O), Madeline Patterson (Senior Manager), Mylene Ployaert (Head of Specialist Support Ope), Ellie Shaw (Project Officer)
**Engineering:** Grant Hearn (Professor of Ocean Engineering), Georges Limbert (Senior Consulting Engineer), Rosalind Mizen (Faculty Executive Engineering), Matthew Praeger (Research, Engineering Staff Me), Ros Stanton (Faculty Education Manager - En), Susanne Ullrich (Engineer)
**Branches:** University Of Southampton, Main Reception, Montefiore House, Southampton, Hampshire SO18 2NU
**US SIC:** 8221 **UK SIC:** 93100
**Auditors:** Mazars LLP
**Bankers:** Fortis Bank London Bch (formerly Generale Bk) (40-52-62)

| | 31-07-13 | 31-07-12 | 31-07-11 |
|---|---|---|---|
| TO | 447,221,000 | 437,873,000 | 436,940,000 |
| P/L | 5,726,000 | 14,230,000 | 15,302,000 |
| NW | 364,516,000 | 325,478,000 | 330,381,000 |
| WC | 17,922,000 | 64,356,000 | 80,433,000 |
| Emp. | 5,190 | 4,992 | 4,868 |

---

DUNS 21-834-9497
### University of Southampton Students Union
Building 48, University Road, Southampton, Hampshire SO17 1BJ
**Tel:** 02380593539
**Web:** www.susu.org
**Reg No:** 8034371 **Estd:** 2012 Private Company Limited By Guarantee
**Line of Business:** Business and management consultancy activities not elsewhere classified
**Directors:** W Yeong, Miss L Butler, Miss R L Thomas, S Bailey, A Aulakh, M R Beattie, Miss K H Lightowler, Miss M A Downing
**Co. Secretary:** John Mills
**Responsibilities**
**Senior:** Peta Ash (Director), Eleanor Cawthera (Director), Nigel Coopey (Director), Jade Head (Director), Nathaniel Jenkins (Director), David Mendoza-Wolfson (Director), Leon Rea (Director)
**US SIC:** 7392 **UK SIC:** 83951
**Bankers:** Lloyds TSB Bank plc (30-90-34)

| | 31-07-14 | 31-07-13 |
|---|---|---|
| TO | 7,512,448 | 7,321,269 |
| P/L | 18,288 | 287,148 |
| NW | 1,399,423 | 1,381,135 |
| WC | 420,387 | 380,056 |
| Emp. | 323 | 315 |

---

DUNS 22-903-8914
### University of St Andrews
79 North Street, St Andrews, Fife KY16 9RJ
**Fax:** 01334-462672
**Web:** www.st375.com
**Estd:** 1999 Incorporate By Act Of Parliament
**Line of Business:** First-degree level higher education
**Director:** Mrs L Richardson
**Responsibilities**
**IT:** Malcolm Bain (Director of IT Services)
**HR:** Marie Stewart (Human Resources Director)
**Health & Safety:** Angus Clark (Health & Safety Director)
**Branches:** University Of St Andrews, College Gate, North Street, St. Andrews, Fife KY16 9AJ
**US SIC:** 8221 **UK SIC:** 93100
**Auditors:** Ernst & Young
**Bankers:** The Royal Bank Of Scotland Plc (83-26-28)
**Employees:** 2,178
**Turnover:** £155,788,000

---

DUNS 49-726-7054
### University of St Andrews Students Association
2 St Marys Place, St Andrews, Fife KY16 9UZ
**Web:** www.yourunion.net
**Estd:** 1970
**Line of Business:** Clubs social and associations
**President:** P Corrigan
**Responsibilities**
**Senior:** David Whitton (General Manager)
**Marketing:** O Walker (Marketing Manager)
**HR:** I Cupples (Personnel Manager)
**US SIC:** 8699 **UK SIC:** 96902
**Employees:** 50

---

DUNS 22-989-3896　　Imp
### University of Stirling
Stirling Campus, Drip Road, Stirling, Stirlingshire FK8 1SE
**Tel:** 01786473171
**Web:** www.stir.ac.uk
**Reg No:** 0000669RC **Estd:** 1967 Incorporate By Act Of Parliament
**Line of Business:** Arts centres
**Trading Style:** Stirling Management Centre Withscotland, University of Stirling Sports Centre, Macrobert Art Centre, Howietown Fishery
**Principals:** Dr D Littlejohn (Chairman), J Gordon (Financial), Professor C Hallett
**Co. Secretary:** Kevin Clarke
**Responsibilities**
**Senior:** Liam Sinclair (Artistic Director)
**Finance:** Liam McCabe (Financial Director)
**Sales:** Liam Spillane (Commercial Director)
**IT:** Brian Bullen (Unix Systems Specialist), Kathleen McCabe (IS Development Manager)
**HR:** Sue Jennings (Deputy Human Resources Directo), Martin Mccrindle (Human Resources Director)
**Facilities:** Karen Plouviez (Estates Director)
**Purchasing:** Colin Elliott (Purchasing Manager)
**Branches:** University Of Stirling, Old Perth Road, Inverness, Inverness-Shire IV2 3JH
**US SIC:** 8221 **UK SIC:** 93100
**Auditors:** KPMG LLP
**Bankers:** Bank Of Scotland (12-02-56)
**Employees:** 1,478
**Turnover:** £101,948,000

---

DUNS 21-029-3103
### The University of Strathclyde
181 St James Road, Glasgow, Lanarkshire G4 0NT
**Tel:** 01415482724
**Web:** www.strath.ac.uk
**VAT No:** 261339762 **Estd:** 1796
**Line of Business:** First-degree level higher education
**Director:** A Hamnett
**Responsibilities**
**Senior:** Jim McDonald (Principal)
**Facilities:** Jim McConnell (Director of Estates Services), Graham Roddick (estates Manager)
**US SIC:** 8221 **UK SIC:** 93100
**Employees:** 3,500

---

DUNS 21-246-5685
### University of Strathclyde
University Of Strathclyde, Gartocharn, Alexandria, Dunbartonshire G83 8NL
**Web:** www.strath.ac.uk
**Estd:** 2002 Proprietorship
**Line of Business:** Clubs social and associations
**Proprietor:** D Upton
**US SIC:** 5813 **UK SIC:** 66200
**Employees:** 98

---

DUNS 23-780-4521
### University of Strathclyde Students Association
John Anderson Campus, Glasgow, Lanarkshire G1 1JH
**Tel:** 01415675000
**Web:** www.strathstudents.com
**Estd:** 1964
**Line of Business:** Education services
**Trading Style:** Strathclyde Students' Association
**Principals:** Ms L Botham (President), G Singh (President), P Whyte, Ms L Fraser, D Macdonald, A Wagner, P Wilson, J Forsyth
**Responsibilities**
**Senior:** Judith Murray (Designated Limited Liability P), Ursula Tereba (Vice President)
**HR:** Meiri Mcdonald (Human Resources Manager)
**US SIC:** 8699 **UK SIC:** 96902
**Bankers:** Bank Of Scotland (80-11-80)
**Employees:** 150

---

DUNS 22-975-2241
### University of Strathclyde Viz Royal College of Science & Technology
Mccance Building, 16 Richmond Street, Glasgow, Lanarkshire G1 1XQ
**Tel:** 01415484078
**Web:** www.strath.ac.uk
**Reg No:** 0000670RC **VAT No:** 261339762
**Estd:** 1796 Incorporate By Act Of Parliament
**Line of Business:** First-degree level higher education institution.
**Trading Style:** The University of Strathclyde
**Principals:** D Coyle (Financial), Sir J Mcdonald, H Hall, K Miller
**Responsibilities**
**Senior:** John Arbuthnott (Principal), Rae Condie (Principal), Allister Ferguson (Principal)
**Marketing:** Audrey Chisholm (Marketing Officer)
**Branches:** University Of Strathclyde Viz Royal College Of Science & Technology, 16 Richmond Street, 50 Richmond St, Glasgow, Lanarkshire G1 1XT
**US SIC:** 8221 **UK SIC:** 93100
**Auditors:** Ernst & Young LLP
**Bankers:** Clydesdale Bank Plc (82-20-00)
**Employees:** 3,625
**Turnover:** £203,994,000

---

DUNS 23-153-0908
### University of Sunderland
Edinburgh Building, Sunderland, Tyne and Wear SR1 3SD
**Tel:** 01915152000 **Fax:** 01915158001
**Web:** www.sunderland.ac.uk
**Estd:** 1969 Incorporate By Act Of Parliament
**Line of Business:** University
**Principals:** S Porteous (Financial), S Porteous (Financial), Prof P Sidler, Prof P Sidler, P Fidler
**Branches:** University Of Sunderland, Sunderland Technical Park, Unit 1-3, Sunderland, Tyne and Wear SR2 7PT
**US SIC:** 8221 **UK SIC:** 93100
**Auditors:** KPMG LLP
**Employees:** 1,700
**Turnover:** £126,195,000

---

DUNS 50-496-4735
### University of Sunderland Enterprises Ltd
The Industry Centre, 1 Colima Avenue, Sunderland Enterprise Park, Sunderland, Tyne and Wear SR5 3XB
**Tel:** 01915152666
**Web:** www.sellingexcellence.co.uk
**Reg No:** 2464641 **Estd:** 1990 Private Limited Company
**Line of Business:** Other business activities not elsewhere classified
**Issued Capital:** £1,010,000
**Directors:** G J Macdonald, Professor P M Fidler, Mrs S A Atkinson
**Co. Secretary:** Mrs Helen Cutting
**Branches:** University Of Sunderland Enterprises Ltd, Backhouse Park, Ashburne House, Sunderland, Tyne and Wear SR2 7EF
**US SIC:** 7399, 8221
**UK SIC:** 83954, 93100
**Auditors:** KPMG LLP

| | 31-07-14 | 31-07-13 | 31-07-12 |
|---|---|---|---|
| TO | 2,240,000 | 2,497,000 | 2,465,000 |
| P/L | (59,000) | (48,000) | (163,000) |
| NW | 198,000 | 254,000 | 289,000 |
| WC | 198,000 | 254,000 | 288,000 |

---

DUNS 22-509-3061　　Imp-Exp
### University of Surrey
University Of Surrey, Guildford, Surrey GU2 7XS
**Web:** www.surrey.ac.uk
**Reg No:** 0000671RC **VAT No:** 688953065
**Estd:** 1891 Incorporate By Act Of Parliament
**Line of Business:** Business services
**Trading Style:** Appleseed Bookshop
**Principals:** D Sharkey (Financial), P N Seaton, P C Snowden, G Melly
**Responsibilities**
**Senior:** Tony Corless (Laboratory and Business Manage)
**Finance:** Shirin Ayandeh (International Officer), Suzanne Owen (Head of Financial Transactions), Belinda Tan (Finance and Administration Man)
**Marketing:** Mike Findlay (Media Relations Manager), Tanya Gubbay (Media Relations Manager), Peter La (Media Relations Officer), R.e. Spier (Editor), Amy Sutton (Media Relations Officer), Samuel Uzzell (?Head of Market Insight and Da)
**Sales:** Celia Gaffney (Business Development Manager), Trevor Hartman (Commercial Manager), Jenny Ritchie (Business Development Officer)

**Admin:** Yoshie Abe *(Administrative Assistant)*, Stefanie Aries *(Secretary - Biochemistry & Phy)*, Nan Bennett *(Postgraduate Research Admissio)*, Zoe Berry *(Senior Faculty Administrator ()*, Jane Bradford *(Admissions Administrator)*, Alex Bryant *(Secretariat Administrative Ass)*, Louise Dams *(Programme Administrator)*, Ferenc Hepp *(Box Office & Front of House Ma)*, Marta Jenner *(Module Administrator)*, Joanna Rodriguez *(Module Administrator)*, Belinda Tan *(Finance and Administration Man)*
**IT:** Martyn Buxton Hoare *(Director Technology)*, Roger Stickland *(Head of IS)*
**Facilities:** Derry Caleb *(Estates Director)*, Dave Hitchcock *(Facilities Manager, Surrey Spo)*
**Operations:** Katy Beaumont *(Projects Officer)*
**Purchasing:** Sonia Amos *(Contracts Manager)*, Nicky Barnard *(Contracts Administrator)*, Rafi Choudhury *(Contracts Manager)*
**Engineering:** Philip Bateman *(Engineer)*, Mark Browton *(Technical Resource Manager)*, Paul Leahy *(Technical Engineer)*, Gary Strudwick *(Technical Engineer)*, Evi Tramantza *(Academic Liaison Librarian - F)*
**Branches:** University Of Surrey, The University Of Surrey, Lrc Building, Guildford, Surrey GU2 7XH
**US SIC:** 8221 **UK SIC:** 93100
**Auditors:** KPMG LLP
**Bankers:** National Westminster Bank Plc (60-09-50)
**Employees:** 2,227
**Turnover:** £193,827,000

DUNS 21-702-4535

## The University of Surrey Students' Union

Union House, University Of Surrey, Guildford, Surrey GU2 7XH
**Web:** www.ussu.co.uk
**Reg No:** 7470232 **Estd:** 2010 Private Company Limited By Guarantee
**Line of Business:** Trade unions
**Directors:** Mrs C M Foord, M T Sadlers, Miss E S Mariuta, H T Alsaidi, H Ap Rees, J E Pattison, M E Hussien, M B Smith
**Responsibilities**
**Senior:** Bob Anderson *(Chief Executive Officer)*, Barry Hitchcock *(Director)*, Daniel Jacobs *(Director)*, Marian Lynch *(Manager)*, Munyaradzi Mudarikiri *(Director)*, Samuel Ratzer *(Manager)*
**US SIC:** 8611 **UK SIC:** 96312
**Bankers:** National Westminster Bank Plc (60-06-03)

| | 31-07-14 | 31-07-13 | 31-07-12 |
|---|---|---|---|
| TO | 3,493,914 | 3,525,651 | 3,533,167 |
| P/L | (31,450) | 5,346 | 6,449 |
| NW | 994,188 | 1,039,769 | 1,020,292 |
| WC | 363,066 | 357,768 | 236,481 |
| Emp. | 145 | 148 | 81 |

DUNS 22-841-9990 **Imp**

## University of Sussex

University Of Sussex, Sussex House, Southern Ring Road, Falmer, Brighton, East Sussex BN1 9RH
**Tel:** 01273 606755
**Web:** www.sussex.ac.uk
**Reg No:** 0000672RC **Estd:** 1981 Incorporate By Act Of Parliament
**Line of Business:** Property shops
**Principals:** A Spencer *(Financial)*, Professor P Layzell, Professor M Farthing, N Gershon, Dr P Harvey
**Responsibilities**
**Senior:** Julie Applin *(Executive)*, Linda Buckham *(Board Member)*, Romi Nijhawan *(Executive)*
**Finance:** Angie Allen *(Finance Assistant)*, Deborah Bonwick *(Finance Coordinator)*, Mathew Bouston *(Finance Assistant)*, Alastair Brand *(Finance Assistant)*, Dawn Buck *(Credit Controller)*, Becky Cameron *(Senior Finance Assistant)*, Anna Charlick *(Credit Controller)*, Marc Eames *(Finance Assistant)*, Jamys Edmunds *(Senior Finance Assistant)*, Sue Fippard *(Finance Assistant)*, Carman Ford *(Finance Assistant)*, Carolyn Gibsey *(Finance Assistant)*, Imogen Gower *(Finance Assistant)*, Elena Greenway *(Finance Assistant)*, Julie Heslop *(Finance Assistant)*, Janet Hood *(Accountant)*, Harriet Howe *(Finance Assistant)*, Catherine Hulme *(Finance Office Manager)*, Jo Kenebel *(Finance Assistant)*, Hazel Orchard *(Finance Assistant)*, Carolyn Pentecost *(Finance Assistant)*, Helen Piniger *(Finance Assistant)*, Mark Raven *(Management Accountant)*, Susan Sacre *(Finance Assistant)*, Elisabeth Saunders *(Management Accountant)*, Lisa Savage *(Management Accountant)*, Lorraine Wall *(Finance Assistant)*, Anita Whedbee *(Finance Assistant)*, Kerry Wilde *(Finance Coordinator)*, Ele Wood *(Senior Finance Assistant)*
**Marketing:** Sara Adamson *(Commissioning Editor)*, Jacqui Bealing *(Senior Press Officer)*, Claudia Biedert *(Prospectus Editor)*, Claire Clinton *(Head of Marketing)*, Melanie Farmer *(Marketing Executive)*, Alison Field *(Senior Communications Officer)*, James Hakner *(Communications Officer)*, Sue Hepburn *(Development Officer: Major Gif)*, Katy Hiles *(Head of Marketing)*, Katherine Jarvis *(PA & Events Coordinator)*, Rachael Miller *(Head of Publications)*, Carrie Prew *(Corporate Editor)*
**Admin:** Katherine Jarvis *(PA & Events Coordinator)*, Beverley Traylen *(PA and Events Coordinator)*, Zoe Varney-Burch *(Personal Assistant)*
**IT:** Julia Darnell *(?Head of Corporate Information)*, James Goodlet *(Assistant Director Infrastruct)*
**HR:** Graham Curry *(HR Adviser)*, Rosemarie Eastham *(HR Adviser)*, Andy Howard *(Career Development Advisor)*, Tracey Llewellyn *(Human Resources Administrator)*, Alasdair MacKay *(HR Adviser)*, Michelle Punter *(Head of HR Advisory Services)*
**Operations:** Chris Leggatt *(Operations Manager)*, Dave Lewney *(Head of Storage)*
**Purchasing:** Iain Monro *(Contracts Manager)*
**Branches:** University Of Sussex, Sportcentre, Sportcentre Road, Brighton, East Sussex BN1 9RB
**US SIC:** 8221, 9121
**UK SIC:** 93100, 91110
**Auditors:** KPMG LLP
**Employees:** 1,880
**Turnover:** £156,665,000

DUNS 39-688-3373

## University of Sussex Students Union Trading Ltd

Falmer House, Falmer, Brighton, East Sussex BN1 9QF
**Tel:** 01273678555 **Fax:** 01273-873329
**Web:** www.sussexstudent.com
**Reg No:** 2146582 **Estd:** 1991 Private Limited Company
**Line of Business:** Education services
**Issued Capital:** £2
**Directors:** R Tata, A A Baldry, N D Tomlinson, Miss M C Steiner, Ms C Mclaughlin, M B Segalov, D J Greenberg
**Co. Secretary:** Paul Newton
**Responsibilities**
**Senior:** Anna Cornish *(Manager)*, Sue Cornsord *(Office Manager)*, Michael Holder *(Manager)*, Mike Riley *(Assistant Director)*
**HR:** Sue Cornsord *(Office Manager)*
**US SIC:** 8299, 5399
**UK SIC:** 93300, 65600
**Auditors:** Mazars Neville Russell
**Bankers:** Barclays Bank Plc (20-49-76)

| | 31-07-14 | 31-07-13 | 31-07-12 |
|---|---|---|---|
| TO | 2,359,014 | 2,059,573 | 2,230,356 |
| NW | 2 | 2 | 2 |
| WC | (40,869) | (38,259) | (58,234) |

DUNS 21-043-0424 **Imp**

## University of Teeside

Borough Road, Middlesbrough, Cleveland TS1 3BA
**Tel:** 01642-218121
**Web:** www.tees.ac.uk
**Estd:** 1989
**Line of Business:** First-degree level higher education
**Proprietor:** G Henderson
**Responsibilities**
**Senior:** Geoff Archer *(Manager)*, Warren Harrison *(Creative Director)*, James Jalalian *(Manager)*, Ashley James *(Manager)*, Wayne Kyte *(Manager)*, Andrew Morwood *(Manager)*, Steve Scott-Marshall *(Chairman)*
**Marketing:** Alison Ferst *(Communications Manager)*, Barbara Gamble *(Journalist)*, Dennis Kelly *(Marketing Director)*, Michelle Ruane *(Communications Coordinator)*
**HR:** Ellie Skene *(PA to HR Director)*, Janet Waine *(Human Resources Manager)*
**US SIC:** 8221 **UK SIC:** 93100
**Auditors:** Deloitte LLP
**Employees:** 1,600
**Turnover:** £141,322,000

DUNS 23-368-3150 **Imp**

## University of the Arts London

272 High Holborn, London WC1V 7EY
**Fax:** 020-7514-6175
**Web:** www.arts.ac.uk
**VAT No:** 510398660 **Estd:** 1940 Incorporate By Act Of Parliament
**Line of Business:** University
**Principals:** Mrs S Douglas *(Financial)*, D Gratton, Sir W Stubbs, R Mcclure, M Bischard
**Responsibilities**
**Senior:** Roger McClure *(Director)*
**Branches:** University of The Arts London, 5 Richbell Place, London WC1N 3LA
**US SIC:** 8221, 8299
**UK SIC:** 93100, 93300
**Auditors:** KPMG LLP
**Bankers:** National Westminster Bank Plc (50-41-06)
**Employees:** 400
**Turnover:** £211,905,000

DUNS 57-195-0591

## University of the Highlands & Islands

12b Ness Walk, Inverness, Inverness-Shire IV3 5SQ
**Tel:** 01463279000
**Web:** www.uhi.ac.uk
**Reg No:** 0148203SC **Estd:** 1996 Private Limited Company
**Line of Business:** Sub-degree level higher education
**Directors:** A A Ross, Mrs V Nairn, M Burr, Professor K Miller, G J Coutts, J D Macdonald, Miss R V Parker, Dr M E Foxley
**Co. Secretary:** Ms Fiona Larg
**Responsibilities**
**Senior:** Gillian Berkeley *(Director)*, Crichton Lang *(Principal)*, Eileen Mackay *(Director)*, Iseabail Mactaggart *(Director)*, Fiona Mclean *(Director)*, William Mulholland *(Director)*, William Printie *(Director)*, David Worthington *(Director)*
**Finance:** Lorna MacDonald *(Finance Director)*
**Marketing:** Alison Lochhead *(Communications and External Re)*, Susan Szymborski *(Communications Officer)*
**Sales:** James Gibbs *(Director of Enterprise)*, Lindsey Moodie *(Business Development - Health)*
**Admin:** Archina Maclellan *(Receptionist)*
**IT:** Mike McDonald *(IT Manager)*
**Purchasing:** Gayle Riddoch *(Contract Administrator)*
**US SIC:** 8221, 8249
**UK SIC:** 93100, 93300
**Auditors:** Ernst & Young
**Bankers:** The Royal Bank Of Scotland Plc (83-23-10)

| | 31-07-14 | 31-07-13 | 31-07-12 |
|---|---|---|---|
| TO | 50,031,000 | 48,308,000 | 43,199,000 |
| P/L | 1,096,000 | 2,270,000 | 146,000 |
| NW | 628,000 | 2,783,000 | 920,000 |
| WC | 6,598,000 | 4,782,000 | 1,920,000 |
| Emp. | 212 | 196 | 188 |

DUNS 21-703-2499 **Imp**

## University of the West of England

Frenchay Campus, Coldharbour Lane, Bristol, Avon BS16 1QY
**Tel:** 01179656261
**Web:** www.uwe.ac.uk
**VAT No:** 520137788 **Estd:** 1969 Incorporate By Act Of Parliament
**Line of Business:** Charities and charitable organisations
**Principals:** W Marshall *(Financial)*, Prof S G West
**Responsibilities**
**Senior:** Alex Isaac *(Head of Sport)*
**IT:** S Grive *(Computer Manager)*
**Operations:** Helen Worboys *(Operations Manager/ Sports)*
**Branches:** University Of The West Of England, Combe Park, Bath, Avon BA1 3NG
**US SIC:** 8221 **UK SIC:** 93100
**Auditors:** Mazars LLP
**Bankers:** National Westminster Bank Plc (60-02-38)
**Employees:** 2,500
**Turnover:** £223,064,000

DUNS 22-845-0003 **Imp**

## University of the West of Scotland

University Avenue, Ayr, Ayrshire KA8 0SX
**Tel:** 01418483000 **Fax:** 01418483751
**Web:** www.uws.ac.uk
**VAT No:** 263824940 **Estd:** 1897 Incorporate By Act Of Parliament
**Line of Business:** University
**Principals:** R W Shaw, J M Fraser
**Responsibilities**
**Senior:** Jane Caffrey *(Executive)*, Maeve Cowper *(General Manager)*, Catherine Czerkawska *(Executive)*, Franzeska Ewart *(Executive)*, Shiona Mcgill *(General Manager)*, Alastair Moodie *(Executive)*, Judith Ramsay *(Executive)*, Lena Robinson *(Chairman)*, Duncan Sim *(Academic Director)*
**Finance:** Audrey Brown *(Payroll Assistant)*, Jackie Cusworth *(Credit Controller)*, Linda Irving *(Credit Controller)*, Helen Liney *(Credit Controller)*, Donald Mathson *(Senior Finance Administrator)*
**Marketing:** Barry Andrew *(European Business Manager)*, Vicky Brown *(Marketing Manager - PR & Publi)*
**Sales:** Karen Kennedy *(Faculty Business Development M)*
**Admin:** Roberta Baird *(Administrative Assistant)*, Maureen Ferguson *(Administrator)*, Alison Gray *(Faculty Administrator)*, Heather Imrie *(Administrator)*, Heather Lambie *(Administrator)*, Thomas Mcginnes *(Administrator)*, Anne Mcglynn *(Clerical, Assistant, Admission)*, Arlene Mcguire *(Administrator)*, Joy Mcleod *(Administrator)*, Kathy Porter *(Office Manager)*, Ann Ralston *(Administrator)*, Kay Shaw *(Administrator)*, Patsy Shiels *(Administrator)*, Paul Snape *(Administrator)*, James fraser *(Secretary)*
**IT:** May Allen *(Senior Infrastructure Support)*, Alan Boyd *(Infrastructure Analyst)*, Greig Glendinning *(ICT Support Analyst)*, Scott Knox *(ICT Support Manager)*, Gerry McCauley *(Assistant Director ICT Service)*, Stewart McGee *(Infrastructure Support Analyst)*, Thomas McSpadyen *(Senior Infrastructure Analyst)*, Neil McTaggart *(Senior Infrastructure Support)*, Stuart Morton *(Web Programmer)*, Derek Osborne *(Technical Development Manager)*, Darren Ricketts *(Campus Enterprise Mobility)*, Willy Summers *(ICT Services Manager)*, Derek Turner *(Senior Lecturer, School of Com)*, Jonathan Warnock *(ICT Services and Media Support)*
**HR:** Susan Gormley *(Human Resources Manager)*, Ray Mcmaster *(HR Executive)*
**Branches:** University Of The West Of Scotland, High Street, Paisley, Renfrewshire PA1 2BE
**US SIC:** 8221 **UK SIC:** 93100
**Auditors:** Ernst & Young LLP
**Bankers:** Bank Of Scotland (80-91-27)
**Employees:** 1,000
**Turnover:** £95,479,000

DUNS 42-440-1057 **Imp**

## University of Ulster

Cromore Road, Coleraine, Co Londonderry BT52 1SA
**Fax:** 028-7032-4933
**Web:** www.ulster.ac.uk
**Reg No:** 0000726RC **VAT No:** 393627128
**Estd:** 1996 Incorporate By Act Of Parliament
**Line of Business:** University
**Trading Style:** Streat Coleraine Campus
**Directors:** D G Cheal, W J Mccourt, Lord T A Smith, P Hope, D Best
**Responsibilities**
**Senior:** William McCourt *(Director)*
**Finance:** Alison Rankin *(Assistant CFO)*
**Marketing:** Lynda Monahan *(Support Assistant, Marketing)*, Fred Morrison *(Lecturer In Communication, Jor)*, Alison Snookes *(Development Services Manager)*
**Admin:** Maria Black *(Clerical Assistant - Informati)*, Claire Bleakley *(Support Assistant (Development)*, Gwen McCracken *(Administrative Manager (Resear)*, Alison Snookes *(Development Services Manager)*
**Branches:** University of Ulster, Magee College, Northland Road, Londonderry, Co Londonderry BT48 7JL
**US SIC:** 8221 **UK SIC:** 93100
**Auditors:** PricewaterhouseCoopers LLP
**Bankers:** Ulster Bank Ltd (98-00-10)
**Employees:** 15
**Turnover:** £205,064,000

DUNS 21-778-7270

## University of Wales

Penglais, Llanon, Dyfed SY23 3FL
**Tel:** 01970623111
**Web:** www.aber.ac.uk
**Estd:** 2011 Proprietorship
**Line of Business:** University
**Proprietor:** R Merrick
**Responsibilities**
**Marketing:** Alice Earp *(Publications Officer)*, Elinor Howells *(Communications Officer)*, Kami Tacickaja *(Senior Web Development)*
**US SIC:** 8221 **UK SIC:** 93100
**Employees:** 1,800

DUNS 36-483-2423

## University of Wales

12 High Street, Cardiff, South Glamorgan CF10 1AX
**Tel:** 02920228205 **Fax:** 02920878625
**Web:** www.wales.ac.uk
**Estd:** 2012 Incorporate By Act Of Parliament
**Line of Business:** Book retailers
**Principals:** D Thomas *(Chairman)*, Ms A Morgan, J Mcnally, Ms L E Williams, P R Johnston, P Jones Evans, H F Hughes, D George
**Responsibilities**
**Senior:** Professor Clement *(Chief Executive Officer)*, John Ennis *(Manager)*, DI George *(Director)*, Medwin Hills *(Vice Chancellor)*
**IT:** Wayne Whittle *(Head of IT)*
**HR:** Kathryn Knowles *(Head of HR)*
**US SIC:** 8221 **UK SIC:** 93100

**Auditors:** PricewaterhouseCoopers LLP
**Employees:** 2
**Turnover:** £15,411,000

DUNS 22-782-1915 **Imp**

## University of Warwick

University House, The University Of Warwick, Coventry, West Midlands CV4 8UW
**Web:** www2.warwick.ac.uk
**Reg No:** 0000678RC **Estd:** 1965 Incorporate By Act Of Parliament
**Line of Business:** First-degree level higher education
**Trading Style:** U.O.W., Warwick Medical School
**Principals:** P Thrift, R Lambert, K Lamberts, K Sloan
**Branches:** University Of Warwick, Scarlman Road, Coventry, West Midlands CV4 7AL
**US SIC:** 8221, 2731
**UK SIC:** 93100, 47532
**Auditors:** KPMG LLP
**Bankers:** Barclays Bank Plc (20-23-55)

| | 31-07-13 | 31-07-12 | 31-07-11 |
|---|---|---|---|
| TO | 459,600,000 | 440,100,000 | 419,100,000 |
| P/L | 19,100,000 | 30,000,000 | 19,600,000 |
| NW | 312,300,000 | 302,200,000 | 286,900,000 |
| WC | 42,100,000 | 19,400,000 | 9,900,000 |
| Emp. | 4,536 | 4,351 | 4,375 |

DUNS 23-210-5460

## University of West London

St Marys Road, Ealing, London W5 5RF
**Tel:** 08000368888
**Web:** www.uwl.ac.uk
**VAT No:** 578337988 **Estd:** 1992 Incorporate By Act Of Parliament
**Line of Business:** Business services
**Trading Style:** Thames Valley University
**Director:** P John
**Responsibilities**
**IT:** Maggie Stephens *(Computer Manager)*
**Branches:** University Of West London, Wellington Street, Slough, Berkshire SL1 1YG
**US SIC:** 8221 **UK SIC:** 93100
**Auditors:** BDO LLP
**Bankers:** Barclays Bank Plc (20-78-58)
**Employees:** 1,800
**Turnover:** £103,745,000

DUNS 22-709-9033

## The University of Westminster

309 Regent Street, London W1B 2HW
**Tel:** 02079115000
**Web:** www.westminster.ac.uk
**Reg No:** 0977818 **Estd:** 1998 Private Company Limited By Guarantee
**Line of Business:** Research and experimental development on natural sciences and engineering
**Directors:** Ms D H Yeo, M C Hogg, S A Courtenage, D F Batchelor, J G Wates, J D Begg, R D Barnes, A Ganguli
**Co. Secretary:** Ms Suzanne Enright
**Responsibilities**
**Senior:** Rita Bellamy James *(Director)*, Karen Dunnell *(Director)*, Nicholas Laws *(Director)*, Kaled Mimouni *(Director)*, Geoffrey Petts *(Director)*, Cameron Thomson *(Assistant Company Secretary)*, Alastair Woods *(Director)*
**Sales:** Brent Holder *(Business Development Officer)*, Valeriya Karuk *(Business Development Manager f)*, Raman Kaur *(Business Development Officer)*, Shanjoy Mairembam *(Business Development Officer)*, Sue Tuttlebury *(Business Development Officer)*
**Admin:** Alice Hsu *(KTP Administrator)*, Eilidh Macdonald *(Associate Director, Knowledge)*
**IT:** Susan Enright *(Director of Information Servic)*, Alice Hsu *(KTP Administrator)*, Jashal Makwana *(Education Technology Specialis)*, Victor Morales *(Computing Information Desk Off)*
**Branches:** The University Of Westminster, 36-37 Featherstone St, London EC1Y 8QZ
**US SIC:** 7391, 8922
**UK SIC:** 94000
**Auditors:** KPMG LLP
**Bankers:** National Westminster Bank Plc (56-00-33)

| | 31-07-14 | 31-07-13 | 31-07-12 |
|---|---|---|---|
| TO | 181,772,000 | 170,437,000 | 165,418,000 |
| P/L | 20,072,000 | 11,098,000 | 10,259,000 |
| NW | 124,320,000 | 55,822,000 | 103,803,000 |
| WC | 46,345,000 | 19,438,000 | 9,604,000 |
| Emp. | 1,793 | 1,774 | 1,753 |

DUNS 23-986-6841

## University of Wolverhampton

City Campus North Administration, 2nd Floor, Camp Street, Wolverhampton, West Midlands WV1 1AD
**Tel:** 01902321000
**Web:** www.wlv.ac.uk
**Line of Business:** First-degree level higher education
**Trading Style:** University of Wolverhampton, The Arena Theatre, School of Sport University of Wolverhampton
**Principals:** J Brooks *(Managing)*, G Sproston *(Financial)*
**Responsibilities**
**Senior:** Jeff Leyar *(Vice Chancellor)*
**Branches:** University Of Wolverhampton, University Of Wolverhampton City Campus, St Peters Square, Wolverhampton, West Midlands WV1 1RH
**US SIC:** 8221 **UK SIC:** 93100
**Auditors:** KPMG LLP
**Employees:** 3,000
**Turnover:** £148,514,000

DUNS 21-185-6138

## University of Wolverhampton (Students Union)

Wulfruna Street, Wolverhampton, West Midlands WV1 1LY
**Tel:** 01902-322021
**Web:** www.wolvesunion.org
**Estd:** 1990
**Line of Business:** Trade unions
**General Manager:** J Elmore
**Responsibilities**
**Senior:** Luke Gilbert *(Manager)*, Ann Gough *(Chief Executive)*, Sophie Williams *(Interim Chief Executive)*
**US SIC:** 8221 **UK SIC:** 93100
**Employees:** 130

DUNS 20-200-0102 **Imp**

## University of Worcester

Henwick Grove, Worcester, Worcestershire WR2 6AJ
**Web:** www.worcester.ac.uk
**Estd:** 2007
**Line of Business:** University
**Director:** Mrs D Urwin
**Responsibilities**
**Senior:** Dominic Crawford *(Executive)*, Catherine Hunt *(Senior Manager)*, Alice Kemble-Davies *(Senior Manager)*, Helen Tabinor *(Manager of the GRS)*, Dominic Upton *(Board Member)*
**Finance:** Rob Bonham *(Director of Finance)*, Donna Obrey *(Finance Officer)*
**Marketing:** Katherine Jones *(Enterprise and Business Partne)*, Kate Moss *(Marketing Manager)*
**Sales:** Tim Maxfield *(Business Development Director)*
**Admin:** Malcolm Claydon *(Administrator)*, Caroline Davies *(Personnel Administrator)*, Stacey Evans *(Administrator)*, John Gardener *(Admissions Tutor)*, Sarah Holland *(Personal Assistant)*, Lindsey Jackson *(Administrator)*, Jill Meadows *(Administrator)*, Donna Obrey *(Finance Officer)*
**IT:** Zeb Amin *(IT Manager)*
**HR:** Caroline Davies *(Personnel Administrator)*, Denise Davis *(Human Resources)*, Esther Floisand *(Training Assistant)*, Alison Simcox *(Personnel Adviser)*, Gill Slater *(Human Resources Manager)*, Anne Steggles *(Human Resources)*, Hilary Woodward *(Deputy Director of Personnel)*
**Health & Safety:** Colin Fry *(Health & Safety Coordinator)*, Gill Slater *(Human Resources Manager)*
**Facilities:** Judith Bick *(Housing Manager)*, Andy Lewis *(Estates Manager)*
**Operations:** Tom Taylor *(Head of Security and Campus Se)*
**Engineering:** James Atkins *(Geography Technician)*, Anne Sinnott *(Technical Support and GIS)*
**US SIC:** 8221 **UK SIC:** 93100
**Auditors:** PricewaterhouseCoopers LLP
**Employees:** 200
**Turnover:** £63,910,000

DUNS 22-807-4605

## The University of York

University Of York, York, North Yorkshire YO10 5DD
**Web:** www.elec.york.ac.uk
**Reg No:** 0000679RC **VAT No:** 647205541
**Estd:** 2001 Incorporate By Act Of Parliament
**Line of Business:** First-degree level higher education
**Principals:** K H Dixon *(Chairman)*, G Gilbert *(Financial)*, D Foster *(Personnel)*, Professor R H Cooke, D Duncan, B Cantor, B Cantor, D Hatliff
**Responsibilities**
**Senior:** Denis Fowler *(Health & Safety Officer)*, Mary Howorth *(Manager)*, R McMeeking *(Principal)*
**HR:** Pat Lofthouse *(Human Resources Director)*
**Health & Safety:** Denis Fowler *(Health & Safety Officer)*
**Branches:** The University Of York, The Students Centre James Colleg, York, North Yorkshire YO10 5NA
**US SIC:** 8221 **UK SIC:** 93100
**Auditors:** Deloitte & Touche LLP
**Turnover:** £216,953,000

DUNS 51-983-2802

## University of York Music Press Ltd

Heslington, York, North Yorkshire YO10 5DD
**Fax:** 01904433704
**Web:** www.york.ac.uk
**Reg No:** 3350729 **Estd:** 1997 Private Limited Company
**Line of Business:** Other publishing
**Directors:** Dr T Simaku, T Ward, Dr R Saxton, Professor D L Blake, Professor N F Lefanu, Dr J C Stringer, P A Boardman, N G King
**Co. Secretary:** Terence Holmes
**Responsibilities**
**Senior:** Rod Peet *(Deputy Finance Director)*, Philip Venables *(Director)*
**Finance:** Rod Peet *(Deputy Finance Director)*
**Marketing:** Sue Abson *(Events Marketing Officer)*, Joan Concannon *(Director of External Relations)*, Sian Fraser *(Marketing Manager)*, Alison Kerwin *(Head of Digital Marketing and)*, Jilly Lovett *(Publications Officer)*, Alex McFarlane *(Communications and Information)*
**Sales:** Philip Kember *(Deputy Director of Commercial)*, Alistair Knock *(Business Intelligence Developm)*, Rena Quarton *(Business Development Manager)*
**Admin:** Gavin Atkinson *(System Administrator/Programme)*, Daryl Bamforth *(Systems Adminstrator/Developer)*, Mary Brooks *(Undergraduate Administrator)*, Rachel Cullivan *(PA to Technology Facility Dire)*, Sarah Dwyer *(PA to Director of Infrastructu)*, Sarah Maynard *(Manager - Support Staff)*, Rebecca Regan *(Secretary)*, Philippa Suret *(PA to the Director of HR)*, Belinda Wade *(PA to Head of Biology Departme)*
**IT:** Helen Adcock *(IT Services Manager)*, Paul Bellwood *(IT Technician)*, Thomas Borgia *(IT Manager)*, Mike Brudenell *(IT Specialist)*, Dawn Cartwright *(Director of Infrastructure and)*, Joanne Casey *(IT Specialist)*, Arthur Clune *(IT Specialist)*, Eleanor Coultish *(IT Services Manager)*, Heidi Fraser-Krauss *(Head of IT Services)*, Peter Halls *(GIS Advisor)*, Alison Kerwin *(Head of Digital Marketing and)*, Stephen Town *(IT Director)*
**HR:** Charlotte Boyce *(HR Officer)*, Jennifer Chubb *(Research Innovation Officer -)*, Sally Daly *(HR Services Operations Manager)*, Glenda Foster *(HR Assistant)*, Rob Hargrave *(HR Services Project Manager)*, Pat Lofthouse *(Director of Human Resources)*, Gail Richmond *(HR and Rewards Administrator)*, Alex Schofield *(HR Officer)*, Helen Selvidge *(Assistant HR Director)*, Paula Tunbridge *(Deputy Director of Human Resou)*
**Facilities:** Dawn Cartwright *(Director of Infrastructure and)*, Sue Final *(Intellectual Property Manager)*
**Purchasing:** Kathy Crocker *(Resources Manager)*, Matthew Just *(Contracts Officer)*
**US SIC:** 2741 **UK SIC:** 47541

| | 30-04-14 | 30-04-13 | 30-04-12 |
|---|---|---|---|
| TA | 23,896 | 23,527 | 26,748 |
| NW | (2,176) | (166) | (179) |
| WC | 59 | 1,780 | 663 |

DUNS 50-639-9687

## Unliever U K

2 Liverpool Road, Warrington, Cheshire WA5 1AA
**Tel:** 01925412035
**Line of Business:** Manufacture of perfumes and toilet preparations
**Trading Style:** Unilever
**US SIC:** 2844 **UK SIC:** 25820
**Employees:** 200

DUNS 22-122-2578

## The Unofficial Tv Company Ltd

**(Subsidiary of:** Shine Pictures Llp)
108 Palace Gardens Terrace, London W8 4RT
**Tel:** 02073138000 **Fax:** 020-8964-7541
**Reg No:** 4141314 **Estd:** 2001 Private Limited Company
**Line of Business:** Media Production
**Issued Capital:** £1
**Directors:** T Hincks, Ms S Turner Laing
**US SIC:** 7814 **UK SIC:** 97111

| | 31-12-13 | 31-12-12 | 31-12-11 |
|---|---|---|---|
| TA | 1 | 1 | 1 |
| NW | 1 | 1 | 1 |

DUNS 39-953-9873 **Exp**

## Unomedical Holdings Ltd

**(Subsidiary of:** Unomedical Holding A/S)
Unit 3 Brunel Way, Stonehouse, Gloucestershire GL10 3SX
**Tel:** 01453-827696
**Web:** www.unomedical.com
**Reg No:** 2259855 **VAT No:** 484795681
**Estd:** 1988 Private Limited Company
**Line of Business:** Manufacture of medical and surgical equipment and orthopaedic appliances
**Export Markets:** Denmark
**Issued Capital:** £9,300,001
**Directors:** S H Cottrill, J Cannon, Ms S J Lewis, R Barratt, R Heginbotham
**Co. Secretary:** Slc Registrars Limited
**Responsibilities**
**Senior:** Timothy Winston *(Manager)*, Adrian Wise *(Plant Director)*
**Admin:** Adrian Wise *(Plant Director)*
**US SIC:** 3841 **UK SIC:** 37201
**Auditors:** Deloitte & Touche LLP
**Bankers:** Barclays Bank Plc (20-33-83)

| | 31-12-11 |
|---|---|
| P/L | (10,192,000) |

DUNS 34-604-2430 **Imp**

## Unruly Group Ltd

**(Subsidiary of:** Unruly Holdings Ltd)
42-46 Princelet Street, London E1 5LP
**Tel:** 02071995800
**Web:** www.unrulymedia.com
**Reg No:** 5411297 **Estd:** 2008 Private Limited Company
**Line of Business:** Motion picture and video distribution
**Export Sales:** £4,255,665
**Issued Capital:** £433
**Director:** S J Button
**Co. Secretary:** Miss Lucy Greggains
**US SIC:** 7829, 7379
**UK SIC:** 97112, 83940

| | 31-03-14 | 31-03-13 | 31-03-12 |
|---|---|---|---|
| TO | 11,199,119 | 12,504,015 | 14,550,487 |
| P/L | (1,309,071) | (2,446,707) | 1,424,262 |
| NW | (1,429,293) | (308,179) | 1,628,908 |
| WC | (1,591,423) | (904,117) | 1,131,100 |
| Emp. | 81 | 78 | 52 |

DUNS 50-493-4662

## Unum European Holding Co Ltd

**(Subsidiary of:** Unum Group)
Milton Court, Dorking, Surrey RH4 3LZ
**Tel:** 01306-887766
**Web:** www.unum.com
**Reg No:** 2461639 **Estd:** 1990 Private Limited Company
**Line of Business:** Financial intermediation not elsewhere classified
**Trading Style:** Unum Provident
**Issued Capital:** £38,903,454
**Directors:** S P Harry, P G O'Donnell, Ms N Ames
**Co. Secretary:** Peter Goddard
**Responsibilities**
**Senior:** Stacey Arnold *(Manager)*
**Sales:** Julia Amy *(Senior Sales Executive)*
**IT:** Matt Fahy *(CIO)*
**Operations:** Paul Hailey *(Head of Production)*, John Trollope *(Database Administration Operat)*
**Engineering:** Steve Harrington *(Head of Change and Testing)*
**Branches:** Unum European Holding Co Ltd, Unum House, Basing View, Basingstoke, Hampshire RG21 4EQ
**US SIC:** 6111, 6411
**UK SIC:** 81501, 83200
**Auditors:** Ernst & Young LLP
**Bankers:** Lloyds TSB Bank plc (30-92-87)

| | 31-12-13 | 31-12-12 | 31-12-11 |
|---|---|---|---|
| TA | 69,370,000 | 71,867,000 | 76,265,000 |
| P/L | (2,385,000) | 5,783,000 | 56,048,000 |
| NW | 55,950,000 | 57,787,000 | 58,874,000 |
| WC | 5,200,000 | 4,556,000 | 1,824,000 |
| Emp. | 921 | 940 | 950 |

DUNS 29-044-3753 **Imp**

## Unum Ltd

**(Subsidiary of:** Unum Group)
Redcliffe Way, Bristol, Avon BS1 6NL
**Tel:** 01179-107-700 **Fax:** 01179107555
**Web:** www.unum.co.uk
**Reg No:** 0983768 **VAT No:** 528473917
**Estd:** 1970 Private Limited Company
**Line of Business:** Life insurance
**Trading Style:** Unum Provident
**Issued Capital:** £12,000,000
**Directors:** E Langston, T R Watjen, Mrs C C Black, S P Harry, P G O'Donnell, D Stewart, R P Mckenney, Dr I B Owen
**Co. Secretary:** Peter Goddard
**Responsibilities**
**Senior:** Stacey Arnold *(Manager)*, Charlotte Birks *(Manager)*, Jack Mcgarry *(Chief Executive)*, Clifton Melvin *(Director)*, Peter O"Donnell *(chief Financial officer)*

**Finance:** Peter O"Donnell *(chief Financial officer)*
**Branches:** Unum Ltd, 15 Blythswood Sq, Glasgow, Lanarkshire G2 4AD
**US SIC:** 6311, 6399
**UK SIC:** 82002, 82001
**Auditors:** Ernst & Young LLP
**Bankers:** Lloyds TSB Bank plc (30-00-48)

| | 31-12-13 | 31-12-12 | 31-12-11 |
|---|---|---|---|
| TO | 356,485,000 | 437,967,000 | 428,463,000 |
| P/L | 61,596,000 | 116,728,000 | 49,695,000 |
| NW | 521,280,000 | 508,413,000 | 494,202,000 |
| WC | 42,037,000 | 28,471,000 | 45,617,000 |

DUNS 21-666-5694
## Unum Select Ltd
(**Subsidiary of:** Unum Group)
Milton Court, Westcott Road, Dorking, Surrey RH4 3LZ
**Tel:** 01306888700
**Web:** www.unum.co.uk
**Reg No:** 7203708 **Estd:** 2010 Private Limited Company
**Line of Business:** Financial intermediation not elsewhere classified
**Issued Capital:** £250,000
**Directors:** P G O'Donnell, M A Forato
**Co. Secretary:** Peter Goddard
**Responsibilities**
**Senior:** Stacey Arnold *(Manager)*
**US SIC:** 6111 **UK SIC:** 81501
**Bankers:** Lloyds TSB Bank plc (30-12-99)

| | 31-12-13 | 31-12-12 | 31-12-11 |
|---|---|---|---|
| TA | 288,666 | 308,311 | 303,409 |
| P/L | 2,637 | 7,882 | 36,889 |
| NW | 283,372 | 283,067 | 277,113 |
| WC | 283,372 | 283,067 | 277,113 |

DUNS 22-730-6602 **Exp**
## Unusual Rigging Ltd
(**Subsidiary of:** Unusual Industries Ltd)
The Wharf, Bugbrooke, Northampton, Northamptonshire NN7 3QB
**Tel:** 01604-830083
**Web:** www.unusual.co.uk
**Reg No:** 1797052 **Estd:** 1983 Private Limited Company
**Line of Business:** Manufacture of cordage, rope, twine and netting
**Export Markets:** Worldwide
**Issued Capital:** £100,000
**Principals:** A M Jacobi *(Managing)*, B H Rose *(Financial)*, D R Elias
**Co. Secretary:** Ms Peta Jacobi
**Responsibilities**
**Operations:** Simon Tiernan *(Senior Project Manager)*
**US SIC:** 2298, 3496
**UK SIC:** 43960, 31694
**Auditors:** MGR Weston Kay LLP
**Bankers:** Lloyds TSB Bank plc (30-90-69)

| | 31-03-14 | 31-03-13 | 31-03-12 |
|---|---|---|---|
| TO | 14,785,748 | 11,313,176 | 7,310,983 |
| P/L | 2,507,244 | 1,501,509 | 120,471 |
| NW | 4,275,327 | 2,363,982 | 1,145,907 |
| WC | 2,349,443 | 936,020 | 106,803 |
| Emp. | 62 | 59 | 59 |

DUNS 42-414-5436
## Unw Llp
Citygate, St James Boulevard, Newcastle-Upon-Tyne, Tyne and Wear NE1 4JE
**Fax:** 01912436060
**Web:** www.unw.co.uk
**Reg No:** 0301800OC **Estd:** 2003 Limited Partnership
**Line of Business:** Book-keeping activities
**Responsibilities**
**Senior:** Paul Kaiser *(Non-designated Limited Liabili)*, Lee Muter *(Non-designated Limited Liabili)*
**US SIC:** 8931 **UK SIC:** 83600
**Auditors:** UNW LLP

| | 31-03-14 | 31-03-13 | 31-03-12 |
|---|---|---|---|
| TA | 2,744,572 | 2,318,845 | 2,531,365 |
| NW | 640,000 | 250,800 | 250,600 |
| WC | 2,047,191 | 1,718,940 | 1,912,800 |

DUNS 21-580-4650
## Unwins
Alconbury Hill, Alconbury Weston, Huntingdon, Cambridgeshire PE28 4HY
**Tel:** 08445738400
**Web:** www.unwins-seeds.co.uk
**Estd:** 2005 Proprietorship
**Line of Business:** Retail sale via mail order house
**Proprietor:** E Conroy
**Responsibilities**
**Senior:** Frank Keenan *(Manager)*
**US SIC:** 5999 **UK SIC:** 65600
**Employees:** 80

DUNS 77-668-7568
## Uoe Accommodation Ltd
St Leonards Hall, 18 Holyrood Park Road, Edinburgh, Midlothian EH16 5AY
**Tel:** 01316512055
**Web:** www.edinburghfirst.com
**Reg No:** 0155192SC **Estd:** 1994 Private Limited Company
**Line of Business:** Hotels
**Trading Style:** Edinburgh First
**Issued Capital:** £2
**Directors:** R M Kington, P G Mcnaull
**Co. Secretary:** David Montgomery
**Responsibilities**
**Senior:** Jonathan Gorringe *(Manager)*
**US SIC:** 7011 **UK SIC:** 66500
**Auditors:** KPMG LLP
**Bankers:** Bank Of Scotland (80-02-24)

| | 31-07-13 | 31-07-12 | 31-07-11 |
|---|---|---|---|
| TO | 13,512,748 | 14,048,145 | 12,715,712 |
| P/L | N/A | 3,407,934 | (57,417) |
| NW | (326,643) | (326,643) | (326,643) |
| WC | (326,643) | (326,643) | (326,643) |

DUNS 21-612-6896 **Imp**
## Uop Ltd
(**Subsidiary of:** Honeywell International Inc.)
Liongate, Ladymead, Guildford, Surrey GU1 1AT
**Tel:** 01483-304848
**Web:** www.uop.com
**Reg No:** 0521570 **Estd:** 1953 Private Limited Company
**Line of Business:** Misc petroleum & coal product mfrs
**Export Sales:** £109,502,000
**Issued Capital:** £1,000,000
**Directors:** N J Orchard, J Pitkin, J G Woodcock, G W Davies, M Preston, P P Piotrowski, J G Bellamy
**Co. Secretary:** Sisec Limited
**Responsibilities**
**Senior:** Tina Pierce *(Vice President / Chief Financi)*
**Finance:** Tina Pierce *(Vice President / Chief Financi)*
**Health & Safety:** Jeff Wells *(Facilities Manager)*
**Facilities:** Jeff Wells *(Facilities Manager)*
**Branches:** Uop Ltd, 1 Jeffreys Road, Enfield, Middlesex EN3 7PN
**US SIC:** 2999, 7399
**UK SIC:** 11150, 83954
**Auditors:** PricewaterhouseCoopers LLP

| | 31-12-13 | 31-12-12 | 31-12-11 |
|---|---|---|---|
| TO | 110,755,000 | 94,406,000 | 85,061,000 |
| P/L | 28,002,000 | 10,938,000 | 18,587,000 |
| NW | 163,545,000 | 135,809,000 | 128,764,000 |
| WC | 151,795,000 | 125,731,000 | 118,922,000 |
| Emp. | 188 | 174 | 164 |

DUNS 34-625-7376
## Up Global Sourcing Holdings Ltd
Manor Mill, Victoria Street Chadderton, Oldham, Lancashire OL9 0DD
**Tel:** 01616271400
**Reg No:** 5432142 **Estd:** 2005 Private Limited Company
**Line of Business:** Management activities of holding companies
**Export Sales:** £6,605,000
**Issued Capital:** £433,463
**Directors:** G P Screawn, S Showman, A J Gossage, B E Franks, D L Bloomfield
**Co. Secretary:** Graham Screawn
**US SIC:** 6711 **UK SIC:** 83962
**Auditors:** PricewaterhouseCoopers LLP
**Bankers:** Barclays Bank Plc (20-35-81)

| | 30-04-14 | 31-07-13 | 31-04-12 |
|---|---|---|---|
| TO | 41,296,000 | 52,560,000 | 56,321,000 |
| P/L | (1,272,000) | (2,593,000) | (4,144,000) |
| NW | (17,824,000) | (17,659,000) | (16,448,000) |
| WC | (328,000) | 383,000 | (1,336,000) |
| Emp. | 179 | 182 | 207 |

DUNS 42-354-7376
## Updata Infrastructure 2012 Ltd
Premier House 1 7 Warren Road, Reigate, Surrey RH2 0BE
**Tel:** 01737-224422 **Fax:** 01737-246571
**Web:** www.urbanconnect.co.uk
**Reg No:** 4342422 **Estd:** 2001 Private Limited Company
**Line of Business:** Other business activities not elsewhere classified
**Issued Capital:** £100
**Directors:** Capita Corporate Director Limite, R J Shearer, F Holm, P Hands
**Co. Secretary:** Capita Group Secretary Limited
**Responsibilities**
**Senior:** Arthur Gormley *(Manager)*, Julian Phipps *(Finance Director)*
**Finance:** Julian Phipps *(Finance Director)*
**Branches:** Round Foundry Media Centre,Leeds, LS11 5QP West Yorkshire
**US SIC:** 7399 **UK SIC:** 83954

**Auditors:** Tenon Audit Ltd

| | 30-06-12 | 30-06-11 |
|---|---|---|
| TO | 23,713,360 | 22,218,284 |
| P/L | (7,821,689) | 3,166,526 |
| NW | N/A | 8,264,942 |
| WC | N/A | 3,765,025 |
| Emp. | 78 | 62 |

DUNS 21-655-7562
## Updata Infrastructure (North) Ltd
(**Subsidiary of:** Capita Plc)
The Omnibus Building, Lesbourne Road, Reigate, Surrey RH2 7LD
**Tel:** 08455650555 **Fax:** 01737246571
**Web:** www.updata.net
**Reg No:** 7126803 **Estd:** 2010 Private Limited Company
**Line of Business:** Telecom services
**Issued Capital:** £1
**Directors:** Capita Corporate Director Limite, R J Shearer, P Hands
**Co. Secretary:** Capita Group Secretary Limited
**Responsibilities**
**Senior:** Arthur Gormley *(Manager)*
**US SIC:** 4899 **UK SIC:** 79020

| | 30-06-12 | 30-06-11 |
|---|---|---|
| TA | N/A | 46,893 |
| P/L | 355,337 | (257,300) |
| NW | N/A | (355,337) |
| WC | N/A | (357,085) |

DUNS 71-933-4208
## Upkeep Shettleston Community Enterprises Ltd
(**Subsidiary of:** Shettleston Housing Association Ltd)
65 Pettigrew Street, Glasgow, Lanarkshire G32 7XR
**Tel:** 01417630511 **Fax:** 0141-778-5278
**Web:** www.shettleston.co.uk
**Reg No:** 0277511SC **Estd:** 1978 Private Limited Company
**Line of Business:** Housing associations societies trusts & co-operatives
**Issued Capital:** £1
**Directors:** J Hastie, S Connor, Ms T Mcintyre, C H Cunningham, Ms A Mcallister, Mrs M Thomas
**Co. Secretary:** Tc Young
**US SIC:** 6531 **UK SIC:** 83400

| | 31-03-14 | 31-03-13 | 31-03-12 |
|---|---|---|---|
| TO | 2,382,675 | 1,798,877 | 1,444,232 |
| P/L | 31,700 | 19,030 | 18,605 |
| NW | 125,019 | 87,395 | 77,313 |
| WC | 63,478 | 44,858 | 35,764 |

DUNS 56-951-4920 **Exp**
## Upl Europe Ltd
(**Subsidiary of:** Bio-Win Corporation Limited)
First Floor The Centre, Birchwood Park, Birchwood, Warrington, Cheshire WA3 6YN
**Tel:** 01925-819-999
**Web:** www.upleurope.com
**Reg No:** 2844616 **Estd:** 1993 Private Limited Company
**Line of Business:** Manufacturers of agricultural chemicals
**Export Markets:** U S A, South America, Italy, France, Spain
**Export Sales:** £76,821,000
**Issued Capital:** £42,565,347
**Directors:** A K Premnath, V Shroff, Ms S Shroff, B Dutia, R Shroff
**Co. Secretary:** Jimmy Dadrewalla
**Responsibilities**
**Senior:** Jai Shroff *(Manager)*
**Marketing:** Chris Hepworth *(Sales & Marketing Manager)*
**Sales:** Chris Hepworth *(Sales & Marketing Manager)*
**Engineering:** Vivek Baidya *(Production Manager)*, Tom Rowlands *(Production Manager)*
**Branches:** Upl Europe Ltd, Hall Lane, Sandbach, Cheshire CW11 3QQ
**US SIC:** 2899 **UK SIC:** 25670
**Auditors:** BDO LLP
**Bankers:** HSBC Bank plc (40-31-24)

| | 31-03-14 | 31-03-13 | 31-03-12 |
|---|---|---|---|
| TO | 92,273,000 | 92,666,000 | 76,648,000 |
| P/L | 3,198,000 | 2,022,000 | 1,006,000 |
| NW | 48,759,000 | 45,772,000 | 43,900,000 |
| WC | 23,986,000 | 29,753,000 | 27,802,000 |
| Emp. | 58 | 56 | 52 |

DUNS 21-033-1354
## Uplands At Oxon Nursing Home
Bicton Heath, Shrewsbury, Shropshire SY3 8GA
**Tel:** 01743282040
**Web:** www.marchescare.co.uk
**Estd:** 2009 Proprietorship
**Line of Business:** Nursing homes
**Proprietor:** Mrs M Thorne
**US SIC:** 8051 **UK SIC:** 95100
**Employees:** 110

DUNS 21-831-9956
## Uplands Educational Trust
Tadpole Lane, Swindon, Wiltshire SN25 2NB
**Tel:** 01793493910
**Web:** www.swindon.schooljotter.com
**Reg No:** 8011951 **Estd:** 2012 Private Company Limited By Guarantee
**Line of Business:** General secondary education
**Directors:** J Smith, T J Mason, Mrs S Hunter, A Segal, A J Stone, Ms N D Parker, Ms J A Smith, D A Dinsey
**Co. Secretary:** Derek Dinsey
**US SIC:** 8211 **UK SIC:** 93200

| | 31-03-14 | 31-03-13 |
|---|---|---|
| TO | 308,931 | 26,590 |
| P/L | 13,608 | 14,499 |
| NW | 28,107 | 14,499 |
| WC | (5,669) | 14,499 |
| Emp. | 14 | N/A |

DUNS 29-889-9378
## Upm-Kymmene (Uk) Ltd
(**Subsidiary of:** Upm-Kymmene Oyj)
Station House Stamford New Road, Altrincham, Cheshire WA14 1EP
**Tel:** 08706 000 876 **Fax:** 08706 060 876
**Web:** www.upm.com
**Reg No:** 0102969SC **VAT No:** 370669530
**Estd:** 2004 Public Limited Company
**Line of Business:** Paper products
**Issued Capital:** £160,000,000
**Director:** Ms M Salmelin
**Co. Secretary:** David Chalmers
**Responsibilities**
**Senior:** Iain Bullimore *(Operations Supervisor)*
**Branches:** Upm-Kymmene (Uk) Limited, Meadowhead Rd, Irvine, Ayrshire KA11 5AT
**US SIC:** 2654 **UK SIC:** 47280
**Auditors:** PricewaterhouseCoopers LLP
**Bankers:** Unibank A/s (40-48-78)

| | 31-12-13 | 31-12-12 | 31-12-11 |
|---|---|---|---|
| TO | 420,810,000 | 635,954,000 | 961,129,000 |
| P/L | (4,739,000) | (68,251,000) | 42,828,000 |
| NW | 186,143,000 | 194,824,000 | 267,086,000 |
| WC | 92,984,000 | 95,544,000 | 74,568,000 |
| Emp. | 951 | 1,018 | 847 |

DUNS 52-035-3806
## Uponor Ltd
(**Subsidiary of:** Uponor Oyj)
Gilmorton Road, Lutterworth, Leicestershire LE17 4DU
**Tel:** 01455550355 **Fax:** 01455551366
**Web:** www.uponor.co.uk
**Reg No:** 3402029 **Estd:** 1997 Private Limited Company
**Line of Business:** Pipes and fittings
**Export Sales:** £426,000
**Issued Capital:** £1,000,100
**Co. Secretary:** Peter Roberts
**Responsibilities**
**Senior:** Reetta H ki *(Director)*, Riitta Palom *(Director)*, Fernando Roses Fernandez *(Vice President)*
**Branches:** Uponor Ltd, Unit 2, Wycliffe Indstl Pk, Leicester Rd, Lutterworth, Leicestershire LE17 4HG
**US SIC:** 1711 **UK SIC:** 50300
**Auditors:** KPMG LLP
**Bankers:** Unibank A/s (40-48-78)

| | 31-12-13 | 31-12-12 | 31-12-11 |
|---|---|---|---|
| TO | 16,260,000 | 19,075,000 | 19,191,000 |
| P/L | (5,732,000) | 358,000 | 889,000 |
| NW | 1,899,000 | 4,886,000 | 4,598,000 |
| WC | 1,826,000 | 2,011,000 | 1,767,000 |
| Emp. | 89 | 84 | 89 |

DUNS 73-758-6573
## Upp Group Holdings Ltd
40 Gracechurch Street, London EC3V 0BT
**Tel:** 02073987200
**Web:** www.upp-ltd.com
**Reg No:** 5016028 **Estd:** 2004 Private Limited Company
**Line of Business:** Management activities of other non-financial holding companies not elsewhere classified
**Issued Capital:** £6,226,593
**Directors:** G S Behr, M A Bryan, S Saggar, R S Mcclatchey, S Guozhuo, J J Wolfs, Ms C B Van Heijningen, J J Wakeford
**Co. Secretary:** Julian Benkel
**Responsibilities**
**Senior:** Hendrik Huizing *(Director)*
**US SIC:** 7399 **UK SIC:** 83954
**Auditors:** Grant Thornton UK LLP

| | 31-08-13 | 31-08-12 | 31-08-11 |
|---|---|---|---|
| TO | 117,558,000 | 105,556,000 | 76,036,000 |
| P/L | (156,602,000) | (24,418,000) | (2,006,000) |
| NW | 70,171,000 | 202,419,000 | 148,600,000 |
| WC | 48,661,000 | (239,212,000) | 44,074,000 |
| Emp. | 645 | 617 | 370 |

DUNS 22-271-7030

## Upp (Nottingham) Ltd

**(Subsidiary of:** Upp Group Holdings Ltd)
Loughborough University, Ashby Road, Loughborough, Leicestershire LE11 3UR
**Tel:** 01509-222256
**Web:** www.upp-ltd.com
**Reg No:** 4288837 **Estd:** 2001 Private Limited Company
**Line of Business:** Other letting of own property
**Issued Capital:** £5,596,747
**Directors:** J S Jackson, R S Bailey-Watts, G S Behr, S O'Shea
**Co. Secretary:** Julian Benkel
**US SIC:** 6519, 6531
**UK SIC:** 85000, 83400
**Auditors:** Grant Thornton UK LLP

| | 31-08-14 | 31-08-13 | 31-08-12 |
|---|---|---|---|
| TO | 12,757,000 | 12,430,000 | 11,959,000 |
| P/L | (4,470,000) | (31,046,000) | (2,029,000) |
| NW | (34,666,000) | (26,794,000) | (1,943,000) |
| WC | (2,709,000) | 734,000 | (93,140,000) |
| Emp. | 101 | 108 | 110 |

DUNS 42-454-8352

## Upper Andersonstown Community Forum Ltd

Tullymore Office, Belfast BT11 8NE
**Tel:** 028-9062-2201 **Fax:** 02890622353
**Web:** www.uacf.info
**Reg No:** 0032258NI **Estd:** 1997 Private Limited Company
**Line of Business:** Activities of other membership organisations not elsewhere classified
**Directors:** P J Maskey, S Lennon, B P Kane, W Groves, G Meehan
**Co. Secretary:** Ms Nuala Lauro
**Responsibilities**
**Senior:** Tish Holland *(Manager)*
**US SIC:** 8999, 8299
**UK SIC:** 83954, 93300
**Auditors:** Lynn Drake & Co
**Bankers:** Ulster Bank Ltd (98-00-15)

| | 31-03-14 | 31-03-13 | 31-03-12 |
|---|---|---|---|
| TO | 1,188,844 | 1,131,233 | 1,004,424 |
| P/L | 23,548 | (47,333) | (6,292) |
| NW | 964,319 | 940,771 | 988,104 |
| WC | 303,148 | 250,329 | 238,559 |
| Emp. | N/A | 48 | 41 |

DUNS 21-160-6350

## Upper Ban Institute of Furthur & Higher Education

34 Lurgan Road, Portadown, Craigavon, Co Armagh BT63 5BL
**Tel:** 028-3839-7777
**Web:** www.src.ac.uk
**Line of Business:** Schools and colleges for further education
**Director:** Dr G Byrne
**US SIC:** 8211, 8221, 8249
**UK SIC:** 93200, 93100, 93300
**Employees:** 150

DUNS 21-590-6519

## Upper Halliford Nursing Home

Charlton Lane, Shepperton, Middlesex TW17 8QN
**Tel:** 01932732600
**Web:** www.upperhallifordnursinghome.co.uk
**Estd:** 2011
**Line of Business:** Medical nursing home activities
**Responsibilities**
**Senior:** Patricia Moon *(Manager)*
**US SIC:** 8051 **UK SIC:** 95100
**Employees:** 50

DUNS 21-591-4009

## Upper St Leonards Family Support Team

Ocean House, 87-89 London Road, St Leonards-On-Sea, East Sussex TN37 6DH
**Estd:** 2011
**Line of Business:** The dss
**Responsibilities**
**Senior:** Karen Baurer *(Operations Manager)*
**US SIC:** 8321 **UK SIC:** 96111
**Employees:** 80

DUNS 21-716-8230

## Uppingham Community College

London Road, Uppingham, Oakham, Leicestershire LE15 9TJ
**Tel:** 01572823631
**Web:** www.ucc.rutland.sch.uk
**Reg No:** 7556159 **Estd:** 2011 Private Company Limited By Guarantee
**Line of Business:** General secondary education
**Directors:** T Gray, Mrs B Mcgregor, H Skannavis, S Berridge, Mrs F C Ryan, Mrs M Topham, Mrs J E Turner, S W Kirk
**Co. Secretary:** Mrs Jane Onn
**Responsibilities**
**Senior:** Sally Allen *(Director)*, Michael Deely *(Director)*, Andrew Gilgrist *(Director)*, Margaret Jennings *(Director)*, Polly Rubinstein *(Director)*, Robert Sawyer *(Director)*, Tony Wilks *(Director)*
**US SIC:** 8211 **UK SIC:** 93200
**Bankers:** HSBC Bank plc (40-35-21)

| | 31-08-14 | 31-08-13 | 31-08-12 |
|---|---|---|---|
| TO | 5,845,532 | 5,528,434 | 14,320,682 |
| P/L | 427,442 | (71,393) | 7,102,163 |
| NW | 6,230,212 | 6,238,770 | 6,280,163 |
| WC | 734,715 | 1,125,031 | 897,245 |
| Emp. | 105 | 130 | 107 |

DUNS 22-669-3133

## Uppingham School

The Bursary, 20-24 High Street West, Uppingham, Oakham, Leicestershire LE15 9QE
**Tel:** 01572-822216 **Fax:** 01572-821872
**Web:** www.uppingham.co.uk
**Estd:** 1584 Incorporate By Act Of Parliament
**Line of Business:** General secondary education
**Director:** Dr S C Winkley
**Responsibilities**
**Finance:** Lindsay Cooper *(Head of Finance)*
**Marketing:** Fiona Bettles *(Sales & Marketing Coordinator)*
**Sales:** Fiona Bettles *(Sales & Marketing Coordinator)*
**IT:** Adam Niblett *(IT Manager)*
**Health & Safety:** Andy Marr *(Health & Safety Officer)*
**Facilities:** Andrew Dyton *(Estates Manager)*, David Hearsum *(Estates Manager)*
**US SIC:** 8211 **UK SIC:** 93200
**Auditors:** Crowe Clark Whitehill LLP
**Bankers:** Barclays Bank Plc (20-63-66)

| | 31-08-13 | 31-08-12 | 31-08-11 |
|---|---|---|---|
| TO | 27,093,959 | 25,948,754 | 24,191,979 |
| P/L | 3,306,818 | 3,183,731 | (311,233) |
| NW | 66,449,251 | 61,182,615 | 59,060,194 |
| WC | 5,383,551 | 9,788,588 | (3,495,495) |
| Emp. | 370 | 364 | 361 |

DUNS 22-565-7121 Imp-Exp

## Ups Ltd

**(Subsidiary of:** United Parcel Service Inc.)
Nobel Road Unit 10a, West Gourdie Industrial Estate, Dundee, Angus DD2 4UH
**Tel:** 08457877877 **Fax:** 01604790689
**Web:** www.ups.co.uk
**Reg No:** 1933173 **VAT No:** 222421710
**Estd:** 1907 Private Limited Company
**Line of Business:** Cargo handling
**Issued Capital:** £2,004
**Directors:** Ms C J Miller, P K Dunstan, H M Mensing, G A Willis
**Co. Secretary:** Peter Dunstan
**Responsibilities**
**Senior:** Mervyn Kelly *(Centre Manager)*
**IT:** G Nugent *(IT Director)*
**Operations:** G Nugent *(IT Director)*
**Branches:** Ups Ltd, 7 St. Albans Road, Gloucester, Gloucestershire GL2 5FW
**US SIC:** 4311, 4511
**UK SIC:** 79010, 75000
**Auditors:** Deloitte LLP
**Bankers:** Barclays Bank Plc (20-32-53)

| | 31-12-13 | 31-12-12 | 31-12-11 |
|---|---|---|---|
| TO | 758,021,000 | 697,347,000 | 669,631,000 |
| P/L | 39,575,000 | 20,368,000 | 14,966,000 |
| NW | 121,411,000 | 100,151,000 | 82,964,000 |
| WC | 32,607,000 | 15,610,000 | 2,159,000 |
| Emp. | 5,114 | 5,274 | 5,046 |

DUNS 73-794-5071 Imp

## Ups Scs (Uk) Ltd

**(Subsidiary of:** United Parcel Service Inc.)
Unit 1 Blackthorne Road, Slough, Berkshire SL3 0DA
**Tel:** 02082606000 **Fax:** 01753 76111
**Web:** www.haulfast.co.uk
**Reg No:** 2928205 **VAT No:** 666255317
**Estd:** 1991 Private Limited Company
**Line of Business:** Freight forwarders
**Export Sales:** £1,574,000
**Issued Capital:** £4,360,012
**Directors:** H M Mensing, M Nightingale, P K Dunstan
**Co. Secretary:** Stewart Wadge
**Branches:** Ups Scs (Uk) Ltd, Wincanton Close,Off Ascot Drive,Osmaston Park Industrial Estate, Derby, Derbyshire DE24 8NB
**US SIC:** 4712 **UK SIC:** 77002
**Auditors:** Deloitte LLP
**Bankers:** Abn Amro Bank Nv (40-50-30)

| | 31-12-13 | 31-12-12 | 31-12-11 |
|---|---|---|---|
| TO | 82,319,000 | 78,140,000 | 74,106,000 |
| P/L | 2,344,000 | 2,298,000 | 2,235,000 |
| NW | 11,186,000 | 14,198,000 | 12,415,000 |
| WC | 10,284,000 | 11,914,000 | 8,596,000 |
| Emp. | 668 | 655 | 667 |

DUNS 22-659-4497

## Upton & Pegg Ltd

Vulcan House, Goliath Road, Coalville, Leicestershire LE67 3FT
**Tel:** 01530-832552 **Fax:** 01530-513594
**Web:** www.uptonandpegg.co.uk
**Reg No:** 0851147 **Estd:** 1961 Private Limited Company
**Line of Business:** Plumbing
**Issued Capital:** £100
**Directors:** S A Upton, K Patrick
**Co. Secretary:** Mrs Nicola Patrick
**US SIC:** 1711 **UK SIC:** 50300
**Auditors:** HLB AV Audit Plc
**Bankers:** HSBC Bank plc (40-18-01)

| | 31-05-14 | 31-05-13 | 31-05-12 |
|---|---|---|---|
| TA | 2,437,213 | 1,991,920 | 2,208,385 |
| NW | 1,385,809 | 1,273,304 | 1,300,707 |
| WC | 1,219,980 | 1,115,877 | 1,148,692 |

DUNS 21-701-4585

## Upton Court Educational Trust

Lascelles Road, Slough, Berkshire SL3 7PR
**Tel:** 01753522892
**Web:** www.sp8.co.uk
**Reg No:** 7462530 **Estd:** 2010 Private Company Limited By Guarantee
**Line of Business:** General secondary education
**Directors:** N Miller, Ms M H Estrada, Ms A L Best, D Kitchener, R L Ford
**Co. Secretary:** Ms Jacqueline Wardle
**Responsibilities**
**Senior:** Resham Manal *(Director)*, David Maitland *(Director)*
**US SIC:** 7399 **UK SIC:** 83954
**Bankers:** HSBC Bank plc (40-42-08)

| | 31-08-13 | 31-08-12 | 31-08-11 |
|---|---|---|---|
| TO | 9,554,000 | 7,638,000 | 21,508,000 |
| P/L | 2,447,000 | 774,000 | 16,822,000 |
| NW | 19,768,000 | 17,383,000 | 16,863,000 |
| WC | 619,000 | 685,000 | 756,000 |
| Emp. | 141 | 139 | 156 |

DUNS 73-303-9601

## Upton Group Ltd

The Vivars, Selby, North Yorkshire YO8 8BE
**Tel:** 01757-291515
**Web:** www.theuptongroup.co.uk
**Reg No:** 4577828 **Estd:** 2002 Private Limited Company
**Line of Business:** Vending machines sale, rental and supply
**Issued Capital:** £1,000
**Directors:** F R Macdonald, A Upton, Mrs T J Macdonald
**Co. Secretary:** Ms Janet Upton
**US SIC:** 5963, 5499
**UK SIC:** 65600, 64100
**Bankers:** HSBC Bank plc (40-40-29)

| | 31-10-13 | 31-10-12 | 31-10-11 |
|---|---|---|---|
| TA | 1,957,972 | 2,237,752 | 1,049,301 |
| NW | 1,295,656 | 1,364,777 | 733,740 |
| WC | 378,606 | 455,555 | (94,716) |

DUNS 28-848-4439

## Upton House School Ltd

115 St Leonards Road, Windsor, Berkshire SL4 3DF
**Tel:** 01753-862610 **Fax:** 01753-621950
**Web:** www.uptonhouse.org.uk
**Reg No:** 0677794 **Estd:** 1960 Private Company Limited By Guarantee
**Line of Business:** Primary education
**Directors:** Mrs B E Stanley, R M Stewart, G E Delaney, A W Warf, Mrs M Breen, R D Smyth, Mrs S C Cairns, Dr P M Warwicker
**Co. Secretary:** Ms Catherine Allies
**Responsibilities**
**Senior:** Mary Ballin *(Manager)*, Madeleine Collins *(Headmistress)*, Thomas Mayhew *(Manager)*, Richard Schooley *(Manager)*, George Story *(Director)*, Carlos Vilares *(Director)*, Emma Wigzell *(Director)*
**Finance:** Kate Allies *(Bursar)*
**IT:** Jamie Day *(IT Manager)*
**Health & Safety:** Kate Allies *(Bursar)*
**Facilities:** Kate Allies *(Bursar)*
**US SIC:** 8211, 6732
**UK SIC:** 93200, 83100
**Auditors:** Menzies
**Bankers:** Barclays Bank Plc (20-97-09)

| | 31-08-13 | 31-08-12 | 31-08-11 |
|---|---|---|---|
| TO | 2,311,854 | 2,305,570 | 2,180,002 |
| P/L | 195,832 | 275,778 | 188,476 |
| NW | 2,708,113 | 2,512,281 | 2,236,503 |
| WC | 80,293 | 60,838 | (243,091) |
| Emp. | 58 | 55 | 50 |

DUNS 39-804-9718 Exp

## Upton McGougan Ltd

Partnership House, Winchester, Hampshire SO23 7RX
**Tel:** 01962-834400 **Fax:** 01962-834411
**Web:** www.uptonmcgougan.com
**Reg No:** 2210227 **Estd:** 1988 Private Limited Company
**Line of Business:** Development and selling of real estate
**Issued Capital:** £37,973
**Directors:** A W O'Hickey, R D Hand, D J Walker, M R Gordon
**Co. Secretary:** Russell Cannings
**Branches:** Upton Mcgougan Ltd, Moorside Road, Winchester, Hampshire SO23 7RX
**US SIC:** 6552 **UK SIC:** 85000
**Auditors:** Baker Tilly
**Bankers:** Barclays Bank Plc (20-05-00)

| | 16-02-14 | 31-03-13 | 31-02-12 |
|---|---|---|---|
| TA | 1,763,362 | 1,515,311 | 1,654,141 |
| NW | 1,129,826 | 878,062 | 872,092 |
| WC | 1,086,103 | 821,834 | 819,197 |

DUNS 21-592-5156

## Upton Primary School

Iris Avenue, Bexley, Kent DA5 1HH
**Tel:** 02083037266
**Web:** www.upton.bexley.sch.uk
**Estd:** 1990
**Line of Business:** Schools (local authority)
**Proprietor:** Mrs O Ramtersad
**US SIC:** 8211 **UK SIC:** 93200
**Employees:** 50

DUNS 54-880-6504

## Ur Cars

5 Lawford Street, Bristol, Avon BS2 0DH
**Tel:** 01179559999
**Estd:** 1994 Proprietorship
**Line of Business:** Taxis and private hire vehicles
**Proprietor:** K Khaliq
**US SIC:** 4121 **UK SIC:** 72200
**Employees:** 50

DUNS 22-112-1960

## Urban Futures London Ltd

Unit A012, The Chocolate Factory, London N22 6XJ
**Tel:** 02083525900
**Web:** www.urbanfutures.org.uk
**Reg No:** 4131420 **Estd:** 2001 Private Limited Company
**Line of Business:** Labour recruitment and provision of personnel
**Directors:** Ms P Jeffery, Dr L P Prince, P D Butler, D S Goddard, S Delaney, D J Wyatt, H N Jones, J A Gray
**Co. Secretary:** Garba Sani
**Responsibilities**
**Senior:** Liz Davies *(Project Manager)*, Paul Head *(Manager)*, Doyle Hector *(General Manager)*
**US SIC:** 7399 **UK SIC:** 83954
**Auditors:** Jeffreys Henry LLP
**Bankers:** The Co-Operative Bank Plc (08-90-37)

| | 31-03-14 | 31-03-13 | 31-03-12 |
|---|---|---|---|
| TO | 4,512,275 | 3,289,333 | 2,709,251 |
| P/L | 412,339 | 130,350 | (136,613) |
| NW | 573,251 | 168,912 | 124,562 |
| WC | 972,251 | 569,912 | 458,562 |
| Emp. | 118 | 69 | 46 |

DUNS 21-146-7420

## Urban Recruitment Group Ltd

Copper House 88 Snakes Lane East, Woodford Green, Essex IG8 7HX
**Tel:** 02085056600 **Fax:** 084 4249 4929
**Web:** www.urbanrec.co.uk
**Reg No:** 6769151 **Estd:** 2008 Private Limited Company
**Line of Business:** Employment service
**Issued Capital:** £10
**Directors:** R C Prince, E Rahman, S C Stedman
**Co. Secretary:** Enamur Rahman
**US SIC:** 7361 **UK SIC:** 83954
**Auditors:** RDP Newmans LLP

| | 31-08-13 | 31-08-12 | 31-08-11 |
|---|---|---|---|
| TO | 15,534,102 | N/A | N/A |
| P/L | 700,423 | N/A | N/A |
| NW | (1,287,757) | (1,581,339) | (1,534,220) |
| WC | 27,955 | (1,629,325) | (1,583,914) |
| Emp. | 48 | N/A | N/A |

DUNS 21-122-1009

## Urban Regeneration Agency

110 Buckingham Palace Road, Westminster, London SW1W 9SA
**Tel:** 020-7881-1600
**Line of Business:** Business services
**Trading Style:** English Partnerships
**Directors:** T Beattie, J Walker
**US SIC:** 7399 **UK SIC:** 83954
**Employees:** 60

DUNS 21-738-3644

## Urban Retreat At Home Llp

13a North Audley Street, London W1K 6ZA
**Tel:** 02076290669
**Web:** www.urbanretreat.co.uk
**Reg No:** 0366851OC **Estd:** 2008
**Line of Business:** Beauty salons

**US SIC:** 7231   **UK SIC:** 98200

| | 30-06-13 | 31-07-12 |
|---|---|---|
| TO | 13,985 | N/A |
| P/L | (50,651) | N/A |
| NW | 219,138 | 163,762 |
| WC | 217,240 | 160,263 |

DUNS 21-033-0703

## Urban Retreat At the Aveda Institute

Alton House 174 177, High Holborn, London WC1V 7AA
**Tel:** 020-7759-7355
**Estd:** 2001 Partnership
**Line of Business:** Activities of professional organisations
**Partners:** S Simmons, Mrs E Kent Smith, R Banks
**US SIC:** 7299   **UK SIC:** 98902
**Employees:** 80

DUNS 56-959-0698     Imp

## Urban Retreats Ltd

(**Subsidiary of:** Urban Retreat Ventures Ltd)
Po Box 372, London SW19 6LH
**Tel:** 02078439012 **Fax:** 02074101899
**Web:** www.urbanretreat.co.uk
**Reg No:** 2849316 **VAT No:** 627575022
**Estd:** 1993 Private Limited Company
**Line of Business:** Hairdressing and other beauty treatment
**Issued Capital:** £3,030,177
**Managing Director:** G C Hammer
**Co. Secretary:** Emile Qadri
**Branches:** Urban Retreats Ltd, Care Of Fenwick, Northumberland St, Newcastle Upon Tyne, Tyne and Wear NE1 7AF
**US SIC:** 7231   **UK SIC:** 98200
**Auditors:** Ashings Ltd
**Bankers:** Barclays Bank Plc (20-67-59)

| | 29-06-13 | 31-12-11 | 30-06-10 |
|---|---|---|---|
| TO | 18,539,558 | 11,680,545 | 10,951,914 |
| P/L | (107,510) | (143,257) | 35,198 |
| NW | 150,078 | 1,597,702 | 1,740,959 |
| WC | (949,702) | 324,002 | 170,798 |
| Emp. | 203 | 203 | 179 |

DUNS 77-956-0556

## Urban Science International Ltd.

(**Subsidiary of:** Urban Science Applications Inc.)
The Blade Abbey Square, Reading, Berkshire RG1 3BE
**Tel:** 01189035300 **Fax:** 01189-035301
**Web:** www.urbanscience.com
**Reg No:** 3059485 **Estd:** 1995 Private Limited Company
**Line of Business:** Management and business consultants
**Export Sales:** £610,282
**Trading Style:** Urban Science
**Issued Capital:** £10,000
**Directors:** P Dillamore, J A Anderson, Ms L Kowalchik
**Co. Secretary:** Francisco Soler Copado
**Responsibilities**
**Senior:** Charles Gardner (Manager), Michael Staebler (Manager)
**US SIC:** 7392   **UK SIC:** 83951
**Auditors:** Grant Thornton UK LLP

| | 31-12-13 | 31-12-12 | 31-12-11 |
|---|---|---|---|
| TO | 4,635,310 | 4,333,166 | 4,417,993 |
| P/L | 319,259 | 115,461 | 632,102 |
| NW | 4,571,403 | 4,298,739 | 4,180,855 |
| WC | 4,362,496 | 4,094,967 | 4,247,446 |
| Emp. | 56 | 54 | 53 |

DUNS 49-426-3437

## Urban Splash Group Ltd

(**Subsidiary of:** Urban Splash Holdings Ltd)
16-22 Worsley Street, Manchester M15 4LD
**Fax:** 0161-839-8999
**Web:** www.urbansplash.co.uk
**Reg No:** 3141013 **Estd:** 1995 Private Limited Company
**Line of Business:** Development and selling of real estate
**Issued Capital:** £2,010,130
**Directors:** T P Bloxham, J P Curnuck, S D Gawthorpe, J M Falkingham
**Co. Secretary:** Mrs Kimberley Essop
**Branches:** Urban Splash Group Ltd, Nore Road, Bristol, Avon BS20 8DW
**US SIC:** 6552, 6531
**UK SIC:** 85000, 83400
**Auditors:** Deloitte LLP
**Bankers:** HSBC Bank plc (40-35-26)

| | 30-09-13 | 31-03-12 | 31-09-11 |
|---|---|---|---|
| TO | 132,603,624 | 33,664,473 | 29,084,720 |
| P/L | 46,738 | (15,431,069) | (9,381,614) |
| NW | (33,658,625) | (17,433,088) | 4,879,663 |
| WC | (130,293,206) | (47,096,241) | (147,768,648) |
| Emp. | 93 | 117 | 142 |

DUNS 39-808-3287

## Urbanfirst Ltd

(**Subsidiary of:** Derwent London Plc)
9 Park Place, London SW1A 1LP
**Tel:** 01786450719
**Reg No:** 2213216 **Estd:** 1989 Private Limited Company
**Line of Business:** Buying and selling of own real estate
**Issued Capital:** £6,362,500
**Directors:** S P Silver, J D Burns, D M Wisniewski, P M Williams, N Q George, D G Silverman
**Co. Secretary:** Timothy Kite
**Branches:** Urbanfirst Ltd, The Broadway, Ealing, London W5 5JY
**US SIC:** 6531, 6519
**UK SIC:** 83400, 85000
**Auditors:** BDO LLP
**Bankers:** National Westminster Bank Plc (60-40-05)

| | 31-12-13 | 31-12-12 | 31-12-11 |
|---|---|---|---|
| TA | 54,250,265 | 51,622,940 | 49,004,077 |
| P/L | 2,625,738 | 2,441,922 | 2,374,345 |
| NW | 47,539,931 | 45,037,193 | 42,418,186 |
| WC | 50,178,623 | 47,845,353 | 45,403,431 |

DUNS 23-590-8097

## Urbaser Ltd

(**Subsidiary of:** Acs Actividades De Construccion Y Servicios Sa)
Unit F, St Margarets Road Pate Court, Cheltenham, Gloucestershire GL50 4DY
**Fax:** 01242261535
**Web:** www.urbaser.co.uk
**Reg No:** 3588422 **Estd:** 1998 Private Limited Company
**Line of Business:** Environmental consultants
**Issued Capital:** £72,300
**Directors:** J D Fernandez, J Peiro Balaguer, C S Mccarthy, J M Sanz, C A Perez
**Co. Secretary:** Christopher Mccarthy
**Responsibilities**
**Senior:** Susana Asin (Manager), Jose Ontanon (Director ( spain ))
**Admin:** Kerry North (Office Manager)
**US SIC:** 8911   **UK SIC:** 83701
**Auditors:** Davies Mayers Barnett LLP
**Bankers:** Barclays Bank Plc (20-98-61)

| | 31-12-13 | 31-12-12 | 31-12-11 |
|---|---|---|---|
| TO | 46,122,867 | 10,108,063 | 5,083,828 |
| P/L | 3,196,650 | (159,867) | 8,165,137 |
| NW | 10,181,964 | 8,704,250 | 8,849,786 |
| WC | 5,847,217 | 8,639,010 | 8,734,931 |
| Emp. | 313 | N/A | 113 |

DUNS 21-198-7573     Imp-Exp

## Urbis Schreder Ltd

(**Subsidiary of:** Schreder Sa)
Saphire House, Basingstoke, Hampshire RG24 8GG
**Web:** www.urbislighting.co.uk
**Reg No:** 1095726 **VAT No:** 240435300
**Estd:** 1973 Private Limited Company
**Line of Business:** Manufacturers of lighting equipment
**Export Markets:** Worldwide
**Issued Capital:** £500,000
**Directors:** I J Pratt, M L Saint-Paul, Mrs M A Velez Vestia, A M Papoular, J S Rubinstein
**Co. Secretary:** Martin Tootill
**Responsibilities**
**Senior:** Patrick Baldrey (Manager)
**Sales:** Mick Glancy (Sales Manager), Simon Perkins (Sales Manager), Ranjit Reehal (Area Sales Manager)
**IT:** Nigel Box (IT Director)
**Engineering:** Jon Gibb (Product Development Manager)
**Branches:** Urbis Schreder Ltd, 1200 Thorpe Park, Century Way, Leeds, West Yorkshire LS15 8ZA
**US SIC:** 3648, 3629
**UK SIC:** 34702, 34350
**Auditors:** KPMG
**Bankers:** Barclays Bank Plc (20-05-00)

| | 31-12-13 | 31-12-12 | 31-12-11 |
|---|---|---|---|
| TO | 36,016,332 | 29,161,267 | 32,077,568 |
| P/L | 1,830,550 | (629,636) | 442,870 |
| NW | 6,212,083 | 5,114,663 | 5,642,052 |
| WC | 4,345,823 | 3,151,082 | 5,209,900 |
| Emp. | 87 | 158 | 209 |

DUNS 49-315-9115     Imp

## Urbn Uk Ltd

(**Subsidiary of:** Uo Netherlands Holding B.V.)
24 Market Place, London W1W 8AN
**Tel:** 020-7908-4960 **Fax:** 020-7908-4999
**Web:** www.urbn.com
**Reg No:** 3124253 **VAT No:** 684936382
**Estd:** 2003 Private Limited Company
**Line of Business:** Retail sale of clothing
**Trading Style:** Urban Outfitters Uk, Anthropologie
**Issued Capital:** £7,974,623
**Directors:** R A Hayne, F J Conforti, G A Bodzy

**Co. Secretary:** Ms Elizabeth Field
**Branches:** Urbn Uk Ltd, 24 Market Place, London W1W 8AN
**US SIC:** 5699, 5621
**UK SIC:** 64500
**Auditors:** Kingston Smith LLP
**Bankers:** First Union National Bank (40-51-33)

| | 31-01-14 | 31-01-13 | 31-01-12 |
|---|---|---|---|
| TO | 152,016,736 | 138,287,279 | 111,549,100 |
| P/L | 1,679,702 | (3,780,334) | 452,043 |
| NW | 42,559,286 | 19,481,708 | 23,262,167 |
| WC | 25,839,557 | (40,558,232) | (31,385,667) |
| Emp. | 1,637 | 1,495 | 1,019 |

DUNS 36-798-7229

## Urdd Gobaith Cymru

Urdd Centre, Llangrannog, Llandysul, Dyfed SA44 6AE
**Web:** www.urdd.org
**Estd:** 1930
**Line of Business:** Children's activity playcentres
**Proprietor:** S Jenkins
**Responsibilities**
**Senior:** Efa Jones (Chief Executive)
**US SIC:** 8321   **UK SIC:** 96111
**Employees:** 90

DUNS 21-814-4772     Imp-Exp

## Uren Food Group Ltd

Wood Park, Chester High Road, Neston, Cheshire CH64 7TB
**Tel:** 01513-530330
**Web:** www.uren.com
**Reg No:** 0517333 **VAT No:** 163415479
**Estd:** 1953 Private Limited Company
**Line of Business:** Frozen foods (wholesale)
**Export Sales:** £17,622,000
**Trading Style:** Uren Food Group Ltd
**Issued Capital:** £5,000
**Principals:** Ms K M Eggleton (Financial), P M Jones, J L Wood, I R Stewart
**Responsibilities**
**Senior:** James Uren (Manager)
**Finance:** Kay Eggleton (Financial Director)
**Engineering:** Tim Brooker (Production Manager)
**US SIC:** 5149   **UK SIC:** 61700
**Auditors:** KPMG LLP
**Bankers:** Barclays Bank Plc (20-51-01)

| | 31-03-14 | 31-03-13 | 31-03-12 |
|---|---|---|---|
| TO | 54,731,000 | 55,087,000 | 57,425,000 |
| P/L | 191,000 | 1,323,000 | 414,000 |
| NW | 11,375,000 | 11,117,000 | 10,361,000 |
| WC | 8,357,000 | 8,113,000 | 7,470,000 |
| Emp. | 283 | 253 | 301 |

DUNS 21-734-0207     Exp

## Urenco Ltd

18 Oxford Road, Marlow, Buckinghamshire SL7 2NL
**Tel:** 01628486941
**Web:** www.urenco.com
**Reg No:** 1022786 **VAT No:** 604005402
**Estd:** 1971 Private Limited Company
**Line of Business:** Processing of nuclear fuel
**Export Markets:** France, Belguim, U S A, Sweden, Switzerland, Brazil, Japan, Korea, Finland, Germany, Netherlands
**Export Sales:** £1,251,238,000
**Issued Capital:** £168,000,000
**Directors:** Dr F Weigand, Dr B E Fischer, R Ter Haar, Dr H H Engelbrecht, Dr J A Hood, R H Nourse, Doctor S R Billingham, V I Goedvolk
**Co. Secretary:** Ms Sarah Newby
**Responsibilities**
**Senior:** George Verberg (Director)
**US SIC:** 2869, 1094
**UK SIC:** 25120, 21000
**Auditors:** Deloitte LLP
**Bankers:** Barclays Bank Plc (20-40-71)
Following financial data are in thousands

| | 31-12-13 | 31-12-12 | 31-12-11 |
|---|---|---|---|
| TO | 1,320,277 | 1,308,984 | 1,133,088 |
| P/L | 404,382 | 438,045 | 400,461 |
| NW | 1,661,023 | 1,468,623 | 1,357,896 |
| WC | 225,159 | 233,940 | 711,079 |
| Emp. | 1,480 | 1,439 | 1,384 |

DUNS 29-383-9114

## Urenco Uk Ltd

(**Subsidiary of:** Urenco Ltd)
Capenhurst Lane, Capenhurst, Chester, Cheshire CH1 6ER
**Tel:** 0151-473-4000
**Web:** www.urenco.com
**Reg No:** 1144899 **Estd:** 1993 Private Limited Company
**Line of Business:** Processing of nuclear fuel
**Issued Capital:** £40,000,000
**Directors:** G O Smith, S C Bowen, C R Chater, Dr H H Engelbrecht
**Co. Secretary:** Ms Sarah Newby
**Responsibilities**
**Senior:** Neil Fagan (Communications Manager), Andrew Stenhoff (Enrichment Operations Director)
**Operations:** Andrew Stenhoff (Enrichment Operations Director)

**Branches:** Urenco Uk Ltd, Central Services Plant Ucl Bldg 711 Stores, Chester, Cheshire CH1 6ER
**US SIC:** 2869, 8922
**UK SIC:** 25120, 94000
**Auditors:** Ernst & Young Llp
**Bankers:** National Westminster Bank Plc (60-07-35)

| | 31-12-13 | 31-12-12 | 31-12-11 |
|---|---|---|---|
| TO | 318,959,000 | 432,223,000 | 420,898,000 |
| P/L | 152,562,000 | 212,750,000 | 203,488,000 |
| NW | 859,189,000 | 739,078,000 | 712,091,000 |
| WC | 901,215,000 | 709,008,000 | 633,094,000 |
| Emp. | 331 | 356 | 357 |

DUNS 50-348-9593

## Uretek (U.K.) Ltd

(**Subsidiary of:** Oy Uretek-Marketing Ltd)
Unit 6, Skelmersdale, Lancashire WN8 9PT
**Tel:** 08000843503
**Web:** www.uretek.co.uk
**Reg No:** 2371014 **VAT No:** 483765406
**Estd:** 1989 Private Limited Company
**Line of Business:** Construction of commercial buildings
**Issued Capital:** £112
**Directors:** R Caldbeck, S Hakkinen, O Lahtinen
**Responsibilities**
**Senior:** Deborah Dudley (Manager), Jussi Karinen (Manager)
**IT:** Bill Short (IT Manager)
**US SIC:** 1541, 1752
**UK SIC:** 50100, 50400
**Auditors:** RSM Tenon Audit Ltd
**Bankers:** National Westminster Bank Plc (60-19-49)

| | 31-12-13 | 31-12-12 | 30-12-12 |
|---|---|---|---|
| TA | 3,202,700 | 2,750,300 | 1,878,712 |
| NW | 1,817,217 | 1,430,991 | 976,221 |
| WC | 1,825,186 | 1,449,638 | 977,907 |

DUNS 42-349-7457     Imp

## Urgo Ltd

(**Subsidiary of:** Laboratoires Urgo)
Sullington Road, Loughborough, Leicestershire LE12 9JG
**Tel:** 01509502051
**Web:** www.urgo.co.uk
**Reg No:** 4337458 **Estd:** 2001 Private Limited Company
**Line of Business:** Medical equipment leasing and rental
**Export Sales:** £368,234
**Issued Capital:** £1
**Directors:** P G Moustial, X L Pelisson, J F Robert, H H Le Lous
**Co. Secretary:** Graeme Francis
**US SIC:** 7394   **UK SIC:** 84000
**Auditors:** KPMG LLP

| | 31-12-13 | 31-12-12 | 31-12-11 |
|---|---|---|---|
| TO | 21,427,209 | 20,783,273 | 20,634,217 |
| P/L | 5,944,360 | 5,166,618 | 5,473,577 |
| NW | 6,410,694 | 5,828,588 | 5,149,044 |
| WC | 3,685,603 | 3,112,128 | 2,525,133 |
| Emp. | 113 | 111 | 118 |

DUNS 21-205-9299

## Uriah Woodhead & Son Ltd

Valley House, Valley Road, Bradford, West Yorkshire BD1 4RY
**Tel:** 01274727528
**Web:** www.uriah-woodhead.co.uk
**Reg No:** 0315622 **Estd:** 1936 Private Limited Company
**Line of Business:** Builders merchants
**Trading Style:** Woodhead Uriah
**Issued Capital:** £1,100
**Principals:** Mrs A O Jaggar (Managing), P R Jaggar
**Co. Secretary:** Mrs Annmarie Jaggar
**Branches:** Uriah Woodhead & Son Ltd, Crown Sawmills Great Northern Rd, Coney La, Keighley, West Yorkshire BD21 5JH
**US SIC:** 5072   **UK SIC:** 61500
**Auditors:** Rawse Varley & Co
**Bankers:** Lloyds TSB Bank plc (30-91-12)

| | 31-12-13 | 31-12-12 | 31-12-11 |
|---|---|---|---|
| TO | N/A | 6,347,791 | 6,536,285 |
| P/L | N/A | 340,050 | 296,036 |
| NW | 6,842,188 | 6,625,534 | 6,367,913 |
| WC | 3,078,687 | 2,896,960 | 3,545,001 |
| Emp. | N/A | 47 | 47 |

DUNS 21-779-5581

## Urmston Information Offices for Advice & Enquiries

Town Hall, 1 Waterside Plaza, Sale, Cheshire M33 7ZF
**Tel:** 01619121212
**Web:** www.trafford.gov.uk
**Estd:** 2011 Proprietorship
**Line of Business:** Adoption and fostering services
**Proprietor:** Mrs J Callendar
**Responsibilities**
**Senior:** Mike Lewis (Director Of Customer Services)
**US SIC:** 8321   **UK SIC:** 96111
**Employees:** 4,000

DUNS 21-581-4177
## Urmston Leisure Centre
Bowfell Road, Urmston, Manchester M41 5RR
**Tel:** 01617492570
**Web:** www.traffordleisure.co.uk
**Estd:** 2011 Proprietorship
**Line of Business:** Leisure centres
**Proprietor:** S Marris
**Responsibilities**
**Senior:** Kevin Henderson *(General Manager)*
**US SIC:** 7999 **UK SIC:** 97913
**Employees:** 50

DUNS 21-932-8291 **Exp**
## Uro Auto Spares Ltd
(**Subsidiary of:** German Swedish & French Car Parts Ltd)
Unit 21-24, Birmingham, West Midlands B35 7AR
**Tel:** 01216267981
**Web:** www.gsfcarparts.com
**Reg No:** 1260044 **Estd:** 1976 Private Limited Company
**Line of Business:** Activities of other transport agencies
**Export Markets:** Rest of Europe, Africa, Asia, America
**Trading Style:** G S F Car Parts Ltd
**Issued Capital:** £26,400
**Director:** S G West
**Co. Secretary:** Diresh De Silva
**Branches:** Uro Auto Spares Ltd, 1283 London Rd, Derby, Derbyshire DE24 8QN
**US SIC:** 4712 **UK SIC:** 77002
**Auditors:** Ernst & Young LLP
**Bankers:** Lloyds TSB Bank plc (30-96-88)

| | 31-12-13 | 31-12-12 | 31-12-11 |
|---|---|---|---|
| TA | 37,800 | 37,800 | 37,800 |
| NW | 37,800 | 37,800 | 37,800 |

DUNS 73-813-9794
## Urquhart-Dykes & Lord Llp
Tower House, Merrion Way, Leeds, West Yorkshire LS2 8PA
**Web:** www.udl.co.uk
**Reg No:** 0307196OC
**Proprietorship**
**Line of Business:** Patent agents
**Export Sales:** £7,184,975
**Responsibilities**
**Senior:** Samantha Chambers *(Practice Manager)*, Gregory Davies *(Designated Limited Liability P)*, Alan Fiddes *(Designated Limited Liability P)*
**Branches:** Urquhart-Dykes & Lord Llp, Canal Rd, Bradford, West Yorkshire BD1 4SP
**US SIC:** 7399 **UK SIC:** 83954
**Bankers:** National Westminster Bank Plc (60-60-05)

| | 30-04-14 | 30-04-13 | 30-04-12 |
|---|---|---|---|
| TO | 16,954,224 | 16,322,813 | 15,607,326 |
| P/L | 649,847 | 673,240 | 608,981 |
| NW | 649,847 | 673,240 | 1,275,560 |
| WC | 4,232,527 | 4,168,090 | 5,090,452 |
| Emp. | 70 | 72 | 78 |

DUNS 21-228-3934
## Urquhart Flooring Contractor
24 Lady Helen Street, Kirkcaldy, Fife KY1 1PR
**Tel:** 01592595253
**Estd:** 2002 Proprietorship
**Line of Business:** Flooring services
**Proprietor:** B Ukhart
**US SIC:** 1752 **UK SIC:** 50400
**Employees:** 53

DUNS 50-381-8601
## Urs Corporation Ltd
(**Subsidiary of:** Aecom)
Citypoint 2, 25 Tyndrum Street, Glasgow, Lanarkshire G4 0JY
**Web:** www.urscorp.eu
**Reg No:** 0118271SC **Estd:** 1957 Private Limited Company
**Line of Business:** Environmental consultants
**Issued Capital:** £1,635,000
**Directors:** A V Marrett, P J Skinner, I Macfadyen
**Responsibilities**
**Senior:** Susan Briggs *(?Regional Director - Eastern E)*, Alan Parry-Jones *(Manager)*
**Finance:** Mhairi McKenna *(Finance Manager)*
**Health & Safety:** Sharon Ross *(Health & Safety Officer)*
**Operations:** Ian Hay *(Head of Rail)*
**Branches:** Urs Corporation Limited, Cawdor Barracks, Bldg 439 Ramsey Wing, Haverfordwest, Dyfed SA62 6NN
**US SIC:** 8911 **UK SIC:** 83701
**Auditors:** PricewaterhouseCoopers LLP

| | 31-12-13 | 31-12-12 | 31-12-11 |
|---|---|---|---|
| TO | 1,056,000 | 201,000 | 17,188,000 |
| P/L | 241,000 | 277,000 | 6,646,000 |
| NW | 11,383,000 | 11,198,000 | 10,989,000 |
| WC | 11,346,000 | 11,161,000 | 10,952,000 |
| Emp. | N/A | N/A | 621 |

DUNS 23-919-5907 **Imp**
## Urs E&C Uk Ltd
(**Subsidiary of:** Aecom)
Washington House, Birchwood Park Avenue, Birchwood, Warrington, Cheshire WA3 6GR
**Tel:** 01925-854500 **Fax:** 01925-854599
**Web:** www.wgint.com
**Reg No:** 3909808 **Estd:** 1954 Private Limited Company
**Line of Business:** Construction of commercial buildings
**Export Sales:** £1,508,000
**Issued Capital:** £17,250,001
**Directors:** G Mcgill, R J Hill, T T Wrenn, A V Marrett
**Co. Secretary:** Ms Jeanne Baughman
**Responsibilities**
**Senior:** David Pethick *(Manager)*, Stuart Thornton *(General Manager)*, Robert Zaist *(Manager)*
**Health & Safety:** Amy Upton *(Health & Safety Officer)*
**Facilities:** Pat Collings *(Facilities Manager)*
**Purchasing:** Pat Collings *(Facilities Manager)*
**Fleet:** Pat Collings *(Facilities Manager)*
**Branches:** Urs E&c Uk Ltd, 20 Bedford Square, London WC1B 3HH
**US SIC:** 1541, 8911
**UK SIC:** 50100, 83701
**Auditors:** Deloitte & Touche
**Bankers:** National Westminster Bank Plc (01-10-01)

| | 31-12-13 | 31-12-12 | 31-12-11 |
|---|---|---|---|
| TO | 39,580,000 | 38,295,000 | 32,763,000 |
| P/L | (2,800,000) | (2,460,000) | (683,000) |
| NW | 1,578,000 | 4,081,000 | 6,233,000 |
| WC | 2,248,000 | 5,821,000 | 8,671,000 |
| Emp. | 61 | 64 | 57 |

DUNS 21-117-0519 **Imp-Exp**
## Urschel International Ltd
(**Subsidiary of:** Urschel Laboratories Inc)
Tiber Way, Meridian Business Park, Leicester, Leicestershire LE19 1QP
**Tel:** 01162-634321
**Web:** www.urschel.com
**Reg No:** 1073957 **VAT No:** 114281405
**Estd:** 1972 Private Limited Company
**Line of Business:** Food processing equipment and supplies
**Export Markets:** Belgium, France, Netherlands, Eire, Denmark, Germany, Switzerland, Austria, East Europe, Portugal
**Export Sales:** £23,280,594
**Issued Capital:** £100,000
**Principals:** R R Urschel *(President)*, Mrs F Le Masle, Mrs H C Gomes, P C Urschel, J G Van Der Horst, H Bruendler, T O'Brien, D Marchetti
**Co. Secretary:** Mrs Teresa Warburton
**Responsibilities**
**Senior:** Richard Cranefield *(Director)*, Patrick Faroux *(Manager)*, Peter Kellam *(Manager)*, Hugh Watson *(Finance Director)*, Florence le Masle *(Director)*
**Finance:** Richard Cranefield *(Director)*, Hugh Watson *(Finance Director)*
**Sales:** Neal Bateman *(Sales Manager)*, Margaret Holtom *(Sales Coordinator)*
**Operations:** Andy Shepherdson *(Plant Manager)*
**US SIC:** 3551 **UK SIC:** 32441
**Auditors:** Horwath Clark Whitehill

| | 31-12-13 | 31-12-12 | 31-12-11 |
|---|---|---|---|
| TO | 27,886,211 | 22,195,617 | 22,016,895 |
| P/L | 2,269,843 | 777,279 | 1,285,188 |
| NW | 10,788,110 | 9,226,956 | 8,559,644 |
| WC | 8,288,583 | 5,977,320 | 5,555,410 |
| Emp. | 75 | 69 | 67 |

DUNS 21-740-5212
## The Ursuline Academy Ilford
Morland Road, Ilford, Essex IG1 4JU
**Tel:** 02085541995
**Web:** www.uai.org.uk
**Reg No:** 7737159 **Estd:** 2011 Private Company Limited By Guarantee
**Line of Business:** Schools (local authority)
**Directors:** R J Mitchell, Mrs D Grant, Ms L Powell, D Burge, Mrs A St Ville, P J Greensmith, Mrs C M Spinner, M W Smith
**Co. Secretary:** Michael King
**Responsibilities**
**Senior:** Sarah Bergin Mccarthy *(Director)*, Alex Burke *(Head Teacher)*, Robert Caldeira *(Director)*, Andrew Headon *(Director)*, John Laviniere *(Director)*, Luke Robertson *(Director)*
**US SIC:** 8211 **UK SIC:** 93200
**Bankers:** National Westminster Bank Plc (60-50-09)

| | 31-08-14 | 31-08-13 | 31-08-12 |
|---|---|---|---|
| TO | 5,334,935 | 4,894,913 | 14,306,270 |
| P/L | 104,832 | (16,729) | 9,566,209 |
| NW | 9,117,312 | 9,318,480 | 9,333,209 |
| WC | (192,151) | 48,630 | (26,727) |
| Emp. | 78 | 73 | 73 |

DUNS 85-618-9618
## Urt Group Ltd
Heath Place, Bognor Regis, West Sussex PO22 9SL
**Web:** www.urtgroupltd.com
**Reg No:** 6212248 **Estd:** 2007 Private Limited Company
**Line of Business:** Management activities of holding companies
**Trading Style:** Urt Group Ltd
**Issued Capital:** £1,133
**Directors:** K R Emmett, P S Walters, D T Weston
**Co. Secretary:** Matthew Cox
**US SIC:** 6711, 8911
**UK SIC:** 83962, 83701

| | 30-06-13 | 30-06-12 | 30-06-11 |
|---|---|---|---|
| TO | 7,237,555 | 10,684,805 | 6,073,433 |
| P/L | (401,383) | 3,093,209 | 2,062,718 |
| NW | 2,952,551 | 3,653,685 | 1,722,871 |
| WC | 1,639,991 | 2,561,730 | 955,043 |
| Emp. | 98 | N/A | N/A |

DUNS 71-904-5812
## Us Two Studio Ltd
62 Shoreditch High Street, London E1 6JJ
**Tel:** 020-7613-0433
**Web:** www.ustwo.co.uk
**Reg No:** 5286528 **VAT No:** 853384704
**Estd:** 2004 Private Limited Company
**Line of Business:** Other computer related activities
**Export Sales:** £8,139,139
**Issued Capital:** £209
**Directors:** M Woxneryd, J Sinclair, J C Ehrhardt
**Co. Secretary:** Matt Miller
**US SIC:** 7379 **UK SIC:** 83940
**Auditors:** RJP LLP
**Bankers:** The Royal Bank Of Scotland Plc (15-10-00)

| | 31-12-13 | 31-12-12 | 31-12-11 |
|---|---|---|---|
| TO | 15,081,227 | 10,529,538 | N/A |
| P/L | 1,803,371 | 1,468,788 | N/A |
| NW | 4,925,040 | 4,466,710 | 2,870,005 |
| WC | 4,685,523 | 4,362,810 | 2,758,630 |
| Emp. | 144 | 108 | N/A |

DUNS 28-851-6099
## Usaa Ltd
(**Subsidiary of:** United Services Automobile Association)
7th Floor, Dashwood House, Old Broad Street, London EC2M 1QS
**Tel:** 02076551831 **Fax:** 020-7655-1849
**Web:** www.usaa.com
**Reg No:** 0730577 **Estd:** 1962 Private Limited Company
**Line of Business:** Non-life insurance
**Issued Capital:** £10,000,000
**Directors:** M J Gaughan, J S Stubbings, A W Krapf, S P Keith, S A Bennett
**Co. Secretary:** Simon Keith
**Responsibilities**
**Senior:** Jennifer Macnaughton *(Manager)*
**Marketing:** Cathy Curry *(Events Planner)*
**HR:** Elizabeth Conklyn *(Human Resource Manager)*
**US SIC:** 6411 **UK SIC:** 83200
**Auditors:** KPMG Audit Plc

| | 31-12-13 | 31-12-12 | 31-12-11 |
|---|---|---|---|
| TO | 51,368,000 | 50,362,000 | 49,394,000 |
| P/L | 5,119,000 | 10,532,000 | 2,841,000 |
| NW | 35,931,000 | 34,811,000 | 27,489,000 |
| WC | 27,003,000 | 26,221,000 | 30,278,000 |
| Emp. | 71 | 69 | 73 |

DUNS 34-671-9573
## Usairtours Holidays Ltd
(**Subsidiary of:** Usairtours Travel Holdings Ltd)
Roxburghe House, 273-287 Regent Street, London W1B 2HA
**Tel:** 08712100500 **Fax:** 02085084992
**Web:** www.usairtours.co.uk
**Reg No:** 5476983 **VAT No:** 862463513
**Estd:** 2005 Private Limited Company
**Line of Business:** Activities of travel agencies
**Trading Style:** Travelplanners, Orlando Villa Experts
**Issued Capital:** £100,000
**Director:** G A Novik
**Responsibilities**
**Senior:** Shirley Saunders *(Manager)*
**Branches:** Usairtours Holidays Ltd, Usairtours, 2 Loughton Business Centre, Langston Road, Essex IG10 3SJ Loughton
**US SIC:** 4722 **UK SIC:** 77001
**Auditors:** King & King
**Bankers:** Allied Irish Bank (gb) (23-84-00)

| | 30-09-13 | 30-09-12 | 30-09-11 |
|---|---|---|---|
| TO | 29,302,365 | 30,750,148 | 29,045,363 |
| P/L | 246,917 | 131,435 | 247,334 |
| NW | 465,011 | 352,050 | 296,821 |
| WC | 1,314,847 | 850,527 | 756,042 |
| Emp. | 60 | 51 | 47 |

DUNS 21-103-4092
## Usay Business Ltd
(**Subsidiary of:** Usay Group Ltd)
Unit A1-A2, Lakeside Business Park, South Cerney, Cirencester, Gloucestershire GL7 5XL
**Tel:** 08458803355 **Fax:** 01285659780
**Web:** www.healthinsurancecompare.co.uk
**Reg No:** 6463920 **Estd:** 2008 Private Limited Company
**Line of Business:** Financial intermediation not elsewhere classified
**Issued Capital:** £2,000
**Directors:** A M Hall, Ms K L Tomkins, P T Carrington
**Co. Secretary:** Mrs Alison Ryder
**US SIC:** 6111 **UK SIC:** 81501
**Bankers:** National Westminster Bank Plc (60-05-41)

| | 31-03-14 | 31-03-13 | 31-03-12 |
|---|---|---|---|
| TA | 2,667,452 | 2,473,509 | 2,233,810 |
| P/L | 1,154,362 | 821,231 | 1,035,335 |
| NW | 866,052 | 1,168,621 | 727,965 |
| WC | 699,666 | 1,051,175 | 628,106 |
| Emp. | 121 | 117 | 100 |

DUNS 21-155-2153 **Imp Exp**
## Usborne Publishing Ltd
Usborne House, London EC1N 8RT
**Tel:** 020-7430-2800 **Fax:** 020-7430-1562
**Web:** www.usborne.com
**Reg No:** 1124359 **VAT No:** 410752682
**Estd:** 1992 Private Limited Company
**Line of Business:** Book publishers
**Export Markets:** Worldwide
**Export Sales:** £28,917,723
**Trading Style:** Usborne Books At Home
**Issued Capital:** £10,000
**Principals:** T P Usborne *(Chairman and Managing)*, M R Robinson
**Co. Secretary:** Mrs Andrea Parsons
**Responsibilities**
**Marketing:** Christian Hereson *(Senior Marketing Executive)*, Anna Howard *(Sales & Marketing Manager)*, Liz Scott *(Sales & Marketing Manager)*
**Sales:** Anna Howard *(Sales & Marketing Manager)*, Liz Scott *(Sales & Marketing Manager)*
**IT:** Steve Bentley *(IT Manager)*
**Branches:** Usborne Publishing Ltd, Chubb Building, Suite 47, Wolverhampton, West Midlands WV1 1HT
**US SIC:** 2731, 2741
**UK SIC:** 47532, 47541
**Auditors:** Nexia Smith & Williamson
**Bankers:** National Westminster Bank Plc (60-00-01)

| | 31-01-14 | 31-01-13 | 31-01-12 |
|---|---|---|---|
| TO | 50,544,656 | 46,780,128 | 44,561,338 |
| P/L | 8,929,787 | 8,836,061 | 8,005,342 |
| NW | 39,154,149 | 35,626,788 | 30,956,712 |
| WC | 39,253,549 | 35,715,105 | 31,013,608 |
| Emp. | 206 | 200 | 187 |

DUNS 21-412-1940
## Usdaw National Helpline
188 Wilmslow Road, Manchester M14 6LJ
**Tel:** 08456060640
**Web:** www.usdaw.org.uk
**Estd:** 2010 Proprietorship
**Line of Business:** Trade unions
**US SIC:** 8611 **UK SIC:** 96312
**Employees:** 400

DUNS 23-597-3372
## Usha Martin U K Ltd
(**Subsidiary of:** Usha Martin Limited)
Unit 5 Blair Court, 5 North Avenue, Clydebank Business Park, Clydebank, Dunbartonshire G81 2LA
**Tel:** 01419518801
**Web:** www.ushamartin.co.uk
**Reg No:** 3594781 **Estd:** 1998 Private Limited Company
**Line of Business:** Manufacturers of wire products
**Export Sales:** £15,938,207
**Issued Capital:** £3,850,000
**Directors:** P Scutt, R Jhawar, P K Jain, S Jodhawat
**Co. Secretary:** Simon Hood
**Responsibilities**
**Senior:** Purandar Bhattacharya *(CEO)*, Graham Steel *(Manager)*
**Branches:** Usha Martin U K Ltd, Mariner Court, Tasman House, Clydebank, Dunbartonshire G81 2NP
**US SIC:** 3357 **UK SIC:** 22470
**Auditors:** Campbell Dallas LLP

**Bankers:** Bank Of Scotland (80-11-80)

| | 31-03-14 | 31-03-13 | 31-03-12 |
|---|---|---|---|
| TO | 40,348,464 | 32,490,352 | 38,150,194 |
| P/L | 3,741,636 | 3,356,598 | 3,811,082 |
| NW | 23,783,030 | 20,876,238 | 18,280,501 |
| WC | 9,036,590 | 10,804,446 | 12,786,813 |
| Emp. | 168 | 142 | 137 |

DUNS 76-751-2502 **Imp-Exp**
## Ushers of Trowbridge Ltd
(**Subsidiary of:** Punch Taverns Plc)
Angel Mill, Westbury, Wiltshire BA13 3DR
**Tel:** 01373828700 **Fax:** 01225-715120
**Web:** http://countyestatepubs.co.uk
**Reg No:** 2597688 **Estd:** 1824 Private Limited Company
**Line of Business:** Malt Beverages
**Export Markets:** European Union (E U); U S A
**Trading Style:** County Estate Pubs Limited
**Issued Capital:** £50,000
**Directors:** E M Bashforth, S P Dando
**Co. Secretary:** Ms Francesca Appleby
**Responsibilities**
**Senior:** Claire Harris *(Manager)*
**Branches:** Ushers Of Trowbridge Ltd, Barley Mow, The Hurst, Hook, Hampshire RG27 8DE
**US SIC:** 2082 **UK SIC:** 42702
**Auditors:** Ernst & Young LLP
**Bankers:** National Westminster Bank Plc (60-21-36)

| | 17-08-13 | 18-08-12 | 20-08-11 |
|---|---|---|---|
| TA | 39,282,000 | 39,282,000 | 39,282,000 |
| NW | 39,282,000 | 39,282,000 | 39,282,000 |

DUNS 73-849-7143
## Uskmouth Power Co Ltd
(**Subsidiary of:** Sse Plc)
Uskmouth Substation A E S Fifoots Power, Station, West Nash Road, Nash, Newport, Gwent NP18 2BZ
**Tel:** 01633 292700 **Fax:** 01633 292701
**Web:** www.sse.com
**Reg No:** 5104786 **Estd:** 2004 Private Limited Company
**Line of Business:** Production of electricity
**Trading Style:** Scottish and Southern Energy
**Issued Capital:** £20,081,417
**Director:** J B Busche
**Responsibilities**
**Senior:** Lawrence Donnelly *(Manager)*
**HR:** Ann Meredith *(Human Resources)*
**US SIC:** 4911 **UK SIC:** 16101
**Auditors:** Deloitte & Touche LLP
**Bankers:** Barclays Bank Plc (20-26-71)

| | 31-03-14 | 31-03-13 | 31-03-12 |
|---|---|---|---|
| TO | 14,700,000 | 24,400,000 | 27,200,000 |
| P/L | (900,000) | 5,500,000 | 111,100,000 |
| NW | 4,500,000 | 2,600,000 | (3,000,000) |
| WC | 14,500,000 | 29,300,000 | 21,900,000 |
| Emp. | 84 | 106 | 106 |

DUNS 42-402-9143
## Usl (Trading) Ltd
(**Subsidiary of:** Britannic Holdings Ltd)
Canal Mill, Botany Bay, Chorley, Lancashire PR6 9AF
**Tel:** 01257-261220
**Web:** www.botanybay.co.uk
**Reg No:** 4390601 **Estd:** 2002 Private Limited Company
**Line of Business:** Other non-store retail sale
**Trading Style:** Usl (Trading) Ltd
**Issued Capital:** £1
**Directors:** T J Knowles, T D Hopkinson
**Co. Secretary:** Miss Claire Sharp
**Responsibilities**
**Senior:** lee holt *(general manager)*
**US SIC:** 5963 **UK SIC:** 65600

| | 31-01-14 | 31-01-13 | 31-01-12 |
|---|---|---|---|
| TO | 1,218,335 | 1,013,686 | 952,223 |
| P/L | 179,101 | 6,649,819 | (841,237) |
| NW | N/A | (179,101) | (6,828,920) |
| WC | (126,256) | (315,970) | (6,969,197) |

DUNS 21-750-9001
## Usual Suspects Ltd
36 High Storrs Drive, Sheffield, South Yorkshire S11 7LL
**Tel:** 01142687409
**Web:** www.usualsuspectscrew.com
**Reg No:** 7814544 **Estd:** 2011 Private Limited Company
**Line of Business:** Operation of arts facilities
**Issued Capital:** £100
**Directors:** B P Morgan, Mrs R Morgan
**Responsibilities**
**Senior:** Amanda Mardelin *(Office Manager)*
**US SIC:** 7911 **UK SIC:** 97913

| | 31-03-14 | 31-03-13 |
|---|---|---|
| TA | 97,868 | 29,233 |
| NW | (18,480) | (18,613) |
| WC | (20,316) | (19,953) |

DUNS 77-106-1058
## Usw Commercial Services Ltd.
Drive William Price Business Centre, Pontypridd, Mid Glamorgan CF37 1DL
**Tel:** 01443480480
**Web:** www.ugcs.co.uk
**Reg No:** 2683025 **Estd:** 1992 Private Company Limited By Guarantee
**Line of Business:** First-degree level higher education
**Export Sales:** £524,155
**Trading Style:** U T C S
**Directors:** H R Williams, M Wahab, J H Francis
**Co. Secretary:** Mrs Lynne Wakefield
**US SIC:** 8221, 7399
**UK SIC:** 93100, 83954
**Auditors:** PricewaterhouseCoopers
**Bankers:** HSBC Bank plc (40-37-08)

| | 31-07-13 | 31-07-12 | 31-07-11 |
|---|---|---|---|
| TO | 4,501,828 | 3,856,056 | 3,590,443 |
| P/L | 252,918 | 222,555 | 321,072 |
| NW | 199,572 | 199,572 | 199,572 |
| WC | 199,572 | 199,572 | 199,572 |

DUNS 23-615-4758
## Uswitch Ltd
(**Subsidiary of:** Uswitch Digital Ltd)
Floor 2 Centro 3, 19 Mandela Street, London NW1 0DU
**Tel:** 02034323894 **Fax:** 020-3214-8417
**Web:** www.uswitch.com
**Reg No:** 3612689 **Estd:** 1999 Private Limited Company
**Line of Business:** Promotion consultants (sales)
**Trading Style:** Forward3d
**Issued Capital:** £100,000
**Director:** S Weller
**Responsibilities**
**Senior:** B Holloway *(Manager)*
**US SIC:** 7319, 4932
**UK SIC:** 83800, 16200
**Auditors:** BDO LLP
**Bankers:** HSBC Bank plc (40-01-13)

| | 31-12-13 | 31-12-12 | 31-12-11 |
|---|---|---|---|
| TO | 34,323,028 | 24,352,195 | 23,490,730 |
| P/L | 11,511,109 | 7,916,745 | 6,975,224 |
| NW | 12,294,894 | 8,294,037 | 15,986,664 |
| WC | 11,798,892 | 8,197,601 | 15,007,211 |
| Emp. | 109 | 88 | 78 |

DUNS 34-607-8939 **Imp**
## Utec Ncs Survey Ltd
14 Abercrombie Court, Arnhall Business Park Prospect Road, Westhill, Aberdeenshire AB32 6FE
**Tel:** 01224749499 **Fax:** 01224-749199
**Web:** www.ncs-survey.com
**Reg No:** 0282769SC **Estd:** 2006 Private Limited Company
**Line of Business:** Other engineering activities
**Issued Capital:** £170,596
**Directors:** Dr B Bruggaier, J W Meaden, C R Erni
**Co. Secretary:** Burness Paull Llp
**US SIC:** 8911 **UK SIC:** 83701
**Auditors:** Williamson & Dunn

| | 31-12-13 | 31-12-12 | 31-12-11 |
|---|---|---|---|
| TO | 15,562,000 | 12,935,000 | 16,723,000 |
| P/L | 1,991,000 | 1,796,000 | 3,941,000 |
| NW | 6,536,000 | 5,201,000 | 3,944,000 |
| WC | 4,300,000 | 1,625,000 | 1,559,000 |
| Emp. | 105 | 82 | 61 |

DUNS 21-154-4644
## Utec Survey Construction Services Ltd
(**Subsidiary of:** Utec International Ltd)
Union Plaza (6th Floor), 1 Union Wynd, Aberdeen, Aberdeenshire AB10 1DQ
**Tel:** 01224636677 **Fax:** 01224636787
**Web:** www.utecsurvey.com
**Reg No:** 0355518SC **Estd:** 2009 Private Limited Company
**Line of Business:** Service activities incidental to oil and gas extraction excluding surveying
**Directors:** Dr B Bruggaier, D Tucker
**Co. Secretary:** Burness Paull Llp
**Responsibilities**
**Senior:** Martin O'Carroll *(Director)*
**US SIC:** 1389, 7399
**UK SIC:** 13000, 83954
**Employees:** 20
**Turnover:** £11,294,724

DUNS 50-395-8175
## Uti Worldwide (Uk) Ltd
(**Subsidiary of:** Uti Belgium Nv)
Reading Cargo Centre, Reading, Berkshire RG2 0JS
**Tel:** 01189-869595 **Fax:** 01189-876074
**Web:** www.go2uti.com
**Reg No:** 2402322 **VAT No:** 641944137
**Estd:** 1989 Private Limited Company
**Line of Business:** Other supporting land transport activities
**Issued Capital:** £1,000,000
**Directors:** D J Van Aalst, Ms S M Mccann, Mrs B Kearney, S G Logan
**Co. Secretary:** Klaus Sichau
**Responsibilities**
**Senior:** John Hextall *(Manager)*, R Mckenna *(Manager)*
**Finance:** Toni Long *(Accounts Team Leader)*
**Branches:** Uti Worldwide (Uk) Ltd, Unit 1 Merlin Park, Barton Dock Road, Stretford, Manchester M32 0TL
**US SIC:** 4789 **UK SIC:** 77002
**Auditors:** Deloitte LLP
**Bankers:** Barclays Bank Plc (20-38-83)

| | 31-01-14 | 31-01-13 | 31-01-12 |
|---|---|---|---|
| TO | 58,231,000 | 123,421,152 | 98,494,448 |
| P/L | 1,454,000 | (582,906) | (816,098) |
| NW | (231,000) | (1,583,484) | (800,078) |
| WC | (584,000) | (2,080,355) | (971,637) |
| Emp. | 266 | 276 | 326 |

DUNS 22-664-8772 **Imp-Exp**
## The Utile Engineering Co. Ltd
(**Subsidiary of:** Utile Holdings Ltd)
New Street, Irthlingborough, Wellingborough, Northamptonshire NN9 5UG
**Web:** www.utileengineering.co.uk
**Reg No:** 1656155 **VAT No:** 119859822
**Estd:** 1982 Private Limited Company
**Line of Business:** Engineers (general)
**Export Markets:** Worldwide
**Issued Capital:** £50,782
**Principals:** T E Poole *(Managing)*, N G Peck, R E Poole
**Co. Secretary:** Ms Julie Rainbow
**Responsibilities**
**Senior:** Francis Sherring *(Technical Sales)*
**Sales:** Francis Sherring *(Technical Sales)*
**Admin:** Sandra Kitchen *(Administration Manager)*
**IT:** Steven Hasdell *(Computer Manager)*
**Facilities:** Sandra Kitchen *(Administration Manager)*
**Engineering:** Graham Swainston *(Service Manager)*
**US SIC:** 8911, 3563
**UK SIC:** 83701, 32831
**Bankers:** Lloyds TSB Bank plc (30-97-78)

| | 31-03-14 | 31-03-13 | 31-03-12 |
|---|---|---|---|
| TA | 2,725,413 | 2,120,038 | 1,980,901 |
| NW | 805,813 | 649,056 | 590,168 |
| WC | 814,090 | 774,357 | 741,227 |

DUNS 73-804-9881
## Utilisoft Ltd
(**Subsidiary of:** Bglobal Plc)
Alliance House, Clayton Green Business Park, Library Road, Clayton-Le-Woods, Chorley, Lancashire PR6 7EN
**Tel:** 01772770280 **Fax:** 01254-588500
**Web:** www.utiligroup.com
**Reg No:** 2931236 **Estd:** 1994 Private Limited Company
**Line of Business:** Computer software sales
**Issued Capital:** £5,000
**Directors:** S P Gosling, J H Furness, M C Hirst, A Green, M H Evans
**Co. Secretary:** Steven Gosling
**Responsibilities**
**Senior:** Timothy Jackson-Smith *(Manager)*, Nicholas Kennedy *(Manager)*
**Finance:** Nick Makinson *(Company Treasurer)*
**Sales:** Nick Antrobus *(Development Director)*, Andrew Humby *(Director, Retail Energy Soluti)*, Vinesh Patel *(Lead Business Consultant)*
**Operations:** Paddy Kay *(Operations Manager)*
**Engineering:** Mark Ashrafi *(Senior Software Engineer)*, Bill Comer *(Senior Software Engineer)*
**US SIC:** 7379 **UK SIC:** 83940
**Auditors:** KPMG
**Bankers:** Barclays Bank Plc (20-09-72)

| | 31-03-14 | 31-03-13 | 31-03-12 |
|---|---|---|---|
| TO | 5,206,239 | 3,208,191 | 4,139,136 |
| P/L | 803,516 | (197,067) | 197,673 |
| NW | 1,065,921 | 1,193,264 | 1,796,559 |
| WC | 954,003 | (137,742) | 1,666,016 |
| Emp. | 66 | 55 | 49 |

DUNS 73-586-3263
## Utilita Group Ltd
(**Subsidiary of:** Secure Meters Limited)
20 Moorside Road, Winchester, Hampshire SO23 7RX
**Tel:** 01962859559 **Fax:** 08457707126
**Web:** www.utilita.co.uk
**Reg No:** 4847763 **Estd:** 2003 Private Limited Company
**Line of Business:** Newspapers publishing
**Issued Capital:** £43,004
**Directors:** W N Bullen, D A Clipsham, K Ghosh, M D Smith, S Singhal, S Singhal
**Co. Secretary:** Michael Smith
**Responsibilities**
**Senior:** Jez Walder *(Manager)*
**US SIC:** 2731 **UK SIC:** 47532

| | 31-03-14 | 31-03-13 | 31-03-12 |
|---|---|---|---|
| TO | 79,918,040 | 46,102,128 | 26,923,705 |
| P/L | 1,832,776 | (1,663,642) | (956,690) |
| NW | (7,023,475) | (7,329,625) | (798,372) |
| WC | (3,883,778) | (2,839,943) | (1,736,938) |
| Emp. | 128 | 76 | N/A |

DUNS 73-687-8120
## Utilita Services Ltd
(**Subsidiary of:** Secure Meters Limited)
Unit 4 Moorside Road, Winchester, Hampshire SO23 7RX
**Fax:** 0845-770-7126
**Web:** www.utilita.co.uk
**Reg No:** 4946848 **Estd:** 2003 Private Limited Company
**Line of Business:** Electricity companies
**Issued Capital:** £2,500,000
**Directors:** W N Bullen, M D Smith
**Co. Secretary:** Michael Smith
**US SIC:** 4911, 7399
**UK SIC:** 16101, 83954
**Auditors:** Unknown Auditor

| | 31-03-14 | 31-03-13 | 31-03-12 |
|---|---|---|---|
| TO | 7,167,053 | 5,647,245 | 3,875,057 |
| P/L | 339,468 | 268,916 | 204,403 |
| NW | 1,102,726 | 763,258 | 494,342 |
| WC | 891,383 | (1,889,746) | (2,099,558) |
| Emp. | 104 | N/A | N/A |

DUNS 73-364-9813
## Utility Management Services (Bcw Group) Ltd
(**Subsidiary of:** Dnb Asa)
Warrington Business Park, Long Lane, Warrington, Cheshire WA2 8TX
**Tel:** 01925635192 **Fax:** 01925635193
**Web:** www.utilityms.co.uk
**Reg No:** 4638477 **Estd:** 2003 Private Limited Company
**Line of Business:** Other business activities not elsewhere classified
**Issued Capital:** £15,000
**Directors:** Ms I H Saunders, Ms J Sharpe, B Mouat, D Waite
**Responsibilities**
**Finance:** John McKenzie *(Finance Manager)*
**US SIC:** 7399 **UK SIC:** 83954
**Auditors:** Baker Tilly
**Bankers:** HSBC Bank plc (40-27-15)

| | 31-12-13 | 31-12-12 | 30-12-12 |
|---|---|---|---|
| TO | 5,467,802 | 2,932,426 | 3,829,000 |
| P/L | (214,850) | (12,267) | 170,000 |
| NW | 386,157 | 555,270 | 565,000 |
| WC | 235,066 | 462,105 | 438,000 |
| Emp. | 99 | 78 | 55 |

DUNS 42-466-0124
## Utility Regulator
Queen House 14 Queen Street, Belfast BT1 6ED
**Tel:** 028-9031-1575
**Web:** www.uregni.gov.uk
**Proprietorship**
**Line of Business:** Trade assoc & regulatory bodies
**Proprietor:** Ms A Boyle
**US SIC:** 4911, 4925
**UK SIC:** 16101, 25670
**Employees:** 70

DUNS 51-568-2461
## Utilitywise Plc
30-31 Long Row, South Shields, Tyne and Wear NE33 1JA
**Tel:** 08706260559
**Web:** www.utilitywise.com
**Reg No:** 5849580 **Estd:** 2006 Public Limited Company
**Line of Business:** Distribution and trade in electricity
**Issued Capital:** £6,187,598
**Directors:** T P Maxfield, J Kempster, A Richardson, J P Middleton, G Thompson, R Feigen, P Hailes
**Co. Secretary:** Jonathan Kempster
**US SIC:** 4911 **UK SIC:** 16101
**Auditors:** BDO LLP

| | 31-07-14 | 31-07-13 | 31-07-12 |
|---|---|---|---|
| TO | 48,641,855 | 25,256,142 | 14,382,806 |
| P/L | 11,367,963 | 6,215,419 | 3,468,072 |
| NW | 14,432,157 | 4,700,402 | 8,499,873 |
| WC | 12,020,759 | 3,647,036 | 6,223,535 |
| Emp. | 745 | 452 | 226 |

DUNS 52-038-8943
## Utilize Plc
Utilize House, Romford, Essex RM3 8XB
**Tel:** 08453666081 **Fax:** 01708-446083
**Web:** www.utilize.co.uk
**Reg No:** 3405211 **VAT No:** 701308779
**Estd:** 1997 Public Limited Company
**Line of Business:** Computer systems and software (sales)
**Issued Capital:** £21,825
**Directors:** D Coates, W S Davies, G R Hocking
**Co. Secretary:** Colin Davies

**Responsibilities**
**Senior:** A Sorrell *(Sales Director)*
**Finance:** Yvonne Creasey *(Accounts Manager)*
**Sales:** A Sorrell *(Sales Director)*
**HR:** Yvonne Creasey *(Accounts Manager)*
**Health & Safety:** Yvonne Creasey *(Accounts Manager)*
**Purchasing:** Yvonne Creasey *(Accounts Manager)*
**US SIC:** 7379 **UK SIC:** 83940
**Auditors:** Hern & Co

| | 30-11-13 | 30-11-12 | 30-11-11 |
|---|---|---|---|
| TO | 6,381,953 | 6,666,492 | 6,276,951 |
| P/L | 141,689 | 79,510 | 150,339 |
| NW | 321,297 | 89,215 | (171,934) |
| WC | 610,817 | 289,114 | 128,555 |
| Emp. | 63 | 68 | 65 |

DUNS 23-933-0314
## Utilyx Ltd
(**Subsidiary of:** Mitie Group Plc)
55 North Wharf Road, London W2 1LA
**Tel:** 02070878622
**Web:** www.utilyx.com
**Reg No:** 3922833 **Estd:** 2000 Private Limited Company
**Line of Business:** Energy conservation consultants
**Issued Capital:** £21,100
**Directors:** G Di-Vita, Ms R Mcgregor-Smith, R M Stokes, P W Stirland, Ms S C Baxter, Ms J L Butlin, P Nisbet
**Co. Secretary:**
Mitie Company Secretarial Servic
**Responsibilities**
**Finance:** Rick Freedman *(Financial Director)*, Helen Protopapas *(Finance Director)*
**Admin:** Claire Keating *(Office Manager)*, Samara Mcrae *(Office Manager)*
**IT:** Adam Belson *(IT Manager)*
**Facilities:** Samara Mcrae *(Office Manager)*
**US SIC:** 4911 **UK SIC:** 16101
**Auditors:** Berg Kaprow Lewis LLP
**Bankers:** Barclays Bank Plc (20-00-00)

| | 31-03-14 | 31-03-13 | 31-03-12 |
|---|---|---|---|
| TO | 10,222,000 | 8,905,000 | 7,261,000 |
| P/L | 2,781,000 | 2,831,000 | 149,000 |
| NW | 6,587,000 | 4,449,000 | 1,835,000 |
| WC | 6,153,000 | 4,912,000 | 1,924,000 |
| Emp. | 98 | 65 | 63 |

DUNS 34-889-0245
## Utopia Furniture Ltd.
(**Subsidiary of:** Utopia Bathroom Group Ltd)
Unit 29 Springvale Way, Bilston, West Midlands WV14 0GL
**Tel:** 01902-406400 **Fax:** 01902-406401
**Web:** www.utopiagroup.com
**Reg No:** 2826071 **VAT No:** 864443215
**Estd:** 1993 Private Limited Company
**Line of Business:** Representative office
**Export Sales:** £285,000
**Issued Capital:** £20,000
**Directors:** M A Oldham, D W Conn, I W Hall
**Co. Secretary:** St Pauls Secretaries Limited
**Responsibilities**
**Senior:** Helen Bray *(Manager)*, Joanne Brooke *(Manager)*
**HR:** Adraina Jones *(Human Resources Manager)*
**US SIC:** 2517 **UK SIC:** 46714
**Auditors:** Ormerod Rutter Ltd
**Bankers:** HSBC Bank plc (40-43-03)

| | 30-06-13 | 30-06-12 | 30-06-11 |
|---|---|---|---|
| TO | 14,827,000 | 15,093,000 | 14,775,822 |
| P/L | (326,000) | 412,000 | 254,832 |
| NW | 6,711,000 | 6,990,000 | 6,217,291 |
| WC | 6,282,000 | 6,612,000 | 5,806,702 |
| Emp. | 163 | 164 | 166 |

DUNS 73-936-4131
## Utopia Leisure Ltd
Rowhill Grange, Rowhill Road, Dartford, Kent DA2 7QH
**Tel:** 01322615136 **Fax:** 01322-615137
**Web:** www.utopialeisure.co.uk
**Reg No:** 2942989 **Estd:** 1994 Private Limited Company
**Line of Business:** Health clubs
**Trading Style:** Rowhill Grange Hotel & Spa
**Issued Capital:** £5,725,002
**Directors:** Ms D Hinchcliffe, P S Hinchcliffe
**Co. Secretary:** Michael Thomas
**Responsibilities**
**Senior:** Karen Crowhurst *(Manager)*
**Marketing:** Lindsey Kinniburgh *(Marketing Manager)*
**US SIC:** 7299 **UK SIC:** 98902
**Auditors:** Arthur Andersen
**Bankers:** Barclays Bank Plc (20-25-69)

| | 29-09-13 | 30-09-12 | 02-09-11 |
|---|---|---|---|
| TO | 12,788,238 | 11,707,020 | 11,415,574 |
| P/L | 2,443,385 | 1,677,339 | 2,195,883 |
| NW | 17,031,910 | 15,177,672 | 13,940,881 |
| WC | (2,124,977) | (2,577,584) | (2,631,343) |
| Emp. | 303 | 291 | 279 |

DUNS 23-951-0766 **Imp**
## Utopia Tableware Ltd
Glass Works, Park Road, Chesterfield, Derbyshire S42 5UY
**Tel:** 01246-858-800 **Fax:** 01246-858-801
**Web:** www.utopia-tableware.com
**Reg No:** 3940440 **Estd:** 2000 Private Limited Company
**Line of Business:** Glass engravers and decorators
**Issued Capital:** £158,400
**Directors:** Ms K A Oldershaw, M T Rammell
**Co. Secretary:**
York Place Company Secretaries L
**Responsibilities**
**Finance:** Chris Wild *(Financial Manager)*
**Sales:** Lee Jones *(National Sales Manager)*
**US SIC:** 3231 **UK SIC:** 24791
**Auditors:** Barber Harrison & Platt
**Bankers:** Hsbc Invoice Finance (uk) Ltd (40-61-35)

| | 31-08-13 | 31-08-12 | 31-08-11 |
|---|---|---|---|
| TO | 27,042,594 | 25,520,031 | 24,161,516 |
| P/L | 2,055,237 | 1,291,137 | 1,149,533 |
| NW | 2,887,321 | 2,572,115 | 1,638,418 |
| WC | 1,758,170 | 1,493,059 | 785,884 |
| Emp. | 68 | 87 | 77 |

DUNS 34-768-6680
## Utopian (One) Ltd
(**Subsidiary of:** Ulysses Leisure Ltd)
Morag Polmear Commercial Lawyer, Newcastle-Upon-Tyne, Tyne and Wear NE2 1NH
**Tel:** 01322-667433
**Reg No:** 5569645 **Estd:** 2005 Private Limited Company
**Line of Business:** Bars
**Issued Capital:** £1
**Directors:** R F Senior, C A Hornsby
**US SIC:** 5813 **UK SIC:** 66200

| | 31-12-13 | 31-12-12 | 31-12-11 |
|---|---|---|---|
| TO | N/A | 2,130,165 | N/A |
| P/L | N/A | (166,957) | N/A |
| NW | (5,025,955) | (5,671,187) | (5,504,230) |
| WC | (4,926,020) | (5,628,798) | (1,736,443) |

DUNS 21-041-4778
## Uttam Direct
13-15 Gorst Road, London NW10 6LA
**Tel:** 02089612299
**Web:** www.yumidirect.co.uk
**Estd:** 2012 Proprietorship
**Line of Business:** Representative office
**Responsibilities**
**Senior:** Uttam Nepal *(Chief Executive Officer)*
**US SIC:** 5961 **UK SIC:** 65600
**Employees:** 200

DUNS 42-442-3242
## Uttlesford District Council
Council Offices, London Road, Saffron Walden, Essex CB11 4ER
**Tel:** 01799510510
**Web:** www.uttlesford.gov.uk
**Estd:** 1974
**Line of Business:** Local government
**Principals:** J B Dickson *(Financial)*, K Ivory
**Responsibilities**
**Senior:** Claire Croft *(Office Manager)*, Jason Dear *(Executive)*, Eileen Evans *(Chairman)*, John Farnell *(Executive)*, Sue Hayden *(Community Development Officer)*, Cllr Hicks *(Chairman)*, Sue Knight *(Animal Warden)*, Sue Russell *(Executive)*, Cllr Sadler *(Member)*, Clive Theobold *(Executive)*, Cllr Walters *(Chairman)*, Peter Wilcock *(Board Member)*, Alyson Wilson *(Manager)*
**Finance:** Philip O'Dell *(Head of Finance)*
**Marketing:** Roger Harborough *(Director of Public Services)*
**Admin:** Claire Croft *(Office Manager)*, J Jonrs *(Office Manager)*
**HR:** Diane Burridge *(Director, Operations)*
**Health & Safety:** Yasser Alromisse *(Health and Safety Executive)*, Martin Ford *(Health and Safety Executive)*
**Operations:** Lisa Lipscombe *(Emergency Planning Officer)*, Ron Pridham *(Head of Street Services)*
**Purchasing:** Claire Croft *(Office Manager)*
**Engineering:** Helen Howells *(Technical Engineer)*, Phil Hunt *(Engineer)*, Richard Snape *(Building Surveyor)*
**Branches:** Uttlesford District Council, Museum Street, Saffron Walden, Essex CB10 1BN
**US SIC:** 9121 **UK SIC:** 91110
**Employees:** 300

DUNS 36-798-7260
## Uttoxeter Leisure Centre
Oldfields Road, Uttoxeter, Staffordshire ST14 7QL
**Tel:** 01283508160
**Web:** www.eaststaffsbc.gov.uk
**Estd:** 1985 Proprietorship
**Line of Business:** Aerobics

**Proprietor:** A Wyles
**Responsibilities**
**Marketing:** Nathan Gallagher *(Sales & Marketing Manager)*
**Sales:** Nathan Gallagher *(Sales & Marketing Manager)*
**US SIC:** 7999 **UK SIC:** 97913
**Employees:** 50

DUNS 21-939-6459
## Utv Media Plc
Ormeau Road, Belfast BT7 1EB
**Tel:** 02890328122 **Fax:** 02890246695
**Web:** www.utvmedia.com
**Reg No:** 0065086NI **Estd:** 2007 Private Limited Company
**Line of Business:** Management activities of other non-financial holding companies not elsewhere classified
**Trading Style:** Utv Media
**Issued Capital:** £4,795,126
**Directors:** Ms R K Brennan, A Anson, Ms H Kirkpatrick, R N Huntingford, C L Mcconville, S W Taunton, J Mccann, S Kirkpatrick
**Co. Secretary:** Norman Mckeown
**Responsibilities**
**Senior:** Heather Beattie *(Business Services Manager)*, John McCann *(Chief Executive Officer)*, John McGuckian *(Non-Executive Chairman)*, Norman McKeown *(Finance Director)*, Ronan McManamy *(Managing Director UTV Radio I)*, Shane Reihill *(Non-Executive Director)*
**Finance:** Norman McKeown *(Finance Director)*, Carmel Mullan *(Group Financial Controller)*
**Marketing:** Judith Hill *(Journalist)*
**US SIC:** 6711, 8811
**UK SIC:** 83962, 99000
**Auditors:** Ernst & Young LLP
**Bankers:** First Trust Bank (aib Group (uk) Plc) (93-84-24)

| | 31-12-13 | 31-12-12 | 31-12-11 |
|---|---|---|---|
| TO | 107,771,000 | 120,105,000 | 121,551,000 |
| P/L | 16,901,000 | 20,981,000 | (21,657,000) |
| NW | (76,611,000) | (88,058,000) | (90,628,000) |
| WC | 5,483,000 | 4,469,000 | (8,843,000) |
| Emp. | 994 | 980 | 942 |

DUNS 21-732-4457
## Uwe Students' Union
Frenchay Campus, Coldharbour Lane, Bristol, Avon BS16 1QY
**Fax:** 01173-282989
**Web:** www.uwe.ac.uk
**Reg No:** 7675253 **Estd:** 2011 Private Company Limited By Guarantee
**Line of Business:** Business and management consultancy activities not elsewhere classified
**Directors:** P J Brasted, Ms S V Oliver, Ms H Khan, C Pocock, C F Roper, Ms R Greenup, Mrs C Sinfield, A Harding
**Responsibilities**
**Senior:** Joshua Clark *(Director)*, James Clune *(Director)*, Nerys Neath *(Membership Services Manager)*
**US SIC:** 7392 **UK SIC:** 83951
**Bankers:** National Westminster Bank Plc (60-02-38)

| | 31-07-14 | 31-07-13 | 31-07-12 |
|---|---|---|---|
| TO | 5,231,224 | 5,183,575 | 5,163,178 |
| P/L | 57,830 | 135,960 | 134,585 |
| NW | 919,644 | 861,813 | 725,853 |
| WC | 302,443 | 380,610 | 414,532 |
| Emp. | 458 | 379 | 99 |

DUNS 22-512-5723
## Uxbridge College
Park Road, Uxbridge, Middlesex UB8 1NQ
**Tel:** 01895853333
**Web:** www.uxbridgecollege.ac.uk
**VAT No:** 627109450 **Estd:** 1998
**Line of Business:** Training services
**Principals:** S Mccormick *(Financial)*, Ms R Davies
**Responsibilities**
**Senior:** Darrell Desouza *(Chairman)*, Larraine Smith *(Principal)*, Doreen West *(Manager)*
**Finance:** Sara Djili *(Director, Finance)*, Stephen McCormick *(Financial Director)*
**Marketing:** Martyn Silver *(Section Manager, Vocational Bu)*, Giles Strachan *(Partnership Manager)*
**Health & Safety:** David Bradford *(Estates Manager)*
**Facilities:** David Bradford *(Estates Manager)*
**Operations:** David Bradford *(Estates Manager)*
**Purchasing:** David Bradford *(Estates Manager)*
**Branches:** Uxbridge College, Movianto Uk Ltd, 1 Progress Park, Bedford, Bedfordshire MK42 9XE
**US SIC:** 8221, 8299
**UK SIC:** 93100, 93300
**Employees:** 494

DUNS 23-680-9950
## Uxbridge High School
The Greenway, Uxbridge, Middlesex UB8 2PR
**Tel:** 01895-234060
**Web:** www.uhs.org.uk
**Estd:** 1900
**Line of Business:** Schools (local authority)
**Directors:** P Lang, M Trowell, Ms M Marshall
**Responsibilities**
**Senior:** Leslie Carroll *(Business Manager)*
**US SIC:** 8211 **UK SIC:** 93200
**Employees:** 100

DUNS 28-836-6107
## Uxbridge Masonic Hall Ltd
Western House, 4a Hercies Road, Uxbridge, Middlesex UB10 9NA
**Tel:** 01895235582
**Web:** www.uxbridge-masonic-centre.co.uk
**Reg No:** 0431979 **Estd:** 1947 Private Limited Company
**Line of Business:** Activities of other membership organisations not elsewhere classified
**Issued Capital:** £14,327
**Directors:** G A Curran, R G Calderwood, G M Collins, M J Owen, P J Craker, R J Paulden, A G Symes
**Co. Secretary:** Michael Owen
**US SIC:** 8999 **UK SIC:** 83954
**Auditors:** P.A. Cook & Co
**Bankers:** Barclays Bank Plc (20-89-16)

| | 31-07-14 | 31-07-13 | 31-07-12 |
|---|---|---|---|
| TO | 236,683 | 228,764 | 228,648 |
| P/L | (6,166) | 7,998 | 8,509 |
| NW | 923,346 | 929,512 | 921,514 |
| WC | 32,268 | 46,500 | 33,292 |

DUNS 23-222-8726
## Uxbridge Technical College
Park Road, Uxbridge, Middlesex UB8 1NQ
**Tel:** 01895853605
**Web:** www.uxbridgecollege.ac.uk
**Reg No:** 0235086 **Estd:** 1964
**Line of Business:** Estate agents
**US SIC:** 8221 **UK SIC:** 93100
**Employees:** 350

DUNS 23-894-4586
## Uyr Ltd
15-17 Langthwaite Road, Pontefract, West Yorkshire WF9 3AP
**Tel:** 01977655899 **Fax:** 01132879878
**Web:** www.uyr.co.uk
**Reg No:** 3885328 **Estd:** 2011 Private Limited Company
**Line of Business:** Printers on plastics and other surfaces
**Trading Style:** Uyr Design
**Issued Capital:** £1
**Director:** A A Wood
**Co. Secretary:** Dan Prescott
**US SIC:** 2752, 7319, 2753
**UK SIC:** 47544, 83800, 47545
**Auditors:** Walker Associates

| | 31-03-14 | 31-03-13 | 31-03-12 |
|---|---|---|---|
| TA | 1,958,850 | 2,054,351 | 1,197,222 |
| NW | 574,806 | 537,384 | 406,425 |
| WC | (223,607) | (295,019) | 13,941 |

DUNS 45-847-7577 **Imp**
## Uys Ltd
(**Subsidiary of:** Honda Motor Co. Ltd.)
Garsington Road, Cowley, Oxford, Oxfordshire OX4 2BW
**Tel:** 01865-334300
**Web:** www.uys.ltd.uk
**Reg No:** 3194438 **Estd:** 1996 Private Limited Company
**Line of Business:** Manufacture of parts and accessories for motor vehicles and their engines
**Issued Capital:** £3,000,000
**Directors:** M Okamoto, K Okamoto, K Tamura, N Maegawa, A Nakamura
**Co. Secretary:** Nigel Smith
**Responsibilities**
**Senior:** Yoichi Ayata *(Manager)*, Takashi Yamamoto *(Manager)*
**Health & Safety:** Bob Stevenson *(Health & Safety Officer)*
**US SIC:** 3714 **UK SIC:** 35300
**Auditors:** Ernst & Young LLP
**Bankers:** The Bank Of Tokyo-Mitsubishi, Ltd (60-01-09)

| | 31-03-14 | 31-03-13 | 31-03-12 |
|---|---|---|---|
| TO | 35,247,000 | 46,785,000 | 39,241,000 |
| P/L | 1,416,000 | 1,781,000 | (161,000) |
| NW | 3,873,000 | 2,873,000 | 1,631,000 |
| WC | 13,969,000 | 13,561,000 | 10,748,000 |
| Emp. | 220 | 270 | 181 |

DUNS 49-426-3551 Imp
## Uyt Ltd
Renown Avenue, Coventry Business Park, Coventry, West Midlands CV5 6UF
**Tel:** 02476-671-400 **Fax:** 02476-671-411
**Web:** www.uyt.ltd.uk
**Reg No:** 3141025 **VAT No:** 663582219
**Estd:** 1995 Private Limited Company
**Line of Business:** Other manufacturing not elsewhere classified
**Issued Capital:** £8,000,000
**Directors:** K Tamura, Y Ota, K Kawase, S Mayumi, T Yoshida, T Arai, A Kaneda, T Enchi
**Responsibilities**
**Senior:** Hiroyuki Houshi *(Manager)*, Tetsuya Kitamura *(Manager)*, Hiroshi Matsumoto *(Manager)*, Noriyuki Miyaoka *(Manager)*, Haruhisa Nihashi *(Manager)*, Yoshimasa Ota *(Manager)*, Mayumi Shaker *(Manager)*, Masahito Taniguchi *(Manager)*
**Purchasing:** Carol Henderson *(Purchasing Manager)*
**US SIC:** 3999 **UK SIC:** 49590
**Auditors:** Deloitte & Touche LLP
**Bankers:** Barclays Bank Plc (20-03-80)

| | 31-03-14 | 31-03-13 | 31-03-11 |
|---|---|---|---|
| TO | 40,007,000 | 67,111,000 | 34,824,000 |
| P/L | (4,582,000) | (1,789,000) | (2,476,000) |
| NW | (8,644,000) | (4,062,000) | (2,273,000) |
| WC | (28,658,000) | (24,997,000) | (24,444,000) |
| Emp. | 380 | 435 | 352 |

# V

DUNS 50-056-3283
## V A Technology Ltd
Halesfield 9, Telford, Shropshire TF7 4QW
**Tel:** 01952-585252 **Fax:** 01952-585288
**Web:** www.vatech.co.uk
**Reg No:** 2316924 **VAT No:** 489059886
**Estd:** 1988 Private Limited Company
**Line of Business:** Manufacture of other special purpose machinery not elsewhere classified
**Export Sales:** £9,570,944
**Issued Capital:** £30,000
**Directors:** S A Bergin, S Byrne, A Hughes
**Co. Secretary:** James Byrne
**Responsibilities**
**IT:** Chris Mark *(IT Manager)*
**US SIC:** 3559 **UK SIC:** 32863
**Auditors:** RSM Tenon Audit Ltd
**Bankers:** Barclays Bank Plc (20-85-46)

| | 31-07-14 | 31-07-13 | 31-07-12 |
|---|---|---|---|
| TO | 13,046,625 | 11,646,803 | 9,942,194 |
| P/L | 3,989,437 | 4,058,038 | 3,556,523 |
| NW | 17,264,943 | 15,821,195 | 13,109,957 |
| WC | 15,825,360 | 14,343,873 | 11,511,475 |
| Emp. | 75 | 72 | 75 |

DUNS 29-672-1301
## V & T (Plumbing & Heating Services) Ltd
Whaley Road, Barugh, Barnsley, South Yorkshire S75 1HT
**Tel:** 01226-243708
**Reg No:** 1998407 **VAT No:** 436593133
**Estd:** 1975 Private Limited Company
**Line of Business:** Plumbers
**Issued Capital:** £60
**Principals:** A J Rhodes *(Managing)*, P D Young, M R Rhodes, A M Ward, D P Rhodes
**Responsibilities**
**Senior:** Beverly Powell *(Manager)*, Anthony Roads *(Manager)*
**Branches:** V & T (Plumbing & Heating Services) Ltd, 16 Troutbeck Gardens, Gateshead, Tyne and Wear NE9 6PU
**US SIC:** 1711 **UK SIC:** 50300
**Auditors:** Reed Smith Accountancy Ltd
**Bankers:** Lloyds TSB Bank plc (30-10-47)

| | 31-03-14 | 31-03-13 | 31-03-12 |
|---|---|---|---|
| TA | 2,550,225 | 2,834,208 | 3,124,516 |
| NW | 2,103,018 | 2,220,633 | 2,191,037 |
| WC | 1,366,261 | 1,475,175 | 1,495,301 |

DUNS 21-313-4653
## V & T (Plumbing Central-Heating & Bathrooms) Ltd
2a Colliers Way, Clayton West, Huddersfield, West Yorkshire HD8 9TR
**Tel:** 01484866866 **Fax:** 01484860123
**Web:** www.aqua-interiors.com
**Reg No:** 1221496 **VAT No:** 182640856
**Estd:** 1975 Private Limited Company
**Line of Business:** Plumbers
**Trading Style:** Aqua Interiors
**Issued Capital:** £9,200
**Principals:** D G Rayner *(Financial)*, R M King, L G Dawson
**Co. Secretary:** Ms Judith Rayner

**Responsibilities**
**IT:** Mathew Dews *(IT Manager)*
**US SIC:** 1711, 1796
**UK SIC:** 50300, 50400
**Auditors:** Deloitte & Touche LLP
**Bankers:** HSBC Bank plc (40-19-17)

| | 31-03-13 | 31-03-12 | 31-03-11 |
|---|---|---|---|
| TO | 15,962,569 | 14,964,837 | 13,221,700 |
| P/L | 159,246 | 107,556 | 22,114 |
| NW | 1,459,518 | 1,342,335 | 1,266,641 |
| WC | 2,251,227 | 2,162,598 | 2,078,640 |
| Emp. | 132 | 143 | 142 |

DUNS 29-492-2976 Exp
## V Band Ltd
**(Subsidiary of:** Silver Lake Partners Ii L.P.)
Retford Hospital North Road, Retford, Nottinghamshire DN22 7XF
**Tel:** 01777701637 **Fax:** 0171-335-1301
**Web:** www.talltreesgpsurgery.co.uk
**Reg No:** 1855636 **VAT No:** 415551763
**Estd:** 1985 Private Limited Company
**Line of Business:** Medical practice activities
**Export Markets:** Europe; Africa; Asia
**Issued Capital:** £50,050
**Directors:** Mrs M Wall, D Hart
**Co. Secretary:** Ms Linda Pennington-Benton
**Branches:** V Band Ltd, Unit 12, 33-34 Eastbury Road, London E6 6GP
**US SIC:** 8011, 1731
**UK SIC:** 95300, 50300
**Auditors:** Ernst & Young LLP
**Bankers:** National Westminster Bank Plc (50-00-00)

| | 30-09-13 | 30-09-12 | 30-09-11 |
|---|---|---|---|
| TA | 880,680 | 880,680 | 880,680 |
| NW | 880,680 | 880,680 | 880,680 |

DUNS 42-366-6606
## V C C P Ltd
**(Subsidiary of:** Chime Communications Plc)
Greencoat House, Francis Street, London SW1P 1DH
**Tel:** 02075929331 **Fax:** 02078025801
**Web:** www.vccpdigital.co.uk
**Reg No:** 4354397 **Estd:** 1902 Private Limited Company
**Line of Business:** Advertising activities not elsewhere classified
**Issued Capital:** £50,000
**Directors:** I M Priest, Ms M J Frost, A M Coleman
**Co. Secretary:** Robert Davison
**US SIC:** 7319 **UK SIC:** 83800
**Auditors:** Roger Lugg & Co

| | 31-12-13 | 31-12-12 | 31-12-11 |
|---|---|---|---|
| TO | N/A | 61,044,059 | 49,574,400 |
| P/L | 158,116 | 1,146,977 | 2,412,819 |
| NW | 50,000 | 900,291 | 1,558,982 |
| WC | N/A | (1,166,156) | 264,801 |
| Emp. | N/A | 220 | 176 |

DUNS 34-625-1619
## V Cars Ltd
Unit 1 Hargreaves Road, Swindon, Wiltshire SN25 5AZ
**Tel:** 01793701701 **Fax:** 01793-701100
**Web:** www.v-cars.com
**Reg No:** 5431537 **Estd:** 2005 Private Limited Company
**Line of Business:** Taxis and private hire vehicles
**Issued Capital:** £25,000
**Director:** Mrs A J Ridings
**Co. Secretary:** Christopher Vaughan
**Responsibilities**
**Senior:** Paul Huntley *(Manager)*, David Scaramanga *(Manager)*, Erwin Vinall *(Manager)*
**Branches:** V Cars Ltd, 11 Cheltenham Street, Bath, Avon BA2 3EX
**US SIC:** 4121 **UK SIC:** 72200

| | 31-03-14 | 30-09-12 | 30-03-11 |
|---|---|---|---|
| TA | 3,578,205 | 3,025,048 | 2,858,747 |
| NW | 64,294 | 516,328 | 641,493 |
| WC | 42,040 | 628,181 | 553,951 |

DUNS 42-449-5534 Imp
## V Group International Ltd
Units 1-7 Erica Road, Stacey Bushes, Milton Keynes, Buckinghamshire MK12 6HS
**Tel:** 08706070196 **Fax:** 01908-220-911
**Web:** www.vgroupinternational.com
**Reg No:** 4437215 **Estd:** 2004 Private Limited Company
**Line of Business:** Other wholesale
**Issued Capital:** £100
**Directors:** Miss G Nash, Ms J Moores, J Nash, B S Ackers
**Co. Secretary:** Martyn Nash
**US SIC:** 5199, 5081
**UK SIC:** 61900, 61490
**Auditors:** Streets Audit LLP
**Bankers:** HSBC Bank plc (40-08-39)

| | 31-12-13 | 31-12-12 | 31-12-11 |
|---|---|---|---|
| TO | 15,227,707 | 8,632,246 | N/A |
| P/L | 843,942 | 1,052,422 | N/A |
| NW | 2,724,794 | 2,102,265 | 1,477,813 |
| WC | 1,571,221 | 1,510,519 | 964,971 |
| Emp. | 100 | 30 | N/A |

DUNS 54-878-5906
## V I P Cabs
160 Market St West, Preston, Lancashire PR1 2EU
**Tel:** 08435156080
**Estd:** 1988 Partnership
**Line of Business:** Taxis and private hire vehicles
**Partners:** W Jones, Mrs C Howorth
**US SIC:** 4121 **UK SIC:** 72200
**Employees:** 50

DUNS 21-230-7386
## V M D
Central Veterinary Laboratory, Woodham Lane, Addlestone, Surrey KT15 3NB
**Tel:** 01932-336911
**Web:** www.vmd.defra.gov.uk
**Estd:** 2002 Proprietorship
**Line of Business:** Central government
**Proprietor:** S Dean
**Responsibilities**
**Senior:** Jackie Atkinson *(Pharmaceutical Licensee)*, Peter Borriello *(Chief Executive Officer)*, Linda Hamilton *(Head of Finance)*
**Finance:** Carol Underhill *(Accounts Administrator)*, Caroline Watson *(Finance Manager)*
**Admin:** Lorraine Oakley *(Directors Support Assistant)*, Natalie Shilling *(Licencing Administration Manag)*, Carol Underhill *(Accounts Administrator)*, Joanne Young *(Licensing Administrative Assis)*
**IT:** Dan Finn *(IT Manager)*, Neil Patterson *(Computer Manager)*, Luke Wakefield *(IT Manager)*
**Operations:** Eric Crutcher *(Head of Residues Surveillance)*, Andrea Ford *(Quality Management)*, Lea Reynolds *(Operations, Legislation Execut)*
**US SIC:** 9121 **UK SIC:** 91110
**Employees:** 150

DUNS 21-231-7729
## V Premchand
Winyates Centre, Redditch, Worcestershire B98 0NR
**Tel:** 01527513888
**Web:** www.winyateshc.co.uk
**Estd:** 1978
**Line of Business:** Doctors
**Responsibilities**
**Senior:** Julie Ingram *(Practice Manager)*
**US SIC:** 8011 **UK SIC:** 95300
**Employees:** 50

DUNS 21-592-5234
## V T Group
Third Floor Motor Point Arena, Mary Ann Street, Cardiff, South Glamorgan CF10 2EQ
**Tel:** 02920239112
**Web:** www.babcock.co.uk
**Estd:** 2011 Proprietorship
**Line of Business:** Training providers
**Proprietor:** Ms A Maguire Lewis
**US SIC:** 8299 **UK SIC:** 93300
**Employees:** 50

DUNS 50-963-8797 Imp
## V W Heritage Parts Centre Ltd
9-11 Consort Way, Burgess Hill, West Sussex RH15 9TJ
**Fax:** 01444254841
**Web:** www.vwheritage.com
**Reg No:** 3294341 **VAT No:** 475767101
**Estd:** 2013 Private Limited Company
**Line of Business:** Sale of motor vehicle parts and accessories
**Export Sales:** £1,975,276
**Trading Style:** Street Style & Power
**Issued Capital:** £1,000
**Directors:** M Rickard, B R Dines, P Howard, D W Ward
**Co. Secretary:** Ms Nicola Swaden
**US SIC:** 5531 **UK SIC:** 65100
**Auditors:** Feist Hedgethorne Ltd
**Bankers:** National Westminster Bank Plc (60-17-01)

| | 30-04-13 | 30-04-12 | 30-04-11 |
|---|---|---|---|
| TO | 7,901,103 | 7,684,671 | N/A |
| P/L | 1,178,824 | 1,078,080 | N/A |
| NW | 3,168,739 | 2,793,251 | 2,372,498 |
| WC | 2,955,878 | 2,571,975 | 2,143,026 |
| Emp. | 51 | 52 | N/A |

DUNS 50-460-5502
## V1 Ltd
**(Subsidiary of:** Advanced Computer Software Group Plc)
Pentland House, Wilmslow, Cheshire SK9 2GH
**Tel:** 01625-856500
**Web:** www.versionone.co.uk
**Reg No:** 2443078 **VAT No:** 548338713
**Estd:** 1989 Private Limited Company
**Line of Business:** Computer software (development)
**Trading Style:** V1 Limited
**Issued Capital:** £100
**Directors:** Ms V Murria, P D Gibson, Mrs B A Firth, G L Millward, Ms B B Firth
**Responsibilities**
**Senior:** Jeanette Martin *(Manager)*
**Marketing:** Liz Ebbrell *(Public Relations Manager)*
**Sales:** Sarah Acton-Hughes *(Sales Manager)*
**HR:** Sarah Coke *(Head of Professional Services)*
**US SIC:** 7379 **UK SIC:** 83940
**Auditors:** A.J. Accountancy Services

| | 28-02-14 | 28-02-13 | 29-02-12 |
|---|---|---|---|
| TO | 7,594,000 | 5,499,000 | 5,220,000 |
| P/L | 2,045,000 | 2,112,000 | 1,904,000 |
| NW | (579,000) | 7,483,000 | 5,796,000 |
| WC | (597,000) | 7,458,000 | 5,764,000 |
| Emp. | 56 | 47 | 43 |

DUNS 23-564-3264 Exp
## Va Tech (Uk) Ltd
**(Subsidiary of:** Siemens Ag)
North Farm Road, Hebburn, Tyne and Wear NE31 1LX
**Tel:** 0191-401-5555 **Fax:** 01914015353
**Reg No:** 3562487 **Estd:** 1998 Private Limited Company
**Line of Business:** Burglar alarm systems
**Issued Capital:** £48,000,000
**Directors:** G S Weir, P Maher
**Co. Secretary:** Ms Helen Carless
**US SIC:** 3643, 3629
**UK SIC:** 34203, 34350
**Auditors:** KPMG Audit PLC
**Bankers:** National Westminster Bank Plc (50-00-00)

| | 30-09-13 | 30-09-12 | 30-09-11 |
|---|---|---|---|
| TA | 118,175,000 | 118,339,000 | 118,196,000 |
| P/L | (745,000) | (953,000) | (748,000) |
| NW | 54,265,000 | 54,836,000 | 55,549,000 |
| WC | (235,000) | 336,000 | (62,451,000) |

DUNS 21-230-2707 Exp
## V.A. Whitley & Co. Ltd
Milward House, Fir Street, Heywood, Lancashire OL10 1NW
**Web:** www.vawhitley.co.uk
**Reg No:** 0474394 **VAT No:** 146755346
**Estd:** 1949 Private Limited Company
**Line of Business:** Catering food and drink suppliers
**Trading Style:** V.A. Whitley & Co. Ltd
**Issued Capital:** £999
**Directors:** Ms E M Rogers, M R Wallace, A M Rogers, Miss C H Rogers
**Co. Secretary:** Christopher Rogers
**Responsibilities**
**Senior:** Peter Towers *(Distribution Manager)*
**Finance:** Kate Rogers *(Financial Director)*
**Sales:** Mike Wallis *(Sales Manager)*
**Admin:** Stephen Ducksbury *(Accounts Manager)*
**IT:** Stephen Ducksbury *(Accounts Manager)*
**HR:** Kate Rogers *(Financial Director)*
**Branches:** V.a. Whitley & Co. Ltd, Affleck House Unit 12, Mochdre Business Park, Colwyn Bay, Clwyd LL28 5HA
**US SIC:** 5149, 5143, 5146
**UK SIC:** 61700
**Auditors:** Baker Tilly
**Bankers:** Barclays Bank Plc (20-72-67)

| | 30-11-13 | 30-11-12 | 30-11-11 |
|---|---|---|---|
| TO | 20,273,998 | 20,359,868 | 20,993,426 |
| P/L | 493,890 | 441,530 | 533,024 |
| NW | 6,639,855 | 6,242,286 | 5,903,422 |
| WC | 3,949,902 | 3,603,361 | 3,507,722 |
| Emp. | 83 | 80 | 81 |

DUNS 34-708-3128
## V.A.C. Media Ltd
32 North Street, Keighley, West Yorkshire BD21 3SE
**Tel:** 08445610487
**Web:** www.vacmedia.co.uk
**Reg No:** 5512439 **VAT No:** 875567274
**Estd:** 2005 Private Limited Company
**Line of Business:** Computer services
**Issued Capital:** £1,000
**Director:** Dr C S Kumar
**Responsibilities**
**Senior:** Janine Sinclair *(Head of Operations)*
**Operations:** Janine Sinclair *(Head of Operations)*
**US SIC:** 7379, 7374
**UK SIC:** 83940
**Auditors:** TaxAssist Accountants

| | 31-10-13 | 31-10-12 | 31-10-11 |
|---|---|---|---|
| TA | 199,961 | 182,945 | 165,885 |
| NW | 28,071 | 6,448 | (18,480) |
| WC | 57,729 | 21,906 | 14,634 |

DUNS 34-551-7176 Imp
## Vacgen Ltd
**(Subsidiary of:** Gd Intressenter Ab)
Maunsell Road, Castleham Industrial Estate, St Leonards-On-Sea, East Sussex TN38 9NN
**Web:** www.vgscienta.com
**Reg No:** 5361640 **VAT No:** 856106722

**Estd:** 1975 Private Limited Company
**Line of Business:** Manufacturers of scientific machinery and instrument
**Export Sales:** £7,212,310
**Issued Capital:** £1
**Directors:** S Y Yeung, S G Tegendal, R J Shenton
**Co. Secretary:** Goodwille Limited
**Responsibilities**
**Senior:** Christer Beckman *(Manager)*, Senay Ciftci *(Marketing Manager)*, Jan Edhall *(Manager)*, Kjell an *(Director)*
**Marketing:** Senay Ciftci *(Marketing Manager)*
**US SIC:** 3829 **UK SIC:** 37100
**Auditors:** BDO LLP
**Bankers:** Svenska Handelsbanken Ab (publ) (40-51-62)

| | 31-12-13 | 31-12-12 | 31-12-11 |
|---|---|---|---|
| TO | 9,369,227 | 11,525,172 | 12,952,857 |
| P/L | (2,158,942) | 231,418 | 1,060,746 |
| NW | 1,434,101 | 3,422,780 | 4,133,691 |
| WC | (94,775) | 2,119,312 | 2,943,497 |
| Emp. | 127 | 136 | 130 |

DUNS 23-302-9383
## Vacherin Ltd
16-18 Hatton Garden, London EC1N 8AT
**Tel:** 02074042277 **Fax:** 020-7404-8833
**Web:** www.vacherin.com
**Reg No:** 4516461 **Estd:** 2002 Private Limited Company
**Line of Business:** Caterers
**Issued Capital:** £100,000
**Directors:** P J Roker, M F Philpott
**Co. Secretary:** Clive Hetherington
**US SIC:** 5812, 5921
**UK SIC:** 66110, 64200
**Auditors:** Simmons Gainsford LLP
**Bankers:** Coutts & Co (18-00-02)

| | 31-08-13 | 31-08-12 | 31-08-11 |
|---|---|---|---|
| TO | 11,522,582 | 10,914,036 | 9,863,065 |
| P/L | 503,275 | 465,507 | 189,227 |
| NW | 583,567 | 441,888 | 169,935 |
| WC | 552,696 | 393,897 | 124,325 |
| Emp. | 221 | 213 | 202 |

DUNS 42-360-1165
## Vaclensa P L C
Service House, 21 Shield Drive, Manchester M28 2QB
**Tel:** 01617281800 **Fax:** 01617288310
**Web:** www.vaclensa.com
**Reg No:** 4347764 **Estd:** 2010 Public Limited Company
**Line of Business:** Manufacturers and suppliers of industrial machinery
**Issued Capital:** £74,941
**Directors:** J J Foggon, P F Ferguson, I P Miller
**Co. Secretary:** Mark Garrahan
**US SIC:** 3559, 8999
**UK SIC:** 32863, 83954
**Bankers:** Lloyds TSB Bank plc (30-13-90)

| | 28-02-14 | 28-02-13 | 29-02-12 |
|---|---|---|---|
| TO | 12,370,109 | 10,783,007 | 11,081,564 |
| P/L | 179,112 | 208,780 | 167,720 |
| NW | 446,165 | 198,552 | (44,086) |
| WC | (658,023) | (557,752) | (1,344,821) |
| Emp. | 121 | 116 | 110 |

DUNS 21-813-1845 **Imp-Exp**
## Vacu-Lug Traction Tyres Ltd
Gonerby Hill Foot, Grantham, Lincolnshire NG31 8HE
**Tel:** 01476-593095
**Web:** www.vaculug.com
**Reg No:** 0488961 **Estd:** 1950 Private Limited Company
**Line of Business:** Manufacture of rubber products
**Export Markets:** Worldwide; E Europe
**Export Sales:** £512,488
**Trading Style:** Vacu-Lug Tyres, Grumac
**Issued Capital:** £1,556,386
**Directors:** T R Hercock, Mrs A E Collins, Mrs D J Parker, J C Langham
**Co. Secretary:** John Parsons
**Responsibilities**
**Senior:** Carl White *(Manager)*, Ian Woodfinden *(Manager)*, Roy Yeomans *(Business Development Manager)*
**Finance:** John Barten *(Finance Director)*
**Sales:** Dave Alsop *(Fleet Sales Director)*
**IT:** Sharon Flaherty *(Head of IT)*
**Operations:** Brian Barron *(Technical, Production Manager)*
**Branches:** Vacu-Lug Traction Tyres Ltd, Diamond Rd, Norwich, Norfolk NR6 6AW
**US SIC:** 3069 **UK SIC:** 48123
**Auditors:** Duncan & Toplis
**Bankers:** HSBC Bank plc (40-22-19)

| | 31-12-13 | 31-12-12 | 31-12-11 |
|---|---|---|---|
| TO | 24,456,488 | 23,258,954 | 23,216,852 |
| P/L | 590,427 | 234,182 | 239,480 |
| NW | 3,284,442 | 2,009,809 | 2,250,022 |
| WC | 3,632,609 | 3,239,207 | 3,009,939 |
| Emp. | 170 | 173 | 172 |

DUNS 77-909-6366 **Exp**
## Vacuumatic Ltd
8 Brunel Way, Severalls Industrial Park, Colchester, Essex CO4 9QX
**Tel:** 01206841100
**Web:** www.vacuumatic.com
**Reg No:** 5812970 **VAT No:** 879760653
**Estd:** 2006 Private Limited Company
**Line of Business:** Manufacture of machinery for paper and paperboard production
**Issued Capital:** £600
**Directors:** S D Boyd, Mrs P E Curtis
**Responsibilities**
**Finance:** Neil Millard *(Financial Director)*
**Marketing:** Sandra Emde *(Head of Sales & Marketing)*
**Sales:** Mark Booth *(Product Manager)*, Judith Channen *(Sales Office Manager)*, Sandra Emde *(Head of Sales & Marketing)*
**Health & Safety:** Brendon Carr *(Health & Safety Officer)*
**Facilities:** Neil Millard *(Financial Director)*
**Operations:** Brendon Carr *(Health & Safety Officer)*
**US SIC:** 3559 **UK SIC:** 32863
**Auditors:** Albert Goodman
**Bankers:** National Westminster Bank Plc (60-24-37)

| | 30-09-13 | 30-09-12 | 30-09-11 |
|---|---|---|---|
| TA | 2,077,183 | 1,773,537 | 1,711,794 |
| NW | 1,224,979 | 1,079,326 | 924,363 |
| WC | 766,003 | 1,070,077 | 904,679 |

DUNS 21-033-0292
## Vail Williams
Unit 4 Peveril Court 6-8, London Road, Crawley, West Sussex RH10 8JE
**Tel:** 01293-612600
**Web:** www.vailwilliams.com
**Estd:** 2010 Proprietorship
**Line of Business:** Real estate agencies
**Proprietor:** A Osborne
**US SIC:** 6531 **UK SIC:** 83400
**Employees:** 160

DUNS 36-526-9583
## Vail Williams Llp
540 Thames Valley Park, Reading, Berkshire RG6 1RA
**Tel:** 01189097400
**Web:** www.vailwilliams.com
**Reg No:** 0319702OC **Estd:** 2006
**Line of Business:** Building consultants and advisors
**Responsibilities**
**Senior:** Christopher Cave *(Non-designated Limited Liabili)*
**Finance:** Adam Robinson *(Finance Manager)*
**Marketing:** Jenine Timms *(Marketing & Communications Man)*
**IT:** Jeremy Bickers *(IT Director)*
**US SIC:** 6531 **UK SIC:** 83400
**Auditors:** BDO LLP
**Bankers:** National Westminster Bank Plc (60-10-43)

| | 31-05-14 | 31-05-13 | 31-05-12 |
|---|---|---|---|
| TO | 12,183,336 | 11,441,191 | 10,207,241 |
| P/L | 38 | (12,369) | (19,113) |
| NW | (79,748) | (79,785) | (67,416) |
| WC | 3,090,294 | 2,769,956 | 2,137,412 |
| Emp. | 116 | 117 | 115 |

DUNS 50-381-3875
## Vaile Office Cleaning Ltd
Haydons Road, London SW19 8TT
**Fax:** 020-8296-5414
**Web:** www.vocltd.co.uk
**Reg No:** 2390420 **Estd:** 1989 Private Limited Company
**Line of Business:** Cleaning activities not elsewhere classified
**Trading Style:** V O C
**Issued Capital:** £2,000
**Principals:** S P Vaile *(Managing)*, Mrs F E Vaile
**Responsibilities**
**Senior:** Vivien Adams *(General Manager)*
**Marketing:** Fran Notermans *(Commercial Director)*
**Sales:** Fran Notermans *(Commercial Director)*
**Health & Safety:** Fran Notermans *(Commercial Director)*
**Facilities:** Vivien Adams *(General Manager)*
**Operations:** Fran Notermans *(Commercial Director)*
**US SIC:** 7349 **UK SIC:** 92300
**Auditors:** Rutter & Co
**Bankers:** HSBC Bank plc (40-43-26)

| | 31-12-13 | 31-12-12 | 31-12-11 |
|---|---|---|---|
| TO | 902,722 | 944,976 | 879,865 |
| P/L | 116,584 | 118,688 | 104,655 |
| NW | 18,818 | 2,955 | (92,733) |
| WC | 68,752 | 37,516 | (25,563) |
| Emp. | 108 | 110 | 108 |

DUNS 21-740-7188 **Imp**
## Vaillant Industrial Uk Ltd
**(Subsidiary of:** Joh. Vaillant Gmbh & Co. Kg)
Nottingham Road, Belper, Derbyshire DE56 1JT
**Tel:** 01773824141
**Web:** www.vaillant.co.uk
**Reg No:** 1064184 **VAT No:** 648152921
**Estd:** 1972 Private Limited Company
**Line of Business:** Manufacture of furnaces and furnace burners
**Export Sales:** £1,539,000
**Trading Style:** Vaillant Industrial Uk Ltd
**Issued Capital:** £8,800,000
**Directors:** J E Moore, N J Partridge, Dr. J Borkowski, Dr. N Schiedeck, K Kock
**Co. Secretary:** Sundip Bhadal
**Branches:** Bradford North Yorkshire
**US SIC:** 3567 **UK SIC:** 32452
**Auditors:** BDO LLP
**Bankers:** National Westminster Bank Plc (56-00-09)

| | 31-12-13 | 31-12-12 | 31-12-11 |
|---|---|---|---|
| TO | 197,988,000 | 151,823,000 | 168,037,000 |
| P/L | 37,069,000 | 14,265,000 | 21,182,000 |
| NW | 50,287,000 | 32,563,000 | 37,280,000 |
| WC | 44,438,000 | 25,738,000 | 31,249,000 |
| Emp. | 164 | 173 | 192 |

DUNS 21-748-3742 **Imp**
## Vaillant Ltd
**(Subsidiary of:** Joh. Vaillant Gmbh & Co. Kg)
Vallant House, Trident Close, Rochester, Kent ME2 4EZ
**Tel:** 08456022922
**Web:** www.vaillant.co.uk
**Reg No:** 1279010 **VAT No:** 226867729
**Estd:** 1976 Private Limited Company
**Line of Business:** Computer systems and software (sales)
**Issued Capital:** £1,500,000
**Directors:** A Bratz, S V Wakely, K Mathers, J E Moore, Dr C Voigtlaender, N J Partridge
**Co. Secretary:** Stephen Wakely
**Responsibilities**
**Marketing:** Katie Cope *(Marketing Director)*
**Facilities:** Tracey Kavell *(Facilities Officer)*
**Branches:** Vaillant Ltd, Unit D1, Elland Riorges Link, Elland, West Yorkshire HX5 9DG
**US SIC:** 5074 **UK SIC:** 61300
**Auditors:** BDO LLP
**Bankers:** National Westminster Bank Plc (60-40-04)

| | 31-12-13 | 31-12-12 | 31-12-11 |
|---|---|---|---|
| TO | 357,281,000 | 299,151,000 | 279,452,064 |
| P/L | 12,381,000 | 14,943,000 | 14,570,670 |
| NW | 10,633,000 | 12,629,000 | 5,106,525 |
| WC | 19,485,000 | 21,524,000 | 13,791,662 |
| Emp. | 324 | 327 | 343 |

DUNS 21-929-9104 **Imp-Exp**
## Vaisala Ltd
**(Subsidiary of:** Vaisala Oyj)
Elm House, 351 Bristol Road, Birmingham, West Midlands B5 7SW
**Tel:** 01216-831200
**Web:** www.vaisala.com
**Reg No:** 1487125 **VAT No:** 336100011
**Estd:** 1979 Private Limited Company
**Line of Business:** Manufacture of medical, precision and optical instruments, watches and clocks
**Export Sales:** £1,296,000
**Issued Capital:** £240,000
**Principals:** A J Harrison *(Financial)*, K Forsen, G D Hart
**Responsibilities**
**Senior:** Jonathan Lister *(Manager)*
**Marketing:** Rachel Adams *(Sales & Marketing Manager)*, Liz Green *(Marketing Director)*
**Sales:** Rachel Adams *(Sales & Marketing Manager)*
**IT:** Jasdeep Attwal *(IT Support Manager)*
**HR:** Nick Johnson *(Training Manager)*
**Health & Safety:** Caroline Heard *(Health & Safety Officer)*
**Facilities:** Steve Laux *(Facilities Manager)*
**Purchasing:** Meena Rai *(Company Buyer)*
**Fleet:** Hira Choudhury *(Stock Control)*
**Engineering:** Megan Harris *(Production Manager)*
**Branches:** Vaisala Ltd, Unit 9, Swan Lane, Newmarket, Suffolk CB8 7FN
**US SIC:** 3829, 8911, 7399
**UK SIC:** 37100, 83701, 83954
**Auditors:** PricewaterhouseCoopers LLP
**Bankers:** Unibank A/s (40-48-78)

| | 31-12-13 | 31-12-12 | 31-12-11 |
|---|---|---|---|
| TO | 7,726,000 | 9,377,000 | 8,422,000 |
| P/L | 903,000 | 878,000 | 797,000 |
| NW | 3,337,000 | 3,694,000 | 4,320,000 |
| WC | 2,809,000 | 3,073,000 | 3,498,000 |
| Emp. | 70 | 67 | 68 |

DUNS 49-145-7792
## Valad Management Services Ltd
**(Subsidiary of:** Valad Europe Ltd)
Valad Property Group, 64 North Row, London W1K 7DA
**Tel:** 02076596666
**Web:** www.valad.eu
**Reg No:** 3112917 **Estd:** 1995 Private Limited Company
**Line of Business:** Development agencies
**Issued Capital:** £2
**Directors:** F J Kennedy, M J Mccarthy
**Co. Secretary:** Valad Secretarial Services Limit
**Branches:** Valad Management Services Ltd, 15 Abercromby Pl, Edinburgh, Midlothian EH3 6LB
**US SIC:** 6552 **UK SIC:** 85000
**Auditors:** PricewaterhouseCoopers LLP
**Bankers:** Bank Of Scotland (80-20-00)

| | 30-06-14 | 30-06-13 | 30-06-12 |
|---|---|---|---|
| TO | 15,380,750 | 12,154,517 | 14,663,049 |
| P/L | 2,968,048 | 501,200 | (1,147,056) |
| NW | 4,810,518 | 1,685,874 | 977,455 |
| WC | 4,660,235 | 1,483,441 | 858,232 |
| Emp. | 80 | 83 | 81 |

DUNS 21-655-5422
## Valdeco Ltd
Time Technology Park, Blackburn Road, Simonstone, Burnley, Lancashire BB12 7TW
**Tel:** 08003345509
**Reg No:** 7125110 **Estd:** 2010 Private Limited Company
**Line of Business:** Manufacturers general
**Issued Capital:** £395,145
**Directors:** P R Siellet, M A Mader-Horne
**US SIC:** 5133 **UK SIC:** 61600

| | 31-12-13 | 31-12-12 | 31-12-11 |
|---|---|---|---|
| TO | 21,242,879 | 20,180,588 | 20,353,314 |
| P/L | 181,500 | 53,782 | (103,292) |
| NW | 3,752,260 | 3,256,368 | 3,127,014 |
| WC | 1,504,147 | 2,742,604 | 2,434,765 |
| Emp. | 137 | 144 | 139 |

DUNS 21-593-0425
## Vale Brothers
William House, Frederick Street, Walsall, West Midlands WS2 9NJ
**Estd:** 1977 Partnership
**Line of Business:** Riding wear and equestrian supplies
**Partners:** Mrs M Hewitt, H Dabbs
**US SIC:** 3161 **UK SIC:** 44201
**Employees:** 67

DUNS 23-970-7136
## Vale Building Services
Cardiff Road, Cardiff, South Glamorgan CF15 7PR
**Tel:** 029-2081-3183
**Web:** www.valebuild.co.uk
**VAT No:** 359435916 **Estd:** 1988 Proprietorship
**Line of Business:** Builders
**Proprietor:** G Vearncombe
**US SIC:** 1522 **UK SIC:** 50100
**Employees:** 50

DUNS 28-917-4385
## Vale Decorators Uk Ltd
Edwards Lane, Liverpool, Merseyside L24 9HY
**Tel:** 0151-486-7120
**Web:** www.valedecs.co.uk
**Reg No:** 1455042 **VAT No:** 319859414
**Estd:** 1979 Private Limited Company
**Line of Business:** Painting and glazing
**Issued Capital:** £100
**Principals:** R Sang *(Managing)*, R Sang *(Financial)*, N Sang, D G Cox
**Responsibilities**
**Marketing:** Viki Duffy *(Marketing & Business Developme)*
**Admin:** Sam Garnett *(Office Manager)*
**IT:** Sam Garnett *(Office Manager)*
**HR:** Sam Garnett *(Office Manager)*
**Facilities:** Sam Garnett *(Office Manager)*
**Operations:** Sam Garnett *(Office Manager)*
**Branches:** Edwards La, Speake, Liverpool, Merseyside L24 9HW
**US SIC:** 1721, 1799
**UK SIC:** 50400, 50000
**Auditors:** BKR Haines Watts
**Bankers:** HSBC Bank plc (40-29-01)

| | 31-12-13 | 31-12-12 | 31-12-11 |
|---|---|---|---|
| TA | 1,414,031 | 1,572,156 | 1,303,866 |
| NW | 1,194,455 | 1,182,591 | 1,085,847 |
| WC | 1,092,795 | 1,079,459 | 967,732 |

DUNS 21-015-4522 **Exp**

### Vale Europe Ltd

(**Subsidiary of:** Caixa De Previdência Dos Funcionários Do Banco Do)
Acton Refinery, Bashley Road, London NW10 6SN
**Tel:** 02089656031
**Web:** www.inco.com
**Reg No:** 0137114 **VAT No:** 778655171
**Estd:** 1914 Private Limited Company
**Line of Business:** Mining of metals
**Export Markets:** Western Europe, Middle East, Africa, South & South East Asia, Far East, Australasia
**Issued Capital:** £4,500,000
**Directors:** K N Williams, K J Strong, M J Cox, R W Kent, S F Rhodes
**Co. Secretary:** Jordan Company Secretaries Limit
**Responsibilities**
**Senior:** James Gosselin *(Manager)*, Iain Guille *(Manager)*
**Branches:** Vale Europe Limited, Clydach Refinery, Glais Road, Swansea, West Glamorgan SA6 5QR
**US SIC:** 1099, 3339
**UK SIC:** 21000, 22470
**Auditors:** PricewaterhouseCoopers LLP
**Bankers:** HSBC Bank plc (40-05-15)

| | 31-12-13 | 31-12-12 | 31-12-11 |
|---|---|---|---|
| TO | 309,019,000 | 245,260,000 | 377,617,000 |
| P/L | 21,297,000 | 14,371,000 | 22,502,000 |
| NW | 45,487,000 | 39,112,000 | 51,620,000 |
| WC | 29,213,000 | 30,931,000 | 39,537,000 |
| Emp. | 312 | 322 | 312 |

DUNS 21-582-0779

### Vale Health Care

Hensol Castle Park, Pontyclun, Mid Glamorgan CF72 8JX
**Tel:** 01443667888
**Web:** www.vale-healthcare.com
**Estd:** 2008 Proprietorship
**Line of Business:** Clinics private
**Proprietor:** Miss K Heeley
**US SIC:** 8051 **UK SIC:** 95100
**Employees:** 70

DUNS 73-397-0052

### Vale Holiday Parks Ltd

Clarach Bay Holiday Village, Clarach Bay, Llanon, Dyfed SY23 3DT
**Tel:** 01970828237 **Fax:** 01970822008
**Web:** www.barkersleisure.com
**Reg No:** 4670394 **Estd:** 2003 Private Limited Company
**Line of Business:** Holiday parks and camps
**Issued Capital:** £100
**Directors:** J W Scarrott, C H Scarrott, T Scarrott, T H Scarrott
**Co. Secretary:** Ms Jacqueline Scarrot
**US SIC:** 7021 **UK SIC:** 66500
**Bankers:** HSBC Bank plc (40-09-19)

| | 31-10-13 | 31-10-12 | 31-10-11 |
|---|---|---|---|
| TO | 6,916,853 | 5,326,942 | 6,005,078 |
| P/L | 1,138,509 | 534,436 | 1,050,826 |
| NW | 8,231,445 | 7,472,190 | 7,068,288 |
| WC | (1,298,847) | (1,081,478) | (1,208,293) |
| Emp. | 83 | 81 | 76 |

DUNS 76-902-8440

### Vale House Oxford

Vale House Oxford, Sandford Road Littlemore, Oxford, Oxfordshire OX4 4XL
**Tel:** 01865718467
**Web:** www.valehouse.org.uk
**Reg No:** 2220564 **Estd:** 1988 Private Limited Company
**Line of Business:** Social work activities with accommodation
**Directors:** Miss J E Cranston, Mrs A R Rooke, E D Wilks, Doctor C Oppenheimer, Mrs L K Wells, J H Barneby
**Co. Secretary:** Hmg Law Secretarial Limited
**Responsibilities**
**Senior:** Nina Hutchins *(Director)*, Trisha O'leary *(Manager)*
**US SIC:** 8321 **UK SIC:** 96111
**Bankers:** Barclays Bank Plc (20-65-18)

| | 31-03-14 | 31-03-13 | 31-03-12 |
|---|---|---|---|
| TO | 1,962,231 | 2,555,059 | 1,948,924 |
| P/L | 202,862 | 1,041,123 | 927,541 |
| NW | 4,172,325 | 3,969,463 | 2,928,340 |
| WC | 205,515 | 386,123 | 327,851 |
| Emp. | 50 | 53 | 35 |

DUNS 23-013-1278

### Vale Housing Association Ltd

The Old Maltings, Vineyard, Abingdon, Oxfordshire OX14 3UG
**Tel:** 01235-536001
**Web:** www.sovereign.org.uk
**Reg No:** 0027916IP **Estd:** 1994 Friendly Society
**Line of Business:** Housing associations societies trusts & co-operatives
**Trading Style:** Sovreign Vale
**Principals:** H Manson *(Chairman)*, Ms K Stratford, N Shaw, G Higham, Mrs B Newport, J Woodford, Ms G E Monaghan, Ms B A Russell
**Co. Secretary:** Michael Roberts
**Responsibilities**
**Senior:** Ian Gilders *(Head of Housing)*, Nicola Hinkley *(Director)*, Raymond Morse *(Director)*, Tina Rey *(Regional Director)*, Ruth Sillitoe *(Director)*
**Marketing:** Karen Blatchley *(Research Manager)*
**HR:** Rebecca Basson *(Personnel Manager)*
**Health & Safety:** Rebecca Basson *(Personnel Manager)*
**Facilities:** Phil Hardy *(Property Services Director)*
**Operations:** Karen Blatchley *(Research Manager)*
**Branches:** Vale Housing Association Ltd, Oxford Road, East Hanney, Wantage, Oxfordshire OX12 0HP
**US SIC:** 8321 **UK SIC:** 96111
**Bankers:** National Westminster Bank Plc (60-01-01)
**Employees:** 183
**Turnover:** £32,730,000

DUNS 21-279-5173 **Imp-Exp**

### Vale Mill (Rochdale) Ltd

Vale Mill, Clifton Street, Rochdale, Lancashire OL16 4HP
**Tel:** 01706-353535 **Fax:** 01706716319
**Web:** www.minky.co.uk
**Reg No:** 0365230 **VAT No:** 145278066
**Estd:** 1941 Private Limited Company
**Line of Business:** Cleaning materials and equipment
**Export Markets:** E U
**Export Sales:** £5,533,913
**Trading Style:** Minky, Minky Homecare Products
**Issued Capital:** £30,000
**Principals:** M Fuchs *(Chairman)*, J Fuchs *(Managing)*, M J Fuchs *(Managing)*, A S Donnelly *(Financial)*
**Co. Secretary:** Martin Fuchs
**Responsibilities**
**Senior:** Graham Chadwick *(Maintenance)*, Shaun Dowling *(Manager)*, Simon Garvey *(IT Manager)*
**Branches:** Vale Mill (Rochdale) Ltd, Bentley Street, Rochdale, Lancashire OL12 6EU
**US SIC:** 5199 **UK SIC:** 61900
**Auditors:** RSM Tenon Audit Ltd
**Bankers:** National Westminster Bank Plc (01-07-44)

| | 30-09-13 | 30-09-12 | 30-09-11 |
|---|---|---|---|
| TO | 35,623,935 | 36,041,529 | 37,582,251 |
| P/L | 2,518,461 | 1,087,265 | 174,587 |
| NW | 22,522,636 | 20,279,750 | 19,615,714 |
| WC | 16,885,103 | 14,404,394 | 13,227,704 |
| Emp. | 330 | 332 | 334 |

DUNS 34-632-7617

### Vale of Aylesbury Housing Trust Ltd

Fairfax House, Aylesbury, Buckinghamshire HP20 2NJ
**Tel:** 01296-732600 **Fax:** 01296-732676
**Web:** www.vaht.co.uk
**Reg No:** 5438914 **Estd:** 2006 Private Company Limited By Guarantee
**Line of Business:** Other letting of own property
**Directors:** G M Kingham, D A Briercliffe, S M Lambert, R Stanway-Williams, V Patel, J R Balshaw, J D Morley, Dr C M O'Sullivan
**Co. Secretary:** Ms Linda Foster
**Responsibilities**
**Senior:** Julian Blundell-Thompson *(Director)*, Lesley Goodman *(Facilities Manager)*, Aziz Rahim *(board memebrs)*, Michael Rand *(Director)*, Ian Silver *(Director of Housing)*
**Finance:** John Lau *(Financial Director)*
**HR:** Rachel Monastyrskyj *(Human Resources Manager)*
**Facilities:** Lesley Goodman *(Facilities Manager)*
**US SIC:** 6519 **UK SIC:** 85000
**Auditors:** Grant Thornton UK LLP
**Bankers:** Barclays Bank Plc (20-00-00)

| | 31-03-14 | 31-03-13 | 31-03-12 |
|---|---|---|---|
| TO | 39,395,000 | 37,802,000 | 34,591,000 |
| P/L | 5,881,000 | 3,853,000 | 1,812,000 |
| NW | (3,262,000) | (7,461,000) | (12,575,000) |
| WC | 5,013,000 | 3,942,000 | (1,625,000) |
| Emp. | 227 | 210 | 188 |

DUNS 23-924-2621

### Vale of Glamorgan Local Health Board

(**Subsidiary of:** Welsh Government)
2 Stanwell Road, Penarth, South Glamorgan CF64 3EA
**Tel:** 01446700111
**Web:** www.valeofglamorgan.gov.uk
**Line of Business:** Other human health activities
**Issued Capital:** £1
**Principals:** I Grist *(Chairman)*, G L Harrhy *(General Manager)*
**Responsibilities**
**Senior:** GEmma Harrhy *(General Manager)*
**Branches:** Vale Of Glamorgan Local Health Board, 213 North Road, Cardiff, South Glamorgan CF14 3AG
**US SIC:** 8091 **UK SIC:** 95200
**Bankers:** National Westminster Bank Plc (56-00-41)
**Employees:** 13,000

DUNS 49-073-8077

### Vale of Mowbray Ltd

(**Subsidiary of:** Vale of Mowbray Holdings Ltd)
20 Leases Road, Northallerton, North Yorkshire DL7 9AW
**Tel:** 01677-422661
**Web:** www.valeofmowbray.co.uk
**Reg No:** 3083593 **VAT No:** 633592040
**Estd:** 1995 Private Limited Company
**Line of Business:** Manufacturers of food products
**Issued Capital:** £1,000
**Director:** J Gatenby
**Responsibilities**
**Senior:** John Gatenbury *(Managing Director)*
**Finance:** Timothy Beatham *(Finance Director)*
**IT:** Jerry Waring *(Technical Manager)*
**Operations:** Jerry Waring *(Technical Manager)*
**US SIC:** 2099 **UK SIC:** 42399
**Auditors:** Clive Owen & Co LLP
**Bankers:** Barclays Bank Plc (20-61-46)

| | 31-03-14 | 31-03-13 | 31-03-12 |
|---|---|---|---|
| TO | 21,011,620 | 20,970,699 | 23,385,116 |
| P/L | 1,041,900 | 457,974 | 337,809 |
| NW | 12,434,608 | 11,623,912 | 11,239,913 |
| WC | 6,847,086 | 5,755,929 | 5,120,226 |
| Emp. | 243 | 242 | 263 |

DUNS 23-667-9353

### Vale of White Horse District Council

Abbey House, Abbey Close, Abingdon, Oxfordshire OX14 3JE
**Tel:** 01235-520202
**Web:** www.whitehorsedc.gov.uk
**Estd:** 2003
**Line of Business:** Local government
**Director:** T Stock
**Responsibilities**
**Senior:** Ann Sadler *(CEO, Managing Director)*
**Admin:** Kate Franklin *(Personal Assistant)*
**HR:** Tim Barnet *(Personnel Manager)*
**Facilities:** Peter Dela *(Facilities Manager)*
**Operations:** Paul Staines *(Head of Housing & Health)*
**Branches:** Vale Of White Horse District Council, Abbey House, Abbey Close, Abingdon, Oxfordshire OX14 3JE
**US SIC:** 9121 **UK SIC:** 91110
**Employees:** 250

DUNS 23-618-0055

### Vale Royal Borough Council

Gilbert Wakefield House, 67 Bewsey Street, Warrington, Cheshire WA2 7JQ
**Tel:** 01925594059 **Fax:** 01606-867514
**Web:** www.caremark.co.uk
**Estd:** 1974 Incorporate By Act Of Parliament
**Line of Business:** General (overall) public service activities
**Directors:** W R Woods, J W Page
**Responsibilities**
**Senior:** John Franklin *(Manager)*
**Branches:** Vale Royal Borough Council, Eaton Road, Tarporley, Cheshire CW6 0BL
**US SIC:** 9121 **UK SIC:** 91110
**Bankers:** HSBC Bank plc (40-35-07)
**Employees:** 952

DUNS 21-331-3810

### Vale U K Ltd

Kitling Road, Knowsley Business Park, Prescot, Merseyside L34 9JA
**Tel:** 0151-546-4684
**Web:** www.valeuk.co.uk
**Reg No:** 1356520 **Estd:** 1978 Private Limited Company
**Line of Business:** Shopfitting contractors
**Issued Capital:** £4,625
**Director:** P Henerty
**Co. Secretary:** Michael Kissack
**Responsibilities**
**Senior:** Thomas Fitzgerald *(Operations Director)*, Frank Fitzgerald *(Manager)*
**Marketing:** Thomas Fitzgerald *(Operations Director)*
**Sales:** Thomas Fitzgerald *(Operations Director)*
**IT:** Thomas Fitzgerald *(Operations Director)*
**Fleet:** Thomas Fitzgerald *(Operations Director)*
**Branches:** Salford
**US SIC:** 2599 **UK SIC:** 46720
**Auditors:** Abrams Ashton
**Bankers:** National Westminster Bank Plc (53-70-21)

| | 30-06-13 | 30-06-12 | 30-06-11 |
|---|---|---|---|
| TO | 14,321,734 | 13,171,422 | 11,866,128 |
| P/L | 1,225,161 | 1,193,999 | 1,189,305 |
| NW | 9,976,215 | 9,074,416 | 8,235,181 |
| WC | 9,046,430 | 8,376,774 | 7,515,717 |
| Emp. | 65 | 62 | 60 |

DUNS 45-827-8488 **Imp-Exp**

### Vale Upholstery Ltd

Unit 1 Greenhill Mills, Hebden Bridge, West Yorkshire HX7 5QF
**Web:** www.valeonline.co.uk
**Reg No:** 3180927 **VAT No:** 399203328
**Estd:** 1958 Private Limited Company
**Line of Business:** Upholstering
**Export Markets:** Far East; Philippines; Vietnam; U S A; Belgium; Italy
**Trading Style:** Vale Bridgecraft
**Issued Capital:** £65,237
**Principals:** S Chadwick *(Managing)*, A R Moore, R P Moore, J Robinson
**Co. Secretary:** John Lister
**Responsibilities**
**Sales:** Lorraine Holt *(Sales Director)*
**Operations:** Lorraine Holt *(Sales Director)*
**Branches:** Vale Upholstery Ltd, Priory Farm, Unit 4, Redhill, Surrey RH1 4EJ
**US SIC:** 2599, 5714, 7699
**UK SIC:** 46720, 64700, 67303
**Auditors:** B.M. Howarth Ltd
**Bankers:** Barclays Bank Plc (20-35-84)

| | 31-12-13 | 31-12-12 | 31-12-11 |
|---|---|---|---|
| TA | 2,763,269 | 2,563,693 | 2,672,270 |
| NW | 1,373,306 | 1,478,393 | 1,428,590 |
| WC | 590,957 | 665,986 | 555,434 |

DUNS 54-425-9914

### Vale Window Co Ltd

Vale House, Warren Way, Forest Town, Mansfield, Nottinghamshire NG19 0FL
**Tel:** 01623633112 **Fax:** 01623633117
**Web:** www.valewindows.co.uk
**Reg No:** 3272115 **Estd:** 2003 Private Limited Company
**Line of Business:** Manufacturers and suppliers of pvc based products
**Issued Capital:** £150
**Directors:** R I Clarke, B Hackett, D Gilberthorpe
**Co. Secretary:** Richard Hackett
**US SIC:** 3079 **UK SIC:** 48360
**Auditors:** Stopford Associates

| | 31-03-14 | 31-03-13 | 31-03-12 |
|---|---|---|---|
| TO | 8,072,305 | N/A | N/A |
| P/L | 845,404 | N/A | N/A |
| NW | 521,185 | 550,793 | 259,033 |
| WC | 89,578 | (148,209) | (364,256) |
| Emp. | 70 | N/A | N/A |

DUNS 34-832-3515 **Imp**

### Valefresco Ltd

Laurels Road, Evesham, Worcestershire WR11 8RE
**Tel:** 0138645867
**Web:** www.valefresco.com
**Reg No:** 5631708 **Estd:** 1979 Private Limited Company
**Line of Business:** Market gardeners
**Issued Capital:** £120
**Directors:** O V Pilade, O V Mauro, G Pilade, G Mauro, V Pilade
**Co. Secretary:** Nicholas Mauro
**US SIC:** 0161 **UK SIC:** 01001

| | 31-12-13 | 31-12-12 | 31-12-11 |
|---|---|---|---|
| TO | 11,862,551 | 11,342,408 | 10,544,162 |
| P/L | 95,354 | 484,847 | 1,159,885 |
| NW | 3,277,209 | 3,183,935 | 2,922,392 |
| WC | 1,055,860 | 347,969 | 557,860 |
| Emp. | 98 | 51 | 34 |

DUNS 22-707-7088 **Imp**

### Valefresh Ltd

(**Subsidiary of:** Fresca Group Ltd)
Enterprise Way, Evesham, Worcestershire WR11 1GT
**Web:** www.valefresh.co.uk
**Reg No:** 1566082 **VAT No:** 245933152
**Estd:** 1981 Private Limited Company
**Line of Business:** Food packers
**Issued Capital:** £555,500
**Principals:** J Marskell *(Managing)*, C P Mack, M J Musk
**Co. Secretary:** Michael Musk
**Branches:** Valefresh Ltd, 424-426 Brushfield St, London Fruit Exchange, London E1 6EL
**US SIC:** 7399 **UK SIC:** 83954
**Auditors:** Kingston Smith
**Bankers:** HSBC Bank plc (40-22-06)

| | 25-04-14 | 26-04-13 | 27-04-12 |
|---|---|---|---|
| TO | 9,814,000 | 9,760,000 | 9,175,000 |
| P/L | (48,000) | 27,000 | 6,000 |
| NW | 3,159,000 | 3,212,000 | 3,206,000 |
| WC | (2,893,000) | (2,643,000) | (2,894,000) |
| Emp. | 68 | 73 | 73 |

DUNS 21-923-3046 **Imp-Exp**
## Valen Fittings Ltd
Valen House, Westgate, Aldridge, Walsall, West Midlands WS9 8DG
**Tel:** 01922454913
**Web:** www.valenfittings.co.uk
**Reg No:** 1288125 **VAT No:** 101793688
**Estd:** 1976 Private Limited Company
**Line of Business:** Manufacturers of pipeline
**Export Markets:** Worldwide
**Issued Capital:** £45,000
**Principals:** L Sandford *(Managing)*, S P Hodgetts
**Co. Secretary:** Ms Valerie Sandford
**Responsibilities**
**Senior:** Nigel Genner *(Operations Director)*, Lance Sandford *(Manager)*
**Marketing:** Michelle Prichard *(E-Business Strategist)*
**IT:** Nigel Genner *(Operations Director)*
**HR:** Nigel Genner *(Operations Director)*
**Operations:** Nigel Genner *(Operations Director)*
**Purchasing:** Nigel Genner *(Operations Director)*
**Engineering:** Nigel Genner *(Operations Director)*
**US SIC:** 4619 **UK SIC:** 72601
**Auditors:** Cox Jerome
**Bankers:** Barclays Bank Plc (20-90-08)

| | 31-12-13 | 31-12-12 | 31-12-11 |
|---|---|---|---|
| TO | 9,823,024 | 11,788,458 | 8,282,506 |
| P/L | 1,448,141 | 1,837,255 | 924,642 |
| NW | 8,900,075 | 7,699,857 | 6,490,665 |
| WC | 6,445,761 | 5,082,662 | 4,308,473 |
| Emp. | 93 | 83 | 80 |

DUNS 23-280-9157
## Valence Junior School
Bonham Road, Dagenham, Essex RM8 3AR
**Tel:** 020-8270-4480
**Web:** www.valenceprimaryschool.com
**Estd:** 2012
**Line of Business:** Schools (local authority)
**Responsibilities**
**Senior:** Elizabeth Chaplin *(Executive Head Teacher)*
**US SIC:** 8211 **UK SIC:** 93200
**Employees:** 50

DUNS 21-322-2594
## Valentines High School
Cranbrook Road, Ilford, Essex IG2 6RG
**Tel:** 020-8554-3608
**Web:** www.valentines-sch.org.uk
**Line of Business:** General secondary education
**Responsibilities**
**Finance:** Barbara May *(Senior Finance Administrator)*
**Admin:** Barbara May *(Senior Finance Administrator)*
**US SIC:** 8211 **UK SIC:** 93200
**Employees:** 120

DUNS 22-620-1812 **Imp-Exp**
## Valeo Service Uk Ltd
(**Subsidiary of:** Valeo)
Unit 53 Heming Road, Redditch, Worcestershire B98 0DZ
**Tel:** 01527838300
**Web:** www.valeoservice.com
**Reg No:** 0956685 **VAT No:** 301669181
**Estd:** 1988 Private Limited Company
**Line of Business:** Sale of motor vehicle parts and accessories
**Export Markets:** Republic of Ireland
**Export Sales:** £3,394,000
**Issued Capital:** £1,315,000
**Directors:** P J Everitt, B J Bassieux, R De La Serve
**US SIC:** 5531 **UK SIC:** 65100
**Auditors:** PricewaterhouseCoopers
**Bankers:** HSBC Bank plc (40-02-50)

| | 31-12-13 | 31-12-12 | 31-12-11 |
|---|---|---|---|
| TO | 39,008,000 | 39,741,000 | 42,632,000 |
| P/L | 2,240,000 | 3,003,000 | 2,577,000 |
| NW | 11,769,000 | 9,742,000 | 7,043,000 |
| WC | 9,698,000 | 7,514,000 | 4,738,000 |
| Emp. | 68 | 69 | 71 |

DUNS 21-870-4493
## Valeport (Holdings) Ltd
Valeport Limited, St Peter's Quay, Totnes, Devon TQ9 5EW
**Tel:** 01803869292
**Reg No:** 8302479 **Estd:** 2012 Private Limited Company
**Line of Business:** Management activities of other non-financial holding companies not elsewhere classified
**Export Sales:** £5,743,015
**Issued Capital:** £1
**Directors:** C P Quartley, M Quartley
**Co. Secretary:** Ms Jennifer Quartley
**US SIC:** 6711 **UK SIC:** 83962

| | 30-11-13 |
|---|---|
| TO | 7,666,315 |
| P/L | 1,743,838 |
| NW | 5,538,018 |
| WC | 3,371,628 |
| Emp. | 65 |

DUNS 21-045-8352 **Imp-Exp**
## Valero Energy Uk Ltd
(**Subsidiary of:** Valero Energy Corporation)
1 Westferry Circus, Canary Wharf, London E14 4HA
**Tel:** 02077-193-000
**Web:** www.chevron.com
**Reg No:** 0145197 **VAT No:** 238924044
**Estd:** 1916 Private Limited Company
**Line of Business:** Oil companies
**Export Sales:** £761,700,000
**Trading Style:** Chevron
**Issued Capital:** £237,153,455
**Directors:** E A Fisher, M E Loeber, N E Roberts
**Co. Secretary:** Intertrust (Uk) Limited
**Responsibilities**
**Senior:** Simon Hammerton *(Manager)*, Duncan McNair *(Manager)*, Graham Townsend *(Stores Manager)*
**Finance:** Malcolm Mitchell *(Accounts Office Manager)*
**IT:** Barry Clough *(Operations Manager)*
**HR:** Sam Hammerton *(Human Resources Manager)*
**Purchasing:** Barry Clough *(Operations Manager)*
**Branches:** Valero Energy Uk Ltd, 430 Holyhead Road, Coventry, West Midlands CV5 8ND
**US SIC:** 2999, 2911
**UK SIC:** 11150, 14010
**Auditors:** KPMG LLP
**Bankers:** National Westminster Bank Plc (50-00-00)
**Following financial data are in thousands**

| | 31-12-13 | 31-12-12 | 31-12-11 |
|---|---|---|---|
| TO | 9,118,400 | 7,883,200 | 3,566,100 |
| P/L | 101,300 | 44,500 | (71,800) |
| NW | 1,439,900 | 1,187,100 | 992,400 |
| WC | 898,800 | 648,200 | 461,600 |
| Emp. | 788 | 858 | 882 |

DUNS 21-937-0355
## Validus-Ivc Ltd
(**Subsidiary of:** Marvel Newco Ltd)
Paston House 11-13, Princes Street, Norwich, Norfolk NR3 1AZ
**Fax:** 08447458201
**Web:** www.validus-ivc.co.uk
**Reg No:** 6233602 **Estd:** 2007 Private Limited Company
**Line of Business:** Activities auxiliary to insurance and pension funding
**Issued Capital:** £10,000
**Director:** E Van Rooyen
**Co. Secretary:** Michael Srokowski
**US SIC:** 6411 **UK SIC:** 83200
**Bankers:** Lloyds Tsb Scotland Plc (30-18-05)

| | 30-04-14 | 30-04-13 | 30-04-12 |
|---|---|---|---|
| TO | 6,839,191 | 6,558,429 | N/A |
| P/L | 616,582 | 66,005 | N/A |
| NW | 1,348,214 | 817,420 | 617,515 |
| WC | 1,250,647 | 897,902 | 642,354 |
| Emp. | 166 | 155 | N/A |

DUNS 22-528-9461 **Exp**
## Valldata Services Ltd
(**Subsidiary of:** Valldata Group Ltd)
2a Halifax Road, Melksham, Wiltshire SN12 6YY
**Tel:** 01225354200 **Fax:** 01594531191
**Web:** www.valldata.co.uk
**Reg No:** 1671518 **Estd:** 1983 Private Limited Company
**Line of Business:** Direct mail service providers
**Issued Capital:** £41,300
**Directors:** H W Horton, A J Moss, T Medcalf, J G Sowler
**Responsibilities**
**Finance:** Simon Hardman *(Financial Director)*
**Admin:** Sue Perrott *(Administration Coordinator)*
**IT:** Paul Doman *(IT Manager)*
**HR:** Sue Perrott *(Administration Coordinator)*
**Health & Safety:** Sue Perrott *(Administration Coordinator)*
**Purchasing:** Sue Perrott *(Administration Coordinator)*
**US SIC:** 7319, 7374
**UK SIC:** 83800, 83940
**Auditors:** Baker Tilly UK Audit LLP
**Bankers:** Lloyds TSB Bank plc (30-98-75)

| | 31-03-13 | 31-03-12 | 31-03-11 |
|---|---|---|---|
| TO | 7,485,555 | 7,083,064 | 6,296,078 |
| P/L | 1,486,323 | 710,073 | 793,290 |
| NW | 2,064,115 | 833,409 | 582,936 |
| WC | 1,349,376 | 389,666 | 269,970 |
| Emp. | 137 | 137 | N/A |

DUNS 51-564-7290
## Vallectric (Holdings) Ltd
3 Hales Road, Leeds, West Yorkshire LS12 4PL
**Tel:** 01132038884
**Web:** www.vallectric.co.uk
**Reg No:** 5846208 **Estd:** 1959 Private Limited Company
**Line of Business:** Electrical contractors and electricians
**Trading Style:** Vallectric (Holdings) Ltd
**Issued Capital:** £449,586
**Director:** C Novotny
**Co. Secretary:** Alan Gardner
**Responsibilities**
**Operations:** Tremayne Vare *(Operations Director)*
**US SIC:** 1731 **UK SIC:** 50300
**Bankers:** Bank Of Scotland (80-02-60)

| | 31-03-14 | 31-03-13 | 31-03-12 |
|---|---|---|---|
| TO | 7,640,464 | 9,904,468 | 8,425,541 |
| P/L | 366,132 | 416,171 | 208,119 |
| NW | 1,132,658 | 1,001,743 | 646,472 |
| WC | 972,131 | 878,799 | 763,603 |
| Emp. | 52 | 53 | 62 |

DUNS 21-320-2117
## Valley Court
Valley Road, Cradley Heath, West Midlands B64 7LT
**Tel:** 01384411299
**Estd:** 1998 Proprietorship
**Line of Business:** Residential care establishments
**Proprietor:** Mrs J Green
**Responsibilities**
**Finance:** Lorraine Greenaway *(CFO)*
**US SIC:** 8321 **UK SIC:** 96111
**Employees:** 75

DUNS 34-616-8250 **Imp**
## Valley Grown Salads Ltd
Nazelow Nursery, Sedge Green, Roydon, Harlow, Essex CM19 5JS
**Tel:** 01992708501 **Fax:** 01992469519
**Reg No:** 5423521 **Estd:** 2005 Private Limited Company
**Line of Business:** Processing and preserving of fruit and vegetables not elsewhere classified
**Issued Capital:** £2
**Director:** V Russo
**Co. Secretary:** Giacomo Russo
**US SIC:** 2033 **UK SIC:** 41473

| | 30-04-14 | 30-04-13 | 30-04-12 |
|---|---|---|---|
| TA | 2 | 2 | 2 |
| NW | 2 | 2 | 2 |

DUNS 23-336-8588
## Valley Hotel
Valley Hotel, London Road, Holyhead, Gwynedd LL65 3DU
**Tel:** 01407-740203
**Web:** www.valley-hotel-anglesey.co.uk
**Estd:** 2002 Proprietorship
**Line of Business:** Hotels
**Proprietor:** D Hall
**Responsibilities**
**Senior:** Paul Snape *(Manager)*
**US SIC:** 7011 **UK SIC:** 66500
**Employees:** 50

DUNS 39-748-1722
## Valley Leisure Ltd
West Street, Andover, Hampshire SP10 1QP
**Tel:** 01264347100
**Web:** www.valleyleisure.com
**Reg No:** 2188010 **Estd:** 1973 Private Company Limited By Guarantee
**Line of Business:** Leisure centres
**Directors:** N C Bravery, P J Horne, M J Cleary, Ms A S Wilbraham, Dr K Blacker, G A Scott Duncan, Dr M Stone, N H Bone
**Co. Secretary:** Wilsons (Company Secretaries) Li
**Branches:** Valley Leisure Ltd, Southampton Road, Romsey, Hampshire SO51 8AF
**US SIC:** 7999 **UK SIC:** 97913
**Auditors:** Beck Randall & Carpenter
**Bankers:** HSBC Bank plc (40-08-28)

| | 31-03-14 | 31-03-13 | 31-03-12 |
|---|---|---|---|
| TO | 5,644,520 | 5,261,772 | 5,085,744 |
| P/L | 346,579 | 179,648 | 119,659 |
| NW | 1,617,927 | 1,385,776 | 1,117,286 |
| WC | 1,224,885 | 967,358 | 614,228 |
| Emp. | 293 | 294 | 275 |

DUNS 23-129-4711
## Valley Manor Nursing Home
Southend Terrace, Bargoed, Mid Glamorgan CF81 9RN
**Tel:** 01685844127
**Web:** www.valleymanor.org
**Estd:** 1990 Proprietorship
**Line of Business:** Nursing homes
**Proprietor:** Dr P Das
**Responsibilities**
**Senior:** Dianne Palmer *(Manager)*
**Branches:** P Das, Pendydarren Rd, Merthyr Tydfil, Mid Glamorgan CF47 8YL
**US SIC:** 8051 **UK SIC:** 95100
**Employees:** 1,500

DUNS 21-042-0282
## Valley Medical Centre
Valley Works, Hebden Bridge, West Yorkshire HX7 7BZ
**Tel:** 0844-477-2477
**Estd:** 2012 Partnership
**Line of Business:** Doctors
**Partners:** Dr E Williams, Dr D Wild, Dr D Burley, Dr M Davies
**Branches:** Valley Medical Centre, Luddendenfoot Surgery, Kershaw Dr, Luddendenfoot, Halifax, West Yorkshire HX2 6PD
**US SIC:** 8011 **UK SIC:** 95300
**Employees:** 60

DUNS 28-835-3535
## The Valley Mill Co Ltd
Plas Iago, Rhoscolyn, Holyhead, Gwynedd LL65 2NQ
**Tel:** 01407860562 **Fax:** 01612035346
**Reg No:** 0391113 **Estd:** 1944 Private Limited Company
**Line of Business:** Accommodation address agents
**Issued Capital:** £12,700
**Directors:** Ms J M Owen, Ms A K Owen
**Co. Secretary:** Ms Anne Owen
**Responsibilities**
**Senior:** Tony Close *(Site Manager)*
**US SIC:** 6519 **UK SIC:** 85000
**Auditors:** Henry R Davis & Co
**Bankers:** National Westminster Bank Plc (53-50-53)

| | 30-06-13 | 30-06-12 | 30-06-11 |
|---|---|---|---|
| TA | 246,911 | 258,696 | 303,180 |
| NW | 225,945 | 237,288 | 283,841 |
| WC | 11,164 | 22,679 | 65,705 |

DUNS 21-205-7400 **Exp**
## Valley Printing Company Ltd
Harden Beck Mill, Bingley, West Yorkshire BD16 1BL
**Tel:** 01535272861
**Web:** www.thevalleygroup.com
**Reg No:** 0098663 **VAT No:** 180091777
**Estd:** 1892 Private Limited Company
**Line of Business:** Marketing consultants
**Export Markets:** Netherlands
**Export Sales:** £3,008,371
**Trading Style:** The Valley Group
**Issued Capital:** £99,396
**Principals:** J S Haggas *(Managing)*, J S Haggas
**Co. Secretary:** Jonathan Haggas
**Branches:** Valley Printing Company Ltd, 1 Heath Villas, Hollywater Rd, Hollywater, Bordon, Hampshire GU35 0AH
**US SIC:** 2794, 2752
**UK SIC:** 47545, 47544
**Auditors:** Baker Tilly
**Bankers:** HSBC Bank plc (40-13-15)

| | 30-06-13 | 30-06-12 | 30-06-11 |
|---|---|---|---|
| TO | 14,888,746 | 14,655,913 | 15,075,551 |
| P/L | 196,064 | 1,087,552 | 1,233,104 |
| NW | 5,405,600 | 5,299,639 | 4,750,362 |
| WC | 4,593,216 | 4,807,775 | 4,301,439 |
| Emp. | 124 | 119 | 112 |

DUNS 21-041-0743
## Valley Road Community Primary School
Corporation Road, Sunderland, Tyne and Wear SR2 8PL
**Tel:** 01915-537750
**Web:** www.schools.sunderland.gov.uk
**Estd:** 2003
**Line of Business:** Schools (local authority)
**Proprietor:** Mrs C Young
**Responsibilities**
**Senior:** Deborah Muschamp *(Proprietor)*
**US SIC:** 8211 **UK SIC:** 93200
**Employees:** 85

DUNS 21-224-8479
## Valley View Care Centre
Dan Y Coed, Cefn Hengoed, Hengoed, Mid Glamorgan CF82 7LP
**Tel:** 01443862217
**Web:** www.fshc.co.uk
**Estd:** 1956
**Line of Business:** Nursing homes
**Proprietor:** Mrs J Williams
**US SIC:** 8051 **UK SIC:** 95100
**Employees:** 60

DUNS 22-703-8759 **Imp**
## Valley Wholesale Carpets Ltd
(**Subsidiary of:** Valley Wholesale Carpets (2004) Ltd)
Turpin Lane, Erith, Kent DA8 2AT
**Tel:** 01322356290 **Fax:** 01322349535
**Reg No:** 1652883 **VAT No:** 205811493

**Estd:** 1982 Private Limited Company
**Line of Business:** Wholesale of textiles
**Issued Capital:** £100
**Director:** S Mitchell
**Co. Secretary:** Kate Mitchell
**Branches:** Valley Wholesale Carpets Ltd, Unit 6B, Stubby Lane, Uttoxeter, Staffordshire ST14 8LP
**US SIC:** 5133, 7399
**UK SIC:** 61600, 83954
**Auditors:** R E Jones
**Bankers:** National Westminster Bank Plc (60-15-28)

| | 30-09-13 | 30-09-12 | 30-09-11 |
|---|---|---|---|
| TO | 26,504,412 | 24,839,461 | 22,544,272 |
| P/L | 1,835,286 | 1,685,251 | 1,501,395 |
| NW | 9,322,054 | 7,918,295 | 7,047,819 |
| WC | 7,958,029 | 6,607,562 | 5,972,445 |
| Emp. | 92 | 87 | 80 |

DUNS 23-723-2249
## Valleys Kids
1 Cross Street, Penygraig, Tonypandy, Mid Glamorgan CF40 1LD
**Tel:** 01443420870 **Fax:** 01443-420877
**Web:** www.valleyskids.org
**Reg No:** 3717865 **Estd:** 1990 Private Company Limited By Guarantee
**Line of Business:** Charities and charitable organisations
**Directors:** Ms M Stokes, P Evans, Ms A Boyce, Ms R L Booth, Ms R Howells, H G Edwards, C Assiratti
**Co. Secretary:** Richard Morgan
**Responsibilities**
**Senior:** Margaret Jervis *(Manager)*
**IT:** Lesley Wilbourne *(IT Manager)*
**HR:** Margaret Jervis *(Manager)*
**Health & Safety:** Katheryn Edwards *(Health & Safety Officer)*
**Operations:** Margaret Jervis *(Manager)*
**Branches:** Valleys Kids, 15 Elm Street, Pontypridd, Mid Glamorgan CF37 5DF
**US SIC:** 8211, 8249, 6732, 8321
**UK SIC:** 93200, 93300, 83100, 96111
**Auditors:** Young & Phillips
**Bankers:** Barclays Bank Plc (20-68-76)

| | 31-03-14 | 31-03-13 | 31-03-12 |
|---|---|---|---|
| TO | 1,775,522 | 2,008,364 | 2,166,699 |
| P/L | (80,033) | (213,002) | 199,679 |
| NW | 3,332,920 | 3,370,313 | 3,583,315 |
| WC | 298,130 | 260,880 | 392,930 |
| Emp. | 57 | 52 | 50 |

DUNS 21-121-3727
## Valleys to Coast Housing Ltd
1 Court Road, Bridgend, Mid Glamorgan CF31 1BE
**Web:** www.v2c.org.uk
**Reg No:** 0030205IP **VAT No:** 811380168
**Estd:** 1900
**Line of Business:** Real estate agencies
**Principals:** C R Thomas *(Chairman)*, A P Rawlins *(Financial)*, S Cook, Ms B I Quennell, S Smith, Ms M A Macintyre, Ms N H Roblin, J Kent
**Responsibilities**
**Senior:** Elwyn Dunster *(Principal)*, Tanya Hicks *(Principal)*, Susan Rhodes *(Vice Chairperson)*, Helen Wooldridge *(Principal)*
**IT:** Nick Meyrick *(IT Manager)*
**US SIC:** 6531 **UK SIC:** 83400
**Auditors:** Mazars LLP
**Bankers:** Lloyds TSB Bank plc (30-00-02)
**Employees:** 214
**Turnover:** £20,204,000

DUNS 57-022-7488 **Imp**
## Vallourec Oil & Gas Uk Ltd.
(**Subsidiary of:** Vallourec)
Mossend, Bellshill, Lanarkshire ML4 2RR
**Tel:** 01698-742300 **Fax:** 01698-742302
**Web:** www.vallourec.com
**Reg No:** 0147386SC **Estd:** 1890 Private Limited Company
**Line of Business:** Oil and gas exploration services
**Trading Style:** Vellourec, V M O G U K
**Issued Capital:** £12,700,000
**Directors:** M Toulemonde, J Michel, B Frischmann, D Hornet, P Carlier
**Co. Secretary:** Kenneth Hall
**Responsibilities**
**Senior:** Daniel Dauron *(Manager)*
**IT:** Ben Patrick *(IT Manager)*
**Branches:** Vallourec Oil & Gas Uk Ltd., 1 Lime St, Aberdeen, Aberdeenshire AB11 5FJ
**US SIC:** 1389 **UK SIC:** 13000
**Auditors:** KPMG LLP
**Bankers:** HSBC Bank plc (40-22-47)

| | 31-12-13 | 31-12-12 | 31-12-11 |
|---|---|---|---|
| TO | 138,361,000 | 172,532,000 | 125,978,000 |
| P/L | 16,425,000 | 26,410,000 | 12,436,000 |
| NW | 39,999,000 | 45,205,000 | 30,670,000 |
| WC | 29,447,000 | 40,030,000 | 27,852,000 |
| Emp. | 266 | 254 | 239 |

DUNS 39-749-2331 **Imp-Exp**
## Valmiera Glass Uk Ltd
Westbury, Sherborne, Dorset DT9 3RB
**Tel:** 01935813722
**Web:** www.atex-membranes.com
**Reg No:** 2189095 **Estd:** 1987 Private Limited Company
**Line of Business:** Manufacture of glass fibres
**Export Markets:** Worldwide
**Export Sales:** £12,846,160
**Trading Style:** Alpha
**Issued Capital:** £7,300,000
**Directors:** C Burt, R W Hallett Andrews, D Senbergs, A H Schwiontek, W Anspach, B Deubel, S Jugel
**Co. Secretary:** Michelmores Secretaries Limited
**Responsibilities**
**Senior:** Heinz Preiss Daimler *(Director)*, Henry Urban *(Manager)*
**Finance:** Karen Loader *(Financial Controller)*
**HR:** Karen Loader *(Financial Controller)*
**Engineering:** Joe Stringer *(Production Manager)*
**US SIC:** 3229, 2269, 2299
**UK SIC:** 24791, 43702, 43992
**Auditors:** Deloitte LLP
**Bankers:** Barclays Bank Plc (20-99-40)

| | 31-12-13 | 31-12-12 | 31-12-11 |
|---|---|---|---|
| TO | 16,435,851 | 16,839,353 | 17,141,028 |
| P/L | 61,467 | 2,291,896 | 2,521,414 |
| NW | 8,082,662 | 8,438,902 | 10,004,301 |
| WC | 9,098,568 | 10,426,428 | 8,659,084 |
| Emp. | 138 | 134 | 134 |

DUNS 23-838-2225 **Imp**
## Valmont Stainton Ltd
(**Subsidiary of:** Valmont Industries Inc.)
Unit 5 Dukesway, Teesside Industrial Estate, Stockton-On-Tees, Cleveland TS17 9LT
**Tel:** 01642766242
**Web:** www.valmont-stainton.com
**Reg No:** 3829923 **Estd:** 1901 Private Limited Company
**Line of Business:** Manufacture of metal structures and parts of structures
**Export Sales:** £781,000
**Issued Capital:** £348,761
**Directors:** D W Tweed, M C Jaksich, N R Stainthorpe, R A Massey, J A Taylor
**Co. Secretary:** Roger Massey
**Responsibilities**
**Senior:** Victor Grizzle *(Manager)*, Edward Meancy *(Manager)*, Philip Plackett *(Manager)*
**US SIC:** 3441, 7397
**UK SIC:** 32042, 83702
**Auditors:** Deloitte LLP
**Bankers:** National Westminster Bank Plc (60-80-09)

| | 28-12-13 | 29-12-12 | 31-12-11 |
|---|---|---|---|
| TO | 15,622,000 | 15,970,000 | 15,898,000 |
| P/L | (217,000) | (760,000) | 522,000 |
| NW | 6,715,000 | 6,661,000 | 6,934,000 |
| WC | 5,336,000 | 5,360,000 | 5,494,000 |
| Emp. | 144 | 149 | 140 |

DUNS 73-727-2380 **Imp**
## Valneva Scotland Ltd
(**Subsidiary of:** Groupe Grimaud La Corbiere)
Oakbank Park Road, Mid Calder, Livingston, West Lothian EH53 0TG
**Tel:** 01506-446600 **Fax:** 01506-446601
**Web:** www.intercell.com
**Reg No:** 0260350SC **Estd:** 2003 Private Limited Company
**Line of Business:** Research and experimental development on natural sciences and engineering
**Issued Capital:** £2,550,000
**Directors:** Dr R Kandera, T Lingelbach
**Co. Secretary:** Morton Fraser Secretaries Limite
**US SIC:** 7391, 2834
**UK SIC:** 94000, 25700
**Auditors:** PricewaterhouseCoopers LLP

| | 31-12-13 | 31-12-12 | 31-12-11 |
|---|---|---|---|
| TO | 17,510,673 | 17,134,857 | 14,862,037 |
| P/L | 821,453 | 658,725 | 653,733 |
| NW | 4,135,915 | 3,475,353 | 3,337,868 |
| WC | (165,736) | (1,699,334) | (2,662,221) |
| Emp. | 99 | 99 | 95 |

DUNS 21-722-2507
## Valpak Holdings Ltd
Unit 4 Stratford Business Park, Banbury Road, Stratford-Upon-Avon, Warwickshire CV37 7GW
**Tel:** 08450682572
**Reg No:** 7597708 **Estd:** 2011 Private Limited Company
**Line of Business:** Holding companies management activities
**Directors:** G Orbell, T P Scriven, A P Hawkes, S A Gough, P A Gale, M D Shenk, P F Schenk Graf Von Stauffenberg, M A Webb

**Co. Secretary:** Philip Gale
**Responsibilities**
**Senior:** John Deben *(Director)*
**US SIC:** 6711 **UK SIC:** 83962

| | 31-12-13 | 31-12-12 | 29-12-12 |
|---|---|---|---|
| TO | 82,122,000 | 54,226,000 | N/A |
| P/L | 2,245,000 | 93,000 | N/A |
| NW | 2,909,000 | 880,000 | 750,000 |
| WC | 1,312,000 | (993,000) | 575,000 |
| Emp. | 127 | 157 | N/A |

DUNS 22-928-8568 **Imp-Exp**
## Valpar Industrial Ltd
(**Subsidiary of:** Ballyliffan Ltd)
13 Balloo Drive, Balloo Industrial Estate, Bangor, Co Down BT19 7QY
**Web:** www.valpar.co.uk
**Reg No:** 0019417NI **VAT No:** 756815889
**Estd:** 1986 Private Limited Company
**Line of Business:** Plastic extruders
**Export Markets:** Worldwide
**Issued Capital:** £47,500
**Directors:** M O'Neill, P O'Neill, P Dooey, J O'Neill, Miss E Rafferty
**Co. Secretary:** Martin O'Neill
**Responsibilities**
**Senior:** Barry Davidson *(Production Manager)*
**Finance:** Gillian Bailie *(Health & Safety Officer)*
**Admin:** Barry Davidson *(Production Manager)*
**IT:** Mervyn Waterworth *(Technical Manager)*
**HR:** Mark Boal *(Engineering Manager)*
**Health & Safety:** Gillian Bailie *(Health & Safety Officer)*, Barry Davidson *(Production Manager)*
**Facilities:** Mervyn Waterworth *(Technical Manager)*
**Operations:** Mervyn Waterworth *(Technical Manager)*
**Engineering:** Mark Boal *(Engineering Manager)*, Barry Davidson *(Production Manager)*
**US SIC:** 3079 **UK SIC:** 48360
**Auditors:** ASM (M) Ltd
**Bankers:** Ulster Bank Ltd (98-11-50)

| | 31-07-13 | 31-07-12 | 31-07-11 |
|---|---|---|---|
| TO | 9,347,185 | 10,348,818 | 8,953,883 |
| P/L | 1,287,328 | 1,055,824 | 960,163 |
| NW | 2,747,913 | 2,385,159 | 3,961,044 |
| WC | 2,482,190 | 2,172,107 | 3,713,057 |
| Emp. | 56 | 51 | 51 |

DUNS 56-958-8825 **Imp-Exp**
## Valspar Powder Coatings Ltd
(**Subsidiary of:** The Valspar Corporation)
95 Aston Church Road, Nechells, Birmingham, West Midlands B7 5RQ
**Tel:** 0121-322-6900 **Fax:** 01213226902
**Web:** www.valspar.com
**Reg No:** 2849106 **VAT No:** 580688795
**Estd:** 1829 Private Limited Company
**Line of Business:** Powder coating specialists
**Export Markets:** Middle East; Belgium; Italy
**Export Sales:** £4,172,000
**Issued Capital:** £8,350,000
**Directors:** E N Braggio, Ms T N Treat
**Co. Secretary:** Nestor Engh
**Responsibilities**
**Senior:** Burt Marchman *(Sales Director)*, Tracy Mccarthy *(Customer Service Manager)*, Bernard Ouimette *(Manager)*, Lori Walker *(Manager)*
**Marketing:** Dan Mathias *(Marketing Manager)*
**Sales:** Burt Marchman *(Sales Director)*
**HR:** Liz Jones *(Human Resources Manager)*
**Facilities:** Peter Beckley *(Maintenance Manager)*
**Engineering:** Peter Beckley *(Maintenance Manager)*
**US SIC:** 2891 **UK SIC:** 25620
**Auditors:** Ernst & Young LLP
**Bankers:** Barclays Bank Plc (20-01-09)

| | 30-09-13 | 30-09-12 | 30-09-11 |
|---|---|---|---|
| TO | 11,647,000 | 11,526,000 | 10,709,000 |
| P/L | (6,116,000) | (239,000) | (535,000) |
| NW | (10,087,000) | 3,630,000 | 3,670,000 |
| WC | (6,909,000) | 2,587,000 | 2,722,000 |
| Emp. | 71 | 68 | 67 |

DUNS 77-937-6854 **Exp**
## The Valspar (Uk) Corporation Ltd
(**Subsidiary of:** The Valspar Corporation)
Unit2/3, Witney, Oxfordshire OX28 4XR
**Tel:** 01993-707400 **Fax:** 01993-775579
**Web:** www.valspar.com
**Reg No:** 3049772 **VAT No:** 656966673
**Estd:** 1966 Private Limited Company
**Line of Business:** Manufacture of mastics and sealants
**Export Markets:** E U; worldwide
**Export Sales:** £45,034,000
**Issued Capital:** £1,000
**Directors:** T N Treat, E N Braggio
**Co. Secretary:** Rolf Engh
**Responsibilities**
**Senior:** Timothy Beastrom *(Manager)*, Lori Walker *(Manager)*
**Branches:** The Valspar (Uk) Corporation Ltd, Parkway, Deeside, Clwyd CH5 2NN
**US SIC:** 2891 **UK SIC:** 25620
**Auditors:** Ernst & Young LLP
**Bankers:** National Westminster Bank Plc (60-24-60)

| | 30-09-13 | 30-09-12 | 30-09-11 |
|---|---|---|---|
| TO | 51,858,000 | 53,244,000 | 53,823,000 |
| P/L | 5,796,000 | 7,929,000 | 6,947,000 |
| NW | 16,954,000 | 15,928,000 | 11,917,000 |
| WC | 14,386,000 | 13,415,000 | 7,927,000 |
| Emp. | 156 | 126 | 122 |

DUNS 49-379-6767
## Valtech Ltd
(**Subsidiary of:** Valtech)
120 Aldersgate Street, London EC1A 4JQ
**Tel:** 020-7014-0800 **Fax:** 020-7014-0801
**Web:** www.valtech.co.uk
**Reg No:** 3127414 **VAT No:** 628656016
**Estd:** 1995 Private Limited Company
**Line of Business:** Management and business consultants
**Trading Style:** Valtech Corporate
**Issued Capital:** £150,000
**Directors:** P Hall, A Dillon, M J Skinner
**Branches:** Valtech Ltd, Suite 902, 8 Exchange Quay, Salford, Lancashire M5 3EJ
**US SIC:** 7379, 7392
**UK SIC:** 83940, 83951
**Auditors:** Deloitte LLP
**Bankers:** HSBC Bank plc (40-03-27)

| | 31-12-13 | 31-12-12 | 31-12-11 |
|---|---|---|---|
| TO | 7,588,350 | 7,459,263 | 6,423,483 |
| P/L | (321,453) | 484,666 | (70,458) |
| NW | 650,865 | 778,083 | 329,132 |
| WC | 766,998 | 1,072,254 | 847,417 |
| Emp. | 49 | 50 | 44 |

DUNS 21-783-0325
## Valuation & Lands Agency Lps Vla
Academy House, 121a Broughshane Street, Ballymena, Co Antrim BT43 6HY
**Tel:** 02825660701
**Web:** www.lpsni.gov.uk
**Estd:** 2010 Proprietorship
**Line of Business:** Other artistic and literary creation and interpretation
**Proprietor:** B Williamson
**US SIC:** 7399 **UK SIC:** 83954
**Employees:** 65

DUNS 49-711-4538
## Valuation Office Agency
Wingate House, 93-107 Shaftesbury Avenue, London W1D 5BU
**Fax:** 03000500453
**Web:** www.voa.gov.uk
**Estd:** 1910 Incorporate By Act Of Parliament
**Line of Business:** Business services
**Trading Style:** Valuation Tribunal Support Group
**Manager:** Ms S Godsell
**Responsibilities**
**Senior:** Penny Ciniewicz *(Chief Executive Officer)*, Mary Hardman *(Operations Director)*, Mark Jorgenson *(Group Valuation Officer)*
**Finance:** Craig Pemberton *(Chief Finance Officer)*
**Sales:** Dyfed Alsop *(Strategy People and Change Dir)*, Marianne Lister *(Head of Organisational Develop)*, Sean Lusk *(Head of Strategy)*
**HR:** Dyfed Alsop *(Strategy People and Change Dir)*
**Health & Safety:** Graham East *(Facilities Manager)*
**Facilities:** Graham East *(Facilities Manager)*
**Operations:** Hayley Butcher *(Head of Measures and Reporting)*
**Branches:** Valuation Office Agency, Whittington Road Block A Government Buildings, Worcester, Worcestershire WR5 2LB
**US SIC:** 9121 **UK SIC:** 91110
**Employees:** 3,990

DUNS 73-464-0613
## Value House Stores Ltd
Unit 3 Seven Brethren Bank, Sticklepath, Barnstaple, Devon EX31 2AS
**Tel:** 01271327966 **Fax:** 01271328051
**Web:** www.valuehousestores.co.uk
**Reg No:** 4728150 **Estd:** 1993 Private Limited Company
**Line of Business:** Garden centres
**Issued Capital:** £20,001
**Directors:** M R Ford, B J Ford
**Co. Secretary:** Richard Ford
**US SIC:** 5999 **UK SIC:** 65600

**Auditors:** Ernst & Young LLP

| | 28-07-13 | 29-07-12 | 31-07-11 |
|---|---|---|---|
| TO | 6,229,457 | 5,866,108 | 7,741,071 |
| P/L | 171,229 | 318,444 | 74,531 |
| NW | 1,476,726 | 1,314,307 | 1,381,753 |
| WC | 1,391,152 | 1,186,968 | 577,776 |
| Emp. | 54 | 54 | 59 |

DUNS 34-955-1163

## Value House Stores (Weymouth) Ltd

Mandeville Road, Wyke Regis, Weymouth, Dorset DT4 9HW
**Tel:** 01305-781141 **Fax:** 01305-766544
**Web:** www.valuehousestores.co.uk
**Reg No:** 5750941 **Estd:** 2007 Private Limited Company
**Line of Business:** Other retail sale in specialised stores not elsewhere classified
**Issued Capital:** £100
**Directors:** B J Ford, M R Ford, R W Ford, A Murdoch
**Co. Secretary:** Keith Herman
**Responsibilities**
**Senior:** Lee Mitchell (Store Manager)
**US SIC:** 5999 **UK SIC:** 65600

| | 28-07-13 | 29-07-12 | 31-07-11 |
|---|---|---|---|
| TA | 825,928 | 959,548 | 986,616 |
| NW | (111,239) | (30,431) | 64,961 |
| WC | (213,319) | (95,082) | (241,188) |

DUNS 57-615-2761

## Value Retail Management (Bicester Village) Ltd

(Subsidiary of: Value Retail Plc)
54-55 Pingle Drive, Bicester, Oxfordshire OX26 6WD
**Tel:** 01869323200
**Web:** www.bicestervillage.com
**Reg No:** 2884096 **Estd:** 1994 Private Limited Company
**Line of Business:** Management of real estate on a fee or contract basis
**Issued Capital:** £2
**Directors:** D F Agar, Ms D Bollier, F W Blanchette, R V Gibbs
**Co. Secretary:** Ms Jane Abrams
**US SIC:** 6531 **UK SIC:** 83400
**Auditors:** Ernst & Young
**Bankers:** National Westminster Bank Plc (56-00-03)

| | 31-12-13 | 31-12-12 | 31-12-11 |
|---|---|---|---|
| TO | 18,646,316 | 16,020,840 | 9,601,606 |
| P/L | 326,181 | 281,586 | 162,708 |
| NW | 969,976 | 730,846 | 527,113 |
| WC | 969,976 | 730,846 | 527,113 |
| Emp. | 50 | 46 | 43 |

DUNS 57-615-4702

## Value Retail Management Ltd

(Subsidiary of: Value Retail Plc)
50 Pingle Drive, Bicester, Oxfordshire OX26 6WD
**Tel:** 01869323757
**Web:** www.valueretail.com
**Reg No:** 2884191 **Estd:** 1994 Private Limited Company
**Line of Business:** Management of real estate on a fee or contract basis
**Issued Capital:** £2
**Directors:** Ms D Bollier, B S Garrison, C D Mackintosh, R V Gibbs, D F Agar
**Co. Secretary:** Ms Jane Abrams
**Responsibilities**
**Marketing:** Elena Foguet (Marketing Director), Helen Gomm (Director of Strategy & Plannin)
**IT:** Tom Thorogood (Head of IT Projects)
**US SIC:** 6531 **UK SIC:** 83400
**Auditors:** Ernst & Young
**Bankers:** National Westminster Bank Plc (56-00-03)

| | 31-12-13 | 31-12-12 | 31-12-11 |
|---|---|---|---|
| TO | 7,102,748 | 5,980,614 | 5,342,159 |
| P/L | 423,036 | 643,063 | 647,153 |
| NW | 1,379,580 | 2,060,074 | 1,579,226 |
| WC | 1,262,269 | 1,942,763 | 1,461,915 |

DUNS 23-621-0063

## Values Academy

College House, 51-54 Hockley Hill, Birmingham, West Midlands B18 5AQ
**Tel:** 01215230222
**Web:** www.valuesacademy.org.uk
**Reg No:** 3618159 **Estd:** 1998 Private Unlimited Company
**Line of Business:** Schools (independent)
**Directors:** P R Lawrie, Ms J A Topping, D C Mcconnell, Dr A Molony, S D Livings, N W Topping, R P Warman
**Co. Secretary:** Patrick Darcy
**Responsibilities**
**Senior:** Estelle Dimelor (Chief Executive Officer)
**US SIC:** 8299 **UK SIC:** 93300

**Auditors:** R A Lea & Co

| | 31-03-14 | 31-12-12 | 31-03-11 |
|---|---|---|---|
| TO | 1,178,537 | 955,889 | 831,520 |
| P/L | (43,450) | 83,498 | 93,095 |
| NW | 131,495 | 174,946 | 91,448 |
| WC | 46,767 | 70,938 | (91,233) |
| Emp. | 45 | 60 | 39 |

DUNS 21-859-1866

## Valueworks Holdings Ltd

1 Smithy Court, Smithy Brook Road, Wigan, Lancashire WN3 6PS
**Tel:** 01942826788
**Web:** www.valueworks.co.uk
**Reg No:** 8218022 **Estd:** 2012 Private Limited Company
**Line of Business:** Other computer related activities
**Issued Capital:** £1
**Directors:** Ms E A Sipiere, M E Brockman, D Issott, A J Macfarlane
**Co. Secretary:** Jarrod Hargreaves
**Responsibilities**
**Senior:** Alan Bell (Manager)
**US SIC:** 7379 **UK SIC:** 83940
**Auditors:** Deloitte LLP
**Bankers:** Barclays Bank Plc (20-69-85)

| | 31-03-14 | 31-03-13 |
|---|---|---|
| TO | 2,812,070 | 1,185,865 |
| P/L | (5,208,029) | (2,038,992) |
| NW | (25,591,073) | (21,244,312) |
| WC | 679,640 | 761,702 |
| Emp. | 75 | 86 |

DUNS 58-447-0629 **Exp**

## Valve Train Components Ltd

(Subsidiary of: Charter Manufacturing Company Inc.)
Unit 9 Attwood Road, Burntwood, Staffordshire WS7 3GJ
**Tel:** 01543272100
**Web:** www.charterautomotive.com
**Reg No:** 2908669 **VAT No:** 580349334
**Estd:** 1994 Private Limited Company
**Line of Business:** Metallurgists
**Export Markets:** E E C and Others
**Export Sales:** £4,190,670
**Issued Capital:** £500,000
**Directors:** Ms S Boeding, T J Glaister, T Endres, J W Mellowes, C Mellowes
**Co. Secretary:** Todd Endres
**US SIC:** 3469 **UK SIC:** 31200
**Auditors:** Dains LLP
**Bankers:** National Westminster Bank Plc (56-00-69)

| | 31-12-13 | 31-12-12 | 31-12-11 |
|---|---|---|---|
| TO | 4,569,978 | N/A | N/A |
| P/L | (3,429,157) | N/A | N/A |
| NW | (665,028) | (2,302,573) | 808,076 |
| WC | 1,123,514 | 5,410,244 | 1,262,335 |
| Emp. | 54 | N/A | N/A |

DUNS 21-406-3240 **Imp**

## Valvona & Crolla Ltd

19 Elm Row, Edinburgh, Midlothian EH7 4AA
**Tel:** 0131-556-6066
**Web:** www.valvonacrolla.co.uk
**Reg No:** 0018060SC **Estd:** 1934 Private Limited Company
**Line of Business:** Retailers of beer, wine and spirits
**Issued Capital:** £1,800
**Principals:** P Contini (Managing), Ms F Contini
**Co. Secretary:** Mrs Mary Contini
**US SIC:** 5921, 5499, 5812
**UK SIC:** 64200, 64100, 66110
**Auditors:** Pricewaterhouse Coopers
**Bankers:** Clydesdale Bank Plc (82-62-28)

| | 28-02-14 | 31-01-13 | 31-02-12 |
|---|---|---|---|
| TO | 4,941,556 | 4,613,889 | 4,506,550 |
| P/L | (182,024) | 85,666 | 85,564 |
| NW | 1,265,712 | 1,302,739 | 1,252,302 |
| WC | (347,239) | (56,010) | (133,278) |
| Emp. | 89 | 87 | 89 |

DUNS 50-564-3452

## Vamw Care

John Thomson House, Motherwell, Lanarkshire ML1 1TT
**Tel:** 01698244344 **Fax:** 01698244345
**Web:** www.vamw.org
**Reg No:** 0125649SC **Estd:** 1990 Private Limited Company
**Line of Business:** Charities and charitable organisations
**Directors:** J Dott, I L Livingstone, Ms J M Proudfoot, G Robertson, S M Duguid, I A Thomson
**Co. Secretary:** Robert Hill
**Responsibilities**
**Senior:** Roddy Thomson (Manager)
**Branches:** Vamw Care, 73 Greenlaw Avenue, Wishaw, Lanarkshire ML2 8QN
**US SIC:** 8811, 8321
**UK SIC:** 99000, 96111
**Auditors:** Robin Wilkie

**Bankers:** The Royal Bank Of Scotland Plc (83-25-45)

| | 31-03-14 | 31-03-13 | 31-03-12 |
|---|---|---|---|
| TO | 4,617,724 | 4,649,389 | 4,741,504 |
| P/L | 59,417 | (38,874) | (78,322) |
| NW | 1,435,266 | 1,375,849 | 1,414,723 |
| WC | 1,075,687 | 997,273 | 1,016,325 |
| Emp. | 286 | 289 | 269 |

DUNS 22-630-3824

## Van Ameyde Uk Ltd

(Subsidiary of: Rwtüv E.V.)
34 The Mall, Bromley, Kent BR1 1TS
**Tel:** 02083150700 **Fax:** 020-8460-1713
**Web:** www.vanameyde.com
**Reg No:** 1106096 **Estd:** 1973 Private Limited Company
**Line of Business:** Representative office
**Issued Capital:** £225,000
**Directors:** K J Berends, P Den Dikken, P Middelkoop, D R Wilson
**Co. Secretary:** Mrs Lisa Caton
**Responsibilities**
**Admin:** Julia Neville (Office Manager)
**HR:** Julia Neville (Office Manager)
**Health & Safety:** Julia Neville (Office Manager)
**Branches:** Van Ameyde Uk Ltd, 50 High St, Ruislip, Middlesex HA4 7AN
**US SIC:** 6111, 6399
**UK SIC:** 81501, 82001
**Auditors:** Cornerstone Accountancy
**Bankers:** National Westminster Bank Plc (60-00-01)

| | 31-12-13 | 31-12-12 | 31-12-11 |
|---|---|---|---|
| TA | 11,681,082 | 11,561,211 | 11,705,346 |
| P/L | 559,271 | 404,772 | 359,234 |
| NW | 849,020 | 706,632 | 598,338 |
| WC | 755,867 | 610,789 | 505,164 |
| Emp. | 67 | 67 | 68 |

DUNS 22-639-1647 **Imp**

## Van Cols Ltd

Old School, School Lane, Colchester, Essex CO6 4BN
**Tel:** 01206-271521
**Web:** www.van-cols.co.uk
**Reg No:** 0789570 **VAT No:** 103396589
**Estd:** 1964 Private Limited Company
**Line of Business:** Photographers (general)
**Issued Capital:** £3,792
**Principals:** A H Van Helfteren (Managing), Ms P C Van Helfteren, A F Van Helfteren
**Co. Secretary:** Ms Margaret King
**Responsibilities**
**Senior:** Mark Misquitta (Senior IT Executive), Janus Van Helfteren (CEO, Managing Director)
**IT:** Mark Misquitta (Senior IT Executive)
**US SIC:** 7333 **UK SIC:** 83953
**Auditors:** Scrutton Bland
**Bankers:** HSBC Bank plc (40-18-51)

| | 31-03-14 | 31-03-13 | 31-03-12 |
|---|---|---|---|
| TA | 1,786,520 | 1,777,581 | 1,571,455 |
| NW | 1,371,152 | 1,273,969 | 1,124,317 |
| WC | 1,065,218 | 978,984 | 773,319 |

DUNS 22-028-6517

## Van Dalen U K Ltd

(Subsidiary of: Stichting Administratiekantoor Aandelen Van Dalen)
Arnold House, Rotherham, South Yorkshire S61 2DW
**Tel:** 01709-560200 **Fax:** 01709-560400
**Web:** www.vandalenrecycling.com
**Reg No:** 4031206 **Estd:** 2001 Private Limited Company
**Line of Business:** Recycling
**Export Sales:** £55,337,262
**Issued Capital:** £12,000
**Director:** J A Van Batenburg
**Responsibilities**
**Senior:** William Bird (Manager)
**Branches:** Van Dalen U K Ltd, Irvines Quay, Hartlepool, Cleveland TS24 0UZ
**US SIC:** 3341 **UK SIC:** 22470
**Auditors:** MGI Watson Buckle
**Bankers:** National Westminster Bank Plc (56-00-36)

| | 31-12-13 | 31-12-12 | 31-12-11 |
|---|---|---|---|
| TO | 67,025,277 | 144,059,696 | 126,823,704 |
| P/L | (9,249,209) | (6,486,672) | 797,684 |
| NW | (19,030,096) | (9,780,887) | (3,294,215) |
| WC | (19,030,096) | (9,780,887) | 5,798,367 |
| Emp. | 76 | 88 | 81 |

DUNS 73-719-8932

## Van Den Bosch Transport Ltd

(Subsidiary of: Stichting Administratiekantoor Aandelen P.J.M.M. V)
Cornwall Court, 19 Cornwall Street, Birmingham, West Midlands B3 2DT
**Tel:** 01214595296 **Fax:** 01214594802
**Web:** www.vandenbosch.com
**Reg No:** 4978319 **Estd:** 2003 Private Limited Company
**Line of Business:** Freight transport by road not elsewhere classified
**Export Sales:** £1,644,551
**Issued Capital:** £15,000
**Director:** P J Van Den Bosch

**Co. Secretary:** Hubertus Van Den Bosch
**US SIC:** 4213, 4411
**UK SIC:** 72300, 74001

| | 31-12-13 | 31-12-12 | 31-12-11 |
|---|---|---|---|
| TO | 5,356,844 | 5,406,337 | 5,541,918 |
| P/L | 295,925 | 397,605 | 588,281 |
| NW | 1,525,071 | 1,305,195 | 1,006,906 |
| WC | 1,525,071 | 1,305,195 | 1,006,906 |

DUNS 21-753-8961

## Van Dyk Hotel

Worksop Road, Clowne, Chesterfield, Derbyshire S43 4TD
**Web:** www.vandykhotel.co.uk
**VAT No:** 772534322 **Estd:** 1969 Proprietorship
**Line of Business:** Hotels
**Proprietor:** M Smith
**Responsibilities**
**Senior:** Gail Eyre (Proprietor)
**US SIC:** 5999 **UK SIC:** 65600
**Bankers:** Allied Irish Bank (gb) (23-84-01)
**Employees:** 70

DUNS 76-687-6726

## Van Elle Ltd

(Subsidiary of: Van Elle 03 Ltd)
Kirkby Lane, Pinxton, Nottingham, Nottinghamshire NG16 6JA
**Web:** www.van-elle.co.uk
**Reg No:** 2590521 **VAT No:** 706373736
**Estd:** 1984 Private Limited Company
**Line of Business:** Engineering services
**Issued Capital:** £2,448
**Directors:** J Fenton, V Handley, M J Mason, C Bosworth, M F Ellis
**Branches:** Van Elle Ltd, Holman HO,36-38 Newport Rd, Caldicot, Gwent NP26 4BQ
**US SIC:** 1799, 8911
**UK SIC:** 50000, 83701
**Auditors:** Grant Thornton U K LLP
**Bankers:** National Westminster Bank Plc (60-02-35)

| | 30-04-14 | 30-04-13 | 30-04-12 |
|---|---|---|---|
| TO | 46,645,000 | 35,680,000 | 33,865,000 |
| P/L | 3,007,000 | 1,738,000 | 1,267,000 |
| NW | 13,213,000 | 10,864,000 | 9,564,000 |
| WC | 6,124,000 | 6,129,000 | 5,765,000 |
| Emp. | 299 | 232 | 243 |

DUNS 21-709-3541 **Imp**

## Van Hage & Co (Holdings) Ltd

Amwell Lane, Ware, Hertfordshire SG12 9SS
**Tel:** 01920870811
**Web:** www.baobabjungle.co.uk
**Reg No:** 0618483 **VAT No:** 214167391
**Estd:** 2012 Private Limited Company
**Line of Business:** Garden centres
**Trading Style:** Van Hage's Garden Company
**Issued Capital:** £7,000
**Directors:** C D Roberts, Mrs M C Charnley
**Co. Secretary:** David Ogilvie
**US SIC:** 5399 **UK SIC:** 65600
**Auditors:** Deloitte & Touche
**Bankers:** Barclays Bank Plc (20-20-37)

| | 31-07-13 | 31-07-12 | 31-07-11 |
|---|---|---|---|
| TO | 17,155,033 | 16,166,279 | 18,553,200 |
| P/L | (591,108) | (479,447) | (1,305,413) |
| NW | 8,401,220 | 9,018,782 | 9,796,644 |
| WC | (258,968) | (2,914,052) | (2,821,946) |
| Emp. | 296 | 300 | 390 |

DUNS 29-665-0088 **Imp-Exp**

## Van Leeuwen Ltd

(Subsidiary of: Van Leeuwen Buizen Groep B.V.)
Nine Lock Works, Mill Street, Brierley Hill, West Midlands DY5 2SX
**Web:** www.vanleeuwen.co.uk
**Reg No:** 1991207 **VAT No:** 439591121
**Estd:** 1986 Private Limited Company
**Line of Business:** Metal merchants
**Export Markets:** European Union (E U); U S A
**Export Sales:** £4,149,000
**Issued Capital:** £8,819,911
**Directors:** J Blakey, Mrs M A Van Engelen
**Co. Secretary:** Michael Davies
**Responsibilities**
**Senior:** Trevor Desmond (Business Manager), Pete Rietberg (Chairman)
**Branches:** Van Leeuwen Ltd, Thorncliffe Park, Sheffield, South Yorkshire S35 2PG
**US SIC:** 5051 **UK SIC:** 61200
**Auditors:** Ernst & Young LLP
**Bankers:** National Westminster Bank Plc (50-00-00)

| | 31-12-13 | 31-12-12 | 31-12-11 |
|---|---|---|---|
| TO | 38,849,000 | 40,272,000 | 41,051,000 |
| P/L | 663,000 | 249,000 | 1,423,000 |
| NW | 11,570,000 | 11,274,000 | 11,224,000 |
| WC | 9,979,000 | 10,029,000 | 9,992,000 |
| Emp. | 125 | 120 | 108 |

DUNS 28-986-9240 **Imp-Exp**

## Van Oord Uk Ltd

(**Subsidiary of:** Merweoord B.V.)
Bankside House, Henfield Road Small Dole, Henfield, West Sussex BN5 9NQ
**Tel:** 01273 494843
**Web:** www.vanoord.com
**Reg No:** 1805156 **VAT No:** 426932245
**Estd:** 1984 Private Limited Company
**Line of Business:** Marine engines and engineering
**Issued Capital:** £100,000
**Directors:** J Martinus De Groot, M Den Broeder, G V Oord
**Co. Secretary:** Pieter-Jan De Wijn
**Responsibilities**
**Senior:** Terry Cripps *(Manager)*, Frederik De Wit *(Manager)*, Joe Wellinc *(Regional Manager)*
**Sales:** John Tharme *(Business Development Manager)*
**Purchasing:** Craig Gilley *(Contracts Manager)*
**Branches:** Van Oord Uk Ltd, Clink Road, Norwich, Norfolk NR12 0UL
**US SIC:** 8911 **UK SIC:** 83701
**Auditors:** Ernst & Young LLP
**Bankers:** Barclays Bank Plc (20-59-14)

| | 31-12-13 | 31-12-12 | 31-12-11 |
|---|---|---|---|
| TO | 89,301,889 | 169,107,239 | 48,670,480 |
| P/L | 17,046,097 | 7,037,117 | 6,771,358 |
| NW | 19,282,442 | 11,201,983 | 10,394,000 |
| WC | 18,956,333 | 11,091,569 | 10,287,215 |
| Emp. | 64 | 72 | 71 |

DUNS 50-007-1352 **Imp-Exp**

## Vanco Uk Ltd

(**Subsidiary of:** Reliance Communications Limited)
Units 5 & 6 Great West Plaza, Riverbank Way, Brentford, Middlesex TW8 9RE
**Tel:** 02086 361700 **Fax:** 02086 361700
**Web:** www.globalcloudxchange.com
**Reg No:** 2296733 **VAT No:** 663124159
**Estd:** 1987 Private Limited Company
**Line of Business:** Telecommunications
**Trading Style:** Global Cloud Xchange, Gcx
**Issued Capital:** £36,690
**Director:** A P Goldie
**Co. Secretary:** Bolaji Taiwo
**Responsibilities**
**Senior:** Punit Garg *(Manager)*, jan Huizeling *(Network Manager)*, Devon Patal *(Facilities Manager)*
**IT:** jan Huizeling *(Network Manager)*
**HR:** Stephen Mansfield *(Human Resources Manager)*
**Health & Safety:** Saida Amar *(Facilities Manager)*
**Facilities:** Saida Amar *(Facilities Manager)*, Devon Patal *(Facilities Manager)*
**US SIC:** 4899 **UK SIC:** 79020
**Auditors:** Nagle James Associates Ltd
**Bankers:** Barclays Bank Plc (20-36-47)

| | 31-03-14 | 31-03-13 | 31-03-12 |
|---|---|---|---|
| TO | 42,273,469 | 46,884,484 | 50,852,366 |
| P/L | 172,105 | 1,014,969 | (645,250) |
| NW | (41,006,678) | (41,178,783) | (42,193,752) |
| WC | (41,359,085) | (41,657,182) | (42,770,253) |
| Emp. | 84 | 96 | 107 |

DUNS 29-629-8276

## V&A Enterprises Ltd

(**Subsidiary of:** Victoria & Albert Museum)
Cromwell Road, London SW7 2RL
**Tel:** 02079422000 **Fax:** 02079422967
**Web:** www.vam.ac.uk
**Reg No:** 1955898 **Estd:** 1986 Private Limited Company
**Line of Business:** Management of the commercial activities of the V&A Museum
**Trading Style:** Victoria and Albert Museum
**Issued Capital:** £202,528
**Directors:** M E Roth, J S Nicoll, T I Reeve, M J Sebba, A Stitt, Ms M Ogundehin
**Co. Secretary:** Ms Heather Francis
**Responsibilities**
**Senior:** Tom Dixon *(Manager)*, Dorota Dominiczak *(Manager)*, Rodney Fitch *(Manager)*, Michelle Oguwdehin *(Director)*, Sarah Sevier *(Joint Managing Director)*
**Finance:** Ian Blatchford *(Finance Director)*, Dorota Dominiczak *(Manager)*
**Marketing:** Annie Wood *(Customer Services Manager)*
**Admin:** Sara Thorpe *(Office Manager)*
**HR:** Dorota Dominiczak *(Manager)*, Michelle Leong *(Human Resources Coordinator)*
**Health & Safety:** Michelle Leong *(Human Resources Coordinator)*
**Facilities:** Michelle Leong *(Human Resources Coordinator)*
**Operations:** Annie Wood *(Customer Services Manager)*
**Branches:** V&a Enterprises Ltd, Cromwell Road, London SW7 2RL
**US SIC:** 5999, 2731
**UK SIC:** 65600, 47532
**Auditors:** haysmacintyre
**Bankers:** Coutts & Co (18-00-02)

| | 31-03-14 | 31-03-13 | 31-03-12 |
|---|---|---|---|
| TO | 15,847,443 | 12,786,485 | 12,427,405 |
| NW | 202,528 | 202,528 | 202,528 |
| WC | 1,016,852 | 901,843 | 880,738 |
| Emp. | 164 | 154 | 148 |

DUNS 23-270-0612

## Vandemoortele Worcester

(**Subsidiary of:** Safinco Nv)
Martley Road, Lower Broadheath, Worcester, Worcestershire WR2 6RF
**Tel:** 01905-641616 **Fax:** 01905-641229
**Reg No:** 0015446FC **Estd:** 1990 Foreign Company
**Line of Business:** Manufacture of bread; manufacture of fresh pastry goods and cakes
**Principals:** G Vandemoortele *(Chairman)*, E L De Muelenaere, Ms J F Vandemoortele, D Durez
**Responsibilities**
**Senior:** Eddy de Muelenaere *(Director)*
**US SIC:** 2051 **UK SIC:** 41960

DUNS 37-842-2539

## Vanderlande Industries United Kingdom Ltd

6050 Knights Court, Solihull Parkway, Birmingham, West Midlands B37 7WY
**Tel:** 01217701888 **Fax:** 01217701131
**Web:** www.vanderlande.com
**Reg No:** 3298374 **Estd:** 1997 Private Limited Company
**Line of Business:** General mechanical engineering
**Export Sales:** £32,000
**Issued Capital:** £1,050,000
**Directors:** H Molenaar, N D Porter, D J Hyslop
**Co. Secretary:** Grahame Bacon
**Responsibilities**
**Admin:** Anne Tansey *(Office Manager)*
**HR:** Anne Tansey *(Office Manager)*
**US SIC:** 8911 **UK SIC:** 83701
**Auditors:** PricewaterhouseCoopers LLP
**Bankers:** National Westminster Bank Plc (60-02-35)

| | 31-03-14 | 31-03-13 | 31-03-12 |
|---|---|---|---|
| TO | 84,274,000 | 82,975,000 | 74,379,000 |
| P/L | 2,272,000 | 2,165,000 | 5,654,000 |
| NW | 1,948,000 | 2,643,000 | 12,958,000 |
| WC | 1,515,000 | 2,234,000 | 12,649,000 |
| Emp. | 275 | 315 | 301 |

DUNS 22-776-9189 **Exp**

## Vanguard Foundry Ltd

Bott Lane, Stourbridge, West Midlands DY9 7AW
**Tel:** 01384422557
**Web:** www.vanguardfoundry.co.uk
**Reg No:** 1743426 **VAT No:** 388610326
**Estd:** 2011 Private Limited Company
**Line of Business:** Foundry machinery and supplies
**Export Markets:** E U, Finland
**Export Sales:** £1,399,344
**Issued Capital:** £45,000
**Principals:** B P Higgins *(Managing)*, C J Mintern, D J Howell, P J Smith
**Co. Secretary:** Brian Higgins
**Responsibilities**
**Engineering:** Natalie Tromans *(Production Controller)*
**US SIC:** 3559 **UK SIC:** 32863
**Auditors:** J.W. Hinks

| | 30-09-13 | 30-09-12 | 30-09-11 |
|---|---|---|---|
| TO | 7,317,008 | 9,437,182 | 9,669,774 |
| P/L | 80,548 | 152,803 | 233,204 |
| NW | 1,968,384 | 1,893,316 | 1,851,133 |
| WC | 1,316,390 | 1,224,825 | 1,046,242 |
| Emp. | 104 | 117 | 123 |

DUNS 21-146-1840

## Vanguard Healthcare Group Ltd

Unit 1411 Charlton Court, Brockworth, Brockworth, Gloucester, Gloucestershire GL3 4AE
**Tel:** 01452-651-850 **Fax:** 01452651852
**Web:** www.vanguardhealthcare.co.uk
**Reg No:** 6764946 **Estd:** 2008 Private Limited Company
**Line of Business:** Medical practice activities
**Export Sales:** £163,000
**Issued Capital:** £12,540
**Directors:** I M Gillespie, I S Wallis, A J Allen
**Co. Secretary:** Mark Spoors
**Responsibilities**
**Senior:** Garland King *(Manager)*, Ian Rudd *(Finance Manager)*
**Marketing:** Mary Smallbone *(Marketing & Operations Directo)*
**Sales:** Ian Monaghan *(Sales Director)*
**HR:** Louise Simmonds *(Human Resources Manager)*
**US SIC:** 8011, 8911, 8091
**UK SIC:** 95300, 83701, 95200
**Auditors:** Deloitte LLP

| | 31-12-13 | 31-12-12 | 31-12-11 |
|---|---|---|---|
| TO | 11,460,000 | 10,490,000 | 11,327,000 |
| P/L | (968,000) | (1,133,000) | (1,036,000) |
| NW | (14,773,000) | (14,319,000) | (13,716,000) |
| WC | (1,504,000) | (2,673,000) | (1,675,000) |
| Emp. | 58 | 58 | 58 |

DUNS 23-604-0189 **Imp**

## Vanguard Logistics Services Ltd

Station House, Station Road, Maldon, Essex CM9 4LQ
**Tel:** 01621-879-200 **Fax:** 01621-879-222
**Web:** www.vls-global.com
**Reg No:** 3601330 **Estd:** 1999 Private Limited Company
**Line of Business:** Freight forwarders
**Trading Style:** Vls Global
**Issued Capital:** £6,100
**Directors:** G A Supre, D Keen, I C Gill
**Responsibilities**
**Finance:** Nigel Fost *(Financial Director)*
**HR:** Nigel Fost *(Financial Director)*
**Health & Safety:** Nigel Fost *(Financial Director)*
**Facilities:** Nigel Fost *(Financial Director)*
**Branches:** Vanguard Logistics Services Ltd, 86 Worsley Road, Manchester M30 8LS
**US SIC:** 4712, 4411
**UK SIC:** 77002, 74001
**Auditors:** BDO LLP

| | 31-12-13 | 31-12-12 | 31-12-11 |
|---|---|---|---|
| TO | 35,593,606 | 35,503,625 | 31,615,062 |
| P/L | 459,302 | 27,204 | 289,226 |
| NW | 750,198 | 381,646 | 324,646 |
| WC | 577,350 | 201,698 | 122,151 |
| Emp. | 111 | 121 | 118 |

DUNS 56-939-6591

## Vanguard Security Services Ltd

Carr Wood Industrial Estate, Carr Wood Road, Castleford, West Yorkshire WF10 4SB
**Tel:** 01977514444 **Fax:** 01977603888
**Web:** www.vanguardsecurity.co.uk
**Reg No:** 2839182 **Estd:** 1993 Private Limited Company
**Line of Business:** Security activities
**Issued Capital:** £3
**Principals:** G Moorby *(Managing)*, Ms C Sutherley
**Responsibilities**
**Senior:** Garry Moorbey *(Managing Director)*, Ian Moorby *(Human Resources Manager)*, Christine Moorby *(Manager)*
**Marketing:** Ian Waite *(Sales Manager)*
**Sales:** Ian Waite *(Sales Manager)*
**HR:** Ian Moorby *(Human Resources Manager)*
**Health & Safety:** Chris Fields *(General Manager)*
**Facilities:** Chris Fields *(General Manager)*
**US SIC:** 7393 **UK SIC:** 83954
**Auditors:** Sochall Smith Ltd
**Bankers:** National Westminster Bank Plc (54-30-64)

| | 31-07-14 | 31-07-13 | 31-07-12 |
|---|---|---|---|
| TA | 630,637 | 406,377 | 470,801 |
| NW | 139,446 | 119,069 | 125,558 |
| WC | (102,388) | (3,700) | 16,850 |

DUNS 37-758-2440

## Vanilla Room

123-125 High Street, Hornchurch, Essex RM11 1TX
**Tel:** 01708-452245
**Web:** www.thevanillaroom.co.uk
**Estd:** 2010 Proprietorship
**Line of Business:** Hairdressers (unisex)
**Proprietor:** Miss K Larcher
**US SIC:** 7231 **UK SIC:** 98200
**Bankers:** Lloyds TSB Bank plc (77-13-12)
**Employees:** 50

DUNS 50-136-1497 **Exp**

## Vanners Ties Ltd

(**Subsidiary of:** Silk Industries Ltd)
Weavers Lane, Sudbury, Suffolk CO10 1BB
**Fax:** 01260-253394
**Web:** www.adamley.com
**Reg No:** 2322023 **VAT No:** 527395424
**Estd:** 1988 Private Limited Company
**Line of Business:** Fabric retailers
**Export Markets:** U K, North America, Europe, Far East
**Trading Style:** David Evans & Co, Adamley, Vanners & Co
**Issued Capital:** £125,588
**Principals:** D E Tooth *(Chairman)*, I R Stevenson
**Responsibilities**
**Senior:** Rick Stevenson *(Manager)*
**Branches:** Vanners Ties Ltd, Adamley Textiles Ltd, River Mills, Macclesfield, Cheshire SK11 0ER
**US SIC:** 5714 **UK SIC:** 64700
**Auditors:** PKF
**Bankers:** HSBC Bank plc (40-19-04)

| | 30-04-14 | 30-04-13 | 30-04-12 |
|---|---|---|---|
| TA | 6,263,000 | 6,263,000 | 6,263,000 |
| NW | 5,476,000 | 5,476,000 | 5,476,000 |
| WC | 4,646,000 | 4,646,000 | 4,646,000 |

DUNS 76-414-2352

## Vanquis Bank Ltd

(**Subsidiary of:** Provident Financial Plc)
1 Godwin Street, Bradford, West Yorkshire BD1 2SU
**Tel:** 0871 770 5555 **Fax:** 02073376301
**Web:** www.vanquis.co.uk
**Reg No:** 2558509 **Estd:** 1990 Private Limited Company
**Line of Business:** Other credit granting not elsewhere classified
**Issued Capital:** £67,200,002
**Directors:** A C Fisher, A T Gosling, P S Crook, R M Van Breda, M C Lenora, J C Roe, A F Reczek, M S Hutko
**Co. Secretary:** Ms Carole Jones
**Responsibilities**
**Marketing:** Lucy Holland *(Head of Marketing)*
**Branches:** Vanquis Bank Ltd, Po Box 399, Chatham, Kent ME4 4WQ
**US SIC:** 6111 **UK SIC:** 81501
**Auditors:** Deloitte LLP

| | 31-12-13 | 31-12-12 | 31-12-11 |
|---|---|---|---|
| TA | 969,800,000 | 714,600,000 | 486,600,000 |
| P/L | 110,700,000 | 71,400,000 | 41,700,000 |
| NW | 210,200,000 | 151,600,000 | 100,600,000 |
| WC | 863,000,000 | 565,300,000 | 413,000,000 |
| Emp. | 909 | 728 | 589 |

DUNS 77-930-0508

## Vanstone Builders Ltd

4a The Rowans, Bude, Cornwall EX23 8PS
**Tel:** 01288-353995 **Fax:** 01288-355706
**Web:** www.vanstonebuildersltd.co.uk
**Reg No:** 3042704 **Estd:** 1965 Private Limited Company
**Line of Business:** Development and selling of real estate
**Issued Capital:** £100
**Directors:** D K Jordan, F A Vanstone, Mrs P M Vanstone
**Co. Secretary:** Mrs Nicola Jordan
**US SIC:** 6552, 1541, 1731
**UK SIC:** 85000, 50100, 50300
**Auditors:** John Harris

| | 31-03-14 | 31-03-13 | 31-03-12 |
|---|---|---|---|
| TA | 164,763 | 163,668 | 202,217 |
| NW | (487,082) | (507,632) | (425,012) |
| WC | (488,358) | (510,947) | (432,350) |

DUNS 21-605-5026

## Vantage 4 Housing

Unit 83 Eurolink Business Centre, 49 Effra Road, London SW2 1BZ
**Tel:** 02086718888
**Estd:** 2011
**Line of Business:** Miscellaneous Business Services
**US SIC:** 7399 **UK SIC:** 83954
**Employees:** 72

DUNS 53-636-0795

## Vantage Insurance Services Ltd

(**Subsidiary of:** Vantage Holdings Ltd)
41 Eastcheap, London EC3M 1DT
**Fax:** 02076558039
**Web:** www.vantageinsurance.co.uk
**Reg No:** 3441136 **Estd:** 1997 Private Limited Company
**Line of Business:** Activities auxiliary to insurance and pension funding
**Issued Capital:** £200
**Directors:** J R Collyear, J M Cooper, J F Corrigan Stuart, P R Friend, S C Wilson
**Co. Secretary:** Nigel Coppen
**US SIC:** 6411 **UK SIC:** 83200
**Auditors:** Mazars LLP

| | 31-12-13 | 31-12-12 | 31-12-11 |
|---|---|---|---|
| TO | 7,918,971 | 7,457,806 | 7,407,368 |
| P/L | 1,626,382 | 1,364,419 | 1,337,928 |
| NW | 3,091,761 | 2,478,927 | 2,022,322 |
| WC | 2,934,421 | 2,358,831 | 1,809,932 |
| Emp. | 81 | 76 | 75 |

DUNS 50-485-2302 **Imp-Exp**

## Vantec Europe Ltd

(**Subsidiary of:** Hitachi Ltd.)
Cherry Blossom Way, Sunderland, Tyne and Wear SR5 3QZ
**Tel:** 01519282552 **Fax:** 0191-416-1970
**Web:** www.vanteceurope.com
**Reg No:** 2458961 **VAT No:** 569306809
**Estd:** 2012 Private Limited Company
**Line of Business:** Road haulage and transport services
**Export Sales:** £5,684,467
**Issued Capital:** £2,000,000
**Directors:** M Kendall, T Sakurai
**Co. Secretary:** Ms Abigail Curry
**Responsibilities**
**Senior:** Robert Goodall *(Manager)*

**Marketing:** Sharon Clinton *(Commercial Manager)*
**Sales:** Sharon Clinton *(Commercial Manager)*
**Admin:** Heather Mayes *(Administrator)*
**IT:** Ian Hepplewhite *(IT Manager)*, Geoffrey Thorpe *(Computer Operations Manager)*
**HR:** Erika Hall *(Human Resources Manager)*
**Facilities:** Michael Deary *(Transport Manager)*
**Operations:** Sharon Clinton *(Commercial Manager)*, Ian Hepplewhite *(IT Manager)*, Neil West *(Senior Project Manager)*
**Purchasing:** Heather Mayes *(Administrator)*
**Fleet:** Michael Deary *(Transport Manager)*
**US SIC:** 4789 **UK SIC:** 77002
**Auditors:** Ernst & Young LLP
**Bankers:** Barclays Bank Plc (20-00-00)

| | 31-03-14 | 31-03-13 | 31-03-11 |
|---|---|---|---|
| TO | 44,449,487 | 43,938,506 | 24,951,062 |
| P/L | 2,811,770 | 4,081,734 | 3,249,036 |
| NW | 13,917,002 | 12,113,279 | 8,194,263 |
| WC | (9,789,215) | (12,191,706) | 6,895,396 |
| Emp. | 883 | 768 | 587 |

DUNS 23-220-9259 **Imp**

## Vantrunk Ltd

(**Subsidiary of:** Uni-Trunk Holdings Ltd)
Swineyard Lane, Knutsford, Cheshire WA16 0SD
**Tel:** 01928-564211
**Web:** www.vantrunk.co.uk
**Reg No:** 0038922NI **VAT No:** 757820307
**Estd:** 2000 Private Limited Company
**Line of Business:** Manufacturers of steel
**Issued Capital:** £1
**Directors:** Mrs H Morrow, M Morrow, M Morrow, K E Campbell
**Co. Secretary:** Michael Clarke
**US SIC:** 3325 **UK SIC:** 31110
**Auditors:** Cunningham, Wilkinson, Maxwell & Co Ltd
**Bankers:** Northern Bank Ltd (95-03-61)

| | 31-12-13 | 31-12-12 | 31-12-11 |
|---|---|---|---|
| TO | 11,177,187 | 18,709,392 | 12,359,978 |
| P/L | 427,230 | 1,299,436 | 883,942 |
| NW | 3,651,862 | 2,960,490 | 2,495,828 |
| WC | 2,293,947 | 2,249,322 | 2,029,534 |
| Emp. | 63 | 65 | 52 |

DUNS 51-583-6810

## Vapiano Ltd

(**Subsidiary of:** Vapiano Se)
19-21 Great Portland Street, London W1W 8QB
**Tel:** 02072680080
**Web:** www.vapiano.com
**Reg No:** 5864690 **Estd:** 2008 Private Limited Company
**Line of Business:** Restaurant - italian
**Issued Capital:** £200,000
**Directors:** S Steinkuhl, G A Gerlach, P B Sermon
**Responsibilities**
**Senior:** Dagmara Salomon *(Manager)*
**US SIC:** 5812 **UK SIC:** 66110

| | 31-12-13 | 31-12-12 | 31-12-11 |
|---|---|---|---|
| TO | 7,532,648 | 6,584,200 | 5,199,076 |
| P/L | 760,778 | 373,633 | 7,096,874 |
| NW | 6,052,412 | 4,941,634 | 4,568,001 |
| WC | 3,369,573 | 2,206,019 | 1,647,842 |
| Emp. | 131 | 139 | 144 |

DUNS 21-606-6522 **Imp-Exp**

## The Vapormatic Co Ltd

(**Subsidiary of:** Deere & Company)
Kestrel Way, Exeter, Devon EX2 7LA
**Tel:** 01392-435461 **Fax:** 01392-438445
**Web:** www.vapormatic.co.uk
**Reg No:** 0538655 **Estd:** 1949 Private Limited Company
**Line of Business:** Suppliers of
**Export Markets:** Worldwide
**Issued Capital:** £3,020,000
**Directors:** P A Brennan, T E Morgan, M C Roberts
**Co. Secretary:** Adam Malik
**Responsibilities**
**Senior:** Gail Leese *(Manager)*
**Finance:** Mark Ashley *(Financial Manager)*
**Sales:** Nick Lee *(Sales Manager)*
**IT:** Rodney Pearman *(IT Manager)*
**US SIC:** 3523, 3711
**UK SIC:** 32113, 35101
**Auditors:** Deloitte LLP
**Bankers:** The Royal Bank Of Scotland Plc (15-00-00)

| | 31-10-13 | 31-10-12 | 31-10-11 |
|---|---|---|---|
| TO | 21,169,000 | 23,247,000 | 22,667,000 |
| P/L | 1,387,000 | 1,492,000 | 2,060,000 |
| NW | 6,501,000 | 5,449,000 | 4,259,000 |
| WC | 9,055,000 | 9,090,000 | 8,779,000 |
| Emp. | 113 | 117 | 115 |

DUNS 77-059-4000

## Varatio Holdings Ltd

752-753 Deal Avenue, Slough, Berkshire SL1 4SH
**Tel:** 01753-526655
**Reg No:** 2670968 **Estd:** 1921 Private Limited Company
**Line of Business:** Management activities of holding companies
**Issued Capital:** £500,002
**Principals:** A M Clinch *(Managing)*, C R Brown
**Co. Secretary:** Alan Clinch
**US SIC:** 6711 **UK SIC:** 83962
**Auditors:** Barnes Roffe LLP

| | 31-03-14 | 31-03-13 | 31-03-12 |
|---|---|---|---|
| TO | N/A | N/A | 4,124,944 |
| P/L | N/A | N/A | 169,861 |
| NW | 1,274,278 | 1,328,176 | 1,206,500 |
| WC | 358,702 | 333,577 | 586,468 |
| Emp. | N/A | N/A | 61 |

DUNS 22-701-9908 **Exp**

## Varian Ltd

(**Subsidiary of:** Agilent Technologies Luxco Sarl)
Magnet Technology Centre, Kidlington, Oxfordshire OX5 1QU
**Tel:** 01865853800 **Fax:** 01865-841945
**Web:** www.variant.inc.com
**Reg No:** 1508692 **VAT No:** 219739337
**Estd:** 1977 Private Limited Company
**Line of Business:** Other business activities not elsewhere classified
**Export Markets:** europe
**Trading Style:** Agilent Ltd
**Issued Capital:** £100
**Directors:** C H Davies, N W Rees
**Branches:** Varian Ltd, Cootehorn Farm, Rooksbridge Rd, Axbridge, Somerset BS26 2UD
**US SIC:** 7399 **UK SIC:** 83954
**Auditors:** PricewaterhouseCoopers LLP
**Bankers:** Barclays Bank Plc (20-90-56)

| | 31-10-13 | 31-10-12 | 31-10-11 |
|---|---|---|---|
| NW | (45,123) | (45,123) | (45,123) |

DUNS 21-610-0040 **Imp-Exp**

## Varian Medical Systems Uk Ltd

(**Subsidiary of:** Varian Medical Systems Uk Holdings Ltd)
Oncology House, Gatwick Road, Crawley, West Sussex RH10 9RG
**Tel:** 01293601200 **Fax:** 01293-510260
**Web:** www.varian.com
**Reg No:** 0558526 **VAT No:** 609233551
**Estd:** 1955 Private Limited Company
**Line of Business:** Manufacturers of medical equipment
**Export Sales:** £49,889,242
**Issued Capital:** £75,000
**Directors:** N R Myles, P J Joda, J W Kuo
**Co. Secretary:** Nicholas Moritz
**Responsibilities**
**Sales:** Nick Lake *(Business Operations Manager -)*
**Operations:** Brian Guy *(Distribution Manager)*, Michael Pennells *(Environmental Manager)*
**Engineering:** Erik Hansen *(Manufacturing Manager)*, Steve Pullen *(Manufacturing Engineering Mana)*
**US SIC:** 3841, 3629
**UK SIC:** 37201, 34350
**Auditors:** PricewaterhouseCoopers LLP
**Bankers:** National Westminster Bank Plc (60-06-20)

| | 27-09-13 | 28-09-12 | 30-09-11 |
|---|---|---|---|
| TO | 100,615,089 | 86,859,094 | 87,069,353 |
| P/L | 13,509,339 | 6,407,736 | 11,277,718 |
| NW | 38,527,909 | 36,217,496 | 39,527,876 |
| WC | 36,571,026 | 35,375,018 | 40,245,212 |
| Emp. | 238 | 233 | 223 |

DUNS 23-810-4058 **Imp-Exp**

## Vario Press Ltd

Marish Wharf, St Marys Road, Middlegreen, Slough, Berkshire SL3 6DA
**Tel:** 01753-548944
**Web:** www.variouk.com
**Reg No:** 3802745 **Estd:** 1963 Private Limited Company
**Line of Business:** Printers general
**Issued Capital:** £900
**Director:** G A Clarke
**Co. Secretary:** David Clarke
**Responsibilities**
**Senior:** Mark Faraday *(Manager)*
**US SIC:** 2752, 6711
**UK SIC:** 47544, 83962
**Auditors:** Haines Watts

| | 30-09-13 | 30-09-12 | 30-09-11 |
|---|---|---|---|
| TA | 3,647,887 | 3,857,431 | 4,014,849 |
| NW | 2,428,418 | 2,343,460 | 2,188,660 |
| WC | 783,053 | 1,038,907 | 751,888 |

DUNS 34-988-3145

## Variohm Holdings Ltd

Williams' Barn Tiffield Road, Towcester, Northamptonshire NN12 6HP
**Tel:** 01327-351004
**Web:** www.variohmholdings.com
**Reg No:** 5783452 **Estd:** 2006 Private Limited Company
**Line of Business:** Management activities of holding companies
**Export Sales:** £6,004,137
**Issued Capital:** £70
**Directors:** Mrs C Donoghue, C Edwards, R Moffatt
**Co. Secretary:** Joan Moffatt
**US SIC:** 6711 **UK SIC:** 83962

| | 30-04-14 | 30-04-13 | 30-04-12 |
|---|---|---|---|
| TO | 18,317,840 | 14,033,066 | 13,322,730 |
| P/L | 791,090 | 1,132,878 | 1,197,441 |
| NW | 1,518,311 | 1,220,035 | 1,518,642 |
| WC | 2,134,245 | 2,387,920 | 1,360,149 |
| Emp. | 174 | 73 | 51 |

DUNS 64-109-3963 **Imp**

## Varlin Storage Ltd

(**Subsidiary of:** Aurum Investments Ltd)
Rookery Estate, West Charlton, Somerton, Somerset TA11 7AL
**Tel:** 01458-224080 **Fax:** 01458-224090
**Web:** www.varlin.co.uk
**Reg No:** 4512757 **Estd:** 1996 Private Limited Company
**Line of Business:** Other storage and warehousing not elsewhere classified
**Trading Style:** Varlin Storage Ltd
**Issued Capital:** £1
**Director:** D J Grindley
**Co. Secretary:** Jason Taylor
**US SIC:** 4226 **UK SIC:** 77003
**Bankers:** HSBC Bank plc (40-17-17)

| | 31-03-14 | 31-03-13 | 31-03-12 |
|---|---|---|---|
| TA | 1,156,857 | 1,078,579 | 705,538 |
| NW | 723,492 | 538,167 | 204,623 |
| WC | 432,526 | 268,901 | (21,010) |

DUNS 23-276-7512

## Varndean College

Surrenden Road, Brighton, East Sussex BN1 6WQ
**Tel:** 01273-508011
**Web:** www.varndean.ac.uk
**Estd:** 1983
**Line of Business:** Colleges (higher education)
**Director:** A Jenkins
**Responsibilities**
**Finance:** Beverley Luck *(Clerk)*
**Admin:** Amber Etherington *(Admissions Coordinator)*
**IT:** Daniel Harman *(Senior Technician)*
**HR:** Hazel O' Donnell *(Instructor)*
**US SIC:** 8221 **UK SIC:** 93100
**Employees:** 200

DUNS 21-419-3249

## The Varsity

19-20 Guildhall Street, Lincoln, Lincolnshire LN1 1TR
**Tel:** 01522-544938
**Web:** www.partyatthepub.co.uk
**Estd:** 1999 Proprietorship
**Line of Business:** Public house management services
**Proprietor:** Ms H Pearce
**Responsibilities**
**Senior:** Matthew Picker *(General Manager)*
**US SIC:** 5813 **UK SIC:** 66200
**Employees:** 47

DUNS 21-738-4740

## Vascroft Holdings Ltd

861 Coronation Road, Park Royal, London NW10 7PT
**Tel:** 020-8963-3400 **Fax:** 020-8963-3401
**Web:** www.vascroft.com
**Reg No:** 7721503 **Estd:** 2011 Private Limited Company
**Line of Business:** Construction of domestic buildings
**Issued Capital:** £10
**Directors:** S K Vekaria, M S Vekaria
**Co. Secretary:** Mrs Chandni Vora
**US SIC:** 1522 **UK SIC:** 50100
**Bankers:** HSBC Bank plc (40-05-23)

| | 31-08-14 | 31-08-13 | 31-08-12 |
|---|---|---|---|
| TO | 39,881,633 | 44,488,296 | 44,553,978 |
| P/L | 2,862,675 | 2,857,213 | 1,441,399 |
| NW | 4,766,967 | 1,888,264 | (930,293) |
| WC | 2,491,644 | 2,546,697 | 1,298,948 |
| Emp. | 134 | 135 | 152 |

DUNS 22-905-3087 **Imp-Exp**

## Vascutek Ltd

(**Subsidiary of:** Terumo Corporation)
Newmains Avenue, Renfrew, Renfrewshire PA4 9RR
**Tel:** 01418125555 **Fax:** 01418127170
**Web:** www.vascutek.com
**Reg No:** 0079773SC **VAT No:** 806391432
**Estd:** 1982 Private Limited Company
**Line of Business:** Manufacture of medical and surgical equipment and orthopaedic appliances
**Export Markets:** Worldwide
**Issued Capital:** £100
**Directors:** K Nishikawa, P Holbrook, A Rogers, S Sato
**Responsibilities**
**Senior:** Hideo Arase *(Manager)*, Timothy Ashton *(Manager)*, Naoyoshi Kitagawa *(Branch Manager)*, Beth-Joy MacLeod *(Manager)*, D McCulloch *(Manager)*, Shogo Ninomiya *(Manager)*, Mac Ritchie *(Vice President)*, Stuart Rodger *(Manager)*, Yutaro Shintaku *(Manager)*, Jim Veitch *(Manager)*
**Finance:** Irene Blackie *(Payroll Manager)*, Frank Carroll *(Financial Director)*
**Marketing:** Amy Heng *(Sales and Marketing Manager)*, Vera Lee *(Marketing Manager)*
**Sales:** Jennifer Carlyle *(Business Manager)*, Amy Heng *(Sales and Marketing Manager)*
**Admin:** Hong Goh *(Administration Manager)*
**Health & Safety:** T Woodruff *(Health and Safety Manager)*
**US SIC:** 3841, 2834
**UK SIC:** 37201, 25700
**Auditors:** KPMG LLP
**Bankers:** Bank Of Scotland (80-18-44)

| | 31-03-14 | 31-03-13 | 31-03-12 |
|---|---|---|---|
| TO | 52,633,000 | 63,812,000 | 58,775,000 |
| P/L | 6,165,000 | 11,847,000 | 10,166,000 |
| NW | 48,810,000 | 51,349,000 | 51,666,000 |
| WC | 35,756,000 | 40,213,000 | 42,232,000 |
| Emp. | 679 | 657 | 574 |

DUNS 39-975-4464

## Vatan Catering Ltd

37-43 Mill Mead Industrial Centre, London N17 9QU
**Tel:** 02088016658 **Fax:** 020 8801 9669
**Web:** www.vatan.com
**Reg No:** 2272123 **Estd:** 1988 Private Limited Company
**Line of Business:** Wholesale of meat and meat products
**Issued Capital:** £25,000
**Principals:** T Ibrahim *(Managing)*, H Ketenci
**Co. Secretary:** Alvin Harris
**Responsibilities**
**Senior:** Alvis Harris *(Manager)*
**Finance:** Alvis Harris *(Manager)*
**Marketing:** Alvis Harris *(Manager)*
**IT:** Ertan Huseyin *(IT Manager)*
**US SIC:** 5147 **UK SIC:** 61700
**Auditors:** Harman & Co
**Bankers:** HSBC Bank plc (40-02-31)

| | 31-03-14 | 31-03-13 | 31-03-12 |
|---|---|---|---|
| TO | 14,216,811 | 14,937,405 | 15,638,188 |
| P/L | 36,330 | (96,230) | (130,755) |
| NW | 1,344,275 | 1,307,945 | 1,404,175 |
| WC | 267,712 | 271,445 | 273,335 |
| Emp. | 96 | 120 | 120 |

DUNS 29-639-7995 **Imp**

## Vatre Terracotta Ltd

(**Subsidiary of:** Vatre Group Ltd)
J1 Dencora Way, Ashford, Kent TN23 4FH
**Web:** www.apta.co.uk
**Reg No:** 1966156 **VAT No:** 680290142
**Estd:** 1978 Private Limited Company
**Line of Business:** Other wholesale
**Trading Style:** A P T A
**Issued Capital:** £2
**Directors:** P A Sykes, Y Hong Wei, Mrs S D Sykes, J R Hoad
**Co. Secretary:** Ernest Clay
**US SIC:** 5199 **UK SIC:** 61900
**Auditors:** Calcutt Matthews
**Bankers:** Barclays Bank Plc (20-02-62)

| | 31-12-13 | 31-12-12 | 31-12-11 |
|---|---|---|---|
| TO | 8,176,774 | 6,711,177 | 6,905,251 |
| P/L | 338,372 | 222,620 | 210,380 |
| NW | 2,981,537 | 2,717,742 | 2,537,646 |
| WC | 2,896,518 | 2,689,886 | 2,476,674 |
| Emp. | 47 | 45 | 47 |

DUNS 85-612-3062

## Vattenfall Wind Power Ltd

(**Subsidiary of:** Vattenfall Ab)
St Andrews House, Hexham, Northumberland NE46 4QQ
**Tel:** 01434611300
**Web:** www.vattenfall.co.uk
**Reg No:** 6205750 **Estd:** 2007 Private Limited Company
**Line of Business:** Utility brokers
**Issued Capital:** £497,000,001
**Directors:** G Groebler, O B Nielsen, Ms I U Mirsch, P B Guy, Mrs A B Pytel, C M Reinholdsson, P H Smink
**Responsibilities**
**Senior:** Anders Dahl *(Manager)*, Veijo Huusko *(Manager)*, Peter Wesslau *(Manager)*
**Marketing:** Jason Ormiston *(Head of UK Media Relations and)*
**Engineering:** Kristin Andersen *(Project manager/R&D Engineer)*, Ronald Donnelly *(Engineering Manager Round 3)*
**US SIC:** 4911, 7399
**UK SIC:** 16101, 83954
**Auditors:** Ernst & Young LLP

| | 31-12-13 | 31-12-12 | 31-12-11 |
|---|---|---|---|
| TO | 12,473,000 | 8,787,000 | 12,117,000 |
| P/L | 9,581,000 | 7,502,000 | 1,393,000 |
| NW | 513,380,000 | 505,661,000 | 499,845,000 |
| WC | 394,261,000 | 417,123,000 | 417,297,000 |
| Emp. | 170 | 137 | 70 |

DUNS 73-802-7213 **Imp**

## Vatukoula Gold Mines Plc

Level 5 2 More London Riverside, London SE1 2AP
**Tel:** 02074400643
**Web:** www.vgmplc.com
**Reg No:** 5059077 **Estd:** 2004 Public Limited Company
**Line of Business:** Quarries
**Issued Capital:** £5,877,917
**Directors:** Y Ng, Z Li, I He, L Sun, Q Cao
**Co. Secretary:** Laytons Secretaries Limited
**US SIC:** 1499 **UK SIC:** 23960
**Auditors:** Mazars LLP

| | 31-08-13 | 31-08-12 | 31-08-11 |
|---|---|---|---|
| TO | 39,080,000 | 54,925,000 | 47,964,000 |
| P/L | (16,853,000) | (8,145,000) | (3,933,000) |
| NW | 32,164,000 | 31,094,000 | 34,481,000 |
| WC | (1,018,000) | 4,276,000 | 16,264,000 |
| Emp. | 1,425 | 1,458 | 1,150 |

DUNS 21-574-0564

## Vaughan Engineering Ltd

(**Subsidiary of:** Rathmore Estates Ltd)
14 Blue Sky Way Monkton Business Park, South, Hebburn, Tyne and Wear NE31 2EQ
**Tel:** 01914952777 **Fax:** 01506-854006
**Web:** www.vaughan-group.co.uk
**Reg No:** 0050679SC **Estd:** 1972 Private Limited Company
**Line of Business:** Plumbing, heating & air cond contractors
**Trading Style:** Vaughan Engineering Ltd
**Issued Capital:** £10,000
**Principals:** A J Vaughan *(Chairman)*, M J Vaughan, B P Vaughan, G W Galletly, D Fraser, C W Paterson, G R Black
**Co. Secretary:** Gavin Vaughan
**Responsibilities**
**Senior:** Darren Charlton *(Branch Manager)*
**Branches:** Vaughan Engineering Ltd, Unit 3, Colne Way, Watford, Hertfordshire WD24 7NE
**US SIC:** 1711, 1796
**UK SIC:** 50300, 50400
**Auditors:** McCreery Turkington Stockman
**Bankers:** Northern Bank Ltd (95-00-05)

| | 31-03-14 | 31-03-13 | 31-03-12 |
|---|---|---|---|
| TO | 36,906,406 | 39,637,805 | 30,348,988 |
| P/L | (17,814) | 213,622 | 244,472 |
| NW | 1,059,669 | 1,178,384 | 1,227,013 |
| WC | 1,022,068 | 1,137,980 | 1,190,247 |
| Emp. | 183 | 158 | 127 |

DUNS 21-714-4810

## Vaughan Lee House

Orchard Vale, Ilminster, Somerset TA19 0EX
**Tel:** 0146052077
**Web:** www.vaughanleehouse.co.uk
**Estd:** 1964
**Line of Business:** Residential care establishments
**Proprietor:** Mrs Y Foulsham
**Responsibilities**
**Senior:** Stella Fuszard *(Manager)*
**US SIC:** 8321 **UK SIC:** 96111
**Employees:** 48

DUNS 57-831-8412

## Vaughan Ltd

Unit G1, Chelsea Harbour Chelsea Harbour Design, Centre, London SW10 0XE
**Tel:** 02073494600
**Web:** www.vaughandesigns.com
**Reg No:** 2889411 **Estd:** 1994 Private Limited Company
**Line of Business:** Agents involved in the sale of a variety of goods
**Export Sales:** £9,127,912
**Trading Style:** Vaughan Ltd
**Issued Capital:** £1,000
**Directors:** Ms L M Vaughan, The Hon M J Vaughan, Ms V C De Lotbiniere, T Coles
**Co. Secretary:** Paul Hillyard
**Branches:** Vaughan Ltd, Units 17-23 Carnwath Road Industrial Estate, Carnwath Road, London SW6 3HR
**US SIC:** 5199, 5064
**UK SIC:** 61900, 61500
**Auditors:** Brebner Allen & Trapp
**Bankers:** National Westminster Bank Plc (50-30-10)

| | 30-04-14 | 30-04-13 | 30-04-12 |
|---|---|---|---|
| TO | 13,188,529 | 13,137,580 | 12,699,515 |
| P/L | 1,372,566 | 1,487,961 | 950,460 |
| NW | 7,958,967 | 7,030,882 | 5,936,963 |
| WC | 8,029,147 | 7,012,064 | 5,917,281 |
| Emp. | 87 | 87 | 81 |

DUNS 23-749-9616

## Vaughans Radio Ltd

21 Quay Street, Haverfordwest, Dyfed SA61 1BD
**Tel:** 01437760101
**Web:** www.vaughans.co.uk
**Reg No:** 3743951 **Estd:** 1970 Private Limited Company
**Line of Business:** Audio visual equipment
**Issued Capital:** £2
**Director:** J A Vaughan
**Co. Secretary:** Mrs Valerie Vaughan
**Branches:** Vaughans Radio Ltd, 10 Thomas Street, Llanelli, Dyfed SA15 3JA
**US SIC:** 3662 **UK SIC:** 34430

| | 31-03-14 | 31-03-13 | 31-03-12 |
|---|---|---|---|
| TO | N/A | N/A | 5,254,056 |
| P/L | N/A | N/A | 55,823 |
| NW | 3,426,536 | 3,414,803 | 3,461,954 |
| WC | 2,489,638 | 2,385,013 | 2,555,137 |
| Emp. | N/A | N/A | 49 |

DUNS 23-699-1399 **Imp**

## Vault-Ic Uk Ltd

Scottish Enterprise Technology Park, Glasgow, Lanarkshire G75 0QR
**Tel:** 01355-803000 **Fax:** 01355242743
**Web:** www.insidesecure.com
**Reg No:** 3693883 **Estd:** 1999 Private Limited Company
**Line of Business:** Design consultants
**Trading Style:** Atmel Secure Products
**Issued Capital:** £1
**Directors:** R V Detourniere, A P Bear
**Co. Secretary:** Jordan Company Secretaries Limit
**Responsibilities**
**Senior:** Patrick Reutens *(Manager)*
**Marketing:** Aloke Sinha *(Marketing Manager)*
**IT:** Cathie Connell *(Risk Manager)*
**HR:** Tom Henery *(Human Resources Manager)*
**US SIC:** 8911, 7391
**UK SIC:** 83701, 94000
**Auditors:** Eacott Worrall
**Bankers:** Bank Of Scotland (80-06-64)

| | 31-12-13 | 31-12-12 | 31-12-11 |
|---|---|---|---|
| TO | 5,866,199 | 6,366,741 | 6,384,084 |
| P/L | 381,030 | 325,654 | 24,096 |
| NW | 4,060,733 | 3,797,198 | 3,644,612 |
| WC | 3,198,163 | 2,774,024 | 2,091,907 |
| Emp. | 57 | 77 | 78 |

DUNS 21-908-8317

## Vauxhall Holiday Park Ltd

Acle New Road, Great Yarmouth, Norfolk NR30 1TB
**Tel:** 01493-857231 **Fax:** 01493-331122
**Web:** www.vauxhallholidays.com
**Reg No:** 0651467 **VAT No:** 104974469
**Estd:** 1960 Private Limited Company
**Line of Business:** Camping site operators
**Issued Capital:** £525,000
**Managing Director:** J S Biss
**Co. Secretary:** Wayne Biss
**Responsibilities**
**Senior:** Roger Finney *(Site Manager)*
**US SIC:** 7033 **UK SIC:** 66701
**Auditors:** Kershen Fairfax
**Bankers:** HSBC Bank plc (40-46-08)

| | 28-02-14 | 28-02-13 | 29-02-12 |
|---|---|---|---|
| TO | 6,578,802 | 6,400,678 | 6,702,975 |
| P/L | 171,696 | 41,327 | 210,298 |
| NW | 4,495,213 | 4,418,374 | 4,357,184 |
| WC | (2,262,050) | (2,172,513) | (1,999,001) |
| Emp. | 110 | 115 | 126 |

DUNS 21-012-5166 **Exp**

## Vauxhall Motors Ltd

(**Subsidiary of:** Gm Automotive Uk)
Osborne Road, Luton, Bedfordshire LU1 3YT
**Tel:** 01582-721122
**Web:** www.vauxhall.co.uk
**Reg No:** 6356274 **Estd:** 1914 Private Limited Company
**Line of Business:** Representative office
**Trading Style:** General Motors Uk
**Issued Capital:** £1
**Directors:** T Tozer, P T Hope, J R Fulcher, Ms R S Nagi
**Responsibilities**
**Senior:** Duncan Aldred *(Manager)*, Richard Molyneux *(Manager)*, Christopher Parfitt *(Chairman)*, Thomas Schmidt *(Manager)*
**Marketing:** Helen Parker *(Direct Marketing Campaigns Man)*, Andy Vincent *(Motability Sales & Marketing M)*
**Sales:** Phil Mackey *(Retail Project Development and)*, Claire Snook *(Regional Fleet Sales Manager)*, Andy Vincent *(Motability Sales & Marketing M)*
**Operations:** Martin Gustard Brown *(Operations Manager)*, Keith Michaels *(Head of Marketing Operations)*
**Fleet:** Claire Snook *(Regional Fleet Sales Manager)*
**Engineering:** Paul Gatland *(Manufacturing Project Engineer)*
**Branches:** Vauxhall Motors Ltd, Kimpton Road, Luton, Bedfordshire LU2 0TY
**US SIC:** 3711 **UK SIC:** 35101

| | 31-12-13 | 31-12-12 | 31-12-11 |
|---|---|---|---|
| TA | 1 | 1 | 1 |
| NW | 1 | 1 | 1 |

DUNS 21-919-0345 **Imp-Exp**

## Vax Ltd

(**Subsidiary of:** Techtronic Industries Co. Ltd.)
Quillgold House, Droitwich, Worcestershire WR9 0QH
**Tel:** 08444128455 **Fax:** 01905799655
**Web:** www.vax.co.uk
**Reg No:** 1341840 **VAT No:** 747878269
**Estd:** 1977 Private Limited Company
**Line of Business:** Wholesale of radio and television goods; wholesale of electrical household appliances not elsewhere classified
**Export Sales:** £7,980,000
**Issued Capital:** £40,000
**Managing Director:** S Lawson
**Co. Secretary:** Michael Raybould
**Responsibilities**
**Senior:** Andy Tyler *(Warehouse Manager)*
**HR:** K Daines *(Human Resources Director)*
**Engineering:** Matt Granger *(Design Engineering Manager)*, Richard Waters *(?Senior Design Engineering Man)*
**Branches:** Vax Ltd, Kingswood Road, Droitwich, Worcestershire WR9 0QH
**US SIC:** 5064, 5732
**UK SIC:** 61500, 64800
**Auditors:** Deloitte LLP
**Bankers:** Barclays Bank Plc (20-07-71)

| | 31-12-13 | 31-12-12 | 31-12-11 |
|---|---|---|---|
| TO | 132,072,000 | 112,234,000 | 83,759,000 |
| P/L | 226,000 | 839,000 | 118,000 |
| NW | 1,031,000 | 2,073,000 | 2,266,000 |
| WC | 11,396,000 | 17,720,000 | 18,234,000 |
| Emp. | 360 | 312 | 264 |

DUNS 22-611-9014 **Imp**

## Vbh (Gb) Ltd

(**Subsidiary of:** Vbh Holding Ag)
Vbh House, Bailey Drive, Gillingham Business Park, Gillingham, Kent ME8 0WG
**Tel:** 01634263300 **Fax:** 01634-263504
**Web:** www.vbhgb.com
**Reg No:** 1634128 **VAT No:** 373550058
**Estd:** 2012 Private Limited Company
**Line of Business:** Door and window furniture
**Export Sales:** £374,964
**Issued Capital:** £3,750,000
**Directors:** Ms F Keddie, P T Rowlands, C Bako, S J Sale
**Co. Secretary:** Ms Fay Keddie
**Responsibilities**
**Senior:** Allan Price *(General Manager)*
**Purchasing:** Robb Crampton *(Purchasing Manager)*
**Branches:** Vbh (Gb) Ltd, 13 Hawbank Road, Glasgow, Lanarkshire G74 5EG
**US SIC:** 4712, 5039
**UK SIC:** 77002, 61300
**Auditors:** MacIntyre Hudson LLP
**Bankers:** HSBC Bank plc (40-39-02)

| | 31-12-13 | 31-12-12 | 31-12-11 |
|---|---|---|---|
| TO | 17,636,851 | 17,569,799 | 18,300,221 |
| P/L | 245,894 | 207,830 | 37,240 |
| NW | 4,538,454 | 4,194,981 | 4,007,758 |
| WC | 3,735,686 | 2,155,007 | 1,945,682 |
| Emp. | 63 | 65 | 71 |

DUNS 42-435-6343

## Vca

1 Eastgate Office Centre, Eastgate Road, Bristol, Avon BS5 6XX
**Tel:** 03003305797
**Web:** www.dft.gov.uk
**Estd:** 1994 Incorporate By Act Of Parliament
**Line of Business:** Central government
**Trading Style:** Vehicle Certification Agency, V C A
**Directors:** D Harvey, A Buckle
**Responsibilities**
**IT:** Nalin Parekh *(Computer Manager)*
**US SIC:** 9121 **UK SIC:** 91110
**Employees:** 85

DUNS 21-669-3529 **Imp**

## Vcg (Holdings) Ltd

Unit 1 Europa Park, Croft Way, Witham, Essex CM8 2FN
**Tel:** 01376533055
**Web:** www.vcg-group.com
**Reg No:** 7224970 **Estd:** 2010 Private Limited Company
**Line of Business:** Management activities of holding companies
**Export Sales:** £4,245,835
**Issued Capital:** £1,000
**Directors:** D J Amber, P J Long, Ms S Ingleson
**Co. Secretary:** Mrs Hannah Wright
**US SIC:** 6711 **UK SIC:** 83962
**Auditors:** Baker Tilly UK Audit LLP

| | 31-12-13 | 31-12-12 | 31-12-11 |
|---|---|---|---|
| TO | 21,998,810 | 24,782,841 | 25,013,747 |
| P/L | 131,897 | (589,895) | 497,550 |
| NW | (1,577,813) | (1,853,959) | (1,465,247) |
| WC | 597,366 | 552,009 | 997,420 |
| Emp. | 299 | 284 | 245 |

DUNS 77-170-1828

## Vdc Trading Ltd

V D C House, 4 Brandon Road, London N7 9AA
**Tel:** 02077002777
**Web:** www.vdctrading.com
**Reg No:** 2708733 **VAT No:** 471832343
**Estd:** 1987 Private Limited Company
**Line of Business:** Manufacture of insulated wire and cable
**Issued Capital:** £430
**Principals:** N J Holden *(Managing)*, A T Higginson, N R Chmara, Ms T J Gould, J Reed
**Co. Secretary:** Ms Sally Holden
**Responsibilities**
**Finance:** Kelly Quidley *(Financial Controller)*
**US SIC:** 3357, 5999
**UK SIC:** 22470, 65600
**Bankers:** National Westminster Bank Plc (60-50-03)

| | 31-12-13 | 31-12-12 | 31-12-11 |
|---|---|---|---|
| TA | 1,961,501 | 2,090,192 | 2,327,143 |
| NW | 334,672 | 689,556 | 1,085,121 |
| WC | 194,000 | 525,944 | 866,697 |

DUNS 21-686-0668

## V.E. Parrott (Oakley) Ltd

(**Subsidiary of:** Parrott Holdings Ltd)
24 Lovell Road, Oakley, Bedford, Bedfordshire MK43 7RZ
**Tel:** 01234824211 **Fax:** 01234-824560
**Web:** www.veparrott.co.uk
**Reg No:** 0940816 **VAT No:** 608727916
**Estd:** 1968 Private Limited Company
**Line of Business:** Building construction contractors
**Issued Capital:** £250,000
**Principals:** M R Parrott *(Chairman and Managing)*, N E Stubbings, D T Moore, C P Layram
**Co. Secretary:** Derek Parrott
**Responsibilities**
**Admin:** Brian Dunlop *(Office Manager)*
**HR:** Roger Mason *(Facilities Manager)*
**Health & Safety:** Roger Mason *(Facilities Manager)*
**Facilities:** Roger Mason *(Facilities Manager)*
**Branches:** V.e. Parrott (Oakley) Ltd, 87 Dallow Rd, Luton, Bedfordshire LU1 1NW
**US SIC:** 1522 **UK SIC:** 50100
**Auditors:** MacIntyre Hudson LLP
**Bankers:** National Westminster Bank Plc (60-02-13)

| | 31-12-13 | 31-12-12 | 31-12-11 |
|---|---|---|---|
| TA | 2,007,494 | 2,206,919 | 2,247,332 |
| NW | 622,067 | 561,323 | 458,444 |
| WC | 537,576 | 459,668 | 349,757 |

DUNS 64-072-6980

## Veale Wasbrough Ltd

(**Subsidiary of:** Veale Wasbrough Vizards Llp)
Orchard Court, Orchard Lane, Bristol, Avon BS1 5WS
**Tel:** 01179-252020 **Fax:** 0117-925-2025
**Web:** www.vwv.co.uk
**Reg No:** 3468094 **Estd:** 1997 Private Limited Company
**Line of Business:** Solicitors
**Issued Capital:** £1
**Directors:** D R Emanuel, S R Heald, G E Philpott, Velocity Company (Holdings) Limi
**Co. Secretary:** Velocity Company Secretarial Ser
**Responsibilities**
**Finance:** M Fice *(Financial Director)*
**Marketing:** Antonia James *(Head of Marketing)*
**US SIC:** 8111, 6531
**UK SIC:** 83500, 83400

| | 30-11-13 | 30-11-12 | 30-11-11 |
|---|---|---|---|
| TA | 1 | 1 | 1 |
| NW | 1 | 1 | 1 |

DUNS 77-936-1732

## Vear Building Services Ltd

(**Subsidiary of:** Vear Holdings Ltd)
3 Mayflower Close, Chandlers Ford, Eastleigh, Hampshire SO53 4AR
**Tel:** 023-8025-2931 **Fax:** 023-8025-4610
**Web:** www.veargroup.co.uk
**Reg No:** 3048253 **VAT No:** 673776879
**Estd:** 1999 Private Limited Company
**Line of Business:** Builders
**Issued Capital:** £3,000
**Directors:** G C Ellison, T C Waters, A J Hammerton, R J Child
**Responsibilities**
**Finance:** Patricia Lupton *(Manager)*
**HR:** Mark Mallon *(Human Resources Manager)*
**US SIC:** 1522 **UK SIC:** 50100
**Auditors:** Fiander Tovell LLP

**Bankers:** Barclays Bank Plc (20-00-62)

| | 31-12-13 | 31-12-12 | 31-12-11 |
|---|---|---|---|
| TO | 8,257,320 | 8,961,527 | 16,199,818 |
| P/L | 24,620 | (317,396) | 168,205 |
| NW | 103,200 | 85,364 | 353,726 |
| WC | (4,710) | (62,377) | 168,229 |
| Emp. | 52 | 63 | 80 |

DUNS 23-411-3699
## Vebego Services Bv
**(Subsidiary of:** Vebego International Nv)
37-39 Manor Road, Romford, Essex RM1 2TL
**Tel:** 01708766977
**Web:** www.vebego.com
**Reg No:** 0022131FC **Estd:** 1995 Foreign Company
**Line of Business:** Cleaning/maintenance Services To Buildings
**US SIC:** 7349 **UK SIC:** 92300

DUNS 51-992-5098
## Vebnet Ltd
**(Subsidiary of:** Standard Life Plc)
Standard Life House, 30 Lothian Road, Edinburgh, Midlothian EH1 2DH
**Tel:** 08453047142
**Web:** www.vebnet.com
**Reg No:** 0207389SC **Estd:** 2000 Private Limited Company
**Line of Business:** Computer services
**Issued Capital:** £11,204
**Directors:** G R Bold, M A Hesketh
**Co. Secretary:** Frances Horsburgh
**US SIC:** 7379 **UK SIC:** 83940
**Auditors:** LWC Audit Ltd
**Bankers:** Clydesdale Bank Plc (82-62-27)

| | 31-12-13 | 31-12-12 | 31-12-11 |
|---|---|---|---|
| TO | 6,996,649 | 7,615,208 | 7,578,491 |
| P/L | 150,901 | 476,316 | (1,135,121) |
| NW | (279,736) | (422,423) | (1,142,659) |
| WC | 1,378,399 | (422,423) | (1,217,141) |
| Emp. | 73 | 91 | 82 |

DUNS 23-929-5137
## Vebra Ltd
**(Subsidiary of:** Shoosmiths Nominees Ltd)
Halifax Way, Pocklington Industrial Estate, Pocklington, York, North Yorkshire YO42 1NP
**Tel:** 01759305374
**Web:** www.vebra.com
**Reg No:** 3919424 **Estd:** 1902 Private Limited Company
**Line of Business:** Management activities of holding companies
**Issued Capital:** £408,260
**Director:** M D Goddard
**Responsibilities**
**Senior:** Steve Tiplady *(Finance Director)*
**Finance:** Steve Tiplady *(Finance Director)*
**US SIC:** 6711 **UK SIC:** 83962
**Auditors:** Smailes Goldie

| | 31-03-14 | 31-03-13 | 01-03-12 |
|---|---|---|---|
| TA | N/A | 203,000 | 877,376 |
| P/L | N/A | (874,000) | N/A |
| NW | (203,000) | (203,000) | 671,206 |
| WC | N/A | (203,000) | N/A |

DUNS 73-256-1480
## Vebra Solutions Ltd
**(Subsidiary of:** Shoosmiths Nominees Ltd)
1 Oxford Court St James Road, Brackley, Northamptonshire NN13 7XY
**Tel:** 08452305333 **Fax:** 08452305777
**Reg No:** 4529917 **Estd:** 2002 Private Limited Company
**Line of Business:** Publishing of software
**Issued Capital:** £1
**Directors:** G N Scott, M D Goddard
**Responsibilities**
**Marketing:** Suzanne Deakins *(Head of Group Marketing)*
**IT:** Ed Mardell *(Chief Technology Officer)*
**US SIC:** 7372, 5081
**UK SIC:** 83940, 61490
**Auditors:** PricewaterhouseCoopers LLP

| | 31-03-14 | 31-03-13 | 01-03-12 |
|---|---|---|---|
| TO | 4,775,000 | 4,497,000 | 4,552,000 |
| P/L | 52,000 | (173,000) | 20,000 |
| NW | 930,000 | 939,000 | 1,560,000 |
| WC | 654,000 | 487,000 | 1,127,000 |
| Emp. | 78 | 78 | 84 |

DUNS 39-694-7400 Imp
## Vectaire Ltd
Lincoln Road, Cressex Business Park, High Wycombe, Buckinghamshire HP12 3RH
**Tel:** 01494522333
**Web:** www.vectaire.co.uk
**Reg No:** 2151635 **Estd:** 1987 Private Limited Company
**Line of Business:** Ventilation systems
**Issued Capital:** £116,000
**Managing Director:** V Gaeta
**Co. Secretary:** Mario Gaeta
**Responsibilities**
**Marketing:** Carol Auster *(Sales & Marketing Manager)*
**Sales:** Carol Auster *(Sales & Marketing Manager)*
**Branches:** Vectaire Ltd, Suite 4D & 5D Epos House, Heage Road, Ripley, Derbyshire DE5 3GH
**US SIC:** 3585 **UK SIC:** 32841
**Auditors:** Saffery Champness
**Bankers:** National Westminster Bank Plc (60-17-31)

| | 31-12-13 | 31-12-12 | 31-12-11 |
|---|---|---|---|
| TO | 7,603,527 | 7,530,107 | 7,834,114 |
| P/L | 329,886 | 296,523 | 426,700 |
| NW | 2,372,612 | 2,113,621 | 1,872,629 |
| WC | 1,982,670 | 1,698,895 | 1,510,314 |
| Emp. | 59 | 58 | 57 |

DUNS 29-432-3985 Imp
## Vectis Holdings Ltd
Blackgang, Ventnor, Isle of Wight PO38 2HN
**Tel:** 01983730330
**Web:** www.vectisholdings.co.uk
**Reg No:** 1552172 **Estd:** 1981 Private Limited Company
**Line of Business:** Fair and amusement park activities
**Issued Capital:** £420
**Directors:** P J Warren, A W Dabell, R C Holgate, Mrs J Dabell
**Co. Secretary:** Robert Holgate
**US SIC:** 7996, 8799
**UK SIC:** 97913, 83954
**Auditors:** Hook & Co Ltd

| | 31-10-13 | 31-10-12 | 31-10-11 |
|---|---|---|---|
| TO | 3,999,461 | 3,540,701 | 3,670,139 |
| P/L | 48,238 | (153,000) | 545,000 |
| NW | 2,578,566 | 4,018,970 | 4,262,191 |
| WC | 1,582,967 | 1,729,120 | 2,197,727 |
| Emp. | 72 | 69 | 50 |

DUNS 21-018-6972 Imp-Exp
## Vector Aerospace International Ltd
**(Subsidiary of:** Airbus Group N.V.)
Fareham Road, Lee-On-The-Solent, Hampshire PO13 0AA
**Tel:** 02392 946100
**Web:** www.vectoraerospace.com
**Reg No:** 6404274 **VAT No:** 924353628
**Estd:** 1940 Private Limited Company
**Line of Business:** Manufacture of aircraft and spacecraft
**Export Sales:** £32,967,000
**Trading Style:** Vector Aerospace
**Issued Capital:** £10,000,100
**Directors:** S G Jones, M K Tyrrell
**Co. Secretary:** Paul Bryant
**Responsibilities**
**Senior:** Randal Levine *(Manager)*, Barry Merrikin *(Manager)*, Declan O'Shea *(Manager)*, Timothy Rice *(Manager)*
**Marketing:** Philip Self *(Head of Sales & Marketing)*
**Sales:** Philip Self *(Head of Sales & Marketing)*
**Facilities:** Kevin Powley *(Engine Manager)*
**Branches:** Vector Aerospace International Ltd, Component Services Uk, Almondbank, PH1 3NQ Perth
**US SIC:** 3721, 7539
**UK SIC:** 36400, 67100
**Auditors:** Ernst & Young LLP
**Bankers:** Bank Of Scotland (80-07-48)

| | 31-12-13 | 31-12-12 | 31-12-11 |
|---|---|---|---|
| TO | 115,250,000 | 103,068,000 | 112,734,000 |
| P/L | 12,500,000 | 408,000 | 8,933,000 |
| NW | 21,852,000 | 13,654,000 | 14,542,000 |
| WC | 1,472,000 | (4,969,000) | (767,000) |
| Emp. | 1,185 | 1,130 | 1,171 |

DUNS 53-613-7748 Imp
## Vectura Group Plc
One Prospect West, Chippenham, Wiltshire SN14 6FH
**Tel:** 01249667700 **Fax:** 01249-667701
**Web:** www.vectura.co.uk
**Reg No:** 3418970 **Estd:** 1997 Private Limited Company
**Line of Business:** Research and experimental development on natural sciences and engineering
**Export Sales:** £33,700,000
**Issued Capital:** £117,913
**Directors:** A J Oakley, Dr C P Blackwell, Dr S E Foden, B F Angelici, Dr T M Phillips, Dr J R Brown, N W Warner
**Co. Secretary:** Andrew Oakley
**Responsibilities**
**Senior:** Colin Dalton *(Director, Intellectual Propert)*
**Marketing:** Siobhan Brown *(Press Officer)*, Doug Smalley *(Marketing Manager)*
**IT:** Ian Attenburrow *(IT Manager)*, Jeremy Benson *(IT Manager)*
**Health & Safety:** Jos Sproot *(Health & Safety Officer)*
**Facilities:** Andy Lilley *(Facilities Manager)*
**Operations:** Martin Shott *(Pharmaceutical Operations Dire)*
**Purchasing:** William Livingstone *(Contracts Director)*
**US SIC:** 7391 **UK SIC:** 94000

**Auditors:** Deloitte LLP
**Bankers:** Barclays Bank Plc (20-17-35)

| | 31-03-14 | 31-03-13 | 31-03-12 |
|---|---|---|---|
| TO | 36,500,000 | 30,500,000 | 33,000,000 |
| P/L | (4,800,000) | (10,400,000) | (13,200,000) |
| NW | 30,500,000 | 68,400,000 | 66,500,000 |
| WC | 79,400,000 | 60,300,000 | 61,700,000 |
| Emp. | 215 | 216 | 209 |

DUNS 73-476-5139 Imp
## Vedanta Resources Plc
5th Floor, London W1J 8DZ
**Tel:** 020-7499-5900
**Web:** www.vedantaresources.com
**Reg No:** 4740415 **Estd:** 2003 Public Limited Company
**Line of Business:** Mining of metals
**Directors:** T Albanese, A Mehta, D Parekh, E R Macdonald, N Agarwal, Ms E N Zotova, G S Green, A Agarwal
**Co. Secretary:** Deepak Kumar
**Responsibilities**
**Senior:** Mahendra Mehta *(Manager)*, A Paliwall *(Manager)*
**Admin:** Preeti Sharma *(CFO Personal Assistant)*
**Operations:** Mansoor Siddiqi *(Group Director - Projects)*
**US SIC:** 1099, 3332
**UK SIC:** 21000, 22470
**Auditors:** Deloitte LLP
**Employees:** 31,171
**Turnover:** £1.294E+10

DUNS 21-158-4868
## Vedbaek Ltd
**(Subsidiary of:** Vedbaek Holdings Ltd.)
3rd Floor, Triton Square, London NW1 3XB
**Web:** www.pc1.co.uk
**Reg No:** 6858712 **VAT No:** 948512207
**Estd:** 2009 Private Limited Company
**Line of Business:** Computer support & services
**Trading Style:** The Nav People
**Issued Capital:** £1,000
**Directors:** M K Dredge, I Humphries, D Walker, G M Wigglesworth, P J Angell, P A Lingham
**Branches:** Vedbaek Ltd, 1 Triton Square, London NW1 3DX
**US SIC:** 7379, 7392
**UK SIC:** 83940, 83951

| | 31-03-14 | 31-03-13 | 31-03-12 |
|---|---|---|---|
| TA | 2,303,678 | 1,817,066 | 1,576,585 |
| NW | (19,024) | (29,821) | (52,556) |
| WC | (62,162) | (204,114) | (187,460) |

DUNS 21-819-8000 Imp-Exp
## Vee Bee Ltd
Old Wharf Road, Stourbridge, West Midlands DY8 4LS
**Tel:** 01384-378884
**Web:** www.veebee.com
**Reg No:** 0586030 **VAT No:** 276901339
**Estd:** 1956 Private Limited Company
**Line of Business:** Manufacture of other special purpose machinery not elsewhere classified
**Export Markets:** Middle East, E U, Japan, U S A,
**Issued Capital:** £109,500
**Principals:** R V Bradley *(Managing)*, Dr W K Bolton, M V Bradley
**Co. Secretary:** John Dalton
**Responsibilities**
**Senior:** Michael Grove *(Partner)*, Simon Hale *(Manager)*
**Finance:** Nikki Reynolds *(Financial Controller)*
**Sales:** Michael Noakes *(Sales Director)*
**US SIC:** 3559 **UK SIC:** 32863
**Auditors:** Felton & Co
**Bankers:** Barclays Bank Plc (20-82-70)

| | 30-09-14 | 30-09-13 | 30-09-12 |
|---|---|---|---|
| TO | 8,360,080 | 9,726,459 | 6,489,669 |
| P/L | 858,553 | 1,012,845 | 310,353 |
| NW | 3,996,447 | 3,341,001 | 2,818,748 |
| WC | 3,709,562 | 3,280,357 | 2,575,795 |
| Emp. | 60 | 61 | 63 |

DUNS 77-932-3849
## Veenus Ltd
Beaufort Court, Admirals Way, London E14 9XL
**Tel:** 01753836600
**Web:** www.veenus.com
**Reg No:** 3044931 **Estd:** 1995 Private Limited Company
**Line of Business:** Tourist information offices
**Issued Capital:** £100
**Director:** R Bhalla
**US SIC:** 7941, 4722
**UK SIC:** 97911, 77001
**Auditors:** RBS Accountants Ltd

| | 30-09-14 | 30-09-13 | 30-09-12 |
|---|---|---|---|
| TA | 749,322 | 639,379 | 916,327 |
| NW | 145,253 | 143,046 | 166,520 |
| WC | 128,205 | 117,813 | 127,404 |

DUNS 34-768-6755 Imp
## Veetee Foods Ltd
Invicta House, Sir Thomas Longley Road, Medway City Estate, Rochester, Kent ME2 4DU
**Tel:** 01634710258 **Fax:** 01634716270
**Web:** www.veetee.com
**Reg No:** 5569652 **Estd:** 2005 Private Limited Company
**Line of Business:** Manufacture of food products and beverages
**Export Sales:** £950,560
**Issued Capital:** £2,000,000
**Directors:** M C Varma, R Varma
**Co. Secretary:** Shashi Surana
**Responsibilities**
**IT:** Andre Ludick *(IT Director)*
**US SIC:** 2099 **UK SIC:** 42399
**Auditors:** Adrian C. Mansbridge & Co

| | 31-12-13 | 31-12-12 | 31-12-11 |
|---|---|---|---|
| TO | 16,157,039 | 12,946,372 | 13,664,895 |
| P/L | 1,476,850 | 1,196,089 | 2,517,357 |
| NW | 7,160,187 | 7,022,224 | 5,826,875 |
| WC | 690,130 | (128,248) | 175,778 |
| Emp. | 66 | 57 | 43 |

DUNS 29-685-4557 Imp-Exp
## Veetee Rice Ltd
**(Subsidiary of:** Veetee Investments Corporation)
Veetee House, Neptune Close, Rochester, Kent ME2 4LT
**Tel:** 01634-290092 **Fax:** 01634-297792
**Web:** www.veetee.com
**Reg No:** 2009019 **VAT No:** 442181866
**Estd:** 1986 Private Limited Company
**Line of Business:** Mills and millers
**Export Markets:** Rest of World
**Export Sales:** £6,716,179
**Trading Style:** V T Rice
**Issued Capital:** £5,000,000
**Principals:** M C Varma *(Managing)*, E Al Muhaidib, R Varma, I M Al-Muhaideb
**Co. Secretary:** Shashi Surana
**Responsibilities**
**Senior:** David Crewe *(Works Manager)*, Andre Ludick *(IT Manager)*, Vikas Magoon *(Chief Executive Officer)*, Moni Varma *(Manager)*
**Marketing:** Gillian Newnham *(Marketing Manager)*, Poneet Thaman *(Brand Manager)*
**IT:** Andre Ludick *(IT Manager)*
**Health & Safety:** Colin O'Connell *(Health & Safety Manager)*
**Facilities:** David Crewe *(Works Manager)*
**Purchasing:** Greg Parmenter *(Purchasing Supply Manager)*
**Engineering:** David Crewe *(Works Manager)*
**US SIC:** 2043 **UK SIC:** 42398
**Auditors:** Adrian C. Mansbridge & Co
**Bankers:** Lloyds TSB Bank plc (30-92-82)

| | 31-12-13 | 31-12-12 | 31-12-11 |
|---|---|---|---|
| TO | 60,911,470 | 55,688,772 | 71,392,702 |
| P/L | 3,501,183 | 2,751,377 | 1,485,593 |
| NW | 19,120,051 | 16,263,341 | 14,230,014 |
| WC | 12,294,176 | 10,003,776 | 7,790,026 |
| Emp. | 128 | 120 | 108 |

DUNS 22-727-5328 Imp-Exp
## Vega Consulting Services Ltd
**(Subsidiary of:** Finmeccanica Spa)
2 Falcon Way, Welwyn Garden City, Hertfordshire AL7 1TW
**Tel:** 01179008975
**Web:** www.vega.co.uk
**Reg No:** 1393778 **Estd:** 1978 Private Limited Company
**Line of Business:** Representative office
**Trading Style:** Vega Skillchange, Vega
**Issued Capital:** £1,098,839
**Directors:** K G Thomsit, C Porter
**Responsibilities**
**Senior:** Kenneth Blyth *(Manager)*, Marco Porfiri *(Manager)*, Heather Quenault Garnham *(Manager)*
**Branches:** Vega Consulting Services Ltd, Second Floor Ardent House, Gates Way, Stevenage, Hertfordshire SG1 3YY
**US SIC:** 7399 **UK SIC:** 83954
**Auditors:** PricewaterhouseCoopers LLP
**Bankers:** Bank Of Scotland (12-01-03)

| | 31-12-13 | 31-12-12 | 31-12-11 |
|---|---|---|---|
| TO | 6,580,000 | 18,196,000 | 21,241,000 |
| P/L | (1,798,000) | (412,000) | 60,000 |
| NW | 14,072,000 | 6,443,000 | 6,181,000 |
| WC | N/A | 5,979,000 | 5,745,000 |
| Emp. | 55 | 111 | 135 |

DUNS 21-145-5409
## The Vehicle Group Ltd
Unit 1 Target, Chartermark Way, Colburn Business Park, Catterick Garrison, North Yorkshire DL9 4QJ
**Tel:** 08450605040
**Web:** www.thevehiclegroup.com
**Reg No:** 6759911 **Estd:** 2008 Private Limited Company
**Line of Business:** Agents specialising in the sale of particular products or ranges of products not elsewhere classified

**Issued Capital:** £100
**Directors:** G M Frankland, Miss C F Palmer
**US SIC:** 5199 **UK SIC:** 61900

| | 31-03-14 | 31-03-13 | 31-03-12 |
|---|---|---|---|
| TO | 5,586,943 | 5,709,415 | 5,623,698 |
| P/L | 438,061 | 108,845 | 19,366 |
| NW | 1,468,871 | 1,166,663 | 1,087,316 |
| WC | 992,860 | 736,114 | 660,969 |

DUNS 23-615-1945
## Vehicle Lease & Service Ltd
Third Floor Centre For Advanced Industry, Coble Dene, North Shields, Tyne and Wear NE29 6DE
**Tel:** 01912937101
**Web:** www.vls-ltd.com
**Reg No:** 3612397 **Estd:** 2012 Private Limited Company
**Line of Business:** Maintenance and repair of motor vehicles
**Issued Capital:** £1,900,000
**Directors:** R I Murray, Ms D Newton, N Rutherford, G D Pearson, J E Mcgovern, D G Keating, O Sutherland, S Hazon
**Co. Secretary:** Mrs Joanne Wheatley
**Responsibilities**
**Senior:** Stephen Lockwood *(Director)*
**US SIC:** 7539, 5511, 7513
**UK SIC:** 67100, 65100, 84802
**Auditors:** Ernst & Young LLP
**Bankers:** Lloyds TSB Bank plc (30-93-71)

| | 31-12-13 | 31-12-12 | 31-12-11 |
|---|---|---|---|
| TO | 14,479,952 | 14,144,680 | 13,670,648 |
| P/L | 1,106,781 | 1,074,719 | 968,175 |
| NW | 6,681,950 | 6,677,341 | 6,568,855 |
| WC | 5,092,676 | 4,230,364 | 5,931,597 |
| Emp. | 71 | 70 | 69 |

DUNS 45-895-2082
## Vehicle Technician Services Ltd
19 Lister Road, North West Industrial Estate, Peterlee, County Durham SR8 2RB
**Fax:** 0191-586-3896
**Reg No:** 3229301 **Estd:** 1996 Private Limited Company
**Line of Business:** Manufacture of bodies (coachwork) for motor vehicles (except caravans)
**Trading Style:** V T S
**Issued Capital:** £2
**Managing Director:** W E Leadbitter
**Co. Secretary:** Ms Pauline Leadbitter
**US SIC:** 3713, 7539
**UK SIC:** 35201, 67100
**Auditors:** Thorne Thurlbeck Russell
**Bankers:** National Westminster Bank Plc (54-21-54)

| | 31-03-14 | 31-03-13 | 31-03-12 |
|---|---|---|---|
| TA | 26,480 | 29,281 | 29,192 |
| NW | 13,194 | 14,939 | 13,455 |
| WC | 7,639 | 7,902 | 5,609 |

DUNS 28-996-6475 Imp
## Veitch Family Holdings Ltd
Unit 2 Travellers Close, Welham Green, North Mymms, Hatfield, Hertfordshire AL9 7JL
**Tel:** 02082753000 **Fax:** 020-8275-3030
**Web:** www.eurocoin.co.uk
**Reg No:** 1847361 **Estd:** 1984 Private Limited Company
**Line of Business:** Management activities of holding companies
**Export Sales:** £14,500
**Issued Capital:** £102
**Director:** N J Veitch
**Co. Secretary:** Colin Veitch
**US SIC:** 6711, 3559
**UK SIC:** 83962, 32863
**Auditors:** William Evans & Partners
**Bankers:** HSBC Bank plc (40-20-23)

| | 31-12-13 | 31-12-12 | 31-12-11 |
|---|---|---|---|
| TO | 19,464,303 | 20,611,946 | 21,602,780 |
| P/L | 1,323,589 | 617,495 | 1,033,198 |
| NW | 5,015,229 | 4,193,006 | 3,676,838 |
| WC | 3,140,037 | 2,365,839 | 2,393,587 |
| Emp. | 73 | 70 | 74 |

DUNS 21-179-2792
## Veitch Penny Llp
1 Manor Court, Dix's Field, Exeter, Devon EX1 1UP
**Tel:** 01392278381
**Web:** www.veitchpenny.co.uk
**Reg No:** 0348623OC **Estd:** 2005 Private Limited Company
**Line of Business:** Solicitors
**US SIC:** 8111 **UK SIC:** 83500

| | 31-03-14 | 31-03-13 | 31-03-12 |
|---|---|---|---|
| TA | 2,297,960 | 2,633,627 | 2,861,441 |
| NW | 840,921 | 1,008,498 | 861,449 |
| WC | 1,098,236 | 1,316,109 | 1,168,939 |

DUNS 21-448-3711
## Veitchi (Holdings) Ltd
15 Bouverie Street, Rutherglen, Glasgow, Lanarkshire G73 2RY
**Tel:** 0141-647-0661 **Fax:** 0141-613-1575
**Web:** www.veitchi.co.uk
**Reg No:** 0009798SC **Estd:** 1917 Private Limited Company
**Line of Business:** Management activities of other non-financial holding companies not elsewhere classified
**Issued Capital:** £181,032
**Directors:** R R Tedeschi, W M Biggart, J J Preston
**Co. Secretary:** James Stewart
**US SIC:** 8999, 1541
**UK SIC:** 83954, 50100
**Auditors:** Geoghegan & Co
**Bankers:** Bank Of Scotland (80-11-80)

| | 30-11-13 | 30-11-12 | 30-11-11 |
|---|---|---|---|
| TO | 38,398,000 | 42,469,000 | 47,077,000 |
| P/L | 845,000 | 475,000 | 115,000 |
| NW | 8,375,000 | 8,243,000 | 8,774,000 |
| WC | 8,229,000 | 8,112,000 | 7,684,000 |
| Emp. | 310 | 342 | 376 |

DUNS 22-852-7917 Imp-Exp
## Veka Plc
**(Subsidiary of:** Laumann Industrie-Holding Gmbh & Co. Kg)
Farrington Road, Burnley, Lancashire BB11 5DA
**Tel:** 01282-716611 **Fax:** 01282725257
**Web:** www.vekauk.com
**Reg No:** 1626563 **VAT No:** 497951576
**Estd:** 1986 Public Limited Company
**Line of Business:** Manufacturers of plastic products
**Export Markets:** Europe
**Export Sales:** £762,000
**Issued Capital:** £23,000,000
**Directors:** A Hartleif, S Gray, M Pattalon, Dr W Schuler, C Torley, D A Jones
**Co. Secretary:** Graham Fitton
**Responsibilities**
**IT:** Pat Parry *(IT Manager)*, Ross Walsh *(IT Manager)*
**US SIC:** 2821 **UK SIC:** 25140
**Auditors:** RSM Tenon Audit Ltd
**Bankers:** Barclays Bank Plc (20-15-70)

| | 31-12-13 | 31-12-12 | 31-12-11 |
|---|---|---|---|
| TO | 76,989,000 | 61,800,000 | 28,913,000 |
| P/L | (3,240,000) | (5,062,000) | (2,534,000) |
| NW | (6,525,000) | (5,841,000) | 13,587,000 |
| WC | (1,352,000) | 3,751,000 | 7,390,000 |
| Emp. | 382 | 271 | 160 |

DUNS 22-718-2037
## Veladail Hotels Ltd
**(Subsidiary of:** Mata Limited)
8-12 Half Moon Street, London W1J 7BH
**Tel:** 02074992964 **Fax:** 020-7629-4063
**Web:** www.flemings.co.uk
**Reg No:** 1023840 **VAT No:** 240873073
**Estd:** 1984 Private Limited Company
**Line of Business:** Hotels
**Trading Style:** Flemings Hotel, Renaissance Hotel, Flemings of Mayfair
**Issued Capital:** £7,756,980
**Principals:** S K Gulhati *(Managing)*, Mrs S Gulhati, S K Gulhati
**Co. Secretary:** Mrs Sudha Gulhati
**Responsibilities**
**Finance:** Varo Thayan *(Accounts Manager)*, A Varothayan *(Financial Manager)*
**IT:** Varo Thayan *(Accounts Manager)*
**HR:** Yolanda Garcia-Morris *(Human Resources Manager)*
**Health & Safety:** Yolanda Garcia-Morris *(Human Resources Manager)*
**Facilities:** Michael Dervan *(Maintenance Manager)*
**Purchasing:** Varo Thayan *(Accounts Manager)*
**Branches:** Veladail Hotels Ltd, Hatfield Heath, Bishops Stortford, Bishop's Stortford, Hertfordshire CM22 7AS
**US SIC:** 7011 **UK SIC:** 66500
**Auditors:** Rakmans
**Bankers:** The Royal Bank Of Scotland Plc (16-00-79)

| | 31-12-13 | 31-12-12 | 31-12-11 |
|---|---|---|---|
| TO | 14,279,993 | 14,331,829 | 13,023,914 |
| P/L | 46,496 | 1,462,586 | 1,233,759 |
| NW | 96,123,734 | 94,215,311 | 68,981,565 |
| WC | 5,647,323 | (2,128,638) | (1,052,537) |
| Emp. | 222 | 224 | 229 |

DUNS 21-896-3981 Exp
## Velcourt Group Plc
Veldt House, Preston Cross, Ledbury, Herefordshire HR8 2LJ
**Tel:** 0193583739
**Web:** www.velcourt.co.uk
**Reg No:** 0718623 **Estd:** 1962 Public Limited Company
**Line of Business:** Farming (arable)
**Export Markets:** W Europe
**Export Sales:** £202,139
**Issued Capital:** £84,191
**Directors:** J R Townshend, S J Ellwood, D J Buckeridge, A O Colburn
**Co. Secretary:** David Teague
**Responsibilities**
**Senior:** Robin Malim *(Chairperson)*, Julian Proctor *(Manager)*
**IT:** Alan Bonehill *(IT Manager)*
**Branches:** Velcourt Group Plc, Broxtead Barns, Broxtead Estate, Woodbridge, Suffolk IP12 3JE
**US SIC:** 0119 **UK SIC:** 01001
**Auditors:** Horwath Clark Whitehill
**Bankers:** Barclays Bank Plc (20-84-58)

| | 30-09-13 | 30-09-12 | 30-09-11 |
|---|---|---|---|
| TO | 28,780,762 | 31,820,787 | 35,284,087 |
| P/L | 1,048,184 | 1,524,136 | 4,561,270 |
| NW | 14,123,957 | 13,846,289 | 13,777,135 |
| WC | 13,438,192 | 13,976,250 | 13,756,882 |
| Emp. | 120 | 124 | 127 |

DUNS 23-259-2659 Imp
## Velfac Ltd
**(Subsidiary of:** Villum Fonden)
The Old Livery, Hildersham, Cambridge, Cambridgeshire CB21 6DR
**Tel:** 01223897100 **Fax:** 01223-897101
**Web:** www.velfac.co.uk
**Reg No:** 2332292 **VAT No:** 493346816
**Estd:** 1989 Private Limited Company
**Line of Business:** Agents involved in the sale of timber and building materials
**Issued Capital:** £1,500,002
**Principals:** F Jespersen *(Managing)*, E Rigby
**Co. Secretary:** Nicholas Brown
**Responsibilities**
**Senior:** Sharen Bard *(Finance Manager)*, Elizabeth Carson *(Manager)*
**Finance:** Sharen Bard *(Finance Manager)*
**Admin:** Sara Goggins *(Office Manager)*
**Health & Safety:** Sara Goggins *(Office Manager)*
**Branches:** Velfac Ltd, 28 Magnaville Road, Bishop's Stortford, Hertfordshire CM23 4DN
**US SIC:** 5072, 7392
**UK SIC:** 61500, 83951
**Auditors:** Price Bailey LLP
**Bankers:** Unibank A/s (40-48-78)

| | 31-12-13 | 31-12-12 | 31-12-11 |
|---|---|---|---|
| TO | 36,587,968 | 31,143,584 | 37,159,459 |
| P/L | 1,062,222 | 1,051,287 | 1,267,953 |
| NW | 3,271,328 | 3,365,718 | 3,474,557 |
| WC | 3,658,190 | 3,727,665 | 3,864,505 |
| Emp. | 57 | 55 | 52 |

DUNS 42-345-2036
## Velindre N H S Trust
Unit 2 Charnwood Court, Heol Billingsley, Parc Nantgarw, Nantgarw, Cardiff, South Glamorgan CF15 7QZ
**Tel:** 02920196161
**Web:** www.velindre-tr.wales.nhs.uk
**VAT No:** 654802433 **Estd:** 2012 Incorporate By Act Of Parliament
**Line of Business:** Hospital activities
**Trading Style:** Velindre Hospital, Welsh Blood Service, National Welsh Informatics Service
**Issued Capital:** £1
**Principals:** S Ham *(Financial)*, Ms A Mcalinden, Dr M Adams, A Lloyd
**Responsibilities**
**Senior:** Simon Dean *(Chief Executive Officer)*, Anne McAlinden *(Director)*
**Branches:** Velindre N H S Trust, Ysbyty Gwynedd, Bangor, Gwynedd LL57 2PW
**US SIC:** 7399 **UK SIC:** 83954
**Bankers:** National Westminster Bank Plc (56-00-41)
**Employees:** 2,000

DUNS 23-325-8800 Imp-Exp
## Velji Bhovan& Sons (Trading) Ltd
V B House, Woodside End, Wembley, Middlesex HA0 1UR
**Tel:** 02089-001355
**Web:** www.vbandsons.net
**Reg No:** 4598252 **VAT No:** 820348061
**Estd:** 2002 Private Limited Company
**Line of Business:** Non-specialised wholesale of food, beverages and tobacco
**Trading Style:** V. B. & Sons
**Issued Capital:** £1,005
**Directors:** M Velji Nathwani, C V Nathwani, M Velji Nathwani, N Velji Nathwani
**Co. Secretary:** Chunilal Velji Nathwani
**Responsibilities**
**Senior:** Natu Nathwanai *(Manager)*
**HR:** Natu Nathwanai *(Manager)*
**US SIC:** 5149, 5399
**UK SIC:** 61700, 65600
**Auditors:** Newman & Partners
**Bankers:** Barclays Bank Plc (20-01-89)

| | 31-07-14 | 31-07-13 | 31-07-12 |
|---|---|---|---|
| TO | 38,042,177 | 36,663,446 | 38,106,418 |
| P/L | 3,481,672 | 2,766,771 | 2,419,665 |
| NW | 14,909,497 | 12,949,988 | 11,402,437 |
| WC | 6,741,876 | 4,934,038 | 4,758,263 |
| Emp. | 196 | 198 | 210 |

DUNS 22-134-1154
## Vellco Ltd
**(Subsidiary of:** Vellco Holdings Ltd)
Suite B2 Josephs Well, Hanover Walk, Leeds, West Yorkshire LS3 1AB
**Tel:** 01944-738715 **Fax:** 01944-738700
**Web:** www.vellcotyrecontrol.co.uk
**Reg No:** 4153063 **Estd:** 2001 Private Limited Company
**Line of Business:** Recycling
**Issued Capital:** £2
**Director:** C G Fell
**Co. Secretary:** Ms Susan Fell
**Responsibilities**
**Senior:** Dave Martin *(General Manager)*
**Branches:** Vellco Ltd, Springfield House, Wold Newton Road, Driffield, North Humberside YO25 3PH
**US SIC:** 3341 **UK SIC:** 22470
**Bankers:** HSBC Bank plc (40-27-10)

| | 31-12-13 | 31-12-12 | 31-12-11 |
|---|---|---|---|
| TA | 3,451,377 | 3,053,309 | 3,087,385 |
| NW | 1,642,266 | 1,536,630 | 1,440,243 |
| WC | 1,256,875 | 1,375,690 | 1,396,515 |

DUNS 21-920-2991 Imp
## Velmore Ltd
**(Subsidiary of:** Velmore Holdings Ltd)
Thornton Road Industrial Estate, Thornton Road, Ellesmere Port, Cheshire CH65 5EU
**Tel:** 01513-571212
**Web:** www.velmore.co.uk
**Reg No:** 1185757 **VAT No:** 707931722
**Estd:** 1974 Private Limited Company
**Line of Business:** Speciality design activities
**Issued Capital:** £30,000
**Directors:** K C Wang, K L Au, X Zhang
**Branches:** Velmore Ltd, Flat 6, 62 Argyle St, Birkenhead, Merseyside CH41 6AF
**US SIC:** 7399 **UK SIC:** 83954
**Auditors:** PKF (UK) LLP
**Bankers:** National Westminster Bank Plc (60-00-01)

| | 31-12-13 | 31-12-12 | 31-12-11 |
|---|---|---|---|
| TO | N/A | 2,667,169 | 2,957,125 |
| P/L | N/A | 127,008 | 140,816 |
| NW | 1,510,702 | 1,430,280 | 1,334,134 |
| WC | 1,484,047 | 1,393,383 | 1,423,063 |
| Emp. | N/A | 26 | 35 |

DUNS 73-795-0928
## Velocity Technology Solutions Uk Ltd
**(Subsidiary of:** Velocity Technology Solutions Uk Holdings Ltd)
39 Cadogan Street, Glasgow, Lanarkshire G2 7AB
**Tel:** 01412026300 **Fax:** 0870-405-2201
**Web:** http://velocity.cc
**Reg No:** 0263817SC **VAT No:** 842750231
**Estd:** 2012 Private Limited Company
**Line of Business:** Other software consultancy and supply
**Trading Style:** Velocity
**Issued Capital:** £20,000
**Directors:** S Shippee, J T Mcinnes, D Smithers
**Co. Secretary:** Burness Paull Llp
**Responsibilities**
**Senior:** Christopher Grier *(Technical Director)*, Katrina Topping *(Office Manager)*
**US SIC:** 7379, 7374
**UK SIC:** 83940
**Auditors:** Wylie & Bisset LLP

| | 31-12-13 | 31-08-12 | 31-12-11 |
|---|---|---|---|
| TA | 2,924,542 | 3,246,439 | 2,634,485 |
| NW | 1,393,935 | 944,100 | 895,552 |
| WC | 668,193 | 307,438 | 437,095 |

DUNS 52-033-7437 Imp
## Velocity Uk Ltd
**(Subsidiary of:** Reece Group Ltd)
Woodbine Street, Hendon, Sunderland, Tyne and Wear SR1 2NL
**Tel:** 0191-565-4400
**Web:** www.velocitypatching.com
**Reg No:** 3400231 **Estd:** 1997 Private Limited Company
**Line of Business:** Road surfacers
**Export Sales:** £1,684,782
**Trading Style:** Velocity
**Issued Capital:** £83,100
**Directors:** J P Reece, D Gardner, R D Anderton, P J Kite
**Responsibilities**
**Senior:** Audrey Hosking *(Management System Manager)*
**Branches:** Velocity Uk Ltd, Tatham Street, Sunderland, Tyne and Wear SR1 2AG
**US SIC:** 1611, 7361, 3711
**UK SIC:** 50200, 83954, 35101
**Auditors:** Pullan Barnes
**Bankers:** National Westminster Bank Plc (55-61-11)

| | 31-12-13 | 31-12-12 | 31-12-11 |
|---|---|---|---|
| TO | 10,438,251 | 7,229,611 | N/A |
| P/L | 220,048 | (405,047) | N/A |
| NW | 432,822 | 236,345 | 600,103 |
| WC | 3,474,131 | 3,321,729 | 157,189 |
| Emp. | 52 | N/A | N/A |

DUNS 34-915-1741

## Velocys Plc

115e Milton Park, Milton, Abingdon, Oxfordshire OX14 4RZ
**Fax:** 01235-841701
**Web:** www.velocys.com
**Reg No:** 5712187 **Estd:** 2006 Public Limited Company
**Line of Business:** Research and experimental development on natural sciences and engineering
**Trading Style:** Velocys
**Issued Capital:** £1,159,856
**Directors:** S M Robertson, Dr P J Jungels, Dr P F Schubert, J Verloop, J D West, Mrs S N Shaw, R Lipski, A Jamieson
**Co. Secretary:** Ms Susan Robertson
**Responsibilities**
**Sales:** Neville Hargreaves *(Business Development Director)*, Jeff McDaniel *(Commercial Director)*
**US SIC:** 7391 **UK SIC:** 94000
**Auditors:** PricewaterhouseCoopers LLP
**Bankers:** Barclays Bank Plc (20-65-18)

| | 31-12-13 | 31-12-12 | 31-12-11 |
|---|---|---|---|
| TO | 4,753,000 | 7,632,000 | 4,722,000 |
| P/L | (18,032,000) | (10,836,000) | (10,437,000) |
| NW | 23,747,000 | 8,540,000 | 16,602,000 |
| WC | 23,087,000 | 7,972,000 | 15,746,000 |
| Emp. | 91 | 79 | 79 |

DUNS 57-055-0087 Exp

## Velosi Europe Ltd

**(Subsidiary of:** Velosi Europe (Luxembourg) Sarl)
Unit 4 Bennet Court, Bennet Road, Reading, Berkshire RG2 0QX
**Tel:** 01189207030
**Web:** www.velosi.com
**Reg No:** 2879999 **VAT No:** 614978704
**Estd:** 1993 Private Limited Company
**Line of Business:** Quality award consultants and procedure assessors
**Export Markets:** Middle East, Far East, U S A and Worldwide
**Export Sales:** £296,396
**Issued Capital:** £200
**Director:** M Coles
**Co. Secretary:** Ben Upton
**Responsibilities**
**Senior:** Matt Stead *(Country Manager)*
**Branches:** Velosi Europe Ltd, Unit 4 Wellheads Way, Aberdeen, Aberdeenshire AB21 7GD
**US SIC:** 7399 **UK SIC:** 83954
**Auditors:** Deloitte LLP
**Bankers:** National Westminster Bank Plc (01-00-04)

| | 31-12-13 | 31-12-12 | 31-12-11 |
|---|---|---|---|
| TO | 14,855,886 | 11,462,083 | 10,130,024 |
| P/L | 415,249 | 696,665 | 424,110 |
| NW | 1,658,758 | 1,429,672 | 1,119,254 |
| WC | (1,002,728) | (1,227,828) | (1,441,806) |
| Emp. | 54 | 38 | 37 |

DUNS 21-586-4091

## Velux Company Ltd.

**(Subsidiary of:** Villum Fonden)
Woodside Way, Glenrothes, Fife KY7 4ND
**Tel:** 01592778225 **Fax:** 08704057701
**Web:** www.velux.co.uk
**Reg No:** 0070286SC **Estd:** 1979 Private Limited Company
**Line of Business:** Roof and skylights
**Trading Style:** Velux Company Ltd.
**Issued Capital:** £1,200,000
**Directors:** P Bang, J Tang-Jensen, Ms M Kann-Rasmussen, J T Schambye, K K Riddle
**Co. Secretary:** Wjm Secretaries Limited
**Responsibilities**
**Senior:** Bjarne Thomsen *(Manager)*, Michael Walter *(Manager)*
**Marketing:** Henrik Bjerregaard *(Public Affairs Manager)*, Clare Macnaugton *(Communications Director)*, Michael Rasmussen *(Marketing Director)*
**Admin:** Laura Protherton *(Human Resources Director)*
**HR:** Laura Protherton *(Human Resources Director)*
**Branches:** Velux Company Ltd., Kettering Parkway, Kettering, Northamptonshire NN15 6XR
**US SIC:** 5199 **UK SIC:** 61900
**Auditors:** KPMG LLP
**Bankers:** Bank Of Scotland (80-08-09)

| | 31-12-13 | 31-12-12 | 31-12-11 |
|---|---|---|---|
| TO | 104,035,947 | 105,246,813 | 107,822,761 |
| P/L | 2,721,970 | 2,546,736 | 3,537,984 |
| NW | 3,693,723 | 2,903,920 | 2,862,688 |
| WC | 3,028,285 | 1,545,115 | 868,011 |
| Emp. | 173 | 167 | 167 |

DUNS 21-678-6937

## Venair Ltd

**(Subsidiary of:** Vfm Sl)
Unit 27 New Albion Trading Estate, Halley Street, Glasgow, Lanarkshire G13 4DJ
**Tel:** 01419524943
**Web:** www.venair.com
**Reg No:** 0381063SC **Estd:** 1986 Private Limited Company
**Line of Business:** Manufacture of other rubber products
**Issued Capital:** £150,000
**Director:** M F Zamora
**Responsibilities**
**Senior:** Alvaro Churruca *(Manager)*
**US SIC:** 3069 **UK SIC:** 48123
**Auditors:** McLay, McAlister & McGibbon LLP

| | 31-12-13 | 31-12-12 | 31-12-11 |
|---|---|---|---|
| TO | 463,691 | N/A | N/A |
| P/L | 13,674 | N/A | N/A |
| NW | (53,177) | (66,842) | (11,668) |
| WC | (69,674) | (87,954) | (43,380) |

DUNS 29-109-8069

## Vencel Resil Ltd

**(Subsidiary of:** Synbra Holding B.V.)
Boothferry Works, Boothferry Road, Howden, Goole, North Humberside DN14 7EA
**Tel:** 08706003666
**Web:** www.jablite.co.uk
**Reg No:** 1530521 **Estd:** 2013 Private Limited Company
**Line of Business:** Cladding and insulation materials
**Trading Style:** Jablite Ltd
**Issued Capital:** £100
**Co. Secretary:** Kenneth Hutchins
**Responsibilities**
**Senior:** Robert Newsum *(Manager)*
**Admin:** Janice Prassby *(Human Resources Manager)*
**HR:** Janice Prassby *(Human Resources Manager)*
**Health & Safety:** Adam Marshall *(Health & Safety)*
**US SIC:** 3079 **UK SIC:** 48360
**Employees:** 60

DUNS 22-226-8752

## Venda Ltd

**(Subsidiary of:** Netsuite Inc.)
101 St Martins Lane, London WC2N 4AZ
**Tel:** 02070707330
**Web:** www.venda.com
**Reg No:** 4244828 **Estd:** 2001 Private Limited Company
**Line of Business:** Internet services
**Issued Capital:** £3,114,113
**Directors:** R S Gill, D P Solomon, D L Andrews
**Co. Secretary:** Miss Natalie Salunke
**Responsibilities**
**Senior:** Eric Abensur *(Chief Executive)*, Alan Docter *(Manager)*, Phil Dur *(Manager)*, Sylvain Hillairaud *(Programme Director & Release O)*, Clifford Siegel *(Manager)*, Daniel Wagner *(Manager)*, Noah Walley *(Manager)*
**Operations:** Sylvain Hillairaud *(Programme Director & Release O)*, Damon Mannion *(Chief Operating Officer)*
**US SIC:** 7379, 7374
**UK SIC:** 83940
**Auditors:** BDO LLP

| | 30-06-13 | 30-06-12 | 30-06-11 |
|---|---|---|---|
| TO | 19,828,000 | 17,033,000 | 13,986,075 |
| P/L | (8,702,000) | (3,472,000) | (7,484,988) |
| NW | (26,533,000) | (18,231,000) | (17,783,928) |
| WC | 1,240,000 | 2,910,000 | 2,384,694 |
| Emp. | 241 | 262 | 244 |

DUNS 21-947-7515

## Venesta Washroom Systems Ltd

**(Subsidiary of:** Intercede Holdco Ltd)
Alder House, Newstead Industrial Trading Estate, Stoke-On-Trent, Staffordshire ST4 8HX
**Tel:** 01782277200 **Fax:** 01782657386
**Web:** www.venesta.co.uk
**Reg No:** 6129513 **Estd:** 2007 Private Limited Company
**Line of Business:** Manufacture of insulated wire and cable
**Export Sales:** £1,474,000
**Issued Capital:** £1
**Directors:** M G Rees, D J Wallis
**Co. Secretary:** Jonathan Sherry
**Responsibilities**
**Senior:** Neil Amphlett *(Transport Manager)*
**IT:** Kamlesh Lad *(Computer Manager)*
**Facilities:** Ian Pimblott *(Maintenance Manager)*
**Fleet:** Neil Amphlett *(Transport Manager)*
**US SIC:** 3357 **UK SIC:** 22470
**Auditors:** Ernst & Young LLP
**Bankers:** HSBC Bank plc (40-18-22)

| | 31-12-13 | 31-12-12 | 31-12-11 |
|---|---|---|---|
| TO | 24,909,000 | 28,007,000 | 30,017,000 |
| P/L | (67,000) | (18,341,000) | (32,456,000) |
| NW | 530,000 | (27,494,000) | (22,845,000) |
| WC | (3,389,000) | (3,559,000) | 1,923,000 |
| Emp. | 195 | 196 | 203 |

DUNS 22-702-3322 Exp

## Venice Simplon-Orient-Express Ltd

1st Floor Shackleton House 4 Battle, Bridge Lane, London SE1 2HP
**Tel:** 08701615060
**Web:** www.orient-express.com
**Reg No:** 1551659 **VAT No:** 802270276
**Estd:** 1982 Private Limited Company
**Line of Business:** Travel agency activities
**Export Markets:** E U, Japan and U.S.A.
**Export Sales:** £6,796,000
**Trading Style:** V S O E
**Issued Capital:** £100,000
**Directors:** G E Franklin, F J Boyen, F Dellepiane, M O'Grady, R M Levine, R M Levine
**Co. Secretary:** Filip Boyen
**Responsibilities**
**Senior:** Vicky Legg *(Manager)*
**Branches:** Venice Simplon-Orient-Express Ltd, 25 London Street, London W2 1HH
**US SIC:** 4722 **UK SIC:** 77001
**Auditors:** Deloitte LLP
**Bankers:** Barclays Bank Plc (20-65-82)

| | 31-12-13 | 31-12-12 | 31-12-11 |
|---|---|---|---|
| TO | 25,203,000 | 27,114,000 | 28,828,000 |
| P/L | (730,000) | 600,000 | (124,000) |
| NW | 402,000 | 1,096,000 | 797,000 |
| WC | (22,012,000) | (3,304,000) | (2,602,000) |
| Emp. | 82 | 87 | 82 |

DUNS 50-325-1472

## Venice Simplon-Orient-Express Tours Ltd

**(Subsidiary of:** Belmond Hotel Holdings (Uk) Ltd)
Lambeth, London, Lambeth, London, London SE1 9PF
**Tel:** 02079214000 **Fax:** 021-2575-7039
**Web:** www.orient-express.com
**Reg No:** 2349958 **Estd:** 1989 Private Limited Company
**Line of Business:** Other transport via railways
**Issued Capital:** £20,000
**Directors:** F J Boyen, M O'Grady
**Co. Secretary:** Filip Boyen
**US SIC:** 4011 **UK SIC:** 71000
**Auditors:** Deloitte & Touche
**Bankers:** The Chase Manhattan Bank (60-92-42)

| | 31-12-13 | 31-12-12 | 31-12-11 |
|---|---|---|---|
| TA | 2,000 | 321,000 | 321,000 |
| P/L | 436,000 | N/A | N/A |
| NW | 2,000 | (434,000) | (434,000) |
| WC | N/A | (434,000) | (434,000) |

DUNS 22-012-5475

## Venn Group Ltd

105-109 Strand, London WC2R 0AA
**Tel:** 020-7557-7667 **Fax:** 02075577666
**Web:** www.venngroup.com
**Reg No:** 4015584 **Estd:** 2000 Private Limited Company
**Line of Business:** Labour recruitment and provision of personnel
**Issued Capital:** £115
**Directors:** D M Moynihan, P S Hanna, A B Badenoch
**Co. Secretary:** Keith Wilmott
**Responsibilities**
**IT:** Tony Randall *(IT Support Manager)*
**Branches:** Venn Group Ltd, Berkshire House, 56 Herschel St, Slough, Berkshire SL1 1PY
**US SIC:** 7361 **UK SIC:** 83954
**Auditors:** Kingston Smith
**Bankers:** HSBC Bank plc (40-02-07)

| | 31-12-13 | 31-12-12 | 31-12-11 |
|---|---|---|---|
| TO | 99,935,141 | 97,563,841 | 98,310,775 |
| P/L | 232,676 | 456,015 | 1,273,353 |
| NW | (4,217,518) | (4,450,995) | (4,674,248) |
| WC | 157,434 | (530,967) | (510,239) |
| Emp. | 302 | 283 | 286 |

DUNS 23-413-8423

## Venner Shipley Llp

200 Aldersgate, London EC1A 4HD
**Tel:** 020-7600-4212 **Fax:** 020-7600-4188
**Web:** www.vennershipley.co.uk
**Reg No:** 0308202OC **Estd:** 1918 Private Limited Company
**Line of Business:** Activities of patent and copyright agents
**Responsibilities**
**Senior:** Gideon Agbanome *(Partner)*, Allie Elend *(Partner)*, Ian Grey *(Non-designated Limited Liabili)*, Jonathan Hewett *(Designated Limited Liability P)*, Paul Jump *(Senior Partner)*, Timothy Jump *(Designated Limited Liability P)*, Paulette Lewis *(Manager)*, Dawn Perkins *(Senior Associate)*, Pawel Piotrowicz *(Partner)*, Sarah Szell *(Designated Limited Liability P)*, Alan Venner *(Partner)*, Jan Walaski *(Designated Limited Liability P)*, Chris Wetherley *(Partner)*
**IT:** Matthew Kent *(IT Manager)*, Simon Pietroni *(IT MANAGER)*
**HR:** Julie Blackford *(Officer Manager)*
**US SIC:** 7399 **UK SIC:** 83954
**Auditors:** Goodman Jones LLP
**Bankers:** National Westminster Bank Plc (50-30-09)

| | 30-06-13 | 30-06-12 | 30-06-11 |
|---|---|---|---|
| TO | 20,476,658 | 17,984,735 | 17,328,568 |
| P/L | 27,127 | 24,499 | 21,314 |
| NW | N/A | N/A | 1,676,951 |
| WC | 1,566,912 | 1,260,510 | 2,487,016 |
| Emp. | 78 | 75 | 71 |

DUNS 21-722-3536 Imp

## Vent-Axia Group Ltd

**(Subsidiary of:** Volution Group Plc)
Fleming Way, Crawley, West Sussex RH10 9YX
**Tel:** 01293842950
**Web:** www.vent-axia.com
**Reg No:** 1102834 **VAT No:** 800739350
**Estd:** 1929 Private Limited Company
**Line of Business:** Manufacture of other electrical equipment not elsewhere classified
**Export Sales:** £5,203,000
**Trading Style:** Elkay Electrical Manufacturing
**Issued Capital:** £70,000
**Directors:** I Dew, R George
**US SIC:** 3629, 3639
**UK SIC:** 34350, 34600
**Auditors:** Ernst & Young LLP
**Bankers:** National Westminster Bank Plc (50-00-00)

| | 31-07-14 | 31-07-13 | 31-07-12 |
|---|---|---|---|
| TO | 52,583,000 | 55,089,000 | 54,479,000 |
| P/L | 13,974,000 | 13,502,000 | 12,524,000 |
| NW | 67,189,000 | 54,277,000 | 52,983,000 |
| WC | 67,586,000 | 54,329,000 | 42,083,000 |
| Emp. | 330 | 313 | 303 |

DUNS 21-712-5012 Imp

## Ventilating Equipment Supply Holdings Ltd

Eagle Close, Chandler's Ford, Eastleigh, Hampshire SO53 4NF
**Tel:** 0844-815-6060 **Fax:** 08702404550
**Web:** www.ves.co.uk
**Reg No:** 1492290 **VAT No:** 314533289
**Estd:** 1966 Private Limited Company
**Line of Business:** Management activities of production holding companies
**Issued Capital:** £181,250
**Principals:** D L Peters *(Chairman and Managing)*, J R Peters *(Managing)*, R M Peters
**Co. Secretary:** Kenneth White
**US SIC:** 6711 **UK SIC:** 83962
**Auditors:** Monahans
**Bankers:** HSBC Bank plc (40-08-28)

| | 30-09-13 | 30-09-12 | 30-09-11 |
|---|---|---|---|
| TO | 21,320,598 | 20,060,244 | 30,160,128 |
| P/L | 1,708,374 | 1,826,296 | 2,632,587 |
| NW | 3,617,892 | 3,045,662 | 1,910,018 |
| WC | 3,013,478 | 2,377,615 | 1,129,724 |
| Emp. | 249 | 249 | 248 |

DUNS 23-022-5315

## Ventilation Hygiene Specialists Ltd

Unit 2, Stockton-On-Tees, Cleveland TS17 7AR
**Tel:** 01642675755
**Reg No:** 3570406 **Estd:** 1996 Private Limited Company
**Line of Business:** Installation of ventilation
**Issued Capital:** £1
**Directors:** P W Healey, M Holliday
**Co. Secretary:** Timothy Kilvington
**US SIC:** 8911, 7349
**UK SIC:** 83701, 92300

| | 31-01-14 | 31-07-13 | 31-01-12 |
|---|---|---|---|
| TA | 36,104 | 3,808 | 100 |
| NW | 8,621 | 423 | 100 |
| WC | 4,932 | (35) | N/A |

DUNS 50-567-5686

## Venture Information Management Ltd

Wessex House, Drake Avenue, Staines, Middlesex TW18 2AP
**Tel:** 02031410500 **Fax:** 01784224131
**Web:** www.venture.co.uk
**Reg No:** 2515314 **VAT No:** 577463891
**Estd:** 1990 Private Limited Company
**Line of Business:** Data processing
**Issued Capital:** £10,800
**Principals:** N D Turner *(Managing)*, D L Ince, Ms S E Rainbow
**Co. Secretary:** Trethowans Services Limited
**US SIC:** 7374, 7392
**UK SIC:** 83940, 83951
**Auditors:** Wheeler & Co

**Bankers:** Lloyds TSB Bank plc (30-95-74)

| | 30-06-14 | 30-06-13 | 30-06-12 |
|---|---|---|---|
| TA | 2,257,389 | 1,947,471 | 1,441,722 |
| NW | 1,037,729 | 1,011,360 | 949,934 |
| WC | 801,948 | 902,372 | 922,763 |

DUNS 39-669-0240

## Venture Marketing Group Ltd
Carlton Plaza, London SW15 2TJ
**Tel:** 020-8394-5100
**Web:** www.venturemarketinggroup.co.uk
**Reg No:** 2135433 **Estd:** 1987 Private
Limited Company
**Line of Business:** Publishing of journals and
periodicals
**Trading Style:** Vmgl
**Issued Capital:** £100
**Directors:** J C Hancock, Mrs T S Shah
**Co. Secretary:** Mrs Barbara Stride
**Responsibilities**
**Senior:** Scott Bannerman (Sales Director)
**Sales:** Scott Bannerman (Sales Director)
**Operations:** Karen Baylis (Operations
Manager)
**US SIC:** 2721, 7374
**UK SIC:** 47522, 83940
**Auditors:** Hughes Spencer

| | 31-12-13 | 31-12-12 | 31-12-11 |
|---|---|---|---|
| TA | 2,912,950 | 3,859,556 | 3,730,849 |
| NW | 1,155,592 | 2,068,249 | 2,137,333 |
| WC | 1,103,984 | 2,015,030 | 2,092,933 |

DUNS 23-898-4269

## Venture Productions Ltd
(**Subsidiary of:** Indigo Venture Capital Ltd)
Premier Park, Road One, Winsford Industrial
Estate, Winsford, Cheshire CW7 3PH
**Tel:** 01606-558-854
**Web:** www.ventureproductions.co.uk
**Reg No:** 3889188 **Estd:** 1999 Private
Limited Company
**Line of Business:** Portrait photographic
activities
**Export Sales:** £754,488
**Trading Style:** Venture Photography
**Issued Capital:** £1
**Director:** M Sweetman
**Responsibilities**
**Senior:** John Peers (Manager)
**Finance:** John Peers (Manager)
**Sales:** Mark Witter (Sales Manager)
**HR:** Helen Tarbatt (Human Resources
Manager)
**Health & Safety:** Jonathan Redden (Quality
Manager)
**Facilities:** Jonathan Redden (Quality
Manager)
**Operations:** Jonathan Redden (Quality
Manager)
**US SIC:** 3999, 7221
**UK SIC:** 49590, 98901
**Auditors:** Deloitte LLP

| | 31-12-13 | 31-12-12 | 31-12-11 |
|---|---|---|---|
| TO | 3,284,674 | 3,918,028 | 5,116,261 |
| P/L | 20,938 | (3,196) | 361,782 |
| NW | 668,541 | 683,725 | 681,893 |
| WC | 533,896 | 477,699 | 523,164 |
| Emp. | 52 | 59 | 73 |

DUNS 22-722-7147

## The Venture Trust
6d Bruntsfield Terrace, Edinburgh, Midlothian
EH10 4EX
**Tel:** 01312287700 **Fax:** 01312-287701
**Web:** www.venturetrust.org.uk
**Reg No:** 1673720 **Estd:** 1982 Private
Company Limited By Guarantee
**Line of Business:** Adult and other education
not elsewhere classified
**Directors:** Ms G F Gray, D E Gunn,
Ms J E Lambert, Ms M E Brackenridge,
Ms J Stevenson, B Cole,
Professor W T Whyte, Professor P Higgins
**Co. Secretary:** Douglas Graham
**Responsibilities**
**Senior:** Alan Mackay (Director - Board
Member)
**Branches:** The Venture Trust, The Historic
Dockyard, Chatham, Kent ME4 4SX
**US SIC:** 8249, 8321
**UK SIC:** 93300, 96111
**Auditors:** Saffery Champness
**Bankers:** National Westminster Bank Plc
(60-40-04)

| | 31-03-14 | 31-03-13 | 31-03-12 |
|---|---|---|---|
| TO | 2,312,067 | 2,904,673 | 2,912,164 |
| P/L | (321,481) | (46,286) | (85,446) |
| NW | 144,720 | 466,201 | 512,487 |
| WC | (62,146) | 157,901 | 156,089 |
| Emp. | 64 | 74 | 71 |

DUNS 29-146-2273

## Venture Wales Ltd
Venture House, Navigation Park, Abercynon,
Mountain Ash, Mid Glamorgan CF45 4SN
**Tel:** 01443742888 **Fax:** 01443-741180
**Web:** www.venturewales.com
**Reg No:** 1716838 **Estd:** 1983 Private
Company Limited By Guarantee
**Line of Business:** Serviced office facilities
**Trading Style:** Venture Wales

**Directors:** Mrs A M Paul, B A Quilter,
H P Cooper, Professor D J Brooksbank,
H J Haines, B J Davies, Ms C M Roberts
**Co. Secretary:** Reginald Baker
**Responsibilities**
**Senior:** Saeed Shad (Manager)
**Branches:** Venture Wales Ltd, Bowen Indstl
Est, Bargoed, Mid Glamorgan CF81 9EP
**US SIC:** 7339 **UK SIC:** 83954
**Auditors:** Deloitte & Touche
**Bankers:** Lloyds TSB Bank plc (30-95-55)

| | 31-03-14 | 31-03-13 | 31-03-12 |
|---|---|---|---|
| TA | 8,905,640 | 8,942,349 | 9,096,603 |
| NW | 4,956,448 | 4,856,420 | 4,785,748 |
| WC | 540,750 | 660,170 | 652,785 |

DUNS 23-686-8944

## Venturethree Ltd
11 Cavalry Square, London SW3 4RB
**Tel:** 020-7290-1950 **Fax:** 020-7290-1955
**Web:** www.venturethree.com
**Reg No:** 3681869 **Estd:** 1998 Private
Limited Company
**Line of Business:** Design consultants
**Export Sales:** £1,190,960
**Issued Capital:** £17,982
**Directors:** G I Jones, P Orwell, P D Townsin,
M J Zur-Szpiro
**Co. Secretary:** Wcphd Secretaries Limited
**US SIC:** 8911, 7399
**UK SIC:** 83701, 83954
**Auditors:** BDO Stoy Hayward LLP

| | 31-12-13 | 31-12-12 | 31-12-11 |
|---|---|---|---|
| TO | 6,893,491 | 7,829,874 | 7,748,673 |
| P/L | 768,932 | 1,492,099 | 1,912,540 |
| NW | 2,855,311 | 3,070,461 | 3,022,763 |
| WC | 1,684,357 | 1,774,722 | 2,704,080 |
| Emp. | 49 | 47 | 41 |

DUNS 21-719-1153

## Venue 360 Ltd
Gipsy Lane, Luton, Bedfordshire LU1 3JH
**Tel:** 01582414264
**Reg No:** 7573682 **Estd:** 2011 Private
Company Limited By Guarantee
**Line of Business:** Operation of sports
arenas and stadiums
**Directors:** R Parmar, D A Carey, C J Angus,
J G Reep, L F Davies, N Jackson,
Mrs R Shah
**US SIC:** 7941 **UK SIC:** 97911

| | 31-03-14 | 31-03-13 | 31-03-12 |
|---|---|---|---|
| TO | 2,056,341 | 2,074,283 | 2,146,806 |
| P/L | (318,977) | (178,522) | 31,654 |
| NW | 3,549,877 | 3,868,854 | 4,049,843 |
| WC | 163,516 | 426,543 | 838,760 |
| Emp. | 79 | 84 | 137 |

DUNS 21-120-8633

## Venue Cymru
Central Promenade, Llandudno, Gwynedd
LL30 1BB
**Tel:** 01492872000
**Web:** www.venuecymru.co.uk
**VAT No:** 636603148 **Estd:** 1994
**Line of Business:** Theatres & concert halls
**Responsibilities**
**Finance:** Amanda Mills (Administrator)
**Facilities:** Amanda Mills (Administrator)
**US SIC:** 6531, 7911
**UK SIC:** 83400, 97913
**Bankers:** Barclays Bank Plc (20-51-23)
**Employees:** 55

DUNS 21-772-7526

## Venue Cymru North Wales Conference Centre
The Promenade, Station Road East,
Penmaenmawr, Gwynedd LL34 6BE
**Tel:** 01492879771
**Web:** www.venuecymru.co.uk
**Estd:** 2011 Proprietorship
**Line of Business:** Conference centres and
facilities
**Proprietor:** Ms S Ecob
**US SIC:** 7999 **UK SIC:** 97913
**Employees:** 76

DUNS 29-859-3781     Imp-Exp

## Venus Properties Ltd
(**Subsidiary of:** Eurovenus Ltd)
Unit A, Brantwood Road, London N17 0YD
**Fax:** 02088016455
**Web:** www.venusplc.com
**Reg No:** 2062694 **VAT No:** 455157345
**Estd:** 1986 Private Limited Company
**Line of Business:** Other letting of own
property
**Export Markets:** E U
**Issued Capital:** £12,000
**Directors:** Mrs L Katsantonis,
P Chrysostomou
**Co. Secretary:** Mrs Valentina Chrysostomou
**US SIC:** 6519, 6531
**UK SIC:** 85000, 83400
**Auditors:** Goodman Lawrence & Co

**Bankers:** HSBC Bank plc (40-03-03)

| | 30-11-13 | 30-11-12 | 30-11-11 |
|---|---|---|---|
| TO | 953,955 | N/A | N/A |
| P/L | (4,489,839) | N/A | N/A |
| NW | 4,258,859 | 8,651,136 | 10,673,164 |
| WC | (843,270) | (489,527) | (970,983) |

DUNS 21-175-6370

## Veolia Energy Services Ni Ltd
(**Subsidiary of:** Veolia Environnement)
115-121 Duncrue Street, Belfast BT3 9AR
**Tel:** 02892-622332 **Fax:** 02892622312
**Web:** www.dalkia.ie
**Reg No:** 0073352NI **Estd:** 2004 Private
Limited Company
**Line of Business:** Electrical contractors and
electricians
**Issued Capital:** £1,000
**Directors:** C C Flanagan, D M Thompson,
P R Gilroy, Mrs S Patton, Miss H Mccarville
**Co. Secretary:** Ms Deborah Nolan
**Responsibilities**
**Senior:** Tony Docherty (General Manager)
**US SIC:** 1731, 7399
**UK SIC:** 50300, 83954

| | 31-12-13 | 31-12-12 | 31-12-11 |
|---|---|---|---|
| TO | 4,469,738 | 3,995,399 | 4,298,045 |
| P/L | 739,010 | 472,161 | 455,323 |
| NW | 1,213,409 | 488,963 | 32,756 |
| WC | 1,201,389 | 434,557 | (125,542) |
| Emp. | 57 | 55 | 55 |

DUNS 21-592-5351

## Veolia Enviromental
Mill Road Depot Mill Road, Esher, Surrey
KT10 8AS
**Tel:** 01372476769
**Web:** www.veoliaenvironmentalservices.co.uk
**Estd:** 2011 Proprietorship
**Line of Business:** Refuse collection
**Proprietor:** J Couthlan
**Responsibilities**
**Senior:** Gary Stammers (Contracts
Manager)
**US SIC:** 7349 **UK SIC:** 92300
**Employees:** 200

DUNS 21-585-0449

## Veolia Environment
Wallasey Bridge Road, Birkenhead,
Merseyside CH41 1EB
**Tel:** 02035674200
**Web:** www.veolia.co.uk
**Estd:** 2011
**Line of Business:** Recycling
**Responsibilities**
**Senior:** Alex Paterson (Manager)
**US SIC:** 7339 **UK SIC:** 83954
**Employees:** 260

DUNS 21-580-3577

## Veolia Environmental
Green Lane, Stewartby, Bedford,
Bedfordshire MK43 9LY
**Tel:** 08704208272
**Estd:** 2011 Proprietorship
**Line of Business:** Collection and treatment
of other waste
**Proprietor:** D Parket
**Responsibilities**
**Senior:** Duncan Pryke (Manager)
**US SIC:** 4953 **UK SIC:** 92110
**Employees:** 80

DUNS 21-607-1243

## Veolia Environmental Services
Southway Drive, Bristol, Avon BS30 5LW
**Tel:** 01179610372
**Web:** www.veolia.co.uk
**Estd:** 2011 Proprietorship
**Line of Business:** Collection and treatment
of other waste
**Proprietor:** P Chewins
**Responsibilities**
**Senior:** Tim Hellings (Manager)
**US SIC:** 4953 **UK SIC:** 92110
**Employees:** 50

DUNS 23-245-9052

## Veolia Environmental Services (Uk) Plc
(**Subsidiary of:** Veolia Environnement)
210 Pentonville Road, London N1 9PE
**Tel:** 01443841200 **Fax:** 020-7812-5001
**Web:** www.veoliaenvironmentalservices.co.uk
**Reg No:** 2215767 **Estd:** 1990 Public Limited
Company
**Line of Business:** Cleaning contracting
commercial
**Issued Capital:** £400,000,000
**Directors:** D A Gerrard, R C Hunt,
Miss C I Kraus, G H Graveson,
Mrs C R Gough, P R Gilroy,
Ms E Brachlianoff
**Co. Secretary:** Mrs Celia Gough

**Responsibilities**
**Senior:** François Bertreau (Director),
Edward Dunsmore (Manager), Kevin
Dunsmore (Manager), Paul Levett (Deputy
Chief Executive Officer), Tom Spaul
(Manager)
**Marketing:** Nick Burchett (Marketing
Communications Manag), Kevin Hurst
(Marketing Director)
**Sales:** Christophe Bellynck (Development
Director), Jennifer Bowan (Business
Development Manager), Paul Cruxton
(National Development Manager), Bockarie
Koroma (Sales Executive), Jack Lavington
(Group Development Director), Brian
Mulholland (Sales & Development Director),
Frank Robertson (Business Improvement
Manager), Chris Sedgley (Business
Development Manager -)
**HR:** Richard Walkland (HR Manager)
**Operations:** Mike Hogan (Operational
Systems Manager), Sarah Moseley (Director
of Hazardous Waste)
**Branches:** Veolia Environmental Services
(Uk) Plc, Lindon Road, Walsall, West
Midlands WS8 7BB
**US SIC:** 6711, 8999
**UK SIC:** 83962, 83954
**Auditors:** Ernst & Young LLP
**Bankers:** Barclays Bank Plc (20-00-00)
**Following financial data are in thousands**

| | 31-12-13 | 30-09-13 | 31-12-12 |
|---|---|---|---|
| TO | 1,285,027 | N/A | 1,288,661 |
| P/L | 29,964 | 355,000 | 43,339 |
| NW | 202,900 | 879,615 | 448,489 |
| WC | 680,600 | 581,497 | 511,627 |
| Emp. | 12,172 | N/A | 13,576 |

DUNS 77-120-1993     Imp

## Veolia Es Birmingham Ltd
Tyseley Incinerator James Road,
Birmingham, West Midlands B11 2BA
**Tel:** 0121-680-2000 **Fax:** 0121-680-2051
**Web:** www.veoliaenvironmentalservices.co.uk
**Reg No:** 2692681 **VAT No:** 614258159
**Estd:** 1994 Private Limited Company
**Line of Business:** Collection and treatment
of other waste
**Issued Capital:** £5,100,099
**Directors:** G H Graveson, R C Hunt,
Ms E K Brachlianoff, D A Gerrard,
Miss C R Gough, D J Macphail
**Co. Secretary:** James Condliffe
**Responsibilities**
**Senior:** Richard Berry (Manager), Laurent
Carrabin (Manager), Sue Thomason
(Manager)
**Branches:** various waste disposal sites
throughout Birmingham
**US SIC:** 4953 **UK SIC:** 92110
**Auditors:** Ernst & Young LLP
**Bankers:** Barclays Bank Plc (20-00-00)

| | 31-12-13 | 31-12-12 | 31-12-11 |
|---|---|---|---|
| TO | 42,502,000 | 42,299,000 | 40,535,000 |
| P/L | 6,409,000 | 6,584,000 | 8,107,000 |
| NW | 78,074,000 | 74,710,000 | 71,133,000 |
| WC | 88,113,000 | 87,104,000 | 90,920,000 |
| Emp. | 188 | 181 | 191 |

DUNS 34-865-9004

## Veolia Es Hampshire Ltd
(**Subsidiary of:** Veolia Environnement)
Transfer Plant, Poles Lane, Winchester,
Hampshire SO21 2EA
**Tel:** 02035673000
**Web:** www.veoliaenvironmentalservices.co.uk
**Reg No:** 2817856 **VAT No:** 530008893
**Estd:** 1993 Private Limited Company
**Line of Business:** Collection and treatment
of other waste
**Trading Style:** Veolia Environmental
Services
**Issued Capital:** £2
**Principals:** G H Graveson (Managing),
B Slater, D A Gerrard, R C Hunt
**Co. Secretary:** Benjamin Lambert
**Responsibilities**
**Senior:** Richard Berry (Manager), Paul
Levett (Manager), Keith Riley (Manager)
**Marketing:** Phil Digweed (IT Manager)
**IT:** Phil Digweed (IT Manager)
**HR:** Cyndi Baker (Human Resources
Manager)
**Operations:** Phil Digweed (IT Manager)
**Branches:** Veolia Es Hampshire Ltd, Marsh
Lane, Lymington, Hampshire SO41 9BX
**US SIC:** 4953 **UK SIC:** 92110
**Auditors:** Ernst & Young LLP

| | 31-12-13 | 31-12-12 | 31-12-11 |
|---|---|---|---|
| TO | 106,784,000 | 102,147,000 | 100,951,000 |
| P/L | 27,517,000 | 27,141,000 | 27,972,000 |
| NW | 26,423,000 | 101,302,000 | 81,099,000 |
| WC | (3,582,000) | 68,213,000 | 49,833,000 |
| Emp. | 395 | 382 | 367 |

DUNS 50-523-9194

## Veolia Es (Uk) Ltd
(**Subsidiary of:** Veolia Environnement)
Kingswood House, Kingswood Crescent,
Cannock, Staffordshire WS11 8JP
**Tel:** 01543452121 **Fax:** 01902798361
**Web:** www.veolia.co.uk
**Reg No:** 2481991 **VAT No:** 530008893

**Estd:** 1990 Private Limited Company
**Line of Business:** Wholesale of waste and scrap
**Trading Style:** Veolia Environmental Services
**Issued Capital:** £75,000,000
**Directors:** P R Gilroy, Ms E Brachlianoff, R C Hunt, Mrs M A Ulrich, G H Graveson, D A Gerrard, Mrs C R Gough, T Spaul
**Co. Secretary:** Mrs Celia Gough
**Responsibilities**
**Senior:** Andrew Reidy *(General Manager - North London)*
**Finance:** Vernon Novy *(Finance Group Controller)*
**Branches:** Veolia Es (Uk) Ltd, Gatehouse Rd, Rotherwas Indstl Est, Hereford, Herefordshire HR2 6RQ
**US SIC:** 5093, 8999
**UK SIC:** 62200, 83954
**Auditors:** Ernst & Young LLP
**Bankers:** Barclays Bank Plc (20-00-00)

| | 31-12-13 | 31-12-12 | 31-12-11 |
|---|---|---|---|
| TO | 800,419,000 | 802,094,000 | 818,820,000 |
| P/L | 9,503,000 | 19,079,000 | 56,933,000 |
| NW | 90,116,000 | 281,004,000 | 276,822,000 |
| WC | (12,590,000) | 191,072,000 | 188,041,000 |
| Emp. | 10,929 | 10,022 | 11,054 |

DUNS 21-099-8827

## Veolia Water Enterprise Ltd

**(Subsidiary of:** Veolia Environnement)
Fifth Floor Kings Place, London N1 9AG
**Tel:** 02078438500 **Fax:** 02078438560
**Web:** www.veoliawater.co.uk
**Reg No:** 6436541 **Estd:** 1987 Private Limited Company
**Line of Business:** Management activities of holding companies
**Trading Style:** Veolia Water Enterprise Limited
**Issued Capital:** £1
**Directors:** D A Gerrard, R C Hunt, Miss C R Gough, A J Dench
**Co. Secretary:** Miss Celia Gough
**Responsibilities**
**Senior:** Olivier Bret *(CEO / Managing Director - UK,)*, Frederic Devos *(Chief Executive)*, Philippe Guitard *(Executive Vice President)*
**Sales:** Roger Lock *(Business Development Manager)*
**US SIC:** 6711 **UK SIC:** 83962
**Auditors:** Ernst & Young LLP

| | 31-12-13 | 31-12-12 | 31-12-12 |
|---|---|---|---|
| TA | 156,936,000 | 111,765,000 | 96,324,000 |
| P/L | (1,210,000) | (2,317,000) | (1,149,000) |
| NW | (6,378,000) | (5,673,000) | (4,969,000) |
| WC | (149,358,000) | (115,253,000) | (99,508,000) |

DUNS 53-601-5977

## Veolia Water Industrial Outsourcing Ltd

**(Subsidiary of:** Veolia Environnement)
The Hub Tamblin Way, Hatfield, Hertfordshire AL10 9EZ
**Tel:** 01707268111 **Fax:** 01923-814398
**Web:** www.affinitywater.co.uk
**Reg No:** 3406788 **Estd:** 2000 Private Limited Company
**Line of Business:** Construction of water projects
**Trading Style:** Affinity Water
**Issued Capital:** £1,429,000
**Directors:** I D Williams, Ms K A Ratcliffe, K H Patton
**Co. Secretary:** Mrs Celia Gough
**Branches:** Veolia Water Industrial Outsourcing Ltd, Trinity Point, New Road, Halesowen, West Midlands B63 3HY
**US SIC:** 1629 **UK SIC:** 50000
**Auditors:** More & Young LLP
**Bankers:** Barclays Bank Plc (20-74-09)

| | 31-12-13 | 31-12-12 | 31-12-11 |
|---|---|---|---|
| TO | 14,403,000 | 13,165,000 | 7,692,000 |
| P/L | (4,526,000) | (1,118,000) | (2,435,000) |
| NW | (6,348,000) | (8,159,000) | (7,837,000) |
| WC | (8,105,000) | 559,000 | (1,411,000) |
| Emp. | 91 | 93 | 65 |

DUNS 39-469-5787

## Veolia Water U K Ltd

**(Subsidiary of:** Veolia Environnement)
Kings Place, 90 York Way, Islington, London N1 9AG
**Tel:** 020-3567-6600
**Web:** www.veoliawater.co.uk
**Reg No:** 2127283 **Estd:** 1987 Private Limited Company
**Line of Business:** Management activities of holding companies
**Issued Capital:** £500,000
**Directors:** Miss C R Gough, R C Hunt, P R Gilroy, N J Paterson, D A Gerrard, S F Shine, Mrs E K Brachlianoff
**Co. Secretary:** Miss Celia Gough
**Responsibilities**
**Senior:** François Bertreau *(Director)*
**Branches:** Veolia Water U K Ltd, Station Road, Mirfield, West Yorkshire WF14 8PT
**US SIC:** 6711 **UK SIC:** 83962

**Auditors:** Ernst & Young LLP
**Bankers:** Banque Nationale De Paris Plc (23-46-35)

| | 31-12-13 | 31-12-12 | 31-12-12 |
|---|---|---|---|
| TO | 1,132,000 | 167,683,000 | 459,414,000 |
| P/L | (19,555,000) | (54,684,000) | 26,928,000 |
| NW | 171,759,000 | 505,194,000 | 443,347,000 |
| WC | 112,428,000 | 590,953,000 | (166,783,000) |
| Emp. | 114 | 1,381 | 2,550 |

DUNS 76-708-5079

## Verase Ltd

11a Albyn Place, Aberdeen, Aberdeenshire AB10 1YE
**Web:** www.verase.co.uk
**Reg No:** 0130656SC **VAT No:** 553218259
**Estd:** 1991 Private Limited Company
**Line of Business:** Other letting of own property
**Trading Style:** Crown Park Consulltans Ltd
**Issued Capital:** £100
**Principals:** I M Finnie *(Managing)*, A Wallace
**Co. Secretary:** Stephen Fairless
**Responsibilities**
**Senior:** Finlay Cran *(Manager)*
**Branches:** Verase Ltd, 44-56 Justice Mill Lane, Aberdeen, Aberdeenshire AB11 6EP
**US SIC:** 6519 **UK SIC:** 85000
**Auditors:** Garden & Marshall

| | 31-12-12 | 31-12-11 | 31-12-10 |
|---|---|---|---|
| TO | 4,682,742 | 4,431,412 | 3,880,009 |
| P/L | 389,089 | (64,909) | (1,573,706) |
| NW | (3,542,179) | (5,530,064) | (5,465,155) |
| WC | (599,573) | (1,579,794) | (2,325,954) |
| Emp. | 84 | 93 | 84 |

DUNS 22-524-6180 **Imp-Exp**

## Verbatim Ltd

**(Subsidiary of:** Mitsubishi Chemical Holdings Corporation)
Prestige House, 23-26 High Street, Egham, Surrey TW20 9DU
**Tel:** 01784-439781 **Fax:** 01784471337
**Web:** www.verbatim-europe.com
**Reg No:** 1669496 **VAT No:** 372714450
**Estd:** 1982 Private Limited Company
**Line of Business:** Wholesale of computers, computer peripheral equipment and software
**Export Markets:** Worldwide
**Export Sales:** £177,177,716
**Issued Capital:** £1,801,400
**Directors:** M J Blonk, T Mutsu, G S Milner, G S Petrausch
**Co. Secretary:** Stephen Colnbrook
**Responsibilities**
**Senior:** Leslie Bacon *(Deputy General Manager, HR and)*, Tracy Collacott *(Office Manager)*, Jurgen Fritz *(President)*
**Finance:** M Oreilly *(Finance & Administration Direc)*
**HR:** Leslie Bacon *(Deputy General Manager, HR and)*
**US SIC:** 5081 **UK SIC:** 61490
**Auditors:** Ernst & Young LLP
**Bankers:** Barclays Bank Plc (20-29-90)

| | 31-12-12 | 31-12-11 | 31-12-10 |
|---|---|---|---|
| TO | 200,402,152 | 252,887,758 | 257,398,735 |
| P/L | 76,438 | (345,384) | 12,596,006 |
| NW | 19,065,262 | 26,408,637 | 59,161,147 |
| WC | 16,305,303 | 23,482,217 | 58,581,471 |
| Emp. | 68 | 67 | 158 |

DUNS 76-347-7460

## Verdant Leisure Ltd

Innerwick, Dunbar, East Lothian EH42 1QT
**Tel:** 01368840643
**Web:** www.thurstonmanor.co.uk
**Reg No:** 2548086 **VAT No:** 553788891
**Estd:** 2002 Private Limited Company
**Line of Business:** Caravan parks
**Trading Style:** Thurston Manor
**Issued Capital:** £400,090
**Directors:** G R Hodgson, A Wall, Ms B J Dixon
**Co. Secretary:** Andrew Wall
**Responsibilities**
**Senior:** Dennis Dunham *(Manager)*, George Hope *(Manager)*
**Finance:** Dennis Dunham *(Manager)*
**Marketing:** Catherine Dunham *(Sales & Marketing Manager)*
**Sales:** Catherine Dunham *(Sales & Marketing Manager)*
**HR:** Dennis Dunham *(Manager)*
**Operations:** Dennis Dunham *(Manager)*
**Purchasing:** Dennis Dunham *(Manager)*
**Branches:** Verdant Leisure Ltd, Pease Bay Caravan Park, Cockburnspath, Berwickshire TD13 5YP
**US SIC:** 7033 **UK SIC:** 66701
**Auditors:** CLB Coopers
**Bankers:** Barclays Bank Plc (20-61-46)

| | 28-02-14 | 28-02-13 | 29-02-12 |
|---|---|---|---|
| TO | 8,642,000 | 8,380,000 | 8,436,216 |
| P/L | 1,899,000 | 1,425,000 | 1,227,556 |
| NW | 10,153,000 | 8,702,000 | 7,676,970 |
| WC | 743,000 | (532,000) | 1,506,380 |
| Emp. | 93 | 77 | 89 |

DUNS 49-494-1750 **Imp-Exp**

## Verder Ltd

**(Subsidiary of:** Verder International B.V.)
Unit 3, Wednesbury, West Midlands WS10 5QH
**Tel:** 01924221001
**Web:** www.verder.co.uk
**Reg No:** 3156345 **Estd:** 1996 Private Limited Company
**Line of Business:** Manufacturers of pump devices
**Export Markets:** Europe
**Export Sales:** £6,962,964
**Trading Style:** Verder Pumping Services
**Issued Capital:** £783,330
**Directors:** M C Heap, K O Mccartney
**Co. Secretary:** David Court
**Responsibilities**
**Senior:** Simon Aspinall *(Marketing Manager)*
**Marketing:** Annalize Davy *(Marketing Manager)*
**Branches:** Verder Ltd, 3 Express Close, Wellingborough, Northamptonshire NN9 5RQ
**US SIC:** 3563, 5084
**UK SIC:** 32831, 61490
**Auditors:** PricewaterhouseCoopers LLP
**Bankers:** Barclays Bank Plc (20-48-46)

| | 31-12-13 | 31-12-12 | 31-12-11 |
|---|---|---|---|
| TO | 12,286,543 | 11,205,451 | 11,165,085 |
| P/L | 1,686,154 | 1,464,440 | 1,620,679 |
| NW | 3,761,200 | 4,445,907 | 3,913,776 |
| WC | 3,418,392 | 4,034,435 | 3,389,911 |
| Emp. | 63 | 60 | 58 |

DUNS 34-625-6105

## Verderg Connectors Ltd

Lansbury Estate Units 5 And 6, Woking, Surrey GU21 2EP
**Tel:** 01483-289300 **Fax:** 01483289301
**Web:** www.verderg.com
**Reg No:** 5432011 **Estd:** 2007 Private Limited Company
**Line of Business:** Engineering services
**Issued Capital:** £3
**Directors:** R W Freeman, G Stalcup, D L Clause, R A Martins Filho
**Responsibilities**
**Senior:** Renato Martins-Filho *(Manager)*, Sarah Pugh *(Office Manager)*
**Finance:** Renato Martins *(Finance Director)*, Renato Martins-Filho *(Manager)*
**Branches:** Verderg Connectors Ltd, Unit B, Tebay Road, Wirral, Merseyside CH62 3AB
**US SIC:** 8911, 3559
**UK SIC:** 83701, 32863
**Auditors:** Target Consulting Ltd

| | 31-03-14 | 31-03-13 | 31-03-12 |
|---|---|---|---|
| TO | 30,518,609 | 22,977,446 | 15,151,657 |
| P/L | 5,784,587 | 2,776,393 | 1,265,866 |
| NW | 10,680,623 | 5,141,761 | 1,876,087 |
| WC | 9,736,042 | 4,824,394 | 1,884,810 |
| Emp. | 105 | 62 | 35 |

DUNS 76-838-2327

## Verdi's Ltd.

Mumbles Road, Mumbles, Swansea, West Glamorgan SA3 4EN
**Tel:** 01792-369135
**Web:** www.verdis-cafe.co.uk
**Reg No:** 2604475 **Estd:** 1991 Private Limited Company
**Line of Business:** Take-away food shops
**Issued Capital:** £50,000
**Directors:** Mrs S E Moruzzi, G Moruzzi, M S Moruzzi
**Co. Secretary:** Marco Moruzzi
**US SIC:** 5812 **UK SIC:** 66110
**Auditors:** Bishop Plimmer Umbleja

| | 30-04-14 | 30-04-13 | 30-04-12 |
|---|---|---|---|
| TA | 938,491 | 886,517 | 933,985 |
| NW | 484,702 | 420,286 | 398,175 |
| WC | (80,395) | (116,725) | (108,996) |

DUNS 77-901-4856

## Verdo Renewables Ltd

West Portway Industrial Estate, Andover, Hampshire SP10 3XW
**Tel:** 01264342000
**Web:** www.verdorenewables.co.uk
**Reg No:** 5806609 **VAT No:** 885099960
**Estd:** 2006 Private Limited Company
**Line of Business:** Other manufacturing not elsewhere classified
**Export Sales:** £975,915
**Issued Capital:** £12,962,001
**Directors:** A D Mcglynn, K Frimer, T W Bornerup, R A Smith, K R Jeppesen, N D Broughton
**US SIC:** 3999, 2421, 5999
**UK SIC:** 49590, 46101, 65600
**Auditors:** Rouse Audit LLP

| | 31-12-13 | 31-12-12 | 31-12-11 |
|---|---|---|---|
| TO | 12,740,402 | 8,891,077 | 5,414,404 |
| P/L | (5,530,099) | (6,837,355) | (5,779,526) |
| NW | 12,392,809 | (4,577,092) | 2,260,263 |
| WC | (9,261,145) | (27,165,691) | (21,766,011) |
| Emp. | 75 | 53 | 51 |

DUNS 23-945-1503

## Verifone Media

21-22 Great Castle Street Lon, London W1G 0HY
**Tel:** 02070911990
**Web:** www.taximedia.co.uk
**Estd:** 2001 Proprietorship
**Line of Business:** Sign and poster site maintenance
**Proprietor:** A Coetzee
**Responsibilities**
**Senior:** Asher Moses *(General Manager)*
**US SIC:** 7319 **UK SIC:** 83800
**Employees:** 52

DUNS 34-606-4967

## Verifone Services Uk & Ireland Ltd

100 Eureka Park, Upper Pemberton, Ashford, Kent TN25 4AZ
**Tel:** 08444828250 **Fax:** 0844-482-8210
**Web:** www.verifone.co.uk
**Reg No:** 2747866 **Estd:** 1992 Private Limited Company
**Line of Business:** Computer software (development)
**Trading Style:** Verifone
**Issued Capital:** £1,000
**Directors:** A Y Liu, M E Rothman
**Co. Secretary:** Albert Liu
**Responsibilities**
**Senior:** Frank Landen *(Head of Sales)*, Ian Rutland *(Manager)*, Tony Saunders *(Manager)*
**Sales:** Frank Landen *(Head of Sales)*
**IT:** Martin Pawley *(Head of IT)*
**US SIC:** 7379, 5081
**UK SIC:** 83940, 61490
**Auditors:** Ersnt & Young LLP
**Bankers:** National Westminster Bank Plc (60-60-08)

| | 31-10-13 | 31-10-12 | 31-10-11 |
|---|---|---|---|
| TO | 24,450,244 | 20,092,286 | 22,689,066 |
| P/L | (163,820) | (2,990,832) | 1,692,264 |
| NW | (699,863) | (1,638,625) | 1,032,231 |
| WC | 2,381,172 | 337,043 | 1,002,132 |
| Emp. | 220 | 236 | 225 |

DUNS 39-905-3982 **Imp-Exp**

## Verifone (U.K.) Ltd

**(Subsidiary of:** Verifone Systems Inc.)
Symphony House, 7 Cowley Business Park, High Street, Cowley, Uxbridge, Middlesex UB8 2AD
**Tel:** 01895275275 **Fax:** 01895275276
**Web:** www.dione.co.uk
**Reg No:** 2230494 **VAT No:** 493920714
**Estd:** 1988 Private Limited Company
**Line of Business:** Other software consultancy and supply
**Export Markets:** Europe, Middle East
**Export Sales:** £6,355,000
**Issued Capital:** £500,000
**Director:** M E Rothman
**Co. Secretary:** Albert Liu
**Responsibilities**
**Sales:** Stanford Rusike *(Account Manager)*
**Branches:** Verifone (U.k.) Ltd, Symphony House, 7 High Street, Uxbridge, Middlesex UB8 2AD
**US SIC:** 7379 **UK SIC:** 83940
**Auditors:** Ernst & Young LLP
**Bankers:** National Westminster Bank Plc (60-10-10)

| | 31-10-13 | 31-10-12 | 31-10-11 |
|---|---|---|---|
| TO | 36,084,000 | 50,465,000 | 41,187,000 |
| P/L | (475,000) | (6,975,000) | (2,072,000) |
| NW | 4,562,000 | 8,601,000 | 15,510,000 |
| WC | 1,716,000 | 5,892,000 | 13,683,000 |
| Emp. | 234 | 215 | 209 |

DUNS 76-816-2786

## Verint Systems U K Ltd

**(Subsidiary of:** Bnr Consulting Llc)
241 Brooklands Road, Weybridge, Surrey KT13 0RH
**Tel:** 01932839500 **Fax:** 01372869005
**Web:** www.verint.com
**Reg No:** 2602824 **Estd:** 1991 Private Limited Company
**Line of Business:** Computer software (development)
**Export Sales:** £23,248,000
**Issued Capital:** £100
**Directors:** K Bain, D E Robinson
**Responsibilities**
**Senior:** David Parcell *(Manager)*
**US SIC:** 7379 **UK SIC:** 83940
**Auditors:** Deloitte & Touche LLP
**Bankers:** HSBC Bank plc (40-49-19)

| | 31-01-14 | 31-01-13 | 31-01-12 |
|---|---|---|---|
| TO | 62,026,000 | 68,344,000 | 53,153,000 |
| P/L | 9,463,000 | 15,665,000 | 18,268,000 |
| NW | 34,931,000 | 26,547,000 | 24,850,000 |
| WC | 36,457,000 | 28,808,000 | 27,686,000 |
| Emp. | 256 | 265 | 238 |

DUNS 76-446-4244 **Exp**

## Verint Witness Systems

**(Subsidiary of:** Bnr Consulting Llc)
Kings Court, Kingston Road, Leatherhead, Surrey KT22 7SL
**Tel:** 08704810050 **Fax:** 08704810055
**Web:** www.verint.com
**Reg No:** 2563800 **VAT No:** 528672518
**Estd:** 1990 Private Unlimited Company
**Line of Business:** Computer software (development)
**Export Markets:** Worldwide
**Issued Capital:** £1
**Directors:** P D Fante, K Bain, D E Robinson
**Responsibilities**
**Facilities:** Harriet McHugh *(Facilities Manager)*
**Branches:** Verint Witness Systems, 4-8 Whites Grounds, London SE1 3LA
**US SIC:** 7379, 5065
**UK SIC:** 83940, 61500
**Auditors:** Deloitte LLP
**Bankers:** National Westminster Bank Plc (60-06-20)
**Employees:** 140

DUNS 21-164-3444

## Veripos Ltd

Prospect Road, Arnhall Business Park, Westhill, Aberdeenshire AB32 6FE
**Tel:** 01224 526375 **Fax:** 01224 527000
**Web:** www.veripos.com
**Reg No:** 0359548SC **Estd:** 1989 Private Limited Company
**Line of Business:** Other business activities not elsewhere classified
**Issued Capital:** £4,000,000
**Directors:** P M Milne, A T Scott, Ms S Hutchinson
**US SIC:** 7399 **UK SIC:** 83954
**Auditors:** PricewaterhouseCoopers LLP

| | 31-12-13 | 31-12-12 | 31-12-11 |
|---|---|---|---|
| TO | 17,822,588 | 19,714,653 | 18,232,409 |
| P/L | 2,482,463 | 4,569,282 | 4,397,753 |
| NW | 22,352,714 | 23,344,444 | 25,563,343 |
| WC | 13,773,377 | 15,490,171 | 16,144,678 |
| Emp. | 73 | 68 | N/A |

DUNS 21-133-5742

## Verisona Ltd

Building 1000 Lakeside North Harbour, Western Road, Portsmouth, Hampshire PO6 3EN
**Tel:** 02392981000 **Fax:** 02392241597
**Web:** www.verisonalaw.com
**Reg No:** 6669970 **Estd:** 2008 Private Limited Company
**Line of Business:** Conveyancing services
**Issued Capital:** £600
**Directors:** N J Cole, Ms A J Cox, C A Allnutt, Ms S J Ball, Ms R A Downie, M C Purdue, N R Oliver, Ms A J Cox
**Co. Secretary:** Michael Dyer
**Responsibilities**
**Senior:** Vincent Cenham *(Chief Executive Officer)*, Timothy Reynolds *(Director)*, Robert Small *(Director)*
**US SIC:** 8111 **UK SIC:** 83500

| | 30-09-13 | 30-09-12 | 30-09-11 |
|---|---|---|---|
| TA | 1,905,701 | 1,960,557 | 2,422,864 |
| NW | 528,546 | 371,200 | 346,867 |
| WC | 409,053 | 240,532 | 220,557 |

DUNS 23-617-4546 **Imp-Exp**

## Veritek Global Ltd

Veritek House, Edgeland Terrace, Eastbourne, East Sussex BN22 9NJ
**Tel:** 01323-500200 **Fax:** 01323-500201
**Web:** www.veritekglobal.com
**Reg No:** 2004704 **VAT No:** 927442514
**Estd:** 1986 Private Limited Company
**Line of Business:** Photographic equipment repair services
**Export Markets:** Netherlands; Russia
**Export Sales:** £666,000
**Issued Capital:** £10,251
**Director:** J R Edgar
**Co. Secretary:** Daren Briant
**Responsibilities**
**HR:** Michelle Walters *(Human Resources Manager)*
**Health & Safety:** Jane Harraway *(Health & Safety Officer)*
**Branches:** Veritek Global Ltd, 10 St. James Ave, Doncaster, South Yorkshire DN7 4DN
**US SIC:** 7699, 3999, 7399
**UK SIC:** 67303, 49590, 83954
**Auditors:** Deloitte LLP
**Bankers:** National Westminster Bank Plc (01-03-87)

| | 31-03-14 | 31-03-13 | 31-03-12 |
|---|---|---|---|
| TO | 15,185,000 | 24,684,000 | 25,412,000 |
| P/L | (2,878,000) | (112,000) | 218,000 |
| NW | 2,397,000 | 2,010,000 | 2,763,000 |
| WC | 163,000 | 1,420,000 | 2,178,000 |
| Emp. | 215 | 299 | 307 |

DUNS 34-678-6171 **Imp**

## Verizon Uk Ltd

**(Subsidiary of:** Verizon International Luxembourg Sarl)
M C I, Reading, Berkshire RG2 6DA
**Tel:** 01189-055-000 **Fax:** 01189-055-711
**Web:** www.verizonbusiness.com
**Reg No:** 2776038 **VAT No:** 823817033
**Estd:** 1990 Private Limited Company
**Line of Business:** Telecom services
**Trading Style:** Verizon Business, Worldcom
**Issued Capital:** £128,263,262
**Directors:** F C De Maio, Miss C B Aitkenhead
**Co. Secretary:** Fox Court Nominees Limited
**Responsibilities**
**Senior:** Farhana Chaudhry *(Head of Strategy, Operations a)*, Dominique Gaillard *(Manager)*
**IT:** Craig Moore *(IT & Networks Sourcing Manager)*
**Operations:** Farhana Chaudhry *(Head of Strategy, Operations a)*, Helen Gill *(International Conferencing Ope)*, Stefana Harding *(Business Operations Manager)*, Nick Johnson *(EMEA Finance Operations Manage)*, Robert McGregor *(Fraud Operations Manager)*
**Branches:** Verizon Uk Ltd, Kirkton Business Centre, Kirk La, Livingston Village, Livingston, West Lothian EH54 7AY
**US SIC:** 4899 **UK SIC:** 79020
**Auditors:** Ernst & Young LLP

| | 31-12-13 | 31-12-12 | 31-12-11 |
|---|---|---|---|
| TO | 440,090,000 | 451,459,000 | 481,289,000 |
| P/L | 27,136,000 | 23,908,000 | 29,592,000 |
| NW | 474,574,000 | 429,650,000 | 405,865,000 |
| WC | 203,380,000 | 128,732,000 | 77,313,000 |
| Emp. | 1,459 | 1,584 | 1,624 |

DUNS 21-548-8839

## Vermont Hotel

Castle Keep, Castle Garth Upon Tyne, Newcastle-Upon-Tyne, Tyne and Wear NE1 1RQ
**Tel:** 0191-233-1010
**Web:** www.vermont-hotel.com
**Estd:** 2003 Proprietorship
**Line of Business:** Hotels
**Proprietor:** A Zivanaris
**Responsibilities**
**Senior:** Teresa Brown *(General Manager)*, Shadia Hernandez *(General Manager)*, Shadia Thanon *(General Manager)*
**HR:** Teresa Brown *(General Manager)*
**Health & Safety:** Teresa Brown *(General Manager)*
**Facilities:** Tracy Robson *(Facilities Manager)*
**Operations:** Teresa Brown *(General Manager)*
**Purchasing:** Teresa Brown *(General Manager)*
**US SIC:** 7011 **UK SIC:** 66500
**Employees:** 70

DUNS 21-101-4887

## Verna Group International Ltd

Folds Road, Bolton, Lancashire BL1 2TX
**Tel:** 01204-529494 **Fax:** 01204521862
**Web:** www.vernagroup.co.uk
**Reg No:** 6449040 **VAT No:** 498097581
**Estd:** 2007 Private Limited Company
**Line of Business:** Manufacture of medical and surgical equipment and orthopaedic appliances
**Export Sales:** £11,730,566
**Issued Capital:** £168,343
**Directors:** D Beeson, M Miller, N Albert
**Co. Secretary:** Matthew Miller
**Responsibilities**
**Senior:** Christopher Attrill *(Financial Director)*, Linda Haslam *(Chief Executive)*
**Finance:** Christopher Attrill *(Financial Director)*
**US SIC:** 3841, 5199
**UK SIC:** 37201, 61900
**Bankers:** Bank Of Scotland (12-01-03)

| | 31-03-14 | 31-03-13 | 31-03-12 |
|---|---|---|---|
| TO | 29,122,661 | 26,702,505 | 29,208,135 |
| P/L | (2,771,632) | (4,320,621) | (8,149,278) |
| NW | (26,748,776) | (25,124,758) | (22,682,026) |
| WC | (30,880,831) | (29,819,385) | (27,667,491) |
| Emp. | 188 | 188 | 209 |

DUNS 45-882-2244

## Vernalis (Cambridge) Ltd

**(Subsidiary of:** Vernalis Plc)
Granta Park, Cambridge, Cambridgeshire CB21 6GB
**Tel:** 01223895555 **Fax:** 01223895556
**Web:** www.vernalis.com
**Reg No:** 3219804 **Estd:** 1997 Private Limited Company
**Line of Business:** Research and laboratory based activities
**Issued Capital:** £2
**Directors:** D Mackney, I Garland, Dr P J Fellner
**Co. Secretary:** Kevin Kissane
**Responsibilities**
**Senior:** Irene Bryce *(Executive Assistant)*
**US SIC:** 7391 **UK SIC:** 94000
**Auditors:** PricewaterhouseCoopers LLP
**Bankers:** National Westminster Bank Plc (60-04-23)

| | 31-12-13 | 31-12-12 | 31-12-11 |
|---|---|---|---|
| TA | 6,995,249 | 6,995,249 | 6,995,249 |
| NW | 6,995,249 | 6,995,249 | 6,995,249 |

DUNS 50-026-7224

## Vernalis Plc

100 Berkshire Place, Wokingham, Berkshire RG41 5RD
**Fax:** 0118-938-0001
**Web:** www.vernalis.com
**Reg No:** 2304992 **Estd:** 1988 Public Limited Company
**Line of Business:** Management activities of holding companies
**Export Sales:** £14,064,000
**Issued Capital:** £4,421,128
**Directors:** D Mackney, Dr P J Fellner, N Sheail, I Garland, Ms C C Ferguson
**Co. Secretary:** Kevin Kissane
**Responsibilities**
**Senior:** Allan Baxter *(Non-Executive Director)*
**Sales:** Tom Parker *(SVP Commercial Operations)*
**Admin:** Paul Greaney *(Head of Information Services)*
**IT:** Paul Greaney *(Head of Information Services)*
**US SIC:** 6711, 5122
**UK SIC:** 83962, 61800
**Auditors:** PricewaterhouseCoopers LLP
**Bankers:** Barclays Bank Plc (20-65-18)

| | 31-12-13 | 31-12-12 | 31-12-11 |
|---|---|---|---|
| TO | 14,084,000 | 14,616,000 | 12,160,000 |
| P/L | (6,274,000) | (6,838,000) | (10,614,000) |
| NW | 75,952,000 | 79,790,000 | 20,420,000 |
| WC | 79,015,000 | 84,391,000 | 25,428,000 |
| Emp. | 89 | 88 | 84 |

DUNS 21-800-3259 **Exp**

## Vernier Springs & Pressings Ltd

**(Subsidiary of:** Worcestershire Metal Holdings Ltd)
Edward Street, Redditch, Worcestershire B97 6HA
**Tel:** 01527-582-950 **Fax:** 01527-584-614
**Web:** www.verniersprings.com
**Reg No:** 0596653 **VAT No:** 110577008
**Estd:** 2012 Private Limited Company
**Line of Business:** Manufacturers of springs
**Issued Capital:** £8,150
**Directors:** I Chatwin, W Hawkins, G J Hawkins, P R Burman
**Responsibilities**
**Senior:** Kevin Stanley *(Works Manager)*
**IT:** Kevin Stanley *(Works Manager)*
**Facilities:** Kevin Stanley *(Works Manager)*
**Engineering:** Kevin Stanley *(Works Manager)*
**US SIC:** 3452, 3499
**UK SIC:** 31371, 31694
**Auditors:** Cottons Accountants LLP
**Bankers:** Lloyds TSB Bank plc (30-96-97)

| | 30-11-13 | 30-11-12 | 30-11-11 |
|---|---|---|---|
| TA | 1,988,584 | 2,814,949 | 2,650,728 |
| NW | 624,794 | 598,957 | 593,374 |
| WC | 237,202 | 208,890 | 66,201 |

DUNS 22-755-2916

## Vernon Building Society

17-19 St Petersgate, Stockport, Cheshire SK1 1HF
**Fax:** 08451297101
**Web:** www.thevernon.co.uk
**Reg No:** 0000625IP **Estd:** 1924 Friendly Society
**Line of Business:** Building societies
**Principals:** A Wainwright *(President)*, G Heywood *(Chairman)*, R D Wainwright, J R Hardy, M H Impey, P G Selby, J K Williams, P J Farley
**Co. Secretary:** J Williams
**Responsibilities**
**Admin:** Jayne Nield *(Office Manager)*
**Purchasing:** Jayne Nield *(Office Manager)*
**US SIC:** 6012 **UK SIC:** 81402
**Bankers:** National Westminster Bank Plc (01-08-38)
**Employees:** 69

DUNS 29-233-6955

## The Vernon Educational Trust Ltd

Leatherhead Road, Leatherhead, Surrey KT22 0JG
**Tel:** 01372842509 **Fax:** 01372-844452
**Web:** www.daneshillschool.co.uk
**Reg No:** 1194206 **Estd:** 1974 Private Company Limited By Guarantee
**Line of Business:** Schools (independent)
**Trading Style:** Danes Hill School
**Directors:** Doctor H F Patel, Mrs S Collard, G H Toms, R G Mansfield, T W Jones, M L Levene, A J Lunn, A H Monro
**Co. Secretary:** William House
**Responsibilities**
**Senior:** Anthony Beadles *(Manager)*, Willie Murdock *(Principal)*, Angela Rumbold *(Manager)*, Rosemary Wood *(Director)*
**Finance:** Anne Welland *(Accounts Manager)*
**IT:** Alistair Forster *(Computer Manager)*
**HR:** Willie Murdock *(Principal)*
**Purchasing:** Willie Murdock *(Principal)*
**Branches:** The Vernon Educational Trust Ltd, School Office & Admissions, Leatherhead Rd, Leatherhead, Surrey KT22 0JG
**US SIC:** 8211 **UK SIC:** 93200
**Auditors:** Mazars Neville Russell
**Bankers:** Lloyds TSB Bank plc (30-97-81)

| | 31-08-13 | 31-08-12 | 31-08-11 |
|---|---|---|---|
| TO | 12,331,459 | 11,450,500 | 10,911,833 |
| P/L | 1,423,912 | 1,414,206 | 1,340,661 |
| NW | 26,056,690 | 24,632,778 | 23,218,572 |
| WC | 1,152,382 | 3,213,625 | (1,113,285) |
| Emp. | 175 | 170 | 171 |

DUNS 53-655-9958

## Vero Software Ltd

**(Subsidiary of:** Hexagon Ab)
Hadley House, Bayshill Road, Cheltenham, Gloucestershire GL50 3AW
**Tel:** 01242542040
**Web:** www.vero-software.com
**Reg No:** 3461213 **VAT No:** 713214185
**Estd:** 1997 Private Limited Company
**Line of Business:** Other software consultancy and supply
**Issued Capital:** £628,292
**Directors:** P Guglielmini, D A Mills
**Responsibilities**
**Finance:** Julie Randall *(Financial Director)*
**Branches:** Vero Software Ltd, 45 Boulton Road, Reading, Berkshire RG2 0NH
**US SIC:** 7379 **UK SIC:** 83940
**Auditors:** Hazlewoods LLP

| | 31-12-13 | 31-12-12 | 31-12-11 |
|---|---|---|---|
| TO | 68,561,000 | 43,470,000 | 21,108,000 |
| P/L | 12,942,000 | 6,617,000 | 184,000 |
| NW | (37,085,000) | (44,727,000) | (37,501,000) |
| WC | 6,245,000 | 767,000 | (4,048,000) |
| Emp. | 589 | 384 | 334 |

DUNS 57-830-0873

## Versalift Distributors (U.K.) Ltd

**(Subsidiary of:** Dark Investment Limited)
1 Altendiez Way, Kettering, Northamptonshire NN15 5YT
**Tel:** 01536-721010 **Fax:** 01536-721111
**Web:** www.versalift.co.uk
**Reg No:** 2888311 **Estd:** 1994 Private Limited Company
**Line of Business:** Manufacture of equipment for concrete crushing and screening and roadworks
**Issued Capital:** £1,300,000
**Principals:** C Mahon *(Financial)*, S O'Flaherty, C D Burnett, N O Flaherty, T O'Dowd
**Co. Secretary:** Ciaran Mahon
**Responsibilities**
**Senior:** Thomas O' Dowd *(Director)*, Nigel O' Flaherty *(Director)*, Stephen O'flaherty *(Director)*
**Marketing:** Lisa Guerin *(Sales & Marketing Manager)*
**Sales:** Lisa Guerin *(Sales & Marketing Manager)*
**Facilities:** Graham Thorley *(Engineering Manager)*
**Operations:** Lisa Guerin *(Sales & Marketing Manager)*
**Engineering:** Graham Thorley *(Engineering Manager)*
**US SIC:** 3531 **UK SIC:** 32541
**Auditors:** KPMG
**Bankers:** The Bank Of Ireland (30-16-07)

| | 31-12-13 | 31-12-12 | 31-12-11 |
|---|---|---|---|
| TO | 15,562,334 | 15,788,880 | 10,171,357 |
| P/L | 223,314 | 482,989 | 330,018 |
| NW | 2,726,521 | 2,570,593 | 2,226,800 |
| WC | 6,741,290 | 6,129,816 | (1,592,957) |
| Emp. | 82 | 78 | 69 |

DUNS 23-265-0957

## Version 1 Ltd

**(Subsidiary of:** Summer 2016 Unlimited)
Heriot Watt Research Park Avenue South, Edinburgh, Midlothian EH14 4AP
**Tel:** 08701004000 **Fax:** 08701-004001
**Web:** www.rocela.com
**Reg No:** 0223430SC **Estd:** 2001 Private Limited Company
**Line of Business:** Hardware consultancy
**Export Sales:** £327,000
**Issued Capital:** £21,053
**Directors:** J Keatinge, J Dooley
**US SIC:** 7379, 7392
**UK SIC:** 83940, 83951
**Auditors:** Baker Tilly

**Bankers:** Bank Of Scotland (80-07-48)

| | 30-11-13 | 30-11-12 | 30-11-11 |
|---|---|---|---|
| TO | 14,350,000 | 14,071,000 | 16,137,000 |
| P/L | 469,000 | 330,000 | (210,000) |
| NW | 819,000 | 433,000 | 107,000 |
| WC | 2,447,000 | 2,044,000 | 1,698,000 |
| Emp. | 54 | 47 | 47 |

DUNS 23-954-9004 **Imp**

## Vertase F L I Ltd

(**Subsidiary of:** F.L.I. Holdings Ltd)
Bristol Road, Bristol, Avon BS20 6PN
**Tel:** 01275-397600 **Fax:** 01275397601
**Web:** www.vertasefli.co.uk
**Reg No:** 3944198 **Estd:** 2000 Private Limited Company
**Line of Business:** Environmental consultants
**Issued Capital:** £100
**Directors:** Dr C Mccarthy, M S Longman, T J Snell, M J Flynn, S Edgar
**Co. Secretary:** Peter Gaynor
**US SIC:** 8911 **UK SIC:** 83701
**Auditors:** PricewaterhouseCoopers
**Bankers:** National Westminster Bank Plc (56-00-05)

| | 31-12-13 | 31-12-12 | 31-12-11 |
|---|---|---|---|
| TO | 17,944,645 | 10,125,784 | 11,899,349 |
| P/L | (626,577) | 232,778 | 479,088 |
| NW | 2,760,611 | 3,387,188 | 3,611,487 |
| WC | 2,514,552 | 3,142,872 | 3,349,042 |
| Emp. | 57 | 61 | 56 |

DUNS 28-893-8921 **Imp-Exp**

## Vertcell Ltd

(**Subsidiary of:** Pendragon Plc)
Centre House, Village Way, Trafford Park, Manchester M17 1QG
**Tel:** 01618727788
**Reg No:** 1304309 **Estd:** 1982 Private Limited Company
**Line of Business:** Sale of motor vehicle parts and accessories
**Export Markets:** European Union (E U)
**Trading Style:** Premier Parts, Sterling Automotive, Express Factors
**Issued Capital:** £500,000
**Directors:** T P Holden, M S Casha, T G Finn, Pendragon Management Services Li
**Co. Secretary:** Ms Hilary Sykes
**Branches:** Vertcell Ltd, Premier Ho, Ring Rd, Beeston, Leeds, West Yorkshire LS12 6PP
**US SIC:** 5531 **UK SIC:** 65100
**Auditors:** KPMG Audit PLC
**Bankers:** National Westminster Bank Plc (01-08-81)

| | 31-12-13 | 31-12-12 | 31-12-11 |
|---|---|---|---|
| TA | 1,000,000 | 1,000,000 | 1,000,000 |
| NW | 221,000 | 221,000 | 221,000 |
| WC | 221,000 | 221,000 | 221,000 |

DUNS 57-007-8642 **Imp-Exp**

## Vertellus Specialties Uk Ltd

(**Subsidiary of:** Vertellus Health & Specialty Products Llc)
Seal Sands Road, Seal Sands, Middlesbrough, Cleveland TS2 1UB
**Tel:** 01642-546546 **Fax:** 01642-546068
**Web:** www.vertellus.com
**Reg No:** 2864354 **Estd:** 1993 Private Limited Company
**Line of Business:** Manufacturers of agricultural chemicals
**Export Markets:** Worldwide
**Export Sales:** £21,148,000
**Issued Capital:** £3,332,003
**Directors:** P R Gillespie, Ms A M Frye, R V Preziotti, J A Steinfink
**Co. Secretary:** Prima Secretary Limited
**Responsibilities**
**Senior:** Stefano Magnani *(Manager)*
**US SIC:** 2899 **UK SIC:** 25670
**Auditors:** Ernst & Young LLP
**Bankers:** National Westminster Bank Plc (54-10-04)

| | 31-12-13 | 31-12-12 | 31-12-11 |
|---|---|---|---|
| TO | 24,216,000 | 23,786,000 | 21,481,000 |
| P/L | (795,000) | (1,213,000) | (1,383,000) |
| NW | 1,649,000 | 2,424,000 | 3,803,000 |
| WC | 3,181,000 | 2,314,000 | 522,000 |
| Emp. | 80 | 82 | 83 |

DUNS 29-492-0236

## Vertex Financial Services Ltd

(**Subsidiary of:** Vtx Holdings Coöperatief U.A.)
Jessop House, Jessop Avenue, Cheltenham, Gloucestershire GL50 3SH
**Tel:** 01242214400 **Fax:** 01242214323
**Web:** www.vertex.co.uk
**Reg No:** 1855353 **Estd:** 1986 Private Limited Company
**Line of Business:** Other business activities not elsewhere classified
**Issued Capital:** £1,500,000
**Directors:** G K James, C Thompson
**Co. Secretary:** Steven Barker
**Responsibilities**
**Sales:** Phil Ashworth *(Commercial Director)*
**HR:** Kirstie Cutler *(Head of Training)*, Zoe Toomey *(Head of HR)*
**Operations:** Teresa Tompkins *(Operations Director)*
**US SIC:** 7399, 7379
**UK SIC:** 83954, 83940
**Auditors:** Deloitte LLP
**Bankers:** Barclays Bank Plc (20-19-90)

| | 31-03-14 | 31-03-13 | 31-03-12 |
|---|---|---|---|
| TO | 1,808,000 | 3,422,000 | 2,471,000 |
| P/L | 729,000 | 717,000 | (5,004,000) |
| NW | (4,004,000) | (28,956,000) | (29,903,000) |
| WC | (2,413,000) | (22,526,000) | (17,335,000) |
| Emp. | 160 | 126 | 111 |

DUNS 67-219-1868

## Vertex Group Ltd

(**Subsidiary of:** Vtx Holdings Coöperatief U.A.)
Jessop House, Jessop Avenue, Cheltenham, Gloucestershire GL50 3SH
**Tel:** 01242214000
**Web:** www.vertex.co.uk
**Reg No:** 6048945 **Estd:** 2007 Private Limited Company
**Line of Business:** Management activities of holding companies
**Export Sales:** £117,789,000
**Issued Capital:** £1,263,569
**Directors:** D Kaden, M Guenther, M E Fairey, G K James
**Co. Secretary:** Gavin James
**Responsibilities**
**Senior:** Robert Coyle *(Manager)*
**US SIC:** 6711 **UK SIC:** 83962
**Auditors:** Deloitte LLP

| | 31-03-14 | 31-03-13 | 31-03-12 |
|---|---|---|---|
| TO | 153,907,000 | 198,353,000 | 340,449,000 |
| P/L | (4,077,000) | 43,213,000 | 9,605,000 |
| NW | (2,393,000) | 7,180,000 | (20,992,000) |
| WC | 23,722,000 | 7,415,000 | (1,822,000) |
| Emp. | 11,857 | 11,155 | 7,083 |

DUNS 58-351-7933 **Imp**

## Vertex Pharmaceuticals (Europe) Ltd

(**Subsidiary of:** Vertex Pharmaceuticals Incorporated)
86-88 Jubilee Avenue, Abingdon, Oxfordshire OX14 4RW
**Tel:** 01235-438800
**Web:** www.vrtx.com
**Reg No:** 2907620 **Estd:** 1994 Private Limited Company
**Line of Business:** Research institutions and organisations
**Export Sales:** £31,147,000
**Issued Capital:** £125,000
**Directors:** I F Smith, J M Leiden
**Co. Secretary:** Mitre Secretaries Limited
**Responsibilities**
**Senior:** Roger Brimblecombe *(Manager)*, Julian Golec *(Vice President)*, Peter Mueller *(President)*
**IT:** Terry Campbell *(Director - IT)*
**US SIC:** 7391 **UK SIC:** 94000
**Auditors:** Ernst & Young LLP
**Bankers:** Barclays Bank Plc (20-02-53)

| | 31-12-13 | 31-12-12 | 31-12-11 |
|---|---|---|---|
| TO | 31,147,000 | 25,925,107 | 21,369,628 |
| P/L | (898,000) | (2,821,751) | (595,827) |
| NW | 6,138,000 | 6,500,532 | 7,115,063 |
| WC | (3,322,000) | (5,146,273) | 628,651 |
| Emp. | 144 | 145 | 119 |

DUNS 21-633-3468

## Vertical Cabinet Co Ltd

Hithercroft Road, Wallingford, Oxfordshire OX10 9DG
**Tel:** 01491-839966
**Web:** www.ver.co.uk
**Reg No:** 0852711 **VAT No:** 434574934
**Estd:** 1984 Private Limited Company
**Line of Business:** Other letting of own property
**Trading Style:** Verco
**Issued Capital:** £11,000
**Principals:** M B Fogden *(Chairman)*, J L Fogden
**Co. Secretary:** Ms Janet Fogden
**Responsibilities**
**Senior:** Stefan Abbott *(Production Director)*
**Health & Safety:** Stefan Abbott *(Production Director)*
**Engineering:** Stefan Abbott *(Production Director)*
**US SIC:** 6519 **UK SIC:** 85000
**Auditors:** Philip Deane
**Bankers:** Lloyds TSB Bank plc (30-96-96)

| | 30-09-13 | 30-09-12 | 30-09-11 |
|---|---|---|---|
| TO | 248,150 | 249,437 | 123,292 |
| P/L | 165,481 | 185,267 | 57,832 |
| NW | 1,224,817 | 1,250,690 | 1,275,881 |
| WC | 640,442 | 686,967 | 706,031 |

DUNS 21-892-2875 **Imp**

## Vertical Pharma Resources Ltd

(**Subsidiary of:** Elysian Capital Llp)
41 Central Avenue, West Molesey, Surrey KT8 2QZ
**Tel:** 02084819721
**Web:** www.vprpharmacy.com
**Reg No:** 6077026 **Estd:** 2007 Private Limited Company
**Line of Business:** Manufacture of medicaments
**Export Sales:** £292,442
**Issued Capital:** £1,000,100
**Director:** D Jones-Owen
**Co. Secretary:** Ashokkumar Patel
**US SIC:** 2834 **UK SIC:** 25700
**Auditors:** John Cumming Ross Ltd

| | 28-02-14 | 28-02-13 | 29-02-12 |
|---|---|---|---|
| TO | 9,962,685 | 8,041,169 | 7,917,032 |
| P/L | 4,107,375 | 3,254,798 | 4,108,305 |
| NW | 19,438,742 | 16,014,615 | 13,268,172 |
| WC | 18,949,210 | 15,488,059 | 12,707,869 |
| Emp. | 48 | 41 | 36 |

DUNS 29-310-8361

## Vertical Systems Ltd

14 Hemmells, Basildon, Essex SS15 6ED
**Tel:** 08009830000
**Web:** www.verticalsystems.co.uk
**Reg No:** 1741340 **VAT No:** 387882483
**Estd:** 1983 Private Limited Company
**Line of Business:** Other software consultancy and supply
**Issued Capital:** £20,001
**Directors:** G Tucker, P L Healey, Mrs N Dilworth, R C Barker, D Gardner
**Responsibilities**
**Senior:** del Comer *(Warehouse Manager)*, Carl Foody *(Manager)*, Tracy Housley *(Manager)*, Mike Russel *(Financial Director)*
**Finance:** Stephanie Cross *(Finance Manager)*, Larry Hanson *(Senior Finance Administrator)*, Mike Russel *(Financial Director)*
**Sales:** Saqib Ahmed *(Head of Sales & Project Manage)*
**Operations:** Katie Creighton *(Project Manager)*, Nyki Dilworth *(Operations Director)*, Scott Lazarus *(Infastructure Manager)*, Matthew Morris *(Project Manager)*
**US SIC:** 7379 **UK SIC:** 83940
**Bankers:** Lloyds TSB Bank plc (30-91-85)

| | 31-01-14 | 31-01-13 | 31-01-12 |
|---|---|---|---|
| TA | 1,784,932 | 2,017,791 | 2,601,155 |
| NW | 888,192 | 824,739 | 709,364 |
| WC | 228,445 | 121,065 | (53,660) |

DUNS 76-973-7461 **Exp**

## Vertik-Al Ltd

Yardley Brook Industrial Park, Lea Ford Road, Birmingham, West Midlands B33 9TX
**Tel:** 01216087171 **Fax:** 0121-693-7787
**Web:** www.vertikal.net
**Reg No:** 2634525 **VAT No:** 580737618
**Estd:** 1991 Private Limited Company
**Line of Business:** Manufacture of paints, varnishes and similar coatings
**Export Markets:** E U, worldwide
**Trading Style:** Vertik-Al Ltd
**Issued Capital:** £2
**Directors:** R Gibbs, W A Lock, M L Lock
**Co. Secretary:** Ms Maxine Lock
**Responsibilities**
**IT:** Marlynn Hill *(Network, Security Manager)*
**US SIC:** 3999 **UK SIC:** 49590
**Auditors:** Barnett Ravenscroft

| | 31-03-14 | 31-03-13 | 31-03-12 |
|---|---|---|---|
| TA | 1,569,506 | 1,128,463 | 1,206,051 |
| NW | 349,849 | 260,291 | 252,086 |
| WC | 349,849 | 260,291 | 252,086 |

DUNS 21-760-6423

## Vertu Corporation Ltd

(**Subsidiary of:** Crown Holdings Ltd)
Beacon Hill Road, Church Crookham, Fleet, Hampshire GU52 8DY
**Tel:** 01252-611-000 **Fax:** 01252-611-300
**Web:** www.vertu.com
**Reg No:** 7753443 **Estd:** 2011 Private Limited Company
**Line of Business:** Manufacture of telegraph and telephone apparatus and equipment
**Issued Capital:** £93,000,001
**Directors:** N A Hooper, Ms J Rouch, J M Leese, M Pogliani
**Co. Secretary:** Anthony Barratt
**Responsibilities**
**Marketing:** Sylwia Tata *(Head of Central Marketing)*
**IT:** Robin H *(IT Programme Manager)*
**US SIC:** 3661 **UK SIC:** 34410
**Auditors:** PricewaterhouseCoopers LLP

| | 27-12-13 | 28-12-12 |
|---|---|---|
| TO | 133,764,000 | 83,987,000 |
| P/L | (23,383,000) | (25,123,000) |
| NW | (56,221,000) | (20,808,000) |
| WC | 13,533,000 | 41,345,000 |
| Emp. | 526 | 566 |

DUNS 67-145-7547 **Imp**

## Vertu Motors Plc

Vertu House, Kingsway North, Team Valley Trading Estate, Gateshead, Tyne and Wear NE11 0JH
**Tel:** 0191-491-2121
**Web:** www.vertumotors.com
**Reg No:** 5984855 **Estd:** 2006 Public Limited Company
**Line of Business:** Car dealers (new & used)
**Issued Capital:** £19,927,803
**Directors:** R T Forrester, N C Stead, M Sherwin, P Jones, D M Forbes, W M Teasdale
**Co. Secretary:** Ms Karen Anderson
**US SIC:** 5511, 6711
**UK SIC:** 65100, 83962
**Auditors:** PricewaterhouseCoopers LLP
**Following financial data are in thousands**

| | 28-02-14 | 28-02-13 | 29-02-12 |
|---|---|---|---|
| TO | 1,684,532 | 1,259,335 | 1,088,262 |
| P/L | 15,842 | 4,525 | 5,541 |
| NW | 120,981 | 84,056 | 78,869 |
| WC | 14,138 | 642 | 5,345 |
| Emp. | 3,488 | 3,059 | 2,822 |

DUNS 73-788-3884

## Verulam Health Care Ltd

Verulam Gardens, 70 Grays Inn Road, London WC1X 8BT
**Tel:** 01727-853991
**Web:** www.verulamhouse.co.uk
**Reg No:** 2927338 **Estd:** 1994 Private Limited Company
**Line of Business:** Healthcare companies
**Issued Capital:** £500,000
**Directors:** Ms P M Jackson, Doctor D P Tominey, Ms B Tominey
**Co. Secretary:** Peter Jackson
**Responsibilities**
**Marketing:** Pam McCarthy *(Marketing Manager)*
**US SIC:** 8091, 8051, 8321
**UK SIC:** 95200, 95100, 96111
**Auditors:** B D O Stoy Hayward

| | 31-05-14 | 31-05-13 | 31-05-12 |
|---|---|---|---|
| TO | 2,499,791 | 2,536,244 | 2,479,229 |
| P/L | 444,939 | 573,778 | 480,809 |
| NW | 3,482,895 | 3,685,567 | 3,679,117 |
| WC | (352,196) | (358,717) | (239,267) |
| Emp. | 92 | 87 | 100 |

DUNS 22-186-3454

## Verve Life Ltd

(**Subsidiary of:** Bourne Care Group Ltd)
97 Broad Lane, Coventry, West Midlands CV5 7AH
**Tel:** 02476677280
**Web:** www.vervelife.co.uk
**Reg No:** 4204572 **Estd:** 2001 Private Limited Company
**Line of Business:** Children's homes
**Issued Capital:** £50,000
**Director:** D M Powell
**Co. Secretary:** Godfrey Brew
**Branches:** Verve Life Ltd, 97 Broad La, Coventry, West Midlands CV5 7AH
**US SIC:** 8321 **UK SIC:** 96111
**Auditors:** Maxwell & Co

| | 30-06-13 | 30-06-12 | 30-06-11 |
|---|---|---|---|
| TA | 1,744,914 | 1,975,484 | 1,956,830 |
| NW | 1,453,582 | 1,367,704 | 1,293,040 |
| WC | 777,121 | 645,273 | 497,576 |

DUNS 21-606-9644

## Verve Ltd

Inch Cross House Standhill, Bathgate, West Lothian EH48 2HT
**Tel:** 01506655522
**Estd:** 2003
**Line of Business:** Sale of new motor vehicles
**Partners:** S Anderson, S Anderson, C Adair
**US SIC:** 5511 **UK SIC:** 65100
**Employees:** 68

DUNS 21-147-3816

## Verve Partners Holdings Ltd

Building 3/4, The Leather Market, Unit 03.2, 11-13 Western Street, London SE1 3ER
**Tel:** 02079284314
**Reg No:** 6774021 **Estd:** 2008 Private Limited Company
**Line of Business:** Market research and public opinion polling
**Issued Capital:** £1,472
**Directors:** N G Brown, A G Cooper, A Harper-Tee, G D Westmore, D J Packford
**Co. Secretary:** David Packford
**Responsibilities**
**Senior:** Mei Chen *(Financial Controller And Offic)*
**US SIC:** 7392 **UK SIC:** 83951

| | 31-12-13 | 31-12-12 | 31-12-11 |
|---|---|---|---|
| TA | 1,329,291 | 1,331,233 | 1,170,690 |
| NW | 683,409 | 684,778 | 552,403 |
| WC | 1,326,117 | 1,327,486 | 1,167,939 |

DUNS 34-981-5113
## Vervia Ltd
Unit F3-F5 The Mayford Centre, Mayford Green, Woking, Surrey GU22 0PP
**Tel:** 01483-727276
**Web:** www.vervia.co.uk
**Reg No:** 5776855 **Estd:** 2006 Private Limited Company
**Line of Business:** Cleaning contracting domestic
**Issued Capital:** £1,000
**Director:** Ms A S Morris
**Co. Secretary:** Kings Mill Practice Ltd
**US SIC:** 7349 **UK SIC:** 92300

| | 30-04-14 | 30-04-13 | 30-04-12 |
|---|---|---|---|
| TA | 100,166 | 88,790 | 73,702 |
| NW | 1,444 | 1,444 | 6,212 |
| WC | (24,786) | (19,227) | (13,466) |

DUNS 21-732-4664
## Verwin Plumbing & Heating Ltd
223 London Road, Reading, Berkshire RG1 3NY
**Tel:** 01189-666049
**Reg No:** 0917733 **VAT No:** 199696964
**Estd:** 1967 Private Limited Company
**Line of Business:** Plumbers
**Issued Capital:** £140
**Principals:** J F Baldwin *(Managing)*, E Oliver, G J Baldwin, S D Oliver
**Co. Secretary:** John Baldwin
**US SIC:** 1711 **UK SIC:** 50300
**Auditors:** Chantrey Vellacott
**Bankers:** The Royal Bank Of Scotland Plc (16-29-25)

| | 31-10-13 | 31-10-12 | 31-10-11 |
|---|---|---|---|
| TA | 1,093,433 | 1,276,790 | 1,097,751 |
| NW | 402,503 | 408,806 | 420,543 |
| WC | 358,165 | 373,580 | 392,546 |

DUNS 42-375-1705
## Verytas Solutions Ltd
**(Subsidiary of:** Verytas Homecare Ltd)
Forest Hill, Downing Road, Whitford, Holywell, Clwyd CH8 9EQ
**Tel:** 01745560295 **Fax:** 01745770220
**Web:** www.verytas.net
**Reg No:** 4362784 **Estd:** 2002 Private Limited Company
**Line of Business:** Home care and help services
**Issued Capital:** £1,006
**Directors:** Ms P C Williams, S P Williams, Ms J E Thomas, G J Paterson
**Co. Secretary:** Anthony Thomas
**US SIC:** 8811, 8321
**UK SIC:** 99000, 96111

| | 31-03-14 | 31-03-13 | 31-03-12 |
|---|---|---|---|
| TA | 144,715 | 170,279 | 166,644 |
| NW | 33,473 | 58,358 | 58,493 |
| WC | 19,975 | 39,714 | 39,783 |

DUNS 71-908-3516
## Vest Construction Ltd
**(Subsidiary of:** Liveco Ltd)
2 Henson Close, South Church Enterprise Park, Bishop Auckland, County Durham DL14 6WA
**Tel:** 01388778822
**Web:** www.vestconstruction.co.uk
**Reg No:** 5290222 **Estd:** 2004 Private Limited Company
**Line of Business:** Building construction contractors
**Issued Capital:** £2
**Director:** D Cooke
**Co. Secretary:** Gavin Vest
**US SIC:** 1799 **UK SIC:** 50000

| | 30-11-14 | 30-11-13 | 30-11-12 |
|---|---|---|---|
| TA | 2 | 2 | 2 |
| NW | 2 | 2 | 2 |

DUNS 22-159-3424
## Vestas-Celtic Wind Technology Ltd.
**(Subsidiary of:** Vestas Wind Systems A/S)
302 Bridgewater Place, Birchwood Park, Warrington, Cheshire WA3 6XG
**Tel:** 01925 857100 **Fax:** 01925 859921
**Web:** www.vestas.com
**Reg No:** 0216807SC **VAT No:** 774728585
**Estd:** 2001 Private Limited Company
**Line of Business:** Manufacture of metal structures and parts of structures
**Issued Capital:** £6,200,000
**Directors:** K S Mortensen, M Samuelsson, S A Pedersen
**Responsibilities**
**Senior:** Ken Fiddes *(Vice President of Sales)*
**Marketing:** Sally Owens *(Head of Marketing)*
**Sales:** Ken Fiddes *(Vice President of Sales)*
**Facilities:** Susan Cartwright *(Head of Facilities)*
**Branches:** Vestas-Celtic Wind Technology Ltd., 302 Bridgewater Place, Warrington, Cheshire WA3 6XG
**US SIC:** 3441, 3621
**UK SIC:** 32042, 34201
**Auditors:** PricewaterhouseCoopers LLP
**Bankers:** Unibank A/s (40-48-78)

| | 31-12-13 | 31-12-12 | 31-12-11 |
|---|---|---|---|
| TO | 223,734,000 | 273,853,000 | 131,940,000 |
| P/L | 1,394,000 | 916,000 | 2,139,000 |
| NW | 16,234,000 | 8,156,000 | 8,321,000 |
| WC | 14,979,000 | 6,889,000 | 7,044,000 |
| Emp. | 282 | 276 | 258 |

DUNS 57-064-9889 Imp-Exp
## Vestas Technology Uk Ltd
**(Subsidiary of:** Vestas Wind Systems A/S)
West Medina Mills, Stag Lane, Newport, Isle of Wight PO30 5TR
**Tel:** 01983288000 **Fax:** 01983288001
**Web:** www.vestas.com
**Reg No:** 2883652 **Estd:** 1993 Private Limited Company
**Line of Business:** Hardware consultancy
**Export Markets:** Worldwide
**Issued Capital:** £90,000
**Directors:** S Sert, A J Vedel, S Moller
**Responsibilities**
**Senior:** Flemming Andersen *(Director)*
**Branches:** Vestas Technology Uk Ltd, Keynes Ho, Chester Pk, Alfreton Rd, Derby, Derbyshire DE21 4AB
**US SIC:** 7379, 7391
**UK SIC:** 83940, 94000
**Auditors:** PricewaterhouseCoopers LLP
**Bankers:** Barclays Bank Plc (20-25-85)

| | 31-12-13 | 31-12-12 | 31-12-11 |
|---|---|---|---|
| TO | 39,242,000 | 30,068,000 | 33,687,000 |
| P/L | (594,000) | (449,000) | (106,000) |
| NW | (4,539,000) | (5,814,000) | (4,730,000) |
| WC | (66,180,000) | (69,528,000) | (66,389,000) |
| Emp. | 168 | 190 | 216 |

DUNS 23-982-1221 Imp-Exp
## Vestey Foods Uk Ltd
**(Subsidiary of:** Western United Investment Company Ltd)
29 Ullswater Crescent, Coulsdon, Surrey CR5 2HR
**Tel:** 02086689344 **Fax:** 020 8655 6921
**Web:** www.vesteyfoods.com
**Reg No:** 3970537 **VAT No:** 644549320
**Estd:** 2000 Private Limited Company
**Line of Business:** Meat wholesalers
**Issued Capital:** £100
**Directors:** N Wakeham, C G Copland, G M Vestey, K Hermansen
**Co. Secretary:** Neil Thornton
**Branches:** Vestey Foods Uk Ltd, 23 Brunel Way, Fareham, Hampshire PO15 5SD
**US SIC:** 5147 **UK SIC:** 61700
**Auditors:** BDO LLP
**Bankers:** Barclays Bank Plc (20-49-76)

| | 31-12-13 | 31-12-12 | 31-12-11 |
|---|---|---|---|
| TO | 182,113,507 | 167,624,241 | 161,131,099 |
| P/L | (7,950,051) | 1,711,546 | (38,570) |
| NW | (599,187) | 8,423,003 | 6,794,457 |
| WC | (2,597,447) | 5,527,809 | 4,497,224 |
| Emp. | 255 | 276 | 102 |

DUNS 21-220-9464
## Vestey Holdings Ltd
**(Subsidiary of:** Western United Investment Company Ltd)
29 Ullswater Crescent, Coulsdon, Surrey CR5 2HR
**Tel:** 02086556920
**Web:** www.vesteyfoods.com
**Reg No:** 0066076 **Estd:** 1830 Private Limited Company
**Line of Business:** Management activities of holding companies
**Export Sales:** £106,660,000
**Trading Style:** Vestey Group
**Issued Capital:** £5,000,000
**Directors:** G M Vestey, C M Fisher, C G Copland, J A Scott, R J Vestey, Lord S G Vestey
**Co. Secretary:** Neil Thornton
**US SIC:** 6711, 7399
**UK SIC:** 83962, 83954
**Auditors:** BDO LLP
**Bankers:** The Royal Bank Of Scotland Plc (15-10-00)

| | 31-12-13 | 31-12-12 | 31-12-11 |
|---|---|---|---|
| TO | 432,474,000 | 535,685,000 | 557,167,000 |
| P/L | (13,084,000) | (34,000) | 7,622,000 |
| NW | 65,071,000 | 76,152,000 | 83,585,000 |
| WC | 60,613,000 | 71,072,000 | 89,686,000 |
| Emp. | 718 | 815 | 835 |

DUNS 21-004-5074
## Vestra Wealth Llp
14 Cornhill, London EC3V 3NR
**Tel:** 020-3207-8000
**Web:** www.vestrawealth.com
**Reg No:** 0329392OC **Estd:** 2007 Private Limited Company
**Line of Business:** Other credit granting not elsewhere classified
**Responsibilities**
**Senior:** Andrew Archer *(Non-designated Limited Liabili)*, David Blanc *(Non-designated Limited Liabili)*, Mark Gheerbrant *(Non-designated Limited Liabili)*, Hugo Heath *(Non-designated Limited Liabili)*, John Jopp *(Non-designated Limited Liabili)*, Ali Sarikhani *(Designated Limited Liability P)*, Benjamin Snee *(Designated Limited Liability P)*
**US SIC:** 6111 **UK SIC:** 81501
**Bankers:** HSBC Bank plc (40-01-08)

| | 30-04-14 | 30-04-13 | 30-04-12 |
|---|---|---|---|
| TA | 28,396,902 | 26,950,270 | 20,630,134 |
| P/L | 8,846,500 | 6,759,493 | 5,138,103 |
| NW | 22,341,653 | 23,140,571 | 16,635,078 |
| WC | 22,501,681 | 22,687,180 | 16,240,596 |
| Emp. | 174 | 128 | 120 |

DUNS 21-584-7499
## Vestry Hall
Vestry Hall, London Road, Mitcham, Surrey CR4 3UD
**Tel:** 02086407274
**Web:** www.merton.gov.uk
**Estd:** 2011
**Line of Business:** Charities and charitable organisations
**Proprietor:** Mrs C Warren
**US SIC:** 8699 **UK SIC:** 96902
**Employees:** 100

DUNS 21-859-1255
## Vesuvius Plc
165 Fleet Street, London EC4A 2AE
**Tel:** 02078-220-000 **Fax:** 02078-220-100
**Web:** www.vesuvius.com
**Reg No:** 8217766 **Estd:** 2012 Public Limited Company
**Line of Business:** Management activities of holding companies
**Export Sales:** £1,431,300,000
**Issued Capital:** £2,784,851
**Directors:** J Mcdonough, Ms I J Hinkley, C G Gardell, C M O'Shea, N J Connors, F C Wanecq, J L Hewitt
**Co. Secretary:** Henry Knowles
**US SIC:** 6711, 3499
**UK SIC:** 83962, 31694
**Auditors:** KPMG LLP
**Following financial data are in thousands**

| | 31-12-13 | 31-12-12 |
|---|---|---|
| TO | 1,510,500 | 1,547,500 |
| P/L | 104,100 | 18,400 |
| NW | 138,900 | 77,300 |
| WC | 272,000 | 368,200 |
| Emp. | 11,496 | 14,767 |

DUNS 21-238-5694 Imp-Exp
## Vesuvius Uk Ltd
**(Subsidiary of:** Vesuvius Plc)
1 Midland Way, Barlborough, Chesterfield, Derbyshire S43 4XA
**Tel:** 01246-571-700 **Fax:** 01246571701
**Web:** www.vesuvius.com
**Reg No:** 0054713 **VAT No:** 662858008
**Estd:** 1897 Private Limited Company
**Line of Business:** Refractory materials
**Export Sales:** £105,141,000
**Trading Style:** Foseco Foundry Division
**Issued Capital:** £12,000,000
**Directors:** Y Nokerman, R M Sykes, M Satterthwaite, H J Knowles, K F Slow
**Co. Secretary:** Michael Satterthwaite
**Responsibilities**
**Senior:** Bart Massant *(Manager)*
**HR:** Heather Hughes *(Human Resources Manager)*, Bart Massant *(Manager)*
**Health & Safety:** Heather Hughes *(Human Resources Manager)*
**Branches:** Vesuvius Uk Limited, A W Nielsen Road, Goole, North Humberside DN14 6UE
**US SIC:** 3269, 3299
**UK SIC:** 24894, 24504
**Auditors:** KPMG Audit PLC
**Bankers:** HSBC Bank plc (40-02-50)

| | 31-12-13 | 31-12-12 | 31-12-11 |
|---|---|---|---|
| TO | 149,351,000 | 148,716,000 | 149,928,000 |
| P/L | 7,899,000 | 6,492,000 | 3,761,000 |
| NW | 39,759,000 | 30,790,000 | 23,234,000 |
| WC | 38,511,000 | 30,145,000 | 24,115,000 |
| Emp. | 382 | 395 | 420 |

DUNS 49-055-7261
## Vet Plus Ltd
**(Subsidiary of:** Tangerine Holdings Ltd)
Docklands, Dock Road, Lytham St Annes, Lancashire FY8 5AQ
**Tel:** 01253-667422 **Fax:** 01772634782
**Web:** www.vetplus.co.uk
**Reg No:** 3076466 **Estd:** 1995 Private Limited Company
**Line of Business:** Manufacturers of veterinary equipment
**Issued Capital:** £100
**Director:** Ms S Haythornthwaite
**Co. Secretary:** David Haythornthwaite
**Responsibilities**
**Senior:** Ayshea Procter *(Business Advisor)*
**US SIC:** 3841 **UK SIC:** 37201
**Auditors:** KPMG LLP

| | 30-06-13 | 30-06-12 | 30-06-11 |
|---|---|---|---|
| TA | 4,047,906 | 3,211,802 | 2,663,999 |
| NW | 2,598,099 | 2,085,074 | 1,759,258 |
| WC | 2,531,785 | 2,031,880 | 1,712,662 |
| Emp. | N/A | 50 | N/A |

DUNS 49-149-4456 Imp-Exp
## Vetco Gray Controls Ltd
**(Subsidiary of:** General Electric Company)
2 High Street, Nailsea, Bristol, Avon BS48 1BS
**Tel:** 01275-810-100
**Web:** www.ge.com
**Reg No:** 3113851 **VAT No:** 664414044
**Estd:** 1995 Private Limited Company
**Line of Business:** Marine engines and engineering
**Export Markets:** Worldwide
**Export Sales:** £150,762,000
**Issued Capital:** £3
**Directors:** D Arnison, N Saunders, N A Dunn
**Responsibilities**
**Senior:** Conrad Apps *(Manager)*, Joanna Dunbar *(Manager)*
**Facilities:** Chris Gough *(Site Services Manager)*
**Operations:** Chris Gough *(Site Services Manager)*
**Branches:** Vetco Gray Controls Ltd, 21-25 Commerce St, Aberdeen, Aberdeenshire AB11 5FE
**US SIC:** 1389 **UK SIC:** 13000
**Auditors:** KPMG Audit PLC
**Bankers:** National Westminster Bank Plc (60-00-01)

| | 31-12-13 | 31-12-12 | 31-12-11 |
|---|---|---|---|
| TO | 188,214,000 | 112,154,000 | 145,420,000 |
| P/L | (8,177,000) | (2,797,000) | 12,564,000 |
| NW | 33,665,000 | 43,329,000 | 44,569,000 |
| WC | 43,367,000 | 40,574,000 | 37,045,000 |
| Emp. | 727 | 576 | 527 |

DUNS 21-580-2348
## Veterans Agency
Tomlinson House, Thornton-Cleveleys, Lancashire FY5 3WP
**Tel:** 08001692277
**Web:** www.veterans-uk.info
**Estd:** 2011
**Line of Business:** Ministry of defence
**US SIC:** 9121 **UK SIC:** 91110
**Employees:** 1,000

DUNS 73-487-1671
## The Veterinary Hospital Ltd
**(Subsidiary of:** Ivc Midco Ltd)
Colwill Road, Plymouth, Devon PL6 8RP
**Tel:** 01752-702646
**Web:** www.plymouthvets.co.uk
**Reg No:** 4750698 **Estd:** 2003 Private Limited Company
**Line of Business:** Veterinary activities
**Issued Capital:** £1,200
**Directors:** Mrs A J Davis, D R Hillier
**Responsibilities**
**Senior:** Hanno Payne *(Practice Manager)*
**US SIC:** 0741 **UK SIC:** 95601

| | 31-01-14 | 31-03-13 | 31-01-12 |
|---|---|---|---|
| TA | 804,960 | 1,366,553 | 1,249,707 |
| NW | 214,785 | (33,307) | (398,594) |
| WC | 160,306 | 70,716 | (280,556) |

DUNS 21-455-9007 Imp-Exp
## Veterinary Surgeons Supply Co. Ltd
29 Enterprise Crescent Ballinderry Road, Lisburn, Co Antrim BT28 2BP
**Tel:** 028-9267-4316 **Fax:** 028-9260-1658
**Web:** www.vssco.co.uk
**Reg No:** 0003708NI **Estd:** 1956 Private Limited Company
**Line of Business:** Agents involved in the sale of agricultural raw materials, live animals, textile raw materials and semi-finished goods
**Export Markets:** Republic of Ireland
**Issued Capital:** £102,250
**Directors:** J Wilson, J Henderson, A J Gordon, G Mcknight, J N Mcmordie, M Maybin
**Co. Secretary:** Mrs Siobhan Mckee
**Responsibilities**
**Senior:** Janet Carson *(Manager)*, Alistair Gibson *(Manager)*, Brian Graham *(Warehouse Manager)*, James Slaine *(Manager)*
**IT:** Tracey Angove *(Computer Manager)*
**HR:** Monica Hickland *(Human Resources Manager)*
**US SIC:** 5159, 5122
**UK SIC:** 61100, 61800
**Auditors:** Hanna Thompson Ltd
**Bankers:** The Bank Of Ireland (90-21-94)

| | 31-08-14 | 31-08-13 | 31-08-12 |
|---|---|---|---|
| TO | 40,098,493 | 38,251,027 | 37,991,475 |
| P/L | 628,320 | 656,405 | 661,757 |
| NW | 4,500,173 | 4,209,815 | 3,900,117 |
| WC | 3,969,974 | 3,720,031 | 3,427,560 |
| Emp. | 46 | 46 | 46 |

DUNS 28-940-9245 **Imp-Exp**

## Vetoquinol U K Ltd

Vetoquinol House, Great Slade, Buckingham Industrial Estate, Buckingham, Buckinghamshire MK18 1PA
**Tel:** 01280-814500
**Web:** www.vetoquinol.co.uk
**Reg No:** 1578434 **VAT No:** 420795356
**Estd:** 1982 Private Limited Company
**Line of Business:** Veterinary pharmacies
**Export Markets:** European Union (E U)
**Export Sales:** £650,000
**Issued Capital:** £291,165
**Principals:** E Frechin *(Chairman)*, M J Frechin
**Responsibilities**
**Senior:** Gilly Macniven *(Finance Manager)*
**HR:** Charlotte Price *(Human Resources Manager)*
**US SIC:** 0741 **UK SIC:** 95601
**Auditors:** PricewaterhouseCoopers LLP
**Bankers:** Lloyds TSB Bank plc (30-96-35)

| | 31-12-13 | 31-12-12 | 31-12-11 |
|---|---|---|---|
| TO | 16,908,000 | 16,718,000 | 16,105,000 |
| P/L | 2,523,000 | 2,654,000 | 2,517,000 |
| NW | 3,038,000 | 3,289,000 | 3,404,000 |
| WC | 2,934,000 | 3,139,000 | 3,166,000 |
| Emp. | 53 | 52 | 46 |

DUNS 23-989-8286

## Vetroseal Ltd

(**Subsidiary of:** Vetroglaze Ltd)
1 Postley Road, Kempston, Bedford, Bedfordshire MK42 7BU
**Fax:** 01234-854553
**Web:** www.vetroseal.co.uk
**Reg No:** 3978078 **Estd:** 2005 Private Limited Company
**Line of Business:** Double glazing suppliers
**Issued Capital:** £70,600
**Director:** E Falisi
**Co. Secretary:** Ms Charlene Dennis
**US SIC:** 1721 **UK SIC:** 50400

| | 30-11-13 | 30-11-12 | 30-11-11 |
|---|---|---|---|
| TA | 1,612,341 | 1,647,687 | 1,535,888 |
| NW | 407,439 | 204,213 | 141,333 |
| WC | 104,029 | (104,292) | (156,330) |

DUNS 22-188-7909

## Vets Now Emergency Ltd

(**Subsidiary of:** Now Group (Europe) Ltd)
Penguin House, Dunfermline, Fife KY11 8SG
**Tel:** 01383620064
**Web:** www.vetsnow.co.uk
**Reg No:** 0218632SC **Estd:** 2003 Private Limited Company
**Line of Business:** Veterinary activities
**Issued Capital:** £100
**Director:** R M Dixon
**Co. Secretary:**
Purple Venture Secretaries Limit
**Responsibilities**
**Senior:** Derek Giblin *(Manager)*
**Sales:** Steve Soden *(New Business Director)*
**US SIC:** 0741 **UK SIC:** 95601
**Auditors:** Thomson Cooper
**Bankers:** Bank Of Scotland (80-22-60)

| | 31-03-14 | 31-03-13 | 31-03-12 |
|---|---|---|---|
| TO | 25,596,040 | 24,528,640 | 22,636,888 |
| P/L | 2,502,516 | 4,343,655 | 945,010 |
| NW | 6,731,693 | 4,825,017 | 1,808,581 |
| WC | 4,748,215 | 3,936,939 | 1,472,327 |
| Emp. | 926 | 919 | 863 |

DUNS 21-112-2423 **Imp**

## Vets Now Ltd

(**Subsidiary of:** Now Group (Europe) Ltd)
1 Lorne Street, Bradford, West Yorkshire BD4 7PS
**Tel:** 01274722721
**Web:** www.vets-now.com
**Reg No:** 0339529SC **Estd:** 2008 Private Limited Company
**Line of Business:** Veterinary activities
**Issued Capital:** £100
**Directors:** Ms F A Dewar, R Brannan, Ms A K Boag, S J Soden, R M Dixon, C Grant
**Co. Secretary:**
Purple Venture Secretaries Limit
**Responsibilities**
**Senior:** Robert Fallow *(Director)*
**US SIC:** 0741 **UK SIC:** 95601
**Auditors:** Thomson Cooper

| | 31-03-14 | 31-03-13 | 31-03-12 |
|---|---|---|---|
| TA | 1,403,176 | 1,284,780 | 78,184 |
| NW | 8,027 | 6,364 | 4,636 |
| WC | 6,942 | 5,280 | 3,552 |

DUNS 53-650-4947

## Vetter U K Ltd

(**Subsidiary of:** Suffolk Partners Corporation)
3 Archway, Manchester M15 5QJ
**Tel:** 01612276400
**Web:** www.vetteruk.com
**Reg No:** 3455837 **VAT No:** 549347706
**Estd:** 1997 Private Limited Company
**Line of Business:** Stone merchants
**Issued Capital:** £1,000
**Directors:** S T Chatwin, C M Tuckett
**Co. Secretary:** Ms Teresa Styant
**Responsibilities**
**Senior:** Nicos Antoniades *(Pecuvremant)*, Bernard Dempsey *(Manager)*, Clive McKenzie *(Manager)*, Alan Sharpley *(Manager)*, David Unsworth *(Manager)*
**US SIC:** 5039, 1752
**UK SIC:** 61300, 50400
**Auditors:** PricewaterhouseCoopers LLP
**Bankers:** Bank Of Scotland (80-11-00)

| | 31-03-14 | 31-03-13 | 31-03-12 |
|---|---|---|---|
| TO | 13,351,000 | 12,041,000 | 7,133,000 |
| P/L | 207,000 | 99,000 | 219,000 |
| NW | 261,000 | 211,000 | 62,000 |
| WC | 261,000 | 211,000 | 62,000 |

DUNS 22-901-9443 **Imp-Exp**

## Vf Northern Europe Services Ltd

(**Subsidiary of:** V.F. Corporation)
Park Road East, Calverton, Nottingham, Nottinghamshire NG14 6GD
**Tel:** 01159656565
**Web:** www.vfcareers.co.uk
**Reg No:** 0081872SC **VAT No:** 406642074
**Estd:** 1983 Private Limited Company
**Line of Business:** Clothing wholesale and suppliers
**Export Markets:** European Union (E U)
**Issued Capital:** £742,168
**Directors:** K H Salzburger, C A Holtz
**Co. Secretary:** Patrick Emmerson
**Branches:** Vf Northern Europe Services Ltd, Little Aynam, Kendal, Cumbria LA9 7AH
**US SIC:** 6711, 2329
**UK SIC:** 83962, 45350
**Auditors:** PricewaterhouseCoopers LLP
**Bankers:** The Royal Bank Of Scotland Plc (83-22-20)

| | 31-12-13 | 31-12-12 | 31-12-11 |
|---|---|---|---|
| TO | 40,128,000 | 25,280,000 | 17,770,000 |
| P/L | 1,662,000 | (3,060,000) | 253,000 |
| NW | (4,929,000) | 3,838,000 | 7,279,000 |
| WC | (7,955,000) | 705,000 | 15,000 |
| Emp. | 718 | 393 | 253 |

DUNS 29-523-3258

## Vfs Financial Services Ltd

(**Subsidiary of:** Ab Volvo)
Wedgnock Lane, Warwick, Warwickshire CV34 5AP
**Tel:** 01926401203 **Fax:** 01926-410278
**Web:** www.vfsco.com
**Reg No:** 0092026SC **VAT No:** 428227159
**Estd:** 1985 Private Limited Company
**Line of Business:** Activities auxiliary to financial intermediation not elsewhere classified
**Issued Capital:** £33,000,000
**Directors:** Mrs T J Carpenter, G L Armitt
**Co. Secretary:** Ms Karen Brown
**Branches:** Vfs Financial Services Ltd, Brick & Stone (Scotland) Ltd, 1 Drovers Road, Broxburn, West Lothian EH52 5ND
**US SIC:** 6111 **UK SIC:** 81501
**Auditors:** PricewaterhouseCoopers
**Bankers:** Barclays Bank Plc (20-23-55)

| | 31-12-13 | 31-12-12 | 31-12-11 |
|---|---|---|---|
| TA | 723,845,000 | 607,275,000 | 576,967,000 |
| P/L | 15,803,000 | 9,676,000 | 6,835,000 |
| NW | 62,927,000 | 53,540,000 | 46,522,000 |
| WC | 131,756,000 | 59,352,000 | 64,029,000 |
| Emp. | 78 | 78 | 76 |

DUNS 54-902-8454 **Exp**

## Vg Systems Ltd

(**Subsidiary of:** Thermo Fisher Scientific Inc.)
Unit 24 Birches Industrial Estate, East Grinstead, West Sussex RH19 1UB
**Tel:** 01342327211
**Web:** www.thermofisher.com
**Reg No:** 3153085 **VAT No:** 787445282
**Estd:** 1996 Private Limited Company
**Line of Business:** Manufacture of other fabricated metal products not elsewhere classified
**Export Markets:** Europe, USA, Asia and Middle East, Rest of the World
**Export Sales:** £19,856,000
**Trading Style:** Thermo Fisher Scientific, Vacuum Generators Thermo Electron Surface Analysis, Thermo Vg Scientific
**Issued Capital:** £2
**Directors:** Ms L M Grant, Ms K R Wright, K N Wheeler
**Co. Secretary:**
Oakwood Corporate Secretary Limi
**Branches:** Vg Systems Ltd, Maunsell Road, Castleham Industrial Estate, St. Leonards-On-Sea, East Sussex TN38 9NN
**US SIC:** 3499, 3829, 3823
**UK SIC:** 31694, 37100
**Auditors:** PricewaterhouseCoopers LLP
**Bankers:** Barclays Bank Plc (20-00-50)

| | 31-12-13 | 31-12-12 | 31-12-11 |
|---|---|---|---|
| TO | 19,902,000 | 20,945,000 | 14,932,000 |
| P/L | 4,440,000 | 3,870,000 | 771,000 |
| NW | 20,260,000 | 16,024,000 | 12,151,000 |
| WC | 20,430,000 | 16,849,000 | 12,324,000 |
| Emp. | 72 | 71 | 65 |

DUNS 34-945-4780

## Vgc Group Ltd

Cardinal House, Bury Street, Ruislip, Middlesex HA4 7GD
**Tel:** 01895671780
**Web:** www.vgcgroup.co.uk
**Reg No:** 5741473 **Estd:** 2007 Private Limited Company
**Line of Business:** Management activities of holding companies
**Issued Capital:** £5,880
**Directors:** S Balasundaram, M J Fitzpatrick, A Rogers, L R Mckidd, Ms C M Pryce, T R Dutton-Wells, R J Cairns, R J Webb
**Co. Secretary:** Ms Olivia Fitzpatrick
**Responsibilities**
**Senior:** Keira Fitzpatrick *(Manager)*
**US SIC:** 6711 **UK SIC:** 83962

| | 31-12-13 | 31-12-12 | 31-12-11 |
|---|---|---|---|
| TO | 42,652,278 | 35,134,592 | 32,383,575 |
| P/L | 1,752,498 | 1,507,313 | 1,493,202 |
| NW | 11,523,487 | 10,389,685 | 9,462,453 |
| WC | 8,284,525 | 7,378,908 | 6,629,214 |
| Emp. | 657 | 426 | 552 |

DUNS 73-928-4313

## Vhe Equipment Services Ltd

Tribal House, Coal Road Hawthorn Park, Leeds, West Yorkshire LS14 1PQ
**Tel:** 01132-739200 **Fax:** 01132739202
**Web:** www.vhe.co.uk
**Reg No:** 2939633 **Estd:** 1994 Private Limited Company
**Line of Business:** Engineering related scientific and technical consulting activities
**Issued Capital:** £1
**Directors:** S Stiff, J W Samuel, Renew Corporate Director Limited
**Co. Secretary:** Renew Nominees Limited
**Responsibilities**
**Senior:** Stiff Stiff *(Manager)*
**US SIC:** 8911, 5082
**UK SIC:** 83701, 61490
**Auditors:** KPMG Audit PLC
**Bankers:** Bank Of Scotland (12-08-83)

| | 30-09-13 | 30-09-12 | 30-09-11 |
|---|---|---|---|
| TO | N/A | N/A | 25,000 |
| NW | (32,000) | (32,000) | (32,000) |
| WC | (32,000) | (32,000) | (32,000) |

DUNS 21-715-0879 **Exp**

## Vi - Spring Ltd

(**Subsidiary of:** Grupo Empresarial Flex Sa)
Inter-City House, Plymouth Station, Plymouth, Devon PL4 6AA
**Tel:** 01752-366311 **Fax:** 01752-355109
**Web:** www.vispring.co.uk
**Reg No:** 0071430 **Estd:** 1901 Private Limited Company
**Line of Business:** Manufacture of mattresses
**Trading Style:** Vi - Spring Ltd
**Issued Capital:** £40,000
**Principals:** T Lay *(Managing)*, Ms J S Johnson, C Harrison, A Rauh, J A Gerety, G Espana, A Moreno, R Gonzalez Betere
**Co. Secretary:** Michael Meehan
**Responsibilities**
**Marketing:** Frances McArthur *(Marketing Director)*
**IT:** Scott Howard *(IT Manager)*
**Purchasing:** A Soughcotp *(Purchasing Manager)*
**US SIC:** 2515, 5133
**UK SIC:** 46715, 61600
**Auditors:** Ernst & Young LLP
**Bankers:** National Westminster Bank Plc (60-02-35)

| | 31-12-13 | 31-12-12 | 31-12-11 |
|---|---|---|---|
| TO | 36,677,000 | 35,457,000 | 34,874,000 |
| P/L | 4,439,000 | 3,480,000 | 3,606,000 |
| NW | 7,472,000 | 6,644,000 | 7,764,000 |
| WC | 4,939,000 | 4,325,000 | 5,732,000 |
| Emp. | 206 | 205 | 204 |

DUNS 67-218-8559

## The Via Partnership Ltd

Chorley House, Centurion Way, Preston, Lancashire PR26 6TT
**Tel:** 08001693361
**Web:** www.via-uk.com
**Reg No:** 6048596 **Estd:** 2007 Private Limited Company
**Line of Business:** Labour recruitment and provision of personnel
**Trading Style:** Career Link
**Issued Capital:** £500,100
**Directors:** M Taplin, Dr D Sanders, M A Kelly, Ms D Park, A W Cavill, A J Walker, Ms K T O'Donoghue, Ms J E Doolan
**Co. Secretary:** Ian Young
**US SIC:** 8999, 7361
**UK SIC:** 83954
**Auditors:** Moore & Smalley LLP
**Bankers:** Lloyds TSB Bank plc (30-90-87)

| | 31-03-14 | 31-03-13 | 31-03-12 |
|---|---|---|---|
| TO | 3,609,174 | 3,991,085 | 4,119,209 |
| P/L | 26,002 | 8,560 | 501,692 |
| NW | (349,853) | (375,855) | (384,316) |
| WC | 615,260 | (325,911) | (171,676) |

DUNS 73-373-2023 **Imp**

## Via-Vox Ltd

1st Floor Vectra House, Richmond, Surrey TW9 1SE
**Tel:** 02079900900 **Fax:** 020 3355 4262
**Web:** www.via-vox.com
**Reg No:** 4646978 **Estd:** 2003 Private Limited Company
**Line of Business:** Telecommunications
**Export Sales:** £1,806,644
**Trading Style:** Via-Vox Ltd
**Issued Capital:** £95,983
**Directors:** J D Stone, T P Schrafft, D R Fairtlough
**Co. Secretary:** Ms Scott Leonard
**Responsibilities**
**Senior:** Paul Lees *(Manager)*, Suresh Rai *(Manager)*, martin rai *(Manager)*
**US SIC:** 4899, 3661
**UK SIC:** 79020, 34410
**Auditors:** Harwood Hutton Ltd

| | 31-12-13 | 31-12-12 | 31-12-11 |
|---|---|---|---|
| TO | 13,156,544 | 10,181,507 | N/A |
| P/L | 1,582,807 | 753,822 | N/A |
| NW | 772,727 | (1,794,837) | 1,433,228 |
| WC | 448,032 | (1,067,293) | 927,188 |
| Emp. | 63 | 58 | N/A |

DUNS 21-769-5446

## Viajante

Patriot Square, London E2 9NF
**Tel:** 02078710461
**Web:** www.viajante.co.uk
**Estd:** 2011 Proprietorship
**Line of Business:** Restaurant - american
**Proprietor:** Mrs K Brown
**US SIC:** 5812 **UK SIC:** 66110
**Employees:** 70

DUNS 22-810-4527

## Viamaster Transport Ltd

Altofts Lane, Castleford, West Yorkshire WF10 5PZ
**Tel:** 01133-076500 **Fax:** 01133-076565
**Web:** www.viamaster.co.uk
**Reg No:** 1011790 **VAT No:** 180844062
**Estd:** 1971 Private Limited Company
**Line of Business:** Other supporting land transport activities
**Issued Capital:** £30,000
**Principals:** A B Warrington *(Managing)*, D K Warrington
**Co. Secretary:** Andrew Warrington
**Responsibilities**
**Marketing:** Craig Hirst *(Senior Marketing Executive)*
**Sales:** Craig Hirst *(Senior Marketing Executive)*
**HR:** Vickey Barret *(Human Resources Manager)*
**Purchasing:** Mark Ingle *(Purchasing Manager)*
**Branches:** Viamaster Transport Ltd, Altofts Lane, Castleford, West Yorkshire WF10 5PZ
**US SIC:** 4789 **UK SIC:** 77002
**Auditors:** Broadhead Peel Rhodes LLP
**Bankers:** National Westminster Bank Plc (60-08-46)

| | 30-09-13 | 30-09-12 | 30-09-11 |
|---|---|---|---|
| TO | 9,617,047 | 9,002,603 | 9,462,439 |
| P/L | 667,340 | 718,333 | 685,495 |
| NW | 2,206,681 | 2,222,880 | 2,222,380 |
| WC | (757,461) | (644,715) | (300,556) |
| Emp. | 98 | 94 | 94 |

DUNS 73-262-5467

## Vianet Fuel Solutions Ltd

(**Subsidiary of:** Vianet Group Plc)
One Surtees Way, Surtees Business Park, Stockton-On-Tees, Cleveland TS18 3HR
**Tel:** 01422317371
**Web:** www.vianetfuelsolutions.com
**Reg No:** 4536379 **Estd:** 2002 Private Limited Company
**Line of Business:** Other business activities not elsewhere classified
**Export Sales:** £78,507
**Issued Capital:** £100
**Director:** J W Dickson
**Co. Secretary:** Mark Foster
**US SIC:** 7399 **UK SIC:** 83954
**Bankers:** Bank Of Scotland (12-09-19)

| | 31-03-14 | 31-03-13 | 31-03-12 |
|---|---|---|---|
| TO | 4,188,247 | 4,815,117 | 1,579,045 |
| P/L | (885,855) | 232,759 | (221,934) |
| NW | (4,149,957) | (2,983,629) | (1,455,461) |
| WC | (4,034,622) | (3,170,138) | (1,493,815) |
| Emp. | 57 | 65 | 25 |

DUNS 34-535-2772

## Vianet Group Plc

One Surtees Way, Stockton-On-Tees, Cleveland TS18 3HR
**Tel:** 01642358800
**Web:** www.vianetplc.com
**Reg No:** 5345684 **Estd:** 2005 Public Limited Company
**Line of Business:** Pre-press activities
**Export Sales:** £486,000
**Issued Capital:** £2,824,816

**Directors:** S C Gilliland, C Williams, S Darling, J W Dickson, M Mcgoun
**Co. Secretary:** Mark Foster
**Responsibilities**
**Marketing:** Phil Prow *(Sales and Marketing Director)*
**Sales:** Phil Prow *(Sales and Marketing Director)*
**US SIC:** 8999 **UK SIC:** 83954
**Auditors:** Grant Thornton UK LLP
**Bankers:** Bank Of Scotland (12-09-19)

|  | 31-03-14 | 31-03-13 | 31-03-12 |
|---|---|---|---|
| TO | 18,335,000 | 21,085,000 | 22,975,000 |
| P/L | 1,563,000 | 1,820,000 | 2,341,000 |
| NW | 4,743,000 | 3,467,000 | 3,505,000 |
| WC | 2,288,000 | 1,425,000 | 993,000 |
| Emp. | 235 | 257 | 260 |

DUNS 77-706-8834
## Viasat Uk Ltd
**(Subsidiary of:** Viasat Inc.)
Unit 22, Wareham, Dorset BH20 4DY
**Tel:** 019295 54400
**Web:** www.viasat.uk.com
**Reg No:** 3007498 **Estd:** 1999 Private Limited Company
**Line of Business:** Manufacture of computers and other information processing equipment
**Export Sales:** £1,268,637
**Issued Capital:** £597
**Directors:** C J Mcintosh, R A Baldridge, K K Lippert, T D Stone
**Co. Secretary:** Keven Lippert
**Responsibilities**
**Senior:** Peter Pridmore *(CFO)*
**Finance:** Peter Pridmore *(CFO)*
**Marketing:** Lara Gillespie *(Digital Marketing Specialist)*
**Admin:** Helen Cosh *(Personal Assistant)*
**IT:** John Fairless *(Chief Technical Architect)*
**HR:** Sara Fuller *(Head of Human Resources)*
**Health & Safety:** Nick Holc-Thompson *(Health & Safety Officer)*
**Purchasing:** Wayne Brown *(Manufacturing Manager)*
**Engineering:** Wayne Brown *(Manufacturing Manager)*
**US SIC:** 3573 **UK SIC:** 33020
**Auditors:** Ward Goodman
**Bankers:** Barclays Bank Plc (20-74-09)

|  | 04-04-14 | 29-03-13 | 30-04-12 |
|---|---|---|---|
| TO | 5,956,044 | 7,800,297 | 7,827,415 |
| P/L | 249,410 | 691,764 | 2,334,642 |
| NW | 4,219,655 | 3,970,245 | 3,242,015 |
| WC | 4,111,565 | 3,899,496 | 3,072,370 |
| Emp. | 63 | 70 | 81 |

DUNS 23-557-9989
## Viatel Belgium Ltd
**(Subsidiary of:** Easynet Enterprise Services Ltd)
Parnell House, 25 Wilton Road, London SW1V 1LW
**Tel:** 01784494200 **Fax:** 0207-8280-1907
**Reg No:** 3556686 **Estd:** 1998 Private Limited Company
**Line of Business:** Telecommunications
**Issued Capital:** £800,001
**Directors:** M G Doyle, C Piercy
**US SIC:** 4899 **UK SIC:** 79020
**Bankers:** Lloyds TSB Bank plc (30-00-01)

|  | 31-12-13 | 31-12-12 | 31-12-11 |
|---|---|---|---|
| TO | N/A | 154,972 | 160,507 |
| P/L | (148,032) | (13,782,885) | 7,867 |
| NW | (13,148,473) | (13,000,441) | 782,444 |
| WC | N/A | N/A | 13,606,171 |

DUNS 55-047-6071
## The Vibe Bar
91-95 Brick Lane, London E1 6QL
**Tel:** 02072476802
**Web:** www.vibe-bar.co.uk
**Estd:** 1999 Proprietorship
**Line of Business:** Public house
**Proprietor:** V Vasan
**Responsibilities**
**Senior:** Lee Dicker *(Manager)*, Gaz Kllokoqi *(Manager)*
**Admin:** Sasha Respinger *(Office Manager)*
**US SIC:** 5813 **UK SIC:** 66200
**Employees:** 47

DUNS 21-605-0182
## Vibert & Valpy
Second Floor International House, 41 The Parade, St Helier, Jersey, Channel Islands JE2 3QQ
**Tel:** 01534737115
**Web:** www.vivattrust.com
**Estd:** 2011 Partnership
**Line of Business:** Investment companies and vehicles
**Trading Style:** Virebets Jersy Laywet, Vivat Trust
**Proprietor:** D Lequesen
**Responsibilities**
**Senior:** David Lequesne *(Manager)*
**US SIC:** 8321 **UK SIC:** 96111
**Employees:** 70

DUNS 21-605-5007
## Viberts Jersey Lawers
Po Box 737 Pirouet House Union S, Jersey, Channel Islands JE4 8ZQ
**Tel:** 01534888666
**Web:** www.viberts.com
**Estd:** 2002
**Line of Business:** Solicitors
**Proprietor:** J Nixon
**Responsibilities**
**Senior:** Christina Hall *(Advocate - Partner)*, Christopher Scholefield *(Partner)*, Stephen Wise *(Manager)*
**IT:** Giles Crouch *(IT Manager)*
**US SIC:** 8111 **UK SIC:** 83500
**Employees:** 80

DUNS 21-608-4616     Imp
## Vibixa Ltd
**(Subsidiary of:** The Central People's Government of the People's Re)
Kingsditch Lane, Cheltenham, Gloucestershire GL51 9NG
**Tel:** 01242-221123
**Web:** www.vibixa.co.uk
**Reg No:** 0314793 **VAT No:** 274344944
**Estd:** 1936 Private Limited Company
**Line of Business:** Manufacturers of boxes and cartons
**Issued Capital:** £250,000
**Directors:** G M Turrell, D A Mcintyre, R W Martin
**Co. Secretary:** Lyne Booth
**Responsibilities**
**IT:** Jonathon Hepplewhite *(Site Services Manager)*
**Facilities:** Jonathon Hepplewhite *(Site Services Manager)*
**Engineering:** Jonathon Hepplewhite *(Site Services Manager)*
**US SIC:** 2651 **UK SIC:** 47253
**Auditors:** KPMG
**Bankers:** Barclays Bank Plc (20-45-77)

|  | 28-12-13 | 29-12-12 | 31-12-11 |
|---|---|---|---|
| TO | 17,475,000 | 18,632,000 | 18,797,000 |
| P/L | 856,000 | 1,641,000 | 1,109,000 |
| NW | 11,439,000 | 10,550,000 | 8,886,000 |
| WC | 8,870,000 | 7,729,000 | 5,821,000 |
| Emp. | 107 | 105 | 105 |

DUNS 21-145-0110
## Vibrant Energy Matters Ltd
2 Foxes Lane, Oakdale Business Park, Blackwood, Gwent NP12 4AB
**Tel:** 01495234300
**Web:** www.vibrantenergymatters.co.uk
**Reg No:** 6755736 **Estd:** 2008 Private Limited Company
**Line of Business:** Technical testing and analysis
**Issued Capital:** £2,247
**Directors:** R J Twigg, A S Gill, M L Stones, M I Wayman, C D Clark
**Responsibilities**
**Senior:** David Newnes *(Manager)*
**US SIC:** 7397 **UK SIC:** 83702

|  | 31-12-13 | 31-12-12 | 31-12-11 |
|---|---|---|---|
| TO | 7,201,000 | 5,264,000 | 3,090,000 |
| P/L | 562,000 | 598,000 | 325,000 |
| NW | 616,000 | 148,000 | (356,000) |
| WC | 380,000 | 5,000 | (578,000) |
| Emp. | 158 | 91 | 68 |

DUNS 51-994-4131     Imp
## Vibrant Media Ltd
**(Subsidiary of:** Vibrant Media Inc.)
3rd Floor, 140 Aldersgate Street, London EC1A 4HY
**Tel:** 02070740000 **Fax:** 02072399396
**Web:** www.vibrantmedia.co.uk
**Reg No:** 4001159 **Estd:** 2000 Private Limited Company
**Line of Business:** Business services
**Export Sales:** £6,851,981
**Issued Capital:** £1,460
**Director:** C A Gooding
**Co. Secretary:** Raymond Berry
**Responsibilities**
**HR:** Carine Pottier *(Human Resources & Recruitment)*
**Health & Safety:** Carine Pottier *(Human Resources & Recruitment)*
**Purchasing:** Carine Pottier *(Human Resources & Recruitment)*
**US SIC:** 7399 **UK SIC:** 83954
**Auditors:** PricewaterhouseCoopers LLP
**Bankers:** The Royal Bank Of Scotland Plc (16-08-05)

|  | 31-12-13 | 31-12-12 | 31-12-11 |
|---|---|---|---|
| TO | 18,443,493 | 21,499,454 | 23,688,513 |
| P/L | 1,417,752 | (261,035) | 3,763,654 |
| NW | 13,749,665 | 12,323,083 | 12,740,155 |
| WC | 13,227,664 | 11,788,644 | 12,188,081 |
| Emp. | 112 | 121 | 112 |

DUNS 39-971-6067
## Vic Young (South Shields) Ltd
19 Newcastle Road, South Shields, Tyne and Wear NE34 9QE
**Tel:** 01914271566
**Web:** www.vicyoung-nissan.co.uk
**Reg No:** 2270866 **VAT No:** 514538846
**Estd:** 1981 Private Limited Company
**Line of Business:** Car dealers (new & used)
**Issued Capital:** £20,000
**Managing Director:** V W Young
**Co. Secretary:** Ms Alicia Young
**US SIC:** 5511 **UK SIC:** 65100
**Auditors:** Charlton & Co
**Bankers:** Lloyds TSB Bank plc (30-97-89)

|  | 30-11-13 | 30-11-12 | 30-11-11 |
|---|---|---|---|
| TO | 20,702,153 | 18,685,572 | 17,597,364 |
| P/L | 1,110,942 | 482,072 | 406,067 |
| NW | 6,671,864 | 5,962,409 | 5,731,449 |
| WC | 2,654,705 | 1,727,305 | 1,580,766 |
| Emp. | 64 | 64 | 65 |

DUNS 50-003-3220
## Vic Young Vehicle Hire Ltd
19 Newcastle Road, South Shields, Tyne and Wear NE34 9QE
**Tel:** 01914545135
**Web:** www.vicyoung.com
**Reg No:** 2293627 **Estd:** 1988 Private Limited Company
**Line of Business:** Sale of new motor vehicles
**Issued Capital:** £2
**Director:** V W Young
**Co. Secretary:** Ms Alicia Young
**Responsibilities**
**Senior:** Steve Hunter *(General Manager)*
**US SIC:** 5511, 4121
**UK SIC:** 65100, 72200

|  | 30-11-13 | 30-11-12 | 30-11-11 |
|---|---|---|---|
| TA | 2 | 2 | 2 |
| NW | 2 | 2 | 2 |

DUNS 50-002-9780
## Vicaima Ltd
**(Subsidiary of:** Vicaima Madeiras (Sgps) S.A.)
Drakes Way Business Centre, Swindon, Wiltshire SN3 3JF
**Tel:** 01793-532333 **Fax:** 01793-530193
**Web:** www.vicaima.com
**Reg No:** 2293275 **Estd:** 1988 Private Limited Company
**Line of Business:** Doors & shutters retails and installers
**Export Sales:** £505,124
**Issued Capital:** £1,000,000
**Directors:** A Da Costa Leite, B J Waddell, P Silva
**Co. Secretary:** Barry Waddell
**Responsibilities**
**Senior:** Humberto Leite *(Manager)*, Simon Snoger *(General Manager)*
**Finance:** Frederico Capela *(Financial Controller)*
**US SIC:** 7399 **UK SIC:** 83954
**Auditors:** Monahans
**Bankers:** Lloyds TSB Bank plc (30-91-74)

|  | 31-12-13 | 31-12-12 | 31-12-11 |
|---|---|---|---|
| TO | 19,730,615 | 17,814,974 | 17,681,735 |
| P/L | 51,728 | 20,244 | 136,496 |
| NW | 913,377 | 899,313 | 904,857 |
| WC | 2,428,531 | 2,267,546 | 2,213,843 |
| Emp. | 75 | 66 | 62 |

DUNS 42-314-1845
## Vicarage House Nursing Home
The Old Vicarage, Hambridge, Langport, Somerset TA10 0BG
**Tel:** 01460-281670
**Web:** www.vicaragehouse.org
**Partnership**
**Line of Business:** Clinics private
**Partners:** D Sutcliffe, Dr L Sutcliffe
**Responsibilities**
**Senior:** Susan Mccallum *(Manager)*
**US SIC:** 8051 **UK SIC:** 95100
**Employees:** 48

DUNS 21-583-6514
## Vicarage Lane Health Centre
10 Vicarage Lane, London E15 4ES
**Tel:** 02085362070
**Web:** www.vlhc.vpweb.co.uk
**Estd:** 2011 Proprietorship
**Line of Business:** Public sector hospital activities, including nhs trusts
**Proprietor:** A Vaja
**Responsibilities**
**Senior:** Michelle Smart *(Centre Manager)*
**US SIC:** 8062 **UK SIC:** 95100
**Employees:** 100

DUNS 73-537-9583
## Vicarage Nursing Home Ltd
Vicarage Cottage, The Common, Shrewsbury, Shropshire SY3 0EA
**Tel:** 01743874030 **Fax:** 01743871095
**Web:** www.ephraimscaregroup.co.uk
**Reg No:** 4800410 **Estd:** 1998 Private Limited Company
**Line of Business:** Medical nursing home activities
**Issued Capital:** £1,000
**Director:** R P Ephraims
**Co. Secretary:** Ms Margaret Ephraims
**US SIC:** 8051 **UK SIC:** 95100

|  | 30-04-14 | 30-04-13 | 30-04-12 |
|---|---|---|---|
| TA | 605,217 | 481,431 | 399,112 |
| NW | 312,209 | 224,505 | 214,741 |
| WC | 256,927 | 175,422 | 164,210 |

DUNS 36-798-7575
## Vicars Moor Lawn Tennis Club
Sherbrook Gardens, London N21 2NU
**Tel:** 020-8360-7497
**Estd:** 1952
**Line of Business:** Racecourses and racetracks
**US SIC:** 7999 **UK SIC:** 97913
**Employees:** 88

DUNS 73-257-6314     Imp
## Vice Uk Ltd
**(Subsidiary of:** Vice Media Inc.)
2-6 New North Place, London EC2A 4JA
**Tel:** 02077497810
**Web:** www.vice.com
**Reg No:** 4531415 **Estd:** 2002 Private Limited Company
**Line of Business:** Publishing of books
**Export Sales:** £22,982,355
**Issued Capital:** £1,320
**Directors:** R Waterlow, S Smith, M Elek, A Creighton
**Co. Secretary:** Richard Waterlow
**Responsibilities**
**Senior:** Suroosh Alvi *(Manager)*
**Finance:** Neeta Shah *(Financial Controller)*
**US SIC:** 2711 **UK SIC:** 47512

|  | 31-12-13 | 31-12-12 | 31-12-11 |
|---|---|---|---|
| TO | 38,189,153 | 27,213,356 | 24,138,041 |
| P/L | 2,983,752 | 2,455,245 | 4,430,424 |
| NW | 2,780,152 | 3,967,883 | 4,457,893 |
| WC | 5,718,876 | 5,192,035 | 3,094,279 |
| Emp. | 349 | 220 | 173 |

DUNS 21-795-4339
## Vickerstock
Unit C 32-38, Lyndon Court, Queen Street, Belfast BT1 6EF
**Tel:** 08458334790
**Web:** www.vickerstock.co.uk
**Estd:** 2011 Proprietorship
**Line of Business:** Employment and recruitment companies and consultants
**Proprietor:** T Hughes
**Responsibilities**
**Senior:** Darren Mcvicker *(Manager)*
**US SIC:** 7361 **UK SIC:** 83954
**Employees:** 185

DUNS 36-814-4259
## Vickerstown Cricket & Tennis Club
Mill Lane, Barrow-In-Furness, Cumbria LA14 3ND
**Tel:** 01229474199
**Line of Business:** Sports clubs
**Principals:** M Mcguire *(Chairman)*, S Reynolds
**US SIC:** 7999 **UK SIC:** 97913
**Employees:** 99

DUNS 21-195-9226     Imp
## Vicomte Bernard De Romanet Ltd
**(Subsidiary of:** Wiv Wein International Ag)
The International Wine Centre, Dallow Road, Luton, Bedfordshire LU1 1UR
**Tel:** 01582-456465 **Fax:** 01582455465
**Web:** www.romanet.co.uk
**Reg No:** 0898375 **Estd:** 1967 Private Limited Company
**Line of Business:** Retailers of beer, wine and spirits
**Issued Capital:** £300,000
**Directors:** D H Samuel, H W Falk
**Co. Secretary:** Ernst Bocker
**Responsibilities**
**Senior:** Craig Michey *(Regional Manager)*
**Branches:** Vicomte Bernard De Romanet Ltd, 212 Fordham Road, Newmarket, Suffolk CB8 7LG
**US SIC:** 5182 **UK SIC:** 61700
**Auditors:** Bdo Stoy Hayward LLP

**Bankers:** Barclays Bank Plc (20-53-30)

| | 31-12-13 | 31-12-12 | 31-12-11 |
|---|---|---|---|
| TO | 6,244,315 | 6,578,822 | 6,927,482 |
| P/L | (235,689) | (135,144) | (82,067) |
| NW | (3,421) | 180,144 | 274,337 |
| WC | (5,279) | 172,270 | 271,067 |
| Emp. | 114 | 109 | 108 |

DUNS 21-621-1383 **Imp-Exp**

## Victa Ltd

(**Subsidiary of:** A.G. Thompson Proprietary Limited)
Unit 25 The Alders, Maidstone, Kent ME18 5JG
**Tel:** 01622812230
**Web:** www.victa.com.au
**Reg No:** 0688654 **VAT No:** 202982377
**Estd:** 1808 Private Limited Company
**Line of Business:** Manufacture of sports goods
**Export Markets:** Worldwide
**Trading Style:** Readersport
**Issued Capital:** £18,899
**Directors:** P Thompson, R E Thompson
**Co. Secretary:** Brett Elliot
**Branches:** Victa Ltd, 2 Wolfe Clo, Parkgate Indust Est, Knutsford, Cheshire WA16 8XJ
**US SIC:** 3949 **UK SIC:** 49420
**Auditors:** Grant Thornton
**Bankers:** National Westminster Bank Plc (60-60-08)

| | 30-06-13 | 30-06-12 | 30-06-11 |
|---|---|---|---|
| TA | 2 | 2 | 2 |
| NW | 2 | 2 | 2 |

DUNS 21-231-6649

## Victim Offender Unit

20-30 Lawefield Lane, Wakefield, West Yorkshire WF2 8SP
**Tel:** 03000487033
**Estd:** 2002 Proprietorship
**Line of Business:** Probation services
**Proprietor:** R Voakes
**Responsibilities**
**Senior:** Gini Wisehead *(Manager)*
**US SIC:** 9121 **UK SIC:** 91110
**Employees:** 50

DUNS 39-706-1771

## Victim Support

56-60hallam Stre Hallam Street House, London W1W 6JL
**Tel:** 02072680200 **Fax:** 02075825712
**Web:** www.victimsupport.org.uk
**Reg No:** 2158780 **Estd:** 1987 Private Company Limited By Guarantee
**Line of Business:** Non-charitable social work activities without accommodation
**Trading Style:** Middlesex Guildhall Witness Service, S A M M
**Directors:** L Mosco, Mrs S M Caldwell, Dr B L Herdan, Ms M D Thomas, W L Sandbrook, Mrs J Cumbley, Mrs C Dugmore, Ms S Miller
**Co. Secretary:** John Castle
**Responsibilities**
**Senior:** Tom Davies *(Director)*, Elizabeth Dymond *(Director)*, Paul Fawcett *(Head Of Marketing & Communicat)*, Gillian Guy *(Chief Executive)*, Geoff Pollard *(Director)*
**Marketing:** Pete Aldridge *(Head of Fundraising)*, Paul Fawcett *(Head Of Marketing & Communicat)*
**Branches:** Victim Support, Lee Ho, Upper Yoden Way, Peterlee, County Durham SR8 1BB
**US SIC:** 8321 **UK SIC:** 96111
**Auditors:** Sayer Vincent
**Bankers:** National Westminster Bank Plc (60-22-27)

| | 31-03-14 | 31-03-13 | 31-03-12 |
|---|---|---|---|
| TO | 50,200,000 | 48,071,000 | 49,504,000 |
| P/L | 234,000 | 860,000 | 814,000 |
| NW | 22,424,000 | 22,299,000 | 21,159,000 |
| WC | 9,793,000 | 7,027,000 | 9,333,000 |
| Emp. | 1,257 | 1,200 | 1,220 |

DUNS 23-044-8552

## Victim Support Northern Ireland

Annsgate House 70 74 Ann Street, Belfast BT1 4EH
**Tel:** 028-9024-4039 **Fax:** 028-9031-3838
**Web:** www.victimsupportni.co.uk
**Reg No:** 0020562NI **Estd:** 1987 Private Company Limited By Guarantee
**Line of Business:** Other service activities not elsewhere classified
**Directors:** Mrs P M Mallon, N B Lavery, B Loughran, Ms M Leonard, J Dunne, Miss K Laverty, Mrs O Hill, Ms U Macauley
**Responsibilities**
**Senior:** Judith Cross *(Director)*
**Branches:** Victim Support Northern Ireland, 45 Oxford Street, Belfast, Belfast BT1 3LL
**US SIC:** 8999 **UK SIC:** 83954
**Auditors:** Crawford Sedgwick & Co

**Bankers:** Ulster Bank Ltd (98-00-60)

| | 31-03-14 | 31-03-13 | 31-03-12 |
|---|---|---|---|
| TA | 352,577 | 547,113 | 508,803 |
| NW | 243,233 | 287,674 | 307,940 |
| WC | 199,930 | 190,675 | 175,514 |

DUNS 39-911-3349

## Victim Support Scotland

15-23 Hardwell Close, Edinburgh, Midlothian EH8 9RX
**Fax:** 01316625424
**Web:** www.victimsupportsco.org.uk
**Reg No:** 0110185SC **Estd:** 1988 Private Limited Company
**Line of Business:** Counselling & advice services
**Directors:** Ms E Taylor, S Delaney, J C Dow, A Dunipace, P D O'Brien, Mrs F J Young, T Peat, I Chisholm
**Co. Secretary:** Dr Anne Dia
**Responsibilities**
**Senior:** Ronald Daniel *(Manager)*, Alan Davie *(Manager)*, Andrew Dempster *(Manager)*, Catherine Findlay *(Committee member)*, Stephen Meighan *(Director)*, Janette Mitchell *(Director)*
**HR:** Michelle Forster *(Personnel Manager)*
**Health & Safety:** Michelle Forster *(Personnel Manager)*
**Facilities:** Duncan Ross *(Facilities Manager)*
**Branches:** Victim Support Scotland, Abbey House, 2ND Floor, Glasgow, Lanarkshire G2 6LU
**US SIC:** 8321 **UK SIC:** 96111
**Auditors:** Whitelaw Wells
**Bankers:** The Royal Bank Of Scotland Plc (83-18-24)

| | 31-03-14 | 31-03-13 | 31-03-12 |
|---|---|---|---|
| TO | 5,084,734 | 5,035,169 | 4,742,867 |
| P/L | (280,144) | 25,703 | (106,860) |
| NW | 203,959 | 484,410 | 458,741 |
| WC | 1,710 | 386,771 | 409,898 |
| Emp. | 149 | 153 | 147 |

DUNS 28-885-2247

## Victor De Banke Ltd

(**Subsidiary of:** Victor De Banke (Northampton) Ltd)
Victor De Bank Ltd, Unit 6, Cirrus Park, Lower Farm Road, Northampton, Northamptonshire NN3 6UR
**Tel:** 01604-648814 **Fax:** 01604-602429
**Web:** www.hgcollins.co.uk
**Reg No:** 1225125 **VAT No:** 121595874
**Estd:** 1975 Private Limited Company
**Line of Business:** Wholesalers of fruit and vegetable
**Trading Style:** H T Collin
**Issued Capital:** £1,000
**Director:** D A Collins
**Co. Secretary:** Ian Williams
**US SIC:** 5148 **UK SIC:** 61700
**Bankers:** National Westminster Bank Plc (54-41-05)

| | 30-11-13 | 30-11-12 | 30-11-11 |
|---|---|---|---|
| TA | 1,252,065 | 1,255,121 | 899,610 |
| NW | 31,713 | 44,036 | 100,423 |
| WC | (89,746) | (34,488) | 25,267 |

DUNS 22-550-1386 **Imp**

## Victor Hugo Ltd

(**Subsidiary of:** Citann Ltd)
Longueville Road, St Saviour, Jersey, Channel Islands JE2 7SA
**Tel:** 01534764044 **Fax:** 01534764067
**Web:** www.victor-hugo-wines.com
**Reg No:** 0019271J **Estd:** 1980 Private Limited Company
**Line of Business:** Retailers of beer, wine and spirits
**Issued Capital:** £1
**Principals:** S J Marie, D M Bralsford, D C Lowe, D P Duff, D Hearne, T H Scott, CIT COSEC LTD
**Responsibilities**
**Senior:** Tim Hubbert *(Manager)*, Alistair Shield-Laignel *(Office Manager)*
**Admin:** Alistair Laignel *(Administrator / Web)*
**Branches:** Victor Hugo Ltd, 8B Quennevias Precinct, Jersey, Channel Islands JE3 8LT
**US SIC:** 5921 **UK SIC:** 64200
**Bankers:** HSBC Bank plc (40-25-34)
**Employees:** 60

DUNS 21-261-7690 **Imp-Exp**

## Victor Manufacturing Ltd

Lonsdale Works, Bradford, West Yorkshire BD3 9TF
**Web:** www.victoronline.co.uk
**Reg No:** 0390738 **VAT No:** 500415508
**Estd:** 1927 Private Limited Company
**Line of Business:** Manufacture of machinery for food, beverage and tobacco processing
**Export Markets:** Cyprus & Eire
**Export Sales:** £242,378
**Issued Capital:** £752
**Principals:** L R Graham *(Chairman)*, M Shaddock, J K Lister, S R Gordon, A M Gibson, P Williams
**Co. Secretary:** Steven Gordon
**Responsibilities**
**Senior:** Graham Healey *(Warehouse Manager)*
**Sales:** Michael Inwood *(National Account Manager)*
**US SIC:** 3551, 3629
**UK SIC:** 32441, 34350
**Auditors:** Ernst & Young
**Bankers:** Barclays Bank Plc (20-11-81)

| | 29-03-14 | 31-03-13 | 31-03-12 |
|---|---|---|---|
| TO | 6,784,449 | 6,218,166 | 6,636,012 |
| P/L | 127,224 | 303,421 | 427,029 |
| NW | 4,992,103 | 4,952,470 | 4,731,776 |
| WC | 4,217,227 | 4,681,103 | 4,329,929 |
| Emp. | 85 | 81 | 79 |

DUNS 21-813-1977

## Victor Wood of Oakham Ltd

(**Subsidiary of:** Victor Wood (Holdings) Ltd)
Spittlegate Level, Grantham, Lincolnshire NG31 7UH
**Tel:** 01476-566110
**Web:** www.victorwood.co.uk
**Reg No:** 0434624 **Estd:** 1949 Private Limited Company
**Line of Business:** Sale of new motor vehicles
**Issued Capital:** £1,002
**Principals:** C J Wood *(Managing)*, T R Griffin, Ms G J Griffin
**Co. Secretary:** Ms Susan Wood
**Responsibilities**
**Senior:** Patrick Oldham *(Dealer Principal)*
**Branches:** Victor Wood Of Oakham Ltd, Spittlegate Level, Grantham, Lincolnshire NG31 7UH
**US SIC:** 5511, 5541
**UK SIC:** 65100, 65200
**Auditors:** Trevor Jones
**Bankers:** HSBC Bank plc (40-28-06)

| | 30-06-14 | 30-06-13 | 30-06-12 |
|---|---|---|---|
| TA | 2,174,868 | 1,983,062 | 1,989,979 |
| NW | 155,807 | 195,658 | 125,737 |
| WC | 61,774 | (15,554) | 69,333 |

DUNS 55-077-8013

## The Victoria

Promenade, Southport, Merseyside PR9 0DS
**Tel:** 01704-541220
**Web:** www.victorialeisure.co.uk
**Estd:** 2012 Proprietorship
**Line of Business:** Other sporting activities not elsewhere classified
**Proprietor:** W Birch
**Branches:** The Victoria, The Cloisters, Liverpool, Merseyside L37 3PX
**US SIC:** 8999 **UK SIC:** 83954
**Employees:** 50

DUNS 21-208-3476

## Victoria Care Home

Memorial Avenue, Worksop, Nottinghamshire S80 2BJ
**Tel:** 01909476416
**Estd:** 1996
**Line of Business:** Medical nursing home activities
**Proprietor:** Mrs M Blower
**Responsibilities**
**Senior:** Graham Cannard *(Manager)*
**US SIC:** 8051 **UK SIC:** 95100
**Employees:** 104

DUNS 21-810-7314

## Victoria Central

Victoria Central Hospital, Mill Lane, Wallasey, Merseyside CH44 5UF
**Tel:** 01516047296
**Estd:** 2012
**Line of Business:** Nhs clinics
**Responsibilities**
**Senior:** Kay Taylor *(Manager)*
**US SIC:** 8062 **UK SIC:** 95100
**Employees:** 117

DUNS 21-185-3366

## The Victoria Club

11 Victoria Avenue, Holmes Chapel, Crewe, Cheshire CW4 7BE
**Estd:** 2002
**Line of Business:** Taxis and private hire vehicles
**Principals:** I Bates *(Chairman)*, H Burgess, S Leake
**Responsibilities**
**Senior:** William Radcliffe *(Proprietor)*
**US SIC:** 8699 **UK SIC:** 96902
**Employees:** 58

DUNS 21-590-6899

## Victoria College

Victoria College, Jersey, Channel Islands JE1 4HT
**Tel:** 01534638200
**Web:** www.victoriacollege.je
**Estd:** 2011 Proprietorship
**Line of Business:** Schools (independent)
**Proprietor:** Mrs C Fletcher
**Responsibilities**
**Senior:** Alun Watkins *(Principal)*
**US SIC:** 8211 **UK SIC:** 93200
**Employees:** 70

DUNS 22-158-7855

## Victoria Community Care Ltd

Ormskirk Road Knowsley, Prescot, Merseyside L34 8HB
**Tel:** 0151-546-4400
**Web:** www.victoriacommunitycare.co.uk
**Reg No:** 4177370 **Estd:** 1998 Private Limited Company
**Line of Business:** Home care service providers
**Issued Capital:** £1
**Director:** Ms B M Thomas
**Co. Secretary:** Ms Gillian Begley
**Responsibilities**
**Senior:** Gillian Cubbin *(Manager)*
**US SIC:** 8091 **UK SIC:** 95200
**Bankers:** National Westminster Bank Plc (60-13-19)

| | 31-03-14 | 31-03-13 | 31-03-12 |
|---|---|---|---|
| TA | 438,435 | 364,917 | 399,473 |
| NW | 205,743 | 199,379 | 229,022 |
| WC | 198,920 | 190,860 | 218,385 |

DUNS 36-802-0798

## Victoria Drive Bowling Association

153 Victoria Drive, Eastbourne, East Sussex BN20 8NH
**Tel:** 01323-738813
**Web:** http://eastbourne-vdel.bowlsclub.info
**Estd:** 1932
**Line of Business:** Sports clubs
**US SIC:** 7999 **UK SIC:** 97913
**Employees:** 189

DUNS 23-827-9756

## The Victoria Foundation

St Davids House, 15 Worple Way, Richmond, Surrey TW10 6DG
**Tel:** 02083321788 **Fax:** 02089499099
**Web:** www.thevictoriafoundation.org.uk
**Reg No:** 1946612 **Estd:** 1985 Private Company Limited By Guarantee
**Line of Business:** Hospital activities
**Directors:** R D Leach, J A Hamblin, H P Hope, C P Lyons
**Co. Secretary:** Graham Ball
**Responsibilities**
**Senior:** John Langan *(Manager)*
**US SIC:** 8062 **UK SIC:** 95100
**Auditors:** Menzies
**Bankers:** HSBC Bank plc (40-34-24)

| | 31-03-14 | 31-03-13 | 31-03-12 |
|---|---|---|---|
| TO | 14,585,000 | 14,400,000 | 15,113,000 |
| P/L | 33,000 | 882,000 | 2,042,000 |
| NW | 27,071,000 | 26,789,000 | 24,060,000 |
| WC | 222,000 | 2,965,000 | 5,048,000 |
| Emp. | 194 | 193 | 189 |

DUNS 21-863-2271

## Victoria Garage (Whitchurch) Ltd

Newport Road, Whitchurch, Shropshire SY13 1QD
**Tel:** 01948663333
**Web:** www.victoriagarage.com
**Reg No:** 0778814 **Estd:** 1956 Private Limited Company
**Line of Business:** Sale of new motor vehicles
**Trading Style:** Cab Motors
**Issued Capital:** £2,000
**Principals:** W A Ball *(Managing)*, C A Ball, W A Ball
**Co. Secretary:** William Ball
**Responsibilities**
**Senior:** Annette-Marie Ball *(Chief Purchasing Officer)*
**Finance:** Annette-Marie Ball *(Chief Purchasing Officer)*
**HR:** Kate Granger *(Human Resources Manager)*
**Purchasing:** Annette-Marie Ball *(Chief Purchasing Officer)*
**US SIC:** 5511, 5541
**UK SIC:** 65100, 65200
**Auditors:** Richard Dyas & Co
**Bankers:** Barclays Bank Plc (20-77-85)

| | 31-03-14 | 31-03-13 | 31-03-12 |
|---|---|---|---|
| TA | 1,411,989 | 1,505,465 | 1,460,649 |
| NW | 1,028,721 | 1,034,145 | 987,716 |
| WC | 210,588 | 191,402 | 184,284 |

DUNS 21-093-8130

## Victoria General Cleaning Services Ltd

The Business Centre, Faringdon Avenue, Romford, Essex RM3 8EN
**Tel:** 08001972953
**Web:** www.victoriacleaning.co.uk
**Reg No:** 0664866 **VAT No:** 248012974
**Estd:** 1945 Private Limited Company

**Line of Business:** Commercial premises cleaning
**Issued Capital:** £10,000
**Co. Secretary:** Michael Rutherford
**US SIC:** 7349, 7341
**UK SIC:** 92300
**Auditors:** Clay Ratnage Strevens & Hills
**Bankers:** Lloyds TSB Bank plc (30-99-08)

|     | 31-07-13 | 31-07-12 | 31-07-11 |
|-----|----------|----------|----------|
| TA  | 1,774,753 | 1,713,015 | 1,576,632 |
| NW  | 1,296,848 | 1,285,039 | 1,308,140 |
| WC  | 150,761 | 66,393 | 412,151 |

DUNS 21-171-6516
## Victoria Group Holdings Ltd
Victoria Wharf, Plymouth, Devon PL4 0RF
**Tel:** 01752663175 **Fax:** 01752313147
**Web:** www.victoriagroup.co.uk
**Reg No:** 6959771 **Estd:** 2009 Private Limited Company
**Line of Business:** Management activities of holding companies
**Issued Capital:** £41,290
**Directors:** A B Luscombe, M A Gatehouse, J H Kearns
**Co. Secretary:** David Martin
**Responsibilities**
**Senior:** G Strickland (Manager)
**US SIC:** 6711 **UK SIC:** 83962

|      | 30-09-13 | 30-09-12 | 30-09-11 |
|------|----------|----------|----------|
| TO   | 25,089,000 | 23,647,000 | 20,754,000 |
| P/L  | 4,293,000 | (1,065,000) | 2,844,000 |
| NW   | 40,534,000 | 34,052,000 | 36,323,000 |
| WC   | 3,049,000 | 657,000 | 752,000 |
| Emp. | 212 | 221 | 218 |

DUNS 21-770-3457
## Victoria Hotel
The Esplanade, Sidmouth, Devon EX10 8RY
**Tel:** 01395512651
**Web:** www.brend-hotels.co.uk
**Estd:** 1984 Proprietorship
**Line of Business:** Hotels
**Proprietor:** M Raistrick
**Responsibilities**
**Senior:** Matthew Raistrick (Area Director)
**IT:** Tony Clark (Senior IT Executive)
**HR:** David Oxley (Human Resources Manager)
**US SIC:** 7011 **UK SIC:** 66500
**Employees:** 100

DUNS 21-222-7217
## Victoria House Home Care
Bath Lane, Stockton-On-Tees, Cleveland TS18 2DX
**Web:** www.schealthcare.co.uk
**Estd:** 1997 Proprietorship
**Line of Business:** Nursing homes
**Proprietor:** Mrs K Thomson
**Responsibilities**
**Senior:** Rob Hearn (Support Manager)
**US SIC:** 8051 **UK SIC:** 95100
**Employees:** 50

DUNS 21-391-5097
## Victoria Lodge Care Home
41 Bent Street, Brierley Hill, West Midlands DY5 1RB
**Tel:** 01384-572567
**Web:** www.selecthealthcaregroup.com
**Estd:** 2009 Proprietorship
**Line of Business:** Non-charitable social work activities with accommodation
**Proprietor:** Mrs D Williams
**Responsibilities**
**Senior:** Avril Nott (Manager)
**US SIC:** 8321 **UK SIC:** 96111
**Employees:** 70

DUNS 21-232-3373
## Victoria Memorial Hospital
Salop Road, Welshpool, Powys SY21 7DU
**Estd:** 2002 Proprietorship
**Line of Business:** Hospitals
**Proprietors:** Ms L Luter, Ms L Luter
**US SIC:** 8062 **UK SIC:** 95100
**Employees:** 136

DUNS 21-592-5746
## Victoria Nursing Home
Victoria Street, Rainford, St Helens, Merseyside WA11 8DA
**Tel:** 01744886225
**Web:** www.fshc.co.uk
**Estd:** 1999
**Line of Business:** Nursing homes
**Proprietor:** Mrs S Dean
**Responsibilities**
**Senior:** Angela Broomhall (Manager), Beverley Taylor (General Manager), Bernie Thomas (Manager)
**US SIC:** 8051 **UK SIC:** 95100
**Employees:** 50

DUNS 28-886-8250
## Victoria Nursing Home Ltd
(Subsidiary of: Mirowe Holdings Ltd)
81 Dyke Road Avenue, Hove, East Sussex BN3 6DA
**Tel:** 01273551355
**Web:** www.vnh.co
**Reg No:** 1241916 **Estd:** 1980 Private Limited Company
**Line of Business:** Nursing homes
**Issued Capital:** £10,000
**Director:** Mrs J M Rowe
**Co. Secretary:** Paul Burns
**Responsibilities**
**Finance:** Susan Knights (Head of Accounts)
**Branches:** Victoria Nursing Home Ltd, 39 Dyke Road Avenue, Hove, East Sussex BN3 6QA
**US SIC:** 8051 **UK SIC:** 95100
**Auditors:** Mazars LLP
**Bankers:** Barclays Bank Plc (20-12-75)

|     | 31-03-14 | 31-03-13 | 31-03-12 |
|-----|----------|----------|----------|
| TA  | 1,242,919 | 953,069 | 659,285 |
| NW  | 1,084,849 | 822,731 | 537,753 |
| WC  | 1,070,440 | 797,029 | 492,948 |

DUNS 73-885-7130
## Victoria Oil & Gas Plc
Hatfield House, 52-54 Stamford Street, London SE1 9LX
**Web:** www.victoriaoilandgas.com
**Reg No:** 5139892 **Estd:** 2004 Public Limited Company
**Line of Business:** Oil and gas exploration services
**Directors:** R S Palmer, J Bryant, K A Foo, G C Manheim, J R Mcburney
**Co. Secretary:** Ms Leena Nagrecha
**Responsibilities**
**Senior:** Philip Rand (Manager)
**Operations:** Radwan Hadi (Chief Operating Officer)
**US SIC:** 1389 **UK SIC:** 13000
**Auditors:** Deloitte & Touche
**Bankers:** Allied Irish Bank (gb) (23-84-82)
**Employees:** 75
**Turnover:** £14,729,000

DUNS 36-802-0806
## Victoria Park Bowling Club
1284 Dumbarton Road, Glasgow, Lanarkshire G14 9EU
**Tel:** 0141-959-5777
**Web:** www.belhaven.co.uk
**Estd:** 2002
**Line of Business:** Operation of other sports arenas and stadiums not elsewhere classified
**Principals:** W Brown (Chairman), P Ross, J Patterson
**Responsibilities**
**Senior:** Allan Cox (President), Ian Gavin (Secretary), Robert Lylle (Treasurer)
**US SIC:** 7999 **UK SIC:** 97913
**Employees:** 75

DUNS 38-779-9604
## Victoria Park Leisure Centre
Manners Road, Ilkeston, Derbyshire DE7 8AT
**Tel:** 01159-440400
**Web:** www.victoriaparkleisurecentre.co.uk
**Estd:** 1975 Partnership
**Line of Business:** Leisure centres
**Partners:** S Bailey, A Gill
**US SIC:** 7999 **UK SIC:** 97913
**Employees:** 50

DUNS 22-047-1218
## Victoria Park Plaza Operator Ltd
(Subsidiary of: Park Plaza Coöperatief U.A.)
239-251 Vauxhall Bridge Road, London SW1V 1EQ
**Tel:** 02077699999 **Fax:** 020-7769-9998
**Web:** www.victoriaparkplaza.com
**Reg No:** 4049387 **Estd:** 2005 Private Limited Company
**Line of Business:** Hotels
**Trading Style:** Park Plaza Victoria London
**Issued Capital:** £2
**Directors:** C C Moravsky, Euro Sea Hotels N V
**Co. Secretary:** Mrs Inbar Zilberman
**Responsibilities**
**Senior:** Robert Flinter (Chief Executive Officer)
**HR:** Laurrenee Barasse (Human Resources Manager)
**Facilities:** Noel Bastianpulle (Chief Engineer)
**US SIC:** 7011 **UK SIC:** 66500

**Auditors:** Mazars LLP

|      | 31-12-13 | 31-12-12 | 31-12-11 |
|------|----------|----------|----------|
| TO   | 18,266,000 | 18,835,000 | 18,003,000 |
| P/L  | 376,000 | 547,000 | 358,000 |
| NW   | (443,000) | (819,000) | (1,366,000) |
| WC   | (443,000) | (819,000) | (1,366,000) |
| Emp. | 141 | 153 | 157 |

DUNS 21-775-2313
## Victoria Park Primary School
Strandburn Street, Belfast BT4 1LX
**Tel:** 02890471274
**Web:** www.victoriaparkprimaryschool.co.uk
**Estd:** 2011 Proprietorship
**Line of Business:** Schools (local authority)
**Proprietor:** Mrs A Gourley
**US SIC:** 8211 **UK SIC:** 93200
**Employees:** 50

DUNS 21-816-1974                                    Exp
## Victoria P.L.C.
Worcester Road, Kidderminster, Worcestershire DY10 1JR
**Tel:** 01562-749300
**Web:** www.victoria.plc.uk
**Reg No:** 0282204 **Estd:** 1933 Public Limited Company
**Line of Business:** Management activities of production holding companies
**Export Markets:** Australia
**Export Sales:** £38,339,000
**Issued Capital:** £1,758,296
**Directors:** G B Wilding, G C Petken, A N Harrison, I A Anton
**Co. Secretary:** Terence Danks
**Responsibilities**
**Senior:** Kevin Mckeith (Landlord), Barry Poynter (Manager)
**Branches:** Victoria P.l.c., 99 Kensington High St, London W8 5SA
**US SIC:** 6711 **UK SIC:** 83962
**Auditors:** Nexia Smith & Williamson
**Bankers:** Barclays Bank Plc (20-46-06)

|      | 29-03-14 | 30-03-13 | 31-03-12 |
|------|----------|----------|----------|
| TO   | 71,386,000 | 70,909,000 | 77,126,000 |
| P/L  | 2,281,000 | (3,520,000) | 1,547,000 |
| NW   | 26,951,000 | 38,225,000 | 39,578,000 |
| WC   | 26,842,000 | 16,537,000 | 16,785,000 |
| Emp. | 585 | 542 | 634 |

DUNS 22-159-0966                                    Imp
## Victoria Plum Ltd
(Subsidiary of: Varnish Bidco Ltd)
Amsterdam Road, Hull, North Humberside HU7 0XF
**Tel:** 08448044545 **Fax:** 01482-212270
**Web:** www.victoriaplumb.com
**Reg No:** 4177694 **VAT No:** 764469784
**Estd:** 2001 Private Limited Company
**Line of Business:** Other retail sale in specialised stores not elsewhere classified
**Trading Style:** Victoria Plumb
**Issued Capital:** £10,000
**Directors:** S M Walker, S M Myers, M Janzarik, J M Walker
**US SIC:** 5999 **UK SIC:** 65600
**Auditors:** Dutton Moore

|      | 28-02-14 | 28-02-13 | 29-02-12 |
|------|----------|----------|----------|
| TO   | 53,785,027 | 26,236,371 | 19,145,633 |
| P/L  | 12,109,109 | 6,007,784 | 4,836,644 |
| NW   | 18,938,955 | 11,472,367 | 6,921,397 |
| WC   | 18,423,102 | 11,079,033 | 6,584,341 |
| Emp. | 100 | 72 | 51 |

DUNS 21-782-6459
## Victoria Primary School
East Street, Newtownards, Co Down BT23 7DD
**Tel:** 02891818783
**Web:** www.victoriaps.co.uk
**Estd:** 1998 Proprietorship
**Line of Business:** Schools (local authority)
**Proprietor:** Mrs M Dunn
**Responsibilities**
**Senior:** Faithe Moffett (Head Teacher)
**US SIC:** 8211 **UK SIC:** 93200
**Employees:** 50

DUNS 21-232-3458
## Victoria Theatre
Fountain Street, Halifax, West Yorkshire HX1 1BP
**Tel:** 01422351156
**Web:** www.victoriatheatre.co.uk
**Estd:** 1988 Proprietorship
**Line of Business:** Theatres & concert halls
**Proprietor:** Miss A Metcalf
**Responsibilities**
**Senior:** Tim Fagan (Theatre Manager)
**Finance:** Lisa Holroyd (Senior Finance Administrator)
**US SIC:** 7911 **UK SIC:** 97913
**Employees:** 40

DUNS 21-011-1752
## Victoria Travel Service Ltd
(Subsidiary of: Risk Capital Partners Llp)
Grosvenor House, Prospect Hill, Redditch, Worcestershire B97 4DL
**Tel:** 01214455656 **Fax:** 08718551191
**Web:** www.victoriatravel.co.uk
**Reg No:** 6346018 **Estd:** 2007 Private Limited Company
**Line of Business:** Travel agents
**Issued Capital:** £1
**Directors:** J M Conlon, A J Gardner
**Responsibilities**
**Senior:** Seamus Conlon (Manager)
**Marketing:** Sukie Rapal (Marketing Manager)
**Facilities:** Seamus Conlon (Manager)
**US SIC:** 4722 **UK SIC:** 77001

|     | 30-11-13 | 30-11-12 | 30-11-11 |
|-----|----------|----------|----------|
| TA  | 1 | 1 | 1 |
| NW  | 1 | 1 | 1 |

DUNS 22-091-2062
## The Victorian Chop House Co Ltd
The Victorian Chop House, 3 St Anns Churchyard, Manchester M2 7LN
**Tel:** 01618321872
**Web:** www.tomschophouse.com
**Reg No:** 4092561 **Estd:** 2000 Private Limited Company
**Line of Business:** Restaurant - english
**Issued Capital:** £57
**Directors:** I J Donald, A D Emmerson
**Co. Secretary:** Roger Ward
**Branches:** The Victorian Chop House Co Ltd, Blackpool Hold, Manchester M2 1HN
**US SIC:** 5812, 5813
**UK SIC:** 66110, 66200

|     | 31-03-14 | 31-03-13 | 31-03-12 |
|-----|----------|----------|----------|
| TA  | 1,358,197 | 1,364,864 | 1,334,516 |
| NW  | 753,623 | 657,415 | 573,347 |
| WC  | 345,660 | 232,369 | 127,276 |

DUNS 77-121-8849
## Victory Fire Ltd
Victory House, Project Park Cody Road, London E16 4TQ
**Tel:** 08454567345
**Web:** www.victoryfire.co.uk
**Reg No:** 2694384 **VAT No:** 577814790
**Estd:** 1992 Private Limited Company
**Line of Business:** Firefighting equipment
**Issued Capital:** £100
**Director:** P Mclaren
**Co. Secretary:** Peter Donovan
**US SIC:** 8911 **UK SIC:** 83701
**Auditors:** David Anthony & Co
**Bankers:** National Westminster Bank Plc (60-40-04)

|     | 31-03-14 | 31-03-13 | 31-03-12 |
|-----|----------|----------|----------|
| TO  | 1,004,281 | 962,805 | 870,044 |
| P/L | 288,011 | 260,429 | 193,533 |
| NW  | 605,796 | 508,522 | 426,303 |
| WC  | 390,246 | 282,243 | 392,553 |

DUNS 71-893-3471
## Victory Housing Trust
Cromer Road, North Walsham, Norfolk NR28 0NB
**Tel:** 08453-006648
**Web:** www.victoryhousing.co.uk
**Reg No:** 5275586 **VAT No:** 874345990
**Estd:** 2004 Private Company Limited By Guarantee
**Line of Business:** Buying and selling of own real estate
**Directors:** T Moore, V Saunders, S B Burke, P J Burton, Ms C Barter, Ms S B Gurrey, J Owen, K Dixon
**Co. Secretary:** Stephen Read
**Responsibilities**
**Senior:** John Rest (Director), John Wollocombe (Director)
**Branches:** Victory Housing Trust, Fakenham Connect, Oak St, Fakenham, NR21 9DY Norfolk
**US SIC:** 6531, 6519
**UK SIC:** 83400, 85000
**Auditors:** Grant Thornton UK LLP
**Bankers:** Lloyds TSB Bank plc (77-91-66)

|      | 31-03-14 | 31-03-13 | 31-03-12 |
|------|----------|----------|----------|
| TO   | 23,117,000 | 21,811,000 | 20,399,000 |
| P/L  | 10,040,000 | 6,013,000 | 3,453,000 |
| NW   | 35,156,000 | 24,451,000 | 52,432,000 |
| WC   | 1,260,000 | 1,660,000 | 8,239,000 |
| Emp. | 73 | 72 | 75 |

DUNS 28-836-5232
## The Victory (Services) Association Ltd
63-79 Seymour Street, London W2 2HF
**Tel:** 020-7723-4474
**Web:** www.vsc.co.uk
**Reg No:** 0429298 **Estd:** 1948 Private Company Limited By Guarantee
**Line of Business:** Clubs social and associations

**Directors:** S P Cass, P R Rossiter, Rear Admiral M Kimmons, Commander M Cox, P Schnepper, Ms S J Bonney, S Chisnall, D K Turnbull
**Co. Secretary:** Air Commodore Nigel Beet, Cbe
**Responsibilities**
**Senior:** Philip Gilby Rm *(Director)*, Brian Kay *(Manager)*, Charles Marment *(Director)*, Clive Martland *(Director)*, Alan Massey Kcb Cbe *(Director)*, Andrew Meek *(Director)*, Julia Routledge *(Manager)*, Gary Wilcox *(Manager)*, Nicola Wood Raf *(Director)*
**Marketing:** Angela Mantzios *(Assistant Marketing Manager)*
**Sales:** Natalie Canavan *(Reservations Manager)*
**US SIC:** 5813 **UK SIC:** 66200
**Auditors:** Hays Allan
**Bankers:** National Westminster Bank Plc (60-16-10)

| | 31-03-14 | 31-03-13 | 31-03-12 |
|---|---|---|---|
| TO | 7,090,875 | 6,695,063 | 6,297,982 |
| P/L | 1,060,090 | 978,532 | 692,445 |
| NW | 10,917,049 | 9,857,381 | 8,833,977 |
| WC | 672,551 | 435,538 | 497,273 |
| Emp. | 111 | 109 | 107 |

DUNS 21-228-4485

## Victory Swimming & Fitness Centre

Station Road, North Walsham, Norfolk NR28 0DZ
**Tel:** 01692-409370
**Web:** www.placesforpeopleleisure.org
**Estd:** 2003 Proprietorship
**Line of Business:** Operation of swimming pools
**Proprietor:** S Jardine
**US SIC:** 7999 **UK SIC:** 97913
**Employees:** 50

DUNS 56-951-9119 **Imp**

## Victrex Manufacturing Ltd

(**Subsidiary of:** Victrex Plc)
Victrex Technology Centre, Hill House International, Thornton-Cleveleys, Lancashire FY5 4QD
**Tel:** 01253861951
**Web:** www.victrex.com
**Reg No:** 2845018 **VAT No:** 604782539
**Estd:** 1993 Private Limited Company
**Line of Business:** Plastics raw materials
**Issued Capital:** £1,000,000
**Principals:** D R Hummel *(Managing)*, L S Burdett, T J Cooper
**Co. Secretary:** Mrs Suzana Koncarevic
**Responsibilities**
**Senior:** Kzunoeo Kawahara *(Manager)*
**Branches:** Victrex Manufacturing Ltd, 41 Colinton Rd, Edinburgh, Midlothian EH10 5EN
**US SIC:** 2821 **UK SIC:** 25140
**Auditors:** KPMG Audit PLC
**Bankers:** National Westminster Bank Plc (01-67-14)

| | 30-09-13 | 30-09-12 | 30-09-11 |
|---|---|---|---|
| TO | 153,500,000 | 156,400,000 | 146,800,000 |
| P/L | 61,200,000 | 68,500,000 | 58,400,000 |
| NW | 237,600,000 | 190,400,000 | 136,900,000 |
| WC | 88,000,000 | 71,900,000 | 36,200,000 |
| Emp. | 464 | 418 | 403 |

DUNS 23-637-7180 **Imp-Exp**

## Victrex Plc

Victrex Technology Centre, Hillhouse International, Thornton-Cleveleys, Lancashire FY5 4QD
**Web:** www.victrex.com
**Reg No:** 2793780 **VAT No:** 604782441
**Estd:** 1993 Public Limited Company
**Line of Business:** Manufacturers of plastic products
**Export Markets:** Worldwide
**Export Sales:** £245,900,000
**Issued Capital:** £846,270
**Directors:** Ms L S Burdett, D R Hummel, Dr P J Kirby, P J De Smedt, T J Cooper, L C Pentz, G F Kerr
**Co. Secretary:** Mrs Suzana Koncarevic
**Responsibilities**
**Senior:** John Grasmeder *(Technical Director)*, Gary Hulme *(Manager)*
**Marketing:** Steve Dougherty *(Marketing Director)*
**IT:** Dean Goodfellow *(Head of Global IT Services)*
**US SIC:** 2821, 3079
**UK SIC:** 25140, 48360
**Auditors:** KPMG Audit PLC
**Bankers:** Barclays Bank Plc (20-10-03)

| | 30-09-14 | 30-09-13 | 30-09-12 |
|---|---|---|---|
| TO | 252,600,000 | 221,900,000 | 219,800,000 |
| P/L | 102,700,000 | 94,600,000 | 94,500,000 |
| NW | 343,300,000 | 303,600,000 | 261,000,000 |
| WC | 134,200,000 | 140,800,000 | 128,300,000 |
| Emp. | 681 | 644 | 607 |

DUNS 21-224-7517

## Victronenergy

Kevin Wadsworth, Huddersfield, West Yorkshire HD9 7AH
**Tel:** 07940244662
**Web:** www.victronenergy.com
**Estd:** 2008 Proprietorship
**Line of Business:** Electronic equipment for vehicles
**Proprietor:** K Wadsworth
**Responsibilities**
**Senior:** Kevin Wadsworth *(Manager)*
**US SIC:** 7539 **UK SIC:** 67100
**Employees:** 55

DUNS 21-579-7272

## Vidal Sassoon Educational Centre

54 Knightsbridge, London SW1X 7JN
**Tel:** 02072351957
**Web:** www.sassoon.com
**Estd:** 1990 Proprietorship
**Line of Business:** Hairdressing schools
**Proprietor:** U Bruer
**Responsibilities**
**Senior:** Josh Gibson *(Manager)*
**US SIC:** 8299 **UK SIC:** 93300
**Employees:** 300

DUNS 49-076-2028 **Imp**

## Videcon Plc

Unit 1 Concept Business Park, Heckmondwike, West Yorkshire WF16 0PN
**Tel:** 01924528000 **Fax:** 01924-528005
**Web:** www.videcon.co.uk
**Reg No:** 3085668 **Estd:** 1995 Public Limited Company
**Line of Business:** Manufacture of television and radio receivers, sound or video recording or reproducing apparatus and associated goods
**Export Sales:** £692,678
**Issued Capital:** £50,005
**Principals:** M D Bradley, A Croston, A Croston *(Proprietor)*
**Co. Secretary:** David Foster
**Responsibilities**
**Senior:** Mike Foster *(Accounts Manager)*
**Sales:** Justin Lindley *(Sales Manager)*
**US SIC:** 3651 **UK SIC:** 34541
**Auditors:** Broadhead Cawley Partnership
**Bankers:** HSBC Bank plc (40-08-20)

| | 31-08-13 | 31-08-12 | 31-08-11 |
|---|---|---|---|
| TO | 14,663,158 | 14,488,635 | 10,882,601 |
| P/L | 1,753,609 | 1,827,562 | 738,403 |
| NW | 3,928,858 | 3,901,975 | 3,749,607 |
| WC | 3,676,012 | 3,631,011 | 3,430,141 |
| Emp. | 55 | 49 | 45 |

DUNS 73-486-0302

## Video Island Entertainment Ltd

(**Subsidiary of:** Amazon.Com Inc.)
9 - 6 Portal Way, London W3 6RU
**Fax:** 02088968110
**Web:** www.lovefilm.com
**Reg No:** 4749640 **Estd:** 2003 Private Limited Company
**Line of Business:** Motion picture and video distribution
**Issued Capital:** £13,418
**Directors:** A J Byrne, K D Ebanks
**Co. Secretary:** Mitre Secretaries Limited
**Responsibilities**
**Operations:** Fern O'Sullivan *(Group Operations Director)*
**Branches:** Video Island Entertainment Ltd, Hook Rd, Chessington, Surrey KT9 1EL
**US SIC:** 7829 **UK SIC:** 97112
**Auditors:** PricewaterhouseCoopers LLP
**Bankers:** Lloyds TSB Bank plc (30-15-57)

| | 31-12-13 | 31-12-12 | 31-12-11 |
|---|---|---|---|
| TA | 220,433,903 | 148,629,275 | 148,187,902 |
| P/L | 415,660 | 452,067 | 30,214 |
| NW | 220,303,611 | 148,464,592 | 148,123,282 |
| WC | 21,104,358 | 365,751 | 20,424,029 |

DUNS 21-411-5351

## Videojug Production & Media

1 Holford Yard, London WC1X 9HD
**Tel:** 02072504300
**Web:** www.videojug.com
**Estd:** 2010 Proprietorship
**Line of Business:** Video production companies
**Proprietor:** A Craven
**Responsibilities**
**Senior:** Tom Laidlaw *(Chief Executive Officer)*, Ben Sinden *(Content Director)*
**US SIC:** 7819 **UK SIC:** 97111
**Employees:** 50

DUNS 21-703-2118

## Videology Ltd

(**Subsidiary of:** Videology Inc.)
Noah's Yard, 10 York Way, London N1 9AA
**Tel:** 02033 181 228 **Fax:** 02076-917-539
**Web:** www.videologygroup.com
**Reg No:** 7476031 **Estd:** 2010 Private Limited Company
**Line of Business:** Hardware consultancy
**Issued Capital:** £2
**Director:** S A Ferber
**Co. Secretary:** Sisec Limited
**Responsibilities**
**Senior:** Yana Eisenstein *(Manager)*
**US SIC:** 7379, 7319
**UK SIC:** 83940, 83800
**Auditors:** Saffery Champness
**Bankers:** HSBC Bank plc (40-06-02)

| | 31-12-13 | 31-12-12 | 31-12-11 |
|---|---|---|---|
| TO | 62,516,000 | 32,101,813 | 13,674,833 |
| P/L | (3,729,000) | (3,477,827) | (2,385,263) |
| NW | (9,490,000) | (5,863,088) | (2,385,261) |
| WC | (9,788,000) | (6,035,210) | (2,401,688) |
| Emp. | 69 | 32 | 13 |

DUNS 21-811-4117

## Videous

29 Landseer Drive, Downham Market, Norfolk PE38 9NG
**Web:** www.videous.co.uk
**Estd:** 2007
**Line of Business:** Motion picture production on film or video
**Proprietor:** S Holloway
**US SIC:** 8999 **UK SIC:** 83954
**Employees:** 80

DUNS 29-579-8995 **Imp-Exp**

## Videx Security Ltd

Unit 1 Osprey House Trinity Park, Trinity Way, London E4 8TD
**Tel:** 0870-300-1240
**Web:** www.videx-security.com
**Reg No:** 1941721 **Estd:** 1985 Private Limited Company
**Line of Business:** Security and related activities
**Export Markets:** Republic of Ireland
**Issued Capital:** £100
**Principals:** J D Rickard *(Managing)*, K E Andrews, R L Sands, Mrs J Bennett
**Co. Secretary:** John Rickard
**Responsibilities**
**Senior:** Kirsty Macrae *(Office Manager)*
**Branches:** Videx Security Ltd, Videx Security Ltd, Unit 4-7, Newcastle Upon Tyne, Tyne and Wear NE6 2XX
**US SIC:** 7393 **UK SIC:** 83954
**Auditors:** Cartwrights
**Bankers:** Lloyds TSB Bank plc (30-98-70)

| | 31-12-13 | 31-12-12 | 31-12-11 |
|---|---|---|---|
| TO | 7,956,092 | 7,799,684 | 7,891,760 |
| P/L | 391,695 | 363,109 | 396,146 |
| NW | 1,803,893 | 1,821,465 | 1,769,212 |
| WC | 757,657 | 988,584 | 923,218 |
| Emp. | 54 | 50 | 45 |

DUNS 23-879-4957

## Vielife Ltd

(**Subsidiary of:** Connecticut General Life Ins. Co.)
62 Threadneedle Street, London EC2R 8HP
**Tel:** 02071832289 **Fax:** 02071834489
**Web:** www.vielife.com
**Reg No:** 3870738 **Estd:** 1999 Private Limited Company
**Line of Business:** Data processing
**Export Sales:** £4,360,350
**Issued Capital:** £12,204,001
**Directors:** K Cotter, G Kemp, Mrs J Silva, J V Quesada
**Co. Secretary:** Miss Sarah Bailey
**Responsibilities**
**Senior:** Jessica Colling *(General Manager)*
**Branches:** Vielife Ltd, 42 Orchard Road, London N6 5TR
**US SIC:** 7374, 8091
**UK SIC:** 83940, 95200
**Auditors:** BDO Stoy Hayward

| | 31-12-13 | 31-12-12 | 31-12-11 |
|---|---|---|---|
| TO | 5,317,500 | 4,836,290 | 4,584,230 |
| P/L | (2,248,012) | (3,668,045) | 10,306,834 |
| NW | (4,311,175) | (2,987,200) | (412,059) |
| WC | (4,498,550) | (3,093,562) | (730,077) |
| Emp. | 65 | 65 | 66 |

DUNS 50-026-8008 **Imp**

## Viessmann Ltd

(**Subsidiary of:** Viessmann Werke Gmbh & Co Kg)
Hortonwood 30, Telford, Shropshire TF1 7YP
**Tel:** 01952-675000
**Web:** www.viessmann.co.uk
**Reg No:** 2305071 **VAT No:** 489218504
**Estd:** 1988 Private Limited Company
**Line of Business:** Wholesale of hardware, plumbing and heating equipment and supplies
**Export Sales:** £1,405,360
**Issued Capital:** £236,517
**Directors:** H Pez, G S Russell
**Co. Secretary:** James Sage
**Responsibilities**
**Senior:** Hans-joachim Pez *(Director)*
**Marketing:** Anja Katz *(Marketing Director)*
**Admin:** Zelia Ward *(Administration Manager)*
**IT:** Zelia Ward *(Administration Manager)*
**HR:** Tony Lobley *(Training Manager)*, Zelia Ward *(Administration Manager)*
**Health & Safety:** Zelia Ward *(Administration Manager)*
**Facilities:** Zelia Ward *(Administration Manager)*
**US SIC:** 5074, 1711
**UK SIC:** 61300, 50300
**Auditors:** PricewaterhouseCoopers
**Bankers:** Barclays Bank Plc (20-85-46)

| | 31-12-13 | 31-12-12 | 31-12-11 |
|---|---|---|---|
| TO | 30,050,298 | 28,131,077 | 31,500,107 |
| P/L | 1,040,849 | 575,717 | 438,132 |
| NW | 2,193,125 | 1,157,917 | 586,525 |
| WC | 195,051 | (924,912) | (1,573,837) |
| Emp. | 88 | 89 | 95 |

DUNS 21-211-9650

## Viewforth School of Healthcare

2 Kenilworth Road, Bridge Of Allan, Stirling, Stirlingshire FK9 4DU
**Tel:** 01786834814
**Estd:** 1998 Proprietorship
**Line of Business:** Colleges Universities & Professional Schools
**Proprietor:** Mrs M Roughead
**US SIC:** 8221 **UK SIC:** 93100
**Employees:** 76

DUNS 23-631-1833

## Viewpoint Housing Association Ltd

4 South Oswald Road, Edinburgh, Midlothian EH9 2HG
**Tel:** 01316684247
**Web:** www.viewpoint.org.uk
**Reg No:** 0001228SP **Estd:** 1947 Friendly Society
**Line of Business:** Other letting of own property
**Principals:** R Duff *(Managing)*, Mrs D Goldie, A F Hay, D I Campbell, Miss E I Macdonald, Mrs R Bell, Miss M Lambert, I W Calder
**Co. Secretary:** Alexander Granton
**Responsibilities**
**Senior:** G Hibbard *(Designated Limited Liability P)*, O Hulme *(Manager)*, A Keymer *(Designated Limited Liability P)*, E MacDonald *(Designated Limited Liability P)*, Dorry McLaughlin *(Manager)*, Doreen Mcluthlin *(Chief Executive)*, E Notman *(Manager)*, P Rendle *(Designated Limited Liability P)*
**Finance:** Jenni Fairbairn *(Finance Director)*
**IT:** Mark Forrester *(IT Manager)*
**Facilities:** Graham Harper *(Estates Director)*
**Branches:** Viewpoint Housing Association Ltd, 2 Croft-An-Righ, Edinburgh, Midlothian EH8 8EG
**US SIC:** 7399 **UK SIC:** 83954
**Auditors:** Coopers & Lybrand
**Bankers:** The Royal Bank Of Scotland Plc (83-00-81)
**Employees:** 194
**Turnover:** £11,529,617

DUNS 49-384-1357 **Imp**

## Viewsonic Europe Ltd

(**Subsidiary of:** Viewsonic Corporation)
4 Level, Tower 42, 25 Old Broad Street, London EC2N 1PB
**Tel:** 020-7382-8250 **Fax:** 02073828251
**Web:** www.viewsoniceurope.com
**Reg No:** 3131161 **VAT No:** 644661429
**Estd:** 1995 Private Limited Company
**Line of Business:** Wholesale of other electronic parts and equipment
**Directors:** Ms C Lin, S Y Yi, Ms S J Pegrum, M R Lufkin, Ms T H Chu, J Chu
**Co. Secretary:** Ms Sue Pegrum
**US SIC:** 5065 **UK SIC:** 61500
**Auditors:** Simmons Gainsford LLP
**Bankers:** Barclays Bank Plc (20-23-97)
**Employees:** 55
**Turnover:** £95,049,000

DUNS 39-707-9690

## Vigcare (Brighton) Ltd

Portland House, 11 Portland Road, Hove, East Sussex BN3 5DR
**Tel:** 01273205879 **Fax:** 01273541130
**Reg No:** 2160626 **Estd:** 1987 Private Limited Company
**Line of Business:** Social work activities with accommodation
**Issued Capital:** £2
**Directors:** P K Vig, J S Vig
**Co. Secretary:** Mrs Beant Vig

US SIC: 8321   UK SIC: 96111
**Auditors:** Bristow Still
**Bankers:** Barclays Bank Plc (20-54-11)

|    | 30-04-14 | 30-04-13 | 30-04-12 |
|----|----------|----------|----------|
| TA | 1,253,017 | 1,255,790 | 1,256,941 |
| NW | 1,252,173 | 1,252,190 | 1,252,443 |
| WC | 1,252,173 | 1,252,190 | 1,252,443 |

DUNS 42-452-7161
## Vigil Security Ltd
1 Eastlands Court, Wade Road, Basingstoke, Hampshire RG24 8PL
**Tel:** 01256463222
**Web:** www.vigil-security.com
**Reg No:** 4440423 **Estd:** 2002 Private Limited Company
**Line of Business:** Security activities
**Issued Capital:** £20
**Directors:** J Goldsworthy, A Binnersley, D J Royal
**Co. Secretary:** William Mortimer
**Responsibilities**
**Senior:** Ellen Mercer (Partner), Michael Mercer (Partner)
**Branches:** Vigil Security Ltd, Eastlands Court, The Beresford Center, Wade Road, Basingstoke, Hampshire RG24 8FA
US SIC: 7393, 1731
UK SIC: 83954, 50300

|    | 31-03-14 | 31-03-13 | 31-03-12 |
|----|----------|----------|----------|
| TA | 148,930 | 139,236 | 87,362 |
| NW | 53,999 | 78,413 | 42,792 |
| WC | 32,834 | 57,248 | 27,121 |

DUNS 77-944-7114
## Vigilant Security Services Uk Ltd
A M C House, 12 Cumberland Avenue, London NW10 7QL
**Tel:** 02071834247 **Fax:** 02089613905
**Web:** www.vigilantsecurityservices.co.uk
**Reg No:** 5914271 **VAT No:** 906370435
**Estd:** 2006 Private Limited Company
**Line of Business:** Security and related activities
**Issued Capital:** £100
**Director:** I Ahmad
**Co. Secretary:** Khalid Mustafa
US SIC: 7393, 7399
UK SIC: 83954

|    | 31-08-13 | 31-08-12 | 31-08-11 |
|----|----------|----------|----------|
| TA | 520,268 | 413,302 | 423,558 |
| NW | 418,796 | 365,683 | 236,189 |
| WC | 200,449 | 188,194 | 168,594 |

DUNS 22-521-6225     Imp
## Viglen Ltd
(**Subsidiary of:** Westcoast (Holdings) Ltd)
7 Hantley Pageway Old Parkbury Lane, St Albans, Hertfordshire AL2 2DQ
**Tel:** 01727201800 **Fax:** 01727201818
**Web:** www.viglen.co.uk
**Reg No:** 1208441 **VAT No:** 217651370
**Estd:** 1975 Private Limited Company
**Line of Business:** Manufacturers of pcs
**Issued Capital:** £10,100
**Principals:** B Tkachuk (Managing), L Hemani, C Littner, S J Madhani
**Co. Secretary:** Michael Ray
**Branches:** Unit 20, Horsenden Lane South, Perivale
US SIC: 3573, 5081, 7379
UK SIC: 33020, 61490, 83940
**Auditors:** Deloitte LLP
**Bankers:** National Westminster Bank Plc (51-50-01)

|    | 30-09-13 | 30-09-12 | 30-09-11 |
|----|----------|----------|----------|
| TO | 73,182,293 | 66,222,589 | 61,821,633 |
| P/L | 3,117,525 | 2,749,300 | 1,781,850 |
| NW | 8,287,233 | 7,754,735 | 7,916,662 |
| WC | 9,836,701 | 9,132,403 | 9,419,407 |
| Emp. | 187 | 176 | 164 |

DUNS 21-783-5591
## Viii City Tower Holdings S A R L
40 Basinghall Street, London EC2V 5DE
**Tel:** 02076382921
**Estd:** 2011 Proprietorship
**Line of Business:** Business and management consultancy activities not elsewhere classified
**Proprietor:** Mrs S Honter
US SIC: 7392   UK SIC: 83951
**Employees:** 1,000

DUNS 21-160-8843
## Viiv Healthcare Ltd
(**Subsidiary of:** Glaxosmithkline Plc)
Gsk House, 980 Great West Road, Brentford, Middlesex TW8 9GS
**Tel:** 02083-806-200
**Web:** www.viivhealthcareeffect.com
**Reg No:** 6876960 **Estd:** 2009 Private Limited Company
**Line of Business:** Management activities of holding companies for HIV treatment development company.
**Trading Style:** Viiv Healthcare

**Issued Capital:** £11,112
**Directors:** Ms D J Limet, Dr I Tomlinson, I Mccubbin, Z Hong, A R Mackenzie, Dr J Shannon, D E Giordano, Dr J A Keller
**Co. Secretary:** Viiv Healthcare Uk Limited
**Responsibilities**
**Senior:** Shah Hussain (Director)
US SIC: 6711, 2834
UK SIC: 83962, 25700
**Auditors:** PricewaterhouseCoopers LLP
*Following financial data are in thousands*

|    | 31-12-13 | 31-12-12 | 31-12-11 |
|----|----------|----------|----------|
| TO | 1,371,000 | 1,337,449 | 1,536,512 |
| P/L | 335,835 | 641,049 | 654,036 |
| NW | (1,656,504) | (1,243,702) | (276,944) |
| WC | 534,573 | 623,116 | 429,730 |
| Emp. | 557 | 491 | 510 |

DUNS 21-175-6066     Imp
## Viiv Healthcare Uk Ltd
(**Subsidiary of:** Glaxosmithkline Plc)
980 Great West Road, Brentford, Middlesex TW8 9GS
**Tel:** 0800221441
**Web:** www.tivicay.com
**Reg No:** 6990358 **Estd:** 2009 Private Limited Company
**Line of Business:** Wholesale of pharmaceutical goods
**Issued Capital:** £2
**Directors:** J C Andries, M R Dawson, Ms D J Limet, N P Shortman
**Co. Secretary:** Ms Laura Hillier
US SIC: 5122   UK SIC: 61800

|    | 31-12-13 | 31-12-12 | 31-12-11 |
|----|----------|----------|----------|
| TO | 471,077,000 | 494,220,000 | 504,993,000 |
| P/L | 396,925,000 | 440,628,000 | 407,945,000 |
| NW | 704,072,000 | 731,267,000 | 320,640,000 |
| WC | 195,072,000 | 353,267,000 | 320,640,000 |
| Emp. | 88 | 67 | 66 |

DUNS 22-199-8805     Imp
## Vijay Fashions Ltd
120 Broughton Street, Manchester M8 8AN
**Tel:** 0161-834-7711
**Web:** www.vijayfashions.com
**Reg No:** 4217882 **Estd:** 2001 Private Limited Company
**Line of Business:** Clothing wholesale and suppliers
**Issued Capital:** £100
**Directors:** S L Jairath, D K Jairath
**Co. Secretary:** Jatinder Jairath
**Responsibilities**
**Senior:** Paul Jairath (Manager)
US SIC: 5136   UK SIC: 61600
**Auditors:** Lopian Gross Barnett & Co

|    | 30-06-13 | 30-06-12 | 30-06-11 |
|----|----------|----------|----------|
| TO | N/A | 5,390,550 | 6,781,545 |
| P/L | N/A | (156,563) | 255,615 |
| NW | 1,101,291 | 872,294 | 1,224,207 |
| WC | 994,250 | 745,459 | 1,075,960 |
| Emp. | N/A | 37 | 37 |

DUNS 52-531-7905     Exp
## Viju Ltd
(**Subsidiary of:** Progressus As)
3 Baird Road, Kirkton Campus, Livingston, West Lothian EH54 7AZ
**Tel:** 01506-591000
**Web:** www.vijugroup.com
**Reg No:** 0167635SC **Estd:** 1996 Private Limited Company
**Line of Business:** Video conferencing
**Issued Capital:** £12,635
**Director:** A J Evans
**Co. Secretary:** Ian Wallace
**Responsibilities**
**Senior:** Odd tlie (Director)
**Facilities:** Valerie Eunson (Personnel Manager)
US SIC: 4899, 7379, 7399
UK SIC: 79020, 83940, 83954
**Auditors:** PKF (UK) LLP
**Bankers:** The Royal Bank Of Scotland Plc (83-19-20)

|    | 31-12-13 | 31-12-12 | 31-12-11 |
|----|----------|----------|----------|
| TO | 29,182,842 | 25,305,850 | 22,501,290 |
| P/L | 611,259 | (544,046) | 1,133,004 |
| NW | 1,913,497 | 1,782,161 | 2,250,563 |
| WC | 1,268,955 | 1,054,507 | 1,933,789 |
| Emp. | 115 | 113 | 111 |

DUNS 22-709-7565     Imp
## Viking River Cruises Uk Ltd
Nelsons House, 83 Wimbledon Park Side, London SW19 5LP
**Tel:** 02087807998
**Web:** www.vikingrivercruises.co.uk
**Reg No:** 1283655 **VAT No:** 242152402
**Estd:** 1976 Private Limited Company
**Line of Business:** Activities of travel organisers
**Issued Capital:** £50,000
**Director:** Ms W C Smith
**Co. Secretary:** Jason Richards
US SIC: 4452, 8999
UK SIC: 74002, 83954
**Auditors:** Bass & Co

**Bankers:** The Royal Bank Of Scotland Plc (16-00-19)

|    | 31-12-13 | 31-12-12 | 31-12-11 |
|----|----------|----------|----------|
| TO | 68,760,328 | 48,709,996 | 23,277,932 |
| P/L | 1,345,667 | 954,894 | 279,727 |
| NW | 2,253,927 | 1,482,124 | 748,708 |
| WC | 4,334,066 | 3,465,667 | 2,852,348 |
| Emp. | 78 | 61 | 47 |

DUNS 73-794-4033     Imp-Exp
## Viking Seatech Ltd
(**Subsidiary of:** Dnb Asa)
Peterseat Drive, Altens Industrial Estate, Aberdeen, Aberdeenshire AB12 3HT
**Tel:** 01224-516516
**Web:** www.viking-moorings.com
**Reg No:** 0150861SC **VAT No:** 875464092
**Estd:** 2012 Private Limited Company
**Line of Business:** Anchor makers
**Export Markets:** Worldwide
**Issued Capital:** £1,000,000
**Directors:** T M Braatz, P Nilsen, J De Koning
**Co. Secretary:** Nicholas Gemmell
**Responsibilities**
**Senior:** William Bayliss (Manager), Mike Main (Manager), Wolfgang Wandl (Manager)
US SIC: 7394   UK SIC: 84000
**Auditors:** KPMG Audit PLC
**Bankers:** Bank Of Scotland (80-05-14)

|    | 31-08-13 | 31-12-12 | 31-08-11 |
|----|----------|----------|----------|
| TO | 11,327,000 | 18,956,000 | 12,588,000 |
| P/L | 24,166,000 | 2,594,000 | 607,000 |
| NW | 40,610,000 | 15,971,000 | 13,355,000 |
| WC | 26,496,000 | 5,614,000 | 90,000 |
| Emp. | 50 | 52 | 50 |

DUNS 49-118-6326
## The Vikings
113 Hamilton Road, Felixstowe, Suffolk IP11 7BL
**Tel:** 01394275111
**Web:** www.thevikings.co.uk
**Reg No:** 3099224 **Estd:** 1971 Private Company Limited By Guarantee
**Line of Business:** Other adult and other education not elsewhere classified
**Directors:** K W Kinrade, S Lines, Ms S D Longlands, T Thorpe, B P Coffin, Ms S E Orchard, M A Talbot, D I Hall
**Responsibilities**
**Senior:** Roger Barry (Director)
**Branches:** The Vikings, 119 Market Street, Rochdale, Lancashire OL12 8SE
US SIC: 8299, 7999
UK SIC: 93300, 97913

|    | 31-01-14 | 31-01-13 | 31-01-12 |
|----|----------|----------|----------|
| TO | 107,350 | N/A | N/A |
| P/L | 8,676 | N/A | N/A |
| NW | 97,694 | 55,207 | 43,926 |
| WC | 97,134 | N/A | N/A |

DUNS 22-955-4886
## Vikoma Holdings Ltd
(**Subsidiary of:** Energy Environmental Technologies Ltd)
Kingston Works Kingston Road, East Cowes, Isle of Wight PO32 6JS
**Tel:** 01983200560
**Web:** www.vikoma.com
**Reg No:** 1601822 **Estd:** 1981 Private Limited Company
**Line of Business:** Other engineering activities
**Issued Capital:** £401,000
**Directors:** P Scholes, R Rooney
**Co. Secretary:** Maclay Murray & Spens Llp
**Responsibilities**
**Senior:** Karen Lucas (Manager Director)
US SIC: 8911   UK SIC: 83701
**Auditors:** Anderson Anderson & Brown LLP
**Bankers:** National Westminster Bank Plc (52-30-04)

|    | 31-03-13 | 31-03-12 | 31-03-11 |
|----|----------|----------|----------|
| TA | 86,290 | 86,290 | 86,290 |
| NW | 86,290 | 86,290 | 86,290 |

DUNS 77-751-1189     Imp-Exp
## Vikoma International Ltd
(**Subsidiary of:** Energy Environmental Technologies Ltd)
Kingston Road, East Cowes, East Cowes, Isle of Wight PO32 6JS
**Tel:** 01983200570
**Web:** www.vikoma.com
**Reg No:** 3015615 **VAT No:** 900542957
**Estd:** 1976 Private Limited Company
**Line of Business:** Manufacture of insulated wire and cable
**Export Markets:** Worldwide
**Trading Style:** Vikoma International Ltd
**Issued Capital:** £1,975,431
**Directors:** P Scholes, R Rooney
**Co. Secretary:** Maclay Murray & Spens Llp
**Responsibilities**
**Senior:** Denis Healy (Manager), Mike King (Manager), Adam Robinson (Operations Director), Peter Tyler (Manager)
**Finance:** Martin Hammond (Financial Manager), Kevan Sturrock (Group Finance Director)

**Marketing:** Guy Downie (Sales & Marketing Director)
**Sales:** Sam Branston (Sales Manager - UK, Eire & Afr), Guy Downie (Sales & Marketing Director)
**HR:** Helen Farrant (HR Officer)
**Operations:** Lorraine Kenyon (Quality Manager), Adam Robinson (Operations Director)
US SIC: 3357, 3542
UK SIC: 22470, 32212
**Auditors:** Anderson Anderson & Brown LLP
**Bankers:** The Royal Bank Of Scotland Plc (83-15-31)

|    | 31-03-13 | 31-03-12 | 31-03-11 |
|----|----------|----------|----------|
| TO | 10,498,801 | 9,702,386 | 14,510,261 |
| P/L | 437,833 | (65,667) | 2,060,077 |
| NW | 6,588,235 | 6,379,312 | 6,491,358 |
| WC | 4,344,222 | 4,016,011 | 3,703,834 |
| Emp. | 75 | 76 | 84 |

DUNS 21-815-6544
## Villa Scalini Ltd
39 University Road, Belfast BT7 1ND
**Tel:** 02890328356
**Web:** www.mocodesign.co.uk
**Reg No:** 0610473NI **Estd:** 2011 Private Limited Company
**Line of Business:** Licensed restaurants
**Issued Capital:** £100
**Directors:** Ms D Giordano, A Giordano
US SIC: 5812   UK SIC: 66110

|    | 31-12-13 | 31-12-12 |
|----|----------|----------|
| TO | 2,877,278 | 3,285,053 |
| P/L | (314,149) | (1,418,343) |
| NW | (3,671,691) | (3,615,922) |
| WC | (2,459,880) | (2,398,677) |
| Emp. | 140 | 126 |

DUNS 28-936-3640
## The Village Bakery (Coedpoeth) Ltd
Ruthin Road, Wrexham, Clwyd LL11 3RD
**Tel:** 01978-720558
**Web:** www.villagebakery.co.uk
**Reg No:** 1555991 **VAT No:** 159140174
**Estd:** 1934 Private Limited Company
**Line of Business:** Retail sale of bread, cakes, flour confectionary and sugar confectionary
**Issued Capital:** £13,137
**Principals:** A E Jones (Managing), C C Jones, R M Jones
**Branches:** The Village Bakery (Coedpoeth) Ltd, 3 High Street, Wrexham, Clwyd LL13 8HP
US SIC: 5462   UK SIC: 64100
**Auditors:** M D Coxey & Co
**Bankers:** HSBC Bank plc (40-47-26)

|    | 31-10-13 | 31-10-12 | 31-10-11 |
|----|----------|----------|----------|
| TO | 11,342,289 | 9,862,915 | 10,191,418 |
| P/L | 2,349,528 | 1,818,469 | 1,008,513 |
| NW | 7,604,189 | 5,889,074 | 4,647,092 |
| WC | 5,353,071 | 4,476,638 | 3,541,908 |
| Emp. | 180 | 175 | 196 |

DUNS 53-648-4850
## Village Green Restaurants Ltd
Broadleaf Farm, Snoad Hill, Bethersden, Ashford, Kent TN26 3DY
**Tel:** 01233820982
**Web:** www.oakonthegreen.com
**Reg No:** 3453858 **Estd:** 1997 Private Limited Company
**Line of Business:** Licensed restaurants
**Issued Capital:** £688,801
**Director:** A V Bensley
**Co. Secretary:** Ms Helen Bensley
**Branches:** Village Green Restaurants Ltd, 79 Offham Road, West Malling, Kent ME19 6RB
US SIC: 5812   UK SIC: 66110
**Bankers:** National Westminster Bank Plc (60-01-21)

|    | 31-10-13 | 31-10-12 | 31-10-11 |
|----|----------|----------|----------|
| TO | 4,091,770 | N/A | N/A |
| P/L | 752,577 | N/A | N/A |
| NW | 3,245,958 | 3,039,917 | 2,835,748 |
| WC | 217,565 | 907,967 | 1,314,559 |
| Emp. | 96 | N/A | N/A |

DUNS 21-226-5428
## The Village Hall
Fallows Way, Whiston, Prescot, Merseyside L35 1RZ
**Tel:** 08712224596
**Proprietorship**
**Line of Business:** Hotels
**Proprietor:** D Walmsley
US SIC: 7011   UK SIC: 66500
**Employees:** 180

DUNS 21-801-0242
## Village Hall Compton Bassett
Old Camp Farm, Compton Bassett, Calne, Wiltshire SN11 8RE
**Tel:** 01249822141
**Web:** www.recycleforwiltshire.com
**Estd:** 2010
**Line of Business:** Waste paper merchants
**Proprietor:** P Hills

**Responsibilities**
**Senior:** Henry Newbery *(Manager)*
**US SIC:** 3031 **UK SIC:** 48123
**Employees:** 200

DUNS 21-812-0424
## Village Home Care Services
30 Uplands Crescent, Uplands, Swansea, West Glamorgan SA2 0PB
**Tel:** 01792643031
**Web:** www.villagehomecare.co.uk
**Estd:** 2012
**Line of Business:** Home care service providers
**US SIC:** 8091 **UK SIC:** 95200
**Employees:** 300

DUNS 21-777-4141
## Village Hotel
Otley Road, Leeds, West Yorkshire LS16 5PR
**Tel:** 08449808031
**Web:** www.village-hotels.co.uk
**Estd:** 2003 Partnership
**Line of Business:** Hotels
**Partner:** S Walmsley
**US SIC:** 7011 **UK SIC:** 66500
**Employees:** 300

DUNS 21-777-3120
## Village Hotel & Leisure Club
Waterfold Park, Bury, Lancashire BL9 7BQ
**Tel:** 01617644444
**Web:** www.village-hotels.co.uk
**Estd:** 2011 Partnership
**Line of Business:** Hotels
**Partners:** Mrs L O'Connor, M Hare
**US SIC:** 7011 **UK SIC:** 66500
**Employees:** 130

DUNS 21-812-2421
## Village Hotel Bournemouth
Deansleigh Road, Bournemouth, Dorset BH7 7DZ
**Tel:** 08712224574
**Web:** www.village-hotels.co.uk
**Estd:** 2012
**Line of Business:** Hotels
**Responsibilities**
**Senior:** Matthew Selch *(General Manager)*
**US SIC:** 7011 **UK SIC:** 66500
**Employees:** 50

DUNS 23-146-0684
## Village Hotel Cheadle
Cheadle Road, Cheadle, Cheshire SK8 1HW
**Tel:** 08712224580
**Web:** www.village-hotels.co.uk
**Proprietorship**
**Line of Business:** Other tourist or short-stay accommodation
**US SIC:** 7021 **UK SIC:** 66500
**Employees:** 160

DUNS 21-583-6756
## Village Hotels
Pinehurst Road, Iq Business Park, Farnborough, Hampshire GU14 7BF
**Tel:** 08712224590
**Web:** www.village-hotels.co.uk
**Estd:** 2011 Proprietorship
**Line of Business:** Hotels and motels without restaurant
**Proprietor:** P Morgan
**US SIC:** 7011 **UK SIC:** 66500
**Employees:** 100

DUNS 21-587-9964
## Village Medical Centre
Browning Street, Derby, Derbyshire DE23 8AL
**Tel:** 01332777080
**Estd:** 2011 Proprietorship
**Line of Business:** Health centres
**Proprietor:** Mrs D Cope
**US SIC:** 8062 **UK SIC:** 95100
**Employees:** 50

DUNS 21-773-9003
## Village Nursing Home
1a The Auld Road, Cumbernauld, Glasgow, Lanarkshire G67 2RF
**Web:** www.hc-one.co.uk
**Estd:** 1996 Partnership
**Line of Business:** Nursing homes
**Partners:** E Milne, I Milne
**US SIC:** 8051 **UK SIC:** 95100
**Employees:** 70

DUNS 21-738-8094
## Village People Ltd
Bowen Industrial Estate, Bargoed, Mid Glamorgan CF81 9EP
**Tel:** 01443879677
**Reg No:** 5740509 **Estd:** 2006 Private Limited Company
**Line of Business:** Other human health activities
**Issued Capital:** £100
**Director:** Mrs M R Stanford
**US SIC:** 8091 **UK SIC:** 95200
**Auditors:** Carston

| | 31-03-14 | 31-03-13 | 31-03-12 |
|---|---|---|---|
| TA | 185,538 | 342,380 | 287,274 |
| NW | 9,369 | 104,476 | (86,176) |
| WC | 2,972 | 95,947 | (97,430) |

DUNS 21-007-2153 Imp
## Villeroy & Boch (Uk) Ltd
**(Subsidiary of:** Villeroy & Boch S.À R.L. Faïencerie De Septfontain)
267 Merton Road, London SW18 5JS
**Tel:** 02088710011
**Web:** www.villeroy-boch.com
**Reg No:** 0339567 **VAT No:** 215980652
**Estd:** 1960 Private Limited Company
**Line of Business:** Manufacturers and suppliers of tableware
**Issued Capital:** £1,104,995
**Directors:** I N Turmes, P U Brocker, M Swan
**Co. Secretary:** Patrick Mcgonigle
**Responsibilities**
**Senior:** Mark Dalton *(Operations Manager)*, Michael Swann *(Managing Director)*
**Finance:** Tina Carman *(Financial Controller)*, Purmgeet Carman *(Financial Controller)*
**Marketing:** Joe Price *(E-Commerce Manager)*
**Sales:** Nick Green *(National Sales Manager)*
**Facilities:** Mark Dalton *(Operations Manager)*
**Operations:** Mark Dalton *(Operations Manager)*
**Branches:** Villeroy & Boch (Uk) Ltd, 32-34 North Promenade Building, Gunwharf Quays, Portsmouth, Hampshire PO1 3TR
**US SIC:** 3421 **UK SIC:** 31621
**Auditors:** Unknown
**Bankers:** HSBC Bank plc (40-06-17)

| | 31-12-13 | 31-12-12 | 31-12-11 |
|---|---|---|---|
| TO | 16,543,000 | 15,655,000 | 15,426,000 |
| P/L | (509,000) | (847,000) | 51,000 |
| NW | (211,000) | 298,000 | 1,215,000 |
| WC | (922,000) | (402,000) | 727,000 |
| Emp. | 235 | 261 | 236 |

DUNS 50-528-1097
## Villiers Hotels Ltd
**(Subsidiary of:** Gw 1244 Ltd)
3 Castle Street, Buckingham, Buckinghamshire MK18 1BS
**Tel:** 01280-822444 **Fax:** 01280-822113
**Web:** www.villiershotels.com
**Reg No:** 2486128 **VAT No:** 581229635
**Estd:** 1990 Private Limited Company
**Line of Business:** Hotels
**Issued Capital:** £4,300,004
**Director:** N R Oddy
**Co. Secretary:** Mrs Susan Oddy
**US SIC:** 7011, 6531
**UK SIC:** 66500, 83400
**Auditors:** Grasso Parker Green
**Bankers:** Investec Bank (uk) Ltd (08-60-68)

| | 31-03-14 | 31-03-13 | 31-03-12 |
|---|---|---|---|
| TA | 4,464,468 | 4,314,541 | 4,157,686 |
| NW | 4,464,468 | 4,314,541 | 4,157,686 |

DUNS 21-733-5140 Imp-Exp
## Vilmorin 2014 (Holdings) Ltd
**(Subsidiary of:** Limagrain Clermont Limagne)
Woodview Road, Paignton, Devon TQ4 7NG
**Tel:** 08702200606 **Fax:** 01803696333
**Web:** www.suttons-seeds.co.uk
**Reg No:** 1341694 **Estd:** 1806 Private Limited Company
**Line of Business:** Management activities of holding companies
**Export Markets:** W Europe, Republic of Ireland, U S A, Canada, Australia & Russia
**Export Sales:** £707,861
**Trading Style:** Suttons Consumer Products Limited
**Issued Capital:** £500,000
**Directors:** J Foucault, S Vidal, M Delsuc, J Petoton, F Heyraud, E Goujon, J Juilliard, B Bejar
**Responsibilities**
**HR:** Dawn Sylvester *(HR Manager)*
**US SIC:** 6711 **UK SIC:** 83962
**Auditors:** KPMG

**Bankers:** National Westminster Bank Plc (55-70-01)

| | 30-06-13 | 30-06-12 | 30-06-11 |
|---|---|---|---|
| TO | 15,037,477 | 16,516,567 | 19,263,057 |
| P/L | (1,520,242) | (1,189,564) | (981,613) |
| NW | (2,519,014) | (1,044,677) | 976,209 |
| WC | (2,207,853) | (349,974) | 857,761 |
| Emp. | 181 | 195 | 204 |

DUNS 21-292-7601
## Vincaffe
11 Multrees Walk, Edinburgh, Midlothian EH1 3DQ
**Tel:** 0131-557-0088
**Web:** www.valvonacrolla.com
**Estd:** 2004 Proprietorship
**Line of Business:** Restaurant - italian
**Proprietor:** Ms F Contini
**Responsibilities**
**Operations:** Tracey Gardener *(Operations Manager)*
**US SIC:** 5812 **UK SIC:** 66110
**Employees:** 76

DUNS 21-639-2407 Imp
## Vincent Davies & Son Ltd
Fishguard Road, Haverfordwest, Dyfed SA62 4BT
**Tel:** 01437-768014
**Web:** www.vincentdavies.co.uk
**Reg No:** 0594706 **Estd:** 1905 Private Limited Company
**Line of Business:** Furniture retail outlets
**Trading Style:** Vincent Davies & Son Ltd
**Issued Capital:** £13,990
**Principals:** Mrs B L Vincent-Davies *(Managing)*, Mrs S John, G John, Dr S Vincent-Davies
**Co. Secretary:** Mrs Lindsey Hughes
**Responsibilities**
**Senior:** Lindsay hughes *(Joint Managing Director)*, sarah john *(Joint Managing Director)*
**Finance:** Lindsay hughes *(Joint Managing Director)*
**Marketing:** sarah john *(Joint Managing Director)*
**Sales:** sarah john *(Joint Managing Director)*
**Admin:** J Ridge *(Office Manager)*
**HR:** Lindsay hughes *(Joint Managing Director)*
**Purchasing:** Lindsay hughes *(Joint Managing Director)*
**Branches:** Vincent Davies & Son Ltd, Fishguard Road, Haverfordwest, Dyfed SA62 4BT
**US SIC:** 5719 **UK SIC:** 64700
**Auditors:** Ashmole & Co

| | 27-01-14 | 28-01-13 | 02-01-12 |
|---|---|---|---|
| TO | 5,888,196 | 5,974,509 | 5,564,024 |
| P/L | 814,736 | 840,667 | 534,890 |
| NW | 4,806,893 | 4,440,814 | 4,064,953 |
| WC | 1,446,697 | 1,037,643 | 939,804 |
| Emp. | 102 | 101 | 101 |

DUNS 29-007-0408 Imp
## Vincent Timber Ltd
**(Subsidiary of:** W.J.Vincent Group Ltd)
8 Montgomery Street, Birmingham, West Midlands B11 1DU
**Tel:** 0121-772-5511
**Web:** www.vincenttimber.co.uk
**Reg No:** 0107182 **Estd:** 1910 Private Limited Company
**Line of Business:** Timber merchants
**Issued Capital:** £870,000
**Principals:** J E Vincent *(Chairman)*, A M Allen
**Co. Secretary:** Nicholas Crespi
**Responsibilities**
**Senior:** Geoffrey Willetts *(Manager)*
**Branches:** Vincent Timber Ltd, 8 Montgomery Street, Birmingham, West Midlands B11 1DU
**US SIC:** 5072 **UK SIC:** 61500
**Auditors:** UHY Hacker Young (Birmingham) LLP
**Bankers:** HSBC Bank plc (40-11-18)

| | 30-09-14 | 30-09-13 | 31-09-13 |
|---|---|---|---|
| TO | 11,174,135 | 5,669,463 | 9,096,730 |
| P/L | 198,919 | 51,446 | (945,352) |
| NW | 1,848,138 | 1,714,361 | 1,666,160 |
| WC | 1,538,002 | 1,379,269 | 1,301,153 |
| Emp. | 49 | 48 | 51 |

DUNS 50-342-7577
## Vinci Park Services Uk Ltd.
**(Subsidiary of:** Vinci Park)
Oak House, Reeds Crescent, Watford, Hertfordshire WD24 4QP
**Tel:** 01908223500 **Fax:** 020-7481-1308
**Web:** www.vincipark.co.uk
**Reg No:** 2362957 **VAT No:** 653551731
**Estd:** 1989 Private Limited Company
**Line of Business:** Other storage and warehousing not elsewhere classified
**Issued Capital:** £1,500,000
**Directors:** G C Pickard, P D Herring, W D Thierry
**Co. Secretary:** Gary Pickard
**Responsibilities**
**Senior:** Jheanell Muir *(Manager)*
**HR:** Debbie Hays *(Human Resources Director)*
**Health & Safety:** Alan Woodison *(Health & Safety Officer)*
**Facilities:** Claire Bacon *(Purchasing Manager)*
**Purchasing:** Claire Bacon *(Purchasing Manager)*
**Branches:** Vinci Park Services Uk Ltd., Skillion Business Centre, Green La, Gateshead, Tyne and Wear NE10 0QH
**US SIC:** 4226 **UK SIC:** 77003
**Auditors:** KPMG LLP
**Bankers:** National Westminster Bank Plc (56-00-33)

| | 31-12-13 | 31-12-12 | 31-12-11 |
|---|---|---|---|
| TO | 18,373,963 | 16,900,189 | 15,980,969 |
| P/L | 1,417,499 | (1,941,279) | 619,866 |
| NW | 3,668,994 | (386,788) | 1,735,004 |
| WC | (977,512) | (5,044,359) | (4,835,291) |
| Emp. | 948 | 626 | 593 |

DUNS 21-221-3854 Imp
## Vinci Plc
**(Subsidiary of:** Vinci)
Astral House, Imperial Way, Watford, Hertfordshire WD24 4WW
**Tel:** 01923233433
**Web:** www.taylorwoodrowinternational.com
**Reg No:** 0737204 **Estd:** 1962 Public Limited Company
**Line of Business:** Management activities of holding companies
**Trading Style:** Vinci Plc, Norwest Holst Engineering
**Issued Capital:** £18,956,000
**Directors:** F Ravery, R M Franciolí, J P Bonnet, B M Dupety, D W Bowler
**Co. Secretary:** Ms Ruth Tilbrook
**Responsibilities**
**Senior:** Jean Rossi *(Director)*, Paul Tuplin *(Manager)*
**HR:** Colin Jellicoe *(Human Resources Director)*
**Branches:** Vinci Plc, Unit 2, Charles Edward Road, Birmingham, West Midlands B26 1BU
**US SIC:** 6711, 1522
**UK SIC:** 83962, 50100
**Auditors:** KPMG LLP
**Bankers:** National Westminster Bank Plc (56-00-03)
**Following financial data are in thousands**

| | 31-12-13 | 31-12-12 | 31-12-11 |
|---|---|---|---|
| TO | 1,255,276 | 1,106,717 | 1,112,694 |
| P/L | 7,149 | 15,327 | 19,812 |
| NW | (54,586) | (21,268) | (32,414) |
| WC | (91,914) | (81,045) | (87,377) |
| Emp. | 3,764 | 4,061 | 4,006 |

DUNS 22-646-8254
## Vindis Group Ltd
4 Washingley Road, Huntingdon, Cambridgeshire PE29 6WP
**Tel:** 01480367182
**Web:** www.vindisgroup.com
**Reg No:** 1879045 **Estd:** 1960 Private Limited Company
**Line of Business:** Car dealers (new & used)
**Issued Capital:** £28,100
**Principals:** G F Vindis *(Managing)*, J F Vindis, Miss T M Vindis
**Co. Secretary:** Stephen Fossey
**Responsibilities**
**Senior:** Jason Packer *(Branch Manager)*, Nigel Vindis *(Manager)*
**Facilities:** Jason Packer *(Branch Manager)*
**Branches:** Vindis Group Ltd, Buckingway Business Park, Rowles Way, Swavesey, Cambridge, Cambridgeshire CB24 4UG
**US SIC:** 5511, 5521, 7539, 5531
**UK SIC:** 65100, 67100
**Auditors:** Peters Elworthy & Moore
**Bankers:** Barclays Bank Plc (20-05-74)

| | 31-12-13 | 31-12-12 | 31-12-11 |
|---|---|---|---|
| TO | 317,882,288 | 287,688,833 | 250,321,643 |
| P/L | 3,520,081 | 1,299,234 | 2,306,418 |
| NW | 11,675,002 | 9,438,445 | 9,263,373 |
| WC | (1,078,537) | (215,586) | 3,109,374 |
| Emp. | 725 | 724 | 700 |

DUNS 28-861-1833
## Vinehall School Ltd
Vinehall Road, Mountfield, Robertsbridge, East Sussex TN32 5JL
**Tel:** 01580880413
**Web:** www.vinehallschool.com
**Reg No:** 0893985 **Estd:** 1966 Private Company Limited By Guarantee
**Line of Business:** Schools (independent)
**Directors:** Mrs H P Kremer, Mrs E A Goodman, P S Redstone, Dr P C Rice Oxley, Ms A J Monro, J M Gilbert, Mrs V E Everett, J M Gordon
**Co. Secretary:** Miss Yvonne Hopkins
**Responsibilities**
**Senior:** Richard Follett *(Headmaster)*, Charles Foster-Kemp *(Director)*, Moira Gammell *(Manager)*, Deanne Thomas *(Director)*
**Finance:** Mike Lewis *(Financial Manager)*

**Purchasing:** Mike Lewis (*Financial Manager*)
**US SIC:** 8211 **UK SIC:** 93200
**Auditors:** Gibbons & Mannington
**Bankers:** National Westminster Bank Plc (60-10-15)

|      | 31-08-14  | 31-08-13  | 31-08-12  |
|------|-----------|-----------|-----------|
| TO   | 4,132,872 | 3,945,400 | 3,871,577 |
| P/L  | 324,461   | 154,017   | 144,438   |
| NW   | 5,162,770 | 4,838,309 | 4,684,291 |
| WC   | 1,606,190 | 1,510,067 | 1,199,884 |
| Emp. | 71        | 72        | 71        |

DUNS 28-997-1400
## Vines Ltd
(**Subsidiary of:** Guildford Portfolios Ltd)
Stephenson Way, Three Bridges, Crawley, West Sussex RH10 1TN
**Tel:** 01293575557 **Fax:** 01293-575500
**Web:** www.vinesgatwickmini.co.uk
**Reg No:** 1849408 **VAT No:** 602611587
**Estd:** 1986 Private Limited Company
**Line of Business:** Car dealers (new & used)
**Trading Style:** Vines of Redhill, Vines of Crawley, Vines of Gatwick
**Issued Capital:** £50,000
**Directors:** B G Moynahan, L Shelly, S P Kelly
**Co. Secretary:** Sean Kelly
**Responsibilities**
**Senior:** Giles Gair (*Principal*), Bob Morris (*Parts Manager*)
**IT:** Rick Penny (*IT Manager*)
**HR:** Sue White (*Human Resources Manager*)
**Purchasing:** Ivan Bell (*Used Car Sales Manager*)
**Branches:** Subject has 2 branches
**US SIC:** 5511 **UK SIC:** 65100
**Auditors:** Deloitte & Touche LLP
**Bankers:** Lloyds TSB Bank plc (30-98-41)

|      | 31-12-13    | 31-12-12    | 31-12-11   |
|------|-------------|-------------|------------|
| TO   | 131,149,061 | 81,704,054  | 84,409,524 |
| P/L  | 1,567,091   | 415,780     | (837,902)  |
| NW   | 338,748     | (1,413,442) | (2,140,133)|
| WC   | (3,493,995) | (2,671,010) | (72,806)   |
| Emp. | 296         | 166         | 167        |

DUNS 21-681-0440
## Vines Model Dairies Ltd
(**Subsidiary of:** Bwp (Cambridge) Ltd)
77-107 Empress Road, Southampton, Hampshire SO14 0YT
**Tel:** 02380221428
**Reg No:** 0550590 **Estd:** 1938 Private Limited Company
**Line of Business:** Eggs and dairy product processors and distributors.
**Issued Capital:** £131,500
**Director:** G J Bishop
**Co. Secretary:** Michael Mitchell
**US SIC:** 0241, 2021
**UK SIC:** 01001, 41302
**Auditors:** Grant Thornton
**Bankers:** HSBC Bank plc (40-42-19)

|    | 31-03-13 | 31-03-12 | 31-03-11 |
|----|----------|----------|----------|
| TA | 131,500  | 131,500  | 131,500  |
| NW | 131,500  | 131,500  | 131,500  |

DUNS 21-749-3910　　Imp
## Vinnolit Hillhouse Ltd
(**Subsidiary of:** Westlake International Holdings Coöperatief U.A.)
Hillhouse International Business Park, Thornton-Cleveleys, Lancashire FY5 4QD
**Tel:** 01253898900
**Web:** www.vinnolit.de
**Reg No:** 6149490 **VAT No:** 917346220
**Estd:** 2007 Private Limited Company
**Line of Business:** Manufacture of other plastic products
**Issued Capital:** £1
**Director:** Dr J Ertl
**Co. Secretary:** Dr Ralph Ottlinger
**Responsibilities**
**Senior:** Dave Boscott (*Site Manager*)
**US SIC:** 3079 **UK SIC:** 48360
**Auditors:** Deloitte LLP

|      | 31-12-13   | 31-12-12   | 31-12-11   |
|------|------------|------------|------------|
| TO   | 32,607,000 | 34,861,000 | 33,730,000 |
| P/L  | 574,000    | 594,000    | 577,000    |
| NW   | 11,469,000 | 10,971,000 | 10,497,000 |
| WC   | 2,835,000  | 3,136,000  | 2,804,000  |
| Emp. | 58         | 58         | 59         |

DUNS 50-380-1649
## Vinshire Plumbing & Heating Ltd
Sinfin Central Business Park, Sinfin Lane, Derby, Derbyshire DE24 9HL
**Tel:** 01332769611 **Fax:** 01332-768865
**Web:** www.vinshire.com
**Reg No:** 2389216 **Estd:** 1989 Private Limited Company
**Line of Business:** Plumbers
**Issued Capital:** £100
**Director:** N J Burdell
**Co. Secretary:** Nicholas Clark
**US SIC:** 1711 **UK SIC:** 50300
**Auditors:** Sibbald & Co

---

**Bankers:** The Royal Bank Of Scotland Plc (16-18-18)

|      | 30-04-14  | 31-10-12  | 31-04-11  |
|------|-----------|-----------|-----------|
| TO   | 17,665,940| 8,377,714 | 7,450,088 |
| P/L  | (73,930)  | 41,304    | 485,481   |
| NW   | 85,027    | 148,441   | 261,636   |
| WC   | (135,989) | 32,838    | 295,208   |
| Emp. | 113       | 73        | 56        |

DUNS 34-840-5130
## Vinspired
Dean Bradley House, Horseferry Road, London SW1P 2AF
**Tel:** 02079607000
**Web:** www.vinspired.com
**Reg No:** 5639682 **Estd:** 2009 Private Company Limited By Guarantee
**Line of Business:** Other business activities not elsewhere classified
**Directors:** Miss L Kerrigan, Miss F Adegbeyeni, R J Levy, D J Harris, Miss J M Watson, D S Frost, J M Taylor
**Co. Secretary:** John Taylor
**Responsibilities**
**Senior:** Terry Ryall (*Chief Executive*), Moira Swimbeak (*Ceo*), Moira Swinbank (*Chief Executive*)
**US SIC:** 7399 **UK SIC:** 83954
**Bankers:** The Co-Operative Bank Plc (08-01-00)

|      | 31-03-14   | 31-03-13   | 31-03-12   |
|------|------------|------------|------------|
| TO   | 7,305,000  | 6,700,000  | 5,322,000  |
| P/L  | (2,530,000)| 209,000    | (3,623,000)|
| NW   | 10,595,000 | 13,125,000 | 12,916,000 |
| WC   | 2,066,000  | 2,715,000  | 2,153,000  |
| Emp. | 71         | 52         | 46         |

DUNS 23-814-0359
## Vintage Financial Ltd
(**Subsidiary of:** Vintage Group Ltd)
Fairchild House, Redbourne Avenue, London N3 2BP
**Tel:** 02083713111
**Web:** www.vintagefinancial.co.uk
**Reg No:** 3806321 **Estd:** 2005 Private Limited Company
**Line of Business:** Financial intermediation not elsewhere classified
**Issued Capital:** £50,000
**Directors:** G D Hartnell, R A Stein
**Branches:** Vintage Financial Ltd, Aztec Financial, Bushey, Hertfordshire WD23 2QJ
**US SIC:** 6111, 6411
**UK SIC:** 81501, 83200
**Auditors:** Leigh & Co

|    | 30-04-14 | 30-04-13 | 30-04-12 |
|----|----------|----------|----------|
| TA | 923,539  | 788,943  | 516,675  |
| NW | 91,958   | 109,365  | 51,852   |
| WC | 37,435   | 56,123   | 2,569    |

DUNS 21-413-7708
## Vintage Inn
West Clyde Street, Helensburgh, Dunbartonshire G84 8ER
**Tel:** 08451126005
**Partnership**
**Line of Business:** Public house
**Partners:** R Kaye, R Patterson
**US SIC:** 5813 **UK SIC:** 66200
**Employees:** 50

DUNS 21-156-1307
## Vintage Services Uk Ltd
174 Brick Lane, London E1 6RU
**Tel:** 020-7247-7779 **Fax:** 02072477779
**Web:** www.vintagecabs.co.uk
**Reg No:** 6840729 **Estd:** 2009 Private Limited Company
**Line of Business:** Taxis and private hire vehicles
**Issued Capital:** £1
**Co. Secretary:** Sharaq Shiraz
**Responsibilities**
**Senior:** Sharaq Haque (*Proprietor*)
**US SIC:** 4121 **UK SIC:** 72200

|    | 31-03-14 | 31-03-13 | 31-03-12 |
|----|----------|----------|----------|
| TA | 8,113    | 10,421   | 5,608    |
| NW | 311      | 269      | 138      |
| WC | (2,802)  | (3,622)  | (4,726)  |

DUNS 23-518-1125
## Vinters Ltd
(**Subsidiary of:** Rolls-Royce Holdings Plc)
Moor Lane, Derby, Derbyshire DE24 8BJ
**Tel:** 02380019490
**Web:** www.venturephotography.com
**Reg No:** 3517200 **Estd:** 1867 Private Limited Company
**Line of Business:** Management activities of holding companies
**Issued Capital:** £57,957,382
**Directors:** R C Orgill, W S Mansfield
**Co. Secretary:** Mrs Delrose Goma
**US SIC:** 6711, 3489
**UK SIC:** 83962, 32901
**Auditors:** KPMG Audit PLC

---

**Bankers:** Lloyds TSB Bank plc (30-00-48)

|      | 31-12-13    | 31-12-12    | 31-12-11    |
|------|-------------|-------------|-------------|
| TA   | 330,812,000 | 330,812,000 | 330,812,000 |
| P/L  | N/A         | 80,000,000  | N/A         |
| NW   | 330,802,000 | 330,802,000 | 330,802,000 |
| Emp. | N/A         | 3           | N/A         |

DUNS 21-585-5605
## Vintners Place
68 Upper Thames Street, London EC4V 3BJ
**Tel:** 02073298410
**Web:** www.vintnershall.co.uk
**Estd:** 1901
**Line of Business:** Business and commerce centres
**Proprietor:** Ms L Rose
**Responsibilities**
**Senior:** Michael Amusu (*Manager*)
**US SIC:** 7392 **UK SIC:** 83951
**Employees:** 3,000

DUNS 21-013-5881　　　　　　　　Imp
## Vinyl Compounds Ltd
Stephanie Works, Chinley, High Peak, Derbyshire SK23 6BT
**Tel:** 01663750221 **Fax:** 01663750912
**Web:** www.vinylcompounds.co.uk
**Reg No:** 6364573 **VAT No:** 914726324
**Estd:** 2007 Private Limited Company
**Line of Business:** Manufacture of other plastic products
**Export Sales:** £5,430,365
**Trading Style:** Vinyl Compounds Ltd
**Issued Capital:** £1,660,000
**Directors:** M D Makin, C M Makin, P Goodinson, A K Beswick, R M Loynes
**US SIC:** 3079 **UK SIC:** 48360
**Auditors:** PKF (UK) LLP
**Bankers:** HSBC Bank plc (40-45-24)

|      | 31-01-14   | 31-01-13   | 31-01-12   |
|------|------------|------------|------------|
| TO   | 20,720,631 | 19,748,062 | 20,246,829 |
| P/L  | 894,266    | 616,773    | 577,071    |
| NW   | 4,434,379  | 3,641,479  | 3,047,718  |
| WC   | 2,732,761  | 2,545,206  | 1,858,835  |
| Emp. | 65         | 61         | 57         |

DUNS 29-063-7693
## Vinyl Graphics Ltd
268 Elgar Road South, Reading, Berkshire RG2 0BT
**Tel:** 01189-221300
**Web:** www.vgl.co.uk
**Reg No:** 1229842 **Estd:** 1975 Private Limited Company
**Line of Business:** Printing not elsewhere classified
**Trading Style:** Vgl
**Issued Capital:** £17,500
**Principals:** E J Ayerst (*Chairman*), M J Ayerst (*Managing*), S D Ayerst (*Sales*), M Elen, R Dadd
**Co. Secretary:** Ms Gillian Makepeace
**Responsibilities**
**Senior:** Mark Ellen (*Production Manager*)
**Finance:** Gillian Ayerst (*Accounts Manager*)
**HR:** Gillian Ayerst (*Accounts Manager*)
**Operations:** Mark Ellen (*Production Manager*)
**Engineering:** Mark Ellen (*Production Manager*)
**Branches:** Vinyl Graphics Ltd, Unit 3-5, Tessa Rd, Reading, Berkshire RG1 8HH
**US SIC:** 2752 **UK SIC:** 47544
**Auditors:** Thickbroom Coventry
**Bankers:** National Westminster Bank Plc (60-13-35)

|      | 31-12-13   | 31-12-12   | 31-12-11   |
|------|------------|------------|------------|
| TO   | 12,004,578 | 13,049,261 | 10,770,744 |
| P/L  | 184,389    | 323,040    | 262,072    |
| NW   | 2,470,989  | 2,406,765  | 2,337,434  |
| WC   | 488,565    | 207,123    | 385,199    |
| Emp. | 97         | 94         | 88         |

DUNS 21-962-7911
## Violets Homecare Services Ltd
Chiltern House, 81 High Street North, Dunstable, Bedfordshire LU6 1JJ
**Tel:** 01582-476044
**Web:** www.violetshomecare.co.uk
**Reg No:** 6144504 **Estd:** 2007 Private Limited Company
**Line of Business:** Other human health activities
**Issued Capital:** £2
**Directors:** A E Noon, Mrs R E Terrey
**Co. Secretary:** Alex Noon
**Responsibilities**
**Senior:** Stephen Terrey (*Manager*)
**US SIC:** 8091 **UK SIC:** 95200

|    | 31-03-14 | 31-03-13 | 31-03-12 |
|----|----------|----------|----------|
| TA | 178,581  | 188,893  | 163,288  |
| NW | 54,728   | (46,731) | (82,032) |
| WC | 52,867   | 30,233   | (83,631) |

---

DUNS 23-637-6740
## Violia Media Services Ltd
Unit 160 Milton Park, Abingdon, Oxfordshire OX14 4SD
**Tel:** 01235465500
**Reg No:** 3634495 **Estd:** 1998 Private Limited Company
**Line of Business:** Graphic designers
**Issued Capital:** £2
**Director:** P J Holloran
**Co. Secretary:** Ross Clayton
**Branches:** Violia Media Services Ltd, 11F Milton Park, Abingdon, Oxfordshire OX14 4RS
**US SIC:** 5199 **UK SIC:** 61900
**Auditors:** Ernst & Young
**Bankers:** Barclays Bank Plc (20-52-74)

|      | 31-12-13  | 31-12-12  | 31-12-11  |
|------|-----------|-----------|-----------|
| TO   | 8,751,731 | 8,782,652 | 9,404,976 |
| P/L  | (144,215) | 44,148    | 713,795   |
| NW   | 3,458,310 | 3,916,242 | 4,222,050 |
| WC   | 2,606,989 | 3,036,441 | 3,549,454 |
| Emp. | 139       | 146       | 150       |

DUNS 21-582-4980
## Vion Halifax
Unit 10 Billet Lane, Scunthorpe, South Humberside DN15 9YH
**Tel:** 01724274000
**Web:** www.vionfood.co.uk
**Estd:** 2011 Partnership
**Line of Business:** Manufacturers of food products
**Trading Style:** Visionary Foods
**Partners:** Mrs B Walton, G Dobson
**Responsibilities**
**Senior:** John Tynan (*Manager*)
**Finance:** Julian Barrett (*Chief Financial Officer - Poul*)
**HR:** Chris Lonnegan (*HR Manager*)
**US SIC:** 2099 **UK SIC:** 42399
**Employees:** 500

DUNS 21-400-2099　　　　　　　　Exp
## Vion Subco Md Ltd
(**Subsidiary of:** Stichting Administratiekantoor Sbt)
Meat Factory, Cookston Road, Portlethen, Aberdeen, Aberdeenshire AB12 4QB
**Tel:** 01224-780381 **Fax:** 01224-782039
**Web:** www.mcintoshdonald.com
**Reg No:** 0030556SC **Estd:** 1955 Private Limited Company
**Line of Business:** Meat wholesalers
**Export Markets:** Europe
**Issued Capital:** £1,978,570
**Director:** L B Abbitt
**Co. Secretary:** Tmf Corporate Administration Ser
**Responsibilities**
**Senior:** Anthony Christiaanse (*Manager*), Mark Steven (*Manager*)
**Sales:** Frank Clark (*Senior Sales Executive*)
**US SIC:** 5147, 2013
**UK SIC:** 61700, 41223
**Auditors:** BDO LLP
**Bankers:** Bank Of Scotland (80-05-14)

|     | 31-12-13   | 31-12-12   | 31-12-11   |
|-----|------------|------------|------------|
| TA  | 16,404,000 | 15,983,000 | 15,541,000 |
| P/L | 421,000    | 441,000    | N/A        |
| NW  | 16,404,000 | 15,983,000 | 15,541,000 |

DUNS 77-894-3688
## Vip Communications (Hull) Ltd
Kennett Building, Hessle, North Humberside HU13 9PD
**Tel:** 01482445665 **Fax:** 01482 330535
**Web:** www.vipcommunications.co.uk
**Reg No:** 3040649 **VAT No:** 647368111
**Estd:** 1995 Private Limited Company
**Line of Business:** Mobile phone suppliers
**Trading Style:** Vip Communications Limited
**Issued Capital:** £100
**Directors:** Mrs C L Lee, J P Wood, I Stainthorp
**Co. Secretary:** Ms Elaine Hubert
**Responsibilities**
**Finance:** Brian Goodrick (*Head and HR and Accounts*)
**HR:** Brian Goodrick (*Head and HR and Accounts*)
**Branches:** Vip Communications (Hull) Ltd, 502 Beverley Road, Hull, North Humberside HU5 1NA
**US SIC:** 5999 **UK SIC:** 65600
**Auditors:** CBA (Accountants) Ltd
**Bankers:** HSBC Bank plc (40-24-34)

|    | 31-12-13 | 31-12-12 | 31-12-11 |
|----|----------|----------|----------|
| TA | 154,800  | 127,246  | 157,030  |
| NW | 23,418   | 22,937   | 19,314   |
| WC | 17,405   | 14,985   | 8,142    |

DUNS 76-374-7425 **Imp-Exp**

### V.I.P. Computer Centre Ltd

Unit 4 Hardwick Grange, Warrington, Cheshire WA1 4RF
**Tel:** 08716227568 **Fax:** 08716227560
**Web:** www.vip-computers.co.uk
**Reg No:** 2552402 **VAT No:** 560305964
**Estd:** 1990 Private Limited Company
**Line of Business:** Wholesale of computers, computer peripheral equipment and software
**Export Markets:** U S A; Dubai; Kuwait
**Export Sales:** £108,844,000
**Issued Capital:** £37,500
**Principals:** J S Sahni *(Managing)*, Mrs A K Sahni, M A Taylor, D J Mcauley, R S Marsden
**Co. Secretary:** Jitenderpal Sahni
**Responsibilities**
**Senior:** Lee Gordon *(Business Manager)*
**Marketing:** Jason D'Cruz *(Marketing Manager)*, Joanne Meredith *(Marketing Manager)*
**HR:** Lynn Barlow *(Group Human Resources Administ)*, Doreen Williams *(Human Resources Administrator)*
**US SIC:** 5081 **UK SIC:** 61490
**Auditors:** Duncan Sheard Glass
**Bankers:** Barclays Bank Plc (20-54-58)

| | 30-06-14 | 30-06-13 | 30-06-12 |
|---|---|---|---|
| TO | 227,005,000 | 204,659,000 | 180,127,000 |
| P/L | 1,447,000 | 1,849,000 | 1,746,000 |
| NW | 13,157,000 | 14,458,000 | 13,759,000 |
| WC | 9,610,000 | 11,279,000 | 10,888,000 |
| Emp. | 264 | 214 | 215 |

DUNS 22-238-2488 **Imp-Exp**

### Vip-Polymers Ltd

St Peters Road, Huntingdon, Cambridgeshire PE29 7DA
**Tel:** 01480-411333
**Web:** www.vip-polymers.com
**Reg No:** 4256307 **VAT No:** 785828959
**Estd:** 2010 Private Limited Company
**Line of Business:** Manufacturers of seals
**Export Sales:** £5,386,786
**Issued Capital:** £100,000
**Principals:** J S Millar *(Managing)*, G Mc Cullum *(Financial)*, S T Casey, T Middleton, L R Litwinowicz
**Co. Secretary:** Glenn Mccullum
**Responsibilities**
**Senior:** Nick Lucken *(Warehouse Manager)*
**HR:** Michele Chopping *(Personnel Manager)*
**Operations:** Michele Chopping *(Personnel Manager)*
**US SIC:** 3559 **UK SIC:** 32863
**Auditors:** MacIntyre Hudson LLP
**Bankers:** Barclays Bank Plc (20-07-71)

| | 31-03-14 | 31-03-13 | 31-03-12 |
|---|---|---|---|
| TO | 12,431,882 | 9,912,961 | 11,723,892 |
| P/L | 166,834 | (453,679) | (261,733) |
| NW | 2,351,042 | 2,184,208 | 2,531,343 |
| WC | 1,275,281 | 1,225,066 | 1,374,807 |
| Emp. | 130 | 109 | 118 |

DUNS 22-908-9032 **Imp**

### Vipond Fire Protection Ltd

**(Subsidiary of:** Api Group Inc.)
10-12 Glenfield Road, Glasgow, Lanarkshire G75 0RA
**Tel:** 01355237588
**Web:** www.vipondfire.co.uk
**Reg No:** 0057058SC **VAT No:** 262326475
**Estd:** 1969 Private Limited Company
**Line of Business:** Other construction work involving special trades
**Issued Capital:** £784,736
**Directors:** L Anderson, J Mccann
**Co. Secretary:** William Beadie
**Responsibilities**
**Senior:** Gregory Keup *(Manager)*
**Sales:** Dave Nelson *(Sales Manager)*
**Facilities:** Scott Crawford *(Maintenance Manager)*
**Branches:** Vipond Fire Protection Ltd, Regus Ho, Fairbourne Dr, Atterbury, Milton Keynes, Buckinghamshire MK10 9RG
**US SIC:** 1799, 7393
**UK SIC:** 50000, 83954
**Auditors:** Campbell Dallas LLP
**Bankers:** The Royal Bank Of Scotland Plc (83-27-34)

| | 31-12-13 | 31-12-12 | 31-12-11 |
|---|---|---|---|
| TO | 8,178,580 | 8,928,728 | 8,790,929 |
| P/L | (165,532) | 300,667 | (116,294) |
| NW | 2,449,961 | 2,573,947 | 2,348,721 |
| WC | 2,007,325 | 2,114,121 | 1,935,786 |
| Emp. | 77 | 78 | 73 |

DUNS 21-915-6023 **Imp**

### Virani Food Products Ltd

10-14 Stewarts Road, Finedon Road Industrial Estate, Wellingborough, Northamptonshire NN8 4RJ
**Tel:** 01933-230500
**Web:** www.virani.com
**Reg No:** 1121605 **VAT No:** 121541613
**Estd:** 1973 Private Limited Company
**Line of Business:** Manufacturers of food products
**Issued Capital:** £750,000
**Directors:** T J Shah, M N Shah
**Co. Secretary:** Nareshbabu Shah
**US SIC:** 2099 **UK SIC:** 42399
**Auditors:** P S J Alexander & Co
**Bankers:** HSBC Bank plc (40-46-03)

| | 31-07-13 | 31-07-12 | 31-07-11 |
|---|---|---|---|
| TO | 10,194,655 | 10,373,434 | 9,549,294 |
| P/L | 251,800 | 578,853 | 370,847 |
| NW | 3,649,671 | 3,482,156 | 3,101,729 |
| WC | 1,425,229 | 1,245,883 | 1,079,854 |
| Emp. | 46 | 46 | 36 |

DUNS 28-873-0591 **Imp**

### Virbac Ltd

**(Subsidiary of:** Virbac Lid 2065 M)
Unit 16 Windmill Avenue Woolpit Business, Park, Bury St Edmunds, Suffolk IP30 9UP
**Tel:** 01359-243243 **Fax:** 01359-243200
**Web:** www.virbac.co.uk
**Reg No:** 1069800 **VAT No:** 445862818
**Estd:** 1972 Private Limited Company
**Line of Business:** Veterinary pharmacies
**Export Sales:** £3,265,022
**Issued Capital:** £2,000
**Directors:** D Ellerton, C Karst, E Maree, H Trentesaux
**Co. Secretary:** Kevin Barton
**US SIC:** 5122 **UK SIC:** 61800
**Auditors:** Gilbert Allen & Co
**Bankers:** National Westminster Bank Plc (60-04-41)

| | 31-12-13 | 31-12-12 | 31-12-11 |
|---|---|---|---|
| TO | 24,181,555 | 22,828,765 | 21,699,632 |
| P/L | 1,570,589 | 654,161 | 279,976 |
| NW | 3,524,562 | 2,855,633 | 2,881,662 |
| WC | 3,453,831 | 2,788,219 | 2,808,860 |
| Emp. | 50 | 51 | 50 |

DUNS 53-642-9905

### Virgin Active Ltd

**(Subsidiary of:** Virgin Group Holdings Limited)
The Water Gardens, College Square, Harlow, Essex CM20 1AJ
**Tel:** 01279634300
**Web:** www.virginactive.co.uk
**Reg No:** 3448441 **Estd:** 1997 Private Limited Company
**Line of Business:** Health clubs
**Issued Capital:** £621
**Directors:** P A Woolf, M P Burrows, M W Bucknall, M G Merrick
**Co. Secretary:** James Archibald
**Responsibilities**
**IT:** Phil Burnett *(IT Manager)*
**HR:** Carol Angel *(Humann Resources Manager)*
**Purchasing:** Louise Lane *(Procurement Officer)*
**Branches:** Virgin Active Limited, 1 Ferris Row, Northampton, Northamptonshire NN3 9HX
**US SIC:** 7299 **UK SIC:** 98902
**Auditors:** KPMG LLP

| | 31-12-13 | 31-12-12 | 31-12-11 |
|---|---|---|---|
| TO | 73,823,000 | 73,120,000 | 71,261,000 |
| P/L | 1,048,000 | (8,515,000) | 4,140,000 |
| NW | (141,716,000) | 91,363,000 | 91,655,000 |
| WC | (322,423,000) | 27,535,000 | 25,457,000 |
| Emp. | 2,045 | 2,013 | 2,001 |

DUNS 50-329-0462

### Virgin Active Management Ltd

**(Subsidiary of:** Virgin Group Holdings Limited)
26-28 Kensington High Street, London W8 4PF
**Tel:** 02077867300 **Fax:** 020-7376-3517
**Web:** www.virginactive.co.uk
**Reg No:** 2353684 **VAT No:** 340192977
**Estd:** 1991 Private Limited Company
**Line of Business:** Operation of sports arenas and stadiums
**Trading Style:** Virgin Active
**Issued Capital:** £100
**Directors:** R P Kay, I J Parkinson
**Responsibilities**
**Senior:** Ashley Aylmer *(Manager)*
**US SIC:** 7941, 7999
**UK SIC:** 97911, 97913
**Auditors:** KPMG LLP
**Bankers:** Barclays Bank Plc (20-35-90)

| | 31-12-13 | 31-12-12 | 31-12-11 |
|---|---|---|---|
| TO | 3,217,000 | 3,232,000 | 3,116,000 |
| P/L | 61,000 | (1,904,000) | 235,000 |
| NW | 2,402,000 | 2,353,000 | 3,643,000 |
| WC | 2,016,000 | 1,792,000 | 920,000 |
| Emp. | 175 | 175 | 177 |

DUNS 39-910-5659

### Virgin Airways Ltd

**(Subsidiary of:** Virgin Group Holdings Limited)
The Office, Manor Royal, Crawley, West Sussex RH10 9NU
**Tel:** 08448110000 **Fax:** 01293-561721
**Web:** www.virgin-atlantic.com
**Reg No:** 2235371 **Estd:** 1988 Private Limited Company
**Line of Business:** Airlines
**Trading Style:** Virgin Atlantic
**Issued Capital:** £100
**Directors:** S J Weiss, C S Kreeger
**Co. Secretary:** Ian De Sousa
**Responsibilities**
**Senior:** Stephen Ridgway *(Chief Executive Officer)*
**US SIC:** 4511 **UK SIC:** 75000

| | 31-12-13 | 28-02-13 | 29-12-12 |
|---|---|---|---|
| TA | 749,182 | 745,660 | 753,666 |
| P/L | N/A | N/A | (596,761) |
| NW | (2,325,591) | (2,329,113) | (2,321,107) |
| WC | (2,325,591) | (2,329,113) | (2,321,107) |

DUNS 23-554-1773

### Virgin Atlantic Two Ltd

**(Subsidiary of:** Virgin Group Holdings Limited)
The Office, Manor Royal, Crawley, West Sussex RH10 9NU
**Tel:** 01293562345
**Web:** www.virgin-atlantic.com
**Reg No:** 3552500 **Estd:** 1998 Private Limited Company
**Line of Business:** Management activities of holding companies
**Issued Capital:** £280,230
**Directors:** C S Kreeger, P M Norris, S Weiss, Sir R C Branson, W I Aaron, G D Mccallum, P A Cantarutti, G W Hauenstein
**Co. Secretary:** Ian De Sousa
**Responsibilities**
**Senior:** Hon Chan *(Baa Administration)*
**US SIC:** 6711, 4511
**UK SIC:** 83962, 75000
**Auditors:** KPMG LLP
**Following financial data are in thousands**

| | 31-12-13 | 28-02-13 | 29-12-12 |
|---|---|---|---|
| TO | 2,570,600 | 2,873,700 | 2,744,900 |
| P/L | (5,100) | (69,900) | (80,200) |
| NW | (15,200) | (7,500) | 27,900 |
| WC | (160,300) | (158,800) | (18,700) |
| Emp. | 9,529 | 9,666 | 9,301 |

DUNS 34-660-6671

### Virgin Care Ltd

**(Subsidiary of:** Virgin Group Holdings Limited)
The Brew House, Warrington, Cheshire WA4 6HL
**Tel:** 01925420660 **Fax:** 01925234503
**Web:** www.assuragroup.co.uk
**Reg No:** 5466033 **VAT No:** 918510332
**Estd:** 2005 Private Limited Company
**Line of Business:** Other letting of own property
**Issued Capital:** £53,805,821
**Directors:** E B Johnson, Dr V M Mcvey
**Responsibilities**
**Senior:** Andrew Darke *(Manager)*, Lianne Holland *(PA to Managing Director - Prop)*
**Facilities:** Simon Gould *(Property Development Manager)*, Amanda Horley *(Property Development Manager)*
**Branches:** Virgin Care Limited, 6400 Daresbury Park, Warrington, Cheshire WA4 4GE
**US SIC:** 6519, 8011
**UK SIC:** 85000, 95300
**Auditors:** KPMG LLP

| | 31-03-14 | 31-03-13 | 31-03-12 |
|---|---|---|---|
| TO | 38,001,986 | 1,166,056 | 1,407,478 |
| P/L | (9,897,041) | (10,933,837) | (9,947,094) |
| NW | (11,289,994) | (206,511) | 10,727,326 |
| WC | (16,371,832) | (4,174,332) | 8,180,094 |
| Emp. | 213 | 120 | 93 |

DUNS 21-728-5343

### Virgin Care Provider Services Ltd

**(Subsidiary of:** Virgin Group Holdings Limited)
Sterling Street, Fairley Medical Centre, Grimsby, South Humberside DN31 3AE
**Tel:** 03003301122
**Web:** www.sexualhealthnortheastlincs.co.uk
**Reg No:** 7645492 **Estd:** 2011 Private Limited Company
**Line of Business:** Medical practice activities
**Issued Capital:** £100
**Directors:** E B Johnson, Dr V M Mcvey
**Responsibilities**
**Senior:** Jill Ladlow *(Service Manager)*
**US SIC:** 8011 **UK SIC:** 95300

| | 31-03-14 | 31-03-13 | 31-03-12 |
|---|---|---|---|
| TO | 7,171,674 | 6,558,472 | N/A |
| P/L | 317,090 | (1,099,651) | (303,494) |
| NW | (1,085,955) | (1,403,045) | (303,394) |
| WC | (1,348,702) | (1,818,394) | (303,394) |
| Emp. | 48 | 11 | N/A |

DUNS 22-065-6008

### Virgin Holidays Cruises Ltd

**(Subsidiary of:** Virgin Group Holdings Limited)
The Office Manor Royal, Crawley, West Sussex RH10 9NU
**Tel:** 08445574321
**Reg No:** 4067240 **Estd:** 2000 Private Limited Company
**Line of Business:** Activities of travel agencies
**Issued Capital:** £50,000
**Directors:** S J Weiss, C S Kreeger
**Co. Secretary:** Ian De Sousa
**Branches:** Virgin Holidays Cruises Ltd, Neighbourhood Centre, High Down Way, Swindon, Wiltshire SN25 4FD
**US SIC:** 4722 **UK SIC:** 77001

| | 31-12-13 | 28-02-13 | 29-12-12 |
|---|---|---|---|
| TO | N/A | N/A | 5,861,000 |
| P/L | N/A | N/A | (624,000) |
| NW | 5,930,000 | 5,930,000 | 5,930,000 |
| Emp. | N/A | N/A | 167 |

DUNS 29-510-5449 **Exp**

### Virgin Holidays Ltd

**(Subsidiary of:** Virgin Group Holdings Limited)
The Galleria, Station Road, Crawley, West Sussex RH10 1WW
**Tel:** 08445575825 **Fax:** 01293536957
**Web:** www.virginholidays.com
**Reg No:** 1873815 **VAT No:** 492268813
**Estd:** 1984 Private Limited Company
**Line of Business:** Activities of travel organisers
**Trading Style:** Virgin Sun
**Issued Capital:** £2,456,774
**Directors:** P A Cantarutti, S Weiss, Sir R C Branson, G W Hauenstein, E H Bastian, G D Mccallum, W I Aaron, C S Kreeger
**Co. Secretary:** Ian De Sousa
**Responsibilities**
**Marketing:** Ed Grimsey *(Group CRM and Social Manager)*
**HR:** Terri Bailey *(Human Resources Manager)*
**Health & Safety:** Terri Bailey *(Human Resources Manager)*
**Branches:** Virgin Holidays Ltd, The Highcross Centre, 1st Floor, Leicester, Leicestershire LE1 4GH
**US SIC:** 4722 **UK SIC:** 77001
**Auditors:** KPMG LLP

| | 31-12-13 | 28-02-13 | 29-12-12 |
|---|---|---|---|
| TO | 467,323,000 | 509,256,000 | 506,765,000 |
| P/L | 2,777,000 | 507,000 | 3,193,000 |
| NW | 55,771,000 | 70,394,000 | 69,266,000 |
| WC | 30,389,000 | 46,433,000 | 47,115,000 |
| Emp. | 1,180 | 1,188 | 1,156 |

DUNS 22-711-8080 **Imp**

### Virgin Management Ltd

**(Subsidiary of:** Virgin Group Holdings Limited)
The School House, 50 Brook Green, London W6 7BJ
**Tel:** 020-7313-2000
**Web:** www.virgin.com
**Reg No:** 1568894 **Estd:** 1970 Private Limited Company
**Line of Business:** Representative office
**Issued Capital:** £15,948,322
**Directors:** N A Fox, R P Blok, I P Woods
**Co. Secretary:** Barry Gerrard
**Responsibilities**
**Senior:** Joshua Bayliss *(Manager)*, John Dealey *(Office Manager)*, Patrick McCall *(Manager)*
**Marketing:** Katherine Salway *(Group Brand Marketing Director)*
**Admin:** John Dealey *(Office Manager)*
**IT:** Wendy Naisby *(Computer Manager)*
**HR:** Angela Smith *(Personnel Director)*
**Health & Safety:** Angela Smith *(Personnel Director)*
**Facilities:** John Dealey *(Office Manager)*
**Operations:** Greg Brash *(Group Procurement Manager)*, Darrell Etherington *(Operations Director)*
**Purchasing:** Greg Brash *(Group Procurement Manager)*, John Dealey *(Office Manager)*
**Fleet:** Greg Brash *(Group Procurement Manager)*
**US SIC:** 7399, 4511
**UK SIC:** 83954, 75000
**Bankers:** Lloyds TSB Bank plc (30-12-18)
**Following financial data are in thousands**

| | 31-12-13 | 31-03-13 | 31-12-12 |
|---|---|---|---|
| TO | 16,592 | 20,990 | 7,204 |
| P/L | 49,006 | 41,498 | 21,584 |
| NW | 1,211,544 | 1,162,623 | 1,049,322 |
| WC | 1,204,733 | 1,159,848 | 1,043,747 |
| Emp. | 84 | 84 | 112 |

DUNS 21-592-5896

### Virgin Media

Fountain House, Fountain Lane, St Mellons, Cardiff, South Glamorgan CF3 0FB
**Web:** www.virginmedia.co.uk
**Estd:** 2011
**Line of Business:** Facsimile machines
**Proprietor:** Ms L Potts
**Responsibilities**
**Senior:** Rayner Carey *(F M C Manager)*, Lee Jones *(Manager)*
**US SIC:** 4899 **UK SIC:** 79020
**Employees:** 150

**DUNS 21-592-5957**

## Virgin Media

Siemens Way, Swansea Enterprise Park, Swansea, West Glamorgan SA7 9BB
**Tel:** 01792613800
**Web:** www.virginmedia.com
**Estd:** 2011
**Line of Business:** Telecom services
**US SIC:** 4899 **UK SIC:** 79020
**Employees:** 1,000

**DUNS 28-982-4328**                                          Exp

## Virgin Media Business Ltd

**(Subsidiary of:** The Depository Trust & Clearing Corporation)
Media House, Peterborough Business Park, Peterborough, Cambridgeshire PE2 6EA
**Tel:** 01733-230666 **Fax:** 01733-230909
**Web:** www.virginmediabusiness.co.uk
**Reg No:** 1785381 **Estd:** 1984 Private Limited Company
**Line of Business:** Television activities
**Export Markets:** Ireland
**Trading Style:** Telewest
**Issued Capital:** £1,000
**Directors:** R D Dunn, T Mockridge, M O Hifzi, Ms D M Strong
**Co. Secretary:** Ms Gillian James
**Responsibilities**
**Senior:** Robert Gale (Executive Director), Pat Megginson (IT Manager)
**IT:** Pat Megginson (IT Manager)
**Purchasing:** Karen Andrew (Head of Complex Order Manageme)
**Branches:** Virgin Media Business Ltd, Crawley Court, Winchester, Hampshire SO21 2QA
**US SIC:** 4833, 4899
**UK SIC:** 97411, 79020
**Auditors:** Ernst & Young LLP
**Bankers:** HSBC Bank plc (40-36-15)

|     | 31-12-13 | 31-12-12 | 31-12-11 |
|-----|----------|----------|----------|
| TO  | 155,652,000 | 145,616,000 | 133,575,000 |
| P/L | 1,789,000 | 13,188,000 | 17,133,000 |
| NW  | 198,209,000 | 196,845,000 | 182,748,000 |
| WC  | 133,042,000 | 142,694,000 | 145,034,000 |

**DUNS 76-691-6738**

## Virgin Media Ltd

**(Subsidiary of:** The Depository Trust & Clearing Corporation)
Spectrum House, Lloyds Court, Manor Royal, Crawley, West Sussex RH10 9QX
**Tel:** 01293400444
**Web:** www.virginmedia.com
**Reg No:** 2591237 **Estd:** 1998 Private Limited Company
**Line of Business:** Telecom services
**Issued Capital:** £1,087,734
**Directors:** T Mockridge, P J Kelly, M O Hifzi, Ms D M Strong, P A Buttery, R D Dunn
**Co. Secretary:** Ms Gillian James
**Branches:** Virgin Media Ltd, Unit 3 Power Industrial Estate, Slade Green Road, Erith, Kent DA8 2HU
**US SIC:** 4899, 7379
**UK SIC:** 79020, 83940
**Auditors:** Ernst & Young LLP
**Following financial data are in thousands**

|     | 31-12-13 | 31-12-12 | 31-12-11 |
|-----|----------|----------|----------|
| TO  | 466,967 | 449,499 | 400,110 |
| P/L | 1,911,396 | 168,908 | 198,759 |
| NW  | 4,110,822 | 2,320,310 | 1,530,549 |
| WC  | 1,898,715 | 837,541 | 188,566 |
| Emp. | 14,074 | 13,352 | 13,087 |

**DUNS 23-712-5344**

## Virgin Mobile Telecoms Ltd

**(Subsidiary of:** The Depository Trust & Clearing Corporation)
Media House, Bartley Wood Business Park, Hook, Hampshire RG27 9UP
**Tel:** 08445571748
**Web:** www.virginmobile.com
**Reg No:** 3707664 **VAT No:** 591819014
**Estd:** 1999 Private Limited Company
**Line of Business:** Telecom services
**Issued Capital:** £19,574
**Directors:** R D Dunn, Ms D M Strong, M O Hifzi, T Mockridge
**Co. Secretary:** Ms Gillian James
**Responsibilities**
**Senior:** Robert Gale (Manager), Joanne Tillbrook (Manager), Caroline Withers (Manager)
**Branches:** Virgin Mobile Telecoms Ltd, Communications House, 48 Leicester Square, London WC2H 7LT
**US SIC:** 4899 **UK SIC:** 79020
**Auditors:** Ernst & Young LLP

|     | 31-12-13 | 31-12-12 | 31-12-11 |
|-----|----------|----------|----------|
| TO  | 536,764,000 | 557,085,000 | 555,785,000 |
| P/L | 24,484,000 | 74,686,000 | 55,659,000 |
| NW  | 329,569,000 | 306,755,000 | 224,584,000 |
| WC  | 313,688,000 | 292,011,000 | 218,368,000 |

**DUNS 49-081-7673**

## Virgin Money Holdings (Uk) Plc

Jubilee House, Gosforth, Newcastle-Upon-Tyne, Tyne and Wear NE3 4PL
**Tel:** 01603-215715 **Fax:** 01603215700
**Web:** www.virginmoney.com
**Reg No:** 3087587 **Estd:** 1995 Public Limited Company
**Line of Business:** Management activities of holding companies
**Trading Style:** Virgin Money Management Services
**Issued Capital:** £40,577
**Directors:** N C Mcluskie, Mrs J Gadhia, Mrs O C Dickson, N C Mcluskie, Ms M H Spearing, L M Rochford, G D Mccallum, P C Mccall
**Co. Secretary:** Ms Katie Marshall
**Responsibilities**
**Senior:** James Lockhart Iii (Director)
**US SIC:** 6711, 6411
**UK SIC:** 83962, 83200
**Auditors:** KPMG LLP

|     | 31-12-13 | 31-12-12 | 31-12-11 |
|-----|----------|----------|----------|
| TO  | 878,900,000 | 778,700,000 | 140,073,000 |
| P/L | 179,400,000 | 150,600,000 | 23,548,000 |
| NW  | 894,400,000 | 720,000,000 | 516,354,000 |
| WC  | 775,100,000 | 811,600,000 | 500,002,000 |
| Emp. | 2,718 | 2,785 | 417 |

**DUNS 21-773-4620**

## Virgin Press Office

179 Harrow Road, London W2 6NB
**Tel:** 02072294738
**Web:** www.virgin.com
**Estd:** 2011 Proprietorship
**Line of Business:** Advertising agency services
**Proprietor:** R Branson
**Responsibilities**
**Senior:** Nick Fox (Manager)
**US SIC:** 7319 **UK SIC:** 83800
**Employees:** 80

**DUNS 37-974-9856**

## Virgin Rail Group Ltd

**(Subsidiary of:** Virgin Group Holdings Limited)
West Wing Offices, Euston Station, London NW1 2DS
**Tel:** 03331031031 **Fax:** 020-7320-0506
**Web:** www.virgintrains.co.uk
**Reg No:** 3282548 **Estd:** 1995 Private Limited Company
**Line of Business:** Transport via railways
**Issued Capital:** £10,026,531
**Directors:** P A Bearpark, G C Leech, P Whittingham
**Co. Secretary:** Barry Gerrard
**Responsibilities**
**Senior:** Tony Collins (Chief Executive Officer)
**Marketing:** Arthur Leathley (Director, Communications)
**Sales:** Penny Munn (Business Development Manager), Elaine Zekavica (Business Development Manager)
**Admin:** Andy Cross (Director, Business Support)
**Operations:** Jill Dyal (Project Manager), Natalie Flaxman (Operations and Safety Manager), Sarah Jeffrey (Project Manager), Malcolm John (Lead Project Manager)
**Fleet:** Andy Grundy (Fleet Delivery Manager), Paul Makepeace (Driver Depot Manager), Kieron Malone (Driver Depot Manager), Daniel Sutton (Driver Depot Manager), Nick Westcott (Driver Depot Manager)
**Engineering:** Hayley Farrar (Service Improvement Engineer), Gary Hambling (Head of Engineering), Greg Newport (Vehicle Engineer), Susan Nichol (Engineering Strategy Manager), Andy Webb (Engineer)
**Branches:** Virgin Rail Group Ltd, Ramada Encore N E C, N E C House, Birmingham, West Midlands B40 1PQ
**US SIC:** 4011 **UK SIC:** 71000
**Auditors:** KPMG LLP

|     | 31-03-14 | 31-03-13 | 05-03-11 |
|-----|----------|----------|----------|
| TA  | 26,465,000 | 28,859,000 | 32,572,000 |
| P/L | 10,945,000 | 42,486,000 | 29,600,000 |
| NW  | 25,001,000 | 26,034,000 | 23,756,000 |
| WC  | 20,885,000 | 21,918,000 | 19,640,000 |

**DUNS 73-620-1216**                                          Imp

## Virgin Strauss Water Uk Ltd

**(Subsidiary of:** Strauss Holdings Ltd)
Unit 3b Henley Business Park, Pirbright Road, Guildford, Surrey GU3 2DX
**Tel:** 08453017700
**Web:** www.virginpure.com
**Reg No:** 4880825 **Estd:** 2003 Private Limited Company
**Line of Business:** Water fresh coolers
**Trading Style:** Virgin Pure
**Issued Capital:** £3,015,184

**Directors:** G Lesin, G Zamir, R Ronen, Y Shirazi, C Everitt, J R Tipple
**Co. Secretary:** Gur Zamir
**Responsibilities**
**Senior:** Toby Coppel (Manager), Barbara Macleod (Manager), Ken Meek (Operations Director)
**Finance:** Alison McWilliams (Financial CO Ordinator)
**IT:** David Milanovic (Computer Manager)
**Purchasing:** Alison McWilliams (Financial CO Ordinator)
**US SIC:** 3559, 7394
**UK SIC:** 32863, 84000
**Auditors:** CMB Partnership
**Bankers:** HSBC Bank plc (40-05-30)

|     | 31-12-12 | 31-12-11 | 31-12-10 |
|-----|----------|----------|----------|
| TO  | 1,652,326 | 1,996,780 | 1,964,134 |
| P/L | (4,488,629) | (1,102,174) | 183,813 |
| NW  | (2,584,262) | (69,289) | 120,127 |
| WC  | (3,038,090) | (681,891) | (206,199) |
| Emp. | 55 | 43 | 40 |

**DUNS 21-409-6051**

## Virgin Trains Disabled Persons Travel Arrangements Journeycare

83 Princes Street, Edinburgh, Midlothian EH2 2ER
**Tel:** 0845-744-3366
**Proprietorship**
**Line of Business:** Retail sale of flowers, plants, seeds, fertilisers, pet animals and pet food in specialised stores
**Proprietor:** J Galbraith
**US SIC:** 5261 **UK SIC:** 65400
**Employees:** 100

**DUNS 23-808-3740**

## Virgin Wine Online Ltd

**(Subsidiary of:** Virgin Wines Holding Co Ltd)
St James Mill, Whitefriars, Norwich, Norfolk NR3 1TN
**Tel:** 08432241001
**Web:** www.virginwines.co.uk
**Reg No:** 3800762 **VAT No:** 732295044
**Estd:** 2000 Private Limited Company
**Line of Business:** E-commerce
**Trading Style:** Virgin Online
**Issued Capital:** £9,900,967
**Directors:** P Adams, J S Wright
**Co. Secretary:** Graeme Weir
**Responsibilities**
**Senior:** Jay White (Manager)
**US SIC:** 5411 **UK SIC:** 64100
**Auditors:** PricewaterhouseCoopers LLP
**Bankers:** The Royal Bank Of Scotland Plc (15-10-00)

|     | 28-06-13 | 29-06-12 | 01-06-11 |
|-----|----------|----------|----------|
| TO  | 34,474,939 | 37,389,702 | 36,803,242 |
| P/L | 1,688,856 | 1,975,489 | 2,230,262 |
| NW  | 776,171 | 2,713,671 | 1,168,623 |
| WC  | 2,310,343 | 6,744,410 | 5,813,449 |
| Emp. | 158 | 156 | 160 |

**DUNS 22-609-5701**                                          Imp

## Virginia Hayward Ltd

Blynfield, Stour Row, Shaftesbury, Dorset SP7 0QW
**Tel:** 01747851515
**Web:** www.virginiahayward.com
**Reg No:** 1842012 **VAT No:** 399031528
**Estd:** 1984 Private Limited Company
**Line of Business:** Other retail sale in specialised stores not elsewhere classified
**Issued Capital:** £17,880
**Principals:** G M Hayward (Chairman), S R Hayward
**Co. Secretary:** Ms Virginia Hayward
**Responsibilities**
**Marketing:** Sarah Cumber (Brand Manager)
**HR:** Tracy Young (Human Resources Manager)
**Fleet:** Tracy Young (Human Resources Manager)
**US SIC:** 5999, 5961
**UK SIC:** 65600
**Auditors:** Stone Osmond Ltd
**Bankers:** HSBC Bank plc (40-41-01)

|     | 31-03-14 | 31-03-13 | 31-03-12 |
|-----|----------|----------|----------|
| TO  | 13,055,494 | 10,695,925 | 9,636,836 |
| P/L | 725,319 | 523,666 | 453,419 |
| NW  | 3,974,793 | 3,424,542 | 3,033,075 |
| WC  | 1,864,312 | 1,529,715 | 1,329,870 |
| Emp. | 65 | 66 | 54 |

**DUNS 73-535-7456**

## Virgo Health Ltd

1-3 Indigo House, Holbrooke Place, Richmond, Surrey TW10 6UD
**Tel:** 020-8939-2450
**Web:** www.virgohealth.com
**Reg No:** 4798253 **Estd:** 2003 Private Limited Company
**Line of Business:** Public relations activities
**Issued Capital:** £100
**Directors:** M A Hamid, Ms A Wiles, B J Beck, Ms S J Matthew
**Co. Secretary:** Ms Louise Bean
**US SIC:** 7392, 8091

**UK SIC:** 83951, 95200
**Auditors:** PricewaterhouseCoopers LLP

|     | 31-12-13 | 31-12-12 | 31-12-11 |
|-----|----------|----------|----------|
| TO  | 8,492,000 | 7,446,000 | 7,635,000 |
| P/L | 777,000 | 47,000 | 1,053,000 |
| NW  | 1,626,000 | 2,841,000 | 2,540,000 |
| WC  | 1,598,000 | 2,778,000 | 2,440,000 |
| Emp. | 65 | 60 | 60 |

**DUNS 23-157-9900**

## Viridian Energy Supply Ltd

**(Subsidiary of:** Viridian Group Fundco Iii Limited)
120 Malone Road, Belfast BT9 5HT
**Tel:** 02890668416 **Fax:** 02890689128
**Web:** www.energia.ie
**Reg No:** 0035800NI **Estd:** 1995 Private Limited Company
**Line of Business:** Distribution and trade in electricity
**Trading Style:** Energia
**Issued Capital:** £2
**Directors:** P J Baillie, J P Newman, T Gillen, Mrs S P Bailey
**Co. Secretary:** Ms Siobhan Bailey
**Branches:** Viridian Energy Supply Ltd, Woodchester House, 62 Newforge La, Belfast, Belfast BT9 5NW
**US SIC:** 4911 **UK SIC:** 16101
**Auditors:** Ernst & Young LLP
**Bankers:** The Bank Of Ireland (90-21-27)

|     | 31-03-14 | 31-03-13 | 31-03-12 |
|-----|----------|----------|----------|
| TO  | 242,120,000 | 186,442,000 | 166,618,000 |
| P/L | 15,972,000 | 11,129,000 | 10,565,000 |
| NW  | 49,470,000 | 35,087,000 | 27,768,000 |
| WC  | 49,194,000 | 33,521,000 | 26,322,000 |
| Emp. | 109 | 110 | 99 |

**DUNS 21-770-5344**

## Viridian Housing

2 Bridge Avenue, Hammersmith, London W6 9JP
**Tel:** 03301230220
**Web:** www.viridianhousing.org.uk
**Estd:** 2004
**Line of Business:** Housing associations societies trusts & co-operatives
**Responsibilities**
**Senior:** Matt Campion (Social Impact Director), Kevin Willetts (Manager)
**Finance:** Iain Bacon (Head of Financial Information), Suzanne Forster (Finance Director)
**Admin:** Iain Bacon (Head of Financial Information), Nicolas Degrandy (Personal Assistant)
**IT:** Sharon Stone (IT Manager)
**Facilities:** Nick Apetroaie (Property Director)
**US SIC:** 8321 **UK SIC:** 96111
**Employees:** 173

**DUNS 22-276-3398**                                          Imp

## Viridian Systems Ltd

Unit 39-41 Wirral Business Centre, Birkenhead, Merseyside CH41 1JW
**Tel:** 01516398666
**Web:** www.viridiansystems.com
**Reg No:** 4294250 **Estd:** 2001 Private Limited Company
**Line of Business:** Electrical contractors and electricians
**Trading Style:** Viridian Air Systems, Viridian Electrical System
**Issued Capital:** £497
**Principals:** R A Dixon (Managing), P A Dabner
**Co. Secretary:** Jacleen Dixon
**Responsibilities**
**Senior:** John Croft (Manager)
**US SIC:** 1731, 5084
**UK SIC:** 50300, 61490

|     | 31-12-13 | 31-12-12 | 31-12-11 |
|-----|----------|----------|----------|
| TA  | 1,217,048 | 909,451 | 769,535 |
| NW  | 260,703 | 136,905 | 67,935 |
| WC  | 185,434 | 105,584 | 64,402 |

**DUNS 21-582-4374**

## The Viridor

Friarton Bridge Park, Friarton Road, Perth, Perthshire PH2 8DD
**Tel:** 01738492950
**Web:** www.viridor.co.uk
**Estd:** 2011 Proprietorship
**Line of Business:** Recycling
**Proprietor:** T Liddell
**US SIC:** 3031 **UK SIC:** 48123
**Employees:** 94

**DUNS 50-482-6769**

## Viridor Ltd

**(Subsidiary of:** Pennon Group Plc)
Viridor House, Priory Bridge Road, Taunton, Somerset TA1 1AP
**Tel:** 01823721400
**Web:** www.viridor.co.uk
**Reg No:** 2456473 **Estd:** 1990 Private Limited Company
**Line of Business:** Management activities of holding companies

**Export Sales:** £56,000,000
**Issued Capital:** £348,234,128
**Directors:** A M Kirkman, I J Mcaulay, R D Holden, Ms S J Davy, P M Ringham, K G Harvey, S L Catford, M Burrows Smith
**Co. Secretary:** Richard Zmuda
**Responsibilities**
**Senior:** Alan Cumming (Director), David Dupont (Director), Felix Schwager (Director)
**Branches:** Viridor Ltd, Manor Furlong, Frome, Somerset BA11 4RJ
**US SIC:** 6711, 7399
**UK SIC:** 83962, 83954
**Auditors:** PricewaterhouseCoopers LLP

|  | 31-03-14 | 31-03-13 | 31-03-12 |
|---|---|---|---|
| TO | 802,000,000 | 703,800,000 | 761,100,000 |
| P/L | (21,000,000) | (152,400,000) | 57,600,000 |
| NW | (98,000,000) | (19,800,000) | (11,800,000) |
| WC | (121,300,000) | (184,700,000) | (164,900,000) |
| Emp. | 3,044 | 3,180 | 3,148 |

DUNS 34-572-5022
## Viridor Waste Disposal Ltd
(**Subsidiary of:** Pennon Group Plc)
42 Kings Hill Avenue, Kings Hill, West Malling, Kent ME19 4AJ
**Tel:** 01732-229200
**Web:** www.viridor.co.uk
**Reg No:** 2722409 **Estd:** 1992 Private Limited Company
**Line of Business:** Sanitation, remediation and similar activities
**Issued Capital:** £4,414
**Directors:** A M Kirkman, M Burrows Smith
**Co. Secretary:** Miss Karen Gale
**Responsibilities**
**IT:** George Ossei (Computer Manager)
**HR:** Debbie Mosley (Human Resources Manager)
**Health & Safety:** Barbara Hutton (Waste Systems Controller)
**Branches:** Viridor Waste Disposal Ltd, Medebridge Road, Grays, Essex RM16 5TZ
**US SIC:** 4959 **UK SIC:** 92110
**Auditors:** PricewaterhouseCoopers
**Bankers:** National Westminster Bank Plc (60-00-01)

|  | 31-03-14 | 31-03-13 | 31-03-12 |
|---|---|---|---|
| TA | 22,321,000 | 22,321,000 | 22,321,000 |
| NW | 22,321,000 | 22,321,000 | 22,321,000 |

DUNS 22-624-4937
## Viridor Waste (Medway) Ltd
(**Subsidiary of:** Pennon Group Plc)
Pelican House, Clipper Close, Medway City Estate, Rochester, Kent ME2 4QP
**Tel:** 01634322400
**Web:** www.viridor.co.uk
**Reg No:** 1067787 **Estd:** 1972 Private Limited Company
**Line of Business:** Waste disposal
**Trading Style:** Medway Quick Skips
**Issued Capital:** £50,100
**Directors:** M Burrows Smith, A M Kirkman
**Co. Secretary:** Richard Zmuda
**Responsibilities**
**Senior:** Steve Kent (Site Manager)
**Branches:** Viridor Waste (Medway) Ltd, Oare Creek, Faversham, Kent ME13 7TX
**US SIC:** 4953 **UK SIC:** 92110
**Auditors:** PricewaterhouseCoopers LLP

|  | 31-03-14 | 31-03-13 | 31-03-12 |
|---|---|---|---|
| NW | (374,000) | (374,000) | (374,000) |

DUNS 28-882-7108
## Viridor Waste Wootton Ltd
(**Subsidiary of:** Pennon Group Plc)
Peninsula House, Rydon Lane, Exeter, Devon EX2 7HR
**Tel:** 01392446699
**Reg No:** 1196767 **Estd:** 1982 Private Limited Company
**Line of Business:** Other service activities not elsewhere classified
**Issued Capital:** £3,500,011
**Directors:** M Burrows Smith, A M Kirkman
**Co. Secretary:** Richard Zmuda
**US SIC:** 8999 **UK SIC:** 83954
**Bankers:** National Westminster Bank Plc (56-00-49)

|  | 31-03-14 | 31-03-13 | 31-03-12 |
|---|---|---|---|
| TA | 3,790,000 | 3,790,000 | 3,790,000 |
| NW | 3,740,000 | 3,740,000 | 3,740,000 |
| WC | 3,740,000 | 3,740,000 | 3,740,000 |

DUNS 23-929-4973
## Virtual College Group PL239294973
Marsel House, Ilkley, West Yorkshire LS29 8DD
**Tel:** 01943-605-976
**Web:** www.virtual-college.co.uk
**Reg No:** 3919407 **Estd:** 2000 Public Limited Company
**Line of Business:** Management activities of holding companies
**Export Sales:** £9,392
**Issued Capital:** £144,925
**Directors:** Dr I R Gomersall, R A Knox

**Co. Secretary:** Paul Dickinson
**Responsibilities**
**Finance:** Caroline Woods (Financial Manager)
**Marketing:** Roger Moore (Sales & Marketing Manager)
**Sales:** Roger Moore (Sales & Marketing Manager)
**IT:** Darren Lawson (Information Technology Manager)
**HR:** Lesley Ord (Operations Manager)
**Health & Safety:** Lesley Ord (Operations Manager)
**Operations:** Lesley Ord (Operations Manager)
**US SIC:** 6711 **UK SIC:** 83962
**Auditors:** BDO LLP
**Bankers:** Barclays Bank Plc (20-11-81)

|  | 31-03-14 | 31-03-13 | 31-03-12 |
|---|---|---|---|
| TO | 5,852,153 | 5,470,409 | 4,228,553 |
| P/L | 22,743 | 208,449 | 219,855 |
| NW | 611,629 | 1,165,670 | 1,066,403 |
| WC | 504,533 | 1,087,781 | 1,025,757 |
| Emp. | 115 | 95 | 79 |

DUNS 77-974-9584
## Virtual Internet Holdings Ltd
(**Subsidiary of:** Stratus (Holdings) Ltd)
Old Truman Brewery, 91 Brick Lane, London E1 6QL
**Tel:** 08000517417
**Web:** www.vi.net
**Reg No:** 5943486 **Estd:** 2006 Private Limited Company
**Line of Business:** Other computer related activities
**Issued Capital:** £180,000
**Directors:** J Morris, A W Kilgour
**Co. Secretary:** Ian Burrell
**US SIC:** 7379 **UK SIC:** 83940
**Bankers:** Barclays Bank Plc (20-97-58)

|  | 31-12-13 | 31-12-12 | 31-12-11 |
|---|---|---|---|
| TA | 180,000 | 180,000 | 180,000 |
| NW | 180,000 | 180,000 | 180,000 |

DUNS 77-961-2027
## Virtual Universe Ltd
(**Subsidiary of:** Amplefuture Group Ltd)
28-39 Amplefuture House, The Quadrant, 135 Salusbury Road, London NW6 6RJ
**Tel:** 08707886060 **Fax:** 020-7264-7981
**Web:** www.virtual-universe.net
**Reg No:** 3064568 **Estd:** 1995 Private Limited Company
**Line of Business:** Telecommunications
**Issued Capital:** £513
**Director:** D W Byrne
**Co. Secretary:** Stephen Bramhall
**US SIC:** 4899 **UK SIC:** 79020
**Auditors:** Calder & Co

|  | 30-06-13 | 30-06-12 | 30-06-11 |
|---|---|---|---|
| TO | N/A | 6,179,914 | 7,241,316 |
| P/L | N/A | 26,896 | (815,892) |
| NW | (2,220,335) | (1,643,733) | (1,722,445) |
| WC | (649,554) | (487,419) | (651,890) |
| Emp. | N/A | 50 | 63 |

DUNS 21-675-8264
## Virtualpie Ltd
11 Broadwells Crescent, Westwood Heath, Coventry, West Midlands CV4 8JD
**Web:** http://virtualpie.co.uk
**Reg No:** 7274578 **Estd:** 2010 Private Limited Company
**Line of Business:** Electrical testing services
**Trading Style:** Bhr Group
**Issued Capital:** £100,000
**Directors:** P A Winstanley, R Chand, K Rutkowski, M J Stevens, J Earl
**Co. Secretary:** Raghbir Chand
**US SIC:** 7397 **UK SIC:** 83702
**Auditors:** Armstrongs Accountancy Ltd
**Bankers:** Barclays Bank Plc (20-49-08)

|  | 30-04-14 | 30-04-13 | 30-04-12 |
|---|---|---|---|
| TO | 5,026,210 | N/A | N/A |
| P/L | 243,108 | N/A | N/A |
| NW | 1,045,452 | 299,956 | 109,352 |
| WC | (105,479) | (181,819) | 187,714 |
| Emp. | 84 | N/A | N/A |

DUNS 73-885-7866 **Imp**
## Visa Europe Ltd
1 Sheldon Square, London W2 6WH
**Tel:** 02079-378-111 **Fax:** 02079-370-877
**Web:** www.visaeurope.com
**Reg No:** 5139966 **Estd:** 2004 Private Limited Company
**Line of Business:** Representative office
**Issued Capital:** £30,970
**Directors:** P Auge, G A Hoffman, L D Matheson, Ms E C Sanz, M Vial, F J Denele, Dr J Evers, C S Rhodes
**Co. Secretary:** Ms Niamh Grogan
**Responsibilities**
**Senior:** Piotr Alicki (Director), Peter Ayliffe (Manager), Joseph Bachar (Director), David Brendl (Senior Manager - Mobile and Co), Fernando De La Rica Goiricelaya (Director), Henning Holtan (Director), Nicolas Huss

(Chief Executive Officer), Amanda Kamin (Head Of Issues Management), Ennio La Monica (Director), Tony Lee (Manager), Jan Liden (Chairman), Carl Renstrom (Director), Nazan Somer Ozelgin (Director), Valerie Soranno Keating (Director)
**Finance:** Nick Mackie (VP - Head of Contactless), Philip Symes (Chief Financial Officer)
**Marketing:** Rich Bolt (Senior Manager - Digital Commu), Ana Jenkins (Online Content Manager), Michelle King (Marketing Executive), Tony Shawcross (E-Commerce Manager), Fiona Wilkinson (Chief Communications Officer), George Yaryura (Head of e-Commerce)
**Sales:** Sandra Alzetta (SVP Innovation New Product & C), Jonathan Vaux (Commercial Director - V.me)
**HR:** Derrick Ahlfeld (Vice President Human Resources)
**US SIC:** 7399 **UK SIC:** 83954
**Auditors:** KPMG LLP
**Bankers:** Barclays Bank Plc (20-90-69)
Following financial data are in thousands

|  | 30-09-14 | 30-09-13 | 30-09-12 |
|---|---|---|---|
| TO | 1,131,116 | 1,044,699 | 883,145 |
| P/L | 299,402 | 230,490 | 206,876 |
| NW | 1,024,258 | 870,604 | 719,194 |
| WC | 884,179 | 657,586 | 504,866 |
| Emp. | 1,952 | 1,884 | 1,609 |

DUNS 22-756-7096 **Imp-Exp**
## Visage Ltd
(**Subsidiary of:** Centennial (Luxembourg) Sarl)
242 Marylebone Road, London NW1 6JQ
**Tel:** 0191 415 1133 **Fax:** 0191 418 8597
**Web:** www.visage-group.com
**Reg No:** 1568110 **VAT No:** 569528882
**Estd:** 1981 Private Limited Company
**Line of Business:** Import and export agents
**Export Markets:** E U; Asia
**Export Sales:** £14,278,000
**Trading Style:** M A Y Trading
**Issued Capital:** £54,100
**Directors:** S Mehan, R S Lister, N A Cottrell
**Responsibilities**
**Senior:** Jim Cox (Manager), Julian Dwyer (Senior Operations Manager), Spencer Fung (Manager), James Hampson (Manager), Anita Mehan (Manager), Raj Sehgal (Manager)
**Branches:** Visage Ltd, 13 Parsons Road, Washington, Tyne and Wear NE37 1EQ
**US SIC:** 4712 **UK SIC:** 77002
**Auditors:** PricewaterhouseCoopers LLP
**Bankers:** The Hongkong And Shanghai Banking Corporation Ltd (40-48-69)

|  | 31-12-13 | 31-12-12 | 31-12-11 |
|---|---|---|---|
| TO | 209,575,000 | 194,963,000 | 194,111,000 |
| P/L | 6,963,000 | 1,227,000 | 2,991,000 |
| NW | 31,976,000 | 30,220,000 | 49,521,000 |
| WC | 33,663,000 | 27,643,000 | 46,489,000 |
| Emp. | 253 | 297 | 393 |

DUNS 29-485-8279 **Imp**
## Viscose Closures Ltd
(**Subsidiary of:** Viscose Holdings Ltd)
Unit 1 Fleming Way Royce Road Business, Park, Crawley, West Sussex RH10 9JY
**Tel:** 01792762085
**Web:** www.viscose.co.uk
**Reg No:** 1848065 **Estd:** 1902 Private Limited Company
**Line of Business:** Other manufacturing not elsewhere classified
**Trading Style:** Viscose Closures
**Issued Capital:** £687,026
**Directors:** Mrs J Royall-Staniforth, Viscose Holdings Ltd
**Co. Secretary:** Paul Evans
**Responsibilities**
**Senior:** William Cartwright (Manager), Keith Foale (Financial Director), Dorothy Gorman (Manager), Duncan Hawkins (Warehouse Coordinator), Gareth Rowlands (Manager)
**Finance:** Redvers Best (Financial Director), Keith Foale (Financial Director)
**Marketing:** Ralph Myer (Marketing Manager)
**Branches:** Viscose Closures Ltd, Unit 22 Ferryboat Close, Swansea, West Glamorgan SA6 8QN
**US SIC:** 3999, 5199
**UK SIC:** 49590, 61900
**Auditors:** PricewaterhouseCoopers LLP
**Bankers:** National Westminster Bank Plc (60-06-20)

|  | 31-07-13 | 31-07-12 | 31-07-11 |
|---|---|---|---|
| TO | 8,805,000 | 9,544,000 | 9,751,161 |
| P/L | 149,000 | 307,000 | 871,773 |
| NW | 457,000 | 309,000 | 1,741,725 |
| WC | 1,135,000 | 969,000 | 1,560,022 |
| Emp. | 57 | 58 | 55 |

DUNS 76-706-6046 **Imp-Exp**
## Vishay Measurements Group Uk Ltd
(**Subsidiary of:** Vishay Precision Group Inc.)
1 Cartel Units, Basingstoke, Hampshire RG24 8FW
**Tel:** 01256-462131
**Web:** www.vishaypg.com
**Reg No:** 2593388 **VAT No:** 582725322
**Estd:** 1966 Private Limited Company
**Line of Business:** Manufacture of electronic instruments and appliances for measuring, checking, testing, navigating and other purposes, except industrial process control equipment
**Export Markets:** Scandinavia: Republic of Ireland
**Export Sales:** £10,337,245
**Issued Capital:** £690,795
**Directors:** M P Deegan, R A Campbell, S C Klausner
**Co. Secretary:** Robert Campbell
**Responsibilities**
**Senior:** Laura Bell (Manager)
**IT:** Stuart Hollocks (IT Manager)
**Operations:** Ziggy Blackwood (Production Manager)
**Purchasing:** P Reece (Purchasing Officer)
**Branches:** Vishay Measurements Group Uk Ltd, C/O T T Group Plc, Clive House, 12-18 Queens Road, Weybridge, Surrey KT13 9XB
**US SIC:** 3829, 5065
**UK SIC:** 37100, 61500
**Auditors:** Ernst & Young LLP
**Bankers:** HSBC Bank plc (40-09-18)

|  | 31-12-13 | 31-12-12 | 31-12-11 |
|---|---|---|---|
| TO | 16,946,303 | 15,852,234 | 15,533,082 |
| P/L | 534,746 | 648,518 | 399,091 |
| NW | 5,667,913 | 5,539,276 | 5,626,682 |
| WC | 5,854,303 | 6,804,777 | 6,496,139 |
| Emp. | 62 | 61 | 57 |

DUNS 77-587-7855
## Vishay Pm Onboard Ltd
(**Subsidiary of:** Vpg Systems Uk Ltd)
Airedale House, Canal Road, Bradford, West Yorkshire BD2 1AG
**Tel:** 01274-771177 **Fax:** 01274-781178
**Web:** www.vishaypg.com
**Reg No:** 3001454 **Estd:** 1989 Private Limited Company
**Line of Business:** Manufacturers of scales
**Issued Capital:** £100
**Directors:** Z Shoshani, J Jackson, M J Burridge
**Co. Secretary:** Edwin Coe Secretaries Limited
**Responsibilities**
**Senior:** Laura Bell (Manager)
**IT:** Richard Simmonds (IT Manager)
**Health & Safety:** Dave Greenwood (Health & Safety Officer)
**Branches:** Cutler House Foundry Lane, Wakefield Road, Bradford, West Yorkshire BD4 7LU
**US SIC:** 3549 **UK SIC:** 32212
**Auditors:** Ernst & Young LLP
**Bankers:** National Westminster Bank Plc (56-00-36)

|  | 31-12-13 | 31-12-12 | 31-12-11 |
|---|---|---|---|
| TO | 8,757,993 | 7,609,107 | 7,741,677 |
| P/L | 1,233,227 | 388,203 | 474,162 |
| NW | 1,402,700 | 339,028 | (171,335) |
| WC | N/A | 2,925,857 | 3,645,363 |
| Emp. | 53 | 52 | 52 |

DUNS 77-932-7642
## Vision 21 (Cyfle Cymru)
Unit 10-12, Field Way, Cardiff, South Glamorgan CF14 4HY
**Tel:** 02920621194
**Web:** www.vision-21.com
**Reg No:** 3045325 **Estd:** 1995 Private Limited Company
**Line of Business:** Adult and other education not elsewhere classified
**Directors:** R S Cooper, A Pursell, M J Winter, Ms C D Cooze, Ms E Gee, M Clarke, B J Shiers
**Co. Secretary:** Robert Larkins
**Branches:** Vision 21 (Cyfle Cymru), Enterprise Centre, Skomer Road, Barry, South Glamorgan CF62 9DA
**US SIC:** 8249, 8321
**UK SIC:** 93300, 96111
**Auditors:** McGarry Worsey & Co
**Bankers:** Lloyds Tsb Private Banking Ltd (30-16-74)

|  | 31-03-14 | 31-03-13 | 31-03-12 |
|---|---|---|---|
| TO | 1,946,753 | 1,825,185 | 1,767,966 |
| P/L | 87,842 | 39,022 | 18,980 |
| NW | 1,185,438 | 1,097,596 | 1,058,574 |
| WC | 515,232 | 527,206 | 456,243 |
| Emp. | 53 | 53 | 52 |

DUNS 57-615-7994 **Imp**

## Vision Alert Automotive Ltd

(**Subsidiary of:** Berwind Corporation)
Unit 3 Victoria Road Victoria Industrial, Park, Leeds, West Yorkshire LS14 2LA
**Tel:** 01132375340 **Fax:** 0113-237-5360
**Web:** www.visionalert.com
**Reg No:** 2884538 **Estd:** 1994 Private Limited Company
**Line of Business:** Safety equipment suppliers
**Export Sales:** £8,855,921
**Trading Style:** Ecco Group
**Issued Capital:** £16,120
**Directors:** C C Thompson, C E Marshall
**Co. Secretary:** Ms Sheila Morgan
**Responsibilities**
**Senior:** Mike Clark *(Manager)*
**IT:** Shomuj Miah *(IT Security Manager)*, Colin Parke *(IT Manager)*
**Health & Safety:** David Winder *(Health & Safety Officer)*
**US SIC:** 5999, 3999
**UK SIC:** 65600, 49590
**Auditors:** Ernst & Young LLP
**Bankers:** Lloyds TSB Bank plc (30-99-99)

| | 31-12-13 | 31-12-12 | 31-12-11 |
|---|---|---|---|
| TO | 16,884,767 | 18,415,254 | 19,397,421 |
| P/L | 2,055,277 | 2,211,311 | 2,203,177 |
| NW | 5,401,968 | 3,526,193 | 1,538,172 |
| WC | 6,789,131 | 5,775,637 | 6,309,571 |
| Emp. | 95 | 104 | 112 |

DUNS 21-661-7317

## Vision Apprentices Ltd

Derby Road, Mansfield, Nottinghamshire NG18 5BH
**Tel:** 08001218317
**Web:** www.visionapprentices.co.uk
**Reg No:** 7172567 **Estd:** 2010 Private Limited Company
**Line of Business:** Technical and industrial schools
**Issued Capital:** £2
**Directors:** Mrs S D Mccarthy, I Baggaley, K R Allsop
**Co. Secretary:** Ms Maxine Bagshaw
**US SIC:** 8249 **UK SIC:** 93300

| | 31-07-13 | 31-07-12 | 31-07-11 |
|---|---|---|---|
| TO | 503,592 | 525,697 | 342,341 |
| P/L | (31,023) | (6,146) | 478 |
| NW | (37,582) | (6,559) | (413) |
| WC | (37,582) | (6,559) | (413) |
| Emp. | 48 | 74 | 69 |

DUNS 21-807-3805

## Vision Critical Research Solutions

2nd Floor, Dominican Court, 17 Hatfields, London SE1 8DJ
**Tel:** 02076332900
**Web:** www.visioncritical.com
**Estd:** 2012
**Line of Business:** Market research and public opinion polling
**Proprietor:** M Stevens
**Responsibilities**
**Admin:** Maggie Ward *(Office Manager)*
**US SIC:** 7392 **UK SIC:** 83951
**Employees:** 58

DUNS 21-636-1212 **Imp-Exp**

## Vision Engineering Ltd

Send Road, Woking, Surrey GU23 7ER
**Tel:** 01483248300 **Fax:** 01483-248301
**Web:** www.visioneng.com
**Reg No:** 0599506 **VAT No:** 211325814
**Estd:** 1956 Private Limited Company
**Line of Business:** Manufacturers of scientific machinery and instrument
**Export Markets:** U.S.A, Germany, France, Japan, E U, India, Pakistan, Korea
**Export Sales:** £15,798,220
**Issued Capital:** £20,000
**Principals:** R J Freeman *(Managing)*, M E Curtis *(Managing)*, S A Mead, Mrs J M Freeman, G P Mercer, Miss J Arnold
**Co. Secretary:** Robin Freeman
**Branches:** Vision Engineering Ltd, Monument House, Monument Way West, Woking, Surrey GU21 5EN
**US SIC:** 3829 **UK SIC:** 37100
**Auditors:** Roffe Swayne
**Bankers:** Bank Of Scotland (12-09-49)

| | 31-03-14 | 31-03-13 | 30-03-12 |
|---|---|---|---|
| TO | 17,770,090 | 16,063,075 | 17,876,281 |
| P/L | 1,434,673 | 1,386,881 | 3,044,571 |
| NW | 21,461,992 | 20,627,006 | 19,274,943 |
| WC | 16,723,606 | 16,389,317 | 15,149,001 |
| Emp. | 106 | 106 | 116 |

DUNS 23-513-1302

## Vision Enhancement Services

Beech House, Park West, Sealand Road, Chester, Cheshire CH1 4RJ
**Tel:** 01244651900 **Fax:** 01244-651909
**Web:** www.vstrading.co.uk
**Reg No:** 3512340 **Estd:** 1998 Private Unlimited Company
**Line of Business:** Social work activities without accommodation
**Directors:** P J Curtis, Mrs L A Davies, Mrs C Blanchard, C Pierce, M K Tutton, Mrs M R Dean, A D Wilson, J M Graham
**Co. Secretary:** Miriam Wright
**Responsibilities**
**Senior:** Joe Dudley *(Director)*
**US SIC:** 8321 **UK SIC:** 96111
**Auditors:** Morris & Co
**Bankers:** National Westminster Bank Plc (60-40-08)

| | 31-03-14 | 31-03-13 | 31-03-12 |
|---|---|---|---|
| TO | 2,846,470 | 2,388,931 | 1,744,114 |
| P/L | 125,138 | (188,615) | (148,578) |
| NW | 1,342,325 | 1,205,187 | 1,382,655 |
| WC | 1,148,112 | 1,040,003 | 979,540 |
| Emp. | 100 | 89 | 73 |

DUNS 77-507-3778

## Vision Express Joint Ventures Ltd

(**Subsidiary of:** Hal Trust)
Abbeyfield Road, Lenton, Nottingham, Nottinghamshire NG7 2SP
**Tel:** 08444771177
**Web:** www.visionexpress.com
**Reg No:** 2981780 **Estd:** 1995 Private Limited Company
**Line of Business:** Management activities of holding companies
**Trading Style:** Vision Express
**Issued Capital:** £113,800
**Directors:** J R Lawson, M Flint
**Co. Secretary:** Simon Hope
**Branches:** Vision Express Joint Ventures Ltd, 24-26 Westgate, Wakefield, West Yorkshire WF1 1JY
**US SIC:** 6711, 5999
**UK SIC:** 83962, 65600
**Auditors:** KPMG
**Bankers:** HSBC Bank plc (40-35-18)

| | 31-12-13 | 31-12-12 | 31-12-11 |
|---|---|---|---|
| TA | 471,000 | 469,000 | 467,000 |
| P/L | 4,000 | 4,000 | 2,000 |
| NW | 471,000 | 468,000 | 465,000 |
| WC | N/A | 468,000 | 465,000 |

DUNS 39-750-0133 **Imp-Exp**

## Vision Express (U K) Ltd

(**Subsidiary of:** Hal Trust)
Abbeyfield Road, Lenton, Nottingham, Nottinghamshire NG7 2SP
**Tel:** 01159865225 **Fax:** 01159-865225
**Web:** www.visionexpress.com
**Reg No:** 2189907 **VAT No:** 520508287
**Estd:** 1987 Private Limited Company
**Line of Business:** Other business activities not elsewhere classified
**Export Markets:** Ireland
**Issued Capital:** £340,012,783
**Directors:** S M Noble, J R Lawson, O Hassan
**Co. Secretary:** Simon Hope
**Responsibilities**
**Finance:** Mark Coverley *(SAP Consultant Finance)*, Carolyn Hesketh *(Financial Controller)*
**Marketing:** Andy Portsmouth *(Head of Marketing)*
**IT:** Kerry Hardy *(IS Support Manager)*
**HR:** Kate Clayton *(Human Resources Manager)*
**Health & Safety:** Kate Clayton *(Human Resources Manager)*
**Branches:** Vision Express (U K) Ltd, 1642 High Street, Solihull, West Midlands B93 0NA
**US SIC:** 7399, 8999, 5999
**UK SIC:** 83954, 65600
**Auditors:** PricewaterhouseCoopers LLP
**Bankers:** Barclays Bank Plc (20-77-67)

| | 31-12-13 | 31-12-12 | 31-12-11 |
|---|---|---|---|
| TO | 216,682,000 | 203,389,000 | 195,818,000 |
| P/L | 18,220,000 | 11,707,000 | 14,243,000 |
| NW | 19,067,000 | 9,937,000 | 8,940,000 |
| WC | (18,897,000) | (24,336,000) | (19,430,000) |
| Emp. | 3,013 | 2,860 | 2,734 |

DUNS 21-099-4276

## Vision for Education Ltd

(**Subsidiary of:** Tes Bidco Ltd)
2 Friar Gate St James Court, Derby, Derbyshire DE1 1BT
**Tel:** 01332372337
**Web:** www.visionforeducation.co.uk
**Reg No:** 6433086 **Estd:** 2008 Private Limited Company
**Line of Business:** Employment and recruitment companies and consultants
**Issued Capital:** £1,360
**Directors:** S H Petherbridge, D Mclaney, Ms L Rogers, M O'Sullivan, P P Schneitter
**Responsibilities**
**Senior:** Navjeet Mclaney *(Manager)*, Sylvia Reid *(Manager)*, Leanne Wainwright *(Manager)*
**Branches:** Vision For Education Ltd, 4 Universal Square, Devonshire Street North, Manchester M12 6JH
**US SIC:** 7361 **UK SIC:** 83954
**Auditors:** Parker Cavendish

| | 31-12-13 | 31-12-12 | 31-12-11 |
|---|---|---|---|
| TO | 21,110,789 | N/A | N/A |
| P/L | 2,112,693 | N/A | N/A |
| NW | 1,938,087 | 1,329,734 | 78,550 |
| WC | 1,891,106 | 1,279,004 | 31,090 |
| Emp. | 56 | N/A | N/A |

DUNS 21-718-6203

## Vision Group (Holdings) Plc

Caxton House, Watermark Way, Hertford, Hertfordshire SG13 7TZ
**Tel:** 08449808700
**Web:** www.visionplc.co.uk
**Reg No:** 7569889 **Estd:** 2011 Public Limited Company
**Line of Business:** Management activities of other non-financial holding companies not elsewhere classified
**Issued Capital:** £51,163
**Directors:** A Bond, E Robinson, P R Bond
**Co. Secretary:** Allen Bond
**US SIC:** 6711 **UK SIC:** 83962
**Auditors:** Wilkins Kennedy LLP

| | 30-09-13 | 30-09-12 | 30-09-11 |
|---|---|---|---|
| TO | 17,171,656 | 12,756,871 | N/A |
| P/L | 745,841 | 204,839 | N/A |
| NW | (2,890,606) | (3,408,978) | 404 |
| WC | (1,267,831) | (1,369,400) | N/A |
| Emp. | 68 | 57 | N/A |

DUNS 34-622-8836

## Vision Homes Association

210 222 Hagley Road West, Oldbury, West Midlands B68 0NP
**Tel:** 0121-434-4644
**Web:** www.visionhomes.org.uk
**Reg No:** 2756733 **Estd:** 1992 Private Company Limited By Guarantee
**Line of Business:** Home care and help services
**Directors:** E Woodhead, R G Wendt, Ms J L Wingrove, A Wood, J R Inglis
**Co. Secretary:** Ewa Stefanowski
**Branches:** Vision Homes Association, The Bungalow Littlelands Court, Bingley, West Yorkshire BD16 1RS
**US SIC:** 8811, 6732
**UK SIC:** 99000, 83100
**Auditors:** Baker Tilly UK Audit LLP
**Bankers:** Barclays Bank Plc (20-53-22)

| | 31-03-14 | 31-03-13 | 31-03-12 |
|---|---|---|---|
| TO | 2,091,453 | 1,908,859 | 2,002,877 |
| P/L | 195,308 | 9,160 | 27,178 |
| NW | 482,044 | 286,736 | 277,576 |
| WC | 470,952 | 274,850 | 261,753 |
| Emp. | 92 | 82 | 115 |

DUNS 50-410-8549 **Imp**

## Vision Labs Ltd.

(**Subsidiary of:** Specsavers International Healthcare Limited)
2 Foley Business Park Foley Grove, Kidderminster, Worcestershire DY11 7PT
**Tel:** 01562-820333 **Fax:** 01562-820500
**Web:** www.visionlabs.co.uk
**Reg No:** 2407981 **VAT No:** 551363849
**Estd:** 1990 Private Limited Company
**Line of Business:** Manufacture of instruments and appliances for measuring, checking, testing, navigating and other purposes, except industrial process control equipment
**Issued Capital:** £100
**Directors:** Specsavers Laboratories Limited, S J Holloway, S D Lawe, A W Tune
**Co. Secretary:**
Specsavers Laboratories Limited
**Responsibilities**
**Senior:** Vivien Hussey *(Human Resources Director)*
**Finance:** Vivien Hussey *(Human Resources Director)*
**HR:** Vivien Hussey *(Human Resources Director)*
**Health & Safety:** Vivien Hussey *(Human Resources Director)*
**US SIC:** 3999 **UK SIC:** 49590
**Auditors:** Deloitte & Touche
**Bankers:** HSBC Bank plc (40-22-25)

| | 28-02-14 | 28-02-13 | 29-02-12 |
|---|---|---|---|
| TO | 23,551,834 | 23,679,428 | 26,151,403 |
| P/L | 1,347,947 | 984,288 | 3,414,511 |
| NW | 1,251,996 | 1,162,898 | 10,621,155 |
| WC | (4,017,183) | (3,201,742) | 5,761,687 |
| Emp. | 233 | 261 | 257 |

DUNS 21-700-8524

## Vision Office & Partners Ltd

23 Wolverhampton Street, Dudley, West Midlands DY1 1DB
**Tel:** 01384451860
**Web:** www.visionumbrella.co.uk
**Reg No:** 7457833 **Estd:** 2013 Private Limited Company
**Line of Business:** Payroll services
**Issued Capital:** £10,300
**Directors:** Mrs B Parsons, J C Shaw
**US SIC:** 8931 **UK SIC:** 83600

| | 31-12-12 | 31-12-11 |
|---|---|---|
| TO | 38,382,276 | 15,774,898 |
| P/L | 1,162,052 | (172,428) |
| NW | 74,368 | (711,534) |
| WC | 63,817 | (717,691) |
| Emp. | 448 | 362 |

DUNS 67-225-2210

## Vision-Redbridge Culture & Leisure

Fullwell Cross Baths, High Street, Ilford, Essex IG6 2EA
**Tel:** 02085590486 **Fax:** 02085-050916
**Web:** www.vision-rcl.org.uk
**Reg No:** 6032714 **Estd:** 2006 Private Company Limited By Guarantee
**Line of Business:** Other sporting activities not elsewhere classified
**Trading Style:** Wanstead Leisure Centre, Redbridge Cycling Centre, Fullwell Cross Leisure Centre, Ashton Playing Fields
**Directors:** B Spinks, D D Kaur-Thiara, M D Solder, K J Pittman, R A Turbefield, M S Gabhari, M A Santos, Ms C J Rowan
**Co. Secretary:** Mrs Pamela Flindall
**Responsibilities**
**Senior:** Sean Northcott *(centre manager)*, Linda Perham *(Director)*, David Thorogood *(Director)*
**US SIC:** 7999, 7941
**UK SIC:** 97913, 97911
**Auditors:** Appleby & Wood

| | 31-03-14 | 31-03-13 | 31-03-12 |
|---|---|---|---|
| TO | 17,979,000 | 17,627,000 | 15,803,000 |
| P/L | 465,000 | (719,000) | 476,000 |
| NW | (2,835,000) | (3,660,000) | (1,090,000) |
| WC | (144,000) | (49,000) | 518,000 |
| Emp. | 644 | 620 | 593 |

DUNS 21-033-5392

## Vision Security

1 Cromac Quay, Belfast BT7 2JD
**Tel:** 028-9044-2280
**Web:** www.vsg.co.uk
**Estd:** 2006 Proprietorship
**Line of Business:** Security activities
**Proprietor:** A Fielding
**Responsibilities**
**Senior:** Jeff Hutchinson *(Manager)*
**US SIC:** 7393 **UK SIC:** 83954
**Employees:** 50

DUNS 51-998-1849

## Vision Security Group Systems Ltd

(**Subsidiary of:** Compass Group Plc)
650 Pavilion Drive, Northampton, Northamptonshire NN4 7SL
**Tel:** 08455192970
**Web:** www.myvsg.co.uk
**Reg No:** 3365236 **Estd:** 1997 Private Limited Company
**Line of Business:** Security and related activities
**Issued Capital:** £27,079
**Directors:** P A Galvin, R K Francis, D M Hogan, N J Reed
**Co. Secretary:**
Compass Secretaries Limited
**Responsibilities**
**Senior:** Keith Francis *(Manager)*
**US SIC:** 7399 **UK SIC:** 83954
**Auditors:** Mercer Lewin
**Bankers:** The Royal Bank Of Scotland Plc (16-26-27)

| | 30-09-13 | 30-09-12 | 30-09-11 |
|---|---|---|---|
| TO | 7,048,955 | 6,556,535 | 11,599,818 |
| P/L | N/A | N/A | 1,140,658 |
| NW | 1,195,029 | 1,195,029 | 1,195,029 |
| WC | N/A | N/A | 1,164,223 |

DUNS 34-786-0640

## Vision Support Services Group Ltd

Darwen House, Blackburn, Lancashire BB1 2QE
**Tel:** 01254589550 **Fax:** 01254589572
**Web:** www.visionss.co.uk
**Reg No:** 5586661 **VAT No:** 876322604
**Estd:** 2005 Private Limited Company
**Line of Business:** Wholesale of textiles
**Export Sales:** £3,287,114
**Issued Capital:** £1,000
**Directors:** L E Thomas, M Doyle, J G Keeling, D P Wright
**Co. Secretary:** Mark Doyle
**Responsibilities**
**Marketing:** Alison Burns *(E-Commerce Marketing Manager)*, Satheesh Menon *(Marketing Manager)*
**Sales:** Rosmin Jose *(Accounts and Logistics Manager)*
**Fleet:** Rosmin Jose *(Accounts and Logistics Manager)*
**US SIC:** 5133, 5081
**UK SIC:** 61600, 61490
**Auditors:** Ernst & Young LLP

**Bankers:** Lloyds TSB Bank plc (30-16-79)

| | 31-03-14 | 31-03-13 | 31-03-12 |
|---|---|---|---|
| TO | 27,395,689 | 31,187,198 | 24,508,210 |
| P/L | 112,668 | 136,993 | (493,442) |
| NW | (127,113) | (361,048) | (473,795) |
| WC | 3,812,170 | 3,150,567 | 3,097,340 |
| Emp. | 74 | 81 | 78 |

DUNS 21-923-4698
## Vision Workforce Skills Ltd
**(Subsidiary of:** West Nottinghamshire College)
C/O West Nottinghamshire College, Derby Road, Mansfield, Nottinghamshire NG18 5BH
**Tel:** 02033089009
**Web:** www.visionworkforceskills.co.uk
**Reg No:** 8387265 **Estd:** 2013 Private Limited Company
**Line of Business:** Technical and vocational secondary education
**Issued Capital:** £100
**Directors:** R I Baggaley, A Martin
**Co. Secretary:** Ms Maxine Bagshaw
**US SIC:** 8249 **UK SIC:** 93300

| | 31-07-13 |
|---|---|
| TO | 4,621,000 |
| P/L | (8,000) |
| NW | (8,000) |
| WC | (81,000) |
| Emp. | 209 |

DUNS 77-919-9731
## ViSION247 Ltd
Medical School, Cleveland Street, London W1T 4JU
**Tel:** 02076367474 **Fax:** 02079087299
**Web:** www.visionip.tv
**Reg No:** 5823060 **Estd:** 2006 Private Limited Company
**Line of Business:** Broadcasting services
**Export Sales:** £9,350,915
**Trading Style:** Vision Iptv Limited
**Issued Capital:** £1,000
**Directors:** M Vidmar, J D Mills
**Co. Secretary:** Ms Petra Oblak
**US SIC:** 7399 **UK SIC:** 83954

| | 31-08-13 | 31-08-12 | 31-08-11 |
|---|---|---|---|
| TO | 10,079,968 | 9,353,023 | 8,447,044 |
| P/L | 599,766 | 396,813 | 1,220,792 |
| NW | 1,448,224 | 987,432 | 656,128 |
| WC | 1,247,391 | 691,277 | 474,653 |
| Emp. | 50 | 25 | N/A |

DUNS 71-927-3836
## Visioncall Ltd
125 Cambuslang Road Investment Park, Glasgow, Lanarkshire G32 8NB
**Tel:** 01417762347 **Fax:** 01418829752
**Web:** www.vision-call.co.uk
**Reg No:** 0277261SC **Estd:** 2004 Private Limited Company
**Line of Business:** Retail sale by opticians
**Issued Capital:** £29,328
**Directors:** B S Mcguire, A G Manson, R Devlin
**Co. Secretary:** Ricky Pooran
**US SIC:** 5999, 8091
**UK SIC:** 65600, 95200
**Bankers:** The Royal Bank Of Scotland Plc (83-18-02)

| | 30-03-14 | 30-03-13 | 30-03-12 |
|---|---|---|---|
| TO | 13,192,509 | 12,500,146 | 12,993,271 |
| P/L | 55,598 | (378,505) | 1,498,934 |
| NW | 1,448,256 | 1,429,818 | 1,829,606 |
| WC | 1,347,317 | 1,114,274 | 1,511,120 |
| Emp. | 211 | 196 | 201 |

DUNS 23-629-6823
## Visiongain Ltd
230 City Road, London EC1V 2QY
**Tel:** 02073366100
**Web:** www.visiongainglobal.com
**Reg No:** 3626739 **VAT No:** 731260861
**Estd:** 1999 Private Limited Company
**Line of Business:** Business information services
**Issued Capital:** £10,000
**Director:** S Glover
**Co. Secretary:** Charles Glover
**Responsibilities**
**Senior:** Sarah Peerun *(Marketing Manager)*
**Marketing:** Sarah Peerun *(Marketing Manager)*
**US SIC:** 2731 **UK SIC:** 47532
**Auditors:** Wadud Patwari & Co

| | 30-09-13 | 30-09-12 | 30-09-11 |
|---|---|---|---|
| TA | 1,225,149 | 2,828,900 | 2,191,288 |
| NW | 883,397 | 2,390,932 | 1,687,915 |
| WC | 873,517 | 2,383,525 | 1,669,902 |

DUNS 73-828-4335
## Visiongroup (Gb) Ltd
6 Barnes Close, Brandon, Suffolk IP27 0NY
**Tel:** 01842816080 **Fax:** 01842813598
**Web:** www.glazinginnovations.co.uk
**Reg No:** 5084155 **Estd:** 2004 Private Limited Company
**Line of Business:** Builders merchants
**Export Sales:** £287,656
**Issued Capital:** £200
**Director:** H Callacher
**Responsibilities**
**Senior:** Ben Snell *(Manager)*
**US SIC:** 6711, 7399
**UK SIC:** 83962, 83954
**Bankers:** The Royal Bank Of Scotland Plc (16-14-98)

| | 30-04-13 | 30-04-12 | 30-04-11 |
|---|---|---|---|
| TO | 8,218,759 | 7,601,774 | 8,096,056 |
| P/L | 904,416 | 1,182,934 | (198,644) |
| NW | 3,224,379 | 2,790,247 | 2,046,336 |
| WC | 2,106,968 | 1,703,186 | 987,308 |
| Emp. | 88 | 95 | 132 |

DUNS 22-905-3707 Imp
## Visit Scotland
5th Floor, Edinburgh, Midlothian EH6 6GH
**Tel:** 08458591006 **Fax:** 01314722250
**Web:** www.visitscotland.com
**VAT No:** 270106107 **Estd:** 2004 Incorporate By Act Of Parliament
**Line of Business:** Tourist information offices
**Trading Style:** Visit Scotland, Visit Scotland
**Principals:** N Chumley *(Marketing)*, Ms L Easton *(Marketing)*, T Band, T Buncle, G Birse, Dr J G Adams, G Inglis, T Oliphant
**Responsibilities**
**Senior:** Mike Cantley *(Chief Executive Officer)*, Jim Clarkson *(Regional Partnership Director)*, Alex Meikleham *(General Manager)*
**Finance:** Mervyn Brown *(Head of Finance)*
**Marketing:** Laura Archibald *(Marketing Manager)*, Lauren Bridges *(Campaigns Manager)*, Noelle Campbell *(Marketing Executive)*, Po Lee *(Marketing Director)*, Kathyrn MacDonald *(Product Manager)*, Elizabeth Milton *(Business Relationship Manager)*, Lorna Reid *(?Local Campaigns Manager)*, Alison Robb *(Corporate Press Manager)*, Lindsay Symington *(Trade Marketing Executive)*, Kerry Thomson *(Press Officer)*
**HR:** Lynn Jack *(Regional Manager - Visitor Ser)*, Fiona Reith *(Human Resources Manager)*
**Facilities:** Neil Dickson *(Facilities Manager)*
**Operations:** Robbie Clyde *(Ryder Cup Project Director)*, Bob Flavell *(Senior Quality Advisor, Qualit)*, John Macphee *(Quality and Tourism Advisor)*
**Branches:** Visit Scotland, Bayfield House, Bayfield Road, Portree, Isle Of Skye IV51 9EL
**US SIC:** 7999 **UK SIC:** 97913
**Bankers:** Bank Of Scotland (80-20-00)
**Employees:** 200

DUNS 73-798-6922
## Visitbritain Ltd
Sanctuary Buildings, Great Smith Street, London SW1P 3BT
**Tel:** 02075781000
**Web:** www.visitbritain.com
**Reg No:** 5055109 **Estd:** 2004 Private Limited Company
**Line of Business:** Market research and public opinion polling
**Issued Capital:** £100
**Director:** Ms R S Carey
**Co. Secretary:** Ms Marcia Oliver
**Responsibilities**
**Senior:** David Parkhill *(Director Of Administration Ser)*
**US SIC:** 7392, 7999
**UK SIC:** 83951, 97913

| | 31-03-14 | 31-03-13 | 31-03-12 |
|---|---|---|---|
| TA | 100 | 100 | 100 |
| NW | 100 | 100 | 100 |

DUNS 21-341-1806
## Visiting Teachers & Support Services
63 Niddrie Mains Terrace, Edinburgh, Midlothian EH16 4NX
**Tel:** 0131-4692850
**Web:** www.educ.edin.gov.uk
**Estd:** 2004 Proprietorship
**Line of Business:** Education agencies and authorities
**Proprietor:** Mrs A Garbett
**Responsibilities**
**Senior:** Geraldine Elliot *(Manager)*, Alison Garbett *(Manager)*, Emily Renner *(Acting Head Of Service)*
**US SIC:** 8299 **UK SIC:** 93300
**Employees:** 60

DUNS 21-391-4796
## Visitscotland
Monteith House, 11 George Square, Glasgow, Lanarkshire G2 1DY
**Web:** www.visitscotland.com
**Estd:** 1996
**Line of Business:** Airline ticket suppliers and agencies
**Proprietor:** N Dixon
**Responsibilities**
**Senior:** David Adams-McGilp *(Regional Director)*
**US SIC:** 7999 **UK SIC:** 97913
**Employees:** 60

DUNS 73-809-5210
## Visitscotland Ltd
94 Ocean Drive, Edinburgh, Midlothian EH6 6JH
**Tel:** 0131-472-2222
**Web:** www.visitscotland.com
**Reg No:** 0264598SC **Estd:** 2004 Private Limited Company
**Line of Business:** Other business activities not elsewhere classified
**Issued Capital:** £1
**Directors:** K W Neilson, M C Roughead
**Co. Secretary:** Leslie Dingley
**Responsibilities**
**IT:** Mike Flack *(Head of IT)*
**US SIC:** 7399 **UK SIC:** 83954

| | 31-03-14 | 31-03-13 | 31-03-12 |
|---|---|---|---|
| TA | 1 | 1 | 1 |
| NW | 1 | 1 | 1 |

DUNS 22-080-7262 Imp-Exp
## Vislink Plc
Marlborough House, Charnham Lane, Hungerford, Berkshire RG17 0EY
**Tel:** 01488-685500
**Web:** www.vislink.com
**Reg No:** 4082188 **Estd:** 2000 Public Limited Company
**Line of Business:** Management activities of holding companies
**Export Sales:** £54,187,000
**Issued Capital:** £2,847,556
**Directors:** J C Varney, O B Ellingham, I G Davies, J E Hawkins, R B Howe
**Co. Secretary:** Ian Davies
**Responsibilities**
**Senior:** Ian Scott-Gall *(Group Chief Executive Officer)*, James Trumper *(Finance Director)*
**Finance:** James Trumper *(Finance Director)*
**US SIC:** 6711, 3679
**UK SIC:** 83962, 34542
**Auditors:** PricewaterhouseCoopers LLP
**Bankers:** Barclays Bank Plc (20-31-52)

| | 31-12-13 | 31-12-12 | 31-12-11 |
|---|---|---|---|
| TO | 59,879,000 | 57,203,000 | 50,314,000 |
| P/L | 3,093,000 | 2,232,000 | (3,617,000) |
| NW | 16,569,000 | 18,701,000 | 16,182,000 |
| WC | 13,208,000 | 16,077,000 | 14,770,000 |
| Emp. | 251 | 251 | 292 |

DUNS 21-034-3834
## Vista
2-6 Simmins Crescent, Leicester, Leicestershire LE2 9AH
**Tel:** 01162781152
**Web:** www.vistablind.org.uk
**Estd:** 2012
**Line of Business:** Disability services
**Responsibilities**
**Senior:** Paul Bott *(Chief Executive)*, Peter Kazakevics *(Manager)*
**US SIC:** 5462 **UK SIC:** 64100
**Employees:** 50

DUNS 22-853-8948 Imp
## Vista Engineering Ltd
Carr Brook Works Elnor Lane, High Peak, Derbyshire SK23 7JN
**Tel:** 01663736700 **Fax:** 01663-736710
**Web:** www.vistaeng.co.uk
**Reg No:** 1439569 **VAT No:** 158021190
**Estd:** 1979 Private Limited Company
**Line of Business:** Wall ties
**Trading Style:** Vista-Fix, Vista-Plas, Vista Scotland
**Issued Capital:** £50,200
**Principals:** D Travis *(Managing)*, P D Travis, Mrs S A Travis
**Co. Secretary:** Mrs Gillian Travis
**Responsibilities**
**Senior:** Neil Barr *(Works Manager)*
**Sales:** Simon Fullard *(National Sales Manager)*
**Health & Safety:** Neil Barr *(Works Manager)*
**Facilities:** Neil Barr *(Works Manager)*
**Engineering:** Neil Barr *(Works Manager)*
**Branches:** Vista Engineering Ltd, Shepley Lane Indstl Est, Stockport, Cheshire SK6 7JN
**US SIC:** 1799, 3496
**UK SIC:** 50000, 31694
**Auditors:** Bennett Verby LLP
**Bankers:** Barclays Bank Plc (20-82-14)

| | 30-11-13 | 30-11-12 | 30-11-11 |
|---|---|---|---|
| TO | 7,923,121 | 7,550,964 | 8,108,226 |
| P/L | 879,092 | 778,740 | 972,222 |
| NW | 5,015,325 | 4,530,706 | 3,980,620 |
| WC | 3,609,997 | 1,963,528 | 996,491 |
| Emp. | 50 | 52 | 53 |

DUNS 77-696-9321
## Vista Panels Ltd
**(Subsidiary of:** Corpacq Ltd)
Prenton Way, Prenton, Merseyside CH43 3DU
**Tel:** 0151-608-1423
**Web:** www.vista-panels.co.uk
**Reg No:** 3006563 **VAT No:** 634086933
**Estd:** 1995 Private Limited Company
**Line of Business:** Manufacturers of domestic doors
**Export Sales:** £385,729
**Issued Capital:** £100
**Directors:** S J Scott, W R Buchan, H W Lau, K G Sadler, W J Anger
**US SIC:** 2431 **UK SIC:** 46300
**Auditors:** Chadwick
**Bankers:** Lloyds TSB Bank plc (30-91-01)

| | 31-12-13 | 31-12-12 | 31-12-11 |
|---|---|---|---|
| TO | 12,057,456 | 10,752,963 | 9,957,533 |
| P/L | 1,077,474 | 997,189 | 887,401 |
| NW | 8,259,568 | 7,439,277 | 6,692,079 |
| WC | 8,092,006 | 7,308,531 | 6,496,687 |
| Emp. | 100 | 98 | 91 |

DUNS 21-722-6739
## Vista Retail Support Holdings Ltd
Unit 1b Pentwyn Business Centre, Wharfedale Road, Cardiff, South Glamorgan CF23 7HB
**Tel:** 02920542487
**Reg No:** 7600905 **Estd:** 1996 Private Limited Company
**Line of Business:** Cash register and epos equipment
**Export Sales:** £43,160
**Issued Capital:** £10,100
**Directors:** K M Brooks, V F Haffenden, Mrs L Humphreys
**Co. Secretary:** Mrs Kara Kerr
**US SIC:** 3579 **UK SIC:** 33010
**Auditors:** PricewaterhouseCoopers LLP

| | 31-08-13 | 31-08-12 |
|---|---|---|
| TO | 12,454,342 | 9,992,424 |
| P/L | 351,877 | 188,811 |
| NW | (1,035,589) | (1,482,491) |
| WC | (296,314) | (222,642) |
| Emp. | 176 | 174 |

DUNS 77-738-2094
## Vista Retail Support Ltd
**(Subsidiary of:** Vista Retail Support Holdings Ltd)
Unit 1b Pentwyn Business Centre, Wharfedale Road, Cardiff, South Glamorgan CF23 7HB
**Tel:** 029-2054-2460 **Fax:** 02920542486
**Web:** www.vistaretail.com
**Reg No:** 3009356 **VAT No:** 741775320
**Estd:** 1995 Private Limited Company
**Line of Business:** Manufacturers of pcs
**Export Sales:** £43,160
**Issued Capital:** £72,391
**Directors:** V F Haffenden, J Pepper, R Cottrell, Mrs L Humphreys, K M Brooks
**Co. Secretary:** Mrs Kara Kerr
**Responsibilities**
**Senior:** Richard Olds *(Manager)*
**Finance:** Richard Olds *(Manager)*
**IT:** David Dwyer *(Network, Security Manager)*
**Operations:** Sean Guy *(Operations)*
**Branches:** Vista Retail Support Ltd, Prospect Ct, Courteenhall Rd, Northampton, Northamptonshire NN7 3DG
**US SIC:** 3573 **UK SIC:** 33020
**Auditors:** PricewaterhouseCoopers LLP
**Bankers:** Barclays Bank Plc (20-97-09)

| | 31-08-13 | 31-08-12 | 31-08-11 |
|---|---|---|---|
| TO | 12,454,342 | 11,968,766 | 11,365,648 |
| P/L | 790,821 | 556,066 | 1,422,817 |
| NW | 2,538,702 | 4,184,518 | 3,456,294 |
| WC | 2,143,509 | 3,923,392 | 3,239,266 |
| Emp. | 176 | 171 | 156 |

DUNS 21-126-7928 Imp
## Vistajet International Ltd
**(Subsidiary of:** Vistajet Group Holding Sa)
5121 Charles Street, Mayfair, London W1J 5EU
**Tel:** 0207 0605 700
**Web:** www.vistajet.com
**Reg No:** 6617647 **Estd:** 2012 Private Limited Company
**Line of Business:** Airports & flying fields
**Trading Style:** Vistajet Holdings
**Issued Capital:** £1
**Director:** I B Moore
**Co. Secretary:** Iain Rubli
**Responsibilities**
**Senior:** Steve Tong *(Finance Director)*
**Finance:** Steve Tong *(Finance Director)*
**US SIC:** 4582, 4712
**UK SIC:** 76400, 77002
**Auditors:** Ernst & Young LLP

**Bankers:** HSBC Bank plc (40-08-21)

| | 31-12-13 | 31-12-12 | 31-12-11 |
|---|---|---|---|
| TO | 13,705,577 | N/A | N/A |
| P/L | 408,714 | N/A | N/A |
| NW | 120,253 | (171,982) | (400,315) |
| WC | (286,953) | (537,347) | (515,319) |
| Emp. | 109 | N/A | N/A |

DUNS 45-847-8716

## Vistastar Leisure Plc

29-30 Fitzroy Square, London W1T 6LQ
**Tel:** 02088400044 **Fax:** 020-8840-0055
**Reg No:** 3194555 **Estd:** 1996 Public Limited Company
**Line of Business:** Other human health activities
**Issued Capital:** £50,002
**Director:** K S Sandhu
**Co. Secretary:** Dharminder Sandhu
**US SIC:** 8091 **UK SIC:** 95200
**Auditors:** Goodman Jones
**Bankers:** Lloyds TSB Bank plc (30-98-91)

| | 31-03-14 | 31-03-13 | 31-03-12 |
|---|---|---|---|
| TO | 6,814,374 | 6,473,780 | 6,150,742 |
| P/L | 1,579,232 | 1,502,114 | 1,464,886 |
| NW | 15,195,738 | 19,593,147 | 18,719,248 |
| WC | 2,605,655 | 321,456 | (696,139) |
| Emp. | 96 | 98 | 92 |

DUNS 21-011-9345

## Visteon Engineering Services Pension Trustees Ltd

1 Springfield Lyons Approach, Springfield, Chelmsford, Essex CM2 5LB
**Tel:** 01245395000
**Web:** www.visteon.com
**Reg No:** 6351852 **Estd:** 2007 Private Limited Company
**Line of Business:** Engineers (general)
**Directors:** Ms B A Quilty, N Hogwood, K A Holland, A Banks, I Scott, P Ewers, J Barham, A S Jullien
**Co. Secretary:**
Squire Patton Boggs Secretarial
**Responsibilities**
**Senior:** Christopher Pond *(Director)*, Bob Swanson *(Manager)*
**IT:** Ilker Giritiliogio *(IT Director)*
**US SIC:** 6371 **UK SIC:** 82002

| | 31-03-14 | 31-03-13 | 31-03-12 |
|---|---|---|---|
| TA | 1 | 1 | 1 |
| NW | 1 | 1 | 1 |

DUNS 39-465-4347

## Vistex (Uk) Ltd

The Forum, London NW1 0EG
**Tel:** 020-7543-7500 **Fax:** 020-7543-7600
**Web:** www.counterp.com
**Reg No:** 2123605 **Estd:** 1987 Private Limited Company
**Line of Business:** Hardware consultancy
**Export Sales:** £5,931,736
**Issued Capital:** £10,000
**Director:** A Biegun
**Responsibilities**
**Senior:** Greg Helland *(Executive Vice President)*, Robert Katovsky *(Manager)*, Laura Katovsky *(Manager)*, Robert Leiper *(Manager)*
**Admin:** Kinga Daszewski *(Office Manager)*
**US SIC:** 7379 **UK SIC:** 83940
**Auditors:** Chantrey Vellacott
**Bankers:** Barclays Bank Plc (20-65-82)

| | 31-12-13 | 31-12-12 | 31-12-11 |
|---|---|---|---|
| TO | 8,455,763 | 7,793,931 | 7,757,864 |
| P/L | (667,549) | (589,469) | 972,197 |
| NW | (357,240) | 295,661 | 852,271 |
| WC | (649,046) | (71,273) | 664,047 |
| Emp. | 106 | 101 | 90 |

DUNS 23-126-0261

## Vistra Trust Company (Jersey) Ltd

**(Subsidiary of:** Vistra Holding Sa)
4th Floor, St Pauls Gate, Jersey, Channel Islands JE1 4TR
**Tel:** 01534-504700 **Fax:** 01534-504701
**Web:** www.vistra.com
**Reg No:** 0025313J **Estd:** 1983 Private Limited Company
**Line of Business:** Book-keeping activities
**Trading Style:** Vistra Trust Company (Jersey) Ltd
**Issued Capital:** £1
**Directors:** R Hodges, A Taylor, C Malet-De-Carteret, B Frith, J Purgal, P Sewell
**Co. Secretary:** Mrs Annette Laffoley
**Responsibilities**
**Senior:** Charles Malet-de-carteret *(Director)*, christopher burton *(Manager)*
**US SIC:** 8931 **UK SIC:** 83600
**Employees:** 60

DUNS 21-828-1000

## Visual Arts Oakwood Academy Technology & Sports College

Chatsworth Road Ellesmere Park, Eccles, Manchester M30 9DY
**Tel:** 01619212894
**Web:** www.oakwoodhighschool.co.uk
**Reg No:** 7982516 **Estd:** 2012 Private Company Limited By Guarantee
**Line of Business:** General secondary education
**Directors:** D C Holland, Miss J Gaskell, Ms J Deadman, Ms A D Nicholson, Ms S Papworth, Ms J Collinson, L Cooper, Ms M Burgin
**US SIC:** 8211 **UK SIC:** 93200
**Bankers:** Lloyds TSB Bank plc (30-00-00)

| | 31-08-14 | 31-08-13 |
|---|---|---|
| TO | 3,247,000 | 4,786,000 |
| P/L | 168,000 | 418,000 |
| NW | 238,000 | 334,000 |
| WC | 900,000 | 791,000 |
| Emp. | 63 | 71 |

DUNS 39-346-8046 **Imp-Exp**

## Visual Impact (U K) Ltd

Units 3&4 Teddington Business Park, Teddington, Middlesex TW11 9BQ
**Tel:** 02089771222 **Fax:** 020-8943-5307
**Web:** www.visuals.co.uk
**Reg No:** 2120497 **VAT No:** 479912689
**Estd:** 1988 Private Limited Company
**Line of Business:** Television activities
**Export Markets:** U.S.A.
**Export Sales:** £25,735,359
**Issued Capital:** £100
**Directors:** G Hawkins, D G Rees, P Jani, T Sparrock
**Responsibilities**
**Senior:** Ian Marsden *(Human Resources Manager)*, John Quincey *(Manager)*
**IT:** Ovi Preda *(Computer Manager)*
**HR:** Ian Marsden *(Human Resources Manager)*
**Health & Safety:** Ian Marsden *(Human Resources Manager)*
**US SIC:** 4833 **UK SIC:** 97411
**Auditors:** Haines Watts
**Bankers:** HSBC Bank plc (40-44-46)

| | 31-07-13 | 31-07-12 | 31-07-11 |
|---|---|---|---|
| TO | 47,395,318 | 47,220,030 | 42,227,495 |
| P/L | 2,453,960 | 2,071,444 | 1,563,871 |
| NW | 16,636,933 | 17,223,832 | 16,416,423 |
| WC | 10,991,819 | 11,499,065 | 9,502,570 |
| Emp. | 149 | 155 | 160 |

DUNS 42-364-1265

## Visual Sort Ltd

117 Ballycastle Road, Coleraine, Co Londonderry BT52 2DZ
**Tel:** 01265-52434
**Reg No:** 0031021NI **Estd:** 1996 Private Limited Company
**Line of Business:** Other service activities not elsewhere classified
**Issued Capital:** £100
**Director:** D N Mc Bride
**Co. Secretary:** William Kane
**US SIC:** 8999 **UK SIC:** 83954
**Auditors:** Price Waterhouse
**Bankers:** Northern Bank Ltd (95-02-77)

| | 30-09-14 | 30-09-13 | 30-09-12 |
|---|---|---|---|
| TA | 783 | 783 | 783 |
| NW | 783 | 783 | 783 |

DUNS 64-080-7418

## Visual Systems Sales Ltd

**(Subsidiary of:** Staging Connections Ltd)
Innovation House, 17-27 Stirling Road, London W3 8DJ
**Tel:** 020-8752-3900 **Fax:** 02087523901
**Web:** www.visualsystems.co.uk
**Reg No:** 3475956 **Estd:** 1997 Private Limited Company
**Line of Business:** Manufacture of other electrical equipment not elsewhere classified
**Issued Capital:** £2
**Director:** A Shah
**Co. Secretary:** Ms Linda Watling
**Responsibilities**
**Senior:** Ray Sappal *(Office Manager)*
**US SIC:** 3629, 3999, 8911
**UK SIC:** 34350, 49590, 83701
**Auditors:** PKF

| | 31-05-13 | 31-05-12 | 30-05-10 |
|---|---|---|---|
| TA | 432,102 | 265,064 | 54,259 |
| NW | 177,793 | 95,865 | (76,819) |
| WC | 170,853 | 85,976 | (85,997) |

DUNS 21-169-6089

## Vit Supermarket Ltd

Airedale Business Centre, Keighley Road, Skipton, North Yorkshire BD23 2TZ
**Tel:** 01756792600
**Reg No:** 6943915 **Estd:** 2009 Private Limited Company
**Line of Business:** Manufacture of other food products not elsewhere classified
**Export Sales:** £4,569,892
**Issued Capital:** £330
**Director:** M J Davies
**Co. Secretary:** Richard Doyle
**US SIC:** 2099, 2834
**UK SIC:** 42399, 25700

| | 31-03-14 | 31-03-13 | 31-03-12 |
|---|---|---|---|
| TO | 20,433,249 | 20,078,339 | 16,224,773 |
| P/L | 1,737,767 | 1,448,670 | 950,839 |
| NW | 2,373,147 | 1,328,601 | 464,687 |
| WC | 2,442,645 | 1,344,866 | 762,567 |
| Emp. | 147 | 137 | 121 |

DUNS 21-806-7833 **Imp**

## Vita Cellular Foams (Uk) Ltd

**(Subsidiary of:** Vita Cayman Limited)
Oldham Road, Middleton, Manchester M24 2DB
**Tel:** 01616538231 **Fax:** 0161 655 3198
**Web:** www.vitec-km.com
**Reg No:** 0621497 **VAT No:** 606342465
**Estd:** 1959 Private Limited Company
**Line of Business:** Chemicals distribution and wholesale
**Export Sales:** £15,364,735
**Trading Style:** Vitafoam
**Issued Capital:** £62,000,000
**Directors:** J H Menendez, G Davids, D J O'Riordan, G L Maundrell, C G King, J M Cheele, J D Meltham
**Co. Secretary:** Vita Industrial (Uk) Limited
**Responsibilities**
**Senior:** John Cheele *(Manager)*
**HR:** Jonathan Frankish *(Human Resources Manager)*
**Branches:** Vita Cellular Foams (Uk) Ltd, Grosvenor Centre, Grosvenor St, Ashton-Under-Lyne, Lancashire OL7 0JY
**US SIC:** 5161 **UK SIC:** 61200
**Auditors:** PricewaterhouseCoopers LLP
**Bankers:** Lloyds TSB Bank plc (30-00-02)

| | 31-12-13 | 31-12-12 | 31-12-11 |
|---|---|---|---|
| TO | 104,201,863 | 99,080,940 | 108,765,662 |
| P/L | 5,236,091 | 3,965,680 | 2,762,032 |
| NW | 64,338,418 | 59,969,700 | 56,412,353 |
| WC | 78,458,647 | 70,931,348 | 75,713,800 |
| Emp. | 521 | 553 | 569 |

DUNS 29-671-3928

## Vita Thermoplastic Sheet Ltd

Cliftonhall Road, Newbridge, Midlothian EH28 8PW
**Tel:** 01313332819 **Fax:** 01313-334603
**Web:** www.vitashetgroup.co.uk
**Reg No:** 0097825SC **VAT No:** 593007542
**Estd:** 1986 Private Limited Company
**Line of Business:** Plastics raw materials
**Export Sales:** £3,630,118
**Trading Style:** Vitasheetgroup
**Issued Capital:** £2,460,733
**Directors:** R J Perkins, T Harkins, W F Schaller
**Co. Secretary:** Vita Services Limited
**Branches:** Vita Thermoplastic Sheet Ltd, Cliftonhall Road, Newbridge, Midlothian EH28 8PW
**US SIC:** 2821 **UK SIC:** 25140
**Auditors:** PricewaterhouseCoopers LLP
**Bankers:** Lloyds TSB Bank plc (30-95-42)

| | 31-12-13 | 31-12-12 | 31-12-11 |
|---|---|---|---|
| TO | 12,515,300 | 12,713,060 | 13,172,110 |
| P/L | (2,153,226) | (970,006) | (950,114) |
| NW | 9,444,177 | 11,763,286 | 12,567,419 |
| WC | 10,568,303 | 14,242,842 | 19,756,453 |
| Emp. | 59 | 66 | 67 |

DUNS 21-724-8079 **Imp-Exp**

## Vitabiotics Ltd

1 Apsley Way, London NW2 7HF
**Fax:** 020-8955-2601
**Web:** www.vitabiotics.com
**Reg No:** 1012146 **VAT No:** 228598325
**Estd:** 1971 Private Limited Company
**Line of Business:** Health food retailers
**Export Markets:** worldwide
**Export Sales:** £50,421,983
**Issued Capital:** £1,025,000
**Principals:** Dr. K S Lalvani *(Managing)*, P S Vaines, R Shelatkar, Professor A Lalvani, R P Taylor, T Lalvani
**Co. Secretary:** Hardip Singh
**Responsibilities**
**Senior:** Arnold Beckett *(Manager)*
**HR:** Kamal Ajwani *(Human Resources Manager)*
**Health & Safety:** Patricia Branley *(Production Manager)*
**Engineering:** Patricia Branley *(Production Manager)*
**US SIC:** 2834, 5122
**UK SIC:** 25700, 61800
**Auditors:** Grant Thornton UK LLP
**Bankers:** Bank Of Baroda (60-93-76)

| | 31-12-13 | 31-12-12 | 31-12-11 |
|---|---|---|---|
| TO | 89,608,877 | 75,496,048 | 64,062,505 |
| P/L | 22,915,094 | 23,014,445 | 13,642,718 |
| NW | 58,065,383 | 45,607,658 | 35,686,223 |
| WC | 47,829,605 | 42,715,855 | 29,587,456 |
| Emp. | 89 | 95 | 88 |

DUNS 21-113-7516

## Vitacress Ltd

**(Subsidiary of:** Siel - S.G.P.S. S.A.)
Lower Link Farm, Lower Link, St Mary Bourne, Andover, Hampshire SP11 6DB
**Tel:** 01264732002
**Web:** www.vitacress.com
**Reg No:** 6544254 **Estd:** 2008 Private Limited Company
**Line of Business:** Secretarial and translation activities
**Export Sales:** £15,535,000
**Issued Capital:** £59,941,593
**Directors:** R T Bastos, Dr S D Rothwell, T J Brinsmead, V J Dos Santos, S Conway, K Fairbrass
**Co. Secretary:** Keith Fairbrass
**Branches:** Vitacress Ltd, Stoneham Gate, Stoneham Lane, Eastleigh, Hampshire SO50 9NW
**US SIC:** 7339 **UK SIC:** 83954
**Auditors:** PricewaterhouseCoopers LLP
**Bankers:** National Westminster Bank Plc (60-10-43)

| | 31-12-13 | 31-12-12 | 31-12-11 |
|---|---|---|---|
| TO | 166,440,000 | 153,567,000 | 148,286,000 |
| P/L | (1,278,000) | (19,000) | (2,758,000) |
| NW | 20,820,000 | 23,902,000 | 21,409,000 |
| WC | (22,471,000) | (18,559,000) | (13,506,000) |
| Emp. | 1,643 | 1,578 | 1,598 |

DUNS 21-716-5075 **Imp Exp**

## Vitacress Salads Ltd

**(Subsidiary of:** Siel - S.G.P.S. S.A.)
London Road, Amesbury, Salisbury, Wiltshire SP4 7RT
**Tel:** 01980676637 **Fax:** 01264-738762
**Web:** www.vitacress.com
**Reg No:** 0689950 **VAT No:** 411574868
**Estd:** 1962 Private Limited Company
**Line of Business:** Wholesalers of fruit and vegetable
**Export Markets:** Europe
**Issued Capital:** £4,935,500
**Principals:** Dr S D Rothwell *(Managing)*, K Fairbrass, S Conway, T J Brinsmead
**Co. Secretary:** Keith Fairbrass
**Responsibilities**
**Senior:** Helen Budgen *(Manager)*
**Branches:** Vitacress Salads Ltd, Lower Link Farm, Lower Link, Andover, Hampshire SP11 6DB
**US SIC:** 0119, 2033
**UK SIC:** 01001, 41473
**Auditors:** PricewaterhouseCoopers LLP
**Bankers:** National Westminster Bank Plc (55-81-26)

| | 31-12-13 | 31-12-12 | 31-12-11 |
|---|---|---|---|
| TO | 54,449,000 | 50,655,000 | 83,009,000 |
| P/L | 1,974,000 | (575,000) | 1,052,000 |
| NW | 24,822,000 | 23,257,000 | 29,859,000 |
| WC | 11,170,000 | 10,188,000 | 11,082,000 |
| Emp. | 571 | 530 | 904 |

DUNS 21-690-1892

## Vitacress Sales Ltd

**(Subsidiary of:** Siel - S.G.P.S. S.A.)
F2-F4 Western International Market, Southall, Middlesex UB2 5XJ
**Tel:** 02085-730568
**Web:** www.freshproduce.org.uk
**Reg No:** 0876767 **VAT No:** 453019862
**Estd:** 1966 Private Limited Company
**Line of Business:** Wholesalers of fruit and vegetable
**Issued Capital:** £60,000
**Principals:** C H Rees *(Managing)*, K Fairbrass, T J Brinsmead
**Co. Secretary:** Keith Fairbrass
**Responsibilities**
**Senior:** Nicholas Stenning *(Chief Executive)*
**Branches:** Vitacress Sales Ltd, 90-92 Wholesale Markets Precinct, Pershore Street, Birmingham, West Midlands B5 6UN
**US SIC:** 5148, 5199
**UK SIC:** 61700, 61900
**Auditors:** PricewaterhouseCoopers LLP
**Bankers:** National Westminster Bank Plc (60-10-43)

| | 31-12-13 | 31-12-12 | 31-12-11 |
|---|---|---|---|
| TO | 20,437,000 | 18,665,000 | 17,736,000 |
| P/L | 133,000 | 97,000 | 115,000 |
| NW | 430,000 | 339,000 | 274,000 |
| WC | 201,000 | 89,000 | (25,000) |
| Emp. | 47 | 46 | 45 |

DUNS 22-047-9542 **Imp**

## Vital Energi Utilities Ltd

**(Subsidiary of:** Vital Holdings Ltd)
Century House, Roman Road, Blackburn, Lancashire BB1 2LD
**Tel:** 01254-296000 **Fax:** 01254296040
**Web:** www.vitalenergi.co.uk
**Reg No:** 4050190 **VAT No:** 764518215
**Estd:** 2014 Private Limited Company
**Line of Business:** Energy management control systems
**Trading Style:** Vital Energi, Vitalenergi
**Issued Capital:** £1

**Directors:** S J Beckett, G Fielding, I Whitelock, S C Webster
**Co. Secretary:** Stephen Beckett
**Responsibilities**
**Senior:** Stewart Mckechnie *(Financial Director)*, Howard Roache *(Manager)*, Helge Wonsbek *(Manager)*
**Finance:** Stewart Mckechnie *(Financial Director)*
**Sales:** Brendan Clancy *(Business Development Manager)*
**HR:** Ella Stokes *(Human Resources Manager)*
**Operations:** Paul Tierney *(Regional Operations Director)*
**Fleet:** Paul Carberry *(Transport Manager)*
**Branches:** Vital Energi Utilities Ltd, 3rd Floor, 20 Little Britain, EC1A 7DH London
**US SIC:** 3643, 7392
**UK SIC:** 34203, 83951
**Auditors:** RSM Tenon Audit Ltd
**Bankers:** The Royal Bank Of Scotland Plc (16-00-06)

| | 30-06-13 | 30-06-12 | 30-06-11 |
|---|---|---|---|
| TO | 42,726,032 | 47,055,094 | 29,221,122 |
| P/L | 1,271,120 | 3,166,951 | 1,640,692 |
| NW | 7,952,520 | 6,978,602 | 4,606,065 |
| WC | 7,710,561 | 6,844,890 | 4,656,308 |
| Emp. | 221 | 186 | 146 |

DUNS 39-414-9389 **Imp-Exp**
## Vital Pet Products Ltd
The Barton, South Tawton, Okehampton, Devon EX20 2BB
**Tel:** 01837-883000 **Fax:** 01837883020
**Web:** www.vitalpetproducts.co.uk
**Reg No:** 2121746 **VAT No:** 456237832
**Estd:** 1987 Private Limited Company
**Line of Business:** Manufacture of prepared pet foods
**Export Markets:** Belgium; Netherlands; Spain
**Trading Style:** Vital Pet Products Ltd
**Issued Capital:** £342,000
**Principals:** D O Steuart *(Managing)*, G M Askew, Mrs A T Steuart, B A Steuart, A P Steuart
**Co. Secretary:** Mrs Audrey Cook
**US SIC:** 2047 **UK SIC:** 42221
**Auditors:** Bishop Fleming

| | 31-12-13 | 31-12-12 | 31-12-11 |
|---|---|---|---|
| TO | 80,769,000 | 106,147,000 | 113,854,000 |
| P/L | 211,000 | 492,000 | 1,275,000 |
| NW | 4,896,000 | 4,885,000 | 4,779,000 |
| WC | 2,615,000 | 2,359,000 | 2,431,000 |
| Emp. | 449 | 492 | 518 |

DUNS 73-843-5606
## Vital Recruitment (Peterborough) Ltd
Endeavour House, Saville Road, Peterborough, Cambridgeshire PE3 7PS
**Tel:** 01733-331155
**Web:** www.vitalrecruitment.com
**Reg No:** 5098864 **Estd:** 2004 Private Limited Company
**Line of Business:** Employment and recruitment companies and consultants
**Issued Capital:** £1
**Director:** B Singh
**Responsibilities**
**Senior:** Terry Waite *(General Manager)*
**US SIC:** 7361 **UK SIC:** 83954

| | 31-03-14 | 31-03-13 | 31-03-12 |
|---|---|---|---|
| TO | 58,749,061 | 40,750,302 | 31,367,736 |
| P/L | 214,054 | 244,860 | 231,853 |
| NW | 898,196 | 809,425 | 624,201 |
| WC | 1,558,628 | 730,908 | 514,659 |
| Emp. | 6,418 | 3,998 | 3,093 |

DUNS 49-372-6277
## Vital Support Consultancy Ltd
6 Salop Road, Oswestry, Shropshire SY11 2NU
**Tel:** 01691-654545 **Fax:** 01691-679449
**Web:** www.morriscook.co.uk
**Reg No:** 3126221 **Estd:** 1995 Private Limited Company
**Line of Business:** Hardware consultancy
**Issued Capital:** £5
**Directors:** A C Clarke, Ms S A Jones, Miss M A Jones
**Responsibilities**
**Senior:** Karen Whitehead *(Manager)*
**Branches:** Vital Support Consultancy Ltd, East Street, Llangollen, Clwyd LL20 8RB
**US SIC:** 7379 **UK SIC:** 83940

| | 31-03-14 | 31-03-13 | 31-03-12 |
|---|---|---|---|
| TA | 24,895 | 29,276 | 39,268 |
| NW | (22,608) | (28,089) | (35,368) |
| WC | (22,608) | (28,089) | (35,368) |

DUNS 77-964-2714
## Vitality Corporate Services Ltd
**(Subsidiary of:** Discovery Ltd)
20 Gracechurch Street, London EC3V 0BG
**Tel:** 02071338600
**Web:** www.pruhealth.co.uk
**Reg No:** 5933141 **Estd:** 2006 Private Limited Company
**Line of Business:** Non-life insurance
**Trading Style:** Pruhealth
**Issued Capital:** £19,000,000
**Directors:** N S Koopowitz, Sir A W Foster, S W Sinclair, Mrs S C Ellen, A Gore, H P Mayers, A Ntsaluba, B Swartzberg
**Co. Secretary:** Mrs Jennifer Thorn
**US SIC:** 6399 **UK SIC:** 82001
**Auditors:** KPMG Audit PLC

| | 30-06-14 | 30-06-13 | 30-06-12 |
|---|---|---|---|
| TO | 158,077,000 | 129,527,000 | 116,371,000 |
| P/L | 2,098,000 | 1,198,000 | 5,533,000 |
| NW | (23,615,000) | 2,504,000 | 6,155,000 |
| WC | (5,096,000) | (2,543,000) | 3,736,000 |
| Emp. | 1,021 | 877 | 774 |

DUNS 39-465-3125
## Vitality Health Insurance Ltd
**(Subsidiary of:** Discovery Ltd)
Standard Life House, 30 Lothian Road, Edinburgh, Midlothian EH1 2DH
**Tel:** 01202292464
**Web:** www.adviserzone.com
**Reg No:** 2123483 **Estd:** 1987 Private Limited Company
**Line of Business:** Non-life insurance
**Trading Style:** Pruhealth
**Issued Capital:** £187,500,000
**Directors:** S W Sinclair, A Ntsaluba, H P Mayers, Mrs S C Ellen, A Gore, B Swartzberg, Sir A W Foster, N S Koopowitz
**Co. Secretary:** Mrs Jennifer Thorn
**Responsibilities**
**Senior:** Alison Gray *(Manager)*
**Branches:** Vitality Health Insurance Ltd, Little Orchard, Lime Tree Avenue, Wetherby, West Yorkshire LS23 6DP
**US SIC:** 6399 **UK SIC:** 82001
**Auditors:** PricewaterhouseCoopers LLP
**Bankers:** HSBC Bank plc (40-03-28)

| | 30-06-14 | 30-06-13 | 30-06-12 |
|---|---|---|---|
| TO | 158,780,000 | 194,232,000 | 225,046,000 |
| P/L | 57,611,000 | 39,224,000 | (30,671,000) |
| NW | 230,112,000 | 176,211,000 | 141,907,000 |
| WC | 43,732,000 | 53,294,000 | 63,306,000 |

DUNS 29-629-8243 **Exp**
## Vitalograph (U K) Ltd
Vitalograph Business Park, Maids Moreton, Buckingham, Buckinghamshire MK18 1SW
**Tel:** 01280827110
**Web:** www.vitalograph.co.uk
**Reg No:** 1955895 **Estd:** 1985 Private Limited Company
**Line of Business:** Manufacturers of medical equipment
**Export Markets:** Worldwide
**Export Sales:** £11,092,361
**Issued Capital:** £139,500
**Principals:** B R Garbe *(Managing)*, M J Garbe *(Managing)*, M J Lindsay *(Managing)*, Ms G Garbe
**Co. Secretary:** Marcus Garbe
**US SIC:** 3841 **UK SIC:** 37201
**Auditors:** Brebner Allen & Trapp
**Bankers:** Barclays Bank Plc (20-03-18)

| | 31-12-13 | 31-12-12 | 31-12-11 |
|---|---|---|---|
| TO | 17,010,066 | 16,613,469 | 11,595,296 |
| P/L | 1,652,019 | 1,316,025 | 652,696 |
| NW | 6,463,018 | 4,857,765 | 4,048,214 |
| WC | 5,373,078 | 3,817,076 | 2,082,228 |
| Emp. | 169 | 151 | 131 |

DUNS 21-808-0380 **Exp**
## The Vitec Group Plc.
Bridge House, Heron Square, Richmond, Twickenham, Middlesex TW9 1EN
**Tel:** 020 8332 4600 **Fax:** 020 8948 8277
**Web:** www.vitecgroup.com
**Reg No:** 0227691 **Estd:** 1928 Public Limited Company
**Line of Business:** Management activities of holding companies
**Export Markets:** Worldwide
**Export Sales:** £288,900,000
**Issued Capital:** £8,762,224
**Directors:** C J Humphrey, Ms C J Fairbaim, M Rollins, S C Bird, P A Hayes, N S Moore, J Mcdonough, Ms L A Rienecker
**Co. Secretary:** Jonathan Bolton
**Responsibilities**
**Senior:** John McDonough *(Chairman)*
**Marketing:** George Kealy *(Senior VP Global Sales & Marke)*
**Sales:** George Kealy *(Senior VP Global Sales & Marke)*
**Operations:** Mauro Lorenzi *(Manager)*
**US SIC:** 6711, 7399
**UK SIC:** 83962, 83954
**Auditors:** KPMG Audit PLC
**Bankers:** HSBC Bank plc (40-15-22)

| | 31-12-13 | 31-12-12 | 31-12-11 |
|---|---|---|---|
| TO | 315,400,000 | 345,300,000 | 351,000,000 |
| P/L | 20,400,000 | 16,100,000 | 23,800,000 |
| NW | 43,900,000 | 46,400,000 | 54,300,000 |
| WC | 62,000,000 | 68,100,000 | 53,000,000 |
| Emp. | 1,898 | 2,085 | 2,052 |

DUNS 28-972-3934 **Imp-Exp**
## Vitec Videocom Ltd
**(Subsidiary of:** The Vitec Group Plc.)
William Vinten Building, 73 Western Way, Bury St Edmunds, Suffolk IP33 3TB
**Tel:** 01284776700 **Fax:** 01284-750560
**Web:** www.vinten.com
**Reg No:** 1738425 **VAT No:** 289503622
**Estd:** 1983 Private Limited Company
**Line of Business:** General mechanical engineering
**Export Markets:** Worldwide
**Export Sales:** £70,994,000
**Issued Capital:** £50,000,000
**Directors:** M J Green, M Danilowicz, P A Hayes, A P Cannon, J M Bolton
**Co. Secretary:** Jonathan Bolton
**Responsibilities**
**Senior:** Johannes Janssen *(Chief Executive)*, Andy Leczycki *(Warehouse Supervisor)*, Jayne Milton *(Manager)*
**Marketing:** Ruth Paskins-Gordon *(Marketing Manager)*
**Sales:** David Monkhouse *(Sales Manager)*
**IT:** Mark Holt *(IT Manager)*
**HR:** Carli Crawford *(Human Resources Advisers)*
**Facilities:** Steve Holstead *(Maintenance Supervisor)*
**US SIC:** 8911 **UK SIC:** 83701
**Auditors:** KPMG Audit PLC
**Bankers:** HSBC Bank plc (40-15-22)

| | 31-12-13 | 31-12-12 | 31-12-11 |
|---|---|---|---|
| TO | 77,714,000 | 75,002,000 | 70,450,000 |
| P/L | 6,095,000 | 8,574,000 | 9,501,000 |
| NW | 119,966,000 | 122,505,000 | 129,273,000 |
| WC | 120,067,000 | 120,842,000 | 123,880,000 |
| Emp. | 248 | 269 | 234 |

DUNS 23-882-1370 **Imp**
## Vitesse Plc
Excelda House, 15 Tennis Street, London SE1 1YD
**Tel:** 02073577888 **Fax:** 02073578855
**Web:** www.vitesse.plc.uk
**Reg No:** 3873327 **Estd:** 1991 Public Limited Company
**Line of Business:** Other computer related activities
**Trading Style:** Laserlife
**Issued Capital:** £250,000
**Directors:** R A Parncutt, C P Mather
**Co. Secretary:** Christopher Hancock
**Responsibilities**
**Senior:** Barbara Lyle *(Manager)*, Barbara palmer *(Manager)*
**IT:** Rayner Baubr *(It Manager)*, Brent McMillan *(Computer Manager)*
**HR:** Lara Woodward *(Human Resources Manager)*
**US SIC:** 7379 **UK SIC:** 83940
**Auditors:** Aston & Co

| | 30-06-14 | 30-06-13 | 30-06-12 |
|---|---|---|---|
| TO | 20,414,191 | 18,984,306 | 17,272,186 |
| P/L | 695,294 | 675,209 | 425,751 |
| NW | 519,596 | 201,283 | (121,908) |
| WC | (620,171) | (820,447) | (860,900) |
| Emp. | 103 | 100 | 105 |

DUNS 73-810-3832
## Vitol Aviation Uk Ltd
**(Subsidiary of:** Stichting Administratiekantoor Vitol Holding Ii)
Belgrave House, 76 Buckingham Palace Road, London SW1W 9TQ
**Tel:** 020-7973-4200
**Web:** www.vitol.com
**Reg No:** 5066574 **Estd:** 1988 Private Limited Company
**Line of Business:** Wholesale of petroleum and petroleum products
**Directors:** J Sterken, R Hardy
**Co. Secretary:** John Martin
**US SIC:** 5171 **UK SIC:** 61200
**Bankers:** Ing Bank Nv (70-13-46)
**Employees:** 100
**Turnover:** £1,088,010,593

DUNS 37-811-9051
## Vittoria Healthcare Ltd
Unit C Eden House, Chester Business Park, Chester, Cheshire CH4 9QT
**Tel:** 01244680558
**Web:** www.vittoriahealthcare.com
**Reg No:** 3298208 **Estd:** 1997 Private Limited Company
**Line of Business:** Dispensing chemists
**Issued Capital:** £9,745
**Directors:** B Downey, G Thomas, P F Murphy
**Co. Secretary:** Robert Cole
**Branches:** Vittoria Healthcare Ltd, Egremont Pharmacy, 9A King Street, Wallasey, Merseyside CH44 8AT
**US SIC:** 5912 **UK SIC:** 64300
**Auditors:** PKF

| | 31-03-14 | 31-03-13 | 31-03-12 |
|---|---|---|---|
| TO | 18,216,127 | 22,385,438 | 26,001,022 |
| P/L | 948,870 | (2,068,712) | (2,731,239) |
| NW | (4,450,604) | (7,905,032) | (8,627,815) |
| WC | (475,855) | (435,721) | (9,542,357) |
| Emp. | 173 | 208 | 228 |

DUNS 22-405-4945
## Vittoria Pharmacy
134 St Anne Street, Birkenhead, Merseyside CH41 3SJ
**Tel:** 0151-647-8679
**Estd:** 1996 Proprietorship
**Line of Business:** Chemists dispensing
**Proprietor:** A Williams
**Responsibilities**
**Senior:** Dave Laughlin *(Manager)*
**US SIC:** 5912 **UK SIC:** 64300
**Employees:** 47

DUNS 29-873-5853 **Imp-Exp**
## Viva Enterprises Ltd
245-247 Cricklewood Broadway, London NW2 6NY
**Tel:** 02084500000
**Web:** www.arrowelectricals.co.uk
**Reg No:** 2076721 **VAT No:** 446177534
**Estd:** 1988 Private Limited Company
**Line of Business:** Electrical wholesalers
**Trading Style:** Arrow Viva Enterprises, Arrow Electrical Trade Discount Centre, Arrow Electric Trade
**Issued Capital:** £1,000
**Principals:** R Dangoor *(Managing)*, N Dangoor
**Co. Secretary:** Nava Dangoor
**Responsibilities**
**Finance:** Dilip Kotcha *(accounts manager)*
**Health & Safety:** Dilip Kotcha *(accounts manager)*
**Branches:** Viva Enterprises Ltd, 38 Goldhawk Road, London W12 8DH
**US SIC:** 5074, 5084
**UK SIC:** 61300, 61490
**Auditors:** Tung Sing & Co Ltd

| | 31-03-14 | 31-03-13 | 31-03-12 |
|---|---|---|---|
| TA | 12,646,828 | 11,139,718 | 9,629,217 |
| P/L | 2,538,525 | 2,814,350 | 284,955 |
| NW | 10,899,293 | 9,248,225 | 7,364,564 |
| WC | 8,615,209 | 8,716,968 | 6,775,737 |
| Emp. | 60 | 57 | 56 |

DUNS 77-956-8849 **Imp**
## Viva Eyewear (U K) Ltd
**(Subsidiary of:** Highmark Inc.)
Milner Court, Hornbeam Square South, Harrogate, North Yorkshire HG2 8NB
**Tel:** 01423874466 **Fax:** 01423-874499
**Web:** www.vivagroup.com
**Reg No:** 3060330 **Estd:** 1995 Private Limited Company
**Line of Business:** Distribution service providers
**Export Sales:** £17,437,000
**Issued Capital:** £2
**Directors:** G Zoppas, M Stefanello
**Co. Secretary:** Ms Julia Bilsland
**Responsibilities**
**Senior:** John Drumm *(Warehouse Manager)*, Brett Moraski *(Manager)*, Frank Rescigna *(Manager)*
**Health & Safety:** John Drumm *(Warehouse Manager)*
**US SIC:** 4712 **UK SIC:** 77002
**Auditors:** PricewaterhouseCoopers LLP
**Bankers:** National Westminster Bank Plc (60-78-81)

| | 31-12-13 | 31-12-12 | 31-12-11 |
|---|---|---|---|
| TO | 22,608,000 | 22,695,000 | 21,901,000 |
| P/L | 4,545,000 | 2,146,000 | 2,298,000 |
| NW | 10,013,000 | 8,837,000 | 7,152,000 |
| WC | 10,224,000 | 9,893,000 | 8,083,000 |
| Emp. | 51 | 49 | 49 |

DUNS 23-859-2658
## Vivalda Ltd
99 Victoria Road, London NW10 6DJ
**Tel:** 02089639999
**Web:** www.vivalda.co.uk
**Reg No:** 3850848 **Estd:** 1999 Private Limited Company
**Line of Business:** Cladding suppliers and contractors
**Export Sales:** £42,020
**Issued Capital:** £100,000
**Directors:** B C Jayes, P Doherty
**Responsibilities**
**Senior:** Jason Mayo *(Manager)*
**Branches:** Vivalda Ltd, Unit 6, Mill Street, Birmingham, West Midlands B6 4BS
**US SIC:** 1799 **UK SIC:** 50000
**Auditors:** P.R. Shah & Co

| | 31-12-13 | 31-12-12 | 31-12-11 |
|---|---|---|---|
| TO | 15,635,324 | 15,015,678 | 18,126,313 |
| P/L | 468,595 | 806,038 | 767,468 |
| NW | 2,839,757 | 2,496,441 | 2,055,764 |
| WC | 1,808,959 | 1,460,909 | 1,515,807 |
| Emp. | 65 | 59 | 52 |

DUNS 29-885-1312

## Vivalis Beauty Ltd

**(Subsidiary of:** Lynch-Staunton Ltd)
Aintree Avenue, White Horse Business Park, Trowbridge, Wiltshire BA14 0XB
**Tel:** 08707551055
**Web:** www.vivalis.co.uk
**Reg No:** 2088080 **Estd:** 1987 Private Limited Company
**Line of Business:** Other retail sale in non-specialised stores
**Issued Capital:** £100
**Directors:** G M Lynch Staunton, J A Thompson, Ms S A Clayton-Smith
**US SIC:** 5399 **UK SIC:** 65600
**Auditors:** BDO LLP
**Bankers:** The Royal Bank Of Scotland Plc (16-00-01)

| | 31-03-14 | 31-03-13 | 16-03-11 |
|---|---|---|---|
| TO | N/A | N/A | 1,288,000 |
| P/L | N/A | N/A | 9,000 |
| NW | 1,419,749 | 721,167 | (4,789,000) |
| WC | 3,220,308 | 2,512,087 | N/A |

DUNS 76-854-8083 **Imp**

## Vivanco U.K. Ltd

**(Subsidiary of:** Xupu Electronics Technology Gmbh)
Vivanco House, Sundon Park Road Luton Enterprise Park, Luton, Bedfordshire LU3 3GU
**Tel:** 01582579333 **Fax:** 01442403030
**Web:** www.vivanco.com
**Reg No:** 2610309 **Estd:** 1992 Private Limited Company
**Line of Business:** Wholesale of computers, computer peripheral equipment and software
**Issued Capital:** £300,000
**Director:** P Gerding
**Co. Secretary:** Miss Deborah Brown
**Responsibilities**
**Senior:** David Bonser *(Commercial Director)*, Philip Gurdin *(Manager)*, Charles Irish *(Manager)*, Paul Irish *(Manager)*
**Operations:** Joe Sweeney *(Operations Manager)*
**Branches:** Vivanco U.k. Ltd, Highfields View, Herne Bay, Kent CT6 6UB
**US SIC:** 7399, 5065
**UK SIC:** 83954, 61500
**Auditors:** PKF
**Bankers:** National Westminster Bank Plc (60-18-11)

| | 31-12-13 | 31-12-12 | 31-12-11 |
|---|---|---|---|
| TO | N/A | N/A | 5,401,600 |
| P/L | N/A | N/A | (618,331) |
| NW | (267,544) | 51,590 | 242,289 |
| WC | (305,544) | (8,028) | 153,707 |
| Emp. | N/A | N/A | 33 |

DUNS 21-664-1059 **Imp**

## Vivat Direct Ltd

**(Subsidiary of:** Regest Ltd)
157 Edgware Road, London W2 2HR
**Tel:** 020-705-34500
**Web:** www.readersdigest.co.uk
**Reg No:** 7184818 **Estd:** 2010 Private Limited Company
**Line of Business:** Publishing of newspapers
**Trading Style:** Reader's Digest
**Issued Capital:** £16,709,603
**Directors:** M S Luckwell, G P Hopkins
**Responsibilities**
**Senior:** Noel Ashman *(Operations Manager)*, Harry Glover *(Customer Service Agent)*, Douglas Nethery *(Manager)*
**US SIC:** 2711, 2741
**UK SIC:** 47512, 47541
**Auditors:** PricewaterhouseCoopers LLP

| | 31-03-14 | 30-06-13 | 30-03-12 |
|---|---|---|---|
| TO | 3,133,835 | 18,505,000 | 62,975,000 |
| P/L | (49,037) | 12,140,000 | (22,304,000) |
| NW | (3,197,206) | (2,183,000) | (32,019,000) |
| WC | (1,769,080) | (894,000) | (12,847,000) |
| Emp. | 33 | 84 | 131 |

DUNS 34-617-9146 **Imp-Exp**

## Vivid Imaginations Ltd

Ashbourne House, Guildford, Surrey GU3 1LS
**Tel:** 01483449944 **Fax:** 01483-446336
**Web:** www.vividtoysandgames.co.uk
**Reg No:** 2755261 **VAT No:** 656543613
**Estd:** 1992 Private Limited Company
**Line of Business:** Manufacturers of games, toys and sporting products
**Issued Capital:** £400,865
**Principals:** N J Austin *(Managing)*, E A Bennie *(Managing)*, P Weston
**Co. Secretary:** Simon Mcintosh
**Responsibilities**
**Senior:** Neil Bandtock *(Manager)*
**Marketing:** E Sherski *(Marketing Director)*, Richard Venner *(Senior Brand Manager - Crayola)*, Mary Wood *(Marketing Director)*
**Sales:** Nic Aldridge *(Senior Brand Manager)*, E Sherski *(Marketing Director)*
**US SIC:** 3949 **UK SIC:** 49420
**Auditors:** PricewaterhouseCoopers LLP
**Bankers:** The Royal Bank Of Scotland Plc (16-29-25)

| | 31-12-13 | 31-12-12 | 31-12-11 |
|---|---|---|---|
| TO | 65,193,000 | 93,089,000 | 78,424,000 |
| P/L | 4,101,000 | 12,425,000 | 8,462,000 |
| NW | 64,808,000 | 62,482,000 | 53,775,000 |
| WC | 63,694,000 | 61,237,000 | 52,900,000 |
| Emp. | 121 | 120 | 111 |

DUNS 21-665-3567

## Vivio Group Holdings Ltd

The Vault, 8 Boughton, Chester, Cheshire CH3 5AG
**Tel:** 01244305100
**Reg No:** 7194376 **Estd:** 2010 Private Limited Company
**Line of Business:** Other letting of own property
**Issued Capital:** £100
**Director:** J Wright
**US SIC:** 6519 **UK SIC:** 85000

| | 31-12-13 | 31-12-12 | 31-12-11 |
|---|---|---|---|
| TO | 9,643,448 | N/A | N/A |
| P/L | 1,413,009 | N/A | N/A |
| NW | 2,297,722 | 100 | 100 |
| WC | 462,055 | N/A | N/A |
| Emp. | 50 | N/A | N/A |

DUNS 57-042-5694 **Imp**

## Vivreau Ltd

**(Subsidiary of:** Hanvest Holding Gmbh)
7-10 Chandos Street, London W1G 9DQ
**Tel:** 0845-674-9655 **Fax:** 08456749655
**Web:** www.vivreau.co.uk
**Reg No:** 2875749 **Estd:** 1993 Private Limited Company
**Line of Business:** Manufacture of other general purpose machinery not elsewhere classified
**Export Sales:** £1,612,594
**Issued Capital:** £202
**Directors:** M R Hankammer, S C Cohen, M Kirschner
**Responsibilities**
**Senior:** Stephen Charles Cohen *(Managing Director)*, Steve Childs *(Manager)*, Debbie Tate *(Corporate Communications)*
**Marketing:** Debbie Tate *(Corporate Communications)*
**US SIC:** 7399 **UK SIC:** 83954
**Auditors:** Shelley Stock Hutter

| | 31-12-13 | 31-12-12 | 31-12-12 |
|---|---|---|---|
| TO | 8,196,903 | 5,079,266 | N/A |
| P/L | 2,612,872 | 1,578,846 | N/A |
| NW | 6,322,197 | 4,949,093 | 3,736,428 |
| WC | 5,288,707 | 4,366,157 | 3,487,622 |
| Emp. | 56 | 54 | N/A |

DUNS 77-888-7018

## Vix Technology Ltd

**(Subsidiary of:** Vix Holdings Ltd)
160 Cowley Road, Acis House, Cambridge, Cambridgeshire CB4 0DL
**Tel:** 01223 728700
**Web:** www.vixuknews.com
**Reg No:** 3039051 **VAT No:** 860209443
**Estd:** 1995 Private Limited Company
**Line of Business:** Other computer related activities
**Export Sales:** £179,000
**Trading Style:** Acis
**Issued Capital:** £2,115,689
**Directors:** M Beeton, S B Gallagher
**Co. Secretary:** Simon Coulthard
**Responsibilities**
**Senior:** Peter Eccleson *(Director Of Uk & Ireland)*
**Branches:** Vix Technology Limited, Unit 10, Stores Rd, Derby, Derbyshire DE21 4BE
**US SIC:** 7379, 7392
**UK SIC:** 83940, 83951
**Auditors:** UHY Hacker Young
**Bankers:** Barclays Bank Plc (20-48-46)

| | 30-06-14 | 30-06-13 | 30-06-12 |
|---|---|---|---|
| TO | 12,684,000 | 12,376,000 | 17,948,000 |
| P/L | 208,000 | 1,225,000 | (1,973,000) |
| NW | 1,548,000 | 1,334,000 | (2,946,000) |
| WC | 1,416,000 | 1,262,000 | (771,000) |
| Emp. | 196 | 197 | 177 |

DUNS 21-629-0964 **Imp**

## Vixen Surface Treatments Ltd

73 Jay Avenue, Teesside Industrial Estate, Stockton-On-Tees, Cleveland TS17 9LZ
**Tel:** 01642769333 **Fax:** 01642769441
**Web:** www.vixen.co.uk
**Reg No:** 7080969 **Estd:** 1990 Private Limited Company
**Line of Business:** Manufacture of other general purpose machinery not elsewhere classified
**Issued Capital:** £1,000
**Director:** A J Mallon
**Responsibilities**
**Finance:** Cheryl Banfield *(Accounts Manager)*, Dorothy Mallon *(Finance Director)*, Gill Stobbs *(Accounts Manager)*
**Sales:** Truda Rogers *(After Sales Manager)*
**Admin:** Debbie Smith *(PA to the Managing Director)*
**Operations:** Andy Scullion *(Factory Manager)*
**US SIC:** 3549 **UK SIC:** 32212
**Auditors:** Eura Audit UK

| | 30-04-14 | 30-04-13 | 30-04-12 |
|---|---|---|---|
| TO | 4,706,025 | 4,133,290 | 4,202,952 |
| P/L | 386,216 | 217,849 | 270,806 |
| NW | 341,858 | 211,488 | 173,777 |
| WC | 120,904 | (51,071) | (43,079) |
| Emp. | 61 | 56 | 64 |

DUNS 50-385-6627

## Vizeum Uk Ltd

**(Subsidiary of:** Dentsu Inc.)
5 Upper St Martin's Lane, London WC2H 9EA
**Tel:** 02073799000 **Fax:** 02074971177
**Web:** www.vizeum.co.uk
**Reg No:** 2394574 **Estd:** 1989 Private Limited Company
**Line of Business:** Advertising activities not elsewhere classified
**Issued Capital:** £59,920
**Directors:** S A Jarrold, M Parry, N C Priday
**Co. Secretary:** Andrew Moberly
**Responsibilities**
**Senior:** Piers Taylor *(Manager)*
**Marketing:** Zoe Schmid *(Sponsorship Manager)*
**US SIC:** 7319 **UK SIC:** 83800
**Auditors:** Deloitte LLP

| | 31-12-13 | 31-12-12 | 31-12-11 |
|---|---|---|---|
| TO | N/A | N/A | 216,848 |
| NW | 59,920 | 59,920 | 59,920 |

DUNS 23-481-7963

## Vizexon Ltd

12 -13 Hassocks Wood, Basingstoke, Hampshire RG24 8UQ
**Tel:** 08442-092533 **Fax:** 01256-470417
**Web:** www.vizexon.co.uk
**Reg No:** 2818598 **VAT No:** 922036164
**Estd:** 1993 Private Limited Company
**Line of Business:** Building of complete constructions or parts thereof; civil engineering
**Issued Capital:** £2
**Directors:** M A Lord-Castle, D R Weston
**US SIC:** 1541, 5161
**UK SIC:** 50100, 61200
**Auditors:** Piper Thompson Chartered Accountants
**Bankers:** Barclays Bank Plc (20-90-56)

| | 31-03-14 | 31-03-13 | 31-03-12 |
|---|---|---|---|
| TO | 125,382 | 71,640 | 232,474 |
| P/L | 99,632 | (81,951) | (47,914) |
| NW | 19,496 | (80,136) | 1,815 |
| WC | 19,493 | (84,635) | (8,880) |

DUNS 34-903-5274

## Viziononline Ltd

64 Birchwood Road, West Byfleet, Surrey KT14 6DP
**Web:** www.viziononline.co.uk
**Reg No:** 5700823 **Estd:** 2006 Private Limited Company
**Line of Business:** Web site design and development
**Issued Capital:** £100
**Director:** H D Coleman
**Co. Secretary:** Mrs Juliet Coleman
**US SIC:** 7379 **UK SIC:** 83940

| | 31-03-14 | 31-03-13 | 31-03-12 |
|---|---|---|---|
| TO | N/A | 329,601 | N/A |
| P/L | N/A | 94,524 | N/A |
| NW | 41,016 | 100 | 5,104 |
| WC | 41,016 | (3,425) | (21) |

DUNS 77-751-4415

## V.J. Donegan & Co. (Plant) Ltd

Europa Way, Stockport, Cheshire SK3 0WT
**Tel:** 0161-495-7300
**Web:** www.donegan.co.uk
**Reg No:** 3015954 **Estd:** 1995 Private Limited Company
**Line of Business:** Other construction work involving special trades
**Issued Capital:** £177
**Directors:** V J Donegan, Ms A Donegan
**Co. Secretary:** Mrs Margarita Ennis
**US SIC:** 1799, 1622
**UK SIC:** 50000, 50200

| | 30-11-13 | 30-11-12 | 30-11-11 |
|---|---|---|---|
| TO | 8,142,379 | 7,362,180 | 6,876,666 |
| P/L | 562,772 | 21,661 | 375,577 |
| NW | 2,215,170 | 2,070,537 | 2,219,868 |
| WC | 946,988 | 609,917 | 695,585 |
| Emp. | 57 | 56 | 51 |

DUNS 21-215-0221 **Imp-Exp**

## Vjs Foods Ltd

**(Subsidiary of:** Tulip International (U K) Ltd)
Beveridge Way, The Hardwick Narrows Industrial Estate, King's Lynn, Norfolk PE30 4NB
**Tel:** 01553-771937 **Fax:** 01553-777139
**Web:** www.tulipltd.co.uk
**Reg No:** 0471630 **Estd:** 2003 Private Limited Company
**Line of Business:** Production of meat products
**Trading Style:** Tulip
**Issued Capital:** £1,500,000
**Co. Secretary:** Herluf Jensen
**Responsibilities**
**Senior:** Stephen Crozier *(Manager)*, Derek Kidd *(Manager)*, Niels Mikkelsen *(Manager)*, Steven Murrells *(CEO)*
**Finance:** Heidi Parton *(Assistant Accountant)*
**IT:** F Power *(IT Manager)*
**US SIC:** 2013, 5147
**UK SIC:** 41223, 61700
**Auditors:** PricewaterhouseCoopers
**Bankers:** Den Danske Bank Aktieselskab (30-12-81)

| | 29-09-13 | 30-09-12 | 02-09-11 |
|---|---|---|---|
| TA | 1,108,000 | 1,108,000 | 1,108,000 |
| NW | 1,108,000 | 1,108,000 | 1,108,000 |

DUNS 28-845-7161

## V.J.Skerry Ltd

72-73 High Street, Huntingdon, Cambridgeshire PE29 3EN
**Tel:** 01480-453524 **Fax:** 01480-433202
**Web:** www.vjskerry.co.uk
**Reg No:** 0628718 **Estd:** 1951 Private Limited Company
**Line of Business:** Electrical contractors and electricians
**Issued Capital:** £1,500
**Principals:** V J Skerry *(Managing)*, P T Wells, Miss J E Skerry
**Co. Secretary:** Ms Jane Skerry
**Responsibilities**
**Senior:** John Skerry *(Managor)*
**US SIC:** 1731 **UK SIC:** 50300
**Auditors:** Bulley Davey, 12 George St, Huntingdon Cambs PE18 6BD.
**Bankers:** National Westminster Bank Plc (60-11-30)

| | 30-06-14 | 30-06-13 | 30-06-12 |
|---|---|---|---|
| TA | 214,967 | 248,747 | 138,733 |
| NW | 111,643 | 114,296 | 18,586 |
| WC | 88,030 | 81,938 | (2,530) |

DUNS 21-104-6406

## Vma Global Resourcing Group Ltd

23 Bedford Square, London WC1B 3HH
**Tel:** 020-7436-4243
**Web:** www.vmagroup.co.uk
**Reg No:** 6473593 **Estd:** 2001 Private Limited Company
**Line of Business:** Labour recruitment and provision of personnel
**Export Sales:** £838,245
**Issued Capital:** £2,000,000
**Directors:** M S Wynn, Miss K Andrews, Ms J Meighan, Ms C E Tuffin
**Co. Secretary:** Martin Wynn
**US SIC:** 7361 **UK SIC:** 83954

| | 31-12-13 | 31-12-12 | 31-12-11 |
|---|---|---|---|
| TO | 8,286,279 | 9,009,079 | 10,152,977 |
| P/L | (224,487) | (326,665) | 311,539 |
| NW | (812,019) | (800,172) | (714,763) |
| WC | (738,876) | (639,055) | (765,464) |
| Emp. | 47 | 47 | 44 |

DUNS 77-490-6879

## Vml London Ltd

**(Subsidiary of:** Wpp Plc)
The Griffin Building, 83 Clerkenwell Road, London EC1R 5AR
**Tel:** 02073-433700 **Fax:** 02073433701
**Web:** http://london.vml.com
**Reg No:** 2974377 **Estd:** 1994 Private Limited Company
**Line of Business:** Hardware consultancy
**Export Sales:** £1,255,000
**Trading Style:** Vml London
**Issued Capital:** £2,600
**Directors:** C Wood, M L Griffiths, S Milliship
**Co. Secretary:** Matthew Griffiths
**US SIC:** 7379 **UK SIC:** 83940
**Auditors:** Deloitte & Touche LLP
**Bankers:** National Westminster Bank Plc (56-00-64)

| | 31-12-13 | 31-12-12 | 31-12-11 |
|---|---|---|---|
| TO | 10,400,451 | 8,786,607 | 8,594,922 |
| P/L | 1,359,652 | 788,282 | 491,734 |
| NW | 1,359,002 | 3,036,856 | 2,243,824 |
| WC | 851,008 | 2,985,924 | 2,176,447 |
| Emp. | 65 | 66 | 72 |

DUNS 42-455-6673 **Imp**

## Vms (Fleet Management) Ltd

**(Subsidiary of:** Vms (Holdings) Ltd)
Stevendale House, Primett Road, Stevenage, Hertfordshire SG1 3EE
**Tel:** 01438731930 **Fax:** 01438-731965
**Web:** www.vmsglobal.co.uk
**Reg No:** 4443331 **Estd:** 2002 Private Limited Company
**Line of Business:** Fleet management
**Issued Capital:** £90
**Directors:** M H James, G C Prentice, R J Horrex
**Co. Secretary:** Richard Horrex
**Responsibilities**
**Senior:** Christopher Oak *(Human Resources Manager)*
**US SIC:** 7399, 7512, 7513
**UK SIC:** 83954, 84801, 84802

**Auditors:** Baker Tilly UK Audit LLP

| | 31-05-13 | 31-05-12 | 31-05-11 |
|---|---|---|---|
| TO | 21,838,476 | 26,439,098 | 23,756,475 |
| P/L | 1,081,138 | 988,182 | 1,434,443 |
| NW | 3,434,331 | 2,724,277 | 2,904,133 |
| WC | (4,091,273) | (3,022,432) | 948,822 |
| Emp. | 58 | 75 | 64 |

DUNS 67-142-3049

## Vmware Uk Ltd

(**Subsidiary of:** Emc Corporation)
Theta Building, Camberley, Surrey GU16 7ER
**Tel:** 01276414300 **Fax:** 01276685018
**Web:** www.vmware.com
**Reg No:** 6001046 **Estd:** 2006 Private Limited Company
**Line of Business:** Computer software (development)
**Trading Style:** Vm Ware
**Issued Capital:** £1,000
**Directors:** P K Krysler, Ms H F Jul Hansen, I Roberts
**Co. Secretary:** Taylor Wessing Secretaries Limit
**Responsibilities**
**Senior:** K Skinnner *(Manager)*
**Marketing:** Jen Gardet *(Marketing Manager)*, Sadrine Leroux-Graves *(?Senior Director, Communicatio)*, Alastair Martin *(Marketing Manager)*
**IT:** Hans Sparkes *(Senior Manager Executive Progr)*
**Engineering:** Joe Baguley *(Chief Technology Officer)*
**US SIC:** 7379 **UK SIC:** 83940
**Auditors:** PricewaterhouseCoopers

| | 31-12-13 | 31-12-12 | 31-12-11 |
|---|---|---|---|
| TO | 85,211,000 | 77,536,000 | 66,316,000 |
| P/L | 5,839,000 | 8,494,000 | 10,275,000 |
| NW | 60,253,000 | 49,313,000 | 35,999,000 |
| WC | 58,503,000 | 48,489,000 | 35,033,000 |
| Emp. | 362 | 344 | 285 |

DUNS 21-884-0916 **Imp**

## V.N. & Britannic Warehouses Ltd

142 Sand Pits, Birmingham, West Midlands B1 3RJ
**Tel:** 01212367271
**Web:** www.britannicwarehouse.co.uk
**Reg No:** 1002902 **Estd:** 1964 Private Limited Company
**Line of Business:** Cash and carry wholesalers
**Trading Style:** Britannic Warehouse
**Issued Capital:** £20,000
**Principals:** K K Laroiya *(Chairman and Managing)*, P D Laroiya, Mrs S D Laroiya, Mrs E A Laroiya
**Co. Secretary:** Kamlesh Laroiya
**Responsibilities**
**Finance:** Mala Higgins *(Financial Controller)*
**Marketing:** Anil Laroiya *(Marketing Manager)*
**HR:** India Laroiya *(Human Resources Manager)*
**Health & Safety:** India Laroiya *(Human Resources Manager)*
**US SIC:** 5199, 5719
**UK SIC:** 61900, 64700
**Auditors:** Bentley Jennison
**Bankers:** HSBC Bank plc (40-05-03)

| | 31-12-13 | 31-12-12 | 31-12-11 |
|---|---|---|---|
| TO | 12,666,652 | 9,943,106 | N/A |
| P/L | 1,436,757 | 1,166,794 | N/A |
| NW | 2,170,599 | 1,897,527 | 1,791,155 |
| WC | 1,251,352 | 999,611 | 1,077,059 |
| Emp. | 81 | 70 | N/A |

DUNS 21-928-8474

## Vocalink Holdings Ltd

Drake House, Homestead Road, Rickmansworth, Hertfordshire WD3 1FX
**Tel:** 0870-165-0019 **Fax:** 0870-920-8711
**Web:** www.vocalink.com
**Reg No:** 6119036 **Estd:** 2007 Private Limited Company
**Line of Business:** Data processing
**Issued Capital:** £142,656,218
**Directors:** P E Horlock, P Emney, Ms C A Hafner, R Hooper, Sir E J Gieve, Ms G Gopalan, J Coyle, D G Yates
**Co. Secretary:** Timothy Ensor-Clinch
**Responsibilities**
**Senior:** Marcelino Castrillo *(Director)*, Marion King *(Chief Executive)*
**Marketing:** Kerry Fraser *(Head of Marketing)*
**IT:** Ian Gausden *(IT Manager)*, Nicholas Masterson-Jones *(IT Officer)*
**HR:** Debbie Longbard *(Human Resources Manager)*
**Health & Safety:** Kaylee Chapman *(Health & Safety Officer)*
**Purchasing:** Rick Hillier *(Purchasing Manager)*
**US SIC:** 7374 **UK SIC:** 83940

**Auditors:** KPMG LLP

| | 31-12-13 | 31-12-12 | 31-12-11 |
|---|---|---|---|
| TO | 190,600,000 | 163,500,000 | 153,400,000 |
| P/L | 27,600,000 | 33,200,000 | 32,100,000 |
| NW | 70,200,000 | 41,600,000 | 25,400,000 |
| WC | 70,000,000 | 35,900,000 | 27,700,000 |
| Emp. | 805 | 776 | 749 |

DUNS 77-777-0140

## The Vocational College Ltd

(**Subsidiary of:** The Vocational College Group Ltd)
1 Dacre Street, Bootle, Merseyside L20 8DN
**Tel:** 01519-441744
**Web:** www.vcoll.ac.uk
**Reg No:** 3023086 **Estd:** 1995 Private Limited Company
**Line of Business:** Training services
**Issued Capital:** £1
**Directors:** J G Mccollah, E Stopforth
**Co. Secretary:** Paul Nilsen
**Responsibilities**
**Senior:** Julian Mcinnerney *(Manager)*
**US SIC:** 8299 **UK SIC:** 93300
**Auditors:** Duncan Sheard Glass

| | 31-07-13 | 31-07-12 | 31-07-11 |
|---|---|---|---|
| TA | 3,380,704 | 3,426,882 | 2,399,625 |
| NW | 1,926,656 | 1,657,485 | 1,245,262 |
| WC | 2,495,304 | 1,926,888 | 1,265,039 |

DUNS 29-847-2457

## Vocational Training Charitable Trust

Eastleigh House, Upper Market Street, Eastleigh, Hampshire SO50 9RD
**Tel:** 02380684500 **Fax:** 023-8065-1493
**Web:** www.vtct.org.uk
**Reg No:** 2050044 **Estd:** 1986 Private Company Limited By Guarantee
**Line of Business:** Charities and charitable organisations
**Directors:** S Dennison, J H Glicher, Dr C Laws, Mrs J A Sworder, Ms B Mitchell, A Lau-Walker, Mrs S C Barnett, Ms V Kay
**Co. Secretary:** Accounting For Charities Ltd
**US SIC:** 8249, 6732
**UK SIC:** 93300, 83100
**Auditors:** Matthews Hanton Ltd
**Bankers:** HSBC Bank plc (40-12-23)

| | 31-07-14 | 31-07-13 | 31-07-12 |
|---|---|---|---|
| TO | 5,609,736 | 5,991,944 | 6,205,038 |
| P/L | (8,453,018) | (207,058) | 852,198 |
| NW | 16,705,354 | 25,002,418 | 23,392,521 |
| WC | (1,192,534) | 7,549,032 | 10,098,884 |
| Emp. | 49 | 48 | 47 |

DUNS 23-296-9076

## Vocus Uk Ltd

Longbow House 20 Chiswell Street, London EC1Y 4TW
**Tel:** 02034-264001 **Fax:** 02072-56284
**Web:** www.whyworkatvocus.co.uk
**Reg No:** 4462780 **Estd:** 2002 Private Limited Company
**Line of Business:** Hardware consultancy
**Trading Style:** Vocus Europe
**Issued Capital:** £100
**Directors:** J Pearlstein, P W Granat
**US SIC:** 7379, 7372
**UK SIC:** 83940
**Auditors:** David G. Simon & Co Ltd
**Bankers:** Lloyds TSB Bank plc (30-00-46)

| | 31-12-13 | 31-12-12 | 31-12-11 |
|---|---|---|---|
| TO | 7,281,795 | N/A | N/A |
| P/L | (2,192,760) | N/A | N/A |
| NW | (7,263,380) | (5,242,497) | (4,157,026) |
| WC | (2,839,122) | (1,646,439) | (817,989) |
| Emp. | 110 | N/A | N/A |

DUNS 29-546-6866

## Vodafone-Central Ltd

(**Subsidiary of:** Vodafone Group Plc)
3 The Maltings, Burton-On-Trent, Staffordshire DE14 1SF
**Web:** www.vodafone-central.com
**Reg No:** 1913537 **VAT No:** 558371123
**Estd:** 1985 Private Limited Company
**Line of Business:** Telecommunications
**Trading Style:** Central Telecom, Telecommunications Europe
**Issued Capital:** £100,000
**Directors:** Ms D Mcintyre, D N Evans, P J Kelly
**Responsibilities**
**Sales:** Adrian Hipkiss *(Sales Manager)*
**IT:** Craig Rogers *(Technical Manager)*
**Health & Safety:** Craig Rogers *(Technical Manager)*
**Facilities:** Craig Rogers *(Technical Manager)*
**Purchasing:** John Banton *(Purchasing Director)*
**Branches:** Vodafone-Central Ltd, 167-169 Eccles New Road, Salford, Lancashire M5 4UD
**US SIC:** 4899, 7399
**UK SIC:** 79020, 83954
**Auditors:** Deloitte LLP

**Bankers:** Lloyds TSB Bank plc (30-91-47)

| | 31-03-14 | 31-03-13 | 31-03-12 |
|---|---|---|---|
| TA | 20,289,757 | 20,289,757 | 20,289,757 |
| NW | 20,289,757 | 20,289,757 | 20,289,757 |

DUNS 22-642-2400 **Exp**

## Vodafone Corporate Ltd

(**Subsidiary of:** Vodafone Group Plc)
The Connection, Vodafone House, Newbury, Berkshire RG14 2FN
**Tel:** 03333040191
**Reg No:** 1786055 **Estd:** 1984 Private Limited Company
**Line of Business:** Telecom consultants
**Export Markets:** Worldwide
**Issued Capital:** £2
**Directors:** D N Evans, Ms D Mcintyre
**Co. Secretary:** Vodafone Corporate Secretaries L
**Branches:** Vodafone Corporate Ltd, 12-14 St. Davids Centre, Cathedral Walk, Cardiff, South Glamorgan CF10 2DS
**US SIC:** 4899 **UK SIC:** 79020
**Bankers:** Barclays Bank Plc (20-00-00)

| | 31-03-14 | 31-03-13 | 31-03-12 |
|---|---|---|---|
| TA | 19,048,000 | 19,048,000 | 19,048,000 |
| NW | 19,048,000 | 19,048,000 | 19,048,000 |

DUNS 22-063-1704

## Vodafone Global Content Services Ltd

(**Subsidiary of:** Vodafone Group Plc)
80 Strand, London WC2R 0RJ
**Tel:** 07717764565
**Web:** www.vodafone.com
**Reg No:** 4064873 **Estd:** 2001 Private Limited Company
**Line of Business:** Business and management consultancy activities not elsewhere classified
**Issued Capital:** £500,466,199
**Directors:** P G Stephenson, N A Wright, J C Morton
**Co. Secretary:** Vodafone Corporate Secretarles L
**US SIC:** 7392 **UK SIC:** 83951
**Auditors:** Arthur Anderson

| | 31-03-14 | 31-03-13 | 31-03-12 |
|---|---|---|---|
| TA | 65,439,000 | 63,216,000 | 62,627,000 |
| P/L | 92,000 | 127,000 | 721,000 |
| NW | (370,959,000) | (358,773,000) | (355,162,000) |
| WC | 65,298,000 | 63,070,000 | 62,327,000 |

DUNS 28-993-6783

## Vodafone Group Plc

Vodafone House, The Connection, Newbury, Berkshire RG14 2FN
**Tel:** 0163533251
**Web:** www.vodafone.com
**Reg No:** 1833679 **Estd:** 1984 Public Limited Company
**Line of Business:** General mechanical engineering
**Issued Capital:** £6,150,892,223
**Directors:** Dame C H Furse, N J Read, G J Kleisterlee, P E Yea, Ms V F Gooding, S C Davis, S C Pusey, S E Jonah
**Co. Secretary:** Ms Rosemary Martin
**Responsibilities**
**Senior:** Jakub Adamczyk *(Manager)*, Tamer Aly *(Manager)*, Denise Anderson *(Team Manager)*, Davide Arzarello *(Executive)*, Patrick Barrett *(Executive)*, Roland Beckmann-Kunz *(Executive)*, Kirsty Bennett *(Manager)*, Ketan Bharati *(Manager)*, Csilla Bodnar *(Manager)*, Amy Oding *(Executive)*, Massimo Pelaia *(Executive)*, Pedro Pena *(Director General)*, Carlo Peretti *(Chairman)*, Debbie Piper *(Manager)*, Francesco Ponticelli *(Manager)*, Andy Reeves *(Chief Technology Officer)*, Ruth Brady *(Manager)*, Kevin Roche *(Manager)*, Francisco Roman *(Chairman)*, Shane Rooney *(Senior Manager)*, Liam Russell *(General Manager)*, Jens Schulte-Bockum *(Chief Executive Officer)*, Ajay Shah *(Assistant Manager)*, Kursten Shalfoon *(General Manager)*, Balesh Sharma *(CEO / Managing Director - Malt)*, Thomas Bruce *(Manager)*, Liliana Solomon *(CEO / Managing Director - Roma)*, Greg Spears *(Spokesman)*, Russell Stanners *(Chief Executive, New Zealand)*, Kendra Stewart *(General manager)*, Joerg Stockinger *(Manager)*, Steve Sumner *(Chairman)*, Ravinder Takkar *(CEO, Vodafone Partner Markets)*, Sandor Tamasi *(Manager)*, Walker Tapia *(Executive)*, Gabor Tarr *(Executive)*, Jakub Buryan *(Manager)*, Ben Threlfall *(Area Manager)*, Serpil Timuray *(Chief Executive of the Africa,)*, Luc Vandevelde *(Director)*, Viswanath Vishy *(Manager)*, Rebecca Webb *(Store Manager)*, Kerry West *(Manager)*, Crispin Westhead *(Manager)*, Oliver Wildblood *(Manager)*, Howard Xia *(General Manager)*, Antonio Caixinha *(Manager)*, Youssef Youssef *(Executive)*, Alaa Zaher *(General Manager)*, Brian Camilleri *(Executive)*, Declan Carew *(Manager)*, Robert Cassar *(Executive)*, Tim Chapman *(Sales Director)*, Ilana Clark *(Director of Communications)*, Mark Clemison *(Executive)*, Daniel Cloke *(HR and Property Director)*, Vittorio Colao *(Chief Executive Officer)*, Niall Cottrill *(Senior Manager Strategy and PI)*, John Coulstock *(Senior Manager)*, David Crown *(General Manager, Business Inno)*, Jouo Cruz *(Manager)*, Rachael Cuschieri *(Executive)*, Mohamed Darwish *(Executive)*, Stephen Deadman *(Executive)*, Nikoleta Dervishi *(Executive)*, Nigel Dews *(Chief Executive Officer)*, Erik Dieteren *(Manager)*, Vassilis Dimos *(Manager)*, Albert Don-Chebe *(Director, Corporate Communicat)*, Hatem Dowidar *(Chairman)*, Pedro Duarte *(Manager)*, Housam El-Dokany *(Manager)*, Bruce Everest *(Executive)*, Salma Farouque *(Executive)*, Daniel Ferrer *(General Manager)*, Marc Fine *(Manager)*, Francesca Fiore *(Manager)*, Nuno Folque *(Manager)*, Susana Fonseca *(Chairman)*, Ralf Forbrig *(Senior Manager OSS Strategy an)*, Wayne Fraser *(Manager)*, Ana Garcia *(Manager)*, Alex Garcia *(Manager)*, Olga Garcia *(Development Officer)*, Max Gasparroni *(Executive)*, Paul Gerlach *(Spokesman)*, Edward Hall *(Executive)*, Sarah Hancy *(Manager)*, Ahmed Hashem *(Executive)*, Gautam Hazari *(Chairman)*, Pablo Herrero *(General Manager)*, Carsten Hess *(Program Manager)*, Dominic Hilton-Foster *(Manager)*, Philipp Humm *(Regional CEO Europe)*, Andrew Hyde *(Manager)*, Renee James *(Non-Executive Director)*, Marcus James *(Manager)*, Andrew Jelley *(Manager)*, Stuart Jordan *(Manager)*, Fritz Joussen *(Chief Executive, Germany)*, Matthias Jungemann *(Partner)*, Dee Kaul *(General Manager)*, Lana Khachan *(Executive)*, Tony Kirkley *(Manager)*, Mohamed Kishk *(Senior Manager)*, Darren Knight *(Manager)*, Ed Large *(Manager)*, Ernest Lefebre *(Executive)*, Peter Lemmens *(Manager)*, Morten Lundal *(Chief Commercial Officer)*, Ruth Maafo *(Manager)*, MAikel Maes *(Manager)*, Craig Marven *(Manager)*, James Moberly *(General Manager)*, Michele Morris *(Executive)*, Mohamed Moshref *(Executive)*, Markus Muenkler *(Manager)*, Rich Neville *(Vice President)*, Fedra Nicholls *(Manager)*
**Finance:** Anna Dimitrova *(Director Finance Enterprise)*, Osama Eldemerdash *(Financial Director)*, Soumitra Ganguly *(General Manager - Finance and)*, neil Garrod *(Treasurer)*, Simon Geyman *(Senior Tax Manager)*, Brian Harris *(Financial Controller)*, David Pursun *(Credit Manager)*, Raj Sethia *(Finance Manager)*, Desmond Webb *(Group Tax Executive)*
**Marketing:** Carlos Avilleira *(Marketing Director)*, Daniela Bagnaschi *(Consumer Marketing Manager)*, Michelle Baguley *(Spokeswoman)*, Carlos Becker *(Marketing Director)*, Deepak Bhatia *(Sales and Marketing Manager)*, Gary Blumgart *(Business Intelligence Manager)*, Ferruccio Borsani *(Head of Business Division)*, Helen Brockett *(Communications Manager)*, Anita Butler *(Business Marketing Manager)*, Antonio Carrico *(Content Services Director)*, David Carro *(Program Manager)*, Naveen Chopra *(Director - Enterprise and Carr)*, Lorena Corinaldesi *(Marketing Manager)*, Mark Corless *(Business Product Manager)*, Rivkah Davidson *(Marketing Manager)*, Caroline Dewing *(Communications Manager)*, Peter Doveren *(Relations Director)*, Blanca Echaniz *(Head of Consumer Marketing)*, Dirk Ellenbeck *(Press Officer)*, Thomas Ellerbeck *(Relations Manager)*, Daryl Fielding *(Director of Brand Marketing)*, Warren Finegold *(Group Strategy and Business De)*, Flaminio Francisci *(Head of Consumer Customer Base)*, Stefano Grianti *(Marketing Director)*, Patrick Harrison-Harvey *(Marketing Manager)*, Kim Hill *(Business Support Manager)*, Juliet Hubert *(Relations Executive)*, Nicola Igusa *(Spokeswoman)*, Martin Jaros *(Head of Marketing Communicatio)*, Ewa Johnson *(Head of Marketing Communicatio)*, Anisa Kaltanji *(Public Relations Specialist)*, Matthew Kirk *(Group External Affairs Directo)*, Jason Knowles *(Business Manager)*, Vangelis Kollias *(Marketing Director)*, Linda Koolman *(Business Channel Manager)*, Ben Lorimer *(Communications Manager)*, Javier Madrono *(Marketing Director)*, Emiliano Maina *(Website Manager)*, Jose Martinez *(Head of Product Development)*, Geraldina Marzolla *(Brand and Advertising Director)*, Debbie Mavis *(Head of Resourcing and Develop)*, Lee Mcdougall *(Marketing Manager)*, Deane Mcintyre *(Head of Campaigns and Online)*, Louise Mifsud *(Relations Manager)*, Claudio Monteverde *(Media and Public Relations)*, Cindy Moussa *(Relations Manager)*, Eadaoin Murphy *(Business Voice Product Manager)*, Mona Nabil *(Communications Manager)*, Rogier Nelissen *(Marketing Director)*, Killian O' Neill *(Business Intelligence Manager)*, Chris Oh *(Relations Executive)*, Gayatri Ojha *(Marketing Manager)*, Shailendra Prasad *(Manager Corporate Affairs)*, Ramanan Ranganathan *(Marketing Director)*, Nils Rouwendal *(Manager Mobile Advertising)*, Jonathan Rutherford *(Marketing Director)*, Manuel Sanchez *(Marketing)*, Nadezda Sobotkova *(Marketing Manager)*, Asit Som

*(Marketing Manager)*, Katelyn Springer *(Business Channel Manager)*, Julie Starley *(Relations Manager)*, Thomas Strehl *(Marketing Manager)*, Sandra Swift *(Relations Manager)*, Ravinder Takkar *(CEO, Vodafone Partner Markets)*, Magdi Tawfiq *(Relations Manager)*, Sylvain Thevenot *(Marketing Director)*, Fiona Turner *(Consultant)*, Uzoni Uzoni *(Head of Customer Base and Expe)*, Nikos Vlachopoulos *(Greece Business Commercial Dir)*, Anka Vollmann *(Press Officer)*, Philippe Weber *(Marketing Director)*, Alard Weisscher *(Relations Executive)*, Alex Windle *(Marketing Director)*, Stephen Wolak *(Website Developer)*
**Sales:** Deepak Bhatia *(Sales and Marketing Manager)*, Cesare Bisio *(Sales Director)*, Haris Broumidis *(Commercial Director Europe)*, Tim Chapman *(Sales Director)*, Simon Cowap *(Sales Delivery Manager)*, Joe Danagher *(Account Manager)*, Jorge Dominguez-Sol *(Head of Wholesale)*, Ana Esposito *(Account Manager)*, Gavin Farnell *(Commercial Manager)*, Ihab Fayed *(Sales Manager)*, Soumitra Ganguly *(General Manager - Finance and)*, Jason Godwin *(Sales Director)*, Jorge Gouveia *(Account Manager)*, Michelle Gray *(Account Manager)*, Carsten Groth *(Account Manager)*, Tyson Hackwood *(Senior Business Development Ma)*, Mike Higham *(Wholesale Business Development)*, Bart Hofker *(Director Consumer Business Uni)*, Pierre Klotz *(Senior Manager, Global Busines)*, Erik Kroon *(Head of Internet Research and)*, Sabrina Lee *(?Customer Management & Commerc)*, John Lillistone *(Business Development Manager)*, Peter Liss *(Senior and Principal Business)*, Morten Lundal *(Chief Commercial Officer)*, Michael Mansour *(Sales Manager)*, Bob Mcninch *(Head of E-Commerce)*, Minnesh Ramdhany *(VGE and Strategic Accounts Man)*, Steve Rieger *(General Manager, Wholesale and)*, Dave Robb *(Senior Sales Executive)*, Jabir Siraz-Ullah *(Commercial Manager)*, Stephen Wareing *(Sales Advisor)*, Darryn Welsh *(Sales Manager)*
**Admin:** Nesreen Fathi *(Executive)*, Kirsten Foster *(Personal Assistant)*, Joost Galema *(Public Relations Manager)*, Moniique Passage *(Secretary)*, Debiie Turton *(Personal Assistant)*
**IT:** Fumagalli Andrea *(Principal Manager Programme &)*, Mark Arnott *(Network Manager)*, Andrea Boccia *(Senior Project Manager)*, Bob Brace *(Head of Information Systems)*, Erik Brenneis *(Head of Global M2M)*, George Bromell *(Technical Manager)*, Andreas Buschmann *(Architect Network and Service)*, Stanley Chia *(Information Technology Directo)*, Andy Dunkin *(Executive)*, Frank Falke *(Executive)*, Mohamed Ghanem *(Information Technology Develop)*, Fiona Gillham *(Enterprise IT & Hosting Catego)*, Kenny Graham *(Head of New Technologies and I)*, Marian Haroon *(Executive)*, Mustafa Komut *(Senior Information Officer)*, Nirupmay Kumar *(Manager, Information Systems a)*, Alan Law *(Manager)*, Fraser Lee *(Director, IT)*, Mike Luntz *(IT Manager)*, Amer Malik *(IT Manager)*, Alessandro Miccono *(Project Manager)*, Wayne Micklethwaite *(Manager, Information Systems a)*, Piergiorgio Mora *(Application Manager)*, Jenifer Mundy *(Technology and Innovation Dire)*, Campbell Murray *(Technology Business Management)*, Mihir Oza *(Vice President - Information T)*, Uday Patil *(Administrator)*, Msrio Reis *(Manager)*, Wael Salem *(Manager)*, Santiago Santo *(Head of Networks)*, Miguel Santos *(IT Director)*, Volkmar Scharf-Katz *(Information Technology Directo)*, Sanjay Sharma *(IT Manager)*, Dipesh Sheth *(Head of Information Technology)*, Sonia Shoesmith *(Manager, Information Systems a)*, Jeffrey Sultana *(Manager, Information Systems a)*, Hazem Tawfik *(Head of Network Development)*, Ken Tunnicliffe *(Information Technology Directo)*, Eric Valentine *(Head of Technology Systems)*, Ivan Zammit *(Manager, Information Systems a)*
**HR:** Terry Cairns *(Human Resources)*, Gabriella Cappitta *(Human Resources)*, Daniel Cloke *(HR and Property Director)*, Carole Driver *(Human Resources)*, Wael El *(Human Resources Director)*, Lorna Farrar *(Head of Employee Experience)*, Michelle Fernandez *(Resourcing Relationship Manage)*, Eugene Gargan *(Manager)*, Sophie Jones *(Technical Recruiter)*, Shammy Joseph *(Associate Vice President Human)*, Sandra Meuter *(HR Consultant)*, Susom Mishra *(Human Resources Manager)*, Neil Porteous *(Human Resources Director)*, Rakesh Ranjan *(Human Resources Manager)*, Menna Samy *(Human Resources)*, Ronald Schellekens *(Group Human Resources Director)*, Vikram Shete *(Human Resources)*, Amit Trivedi *(Human Resources Manager)*, Ranjan Tyagi *(Human Resources Manager)*
**Facilities:** Roger Wakelin *(Group Property Strategy Manage)*
**Operations:** Claire Alexandre *(Production and Operations Mana)*, Rachel Andrews *(Head of Service Operations)*, Paolo Bertoluzzo *(Group Chief Commercial and Ope)*, Julian Bessey *(Product Manager)*, Thomas Born *(Head of ICT Security)*, Katerina Bourgani *(Manager)*, Declan Brennan *(Head of Product and Services D)*, Liam Butler *(Operations Director)*, Scott Carrick *(Product Manager)*, Dimitris Chrysakopoulos *(Project Executive)*, Maurizio Conti *(Senior Quality Specialist)*, Denise D' Elia *(Director, Services)*, Fabrizio De Liberali *(Senior Product Manager)*, Vassilis Emmanuilidis *(Operations Manager)*, Francesco Foglia *(Project Executive)*, Martin Griese *(Manager)*, Thomas Hollwedel *(Product Manager)*, Maya Iyer *(Senior Project Manager)*, Katerina Kalogeratou *(Product Manager)*, Liz Kendall-Jones *(Production and Operations Mana)*, Edward Kuijk *(Head of Operations)*, Pradeep Lal *(Chief Operating Officer)*, Stefan Langkamp *(Operations Director)*, Gianluca Marini *(Operations Manager)*, Simon Mendham *(Energy Manager)*, Martin Meyners *(Engineering Manager)*, Sean Mills *(Production and Operations Mana)*, Tamer Nasr *(Planning Manager)*, Jose Oliveira *(Operations Director)*, Takis Papadakis *(Manager)*, Sunil Sood *(Operations Director)*, Anna Tomkins *(Resourcing Operations Manager)*, Charlie Wade *(Head of Product)*
**Purchasing:** Bart Borchardt *(Head of Supply Chain Managemen)*, Laurent Bouvier *(Head of Purchasing)*, Vanessa Fonseca *(Procurement)*, Frank Redmer *(Purchasing Manager)*
**Fleet:** Ahmed Nabil *(Data Manager)*, Daudi Turya *(Logistics Manager)*
**Engineering:** Ahmed Akl *(Switching Planning Engineer)*, Daniel Appelquist *(Senior Technical)*, David Ashbrook *(Engineer)*, Ehab Azzam *(Engineer)*, Edin Bektesevic *(Senior Technical)*, Nadia Benabdallah *(Director, Engineering)*, Nick Bone *(Chief Engineer)*, Elizabeth Boyle *(Program Manager)*, Stefano Brivio *(Engineer)*, Luca Crosti *(Executive)*, Mairead Cullen *(Head of Network Development)*, Frank Curulli *(Design Engineer)*, Maria Farrugia *(Core Network and FMC Architect)*, Chiara Ferrero *(Engineer)*, Matthias Fischer *(Technology Manager)*, Raquel Frisa *(Engineer)*, Stefano Galli *(Innovation Technology Manager)*, Jorge Gato *(Director, Engineering)*, Alfred Gega *(Engineering Manager)*, Nicola Greco *(Engineer)*, Terji Hansen *(Engineer)*, Mike Hyland *(Technical Support Manager)*, David Kayes *(Engineer)*, Pavel Kos *(Chief Technology Officer)*, Antonio Luna *(Engineer)*, Miguel Martins *(Chief Technology Officer)*, Nikos Mastorakis *(Technical Director)*, Ana Migueis *(Engineering Manager)*, Ahmed Momtaz *(Engineer)*, Fiona Nee *(Program Manager)*, Hugh Nolan *(Technology)*, Nikos Plevris *(Engineering Manager)*, David Pollington *(Head of Technical Research - C)*, Carlos Prados *(Engineer)*, Andy Reeves *(Chief Technology Officer)*, Tony Sammut *(Chief Engineer)*, Mohamed Selim *(Engineer)*, Mats Svardh *(Chief Technical Officer)*, Peter Weingart *(Engineering Manager)*
**Branches:** Vodafone Group Plc, 42 Princess Alexandra Walk, Queensgate Market Arcade, Huddersfield, West Yorkshire HD1 2UJ
**US SIC:** 8911, 4899, 6711
**UK SIC:** 83701, 79020, 83962
**Auditors:** Deloitte LLP
**Following financial data are in thousands**

| | 31-03-14 | 31-03-13 | 31-03-12 |
|---|---|---|---|
| TO | 38,346,000 | 44,445,000 | 46,417,000 |
| P/L | (5,270,000) | 3,255,000 | 9,549,000 |
| NW | 24,114,000 | 19,080,000 | 17,421,000 |
| WC | (317,000) | (7,937,000) | (4,000,000) |
| Emp. | 89,146 | 91,272 | 86,373 |

DUNS 23-809-6411
## Vodafone Group Services Ltd
(**Subsidiary of:** Vodafone Group Plc)
Vodafone House, The Connection, Newbury, Berkshire RG14 2FN
**Tel:** 08700700191
**Web:** www.mpc-mobiles.co.uk
**Reg No:** 3802001 **Estd:** 1984 Private Limited Company
**Line of Business:** Telecommunications
**Export Sales:** £1,178,121,000
**Issued Capital:** £601
**Directors:** K A Salvadori, N O'Sullivan, Ms R E Martin, Ms D Isaia, J Mccoy, P Chomet, Ms M Della Valle
**Co. Secretary:** Ms Rosemary Martin
**Responsibilities**
**Senior:** Gudrun Evans *(Manager)*, Francinne Hansen *(Manager)*, Albert Hitchcock *(Manager)*
**Branches:** Vodafone Group Service Ltd, One Kingdom St, London W2 6BY Paddington
**US SIC:** 4899 **UK SIC:** 79020
**Auditors:** Deloitte LLP
**Following financial data are in thousands**

| | 31-03-14 | 31-03-13 | 31-03-12 |
|---|---|---|---|
| TO | 1,852,614 | 1,640,651 | 1,391,652 |
| P/L | 37,172 | 11,535 | 14,895 |
| NW | 655,286 | 316,782 | 223,835 |
| WC | 162,080 | (90,389) | (121,206) |
| Emp. | 2,317 | 1,440 | 1,403 |

DUNS 28-984-8129
## Vodafone Multimedia Ltd
(**Subsidiary of:** Vodafone Group Plc)
Dower House, London Road, Newbury, Berkshire RG14 1LA
**Tel:** 07836191191 **Fax:** 01635-673936
**Reg No:** 1795704 **Estd:** 1984 Private Limited Company
**Line of Business:** Telecom consultants
**Issued Capital:** £2
**Directors:** Ms D Mcintyre, D N Evans, M J Purkess
**Co. Secretary:** Vodafone Corporate Secretaries L
**US SIC:** 4899, 7399
**UK SIC:** 79020, 83954
**Bankers:** Barclays Bank Plc (20-00-00)

| | 31-03-14 | 31-03-13 | 31-03-12 |
|---|---|---|---|
| TA | 300,271,000 | 300,271,000 | 300,271,000 |
| NW | 300,271,000 | 300,271,000 | 300,271,000 |

DUNS 39-888-2498
## Vodafone U K Ltd
(**Subsidiary of:** Vodafone Group Plc)
Vodafone House, The Connection, Newbury, Berkshire RG14 2FN
**Tel:** 01635550000
**Web:** www.vodafone.co.uk
**Reg No:** 2227940 **Estd:** 1988 Private Limited Company
**Line of Business:** Management activities of holding companies
**Issued Capital:** £2
**Directors:** Ms H Lamprell, H J Hoencamp, D Galli
**Co. Secretary:** Vodafone Corporate Secretaries L
**Responsibilities**
**Senior:** Daniel Cloke *(Manager)*, Danielle Crook *(Director of Brands Marketing)*, Philip Howie *(Manager)*
**HR:** Daniel Cloke *(Manager)*
**US SIC:** 6711, 4899
**UK SIC:** 83962, 79020
**Bankers:** Barclays Bank Plc (20-00-00)
**Following financial data are in thousands**

| | 31-03-14 | 31-03-13 | 31-03-12 |
|---|---|---|---|
| TA | 3,929,467 | 3,919,882 | 3,903,631 |
| P/L | 9,088 | 10,041 | (9,280) |
| NW | 2,675,693 | 2,668,695 | 2,661,136 |
| WC | 1,685,139 | 1,678,141 | 1,670,571 |

DUNS 45-869-4031
## Voel Coaches Ltd
Long Acres Road, Dyserth, Rhyl, Clwyd LL18 6BP
**Tel:** 01745570309
**Web:** www.voelcoaches.com
**Reg No:** 3211899 **VAT No:** 691615028
**Estd:** 1948 Private Limited Company
**Line of Business:** Coach and bus hire
**Issued Capital:** £2
**Directors:** W M Kerfoot-Davies, Ms M Kerfoot Higginson, M Higginson, G Kerfoot Ashton
**Co. Secretary:** Ms Mavis Kerfoot-Davies
**Branches:** Voel Coaches Ltd, The Garage, Holyhead, Gwynedd LL65 4NW
**US SIC:** 4119 **UK SIC:** 72200
**Auditors:** John Graham & Co
**Bankers:** Barclays Bank Plc (20-25-76)

| | 31-03-14 | 31-03-13 | 31-03-12 |
|---|---|---|---|
| TA | 2,853,052 | 2,816,309 | 3,515,615 |
| NW | 537,339 | 479,677 | 823,780 |
| WC | (670,066) | (755,791) | (1,523,954) |

DUNS 21-927-4669 **Imp-Exp**
## Voestalpine Rotec Ltd
(**Subsidiary of:** Voestalpine Ag)
2 Jacknell Road, Dodwells Bridge Industrial Estate, Hinckley, Leicestershire LE10 3BS
**Web:** www.voestalpine.com
**Reg No:** 1339039 **VAT No:** 316026983
**Estd:** 1977 Private Limited Company
**Line of Business:** Manufacturers of automotive components
**Export Markets:** Germany, France & U S A
**Export Sales:** £4,243,884
**Issued Capital:** £200,000
**Director:** G A Hitchman
**Responsibilities**
**Senior:** Rowland Braeuer *(Manager)*, Peter Schneider *(Group Md)*
**US SIC:** 3714 **UK SIC:** 35300
**Auditors:** Deloitte & Touche LLP
**Bankers:** Barclays Bank Plc (20-49-11)

| | 31-03-14 | 31-03-13 | 31-03-12 |
|---|---|---|---|
| TO | 10,352,311 | 12,842,322 | 16,337,750 |
| P/L | (245,870) | (126,951) | (39,909) |
| NW | 3,249,102 | 3,629,084 | 3,731,601 |
| WC | (646,056) | (712,982) | (719,215) |
| Emp. | 83 | 94 | 95 |

DUNS 34-747-6764 **Imp**
## Vogue Beds Ltd
Kingsfield House, Arthur Street, Leicester, Leicestershire LE9 8GZ
**Tel:** 01455-841257 **Fax:** 01455-841259
**Web:** www.voguebeds.co.uk
**Reg No:** 2783102 **VAT No:** 536287720
**Estd:** 1994 Private Limited Company
**Line of Business:** Other manufacturing not elsewhere classified
**Issued Capital:** £1,000
**Directors:** E M Patel, M Jennings
**Co. Secretary:** Ms Zareen Patel
**Responsibilities**
**Sales:** Nic Houslip *(Sales Manager)*
**Health & Safety:** Peter Toms *(Production Manager)*
**Facilities:** Peter Toms *(Production Manager)*
**Purchasing:** Jim Day *(Buyer)*
**Engineering:** Peter Toms *(Production Manager)*
**Branches:** Vogue Beds Ltd, 100 Kirby Road, Leicester, Leicestershire LE9 8FN
**US SIC:** 3999 **UK SIC:** 49590
**Auditors:** Clear & Lane Ltd
**Bankers:** National Westminster Bank Plc (56-00-55)

| | 31-12-13 | 31-12-12 | 31-12-11 |
|---|---|---|---|
| TA | 1,403,073 | 1,278,434 | 1,083,035 |
| NW | 475,229 | 441,187 | 358,598 |
| WC | 321,638 | 262,565 | 157,830 |
| Emp. | N/A | 65 | N/A |

DUNS 21-559-7006
## Vogue House Furnishers Ltd
(**Subsidiary of:** Sterling Furniture Group Ltd)
6 Whitehill Road, Edinburgh, Midlothian EH15 3HR
**Tel:** 01316576000 **Fax:** 01316576001
**Web:** www.sterlingfurniture.co.uk
**Reg No:** 0040525SC **VAT No:** 268742325
**Estd:** 1941 Private Limited Company
**Line of Business:** Retail sale of furniture, lighting equipment and household articles not elsewhere classified
**Trading Style:** Sterling Furniture
**Issued Capital:** £35,954
**Director:** G L Mearns
**Co. Secretary:** Stuart Logan
**Responsibilities**
**Senior:** John Heyward *(General Manager)*
**Branches:** Vogue House Furnishers Ltd, 2129 London Road, Glasgow, Lanarkshire G32 8XQ
**US SIC:** 5719 **UK SIC:** 64700
**Auditors:** Geoghegan & Co
**Bankers:** The Royal Bank Of Scotland Plc (83-06-08)

| | 28-02-14 | 28-02-13 | 29-02-12 |
|---|---|---|---|
| TA | 11,084,704 | 11,084,704 | 11,084,704 |
| P/L | N/A | N/A | (113) |
| NW | 11,074,704 | 11,074,704 | 11,074,704 |
| WC | N/A | N/A | 9,970,205 |

DUNS 21-557-8492
## Vogue Interiors
Unit 7 Springfield Business Park Adams, Way, Alcester, Warwickshire B49 6PU
**Tel:** 01789-767-075
**Web:** www.vogue-interiors.co.uk
**VAT No:** 695943080 **Estd:** 2010 Partnership
**Line of Business:** Interior designers
**Trading Style:** Vogue Flooring
**Partners:** M Dowling, A G Winter
**Responsibilities**
**Senior:** Emily Carr *(Director Secretary)*, Di Earnshaw *(Manager)*
**Branches:** Vogue Interiors, Great Bramshot Farm Barns, Unit 8, Fleet, Hampshire GU51 2SF
**US SIC:** 1799, 5719
**UK SIC:** 50000, 64700
**Employees:** 50

DUNS 50-481-6299 **Imp-Exp**
## Vogue (U K) Ltd
Unit 8 Strawberry Lane Strawberry Lane, Industrial Estate, Willenhall, West Midlands WV13 3RS
**Tel:** 01902387000 **Fax:** 01902-387001
**Web:** www.vogueuk.co.uk
**Reg No:** 2455446 **Estd:** 1990 Private Limited Company
**Line of Business:** Other manufacturing not elsewhere classified
**Export Markets:** E U
**Issued Capital:** £20,000
**Principals:** R M Tunks *(Managing)*, R W Kelley
**Co. Secretary:** Raymond Tunks
**US SIC:** 3999, 5074
**UK SIC:** 49590, 61300
**Auditors:** Bloomer Heaven
**Bankers:** National Westminster Bank Plc (60-02-35)

| | 31-03-14 | 31-03-13 | 31-03-12 |
|---|---|---|---|
| TA | 2,067,842 | 2,314,116 | 2,440,627 |
| NW | 926,749 | 853,001 | 801,918 |
| WC | 793,829 | 699,376 | 656,780 |

DUNS 22-123-5125

## Vohkus Ltd

3b, Napier House, 2 Cranwood Street, London EC1V 9PE

**Tel:** 08456470100 **Fax:** 08456470401

**Web:** www.vohkus.com

**Reg No:** 4142508 **Estd:** 2011 Private Limited Company

**Line of Business:** Computer systems and software (sales)

**Export Sales:** £2,417,607

**Issued Capital:** £40,000

**Directors:** F R O Leary, I D Hounsome, U K Sharma, L Lawrence, L Forster, S Brand, C B Compton

**Co. Secretary:** Ivor Davis

**Responsibilities**

**Senior:** James Lythe *(Manager)*, Richie Sharma *(Manager)*

**Branches:** Vohkus Ltd, Centurion House, Barnes Wallis Road, Fareham, Hampshire PO15 5TT

**US SIC:** 7379 **UK SIC:** 83940

**Auditors:** BDO LLP

**Bankers:** Lloyds TSB Bank plc (30-90-02)

| | 31-05-13 | 31-05-12 | 31-05-11 |
|---|---|---|---|
| TO | 39,628,632 | 36,797,832 | 33,190,114 |
| P/L | 319,129 | 431,316 | 538,043 |
| NW | 1,507,945 | 1,406,660 | 1,229,071 |
| WC | 1,184,652 | 1,112,738 | 899,242 |
| Emp. | 88 | 83 | 71 |

DUNS 77-916-9262

## Voice Marketing Ltd

Chantrey House, 798 Chesterfield Road, Sheffield, South Yorkshire S8 0SF

**Tel:** 01143-210000 **Fax:** 01143211111

**Web:** www.voicegroup.co.uk

**Reg No:** 5820091 **Estd:** 2007 Private Limited Company

**Line of Business:** Call centre activities

**Issued Capital:** £167,477

**Directors:** J Flint, H Seaton, J D Robinson, P J Kitchen, Ms A Whitehead

**Co. Secretary:** James Hinchliffe

**Responsibilities**

**Marketing:** Jonathan Wall *(Marketing director)*

**US SIC:** 7399, 7311

**UK SIC:** 83954, 83800

| | 31-07-14 | 31-12-13 | 31-07-12 |
|---|---|---|---|
| TO | 7,142,382 | 12,259,004 | 7,313,049 |
| P/L | 625,975 | (467,883) | 41,563 |
| NW | 413,474 | (85,572) | 296,776 |
| WC | (53,161) | (600,965) | (257,384) |
| Emp. | 527 | 438 | 334 |

DUNS 23-806-4005

## Voiceability Advocacy

Mount Pleasant House, Mount Pleasant, Cambridge, Cambridgeshire CB3 0RN

**Tel:** 01223555800

**Web:** www.voiceability.org

**Reg No:** 3798884 **VAT No:** 834575703

**Estd:** 2000 Private Company Limited By Guarantee

**Line of Business:** Non-charitable social work activities with accommodation

**Directors:** A Fox, P A Letley, M N Vivian, Ms K Markey, Miss G S Ferris, J M Willis, C Broadhurst, P Tatt

**Co. Secretary:** Ms Genevieve Cowcher

**Responsibilities**

**Senior:** Jonathan Senco *(Chief Executive)*

**US SIC:** 8321 **UK SIC:** 96111

**Auditors:** Chater Allan LLP

**Bankers:** National Westminster Bank Plc (60-04-23)

| | 31-03-14 | 31-03-13 | 31-03-12 |
|---|---|---|---|
| TO | 9,051,344 | 6,922,897 | 7,889,154 |
| P/L | 525,588 | 203,998 | 226,531 |
| NW | 3,146,872 | 2,621,286 | 2,384,364 |
| WC | 3,156,310 | 2,672,706 | 2,522,721 |
| Emp. | 199 | 141 | 183 |

DUNS 22-717-6245 **Imp-Exp**

## Voicevale Ltd

Dove House Arcadia Avenue, London N3 2JU

**Fax:** 02083710208

**Web:** www.voicevale.com

**Reg No:** 1565241 **VAT No:** 340851079

**Estd:** 1981 Private Limited Company

**Line of Business:** Import and export agents

**Export Markets:** Europe

**Export Sales:** £135,944,926

**Issued Capital:** £420,170

**Principals:** R T Danon *(Chairman and Managing)*, M O'Toole, C Y Ho, H Umino, Ms N Danon

**Co. Secretary:** Ms Linda Barrett

**US SIC:** 4712, 5153

**UK SIC:** 77002, 61100

**Auditors:** Westbury

**Bankers:** Barclays Bank Plc (20-29-37)

| | 31-12-13 | 31-12-12 | 31-12-11 |
|---|---|---|---|
| TO | 178,844,926 | 157,926,490 | 152,791,602 |
| P/L | 4,756,696 | 3,871,996 | 3,998,784 |
| NW | 12,650,767 | 11,164,239 | 10,445,160 |
| WC | 13,612,083 | 11,845,990 | 10,938,947 |
| Emp. | 53 | 52 | 45 |

DUNS 50-468-5678 **Imp**

## Voiteq Ltd

(**Subsidiary of:** Centriq Group Ltd)

Unit 1 Neptune Court, Hallam Way, Blackpool, Lancashire FY4 5LZ

**Tel:** 08448940322 **Fax:** 0870-300-0481

**Web:** www.voiteq.com

**Reg No:** 2447508 **Estd:** 2001 Private Limited Company

**Line of Business:** Hardware consultancy

**Export Sales:** £57,000

**Issued Capital:** £202,000

**Directors:** P G Morgan, D F Webb, F I Heald, A Du Preez, J Gylanders

**Co. Secretary:** David Stanhope

**Branches:** Voiteq Ltd, 40 King Street, Bacup, Lancashire OL13 0AH

**US SIC:** 7379 **UK SIC:** 83940

**Auditors:** John Potter & Harrison

| | 31-12-13 | 31-12-12 | 31-12-11 |
|---|---|---|---|
| TO | 7,161,000 | 6,731,000 | 5,861,000 |
| P/L | 502,000 | 562,000 | 355,000 |
| NW | 3,627,000 | 3,017,000 | 2,404,000 |
| WC | 1,928,000 | 1,504,000 | 953,000 |
| Emp. | 65 | 59 | 60 |

DUNS 53-636-2445

## Voith Industrial Services Ltd

Tournament Court, Edgehill Drive, Warwick, Warwickshire CV34 6LG

**Tel:** 01926-623-550 **Fax:** 01926-623-551

**Web:** www.uk.voithindustrialservices.com

**Reg No:** 3441005 **Estd:** 1997 Private Limited Company

**Line of Business:** Management of real estate on a fee or contract basis

**Issued Capital:** £50,000

**Principals:** L A Cheek *(Financial)*, P A Nicholson, Mrs M Kitchingman, P J Spencer, G G Quinn

**Co. Secretary:** Paul Griffiths

**Branches:** Voith Industrial Services Ltd, Kimtton Road, Luton, Bedfordshire LU2 0TY

**US SIC:** 3999, 6531

**UK SIC:** 49590, 83400

**Auditors:** KPMG LLP

| | 30-09-13 | 30-09-12 | 30-09-11 |
|---|---|---|---|
| TO | 39,125,000 | 37,718,000 | 28,625,000 |
| P/L | 896,000 | 1,813,000 | 1,747,000 |
| NW | 218,000 | 370,000 | 3,227,000 |
| WC | 296,000 | 489,000 | 3,377,000 |
| Emp. | 1,196 | 1,071 | 720 |

DUNS 21-639-0294 **Exp**

## Voith Paper Fabrics Stubbins Ltd

(**Subsidiary of:** Voith Familien Verwaltung Gmbh)

Stubbins Vale Mill, Stubbins Vale Road, Ramsbottom, Bury, Lancashire BL0 0NT

**Tel:** 01706-822951 **Fax:** 01706-283401

**Web:** www.voith.com

**Reg No:** 0071121 **VAT No:** 431198462

**Estd:** 1901 Private Limited Company

**Line of Business:** Textile weaving

**Export Markets:** Worldwide

**Export Sales:** £5,658,087

**Issued Capital:** £160,000

**Director:** D H Hecht

**Co. Secretary:** David Connett

**Responsibilities**

**Senior:** Markus Maier *(Manager)*

**Health & Safety:** Daniel Knight *(Health & Safety & IT Manager)*

**Facilities:** Stefan Hetlof *(Maintaenance Manager)*

**US SIC:** 2269 **UK SIC:** 43702

**Auditors:** BDO Stoy Hayward

**Bankers:** HSBC Bank plc (40-12-04)

| | 30-09-13 | 30-09-12 | 30-09-11 |
|---|---|---|---|
| TO | 5,796,483 | 5,502,038 | 5,897,165 |
| P/L | 35,466 | (403,733) | 164,602 |
| NW | 4,630,329 | 4,872,655 | 5,011,931 |
| WC | 1,692,091 | 1,488,256 | 1,292,196 |
| Emp. | 70 | 76 | 51 |

DUNS 21-443-2080 **Imp-Exp**

## Voith Turbo Ltd

(**Subsidiary of:** Voith Familien Verwaltung Gmbh)

6 Beddington Farm Road, Croydon, Surrey CR0 4XB

**Tel:** 02086670333 **Fax:** 02085691726

**Web:** www.uk.voithturbo.com

**Reg No:** 0038144SC **VAT No:** 218538062

**Estd:** 1962 Private Limited Company

**Line of Business:** General mechanical engineering

**Export Markets:** Europe

**Export Sales:** £6,400,982

**Issued Capital:** £5,000,000

**Directors:** J Hagemann, K M Sanders, V R Jarvis

**Co. Secretary:** Richard Skinner

**Responsibilities**

**Senior:** William Boyd *(Manager)*, Francisco Halffter Gonzalez-Parrado *(Manager)*, Reece Jarvis *(Manager)*, Keith Lane *(General Manager)*, Martin Wawra *(Manager)*, Edgar Wolf *(Manager)*

**Marketing:** John Domigan *(Sales & Marketing Manager)*, Roger Everest *(Sales & Marketing Manager - Ra)*, Andreas Fecht *(Marketing Manager)*

**Sales:** John Domigan *(Sales & Marketing Manager)*, Roger Everest *(Sales & Marketing Manager - Ra)*, Andreas Fecht *(Marketing Manager)*

**Operations:** Carlo Ferri *(Operations Manager)*

**Branches:** Voith Turbo Ltd, 7 Abbotsford Drive, Dudley, West Midlands DY1 2HD

**US SIC:** 8911, 3799

**UK SIC:** 83701, 36502

**Auditors:** Ernst & Young LLP

**Bankers:** HSBC Bank plc (40-44-15)

| | 30-09-13 | 30-09-12 | 30-09-11 |
|---|---|---|---|
| TO | 39,541,280 | 39,095,401 | 32,769,250 |
| P/L | 3,848,519 | 5,359,367 | 3,897,264 |
| NW | 12,796,215 | 11,915,397 | 10,136,048 |
| WC | 9,764,661 | 8,048,913 | 6,896,663 |
| Emp. | 162 | 144 | 122 |

DUNS 21-748-9475 **Exp**

## Voith Turbo Rail Systems Ltd

(**Subsidiary of:** Voith Familien Verwaltung Gmbh)

6 Beddington Farm Road, Croydon, Surrey CR0 4XB

**Tel:** 020-8561-2131 **Fax:** 020-8569-1726

**Web:** www.uk.voithturbo.com

**Reg No:** 1416138 **VAT No:** 225291673

**Estd:** 1979 Private Limited Company

**Line of Business:** General mechanical engineering

**Issued Capital:** £12,000

**Director:** V R Jarvis

**Co. Secretary:** Richard Skinner

**Responsibilities**

**Senior:** Roger Everest *(Sales Manager)*

**Sales:** Roger Everest *(Sales Manager)*

**Operations:** Carlo Ferri *(Operations Manager)*

**Purchasing:** Jardel Senno *(Purchasing Manager)*

**US SIC:** 8911, 5084

**UK SIC:** 83701, 61490

**Bankers:** National Westminster Bank Plc (60-00-01)

| | 30-09-14 | 30-09-13 | 30-09-12 |
|---|---|---|---|
| TA | 12,000 | 12,000 | 12,000 |
| NW | 12,000 | 12,000 | 12,000 |

DUNS 22-531-9672 **Imp-Exp**

## Vokera Ltd

(**Subsidiary of:** Riello Group Spa)

Unit 6a Riverside Industrial Estate, St Albans, Hertfordshire AL2 1HG

**Tel:** 08443910999 **Fax:** 0172-774-4001

**Web:** www.vokera.co.uk

**Reg No:** 1047779 **Estd:** 1972 Private Limited Company

**Line of Business:** Wholesale of hardware, plumbing and heating equipment and supplies

**Export Markets:** Ireland

**Export Sales:** £4,582,000

**Issued Capital:** £4,800

**Directors:** A Nigro, U P Ferretti

**Co. Secretary:** Tiow Ng

**Responsibilities**

**Senior:** Steve Cipriano *(Manager)*

**Branches:** Vokera Ltd, Unit 6A, London Colney By Pass, St. Albans, Hertfordshire AL2 1HG

**US SIC:** 5074 **UK SIC:** 61300

**Auditors:** PricewaterhouseCoopers LLP

**Bankers:** Barclays Bank Plc (20-29-77)

| | 31-12-13 | 31-12-12 | 31-12-11 |
|---|---|---|---|
| TO | 32,122,000 | 31,266,000 | 38,562,000 |
| P/L | 2,649,000 | 2,540,000 | 2,744,000 |
| NW | 10,169,000 | 16,102,000 | 14,119,000 |
| WC | 9,580,000 | 15,461,000 | 13,412,000 |
| Emp. | 105 | 104 | 107 |

DUNS 76-605-0488 **Exp**

## Volac International Ltd

(**Subsidiary of:** Woodford Holdings Ltd)

Orwell, Royston, Hertfordshire SG8 5QX

**Tel:** 01223-208021 **Fax:** 01223-207629

**Web:** www.volac.com

**Reg No:** 2576295 **VAT No:** 842935214

**Estd:** 1991 Private Limited Company

**Line of Business:** Manufacture of other milk products

**Export Markets:** Europe; Worldwide

**Trading Style:** Volac

**Issued Capital:** £3,427,992

**Directors:** M R Neville, G C Stone, J R Neville, W S Mcbride, N F Franklin, D C Neville, P D Pearson

**Responsibilities**

**Senior:** Peter Constable *(Site Manager)*

**Finance:** Mary Paxman *(Finance Director)*

**Marketing:** Mike Rogers *(Marketing Manager)*

**Sales:** Richard Allum *(Sales Manager)*

**IT:** Stuart Garrick *(Computer Manager)*

**HR:** Lynne Koch *(Human Resources Manager)*

**Health & Safety:** Peter Constable *(Site Manager)*

**Facilities:** Peter Constable *(Site Manager)*

**Purchasing:** Peter Constable *(Site Manager)*

**Engineering:** Neville Chapman *(Production Manager)*

**Branches:** Volac International Ltd, South Canada Dock, Bootle, Liverpool, Merseyside L20 1DE

**US SIC:** 2023, 2048

**UK SIC:** 41303, 42210

**Auditors:** Deloitte LLP

**Bankers:** National Westminster Bank Plc (60-04-02)

| | 28-02-14 | 28-02-13 | 29-02-12 |
|---|---|---|---|
| TO | 197,396,000 | 143,118,000 | 120,803,000 |
| P/L | 18,315,000 | 23,170,000 | 16,522,000 |
| NW | 61,623,000 | 51,053,000 | 35,370,000 |
| WC | 34,520,000 | 29,727,000 | 16,796,000 |
| Emp. | 382 | 290 | 241 |

DUNS 22-562-5128

## Volaw Trust & Corporate Services Ltd

Templar House, Jersey, Channel Islands JE1 2TR

**Tel:** 01534-500400 **Fax:** 01534-500450

**Web:** www.volaw.com

**Reg No:** 0024415J **Estd:** 2010 Private Limited Company

**Line of Business:** Activities auxiliary to financial intermediation not elsewhere classified

**Issued Capital:** £30,000

**Director:** R Christensen

**Responsibilities**

**Senior:** Robert Christiansen *(CEO, Managing Director)*, Debbie Du Feu *(Senior Manager - Wealth Struct)*, Philip Duffin *(Senior Manager - Investment Su)*, Karen Grieve *(Senior Manager - Wealth Struct)*, Ashley Le Feuvre *(Senior Manager - Fund Services)*, Trevor Norman *(Manager)*, Simon Perchard *(Company Director)*, Suzanne Young *(Senior Manager - Wealth Struct)*

**Finance:** Mike Gardner *(Senior Manager - Accounts)*, Denise Marett *(Senior Finance Administrator)*, Eleanor Monaghan *(Senior Manager - Client Accoun)*

**Marketing:** Georgina Jeffries *(Head of Marketing)*

**Admin:** Paul Bulstrode *(Client Administrator - Fund Se)*, Dominic Coyne *(Client Administrator - Fund Se)*, Paula Evans *(Client Administrator - Fund Se)*, Stuart Fell *(Senior Trust & Company Adminis)*, Jill Guilleaume *(Client Administrator - Funds S)*, Angela Hutchings *(Group Company Secretary)*, Elly Le Cornu *(Trust Administrator - Employee)*, Jessica Riley *(Client Administrator - Fund Se)*

**HR:** Emma Stewart *(Head of Human Resources)*

**Operations:** Jodie Gray *(Team Leader - Wealth Structuri)*

**US SIC:** 7399 **UK SIC:** 83954

**Employees:** 100

DUNS 36-541-6684

## Volcke Aerosol Connection Plc

Unit 54-56 Llantarnam Industrial Estate, Cwmbran, Gwent NP44 3AW

**Web:** www.goodmarkgroup.com

**Reg No:** 3292542 **Estd:** 1995 Public Limited Company

**Line of Business:** Manufacture of light metal packaging

**Export Sales:** £17,943,000

**Issued Capital:** £500,000

**Directors:** S C Volcke Jr, J R Volcke, M Rhodes

**Co. Secretary:** Stephan Volcke

**Responsibilities**

**Senior:** Pierre Van Keirsblick *(Manager)*, Stefan Volcke *(Director)*

**US SIC:** 3999, 2649

**UK SIC:** 49590, 47280

**Auditors:** KPMG LLP

| | 30-06-14 | 30-06-13 | 30-06-12 |
|---|---|---|---|
| TO | 27,092,000 | 24,614,000 | 40,240,000 |
| P/L | 238,000 | (584,000) | 1,472,000 |
| NW | 4,762,000 | 4,892,000 | 5,118,000 |
| WC | 4,500,000 | 4,524,000 | 6,459,000 |
| Emp. | 120 | 130 | 91 |

DUNS 21-230-1535 **Exp**

## Volex Plc

10 Eastbournce Terrace, Paddington, London W2 6LG

**Tel:** 02033708830

**Web:** www.volex.com

**Reg No:** 0158956 **VAT No:** 145101807

**Estd:** 1919 Public Limited Company

**Line of Business:** Misc elec industrial apparatus mfrs

**Trading Style:** Volex Power Cords, Volex Wiring Systems, Volex

**Directors:** Mrs K Slatford, D J Morris, M T Geh, C Eisenhardt, G Anderson

**Co. Secretary:** Ms Nicole Pask

**Responsibilities**
**Senior:** Richard Arkle *(Manager)*, Robert McTighe *(Manager)*
**Finance:** Wendy Tate *(Finance Director)*
**Branches:** Volex Plc, Unit 4 Triangle Business Pk, Merthyr Tydfil, Mid Glamorgan CF48 4TQ
**US SIC:** 3629 **UK SIC:** 34350
**Auditors:** PricewaterhouseCoopers LLP
**Bankers:** Lloyds TSB Bank plc (30-00-02)
**Employees:** 20
**Turnover:** £400,177,000

DUNS 23-826-8416     Imp
## Volga-Dnepr Uk Ltd.
**(Subsidiary of:** Volga-Dnepr Logistics B.V.)
Endeavour House, Coopers End Road, London Stansted Airport, Stansted, Essex CM24 1AL
**Tel:** 01279661166
**Web:** www.volga-dnepr.com
**Reg No:** 3818835 **Estd:** 2000 Private Limited Company
**Line of Business:** Airlines
**Directors:** D A Gliznoutsa, A I Isaykin
**Co. Secretary:** Mikhail Arzamaskin
**Responsibilities**
**Senior:** Tatyana Arslanova *(Manager)*, Dimitry Grishin *(Sales Vice President)*, Nikolay Makarov *(Manager)*
**Finance:** Derek Wade *(Finance Manager)*
**Marketing:** Natalia Ivanes *(Head of Marketing)*
**HR:** Enza Andrews *(Human Resources Manager)*
**US SIC:** 4511, 4582
**UK SIC:** 75000, 76400
**Auditors:** Ernst & Young LLP
**Bankers:** National Westminster Bank Plc (60-18-10)
**Employees:** 40
**Turnover:** £93,758,681

DUNS 51-606-1061
## Volga Gas Plc
17-19 Rochester Row, London SW1P 1QT
**Web:** www.volgagas.com
**Reg No:** 5886534 **Estd:** 2006 Public Limited Company
**Line of Business:** Oil and gas extraction
**Directors:** M Y Ivanov, V A Koshcheev, S Ogden, R M Freeman, M Calvey, A Kalinin
**Co. Secretary:** Antonio Alves
**US SIC:** 1311 **UK SIC:** 13000
**Auditors:** PricewaterhouseCoopers LLP
**Employees:** 151
**Turnover:** £34,621,000

DUNS 21-600-9322
## Volker Highways
Jeffreys Road, Enfield, Middlesex EN3 7UA
**Tel:** 02083449860
**Web:** www.gabrielceng.co.uk
**Estd:** 1959
**Line of Business:** Civil engineers
**Partners:** A Robertson, P Hyde, Mrs A Foster, D Waller
**US SIC:** 8911 **UK SIC:** 83701
**Employees:** 200

DUNS 45-833-5718     Imp
## Volkerrail Ltd
**(Subsidiary of:** Storm Investments B.V.)
Unit 1 Carolina Court, Doncaster, South Yorkshire DN4 5RA
**Tel:** 01302-791100 **Fax:** 01302791200
**Web:** www.volkerrail.co.uk
**Reg No:** 3184313 **VAT No:** 678953268
**Estd:** 1996 Private Limited Company
**Line of Business:** Public works contractors
**Issued Capital:** £4,000,000
**Directors:** Volkerwessels Uk Limited, P H Nolan, M G Woods, S J Cocliff, Ms N A Connell, A M Wilkins, A R Robertson
**Responsibilities**
**IT:** Steve Lount *(Business Systems Manager)*
**HR:** Bryan Webster *(Human Resources Manager)*
**Health & Safety:** Chris Hext *(Head of Corporate Safety)*
**Purchasing:** Ron Abbotts *(Purchasing Manager)*
**Branches:** Volkerrail Ltd, British Steel Site, Llanwern Wks, Newport, Gwent NP6 1XX
**US SIC:** 4011, 1622
**UK SIC:** 71000, 50200
**Auditors:** KPMG LLP
**Bankers:** HSBC Bank plc (40-40-24)

| | 31-12-13 | 31-12-12 | 31-12-11 |
|---|---|---|---|
| TO | 83,031,000 | 79,844,000 | 76,221,000 |
| P/L | 5,839,000 | 2,787,000 | 2,520,000 |
| NW | 12,110,000 | 7,757,000 | 11,072,000 |
| WC | 10,725,000 | 5,038,000 | 10,152,000 |
| Emp. | 195 | 180 | 198 |

DUNS 21-606-8502
## Volkerstevin Ltd
**(Subsidiary of:** Storm Investments B.V.)
The Hub, Brian Johnson Way, Preston, Lancashire PR2 5PE
**Tel:** 01772 708620 **Fax:** 01772708621
**Web:** www.volkerstevin.co.uk
**Reg No:** 0288392 **VAT No:** 178820433
**Estd:** 1934 Private Limited Company
**Line of Business:** Civil engineers
**Issued Capital:** £8,000,000
**Directors:** Ms N A Connell, A R Robertson, R D Coupe, M G Woods, A R Towse, Volkerwessels Uk Limited
**Responsibilities**
**Senior:** Alan Gerrett *(Manager)*, John Hume *(Manager)*, James McNeilly *(Manager)*, Christopher O'Donnell *(Manager)*
**HR:** Carol Bold *(Human Resources Manager)*
**Branches:** Volkerstevin Ltd, Bank Chambers, 25 Crossgate, Otley, West Yorkshire LS21 1BE
**US SIC:** 1541, 5051, 1622, 1799
**UK SIC:** 50100, 61200, 50200, 50000
**Auditors:** KPMG LLP
**Bankers:** HSBC Bank plc (40-22-04)

| | 31-12-13 | 31-12-12 | 31-12-11 |
|---|---|---|---|
| TO | 68,087,000 | 73,704,000 | 62,388,000 |
| P/L | 204,000 | 3,336,000 | 7,887,000 |
| NW | 13,964,000 | 13,354,000 | 11,662,000 |
| WC | 13,242,000 | 12,663,000 | 9,987,000 |
| Emp. | 205 | 199 | 194 |

DUNS 22-508-1249
## Volkerwessels Uk Ltd
**(Subsidiary of:** Storm Investments B.V.)
Hertford Road, Hoddesdon, Hertfordshire EN11 9BX
**Tel:** 01992 305000 **Fax:** 01992 305001
**Web:** www.volkerwessels.co.uk
**Reg No:** 1179305 **Estd:** 1974 Private Limited Company
**Line of Business:** Construction of commercial buildings
**Trading Style:** Brookes Contracting, Volkerstevin
**Issued Capital:** £27,127,000
**Directors:** H H Janssen, A Vos, A R Robertson
**Co. Secretary:** Ms Naomi Connell
**Branches:** Volkerwessels Uk Ltd, Springwell Road, Gateshead, Tyne and Wear NE9 7SP
**US SIC:** 1541, 6711
**UK SIC:** 50100, 83962
**Auditors:** KPMG LLP
**Bankers:** National Westminster Bank Plc (53-61-38)

| | 31-12-13 | 31-12-12 | 31-12-11 |
|---|---|---|---|
| TO | 696,916,000 | 690,978,000 | 666,194,000 |
| P/L | 11,507,000 | 11,677,000 | 12,227,000 |
| NW | 47,625,000 | 38,375,000 | 30,529,000 |
| WC | 17,504,000 | 9,782,000 | (5,000) |
| Emp. | 2,059 | 2,055 | 2,031 |

DUNS 21-676-3180
## Volkswagen
Sheepbridge Industrial Estate, Broombank Road, Chesterfield, Derbyshire S41 9QJ
**Tel:** 08448446719
**Web:** www.jct600.co.uk
**Estd:** 1999 Proprietorship
**Line of Business:** Car dealers (new & used)
**Proprietor:** R B Evans
**Responsibilities**
**Senior:** Jack Bryson *(Branch Manager)*
**US SIC:** 5511, 5521
**UK SIC:** 65100
**Employees:** 50

DUNS 51-597-5985
## Volkswagen Audi Specialist
186 Deane Road, Bolton, Lancashire BL3 5DP
**Tel:** 01204-535152
**Estd:** 2002 Partnership
**Line of Business:** Maintenance and repair of motor vehicles
**Partners:** P Cleworth, Mrs J Cleworth
**US SIC:** 7539, 5531
**UK SIC:** 67100, 65100
**Employees:** 52

DUNS 21-030-6932     Imp
## Volkswagen Group United Kingdom Ltd
**(Subsidiary of:** Volkswagen Ag)
Yeomans Drive, Blakelands, Milton Keynes, Buckinghamshire MK14 5AN
**Tel:** 01908548000 **Fax:** 01908663936
**Web:** www.skoda.co.uk
**Reg No:** 0514809 **VAT No:** 217990930
**Estd:** 1953 Private Limited Company
**Line of Business:** Sale of new motor vehicles
**Trading Style:** Audi Uk, Volkswagen
**Issued Capital:** £517,380,000
**Directors:** H Schmitt, S B Mund, J T Willis, J M Muir, Dr W S Specht, M A Frisch, C Klingler, M J Renz
**Co. Secretary:** Stephen Mund
**Responsibilities**
**Senior:** Uwe Baunack *(Director)*, Robert Hazel-Wood *(Director of Skoda)*, Spichalsky India *(Manager)*, Oliver Luchs *(Executive)*, Andreas Offermann *(Director)*, Hans Poetsch *(Manager)*, Ralph Weyler *(Manager)*
**Finance:** Juergen Ibach *(Director and Company Secretary)*, David Perez *(Finance Manager)*
**Marketing:** Heidi Cartledge *(Head of Marketing)*, Nicki Finlayson *(Press Officer)*, Natalie Lamont *(Communications Manager)*, Charlie Taylor *(Marketing Manager)*
**Sales:** Casey Fouts *(Sales Manager)*, Hal Smulson *(Sales Manager)*, Marc Thaler *(Sales Executive)*
**IT:** Nick Gaines *(Group Information Systems Dire)*
**HR:** Fiona Roberts *(Head of Human Resources)*
**Facilities:** Nick Laws *(Facilities Manager)*
**Operations:** Curt Chamberlain *(General Manager)*, Pete Georgievski *(Fixed Operations Manager)*, Alistair Hemmings *(National Operations Manager)*, Marc-Michael Meinecke *(Project Executive)*, Ryan Smith *(Service Manager and Service Ad)*
**Purchasing:** Thomas Loafman *(Director, Purchasing)*
**Fleet:** Tangam Agnihotri *(Logistics)*, Sean Maynard *(Fleet Manager)*
**Engineering:** David Bodily *(Technical Engineer)*, Marcial Hernandez *(Senior Engineer)*
**Branches:** Volkswagen Group United Kingdom Ltd, Dovercourt Motor Co Ltd, 98 York Road, London SW11 3RD
**US SIC:** 5511 **UK SIC:** 65100
**Auditors:** PricewaterhouseCoopers LLP
**Bankers:** Lloyds TSB Bank plc (30-15-53)
**Following financial data are in thousands**

| | 31-12-13 | 31-12-12 | 31-12-11 |
|---|---|---|---|
| TO | 7,619,500 | 6,667,600 | 6,363,600 |
| P/L | 130,000 | 105,100 | 110,500 |
| NW | 699,800 | 695,400 | 667,800 |
| WC | 707,800 | 704,700 | 695,600 |
| Emp. | 908 | 539 | 524 |

DUNS 21-583-5036
## Volkswagen National Learning Centre
Garamonde Drive, Wymbush, Milton Keynes, Buckinghamshire MK8 8DF
**Tel:** 01908601595
**Estd:** 2011 Proprietorship
**Line of Business:** Training centres
**Proprietor:** Miss M Newcombe
**Responsibilities**
**Senior:** David Sterling *(Manager)*
**US SIC:** 8299 **UK SIC:** 93300
**Employees:** 300

DUNS 21-029-5660
## Volkswagen Uk
277 Finchley Road, London NW3 6LT
**Web:** www.alandayvolkswagen.co.uk
**Estd:** 2007 Proprietorship
**Line of Business:** Car dealers (new & used)
**Proprietor:** P Tanner
**US SIC:** 5511 **UK SIC:** 65100
**Employees:** 90

DUNS 34-690-4709     Imp
## Volt Delta International Ltd
**(Subsidiary of:** Volt Information Sciences Inc)
Dolphin House, 140 Windmill Road, Sunbury-On-Thames, Middlesex TW16 7HT
**Tel:** 01932-755555
**Web:** www.voltdelta.net
**Reg No:** 2775288 **VAT No:** 584686777
**Estd:** 1993 Private Limited Company
**Line of Business:** Directory enquiries services
**Export Sales:** £4,284,820
**Issued Capital:** £100
**Managing Director:** N Hughes
**Co. Secretary:** Cyril Morgan
**Responsibilities**
**Senior:** Bridget Aujla *(Office Manager)*, James Schmitt *(Manager)*, James Schmitt *(Manager)*, Howard Weinreich *(Manager)*
**Finance:** Steve Lovejoy *(Finance Manager)*
**Sales:** Rob Blomfield *(Account Director)*, Andy Minshaw *(Business Development Director)*
**IT:** Jeff Haggi *(Computer Manager)*
**HR:** Dushy Stevanic *(Human Resources Manager)*
**Operations:** Jeff Haggi *(Computer Manager)*
**US SIC:** 7399 **UK SIC:** 83954
**Auditors:** Ernst & Young LLP

**Bankers:** Barclays Bank Plc (20-81-11)

| | 03-11-13 | 28-10-12 | 30-11-11 |
|---|---|---|---|
| TO | 6,077,399 | 5,757,505 | 11,784,575 |
| P/L | 1,424,487 | (2,115,271) | 3,655,878 |
| NW | 13,412,917 | 12,323,182 | 13,920,324 |
| WC | 13,135,914 | 12,973,503 | 13,644,646 |
| Emp. | 56 | 64 | 64 |

DUNS 29-464-5940     Imp-Exp
## Volt Europe Ltd
**(Subsidiary of:** Volt Information Sciences Inc)
Betchworth House, 57-65 Station Road, Redhill, Surrey RH1 1DL
**Tel:** 01737-774100 **Fax:** 01737772949
**Web:** www.volt.eu.com
**Reg No:** 1739576 **VAT No:** 394695785
**Estd:** 1983 Private Limited Company
**Line of Business:** Labour recruitment and provision of personnel
**Export Markets:** E U
**Export Sales:** £311,220
**Trading Style:** Volt Europe
**Issued Capital:** £2
**Director:** R H Herring
**Co. Secretary:** Miss Dawn Lock
**US SIC:** 7361 **UK SIC:** 83954
**Auditors:** BDO LLP
**Bankers:** Lloyds TSB Bank plc (30-93-23)

| | 31-10-13 | 31-10-12 | 31-10-11 |
|---|---|---|---|
| TO | 59,147,526 | 56,276,104 | 55,073,501 |
| P/L | 952,412 | 895,722 | 231,994 |
| NW | 3,270,683 | 2,463,441 | 1,717,606 |
| WC | 3,027,388 | 23,478,897 | 1,221,183 |
| Emp. | 121 | 126 | 122 |

DUNS 34-837-1720
## Voltcom Construction Ltd
Unit 3 Sovereign Court, Sterling Drive, Pontyclun, Mid Glamorgan CF72 8YX
**Web:** www.voltcomgroup.com
**Reg No:** 5636414 **Estd:** 2005 Private Limited Company
**Line of Business:** Electrical distribution companies
**Issued Capital:** £111
**Directors:** J Nash, S W Watt, M A Wright
**US SIC:** 7539, 8911
**UK SIC:** 67100, 83701

| | 31-03-14 | 31-03-13 | 31-03-12 |
|---|---|---|---|
| TO | 13,609,181 | N/A | N/A |
| P/L | 971,019 | N/A | N/A |
| NW | 1,221,505 | 484,508 | 206,291 |
| WC | 8,318 | 475,402 | 121,044 |
| Emp. | 203 | N/A | N/A |

DUNS 28-831-1145
## Voluntary Action Sheffield
The Circle, 33 Rockingham Lane, Sheffield, South Yorkshire S1 4FW
**Tel:** 01142536600 **Fax:** 01142536601
**Web:** www.vas.org.uk
**Reg No:** 0215695 **Estd:** 1926 Private Limited Company
**Line of Business:** Charities and charitable organisations
**Directors:** Miss R Boyce, Ms D J Mathews, E Eruero, Ms S L Gill, N M Booth, M Hassan, R J Walton, Mrs S L Williamson
**Co. Secretary:** Mrs Susan White
**Responsibilities**
**Senior:** Ahmed Al Aagam *(Trustee)*, Wendy Bussey *(Manager)*, Daljit Kaur *(Manager)*, Luke Kenny *(Manager)*, Jane Leathley *(Manager)*, Roy Love *(Manager)*, Uriah Rennie *(Director)*
**Branches:** Voluntary Action Sheffield, The Circle, 33 Rockingham Lane, Sheffield, South Yorkshire S1 4FW
**US SIC:** 8699 **UK SIC:** 96902
**Auditors:** Barber Harrison & Platt
**Bankers:** Bank Of Scotland (12-18-68)

| | 31-03-14 | 31-03-13 | 31-03-12 |
|---|---|---|---|
| TO | 1,584,243 | 1,770,935 | 1,863,798 |
| P/L | (203,397) | (121,394) | (23,800) |
| NW | 1,611,268 | 1,814,665 | 1,936,059 |
| WC | 301,188 | 492,983 | 597,256 |
| Emp. | 46 | 52 | 56 |

DUNS 52-307-0076
## Voluntary Norfolk
St Clements House, 2-16 Colegate, Norwich, Norfolk NR3 1BQ
**Tel:** 01603-614474
**Web:** www.voluntarynorfolk.org.uk
**Reg No:** 5616120 **Estd:** 2005 Private Limited Company
**Line of Business:** Charities and charitable organisations
**Directors:** Mrs P A Seligman Obe, Jp Dl, T G Williams, J K Archibald, Ms V H Clifford-Jackson, Ms H Johnson, C R Bland, R Hetherington, Ms J L Chambers
**Responsibilities**
**Senior:** William Armstrong Obe *(Director)*, Frances Harrold *(Director)*, Richard Packham *(Director)*, Antony Parke *(Enterprise And Funding Develop)*, Penelope Seligman Obe Jp Dl *(Director)*
**US SIC:** 7392, 8321
**UK SIC:** 83951, 96111

**Bankers:** Bank Of Scotland (80-11-80)

| | 31-03-14 | 31-03-13 | 31-03-12 |
|---|---|---|---|
| TO | 1,445,119 | 1,673,468 | 1,810,990 |
| P/L | (113,242) | (14,843) | (401,705) |
| NW | 178,722 | 291,965 | 306,808 |
| WC | 121,027 | 288,173 | 271,376 |
| Emp. | 51 | 52 | 63 |

DUNS 22-706-6735 **Exp**

## Voluntary Service Overseas

100 London Road, Kingston-Upon-Thames, Surrey KT2 6QJ
**Web:** www.vso.org.uk
**Reg No:** 0703509 **Estd:** 1961 Private Company Limited By Guarantee
**Line of Business:** Adult and other education not elsewhere classified
**Trading Style:** V S O
**Directors:** R Choudhury, Dr N Kaleeba, T Carver, W Vota, Ms A Sen, S Pidgeon, J G Bason, Ms P Culpepper
**Co. Secretary:** Miss Jennifer Owen
**Responsibilities**
**Senior:** Marg Mayne (Chief Executive), Angela Salt (Company Director), Mari Simonen (Director), James Younger (Director)
**HR:** Kathryn Gordon (Human Resources Manager)
**Branches:** Voluntary Service Overseas, 34 Shaftesbury Sq, Belfast, Belfast BT2 7DB
**US SIC:** 8249, 8091
**UK SIC:** 93300, 95200
**Auditors:** BDO LLP
**Bankers:** HSBC Bank plc (40-03-17)

| | 31-03-14 | 31-03-13 | 31-03-12 |
|---|---|---|---|
| TO | 68,713,000 | 57,080,000 | 55,981,000 |
| P/L | 486,000 | (2,339,000) | 1,660,000 |
| NW | 15,161,000 | 14,675,000 | 17,009,000 |
| WC | 17,137,000 | 21,498,000 | 15,740,000 |
| Emp. | 760 | 717 | 723 |

DUNS 45-863-8293

## The Volunteer Centre - the Centre for Volunteering Community Action & Employment Initiat

84 Miller Street, Glasgow, Lanarkshire G1 1DT
**Tel:** 0141-226-3431
**Web:** www.volunteerglasgow.org
**Reg No:** 0166042SC **Estd:** 1996 Private Limited Company
**Line of Business:** Management activities of holding companies
**Directors:** Mrs A C Macdonald, A Kirkwood, Ms R Shah, Ms S R Kinn, B Bogle, Mrs S J Brimelow, Ms R J Findlater, N S Stewart
**Co. Secretary:** Julian Clarke
**Responsibilities**
**Admin:** Angela Kane (Admin Officer)
**Branches:** The Volunteer Centre - The Centre For Volunteering Community Action &, 143 Vanguard St, Clydebank, Dunbartonshire G81 2LZ
**US SIC:** 6711 **UK SIC:** 83962
**Auditors:** Deloitte & Touche
**Bankers:** Bank Of Scotland (80-07-60)

| | 31-03-14 | 31-03-13 | 31-03-12 |
|---|---|---|---|
| TO | 1,515,698 | 1,498,299 | 1,505,400 |
| P/L | 17,631 | 72,928 | 15,874 |
| NW | 385,378 | 367,747 | 294,819 |
| WC | 329,759 | 367,747 | 294,819 |
| Emp. | 54 | 56 | 51 |

DUNS 39-715-3644

## Volunteer Development Scotland Ltd

Jubilee House, Forthside Way, Stirling, Stirlingshire FK8 1QZ
**Tel:** 01786-479593
**Web:** www.volunteerscotland.org.uk
**Reg No:** 0106743SC **Estd:** 1987 Private Company Limited By Guarantee
**Line of Business:** Social work activities
**Directors:** S Laidlaw, D M Little, C Horne, Ms G Mccreath, K Yates, Dr R Jennings, Ms R Harper, Ms J Judson
**Co. Secretary:** George Thomson
**Responsibilities**
**Senior:** Delia Hendry (Director), Colin Lee (Manager), Phyl Meyer (Manager), george thomson (Chief Executive)
**Branches:** Volunteer Development Scotland Ltd, 146 Argyle St, Glasgow, Lanarkshire G2 8BL
**US SIC:** 7399 **UK SIC:** 83954
**Auditors:** Messrs Macfarlane Gray
**Bankers:** The Royal Bank Of Scotland Plc (83-48-00)

| | 31-03-14 | 31-03-13 | 31-03-12 |
|---|---|---|---|
| TO | 1,993,356 | 2,513,788 | 2,503,859 |
| P/L | (232,052) | 72,545 | 60,961 |
| NW | 1,564,783 | 1,796,835 | 1,724,290 |
| WC | 765,060 | 1,042,257 | 999,379 |
| Emp. | 54 | 53 | 49 |

DUNS 21-663-3455

## Volunteer Now

129 Ormeau Road, Belfast BT7 1SH
**Tel:** 02890236100
**Web:** www.volunteernow.co.uk
**Reg No:** 0602399NI **Estd:** 2010 Private Company Limited By Guarantee
**Line of Business:** Activities of other membership organisations not elsewhere classified
**Directors:** Ms J Mcstay, Ms C E Houston, C P Preen, A Coen, J Lowry, Ms E Mccrory, Ms W O Neilly, Ms J Baskin
**Co. Secretary:** Ms Wendy Osborne
**Responsibilities**
**Senior:** Martin Busch (Director), Paul Mccarroll (Director), Joe Mcvey (Director), Jayne Thompson (Director)
**US SIC:** 8699 **UK SIC:** 96902
**Bankers:** Ulster Bank Ltd (98-00-00)

| | 31-03-14 | 31-03-13 | 31-03-12 |
|---|---|---|---|
| TO | 2,138,608 | 2,755,161 | 2,687,935 |
| P/L | (277,109) | (65,948) | 78,864 |
| NW | 103,350 | 380,459 | 446,407 |
| WC | 88,653 | 347,250 | 438,291 |
| Emp. | 66 | 73 | 64 |

DUNS 29-933-0092

## Volunteer Reading Help

6 Middle Street, London EC1A 7JA
**Tel:** 020-7729-4087
**Web:** www.beanstalkcharity.org.uk
**Reg No:** 2101719 **Estd:** 1987 Private Limited Company
**Line of Business:** Activities of other membership organisations not elsewhere classified
**Trading Style:** Beanstalk
**Directors:** Ms S M Floyer, J R Pike, J G Murray, Ms J P Pay, P D Dean, Ms C M Roe, J K Brading, Miss S Kenny
**Responsibilities**
**Senior:** Suzanne Davies (Chief Executive Officer), Sue Porto (Chief Executive)
**Admin:** Paul O'brien (Office Manager)
**HR:** Victoria Dobos (Human Resources Manager)
**Branches:** Volunteer Reading Help, Kings Manor School, Southway, Guildford, Surrey GU2 8DU
**US SIC:** 7399, 8999
**UK SIC:** 83954
**Auditors:** haysmacintyre
**Bankers:** Cafcash Ltd (40-52-40)

| | 31-08-14 | 31-08-13 | 31-08-12 |
|---|---|---|---|
| TO | 2,815,139 | 2,185,287 | 1,883,654 |
| P/L | 178,050 | (100,409) | (35,698) |
| NW | 754,035 | 575,985 | 676,394 |
| WC | 702,540 | 570,985 | 663,839 |
| Emp. | 53 | 47 | 46 |

DUNS 73-295-5393 **Imp**

## Volution Ventilation Group Ltd

(**Subsidiary of:** Volution Group Plc)
Fleming Way, Crawley, West Sussex RH10 9YX
**Tel:** 08448560580 **Fax:** 01293418681
**Web:** www.vent-axia.com
**Reg No:** 4569321 **Estd:** 1933 Private Limited Company
**Line of Business:** Manufacture of other electrical equipment not elsewhere classified
**Trading Style:** Vent-Axia
**Issued Capital:** £1
**Directors:** I Dew, R George
**Responsibilities**
**Senior:** Frank Quinn (Manager), Kevin Sargeant (Manager)
**Finance:** Laurie Shelton (Finance Director)
**Marketing:** Chloe Griffin (Marketing Assistant), Lee Nurse (Marketing Director), Daniel Rollings (?Assistant Product Marketing M), Jenny Smith (Marketing Services Manager)
**Admin:** Kayrn Stevens (PA to Managing Director)
**IT:** Sanjay Sandhar (?IT Technician)
**US SIC:** 3629 **UK SIC:** 34350

| | 31-07-14 | 31-07-13 | 31-07-12 |
|---|---|---|---|
| TO | 2,716,000 | 155,000 | 128,000 |
| P/L | (2,752,000) | (1,641,000) | (1,382,000) |
| NW | 86,897,000 | 88,901,000 | 82,283,000 |
| WC | 60,788,000 | N/A | N/A |
| Emp. | 4 | N/A | N/A |

DUNS 64-075-3252

## Volvere Plc

York House, London EC4N 4SJ
**Tel:** 02076349707
**Web:** www.volvere.co.uk
**Reg No:** 4478674 **Estd:** 2002 Public Limited Company
**Line of Business:** Holding companies management activities
**Export Sales:** £911,000
**Trading Style:** Volvere
**Issued Capital:** £50,001
**Directors:** D J Buchler, J E Lander
**Co. Secretary:** Nicholas Lander
**Branches:** Volvere Plc, 631 Warwick Road, Solihull, West Midlands B91 1AR

**US SIC:** 6711 **UK SIC:** 83962
**Auditors:** Grant Thornton UK LLP

| | 31-12-13 | 31-12-12 | 31-12-11 |
|---|---|---|---|
| TO | 16,137,000 | 15,341,000 | 12,221,000 |
| P/L | 508,000 | (130,000) | 1,154,000 |
| NW | 17,041,000 | 17,257,000 | 18,360,000 |
| WC | 13,915,000 | 14,325,000 | 14,268,000 |
| Emp. | 232 | 123 | 169 |

DUNS 22-626-4992 **Imp-Exp**

## Volvo Construction Equipment Ltd

(**Subsidiary of:** Ab Volvo)
Leicester House, Moorfield Road, Cambridge, Cambridgeshire CB22 4PS
**Web:** www.volvoce.com
**Reg No:** 1673954 **VAT No:** 599304108
**Estd:** 1982 Private Limited Company
**Line of Business:** Plant dealers
**Issued Capital:** £300,000
**Directors:** V P Ledden, S D Villanueva
**Co. Secretary:** Simon Villanueva
**Responsibilities**
**Senior:** Per Barreng (Manager), Paul Fennessy (Manager)
**Finance:** Nick Allen (Chief Finance Officer), Paul Humphrey (Accountant)
**Marketing:** Mark Gunns (Marketing Manager)
**HR:** Graham Paflin (Training Manager), Marko Simic (Human Resources Director)
**Branches:** Volvo Construction Equipment Ltd, Portobello Road, Chester Le Street, County Durham DH3 2RR
**US SIC:** 5084, 5082
**UK SIC:** 61490

| | 31-12-13 | 31-12-12 | 31-12-11 |
|---|---|---|---|
| TA | 1,945,000 | 1,945,000 | 25,945,000 |
| NW | 1,945,000 | 1,945,000 | 25,945,000 |

DUNS 39-751-5404 **Imp**

## Volvo Group Uk Ltd

(**Subsidiary of:** Ab Volvo)
Wedgnock Lane, Warwick, Warwickshire CV34 5YA
**Tel:** 01926 401777 **Fax:** 01926 490991
**Web:** www.volvo.com
**Reg No:** 2190944 **Estd:** 1987 Private Limited Company
**Line of Business:** Sale of motor vehicles
**Export Sales:** £51,041,000
**Issued Capital:** £75,843,601
**Directors:** N J Allen, S Villanueva, S D Villanueva, Ms S Jannesson, R E Ericsson, J Wergeland, G Costa, A Knaben
**Co. Secretary:** Simon Villanueva
**Responsibilities**
**Senior:** Stefan Carlsson (Manager), Gustaf Engstrom (Manager), Jorn Kullberg (Manager), Anthony Mcgreal (Manager), Claes Nilsson (Manager), Goran Nyberg (Manager)
**Marketing:** Amanda Hiatt (Director Public Relations)
**Branches:** Volvo Group Uk Ltd, Banbury Rd, Souldern, Bicester, Oxfordshire OX27 8TG
**US SIC:** 5511 **UK SIC:** 65100
**Auditors:** PricewaterhouseCoopers LLP
**Bankers:** Barclays Bank Plc (20-23-55)
Following financial data are in thousands

| | 31-12-13 | 31-12-12 | 31-12-11 |
|---|---|---|---|
| TO | 571,757 | 1,291,060 | 1,471,011 |
| P/L | 7,473 | 9,230 | 14,263 |
| NW | 87,335 | 102,404 | 106,198 |
| WC | 58,702 | 67,271 | 65,534 |
| Emp. | 1,656 | 1,760 | 1,809 |

DUNS 34-586-5732

## Volvox Group Ltd

(**Subsidiary of:** Elysian Capital I Lp)
Volvox House, Gelderd Road, Leeds, West Yorkshire LS12 6NA
**Tel:** 01132-137300
**Reg No:** 5394180 **Estd:** 1972 Private Limited Company
**Line of Business:** Holding companies management activities
**Issued Capital:** £460,000
**Directors:** Ms K N Hawkins, J M Hall
**US SIC:** 6711, 5531
**UK SIC:** 83962, 65100
**Auditors:** KPMG LLP
**Bankers:** National Westminster Bank Plc (60-60-05)

| | 30-09-13 | 30-09-12 | 30-09-11 |
|---|---|---|---|
| TO | N/A | N/A | 43,686,000 |
| P/L | 1,161,000 | 1,202,000 | 2,980,000 |
| NW | 3,640,000 | 3,629,000 | 9,133,000 |
| WC | 2,920,000 | 74,000 | 8,426,000 |
| Emp. | N/A | 5 | 205 |

DUNS 34-879-7007 **Imp**

## Volz Filters Uk Ltd

1 Canary Way, Manchester M27 8AW
**Tel:** 0161-743-4190 **Fax:** 01617433190
**Web:** www.volzfilters.com
**Reg No:** 5677689 **Estd:** 2006 Private Limited Company
**Line of Business:** Air purification systems
**Issued Capital:** £1,000

**Directors:** J Thornton, R Volz
**Co. Secretary:** Mrs Tatiana Vaganova
**Responsibilities**
**Senior:** Bernard Moat (Manager)
**US SIC:** 3585 **UK SIC:** 32841

| | 31-12-13 | 31-12-12 | 31-12-11 |
|---|---|---|---|
| TA | 4,236,723 | 3,707,905 | 3,459,282 |
| NW | 1,403,813 | 986,767 | 587,122 |
| WC | 1,488,218 | 1,109,410 | 621,501 |

DUNS 23-323-0940

## Vopak Terminal London B V Ltd

(**Subsidiary of:** Koninklijke Vopak N.V.)
Oliver Road, Grays, Essex RM20 3ED
**Tel:** 01708-863399 **Fax:** 01708-683700
**Web:** www.vopak.com
**Reg No:** 0006133FC **VAT No:** 761281829
**Estd:** 1967 Foreign Company
**Line of Business:** Manufacture of gas
**Principals:** C Van Seventer (Managing), I Cochrane, C Scott, F E Erkelens, D A Van Slooten, H C Van Westenbrugge
**Co. Secretary:** C Jones
**Responsibilities**
**Senior:** Cornelis van Seventer (Director), Dirk van Slooten (Director), Hendrikus van Westenbrugge (Director)
**US SIC:** 4925 **UK SIC:** 25670
**Bankers:** The Royal Bank Of Scotland Plc (16-01-01)

DUNS 21-292-2264

## Vopak Terminal Teesside Ltd

(**Subsidiary of:** Koninklijke Vopak N.V.)
Seal Sands, Middlesbrough, Cleveland TS2 1UA
**Tel:** 01642-546767 **Fax:** 01642546300
**Web:** www.vopak.com
**Reg No:** 0829104 **VAT No:** 258184242
**Estd:** 1964 Private Limited Company
**Line of Business:** Storage and warehousing
**Issued Capital:** £100,000
**Directors:** F E Erkelens, I Cochrane
**Co. Secretary:** Robert Goldsmid
**Responsibilities**
**Finance:** Ian Saul (Accountant)
**Admin:** Ian Saul (Accountant)
**Facilities:** Donald Levelle (Maintenance Coordinator)
**Purchasing:** Colin Lines (Purchasing Manager)
**Fleet:** Donald Levelle (Maintenance Coordinator)
**US SIC:** 4226 **UK SIC:** 77003
**Auditors:** PricewaterhouseCoopers LLP
**Bankers:** Barclays Bank Plc (20-56-74)

| | 31-12-13 | 31-12-12 | 31-12-11 |
|---|---|---|---|
| TO | 22,186,000 | 21,633,000 | 19,530,000 |
| P/L | 8,106,000 | 8,061,000 | 6,323,000 |
| NW | 19,958,000 | 17,318,000 | 17,948,000 |
| WC | (13,312,000) | (15,324,000) | (11,822,000) |
| Emp. | 71 | 71 | 75 |

DUNS 21-602-0927

## Vosa

Berkeley House, Croydon Street, Bristol, Avon BS5 0DA
**Web:** www.vosa.gov.uk
**Estd:** 1964
**Line of Business:** Department of transport
**Partners:** A Peebles, M Giles, Mrs M Roberts, Ms J Fordham, J Bell
**US SIC:** 9121 **UK SIC:** 91110
**Employees:** 3,500

DUNS 21-223-8458

## Vosa Enforcement

Grange Road, Houstoun Industrial Estate, Livingston, West Lothian EH54 5DE
**Tel:** 01506-445200
**Estd:** 1975 Proprietorship
**Line of Business:** Vehicle inspection services
**Proprietor:** D Gibbson
**US SIC:** 7539 **UK SIC:** 67100
**Employees:** 100

DUNS 22-955-8275

## Vospers of Plymouth Ltd

Marsh Mills Park, Longbridge Road, Plymouth, Devon PL6 8AY
**Tel:** 01752-636363
**Web:** www.vospers.com
**Reg No:** 1019172 **Estd:** 1971 Private Limited Company
**Line of Business:** Sale of new motor vehicles
**Issued Capital:** £4,005,302
**Principals:** P G Vosper (Chairman and Managing), N J Vosper, Ms D E Vosper
**Co. Secretary:** Paul Rogers
**Responsibilities**
**Senior:** Bob Widdecombe (Property Director)
**Sales:** Ben Darnell (Used Car Director)
**IT:** Gordon Boyce (Group IT Manager), Trevor Hoy (IT Technician)
**Facilities:** Bob Widdecombe (Property Director)

**Operations:** Gordon Boyce *(Group IT Manager)*
**Engineering:** Olivia Weaving *(Technical Service Manager)*
**US SIC:** 5511, 7539
**UK SIC:** 65100, 67100
**Auditors:** PricewaterhouseCoopers
**Bankers:** Lloyds TSB Bank plc (30-96-68)

| | 31-12-13 | 31-12-12 | 31-12-11 |
|---|---|---|---|
| TO | 207,900,407 | 174,143,971 | 179,497,935 |
| P/L | 2,426,015 | 117,476 | 1,004,073 |
| NW | 17,231,001 | 14,960,645 | 14,949,376 |
| WC | (12,597,010) | (14,928,096) | (13,355,777) |
| Emp. | 663 | 650 | 682 |

DUNS 64-114-2310 **Exp**

## Vossloh Cogifer Uk Ltd

**(Subsidiary of:** Vossloh Ag)
80a Scotter Road, Scunthorpe, South Humberside DN15 8EF
**Tel:** 01724-862131 **Fax:** 01724-295243
**Web:** www.vossloh-cogifer.com
**Reg No:** 4114382 **VAT No:** 763990780
**Estd:** 2000 Private Limited Company
**Line of Business:** Manufacturers of railway equipment and related system
**Export Sales:** £1,106,120
**Issued Capital:** £2,000,001
**Directors:** G Thorez, D Redda, J Toubeau, I S Lindsay
**Co. Secretary:** Ms Wendy Preston
**US SIC:** 3743 **UK SIC:** 36201
**Auditors:** Ernst & Young LLP
**Bankers:** The Royal Bank Of Scotland Plc (16-31-15)

| | 31-12-13 | 31-12-12 | 31-12-11 |
|---|---|---|---|
| TO | 14,153,131 | 13,410,516 | 13,318,213 |
| P/L | 1,868,442 | 1,324,852 | 1,914,679 |
| NW | 4,996,800 | 7,573,927 | 7,636,910 |
| WC | 1,588,066 | 5,458,177 | 5,285,877 |
| Emp. | 92 | 84 | 70 |

DUNS 22-811-1639 **Imp**

## Vow Europe Ltd

**(Subsidiary of:** Vasanta Group Holdings Ltd)
K House, Sheffield, South Yorkshire S9 1XU
**Fax:** 01142566014
**Web:** www.kingfieldheath.co.uk
**Reg No:** 1204488 **VAT No:** 391085740
**Estd:** 1975 Private Limited Company
**Line of Business:** Wholesale of other household goods not elsewhere classified
**Issued Capital:** £580,385
**Directors:** A P Butler, J S Burkill, S Haworth, A P Gale, R R Baldrey
**Responsibilities**
**Senior:** Steve Blowers *(Regional Director Midlands, E.)*, Ashley Coleman *(Regional Director Ireland)*, Carol Houston *(Personal Assistant)*, Ian Newton *(Director)*
**Branches:** Vow Europe Ltd, Phase 11 Dene Way, Seaham, County Durham SR7 7BW
**US SIC:** 5199, 5999
**UK SIC:** 61900, 65600
**Auditors:** Deloitte LLP
**Bankers:** The Royal Bank Of Scotland Plc (16-00-08)

| | 31-12-13 | 31-12-12 | 31-12-11 |
|---|---|---|---|
| TO | 297,764,000 | 270,414,000 | 258,586,000 |
| P/L | 824,000 | (1,260,000) | (2,334,000) |
| NW | 9,958,000 | 9,115,000 | 12,188,000 |
| WC | 52,776,000 | 49,144,000 | 86,982,000 |
| Emp. | 849 | 835 | 863 |

DUNS 21-663-8579

## Vow Ltd

Flat 12 Berkeley House, 14 Wellington Way, London E3 4NG
**Fax:** 01455200174
**Web:** www.voweurope.com
**Reg No:** 7182917 **Estd:** 2010 Private Limited Company
**Line of Business:** Other computer related activities
**Issued Capital:** £100
**Director:** Miss R R Sankarappan
**US SIC:** 7379 **UK SIC:** 83940

| | 31-03-14 | 31-03-13 | 31-03-12 |
|---|---|---|---|
| TO | 17,360 | N/A | N/A |
| P/L | 4,200 | N/A | N/A |
| NW | 3,460 | 1 | 1,167 |
| WC | 3,460 | N/A | 1,167 |

DUNS 39-816-8989

## Voyage 1 Ltd

**(Subsidiary of:** Voyage Mezzco Ltd)
Voyage Care, Wall Island, Birmingham Road, Lichfield, Staffordshire WS14 0QP
**Tel:** 01543 484500 **Fax:** 01543-442518
**Web:** www.voyagecare.com
**Reg No:** 2215899 **Estd:** 1989 Private Limited Company
**Line of Business:** Other human health activities
**Issued Capital:** £2,210,000
**Director:** A Winning
**Co. Secretary:** Philip Sealey
**Responsibilities**
**Senior:** James Mckendrick *(Ceo)*, Chris Summers *(Manager)*
**Branches:** Voyage 1 Ltd, 21 Roundshead Drive, Bracknell, Berkshire RG42 3RZ
**US SIC:** 8091, 8321
**UK SIC:** 95200, 96111
**Auditors:** KPMG LLP
**Bankers:** Barclays Bank Plc (20-08-44)

| | 31-03-14 | 31-03-13 | 31-03-12 |
|---|---|---|---|
| TO | 74,528,000 | 76,330,000 | 76,910,000 |
| P/L | 22,556,000 | 22,176,000 | 19,694,000 |
| NW | 162,068,000 | 139,553,000 | 84,175,000 |
| WC | 235,049,000 | 152,158,000 | 88,157,000 |
| Emp. | 3,622 | 3,667 | 3,881 |

DUNS 21-155-5518

## Voyage Holdings Ltd

Voyage Care Wall Island, Birmingham Road, Lichfield, Staffordshire WS14 0QP
**Tel:** 0800 021 3232
**Web:** www.voyagecare.com
**Reg No:** 6836245 **Estd:** 2009 Private Limited Company
**Line of Business:** Management activities of holding companies
**Issued Capital:** £554
**Directors:** A Winning, P A Sealey
**Co. Secretary:** Philip Sealey
**US SIC:** 6711 **UK SIC:** 83962
**Auditors:** KPMG LLP

| | 31-03-14 | 31-03-13 | 31-03-12 |
|---|---|---|---|
| TO | 196,056,000 | 181,384,000 | 142,234,000 |
| P/L | (64,941,000) | (55,273,000) | (34,504,000) |
| NW | (301,593,000) | (247,779,000) | (199,288,000) |
| WC | (6,104,000) | 490,000 | 11,524,000 |
| Emp. | 8,252 | 7,496 | 6,353 |

DUNS 34-732-8499

## Voyage Specialist Healthcare Ltd

**(Subsidiary of:** Voyage Mezzco Ltd)
Innovation Centre, Venture Court, Queens Meadow Business Park, Hartlepool, Cleveland TS25 5TG
**Tel:** 01429-239616 **Fax:** 01429-239600
**Web:** www.voyagespecialisthealthcare.com
**Reg No:** 5534994 **Estd:** 2005 Private Limited Company
**Line of Business:** Other human health activities
**Issued Capital:** £100
**Directors:** P A Sealey, A Winning
**Co. Secretary:** Philip Sealey
**Responsibilities**
**Senior:** Alison Langthorne *(Manager)*, Marie Mason-Begbie *(Operations Director)*, Bruce Mckendrick *(Group Director)*, Mo Nazir *(Manager)*
**US SIC:** 8091 **UK SIC:** 95200

| | 31-03-14 | 31-03-13 | 31-03-12 |
|---|---|---|---|
| TO | 2,890,000 | 2,931,000 | 2,756,000 |
| P/L | (166,000) | (382,000) | 263,000 |
| NW | 708,000 | 869,000 | 1,115,000 |
| WC | 2,328,000 | 1,526,000 | 1,742,000 |
| Emp. | 206 | 192 | 154 |

DUNS 22-232-3375

## Voyager Networks Ltd

Voyager House, Coventry, West Midlands CV4 7EZ
**Tel:** 01189408510
**Web:** www.voyager.net.uk
**Reg No:** 4250304 **Estd:** 1993 Private Limited Company
**Line of Business:** Telecommunications
**Issued Capital:** £1,900,000
**Director:** N P Williams
**Co. Secretary:** Jonathan Shaw
**Responsibilities**
**Senior:** Lesley Ayres *(Human Resources Manager)*, Sean Huggett *(Director)*, C Key *(Manager)*
**Marketing:** S Baden *(Marketing Manager)*
**IT:** Eddie Ringrose *(Computer Manager)*
**HR:** Lesley Ayres *(Human Resources Manager)*
**Branches:** Voyager Networks Ltd, Voyager House, Unit 9, Coventry, West Midlands CV4 7EZ
**US SIC:** 4899, 7379
**UK SIC:** 79020, 83940
**Auditors:** Baker Tilly

| | 31-12-13 | 31-12-12 | 31-12-11 |
|---|---|---|---|
| TA | 945,900 | 2,606,414 | 2,902,241 |
| NW | (1,330,716) | (449,130) | (188,193) |
| WC | 166,579 | (1,662,777) | (1,388,503) |

DUNS 22-064-5084

## Voyager Pub Group Ltd

**(Subsidiary of:** Enterprise Inns Plc)
Voyager Transition Team, Unique Pub Co Ltd, Mill House, Aylesbury Road, Thame, Oxfordshire OX9 3AT
**Tel:** 01229825809
**Reg No:** 4066191 **Estd:** 2000 Private Limited Company
**Line of Business:** Management activities of other non-financial holding companies not elsewhere classified
**Issued Capital:** £1
**Directors:** W S Townsend, N R Smith, D C George
**Co. Secretary:** Ms Loretta Togher
**Branches:** Voyager Pub Group Ltd, 605 Gorton Road, Stockport, Cheshire SK5 6NX
**US SIC:** 6711 **UK SIC:** 83962
**Auditors:** Ernst & Young LLP

| | 30-09-13 | 30-09-12 | 30-09-11 |
|---|---|---|---|
| TA | 529,742,000 | 529,288,000 | 528,873,000 |
| P/L | 54,907,000 | 54,868,000 | 54,833,000 |
| NW | 188,774,000 | 188,427,000 | 188,116,000 |
| WC | (71,276,000) | (71,623,000) | (71,934,000) |

DUNS 77-887-7100

## Voyages-Sncf Uk Ltd

**(Subsidiary of:** Soc Nat Des Chemins De Fer Franc)
34 Tower View, Kings Hill, West Malling, Kent ME19 4ED
**Tel:** 01732-526700 **Fax:** 01732-526799
**Web:** http://uk.voyages-sncf.com
**Reg No:** 3038075 **Estd:** 1937 Private Limited Company
**Line of Business:** Tour operators
**Trading Style:** Voyages Sncf Uk Ltd
**Issued Capital:** £500,000
**Directors:** J Nicolas, O Jolly, N G Moser, O J Pinna, Miss S S Hocquez
**Co. Secretary:** Nicholas Moser
**Responsibilities**
**Senior:** Vincent Dedecker *(Manager)*, Frederic Langlois *(President and Chief Executive)*, Karen Mcclellan *(Financial Director)*, Fabien Soulet *(Manager)*
**Finance:** Karen Mcclellan *(Financial Director)*
**Marketing:** Lorna Bartholomew *(Senior Marketing Executive)*, Beth De Marte *(Marketing Director)*, Amanda Monroe *(Relations Manager)*, Joanne Woolcock *(Marketing Director)*, victoria fraser *(Marketing Manager)*
**IT:** rob harrison *(IT manager)*
**HR:** Alison Ryan *(Human Resources Manager)*
**Health & Safety:** Alison Ryan *(Human Resources Manager)*
**Facilities:** Alison Ryan *(Human Resources Manager)*
**Purchasing:** Karen Mcclellan *(Financial Director)*
**US SIC:** 4141 **UK SIC:** 72102
**Auditors:** Mazars Neville Russell

| | 31-12-13 | 31-12-12 | 31-12-11 |
|---|---|---|---|
| TO | 8,041,000 | 6,851,000 | 6,789,000 |
| P/L | 1,631,000 | 613,000 | 415,000 |
| NW | 2,541,000 | 1,312,000 | 1,327,000 |
| WC | 2,879,000 | 1,703,000 | 1,372,000 |
| Emp. | 96 | 93 | 91 |

DUNS 28-838-3839 **Imp**

## Vp Plc

Central House, Harrogate, North Yorkshire HG3 5QY
**Tel:** 01423533400
**Web:** www.vpplc.com
**Reg No:** 0481833 **VAT No:** 169406444
**Estd:** 1973 Public Limited Company
**Line of Business:** Plant hire and leasing
**Trading Style:** Groundforce, Hire Station Midlands, Airpac Bukom Oilfield Services
**Issued Capital:** £2,007,713
**Principals:** J F Pilkington *(Chairman)*, N A Stothard *(Managing)*, P M White, S Rogers
**Co. Secretary:** Mrs Allison Bainbridge
**Responsibilities**
**Marketing:** Anil Govind *(Marketing Coordinator)*
**HR:** Denise Stonard *(Human Resources Director)*
**Branches:** Vp Plc, Maynard Road, Wincheap Industrial Estate, Canterbury, Kent CT1 3RH
**US SIC:** 7394 **UK SIC:** 84000
**Auditors:** KPMG Audit PLC

| | 31-03-14 | 31-03-13 | 31-03-12 |
|---|---|---|---|
| TO | 183,064,000 | 167,034,000 | 163,563,000 |
| P/L | 18,933,000 | 16,402,000 | 15,328,000 |
| NW | 66,606,000 | 61,616,000 | 52,068,000 |
| WC | 7,641,000 | (12,730,000) | (3,726,000) |
| Emp. | 1,629 | 1,580 | 1,529 |

DUNS 73-574-1287

## Vps Holdings Ltd.

**(Subsidiary of:** Tdr Capital Llp)
Elstree Business Centre, Borehamwood, Hertfordshire WD6 1RX
**Tel:** 08706087062
**Web:** www.vpspecialists.co.uk
**Reg No:** 4835721 **Estd:** 2003 Private Limited Company
**Line of Business:** Management activities of holding companies
**Export Sales:** £84,428,000
**Issued Capital:** £3,600
**Directors:** K A Reid, M J Silver
**Co. Secretary:** Timothy O'Gorman
**Responsibilities**
**Senior:** Ian Quinlan *(Manager)*
**US SIC:** 6711 **UK SIC:** 83962
**Auditors:** KPMG LLP
**Bankers:** National Westminster Bank Plc (60-00-01)

| | 31-03-14 | 31-03-13 | 31-03-11 |
|---|---|---|---|
| TO | 121,581,000 | 201,880,000 | 139,694,000 |
| P/L | 40,282,000 | (8,019,000) | (16,954,000) |
| NW | (84,825,000) | (132,909,000) | (101,960,000) |
| WC | 2,831,000 | 12,119,000 | (3,189,000) |
| Emp. | 1,241 | 1,890 | 1,253 |

DUNS 77-506-8984

## Vroon Offshore Services Ltd

**(Subsidiary of:** Vroon Offshore B.V.)
Annat House, South Quay, Ferryden, Montrose, Angus DD10 9UG
**Tel:** 01224578750 **Fax:** 01224-578751
**Web:** www.vroonoffshore.com
**Reg No:** 0153759SC **Estd:** 1994 Private Limited Company
**Line of Business:** Service activities incidental to oil and gas extraction excluding surveying
**Issued Capital:** £6,500,000
**Directors:** S G Thom, E D Maandag, G P Sheach
**Co. Secretary:** Graeme Sheach
**Responsibilities**
**Senior:** Johannes Baars *(Manager)*, Jan-Piet Barrs *(Manager)*, Graham Philips *(Chief Executive)*
**Health & Safety:** Derek Leiper *(Health & Safety Officer)*
**US SIC:** 1389, 4469
**UK SIC:** 13000, 76300
**Auditors:** Deloitte & Touche LLP
**Bankers:** Bank Of Scotland (80-05-14)

| | 31-12-13 | 31-12-12 | 31-12-11 |
|---|---|---|---|
| TO | 26,773,000 | 33,316,000 | 33,570,000 |
| P/L | 4,476,000 | 4,901,000 | 4,962,000 |
| NW | 12,345,000 | 10,732,000 | 20,833,000 |
| WC | 2,386,000 | (18,653,000) | 661,000 |
| Emp. | 55 | 50 | 52 |

DUNS 21-169-3463

## Vrs Vericlaim Uk Ltd

1 Alie Street, London E1 8DE
**Tel:** 02077094040 **Fax:** 01619058529
**Web:** www.vrsvericlaim.co.uk
**Reg No:** 6941936 **Estd:** 2009 Private Limited Company
**Line of Business:** Insurance claims investigators
**Issued Capital:** £872,133
**Directors:** C J Ackerman, M Arbour, S C Steel, R Hogue
**US SIC:** 7393 **UK SIC:** 83954

| | 30-06-13 | 30-06-12 | 30-06-11 |
|---|---|---|---|
| TO | 6,892,037 | N/A | N/A |
| P/L | 826,368 | N/A | N/A |
| NW | 2,352,245 | 1,691,478 | 1,167,145 |
| WC | 2,354,539 | 1,848,470 | 1,931,177 |
| Emp. | 66 | N/A | N/A |

DUNS 22-917-4321

## V.Ships Uk Ltd

**(Subsidiary of:** Vouvray Holdings Limited)
8 Elliot Place, Glasgow, Lanarkshire G3 8EP
**Tel:** 01412-432435 **Fax:** 01412-432436
**Web:** www.vships.com
**Reg No:** 2268506 **VAT No:** 002255432
**Estd:** 1988 Private Limited Company
**Line of Business:** Other supporting water transport activities
**Issued Capital:** £100
**Directors:** Captain R M Bishop, J H Brechin
**Co. Secretary:** James Fairfield
**Responsibilities**
**Senior:** Philip Naylor *(Director)*
**Branches:** V.ships Uk Ltd, 20 Rutland Sq, Edinburgh, Midlothian EH1 2BB
**US SIC:** 4469 **UK SIC:** 76300
**Auditors:** Deloitte LLP
**Bankers:** Bank Of Scotland (80-11-80)

| | 31-12-13 | 31-12-12 | 31-12-11 |
|---|---|---|---|
| TO | 65,314,390 | 52,307,933 | 14,091,209 |
| P/L | 7,593,779 | 5,656,704 | 5,811,791 |
| NW | 8,084,925 | 2,286,282 | 1,058,306 |
| WC | 7,444,612 | 1,413,994 | 134,873 |
| Emp. | 222 | 236 | 227 |

DUNS 21-020-8609 **Imp**

## Vtb Capital Plc

14 Cornhill, London EC3V 3ND
**Tel:** 020 3334 8000
**Web:** www.vtbcapital.com
**Reg No:** 0159752 **VAT No:** 524765336
**Estd:** 1919 Public Limited Company
**Line of Business:** Banks and financial institutions
**Trading Style:** Vtb Group
**Directors:** O Pankratov, R P Munger, N J Hutt, S G Rice, N Joseph, P J Dayer, G S Russell, H Moos
**Co. Secretary:** Roger Munger
**Responsibilities**
**Senior:** David Brawn *(Manager)*, Sergey Dubinin *(Manager)*, Julian Simmonds *(Director)*
**US SIC:** 6012 **UK SIC:** 81402
**Auditors:** Ernst & Young LLP

**Bankers:** HSBC Bank plc (40-05-15)
**Employees:** 400
**Turnover:** £540,498,000

DUNS 22-232-1015
## Vtl Group (Holdings) Ltd
St Thomas? Road, Huddersfield, West Yorkshire HD1 3LG
**Tel:** 01484478790
**Web:** www.vtl-group.com
**Reg No:** 4250061 **Estd:** 2001 Private Limited Company
**Line of Business:** Management activities of holding companies
**Export Sales:** £18,150,000
**Issued Capital:** £90,000
**Directors:** A N Gregory, M J Baunton, C T Elliott, D R Myers
**Co. Secretary:** Bruno Jouan
**Responsibilities**
**Senior:** Steve Robins *(Managing Director Global Opera)*
**Finance:** Norah Redman *(Finance Administrator)*
**Marketing:** Stephanie Sayers *(Sales & Business Development M)*
**Sales:** Stephanie Sayers *(Sales & Business Development M)*
**Admin:** Norah Redman *(Finance Administrator)*, Kristy Simpson *(Group HR Administrator)*
**IT:** Mark Strutz *(IT Manager)*, Robert Wilkin *(Project Manager)*
**HR:** Kristy Simpson *(Group HR Administrator)*
**Engineering:** Steve Eeles *(Group Technical and Engineerin)*
**US SIC:** 6711 **UK SIC:** 83962
**Bankers:** HSBC Bank plc (40-00-00)

| | 31-12-13 | 31-12-12 | 31-12-11 |
|---|---|---|---|
| TO | 49,938,000 | 62,940,000 | 65,552,157 |
| P/L | (1,447,000) | 543,000 | 2,403,904 |
| NW | 3,949,000 | 6,240,000 | 5,522,923 |
| WC | 512,000 | 192,000 | (602,741) |
| Emp. | 347 | 418 | 400 |

DUNS 73-446-6597
## Vue Entertainment Ltd
**(Subsidiary of:** Allen & Overy Llp)
Building 10 Chiswick Park, 566 Chiswick High Road, London W4 5XS
**Tel:** 020-8396-0100 **Fax:** 020-8396-0100
**Web:** www.myvue.com
**Reg No:** 4699504 **Estd:** 2003 Private Limited Company
**Line of Business:** Motion picture projection
**Issued Capital:** £1,301
**Directors:** J T Richards, S J Knibbs, A E Mcnair
**Responsibilities**
**Senior:** Charlotte Driessen *(Office Manager)*, Anne Whalley *(Manager)*
**Branches:** Vue Entertainment Ltd, Doncaster Leisure Park, Bawtry Road, Doncaster, South Yorkshire DN4 7PD
**US SIC:** 7399 **UK SIC:** 83954
**Auditors:** PricewaterhouseCoopers LLP

| | 28-11-13 | 29-11-12 | 24-11-11 |
|---|---|---|---|
| TO | 258,111,000 | 257,952,000 | 242,565,000 |
| P/L | 28,034,000 | 28,893,000 | 27,279,000 |
| NW | 188,736,000 | 168,258,000 | 147,695,000 |
| WC | 41,049,000 | 20,145,000 | (148,000) |
| Emp. | 2,490 | 2,482 | 2,640 |

DUNS 23-820-1516
## Vue Services Ltd
**(Subsidiary of:** Allen & Overy Llp)
10 Chiswick Park, London W4 5XS
**Tel:** 08712240240 **Fax:** 0208-396-0199
**Web:** www.myvue.com
**Reg No:** 3812286 **Estd:** 1999 Private Limited Company
**Line of Business:** Film production services and studios
**Issued Capital:** £100
**Directors:** S J Knibbs, A E Mcnair, J T Richards
**Responsibilities**
**HR:** Rachel Daniel *(HR Operations Manager)*
**US SIC:** 6711 **UK SIC:** 83962
**Auditors:** PricewaterhouseCoopers LLP

| | 28-11-13 | 29-11-12 | 24-11-11 |
|---|---|---|---|
| TO | 9,580,000 | 7,412,000 | 7,602,000 |
| P/L | 410,000 | 14,000 | N/A |
| NW | 7,530,000 | 7,235,000 | 7,253,000 |
| WC | 6,842,000 | 6,682,000 | 6,558,000 |
| Emp. | 114 | 108 | 110 |

DUNS 22-138-2000
## Vuk Pharmaceuticals Ltd
**(Subsidiary of:** Meda Ab)
Skyway House, Parsonage Road, Takeley, Bishops Stortford, Hertfordshire CM22 6PU
**Fax:** 0845-460-0002
**Web:** www.meda.se
**Reg No:** 4157106 **Estd:** 2001 Private Limited Company
**Line of Business:** Wholesale of pharmaceutical goods
**Issued Capital:** £1

**Directors:** O Mckeon, H J Kromp
**Responsibilities**
**Senior:** Anthonius Van T Hullenaar *(Director)*
**US SIC:** 5122 **UK SIC:** 61800
**Auditors:** KPMG
**Bankers:** Lloyds TSB Bank plc (30-13-55)

| | 31-12-13 | 31-12-12 | 31-12-11 |
|---|---|---|---|
| TA | 4,437,000 | 4,437,000 | 4,437,000 |
| NW | 4,437,000 | 4,437,000 | 4,437,000 |

DUNS 53-652-4309
## Vulcan Aluminium Ltd
**(Subsidiary of:** Basicbonus Ltd)
37a Copenhagen Road, Hull, North Humberside HU7 0XQ
**Tel:** 01482-830500
**Reg No:** 3457722 **Estd:** 1993 Private Limited Company
**Line of Business:** Painting and glazing
**Issued Capital:** £2
**Directors:** D H Walker, T D Brown
**Co. Secretary:** David Bell
**US SIC:** 1721 **UK SIC:** 50400
**Auditors:** Norrie Gibson & Co Ltd

| | 30-11-13 | 30-11-12 | 30-11-11 |
|---|---|---|---|
| TA | 1,182,414 | 1,300,360 | 1,688,067 |
| NW | 516,247 | 451,455 | 399,488 |
| WC | 516,247 | 451,455 | 399,488 |

DUNS 21-689-2364
## Vur Village Trading No 1 Ltd
**(Subsidiary of:** Starwood Capital Group Global L.P.)
Henry Boot Way Priory Park, Hull, North Humberside HU4 7DY
**Tel:** 01482642422 **Fax:** 02476719100
**Web:** www.devere.co.uk
**Reg No:** 0418878 **Estd:** 2006 Private Limited Company
**Line of Business:** Other tourist assistance activities not elsewhere classified
**Trading Style:** Village Hotel and Leisure Club
**Issued Capital:** £10,500
**Directors:** G R Davis, C J Brenan
**Responsibilities**
**Senior:** Mark Nesbitt *(General Manager)*
**Finance:** Gerald Holden *(Financial Controller)*
**Marketing:** Mark Nesbitt *(General Manager)*
**HR:** Debbie Nolan *(People Development Officer)*
**Health & Safety:** Mark Nesbitt *(General Manager)*
**Facilities:** Mark Nesbitt *(General Manager)*
**Purchasing:** Mark Nesbitt *(General Manager)*
**Branches:** Vur Village Trading No 1 Ltd, Regent Street, Cambridge, Cambridgeshire CB2 1AD
**US SIC:** 7999 **UK SIC:** 97913
**Auditors:** Ernst & Young LLP
**Bankers:** National Westminster Bank Plc (01-09-17)

| | 31-12-13 | 31-12-12 | 31-12-11 |
|---|---|---|---|
| TO | 106,594,000 | 112,929,000 | 113,388,000 |
| P/L | (17,420,000) | (2,487,000) | (22,813,000) |
| NW | 86,825,000 | 98,156,000 | 407,442,000 |
| WC | 66,651,000 | 72,737,000 | 379,205,000 |
| Emp. | 2,333 | 2,366 | 2,412 |

DUNS 34-604-9799
## Vvb Engineering Services Ltd
**(Subsidiary of:** Hinde Holdings Ltd)
Church Road, Ramsden Heath, Billericay, Essex CM11 1PW
**Tel:** 01268711845
**Web:** www.vvb-eng.com
**Reg No:** 5411931 **Estd:** 2005 Private Limited Company
**Line of Business:** Installation of electrical wiring and fittings
**Issued Capital:** £2
**Directors:** S K Hinde, G J Race, S Wilson
**Co. Secretary:** Ms Rosemary Hinde
**US SIC:** 1731, 1796
**UK SIC:** 50300, 50400
**Auditors:** Moore & Smalley LLP
**Bankers:** National Westminster Bank Plc (01-01-75)

| | 30-04-14 | 30-04-13 | 30-04-12 |
|---|---|---|---|
| TO | 26,954,397 | 24,570,342 | 32,801,701 |
| P/L | 359,096 | 1,082,981 | (3,260,711) |
| NW | (147,451) | (506,547) | (1,589,528) |
| WC | (147,451) | 906,920 | (1,589,528) |
| Emp. | 65 | 69 | 69 |

DUNS 29-571-0289 Imp
## Vwr International Ltd
**(Subsidiary of:** Madison Dearborn Partners Llc)
Unit 3310 Hunter Boulevard, Lutterworth, Leicestershire LE17 4XN
**Tel:** 01455 558 600 **Fax:** 01455 558 586
**Web:** www.vwr.com
**Reg No:** 1932827 **VAT No:** 823853225
**Estd:** 1985 Private Limited Company
**Line of Business:** Pharmaceutical suppliers and wholesalers
**Issued Capital:** £16,700,000

**Directors:** B Hogan, Ms K Pulford, H Russmann
**Co. Secretary:** Ms Karen Pulford
**Responsibilities**
**Sales:** Elidh Robertson *(Sales Director)*
**Operations:** Martin Glover *(Operations Director)*
**Branches:** Vwr International Ltd, Unit 15, The Birches, Willard Way, Inberhourne Indstl Est, East Grinstead, West Sussex RH19 1XZ
**US SIC:** 5122, 5199
**UK SIC:** 61800, 61900
**Auditors:** KPMG LLP
**Bankers:** National Westminster Bank Plc (56-00-35)

| | 31-12-13 | 31-12-12 | 31-12-11 |
|---|---|---|---|
| TO | 118,484,000 | 104,017,000 | 100,381,000 |
| P/L | 4,190,000 | 5,825,000 | 765,000 |
| NW | 222,000 | (4,497,000) | (5,750,000) |
| WC | 14,911,000 | 14,383,000 | 13,203,000 |
| Emp. | 356 | 314 | 313 |

DUNS 21-617-2361 Imp
## Vws (Uk) Ltd
**(Subsidiary of:** Veolia Environnement)
Windsor Court, Kingsmead Business Park, High Wycombe, Buckinghamshire HP11 1JU
**Tel:** 01628897000 **Fax:** 01628897001
**Web:** www.veolia.com
**Reg No:** 0327847 **Estd:** 2012 Private Limited Company
**Line of Business:** Business services
**Export Sales:** £23,101,000
**Trading Style:** Veolia Water, Veolia Water Solutions & Technologies, Elga Lab Water
**Issued Capital:** £115,876
**Directors:** M P Fisher, F G Thery, P J Addington, Ms N Ikene, S K Lakhenpaul, N V Gallagher, P A Chattle
**Responsibilities**
**Senior:** Anita Sayer *(Sustainability Director)*
**Marketing:** Tina Desimone *(Senior Marketing Executive)*
**HR:** Beverley Eagle *(Human Resources Manager)*
**Purchasing:** David Swell *(Purchasing Manager)*
**Branches:** Vws (Uk) Ltd, Derby Road, Matlock, Derbyshire DE4 4BG
**US SIC:** 4941 **UK SIC:** 17000
**Auditors:** Ernst & Young LLP
**Bankers:** HSBC Bank plc (40-03-15)

| | 31-12-13 | 31-12-12 | 31-12-11 |
|---|---|---|---|
| TO | 79,231,000 | 79,289,000 | 72,804,000 |
| P/L | 7,189,000 | 2,559,000 | 2,610,000 |
| NW | 14,612,000 | 7,302,000 | 7,748,000 |
| WC | 15,930,000 | 9,048,000 | 6,834,000 |
| Emp. | 427 | 457 | 467 |

DUNS 21-726-9265 Imp-Exp
## Vygon (U.K.) Ltd
Gateway North, Latham Road, Swindon, Wiltshire SN25 4DL
**Tel:** 01793-748800 **Fax:** 01793-748899
**Web:** www.vygonvet.co.uk
**Reg No:** 1131530 **VAT No:** 484930515
**Estd:** 1978 Private Limited Company
**Line of Business:** Manufacture of medical and surgical equipment and orthopaedic appliances
**Issued Capital:** £311,000
**Principals:** L C Davies *(Managing)*, B Cuny, S Regnault
**Co. Secretary:** Ms Susan Power
**US SIC:** 3841, 5199
**UK SIC:** 37201, 61900
**Auditors:** Ernst & Young LLP
**Bankers:** National Westminster Bank Plc (60-05-41)

| | 31-12-13 | 31-12-12 | 31-12-11 |
|---|---|---|---|
| TO | 53,698,000 | 54,323,000 | 54,067,000 |
| P/L | 12,309,000 | 9,301,000 | 11,708,000 |
| NW | 37,748,000 | 35,474,000 | 36,714,000 |
| WC | 23,495,000 | 20,333,000 | 21,454,000 |
| Emp. | 142 | 137 | 136 |

DUNS 21-748-5907
## Vyners Learning Trust
Warren Road, Uxbridge, Middlesex UB10 8AB
**Tel:** 01895234342
**Web:** www.hillingdongrid.org
**Reg No:** 7796938 **Estd:** 2011 Private Company Limited By Guarantee
**Line of Business:** Schools (local authority)
**Directors:** P W Davies, W H Gardner, D P Trood, H Mcveigh, Mrs N C Forster, J Heale, D Thandrayen, M Hague
**Co. Secretary:** Ms Janet Beater
**Responsibilities**
**Senior:** Susan Baraban *(Director)*, Michelina Becker *(Assistant Head Teacher)*, Harjit Chaggar *(Director)*, Carolyn Crouchman *(Director)*, Jane Culley *(Key Stage Learning Mentor)*, Heather Danpure *(Director)*, David Dent *(Director)*, Kieran Dineen *(Director)*, Jillian Hayward *(Director)*, James Hockin *(Director)*, Aaron Shufflebotham *(Director)*, Janaki Try *(Director)*, Andrew Wilcock *(Director)*
**US SIC:** 8211 **UK SIC:** 93200

**Bankers:** Lloyds TSB Bank plc (30-98-91)

| | 31-08-13 | 31-08-12 |
|---|---|---|
| TO | 6,541,000 | 17,705,000 |
| P/L | 51,000 | 12,416,000 |
| NW | 12,370,000 | 12,308,000 |
| WC | 1,373,000 | 1,230,000 |
| Emp. | 121 | 125 |

DUNS 73-262-2811
## Vyre Ltd
**(Subsidiary of:** North Plains (Uk) Ltd)
House 5, 5-25 Scrutton Street, London EC2A 4HJ
**Tel:** 020-7749-1800 **Fax:** 02077498101
**Web:** www.northplains.com
**Reg No:** 4536106 **Estd:** 2003 Private Limited Company
**Line of Business:** Computer software (development)
**Issued Capital:** £1,984
**Directors:** Miss B Gerety, D Jacobson
**Responsibilities**
**Senior:** Shehzada Munir *(Consultant)*, Rich Upshall *(Consultant)*
**US SIC:** 7379 **UK SIC:** 83940

| | 31-12-13 | 31-12-12 | 31-12-11 |
|---|---|---|---|
| TO | 4,271,019 | 5,066,338 | 3,999,943 |
| P/L | (786,624) | (35,909) | (737,719) |
| NW | (441,425) | 308,271 | (1,626,261) |
| WC | (709,623) | 171,328 | (677,713) |
| Emp. | N/A | 56 | 62 |

DUNS 23-541-3619
## Vysionics Its Ltd
**(Subsidiary of:** Jenoptik Ag)
4.8 Frimley Business Park, Frimley, Camberley, Surrey GU16 7SG
**Tel:** 01276-698980
**Web:** www.speedcheck.co.uk
**Reg No:** 3540380 **Estd:** 1999 Private Limited Company
**Line of Business:** Technical testing and analysis
**Issued Capital:** £400,000
**Directors:** K Chevis, R Gorringe, C Biermann, S F Oelert
**Co. Secretary:** Shoosmiths Secretaries Limited
**Responsibilities**
**Senior:** Bruce Brain *(Manager)*, Graeme Southwood *(Manager)*
**US SIC:** 7397 **UK SIC:** 83702
**Auditors:** Deloitte LLP

| | 31-12-13 | 31-12-12 | 31-12-11 |
|---|---|---|---|
| TO | 9,305,119 | 7,825,441 | 6,656,994 |
| P/L | 1,143,530 | 333,485 | 84,874 |
| NW | 5,437,073 | 5,025,741 | 4,859,674 |
| WC | 3,255,696 | 2,790,062 | 2,353,764 |
| Emp. | 48 | 44 | 45 |

# W

DUNS 21-781-9995
## W A Printers
Cowden Close Horns Road, Cranbrook, Kent TN18 4QQ
**Tel:** 01580754847
**Web:** www.wealdenad.co.uk
**Estd:** 2011 Proprietorship
**Line of Business:** Newspapers publishing
**Proprietor:** G Thorn
**Responsibilities**
**Senior:** Robert Mitham *(Manager)*
**US SIC:** 2711 **UK SIC:** 47512
**Employees:** 50

DUNS 21-170-7661
## W & A S Bruce
Bruce House, 15-17 Chalmers Street, Dunfermline, Fife KY12 8AT
**Tel:** 01383738000
**Web:** www.wasbruce.co.uk
**Estd:** 1978 Partnership
**Line of Business:** Solicitors
**Partners:** K Kordula, C Campbell
**Branches:** W & A S Bruce, W & A S Bruce, 6-8 Hunter Street, Kirkcaldy, Fife KY1 1ED
**US SIC:** 8111, 6531
**UK SIC:** 83500, 83400
**Employees:** 47

DUNS 22-930-3821
## W & D Fraser Ltd
**(Subsidiary of:** William J M Fraser & Co Ltd)
19 Beechmount Road, Belfast BT8 8AD
**Tel:** 02890814941
**Web:** www.fraserhomes.co.uk
**Reg No:** 0017189NI **Estd:** 1984 Private Limited Company
**Line of Business:** Activities of households as employers of domestic staff
**Issued Capital:** £3,600,905

**Directors:** Ms C A Hill, Ms P F Maconaghie, Ms D S Steele, D Fraser, Ms M M Fraser, Ms A M Haslett
**Co. Secretary:** David Fraser
**Responsibilities**
**IT:** Mark Gilmore *(Technical Manager)*
**US SIC:** 8811 **UK SIC:** 99000
**Auditors:** Crawford Sedgwick & Co
**Bankers:** First Trust Bank (aib Group (uk) Plc) (93-80-92)

| | 31-03-14 | 31-03-13 | 31-03-12 |
|---|---|---|---|
| TA | 3,600,905 | 7,083,207 | 7,083,207 |
| NW | 3,600,905 | 7,083,207 | 7,083,207 |

DUNS 21-010-9252 Imp
## W. & G. Foyle Ltd
107 Charing Cross Road, London WC2H 0EB
**Tel:** 020-7437-5660
**Web:** www.foyles.co.uk
**Reg No:** 0945131 **Estd:** 1903 Private Limited Company
**Line of Business:** Book retailers
**Trading Style:** Foyles Bookstores, Rays Jazz At Foyles
**Issued Capital:** £600
**Directors:** W R Foyle, R K Burnett, S Hamilton, Mrs B A Aspinall, S Husain, W E Samuel
**Co. Secretary:** John Browne
**Responsibilities**
**Senior:** Frank Binsbergen *(Manager)*, Sam Husain *(Chief Executive)*
**Marketing:** Gavin Read *(Marketing Manager)*
**US SIC:** 5732, 5999
**UK SIC:** 64800, 65600
**Auditors:** Baker Tilly UK Audit LLP
**Bankers:** Barclays Bank Plc (20-78-98)

| | 30-06-13 | 30-06-12 | 30-06-11 |
|---|---|---|---|
| TO | 22,924,068 | 23,492,891 | 22,848,251 |
| P/L | 83,294 | 152,552 | 204,681 |
| NW | 4,904,646 | 2,829,317 | 2,747,136 |
| WC | 3,464,263 | 1,841,852 | 2,008,828 |
| Emp. | 198 | 204 | 183 |

DUNS 21-315-6367
## W. & G. Harrison Ltd
**(Subsidiary of:** Dowbridge Ltd)
Ribby Road, Preston, Lancashire PR4 2PR
**Tel:** 01772671111
**Web:** www.ribbyhall.com
**Reg No:** 1032929 **VAT No:** 155255958
**Estd:** 1971 Private Limited Company
**Line of Business:** Hairdressers (unisex)
**Trading Style:** Ribby Hall Holiday Village
**Issued Capital:** £1,000,000
**Directors:** Mrs S Holloway, Mrs J P Livock, M R Partington, J A Atkinson
**Co. Secretary:** Paul Harrison
**Responsibilities**
**Senior:** Karen Thompson *(Proprietor)*
**Health & Safety:** John Mcilwham *(Health & Safety Officer)*
**US SIC:** 7231, 7032
**UK SIC:** 98200, 66702
**Auditors:** Haworth Moore
**Bankers:** HSBC Bank plc (40-26-19)

| | 29-12-13 | 30-12-12 | 01-12-12 |
|---|---|---|---|
| TO | 20,308,000 | 20,031,663 | 18,115,006 |
| P/L | 799,000 | 1,569,093 | 1,017,045 |
| NW | 11,629,000 | 11,089,100 | 10,001,788 |
| WC | (5,316,000) | (4,132,017) | (4,301,848) |
| Emp. | 375 | 359 | 326 |

DUNS 22-049-2842
## W & H Peacock Auction Ltd
**(Subsidiary of:** Akmb Holdings Ltd)
26 Newnham Street, Bedford, Bedfordshire MK40 3JR
**Tel:** 01234266366
**Web:** www.peacockauction.co.uk
**Reg No:** 4051468 **VAT No:** 746216042
**Estd:** 1901 Private Limited Company
**Line of Business:** Other business activities not elsewhere classified
**Issued Capital:** £1
**Director:** M N Baker
**Responsibilities**
**Senior:** Edward Crawshay *(Manager)*
**Marketing:** Tim Brophy *(Marketing Department)*
**Sales:** Ben Adams *(Sales & Valuation Advice)*, Nikki Bell *(Sales & Valuation Advice)*, Nigel Croskell *(Consultant Valuer)*, Rod Sancto *(Consultant Valuer))*
**Admin:** Georgina Grant *(Secretary)*
**US SIC:** 7399 **UK SIC:** 83954

| | 31-08-13 | 31-08-12 | 31-08-11 |
|---|---|---|---|
| TA | 1 | 1 | 1 |
| NW | 1 | 1 | 1 |

DUNS 21-619-7442
## W & H (Roads)Ltd
Stock Road Industrial Estate, Southend-On-Sea, Essex SS2 5QF
**Tel:** 01702-442010
**Web:** www.whroads.co.uk
**Reg No:** 0590714 **VAT No:** 250627868
**Estd:** 1957 Private Limited Company
**Line of Business:** Construction of motorways, roads, railways, airfields and sports facilities
**Issued Capital:** £5,100
**Principals:** M L Hardy *(Managing)*, D M Hardy *(Financial)*, G A Churn, P E Cook
**Co. Secretary:** Ms Lynne Betts
**US SIC:** 1611, 7394
**UK SIC:** 50200, 84000
**Auditors:** Barrons
**Bankers:** Barclays Bank Plc (20-79-73)

| | 30-04-14 | 30-04-13 | 30-04-12 |
|---|---|---|---|
| TA | 2,807,442 | 2,538,326 | 2,506,760 |
| NW | 1,114,146 | 952,230 | 768,659 |
| WC | 342,193 | 120,917 | 64,299 |

DUNS 21-112-9131
## W & H (Romac) Ltd
Stock Road, Southend-On-Sea, Essex SS2 5QG
**Tel:** 01702469777 **Fax:** 01702442016
**Web:** www.whroads.co.uk
**Reg No:** 6538140 **Estd:** 1957 Private Limited Company
**Line of Business:** Other engineering activities
**Issued Capital:** £100
**Directors:** P E Cook, R Mcdonald, D M Hardy
**Co. Secretary:** Ms Suzanne Mcdonald
**US SIC:** 8911 **UK SIC:** 83701

| | 30-04-14 | 30-04-13 | 30-04-12 |
|---|---|---|---|
| TA | 222,347 | 195,832 | 255,577 |
| NW | 71,489 | 45,237 | 30,193 |
| WC | 33,190 | 13,398 | (4,059) |

DUNS 23-221-3090 Exp
## W. & J. Chambers Ltd
91 Glenshane Road, Londonderry, Co Londonderry BT47 3SG
**Tel:** 02871301239
**Web:** www.wjchambers.com
**Reg No:** 0028587NI **Estd:** 1935 Private Limited Company
**Line of Business:** Manufacture of concrete products for construction purposes
**Export Markets:** Republic of Ireland
**Issued Capital:** £600,000
**Directors:** A R Chambers, J M Chambers, W A Chambers, D W Chambers, W A Chambers, G A Chambers
**Co. Secretary:** Mrs Kathleen Chambers
**Branches:** Claudy
**US SIC:** 3271 **UK SIC:** 24370
**Auditors:** W S Sterritt & Co
**Bankers:** Ulster Bank Ltd (98-09-85)

| | 30-06-13 | 30-06-12 | 30-06-11 |
|---|---|---|---|
| TO | 7,699,027 | N/A | N/A |
| P/L | (103,832) | (248,057) | (185,550) |
| NW | 4,706,651 | 4,829,516 | 5,030,426 |
| WC | 190,783 | 368,827 | 191,166 |
| Emp. | 55 | N/A | N/A |

DUNS 21-402-4101
## W & J Cruickshank & Co Ltd
Cunningholes Industrial Estate, Buckie, Banffshire AB56 4DA
**Tel:** 01542832132 **Fax:** 01542835573
**Reg No:** 0064823SC **VAT No:** 296789180
**Estd:** 2010 Private Limited Company
**Line of Business:** Manufacture of mineral waters and soft drinks
**Issued Capital:** £50,000
**Managing Director:** W Cruickshank
**Co. Secretary:**
Grigor & Young Trustees Limited
**Branches:** W & J Cruickshank & Co Ltd, 31 Telford St, Wick, Caithness KW1 5EQ
**US SIC:** 2086, 5182
**UK SIC:** 42831, 61700
**Bankers:** Clydesdale Bank Plc (82-61-14)

| | 31-03-14 | 31-03-13 | 31-03-12 |
|---|---|---|---|
| TA | 1,788,710 | 1,827,693 | 1,830,844 |
| NW | 1,775,443 | 1,804,106 | 1,809,229 |
| WC | 1,353,441 | 1,358,379 | 1,319,616 |

DUNS 50-659-4985
## W & J Kirk
Buxton Road, Blackshaw Moor, Leek, Staffordshire ST13 8TW
**Tel:** 01538-300296
**Web:** www.threeshoesin.co.uk
**Estd:** 1982 Partnership
**Line of Business:** Public house and hotel
**Trading Style:** Three Horseshoes Inn
**Partners:** Mrs J Kirk, W Kirk
**US SIC:** 5812, 7399
**UK SIC:** 66110, 83954
**Employees:** 62

DUNS 73-957-3702 Imp-Exp
## W & J Knox Ltd
**(Subsidiary of:** Macrocom (1030) Ltd)
Mill Road, Kilbirnie, Ayrshire KA25 7GY
**Tel:** 01505-682511
**Web:** www.wjknox.co.uk
**Reg No:** 0272146SC **VAT No:** 847785565
**Estd:** 2004 Private Limited Company
**Line of Business:** Manufacturers of netting and netting product
**Export Sales:** £1,341,999
**Issued Capital:** £110,103
**Directors:** J Traynor, J Borrows, J R Dehany
**Co. Secretary:** David Sloan
**Responsibilities**
**Senior:** James Templeton *(Production Manager)*
**Engineering:** James Templeton *(Production Manager)*
**US SIC:** 2298 **UK SIC:** 43960
**Bankers:** Clydesdale Bank Plc (82-20-00)

| | 31-12-13 | 31-12-12 | 31-12-11 |
|---|---|---|---|
| TO | 8,638,614 | 10,566,645 | 9,959,882 |
| P/L | 326,539 | 681,823 | 520,527 |
| NW | 1,649,457 | 2,249,990 | 1,754,090 |
| WC | 843,752 | 1,100,605 | 599,404 |
| Emp. | 115 | 112 | 104 |

DUNS 21-820-4733 Imp
## W & J Linney Ltd
Adamsway, Mansfield, Nottinghamshire NG18 4FL
**Tel:** 01623450460 **Fax:** 01623-450451
**Web:** www.linney.com
**Reg No:** 0137552 **VAT No:** 116932276
**Estd:** 1914 Private Limited Company
**Line of Business:** Management activities of holding companies
**Trading Style:** Linney Direct Business Magazine Group, Linney Print
**Issued Capital:** £186,000
**Principals:** N S Linney *(Managing)*, R R Munro *(Financial)*, M J Linney, P R Biddle, G Fryett, C H Linney
**Co. Secretary:** Carl Drake
**Responsibilities**
**Senior:** Ian Linney *(Manager)*
**Branches:** W.& J.linney,Ltd, Adamsway, Mansfield, Nottinghamshire NG18 4FW
**US SIC:** 6711, 7339
**UK SIC:** 83962, 83954
**Auditors:** Cooper Parry LLP
**Bankers:** National Westminster Bank Plc (60-14-03)

| | 04-05-14 | 05-05-13 | 29-05-12 |
|---|---|---|---|
| TO | 80,089,000 | 71,074,000 | 68,866,000 |
| P/L | 3,208,000 | 2,682,000 | 2,983,000 |
| NW | 15,763,000 | 15,679,000 | 15,943,000 |
| WC | (1,307,000) | (401,000) | 1,425,000 |
| Emp. | 714 | 607 | 554 |

DUNS 50-566-6461 Exp
## W & J Tod Holdings Ltd
**(Subsidiary of:** Acorn Growth Companies Llc)
8 Cropmead, Crewkerne, Somerset TA18 7HQ
**Tel:** 01460-77666
**Web:** www.tods.co.uk
**Reg No:** 2514416 **Estd:** 1991 Private Limited Company
**Line of Business:** Manufacture of other plastic products
**Export Markets:** E U, Asia, North America
**Issued Capital:** £98,500
**Principals:** S T Finch *(Managing)*, R R Nagel
**Co. Secretary:** Vp Secretarial Limited
**Responsibilities**
**Senior:** Shirley Bowley *(Manager)*, Matthew Molyneux *(Manager)*, Richard Ripper *(Chairman)*
**Finance:** Phil Louch *(Head of Finance)*
**US SIC:** 3079 **UK SIC:** 48360
**Auditors:** Francis Clark LLP
**Bankers:** National Westminster Bank Plc (60-14-55)

| | 31-12-13 | 30-09-12 | 30-12-11 |
|---|---|---|---|
| TO | N/A | 15,810,000 | 15,557,000 |
| P/L | N/A | 1,967,000 | 1,375,000 |
| NW | 1,223,000 | 4,226,000 | 2,651,000 |
| WC | N/A | 2,526,000 | 778,000 |
| Emp. | N/A | 177 | 162 |

DUNS 76-851-6031
## W & M Wholesale Ltd
**(Subsidiary of:** W & M Holding Co Ltd)
Unit 3c Admiral Business Park, Cramlington, Northumberland NE23 1WG
**Tel:** 01670 700030
**Web:** www.startfitness.co.uk
**Reg No:** 2607133 **Estd:** 1985 Private Limited Company
**Line of Business:** Manufacture of sports goods
**Export Sales:** £5,628,443
**Issued Capital:** £217,966
**Directors:** G Middlemiss, A Wallett
**Co. Secretary:** Gary Middlemiss
**Branches:** W & M Wholesale Limited, Homestead Farm, Darwell Hill, Battle, East Sussex TN33 9QL
**US SIC:** 5136, 5941, 5961, 5139
**UK SIC:** 61600, 65400, 65600
**Auditors:** RSM Tenon Audit Ltd
**Bankers:** Lloyds TSB Bank plc (30-93-55)

| | 31-07-13 | 31-07-12 | 31-07-11 |
|---|---|---|---|
| TO | 19,287,801 | 15,795,259 | 12,703,403 |
| P/L | 2,279,395 | 1,819,940 | 1,078,746 |
| NW | 6,268,239 | 4,589,588 | 2,706,538 |
| WC | 3,383,232 | 2,427,843 | 1,510,950 |
| Emp. | 84 | 74 | 62 |

DUNS 21-454-2268 Imp
## W & R Barnett Ltd
Clarendon House, Belfast BT1 3BG
**Web:** www.wrbarnett.com
**Reg No:** 0000166NI **Estd:** 1924 Private Limited Company
**Line of Business:** Farming of sheep, goats, horses, asses, mules and hinnies
**Issued Capital:** £87,500
**Directors:** D G Billington, B N Mcdonnell, Ms C J Heron, W B Barnett, R Barnett, C F Roberts
**Co. Secretary:** Geoffrey Jordan
**Responsibilities**
**Senior:** Michael Mc Aree *(Manager)*
**Sales:** Ryan Mcauley *(Commodity Trader)*
**IT:** Ryan Mcauley *(Commodity Trader)*
**Branches:** W & R Barnett Ltd, Dufferin Road, Belfast, Belfast BT3 9AA
**US SIC:** 0214, 6711
**UK SIC:** 01001, 83962
**Auditors:** PricewaterhouseCoopers LLP
**Bankers:** The Bank Of Ireland (90-21-27)

| | 31-07-13 | 31-07-12 | 31-07-11 |
|---|---|---|---|
| TO | 199,727,651 | 417,727,464 | 350,744,084 |
| P/L | 22,279,563 | 20,708,955 | 17,687,979 |
| NW | 167,325,918 | 140,393,719 | 127,953,675 |
| WC | 114,706,350 | 101,829,134 | 76,777,708 |
| Emp. | 278 | 256 | 236 |

DUNS 73-537-6852
## W & R Buxton Contracting Ltd
Cedar House, 91 High Street, Caterham, Surrey CR3 5UH
**Tel:** 01883-348921 **Fax:** 01883340964
**Reg No:** 4800129 **Estd:** 2003 Private Limited Company
**Line of Business:** Development and selling of real estate
**Issued Capital:** £622
**Directors:** S W Buxton, G J Davies, D W Buxton, Miss M Buxton, Mrs G S Buxton
**Co. Secretary:** Mark Freeland
**US SIC:** 6552, 6711
**UK SIC:** 85000, 83962

| | 31-07-13 | 31-07-12 | 31-07-11 |
|---|---|---|---|
| TO | 40,849,601 | 38,149,972 | 30,424,277 |
| P/L | 53,438 | 21,295 | (629,331) |
| NW | 1,617,402 | 1,563,964 | 1,518,402 |
| WC | 1,394,218 | 1,329,455 | 1,271,660 |
| Emp. | 69 | 54 | 57 |

DUNS 53-565-0949
## W & W H Pettit
Cowbit Road, Spalding, Lincolnshire PE12 6AB
**Estd:** 2002 Partnership
**Line of Business:** Blast cleaning
**Partners:** R Pettit, J Pettit
**US SIC:** 0729 **UK SIC:** 01003
**Bankers:** HSBC Bank plc (40-43-01)
**Employees:** 74

DUNS 23-283-6648
## W B B Minerals
Brookside Hall, Sandbach, Cheshire CW11 4TF
**Tel:** 01270752777
**Web:** www.sibelco.co.uk
**Line of Business:** Other mining and quarrying not elsewhere classified
**Trading Style:** Sibelco Uk Ltd
**Responsibilities**
**Engineering:** Mick Higgins *(Technical Manager)*
**Branches:** W B B Minerals, Cove Rd, Doncaster, South Yorkshire DN9 2BB
**US SIC:** 1499 **UK SIC:** 23960
**Employees:** 1,300

DUNS 28-828-4524
## W B Penman Ltd
**(Subsidiary of:** W B Penman Holdings Ltd)
5 7 William Street, Johnstone, Renfrewshire PA5 8DP
**Tel:** 01505-320116
**Reg No:** 0089151SC **VAT No:** 789794434
**Estd:** 1984 Private Limited Company
**Line of Business:** Chemists dispensing
**Trading Style:** Penmans Pharmacy
**Issued Capital:** £1,000
**Directors:** D P Penman, M Penman
**Co. Secretary:** Mrs Elaine Penman
**Branches:** W B Penman Ltd, 72 High Street, Johnstone, Renfrewshire PA5 8SG
**US SIC:** 5912 **UK SIC:** 64300
**Auditors:** Milne Craig
**Bankers:** The Royal Bank Of Scotland Plc (83-23-16)

| | 30-11-13 | 30-11-12 | 30-11-11 |
|---|---|---|---|
| TA | 2,086,063 | 2,152,210 | 2,362,268 |
| NW | 820,262 | 738,630 | 653,539 |
| WC | 922,056 | 737,530 | 867,176 |

DUNS 39-346-3591 Exp
## W B Power Services Ltd
Manners Avenue, Manners Industrial Estate, Ilkeston, Derbyshire DE7 8EF
**Tel:** 01159444422 **Fax:** 01132-453255
**Web:** www.wbpsltd.co.uk
**Reg No:** 2120023 **VAT No:** 411219892
**Estd:** 1987 Private Limited Company
**Line of Business:** Sales and servicing of generators
**Export Markets:** Yemen
**Issued Capital:** £5,000
**Directors:** C M Wilmott, D Buttar, K R Wilmott, Ms V A Wilmott
**Co. Secretary:** Andrew Wilmott
**Responsibilities**
**Senior:** Steve Rake *(Operations Director)*
**US SIC:** 3621, 3743
**UK SIC:** 34201, 36201
**Auditors:** BW Business Services Ltd
**Bankers:** Yorkshire Bank Plc (05-05-31)

| | 30-04-14 | 30-04-13 | 30-04-12 |
|---|---|---|---|
| TO | 11,821,459 | 10,020,162 | 9,221,973 |
| P/L | 270,234 | 577,240 | 523,307 |
| NW | 799,934 | 923,075 | 805,528 |
| WC | (570,142) | (71,733) | (73,243) |
| Emp. | 76 | 65 | 67 |

DUNS 21-404-2129 Exp
## W. B. S. Keillor Ltd
**(Subsidiary of:** W.B.S. Keillor Holdings Ltd)
Unit 2 Fowler Road, West Pitkerro Industrial Estate, Broughty Ferry, Dundee, Angus DD5 3RU
**Tel:** 01382-737744
**Web:** www.keillor.net
**Reg No:** 0037549SC **VAT No:** 269228138
**Estd:** 1948 Private Limited Company
**Line of Business:** Manufacturers of joinery
**Export Markets:** Republic of Ireland
**Issued Capital:** £10,000
**Directors:** M C Smith, J M Livie
**Responsibilities**
**Senior:** Allan Keillor *(Manager)*
**US SIC:** 2431 **UK SIC:** 46300
**Auditors:** Henderson Loggie
**Bankers:** Bank Of Scotland (80-73-31)

| | 31-05-14 | 31-05-13 | 31-05-12 |
|---|---|---|---|
| TA | 1,000,203 | 1,266,064 | 716,123 |
| NW | 377,835 | 320,038 | 232,497 |
| WC | 325,451 | 288,890 | 207,453 |

DUNS 21-237-3468 Imp
## W Boyes & Co Ltd
**(Subsidiary of:** Boyes Holdings (Scarborough) Ltd)
33 North Parade, Bradford, West Yorkshire BD1 3JH
**Tel:** 01274732247
**Web:** www.boyes.co.uk
**Reg No:** 0066251 **VAT No:** 166846720
**Estd:** 1881 Private Limited Company
**Line of Business:** Departmental stores
**Trading Style:** Boyes Stores, Boyes W
**Issued Capital:** £396,718
**Principals:** A P Boyes *(Managing)*, T J Boyes *(Managing)*, R Van Der Heijden, R M Boyes, E Gee
**Co. Secretary:** Ms Diane Shortland
**Responsibilities**
**Senior:** Mike Gaines *(Warehouse Manager)*
**Facilities:** Kevin Marson *(Maintenance Manager)*
**Branches:** W.boyes & Co.,Ltd, 5-13 West Row, Stockton-On-Tees, Cleveland TS18 1BT
**US SIC:** 5399 **UK SIC:** 65600
**Auditors:** Coulsons
**Bankers:** HSBC Bank plc (40-40-22)

| | 25-01-14 | 26-01-13 | 28-01-12 |
|---|---|---|---|
| TO | 70,148,635 | 65,879,723 | 63,428,081 |
| P/L | 4,836,103 | 4,281,440 | 4,518,290 |
| NW | 33,821,041 | 31,399,118 | 29,384,431 |
| WC | 13,347,524 | 12,574,366 | 11,324,764 |
| Emp. | 1,444 | 1,344 | 1,325 |

DUNS 21-390-1117
## W C V A
Unit 2, Llanon, Dyfed SY23 3AH
**Tel:** 08002888329
**Web:** www.wcva.org.uk
**Proprietorship**
**Line of Business:** Non-charitable social work activities without accommodation
**Proprietor:** R Jones
**US SIC:** 8321 **UK SIC:** 96111
**Employees:** 130

DUNS 21-229-8622
## W Carswell
Hartley Avenue, London NW7 2HX
**Tel:** 02089590888
**Estd:** 1972
**Line of Business:** Cosmetic surgery
**Trading Style:** Mgp Surgery
**US SIC:** 8011 **UK SIC:** 95300
**Employees:** 46

DUNS 21-228-2168
## W Chadwick
Rievaulx Road, Whitby, North Yorkshire YO21 1SD
**Tel:** 01947600995
**Web:** www.rowlandspharmacy.co.uk
**Estd:** 2009
**Line of Business:** Chemists dispensing
**Responsibilities**
**Senior:** Trish Rutland *(Practice Manager)*
**US SIC:** 8011 **UK SIC:** 95300
**Employees:** 49

DUNS 21-833-2468 Imp
## W. Corbett & Co. (Galvanizing) Ltd
New Alexandra Works, Haldane Halesfield 1, Telford, Shropshire TF7 4QQ
**Tel:** 01952-412777 **Fax:** 01952-412888
**Web:** www.wcorbett.co.uk
**Reg No:** 0490482 **Estd:** 1951 Private Limited Company
**Line of Business:** Treatment and coating of metals
**Issued Capital:** £31,389
**Principals:** A S Rai *(Managing)*, T Ward, Miss S L Boothroyd
**Co. Secretary:** Mrs Baksho Rai
**Responsibilities**
**Senior:** Mark Statham *(Manager)*
**Sales:** Joe Rai *(Sales Director)*
**HR:** Mark Statham *(Manager)*
**Purchasing:** Mark Statham *(Manager)*
**Engineering:** Ian Hayles *(Production Manager)*
**US SIC:** 3398 **UK SIC:** 31380
**Auditors:** Davies Grindrod & Co
**Bankers:** Lloyds TSB Bank plc (30-18-55)

| | 31-03-14 | 31-03-13 | 31-03-12 |
|---|---|---|---|
| TO | 9,798,795 | 10,736,512 | 10,266,403 |
| P/L | 517,750 | 711,531 | 709,887 |
| NW | 3,389,763 | 3,367,843 | 3,263,872 |
| WC | 1,172,272 | 1,475,962 | 1,175,958 |
| Emp. | 127 | 131 | 131 |

DUNS 21-814-8104 Imp-Exp
## W Crowder & Sons Ltd
Thimbleby Nurseries Lincoln Road, Thimbleby, Horncastle, Lincolnshire LN9 5LZ
**Tel:** 01507-525000 **Fax:** 01507-524000
**Web:** www.crowders.co.uk
**Reg No:** 1069525 **VAT No:** 127729844
**Estd:** 1972 Private Limited Company
**Line of Business:** Florists wholesale
**Export Markets:** Germany, Switzerland, France, Sweden
**Export Sales:** £272,878
**Trading Style:** Crowders Nurseries, Crowders Garden Centre
**Issued Capital:** £255,565
**Principals:** W K Crowder *(Managing)*, K D Lee, M T Dugdale
**Co. Secretary:** Neil Rudkin
**Branches:** W.crowder & Sons,Ltd, Lincoln Road, Horncastle, Lincolnshire LN9 5LZ
**US SIC:** 5199, 5999
**UK SIC:** 61900, 65600
**Auditors:** Dexter & Sharpe Audit Services Ltd
**Bankers:** Lloyds TSB Bank plc (77-30-30)

| | 30-09-13 | 30-09-12 | 30-09-11 |
|---|---|---|---|
| TO | 5,652,418 | 5,414,464 | 4,789,864 |
| P/L | (39,172) | (40,716) | 35,786 |
| NW | 2,173,011 | 2,190,448 | 1,313,222 |
| WC | 5,895 | 70,506 | 152,845 |
| Emp. | 77 | 83 | 79 |

DUNS 28-975-8997 Exp
## W D-40 Co Ltd
**(Subsidiary of:** Wd-40 Holdings Ltd)
Po Box440, Milton Keynes, Buckinghamshire MK11 3LF
**Tel:** 01908555400
**Web:** www.wd40.co.uk
**Reg No:** 1755958 **VAT No:** 844274910
**Estd:** 2004 Private Limited Company
**Line of Business:** Manufacturers of lubricating oils
**Export Markets:** E U, Middle East, Africa
**Export Sales:** £72,194,000
**Issued Capital:** £250,100
**Principals:** W B Noble *(Managing)*, G O Ridge
**Co. Secretary:**
Bird & Bird Company Secretaries
**Responsibilities**
**Marketing:** Simon Daw *(Marketing Director)*
**IT:** Jonathan McCoy *(IT Manager)*
**HR:** Sonya Jenkins *(Human Resources Manager)*
**US SIC:** 2999 **UK SIC:** 11150
**Auditors:** PricewaterhouseCoopers LLP
**Bankers:** Barclays Bank Plc (20-57-40)

| | 31-08-13 | 31-08-12 | 31-08-11 |
|---|---|---|---|
| TO | 89,483,000 | 76,023,000 | 80,618,000 |
| P/L | 10,617,000 | 6,647,000 | 8,763,000 |
| NW | 56,620,000 | 47,809,000 | 42,164,000 |
| WC | 54,414,000 | 45,840,000 | 40,533,000 |
| Emp. | 149 | 140 | 134 |

DUNS 73-807-4405
## W D Lewis (Holdings) Ltd
Stuart Quarry, Chapel Road, Penderyn, Aberdare, Mid Glamorgan CF44 9JY
**Tel:** 01685-811975
**Web:** www.wdlewis.co.uk
**Reg No:** 5063704 **Estd:** 2004 Private Limited Company
**Line of Business:** Management activities of holding companies
**Issued Capital:** £23,656,290
**Director:** R A Lewis
**Co. Secretary:** Martin Lewis
**US SIC:** 6711, 7392
**UK SIC:** 83962, 83951

| | 31-03-14 | 31-03-13 | 31-03-12 |
|---|---|---|---|
| TO | 28,005,676 | 21,446,950 | 19,730,676 |
| P/L | 353,594 | (1,427,632) | (1,173,804) |
| NW | 1,046,489 | 64,266 | (165,182) |
| WC | 7,226,043 | 5,120,942 | 4,531,257 |
| Emp. | 196 | 186 | 162 |

DUNS 21-589-9055 Exp
## W D Meats
**(Subsidiary of:** Kilda Limited)
Newmills Road Lower, Coleraine, Co Londonderry BT52 2JR
**Tel:** 028-7035-6111 **Fax:** 028-7035-4903
**Web:** www.wd-meats.co.uk
**Reg No:** 0013845NI **VAT No:** 331747855
**Estd:** 1979 Private Unlimited Company
**Line of Business:** Animal by-product processing
**Export Markets:** Europe
**Issued Capital:** £200,100
**Directors:** Miss G Dillon, F J Dillon, A J Dillon, Miss C M Dillon, Miss M F Dillon, Ms H Dillon
**Co. Secretary:** Mrs Helen Dillon
**Responsibilities**
**Senior:** Tony Butler *(General Manager)*
**Sales:** Melvyn Pollock *(Sales Manager)*
**HR:** Sharon Finley *(Personnel Officer)*
**Facilities:** Eamon Turner *(Maintenance Manager)*
**Operations:** Tony Butler *(General Manager)*
**US SIC:** 2013, 5148
**UK SIC:** 41223, 61700
**Auditors:** Moore Stephens
**Bankers:** Northern Bank Ltd (95-01-31)
**Employees:** 330
**Turnover:** £52,581,340

DUNS 22-841-3332
## W D R & R T Taggart
Laganwood House, 44 Newforge Lane, Belfast BT9 5NX
**Tel:** 028-9066-2121
**Web:** www.wdr-rt-taggart.com
**VAT No:** 252523971 **Estd:** 1902 Partnership
**Line of Business:** Architects
**Principals:** D H Adams, A J Allen, A J Giffen *(Partner)*, T A Mcneill *(Partner)*
**Responsibilities**
**Senior:** Alan McNeil *(Partner)*
**Engineering:** Trudy Harbinson *(Associate)*
**Branches:** Londonderry
**US SIC:** 8911, 7392, 0729
**UK SIC:** 83701, 83951, 01003
**Bankers:** First Trust Bank (aib Group (uk) Plc) (93-80-92)
**Employees:** 45

DUNS 21-627-9927
## W Davis & Sons (Sevenoaks) Ltd
**(Subsidiary of:** Gillham Hayward Ltd)
Otford Road, Sevenoaks, Kent TN14 5EG
**Tel:** 01732-455174 **Fax:** 01732-457361
**Web:** www.haywardsmotorgroup.com
**Reg No:** 0406113 **VAT No:** 209549644
**Estd:** 1946 Private Limited Company
**Line of Business:** Sale of new motor vehicles
**Trading Style:** Haywards Motor Group
**Issued Capital:** £100,000
**Director:** D R Hayward
**Co. Secretary:** Neil Davis
**Responsibilities**
**Senior:** John Brookwell *(Parts Manager)*, Richard Collison *(General Manager)*
**Branches:** Branches: 1 in Sevenoaks
**US SIC:** 5511, 5521
**UK SIC:** 65100
**Bankers:** National Westminster Bank Plc (60-19-02)

| | 31-12-13 | 31-12-12 | 31-12-11 |
|---|---|---|---|
| TA | 3,664,127 | 3,563,801 | 3,246,586 |
| NW | 1,538,620 | 1,337,550 | 1,064,558 |
| WC | 248,747 | 436,194 | 202,528 |

DUNS 73-590-7623
## W Denis (Holdings) Plc
86 Kirkstall Road, Leeds, West Yorkshire LS3 1LQ
**Tel:** 02035444770
**Web:** www.wdenis.co.uk
**Reg No:** 4852098 **Estd:** 2003 Public Limited Company
**Line of Business:** Financial management
**Issued Capital:** £52,649
**Directors:** S R Thew, H A Thew, C H Thurston
**Co. Secretary:** Ian Desbottes
**US SIC:** 7392 **UK SIC:** 83951
**Bankers:** HSBC Bank plc (40-27-15)

| | 30-06-14 | 30-06-13 | 30-06-12 |
|---|---|---|---|
| TO | 4,703,003 | 4,049,826 | 3,899,080 |
| P/L | 396,132 | 312,873 | 356,709 |
| NW | 4,242,580 | 4,562,040 | 4,372,208 |
| WC | 1,176,911 | 1,663,050 | 1,506,614 |
| Emp. | 61 | 56 | 53 |

DUNS 21-618-1081 Exp
## W F E L Ltd
**(Subsidiary of:** Krauss-Maffei Wegmann Gmbh & Co. Kg)
Heaton Chapel, Stockport, Cheshire SK4 5BF
**Tel:** 01619755700
**Web:** www.wfel.com
**Reg No:** 0310308 **Estd:** 1936 Private Limited Company
**Line of Business:** Manufacture of metal structures and parts of structures
**Export Markets:** Western Europe, Middle East, U S A, S America, Africa, South & South East Asia, Australasia & Canada
**Export Sales:** £49,234,000
**Issued Capital:** £18,819,000
**Directors:** H Rieder, J Weber, R Ketzel, P N Grady, M G Houghton, J A Field, M Sheridan, I G Wilson
**Co. Secretary:** Patrick Grady
**Responsibilities**
**Senior:** Clifford Richards *(Manager)*
**IT:** Mal Haddad *(IT manager)*
**Health & Safety:** Wayne Scholfield *(Health & Safety Officer)*
**US SIC:** 3441 **UK SIC:** 32042
**Auditors:** Deloitte LLP
**Bankers:** Barclays Bank Plc (20-25-85)

| | 31-12-13 | 31-12-12 | 31-12-11 |
|---|---|---|---|
| TO | 51,963,000 | 39,659,000 | 36,168,000 |
| P/L | 17,478,000 | 11,125,000 | 7,223,000 |
| NW | 29,329,000 | 26,588,000 | 39,838,000 |
| WC | 37,429,000 | 23,158,000 | 46,508,000 |
| Emp. | 81 | 83 | 87 |

DUNS 21-600-9523
## W F S
Building 550, Hounslow, Middlesex TW6 3UA
**Tel:** 02085645330
**Web:** www.wfs.aero
**Estd:** 2011 Proprietorship
**Line of Business:** Cargo handling
**Proprietor:** P Roberts
**US SIC:** 4712 **UK SIC:** 77002
**Employees:** 500

DUNS 53-549-1146
## W Fairlie & Son
West Pittendriech Farm, Brechin, Angus DD9 6RD
**Estd:** 2002 Proprietorship
**Line of Business:** Livestock breeders
**Proprietor:** W Farlie
**Responsibilities**
**Senior:** David Fairlie *(Proprietor)*
**US SIC:** 0214 **UK SIC:** 01001
**Employees:** 91

DUNS 21-831-5836
## W G Allen & Sons (Tipton) Ltd
Princess End Works, Tipton, West Midlands DY4 9EX
**Tel:** 0121-557-3977
**Reg No:** 0103370 **Estd:** 1850 Public Limited Company
**Line of Business:** Holding company for agroup engaged in manufacture of boilers, conveyors, hoists (50%) and sheet metal and steel fabrication work.
**US SIC:** 6711, 3443, 3535, 3441, 3444
**UK SIC:** 83962, 32051, 32551, 32042, 31694
**Employees:** 356

DUNS 77-009-9588
## W G & R U K Ltd
Signal House, Huddersfield, West Yorkshire HD4 5NS
**Web:** www.wgr.co.uk
**Reg No:** 2660215 **VAT No:** 516372650
**Estd:** 1986 Private Limited Company
**Line of Business:** Assembling and wiring
**Issued Capital:** £100
**Managing Director:** S Puckering
**Co. Secretary:** Ms Katherine Puckering

**Responsibilities**
**Senior:** Stephen Puckering *(Managing Director)*
**Finance:** Rachel Brooke *(Accountant)*
**IT:** Rachel Brooke *(Accountant)*
**Branches:** W G & R U K Ltd, Unit C15, Prestons Road, London E14 9RL
**US SIC:** 1731 **UK SIC:** 50300
**Auditors:** Mazars LLP
**Bankers:** National Westminster Bank Plc (53-61-07)

| | 30-09-13 | 30-09-12 | 30-09-11 |
|---|---|---|---|
| TO | 4,181,477 | 6,900,688 | N/A |
| P/L | (88,636) | 540,310 | N/A |
| NW | 1,656,453 | 2,031,658 | 1,924,248 |
| WC | 1,085,263 | 1,716,853 | 1,618,209 |
| Emp. | 50 | 58 | N/A |

DUNS 28-886-2691 **Imp**

## W G Jones Ltd

22-24 Black Moor Road, Verwood, Dorset BH31 6BD
**Tel:** 01202-825467 **Fax:** 01202-823944
**Web:** www.wgjones.co.uk
**Reg No:** 1235895 **Estd:** 1975 Private Limited Company
**Line of Business:** Animal husbandry service activities, except veterinary activities, not elsewhere classified
**Trading Style:** W G Jones Limited
**Issued Capital:** £33,500
**Directors:** B C Evans, Miss L A Evans, P J Evans
**Co. Secretary:** Elson Geaves Business Services L
**Responsibilities**
**Finance:** Phil Forbes *(Accounts Manager)*
**IT:** Steve Bartlett *(Computer Manager)*
**Operations:** Garry Bungay *(Production Manager)*
**Engineering:** Ray Leake *(Production Manager)*
**US SIC:** 0751 **UK SIC:** 01003
**Auditors:** T.R. Hammond
**Bankers:** HSBC Bank plc (40-19-30)

| | 31-12-13 | 31-12-12 | 31-12-11 |
|---|---|---|---|
| TA | 3,100,526 | 2,851,361 | 2,678,127 |
| NW | 1,306,022 | 1,077,497 | 1,098,881 |
| WC | 68,837 | (11,625) | 29,933 |

DUNS 21-562-8732

## W G Sheds

The Grove, Three Gates Road, Fawkham, Longfield, Kent DA3 8NZ
**Tel:** 01474700160
**Proprietorship**
**Line of Business:** Prefab wood bldgs/ components
**Proprietor:** D Perrott
**US SIC:** 2499 **UK SIC:** 46500
**Employees:** 60

DUNS 73-304-5186

## W. Grose Northampton Ltd

(**Subsidiary of:** W. Grose Holdings Ltd)
The Granary Tithe Farm, Moulton Road, Northampton, Northamptonshire NN6 9SH
**Tel:** 01604-712525
**Web:** www.wgrose.co.uk
**Reg No:** 4578329 **Estd:** 2002 Private Limited Company
**Line of Business:** Maintenance and repair of motor vehicles
**Issued Capital:** £1,700,000
**Directors:** Ms G M Harris, P W Grose
**US SIC:** 5521 **UK SIC:** 65100
**Bankers:** HSBC Bank plc (40-00-00)

| | 30-06-13 | 30-06-12 | 31-06-10 |
|---|---|---|---|
| TO | N/A | 20,643,554 | 20,757,387 |
| P/L | N/A | (883,888) | 166,691 |
| NW | 680,455 | 680,455 | 2,100,043 |
| WC | N/A | 1,054,155 | 2,983,794 |
| Emp. | N/A | 74 | 104 |

DUNS 52-536-5086

## W H Bond & Sons Ltd

(**Subsidiary of:** Bond Holdings Ltd)
Trerulefoot, Saltash, Cornwall PL12 5BL
**Tel:** 01503240304
**Web:** www.whbond.co.uk
**Reg No:** 3240088 **Estd:** 1957 Private Limited Company
**Line of Business:** Growing of cereals and other crops not elsewhere classified
**Issued Capital:** £1,000
**Directors:** M S Bond, C I Bond, J M Bond
**Co. Secretary:** Alison Bond
**Branches:** W H Bond & Sons Ltd, Broadmoor Farm, Saltash, Cornwall PL12 4SA
**US SIC:** 0119, 7391
**UK SIC:** 01001, 94000
**Auditors:** Riley
**Bankers:** Barclays Bank Plc (20-50-40)

| | 30-04-14 | 30-04-13 | 30-04-12 |
|---|---|---|---|
| TO | 16,013,049 | 12,568,176 | 12,483,861 |
| P/L | 845,619 | 291,316 | 296,228 |
| NW | 4,809,157 | 4,139,764 | 3,913,084 |
| WC | (1,811,265) | (983,794) | (897,832) |
| Emp. | 62 | 61 | 64 |

DUNS 29-675-7115

## W H Ireland Ltd

(**Subsidiary of:** Lloyds Banking Group Plc)
11 St James's Square, Manchester M2 6WH
**Tel:** 01618326644
**Web:** www.wh-ireland.co.uk
**Reg No:** 2002044 **Estd:** 2002 Private Limited Company
**Line of Business:** Stockbrokers
**Trading Style:** W H Allan
**Issued Capital:** £691,339
**Directors:** R J Lowe, S J Cooper, T M Steel, R W Killingbeck, R E Lee, D J Cowland
**Co. Secretary:** Miss Katy Mitchell
**Responsibilities**
**Senior:** Daniel Bate *(Manager)*, Christopher Compton *(Manager)*, Alan Kershaw *(Manager)*
**Finance:** Daniel Bate *(Manager)*, Alan Kershaw *(Manager)*, Zoltan Molnar *(Finance Manager)*
**Branches:** W H Ireland Ltd, April House, The Purlieu, Malvern, Worcestershire WR14 4DJ
**US SIC:** 6211 **UK SIC:** 83100
**Auditors:** KPMG Audit Plc

| | 30-11-13 | 30-11-12 | 30-11-11 |
|---|---|---|---|
| TA | 45,779,731 | 46,688,272 | 36,344,336 |
| P/L | 1,305,767 | (323,548) | 604,934 |
| NW | 7,848,930 | 6,861,925 | 7,826,800 |
| WC | 7,263,584 | 5,607,076 | 6,858,043 |
| Emp. | 229 | 214 | 182 |

DUNS 21-727-4604 **Exp**

## W H Rowe Ltd

Quayside Road, Bitterne Manor, Southampton, Hampshire SO18 1DH
**Tel:** 023-8022-5636
**Web:** www.whrowe.com
**Reg No:** 1172026 **VAT No:** 189959473
**Estd:** 1932 Private Limited Company
**Line of Business:** Manufacture of basic iron and steel and of ferro-alloys
**Export Markets:** E U, U S A
**Issued Capital:** £5,556
**Principals:** I R Fowler *(Managing)*, C Theoharis
**Co. Secretary:** David Bartlett
**Responsibilities**
**Senior:** Penelope Harris *(Manager)*, Shirley Rowe *(Manager)*
**Branches:** Bond St, Southampton
**US SIC:** 3325, 3499
**UK SIC:** 31110, 31694
**Auditors:** Blueprint Audit Ltd
**Bankers:** National Westminster Bank Plc (56-00-68)

| | 30-04-14 | 30-04-13 | 30-04-12 |
|---|---|---|---|
| TA | 2,089,827 | 2,269,585 | 2,540,407 |
| NW | 783,228 | 692,188 | 816,123 |
| WC | 12,994 | (101,668) | 83,292 |

DUNS 50-640-5583

## W H Smith News

Javelin Park, Black Country New Road, Wednesbury, West Midlands WS10 7ND
**Tel:** 0845-126-2700
**Web:** www.connect2u.co.uk
**Estd:** 2010 Proprietorship
**Line of Business:** Newspapers publishing
**Proprietor:** P Hancher
**Responsibilities**
**Senior:** Rashid Qureshi *(Distribution Manager)*
**HR:** Carol Cullum *(Human Resources Administrator)*
**Health & Safety:** Rashid Qureshi *(Distribution Manager)*
**Facilities:** Rashid Qureshi *(Distribution Manager)*
**US SIC:** 2711 **UK SIC:** 47512
**Employees:** 150

DUNS 21-820-1739 **Imp-Exp**

## W. Hargreaves & Co. (Property) Ltd

Howardson Works, Ashbourne Road, Kirk Langley, Ashbourne, Derbyshire DE6 4NJ
**Tel:** 01332824777 **Fax:** 01625-427426
**Web:** www.dennisuk.com
**Reg No:** 0262618 **VAT No:** 157667034
**Estd:** 1932 Private Limited Company
**Line of Business:** Other letting of own property
**Export Markets:** Worldwide
**Issued Capital:** £85,417
**Managing Director:** J W Hargreaves
**Co. Secretary:** Derek Cronshaw
**Responsibilities**
**Senior:** John Brocklebank *(Manager)*, Roger Hargreaves *(Manager)*
**Branches:** W. Hargreaves & Co. (Property) Ltd, Unit J, The Roundel, Falkirk, Stirlingshire FK2 9HG
**US SIC:** 6519 **UK SIC:** 85000
**Auditors:** Booth Ainsworth
**Bankers:** National Westminster Bank Plc (01-10-01)

| | 30-06-13 | 30-06-12 | 30-06-11 |
|---|---|---|---|
| TO | N/A | N/A | 3,331,570 |
| P/L | N/A | N/A | (344,275) |
| NW | 1,130,832 | 701,916 | 1,068,702 |
| WC | (109,207) | (105,358) | 94,265 |
| Emp. | N/A | N/A | 51 |

DUNS 21-327-1398

## W. Harrison & Sons (Carriers) Ltd

Grimshaw Lane, Manchester M24 2AA
**Tel:** 01616532200
**Web:** www.expressparcels.co.uk
**Reg No:** 0729701 **Estd:** 1920 Private Limited Company
**Line of Business:** Storage and warehousing
**Trading Style:** Express Parcel Services, B S T Carriers
**Issued Capital:** £7,000
**Principals:** B Taylor *(Managing)*, A Taylor, J Taylor, A Taylor
**Co. Secretary:** Alistair Taylor
**Responsibilities**
**Senior:** Brian Steventon *(Manager)*
**US SIC:** 4226, 4213
**UK SIC:** 77003, 72300
**Auditors:** Grundy Anderson & Kershaw
**Bankers:** The Royal Bank Of Scotland Plc (16-27-11)

| | 31-05-14 | 31-05-13 | 31-05-12 |
|---|---|---|---|
| TO | 7,346,466 | 7,669,412 | 7,582,774 |
| P/L | 365,112 | 417,846 | 454,383 |
| NW | 1,981,175 | 2,332,209 | 2,000,847 |
| WC | 622,208 | 1,002,723 | 665,216 |
| Emp. | 184 | 200 | 198 |

DUNS 21-682-0761 **Exp**

## W Harvey & Sons

The Coombe, Newlyn, Penzance, Cornwall TR18 5HF
**Web:** www.crabmeat.co.uk
**VAT No:** 131840202 **Estd:** 1955 Partnership
**Line of Business:** Shell fish suppliers and processors
**Export Markets:** Sweden, France & Spain
**Partners:** M R Harvey, Ms E C Harvey, Ms M Harvey, R P Harvey, J A Harvey
**US SIC:** 0912 **UK SIC:** 03001
**Employees:** 60

DUNS 22-161-2422

## W Howard Group Ltd

Phillips Sawmill, Lower Green Lane, Manchester M29 7JZ
**Tel:** 01942-881900 **Fax:** 01942891544
**Web:** www.whowardtimber.co.uk
**Reg No:** 4179813 **Estd:** 2001 Private Limited Company
**Line of Business:** Management activities of holding companies
**Export Sales:** £768,024
**Issued Capital:** £31,600
**Directors:** Mrs F B Grant, J A Grant
**Co. Secretary:** Jonathan Grant
**US SIC:** 6711 **UK SIC:** 83962
**Bankers:** National Westminster Bank Plc (01-05-31)

| | 31-12-13 | 31-12-12 | 31-12-11 |
|---|---|---|---|
| TO | 15,109,222 | 17,034,136 | 15,262,186 |
| P/L | 463,080 | 368,405 | 527,837 |
| NW | 3,075,188 | 2,908,537 | 2,839,414 |
| WC | 559,442 | 285,588 | 284,660 |
| Emp. | 94 | 110 | 103 |

DUNS 49-484-7916

## W J E C C B A C Ltd

245 Western Avenue, Cardiff, South Glamorgan CF5 2YX
**Tel:** 02920265000 **Fax:** 02920575987
**Web:** www.wjec.co.uk
**Reg No:** 3149686 **Estd:** 1996 Private Limited Company
**Line of Business:** Education agencies and authorities
**Director:** Nqh Ltd
**Co. Secretary:** Nqh (Co Sec) Ltd
**Responsibilities**
**Senior:** Elaine Carlile *(Executive)*, Elaine Chard *(General Manager)*, Leah Crowley *(Executive)*, Jodie Mearing-Lane *(General Manager)*, Gavin Naish *(Executive)*, Brigid O' Regan *(Assistant Director Development)*, Matthew Oatley *(Executive)*, Angela Perkins *(General Manager)*, Gareth Pierce *(Chief Executive Officer)*
**Marketing:** Brigid O' Regan *(Assistant Director Development)*, Catherine Roberts-Straw *(Assistant Director of Strategy)*, Ross Thomas *(Development Officer)*, Dafydd Wyn *(Communications Officer)*
**Sales:** Hugh Lester *(Assistant Director Business De)*, Caroline Morgan *(Development Officer)*, Caroline Redman *(Bookshop Manager)*
**Admin:** Kieran Mcdonnell *(Administrator)*
**IT:** Steve Howells *(IT Manager)*, Kim Morgan *(Project Manager)*
**HR:** Allison Candy *(Course Trainer)*, Beverley Green *(Human Resources Manager)*, Jeana Hayes *(Course Trainer)*
**Operations:** Bob Childs *(Assistant Director Quality Ass)*
**US SIC:** 8299 **UK SIC:** 93300
**Employees:** 300

DUNS 22-786-9237

## W J G Evans & Sons

Unit 1 2 Snowdrop Lane, Haverfordwest, Dyfed SA61 1JB
**Tel:** 01437762294
**VAT No:** 123840588 **Estd:** 1967 Partnership
**Line of Business:** Builders
**Partner:** M Evans
**US SIC:** 1521 **UK SIC:** 50100
**Bankers:** HSBC Bank plc (40-23-21)
**Employees:** 50

DUNS 57-007-0979

## W K B Havant Ltd

(**Subsidiary of:** Wkb Waterlooville Ltd)
Eletra Avenue, Hambledown Road, Waterlooville, Hampshire PO7 7XW
**Tel:** 02392320320
**Web:** www.wkbwaterloovill.toyota.co.uk
**Reg No:** 2863605 **Estd:** 1994 Private Limited Company
**Line of Business:** Car dealers (used)
**Issued Capital:** £250,000
**Principals:** D N Kilby *(Managing)*, S T Wood, M W Fenlon, G G Harmar
**Co. Secretary:** Mrs Tracey Gibbs
**US SIC:** 5511, 5521, 7539, 5531
**UK SIC:** 65100, 67100
**Auditors:** Brooking Knowles & Lawrence
**Bankers:** Barclays Bank Plc (20-11-39)

| | 31-12-13 | 31-12-12 | 31-12-11 |
|---|---|---|---|
| TO | 29,212,106 | 24,581,028 | 16,316,547 |
| P/L | 207,457 | 268,898 | 331,451 |
| NW | 586,714 | 401,801 | 665,605 |
| WC | 976,081 | 814,148 | (434,507) |
| Emp. | 70 | 69 | 59 |

DUNS 28-871-1591

## W K Webster & Co Ltd

Webster House, 207 Longlands Road, Sidcup, Kent DA15 7JH
**Tel:** 020 8300 7744 **Fax:** 020 8309 1266
**Web:** www.wkwebster.com
**Reg No:** 1043671 **Estd:** 1972 Private Limited Company
**Line of Business:** Marine services
**Export Sales:** £15,232,813
**Issued Capital:** £120,120
**Principals:** J W Martin *(Managing)*, A P Joannou, G V Newman, C J Osman, A S Smith
**Co. Secretary:** John Martin
**Responsibilities**
**Senior:** Frank Holden *(General Manager)*, Steve Jarrett *(Cargo Claims - Assistant Gener)*
**Admin:** Ann Castle *(Administrator)*, Hans-Christian Kuepers *(Administrator)*
**IT:** Les Dean *(Computer Manager)*
**Fleet:** Keith Ackland *(Head of Recoveries)*
**US SIC:** 7399 **UK SIC:** 83954
**Auditors:** Barnes Roffe LLP
**Bankers:** Lloyds TSB Bank plc (30-16-87)

| | 28-02-14 | 28-02-13 | 29-02-12 |
|---|---|---|---|
| TO | 17,920,956 | 17,003,232 | 16,020,207 |
| P/L | 6,017,789 | 3,787,721 | 3,510,543 |
| NW | 3,999,023 | 5,977,194 | 3,149,206 |
| WC | 4,246,221 | 6,549,683 | 3,907,442 |
| Emp. | 183 | 183 | 182 |

DUNS 56-995-1577

## W. Liddy & Company Ltd

23 Northumberland Square, North Shields, Tyne and Wear NE30 1PW
**Tel:** 01912591570
**Web:** www.mcdonalds.co.uk
**Reg No:** 2860364 **Estd:** 1993 Private Limited Company
**Line of Business:** Caterers
**Trading Style:** McDonalds
**Issued Capital:** £316,400
**Managing Director:** W Liddy
**Co. Secretary:** Mrs Emma Vieira
**Branches:** W. Liddy & Company Ltd, Tyneside Retail Park, Coast Road, Wallsend, Tyne and Wear NE28 9HP
**US SIC:** 5812 **UK SIC:** 66110
**Auditors:** Ryecroft Glenton
**Bankers:** The Royal Bank Of Scotland Plc (16-26-21)

| | 31-12-13 | 31-12-12 | 31-12-11 |
|---|---|---|---|
| TO | 12,798,366 | 12,540,225 | 11,300,744 |
| P/L | 212,271 | 461,225 | 148,350 |
| NW | 1,112,498 | 915,902 | 841,707 |
| WC | (305,344) | (181,663) | (384,913) |
| Emp. | 402 | 384 | 432 |

DUNS 77-888-0211
## W M Donald Ltd
Marlaine, Netherley, Stonehaven, Kincardineshire AB39 3QP
**Fax:** 01569-731315
**Web:** www.wmdonald.co.uk
**Reg No:** 0156961SC **VAT No:** 723965512
**Estd:** 1995 Private Limited Company
**Line of Business:** Civil engineers
**Issued Capital:** £10,000
**Principals:** W M Donald *(Managing)*, D G Morrison, E Riddoch
**Co. Secretary:** Ms Elaine Donald
**US SIC:** 8911, 1629
**UK SIC:** 83701, 50000
**Auditors:** Simpson Forsyth & Co
**Bankers:** Bank Of Scotland (80-09-68)

| | 31-03-14 | 31-03-13 | 30-03-11 |
|---|---|---|---|
| TO | 30,363,405 | 26,141,461 | 15,486,924 |
| P/L | 4,107,654 | 1,479,226 | 1,497,245 |
| NW | 13,381,671 | 13,023,046 | 12,074,890 |
| WC | 11,450,856 | 11,685,774 | 10,993,527 |
| Emp. | 71 | 62 | 53 |

DUNS 21-708-1772
## W M Morrison Supermarkets
Poplar Way, Catcliffe, Rotherham, South Yorkshire S60 5TR
**Web:** www.morrisons.com
**Estd:** 2011 Proprietorship
**Line of Business:** Supermarkets
**Proprietor:** M Foster
**US SIC:** 5411 **UK SIC:** 64100
**Employees:** 83

DUNS 28-881-1219
## W. Maher and Sons Ltd
Soapstone Way, Manchester M44 6RA
**Tel:** 0161-776-2200 **Fax:** 01618487357
**Web:** www.wmaherandsons.com
**Reg No:** 1178587 **VAT No:** 638929290
**Estd:** 2008 Private Limited Company
**Line of Business:** Groundwork contractors
**Issued Capital:** £10,000
**Directors:** V J Maher, G M Maher
**Co. Secretary:** Brendan Maher
**US SIC:** 1622 **UK SIC:** 50200
**Auditors:** McKellens Ltd
**Bankers:** HSBC Bank plc (40-43-20)

| | 30-06-13 | 30-06-12 | 30-06-11 |
|---|---|---|---|
| TO | 7,333,071 | 7,482,906 | 9,386,503 |
| P/L | 378,175 | 916,650 | 175,786 |
| NW | 14,435,888 | 14,189,540 | 13,535,363 |
| WC | 418,329 | 781,274 | (224,471) |
| Emp. | 75 | 79 | 79 |

DUNS 28-829-7716 **Imp-Exp**
## W Moorcroft Ltd
(**Subsidiary of:** W. Moorcroft Holdings Ltd)
Sandbach Road, Stoke-On-Trent, Staffordshire ST6 2DQ
**Fax:** 01782820502
**Web:** www.moorcroft.com
**Reg No:** 0128500 **VAT No:** 278343629
**Estd:** 1913 Private Limited Company
**Line of Business:** Manufacture of other ceramic products
**Export Markets:** U S A; Australia; Canada
**Export Sales:** £948,208
**Issued Capital:** £129,432
**Principals:** H R Edwards *(Chairman)*, Ms E W Adams, E Knowles, Mrs C M Gage, D A Johnson, Mrs H Hughes, K Thompson
**Co. Secretary:** Mrs Maureen Edwards
**Responsibilities**
**Health & Safety:** Gloria Withington *(Factory Manager)*
**Facilities:** Gloria Withington *(Factory Manager)*
**Branches:** W Moorcroft Ltd, Hot Ln, Hot Ln Indstl Est, Stoke-On-Trent, Staffordshire ST6 2BN
**US SIC:** 3269 **UK SIC:** 24894
**Auditors:** Baker Tilly UK Audit LLP
**Bankers:** National Westminster Bank Plc (01-01-38)

| | 31-08-13 | 31-08-12 | 31-08-11 |
|---|---|---|---|
| TO | 5,550,482 | 6,051,224 | 5,626,285 |
| P/L | 109,547 | 420,146 | 333,338 |
| NW | 2,791,640 | 2,893,545 | 2,610,266 |
| WC | 462,066 | 449,388 | 135,677 |
| Emp. | 113 | 121 | 115 |

DUNS 21-607-1882
## W Moorcroft Plc
Phoenix Works, Nile Street, Stoke-On-Trent, Staffordshire ST6 2BH
**Web:** www.moorcroft.com
**Estd:** 1913
**Line of Business:** Potteries
**US SIC:** 3269 **UK SIC:** 24894
**Employees:** 150

DUNS 21-226-8674
## W Mutch
9 Auchinlea Road, Glasgow, Lanarkshire G34 9HQ
**Tel:** 01415318180
**Web:** www.nhs.net
**Estd:** 1983
**Line of Business:** Doctors
**Trading Style:** Easterhouse Health Centre & Pharmacy
**Responsibilities**
**Senior:** Eileen Sword *(Practice Manager)*, Irene Sword *(Practice Manager)*
**US SIC:** 8011 **UK SIC:** 95300
**Employees:** 56

DUNS 22-752-8585 **Imp-Exp**
## W Oliver (Exorna) Ltd
Hillmans Way, Coleraine, Co Londonderry BT52 2EB
**Tel:** 02870356501 **Fax:** 028-7035-3674
**Web:** www.oliverexorna.co.uk
**Reg No:** 0016697NI **VAT No:** 393596891
**Estd:** 2004 Private Limited Company
**Line of Business:** Furniture (fitted)
**Export Markets:** Republic of Ireland
**Trading Style:** Exorna Kitchens
**Issued Capital:** £20,000
**Directors:** Ms A Bell, R W Oliver, W Oliver, Mrs M E Oliver
**Co. Secretary:** William Oliver
**Branches:** Duncrue Rd, Belfast
**US SIC:** 2599 **UK SIC:** 46720
**Auditors:** E & M Associates
**Bankers:** First Trust Bank (aib Group (uk) Plc) (93-82-46)

| | 31-03-14 | 31-03-13 | 31-03-12 |
|---|---|---|---|
| TA | 2,188,120 | 2,207,631 | 2,146,560 |
| NW | 1,481,246 | 1,389,724 | 1,329,404 |
| WC | 336,045 | 331,883 | 301,129 |

DUNS 21-620-5617
## W Portsmouth & Co Ltd
69 Havelock Road, Luton, Bedfordshire LU2 7PW
**Tel:** 01582-731517 **Fax:** 01582-401920
**Web:** www.wportsmouth.co.uk
**Reg No:** 0610757 **VAT No:** 197000865
**Estd:** 1956 Private Limited Company
**Line of Business:** Electrical contractors and electricians
**Issued Capital:** £2,100
**Directors:** J C Shanahan, Ms M F Norsworthy, D W Norsworthy, Ms H V Shanahan
**Responsibilities**
**Senior:** Merv Kirwin *(Contracts Manager)*
**Engineering:** Michael Falon *(Contracts Manager)*, Mike Flemming *(Contracts Manager)*, Merv Kirwin *(Contracts Manager)*, Terry Showell *(Contracts Manager)*
**Branches:** W Portsmouth & Co Ltd, 4 Liddell Road, London NW6 2EW
**US SIC:** 1731 **UK SIC:** 50300
**Auditors:** Nagler Wolfson
**Bankers:** Barclays Bank Plc (20-37-16)

| | 31-01-14 | 31-01-13 | 31-01-12 |
|---|---|---|---|
| TO | 14,839,647 | 9,368,759 | 9,460,648 |
| P/L | 149,265 | 102,167 | 45,893 |
| NW | 1,207,847 | 1,903,716 | 1,826,079 |
| WC | 1,139,784 | 1,846,953 | 1,765,544 |
| Emp. | 77 | 71 | 69 |

DUNS 77-470-9489
## W R B Gas (Contracts) Ltd
40 North Ellen Street, Dundee, Angus DD3 7DH
**Tel:** 01382204030 **Fax:** 01382-204185
**Web:** www.wrbgas.co.uk
**Reg No:** 0153084SC **Estd:** 1994 Private Limited Company
**Line of Business:** Central heating supplies
**Issued Capital:** £12,000
**Directors:** D Murray, N D Campbell
**Co. Secretary:** Robert Ward
**Branches:** W R B Gas (Contracts) Ltd, 40 North Ellen Street, Dundee, Angus DD3 7DH
**US SIC:** 5074, 1711
**UK SIC:** 61300, 50300
**Auditors:** Findlay & Co
**Bankers:** Clydesdale Bank Plc (82-62-14)

| | 31-10-13 | 31-10-12 | 31-10-11 |
|---|---|---|---|
| TA | 1,551,472 | 1,406,187 | 1,517,972 |
| NW | 376,933 | 254,531 | 227,824 |
| WC | 99,723 | (82,042) | (28,634) |

DUNS 21-119-6595
## W. R. Berkley Syndicate Ltd
(**Subsidiary of:** W. R. Berkley Syndicate Holdings Ltd)
34 Lime Street, London EC3M 7AT
**Reg No:** 6589648 **Estd:** 2008 Private Limited Company
**Line of Business:** Business services
**Issued Capital:** £100
**Directors:** E G Ballard, A Blades, S W Taylor, W R Berkley Jr, I S Lederman
**Co. Secretary:** Clyde Secretaries Limited
**Responsibilities**
**Senior:** William Berkley *(Director)*
**US SIC:** 7399 **UK SIC:** 83954

| | 31-12-13 | 31-12-12 | 31-12-11 |
|---|---|---|---|
| TO | 15,000,000 | 10,800,000 | 6,800,000 |
| P/L | 1,462,390 | (924,314) | 132,807 |
| NW | 2,156,894 | 981,848 | 1,018,145 |
| WC | 1,455,878 | 219,739 | 413,129 |
| Emp. | 55 | 44 | 24 |

DUNS 21-592-6076
## W R Davies
Industrial Estate Road, Llangefni, Gwynedd LL77 7JA
**Tel:** 01248750142
**Web:** www.wrdavies.co.uk
**Estd:** 2011 Proprietorship
**Line of Business:** Sale of new motor vehicles
**Proprietor:** G Jones
**Responsibilities**
**Senior:** Geranint Jones *(Dealer Principal)*
**Marketing:** Sara Ballam *(Group Marketing Executive)*
**US SIC:** 5511 **UK SIC:** 65100
**Employees:** 58

DUNS 22-530-3239 **Imp**
## W R Ferris Ltd
Whitgift Centre, Croydon, Surrey CR0 1LP
**Tel:** 02086887646
**Web:** www.swaguk.co.uk
**Reg No:** 1365542 **VAT No:** 217789917
**Estd:** 1974 Private Limited Company
**Line of Business:** Manufacture of jewellery and related articles not elsewhere classified
**Trading Style:** Swag Jewellers
**Issued Capital:** £100
**Principals:** W R Ferris *(Managing)*, E W Ferris
**Co. Secretary:** Thomas Ferris
**Branches:** W R Ferris Ltd, Unit G12A Bentalls Shopping Cent, Wood Street, Kingston Upon Thames, Surrey KT1 1TR
**US SIC:** 3911 **UK SIC:** 49101
**Auditors:** Perrys
**Bankers:** HSBC Bank plc (40-39-05)

| | 30-04-14 | 30-04-13 | 30-04-12 |
|---|---|---|---|
| TO | 31,458,397 | 26,517,935 | 25,667,935 |
| P/L | 1,461,127 | 1,005,270 | 815,267 |
| NW | 5,763,837 | 4,794,843 | 5,250,787 |
| WC | 5,251,812 | 4,261,349 | 4,393,682 |
| Emp. | 115 | 125 | 144 |

DUNS 77-826-7419
## W R Simmers Ltd
Backmuir, Keith, Banffshire AB55 5PE
**Tel:** 01542-882543
**Reg No:** 0156505SC **Estd:** 1995 Private Limited Company
**Line of Business:** Other engineering activities
**Issued Capital:** £40,000
**Principals:** S E Simmers *(Managing)*, P Simmers
**US SIC:** 8911 **UK SIC:** 83701
**Auditors:** Scott-Moncrieff & Co CA
**Bankers:** The Royal Bank Of Scotland Plc (83-20-06)

| | 31-12-13 | 30-06-12 | 30-12-11 |
|---|---|---|---|
| TA | 10,082,195 | 9,630,487 | 9,072,555 |
| NW | 9,335,102 | 8,857,242 | 7,953,749 |
| WC | 8,553,654 | 8,067,963 | 7,088,330 |

DUNS 21-822-7965
## W S Lusher & Son Ltd
School Lane, Sprowston, Norwich, Norfolk NR7 8TH
**Tel:** 01603-426363
**Web:** www.wslusherandson.co.uk
**Reg No:** 1006277 **VAT No:** 105080321
**Estd:** 1924 Private Limited Company
**Line of Business:** Other construction work involving special trades
**Issued Capital:** £26,000
**Principals:** M N Lusher *(Managing)*, R C Doughty
**Co. Secretary:** Ms Sarah Lusher
**Responsibilities**
**Finance:** James Sharpe *(Finance Manager)*
**US SIC:** 1799, 1541
**UK SIC:** 50000, 50100
**Auditors:** Sexty & Co
**Bankers:** Barclays Bank Plc (20-62-68)

| | 30-04-14 | 30-04-13 | 30-04-12 |
|---|---|---|---|
| TA | 845,916 | 691,816 | 845,922 |
| NW | 231,300 | 196,508 | 345,958 |
| WC | 263,838 | 139,664 | 291,563 |

DUNS 21-781-7034
## W S P
Colston 33, 33 Colston Avenue, Bristol, Avon BS1 4UA
**Tel:** 01179302000
**Estd:** 2004 Partnership
**Line of Business:** Other engineering activities
**Partners:** N Rye, D Dugan
**US SIC:** 8911 **UK SIC:** 83701
**Employees:** 100

DUNS 21-582-9311
## W S P Buildings
Mountbatten House, Basing View, Basingstoke, Hampshire RG21 4HG
**Tel:** 01256318800
**Web:** www.wspgroup.com
**Estd:** 2011 Proprietorship
**Line of Business:** Property developers
**Proprietor:** J Harvey
**Responsibilities**
**Senior:** Mark Kretowicz *(Regional Head Of Building Stru)*
**IT:** Neil Croman *(IT manager)*
**Engineering:** Mark Kretowicz *(Regional Head Of Building Stru)*
**US SIC:** 6552 **UK SIC:** 85000
**Employees:** 500

DUNS 21-393-4871
## W S P Consulting Engineers
4-5 Lochside View, Edinburgh, Midlothian EH12 9DH
**Tel:** 01382225308
**Partnership**
**Line of Business:** Aeronautical engineers
**Partners:** K Mckenzie, Ms H Smith, D Gray
**Responsibilities**
**Senior:** Kyle McKenzie *(Partner)*
**US SIC:** 8911 **UK SIC:** 83701
**Employees:** 130

DUNS 21-579-8183
## W S P Group
White Grove, Leeds, West Yorkshire LS8 1LB
**Web:** www.wspgroup.com
**Estd:** 2011 Proprietorship
**Line of Business:** Engineers (consulting)
**Proprietor:** C Fuller
**US SIC:** 8911 **UK SIC:** 83701
**Employees:** 106

DUNS 21-622-3941 **Exp**
## W Stevenson & Sons
Harbour Offices, Penzance, Cornwall TR18 5HB
**Tel:** 01736-362982
**Web:** www.btclick.com
**Estd:** 1850 Partnership
**Line of Business:** Freight sea and coastal water transport
**Export Markets:** France, Spain, Netherlands
**Partners:** A Stevenson, Ms S C Stevenson, W S Stevenson, W Stevenson, A B Stevenson, Ms E C Stevenson, Ms M C Stevenson, Ms L J Stevenson
**Responsibilities**
**Senior:** Andy Manza *(General Manager)*
**Finance:** Andy Manza *(General Manager)*
**Health & Safety:** Andy Manza *(General Manager)*
**US SIC:** 4411, 5199
**UK SIC:** 74001, 61900
**Bankers:** Barclays Bank Plc (20-67-19)
**Employees:** 100

DUNS 23-571-1848
## W. Stevenson & Sons Ltd
Harbour Offices, Newlyn, Penzance, Cornwall TR18 5HB
**Tel:** 01736362998
**Web:** www.newlynfreshfish.co.uk
**Reg No:** 3569268 **Estd:** 1998 Private Limited Company
**Line of Business:** Fishing
**Export Sales:** £431,344
**Issued Capital:** £5
**Directors:** Miss E C Stevenson, A B Stevenson, W Stevenson, W M Waddington, Mrs J E Piper
**Co. Secretary:** Mrs Judith Piper
**Responsibilities**
**Senior:** Andrew Mamza *(Manager)*, John Tucker *(Manager)*
**US SIC:** 0912 **UK SIC:** 03001
**Auditors:** Old Mill Audit LLP

| | 31-12-13 | 31-12-12 | 31-12-11 |
|---|---|---|---|
| TO | 10,710,687 | N/A | N/A |
| P/L | 163,889 | N/A | N/A |
| NW | 1,971,740 | (9,335,559) | 2 |
| WC | (468,682) | (11,907,122) | N/A |
| Emp. | 59 | N/A | N/A |

DUNS 21-768-7570
## W T Prima
Prima Business & Technology Centre, Radway Green, Crewe, Cheshire CW2 5PR
**Tel:** 01270879448
**Estd:** 2011 Proprietorship
**Line of Business:** Distribution service providers
**Proprietor:** R Halford
**US SIC:** 4712 **UK SIC:** 77002
**Employees:** 150

DUNS 23-997-2149

### W. Wing Yip & Brothers Trading Group Ltd

The Wing Yip Centre, 375 Nechells Park Road, Birmingham, West Midlands B7 5NT
**Tel:** 01213-276618
**Web:** www.wingyip.com
**Reg No:** 3985372 **Estd:** 2000 Private Limited Company
**Line of Business:** Management activities of holding companies
**Export Sales:** £166,011
**Issued Capital:** £100,000
**Directors:** B J Yip, H Y Yap, G Y Yap, A S Yip, W W Yip, M J Newport
**Co. Secretary:** Robert Brittain
**Responsibilities**
**Senior:** Christopher Torbe *(Manager)*
**US SIC:** 6711 **UK SIC:** 83962
**Auditors:** Clement Keys
**Bankers:** HSBC Bank plc (40-37-27)

| | 30-09-13 | 30-09-12 | 30-09-11 |
|---|---|---|---|
| TO | 96,873,351 | 99,107,695 | 101,499,284 |
| P/L | 4,611,878 | 4,914,804 | 6,918,880 |
| NW | 38,784,456 | 36,743,853 | 34,565,492 |
| WC | 15,375,448 | 13,413,105 | 16,147,260 |
| Emp. | 355 | 363 | 360 |

DUNS 21 795 6582

### W Y G

Longcross Court, 47 Newport Road, Cardiff, South Glamorgan CF24 0AD
**Web:** www.wyg.com
**Estd:** 2011
**Line of Business:** Aeronautical engineers
**US SIC:** 8911 **UK SIC:** 83701
**Employees:** 70

DUNS 45-848-8491

### W Y G International Ltd

(**Subsidiary of:** Wyg Plc)
Geneva Building, Lakeview Drive, Sheerwood Business Park, Nottingham, Nottinghamshire NG15 0ED
**Tel:** 01623-684500 **Fax:** 01623-684545
**Web:** www.wyg.com
**Reg No:** 3195485 **Estd:** 2005 Private Limited Company
**Line of Business:** Management and business consultants
**Issued Capital:** £100,002
**Directors:** S V Cummins, A S Dziurdzik, G N Lamond, G D Olver, P C Hamer, K J Cook
**Co. Secretary:** Benjamin Whitworth
**Responsibilities**
**Health & Safety:** Christopher Flint *(Health & Safety Coordinator)*
**US SIC:** 7392, 8911
**UK SIC:** 83951, 83701
**Auditors:** PricewaterhouseCoopers LLP
**Bankers:** National Westminster Bank Plc (55-61-17)

| | 31-03-14 | 31-03-13 | 31-03-12 |
|---|---|---|---|
| TO | 53,762,000 | 50,545,000 | 58,979,000 |
| P/L | 1,947,000 | 359,000 | (39,400,000) |
| NW | 10,498,000 | 11,742,000 | 11,701,000 |
| WC | 10,954,000 | 11,562,000 | 11,298,000 |
| Emp. | 747 | 669 | 410 |

DUNS 42-482-1846

### W.A. Baxter & Sons (Holdings) Ltd

Highland Village, Fochabers, Morayshire IV32 7LD
**Tel:** 01343820666
**Web:** www.baxters.com
**Reg No:** 0233302SC **Estd:** 2002 Private Limited Company
**Line of Business:** Manufacturers of food products
**Export Sales:** £58,942,000
**Trading Style:** Baxter Food Group Limited
**Issued Capital:** £636,548
**Directors:** Miss A C Baxter, R Davis, A G Baxter, E Hagman, Mrs H M Metcalfe, W King, J E Sugden, E D Murray
**Co. Secretary:** Peter Mcluckie
**Responsibilities**
**Senior:** Andrew Tough *(Manager)*, Trevor Ware *(Non Executive Director)*
**Branches:** W.a. Baxter & Sons (Holdings) Limited, Unit 8 Centurian Business Park, Seaward Place, Glasgow, Lanarkshire G41 1HH
**US SIC:** 2099 **UK SIC:** 42399
**Auditors:** Johnston Carmichael

| | 31-05-14 | 01-06-13 | 02-05-12 |
|---|---|---|---|
| TO | 160,689,000 | 156,993,000 | 136,759,000 |
| P/L | 146,000 | 1,785,000 | 4,606,000 |
| NW | 37,370,000 | 39,530,000 | 35,037,000 |
| WC | 5,686,000 | 2,208,000 | 10,362,000 |
| Emp. | 1,154 | 994 | 908 |

DUNS 28-939-9909

### W.A. Cooke & Sons (Site Services) Ltd

(**Subsidiary of:** W.A. Cooke & Sons Engineers (Established 1926) Ltd)
Southern Street, Worsley, Manchester M28 3QN
**Web:** www.wacooke.co.uk
**Reg No:** 1573639 **Estd:** 1981 Private Limited Company
**Line of Business:** Engineering services
**Issued Capital:** £100
**Directors:** W G Cooke, J D Cooke, S A Cooke
**Co. Secretary:** Mrs Gwyneth Cooke
**Responsibilities**
**Engineering:** Darren Dolega *(Production Manager)*
**Branches:** W.a. Cooke & Sons (Site Services) Ltd, Bankfield Wks, Emlyn St, Bolton, Lancashire BL4 7EB
**US SIC:** 8911 **UK SIC:** 83701
**Auditors:** Jennings & Gilchreaste
**Bankers:** Barclays Bank Plc (20-10-71)

| | 31-12-13 | 31-12-12 | 31-12-11 |
|---|---|---|---|
| TA | 629,311 | 712,353 | 732,093 |
| NW | 339,074 | 341,835 | 144,674 |
| WC | 302,263 | 297,551 | 116,146 |

DUNS 49-094-6928

### W.A. Fairhurst (U.K.) Ltd

(**Subsidiary of:** Fairhurst)
225 Bath Street, Glasgow, Lanarkshire G2 4GZ
**Tel:** 01412048800 **Fax:** 01412048801
**Web:** www.fairhurst.co.uk
**Reg No:** 0159839SC **Estd:** 1995 Private Limited Company
**Line of Business:** Civil engineers
**Issued Capital:** £10,000
**Directors:** A J Connell, R Bryson
**Co. Secretary:** Martin Cullen
**Responsibilities**
**Senior:** R. Mccracken *(Partner)*, N Mcspadden *(Partner)*, J Message *(Partner)*, A Scott-kiddie *(Partner)*
**Admin:** Rhona McNeil *(Senior Partner'S Secretary)*, Marlyn Robertson *(Senior Partner'S Secretary)*
**Engineering:** Kenneth Barr *(Technical Director)*, Alan Blair *(Technical Director)*
**US SIC:** 1541, 8999
**UK SIC:** 50100, 83954
**Auditors:** BDO Stoy Hayward

| | 31-12-13 | 31-12-12 | 31-12-11 |
|---|---|---|---|
| TA | 10,001 | 10,001 | 10,001 |
| P/L | N/A | 800,000 | N/A |
| NW | 10,000 | 10,000 | 10,000 |
| WC | 9,999 | 9,999 | 9,999 |

DUNS 34-856-6899

### Wa Products (Uk) Ltd

Midas House Units 8 And 9, Burnham Business Park, Springfie, Southminster, Essex CM0 8TE
**Tel:** 01621786654 **Fax:** 0870-116-1000
**Web:** www.waproducts.net
**Reg No:** 5655413 **Estd:** 2005 Private Limited Company
**Line of Business:** Packaging activities
**Export Sales:** £788,979
**Issued Capital:** £905
**Directors:** D E Wiseman, S R Wiseman, M Hopson, J H Carpenter
**Co. Secretary:** Ms Julie Smith
**US SIC:** 7399 **UK SIC:** 83954

| | 31-10-13 | 31-10-12 | 31-10-11 |
|---|---|---|---|
| TO | 8,490,176 | 7,065,923 | 6,785,399 |
| P/L | 873,964 | 815,924 | 535,443 |
| NW | 554,172 | (660,892) | (1,581,530) |
| WC | 2,512,835 | 1,708,126 | 1,470,671 |
| Emp. | 55 | 44 | 43 |

DUNS 21-828-0204

### W.A. Rainbow & Sons Ltd

Quibells Lane, Newark, Nottinghamshire NG24 2AL
**Tel:** 01636812276 **Fax:** 01752849016
**Web:** www.nightfreight.co.uk
**Reg No:** 1783207 **VAT No:** 116945459
**Estd:** 1921 Private Limited Company
**Line of Business:** Freight services
**Trading Style:** Nightfreight (South West)
**Issued Capital:** £50,000
**Director:** D P Rainbow
**Co. Secretary:** Andrew Rainbow
**Branches:** W.a. Rainbow & Sons Ltd, The Parcel Centre, Exchange Road, Lincoln, Lincolnshire LN6 3JZ
**US SIC:** 4213 **UK SIC:** 72300
**Auditors:** BDO Stoy Hayward
**Bankers:** National Westminster Bank Plc (60-20-15)

| | 30-04-14 | 30-04-13 | 30-04-12 |
|---|---|---|---|
| TO | 11,368,172 | 11,845,572 | 10,980,597 |
| P/L | 22,692 | 149,949 | 288,493 |
| NW | 2,248,967 | 2,270,263 | 2,189,452 |
| WC | 345,073 | 1,291,418 | 1,218,159 |
| Emp. | 153 | 158 | 147 |

DUNS 21-631-0813

### W.A. Truelove & Son Ltd

118 Carshalton Road, Sutton, Surrey SM1 4RL
**Web:** www.watltd.co.uk
**Reg No:** 0293103 **Estd:** 1934 Private Limited Company
**Line of Business:** Funeral and related activities
**Trading Style:** Drewett Donald S & Sons, Magnificent Marble
**Issued Capital:** £1,000
**Principals:** S A Truelove *(Managing)*, G M Peck
**Co. Secretary:** David Truelove
**Responsibilities**
**Senior:** Steven Lapper *(General Manager)*
**Branches:** W.a. Truelove & Son Ltd, Leslie House, 187 Croydon Road, Caterham, Surrey CR3 6PH
**US SIC:** 7399 **UK SIC:** 83954
**Auditors:** BDO LLP
**Bankers:** Barclays Bank Plc (20-84-17)

| | 31-03-14 | 31-03-13 | 31-03-12 |
|---|---|---|---|
| TO | 5,224,766 | 4,969,993 | 4,590,616 |
| P/L | 479,156 | 279,109 | 196,087 |
| NW | 4,172,040 | 4,277,225 | 4,351,619 |
| WC | (640,606) | (706,772) | (660,298) |
| Emp. | 60 | 60 | 60 |

DUNS 21-818-7730 **Imp-Exp**

### Wabco Automotive U.K. Ltd

(**Subsidiary of:** Wabco Holdings Inc.)
Unit A1 Grange Valley Road, Batley, West Yorkshire WF17 6GH
**Tel:** 01924-595400
**Web:** www.wabco-auto.com
**Reg No:** 0709827 **VAT No:** 307663261
**Estd:** 1961 Private Limited Company
**Line of Business:** Manufacturers of automotive components
**Export Markets:** E U, Middle East, Canada, South America, Africa, South & South East Asia, Australasia & U S A
**Export Sales:** £1,371,000
**Issued Capital:** £3,000,000
**Director:** D T Rickell
**Co. Secretary:** Derek Colquhoun
**Responsibilities**
**Finance:** Mike Harris *(Senior Finance Administrator)*
**HR:** Colleen Bosworth *(HR)*
**Operations:** julian wedgery *(Operations Manager)*
**Branches:** Wabco Automotive U.k. Ltd, Po Box 9, Titanic Wks, Lincoln, Lincolnshire LN5 7JL
**US SIC:** 3714, 7399
**UK SIC:** 35300, 83954
**Auditors:** Ernst & Young LLP
**Bankers:** National Westminster Bank Plc (60-13-15)

| | 31-12-13 | 31-12-12 | 31-12-11 |
|---|---|---|---|
| TO | 37,019,000 | 37,658,000 | 41,178,000 |
| P/L | (317,000) | 2,315,000 | 1,515,000 |
| NW | (762,000) | 6,056,000 | 6,208,000 |
| WC | (6,550,000) | (2,023,000) | (772,000) |
| Emp. | 50 | 50 | 49 |

DUNS 73-746-9585 **Imp-Exp**

### Wabtec Rail Ltd

(**Subsidiary of:** Wabtec Uk Holdings Ltd)
Po Box 400, Doncaster Works, Hexthorpe Road, Doncaster, South Yorkshire DN1 1SL
**Tel:** 01302 340700 **Fax:** 01302 790058
**Web:** www.wabtecrail.co.uk
**Reg No:** 2923485 **VAT No:** 642789893
**Estd:** 1994 Private Limited Company
**Line of Business:** Other transport via railways
**Issued Capital:** £1,756,000
**Directors:** D J Meyer, D I Woolhouse, K P Hildum, C J Weatherall, R T Betler
**Co. Secretary:** Michael Isaac
**Responsibilities**
**Senior:** Dave Brennen *(Engineering Manager)*, Martin Sutton *(Fleetcare Director)*
**Health & Safety:** Kristine Bark *(Health & Safety Administrator)*
**Operations:** Kristine Bark *(Health & Safety Administrator)*, Darran Gleave *(Project Manager)*
**Fleet:** Gordon Innes *(Fleet care Business Director)*, Martin Sutton *(Fleetcare Director)*
**Engineering:** Dave Brennen *(Engineering Manager)*
**Branches:** Wabtec Rail Ltd, Eastleigh Works, Campbell Road, Eastleigh, Hampshire SO50 5AD
**US SIC:** 4011, 3799
**UK SIC:** 71000, 36502
**Auditors:** Ernst & Young LLP
**Bankers:** National Westminster Bank Plc (60-06-39)

| | 31-12-13 | 31-12-12 | 30-12-11 |
|---|---|---|---|
| TO | 123,399,000 | 120,007,000 | 102,845,000 |
| P/L | 12,913,000 | 13,387,000 | 12,541,000 |
| NW | 48,034,000 | 38,483,000 | 25,089,000 |
| WC | 41,457,000 | 32,063,000 | 18,908,000 |
| Emp. | 913 | 908 | 749 |

DUNS 21-018-2750

### Wabtec Rail Scotland Ltd

(**Subsidiary of:** Wabtec Uk Holdings Ltd)
Caledonia Works, West Langlands Street, Kilmarnock, Ayrshire KA1 2QD
**Tel:** 01563 523573
**Web:** www.wabtecrail.co.uk
**Reg No:** 6401040 **Estd:** 2007 Private Limited Company
**Line of Business:** Business services
**Issued Capital:** £1
**Directors:** C J Weatherall, K P Hildum, R T Betler
**Co. Secretary:** Michael Isaac
**Responsibilities**
**Senior:** Martin Sutton *(Manager)*
**Operations:** Paul Nisbett *(Operations Manager)*
**US SIC:** 3629 **UK SIC:** 34350
**Bankers:** Barclays Bank Plc (20-11-81)

| | 31-12-13 | 31-12-12 | 29-12-12 |
|---|---|---|---|
| TO | N/A | N/A | 7,116,463 |
| P/L | N/A | N/A | (113,802) |
| NW | (1,971,361) | (1,971,361) | (1,971,361) |
| WC | N/A | (1,971,361) | (1,971,361) |
| Emp. | N/A | N/A | 82 |

DUNS 21-717-6452 **Imp-Exp**

### Wacker Neuson Ltd

Lea Road, Waltham Abbey, Essex EN9 1AW
**Tel:** 01992707200 **Fax:** 01495718162
**Web:** www.wackerneuson.com
**Reg No:** 0721483 **VAT No:** 220846874
**Estd:** 1962 Private Limited Company
**Line of Business:** Plant dealers
**Export Markets:** Worldwide
**Export Sales:** £134,849
**Issued Capital:** £1,000,000
**Director:** R F Harrison
**Co. Secretary:** Richard Harrison
**Responsibilities**
**Senior:** Hans Neunteufel *(Manager)*, Jonathan Vaines *(Manager)*, Johnathon Vains *(Manager)*
**Finance:** Christine Hatley *(Financial Manager)*
**IT:** E Canti *(IT Manager)*
**HR:** Christine Hatley *(Financial Manager)*
**Health & Safety:** Christopher Pearce *(Customer Services Manager)*
**Operations:** Christopher Pearce *(Customer Services Manager)*
**Purchasing:** R Tenby *(Purchasing Manager)*
**Branches:** Wacker Neuson Ltd, Unit 1, Swangate, Hungerford, Berkshire RG17 0YX
**US SIC:** 5084 **UK SIC:** 61490
**Auditors:** Saffery Champness
**Bankers:** Barclays Bank Plc (20-77-67)

| | 31-12-13 | 31-12-12 | 31-12-11 |
|---|---|---|---|
| TO | 24,080,244 | 13,988,924 | 14,211,561 |
| P/L | 356,294 | 411,189 | 291,822 |
| NW | 4,489,916 | 4,234,428 | 3,814,489 |
| WC | 1,663,308 | 3,347,582 | 3,084,400 |
| Emp. | 50 | 45 | 48 |

DUNS 23-853-0265 **Exp**

### Waco Uk Ltd

(**Subsidiary of:** Waco Sa Security (Pty) Ltd)
Catfoss Airfield, Brandesburton, Driffield, North Humberside YO25 8EJ
**Tel:** 01964545000 **Fax:** 01964544377
**Web:** www.waco.co.uk
**Reg No:** 2487565 **VAT No:** 572302366
**Estd:** 1989 Private Limited Company
**Line of Business:** Building construction contractors
**Trading Style:** Premier Interlink
**Issued Capital:** £16,504,993
**Directors:** E P De Sa, C Glover
**Co. Secretary:** Craig Glover
**Responsibilities**
**Senior:** Jenny O'connor *(Marketing Coordinator)*, Mick Webb *(Engineering Manager)*
**Finance:** Riaan Krumholectski *(Financial Director)*
**Marketing:** Jenny O'connor *(Marketing Coordinator)*
**HR:** Sherli Tarry-Smith *(Human Resources Manager)*
**Purchasing:** Judy Neill *(Buyer)*
**Engineering:** Mick Webb *(Engineering Manager)*
**Branches:** Waco Uk Ltd, Townsend Centre, Unit 2, Dunstable, Bedfordshire LU5 5BQ
**US SIC:** 1522, 7394
**UK SIC:** 50100, 84000
**Auditors:** KPMG LLP
**Bankers:** HSBC Bank plc (40-13-15)

| | 30-06-14 | 30-06-13 | 30-06-12 |
|---|---|---|---|
| TO | 34,384,000 | 26,848,000 | 29,765,000 |
| P/L | 86,000 | (2,919,000) | (22,142,000) |
| NW | 4,569,000 | (4,292,000) | (1,373,000) |
| WC | (917,000) | (2,357,000) | (3,702,000) |
| Emp. | 168 | 136 | 136 |

DUNS 21-619-4175 **Imp-Exp**

## Wacoal Emea Ltd

(**Subsidiary of:** Wacoal Holdings Corp.)
The Corsetry Factory, Kettering, Northamptonshire NN14 2PG
**Tel:** 01536 760282
**Web:** www.eveden.com
**Reg No:** 0171167 **VAT No:** 638287602
**Estd:** 1920 Private Limited Company
**Line of Business:** Manufacturers of lingerie
**Export Markets:** Worldwide
**Export Sales:** £16,182,000
**Trading Style:** Fantasie, Key Brands, Freya, Fauve
**Issued Capital:** £250,000
**Directors:** S Nicholls, D Laing, Ms T Lewis
**Co. Secretary:** Geoffrey Embley
**Responsibilities**
**Senior:** Ruth Skinner *(Manager)*, Robert Underhill *(Manager)*
**Marketing:** Heather McHattie *(Marketing Executive)*
**Sales:** Michaela Pinch *(Head of Customer Service and D)*
**IT:** Bill Phelan *(Head of Group IT)*
**Branches:** Eveden Ltd, Corset Factory, Rothwell Rd, Desborough, Kettering, Northamptonshire NN14 2PG
**US SIC:** 2341 **UK SIC:** 45362
**Auditors:** Deloitte LLP
**Bankers:** Lloyds TSB Bank plc (30-94-97)

| | 31-03-14 | 30-06-13 | 30-03-12 |
|---|---|---|---|
| TO | 38,660,000 | 51,646,000 | 50,769,000 |
| P/L | 4,841,000 | 6,160,000 | (8,154,000) |
| NW | 11,072,000 | 7,272,000 | 6,862,000 |
| WC | 6,938,000 | 3,294,000 | 2,747,000 |
| Emp. | 342 | 345 | 354 |

DUNS 21-343-7465 **Imp**

## Waddesdon Manor National Trust

Waddesdon Manor Estate, Waddesdon, Aylesbury, Buckinghamshire HP18 0JH
**Tel:** 01296653203
**Web:** www.waddesdon.org.uk
**Estd:** 2002
**Line of Business:** Hotels
**Responsibilities**
**Senior:** Fabaia Bromovsky *(Chief Executive)*
**Finance:** Dave Silvester *(Senior Finance Administrator)*
**Marketing:** Suzy Barron *(Marketing Executive)*, Samantha Lochhead *(Press Officer)*
**Sales:** Sheena Cox *(Sales Manager)*
**Admin:** Diane Bellis *(Collection Administrator)*, Dave Silvester *(Senior Finance Administrator)*
**HR:** Bonnie Bennett *(Personnel Manager)*
**Health & Safety:** Les Duff *(Property Manager)*
**Facilities:** Les Duff *(Property Manager)*
**Operations:** Bonnie Bennett *(Personnel Manager)*
**US SIC:** 8699 **UK SIC:** 96902
**Employees:** 350

DUNS 21-729-5027 **Imp**

## Waddington & Ledger Group Ltd

Lowfields Way, Elland, West Yorkshire HX5 9DA
**Tel:** 01422315000
**Reg No:** 7652863 **Estd:** 2011 Private Limited Company
**Line of Business:** Management activities of holding companies
**Issued Capital:** £100,000
**Directors:** G Mortimer, P Moreland, B Cameron, M H Smith, Mrs R Smith, S R Chambers
**US SIC:** 6711 **UK SIC:** 83962

| | 30-06-14 | 30-06-13 | 31-06-12 |
|---|---|---|---|
| TO | 17,644,982 | 17,638,489 | N/A |
| P/L | 837,036 | 283,831 | N/A |
| NW | 6,723,791 | 7,050,091 | 1 |
| WC | 1,877,521 | 1,572,473 | N/A |
| Emp. | 105 | 106 | N/A |

DUNS 21-779-5204

## Wade & Co

King Edward House, 1 Jordangate, Macclesfield, Cheshire SK10 1EE
**Tel:** 01625501900
**Web:** www.wadeclaims.com
**Estd:** 2011 Proprietorship
**Line of Business:** Legal services
**Proprietor:** A Davidson
**US SIC:** 8111 **UK SIC:** 83500
**Employees:** 60

DUNS 21-830-2495 **Imp-Exp**

## Wade Ceramics Ltd.

(**Subsidiary of:** Wade Allied Holdings Ltd)
Bessemer Drive, Stoke-On-Trent, Staffordshire ST1 5GR
**Tel:** 01782277000 **Fax:** 0845-481-0207
**Web:** www.eatingout-athome.com
**Reg No:** 0156368 **VAT No:** 278599972
**Estd:** 1919 Private Limited Company
**Line of Business:** Manufacturers and suppliers of ceramics
**Export Markets:** Europe, U S A, Canada and The Rest of the World
**Export Sales:** £1,239,000
**Issued Capital:** £20,000
**Director:** E Duke
**Co. Secretary:** Paul Farmer
**Responsibilities**
**Finance:** C Mannering *(Financial Director)*
**Branches:** Wade Ceramics Ltd., Bessemer Drive, Stoke-On-Trent, Staffordshire ST1 5GR
**US SIC:** 3269 **UK SIC:** 24894
**Auditors:** Deloitte LLP
**Bankers:** National Westminster Bank Plc (01-01-38)

| | 31-12-13 | 31-12-12 | 31-12-11 |
|---|---|---|---|
| TO | 10,324,000 | 15,681,000 | 13,123,000 |
| P/L | 175,000 | 2,432,000 | 1,757,000 |
| NW | 6,169,000 | 5,748,000 | 3,345,000 |
| WC | 988,000 | 788,000 | (616,000) |
| Emp. | 145 | 169 | 141 |

DUNS 42-410-5026 **Imp-Exp**

## Wade International Ltd

3 Third Avenue, Halstead, Essex CO9 2SX
**Tel:** 01787-475151 **Fax:** 01787-475579
**Web:** www.wade.eu
**Reg No:** 4398143 **Estd:** 2002 Private Limited Company
**Line of Business:** Drainage contractors
**Trading Style:** Wade International Ltd
**Issued Capital:** £50,000
**Managing Director:** R Thomas
**Co. Secretary:** Ms Dawn Lewis
**Responsibilities**
**Sales:** Pat Rawlinson *(Customer Services Manager)*
**Operations:** Pat Rawlinson *(Customer Services Manager)*
**Engineering:** Ron Blackburn *(Engineering Manager)*
**US SIC:** 3321, 3339
**UK SIC:** 31110, 22470
**Bankers:** Barclays Bank Plc (20-22-67)

| | 30-06-14 | 30-06-13 | 30-06-12 |
|---|---|---|---|
| TO | 5,581,995 | 5,470,947 | 6,519,670 |
| P/L | 1,075,120 | 927,972 | 1,666,393 |
| NW | 11,294,534 | 10,467,681 | 9,777,428 |
| WC | 7,877,145 | 6,837,747 | 6,249,801 |
| Emp. | 64 | 68 | 67 |

DUNS 21-799-4735

## The Wadebridge Charity

County Hall, Treyew Road, Truro, Cornwall TR1 3AY
**Web:** www.cornwall.gov.uk
**Estd:** 1964
**Line of Business:** Charities and charitable organisations
**Trading Style:** Cornwall County Council
**Partners:** I Kennaway, R Fish, D Bailey, F Twyning
**Responsibilities**
**Senior:** Jenny Christie *(Registration Officer)*, Martin Cookman *(Senior Manager)*, Sheena Davey *(Senior Manager)*, Pat Harvey *(Chairman)*, Helen Sinclair *(Team Manager)*, Shirley Trebilcock *(General Manager)*
**Finance:** Cath Robinson *(Head of Finance)*, Sandra Rothwell *(Head of Economic Development)*
**Marketing:** Carole Theobald *(Head of Strategy, Localism and)*
**IT:** Adrian Busby *(Senior Technician)*, Tracey Carter *(Infrastructure Technician)*, Sarah Sims *(Community Network Manager)*
**Health & Safety:** Chris Billing *(Health and Safety Executive)*, Tamsin Ferris *(Health and Safety Executive)*
**Facilities:** Sharon Bundy *(Estate Road Adoptions Officer)*, Simon Lowry *(Infrastructure Asset Coordinat)*
**Operations:** Kate Martin *(Project Coordinator)*
**Purchasing:** Sharon Hamilton *(Category Manager)*, Rebecca Yorke *(Category Manager)*
**Fleet:** Nigel Blackler *(Head of Transport, Waste and E)*
**Engineering:** Scott Perry *(Civil Engineer)*
**US SIC:** 6732 **UK SIC:** 83100
**Employees:** 1,500

DUNS 21-773-5330

## Wadebridge Community Primary

Gonvena Hill, Wadebridge, Cornwall PL27 6BL
**Tel:** 01208814560
**Web:** www.wadebridgeprimary.co.uk
**Estd:** 2007 Proprietorship
**Line of Business:** Schools (foundation)
**Proprietor:** G Leend
**Responsibilities**
**Senior:** Adrian Massey *(Head Teacher)*
**US SIC:** 8211 **UK SIC:** 93200
**Employees:** 60

DUNS 21-830-4143

## Wadebridge School

Wadebridge School, Gonvena Hill, Sladesbridge, Wadebridge, Cornwall PL27 6BU
**Tel:** 01208812881
**Web:** www.wadebridge.cornwall.sch.uk
**Reg No:** 7999988 **Estd:** 2012 Private Company Limited By Guarantee
**Line of Business:** Schools (local authority)
**Directors:** P M Howard, Mrs B Lyle, D R Abbiss, Mrs N M Brooks, D Constance, Ms V A Crabb, Ms T Yardley, S J Robertson
**Co. Secretary:** Christopher Wilson
**Responsibilities**
**Senior:** Jan Everitt *(Director)*, Rosslyn Franks *(Director)*, Matthew Gibbons *(Director)*, Katy Holmes *(Director)*, Ian Thurtle *(Director)*
**US SIC:** 8211 **UK SIC:** 93200
**Bankers:** Lloyds TSB Bank plc (30-17-03)

| | 31-08-14 | 31-08-13 |
|---|---|---|
| TO | 6,402,167 | 30,660,136 |
| P/L | (199,233) | 21,881,008 |
| NW | 20,868,775 | 21,502,008 |
| WC | 1,396,489 | 1,226,798 |
| Emp. | 123 | 122 |

DUNS 21-611-3365 **Imp**

## Wadworth & Company Ltd

Northgate Brewery, Devizes, Wiltshire SN10 1JW
**Tel:** 01380-723361
**Web:** www.wadworth.co.uk
**Reg No:** 0030177 **VAT No:** 137487246
**Estd:** 1887 Private Limited Company
**Line of Business:** Manufacture of beer
**Trading Style:** Giddings Edwin, The Canal Tavern, The Bungalow Inn, The Bell Inn
**Issued Capital:** £12,460,217
**Principals:** C J Bartholomew *(Chairman and Managing)*, R I Gordon Finlayson *(Financial)*, Sir J Butler, N J Atkinson, J P Sullivan, L J Stephens
**Co. Secretary:** Andrew Percy
**Responsibilities**
**Marketing:** Tricia Hurle *(Marketing Administrator)*, Jo Skuse *(?Tenanted Trade Manager)*
**Sales:** Anthony West *(Sales Director)*
**Admin:** Tricia Hurle *(Marketing Administrator)*
**HR:** Dawn Youngman *(Human Resources Manager)*
**Health & Safety:** Colin Oke *(Health & Safety Officer)*
**Facilities:** Bob Tyre *(Chief Engineer)*
**Operations:** Colin Oke *(Health & Safety Officer)*, Bob Tyre *(Chief Engineer)*
**Branches:** Wadworth & Company Ltd, Abbotswell Road, Fordingbridge, Hampshire SP6 2JA
**US SIC:** 2082, 5182, 5813
**UK SIC:** 42702, 61700, 66200
**Auditors:** David Owen & Co
**Bankers:** Lloyds TSB Bank plc (30-92-63)

| | 30-09-13 | 30-09-12 | 30-09-11 |
|---|---|---|---|
| TO | 56,111,000 | 55,231,000 | 55,027,000 |
| P/L | 3,987,000 | 3,438,000 | 4,176,000 |
| NW | 78,880,000 | 77,111,000 | 76,530,000 |
| WC | 50,000 | (909,000) | (620,000) |
| Emp. | 621 | 623 | 647 |

DUNS 23-728-8977

## Waer Systems Ltd

(**Subsidiary of:** Waer Holdings Ltd)
Unit 8, The Quadrant, 60 Marlborough Road, Lancing, West Sussex BN15 8UW
**Tel:** 01903-768010
**Web:** www.waersystems.com
**Reg No:** 3723453 **Estd:** 1999 Private Limited Company
**Line of Business:** Computer software (development)
**Export Sales:** £48,668
**Issued Capital:** £32,600
**Directors:** D Snelson, R M Scott, D J Mockler
**Co. Secretary:** David Mockler
**US SIC:** 7379 **UK SIC:** 83940
**Auditors:** Manser Hunot

| | 31-12-13 | 31-12-12 | 31-12-11 |
|---|---|---|---|
| TO | 705,328 | 689,851 | 820,759 |
| P/L | (48,257) | (144,720) | (258,812) |
| NW | 456,471 | 377,853 | 363,118 |
| WC | 159,567 | 91,577 | 81,245 |

DUNS 21-600-7587

## Wagamama

46 Wimbledon Hill Road, Wimbledon, London SW19 7PA
**Tel:** 02088797280
**Web:** www.wagamama.com
**Estd:** 2011 Proprietorship
**Line of Business:** Licensed restaurants
**Proprietor:** M Medina
**Responsibilities**
**Senior:** Patrycja Krupa *(General Manager)*
**US SIC:** 5812 **UK SIC:** 66110
**Employees:** 50

DUNS 76-846-1550

## Wagamama Ltd

(**Subsidiary of:** Mabel Topco Ltd)
Waverley House, 7-12 Noel Street, London W1F 8GQ
**Tel:** 02070093600
**Web:** www.wagamama.com
**Reg No:** 2605751 **VAT No:** 681447517
**Estd:** 1992 Private Limited Company
**Line of Business:** Licensed restaurants
**Trading Style:** Wagamama Ltd
**Issued Capital:** £25,000
**Directors:** Mrs J S Holbrook, G M House, D Campbell
**Responsibilities**
**Finance:** Antony Perring *(Finance Director)*
**Marketing:** Ingrid Kelly *(Marketing Director)*
**Branches:** Wagamama Ltd, 26A Kensington High Street, London W8 4PW
**US SIC:** 7399 **UK SIC:** 83954
**Auditors:** PricewaterhouseCoopers LLP
**Bankers:** The Royal Bank Of Scotland Plc (16-00-19)

| | 27-04-14 | 28-04-13 | 29-04-12 |
|---|---|---|---|
| TO | 159,233,000 | 141,170,000 | 124,392,000 |
| P/L | 15,942,000 | 17,575,000 | 17,388,000 |
| NW | 54,531,000 | 39,346,000 | 82,509,000 |
| WC | (11,626,000) | (20,642,000) | 30,478,000 |
| Emp. | 3,395 | 2,927 | 2,538 |

DUNS 22-160-7646

## Wage Day Advance Ltd

(**Subsidiary of:** Src Transatlantic Ltd)
Unit 7 Acorn Business Park, Keighley Road, Skipton, North Yorkshire BD23 2UE
**Tel:** 08717037777 **Fax:** 08435153921
**Web:** www.wagedayadvance.co.uk
**Reg No:** 4179322 **Estd:** 2000 Private Limited Company
**Line of Business:** Financial intermediation not elsewhere classified
**Issued Capital:** £156
**Directors:** D F Gayhardt, J M Graham-Rack, P L Mazzini
**Responsibilities**
**Senior:** Ross Chapman *(Business Development/Marketing)*, Dale Chapman *(Manager)*
**Sales:** Ross Chapman *(Business Development/Marketing)*
**US SIC:** 6111 **UK SIC:** 81501
**Auditors:** Walker & Co
**Bankers:** Barclays Bank Plc (20-45-14)

| | 31-12-13 | 31-12-12 | 31-12-11 |
|---|---|---|---|
| TA | 21,732,578 | 27,528,874 | 22,083,884 |
| P/L | 11,475,002 | 19,005,032 | 16,395,481 |
| NW | 19,262,055 | 24,131,529 | 18,677,803 |
| WC | 18,886,925 | 23,613,495 | 18,227,735 |
| Emp. | 147 | 144 | 105 |

DUNS 21-113-1539

## Wagg Foods Holdings Ltd

Dalton Airfield, Thirsk, North Yorkshire YO7 3HE
**Tel:** 01845-578111
**Web:** www.waggfoods.com
**Reg No:** 6539733 **Estd:** 2008 Private Limited Company
**Line of Business:** Management activities of holding companies
**Export Sales:** £2,045,947
**Issued Capital:** £220,000
**Directors:** W H Page, R H Page, T G Page, J S Lambert, W G Page
**Co. Secretary:** William Page
**US SIC:** 6711 **UK SIC:** 83962

| | 30-06-14 | 30-06-13 | 30-06-12 |
|---|---|---|---|
| TO | 58,998,502 | 57,095,351 | 49,987,030 |
| P/L | 6,050,632 | 5,613,160 | 4,095,884 |
| NW | 18,183,543 | 14,751,878 | 12,138,291 |
| WC | 2,848,845 | 4,562,830 | 2,666,621 |
| Emp. | 121 | 120 | 118 |

DUNS 22-134-5551

## Waggener Edstrom Worldwide Ltd.

(**Subsidiary of:** Waggener Edstrom Worldwide Inc.)
Fourth Floor Tower House, 10 Southampton Street, London WC2E 7HA
**Tel:** 020-7632-3800 **Fax:** 020-7632-3801
**Web:** www.waggeneredstrom.co.uk
**Reg No:** 4153480 **Estd:** 2001 Private Limited Company

**Line of Business:** Public relations consultants
**Issued Capital:** £900
**Directors:** Mrs M Waggener Zorkin, C W Kalbfleisch
**Co. Secretary:** Michael Bigelow
**Responsibilities**
**Senior:** Chris Talago (Vice President), Sam Whitby (Operations Manager)
**Finance:** Julie Curtis (Operations Manager)
**IT:** Paul Middleton (IT Manager)
**Health & Safety:** Julie Curtis (Operations Manager)
**Facilities:** Julie Curtis (Operations Manager), Chris Talago (Vice President)
**US SIC:** 7392 **UK SIC:** 83951

|  | 31-12-13 | 31-12-12 | 31-12-11 |
| --- | --- | --- | --- |
| TO | 4,569,000 | 4,480,000 | 5,284,000 |
| P/L | (358,000) | (12,000) | 237,000 |
| NW | 833,000 | 1,182,000 | 1,201,000 |
| WC | 772,000 | 1,091,000 | 1,031,000 |
| Emp. | 61 | 52 | 51 |

DUNS 39-465-8744   Imp-Exp
## Wagner Spraytech (Uk) Ltd
Opus Park, Moorfield Road, Slyfield Industrial Estate, Guildford, Surrey GU1 1SZ
**Tel:** 01483-454666
**Web:** www.earlex.co.uk
**Reg No:** 2124076 **VAT No:** 413985437
**Estd:** 1987 Private Limited Company
**Line of Business:** Diy wholesalers
**Export Markets:** Worlwide
**Export Sales:** £10,324,914
**Issued Capital:** £109,999
**Principals:** K F Pavia (Financial), D K Barron, A Aepli, I Mullaney
**Co. Secretary:** Kevin Pavia
**Responsibilities**
**Sales:** Steve Darbeyshire (Senior Sales Executive)
**IT:** Tim Hopper (Computer Operations Manager)
**Branches:** Earlex Ltd, Varey Road, Congleton, Cheshire CW12 1PJ
**US SIC:** 5039 **UK SIC:** 61300
**Auditors:** Roffe Swayne
**Bankers:** National Westminster Bank Plc (60-09-21)

|  | 31-01-14 | 31-07-12 | 31-01-11 |
| --- | --- | --- | --- |
| TO | 20,635,951 | 17,668,152 | 19,864,076 |
| P/L | (2,333,999) | (182,980) | 704,493 |
| NW | 397,015 | 1,666,377 | 1,820,632 |
| WC | 226,904 | 1,262,331 | 1,724,182 |
| Emp. | 150 | 163 | 160 |

DUNS 50-538-1012   Imp
## Wago Ltd
Triton Park, Rugby, Warwickshire CV21 1SG
**Tel:** 01788-568008 **Fax:** 01788-568050
**Web:** www.wago.com
**Reg No:** 2495884 **VAT No:** 528502355
**Estd:** 1990 Private Limited Company
**Line of Business:** Manufacturers and distributiors of electronic components
**Export Sales:** £3,105,000
**Issued Capital:** £100,000
**Directors:** A D Hoyle, S Hohorst, A C Borner
**Co. Secretary:** David Tarlton
**Responsibilities**
**Senior:** Nick Tarlton (IT Manager)
**IT:** Nick Tarlton (IT Manager)
**US SIC:** 3679 **UK SIC:** 34542
**Bankers:** HSBC Bank plc (40-39-11)

|  | 31-12-13 | 31-12-12 | 31-12-11 |
| --- | --- | --- | --- |
| TO | 14,037,000 | 12,063,000 | 11,340,000 |
| P/L | 1,021,000 | 485,000 | 381,000 |
| NW | 3,728,000 | 2,952,000 | 2,590,000 |
| WC | 3,560,000 | 2,774,000 | 2,530,000 |
| Emp. | 85 | 69 | 65 |

DUNS 21-030-7773   Imp
## Wagstaff Bros Ltd
The Wagstaff Centre, 15 Wharfside Rosemont Road, Wembley, Middlesex HA0 4PE
**Tel:** 02084321004 **Fax:** 020-8432-1111
**Web:** www.wagstaffgroup.co.uk
**Reg No:** 0295393 **VAT No:** 244019585
**Estd:** 1934 Private Limited Company
**Line of Business:** Office furniture and equipment suppliers
**Trading Style:** Wagstaff Office Interiors
**Issued Capital:** £1,188,750
**Principals:** R G Ansell (Managing), Mrs C N Batsford, Mrs E D Ansell
**Co. Secretary:** David Smith
**Responsibilities**
**Senior:** Darren Miles (Sales Director)
**Finance:** Austin Arafiena (Human Resources Manager)
**Marketing:** Michael Selman (Marketing Director)
**Sales:** Darren Miles (Sales Director)
**HR:** Austin Arafiena (Human Resources Manager)
**Branches:** Wagstaff Bros.,Ltd, Stuart House, The Back, Chepstow, Gwent NP16 5HH
**US SIC:** 2599 **UK SIC:** 46720
**Auditors:** RSM Bentley Jennison

**Bankers:** HSBC Bank plc (40-03-27)

|  | 31-12-13 | 31-12-12 | 31-12-11 |
| --- | --- | --- | --- |
| TO | 40,646,180 | 31,396,125 | 35,704,968 |
| P/L | 129,923 | 113,737 | 904,650 |
| NW | 4,488,244 | 4,426,935 | 4,637,273 |
| WC | 4,336,453 | 4,345,432 | 4,648,605 |
| Emp. | 109 | 97 | 105 |

DUNS 21-629-0726
## Wagstaff Foundries Ltd
(**Subsidiary of:** Wagstaff Foundries (Holdings) Ltd)
7 David Road, Slough, Berkshire SL3 0DB
**Tel:** 01753-683356
**Web:** www.wagstafffoundries.com
**Reg No:** 0563260 **VAT No:** 208051304
**Estd:** 1946 Private Limited Company
**Line of Business:** Casting of iron
**Issued Capital:** £14,404
**Principals:** J W Wagstaff (Managing), A J Wagstaff
**Co. Secretary:** James Wagstaff
**Responsibilities**
**Senior:** Roger Gearing (Manager)
**US SIC:** 3321 **UK SIC:** 31110
**Auditors:** Orr Shotliff
**Bankers:** HSBC Bank plc (40-42-09)

|  | 30-09-13 | 01-10-12 | 31-09-11 |
| --- | --- | --- | --- |
| TA | 1,187,305 | 868,020 | 1,105,086 |
| NW | 507,827 | 465,798 | 607,234 |
| WC | 485,664 | 433,466 | 561,886 |

DUNS 21-370-6577
## Wahaca
66 Chandos Place, London WC2N 4HG
**Tel:** 020-72401883
**Web:** www.wahaca.co.uk
**Estd:** 2009 Proprietorship
**Line of Business:** Licensed restaurants
**Proprietor:** A Whitney
**Responsibilities**
**Senior:** Ronan Andre (Manager)
**US SIC:** 5812 **UK SIC:** 66110
**Employees:** 70

DUNS 39-744-1080   Imp-Exp
## Wahl (Uk) Ltd
Unit 3-10 Herne Bay West Industrial Park, Sea Street, Herne Bay, Kent CT6 8JZ
**Tel:** 01227740066 **Fax:** 01227-367550
**Web:** www.wahl.co.uk
**Reg No:** 2184515 **VAT No:** 472798495
**Estd:** 1987 Private Limited Company
**Line of Business:** Hairdressing and other beauty treatment
**Export Markets:** European Union (E U); E Europe; Middle East
**Issued Capital:** £30,000
**Principals:** D M Goodman (Financial), G S Wahl, K T Wahl
**Co. Secretary:** Matthew Smith
**Responsibilities**
**Senior:** Neil Mancais (Sales And Marketing Manager)
**Marketing:** Neil Mancais (Sales And Marketing Manager)
**Sales:** Neil Mancais (Sales And Marketing Manager)
**Admin:** Nikki Darling (Personal Assistant To Administ)
**US SIC:** 7231 **UK SIC:** 98200
**Auditors:** Barnes Roffe
**Bankers:** Barclays Bank Plc (20-17-92)

|  | 31-12-13 | 31-12-12 | 31-12-11 |
| --- | --- | --- | --- |
| TO | 22,204,396 | 19,859,473 | 18,586,641 |
| P/L | 3,518,734 | 3,284,905 | 3,228,015 |
| NW | 12,707,063 | 14,002,386 | 11,515,188 |
| WC | 11,000,724 | 12,242,686 | 9,924,117 |
| Emp. | 63 | 66 | 61 |

DUNS 73-720-1454
## Wainhomes (North West) Ltd
(**Subsidiary of:** Wain Group Holdings Ltd)
2 Kelvin Close, Warrington, Cheshire WA3 7PB
**Tel:** 01925859650
**Reg No:** 4978580 **Estd:** 2003 Private Limited Company
**Line of Business:** Construction of domestic buildings
**Issued Capital:** £10,001,000
**Directors:** P Barlow, S J Owen, S T Toghill, W Ainscough
**Co. Secretary:** Andrew Savage
**Responsibilities**
**Senior:** Linda Collins (Sales Executive)
**Sales:** Linda Collins (Sales Executive)
**US SIC:** 1522 **UK SIC:** 50100
**Auditors:** KPMG LLP

|  | 30-06-13 | 30-06-12 | 30-06-11 |
| --- | --- | --- | --- |
| TO | 53,369,000 | 39,596,000 | 34,490,000 |
| P/L | 4,711,000 | 3,013,000 | 2,449,000 |
| NW | 20,805,000 | 17,234,000 | 14,989,000 |
| WC | 21,684,000 | 19,958,000 | 14,099,000 |
| Emp. | 82 | 75 | 65 |

DUNS 22-168-5808
## Wainhomes (South West) Holdings Ltd
(**Subsidiary of:** Wain Group Holdings Ltd)
Owlsfoot Business Centre, Sticklepath, Okehampton, Devon EX20 2PA
**Tel:** 01837-841000 **Fax:** 01837841019
**Web:** www.wainhomes.net
**Reg No:** 4187073 **Estd:** 1995 Private Limited Company
**Line of Business:** Construction of domestic buildings
**Issued Capital:** £133,803
**Directors:** R M Taylor, A M Dyer, M J Upton, S J Owen, W Ainscough
**Co. Secretary:** Roger Treweek
**Responsibilities**
**Senior:** Sarah Ascott (Office Manager), Irving Bunt (Health & Safety Officer)
**Health & Safety:** Irving Bunt (Health & Safety Officer)
**Branches:** Wainhomes (South West) Holdings Ltd, Plot 1 Wainhomes Dev Off Old Rosely Rd, Par, Cornwall PL24 1AZ
**US SIC:** 1522 **UK SIC:** 50100
**Auditors:** KPMG LLP

|  | 30-06-13 | 30-06-12 | 30-06-11 |
| --- | --- | --- | --- |
| TO | 66,827,000 | 54,667,000 | 47,120,000 |
| P/L | 16,218,000 | 10,486,000 | 8,690,000 |
| NW | 71,244,000 | 59,748,000 | 52,540,000 |
| WC | 70,577,000 | 60,214,000 | 52,973,000 |
| Emp. | 81 | 83 | 75 |

DUNS 21-030-7906
## Waitrose Ltd
(**Subsidiary of:** John Lewis Partnership Trust Ltd)
The Rosebird Centre, Shipston Road, Stratford-Upon-Avon, Warwickshire CV37 8LU
**Tel:** 01789263465 **Fax:** 0800-188-888
**Web:** www.waitrose.com
**Reg No:** 0099405 **VAT No:** 232457280
**Estd:** 1908 Private Limited Company
**Line of Business:** Supermarkets
**Trading Style:** Leckford Estate
**Issued Capital:** £1,000,000
**Directors:** M I Price, A C Mayfield, M R Williamson, Ms L Woodhouse, N Keen, T C Athron
**Co. Secretary:** Keith Hubber
**Responsibilities**
**Marketing:** Rupert Thomas (Marketing Director)
**Branches:** Waitrose Ltd, Waitrose Ltd, 6 Cherry Tree Walk, London EC1Y 8NX
**US SIC:** 5411 **UK SIC:** 64100
**Auditors:** PricewaterhouseCoopers LLP
**Bankers:** National Westminster Bank Plc (60-40-02)
Following financial data are in thousands

|  | 25-01-14 | 26-01-13 | 28-01-12 |
| --- | --- | --- | --- |
| TO | 5,640,900 | 5,416,100 | 5,072,300 |
| P/L | 109,100 | 147,500 | 148,100 |
| NW | 796,600 | 1,202,500 | 1,150,000 |
| WC | (1,483,000) | (914,800) | (944,800) |
| Emp. | 54,335 | 51,000 | 48,400 |

DUNS 21-702-0257
## Wake Smith Llp
68 Clarkehouse Road, Sheffield, South Yorkshire S10 2LJ
**Tel:** 01142666660
**Web:** www.wake-smith.co.uk
**Reg No:** 0360229OC **Estd:** 1934
**Line of Business:** Solicitors
**Responsibilities**
**Senior:** Lindsey Canning (Partner), Amanda Cowley (Partner), Michelle Hayward (Partner), Glenn Jaques (Partner), Jonathan Knight (Partner), Roger Swift (Manager)
**US SIC:** 8111 **UK SIC:** 83500

|  | 30-04-14 | 30-04-13 | 30-04-12 |
| --- | --- | --- | --- |
| TO | 5,542,910 | 5,238,507 | 5,730,810 |
| P/L | 1,008,322 | 710,832 | 1,135,354 |
| NW | 1,008,322 | 710,832 | 1,135,354 |
| WC | 1,315,533 | 936,947 | 1,420,837 |
| Emp. | 111 | 103 | 116 |

DUNS 73-689-5157
## Wakefield & District Housing Ltd
Merefield House, Castleford, West Yorkshire WF10 5HX
**Web:** www.wdh.co.uk
**Reg No:** 4948519 **Estd:** 2012 Private Company Limited By Guarantee
**Line of Business:** Other letting of own property
**Directors:** W Clift Mbe, J S Hemingway, D N Bailey, Ms K E Harness, K A Wright, D M Jeffery, S Green, Ms A Cuthbert
**Co. Secretary:** Mrs Juliet Craven
**Responsibilities**
**Senior:** Colleen Adamson (Manager), Kay Binnersley (Board Member), Graham Haslam (Senior Manager), Elaine Rank (Director), Sandra Stephenson (Manager), Rachel Willoughby (Area Manager)
**Finance:** Clare Barnard (Exchequer Manager)

**Marketing:** Lisa Mason (Communications manager)
**IT:** Eric Backhouse (ICT Infrastructure and Custome), Chris Savage (IT Support Officer)
**HR:** Tracy Tallant (Human Resources Director)
**Health & Safety:** Dave Tierney (Health & Safety Manager)
**Facilities:** Sharon France (New Tenancy Manager), Eric Gilchrist (Maintenance Manager), Kaye Thompson (Facilities Officer), Pauline Wall (Facilities Officer)
**Operations:** Steve Rawson (Executive Director of Operatio)
**Engineering:** Andy Melvin (Technical Engineer)
**US SIC:** 6519 **UK SIC:** 85000
**Auditors:** RSM Robson Rhodes LLP
**Bankers:** The Royal Bank Of Scotland Plc (16-00-07)

|  | 31-03-14 | 31-03-13 | 31-03-12 |
| --- | --- | --- | --- |
| TO | 137,833,000 | 130,613,000 | 118,206,000 |
| P/L | 17,630,000 | 12,507,000 | (5,909,000) |
| NW | 470,183,000 | 354,936,000 | 321,612,000 |
| WC | 11,493,000 | (9,315,000) | (11,623,000) |
| Emp. | 1,281 | 1,278 | 1,268 |

DUNS 23-998-5799
## Wakefield College
Margaret Street, Wakefield, West Yorkshire WF1 2DH
**Tel:** 01924-789780
**Web:** www.wakefield.ac.uk
**VAT No:** 590939594 **Estd:** 1867
**Line of Business:** Further education schools and colleges
**Principals:** I Fitzgerald (Financial), J Muskett
**Responsibilities**
**Senior:** Stuart Parton (Marketing Manager)
**Purchasing:** Julian Andrews (Management Accountant)
**Branches:** Wakefield College, Thornes Park, Wakefield, West Yorkshire WF2 8QZ
**US SIC:** 8221 **UK SIC:** 93100
**Bankers:** The Co-Operative Bank Plc (08-90-20)
**Employees:** 700

DUNS 21-031-9008
## Wakefield Girls High School
Wentworth Street, Wakefield, West Yorkshire WF1 2QU
**Tel:** 01924372490
**Web:** www.wgsf.org.uk
**Estd:** 2002 Partnership
**Line of Business:** Schools (independent)
**Partners:** Mrs J Wallwork, Mrs G Wallwork
**Responsibilities**
**Finance:** Alison Binns (Financial Coordinator)
**Marketing:** Camilla Field (Marketing Manager)
**IT:** Stephen Paget (Head of IT)
**HR:** Annette Casey (Human Resources Manager)
**Health & Safety:** David Butterfield (Health & Safety Officer)
**Purchasing:** Alison Binns (Financial Coordinator)
**US SIC:** 8211 **UK SIC:** 93200
**Employees:** 200

DUNS 22-240-2906
## Wakefield Grammar School Foundation
154 Northgate, Wakefield, West Yorkshire WF1 3QX
**Tel:** 01924231600 **Fax:** 01924231605
**Web:** www.wgsf.org.uk
**Reg No:** 4258359 **Estd:** 2001 Private Company Limited By Guarantee
**Line of Business:** Schools (independent)
**Directors:** D A Young, A M Hofbauer, Ms R L Hannan, C R Blair, M G Patel, M Golightly, Ms S M Brown, J P Mcleod
**Co. Secretary:** Laurence Perry
**Responsibilities**
**Senior:** Angela Byram (Director), Thomas Garner (Director), Marie Green (Director), Michael Hird (Director), George Holmes (Director), Douglas Metcalfe (Manager), Patricia Stark (Manager), Dennis Wheatley (Manager)
**Finance:** Brenda Whiteley (Financial Director)
**Marketing:** Camilla Field (Marketing Director)
**Admin:** Christina Hastings (Administration Manager)
**HR:** Annette Casey (Human Resources Manager)
**US SIC:** 8211 **UK SIC:** 93200
**Bankers:** Barclays Bank Plc (20-89-68)

|  | 31-07-13 | 31-07-12 | 31-07-11 |
| --- | --- | --- | --- |
| TO | 19,350,717 | 19,042,787 | 18,626,697 |
| P/L | (216,870) | (459,874) | 165,810 |
| NW | 25,457,200 | 25,359,254 | 25,866,334 |
| WC | 4,027,336 | 4,035,907 | 3,728,581 |
| Emp. | 488 | 484 | 468 |

**DUNS 23-413-8337**
## Wakefield Hospice
Wakefield Hospice, Wakefield, West Yorkshire WF1 4TS
**Tel:** 01924213900
**Web:** www.wakefieldhospice.co.uk
**Estd:** 1986
**Line of Business:** Other human health activities
**Partners:** J Gill, Mrs B Baker, Mrs K Crawshaw, J Firth, G Mortimer, J Chapman, S Hastings
**Branches:** Wakefield Hospice, 97 Queen Street, Leeds, West Yorkshire LS27 8DW
**US SIC:** 8091 **UK SIC:** 95200
**Employees:** 80

**DUNS 22-810-2620**
## Wakefield Metropolitan District Council
Town Hall, Wakefield, West Yorkshire WF1 2HQ
**Tel:** 01924306090
**Web:** www.wakefield.gov.uk
**Estd:** 1974 Incorporate By Act Of Parliament
**Line of Business:** Local council
**Trading Style:** Normanton Market, Wmdc Market, Wmdc Metroglaze, Wmdc Homecare
**Principals:** M Pullan (Financial), P Box
**Responsibilities**
**Senior:** Nasim Aslam (Executive), Jane Bragg (Manager), Janet Burhouse (Chairman), Jayne Dowding (Manager), Cheryl Hobson (Partner), Cllr Hudson (Board Member), Wendy Jewitt (Manager), Sharron Limb (Manager), Christine Mason (General Manager), Darren Pollington (Manager), Susie Richmond (Senior Manager), Joanne Roney (Chief Executive Officer), Vicky Shearman (Executive), Vicky Staveley (Manager), Zoe Styles (Manager), Neil Whitehouse (Manager), Ian Wiper (Manager)
**Finance:** Judith Badger (Head of Finance), Judy Billings (Treasurer), Terry Crook (Finance Manager), Julia Ford (Finance Manager)
**Marketing:** Stacey Burliet (Marketing Manager)
**IT:** Mick O'Malley (Non-pc Systems Manager)
**HR:** Hilary Brearley (Head of Human Resources), Cllr Jenkins (Board Member), Cath O'Malley (Workforce Development Coordina)
**Health & Safety:** Cllr Rowley (Health and Safety Executive), Jane Stark (Health and Safety Executive), Angela Vine (Environmental Health Manager,)
**Facilities:** Bernard Boyle (Senior Facilities Officer)
**Operations:** Ian Copley (Aimhigher Project Officer), Sam Townend (Production and Operations Mana)
**Purchasing:** Colin Woods (Procurement Officer)
**Fleet:** Dale Hick (Executive), Brendan McNamara (Transport Operations Manager)
**Engineering:** Kath Walkington (Technical Engineer)
**Branches:** Wakefield Metropolitan District Council, 9 Bull Ring, Wakefield, West Yorkshire WF1 1HB
**US SIC:** 9121 **UK SIC:** 91110
**Bankers:** The Co-Operative Bank Plc (08-90-20)
**Employees:** 20,000

**DUNS 21-810-6090**
## Wakefield Placement & Adoption Services
Unit 21, Calder Vale Road, Wakefield, West Yorkshire WF1 5PE
**Tel:** 01924302160
**Web:** www.wakefield.gov.uk
**Estd:** 2012
**Line of Business:** Adoption and fostering services
**Responsibilities**
**Senior:** Julie Chew (Adoption Team Manager)
**US SIC:** 8321 **UK SIC:** 96111
**Employees:** 140

**DUNS 21-242-9070** *Imp-Exp*
## Wakefield Shirt Co Ltd
Thornes Wharf Lane, Wakefield, West Yorkshire WF1 5RL
**Web:** www.doubletwo.co.uk
**Reg No:** 0361629 **Estd:** 1940 Private Limited Company
**Line of Business:** Management activities of holding companies
**Export Markets:** Worldwide
**Export Sales:** £5,784,944
**Trading Style:** Double Two Ltd
**Issued Capital:** £1,174,504
**Principals:** R J Donner (Managing), R J Donner

**Co. Secretary:** Kevin Mellor
**Responsibilities**
**HR:** Barbara Lawton (Personnel Manager)
**Health & Safety:** Barbara Lawton (Personnel Manager)
**Facilities:** Bernard Dews (Maintenance Manager)
**Operations:** Barbara Lawton (Personnel Manager)
**Purchasing:** Cheryl Bayliss (Buyer)
**Branches:** Wakefield Shirt Co Ltd, Park Lane, Newcastle Upon Tyne, Tyne and Wear NE27 0BS
**US SIC:** 6711, 2328
**UK SIC:** 83962, 45340
**Auditors:** Jolliffe Cork LLP
**Bankers:** HSBC Bank plc (40-45-11)

|     | 31-12-13 | 31-12-12 | 31-12-11 |
| --- | --- | --- | --- |
| TO | 17,559,602 | 16,636,174 | 24,042,906 |
| P/L | 153,946 | 273,463 | 495,215 |
| NW | 8,454,054 | 8,302,125 | 8,229,908 |
| WC | 4,939,565 | 4,803,031 | 4,593,875 |
| Emp. | 141 | 139 | 138 |

**DUNS 23-508-1663**
## Wakemans Ltd
**(Subsidiary of:** Wakemans Holdings Ltd)
11-12 Highfield Road, Birmingham, West Midlands B15 3EB
**Tel:** 0121-454-4581 **Fax:** 0121-454-5206
**Web:** www.wakemans.com
**Reg No:** 3507404 **Estd:** 1998 Private Limited Company
**Line of Business:** Quantity surveyors
**Trading Style:** Wakemans Ltd
**Issued Capital:** £100,151
**Principals:** J D Woodhall (Managing), D R Howles, D M Watson, O O Balogun, A R Aston, S M Baugh
**Co. Secretary:** Ms Michelle Golding
**Responsibilities**
**Health & Safety:** Andrew Pennell (Health & Safety Officer)
**Purchasing:** Donna Clayton (Purchasing Manager)
**Branches:** Wakemans Ltd, 16 Whiteladies Road, Bristol, Avon BS8 2LG
**US SIC:** 6552, 7399
**UK SIC:** 85000, 83954
**Auditors:** Haslehursts
**Bankers:** Allied Irish Bank (gb) (23-83-99)

|     | 30-09-13 | 30-09-12 | 30-09-11 |
| --- | --- | --- | --- |
| TA | 1,449,620 | 1,347,638 | 1,393,052 |
| NW | 413,674 | 377,037 | 363,798 |
| WC | 400,125 | 357,179 | 334,481 |

**DUNS 23-300-2372**
## Walberton Nursery
Yapton Lane, Walberton, Arundel, West Sussex BN18 0AS
**Web:** www.walberton-nursery.co.uk
**VAT No:** 193586814 **Estd:** 1973 Proprietorship
**Line of Business:** Nurseries wholesale
**Proprietor:** D L Tristran
**US SIC:** 0291, 8211
**UK SIC:** 01001, 93200
**Bankers:** National Westminster Bank Plc (60-05-24)
**Employees:** 50

**DUNS 21-391-5962**
## Walby Farm Park
Walby, Crosby-On-Eden, Carlisle, Cumbria CA6 4QL
**Tel:** 01228-573056
**Web:** www.walbyfarmpark.co.uk
**Estd:** 2009 Proprietorship
**Line of Business:** Preservation of historical sites and buildings
**Proprietor:** N Milborn
**Responsibilities**
**Senior:** Neil Milbourn (Proprietor)
**US SIC:** 8411 **UK SIC:** 97700
**Employees:** 50

**DUNS 21-722-6562**
## Walcon Marine Ltd
**(Subsidiary of:** Walcon Ltd)
Cockerell Close, Segensworth West, Fareham, Hampshire PO15 5SR
**Fax:** 01489-579988
**Web:** www.walconmarine.com
**Reg No:** 1143519 **Estd:** 1973 Private Limited Company
**Line of Business:** Building of complete constructions or parts thereof; civil engineering
**Export Sales:** £1,138,925
**Issued Capital:** £10,000
**Principals:** R G Walters (Chairman), J H Walters (Managing), C Kemp (Commercial), D Philbrow, J D Donald
**Co. Secretary:** James Walters
**US SIC:** 1541, 7399
**UK SIC:** 50100, 83954
**Auditors:** BDO Stoy Hayward LLP

**Bankers:** National Westminster Bank Plc (56-00-68)

|     | 30-04-14 | 30-04-13 | 30-04-12 |
| --- | --- | --- | --- |
| TO | 8,436,097 | 8,070,464 | 7,581,996 |
| P/L | 32,212 | 76,291 | 274,803 |
| NW | 1,321,710 | 1,307,537 | 1,385,391 |
| WC | 1,092,886 | 1,147,546 | 1,337,730 |
| Emp. | 50 | 46 | 50 |

**DUNS 54-851-7903**
## Walde & Bushnell
47a High Street, Wheatley, Oxford, Oxfordshire OX33 1XX
**Tel:** 01865872425
**Web:** www.whitepostfarm.co.uk
**Estd:** 1998 Partnership
**Line of Business:** Chauffeur driven car hire
**Partners:** R Bushnell, Mrs B Bushnell
**US SIC:** 8411 **UK SIC:** 97700
**Bankers:** National Westminster Bank Plc (60-24-60)
**Employees:** 114

**DUNS 21-749-0488**
## Walderslade Girls' School
Bradfields Avenue, Chatham, Kent ME5 0LE
**Tel:** 01634301120
**Web:** www.walderslade girls.org.uk
**Reg No:** 7800431 **Estd:** 2011 Private Company Limited By Guarantee
**Line of Business:** General secondary education
**Directors:** A M Frith, R J Lincoln, Ms L Mcgowan, Miss S K Kay, Ms L J Mcconnell, Dr J N Mount, N C Scott, S Willshire
**Co. Secretary:** Mrs Coral Gammon
**Responsibilities**
**Senior:** Pamela Burborough (Director), Louise McGowan (Head Teacher), Barbara Uden (Director), Christina Williams (Director)
**Admin:** Maggie Taylor (Office Manager)
**US SIC:** 8211 **UK SIC:** 93200

|     | 31-08-13 | 31-08-12 |
| --- | --- | --- |
| TO | 4,825,037 | 16,401,846 |
| P/L | (451,203) | 12,337,251 |
| NW | 10,614,048 | 11,112,251 |
| WC | 307,408 | 587,295 |
| Emp. | 127 | 95 |

**DUNS 34-846-0494** *Imp-Exp*
## Waldon Ltd.
Unit A, Porth, Mid Glamorgan CF39 8WA
**Tel:** 01443671315 **Fax:** 01443 67 5219
**Web:** www.soehnergroup.com
**Reg No:** 2809288 **VAT No:** 615572344
**Estd:** 1993 Private Limited Company
**Line of Business:** Plastic injection moulding
**Export Markets:** Germany; Spain
**Export Sales:** £5,012,097
**Issued Capital:** £300,000
**Principals:** W Sohner (Managing), Ms R Sohner
**Co. Secretary:** Albrecht Heege
**Responsibilities**
**IT:** Gareth James (IT Manager)
**US SIC:** 3079 **UK SIC:** 48360
**Auditors:** Agincourt Chartered Accountants
**Bankers:** Barclays Bank Plc (20-18-15)

|     | 31-12-13 | 31-12-12 | 31-12-11 |
| --- | --- | --- | --- |
| TO | 10,178,485 | 10,090,813 | 14,473,033 |
| P/L | 1,165,653 | 199,373 | 547,337 |
| NW | 4,731,113 | 3,693,922 | 3,499,663 |
| WC | 3,112,301 | 1,891,229 | 1,492,588 |
| Emp. | 66 | 85 | 118 |

**DUNS 22-841-1989**
## The Waldorf Hilton Hotel
Aldwych, London WC2B 4DD
**Tel:** 020-7836-2400
**Web:** www.hilton.com
**VAT No:** 863147028 **Estd:** 2003 Proprietorship
**Line of Business:** Hotels and motels without restaurant
**Proprietors:** P Nesbett, M Nash, P Littlehouse, A Scott
**Responsibilities**
**Senior:** Peter Beckwith (General Manager), P LITTLEHOUSE (Proprietor), Pierre-Antoine Lhommet (Restaurant Manager), M NASH (Proprietor), Alison Palin (General Manager)
**Marketing:** Yoori Koo (Marketing Manager)
**Sales:** M NASH (Proprietor)
**Admin:** Kara Monteir (Office Manager)
**HR:** Anja Henschel (Human Resources Manager)
**Health & Safety:** Ben Reeves (Health & Safety Officer)
**Facilities:** Exnoll Harris (Maintenance Manager)
**US SIC:** 7011 **UK SIC:** 66500
**Employees:** 200

**DUNS 23-995-2641**
## Wales & West Housing Association Ltd
Alexandra Gate, Ffordd Pengam, Tremorfa, Cardiff, South Glamorgan CF24 2UD
**Fax:** 029-2041-5380
**Web:** www.wwha.co.uk
**Reg No:** 0021114IP **VAT No:** 655752118
**Estd:** 1965 Friendly Society
**Line of Business:** Non-charitable social work activities with accommodation
**Principals:** Mrs A Mainwaring (Chairman), D Taylor, Mrs J Maw, I Williams, W Radley, M Lloyd, Dr A Burrowes, J C Bowen
**Responsibilities**
**Senior:** Ivor Gittens (Chair of Association)
**Finance:** Stuart Epps (Head of Finance)
**Marketing:** Nikki Cole (Head of Development)
**IT:** Marc Pensom (Senior Infrastructure Speciali), Richard Troote (Head of ICT)
**US SIC:** 8321 **UK SIC:** 96111
**Auditors:** Coopers & Lybrand
**Bankers:** National Westminster Bank Plc (01-01-55)
**Employees:** 602
**Turnover:** £32,688,000

**DUNS 73-790-1533**
## Wales & West Utilities Ltd
**(Subsidiary of:** Wales & West Gas Networks (Holdings) Ltd)
Wales & West House, Spooner Close, Newport, Gwent NP10 8FZ
**Tel:** 08701650597 **Fax:** 01912 163435
**Web:** www.wwutilities.co.uk
**Reg No:** 5046791 **Estd:** 2004 Private Limited Company
**Line of Business:** Pipework contractors
**Issued Capital:** £30,675,000
**Directors:** T C Ip, N D Mcgee, N S Henson, M J Pavia, G W Edwards, L S Chan, A J Hunter, C C Tsai
**Co. Secretary:** Paul Millar
**Responsibilities**
**Senior:** Grant Hawkins (Director)
**Finance:** Adrian Breakspear (Treasury)
**Admin:** Gloria Hall (PA to CEO)
**IT:** Ralph Evans (Network Operations Manager)
**Facilities:** Ian Kirkhope (Facilities Manager)
**Operations:** Christopher Boughton (Lead Project Manager), Paul Breakey (Operations Manager), Trevor Clark (Contract Operations Manager), Stephen Hanman (Commercial Operations Manager), Allan Paul (Contract Operations Manager)
**Purchasing:** Andrew Studley (Purchasing Manager)
**Fleet:** Jeanette Morgan (Fleet Manager), Andrew Petiford (Transport Manager)
**Engineering:** Nicci Birchall (Engineer)
**US SIC:** 1711 **UK SIC:** 50300
**Auditors:** PricewaterhouseCoopers LLP

|     | 31-12-13 | 31-12-12 | 31-12-12 |
| --- | --- | --- | --- |
| TO | 406,300,000 | 277,000,000 | 350,900,000 |
| P/L | (54,100,000) | (87,400,000) | (127,200,000) |
| NW | (909,100,000) | (833,800,000) | (737,400,000) |
| WC | (594,500,000) | (542,300,000) | (468,900,000) |
| Emp. | 1,376 | 1,462 | 1,468 |

**DUNS 21-038-0567**
## Wales Audit Office
24 Cathedral Road, Cardiff, South Glamorgan CF11 9LJ
**Tel:** 029-2032-0500
**Web:** www.wao.gov.uk
**Estd:** 2005
**Line of Business:** Accounting and auditing activities
**Director:** H Vaughan Thomas
**Responsibilities**
**Senior:** Rachel Moss (Head Of Communications)
**Marketing:** Rachel Moss (Head Of Communications)
**US SIC:** 8931 **UK SIC:** 83600
**Auditors:** KTS Owens Thomas Ltd
**Employees:** 5
**Turnover:** £25,623,000

**DUNS 22-779-5309**
## The Wales Council for Voluntary Action
Baltic House, Mount Stuart Square, Cardiff, South Glamorgan CF10 5FH
**Tel:** 02920431700 **Fax:** 029-2043-1701
**Web:** www.cnp.org.uk
**Reg No:** 0425299 **Estd:** 1946 Private Company Limited By Guarantee
**Line of Business:** Social work activities without accommodation
**Trading Style:** W C V A
**Directors:** W E Dickie, F M Targett, Mrs J L Leering, S Harris, Ms R Cifuentes, Mrs P L Boyd, Mrs M A Lockitt, S Mohamed
**Co. Secretary:** Mrs Tracey Lewis

**Responsibilities**
**Senior:** Philip Avery *(Director)*, Louise Bennett *(Director)*, Eurwen Edwards *(Director)*, Cherrie Galvin *(Director)*, Paul Glaze *(Director)*, Catherine Gwynant *(Director)*, Sioned Hughes *(Director)*, Lydia Stephens *(Director)*, Catriona Williams *(Director)*
**Finance:** Wilma Thomas *(Financial Controller)*
**IT:** Sarah Hatton *(IS Director)*
**Health & Safety:** Julie Cull *(Facilities Manager)*
**Facilities:** Julie Cull *(Facilities Manager)*
**Purchasing:** Julie Cull *(Facilities Manager)*
**Branches:** The Wales Council For Voluntary Action, 11-12 King St, Carmarthen, Dyfed SA31 1BH
**US SIC:** 8321 **UK SIC:** 96111
**Auditors:** KPMG LLP
**Bankers:** HSBC Bank plc (40-16-03)

| | 31-03-14 | 31-03-13 | 31-03-12 |
|---|---|---|---|
| TO | 23,212,229 | 20,631,270 | 43,135,498 |
| P/L | (1,076,334) | (7,497,299) | (4,368,393) |
| NW | 10,199,245 | 8,004,593 | 15,849,628 |
| WC | 7,628,343 | 8,702,685 | 16,279,413 |
| Emp. | 116 | 136 | 144 |

DUNS 21-392-8502
## Wales Further Education Centre
Wales High School, Storth Lane, Kiveton Park, Sheffield, South Yorkshire S26 5QQ
**Tel:** 01909771504
**Proprietorship**
**Line of Business:** Miscellaneous Vocational Schools
**US SIC:** 8249 **UK SIC:** 93300
**Employees:** 100

DUNS 45-884-3588
## Wales Millennium Centre
Bute Place, Cardiff, South Glamorgan CF10 5AL
**Tel:** 02920636400
**Web:** www.wmc.org.uk
**Reg No:** 3221924 **Estd:** 2004 Private Limited Company
**Line of Business:** Operation of other sports arenas and stadiums not elsewhere classified
**Directors:** F E Morris, R K Aggarwal, E P Jones, S J Luke, B G Phillips, H Child, L Fletcher, E Jones Parry
**Co. Secretary:** Huw Williams
**Responsibilities**
**Senior:** Mathew Milsom *(General Manager)*, Marie Wood *(Development Director)*
**Finance:** Mathew Milsom *(General Manager)*
**Marketing:** Nia Jones *(Press Officer)*, Dylan Tozer *(Marketing Manager)*, Marie Wood *(Development Director)*
**HR:** Jeremy Ashdown *(Human Resources Manager)*
**Facilities:** Dave Bonney *(Maintenance Manager)*
**Operations:** Sarah Pellow *(Project Officer)*
**US SIC:** 7999, 6531
**UK SIC:** 97913, 83400
**Bankers:** HSBC Bank plc (40-16-13)

| | 31-03-14 | 31-03-13 | 31-03-12 |
|---|---|---|---|
| TO | 19,461,000 | 22,054,000 | 18,657,000 |
| P/L | (2,934,000) | (2,738,000) | (2,395,000) |
| NW | 65,751,000 | 68,685,000 | 71,423,000 |
| WC | 3,742,000 | 4,214,000 | 3,615,000 |
| Emp. | 204 | 227 | 215 |

DUNS 42-349-0601
## Wales National Pool Swansea
Sketty Lane, Swansea, West Glamorgan SA2 8QG
**Web:** www.walesnationalpoolswansea.co.uk
**Reg No:** 4336723 **Estd:** 2003 Private Company Limited By Guarantee
**Line of Business:** Operation of sports arenas and stadiums
**Directors:** R Francis Davies, Ms A Ellis, R V Smith, Ms J E Burgess, M C Child, R Ciborowski, C J Nowell
**Co. Secretary:** Mrs Helen Van Willegen
**Responsibilities**
**Senior:** Lewis Thomas *(Board Member)*, Noel Thompson *(Board Member)*
**Marketing:** Sian Gillies *(Marketing Coordinator)*
**Health & Safety:** Mike Rees *(Health & Safety Officer)*
**US SIC:** 7941 **UK SIC:** 97911

| | 31-07-14 | 31-07-13 | 31-07-12 |
|---|---|---|---|
| TO | 1,125,000 | 1,077,000 | 1,040,000 |
| WC | 570,000 | 500,000 | 507,000 |

DUNS 45-806-2924
## Wales Pre-School Providers Association
Unit 1, The Lofts, 9 Hunter Street, Cardiff, South Glamorgan CF10 5GX
**Web:** www.walesppa.org
**Reg No:** 3164233 **Estd:** 2002 Private Company Limited By Guarantee
**Line of Business:** Pre school education
**Directors:** M F Thorne, Mrs D Crimmins, Ms J M Howells, Mrs C W George, Mrs T Minett, Mrs B Davies, Ms L Bell, Ms W M Montague
**Co. Secretary:** Ms Jane Alexander
**Responsibilities**
**Senior:** Julie Besley *(Manager)*, Suzanne Rowlands *(Trustee)*
**Branches:** Wales Pre-School Providers Association, Cardiff Play Resource Centre, Ely Bridge Indstl Est, Cardiff, South Glamorgan CF5 4AQ
**US SIC:** 8211, 8699
**UK SIC:** 93200, 96902
**Auditors:** Allwoods

| | 31-03-14 | 31-03-13 | 31-03-12 |
|---|---|---|---|
| TO | 1,465,438 | 1,468,439 | 1,551,887 |
| P/L | 242,005 | 119,294 | 178,986 |
| NW | 1,454,033 | 1,212,029 | 1,092,737 |
| WC | 1,449,232 | 1,211,199 | 1,088,309 |
| Emp. | 65 | 68 | 80 |

DUNS 76-936-7947
## Wales the National Federation of Women's Institutes of England Jersey Guernsey
Home & Country Magazine, London SW6 4LY
**Tel:** 02073719300
**Web:** www.thewi.org.uk
**Reg No:** 2517690 **Estd:** 1990 Private Company Limited By Guarantee
**Line of Business:** Charities and charitable organisations
**Directors:** Mrs L M Andrews, J Thomson, Mrs J M Roberts, Mrs A M Jones, Ms P Tulip, Mrs S Fort, Mrs J Langley, Dr E J Probitts
**Co. Secretary:** Ms Anne Wheeler
**Responsibilities**
**Senior:** Catriona Adams *(Director)*, Diana Birch *(Director)*, Mary Clarke *(Director)*, Marylyn Haines Evans *(Director)*, Jana Osbourne *(General Secretary)*, Margaret Simons *(Director)*, Lynne Stubbings *(Director)*
**Admin:** Jana Osbourne *(General Secretary)*
**Branches:** The National Federation Of Women's Institutes Of England, Wales, Jerse, 11 Middle Way, Oxford, Oxfordshire OX2 7LH
**US SIC:** 8699 **UK SIC:** 96902
**Auditors:** Knox Cropper
**Bankers:** National Westminster Bank Plc (60-07-29)

| | 30-09-13 | 30-09-12 | 30-09-11 |
|---|---|---|---|
| TO | 7,443,815 | 5,932,894 | 5,801,226 |
| P/L | 843,228 | (751,804) | (361,472) |
| NW | 9,621,482 | 8,566,338 | 8,935,251 |
| WC | 3,598,777 | 2,783,656 | 2,193,337 |
| Emp. | 71 | 69 | 71 |

DUNS 22-791-9784
## The Wales Tourist Board
Brunel House, Cardiff, South Glamorgan CF24 0UY
**Tel:** 08450103300
**Web:** www.visitwales.co.uk
**VAT No:** 133814385 **Estd:** 1969 Incorporate By Act Of Parliament
**Line of Business:** National Authority for tourism in Wales
**Principals:** T Lewis *(Chairman)*, J Jones *(Managing)*, J P Cory *(Financial)*, R Pride *(Marketing)*, N Poole, P Loveluck, J Pride, E Owen
**Co. Secretary:** John Cory
**Branches:** The Wales Tourist Board, High St, Newport, Gwent NP18 1AG
**US SIC:** 7999 **UK SIC:** 97913
**Bankers:** HSBC Bank plc (40-16-15)
**Employees:** 100

DUNS 23-680-6774
## Walford and North Shropshire College
Walford Manor, Walford, Baschurch, Shrewsbury, Shropshire SY4 2HL
**Tel:** 01939262100
**Web:** www.wnsc.ac.uk
**Estd:** 1949
**Line of Business:** First-degree level higher education
**Trading Style:** Walford and North Shropshire College
**Director:** K W Dann
**Responsibilities**
**Finance:** Jim Godfrey *(Senior Finance Administrator)*
**IT:** Tim Harding *(Senior IT Executive)*
**Branches:** Walford College, Unit 6 Burway Trading Estate, Bromfield Road, Ludlow, Shropshire SY8 1EN
**US SIC:** 8221 **UK SIC:** 93100
**Bankers:** National Westminster Bank Plc (55-50-05)
**Employees:** 100

DUNS 23-225-5547
## Walfords Partnership
25-27 Castle Street, Liverpool, Merseyside L2 4TA
**Tel:** 01512360946
**Estd:** 1936 Partnership
**Line of Business:** Commercial Testing Services
**Principals:** M W Hardy, B M Woodman, Ms S Tan *(Partner)*, C E Thompson *(Partner)*, R G Chadwick *(Partner)*, J C Huston *(Partner)*, K Flemming *(Partner)*
**Branches:** Walfords Partnership, The Town House 3 Park Terrace, Manor Road, Luton, Bedfordshire LU1 3HN
**US SIC:** 7397 **UK SIC:** 83702
**Employees:** 49

DUNS 28-859-9384
## Walhampton School Trust Ltd
Walhampton School, Walhampton, Lymington, Hampshire SO41 5ZG
**Tel:** 01590 613 300
**Web:** www.walhampton.com
**Reg No:** 0871641 **Estd:** 2012 Private Company Limited By Guarantee
**Line of Business:** Primary education
**Directors:** S P Williams, The Honourable R Montagu, Mrs S Keen, D A Shakespeare, J R Cook, C Knox, Mrs K Host-Verbraak, J J Bennett
**Co. Secretary:** Daniel Boswell
**Responsibilities**
**Senior:** Neil Chippington *(Director)*, William Land *(Director)*, Neil Mcgrigor *(Director)*, Titus Mills *(Head Teacher)*, Beth Morris *(Head Teacher)*, Matthew Winter *(Director)*
**US SIC:** 8211 **UK SIC:** 93200
**Auditors:** Saffery Champness
**Bankers:** Lloyds TSB Bank plc (30-97-41)

| | 31-08-13 | 31-08-12 | 31-08-11 |
|---|---|---|---|
| TO | 3,494,867 | 3,443,824 | 3,360,429 |
| P/L | (175,487) | (53,291) | 32,825 |
| NW | 3,244,602 | 3,418,073 | 3,467,433 |
| WC | (157,148) | (56,788) | 6,671 |
| Emp. | 81 | 81 | 79 |

DUNS 21-413-6344
## Walkabout
266-271 Broad Street, Birmingham, West Midlands B1 2DS
**Tel:** 0121-6325712
**Web:** www.walkabout.eu.com
**Estd:** 2003 Proprietorship
**Line of Business:** Public house
**Proprietor:** G Keen
**Responsibilities**
**Senior:** Vincent Brown *(Proprietor)*
**US SIC:** 5813 **UK SIC:** 66200
**Employees:** 75

DUNS 21-761-9481
## Walkabout Ltd
The Outback, Barrack Street, Douglas, Isle of Man IM1 2AF
**Tel:** 01624-661547
**Reg No:** 0103795M **Estd:** 2001 Private Limited Company
**Line of Business:** Business services
**US SIC:** 7399 **UK SIC:** 83954
**Employees:** 430

DUNS 21-831-8467
## Walker & Son (Hauliers) Ltd
Ollerton Road, Tuxford, Newark, Nottinghamshire NG22 0PQ
**Tel:** 01777-870431
**Web:** www.walker-tuxford.co.uk
**Reg No:** 0533089 **VAT No:** 125301615
**Estd:** 1954 Private Limited Company
**Line of Business:** Representative office
**Issued Capital:** £47,350
**Managing Director:** R E Walker
**Co. Secretary:** Lee Bartrop
**US SIC:** 6519, 7394
**UK SIC:** 85000, 84000
**Auditors:** Landin Wilcock & Co
**Bankers:** Barclays Bank Plc (20-55-62)

| | 30-06-13 | 30-06-12 | 30-06-11 |
|---|---|---|---|
| TO | 11,911,939 | 9,862,447 | 9,958,316 |
| P/L | 1,799,968 | 810,407 | 1,472,453 |
| NW | 19,658,549 | 19,627,164 | 21,370,710 |
| WC | 7,053,088 | 7,502,786 | 9,245,782 |
| Emp. | 85 | 89 | 87 |

DUNS 21-890-4415
## Walker & Son (Leicester) Ltd
**(Subsidiary of:** Samworth Brothers (Holdings) Ltd)
Charnwood Bakery, 200 Madeline Road, Leicester, Leicestershire LE4 1EX
**Tel:** 01162-340033 **Fax:** 01162-340084
**Web:** www.samworthbrothers.co.uk
**Reg No:** 0988978 **Estd:** 1820 Private Limited Company
**Line of Business:** Manufacturers of food products
**Trading Style:** Walkers Charnwood Bakery
**Issued Capital:** £40,000
**Director:** R J Armitage
**Co. Secretary:** Timothy Barker
**Responsibilities**
**Senior:** Ian Beale *(Manager)*, Tracey McLoughlin *(Manager)*
**Finance:** Tom Lin *(Finance Manager)*
**IT:** Charles Dalby *(IT Manager)*
**Branches:** Walker & Son (Leicester) Ltd, 4A Cheapside, Melton Mowbray, Leicestershire LE13 0TP
**US SIC:** 2099 **UK SIC:** 42399
**Bankers:** HSBC Bank plc (40-11-18)

| | 31-12-13 | 31-12-12 | 31-12-11 |
|---|---|---|---|
| TA | 130,000 | 130,000 | 130,000 |
| NW | 130,000 | 130,000 | 130,000 |

DUNS 21-159-5392 **Imp-Exp**
## Walker Books Ltd
87 Vauxhall Walk, London SE11 5HJ
**Tel:** 020-7793-0909 **Fax:** 020-7587-1123
**Web:** www.walkerbooks.co.uk
**Reg No:** 1378601 **VAT No:** 235379449
**Estd:** 1978 Private Limited Company
**Line of Business:** Publishing of books
**Export Markets:** E U; U S A
**Export Sales:** £44,048,000
**Issued Capital:** £1,000,000
**Directors:** Mrs J L Winterbotham, Mrs K E Lotz, R M Alexander, Ms H Berkman, A Lee, Ms H Mcaleer, I D Mablin, Miss A Van Den Belt
**Responsibilities**
**Senior:** David Heatherwick *(Manager)*, John Mendelson *(Director)*, Mohanie Mohariff *(Manager)*
**Finance:** David Heatherwick *(Manager)*
**Marketing:** Gill Evans *(Publishing Director)*, Denise Johnstone-Burt *(Publisher)*, Molly Main *(Marketing Manager)*
**IT:** Gudrun Claeys *(IT Manager)*
**Facilities:** Bob Wharton *(Facilities Manager)*
**Branches:** Walker Books Ltd, 184-192 Drummond Street, London NW1 3HP
**US SIC:** 2731 **UK SIC:** 47532
**Auditors:** Blick Rothenberg
**Bankers:** HSBC Bank plc (40-03-05)

| | 31-12-13 | 31-12-12 | 31-12-11 |
|---|---|---|---|
| TO | 56,022,000 | 50,856,000 | 50,011,000 |
| P/L | 1,357,000 | 1,151,000 | 1,517,000 |
| NW | 21,273,000 | 20,811,000 | 20,223,000 |
| WC | 20,514,000 | 17,299,000 | 16,708,000 |
| Emp. | 245 | 243 | 237 |

DUNS 29-652-8565
## Walker Bros. Electrical Engineers Ltd
12 Watlington Road, Oxford, Oxfordshire OX4 6NF
**Tel:** 01865-718222
**Reg No:** 1979125 **VAT No:** 434657046
**Estd:** 1986 Private Limited Company
**Line of Business:** Electrical engineers
**Issued Capital:** £1,000
**Director:** R H Pryor
**Co. Secretary:** Martin Clifford
**Responsibilities**
**Finance:** Anita Crawford *(Financial Controller)*
**US SIC:** 8911 **UK SIC:** 83701
**Auditors:** Chapman Worth LLP
**Bankers:** National Westminster Bank Plc (60-70-03)

| | 31-03-14 | 31-03-13 | 31-03-12 |
|---|---|---|---|
| TO | N/A | N/A | 4,442,403 |
| P/L | N/A | N/A | (101,061) |
| NW | 348,847 | 344,604 | 299,525 |
| WC | 256,365 | 236,701 | 214,455 |

DUNS 21-613-9550
## Walker Construction (U.K.) Ltd
Park Farm Road, Folkestone, Kent CT19 5DY
**Tel:** 01303-851-111 **Fax:** 01303-259-439
**Web:** www.walker-construction.co.uk
**Reg No:** 0818974 **VAT No:** 702936639
**Estd:** 1964 Private Limited Company
**Line of Business:** Construction of commercial buildings
**Issued Capital:** £51,511
**Directors:** D A Marshall, S R Walker, P A Webb, P S King
**Co. Secretary:** Paul King
**Responsibilities**
**Senior:** Peter Maddox *(Director)*
**Marketing:** Sue Sharman *(Marketing Coordinator)*
**HR:** Pamela Lilley *(HR Manager)*
**Health & Safety:** Chris Gadd *(Health & Safety Officer)*
**Branches:** Walker Construction (U.k.) Ltd, Park Farm Road, Folkestone, Kent CT19 5DY
**US SIC:** 1541, 1611
**UK SIC:** 50100, 50200
**Auditors:** Donald Jacobs & Partners

**Bankers:** National Westminster Bank Plc (50-41-06)

| | 31-03-14 | 31-03-13 | 31-03-12 |
|---|---|---|---|
| TO | 42,019,044 | 28,492,918 | 28,253,954 |
| P/L | 463,607 | 365,042 | 313,433 |
| NW | 2,580,884 | 2,376,084 | 2,185,636 |
| WC | 2,255,780 | 2,303,969 | 2,259,534 |
| Emp. | 333 | 224 | 218 |

DUNS 28-913-4330
## Walker Crips Group Plc
Finsbury Tower, London EC1Y 8LZ
**Tel:** 020-3100-8000 **Fax:** 02031008001
**Web:** www.wcwb.co.uk
**Reg No:** 1432059 **VAT No:** 333329081
**Estd:** 1979 Public Limited Company
**Line of Business:** Stockbrokers
**Issued Capital:** £2,470,879
**Principals:** R A Fitzgerald *(Financial)*, H M Lim, R A Elliott, M J Rushton, S K Lam, D Gelber, M J Wright, D Hetherton
**Co. Secretary:** David Hall
**Responsibilities**
**Admin:** Martin Fairburn *(Administration Manager)*, Sarah Longstaff *(Administration Manager)*
**Branches:** Walker Crips Group Plc, 1705 High Street, Solihull, West Midlands B93 0LN
**US SIC:** 6211, 6111
**UK SIC:** 83100, 81501
**Auditors:** Deloitte LLP
**Bankers:** HSBC Bank plc (40-05-30)

| | 31-03-14 | 31-03-13 | 31-03-12 |
|---|---|---|---|
| TA | 63,874,000 | 55,682,000 | 66,150,000 |
| P/L | 2,529,000 | 9,103,000 | 769,000 |
| NW | 17,402,000 | 15,355,000 | 8,294,000 |
| WC | 14,088,000 | 8,896,000 | 6,900,000 |
| Emp. | 167 | 142 | 133 |

DUNS 22-810-0079 **Imp-Exp**
## Walker Filtration Ltd
Birtley Road, Washington, Tyne and Wear NE38 9DA
**Tel:** 0191 417 7816
**Web:** www.walkerfiltration.com
**Reg No:** 1726079 **VAT No:** 389626787
**Estd:** 1983 Private Limited Company
**Line of Business:** Manufacturers of filters
**Export Markets:** Worldwide
**Export Sales:** £18,814,126
**Issued Capital:** £153,500
**Principals:** B Walker *(Managing)*, C J Gill, Mrs C A Walker, Ms L Powell
**Co. Secretary:** Robert Welsh
**Branches:** Walker Filtration Ltd, Glover Industrial Estate, Spire Road, Washington, Tyne and Wear NE37 3ES
**US SIC:** 3559, 3542
**UK SIC:** 32863, 32212
**Auditors:** TTR Barnes Ltd
**Bankers:** Lloyds TSB Bank plc (30-98-34)

| | 31-08-13 | 31-08-12 | 31-08-11 |
|---|---|---|---|
| TO | 21,059,892 | 20,311,292 | 19,292,408 |
| P/L | 1,284,678 | 160,741 | 1,238,442 |
| NW | 9,683,859 | 8,542,542 | 8,124,757 |
| WC | 8,850,843 | 7,707,989 | 7,427,556 |
| Emp. | 210 | 204 | 189 |

DUNS 29-279-5127
## Walker Fire (Uk) Ltd
**(Subsidiary of:** Printbetter Ltd)
Unit 2 Roman Way, Preston, Lancashire PR2 5BB
**Tel:** 01772693777 **Fax:** 01772-693760
**Web:** www.walkerfire.com
**Reg No:** 1554539 **VAT No:** 349931126
**Estd:** 1981 Private Limited Company
**Line of Business:** Other retail sale in non-specialised stores
**Issued Capital:** £1,000
**Director:** A J Cosgrove
**Co. Secretary:** David Cosgrove
**Responsibilities**
**Senior:** Stephanie Higgins *(General Manager)*
**Branches:** Walker Fire (Uk) Ltd, Brock House, Walker House, Broxburn, West Lothian EH52 5NB
**US SIC:** 5399 **UK SIC:** 65600
**Auditors:** Moore & Smalley LLP
**Bankers:** The Royal Bank Of Scotland Plc (16-28-33)

| | 31-12-13 | 31-12-12 | 31-12-11 |
|---|---|---|---|
| TO | 5,140,382 | N/A | N/A |
| P/L | 120,233 | 91,215 | (197,484) |
| NW | (1,169,774) | (2,828) | (248,715) |
| WC | 3,651,198 | 3,367,035 | 2,655,834 |
| Emp. | 89 | 52 | 53 |

DUNS 21-833-3052 **Imp-Exp**
## Walker Greenbank Plc.
Gilbert Road, London SW19 1BP
**Tel:** 08002802575 **Fax:** 01908658077
**Web:** www.walkergreenbank.com
**Reg No:** 0061880 **Estd:** 1899 Public Limited Company
**Line of Business:** Management activities of holding companies
**Export Markets:** America, Norway, Continental Europe and the Far East
**Export Sales:** £28,244,000
**Trading Style:** Standfast & Barracks
**Issued Capital:** £590,062
**Principals:** J D Sach *(Financial)*, M D Gant, M S Goldsmith, T G Stannard, D H Smallridge
**Co. Secretary:** Ms Caroline Geary
**Responsibilities**
**Finance:** Dawn Knight *(Accounts Manager)*
**Branches:** Walker Greenbank Plc., Greenbank, Stockport, Cheshire SK4 5NR
**US SIC:** 6711, 2649
**UK SIC:** 83962, 47280
**Auditors:** PricewaterhouseCoopers LLP
**Bankers:** Barclays Bank Plc (20-37-75)

| | 31-01-14 | 31-01-13 | 31-01-12 |
|---|---|---|---|
| TO | 78,434,000 | 75,725,000 | 74,014,000 |
| P/L | 5,495,000 | 4,934,000 | 4,894,000 |
| NW | 19,563,000 | 17,499,000 | 16,941,000 |
| WC | 15,860,000 | 15,278,000 | 14,337,000 |
| Emp. | 592 | 589 | 582 |

DUNS 23-936-8942
## Walker Logistics Ltd
**(Subsidiary of:** Walker Logistics (Holdings) Ltd)
Ramsbury Road, Hungerford, Berkshire RG17 7TG
**Tel:** 0148873848
**Web:** www.walkerlogistics.com
**Reg No:** 3926608 **Estd:** 2000 Private Limited Company
**Line of Business:** Freight transport by road not elsewhere classified
**Issued Capital:** £100
**Directors:** R Montague, P N Walker, W J Walker, Ms A J Hall
**Branches:** Walker Logistics Ltd, Membury Logistics Centre, Hungerford, Berkshire RG17 7TQ
**US SIC:** 4213 **UK SIC:** 72300
**Auditors:** Masons

| | 31-08-13 | 31-08-12 | 31-08-11 |
|---|---|---|---|
| TO | 6,624,392 | N/A | N/A |
| P/L | 533,941 | N/A | N/A |
| NW | 1,135,422 | 965,005 | 920,973 |
| WC | 692,687 | 444,187 | 349,731 |
| Emp. | 53 | N/A | N/A |

DUNS 42-366-8698
## Walker Love
Galgorm Road, Ballymena, Co Antrim BT42 1AD
**Tel:** 02825652214
**Web:** www.walkerlove.com
**VAT No:** 624093455 **Estd:** 1946 Partnership
**Line of Business:** Other scheduled passenger land transport not elsewhere classified
**Partners:** H Hepner, A Walker, D A Walker, B A Walker, J A Walker, J S Hamilton, W P Dolier
**Branches:** Walker Love, 5 South Fergus Place, Kirkcaldy, Fife KY1 1YA
**US SIC:** 4119, 9221
**UK SIC:** 72200, 91300
**Bankers:** Bank Of Scotland (80-54-01)
**Employees:** 70

DUNS 22-901-2018
## Walker Macleod Ltd
8-36 Bulldale Street, Glasgow, Lanarkshire G14 0NU
**Fax:** 0141-950-1351
**Web:** www.walkermacleod.co.uk
**Reg No:** 0075070SC **VAT No:** 353651554
**Estd:** 1981 Private Limited Company
**Line of Business:** Sheet metal fabricators
**Trading Style:** Walker Macleod Ltd
**Issued Capital:** £5,000
**Director:** A R Walker
**Co. Secretary:** Mrs Ellen Walker
**Responsibilities**
**Senior:** Janice Calder *(Finance Manager)*
**Finance:** Janice Calder *(Finance Manager)*
**US SIC:** 3469, 8911
**UK SIC:** 31200, 83701
**Auditors:** Bannerman Johnstone MacLey
**Bankers:** Bank Of Scotland (80-91-27)

| | 31-12-13 | 31-12-12 | 31-12-11 |
|---|---|---|---|
| TO | 4,252,732 | 7,624,626 | N/A |
| P/L | (501,101) | 371,173 | N/A |
| NW | 793,295 | 1,184,511 | 972,113 |
| WC | 492,636 | 811,774 | 716,812 |
| Emp. | 58 | 83 | |

DUNS 51-589-8455
## Walker Modular Ltd
Westmoreland House, Hull, North Humberside HU2 0DJ
**Tel:** 01482586812 **Fax:** 01482590739
**Web:** www.walkermodular.com
**Reg No:** 5870616 **Estd:** 2006 Private Limited Company
**Line of Business:** Other manufacturing not elsewhere classified
**Issued Capital:** £85
**Directors:** P A Trotter, M C Walker, J M Walker, S M Walker
**Co. Secretary:** Lee Davies
**US SIC:** 3999, 2431
**UK SIC:** 49590, 46300

| | 31-03-14 | 31-03-13 | 31-03-12 |
|---|---|---|---|
| TO | 34,819,567 | 19,295,788 | 29,307,517 |
| P/L | 4,454,736 | 3,290,866 | 5,131,510 |
| NW | 12,752,631 | 10,285,975 | 7,670,838 |
| WC | 11,090,753 | 8,774,401 | 6,942,007 |
| Emp. | 154 | 137 | 119 |

DUNS 57-840-0087
## Walker Morris Resources Ltd
Kings Court, 12 King Street, Leeds, West Yorkshire LS1 2HL
**Tel:** 01132832500 **Fax:** 01132-459412
**Web:** www.walkermorris.co.uk
**Reg No:** 2893065 **Estd:** 1994 Private Limited Company
**Line of Business:** Solicitors
**Issued Capital:** £1
**Directors:** P J Mudd, I M Gilbert, D A Smedley
**Co. Secretary:** David Auty
**US SIC:** 8111, 7399
**UK SIC:** 83500, 83954
**Auditors:** PricewaterhouseCoopers

| | 30-04-14 | 30-04-13 | 30-04-12 |
|---|---|---|---|
| TO | 16,786,874 | 14,898,420 | 14,389,778 |
| P/L | 472,079 | N/A | N/A |
| NW | 280,553 | 13,455 | 13,468 |
| WC | 280,549 | 13,451 | 13,464 |
| Emp. | 431 | 413 | 403 |

DUNS 22-905-8482 **Imp**
## Walker Precision Engineering Ltd
4 Fullarton Drive, Glasgow East Investment Park, Glasgow, Lanarkshire G32 8FA
**Tel:** 0141-641-9641 **Fax:** 0141-646-2060
**Web:** www.walkerprecision.com
**Reg No:** 0068820SC **VAT No:** 328725246
**Estd:** 1979 Private Limited Company
**Line of Business:** Manufacture of other machine tools not elsewhere classified
**Issued Capital:** £20,000
**Principals:** J B Walker *(Managing)*, G S Walker, Ms J R Walker
**Co. Secretary:** Mark Walker
**Responsibilities**
**Senior:** fank O'reilly *(Buyer)*
**US SIC:** 3545, 3534
**UK SIC:** 32223, 32553
**Auditors:** BDO Stoy Hayward
**Bankers:** Bank Of Scotland (80-54-01)

| | 30-09-13 | 30-09-12 | 30-09-11 |
|---|---|---|---|
| TO | 15,358,711 | 13,882,453 | 13,947,829 |
| P/L | 516,913 | (42,744) | 575,188 |
| NW | 5,046,065 | 4,688,562 | 4,647,866 |
| WC | 826,180 | 430,851 | 918,391 |
| Emp. | 152 | 150 | 143 |

DUNS 21-579-7477
## Walker Road Primary School
Walker Road, Aberdeen, Aberdeenshire AB11 8DL
**Tel:** 01224879720
**Web:** www.walkerroad.aberdeen.sch.uk
**Estd:** 1990 Partnership
**Line of Business:** General secondary education
**Partners:** Ms C Mcguigan, Mrs J Merchant
**Responsibilities**
**Senior:** Celia McGuigan *(Partner)*
**US SIC:** 8211 **UK SIC:** 93200
**Employees:** 60

DUNS 21-179-0015
## Walker Smith Way Ltd
26-28 Nicholas Street, Chester, Cheshire CH1 2PQ
**Fax:** 01244357444
**Web:** www.walkersmithway.com
**Reg No:** 7016439 **Estd:** 2009 Private Limited Company
**Line of Business:** Solicitors
**Issued Capital:** £50,000
**Directors:** H E Davies, Ms A Woods, B M Dawson, N H Turnbull, D C Rudd, A J Clark, A P Britlin, J Sharples
**Co. Secretary:** Neil Turnbull
**Responsibilities**
**Senior:** Katie Brassington *(Partner)*, Jonathen Clark *(Partner)*, Holly Nelson *(Marketing Manager)*, G Prest *(Senior Partner)*, Toni Ryder *(Marketing Manager)*
**Finance:** Judith Newton *(Accounts Manager)*
**Marketing:** Holly Nelson *(Marketing Manager)*, Elen Rowlands *(Marketing Manager)*
**Sales:** Holly Nelson *(Marketing Manager)*
**IT:** Val Leeming *(IT Executive)*
**Facilities:** A O'Donald *(Facilities Manager)*, Ann O'Donnell *(Facilities Manager)*
**US SIC:** 8111 **UK SIC:** 83500

| | 31-03-14 | 31-03-13 | 31-03-12 |
|---|---|---|---|
| TO | 12,425,948 | 11,715,990 | 12,115,320 |
| P/L | 1,288,291 | 3,017,308 | 3,227,445 |
| NW | 1,573,402 | 138,123 | (3,062,407) |
| WC | 3,891,818 | 3,251,260 | 2,669,005 |
| Emp. | 173 | 179 | 182 |

DUNS 21-809-1293
## Walker Technology College
Waverdale Avenue, Newcastle-Upon-Tyne, Tyne and Wear NE6 4AW
**Tel:** 01912958660
**Web:** www.walkertechnologycollege.co.uk
**Estd:** 2012
**Line of Business:** Higher education
**Responsibilities**
**IT:** Nigel Rackstraw *(Senior Technician/ ICT Analyst)*
**US SIC:** 7399 **UK SIC:** 83954
**Employees:** 130

DUNS 34-850-9600
## Walkerpack Ltd
34 Liliput Road, Brackmills Industrial Estate, Northampton, Northamptonshire NN4 7DT
**Tel:** 01604760529
**Web:** www.walkerpack.co.uk
**Reg No:** 5649769 **Estd:** 2005 Private Limited Company
**Line of Business:** Packagers
**Issued Capital:** £100,100
**Directors:** L S Moss, Ms C A Clarke, Ms J Moss
**Co. Secretary:** Leslie Clarke
**Responsibilities**
**Senior:** Chloe Earle *(Manager)*, Lavinia Walker *(Manager)*, Sophie Walker *(Manager)*
**US SIC:** 7399 **UK SIC:** 83954

| | 31-03-14 | 31-03-13 | 31-03-12 |
|---|---|---|---|
| TA | 1,964,065 | 2,255,069 | 2,179,594 |
| NW | 390,293 | 1,054,280 | 905,089 |
| WC | 310,618 | 587,168 | 519,084 |

DUNS 21-101-9794
## Walkers Fish Restaurants
West Quay, Padstow, Cornwall PL28 8AQ
**Tel:** 01841-532915
**Estd:** 1984 Proprietorship
**Line of Business:** Take away meal outlets - indian
**Proprietor:** R Walker
**US SIC:** 5812 **UK SIC:** 66110
**Bankers:** National Westminster Bank Plc (60-21-37)
**Employees:** 50

DUNS 21-584-5082 **Imp-Exp**
## Walkers Shortbread Ltd
Aberlour House, Aberlour, Banffshire AB38 9LD
**Tel:** 01340-871-555 **Fax:** 01340-871-355
**Web:** www.walkers-shortbread.co.uk
**Reg No:** 0063233SC **VAT No:** 296814415
**Estd:** 1977 Private Limited Company
**Line of Business:** Manufacturers of biscuits
**Export Markets:** Worldwide
**Export Sales:** £58,058,000
**Issued Capital:** £91,908
**Principals:** J N Walker *(Managing)*, Ms M H Walker *(Managing)*, J Walker *(Managing)*, R J Walker, D J Edwards, J N Walker, J B Walker, M J Walker
**Co. Secretary:** Kenneth Fraser
**Responsibilities**
**Senior:** Dennis Allan *(Factory Manager)*
**Facilities:** Alan McTavish *(Engineering Manager)*
**Operations:** Dennis Allan *(Factory Manager)*
**Purchasing:** Joan Grant *(Buyer)*
**Branches:** Walkers Shortbread Ltd, Edgar Road, Elgin, Morayshire IV30 6YQ
**US SIC:** 2052 **UK SIC:** 41970
**Auditors:** Johnston Carmichael LLP
**Bankers:** Clydesdale Bank Plc (82-60-16)

| | 31-12-13 | 31-12-12 | 31-12-11 |
|---|---|---|---|
| TO | 137,139,000 | 123,697,000 | 119,113,000 |
| P/L | 14,473,000 | 14,631,000 | 8,932,000 |
| NW | 72,783,000 | 64,573,000 | 56,479,000 |
| WC | 44,880,000 | 41,176,000 | 35,490,000 |
| Emp. | 1,394 | 1,326 | 1,302 |

DUNS 23-255-1333 **Imp-Exp**
## Walkers Snack Foods Ltd
**(Subsidiary of:** Pepsico Inc.)
1600 Arlington Business Park, Theale, Reading, Berkshire RG7 4SA
**Tel:** 01189-306666 **Fax:** 01189303152
**Web:** www.pepsico.co.uk
**Reg No:** 2333074 **VAT No:** 570065850
**Estd:** 1989 Private Limited Company
**Line of Business:** Manufacture of other food products not elsewhere classified
**Trading Style:** Pepsico Uk & Ireland, Pepsico Uk
**Issued Capital:** £141,370,792
**Directors:** Ms J K Averiss, Ms C E Stone, I L Ellington, Ms V E Evans, A Macdonald, A J Macleod
**Co. Secretary:** Ms Holly King

**Responsibilities**
**Senior:** Simon Ely *(Manufacturing Director)*, Stephen Hendry *(Customer Business Manager)*, Catherine Lentz *(R&D Director)*, Angus MacDonald *(Sales Strategy & Channel Marke)*, John Sigalos *(CFO and Senior Vice President)*, James Stillman *(R&D Director)*, Walter Todd *(Senior Vice President)*
**Finance:** Anwar Ahmed *(Finance Manager)*, John Sigalos *(CFO and Senior Vice President)*
**Marketing:** Laurent Grandet *(Head of Marketing & Innovation)*, Patrick Kalotis *(Head of Marketing & Innovation)*, Angus MacDonald *(Sales Strategy & Channel Marke)*, Neil Macfarlane *(Insights Controller)*, Sebastian Micozzi *(Head of Marketing)*, Evrim Sen *(Marketing Director)*
**Sales:** Graham Essex *(Business Intelligence solution)*, Angus MacDonald *(Sales Strategy & Channel Marke)*, Brynn Zais *(Commercialisation Change Manag)*
**IT:** Ian Shields *(Chief Information Officer)*
**Operations:** Simon Ely *(Manufacturing Director)*, Steve Hills *(?European Contract Manufacturi)*, Mike Jolley *(Technical Operations Manager)*
**Engineering:** Martin Beckford *(Engineering Manager)*, Ian Belton *(Engineering Manager)*
**Branches:** Walkers Snack Foods Ltd, Unit 7, Northfield Way, Newton Aycliffe, County Durham DL5 6EJ
**US SIC:** 7399 **UK SIC:** 83954
**Auditors:** KPMG LLP
**Bankers:** National Westminster Bank Plc (60-00-01)

| | 28-12-13 | 29-12-12 | 31-12-11 |
|---|---|---|---|
| TO | 256,309,000 | 273,089,000 | 256,433,000 |
| P/L | 12,860,000 | 208,000 | 21,620,000 |
| NW | 116,538,000 | 111,574,000 | 110,819,000 |
| WC | 37,167,000 | 61,213,000 | 97,778,000 |
| Emp. | 3,353 | 3,432 | 3,244 |

DUNS 64-079-7130

## Walkers Snacks Ltd

(**Subsidiary of:** Pepsico Inc.)
Pepsico Uk & Ireland, 1600 Arlin, Reading, Berkshire RG7 4SA
**Tel:** 02030036362 **Fax:** 01189-303152
**Web:** www.walkers.co.uk
**Reg No:** 3474989 **Estd:** 1989 Private Limited Company
**Line of Business:** Wholesale of other machinery for use in industry, trade and navigation
**Export Sales:** £4,497,000
**Trading Style:** Pepsico
**Issued Capital:** £500,002
**Directors:** Ms V E Evans, Ms J K Averiss, Ms C E Stone, I L Ellington, A J Macleod, A Macdonald
**Co. Secretary:** Ms Sharon Dean
**Branches:** Walkers Snacks Ltd, Unit 6, Northfield Way, Newton Aycliffe, County Durham DL5 6EJ
**US SIC:** 7399, 5146
**UK SIC:** 83954, 61700
**Auditors:** KPMG LLP

| | 28-12-13 | 29-12-12 | 31-12-11 |
|---|---|---|---|
| TO | 166,282,000 | 170,865,000 | 150,733,000 |
| P/L | 35,740,000 | 274,000 | 83,015,000 |
| NW | 51,223,000 | 26,220,000 | 27,446,000 |
| WC | 54,085,000 | 29,705,000 | 29,344,000 |
| Emp. | 422 | 378 | 328 |

DUNS 21-807-0878 **Imp-Exp**

## Wall Colmonoy Ltd

(**Subsidiary of:** Wall Co. Incorporated)
Alloy Industrial Estate, Pontardawe, Swansea, West Glamorgan SA8 4HL
**Tel:** 01792-862287
**Web:** www.wallcolmonoy.com
**Reg No:** 0788765 **VAT No:** 122359001
**Estd:** 1938 Private Limited Company
**Line of Business:** Other non-ferrous metal production
**Trading Style:** Wall Colmonoy Ltd
**Issued Capital:** £45,000
**Directors:** W P Clark, N Clark, R Verstraete, E Ridge, S J Curtis, Ms A Clark
**Co. Secretary:** Nicholas Clark
**Responsibilities**
**Senior:** Byron Davies *(Warehouse Supervisor)*, Noel Rees *(Warehouse Manager)*, philip tiltson *(Financial director)*, Noel wreath *(Warehouse Manager)*
**Finance:** philip tiltson *(Financial director)*
**Sales:** Gabriele Adams *(Senior Sales Executive)*
**IT:** Peter Skelley *(IT Manager)*
**HR:** Angela Smith *(Human Resources Manager)*
**Facilities:** Noel wreath *(Warehouse Manager)*
**Operations:** Noel wreath *(Warehouse Manager)*
**US SIC:** 3339 **UK SIC:** 22470
**Auditors:** Broomfield & Alexander Ltd

**Bankers:** Barclays Bank Plc (20-84-41)

| | 31-12-13 | 31-12-12 | 31-12-11 |
|---|---|---|---|
| TO | 33,197,000 | 37,713,000 | 43,650,000 |
| P/L | 294,000 | (808,000) | 3,681,000 |
| NW | 14,605,000 | 13,933,000 | 14,864,000 |
| WC | 7,810,000 | 7,794,000 | 9,171,000 |
| Emp. | 232 | 248 | 256 |

DUNS 21-822-3667 **Exp**

## The Wall Engineering Co Ltd

Cromer Road, North Walsham, Norfolk NR28 0NB
**Tel:** 01692-403701
**Web:** www.wallengineering.co.uk
**Reg No:** 0471090 **VAT No:** 105853675
**Estd:** 1949 Private Limited Company
**Line of Business:** Engineers (structural)
**Export Markets:** E U
**Issued Capital:** £85,743
**Principals:** A R Bell *(Managing)*, P B Hemstock *(Commercial)*, R S Mcculloch, S C Tully, T J Ford
**Co. Secretary:** Keith Bindley
**US SIC:** 1622, 1799
**UK SIC:** 50200, 50000
**Auditors:** Grant Thornton UK LLP
**Bankers:** The Royal Bank Of Scotland Plc (15-10-00)

| | 31-03-14 | 31-03-13 | 31-03-12 |
|---|---|---|---|
| TO | 7,682,235 | 4,668,817 | 7,565,166 |
| P/L | 200,017 | (352,568) | 136,367 |
| NW | 3,592,901 | 3,385,277 | 3,668,681 |
| WC | 3,335,125 | 3,109,477 | 3,361,040 |
| Emp. | 59 | 54 | 57 |

DUNS 73-924-0146

## Wall Family Europe Ltd

Grange House, Geddings Road, Hoddesdon, Hertfordshire EN11 0NT
**Tel:** 01992454500 **Fax:** 01992454560
**Web:** www.demcoeurope.eu
**Reg No:** 5177177 **Estd:** 2004 Private Limited Company
**Line of Business:** Business and management consultancy activities not elsewhere classified
**Export Sales:** £5,371,000
**Issued Capital:** £9,315,121
**Directors:** Ms A M Wall, P Wall, Ms L J Cross, Ms L M Mcdonald, Ms S Brandmeier, P Wall, S Holdeman, R Conway
**Co. Secretary:** Hs Secretarial Limited
**Responsibilities**
**Senior:** David Southern *(Manager)*
**HR:** Sue Armes *(HR Manager)*
**US SIC:** 7392 **UK SIC:** 83951

| | 31-12-13 | 31-12-12 | 31-12-11 |
|---|---|---|---|
| TO | 47,887,000 | 44,635,000 | 23,963,000 |
| P/L | 901,000 | 813,000 | 632,000 |
| NW | 4,438,000 | 4,672,000 | (132,000) |
| WC | 2,843,000 | 2,967,000 | 1,550,000 |
| Emp. | 317 | 302 | 179 |

DUNS 21-930-9259

## Wall Lag (Wales) Ltd

Bromfield Lane, Bromfield Industrial Estate, Mold, Clwyd CH7 1HA
**Fax:** 01352755643
**Web:** www.printcentrewales.co.uk
**Reg No:** 1301528 **VAT No:** 479094011
**Estd:** 1974 Private Limited Company
**Line of Business:** Painting and glazing
**Trading Style:** Snowdonia Windows & Doors
**Issued Capital:** £25,000
**Principals:** A J Wheatley *(Managing)*, R C Griffiths
**Co. Secretary:** Alan Wheatley
**Responsibilities**
**Senior:** James Flanagan *(Manager)*
**US SIC:** 1721, 1799
**UK SIC:** 50400, 50000
**Auditors:** Guy Walmsley & Co
**Bankers:** Lloyds TSB Bank plc (30-99-95)

| | 31-03-14 | 31-03-13 | 31-03-12 |
|---|---|---|---|
| TA | 1,660,805 | 1,857,516 | 1,882,400 |
| NW | 793,598 | 1,243,398 | 1,096,518 |
| WC | 421,622 | 844,744 | 677,609 |

DUNS 21-525-6608

## Wall Street Systems

50 Victoria Embankment, London EC4Y 0DW
**Tel:** 02031703000
**Web:** www.wallstreetsystems.com
**Estd:** 1994
**Line of Business:** Computer software (development)
**Director:** S Middlehurst
**Responsibilities**
**Health & Safety:** Lindsay Clayden *(Facilities Manager)*
**Facilities:** Lindsay Clayden *(Facilities Manager)*
**US SIC:** 7379 **UK SIC:** 83940
**Employees:** 150

DUNS 42-435-0262 **Imp**

## Wall Street Systems Services Corp

(**Subsidiary of:** Itt Sa)
160 Queen Victoria Street, London EC4V 4BF
**Tel:** 020 3170 3000 **Fax:** 020 3170 3001
**Web:** www.wallstreetsystems.com
**Reg No:** 0017941FC **Estd:** 1994 Foreign Company
**Line of Business:** IT solutions provider
**Directors:** A Triplett, J M Patrina, J W Strouss, J A Patrina
**Co. Secretary:** Lucien Kneip
**Responsibilities**
**Senior:** Tony White *(Manager)*
**US SIC:** 7379 **UK SIC:** 83940

DUNS 22-189-2362

## Wall to Wall Media Ltd

(**Subsidiary of:** Shed Media Ltd)
85 Grays Inn Road, London WC1X 8TX
**Tel:** 02074857424
**Web:** www.walltowall.co.uk
**Reg No:** 4207414 **Estd:** 2001 Private Limited Company
**Line of Business:** Television activities
**Export Sales:** £7,466,000
**Issued Capital:** £2
**Directors:** T W Downing, Miss C E Hungate
**Responsibilities**
**Senior:** Helena Ely *(Manager)*, Nicholas Southgate *(Manager)*
**US SIC:** 4833 **UK SIC:** 97411
**Auditors:** Baker Tilly UK Audit LLP
**Bankers:** Barclays Bank Plc (20-71-74)

| | 31-12-13 | 31-12-12 | 31-12-11 |
|---|---|---|---|
| TO | 42,729,000 | 41,044,000 | 25,246,509 |
| P/L | 8,680,000 | 5,619,000 | 4,152,983 |
| NW | 10,360,000 | 7,449,000 | 7,165,380 |
| WC | 10,882,000 | 7,813,000 | 4,542,481 |
| Emp. | 140 | 115 | 73 |

DUNS 54-895-5327 **Imp**

## The Wallace Collection

Hertford House, Manchester Square, London W1U 3BN
**Tel:** 02075639500
**Web:** www.wallacecollection.org
**Estd:** 2000
**Line of Business:** Operation of arts facilities
**Trading Style:** Hertford House Marketing
**Principals:** Hon S Sainsbury *(Chairman)*, J Lewis, L Egremont
**Responsibilities**
**Senior:** Christoph Vogtherr *(Head of Collections and Curato)*
**Finance:** Clare Obrien *(Finance Advisor)*, Phil Walsh *(Financial Director)*
**Facilities:** Keith Welch *(Facilities Manager)*
**US SIC:** 7911 **UK SIC:** 97913
**Employees:** 200

DUNS 64-721-1655

## Wallace Engineering

50 Soldierstown Road, Aghalee, Craigavon, Co Armagh BT67 0ET
**Web:** www.wallace-engineering.co.uk
**Estd:** 1995 Proprietorship
**Line of Business:** Engineers (general)
**Proprietor:** G Rogan
**US SIC:** 8911 **UK SIC:** 83701
**Employees:** 172

DUNS 21-777-7132

## Wallace Hall Academy

Station Road, Thornhill, Thornhill, Dumfriesshire DG3 5DS
**Tel:** 01848332120
**Web:** www.wallacehallacademy.co.uk
**Estd:** 2002 Proprietorship
**Line of Business:** Schools (local authority)
**Proprietor:** B Graham
**Responsibilities**
**Finance:** Diana Jarvre *(Finance Manager)*
**Admin:** Ann-Marie Smith *(Office Manager)*
**IT:** Simon Myatt *(ICT Manager)*
**US SIC:** 8211 **UK SIC:** 93200
**Employees:** 100

DUNS 23-664-6758

## Wallace High School

12a Clonevin Park, Lisburn, Co Antrim BT28 3AD
**Tel:** 028-9267-2311
**Web:** www.wallacehigh.org
**Estd:** 2002 Partnership
**Line of Business:** General secondary education
**Principals:** G K Sutton *(Chairman)*, E G Taylor, Mrs D O'Hare *(Partner)*, Mrs D O'Hare *(Partner)*
**Responsibilities**
**Senior:** Deborah O' Hare *(CEO, Managing Director)*, Greaham Sutton *(Chairperson)*, Greaham Sutton *(Chairperson)*
**IT:** Colin Napier *(ICT Technician)*
**US SIC:** 8211 **UK SIC:** 93200
**Bankers:** Ulster Bank Ltd (98-09-60)
**Employees:** 100

DUNS 21-401-5331 **Imp**

## Wallace McDowall Ltd

(**Subsidiary of:** Wmd Holdings Ltd)
Spirit Aerosystems, Tarbolton Road, Prestwick, Ayrshire KA9 2RR
**Tel:** 01292670500
**Web:** www.wallacemcdowall.com
**Reg No:** 0046491SC **VAT No:** 264001795
**Estd:** 1960 Private Limited Company
**Line of Business:** Manufacture of metal structures and parts of structures
**Export Sales:** £613,823
**Trading Style:** Solder Pallet Solutions
**Issued Capital:** £487,176
**Principals:** J Wilson *(Managing)*, L Collins
**Co. Secretary:** Ms Yvonne Ward
**Responsibilities**
**Senior:** Martin Doolan *(Manager)*
**US SIC:** 3441, 3499
**UK SIC:** 32042, 31694
**Auditors:** William Duncan & Co
**Bankers:** Bank Of Scotland (80-12-39)

| | 31-12-13 | 31-12-12 | 31-12-11 |
|---|---|---|---|
| TO | 9,182,999 | 9,081,533 | 8,528,961 |
| P/L | 198,362 | 175,924 | 372,973 |
| NW | 1,828,095 | 1,522,877 | 1,672,997 |
| WC | 235,384 | 131,617 | 434,810 |
| Emp. | 159 | 155 | 140 |

DUNS 21-389-3087

## Wallace View Care Home

77 Westhaugh Road, Stirling, Stirlingshire FK9 5GF
**Tel:** 01786241339
**Web:** www.countrywidecarehomes.co.uk
**Estd:** 2008
**Line of Business:** Residential care establishments
**Partners:** Mrs J Mcgregor, G Downie
**US SIC:** 8321 **UK SIC:** 96111
**Employees:** 50

DUNS 39-974-4127

## Wallace Whittle Ltd

(**Subsidiary of:** Tüv Süd E.V.)
8 Elmbank Gardens, Glasgow, Lanarkshire G2 4NQ
**Tel:** 01412219866 **Fax:** 0141-221-6088
**Web:** www.wallacewhittle.com
**Reg No:** 0111930SC **Estd:** 1988 Private Limited Company
**Line of Business:** Engineers (consulting)
**Issued Capital:** £1,140,999
**Directors:** W J Mcknight, B R Mayberry, M Valente
**Co. Secretary:** William Mcknight
**Responsibilities**
**Senior:** David Clabby *(Manager)*, Ian Docherty *(Manager)*, Keith Howell *(Manager)*, Alan Mcgill *(Manager)*
**Branches:** Wallace Whittle Ltd, 166 Great Western Road, Aberdeen, Aberdeenshire AB10 6QE
**US SIC:** 8911 **UK SIC:** 83701
**Auditors:** Gerber Landa & Gee
**Bankers:** Clydesdale Bank Plc (82-64-34)

| | 31-12-13 | 31-12-12 | 31-12-11 |
|---|---|---|---|
| TO | N/A | N/A | 9,795,000 |
| P/L | N/A | N/A | (1,494,000) |
| NW | 5,269,000 | 5,269,000 | 5,269,000 |
| Emp. | N/A | N/A | 123 |

DUNS 64-105-3991

## Wallasey Cars Ltd

20 Liscard Village, Wallasey, Merseyside CH45 4JP
**Fax:** 0151-201-3020
**Web:** www.wallaseycars.co.uk
**Reg No:** 4508871 **Estd:** 1988 Private Limited Company
**Line of Business:** Taxis and private hire vehicles
**Issued Capital:** £3,125
**Directors:** J Robinson, S J Spence, G Graham
**Responsibilities**
**Senior:** Damian Grealis *(Manager)*
**US SIC:** 4121 **UK SIC:** 72200

| | 30-09-14 | 30-09-13 | 30-09-12 |
|---|---|---|---|
| TA | 138,458 | 136,675 | 148,362 |
| NW | (28,584) | (31,537) | (28,485) |
| WC | (56,917) | (62,223) | (60,513) |

DUNS 21-779-3224

## The Walled Garden of Cannington

Church Street, Cannington, Cannington, Bridgwater, Somerset TA5 2HA
**Tel:** 01278655042
**Web:** www.canningtonwalledgardens.co.uk
**Estd:** 2010 Proprietorship
**Line of Business:** Places of interest
**Proprietor:** Mrs J Wagner
**US SIC:** 8411 **UK SIC:** 97700
**Employees:** 160

DUNS 84-694-8271

## Wallenius Wilhelmsen Logistics Terminals (Uk) Ltd

(**Subsidiary of:** Wallenius Wilhelmsen Logistics As)
Dock Gate 4, Southampton, Hampshire SO14 3GG
**Tel:** 02380637233
**Web:** www.2wglobal.com
**Reg No:** 6226290 **Estd:** 2007 Private Limited Company
**Line of Business:** Distribution service providers
**Issued Capital:** £100
**Directors:** J P Speakman, Captain M A Bookham, J A Boman, T K Fritzen
**Co. Secretary:** Ms Caroline Marshall
**Responsibilities**
**Senior:** Paul reeves *(Manager)*
**Branches:** Wallenius Wilhelmsen Logistics Terminals (Uk) Ltd, Po Box 4, Export Car Pk, Seaforth, Liverpool, Merseyside L21 1JH
**US SIC:** 4712 **UK SIC:** 77002

| | 31-12-13 | 31-12-12 | 31-12-11 |
|---|---|---|---|
| TA | 1 | 1 | 1 |
| NW | 1 | 1 | 1 |

DUNS 42-438-5482

## Walletts Ltd

Adventure Place, Stoke-On-Trent, Staffordshire ST1 3AF
**Tel:** 01782-212326
**Web:** www.walletts.co.uk
**Reg No:** 3304471 **Estd:** 1997 Private Limited Company
**Line of Business:** Accounting activities
**Issued Capital:** £100
**Directors:** D L Bould, M Tatton, D Fox
**Co. Secretary:** Keith Salt
**Branches:** Walletts Ltd, 3 Adventure Pl, Stoke-On-Trent, Staffordshire ST1 3AG
**US SIC:** 8931 **UK SIC:** 83600

| | 31-03-14 | 31-03-13 | 31-03-12 |
|---|---|---|---|
| TA | 28,000 | 31,000 | 94,000 |
| NW | (100,650) | (100,650) | (100,650) |

DUNS 21-717-9340 **Exp**

## Wallgate Ltd

(**Subsidiary of:** E.V. Naish Ltd)
Crow Lane, Wilton, Salisbury, Wiltshire SP2 0HB
**Tel:** 01722-744594
**Web:** www.wallgate.com
**Reg No:** 0156022 **VAT No:** 188203945
**Estd:** 1869 Private Limited Company
**Line of Business:** Sanitary services
**Export Markets:** Europe; Australia; U S A; Middle East
**Export Sales:** £988,164
**Issued Capital:** £10,000
**Directors:** D J Beale, G D Naish, T F Powell
**Co. Secretary:** Mrs Melissa Poore
**Responsibilities**
**Senior:** Phil Pawn *(Commercial Manager)*, Philip Thorne *(Commercial Manager)*
**Sales:** Marie Ashton *(Sales Order Processor)*, Jean Donovan *(Business Development Manager)*
**Purchasing:** Barry Gollins *(Purchasing Manager)*
**US SIC:** 2647, 3999
**UK SIC:** 47220, 49590
**Auditors:** Fawcetts
**Bankers:** Lloyds TSB Bank plc (30-97-41)

| | 30-09-13 | 30-09-12 | 30-09-11 |
|---|---|---|---|
| TO | 6,022,913 | 5,579,355 | 7,323,264 |
| P/L | 785,738 | 610,123 | 732,218 |
| NW | 2,519,616 | 2,208,611 | 1,984,229 |
| WC | 2,058,962 | 1,821,502 | 1,459,051 |
| Emp. | 50 | 51 | 56 |

DUNS 76-984-8888

## Wallich-Clifford Community

The Wallich Centre, Cathedral Road, Cardiff, South Glamorgan CF11 9JF
**Tel:** 029-2066-8464
**Web:** www.thewallich.com
**Reg No:** 2642780 **Estd:** 1978 Private Limited Company
**Line of Business:** Charities and charitable organisations
**Directors:** Mrs S E Cleverley, Ms S L Botterill, Ms A J Clarke, D J Hampson, R P Dubrow-Marshall, M J Thomas, Mrs H C Phillips, S Sanders
**Co. Secretary:** Darren Pritchard
**Responsibilities**
**Senior:** Albert Bates *(Manager)*, Antonia Watson *(Chief Executive)*
**Branches:** Wallich-Clifford Community, 30 Bridge Street, Newport, Gwent NP20 4BG
**US SIC:** 7021, 8321
**UK SIC:** 66500, 96111
**Auditors:** John Smart
**Bankers:** Allied Irish Bank (gb) (23-85-86)

| | 31-03-14 | 31-03-13 | 31-03-12 |
|---|---|---|---|
| TO | 9,813,814 | 10,068,916 | 9,247,182 |
| P/L | 468,600 | 1,317,783 | 337,584 |
| NW | 8,453,267 | 7,984,667 | 6,666,884 |
| WC | 2,663,742 | 2,141,752 | 1,696,805 |
| Emp. | 227 | 238 | 243 |

DUNS 23-590-2434 **Imp**

## Wallingford Systems Ltd

(**Subsidiary of:** H R Wallingford Group Ltd)
Howbery Park, Wallingford, Oxfordshire OX10 8BA
**Tel:** 01491835381
**Web:** www.hrwallingford.co.uk
**Reg No:** 2288719 **Estd:** 2007 Private Limited Company
**Line of Business:** Research and laboratory based activities
**Trading Style:** H R Wallingford
**Issued Capital:** £2
**Directors:** Dr S W Huntington, Mrs L K Patterson
**Co. Secretary:** Ms Nicole Norris
**Responsibilities**
**Senior:** Stuart Stripling *(Project Manager)*
**IT:** David Ramsbottom *(Technical Director)*
**Branches:** Wallingford Systems Ltd, 8 Boyd Orr Cr, Kilmarnock, Ayrshire KA3 2QB
**US SIC:** 8911 **UK SIC:** 83701
**Auditors:** Grant Thornton UK LLP
**Bankers:** Lloyds TSB Bank plc (30-91-31)

| | 31-03-14 | 31-03-12 |
|---|---|---|
| TA | 2 | 100,000 |
| P/L | N/A | (899,000) |
| NW | 2 | 100,000 |

DUNS 49-388-6840

## Wallington Cars & Couriers Ltd

Jane Seymour House, 23 Ewell Road, Cheam, Sutton, Surrey SM3 8DD
**Tel:** 02084010203 **Fax:** 02084086880
**Web:** www.wallingtoncars.com
**Reg No:** 3135724 **VAT No:** 681672706
**Estd:** 1981 Private Limited Company
**Line of Business:** Couriers
**Issued Capital:** £1,000
**Managing Director:** C M Palmer
**Co. Secretary:** Ms Rebecca Palmer
**Responsibilities**
**Finance:** Steve Duncan *(Financial Manager)*
**Health & Safety:** Dave Palmer *(Operations Manager)*
**US SIC:** 4213 **UK SIC:** 72300
**Auditors:** Finerty Brice
**Bankers:** National Westminster Bank Plc (56-00-46)

| | 30-09-14 | 30-09-13 | 30-09-12 |
|---|---|---|---|
| TO | 4,520,988 | 4,270,195 | 4,372,683 |
| P/L | 223,381 | 262,392 | 268,965 |
| NW | 1,061,186 | 1,033,279 | 962,001 |
| WC | 694,692 | 763,699 | 740,495 |

DUNS 21-726-1391

## Wallington County Grammar School

Croydon Road, Wallington, Surrey SM6 7PH
**Tel:** 02086472235
**Web:** www.wcgs.org.uk
**Reg No:** 7627302 **Estd:** 2011 Private Company Limited By Guarantee
**Line of Business:** General secondary education
**Directors:** J J Wilden, P Huitson, A Ghazanfar, H Ruparelia, J R Diamond, Mrs A Ali, A J Andre, N J Mogridge
**Co. Secretary:** Richard Baker
**Responsibilities**
**Senior:** Folashade Ambrose *(Director)*, Kevin Plummer *(Chairman)*, Anne Rodrigues *(Chairwoman)*, Suresh Sundaramurthy *(Director)*
**US SIC:** 8211 **UK SIC:** 93200
**Bankers:** Lloyds TSB Bank plc (30-00-00)

| | 31-08-13 | 31-08-12 |
|---|---|---|
| TO | 6,431,000 | 21,423,000 |
| P/L | 921,000 | 14,169,000 |
| NW | 14,975,000 | 14,060,000 |
| WC | 27,000 | 81,000 |
| Emp. | 90 | 96 |

DUNS 21-166-5265

## Wallington High School for Girls

Woodcote Road, Wallington, Surrey SM6 0PH
**Tel:** 02086472380
**Web:** www.wallingtongirls.sutton.sch.uk
**Estd:** 1978 Proprietorship
**Line of Business:** Schools (foundation)
**Proprietor:** Mrs B Greatorex
**Responsibilities**
**Senior:** Athar Akram *(Manager)*, Justine Allen *(Manager)*, Rosemary Allotey *(Manager)*, Hamza Aumeer *(Manager)*, Robert Etchell *(Manager)*, David Forsdyke *(Manager)*, Sandra Gillett *(Manager)*, Barbara Greatorex *(Head Teacher)*, Frederick Mundle *(Manager)*, Alison Myerscough *(Manager)*, Nigel Pepper *(Manager)*, Eveline Reynolds-Boison *(Manager)*, Ramakrishnan Venkatakrishna *(Manager)*, Victoria Watson *(Manager)*
**US SIC:** 8211 **UK SIC:** 93200
**Employees:** 150

DUNS 22-232-8812

## Wallis Retail Ltd

(**Subsidiary of:** Taveta Ltd)
Colegrave House, 68-70 Berners Street, London W1T 3NL
**Tel:** 01419527786
**Web:** www.wallis.co.uk
**Reg No:** 4250825 **Estd:** 2003 Private Limited Company
**Line of Business:** Ladies fashionwear (retail)
**Export Sales:** £8,151,000
**Trading Style:** Arcadia Group Plc
**Issued Capital:** £6,700
**Directors:** Ms M J Gammon, Mrs S Wightman, R L Burchill, R Dedombal, Mrs G Hague
**Co. Secretary:** Ms Rebecca Flaherty
**Responsibilities**
**Senior:** Gurpal Premi *(Manager)*, Aisha Waldron *(Manager)*
**Branches:** Wallis Retail Ltd, 4 Risman Place, Workington, Cumbria CA14 3DU
**US SIC:** 5621 **UK SIC:** 64500
**Auditors:** PricewaterhouseCoopers LLP

| | 31-08-13 | 25-08-12 | 27-08-11 |
|---|---|---|---|
| TO | 167,270,000 | 167,406,000 | 175,911,000 |
| P/L | (233,000) | 303,000 | (9,541,000) |
| NW | 99,040,000 | 96,487,000 | 93,560,000 |
| WC | 100,658,000 | 94,982,000 | 88,755,000 |
| Emp. | 2,502 | 2,623 | 3,005 |

DUNS 21-613-3868 **Imp**

## Wallop Defence Systems Ltd

(**Subsidiary of:** Esterline Technologies Corp)
Craydown Lane, Middle Wallop, Stockbridge, Hampshire SO20 8DX
**Tel:** 01264781456
**Web:** www.wallopdefence.com
**Reg No:** 0675623 **VAT No:** 107893353
**Estd:** 1960 Private Limited Company
**Line of Business:** Manufacturers of security equipment suppliers and
**Export Sales:** £7,363,000
**Trading Style:** Wdsl, Esterline Corporation
**Issued Capital:** £30,800
**Directors:** J D Brandt, R D George, J R Etherton, J P Hunt, K J Smart
**Co. Secretary:** Taylor Wessing Secretaries Limit
**Responsibilities**
**Senior:** John Grey *(Maintenance Manager)*, Ian Sandell *(Warehouse Officer)*
**US SIC:** 7393 **UK SIC:** 83954
**Auditors:** Ernst & Young LLP
**Bankers:** HSBC Bank plc (40-21-03)

| | 25-10-13 | 26-10-12 | 28-10-11 |
|---|---|---|---|
| TO | 14,936,000 | 11,624,000 | 16,699,000 |
| P/L | (2,106,000) | (4,241,000) | (4,671,000) |
| NW | 7,336,000 | 8,885,000 | 12,190,000 |
| WC | (7,964,000) | (7,483,000) | (4,782,000) |
| Emp. | 151 | 143 | 193 |

DUNS 73-379-1680

## Walls & Floors Ltd

Garrard Way, Telford Way Industrial Estate, Kettering, Northamptonshire NN16 8TD
**Tel:** 01536410484
**Web:** www.wallsandfloors.co.uk
**Reg No:** 4652706 **Estd:** 2003 Private Limited Company
**Line of Business:** Tile wholesalers and suppliers
**Issued Capital:** £100,000
**Directors:** J P Steel, R W Greenbank, G Spencer
**Co. Secretary:** Duncan Lewin
**US SIC:** 5039 **UK SIC:** 61300

| | 31-03-14 | 31-03-13 | 31-03-12 |
|---|---|---|---|
| TO | 24,406,492 | 19,085,306 | 18,631,726 |
| P/L | 937,920 | (1,298,521) | 773,726 |
| NW | 1,506,452 | 863,185 | 776,796 |
| WC | 1,277,830 | 556,011 | 535,867 |
| Emp. | 125 | 118 | 113 |

DUNS 21-862-7792 **Imp**

## Wallwork Heat Treatment Ltd

(**Subsidiary of:** Wht Holdings Ltd)
Lord Street, Bury, Lancashire BL9 0RE
**Tel:** 0161-797-9111
**Web:** www.wallworkht.com
**Reg No:** 0640305 **Estd:** 1959 Private Limited Company
**Line of Business:** Heat treatment (metals)
**Export Sales:** £196,179
**Issued Capital:** £2,629
**Directors:** I C Griffin, S P Collins, R P Carpenter, M Jarvis, Miss S J Wallwork, H A Wallwork
**Co. Secretary:** Mrs Carole Chettoe
**Responsibilities**
**Senior:** Chris Stretton *(Manager)*
**Sales:** John Copple *(Internal Sales)*, Ian Lacey *(Technical Sales)*, Howard Maher *(Sales Manager)*
**Admin:** Wendy Boniface *(Administration Manager)*
**HR:** Wendy Boniface *(Administration Manager)*
**Operations:** Chris Stretton *(Manager)*
**Fleet:** Gary Bannister *(Transport Manager)*
**US SIC:** 3398 **UK SIC:** 31380
**Auditors:** Ajp
**Bankers:** National Westminster Bank Plc (01-05-31)

| | 31-03-14 | 31-03-13 | 31-03-12 |
|---|---|---|---|
| TO | 8,430,712 | 7,622,262 | 7,608,771 |
| P/L | 470,288 | 318,148 | 521,748 |
| NW | 2,017,116 | 1,638,533 | 1,398,914 |
| WC | 652,050 | 184,121 | (34,422) |
| Emp. | 107 | 101 | 101 |

DUNS 36-511-5828

## Walmley Infant School

Walmley Ash Road, Sutton Coldfield, West Midlands B76 1JB
**Tel:** 0121-351-1355
**Web:** www.walmleyinfantschool.co.uk
**Estd:** 1996
**Line of Business:** Schools (local authority)
**Proprietor:** Miss C Allens
**Responsibilities**
**Senior:** Helen Murphy *(Head Teacher)*
**US SIC:** 8211 **UK SIC:** 93200
**Employees:** 50

DUNS 22-282-1055

## Walnut Care Ltd

Northorpe Road, Spilsby, Lincolnshire PE23 5NZ
**Tel:** 07747011138 **Fax:** 01790-755613
**Web:** www.walnutcare.co.uk
**Reg No:** 4300065 **Estd:** 2002 Private Limited Company
**Line of Business:** Home care service providers
**Trading Style:** Walnut Care At Home
**Issued Capital:** £5,000
**Director:** D A Weatherley
**Co. Secretary:** Mrs Melanie Weatherley
**Branches:** Walnut Care Ltd, Walnut Cottage, Copping Syke, Boston, Lincolnshire PE22 7AP
**US SIC:** 8091 **UK SIC:** 95200
**Auditors:** Duncan & Toplis
**Bankers:** The Royal Bank Of Scotland Plc (16-18-18)

| | 07-02-14 | 08-02-13 | 06-02-12 |
|---|---|---|---|
| TA | 504,363 | 487,446 | 436,189 |
| NW | 57,285 | 17,537 | (22,162) |
| WC | 207,083 | 188,523 | 179,724 |

DUNS 22-952-4863 **Imp-Exp**

## Walraven Ltd

(**Subsidiary of:** Stichting Administratiekantoor J. Van Walraven Hol)
Thorpe Way, Banbury, Oxfordshire OX16 4UU
**Tel:** 01295-753400 **Fax:** 01295-753428
**Web:** www.walraven.com
**Reg No:** 1352033 **Estd:** 1978 Private Limited Company
**Line of Business:** Fabricated metal products
**Export Markets:** E U, Middle East
**Issued Capital:** £2,981,624
**Directors:** J Van Walraven Holding Bv, G A Gardner
**Responsibilities**
**Senior:** Brian Boxer *(Manager)*
**Finance:** Katherine Humphries *(Finance Manager)*
**Marketing:** Sarah Johnstone *(Marketing & Communications Man)*
**Sales:** Stephen Duck *(Regional Sales Manager)*, Andy Hird *(Regional Sales Manager)*, Terry Oliver *(Business Development Manager)*, Dean Shotton *(Regional Sales Manager)*, Rob Staniforth *(Regional Sales Manager)*, Rod Tay *(Regional Sales Manager)*, Rachel Watts *(Sales Office Manager)*
**Admin:** Rachel Watts *(Sales Office Manager)*
**Branches:** Walraven Ltd, Ringlestone Farm, Warbury La, Woking, Surrey GU21 2TX
**US SIC:** 3441, 5084
**UK SIC:** 32042, 61490
**Auditors:** Burgis & Bullock
**Bankers:** National Westminster Bank Plc (60-01-35)

| | 31-12-13 | 31-12-12 | 31-12-11 |
|---|---|---|---|
| TA | 2,918,761 | 2,611,616 | 2,731,868 |
| NW | 2,193,352 | 2,008,631 | 1,927,355 |
| WC | 2,099,350 | 1,910,139 | 1,798,506 |

DUNS 22-233-3028
## Walsall City Academy Trust
Lichfield Road, Walsall, West Midlands WS3 3LX
**Tel:** 01922-493910
**Web:** www.walsallacademy.com
**Reg No:** 4251277 **Estd:** 2001 Private Company Limited By Guarantee
**Line of Business:** Schools (independent)
**Trading Style:** Walsall City Academy Trust
**Directors:** Ms N L Latham, C H Whittington, Ms T M Littlefield, S P Murray, M S Parker, G J Smith, Mrs S C Percox, T D Watney
**Co. Secretary:** Mrs Michelle Davies
**Responsibilities**
**Senior:** Vivienne Evans *(Headmistress)*, Georgina Ruoss *(Director)*
**US SIC:** 8211 **UK SIC:** 93200

| | 31-08-14 | 31-08-13 | 31-08-12 |
|---|---|---|---|
| TO | 6,993,054 | 6,942,356 | 6,737,805 |
| P/L | (468,900) | (434,178) | (450,211) |
| NW | 12,945,612 | 13,238,512 | 13,583,690 |
| WC | 755,864 | 736,326 | 712,515 |
| Emp. | 141 | 156 | 159 |

DUNS 23-082-8373
## Walsall College of Arts & Technology
Littleton Street West, Walsall, West Midlands WS2 8ES
**Tel:** 01922-657000
**Web:** www.walcat.ac.uk
**Estd:** 1993
**Line of Business:** First-degree level higher education
**Directors:** Mrs R Gray, Mrs R Gray
**Branches:** Walsall College Of Arts & Technology, 14 Caldmore Grn, Walsall, West Midlands WS1 3RL
**US SIC:** 8221 **UK SIC:** 93100
**Employees:** 577

DUNS 21-773-1703
## Walsall Council - Parks & Open Spaces
Environmental Depot, 200 Pelsall Road, Brownhills, Walsall, West Midlands WS8 7EN
**Tel:** 01922653344
**Web:** www.walsall.gov.uk
**Estd:** 2011 Proprietorship
**Line of Business:** Parks & gardens
**Proprietor:** N Ilsley
**US SIC:** 8411 **UK SIC:** 97700
**Employees:** 100

DUNS 28-830-4397
## The Walsall Football Club Ltd
Bescot Crescent, Walsall, West Midlands WS1 4SA
**Tel:** 01922622791 **Fax:** 01922-613202
**Web:** www.walsallfc.co.uk
**Reg No:** 0171970 **VAT No:** 100722236
**Estd:** 1920 Private Limited Company
**Line of Business:** Retail sale of sports goods, games and toys, stamps and coins
**Issued Capital:** £50,000
**Principals:** K R Whalley *(Commercial)*, N C Bond, J W Bonser, L M Pomlett, R E Tisdale, S Gamble, P J Gilman
**Co. Secretary:** Stefan Gamble
**Responsibilities**
**Health & Safety:** Dave Storr *(Stadium Manager)*
**Facilities:** Ian Hibkiss *(Facilities Manager)*, Dave Storr *(Stadium Manager)*
**Branches:** The Walsall Football Club Ltd, 1 Bradford Street, Walsall, West Midlands WS1 1NX
**US SIC:** 5941, 5812
**UK SIC:** 65400, 66110
**Auditors:** BDO Stoy Hayward
**Bankers:** Barclays Bank Plc (20-90-08)

| | 31-05-14 | 31-05-13 | 31-05-12 |
|---|---|---|---|
| TO | 5,298,000 | 4,759,000 | 5,049,000 |
| P/L | 19,000 | 23,000 | 10,000 |
| NW | 3,049,000 | 3,030,000 | 3,007,000 |
| WC | (790,000) | (739,000) | (745,000) |
| Emp. | 126 | 113 | 112 |

DUNS 23-999-3975
## Walsall Healthcare Nhs Trust
Manor Hospital, Moat Road, Walsall, West Midlands WS2 9PS
**Tel:** 01922-721-172
**Web:** www.walsallhealthcare.nhs.uk
**Estd:** 1991
**Line of Business:** Local government
**Trading Style:** Manor Hospital
**Issued Capital:** £1
**Director:** Ms S James
**Responsibilities**
**Senior:** Susan James *(Chief Executive)*
**Branches:** Walsall Healthcare Nhs Trust, Bilston Street, Wednesbury, West Midlands WS10 8EY
**US SIC:** 9121, 8062

**UK SIC:** 91110, 95100
**Bankers:** National Westminster Bank Plc (60-22-22)
**Employees:** 3,800

DUNS 22-012-5954
## Walsall Housing Group Ltd
100 Hatherton Street, Walsall, West Midlands WS1 1AB
**Tel:** 03005556666
**Web:** www.whg.uk.com
**Reg No:** 4015633 **Estd:** 2003 Private Company Limited By Guarantee
**Line of Business:** Other letting of own property
**Trading Style:** Walsall Housing Group, W H G
**Directors:** Mrs G Bateman, E Hughes, S Wade, Dr H Harnisch, N F Maxwell, Mrs T E Mingay, D Barker, P I Murray
**Co. Secretary:** Ms Jane Preece
**Responsibilities**
**Senior:** Frederick Bell *(Chairman)*, Linda Cole *(Director)*, Robert Gilham *(Director, Housing Services)*, Michael Hew *(Director)*, Neville Styles *(Board of Directors)*, Amanda Tomlinson *(Director)*
**IT:** Tony Holland *(IT Manager)*, Phil Pettifer *(IT Manager)*
**HR:** Mike Sutton *(Human Resources Manager)*
**Facilities:** Robert Gilham *(Director, Housing Services)*, Fay Wood *(Facilities Manager)*
**Branches:** Walsall Housing Group Ltd, Elmore Court, Bloxwich Hall, Walsall, West Midlands WS3 2QW
**US SIC:** 6519 **UK SIC:** 85000

| | 31-03-14 | 31-03-13 | 31-03-12 |
|---|---|---|---|
| TO | 86,484,000 | 80,697,000 | 75,518,000 |
| P/L | 11,886,000 | 8,923,000 | 10,599,000 |
| NW | 25,459,000 | 6,235,000 | 2,550,000 |
| WC | 12,061,000 | 4,252,000 | 2,497,000 |
| Emp. | 625 | 627 | 633 |

DUNS 22-765-0066
## Walsall Metropolitan Borough Council
Civic Centre, Darwall Street, Walsall, West Midlands WS1 1TP
**Tel:** 01922650000
**Web:** www.walsall.gov.uk
**Estd:** 1974
**Line of Business:** General (overall) public service activities
**Trading Style:** Alumwell Business & Enterprise College, Mossley Primary School, Highways D S O
**Directors:** H Bhogal, W J Kirkham, G Porter-Williams
**Responsibilities**
**Senior:** Paul shieehan *(Chief Executive)*
**Purchasing:** Lawrence Brazier *(Procurement Manager)*
**Branches:** Walsall Metropolitan Borough Council, Lord Hill House, Darwall Street, Walsall, West Midlands WS1 1DA
**US SIC:** 9121 **UK SIC:** 91110
**Bankers:** National Westminster Bank Plc (60-22-22)
**Employees:** 1,000

DUNS 21-832-6874 **Imp-Exp**
## Walsall Pressings Co Ltd
Wednesbury Road, Walsall, West Midlands WS1 4JW
**Tel:** 01922-721152 **Fax:** 01922-721106
**Web:** www.walpres.co.uk
**Reg No:** 0888236 **VAT No:** 100118154
**Estd:** 1966 Private Limited Company
**Line of Business:** Metal spinners
**Export Markets:** European Union (E U); Middle East; Far East
**Export Sales:** £3,132,997
**Issued Capital:** £30,000
**Managing Director:** P Woolley
**Responsibilities**
**Senior:** Margaret Woolley *(Manager)*
**Marketing:** Graham Boyd *(Sales Manager)*
**Sales:** Graham Boyd *(Sales Manager)*
**HR:** John Dwyer *(General Manager)*, Christopher Mountford *(Training Manager)*
**Health & Safety:** John Dwyer *(General Manager)*
**Facilities:** John Dwyer *(General Manager)*
**Operations:** John Dwyer *(General Manager)*
**Purchasing:** Graham Boyd *(Sales Manager)*, Paul Chester *(Purchasing Manager)*
**Engineering:** John Dwyer *(General Manager)*, Steven Lowbridge *(Production Manager)*
**US SIC:** 3398 **UK SIC:** 31380
**Auditors:** Horwath Calrk Whitehill
**Bankers:** Lloyds TSB Bank plc (30-99-06)

| | 30-06-13 | 30-06-12 | 30-06-11 |
|---|---|---|---|
| TO | 39,758,661 | 33,505,464 | 23,411,568 |
| P/L | 639,183 | (62,664) | (152,300) |
| NW | 6,868,168 | 6,365,640 | 6,415,304 |
| WC | 5,834,674 | 5,253,700 | 5,373,654 |
| Emp. | 330 | 303 | 170 |

DUNS 22-777-6028 **Imp-Exp**
## Walsall Security Printers Ltd
**(Subsidiary of:** B & W Holdings Ltd)
Unit G3, Valiant Way, Wolverhampton, West Midlands WV9 5GB
**Tel:** 01922-721331
**Web:** www.wsp.co.uk
**Reg No:** 0870128 **VAT No:** 100372628
**Estd:** 1966 Private Limited Company
**Line of Business:** Printing not elsewhere classified
**Export Markets:** Worldwide
**Issued Capital:** £100,000
**Directors:** I R Brigham, P T White
**Co. Secretary:** Martin French
**Responsibilities**
**Purchasing:** Angie Heathcote *(Purchasing Manager)*
**US SIC:** 2752 **UK SIC:** 47544
**Auditors:** Horwath Clark Whitehill LLP
**Bankers:** HSBC Bank plc (40-45-19)

| | 30-09-13 | 30-09-12 | 30-09-11 |
|---|---|---|---|
| TO | 8,286,074 | 9,570,994 | 8,749,293 |
| P/L | 358,231 | 668,957 | 726,269 |
| NW | 2,716,194 | 2,905,803 | 3,096,798 |
| WC | 1,183,729 | 2,232,977 | 2,120,649 |
| Emp. | 79 | 78 | 72 |

DUNS 54-864-0853
## Walsall Teaching Pct
Jubilee House, Bloxwich Lane, Walsall, West Midlands WS2 7JL
**Tel:** 01922-618388
**Web:** www.walsall.nhs.uk
**Estd:** 2002
**Line of Business:** Primary care trust headquarters
**Issued Capital:** £1
**Principals:** Dr G Archenhold *(Chairman)*, Ms T Skitt *(Managing)*, Ms Y Sheward, J Rainsford, S Darkes, R Mackie, Ms Y Thomas, Dr S Ramaiah
**Responsibilities**
**Senior:** Anne Baines *(Director)*, David Heggarty *(Chairman)*
**Admin:** Ruth Hall *(PA Public Health Director/ Medi)*, Sharon Lawton *(Personal Assistant)*
**Health & Safety:** Sara Saville *(Health & Safety Officer)*
**Branches:** Walsall Teaching Pct, 40 Beacon Rd, Gt Barr, Birmingham, West Midlands B43 7BW
**US SIC:** 8321 **UK SIC:** 96111
**Employees:** 180

DUNS 23-771-0785
## Walsh Associates Ltd
32 Lafone Street, London SE1 2LX
**Tel:** 02070896800 **Fax:** 020-7089-6801
**Web:** www.walshgroup.eu.com
**Reg No:** 2339267 **VAT No:** 493763405
**Estd:** 1989 Private Limited Company
**Line of Business:** Civil engineers
**Issued Capital:** £2,126
**Directors:** C P Bean, T M Finbow, B C Ume, A Stanford, B Ransom, I Welsh, P Modarres
**Co. Secretary:** Timothy Finbow
**US SIC:** 8911 **UK SIC:** 83701
**Auditors:** Baker & Co
**Bankers:** Barclays Bank Plc (20-32-29)

| | 31-12-13 | 31-12-12 | 31-12-11 |
|---|---|---|---|
| TA | 4,252,372 | 2,577,726 | 2,159,365 |
| NW | 2,425,435 | 1,559,178 | 1,530,631 |
| WC | 1,874,749 | 1,477,580 | 1,441,342 |

DUNS 21-820-3388
## Walsh Construction Ltd
**(Subsidiary of:** Aliam Ltd)
The Byre, Woodbury Lane, Norton, Worcester, Worcestershire WR5 2PT
**Tel:** 01905-350053
**Web:** www.walshconstruction.co.uk
**Reg No:** 0657545 **VAT No:** 274440755
**Estd:** 1944 Private Limited Company
**Line of Business:** Building construction contractors
**Issued Capital:** £12,002
**Directors:** P G Crosby, N Mason, J P Bird, Mrs E V Bird
**Co. Secretary:** Ms Emily Bird
**Responsibilities**
**Senior:** Adrian Procker *(Manager)*
**US SIC:** 8911 **UK SIC:** 83701
**Auditors:** Crombies
**Bankers:** Lloyds TSB Bank plc (30-95-41)

| | 31-12-13 | 31-12-12 | 31-12-11 |
|---|---|---|---|
| TA | 927,491 | 907,425 | 753,644 |
| NW | 487,598 | 464,008 | 455,240 |
| WC | 263,615 | 212,913 | 182,951 |

DUNS 50-542-6866
## Walsh Integrated Building Services Ltd
Chardec House, 27 Kenyon Road, Nelson, Lancashire BB9 5SP
**Fax:** 01282-619910
**Web:** www.walsh-ibs.co.uk
**Reg No:** 2496955 **VAT No:** 458011758

**Estd:** 1990 Private Limited Company
**Line of Business:** Electrical contractors and electricians
**Issued Capital:** £500
**Managing Director:** I C Walsh
**Co. Secretary:** Ms Tracey Finnerty
**US SIC:** 1731 **UK SIC:** 50300
**Auditors:** Pierce C A Ltd
**Bankers:** The Royal Bank Of Scotland Plc (16-14-32)

| | 30-11-13 | 30-11-12 | 30-11-11 |
|---|---|---|---|
| TO | 8,429,304 | 9,366,279 | 8,484,402 |
| P/L | 370,545 | (218,622) | (34,479) |
| NW | 579,995 | 248,674 | 642,200 |
| WC | 196,587 | (144,874) | 250,974 |
| Emp. | 52 | 63 | 60 |

DUNS 29-692-6355
## Walsingham
Walsingham House, 1331-1337 High Road, London N20 9HR
**Tel:** 02083463860
**Web:** www.walsingham.com
**Reg No:** 2016251 **Estd:** 1986 Private Company Limited By Guarantee
**Line of Business:** Other human health activities
**Directors:** Mrs L A Tarpey, Ms J Desmond, Ms M Thomson, R Keagan-Bull, Mrs J Barrowcliffe, Ms D Boakye, Ms A R Johnson, Mrs D Clark
**Co. Secretary:** Mrs Ravanti Halai
**Responsibilities**
**Senior:** Conall Bullock *(Trustee)*, Mabel Cooper *(Trustee)*, Anita Grant *(Manager)*, Geoffrey Ravalde *(Director)*, Joy Small *(Manager)*
**HR:** Caroline Biddle *(Human Resources Director)*, Clare Worrell *(HR Manager)*
**Facilities:** Lizzie Northcott *(Facilities Manager)*
**Operations:** Sarah Macey *(Director Operations & Developm)*
**Branches:** Walsingham, 19 Crummock Road, Workington, Cumbria CA14 3RP
**US SIC:** 8091 **UK SIC:** 95200
**Auditors:** Maurice Apple
**Bankers:** National Westminster Bank Plc (60-23-36)

| | 31-03-14 | 31-03-13 | 31-03-12 |
|---|---|---|---|
| TO | 18,057,151 | 15,259,402 | 15,249,376 |
| P/L | 693,618 | 362,835 | 254,400 |
| NW | 9,648,368 | 8,954,750 | 8,591,915 |
| WC | 4,944,914 | 3,703,928 | 3,051,947 |
| Emp. | 622 | 681 | 640 |

DUNS 39-742-1942
## Walsingham College Trust Association Ltd
The Shrine Office, 2 Common Place, Walsingham, Norfolk NR22 6EE
**Tel:** 01328820239
**Web:** www.walsinghamanglican.org.uk
**Reg No:** 0318358 **Estd:** 1936 Private Limited Company
**Line of Business:** Places of worship
**Trading Style:** Shrine of Our Lady
**Issued Capital:** £5
**Directors:** A Roberts, Ms R S Ward, The Reverend J M Baker, The Reverend H C Stoker, J S Downing, M C Warner, R J Mantle, Reverend K Smith
**Co. Secretary:** Dr Brian Hanson
**Responsibilities**
**Senior:** Ian Garden *(Manager)*, Martin Kiddle *(Manager)*, Barbara Marlow *(Manager)*, Lindsay Urwin *(Priests Administrator)*
**Health & Safety:** Tracey Anderson *(Domestic Bursar)*
**Facilities:** Tracey Anderson *(Domestic Bursar)*
**US SIC:** 8661 **UK SIC:** 96600
**Auditors:** Larking Gowen
**Bankers:** Barclays Bank Plc (20-30-81)

| | 31-12-13 | 31-12-12 | 31-12-11 |
|---|---|---|---|
| TO | 4,826,307 | 2,961,382 | 2,547,081 |
| P/L | 485,277 | 420,353 | 76,457 |
| NW | 19,473,560 | 13,985,087 | 13,191,287 |
| WC | 945,070 | 829,740 | 674,317 |
| Emp. | 116 | 69 | 74 |

DUNS 21-712-9626
## Walston Holdings Ltd
East Down Farm, Blandford Forum, Dorset DT11 9AS
**Tel:** 01258450973 **Fax:** 01258456542
**Reg No:** 0527298 **Estd:** 1953 Private Limited Company
**Line of Business:** Farming of poultry
**Issued Capital:** £800
**Principals:** Mrs B G Friend *(Managing)*, I G Friend
**Co. Secretary:** Mrs Betty Friend
**Responsibilities**
**Facilities:** Charles Bullock *(Facilities Manager)*
**Branches:** Walston Holdings Ltd, Yearlings Fm, Dorset Wareham
**US SIC:** 0259 **UK SIC:** 01001
**Auditors:** Smith & Williamson

Bankers: National Westminster Bank Plc (56-00-35)

| | 30-04-14 | 30-04-13 | 30-04-12 |
|---|---|---|---|
| TO | 8,360,706 | 10,858,431 | 9,105,393 |
| P/L | (629,910) | 1,735,414 | 172,821 |
| NW | 9,881,306 | 10,469,532 | 9,171,759 |
| WC | 1,742,675 | 2,371,065 | 1,490,828 |
| Emp. | 66 | 67 | 66 |

DUNS 21-198-2897 Imp-Exp

## The Walt Disney Co Ltd

(**Subsidiary of:** The Walt Disney Company)
3 Queen Caroline Street, London W6 9PE
**Tel:** 02082221000 **Fax:** 02082222795
**Web:** www.disney.co.uk
**Reg No:** 0530051 **VAT No:** 539293808
**Estd:** 1954 Private Limited Company
**Line of Business:** Other artistic and literary creation and interpretation
**Trading Style:** Walt Disney Records
**Issued Capital:** £16
**Directors:** M Endemano, D J Lerner, P L Wiley, A T Widger, S U Bailey
**Co. Secretary:** Andrew Widger
**Branches:** The Walt Disney Co Ltd, Walmer House, 296 Regent St, London W1B 3AW
**US SIC:** 8999, 5042
**UK SIC:** 83954, 61900
**Auditors:** PricewaterhouseCoopers LLP
**Bankers:** Barclays Bank Plc (20-35-90)

**Following financial data are in thousands**

| | 28-09-13 | 29-09-12 | 01-09-11 |
|---|---|---|---|
| TO | 1,487,679 | 1,511,875 | 1,330,769 |
| P/L | 129,494 | 181,051 | 182,350 |
| NW | 941,177 | 835,713 | 932,649 |
| WC | 371,134 | 271,593 | 372,649 |
| Emp. | 1,506 | 1,426 | 1,435 |

DUNS 42-338-9761

## Walter Black (Holdings) Ltd

3 Drumhead Road, Glasgow East Investment Park, Glasgow, Lanarkshire G32 8EX
**Tel:** 01416410000
**Web:** www.walterblack.co.uk
**Reg No:** 0225571SC **Estd:** 2001 Private Limited Company
**Line of Business:** Management activities of holding companies
**Issued Capital:** £15,000
**Director:** S S Black
**Co. Secretary:** Walter Black
**US SIC:** 6711 **UK SIC:** 83962
**Bankers:** The Royal Bank Of Scotland Plc (83-22-27)

| | 11-03-14 | 11-03-13 | 11-03-12 |
|---|---|---|---|
| TO | 9,970,611 | 10,586,392 | 9,528,498 |
| P/L | 268,521 | 107,254 | (396,162) |
| NW | 5,256,749 | 5,025,335 | 5,016,337 |
| WC | 2,409,271 | 2,314,427 | 2,493,306 |
| Emp. | 84 | 95 | 73 |

DUNS 39-345-4046

## Walter C Parson Ltd

The Firs, 702 Budshead Road, Plymouth, Devon PL6 5DY
**Web:** www.wcpltd.com
**Reg No:** 2119023 **Estd:** 1987 Private Limited Company
**Line of Business:** Funeral directors
**Issued Capital:** £10,000
**Principals:** S J Ware *(Managing)*, G P May, D J Parslow
**Responsibilities**
**HR:** Angie Pender *(Head of Personnel)*
**Branches:** Walter C Parson Ltd, 11 Tothill Avenue, Plymouth, Devon PL4 8PJ
**US SIC:** 7261 **UK SIC:** 98902
**Auditors:** Riley
**Bankers:** Lloyds TSB Bank plc (30-96-68)

| | 31-03-14 | 31-03-13 | 31-03-12 |
|---|---|---|---|
| TO | 4,367,159 | 4,305,605 | 3,812,912 |
| P/L | 637,603 | 509,140 | 160,566 |
| NW | 2,977,521 | 2,554,477 | 2,126,052 |
| WC | 154,448 | 103,230 | 23,615 |
| Emp. | 66 | 66 | 65 |

DUNS 22-852-8576

## Walter Craven Ltd

Craven Lodge, 14 Broad Green Road, Liverpool, Merseyside L13 5SG
**Tel:** 01512283900
**Web:** www.cravens-funerals.com
**Reg No:** 0528142 **Estd:** 1954 Private Limited Company
**Line of Business:** Funeral directors
**Issued Capital:** £9,088
**Director:** D R Craven
**Co. Secretary:** Charles Craven
**Branches:** Walter Craven Ltd, 48-50 Lark Lane, Liverpool, Merseyside L17 8UU
**US SIC:** 7261 **UK SIC:** 98902
**Auditors:** PKF
**Bankers:** HSBC Bank plc (40-29-26)

| | 31-12-13 | 31-12-12 | 31-12-11 |
|---|---|---|---|
| TO | 3,810,375 | 3,592,977 | 3,047,208 |
| P/L | 765,532 | 1,091,124 | 471,082 |
| NW | 3,145,157 | 3,297,332 | 2,483,271 |
| WC | 1,401,786 | 1,409,322 | 809,436 |
| Emp. | 65 | 65 | 68 |

DUNS 21-402-0760

## Walter Davidson & Sons Ltd

21-23 Wellmeadow, Blairgowrie, Perthshire PH10 6AT
**Tel:** 01250872655
**Web:** www.wdavidson.com
**Reg No:** 0029652SC **VAT No:** 268564321
**Estd:** 1897 Private Limited Company
**Line of Business:** Chemists dispensing
**Trading Style:** Davidson Chemists, Davidson Veterinary Supply
**Issued Capital:** £39,000
**Principals:** D W Davidson *(Chairman)*, T H Lonsdale, Ms K H Gordon, G W Davidson
**Co. Secretary:** Allan Gordon
**Branches:** Walter Davidson & Sons Ltd, 94 South Street, Perth, Perthshire PH2 8PD
**US SIC:** 5912 **UK SIC:** 64300
**Auditors:** Wm Inverarity & Co
**Bankers:** Bank Of Scotland (80-05-68)

| | 31-01-14 | 31-01-13 | 31-01-12 |
|---|---|---|---|
| TO | 33,010,420 | 32,340,396 | 33,955,476 |
| P/L | 1,231,086 | 1,493,535 | 941,683 |
| NW | 10,080,823 | 9,403,496 | 7,593,694 |
| WC | 4,708,095 | 3,835,047 | 3,313,125 |
| Emp. | 284 | 290 | 283 |

DUNS 21-818-3408

## Walter E. Sturgess & Sons Ltd

Aylestone Road, Leicester, Leicestershire LE2 7QN
**Tel:** 01162541717
**Web:** www.sturgessgroup.co.uk
**Reg No:** 0340309 **VAT No:** 114155606
**Estd:** 1897 Private Limited Company
**Line of Business:** Sale of new motor vehicles
**Trading Style:** Nissan Leicester, Jaguar Leicester, Land Rover Leicester, Volvo Leicester
**Issued Capital:** £89,142
**Principals:** R P Sturgess *(Chairman)*, B G Sturgess, I W Smith, C M Sturgess
**Co. Secretary:** Ms Valerie Sturgess
**Responsibilities**
**Senior:** Stuart Bushell *(Parts Manager)*
**Health & Safety:** George Waistell *(Health & Safety Officer)*
**US SIC:** 5511, 7539
**UK SIC:** 65100, 67100
**Auditors:** Newby Castleman
**Bankers:** National Westminster Bank Plc (56-00-55)

| | 31-12-13 | 31-12-12 | 31-12-11 |
|---|---|---|---|
| TO | 94,158,705 | 81,908,584 | 66,075,013 |
| P/L | 1,073,087 | 900,193 | 702,003 |
| NW | 8,843,391 | 8,013,391 | 7,340,049 |
| WC | 1,358,762 | 1,392,486 | 1,135,654 |
| Emp. | 261 | 236 | 197 |

DUNS 21-322-5188

## Walter Edmundson(Haulage)Ltd

(**Subsidiary of:** Manx Independent Carriers Ltd)
Unit 8, Prospect Place, Skelmersdale, Lancashire WN8 9QD
**Tel:** 01695711670 **Fax:** 01772-204458
**Web:** www.edmundson.co.im
**Reg No:** 0970056 **Estd:** 1970 Private Limited Company
**Line of Business:** Freight transport by road not elsewhere classified
**Trading Style:** Walter Edmundson(Haulage)ltd
**Issued Capital:** £1,800
**Directors:** J Quaye, J Jones, N C Freeland
**Co. Secretary:** Ms Gillian Charnley
**Branches:** Walter Edmundson(Haulage)ltd, 1 Douglas Head Rd, IM1 5BD Isle Of Man
**US SIC:** 4213 **UK SIC:** 72300
**Auditors:** Wallwork Nelson & Johnson
**Bankers:** HSBC Bank plc (40-37-25)

| | 30-06-14 | 30-06-13 | 30-06-12 |
|---|---|---|---|
| TA | 963,414 | 621,162 | 652,765 |
| NW | 378,022 | 124,732 | 138,214 |
| WC | 424,173 | 113,108 | 16,543 |

DUNS 23-824-4607

## Walter Forshaw Holdings Ltd

King House, Bolton, Lancashire BL5 3QR
**Tel:** 01942813188 **Fax:** 01942-814039
**Web:** www.walterforshaw.co.uk
**Reg No:** 3816485 **Estd:** 1921 Private Limited Company
**Line of Business:** Management activities of holding companies
**Issued Capital:** £2,250
**Directors:** C Forshaw, A J Forshaw, Ms K L Forshaw-Jones, Mrs K L Jones
**Co. Secretary:** Mrs Karen Jones
**Responsibilities**
**IT:** Jeremy Wolstencroft *(IT Manager)*
**Facilities:** Sue Ahern *(Faculties Manager)*
**Purchasing:** Sue Ahern *(Faculties Manager)*
**US SIC:** 6711 **UK SIC:** 83962
**Auditors:** Cowgill Holloway LLP

**Bankers:** National Westminster Bank Plc (60-23-30)

| | 30-11-13 | 30-11-12 | 30-11-11 |
|---|---|---|---|
| TO | 7,604,374 | 5,703,342 | 4,951,902 |
| P/L | 569,114 | 480,530 | 429,585 |
| NW | 1,210,378 | 1,128,672 | 1,107,306 |
| WC | (141,219) | (157,987) | (723,465) |
| Emp. | 55 | 51 | 56 |

DUNS 28-832-2456

## Walter Holland & Sons Ltd

(**Subsidiary of:** Boparan Holdco Ltd)
Blackburn Road, Accrington, Lancashire BB5 2SA
**Tel:** 01706213591 **Fax:** 01706-228044
**Web:** www.hollandspies.co.uk
**Reg No:** 0271252 **Estd:** 1932 Private Limited Company
**Line of Business:** Bakers shops
**Trading Style:** Walter Holland & Sons Ltd
**Issued Capital:** £16,210
**Directors:** D S Morgan, S P Leadbeater
**Responsibilities**
**Senior:** Jack O'Brien *(Manager)*
**Marketing:** Leanne Holcroft *(Sales & Marketing Manager)*
**Sales:** Leanne Holcroft *(Sales & Marketing Manager)*
**HR:** Sarah Oldham *(HR Business Partner)*, D Summons *(Personnel Manager)*
**US SIC:** 5462 **UK SIC:** 64100

| | 27-07-13 | 28-07-12 | 02-07-11 |
|---|---|---|---|
| TA | 13,929 | 13,929 | 13,929 |
| NW | 13,929 | 13,929 | 13,929 |

DUNS 28-890-9302

## Walter John Cook & Sons Ltd

Richmond Drive, Skegness, Lincolnshire PE25 3TQ
**Tel:** 01754762097 **Fax:** 01754-765631
**Web:** www.richmondholidays.com
**Reg No:** 1279150 **VAT No:** 310804504
**Estd:** 2009 Private Limited Company
**Line of Business:** Caravan parks
**Trading Style:** The Richmond Holiday Centre
**Issued Capital:** £10,001
**Principals:** M R Williams *(Managing)*, S J Parish *(Financial)*, A W Downing
**Co. Secretary:** Mark Williams
**Responsibilities**
**Admin:** Joan Stephens *(Office Manager)*
**US SIC:** 7033 **UK SIC:** 66701
**Auditors:** Montepelier Audit Ltd
**Bankers:** National Westminster Bank Plc (55-50-09)

| | 31-12-13 | 31-12-12 | 31-12-11 |
|---|---|---|---|
| TA | 14,645,003 | 14,280,653 | 14,462,142 |
| NW | 11,412,106 | 11,324,557 | 11,193,999 |
| WC | (1,575,559) | (1,425,477) | (1,198,211) |

DUNS 22-903-0390

## Walter Scott & Partners Ltd

(**Subsidiary of:** The Bank of New York Mellon Corporation)
1-3 Charlotte Square, Edinburgh, Midlothian EH2 4DR
**Tel:** 01312251357 **Fax:** 01312227997
**Web:** www.walterscott.com
**Reg No:** 0093685SC **Estd:** 1983 Private Limited Company
**Line of Business:** Financial intermediation not elsewhere classified
**Issued Capital:** £25,126
**Directors:** R M Leckie, C E Macquaker, Ms J E Henderson, M E Harris, Mrs E L Pearston, J D Smith, R H Nisbet
**Co. Secretary:** Colin Wood
**Responsibilities**
**HR:** Diane Crichton *(Human Resources Manager)*
**Facilities:** John Fernie *(Facilities Manager)*
**US SIC:** 6111 **UK SIC:** 81501
**Auditors:** KPMG Audit PLC
**Bankers:** Clydesdale Bank Plc (82-45-05)

| | 31-12-13 | 31-12-12 | 31-12-11 |
|---|---|---|---|
| TA | 338,499,703 | 218,317,701 | 175,568,313 |
| P/L | 144,025,710 | 93,087,769 | 94,066,295 |
| NW | 242,744,036 | 136,435,580 | 108,312,502 |
| WC | 240,905,207 | 159,037,638 | 127,264,624 |
| Emp. | 99 | 106 | 101 |

DUNS 22-900-2258 Imp-Exp

## Walter Shearer Ltd

23 Robert Street, Govan, Glasgow, Lanarkshire G51 3HB
**Tel:** 0141-445-1066 **Fax:** 0141-445-1061
**Web:** www.shearer-candles.com
**Reg No:** 0049776SC **VAT No:** 260433095
**Estd:** 1972 Private Limited Company
**Line of Business:** Other treatment of petroleum products (excluding petrochemicals manufacture)
**Export Markets:** Worldwide
**Trading Style:** Shearer Candles
**Issued Capital:** £100,000
**Principals:** J G Barnet *(Managing)*, J F Lane, L J Barnet
**Co. Secretary:** John Barnet
**Responsibilities**
**Operations:** Anne Burnett *(Production Manager)*
**Engineering:** Anne Burnett *(Production Manager)*
**US SIC:** 2999, 3999, 6711
**UK SIC:** 11150, 49590, 83962
**Bankers:** The Royal Bank Of Scotland Plc (83-06-08)

| | 31-03-14 | 31-03-13 | 31-03-12 |
|---|---|---|---|
| TA | 3,050,272 | 2,971,502 | 2,362,964 |
| NW | 913,211 | 831,474 | 782,505 |
| WC | 652,837 | 522,944 | 479,321 |

DUNS 21-818-7169 Imp

## Walter Tipper Ltd

Unit 23 Europa Way, Britannia Enterprise Park, Lichfield, Staffordshire WS14 9TZ
**Tel:** 01543419696 **Fax:** 01543419696
**Web:** www.tippersbm.co.uk
**Reg No:** 0425545 **Estd:** 1929 Private Limited Company
**Line of Business:** Agents involved in the sale of timber and building materials
**Trading Style:** Tippers
**Issued Capital:** £738,600
**Principals:** A W Tipper *(Managing)*, A J Tunstall, P L Sampson, Miss A J Tipper, W A Tipper, J W Tipper
**Co. Secretary:** Mrs Jennifer Tipper
**Branches:** Walter Tipper Ltd, Speedwell Road, Birmingham, West Midlands B25 8HH
**US SIC:** 5072 **UK SIC:** 61500
**Auditors:** Dains
**Bankers:** National Westminster Bank Plc (53-70-15)

| | 31-12-13 | 31-12-12 | 31-12-11 |
|---|---|---|---|
| TO | 26,208,032 | 22,389,340 | 22,600,441 |
| P/L | 913,189 | 367,771 | 1,019,266 |
| NW | 10,489,678 | 9,838,091 | 9,724,117 |
| WC | 3,796,432 | 3,610,552 | 4,147,019 |
| Emp. | 151 | 140 | 143 |

DUNS 21-565-4070 Imp

## Walter Watson Ltd

Ballylough Road, Castlewellan, Co Down BT31 9JQ
**Tel:** 028-4377-8711
**Web:** www.walter-watson.co.uk
**Reg No:** 0010745NI **Estd:** 1965 Private Limited Company
**Line of Business:** Steel stockholders
**Issued Capital:** £147,369
**Directors:** W Watson, D W Barr
**Co. Secretary:** Mrs Sarah Watson
**Responsibilities**
**Finance:** Kathryn Hanna *(Financial Director)*
**Branches:** Walter Watson Ltd, 2 Edison House, Fullerton Road, Glenrothes, Fife KY7 5QR
**US SIC:** 5051, 3317
**UK SIC:** 61200, 22200
**Auditors:** PricewaterhouseCoopers LLP
**Bankers:** Northern Bank Ltd (95-02-66)

| | 31-12-13 | 31-12-12 | 31-12-11 |
|---|---|---|---|
| TO | 30,242,601 | 36,311,585 | 35,758,037 |
| P/L | 445,449 | 147,521 | 306,525 |
| NW | 7,919,408 | 7,404,218 | 7,230,706 |
| WC | 2,542,689 | 1,870,240 | 1,893,214 |
| Emp. | 189 | 194 | 183 |

DUNS 67-152-4044

## Walters Group Holdings Ltd

(**Subsidiary of:** Walters Electronics Ltd)
Acre House 11 15, William Road, London NW1 3ER
**Tel:** 01865855085
**Web:** www.waltersgroup.co.uk
**Reg No:** 6010857 **Estd:** 2006 Private Limited Company
**Line of Business:** Management activities of holding companies
**Export Sales:** £829,385
**Issued Capital:** £535,086
**Director:** C J Walters
**Co. Secretary:** Mark Newell
**Branches:** Walters Group Holdings Ltd, Walters House, 12 Lancaster Road, High Wycombe, Buckinghamshire HP12 3TB
**US SIC:** 6711 **UK SIC:** 83962
**Bankers:** Barclays Bank Plc (20-40-71)

| | 30-06-13 | 31-12-11 | 31-06-10 |
|---|---|---|---|
| TO | 11,845,718 | 9,400,277 | 8,973,279 |
| P/L | (724,311) | 200,634 | 110,867 |
| NW | (1,081,411) | (693,979) | (831,376) |
| WC | (436,921) | 287,003 | 133,251 |
| Emp. | 78 | 79 | 77 |

DUNS 21-114-5836

## Waltet Ltd

Unit 4 Andes Road, Nursling, Southampton, Hampshire SO16 0YZ
**Tel:** 02380748826
**Web:** www.waltet.co.uk
**Reg No:** 6550655 **Estd:** 2008 Private Limited Company
**Line of Business:** Management activities of holding companies
**Issued Capital:** £200
**Directors:** D B Newbold, M Howard

**US SIC:** 6711   **UK SIC:** 83962

| | 31-07-14 | 31-07-13 | 31-07-12 |
|---|---|---|---|
| TO | 8,906,492 | 7,895,671 | 6,010,920 |
| P/L | 169,467 | 427,671 | 1,019,462 |
| NW | 1,262,628 | 1,370,453 | 1,221,288 |
| WC | (1,062,854) | (673,240) | (480,295) |
| Emp. | 76 | 61 | 47 |

DUNS 21-801-2461

## Waltham Forest Asian Seniors' Club
94 Wood Street, London E17 3HX
**Tel:** 02085093556
**Web:** www.wfasc.org.uk
**Estd:** 2009 Proprietorship
**Line of Business:** Clubs social and associations
**Proprietor:** Mrs S Syed
**US SIC:** 5813, 6732
**UK SIC:** 66200, 83100
**Employees:** 250

DUNS 22-841-6152

## Waltham Forest College
Forest Road, London E17 4JB
**Tel:** 020-8501-8000
**Web:** www.waltham.ac.uk
**Estd:** 1963
**Line of Business:** Further education schools and colleges
**Director:** J Card
**Responsibilities**
**Finance:** Peter Doble (CFO), Debbie Greenage (Financial Manager)
**IT:** Kalim Uddin (Head of IT)
**HR:** Jeanette Cozzi (Training Manager), Annette Evans (Head of HR)
**Purchasing:** Debbie Greenage (Financial Manager)
**Branches:** Waltham Forest College, Unit 3, Lockwood Way, London E17 5RB
**US SIC:** 8221 **UK SIC:** 93100
**Bankers:** Lloyds TSB Bank plc (30-99-08)
**Employees:** 450

DUNS 21-581-6355

## Waltham Forest Community Learning & Skills Service
398 Hoe Street, London E17 9AA
**Web:** www.walthamforest.gov.uk
**Estd:** 2011 Proprietorship
**Line of Business:** Non-charitable social work activities without accommodation
**Proprietor:** Mrs A Perez
**US SIC:** 8321 **UK SIC:** 96111
**Employees:** 100

DUNS 23-707-2863

## Waltham Hall Nursing Home
Melton Road, Waltham On The Wolds, Melton Mowbray, Leicestershire LE14 4AJ
**Tel:** 01664-464865
**Web:** www.walthamhall.com
**Estd:** 1990 Proprietorship
**Line of Business:** Nursing homes
**Proprietor:** P M Robinson
**Responsibilities**
**HR:** Jane Fielder (Matron)
**Health & Safety:** Jane Fielder (Matron)
**Facilities:** Jane Fielder (Matron)
**Purchasing:** Jane Fielder (Matron)
**US SIC:** 8051 **UK SIC:** 95100
**Employees:** 70

DUNS 21-801-2537

## Waltham Village Institute
Goadby Road, Waltham On The Wolds, Waltham On The Wolds, Melton Mowbray, Leicestershire LE14 4AJ
**Tel:** 07896929692
**Web:** www.walthamvillagehall.co.uk
**Estd:** 2006
**Line of Business:** Corporate entertainment and hospitality
**Proprietor:** M Robinson
**US SIC:** 7999 **UK SIC:** 97913
**Employees:** 70

DUNS 52-556-6980

## Walthamstow Hall
Holly Bush Lane, Sevenoaks, Kent TN13 3UL
**Tel:** 01732-451334
**Web:** www.walthamstow-hall.co.uk
**Reg No:** 3245514 **Estd:** 1898 Private Company Limited By Guarantee
**Line of Business:** General secondary education
**Principals:** I E Philip (Financial), Dr J C Kevis, S T Hussain, P A Gloyne, Mrs J B Adams, Dr A G Pigot, Mrs S Quirk, Dr N W Jepps
**Co. Secretary:** Malcolm Browning
**Responsibilities**
**Senior:** Alun Evans (Director), Roger Evernden (Director), Isabel Heald (Director), Denize Wallace (Director)

**Marketing:** S Pelling (Marketing Manager)
**Sales:** S Pelling (Marketing Manager)
**US SIC:** 8211 **UK SIC:** 93200
**Auditors:** Wilkins Kennedy
**Bankers:** Barclays Bank Plc (20-76-55)

| | 31-08-13 | 31-08-12 | 31-08-11 |
|---|---|---|---|
| TO | 7,531,262 | 7,323,335 | 7,052,625 |
| P/L | 310,072 | 496,228 | 353,890 |
| NW | 13,294,862 | 12,984,790 | 12,488,562 |
| WC | (980,396) | (986,823) | (776,627) |
| Emp. | 171 | 170 | 161 |

DUNS 21-773-1542

## Walthamstow School for Girls
58-60 Church Hill, London E17 9RZ
**Tel:** 02085099446
**Web:** www.wsfg.waltham.sch.uk
**Estd:** 2000 Proprietorship
**Line of Business:** Schools (local authority)
**Proprietor:** Miss R Macfarlane
**US SIC:** 8211 **UK SIC:** 93200
**Employees:** 100

DUNS 21-663-6147

## Walton Audi
Station Avenue, Walton-On-Thames, Surrey KT12 1NR
**Tel:** 01932220404
**Web:** www.walton.audi.co.uk
**Estd:** 1938 Partnership
**Line of Business:** Car dealers (new & used)
**Trading Style:** Walton Audi
**Partners:** M Rigley, J Frost
**Responsibilities**
**Senior:** Ann Harting (Manager), Neil Harting (Manager), M Wrighley (Manager)
**Finance:** Nick Karanikki (Financial Director)
**US SIC:** 5511 **UK SIC:** 65100
**Employees:** 60

DUNS 49-137-3148

## Walton Care Ltd
188 Chorley Road, Walton-Le-Dale, Preston, Lancashire PR5 4PD
**Tel:** 01772-628514
**Web:** www.waltoncare.co.uk
**Reg No:** 3107895 **Estd:** 1995 Private Limited Company
**Line of Business:** Residential care establishments
**Trading Style:** Walton House Nursing Home
**Issued Capital:** £50,000
**Director:** D H Haslam
**Responsibilities**
**Senior:** Patricia Dickson (Senior Marketing Executive), Oliver Haslam (Manager), Paul Semans (Manager), pat dixson (manager)
**Marketing:** Patricia Dickson (Senior Marketing Executive)
**US SIC:** 8321, 8091
**UK SIC:** 96111, 95200
**Auditors:** Hayes & Co

| | 30-11-13 | 30-11-12 | 30-11-11 |
|---|---|---|---|
| TA | 2,422,684 | 2,516,028 | 2,517,763 |
| NW | 1,675,147 | 1,587,259 | 1,325,411 |
| WC | (249,861) | (148,478) | (145,662) |

DUNS 54-864-0960    **Imp**

## The Walton Centre Nhs Foundation Trust
Lower Lane, Liverpool, Merseyside L9 7LJ
**Tel:** 0151-525-3611
**Web:** www.thewaltoncentre.nhs.uk
**Estd:** 2011
**Line of Business:** Hospitals
**Principals:** K Hoskission (Chairman), C Harrop (Financial), Ms A Oates (Personnel), Ms S Hill, M Pickup, G Clarke, Ms C Lee-Jones, Ms J Rosser
**Responsibilities**
**Senior:** Caroline Kenyon (Communications Manager), Christine Lee-jones (Non Executive Member), Melanie Pickup (CEO, Managing Director), Leslie Porter (Non Executive Member)
**Health & Safety:** D Sinclaire (Health & Safety Advisor)
**Facilities:** Mike Hill (Maintenance Manager)
**Operations:** Jayne Wood (Director of Operations and Per)
**US SIC:** 8062 **UK SIC:** 95100
**Auditors:** Julian Farmer

| | 31-03-14 | 31-03-13 | 31-03-12 |
|---|---|---|---|
| TO | 97,785,000 | 102,515,000 | 73,554,000 |
| P/L | 1,342,000 | 13,921,000 | 2,399,000 |
| NW | 54,662,000 | 51,463,000 | 45,642,000 |
| WC | 12,110,000 | 15,825,000 | 5,564,000 |
| Emp. | 1,159 | 1,030 | 909 |

DUNS 53-652-5850

## Walton Civil Engineering & Surfacing Contractors Ltd
Yelling Mill Lane, Downside, Shepton Mallet, Somerset BA4 4JT
**Tel:** 01749333800
**Web:** www.waltonltd.com
**Reg No:** 3457890 **Estd:** 2002 Private Limited Company

**Line of Business:** Construction of motorways, roads, railways, airfields and sports facilities
**Issued Capital:** £100,364
**Directors:** T M Payne, A Walton
**Co. Secretary:** Ms Beverly Walton
**Responsibilities**
**Senior:** Matthew Payne (Manager), Teresa Payne (General Manager), Kenneth Walton (Manager)
**Sales:** Andrew Britten (Commercial Manager)
**Operations:** Chris Douglas (Operations Manager), Mike Pickard (Depot Manager)
**Fleet:** John Binding (Logistics Director)
**US SIC:** 1611 **UK SIC:** 50200

| | 31-03-14 | 31-03-13 | 31-03-12 |
|---|---|---|---|
| TO | 12,380,107 | 13,244,529 | 13,098,685 |
| P/L | 626,323 | (23,870) | 768,160 |
| NW | 3,478,233 | 3,116,070 | 3,276,990 |
| WC | 1,567,940 | 1,188,578 | 1,663,759 |
| Emp. | 120 | 157 | 142 |

DUNS 21-779-8697

## Walton Community Hospital
Rodney Road, Walton-On-Thames, Surrey KT12 3LD
**Tel:** 01932228999
**Web:** www.virgincare.co.uk
**Estd:** 1993 Proprietorship
**Line of Business:** Hospitals
**Proprietor:** Mrs S Smith
**Responsibilities**
**Senior:** Claire Hooper (Acting Manager)
**US SIC:** 8062 **UK SIC:** 95100
**Employees:** 100

DUNS 23-850-5010

## Walton Hall
Walton Hall, Warwick, Warwickshire CV35 9HU
**Tel:** 01789472500
**Web:** www.wthehotelcollection.co.uk
**Estd:** 2013
**Line of Business:** Hotels
**Responsibilities**
**Senior:** Nigel Hadfield (Food & Beverage Manager), Peter Montague (General Manager), Ron Terry (General Manager)
**Marketing:** Peter Watkins (Operations Manager)
**Health & Safety:** Peter Montague (General Manager)
**Operations:** Joel Fagg (Operations Manager), Peter Watkins (Operations Manager)
**US SIC:** 7011 **UK SIC:** 66500
**Employees:** 140

DUNS 21-225-6925

## Walton Homecare
206 Station Road, Bamber Bridge, Preston, Lancashire PR5 6TQ
**Web:** www.waltoncare.co.uk
**Estd:** 1999 Proprietorship
**Line of Business:** Home care service providers
**Proprietor:** Mrs J Kelly
**Responsibilities**
**Senior:** Patricia Tedesto (Manager)
**US SIC:** 8091 **UK SIC:** 95200
**Employees:** 75

DUNS 22-284-1335

## Walton Lodge Ltd
316 Bawtry Road, Bessacarr, Doncaster, South Yorkshire DN4 7PD
**Tel:** 01302-868897 **Fax:** 01302-868897
**Web:** www.waltonlodge.net
**Reg No:** 4302089 **Estd:** 2001 Private Limited Company
**Line of Business:** Other service activities not elsewhere classified
**Issued Capital:** £20,000
**Directors:** P J Walton, A D Kamara
**Co. Secretary:** Secretary Solutions Ltd
**Responsibilities**
**Senior:** Barbara Walton (Manager)
**Finance:** Ros Grady (Finance Administrator)
**US SIC:** 8999 **UK SIC:** 83954

| | 31-03-14 | 31-03-13 | 31-03-12 |
|---|---|---|---|
| TA | 2,197,535 | 1,940,365 | 1,791,554 |
| NW | 1,853,650 | 1,699,099 | 1,578,453 |
| WC | 601,246 | 440,128 | 324,483 |

DUNS 22-549-5936

## Walton-on-Thames Charity
Mayfield, 74 Hersham Road, Hersham, Walton-On-Thames, Surrey KT12 5NU
**Web:** www.waltoncharity.careforfree.net
**Estd:** 1970
**Line of Business:** Activities of other membership organisations not elsewhere classified
**Principals:** J S Harding, N Lucas, L G James, V Cass (General Manager)
**Responsibilities**
**Senior:** Jackie Lodge (Chief Executive)

**Branches:** Walton-On-Thames Charity, Hylton Lodge, 40 Trenchard Clo, Walton-On-Thames, Surrey KT12 5JN
**US SIC:** 8699 **UK SIC:** 96902
**Auditors:** Kingsmill Partnership
**Bankers:** Barclays Bank Plc (20-90-56)

| | 31-03-12 | 31-03-11 | 31-03-10 |
|---|---|---|---|
| TO | 1,947,934 | 1,967,493 | 1,898,102 |
| P/L | 3,653,013 | 173,200 | 753,565 |
| NW | 23,268,929 | 19,393,715 | 18,594,572 |
| WC | 5,155,956 | 619,740 | 904,598 |
| Emp. | 49 | 51 | 45 |

DUNS 54-835-2855

## Walton Park Hotel
Wellington Terrace, Clevedon, Avon BS21 7BL
**Tel:** 01275-874253
**Web:** www.waltonparkhotel.co.uk
**Estd:** 1976 Proprietorship
**Line of Business:** Hotels
**Proprietor:** M Brigss
**Responsibilities**
**Senior:** Brenda Cobb (Restaurant Manager), Patricia Mccarthy (General Manager), Patricia Turner (General Manager)
**Marketing:** Steve Crawley (Marketing Manager), Patricia Mccarthy (General Manager)
**HR:** Marie Keay (Operations Manager), Patricia Mccarthy (General Manager)
**Health & Safety:** Marie Keay (Operations Manager)
**Operations:** Marie Keay (Operations Manager)
**US SIC:** 7011 **UK SIC:** 66500
**Employees:** 85

DUNS 22-867-1418

## Walton Summit Truck Centre Ltd
Canal Works, Plox Brow, Tarleton, Preston, Lancashire PR4 6HE
**Tel:** 01772334006 **Fax:** 01772-627607
**Web:** www.waltonsummit.co.uk
**Reg No:** 1410737 **VAT No:** 322861077
**Estd:** 1979 Private Limited Company
**Line of Business:** Commercial vehicle servicing repairs parts & accessories
**Issued Capital:** £10,000
**Principals:** G Perplus (Managing), N G Perplus, Mrs P Perplus
**Responsibilities**
**Finance:** Duncan Fleming (Financial Director), Elaine Wignall (Financial Director)
**Admin:** John Ainsworth (Office Manager)
**IT:** Duncan Fleming (Financial Director)
**Health & Safety:** John Ainsworth (Office Manager)
**Purchasing:** John Ainsworth (Office Manager)
**US SIC:** 5511, 7539, 5531
**UK SIC:** 65100, 67100
**Auditors:** Warr & Co

| | 28-02-14 | 28-02-13 | 29-02-12 |
|---|---|---|---|
| TO | 15,138,066 | 16,044,207 | 12,067,235 |
| P/L | 240,437 | 241,436 | 232,075 |
| NW | 1,145,941 | 1,011,171 | 825,708 |
| WC | 727,696 | 864,343 | 594,170 |
| Emp. | 56 | 57 | 53 |

DUNS 50-640-7175

## Walworth Upper School
Shorncliffe Road, London SE1 5UJ
**Tel:** 020-7450-9570
**Web:** www.walworthacademy.org
**Estd:** 2002 Proprietorship
**Line of Business:** Schools (local authority)
**Proprietor:** D Hanson
**US SIC:** 8211 **UK SIC:** 93200
**Employees:** 80

DUNS 56-977-7840

## Wam Care Homes Ltd
(**Subsidiary of:** Wam Group Holdings Ltd)
113a Bolgoed Road, Pontarddulais, Swansea, West Glamorgan SA4 8JP
**Tel:** 01792883671
**Web:** www.tymair.co.uk
**Reg No:** 2854128 **Estd:** 1993 Private Limited Company
**Line of Business:** Builders
**Issued Capital:** £50,000
**Director:** P J Michael
**Co. Secretary:** Ms Kerry Richards
**Responsibilities**
**Senior:** Evelyn Hughes (Manager)
**US SIC:** 8051 **UK SIC:** 95100
**Auditors:** Bevan & Buckland
**Bankers:** Barclays Bank Plc (20-51-32)

| | 31-07-13 | 31-07-12 | 31-07-11 |
|---|---|---|---|
| TA | 769,839 | 660,443 | 686,459 |
| NW | 494,164 | 490,426 | 465,991 |
| WC | 338,004 | 434,950 | 408,376 |

DUNS 21-608-1299

## W.& H.Marriage & Sons Ltd

Chelmer Mills, New Street, Chelmsford, Essex CM1 1PN
**Tel:** 01245354455
**Web:** www.marriagefeeds.co.uk
**Reg No:** 0690479 **VAT No:** 102662017
**Estd:** 1824 Private Limited Company
**Line of Business:** Mills and millers
**Issued Capital:** £44,400
**Principals:** S H Marriage *(Chairman)*, G D Marriage, Miss H L Marriage, S J Marriage, J H Marriage, S P Marriage
**Co. Secretary:** Ms Kathryn Lee
**Responsibilities**
**Marketing:** Ian Whymark *(Sales & Marketing Manager)*
**Sales:** Ian Whymark *(Sales & Marketing Manager)*
**Branches:** W.& H.marriage & Sons Ltd, C1-C2 The Cowdray Centre, Colchester, Essex CO1 1BN
**US SIC:** 2043, 2048
**UK SIC:** 42398, 42210
**Auditors:** HLB Kidsons
**Bankers:** Barclays Bank Plc (20-19-95)

| | 26-04-14 | 27-04-13 | 28-04-12 |
|---|---|---|---|
| TO | 46,435,148 | 38,073,651 | 26,982,844 |
| P/L | (503,719) | (330,024) | 757,954 |
| NW | 7,660,522 | 6,468,548 | 8,020,076 |
| WC | 6,258,914 | 7,144,655 | 8,418,178 |
| Emp. | 144 | 125 | 105 |

DUNS 22-536-4850

## Wandle Housing Association Ltd

232 Mitcham Road, London SW17 9NN
**Tel:** 02086821177
**Web:** www.wandle.com
**Reg No:** 0019225IP **VAT No:** 561848712
**Estd:** 2002 Friendly Society
**Line of Business:** Housing associations societies trusts & co-operatives
**Directors:** J Evanson, S Battersby, S Ellenby, R Byng, A Thompson, K P Exford, J Evans, E Arnold
**Co. Secretary:** D Lawson
**Responsibilities**
**Senior:** E Hindmarsh *(Director)*, D Newsam *(Director)*, Sarah Thakker *(Chief Executive)*
**US SIC:** 8699 **UK SIC:** 96902
**Auditors:** BDO Stoy Hayward LLP
**Bankers:** The Royal Bank Of Scotland Plc (16-00-93)

| | 31-03-12 | 31-03-11 | 31-03-10 |
|---|---|---|---|
| TO | 36,556,000 | 38,190,000 | 42,208,000 |
| P/L | 3,463,000 | 6,165,000 | 4,914,000 |
| NW | 85,547,000 | 93,907,000 | 86,836,000 |
| WC | 22,108,000 | 16,504,000 | 25,906,000 |
| Emp. | 135 | 152 | 151 |

DUNS 42-468-4298

## W&S Recycling

14-16 Nuffield Road, Poole, Dorset BH17 0RB
**Tel:** 01202-675-564
**Web:** www.wsrecycling.co.uk
**VAT No:** 541630274 **Estd:** 2001 Proprietorship
**Line of Business:** Representative office
**Trading Style:** Weymouth & Sherbourne Recycling
**Proprietors:** G D Thompson, G D Thompson
**Responsibilities**
**IT:** Ian Squires *(Senior IT Executive)*
**Branches:** W+s Recycling Services, 41 Balena Cl, Poole, Dorset BH17 7DY
**US SIC:** 5093, 4911, 3031
**UK SIC:** 62200, 16101, 48123
**Auditors:** Thomas Harvey

| | 31-03-13 | 31-03-12 |
|---|---|---|
| TO | 15,460,357 | 17,350,609 |
| P/L | 944,286 | 1,724,936 |
| NW | 2,067,157 | 851,850 |
| WC | 1,925,146 | 1,828,228 |
| Emp. | 250 | 250 |

DUNS 23-568-3851

## Wandsworth Council

Town Hall, Wandsworth High Street, London SW18 2PU
**Web:** www.wandsworth.gov.uk
**Estd:** 1980
**Line of Business:** Local government
**Trading Style:** Wandsworth School
**Directors:** G K Jones, H J Heywood
**Responsibilities**
**Senior:** Judith Arkwright *(Training Director)*, Brian Reilly *(Manager)*
**Finance:** Nancy Aldred *(Finance Officer)*, Chris Buss *(Financial Director)*, Suzanne Lancaster *(Tax Manager)*
**Marketing:** Joanna Kettle *(Marketing Officer)*, Simon Whitworth *(Website Manager)*
**Admin:** Frankie Belloli *(Administrator)*, Meghan Bison *(Administrative Officer)*
**IT:** Pauline Mc Dermott *(Computer Operations Manager)*, Frank McGeady *(Head of Corporate IT)*
**HR:** Judith Arkwright *(Training Director)*, Paula Brown *(Workforce Training Manager)*
**Facilities:** Cllr Johnson *(Estate Manager)*
**Operations:** Stephen Jiggins *(Senior Projects Manager)*, Gareth Llywelyn-Roberts *(Environmental Manager)*, Don Ogunyemi *(Manager, Roads)*, Steve Tucker *(Operations Manager)*
**Branches:** Wandsworth Council, Hollman Gardens, London SW16 3SJ
**US SIC:** 9121 **UK SIC:** 91110
**Bankers:** Barclays Bank Plc (20-90-69)
**Employees:** 2,000

DUNS 21-636-1238 Imp-Exp

## The Wandsworth Group Ltd

**(Subsidiary of:** Artillery Partners Ltd)
Albert Drive, Woking, Surrey GU21 5SE
**Tel:** 01483740740
**Web:** www.wandsworthgroup.com
**Reg No:** 0084301 **VAT No:** 211494783
**Estd:** 1905 Private Limited Company
**Line of Business:** Electricity generating equipment
**Export Markets:** Worldwide
**Export Sales:** £699,213
**Issued Capital:** £228,684
**Directors:** A P Sherry, C E Salter, D R Swinnerton
**Co. Secretary:** David Swinnerton
**Responsibilities**
**Senior:** Richard Mockitt *(Manager)*
**Marketing:** Gary Duarte *(Sales & Marketing Manager)*
**Sales:** Gary Duarte *(Sales & Marketing Manager)*, Gerry Thornton *(Customer Services Manager)*
**Operations:** Gerry Thornton *(Customer Services Manager)*
**US SIC:** 3643 **UK SIC:** 34203
**Auditors:** Moore Stephens (Guildford) LLP
**Bankers:** Lloyds TSB Bank plc (30-00-03)

| | 31-03-14 | 31-03-13 | 31-03-12 |
|---|---|---|---|
| TO | 9,455,239 | 10,520,077 | 17,061,169 |
| P/L | (158,296) | 2,069,143 | 249,589 |
| NW | 3,881,080 | 6,966,390 | 5,045,667 |
| WC | 3,397,020 | 6,466,628 | 1,038,919 |
| Emp. | 100 | 125 | 134 |

DUNS 39-720-1674

## W&We (Wales & West England) Ltd

**(Subsidiary of:** Amber Real Estate Investments Ltd)
100 Commercial Street, Malton, North Yorkshire YO17 9EU
**Tel:** 01653693031
**Web:** www.vionfood.co.uk
**Reg No:** 2169077 **VAT No:** 464849013
**Estd:** 1987 Private Limited Company
**Line of Business:** Other letting of own property
**Export Sales:** £19,499,000
**Issued Capital:** £45,327,327
**Directors:** R J Rafferty, Ms J A Charles
**Branches:** W&we (Wales & West England) Ltd, Victoria Business Pk, St. Austell, Cornwall PL26 8LX
**US SIC:** 6519 **UK SIC:** 85000
**Auditors:** BDO LLP
**Bankers:** Bank Of Scotland (12-21-37)

| | 31-12-12 | 31-12-11 | 31-12-10 |
|---|---|---|---|
| TO | 754,883,000 | 755,372,000 | 684,993,000 |
| P/L | 3,329,000 | 12,127,000 | 17,421,000 |
| NW | 97,300,000 | 97,067,000 | 64,421,000 |
| WC | (20,475,000) | 9,727,000 | 7,465,000 |
| Emp. | 3,257 | 3,033 | 3,604 |

DUNS 21-813-8371

## Wannops Llp

South Pallant House, South Pallant, Chichester, West Sussex PO19 1TH
**Tel:** 01243-778-844 **Fax:** 01243788349
**Web:** www.wfsblaw.co.uk
**Reg No:** 0370590OC **Estd:** 2011 Private Limited Company
**Line of Business:** Corporate and personal solicitors' office.
**Responsibilities**
**Senior:** Martin Beames *(Non-designated Limited Liabili)*, Peter Byfield *(Non-designated Limited Liabili)*, Maria Haywood *(Non-designated Limited Liabili)*, Mark Kessler *(Matrimonial and Family)*, Robert Stangroom *(Non-designated Limited Liabili)*
**Sales:** Damien Newton *(Commercial Team)*
**Branches:** WANNOPS LLP: York Road Chambers, York Road, Bognor Regis, PO21 1LT, WEST SUSSEX.
**US SIC:** 8111, 7399
**UK SIC:** 83500, 83954
**Auditors:** Carpenter Box LLP

| | 31-03-14 | 31-03-13 |
|---|---|---|
| TA | 2,775,599 | 2,784,110 |
| NW | 847,117 | 682,905 |
| WC | 1,841,513 | 1,399,061 |

DUNS 21-121-2953

## Wansbeck Homes Ltd

East View, Stakeford, Choppington, Northumberland NE62 5TR
**Tel:** 01670844200 **Fax:** 01670 844280
**Reg No:** 0003007IP **Estd:** 2008 Private Limited Company
**Line of Business:** Charitable organisation (registered for social landlord)
**US SIC:** 6732 **UK SIC:** 83100
**Bankers:** Barclays Bank Plc (20-59-42)

| | 31-03-12 | 31-03-11 | 31-03-10 |
|---|---|---|---|
| TO | 19,513,000 | 18,178,000 | 17,061,000 |
| P/L | 4,904,000 | 1,391,000 | 162,000 |
| NW | 19,728,000 | 3,296,000 | (110,000) |
| WC | 68,543,000 | 80,409,000 | 99,419,000 |
| Emp. | 186 | 195 | 205 |

DUNS 21-777-6014

## Wantage Hospital

Garston Lane, Wantage, Oxfordshire OX12 7AS
**Tel:** 01235205801
**Estd:** 2011 Partnership
**Line of Business:** Public sector hospital activities, including nhs trusts
**Partners:** Mrs W Jeffs, Mrs J Beckling
**US SIC:** 8062 **UK SIC:** 95100
**Employees:** 100

DUNS 22-765-0884 Imp

## Wanzl Ltd

**(Subsidiary of:** Wanzl Gmbh & Co. Holding Kg)
Europa House, Heathcote Lane, Heathcote, Warwick, Warwickshire CV34 6SP
**Tel:** 01926451951 **Fax:** 01926-451952
**Web:** www.wanzl.co.uk
**Reg No:** 1403566 **Estd:** 1978 Private Limited Company
**Line of Business:** Other building installation
**Export Sales:** £2,908,840
**Issued Capital:** £1,100,000
**Directors:** G Wanzl, D M Rolland
**Responsibilities**
**Senior:** Rudolf Wanzl *(Manager)*
**HR:** Beverley Christoferson *(Human Resources Manager)*
**Health & Safety:** Beverley Christoferson *(Human Resources Manager)*
**Facilities:** Ian Carden *(Facilities Manager)*
**US SIC:** 1796 **UK SIC:** 50400
**Auditors:** Deloitte & Touche LLP
**Bankers:** Barclays Bank Plc (20-48-08)

| | 31-12-13 | 31-12-12 | 31-12-11 |
|---|---|---|---|
| TO | 51,192,504 | 52,246,850 | 35,590,084 |
| P/L | 3,422,936 | 4,871,811 | 1,456,642 |
| NW | 20,225,364 | 18,605,313 | 14,861,473 |
| WC | 9,534,496 | 8,604,273 | 5,631,869 |
| Emp. | 109 | 92 | 75 |

DUNS 23-803-9924

## Wapping Restaurants Ltd

Wapping Wall, London E1W 3SG
**Tel:** 02076802080
**Web:** www.thewappingproject.com
**Reg No:** 3796531 **Estd:** 2000 Private Limited Company
**Line of Business:** Restaurant - english
**Trading Style:** Wapping Food
**Issued Capital:** £2
**Director:** Ms J Wright
**Co. Secretary:** Ian James
**Responsibilities**
**Senior:** Beverly Fernando *(Practice Manager)*
**US SIC:** 5812, 5813
**UK SIC:** 66110, 66200
**Auditors:** Audit Assure

| | 31-03-14 | 31-03-13 | 31-03-12 |
|---|---|---|---|
| TA | 28,914 | 254,956 | 227,923 |
| NW | (284,130) | 10,081 | 23,332 |
| WC | (284,130) | 10,081 | 3,962 |

DUNS 23-612-5683

## War Child

Unit 3 5-7 Anglers Lane, London NW5 3DG
**Tel:** 02079169276
**Web:** www.warchild.org.uk
**Reg No:** 3610100 **Estd:** 1998 Private Unlimited Company
**Line of Business:** Charities and charitable organisations
**Directors:** N R Fenton, Ms S Maguire, T Davis, N Wilson, Ms P Richards, Mrs J A Weston, R A Longbottom, J Tas
**Co. Secretary:** John Macauslan
**Responsibilities**
**Senior:** Lydia Lee *(Board Member)*, Nicholas Rolfe *(Director)*
**Marketing:** Gemma Cropper *(Media & PR Manager)*
**IT:** Dan Collison *(Programmes Director)*
**US SIC:** 9111 **UK SIC:** 91110
**Auditors:** Crowe Clark Whitehill LLP
**Bankers:** The Co-Operative Bank Plc (08-02-28)

| | 31-12-13 | 31-12-12 | 31-12-11 |
|---|---|---|---|
| TO | 5,535,000 | 4,971,000 | 3,667,102 |
| P/L | 268,000 | 451,000 | 560,019 |
| NW | 2,138,000 | 1,870,000 | 1,418,844 |
| WC | 1,936,000 | 1,683,000 | 1,296,132 |
| Emp. | 192 | 149 | 116 |

DUNS 54-864-0267

## War Memorial Community Hospital

Charlton Road, Andover, Hampshire SP10 3LB
**Tel:** 01264-358811
**Web:** www.wehct.nhs.uk
**Proprietorship**
**Line of Business:** Hospitals
**Principals:** R P Sloane, R Sloane *(Proprietor)*
**Responsibilities**
**Senior:** Steven Beasley *(Project Manager)*
**US SIC:** 8062 **UK SIC:** 95100
**Employees:** 250

DUNS 21-230-5588

## War Memorial Hospital

Love Lane, Burnham-On-Sea, Somerset TA8 1ED
**Tel:** 01278-773100
**Web:** www.somersetpct.nhs.uk
**Estd:** 2003 Proprietorship
**Line of Business:** Hospitals
**Proprietor:** Mrs C Turberville
**Responsibilities**
**Senior:** Angela Conway *(Matron)*
**US SIC:** 8062 **UK SIC:** 95100
**Employees:** 100

DUNS 39-790-0861 Imp

## Warburg Pincus International Llc

**(Subsidiary of:** Warburg Pincus Llc)
Almack House, 26-28 King Street, London SW1Y 6QW
**Tel:** 020-7306-0306
**Web:** www.warburgpincus.com
**Reg No:** 0014240FC **Estd:** 1987 Foreign Company
**Line of Business:** Activities auxiliary to financial intermediation not elsewhere classified
**Principals:** E Mckinley *(President)*, J P Landy, S G Schneider, C R Kaye, C R Kaye, J P Landy, J C Schull, D Pathak
**Responsibilities**
**Senior:** Scott Arenare *(Director)*, Timothy Curt *(Director)*, E McKinley *(President)*
**Marketing:** Sarah Gestetner *(Director, Communications)*
**US SIC:** 6111 **UK SIC:** 81501
**Bankers:** Lloyds TSB Bank plc (30-00-08)

DUNS 21-746-4130

## Warburton Building Services Ltd

Chandler House, Cumnor Road, Farmoor, Oxford, Oxfordshire OX2 9NS
**Tel:** 01865-864040
**Web:** www.warburton.co.uk
**Reg No:** 1422905 **VAT No:** 332716374
**Estd:** 1979 Private Limited Company
**Line of Business:** Plumbing
**Issued Capital:** £3,914
**Directors:** S B Lee, J C Warburton, P J Burt
**Responsibilities**
**Senior:** Margaret Warburton *(Manager)*
**Finance:** Simon Whitehead *(Finance Manager)*
**US SIC:** 1711 **UK SIC:** 50300
**Auditors:** Grant Thornton UK LLP
**Bankers:** Barclays Bank Plc (20-01-09)

| | 30-11-13 | 30-11-12 | 30-11-11 |
|---|---|---|---|
| TO | 10,242,248 | 8,401,893 | 8,442,895 |
| P/L | 19,178 | 25,831 | 11,021 |
| NW | 531,156 | 508,350 | 486,147 |
| WC | 446,933 | 424,746 | 315,437 |
| Emp. | 99 | 86 | 77 |

DUNS 51-577-5299

## Warburton Funerals Ltd

**(Subsidiary of:** Dignity Plc)
Beverley Veneers Limited, Grovehill Road, Beverley, North Humberside HU17 0JJ
**Tel:** 01914103863
**Reg No:** 5858729 **Estd:** 2006 Private Limited Company
**Line of Business:** Funeral services
**Issued Capital:** £1
**Directors:** S L Whittern, A R Davies, R H Portman, M K Mccollum
**Co. Secretary:** Richard Portman
**US SIC:** 7261 **UK SIC:** 98902

**Auditors:** PricewaterhouseCoopers LLP

| | 27-12-13 | 25-01-13 | 31-12-12 |
|---|---|---|---|
| TO | 2,038,791 | 13,011,236 | 26,323,859 |
| P/L | 22,848,566 | 11,483,368 | 1,293,156 |
| NW | 37,490,760 | 7,427,315 | (11,188,048) |
| WC | 37,306,100 | 16,703,381 | 1,024,700 |
| Emp. | 104 | 151 | 149 |

DUNS 21-203-9309 Imp

## Warburtons Ltd

(**Subsidiary of:** Warburtons 1876 Ltd)
Hereford House, Bolton, Lancashire BL1 8JB
**Tel:** 01204523551 **Fax:** 01204523361
**Web:** www.warburtons.co.uk
**Reg No:** 0178711 **VAT No:** 337588320
**Estd:** 2008 Private Limited Company
**Line of Business:** Manufacturers general
**Issued Capital:** £2,376,497
**Principals:** W B Warburton *(Chairman and Managing)*, J Warburton *(Managing)*, W R Warburton, D A Light, A N Campbell, N W Dunlop
**Co. Secretary:** John Healey
**Responsibilities**
**Finance:** Veronica Lomax *(Finance Manager)*
**Marketing:** Tearmh France *(Corporate Communications Manag)*, Andrea Hayes *(Market Analysis Manager)*, Jill Kippax *(Corporate Affairs Director)*, Darren Littler *(Innovation & Renovation Direct)*, Mark Simester *(Marketing Director)*
**Sales:** Sean Dand *(Business Development Manager)*, Damien Ghee *(IT Director)*, John Smethurst *(Sales Director)*
**IT:** David Adamson *(Infrastructure Analyst)*, Damien Ghee *(IT Director)*
**HR:** Sheila Downward *(HR)*, Mark Eccles *(Human Resources Manager)*, Jane Tomlinson *(Human Resources Manager)*, D Warburton *(Human Resources Manager)*
**Health & Safety:** Paul Fenner *(Health & Safety Director)*
**Purchasing:** Adam Marson *(Supply Chain & Procurement Dir)*
**Branches:** Warburtons Ltd, 11 Moorcroft Pk, Smethwick, West Midlands B66 1BT
**US SIC:** 3999, 5149
**UK SIC:** 49590, 61700
**Auditors:** Deloitte LLP
**Bankers:** National Westminster Bank Plc (01-30-99)

| | 28-09-13 | 29-09-12 | 24-09-11 |
|---|---|---|---|
| TO | 562,139,000 | 523,653,000 | 495,465,000 |
| P/L | 36,327,000 | 75,904,000 | 19,553,000 |
| NW | 344,990,000 | 334,150,000 | 330,403,000 |
| WC | 109,562,000 | 92,587,000 | 137,898,000 |
| Emp. | 4,534 | 4,546 | 4,659 |

DUNS 21-006-2750

## Ward Bros Holdings (North East) Ltd

Cleveland House, Cleveland Street, Darlington, County Durham DL1 2PE
**Tel:** 01325460831
**Web:** www.wardbrothenssteel.co.uk
**Reg No:** 6307645 **Estd:** 2007 Private Limited Company
**Line of Business:** Management activities of other non-financial holding companies not elsewhere classified
**Issued Capital:** £12,000
**Director:** R Ward
**Co. Secretary:** Robert Ward Junior
**US SIC:** 6711 **UK SIC:** 83962

| | 30-09-13 | 30-09-12 | 30-09-11 |
|---|---|---|---|
| TO | 33,048,243 | 29,970,603 | 32,619,237 |
| P/L | 69,595 | 232,930 | 592,653 |
| NW | 2,204,976 | 2,122,236 | 1,624,972 |
| WC | (1,473,285) | (715,773) | (592,705) |
| Emp. | 63 | 54 | 48 |

DUNS 21-308-1193 Exp

## Ward Bros (Plant Hire) Ltd

Littleburn Industrial Estate, Langley Moor, Durham, County Durham DH7 8HJ
**Tel:** 01913781776 **Fax:** 0191-378-9024
**Web:** www.skip-hire-durham.co.uk
**Reg No:** 1006015 **VAT No:** 177032175
**Estd:** 1971 Private Limited Company
**Line of Business:** Plant hire and leasing
**Export Markets:** E U
**Trading Style:** Ward Bros Skip Hire
**Issued Capital:** £66,667
**Principals:** A W Plumb *(Financial)*, A M Ward, J S Ward
**US SIC:** 7394, 1799
**UK SIC:** 84000, 50000
**Auditors:** Tait Walker
**Bankers:** Barclays Bank Plc (20-27-41)

| | 30-04-13 | 30-04-12 | 30-04-11 |
|---|---|---|---|
| TO | N/A | N/A | 3,831,916 |
| P/L | N/A | N/A | 12,849 |
| NW | 1,037,366 | 856,744 | 549,103 |
| WC | (372,909) | (648,780) | (689,723) |
| Emp. | N/A | N/A | 36 |

DUNS 21-761-3107

## Ward Gethin Archer Ltd

Manor House, 8 Dereham Road, Thetford, Norfolk IP25 6ER
**Tel:** 01953880800
**Web:** www.wardgethinarcher.co.uk
**Reg No:** 7869806 **Estd:** 2011 Private Limited Company
**Line of Business:** Solicitors
**Issued Capital:** £1
**Directors:** Mrs C L Page, Ms S L Scott, R W Pennington, M J Judkins, Mrs R J Molony, D N Humberston, C R Dewey, S D Wilson
**Responsibilities**
**Senior:** Cameron Green *(Director)*, Julie Sheldrake *(Office Manager)*, John Thorogood *(Director)*
**US SIC:** 8111 **UK SIC:** 83500

| | 31-03-14 | 31-03-13 |
|---|---|---|
| TO | 6,514,943 | 5,744,488 |
| P/L | 1,589,831 | 1,393,735 |
| NW | 370,563 | (1,002,287) |
| WC | 289,866 | (743,416) |
| Emp. | 122 | 122 |

DUNS 21-324-2394

## Ward Gethin Solicitors

10-12 Tuesday Market Place, King's Lynn, Norfolk PE30 1JT
**Tel:** 01553660033
**Web:** www.wardgethinarcher.co.uk
**Estd:** 1996 Partnership
**Line of Business:** Solicitors
**Partners:** R Pennington, C Gewey
**Responsibilities**
**Senior:** Lynn Bowler *(Legal Executive and Partner)*, Cameron Green *(Partner)*, Penny Lees *(Solicitor and Partner)*
**Branches:** Ward Gethin Solicitors, 11 London Street, Swaffham, Norfolk PE37 7BW
**US SIC:** 8111 **UK SIC:** 83500
**Employees:** 100

DUNS 50-537-1856

## Ward Goodman Ltd

4 Cedar Park, Cobham Road, Ferndown Industrial Estate, Wimborne, Dorset BH21 7SF
**Tel:** 01202-875900 **Fax:** 01202-876288
**Web:** www.wardgoodman.co.uk
**Reg No:** 2494983 **VAT No:** 541997116
**Estd:** 2001 Private Limited Company
**Line of Business:** Accounting and auditing activities
**Trading Style:** C T C
**Issued Capital:** £50,329
**Directors:** E S Battey, I M Rodd, R S Dare, T D Riley, G Simon, D E Lapthorn
**Co. Secretary:** Roger Duckworth
**Responsibilities**
**Senior:** Ward Goodman *(Principal Departments)*, Simon Willcox *(Manager)*
**Marketing:** Carl Wilson *(Marketing Manager)*
**HR:** Bob Cox *(HR Manager)*
**US SIC:** 8931 **UK SIC:** 83600
**Auditors:** Ward Goodman
**Bankers:** National Westminster Bank Plc (54-41-19)

| | 31-03-14 | 31-03-13 | 31-03-12 |
|---|---|---|---|
| TA | 2,341,923 | 2,426,331 | 2,404,242 |
| NW | 273,429 | 365,380 | 223,001 |
| WC | 83,782 | 135,643 | 57,124 |

DUNS 23-809-9696

## Ward Hadaway Incorporations Ltd

Sandgate House, 102 Quayside, Newcastle-Upon-Tyne, Tyne and Wear NE1 3DX
**Tel:** 0191-204-4000 **Fax:** 01912044001
**Web:** www.wardhadaway.com
**Reg No:** 3802333 **Estd:** 1999 Private Limited Company
**Line of Business:** Solicitors
**Issued Capital:** £2
**Director:** C T Hewitt
**Co. Secretary:** Nigel Martin
**Responsibilities**
**Senior:** Lisa Davies *(Personal Manager)*
**Finance:** Keith Milton *(Financial Director)*
**Marketing:** Elaine Magnani *(Marketing Manager)*
**HR:** Lisa Davies *(Personal Manager)*
**Health & Safety:** Norma Tullock *(Facilities Manager)*
**Facilities:** Norma Tullock *(Facilities Manager)*
**Operations:** Elaine Magnani *(Marketing Manager)*, Norma Tullock *(Facilities Manager)*
**US SIC:** 7399, 8111
**UK SIC:** 83954, 83500

| | 30-04-14 | 30-04-13 | 30-04-12 |
|---|---|---|---|
| TA | 2 | 2 | 4 |
| NW | 2 | 2 | 2 |
| WC | N/A | N/A | 2 |

DUNS 21-614-2604

## Ward Homes Ltd

(**Subsidiary of:** Barratt Developments Plc)
88 Main Road, Willed House, Sundridge, Kent, Sevenoaks, Kent TN14 6ER
**Tel:** 01959568400 **Fax:** 01634-577172
**Web:** www.wardhomes.co.uk
**Reg No:** 0329622 **Estd:** 1937 Private Limited Company
**Line of Business:** Development and selling of real estate
**Issued Capital:** £888
**Directors:** S J Boyes, M S Clare, D F Thomas
**Co. Secretary:** Barratt Corporate Secretarial Se
**Responsibilities**
**Senior:** Natalie Perry *(Sales Manager)*
**Branches:** Ward Homes Ltd, Whitesand Sales Office Scotts Acre, Rye, East Sussex TN31 7RQ
**US SIC:** 6552, 1541
**UK SIC:** 85000, 50100
**Auditors:** Deloitte LLP
**Bankers:** HSBC Bank plc (40-17-05)

| | 30-06-13 | 30-06-12 | 30-06-11 |
|---|---|---|---|
| TA | 2,000 | 65,834 | 25,102,000 |
| P/L | N/A | 250,330 | 249,000 |
| NW | 2,000 | 2,000 | 25,034,000 |
| WC | N/A | 2,000 | 25,034,000 |

DUNS 23-415-4339

## Ward House Ltd

Admark House, 2 West Street, Ewell, Ewell, Epsom, Surrey KT17 1UY
**Tel:** 02087865780
**Web:** www.godavri.com
**Reg No:** 5549599 **Estd:** 2005 Private Limited Company
**Line of Business:** Medical nursing home activities
**Issued Capital:** £99
**Directors:** M Bharkhda, N Bharkhda, H Bharkhda
**US SIC:** 8051 **UK SIC:** 95100
**Bankers:** Abbey National Plc (09-00-28)

| | 31-12-13 | 31-12-12 | 31-12-11 |
|---|---|---|---|
| TA | 1,270,731 | 1,170,153 | 1,177,471 |
| NW | (188,225) | (259,650) | (312,988) |
| WC | 212,091 | 211,407 | 156,604 |

DUNS 42-385-6249

## Ward Recycling Ltd

Wilson House, Puddlers Road South Tees Industrial, Estate, Middlesbrough, Cleveland TS6 6TX
**Tel:** 01642458666 **Fax:** 01642456274
**Web:** www.wardrecyclingltd.co.uk
**Reg No:** 4373217 **VAT No:** 789407084
**Estd:** 2002 Private Limited Company
**Line of Business:** Recycling
**Trading Style:** Ward Recycling Ltd
**Issued Capital:** £1,000
**Director:** M Ward
**Co. Secretary:** Mark Ward
**Responsibilities**
**Senior:** Ron Humphreys *(Manager)*, Thomas Neckenig *(Manager)*, Mel Thompson *(Area Manager)*
**Branches:** Ward Recycling Ltd, Unit 5, Sketchley Meadows, Hinckley, Leicestershire LE10 3EN
**US SIC:** 3031 **UK SIC:** 48123
**Auditors:** Lawson & Co

| | 31-01-14 | 31-01-13 | 31-01-12 |
|---|---|---|---|
| TO | 6,404,540 | 7,059,818 | 8,042,458 |
| P/L | 246,528 | 362,375 | 188,450 |
| NW | 3,019,191 | 2,720,201 | 2,527,755 |
| WC | 349,857 | 70,591 | (239,379) |
| Emp. | 120 | 196 | 204 |

DUNS 34-807-2708

## Ward Security Ltd

(**Subsidiary of:** Ward Security Holdings Ltd)
A9-A10 Spectrum Business Centre, Rochester, Kent ME2 4NP
**Tel:** 01634225100 **Fax:** 01634-225101
**Web:** www.ward-security.co.uk
**Reg No:** 5607258 **Estd:** 2005 Private Limited Company
**Line of Business:** Security and related activities
**Issued Capital:** £396,814
**Directors:** K M Ward, D G Ward
**Co. Secretary:** Benjamin Draper
**Responsibilities**
**HR:** Samantha Pullen *(Associate Director)*
**Facilities:** Samantha Pullen *(Associate Director)*
**Operations:** Liz Buys *(Operations Director)*, Paul Hearne *(Operations Manager)*, Lewis Roberts *(Operations Director)*
**US SIC:** 7399 **UK SIC:** 83954
**Auditors:** Burgess Hodgson

| | 31-12-13 | 31-12-12 | 31-12-11 |
|---|---|---|---|
| TO | 13,485,032 | 11,626,083 | 9,784,518 |
| P/L | (110,139) | 131,353 | 79,967 |
| NW | 501,727 | 597,366 | 445,990 |
| WC | (70,765) | 297,115 | 403,179 |
| Emp. | 453 | 390 | 337 |

DUNS 73-914-1476 Imp

## Ward Thomas Removals Ltd

Unit 1 Interface Business Park, Royal Wootton Bassett, Swindon, Wiltshire SN4 8GL
**Tel:** 01793 859 010
**Web:** www.wardthomas.co.uk
**Reg No:** 5167541 **Estd:** 2005 Private Limited Company
**Line of Business:** Removals and storage activities (domestic)
**Trading Style:** Bishopsgate Specialist Installations
**Issued Capital:** £3,676,303
**Directors:** T Bloch, C Rickards, A Ward Thomas, C Parry, W E Karslake
**Co. Secretary:** Joseph Kok
**US SIC:** 4214 **UK SIC:** 72300
**Auditors:** Fawcetts

| | 30-09-13 | 30-09-12 | 30-09-11 |
|---|---|---|---|
| TO | 12,168,918 | 10,982,847 | 11,049,674 |
| P/L | 1,656,431 | 1,257,249 | 1,896,343 |
| NW | 5,967,439 | 5,034,495 | 4,276,968 |
| WC | 1,877,287 | 1,640,500 | 902,582 |
| Emp. | 160 | 140 | 137 |

DUNS 22-766-5767

## Wardell Armstrong

2 The Avenue, Leigh, Lancashire WN7 1ES
**Web:** www.wardell-armstrong.com
**Estd:** 1992 Partnership
**Line of Business:** Environmental consultants
**Partners:** P G Morgan, S D Barry, D P Mcnicholl, J D Pears, T Bason, K E Sizer, S S Hake, P R Ainsworth
**Responsibilities**
**Senior:** Trevor Cooper *(Partner)*, Nicholas Coppin *(Partner)*, Michael Hassall *(Partner)*, Denis McNicholl *(Partner)*, Christopher Rigby *(Regional Director)*, Nicholas Tovey *(Partner)*, David Wilshaw *(Partner)*
**Branches:** Wardell Armstrong, Thynne Court, Thynne Street, West Bromwich, West Midlands B70 6PH
**US SIC:** 8911 **UK SIC:** 83701
**Bankers:** National Westminster Bank Plc (54-10-27)
**Employees:** 46

DUNS 73-806-9728 Exp

## Wardell Armstrong L L P

Sir Henry Doulton House, Forge Lane, Stoke-On-Trent, Staffordshire ST1 5BD
**Tel:** 0845-111-7777
**Web:** www.wardell-armstrong.com
**Reg No:** 0307138OC **Estd:** 1837
**Line of Business:** Engineering consultative and design activities
**Export Sales:** £7,936,639
**Responsibilities**
**Senior:** Phil Newall *(Non-designated Limited Liabili)*
**Admin:** Hazel Paynter *(Office Manager)*
**IT:** Paul Forrester *(IT Manager)*
**Facilities:** Hazel Paynter *(Office Manager)*
**Purchasing:** Hazel Paynter *(Office Manager)*
**Branches:** Wardell Armstrong L L P, 2 The Avenue, Leigh, Manchester WM7 1ES
**US SIC:** 8911 **UK SIC:** 83701
**Auditors:** Baker Tilly UK Audit LLP

| | 31-03-14 | 31-03-13 | 31-03-12 |
|---|---|---|---|
| TO | 26,897,907 | 26,234,226 | 25,062,505 |
| P/L | 62,292 | 752,000 | 1,502,000 |
| NW | 225,178 | (2,298,530) | (3,264,528) |
| WC | 2,075,352 | 2,992,171 | 2,509,500 |
| Emp. | 452 | 445 | 371 |

DUNS 21-458-2868

## Warden Brothers (Newtownards) Ltd

45-47 High Street, Newtownards, Co Down BT23 7HS
**Tel:** 02891812147 **Fax:** 028-9182-0226
**Web:** www.wardenbros.com
**Reg No:** 0003087NI **Estd:** 1952 Private Limited Company
**Line of Business:** Departmental stores
**Issued Capital:** £51,667
**Directors:** R J Brown, K Irvine
**Co. Secretary:** Mrs Helen Campbell
**US SIC:** 5399 **UK SIC:** 65600
**Auditors:** McKeague Morgan & Co
**Bankers:** Ulster Bank Ltd (98-11-50)

| | 31-01-14 | 31-01-13 | 31-01-12 |
|---|---|---|---|
| TO | 3,493,868 | 3,446,115 | 3,365,376 |
| P/L | (123,673) | (20,334) | (282,216) |
| NW | 3,035,919 | 3,163,334 | 3,187,410 |
| WC | 2,481,533 | 2,690,578 | 2,698,982 |
| Emp. | 55 | 61 | 63 |

DUNS 22-512-3884

## Warden Housing Association Ltd

Malt House, 281 Field End Road, Ruislip, Middlesex HA4 9XQ
**Tel:** 020-8868-9000
**Web:** www.homegroup.org.uk
**Reg No:** 0019489IP **VAT No:** 225893441

**Estd:** 1996 Private Company Limited By Guarantee
**Line of Business:** Social work activities
**Trading Style:** Home Group
**Principals:** Sir A W Pearce *(Chairman)*, Ms P M Scott, D M Tuft, Z Raniwala, P Shirley, J C Sledge, C G Chester, Ms C A Turner
**Co. Secretary:** M Jeffrey
**Responsibilities**
**Senior:** Peter Welborn *(Director)*
**IT:** Micheal Bamford *(Senior IT Executive)*
**Branches:** Warden Housing Association Ltd, Norton Clo, Borehamwood, Hertfordshire WD6 5DW
**US SIC:** 6732, 7021
**UK SIC:** 83100, 66500
**Employees:** 290

DUNS 21-707-8252 Exp
## Warden Plastics Ltd
Unit 31, Sundon Industrial Estate, Dencora Way, Luton, Bedfordshire LU3 3HP
**Tel:** 01582-573030
**Web:** www.wardenplastics.co.uk
**Reg No:** 0585969 **VAT No:** 196502742
**Estd:** 1957 Private Limited Company
**Line of Business:** Manufacture of other plastic products
**Export Markets:** Europe and Worldwide
**Trading Style:** Amity, Plasticut
**Issued Capital:** £1,046
**Managing Director:** M Barrett
**Co. Secretary:** Ms Denise Piper
**Responsibilities**
**Senior:** Lee George *(Warehouse Manager)*
**Marketing:** Mel Bellingham *(Sales & Marketing Manager)*
**Sales:** Mel Bellingham *(Sales & Marketing Manager)*
**IT:** Dave House *(IT Manager)*
**Facilities:** Steve Jenkins *(Maintenance Engineer)*
**US SIC:** 3079 **UK SIC:** 48360
**Auditors:** GKP Ltd

| | 30-06-13 | 30-06-12 | 30-06-11 |
|---|---|---|---|
| TO | 2,054,860 | 2,321,990 | N/A |
| P/L | 4,193 | (44,288) | N/A |
| NW | 363,382 | 365,989 | 443,517 |
| WC | (45,057) | (76,433) | (3,972) |

DUNS 22-539-1747
## The Wardens & Commonalty of the Mystery of Goldsmiths of the City of London
Goldsmiths Hall, 13 Foster Lane, London EC2V 6BN
**Web:** www.thegoldsmiths.co.uk
**VAT No:** 657101649 **Estd:** 1327
**Line of Business:** Livery company. Founded to regulate the craft or trade of the goldsmith, responsible since 1300 for testing the quality of gold, silver and, from 1975, platinum articles. One of Twelve Great Livery Companies of the City of London, it has been responsible for hallmarking since 1300 and, operates the Assay Office London and supports the craft and industry of silversmithing and precious metal jewellery.
**Trading Style:** Assay Office London
**Directors:** S Bailey, R G Melly
**Branches:** The Wardens & Commonalty Of The Mystery Of Goldsmiths Of The City Of L, Gutter Lane, London EC2V 8AQ
**US SIC:** 8699 **UK SIC:** 96902
**Bankers:** The Royal Bank Of Scotland Plc (16-00-32)
**Employees:** 105

DUNS 21-038-0439
## Wardington House Nursing Home
Wardington House, Wardington, Banbury, Oxfordshire OX17 1SD
**Web:** www.wardington.com
**Estd:** 1979 Partnership
**Line of Business:** Nursing homes
**Proprietor:** G Tuthill
**Responsibilities**
**HR:** Karl Jelff *(Facilities Manager)*, Maggie Rampley *(Matron)*, Reg Tipping *(General Manager)*
**Health & Safety:** Karl Jelff *(Facilities Manager)*, Reg Tipping *(General Manager)*
**Facilities:** Karl Jelff *(Facilities Manager)*, Reg Tipping *(General Manager)*
**US SIC:** 8051 **UK SIC:** 95100
**Employees:** 100

DUNS 73-437-9543 Exp
## Wardle Storeys (Earby) Ltd
**(Subsidiary of:** Invisa Inc.)
West Craven Business Park, Earby, Barnoldswick, Lancashire BB18 6JZ
**Tel:** 01282842511 **Fax:** 01282-843170
**Web:** www.wardlestoreys.com
**Reg No:** 4710820 **VAT No:** 815368030
**Estd:** 2012 Private Limited Company
**Line of Business:** Manufacturers and suppliers of pvc based products
**Export Sales:** £23,963,000
**Issued Capital:** £1
**Directors:** G Sanchez, H R Curd, H F Curd
**Co. Secretary:** Stewart Quinn
**Responsibilities**
**Senior:** Alun Hall *(Manager)*
**US SIC:** 3079, 2392
**UK SIC:** 48360, 45550
**Auditors:** KPMG LLP
**Bankers:** Bank Of Scotland (12-01-03)

| | 31-12-13 | 31-12-12 | 31-12-11 |
|---|---|---|---|
| TO | 32,584,000 | 26,767,000 | 38,213,000 |
| P/L | 1,722,000 | 826,000 | 1,317,000 |
| NW | 6,227,000 | 4,647,000 | 3,943,000 |
| WC | 4,153,000 | 5,663,000 | 5,730,000 |
| Emp. | 242 | 243 | 244 |

DUNS 42-359-1502
## Wardour Communications Ltd
**(Subsidiary of:** Wardour Publishing & Design Ltd)
5th Floor, Drury House, 34-43 Russell Street, London WC2B 5HA
**Tel:** 02070100999 **Fax:** 020-7907-4820
**Web:** www.wardour.co.uk
**Reg No:** 3189306 **Estd:** 2007 Private Limited Company
**Line of Business:** Publishers
**Trading Style:** Wardour
**Issued Capital:** £1,033
**Directors:** R J Merson, M D Macconnol, Ms H C Oldfield
**Co. Secretary:** Richard Payn
**Responsibilities**
**Admin:** Fiona Forbes-Hunter *(Office Manager)*
**Health & Safety:** Fiona Forbes-Hunter *(Office Manager)*
**Facilities:** Fiona Forbes-Hunter *(Office Manager)*
**Purchasing:** Fiona Forbes-Hunter *(Office Manager)*
**US SIC:** 2731, 7311
**UK SIC:** 47532, 83800
**Auditors:** BDO Stoy Hayward LLP
**Bankers:** Barclays Bank Plc (20-19-90)

| | 30-04-14 | 30-04-13 | 30-04-12 |
|---|---|---|---|
| TA | 3,951,637 | 3,715,892 | 2,710,523 |
| NW | 1,557,783 | 1,482,860 | 1,411,988 |
| WC | 1,403,693 | 1,277,812 | 1,201,338 |

DUNS 29-011-2572 Imp-Exp
## Wardray Premise Ltd
3 Hampton Court Estate, Summer Road, Thames Ditton, Surrey KT7 0SP
**Tel:** 020-8398-9911
**Web:** www.wardray-premise.com
**Reg No:** 0347881 **VAT No:** 234520884
**Estd:** 1938 Private Limited Company
**Line of Business:** X-ray facilities and services
**Export Sales:** £2,006,559
**Issued Capital:** £16,124
**Principals:** R B Wardley *(Managing)*, A B Wardley, Mrs S M Wardley
**Co. Secretary:** Mrs Justine Colquhoun
**Responsibilities**
**Senior:** John Cobbing *(Warehouse Manager)*, Anne Leach *(Silent Director)*, John Wardley *(Manager)*, Jeremy Wardley *(Manager)*
**Finance:** Lynn Edwards *(Accounts Manager)*
**Engineering:** Gary Colquhoun *(Production Manager)*
**Branches:** Wardray Premise Ltd, Unit 8, Southdown Road, Harpenden, Hertfordshire AL5 1PW
**US SIC:** 3999, 3559
**UK SIC:** 49590, 32863
**Auditors:** Baker Tilly UK Audit LLP
**Bankers:** Barclays Bank Plc (20-98-21)

| | 31-12-13 | 31-12-12 | 31-12-11 |
|---|---|---|---|
| TO | 5,756,049 | 5,988,100 | 6,325,392 |
| P/L | (184,217) | (117,651) | 18,248 |
| NW | 1,431,082 | 1,609,385 | 1,701,145 |
| WC | 568,267 | 761,506 | 840,248 |
| Emp. | N/A | N/A | 75 |

DUNS 21-061-6723
## Wards Solicitors
52 Broad Street, Bristol, Avon BS1 2EP
**Web:** www.wards.uk.com
**Estd:** 2000 Partnership
**Line of Business:** Solicitors
**Partner:** D Sheridan
**Responsibilities**
**Senior:** Alison Bradley *(Partner)*, Elizabeth Fry *(Partner)*, Bridget Juckes *(Partner)*, Alison Underhill *(Partner)*
**Finance:** David Vernalls *(Finance Director)*
**Marketing:** Sadie Francis *(Marketing Assistant)*, Jane Sanger *(Marketing Coordinator)*
**Branches:** Wards Solicitors, 195 197 High Street, Weston-Super-Mare, Avon BS22 6JS
**US SIC:** 8111 **UK SIC:** 83500
**Employees:** 135

DUNS 21-520-7981
## Wardue High School
Birch Road, Wardle, Rochdale, Lancashire OL12 9RD
**Tel:** 01706-373911
**Web:** www.wardlehigh.co.uk
**Estd:** 2002 Proprietorship
**Line of Business:** Schools (foundation)
**Proprietor:** G Wright
**US SIC:** 8211 **UK SIC:** 93200
**Employees:** 142

DUNS 51-999-9841 Imp
## Warehouse Express Ltd
**(Subsidiary of:** Barclays Plc)
13 Frensham Road, Sweey Briar Industrial Estate, Norwich, Norfolk NR3 2BT
**Tel:** 01603-486413 **Fax:** 01603258950
**Web:** www.warehouseexpress.co.uk
**Reg No:** 3366976 **Estd:** 1997 Private Limited Company
**Line of Business:** Retail of photographic equipment and supplies
**Export Sales:** £1,859,090
**Issued Capital:** £100
**Directors:** L E Wahl, A J Morrissey, D H Garratt, B C Hewitt
**Co. Secretary:** David Garratt
**Responsibilities**
**Senior:** Karen Dyson *(Accounts Manager)*, Lee Flynn *(General Manager)*
**Finance:** Karen Dyson *(Accounts Manager)*
**Health & Safety:** Lee Flynn *(General Manager)*
**Facilities:** Lee Flynn *(General Manager)*
**Purchasing:** Phil Munnings *(Purchasing Manager)*
**US SIC:** 5946 **UK SIC:** 65400

| | 30-06-14 | 30-06-13 | 30-06-12 |
|---|---|---|---|
| TO | 55,496,492 | 50,089,132 | 41,086,109 |
| P/L | 1,107,399 | 1,211,502 | 660,875 |
| NW | 6,911,264 | 6,067,701 | 5,133,980 |
| WC | 6,111,444 | 5,494,186 | 4,649,365 |
| Emp. | 107 | 87 | 82 |

DUNS 21-014-2390
## Warehouse One Distribution Ltd
Unit 11 Smokehall Lane, Winsford, Cheshire CW7 3BE
**Tel:** 01606869696
**Web:** www.warehouseone.co.uk
**Reg No:** 6369589 **Estd:** 2007 Private Limited Company
**Line of Business:** Warehouses
**Issued Capital:** £102
**Directors:** L Lee, S Lee
**Co. Secretary:** Anthony Dodd
**Responsibilities**
**Senior:** Willam Lee *(Manager)*
**US SIC:** 4226 **UK SIC:** 77003

| | 31-07-13 | 31-07-12 | 31-07-11 |
|---|---|---|---|
| TA | 1,196,624 | 1,213,122 | 1,074,289 |
| NW | 1,928 | 23,801 | 38,821 |
| WC | (140,445) | (33,569) | (60,099) |

DUNS 23-907-7014
## The Warehouse Wine Co Ltd
**(Subsidiary of:** Virgin Wines Holding Co Ltd)
39 Roman Way Industrial Estate, Ribbleton, Preston, Lancashire PR2 5BD
**Tel:** 01772-707700 **Fax:** 01772-707701
**Web:** www.winebymailorder.com
**Reg No:** 3898259 **Estd:** 1999 Private Limited Company
**Line of Business:** Retail sale of alcoholic and other beverages
**Trading Style:** Virgin Wines
**Issued Capital:** £178,714
**Directors:** P Adams, J S Wright
**Co. Secretary:** Graeme Weir
**Responsibilities**
**Senior:** Jay Wright *(Manager)*
**US SIC:** 5921 **UK SIC:** 64200
**Auditors:** PricewaterhouseCoopers LLP
**Bankers:** Barclays Bank Plc (20-71-02)

| | 28-06-13 | 29-06-12 | 01-06-11 |
|---|---|---|---|
| TA | 1,800,000 | 1,800,000 | 1,800,000 |
| NW | 1,800,000 | 1,800,000 | 1,800,000 |

DUNS 28-913-8950
## Waremoss Ltd
6 Bolton Close Bellbrook Industrial Park, Uckfield, East Sussex TN22 1PH
**Tel:** 01825-761349
**Web:** www.kamsons.co.uk
**Reg No:** 1434575 **Estd:** 2010 Private Limited Company
**Line of Business:** Representative office
**Trading Style:** Kamsons Pharmacy, Stallion's Pharmacy
**Issued Capital:** £30,000
**Principals:** B K Chotai *(Managing)*, P K Chotai *(Financial)*
**Co. Secretary:** Anna Chotai
**Responsibilities**
**Operations:** Paul Antenen *(Operations Manager)*, Bharat Chotai *(Operations Director)*
**Branches:** Waremoss Ltd, Health Centre, Milfoil Rd, Eastbourne, East Sussex BN23 8ED
**US SIC:** 5912 **UK SIC:** 64300
**Auditors:** Sterling

| | 31-08-13 | 31-08-12 | 31-08-11 |
|---|---|---|---|
| TO | 55,633,078 | 53,907,045 | 50,146,701 |
| P/L | 3,232,011 | 3,417,212 | 3,849,244 |
| NW | 4,753,815 | 4,825,923 | 5,148,291 |
| WC | 9,537,164 | 8,230,342 | 6,740,337 |
| Emp. | 546 | 462 | 376 |

DUNS 73-812-2659
## Wargrave House Ltd
Wargrave Road, Newton-Le-Willows, Merseyside WA12 8RS
**Tel:** 01925-224899
**Web:** www.wargravehouse.com
**Reg No:** 5068428 **Estd:** 2004 Private Company Limited By Guarantee
**Line of Business:** Schools (independent)
**Directors:** P N Berman, J R Hawkins, R K Booth, Ms C M Galligan, Ms J A Warner, W Duncan, S D Whalley
**Co. Secretary:** Ms Helen Whitehead
**Responsibilities**
**Senior:** Sheila Jaeger *(Director of Services)*, Catherine Whitehead *(Manager)*
**US SIC:** 8211 **UK SIC:** 93200
**Bankers:** Lloyds TSB Bank plc (30-99-14)

| | 31-08-13 | 31-08-12 | 31-08-11 |
|---|---|---|---|
| TO | 3,372,586 | 3,257,844 | 3,366,975 |
| P/L | 119,660 | 296,005 | 245,581 |
| NW | 3,517,580 | 3,488,920 | 3,451,915 |
| WC | 1,634,045 | 1,584,321 | 1,385,029 |
| Emp. | 90 | 94 | 98 |

DUNS 21-624-8708
## Warings Contractors Ltd
**(Subsidiary of:** Bouygues)
1000 Lakeside, North Harbour, Portsmouth, Hampshire PO6 3EN
**Tel:** 02392694900
**Web:** www.waringsgroup.com
**Reg No:** 0326584 **Estd:** 1933 Private Limited Company
**Line of Business:** Construction of commercial buildings
**Trading Style:** Bouygues Uk
**Issued Capital:** £1,499,000
**Directors:** P D Jouy, M Sow, L Christolomme
**Co. Secretary:** Mrs Charissa Shears
**Responsibilities**
**Senior:** Alison Durkin *(Manager)*, Daniel Rigout *(Manager)*, Leonard Salter *(Manager)*
**IT:** David Tippett *(IT Support Services)*
**Branches:** Warings Contractors Ltd, Tampla Ho, Tampla Qy, Bristol, Avon BS1 6HG
**US SIC:** 1541 **UK SIC:** 50100
**Auditors:** Ernst & Young LLP
**Bankers:** Lloyds TSB Bank plc (30-93-17)

| | 31-12-13 | 31-12-12 | 31-12-11 |
|---|---|---|---|
| TO | 36,780,000 | 42,519,000 | 79,593,000 |
| P/L | 1,900,000 | 1,510,000 | 1,801,000 |
| NW | 1,000 | 1,095,000 | 18,000 |
| WC | 551,000 | 1,431,000 | 373,000 |
| Emp. | 120 | 155 | 191 |

DUNS 21-863-1442
## Warlingham School
Tithepit Shaw Lane, Warlingham, Surrey CR6 9YB
**Tel:** 01883624067
**Web:** www.warlinghamschool.co.uk
**Reg No:** 8248059 **Estd:** 2012 Private Company Limited By Guarantee
**Line of Business:** Schools (foundation)
**Directors:** R J Toop, S Burn, P D Jones, Miss C A Jones, J E Kite, G R Bull, N Bradwell, A Ghattas
**Co. Secretary:** Ms Jane Pocock
**Responsibilities**
**Senior:** Sarah Berke *(Director)*, Linda Bowers *(Director)*, Graham Knott *(Director)*, Karen Quinton *(Director)*
**US SIC:** 8211 **UK SIC:** 93200
**Bankers:** Lloyds TSB Bank plc (30-92-45)

| | 31-08-13 |
|---|---|
| TO | 26,154,000 |
| P/L | 19,286,000 |
| NW | 19,211,000 |
| WC | 1,291,000 |
| Emp. | 120 |

DUNS 22-104-8999
## Warm Zones C.I.C
Pure Offices, Broadwell Road, Oldbury, West Midlands B69 4BY
**Tel:** 01215444689 **Fax:** 01912-325143
**Web:** www.warmzones.co.uk
**Reg No:** 4124262 **VAT No:** 755456701
**Estd:** 2000 Private Limited Company
**Line of Business:** Other service activities not elsewhere classified
**Directors:** I Belfield, W W Gillis, R Fraser, Dr R C Dobbie, D Connor, W E Jones, G N Fernie

**Co. Secretary:** Mrs Toni Dawson
**Responsibilities**
**Senior:** Lorraine Gumbs *(Manager)*
**Branches:** Warm Zones C.i.c, Blue Post Yard, Stockton-On-Tees, Cleveland TS18 1DA
**US SIC:** 8999 **UK SIC:** 83954
**Auditors:** H W
**Bankers:** National Westminster Bank Plc (54-10-58)

| | 31-03-14 | 31-03-13 | 31-03-12 |
|---|---|---|---|
| TO | 7,655,075 | 16,321,161 | 13,314,736 |
| WC | (59,783) | (77,570) | (82,134) |
| Emp. | 54 | 62 | 65 |

DUNS 49-130-5470 **Imp**
## Warmafloor (G B) Ltd
(**Subsidiary of:** Grupo Empresarial Kaluz S.A. De C.V.)
Concorde House, Concorde Way, Fareham, Hampshire PO15 5RL
**Tel:** 01489-581787
**Web:** www.warmafloor.co.uk
**Reg No:** 3104571 **Estd:** 1995 Private Limited Company
**Line of Business:** Heating equipment sales and service
**Issued Capital:** £17,852
**Directors:** P Maclaurin, A B Nicholls, M K Lamb, C R King
**Co. Secretary:** Paul Taylor
**Responsibilities**
**Senior:** Malcolm Jaques *(Manager)*, Mathew Norris *(Marketing Manager)*
**Marketing:** Malcolm Jaques *(Manager)*, Mathew Norris *(Marketing Manager)*
**IT:** Tony Davis *(It Manager)*
**US SIC:** 1711 **UK SIC:** 50300
**Auditors:** KPMG LLP

| | 31-12-12 | 31-12-11 | 31-12-10 |
|---|---|---|---|
| TO | 7,273,000 | 13,109,000 | 10,802,000 |
| P/L | 835,000 | 787,000 | 774,000 |
| NW | 4,246,000 | 3,617,000 | 3,039,000 |
| WC | 4,221,000 | 3,575,000 | 2,953,000 |
| Emp. | 65 | 72 | 72 |

DUNS 22-249-7914
## Warmer Energy Services Ltd
Unit B2, Senator Point, South Boundary Road, Knowsley Industrial Park, Liverpool, Merseyside L33 7RR
**Tel:** 08000 282373 **Fax:** 01515 466723
**Web:** www.warmerenergyservices.com
**Reg No:** 4267794 **Estd:** 2001 Private Limited Company
**Line of Business:** Heating contractors
**Issued Capital:** £100
**Directors:** Ms S A Warren, P Warren, C J Mullan, M Thomas, Ms N L Bennett
**Co. Secretary:** Ms Sarah Warren
**Responsibilities**
**Finance:** Richard Cassry *(Financial Director)*
**HR:** Lorraine Allen *(Human Resources Manager)*
**Facilities:** Bernard Keating *(Operations Manager)*
**Operations:** Bernard Keating *(Operations Manager)*
**US SIC:** 1711 **UK SIC:** 50300
**Auditors:** Malthouse & Co
**Bankers:** HSBC Bank plc (40-29-08)

| | 31-03-14 | 31-03-13 | 30-03-12 |
|---|---|---|---|
| TO | 15,103,822 | 11,581,808 | 10,522,800 |
| P/L | 2,089,377 | 1,390,346 | 643,666 |
| NW | 2,981,082 | 1,451,367 | 493,869 |
| WC | 2,857,393 | 1,390,330 | 412,539 |
| Emp. | 116 | 92 | 85 |

DUNS 21-812-1041
## Warmley House Care Home
Tower Road North, Bristol, Avon BS30 8XN
**Tel:** 01179674872
**Web:** www.fshc.co.uk
**Estd:** 2012
**Line of Business:** Children's homes
**US SIC:** 8321 **UK SIC:** 96111
**Employees:** 80

DUNS 21-464-1032
## Warmley House Nursing Home
Tower Road North, Bristol, Avon BS30 8XN
**Tel:** 01179674873
**Web:** www.fshc.co.uk
**Estd:** 1996 Proprietorship
**Line of Business:** Nursing homes
**Proprietor:** Mrs J Goodfellow
**Responsibilities**
**Senior:** Sue Horsewell *(Home Manager)*
**Finance:** Sue Horsewell *(Home Manager)*
**HR:** Sue Horsewell *(Home Manager)*
**Health & Safety:** Sue Horsewell *(Home Manager)*
**US SIC:** 8051 **UK SIC:** 95100
**Employees:** 84

DUNS 73-679-8997 **Imp**
## Warmseal Windows (Newcastle) Ltd
Unit 2 Westway Industrial Park, Throckley, Newcastle-Upon-Tyne, Tyne and Wear NE15 9HW
**Tel:** 0191-264-8383 **Fax:** 01912-648585
**Web:** www.warmseal.co.uk
**Reg No:** 4939152 **Estd:** 2003 Private Limited Company
**Line of Business:** Double glazing installers
**Issued Capital:** £110,191
**Directors:** S Flint, H J Samson
**Co. Secretary:** Paul Jennison
**US SIC:** 1721, 3079
**UK SIC:** 50400, 48360
**Auditors:** Ernst & Young LLP
**Bankers:** Barclays Bank Plc (20-59-42)

| | 31-12-13 | 31-12-12 | 31-12-11 |
|---|---|---|---|
| TO | 11,417,786 | 9,419,391 | 15,296,163 |
| P/L | 1,231 | (1,321,782) | (126,329) |
| NW | (3,039,396) | (3,284,893) | (2,200,284) |
| WC | (468,022) | (540,793) | 531,441 |
| Emp. | 96 | N/A | 120 |

DUNS 77-446-1313
## Warmup Plc
Unit 702, Tudor Estate, Abbey Road, London NW10 7UW
**Tel:** 08453452288 **Fax:** 02084536869
**Web:** www.warmup.co.uk
**Reg No:** 2955213 **VAT No:** 648958960
**Estd:** 1994 Public Limited Company
**Line of Business:** Wholesale of hardware, plumbing and heating equipment and supplies
**Export Sales:** £4,356,000
**Issued Capital:** £373,303
**Directors:** A Stimpson, S D Sheen, D F Read, D Stimpson, G P Parsons, J B Stokes, C F Mathias
**US SIC:** 5074 **UK SIC:** 61300
**Auditors:** Davis Grant
**Bankers:** National Westminster Bank Plc (60-15-42)

| | 31-12-13 | 31-12-12 | 31-12-11 |
|---|---|---|---|
| TO | 14,331,000 | 13,978,000 | 13,006,000 |
| P/L | 147,000 | 302,000 | 415,000 |
| NW | 1,918,000 | 1,835,000 | 1,664,000 |
| WC | 1,484,000 | 1,585,000 | 1,499,000 |
| Emp. | 141 | 134 | 124 |

DUNS 21-579-7524
## Warmwell Leisure Resort
Warmwell, Dorchester, Dorset DT2 8JE
**Tel:** 01305851080
**Web:** www.parkdeanholidays.co.uk
**Estd:** 1986 Partnership
**Line of Business:** Other tourist or short-stay accommodation
**Partners:** P George, D Trieharne
**US SIC:** 7033 **UK SIC:** 66701
**Employees:** 71

DUNS 22-566-0943 **Imp**
## Warndell Investments P L C
Mercury House, Waltham Abbey, Essex EN9 1AT
**Tel:** 01992769612
**Web:** www.ghwarnerfootwear.co.uk
**Reg No:** 1252396 **Estd:** 1976 Public Limited Company
**Line of Business:** Wholesale of clothing and footwear
**Export Sales:** £917,554
**Trading Style:** Mercury Sports Footwear, G H Warner Footwear
**Issued Capital:** £400,000
**Principals:** M G Warner *(Managing)*, C D Hollamby *(Financial)*, G H Warner, Ms H J Hollamby
**Co. Secretary:** Ms Josephine Warner
**Responsibilities**
**Finance:** Derek Hollanby *(Finance Director)*
**Sales:** Debby Ayres *(Account Coordinator)*
**US SIC:** 5136 **UK SIC:** 61600
**Auditors:** Meyer Williams
**Bankers:** Fortis Bank London Bch (formerly Generale Bk) (40-52-62)

| | 31-12-13 | 31-12-12 | 31-12-11 |
|---|---|---|---|
| TO | 11,863,519 | 12,944,724 | 11,411,945 |
| P/L | (292,961) | (36,928) | 32,010 |
| NW | 3,347,033 | 3,633,715 | 3,663,386 |
| WC | 1,993,548 | 2,285,265 | 2,322,601 |
| Emp. | 46 | 45 | 41 |

DUNS 21-580-4784
## Warner Bros Records
12 Lancer Square, Kensington, London W8 4EH
**Tel:** 02073683500
**Web:** www.wmg.com
**Estd:** 2006 Proprietorship
**Line of Business:** Record publishing
**Proprietor:** K Marshall
**Responsibilities**
**Senior:** Christian Tattersfield *(Chairman)*
**US SIC:** 8999 **UK SIC:** 83954
**Employees:** 50

DUNS 21-151-1845 **Imp**
## Warner Bros. Entertainment Uk Ltd
(**Subsidiary of:** Time Warner Inc.)
98 Theobalds Road, London WC1X 8WB
**Tel:** 02079846400 **Fax:** 01773829938
**Web:** www.ultimatestagdo.com
**Reg No:** 0259661 **Estd:** 1931 Private Limited Company
**Line of Business:** Motion picture and video distribution
**Trading Style:** Warner Bros. Entertainment Uk Ltd
**Issued Capital:** £1,100
**Directors:** M Emanuele, S W Mertz, T H Creighton
**Responsibilities**
**Senior:** John Rogovin *(Director)*, Edward Romano *(Director)*
**Finance:** Suzanne Shine *(Financial Director)*
**Marketing:** Noreen McConigley *(Marketing Coordinator EMEA)*
**Branches:** Warner Bros. Entertainment Uk Ltd, First Chicago Ho, 90 Long Acre, London WC2E 9RA
**US SIC:** 7829 **UK SIC:** 97112
**Auditors:** Ernst & Young LLP
**Bankers:** Barclays Bank Plc (20-36-47)

| | 31-12-13 | 31-12-12 | 31-12-11 |
|---|---|---|---|
| TO | 291,976,000 | 284,613,000 | 383,241,000 |
| P/L | 23,322,000 | 18,787,000 | 20,882,000 |
| NW | 46,656,000 | 53,079,000 | 40,510,000 |
| WC | 40,829,000 | 46,770,000 | 38,622,000 |
| Emp. | 455 | 444 | 448 |

DUNS 21-682-7174
## Warner Bros. Television Production Uk Ltd
98 Theobalds Road, London WC1X 8WB
**Tel:** 02079846100
**Web:** www.warnerbros.com
**Reg No:** 7329044 **Estd:** 2010 Private Limited Company
**Line of Business:** Other motion picture and video production activities
**Export Sales:** £5,974,000
**Issued Capital:** £71,719,672
**Directors:** Ms C E Hungate, N A Emmerson, T W Downing, A W Ogilvie, R Goes
**Responsibilities**
**Senior:** Craig Hunegs *(Director)*, Jeffrey Schlesinger *(Director)*
**US SIC:** 7819, 7829, 6711
**UK SIC:** 97111, 97112, 83962
**Auditors:** Ernst & Young LLP

| | 31-12-13 | 31-12-12 | 31-12-11 |
|---|---|---|---|
| TO | 11,933,000 | 13,522,000 | 14,312,000 |
| P/L | (6,372,000) | (220,000) | (6,327,000) |
| NW | 64,357,000 | 69,239,000 | 67,880,000 |
| WC | 27,920,000 | 29,994,000 | 27,361,000 |
| Emp. | 77 | 63 | 49 |

DUNS 73-387-4502
## Warner Bros. Uk Services Ltd
(**Subsidiary of:** Time Warner Inc.)
98 Theobalds Road, London WC1X 8WB
**Tel:** 020-7984-5400 **Fax:** 02079845001
**Web:** www.warnerbros.com
**Reg No:** 4660932 **Estd:** 2003 Private Limited Company
**Line of Business:** Audio/visual production services
**Issued Capital:** £1
**Directors:** M Emanuele, D J Blaikley
**Co. Secretary:** Ms Tina Hammond
**Responsibilities**
**Finance:** Rose Jensen *(Financial Director)*
**US SIC:** 7819 **UK SIC:** 97111

| | 31-12-13 | 31-12-12 | 31-12-11 |
|---|---|---|---|
| TO | 25,000 | 54,000 | 103,530,843 |
| P/L | 20,000 | 48,000 | 3,854 |
| NW | 197,000 | 177,000 | 129,393 |
| WC | 197,000 | 177,000 | 129,393 |

DUNS 23-620-1174 **Imp**
## Warner Chilcott Uk Ltd
(**Subsidiary of:** Warner Chilcott Acquisition Ltd)
Old Belfast Road, Millbrook, Larne, Co Antrim BT40 2SH
**Tel:** 028 28267222
**Web:** www.wcrx.com
**Reg No:** 0023272NI **VAT No:** 575488586
**Estd:** 1989 Private Limited Company
**Line of Business:** Health food retailers
**Trading Style:** Actavis
**Issued Capital:** £201,003
**Directors:** R Whitford, Dr C Gilligan
**Co. Secretary:** Robert Whitford
**Responsibilities**
**Senior:** Robert Whiteford *(Finance Director)*
**Finance:** Robert Whiteford *(Finance Director)*
**IT:** Gareth Reilly *(IT Manager)*
**Health & Safety:** Willis Millar *(Health & Safety Officer)*
**Operations:** Tom Hagarty *(Technical, Production Manager)*
**US SIC:** 5499 **UK SIC:** 64100

**Auditors:** PricewaterhouseCoopers LLP
**Bankers:** The Bank Of Ireland (90-23-54)

| | 31-12-13 | 31-12-12 | 31-12-11 |
|---|---|---|---|
| TO | 65,577,659 | 60,798,387 | 61,311,439 |
| P/L | 2,435,462 | 2,313,726 | 3,251,207 |
| NW | 71,147,641 | 66,534,687 | 54,125,008 |
| WC | 34,173,351 | 29,327,549 | 16,393,816 |
| Emp. | 225 | 211 | 214 |

DUNS 23-907-1660
## Warner Electric Uk Group Ltd
(**Subsidiary of:** Altra Industrial Motion Corp.)
Wichita Company Ltd, Bedford, Bedfordshire MK42 9RD
**Tel:** 01234350311
**Web:** www.wichita.co.uk
**Reg No:** 3897757 **Estd:** 1999 Private Limited Company
**Line of Business:** Management activities of holding companies
**Issued Capital:** £1
**Directors:** C Storch, C R Christenson
**Co. Secretary:** Richard Laws
**US SIC:** 6711 **UK SIC:** 83962
**Auditors:** BDO LLP
**Bankers:** Bank Of Scotland (80-11-45)

| | 31-12-13 | 31-12-12 | 31-12-11 |
|---|---|---|---|
| TA | 33,686,509 | 36,513,151 | 34,968,492 |
| P/L | 11,029,952 | 17,027,985 | (2,189,942) |
| NW | 12,384,334 | 14,462,507 | (3,318,221) |
| WC | N/A | 3,360,915 | 2,597,382 |

DUNS 67-204-9330
## Warner Goodman Llp
Portland Chambers, Fareham, Hampshire PO16 0JR
**Tel:** 01329-288121 **Fax:** 01329-822714
**Web:** www.warnergoodman.co.uk
**Reg No:** 0325046OC **Estd:** 2006 Private Limited Company
**Line of Business:** Solicitors
**Responsibilities**
**Senior:** Graeme Barclay *(Non-designated Limited Liabili)*, Sarah Brooks *(Non-designated Limited Liabili)*, Jane Cox *(Non-designated Limited Liabili)*, Navdeep Dulai *(Head of Finance)*, Kevin Horn *(Non-designated Limited Liabili)*, Samantha Miles *(Non-designated Limited Liabili)*, Paul Winslade *(Non-designated Limited Liabili)*
**Finance:** Navdeep Dulai *(Head of Finance)*
**US SIC:** 8111 **UK SIC:** 83500
**Bankers:** Lloyds TSB Bank plc (30-93-17)

| | 30-04-14 | 30-04-13 | 31-04-12 |
|---|---|---|---|
| TO | N/A | N/A | 4,704,804 |
| NW | (45,000) | N/A | N/A |
| WC | 1,761,898 | 1,065,834 | 517,127 |
| Emp. | N/A | N/A | 112 |

DUNS 22-055-6406
## Warner Howard Group Ltd
(**Subsidiary of:** Phs Group Holdings Ltd)
Warner Howard House, Harrow, Middlesex HA3 0XD
**Tel:** 02089270100 **Fax:** 01484401454
**Web:** www.warnerhoward.co.uk
**Reg No:** 4057631 **Estd:** 2000 Private Limited Company
**Line of Business:** Washroom services
**Issued Capital:** £138,600
**Director:** S A Woods
**Co. Secretary:** David Finlayson
**Responsibilities**
**Senior:** Jan Henley *(Chief Executive PA)*, Debbie Mayo *(Chief Executive PA)*
**Branches:** Warner Howard Group Ltd, 313 Blochairn Road, Glasgow, Lanarkshire G21 2RX
**US SIC:** 7219 **UK SIC:** 98110
**Auditors:** BDO Stoy Hayward LLP

| | 31-03-14 | 31-03-13 | 31-03-12 |
|---|---|---|---|
| TA | 125,676,000 | 125,676,000 | 125,676,000 |
| NW | 186,000 | 186,000 | 186,000 |
| WC | (80,284,000) | (80,284,000) | (80,284,000) |

DUNS 73-946-5128
## Warner Land Surveys Ltd
Beaumont House, 59 High Street, Theale, Theale, Reading, Berkshire RG7 5AL
**Tel:** 01189-303314
**Web:** www.warnerlandsurveys.com
**Reg No:** 2945461 **VAT No:** 314325787
**Estd:** 1994 Private Limited Company
**Line of Business:** Architects
**Issued Capital:** £71,000
**Directors:** S G Wilkinson, D D Hutson, P J Field
**Co. Secretary:** Martin Green
**Responsibilities**
**Senior:** Kristian Nixon *(Manager)*
**Branches:** Warner Land Surveys Ltd, Dashwood House, 69 Old Broad Street, London EC2M 1NA
**US SIC:** 8911 **UK SIC:** 83701
**Auditors:** Griffins
**Bankers:** HSBC Bank plc (40-35-34)

| | 31-07-13 | 31-07-12 | 31-07-11 |
|---|---|---|---|
| TA | 1,498,003 | 1,334,986 | 1,269,342 |
| NW | 617,332 | 698,025 | 848,628 |
| WC | 659,927 | 685,461 | 812,278 |

DUNS 39-952-7548

## Warner Music International Services Ltd

**(Subsidiary of:** Access Industries Inc.)
Warner Building, 28 Kensington Church Street, London W8 4EP
**Tel:** 02079380000 **Fax:** 0207-368-2777
**Web:** www.warnermusic.co.uk
**Reg No:** 2258593 **Estd:** 1988 Private Limited Company
**Line of Business:** Holding companies management activities
**Export Sales:** £41,657,000
**Issued Capital:** £242,361,742
**Directors:** J M Morris, C J Ancliff, P M Robinson, R D Booker
**Co. Secretary:** Olswang Cosec Limited
**Responsibilities**
**Senior:** Edgar Bronfman *(Manager)*
**Health & Safety:** Geraldine Allen *(facilities & building Coordina)*
**Facilities:** Geraldine Allen *(facilities & building Coordina)*
**Branches:** Warner Music International Services Ltd, 35-38 Portman Sq, London W1H 6LF
**US SIC:** 6711, 3652
**UK SIC:** 83962, 34520
**Auditors:** Ernst & Young LLP
**Bankers:** Barclays Bank Plc (20-36-47)

| | 27-09-13 | 30-09-12 | 30-09-11 |
|---|---|---|---|
| TO | 45,632,000 | 39,616,000 | 40,266,000 |
| P/L | 2,103,000 | 2,229,000 | 2,047,000 |
| NW | 127,692,000 | 126,616,000 | 124,973,000 |
| WC | (4,040,000) | (5,720,000) | (6,047,000) |
| Emp. | 107 | 85 | 87 |

DUNS 28-848-6103

## Warner Music (U K) Ltd

**(Subsidiary of:** Access Industries Inc.)
Warner Building, 28 Kensington Church Street, London W8 4EP
**Tel:** 020-7368-2500 **Fax:** 020-7368-2770
**Web:** www.wmg.com
**Reg No:** 0680511 **Estd:** 1961 Private Limited Company
**Line of Business:** Wholesale of gramophone records, audio tapes, compact discs and video tapes and of the equipment on which these are played
**Export Sales:** £23,264,000
**Issued Capital:** £400
**Directors:** P M Robinson, R D Booker, C J Ancliff, S K Robson
**Co. Secretary:** Olswang Cosec Limited
**Responsibilities**
**Senior:** Richard Manners *(Proprietor)*
**IT:** Frank Jaschinski *(IT Director)*, Johnathon Smallwood *(It Customer Services Director)*
**Branches:** Warner Music (U K) Ltd, 74-80 Camden St, London NW1 0EG
**US SIC:** 5064, 3652
**UK SIC:** 61500, 34520
**Auditors:** Ernst & Young LLP
**Bankers:** Barclays Bank Plc (20-03-80)

| | 27-09-13 | 30-09-12 | 30-09-11 |
|---|---|---|---|
| TO | 150,893,000 | 134,116,000 | 143,822,000 |
| P/L | (3,351,000) | (7,030,000) | 4,108,000 |
| NW | (29,235,000) | (27,464,000) | (23,196,000) |
| WC | (41,702,000) | (42,442,000) | (39,715,000) |
| Emp. | 232 | 251 | 261 |

DUNS 21-158-0915 Exp

## Warner/Chappell Music Ltd

**(Subsidiary of:** Access Industries Inc.)
Griffin House, 161 Hammersmith Road, London W6 8BS
**Tel:** 02085635800
**Web:** www.warnerchappell.com
**Reg No:** 0488466 **Estd:** 1950 Private Limited Company
**Line of Business:** Business services
**Export Markets:** Worldwide
**Export Sales:** £31,185,145
**Issued Capital:** £100
**Principals:** J R Manners *(Managing)*, M A Lavin *(Financial)*, C A Strang, W S Mcdowell Iii, R D Booker, Ms J S Smith
**Co. Secretary:** Olswang Cosec Limited
**US SIC:** 8999 **UK SIC:** 83954
**Auditors:** Ernst & Young LLP
**Bankers:** Barclays Bank Plc (20-36-47)

| | 30-09-13 | 30-09-12 | 30-09-11 |
|---|---|---|---|
| TO | 69,065,147 | 67,463,599 | 70,626,588 |
| P/L | 10,484,376 | 10,118,874 | 9,190,964 |
| NW | 11,771,541 | 3,529,679 | 667,936 |
| WC | (18,948,961) | (27,626,899) | (30,916,297) |
| Emp. | 69 | 68 | 63 |

DUNS 64-252-5612

## Warners

22 St Patrick Square, Edinburgh, Midlothian EH8 9EY
**Web:** www.warnersol.com
**Estd:** 1982 Partnership
**Line of Business:** Solicitors
**Partners:** S Craig, S Brown
**Responsibilities**
**Senior:** Garry Alen *(Office Manager)*, Bill Gibson *(Partner)*, Craig Innes *(Partner)*, Ross Kennedy *(Partner)*
**Finance:** Bob Clephane *(Financial Director)*
**Marketing:** Garry Alen *(Office Manager)*
**Sales:** Garry Alen *(Office Manager)*
**Admin:** Garry Alen *(Office Manager)*
**HR:** Garry Alen *(Office Manager)*
**Health & Safety:** Garry Alen *(Office Manager)*
**Facilities:** Garry Alen *(Office Manager)*
**Operations:** Garry Alen *(Office Manager)*
**Branches:** Warners, 176 Portobello High Street, Edinburgh, Midlothian EH15 1EX
**US SIC:** 8111, 6531
**UK SIC:** 83500, 83400
**Employees:** 67

DUNS 77-933-4684

## Warners Law Llp

Bank House, Bank Street, Tonbridge, Kent TN9 1BL
**Tel:** 01732770660
**Web:** www.warners-solicitors.co.uk
**Reg No:** 0320151OC **Estd:** 2006 Private Limited Company
**Line of Business:** Company formation services
**Responsibilities**
**Senior:** Matthew Aves *(Non-designated Limited Liabili)*, Rayma Collins *(Non-designated Limited Liabili)*, John Mcauliffe *(Non-designated Limited Liabili)*, Angela Rowe *(Non-designated Limited Liabili)*, Matthew Sabine *(Non-designated Limited Liabili)*, Robert Twining *(Non-designated Limited Liabili)*
**US SIC:** 8111 **UK SIC:** 83500
**Bankers:** National Westminster Bank Plc (60-01-21)

| | 30-09-13 | 30-09-12 | 30-09-11 |
|---|---|---|---|
| TA | 2,156,404 | 2,327,363 | 2,251,917 |
| NW | N/A | 117,705 | 103,878 |
| WC | 1,072,248 | 836,814 | 798,665 |

DUNS 21-807-0548

## Warners (Midlands)Plc

The Maltings, West Street, Bourne, Lincolnshire PE10 9PH
**Tel:** 01778-391000 **Fax:** 01778-425888
**Web:** www.warners.co.uk
**Reg No:** 0223519 **VAT No:** 119147769
**Estd:** 1926 Public Limited Company
**Line of Business:** Printing not elsewhere classified
**Issued Capital:** £54,800
**Principals:** P A Warner *(Managing)*, Ms J M Warner
**Co. Secretary:** Stephen Warner
**Responsibilities**
**Senior:** Tom Brown *(Distribution Manager)*, Collette Dimbleby *(Manager)*, Ian Greenfield *(General Manager)*
**Marketing:** Andrea Kettle *(Relations Manager)*, Vicki Stevenson *(Relations Manager)*, Andrew York *(Sales & Marketing Manager)*
**Sales:** Michelle Harris *(Key Account Manager)*, Tracy Henson *(Key Account Manager)*, Andrew York *(Sales & Marketing Manager)*
**IT:** Ben Issit *(IT Manager)*
**HR:** Mark Lynch *(Personnel Manager)*
**Operations:** Andrew York *(Sales & Marketing Manager)*
**Branches:** Warners (Midlands)public Limited Company, 3rd Flr Grant Ho, 56-60 St John St, London EC1M 4HG
**US SIC:** 2752 **UK SIC:** 47544
**Auditors:** Saffery Champness
**Bankers:** HSBC Bank plc (40-12-32)

| | 30-09-14 | 30-09-13 | 30-09-12 |
|---|---|---|---|
| TO | 34,200,349 | 32,793,083 | 34,599,036 |
| P/L | 2,146,015 | 2,249,174 | 2,498,524 |
| NW | 18,789,803 | 18,000,251 | 16,802,546 |
| WC | 1,664,049 | 2,254,700 | 2,120,507 |
| Emp. | 243 | 247 | 251 |

DUNS 29-765-4535

## Warners of Gloucester Ltd

Eastern Avenue, Gloucester, Gloucestershire GL4 3BS
**Tel:** 01452529755
**Web:** www.warnerscars.co.uk
**Reg No:** 2028470 **Estd:** 1986 Private Limited Company
**Line of Business:** Car dealers (new & used)
**Issued Capital:** £950,125
**Directors:** C Smart, D Ryland, M D Warner, G D Warner, M Jones
**Co. Secretary:** Ms Anita Jenkins
**Branches:** Warners Of Gloucester Ltd, 333 Bristol Rd, Gloucester, Gloucestershire GL2 5DN
**US SIC:** 5511, 7539
**UK SIC:** 65100, 67100
**Auditors:** Hazlewoods
**Bankers:** Lloyds TSB Bank plc (30-93-48)

| | 30-09-13 | 30-09-12 | 30-09-11 |
|---|---|---|---|
| TO | 25,968,612 | 23,804,030 | 22,394,617 |
| P/L | 124,320 | 2,084 | (7,753) |
| NW | 534,782 | 445,237 | 453,516 |
| WC | 285,113 | 194,122 | 175,469 |
| Emp. | 87 | 86 | 86 |

DUNS 28-891-2611

## Warners Retail Ltd

**(Subsidiary of:** Warners Retail Group Ltd)
Bredon Road, Tewkesbury, Gloucestershire GL20 5DA
**Tel:** 01684294223
**Web:** www.shell.co.uk
**Reg No:** 1282570 **Estd:** 1976 Private Limited Company
**Line of Business:** Retail sale of automotive fuel
**Issued Capital:** £100
**Principals:** M D Warner *(Managing)*, G D Warner, Ms M A Warner
**Co. Secretary:** Ms Anita Jenkins
**Responsibilities**
**Senior:** Oliver Strade *(Manager)*
**Branches:** Warners Retail Ltd, 121 Bristol Road, Gloucester, Gloucestershire GL2 4NB
**US SIC:** 5541 **UK SIC:** 65200
**Auditors:** Hazlewoods

| | 30-09-13 | 30-09-12 | 30-09-11 |
|---|---|---|---|
| TO | 12,483,464 | 11,583,162 | 11,312,153 |
| P/L | 190,707 | 162,842 | 185,159 |
| NW | 160,556 | 61,016 | 113,291 |
| WC | (795,613) | (718,466) | (597,382) |
| Emp. | 80 | 81 | 80 |

DUNS 67-212-5176

## Warners Retail (Moreton) Ltd

**(Subsidiary of:** Warners Retail Group Ltd)
Unit 2, 130 Bristol Road, Gloucester, Gloucestershire GL1 5SQ
**Tel:** 01608651854
**Web:** www.warnersbudgens.co.uk
**Reg No:** 6020641 **Estd:** 2006 Private Limited Company
**Line of Business:** Retail sale in non-specialised stores with food, beverages or tobacco predominating
**Issued Capital:** £100
**Directors:** M D Warner, G D Warner, Ms M A Warner
**Co. Secretary:** Ms Anita Jenkins
**US SIC:** 5411 **UK SIC:** 64100

| | 30-09-13 | 30-09-12 | 30-09-11 |
|---|---|---|---|
| TO | 6,774,825 | 6,716,021 | 6,551,017 |
| P/L | 115,080 | 112,016 | 35,232 |
| NW | 668,610 | 479,215 | 314,612 |
| WC | (485,221) | (351,554) | (420,269) |
| Emp. | 56 | 52 | 55 |

DUNS 21-631-7594

## Warners Trust Plc

Eastern Avenue, Gloucester, Gloucestershire GL4 3BS
**Tel:** 08453133810
**Web:** www.warnerscars.co.uk
**Reg No:** 0413728 **Estd:** 1920 Public Limited Company
**Line of Business:** Management activities of holding companies
**Issued Capital:** £50,006
**Principals:** M D Warner *(Managing)*, Ms R A Warner
**Co. Secretary:** Ms Anita Jenkins
**Branches:** Warners Trust Plc, Blaisdon Way, Cheltenham, Gloucestershire GL51 0WH
**US SIC:** 6711 **UK SIC:** 83962
**Auditors:** Hazlewoods
**Bankers:** Lloyds TSB Bank plc (30-93-48)

| | 30-09-13 | 30-09-12 | 30-09-11 |
|---|---|---|---|
| TO | 25,968,612 | 23,804,030 | 22,394,617 |
| P/L | 173,543 | (43,240) | 38,554 |
| NW | 2,934,832 | 2,847,150 | 2,951,885 |
| WC | (395,658) | (398,084) | (599,207) |
| Emp. | 90 | 89 | 89 |

DUNS 21-043-2091

## Waroughton Parish Church

The Vicarage, Church Hill, Wroughton, Swindon, Wiltshire SN4 9JS
**Web:** www.wroughton.com
**Estd:** 2002 Proprietorship
**Line of Business:** Places of worship
**Proprietor:** M Johnson
**US SIC:** 8661 **UK SIC:** 96600
**Employees:** 100

DUNS 21-809-6481

## Warranty Wise Insurance Services

Petre Court, Accrington, Lancashire BB5 5HY
**Tel:** 08000014990
**Web:** www.warrantywise.co.uk
**VAT No:** 994091485 **Estd:** 2012 Partnership
**Line of Business:** Insurance services
**Trading Style:** Warrantywise
**Partners:** A Whittaker, Ms A Keenan, Ms A Whittaker, L Whittaker
**Responsibilities**
**IT:** Scott Baxter *(IT Manager)*
**US SIC:** 6411, 7539
**UK SIC:** 83200, 67100
**Employees:** 55

DUNS 22-726-2847

## Warren Adams

96-122 Uxbridge Road, London W13 8RA
**Tel:** 02082809900
**Web:** www.warrenevans.com
**Estd:** 1995 Proprietorship
**Line of Business:** Beds and bedding
**Proprietor:** W Adams
**Responsibilities**
**Senior:** Warren Evans *(Proprietor)*
**Branches:** 1A Hawley Rd Camden Lock London NW1
**US SIC:** 2392, 5719
**UK SIC:** 45550, 64700
**Bankers:** Lloyds TSB Bank plc (30-96-29)
**Employees:** 80

DUNS 21-233-6425

## Warren Childrens Centre

Woodland Park, Lisburn, Co Antrim BT28 1LQ
**Tel:** 028-92607528
**Web:** www.setrust.hscni.net
**Estd:** 1996 Proprietorship
**Line of Business:** Health centres
**Proprietor:** Mrs W Sherlock
**Responsibilities**
**Senior:** Susan Barr *(Administration Manager)*
**US SIC:** 8091 **UK SIC:** 95200
**Employees:** 50

DUNS 21-478-2939

## Warren Evans

Unit 4 Uplands Business Park, Blackhorse Lane, London E17 5QJ
**Tel:** 02085018995
**Web:** www.warrenevans.com
**Estd:** 2011
**Line of Business:** Manufacturers of household furnishings
**Responsibilities**
**Senior:** Christine Sim *(Manager)*
**US SIC:** 2517 **UK SIC:** 46714
**Employees:** 100

DUNS 21-317-8226

## Warren Grange Nursing Home

66 Warren Road, Liverpool, Merseyside L23 6UG
**Tel:** 0151-932-0286
**Web:** www.warrencare.co.uk
**Estd:** 1988 Proprietorship
**Line of Business:** Nursing homes
**Proprietor:** J Lysaght
**Responsibilities**
**Senior:** Margaret Sadi *(Home Manager)*
**Branches:** 14 Warren Rd, Liverpool
**US SIC:** 8051 **UK SIC:** 95100
**Employees:** 60

DUNS 34-734-8570

## Warren House Conference Centre Ltd

Warren Road, Kingston-Upon-Thames, Surrey KT2 7HY
**Tel:** 02085471777
**Web:** www.warrenhouse.com
**Reg No:** 5537011 **Estd:** 1954 Private Limited Company
**Line of Business:** Hotels
**Issued Capital:** £14,000,000
**Directors:** O L O'Callaghan-Brown, Dr P J Brown, Mrs V K Good
**Co. Secretary:** Mrs Patricia Brown
**Responsibilities**
**Senior:** Colin Dunnicliffe *(Partner)*, Tony Hearsfield *(Partner)*, Carolyn Henderson *(House Manager)*
**IT:** Karen Coomber *(Accounts Manager)*
**Health & Safety:** Carolyn Henderson *(House Manager)*
**US SIC:** 7011, 6531
**UK SIC:** 66500, 83400

| | 31-03-14 | 31-03-13 | 31-03-12 |
|---|---|---|---|
| TO | 2,923,597 | 2,654,116 | N/A |
| P/L | (174,753) | (181,873) | N/A |
| NW | 9,427,510 | 9,382,616 | 9,370,372 |
| WC | 1,391,086 | 1,383,425 | 1,382,507 |
| Emp. | 68 | 65 | N/A |

DUNS 28-913-4389

## Warren James (Jewellers) Ltd

7 Merseyway, Stockport, Cheshire SK1 1PN
**Tel:** 01614-771-814
**Web:** www.warrenjames.co.uk
**Reg No:** 1432090 **VAT No:** 696372683
**Estd:** 1979 Private Limited Company
**Line of Business:** Jewellery retailers
**Issued Capital:** £100,000
**Managing Director:** J Coulter

**Co. Secretary:** Ms Ann Jones
**Responsibilities**
**Senior:** Dawn Delaney *(Branch Manager)*
**Branches:** Warren James (Jewellers) Ltd, 10A Metrocentre, Cameron Walk, Gateshead, Tyne and Wear NE11 9YR
**US SIC:** 5944 **UK SIC:** 65400
**Auditors:** RSM Tenon Audit Ltd
**Bankers:** Barclays Bank Plc (20-82-14)

| | 31-03-14 | 31-03-13 | 31-03-12 |
|---|---|---|---|
| TO | 73,630,000 | 58,606,373 | 59,039,848 |
| P/L | 26,239,000 | 17,109,396 | 15,887,174 |
| NW | 119,833,000 | 100,000,220 | 87,071,311 |
| WC | 101,222,000 | 81,853,213 | 72,345,275 |
| Emp. | 878 | 828 | 795 |

DUNS 21-094-5445
## The Warren Medical Centre
The Warren, Hayes, Middlesex UB4 0SG
**Tel:** 02085732476
**Web:** www.redpublish.co.uk
**Estd:** 1997 Partnership
**Line of Business:** Doctors
**Partners:** Dr T O'Kane, Dr I Caie
**Responsibilities**
**Senior:** Michelle Lyon *(Manager)*, T O' Kane *(Partner)*
**US SIC:** 8062 **UK SIC:** 95100
**Employees:** 50

DUNS 21-579-7529
## Warren Park
White Lane, Chapeltown, Sheffield, South Yorkshire S35 2YH
**Tel:** 01142570595
**Web:** www.mimosahealthcare.com
**Estd:** 1995 Partnership
**Line of Business:** Medical nursing home activities
**Partner:** J Cranmer
**Responsibilities**
**Senior:** Jonathan Hoyle *(Manager)*, Michelle Mehca *(Manager)*
**US SIC:** 8051 **UK SIC:** 95100
**Employees:** 55

DUNS 21-728-5679
## Warren Road Primary School
Warren Road, Orpington, Kent BR6 6JF
**Tel:** 01689853798
**Web:** www.warrenroad.bromley.sch.uk
**Reg No:** 7645774 **Estd:** 1937 Private Company Limited By Guarantee
**Line of Business:** General secondary education
**Directors:** Ms S V Fernando, R T Hulme, Ms C M Knowles, Ms J S English, Ms T L Harvey, F Musanhu, H Yu, R A Jackson
**Responsibilities**
**Senior:** Mary Barette *(Director)*, Justine Keene *(Director)*, Malcolm Leng *(Director)*, Susan Meckiff *(Head Teacher)*, Paula Reddin *(Director)*, Vathana Sackett *(Director)*, Carol Tarhan *(Director)*
**US SIC:** 8211 **UK SIC:** 93200
**Bankers:** Lloyds TSB Bank plc (30-94-66)

| | 31-08-14 | 31-08-13 | 31-08-12 |
|---|---|---|---|
| TO | 3,364,201 | 3,608,884 | 11,681,301 |
| P/L | (18,001) | 407,714 | 8,128,804 |
| NW | 8,347,517 | 8,329,518 | 7,921,804 |
| WC | 262,617 | 344,862 | 269,274 |
| Emp. | 127 | 72 | 120 |

DUNS 49-072-0547
## Warren Services Ltd
**(Subsidiary of:** Rawner Ltd)
4 Fison Way, Thetford, Norfolk IP24 1HT
**Tel:** 01842-760850
**Web:** www.warrenservices.co.uk
**Reg No:** 3081991 **Estd:** 1995 Private Limited Company
**Line of Business:** Other engineering activities
**Issued Capital:** £1,000
**Directors:** C E Poyner, Mrs C L Bridgman, W R Bridgman, R Bridgman, Mrs R S Mason
**Co. Secretary:** Mrs Sharon Bridgman
**Responsibilities**
**Senior:** Martin Rickard *(Manager)*, Estee Ross *(Manager)*
**US SIC:** 8911 **UK SIC:** 83701

| | 31-12-13 | 31-12-12 | 31-12-11 |
|---|---|---|---|
| TA | 2,842,561 | 2,831,481 | 2,682,658 |
| NW | 928,912 | 968,520 | 923,077 |
| WC | 348,063 | 377,770 | 346,835 |

DUNS 22-741-7581 **Imp-Exp**
## Warrenpoint Harbour Authority
The Docks, Warrenpoint, Newry, Co Down BT34 3JR
**Tel:** 02841773381 **Fax:** 028-4177-3962
**Web:** www.warrenpointharbour.co.uk
**Estd:** 1971 Incorporate By Act Of Parliament
**Line of Business:** Operation of habours and ports
**Export Markets:** E E C
**Principals:** D Connolly *(Chairman)*, D Wheeler *(Financial)*, Q Goldie, T Stephenson
**Responsibilities**
**Senior:** Kieren Grant *(Finance Director)*
**Finance:** Kieren Grant *(Finance Director)*
**US SIC:** 4469, 4411
**UK SIC:** 76300, 74001
**Bankers:** Ulster Bank Ltd (98-11-40)
**Employees:** 51

DUNS 28-916-8494
## Warrens Bakery Ltd
Boswedden Road, St Just, St Just, Penzance, Cornwall TR19 7JP
**Tel:** 01736-788538 **Fax:** 01736788354
**Web:** www.warrensbakery.co.uk
**Reg No:** 1451668 **VAT No:** 383931820
**Estd:** 1977 Private Limited Company
**Line of Business:** Manufacture of bread; manufacture of fresh pastry goods and cakes
**Trading Style:** Warrens Traditional Bakery
**Issued Capital:** £30,000
**Directors:** M Sullivan, J Jobling, S D Toft, Ms A L Martin, N B Straw
**Branches:** Warrens Bakery Ltd, 95 Wolseley Road, Plymouth, Devon PL2 3BL
**US SIC:** 2051, 5462
**UK SIC:** 41960, 64100
**Auditors:** Walker Moyle
**Bankers:** Barclays Bank Plc (20-67-19)

| | 30-06-14 | 30-06-13 | 30-06-12 |
|---|---|---|---|
| TO | 12,284,343 | 11,684,714 | 12,640,610 |
| P/L | (307,677) | (869,167) | (706,946) |
| NW | (404,644) | (296,967) | 335,066 |
| WC | (1,338,571) | (1,979,743) | (1,345,065) |
| Emp. | 466 | 440 | 455 |

DUNS 34-631-9296
## Warrens' Warehousing & Distribution (Midlands) Ltd
**(Subsidiary of:** Warrens Warehousing Group Ltd)
40 Victoria Way Charlton, London SE7 7QS
**Tel:** 020-8858-2356 **Fax:** 020-8858-4888
**Web:** www.warrens-midlands.co.uk
**Reg No:** 2765595 **Estd:** 1992 Private Limited Company
**Line of Business:** Road haulage and transport services
**Issued Capital:** £1,111
**Director:** M R Warren
**Co. Secretary:** Mark Allen
**Responsibilities**
**Senior:** Douglas Warren *(Manager)*
**Branches:** 5 Chariot Way, Glebe Farm Est, Rugby Warwickshire CV21 1DA (Tel: 0788-575600 Fax: 0788-575976)
**US SIC:** 4789 **UK SIC:** 77002
**Auditors:** Blumire & Associates
**Bankers:** Barclays Bank Plc (20-98-57)

| | 31-12-13 | 31-12-12 | 31-12-11 |
|---|---|---|---|
| TO | 31,350,870 | 29,444,981 | 26,112,515 |
| P/L | 769,849 | 1,123,275 | 856,264 |
| NW | 4,379,295 | 3,787,558 | 2,644,260 |
| WC | 3,099,852 | 2,674,800 | 3,405,039 |
| Emp. | 361 | 330 | 300 |

DUNS 23-256-8852
## Warrington and Halton Hospitals Nhs Foundation Trust
Warrington Hospital, Lovely Lane, Warrington, Cheshire WA5 1QG
**Web:** www.warringtonandhaltonhospitals.nhs.uk
**Estd:** 2002
**Line of Business:** Hospitals
**Trading Style:** Warrington Hospital, Halton General Hospital, Cheshire and Merseyside Treatment Centre
**Principals:** A Massey *(Chairman)*, J Stephens *(Financial)*, Ms S Samuals, Ms C Beardshaw, R Adam, Ms C Withenshaw, Ms M Banner, Ms C Briegal
**Responsibilities**
**Senior:** Allan Mackie *(Non-Executive Director)*, Melanie Pickup *(Chief Executive)*
**Branches:** Warrington and Halton Hospitals Nhs Foundation Trust, West Bank Medical Centre, 2 Lower Church Street, Widnes, Cheshire WA8 0NG
**US SIC:** 8062, 8091, 9121
**UK SIC:** 95100, 95200, 91110
**Auditors:** PriceWaterhouseCoopers LLP

| | 31-03-14 | 31-03-13 | 31-03-12 |
|---|---|---|---|
| TO | 194,633,000 | 190,654,000 | 183,784,000 |
| P/L | (2,849,000) | (1,109,000) | 926,000 |
| NW | 135,153,000 | 133,050,000 | 115,995,000 |
| WC | 2,904,000 | 2,495,000 | 677,000 |
| Emp. | 3,599 | 3,463 | 3,466 |

DUNS 21-330-0571
## Warrington Borough Council
Palmyra House, Palmyra Square North, Warrington, Cheshire WA1 1JN
**Tel:** 01925443322
**Web:** www.warrington.gov.uk
**Line of Business:** Social work activities
**Trading Style:** Warrington Borough Council
**Responsibilities**
**Senior:** Alastair Elder *(PC Manager)*
**US SIC:** 8999 **UK SIC:** 83954
**Employees:** 8,000

DUNS 29-664-2168
## Warrington Borough Transport Ltd
**(Subsidiary of:** Warrington Borough Council)
Wilderspool Causeway, Warrington, Cheshire WA4 6PT
**Tel:** 01925-634296 **Fax:** 01925-418382
**Web:** www.warringtonboroughtransport.co.uk
**Reg No:** 1990371 **VAT No:** 428943030
**Estd:** 1902 Private Limited Company
**Line of Business:** Other passenger land transport
**Issued Capital:** £888,000
**Directors:** Rev S Parish, J Burke, T Higgins, Ms P Nelson, D Graham, D Price, Ms M Banner, Dr B Axcell
**Co. Secretary:** Damian Graham
**Responsibilities**
**Senior:** Peter Carey *(Director)*, Thomas Hoyle *(Manager)*, Alastair Nuttall *(Director)*, Annmarie Slabin *(Interim Managing Director)*
**US SIC:** 4141 **UK SIC:** 72102
**Auditors:** PricewaterhouseCoopers
**Bankers:** HSBC Bank plc (40 45 21)

| | 31-03-14 | 31-03-13 | 31-03-12 |
|---|---|---|---|
| TO | 11,288,900 | 11,632,900 | 11,530,922 |
| P/L | (725,400) | 708,403 | (131,736) |
| NW | 3,492,660 | 3,958,577 | 2,582,577 |
| WC | (809,217) | (2,229,154) | (635,202) |
| Emp. | 255 | 272 | 265 |

DUNS 34-517-3582
## Warrington Business School Ltd
**(Subsidiary of:** Warrington Collegiate)
Winwick Road Campus, Winwick Road, Warrington, Cheshire WA2 8QA
**Tel:** 0845-849-0020
**Web:** www.thewbs.co.uk
**Reg No:** 5328120 **Estd:** 2005 Private Limited Company
**Line of Business:** Sub-degree level higher education
**Issued Capital:** £100
**Directors:** J E Mccrudden, C Daniels, Mrs M D Seeley
**Co. Secretary:** Frank Hardman
**Responsibilities**
**Senior:** Paul Hafren *(Director)*
**US SIC:** 8221 **UK SIC:** 93100

| | 31-07-14 | 31-07-13 | 31-07-12 |
|---|---|---|---|
| TA | 100 | 100 | 100 |
| NW | 100 | 100 | 100 |

DUNS 22-001-8984
## Warrington Clinical Commissioning Group
Arpley House, 110 Birchwood Boulevard, Warrington, Cheshire WA4 7QH
**Web:** ww.warringtonccg.nhs.uk
**Estd:** 2012
**Line of Business:** Clinical Commissioning Group
**Trading Style:** Warrington Ccg
**US SIC:** 8091 **UK SIC:** 95200
**Employees:** 100

DUNS 76-717-0558
## Warrington Community Living
The Gateway, 85 Sankey Street, Warrington, Cheshire WA1 1SR
**Tel:** 01925-246870 **Fax:** 01925246879
**Web:** www.wcl.uk.net
**Reg No:** 2595601 **Estd:** 2010 Private Limited Company
**Line of Business:** Activities of other membership organisations not elsewhere classified
**Trading Style:** Heathside Residential Care Home
**Directors:** T J Ennis, A Kemp, Ms J L Wycherley, Ms H A Whitfield, Ms M Sudlow, G Spenley
**Co. Secretary:** Michael Finlay
**Responsibilities**
**Senior:** Mark Leah *(Manager)*
**Branches:** Warrington Community Living, 28 Station Road South, Warrington, Cheshire WA2 0QS
**US SIC:** 8999 **UK SIC:** 83954
**Auditors:** Livesey Spottiswood
**Bankers:** Barclays Bank Plc (20-91-48)

| | 31-03-14 | 31-03-13 | 31-03-12 |
|---|---|---|---|
| TO | 2,888,050 | 4,218,804 | 4,253,024 |
| P/L | 142,791 | 47,576 | 118,789 |
| NW | 4,377,604 | 3,414,813 | 3,921,237 |
| WC | 3,271,501 | 3,020,046 | 2,890,225 |
| Emp. | 128 | 206 | 213 |

DUNS 21-931-3632
## Warrington Fabrication Co Ltd
Athertons Quay, Liverpool Road, Warrington, Cheshire WA5 1AH
**Fax:** 01925-411604
**Web:** www.warrfabs.co.uk
**Reg No:** 1382523 **VAT No:** 295060159
**Estd:** 1978 Private Limited Company
**Line of Business:** Construction of civil engineering constructions
**Issued Capital:** £114
**Managing Director:** M Simcock
**Co. Secretary:** Robert Backhouse
**Responsibilities**
**HR:** Rachael Pettitt *(Human Resources Manager)*
**Facilities:** Phil Dowling *(Facilities)*
**US SIC:** 1622 **UK SIC:** 50200
**Bankers:** National Westminster Bank Plc (01-09-17)

| | 31-12-13 | 31-12-12 | 31-12-11 |
|---|---|---|---|
| TO | 7,692,979 | 7,645,457 | 6,911,005 |
| P/L | 752,509 | 159,236 | 240,907 |
| NW | 1,590,421 | 1,173,091 | 1,062,494 |
| WC | 797,593 | 316,922 | 117,321 |
| Emp. | 65 | 67 | 63 |

DUNS 28-834-7206
## The Warrington Football Club Ltd
**(Subsidiary of:** Warrington Sports Holdings Ltd)
Halliwell Jones Stadium, Winwick Road, Warrington, Cheshire WA2 7NE
**Tel:** 01925248880
**Web:** www.warringtonwolves.org
**Reg No:** 0370871 **VAT No:** 152685258
**Estd:** 1941 Private Limited Company
**Line of Business:** Sports clubs
**Trading Style:** Warrington Rugby League Football Club
**Issued Capital:** £1,723,000
**Directors:** S J Broomhead, A J Gatcliffe
**Co. Secretary:** Charles Agar
**Responsibilities**
**HR:** Deborah Henderson *(HR Manager)*
**US SIC:** 7999 **UK SIC:** 97913
**Auditors:** Moores Rowland Warrington
**Bankers:** Barclays Bank Plc (20-91-48)

| | 30-11-13 | 30-11-12 | 30-11-11 |
|---|---|---|---|
| TA | 1,526,125 | 1,137,499 | 1,021,945 |
| NW | (1,714,887) | (1,728,826) | (2,238,005) |
| WC | (1,437,749) | (1,451,315) | (1,623,511) |

DUNS 28-893-6628
## The Warrington Homes Ltd
Linleys, Corsham, Wiltshire SN13 9PD
**Fax:** 01249280051
**Web:** www.warringtonresidentialcare.org.uk
**Reg No:** 1302478 **Estd:** 1977 Private Limited Company
**Line of Business:** Residential care establishments
**Directors:** M C Shirley, Dr N J Davis, J G Brown, Ms G C Stafford, Ms C Reid, J M Chatwin, Doctor R C Drummond, K V Hoffman
**Co. Secretary:** Richard Mauldon
**Responsibilities**
**Senior:** Jodie Llewellyn *(Manager)*
**US SIC:** 8321 **UK SIC:** 96111

| | 31-10-13 | 31-10-12 | 31-10-11 |
|---|---|---|---|
| TO | 1,825,288 | 1,780,570 | 1,125,626 |
| P/L | 156,532 | 221,890 | 7,835 |
| NW | 4,114,659 | 3,958,127 | 3,736,237 |
| WC | 421,493 | 365,463 | 146,932 |
| Emp. | 79 | 72 | 63 |

DUNS 21-723-8112 **Imp-Exp**
## Wartsila Uk Ltd
**(Subsidiary of:** Wärtsilä Technology Oy Ab)
4 Marples Way, Havant, Hampshire PO9 1NX
**Web:** www.wartsila.com
**Reg No:** 1004816 **VAT No:** 107305311
**Estd:** 1971 Private Limited Company
**Line of Business:** Manufacture, supply and engineering design of seals and other specialist equipment used by the marine and power plant industries.
**Export Markets:** Worldwide
**Issued Capital:** £3
**Directors:** A D Dickinson, G G Van Beers, T E Koponen, C D Rowlands
**Co. Secretary:** John Henshaw
**Responsibilities**
**Senior:** Terence Eaves *(Manager)*, Colin Langridge *(Business Development Director)*
**Branches:** WARTSILA UK LTD: Wartsila Specialist Propulsion Services, Inchinnan Business Park, Cartside Avenue, Paisley, PA4 9RX, RENFREWSHIRE.
**US SIC:** 3494 **UK SIC:** 32880
**Auditors:** KPMG LLP
**Bankers:** HSBC Bank plc (40-05-15)

| | 31-12-13 | 31-12-12 | 31-12-11 |
|---|---|---|---|
| TO | 105,757,717 | 102,975,370 | 93,807,542 |
| P/L | 9,336,834 | 7,850,856 | 6,666,858 |
| NW | (9,209,263) | (9,322,832) | (10,825,424) |
| WC | (6,147,413) | (7,031,719) | (9,207,911) |
| Emp. | 353 | 370 | 375 |

DUNS 50-593-8597
## Wartsila Valves Ltd
(**Subsidiary of:** Wärtsilä Technology Oy Ab)
Hawthorn Avenue, Hull, North Humberside HU3 5JX
**Tel:** 01482323163 **Fax:** 01482-224-057
**Web:** www.wartsila.com
**Reg No:** 2532854 **VAT No:** 847752586
**Estd:** 2012 Private Limited Company
**Line of Business:** Manufacturers of valves
**Export Sales:** £20,327,311
**Trading Style:** Shipham Valves, Leeds Valve, Conflow
**Issued Capital:** £422,166
**Directors:** T Koponen, P A Fleetwood
**Co. Secretary:** Peter Dawes
**Responsibilities**
**Senior:** Donald Hammond *(Director)*
**Finance:** Marie Bellamy *(Financial Director)*
**HR:** Marie Bellamy *(Financial Director)*
**Health & Safety:** Dave Sylvester *(Maintenance Manager)*
**Facilities:** Dave Sylvester *(Maintenance Manager)*
**Operations:** Dave Sylvester *(Maintenance Manager)*
**US SIC:** 3494, 8999
**UK SIC:** 32880, 83954
**Auditors:** KPMG LLP
**Bankers:** Lloyds TSB Bank plc (30-97-80)

| | 31-12-13 | 31-12-12 | 31-12-12 |
|---|---|---|---|
| TO | 26,650,853 | 20,830,925 | 32,444,129 |
| P/L | 7,107,334 | 7,999,947 | 2,307,869 |
| NW | 11,100,010 | 0,001,400 | 11,007,011 |
| WC | 12,785,966 | 7,387,821 | 10,426,811 |
| Emp. | 138 | 93 | 109 |

DUNS 29-204-3825
## Wartsila Water Systems Ltd
(**Subsidiary of:** Wärtsilä Technology Oy Ab)
Fleets Corner, Poole, Dorset BH17 0JT
**Tel:** 01202662600
**Web:** www.hamworthy.com
**Reg No:** 0713227 **Estd:** 1962 Private Limited Company
**Line of Business:** Manufacture of machinery for the production and use of mechanical power, except aircraft, vehicle and cycle engines
**Export Sales:** £33,768,000
**Issued Capital:** £25,000
**Directors:** J K Kytola, T Koponen, Dr J Thomas
**Co. Secretary:** Peter Dawes
**US SIC:** 3519, 3559
**UK SIC:** 32811, 32863
**Auditors:** PricewaterhouseCoopers LLP
**Bankers:** National Westminster Bank Plc (50-00-00)

| | 31-12-13 | 31-12-12 | 31-12-12 |
|---|---|---|---|
| TO | 46,827,000 | 25,690,000 | 38,238,000 |
| P/L | 8,943,000 | 5,185,000 | 4,732,000 |
| NW | 6,560,000 | 3,610,000 | (581,000) |
| WC | 7,094,000 | 4,558,000 | 391,000 |
| Emp. | 165 | 158 | 155 |

DUNS 21-030-7707
## Warwick Arts Centre
Gibbet Hill Road, Coventry, West Midlands CV4 7AL
**Tel:** 02476524524
**Web:** www.warwickartcentre.co.uk
**Estd:** 1975 Proprietorship
**Line of Business:** Other artistic and literary creation and interpretation
**Proprietor:** Professor M Taylor
**Responsibilities**
**Senior:** Katie Anderson *(Marketing Director)*, Howard Potts *(Technical Director)*, Andrea Pulford *(Director Planning and Operatio)*, Alan Rivett *(Manager)*
**Marketing:** Katie Anderson *(Marketing Director)*
**Operations:** Andrea Pulford *(Director Planning and Operatio)*
**US SIC:** 8999 **UK SIC:** 83954
**Employees:** 300

DUNS 21-600-2543 **Imp-Exp**
## Warwick Bros.(Alresford)Ltd
(**Subsidiary of:** Ceejay Holdings Ltd)
The Dean, Alresford, Hampshire SO24 9BN
**Tel:** 01962-732681
**Web:** www.warwicktrailers.co.uk
**Reg No:** 0604875 **VAT No:** 188676691
**Estd:** 1958 Private Limited Company
**Line of Business:** General mechanical engineering
**Export Markets:** Worldwide
**Issued Capital:** £1,000
**Director:** C J Jones
**Co. Secretary:** Ms Linda Jones
**US SIC:** 8911 **UK SIC:** 83701

| | 30-04-14 | 30-04-13 | 30-04-12 |
|---|---|---|---|
| TA | 1,501,052 | 1,554,438 | 1,656,998 |
| NW | 1,204,108 | 1,171,062 | 1,105,605 |
| WC | 1,177,518 | 1,137,855 | 1,062,563 |

DUNS 21-775-6315
## Warwick Business School
The University Of Warwick, Coventry, West Midlands CV4 7AL
**Tel:** 02476524306
**Web:** www.wbs.ac.uk
**Estd:** 2002 Proprietorship
**Line of Business:** Colleges (higher education)
**Proprietor:** Professor M Taylor
**Responsibilities**
**Finance:** Joanne Harrison *(Management Accountant)*
**Marketing:** Cara Curran *(Marketing Manager)*, Rachel Goldsby *(Marketing Manager)*, Clare Hudson *(Marketing Manager)*, Tracy Lynch *(Relationships Manager)*
**IT:** Martin Chandler *(IT Director)*
**US SIC:** 8221 **UK SIC:** 93100
**Employees:** 300

DUNS 21-579-7561
## Warwick Girls Marching Band
9 Station Avenue, Warwick, Warwickshire CV34 5HJ
**Tel:** 01926492327
**Estd:** 1979 Proprietorship
**Line of Business:** Musicians and orchestras
**Proprietor:** R Everrett
**US SIC:** 7922 **UK SIC:** 97412
**Employees:** 55

DUNS 77-867-9555
## Warwick Holdings Ltd
Penn Road, Inner Ring Road, Wolverhampton, West Midlands WV2 4HD
**Tel:** 01902427897
**Web:** www.draytongroup.co.uk
**Reg No:** 3034706 **Estd:** 1995 Private Limited Company
**Line of Business:** Management activities of holding companies
**Trading Style:** Drayton Group
**Issued Capital:** £104,313
**Directors:** D F Guest, A J Guest, K R Forbes
**Co. Secretary:** Simon Miles
**US SIC:** 6711, 5511
**UK SIC:** 83962, 65100
**Auditors:** Clement Keys

| | 31-12-13 | 31-12-12 | 31-12-11 |
|---|---|---|---|
| TO | 190,546,944 | 172,944,634 | 150,637,548 |
| P/L | 2,743,631 | 2,183,112 | 88,348 |
| NW | 19,268,867 | 18,800,174 | 18,469,911 |
| WC | 5,334,592 | 7,169,198 | 6,921,895 |
| Emp. | 378 | 366 | 355 |

DUNS 22-234-3183
## Warwick Independent Schools Foundation
Warwick School, Warwick, Warwickshire CV34 6PP
**Tel:** 01926735400
**Web:** www.warwickindependentschools.org
**Reg No:** 4252305 **Estd:** 2001 Private Company Limited By Guarantee
**Line of Business:** Schools (independent)
**Directors:** R M Griffiths, Ms J Marshall, C R Gibbons, Mrs P A Snape, Ms P A Goddard, Professor D Grammatopoulos, R M Dancey, Mrs C A Sawdon
**Co. Secretary:** Simon Jones
**Responsibilities**
**Senior:** John Cavanagh *(Non Executive Director)*, Jennifer Edwards *(Non Executive Director)*, Moira Grainger *(Director)*, Nicholas Keegan *(Director)*, Susan Lampitt *(Director)*, Elizabeth Lillyman *(Director)*, Kathryn Parr *(Director)*
**US SIC:** 8211 **UK SIC:** 93200
**Auditors:** Horwath Clark Whitehill
**Bankers:** Lloyds TSB Bank plc (30-99-15)

| | 31-08-13 | 31-07-12 | 31-08-11 |
|---|---|---|---|
| TO | 27,113,000 | 25,718,000 | 24,412,000 |
| P/L | 1,331,000 | 2,577,000 | 1,191,000 |
| NW | 50,710,000 | 47,813,000 | 46,391,000 |
| WC | 2,533,000 | 3,788,000 | 3,198,000 |
| Emp. | 611 | 403 | 384 |

DUNS 77-509-4154
## Warwick International Group Ltd
(**Subsidiary of:** Cbpe Capital Llp)
Mostyn Road, Holywell, Clwyd CH8 7EJ
**Tel:** 01745-560651 **Fax:** 01745-561353
**Web:** www.warwickint.com
**Reg No:** 2982784 **Estd:** 1994 Private Limited Company
**Line of Business:** Manufacture of other inorganic basic chemicals
**Issued Capital:** £100
**Directors:** A M Smits, Lubrizol Holdings France Sas
**Co. Secretary:** John Davies
**Responsibilities**
**Senior:** Steven Pipe *(Director)*, Mark Strickland *(Director)*
**Finance:** Graeme Bragger *(Head of Finance and IT)*
**HR:** Philip Kelsall *(Head of HR)*
**Health & Safety:** Peter Bryant *(Health & Safety Officer)*, Chris Hickman *(Head of Health, Safety and Env)*
**Operations:** Tony Beck *(Head of Manufacturing)*, Steven Pipe *(Director)*
**Engineering:** Jane Mathews *(Head of Technical Services)*
**US SIC:** 2819 **UK SIC:** 25110
**Auditors:** Deloitte LLP
**Bankers:** HSBC Bank plc (40-27-15)

| | 31-12-13 | 31-12-12 | 31-12-11 |
|---|---|---|---|
| TO | 90,024,000 | 80,566,000 | 78,824,000 |
| P/L | (1,506,000) | 15,898,000 | 17,236,000 |
| NW | 22,456,000 | 20,914,000 | 84,550,000 |
| WC | 5,891,000 | 1,563,000 | 73,382,000 |
| Emp. | 233 | 224 | 225 |

DUNS 21-333-1304
## Warwick Park House
17 Butt Park Road, Plymouth, Devon PL5 3NW
**Web:** www.warwickpark.co.uk
**Estd:** 1993 Partnership
**Line of Business:** Nursing homes
**Partners:** R Jones, C Jones, P Jones
**Responsibilities**
**Senior:** Peter Coterall *(Partner)*
**US SIC:** 8051, 6732
**UK SIC:** 95100, 83100
**Employees:** 55

DUNS 23-082-9611
## Warwick Preparatory School
Bridge Field, Banbury Road, Warwick, Warwickshire CV34 6PL
**Tel:** 01926-491545
**Web:** www.warwickprep.com
**Estd:** 1964
**Line of Business:** General secondary education
**Director:** Mrs D M Robinson
**Responsibilities**
**IT:** Steve Emmerson *(IT Manager)*
**US SIC:** 8211 **UK SIC:** 93200
**Employees:** 90

DUNS 29-669-6172
## Warwick Printing Co Ltd
Caswell Road, Leamington Spa, Warwickshire CV31 1QD
**Tel:** 01926-883355
**Web:** www.warwickprinting.co.uk
**Reg No:** 1995758 **VAT No:** 418870039
**Estd:** 1946 Private Limited Company
**Line of Business:** Printing not elsewhere classified
**Issued Capital:** £10,000
**Managing Director:** A J Young
**Co. Secretary:** Mrs Gillian Young
**Responsibilities**
**Senior:** Dave Hastie *(Works Manager)*
**Health & Safety:** Dave Hastie *(Works Manager)*
**Facilities:** Dave Hastie *(Works Manager)*
**US SIC:** 2752 **UK SIC:** 47544
**Auditors:** Deloitte & Touche
**Bankers:** Lloyds TSB Bank plc (30-00-06)

| | 31-03-14 | 31-03-13 | 31-03-12 |
|---|---|---|---|
| TO | N/A | N/A | 5,790,787 |
| P/L | N/A | N/A | 290,135 |
| NW | 1,592,773 | 1,553,259 | 1,408,328 |
| WC | 512,403 | 464,726 | 381,226 |
| Emp. | N/A | N/A | 66 |

DUNS 64-726-9083
## Warwick School
Warwick School, Myton Road, Warwick, Warwickshire CV34 6UE
**Tel:** 01926-776400
**Web:** www.warwickschool.org
**Estd:** 2001
**Line of Business:** Schools (independent)
**Director:** Doctor P J Cheshire
**Responsibilities**
**Senior:** Ed Halse *(Principal)*, G.a. Tedstone *(Manager)*
**Marketing:** Alison Hartin *(Marketing Manager)*
**IT:** Martyn Colliver *(Head of IT)*, Andrew Joubert *(IT Manager)*, Scott Shreeve *(IT Manager)*
**HR:** Baly Bannister *(Human Resources Manager)*
**Health & Safety:** Lee Hartingan *(Estates Manager)*
**Facilities:** Lee Hartingan *(Estates Manager)*
**Operations:** Alison Hartin *(Marketing Manager)*, Lee Hartingan *(Estates Manager)*
**US SIC:** 8211 **UK SIC:** 93200
**Employees:** 250

DUNS 34-551-2508
## Warwick Street (Ks) Llp
30 Warwick Street, London W1B 5NH
**Tel:** 02074934933
**Web:** www.joneslanglasalle.co.uk
**Reg No:** 0311501OC **Estd:** 2005
**Line of Business:** Chartered surveyors and international property consultants
**Trading Style:** Jll
**Responsibilities**
**Senior:** Jeremy Attfield *(Non-designated Limited Liabili)*, James Beckham *(Non-designated Limited Liabili)*, Mark Bourne *(Non-designated Limited Liabili)*, Melanie Brandon *(Non-designated Limited Liabili)*, John Callander *(Non-designated Limited Liabili)*, Ian Cornock *(Non-designated Limited Liabili)*, Martin Crossley *(Non-designated Limited Liabili)*, Patrick Cryer *(Non-designated Limited Liabili)*, Richard Fiddes *(Non-designated Limited Liabili)*
**Branches:** Warwick Street (Ks) Llp, 40 Berkeley Square, Bristol, Avon BS8 1HU
**US SIC:** 6531, 8911
**UK SIC:** 83400, 83701
**Auditors:** PricewaterhouseCoopers LLP

| | 31-03-14 | 31-03-13 | 31-03-12 |
|---|---|---|---|
| TO | N/A | N/A | 7,846,000 |
| P/L | (4,374,000) | (2,965,000) | N/A |
| NW | (7,339,000) | (2,965,000) | 108,401,000 |
| WC | 69,302,000 | 89,464,000 | 112,463,000 |

DUNS 21-678-8766
## Warwick Students' Union
University Of Warwick, Coventry, West Midlands CV4 7AL
**Tel:** 02476572777 **Fax:** 02476572759
**Web:** www.warwicksu.com
**Reg No:** 7297865 **Estd:** 2012 Private Company Limited By Guarantee
**Line of Business:** Activities of other membership organisations not elsewhere classified
**Directors:** H Gould, Miss N C Pitt, I A Leigh, T Leek, Miss A Husakova, A Thompson, S N Fry, Miss M E Beatty
**Co. Secretary:** Mrs Jacqueline Clements
**Responsibilities**
**Senior:** Robert Ankorn *(Director)*, Ruby Compton-Davies *(Director)*, Emma Cox *(Director)*, Christiane Durr *(Doctor)*, Maahwish Mirza *(Director)*, Judith Ryder *(Director)*, Nathaniel Shiers *(Director)*, Rachel Strudwick *(Director)*, Cathryn Turhan *(Director)*
**Marketing:** Jackie Smyth *(Marketing Manager)*
**US SIC:** 8699 **UK SIC:** 96902
**Bankers:** National Westminster Bank Plc (56-00-45)

| | 31-07-13 | 31-07-12 | 31-07-11 |
|---|---|---|---|
| TO | 7,059,300 | 6,871,153 | 6,689,923 |
| P/L | 196,164 | 214,353 | 265,297 |
| NW | 738,381 | 542,155 | 327,727 |
| WC | 540,392 | 405,917 | 193,673 |
| Emp. | 554 | 582 | 136 |

DUNS 21-309-3776 **Imp-Exp**
## Warwick Ward (Machinery) Ltd
Blacker Hill Sidings, Blacker Hill, Barnsley, South Yorkshire S74 0RE
**Tel:** 01226-747260
**Web:** www.warwick-ward.com
**Reg No:** 0988708 **VAT No:** 172950550
**Estd:** 1970 Private Limited Company
**Line of Business:** Plant dealers
**Export Markets:** Europe, E U & Middle East
**Export Sales:** £2,457,559
**Issued Capital:** £10,000
**Directors:** M Ward, A Ward, Ms B Ward
**Co. Secretary:** Ashley Ward
**Responsibilities**
**Senior:** Paul Ronksley *(Workshop Manager)*
**US SIC:** 5084 **UK SIC:** 61490
**Auditors:** Hawsons
**Bankers:** National Westminster Bank Plc (51-61-35)

| | 30-09-13 | 30-09-12 | 30-09-11 |
|---|---|---|---|
| TO | 15,758,317 | 13,629,548 | 14,686,833 |
| P/L | 1,077,122 | 597,814 | 749,543 |
| NW | 3,741,829 | 3,243,371 | 2,791,445 |
| WC | 3,462,885 | 2,631,695 | 2,266,882 |
| Emp. | 53 | 53 | 48 |

DUNS 21-447-5923
## Warwick Woollen Co Ltd
(**Subsidiary of:** Tom James Company)
Venlaw Road, Peebles, Peeblesshire EH45 8AY
**Tel:** 01721720101
**Web:** www.hollandandsherry.com
**Reg No:** 0575664 **Estd:** 1956 Private Limited Company
**Line of Business:** Woolen Merchants
**Issued Capital:** £100,000
**Co. Secretary:** Frank O'Reilly
**US SIC:** 2231 **UK SIC:** 43103

**Bankers:** The Royal Bank Of Scotland Plc (83-26-09)

| | 31-12-13 | 31-12-12 | 31-12-11 |
|---|---|---|---|
| TA | 550,133 | 550,133 | 550,133 |
| NW | 550,133 | 550,133 | 550,133 |

DUNS 23-992-6520
## Warwickshire College
Leamington Centre, Leamington Spa, Warwickshire CV32 5JE
**Tel:** 03004560047
**Web:** www.warwickshire.ac.uk
**Estd:** 2002
**Line of Business:** Further education schools and colleges
**Principals:** S Patey *(Financial)*, I Morgan
**Responsibilities**
**Senior:** Tanya Carey *(Board Member)*, Sue Georgious *(Principal)*, John Ledgwidge *(Executive)*
**Marketing:** Kate Atwell *(Marketing Manager)*, Mike Bradley *(Web Master)*, Jane Murphy *(Business Relationship Manager)*
**Sales:** Sarah Liu *(Director of International)*, Gary Marston *(International Business Develop)*
**Admin:** Sarah Norton *(Office Administrator)*
**IT:** Matt Tennant *(Infrastructure Manager)*
**HR:** Peter Husband *(Head of Employer Services)*, Lorreine Smith *(Human Resources Manager)*
**Operations:** Richard Trigg *(Production and Operations Mana)*, Diane Whitehouse *(Program Manager)*
**Branches:** Warwickshire College, Moreton Morrell Centre, Moreton Hall, Moreton Morrell, Warwick, Warwickshire CV35 9BL
**US SIC:** 8211 **UK SIC:** 93200
**Bankers:** HSBC Bank plc (40-27-06)
**Employees:** 1,400

DUNS 23-260-0452
## Warwickshire County Council
Shire Hall, Warwick, Warwickshire CV34 4RL
**Tel:** 01926-410-410
**Web:** www.warwickshire.gov.uk
**VAT No:** 272426659 **Estd:** 1888 Incorporate By Act Of Parliament
**Line of Business:** General (overall) public service activities
**Trading Style:** Warwickshire Legal Services
**Directors:** J Graham, J Graham
**Branches:** Warwickshire County Council, Four Acres, Archer Close, Studley, Warwickshire B80 7HX
**US SIC:** 9121 **UK SIC:** 91110
**Bankers:** Lloyds TSB Bank plc (30-99-15)
**Employees:** 13,000

DUNS 23-230-5755
## Warwickshire County Cricket Club Ltd
County Ground, Edgbaston Road, Birmingham, West Midlands B5 7QU
**Tel:** 08446351902 **Fax:** 0121-446-4544
**Web:** www.thebears.co.uk
**Reg No:** 0027221IP **Estd:** 1886 Friendly Society
**Line of Business:** Property developers
**Principals:** M J Smith *(Chairman)*, J Winspear, G Williamson, D C Bryant, R Ball, A L Burn, W N Houghton, H Cherry
**Co. Secretary:** D Amiss
**Responsibilities**
**Senior:** J Bridgman *(Director)*, Claire Daniel *(Catering Manager)*, Mr Dodge *(Director)*, F Graves *(Director)*, J McDowall *(Director)*, A Tickle *(Director)*
**US SIC:** 7999 **UK SIC:** 97913
**Auditors:** Pricewaterhousecoopers
**Bankers:** Lloyds TSB Bank plc (30-92-99)
**Employees:** 50

DUNS 42-487-2786
## Warwickshire Fire & Rescue Service
Fire Station, Warwick Street, Leamington Spa, Warwickshire CV32 5LH
**Tel:** 01926423231
**Web:** www.warwickshire.co.uk
**Estd:** 1974 Incorporate By Act Of Parliament
**Line of Business:** Representative office
**Director:** W W Redford
**Responsibilities**
**Senior:** Gary Phillips *(Deputy Chief Fire Officer)*
**Finance:** Helen Murphy *(Financial Services Manager)*
**IT:** Abdul Rashid *(IT Manager)*
**HR:** David Vazquez *(Training Officer)*
**Facilities:** Keith Gilks *(Facilities Manager)*
**Operations:** David Vazquez *(Training Officer)*
**Branches:** Warwickshire Fire & Rescue Service, Newtown Road, Nuneaton, Warwickshire CV11 4HR
**US SIC:** 9224 **UK SIC:** 91400
**Employees:** 200

DUNS 34-840-9707
## The Warwickshire Nursing & Residential Home Ltd
Main Street, Thurlaston, Thurlaston, Rugby, Warwickshire CV23 9JS
**Tel:** 01788-522405
**Web:** www.warwickshire.co.uk
**Reg No:** 2804460 **Estd:** 1993 Private Limited Company
**Line of Business:** Nursing homes
**Trading Style:** The Warwickshire Nursing & Residential Home Ltd
**Issued Capital:** £200
**Directors:** R A Perry, J Perry
**Co. Secretary:** Boston International Investments
**Responsibilities**
**Senior:** Sharon Belsey *(Home Manager)*, Jeanette Corby *(Home Manager)*, Allan Fairweather *(Home Manager)*, Norr Khan *(Manager)*, Julie Leadbetter *(Financial Director)*, Pauline Starrs *(Home Manager)*
**Finance:** Julie Leadbetter *(Financial Director)*
**Admin:** Julie Leadbetter *(Financial Director)*
**US SIC:** 8051, 6732
**UK SIC:** 95100, 83100
**Auditors:** Fox Evans

| | 30-04-14 | 30-04-13 | 30-04-12 |
|---|---|---|---|
| TA | 181,324 | 218,407 | 212,257 |
| NW | 68,748 | 59,418 | 48,699 |
| WC | (8,316) | (29,819) | (52,475) |

DUNS 23-261-2002
## Warwickshire Police
Police Station, Shipston-On-Stour, Warwickshire CV36 4HD
**Tel:** 01608661415
**Web:** www.warwickshire.police.uk
**Estd:** 1974 Incorporate By Act Of Parliament
**Line of Business:** Police support services
**Principals:** S Pamley *(Financial)*, B Holland, A Parker, K Bristow, L Benjamin
**Responsibilities**
**Finance:** Richard Elkin *(Director of Resources)*
**Marketing:** Carl Baldacchino *(Public Relations Manager)*
**Health & Safety:** Natassia James *(Health & Safety Officer)*
**Operations:** Carl Baldacchino *(Public Relations Manager)*
**Branches:** Warwickshire Police, Police Station, Rother Street, Stratford-Upon-Avon, Warwickshire CV37 6RD
**US SIC:** 9221 **UK SIC:** 91300
**Bankers:** Lloyds TSB Bank plc (30-99-15)
**Employees:** 500

DUNS 21-294-3399
## Warwickshire Police Federation
Smalley Place, Kenilworth, Warwickshire CV8 1QG
**Tel:** 01926851111
**Web:** www.warwickshire.police.uk
**Estd:** 1978 Partnership
**Line of Business:** Police forces
**Partners:** R Woodcock, R Woodcock
**US SIC:** 9221 **UK SIC:** 91300
**Employees:** 80

DUNS 22-777-9766
## Warwickshire Wildlife Trust Ltd
Brandon Marsh Nature Centre, Brandon Lane, Coventry, West Midlands CV3 3GW
**Tel:** 024-7630-2912
**Web:** www.warwickshirewildlifetrust.org.uk
**Reg No:** 0585247 **Estd:** 1957 Private Company Limited By Guarantee
**Line of Business:** Activities of other membership organisations not elsewhere classified
**Directors:** Ms S Pentreath, R G Gibbs, R W Hill, R V Cadbury, Mrs C P Waring, G R Harrison, B P Whittington, M Bunney
**Co. Secretary:** Ms Kathryn Reeve
**Responsibilities**
**Senior:** Stephen Batt *(Director)*, Martyn Bradley *(Manager)*, Sophie Leszczynska *(General Manager)*, Alistair Lorimer *(Director)*, Valentine Roberts *(Director)*
**Marketing:** Emma Richmond *(Marketing and Communications O)*
**Branches:** Warwickshire Wildlife Trust Ltd, Common Lane Industrial Estate, Kenilworth, Warwickshire CV8 2EL
**US SIC:** 8699 **UK SIC:** 96902
**Bankers:** National Westminster Bank Plc (56-00-45)

| | 31-12-13 | 31-12-12 | 31-12-11 |
|---|---|---|---|
| TO | 4,903,731 | 4,104,767 | 4,152,307 |
| P/L | 366,197 | 271,335 | 165,465 |
| NW | 4,085,570 | 3,715,723 | 3,431,857 |
| WC | 2,524,454 | 2,154,068 | 1,932,243 |
| Emp. | 103 | 97 | 103 |

DUNS 21-878-7327
## Warwickshire Youth Justice Service
Justice Building, Newbold Terrace, Leamington Spa, Warwickshire CV32 4EL
**Tel:** 01926682650
**Web:** www.warwickshire.gov.uk
**Estd:** 2012
**Line of Business:** Courts
**Proprietor:** L Tregear
**US SIC:** 9211 **UK SIC:** 91200
**Employees:** 50

DUNS 21-614-4322
## Wasabi
Platform 14, Victoria Station, London SW1V 1JT
**Tel:** 02076300311
**Web:** www.wasabi.uk.com
**Estd:** 2011
**Line of Business:** Take away meal outlets
**Responsibilities**
**Senior:** Eduardo Acleto *(Branch Manager)*
**US SIC:** 5812 **UK SIC:** 66110
**Employees:** 60

DUNS 42-443-3741
## Wasabi Co. Ltd
(**Subsidiary of:** Wasabi Sushi Bento Ltd)
4 Rochester Mews, London NW1 9JB
**Tel:** 020 7428 1550
**Web:** www.wasabi.uk.com
**Reg No:** 4431046 **Estd:** 2002 Private Limited Company
**Line of Business:** Restaurant - japanese
**Issued Capital:** £100
**Director:** D H Kim
**Co. Secretary:** Ms Jinhee Park
**Responsibilities**
**Senior:** Kyrrie Kleanthous *(Manager)*
**US SIC:** 5812 **UK SIC:** 66110
**Auditors:** Nexia Smith & Williamson
**Bankers:** HSBC Bank plc (40-17-16)

| | 31-12-13 | 31-08-12 | 31-12-11 |
|---|---|---|---|
| TO | 70,113,138 | 40,741,577 | 32,594,368 |
| P/L | 480,557 | 2,402,042 | 1,022,895 |
| NW | 4,805,984 | 4,295,572 | 2,611,930 |
| WC | (6,602,764) | (2,512,754) | (2,492,366) |
| Emp. | 1,126 | 961 | 946 |

DUNS 21-330-0619
## W.A.Salter (Chemists) Ltd
7 Ince Green Lane, Ince, Wigan, Lancashire WN2 2AR
**Tel:** 01942245652
**Reg No:** 0486347 **VAT No:** 151638373
**Estd:** 1950 Private Limited Company
**Line of Business:** Chemists dispensing
**Issued Capital:** £5,250
**Director:** S J Heaton
**Responsibilities**
**Senior:** Mark Layland *(Pharmacist)*
**Branches:** W.a.salter (Chemists) Ltd, W A Salter Chemist, 28 Blackhorse Street, Bolton, Lancashire BL6 5EW
**US SIC:** 5912 **UK SIC:** 64300
**Auditors:** John Fairhurst & Co
**Bankers:** National Westminster Bank Plc (60-24-02)

| | 30-09-13 | 30-09-12 | 30-09-11 |
|---|---|---|---|
| TO | 5,891,614 | 6,206,821 | 6,500,757 |
| P/L | (283,660) | (93,284) | (62,418) |
| NW | (210,634) | 3,478 | (16,388) |
| WC | 267,358 | 966,276 | 1,072,451 |
| Emp. | 78 | 78 | 84 |

DUNS 21-735-1428 **Imp-Exp**
## Wasdell Packaging Ltd
(**Subsidiary of:** Wasdell Holdings Ltd)
Euro Way, Blagrove, Swindon, Wiltshire SN5 8YW
**Tel:** 01793777560 **Fax:** 01793777599
**Web:** www.wasdell.co.uk
**Reg No:** 0956939 **VAT No:** 892217020
**Estd:** 1969 Private Limited Company
**Line of Business:** Manufacture of machinery for food, beverage and tobacco processing
**Export Markets:** Worldwide
**Issued Capital:** £57,700
**Director:** M J Tedham
**Responsibilities**
**Senior:** James Wasdell *(Manager)*
**US SIC:** 3551, 7399
**UK SIC:** 32441, 83954
**Auditors:** Griffiths Marshall
**Bankers:** Lloyds TSB Bank plc (30-00-03)

| | 30-04-14 | 30-04-13 | 30-04-12 |
|---|---|---|---|
| TO | 13,254,018 | 9,548,814 | 9,433,666 |
| P/L | 1,504,123 | 357,124 | (110,174) |
| NW | 3,863,164 | 2,533,210 | 2,176,086 |
| WC | 1,592,569 | 380,081 | (313,278) |
| Emp. | 205 | 170 | 180 |

DUNS 77-100-9909
## Waseley (Cvs) Ltd
(**Subsidiary of:** Compass Group Plc)
1 Steuart Road, Bridge Of Allan, Stirling, Stirlingshire FK9 4JG
**Tel:** 01786834060
**Reg No:** 0135998SC **VAT No:** 607458040
**Estd:** 1964 Private Limited Company
**Line of Business:** Schools & educational services
**Issued Capital:** £2,175,001
**Directors:** R A Downing, P A Galvin
**Co. Secretary:** Compass Secretaries Limited
**Branches:** Waseley (Cvs) Ltd, Parsons Ho, Parsons Rd, Washington, Tyne and Wear NE37 1EZ
**US SIC:** 8299, 6732
**UK SIC:** 93300, 83100
**Bankers:** The Royal Bank Of Scotland Plc (83-07-06)

| | 30-09-13 | 30-09-12 | 30-09-11 |
|---|---|---|---|
| TA | 2,275,002 | 2,275,002 | 2,275,002 |
| NW | 2,275,002 | 2,275,002 | 2,275,002 |

DUNS 29-675-5242 **Imp**
## Washington Green Fine Art Publishing Co Ltd
(**Subsidiary of:** Halcyon Fine Art Group Holdings Ltd)
44 Upper Gough Street, Birmingham, West Midlands B1 1JL
**Tel:** 01216161313
**Web:** www.washingtongreen.co.uk
**Reg No:** 2001847 **Estd:** 1986 Private Limited Company
**Line of Business:** Publishers
**Export Sales:** £159,813
**Issued Capital:** £100
**Directors:** P J Green, G Washington, R Green
**Co. Secretary:** Trevor Dawson
**Responsibilities**
**Senior:** Mick Mitchell *(Warehouse Manager)*
**Health & Safety:** Mick Mitchell *(Warehouse Manager)*
**Facilities:** Mick Mitchell *(Warehouse Manager)*
**Branches:** Washington Green Fine Art Publishing Co Ltd, St. Georges Street, Canterbury, Kent CT1 2TB
**US SIC:** 2731, 8999
**UK SIC:** 47532, 83954
**Auditors:** H W Fisher & Co
**Bankers:** Barclays Bank Plc (20-07-71)

| | 30-04-13 | 30-04-12 | 30-04-11 |
|---|---|---|---|
| TO | 9,124,982 | 10,025,866 | 9,702,961 |
| P/L | 881,367 | 1,456,642 | 869,186 |
| NW | 827,183 | 11,915 | (1,056,821) |
| WC | (4,179,437) | (4,942,498) | (1,185,576) |
| Emp. | 62 | 62 | 62 |

DUNS 21-165-1953
## Washington Green Retail Ltd
(**Subsidiary of:** Halcyon Fine Art Group Holdings Ltd)
44 Upper Gough Street, Birmingham, West Midlands B1 1JL
**Tel:** 01216550003
**Web:** www.castlegalleries.com
**Reg No:** 6910082 **Estd:** 2009 Private Limited Company
**Line of Business:** Other retail sale in specialised stores not elsewhere classified
**Issued Capital:** £10,000
**Director:** E Sheleg
**Co. Secretary:** Glyn Washington
**Branches:** Washington Green Retail Ltd, 40-42 Parliament Street, Harrogate, North Yorkshire HG1 2RL
**US SIC:** 7399 **UK SIC:** 83954

| | 30-04-13 | 30-04-12 | 30-04-11 |
|---|---|---|---|
| TO | 14,909,667 | 15,905,129 | 14,483,282 |
| P/L | (1,358,702) | (599,795) | (1,733,422) |
| NW | (1,164,826) | 886,408 | (3,558,674) |
| WC | (1,648,748) | 839,684 | (3,787,567) |
| Emp. | 144 | 130 | 137 |

DUNS 22-086-6383 **Imp**
## Washington Inventory Service Ltd
(**Subsidiary of:** American Capital Ltd.)
Marlborough House Westminster Place, York Business Park, Nether Poppleton, York, North Yorkshire YO26 6RW
**Tel:** 01904-795550 **Fax:** 01904-520070
**Web:** www.countonwis.com
**Reg No:** 4088001 **Estd:** 2001 Private Limited Company
**Line of Business:** Telecommunications
**Export Sales:** £1,579,737
**Trading Style:** Wis International
**Issued Capital:** £100
**Director:** G D Chaplin
**Co. Secretary:** Thomas Compogiannis
**Responsibilities**
**Senior:** Sean Davoren *(Manager)*

**Branches:** Washington Inventory Service Ltd, Hollies Ave, Cannock, Staffordshire WS11 1DW
**US SIC:** 7399 **UK SIC:** 83954
**Auditors:** Garbutt & Elliott Ltd

| | 31-03-14 | 31-03-13 | 31-03-12 |
|---|---|---|---|
| TO | 6,025,982 | 4,646,923 | 4,449,953 |
| P/L | 663,386 | 331,566 | 207,027 |
| NW | (72,529) | (721,415) | (1,056,147) |
| WC | (287,362) | (897,840) | (1,219,996) |
| Emp. | 385 | 322 | 352 |

DUNS 29-521-6824
## Washington Metal Works Ltd
Bath Road, Gateshead, Tyne and Wear NE10 0LH
**Tel:** 0191-469-4466 **Fax:** 01914694469
**Web:** www.washington-metalworks.co.uk
**Reg No:** 1884797 **VAT No:** 425937432
**Estd:** 1985 Private Limited Company
**Line of Business:** Forging, pressing, stamping and roll forming of metal; powder metallurgy
**Issued Capital:** £1,000
**Managing Directors:** S J Tate, R Barella
**Co. Secretary:** Stephen Tate
**Responsibilities**
**Purchasing:** Tony Corner *(Purchasing Manager)*
**US SIC:** 3469 **UK SIC:** 31200
**Auditors:** Joseph Miller & Co
**Bankers:** National Westminster Bank Plc (60-22-52)

| | 31-03-14 | 31-03-13 | 31-03-12 |
|---|---|---|---|
| TO | 10,171,112 | 9,622,262 | 11,209,106 |
| P/L | 590,727 | 697,077 | 1,003,720 |
| NW | 3,520,770 | 3,184,933 | 2,877,115 |
| WC | 1,310,282 | 1,362,312 | 1,300,621 |
| Emp. | 166 | 157 | 156 |

DUNS 55-060-0498
## Washington Multi Purpose Centre
Ayton Road Oxclose Villages, Washington, Tyne and Wear NE38 0LR
**Tel:** 01912193530
**Proprietorship**
**Line of Business:** Day and care centres
**Proprietor:** Ms F Everett
**US SIC:** 8321 **UK SIC:** 96111
**Employees:** 50

DUNS 29-822-0492 **Imp**
## Washtec (U K) Ltd
**(Subsidiary of:** Washtec Ag)
14a Chelmsford Road Oak Industrial Park, Dunmow, Essex CM6 1XN
**Tel:** 01371-878800 **Fax:** 01371-878810
**Web:** www.washtec-uk.com
**Reg No:** 2040161 **VAT No:** 448973689
**Estd:** 1986 Private Limited Company
**Line of Business:** Car washing and polishing equipment and supplies
**Issued Capital:** £250,000
**Directors:** A Wessels, M J Fleetham
**Co. Secretary:** David Halls
**Responsibilities**
**IT:** Chris Sampson *(IT Manager)*
**US SIC:** 3549 **UK SIC:** 32212
**Auditors:** PricewaterhouseCoopers LLP
**Bankers:** National Westminster Bank Plc (56-00-29)

| | 31-12-13 | 31-12-12 | 31-12-11 |
|---|---|---|---|
| TO | 10,444,735 | 9,655,493 | 8,087,088 |
| P/L | 412,299 | 236,962 | (896,329) |
| NW | 1,757,073 | 1,466,852 | 1,241,553 |
| WC | 1,575,535 | 1,257,337 | 888,694 |
| Emp. | 94 | 90 | 94 |

DUNS 21-783-5845
## Washwood Heath Technology College
Burney Lane, Birmingham, West Midlands B8 2AS
**Tel:** 01216757272
**Estd:** 1972 Proprietorship
**Line of Business:** Schools (local authority)
**Proprietor:** Mrs B Mabey
**US SIC:** 8211 **UK SIC:** 93200
**Employees:** 170

DUNS 42-433-7327 **Exp**
## Wassenburg Ltd
**(Subsidiary of:** Wassenburg Medical B.V.)
1 Smithy Wood Drive, Chapeltown, Sheffield, South Yorkshire S35 1QN
**Tel:** 01142-454282 **Fax:** 01142328234
**Web:** www.wassenburgmedical.co.uk
**Reg No:** 3430686 **Estd:** 2011 Private Limited Company
**Line of Business:** Manufacture of other special purpose machinery not elsewhere classified
**Issued Capital:** £23,013
**Directors:** R Wassenburg, R Salter, A Wassenburg
**Responsibilities**
**Senior:** John Crispin *(Manager)*
**US SIC:** 3559, 3629

**UK SIC:** 32863, 34350
**Auditors:** KPMG LLP

| | 31-03-14 | 31-12-12 | 31-03-11 |
|---|---|---|---|
| TO | 14,360,456 | 9,346,358 | 8,752,234 |
| P/L | 3,273,713 | 1,827,505 | 1,114,143 |
| NW | 3,279,211 | 2,514,052 | 2,315,745 |
| WC | 3,088,133 | 2,346,002 | 2,081,015 |
| Emp. | 65 | 68 | 67 |

DUNS 22-106-4483
## The Waste & Resources Action Programme
21 Horse Fair, Banbury, Oxfordshire OX16 0AH
**Tel:** 01295819900 **Fax:** 01295819911
**Web:** www.wrap.org.uk
**Reg No:** 4125764 **Estd:** 2000 Private Company Limited By Guarantee
**Line of Business:** Recycling
**Trading Style:** Wrap
**Directors:** Ms M Jones, Mrs A M Austin, A P Hinton, Dr R Chilton, D Palmer-Jon, Dr E J Goodwin, J D Lea, Ms J E Hill
**Co. Secretary:** Jonathan Lea
**US SIC:** 3031, 7391, 9121
**UK SIC:** 48123, 94000, 91110
**Auditors:** KPMG LLP
**Bankers:** Barclays Bank Plc (20-00-50)

| | 31-03-14 | 31-03-13 | 31-03-12 |
|---|---|---|---|
| TO | 65,411,000 | 63,155,000 | 65,582,000 |
| P/L | 656,000 | 899,000 | 514,000 |
| NW | 8,855,000 | 8,257,000 | 7,544,000 |
| WC | 38,376,000 | 38,202,000 | 22,547,000 |
| Emp. | 270 | 249 | 252 |

DUNS 42-431-2424
## Waste Management Systems Ltd
Lakeside, Western Road, Portsmouth, Hampshire PO6 3EN
**Tel:** 08708802430 **Fax:** 01329894538
**Web:** www.hippowaste.co.uk
**Reg No:** 4418836 **Estd:** 1902 Private Limited Company
**Line of Business:** Waste disposal
**Trading Style:** Hippowaste
**Issued Capital:** £15,702,060
**Directors:** E Wallner, A Mcguinness, S J Noar, D G Jones, R Last, Ms J M Helson
**Co. Secretary:** Richard Scarrott
**Responsibilities**
**Senior:** Lisa Barber *(Manager)*
**Health & Safety:** Nicky Mercer *(Health & Safety Officer)*
**US SIC:** 4953 **UK SIC:** 92110
**Auditors:** CW Fellowes Ltd
**Bankers:** HSBC Bank plc (40-46-39)

| | 31-12-13 | 31-12-12 | 31-12-11 |
|---|---|---|---|
| TO | 11,064,337 | N/A | N/A |
| P/L | (1,170,599) | N/A | N/A |
| NW | (4,556,538) | (3,386,189) | (2,338,173) |
| WC | (851,699) | (809,426) | (115,461) |
| Emp. | 99 | N/A | N/A |

DUNS 21-712-3772
## Waste Recycling
New Office, Lewes, East Sussex BN8 6JN
**Tel:** 01273-486848
**Web:** www.lightbros.co.uk
**Partnership**
**Line of Business:** Recycling
**Trading Style:** Mdj Lighte Brothers
**Partners:** M D Lighte, J Lighte
**US SIC:** 5093 **UK SIC:** 62200
**Employees:** 100

DUNS 51-993-2771
## Waste Recycling Group (Central) Ltd
**(Subsidiary of:** Fomento De Construcciones Y Contratas Sa)
Po Box 637, Doncaster, South Yorkshire DN4 5WZ
**Tel:** 01302-303030 **Fax:** 01302303040
**Web:** www.wrg.co.uk
**Reg No:** 4000033 **Estd:** 1994 Private Limited Company
**Line of Business:** Recycling
**Trading Style:** Fcc Environment
**Issued Capital:** £14,500,010
**Directors:** V F Orts-Llopis, P Taylor, A Serrano Mi
**Co. Secretary:** Miss Carol Nunn
**Responsibilities**
**Senior:** Claire Favier Tilston *(Manager)*, Esther Juseu *(Manager)*, Patrick Mainprize *(Financial Controller)*, Jose Sanchez *(Manager)*, Tomas Vega *(Manager)*
**Finance:** Leslie Cassells *(Finance Director)*
**Branches:** Waste Recycling Group (Central) Ltd, Tuttle Hill, Nuneaton, Warwickshire CV10 0HU
**US SIC:** 3031 **UK SIC:** 48123
**Auditors:** Deloitte LLP

| | 31-12-13 | 31-12-12 | 31-12-11 |
|---|---|---|---|
| TO | 63,008,000 | 58,132,000 | 57,705,000 |
| P/L | (463,000) | 1,176,000 | 2,846,000 |
| NW | 151,537,000 | 144,318,000 | 135,545,000 |
| WC | 135,529,000 | 137,657,000 | 133,684,000 |
| Emp. | 134 | 146 | 128 |

DUNS 37-973-0278
## Wastecare Group Ltd
Richmond Works, Selby Road, Garforth, Leeds, West Yorkshire LS25 1NB
**Tel:** 08000910000
**Web:** www.wastecare.co.uk
**Reg No:** 3280384 **Estd:** 1996 Private Limited Company
**Line of Business:** Management activities of holding companies
**Trading Style:** Waste Care
**Issued Capital:** £40,671
**Directors:** S R Price, M Owen, R Scott, Ms R M Hunt, P T Hunt
**Responsibilities**
**Senior:** Rachel Denton *(Manager)*, Duncan Mclaren *(Manager)*
**HR:** Vicky Flower *(Human Resources Manager)*
**Branches:** Wastecare Group Ltd, Willenhall Lane Industrial Estate, Willenhall Lane, Walsall, West Midlands WS3 2XN
**US SIC:** 6711 **UK SIC:** 83962
**Auditors:** Lloyd & Co
**Bankers:** National Westminster Bank Plc (50-30-09)

| | 31-03-14 | 31-03-13 | 31-03-12 |
|---|---|---|---|
| TO | 30,921,902 | 28,446,930 | 27,265,621 |
| P/L | 947,718 | 1,120,974 | 1,082,349 |
| NW | 7,814,425 | 7,122,867 | 6,330,431 |
| WC | 940,708 | (310,942) | 381,397 |
| Emp. | 399 | 380 | 347 |

DUNS 53-644-8590
## Wastecycle Ltd
**(Subsidiary of:** Dcc Plc)
Private Road 4, Colwick Industrial Estate, Nottingham, Nottinghamshire NG4 2JT
**Tel:** 01159403111
**Web:** www.wastecycle.co.uk
**Reg No:** 3450311 **VAT No:** 828109918
**Estd:** 1997 Private Limited Company
**Line of Business:** Refuse systems
**Issued Capital:** £50,000
**Principals:** P A Clements, N B Cole, M T Tracey, T Davy, K Wilcockson, P R Needham
**Co. Secretary:** Nathan Cole
**US SIC:** 4953, 3341
**UK SIC:** 92110, 22470
**Auditors:** PricewaterhouseCoopers LLP
**Bankers:** HSBC Bank plc (40-19-15)

| | 31-03-14 | 31-03-13 | 31-03-12 |
|---|---|---|---|
| TO | 31,077,000 | 25,057,000 | 20,174,000 |
| P/L | 1,233,000 | (206,000) | 1,090,000 |
| NW | 8,745,000 | 7,713,000 | 7,649,000 |
| WC | 1,237,000 | (661,000) | 1,078,000 |
| Emp. | 223 | 204 | 169 |

DUNS 22-210-4874
## Wastesaver Ltd
Grafton House, 15-17 Russell Road, Ipswich, Suffolk IP1 2DE
**Tel:** 01473-433084
**Web:** www.wastesavers.co.uk
**Reg No:** 4228600 **Estd:** 2001 Private Limited Company
**Line of Business:** Refuse collection
**Issued Capital:** £2
**Directors:** L Collins, A G Martin
**Co. Secretary:** Ms Claire Barritt Hayes
**Responsibilities**
**Senior:** Debbie Reeves *(Operations Manager)*
**Marketing:** Max Stocker *(Marketing Director)*
**Operations:** Debbie Reeves *(Operations Manager)*
**US SIC:** 9121 **UK SIC:** 91110

| | 30-06-13 | 30-06-12 | 30-06-11 |
|---|---|---|---|
| TA | 2 | 2 | 2 |
| NW | 2 | 2 | 2 |

DUNS 23-825-6502
## Wastesolve Ltd
Silbury Court, 420 Silbury Boulevard, Milton Keynes, Buckinghamshire MK9 2AF
**Tel:** 0845-130-7484
**Web:** www.wastesolve.co.uk
**Reg No:** 3817642 **Estd:** 1999 Private Limited Company
**Line of Business:** Sanitation, remediation and similar activities
**Issued Capital:** £106
**Directors:** J Cawley, Mrs A L Pegg, Mrs H E Cawley, S Platt, Ms K E Cawley, A T Goodman
**Co. Secretary:** Simon Platt
**US SIC:** 4959 **UK SIC:** 92110
**Bankers:** HSBC Bank plc (40-30-32)

| | 30-09-13 | 30-09-12 | 30-09-11 |
|---|---|---|---|
| TA | 1,056,961 | 1,260,882 | 968,002 |
| NW | 117,546 | 241,868 | 198,962 |
| WC | 60,404 | 179,521 | 176,279 |

DUNS 29-631-6748
## The Watch Security Ltd
**(Subsidiary of:** Mitie Group Plc)
Security House, Nelson Lane, Warwick, Warwickshire CV34 5JB
**Web:** www.watchsecurity.co.uk
**Reg No:** 1957715 **VAT No:** 418729723
**Estd:** 1985 Private Limited Company
**Line of Business:** Security and related activities
**Issued Capital:** £10,000
**Directors:** P I Skoulding, J P Flanagan
**Co. Secretary:** Mitie Company Secretarial Servic
**US SIC:** 7393 **UK SIC:** 83954
**Auditors:** Deloitte & Touche LLP
**Bankers:** Barclays Bank Plc (20-48-08)

| | 31-03-13 | 31-03-12 | 31-03-11 |
|---|---|---|---|
| TA | 1,492,657 | 1,492,657 | 1,492,657 |
| NW | 1,492,657 | 1,492,657 | 1,492,657 |

DUNS 21-008-3102
## Watch Shop Ltd
**(Subsidiary of:** Jewel Holdco Sarl)
27-29 Cross Street, Reading, Berkshire RG1 1ST
**Tel:** 01189500937 **Fax:** 01189-585202
**Web:** www.watchshop.com
**Reg No:** 6323462 **VAT No:** 913559907
**Estd:** 1991 Private Limited Company
**Line of Business:** Retail sale of jewellery, clocks and watches
**Trading Style:** G D K Jewellers
**Issued Capital:** £100
**Directors:** H B Duffy, L A Romberg, A J Broderick
**Responsibilities**
**Senior:** Sham Naib *(Manager)*, Karl Schroedr *(Manager)*
**Branches:** Watch Shop Ltd, 27 Cross Street, Reading, Berkshire RG1 1ST
**US SIC:** 5944, 5961
**UK SIC:** 65400, 65600
**Auditors:** James Cowper LLP

| | 28-02-14 | 28-02-13 | 29-02-12 |
|---|---|---|---|
| TO | 30,428,419 | 17,468,275 | 13,320,204 |
| P/L | 4,511,699 | 1,277,607 | 679,705 |
| NW | 5,580,353 | 2,122,398 | 1,173,818 |
| WC | 5,346,450 | 1,966,652 | 984,917 |
| Emp. | 73 | 50 | 48 |

DUNS 23-866-5868 **Imp**
## Watch Tower Bible & Tract Society of Britain
Ibsa House, The Ridgeway, London NW7 1RN
**Tel:** 020-8906-2211
**Web:** www.jw.org
**Reg No:** 3858051 **Estd:** 1884 Private Company Limited By Guarantee
**Line of Business:** Religious organisations and places of worship
**Trading Style:** Kingdom Hall of Jehovahs Witnesses, 1hull Newland Congregation of Jehovahs Witnesses
**Directors:** B J Vigo, P Longstaff, P P Bell
**Responsibilities**
**Senior:** Jack Dowson *(Manager)*, Ronald Drage *(Manager)*
**Branches:** Watch Tower Bible & Tract Society Of Britain, Kingdom Hall, Elmstead Rd, Colchester, Essex CO4 0LG
**US SIC:** 2741 **UK SIC:** 47541
**Auditors:** Calcutt Matthews
**Bankers:** Barclays Bank Plc (20-00-30)

| | 31-08-13 | 31-08-12 | 31-08-11 |
|---|---|---|---|
| TO | 30,560,270 | 35,925,958 | 30,433,582 |
| P/L | (966,469) | (3,622,364) | (7,037,535) |
| NW | 36,830,344 | 37,215,202 | 40,351,331 |
| WC | 13,603,158 | 6,821,361 | 3,967,135 |

DUNS 23-998-5208 **Imp**
## Watchet Harbour Marina Ltd
10 The Esplanade, Harbour Road, Watchet, Somerset TA23 0AJ
**Tel:** 01984631264
**Web:** www.watchet-harbour-marina.com
**Reg No:** 3986667 **Estd:** 2000 Private Limited Company
**Line of Business:** Other supporting water transport activities
**Issued Capital:** £100
**Director:** T J Taylor
**US SIC:** 8999 **UK SIC:** 83954
**Auditors:** KPMG LLP

| | 31-03-14 | 31-03-13 | 31-03-12 |
|---|---|---|---|
| TA | 1,757,295 | 1,398,019 | 1,393,546 |
| NW | 1,020,715 | 670,136 | 680,451 |
| WC | (240,319) | (141,858) | (111,768) |

DUNS 34-612-7660
## Water & Sanitation for the Urban Poor
91 Waterloo Road, London SE1 8RT
**Tel:** 020 3170 0935
**Reg No:** 5419428 **Estd:** 2005 Private Limited Company
**Line of Business:** Publishing services
**Trading Style:** Www.Wsup.Com

**Directors:** Ms D Wiplinger, W M Day, D D Scott, D R Birch, Mrs R L Marmot, Dr E Cartmell, Ms H Newman, G K Menon
**Co. Secretary:** David Woodbine
**Responsibilities**
**Senior:** Edward Mitchell *(Director)*, Mark Salway *(Director)*, Marco Schouten *(Director)*
**US SIC:** 2741, 8911
**UK SIC:** 47541, 83701
**Auditors:** Sayer Vincent
**Bankers:** HSBC Bank plc (40-05-20)

| | 31-03-14 | 31-03-13 | 31-03-12 |
|---|---|---|---|
| TO | 7,339,331 | 7,532,300 | 2,680,782 |
| P/L | (677,385) | 3,341,722 | (2,075,444) |
| NW | 3,720,655 | 4,617,619 | 1,217,785 |
| WC | 3,403,835 | 4,475,613 | 1,195,148 |
| Emp. | 70 | 46 | 36 |

DUNS 50-423-7728
## Water At Work Ltd
**(Subsidiary of:** Hydra Dutch Holdings 2 B.V.)
3 Livingstone Boulevard, Glasgow, Lanarkshire G72 0BP
**Tel:** 01624661321
**Web:** www.wateratworkmidlands.co.uk
**Reg No:** 0119721SC **VAT No:** 481347244
**Estd:** 1998 Private Limited Company
**Line of Business:** Manufacture of ceramic sanitary fixtures
**Issued Capital:** £81,100
**Directors:** Y Shapira, O Plouvin
**Co. Secretary:** Maclay Murray & Spens Llp
**Responsibilities**
**Senior:** Eddie Joyce *(Manager)*, Gaynor Joyce *(Director of accounts)*
**Branches:** Water At Work Ltd, 3 Pine St, Dunbar, East Lothian EH42 1PU
**US SIC:** 7399 **UK SIC:** 83954
**Auditors:** PricewaterhouseCoopers LLP
**Bankers:** The Royal Bank Of Scotland Plc (83-21-08)

| | 31-12-13 | 31-12-12 | 31-12-11 |
|---|---|---|---|
| TA | 8 | 8 | 8 |
| NW | 8 | 8 | 8 |

DUNS 21-741-7617 **Imp-Exp**
## Water for Work and Home Ltd
Conway House, Pattenden Lane, Marden, Tonbridge, Kent TN12 9QJ
**Tel:** 01622834800 **Fax:** 01622-832702
**Web:** www.edgarswater.co.uk
**Reg No:** 1327099 **VAT No:** 205190206
**Estd:** 1977 Private Limited Company
**Line of Business:** Water fresh coolers
**Export Markets:** Worldwide
**Trading Style:** Edgars Water, Water Line
**Issued Capital:** £52,151
**Principals:** B R Mcgannan *(Managing)*, S G Hill, S T Edgar, N G Ackerman, A Vickers
**Co. Secretary:** Benjamin Mcgannan
**Responsibilities**
**Senior:** Mike Beaumont *(General Manager)*, Elizabeth Mcgannan *(Manager)*, Shiobhan Payne *(Sales Manager & Customer Servi)*
**Marketing:** Holly Blencowe *(Marketing Manager)*
**Sales:** Jackie Betts *(Sales Manager)*, Kathy Martin *(Sales Manager)*, Shiobhan Payne *(Sales Manager & Customer Servi)*
**Operations:** Jackie Betts *(Sales Manager)*
**US SIC:** 5149, 4941
**UK SIC:** 61700, 17000
**Bankers:** National Westminster Bank Plc (60-60-08)

| | 31-03-14 | 31-03-13 | 31-03-11 |
|---|---|---|---|
| TO | 7,374,525 | N/A | N/A |
| P/L | 475,212 | N/A | N/A |
| NW | 467,806 | 236,281 | 160,957 |
| WC | (983,551) | (1,276,235) | (962,297) |
| Emp. | 145 | N/A | N/A |

DUNS 73-267-9043
## Water Marc Ltd
North Fairlee Farm, Fairlee Road, Newport, Isle of Wight PO30 2JU
**Tel:** 01962716631 **Fax:** 01983-533972
**Web:** www.southernwater.co.uk
**Reg No:** 4541675 **Estd:** 2003 Private Limited Company
**Line of Business:** Forestry and logging related service activities
**Issued Capital:** £30
**Director:** P S Debenham
**Co. Secretary:** Trevor Debenham
**Responsibilities**
**Finance:** H Goodbone *(Financial Director)*
**US SIC:** 0851, 4941
**UK SIC:** 02000, 17000

| | 31-05-14 | 31-05-13 | 31-05-12 |
|---|---|---|---|
| TA | 67,086 | 73,291 | 85,936 |
| NW | (35,891) | (54,508) | (42,212) |
| WC | (70,256) | (102,980) | (88,327) |

DUNS 21-779-8344
## Water Pollution Hotline
Howard Davis Farm, Lane Route De Lane Trinite, Trinity, Jersey, Channel Islands JE3 5JP
**Tel:** 01534709535
**Web:** www.gov.je
**Estd:** 2011
**Line of Business:** Manufacture of non-domestic cooling and ventilation equipment
**Responsibilities**
**Senior:** Shelley Hawkins *(Environmental Protection Offic)*
**US SIC:** 7399 **UK SIC:** 83954
**Employees:** 65

DUNS 73-249-8360
## Water Process Ltd
**(Subsidiary of:** Xylem Inc.)
I T T Industries, Viables Industrial Estate, Jays Close, Basingstoke, Hampshire RG22 4BA
**Tel:** 01256-311800 **Fax:** 01256-303801
**Web:** www.xylemflowcontrol.com
**Reg No:** 4523662 **VAT No:** 803824738
**Estd:** 2002 Private Limited Company
**Line of Business:** Manufacture of other special purpose machinery not elsewhere classified
**Export Sales:** £13,503,000
**Trading Style:** P C I Membrance Systems, Portacel
**Issued Capital:** £7,001,200
**Directors:** J E Mowbray, M R Skilling
**Co. Secretary:** Mrs Linda Frawley
**US SIC:** 3559, 5199
**UK SIC:** 32863, 61900
**Auditors:** Deloitte & Touche LLP
**Bankers:** National Westminster Bank Plc (50-42-28)

| | 31-12-13 | 31-12-12 | 31-12-11 |
|---|---|---|---|
| TO | 30,027,000 | 40,872,000 | 21,267,000 |
| P/L | (3,230,000) | (10,470,000) | (14,158,000) |
| NW | 1,763,000 | (3,456,000) | 830,000 |
| WC | (2,275,000) | (8,126,000) | (4,373,000) |
| Emp. | 127 | 181 | 191 |

DUNS 28-982-8550 **Exp**
## Wateraid
47-49 Durham Street, London SE11 5JD
**Tel:** 020-7793-4500
**Web:** www.wateraid.org
**Reg No:** 1787329 **Estd:** 1984 Private Company Limited By Guarantee
**Line of Business:** Representative office
**Export Markets:** Countries worldwide.
**Directors:** Ms C Brocklehurst, Ms C Wuillamie, P J Newman, S Katwala, T N Clark, P J Millward, R D Flint, C Loughlin
**Co. Secretary:** Ms Barbara Frost
**Responsibilities**
**Senior:** Dominique Abranson *(Executive)*, Sanjaya Adhikary *(Country Representative)*, Nancy Bikson *(Board Member)*, Tom Burgess *(Executive)*, Heike Gloeckner *(Executive)*, Fatoumata Haidara *(Country Representative)*, Rona Higgins *(Board Member)*, Khairul Islam *(Country Representative)*, Indira Khurana *(Director of Partnerships)*, Joe Lambongang *(Partner)*, Yerefolo Malle *(Country Representative)*, Anna Segall *(Director)*, Beverley Wall *(Executive)*, Christianne Wuillamie *(Director)*
**Finance:** Marta Barcelo *(Governance and Transparency Fu)*
**Marketing:** Fiona Blake *(Development Manager)*, Bankole Ebemesi *(Head of the Communication and)*, Daniel Holking *(Communications Officer)*, Kate Holme *(Corporate Partnerships Team Le)*, Brenda Mcilwraith *(?Partnership Communications Ma)*, Libby Plumb *(Communications Manager)*, Samantha Weir *(Communications Services Assist)*
**Sales:** Chloe Bayram *(Regional Development Manager)*, Cara Keane *(Corporate Account Manager)*
**Admin:** Lydia Zigomo *(Head of Programmes)*
**IT:** Papa Diouf *(Programme Support and Systems)*, Harjit Sandhu *(Computer Manager)*
**Health & Safety:** Emma Downie *(Facilities Manager)*
**Facilities:** Emma Downie *(Facilities Manager)*
**Operations:** Erik Harvey *(Head Programme Support Unit)*, Moses Mumba *(Programme Officer)*
**Engineering:** Abdul Hafeez *(Program Manager)*
**Branches:** Wateraid, 419 Balmore Road, Glasgow, Lanarkshire G22 6NU
**US SIC:** 7399, 8922
**UK SIC:** 83954, 94000
**Auditors:** PricewaterhouseCoopers LLP

**Bankers:** Barclays Bank Plc (20-94-48)

| | 31-03-14 | 31-03-13 | 31-03-12 |
|---|---|---|---|
| TO | 73,695,000 | 65,648,000 | 55,807,000 |
| P/L | 1,772,000 | 4,316,000 | 1,846,000 |
| NW | 22,634,000 | 21,033,000 | 16,895,000 |
| WC | 22,642,000 | 21,088,000 | 15,913,000 |
| Emp. | 719 | 671 | 670 |

DUNS 21-770-9394
## Watercliffe Meadow County Primary School
Boynton Road, Sheffield, South Yorkshire S5 7HL
**Tel:** 01142326603
**Estd:** 2011 Proprietorship
**Line of Business:** Primary education
**Proprietor:** Mrs L Kingdon
**US SIC:** 8211 **UK SIC:** 93200
**Employees:** 85

DUNS 64-082-0841
## Waterdale Associates Ltd
Arden House, 25 The Courtyard, Gorsey Lane, Birmingham, West Midlands B46 1JA
**Tel:** 0844-880-6140
**Web:** www.waterdale.co.uk
**Reg No:** 3477263 **Estd:** 1990 Private Limited Company
**Line of Business:** Management activities of holding companies
**Issued Capital:** £161,535
**Principals:** A J Watkinson *(Managing)*, Miss L A Blakeman, A D Cobbald
**Co. Secretary:** Roger Fleury
**US SIC:** 6711, 5732
**UK SIC:** 83962, 64800
**Auditors:** Somerbys
**Bankers:** HSBC Bank plc (40-11-36)

| | 30-06-13 | 30-06-12 | 30-06-11 |
|---|---|---|---|
| TO | 7,988,371 | 8,823,080 | 7,468,142 |
| P/L | (297,404) | (87,617) | (110,255) |
| NW | (1,045,660) | (891,197) | (959,033) |
| WC | (853,237) | (701,282) | (835,727) |
| Emp. | 72 | 73 | 64 |

DUNS 36-821-1595
## Waterfield Leisure Pool
Waterfield Baths, Dalby Road, Melton Mowbray, Leicestershire LE13 0BG
**Tel:** 01664-563550
**Web:** www.everyoneactive.com
**Estd:** 1965 Proprietorship
**Line of Business:** Health clubs
**Proprietor:** T Alsopp
**Responsibilities**
**Senior:** Ian Bradgate *(Regional Manager)*, Matthew Hopkin *(Branch Manager)*
**US SIC:** 7299 **UK SIC:** 98902
**Employees:** 75

DUNS 22-853-5944
## Waterfields (Leigh) Ltd
Manchester Road, Leigh, Lancashire WN7 2LX
**Tel:** 01942740000 **Fax:** 01942-740245
**Web:** www.waterfields.co.uk
**Reg No:** 0337210 **VAT No:** 437620355
**Estd:** 1926 Private Limited Company
**Line of Business:** Manufacturers general
**Trading Style:** Waterfields Bakers and Confectioners
**Issued Capital:** £52,200
**Principals:** W J Waterfield *(Technical)*, C Harris
**Co. Secretary:** Albert Waterfield
**Responsibilities**
**Senior:** John Waterfield *(Manager)*
**Facilities:** Derrick Palleo *(Chief Engineer)*
**Branches:** Waterfields (Leigh) Ltd, 572 Warrington Road, Prescot, Merseyside L35 4LZ
**US SIC:** 3999 **UK SIC:** 49590
**Auditors:** Jackson Stephen
**Bankers:** National Westminster Bank Plc (60-13-04)

| | 05-04-14 | 05-04-13 | 05-04-12 |
|---|---|---|---|
| TO | 14,034,974 | 13,371,975 | 13,358,874 |
| P/L | (626,907) | (214,762) | (3,306) |
| NW | 377,806 | 1,052,836 | 1,313,633 |
| WC | (625,447) | (584,665) | (435,277) |
| Emp. | 619 | 585 | 610 |

DUNS 22-931-5395
## Waterfoot Inn
14 Clooney Road, Londonderry, Co Londonderry BT47 6TB
**Tel:** 028-7134-5500
**Web:** www.waterfoothotel.com
**Estd:** 1984 Partnership
**Line of Business:** Hotels
**Partners:** Another, H C Sherrard
**US SIC:** 7011 **UK SIC:** 66500
**Bankers:** Ulster Bank Ltd (98-09-85)
**Employees:** 200

DUNS 23-492-2144
## Waterfront-Student Union Services Ltd
139-141 King Street, Norwich, Norfolk NR1 1QH
**Tel:** 01603-632717
**Web:** www.waterfrontnorwich.com
**Reg No:** 2834353 **Estd:** 2002 Private Limited Company
**Line of Business:** Artistic and literary creation and interpretation
**Trading Style:** The Waterfront
**Issued Capital:** £4
**Directors:** L Mccafferty, Y Yu, Ms R Mckenzie, Miss R S Handforth, C Rand, Ms H Staynor, C Jarvis
**Co. Secretary:** Anthony Moore
**Responsibilities**
**Senior:** Johan Bolling *(Director)*, Lesley Hanner *(Manager)*, E Idahosa *(Manager)*, Christopher Matheson *(Manager)*, Leslie Morrell *(Director)*, Leander Platten *(venue manager)*, Andrew Pott *(Manager)*, Michelle Pratt *(Manager)*, Paul Waugh *(Director)*
**US SIC:** 7999 **UK SIC:** 97913
**Auditors:** BKR Haines Watts

| | 30-04-13 | 30-04-12 | 31-04-11 |
|---|---|---|---|
| TO | 1,134,405 | 1,017,119 | 1,144,211 |
| P/L | 6,966 | 1,082 | (10,130) |
| NW | 140,456 | 133,490 | 132,408 |
| WC | 129,844 | 120,907 | 112,276 |
| Emp. | 48 | 45 | 49 |

DUNS 21-766-5078
## Waterfront Studios
Waterfront Studios Business Centre, 1 Dock Road, London E16 1AG
**Tel:** 02074769707
**Web:** www.waterfrontstudios.biz
**Estd:** 2011 Proprietorship
**Line of Business:** Business and commerce centres
**Proprietor:** D Cowley
**Responsibilities**
**Senior:** Daniel Cowling *(Manager)*, Daniel Forsyth *(Manager)*
**US SIC:** 7392 **UK SIC:** 83951
**Employees:** 400

DUNS 23-714-2182
## Watergate Bay Hotel Ltd
Watergate Bay Hotel, Watergate Bay, Newquay, Cornwall TR8 4AA
**Tel:** 01637860543 **Fax:** 01637-860333
**Web:** www.watergatebay.co.uk
**Reg No:** 3709185 **Estd:** 1999 Private Limited Company
**Line of Business:** Hotels
**Issued Capital:** £128,314
**Directors:** Mrs R E Ashworth, H W Ashworth, Mrs M A Ashworth, Ms J A Blakeburn, C J Hugo, W J Ashworth, A M Young
**Co. Secretary:** John Ashworth
**US SIC:** 7011, 5812
**UK SIC:** 66500, 66110
**Auditors:** KPMG

| | 28-02-14 | 28-02-13 | 29-02-12 |
|---|---|---|---|
| TO | 10,725,435 | 6,480,916 | 7,890,959 |
| P/L | 1,052,294 | 392,397 | 1,259,783 |
| NW | 4,181,869 | 2,918,453 | 2,548,798 |
| WC | (1,405,689) | (3,427,036) | (1,093,183) |
| Emp. | 196 | 172 | 145 |

DUNS 21-780-8087
## Wateringbury Ce Primary School
147 Bow Road, Maidstone, Kent ME18 5EA
**Tel:** 01622812199
**Estd:** 2011
**Line of Business:** Schools (local authority)
**Responsibilities**
**Senior:** Noreen Vinall *(Head Teacher)*
**US SIC:** 8211 **UK SIC:** 93200
**Employees:** 243

DUNS 21-605-5250
## Waterlane Leisure Centre
Water Lane, Lowestoft, Suffolk NR32 2NH
**Tel:** 01502532540
**Web:** www.sentinelleisuretrust.co.uk
**Estd:** 1976
**Line of Business:** Leisure centres
**Proprietor:** S Bellamy
**US SIC:** 7999 **UK SIC:** 97913
**Employees:** 60

DUNS 21-810-8883
## Waterlees Court Supported Living
Aylestone Lane, Wigston, Leicestershire LE18 1AR
**Estd:** 2012
**Line of Business:** Home care and help services
**US SIC:** 8811 **UK SIC:** 99000
**Employees:** 50

DUNS 21-014-5637

## Waterline Ltd

**(Subsidiary of:** Crown Products (Kent) Ltd)
Jenna House, North Crawley Road, North Crawley, Newport Pagnell, Buckinghamshire MK16 9TG
**Tel:** 0844-412-2524 **Fax:** 0800 585 531
**Web:** www.waterline.co.uk
**Reg No:** 0428931 **VAT No:** 229827531
**Estd:** 1947 Private Limited Company
**Line of Business:** Wholesale of radio and television goods; wholesale of electrical household appliances not elsewhere classified
**Issued Capital:** £7,064
**Directors:** M J Head, Ms K E Sturgess, R B Taylor, A C Davidson, B J Head, V V Zaheer
**Responsibilities**
**Health & Safety:** Terry Barker *(Operations Manager)*
**Facilities:** Terry Barker *(Operations Manager)*
**Operations:** Terry Barker *(Operations Manager)*
**Branches:** Waterline Ltd, Unit 10-12, Plodder Lane, Bolton, Lancashire BL4 0LR
**US SIC:** 5064, 5021
**UK SIC:** 61500
**Auditors:** BDO Stoy Hayward LLP
**Bankers:** Barclays Bank Plc (20-57-40)

| | 31-03-14 | 31-03-13 | 31-03-12 |
|---|---|---|---|
| TO | 51,573,890 | 51,408,801 | 44,387,510 |
| P/L | 797,662 | 291,498 | 481,998 |
| NW | 1,405,238 | 804,042 | 778,245 |
| WC | 3,857,176 | 319,262 | (3,267,278) |
| Emp. | 211 | 209 | 180 |

DUNS 73-651-9617 Imp

## Waterloo Air Products Plc

**(Subsidiary of:** Waterloo Group Ltd)
Quarrywood Industrial Estate, Mills Road, Aylesford, Kent ME20 7NB
**Tel:** 01622717861
**Web:** www.waterloo.co.uk
**Reg No:** 4911865 **Estd:** 2003 Public Limited Company
**Line of Business:** Ventilation systems
**Export Sales:** £147,807
**Issued Capital:** £100,000
**Directors:** R H Edmondson, S P Marshall, R H Edmondson, J E Tiernan
**Co. Secretary:** Miss Kate Searles
**Responsibilities**
**Finance:** Jenny Stolworthy *(Management Accountant)*
**HR:** Nick Bailey *(Human Resources Manager)*
**Engineering:** Dave Martin *(Systems Manager)*
**US SIC:** 3585 **UK SIC:** 32841
**Bankers:** Lloyds TSB Bank plc (30-95-37)

| | 31-12-13 | 31-12-12 | 31-12-11 |
|---|---|---|---|
| TO | 6,941,669 | 6,086,260 | 6,647,504 |
| P/L | 55,088 | (280,336) | 27,712 |
| NW | 330,577 | 153,693 | 395,073 |
| WC | (88,336) | (184,095) | (42,739) |
| Emp. | 86 | 80 | 74 |

DUNS 23-230-6225

## Waterloo Housing Association Ltd

1700 Solihull Parkway, Birmingham, West Midlands B37 7YD
**Tel:** 01217887620
**Web:** www.waterloo.org.uk
**Reg No:** 0019741IP **Estd:** 1971 Friendly Society
**Line of Business:** Housing associations societies trusts & co-operatives
**Trading Style:** West Midlands Housing
**Principals:** A E Taylor *(President)*, M Dufty *(Chairman)*, Ms S Harris
**Responsibilities**
**Senior:** Marion Dufty *(?Director of Operations)*, Dermot McRoberts *(Group Finance Director/Group C)*, david pickering *(chief executive)*
**Finance:** Andrew Brook *(Head of Treasury and Capital F)*, Liz Casey *(Deputy Finance Director)*, Dermot McRoberts *(Group Finance Director/Group C)*, Malkit Sagoo *(Director of Asset Management)*
**Admin:** Rachel Case *(Personal Secretary)*
**HR:** Claire Durnin *(HR and Business Services Direc)*
**Health & Safety:** Debbie allen *(h&S)*
**Facilities:** Neil Adie *(Group Head of Development)*, Malcolm Kazics *(Maintenance Manager)*, Roy Mowbray *(Regeneration Manager)*, Helen Newbury *(Group Head of Programme and Pe)*
**Operations:** Marion Dufty *(?Director of Operations)*, Anthony Riley *(Group Director of Development)*, Gurmeet Virdi *(Housing Operations Director)*
**Branches:** Waterloo Housing Association Ltd, 25 Bradegate Drive, Peterborough, Cambridgeshire PE1 4SP
**US SIC:** 6531 **UK SIC:** 83400
**Auditors:** Beever & Struthers
**Bankers:** National Westminster Bank Plc (60-21-07)

| | 31-03-12 | 31-03-11 | 31-03-10 |
|---|---|---|---|
| TO | 24,457,000 | 22,860,000 | 23,515,000 |
| P/L | 8,874,000 | 3,552,000 | 1,635,000 |
| NW | 33,160,000 | 32,915,000 | 18,009,000 |
| WC | 15,954,000 | 914,000 | 3,341,000 |
| Emp. | 112 | 109 | 125 |

DUNS 21-605-5208

## Waterloo Manor

Selby Road, Garforth, Leeds, West Yorkshire LS25 1NA
**Tel:** 01132876660
**Web:** www.inmind.co.uk
**Estd:** 2004
**Line of Business:** Mental health centres
**Proprietor:** A Saquir
**Responsibilities**
**Senior:** Diane Dolman *(Chief Executive)*
**US SIC:** 8091 **UK SIC:** 95200
**Employees:** 60

DUNS 73-516-4415

## Waterloo Manor Ltd

**(Subsidiary of:** Cayes (Uk) Ltd)
Ground Floor Management Training, Badgemore Park Golf Club, Henley-On-Thames, Oxfordshire RG9 4NR
**Tel:** 02086439738
**Web:** www.inmind.co.uk
**Reg No:** 4779350 **Estd:** 2003 Private Limited Company
**Line of Business:** Other human health activities
**Issued Capital:** £82
**Director:** Dr A J Faqir
**Co. Secretary:** Assad Sheikh
**US SIC:** 8091 **UK SIC:** 95200

| | 31-12-13 | 31-12-12 | 31-12-11 |
|---|---|---|---|
| TO | 6,095,216 | 3,150,419 | 3,497,377 |
| P/L | 501,061 | (751,394) | 115,571 |
| NW | 939,730 | 415,879 | 1,133,396 |
| WC | (640,874) | (1,118,211) | (379,009) |
| Emp. | 159 | 87 | 90 |

DUNS 21-215-3076

## Waterloo (Motor Trade) Ltd

**(Subsidiary of:** Waterloo (Motor Trade) Holdings Ltd)
Main Street, Hull, North Humberside HU2 0JX
**Tel:** 01482328308 **Fax:** 01482-386974
**Web:** www.waterloo-mt.co.uk
**Reg No:** 0396347 **Estd:** 1928 Private Limited Company
**Line of Business:** Sale of motor vehicle parts and accessories
**Issued Capital:** £12,600
**Principals:** J W Munday *(Managing)*, Mrs J P Munday
**Co. Secretary:** Mrs Judith Munday
**Branches:** Waterloo (Motor Trade) Ltd, Bessingby Industrial Estate, Bridlington, North Humberside YO16 4SJ
**US SIC:** 5531 **UK SIC:** 65100
**Auditors:** Sadofskys
**Bankers:** National Westminster Bank Plc (56-00-06)

| | 31-12-13 | 30-06-12 | 30-12-11 |
|---|---|---|---|
| TA | 892,634 | 893,602 | 941,065 |
| NW | 453,870 | 483,372 | 479,774 |
| WC | 357,830 | 423,971 | 390,466 |

DUNS 57-039-7026

## Waterloo Quay Properties Ltd

Steadfast House, Greenwell Road East Tullos Industrial, Estate, Aberdeen, Aberdeenshire AB12 3AX
**Tel:** 01224-357100 **Fax:** 01224-357101
**Web:** www.waterlooquay.com
**Reg No:** 2873885 **VAT No:** 474107749
**Estd:** 1993 Private Limited Company
**Line of Business:** Other tourist or short-stay accommodation
**Issued Capital:** £100
**Directors:** S N Eardley, B R Lewis
**Co. Secretary:** Ms Anna Eardley
**US SIC:** 7021 **UK SIC:** 66500
**Auditors:** PKF
**Bankers:** The Royal Bank Of Scotland Plc (83-15-31)

| | 30-11-13 | 30-11-12 | 30-11-11 |
|---|---|---|---|
| TA | 14,154,809 | 13,554,202 | 13,240,396 |
| NW | 3,826,845 | 2,868,543 | 2,481,765 |
| WC | (1,778,217) | (1,467,675) | (1,798,995) |

DUNS 22-105-7719

## Waterlooville Conservatory Blind & Awnings Ltd

**(Subsidiary of:** Hunter Douglas N.V.)
7 Waterberry Drive Brambles Enterprise, Centre, Waterlooville, Hampshire PO7 7TH
**Tel:** 02392231109 **Fax:** 02392232700
**Web:** www.thomas-sanderson.co.uk
**Reg No:** 4125067 **Estd:** 2000 Private Limited Company
**Line of Business:** Other manufacturing not elsewhere classified
**Trading Style:** Thomas Sanderson Ltd
**Issued Capital:** £1,650,002
**Director:** N J Campkin
**Co. Secretary:** James Curley
**Responsibilities**
**IT:** Dave Oakley *(Head of IT)*
**US SIC:** 3999 **UK SIC:** 49590
**Bankers:** Bank Of Scotland (80-07-48)

| | 31-12-13 | 31-12-12 | 31-12-11 |
|---|---|---|---|
| TA | 4,373,000 | 4,373,000 | 4,373,000 |
| NW | 2,943,000 | 2,943,000 | 2,943,000 |
| WC | 1,513,000 | 1,513,000 | 1,513,000 |

DUNS 21-091-6636

## Waterlooville Health Centre

Dryden Close, Waterlooville, Hampshire PO7 6AL
**Tel:** 023-9224-0340
**Estd:** 1978 Partnership
**Line of Business:** Hospitals
**Partners:** Dr J K Pringle, Dr I Sheikh
**Responsibilities**
**Senior:** Alison Grout *(Manager)*
**US SIC:** 8062 **UK SIC:** 95100
**Employees:** 100

DUNS 21-228-6584

## Waterlooville Leisure Centre

Waterberry Drive, Waterlooville, Hampshire PO7 7UW
**Tel:** 02392245900
**Web:** www.horizonlc.com
**Estd:** 1991 Proprietorship
**Line of Business:** Leisure centres
**Proprietor:** Mrs M Wilkinson
**US SIC:** 7999 **UK SIC:** 97913
**Employees:** 50

DUNS 28-835-6785

## The Waterlooville (Portsmouth) Golf Club Ltd

**(Subsidiary of:** Waterlooville Golfers Ltd)
Cherry Tree Avenue, Cowplain, Waterlooville, Hampshire PO8 8AP
**Tel:** 02392263388
**Web:** www.waterloovillegolfclub.co.uk
**Reg No:** 0401492 **Estd:** 1945 Private Limited Company
**Line of Business:** Operation of sports arenas and stadiums
**Issued Capital:** £2,000
**Directors:** C Ashman, B W Chambers, R C Stokes
**Co. Secretary:** John Hay
**US SIC:** 7941 **UK SIC:** 97911
**Auditors:** Business & Tax Advisors
**Bankers:** Lloyds TSB Bank plc (30-99-20)

| | 31-12-13 | 31-12-12 | 31-12-11 |
|---|---|---|---|
| TA | 801,997 | 801,977 | 801,967 |
| NW | 801,367 | 801,367 | 801,367 |
| WC | 1,367 | 1,367 | 1,367 |

DUNS 39-791-2718 Exp

## Waterman Aspen Ltd

**(Subsidiary of:** Waterman Group Plc)
Dippen Hall, Eastbourne Road, Blindley Heath, Lingfield, Surrey RH7 6JX
**Tel:** 01342893800 **Fax:** 03333444501
**Web:** www.watermangroup.com
**Reg No:** 2203474 **VAT No:** 491408441
**Estd:** 1987 Private Limited Company
**Line of Business:** Engineers (consulting)
**Export Markets:** Worldwide
**Trading Style:** Waterman Group
**Issued Capital:** £200,075
**Principals:** C J Chaplin *(Managing)*, N Humphrey, M A Emberton, R C Bellm
**Co. Secretary:** Graham Hiscocks
**Responsibilities**
**Senior:** Linda McGregor *(Divisional Director)*, Craig Ridley *(Manager)*, John Waiting *(Manager)*
**HR:** Cy Turner *(Human Resources Manager)*
**Branches:** Waterman Aspen Ltd, Lockington Hall, Derby, Derbyshire DE74 2RH
**US SIC:** 7361, 7399
**UK SIC:** 83954
**Auditors:** PricewaterhouseCoopers LLP
**Bankers:** Lloyds TSB Bank plc (30-92-92)

| | 30-06-13 | 30-06-12 | 30-06-11 |
|---|---|---|---|
| TO | 9,789,000 | 7,818,000 | 9,493,000 |
| P/L | 315,000 | (576,000) | (411,000) |
| NW | 3,001,000 | 2,802,000 | 3,358,000 |
| WC | 2,991,000 | 2,801,000 | 3,356,000 |
| Emp. | 119 | 118 | 142 |

DUNS 39-748-9873

## Waterman Group Plc

Pickfords Wharf, Clink Street, Lambeth, London SE1 9DG
**Tel:** 020 7928 7888
**Web:** www.watermangroup.com
**Reg No:** 2188844 **Estd:** 1952 Public Limited Company
**Line of Business:** Management activities of holding companies
**Export Sales:** £9,048,000
**Issued Capital:** £3,075,882
**Directors:** N J Taylor, G H Wright, M P Baker, C W Beresford, A Steele, R J Piper, G R Hiscocks
**Responsibilities**
**Senior:** John Towers *(stuctial Director)*
**Engineering:** John Towers *(stuctial Director)*
**Branches:** Waterman Group Plc, Civic House, Birmingham, West Midlands B3 3HN
**US SIC:** 6711 **UK SIC:** 83962
**Auditors:** PricewaterhouseCoopers LLP
**Bankers:** HSBC Bank plc (40-07-13)

| | 30-06-14 | 30-06-13 | 30-06-12 |
|---|---|---|---|
| TO | 68,840,000 | 66,759,000 | 68,840,000 |
| P/L | 810,000 | 353,000 | 530,000 |
| NW | 10,548,000 | 14,287,000 | 14,137,000 |
| WC | 10,324,000 | 14,955,000 | 15,945,000 |
| Emp. | 907 | 837 | 914 |

DUNS 22-075-9513

## Watermelon Ltd

66 Porchester Road, 1st Floor, London W2 6ET
**Tel:** 02078810060
**Web:** www.watermelon.com
**Reg No:** 4077391 **Estd:** 1998 Private Limited Company
**Line of Business:** Speciality design activities
**Issued Capital:** £2
**Director:** J D Sieff
**Co. Secretary:** Miss Alice Wishart
**Responsibilities**
**Senior:** Charlotte Rakowski *(Creative Director)*
**US SIC:** 7399 **UK SIC:** 83954

| | 31-03-14 | 31-03-13 | 30-03-12 |
|---|---|---|---|
| TA | 411,408 | 754,058 | 600,464 |
| NW | 42,702 | 117,759 | 94,932 |
| WC | (35,678) | 31,592 | 3,772 |

DUNS 21-609-2395

## Watermoor Meat Supply Ltd

Unit 13a, Cirencester, Gloucestershire GL7 1YG
**Tel:** 01285653352
**Web:** www.watermoormeats.co.uk
**Reg No:** 0508027 **Estd:** 1952 Private Limited Company
**Line of Business:** Retail sale of meat and meat products
**Issued Capital:** £1,000
**Managing Director:** R S Hawes
**Co. Secretary:** Ms Nesta Hawes
**Branches:** Watermoor Meat Supply Ltd, W J Castle Ltd, 111 High Street, Burford, Oxfordshire OX18 4RG
**US SIC:** 5423, 6531, 6519
**UK SIC:** 64100, 83400, 85000
**Auditors:** Bronsens
**Bankers:** Lloyds TSB Bank plc (30-92-06)

| | 31-08-13 | 31-08-12 | 31-08-11 |
|---|---|---|---|
| TA | 3,052,058 | 2,970,352 | 3,253,687 |
| NW | 1,242,796 | 1,275,055 | 1,420,460 |
| WC | (259,760) | (974,196) | (1,022,342) |

DUNS 39-908-5521

## Waterperry Gardens Ltd

Waterperry, Oxford, Oxfordshire OX33 1JZ
**Tel:** 01844339226
**Web:** www.waterperrygardens.co.uk
**Reg No:** 2233285 **Estd:** 1988 Private Limited Company
**Line of Business:** Growing of other fruit, nuts and spice crops; growing of other beverage crops
**Trading Style:** The Pear Tree Teashop
**Issued Capital:** £357,002
**Directors:** R J Edmunds, J Hubbersgilt, G N Pearce, S N Buchanan, R Jacobs, P P Watson, I D Mason
**Responsibilities**
**Senior:** Dawn Stott *(Manager)*
**US SIC:** 0179, 0119, 2033, 5999
**UK SIC:** 01002, 01001, 41473, 65600
**Auditors:** Gorman Seaton & Co

| | 31-12-13 | 31-12-12 | 31-12-11 |
|---|---|---|---|
| TO | 1,539,129 | 1,545,960 | 1,766,732 |
| P/L | (105,989) | (167,833) | (81,881) |
| NW | 169,419 | 275,408 | 443,241 |
| WC | (9,310) | 45,073 | 193,509 |

DUNS 52-035-3814

## Waters Park House Ltd

Exmouth Road, Plymouth, Devon PL1 4QQ
**Tel:** 01752-567755
**Web:** www.waterspark.co.uk
**Reg No:** 3402064 **Estd:** 1997 Private Limited Company
**Line of Business:** Non-charitable social work activities with accommodation
**Issued Capital:** £1,000
**Director:** Ms E A Waters
**Co. Secretary:** Ms Hayley Bowden
**Responsibilities**
**Purchasing:** Joy Geech *(Purchasing Manager)*
**US SIC:** 8321 **UK SIC:** 96111

**Auditors:** SCOTT

| | 31-07-13 | 31-07-12 | 31-07-11 |
|---|---|---|---|
| TO | 2,379,711 | N/A | N/A |
| P/L | 143,104 | N/A | N/A |
| NW | 1,552,817 | 1,445,944 | 1,326,174 |
| WC | 1,921,671 | 1,895,707 | 1,924,188 |
| Emp. | 95 | N/A | N/A |

DUNS 21-039-3487
## Watershed
1 Canons Road, Bristol, Avon BS1 5TX
**Tel:** 01179275100
**Web:** www.watershed.co.uk
**Estd:** 1982 Partnership
**Line of Business:** Cinemas
**Partners:** S Williams, W Bowen, D Price
**Responsibilities**
**Senior:** Dick Penny *(Manager)*
**US SIC:** 6531 **UK SIC:** 83400
**Employees:** 250

DUNS 28-947-2474
## The Watershed Arts Trust Ltd
1 Canons Road, Bristol, Avon BS1 5TX
**Tel:** 01179-276444
**Web:** www.watershed.co.uk
**Reg No:** 1608779 **Estd:** 1982 Private Company Limited By Guarantee
**Line of Business:** Operation of arts facilities
**Trading Style:** The Watershed Arts Trust Limited
**Directors:** Dr J Chakrabarti Gallemore, Miss S Luton, Ms D E Bunyan, J G Touzel, Ms L M Bilbe, S J Gatfield, S Wilson, P M Appleby
**Co. Secretary:** Ms Lisa Bilbe
**Responsibilities**
**Senior:** Alex Gilkison *(Director)*, Estella Tincknell *(Director)*
**Finance:** James Flintoff *(Finance Director)*
**Marketing:** Louise Gardner *(Marketing Manager)*, Richard Grafton *(Senior Developer)*
**Sales:** Charlie McKinnon *(Sales Manager)*
**HR:** Laura Walder *(Operations Manager)*
**Health & Safety:** Laura Walder *(Operations Manager)*
**Facilities:** Laura Walder *(Operations Manager)*
**Operations:** Layla Barron *(Head of Operations)*, Roberta Walker *(Technical, Production Manager)*
**Branches:** The Watershed Arts Trust Ltd, 1 Canons Road, Bristol, Avon BS1 5TX
**US SIC:** 7911 **UK SIC:** 97913
**Auditors:** KPMG
**Bankers:** Barclays Bank Plc (20-13-42)

| | 31-03-14 | 31-03-13 | 31-03-12 |
|---|---|---|---|
| TO | 4,513,908 | 4,184,788 | 3,707,038 |
| P/L | (156,609) | (233,641) | (150,142) |
| NW | 7,685,144 | 7,841,753 | 8,075,394 |
| WC | 65,898 | 54,813 | 132,442 |
| Emp. | 83 | 77 | 77 |

DUNS 57-044-7177 **Imp-Exp**
## Watershed Packaging Ltd
Westland House, Westland Square, Leeds, West Yorkshire LS11 5SS
**Tel:** 01132770606 **Fax:** 0113 277 7174
**Web:** www.watershed-packaging.co.uk
**Reg No:** 2877836 **VAT No:** 548793487
**Estd:** 1993 Private Limited Company
**Line of Business:** Packaging equipment
**Export Markets:** Russia, Middle East, Liberia
**Issued Capital:** £1,000
**Principals:** J Waters *(Managing)*, S Waters
**Co. Secretary:** Miss Anna Wood
**Branches:** Watershed Packaging Ltd, Unit 2, Bryn Brithdir, Blackwood, Gwent NP12 4AA
**US SIC:** 3551, 2648
**UK SIC:** 32441, 47231
**Auditors:** Atkinsons (Hull)
**Bankers:** The Bank Of Ireland (30-11-42)

| | 31-12-13 | 31-12-12 | 31-12-11 |
|---|---|---|---|
| TO | 9,717,248 | 8,637,608 | 8,067,184 |
| P/L | 435,453 | 310,544 | 106,864 |
| NW | 1,549,716 | 1,143,561 | 892,483 |
| WC | 66,978 | 287,790 | 142,161 |
| Emp. | 73 | 63 | 59 |

DUNS 50-150-5515
## Waterside Holiday Group Ltd
Bowleaze Coveway, Weymouth, Dorset DT3 6PP
**Tel:** 01305-833-103
**Web:** www.watersideholidays.co.uk
**Reg No:** 2328741 **VAT No:** 515792334
**Estd:** 1965 Private Limited Company
**Line of Business:** Holiday parks and camps
**Trading Style:** Waterside Holiday Park & Spa, Chesil Vista Holiday Park, Osmington Holiday Park
**Issued Capital:** £20,000
**Principals:** G C Frampton *(Managing)*, Miss C V Jacobs, Miss O J Jacobs, Miss M L Jacobs, Ms J H Jacobs
**Co. Secretary:** Philip Jacobs
**Responsibilities**
**Sales:** Louise Rooks *(Senior Sales Executive)*
**Branches:** Waterside Holiday Group Limited, Chesil Beach Car Park, Chesil Beach Centre, Weymouth, Dorset DT4 9XE
**US SIC:** 7021, 7032
**UK SIC:** 66500, 66702
**Auditors:** Filer Knapper LLP
**Bankers:** Barclays Bank Plc (20-26-62)

| | 31-10-13 | 31-10-12 | 31-10-11 |
|---|---|---|---|
| TO | 12,796,935 | 11,489,594 | 10,234,047 |
| P/L | 2,308,135 | 1,903,962 | 1,532,504 |
| NW | 13,227,534 | 11,807,471 | 10,707,327 |
| WC | 84,363 | (108,833) | (1,361,203) |
| Emp. | 145 | 139 | 132 |

DUNS 21-130-9856
## Waterside Inn
Ferry Road, Shoreham-By-Sea, West Sussex BN43 5RA
**Web:** www.waterside-inn.co.uk
**Estd:** 1972 Proprietorship
**Line of Business:** Public house
**Proprietor:** M Roux
**Responsibilities**
**Senior:** Mick Cross *(Licensee)*, Sarah Jeram *(Manager)*
**US SIC:** 5813 **UK SIC:** 66200
**Employees:** 60

DUNS 21-586-2285
## Waterside Inns Ltd
(**Subsidiary of:** Mref Hotels Limited)
Fraserburgh Road, Peterhead, Peterhead, Aberdeenshire AB42 3BN
**Tel:** 08712210241 **Fax:** 01779-470670
**Web:** www.britanniahotels.com
**Reg No:** 0063327SC **Estd:** 1977 Private Limited Company
**Line of Business:** Hotels and motels without restaurant
**Trading Style:** The Waterside Inn
**Issued Capital:** £825,000
**Directors:** N W Edwards, C J Ferguson Davie, H Figge, M E Gilbard, S Hall
**Responsibilities**
**Senior:** Hilda Reid *(Food & Beverage Manager)*, Timothy Sanderson *(Manager)*
**Finance:** Verity Wilson *(Financial Controller)*
**HR:** Karen Higgins *(Assistant Operations Manager)*
**Health & Safety:** Karen Higgins *(Assistant Operations Manager)*
**Facilities:** Karen Higgins *(Assistant Operations Manager)*
**Branches:** Ardoe House Hotel, Blairs, Aberdeen.
**US SIC:** 7011, 6531
**UK SIC:** 66500, 83400
**Bankers:** Bank Of Scotland (80-09-38)

| | 31-12-13 | 31-12-12 | 31-12-11 |
|---|---|---|---|
| TA | 3,474,000 | 3,373,000 | 3,275,000 |
| P/L | 101,000 | 98,000 | 95,000 |
| NW | 3,474,000 | 3,373,000 | 3,275,000 |

DUNS 21-579-0483
## Waterside School
Robert Street, London SE18 7NB
**Tel:** 020-83177659
**Web:** www.watersideschool.ik.org
**Proprietorship**
**Line of Business:** Schools (local authority)
**Proprietor:** Miss S Vernoit
**US SIC:** 8211 **UK SIC:** 93200
**Employees:** 60

DUNS 49-419-2123
## Waterside Training Ltd
Technology Campus, Waterside, Pocket Nook Street, St Helens, Merseyside WA9 1TW
**Tel:** 01744-616837
**Web:** www.waterside-training.co.uk
**Reg No:** 3140204 **Estd:** 1996 Private Limited Company
**Line of Business:** Activities of private training providers
**Trading Style:** Waterside Training Ltd
**Issued Capital:** £1,125
**Directors:** N A Shore, R Molloy, D Holt, Ms S Jee, Dr D Mcareavey
**Co. Secretary:** Ms Susan Brooks
**Responsibilities**
**Senior:** Anis Ahmed *(Manager)*, Patricia Bacon *(Manager)*, Karl Brogan *(Manager)*
**US SIC:** 8299 **UK SIC:** 93300
**Auditors:** Wheawill & Sudworth

| | 31-03-14 | 31-03-13 | 31-03-12 |
|---|---|---|---|
| TA | 421,271 | 528,550 | 544,994 |
| NW | 56,505 | 60,082 | 43,360 |
| WC | 42,334 | 44,876 | 39,138 |

DUNS 23-826-4373
## Waterstons Ltd
Liddon House, Belmont Business Park, Durham, County Durham DH1 1TW
**Tel:** 01913845891 **Fax:** 08450940946
**Web:** www.waterstons.co.uk
**Reg No:** 3818424 **Estd:** 1999 Private Limited Company
**Line of Business:** Management and business consultants
**Issued Capital:** £1,177,783
**Directors:** Dr R M Waterston, Miss S J Bell, A Mcleod, M P Stirrup, A Singh, Ms S A Waterston, Mrs L Cullen, R Morrow
**Co. Secretary:** Michael Stirrup
**Responsibilities**
**Senior:** Gabriel Radu *(Board Member)*, Mike Waterston *(Manager)*
**Finance:** Mike Waterston *(Manager)*
**Marketing:** Amy Crimmens *(Marketing Officer)*
**Sales:** Mike Waterston *(Manager)*
**IT:** Chris Fenly *(Information Technology Consult)*
**HR:** Lesley Renteurs *(HR Manager)*
**Health & Safety:** Mike Waterston *(Manager)*
**Purchasing:** Ray Renteurs *(Purchasing Manager)*
**US SIC:** 7379, 7374
**UK SIC:** 83940
**Auditors:** Deloitte & Touche LLP
**Bankers:** Lloyds TSB Bank plc (30-92-79)

| | 30-06-14 | 30-06-13 | 30-06-12 |
|---|---|---|---|
| TA | 2,344,042 | 2,288,513 | 2,320,586 |
| NW | 1,278,290 | 1,082,717 | 1,036,480 |
| WC | 819,516 | 603,645 | 412,736 |

DUNS 23-779-2874
## Watertite Heating Ltd
Unit 10 Bartlett Court, Sea King Road, Lynx Trading Estate, Yeovil, Somerset BA20 2NZ
**Web:** www.watertiteheating.co.uk
**Reg No:** 2335007 **VAT No:** 453799207
**Estd:** 1989 Private Limited Company
**Line of Business:** Heating contractors
**Issued Capital:** £1,600
**Principals:** M N Rowswell *(Managing)*, J R Newbury, Mrs H D Rowswell, Mrs S Wintersgill, J D Wintersgill
**Co. Secretary:** Marcus Rowswell
**Responsibilities**
**Engineering:** Peter Hoppe *(Contracts Manager)*
**Branches:** Watertite Heating Ltd, 124 Imber Rd, Warminster, Wiltshire BA12 0BR
**US SIC:** 1711 **UK SIC:** 50300
**Auditors:** Milsted Langdon
**Bankers:** National Westminster Bank Plc (60-24-37)

| | 31-07-14 | 31-07-13 | 31-07-12 |
|---|---|---|---|
| TA | 1,630,704 | 1,891,714 | 1,617,936 |
| NW | 487,683 | 351,836 | 371,093 |
| WC | 427,404 | 285,994 | 319,772 |

DUNS 23-365-3620
## Waterways Ireland
5 Darling Street, Enniskillen, Co Fermanagh BT74 7DP
**Tel:** 028-6632-3004
**Web:** www.waterwaysireland.org
**Estd:** 1999 Proprietorship
**Line of Business:** Water Supply
**Director:** J Marton
**Branches:** WATERWAYS IRELAND,17/19 LWR HATCH ST,DUBLIN 2
**US SIC:** 4941 **UK SIC:** 17000
**Employees:** 70

DUNS 23-733-7030
## The Waterways Trust
Llanthony Warehouse, The Docks, Gloucester, Gloucestershire GL1 2EH
**Tel:** 01452318200 **Fax:** 01452-318202
**Web:** www.canalrivertrust.org.uk
**Reg No:** 3728156 **Estd:** 1999 Private Company Limited By Guarantee
**Line of Business:** Museum activities
**Trading Style:** Canal and River Trust
**Directors:** R G Hanbury, V P Moran, Ms J A Lewis, S Pullinger
**Co. Secretary:** Yetunde Salami
**Responsibilities**
**Senior:** Doreen Davies *(Manager)*, Peter Juniper *(Manager)*
**US SIC:** 8411 **UK SIC:** 97700
**Auditors:** Griffiths Marshall
**Bankers:** National Westminster Bank Plc (60-00-01)

| | 31-03-14 | 31-03-13 | 31-03-12 |
|---|---|---|---|
| TO | N/A | 3,560,298 | 4,551,695 |
| P/L | (539,650) | (2,406,866) | (83,612) |
| NW | (1,987,331) | (1,583,744) | 823,122 |
| WC | N/A | (1,857,784) | 325,078 |
| Emp. | N/A | 62 | 76 |

DUNS 73-972-4685
## Waterworld 2000 Ltd
(**Subsidiary of:** Waterworld Group (Staffs) Ltd)
Stoke Ski Centre, Festival Way, Stoke-On-Trent, Staffordshire ST1 5PU
**Tel:** 01782-205747 **Fax:** 01782-201815
**Web:** www.waterworld.co.uk
**Reg No:** 5223326 **Estd:** 1990 Private Limited Company
**Line of Business:** Operation of swimming pools
**Issued Capital:** £101
**Principals:** M I Chaudry *(Managing)*, T Kiely
**Co. Secretary:** Mrs Ann Chaudry
**US SIC:** 7999 **UK SIC:** 97913

| | 31-07-13 | 31-07-12 | 31-07-11 |
|---|---|---|---|
| TA | 868,743 | 1,123,981 | 1,038,414 |
| NW | 453,220 | 704,092 | 566,232 |
| WC | 436,900 | 313,963 | 546,867 |

DUNS 28-991-6413
## Wates Group Ltd
Wates House, Station Approach, Leatherhead, Surrey KT22 7SW
**Tel:** 01372-861000 **Fax:** 01372861267
**Web:** www.wates.co.uk
**Reg No:** 1824828 **Estd:** 1986 Private Limited Company
**Line of Business:** Building construction contractors
**Trading Style:** Wates Construction
**Issued Capital:** £9,777,848
**Directors:** A E Wates, A J G Wates, C W Wates, G Mcfaull, Ms D E Mattar, T A Wates, A O Davies, J G Wates
**Co. Secretary:** David Davies
**Responsibilities**
**Senior:** Richard Girdlestone *(Manager)*
**Marketing:** Radhika Kapur *(Personal Corporate Strategy Ma)*
**Sales:** Natasha Cottell *(Business Development Manager)*, Ben DeSanges *(Regional Commercial Director)*, Ross Green *(Business Development Manager)*, Nick Horton *(Commercial Manager)*, Maria Joyce *(Regional Commercial Manager)*, Gareth Peerman *(Commercial Manager)*, Fred Syed *(Commercial Manager)*, Chelsea Walters *(Commercial Legal Advisor)*, Mick Worrell *(Commercial Manager)*
**Admin:** Ellen Costello *(Personal Assistant)*
**Purchasing:** Nigel Holzer *(Contracts Manager)*
**Branches:** Wates Group Ltd, 353 Altrincham Road, Manchester M22 4BJ
**US SIC:** 6711 **UK SIC:** 83962
**Auditors:** PricewaterhouseCoopers LLP
**Bankers:** HSBC Bank plc (40-02-50)
**Following financial data are in thousands**

| | 31-12-13 | 31-12-12 | 31-12-11 |
|---|---|---|---|
| TO | 851,695 | 1,096,991 | 1,033,929 |
| P/L | 22,340 | 25,735 | 40,144 |
| NW | 54,499 | 43,989 | 36,456 |
| WC | 32,411 | 27,637 | 12,603 |
| Emp. | 2,074 | 2,367 | 2,650 |

DUNS 42-443-0846
## Watford & District Ymca
Charter House, Charter Place, Watford, Hertfordshire WD17 2RT
**Web:** www.watfordymca.com
**Reg No:** 4430743 **Estd:** 1980 Private Company Limited By Guarantee
**Line of Business:** Youth hostels and mountain refuges
**Directors:** A Newell, J Moxham, J G Hyde, Ms D Morrad, Ms T J Barnard, Ms C M Neyndorff, R K Green, J N Robinson
**Co. Secretary:** David Martin
**Responsibilities**
**Senior:** W Craddock-Jones *(Principal)*, Guy Foxell *(Manager)*, K Lees *(Principal)*, G Swinscoe *(Principal)*
**Branches:** Watford & District Ymca, Linnet Road, Abbots Langley, Hertfordshire WD5 0GN
**US SIC:** 7021, 7999, 8321, 8699
**UK SIC:** 66500, 97913, 96111, 96902
**Bankers:** Barclays Bank Plc (20-91-79)

| | 31-03-14 | 31-03-13 | 31-03-12 |
|---|---|---|---|
| TO | 8,939,660 | 5,263,897 | 5,390,811 |
| P/L | (129,706) | 26,852 | 294,871 |
| NW | 5,491,222 | 4,591,728 | 4,306,701 |
| WC | 649,930 | 712,685 | 569,296 |
| Emp. | 213 | 123 | 148 |

DUNS 22-633-7459 **Imp**
## The Watford Association Football Club Ltd
Vicarage Road Stadium, Watford, Hertfordshire WD18 0ER
**Tel:** 01923496000 **Fax:** 01923-496001
**Web:** www.watfordfc.com
**Reg No:** 0104194 **VAT No:** 197736995
**Estd:** 1997 Private Limited Company
**Line of Business:** Operation of other sports arenas and stadiums not elsewhere classified
**Trading Style:** The Watford Association Football Club Ltd
**Issued Capital:** £1,072,852
**Directors:** Professor S R Timperley, R Riva, S I Duxbury, D B Fransen
**Co. Secretary:** Peter Wastall
**Responsibilities**
**Senior:** Jackie Sheppard *(Personal Assistant)*
**US SIC:** 7999 **UK SIC:** 97913
**Auditors:** Chantrey Vellacott DFK LLP

**Bankers:** Barclays Bank Plc (20-91-79)

| | 30-06-14 | 30-06-13 | 30-06-12 |
|---|---|---|---|
| TO | 16,690,000 | 18,133,000 | 11,184,000 |
| P/L | (344,000) | 190,000 | (2,648,000) |
| NW | (4,508,000) | (4,344,000) | (4,851,000) |
| WC | (7,619,000) | (4,829,000) | (9,182,000) |
| Emp. | 158 | 164 | 207 |

DUNS 21-560-9963
## Watford Audi
The Grange, Watford Heath, Watford, Hertfordshire WD19 4EU
**Tel:** 01923202800
**Web:** www.m25audi.co.uk
**Estd:** 2006 Proprietorship
**Line of Business:** Car dealers (new & used)
**Proprietor:** P Greenberg
**US SIC:** 5511 **UK SIC:** 65100
**Employees:** 70

DUNS 23-782-5344
## Watford Borough Council
The Brow, Watford, Hertfordshire WD25 7NX
**Tel:** 01923678240
**Web:** www.albanwood.herts.sch.uk
**Estd:** 2012
**Line of Business:** General secondary education
**Principals:** A R Garman *(Financial)*, R B Mcmillan, R Carter
**Responsibilities**
**Senior:** Rachel Kirk *(Head Teacher)*, R McMillan *(Chief Executive Officer)*
**Branches:** Watford Borough Council, 194 High Street, Watford, Hertfordshire WD17 2DT
**US SIC:** 8211 **UK SIC:** 93200
**Employees:** 1,100

DUNS 21-685-2437
## Watford Grammar School for Boys
Rickmansworth Road, Watford, Hertfordshire WD18 7JF
**Tel:** 01923521786
**Web:** www.minibuswatford.co.uk
**Reg No:** 7348288 **Estd:** 2010 Private Company Limited By Guarantee
**Line of Business:** General secondary education
**Directors:** Mrs S V Smith, Mrs C Cox, Mrs S M Branch, B Speel, T Sweeney, Mrs A Dawkins, Ms S Scott, Professor J Hoppit
**Co. Secretary:** Ms Caroline Brown
**Responsibilities**
**Senior:** Mark Allchorn *(Director)*, Len Arlow *(Director)*, Jessica Callow *(Director)*, Paul Shearring *(Director)*, Lana Wood *(Director)*
**US SIC:** 8211 **UK SIC:** 93200
**Bankers:** Lloyds TSB Bank plc (30-99-21)

| | 31-08-13 | 31-08-12 | 31-08-11 |
|---|---|---|---|
| TO | 8,028,247 | 8,476,703 | 15,063,045 |
| P/L | (183,907) | 305,788 | 6,450,514 |
| NW | 15,440,836 | 10,683,922 | 6,573,514 |
| WC | 768,925 | 607,174 | 305,516 |
| Emp. | 136 | 134 | 170 |

DUNS 21-685-2395
## Watford Grammar School for Girls
Ladys Close, Watford, Hertfordshire WD18 0AE
**Tel:** 01923223403
**Web:** www.watfordgrammarschoolforgirls.org.uk
**Reg No:** 7348254 **Estd:** 2010 Private Company Limited By Guarantee
**Line of Business:** Schools (foundation)
**Directors:** Mrs G R Collison, Mrs J Willis, P Baird, Ms H Hyde, L M Renak, P Mccloskey, Ms Y Bateson, A W Rindl
**Co. Secretary:** Philip Beasley
**Responsibilities**
**Senior:** Marianne Cordingley *(Governor)*, Russell Deane *(Director)*, Richard Farmery *(Director)*, Jeffrey Herman *(Director)*, Percy McCloskey *(Governor)*, Sreedhara Naidu *(Director)*, Anthony Perrott *(Director)*, Fiona Shore *(Governor)*, Camilla Woods *(Director)*
**US SIC:** 8211 **UK SIC:** 93200
**Bankers:** Clydesdale Bank Plc (82-61-15)

| | 31-08-14 | 31-08-13 | 31-08-12 |
|---|---|---|---|
| TO | 7,713,071 | 8,438,649 | 7,899,771 |
| P/L | 93,880 | 812,109 | 650,547 |
| NW | 1,139,219 | 1,359,341 | 496,233 |
| WC | 678,237 | 757,807 | 390,826 |
| Emp. | 132 | 127 | 126 |

DUNS 21-634-1982
## Watford Launderers & Cleaners Ltd
45-69 Sydney Road, Watford, Hertfordshire WD18 7QA
**Tel:** 01923227702
**Web:** www.watfordonline.co.uk
**Reg No:** 0239593 **VAT No:** 382402370
**Estd:** 1907 Private Limited Company
**Line of Business:** Laundries
**Issued Capital:** £60,000
**Directors:** R M Ross, A J Ross, M S Johnson, G M Ross, Ms K E Cort, S R Ross
**Co. Secretary:** Mrs Penelope Ross
**Responsibilities**
**HR:** Elaine Thorn *(Human Resources Manager)*
**US SIC:** 7219 **UK SIC:** 98110
**Auditors:** Myers Clark
**Bankers:** National Westminster Bank Plc (60-00-08)

| | 28-09-13 | 29-09-12 | 01-09-11 |
|---|---|---|---|
| TO | N/A | 4,469,524 | 4,149,288 |
| P/L | N/A | 216,563 | 91,778 |
| NW | 6,198,938 | 6,113,021 | 6,033,706 |
| WC | 2,783,098 | 2,733,288 | 2,608,583 |
| Emp. | N/A | 170 | 174 |

DUNS 23-980-5638
## Watford New Hope Trust
67 Queens Road, Watford, Hertfordshire WD17 2QN
**Tel:** 01923210680 **Fax:** 01923-210680
**Web:** www.newhope.org.uk
**Reg No:** 3969063 **Estd:** 2000 Private Company Limited By Guarantee
**Line of Business:** Retail sale of furniture, lighting equipment and household articles not elsewhere classified
**Directors:** I J Peck, Mrs M J Sills, Ms S E Meaning, K R Stevens, J R Ford, H G Lloyd
**Co. Secretary:** Derek Heasman
**Responsibilities**
**Senior:** Matthew Heasman *(Chief Executive Officer)*, Frederick Langley *(Manager)*, Philippa Leese *(Manager)*
**Marketing:** Wil Berdinner *(Fund Raising And Communication)*
**Branches:** Watford New Hope Trust, 124 Exchange Road, Watford, Hertfordshire WD18 0PP
**US SIC:** 8999 **UK SIC:** 83954
**Auditors:** Cansdales
**Bankers:** Cafcash Ltd (40-52-40)

| | 31-03-14 | 31-03-13 | 31-03-12 |
|---|---|---|---|
| TO | 2,268,390 | 2,092,959 | 1,904,535 |
| P/L | 29,719 | (21,499) | 6,107 |
| NW | 809,872 | 780,153 | 801,652 |
| WC | 424,190 | 383,918 | 415,052 |
| Emp. | 50 | 259 | 51 |

DUNS 76-236-0907
## Watkin Jones & Son Ltd
**(Subsidiary of:** Watkin Jones Group Ltd)
Llandygai Industrial Estate, Llandygai, Bangor, Gwynedd LL57 4YH
**Tel:** 01248-362516 **Fax:** 01248352860
**Web:** www.watkinjones.com
**Reg No:** 2539870 **VAT No:** 560001208
**Estd:** 1791 Private Limited Company
**Line of Business:** Building construction contractors
**Trading Style:** Watkin Jones & Son Ltd
**Issued Capital:** £250,000
**Principals:** G Watkin Jones *(Managing)*, N L Bingham, A Pease, M Watkin Jones, G Morgan, J M Davies, B Evans, G Davies
**Co. Secretary:** Philip Byrom
**Responsibilities**
**Senior:** Andrew Mcdonough *(Director)*
**Branches:** Watkin Jones & Son Ltd, Unit 2 Wellfield, Business Park, Runcorn, Cheshire WA7 3FR
**US SIC:** 1522 **UK SIC:** 50100
**Auditors:** Ernst & Young LLP
**Bankers:** HSBC Bank plc (40-09-03)

| | 30-09-13 | 30-09-12 | 30-09-11 |
|---|---|---|---|
| TO | 113,006,000 | 107,515,000 | 124,754,000 |
| P/L | 4,495,000 | 2,767,000 | 18,094,000 |
| NW | 86,820,000 | 82,788,000 | 81,798,000 |
| WC | 90,031,000 | 75,031,000 | 73,877,000 |
| Emp. | 273 | 239 | 245 |

DUNS 22-082-8961
## Watkin Jones Group Ltd
Unit 2 Wellfield Business Park, Chester Road, Preston Brook, Runcorn, Cheshire WA7 3FR
**Tel:** 01928785900 **Fax:** 01248352860
**Web:** www.watkinjones.com
**Reg No:** 4084303 **VAT No:** 741531554
**Estd:** 1971 Private Limited Company
**Line of Business:** Builders
**Issued Capital:** £1,000,000
**Directors:** G Watkin Jones, Ms J A Watkin Jones, M Watkin Jones, P M Byrom
**Responsibilities**
**Senior:** Gwyn Pritchard *(Regional Director)*
**US SIC:** 1522, 1541
**UK SIC:** 50100
**Auditors:** Ernst & Young LLP
**Bankers:** Bank Of Scotland (12-08-95)

| | 30-09-13 | 30-09-12 | 30-09-11 |
|---|---|---|---|
| TO | 138,013,000 | 145,563,000 | 185,839,000 |
| P/L | 5,030,000 | 9,017,000 | 11,066,000 |
| NW | 77,384,000 | 72,731,000 | 64,961,000 |
| WC | 99,224,000 | 74,924,000 | 70,760,000 |
| Emp. | 273 | 239 | 245 |

DUNS 28-879-8945
## Watkins & Sole Ltd
Unit 11, Galleymead Road, Colnbrook, Slough, Berkshire SL3 0EN
**Tel:** 01753683647 **Fax:** 01753682405
**Web:** www.wasuk.net
**Reg No:** 1163741 **Estd:** 1974 Private Limited Company
**Line of Business:** Road haulage and transport services
**Issued Capital:** £100
**Principals:** J E Watkins *(Managing)*, Ms J E Watkins, M Higgins, A A Watkins
**Co. Secretary:** Mrs Anita Watkins
**US SIC:** 4789 **UK SIC:** 77002
**Auditors:** Hurst Morrison Thomson
**Bankers:** HSBC Bank plc (40-43-04)

| | 31-01-14 | 31-01-13 | 31-01-12 |
|---|---|---|---|
| TO | 4,059,795 | 4,420,500 | 4,636,700 |
| P/L | (70,707) | 17,901 | 131,243 |
| NW | (107,171) | (33,452) | (43,873) |
| WC | (152,077) | (107,728) | (7,953) |

DUNS 42-418-0375
## Watkins Gray International L L P
Colechurch House, 1 London Bridge Walk, London SE1 2SX
**Tel:** 020-7940-8400
**Web:** www.wgi.co.uk
**Reg No:** 0301851OC **Estd:** 1900 Limited Partnership
**Line of Business:** Engineering consultative and design activities
**US SIC:** 8911 **UK SIC:** 83701
**Auditors:** Wilkins Kennedy

| | 31-03-14 | 31-03-13 | 31-03-12 |
|---|---|---|---|
| TA | 1,083,420 | 1,192,915 | 1,676,580 |
| NW | 3,830 | (17,537) | 164,676 |
| WC | 508,973 | 432,488 | 513,825 |

DUNS 23-601-9662
## Watkins Hire Ltd
Ward Industrial Estate, Church Road, Lydney, Gloucestershire GL15 5EL
**Tel:** 01594 840025 **Fax:** 01594 840026
**Web:** www.watkinshire.co.uk
**Reg No:** 3599314 **VAT No:** 762707518
**Estd:** 1998 Private Limited Company
**Line of Business:** Plant and tool hire
**Issued Capital:** £11,496
**Directors:** P B O'Kelly, S E Platt, S J Blaby, R S Williams, M A Walton, T V Stevens-Smith
**Co. Secretary:** Steven Blaby
**Responsibilities**
**Senior:** Mark Hills *(Manager)*, Bill Watkins *(Proprietor)*
**Branches:** Watkins Hire Ltd, L C P Ho, 36 First Ave, Kingswinford, West Midlands DY6 7NA
**US SIC:** 7394 **UK SIC:** 84000
**Auditors:** Dunkley''s
**Bankers:** Yorkshire Bank Plc (05-04-37)

| | 30-06-13 | 30-06-12 | 30-06-11 |
|---|---|---|---|
| TO | 11,658,664 | 9,972,488 | 11,681,263 |
| P/L | 520,427 | (87,095) | 778,787 |
| NW | 11,010,791 | 10,776,014 | 10,793,501 |
| WC | 4,918,008 | 3,645,965 | 3,327,977 |
| Emp. | 62 | 43 | 65 |

DUNS 21-718-3318 Imp-Exp
## Watkiss Automation Ltd
Watkiss House, 1 Blaydon Road, Sandy, Bedfordshire SG19 1RZ
**Tel:** 01767685700 **Fax:** 01767-689902
**Web:** www.watkiss.com
**Reg No:** 1222069 **VAT No:** 283685125
**Estd:** 1968 Private Limited Company
**Line of Business:** Manufacture of machinery for paper and paperboard production
**Export Markets:** Worldwide
**Export Sales:** £4,421,608
**Issued Capital:** £12,000
**Principals:** C R Watkiss *(Chairman)*, Ms B A Watkiss *(Managing)*, M C Watkiss *(Financial)*
**Co. Secretary:** Ms Barbara Watkiss
**Responsibilities**
**Senior:** Susan Atchew *(Financial Director)*, Zoe Mortimer *(Senior Export Coordinator)*, Jo Watkiss *(Communications Director)*
**Finance:** Susan Atchew *(Financial Director)*
**Marketing:** Jo Watkiss *(Communications Director)*
**Sales:** Jo Watkiss *(Communications Director)*
**Branches:** Watkiss Automation Ltd, 2A Blacksmiths Lane, Fakenham, Norfolk NR21 0QB
**US SIC:** 3554 **UK SIC:** 32754
**Auditors:** Bradshaw Johnson
**Bankers:** Lloyds TSB Bank plc (30-94-30)

| | 28-02-14 | 28-02-13 | 29-02-12 |
|---|---|---|---|
| TO | 5,542,787 | 5,113,584 | 6,983,953 |
| P/L | 34,505 | (331,734) | 302,724 |
| NW | 2,091,708 | 1,964,132 | 2,190,966 |
| WC | 574,272 | 643,589 | 864,444 |
| Emp. | 70 | 73 | 76 |

DUNS 21-605-5233
## Watling View School
Watling View, St Albans, Hertfordshire AL1 2NU
**Tel:** 01727850560
**Estd:** 1988
**Line of Business:** Schools (special)
**Partners:** T Owen Jackson, T Jackson-Owens
**Responsibilities**
**Senior:** William Fletcher *(Acting Head Teacher)*
**US SIC:** 8299 **UK SIC:** 93300
**Employees:** 80

DUNS 21-227-4949
## Watlington & District Care Home
Hill Road, Watlington, Oxfordshire OX49 5AE
**Tel:** 01491-613400
**Web:** www.sanctuary-care.co.uk
**Estd:** 2004 Partnership
**Line of Business:** Nursing homes
**Partners:** Mrs J Cooper, Mrs A Morely
**US SIC:** 8051 **UK SIC:** 95100
**Employees:** 89

DUNS 21-705-2825
## Watmos Community Homes
116-120 Lichfield Street, Walsall, West Midlands WS1 1SZ
**Tel:** 01922 471010
**Web:** www.watmos.org.uk
**Reg No:** 0029338IP **VAT No:** 806639319
**Estd:** 2003
**Line of Business:** Housing associations societies trusts & co-operatives
**Proprietor:** Ms U Barrington
**Responsibilities**
**Senior:** Tom Hopkins *(Chief Executive)*
**US SIC:** 8699 **UK SIC:** 96902
**Bankers:** Lloyds TSB Bank plc (30-99-06)

| | 31-03-12 | 31-03-11 | 31-03-10 |
|---|---|---|---|
| TO | 6,817,000 | 6,363,000 | 6,286,000 |
| P/L | 1,590,000 | 1,091,000 | 1,177,000 |
| NW | 9,378,000 | 8,093,000 | 5,809,000 |
| WC | (2,745,000) | 2,816,000 | 2,297,000 |
| Emp. | 84 | 80 | 81 |

DUNS 21-715-9680
## Watret & Co Ltd
65-67 Park St Albans, St Albans, Hertfordshire AL2 2PE
**Tel:** 01727-873765 **Fax:** 01727-875304
**Web:** www.watret.co.uk
**Reg No:** 1023740 **VAT No:** 214197477
**Estd:** 1968 Private Limited Company
**Line of Business:** Plumbing
**Issued Capital:** £26,000
**Managing Director:** K R Watret
**Co. Secretary:** Ms Joan Watret
**US SIC:** 1711 **UK SIC:** 50300
**Auditors:** Rayner Essex LLP

| | 31-03-14 | 31-03-13 | 31-03-12 |
|---|---|---|---|
| TA | 1,554,009 | 1,471,985 | 1,269,034 |
| NW | 774,675 | 771,429 | 617,193 |
| WC | 698,143 | 714,967 | 583,032 |

DUNS 73-714-5776
## Watson Burton Llp
1 St James' Gate, Newcastle-Upon-Tyne, Tyne and Wear NE99 1YQ
**Tel:** 01912444444
**Web:** www.watsonburton.com
**Reg No:** 0306105OC **Estd:** 1842
**Line of Business:** Solicitors
**Responsibilities**
**Senior:** Andrew Francey *(Non-designated Limited Liabili)*, Roddy Gordon *(Partner)*, Sam Jardine *(Non-designated Limited Liabili)*, Patrick Kemp *(Associate)*, Warren Kemp *(Partner)*, George Parker Fuller *(Partner)*, Andrew Poyner *(Non-designated Limited Liabili)*, Doreen Reveley *(Compliance Director)*, Bryan Riley *(Non-designated Limited Liabili)*, Richard Sowler *(Partner)*, David Spires *(Associate)*
**Finance:** Christine Hannant *(Finance Office Manager)*
**Marketing:** Claire Brunton *(Marketing Manager)*
**Admin:** Heather Topham *(Administration Manager)*
**US SIC:** 8111 **UK SIC:** 83500
**Auditors:** Ernst & Young LLP

| | 30-04-14 | 30-04-13 | 30-04-12 |
|---|---|---|---|
| TO | 10,760,313 | 11,092,794 | 12,113,154 |
| P/L | 1,628,506 | 1,388,659 | 1,428,206 |
| NW | N/A | 2,266,453 | N/A |
| WC | 2,598,555 | 3,009,188 | 2,465,584 |
| Emp. | 117 | 122 | 145 |

DUNS 21-810-2681
## Watson Card Services
Lindum House, Causeway End, Brinkworth, Chippenham, Wiltshire SN15 5DN
**Tel:** 01666511230
**Web:** www.watsonfuels.co.uk
**Estd:** 2012

**Line of Business:** Fuel and oil distributors
**US SIC:** 5052 **UK SIC:** 61200
**Employees:** 50

DUNS 34-587-8479
### Watson Farley & Williams Llp
15 Appold Street, London EC2A 2HB
**Tel:** 020-7814-8000
**Web:** www.wfw.com
**Reg No:** 0312252OC **Estd:** 1980
**Line of Business:** Other legal activities not elsewhere classified
**Export Sales:** £28,723,745
**Responsibilities**
**Senior:** Liz Buchan *(Partner)*, Charles Buss *(Partner)*, Ivan Chia *(Non-designated Limited Liabili)*, Nicholas Fothergill *(Partner)*, Celia Gardiner *(Partner)*, Angharad Harris *(Partner)*, Nikolaus Holzinger *(Non-designated Limited Liabili)*, Christina Howard *(Partner)*, Andrew Hutcheon *(Partner Ligiation)*, Simon Kavanagh *(Partner)*, Ahmad Khonsari *(Non-designated Limited Liabili)*, Patrick Kirkby *(Partner)*, Anne Kleffmann *(Non-designated Limited Liabili)*, Joseph Levin *(Non-designated Limited Liabili)*, Maria Llewellyn *(Partner)*, Axel Lohde *(Non-designated Limited Liabili)*, Daniel Marhewka *(Non-designated Limited Liabili)*, Ivana Mikesic *(Non-designated Limited Liabili)*, Andrew Nimmo *(Non-designated Limited Liabili)*, James Penn *(Partner)*, Mark Prevezer *(Partner, Real Estate / Propert)*, Jahnavi Ramachandran *(Non-designated Limited Liabili)*, Gary Ritter *(Partner)*, Torsten Rosenboom *(Non-designated Limited Liabili)*, Kavita Shah *(Non-designated Limited Liabili)*, Evan Stergoulis *(Partner)*, Henry Stewart *(Non-designated Limited Liabili)*, Mark Tooke *(Partner)*, Charles Walford *(Partner)*, David Warder *(Partner)*
**Admin:** Barry Waite *(Office Manager)*
**IT:** Sam Luxford-Watts *(IT Manager)*
**HR:** Eleanor Hogg *(Training Director)*
**Health & Safety:** Barry Waite *(Office Manager)*
**Facilities:** Felicity Jones *(Head of Hotel & Leisure)*
**Operations:** David Greening *(Director of Operations)*
**US SIC:** 8111 **UK SIC:** 83500
**Auditors:** PricewaterhouseCoopers LLP

| | 30-04-14 | 30-04-13 | 30-04-12 |
|---|---|---|---|
| TO | 76,106,664 | 67,655,725 | 67,061,091 |
| P/L | 24,388,752 | 18,661,512 | 21,203,532 |
| NW | 14,254,200 | 11,361,795 | 13,015,549 |
| WC | 11,150,302 | 8,217,355 | 9,821,761 |
| Emp. | 459 | 382 | 340 |

DUNS 21-588-0740
### Watson Group
N1 Building, Euxton Lane, Euxton, Chorley, Lancashire PR7 6TE
**Tel:** 03333210954
**Web:** www.kuk.com
**Estd:** 2001 Proprietorship
**Line of Business:** Activities of households as employers of domestic staff
**Proprietor:** Mrs J Silver
**US SIC:** 8811 **UK SIC:** 99000
**Employees:** 200

DUNS 39-466-4502
### Watson Ltd
17 The Crescent, Taunton, Somerset TA1 4EB
**Tel:** 01823336400
**Web:** www.setsquare.uk.com
**Reg No:** 2124693 **Estd:** 1987 Private Limited Company
**Line of Business:** Employment and recruitment companies and consultants
**Export Sales:** £269,976
**Trading Style:** Setsquare
**Issued Capital:** £99
**Managing Director:** R B Watson
**Co. Secretary:** Murray Watson
**Branches:** Watson Ltd, South Lodge, Unit 7, Reigate, Surrey RH2 8QG
**US SIC:** 7361, 7392
**UK SIC:** 83954, 83951
**Auditors:** Whites

| | 30-09-13 | 30-09-12 | 30-09-11 |
|---|---|---|---|
| TO | 9,516,784 | 10,525,970 | 14,016,003 |
| P/L | (270,488) | (270,355) | 261,068 |
| NW | 687,541 | 978,801 | 1,253,665 |
| WC | 481,512 | 774,780 | 1,053,500 |
| Emp. | 186 | 206 | 342 |

DUNS 50-513-1664 **Imp-Exp**
### Watson-Marlow Ltd
Bickland Water Road, Tregoniggie, Falmouth, Cornwall TR11 4RU
**Tel:** 01326 370370
**Web:** www.watson-marlow.co.uk
**Reg No:** 2481019 **Estd:** 1990 Private Limited Company
**Line of Business:** Manufacturers of pump devices
**Export Markets:** worldwide
**Trading Style:** Watson-Marlow Pumps Group
**Issued Capital:** £1,000,000
**Principals:** Mrs S M Godzicz *(Financial)*, J L Whalen, D J Meredith, S Nicholson, M J Johnston, C A Magor, A J Green, Ms R Pallett
**Co. Secretary:** Steven Pearsall
**Responsibilities**
**Senior:** Darren Etherington *(Director)*, Christopher Gadsden *(Manager)*, Cindy Gray *(Manager)*, Mark Rawet *(Director)*
**Marketing:** Mike Sullivan *(Marketing Manager)*
**Sales:** Rick Balek *(Sales Director, US and Canada)*, Joakim Cederqvist *(District Sales Manager)*, Ashley Shepherd *(Manager)*, Rodd Turnquist *(National Sales Manager)*
**IT:** Darren Jeffery *(IT Manager)*
**Operations:** Mark Rawet *(Director)*
**US SIC:** 3561 **UK SIC:** 32870
**Auditors:** KPMG Audit PLC
**Bankers:** Barclays Bank Plc (20-20-15)

| | 31-12-13 | 31-12-12 | 31-12-11 |
|---|---|---|---|
| TO | 39,185,833 | 36,106,371 | 33,337,940 |
| P/L | 9,294,536 | 8,094,189 | 7,621,651 |
| NW | 3,859,568 | 3,559,202 | 4,781,016 |
| WC | (9,994,194) | (6,993,641) | (4,158,428) |
| Emp. | 236 | 217 | 199 |

DUNS 21-578-9090
### Watson-Towers (Holdings) Ltd
Waverley Street, Coatbridge, Lanarkshire ML5 2BE
**Web:** www.watson-towers.co.uk
**Reg No:** 0052812SC **Estd:** 1973 Private Limited Company
**Line of Business:** Management activities of holding companies
**Issued Capital:** £200
**Principals:** D H Towers *(Managing)*, R B Watson *(Marketing)*, N Watson, F M Towers
**Co. Secretary:** Fraser Towers
**Responsibilities**
**Finance:** Campbell Gillan *(Financial Director)*
**US SIC:** 6711, 5051
**UK SIC:** 83962, 61200
**Auditors:** Robb Ferguson
**Bankers:** Clydesdale Bank Plc (82-68-28)

| | 31-03-14 | 31-03-13 | 31-03-12 |
|---|---|---|---|
| TO | 11,597,802 | 11,540,933 | 18,542,308 |
| P/L | 450,245 | 653,041 | 373,822 |
| NW | 2,490,262 | 2,396,739 | 2,174,439 |
| WC | 1,632,071 | 1,890,558 | 1,637,624 |
| Emp. | 86 | 91 | 97 |

DUNS 34-571-5242
### Watson Wyatt (Uk) Acquisitions 1 Ltd
**(Subsidiary of:** Watson Wyatt European Investment Lp)
21 Tothill Street, London SW1H 9LL
**Tel:** 020-7222-8033
**Web:** www.towerswatson.com
**Reg No:** 5379696 **Estd:** 2005 Private Limited Company
**Line of Business:** Management activities of holding companies
**Trading Style:** Towers Watson Ltd
**Directors:** P G Morris, V J Raimondo, Ms T A Rhodes
**Co. Secretary:** David Loveridge
**Responsibilities**
**Senior:** Babloo Ramamurthy *(Regional Manager Europe)*
**HR:** Eloise Martin *(Human Resources Director)*, Naomi Sutcliffe *(Human Resources Manager)*
**US SIC:** 6711 **UK SIC:** 83962
**Auditors:** Deloitte LLP
**Employees:** 300

DUNS 21-443-2692
### Watt Brothers (Glasgow & Edinburgh) Ltd
119-121 Sauchiehall Street, Glasgow, Lanarkshire G2 3EW
**Tel:** 01413325831 **Fax:** 0141-353-2118
**Web:** www.wattbros.co.uk
**Reg No:** 0009379SC **VAT No:** 260128393
**Estd:** 1915 Private Limited Company
**Line of Business:** Departmental stores
**Issued Capital:** £3,835
**Managing Director:** W Watt
**Co. Secretary:** Ms Sandra Watt
**Responsibilities**
**Senior:** Jim Barrie *(Store Manager)*
**Finance:** Pam Nelson *(Finance Director)*
**Sales:** Paul Bowers *(Senior Sales Executive)*
**IT:** Jack Carruthers *(IT Systems Administrator)*
**Operations:** Jim Barrie *(Store Manager)*
**Branches:** Watt Brothers (Glasgow & Edinburgh) Ltd, 2 Broomgate, Lanark, Lanarkshire ML11 9EE
**US SIC:** 5399 **UK SIC:** 65600
**Auditors:** Ernst & Young LLP
**Bankers:** Bank Of Scotland (80-07-48)

| | 31-01-14 | 31-01-13 | 31-01-12 |
|---|---|---|---|
| TO | 18,602,504 | 17,311,821 | 17,234,409 |
| P/L | 143,800 | 59,509 | 64,545 |
| NW | 4,976,275 | 4,878,457 | 4,860,792 |
| WC | 2,387,388 | (223,854) | 2,423,753 |
| Emp. | 302 | 356 | 395 |

DUNS 21-881-4655
### Watts Clift Holdings Ltd
Westgate, Aldridge, Walsall, West Midlands WS9 8DJ
**Fax:** 01922-743362
**Web:** www.wattscliftholdingsltd.com
**Reg No:** 0751983 **Estd:** 1961 Private Limited Company
**Line of Business:** Wholesale of metals and ores
**Export Sales:** £300,585
**Issued Capital:** £79,178
**Principals:** E B Watts *(Managing)*, J H Rimmer, P M Doyle, P B Burns, Ms S M Ursell
**Co. Secretary:** Paul Burns
**Responsibilities**
**Senior:** Christopher Blakemore *(Manager)*
**Finance:** Christopher Blakemore *(Manager)*
**IT:** Jon Hartle *(IT Manager)*
**US SIC:** 8999, 5051
**UK SIC:** 83954, 61200
**Auditors:** Bamford Tiffen
**Bankers:** National Westminster Bank Plc (60-07-41)

| | 30-04-14 | 30-04-13 | 30-04-12 |
|---|---|---|---|
| TO | 12,946,446 | 11,485,116 | 12,805,314 |
| P/L | 187,725 | (270,960) | 171,787 |
| NW | 3,177,625 | 2,961,348 | 3,023,002 |
| WC | (1,026,083) | (956,576) | (538,962) |
| Emp. | 61 | 61 | 60 |

DUNS 67-239-6405
### Watts Gregory Llp
Oak Tree Court, Mulberry Drive, Cardiff, South Glamorgan CF23 8RS
**Tel:** 029-2054-6600 **Fax:** 029-2054-6611
**Web:** www.watts-gregory.co.uk
**Reg No:** 0326248OC **Estd:** 2007 Private Limited Company
**Line of Business:** Accounting and auditing activities
**US SIC:** 8931 **UK SIC:** 83600

| | 05-04-14 | 05-04-13 | 05-04-12 |
|---|---|---|---|
| TA | 1,329,668 | 1,395,466 | 1,364,262 |
| WC | 821,589 | 940,319 | 875,820 |

DUNS 34-932-0072
### Watts Group Plc
1 Great Tower Street, London EC3R 5AA
**Fax:** 02072808001
**Web:** www.watts.co.uk
**Reg No:** 5728557 **VAT No:** 205960961
**Estd:** 1967 Public Limited Company
**Line of Business:** Surveyors and valuers
**Issued Capital:** £3,100,851
**Directors:** N P Winks, I T Ford, T Rushton
**Co. Secretary:** Miss Lisa Bonney
**Responsibilities**
**Senior:** Robert Burke *(Manager)*, Jane Dalgliesh *(Manager)*, Mark Rabbett *(Manager)*
**US SIC:** 8911 **UK SIC:** 83701
**Auditors:** H W Fisher & Co
**Bankers:** HSBC Bank plc (40-05-20)

| | 25-04-14 | 26-04-13 | 27-04-12 |
|---|---|---|---|
| TO | 11,770,656 | 11,364,006 | 12,553,931 |
| P/L | 1,097,039 | 283,711 | 966,528 |
| NW | 1,255,388 | 345,000 | 93,657 |
| WC | 1,229,829 | 318,220 | 86,810 |
| Emp. | 127 | 125 | 144 |

DUNS 21-620-6979 **Imp**
### Watts of Lydney Group Ltd
Althorpe House, High Street, Lydney, Gloucestershire GL15 5DD
**Web:** www.wattsonline.co.uk
**Reg No:** 0172209 **Estd:** 1950 Private Limited Company
**Line of Business:** Holding companies management activities
**Export Sales:** £1,623,000
**Trading Style:** Watts Group
**Issued Capital:** £1,917,282
**Principals:** J C Thurston *(Managing)*, J P Thurston, P J Rilett, S Charters
**Branches:** Watts Of Lydney Group Ltd, Church Rd, Lydney, Gloucestershire GL15 5EN
**US SIC:** 6711 **UK SIC:** 83962
**Auditors:** Grant Thornton UK LLP
**Bankers:** National Westminster Bank Plc (53-81-21)

| | 31-12-13 | 31-12-12 | 31-12-11 |
|---|---|---|---|
| TO | 25,930,000 | 31,679,000 | 56,363,000 |
| P/L | 462,000 | 2,408,000 | 2,897,000 |
| NW | 12,777,000 | 13,955,000 | 12,943,000 |
| WC | 3,997,000 | 5,145,000 | 3,963,000 |
| Emp. | 175 | 194 | 335 |

DUNS 22-876-0492
### Watts Truck & Van Ltd
Ctc House, Whittle Road, Leckwith, Cardiff, South Glamorgan CF11 8AT
**Fax:** 02920367898
**Web:** www.cardifftruck.co.uk
**Reg No:** 2041427 **VAT No:** 433298249
**Estd:** 1986 Private Limited Company
**Line of Business:** Van and truck dealers
**Trading Style:** Cardiff Truck & Van Centre
**Issued Capital:** £100,000
**Directors:** S Charters, J C Thurston
**Responsibilities**
**Senior:** Simon Griffin *(Dealer Principal)*, Mike Hole *(General Manager)*, T Nessbert *(Manager)*
**Health & Safety:** Mike Hole *(General Manager)*
**Operations:** Mike Hole *(General Manager)*
**Branches:** Watts Truck & Van Ltd, Unit 4, Afon Ebbw Road, Newport, Gwent NP10 9HZ
**US SIC:** 5511 **UK SIC:** 65100
**Auditors:** Grant Thornton UK LLP
**Bankers:** HSBC Bank plc (40-16-18)

| | 31-12-13 | 31-12-12 | 31-12-11 |
|---|---|---|---|
| TO | 18,218,000 | 15,141,000 | 17,640,000 |
| P/L | (385,000) | 257,000 | (182,000) |
| NW | 452,000 | 837,000 | 578,000 |
| WC | 404,000 | 306,000 | 295,000 |
| Emp. | 110 | 72 | 86 |

DUNS 21-773-8636
### Wattville Primary School
Wattville Road, Birmingham, West Midlands B21 0DP
**Tel:** 01215542768
**Web:** www.wattvilleprimary.bham.sch.uk
**Estd:** 2011
**Line of Business:** Schools (local authority)
**Responsibilities**
**Senior:** Joanne Roach *(Head Teacher)*
**US SIC:** 8211 **UK SIC:** 93200
**Employees:** 50

DUNS 73-551-5202
### W.A.Turner Ltd
**(Subsidiary of:** Fane Unlimited)
Broadwater Lane, Tunbridge Wells, Kent TN2 5RD
**Tel:** 01892515215 **Fax:** 01892-510028
**Web:** www.waturner.co.uk
**Reg No:** 4813576 **VAT No:** 811417856
**Estd:** 2003 Private Limited Company
**Line of Business:** Production of sausages
**Trading Style:** W.A.Turner
**Issued Capital:** £250,000
**Director:** P J Finnerty
**Co. Secretary:** John Mclaughlin
**Responsibilities**
**Senior:** Ian Backnall *(Manager)*
**US SIC:** 2013 **UK SIC:** 41223
**Auditors:** PKF (UK) LLP

| | 30-03-14 | 31-03-13 | 01-03-12 |
|---|---|---|---|
| TA | 12,944,336 | 12,944,336 | 12,971,225 |
| P/L | N/A | (26,889) | N/A |
| NW | 586,709 | 586,709 | 613,598 |
| WC | 586,709 | 586,709 | 613,598 |

DUNS 22-185-2218
### Waukesha Bearings Ltd
**(Subsidiary of:** Dover Corporation)
Unit K, Lyons Way Downland Business Park, Worthing, West Sussex BN14 9LA
**Web:** www.waukeshabearing.com
**Reg No:** 4203526 **Estd:** 1990 Private Limited Company
**Line of Business:** Manufacturers and suppliers of industrial machinery
**Export Sales:** £35,089,908
**Trading Style:** Waukesha Magnetic Bearings
**Issued Capital:** £1
**Financial Director:** D T Arbuckle
**Co. Secretary:** David Arbuckle
**Responsibilities**
**Senior:** Colin Ray *(Manager)*
**IT:** Andy Pearce *(Network Manager)*
**Branches:** Waukesha Bearings Ltd, Riverside Business Centre Brighton Rd, Shoreham-By-Sea, West Sussex BN43 6RE
**US SIC:** 3559, 3573
**UK SIC:** 32863, 33020
**Auditors:** PricewaterhouseCoopers LLP
**Bankers:** National Westminster Bank Plc (56-00-20)

| | 31-12-13 | 31-12-12 | 31-12-11 |
|---|---|---|---|
| TO | 39,582,402 | 40,216,286 | 30,889,114 |
| P/L | 9,726,037 | 10,933,427 | 7,057,120 |
| NW | 31,446,765 | 23,936,430 | 30,790,550 |
| WC | 28,176,382 | 20,067,174 | 26,477,210 |
| Emp. | 242 | 234 | 220 |

DUNS 34-821-7592

## Wave Leisure Trust Ltd

Sutton Road, Seaford, East Sussex BN25 4QW
**Tel:** 01323490011
**Web:** www.waveleisure.co.uk
**Reg No:** 5621359 **Estd:** 2005 Private Company Limited By Guarantee
**Line of Business:** Operation of sports arenas and stadiums
**Directors:** Mrs C Miller, D H Marshall, D R Kerr, S Dawson, M J Saunders, D Hearn, Mrs J M Armstrong, R O'Keeffe
**Co. Secretary:** Stephen Wingate
**US SIC:** 7941 **UK SIC:** 97911
**Bankers:** The Co-Operative Bank Plc (08-90-25)

| | 31-03-14 | 31-03-13 | 31-03-12 |
|---|---|---|---|
| TO | 4,583,393 | 4,460,860 | 4,241,755 |
| P/L | 182,688 | 168,735 | 225,199 |
| NW | 105,932 | 626,244 | 801,509 |
| WC | 1,045,806 | 842,230 | 728,578 |
| Emp. | 246 | 241 | 231 |

DUNS 23-039-2656 Imp

## Wavecrest (Uk) Ltd

**(Subsidiary of:** Marr T & T Limited)
4-12 Norton Folgate, London E1 6DB
**Tel:** 0207-097-4000 **Fax:** 0207-097-4001
**Web:** www.wavecrest.eu
**Reg No:** 3042254 **VAT No:** 685286391
**Estd:** 1995 Private Limited Company
**Line of Business:** Telecommunications
**Export Sales:** £15,104,000
**Trading Style:** Wavecrest, First Number, Go Talk, Fntele
**Issued Capital:** £941,130
**Directors:** R C Jennings, C J Adams, J Kirkpatrick
**Co. Secretary:** Tmf Corporate Administration Ser
**Responsibilities**
**Sales:** Joe Rothstein *(SVP Commercial Operations)*
**IT:** Rhys Williams *(Chief Technology Officer)*
**HR:** Heidi Baxter-Smith *(HR Assistant)*, Caroline Gardiner *(Head of Human Resources)*
**Operations:** Lyndon Clements *(Network Operations Manager)*
**US SIC:** 4899 **UK SIC:** 79020
**Auditors:** Mazars LLP
**Bankers:** National Westminster Bank Plc (60-50-06)

| | 31-12-13 | 31-12-12 | 31-12-11 |
|---|---|---|---|
| TO | 75,521,000 | 77,666,000 | 60,553,000 |
| P/L | (316,000) | (489,000) | (1,877,000) |
| NW | (8,111,000) | (8,387,000) | (7,778,000) |
| WC | 1,195,000 | 634,000 | 430,000 |
| Emp. | 77 | 76 | 74 |

DUNS 21-753-6465

## Wavendon Allmusic Plan Ltd

The Stables, Milton Keynes, Buckinghamshire MK17 9EG
**Tel:** 01908282395 **Fax:** 01908-281024
**Web:** www.stables.org
**Reg No:** 0979681 **Estd:** 1973 Private Company Limited By Guarantee
**Line of Business:** Operation of arts facilities
**Trading Style:** The Stables
**Directors:** Dr P H Smith, A W Dankworth, R G French, D R Dean, Mrs C D Dankworth, Dr A G Limb, S P Clarke, Ms C Teal
**Co. Secretary:** Mrs Kirsti Roberts
**Responsibilities**
**Senior:** Stephen Hasson *(Director)*
**US SIC:** 7911 **UK SIC:** 97913
**Auditors:** Macintyre Hudson
**Bankers:** National Westminster Bank Plc (60-24-19)

| | 31-03-14 | 31-03-13 | 31-03-12 |
|---|---|---|---|
| TO | 2,616,623 | 3,204,518 | 2,621,542 |
| P/L | 69,244 | 146,324 | 90,311 |
| NW | 3,116,957 | 3,047,713 | 2,901,389 |
| WC | 784,318 | 686,387 | 496,673 |
| Emp. | 49 | 49 | 49 |

DUNS 22-974-0980

## Waveney District Council

Town Hall, High Street, Lowestoft, Suffolk NR32 1HS
**Tel:** 01502523470
**Web:** www.waveney.gov.uk
**Estd:** 1974
**Line of Business:** Local government
**Principals:** Ms M Mclean *(Managing)*, T Oakes, J Johnstone, G Jermyn, L Monkhouse, M Berridge
**Responsibilities**
**Senior:** Tony Burgess *(Chairman)*, Linda Grainge *(Administration Manager)*, Donna Offord *(Chairman)*, Paul Patterson *(Chairman)*, Dick Woodrow *(Executive)*
**Finance:** Cheryl Stockwell *(Economic Development Assistant)*, andrew cook *(finance manager)*
**Marketing:** Stuart Halsey *(Community Development Officer)*
**Admin:** Tina Crisp *(Administrator)*, Linda Grainge *(Administration Manager)*
**Facilities:** Robert Prince *(Head of Strategic Housing)*
**Operations:** Claire Henwood *(Service Manager ( Sports and L)*, Jim Rowley *(Production and Operations Mana)*
**Purchasing:** Linda Grainge *(Administration Manager)*, Debra Mcmurtry *(Senior Procurement Officer)*
**Branches:** Waveney District Council, Meadowlands, Beccles, Suffolk NR34 7HG
**US SIC:** 9121 **UK SIC:** 91110
**Bankers:** Barclays Bank Plc (20-53-06)
**Employees:** 200

DUNS 23-642-9064

## Waverley Borough Council

The Burys, Godalming, Surrey GU7 1HR
**Tel:** 01483523333
**Web:** www.waverley.gov.uk
**Estd:** 1974 Incorporate By Act Of Parliament
**Line of Business:** Local government
**Directors:** Miss C Pointer, T Carter, S Clutterbuck, F Ansell
**Responsibilities**
**Admin:** Roger Standing *(Office Manager)*
**IT:** Roger Standing *(Office Manager)*
**Health & Safety:** Aaron Carter *(Health & Safety Officer)*
**Facilities:** Roger Standing *(Office Manager)*
**Branches:** Waverley Borough Council, Blunden Ct, High St, Bramley, Guildford, Surrey GU5 0HL
**US SIC:** 9121 **UK SIC:** 91110
**Bankers:** Lloyds TSB Bank plc (30-93-49)
**Employees:** 400

DUNS 21-879-7859

## Waverley C M H R S

Berkeley House, 11-13 Ockford Road, Godalming, Surrey GU7 1QU
**Tel:** 01483528100
**Web:** www.sabp.nhs.uk
**Estd:** 2012
**Line of Business:** Nhs clinics
**Responsibilities**
**Senior:** Karen Duckenfield *(Manager)*
**US SIC:** 8062 **UK SIC:** 95100
**Employees:** 60

DUNS 73-576-7373

## Waverley Care

1-3 Mansfield Place, Edinburgh, Midlothian EH3 6NB
**Tel:** 01315581425 **Fax:** 01314669883
**Web:** www.waverleycare.org
**Reg No:** 0253043SC **Estd:** 2003 Private Company Limited By Guarantee
**Line of Business:** Charities and charitable organisations
**Directors:** Ms A C Mowat, Ms A S Park, Ms L Taylor, I Arnot, B C West, Bishop J Armes, Dr A M Richardson, G Walker
**Co. Secretary:** Grant Sugden
**Responsibilities**
**Senior:** Karin Froebel *(Manager)*, Andrew Marshall-Roberts *(Manager)*, Gillian Stewart *(Manager)*, Helen Zealley *(Chairman)*
**Marketing:** Karen Docwra *(Fundraising Manager)*, Kapulu Simonde *(African Health Project)*, Jonathan Ssentamu *(African Health Project)*
**US SIC:** 8321 **UK SIC:** 96111

| | 31-03-14 | 31-03-13 | 31-03-12 |
|---|---|---|---|
| TO | 2,467,840 | 2,283,559 | 2,303,508 |
| P/L | (142,285) | (48,797) | 145,968 |
| NW | 1,222,329 | 1,120,689 | 1,321,113 |
| WC | 788,168 | 876,196 | 984,892 |
| Emp. | 61 | 60 | 52 |

DUNS 50-146-1628

## Waverley Housing

27 North Bridge Street, Newcastleton, Roxburghshire TD9 9BD
**Tel:** 01450-364200
**Web:** www.waverley-housing.co.uk
**Reg No:** 0115066SC **Estd:** 1988 Private Company Limited By Guarantee
**Line of Business:** Other letting of own property
**Directors:** I S Baxter, D Thomson, N A White, G Thomas, W A Robson, Ms M Stenhouse, G H Young
**Co. Secretary:** Haddon And Turnbull Ws
**Responsibilities**
**Senior:** Russell Pearson *(Director)*, Margaret Spalding *(Chairperson)*
**HR:** Elaine Turnbull *(Personnel Manager)*
**US SIC:** 6519 **UK SIC:** 85000
**Auditors:** Findlay & Co
**Bankers:** Clydesdale Bank Plc (82-62-27)

| | 31-03-14 | 31-03-13 | 31-03-12 |
|---|---|---|---|
| TO | 5,451,657 | 5,264,949 | 4,997,464 |
| P/L | 316,547 | 626,717 | 281,945 |
| NW | 21,226,061 | 20,410,906 | 17,508,927 |
| WC | 3,261,271 | 3,922,741 | 3,989,730 |
| Emp. | 50 | 47 | 85 |

DUNS 21-773-3789

## Waverley Medical Centre

Dalrymple Street, Stranraer, Wigtownshire DG9 7DW
**Tel:** 01776707814
**Web:** www.waverleymedicalcentre.org
**Estd:** 2011 Proprietorship
**Line of Business:** Nhs clinics
**Proprietor:** Mrs K Irbing
**US SIC:** 8062 **UK SIC:** 95100
**Employees:** 60

DUNS 29-824-2140

## Waverton Investment Management Ltd

**(Subsidiary of:** Credit Suisse Group Ag)
21 St James's Square, London SW1Y 4HB
**Tel:** 020-7484-7484 **Fax:** 020-7484-7400
**Web:** www.johim.co.uk
**Reg No:** 2042285 **Estd:** 1986 Private Limited Company
**Line of Business:** Financial intermediation not elsewhere classified
**Issued Capital:** £22,644
**Directors:** C M Rose, H J Grootenhuis, Ms V M Gould, P J Troughton, Sir R B Williamson, C D Jillings, D J Morgan, J A Anderson
**Co. Secretary:** Ms Lucy Tavener
**Responsibilities**
**Senior:** Richard Bonsor *(Non-Executive Director)*, William Francklin *(Director)*, Christopher Keljik *(Director)*, Warren Mcleland *(Director)*, Algernon Percy *(Director & Head of Private Cli)*
**Finance:** Mark Barrington *(Head of Distribution & Managed)*, Alan Gibbs *(Head of Funds)*, Jeff Keen *(Fund Manager)*
**Marketing:** Steven Browne *(Marketing Director)*, Francesca McSloy *(Charities Marketing Manager)*
**IT:** Mudassar Ulhaq *(Head of IT)*
**Operations:** Mark Geduldt *(Head of Operations)*
**US SIC:** 6111 **UK SIC:** 81501
**Auditors:** KPMG Audit PLC
**Bankers:** Bank Of Scotland (12-01-03)

| | 31-12-13 | 31-12-12 | 31-12-11 |
|---|---|---|---|
| TA | 25,260,000 | 42,561,000 | 38,300,000 |
| P/L | 7,171,000 | 6,747,000 | 6,288,000 |
| NW | 12,119,000 | 29,375,000 | 25,390,000 |
| WC | 12,013,000 | 29,155,000 | 27,593,000 |
| Emp. | 109 | 109 | 107 |

DUNS 22-240-4712

## Wavex Technology Ltd

**(Subsidiary of:** It Services Livonia Ltd)
Livonia Street, London W1F 8AF
**Tel:** 08452268182 **Fax:** 0845 838 6870
**Web:** www.wavex.co.uk
**Reg No:** 4258498 **Estd:** 2001 Private Limited Company
**Line of Business:** Computer support & services
**Issued Capital:** £27,915
**Directors:** Ms L Price, M B Williams, G R Russell
**Co. Secretary:** Mrs Linda Price
**Responsibilities**
**Senior:** Peter Sweetband *(Manager)*
**US SIC:** 7379 **UK SIC:** 83940
**Auditors:** Deloitte LLP
**Bankers:** National Westminster Bank Plc (50-30-10)

| | 30-09-13 | 30-09-12 | 30-09-11 |
|---|---|---|---|
| TO | 9,415,790 | 9,859,261 | 9,673,447 |
| P/L | 491,831 | 369,450 | 874,277 |
| NW | 3,168,758 | 2,598,415 | 2,236,885 |
| WC | 2,986,065 | 2,297,415 | 1,843,290 |
| Emp. | 111 | 109 | 107 |

DUNS 21-715-6835 Imp-Exp

## Wavin Ltd

**(Subsidiary of:** Grupo Empresarial Kaluz S.A. De C.V.)
Parsonage Way, Chippenham, Wiltshire SN15 5PN
**Tel:** 01249-766600
**Web:** www.wavin.co.uk
**Reg No:** 0405836 **Estd:** 1946 Private Limited Company
**Line of Business:** Manufacturers of plastic products
**Export Sales:** £10,386,000
**Trading Style:** Wavin Building Products, Wavin Industrial Products, Polybau
**Issued Capital:** £500,000
**Directors:** A B Nicholls, P Maclaurin, B M Jonkhoff, C R King
**Co. Secretary:** Paul Taylor
**Responsibilities**
**Senior:** Michael Curnyn *(Manager)*, Brent Nichols *(Manager)*, John Sage *(Human Resource Director)*
**Finance:** Paul Ramsey *(Financial Director)*
**Marketing:** Karen Stables *(Marketing Manager)*
**Branches:** Wavin Ltd, Dart Building, Grenadier Road, Exeter Business Park, Exeter, Devon EX1 3QF
**US SIC:** 2821, 3272
**UK SIC:** 25140, 24370
**Auditors:** Deloitte LLP
**Bankers:** Lloyds TSB Bank plc (30-00-02)

| | 31-12-12 | 31-12-11 | 31-12-10 |
|---|---|---|---|
| TO | 154,651,000 | 172,497,000 | 176,249,000 |
| P/L | (13,109,000) | (136,000) | 9,548,000 |
| NW | (4,461,000) | 14,213,000 | 24,524,000 |
| WC | (27,523,000) | (18,352,000) | (13,760,000) |
| Emp. | 1,054 | 1,130 | 1,146 |

DUNS 22-802-1820 Imp-Exp

## Wax Lyrical Ltd

**(Subsidiary of:** Lighthouse Holdings Ltd)
London Road, Ulverston, Cumbria LA12 0LD
**Tel:** 01229469404
**Web:** www.wax-lyrical.com
**Reg No:** 1499611 **VAT No:** 659895945
**Estd:** 1995 Private Limited Company
**Line of Business:** Manufacturers and suppliers of candles
**Export Markets:** Worldwide
**Trading Style:** Colony
**Issued Capital:** £2,220,070
**Directors:** R C Wood, Ms J M Barber, M B Armstead
**Co. Secretary:** Pinsent Masons Secretarial Limit
**Responsibilities**
**Senior:** Tarja Barnes *(Financial Director)*, Liz Kerr *(Financial Director)*
**Finance:** Tarja Barnes *(Financial Director)*, Liz Kerr *(Financial Director)*
**HR:** Jemma Rawlings *(Human Resources Manager)*
**Health & Safety:** Andy Kerr *(Maintenance Manager)*
**Facilities:** Andy Kerr *(Maintenance Manager)*
**Operations:** Andy Kerr *(Maintenance Manager)*
**Engineering:** Wayne Barclay *(Operations Manager)*
**Branches:** Wax Lyrical Ltd, 2C Clarks Village, Street, Somerset BA16 0BB
**US SIC:** 2899, 5199
**UK SIC:** 25670, 61900
**Auditors:** Deloitte & Touche LLP
**Bankers:** Barclays Bank Plc (20-04-68)

| | 31-12-13 | 31-12-12 | 31-12-11 |
|---|---|---|---|
| TO | 12,964,000 | 12,249,000 | 11,016,000 |
| P/L | 1,546,000 | 467,000 | 304,000 |
| NW | 7,774,000 | 7,245,000 | 6,791,000 |
| WC | 6,280,000 | 4,999,000 | 4,473,000 |
| Emp. | 131 | 132 | 136 |

DUNS 77-534-4245 Imp-Exp

## Waxman Ceramics Ltd

Grove Mills, Elland Lane, Elland, West Yorkshire HX5 9DZ
**Tel:** 01422-311-331 **Fax:** 01422-310-654
**Web:** www.waxmanceramics.co.uk
**Reg No:** 2992383 **VAT No:** 640603569
**Estd:** 1981 Private Limited Company
**Line of Business:** Tile wholesalers and suppliers
**Export Markets:** European Union (E U)
**Export Sales:** £98,329
**Trading Style:** Waxman Group, Waxman Ceramic Tiles
**Issued Capital:** £16,250
**Principals:** M J Pape *(Managing)*, Ms J Waxman, D J Garlick, M Thomas, R D Waxman
**Co. Secretary:** Stephen John
**Responsibilities**
**Senior:** Janet Bassinder *(Office Manager)*, Margaret Birch *(Maintenance Manager)*
**Facilities:** Margaret Birch *(Maintenance Manager)*
**Branches:** Waxman Ceramics Ltd, Unit 2-3, Bonville Road, Bristol, Avon BS4 5NZ
**US SIC:** 5039 **UK SIC:** 61300
**Auditors:** KPMG LLP

| | 31-05-14 | 31-05-13 | 31-05-12 |
|---|---|---|---|
| TO | 6,644,234 | 6,616,573 | 7,467,364 |
| P/L | 63,938 | 26,402 | (128,766) |
| NW | 1,744,424 | 1,685,734 | 1,674,152 |
| WC | 1,596,030 | 1,725,181 | 1,533,607 |
| Emp. | 58 | 56 | 63 |

DUNS 64-083-0204

## Waxman Group Ltd

Grove Mills, Elland Lane, Elland, West Yorkshire HX5 9DZ
**Tel:** 01422-371-811
**Web:** www.waxmangroup.co.uk
**Reg No:** 3478242 **VAT No:** 640603569
**Estd:** 1997 Private Limited Company
**Line of Business:** Distribution service providers.
**Export Sales:** £12,827,000
**Trading Style:** The Waxman Group
**Issued Capital:** £1,520
**Directors:** M J Pape, S M Waxman, R D Waxman, Ms J Waxman, G J Cluskey, S M John, A A Waxman
**Co. Secretary:** Stephen John
**Responsibilities**
**Senior:** Julie Boustead *(Office Manager)*
**US SIC:** 4712 **UK SIC:** 77002

**Auditors:** KPMG LLP

| | 31-05-14 | 31-05-13 | 31-05-12 |
|---|---|---|---|
| TO | 35,052,000 | 30,924,000 | 48,714,000 |
| P/L | 766,000 | 666,000 | 2,116,000 |
| NW | 7,537,000 | 6,979,000 | 6,470,000 |
| WC | 7,723,000 | 6,814,000 | 6,397,000 |
| Emp. | 88 | 91 | 102 |

DUNS 49-196-2619

## Way Ahead Community Services Ltd

(**Subsidiary of:** Wayside Properties Ltd)
1-3 The Courtyard, Higher Comeytrowe, Taunton, Somerset TA4 1EQ
**Tel:** 01823 462804 **Fax:** 01823 462905
**Web:** www.wayaheadcare.co.uk
**Reg No:** 3116636 **Estd:** 1995 Private Limited Company
**Line of Business:** Social work activities without accommodation
**Trading Style:** Way Ahead Care
**Issued Capital:** £4
**Directors:** Ms P D Smith, Ms C Bosley, R L Smith
**Co. Secretary:** Miss Carol Evans
**US SIC:** 8321 **UK SIC:** 96111
**Bankers:** National Westminster Bank Plc (60-80-06)

| | 31-10-13 | 31-10-12 | 31-10-11 |
|---|---|---|---|
| TA | 1,075,862 | 962,007 | 944,931 |
| NW | 440,965 | 417,932 | 382,928 |
| WC | 398,333 | 382,127 | 342,339 |

DUNS 23-556-1466

## The Way Ahead Group Ltd

(**Subsidiary of:** Uk Ticketing Ltd)
The Hollows, 5 St James's Terrace, Nottingham, Nottinghamshire NG1 6FW
**Tel:** 01908232888
**Web:** www.thewayaheadgroup.com
**Reg No:** 3554468 **Estd:** 1998 Private Limited Company
**Line of Business:** Other entertainment activities not elsewhere classified
**Trading Style:** The Way Ahead Box Office, Ticket Line Way Ahead
**Issued Capital:** £1,563
**Directors:** J C Bonamy, C Sere-Annichini, R I Wilmshurst, S Gillham
**Co. Secretary:** Mrs Leanne Lipscombe
**Responsibilities**
**Senior:** Stephanie Hosman *(Manager)*
**Branches:** The Way Ahead Group Ltd, 37 Castlefields Main Centre, Derby, Derbyshire DE1 2PE
**US SIC:** 7999 **UK SIC:** 97913
**Auditors:** Deloitte & Touche LLP
**Bankers:** Bank Of Scotland (80-11-45)

| | 31-12-13 | 31-12-12 | 31-12-11 |
|---|---|---|---|
| TO | 20,505,000 | 21,352,000 | 27,297,000 |
| P/L | 6,530,000 | 6,165,000 | 8,733,000 |
| NW | 20,281,000 | 14,951,000 | 10,393,000 |
| WC | 18,829,000 | 13,313,000 | 8,533,000 |
| Emp. | 180 | 200 | 196 |

DUNS 21-233-2335

## Way Ahead Support Services

4 Scar Bank, Warwick, Warwickshire CV34 5DB
**Tel:** 01926622980
**Web:** www.wayaheaduk.org
**Estd:** 1997
**Line of Business:** Charities and charitable organisations
**Partners:** P Cullen, D Harvey, D Harvey
**US SIC:** 8811 **UK SIC:** 99000
**Employees:** 50

DUNS 29-492-9427 **Imp-Exp**

## Waymade Plc

(**Subsidiary of:** Verdot Ltd)
Sovereign House, Miles Gray Road, Basildon, Essex SS14 3FR
**Tel:** 08081080228 **Fax:** 01268 535 299
**Web:** www.waymade.co.uk
**Reg No:** 1856320 **Estd:** 2010 Public Limited Company
**Line of Business:** Dental equipment suppliers
**Trading Style:** Waymade, Sovereign Medical
**Issued Capital:** £2,000,000
**Principals:** B C Patel *(Managing)*, M J Cotterill, V K Patel
**Co. Secretary:** Dipen Patel
**Responsibilities**
**Senior:** Peter Lumm *(Warehouse Manager)*, Brian Mcewan *(General Manager)*, Daisy Webb *(Team Leader)*
**Marketing:** Brian Mcewan *(General Manager)*
**Health & Safety:** Jenny Falcone *(Facilities Manager)*
**Facilities:** Jenny Falcone *(Facilities Manager)*
**Operations:** Brian Wyatt *(Operations Director)*
**Fleet:** Peter Lumm *(Warehouse Manager)*
**Branches:** Waymade Plc, 4 South St, Rochford, Essex SS4 1BQ
**US SIC:** 3841, 7399
**UK SIC:** 37201, 83954
**Auditors:** KPMG LLP
**Bankers:** Barclays Bank Plc (20-19-95)

| | 31-12-13 | 31-12-12 | 31-12-11 |
|---|---|---|---|
| TO | 105,933,000 | 115,697,000 | 112,389,000 |
| P/L | 2,024,000 | 2,037,000 | (5,227,000) |
| NW | 46,169,000 | 44,095,000 | 74,433,000 |
| WC | 29,292,000 | 25,003,000 | 61,217,000 |
| Emp. | 379 | 384 | 376 |

DUNS 21-747-2646

## Wayside Garages Ltd

(**Subsidiary of:** Jardine Matheson Holdings Limited)
3 Denbigh Road, Bletchley, Milton Keynes, Buckinghamshire MK1 1DF
**Tel:** 01908840000
**Web:** www.waysidegroup.co.uk
**Reg No:** 1204741 **VAT No:** 727868091
**Estd:** 1975 Private Limited Company
**Line of Business:** Sale of new motor vehicles
**Trading Style:** Milton Keynes Audi
**Issued Capital:** £250
**Directors:** C A Beattie, M P Herbert
**Co. Secretary:** Mark Finch
**Responsibilities**
**Senior:** Mike Lishman *(Head of Business)*
**Sales:** Chris Springer *(New Care Sales Manager)*
**Branches:** Wayside Garages Ltd, Main Road, Crediton, Devon EX17 6EZ
**US SIC:** 5511, 7539, 5531
**UK SIC:** 65100, 67100
**Auditors:** Grant Thornton UK LLP
**Bankers:** Barclays Bank Plc (20-74-09)

| | 31-12-13 | 31-12-12 | 31-12-11 |
|---|---|---|---|
| TO | N/A | N/A | 148,287,000 |
| P/L | N/A | 56,000 | 543,000 |
| NW | 4,036,000 | 4,036,000 | 4,048,000 |
| WC | N/A | N/A | 4,291,000 |
| Emp. | N/A | N/A | 182 |

DUNS 21-817-2351 **Imp-Exp**

## W.Brewin & Company Ltd

145-151 Parker Drive, Leicester, Leicestershire LE4 0JP
**Tel:** 01162-362020 **Fax:** 01162-350969
**Web:** www.wbsocks.co.uk
**Reg No:** 0259857 **Estd:** 1926 Private Limited Company
**Line of Business:** Manufacture of knitted and crocheted hosiery
**Export Markets:** Middle & Far East & Scandinavia
**Trading Style:** Pearlustra
**Issued Capital:** £106,260
**Directors:** A C Bexon, M C Brewin, Ms M R Brewin, Ms P L Brewin, J M Kendall, P J Brewin, T C Tilly
**Co. Secretary:** Edward Spence
**Responsibilities**
**Senior:** Andrew Kendall *(Manager)*
**Branches:** W.brewin & Company Ltd, 145-151 Parker Drive, Leicester, Leicestershire LE4 0JP
**US SIC:** 2251 **UK SIC:** 43631
**Auditors:** Thomas May & Co
**Bankers:** Barclays Bank Plc (20-49-08)

| | 31-10-13 | 31-10-12 | 31-10-11 |
|---|---|---|---|
| TA | 3,649,623 | 3,293,868 | 3,110,225 |
| NW | 3,122,571 | 2,920,893 | 2,894,302 |
| WC | 1,966,680 | 1,689,699 | 1,484,215 |

DUNS 21-834-6278

## W.Brindley (Garages) Ltd

55 Penn Road, Wolverhampton, West Midlands WV2 4WW
**Tel:** 01902310666 **Fax:** 01902-712111
**Web:** www.brindley.co.uk
**Reg No:** 0333492 **Estd:** 1998 Private Limited Company
**Line of Business:** Sale of motor vehicles
**Trading Style:** Brincars, Brindley Vauxhall
**Issued Capital:** £12,000
**Principals:** R G Brindley *(Managing)*, P M Ashcroft, S R Grosvenor, G E Reed, W C Watson, Ms A E Philipson, C H Adams, T A Butcher
**Co. Secretary:** Paul Ashcroft
**Responsibilities**
**Senior:** James Elkes *(Dealer Principal)*, David Tolley *(Financial Director)*
**Finance:** David Tolley *(Financial Director)*
**Branches:** W.brindley (Garages) Ltd, Brindley Honda, Millennium Park, West Bromwich, West Midlands B70 0NR
**US SIC:** 7399, 5521, 7539, 5531
**UK SIC:** 83954, 65100, 67100
**Auditors:** Price Pearson
**Bankers:** HSBC Bank plc (40-47-11)

| | 30-11-13 | 30-11-12 | 30-11-11 |
|---|---|---|---|
| TO | 146,999,205 | 129,652,878 | 129,970,503 |
| P/L | 1,043,197 | 679,863 | (348,860) |
| NW | 23,324,963 | 22,627,446 | 22,162,689 |
| WC | 9,287,750 | 8,027,244 | 8,463,953 |
| Emp. | 365 | 345 | 341 |

DUNS 21-153-1200

## Wbw Solicitors Llp

Church House, Queen Street, Newton Abbot, Devon TQ12 2QP
**Tel:** 01626202404
**Web:** www.wbw.co.uk
**Reg No:** 0343339OC **Estd:** 2009 Private Limited Company
**Line of Business:** Solicitors
**Trading Style:** Wbw Solicitors Llp
**Responsibilities**
**Senior:** Sarah Couch *(Non-designated Limited Liabili)*, Francis Goddard *(Designated Limited Liability P)*
**US SIC:** 8111 **UK SIC:** 83500
**Bankers:** Barclays Bank Plc (20-87-94)

| | 30-04-14 | 30-04-13 | 30-04-12 |
|---|---|---|---|
| TO | 5,355,765 | 4,648,572 | 4,579,614 |
| NW | N/A | N/A | (19,805) |
| WC | 1,834,085 | 1,492,746 | (605,452) |
| Emp. | 159 | 118 | 111 |

DUNS 21-613-3561

## W.C. Rowe (Falmouth) Ltd

Parkengue, Penryn, Cornwall TR10 9EP
**Tel:** 01326372380
**Web:** www.wcrowe.co.uk
**Reg No:** 1238149 **Estd:** 1950 Private Limited Company
**Line of Business:** Manufacture of bread; manufacture of fresh pastry goods and cakes
**Issued Capital:** £40,000
**Principals:** A H Pearce *(Managing)*, M Rowe *(Financial)*, K Lynch, P W Pearce, K Devoy, M Matthews, M B Parsons
**Co. Secretary:** Matthew Pearce
**Responsibilities**
**Health & Safety:** David Bodinar *(Health & Safety Officer)*
**Operations:** David Bodinar *(Health & Safety Officer)*
**Branches:** W.c. Rowe (Falmouth) Ltd, 54 Market Street, Falmouth, Cornwall TR11 3AB
**US SIC:** 2051 **UK SIC:** 41960
**Auditors:** Wills Bingley Ltd

| | 28-12-13 | 29-12-12 | 31-12-11 |
|---|---|---|---|
| TO | 20,386,805 | 25,093,883 | 28,708,916 |
| P/L | (608,040) | (938,050) | (90,727) |
| NW | 4,228,312 | 4,766,978 | 5,372,268 |
| WC | (578,255) | (1,172,177) | (604,620) |
| Emp. | 393 | 493 | 540 |

DUNS 39-962-9997 **Imp**

## Wcf Ltd.

Crawhall, Brampton, Cumbria CA8 1TN
**Tel:** 01697-745-050 **Fax:** 01697-745-055
**Web:** www.wcf.co.uk
**Reg No:** 2263148 **VAT No:** 442814556
**Estd:** 1988 Private Limited Company
**Line of Business:** Mail order houses
**Trading Style:** W C F Farm Produce, W C F Distribution, W C F Country Centres, W C F Country Collection
**Issued Capital:** £3,773,352
**Principals:** A I Stewart *(Managing)*, M S Ward, D J Biggar, D A Routledge
**Co. Secretary:** Mrs Joanne Ritzema
**Responsibilities**
**Senior:** Debbie Brimicombe *(Purchasing Manager)*, Tracey Cannon *(Sales & Marketing Manager)*
**Marketing:** Tracey Cannon *(Sales & Marketing Manager)*
**Sales:** Tracey Cannon *(Sales & Marketing Manager)*
**Purchasing:** Debbie Brimicombe *(Purchasing Manager)*
**Branches:** Wcf Ltd., Burn Lane, Hexham, Northumberland NE46 3HJ
**US SIC:** 5921, 5499, 5699, 4213
**UK SIC:** 64200, 64100, 64500, 72300
**Auditors:** KPMG LLP
**Bankers:** HSBC Bank plc (40-16-22)

| | 31-05-14 | 01-06-13 | 02-05-12 |
|---|---|---|---|
| TO | 158,428,000 | 148,857,000 | 118,530,000 |
| P/L | 3,049,000 | (3,198,000) | 3,424,000 |
| NW | 28,616,000 | 27,206,000 | 31,829,000 |
| WC | 20,373,000 | 19,440,000 | 25,881,000 |
| Emp. | 303 | 297 | 240 |

DUNS 21-712-6047

## Wcl Ebt Ltd

(**Subsidiary of:** Nord Anglia Education Inc)
6th Floor, 18 King William Street, London EC4N 7BP
**Tel:** 02075319696
**Web:** www.greatlearning.com
**Reg No:** 7523953 **Estd:** 2011 Private Limited Company
**Line of Business:** Other service activities not elsewhere classified
**Issued Capital:** £1
**Directors:** A Fitzmaurice, G R Halder
**US SIC:** 8999 **UK SIC:** 83954

| | 31-08-13 | 31-08-12 |
|---|---|---|
| TA | 100 | 100 |
| NW | 100 | 100 |

DUNS 21-206-1048

## W.Clifford Watts Ltd

118-122 Scarborough Road, Bridlington, North Humberside YO16 7NU
**Tel:** 01262-675383 **Fax:** 01262-604629
**Web:** www.wcwatts.co.uk
**Reg No:** 0391968 **Estd:** 1939 Private Limited Company
**Line of Business:** Retail sale of automotive fuel
**Issued Capital:** £293
**Directors:** D C Watts, W R Watts, Ms C Watts
**Co. Secretary:** Paul Thompson
**US SIC:** 5541, 1795
**UK SIC:** 65200, 50000
**Auditors:** Ashby Berry & Co
**Bankers:** Bank Of Scotland (12-16-30)

| | 31-03-14 | 31-03-13 | 31-03-12 |
|---|---|---|---|
| TA | 5,356,530 | 4,517,039 | 4,334,216 |
| NW | 2,750,318 | 2,453,006 | 2,269,524 |
| WC | 65,646 | (44,379) | 25,443 |

DUNS 34-750-3794 **Imp**

## Wcm Europe Ltd

10-11 Westmayne Industrial Park, Bramston Way, Laindon, Basildon, Essex SS15 6TP
**Tel:** 01268-564-611 **Fax:** 01268-410-744
**Web:** www.wcmeurope.com
**Reg No:** 5551941 **Estd:** 2010 Private Limited Company
**Line of Business:** Manufacturers of car accessories
**Issued Capital:** £100
**Directors:** Mrs K Burden, A R Anderson, Mrs R Mcgee, Mrs L T Reading, A Long, I E Hammond
**Co. Secretary:** Karl Mcgee
**US SIC:** 3714, 3316
**UK SIC:** 35300, 22350
**Auditors:** Fox Evans Ltd

| | 31-12-13 | 31-12-12 | 31-12-11 |
|---|---|---|---|
| TO | N/A | 5,877,295 | N/A |
| P/L | N/A | 332,000 | N/A |
| NW | 1,341,676 | 909,276 | 586,276 |
| WC | 20,695 | 349,555 | 139,512 |

DUNS 77-262-1264

## Wcs Care Group Ltd

Newlands, Whites Row, Kenilworth, Warwickshire CV8 1HW
**Tel:** 01926864242
**Web:** www.wcscare.co.uk
**Reg No:** 2713150 **Estd:** 1992 Private Company Limited By Guarantee
**Line of Business:** Social work activities with accommodation
**Issued Capital:** £11
**Directors:** K J Nurcombe, R D Brookes, A S Fossey, B C Cressey, K W Demian, Mrs P J Southeard, Ms J E Deeley, A T Last
**Co. Secretary:** Nicholas Wood
**Responsibilities**
**Senior:** Christine Asbury *(Chief Executive)*, Laurence Lodge *(Manager)*, Mary Malloy *(Director)*, Howell Merchant *(Manager)*, Lee Middleburgh *(Director)*
**Branches:** Wcs Care Group Ltd, Alcester Road, Stratford-Upon-Avon, Warwickshire CV37 6PH
**US SIC:** 8321 **UK SIC:** 96111
**Auditors:** PricewaterhouseCoopers
**Bankers:** Allied Irish Bank (gb) (23-83-93)

| | 31-03-14 | 31-03-13 | 31-03-12 |
|---|---|---|---|
| TO | 11,214,000 | 11,200,000 | 11,102,000 |
| P/L | 870,000 | 887,000 | 988,000 |
| NW | 7,083,000 | 6,154,000 | 5,695,000 |
| WC | 1,005,000 | 703,000 | 1,709,000 |
| Emp. | 547 | 576 | 588 |

DUNS 39-744-2377

## Wcs Environmental Ltd

(**Subsidiary of:** Wcs Environmental Group Ltd)
Sturmi Way, Village Farm Industrial Estate, Pyle, Bridgend, Mid Glamorgan CF33 6BZ
**Tel:** 01656-741359 **Fax:** 01656-742471
**Web:** www.wcsenvironmental.co.uk
**Reg No:** 2184649 **VAT No:** 452885812
**Estd:** 1987 Private Limited Company
**Line of Business:** Water treatment services
**Issued Capital:** £1,000
**Principals:** M R Sullivan *(Managing)*, A W Champion, A M Poole, P E Dorey
**Co. Secretary:** Ian Butcher
**Responsibilities**
**Senior:** Paul Hole *(Manager)*, Tony Price *(Projects Manager)*
**US SIC:** 4441, 7399
**UK SIC:** 72603, 83954
**Auditors:** Broomfield & Alexander Ltd
**Bankers:** Lloyds TSB Bank plc (30-95-46)

| | 31-12-13 | 31-12-12 | 31-12-11 |
|---|---|---|---|
| TO | 6,741,230 | 7,009,051 | N/A |
| P/L | 533,961 | 642,249 | N/A |
| NW | 2,286,471 | 2,215,672 | 1,629,613 |
| WC | 2,518,363 | 2,385,682 | 1,867,710 |
| Emp. | 123 | 115 | N/A |

DUNS 29-768-9259

## W.D. Close & Sons Ltd

Valentia Avenue, Newcastle-Upon-Tyne, Tyne and Wear NE6 4QR
**Tel:** 0191-224-4552 **Fax:** 0191-276-4078
**Web:** www.wdclose.co.uk
**Reg No:** 2031962 **VAT No:** 376461136
**Estd:** 1983 Private Limited Company
**Line of Business:** Architects
**Export Sales:** £213,011
**Issued Capital:** £10,000
**Principals:** W D Close *(Managing)*, D W Close, K Scott
**Co. Secretary:** Ms Ann Close
**Responsibilities**
**Senior:** Kimberly Close *(Purchasing Manager)*
**Operations:** Kevin Ireland *(Quality Manager)*
**Engineering:** Jim Storrar *(Contracts Manager)*
**US SIC:** 8911 **UK SIC:** 83701
**Auditors:** Rowlands
**Bankers:** The Co-Operative Bank Plc (08-90-06)

| | 31-03-14 | 31-03-13 | 31-03-12 |
|---|---|---|---|
| TO | 16,770,477 | 17,044,089 | 13,969,841 |
| P/L | 2,364,745 | 784,909 | 1,476,736 |
| NW | 5,974,766 | 4,179,707 | 3,581,566 |
| WC | 4,113,363 | 2,749,856 | 2,490,317 |
| Emp. | 130 | 116 | 104 |

DUNS 21-881-0315

## W.D. Coe Ltd

20-28 Norwich Road, Ipswich, Suffolk IP1 2NH
**Tel:** 01473-256061
**Web:** www.coes.co.uk
**Reg No:** 0671546 **VAT No:** 102122548
**Estd:** 1928 Private Limited Company
**Line of Business:** Retail sale of clothing
**Trading Style:** W.D. Coe Limited, Goddards of Kings Lynn, Golding of Newmarket
**Issued Capital:** £91,800
**Principals:** D J Coe *(Managing)*, M Rawlings, W D Coe, P P Hubka, Mrs C R Rowlands, Ms B J Coe
**Co. Secretary:** Mrs Charlotte Rowlands
**Branches:** W.d. Coe Ltd, 67 High Street, Newmarket, Suffolk CB8 8NA
**US SIC:** 5699, 5621
**UK SIC:** 64500
**Auditors:** Ensors
**Bankers:** Lloyds TSB Bank plc (30-94-55)

| | 02-03-14 | 03-03-13 | 26-03-12 |
|---|---|---|---|
| TO | 9,542,000 | 9,614,000 | 9,247,000 |
| P/L | 247,000 | 103,000 | 35,000 |
| NW | 5,162,000 | 4,512,000 | 4,541,000 |
| WC | 1,103,000 | 1,316,000 | 1,324,000 |
| Emp. | 226 | 217 | 221 |

DUNS 73-446-9393

## W.D. Davison & Sons Ltd

Collingwood House, 1 Collingwood Street, Gateshead, Tyne and Wear NE10 9NA
**Tel:** 01914204400 **Fax:** 0191-420-0367
**Web:** www.wddavison.co.uk
**Reg No:** 4699847 **Estd:** 1964 Private Limited Company
**Line of Business:** Painters and decorators
**Issued Capital:** £100
**Directors:** W D Davison (Jnr), W D Davison (Snr), P A Davison
**Co. Secretary:** Ms Lynn Boddy
**Responsibilities**
**Senior:** William Davison *(Director)*
**US SIC:** 1721, 7399
**UK SIC:** 50400, 83954
**Auditors:** Robson Laidler LLP

| | 31-03-14 | 31-03-13 | 31-03-12 |
|---|---|---|---|
| TA | 414,314 | 539,070 | 450,145 |
| NW | (187,053) | (225,929) | (213,842) |
| WC | (151,422) | (183,910) | (163,365) |

DUNS 21-743-7875

## W.D.Irwin & Sons Ltd

(**Subsidiary of:** W.D. Irwin & Sons (Portadown) Ltd)
55 Gortgonis Road, Dungannon, Co Tyrone BT71 4QG
**Tel:** 02887740362 **Fax:** 028-8774-7473
**Web:** www.irwin-aggregates.com
**Reg No:** 0059204NI **Estd:** 2006 Private Limited Company
**Line of Business:** Manufacture of bread; manufacture of fresh pastry goods and cakes
**Issued Capital:** £9,200
**Directors:** R K Irwin, K Davenport, D M Holmes, P L Johnston, J Hopkins, B H Irwin, E W Graham, M Murphy
**Co. Secretary:** Brian Irwin
**US SIC:** 2051 **UK SIC:** 41960
**Auditors:** PricewaterhouseCoopers LLP
**Bankers:** Ulster Bank Ltd (98-00-00)

| | 30-03-14 | 31-03-13 | 26-03-12 |
|---|---|---|---|
| TO | 32,837,516 | 19,772,445 | 51,292,093 |
| P/L | (543,032) | 1,099,476 | (3,597,838) |
| NW | 380,844 | 1,051,917 | (568,815) |
| WC | (4,254,320) | (3,941,061) | (5,686,650) |
| Emp. | 374 | 385 | 396 |

DUNS 76-477-2422 **Exp**

## Wdm 2012 Ltd

Market Abattoir, Okehampton, Devon EX20 3HT
**Tel:** 01837-810491 **Fax:** 01837-810036
**Web:** www.westdevonmeat.co.uk
**Reg No:** 2564443 **VAT No:** 585513716
**Estd:** 1990 Private Limited Company
**Line of Business:** Abattoirs
**Export Markets:** France
**Issued Capital:** £506,000
**Directors:** J Queally, P Queally, D Browne
**Co. Secretary:** Daniel Browne
**Responsibilities**
**Senior:** Arthur Cleave *(Manager)*, Pat Walsh *(Manager)*
**Finance:** Peter Bowyer *(Operations Manager)*
**Marketing:** Peter Bowyer *(Operations Manager)*
**Sales:** Peter Bowyer *(Operations Manager)*
**IT:** Arthur Cleave *(Manager)*
**HR:** Peter Bowyer *(Operations Manager)*
**Purchasing:** Peter Bowyer *(Operations Manager)*
**US SIC:** 2013 **UK SIC:** 41223
**Auditors:** Simpkins Edwards
**Bankers:** Barclays Bank Plc (20-30-47)

| | 31-12-13 | 31-12-12 | 31-12-12 |
|---|---|---|---|
| TO | N/A | N/A | 54,566,122 |
| P/L | N/A | N/A | 1,697,025 |
| NW | 5,000 | 151,045 | 652,045 |
| Emp. | N/A | N/A | 52 |

DUNS 21-606-1382 **Exp**

## W.D.M.Ltd

North View, Staple Hill, Bristol, Avon BS16 5RU
**Tel:** 01179567233
**Web:** www.wdm.co.uk
**Reg No:** 0403583 **VAT No:** 433825942
**Estd:** 1946 Private Limited Company
**Line of Business:** Manufacture of other special purpose machinery not elsewhere classified
**Export Markets:** E U, N America, Asia, Austrialia.
**Export Sales:** £1,621,000
**Issued Capital:** £100,000
**Principals:** J L Gardiner *(Managing)*, C J Gardiner
**Co. Secretary:** Stuart Smith
**Responsibilities**
**Health & Safety:** Anthony Szerencses *(Health & Safety Officer)*
**US SIC:** 3559, 8911
**UK SIC:** 32863, 83701
**Auditors:** Grant Thornton UK LLP
**Bankers:** Barclays Bank Plc (20-13-42)

| | 31-03-14 | 31-03-13 | 31-03-12 |
|---|---|---|---|
| TO | 11,360,000 | 10,933,000 | 11,876,000 |
| P/L | 295,000 | 420,000 | 925,000 |
| NW | 11,392,000 | 11,198,000 | 10,917,000 |
| WC | 6,825,000 | 6,453,000 | 6,100,000 |
| Emp. | 138 | 149 | 140 |

DUNS 76-960-8167

## Wdr Ltd

60 London Road, Horsham, West Sussex RH12 1AY
**Tel:** 01403-268251
**Web:** www.wdr.co.uk
**Reg No:** 2625137 **Estd:** 1991 Private Limited Company
**Line of Business:** Training services
**Issued Capital:** £100
**Principals:** J M Dennis *(Managing)*, Ms C J Dennis
**Co. Secretary:** John Dennis
**US SIC:** 8299, 8249
**UK SIC:** 93300
**Auditors:** Baker Tilly

| | 30-06-13 | 30-06-12 | 30-06-11 |
|---|---|---|---|
| TA | 1,474,256 | 1,481,515 | 1,967,202 |
| NW | 329,876 | 239,757 | 81,209 |
| WC | 575,106 | 490,665 | 340,606 |

DUNS 21-688-5079

## W.D.Smith & Son

Woodham Road, Wickford, Essex SS11 7QU
**Tel:** 01245320220
**Web:** www.wdsmith.com
**Reg No:** 0750120 **Estd:** 1938 Private Unlimited Company
**Line of Business:** Nurseries wholesale
**Trading Style:** Meadow Croft Garden Centre
**Issued Capital:** £10,000
**Principals:** R W Smith *(Managing)*, M J Smith, Mrs L Smith
**Co. Secretary:** Roland Smith
**US SIC:** 0161, 5999
**UK SIC:** 01001, 65600
**Bankers:** Barclays Bank Plc (20-19-95)
**Employees:** 60
**Turnover:** £2,822,554

DUNS 21-128-3512

## We Are Social Ltd

(**Subsidiary of:** We Are Very Social Ltd)
1 Saint John's Square, London EC1M 4PN
**Tel:** 02031951700
**Web:** http://wearesocial.net
**Reg No:** 6629464 **Estd:** 2008 Private Limited Company
**Line of Business:** Advertising
**Export Sales:** £3,715,036
**Issued Capital:** £102
**Directors:** N A Mcdonald, R O Grant
**Co. Secretary:** Lee (Secretari
**Responsibilities**
**Senior:** Jim Coleman *(Managing Partner - London)*, Gabriele Cucinella *(Managing Partner - Milan)*, Simon Kemp *(Managing Director - Singapore)*, Guillaume Lalu *(Deputy Managing Director - Par)*, Stefano Maggi *(Managing Partner - Milan)*, Ottavio Nava *(Managing Partner - Milan)*, Tom Ollerton *(Marketing Director)*, Leslie Orsioli *(Managing Director - Sao Paulo)*, Sandrine Plasseraud *(Managing Director - Paris)*, Bastian Sherbeck *(Managing Director - Munich)*, Leila Thabet *(Managing Director - New York)*
**Finance:** Pippa Strong *(Finance Director)*
**Marketing:** Alex Hobhouse *(New Business & Marketing Manag)*
**Sales:** Joe Weston *(Senior Account Director)*
**US SIC:** 7311 **UK SIC:** 83800

| | 30-06-13 | 30-06-12 | 30-06-11 |
|---|---|---|---|
| TO | 10,107,389 | N/A | N/A |
| P/L | 1,979,470 | N/A | N/A |
| NW | 3,771,057 | 1,862,038 | 858,339 |
| WC | 3,477,437 | 1,780,573 | 769,429 |
| Emp. | 91 | N/A | N/A |

DUNS 37-991-9418

## We Are Vista Ltd

Carlton Mills, Pickering Street, Leeds, West Yorkshire LS12 2QG
**Tel:** 01132-244800
**Web:** www.logistikgroup.com
**Reg No:** 3293747 **VAT No:** 698560965
**Estd:** 2007 Private Limited Company
**Line of Business:** Exhibition and trade fair organisers
**Issued Capital:** £94,000
**Directors:** J G Wilkins, K J Walsh, M S Evans, D Hunter
**Co. Secretary:** Joseph Yates
**Responsibilities**
**Senior:** Dirk Mischendahl *(Manager)*
**HR:** alana cottier *(HR manager)*
**Facilities:** Christine Catterall *(Facilities Manager)*
**US SIC:** 7999 **UK SIC:** 97913
**Auditors:** KPMG LLP
**Bankers:** Lloyds TSB Bank plc (30-00-05)

| | 31-10-13 | 31-10-12 | 31-10-11 |
|---|---|---|---|
| TO | 18,296,222 | 13,485,860 | 14,615,023 |
| P/L | 495,917 | 744,651 | 701,286 |
| NW | 2,164,393 | 1,791,373 | 1,208,810 |
| WC | 1,638,401 | 1,377,290 | 914,517 |
| Emp. | 92 | 88 | 84 |

DUNS 34-931-4265

## We Buy Any Car Ltd

(**Subsidiary of:** Cdr Osprey (Cayman) Partners L.P.)
Headway House, Crosby Way, Farnham, Surrey GU9 7XG
**Tel:** 01706391379
**Web:** www.webuyanycar.com
**Reg No:** 5727953 **Estd:** 2006 Private Limited Company
**Line of Business:** Car dealers (used)
**Issued Capital:** £100
**Directors:** S R Nobes, D T Mckee, N F Mckee, S C Hosking, J R Olsen
**Co. Secretary:** Ian Farrelly
**Branches:** We Buy Any Car, 20 Shaw Road, Lancashire OL1 3HZ Oldham
**US SIC:** 5521 **UK SIC:** 65100
**Auditors:** PricewaterhouseCoopers LLP
**Bankers:** The Royal Bank Of Scotland Plc (15-00-00)

| | 31-12-13 | 30-09-12 | 30-12-11 |
|---|---|---|---|
| TO | 513,106,000 | 289,317,000 | 263,747,000 |
| P/L | 3,743,000 | 1,811,000 | 3,473,000 |
| NW | 1,110,000 | 2,120,000 | 2,723,000 |
| WC | (527,000) | 1,807,000 | 2,672,000 |
| Emp. | 270 | 188 | 225 |

DUNS 21-683-0166 **Exp**

## W.E. Deane Ltd

Mayesbrook House, Lyon Business Park, Barking, Essex IG11 0EU
**Tel:** 020-8532-6400 **Fax:** 020-8532-6497
**Web:** www.deanefreight.com
**Reg No:** 0768571 **VAT No:** 246346555
**Estd:** 1963 Private Limited Company
**Line of Business:** Freight forwarders
**Issued Capital:** £105,000
**Principals:** C M Fitch *(Managing)*, R A Falconer *(Managing)*, Mrs J R Brown
**Responsibilities**
**Senior:** Roger Adamson *(Manager)*, Alan Pitts *(Manager)*
**Finance:** A Doctors *(Manager)*
**Branches:** W.e. Deane Ltd, Unit 8, Eversley Way, Egham, Surrey TW20 8RG
**US SIC:** 4712, 4226
**UK SIC:** 77002, 77003
**Auditors:** The Leaman Partnership LLP
**Bankers:** Barclays Bank Plc (20-72-89)

| | 31-07-13 | 31-07-12 | 31-07-11 |
|---|---|---|---|
| TO | 19,158,906 | 24,431,890 | 27,210,501 |
| P/L | 85,209 | 519,154 | 414,893 |
| NW | 4,126,111 | 4,950,861 | 2,505,504 |
| WC | 3,550,325 | 5,227,173 | 2,488,981 |
| Emp. | 104 | 108 | 114 |

DUNS 23-518-1419

## W.E. Dowds (Shipping) Ltd

2 Alexandra Road, Newport, Gwent NP20 2GY
**Tel:** 01633-779900 **Fax:** 01633779901
**Web:** www.wedowds.co.uk
**Reg No:** 0770578 **Estd:** 1960 Private Limited Company
**Line of Business:** Shipping companies
**Issued Capital:** £100
**Principals:** A C Davies *(Managing)*, C W Dowds, Ms L M Dowds
**Co. Secretary:** Ms Barbara Gilfillan
**Responsibilities**
**Senior:** Julie Boycott *(Human Resources Manager)*
**HR:** Julie Boycott *(Human Resources Manager)*
**US SIC:** 4712, 4226
**UK SIC:** 77002, 77003
**Auditors:** McGuire & Farry Ltd

| | 31-08-13 | 31-08-12 | 31-08-11 |
|---|---|---|---|
| TO | 6,893,090 | 9,312,044 | 8,068,544 |
| P/L | 153,488 | 708,873 | 449,539 |
| NW | 2,621,087 | 2,519,167 | 1,964,589 |
| WC | 1,655,529 | 1,520,344 | 906,078 |
| Emp. | 60 | 60 | 55 |

DUNS 28-988-8893 **Imp**

## W.E. Roberts (Holdings) Ltd

Thamesworks, Grove Road, North Fleet, Gravesend, Kent DA11 9AX
**Tel:** 01474574648
**Web:** www.wer.co.uk
**Reg No:** 1812607 **Estd:** 1984 Private Limited Company
**Line of Business:** Holding companies management activities
**Issued Capital:** £1,000
**Principals:** A W Roberts *(Managing)*, Ms S T Roberts, P T Roberts, R J Puffette, S W Roberts
**Co. Secretary:** Alan Roberts
**Responsibilities**
**Marketing:** B Wilkes *(Sales & Marketing Manager)*
**Sales:** B Wilkes *(Sales & Marketing Manager)*
**HR:** Andrew Brockman *(Production Manager)*, Claire Probets *(Human Resources Manager)*
**Health & Safety:** Ian McAllister *(Facilities Manager)*
**Facilities:** Ian McAllister *(Facilities Manager)*
**Engineering:** Andrew Brockman *(Production Manager)*
**US SIC:** 6711 **UK SIC:** 83962
**Auditors:** Deeks Evans
**Bankers:** Lloyds TSB Bank plc (30-98-63)

| | 31-12-13 | 31-12-12 | 31-12-11 |
|---|---|---|---|
| TO | 15,945,635 | 15,053,068 | 14,375,166 |
| P/L | 165,791 | 527,171 | 67,247 |
| NW | 578,513 | 649,440 | 422,193 |
| WC | (1,748,921) | (1,469,811) | (1,403,560) |
| Emp. | 157 | 139 | 126 |

DUNS 49-139-5695

## Wea Cymru (Cymdeithas Addysg Y Gweithwyr Cymru the Workers' Edu

7 Iard Y Cowper / Coopers Yard, Ffordd Curran / Curran Road, Cardiff, South Glamorgan CF10 5NB
**Tel:** 08435385964
**Reg No:** 3109524 **Estd:** 1995 Private Limited Company
**Line of Business:** Technical and vocational secondary education
**Directors:** N Davies, Mrs J D Jeremy, Ms A Hill, V P Davies, G D Price, Ms R Rumbul, J I Gass, R O Humphreys
**Co. Secretary:** Stephen Thomas
**Responsibilities**
**Senior:** Cathrine Clark *(Director)*, Derek Edwards *(Director)*, Philip Elias *(Director)*, Christopher Franks *(Director)*, Gerry Jenson *(Director)*, Jennifer Jones Annetts *(Director)*, David Macmanus *(Director)*, Toni Schiavone *(Director)*, Nick Taylor *(Director)*, Christine Topham *(Director)*
**US SIC:** 8249, 8221
**UK SIC:** 93300, 93100

**Bankers:** The Co-Operative Bank Plc (08-90-03)

| | 31-07-13 | 31-07-12 | 31-07-11 |
|---|---|---|---|
| TO | 3,513,468 | 3,573,763 | 2,782,574 |
| P/L | 123,422 | 293,673 | 32,537 |
| NW | 648,728 | 447,040 | 435,133 |
| WC | 784,493 | 693,088 | 504,768 |
| Emp. | 84 | 85 | 65 |

DUNS 23-268-8697

## Wealden District Council

Vicarage Lane, Hailsham, East Sussex BN27 2AX

**Tel:** 01323443322

**Web:** www.wealden.gov.uk

**VAT No:** 210898561 **Estd:** 1974 Incorporate By Act Of Parliament

**Line of Business:** Local government

**Directors:** D Holness, Ms S Douglas, B A Moss, G Parish, A Wallwork

**Branches:** Wealden District Council, Tunbridge Wells Road, Mayfield, East Sussex TN20 6PJ

**US SIC:** 9121 **UK SIC:** 91110

**Bankers:** National Westminster Bank Plc (60-09-25)

**Employees:** 600

DUNS 21-746-7260

## Wealden Leisure Ltd

The Paddock, 1-6 Carriers Way, (Off Juziers Drive), East Hoathly, Lewes, East Sussex BN8 6AG

**Tel:** 01825765002

**Web:** www.freedom-leisure.co.uk

**Reg No:** 0029336IP **VAT No:** 791125041

**Estd:** 2002 Friendly Society

**Line of Business:** Charities and charitable organisations

**Trading Style:** Freedom Leisure

**Principals:** J Hart *(Managing)*, D Talbut *(Financial)*, Ms K Burrel *(Marketing)*, Ms N Bonetti *(Personnel)*, I Horsfall-Turner, G Freeborn

**US SIC:** 7999 **UK SIC:** 97913

**Auditors:** McCabe Ford Williams

**Employees:** 971

**Turnover:** £15,944,473

DUNS 21-007-6544 **Imp**

## Wealmoor Atherstone Ltd

Jehta House, Springfield Road, Hayes, Middlesex UB4 0JT

**Tel:** 020-8867-3700 **Fax:** 02088673770

**Web:** www.wealmoor.co.uk

**Reg No:** 6318423 **Estd:** 2007 Private Limited Company

**Line of Business:** Other letting of own property

**Issued Capital:** £1

**Director:** Ms L A Malde

**Co. Secretary:** Avnish Malde

**US SIC:** 6519 **UK SIC:** 85000

| | 31-03-14 | 31-03-13 | 31-03-12 |
|---|---|---|---|
| TA | 1,286,730 | 1,392,108 | 1,541,496 |
| NW | 192,802 | 184,910 | 175,286 |
| WC | (1,079,350) | (1,184,677) | (1,310,133) |

DUNS 21-164-1273

## Wealth At Work Holdings Ltd

5 Temple Square, Temple Street, Liverpool, Merseyside L2 5RH

**Tel:** 08000283200

**Reg No:** 6901909 **Estd:** 2009 Private Limited Company

**Line of Business:** Management activities of other non-financial holding companies not elsewhere classified

**Issued Capital:** £2,430,627

**Directors:** S Payne, I Copelin, G W Tipper, A K Whalley, P E Morton, D Cassidy, Ms B C Houghton, J R Watts-Lay

**Co. Secretary:** Mark Hutchinson

**US SIC:** 7399 **UK SIC:** 83954

**Auditors:** Deloitte LLP

**Bankers:** Lloyds TSB Bank plc (30-17-48)

| | 31-12-13 | 31-12-12 | 31-12-11 |
|---|---|---|---|
| TO | 5,753,000 | 3,320,000 | 2,820,000 |
| P/L | (1,683,000) | (2,532,000) | (2,268,000) |
| NW | 4,412,000 | 2,382,000 | 4,615,000 |
| WC | 4,300,000 | 2,266,000 | 4,599,000 |
| Emp. | 98 | 64 | 51 |

DUNS 73-975-0045

## Wealth At Work Ltd

(**Subsidiary of:** Wealth At Work Holdings Ltd)

5 Temple Square, Temple Street, Liverpool, Merseyside L2 5RH

**Tel:** 01512553400

**Web:** www.wealthatwork.co.uk

**Reg No:** 5225819 **Estd:** 2004 Private Limited Company

**Line of Business:** Activities auxiliary to financial intermediation not elsewhere classified

**Issued Capital:** £19,530,293

**Directors:** P Morton, S Payne, I Copelin, J R Watts Lay, D Cassidy, A K Whalley

**Co. Secretary:** Mark Hutchinson

**US SIC:** 7399 **UK SIC:** 83954

**Auditors:** Deloitte LLP

| | 31-12-13 | 31-12-12 | 31-12-11 |
|---|---|---|---|
| TO | 5,329,000 | 3,102,000 | 2,820,000 |
| P/L | (1,721,000) | (2,531,000) | (2,028,000) |
| NW | 2,913,000 | 2,871,000 | 2,677,000 |
| WC | 2,051,000 | 2,029,000 | 2,661,000 |
| Emp. | 88 | 64 | 51 |

DUNS 23-084-3679

## Wearcheck Laboratory

Robertsons Research Unit 6, Conwy Morfa Enterprise Park Parc Caer, Seion, Conwy, Gwynedd LL32 8FA

**Tel:** 01492574803

**Proprietorship**

**Line of Business:** Oil sample analysis

**Responsibilities**

**Senior:** Bob Culter *(Manager)*

**US SIC:** 1389 **UK SIC:** 13000

**Employees:** 70

DUNS 29-324-9033 **Exp**

## Wearmouth Construction & Plant Ltd

Wearmouth House, Yarm Road, Innovation Court, Stockton-On-Tees, Cleveland TS18 3DA

**Tel:** 01642-601354 **Fax:** 01642601388

**Web:** www.rawearmouth.co.uk

**Reg No:** 1812961 **Estd:** 1984 Private Limited Company

**Line of Business:** Groundwork contractors

**Issued Capital:** £70

**Directors:** G K Humphreys, R A Wearmouth

**Co. Secretary:** Ms Susan Wearmouth

**Responsibilities**

**Senior:** David Wearmouth *(Assistant Site Manager)*

**Health & Safety:** Bill Newton *(Health & Safety Manager)*

**Facilities:** Barbara Roger *(Facilities Manager)*

**US SIC:** 1622 **UK SIC:** 50200

**Auditors:** King Hope & Co

| | 31-03-14 | 31-03-13 | 31-03-12 |
|---|---|---|---|
| TO | 25,534,524 | 16,513,042 | 19,475,391 |
| P/L | 1,522,738 | 430,315 | (116,999) |
| NW | 4,061,811 | 3,096,939 | 2,929,497 |
| WC | 2,133,908 | 1,457,411 | 1,322,046 |
| Emp. | 289 | 164 | 169 |

DUNS 21-808-0638 **Imp-Exp**

## Wearnes Cambion Ltd

(**Subsidiary of:** Wbl Corporation Limited)

Peveril House, Mill Bridge, Hope Valley, South Yorkshire S33 8WR

**Tel:** 01433621555

**Web:** www.cambion.co.uk

**Reg No:** 0703283 **VAT No:** 157241864

**Estd:** 1961 Private Limited Company

**Line of Business:** Manufacturers and distributors of electronic components

**Export Markets:** Worldwide

**Export Sales:** £2,486,677

**Issued Capital:** £2,800,586

**Directors:** K T Ong, M P Stoneman

**Co. Secretary:** William Rowland

**Responsibilities**

**HR:** Jane Taylor-Dutton *(HR Manager)*

**Engineering:** Dave Howard *(Production Manager)*

**Branches:** Wearnes Cambion Ltd, Mill Bridge, Sheffield, South Yorkshire S35 0FL

**US SIC:** 3679 **UK SIC:** 34542

**Auditors:** PricewaterhouseCoopers LLP

**Bankers:** National Westminster Bank Plc (56-00-09)

| | 31-12-13 | 30-09-12 | 30-12-11 |
|---|---|---|---|
| TO | 4,324,872 | 3,907,921 | 3,911,897 |
| P/L | 220,858 | 343,764 | 241,970 |
| NW | 3,120,025 | 2,096,077 | 2,429,890 |
| WC | 2,252,450 | 2,310,791 | 2,280,745 |
| Emp. | 60 | 63 | 67 |

DUNS 64-118-8248

## Weartech International Ltd

(**Subsidiary of:** Lincoln Electric Holdings Inc.)

Moor Road, Baglan Industrial Estate, Port Talbot, West Glamorgan SA12 7BJ

**Tel:** 01639 812 900 **Fax:** 01639 825 190

**Web:** www.weartecheurope.co.uk

**Reg No:** 4118871 **VAT No:** 771784493

**Estd:** 2000 Private Limited Company

**Line of Business:** Other non-ferrous metal production

**Export Sales:** £8,057,997

**Issued Capital:** £100,000

**Directors:** G Allman, G Blankenship

**Co. Secretary:** Beach Secretaries Limited

**Responsibilities**

**Senior:** David Estall *(Manager)*, Dean Thomas *(Operations Director)*

**Operations:** Dean Thomas *(Operations Director)*

**Branches:** WEARTECH INTERNATIONAL LTD: Moor Road, Baglan Industrial Estate, Port Talbot, SA12 7BJ. Tel: 01639-814-907.

**US SIC:** 3339, 3829

**UK SIC:** 22470, 37100

**Auditors:** WBV Ltd

| | 31-12-13 | 31-12-12 | 30-12-11 |
|---|---|---|---|
| TO | 8,810,007 | 9,377,628 | N/A |
| P/L | 689,550 | (155,211) | N/A |
| NW | 1,595,169 | 1,101,621 | 1,239,528 |
| WC | 1,363,567 | 1,405,806 | (346,634) |
| Emp. | 66 | 51 | N/A |

DUNS 77-535-6074 **Imp**

## Wearwell (U K) Ltd

(**Subsidiary of:** Wearwell Group Ltd)

Gargarin, Lichfield Road, Tamworth, Staffordshire B79 7TR

**Tel:** 0182763651

**Web:** www.wearwell.co.uk

**Reg No:** 2993093 **Estd:** 1994 Private Limited Company

**Line of Business:** Manufacture of other wearing apparel and accessories not elsewhere classified

**Issued Capital:** £146,178

**Directors:** G Clayton, C Rooney

**Co. Secretary:** Ms Beate Greasley

**Responsibilities**

**Senior:** Judy Smith *(Warehouse Manager)*

**Sales:** Paul Danby *(Sales Director)*

**HR:** Rosemarie Watterson *(Personnel Manager)*

**Health & Safety:** Rosemarie Watterson *(Personnel Manager)*

**Facilities:** Rosemarie Watterson *(Personnel Manager)*

**Operations:** Rosemarie Watterson *(Personnel Manager)*

**Purchasing:** Nicola Morgan *(Purchasing Clerk)*

**US SIC:** 2389 **UK SIC:** 45393

**Auditors:** Smith Cooper

**Bankers:** HSBC Bank plc (40-19-15)

| | 31-12-13 | 31-12-12 | 31-12-11 |
|---|---|---|---|
| TO | 5,604,931 | 5,431,432 | 6,245,331 |
| P/L | 227,473 | 427,022 | 289,762 |
| NW | 3,260,529 | 3,089,832 | 3,036,235 |
| WC | 3,086,223 | 3,049,827 | 2,983,989 |
| Emp. | 58 | 57 | 59 |

DUNS 23-512-4570

## Weatherall Green & Smith North Ltd

(**Subsidiary of:** Sanderson Weatherall Group Ltd)

Brook House, Manchester M2 2BQ

**Web:** www.sandersonweatherall.com

**Reg No:** 3511647 **Estd:** 1998 Private Limited Company

**Line of Business:** Real estate agencies

**Trading Style:** Sanderson Weatherall

**Issued Capital:** £600,005

**Director:** M W Archer

**Branches:** Weatherall Green & Smith North Ltd, Neville St, Newcastle-Upon-Tyne, Newcastle Upon Tyne, Tyne and Wear NE1 5DL

**US SIC:** 6531, 8911

**UK SIC:** 83400, 83701

**Auditors:** Baker Tilly UK Audit LLP

| | 31-03-14 | 31-03-13 | 31-03-12 |
|---|---|---|---|
| TA | 482,919 | 482,919 | 482,919 |
| NW | 482,919 | 482,919 | 482,919 |

DUNS 77-702-9448

## Weatherbeeta Ltd

(**Subsidiary of:** Alistair Somerset Pty Ltd)

Unit 9 Somerville Court, Banbury Business Park, Adderbury, Banbury, Oxfordshire OX17 3SN

**Tel:** 01295-226905

**Web:** www.weatherbeeta.com

**Reg No:** 3006765 **VAT No:** 623911356

**Estd:** 1995 Private Limited Company

**Line of Business:** Equestrian supplies

**Export Sales:** £305,972

**Issued Capital:** £965,746

**Directors:** R G Bates, A J Bucknell, J H Kennard, J M Bucknell

**Co. Secretary:** Mark Abrahart

**Responsibilities**

**Senior:** Ellen Bates *(General Manager)*

**Marketing:** Rachel Beckham *(Marketing Manager)*

**Sales:** Lynne Westwood *(Sales Manager)*

**Operations:** Lynne Westwood *(Sales Manager)*

**US SIC:** 5948 **UK SIC:** 64600

**Auditors:** Breslin Banbury Ltd

**Bankers:** National Westminster Bank Plc (60-01-35)

| | 30-06-13 | 30-06-12 | 30-06-11 |
|---|---|---|---|
| TO | 11,908,040 | 12,573,219 | 12,585,852 |
| P/L | (175,385) | 153,131 | 313,322 |
| NW | 2,748,396 | 2,886,314 | 2,776,728 |
| WC | 3,508,209 | 3,729,226 | 3,562,015 |
| Emp. | 58 | 68 | 71 |

DUNS 34-860-6059

## Weatherbys Bank Holdings Ltd

52-60 Sanders Road, Finedon Road Industrial Estate, Wellingborough, Northamptonshire NN8 4NL

**Web:** www.weatherbys.co.uk

**Reg No:** 5659237 **Estd:** 2005 Private Limited Company

**Line of Business:** Management activities of other non-financial holding companies not elsewhere classified

**Issued Capital:** £10,660,000

**Directors:** J R Weatherby, R N Weatherby

**Co. Secretary:** Adrian Mcglynn

**US SIC:** 6711 **UK SIC:** 83962

| | 31-12-13 | 31-12-12 | 31-12-11 |
|---|---|---|---|
| TO | 22,105,974 | 19,649,449 | 18,289,815 |
| P/L | 3,711,088 | 3,088,913 | 2,666,153 |
| NW | 24,334,493 | 22,685,028 | 20,861,934 |
| WC | 21,490,550 | 19,156,214 | 37,061,050 |
| Emp. | 106 | 99 | 92 |

DUNS 22-759-3480 **Imp**

## Weatherbys Thoroughbred Ltd

(**Subsidiary of:** Weatherbys Thoroughbred Holdings Ltd)

Sanders Road, Finedon Road Industrial Estate, Wellingborough, Northamptonshire NN8 4BX

**Web:** www.statisticsonline.co.uk

**Reg No:** 0526599 **VAT No:** 387521624

**Estd:** 2006 Private Limited Company

**Line of Business:** Other publishing

**Export Sales:** £651,753

**Trading Style:** Weatherbys

**Issued Capital:** £100

**Principals:** J R Weatherby *(Chairman)*, G W Ayres, N D Craven, C G Coles, Mrs J Abraham, R N Weatherby

**Co. Secretary:** Adrian Mcglynn

**Responsibilities**

**Senior:** Joanne Abrams *(Manager)*, Gary Eldershaw *(Facilities Manager)*, Rachel Flynn *(Director)*

**Finance:** Carol Church *(Financial Director)*

**IT:** Alicia Aldis *(IT Director)*

**HR:** Jane Olds *(Human Resources Officer)*

**US SIC:** 2741, 7374, 5961

**UK SIC:** 47541, 83940, 65600

**Auditors:** Deloitte & Touche LLP

**Bankers:** Coutts & Co (18-00-14)

| | 31-12-13 | 31-12-12 | 31-12-11 |
|---|---|---|---|
| TO | 15,177,071 | 15,006,624 | 15,309,523 |
| P/L | 1,117,470 | 1,082,274 | 1,129,103 |
| NW | 3,253,564 | 2,703,661 | 1,688,645 |
| WC | (1,508,242) | 238,432 | 974,250 |
| Emp. | 232 | 226 | 233 |

DUNS 39-842-2931 **Exp**

## Weatherford Completion Systems (Uk) Ltd

(**Subsidiary of:** Weatherford (G.B.) Llp)

Kirkton Drive Weatherford Pss, Aberdeen, Aberdeenshire AB21 0BG

**Tel:** 01224767015 **Fax:** 01224-767104

**Web:** www.weatherford.com

**Reg No:** 0109200SC **VAT No:** 498197968

**Estd:** 1988 Private Limited Company

**Line of Business:** Service activities incidental to oil and gas extraction excluding surveying

**Trading Style:** Weatherford Pss

**Issued Capital:** £100,000

**Directors:** N A Macleod, E R Prentice, Ms J M Thomson

**Co. Secretary:** Mrs Gemma Rose-Garvie

**Responsibilities**

**Senior:** Murray Dowsett *(Engineering Director)*

**Engineering:** Murray Dowsett *(Engineering Director)*

**Branches:** Weatherford Completion Systems (Uk) Ltd, James Chalmers Rd, Kirkton Indstl Est, Arbroath, Angus DD11 3LR

**US SIC:** 1389 **UK SIC:** 13000

**Auditors:** Ernst & Young LLP

**Bankers:** The Royal Bank Of Scotland Plc (83-49-40)

| | 31-12-13 | 31-12-12 | 31-12-11 |
|---|---|---|---|
| TA | 10,917,000 | 10,651,000 | 10,375,000 |
| P/L | 266,000 | 275,000 | 317,000 |
| NW | 10,333,000 | 10,014,000 | 9,807,000 |
| WC | 10,333,000 | 10,014,000 | 9,807,000 |

DUNS 21-755-1594

## Weatherhead High School

Weatherhead High School, Breck Road, Wallasey, Merseyside CH44 3HS

**Tel:** 01516314400

**Web:** www.weatherhead.wirral.sch.uk

**Reg No:** 7847190 **Estd:** 2011 Private Company Limited By Guarantee

**Line of Business:** General secondary education

**Directors:** Miss K J Coates, A S Beere, Mrs J H Owens, N R Dyment, Mrs H O'Brien, Ms B J Weir, A B Clare, B Clark

**Co. Secretary:** Ms Karen Mcardle

**Responsibilities**
**Senior:** Samantha Ashby (*Director*), Anne Barker (*Director*), Kathleen Hackett (*Director*), Karen Hayes (*Director*), Rebecca Jones (*Director*), Katherine Stuart (*Director*)
**US SIC:** 8211 **UK SIC:** 93200

| | 31-08-13 | 31-08-12 |
|---|---|---|
| TO | 8,704,000 | 6,845,000 |
| P/L | 53,000 | (869,000) |
| NW | (860,000) | (969,000) |
| WC | 1,062,000 | 1,089,000 |
| Emp. | 171 | 161 |

DUNS 23-623-8601 **Imp**
## Weatherite Holdings Ltd
Weatherite House, Credenda Road, West Bromwich, West Midlands B70 7JE
**Tel:** 0121-665-2266
**Web:** www.weatherite-group.com
**Reg No:** 3621010 **VAT No:** 705336259
**Estd:** 1997 Private Limited Company
**Line of Business:** Air conditioning equipment
**Export Sales:** £279,046
**Issued Capital:** £7,250
**Directors:** R Boswell, J S Whitehouse, T J Whitehouse, M Kordbacheh, Ms J Whitehouse
**Co. Secretary:** Stephen Lander
**Responsibilities**
**Senior:** Jim Gale (*Manager*)
**US SIC:** 3585 **UK SIC:** 32841
**Auditors:** Henn & Westwood
**Bankers:** Lloyds TSB Bank plc (30-93-75)

| | 28-02-14 | 28-02-13 | 29-02-12 |
|---|---|---|---|
| TO | 23,848,682 | 27,119,559 | 33,202,044 |
| P/L | 157,065 | 867,842 | 928,529 |
| NW | 7,464,709 | 7,406,413 | 6,722,426 |
| WC | 2,915,482 | 2,647,344 | 1,979,273 |
| Emp. | 171 | 194 | 203 |

DUNS 29-933-5216
## Weatherproofing Advisors Ltd
Advisor House, Block 13 West Avenue, Blantyre, Glasgow, Lanarkshire G72 0UZ
**Tel:** 01698-826928 **Fax:** 01698-824616
**Web:** www.weatherproofing.co.uk
**Reg No:** 0103301SC **Estd:** 1987 Private Limited Company
**Line of Business:** Roofing contracting services
**Issued Capital:** £7,500
**Principals:** J M Kelly (*Managing*), F Gaskell, C R Henderson, S Mccartney, J S Turner, A A Grieve
**Responsibilities**
**Health & Safety:** Sid McCartney (*Health & Safety Officer*)
**Branches:** Weatherproofing Advisors Ltd, 2 Mill Lane, Mill Brook Business Park, St. Helens, Merseyside WA11 8LZ
**US SIC:** 1761, 5039, 1799
**UK SIC:** 50400, 61300, 50000
**Auditors:** Iain M Neilson
**Bankers:** The Royal Bank Of Scotland Plc (83-25-45)

| | 31-03-14 | 31-03-13 | 31-03-12 |
|---|---|---|---|
| TO | 11,007,431 | 10,042,297 | 9,000,436 |
| P/L | 541,823 | 237,003 | (199,629) |
| NW | 2,473,682 | 2,046,068 | 2,057,144 |
| WC | 2,345,601 | 1,913,631 | 1,763,366 |
| Emp. | 89 | 82 | 83 |

DUNS 73-538-3130
## Weatherseal Holdings Ltd
Road One, Winsford Industrial Estate, Winsford Industrial Estate, Winsford, Cheshire CW7 3PZ
**Tel:** 01606866500
**Web:** www.weatherseal.co.uk
**Reg No:** 4800670 **Estd:** 2003 Private Limited Company
**Line of Business:** Double glazing installers
**Issued Capital:** £100
**Director:** K A Brookman
**Co. Secretary:** Martin Del Manso
**Responsibilities**
**Senior:** Tony Riley (*Manager*)
**Finance:** Joseph Howarth (*Financial Director*)
**Sales:** Tony Riley (*Manager*)
**Branches:** Weatherseal Holdings Ltd, Friars House, 2 Falcon Street, Ipswich, Suffolk IP1 1SL
**US SIC:** 1721, 7399
**UK SIC:** 50400, 83954
**Auditors:** KPMG LLP
**Bankers:** Barclays Bank Plc (20-35-81)

| | 31-10-13 | 31-10-12 | 31-10-11 |
|---|---|---|---|
| TA | 1,388,363 | 1,253,496 | 839,000 |
| NW | (1,068,642) | (1,062,219) | (1,064,000) |
| WC | (1,035,642) | (1,029,219) | (1,031,000) |

DUNS 22-209-7698
## Weaver Vale Housing Trust Ltd
Gadbrook Point, Rudheath Way, Northwich, Cheshire CW9 7LL
**Tel:** 01606813300 **Fax:** 01606813301
**Web:** www.wvht.co.uk
**Reg No:** 4227894 **Estd:** 2001 Private Company Limited By Guarantee

**Line of Business:** Non-charitable social work activities with accommodation
**Directors:** Mrs J A Chatwood, Mrs M Shaw, Miss R Radway, A Ball, Mrs L C Reilly-Cooper, I D Moston, G R Miller, Ms A C Miller
**Co. Secretary:** Andrew White
**Responsibilities**
**Senior:** James Boyd (*Director*), Alan Kie (*Manager*), Sue Malek (*Chairman*), Edith Morgan (*Manager*), Christine Pickthall (*Manager*), Edna Samlofski (*Manager*), Kenton Surveyor (*Executive*)
**Finance:** Sabine Isaac (*?Money Management Officer*), Heather Maddock (*Housing Benefit Liaison Office*)
**Marketing:** Lucy Goldsmith (*PR & Communications Officer*)
**HR:** Marianne Richards (*Director of Organisation and P*)
**Facilities:** Lauren Hancox (*Property Services and Faciliti*)
**Engineering:** Kenton Surveyor (*Executive*)
**Branches:** Weaver Vale Housing Trust Ltd, 38-44 Cotswold Way, Winsford, Cheshire CW7 1QW
**US SIC:** 8321 **UK SIC:** 96111
**Auditors:** Baker Tilly UK Audit LLP
**Bankers:** National Westminster Bank Plc (60-15-29)

| | 31-03-14 | 31-03-13 | 31-03-12 |
|---|---|---|---|
| TO | 30,934,000 | 31,264,000 | 27,220,000 |
| P/L | 3,078,000 | 3,898,000 | 3,014,000 |
| NW | (1,538,000) | (7,068,000) | (7,826,000) |
| WC | 1,887,000 | 2,916,000 | (1,953,000) |
| Emp. | 325 | 317 | 325 |

DUNS 22-655-1281 **Imp**
## Weavers Close Ltd
Temple Walk, Matlock Bath, Matlock, Derbyshire DE4 3PG
**Tel:** 01629580540
**Web:** www.gulliversfun.co.uk
**Reg No:** 1117258 **Estd:** 1973 Private Limited Company
**Line of Business:** Other service activities not elsewhere classified
**Trading Style:** Gullivers Kingdom, Gullivers World, Gullivers Land
**Issued Capital:** £800
**Principals:** Dr R C Phillips (*Managing*), N G Phillips, Ms H J Phillips
**Co. Secretary:** Ms Julie Dalton
**US SIC:** 8999 **UK SIC:** 83954
**Auditors:** Johnson Tidsall
**Bankers:** National Westminster Bank Plc (60-40-09)

| | 31-12-13 | 31-12-12 | 31-12-11 |
|---|---|---|---|
| TO | 3,239,390 | 2,821,165 | 2,750,849 |
| P/L | (8,363) | 99,539 | 199,725 |
| NW | 2,292,937 | 1,778,995 | 1,711,673 |
| WC | (504,433) | (274,907) | (470,334) |
| Emp. | 89 | 91 | 80 |

DUNS 22-069-0668
## Web Applications Uk Ltd
(**Subsidiary of:** General Commercial Objects Ltd)
Unit 2-3 Windsor Works, Hall Street, Oldham, Lancashire OL4 1TD
**Tel:** 01616826565
**Web:** www.webapplicationsuk.com
**Reg No:** 4070605 **Estd:** 2000 Private Limited Company
**Line of Business:** Computer software (development)
**Issued Capital:** £151
**Directors:** L Tudor, C T Kennedy, C A Dean
**Co. Secretary:** Gordon Pearce
**Responsibilities**
**Senior:** Kamal Choudhury (*Manager*), Jon Cockerill (*Manager*), Naomi Mckenna (*Administrator*)
**US SIC:** 7379 **UK SIC:** 83940

| | 28-02-14 | 28-02-13 | 29-02-12 |
|---|---|---|---|
| TA | 918,922 | 1,540,463 | 1,311,483 |
| NW | 94,612 | 89,293 | 184,514 |
| WC | (132,503) | (198,221) | (15,062) |

DUNS 76-981-2520 **Exp**
## Webasto Roof Systems Ltd
(**Subsidiary of:** Werner Baier Und Gerhard Mey)
Unit 7, Sutton Coldfield, West Midlands B76 9DL
**Tel:** 01213135600
**Web:** www.webasto.com
**Reg No:** 2630029 **VAT No:** 486672789
**Estd:** 1991 Private Limited Company
**Line of Business:** Manufacturers of car accessories
**Export Markets:** Countries Worldwide
**Export Sales:** £934,000
**Issued Capital:** £3,876,100
**Directors:** J M Castle, T Deisenhoter, A Hoermann, M E Arleth
**Co. Secretary:** Kevin Green
**Responsibilities**
**Senior:** Emma Markham (*Manager*), Reinhard Strahanner (*Manager*), Reinhard Straihammer (*?Director of Operations*)
**IT:** Steve Withington (*IT Manager*)

**Operations:** Reinhard Straihammer (*?Director of Operations*), Steve Withington (*IT Manager*)
**Branches:** Webasto Roof Systems Ltd, Minworth Ind Est, Fulford Dv, Sutton Coldfield, West Midlands B76 1DJ
**US SIC:** 3714 **UK SIC:** 35300
**Auditors:** KPMG LLP
**Bankers:** Bayerische Vereinsbank Ag (30-10-61)

| | 31-12-13 | 31-12-12 | 31-12-11 |
|---|---|---|---|
| TO | 94,940,000 | 66,921,000 | 55,098,000 |
| P/L | 629,000 | (8,065,000) | (3,293,000) |
| NW | 3,591,000 | 1,151,000 | 4,596,000 |
| WC | (231,000) | (1,290,000) | 3,030,000 |
| Emp. | 337 | 325 | 272 |

DUNS 23-658-1232
## Webb Hotels and Travel Ltd
Moor Hall Drive, Sutton Coldfield, West Midlands B75 6LN
**Tel:** 01903879494 **Fax:** 01213-088-974
**Web:** www.moorhallhotel.co.uk
**Reg No:** 3653076 **Estd:** 1998 Private Limited Company
**Line of Business:** Hotels
**Trading Style:** Moor Hall Hotel & Spa, The George Hotel, The Gables Hotel, Broads Travel Group
**Issued Capital:** £11,000
**Directors:** M J Webb, Miss S L Webb, Mrs H Griffiths, S Ledbrooke, Mrs A C Burns
**Co. Secretary:** Nigel Saunders
**Responsibilities**
**Senior:** Maggie Parsons (*General Manager*)
**US SIC:** 7011 **UK SIC:** 66500
**Auditors:** Bloomer Heaven Ltd
**Bankers:** Barclays Bank Plc (20-77-62)

| | 31-12-13 | 31-12-12 | 31-12-11 |
|---|---|---|---|
| TO | 14,839,239 | 15,340,269 | 14,737,367 |
| P/L | 593,831 | (98,216) | 165,107 |
| NW | 6,497,597 | 6,120,114 | 8,176,930 |
| WC | (1,511,220) | (1,568,969) | (1,620,598) |
| Emp. | 315 | 309 | 308 |

DUNS 21-579-7617
## Webb Ivory Catalogue
Clayton Business Park, Clayton Le Moors, Accrington, Lancashire BB5 5JY
**Tel:** 08713769977
**Estd:** 2011 Proprietorship
**Line of Business:** Call centres
**Proprietor:** Mrs A Yates
**US SIC:** 7399 **UK SIC:** 83954
**Employees:** 431

DUNS 54-426-3163
## Webb One Ltd
124-125 High Street, Uxbridge, Middlesex UB8 1JT
**Tel:** 01895-252868
**Web:** www.mcdonalds.co.uk
**Reg No:** 3272447 **Estd:** 1996 Private Limited Company
**Line of Business:** Licensed restaurants
**Trading Style:** McDonalds Fast Food Restaurant
**Issued Capital:** £100
**Managing Director:** C Webb
**Co. Secretary:** Ms Noreeza Webb
**Branches:** Webb One Ltd, 37 Oxford Road, Gerrards Cross, Buckinghamshire SL9 8AA
**US SIC:** 5812 **UK SIC:** 66110
**Auditors:** Hazlems Fenton

| | 31-12-13 | 31-12-12 | 31-12-11 |
|---|---|---|---|
| TO | 18,581,482 | 17,592,129 | 16,236,341 |
| P/L | 905,490 | 1,481,814 | 925,153 |
| NW | 2,786,783 | 3,343,364 | 2,454,434 |
| WC | 1,060,587 | 2,370,125 | 1,639,671 |
| Emp. | 477 | 465 | 450 |

DUNS 23-841-8177
## Webber Independent School Ltd
(**Subsidiary of:** Global Education Management Systems Ltd)
Soskin Drive, Stantonbury Fields, Milton Keynes, Buckinghamshire MK14 6DP
**Tel:** 01908574740 **Fax:** 01908-574741
**Web:** www.webberindependentschool.co.uk
**Reg No:** 3833450 **Estd:** 2012 Private Limited Company
**Line of Business:** Pre school education
**Issued Capital:** £10,000
**Directors:**
Global Education Management Syst, D S Varkey
**Co. Secretary:**
M&R Secretarial Services Limited
**Responsibilities**
**Senior:** Sue Vig (*Principal*)
**US SIC:** 8211 **UK SIC:** 93200
**Auditors:** Nigle Wilson & Co
**Bankers:** Barclays Bank Plc (20-03-18)

| | 31-03-14 | 31-03-13 | 31-03-12 |
|---|---|---|---|
| TO | 1,259,685 | 1,499,264 | 1,795,483 |
| P/L | (903,558) | (1,388,562) | (424,196) |
| NW | (3,106,961) | (2,203,403) | (632,841) |
| WC | (5,615,030) | (4,806,103) | (4,051,626) |
| Emp. | 55 | 75 | 74 |

DUNS 73-875-9682
## Webberbus Ltd
Unit 8 Beech Business Park, Bristol Road, Bridgwater, Somerset TA6 4FF
**Tel:** 08000963039
**Web:** www.webberbus.com
**Reg No:** 5130334 **Estd:** 2004 Private Limited Company
**Line of Business:** Bus operators and stations
**Issued Capital:** £62,500
**Directors:** M C Pedlar, R D Plunkett, T J Gardner, D J Webber
**Co. Secretary:** Ms Elaine Gardner
**US SIC:** 4119 **UK SIC:** 72200

| | 31-03-14 | 31-03-13 | 31-03-12 |
|---|---|---|---|
| TA | 3,044,457 | 3,131,111 | 3,147,855 |
| NW | 498,843 | 456,786 | 366,944 |
| WC | (535,983) | (540,723) | (565,387) |

DUNS 58-399-3266
## Webbers Property Services Ltd
39-41 Boutport Street, Barnstaple, Devon EX31 1SA
**Tel:** 01271373404
**Web:** www.webbers.co.uk
**Reg No:** 2908137 **Estd:** 1921 Private Limited Company
**Line of Business:** Estate agents
**Issued Capital:** £995
**Directors:** G G Harrison, M E Prescott, N C Wilcox, P H Mchugh
**Co. Secretary:** Gary Holder
**Branches:** Webbers Property Services Ltd, 9 The Square, Braunton, Devon EX33 2JF
**US SIC:** 6531 **UK SIC:** 83400
**Auditors:** Sully & Co
**Bankers:** National Westminster Bank Plc (60-02-03)

| | 31-03-14 | 31-03-13 | 31-03-12 |
|---|---|---|---|
| TO | 5,230,321 | 4,456,786 | 4,541,102 |
| P/L | 316,916 | 112,899 | 218,636 |
| NW | 2,327,273 | 2,208,044 | 2,362,556 |
| WC | 1,112,439 | 977,972 | 1,048,850 |
| Emp. | 142 | 124 | 152 |

DUNS 34-806-2548
## Webbs Cleaning Ltd
10 Farleigh Road, Backwell, Bristol, Avon BS48 3PA
**Tel:** 01275-463993
**Web:** www.webbscleaning.co.uk
**Reg No:** 2790970 **Estd:** 1992 Private Limited Company
**Line of Business:** Cleaning contracting commercial
**Issued Capital:** £1,000
**Directors:** Ms S Webb, D E Webb, A M Webb
**Co. Secretary:** Mrs Lynn Webb
**US SIC:** 7349 **UK SIC:** 92300
**Auditors:** Stanley Joseph Ltd
**Bankers:** National Westminster Bank Plc (56-00-40)

| | 31-12-13 | 31-12-12 | 31-12-11 |
|---|---|---|---|
| TO | N/A | N/A | 679,995 |
| P/L | N/A | N/A | 151,428 |
| NW | 131,995 | 72,799 | 77,896 |
| WC | 119,242 | 63,160 | 63,402 |

DUNS 21-914-6669 **Imp**
## Webbs Garden Centres Ltd
38 Worcester Road, Droitwich, Worcestershire WR9 0DG
**Web:** http://info.webbsdirect.co.uk
**Reg No:** 0777596 **VAT No:** 276820633
**Estd:** 2002 Private Limited Company
**Line of Business:** Garden centres
**Trading Style:** Webbs, Webbs of Wychbold
**Issued Capital:** £713
**Director:** E A Webb
**Co. Secretary:** Richard Brown
**Responsibilities**
**Senior:** Boyd Douglas-Davies (*Chief Executive*)
**Marketing:** Jacqui Sheard (*Human Resources Manager*), Claire Wilson (*Marketing Manager*)
**IT:** Paul Humphries (*Computer Manager*)
**HR:** Jackie Cheard (*Human Resources Manager*), Jacqui Sheard (*Human Resources Manager*)
**Health & Safety:** Nick bolder (*Health & Safety Officer*)
**Facilities:** Paul Maycroft (*Maintenance Manager*)
**Purchasing:** Alan Docherty (*Head Buyer*)
**US SIC:** 5999 **UK SIC:** 65600
**Auditors:** John Yelland & Co
**Bankers:** HSBC Bank plc (40-43-17)

| | 31-12-13 | 31-12-12 | 31-12-11 |
|---|---|---|---|
| TO | 13,605,872 | 13,592,652 | 14,045,001 |
| P/L | 528,066 | (108,757) | 200,217 |
| NW | 9,221,958 | 8,617,467 | 8,564,754 |
| WC | 39,119 | (36,356) | 83,263 |
| Emp. | 290 | 289 | 303 |

DUNS 21-140-0490 **Imp**

## Webcertain Group Ltd

World Language Hub, Northminster Business Park, Upper Poppleton, York, North Yorkshire YO26 6QW
**Tel:** 01904780030
**Web:** www.webcertain.com
**Reg No:** 6721395 **Estd:** 2008 Private Limited Company
**Line of Business:** Marketing consultants
**Issued Capital:** £100
**Directors:** A R Atkins-Krueger, P M Hopkinson
**Co. Secretary:** Philip Hopkinson
**US SIC:** 7392, 6711
**UK SIC:** 83951, 83962

| | 31-12-13 | 31-12-12 | 31-12-11 |
|---|---|---|---|
| TA | 1,924,230 | 989,187 | 629,979 |
| NW | 72,595 | 16,667 | (16,250) |
| WC | (27,926) | (91,783) | (121,493) |

DUNS 37-973-4270 **Imp-Exp**

## Weber Marking Ltd

**(Subsidiary of:** Weber Marking Systems Inc)
Macmerry Industrial Estate, Macmerry, Tranent, East Lothian EH33 1HD
**Tel:** 01875611111
**Web:** www.webermarking.ie
**Reg No:** 0169985SC **Estd:** 1932 Private Limited Company
**Line of Business:** Labels finishing and supply
**Export Sales:** £1,323,693
**Issued Capital:** £50
**Directors:** D A Weber, J A Weber
**Co. Secretary:** Jordan Company Secretaries Limit
**Responsibilities**
**Marketing:** Derek Mack *(Sales & Marketing Director)*
**Sales:** Derek Mack *(Sales & Marketing Director)*
**Admin:** Michele Cleland *(Administration Manager)*
**IT:** Margaret Swan *(IT Manager)*
**HR:** Michele Cleland *(Administration Manager)*
**Purchasing:** Michele Cleland *(Administration Manager)*
**US SIC:** 2752 **UK SIC:** 47544
**Auditors:** Condie & Co
**Bankers:** The Royal Bank Of Scotland Plc (83-27-25)

| | 31-12-13 | 31-12-12 | 31-12-11 |
|---|---|---|---|
| TO | 6,246,648 | 6,026,512 | 5,823,099 |
| P/L | 150,694 | 100,111 | (265,107) |
| NW | 2,487,860 | 2,228,920 | 2,121,610 |
| WC | 1,289,105 | 1,228,352 | 1,065,722 |
| Emp. | 47 | 45 | 50 |

DUNS 23-519-7758 **Imp**

## Weber-Stephen Products (U.K.) Ltd

**(Subsidiary of:** Weber-Stephen Products Llc)
Weber Stephen Products (Uk) Ltd, Skipton, North Yorkshire BD23 3AE
**Tel:** 01756-692600 **Fax:** 01756-692610
**Web:** www.weberbbq.co.uk
**Reg No:** 3518831 **Estd:** 2003 Private Limited Company
**Line of Business:** Barbecue & grilling equipment and accessories
**Export Sales:** £118,841,022
**Issued Capital:** £2
**Directors:** T Koos, Ms M L Hansen, J C Bindslev, J C Stephen
**Co. Secretary:** Ms Pauline Feather
**US SIC:** 5021, 5199
**UK SIC:** 61500, 61900
**Auditors:** Ainsworths Ltd

| | 30-09-13 | 30-09-12 | 30-09-11 |
|---|---|---|---|
| TO | 137,025,509 | 108,795,217 | 15,275,942 |
| P/L | 9,575,152 | 6,011,418 | 863,620 |
| NW | 22,974,169 | 16,989,698 | 3,339,209 |
| WC | 21,147,316 | 14,829,664 | 3,189,571 |
| Emp. | 183 | 159 | 34 |

DUNS 73-339-8114

## Webfold Communications Ltd

26 York Street, London W1U 6PZ
**Tel:** 08451300080 **Fax:** 08701359784
**Web:** www.webfold.co.uk
**Reg No:** 4613601 **Estd:** 2002 Private Limited Company
**Line of Business:** Telecommunication networks
**Issued Capital:** £1
**Director:** K Lawrence
**Co. Secretary:** Ms Deborah Lawrence
**US SIC:** 7379 **UK SIC:** 83940

| | 31-12-13 | 31-12-12 | 31-12-11 |
|---|---|---|---|
| TA | 1,921 | 1,655 | 3,656 |
| NW | 357 | 953 | 2,736 |
| WC | (13) | 400 | 1,570 |

DUNS 71-925-3697

## Webfusion Ltd

**(Subsidiary of:** Host Europe Investments Ltd)
5 Stockley Park Roundwood Avenue, Uxbridge, Middlesex UB11 1FF
**Tel:** 08454502310 **Fax:** 02088135911
**Web:** www.vialtus.com
**Reg No:** 5306504 **Estd:** 2004 Private Limited Company
**Line of Business:** Data processing
**Trading Style:** Vialtus Solutions
**Issued Capital:** £377
**Directors:** R A Winslow, J Shutler
**Co. Secretary:** James Shutler
**US SIC:** 7374 **UK SIC:** 83940
**Auditors:** KPMG Audit PLC

| | 31-12-13 | 31-12-12 | 31-12-11 |
|---|---|---|---|
| TO | 43,092,000 | 39,749,000 | 34,023,000 |
| P/L | 16,611,000 | 28,988,000 | 13,022,000 |
| NW | 68,720,000 | 96,856,000 | 85,407,000 |
| WC | 9,822,000 | 96,139,000 | 54,236,000 |
| Emp. | 146 | 168 | 169 |

DUNS 34-543-4513

## Webgains Ltd

**(Subsidiary of:** Ad Pepper Media International N.V.)
20 Farringdon Road, London EC1M 3HE
**Tel:** 02072691230
**Web:** www.webgains.com
**Reg No:** 5353649 **Estd:** 2005 Private Limited Company
**Line of Business:** Marketing consultants
**Export Sales:** £1,096,704
**Issued Capital:** £560,948
**Directors:** Ms U Handel, P E Dunham, S T Kerin
**Co. Secretary:** Ms Katharine Woo
**Responsibilities**
**Senior:** Jens K rner *(Director)*, Jessica Tait *(Office Manager)*
**US SIC:** 7392 **UK SIC:** 83951
**Bankers:** HSBC Bank plc (40-46-39)

| | 31-12-13 | 31-12-12 | 31-12-11 |
|---|---|---|---|
| TO | 16,203,608 | 12,535,744 | 11,080,867 |
| P/L | 175,535 | 105,268 | 530,282 |
| NW | 473,710 | 666,216 | 1,039,419 |
| WC | 460,198 | 637,570 | 1,017,253 |
| Emp. | 58 | 52 | 40 |

DUNS 23-684-6759

## WeBNET2000 Ltd

15 Consort House, De Montfort Place, Leicester, Leicestershire LE1 7GZ
**Tel:** 01162852444 **Fax:** 01162544901
**Web:** www.webnet2000.net
**Reg No:** 3679708 **Estd:** 1998 Private Limited Company
**Line of Business:** Other computer related activities
**Issued Capital:** £23
**Director:** K Farrington
**Co. Secretary:** Ms Deborah Farrington
**US SIC:** 7379 **UK SIC:** 83940
**Auditors:** Kemp Taylor
**Bankers:** HSBC Bank plc (40-28-06)

| | 31-12-12 | 31-12-11 | 31-12-10 |
|---|---|---|---|
| TA | 168,692 | 166,908 | 199,230 |
| NW | 32,079 | 26,371 | 12,895 |
| WC | 23,746 | (7,667) | (47,874) |

DUNS 22-109-5933 **Imp**

## Websense Uk Ltd

**(Subsidiary of:** Vista Equity Partners Llc)
420 Thames Valley Park Drive, Reading, Berkshire RG6 1PU
**Tel:** 01189388600 **Fax:** 01189388697
**Web:** www.websense.com
**Reg No:** 4128869 **Estd:** 2000 Private Limited Company
**Line of Business:** Other computer related activities
**Export Sales:** £19,170,942
**Issued Capital:** £6,415
**Directors:** J P Borgerding, D L Cochenour, J M Hagan, B Lemay, Ms M E Rodriquez
**Co. Secretary:** Jordan Company Secretaries Limit
**Responsibilities**
**Senior:** Michelle Gipson *(Manager)*, John Mccormack *(Manager)*, Michael Newman *(Manager)*
**Marketing:** Rebecca Eastwood *(Public Relations Director)*, Ben Ross *(Marketing Manager)*
**IT:** Nicole Sanders *(Senior Manager, Global Technic)*
**HR:** Natalie Chotai *(Human Resources Director)*
**US SIC:** 7379 **UK SIC:** 83940
**Auditors:** Ernst & Young
**Bankers:** The Bank Of Ireland (30-11-55)

| | 31-12-13 | 31-12-12 | 31-12-11 |
|---|---|---|---|
| TO | 19,170,942 | 17,007,199 | 18,051,864 |
| P/L | 2,062,138 | (3,938,383) | 3,006,696 |
| NW | (8,064,929) | (8,611,265) | (5,236,653) |
| WC | (8,307,718) | (8,829,625) | (5,494,927) |
| Emp. | 155 | 143 | 149 |

DUNS 21-806-2883 **Imp-Exp**

## Webster & Horsfall Ltd

**(Subsidiary of:** Webster & Horsfall (Holdings) Ltd)
Hay Mills, Birmingham, West Midlands B25 8DW
**Tel:** 01217722555
**Web:** www.websterandhorsfall.co.uk
**Reg No:** 0035630 **VAT No:** 110165430
**Estd:** 1892 Private Limited Company
**Line of Business:** Manufacture of wire products
**Export Markets:** Africa, Middle East, U S A, S & S E Asia, Australasia, Canada
**Issued Capital:** £232,805
**Principals:** C A Horsfall *(Managing)*, R H Horsfall, G M Stokes, J C Horsfall, G R Coshan, M J Sewell
**Co. Secretary:** Harpal Dulai
**Responsibilities**
**Senior:** Darren Jenkins *(Warehouse Manager)*, Elaine Ostroumoff *(Owner)*
**Marketing:** Alison Parkinson *(Buyer)*
**Sales:** Anne Westwood *(Sales Coordinator)*
**IT:** Alison Parkinson *(Buyer)*
**Facilities:** Darren Jenkins *(Warehouse Manager)*
**Purchasing:** Alison Parkinson *(Buyer)*
**Engineering:** Kevin Garner *(Production Manager)*, Jed Stokes *(Engineering Manager)*
**US SIC:** 3406 **UK SIC:** 31694
**Auditors:** Jerroms LLP
**Bankers:** National Westminster Bank Plc (60-02-35)

| | 30-06-14 | 30-06-13 | 30-06-12 |
|---|---|---|---|
| TO | 5,654,559 | 5,748,489 | 9,775,306 |
| P/L | (73,532) | (207,715) | (56,423) |
| NW | 3,292,739 | 3,247,496 | 3,349,801 |
| WC | 1,842,613 | 1,978,982 | 1,980,577 |
| Emp. | 78 | 85 | 87 |

DUNS 21-406-9718

## Webster Contracts Ltd

**(Subsidiary of:** Scotia Homes Ltd)
Kingsmuir, Forfar, Angus DD8 2NS
**Tel:** 01307466161
**Web:** www.scotia-homes.co.uk
**Reg No:** 0049656SC **VAT No:** 268755410
**Estd:** 1946 Private Limited Company
**Line of Business:** Building services
**Issued Capital:** £40,000
**Directors:** Z Michael Luigi, B William Henry, R S Dryburgh
**Co. Secretary:** Michael Zanre
**Responsibilities**
**Senior:** Bill Livingston *(Supervisor)*
**Purchasing:** Malcom Nicholl *(Purchasing Manager)*
**US SIC:** 1622 **UK SIC:** 50200
**Auditors:** Bell & Co
**Bankers:** The Royal Bank Of Scotland Plc (83-20-13)
**Employees:** 60

DUNS 21-730-3551

## Webster Miller Ltd

Unit 3 Burnley Road, Grays, Essex RM20 3EG
**Tel:** 01708-867171
**Web:** www.webstermiller.co.uk
**Reg No:** 0987479 **Estd:** 1970 Private Limited Company
**Line of Business:** Crane sales, service and hire
**Issued Capital:** £2,000
**Directors:** S Steptoe, J Miller
**Co. Secretary:** Ms Linda Miller
**US SIC:** 7394 **UK SIC:** 84000
**Auditors:** Tayler Viney & Marlow
**Bankers:** National Westminster Bank Plc (60-22-06)

| | 31-08-14 | 31-08-13 | 31-08-12 |
|---|---|---|---|
| TA | 1,317,388 | 1,311,277 | 1,184,696 |
| NW | 148,209 | 157,796 | 158,378 |
| WC | (197,232) | (208,792) | (186,612) |

DUNS 22-761-9434 **Imp-Exp**

## Webster-Wilkinson Ltd

**(Subsidiary of:** Melrace Ltd)
Unit A, Halesfield 10, Telford, Shropshire TF7 4QP
**Tel:** 01952-585701 **Fax:** 01952-581901
**Web:** www.webster-wilkinson.com
**Reg No:** 0892102 **VAT No:** 159289812
**Estd:** 1966 Private Limited Company
**Line of Business:** Distribution and trade in electricity
**Export Markets:** Worldwide
**Trading Style:** Webster-Wilkinson & Component Developments
**Issued Capital:** £10,000
**Directors:** T Greenfield, J Russell, K Allison
**Co. Secretary:** Martyn Webster
**Responsibilities**
**Senior:** Leslie Jux *(Manager)*
**US SIC:** 8911, 3643
**UK SIC:** 83701, 34203
**Bankers:** HSBC Bank plc (40-46-04)

| | 31-12-13 | 31-12-12 | 31-12-11 |
|---|---|---|---|
| TA | 2,087,482 | 2,604,419 | 2,787,080 |
| NW | 1,046,968 | 1,017,196 | 1,067,640 |
| WC | 738,280 | 658,948 | 705,945 |

DUNS 28-987-1048 **Imp-Exp**

## Websters International Publishers Ltd

**(Subsidiary of:** Trio Multimedia Ltd)
70 Newcomen Street, London SE1 1YT
**Tel:** 02074037224
**Web:** www.websters.co.uk
**Reg No:** 1805852 **VAT No:** 394596885
**Estd:** 1984 Private Limited Company
**Line of Business:** Other business activities not elsewhere classified
**Export Markets:** Europe and worldwide
**Issued Capital:** £100
**Principals:** A E Webster *(Managing)*, J L Barbanneau, D J Skinner
**Co. Secretary:** Alan Fennell
**US SIC:** 7399, 2741
**UK SIC:** 83954, 47541
**Auditors:** FMCB
**Bankers:** The Royal Bank Of Scotland Plc (16-00-30)

| | 30-06-14 | 30-06-13 | 30-06-12 |
|---|---|---|---|
| TA | 1,160,649 | 1,604,900 | 1,434,403 |
| NW | 784,332 | 827,529 | 878,483 |
| WC | 780,577 | 823,749 | 872,131 |

DUNS 21-913-2172 **Imp-Exp**

## Webtec Products Ltd

Nuffield Road, St Ives, Cambridgeshire PE27 3LZ
**Fax:** 01480-466555
**Web:** www.webtec.co.uk
**Reg No:** 0832125 **VAT No:** 213814489
**Estd:** 1964 Private Limited Company
**Line of Business:** Manufacture of other plastic products
**Export Markets:** Worldwide
**Export Sales:** £4,872,083
**Trading Style:** Webtec Hydraulics, Webster Instruments
**Issued Capital:** £250,000
**Directors:** D C Wassell, N G Moore, S A Cuthbert, G A Watts, M R Cuthbert
**Co. Secretary:** Dhananjay Pandya
**Responsibilities**
**HR:** Peck Howe *(Head of Human Resources)*
**Health & Safety:** Peck Howe *(Head of Human Resources)*
**Engineering:** Andy Peacock *(Engineering Manager)*
**US SIC:** 3999, 3494
**UK SIC:** 49590, 32880
**Auditors:** Deloitte & Touche
**Bankers:** Barclays Bank Plc (20-43-63)

| | 31-10-13 | 31-10-12 | 31-10-11 |
|---|---|---|---|
| TO | 6,099,401 | 6,141,183 | N/A |
| P/L | 850,843 | 1,072,268 | N/A |
| NW | 2,832,940 | 2,535,563 | 1,989,662 |
| WC | 1,994,066 | 1,968,211 | 1,669,389 |
| Emp. | 56 | 52 | N/A |

DUNS 39-780-4675

## Wec Group Ltd

**(Subsidiary of:** Burnhart Holdings Ltd)
Britannia House, Junction Street, Darwen, Lancashire BB3 2RB
**Tel:** 01254773718 **Fax:** 01254700254
**Web:** www.wec-group.com
**Reg No:** 2141828 **Estd:** 2010 Private Limited Company
**Line of Business:** Manufacturers of aerials
**Export Sales:** £685,156
**Issued Capital:** £8,332
**Principals:** J S Hartley *(Managing)*, A B Sedgley, Mrs M A Wild, Ms M B Halliwell, D J Connolly, Ms M G Hartley, W A Wild
**Responsibilities**
**Senior:** Mike Allison *(Sales Manager)*
**US SIC:** 3651, 8911
**UK SIC:** 34541, 83701
**Auditors:** PM&M Solutions for Business LLP
**Bankers:** National Westminster Bank Plc (01-02-57)

| | 31-12-13 | 31-12-12 | 31-12-11 |
|---|---|---|---|
| TO | 28,739,688 | 37,646,812 | 31,783,907 |
| P/L | 2,702,765 | 5,831,050 | 4,102,966 |
| NW | 17,710,026 | 17,107,322 | 12,657,584 |
| WC | 3,480,526 | 5,687,847 | 3,885,438 |
| Emp. | 334 | 402 | 336 |

DUNS 21-586-8750

## Wedgwood Visitor Centre

Wedgwood Drive, Barlaston, Stoke-On-Trent, Staffordshire ST12 9ER
**Tel:** 01782282986
**Web:** www.wedgwoodvisitorcentre.com
**Estd:** 2011 Proprietorship
**Line of Business:** Preservation of historical sites and buildings
**Proprietor:** Miss J Gibson
**Responsibilities**
**Senior:** Lyn Mountford *(Supervisor)*
**US SIC:** 8411 **UK SIC:** 97700
**Employees:** 50

DUNS 21-657-6100

## Wedlake Bell Llp

52 Bedford Row, London WC1R 4LR
**Tel:** 02073953000
**Web:** www.wedlakebell.com
**Reg No:** 0351980OC **Estd:** 2002 Partnership
**Line of Business:** Legal services
**Export Sales:** £4,037,026
**Responsibilities**
**Senior:** Thomas Allfree *(Non-designated Limited Liabili)*, Fay Copeland *(Non-designated Limited Liabili)*, Justin Lewis Vivas *(Non-designated Limited Liabili)*, Matthew Lindsay *(Designated Limited Liability P)*, Malcolm Macfarlane *(Non-designated Limited Liabili)*, Ravinder Mahal *(Non-designated Limited Liabili)*, Eleanor Metcalf *(Designated Limited Liability P)*, John Muncey *(Non-designated Limited Liabili)*, Hilary Platt *(Non-designated Limited Liabili)*, Suzanne Reeves *(Non-designated Limited Liabili)*, Michael Ridsdale *(Non-designated Limited Liabili)*, Michael Sinha *(Designated Limited Liability P)*
**Finance:** Iain Hooper *(Head of Accounts)*
**US SIC:** 8111 **UK SIC:** 83500

| | 31-03-14 | 31-03-13 | 31-03-12 |
|---|---|---|---|
| TO | 27,421,326 | 26,742,188 | 17,964,622 |
| P/L | 6,446,678 | 6,682,710 | 1,863,276 |
| NW | 1,740,476 | 2,421,369 | N/A |
| WC | 10,215,507 | 9,476,825 | 6,060,792 |
| Emp. | 193 | 192 | 163 |

DUNS 20-007-2940

## Weedfree Ltd

**(Subsidiary of:** Railclear Ltd)
Holly Tree Farm, Park Lane, Balne, Goole, North Humberside DN14 0EP
**Tel:** 01405860022 **Fax:** 01405862283
**Web:** www.weedfree.co.uk
**Reg No:** 1246411 **Estd:** 1976 Private Limited Company
**Line of Business:** Agricultural and farm contractors
**Issued Capital:** £400
**Directors:** N Bangham, I C Hornsby
**Co. Secretary:** Richard Stow
**Responsibilities**
**Senior:** Mike Butler *(Sales Manager)*
**Branches:** Weedfree Ltd, Ladds Garden Village, Bath Road, Hare Hatch, Reading, Berkshire RG10 9SB
**US SIC:** 0729, 1795, 8999
**UK SIC:** 01003, 50000, 83954
**Auditors:** Brown Butler
**Bankers:** National Westminster Bank Plc (53-61-07)

| | 31-12-13 | 31-12-12 | 31-12-11 |
|---|---|---|---|
| TA | 2,618,591 | 1,925,973 | 1,660,488 |
| NW | 297,476 | 227,881 | 206,636 |
| WC | 155,012 | 82,975 | 73,337 |

DUNS 21-911-7769 Imp

## Weedon Packaging Solution Centre Ltd

**(Subsidiary of:** Weedon Holdings Ltd)
110 Anglesey Business Park, Cannock, Staffordshire WS12 1NR
**Tel:** 01543-423838 **Fax:** 01543871451
**Web:** www.weedonpsc.com
**Reg No:** 1208323 **Estd:** 1973 Private Limited Company
**Line of Business:** Manufacture of other containers
**Trading Style:** Weedon P S C Groop
**Issued Capital:** £100
**Managing Director:** J D Weedon
**Co. Secretary:** Peter Weedon
**Responsibilities**
**Senior:** John Blackmore *(Senior Finance Administrator)*
**Finance:** Iain Blackmore *(Senior Finance Administrator)*
**US SIC:** 2654 **UK SIC:** 47280
**Auditors:** Baldwins
**Bankers:** Lloyds TSB Bank plc (30-92-59)

| | 31-12-13 | 31-12-12 | 31-12-11 |
|---|---|---|---|
| TO | 9,922,618 | 9,978,505 | 10,895,507 |
| P/L | 182,071 | 256,189 | 558,403 |
| NW | 969,046 | 887,825 | 734,744 |
| WC | 323,201 | 231,770 | (2,153) |
| Emp. | 93 | 103 | 105 |

DUNS 21-880-6958 Imp-Exp

## Weetabix Ltd

**(Subsidiary of:** The Central People's Government of the People's Re)
Weetabix Mills, Kettering, Northamptonshire NN15 5JR
**Tel:** 01536-722-181
**Web:** www.weetabix.co.uk
**Reg No:** 0267687 **VAT No:** 823839803
**Estd:** 1932 Private Limited Company
**Line of Business:** Representative office
**Export Sales:** £55,091,000
**Trading Style:** Weetabix Food Company
**Issued Capital:** £2,969,004
**Directors:** R J Schofield, L Lin, R W Martin, V F Benazach, G M Turrell, W Lili, C Xiaofeng, D Halstenberg
**Co. Secretary:** Lyne Booth
**Responsibilities**
**Senior:** Kelvin Jinjell *(Distribution Manager)*
**Marketing:** Tony Corp *(Marketing Controller)*
**Sales:** David Revell *(Sales Director)*
**IT:** Bruce Langford *(IT Infrastructure Specialist)*, Logan Tweedie *(ITand Business Systems Manage)*
**HR:** Noel Burton *(Training Manager)*, John Evoy *(Human Resources Director)*
**Health & Safety:** Micahel Emery *(Health & Safety Officer)*
**Facilities:** Damian McGill *(Engineering Manager)*
**Operations:** David Revell *(Sales Director)*
**Fleet:** Kelvin Jinjell *(Distribution Manager)*
**Branches:** Weetabix Ltd, Fatory 1 Earlstree Industrial Estate, Earlstrees Road, Earlstrees Industrial Estate, Corby, Northamptonshire NN17 4AZ
**US SIC:** 2099 **UK SIC:** 42399
**Auditors:** PricewaterhouseCoopers LLP
**Bankers:** Barclays Bank Plc (20-45-77)

| | 28-12-13 | 29-12-12 | 31-12-11 |
|---|---|---|---|
| TO | 366,398,000 | 354,652,000 | 335,005,000 |
| P/L | 116,039,000 | 95,690,000 | 86,177,000 |
| NW | 610,831,000 | 524,215,000 | 741,383,000 |
| WC | 487,898,000 | 407,217,000 | 630,596,000 |
| Emp. | 1,063 | 1,076 | 1,102 |

DUNS 76-853-5064

## Weetwood Hall Ltd

Weetwood Hall Hotel Training &, Conference Centre, Otley Road, Leeds, West Yorkshire LS16 5PS
**Tel:** 01132306000 **Fax:** 01132226095
**Web:** www.weetwood.co.uk
**Reg No:** 2609047 **VAT No:** 545699003
**Estd:** 1991 Private Limited Company
**Line of Business:** Hotels
**Trading Style:** Weetwood Hall Conference Centre & Hotel
**Issued Capital:** £130,100
**Principals:** M L Hicks *(Managing)*, Professor P Moizer, D Hopper, A C Roberts, O T Morton, J D Stoddart-Scott
**Co. Secretary:** Ms Helena Smith
**Responsibilities**
**Senior:** Michael Longstaff *(Facilities Manager)*
**Facilities:** Michael Longstaff *(Facilities Manager)*
**US SIC:** 7011 **UK SIC:** 66500
**Auditors:** Deloitte LLP
**Bankers:** Barclays Bank Plc (20-48-46)

| | 31-07-14 | 31-07-13 | 31-07-12 |
|---|---|---|---|
| TO | 4,925,165 | 4,856,753 | 4,411,947 |
| P/L | 301,350 | 233,044 | 133,018 |
| NW | 4,094,192 | 3,888,857 | 3,726,331 |
| WC | (775,035) | (685,693) | (716,087) |
| Emp. | 123 | 125 | 122 |

DUNS 21-329-8599 Imp-Exp

## Weidmann Whiteley Ltd

**(Subsidiary of:** Wicor Holding Ag)
Pool Road In-Wharfedale, Otley, West Yorkshire LS21 1RP
**Tel:** 01132027000
**Web:** www.weidmannelectrical.com
**Reg No:** 1531157 **VAT No:** 343199056
**Estd:** 1981 Private Limited Company
**Line of Business:** Manufacture of other containers
**Export Sales:** £9,067,829
**Issued Capital:** £5,000,000
**Director:** J Brunner
**Co. Secretary:** John Briggs
**Responsibilities**
**Senior:** Toby Albrecht *(Sales & Marketing Manager)*, Ron Pegg *(Computer Systems Administrator)*
**Marketing:** Toby Albrecht *(Sales & Marketing Manager)*
**Sales:** Toby Albrecht *(Sales & Marketing Manager)*
**IT:** Ron Pegg *(Computer Systems Administrator)*
**Health & Safety:** Brian Richerby *(Health & Safety Manager)*
**Operations:** Toby Albrecht *(Sales & Marketing Manager)*, Mike Gosling *(Technical Manager)*
**US SIC:** 2654 **UK SIC:** 47280
**Auditors:** Ernst & Young LLP
**Bankers:** National Westminster Bank Plc (54-21-20)

| | 31-12-13 | 31-12-12 | 31-12-11 |
|---|---|---|---|
| TO | 13,941,337 | 14,963,494 | 17,202,758 |
| P/L | (1,458,963) | (996,893) | 431,222 |
| NW | 826,878 | 1,450,841 | 2,561,918 |
| WC | 2,728,589 | 2,678,781 | 4,060,590 |
| Emp. | 103 | 101 | 109 |

DUNS 28-886-9936

## Weight Watchers (Exercise) Ltd.

**(Subsidiary of:** Weight Watchers International Inc.)
Millenium House, Ludlow Road, Maidenhead, Berkshire SL6 2SL
**Tel:** 08453451500 **Fax:** 01628-415205
**Web:** www.weightwatchers.co.uk
**Reg No:** 1243290 **Estd:** 1976 Private Limited Company
**Line of Business:** Sports clubs
**Issued Capital:** £2
**Directors:** Ms J Lemmens, J Chambers, N Hotchkin
**US SIC:** 7999 **UK SIC:** 97913
**Bankers:** Barclays Bank Plc (20-66-11)

| | 31-12-13 | 31-12-12 | 31-12-11 |
|---|---|---|---|
| TA | 9,385 | 9,385 | 9,385 |
| NW | (574,099) | (574,099) | (574,099) |
| WC | (574,099) | (574,099) | (574,099) |

DUNS 28-887-5149 Imp

## Weight Watchers (U.K.) Ltd

**(Subsidiary of:** Weight Watchers International Inc.)
Millennium House, Ludlow Road, Maidenhead, Berkshire SL6 2SL
**Tel:** 01628777077
**Web:** www.weightwatchers.co.uk
**Reg No:** 1248588 **VAT No:** 578384585
**Estd:** 1976 Private Limited Company
**Line of Business:** Physical well-being activities
**Trading Style:** Weight Watcher At Home
**Issued Capital:** £50,000
**Directors:** N Hotchkin, Ms J Lemmens, J Chambers
**Responsibilities**
**Senior:** Jeffrey Fiarman *(Manager)*, Melanie Stubbings *(International President)*, Louise Timms *(Brand Manager)*
**Finance:** Sarah Scammell *(Financial Director)*
**IT:** Sanjeev Dhalla *(Computer Manager)*
**HR:** Louisa Chipperfield *(Human Resources Manager)*, Susi Petherick *(Training Manager)*
**Branches:** Weight Watchers (U.k.) Ltd, 10 The Moore, Melborn, Royston, Hertfordshire SG8 6ED
**US SIC:** 7399 **UK SIC:** 83954
**Auditors:** PricewaterhouseCoopers LLP
**Bankers:** National Westminster Bank Plc (60-19-28)

| | 31-12-13 | 31-12-12 | 31-12-11 |
|---|---|---|---|
| TO | 78,590,000 | 96,902,000 | 110,083,000 |
| P/L | 4,416,000 | 14,826,000 | 17,263,000 |
| NW | 67,282,000 | 63,815,000 | 53,173,000 |
| WC | 66,041,000 | 62,481,000 | 51,570,000 |
| Emp. | 2,091 | 2,212 | 1,183 |

DUNS 21-919-7324 Imp

## Weightlifter Bodies Ltd

**(Subsidiary of:** New Month Ltd)
Grange Lane North, Scunthorpe, South Humberside DN16 1BN
**Tel:** 01724-872444
**Web:** http://weightlifterbodies.com
**Reg No:** 1431854 **VAT No:** 317359451
**Estd:** 1977 Private Limited Company
**Line of Business:** Manufacture of bodies (coachwork) for motor vehicles (except caravans)
**Issued Capital:** £1,572
**Directors:** R A Nichols, G R Simons
**Co. Secretary:** Keith Hunt
**Responsibilities**
**Senior:** Frederick Mollon *(Manager)*, P Weightman *(Manager)*
**Engineering:** Luke Richardson *(Design Engineer)*
**US SIC:** 3713, 3715
**UK SIC:** 35201, 35220
**Auditors:** Streets Audit LLP
**Bankers:** HSBC Bank plc (40-40-24)

| | 31-03-14 | 30-06-13 | 30-03-12 |
|---|---|---|---|
| TO | 7,534,262 | 8,469,636 | 12,493,534 |
| P/L | 139,040 | (350,609) | (890,832) |
| NW | 2,867,714 | 3,215,067 | 3,400,906 |
| WC | 852,628 | 1,178,444 | 1,379,433 |
| Emp. | 84 | 86 | 89 |

DUNS 21-924-0434

## Weightmans Llp

100 Old Hall Street, Liverpool, Merseyside L3 9QJ
**Tel:** 08450739900
**Web:** www.weightmans.com
**Reg No:** 0326117OC **VAT No:** 974825769
**Estd:** 2007
**Line of Business:** Solicitors
**Responsibilities**
**Senior:** Carole Atkinson *(Head of Legal)*, Kiran Bhogal *(Non-designated Limited Liabili)*, Clive Bleasdale *(Non-designated Limited Liabili)*, Beth Buchanan *(Non-designated Limited Liabili)*, James Byard *(Non-designated Limited Liabili)*, Elaine Chapman *(Non-designated Limited Liabili)*, Victoria Coleman *(Non-designated Limited Liabili)*, Robert Crossingham *(Non-designated Limited Liabili)*, Paul Debney *(Non-designated Limited Liabili)*, Sarah Ellington *(Non-designated Limited Liabili)*, Rena Field *(Non-designated Limited Liabili)*, Martin Forshaw *(Non-designated Limited Liabili)*, Mark Hatfield *(Partner - Employment)*, Sarah Howitt *(Marketing Director)*, Roland Hutchins *(Partner, Firm's Corporate and)*, Nicholas Peel *(Partner - Police Team)*, Paul Raftery *(Head of Department)*, Joanne Shelston *(Associate)*, Dominic Vincent *(Partner)*, Janice Weatherly *(Partner - Real Estate)*, Emlyn Williams *(Partner)*, Bernadette Worthington *(Partner)*
**Marketing:** Sarah Howitt *(Marketing Director)*
**HR:** Sam Airey *(Human Resources Director)*
**Facilities:** Malcolm Boardman *(Project Manager)*, Andrea Steventon *(Property Services and Faciliti)*
**Operations:** Sarah Howitt *(Marketing Director)*
**Purchasing:** Malcolm Boardman *(Project Manager)*
**Branches:** Weightmans Llp, 47 Cannon Street City Plaza, Birmingham, West Midlands B2 5EF
**US SIC:** 8111, 7399
**UK SIC:** 83500, 83954
**Auditors:** Deloitte LLP
**Bankers:** Allied Irish Bank (gb) (23-84-03)

| | 30-04-14 | 30-04-13 | 30-04-12 |
|---|---|---|---|
| TO | 87,603,000 | 81,679,000 | 77,480,000 |
| P/L | 24,898,000 | 23,914,000 | 21,080,000 |
| NW | 11,393,000 | 10,818,000 | 7,521,000 |
| WC | 27,170,000 | 21,655,000 | 22,651,000 |
| Emp. | 1,236 | 994 | 1,079 |

DUNS 22-867-0915 Imp-Exp

## Weilburger Coatings (Uk) Ltd

**(Subsidiary of:** Stretford Holdings Ltd)
9 Stuart Road, Runcorn, Cheshire WA7 1SF
**Tel:** 01928-570900 **Fax:** 01928-579235
**Web:** www.trimite.com
**Reg No:** 1564257 **VAT No:** 344058172
**Estd:** 1981 Private Limited Company
**Line of Business:** Coating companies
**Export Markets:** Worldwide
**Trading Style:** Weilburger
**Issued Capital:** £926,370
**Directors:** Grebe Financial Services Gmbh, S Mountain, D G Roberts, M B Franckel
**Co. Secretary:** Jonathan Irwin
**Responsibilities**
**Senior:** Christopher Heywood *(Financial Controller)*
**Finance:** Christopher Heywood *(Financial Controller)*
**US SIC:** 2891 **UK SIC:** 25620
**Auditors:** Bennett Brooks & Co Ltd
**Bankers:** National Westminster Bank Plc (01-09-17)

| | 31-03-14 | 31-03-13 | 31-03-12 |
|---|---|---|---|
| TO | 11,547,727 | 10,508,054 | 9,128,653 |
| P/L | 103,400 | (757,098) | (1,208,954) |
| NW | (2,724,721) | (2,942,168) | (2,110,273) |
| WC | (2,448,680) | (2,642,094) | (2,185,967) |
| Emp. | 77 | 79 | 80 |

DUNS 21-585-4764

## Weima Uk

Unit 1 Old Mill Lane, Aylesford, Kent ME20 7DT
**Tel:** 08704282688
**Web:** www.weima.com
**Estd:** 1977 Proprietorship
**Line of Business:** Document disposal and shredding equipment
**Proprietor:** M Fletcher
**US SIC:** 3579 **UK SIC:** 33010
**Employees:** 50

DUNS 21-583-3518

## Weir & McQuiston (Scotland) Ltd

Mcarthur House, 201 Netherton Street, Wishaw, Lanarkshire ML2 0EF
**Tel:** 01698-372113 **Fax:** 01698377269
**Web:** www.wmq.biz
**Reg No:** 0060469SC **VAT No:** 262751752
**Estd:** 1976 Private Limited Company
**Line of Business:** Installation of electrical wiring and fittings
**Trading Style:** W M Q Building Services
**Issued Capital:** £2,042
**Principals:** J Mcarthur *(Managing)*, D Mcneill, G Mcarthur, J Crossar
**Co. Secretary:** Ms Jacqueline Mcarthur
**Responsibilities**
**Senior:** Andrew Eadie *(Manager)*, Calum Shields *(Purchasing Manager)*
**HR:** Joanne Whiteford *(Human Resources Manager)*
**Health & Safety:** Heidi Campbell *(Health & Safety Officer)*
**Purchasing:** Calum Shields *(Purchasing Manager)*
**US SIC:** 1731 **UK SIC:** 50300
**Auditors:** Gillespie & Anderson

**Bankers:** The Royal Bank Of Scotland Plc (83-25-45)

| | 31-05-14 | 31-05-13 | 31-05-12 |
|---|---|---|---|
| TO | 11,413,559 | 9,881,218 | 9,295,866 |
| P/L | 549,418 | (43,083) | (632,380) |
| NW | 2,361,142 | 1,938,733 | 1,988,392 |
| WC | 1,650,685 | 1,236,460 | 1,261,119 |
| Emp. | 91 | 99 | 93 |

DUNS 21-443-2858 **Exp**

## The Weir Group Plc

Clydesdale Bank Exchange, Glasgow, Lanarkshire G2 6DB

**Tel:** 01416-377111 **Fax:** 01412-218789

**Web:** www.weir.co.uk

**Reg No:** 0002934SC **Estd:** 2013 Public Limited Company

**Line of Business:** Management activities of holding companies

**Export Sales:** £2,325,000,000

**Trading Style:** Weir Oil & Gas, Weir Power & Industrial

**Issued Capital:** £26,700,331

**Directors:** R P Menell, J A Stanton, Ms M J Jacobi, J Mcdonald, J Mogford, A M Ferguson, Ms M Gee, C A Berry

**Co. Secretary:** Keith Ruddock

**Responsibilities**

**Senior:** Keith Cochrane *(Director)*

**Finance:** Keith Cochrane *(Director)*, John Stanton *(Finance Director)*

**Marketing:** Joan McIntosh *(Marketing Manager)*

**IT:** Leslie Powell *(Group Head of Information Serv)*

**Health & Safety:** David Beard *(Health & Safety Director)*

**Branches:** The Weir Group Plc, Bramah Avenue, Glasgow, Lanarkshire G75 0RD

**US SIC:** 6711, 8911

**UK SIC:** 83962, 83701

**Auditors:** Ernst & Young LLP

**Bankers:** The Royal Bank Of Scotland Plc (83-07-06)

**Following financial data are in thousands**

| | 03-01-14 | 28-12-12 | 30-01-11 |
|---|---|---|---|
| TO | 2,429,800 | 2,538,300 | 2,292,000 |
| P/L | 431,200 | 424,000 | 391,500 |
| NW | (132,300) | (147,000) | (216,600) |
| WC | 512,300 | 766,800 | 342,700 |
| Emp. | 13,750 | 13,245 | 13,996 |

DUNS 21-360-5873 **Exp**

## Weir Lge Process

42 Research Park, Edinburgh, Midlothian EH14 4AP

**Tel:** 0131-3178787

**Web:** www.lgeprocess.com

**Estd:** 1992 Proprietorship

**Line of Business:** Design engineers

**Proprietor:** R Davis

**Responsibilities**

**Marketing:** Alan Duckett *(Sales & Marketing Director)*

**Sales:** Alan Duckett *(Sales & Marketing Director)*

**IT:** Martin Halcrow *(IT Manager)*

**Health & Safety:** Maurice Turner *(Facilities Manager)*

**Facilities:** Maurice Turner *(Facilities Manager)*

**Purchasing:** Fiona Kane *(Purchasing Manager)*

**US SIC:** 8911 **UK SIC:** 83701

**Employees:** 80

DUNS 21-242-3768 **Imp-Exp**

## Weir Minerals Europe Ltd

(**Subsidiary of:** The Weir Group Plc)

Halifax Road, Todmorden, Lancashire OL14 5RT

**Tel:** 01706814251

**Web:** www.weirminerals.com

**Reg No:** 0076959 **VAT No:** 183592731

**Estd:** 1893 Private Limited Company

**Line of Business:** Wholesale of other machinery for use in industry, trade and navigation

**Export Markets:** Europe, U S A, Canada, E Europe, Middle East

**Export Sales:** £118,043,000

**Issued Capital:** £1,600,000

**Directors:** C Zaalberg, A G Locke

**Co. Secretary:** David Stephenson

**Responsibilities**

**Senior:** Samuel Crossley *(Manager)*

**IT:** Tayler Moreland *(IT Technician)*

**US SIC:** 5084 **UK SIC:** 61490

**Auditors:** Ernst & Young LLP

**Bankers:** The Royal Bank Of Scotland Plc (83-07-06)

| | 03-01-14 | 28-12-12 | 30-01-11 |
|---|---|---|---|
| TO | 130,122,000 | 121,130,000 | 83,220,000 |
| P/L | 18,175,000 | 20,349,000 | 13,968,000 |
| NW | 54,469,000 | 46,208,000 | 38,331,000 |
| WC | 46,315,000 | 35,337,000 | 31,623,000 |
| Emp. | 518 | 508 | 493 |

DUNS 21-860-4163 **Imp**

## Weir Minor and Willis Ltd

(**Subsidiary of:** Enghouse Systems Limited)

241 Wellington Road, Birmingham, West Midlands B20 2EA

**Tel:** 01213-444-554

**Web:** www.mww.co.uk

**Reg No:** 0776793 **VAT No:** 110223251

**Estd:** 1963 Private Limited Company

**Line of Business:** Food import and exporters and agents

**Export Sales:** £977,724

**Issued Capital:** £7,500

**Principals:** P K Mehta *(Financial)*, S K Mehta *(Marketing)*, S K Mehta, R S Gill

**Co. Secretary:** Stephen Vale

**Responsibilities**

**Senior:** Abdul Saleem *(Warehouse Manager)*

**IT:** Paul Swan *(IT Manager)*

**Health & Safety:** Mark Driver *(Health & Safety Officer)*

**Operations:** Mark Driver *(Health & Safety Officer)*

**Branches:** Minor, Weir and Willis Ltd, Smithfield Market, Wholesale Markets Precinct, Pershore Street, Birmingham, West Midlands B5 6UN

**US SIC:** 5149 **UK SIC:** 61700

**Auditors:** Grant Thornton UK LLP

**Bankers:** National Westminster Bank Plc (52-30-02)

| | 31-12-13 | 31-12-12 | 31-12-11 |
|---|---|---|---|
| TO | 137,378,503 | 123,571,210 | 108,103,908 |
| P/L | 3,108,007 | 2,155,848 | 2,108,724 |
| NW | 13,496,482 | 12,862,859 | 11,196,427 |
| WC | 12,557,659 | 11,780,127 | 10,322,026 |
| Emp. | 210 | 207 | 208 |

DUNS 21-213-7657 **Imp-Exp**

## Weir Valves & Controls Uk Ltd

(**Subsidiary of:** The Weir Group Plc)

Britannia House, Huddersfield Road, Elland, West Yorkshire HX5 9JR

**Tel:** 01422-282000 **Fax:** 01422-282100

**Web:** www.weirpowerindustrial.com

**Reg No:** 0869208 **VAT No:** 183349544

**Estd:** 1966 Private Limited Company

**Line of Business:** Other manufacturing not elsewhere classified

**Trading Style:** Hopkinsons Engineering Services, Blakeborough Control Valves

**Issued Capital:** £11,264,000

**Directors:** M N Mannion, P J Crookes, Ms J G Magowan, J Heasley, R Griffin

**Co. Secretary:** Walter Clark

**Responsibilities**

**Senior:** Janice Kelly *(Logistics Manager)*, Katie Lewis *(Logistics Manager)*

**HR:** Colin Somers *(Human Resources Manager)*

**Health & Safety:** Colin Somers *(Human Resources Manager)*

**Facilities:** Colin Somers *(Human Resources Manager)*

**Operations:** Colin Somers *(Human Resources Manager)*

**Fleet:** Janice Kelly *(Logistics Manager)*

**Branches:** Weir Valves & Controls Uk Ltd, Unit 5 and 11 Llandough Trad Est, Penarth Rd, Cardiff, South Glamorgan CF11 8RR

**US SIC:** 3999 **UK SIC:** 49590

**Auditors:** Ernst & Young LLP

**Bankers:** The Royal Bank Of Scotland Plc (83-07-06)

| | 03-01-14 | 28-12-12 | 30-01-11 |
|---|---|---|---|
| TO | 47,773,000 | 36,590,000 | 35,309,000 |
| P/L | (1,885,000) | (1,024,000) | 1,717,000 |
| NW | 11,039,000 | 14,262,000 | 15,621,000 |
| WC | 10,203,000 | 14,025,000 | 14,884,000 |
| Emp. | 229 | 220 | 211 |

DUNS 23-784-1361

## Weir Waste Services Ltd

Fawdry House, Birmingham, West Midlands B7 4TS

**Tel:** 0121-772-6726 **Fax:** 0121-773-1244

**Web:** www.weirwaste.co.uk

**Reg No:** 3777183 **Estd:** 1994 Private Limited Company

**Line of Business:** Collection and treatment of other waste

**Issued Capital:** £100,000

**Directors:** D J Weir, A N Veal

**Co. Secretary:** Mrs Pamela Weir

**Responsibilities**

**Admin:** Louise Mumford *(Office Manager)*

**US SIC:** 4953, 3341

**UK SIC:** 92110, 22470

**Auditors:** R K Thomas & Co

**Bankers:** Lloyds TSB Bank plc (77-85-65)

| | 31-05-13 | 31-05-12 | 31-05-11 |
|---|---|---|---|
| TO | 11,797,130 | 11,119,954 | 10,505,260 |
| P/L | 533,325 | 626,604 | 815,694 |
| NW | 2,543,971 | 2,373,616 | 2,149,784 |
| WC | 55,614 | (425,533) | (668,029) |
| Emp. | 98 | 95 | 93 |

DUNS 21-628-5076

## Weird Fish Holdings Ltd

Unit 2 Rutherford Way, Swindon Village, Swindon Village, Cheltenham, Gloucestershire GL51 9TU

**Tel:** 01786825797

**Web:** www.weirdfish.co.uk

**Reg No:** 7076354 **Estd:** 2009 Private Limited Company

**Line of Business:** Management activities of holding companies

**Export Sales:** £444,934

**Issued Capital:** £666,119

**Directors:** C J Curry, Ms E Gibson, G S Dawson, J Stockton, A Stafford

**Co. Secretary:** Jon Goodwin

**Responsibilities**

**Senior:** Spencer Marriott-Dodington *(Manager)*

**US SIC:** 6711 **UK SIC:** 83962

| | 31-12-13 | 31-12-12 | 31-12-11 |
|---|---|---|---|
| TO | 13,792,532 | 12,979,202 | 11,897,730 |
| P/L | (1,319,256) | (1,458,585) | (1,054,909) |
| NW | (10,274,147) | (9,343,218) | (8,287,465) |
| WC | 360,530 | 553,725 | 141,926 |
| Emp. | 123 | 113 | 92 |

DUNS 23-664-3057

## Weiss Technik Uk Ltd

(**Subsidiary of:** Ludwig Schunk-Stiftung E.V.)

Unit 37-38 Loughborough Technology, Centre, Epinal Way, Loughborough, Leicestershire LE11 3GE

**Web:** www.weiss-uk.com

**Reg No:** 3659232 **Estd:** 1998 Private Limited Company

**Line of Business:** Refrigeration equipment (commercial and industrial)

**Export Sales:** £3,347,186

**Trading Style:** Weiss Technik

**Issued Capital:** £1,500,000

**Directors:** P A Downes, T Joerdens, P Manolopoulos

**Co. Secretary:** Alison Fox

**Responsibilities**

**Senior:** Arno Roth *(Manager)*

**Marketing:** Garry Taylor *(Sales & Marketing Manager)*

**Sales:** Julie Chinn *(Sales Executive)*, Garry Taylor *(Sales & Marketing Manager)*

**US SIC:** 3585, 8999

**UK SIC:** 32841, 83954

**Auditors:** Clough & Co LLP

**Bankers:** Lloyds TSB Bank plc (30-99-21)

| | 31-12-13 | 31-12-12 | 31-12-11 |
|---|---|---|---|
| TO | 11,390,137 | 7,505,673 | 7,152,821 |
| P/L | (358,916) | (187,377) | 228,775 |
| NW | 723,127 | 1,480,140 | 1,926,187 |
| WC | 77,322 | 1,222,264 | 1,683,298 |
| Emp. | 94 | 34 | 33 |

DUNS 21-919-1749

## The Welbeck Estates Co Ltd

Portland Estate Office, Cavendish House, Welbeck, Worksop, Nottinghamshire S80 3LL

**Tel:** 01909-500211

**Web:** www.welbeck.co.uk

**Reg No:** 0689754 **Estd:** 1961 Private Limited Company

**Line of Business:** Other letting of own property

**Issued Capital:** £821,200

**Directors:** H J Parente, M P Swan, Ms D M Parente, W H Parente

**Co. Secretary:** Robin Brown

**Responsibilities**

**Finance:** Bryan Chambers *(Financial Controller)*

**IT:** Sue Beaumont *(Senior IT Executive)*

**Branches:** The Welbeck Estates Co Ltd, Portland Estate Office, Berriedale, Caithness KW7 6HB

**US SIC:** 6519, 6531

**UK SIC:** 85000, 83400

**Auditors:** Saffery Champness

**Bankers:** Yorkshire Bank Plc (05-09-89)

| | 31-03-14 | 28-02-13 | 29-03-12 |
|---|---|---|---|
| TO | 14,534,000 | 11,489,000 | 11,170,000 |
| P/L | 10,668,000 | (999,000) | 1,440,000 |
| NW | 184,436,000 | 174,009,000 | 84,172,000 |
| WC | 2,021,000 | (1,511,000) | 8,664,000 |
| Emp. | 130 | 112 | 108 |

DUNS 21-592-1267

## Welbeck Group

4th Floor City Place House, 55 Basinghall Street, London EC2V 5DX

**Tel:** 020 7776 2000

**Web:** www.welbeckgroup.co.uk

**Estd:** 2011 Proprietorship

**Line of Business:** Credit and finance companies

**Proprietor:** Mrs K Booth

**US SIC:** 6111 **UK SIC:** 81501

**Employees:** 80

DUNS 21-770-6854

## Welbeck Primary School

Flodden Street, Newcastle-Upon-Tyne, Tyne and Wear NE6 2QL

**Tel:** 01912655362

**Web:** www.welbeckacademy.co.uk

**Estd:** 1990 Proprietorship

**Line of Business:** Schools (local authority)

**Proprietor:** Mrs B Redhead

**US SIC:** 8211 **UK SIC:** 93200

**Employees:** 50

DUNS 21-032-5434

## Welbeck the Defence Sixth Form College

Forest Road, Woodhouse, Loughborough, Leicestershire LE12 8WD

**Tel:** 01509891700

**Web:** www.dsfc.ac.uk

**Line of Business:** Sixth form colleges

**Responsibilities**

**Senior:** Tony Halliwell *(Principal)*

**US SIC:** 8221 **UK SIC:** 93100

**Employees:** 500

DUNS 23-005-4525

## Welbourn Hall Nursing Home

Hall Lane, Welbourn, Lincoln, Lincolnshire LN5 0NN

**Tel:** 01400272771

**Web:** www.welbournhall.co.uk

**Estd:** 1989 Proprietorship

**Line of Business:** Nursing homes

**Proprietor:** Mrs J Lawton

**Responsibilities**

**Senior:** Cathy Browne *(Manager)*, Jayne Finnis *(Business Manager)*

**US SIC:** 8051 **UK SIC:** 95100

**Employees:** 50

DUNS 22-801-9436 **Exp**

## Welch's Group Holdings Ltd

Granta Terrace, Cambridge, Cambridgeshire CB22 5DL

**Tel:** 01223-843011

**Web:** www.welchgroup.co.uk

**Reg No:** 1554970 **Estd:** 1981 Private Limited Company

**Line of Business:** Freight transport by road not elsewhere classified

**Issued Capital:** £16,221

**Principals:** R N Welch *(Managing)*, A G Welch

**Co. Secretary:** James Welch

**Responsibilities**

**Sales:** Ian Lawton *(Business Development Manager)*

**Health & Safety:** Ian Lawton *(Business Development Manager)*

**Purchasing:** Ian Lawton *(Business Development Manager)*

**US SIC:** 4213 **UK SIC:** 72300

**Auditors:** Peters Elworthy & Moore

**Bankers:** Barclays Bank Plc (20-17-19)

| | 31-12-13 | 31-12-12 | 31-12-11 |
|---|---|---|---|
| TO | 12,304,742 | 12,721,501 | 13,273,025 |
| P/L | 5,044,830 | (30,613) | 133,227 |
| NW | 15,985,498 | 10,942,822 | 10,826,969 |
| WC | 8,731,022 | 2,999,000 | 2,753,631 |
| Emp. | 143 | 148 | 147 |

DUNS 34-519-7805 **Exp**

## Welcom Software Holdings Ltd

The Exchange, Station Parade, Harrogate, North Yorkshire HG1 1TS

**Tel:** 08454565859 **Fax:** 0845-456-5253

**Web:** www.welcom.co.uk

**Reg No:** 5330495 **Estd:** 2005 Private Limited Company

**Line of Business:** Management activities of other non-financial holding companies not elsewhere classified

**Issued Capital:** £10,000

**Directors:** N A Welch, Mrs K J Welch

**US SIC:** 6711 **UK SIC:** 83962

| | 31-03-14 | 31-03-13 | 31-03-12 |
|---|---|---|---|
| TO | N/A | N/A | 454,874 |
| P/L | N/A | N/A | 436,128 |
| NW | 5,276,953 | 5,427,771 | 5,011,711 |
| WC | 2,496,009 | 2,646,827 | N/A |

DUNS 21-891-8816

## Welcom Software Llp

The Exchange, Station Parade, Harrogate, North Yorkshire HG1 1TS

**Tel:** 01423851170

**Web:** www.welcom.co.uk

**Reg No:** 0325626OC **Estd:** 2007 Private Limited Company

**Line of Business:** Publishing of software

**Principals:** S Sutherland, Mrs J Paterson, N Jheeta, I Dugdale, I N Corp, N A Welch, Welcom Software Holdings Limited, Welcom Digital Limited

**Responsibilities**
**Senior:** Frances Chalmers *(Non-designated Limited Liabili)*, Catherine Corp *(Non-designated Limited Liabili)*, Jonathan Meller *(Non-designated Limited Liabili)*, Sylvester Morgan *(Non-designated Limited Liabili)*, Alyas Razzaq *(Non-designated Limited Liabili)*, Fiona Rule *(Non-designated Limited Liabili)*
**US SIC:** 7372 **UK SIC:** 83940

| | 31-03-14 | 31-03-13 | 31-03-12 |
|---|---|---|---|
| TO | N/A | 4,942,435 | 5,279,333 |
| NW | 14,700 | 14,200 | 14,400 |
| WC | 2,683,052 | 3,164,946 | 2,721,562 |
| Emp. | N/A | 48 | 16 |

DUNS 22-098-0069
## Welcome Break Holdings (1) Ltd
(**Subsidiary of:** Appia Group Limited)
2 Vantage Court, Pickford Street, Newport Pagnell, Buckinghamshire MK16 9EZ
**Tel:** 01908299700 **Fax:** 01908299701
**Web:** www.welcomebreak.co.uk
**Reg No:** 4099287 **Estd:** 1996 Private Limited Company
**Line of Business:** Management activities of other non-financial holding companies not elsewhere classified
**Issued Capital:** £1,000
**Directors:** D A Love, Ms A Grandin, R W Mckie, A T Kawonczyk, Mrs L M Parsons, N D Wright, D S Kyte, M D Canham
**US SIC:** 6711 **UK SIC:** 00902
**Auditors:** PricewaterhouseCoopers LLP

| | 28-01-14 | 29-01-13 | 31-01-12 |
|---|---|---|---|
| TO | 620,259,000 | 611,706,000 | 606,945,000 |
| P/L | 10,127,000 | 13,213,000 | 5,007,000 |
| NW | 402,410,000 | 400,701,000 | 403,338,000 |
| WC | 352,821,000 | 351,665,000 | 440,660,000 |
| Emp. | 4,087 | 4,063 | 4,010 |

DUNS 21-332-5053
## Welcome Financial Services Ltd
(**Subsidiary of:** Sfm Holdings Ltd)
Ruddington Fields Business Park Mere Way, Nottingham, Nottinghamshire NG11 6NZ
**Tel:** 01159849200 **Fax:** 01159-778892
**Web:** www.wfs.co.uk
**Reg No:** 0133540 **Estd:** 1990 Private Limited Company
**Line of Business:** Credit granting by non-deposit taking finance houses and other specialist consumer credit grantors
**Trading Style:** Shoppercheck, Welcome Car Finance, Welcomefinance
**Issued Capital:** £101,139,767
**Directors:** J M Briggs, R D East, R S Johnson, J R Drummond Smith
**Co. Secretary:** Roland Todd
**Responsibilities**
**HR:** Lynne Farrage *(Hr Director)*
**Branches:** Welcome Financial Services Ltd, Swan Depot Swan Road, Washington, Tyne and Wear NE38 8JJ
**US SIC:** 6111 **UK SIC:** 81501
**Auditors:** Grant Thornton UK LLP
**Bankers:** The Royal Bank Of Scotland Plc (16-22-11)
**Following financial data are in thousands**

| | 31-12-13 | 31-12-12 | 31-12-11 |
|---|---|---|---|
| TA | 390,007 | 471,067 | 625,778 |
| P/L | (28,498) | (172,719) | 1,943,177 |
| NW | 90,131 | 118,493 | 290,719 |
| WC | (51,988) | 110,415 | 149,765 |
| Emp. | 952 | 1,159 | 1,476 |

DUNS 21-625-5853
## Welcome Furniture (Sales) Ltd
Welcome Furniture, 1 Cibyn Industrial Estate, Caernarfon, Gwynedd LL55 2BD
**Tel:** 08445883353
**Reg No:** 7053896 **Estd:** 2009 Private Limited Company
**Line of Business:** Manufacture of other furniture
**Issued Capital:** £100
**Directors:** J Peterson, R Matthews
**Co. Secretary:** Simon Montague
**US SIC:** 2517 **UK SIC:** 46714

| | 31-03-14 | 31-03-13 | 31-03-12 |
|---|---|---|---|
| TO | 12,332,771 | 12,417,994 | 12,630,319 |
| P/L | 896,889 | 693,114 | 696,609 |
| NW | 1,698,250 | 1,553,779 | 1,394,270 |
| WC | (30,813) | (249,308) | (477,964) |
| Emp. | 149 | 149 | 133 |

DUNS 23-720-9361
## Weld-A-Rail Ltd
Lockwood Close, Top Valley, Nottingham, Nottinghamshire NG5 9JN
**Tel:** 01159268797
**Web:** www.weldarail.co.uk
**Reg No:** 3715671 **Estd:** 1999 Private Limited Company
**Line of Business:** Public works contractors
**Issued Capital:** £300
**Director:** K Mckeown
**Co. Secretary:** Alan Mckeown
**US SIC:** 1796 **UK SIC:** 50400

| | 31-03-14 | 31-03-13 | 31-03-12 |
|---|---|---|---|
| TA | 2,749,968 | 2,531,735 | 2,359,119 |
| NW | 1,253,332 | 1,028,086 | 1,003,868 |
| WC | 727,121 | 604,198 | 638,044 |

DUNS 21-724-7691
## Weld Enterprises Ltd
Estate Office, East Lulworth, Wareham, Dorset BH20 5QS
**Tel:** 01929400870
**Web:** www.lulworth.com
**Reg No:** 0843286 **VAT No:** 187039147
**Estd:** 1965 Private Limited Company
**Line of Business:** Other provision of lodgings not elsewhere classified
**Issued Capital:** £205,000
**Directors:** W J Weld, Mrs E S Weld
**Co. Secretary:** James Weld
**Branches:** Weld Enterprises Ltd, West Lulworth, Wareham, Dorset BH20 5PU
**US SIC:** 7011, 4712
**UK SIC:** 66500, 77002
**Auditors:** Edwards & Keeping
**Bankers:** HSBC Bank plc (40-19-21)

| | 31-01-14 | 31-01-13 | 31-01-12 |
|---|---|---|---|
| TA | 2,801,513 | 2,875,204 | 2,904,490 |
| NW | (1,893,663) | (1,845,412) | (1,847,995) |
| WC | (3,082,878) | (2,907,685) | (2,786,619) |

DUNS 23-576-3836
## Weld Farms Ltd
The Estate Office, East Lulworth, Wareham, Dorset BH20 5QS
**Tel:** 01929400580
**Web:** www.lulworth.com
**Reg No:** 0770026 **Estd:** 1963 Private Limited Company
**Line of Business:** Estate agents
**Trading Style:** Weld Estate
**Issued Capital:** £100
**Director:** W J Weld
**Co. Secretary:** James Weld
**US SIC:** 6531 **UK SIC:** 83400
**Auditors:** Edwards & Keeping
**Bankers:** HSBC Bank plc (40-19-21)

| | 05-04-14 | 05-04-13 | 05-04-12 |
|---|---|---|---|
| TA | 72,642 | 72,540 | 72,807 |
| P/L | N/A | (3) | N/A |
| NW | 71,830 | 71,830 | 71,833 |
| WC | 71,830 | 71,830 | 71,833 |

DUNS 22-768-0121
## Welded Presswork (1982) Ltd
(**Subsidiary of:** Ron Jeavons (Steels) Ltd)
Stafford Road, Wednesbury, West Midlands WS10 8SZ
**Tel:** 01215262022
**Web:** www.wpw-uk.com
**Reg No:** 1653313 **Estd:** 1953 Private Limited Company
**Line of Business:** Manufacture of metal structures and parts of structures
**Issued Capital:** £100
**Directors:** D Eaglesfield, R Jeavons
**Co. Secretary:** Mrs Diane Proffitt
**Responsibilities**
**Senior:** Eric Russon *(Sales & Marketing Director)*
**Marketing:** Eric Russon *(Sales & Marketing Director)*
**Sales:** Eric Russon *(Sales & Marketing Director)*
**Branches:** Welded Presswork (1982) Ltd, Pedmore Rd Industrial Estate, Pedmore Road, Brierley Hill, West Midlands DY5 1TJ
**US SIC:** 3441, 8911
**UK SIC:** 32042, 83701
**Auditors:** Cox & Co
**Bankers:** HSBC Bank plc (40-19-02)

| | 31-08-13 | 31-08-12 | 31-08-11 |
|---|---|---|---|
| TA | 1,683,605 | 1,898,741 | 1,714,178 |
| NW | 1,220,782 | 1,179,843 | 1,062,134 |
| WC | 721,592 | 635,636 | 488,830 |

DUNS 21-677-4571
## Weldex (International) Offshore Holdings Ltd
18-20 Harbour Road, Inverness, Inverness-Shire IV1 1UA
**Tel:** 01463220333
**Reg No:** 0380577SC **Estd:** 2010 Private Limited Company
**Line of Business:** Other construction work involving special trades
**Export Sales:** £2,262,000
**Issued Capital:** £19,136,847
**Directors:** W Caplan, D M Mcgilvray, I M Mcgilvray, N R Fraser, Ms M J Mcgilvray, N M Yarrow
**Co. Secretary:** Ms Margaret Mcgilvray
**US SIC:** 1799 **UK SIC:** 50000

| | 30-11-13 | 30-11-12 | 30-11-11 |
|---|---|---|---|
| TO | 23,063,000 | 25,172,000 | 36,795,000 |
| P/L | (1,896,000) | (738,000) | 2,266,000 |
| NW | (24,056,000) | (24,664,000) | (26,097,000) |
| WC | (8,767,000) | (5,916,000) | (6,983,000) |
| Emp. | 122 | 124 | 120 |

DUNS 22-126-3150
## Weldglobe Ltd
Crouch Street, Colchester, Essex CO3 3HA
**Tel:** 01206572647
**Reg No:** 4145315 **Estd:** 2001 Private Limited Company
**Line of Business:** Social work activities with accommodation
**Issued Capital:** £100
**Directors:** Mrs H R Odedra, R K Odedra
**Co. Secretary:** Krishen Odedra
**US SIC:** 8321 **UK SIC:** 96111
**Auditors:** Nigel Pratt & Co
**Bankers:** The Royal Bank Of Scotland Plc (16-18-18)

| | 31-01-14 | 31-01-13 | 31-01-12 |
|---|---|---|---|
| TO | 871,426 | 847,937 | 1,578,911 |
| P/L | 97,473 | 79,125 | 1,951,120 |
| NW | 3,769,642 | 3,695,942 | 3,512,469 |
| WC | 2,526,631 | 2,478,131 | 2,672,713 |
| Emp. | N/A | 28 | 57 |

DUNS 21-892-0338 Imp-Exp
## Welding Alloys Ltd
(**Subsidiary of:** Welding Alloys Group Ltd)
The Way, Fowlmere, Royston, Hertfordshire SG8 7QS
**Tel:** 01763207500
**Web:** www.welding-alloys.com
**Reg No:** 0793416 **VAT No:** 213817284
**Estd:** 1964 Private Limited Company
**Line of Business:** Manufacturers of welding machines and equipment
**Export Markets:** U.S.A., Scandinavia, Russia
**Export Sales:** £8,985,851
**Issued Capital:** £1,250
**Directors:** K D Thomson, J A Vicente Herrero, D C Stekly, J G Boot
**Responsibilities**
**Senior:** Graham Bonnet *(Sales Manager)*, Catherine Stekly *(Manager)*, Victor Stekly *(Manager)*, Dorival Tecco *(Manager)*
**Marketing:** Iain Pickles *(UK Marketing Executive)*
**Sales:** Mike Hibberd *(Sales Manager)*
**IT:** Damien Marsh *(IT Manager)*
**HR:** Sally Hopkins *(Human Resources Manager)*
**Purchasing:** Chris Goates *(Purchasing Manager)*
**US SIC:** 3629, 3499
**UK SIC:** 34350, 31694
**Auditors:** Gibson Booth
**Bankers:** Barclays Bank Plc (20-17-19)

| | 31-12-13 | 31-12-12 | 31-12-11 |
|---|---|---|---|
| TO | 12,116,018 | 11,525,327 | 13,602,477 |
| P/L | (84,771) | (44,017) | 49,062 |
| NW | 4,195,389 | 4,226,854 | 4,256,682 |
| WC | 601,433 | 944,841 | 1,050,941 |
| Emp. | 89 | 90 | 86 |

DUNS 22-079-0005
## Welding Engineers (Holdings) Ltd
38 Dalness Street, Glasgow, Lanarkshire G32 7RF
**Tel:** 0141-778-8461
**Web:** www.weldingengineers.co.uk
**Reg No:** 0211502SC **Estd:** 2001 Private Limited Company
**Line of Business:** Fabricated metal products
**Trading Style:** Welding Engineers (Holdings) Ltd
**Issued Capital:** £40,000
**Directors:** J Cassells, R A Holmes, S Austin, G Nicol
**Co. Secretary:** Ms Pauline Wilson
**US SIC:** 1799, 7699
**UK SIC:** 50000, 67303
**Auditors:** William Duncan & Co
**Bankers:** Bank Of Scotland (80-83-33)

| | 31-12-13 | 31-12-12 | 31-12-11 |
|---|---|---|---|
| TO | 10,924,469 | 10,806,823 | 9,881,611 |
| P/L | 991,251 | 1,291,936 | 1,201,665 |
| NW | 1,790,126 | 1,594,839 | 1,275,041 |
| WC | 1,663,673 | 1,491,220 | 1,165,672 |
| Emp. | 150 | 153 | 145 |

DUNS 21-926-7853 Exp
## The Welding Institute
Abington Hall, Pampisford Road, Cambridge, Cambridgeshire CB21 6AH
**Tel:** 01223899000
**Web:** www.twi.co.uk
**Reg No:** 0405555 **VAT No:** 700170889
**Estd:** 1946 Private Company Limited By Guarantee
**Line of Business:** Research institutions and organisations
**Export Markets:** Worldwide
**Export Sales:** £36,409,000
**Directors:** J G Beasley, G R Nix, P J Tooms, D Millar, N I Cooper, Professor S A Lockyer, S E Webster, Professor R L Jones
**Co. Secretary:** Mrs Gillian Leech
**Responsibilities**
**Senior:** Alan Denney *(Director)*, Jeffrey Garner *(Director)*, Maxwell George *(Director)*, Paul Jordinson *(Director)*, Johann Krancioch *(Director)*, James Lochhead *(Director)*, Jerzy Nowicki *(Director)*, Robert Rivett *(Director)*, Robert Sawdon *(Director)*, Julio Tolaini *(Director)*, Christoff Wienser *(Manager)*, christoph wisner *(Manager)*
**Branches:** The Welding Institute, 55 Grosmont, Chester Le Street, County Durham DH3 4NQ
**US SIC:** 7391, 7399, 8211, 8621
**UK SIC:** 94000, 83954, 93200, 96311
**Auditors:** Peters, Elworthy & Moore
**Bankers:** Barclays Bank Plc (20-74-05)

| | 31-12-13 | 31-12-12 | 31-12-11 |
|---|---|---|---|
| TO | 75,688,000 | 69,092,000 | 59,896,000 |
| P/L | 2,676,000 | 4,476,000 | 966,000 |
| NW | 67,232,000 | 66,605,000 | 54,753,000 |
| WC | 9,322,000 | 11,936,000 | 7,839,000 |
| Emp. | 803 | 746 | 691 |

DUNS 21-320-7459 Exp
## Welding Units (U.K.) Ltd
(**Subsidiary of:** Ameriforge Uk Ltd)
Mill Lane, Rainford, St Helens, Merseyside WA11 8LR
**Web:** www.weldingunits.com
**Reg No:** 1138116 **Estd:** 1973 Private Limited Company
**Line of Business:** Engineers (general)
**Export Markets:** E U, S America, Australasia, S & S E Asia.
**Export Sales:** £5,567,908
**Issued Capital:** £107,200
**Directors:** M C Peat, G Stalcup
**Co. Secretary:** Brian Fontana
**Responsibilities**
**Senior:** Alan Bradshaw *(Production Manager)*
**Finance:** Christopher Hodgkins *(Financial Director)*
**Marketing:** Bernard Stanway *(Sales Manager)*
**Sales:** Bernard Stanway *(Sales Manager)*
**Health & Safety:** Len Marsh *(Quality Manager)*
**Facilities:** Alan Bradshaw *(Production Manager)*
**Engineering:** Alan Bradshaw *(Production Manager)*
**Branches:** Welding Units (U.k.) Ltd, Skene House, 96 Rosemount Viaduct, Aberdeen, Aberdeenshire AB25 1NX
**US SIC:** 3441 **UK SIC:** 32042
**Auditors:** Langtons
**Bankers:** Barclays Bank Plc (20-51-01)

| | 31-12-13 | 31-12-12 | 31-12-11 |
|---|---|---|---|
| TO | 9,392,923 | 11,712,153 | 9,954,832 |
| P/L | 2,064,877 | 3,297,299 | 2,250,353 |
| NW | 91,331,563 | 5,671,351 | 4,178,440 |
| WC | 18,973,707 | 4,727,489 | 3,172,684 |
| Emp. | 51 | 46 | 40 |

DUNS 50-572-7693
## Weldmar Hospicecare Trust
Herrington Road, Dorchester, Dorset DT1 2SL
**Tel:** 01305215300
**Web:** www.cancercaredorset.org
**Reg No:** 2520727 **Estd:** 1990 Private Limited Company
**Line of Business:** Hospices
**Directors:** Mrs D L Smith, S Baynard, J D Joicey-Cecil, Ms S M Davies, Ms F Leaper, I R Stone, Viscount J H Fitzharris
**Co. Secretary:** Mrs Sheena Keep
**Responsibilities**
**Senior:** Alison Ryan *(Chief Executive)*
**Admin:** Liz Billingham *(Office Manager)*, Nikki Grattan *(Administrator)*
**IT:** Joe Higgs *(IT Manager)*
**Facilities:** Brian Barnicoat *(Facilities Manager)*, Steve Whyte *(Head of Buildings)*
**Branches:** Weldmar Hospicecare Trust, 93 Cheap Street, Sherborne, Dorset DT9 3LS
**US SIC:** 8091, 8321
**UK SIC:** 95200, 96111
**Auditors:** Perks Simm
**Bankers:** Cafcash Ltd (40-52-40)

| | 31-03-14 | 31-03-13 | 31-03-12 |
|---|---|---|---|
| TO | 7,978,521 | 5,946,418 | 6,577,693 |
| P/L | 100,514 | (1,310,290) | (397,912) |
| NW | 13,391,120 | 13,045,933 | 13,640,046 |
| WC | 1,370,868 | 492,260 | 1,373,255 |
| Emp. | 200 | 211 | 198 |

DUNS 21-611-7796 Imp-Exp
## Weleda (U.K.) Ltd
(**Subsidiary of:** Weleda Ag)
Heanor Road, Ilkeston, Derbyshire DE7 8DR
**Tel:** 01159-448200 **Fax:** 01159-448210
**Web:** www.weleda.co.uk
**Reg No:** 0203230 **VAT No:** 209542665
**Estd:** 1925 Private Limited Company
**Line of Business:** Manufacture of medicaments
**Export Markets:** Republic of Ireland, Australia
**Export Sales:** £578,308

**Issued Capital:** £2,215,000
**Directors:** A O Sommer, P Brandle
**Responsibilities**
**Senior:** Morite Aebersold *(Manager)*, Mary Carroll *(Warehouse Manager)*, Orjan Liebendorfer *(Manager)*, Jayne Sterland *(Manager)*, Ian Wiggle *(Manager)*
**Marketing:** Roger Barsby *(General Manager)*
**Sales:** Roger Barsby *(General Manager)*
**US SIC:** 2834, 5912
**UK SIC:** 25700, 64300
**Auditors:** Ernst & Young LLP
**Bankers:** HSBC Bank plc (40-25-29)

| | 31-12-13 | 31-12-12 | 31-12-11 |
|---|---|---|---|
| TO | 5,843,070 | 5,988,407 | 5,569,870 |
| P/L | (69,589) | 126,981 | (212,172) |
| NW | 617,143 | 550,133 | 1,326,954 |
| WC | 1,025,780 | 1,246,901 | 1,178,683 |
| Emp. | 72 | 78 | 86 |

DUNS 21-601-7822 Imp-Exp

## Wella (U.K.) Ltd

(**Subsidiary of:** The Procter & Gamble Company)
Brooklands The Heights, Weybridge, Surrey KT13 0XP
**Web:** www.wella.co.uk
**Reg No:** 0271363 **Estd:** 1932 Private Limited Company
**Line of Business:** Beauty products
**Issued Capital:** £10,092,100
**Directors:** B D Young, D Minney
**Co. Secretary:** Anthony Appleton
**Responsibilities**
**HR:** S Hayden *(Human Resources Manager)*
**Branches:** Wella (U.k.) Ltd, Wella Word Studio London, 93 Mortimer Street, London W1W 7SS
**US SIC:** 5999, 5122
**UK SIC:** 65600, 61800
**Auditors:** Deloitte LLP
**Bankers:** HSBC Bank plc (40-09-18)

| | 30-06-13 | 30-06-12 | 30-06-11 |
|---|---|---|---|
| TO | 110,191,000 | 106,667,000 | 106,378,000 |
| P/L | 1,151,000 | 4,002,000 | 3,200,000 |
| NW | 12,588,000 | 12,660,000 | 11,302,000 |
| WC | 20,269,000 | 19,287,000 | 18,448,000 |
| Emp. | 257 | 276 | 284 |

DUNS 21-691-5292

## Wellacre Technology Academy Trust

Irlam Road, Urmston, Manchester M41 6AP
**Tel:** 01617485011 **Fax:** 01617553234
**Web:** www.wellacre.org
**Reg No:** 7386228 **Estd:** 1997 Private Company Limited By Guarantee
**Line of Business:** Schools (foundation)
**Directors:** Ms H L Walsh, J M Whitby, Ms B Williams, Ms E Johnson, M D Sherwin, Ms M D Wicks, Ms J Richens, G Turner
**Co. Secretary:** Mrs Christine Ellis
**US SIC:** 8211 **UK SIC:** 93200
**Bankers:** Lloyds TSB Bank plc (30-95-42)

| | 31-08-14 | 31-08-13 | 31-08-12 |
|---|---|---|---|
| TO | 6,059,000 | 6,360,000 | 6,135,000 |
| P/L | (768,000) | (1,097,000) | (1,235,000) |
| NW | 25,416,000 | 26,548,000 | 27,573,000 |
| WC | 1,524,000 | 1,363,000 | 1,040,000 |
| Emp. | 121 | 136 | 126 |

DUNS 21-233-8590

## Welland House

Poplar Avenue, Peterborough, Cambridgeshire PE1 4QG
**Estd:** 1984
**Line of Business:** Children's homes
**Proprietor:** Mrs C Wiseman
**Responsibilities**
**Senior:** Catherine Wiseman *(CEO, Managing Director)*
**US SIC:** 8321 **UK SIC:** 96111
**Employees:** 66

DUNS 21-208-3757

## Welland House Nursing Home

Lime Grove, Welland, Malvern, Worcestershire WR13 6LY
**Tel:** 01684-310840
**Web:** www.wellandhousecarecentre.co.uk
**Estd:** 1985 Partnership
**Line of Business:** Medical nursing home activities
**Partners:** Mrs J Carroll, M Stone
**Responsibilities**
**Senior:** Jeanette Bedford *(Manager)*
**US SIC:** 8051 **UK SIC:** 95100
**Employees:** 52

DUNS 34-786-8973

## Wellbeing Residential Ltd

Planet World 1st Floor, Northgate Aldridge, Walsall, West Midlands WS9 8TH
**Tel:** 08448247788
**Web:** www.wellbeingresidential.co.uk
**Reg No:** 5587420 **Estd:** 2004 Private Limited Company
**Line of Business:** Social work activities with accommodation
**Issued Capital:** £1,000
**Director:** B H Dhaliwal
**US SIC:** 8321 **UK SIC:** 96111

| | 30-06-13 | 30-06-12 | 30-06-11 |
|---|---|---|---|
| TA | 815,804 | 844,184 | 859,183 |
| NW | (29,670) | (121,411) | (181,044) |
| WC | (7,562) | (12,862) | (23,896) |

DUNS 22-844-8262

## Wellburn Care Homes Ltd

9 Grange Road, Newcastle-Upon-Tyne, Tyne and Wear NE15 8ND
**Web:** www.wellburncare.co.uk
**Reg No:** 1965619 **Estd:** 1995 Private Limited Company
**Line of Business:** Social work activities with accommodation
**Issued Capital:** £19,895
**Principals:** S W Beckett *(Managing)*, C J Davey, S W Buckland, D P Smith, Mrs R Buckland
**Co. Secretary:** Ms Sharon Burns
**Branches:** Wellburn Care Homes Ltd, Wellburn Home, 118 Liff Road, Dundee, Angus DD2 2QT
**US SIC:** 7399 **UK SIC:** 83954
**Auditors:** Horwath Clark Whitehill
**Bankers:** Bank Of Scotland (12-09-19)

| | 31-03-14 | 31-03-13 | 31-03-12 |
|---|---|---|---|
| TO | 15,224,322 | 14,442,206 | 14,129,668 |
| P/L | 1,114,568 | 720,248 | 943,854 |
| NW | 21,359,343 | 20,750,822 | 20,429,705 |
| WC | (2,425,959) | (2,558,392) | (1,745,168) |
| Emp. | 598 | 604 | 599 |

DUNS 21-605-5259

## Wellburn House

Wellburn Road, Stockton-On-Tees, Cleveland TS19 7PP
**Tel:** 01642647400
**Estd:** 1998
**Line of Business:** Residential care establishments
**Proprietor:** A Underwood
**US SIC:** 8321 **UK SIC:** 96111
**Employees:** 70

DUNS 21-196-0240 Imp

## Wellcom London Ltd

7 Curtain Road, London EC2A 3LT
**Tel:** 020 7655 8250 **Fax:** 02070929769
**Web:** www.wellcom.com.au
**Reg No:** 0979521 **VAT No:** 752203268
**Estd:** 1970 Private Limited Company
**Line of Business:** Advertising, radio, tv and other media
**Trading Style:** Wellcom London
**Issued Capital:** £1,700
**Directors:** C A Anzarut, A S Lumsden, W W Sidwell
**Co. Secretary:** Andrew Lumsden
**Responsibilities**
**Senior:** Julian Graham *(Manager)*, Christopher Grawe *(The Managing Director)*
**Finance:** Richard Sayers *(Finance Manager)*
**Branches:** Wellcom London Ltd, Walworth Enterprise Centre, Unit 3B, Andover, Hampshire SP10 5AS
**US SIC:** 7319 **UK SIC:** 83800
**Auditors:** Sayers Butterworth LLP
**Bankers:** Lloyds TSB Bank plc (30-94-31)

| | 30-06-14 | 30-06-13 | 30-06-12 |
|---|---|---|---|
| TO | 5,898,160 | 5,935,227 | 6,562,630 |
| P/L | 422,293 | 705,082 | 1,030,357 |
| NW | 1,558,498 | 1,238,322 | 709,692 |
| WC | 1,316,544 | 960,306 | 910,056 |
| Emp. | 51 | 53 | 59 |

DUNS 22-537-0006 Imp

## The Wellcome Trust

Gibbs Building 215 Euston Road, London NW1 2BE
**Tel:** 020-7611-8888
**Web:** www.wellcome.ac.uk
**Estd:** 1936
**Line of Business:** Charitable social work activities without accommodation
**Trading Style:** The Wellcome Trust, The European Bioinformatics Institute
**Principals:** Sir W Castell *(Chairman)*, Sir M Walport, P Rigby, Baroness E Manningham-Buller, Ms A Johnson, P Smith, R Hynes, R Kent
**Branches:** The Wellcome Trust, Wellcome Trust Genome Campus, Saffron Walden, Essex CB10 1SA
**US SIC:** 6732 **UK SIC:** 83100
**Auditors:** PricewaterhouseCoopers LLP
**Bankers:** HSBC Bank plc (40-03-28)
**Following financial data are in thousands**

| | 30-09-13 | 30-09-12 | 30-09-11 |
|---|---|---|---|
| TO | 281,500 | 242,400 | 254,400 |
| P/L | (590,800) | (594,700) | (473,700) |
| NW | 15,041,200 | 13,329,700 | 12,438,400 |
| WC | (983,000) | (834,000) | (802,500) |
| Emp. | 1,452 | 1,413 | 1,354 |

DUNS 21-705-9557

## The Wellcome Trust Centre for Stem Cell Research

Gurdon Institute, Tennis Court Road, Cambridge, Cambridgeshire CB2 1QN
**Web:** www.gurdon.cam.ac.uk
**Estd:** 2012
**Line of Business:** Research and laboratory based activities
**Director:** A Smith
**Responsibilities**
**Senior:** Anne Cartwright *(Administrator)*
**US SIC:** 7391 **UK SIC:** 94000
**Employees:** 100

DUNS 36-489-0199

## Wellcome Trust Hg Centre

Roosevelt Drive, Headington, Oxford, Oxfordshire OX3 7BN
**Web:** www.well.ox.ac.uk
**Proprietorship**
**Line of Business:** Research and experimental development on natural sciences and engineering
**Proprietor:** J Flint
**Responsibilities**
**IT:** Tim Barsley *(Computer Manager)*
**HR:** Nina Gartside *(Personnel Officer)*
**Facilities:** Gerry Condon *(Facilities Manager)*
**US SIC:** 7391 **UK SIC:** 94000
**Employees:** 400

DUNS 34-583-6907

## Wellcome Trust Investments 3 Unlimited

215 Euston Road, London NW1 2BE
**Tel:** 02076112222
**Reg No:** 5391431 **Estd:** 2005 Private Unlimited Company
**Line of Business:** Activities of investment trusts
**Issued Capital:** £115,015,164
**Directors:** D F Truell, N D Moakes, Ms S J Wallcraft, P J Pereira Gray
**Co. Secretary:** Andrew Cossar
**US SIC:** 8999 **UK SIC:** 83954
**Auditors:** PricewaterhouseCoopers LLP
**Bankers:** HSBC Bank plc (40-03-28)

| | 30-09-13 | 30-09-12 | 30-09-11 |
|---|---|---|---|
| TO | 596,119 | 1,706 | 131,285 |
| P/L | (9,725,161) | 119,535 | 123,995 |
| NW | 148,320,504 | 110,244,217 | 69,071,065 |
| WC | 2,801,562 | 1,615,729 | 1,459,397 |

DUNS 28-859-1845

## Wellesley House & St. Peter's Court Educational Trust Ltd

114 Ramsgate Road, Broadstairs, Kent CT10 2DG
**Tel:** 01843-862991 **Fax:** 01843-602068
**Web:** www.wellesley.kent.sch.uk
**Reg No:** 0859223 **Estd:** 1900 Private Limited Company
**Line of Business:** Primary education
**Trading Style:** Wellesey House School
**Directors:** Mrs S J Ashton, S R Mays Smith, B R Moorhead, G D Mann, T E Nolan, J B Hawkins, P J Woodhouse, S E Munir
**Co. Secretary:** Mrs Barbara Parsons
**Responsibilities**
**Senior:** Kate Fenwick *(Director)*, Michelle Humpreys *(Assistant Head Master)*, Louise Martine *(Director)*, Simon O'Malley *(Head Master)*, Sophia Ratcliffe *(Director)*, Jonathan Sale *(Director)*
**US SIC:** 8211 **UK SIC:** 93200
**Auditors:** Saffery Champness
**Bankers:** HSBC Bank plc (40-15-02)

| | 31-08-13 | 31-08-12 | 31-08-11 |
|---|---|---|---|
| TO | 2,892,046 | 2,914,437 | 2,510,457 |
| P/L | 14,673 | 140,456 | 60,874 |
| NW | 6,280,429 | 6,258,375 | 6,113,028 |
| WC | (53,317) | (736,656) | (874,300) |
| Emp. | 57 | 58 | 60 |

DUNS 73-671-5587

## Wellingborough School

Wellingborough School, Wellingborough, Northamptonshire NN8 2BX
**Tel:** 01933222698
**Web:** www.wellingboroughschool.org
**Reg No:** 4931009 **Estd:** 2003 Private Company Limited By Guarantee
**Line of Business:** General secondary education
**Directors:** Ms A M Coles, Mrs D A Line, A W Bailey, Lt Col J K Cox, S Marriott, T Baldry, Ms P A Perkins, D K Exham
**Co. Secretary:** Colin Evans
**Responsibilities**
**Senior:** Neil Lyon *(Director)*, Peter Tyldesley *(Director)*
**US SIC:** 8211 **UK SIC:** 93200
**Bankers:** National Westminster Bank Plc (55-70-37)

| | 31-08-14 | 31-08-13 | 31-08-12 |
|---|---|---|---|
| TO | 10,578,716 | 10,426,997 | 10,348,470 |
| P/L | 651,657 | 626,226 | 744,193 |
| NW | 19,437,522 | 18,785,865 | 17,911,002 |
| WC | 1,443,310 | 1,518,044 | 1,296,640 |
| Emp. | 189 | 190 | 187 |

DUNS 53-645-4754

## Wellingborough Specsavers Ltd

26-27 Spring Lane, Wellingborough, Northamptonshire NN8 1EY
**Tel:** 01933228600
**Web:** www.specsavers.co.uk
**Reg No:** 3450905 **Estd:** 1998 Private Limited Company
**Line of Business:** Other retail sale in specialised stores not elsewhere classified
**Issued Capital:** £100
**Directors:** J D Perkins, D J Williams, R Chauhan, P V Cunningham, Mrs M L Perkins
**Co. Secretary:**
Specsavers Optical Group Limited
**US SIC:** 5999 **UK SIC:** 65600
**Auditors:** Newland Mallett Garner

| | 30-04-14 | 30-04-13 | 30-04-12 |
|---|---|---|---|
| TA | 250,752 | 126,973 | 124,022 |
| NW | 109,638 | (327,148) | (70,470) |
| WC | 54,605 | (379,664) | (137,868) |

DUNS 21-683-6840

## Wellington College Academy Enterprises Ltd

The Wellington Academy, Ludgersall, Andover, Hampshire SP11 9RR
**Tel:** 01264405060
**Reg No:** 7336441 **Estd:** 2010 Private Limited Company
**Line of Business:** Operation of arts facilities
**Issued Capital:** £1
**Directors:** S J Crouch, D J Cowley, Dr M J Milner
**Co. Secretary:** Ms Sandra Richardson
**US SIC:** 7911, 7941
**UK SIC:** 97913, 97911

| | 31-08-13 | 31-08-12 | 31-08-11 |
|---|---|---|---|
| TO | 161,298 | 101,936 | 48,607 |
| P/L | 1 | (18) | 1,132 |
| NW | 1,116 | 1,115 | 1,133 |
| WC | 702 | 287 | (109) |

DUNS 28-888-9025

## Wellington College Enterprises Ltd

(**Subsidiary of:** Wellington College)
Dukes Ride, Crowthorne, Berkshire RG45 6ND
**Tel:** 01344444000
**Web:** www.wellingtoncollege.org.uk
**Reg No:** 1259773 **Estd:** 1976 Private Limited Company
**Line of Business:** Other sporting activities not elsewhere classified
**Trading Style:** Wellington College Enterprises Ltd
**Issued Capital:** £20,000
**Directors:** S Crouch, P F Thompson, M M Rickards, S J Blosse, G M Burbidge, D S Ritchie
**Co. Secretary:** Paul Thompson
**Responsibilities**
**Senior:** D.C Arnold *(Domestic general Manager)*, Rosemary Groves *(Board Member)*, Roland Rudd *(Board Member)*, A Sachdev *(College Doctor)*, Andy Schofield *(Principal)*, Elizabeth Sidwell *(Board Member)*, Howard Veary *(Board Member)*
**IT:** Tom Whelton *(IT Director)*
**US SIC:** 7999, 8221
**UK SIC:** 97913, 93100
**Auditors:** Crowe Clark Whitehill LLP

| | 31-07-14 | 31-07-13 | 31-07-12 |
|---|---|---|---|
| TO | 2,354,765 | 3,972,248 | 5,616,791 |
| P/L | 31,682 | N/A | (39,192) |
| NW | 1,431,038 | 1,413,176 | 1,413,176 |
| WC | (106,025) | (163,047) | 66,393 |

DUNS 34-979-0498

## Wellington House Nursing Home Ltd

82-84 Kirkgate, Shipley, West Yorkshire BD18 3LU
**Tel:** 01274-531244 **Fax:** 01274-596573
**Web:** www.wellingtonhousenursinghome.co.uk
**Reg No:** 5774448 **Estd:** 1987 Private Limited Company
**Line of Business:** Nursing homes
**Issued Capital:** £100,132
**Director:** Miss A J Pitts
**Co. Secretary:** Miss Sally Pitts
**US SIC:** 8051 **UK SIC:** 95100

| | 30-06-14 | 30-06-13 | 30-06-12 |
|---|---|---|---|
| TA | 1,393,310 | 1,309,934 | 1,332,739 |
| NW | 291,409 | 172,075 | 118,935 |
| WC | (68,425) | (94,842) | (85,008) |

DUNS 21-030-1375
## The Wellington Inn
19 The Green, Lund, Driffield, North Humberside YO25 9TE
**Web:** www.thewellingtoninn.co.uk
**Estd:** 1995 Proprietorship
**Line of Business:** Bars
**Proprietor:** R Jeffrey
**US SIC:** 5813 **UK SIC:** 66200
**Employees:** 49

DUNS 22-265-5289 **Imp**
## Wellington Management International Ltd
(**Subsidiary of:** Wellington Management Co L.L.P.)
80 Victoria Street, London SW1E 5JL
**Fax:** 02071266500
**Web:** www.wellington.com
**Reg No:** 4283513 **Estd:** 2001 Private Limited Company
**Line of Business:** Book retailers
**Export Sales:** £2,071,000
**Issued Capital:** £10,000
**Directors:** J M Hynes, K J Blake, J E Butler, P H Perelmuter, M J Boudens, P L Bradley, E B Baldini, M D Jordy
**Co. Secretary:** Abogado Nominees Limited
**Responsibilities**
**Senior:** Cynthia Clarke *(Director)*, David Cushing *(Director)*, Mark Flaherty *(Manager)*, Stephen Klar *(Manager)*, Nancy Lukitsh *(Manager)*, Diane Nordin *(Manager)*, Edward Steinborn *(Director)*
**Marketing:** Andrea Keatinge *(Marketing Manager)*
**IT:** Quentin Bradley *(IT Manager)*
**US SIC:** 6371, 7392
**UK SIC:** 82002, 83951
**Auditors:** PricewaterhouseCoopers LLP

| | 31-12-13 | 31-12-12 | 31-12-11 |
|---|---|---|---|
| TO | 192,507,000 | 167,701,000 | 120,268,000 |
| P/L | 52,900,000 | 44,524,000 | 17,876,000 |
| NW | 70,536,000 | 65,079,000 | 31,733,000 |
| WC | (258,000) | 62,276,000 | 27,373,000 |
| Emp. | 223 | 201 | 173 |

DUNS 49-344-2248
## Wellington Motors Ltd
Taunton Vale House, Summerfield Way, Chelston Business Park, Wellington, Somerset TA21 9JE
**Tel:** 01823-667511
**Web:** www.wellington-nissan.co.uk
**Reg No:** 3125962 **Estd:** 1995 Private Limited Company
**Line of Business:** Car dealers (new & used)
**Issued Capital:** £69,160
**Directors:** M Holcombe, M J Finn
**Co. Secretary:** Ms Lorraine Hector
**US SIC:** 5511, 7539, 5531
**UK SIC:** 65100, 67100
**Auditors:** Milsted Langdon

| | 31-12-13 | 31-12-12 | 31-12-11 |
|---|---|---|---|
| TO | 36,147,122 | 30,572,142 | 28,088,330 |
| P/L | 1,240,106 | 732,717 | (185,296) |
| NW | 2,597,551 | 1,971,977 | 1,519,157 |
| WC | 799,459 | 283,166 | (718,280) |
| Emp. | 89 | 81 | 90 |

DUNS 21-146-3999
## Wellington Park (2000) Ltd
(**Subsidiary of:** Leyland Masonic Properties Ltd)
Wellington Park, Church Road, Preston, Lancashire PR25 3AB
**Tel:** 01772-432881
**Web:** www.wellingtonpark.com
**Reg No:** 6766584 **Estd:** 2008 Private Limited Company
**Line of Business:** Catering
**Issued Capital:** £100
**Directors:** V S Parker, H E Bracegirdle, G H Lee, J H Mayor, W F Fairman
**Co. Secretary:** William Fairman
**Responsibilities**
**Senior:** Joy Briggs *(Manager)*, Jacqueline Cobham *(Manager)*, June Matthews *(Manager)*
**US SIC:** 5812 **UK SIC:** 66110

| | 31-03-14 | 31-03-13 | 31-03-12 |
|---|---|---|---|
| TA | 76,262 | 37,314 | 29,800 |
| NW | 4,754 | 1,697 | 1,617 |
| WC | 4,754 | 1,697 | 1,617 |

DUNS 42-397-4443
## Wellington School
Wellington School, South Street, Wellington, Somerset TA21 8NZ
**Tel:** 01823668800
**Web:** www.wellington-school.org.uk
**Estd:** 1995
**Line of Business:** Schools (independent)
**Directors:** A J Rogers, R Coupe, R T Homeshaw
**Responsibilities**
**Senior:** Henry Price *(Headmaster)*
**Marketing:** Rebecca Langden *(Marketing Manager)*, Carol Loftuowen *(Marketing Manager)*
**US SIC:** 8211 **UK SIC:** 93200
**Employees:** 280

DUNS 22-913-4671
## Wellington School (Ayr) Ltd
Carleton Turrets, 1 Craigweil Road, Ayr, Ayrshire KA7 2XH
**Tel:** 01292269321 **Fax:** 01292-272161
**Web:** www.wellingtonschool.org
**Reg No:** 0026589SC **Estd:** 1836 Private Company Limited By Guarantee
**Line of Business:** Schools (independent)
**Directors:** Ms J E Simpson, A Wilson, P J Lorimer, Ms E M Napier, K A Swinley, Ms B E Stewart, Ms A C Brodie, Ms J K Fergusson
**Co. Secretary:** John Mccolgan
**Responsibilities**
**Senior:** Gilbert Andrew *(Director)*, Mary Foran *(Director)*, Dianne Gardner *(Director)*
**Health & Safety:** Lysanne McMahon *(Health & Safety Officer)*
**Branches:** Hartfield Ho, Racecourse View, Ayr
**US SIC:** 8211 **UK SIC:** 93200
**Auditors:** William Duncan & Co
**Bankers:** Bank Of Scotland (80-12-39)

| | 30-06-13 | 30-06-12 | 30-06-11 |
|---|---|---|---|
| TO | 4,768,184 | 4,619,945 | 4,614,398 |
| P/L | (265,985) | 17,367 | 126,988 |
| NW | 4,794,380 | 5,060,365 | 5,042,998 |
| WC | 1,000,004 | 1,784,642 | 1,714,578 |
| Emp. | 111 | 111 | 108 |

DUNS 71-908-5974
## Wellness Foods Ltd
(**Subsidiary of:** Lydian Capital Partners L.P.)
3000 Hillswood Drive, Chertsey, Surrey KT16 0RS
**Tel:** 02035890200 **Fax:** 01344 887604
**Web:** www.wellnessfoods.co.uk
**Reg No:** 5290486 **Estd:** 2004 Private Limited Company
**Line of Business:** Manufacturers of food products
**Export Sales:** £10,873,000
**Issued Capital:** £79,504,111
**Directors:** E F Mcelroy, G V Magee, N O'Callaghan, M J Lane
**Co. Secretary:** Mark Lane
**Responsibilities**
**Senior:** Bernadette Ford *(Personal Assistant)*
**US SIC:** 2099, 5149
**UK SIC:** 42399, 61700
**Auditors:** PricewaterhouseCoopers LLP

| | 31-12-13 | 31-12-12 | 31-12-11 |
|---|---|---|---|
| TO | 239,075,000 | 214,536,000 | 221,641,000 |
| P/L | 7,090,000 | 5,170,000 | 3,732,000 |
| NW | (62,534,000) | (75,143,000) | (85,158,000) |
| WC | 32,215,000 | 27,670,000 | 23,487,000 |
| Emp. | 1,494 | 1,412 | 1,485 |

DUNS 49-316-8744 **Imp**
## Wellpak (Uk) Ltd
(**Subsidiary of:** Wellpak Group Ltd)
Enterprise Way, Evesham, Worcestershire WR11 1GS
**Tel:** 01386-768-200 **Fax:** 01386-768-300
**Web:** www.wellpak.co.uk
**Reg No:** 3124635 **VAT No:** 661067935
**Estd:** 1995 Private Limited Company
**Line of Business:** Retail sale of fruit and vegetables
**Issued Capital:** £20,000
**Directors:** P B Simian, A Padoan, R C Jones, G R Thomas, Ms L K Moore, R D Kelly
**US SIC:** 5431, 7399
**UK SIC:** 64100, 83954
**Auditors:** BDO LLP
**Bankers:** Barclays Bank Plc (20-98-61)

| | 01-12-13 | 07-12-12 | 27-12-11 |
|---|---|---|---|
| TO | 38,275,104 | 46,730,412 | 37,698,189 |
| P/L | 846,704 | 548,226 | 1,090,368 |
| NW | 1,402,659 | 1,293,669 | 1,260,594 |
| WC | (329,780) | (326,801) | (11,679) |
| Emp. | 70 | 89 | 75 |

DUNS 28-849-2044
## Wells & Root (Shipping) Ltd
Parker Drive, Leicester, Leicestershire LE4 0JP
**Tel:** 01162-353535
**Web:** www.wellsandroot.co.uk
**Reg No:** 0690876 **Estd:** 1961 Private Limited Company
**Line of Business:** Freight forwarders
**Issued Capital:** £5,000
**Director:** Mrs S M Green
**Co. Secretary:** Mrs Janice Langley
**US SIC:** 4712 **UK SIC:** 77002
**Auditors:** Godkin & Co

| | 31-05-14 | 31-05-13 | 31-05-12 |
|---|---|---|---|
| TA | 6,357 | 6,357 | 6,357 |
| NW | 6,357 | 6,357 | 6,357 |

DUNS 28-868-5241
## Wells Cathedral Publications Ltd
Wells Cathedral, Wells, Somerset BA5 2PA
**Tel:** 01749672773 **Fax:** 01749-676543
**Web:** www.wellscathedral.org.uk
**Reg No:** 1007081 **Estd:** 1971 Private Limited Company
**Line of Business:** Gift shops
**Issued Capital:** £40
**Directors:** Ms K A Nichols, Miss C J Mead, Mrs F J Good, M R Blandford, Mrs B C Bates
**Co. Secretary:** Mrs Frances Good
**Responsibilities**
**Senior:** Paul Richard *(Manager)*
**US SIC:** 5399, 5942
**UK SIC:** 65600, 65300
**Auditors:** Blueprint Audit Ltd
**Bankers:** National Westminster Bank Plc (60-23-06)

| | 31-12-13 | 31-12-12 | 31-12-11 |
|---|---|---|---|
| TO | 281,879 | 278,651 | 290,541 |
| P/L | 17,653 | 106 | N/A |
| NW | 18,342 | 18,342 | 18,342 |
| WC | 14,645 | 13,413 | 11,770 |

DUNS 34-840-9988
## The Wells Cathedral School Foundation
School Office, 15 The Liberty, Wells, Somerset BA5 2ST
**Tel:** 01749834200 **Fax:** 01749834421
**Web:** www.wellscathedralschool.org
**Reg No:** 2804495 **Estd:** 1993 Private Limited Company
**Line of Business:** Schools (independent)
**Directors:** J J Brade, Dr J M Kingston, J S Baxter, M Costantini, T W Lewis, C I Jackson, P G Brown, P R Lemanski
**Co. Secretary:** Peter Knell
**Responsibilities**
**Senior:** Charles Cain *(Deputy Head)*, Elizabeth Cairncroftt *(Head Teacher)*, Elizabeth Cairncross *(Director)*, Stella Clarke *(Director)*, Ann Gummer *(Director)*, Christopher Seaton *(Director)*, Steven Webber *(Bursar)*, Patrick Woodhouse *(Manager)*, Elsa Zee *(Manager)*
**Finance:** Steven Webber *(Bursar)*
**Marketing:** Julia Thurling *(Marketing Officer)*
**IT:** Jonathan Peace *(Head of IT)*
**US SIC:** 8211, 8299
**UK SIC:** 93200, 93300
**Auditors:** KPMG
**Bankers:** National Westminster Bank Plc (60-23-06)

| | 31-07-14 | 31-07-13 | 31-07-12 |
|---|---|---|---|
| TO | 675,416 | 1,005,834 | 1,034,609 |
| P/L | 434,659 | 784,464 | 706,795 |
| NW | 2,939,348 | 2,508,135 | 1,723,671 |
| WC | 2,692,794 | 2,508,135 | 1,723,671 |

DUNS 28-842-3486
## Wells Cathedral School Ltd
Cathedral Green, Wells, Somerset BA5 2UE
**Tel:** 01749834450
**Web:** www.wells-cathedral-school.com
**Reg No:** 0564883 **Estd:** 1933 Private Company Limited By Guarantee
**Line of Business:** Schools
**Directors:** J A Vaughan, A Featherstone, N L Jepson-Biddle, Ms H M Ball, R Sommers, D W Pretty, D A Brown, M J Smout
**Co. Secretary:** Peter Knell
**Responsibilities**
**Senior:** Elizabeth Cairncross *(Principal)*
**Finance:** Steven Webber *(Bursar)*
**Marketing:** Julia Thurling *(Marketing Officer)*
**IT:** Jonathan Peace *(Head of IT)*
**HR:** Steven Webber *(Bursar)*
**Health & Safety:** Steven Webber *(Bursar)*
**Facilities:** Steven Webber *(Bursar)*
**Purchasing:** Elizabeth Cairncross *(Principal)*
**Branches:** Wells Cathedral School Ltd, Junior School, 8 New Street, Wells, Somerset BA5 2LQ
**US SIC:** 8211, 8299
**UK SIC:** 93200, 93300
**Auditors:** KPMG
**Bankers:** National Westminster Bank Plc (60-23-06)

| | 31-07-14 | 31-07-13 | 31-07-12 |
|---|---|---|---|
| TO | 15,185,000 | 15,177,000 | 14,678,000 |
| P/L | 211,000 | 831,000 | 2,092,000 |
| NW | 16,672,000 | 16,464,000 | 15,633,000 |
| WC | 5,295,000 | 6,074,000 | 6,902,000 |
| Emp. | 233 | 224 | 208 |

DUNS 73-308-3070 **Imp**
## Wellstream International Ltd
(**Subsidiary of:** Wellstream Holdings Ltd)
Wellstream House, Wincomblee Road Walker Riverside, Newcastle-Upon-Tyne, Tyne and Wear NE6 3PF
**Tel:** 01912959000 **Fax:** 0191-295-9001
**Web:** www.ge.com
**Reg No:** 4582101 **Estd:** 2002 Private Limited Company
**Line of Business:** Other business activities not elsewhere classified
**Trading Style:** Ge Oil & Gas
**Issued Capital:** £1,000
**Directors:** F Romani, B M Heppenstall
**Responsibilities**
**Senior:** Marcio Perillo *(Director)*
**Sales:** Keith Robertshaw *(Sales Manager)*
**IT:** Kevin Gribben *(Senior IT Support Technician)*
**US SIC:** 7399 **UK SIC:** 83954
**Auditors:** KPMG LLP

| | 31-12-13 | 31-12-12 | 31-12-11 |
|---|---|---|---|
| TO | 200,834,000 | 196,061,000 | 141,703,000 |
| P/L | 7,846,000 | 40,730,000 | 3,295,000 |
| NW | 81,577,000 | 16,018,000 | (21,470,000) |
| WC | 240,000 | 36,158,000 | 70,079,000 |
| Emp. | 593 | 569 | 493 |

DUNS 21-741-7818
## Wellsway Multi Academy Trust
Chandag Road, Keynsham, Bristol, Avon BS31 1PH
**Web:** www.wellsway.bathnes.sch.uk
**Reg No:** 7746787 **Estd:** 1995 Private Company Limited By Guarantee
**Line of Business:** Schools (local authority)
**Directors:** A W Inker, Mrs A J Arlidge, Ms C M Whitfield, K J Reynolds, A J Williams, Ms I H Arnold, M J Atkinson, Ms M Morley
**Co. Secretary:** Timothy Howes
**Responsibilities**
**Senior:** Stuart Bradfield *(Director)*
**US SIC:** 8211 **UK SIC:** 93200

| | 31-08-14 | 31-08-13 | 31-08-12 |
|---|---|---|---|
| TO | 10,534,283 | 9,140,213 | 20,958,406 |
| P/L | 2,585,015 | 2,479,562 | 14,926,757 |
| NW | 19,882,334 | 17,375,319 | 14,825,757 |
| WC | 1,839,168 | 1,251,683 | 1,024,097 |
| Emp. | 158 | 128 | 142 |

DUNS 23-952-8248 **Imp**
## Welltec (Uk) Ltd.
(**Subsidiary of:** Jh Holding. Allerød Aps)
Silverburn Crescent, Bridge Of Don Industrial Estate, Aberdeen, Aberdeenshire AB23 8EW
**Tel:** 01224708705
**Web:** www.welltec.com
**Reg No:** 0204742SC **Estd:** 2000 Private Limited Company
**Line of Business:** Service activities incidental to oil and gas extraction excluding surveying
**Issued Capital:** £1
**Directors:** J Hallundbaek, M Skovbjerg
**Co. Secretary:** Burness Paull Llp
**Responsibilities**
**Senior:** Mike Affleck *(General Manager)*
**US SIC:** 1389 **UK SIC:** 13000
**Bankers:** The Royal Bank Of Scotland Plc (83-15-31)

| | 31-12-13 | 31-12-12 | 31-12-11 |
|---|---|---|---|
| TO | 11,734,849 | 12,304,657 | 7,318,256 |
| P/L | 671,513 | 614,406 | 425,253 |
| NW | 5,660,220 | 5,165,462 | 4,707,729 |
| WC | 5,532,222 | 5,002,837 | 4,601,512 |
| Emp. | 55 | 48 | 40 |

DUNS 21-604-9566
## Wellway Medical
The Health Centre, Buteland Terrace, Newbiggin-By-The-Sea, Northumberland NE64 6NS
**Tel:** 01670816921
**Web:** www.wellway.co.uk
**Estd:** 2002 Proprietorship
**Line of Business:** Doctors
**Proprietor:** Mrs F Smallwood
**Responsibilities**
**Senior:** Christopher Marr *(Senior Partner)*, R Toot *(Senior Partner)*
**US SIC:** 8062 **UK SIC:** 95100
**Employees:** 64

DUNS 23-895-7489
## Wellwork Ltd
High Street, Croydon, Surrey CR9 1PD
**Tel:** 08456101202
**Web:** www.audiotesting.info
**Reg No:** 3886565 **Estd:** 1999 Private Limited Company
**Line of Business:** Occupational health
**Trading Style:** Well Work
**Issued Capital:** £115
**Directors:** Ms J Murray, Dr G M Helliwell
**Co. Secretary:** Ms Diane Helliwell
**Branches:** Wellwork Ltd, Port Of Liverpool Building, Pier Head, Liverpool, Merseyside L3 1DA
**US SIC:** 8091, 8011
**UK SIC:** 95200, 95300
**Auditors:** RSM Tenon Ltd
**Bankers:** National Westminster Bank Plc (53-50-46)

| | 30-06-13 | 30-06-12 | 30-06-11 |
|---|---|---|---|
| TA | 781,638 | 542,142 | 582,151 |
| NW | 7,972 | 31,565 | 3,708 |
| WC | (161,368) | (132,677) | (37,359) |

DUNS 21-040-4333
## Welly Club
105-107 Beverley Road, Hull, North Humberside HU3 1TS
**Tel:** 01482-221113
**Web:** www.giveitsomewelly.com
**Estd:** 2000
**Line of Business:** Managed public houses and bars
**US SIC:** 5813, 5812
**UK SIC:** 66200, 66110
**Employees:** 50

DUNS 34-745-6550
## Welplan Ltd
**(Subsidiary of:** B&Esa Ltd)
Old Mansion House, Eamont Bridge, Penrith, Cumbria CA10 2BX
**Tel:** 01768-860400
**Web:** www.welplan.co.uk
**Reg No:** 2782737 **Estd:** 1993 Private Limited Company
**Line of Business:** Other business activities not elsewhere classified
**Issued Capital:** £50,000
**Directors:** A J Miller, M V Mccloskey, P G Lewis, R J Read, G Robinson
**Co. Secretary:** Richard Kirton
**Responsibilities**
**Senior:** Robin Scoley *(Manager)*
**Marketing:** Mike Jenkins *(Marketing Manager)*
**US SIC:** 7399 **UK SIC:** 83954
**Auditors:** BDO Stoy Hayward
**Bankers:** Barclays Bank Plc (20-66-97)

| | 28-02-14 | 28-02-13 | 29-02-12 |
|---|---|---|---|
| TO | N/A | N/A | 2,479,197 |
| P/L | N/A | N/A | 425,698 |
| NW | 3,017,831 | 3,273,355 | 3,208,690 |
| WC | 1,628,231 | 1,896,268 | 1,687,751 |
| Emp. | N/A | N/A | 69 |

DUNS 22-034-0959
## Welsh Air Ambulance Charitable Trust
57 Regent Street, Wrexham, Clwyd LL11 1PF
**Tel:** 08448584999
**Web:** www.walesairambulance.com
**Reg No:** 4036600 **Estd:** 2000 Private Company Limited By Guarantee
**Line of Business:** Charities and charitable organisations
**Directors:** R M James, D Jones-Morris, J Wagstaffe, D R Kitto, S J Curtis, Ms M P Hurst Di Pasquale, P L Morgan, D Gilbert
**Co. Secretary:** Ms Angela Hughes
**Responsibilities**
**Senior:** Kyle Jacques *(Director)*
**Branches:** Welsh Air Ambulance Charitable Trust, Regent House, Nott Square, Carmarthen, Dyfed SA31 1PG
**US SIC:** 8699 **UK SIC:** 96902
**Auditors:** KPMG
**Bankers:** Barclays Bank Plc (20-97-09)

| | 31-07-13 | 31-07-12 | 31-07-11 |
|---|---|---|---|
| TO | 6,894,917 | 6,094,321 | 5,736,625 |
| P/L | (52,719) | 55,467 | 182,544 |
| NW | 1,606,614 | 1,659,333 | 1,603,866 |
| WC | 1,547,662 | 1,600,141 | 1,559,517 |
| Emp. | 70 | 66 | 58 |

DUNS 21-226-3171
## Welsh Ambulance
Aber Road, Llanfairfechan, Gwynedd LL33 0HH
**Tel:** 01248689089
**Web:** www.wales.nhs.uk
**Estd:** 1986 Proprietorship
**Line of Business:** Other human health activities
**Proprietor:** H Davies
**Responsibilities**
**Senior:** Gillian Pleming *(Manager)*
**US SIC:** 8091, 7399
**UK SIC:** 95200, 83954
**Employees:** 60

DUNS 54-849-6967
## Welsh Ambulance N H S Trust
Cefn Coed Hospital, Swansea, West Glamorgan SA2 0GP
**Tel:** 01792562900
**Web:** www.ambulance.wales.nhs.uk
**Estd:** 1995
**Line of Business:** Ambulance and medical transportation services
**Director:** J E Bottell
**Branches:** Welsh Ambulance N H S Trust, Withybush Hospital, Fishguard Rd, Haverfordwest, Dyfed SA61 2PZ
**US SIC:** 8091 **UK SIC:** 95200
**Employees:** 70

DUNS 23-293-7511
## Welsh Ambulance Services Nhs Trust
H M Stanley Hospital, St Asaph, Clwyd LL17 0RS
**Tel:** 01745-532-900
**Web:** www.ambulance.wales.nhs.uk
**Estd:** 2003
**Line of Business:** Ambulance and medical transportation services
**Trading Style:** Was
**Issued Capital:** £1
**Principals:** S Fletcher *(Chairman)*, Ms L Meadows, M Cassidy, T Woodhead, D Jackland, Ms S Jones, A Murray
**Responsibilities**
**Senior:** Elwyn Price-Morris *(Chief Executive)*
**Facilities:** Derek Johns *(National Estates Manager)*
**Branches:** Welsh Ambulance Services Nhs Trust, Abergwili Road, Carmarthen, Dyfed SA31 2HG
**US SIC:** 8091 **UK SIC:** 95200
**Employees:** 70

DUNS 21-713-7611
## Welsh Bros Foods Ltd
Unit 1, Leeway Industrial Estate, Queensway Meadows Industrial E, Newport, Gwent NP19 4SL
**Tel:** 01633-273344 **Fax:** 01633-278844
**Web:** www.welshbros.co.uk
**Reg No:** 0821597 **VAT No:** 135804573
**Estd:** 1964 Private Limited Company
**Line of Business:** Butchers
**Issued Capital:** £135,000
**Directors:** C W Blackburn, D A Heycock, S P Burns, M P Welsh
**Co. Secretary:** Ms Julie Heycock
**Responsibilities**
**Senior:** Alan Haycock *(Manager)*, A Heycock *(Manager)*, Alan Welsh *(Manager)*, George Welsh *(Manager)*
**Facilities:** Alan Haycock *(Manager)*
**Fleet:** Alan Haycock *(Manager)*
**US SIC:** 5147 **UK SIC:** 61700
**Auditors:** Tee & Co
**Bankers:** National Westminster Bank Plc (52-21-54)

| | 01-03-14 | 03-03-13 | 03-03-12 |
|---|---|---|---|
| TO | 7,739,137 | 8,465,650 | 8,759,149 |
| P/L | 67,634 | 200,556 | 224,320 |
| NW | 445,141 | 519,990 | 524,846 |
| WC | (384,879) | (292,997) | (227,759) |
| Emp. | 49 | 58 | 56 |

DUNS 21-035-4618
## Welsh College of Horticulture Coleg Garddwriaeth Cymru
Holywell Road, Northop, Mold, Clwyd CH7 6AA
**Tel:** 01352841000
**Web:** www.cambria.ac.uk
**Estd:** 1992 Partnership
**Line of Business:** Colleges Universities & Professional Schools
**Trading Style:** Deeside College
**US SIC:** 8221 **UK SIC:** 93100
**Employees:** 49

DUNS 22-783-5105 Imp
## Welsh Fourth Channel Authority
Parc Ty Glas, Llanishen, Cardiff, South Glamorgan CF14 5DU
**Tel:** 08706004141 **Fax:** 029-2075-4444
**Web:** www.s4c.co.uk
**Estd:** 1982 Incorporate By Act Of Parliament
**Line of Business:** Television activities
**Principals:** I P Edwards *(Chairman)*, Mrs K Morris *(Financial)*, I Roberts *(Personnel)*, D Rhys, I Jones, D Williams, C Grace, R Fuse
**Co. Secretary:** Emyr Hughes
**Responsibilities**
**Senior:** Gwenllian Awbery *(Designated Limited Liability P)*, Miah Jones *(Designated Limited Liability P)*, Dyfrig Jones *(Designated Limited Liability P)*, Janet Lewis-Jones *(Designated Limited Liability P)*, Janice Rowlands *(Partner)*
**Branches:** Welsh Fourth Channel Authority, Doc Fictoria, Caernarfon, Gwynedd LL55 1TH
**US SIC:** 4833 **UK SIC:** 97411
**Employees:** 180

DUNS 21-486-6704
## Welsh Government
Crown Buildings, Cathays Park, Cardiff, South Glamorgan CF10 3NQ
**Tel:** 02920 898734
**Web:** www.wales.gov.uk
**Estd:** 1999
**Line of Business:** Central government
**Trading Style:** The Welsh Ministers, Www.Wales1000things.Com
**Directors:** L Elis-Thomas, Ms R Butler, I W Jones, Ms C Jones, Ms E Jones, Ms E Hart, Dr B Gibbons, Ms J Hutt
**Responsibilities**
**Senior:** Claire Clancy *(Chief Executive)*, Jane Davidson *(Principal)*, Lord Elis-thomas *(Chair of Environment and Susta)*, Sara Moseley *(Director Of Communications)*
**Finance:** Anna Meyer *(Business Development Manager)*
**Marketing:** Pippa Duggan *(Marketing Manager)*, Paul Landricombe *(Head of Business Marketing)*, Sara Moseley *(Director Of Communications)*
**Sales:** Tony Godfrey *(Business Development Director)*, Anna Meyer *(Business Development Manager)*, Kathryn Thurlow *(Business Development Manager)*
**IT:** Brian Davidge *(Head of IT)*
**HR:** Peter Kennedy *(Human Resources Manager)*
**Health & Safety:** Jurgen Dreyer *(Health & Safety Officer)*
**Branches:** Welsh Government, Tyr Llyn, Unit 3, Swansea, West Glamorgan SA6 8AH
**US SIC:** 9121, 8091
**UK SIC:** 91110, 95200
**Employees:** 5,000

DUNS 21-067-1122
## Welsh Health Supplies
Central Stores, Coity Road, Bridgend, Mid Glamorgan CF31 1UZ
**Tel:** 01656641200
**Web:** www.procurementservices.co.uk
**Estd:** 1983 Proprietorship
**Line of Business:** Medical equipment leasing and rental
**Proprietor:** P Atkinson
**US SIC:** 7394 **UK SIC:** 84000
**Employees:** 75

DUNS 28-992-9341
## Welsh Housing Aid Ltd
25 Walter Road, Swansea, West Glamorgan SA1 5NN
**Tel:** 01792469400
**Reg No:** 1830262 **Estd:** 1984 Private Limited Company
**Line of Business:** Social work activities without accommodation
**Trading Style:** Sheltered Cymru
**Directors:** Ms D Mccrea, S Davison, Dr S I Lloyd-Jones, A L Weltch, Ms N Langrish, Ms E C Howells, D J Childs, N S Colbourne
**Co. Secretary:** John Puzey
**Responsibilities**
**Senior:** Terence Brenig-Jones *(Director)*, John Killion *(Director)*, Ana Palazon *(Director)*, Ray Pritchard *(Director)*
**US SIC:** 8321 **UK SIC:** 96111
**Bankers:** Unity Trust Bank Plc (08-60-01)

| | 30-09-13 | 30-09-12 | 30-09-11 |
|---|---|---|---|
| TO | 3,913,813 | 3,825,042 | 3,853,792 |
| P/L | 400,524 | 64,334 | (78,958) |
| NW | 1,043,438 | 642,914 | 578,580 |
| WC | 973,967 | 590,101 | 532,593 |
| Emp. | 103 | 108 | 124 |

DUNS 23-996-4067
## Welsh Joint Education Committee
245 Western Avenue, Cardiff, South Glamorgan CF5 2YX
**Tel:** 02920265189
**Web:** www.wjec.co.uk
**Estd:** 1948
**Line of Business:** Other adult and other education not elsewhere classified
**Trading Style:** Wjec
**Principals:** L Bence *(Financial)*, South Glamorgan County Council, Powys County Council, Gwynedd County Council, Gwent, Clwydd County Council, Dyfed County Council, West Glamorgan County Council
**Branches:** Welsh Joint Education Committee, Unit A16-17 Gwaelod-Y-Garth Rd, Treforest Indstl Est, Pontypridd, Mid Glamorgan CF37 5XF
**US SIC:** 8299 **UK SIC:** 93300
**Bankers:** Lloyds TSB Bank plc (30-91-63)
**Employees:** 300

DUNS 21-782-2182
## Welsh Local Government Association
Local Government House, Drake Walk, Brigantine Place, Cardiff, South Glamorgan CF10 4LG
**Tel:** 02920468600
**Web:** www.wlga.gov.uk
**Estd:** 2002 Partnership
**Line of Business:** Central government
**Partners:** Ms L D'Agnilli, S Thomas
**Responsibilities**
**Senior:** Lorraine D'agnilli *(HR Manager)*
**HR:** Lorraine D'agnilli *(HR Manager)*
**US SIC:** 9121 **UK SIC:** 91110
**Employees:** 70

DUNS 22-759-8356
## Welsh National Opera Ltd
Wales Millennium Centre, Cardiff, South Glamorgan CF10 5AL
**Tel:** 02920635000
**Web:** www.wno.org.uk
**Reg No:** 0454297 **Estd:** 1948 Private Company Limited By Guarantee
**Line of Business:** Theatres & concert halls
**Directors:** G A Watts, A W Wyatt, D G Evans, Ms H Boulding, G T Davies, A G Bunker, Ms E Ap Robert, Sir P J Davis
**Co. Secretary:** Peter Bellingham
**Responsibilities**
**Senior:** Cathy Cole *(Deputy Company Manager)*, Awen Jones *(Director)*, Sally Osman *(Director)*, David Pountney *(Chief Executive and Artistic D)*
**Finance:** Becky Wright *(Senior Development Manager (Tr)*
**Marketing:** Rachel Bowyer *(Public Affairs Manager)*, David Massey *(Digital Manager)*, Siobhan Neil *(Marketing Manager)*, Ed Newsome *(Head of Marketing)*, Lowri Pugh-Morgan *(Press Officer)*, Michael Took *(Marketing Officer)*
**Sales:** Hannah Beadsworth *(Development Assistant)*, Amber Bell *(Corporate Development Officer)*, Georgia Butters *(Senior Development Manager)*, Alison Dunnett *(Director of Development and Co)*
**Admin:** Ruth Lepper *(Technical Office Administrator)*
**IT:** Daniel Bertelli *(IT Support)*
**Health & Safety:** Liz Walker *(Senior Deputy Stage Manager an)*
**Operations:** Llinos Beasley *(Scheduling Coordinator)*, Matt Broom *(Head of Planning)*, Sarah Crisp *(Revival Director)*, Hywel Evans *(Operations Manager)*, Robert Pagett *(Head of Production)*
**Purchasing:** Jenna Shiells *(Buyer of Office Products)*
**Engineering:** David Flinn *(Technical Manager)*, Chris Macauley *(Technical Engineer)*, Jan Michaelis *(Technical Director)*, Robert Pagett *(Head of Production)*
**US SIC:** 7911 **UK SIC:** 97913
**Auditors:** PricewaterhouseCoopers
**Bankers:** National Westminster Bank Plc (53-70-30)

| | 31-08-14 | 31-08-13 | 31-08-12 |
|---|---|---|---|
| TO | 18,123,000 | 16,999,000 | 17,780,000 |
| P/L | (291,000) | (236,000) | 102,000 |
| NW | 6,971,000 | 7,245,000 | 7,014,000 |
| WC | 2,910,000 | 5,621,000 | 5,856,000 |
| Emp. | 207 | 204 | 212 |

DUNS 51-689-8061
## The Welsh Pantry
Unit 10 Llantrisant Business Park, Llantrisant, Pontyclun, Mid Glamorgan CF72 8LF
**Tel:** 01443233991
**Web:** www.welshpantry.com
**Estd:** 1992 Proprietorship
**Line of Business:** Manufacture of other food products not elsewhere classified
**Proprietor:** E Parry
**Responsibilities**
**Finance:** Paul Anzani *(Site Director)*, Mike Brennan *(Site Director)*
**Marketing:** Paul Anzani *(Site Director)*, Mike Brennan *(Site Director)*
**Sales:** Geraint Parry *(Sales Manager)*
**IT:** Paul Anzani *(Site Director)*, Mike Brennan *(Site Director)*
**HR:** Wesley Ap-Carreg *(Quality Assurance Manager)*
**Health & Safety:** Wesley Ap-Carreg *(Quality Assurance Manager)*
**Operations:** Wesley Ap-Carreg *(Quality Assurance Manager)*
**US SIC:** 2099 **UK SIC:** 42399
**Employees:** 65

DUNS 53-614-1096 Imp
## The Welsh Rugby Union Ltd
Westgate Street, Cardiff, South Glamorgan CF10 1NS
**Tel:** 0870-013-8600 **Fax:** 029-2082-2474
**Web:** www.wru.co.uk
**Reg No:** 3419514 **VAT No:** 133854663
**Estd:** 1897 Private Company Limited By Guarantee
**Line of Business:** Other sporting activities not elsewhere classified
**Trading Style:** W R U, Welsh Rugby Union
**Directors:** C G Morgan, H Evans, W A Jones, K J Hewitt, A K Jones, G Edwards, M R Davies, B Fowler
**Co. Secretary:** Gareth Williams

**Responsibilities**
**Senior:** Maldwyn Beynon *(Director)*, Gordon Eynon *(Director)*, Roy Giddings *(Manager)*, Richard Gwynn *(Director)*, Daniel Howell *(Director)*, Anthony John *(Director)*, Raymond Wilton *(Director)*
**Marketing:** Craig Maxwell *(Group Sales & Marketing Manage)*, Alex Saul *(Marketing Manager)*
**Sales:** Craig Maxwell *(Group Sales & Marketing Manage)*
**IT:** Craig Phillips *(IT Manager)*
**Facilities:** Gerry Toms *(Stadium Manager)*
**Branches:** The Welsh Rugby Union Ltd, Morfa Athletics Stadium, Upr Bank, Swansea, West Glamorgan SA1 7DB
**US SIC:** 7999 **UK SIC:** 97913
**Auditors:** Walter Hunter & Co Ltd
**Bankers:** Barclays Bank Plc (20-18-27)

| | 30-06-14 | 30-06-13 | 30-06-12 |
|---|---|---|---|
| TO | 58,493,000 | 60,962,000 | 63,183,000 |
| P/L | 2,382,000 | 2,333,000 | 2,386,000 |
| NW | 50,576,000 | 50,594,000 | 46,838,000 |
| WC | (20,267,000) | (21,648,000) | (25,815,000) |
| Emp. | 211 | 215 | 194 |

DUNS 21-017-0116 **Imp-Exp**
## Welsh Slate Ltd
Penrhyn Quarry, Bethesda, Bangor, Gwynedd LL57 4YG
**Tel:** 01248 600656
**Web:** www.welshslate.com
**Reg No:** 6391123 **Estd:** 1800 Private Limited Company
**Line of Business:** Slate quarried products
**Issued Capital:** £17,010,000
**Directors:** Mrs N Oakes, J P Lagan, M Hodgkinson, P Lagan, C J Allwood
**Co. Secretary:** Declan Canavan
**Responsibilities**
**Senior:** Edward Griffiths *(Purchasing Manager)*
**Finance:** Danielle Blyth *(Finance Manager)*, Wendy Davies *(Accounts/Finance Administrator)*
**Admin:** Moses Chinyama *(Accounting Technician)*
**HR:** Rhian Williams *(Human Resources Manager)*
**Purchasing:** Edward Griffiths *(Purchasing Manager)*
**Engineering:** Andy Smith *(Engineering Manager)*
**US SIC:** 1429, 3281
**UK SIC:** 23102, 24503
**Auditors:** Ernst & Young LLP
**Bankers:** Ulster Bank Ltd (98-00-00)

| | 31-12-13 | 31-12-12 | 31-12-11 |
|---|---|---|---|
| TO | 19,330,707 | 17,744,480 | 17,962,279 |
| P/L | 2,238,355 | 341,149 | 272,773 |
| NW | (672,575) | (3,366,061) | (20,918,444) |
| WC | (14,271,919) | 496,652 | (14,971,172) |
| Emp. | 203 | 205 | 204 |

DUNS 42-341-0724
## Welsh Water Pension Trustee Ltd
Pentwyn Road, Nelson, Treharris, Mid Glamorgan CF46 6LY
**Tel:** 08000853968
**Reg No:** 4328831 **Estd:** 2001 Private Limited Company
**Line of Business:** Pension funding
**Issued Capital:** £1
**Directors:** J Sampson, P M Davis, Miss M F Jones, P J Edwards, M P Henderson, T P Jones
**Co. Secretary:** Ms Nicola Williams
**US SIC:** 6371 **UK SIC:** 82002

| | 31-03-14 | 31-03-13 | 31-03-12 |
|---|---|---|---|
| TA | 1 | 1 | 1 |
| NW | 1 | 1 | 1 |

DUNS 21-781-0101
## Welshpool High School
Salop Road, Welshpool, Powys SY21 7RE
**Tel:** 01938552014
**Web:** www.welshpool-hs.powys.sch.uk
**Estd:** 2011 Proprietorship
**Line of Business:** Schools (local authority)
**Proprietor:** J Toal
**Responsibilities**
**IT:** Bob Cannon *(IT Teacher)*, Mark Fellows *(IT Systems Manager)*
**US SIC:** 8211 **UK SIC:** 93200
**Employees:** 100

DUNS 23-912-3149
## Welspun Uk Ltd
(**Subsidiary of:** Welspun Holdings Private Limited)
Park Square, Stockport, Cheshire SK3 0XF
**Tel:** 01613675800 **Fax:** 01613675869
**Web:** www.welspun.com
**Reg No:** 3902741 **VAT No:** 727144049
**Estd:** 2000 Private Limited Company
**Line of Business:** Wholesale of textiles
**Export Sales:** £2,115,000
**Trading Style:** Christy
**Issued Capital:** £1
**Directors:** R R Mandawewala, M Bansal, G M Naismith, R J Walker
**Co. Secretary:** Manish Bansal
**Branches:** Welspun Uk Ltd, 94 Kinsey Road, Cheshire Oaks Outlet Village, Ellesmere Port, Cheshire CH65 9LA
**US SIC:** 5133, 5199
**UK SIC:** 61600, 61900
**Auditors:** PricewaterhouseCoopers LLP
**Bankers:** Bank Of India (60-92-91)

| | 31-03-14 | 31-03-13 | 31-03-12 |
|---|---|---|---|
| TO | 26,974,000 | 22,327,000 | 24,180,000 |
| P/L | 694,000 | (173,000) | (777,000) |
| NW | 3,058,000 | 2,460,000 | 1,006,000 |
| WC | (8,965,000) | 10,240,000 | 8,774,000 |
| Emp. | 261 | 285 | 318 |

DUNS 73-686-9848 **Imp**
## Welton Bibby & Baron Ltd
(**Subsidiary of:** Welton Bibby & Baron Holdings Limited)
1 Quartermaster Road, West Wilts Trading Estate, Westbury, Wiltshire BA13 4JT
**Tel:** 01373-860-200
**Web:** www.welton.co.uk
**Reg No:** 4946078 **VAT No:** 821740451
**Estd:** 1997 Private Limited Company
**Line of Business:** Sppliers of bags various types
**Export Sales:** £3,197,000
**Issued Capital:** £1,000
**Directors:** M M Mettler, M D Ross, J Goudie, N R Tomkins
**Responsibilities**
**Senior:** Raymond Brooksbank *(Manager)*, Jamie Goudie *(Operations Director)*
**IT:** C Postalethwaite *(IT Manager)*
**Operations:** Jamie Goudie *(Operations Director)*
**US SIC:** 2645 **UK SIC:** 47280
**Auditors:** Baker Tilly UK Audit LLP

| | 31-12-13 | 31-12-12 | 31-12-11 |
|---|---|---|---|
| TO | 47,147,000 | 50,471,000 | 44,594,000 |
| P/L | 1,131,000 | 2,476,000 | 2,773,000 |
| NW | 15,050,000 | 14,076,000 | 11,574,000 |
| WC | 504,000 | 2,735,000 | 682,000 |
| Emp. | 331 | 337 | 306 |

DUNS 21-317-7207 **Exp**
## Weltonhurst Ltd
Centurion Way, Roman Road, Blackburn, Lancashire BB1 2LD
**Tel:** 01254-671177 **Fax:** 01254-671717
**Web:** www.weltonhurst.co.uk
**Reg No:** 0894340 **VAT No:** 628767787
**Estd:** 1966 Private Limited Company
**Line of Business:** Plastic injection moulding
**Export Markets:** Worldwide
**Export Sales:** £440,742
**Issued Capital:** £1,357,250
**Principals:** H A Cann *(Chairman)*, A Hutchinson, S R Watts, P Wareing
**Co. Secretary:** Richard Howarth
**Responsibilities**
**Senior:** Andrew Fish *(Manager)*, Chris Slinger *(Works Manager)*
**Facilities:** Chris Slinger *(Works Manager)*
**Operations:** Chris Slinger *(Works Manager)*
**Purchasing:** Stephen Wilding *(Purchasing Manager)*
**US SIC:** 3079 **UK SIC:** 48360
**Auditors:** KPMG LLP
**Bankers:** National Westminster Bank Plc (01-00-85)

| | 31-12-13 | 31-12-12 | 31-12-11 |
|---|---|---|---|
| TO | 9,672,010 | 11,111,953 | 9,873,458 |
| P/L | 76,263 | 564,924 | 181,682 |
| NW | 2,157,852 | 1,980,672 | 1,542,217 |
| WC | (317,220) | (311,386) | (694,233) |
| Emp. | 110 | 110 | 98 |

DUNS 64-266-8552
## Welwyn Garden City Housing Association Ltd
10 Parkway, Welwyn Garden City, Hertfordshire AL8 6HG
**Tel:** 01707-390044
**Reg No:** 0016067IP **Estd:** 1962
**Line of Business:** Charitable social work activities with accommodation
**Principals:** G Vaughan *(Chairman)*, S Godshaw
**Responsibilities**
**Senior:** R Bek *(Chief Executive)*
**HR:** Maria Bellis *(Personnel Coordinator)*
**Branches:** Welwyn Garden City Housing Association Ltd, Greenfields South Drive, Potters Bar, Hertfordshire EN6 4HW
**US SIC:** 6111 **UK SIC:** 81501
**Auditors:** Nexia Smith & Williamson
**Bankers:** Barclays Bank Plc (20-87-46)

| | 31-03-12 | 31-03-11 | 31-03-10 |
|---|---|---|---|
| TA | 8,756,157 | 7,751,372 | 6,744,318 |
| P/L | 171,888 | 176,128 | 158,920 |
| NW | 2,185,197 | 1,859,775 | 1,683,647 |
| WC | 722,005 | (120,096) | 495,239 |
| Emp. | 77 | 73 | 74 |

DUNS 21-121-4929
## Welwyn Hatfield Council
Council Offices, The Campus, Welwyn Garden City, Hertfordshire AL8 6AE
**Web:** www.welhat.gov.uk
**VAT No:** 214558764 **Estd:** 1974 Partnership
**Line of Business:** Local government
**Principals:** Mrs L Mendez *(Chairman)*, D Irving *(Technical)*, M Saminaden, B Worthington, A Gray, M Saminaden, D Irving, J Anderson
**Responsibilities**
**Senior:** Laurence Hart *(Manager)*
**IT:** Warwick Turnbull *(IT Manager)*
**Branches:** Welwyn Hatfield Council, Howardsgate, Welwyn Garden City, Hertfordshire AL8 6BH
**US SIC:** 9121 **UK SIC:** 91110
**Employees:** 1,000

DUNS 23-400-2728
## Welwyn Hatfield Leisure Ltd
4th Floor, Campus West, The Campus, Welwyn Garden City, Hertfordshire AL8 6BX
**Tel:** 01707276276 **Fax:** 01707-336162
**Web:** www.finesseleisure.com
**Reg No:** 0029635IP **VAT No:** 828368005
**Friendly Society**
**Line of Business:** Other sporting activities not elsewhere classified
**Trading Style:** Finesse Leisure Partnership
**Principals:** A Ashby, P Nye
**US SIC:** 7000 **UK SIC:** 97913
**Bankers:** HSBC Bank plc (40-46-08)
**Employees:** 105

DUNS 52-021-9361 **Imp**
## Wembley National Stadium Ltd
(**Subsidiary of:** Football Association Ltd)
Wembley Stadium, Wembley, Middlesex HA9 0WS
**Tel:** 08449808001 **Fax:** 02087-955050
**Web:** www.wembleystadium.com
**Reg No:** 3388437 **Estd:** 1997 Private Limited Company
**Line of Business:** Operation of sports arenas and stadiums
**Trading Style:** English National Stadium Trust
**Issued Capital:** £101
**Directors:** P A Gartside, R Maslin, A J Horne, M J Benn, G Burr, W S Martin, C L Mcconville
**Responsibilities**
**Senior:** Rodger Madalin *(Manager)*
**HR:** Melanie Millner *(Human Resources Director)*
**Health & Safety:** Nick Woodhouse *(Head of Health & Safety Compli)*
**Facilities:** Greg Gillin *(Facilities Director)*
**US SIC:** 7941, 6531
**UK SIC:** 97911, 83400
**Auditors:** Deloitte LLP
**Bankers:** National Westminster Bank Plc (60-23-09)

| | 31-07-13 | 31-12-12 | 31-07-11 |
|---|---|---|---|
| TO | 58,108,000 | 89,821,000 | 99,639,000 |
| P/L | (7,288,000) | (7,834,000) | 83,000 |
| NW | 53,729,000 | 168,705,000 | 174,189,000 |
| WC | (14,603,000) | (9,200,000) | (13,651,000) |
| Emp. | 109 | 104 | 104 |

DUNS 76-975-7402
## Wembley Sports Arena Ltd
(**Subsidiary of:** Compass Group Plc)
Elvin House, Stadium Way, Wembley, Middlesex HA9 0DW
**Tel:** 02089035812
**Web:** www.keithprowse.co.uk
**Reg No:** 2637323 **Estd:** 1991 Private Limited Company
**Line of Business:** Other service activities not elsewhere classified
**Trading Style:** Keith Prowse
**Issued Capital:** £2
**Directors:** P A Galvin, R A Downing
**Co. Secretary:**
Compass Secretaries Limited
**Branches:** Wembley Sports Arena Ltd, The Links, St Andrews, St. Andrews, Fife KY16 9JB
**US SIC:** 8999, 7999
**UK SIC:** 83954, 97913
**Auditors:** Hurst Morrison Thomson LLP
**Bankers:** Barclays Bank Plc (20-03-53)

| | 30-09-13 | 30-09-12 | 30-09-11 |
|---|---|---|---|
| TA | 2 | 2 | 2 |
| NW | 2 | 2 | 2 |

DUNS 22-729-8882
## The Wemyss Development Company Ltd
4 Melville Crescent, Edinburgh, Midlothian EH3 7JA
**Tel:** 01312259305
**Reg No:** 0003626SC **VAT No:** 401013634
**Estd:** 1897 Private Limited Company
**Line of Business:** Management activities of holding companies
**Issued Capital:** £496,500
**Directors:** M B Mackay, A M Wemyss, Ms I A Wemyss, D R Ashe, Dr. A G Rutherford, R B Waller, W J Wemyss, M J Wemyss
**Co. Secretary:** James Robertson
**US SIC:** 6711, 6531
**UK SIC:** 83962, 83400
**Auditors:** Ernst & Young
**Bankers:** The Royal Bank Of Scotland Plc (83-24-24)

| | 31-03-14 | 31-03-13 | 31-03-12 |
|---|---|---|---|
| TO | 31,988,463 | 31,703,478 | 27,979,003 |
| P/L | 3,947,159 | 8,436,464 | 6,572,703 |
| NW | 38,200,306 | 39,888,906 | 36,588,781 |
| WC | 21,605,813 | 24,089,016 | 21,607,034 |
| Emp. | 2,683 | 2,709 | 2,978 |

DUNS 73-323-9466
## Wemyss Lodge Ltd
Wemyss Lodge, Ermin Street, Swindon, Wiltshire SN3 4LH
**Tel:** 01793828227
**Web:** www.wemysslodge.com
**Reg No:** 4597794 **Estd:** 2002 Private Limited Company
**Line of Business:** Medical nursing home activities
**Issued Capital:** £800
**Director:** M Freeland
**Co. Secretary:** Ms Lucinda Freeland
**US SIC:** 8051, 6732
**UK SIC:** 95100, 83100
**Bankers:** National Westminster Bank Plc (56-00-63)

| | 31-10-13 | 31-10-12 | 31-10-11 |
|---|---|---|---|
| TO | 6,043,275 | 5,682,542 | 5,677,930 |
| P/L | 1,458,844 | 1,239,766 | 1,299,830 |
| NW | 2,130,385 | 1,597,468 | 1,050,096 |
| WC | 1,466,063 | 1,286,154 | 506,449 |
| Emp. | 199 | 192 | 186 |

DUNS 21-636-5650 **Imp**
## Wenban-Smith Ltd
14 Newland Road, Worthing, West Sussex BN11 1JT
**Web:** www.wenbans.com
**Reg No:** 0233418 **VAT No:** 192980720
**Estd:** 1876 Private Limited Company
**Line of Business:** Agents involved in the sale of timber and building materials
**Issued Capital:** £12,559
**Directors:** M Kemp-Potter, J A Kemp Potter, P B Kemp Potter, J R Kemp-Potter, Ms N E Abraham, D Parry
**Co. Secretary:** Ms Nadia Abraham
**Responsibilities**
**Senior:** Nadia Tooth *(Computer Manager)*
**IT:** Nadia Tooth *(Computer Manager)*
**Branches:** Wenban-Smith Ltd, Unit 14, 14-15 Phoenix Place, Lewes, East Sussex BN7 2QJ
**US SIC:** 5072, 3841
**UK SIC:** 61500, 37201
**Auditors:** Breeze & Associates Ltd
**Bankers:** Barclays Bank Plc (20-98-74)

| | 31-03-14 | 31-03-13 | 31-03-12 |
|---|---|---|---|
| TO | 6,616,235 | 6,326,005 | 6,589,915 |
| P/L | 136,533 | 52,025 | 166,336 |
| NW | 2,838,372 | 2,768,426 | 2,733,315 |
| WC | 1,870,696 | 1,777,605 | 1,773,826 |
| Emp. | 71 | 73 | 73 |

DUNS 34-898-6576
## Wenn Townsend Accountants Ltd
(**Subsidiary of:** Wenn Townsend Consultants Ltd)
30 St Giles, Oxford, Oxfordshire OX1 3LE
**Tel:** 01865559900
**Web:** www.wenntownsend.co.uk
**Reg No:** 5696146 **Estd:** 1876 Private Limited Company
**Line of Business:** Accounting and auditing activities
**Trading Style:** Wenn Townsend
**Issued Capital:** £100
**Directors:** J V Gould, Miss R L Herbert
**Co. Secretary:** Miss Ruth Herbert
**Responsibilities**
**Senior:** Stuart Bates *(Manager)*, Jacqueline Layzell *(Manager)*, Keith Middleton *(Manager)*, Stephen Shelley *(Manager)*
**US SIC:** 8931 **UK SIC:** 83600

| | 30-04-14 | 30-04-13 | 30-04-12 |
|---|---|---|---|
| TA | 206,212 | 252,583 | 303,888 |
| NW | (91,441) | (127,404) | (163,367) |
| WC | (91,441) | (127,404) | (163,367) |

DUNS 21-879-3775
## Wensley Group
The Works, Alcester Road, Beoley, Redditch, Worcestershire B98 9EJ
**Tel:** 01564742465
**Web:** www.wensleygroup.co.uk
**Estd:** 2012
**Line of Business:** Other construction work involving special trades

**Responsibilities**
**Senior:** Ann Grainger *(Manager)*
**US SIC:** 1799   **UK SIC:** 50000
**Employees:** 50

**DUNS 21-811-9069**
## Wensley Street Care Home
142 Wensley Street, Sheffield, South
Yorkshire S4 8HN
**Tel:** 01142424359
**Estd:** 2012
**Line of Business:** Residential care
establishments
**Responsibilities**
**Senior:** Mandy Mason *(Manager)*
**US SIC:** 8321   **UK SIC:** 96111
**Employees:** 58

**DUNS 34-591-2968**       Exp
## Wensleydale Dairy Products Ltd
Gayle Lane, Leyburn, North Yorkshire DL8
3RN
**Tel:** 01969-667664 **Fax:** 01969-667638
**Web:** www.wensleydale.co.uk
**Reg No:** 2735431 **VAT No:** 602089957
**Estd:** 1992 Private Limited Company
**Line of Business:** Dairy produce merchants
**Trading Style:** Wensleydale Creamery
**Issued Capital:** £116,500
**Principals:** D A Hartley *(Managing)*,
R Clarke, M Gribbin, R A Jones
**Co. Secretary:** Paul Birnie
**Responsibilities**
**Marketing:** Sandra Bell *(Marketing Manager)*
**HR:** Lynn Starsmore *(Human Resources Manager)*
**Facilities:** Donna Brodie *(Production Manager)*
**Purchasing:** Donna Brodie *(Production Manager)*
**Engineering:** Donna Brodie *(Production Manager)*
**Branches:** Wensleydale Dairy Products Ltd,
Ripon Road, Ripon, North Yorkshire HG4
3QD
**US SIC:** 5199, 5143
**UK SIC:** 61900, 61700
**Auditors:** Benson Wood Ltd
**Bankers:** HSBC Bank plc (40-33-01)

| | 31-03-14 | 31-03-13 | 31-03-12 |
|---|---|---|---|
| TO | 26,300,860 | 25,617,842 | 23,458,452 |
| P/L | 889,020 | 872,277 | 603,431 |
| NW | 4,650,546 | 4,035,645 | 3,404,786 |
| WC | 1,635,997 | 903,656 | 355,805 |
| Emp. | 235 | 239 | 233 |

**DUNS 28-830-8901**       Imp
## Wentworth Club Ltd
*(Subsidiary of:* Wentworth Group Holdings
Ltd*)*
Wentworth Drive, Virginia Water, Surrey
GU25 4LS
**Tel:** 01344846360 **Fax:** 01344-842804
**Web:** www.wentworthclub.com
**Reg No:** 0201357 **Estd:** 2012 Private
Limited Company
**Line of Business:** Health clubs
**Issued Capital:** £30,000
**Directors:** W Ruayrungruang, S Ni,
Dr C Ruayrungruang, R A Caring
**Co. Secretary:** Forsters Secretaries Limited
**Responsibilities**
**Senior:** Paulina Dimitrov *(Manager)*, Justin
Ellis *(Director of Operations)*, Jane Seaman
*(Manager)*, Julian Small *(Manager)*
**Marketing:** Annie Nicholson *(Director of
Marketing & Commun)*
**Sales:** Annie Nicholson *(Director of
Marketing & Commun)*
**Operations:** Annie Nicholson *(Director of
Marketing & Commun)*
**US SIC:** 7299   **UK SIC:** 98902
**Auditors:** KPMG Audit Plc
**Bankers:** Lloyds TSB Bank plc (30-90-24)

| | 31-03-14 | 31-03-13 | 31-03-12 |
|---|---|---|---|
| TO | 19,387,000 | 18,806,000 | 19,001,000 |
| P/L | 3,764,000 | 8,970,000 | 6,705,000 |
| NW | 32,307,000 | 29,424,000 | 21,644,000 |
| WC | 6,665,000 | 3,228,000 | (5,696,000) |
| Emp. | 231 | 230 | 228 |

**DUNS 23-268-7285**
## Wentworth Garden Centre
Hague Lane, Wentworth, Rotherham, South
Yorkshire S62 7TF
**Tel:** 01226-744842
**Web:** www.wentworthgardencentre.co.uk
**VAT No:** 308466746 **Estd:** 1976 Partnership
**Line of Business:** Garden centres
**Partners:** Ms S Airey, A Airey
**US SIC:** 5999   **UK SIC:** 65600
**Bankers:** Lloyds TSB Bank plc (30-17-16)
**Employees:** 60

**DUNS 21-209-7971**
## Wentworth Grange Nursing Home
Underwood Hall, Riding Mill, Northumberland
NE44 6DZ
**Web:** www.wentworthgrange.com
**Estd:** 1980 Partnership
**Line of Business:** Nursing homes
**Partners:** R L Lee, Mrs P R Lee
**US SIC:** 8051   **UK SIC:** 95100
**Bankers:** Allied Irish Bank (gb) (23-92-82)
**Employees:** 60

**DUNS 21-776-0738**
## Wentworth Leisure Centre
Wentworth Park, Hexham, Northumberland
NE46 3PD
**Tel:** 01434607080
**Web:** www.northcountryleisure.org.uk
**Estd:** 1986 Proprietorship
**Line of Business:** Leisure centres
**Proprietor:** J Maude
**US SIC:** 7999   **UK SIC:** 97913
**Employees:** 200

**DUNS 55-063-7201**
## Wepre Villa Home Care
Holywell Road, Ewloe, Deeside, Clwyd CH5
3RS
**Tel:** 01244-537733
**Estd:** 1992 Proprietorship
**Line of Business:** Home care and help
services
**Proprietor:** N Massey
**Responsibilities**
**Senior:** Iraj Forooghian *(Manager)*
**Finance:** Carole Forooghian *(Finance
Director)*
**US SIC:** 8811   **UK SIC:** 99000
**Employees:** 60

**DUNS 21-305-6617**       Imp
## Werfen Ltd
*(Subsidiary of:* Werfen Life Group Sa*)*
Kelvin Close, Warrington, Cheshire WA3
7PB
**Tel:** 01925-810141 **Fax:** 01925-826708
**Web:** http://uk.instrumentationlaboratory.com
**Reg No:** 1040034 **VAT No:** 147447059
**Estd:** 1972 Private Limited Company
**Line of Business:** Measuring instruments
and appliances
**Export Sales:** £1,076,664
**Issued Capital:** £100,000
**Principals:** A J Grant *(Managing)*,
C Pascual Sancho
**Co. Secretary:** Stephen Calderbank
**Responsibilities**
**Senior:** Ron Thornton *(Manager)*
**US SIC:** 3829, 3841
**UK SIC:** 37100, 37201
**Auditors:** BDO Stoy Hayward LLP
**Bankers:** Barclays Bank Plc (20-01-96)

| | 31-12-13 | 31-12-12 | 31-12-11 |
|---|---|---|---|
| TO | 27,480,587 | 26,727,320 | 25,415,417 |
| P/L | 6,419,980 | (4,417,842) | (3,068,135) |
| NW | 30,013,894 | 22,381,185 | 15,957,811 |
| WC | 27,889,176 | 24,850,266 | 18,542,388 |
| Emp. | 62 | 62 | 59 |

**DUNS 23-676-8490**
## Wernick Group (Holdings) Ltd
Russell Gardens, Wickford, Essex SS11 8BL
**Tel:** 01268-735544
**Web:** www.wernick.co.uk
**Reg No:** 3671447 **Estd:** 1998 Private
Limited Company
**Line of Business:** Erection of roof covering
and frames
**Trading Style:** Wernick Hire, Wernick
Constructions, S Warnick & Sons
**Issued Capital:** £32,759
**Directors:** L R Wernick, D M Wernick,
S M Doran
**Co. Secretary:** John Jaggon
**Responsibilities**
**Senior:** Leigh Fennell *(Marketing Manager)*
**Marketing:** Jeff Bownds *(Marketing
Manager)*
**US SIC:** 1761   **UK SIC:** 50400
**Auditors:** Tiffin Green

| | 31-12-13 | 31-12-12 | 31-12-11 |
|---|---|---|---|
| TO | 81,750,273 | 76,286,968 | 65,560,282 |
| P/L | 9,592,197 | 8,533,031 | 7,238,245 |
| NW | 53,136,112 | 43,656,580 | 36,669,230 |
| WC | (16,804,917) | (12,961,943) | (13,091,402) |
| Emp. | 537 | 502 | 481 |

**DUNS 21-750-7201**
## Wernick Hire Ltd
*(Subsidiary of:* Wernick Group (Holdings)
Ltd*)*
Roall Lane Industrial Estate, Goole, North
Humberside DN14 0NY
**Tel:** 01977663100
**Web:** www.wernick.co.uk
**Reg No:** 0633778 **VAT No:** 250557077
**Estd:** 2002 Private Limited Company

**Line of Business:** Portable buildings
**Issued Capital:** £1,800
**Principals:** L R Wernick *(Chairman)*,
D M Wernick, S M Doran, M Thistlethwaite
**Co. Secretary:** John Jaggon
**Branches:** Wernick Hire Ltd, Joseph House,
Northgate Way, Aldridge, Walsall, West
Midlands WS9 8ST
**US SIC:** 1761, 6531, 7394
**UK SIC:** 50400, 83400, 84000
**Auditors:** Tiffin Green
**Bankers:** National Westminster Bank Plc
(60-03-25)

| | 31-12-13 | 31-12-12 | 31-12-11 |
|---|---|---|---|
| TO | 54,125,011 | 49,966,880 | 43,953,795 |
| P/L | 7,342,099 | 4,198,606 | 5,517,183 |
| NW | 35,973,695 | 29,845,047 | 26,211,906 |
| WC | (8,913,815) | (7,036,533) | (9,262,864) |
| Emp. | 327 | 307 | 297 |

**DUNS 21-034-6432**
## Wesco Aircraft
Park Mill Way, Clayton West, Huddersfield,
West Yorkshire HD8 9XJ
**Web:** www.wescoair.com
**Estd:** 1984 Proprietorship
**Line of Business:** Aviation supplies
**Proprietor:** F Short
**Responsibilities**
**Senior:** Fred Short *(Director)*
**US SIC:** 4582   **UK SIC:** 76400
**Employees:** 175

**DUNS 22-815-7624**       Imp-Exp
## Wesco Aircraft Europe Ltd
*(Subsidiary of:* Wesco Aircraft Holdings
Inc.*)*
Unit 1 Park Mill Way, Huddersfield, West
Yorkshire HD8 9XJ
**Fax:** 01484-867711
**Web:** www.wescoair.com
**Reg No:** 1857310 **VAT No:** 640632560
**Estd:** 1984 Private Limited Company
**Line of Business:** Wholesale of other
intermediate products
**Export Markets:** Western Europe, U S A, S
America
**Export Sales:** £124,983,000
**Issued Capital:** £20,001
**Directors:** J Holland, J A Dobrucki,
A Murray, G Capell
**Co. Secretary:** John Holland
**Responsibilities**
**Senior:** Randy Snyder *(Manager)*
**IT:** Robert Lea *(Network Manager)*
**HR:** Julia Langton *(Human Resources
Manager)*
**US SIC:** 5199   **UK SIC:** 61900
**Auditors:** PricewaterhouseCoopers LLP
**Bankers:** Lloyds TSB Bank plc (30-93-76)

| | 30-09-13 | 30-09-12 | 30-09-11 |
|---|---|---|---|
| TO | 162,390,000 | 107,589,000 | 70,022,000 |
| P/L | 25,863,000 | 10,485,000 | 5,878,000 |
| NW | 55,543,000 | (1,563,000) | 37,588,000 |
| WC | 53,290,000 | (3,822,000) | 36,703,000 |
| Emp. | 196 | 185 | 165 |

**DUNS 23-538-7094**
## Wesco Distribution-International Ltd
*(Subsidiary of:* Wesco Distribution NI B.V.*)*
Unit 2 Park Seventeen, Moss Lane,
Whitefield, Manchester M45 8FJ
**Web:** www.wesco.com
**Reg No:** 3537564 **VAT No:** 711073676
**Estd:** 1998 Private Limited Company
**Line of Business:** Outsource company for
indirect materials and supply chain services.
**Export Sales:** £17,870,881
**Trading Style:** Wesco Sourcing &
Procurment Services, Bruckner Supply
Company, Wesco Sps
**Issued Capital:** £1,000
**Directors:** K S Parks, B M Begg
**Co. Secretary:** Daniel Brailer
**Responsibilities**
**Senior:** Joe Bachegalup *(UK Manager)*, Paul
Jenner *(Manager)*
**Branches:** WESCO DISTRIBUTION-
INTERNATIONAL LTD: Unit 2 Park
Seventeen, Moss Lane, M45 8FJ,
MANCHESTER.
**US SIC:** 7399, 7392
**UK SIC:** 83954, 83951
**Auditors:** PricewaterhouseCoopers LLP
**Bankers:** Barclays Bank Plc (20-72-17)

| | 31-12-13 | 31-12-12 | 31-12-11 |
|---|---|---|---|
| TO | 30,570,031 | 33,282,235 | 25,820,477 |
| P/L | 199,197 | 1,388,503 | 360,201 |
| NW | 3,504,058 | 3,371,449 | 2,295,304 |
| WC | 3,440,624 | 3,306,488 | 2,222,700 |
| Emp. | 52 | 44 | 37 |

**DUNS 22-774-3952**       Imp-Exp
## Wescol Ltd
Unit 7, Wolverhampton, West Midlands WV1
2RZ
**Tel:** 01902-351283
**Web:** www.wescol.com
**Reg No:** 0490107 **VAT No:** 100293524

**Estd:** 1951 Private Limited Company
**Line of Business:** Manufacture of other
electrical equipment not elsewhere classified
**Export Markets:** E U, Middle East, Far East,
Africa
**Issued Capital:** £245,003
**Directors:** R T Jervis, S R Jervis, G H Jervis
**Co. Secretary:** Andrew Cross
**US SIC:** 3629   **UK SIC:** 34350
**Auditors:** Thorpe Thompson
**Bankers:** Barclays Bank Plc (20-97-78)

| | 31-03-14 | 31-03-13 | 31-03-12 |
|---|---|---|---|
| TA | 731,244 | 862,582 | 917,271 |
| NW | 287,502 | 361,279 | 377,770 |
| WC | 101,942 | 172,832 | 199,853 |

**DUNS 34-657-6999**
## Wescot Topco Ltd
The Mash, Jarratt Street, Hull, North
Humberside HU1 3HB
**Tel:** 01482590590
**Web:** www.wescot.co.uk
**Reg No:** 5463121 **Estd:** 2005 Private
Limited Company
**Line of Business:** Credit reporting and
collection agency activities
**Issued Capital:** £103,600
**Directors:** A R Punch, J A Graham,
P Jenkins, S G Bodger
**US SIC:** 7321   **UK SIC:** 83954

| | 28-02-14 | 28-02-13 | 29-02-12 |
|---|---|---|---|
| TO | 28,177,000 | 35,682,000 | 36,557,000 |
| P/L | (491,000) | 2,917,000 | 1,262,000 |
| NW | (40,984,000) | (42,191,000) | (55,177,000) |
| WC | 8,272,000 | 31,668,000 | 15,934,000 |
| Emp. | 550 | 561 | 612 |

**DUNS 21-635-8614**       Imp
## Wesley Barrell (Witney) Ltd
*(Subsidiary of:* Wessex Bristol Investments
Ltd*)*
Ducklington Mill, Standlake Road, Witney,
Oxfordshire OX29 7YR
**Tel:** 01993-893100
**Web:** www.wesley-barrell.co.uk
**Reg No:** 0286568 **VAT No:** 479290992
**Estd:** 1934 Private Limited Company
**Line of Business:** Furniture for home and
office
**Issued Capital:** £17,954
**Directors:** Ms J T Crisp, Ms N Babar,
A A Ahmed, T M Cook, Ms I M Barrell
**Co. Secretary:** Ms Eugenie Barrell
**Responsibilities**
**HR:** Pauline Bowes *(Human Resources
Manager)*
**Branches:** Wesley Barrell (Witney) Ltd, 3
Queens Circus, Cheltenham,
Gloucestershire GL50 1RX
**US SIC:** 5719   **UK SIC:** 64700
**Auditors:** H.W. Fisher & Co
**Bankers:** Barclays Bank Plc (20-97-48)

| | 29-12-13 | 30-12-12 | 25-12-11 |
|---|---|---|---|
| TO | 6,149,366 | 6,085,918 | 6,441,674 |
| P/L | 21,867 | (221,967) | (157,528) |
| NW | 1,951,204 | 1,940,810 | 2,038,944 |
| WC | 319,716 | 337,165 | 589,985 |
| Emp. | 100 | 104 | 104 |

**DUNS 21-808-4762**       Imp-Exp
## Wesley Coe (Cambridge) Ltd
*(Subsidiary of:* Coebros Ltd*)*
Gas Lane, Ely, Cambridgeshire CB7 4GH
**Tel:** 01353-667914 **Fax:** 01353661471
**Web:** www.wesleycoe.com
**Reg No:** 0502988 **VAT No:** 213504019
**Estd:** 1952 Private Limited Company
**Line of Business:** Manufacturers of medical
equipment
**Export Markets:** E U
**Export Sales:** £350,279
**Issued Capital:** £15,750
**Director:** S J Coe
**Co. Secretary:** Adam Coe
**Responsibilities**
**HR:** Hannah Coe *(Human Resources
Manager)*
**US SIC:** 3841   **UK SIC:** 37201
**Auditors:** Ernst & Young LLP
**Bankers:** Barclays Bank Plc (20-17-35)

| | 31-03-14 | 31-03-13 | 31-03-12 |
|---|---|---|---|
| TO | 4,608,937 | 4,208,691 | 4,208,139 |
| P/L | 997,212 | 828,167 | 333,415 |
| NW | 2,243,280 | 3,362,335 | 3,159,229 |
| WC | 992,214 | 2,163,487 | 1,925,410 |
| Emp. | 52 | 48 | 54 |

**DUNS 21-922-3799**
## Wesley Coe Ltd
*(Subsidiary of:* Coebros Investments Ltd*)*
Gas Lane, Ely, Cambridgeshire CB7 4GH
**Tel:** 01223363252 **Fax:** 01223356693
**Web:** www.wesley-coe.com
**Reg No:** 0988564 **Estd:** 1970 Private
Limited Company
**Line of Business:** Management activities of
holding companies
**Issued Capital:** £43,695
**Director:** S J Coe
**Co. Secretary:** Adam Coe
**US SIC:** 6711, 3229

**UK SIC:** 83962, 24791
**Auditors:** Ernst & Young LLP
**Bankers:** Barclays Bank Plc (20-17-35)

| | 31-03-14 | 31-03-13 | 31-03-12 |
|---|---|---|---|
| TO | 183,702 | 4,213,114 | 4,213,455 |
| P/L | 1,793,177 | 899,662 | 411,695 |
| NW | 4,056,853 | 5,647,070 | 5,336,824 |
| WC | 4,056,853 | 4,448,222 | 4,103,005 |
| Emp. | N/A | 48 | 56 |

DUNS 76-912-1989
## Wesleyan Assurance Society
Colmore Circus, Birmingham, West Midlands B4 6AR
**Tel:** 01212003003
**Web:** www.wesleyan.co.uk
**Reg No:** 0000145ZC **VAT No:** 487282114
**Estd:** 2000 Incorporate By Act Of Parliament
**Line of Business:** Life assurance services
**Trading Style:** Wesleyan Financial Services
**Directors:** C Bridge, Ms E L Mckenzie, R H Green, M W Bryant, A F Neden, B S Jackson, C D Brinsmead, C W Errington
**Co. Secretary:** Doug Bright
**Responsibilities**
**Senior:** Andrew D' Arcy *(Managing Director of Practice)*, Steve Deutsch *(Commercial Director)*, Lowry Maclean *(Chairman)*, Matthew Rodhouse *(Manager)*
**Marketing:** Donna Owens *(Marketing Content Manager)*, Sunny Rai *(Data Analyst)*
**Sales:** Steve Deutsch *(Commercial Director)*
**IT:** Gareth Jackson *(IT Architect)*, Dave Turner *(Strategic Delivery Manager)*
**HR:** Matthew Beeston *(Training Manager)*
**Branches:** Wesleyan Assurance Society, 165 High St, Sevenoaks, Kent TN13 1XJ
**US SIC:** 6411 **UK SIC:** 83200
**Auditors:** PricewaterhouseCoopers LLP
**Bankers:** Lloyds TSB Bank plc (30-00-03)

| | 31-12-13 | 31-12-12 | 31-12-11 |
|---|---|---|---|
| TO | 234,600,000 | 303,400,000 | 259,400,000 |
| P/L | 16,300,000 | 7,600,000 | (2,400,000) |
| NW | 589,100,000 | 651,100,000 | 582,700,000 |
| WC | (124,200,000) | (124,200,000) | (57,600,000) |
| Emp. | 1,214 | 1,144 | 1,032 |

DUNS 39-230-2477
## Wesleyan Unit Trust Managers Ltd
**(Subsidiary of:** Wesleyan Assurance Society)
Colmore Circus Queensway, Birmingham, West Midlands B4 6AR
**Tel:** 01212003003
**Web:** www.wesleyan.co.uk
**Reg No:** 2114859 **Estd:** 1987 Private Limited Company
**Line of Business:** Life assurance services
**Issued Capital:** £1,000,000
**Directors:** C Bridge, C C Ward, C W Errington, Mrs S J Porter
**Co. Secretary:** Doug Bright
**Branches:** Wesleyan Unit Trust Managers Ltd, Windsor Ho, Britannia Rd, Queens Gate, Waltham Cross, Hertfordshire EN8 7TF
**US SIC:** 6111 **UK SIC:** 81501
**Auditors:** PricewaterhouseCoopers
**Bankers:** Bank Of Cyprus (london) Ltd (30-00-43)

| | 31-12-13 | 31-12-12 | 31-12-11 |
|---|---|---|---|
| TA | 5,214,186 | 4,981,001 | 5,111,964 |
| P/L | 403,926 | 405,944 | 540,693 |
| NW | 4,770,795 | 4,735,782 | 4,839,857 |
| WC | 4,770,795 | 4,735,782 | 4,839,857 |

DUNS 34-616-5483
## Weslo Housing Management
66 North Bridge Street, Bathgate, West Lothian EH48 4PP
**Tel:** 01506-634060 **Fax:** 01506-639122
**Web:** www.weslo-housing.org
**Reg No:** 0140597SC **Estd:** 1992 Private Company Limited By Guarantee
**Line of Business:** Other letting of own property
**Principals:** D W Drummond *(Financial)*, Ms E Porter, J Spraggon, Ms M Mcintyre, Ms A A Jackson, M S Crozier, C S Torrie, M A Bruce
**Co. Secretary:** Hbjg Secretarial Limited
**Responsibilities**
**Senior:** Frank Anderson *(Manager)*, Katherine Dewar *(Director)*, Andrew Sneddon *(Manager)*, Janette Wallace *(Board Member)*
**Admin:** David McLaren *(Office Manager)*
**IT:** Kevin Cairns *(Computer Manager)*
**Health & Safety:** Margaret Walker *(Health & Safety Officer)*
**Branches:** Weslo Housing Management, Weslo Housing Management, 15 North Street, Bo'ness, West Lothian EH51 0AQ
**US SIC:** 7399 **UK SIC:** 83954
**Auditors:** Baker Tilly UK Audit LLP
**Bankers:** Bank Of Scotland (80-07-14)

| | 28-02-14 | 28-02-13 | 29-02-12 |
|---|---|---|---|
| TO | 8,598,483 | 8,014,218 | 7,482,802 |
| P/L | 117,222 | 17,384 | 24,172 |
| NW | 926,367 | 1,306,145 | 1,256,457 |
| WC | 5,047,130 | 4,980,019 | 1,804,372 |
| Emp. | 79 | 75 | 71 |

DUNS 23-855-0276
## Wessex Advanced Switching Products Ltd
**(Subsidiary of:** Be Aerospace Europe Holding Llp)
Alexandria Park, 1 Penner Road, Havant, Hampshire PO9 1QY
**Tel:** 02392457000 **Fax:** 023-9247-3918
**Web:** www.waspswitches.co.uk
**Reg No:** 3846820 **Estd:** 2002 Private Limited Company
**Line of Business:** Manufacturers and distributiors of electronic components
**Export Sales:** £7,919,463
**Issued Capital:** £86,637
**Principals:** R D Middleton *(Managing)*, J P Martyn *(Financial)*, R M Patch, W R Exton
**Co. Secretary:**
Hackwood Secretaries Limited
**Responsibilities**
**Senior:** Derek Beecher *(Manager)*
**Health & Safety:** Les Tregeas *(production manager)*
**US SIC:** 3679 **UK SIC:** 34542
**Auditors:** BDO Stoy Hayward

| | 31-12-13 | 31-12-12 | 31-12-11 |
|---|---|---|---|
| TO | 13,044,177 | 9,909,417 | 8,132,991 |
| P/L | 1,561,059 | 1,012,864 | 428,550 |
| NW | 3,831,807 | 2,977,798 | 2,889,521 |
| WC | 3,184,739 | 2,429,163 | 2,327,187 |
| Emp. | 135 | 98 | 88 |

DUNO 21-793-8076
## Wessex Archaeology
Bridgewood House, 8 Rochester Airport Industrial Estate, Laker Road, Rochester, Kent ME1 3QX
**Tel:** 01634868834
**Web:** www.wessexarch.co.uk
**Estd:** 2011 Proprietorship
**Line of Business:** Archaeologists
**Proprietor:** A Fitzpatrick
**US SIC:** 7391 **UK SIC:** 94000
**Employees:** 120

DUNS 28-967-4038
## Wessex Archaeology Ltd
Portway House, Salisbury, Wiltshire SP4 6JX
**Tel:** 01722-326867 **Fax:** 01722-337562
**Web:** www.wessexarch.co.uk
**Reg No:** 1712772 **Estd:** 1983 Private Company Limited By Guarantee
**Line of Business:** Archaeologists
**Directors:** C Watson, C M Brayne, Dr I C Selby, Mrs J N Johnson, G A Allison, Ms R K Cook, P D Dean, Mrs E C Turton
**Co. Secretary:** Ian Phillips
**Responsibilities**
**Senior:** Paul Baggaley *(Manager)*, Robert Beattie *(Manager)*, Susan Clelland *(Executive)*, Robert Key *(Manager)*
**Finance:** Matt Leivers *(Finance Manager)*
**IT:** Andy Crockett *(Project Manager)*, Tom Goskar *(Archaeological Multimedia Deve)*, Paul Mcculloch *(Project Manager)*, Paul Middleton-Jones *(Senior IT Executive)*
**Operations:** Jonathan Benjamin *(Project Manager (Coastal & Mar)*, Richard Greatorex *(Production and Operations Mana)*
**Fleet:** Euan McNeill *(Director Coastal & Marine)*
**US SIC:** 7391, 8999
**UK SIC:** 94000, 83954
**Auditors:** Langdowns DFK
**Bankers:** The Co-Operative Bank Plc (08-90-26)

| | 31-03-14 | 31-03-13 | 31-03-12 |
|---|---|---|---|
| TO | 6,778,420 | 6,115,644 | 6,571,886 |
| P/L | (78,282) | (644,740) | (293,829) |
| NW | 912,529 | 990,811 | 1,548,243 |
| WC | 310,071 | 366,024 | 925,231 |
| Emp. | 181 | 175 | 189 |

DUNS 73-404-8668
## Wessex Care Ltd
11 Tollgate Road, Salisbury, Wiltshire SP1 2JA
**Tel:** 01722336933 **Fax:** 01722-337347
**Web:** www.wessexcare.com
**Reg No:** 4677336 **Estd:** 1903 Private Limited Company
**Line of Business:** Nursing homes
**Issued Capital:** £100
**Director:** Ms P M Airey
**Co. Secretary:** Matthew Airey
**Responsibilities**
**Senior:** Kim Donnelly *(Human Resources Admin)*
**US SIC:** 8051 **UK SIC:** 95100

| | 31-03-13 | 31-03-12 | 31-03-11 |
|---|---|---|---|
| TO | 4,068,473 | 3,948,405 | 3,944,008 |
| P/L | 277,600 | 397,570 | 276,933 |
| NW | 921,835 | 845,659 | 627,049 |
| WC | (160,821) | (83,024) | (397,038) |
| Emp. | 150 | 144 | 143 |

DUNS 23-679-2771
## Wessex Catering Maintenance Ltd.
Wincombe Lane, Shaftesbury, Dorset SP7 8PJ
**Tel:** 01747850735 **Fax:** 01747-855117
**Reg No:** 3673821 **Estd:** 1998 Private Limited Company
**Line of Business:** General mechanical engineering
**Issued Capital:** £2
**Directors:** G A Mitchell, Mrs N Taylor
**Co. Secretary:** Geoffrey Mitchell
**US SIC:** 8911 **UK SIC:** 83701
**Auditors:** Rutter & Allhusen
**Bankers:** National Westminster Bank Plc (55-50-21)

| | 28-02-14 | 28-02-13 | 29-02-12 |
|---|---|---|---|
| TO | N/A | 4,112,605 | 2,387,443 |
| P/L | N/A | (38,370) | (157,575) |
| NW | (336,903) | (641,138) | (602,268) |
| WC | 376,695 | (953,650) | (751,732) |
| Emp. | N/A | 54 | 24 |

DUNS 76-837-2690
## Wessex Children's Hospice Trust
Naomi House, Stockbridge Road, Sutton Scotney, Winchester, Hampshire SO21 3JE
**Tel:** 01962843513
**Web:** www.naomihouse.org.uk
**Reg No:** 2601495 **Estd:** 1991 Private Company Limited By Guarantee
**Line of Business:** Charities and charitable organisations
**Trading Style:** Naomi House
**Directors:** J R Lear, C R Kenny, D C Holmes, Mrs E M Wallace, Dr D Schapira, Mrs J Gillow, J J Grew, N Kinghan
**Co. Secretary:** Thomas Craig
**Responsibilities**
**Senior:** Lesley Brook *(Director of Care)*, David D Arcy Hughes *(Director)*, Janette Hollingbery *(Manager)*, Stevo Radjen *(Director)*, Faith Ramsay *(Director)*
**HR:** June Morton *(Human Resources Manager)*
**Branches:** Wessex Children's Hospice Trust, 74 Market Street, Eastleigh, Hampshire SO50 5RD
**US SIC:** 8321, 6732
**UK SIC:** 96111, 83100
**Auditors:** Blueprint Audit Ltd
**Bankers:** The Royal Bank Of Scotland Plc (16-34-25)

| | 31-03-14 | 31-03-13 | 31-03-12 |
|---|---|---|---|
| TO | 7,304,656 | 6,909,568 | 6,192,533 |
| P/L | 339,478 | 723,173 | 124,997 |
| NW | 24,095,185 | 23,618,180 | 22,142,655 |
| WC | 1,798,008 | 1,460,152 | 2,146,904 |
| Emp. | 126 | 121 | 120 |

DUNS 22-555-0284
## Wessex Eagle Ltd
**(Subsidiary of:** Hay Bluff Ltd)
Howden Industrial Estate, Tiverton, Devon EX16 5HW
**Tel:** 01884 254601
**Web:** www.eagleplant.co.uk
**Reg No:** 1540286 **Estd:** 1976 Private Limited Company
**Line of Business:** Renting of construction and civil engineering machinery and equipment
**Trading Style:** Eagle Plant, County Cabins
**Issued Capital:** £70,002
**Principals:** M J Grimoldby *(Chairman and Managing)*, R W Carter, N P Cox, A J Cradock
**Co. Secretary:** Gary Parfoot
**Responsibilities**
**Senior:** Nicholas Barrow *(Manager)*, Vivien Grimoldby *(Manager)*, Hazel Lewis *(Manager)*
**Branches:** Wessex Eagle Ltd, Cornishway West, Taunton, Somerset TA1 5NA
**US SIC:** 7394 **UK SIC:** 84000
**Auditors:** Albert Goodman LLP
**Bankers:** Barclays Bank Plc (20-85-26)

| | 31-12-13 | 31-12-12 | 31-12-11 |
|---|---|---|---|
| TO | 20,741,744 | 17,442,581 | 13,804,768 |
| P/L | 2,746,693 | 2,248,941 | 1,311,789 |
| NW | 15,131,709 | 13,014,824 | 11,232,225 |
| WC | (5,652,656) | (2,838,277) | (1,427,496) |
| Emp. | 199 | 187 | 163 |

DUNS 50-398-3918
## Wessex G S Ltd
Roundhead Road, Newton Abbot, Devon TQ12 6UE
**Tel:** 01626833737 **Fax:** 01626-837878
**Web:** www.wessexgsnewtonabbot.co.uk
**Reg No:** 2404860 **VAT No:** 631044875
**Estd:** 1989 Private Limited Company
**Line of Business:** Sale of new motor vehicles
**Trading Style:** Wessex Daf, Daf Ldv
**Issued Capital:** £143
**Directors:** Ms M H Kingdon, N P Kingdon

**Responsibilities**
**Senior:** Henry Kingdom *(Manager)*
**Branches:** Wessex G S Ltd, Bojea Sidings, Trethowel, St Austell, Cornwall PL25 5RT
**US SIC:** 5511, 7539, 5531
**UK SIC:** 65100, 67100
**Auditors:** Simpkins Edwards
**Bankers:** National Westminster Bank Plc (56-00-49)

| | 31-08-12 | 31-08-13 | 31-08-11 |
|---|---|---|---|
| TO | 21,930,151 | 24,629,658 | 19,925,373 |
| P/L | 296,098 | 404,080 | 248,719 |
| NW | 3,247,994 | 3,165,178 | 3,053,374 |
| WC | 1,773,015 | 1,705,513 | 1,479,522 |
| Emp. | 116 | 117 | 116 |

DUNS 76-980-9880
## Wessex Garages Holdings Ltd
Pennywell Road, Bristol, Avon BS5 0TT
**Tel:** 01172449242
**Web:** www.wessexgarages.com
**Reg No:** 2639755 **VAT No:** 567778570
**Estd:** 1991 Private Limited Company
**Line of Business:** Car dealers (new & used)
**Trading Style:** The Business Car Leasing Co
**Issued Capital:** £108,889
**Principals:** S M Patch *(Managing)*, Mrs L Patch, K B Brock
**Co. Secretary:** David Taylor
**Branches:** Wessex Garages Holdings Ltd, Mercia Road, Gloucester, Gloucestershire CL1 £0Q
**US SIC:** 5511, 7539
**UK SIC:** 65100, 67100
**Auditors:** Millener Davies
**Bankers:** Lloyds TSB Bank plc (30-94-80)

| | 31-12-13 | 31-12-12 | 31-12-11 |
|---|---|---|---|
| TO | 121,625,991 | 102,395,917 | 85,394,554 |
| P/L | 1,705,238 | 1,394,623 | 742,614 |
| NW | 10,753,692 | 9,514,305 | 8,463,079 |
| WC | 5,616,173 | 4,459,604 | 3,087,562 |
| Emp. | 231 | 198 | 185 |

DUNS 50-483-3492
## Wessex Group Ltd
Wincombe Lane, Shaftesbury, Dorset SP7 8PJ
**Tel:** 01747-855406 **Fax:** 01747850996
**Web:** www.wessex.org
**Reg No:** 2457125 **Estd:** 1990 Private Limited Company
**Line of Business:** Management of real estate on a fee or contract basis
**Issued Capital:** £2,800
**Directors:** R M Hall, A Morgan, A J Brunt
**Co. Secretary:** Simon Morgan
**Responsibilities**
**Facilities:** Dave Clasby *(Facilities Manager)*
**US SIC:** 6531 **UK SIC:** 83400
**Auditors:** Messrs Rutter & Allhusen
**Bankers:** HSBC Bank plc (40-41-01)

| | 28-02-14 | 28-02-13 | 29-02-12 |
|---|---|---|---|
| TO | 31,266,055 | 32,948,423 | 31,302,978 |
| P/L | 1,032,576 | 324,576 | 1,177,341 |
| NW | 5,709,218 | 5,064,262 | 5,286,277 |
| WC | 3,324,595 | 2,251,744 | 2,734,145 |
| Emp. | 337 | 405 | 333 |

DUNS 64-227-6307
## Wessex Hotel
West Cliff Road, Bournemouth, Dorset BH4 8BE
**Tel:** 01202-551911
**Web:** www.forestdale.com
**Estd:** 2002 Proprietorship
**Line of Business:** Hotels and motels without restaurant
**Proprietor:** R Collins
**Responsibilities**
**Senior:** James Brent *(Manager)*, Philip Welbourn *(Manager)*
**US SIC:** 7011 **UK SIC:** 66500
**Bankers:** National Westminster Bank Plc (60-03-14)
**Employees:** 70

DUNS 36-517-1441
## Wessex Housing Partnership Ltd
Saxon Court, Sarum Hill, Basingstoke, Hampshire RG21 8SR
**Tel:** 01256-865800
**Estd:** 2006
**Line of Business:** Business services
**Principals:** M Thompson *(Chairman)*, B Hutchinson, T Sullivan
**US SIC:** 7399 **UK SIC:** 83954
**Auditors:** PricewaterhouseCoopers LLP
**Employees:** 282
**Turnover:** £44,238,000

DUNS 29-644-2973
## Wessex Office Cleaning Services Ltd
Om, The Roundway, Littlehampton, West Sussex BN16 2BW
**Tel:** 01903850353
**Web:** www.wessexofficecleaning.com
**Reg No:** 1970623 **Estd:** 1985 Private Limited Company
**Line of Business:** Cleaning contracting commercial
**Issued Capital:** £4
**Managing Director:** M J Ketcher
**Co. Secretary:** Ms June Ketcher
**Branches:** Wessex Office Cleaning Services Ltd, Central Ho, Medwin Walk, Horsham, West Sussex RH12 1AG
**US SIC:** 7349 **UK SIC:** 92300
**Auditors:** Michael Finn & Co
**Bankers:** Lloyds TSB Bank plc (30-94-41)

| | 31-12-13 | 31-12-12 | 31-12-11 |
|---|---|---|---|
| TA | 104,950 | 107,676 | 106,040 |
| NW | 52,509 | 48,223 | 43,572 |
| WC | 25,819 | 19,843 | 13,496 |

DUNS 23-776-0517
## Wessex Water Ltd
**(Subsidiary of:** Ytl Corporation Berhad)
Operations Centre, Claverton Down Road, Bath, Avon BA2 7WW
**Tel:** 03456004600 **Fax:** 01225-528000
**Web:** www.wessexwater.co.uk
**Reg No:** 2366633 **Estd:** 2012 Private Limited Company
**Line of Business:** Water companies
**Issued Capital:** £131,751,592
**Principals:** C F Skellett *(Chairman and Managing)*, P K Chin, S H Yeoh, S A Cater, S K Yeoh, S K Yeoh, F S Yeoh, A F Pymer
**Co. Secretary:** Andrew Phillips
**Responsibilities**
**Senior:** Lesley Bennett *(Non-Executive Director)*, Kathleen Chew *(Non-Executive Director)*, Peter Costain *(Non-Executive Director)*, Nick Mitchell *(Senior Manager)*, Choong Tan *(Director)*, Tiong Yeoh *(Director)*
**Marketing:** Steve Arthur *(Strategic Planning Manager)*, Ian Drury *(Press Office Manager)*
**Admin:** Paul Acres *(Administrator)*
**IT:** Richie Chandler *(IT Support)*, Kate Hayden *(IT Service Performance and Sup)*, Andy Nicholson *(Asset Data Manager)*, Charles Uppington *(I.T. Technical Support Manager)*
**Health & Safety:** Ian Blair *(Health & Safety Officer)*
**Facilities:** Mike Caple *(Facilities Manager)*
**Operations:** Andrew Chatterley *(Operational Services Manager)*, Dave Durkin *(Production and Operations Mana)*, Richard Soloman *(Principal Project Manager)*
**Purchasing:** Ashley Mee *(Purchasing Manager)*
**Engineering:** Dan Bown *(Design Engineer)*, Barry Burtenshaw *(Engineer)*, Nathan Dove *(Engineer)*, Leanne Ford *(Critical Sewers Technician)*, Anne Hipperson *(Engineer)*, Mandy Westlake *(Group Treatment Director)*
**Branches:** Wessex Water Ltd, Po Box 2870, Bath, Avon BA2 7YB
**US SIC:** 4941, 4939
**UK SIC:** 17000, 16300
**Auditors:** KPMG Audit PLC
**Bankers:** HSBC Bank plc (40-14-13)

| | 30-06-14 | 30-06-13 | 30-06-12 |
|---|---|---|---|
| TO | 546,800,000 | 516,700,000 | 489,900,000 |
| P/L | 164,500,000 | 147,100,000 | 139,100,000 |
| NW | 351,300,000 | 297,000,000 | 257,000,000 |
| WC | 143,900,000 | 180,300,000 | 168,900,000 |
| Emp. | 2,244 | 2,174 | 2,106 |

DUNS 39-982-5041
## Wessex Water Trustee Co Ltd
**(Subsidiary of:** Ytl Corporation Berhad)
Operations Centre, Claverton Down Road, Claverton Down, Bath, Avon BA2 7WW
**Tel:** 07748761237 **Fax:** 01225-528000
**Reg No:** 2278257 **Estd:** 1988 Private Limited Company
**Line of Business:** Collection, purification and distribution of water
**Issued Capital:** £100
**Directors:** M T Watts, C F Skellett
**Co. Secretary:** Andrew Phillips
**Branches:** Wessex Water Trustee Co Ltd, Wessex Water Depot, Lower Wharf, Devizes, Wiltshire SN10 1JP
**US SIC:** 4941, 4952
**UK SIC:** 17000, 92120

| | 30-06-14 | 30-06-13 | 30-06-12 |
|---|---|---|---|
| TA | 100 | 100 | 100 |
| NW | 100 | 100 | 100 |

DUNS 21-476-8298
## Wessex Youth Offending Team
Dame Mary Fagan House, Lutyens Close, Lychpit, Basingstoke, Hampshire RG24 8AG
**Tel:** 01256-464034
**Proprietorship**
**Line of Business:** Local government
**Proprietors:** M Evans, M Evans
**Branches:** 62 Crocker St, Newport, Isle Of Wight PO30 5DA
**US SIC:** 9121 **UK SIC:** 91110
**Employees:** 100

DUNS 28-957-6431
## West & Coe Ltd
620-626 Rainham Road South, Dagenham, Essex RM10 8YP
**Tel:** 020-8592-0164
**Web:** www.westcoe.co.uk
**Reg No:** 1663282 **Estd:** 1903 Private Limited Company
**Line of Business:** Funeral directors
**Issued Capital:** £1,000
**Principals:** E J West *(Managing)*, Mrs D M West, Ms J Gillanders
**Co. Secretary:** William Gillanders
**Branches:** West & Coe Ltd, 26 Broadway, Rainham, Essex RM13 9YW
**US SIC:** 7261 **UK SIC:** 98902
**Auditors:** Kingston Smith
**Bankers:** National Westminster Bank Plc (60-18-01)

| | 31-12-13 | 31-12-12 | 31-12-11 |
|---|---|---|---|
| TO | 8,504,155 | 7,374,110 | 6,947,186 |
| P/L | 1,049,803 | 564,025 | 535,427 |
| NW | 3,907,356 | 3,498,866 | 3,708,142 |
| WC | 1,082,712 | 230,157 | 602,356 |
| Emp. | 62 | 62 | 64 |

DUNS 21-230-2277 Imp-Exp
## West & Senior Ltd
Milltown Street, Radcliffe, Manchester M26 1WE
**Web:** www.westsenior.co.uk
**Reg No:** 0508673 **VAT No:** 147895025
**Estd:** 1952 Private Limited Company
**Line of Business:** Manufacturers of colours
**Export Markets:** Europe, Asia
**Export Sales:** £5,990,589
**Issued Capital:** £75,001
**Principals:** S R Senior *(Managing)*, N Wright, B J Daniels
**Co. Secretary:** David Brown
**Responsibilities**
**Admin:** Natalie Dickinson *(Purchasing Manager)*
**Purchasing:** Natalie Dickinson *(Purchasing Manager)*
**US SIC:** 2851 **UK SIC:** 25510
**Auditors:** PKF (UK) LLP
**Bankers:** Barclays Bank Plc (20-16-08)

| | 31-05-14 | 31-05-13 | 31-05-12 |
|---|---|---|---|
| TO | 11,504,015 | 11,031,801 | 12,290,737 |
| P/L | 612,435 | 502,439 | 682,434 |
| NW | 3,376,648 | 3,000,188 | 2,717,414 |
| WC | 1,804,120 | 1,508,149 | 1,291,922 |
| Emp. | 55 | 54 | 53 |

DUNS 42-392-3015
## West Anglia Crossroads Caring for Carers
4 The Meadow, St Ives, Cambridgeshire PE27 4LG
**Tel:** 0845-241-0954
**Web:** www.westangliacrossroads.org.uk
**Reg No:** 4379948 **Estd:** 2002 Private Company Limited By Guarantee
**Line of Business:** Activities of households as employers of domestic staff
**Directors:** Dr M J Pye, Mrs G L West, Ms L Collumbell, Ms A Braithwaite, R P Rhodes, M Van Der Hart, W R Weedon, Mrs A J Davis
**Responsibilities**
**Senior:** Margaret Pearce Higgins *(Director)*, Adam Rowles *(Director)*
**US SIC:** 8811, 8321
**UK SIC:** 99000, 96111
**Bankers:** Cafcash Ltd (40-52-40)

| | 31-03-14 | 31-03-13 | 31-03-12 |
|---|---|---|---|
| TO | 2,610,264 | 2,241,842 | 2,230,001 |
| P/L | (50,511) | (135,462) | (141,102) |
| NW | 607,292 | 594,559 | 683,886 |
| WC | 550,394 | 510,407 | 647,559 |
| Emp. | 87 | 82 | 95 |

DUNS 23-231-6158
## West Bay Housing Society Ltd
Harbour House, George Street, Bridport, Dorset DT6 4EY
**Tel:** 01308-423277
**Web:** www.westbayhousing.co.uk
**Reg No:** 0016230IP **Estd:** 2002 Friendly Society
**Line of Business:** Rest and retirement homes
**Responsibilities**
**Senior:** Jean Adams *(Manager)*, Anna Filsell *(Manager)*
**US SIC:** 8321 **UK SIC:** 96111
**Employees:** 50

DUNS 23-644-3610
## West Berkshire Council
Council Office, Market Street, Newbury, Berkshire RG14 5LD
**Tel:** 01635519111
**Web:** www.westberks.gov.uk
**Estd:** 2002
**Line of Business:** Local government
**Principals:** G Past *(Chairman)*, N Carter
**Responsibilities**
**Senior:** Theresa Bashford *(Chairman)*, Derek Carnegie *(Executive)*, Hilary Fabry *(Executive)*, Moira Fraser *(General Manager)*, Amanda Loaring *(Manager)*, Bryan Lyttle *(Head of Planning and Transport)*, Carolyn Murison *(Chairman)*, Alyson Paisley *(General Manager)*, Maureen Sheridan *(Executive)*, Anna Shiner *(Chairman)*, Gaye Sumner *(Executive)*, Johanna Watt *(Board Member)*, Quentin Webb *(Vice Chairman)*
**Finance:** Andy Walker *(Senior Financial Executive)*
**Marketing:** Peta Stoddart-Crompton *(Public Relations Officer)*, Keith Ulyatt *(Public Relations Manager)*
**Admin:** Alison Redmond *(Office Manager)*
**IT:** Andy Best *(IT Operations Manager)*
**HR:** Robert O'Reilly *(Human Resources Manager)*
**Health & Safety:** Andrew Garratt *(Principal Traffic & Road Safet)*
**Facilities:** Paul Hendry *(Countryside, Rights of Way Gro)*
**Operations:** Bill Bagnell *(Construction Project Manager)*, Greg Bowman *(Construction Project Manager)*, Tara Coulson *(Parking Enforcement Officer)*
**Purchasing:** Mike Sullivan *(Procurement Officer)*
**Fleet:** Bryan Lyttle *(Head of Planning and Transport)*
**Engineering:** Andrew Garratt *(Principal Traffic & Road Safet)*, Stewart Souden *(Technical Manager)*, Jon Winstanley *(Officer)*
**Branches:** West Berkshire Council, The Town Hall, Market Place, Newbury, Berkshire RG14 5AA
**US SIC:** 9121 **UK SIC:** 91110
**Bankers:** National Westminster Bank Plc (60-15-07)
**Employees:** 3,450

DUNS 23-842-4329
## West Berkshire Health Authority
West St The Ironstone Centre, Scunthorpe, South Humberside DN15 6HX
**Tel:** 01724292120
**Line of Business:** Dentists
**Trading Style:** Community Dental Services
**Branches:** West Berkshire Health Authority, 118 Bath Road, Thatcham, Berkshire RG18 3HH
**US SIC:** 8021 **UK SIC:** 95400
**Employees:** 80

DUNS 23-231-6315
## West Berkshire Housing Consortium Ltd
9-10 Brunel Road Commerce Park, Reading, Berkshire RG7 4AB
**Tel:** 01189302979 **Fax:** 01182-97958
**Web:** www.whbc.co.uk
**Reg No:** 0026554IP **Estd:** 1989 Friendly Society
**Line of Business:** Housing association.
**Principals:** Ms R Monbiot *(Chairman)*, J Clay, R Morcom, G Collings, K Tibbs, S Collins, R Cane, D Smith
**Co. Secretary:** S Inch
**Branches:** West Berkshire Housing Consortium Ltd, 22 Hollow La, Reading, Berkshire RG2 9BT
**US SIC:** 6531, 9121
**UK SIC:** 83400, 91110
**Auditors:** Binder Hamlyn
**Bankers:** National Westminster Bank Plc (60-17-21)
**Employees:** 640

DUNS 23-926-6203
## West Bromwich African Caribbean Resource Centre
Thomas Street, West Bromwich, West Midlands B70 6LY
**Tel:** 0121-525-9177
**Web:** www.wbacrc.org.uk
**Reg No:** 3916617 **Estd:** 2000 Private Company Limited By Guarantee
**Line of Business:** Community centres
**Directors:** R Ross, K James, Mrs H Jarrett
**Co. Secretary:** Clarence Cameron
**Responsibilities**
**Senior:** Shane Ward *(Ceo)*
**Branches:** West Bromwich African Caribbean Resource Centre, Landchard House, Victoria Street, West Bromwich, West Midlands B70 8ER
**US SIC:** 8811 **UK SIC:** 99000
**Auditors:** Gary Peter Brookes
**Bankers:** HSBC Bank plc (40-42-11)

| | 31-03-14 | 31-03-13 | 31-03-12 |
|---|---|---|---|
| TO | 715,629 | 765,463 | 1,058,799 |
| P/L | (3,022) | (71,192) | (88,066) |
| NW | 13,161 | 16,183 | 87,375 |
| WC | 10,099 | 9,752 | 77,575 |
| Emp. | 52 | 63 | 75 |

DUNS 50-964-4027
## West Bromwich Albion Football Club Ltd
**(Subsidiary of:** West Bromwich Albion Holdings Ltd)
The Hawthorns, Halfords Lane, West Bromwich, West Midlands B71 4LF
**Tel:** 0871-271-1100 **Fax:** 08712719861
**Web:** www.wba.co.uk
**Reg No:** 3295063 **Estd:** 1996 Private Limited Company
**Line of Business:** Other sporting activities not elsewhere classified
**Trading Style:** W B A A F C
**Issued Capital:** £2
**Directors:** A D Wright, R P Garlick, M J Jenkins, J R Peace
**Co. Secretary:** Richard Garlick
**Responsibilities**
**Marketing:** Katy Barton *(Head Of Marketing)*
**Branches:** West Bromwich Albion Football Club Ltd, Savacentre Freeth Street, Oldbury, West Midlands B69 3DB
**US SIC:** 7999 **UK SIC:** 97913
**Auditors:** Clement Keys

| | 30-06-13 | 30-06-12 | 30-06-11 |
|---|---|---|---|
| TO | 69,734,000 | 66,660,000 | 65,086,000 |
| P/L | 6,044,000 | 399,000 | 18,934,000 |
| NW | 26,516,000 | 18,722,000 | 16,106,000 |
| WC | 3,051,000 | (1,916,000) | (3,766,000) |
| Emp. | 150 | 139 | 135 |

DUNS 22-768-2309
## West Bromwich Building Society
374 High Street, Town Centre, West Bromwich, West Midlands B70 8LR
**Tel:** 01215257070
**Web:** www.westbrom.co.uk
**Reg No:** 0000651I **VAT No:** 648668579
**Estd:** 1849 Friendly Society
**Line of Business:** Building societies
**Directors:** C Walklin, M Ritchley, C Hafner, J Westhoff, M Nicholls, R Sommers, M Gibbard
**Co. Secretary:** Mark Preston
**Responsibilities**
**Senior:** Chris Behan *(Warehouse Manager)*
**Finance:** Jeff Ball *(Treasury Accountant)*
**Marketing:** Jane Hancher *(Marketing Manager)*, Sarah Hemmings *(Head of Communications)*, Ian Kilmartin *(Divisional Director-Transforma)*, Jim King *(Communications Manager)*, Elaine Marson *(Communications Manager)*
**IT:** Dave Archer *(Senior IT Project Manager)*
**Health & Safety:** Chris Behan *(Warehouse Manager)*
**Operations:** Chris Behan *(Warehouse Manager)*
**US SIC:** 6111 **UK SIC:** 81501
**Auditors:** KPMG Audit PLC
**Bankers:** HSBC Bank plc (40-46-13)

**Following financial data are in thousands**

| | 31-03-14 | 31-03-13 | 31-03-12 |
|---|---|---|---|
| TA | 5,650,500 | 6,203,600 | 7,417,100 |
| P/L | 2,100 | (9,400) | (9,500) |
| NW | 483,800 | 489,900 | 488,400 |
| WC | 336,500 | (3,664,400) | (4,225,200) |
| Emp. | 763 | 761 | 752 |

DUNS 21-585-7912
## West Bromwich Fire Station
Station D8, Hargate Lane, West Bromwich, West Midlands B71 1PD
**Tel:** 01213807548
**Web:** www.wmfs.net
**Estd:** 2011 Proprietorship
**Line of Business:** Fire stations
**Proprietor:** C Shaffrey
**Responsibilities**
**Senior:** Andrew Rainey *(Station Commander)*
**US SIC:** 9224 **UK SIC:** 91400
**Employees:** 70

DUNS 50-572-8501
## West Buckland Activities Ltd
West Buckland, Barnstaple, Devon EX32 0SX
**Tel:** 01598760100
**Web:** www.westbuckland.com
**Reg No:** 2520795 **Estd:** 1990 Private Limited Company
**Line of Business:** Schools (independent)
**Trading Style:** West Buckland School
**Directors:** J F Vick, C D Phillips

**Co. Secretary:** Commander Alan Jackson
**US SIC:** 8211, 7021
**UK SIC:** 93200, 66500
**Auditors:** Sully & Co
**Bankers:** Lloyds TSB Bank plc (30-90-49)

|    | 31-07-14 | 31-07-13 | 31-07-12 |
|----|----------|----------|----------|
| TA | 26,408   | 38,757   | 33,842   |
| NW | 15,193   | 16,050   | 16,908   |
| WC | 12,007   | 12,007   | 12,007   |

DUNS 21-588-5014
## West Centre
60 Kinfauns Drive, Glasgow, Lanarkshire G15 7TS
**Tel:** 01412077100
**Estd:** 2011 Proprietorship
**Line of Business:** Hospitals
**Proprietor:** B Frazer
**Responsibilities**
**Senior:** Cathy Holden (Practice Manager)
**US SIC:** 8062 **UK SIC:** 95100
**Employees:** 60

DUNS 22-987-4565
## West Cheshire College
Eaton Road, Handbridge, Chester, Cheshire CH4 7ER
**Tel:** 01244656555
**Web:** www.west-cheshire.ac.uk
**Estd:** 2002
**Line of Business:** Further education schools and colleges
**Financial Director:** B Pearson
**Responsibilities**
**Senior:** Nicola Southern (Assistant Manager)
**Branches:** West Cheshire College, Stanney La, Ellesmere Port, Cheshire CH65 9DB
**US SIC:** 8221 **UK SIC:** 93100
**Bankers:** National Westminster Bank Plc (60-40-08)
**Employees:** 500

DUNS 21-582-3358
## West Coast
Tongwell Street, Fox Milne, Milton Keynes, Buckinghamshire MK15 0SF
**Tel:** 01908685800
**Web:** www.westcoast.co.uk
**Estd:** 2011 Proprietorship
**Line of Business:** Computer stationery
**Proprietor:** L Watson
**US SIC:** 5942 **UK SIC:** 65300
**Employees:** 136

DUNS 76-348-7311     Imp
## West Coast Corrugated Ltd
Hornhouse Lane, Deacon Park, Knowsley Industrial Park, Liverpool, Merseyside L33 7YQ
**Tel:** 01515-491002
**Web:** www.westcoastcorr.co.uk
**Reg No:** 2548538 **Estd:** 1993 Private Limited Company
**Line of Business:** Manufacturers of boxes and cartons
**Issued Capital:** £75
**Directors:** D A Graham, C W Graham
**Co. Secretary:** Paul Norman
**Responsibilities**
**Senior:** Sharon Baynes (Warehouse Manager)
**Sales:** Tony Wigfield (Sales Manager)
**Admin:** Sharon Baynes (Warehouse Manager)
**HR:** Paul Baynes (Production Manager)
**Facilities:** Tommy James (Engineer)
**Operations:** Paul Baynes (Production Manager)
**Engineering:** Paul Baynes (Production Manager)
**US SIC:** 2651 **UK SIC:** 47253
**Auditors:** Edward Robinson & Co
**Bankers:** The Royal Bank Of Scotland Plc (16-32-10)

|     | 31-12-13  | 31-12-12  | 31-12-11  |
|-----|-----------|-----------|-----------|
| TO  | 8,461,104 | 7,855,379 | 8,631,985 |
| P/L | 569,364   | 652,058   | 658,690   |
| NW  | 2,323,943 | 2,147,567 | 1,868,016 |
| WC  | 612,335   | 442,389   | 391,375   |
| Emp.| 70        | 71        | 65        |

DUNS 49-101-2274
## West Coast Energy Ltd
(Subsidiary of: Gdf Suez)
Mynydd Awel, Mold, Clwyd CH7 1XN
**Tel:** 01352757604
**Web:** www.westcoastenergy.co.uk
**Reg No:** 3094654 **Estd:** 1996 Private Limited Company
**Line of Business:** Business and management consultancy activities not elsewhere classified
**Issued Capital:** £964
**Directors:** R P Tate, Ms H S Berger, S D Pinnell, M M Maino, C J Warden
**Co. Secretary:** Ms Hillary Berger

**Responsibilities**
**Senior:** Stephen Salt (Manager), Michael Tough (Technical Director), Neil Wyn-Jones (Manager)
**Marketing:** Stephen Salt (Manager)
**IT:** Michael Tough (Technical Director)
**HR:** Yvonne Stamp (Human Resources Manager)
**Health & Safety:** Mike Finlow (Health & Safety Officer)
**Branches:** West Coast Energy Ltd, 48 Cassillis Rd, Maybole, Ayrshire KA19 7HF
**US SIC:** 7392 **UK SIC:** 83951
**Auditors:** McLintocks Partnership Ltd

|     | 31-03-14     | 31-03-13   | 31-03-12   |
|-----|--------------|------------|------------|
| TO  | 2,884,904    | 3,571,266  | 3,710,603  |
| P/L | (12,283,653) | 19,840,634 | 9,223,882  |
| NW  | 26,871,937   | 40,396,686 | 27,031,446 |
| WC  | 23,960,274   | 34,921,052 | 17,179,869 |
| Emp.| 97           | 105        | 98         |

DUNS 21-569-1015     Exp
## West Coast Sea Products Ltd
Dee Walk, Kirkcudbright, Kirkcudbrightshire DG6 4DQ
**Tel:** 01557-330789
**Web:** www.wcspltd.co.uk
**Reg No:** 0048969SC **Estd:** 1971 Private Limited Company
**Line of Business:** Shell fish suppliers and processors
**Export Markets:** U S A, France, German etc.
**Export Sales:** £10,441,079
**Issued Capital:** £10,800
**Director:** J W King
**Co. Secretary:** Ms Jacqueline King
**Responsibilities**
**Health & Safety:** Matthew Atkin (Health & Safety Officer)
**Branches:** Dee Walk, Kirkcudbright, Kirkcudbrightshire DG6
**US SIC:** 0912 **UK SIC:** 03001
**Auditors:** BDO Stoy Hayward
**Bankers:** The Royal Bank Of Scotland Plc (83-24-02)

|     | 30-04-14   | 30-04-13   | 30-04-12   |
|-----|------------|------------|------------|
| TO  | 13,519,460 | 16,425,607 | 19,811,000 |
| P/L | 155,577    | 091,841    | 2,568,048  |
| NW  | 9,594,711  | 9,552,751  | 11,031,279 |
| WC  | 5,550,723  | 5,043,199  | 6,595,868  |
| Emp.| 162        | 180        | 180        |

DUNS 77-719-8748
## West Coast Trains Ltd
(Subsidiary of: Virgin Group Holdings Limited)
Jesson Way, Crag Bank, Carnforth, Lancashire LA5 9UR
**Tel:** 08448504685 **Fax:** 0121-654-3252
**Web:** www.westcoastrailways.co.uk
**Reg No:** 3007940 **Estd:** 1995 Private Limited Company
**Line of Business:** Rail transport services
**Trading Style:** West Coast Railways, Virgin Trains, Virgin Rail, Virgin West Coast
**Issued Capital:** £1
**Directors:** G C Leech, P A Bearpark, P Whittingham
**Co. Secretary:** Barry Gerrard
**Branches:** West Coast Trains Ltd, New Street Station, Birmingham, West Midlands B2 4QA
**US SIC:** 4141 **UK SIC:** 72102
**Auditors:** KPMG LLP

|     | 31-03-14    | 31-03-13    | 31-03-12    |
|-----|-------------|-------------|-------------|
| TO  | 951,132,000 | 895,750,000 | 929,246,000 |
| P/L | 9,292,000   | 24,911,000  | 40,775,000  |
| NW  | 1,828,000   | 4,223,000   | 25,738,000  |
| WC  | 23,925,000  | 26,293,000  | 48,987,000  |
| Emp.| 2,973       | 2,915       | 2,886       |

DUNS 22-002-3564
## West College Scotland
College Square, Queen's Quay, Clydebank, Dunbartonshire G81 1BF
**Tel:** 01415-812-286
**Web:** www.westcollegescotland.ac.uk
**VAT No:** 845353028 **Estd:** 2013
**Line of Business:** Third-level college education.
**Trading Style:** Wcs
**Principals:** K Mckellar (Chairman), A Ritchie (Financial), D Alexander, Ms A Cumberford, G Kelly, Ms G Mcarthur
**Responsibilities**
**Senior:** Keith McKellar (Chairperson)
**Admin:** Gwen McArthur (Secretary of the Board)
**US SIC:** 8221 **UK SIC:** 93100
**Employees:** 1,200

DUNS 21-995-4824
## West College Scotland Foundation
Renfrew Road, Paisley, Renfrewshire PA3 4DR
**Tel:** 01415812222
**Web:** www.reidkerr.ac.uk
**Reg No:** 0472412SC **VAT No:** 845353028
**Estd:** 1991 Private Company Limited By Guarantee

**Line of Business:** Provide FE and HE education
**Directors:** W D Robertson, Ms A M O'Hagan, Ms A Cumberford, G A Mcguinness, B Humphrey, D Alexander, J Mcmillan, Dr D Little
**Co. Secretary:** Alexander Nelson
**Responsibilities**
**Marketing:** Irene Allan (Marketing Manager), Sharon Gardiner (Head of Business)
**IT:** Bill Gallacher (?Head of Business and Computin), Bernadette O' Donnell (IT Manager)
**HR:** Maureen Scott (HR Manager)
**Engineering:** Tommy Campbell (Head of Construction)
**US SIC:** 6732 **UK SIC:** 83100
**Employees:** 1,200

DUNS 33-945-5826
## West Cornwall Nursing Agency
Long Rock Industrial Estate, Long Rock, Long Rock, Penzance, Cornwall TR20 8HX
**Tel:** 01736333177
**Estd:** 1984 Proprietorship
**Line of Business:** Nursing agencies
**Proprietor:** Ms J O'Dwyer
**US SIC:** 7361 **UK SIC:** 83954
**Employees:** 55

DUNS 52-021-4248
## West Country Business Systems (Holdings) Ltd
(Subsidiary of: Westleigh Investments Holdings Ltd)
Somerset House, Magdalene Street, Glastonbury, Somerset BA6 9EJ
**Tel:** 01458-833344
**Web:** www.wcbs.co.uk
**Reg No:** 3387976 **Estd:** 1997 Private Limited Company
**Line of Business:** Educational equipment and supplies
**Export Sales:** £220,440
**Trading Style:** W C B S
**Issued Capital:** £133,500
**Directors:** C G Clarke, I Santamaria, C Race, T C Berry, J N Harrison
**Co. Secretary:** Mrs Deborah Jewell
**Responsibilities**
**Senior:** Anthony Child (Manager), Peter Heginbotham (Manager)
**US SIC:** 7379 **UK SIC:** 83940
**Auditors:** Grant Thornton UK LLP
**Bankers:** Barclays Bank Plc (20-99-40)

|     | 31-08-13  | 31-08-12  | 31-08-11  |
|-----|-----------|-----------|-----------|
| TO  | 3,643,807 | 3,550,173 | 3,537,722 |
| P/L | 717,322   | 642,563   | 892,899   |
| NW  | 1,298,196 | 1,375,696 | 1,525,080 |
| WC  | 631,888   | 716,606   | 867,225   |
| Emp.| 62        | 65        | 57        |

DUNS 28-917-4195
## West Country Motor Homes Ltd
Bristol Road, Brent Knoll, Highbridge, Somerset TA9 4HG
**Tel:** 01278761200 **Fax:** 01278761214
**Web:** www.westcountrymotorhomes.co.uk
**Reg No:** 1454914 **Estd:** 1979 Private Limited Company
**Line of Business:** Mobile homes
**Issued Capital:** £863,000
**Directors:** P R Shaw, S G Pike
**Branches:** West Country Motor Homes Ltd, Bristol Road, Highbridge, Somerset TA9 4HG
**US SIC:** 7033, 7539
**UK SIC:** 66701, 67100
**Auditors:** Webb & Co Ltd
**Bankers:** National Westminster Bank Plc (60-11-38)

|     | 31-12-13   | 31-12-12   | 31-12-11   |
|-----|------------|------------|------------|
| TO  | 15,996,187 | 18,119,069 | 20,962,441 |
| P/L | 278,485    | 364,219    | 603,647    |
| NW  | 8,800,764  | 8,949,804  | 8,934,758  |
| WC  | 8,467,580  | 8,614,030  | 8,591,903  |
| Emp.| 46         | 50         | 49         |

DUNS 21-716-5760
## West Country Vending Service Ltd
Bath Road Peasedown St John, Bath, Avon BA2 8DH
**Tel:** 0870-225-0005 **Fax:** 01225444936
**Web:** www.wcvs.co.uk
**Reg No:** 0923301 **Estd:** 1967 Private Limited Company
**Line of Business:** Vending machines sale, rental and supply
**Issued Capital:** £329,100
**Principals:** W H Booty (Chairman and Managing), N P Fowler, G S Currer, B E Tustain, Mrs B J Booty
**Co. Secretary:** Douglas Stembridge
**Responsibilities**
**Sales:** Coleen Cook (Business Development Manager), Paul Tweed (Business Development Manager)

**US SIC:** 5963, 3542
**UK SIC:** 65600, 32212
**Auditors:** Deloitte & Touche LLP
**Bankers:** National Westminster Bank Plc (60-02-05)

|     | 31-12-13   | 31-12-12  | 31-12-11  |
|-----|------------|-----------|-----------|
| TO  | 10,414,744 | 9,985,560 | 9,905,599 |
| P/L | 800,764    | 729,863   | 1,338,721 |
| NW  | 2,988,732  | 2,743,492 | 2,568,470 |
| WC  | 644,440    | 430,039   | 231,073   |
| Emp.| 175        | 174       | 176       |

DUNS 50-709-1338
## West Cumbria Care & Support
26 Stanley Street, Workington, Cumbria CA14 2JD
**Tel:** 01900-67777 **Fax:** 0190068137
**Web:** www.westhouse.org.uk
**Reg No:** 0028282IP **Estd:** 1986 Friendly Society
**Line of Business:** Charities and charitable organisations
**Trading Style:** West House
**Principals:** Reverend J Martin (Chairman), M Devlin, E Rushpal, E Jansen, C Shaw, R John, M Yuir
**Co. Secretary:** Keith Fitton
**Responsibilities**
**Finance:** Susan McKaa (Financial Officer)
**HR:** Cathy Parker (Human Resources Manager)
**Health & Safety:** Cathy Parker (Human Resources Manager)
**Branches:** West Cumbria Care & Support, Main St, Cockermouth, Cumbria CA13 9LU
**US SIC:** 6732, 6733
**UK SIC:** 83100
**Auditors:** Michael Craig Consultancy
**Bankers:** Clydesdale Bank Plc (82-68-25)
**Employees:** 137

DUNS 21-891-6377
## West Cumbria College
Hallwood Road Lillyhall Industrial, Estate, Workington, Cumbria CA14 4JN
**Tel:** 01946-839300
**Web:** www.lcwc.ac.uk
**Estd:** 1999
**Line of Business:** First-degree level higher education
**Trading Style:** Lakes College
**Principals:** Ms H Bland (Financial), Dr B Taylor
**Responsibilities**
**Senior:** Cathrene Richardson (Principal)
**IT:** Neil Hamblin (IT Manager)
**HR:** Joan Bayliff (Human Resources Manager)
**Branches:** West Cumbria College, Flatt Walks, Whitehaven, Cumbria CA28 7RN
**US SIC:** 8221 **UK SIC:** 93100
**Employees:** 350

DUNS 54-900-3671
## West Derby School
West Derby Road, Liverpool, Merseyside L13 7HQ
**Tel:** 0151-235-1333
**Web:** www.westderbyschool.co.uk
**Estd:** 2012
**Line of Business:** Schools (local authority)
**Director:** P Fraser
**Responsibilities**
**Senior:** Margaret Rannard (Head Teacher)
**Finance:** Sue Dardis (Bursar)
**Health & Safety:** Tom Butterworth (Site Manager)
**Facilities:** Tom Butterworth (Site Manager)
**US SIC:** 8211 **UK SIC:** 93200
**Employees:** 120

DUNS 22-971-9877
## West Dunbartonshire Council
Garshake Road, Dumbarton, Dunbartonshire G82 3PU
**Web:** www.west-dunbarton.gov.uk
**Estd:** 1996
**Line of Business:** Local government
**Trading Style:** Dumbarton District Unemployed Initiative Group, Dumbarton Adult Training Centre, Dalreoch House
**Principals:** C Howett (Financial), T Huntingford, E Walker
**Responsibilities**
**Senior:** David McMillan (Chief Executive)
**Marketing:** Malcolm Bennie (Marketing Officer)
**Operations:** Ronald Dinnie (Environmental Manager)
**Branches:** West Dunbartonshire Council, Clydebank Area Team Rosebery Place, Clydebank, Dunbartonshire G81 1TG
**US SIC:** 9121 **UK SIC:** 91110
**Employees:** 800

## DUNS 28-853-7640
### West End Motors (Bodmin) Ltd
Bodmin Business Park, Launceston Road, Bodmin, Cornwall PL31 2RJ
**Tel:** 01208261111 **Fax:** 01208261112
**Web:** www.westendmotorsbodmin.co.uk
**Reg No:** 0767465 **VAT No:** 143945358
**Estd:** 2009 Private Limited Company
**Line of Business:** Car dealers (new & used)
**Issued Capital:** £6,500
**Principals:** B A Cook (Managing), A P Martin
**Co. Secretary:** Antony Cook
**Responsibilities**
**Senior:** Ryan Cook (Dealer Principal), David Culverhouse (Parts Manager)
**Finance:** Terri Vanderplank (Accountant)
**Sales:** Andy Coppin (Vauxhall Sales Manager)
**Branches:** West End Motors (Bodmin) Ltd, 7-13 Normandy Way, Bodmin, Cornwall PL31 1EU
**US SIC:** 5511, 7539
**UK SIC:** 65100, 67100
**Auditors:** Phillips Frith
**Bankers:** HSBC Bank plc (40-12-22)

|      | 31-12-13   | 31-12-12   | 31-12-11    |
|------|------------|------------|-------------|
| TO   | 16,388,275 | 13,341,106 | 11,623,108  |
| P/L  | 367,769    | 41,618     | 30,297      |
| NW   | 3,004,652  | 2,728,911  | 2,704,711   |
| WC   | (577,627)  | (932,902)  | (1,054,059) |
| Emp. | 60         | 58         | 57          |

## DUNS 23-775-6072
### West End Operatic Society Ltd
5 Magenta Crescent, Newcastle-Upon-Tyne, Tyne and Wear NE5 1YL
**Tel:** 01912670890
**Web:** www.westendoperaticsociety.com
**Reg No:** 3768900 **Estd:** 1999 Private Limited Company
**Line of Business:** Operation of arts facilities
**Directors:** F L Saxby, Miss S J Noutch, L Gilbert, D Coleman, Ms C J Grey, S Wooley, M Armstrong
**Co. Secretary:** Ms Dorothy Coleman
**Responsibilities**
**Senior:** Vivien Edington (Manager), Valerie Shield (Manager)
**US SIC:** 7911 **UK SIC:** 97913

|    | 30-06-13 | 30-06-12 | 30-06-11 |
|----|----------|----------|----------|
| TA | 10,458   | 37,294   | 41,617   |
| NW | 9,453    | 36,040   | 41,200   |
| WC | 9,152    | 35,639   | 40,666   |

## DUNS 22-606-8922   Imp-Exp
### West End Precision Ltd
Unit 1, Caddsdown Business Support Centre, Caddsdown Industrial Park, Clovelly Road, Bideford, Devon EX39 3DX
**Web:** www.wepl.co.uk
**Reg No:** 1458714 **Estd:** 1967 Private Limited Company
**Line of Business:** Other engineering activities
**Issued Capital:** £25,000
**Managing Director:** L P Dziurzynski
**Co. Secretary:** Ms Dawn Dziurzynski
**Responsibilities**
**Senior:** Warren Rhode (Production Manager)
**IT:** Warren Rhode (Production Manager)
**HR:** Warren Rhode (Production Manager)
**Health & Safety:** Warren Rhode (Production Manager)
**Purchasing:** Warren Rhode (Production Manager)
**Engineering:** Warren Rhode (Production Manager)
**US SIC:** 8911, 3423
**UK SIC:** 83701, 31612
**Auditors:** Perrins Ltd

|      | 31-03-14  | 31-03-13  | 31-03-12  |
|------|-----------|-----------|-----------|
| TO   | 3,957,051 | 3,760,602 | N/A       |
| P/L  | 382,432   | 586,251   | N/A       |
| NW   | 3,479,034 | 3,206,862 | 2,802,300 |
| WC   | 725,898   | 970,508   | 1,104,560 |
| Emp. | 64        | 62        | N/A       |

## DUNS 54-864-5589
### West Essex Clinical Commissioning Group Offices
Building 4, Spencer Close, St Margarets Hospital, The Plain, Epping, Essex CM16 6TN
**Tel:** 01992 566140
**Web:** www.westessexccg.nhs.uk/
**Estd:** 2013
**Line of Business:** Health authority
**Trading Style:** Nhs West Sussex
**Issued Capital:** £2
**Director:** Ms C Morris
**Responsibilities**
**Senior:** Laura Robertson (Senior Communications Manager)
**Branches:** West Essex Clinical Commissioning Group Offices, Langley House, 27 West Street, Chichester, West Sussex PO19 1QS
**US SIC:** 8091 **UK SIC:** 95200
**Employees:** 200

## DUNS 29-670-9405
### West Ferry Printers Ltd
(**Subsidiary of:** Northern & Shell Media Group Ltd)
235 Westferry Road, London E14 8NX
**Tel:** 020-7538-3100
**Web:** www.northernandshell.co.uk
**Reg No:** 1997219 **VAT No:** 506962631
**Estd:** 1986 Private Limited Company
**Line of Business:** Printers general
**Trading Style:** West Ferry
**Issued Capital:** £7,000,000
**Directors:** S Myerson, M S Ellice, R Sanderson, R C Desmond
**Co. Secretary:** Robert Sanderson
**Responsibilities**
**Senior:** David Broadhurst (Chief Executive), Thomas Pannett (Manager), John Wenman (Manager)
**Finance:** John Higginbottom (Finance Manager)
**Engineering:** Phil Sweetman (Engineering Manager)
**Branches:** West Ferry Printers Ltd, 1 Canada Square, London E14 5AB
**US SIC:** 2794 **UK SIC:** 47545
**Auditors:** KPMG LLP
**Bankers:** National Westminster Bank Plc (60-80-08)

|      | 31-12-13     | 31-12-12     | 31-12-11     |
|------|--------------|--------------|--------------|
| TO   | 20,204,000   | 22,187,000   | 24,664,000   |
| P/L  | 2,279,000    | 2,628,000    | 3,356,000    |
| NW   | 8,751,000    | 10,558,000   | 11,071,000   |
| WC   | (13,906,000) | (12,372,000) | (11,440,000) |
| Emp. | 84           | 103          | 182          |

## DUNS 23-480-7642
### West Fife Enterprise Ltd
Forth View Learning Centre, Forth View Industrial Estate, Newmills, Dunfermline, Fife KY12 8TL
**Tel:** 01383-881364
**Web:** www.westfifeenterprise.org.uk
**Reg No:** 0131467SC **Estd:** 1984 Private Company Limited By Guarantee
**Line of Business:** Adult and other education not elsewhere classified
**Directors:** Mrs J A Mccauslin, M G Laidlaw, Mrs C Paterson, T Douglas, G Mclaren, Miss C Maher
**Co. Secretary:** Alan Boyle
**Responsibilities**
**Senior:** William Sheilds (Manager)
**Finance:** Joyce Cambell (Financial Controller)
**US SIC:** 8249 **UK SIC:** 93300
**Auditors:** Convyclark Ltd
**Bankers:** Clydesdale Bank Plc (82-62-19)

|      | 30-04-14  | 30-04-13  | 30-04-12 |
|------|-----------|-----------|----------|
| TO   | 710,081   | 765,669   | 866,852  |
| P/L  | (118,541) | (129,378) | 32,885   |
| NW   | (23,166)  | 95,375    | 224,753  |
| WC   | (26,964)  | 83,990    | 212,028  |
| Emp. | 59        | 59        | 59       |

## DUNS 23-016-6485
### West Glamorgan Health
Gowerton Medical Centre, Mill Street, Gowerton, Swansea, West Glamorgan SA4 3ED
**Tel:** 01792872404
**Web:** www.gowertondentalpractice.co.uk
**Estd:** 1979 Partnership
**Line of Business:** Doctors surgery
**Trading Style:** Gowerton Medical Practice
**Partners:** Dr P Evans, Dr N Acton, Dr E Jones, Dr D Edwards, Dr C R Morgan
**Branches:** West Glamorgan Health, Mansel Road, Swansea, West Glamorgan SA1 7JR
**US SIC:** 8011 **UK SIC:** 95300
**Employees:** 50

## DUNS 22-602-2259   Imp
### The West Group (Fluid Power) Ltd
29 Aston Road, Waterlooville, Hampshire PO7 7XJ
**Tel:** 023-9226-6031 **Fax:** 02392240323
**Web:** www.westgroup.co.uk
**Reg No:** 1661106 **Estd:** 1982 Private Limited Company
**Line of Business:** General mechanical engineering
**Issued Capital:** £52,000
**Principals:** B E West (Managing), M T Middleton, P M Brown
**Branches:** The West Group (Fluid Power) Ltd, 29 Aston Road, Waterlooville, Hampshire PO7 7XJ
**US SIC:** 8911 **UK SIC:** 83701

|      | 31-08-13   | 31-08-12  | 31-08-11  |
|------|------------|-----------|-----------|
| TO   | 11,000,941 | N/A       | N/A       |
| P/L  | 530,001    | N/A       | N/A       |
| NW   | 955,289    | 379,375   | 379,375   |
| WC   | (59,277)   | (672,275) | (672,275) |
| Emp. | 76         | N/A       | N/A       |

## DUNS 22-716-5396
### West Ham United Football Club Ltd
(**Subsidiary of:** Wh Holding Ltd)
Boleyn Ground, Green Street, London E13 9AZ
**Tel:** 02085482748 **Fax:** 02085482758
**Web:** www.whufc.com
**Reg No:** 0066516 **VAT No:** 248500077
**Estd:** 1900 Private Limited Company
**Line of Business:** Sports clubs
**Issued Capital:** £5,500,000
**Directors:** A Bernhardt, A J Mollett, D Gold, D Sullivan, Ms K R Brady, A Kinnear
**Co. Secretary:** Andrew Mollett
**Responsibilities**
**Senior:** Liz Coley (Club Secretary), Mick King (Chief Executive Officer), Julie Pidgeon (Executive)
**Marketing:** Dan Huson (Marketing and CRM Manager), Tara Warren (?Executive Director Marketing)
**Admin:** Amanda Ayres (Administration Officer)
**HR:** Rashid Abba (Training Director)
**Branches:** West Ham United Football Club Ltd, Training Ground, Saville Road, Romford, Essex RM6 6DS
**US SIC:** 7999 **UK SIC:** 97913
**Auditors:** PricewaterhouseCoopers LLP
**Bankers:** Barclays Bank Plc (20-67-88)

|      | 31-05-14      | 31-05-13      | 31-05-12     |
|------|---------------|---------------|--------------|
| TO   | 114,852,000   | 89,815,000    | 46,165,000   |
| P/L  | 10,345,000    | (3,511,000)   | (25,480,000) |
| NW   | (148,912,000) | (143,111,000) | (92,730,000) |
| WC   | (104,346,000) | (172,228,000) | (97,674,000) |
| Emp. | 609           | 580           | 586          |

## DUNS 53-602-4953
### West Ham United Ltd
(**Subsidiary of:** Wh Holding Ltd)
Boleyn Ground, Green Street, Plaistow, London E13 9AZ
**Fax:** 020-8548-2758
**Web:** www.westhamhotel.co.uk
**Reg No:** 3407691 **Estd:** 1900 Private Limited Company
**Line of Business:** Operation of other sports arenas and stadiums not elsewhere classified
**Issued Capital:** £16,808,738
**Directors:** Ms K R Brady, A Bernhardt, D Gold, A J Mollett, D Sullivan
**Co. Secretary:** Andrew Mollett
**Responsibilities**
**Senior:** Nicholas Igoe (Financial Director)
**Finance:** Nicholas Igoe (Financial Director)
**Marketing:** Tara Warren (Communications Manager)
**Sales:** Tara Warren (Communications Manager)
**HR:** Ron Pearce (Stadium Manager)
**Health & Safety:** Ron Pearce (Stadium Manager)
**Facilities:** Ron Pearce (Stadium Manager)
**Operations:** Debbie Silver (Head of Retail), Tara Warren (Communications Manager)
**Purchasing:** Debbie Silver (Head of Retail)
**US SIC:** 7011 **UK SIC:** 66500
**Auditors:** Deloitte LLP
**Bankers:** Bank Of Scotland (80-20-00)

|    | 31-05-14   | 31-05-13   | 31-05-12   |
|----|------------|------------|------------|
| TA | 41,903,000 | 41,903,000 | 41,903,000 |
| NW | 41,463,000 | 41,463,000 | 41,463,000 |
| WC | 35,913,000 | 35,913,000 | 35,913,000 |

## DUNS 21-812-7097
### West Hampshire Clinical Commissioning Group
Omega House 112, Southampton Road, Eastleigh, Hampshire SO50 5PB
**Tel:** 02380 627 444
**Web:** www.westhampshireccg.nhs.uk
**Estd:** 2014 Incorporate By Act Of Parliament
**Line of Business:** Nhs clinics
**Trading Style:** West Hampshire Ccg
**Responsibilities**
**Senior:** Heather Hauschild (Ceo)
**US SIC:** 9121 **UK SIC:** 91110
**Employees:** 160

## DUNS 28-831-0329
### The West Hants Lawn Tennis Company (Bournemouth) Ltd
Roslin Road South, Bournemouth, Dorset BH3 7EF
**Tel:** 01202-519455
**Web:** www.westhants.co.uk
**Reg No:** 0210654 **VAT No:** 186325742
**Estd:** 1925 Private Limited Company
**Line of Business:** Sports clubs
**Issued Capital:** £11
**Directors:** S G Smith, Mrs M S Bray, M A Smith, N W Humby, Dr D R Richards, Mrs K F Cooper, E Dry, E C Bessant
**Co. Secretary:** Colin Wise

## Responsibilities
**Senior:** Richard Atkin (Manager), Robert Booth (Manager), Peter Elvis (Chief Executive)
**US SIC:** 7999 **UK SIC:** 97913
**Auditors:** Mazars Neville Russell
**Bankers:** National Westminster Bank Plc (51-81-20)

|      | 31-12-13  | 31-12-12  | 31-12-11  |
|------|-----------|-----------|-----------|
| TO   | 2,802,206 | 2,678,935 | 2,569,729 |
| P/L  | 93,651    | 70,267    | 67,517    |
| NW   | 1,141,779 | 1,049,150 | 979,851   |
| WC   | (185,106) | (222,940) | (162,741) |
| Emp. | 118       | 134       | 128       |

## DUNS 21-726-3583
### West Hatch High School Academy Trust
West Hatch High School, High Road, Chigwell, Essex IG7 5BT
**Tel:** 02085048216
**Reg No:** 7628943 **Estd:** 2011 Private Company Limited By Guarantee
**Line of Business:** General secondary education
**Directors:** C F Hansen, Mrs S Weeden, M S Sait, S Treacher, D P Solomons, Ms S Trickey, J W Haley, Ms S A Avery
**Co. Secretary:** Ms Lisa Barker
**Responsibilities**
**Senior:** Alan Drake (Director), Frances Howarth (Director), Ashley Russell (Director), Kiran Suri (Director), Barbara Trister (Director)
**US SIC:** 8211 **UK SIC:** 93200
**Bankers:** The Royal Bank Of Scotland Plc (16-12-21)

|      | 31-08-14   | 31-08-13   | 31-08-12   |
|------|------------|------------|------------|
| TO   | 7,799,000  | 9,079,000  | 21,269,000 |
| P/L  | 11,000     | 1,423,000  | 12,084,000 |
| NW   | 13,168,000 | 12,906,000 | 11,601,000 |
| WC   | 1,401,000  | 1,258,000  | 1,063,000  |
| Emp. | 140        | 147        | 143        |

## DUNS 23-223-2165
### West Health & Social Service Board
Gransha Hospital, Clooney Road, Londonderry, Co Londonderry BT47 6YZ
**Tel:** 02871865228
**Web:** www.westerntrust.hscni.net
**Line of Business:** Healthcare companies
**Trading Style:** West Health & Social Care Trust
**Responsibilities**
**Senior:** Helena Doherty (Service Manager)
**Branches:** West Health & Social Service Board, 51 Chanterhill Road, Enniskillen, Co Fermanagh BT74 6DE
**US SIC:** 8091 **UK SIC:** 95200
**Employees:** 60

## DUNS 23-573-1770
### West Heath 2000
Ashgrove Road, Sevenoaks, Kent TN13 1SR
**Tel:** 01732468993
**Web:** www.westheathschool.com
**Reg No:** 3571239 **Estd:** 1998 Private Unlimited Company
**Line of Business:** Schools
**Directors:** S A Crookshank, Mrs M E Crabtree, L Harris, Mrs M M Boyle, D S Crawford, R J Fallowfield, R Vogt, Ms M Corbett
**Co. Secretary:** Mrs Joanne Flanagan
**Responsibilities**
**Senior:** Glenn Campbell (Director), Jean Canet (Director), Victoria Furneaux (Director)
**US SIC:** 8211, 8321
**UK SIC:** 93200, 96111
**Auditors:** Levy Gee
**Bankers:** HSBC Bank plc (40-05-22)

|      | 31-08-14  | 31-08-13  | 31-08-12  |
|------|-----------|-----------|-----------|
| TO   | 5,873,840 | 6,443,895 | 5,702,755 |
| P/L  | 37,600    | 971,025   | 272,562   |
| NW   | 4,486,086 | 4,448,486 | 3,477,261 |
| WC   | 2,058,977 | 2,493,880 | 1,778,867 |
| Emp. | 128       | 124       | 124       |

## DUNS 42-393-8505
### West Herefordshire Community N H S Trust
99 Waverley Road, St Albans, Hertfordshire AL3 5TL
**Tel:** 03007770707
**Estd:** 1994 Incorporate By Act Of Parliament
**Line of Business:** N H S Trust.
**Branches:** West Herefordshire Community N H S Trust, 45 Barton Road, Hereford, Herefordshire HR4 0AY
**US SIC:** 8062, 8091
**UK SIC:** 95100, 95200
**Employees:** 200

DUNS 54-864-3915 **Imp**

## West Hertfordshire Hospitals Nhs Trust

Vicarage Road, Watford, Hertfordshire WD18 0HB

**Tel:** 01923217392

**Web:** www.westhertshospitals.nhs.uk

**Estd:** 2000

**Line of Business:** Public sector hospital activities, including nhs trusts

**Trading Style:** Whht, Watford General Hospital, Hemel Hempstead Hospital, St. Albans City Hospital

**Issued Capital:** £1

**Principals:** P Hanahoe *(Chairman)*, D Mcneil, Ms S Wiles, N Evans, R Harrison, Ms S Childerstone, J Filochowski, Dr C Johnston

**Responsibilities**

**Senior:** Osi Ajaegbu *(Services Manager)*, David McNeil *(Director)*

**Branches:** West Hertfordshire Hospitals Nhs Trust, Hemel Hempstead General Hospital, Hillfield Rd, Hemel Hempstead, Hertfordshire HP2 4AD

**US SIC:** 9121, 8062, 8091

**UK SIC:** 91110, 95100, 95200

**Auditors:** Grant Thornton UK LLP

**Turnover:** £260,398,000

DUNS 23-210-8332

## West Herts College

Watford Campus, Hempstead Road, Watford, Hertfordshire WD17 3EZ

**Tel:** 01923812000

**Web:** www.westherts.ac.uk

**Estd:** 1890

**Line of Business:** Colleges (technical and agricultural)

**Trading Style:** Watford Campus, Casio Campus, Dacorum

**Principals:** Ms R Prinderville *(Financial)*, A Bragg

**Responsibilities**

**Senior:** Ellen Alexander *(Site Manager)*, Jill Worgan *(Principal)*

**HR:** Coral Dean *(HR Manager)*

**Facilities:** Kim Murphy *(Facilities Manager)*

**Branches:** West Herts College, 179 High St, Berkhamsted, Hertfordshire HP4 3HB

**US SIC:** 8221 **UK SIC:** 93100

**Bankers:** Lloyds TSB Bank plc (30-99-21)

**Employees:** 300

DUNS 77-511-7120

## West Highland College Uhi

West Highland College Uhi - Fort William, Carmichae, Fort William, Inverness-Shire PH33 6FF

**Tel:** 01397-874000

**Web:** www.whc.uhi.ac.uk

**Reg No:** 0153921SC **Estd:** 1994 Private Limited Company

**Line of Business:** First-degree level higher education

**Issued Capital:** £2

**Directors:** G H Bushnell, Ms L D Rohmer, A C Shepherd, Ms R J Bradley, Ms K J Macgregor, D J Ferguson, N Ababurko, G M Semler

**Co. Secretary:** Anthony Humphreys

**Responsibilities**

**Senior:** Alan Ashworth *(Manager)*, Alice Cameron *(Director)*, Kevin Peach *(Director)*, Hilary Stubbs *(Director)*

**US SIC:** 8221, 8249

**UK SIC:** 93100, 93300

**Auditors:** R A Clement Associates

**Bankers:** Bank Of Scotland (80-06-84)

| | 31-07-14 | 31-07-13 | 31-07-12 |
|---|---|---|---|
| TO | 3,721,620 | 3,468,464 | 3,225,986 |
| P/L | (33,813) | 39,449 | 121,421 |
| NW | 5,929,682 | 807,807 | 4,136,348 |
| WC | 191,352 | 424,022 | 586,133 |
| Emp. | 139 | 153 | 144 |

DUNS 23-082-9223

## West Hill School

Stamford Street, Stalybridge, Cheshire SK15 1LX

**Tel:** 0161-338-2193

**Estd:** 1927

**Line of Business:** Schools (local authority)

**Director:** R J Hewitt

**US SIC:** 8211 **UK SIC:** 93200

**Employees:** 100

DUNS 23-653-8773

## West Hill School Trust Ltd

Saint Margarets Lane, Fareham, Hampshire PO14 4BS

**Web:** www.westhillpark.com

**Reg No:** 0633736 **Estd:** 1920 Private Company Limited By Guarantee

**Line of Business:** Primary education

**Trading Style:** West Park School

**Directors:** Mrs M Breen, Mrs B Worsley, R G Walters, D R Llewellyn, A M Sears, Ms S C Mclaren, P L Coote, Mrs F C Knight

**Co. Secretary:** Timothy Rogerson

**Responsibilities**

**Senior:** John Lever *(Manager)*, Sally Mostyn *(Director)*

**Marketing:** Kay Ramsay *(Marketing Manager)*

**US SIC:** 8211, 7392

**UK SIC:** 93200, 83951

**Auditors:** BDO Stoy Hayward LLP

**Bankers:** Lloyds TSB Bank plc (30-93-17)

| | 31-07-13 | 31-07-12 | 31-07-11 |
|---|---|---|---|
| TO | 3,167,804 | 3,205,117 | 2,964,133 |
| P/L | (130,523) | (28,889) | (86,841) |
| NW | 860,073 | 990,596 | 1,019,485 |
| WC | (1,126,342) | (711,763) | (781,506) |
| Emp. | 109 | 101 | 102 |

DUNS 49-492-5233

## West Horsley Dairy Ltd

Kingswey Business Park, Forsyth Road, Woking, Surrey GU21 5SF

**Tel:** 01483-725000

**Web:** www.westhorsleydairy.co.uk

**Reg No:** 3154768 **Estd:** 1996 Private Limited Company

**Line of Business:** Distribution service providers

**Issued Capital:** £1,000

**Director:** P H Colton

**Co. Secretary:** Ms Catherine Colton

**Responsibilities**

**Senior:** Catherine Entwistle *(partner)*

**Sales:** Catherine Entwistle *(partner)*

**Operations:** Roger Heels *(Manager)*

**US SIC:** 4712, 4222, 5143, 5149, 5146

**UK SIC:** 77002, 77003, 61700

**Bankers:** Barclays Bank Plc (27-99-00)

| | 26-04-14 | 27-04-13 | 28-04-12 |
|---|---|---|---|
| TO | 16,532,619 | 15,849,495 | 15,193,619 |
| P/L | 925,902 | 799,901 | 654,508 |
| NW | 1,562,277 | 945,353 | 453,939 |
| WC | 788,342 | 364,785 | 393,444 |
| Emp. | 92 | 93 | 93 |

DUNS 28-846-0520

## West House School

24 St James Road, Birmingham, West Midlands B15 2NX

**Tel:** 0121-440-4097

**Web:** www.westhouse.bham.sch.uk

**Reg No:** 0634981 **Estd:** 1959 Private Limited Company

**Line of Business:** Schools (independent)

**Trading Style:** West House Nusery

**Directors:** Ms S H Evans, S T Heathcote, K D Phillips, R A Middleton, Ms A M Tonks, J R Gittins, E J Rutledge, C S Smith

**Co. Secretary:** Ms Ann Doyle

**Responsibilities**

**Senior:** Celia Bell *(Director)*, Alistair Lyttle *(Headmaster)*

**Marketing:** Alistair Lyttle *(Headmaster)*

**HR:** Alistair Lyttle *(Headmaster)*

**Health & Safety:** Alistair Lyttle *(Headmaster)*

**Purchasing:** Sarah Todd *(Purchasing Manager)*

**US SIC:** 8211 **UK SIC:** 93200

**Auditors:** John W Hinks & Co

**Bankers:** Lloyds TSB Bank plc (30-92-99)

| | 31-08-13 | 31-08-12 | 31-08-11 |
|---|---|---|---|
| TO | 2,233,636 | 2,036,553 | 1,808,657 |
| P/L | 241,504 | 163,038 | 116,572 |
| NW | 1,888,001 | 1,646,152 | 1,482,904 |
| WC | 1,209,091 | 1,081,187 | 915,689 |
| Emp. | 54 | 57 | 52 |

DUNS 50-583-1719

## West House Transport (S & G) Ltd

20 Whitehouse Street, Bristol, Avon BS3 4AY

**Tel:** 01179634000

**Web:** www.whtransport.com

**Reg No:** 2525856 **VAT No:** 567546794

**Estd:** 1990 Private Limited Company

**Line of Business:** Other business activities not elsewhere classified

**Issued Capital:** £16,000

**Directors:** R M Gallop, P H Chapman

**Co. Secretary:** Ian Dunbar

**Responsibilities**

**Senior:** Michael Stafford *(Manager)*

**Branches:** West House Transport (S & G) Ltd, Unit 4, Telford Gate, Andover, Hampshire SP10 3SF

**US SIC:** 4789 **UK SIC:** 77002

**Auditors:** Solomon Hare

**Bankers:** Lloyds TSB Bank plc (30-00-01)

| | 30-09-13 | 30-09-12 | 30-09-11 |
|---|---|---|---|
| TO | 11,669,373 | 11,470,281 | 11,264,479 |
| P/L | 968,541 | 897,541 | 725,594 |
| NW | 1,372,604 | 1,081,367 | 833,250 |
| WC | 674,080 | 520,000 | 354,326 |
| Emp. | 238 | 216 | 216 |

DUNS 21-579-7716

## West Jesmond Primary School

Tankerville Terrace, Newcastle-Upon-Tyne, Tyne and Wear NE2 3AJ

**Tel:** 01912810000

**Web:** www.westjesmond.newcastle.sch.uk

**Estd:** 2011 Proprietorship

**Line of Business:** Primary education

**Proprietor:** Mrs V Lyons

**Responsibilities**

**Senior:** Gary Wallis-Clarke *(Head Teacher)*

**US SIC:** 8211 **UK SIC:** 93200

**Employees:** 50

DUNS 23-616-8373

## West Kent Housing Association

101 London Road, Sevenoaks, Kent TN13 1AX

**Tel:** 01732-749400

**Web:** www.westkent.org

**Reg No:** 0026278IP **Estd:** 1988 Friendly Society

**Line of Business:** Housing associations societies trusts & co-operatives

**Principals:** D Bootle *(Chairman)*, M Minett, R J Brown, R Parker, A Copleston, A M Mickleburgh, R Nalder, D Trigg

**Co. Secretary:** Michael Annan

**Responsibilities**

**Senior:** H Cash *(Director)*, K Hargreaves *(Director)*, C Malcolm *(Director)*, Nora Pienkoss *(Director)*, Barbara Thorndick *(Chief Executive)*

**US SIC:** 6531 **UK SIC:** 83400

**Auditors:** BDO LLP

**Bankers:** National Westminster Bank Plc (60-19-02)

**Employees:** 193

**Turnover:** £35,018,000

DUNS 21-514-4150

## West Kent N H S & Social Care Trust

Units 4-6 Nene Court, The Embankment, Wellingborough, Northamptonshire NN8 1LD

**Web:** www.floorsworlddirect.com

**Estd:** 2002

**Line of Business:** Healthcare companies

**Trading Style:** Child & Family Therapy Unit

**Director:** J Wilkes

**Branches:** West Kent N H S & Social Care Trust, 41 Church Road, Tunbridge Wells, Kent TN1 1JU

**US SIC:** 8091 **UK SIC:** 95200

**Employees:** 150

DUNS 21-584-9271

## West Kent Primary Care Trust

Foster St Clinic, Foster Street, Maidstone, Kent ME15 6NH

**Tel:** 01622227478

**Web:** www.kentcht.nhs.uk

**Estd:** 2011 Proprietorship

**Line of Business:** Linen retail

**Proprietor:** Mrs A Evans

**US SIC:** 8091 **UK SIC:** 95200

**Employees:** 500

DUNS 21-801-9239

## West Kidlington Primary Nursery School

Oxford Road, Kidlington, Oxfordshire OX5 1EA

**Tel:** 01865373369

**Web:** www.west-kidlington.oxon.sch.uk

**Estd:** 2011

**Line of Business:** Schools (local authority)

**Responsibilities**

**Senior:** Eugene Simons *(Head Teacher)*

**US SIC:** 8211 **UK SIC:** 93200

**Employees:** 94

DUNS 36-814-4804

## West Kilbride Golf Club

33 Fullerton Drive, Seamill, West Kilbride, Ayrshire KA23 9HT

**Tel:** 01294823042

**Web:** www.westkilbridegolfclub.com

**Estd:** 1900

**Line of Business:** Golf equipment

**US SIC:** 7999 **UK SIC:** 97913

**Employees:** 65

DUNS 21-735-3246

## West Kirby Grammar School

Graham Road, Wirral, Merseyside CH48 5DP

**Tel:** 01516323449

**Web:** www.westkirby-grammar.wirral.sch.uk

**Reg No:** 7697158 **Estd:** 2011 Private Company Limited By Guarantee

**Line of Business:** General secondary education

**Directors:** L P Hayes, Dr A M Waller, S M Rampton, Mrs S E Wallis, Mrs C L Bilton, J P Young, Ms S Mcclennon, Mrs S A Boyd

**Responsibilities**

**Senior:** Lesley Broadbere *(Director)*, Alison Duffy *(Director)*, Darryl Ellson *(Director)*, Deborah Favager *(Director)*, Teresa Janikiewicz *(Director)*, Keith Jones Ceng Beng Mice *(Director)*, Glenice Robinson *(Head Teacher)*, Malcolm Simmons *(Director)*

**IT:** Neil Attwood *(Computer Networks Manager)*

**US SIC:** 8211 **UK SIC:** 93200

**Bankers:** Lloyds TSB Bank plc (77-17-19)

| | 31-08-13 | 31-08-12 |
|---|---|---|
| TO | 6,137,000 | 16,922,000 |
| P/L | 103,000 | 9,661,000 |
| NW | 9,688,000 | 9,517,000 |
| WC | 810,000 | 610,000 |
| Emp. | 105 | 105 |

DUNS 28-830-8646

## West Kirby Residential School

Meols Drive, Wirral, Merseyside CH48 5DA

**Tel:** 0151-632-3201 **Fax:** 0151-632-0621

**Web:** www.wkrs.co.uk

**Reg No:** 0200018 **Estd:** 1924 Private Company Limited By Guarantee

**Line of Business:** Schools (special)

**Directors:** B K Boumphrey, P J Wilson, S M Dickinson, N G Lumb, Ms K A Thomas, Mrs G M Moore, J M Wylie

**Co. Secretary:** Mrs Rachel Kennedy

**Responsibilities**

**Senior:** Erica Bastow *(Manager)*, Jane Corlett *(Manager)*

**US SIC:** 8299 **UK SIC:** 93300

**Auditors:** Moore Stephans

**Bankers:** Barclays Bank Plc (20-50-36)

| | 31-03-14 | 31-03-13 | 31-03-12 |
|---|---|---|---|
| TO | 4,890,719 | 4,573,345 | 4,353,130 |
| P/L | 576,281 | 356,190 | 500,378 |
| NW | 6,169,998 | 5,660,197 | 5,694,335 |
| WC | 2,906,123 | 2,539,668 | 2,501,630 |
| Emp. | 123 | 118 | 120 |

DUNS 21-128-0890

## West Lakes Academy

90 Main Street, Egremont, Cumbria CA22 2DJ

**Tel:** 01946822858

**Web:** www.westlakesacademy.org.uk

**Reg No:** 6627459 **Estd:** 2008 Private Company Limited By Guarantee

**Line of Business:** Laundries

**Directors:** Mrs A A Le Jeune, Ms A Butterfield, R Wylie, D E Southward, A N Thompson, C D Nattress, Mrs V Ray, Mrs S J Alderson

**Co. Secretary:** Ms Karen Forsyth

**Responsibilities**

**Senior:** Ian Curwen *(Director)*, Amy Finn *(Director)*, Michelle Pearse *(Director)*, Deborah Plews *(Director)*, Catherine Whitfield *(Partner)*

**US SIC:** 7219, 8211

**UK SIC:** 98110, 93200

**Bankers:** HSBC Bank plc (40-20-17)

| | 31-08-14 | 31-08-13 | 31-08-12 |
|---|---|---|---|
| TO | 5,854,000 | 5,692,000 | 31,777,000 |
| P/L | (733,000) | (804,000) | 25,196,000 |
| NW | 26,557,000 | 27,116,000 | 27,525,000 |
| WC | 1,710,000 | 1,356,000 | 1,166,000 |
| Emp. | 120 | 120 | 123 |

DUNS 23-224-0978

## West Lancashire Borough Council

52 Derby Street, Ormskirk, Lancashire L39 2DF

**Tel:** 01695-577177

**Web:** www.westlancsdc.gov.uk

**Estd:** 2002

**Line of Business:** Local government

**Director:** W J Taylor

**Responsibilities**

**Senior:** Dominic Carr *(Executive)*, Mike Dutton *(Manager)*, Gill Rowe *(Managing Director (People and))*, Bill Taylor *(Chief Executive)*

**Finance:** Shirley Stankowski *(Tax Manager)*

**Marketing:** Edwina Leigh *(Head of Public Relations)*

**Sales:** William Berkley *(Business Development Manager)*

**Health & Safety:** Cliff Owens *(Health and Safety Executive)*

**Facilities:** Graham Concannon *(Assistant Director of Street S)*, Rachel Kneale *(Estates & Valuation Manager.)*, Bob Livermore *(Assistant Director of Housing)*

**Operations:** Stephen Benge *(Planning Manager)*, Phil Samosa *(Contracts Performance Manager)*, Shaun Walsh *(Transformation Manager)*

**Branches:** West Lancashire Borough Council, Mere Court, Burscough, Ormskirk, Lancashire L40 0TQ

**US SIC:** 9121 **UK SIC:** 91110

**Employees:** 700

**DUNS 21-879-9891**
## West Lancashire College
Northway Campus, College Way, Skelmersdale, Lancashire WN8 6DX
**Tel:** 01695577140
**Web:** www.skelmersdale.ac.uk
**Estd:** 2012
**Line of Business:** Universities, Colleges, Prof. Schools
**Responsibilities**
**Senior:** Louise Dawson (Principal)
**HR:** Vicky Bosward (Human Resources Manager)
**US SIC:** 8221  **UK SIC:** 93100
**Employees:** 400

**DUNS 23-043-1330**
## West Lancashire Heating Co
Dunnisher Road, Wythenshawe, Manchester M23 2YN
**Tel:** 07821737488
**Web:** www.lancashireheating.com
**Estd:** 1968 Partnership
**Line of Business:** Gas installers
**Trading Style:** West Lancs Heating Co
**Partners:** C P Cleary, Mrs G A Cleary
**US SIC:** 1799  **UK SIC:** 50000
**Employees:** 70

**DUNS 23-216-5944**
## West Lancashire Primary Care Trust
22 Wigan Road, Ormskirk, Lancashire L39 2AU
**Tel:** 01695577111
**Web:** www.chemist-4-u.com
**Estd:** 1990
**Line of Business:** Chemists dispensing
**Trading Style:** Ormskirk & District General Hospital
**Director:** Mrs J Thompson
**Responsibilities**
**Senior:** M Iskander (Medical Director)
**Branches:** West Lancashire Primary Care Trust, 137 Cambridge Road, Southport, Merseyside PR9 7LT
**US SIC:** 8062  **UK SIC:** 95100
**Employees:** 1,000

**DUNS 54-864-0762**
## West Lane Hospital
Acklam Road, Middlesbrough, Cleveland TS5 4EE
**Web:** www.tewv.nhs.uk
**Estd:** 2002
**Line of Business:** Hospitals
**Trading Style:** West Lane Hospital
**Directors:** Mrs M J Britton, Mrs M J Britton
**Responsibilities**
**Senior:** Leah Allinson (Matron)
**Branches:** West Lane Hospital, 20 Cleveland Centre, Cleveland Sq, Middlesbrough, Cleveland TS1 2NX
**US SIC:** 8091  **UK SIC:** 95200
**Employees:** 100

**DUNS 21-031-4258**                                          Imp
## West Leigh Ltd
11-13 Spa Road, London SE16 3RB
**Tel:** 020-7232-0030  **Fax:** 020-7232-1763
**Web:** www.west-leigh.co.uk
**Reg No:** 0384694  **VAT No:** 662844122
**Estd:** 1944 Private Limited Company
**Line of Business:** Other construction work involving special trades
**Trading Style:** West Leigh Southern
**Issued Capital:** £50,000
**Principals:** B M Briggs (Managing), T A Woskett
**Co. Secretary:** David Grew
**Responsibilities**
**Senior:** Alan Hart (Works Manager), Tom London (Contracts Manager)
**Branches:** West Leigh Ltd, Unit 3 Fourdry Rd, Horsham, West Sussex RH13 5PX
**US SIC:** 1799  **UK SIC:** 50000
**Auditors:** Baker Tilly UK Audit LLP
**Bankers:** HSBC Bank plc (40-02-50)

|     | 31-03-14  | 31-03-13  | 31-03-12  |
| --- | --------- | --------- | --------- |
| TO  | 4,889,000 | 4,101,000 | 5,219,000 |
| P/L | 107,000   | 20,000    | 22,000    |
| NW  | 2,552,000 | 2,471,000 | 2,460,000 |
| WC  | 1,677,000 | 1,721,000 | 1,730,000 |
| Emp.| 54        | 54        | 60        |

**DUNS 22-747-1026**
## West Lindsey District Council
Guildhall, Marshalls Yard, Gainsborough, Lincolnshire DN21 9SB
**Tel:** 01427-676-676
**Web:** www.west-lindsey.gov.uk
**VAT No:** 129383062  **Estd:** 1974
**Line of Business:** Local government
**Directors:** R W Nelsey, A G Biggs
**Responsibilities**
**Admin:** Roger Vine (Director of Administration)

**Branches:** West Lindsey District Council, Guildhall, Marshalls Yard, Gainsborough, Lincolnshire DN21 9SB
**US SIC:** 9111  **UK SIC:** 91110
**Bankers:** The Co-Operative Bank Plc (08-90-32)
**Employees:** 200

**DUNS 21-754-8888**
## West Link Helicopters Ltd
50 Brook Street, London W1K 5DR
**Tel:** 02070609933
**Web:** www.westlinkhelicopters.net
**Reg No:** 7845141  **Estd:** 2011 Private Limited Company
**Line of Business:** Aircraft rental leasing and charter services
**Issued Capital:** £1,000
**Director:** A G Mallet
**US SIC:** 4582  **UK SIC:** 76400

|    | 31-12-13 | 31-12-12 |
| -- | -------- | -------- |
| TA | 40,305   | 40,305   |
| NW | 24,444   | 24,444   |
| WC | 24,444   | 24,444   |

**DUNS 45-838-3809**
## West Lodge Care Homes Ltd
(**Subsidiary of:** West Lodge Holdings Ltd)
Salisbury House 2 3, Salisbury Villas, Cambridge, Cambridgeshire CB1 2LA
**Tel:** 01388763650  **Fax:** 01388-768368
**Web:** www.westlodgecarehomes.co.uk
**Reg No:** 3188635  **Estd:** 1996 Private Limited Company
**Line of Business:** Other human health activities
**Issued Capital:** £100,000
**Directors:** Ms C Higginbotham, S M Higginbotham
**Co. Secretary:** Mrs Julie Price
**US SIC:** 8091  **UK SIC:** 95200

|    | 31-03-14 | 31-03-13 | 31-03-12 |
| -- | -------- | -------- | -------- |
| TA | 615,612  | 507,569  | 563,874  |
| NW | 363,305  | 298,257  | 368,522  |
| WC | 431,115  | 366,414  | 436,183  |

**DUNS 23-227-9567**
## West London Mental Health N H S Trust
St Bernard'S Hospital, Southall, Middlesex UB1 3EU
**Tel:** 020-8354-8354
**Web:** www.wlmht.nhs.uk
**Estd:** 2005
**Line of Business:** Nhs clinics
**Issued Capital:** £1
**Principals:** Ms B Byrne (Financial), L Mcgee, Ms R Lewis, P Cubbon, I Kent, S Trenchard, Ms E Fellow-Smith
**Responsibilities**
**Senior:** Miriam Byfield (Manager), Leeanne McGee (Director), Nigel Mccorkell (Non-Executive Director), Eamon Walsh (Team Manager)
**Marketing:** Tara Ferguson-Jones (Director, Communications)
**Branches:** West London Mental Health N H S Trust, 304 Westbourne Gro, London W11 2PS
**US SIC:** 9121, 8091
**UK SIC:** 91110, 95200
**Employees:** 4,000

**DUNS 21-031-4937**
## West London Mental Health Trust
1 Edgecote Close, London W3 8PH
**Tel:** 02084831700
**Web:** www.wlmht.nhs.uk
**Line of Business:** General medical & surgical hospitals
**US SIC:** 8091  **UK SIC:** 95200
**Employees:** 80

**DUNS 52-555-9092**
## West London Y M C A
25 St Marys Road, Ealing, London W5 5RE
**Tel:** 03001111500
**Web:** www.westlondonymca.org
**Reg No:** 3244611  **Estd:** 1996 Private Limited Company
**Line of Business:** Other tourist or short-stay accommodation
**Directors:** A Thomson, J M Kelly, C D Horne, G C Lockhart, I R North, B M Laryea, A ( Stadtmiller, J P Lazarus
**Co. Secretary:** Ms Clare Scott Booth
**Responsibilities**
**Senior:** Monica Bolley (Manager), Froukje Cradock (Manager), Elizabeth Griffiths (Manager), Barbara Quartey (Manager), Hazel Vinson (Manager)
**US SIC:** 7021, 8321
**UK SIC:** 66500, 96111
**Auditors:** Jacob Cavenagh & Skeet

**Bankers:** Barclays Bank Plc (20-37-75)

|      | 31-03-14   | 31-03-13   | 31-03-12   |
| ---- | ---------- | ---------- | ---------- |
| TO   | 6,452,196  | 6,692,784  | 6,773,047  |
| P/L  | (399,824)  | 35,821     | 214,175    |
| NW   | 13,786,570 | 14,186,394 | 14,150,573 |
| WC   | 608,036    | 846,684    | 1,054,115  |
| Emp. | 135        | 140        | 152        |

**DUNS 21-782-3312**
## West Lothian Community Health & Care Partnership
Howden South Road, Livingston, West Lothian EH54 6FF
**Web:** www.westlothianchcp.org.uk
**Estd:** 2011 Proprietorship
**Line of Business:** Health authorities
**Proprietor:** Mrs R Anderson
**US SIC:** 8062  **UK SIC:** 95100
**Employees:** 2,000

**DUNS 23-982-2521**
## West Lothian Council
Guildiehaugh Depot, Blackburn Road, Bathgate, West Lothian EH48 2EB
**Tel:** 01506776666
**Web:** www.westlothian.gov.uk
**VAT No:** 271632173  **Estd:** 1995
**Line of Business:** General (overall) public service activities
**Trading Style:** Newton Community Education Centre
**Directors:** G Blair, A Logan, A M Linkston
**Branches:** West Lothian Council, 5-6 Dunlop Square, Livingston, West Lothian EH54 8SB
**US SIC:** 9121, 7699
**UK SIC:** 91110, 67303
**Bankers:** Bank Of Scotland (80-08-80)
**Employees:** 400

**DUNS 23-730-5461**
## West Mercia Constabulary
Hindlip Hall, Hindlip, Hindlip, Worcester, Worcestershire WR3 8SP
**Tel:** 08457444888  **Fax:** 01432346729
**Web:** www.westmercia.police.uk
**Estd:** 1967 Incorporate By Act Of Parliament
**Line of Business:** Police forces
**Director:** D C Blakey
**Responsibilities**
**Senior:** Dave Richardson (Supplies Officer)
**Marketing:** Kate Tonge (Press Officer)
**Facilities:** Jim Stobie (Head of Estates Services)
**Purchasing:** Dave Richardson (Supplies Officer)
**Branches:** West Mercia Constabulary, Divisional Police Headquarters, Bath Street, Hereford, Herefordshire HR1 2HT
**US SIC:** 9221  **UK SIC:** 91300
**Employees:** 750

**DUNS 21-584-2794**
## West Mercia Probatin Services
3-4 Shaw Street, Worcester, Worcestershire WR1 3QQ
**Tel:** 01905743100
**Estd:** 2011 Proprietorship
**Line of Business:** Probation services
**Proprietor:** Mrs G Bearcroft
**US SIC:** 9121  **UK SIC:** 91110
**Employees:** 80

**DUNS 23-845-0402**
## West Mercia Women's Aid
Po Box 74, Hereford, Herefordshire HR4 9WB
**Web:** www.westmerciawomensaid.org
**Reg No:** 3837084  **Estd:** 1999 Private Company Limited By Guarantee
**Line of Business:** Social work activities without accommodation
**Directors:** Dr J Liddle, Ms N C Griffiths, Ms A Lewis, Ms C M Hinton, Ms N K Fisher, Ms K V Bentham, Ms S Gorbing, Ms L Proctor
**US SIC:** 8321  **UK SIC:** 96111
**Bankers:** Unity Trust Bank Plc (08-60-01)

|      | 31-03-14  | 31-03-13  | 31-03-12  |
| ---- | --------- | --------- | --------- |
| TO   | 1,407,201 | 1,396,682 | 1,549,973 |
| P/L  | 10,074    | 16,671    | 223,756   |
| NW   | 911,427   | 901,353   | 890,692   |
| WC   | 901,116   | 886,464   | 878,225   |
| Emp. | 3,032     | 38        | 33        |

**DUNS 54-864-0994**
## West Middlesex University Hospital N H S Trust
Twickenham Road, Isleworth, Middlesex TW7 6AF
**Tel:** 02085683679
**Web:** www.west-middlesex-hospital.nhs.uk
**Line of Business:** Hospitals
**Issued Capital:** £1
**Principals:** Ms S Ellen (Chairman), S Marshall (Financial), Ms A Gibbs, Ms N Singh, D Docherty, A Mcintosh, G Head, A Winning

**Responsibilities**
**Senior:** Alison McIntosh (Deputy Chief Executive Officer)
**Marketing:** Jane Brennan (Corporate Affairs Director)
**IT:** Karl Minhas (Computer Manager)
**Operations:** Jane Brennan (Corporate Affairs Director)
**Purchasing:** M Loucaidou (Purchasing Manager)
**Branches:** West Middlesex University Hospital N H S Trust, West Middlesex University Hospital, Twickenham Road, Isleworth, Middlesex TW7 6AF
**US SIC:** 8062  **UK SIC:** 95100
**Employees:** 2,000

**DUNS 21-614-6118**
## West Midland Farmers Association Ltd
Bradford Road, Melksham, Wiltshire SN12 8LQ
**Reg No:** 0010257IP  **VAT No:** 274207466
**Estd:** 2012 Friendly Society
**Line of Business:** Supermarkets
**Issued Capital:** £2
**Principals:** J B Bush (Chairman), R A Godwin, G E Osbourne, J A Rutherford, S A Hurd, J W Nichols, R M Ecroyd, D C Gamberoni
**Responsibilities**
**Senior:** John Arthur (Director), William Bullock (Director), Dennis McCausland (Director), G Pow (Vice Chairperson)
**Branches:** West Midland Farmers Association Ltd, Llanthony Mills, Merchants Road, Gloucester, Gloucestershire GL1 5RJ
**US SIC:** 8699  **UK SIC:** 96902
**Bankers:** National Westminster Bank Plc (60-09-02)
**Employees:** 14

**DUNS 77-267-7399**
## West Midland Fencing Ltd
(**Subsidiary of:** Crh Plc)
Mesty Croft Clinic, Alma Street, Wednesbury, West Midlands WS10 0QB
**Tel:** 01215051027  **Fax:** 01215051022
**Web:** www.westmidlandfencing.com
**Reg No:** 2714432  **VAT No:** 610915663
**Estd:** 1992 Private Limited Company
**Line of Business:** Saw milling and planing of wood, impregnation of wood
**Issued Capital:** £100
**Directors:** J V Gardom, S A Towers
**Co. Secretary:** Philip Chadwick
**US SIC:** 2421, 1799
**UK SIC:** 46101, 50000
**Auditors:** Baldwin & Co (Bilston) LLP
**Bankers:** Lloyds TSB Bank plc (30-99-25)

|     | 31-12-13 | 31-12-11  |
| --- | -------- | --------- |
| TA  | 1,330    | 2,531,000 |
| P/L | N/A      | 287,000   |
| NW  | 100      | 2,509,000 |
| WC  | 100      | 2,509,000 |

**DUNS 21-101-5459**                                          Imp
## West Midland Safari Park Ltd
(**Subsidiary of:** Safariworld Holdings Ltd)
Spring Grove, Bewdley, Worcestershire DY12 1LF
**Tel:** 01299402114  **Fax:** 01299404519
**Web:** www.wmsp.co.uk
**Reg No:** 6449517  **Estd:** 2007 Private Limited Company
**Line of Business:** Fair and amusement park activities
**Issued Capital:** £1,100
**Directors:** I Knezovich, D D Chorley
**Co. Secretary:** Robert Kilby
**US SIC:** 7996  **UK SIC:** 97913

|      | 31-03-14   | 31-03-13   | 31-03-12   |
| ---- | ---------- | ---------- | ---------- |
| TO   | 12,108,407 | 11,327,054 | 11,534,890 |
| P/L  | 506,624    | 319,592    | 470,575    |
| NW   | 3,045,721  | 2,766,824  | 2,526,823  |
| WC   | 122,533    | (206,828)  | (520,497)  |
| Emp. | 373        | 374        | 377        |

**DUNS 23-265-7705**
## West Midlands Ambulance Service Nhs Foundation
Unit 9, Waterfront Business Park, Dudley Road, Brierley Hill, West Midlands DY5 1LX
**Tel:** 01384-215555
**Web:** www.wmas.nhs.uk
**Estd:** 2006
**Line of Business:** N H S trust, ambulance service
**Issued Capital:** £1
**Director:** A Marsh
**US SIC:** 9121, 8062
**UK SIC:** 91110, 95100

|      | 31-03-13    |
| ---- | ----------- |
| TO   | 53,073,000  |
| P/L  | (1,625,000) |
| NW   | 43,418,000  |
| WC   | 21,871,000  |
| Emp. | 3,795       |

**DUNS 23-231-3437**

## West Midlands Co-Operative Chemists Ltd

27 Market Hall Street, Cannock, Staffordshire WS11 1EB
**Fax:** 01926-516-094
**Web:** www.wmcs.coop
**Reg No:** 0012713IP **Estd:** 1945 Friendly Society
**Line of Business:** Dispensing chemists
**Trading Style:** Minster Pharmacy
**Principals:** H Witunan (*Chairman*), N E Heywood, G J Taylor, H S Minten, B Naylor, G E Hough, J T Boot, I Edean
**Responsibilities**
**Senior:** F Bate (*Director*), G Hurmson (*Director*), D Suaw (*Director*), B Swan (*Director*)
**US SIC:** 5912 **UK SIC:** 64300
**Auditors:** Horwath Clark Whitehill
**Employees:** 415

**DUNS 23-291-3731**

## West Midlands Fire Service

99 Vauxhall Road, Nechells, Birmingham, West Midlands B7 4HW
**Tel:** 01213595161
**Web:** www.wmss.net
**Estd:** 1974 Incorporate By Act Of Parliament
**Line of Business:** Fire stations
**Director:** K Knight
**Responsibilities**
**Finance:** kal Shoker (*Finance Director*)
**Marketing:** Neil Spencer (*Senior Media Relations Officer*)
**Operations:** Phil Loach (*Operations Manager*)
**Branches:** West Midlands Fire Service, Hagley Rd, Halesowen, West Midlands B63 4JP
**US SIC:** 9224 **UK SIC:** 91400
**Employees:** 63

**DUNS 23-600-1616**

## West Midlands Passenger Transport Executive

Centro House, Birmingham, West Midlands B19 3SD
**Tel:** 01212002787 **Fax:** 0121-233-1841
**Web:** www.centro.org.uk
**Estd:** 1969 Incorporate By Act Of Parliament
**Line of Business:** Freight Forwarders
**Principals:** R J Tarr (*Chairman*), P R Evans (*Financial*), P Severs (*Financial*), R Donald, A Pitts, P Cordle
**Co. Secretary:** Clive Sayer
**US SIC:** 4712 **UK SIC:** 77002
**Auditors:** Tony Corcoran
**Bankers:** HSBC Bank plc (40-11-18)
**Employees:** 6
**Turnover:** £141,712,000

**DUNS 21-355-5045**

## West Midlands Police

199 Park Lane, Aston, Birmingham, West Midlands B6 5DD
**Tel:** 0121-626-5154
**Web:** www.west-midlands.pnn.police.uk
**Line of Business:** Maintenance and repair of motor vehicles
**Trading Style:** West Midlands Police
**US SIC:** 7539 **UK SIC:** 67100
**Employees:** 104

**DUNS 21-279-2382**

## West Midlands Probation Service

52 Newton Street, Birmingham, West Midlands B4 6NF
**Tel:** 01212486100
**Web:** www.swmprobation.gov.uk
**Estd:** 2002 Proprietorship
**Line of Business:** Central government
**Proprietor:** P Derby
**Responsibilities**
**Senior:** Emma Penton (*Manager*)
**US SIC:** 9121 **UK SIC:** 91110
**Employees:** 1,000

**DUNS 21-772-4043**

## West Midlands Special Needs Transport

Unit 2 Smith Road, Wednesbury, Wednesbury, West Midlands WS10 0PD
**Tel:** 01215056468
**Web:** www.ringandride.org
**Estd:** 2011 Proprietorship
**Line of Business:** Community networks
**Proprietor:** Mrs S Cozens
**Responsibilities**
**Senior:** Jason Hall (*Contract Supervisor*)
**US SIC:** 4119 **UK SIC:** 72200
**Employees:** 125

**DUNS 50-709-1346**

## West Norfolk Community Transport Project

Columbia Way, King's Lynn, Norfolk PE30 2LB
**Tel:** 01553776971
**Web:** www.wnct.co.uk
**Estd:** 1993
**Line of Business:** Charities and charitable organisations
**Responsibilities**
**Senior:** Marion Coleman (*Manager*), Dee Jackson (*Manager*), Denise Jackson (*CEO*), Jackie Nurse (*Trustee*), Sylvia Pomeroy (*Manager*)
**Fleet:** Fiona Matchett (*Transport Manager*)
**US SIC:** 6732, 4712
**UK SIC:** 83100, 77002
**Auditors:** Mapus-Smith & Lemmon LLP
**Employees:** 75
**Turnover:** £1,051,078

**DUNS 67-224-0066**

## West North West Homes Leeds Ltd

Westfield House, Lower Wortley Road, Leeds, West Yorkshire LS12 4PT
**Tel:** 01132477058
**Web:** www.leeds.gov.uk
**Reg No:** 6031549 **Estd:** 2006 Private Company Limited By Guarantee
**Line of Business:** Housing associations societies trusts & co-operatives
**Directors:** Ms A Lowe, A Mann
**Responsibilities**
**Senior:** Claire Warren (*Chief Executive Officer*)
**US SIC:** 8321 **UK SIC:** 96111
**Auditors:** BDO LLP
**Bankers:** National Westminster Bank Plc (60-60-05)

| | 31-03-14 | 31-03-13 | 31-03-12 |
|---|---|---|---|
| TO | 18,423,258 | 36,107,795 | 33,345,830 |
| P/L | (6,005,902) | (3,335,923) | (8,301,034) |
| NW | N/A | (420,874) | 4,615,787 |
| WC | N/A | 7,638,553 | 10,950,435 |
| Emp. | 441 | 424 | 426 |

**DUNS 23-223-3846**

## West Nottinghamshire College

Derby Road, Mansfield, Nottinghamshire NG18 5BH
**Tel:** 01623627191
**Web:** www.westnotts.ac.uk
**Estd:** 2002
**Line of Business:** Training services
**Trading Style:** Vision West Nottinghamshire College
**Director:** J Aleander
**Responsibilities**
**Senior:** Asha Khemka (*Principal*), Dani Mackinnon (*General Manager*), James Stafford (*President*), Tom Stevens (*Executive Director-Capital Pro*)
**Finance:** Wendy Barratt (*Finance Manager*)
**Marketing:** Sue Armstrong (*Connexions Advisor*), Cate Hunt (*Entitlement Enterprise and Emp*), Louise Knott (*Communications and Marketing D*), Rebecca Short (*Press and PR Officer*), Richard Skelhorn (*Communications Manager*)
**Sales:** Sacha McCarthy (*Business Development Director*), Angie Pilgrim (*Sales Manager*)
**Admin:** Gemma Stevenson (*Administration*)
**IT:** Colin Gilbert (*Senior IT Executive*), Gavin Peake (*IT Director*)
**HR:** Edina Baines (*Careers Advisor*), Lucy Bunting (*HR Team Leader*)
**Health & Safety:** Susan Fretwell (*Health & Safety Officer*)
**Operations:** Roger Martin (*Operations Manager*)
**Purchasing:** Garry Checklin (*Purchasing Officer*)
**US SIC:** 8299, 8221, 8249, 7231
**UK SIC:** 93300, 93100, 98200
**Employees:** 200

**DUNS 21-941-2678**

## West of England Insurance Services (Luxembourg) Sa

(**Subsidiary of:** West of England Insurance Services (Luxembourg) Sa)
Tower Bridge Court, 224-226 Tower Bridge Road, London SE1 2UP
**Web:** www.westpandi.com
**Reg No:** 0025878FC **Estd:** 2005 Foreign Company
**Line of Business:** Insurance services
**Directors:** Ms F C Emmerson, T J Bowsher, Ms S Byrne, S G Parrott, T L Brevet, C Q Drew, A Paulson
**Co. Secretary:** Thierry Brevet
**Responsibilities**
**Senior:** Carolina Lockwood (*Manager*), Jerry Westmore (*Manager*)
**US SIC:** 6411 **UK SIC:** 83200

**DUNS 50-437-7862**

## West of England Language Services Ltd

(**Subsidiary of:** Graham Holdings Company)
International House, 30 Ash Hill Road, Torquay, Devon TQ1 3HZ
**Tel:** 01803210940
**Web:** www.kaplaninternational.com
**Reg No:** 2425769 **Estd:** 1991 Private Limited Company
**Line of Business:** Language schools
**Trading Style:** Kaplan International
**Issued Capital:** £800
**Directors:** A V Thick, D Jones, G R Isaac
**Responsibilities**
**Senior:** Martin Lemon (*Manager*), Anna Robinson (*Principal*)
**Finance:** Elaine Calcutt (*Head of Finance*)
**Marketing:** Anya Jones (*Marketing Administrator*)
**Branches:** West Of England Language Services Ltd, 5 Trim Street, Bath, Avon BA1 1HB
**US SIC:** 8249 **UK SIC:** 93300
**Auditors:** Bishop Fleming
**Bankers:** Barclays Bank Plc (20-60-88)

| | 31-12-13 | 31-12-12 | 31-12-11 |
|---|---|---|---|
| TO | N/A | 1,135,925 | 4,612,989 |
| P/L | N/A | (208,004) | (99,520) |
| NW | (88,694) | (88,694) | 85,208 |
| WC | (88,694) | (88,694) | 26,240 |
| Emp. | N/A | 47 | 67 |

**DUNS 21-160-7648**

## West of England School for Children With Little Or No Sight

Countess Wear, Exeter, Devon EX2 6HA
**Web:** www.westengland.ac.uk
**Estd:** 1865
**Line of Business:** Educational training
**US SIC:** 8299, 6732
**UK SIC:** 93300, 83100
**Employees:** 250

**DUNS 22-525-6049**

## The West of England Trust Ltd

21 St Thomas Street, Bristol, Avon BS1 6JS
**Tel:** 01179299292
**Web:** www.jordans.co.uk
**Reg No:** 1636508 **Estd:** 1863 Private Limited Company
**Line of Business:** Management activities of other non-financial holding companies not elsewhere classified
**Issued Capital:** £1,078,200
**Principals:** I A Harbottle (*Chairman*), R Templeton (*Chairman*), P B Heal, N W Owen, P N Randall, M Whitwell, H G Leighton
**Co. Secretary:** Ian Harbottle
**Responsibilities**
**Senior:** George Cusworth (*Manager*)
**US SIC:** 2741, 7392
**UK SIC:** 47541, 83951
**Auditors:** PricewaterhouseCoopers LLP
**Bankers:** Barclays Bank Plc (20-13-42)

| | 31-03-14 | 31-03-13 | 31-03-12 |
|---|---|---|---|
| TO | 25,137,000 | 25,151,000 | 26,153,000 |
| P/L | 2,895,000 | 3,334,000 | 4,221,000 |
| NW | 10,571,000 | 9,992,000 | 8,798,000 |
| WC | 8,060,000 | 8,183,000 | 7,862,000 |
| Emp. | 237 | 252 | 246 |

**DUNS 42-367-5883**

## West of Scotland Housing Association

252 Keppochhill Road, Glasgow, Lanarkshire G21 1HG
**Tel:** 01415586336 **Fax:** 01415576377
**Web:** www.westscot.co.uk
**Reg No:** 0001828IP **Estd:** 1965 Friendly Society
**Line of Business:** Housing associations societies trusts & co-operatives
**Principals:** K Kintrea (*Chairman*), Ms J Smyllie, W Gowrie, N Craig, J Loran
**Co. Secretary:** Mark Logan
**Responsibilities**
**Senior:** Brendan McGeever (*Housing Manager*)
**Sales:** Colin Turnbull (*Senior Sales Executive*)
**Branches:** West Of Scotland Housing Association, 24 Crofthead Street, Glasgow, Lanarkshire G71 7JP
**US SIC:** 8321 **UK SIC:** 96111
**Auditors:** Downie Wilson
**Bankers:** Clydesdale Bank Plc (82-65-00)
**Employees:** 79
**Turnover:** £10,644,212

**DUNS 21-618-5857**

## West One Bathrooms

140 Garratt Lane, London SW18 4EE
**Tel:** 02087044000
**Web:** www.westonebathrooms.com
**Estd:** 2007

**Line of Business:** Bathroom fixtures and fittings
**US SIC:** 3499 **UK SIC:** 31694
**Employees:** 54

**DUNS 21-156-6609** Imp-Exp

## West One Bathrooms Ltd

(**Subsidiary of:** West One Bathrooms Group Ltd)
Unit 5 Kimber Centre, 54 Kimber Road, London SW18 4PP
**Tel:** 02088702121 **Fax:** 020-8874-4141
**Web:** www.westonebathrooms.co.uk
**Reg No:** 1356065 **VAT No:** 242381676
**Estd:** 1978 Private Limited Company
**Line of Business:** Other retail sale in specialised stores not elsewhere classified
**Export Markets:** worldwide
**Export Sales:** £159,759
**Issued Capital:** £30,000
**Directors:** D J Waters, K A Waters, S J Farrington
**Branches:** West One Bathrooms Ltd, 45-46 South Audley Street, London W1K 2PY
**US SIC:** 3499, 5122
**UK SIC:** 31694, 61800
**Auditors:** Target Winters Ltd
**Bankers:** HSBC Bank plc (40-05-01)

| | 31-03-14 | 31-03-13 | 31-03-12 |
|---|---|---|---|
| TO | 14,175,837 | 11,513,354 | 11,836,127 |
| P/L | 766,300 | 305,826 | 142,293 |
| NW | 802,205 | 777,351 | 772,528 |
| WC | (936,443) | (880,345) | (734,352) |
| Emp. | 63 | 57 | 55 |

**DUNS 77-903-7261**

## West One Foods Ltd

Room 12 Chiltern House, Thame Road Haddenham, Aylesbury, Buckinghamshire HP17 8BY
**Tel:** 02076387787
**Web:** www.westonefoods.co.uk
**Reg No:** 5808791 **Estd:** 2006 Private Limited Company
**Line of Business:** Unlicensed restaurants and cafes
**Issued Capital:** £100
**Directors:** R P Forte, P Sullivan, T J Bull
**Co. Secretary:** Ms Pauline Sullivan
**Branches:** West One Foods Ltd, 302-304 Pentonville Road, London N1 9NR
**US SIC:** 5812 **UK SIC:** 66110
**Bankers:** The Royal Bank Of Scotland Plc (16-01-00)

| | 31-12-13 | 31-12-12 | 31-12-11 |
|---|---|---|---|
| TO | 64,418,392 | 61,110,145 | 57,860,069 |
| P/L | 2,809,872 | 1,986,716 | 2,311,520 |
| NW | 4,110,793 | 3,693,528 | 3,061,877 |
| WC | (851,111) | (1,683,761) | (177,283) |
| Emp. | 1,765 | 1,749 | 1,650 |

**DUNS 77-909-6200**

## West One Restaurants Ltd

11-59 High Road, London N2 8AW
**Tel:** 02078286911
**Reg No:** 5812954 **Estd:** 2006 Private Limited Company
**Line of Business:** Canteens and catering
**Issued Capital:** £704,592
**Directors:** T J Bull, N J Hindle
**Branches:** West One Restaurants Ltd, Macmillan House, Unit 55, London W2 1HD
**US SIC:** 5812 **UK SIC:** 66110
**Auditors:** Manex Accountants Ltd

| | 31-12-12 | 31-12-11 | 31-12-10 |
|---|---|---|---|
| TO | 50,162,045 | 47,054,238 | 44,055,702 |
| P/L | 159,064 | 465,000 | 992,952 |
| NW | (31,318) | 950,319 | 647,989 |
| WC | (2,337,796) | (894,286) | (916,988) |
| Emp. | 1,295 | 1,278 | 1,257 |

**DUNS 21-584-1686**

## West Oxfordshire District Council

Council Offices, Woodgreen, Witney, Oxfordshire OX28 1NB
**Tel:** 01993861020
**Web:** www.westoxon.gov.uk
**Estd:** 2011 Proprietorship
**Line of Business:** Local government
**Proprietor:** D Neudegg
**US SIC:** 9121 **UK SIC:** 91110
**Employees:** 200

**DUNS 64-263-1881**

## West Park Community School

West Road, Derby, Derbyshire DE21 7BT
**Tel:** 01332-662337
**Web:** www.westpark.derby.sch.uk
**Estd:** 1964
**Line of Business:** Schools (foundation)
**Director:** B Walker
**US SIC:** 8211 **UK SIC:** 93200
**Employees:** 103

DUNS 21-711-2291　　Imp-Exp
## West Pharmaceutical Services Cornwall Ltd
(Subsidiary of: West Pharmaceutical Services Inc.)
Bucklers Lane, St Austell, Cornwall PL25 3JU
Tel: 01726635633 Fax: 01726-223219
Web: www.westpharma.com
Reg No: 0930319 VAT No: 132307706
Estd: 1968 Private Limited Company
Line of Business: Manufacturers of pharmaceutical products
Export Markets: Ireland; Germany; South Africa
Export Sales: £25,713,000
Issued Capital: £12,292,528
Directors: H Lennartz, S P Parish, D Elliott, A Smith
Co. Secretary: Darren Pope
Responsibilities
Senior: Rachel Bushey (Director), Tom Gribbin (Operations Director Uk)
Branches: West Pharmaceutical Services Cornwall Ltd, Windwhistle, 15 Cooksland Road, Bodmin, Cornwall PL31 2RH
US SIC: 2834 UK SIC: 25700
Auditors: PricewaterhouseCoopers LLP
Bankers: National Westminster Bank Plc (54-41-12)

| | 31-12-13 | 31-12-12 | 31-12-11 |
|---|---|---|---|
| TO | 29,690,000 | 34,596,000 | 33,223,000 |
| P/L | (6,491,000) | 36,000 | 1,763,000 |
| NW | 9,583,000 | 19,165,000 | 19,916,000 |
| WC | 8,933,000 | 13,754,000 | 11,953,000 |
| Emp. | 168 | 313 | 361 |

DUNS 29-364-6774
## West Properties Holdings Ltd
51 Gloucester Terrace, London W2 3DQ
Tel: 02072623194
Web: www.jjmlondonlettings.co.uk
Reg No: 0812524 Estd: 1964 Private Limited Company
Line of Business: Development and selling of real estate
Issued Capital: £100,000
Principals: J Singh Gill (Chairman and Managing), Mrs A Kaur
Responsibilities
Senior: Jack Gill (Proprietor), Jagmail Gill (Manager)
Branches: West Properties Holdings Ltd, 12 Osborn Street, London E1 6TE
US SIC: 6552, 6531
UK SIC: 85000, 83400
Auditors: Silver Levene Audit Ltd
Bankers: National Westminster Bank Plc (56-00-29)

| | 31-12-13 | 31-12-12 | 30-12-12 |
|---|---|---|---|
| TO | N/A | N/A | 10,790,296 |
| P/L | N/A | (2,186,704) | 571,106 |
| NW | 11,918,205 | 11,889,592 | 14,076,296 |
| WC | 405,183 | 376,570 | 804,774 |
| Emp. | N/A | 1 | 149 |

DUNS 34-562-8379
## West Retford Hotel Ltd
24 North Road, Retford, Nottinghamshire DN22 7XG
Tel: 01777-706333
Web: www.bestwestern.co.uk
Reg No: 5372392 Estd: 1982 Private Limited Company
Line of Business: Hotels and motels without restaurant
Trading Style: West Retford Hotel Ltd
Issued Capital: £100
Director: A J Lavin
Co. Secretary: Ms Patricia Lavin
Responsibilities
Operations: Nick Finlay (Operations Manager)
US SIC: 7011 UK SIC: 66500
Bankers: National Westminster Bank Plc (60-17-28)

| | 28-02-14 | 28-02-13 | 29-02-12 |
|---|---|---|---|
| TO | 1,938,449 | 2,026,434 | 1,887,981 |
| P/L | 266,803 | 452,702 | 390,302 |
| NW | 3,527,637 | 3,303,172 | 2,678,592 |
| WC | 347,077 | 265,910 | (19,489) |
| Emp. | 56 | 51 | 47 |

DUNS 42-462-7011
## West Scottish Lamb Ltd
Carlisle Abattoir, Carlisle, Cumbria CA3 0EH
Tel: 01228-819805 Fax: 01228515998
Web: www.westscottishlamb.co.uk
Reg No: 4450315 VAT No: 790239124
Estd: 2002 Private Limited Company
Line of Business: Retail sale of meat and meat products
Export Sales: £31,486,522
Issued Capital: £300,120
Directors: J F Errington, C M Kirk Patrick, D Burton
Co. Secretary: Ms Amanda Burton
Responsibilities
Health & Safety: Ewan Hind (Health & Safety Officer)

Facilities: Ewan Hind (Health & Safety Officer)
US SIC: 2013 UK SIC: 41223
Bankers: Barclays Bank Plc (20-18-47)

| | 31-03-14 | 31-03-13 | 31-03-12 |
|---|---|---|---|
| TO | 44,851,627 | 42,044,440 | 43,880,668 |
| P/L | 248,730 | 367,544 | 360,578 |
| NW | 1,212,552 | 1,015,624 | 728,182 |
| WC | 879,031 | 716,113 | 463,556 |
| Emp. | 86 | 74 | 60 |

DUNS 21-490-7927
## West Somerset Community College
Bircham Road, Minehead, Somerset TA24 6AY
Tel: 01643-706061
Web: www.westsomersetcollege.org
Estd: 2011
Line of Business: Sixth form colleges
Responsibilities
Senior: Nick Swann (Head Teacher)
US SIC: 7999 UK SIC: 97913
Employees: 130

DUNS 21-905-2248
## West Somerset Council
West Somerset House, Killick Way, Williton, Taunton, Somerset TA4 4QA
Tel: 01643-703-704 Fax: 01643633022
Web: www.westsomerset.gov.uk
Estd: 1974 Incorporate By Act Of Parliament
Line of Business: General (overall) public service activities
Directors: A Dyer, H Close, R Bullen, P Jackson
Responsibilities
Senior: Penny James (CEO, Managing Director)
IT: Steve Farmer (Computer Manager)
HR: Martin Grissyn (Human Resources Manager), Alex Groves (Human Resources Officer)
Health & Safety: Ian Timms (Environmental Health Manager)
Operations: Ian Timms (Environmental Health Manager)
Purchasing: Steve Farmer (Computer Manager)
Branches: West Somerset Council, Po Box 618, Queens St, Taunton, Somerset TA1 3WF
US SIC: 9121 UK SIC: 91110

| | 31-03-13 |
|---|---|
| TO | 19,426,000 |
| P/L | (7,402,000) |
| NW | (1,695,000) |
| WC | 2,412,000 |
| Emp. | 96 |

DUNS 23-750-1825
## West Street Potters
Barnfield The Avenue, Farnham, Surrey GU10 4AL
Tel: 01483417756
Reg No: 3744174 Estd: 1999 Private Limited Company
Line of Business: Training centres
Directors: Mrs G Anderson, D Pratap, Dr. I L Chrystie, Ms K E Mason, K C Broadhead, Miss C M Phillips, Ms A P Watson
Co. Secretary: Miss Caroline Phillips
US SIC: 8299 UK SIC: 93300
Auditors: The Southhill Partnership

| | 31-07-13 | 31-07-12 | 31-07-11 |
|---|---|---|---|
| TO | 78,502 | 78,177 | 66,649 |
| P/L | 18,975 | 18,900 | 18,216 |
| NW | 91,199 | 70,791 | 51,891 |
| WC | 78,763 | 69,011 | 49,597 |

DUNS 22-984-1838
## West Suffolk College
Out Risbygate, Bury St Edmunds, Suffolk IP33 3RL
Tel: 01284701301
Web: www.westsuffolk-ac.co.uk
Estd: 1925
Line of Business: Further education schools and colleges
Director: N Foster
Responsibilities
Senior: Nikos Savvas (Principal)
Marketing: Sharon Caine (Marketing Executive), Emmanuelle Durand (Sales & Marketing Manager)
Sales: Emmanuelle Durand (Sales & Marketing Manager)
IT: Rudy Berongoy (Computer Operations Manager), Scott Gerber (IT Manager)
Purchasing: Julia Moore (Purchasing Manager)
Branches: West Suffolk College, Health Centre, Camps Road, Haverhill, Suffolk CB9 8HF
US SIC: 8221 UK SIC: 93100
Bankers: National Westminster Bank Plc (60-04-16)
Employees: 500

DUNS 22-223-3145
## West Suffolk Crossroads Caring for Carers
West Suffolk Crossroads Care, Bury St Edmunds, Suffolk IP32 7BX
Tel: 01284718686
Web: www.dawnstackbox.co.uk
Reg No: 4241235 Estd: 2001 Private Company Limited By Guarantee
Line of Business: Riding wear and equestrian supplies
Directors: D J Taylor, B R Wesley, M A Jesky, Ms C M Scott, G C Elliot, T E Cook, Ms O M Anderson
Responsibilities
Senior: Wendy Cullingworth (Manager), Andrew Mildren (Partner)
Branches: West Suffolk Crossroads Caring For Carers, Unit 4, Bunting Road, Bury St. Edmunds, Suffolk IP32 7BX
US SIC: 3161, 8321
UK SIC: 44201, 96111
Bankers: Cafcash Ltd (40-52-40)

| | 31-03-13 | 31-03-12 | 31-03-11 |
|---|---|---|---|
| TO | N/A | 454,862 | 612,863 |
| P/L | (202,887) | (55,762) | 87,033 |
| NW | N/A | 202,886 | 258,648 |
| WC | N/A | 196,413 | 254,018 |
| Emp. | N/A | 71 | 67 |

DUNS 42-393-9016
## West Suffolk Nhs Foundation Trust
Hardwick Lane, Bury St Edmunds, Suffolk IP33 2QZ
Tel: 01284-713000
Web: www.wsh.nhs.uk
Estd: 1993
Line of Business: Hospitals
Issued Capital: £1
Principals: C Bown, G Corser, D O'Riordan, Ms G Nuttall, J Bloomfield, Ms L Potter, Ms N Day
Responsibilities
Senior: Nigel Beeton (Manager), Clare Laroche (Clinical Director), Stephen Myers (General Manager for Surgery &)
Sales: Craig Black (Executive Director of Resource)
Admin: Virginia Eden (Administrator), Ann Southgate (Administrator)
IT: Nick Mcdonnell (Head of IT)
Operations: Andy Graham (Director of Major Projects), Jim Pretty (Security Manager)
Purchasing: Debbie Stevenson (Chief Purchasing Officer)
Branches: West Suffolk Nhs Foundation Trust, Walnuttree Lane, Sudbury, Suffolk CO10 1BE
US SIC: 8062 UK SIC: 95100
Auditors: BDO LLP

| | 31-03-14 | 31-03-13 |
|---|---|---|
| TO | 172,283,000 | 165,564,000 |
| P/L | (3,639,000) | 1,512,000 |
| NW | 69,440,000 | 72,288,000 |
| WC | (1,426,000) | 235,000 |
| Emp. | 2,816 | 2,741 |

DUNS 21-122-7657
## West Sussex County Council
County Hall, West Street, Chichester, West Sussex PO19 1RQ
Tel: 01243777100
Web: www.westsussex.gov.uk
Estd: 1898
Line of Business: Representative office
Trading Style: St Philip Howard Catholic High School, West Sussex Health
Principals: I Elliot (Chairman), P Rigg, P Rigg, B Robinson, M Holdsworth
Responsibilities
Admin: Lesley Gibbs (Leader Programme Administrator)
IT: Mike Branson (IT Services Manager)
Branches: West Sussex County Council, Canterbury Road, Crawley, West Sussex RH10 5EZ
US SIC: 9121 UK SIC: 91110
Bankers: Barclays Bank Plc (20-20-62)
Employees: 2,000

DUNS 21-582-5583
## West Sussex Crossroads
Tele Cottage, Horsemere Green Lane, Climping, Littlehampton, West Sussex BN17 5QZ
Tel: 01903790270
Web: www.crossroadscarewestsussex.org
Estd: 2011 Partnership
Line of Business: Activities of households as employers of domestic staff
Partners: Mrs M Burnett, E Geddes
US SIC: 8811 UK SIC: 99000
Employees: 100

DUNS 42-487-2828
## West Sussex Fire and Rescue Services
Fire Brigade Headquarters, Northgate, Chichester, West Sussex PO19 1BD
Tel: 01243642142
Web: www.westsussex.gov.uk
Estd: 2014 Incorporate By Act Of Parliament
Line of Business: Fire stations
Director: K J Lloyd
Responsibilities
Senior: Sean Ruth (Chief Fire Officer)
Finance: Matt Starling (Senior Finance Administrator)
Branches: West Sussex Fire and Rescue Services, Hurst Rd, Horsham, West Sussex RH12 2DN
US SIC: 9224 UK SIC: 91400
Employees: 50

DUNS 29-084-6724
## West Sussex Newspapers Ltd.
(Subsidiary of: Johnston Press Plc)
14-16 Market Square, Horsham, West Sussex RH12 1EU
Tel: 01403-751200 Fax: 01403751248
Web: www.horesorshamtoday.co.uk
Reg No: 1386925 Estd: 1978 Private Limited Company
Line of Business: Newspapers publishing
Trading Style: Sussex Newspapers
Issued Capital: £20,000
Directors: D J King, A G Highfield
Co. Secretary: Peter Mccall
Responsibilities
Senior: Gary Shipton (Editor)
US SIC: 2711 UK SIC: 47512

| | 28-12-13 | 29-12-12 | 31-12-11 |
|---|---|---|---|
| TA | 87,000 | 87,000 | 87,000 |
| NW | (822,000) | (822,000) | (822,000) |
| WC | N/A | N/A | (822,000) |

DUNS 21-778-4950
## West Sussex P C T
44-45 West Street, Chichester, West Sussex PO19 1RP
Tel: 01243770770
Web: www.wsx-pct.nhs.uk
Estd: 2011 Partnership
Line of Business: Home care service providers
Partners: J Wilderspin, Mrs C Holloway
US SIC: 8062 UK SIC: 95100
Employees: 125

DUNS 22-988-9399
## West Thames College
London Road, Isleworth, Middlesex TW7 4HS
Tel: 02083262000
Web: www.west-thames.ac.uk
VAT No: 625887890 Estd: 1980
Line of Business: Further education schools and colleges
Directors: G O'Donnel, Ms K Marriott
Responsibilities
Senior: Jane Clifford (Chairman), Taz Khusal (Senior Manager), John Kisby (Manager), Marjorie Semple (Principal), Pam Singer (Senior Manager)
Marketing: Shazia Hasnain (Sales & Marketing Manager), Nicola Ingle (Head of Strategic Marketing an)
Sales: Shazia Hasnain (Sales & Marketing Manager)
IT: Michael Michaelides (Head of IT Services)
HR: Marion Perkins (Human Resources Manager)
Engineering: Jamila Ebberson (Lecturer in Construction), Julian Shapter (Theatre Technical Manager)
Branches: London Rd, Isleworth, Middlesex TW7 4HS
US SIC: 8221 UK SIC: 93100
Employees: 200

DUNS 21-864-5969
## West Thurrock Academy
West Thurrock Academy, Schoolfield Road, Grays, Essex RM20 3HR
Tel: 01708863559
Reg No: 8259069 Estd: 2012 Private Company Limited By Guarantee
Line of Business: Primary education
Directors: D Jethwa, Ms E Henderson, Ms J A Eillis, Ms V Simmonds, A J Wright, R O Dawodu, M Antai, Ms L J Fishleigh
Responsibilities
Senior: Michael Prue (Director), Michelle Reynolds (Director)
US SIC: 8211 UK SIC: 93200
Bankers: HSBC Bank plc (40-17-08)

| | 31-08-14 | 31-08-13 |
|---|---|---|
| TO | 2,374,764 | 7,989,099 |
| P/L | (58,761) | 7,813,782 |
| NW | 5,811,522 | 7,813,783 |
| WC | 245,760 | 38,038 |
| Emp. | 61 | 65 |

DUNS 21-781-7906
## West View Intergrated Care Centre I C T
Plummer Lane, Tenterden, Kent TN30 6TX
**Tel:** 01580261500
**Web:** www.kent.gov.uk
**Estd:** 2005 Proprietorship
**Line of Business:** Residential care establishments
**Proprietor:** Ms C Shorter
**US SIC:** 8321 **UK SIC:** 96111
**Employees:** 120

DUNS 21-324-6650
## West Villa Nursing Home
Westfield Road, Retford, Nottinghamshire DN22 7BT
**Tel:** 01777701636
**Web:** www.westvilla.weebly.com
**Estd:** 1990
**Line of Business:** Nursing homes
**Proprietor:** E Walton
**Responsibilities**
**Senior:** Karen Bowler (Manager), Julie Spurr (Unit Manager)
**US SIC:** 8051 **UK SIC:** 95100
**Employees:** 55

DUNS 22-864-4696
## West Wallasey Car Hire Ltd
(Subsidiary of: Fleethire Services Ltd)
75 Leasowe Road, Wallasey, Merseyside CH45 8NZ
**Tel:** 01516303000 **Fax:** 0151-639-1958
**Web:** www.a1nationalvanhire.co.uk
**Reg No:** 1172466 **VAT No:** 165854238
**Estd:** 1974 Private Limited Company
**Line of Business:** Vehicle rental (car)
**Trading Style:** John Howarth & Son
**Issued Capital:** £50,000
**Principals:** M A Kenny (Managing), J P Kinney, J R Darke
**Co. Secretary:** Ms Dora Lynchehaun
**US SIC:** 7512 **UK SIC:** 84801
**Auditors:** Grant Thornton
**Bankers:** National Westminster Bank Plc (60-13-16)

|      | 30-09-13 | 30-09-12 | 30-09-11 |
|------|----------|----------|----------|
| TO   | 44,399,721 | 36,962,283 | 35,355,057 |
| P/L  | 5,206,446 | 3,809,408 | 4,525,030 |
| NW   | 30,138,279 | 25,225,061 | 21,522,914 |
| WC   | 7,596,585 | 6,806,077 | 951,340 |
| Emp. | 186 | 183 | 180 |

DUNS 21-131-9264
## West Way Development Trust
1 Thorpe Close, London W10 5XL
**Tel:** 020-8962-5720
**Web:** www.westwayproperty.co.uk
**VAT No:** 340040225 **Estd:** 1971
**Line of Business:** Charities and charitable organisations
**Principals:** J Rayman (Chairman), M Lockhart (Financial), R Matland
**Responsibilities**
**Senior:** Angela Mcconville (Chief Executive Officer)
**Facilities:** Paul Kusikwenyu (Maintenance Manager)
**Branches:** West Way Development Trust, 1 Crowthorne Road, London W10 6RP
**US SIC:** 6732 **UK SIC:** 83100
**Bankers:** Barclays Bank Plc (20-96-55)
**Employees:** 100

DUNS 28-839-5700 Imp
## West Wittering Estate Plc
Pound Road, West Wittering, Chichester, West Sussex PO20 8AJ
**Web:** www.westwitteringbeach.co.uk
**Reg No:** 0508519 **VAT No:** 193186148
**Estd:** 1952 Public Limited Company
**Line of Business:** Museums & art galleries
**Issued Capital:** £110,696
**Directors:** Ms A M Carnegie, S B Hammett, D F Swayne, R G Pike, M A Ralf, M Irwin-Brown, V P Byrne, G A Pettit
**Co. Secretary:** Thomas Eggar Secretaries Limited
**Responsibilities**
**Senior:** Clifford Hodgetts (Manager), Richard Melville (Director), Susan Trayler (Manager)
**US SIC:** 8411, 6531
**UK SIC:** 97700, 83400
**Auditors:** Jones Avens Ltd
**Bankers:** Lloyds TSB Bank plc (30-91-97)

|      | 31-12-13 | 31-12-12 | 31-12-11 |
|------|----------|----------|----------|
| TO   | 1,825,670 | 1,368,884 | 1,595,099 |
| P/L  | 364,840 | 159,780 | 293,475 |
| NW   | 5,966,868 | 5,710,078 | 5,652,700 |
| WC   | 18,999 | 165,712 | 25,772 |
| Emp. | 62 | 61 | 58 |

DUNS 21-776-4873
## West Yorkshire Central Services Agency
Brunswick Court, 2-8 Bridge Street, Leeds, West Yorkshire LS2 7RJ
**Tel:** 01132952500
**Web:** www.wycsa.nhs.uk
**Estd:** 1997
**Line of Business:** Community projects
**Responsibilities**
**Senior:** Gary Snowball (Assistant Director)
**IT:** Michael Dewhurst (Senior IT Executive)
**US SIC:** 8062 **UK SIC:** 95100
**Employees:** 90

DUNS 22-801-6648
## West Yorkshire Combined Authority
Wellington House, 40-50 Wellington Street, Leeds, West Yorkshire LS1 2DE
**Tel:** 01132517272 **Fax:** 0113 251 7373
**Web:** www.wypte.gov.uk
**VAT No:** 457507627 **Estd:** 1974 Incorporate By Act Of Parliament
**Line of Business:** Scheduled passenger air transport
**Trading Style:** Metro
**Principals:** P Box (Chairman), T Swift, J Alexander
**Responsibilities**
**Senior:** Anne Barwell (Manager), John Carr (Principal), Rachel Murphy (Manager), Roger Pickup (Manager), James Rawnsley (Non Executive Member), Mike Woodhall (Manager)
**HR:** Lisa Secker (Human Resources Manager)
**Branches:** Metro Change House, 61 Hall Ings, Bradford
**US SIC:** 7399, 9121
**UK SIC:** 83954, 91110
**Bankers:** Lloyds TSB Bank plc (30-00-05)
**Employees:** 250

DUNS 22-810-1507 Exp
## West Yorkshire Fellmongers Ltd
Halfords Ltd, Bradford, West Yorkshire BD1 4RH
**Tel:** 01274-731405
**Web:** www.westyorkshirefellmongers.co.uk
**Reg No:** 1693249 **VAT No:** 381249839
**Estd:** 1983 Private Limited Company
**Line of Business:** Hide dealers and merchants
**Export Markets:** E U, Far East.
**Issued Capital:** £1,000
**Principals:** C N Newton (Managing), B P Bailey, R A Brady, Miss S A Ward, Mrs J L Byrne
**Responsibilities**
**Senior:** Hugh Byrne (Manager)
**Health & Safety:** Ken Beestin (Health & Safety Manager)
**Branches:** West Yorkshire Fellmongers Ltd, 66-68 London Road, Gloucester, Gloucestershire GL1 3PB
**US SIC:** 3111 **UK SIC:** 44101
**Auditors:** Tayabali Tomlin
**Bankers:** Lloyds TSB Bank plc (30-91-74)

|      | 28-02-14 | 28-02-13 | 28-02-12 |
|------|----------|----------|----------|
| TO   | 34,223,712 | 34,715,130 | 46,985,246 |
| P/L  | 231,147 | 208,836 | 310,372 |
| NW   | 3,412,211 | 3,242,642 | 3,135,467 |
| WC   | 966,008 | 1,039,217 | 938,919 |
| Emp. | 62 | 64 | 54 |

DUNS 21-772-4476
## West Yorkshire Fire & Rescue Service
Outcote Bank, Huddersfield, West Yorkshire HD1 2JT
**Tel:** 01484551800
**Web:** www.wyfs.co.uk
**Estd:** 2011 Proprietorship
**Line of Business:** Fire stations
**Proprietor:** C Curby
**US SIC:** 9224 **UK SIC:** 91400
**Employees:** 100

DUNS 23-260-3761
## West Yorkshire Police
The Old Coach House, Laburnum Road, Wakefield, West Yorkshire WF1 3QS
**Tel:** 01924375222
**Web:** www.westyorkshire.police.uk
**Incorporate By Act Of Parliament**
**Line of Business:** Police Force
**Trading Style:** E-Crime Unit
**Director:** C Cramphorn
**Responsibilities**
**Health & Safety:** Christopher Shinn (Force Medical Officer)
**Branches:** West Yorkshire Police, Hard Ings Road, Keighley, West Yorkshire BD21 3NH
**US SIC:** 9221 **UK SIC:** 91300
**Employees:** 2,000

DUNS 21-224-6406
## West Yorkshire Probation Trust
Waterloo House, 58 Wellington Street, Leeds, West Yorkshire LS1 2EE
**Tel:** 01132430601
**Web:** www.westyorksprobation.org.uk
**Estd:** 2013
**Line of Business:** General (overall) public service activities
**Director:** Ms J King
**Branches:** WEST YORKSHIRE PROBATION TRUST - Harropwell Lane, Off Southgate, Pontefract.
**US SIC:** 9121, 6732
**UK SIC:** 91110, 83100
**Employees:** 1,260

DUNS 45-869-5459
## West Yorkshire Windows Ltd
Unit 17 Headway Business Park, Denby Dale Road, Wakefield, West Yorkshire WF2 7AZ
**Tel:** 01924299600
**Web:** www.westyorkshirewindows.co.uk
**Reg No:** 3212045 **Estd:** 1996 Private Limited Company
**Line of Business:** Other building installation
**Issued Capital:** £2,000
**Co. Secretary:** Andrew Glover
**Responsibilities**
**Senior:** Dereck Gedman (Store Manager)
**Branches:** West Yorkshire Windows Ltd, Unit 4 Brunel Road, Doncaster, South Yorkshire DN5 8PT
**US SIC:** 1796, 1751
**UK SIC:** 50400
**Auditors:** Bell Brown & Co
**Bankers:** HSBC Bank plc (40-36-08)

|      | 31-05-13 | 31-05-12 | 31-05-11 |
|------|----------|----------|----------|
| TA   | 1,238,760 | 1,416,784 | 1,356,400 |
| NW   | 63,256 | 185,436 | 196,458 |
| WC   | (195,470) | (121,026) | (128,790) |

DUNS 23-276-4139
## West Yorkshire Workforce Development Confederation
Blenheim House, Duncombe Street, Leeds, West Yorkshire LS1 4PL
**Tel:** 01132952000
**Web:** www.yorksandhumber.nhs.uk
**Estd:** 2012
**Line of Business:** Health authorities
**Director:** G Saunders
**Responsibilities**
**Senior:** Tony Dudson (Manager)
**US SIC:** 7999 **UK SIC:** 97913
**Employees:** 150

DUNS 21-778-7020
## Westacre Middle School
Ombersley Way, Droitwich, Worcestershire WR9 0AA
**Tel:** 01905772795
**Web:** www.westacre-middle-school.co.uk
**Estd:** 2002 Partnership
**Line of Business:** Schools (local authority)
**Partner:** Mrs D Evans
**US SIC:** 8211 **UK SIC:** 93200
**Employees:** 55

DUNS 21-557-7623
## Westacre Nursing Home
Sleepers Hill, Winchester, Hampshire SO22 4NE
**Tel:** 01962-855188
**Web:** www.fernsidehealthcare.com
**Estd:** 1983 Proprietorship
**Line of Business:** Medical nursing home activities
**Proprietor:** J Sargeant
**Responsibilities**
**Senior:** Syvia Carter (Manager), Oliver Sargent (CEO, Managing Director), Liz Stewart (Home Manager)
**Finance:** Sue Watson (Senior Finance Administrator)
**US SIC:** 8051 **UK SIC:** 95100
**Employees:** 65

DUNS 22-354-3039
## Westbank Healthy Living Centre
Farmhouse Rise, Exminster, Exeter, Devon EX6 8AT
**Web:** www.westbank.org.uk
**Estd:** 2010 Proprietorship
**Line of Business:** Community centres
**Proprietor:** Mrs J Dunster
**Responsibilities**
**Senior:** Mary Nistett (Ceo)
**US SIC:** 8091 **UK SIC:** 95200
**Employees:** 70

DUNS 28-861-6857
## Westbourne House School Educational Trust Ltd
Coach Road, Shopwyke, Chichester, West Sussex PO20 2BH
**Tel:** 01243782739
**Web:** www.westbournehouse.org
**Reg No:** 0902869 **Estd:** 1967 Private Company Limited By Guarantee
**Line of Business:** Schools (foundation)
**Directors:** K W Langmead, R A Hill, B A Vessey, C E Snell, N P Backhouse, Mrs D J Alun-Jones, Mrs G M Hooker, C M Keville
**Co. Secretary:** Andrew Wilkinson
**Responsibilities**
**Senior:** Martin Barker (Head Master), John Broad (Manager), Rosemary Groves (Governor), Leah Hamblett (Director), Juliet Matthews (Director), Michael Perkins (Manager)
**US SIC:** 8211 **UK SIC:** 93200
**Auditors:** Jones Avens
**Bankers:** National Westminster Bank Plc (60-05-24)

|      | 31-08-14 | 31-08-13 | 31-08-12 |
|------|----------|----------|----------|
| TO   | 5,715,171 | 5,462,011 | 5,228,057 |
| P/L  | 616,167 | 698,893 | 664,339 |
| NW   | 10,834,154 | 10,217,987 | 9,519,094 |
| WC   | 1,645,946 | 1,254,638 | 1,850,488 |
| Emp. | 101 | 100 | 97 |

DUNS 21-210-8687
## Westbourne Nursing Home
190 Reservoir Road, Gloucester, Gloucestershire GL4 6SB
**Tel:** 01452506106
**Estd:** 1987 Proprietorship
**Line of Business:** Nursing homes
**Proprietor:** Ms A Harris
**Responsibilities**
**Senior:** Josie Dalli (Proprietor)
**US SIC:** 8051 **UK SIC:** 95100
**Employees:** 50

DUNS 22-271-8699 Imp-Exp
## Westbridge Foods (Haydock) Ltd
(Subsidiary of: Westbridge Food Group Ltd)
5 Bahama Road, Haydock Industrial Estate, St Helens, Merseyside WA11 9XB
**Fax:** 01942-722265
**Web:** www.westbridgefoods.com
**Reg No:** 4289793 **Estd:** 2002 Private Limited Company
**Line of Business:** Canteens and catering
**Issued Capital:** £252,855
**Directors:** N C Shaw, J Middleton, P J Mcneil
**Co. Secretary:** Philip Turtle
**Responsibilities**
**Senior:** Derek Wignall (Manager)
**US SIC:** 5812, 5147
**UK SIC:** 66110, 61700
**Auditors:** Grant Thornton UK LLP
**Bankers:** The Royal Bank Of Scotland Plc (16-08-84)

|      | 31-12-13 | 31-12-12 | 31-12-11 |
|------|----------|----------|----------|
| TO   | 65,698,955 | 48,030,925 | 53,107,878 |
| P/L  | 3,212,590 | 2,356,496 | 2,038,933 |
| NW   | 12,311,779 | 9,105,651 | 7,347,538 |
| WC   | 11,593,117 | 8,418,562 | 6,947,513 |
| Emp. | 49 | 47 | 51 |

DUNS 51-980-7619 Imp
## Westbridge Foods Ltd
(Subsidiary of: Westbridge Food Group Ltd)
Polonia House, Enigma Commercial Centre, Malvern, Worcestershire WR14 1JJ
**Tel:** 01684-581800
**Web:** www.westbridgefoods.com
**Reg No:** 3443712 **VAT No:** 696155105
**Estd:** 1998 Private Limited Company
**Line of Business:** Canteens and catering
**Issued Capital:** £100
**Directors:** J J Mcneil, M Whaley, P J Mcneil, J Middleton, N C Shaw
**Responsibilities**
**Senior:** Sara Barnard (Operations Director), Derek Wignall (Manager)
**Operations:** Sara Barnard (Operations Director)
**US SIC:** 5812, 5149
**UK SIC:** 66110, 61700
**Auditors:** Knipe Whiting Heath Ltd
**Bankers:** Lloyds TSB Bank plc (30-94-14)

|      | 31-12-13 | 31-12-12 | 31-12-11 |
|------|----------|----------|----------|
| TO   | 381,949,148 | 284,720,401 | 230,292,720 |
| P/L  | (3,439,383) | 6,252,490 | 5,746,647 |
| NW   | 15,812,267 | 28,760,306 | 24,623,282 |
| WC   | 23,187,689 | 25,562,212 | 21,350,635 |
| Emp. | 64 | 49 | 35 |

DUNS 21-227-9250
## Westbrook Centre
1-7 Milton Road, Cambridge, Cambridgeshire CB4 1UY
**Tel:** 01223-324425
**Web:** www.greenpropertyplc.com
**Estd:** 2003 Proprietorship
**Line of Business:** Business and commerce centres
**Proprietor:** Mrs S Ganisord
**US SIC:** 7392 **UK SIC:** 83951
**Employees:** 523

DUNS 22-841-6616
## Westbury
145/157 St John Street, London EC1V 4PY
**Tel:** 020-7253-7272
**Web:** www.westbury.co.uk
**Estd:** 1930 Partnership
**Line of Business:** Accounting activities primarily bookkeeping
**Partners:** K Graham, P B Klinger, J Gubby, R D Lele, N Springer, S D Clarke, H Graham
**Responsibilities**
**Senior:** Adrian Keo *(Manager)*, Ratan Lele *(Partner)*, Ihab Serafi *(Manager)*
**Finance:** Catherine Corti *(Payroll Manager)*, Miranda Lastic *(Tax Department Manager)*
**US SIC:** 8931 **UK SIC:** 83600
**Employees:** 50

DUNS 45-835-1731
## Westbury Care Ltd
Falcondale Road, Bristol, Avon BS9 3JH
**Tel:** 01179079970
**Web:** http://westburycare.co.uk
**Reg No:** 3185917 **Estd:** 1996 Private Limited Company
**Line of Business:** Nursing homes
**Trading Style:** The Westbury Nursing Home
**Issued Capital:** £100
**Principals:** Ms J M Phillips *(Managing)*, Ms S J Wilson
**Co. Secretary:** Gordon Brooking
**Responsibilities**
**Senior:** Derek Marsh *(Manager)*
**Finance:** Norman Brookes *(Financial Director)*
**HR:** Penny Brown *(Matron)*
**Health & Safety:** Penny Brown *(Matron)*
**US SIC:** 8051 **UK SIC:** 95100
**Auditors:** Houghton Stone
**Bankers:** National Westminster Bank Plc (52-10-05)

| | 31-03-14 | 31-03-13 | 31-03-12 |
|---|---|---|---|
| TO | 3,351,808 | 3,034,039 | 2,844,911 |
| P/L | 339,629 | 588,798 | 476,625 |
| NW | 3,370,269 | 3,107,335 | 2,737,722 |
| WC | 400,161 | 564,142 | 454,618 |
| Emp. | 109 | 123 | 119 |

DUNS 23-897-4708
## Westbury Control Systems Ltd
Unit 5 Wylam Court, Telford Way, Coalville, Leicestershire LE67 3HE
**Tel:** 01530510751
**Web:** www.westbury-uk.com
**Reg No:** 3888243 **Estd:** 1999 Private Limited Company
**Line of Business:** Manufacture of electronic valves and tubes and other electronic components
**Issued Capital:** £100
**Directors:** G Westbury, P Tongue
**Co. Secretary:** Ms Lucy Westbury
**US SIC:** 3679 **UK SIC:** 34542

| | 31-03-14 | 31-03-13 | 31-03-12 |
|---|---|---|---|
| TA | 3,084,003 | 2,566,951 | 2,264,376 |
| NW | 1,017,373 | 901,172 | 576,292 |
| WC | 658,088 | 1,085,197 | 522,296 |

DUNS 21-208-3831
## Westbury House
West Meon, Petersfield, Hampshire GU32 1HY
**Web:** www.westburyhouse.net
**Estd:** 1994 Partnership
**Line of Business:** Nursing homes
**Partners:** Dr V Naqvi, I N Naqvi
**Responsibilities**
**Senior:** Irvine Naqvi *(Marketing Manager)*
**Marketing:** Irvine Naqvi *(Marketing Manager)*
**Branches:** 6 Rempstone Road, Swanage, Dorset BH19 1DW
**US SIC:** 8051 **UK SIC:** 95100
**Employees:** 60

DUNS 21-712-5539
## Westbury Street Holdings Ltd
(**Subsidiary of:** Boxford Investments Limited)
Tvp 2, 300 Thames Valley Park Drive, Reading, Berkshire RG6 1PT
**Tel:** 01189356705
**Web:** www.wshlimited.com
**Reg No:** 7523520 **Estd:** 2011 Private Limited Company
**Line of Business:** Management activities of other non-financial holding companies not elsewhere classified
**Export Sales:** £28,932,000
**Issued Capital:** £94,712,317
**Directors:** A D Storey, M Bradley
**Co. Secretary:** Marc Bradley
**US SIC:** 6711 **UK SIC:** 83962

| | 27-12-13 | 28-12-12 | 30-12-11 |
|---|---|---|---|
| TO | 534,818,000 | 466,062,000 | 353,188,000 |
| P/L | 1,994,000 | 6,181,000 | (1,667,000) |
| NW | (95,362,000) | (106,521,000) | (110,466,000) |
| WC | (6,039,000) | (29,784,000) | (16,927,000) |
| Emp. | 11,840 | 10,370 | 9,643 |

DUNS 23-790-1199
## Westcars Ltd
(**Subsidiary of:** Eastern Holdings Ltd)
Lexus Scotland 100 West Street, Glasgow, Lanarkshire G5 8AW
**Tel:** 01414297222
**Web:** www.lexusscotland.co.uk
**Reg No:** 0196894SC **Estd:** 2013 Private Limited Company
**Line of Business:** Car dealers (new & used)
**Trading Style:** Lexus Glasgow
**Issued Capital:** £1
**Director:** D J Brown
**Co. Secretary:** Nasser Mohammed
**US SIC:** 7699, 5511
**UK SIC:** 67303, 65100
**Auditors:** Gilchrist & Co

| | 31-12-13 | 31-12-12 | 31-12-11 |
|---|---|---|---|
| TA | 1 | 1 | 1 |
| NW | 1 | 1 | 1 |

DUNS 34-578-6677
## Westcity Property Development Ltd
(**Subsidiary of:** Westcity Ltd)
46 Blandford Street, London W1U 7HT
**Tel:** 02075355242
**Web:** www.westcity.co.uk
**Reg No:** 2725831 **Estd:** 1992 Private Limited Company
**Line of Business:** Buying and selling of own real estate
**Issued Capital:** £2
**Director:** I S Rapp
**Co. Secretary:** Michael Tannenbaum
**US SIC:** 6531 **UK SIC:** 83400
**Auditors:** BDO Stoy Hayward
**Bankers:** Lloyds TSB Bank plc (30-12-18)

| | 31-12-14 | 31-12-13 | 31-12-12 |
|---|---|---|---|
| NW | (6,377,377) | (6,377,377) | (6,377,377) |

DUNS 57-807-5079
## Westcliff Casino Ltd
(**Subsidiary of:** Genting Bhd.)
Western Esplanade, Westcliff-On-Sea, Essex SS0 7QY
**Tel:** 01702435535 **Fax:** 01702332465
**Web:** www.gentingcasinos.co.uk
**Reg No:** 2886476 **Estd:** 1970 Private Limited Company
**Line of Business:** Casinos
**Issued Capital:** £2
**Directors:** P M Brooks, R R Salmond
**Co. Secretary:** Ms Elizabeth Tarn
**Responsibilities**
**Senior:** Simon Woodford *(General Manager)*
**Marketing:** John Harland *(Marketing Manager)*
**US SIC:** 7999 **UK SIC:** 97913
**Auditors:** PricewaterhouseCoopers LLP
**Bankers:** Barclays Bank Plc (20-77-67)

| | 31-12-13 | 31-12-12 | 31-12-11 |
|---|---|---|---|
| TA | 3,497,000 | 3,497,000 | 3,497,000 |
| NW | 3,497,000 | 3,497,000 | 3,497,000 |

DUNS 21-685-2008
## Westcliff High School for Boys Ltd
Kenilworth Gardens, Westcliff-On-Sea, Essex SS0 0BP
**Tel:** 01702475443 **Fax:** 01702470495
**Web:** www.whsb.essex.sch.uk
**Reg No:** 7347930 **Estd:** 1990 Private Company Limited By Guarantee
**Line of Business:** Schools (foundation)
**Directors:** M A Skelly, S J Johnson, I Croxford, J H Gershinson
**Co. Secretary:** Ms Fiona Colwell
**Responsibilities**
**Senior:** Howard Briggs *(Governor)*
**Finance:** Carol Shirlin *(Bursar)*
**US SIC:** 8211 **UK SIC:** 93200

| | 31-08-14 | 31-08-13 | 31-08-12 |
|---|---|---|---|
| TO | 7,126,330 | 6,667,484 | 5,688,610 |
| P/L | 1,553,136 | 1,162,396 | 420,769 |
| NW | 21,595,792 | 20,114,656 | 18,975,260 |
| WC | 3,419,889 | 3,110,822 | 1,834,067 |
| Emp. | 122 | 117 | 111 |

DUNS 29-660-1404
## Westco Floorcoverings Ltd
Penarth Road, Cardiff, South Glamorgan CF11 8YN
**Web:** www.westcofloors.co.uk
**Reg No:** 1986386 **Estd:** 1986 Private Limited Company
**Line of Business:** Wholesale of furniture
**Trading Style:** Glue London
**Issued Capital:** £2
**Principals:** N G Gibbs *(Managing)*, N C Gibbs *(Marketing)*
**Co. Secretary:** Timothy Thomas
**US SIC:** 5021, 5199
**UK SIC:** 61500, 61900
**Auditors:** PricewaterhouseCoopers
**Bankers:** National Westminster Bank Plc (01-01-55)

| | 31-01-14 | 31-01-13 | 31-01-12 |
|---|---|---|---|
| TA | 2 | 2 | 2 |
| NW | 2 | 2 | 2 |

DUNS 22-851-2869 **Imp**
## Westco Flow Control Ltd
(**Subsidiary of:** Aalberts Industries N.V.)
Unit C6 - William Way, Leigh, Lancashire WN7 3PT
**Tel:** 01942-603351 **Fax:** 01942-607780
**Web:** www.comap.co.uk
**Reg No:** 1322734 **Estd:** 1977 Private Limited Company
**Line of Business:** Heating system consultants
**Export Sales:** £77,000
**Issued Capital:** £7,500
**Directors:** S Anderson, I M Howarth, N J Johnston
**Co. Secretary:** Andrew Mitchell
**Responsibilities**
**IT:** Philip Prince *(Computer Manager)*
**Branches:** Westco Flow Control Ltd, Mount Pleasant Business Centre, Jackson St, Oldham, Lancashire OL4 1HU
**US SIC:** 4712 **UK SIC:** 77002
**Auditors:** PricewaterhouseCoopers LLP
**Bankers:** Bank Of Scotland (80-54-01)

| | 31-12-13 | 31-12-12 | 31-12-11 |
|---|---|---|---|
| TO | 22,401,000 | 22,062,000 | 23,790,000 |
| P/L | 1,137,000 | 1,599,000 | 1,595,000 |
| NW | 875,000 | 1,206,000 | 1,169,000 |
| WC | 819,000 | 1,154,000 | 1,114,000 |
| Emp. | 74 | 74 | 78 |

DUNS 51-992-6455
## Westcoast (Holdings) Ltd
Arrowhead Park, Arrowhead Road, Theale, Reading, Berkshire RG7 4AH
**Tel:** 07900-218-666 **Fax:** 01189-521-700
**Web:** www.kelido.co.uk
**Reg No:** 3359843 **Estd:** 1997 Private Limited Company
**Line of Business:** Holding companies management activities
**Export Sales:** £109,937,000
**Issued Capital:** £1,344,001
**Directors:** S J Madhani, D G Forsyth, A Hemani, L Hemani, B Tkachuk
**Co. Secretary:** Ms Christine Batchelor
**US SIC:** 6711, 5081
**UK SIC:** 83962, 61490
**Auditors:** PricewaterhouseCoopers LLP
**Bankers:** Lloyds TSB Bank plc (30-96-96)

**Following financial data are in thousands**

| | 31-12-13 | 31-12-12 | 31-12-11 |
|---|---|---|---|
| TO | 1,199,394 | 1,047,331 | 942,413 |
| P/L | 7,883 | 6,333 | 6,216 |
| NW | 25,665 | 18,764 | 15,121 |
| WC | 36,183 | 27,223 | 26,844 |
| Emp. | 829 | 793 | 755 |

DUNS 22-642-7821 **Imp-Exp**
## Westcoast Ltd
(**Subsidiary of:** Westcoast (Holdings) Ltd)
Unit A Arrowhead Park, Reading, Berkshire RG7 4AH
**Tel:** 0118-912-6000 **Fax:** 0118-912-6200
**Web:** www.westcoast.co.uk
**Reg No:** 1816587 **VAT No:** 569976554
**Estd:** 1984 Private Limited Company
**Line of Business:** Clothing retailers
**Export Sales:** £29,141,000
**Issued Capital:** £10,000
**Principals:** D G Forsyth *(Managing)*, A Tatham, A Hunt, A Hemani, A P Newberry, S Madhani, C J Oxley, P Heath
**Co. Secretary:** Ms Christine Batchelor
**Responsibilities**
**IT:** Ryan Hemani *(Computer Operations Manager)*
**Branches:** Westcoast Ltd, Wilford Industrial Estate, Ruddington Lane, Wilford, Nottingham, Nottinghamshire NG11 7EP
**US SIC:** 5065, 7379
**UK SIC:** 61500, 83940
**Auditors:** PricewaterhouseCoopers LLP

**Following financial data are in thousands**

| | 31-12-13 | 31-12-12 | 31-12-11 |
|---|---|---|---|
| TO | 1,120,854 | 960,441 | 826,104 |
| P/L | 8,120 | 6,918 | 5,583 |
| NW | 47,785 | 45,421 | 44,351 |
| WC | 50,706 | 49,571 | 50,128 |
| Emp. | 510 | 474 | 448 |

DUNS 42-423-7001 **Imp**
## Westcon Group European Operations Ltd
(**Subsidiary of:** Datatec Ltd)
Astral Towers, Betts Way, Crawley, West Sussex RH10 9UY
**Tel:** 01753797800 **Fax:** 01753797801
**Web:** www.westcon.co.uk
**Reg No:** 4411285 **VAT No:** 911018375
**Estd:** 2002 Private Limited Company
**Line of Business:** Computer systems and software (sales)
**Trading Style:** Westcon Group
**Directors:** R Hodgetts, J Butt, Ms C K Jessup
**Co. Secretary:** Daniel Jones
**Branches:** Westcon Group European Operations Ltd, Chandlers House, Wilkinson Road, Cirencester, Gloucestershire GL7 1YT
**US SIC:** 7379, 4899
**UK SIC:** 83940, 79020
**Auditors:** Deloitte LLP
**Employees:** 878
**Turnover:** £1,417,320,000

DUNS 21-561-1863
## Westcott House
Guildford Road, Westcott, Dorking, Surrey RH4 3QD
**Web:** www.westcotthouse.co.uk
**Proprietorship**
**Line of Business:** Medical nursing home activities
**Proprietor:** Y Charalambous
**Responsibilities**
**Senior:** Julie Charalambous *(Home Manager)*
**US SIC:** 8051 **UK SIC:** 95100
**Employees:** 60

DUNS 21-700-1296
## Westcountry Fruit Sales Ltd
Higher Argal, Argal, Falmouth, Cornwall TR11 5PE
**Tel:** 01326372304
**Web:** www.thegreengrocery.co.uk
**Reg No:** 0980586 **VAT No:** 434454065
**Estd:** 2000 Private Limited Company
**Line of Business:** Retail sale of fruit and vegetables
**Issued Capital:** £100,000
**Principals:** S H Williams *(Managing)*, R B Rossignol
**Co. Secretary:** Lee Bartholomew
**Responsibilities**
**Finance:** Jack Griffiths *(Senior Finance Administrator)*
**HR:** Adrian Bailey *(Human Resources Manager)*
**Branches:** Westcountry Fruit Sales Ltd, Unit 20 St. Austell Bay Business Park, Par Moor Road, St Austell, St. Austell, Cornwall PL25 3RF
**US SIC:** 5148 **UK SIC:** 61700
**Auditors:** Hodgsons
**Bankers:** Barclays Bank Plc (20-87-94)

| | 28-12-13 | 29-12-12 | 31-12-11 |
|---|---|---|---|
| TO | 12,123,468 | 11,429,685 | 11,665,892 |
| P/L | 276,988 | 262,587 | 318,278 |
| NW | 1,981,995 | 1,836,071 | 1,633,937 |
| WC | 1,404,493 | 1,114,601 | 888,519 |
| Emp. | 89 | 97 | 107 |

DUNS 77-109-0693
## Westcountry Garden Centres Ltd
Flitwick Road, Westoning, Bedford, Bedfordshire MK45 5AA
**Tel:** 01525-712484
**Web:** www.flitvale.com
**Reg No:** 2685960 **Estd:** 1992 Private Limited Company
**Line of Business:** Garden centres
**Trading Style:** Flittvale Garden Centre
**Issued Capital:** £2
**Principals:** M I Hassall *(Managing)*, Mrs J R Hassall
**US SIC:** 5999 **UK SIC:** 65600
**Auditors:** B W Holman & Co
**Bankers:** The Royal Bank Of Scotland Plc (16-00-63)

| | 31-12-13 | 31-12-12 | 31-12-11 |
|---|---|---|---|
| TO | 3,702,126 | N/A | N/A |
| P/L | 559,937 | N/A | N/A |
| NW | 3,944,819 | 1,702,826 | 1,623,647 |
| WC | 941,465 | (111,606) | (191,006) |
| Emp. | 73 | N/A | N/A |

DUNS 52-556-6279

## Westcountry Home Care Ltd

**(Subsidiary of:** South West Care Solutions Ltd)
6 Scarne Court, Hurdon Road, Launceston, Cornwall PL15 9LR
**Tel:** 01566-775960
**Reg No:** 3245318 **Estd:** 1996 Private Limited Company
**Line of Business:** Home care service providers
**Issued Capital:** £15,000
**Directors:** Mrs V Saraogi, G K Saraogi
**Responsibilities**
**Senior:** Mariane Greenerway *(Care Manager)*
**US SIC:** 8321 **UK SIC:** 96111
**Bankers:** Lloyds TSB Bank plc (30-94-91)

| | 31-10-13 | 31-10-12 | 31-10-11 |
|---|---|---|---|
| TA | 778,605 | 328,472 | 565,414 |
| NW | 250,357 | 9,776 | (167,519) |
| WC | 204,678 | 171,026 | (29,337) |

DUNS 23-208-7270

## Westcountry Housing Association Ltd

Templar House, Collett Way, Newton Abbot, Devon TQ12 4PH
**Tel:** 03001001011
**Web:** www.westwardhousing.org.uk
**Reg No:** 0019141IP **Estd:** 1993 Friendly Society
**Line of Business:** Housing associations societies trusts & co-operatives
**Trading Style:** Westward Housing Group
**Principals:** P Bevan, R Almy, C Born, B F Chudley, P G Wilde, J Tuck
**Responsibilities**
**Senior:** Barabara Shaw *(Chief Executive)*
**Finance:** Mike Sennitt *(Financial Director)*
**Marketing:** Vanessa Gray *(Marketing Manager)*, Terry Leech *(Resident Involvement Officer)*
**Facilities:** Malcolm Quantick *(Housing Services Manager)*
**Branches:** Westcountry Housing Association Ltd, Bethany House, St. Sidwells Avenue, Exeter, Devon EX4 6QW
**US SIC:** 8321 **UK SIC:** 96111
**Auditors:** Grant Thornton UK LLP
**Bankers:** The Royal Bank Of Scotland Plc (16-19-25)

| | 31-03-12 | 31-03-11 | 31-03-10 |
|---|---|---|---|
| TO | 25,241,000 | 23,471,000 | 28,183,000 |
| P/L | 2,378,000 | 2,372,000 | 1,331,000 |
| NW | 39,018,000 | 37,236,000 | 32,253,000 |
| WC | 22,773,000 | 7,866,000 | 8,143,000 |
| Emp. | 284 | 290 | 332 |

DUNS 29-755-3711 Imp

## Westcrowns Ltd

Quay House, Quay Road North, Rutherglen, Glasgow, Lanarkshire G73 1LD
**Tel:** 01416134700 **Fax:** 0141-613-1216
**Web:** www.westcrownsgroup.com
**Reg No:** 0098991SC **Estd:** 1986 Private Limited Company
**Line of Business:** Management activities of holding companies
**Export Sales:** £25,000
**Issued Capital:** £576,356
**Principals:** J F Haran *(Managing)*, Ms S Haran, W A Mcbride, J W Haran, J Devine, L E Haran
**Co. Secretary:** Ian Finlayson
**US SIC:** 6711, 5039
**UK SIC:** 83962, 61300
**Auditors:** Ernst & Young LLP
**Bankers:** Clydesdale Bank Plc (82-20-00)

| | 31-03-14 | 31-03-13 | 31-03-12 |
|---|---|---|---|
| TO | 30,797,000 | 29,234,000 | 30,560,000 |
| P/L | 922,000 | 791,000 | 451,000 |
| NW | 4,351,000 | 3,878,000 | 4,143,000 |
| WC | 4,525,000 | 3,492,000 | 3,145,000 |
| Emp. | 377 | 361 | 351 |

DUNS 29-161-3685

## The Westdale Press Ltd

**(Subsidiary of:** Westdale Printing Group Ltd)
Unit 70 Portmanmoor Road Industrial, Estate, Cardiff, South Glamorgan CF24 5HB
**Tel:** 02920662600
**Web:** www.westdale.co.uk
**Reg No:** 1787743 **VAT No:** 402518000
**Estd:** 1984 Private Limited Company
**Line of Business:** Printing not elsewhere classified
**Issued Capital:** £25,946
**Principals:** A J Padbury *(Managing)*, Ms J C Cundy, D J Pike, D B Deere
**Co. Secretary:** Bernard Atkins
**Responsibilities**
**Senior:** Wayne Bray *(Transport Manager)*
**IT:** Neill Hamblyn *(Production Manager)*
**HR:** Katie Pottinger *(Human Resources Manager)*
**Fleet:** Wayne Bray *(Transport Manager)*
**Engineering:** Neill Hamblyn *(Production Manager)*
**US SIC:** 2752 **UK SIC:** 47544
**Auditors:** Bowker Orford
**Bankers:** Barclays Bank Plc (20-36-47)

| | 30-04-14 | 30-04-13 | 30-04-12 |
|---|---|---|---|
| TO | 17,052,691 | 19,081,455 | 19,432,534 |
| P/L | 222,649 | 378,262 | 270,435 |
| NW | 2,466,259 | 2,231,666 | 2,020,559 |
| WC | 330,847 | 25,563 | 256,096 |
| Emp. | 46 | 52 | 51 |

DUNS 76-374-9629

## Westender Ltd

25 Horsell Road, London N5 1XL
**Tel:** 02076076060
**Reg No:** 2552626 **Estd:** 1990 Private Limited Company
**Line of Business:** Publishing of newspapers
**Issued Capital:** £2
**Director:** D A Connolley
**Co. Secretary:** Robert Denton
**US SIC:** 2711 **UK SIC:** 47512
**Employees:** 50

DUNS 34-917-3141 Imp

## Wester Ross Fisheries Ltd.

Kinsteary, Nairn, Nairnshire IV12 5NZ
**Tel:** 01667455222 **Fax:** 01667455184
**Web:** www.wrs.co.uk
**Reg No:** 0297376SC **Estd:** 2010 Private Limited Company
**Line of Business:** Fish farms
**Export Sales:** £4,019,664
**Issued Capital:** £50,200
**Directors:** D A Robinson, C W Milne, J R Bradley, H J Richards
**Co. Secretary:** Eagle Consulting
**US SIC:** 0921 **UK SIC:** 03002
**Auditors:** Saffery Champness

| | 31-12-13 | 31-12-12 | 31-12-11 |
|---|---|---|---|
| TO | 8,028,457 | 7,801,092 | 6,534,347 |
| P/L | 352,300 | 253,162 | 87,054 |
| NW | 1,493,883 | 1,396,789 | 1,336,931 |
| WC | 1,587,341 | 1,414,944 | 1,122,138 |
| Emp. | 51 | 51 | 50 |

DUNS 21-484-7217

## Westerleigh Nursing Home

18 Corsica Road, Seaford, East Sussex BN25 1BD
**Tel:** 01323-892335
**Web:** www.westerleigh.info
**Estd:** 1986 Partnership
**Line of Business:** Nursing homes
**Partner:** Mrs C Whelan
**Responsibilities**
**Senior:** Tracey Austin *(Manager)*
**US SIC:** 8051 **UK SIC:** 95100
**Employees:** 60

DUNS 21-717-1640

## Western & Oriental Travel Ltd

**(Subsidiary of:** Furze International Limited)
Layden House, 76-86 Turnmill Street, London EC1M 5QU
**Tel:** 0207 6661234
**Web:** www.wandotravel.com
**Reg No:** 7558669 **Estd:** 2011 Private Limited Company
**Line of Business:** Activities of travel organisers
**Trading Style:** Western & Oriental Travel Limited
**Issued Capital:** £100,000
**Directors:** R R Kumar, Mrs M F Kumar
**Responsibilities**
**Senior:** Matthew Rushbrooke *(Centre Manager)*
**US SIC:** 4722 **UK SIC:** 77001

| | 31-03-14 | 31-03-13 | 31-03-12 |
|---|---|---|---|
| TO | 27,285,796 | 26,839,464 | 25,432,653 |
| P/L | (627,754) | (868,612) | (1,071,337) |
| NW | (3,448,081) | (2,960,383) | (1,961,346) |
| WC | (388,264) | 36,202 | 1,386,091 |
| Emp. | 86 | 82 | 87 |

DUNS 50-511-8117 Exp

## Western Asset Management Co Ltd

**(Subsidiary of:** Lm International Holding L.P.)
10 Primrose Street Exchange Square, London EC2A 2EN
**Tel:** 020-7422-3000 **Fax:** 02074223100
**Web:** www.westernasset.com
**Reg No:** 2479672 **Estd:** 1984 Private Limited Company
**Line of Business:** Financial intermediation not elsewhere classified
**Export Markets:** Worldwide
**Directors:** M B Zelouf, C A Ruys De Perez, T C Merchant
**Co. Secretary:** Ms Kate Blackledge
**Responsibilities**
**Finance:** Suzanne Taylor-King *(Financial Officer)*
**Facilities:** Portia Perry *(Facilities Manager)*
**US SIC:** 6111 **UK SIC:** 81501
**Auditors:** PricewaterhouseCoopers LLP
**Bankers:** American Express Bank Limited (60-92-00)
**Employees:** 75

DUNS 57-842-5969

## Western Automobile Company Ltd

**(Subsidiary of:** Eastern Holdings Ltd)
1 Corstorphine Road, Edinburgh, Midlothian EH12 6DD
**Tel:** 01313130500 **Fax:** 01314665577
**Web:** www.western-mazda.co.uk
**Reg No:** 0148914SC **Estd:** 2011 Private Limited Company
**Line of Business:** Sale of new motor vehicles
**Trading Style:** Western Mercedes Passenger Car
**Issued Capital:** £250,000
**Principals:** D J Brown *(Managing)*, P J Collin, K Robb
**Co. Secretary:** Nasser Mohammed
**Responsibilities**
**Senior:** Graham Affleck *(Market Area Director)*, Roy Blackley *(Parts Manager)*, John La-Trobe *(Dealer Principal)*
**Marketing:** Graham Affleck *(Market Area Director)*
**Branches:** Western Commercials, 51 Bridge St, Newbridge
**US SIC:** 5511 **UK SIC:** 65100
**Auditors:** Deloitte & Touche
**Bankers:** The Royal Bank Of Scotland Plc (83-06-08)

| | 31-12-13 | 31-12-12 | 31-12-11 |
|---|---|---|---|
| TO | 139,092,000 | 114,399,000 | 106,932,000 |
| P/L | 1,197,000 | 21,000 | 571,000 |
| NW | 3,688,000 | 2,750,000 | 2,764,000 |
| WC | 2,219,000 | 1,222,000 | 1,196,000 |
| Emp. | 352 | 332 | 321 |

DUNS 52-305-5317

## Western Brand Poultry Products (N I) Ltd

**(Subsidiary of:** Western Brand Poultry Products Ltd)
Screevagh, Lisnaskea, Enniskillen, Co Fermanagh BT92 0FA
**Tel:** 028-6772-1999 **Fax:** 02867722422
**Web:** http://westernbrandni.com
**Reg No:** 0061909NI **Estd:** 1991 Private Limited Company
**Line of Business:** Poultry farmers
**Issued Capital:** £1
**Directors:** Mrs C Lannon, E Lannon
**Co. Secretary:** Eugene Lannon
**US SIC:** 2099, 2013
**UK SIC:** 42399, 41223
**Auditors:** FPM Accountants LLP

| | 31-12-13 | 31-12-11 | 31-12-10 |
|---|---|---|---|
| TO | 14,185,246 | 13,763,088 | 14,960,598 |
| P/L | 695,680 | 834,846 | 876,267 |
| NW | 1,601,675 | 1,650,977 | 872,082 |
| WC | 1,548,681 | 1,477,730 | 1,319,186 |
| Emp. | 139 | 120 | 106 |

DUNS 51-996-7926 Imp

## Western Commodities Ltd

South View Estate, Cullompton, Devon EX15 2QU
**Tel:** 01884839710
**Web:** www.westcommorganics.com
**Reg No:** 4101382 **Estd:** 2011 Private Limited Company
**Line of Business:** Manufacturers of food products
**Issued Capital:** £1
**Directors:** R A Stoker, P Collier
**Responsibilities**
**Senior:** Nigel Tarrant *(Manager)*
**US SIC:** 2099 **UK SIC:** 42399

| | 31-03-14 | 31-03-13 | 31-03-12 |
|---|---|---|---|
| TA | 4,673,684 | 2,892,471 | 2,983,474 |
| NW | 292,459 | 327,204 | 123,746 |
| WC | 286,445 | 229,536 | (225,040) |

DUNS 21-229-1636

## Western Computer Apple Premium Retailer

Unit 7, Beechwood Shopping Centre, 123 High Street, Cheltenham, Gloucestershire GL50 1DQ
**Tel:** 01242234700
**Web:** www.western.co.uk
**Proprietorship**
**Line of Business:** Computer systems and software (sales)
**Proprietor:** P Mills
**Responsibilities**
**Senior:** D Doobie *(Branch Manager)*
**US SIC:** 7379 **UK SIC:** 83940
**Employees:** 46

DUNS 22-762-3154

## Western Computer Group Ltd

Victoria House, Temple Gate, Bristol, Avon BS1 6PW
**Tel:** 01179225661
**Web:** www.western.co.uk
**Reg No:** 1850885 **VAT No:** 329014674
**Estd:** 1984 Private Limited Company
**Line of Business:** Other software consultancy and supply
**Trading Style:** Applecentre West
**Issued Capital:** £350,000
**Principals:** K J Courtman *(Managing)*, J R Smith, A Dobson
**Co. Secretary:** Lee Ford
**Branches:** Western Computer Group Ltd, Victoria House, Unit 4, Bristol, Avon BS1 6PW
**US SIC:** 7379 **UK SIC:** 83940
**Auditors:** Davis Williams
**Bankers:** Lloyds TSB Bank plc (77-62-01)

| | 06-01-14 | 02-01-13 | 03-01-12 |
|---|---|---|---|
| TO | 13,573,819 | 13,347,311 | 10,984,471 |
| P/L | 179,387 | 247,581 | 270,849 |
| NW | 1,439,629 | 1,340,840 | 1,182,734 |
| WC | 1,117,458 | 1,029,491 | 998,953 |
| Emp. | 66 | N/A | N/A |

DUNS 22-531-2586 Imp-Exp

## Western Digital (U K) Ltd

**(Subsidiary of:** Western Digital Corporation)
Hamilton House, Regent Park, Kingston Road, Leatherhead, Surrey KT22 7PL
**Tel:** 01372366000 **Fax:** 01372360391
**Web:** www.wdc.com
**Reg No:** 1827612 **VAT No:** 395278603
**Estd:** 1984 Private Limited Company
**Line of Business:** Wholesale of computers, computer peripheral equipment and software
**Directors:** G L Holmes, P J Dyson, M C Ray, B T Bailey
**Co. Secretary:** Michael Ray
**Responsibilities**
**Senior:** Alex Blackwell *(Technical Manager)*
**IT:** Alex Blackwell *(Technical Manager)*
**Branches:** Western Digital (U K) Ltd, 8 Minerva Way, Glasgow, Lanarkshire G3 8AU
**US SIC:** 5081, 7379
**UK SIC:** 61490, 83940
**Auditors:** KPMG
**Bankers:** Lloyds TSB Bank plc (30-93-08)
**Employees:** 76
**Turnover:** £424,006,000

DUNS 22-753-5515

## Western Education & Library Board

1 Hospital Road, Omagh, Co Tyrone BT79 0AW
**Tel:** 02882-411-411
**Web:** www.welbni.org
**Estd:** 1973
**Line of Business:** Representative office
**Trading Style:** Western Board, Magilligan Field Centre
**Principals:** P O'Kane *(Chairman)*, K Doran *(Financial)*, J Martin, M H Murphy, B Faulkner
**Responsibilities**
**Senior:** Barry Mulholland *(Chief Executive Officer)*, Pat O' Kane *(Chairman)*
**IT:** Joseph McQuaid *(IT Coordinator)*
**Branches:** Western Education & Library Board, Main Street, Enniskillen, Co Fermanagh BT94 4EZ
**US SIC:** 9121, 8231, 8299
**UK SIC:** 91110, 97700, 93300
**Bankers:** First Trust Bank (aib Group (uk) Plc) (93-81-30)
**Employees:** 315

DUNS 29-636-5075 Imp

## Western Electrical Ltd

**(Subsidiary of:** Marlowe Holdings Ltd)
32 Macadam Road, Plymouth, Devon PL4 0RU
**Web:** www.western-electrical.co.uk
**Reg No:** 1962789 **VAT No:** 434378736
**Estd:** 1985 Private Limited Company
**Line of Business:** Wholesale of radio and television goods; wholesale of electrical household appliances not elsewhere classified
**Issued Capital:** £2,000
**Directors:** P G Elsegood, D T Mcnair, W S Woof, R D Goddard
**Co. Secretary:** Philip Elsegood
**Responsibilities**
**Finance:** Dorothy Hockley *(Financial Manager)*
**HR:** Allyson Morrison *(Human Resources Manager)*
**Branches:** Western Electrical Ltd, Unit G, Treliske Industrial Estate, Truro, Cornwall TR1 3LP
**US SIC:** 5064 **UK SIC:** 61500
**Auditors:** Thompson Jenner LLP

**Bankers:** Lloyds TSB Bank plc (30-96-68)

| | 31-12-13 | 31-01-13 | 31-12-12 |
|---|---|---|---|
| TO | 19,774,426 | 25,093,922 | 26,563,790 |
| P/L | (3,512,446) | 346,703 | 352,734 |
| NW | (1,503,401) | 1,996,439 | 1,772,712 |
| WC | (1,357,064) | 1,781,090 | 1,444,685 |
| Emp. | 136 | 143 | 140 |

DUNS 22-780-2345 **Imp**

## Western Expanded Metal Industries Co. Ltd

(**Subsidiary of:** Protektorwerk Florenz Maisch Gesellschaft Mit Besc)
Matthew Lane, Kidderminster, Worcestershire DY11 7RA
**Tel:** 01562-820123 **Fax:** 01562-822012
**Web:** www.wemico.com
**Reg No:** 1798633 **VAT No:** 396220739
**Estd:** 1984 Private Limited Company
**Line of Business:** Base metal industries
**Export Sales:** £1,517,514
**Trading Style:** W E M I C O
**Issued Capital:** £100
**Directors:** Dr C Maisch, Ms R Hill
**Co. Secretary:** Ms June Phillips
**US SIC:** 3325, 8911
**UK SIC:** 31110, 83701
**Auditors:** Folkes Worton
**Bankers:** HSBC Bank plc (40-45-19)

| | 31-12-13 | 31-12-12 | 31-12-11 |
|---|---|---|---|
| TO | 10,697,102 | N/A | N/A |
| P/L | (531,198) | N/A | N/A |
| NW | 3,293,946 | 3,941,323 | 3,614,824 |
| WC | 1,322,452 | 1,717,956 | 1,614,181 |
| Emp. | 90 | N/A | N/A |

DUNS 76-909-9623

## Western Ferries (Clyde) Ltd

Marine Parade, Hunters Quay, Dunoon, Argyll PA23 8HJ
**Tel:** 01369-704452
**Web:** www.western-ferries.co.uk
**Reg No:** 0091850SC **Estd:** 1985 Private Limited Company
**Line of Business:** Passenger sea and coastal water transport
**Issued Capital:** £70,000
**Directors:** A F Ross, The Rt Hon Lord G I Robertson, D R Harris, J L Denham, G Ross, G J Fletcher
**Co. Secretary:** Ms Marjorie Beattie
**Responsibilities**
**Senior:** Margerie Beattie *(Finance Director)*
**Finance:** Margerie Beattie *(Finance Director)*
**US SIC:** 4452 **UK SIC:** 74002
**Auditors:** French Duncan

| | 31-03-14 | 31-03-13 | 31-03-12 |
|---|---|---|---|
| TO | 7,310,000 | 7,272,000 | 6,978,000 |
| P/L | 2,043,000 | 2,234,000 | 1,900,000 |
| NW | 7,127,000 | 5,932,000 | 4,716,000 |
| WC | (4,042,000) | (1,765,000) | 93,000 |
| Emp. | 66 | 66 | 65 |

DUNS 50-641-1201

## Western General Hospital

Crewe Road South, Edinburgh, Midlothian EH4 2XU
**Tel:** 01315371000
**Web:** www.nhslothian.scot.nhs.uk
**Line of Business:** Public sector hospital activities, including nhs trusts
**Responsibilities**
**Senior:** George Curley *(Warehouse Manager)*
**HR:** Judith Gaskell *(Human Resources Manager)*, Jim Paterson *(Training Manager)*
**Facilities:** Ernie Bain *(Estates Manager)*
**US SIC:** 8062 **UK SIC:** 95100
**Employees:** 3,800

DUNS 34-618-7003 **Imp**

## Western Global Ltd

(**Subsidiary of:** Western Global Holdings Ltd)
Western House, Broad Lane, Yale, Bristol, Avon BS37 7LB
**Tel:** 01454 227 277 **Fax:** 01454 227 549
**Web:** www.westernenvironmental.co.uk
**Reg No:** 5425318 **Estd:** 2005 Private Limited Company
**Line of Business:** Manufacture of other general purpose machinery not elsewhere classified
**Export Sales:** £4,818,670
**Trading Style:** Western Environmental
**Issued Capital:** £1,160
**Directors:** F T Nunn, J Davies, N Davies, R Critchley, G M Cornell
**US SIC:** 3999 **UK SIC:** 49590
**Auditors:** Butterworth Jones

| | 31-12-13 | 31-10-08 | 31-12-07 |
|---|---|---|---|
| TO | 14,916,299 | N/A | N/A |
| P/L | 1,618,689 | N/A | N/A |
| NW | 2,376,396 | (55,367) | 98 |
| WC | 2,491,198 | 659,544 | N/A |
| Emp. | 51 | N/A | N/A |

DUNS 23-740-5597

## Western Green Ltd

(**Subsidiary of:** Eastern Green Ltd)
1 Ashley Road, Altrincham, Cheshire WA14 2DT
**Tel:** 01619287171
**Reg No:** 3734820 **Estd:** 1999 Private Limited Company
**Line of Business:** Other letting of own property
**Issued Capital:** £100
**Managing Director:** S E Elias
**Co. Secretary:** Norman Denton
**US SIC:** 6519 **UK SIC:** 85000
**Auditors:** Lopian Gross Barnett & Co

| | 31-03-14 | 31-03-13 | 31-03-12 |
|---|---|---|---|
| TA | 2,941,786 | 2,916,012 | 3,164,811 |
| NW | 1,803,844 | 1,764,826 | 1,649,818 |
| WC | 1,033,844 | 784,826 | 1,069,818 |

DUNS 52-021-4990

## Western Greyhound Ltd.

Western House, St Austell Street, Newquay, Cornwall TR8 5DR
**Web:** www.westerngreyhound.com
**Reg No:** 3388055 **Estd:** 1997 Private Limited Company
**Line of Business:** Other scheduled passenger land transport not elsewhere classified
**Issued Capital:** £200
**Director:** M J Bishop
**Responsibilities**
**Senior:** Robin Orbell *(Manager)*
**US SIC:** 4119 **UK SIC:** 72200
**Bankers:** National Westminster Bank Plc (54-10-38)

| | 30-09-13 | 30-09-12 | 30-09-11 |
|---|---|---|---|
| TO | 9,718,677 | 11,100,409 | 11,367,755 |
| P/L | (506,857) | 111,029 | 384,541 |
| NW | 1,281,831 | 1,704,718 | 1,817,240 |
| WC | (615,688) | (1,032,242) | (959,800) |
| Emp. | 256 | 285 | 286 |

DUNS 21-124-2824

## Western Health & Social Care Trust

Altnagelvin, Londonderry, Co Londonderry BT47 6SB
**Tel:** 02871345171
**Web:** www.westerntrust.hscni.net
**Estd:** 2012
**Line of Business:** Nhs clinics
**Principals:** G Guckian *(Chairman)*, Ms E Way, J Lusby
**Responsibilities**
**Senior:** Grainne Concannon *(Team Leader)*
**Branches:** Western Health & Social Care Trust, 124 Irvinestown Road, Enniskillen, Co Fermanagh BT74 6DN
**US SIC:** 8062, 9121
**UK SIC:** 95100, 91110
**Employees:** 12,500

DUNS 21-287-2870

## Western House Primary School

Richards Way, Slough, Berkshire SL1 5TJ
**Tel:** 01753-526326
**Web:** www.westernhouse.slough.sch.uk
**Estd:** 2006
**Line of Business:** Primary education
**Proprietor:** Mrs G Bodman
**US SIC:** 8211 **UK SIC:** 93200
**Employees:** 76

DUNS 22-916-9776

## Western Isles Islands Council

Council Offices, Sandwick Road, Stornoway, Isle of Lewis HS1 2BW
**Tel:** 01851703773
**Web:** www.cne-siar.gov.uk
**Estd:** 1975
**Line of Business:** Local government
**Trading Style:** Comhairle Nan Eilean-Siar
**Principals:** R W Bennie *(Financial)*, B Howat, B W Stewart, A Lamont
**Branches:** Western Isles Islands Council, 4 South Beach, Stornoway, Isle Of Lewis HS1 2XY
**US SIC:** 9121, 8299
**UK SIC:** 91110, 93300
**Bankers:** The Royal Bank Of Scotland Plc (83-27-12)
**Employees:** 1,000

DUNS 52-014-8669

## Western Leisure & Amusements Ltd

(**Subsidiary of:** Case Concepts Ltd)
Case Concepts Ltd, Countgrade House, Port Talbot, West Glamorgan SA13 2PE
**Tel:** 01656745444
**Reg No:** 3381549 **Estd:** 1997 Private Limited Company
**Line of Business:** Gambling and betting activities
**Trading Style:** Case Amusements, Case Concepts, Court Grade, Ensour
**Issued Capital:** £378,020
**Director:** R P Case
**Co. Secretary:** Philip Case
**Branches:** Western Leisure & Amusements Ltd, 43 Quay Street, Ammanford, Dyfed SA18 3BS
**US SIC:** 7999 **UK SIC:** 97913
**Auditors:** PricewaterhouseCoopers

| | 31-10-13 | 31-10-12 | 31-10-11 |
|---|---|---|---|
| TA | 961,229 | 961,358 | 955,035 |
| NW | 238,872 | 240,800 | 234,477 |
| WC | 238,872 | 240,800 | 234,477 |

DUNS 22-719-9171

## Western Mail & Echo Ltd

(**Subsidiary of:** Trinity Mirror Plc)
Brookman House, 62-65 Chandos Place, London WC2N 4LP
**Tel:** 02920223333 **Fax:** 020-7845-0101
**Reg No:** 0326067 **Estd:** 1937 Private Limited Company
**Line of Business:** Regional publishing agents.
**Issued Capital:** £400,000
**Directors:** T M Directors Limited, V L Vaghela, S R Fox
**Co. Secretary:** T M Secretaries Limited
**Branches:** Western Mail & Echo Ltd, Unit 12 The Office Village, Exchange Quay, Salford, Lancashire M5 3EQ
**US SIC:** 2741 **UK SIC:** 47541
**Auditors:** Deloitte & Touche
**Bankers:** HSBC Bank plc (40-06-03)

| | 29-12-13 | 30-12-12 | 01-12-12 |
|---|---|---|---|
| TA | 1,056,000 | 1,056,000 | 1,056,000 |
| NW | 1,056,000 | 1,056,000 | 1,056,000 |

DUNS 64-095-7770

## The Western Meeting Club Ltd

(**Subsidiary of:** The Western Meeting Club 2003 Ltd)
Ayr Racecourse, 2 Whitletts Road, Ayr, Ayrshire KA8 0JE
**Tel:** 01292264179
**Web:** www.ayr-racecourse.co.uk
**Reg No:** 0234779SC **Estd:** 2002 Private Limited Company
**Line of Business:** Other sporting activities not elsewhere classified
**Issued Capital:** £1,120
**Directors:** B N Macdonald, A G Macdonald, J S Morrison, R B Johnstone
**Co. Secretary:** David Brown
**US SIC:** 7999 **UK SIC:** 97913

| | 31-12-13 | 31-12-12 | 31-12-11 |
|---|---|---|---|
| TO | 6,888,328 | 6,240,701 | 6,231,828 |
| P/L | 676,535 | 181,460 | 276,448 |
| NW | 6,915,294 | 6,212,750 | 6,084,083 |
| WC | 5,132,351 | 3,448,495 | 2,516,582 |
| Emp. | 63 | 69 | 75 |

DUNS 76-626-0590

## Western Power Investments Ltd

(**Subsidiary of:** Mtglq Investors L.P.)
Avonbank, Feeder Road, Bristol, Avon BS2 0TB
**Tel:** 01179252377
**Web:** www.westernpower.co.uk
**Reg No:** 2579329 **Estd:** 1991 Private Limited Company
**Line of Business:** Financial intermediation not elsewhere classified
**Issued Capital:** £2,644,878
**Directors:** M Holmes, G P Minson, J A Wiltshire
**Co. Secretary:** Ms Clare Richards
**US SIC:** 6111 **UK SIC:** 81501
**Auditors:** Arthur Andersen

| | 31-12-13 | 31-12-12 | 31-12-11 |
|---|---|---|---|
| TA | 3,051,403 | 2,988,492 | 2,918,475 |
| P/L | 6,556 | 74,989 | 53,608 |
| NW | 2,961,070 | 2,954,519 | 2,912,105 |
| WC | 2,961,070 | 2,954,519 | 2,912,105 |

DUNS 22-503-4552

## Western Provident Association Ltd

Rivergate House, Taunton, Somerset TA1 2PE
**Web:** www.wpa.org.uk
**Reg No:** 0475557 **VAT No:** 567681788
**Estd:** 1901 Private Company Limited By Guarantee
**Line of Business:** Non-life insurance
**Principals:** J C Stainton *(Managing)*, R A Bramston, R E Lee, E R Cromer, K Y Butler, J F Chester, M C Kramer, C D Collins
**Co. Secretary:** Andrew Haworth
**Responsibilities**
**Senior:** Michael Foden *(Director)*, Nathan Irwin *(Director)*, Rachel Riley *(Director)*, Mark Southern *(General Manager)*, Jane Willcox *(General Manager)*
**Finance:** Nathan Irwin *(Director)*
**Sales:** Rachel Riley *(Director)*
**Branches:** Western Provident Association Ltd, Main St, Church Langton, Market Harborough, Leicestershire LE16 7SY
**US SIC:** 6399 **UK SIC:** 82001
**Auditors:** PricewaterhouseCoopers LLP

| | 31-12-13 | 31-12-12 | 31-12-11 |
|---|---|---|---|
| TO | 100,636,000 | 97,544,000 | 95,215,000 |
| P/L | 11,546,000 | 4,038,000 | (1,958,000) |
| NW | 172,510,000 | 163,371,000 | 160,275,000 |
| WC | 22,825,000 | 25,486,000 | 25,115,000 |
| Emp. | 304 | 302 | 303 |

DUNS 21-558-1522

## Western Sussex Hospitals Nhs Foundation Trust

St Richards Hospital, Spitalfield Lane, Chichester, West Sussex PO19 6SE
**Web:** www.rwst.nhs.uk
**VAT No:** 654439322 **Estd:** 2009
**Line of Business:** Alternative medical treatments and therapies
**Trading Style:** St Richard's Hospital
**Principals:** M Viggers *(Chairman)*, Ms M Griffiths, P Barnes
**Responsibilities**
**Senior:** Emma Rutland *(Consultant)*, Mitch Thomas *(General Manager)*
**Admin:** Carol McGowan *(Administrator)*, Natalie Piggott *(Administrator)*, Kevin Ravera *(Administration Manager)*
**Branches:** Western Sussex Hospitals Nhs Foundation Trust, Southlands Hospital, Upper Shoreham Road, Shoreham-By-Sea, West Sussex BN43 6TQ
**US SIC:** 8062 **UK SIC:** 95100
**Employees:** 2,400

DUNS 29-544-1547

## Western Thermal Ltd

Unit 14 Springfield Business Centre, Brunel Way, Stroudwater Business Park, Stonehouse, Gloucestershire GL10 3SX
**Tel:** 01453-791232 **Fax:** 01453-791305
**Web:** www.westernthermal.co.uk
**Reg No:** 1910892 **VAT No:** 401894166
**Estd:** 1985 Private Limited Company
**Line of Business:** Insulation installers
**Issued Capital:** £5,000
**Principals:** T M Horsley *(Managing)*, R L Cardiss, P A Jones
**Co. Secretary:** Trevor Horsley
**Branches:** Western Thermal Ltd, Walkham Business Pk, Plymouth, Devon PL5 3LS
**US SIC:** 1742, 1799
**UK SIC:** 50400, 50000
**Auditors:** Baldwins (Ashby) Ltd
**Bankers:** HSBC Bank plc (40-43-42)

| | 31-03-14 | 31-03-13 | 31-03-12 |
|---|---|---|---|
| TO | 9,086,790 | 11,396,576 | 8,566,295 |
| P/L | 569,099 | 838,205 | 494,002 |
| NW | 422,865 | 359,968 | 169,677 |
| WC | 97,666 | 56,951 | (27,068) |
| Emp. | 62 | 64 | 66 |

DUNS 56-987-4084

## Western Union Business Solutions (Uk) Ltd

Worldwide House, Thorpe Wood, Peterborough, Cambridgeshire PE3 6SB
**Tel:** 0870 905 5000 **Fax:** 0173 350 2930
**Web:** www.ruesch.com
**Reg No:** 2854737 **Estd:** 1994 Private Limited Company
**Line of Business:** Financial intermediation not elsewhere classified
**Issued Capital:** £500
**Directors:** I C Jeffrey, C H Fischer, K A Timbers
**Responsibilities**
**Senior:** Else Hamilton *(Director)*
**US SIC:** 6111 **UK SIC:** 81501
**Auditors:** Ernst & Young
**Bankers:** National Westminster Bank Plc (50-00-00)

| | 31-12-13 | 31-12-12 | 31-12-11 |
|---|---|---|---|
| TA | 158,252,978 | 204,820,000 | 189,318,000 |
| P/L | 3,742,008 | 3,444,000 | 5,926,000 |
| NW | 64,780,715 | 61,151,000 | 49,390,000 |
| WC | 54,537,423 | 50,268,000 | 38,037,000 |
| Emp. | 325 | 291 | 267 |

DUNS 50-368-8244 **Imp**

## Western Union Retail Services Gb Ltd

(**Subsidiary of:** Fexco Holdings (Bvi) Limited)
Po Box 8252, London W6 0BX
**Tel:** 0800833833 **Fax:** 020-8741-4612
**Web:** www.westernunion.com
**Reg No:** 2383761 **Estd:** 1924 Private Limited Company
**Line of Business:** Financial services
**Trading Style:** Western Union Money Transfer
**Issued Capital:** £1,950,000
**Directors:** M J O'Sullivan, M Alvisini
**Co. Secretary:** Patrick Schumacher
**US SIC:** 6111, 7399
**UK SIC:** 81501, 83954
**Auditors:** Ernst & Young

**Bankers:** HSBC Bank plc (40-01-13)

| | 31-12-13 | 31-12-12 | 31-12-11 |
|---|---|---|---|
| TA | 58,375,739 | 43,318,086 | 37,742,897 |
| P/L | 2,416,653 | 6,059,928 | 2,813,978 |
| NW | 22,396,834 | 20,639,321 | 18,574,119 |
| WC | (5,359,362) | 2,600,306 | 952,710 |
| Emp. | 78 | 63 | 50 |

DUNS 21-584-6892
## Westerwoodthe
St Andrews Drive, Cumbernauld, Glasgow, Lanarkshire G68 0EW
**Web:** www.qhotels.co.uk
**Estd:** 2011 Proprietorship
**Line of Business:** Hotels
**Proprietor:** Miss L Barr
**US SIC:** 7011 **UK SIC:** 66500
**Employees:** 180

DUNS 22-706-2593    **Imp**
## Westex Ltd
(**Subsidiary of:** Westex Distribution Ltd)
7 St Andrews Way, Bow, London E3 3PA
**Tel:** 020-7510-0100 **Fax:** 02079876505
**Web:** www.westex.co.uk
**Reg No:** 1475497 **VAT No:** 250101626
**Estd:** 1980 Private Limited Company
**Line of Business:** Business and management consultancy activities not elsewhere classified
**Export Sales:** £315,326
**Issued Capital:** £80,000
**Director:** R Keable
**Co. Secretary:** Roy Vesey
**US SIC:** 7392 **UK SIC:** 83951
**Auditors:** Barnes Roffe LLP
**Bankers:** National Westminster Bank Plc (60-40-05)

| | 31-08-13 | 31-08-12 | 29-08-12 |
|---|---|---|---|
| TO | 11,211,171 | 5,167,126 | 10,408,071 |
| P/L | 196,380 | 92,047 | 208,852 |
| NW | 333,482 | 165,499 | 87,591 |
| WC | (26,115) | (120,092) | (197,917) |
| Emp. | 173 | 175 | 176 |

DUNS 21-807-8206
## Westfield Care Centre
30 High Calside, Paisley, Renfrewshire PA2 6BE
**Tel:** 01418401110
**Estd:** 2012
**Line of Business:** Medical nursing home activities
**Responsibilities**
**Senior:** Annette Mcconnachie (Home Manager)
**US SIC:** 8051 **UK SIC:** 95100
**Employees:** 65

DUNS 28-832-9576
## Westfield Contributory Health Scheme Ltd
Westfield House, 87 Division Street, Sheffield, South Yorkshire S1 1HT
**Tel:** 01142729521
**Web:** www.sheffieldct.co.uk
**Reg No:** 0303523 **Estd:** 1919 Private Company Limited By Guarantee
**Line of Business:** Non-life insurance
**Principals:** G Moore (Chairman and Managing), Mrs J Davies, Ms P A Cantrill, P R Shires, D E Palmer, K Bardsley, N J Hutton, D J Whitney
**Co. Secretary:** Mrs Julie Gill
**Responsibilities**
**Senior:** Audrey Mcfarlane (Senior Business Consultant), Claire Ward (Senior Manager), Lesley Welton (Director)
**Sales:** Steve Sharrock (Head of Intermediary Sales)
**Admin:** Heather Bamford (PA to the Chief Executive)
**HR:** Fiona Lowe (Human Resources Manager)
**Purchasing:** Tony Plusa (Purchasing Manager)
**Branches:** Westfield Contributory Health Scheme Ltd, 12-13 Sussex St, Plymouth, Devon PL1 2HR
**US SIC:** 6399 **UK SIC:** 82001
**Auditors:** BDO LLP

| | 31-03-14 | 31-03-13 | 31-03-12 |
|---|---|---|---|
| TO | 52,934,249 | 51,306,652 | 51,764,714 |
| P/L | 99,384 | 5,792,310 | 5,506,504 |
| NW | 84,282,427 | 83,097,043 | 79,102,215 |
| WC | 4,747,818 | 13,172,067 | 13,569,420 |
| Emp. | 206 | 201 | 195 |

DUNS 23-922-0234    **Imp**
## Westfield Europe Ltd
(**Subsidiary of:** Scentre Group Limited)
Centre Management Suite, Unit 4006, Ariel Way, London W12 7GF
**Tel:** 02070611400
**Web:** http://uk.westfield.com
**Reg No:** 3912122 **VAT No:** 815032663
**Estd:** 1960 Private Limited Company
**Line of Business:** Development and selling of real estate
**Issued Capital:** £119,000,000

**Directors:** E C Rusanow, M J Gutman, J A Hodes, P S Slavin, P Miller
**Co. Secretary:** Leon Shelley
**Responsibilities**
**Senior:** Dennis Carruthers (Centre Management Director), Sarah Warrington (Facilities Manager)
**Branches:** Westfield Europe Ltd, Management Suite 29A The Plaza, Swindon, Wiltshire SN1 1HE
**US SIC:** 6552, 6711
**UK SIC:** 85000, 83962
**Auditors:** Ernst & Young LLP
**Bankers:** Barclays Bank Plc (20-32-53)

| | 31-12-13 | 31-12-12 | 31-12-11 |
|---|---|---|---|
| TO | N/A | 172,176,000 | 401,033,000 |
| P/L | (8,969,000) | (5,315,000) | (4,641,000) |
| NW | 69,763,000 | 28,874,000 | 35,267,000 |
| WC | (114,682,000) | (115,191,000) | (91,814,000) |
| Emp. | 471 | 591 | 639 |

DUNS 23-082-9983
## Westfield Grant Maintained School
Littlemoor Road, Weymouth, Dorset DT3 6AA
**Web:** www.westfield.dorset.sch.uk
**Estd:** 1976
**Line of Business:** Schools (special)
**Trading Style:** Westfield Technology College
**Principals:** Mrs C Gould (Chairman), P Silvester
**Responsibilities**
**Senior:** Andrew Penman (Head Teacher)
**Finance:** Jenny Savage (Finance and Business Manager)
**IT:** Yvonne Aylott (Head of ICT)
**HR:** Dawn Brooks (Human Resources Manager)
**US SIC:** 8299 **UK SIC:** 93300
**Employees:** 100

DUNS 21-775-6955
## Westfield Park Nursing Home
Westfield Lane, Hook, Goole, North Humberside DN14 5PW
**Tel:** 01405761021
**Web:** www.westfieldparkcare.co.uk
**Estd:** 2010 Proprietorship
**Line of Business:** Nursing homes
**Proprietor:** Miss S Rollinson
**US SIC:** 8051 **UK SIC:** 95100
**Employees:** 50

DUNS 21-223-4265
## Westgate Casino
Wellington Bridge Street, Leeds, West Yorkshire LS3 1LW
**Tel:** 0113-3893700
**Web:** www.galacasino.co.uk
**Proprietorship**
**Line of Business:** Casinos
**Responsibilities**
**Senior:** David Croft (CEO, Managing Director)
**US SIC:** 7999 **UK SIC:** 97913
**Employees:** 129

DUNS 42-407-5856
## Westgate Cleaning Services Ltd
37 College Road, Bromley, Kent BR1 3PU
**Tel:** 02082906665 **Fax:** 02083256565
**Web:** www.westgatecleaning.co.uk
**Reg No:** 4395264 **Estd:** 2002 Private Limited Company
**Line of Business:** Cleaning activities not elsewhere classified
**Issued Capital:** £100
**Directors:** Mrs S J Evans, S M Evans, Velocity Company Secretarial Ser
**US SIC:** 7349, 7399
**UK SIC:** 92300, 83954

| | 31-03-14 | 31-03-13 | 31-03-12 |
|---|---|---|---|
| TA | 89,493 | 91,235 | 53,059 |
| NW | 5,873 | 1,708 | (19,835) |
| WC | 4,146 | (8,006) | (22,735) |

DUNS 77-917-1680
## Westgate Efi Ltd
Little Park Cottages, Breach Lane, Wootton Bassett, Swindon, Wiltshire SN4 7QW
**Tel:** 01303 872277
**Web:** www.wefi.co.uk
**Reg No:** 5820341 **Estd:** 2006 Private Limited Company
**Line of Business:** Other business activities not elsewhere classified
**Export Sales:** £604,910
**Issued Capital:** £100
**Directors:** B G Heusch, D Mcconnell
**Co. Secretary:** Edward Vant
**Responsibilities**
**Senior:** Daimien McConnell (Director)
**Branches:** Westgate Efi Ltd, Bentley Lane Industrial Park Bentley Lane, Walsall, West Midlands WS2 8TL
**US SIC:** 7399, 2389

**UK SIC:** 83954, 45393
**Auditors:** Spain Brothers & Co

| | 31-12-13 | 31-12-12 | 31-12-11 |
|---|---|---|---|
| TO | 9,376,926 | 9,947,591 | 9,379,639 |
| P/L | 77,835 | 742,229 | 621,405 |
| NW | 97,727 | 167,970 | 22,164 |
| WC | 512,217 | 191,951 | 743,251 |
| Emp. | 57 | 60 | 63 |

DUNS 21-589-3847
## Westgate Health Care
Tower Road, Ware, Hertfordshire SG12 7LP
**Tel:** 01920468079
**Web:** www.westgatehc.co.uk
**Estd:** 2011 Proprietorship
**Line of Business:** Residential care establishments
**Proprietor:** Mrs F Massey
**Responsibilities**
**Senior:** Shiji Mathew (Manager), Angie Patel (CEO, Managing Director)
**US SIC:** 8321 **UK SIC:** 96111
**Employees:** 125

DUNS 34-578-2726
## Westgate Healthcare Ltd
(**Subsidiary of:** Westgate Healthcare Group Ltd)
Devonshire House 1, Devonshire Street, London W1W 5DR
**Tel:** 02085306211
**Web:** www.westgatehealthcare.co.uk
**Reg No:** 2725412 **Estd:** 1992 Private Limited Company
**Line of Business:** Other human health activities
**Issued Capital:** £1,000
**Directors:** A P Patel, Ms S P Patel, Ms T D Teubner, P S Patel, S C Patel
**Co. Secretary:** Ms Tara Teubner
**US SIC:** 8091 **UK SIC:** 95200

| | 31-12-13 | 31-12-12 | 30-12-11 |
|---|---|---|---|
| TO | 6,664,051 | 7,803,874 | 6,188,205 |
| P/L | 162,871 | (253,158) | 95,316 |
| NW | 12,915,362 | 13,082,934 | 13,709,142 |
| WC | (690,893) | 104,293 | 499,791 |
| Emp. | 216 | 185 | 190 |

DUNS 21-587-3988
## Westgate House Care Centre
Tower Road, Ware, Hertfordshire SG12 7LP
**Tel:** 01920426100
**Estd:** 2011 Proprietorship
**Line of Business:** Other human health activities
**Proprietor:** Mrs F Ilogon
**US SIC:** 8091 **UK SIC:** 95200
**Employees:** 100

DUNS 21-324-1131
## Westgate Junior School
Westgate, Lincoln, Lincolnshire LN1 3BQ
**Web:** www.westgate.lincs.sch.uk
**Estd:** 1993
**Line of Business:** Schools (foundation)
**Director:** R Ingram
**Responsibilities**
**Senior:** Tim Culpin (Head Teacher)
**US SIC:** 8211 **UK SIC:** 93200
**Employees:** 50

DUNS 39-739-2697    **Imp**
## Westgate Motors Ltd
West Coates Road, Grimsby, South Humberside DN31 2SU
**Tel:** 01472349045
**Web:** www.westgateskoda.co.uk
**Reg No:** 2180511 **VAT No:** 455592030
**Estd:** 1987 Private Limited Company
**Line of Business:** Sale of new motor vehicles
**Trading Style:** Westgate Honda
**Issued Capital:** £100,000
**Managing Director:** R C Addison
**Co. Secretary:** Mrs Norma Addison
**Responsibilities**
**Sales:** Mick Carr (After Sales Director)
**Facilities:** Mick Carr (After Sales Director)
**US SIC:** 5511, 7539
**UK SIC:** 65100, 67100
**Auditors:** Forrester Boyd
**Bankers:** Barclays Bank Plc (20-35-27)

| | 31-12-13 | 31-12-12 | 31-12-11 |
|---|---|---|---|
| TO | 20,844,849 | N/A | N/A |
| P/L | 454,260 | N/A | N/A |
| NW | 1,698,488 | 1,445,403 | 1,246,240 |
| WC | 559,473 | 301,156 | 756,965 |
| Emp. | 48 | N/A | N/A |

DUNS 21-098-0095
## Westgate Practice
Church Street, Lichfield, Staffordshire WS13 6JL
**Tel:** 01543414311
**Web:** www.westgatepractice.co.uk
**Estd:** 1841 Partnership
**Line of Business:** Doctors

**Partners:** Dr T Herbert, Dr G Southall, Dr E J Muller, Dr N Flanagan, Dr R Walsh, Dr P Cooper, Dr J Rocket, Dr J James
**Responsibilities**
**Senior:** Claire Bennett (Doctor), Lorne Thomson (Practice Manager)
**US SIC:** 8011 **UK SIC:** 95300
**Employees:** 50

DUNS 23-601-9324
## Westgrove Cleaning Services Ltd
940 Centre Park, Warrington, Cheshire WA1 1QY
**Tel:** 01925-414190
**Web:** www.westgrove.co.uk
**Reg No:** 3599280 **VAT No:** 713237168
**Estd:** 1998 Private Limited Company
**Line of Business:** Traditional cleaning activities
**Issued Capital:** £15,000
**Director:** S P Fives
**Co. Secretary:** Simon Whittle
**US SIC:** 7349 **UK SIC:** 92300
**Auditors:** Alextra Accountants Ltd

| | 31-12-13 | 31-12-12 | 31-12-11 |
|---|---|---|---|
| TO | N/A | N/A | 5,809,104 |
| P/L | N/A | N/A | 350 |
| NW | (103,196) | (62,162) | 67,842 |
| WC | (879,984) | (761,874) | (457,101) |
| Emp. | N/A | N/A | 375 |

DUNS 77-545-3970
## Westhampnett Motor Co Ltd
(**Subsidiary of:** Chichester Motor Group Ltd)
28-29 Westhampnett Road, Chichester, West Sussex PO19 7HH
**Tel:** 01243531335
**Reg No:** 2997981 **Estd:** 1994 Private Limited Company
**Line of Business:** Sale of new motor vehicles
**Issued Capital:** £1,200,000
**Directors:** G R Walker, A J Wickins
**Responsibilities**
**Senior:** Nigel Littler (Manager)
**US SIC:** 5511 **UK SIC:** 65100
**Auditors:** BDO LLP
**Bankers:** National Westminster Bank Plc (60-05-24)

| | 31-12-13 | 31-12-12 | 31-12-11 |
|---|---|---|---|
| TO | 21,763,000 | N/A | N/A |
| P/L | (19,000) | N/A | N/A |
| NW | 655,000 | 657,000 | 523,000 |
| WC | 448,000 | 461,000 | 517,000 |
| Emp. | 63 | N/A | N/A |

DUNS 29-510-3758
## Westholme Ltd
(**Subsidiary of:** Prism Medical Ltd)
Unit 4 Jubilee Way, Grange Moor, Wakefield, West Yorkshire WF4 4TD
**Tel:** 08449802260 **Fax:** 01422370572
**Web:** www.westhomes.co.uk
**Reg No:** 1873637 **VAT No:** 399389272
**Estd:** 1984 Private Limited Company
**Line of Business:** Hospital equipment
**Trading Style:** Westholme
**Issued Capital:** £852,917
**Directors:** S Meldrum, A J Walker
**Responsibilities**
**Senior:** Graham Appleyard (Manager), Andrew McIntyre (Manager)
**Branches:** Westholme Ltd, Unit 12, Golden Acres Lane, Coventry, West Midlands CV3 2SY
**US SIC:** 8321, 1796
**UK SIC:** 96111, 50400
**Auditors:** Deloitte LLP
**Bankers:** Yorkshire Bank Plc (05-09-24)

| | 30-11-13 | 30-11-12 | 30-11-11 |
|---|---|---|---|
| TA | 1 | 1 | 921,210 |
| NW | 1 | 1 | 921,210 |
| WC | N/A | 1 | N/A |
| Emp. | N/A | 55 | N/A |

DUNS 22-754-7478
## Westholme School Ltd
Wilmar Lodge, Meins Road, Pleasington, Blackburn, Lancashire BB2 6QU
**Tel:** 01254506070
**Web:** www.westholmeschool.com
**Reg No:** 0926692 **Estd:** 1968 Private Company Limited By Guarantee
**Line of Business:** General secondary education
**Directors:** K J Ainsworth, J R Yates, Ms J M Meadows, Mrs P Whittle, B C Marsden, D J Berry, E Slinger, Mrs J V Ashcroft
**Co. Secretary:** Jonathon Backhouse
**Responsibilities**
**Senior:** Anne Booth (Chairman), Peter Forrest (Director), Lynne Horner (Principal), Sally Sharples (Manager)
**Purchasing:** J Mackereth (Purchase Ledger Clerk)
**Branches:** Westholme School Ltd, Beardwood House, Wycollar Rd, Blackburn, Lancashire BB2 7AF

**US SIC:** 8211   **UK SIC:** 93200
**Auditors:** Waterworths
**Bankers:** National Westminster Bank Plc (01-00-85)

| | 31-08-14 | 31-08-13 | 31-08-12 |
|---|---|---|---|
| TO | 7,031,864 | 7,208,543 | 7,151,415 |
| P/L | (272,802) | (454,137) | (299,111) |
| NW | 9,346,980 | 9,619,782 | 10,073,919 |
| WC | (828,074) | (771,199) | (527,437) |
| Emp. | 214 | 219 | 220 |

DUNS 51-579-9513

## Westhouse Securities Holdings Ltd

(**Subsidiary of:** Westhouse Group Ltd)
Heron Tower 20th Floor, 110 Bishopsgate, London EC2N 4AY
**Tel:** 02076016100
**Web:** www.hansonwesthouse.com
**Reg No:** 5861129   **Estd:** 2003 Private Limited Company
**Line of Business:** Financial intermediation not elsewhere classified
**Issued Capital:** £238,515
**Director:** C D Getley
**Co. Secretary:** Ms Nicola Butler
**US SIC:** 6111   **UK SIC:** 81501

| | 31-12-13 | 31-12-12 | 31-12-11 |
|---|---|---|---|
| TA | 16,000 | 4,586,000 | 6,449,891 |
| P/L | (1,046,000) | 79,000 | (3,023,746) |
| NW | N/A | 1,046,000 | 595,068 |
| WC | N/A | N/A | 3,792,461 |
| Emp. | N/A | 52 | 49 |

DUNS 21-036-0855      **Exp**

## Westhouse Securities Ltd

(**Subsidiary of:** Westhouse Holdings Plc)
Arbuthnot House, 20 Ropemaker Street, London EC2Y 9AR
**Tel:** 020-7012-2000
**Web:** www.arbuthnot.co.uk
**Reg No:** 0762818   **Estd:** 1963 Private Limited Company
**Line of Business:** Financial intermediation not elsewhere classified
**Issued Capital:** £14,459,429
**Directors:** C D Getley, A B Proctor, R K Butler, S Wickham, R J Finlay, Ms J T Parsons
**Co. Secretary:** Ms Nicola Butler
**US SIC:** 6111   **UK SIC:** 81501
**Auditors:** PricewaterhouseCoopers LLP
**Bankers:** The Royal Bank Of Scotland Plc (15-20-25)

| | 30-09-14 | 31-12-13 | 31-09-12 |
|---|---|---|---|
| TA | 16,402,000 | 12,461,000 | 9,294,000 |
| P/L | (1,515,000) | (2,893,000) | (6,210,000) |
| NW | 1,548,000 | (296,000) | 4,012,000 |
| WC | 2,173,000 | (1,615,000) | 2,579,000 |
| Emp. | 57 | 59 | 68 |

DUNS 42-367-5867

## Westlakes Research Institute

Princess Royal Building, Ingwell Drive, Moor Row, Cumbria CA24 3JZ
**Tel:** 01946514000
**Web:** www.westlakes.ac.uk
**Estd:** 1992
**Line of Business:** Environmental and life science research consultants and registered charity.
**Directors:** Dr G Butler, Professor J Fife
**US SIC:** 7392, 8999, 7391
**UK SIC:** 83951, 83954, 94000
**Bankers:** National Westminster Bank Plc (01-09-54)
**Employees:** 80

DUNS 21-029-7777

## Westland Conference & Leisure Complex

Westbourne Close, Yeovil, Somerset BA20 2DD
**Tel:** 01935-848380
**Web:** www.westlandleisure.com
**Estd:** 1975 Proprietorship
**Line of Business:** Function halls and rooms for hire
**Proprietor:** D Pitman
**Responsibilities**
**Senior:** David Pitman (Assistant Manager)
**US SIC:** 7011   **UK SIC:** 66500
**Employees:** 55

DUNS 42-359-3693

## Westland Estates (Uk) Ltd

(**Subsidiary of:** Westland Holdings (Uk) Ltd)
Unit 12, Tait Road Industrial Estate, Croydon, Surrey CR0 2DP
**Tel:** 01689-855069
**Web:** www.westlandgroup.co.uk
**Reg No:** 4347010   **Estd:** 2002 Private Limited Company
**Line of Business:** Management of real estate on a fee or contract basis
**Issued Capital:** £2
**Directors:** P S Jeal, J R Kelly, G A Jeal
**Co. Secretary:** Gary Jeal

---

**Responsibilities**
**Senior:** Cathryn Kelly (Manager)
**US SIC:** 6531, 7399
**UK SIC:** 83400, 83954
**Auditors:** Maths Partnership

| | 31-12-13 | 31-12-12 | 31-12-11 |
|---|---|---|---|
| TA | 762,796 | 671,374 | 635,893 |
| NW | 371,282 | 321,746 | 274,305 |
| WC | 207,877 | 174,405 | 136,481 |

DUNS 23-718-8750      **Imp-Exp**

## Westland Horticulture Ltd

Granville Industrial Estate, Dungannon, Co Tyrone BT70 1NJ
**Tel:** 02887727500
**Web:** www.gardenhealth.com
**Reg No:** 0027321NI   **Estd:** 1993 Private Limited Company
**Line of Business:** Horticultural supplies
**Export Markets:** Europe and Republic of Ireland
**Trading Style:** Westland Horticulture
**Issued Capital:** £8,422
**Directors:** E J Conroy, K Nicholson, S Dougherty, P Madden, R H Lavery, J Mcdowell, J B Mcveigh
**Co. Secretary:** John Mcveigh
**Responsibilities**
**Marketing:** Dympna Carron (Marketing Manager)
**IT:** Finbarr McNamee (IT Director)
**HR:** Caroline Blackburn (Personnel Manager)
**Health & Safety:** Michael McVey (Health & Safety Officer)
**Facilities:** Cliff Cairns (Maintenance Manager)
**Branches:** Westland Horticulture Ltd, 220 Camlough Road, Dungannon, Co Tyrone BT70 2ST
**US SIC:** 5999   **UK SIC:** 65600
**Auditors:** McKeague Morgan & Co
**Bankers:** Ulster Bank Ltd (98-00-10)

| | 29-12-13 | 31-12-12 | 31-12-11 |
|---|---|---|---|
| TO | 102,427,390 | 93,839,006 | 68,084,409 |
| P/L | 6,598,212 | 5,563,851 | 4,578,569 |
| NW | 17,655,337 | 10,361,921 | 13,621,605 |
| WC | 10,371,528 | 8,713,788 | 6,320,226 |
| Emp. | 431 | 422 | 300 |

DUNS 28-995-6567

## Westland Nurseries (Offenham) Ltd

Ferry Lane, Offenham, Evesham, Worcestershire WR11 8RT
**Tel:** 0138641436
**Reg No:** 1843037   **Estd:** 1947 Private Limited Company
**Line of Business:** Growing of cereals and other crops not elsewhere classified
**Issued Capital:** £200
**Director:** M Boers
**Co. Secretary:** Ms Jayne Boers
**US SIC:** 0119   **UK SIC:** 01001
**Auditors:** Allchurch Bailey & Co
**Bankers:** Lloyds TSB Bank plc (30-93-11)

| | 31-12-13 | 31-12-12 | 31-12-11 |
|---|---|---|---|
| TO | 7,839,121 | 6,928,515 | 6,367,407 |
| P/L | 737,537 | 483,410 | 588,195 |
| NW | 2,843,654 | 2,432,030 | 2,149,243 |
| WC | 1,323,031 | 931,833 | 1,405,794 |
| Emp. | 84 | 53 | 64 |

DUNS 21-163-9518

## The Westlands School

Westlands Avenue, Sittingbourne, Kent ME10 1PF
**Tel:** 01795-477475
**Web:** www.westlands.org.uk
**Estd:** 1994
**Line of Business:** Schools (local authority)
**Director:** A Burchett
**US SIC:** 8211   **UK SIC:** 93200
**Employees:** 220

DUNS 21-783-8038

## Westlea Care Home

Donnies Brae, Neilston, Glasgow, Lanarkshire G78 3PT
**Estd:** 1984 Proprietorship
**Line of Business:** Nursing homes
**Proprietor:** Mrs E Holland
**US SIC:** 8051   **UK SIC:** 95100
**Employees:** 68

DUNS 39-716-1589

## Westleigh Developments Ltd

Tudor Gate, Grange Business Park, Enderby Road, Whetstone, Leicester, Leicestershire LE8 6EP
**Tel:** 01162-773324
**Web:** www.westleigh.co.uk
**Reg No:** 2165362   **VAT No:** 477984471
**Estd:** 1987 Private Limited Company
**Line of Business:** Construction of domestic buildings
**Issued Capital:** £27,500
**Principals:** C M Beighton (Managing), T L Keable, M R Rockley, I M Jones, M N Moore

---

**Co. Secretary:** Mrs Judy Beighton
**Branches:** Westleigh Developments Ltd, Church Lane, Sleaford, Lincolnshire NG34 7DF
**US SIC:** 1522, 1541
**UK SIC:** 50100
**Auditors:** Thomas May & Co
**Bankers:** National Westminster Bank Plc (56-00-55)

| | 31-03-14 | 31-03-13 | 31-03-12 |
|---|---|---|---|
| TO | 73,150,000 | 40,968,000 | 53,469,000 |
| P/L | 5,051,000 | 1,871,000 | 3,148,000 |
| NW | 25,461,000 | 21,661,000 | 20,293,000 |
| WC | 25,269,000 | 22,728,000 | 19,291,000 |
| Emp. | 250 | 185 | 200 |

DUNS 34-894-8840

## Westleigh Investments Holdings Ltd

Lakeside, Fountain Lane, St Mellons, Cardiff, South Glamorgan CF3 0FB
**Tel:** 03303338240   **Fax:** 03303338241
**Web:** www.westleighuk.com
**Reg No:** 5692439   **Estd:** 2006 Private Limited Company
**Line of Business:** Management activities of holding companies
**Export Sales:** £220,440
**Issued Capital:** £193,825
**Directors:** Mrs J A Clarke, J N Harrison, Mrs H Harrison, C G Clarke
**Co. Secretary:** William James
**US SIC:** 6711   **UK SIC:** 83962
**Bankers:** HSBC Bank plc (40-16-13)

| | 31-08-13 | 31-08-12 | 31-08-11 |
|---|---|---|---|
| TO | 5,283,707 | 5,782,162 | 5,317,292 |
| P/L | 10,093 | (125,552) | 198,789 |
| NW | 3,918,141 | 701,209 | 461,705 |
| WC | 5,483,553 | 1,104,574 | 1,017,956 |
| Emp. | 81 | 93 | 80 |

DUNS 21-231-7365

## Westleigh Lodge

Nel Pan Lane, Leigh, Lancashire WN7 5JT
**Web:** www.hc-one.co.uk
**Estd:** 2000 Proprietorship
**Line of Business:** Nursing homes
**Proprietor:** Mrs S Tanham
**Responsibilities**
**Senior:** Beryl Cauldwell (Manager)
**US SIC:** 8051   **UK SIC:** 95100
**Employees:** 50

DUNS 22-954-3129      **Imp-Exp**

## Westley Group Ltd

Po Box 1, Cradley Heath, West Midlands B64 5QS
**Tel:** 01384410111   **Fax:** 01384-410116
**Web:** www.westleygroup.co.uk
**Reg No:** 1150600   **Estd:** 1973 Private Limited Company
**Line of Business:** Production of non ferrous metals
**Export Sales:** £7,791,471
**Issued Capital:** £60,646
**Principals:** P A Hine (Chairman), J M Salisbury (Managing), R J Salisbury, M J Richards, T P Westley
**Co. Secretary:**
Newfield Trust Services Limited
**Responsibilities**
**Senior:** Adrian Shaw (Works Manager)
**Marketing:** Ian McWhirter (Business Development Director)
**Sales:** Ian McWhirter (Business Development Director)
**Facilities:** Tony Dawes (Maintenance Manager)
**Operations:** Ian McWhirter (Business Development Director)
**Branches:** Westley Group Ltd, 1 Wentloog Rd, Cardiff, South Glamorgan CF3 1YD
**US SIC:** 3339, 3369
**UK SIC:** 22470, 31120
**Auditors:** Walker Hubble
**Bankers:** Barclays Bank Plc (20-97-78)

| | 31-08-13 | 31-08-12 | 31-08-11 |
|---|---|---|---|
| TO | 32,843,070 | 34,557,131 | 42,426,367 |
| P/L | (422,292) | 1,791,036 | (1,186,338) |
| NW | 8,434,890 | 8,876,544 | 7,492,817 |
| WC | 3,861,036 | 5,005,641 | 4,152,238 |
| Emp. | 330 | 334 | 455 |

DUNS 77-737-4133

## Westley Richards (Holdings) Ltd

120 Pritchett Street, Birmingham, West Midlands B6 4EH
**Fax:** 01213331901
**Web:** www.westleyrichards.co.uk
**Reg No:** 3009015   **Estd:** 1812 Private Limited Company
**Line of Business:** Other letting of own property
**Issued Capital:** £250
**Directors:** S D Clode, S B Al Thani
**Co. Secretary:** Tom Zjalic
**Responsibilities**
**Senior:** Neil Portman (Manager), Tommy Zjalic (IT Manager)

---

**IT:** Tommy Zjalic (IT Manager)
**US SIC:** 6519   **UK SIC:** 85000
**Auditors:** Austral Ryley

| | 30-09-13 | 30-09-12 | 30-09-11 |
|---|---|---|---|
| TA | 5,241,836 | 4,815,610 | 4,718,673 |
| NW | 4,604,782 | 4,251,867 | 4,221,210 |
| WC | 659,225 | 625,974 | 564,198 |

DUNS 50-343-3336

## Westlive Ltd

Wilson Square, Thornton-Cleveleys, Lancashire FY5 1RF
**Tel:** 01253864309
**Web:** www.farthingsnursinghome.co.uk
**Reg No:** 2363511   **Estd:** 1989 Private Limited Company
**Line of Business:** Medical nursing home activities
**Trading Style:** Farthings Nursing Home
**Issued Capital:** £100
**Directors:** R C Walsh, Mrs C J Davey, D J Walsh, Mrs M A Walsh
**Co. Secretary:** Ms Maureen Walsh
**US SIC:** 8051   **UK SIC:** 95100
**Auditors:** Crossley & Davis
**Bankers:** Yorkshire Bank Plc (05-02-63)

| | 31-07-13 | 31-07-12 | 31-07-11 |
|---|---|---|---|
| TA | 1,266,126 | 1,448,504 | 1,386,655 |
| NW | 1,095,117 | 932,298 | 886,448 |
| WC | 187,612 | (3,019) | (76,780) |

DUNS 21-917-4372      **Imp-Exp**

## Westmill Foods Ltd

(**Subsidiary of:** Wittington Investments Ltd)
26 Crown Road, Enfield, Middlesex EN1 1DZ
**Tel:** 020-8345-8100   **Fax:** 020-8804-9977
**Web:** www.westmill.co.uk
**Reg No:** 0044394   **Estd:** 1987 Private Limited Company
**Line of Business:** Chinese food wholesalers and suppliers
**Trading Style:** Pataks / Stokely's / Asli Atta, Hp / Lea & Perrins / Lucky Boat Noodles, Amoy / Green Dragon / Guru / Rajah, Elephant Atta / Fassal / Habib
**Issued Capital:** £32,250
**Directors:** P Kenward, J P Willis
**Co. Secretary:** Mrs Rosalyn Schofield
**Responsibilities**
**Senior:** Bob Amon (Logistics Manager), Tim Borman (Warehouse Manager)
**Marketing:** Mark Jaffe (Marketing Director)
**Branches:** Westmill Foods Ltd, Unit 2, Main Avenue, Manchester M17 1FD
**US SIC:** 5149, 2099, 2033
**UK SIC:** 61700, 42399, 41473

| | 14-09-13 | 15-09-12 | 17-09-11 |
|---|---|---|---|
| TA | 32,250 | 32,250 | 32,250 |
| NW | 32,250 | 32,250 | 32,250 |

DUNS 21-620-2001

## Westminster Abbey Shop

The Sanctuary, London SW1P 3JS
**Web:** www.westminster-abbey.org
**Estd:** 2011
**Line of Business:** Gift shops
**Responsibilities**
**Senior:** Kirsty Mcdonald-West (Retail Manager)
**Purchasing:** Vicky Prodrick (Purchasing Manager)
**US SIC:** 5399   **UK SIC:** 65600
**Employees:** 300

DUNS 73-847-7780

## The Westminster Academy (Westbourne Green)

255 Harrow Road, London W2 5EZ
**Tel:** 02071210642   **Fax:** 02071210601
**Web:** www.westminsteracademy.net
**Reg No:** 5102934   **Estd:** 2004 Private Company Limited By Guarantee
**Line of Business:** Leisure centres
**Directors:** Ms M T Amayo, D A Dangoor, Ms H P Bunch, D G Harman-Wilson, W N Hugill, N Mcnaughton, S A Randeree, M Furlonger
**Responsibilities**
**Senior:** Jamie Armstrong (Line Manager), Smita Bora (Director), Elizabeth Dangoor (Director), Judy Dangoor (Director), Jeremy Witts (Director)
**US SIC:** 7999   **UK SIC:** 97913
**Bankers:** Barclays Bank Plc (20-40-18)

| | 31-08-14 | 31-08-13 | 31-08-12 |
|---|---|---|---|
| TO | 10,774,289 | 10,897,280 | 10,614,568 |
| P/L | (607,538) | 332,514 | (759,297) |
| NW | 27,366,409 | 27,423,947 | 26,848,433 |
| WC | 648,064 | 543,746 | 98,715 |
| Emp. | 152 | 114 | 168 |

DUNS 64-260-4094

## Westminster Adult Education Service

Amberley Road, London W9 2JJ
**Tel:** 020-7297-7297
**Web:** www.waes.ac.uk
**Proprietorship**
**Line of Business:** Adult education locations

**Proprietor:** Ms B Holme
**Responsibilities**
**Senior:** Barbara Holmes *(Manager)*
**US SIC:** 8221, 8249
**UK SIC:** 93100, 93300
**Employees:** 100

DUNS 21-771-0443
## Westminster City Boys School
55 Palace Street, London SW1E 5HJ
**Tel:** 02079636300
**Web:** www.wcsch.com
**Estd:** 1998 Proprietorship
**Line of Business:** Schools (foundation)
**Proprietor:** D Maloney
**US SIC:** 8211 **UK SIC:** 93200
**Employees:** 90

DUNS 21-843-6701
## Westminster City School
55a Catherine Place, London SW1E 6DY
**Tel:** 02078341731
**Web:** www.wcsch.com
**Reg No:** 8100409 **Estd:** 2012 Private Company Limited By Guarantee
**Line of Business:** General secondary education
**Directors:** R Blanchett, Ms M Parsons, Ms H M Brooks, B F Baughan, Ms B D Drummond, Ms T J Douglas-Home, Ms C A Rider, S L Oliver
**Co. Secretary:** Roy Blackwell
**Responsibilities**
**Senior:** Francis Abbott *(Director)*, Colin Nash *(Director)*, Canon Tremlett *(Director)*, Brian Weaver *(Director)*
**US SIC:** 8211 **UK SIC:** 93200
**Bankers:** Lloyds TSB Bank plc (30-98-97)

| | 31-08-14 | 31-08-13 |
|---|---|---|
| TO | 6,027,000 | 7,403,000 |
| P/L | (322,000) | 296,000 |
| NW | 609,000 | 539,000 |
| WC | 901,000 | 1,467,000 |
| Emp. | 88 | 86 |

DUNS 22-805-6644
## Westminster Controls Ltd
Unit 3, Leeds, West Yorkshire LS10 1PG
**Tel:** 01132884500
**Web:** www.westminstercontrols.com
**Reg No:** 1621972 **VAT No:** 371991717
**Estd:** 1982 Private Limited Company
**Line of Business:** Manufacture of electronic valves and tubes and other electronic components
**Issued Capital:** £28,000
**Managing Director:** J Quinn
**Co. Secretary:** Ms Laura Rook
**US SIC:** 3679, 1731
**UK SIC:** 34542, 50300
**Auditors:** Kirk Newsholme
**Bankers:** Bank Of Scotland (12-08-83)

| | 30-09-13 | 30-09-12 | 30-09-11 |
|---|---|---|---|
| TA | 1,140,729 | 1,316,239 | 1,149,040 |
| NW | 377,609 | 334,259 | 265,193 |
| WC | 259,906 | 242,926 | 208,444 |

DUNS 34-844-6022
## Westminster Drug Project
103 Kingsway, London WC2B 6QX
**Fax:** 01582417817
**Web:** www.wdp-drugs.org.uk
**Reg No:** 2807934 **Estd:** 2003 Private Limited Company
**Line of Business:** Social work activities without accommodation
**Trading Style:** Wdp
**Directors:** Mrs G Benning, Ms Y Batliwala, R J Paul, Doctor G Dhanani, L Boyjoonauth, M Eaton, J N Saunders
**Co. Secretary:** Mrs Karin Read
**Responsibilities**
**Senior:** Julian Mockridge *(Senior Practitioner)*
**Branches:** Westminster Drug Project, Kingsway House, 103 Kingsway, London WC2B 6QX
**US SIC:** 8321, 8091
**UK SIC:** 96111, 95200
**Auditors:** Hillier Hopkins
**Bankers:** The Royal Bank Of Scotland Plc (16-00-48)

| | 31-03-14 | 31-03-13 | 31-03-12 |
|---|---|---|---|
| TO | 19,764,933 | 15,766,781 | 15,594,054 |
| P/L | 1,597,138 | (470,279) | (5,741) |
| NW | 5,575,595 | 3,828,457 | 4,298,736 |
| WC | 3,435,284 | 2,969,221 | 3,497,239 |
| Emp. | 363 | 361 | 344 |

DUNS 23-979-1291 Imp
## Westminster Group Plc
Westminster House, Blacklocks Hill, Banbury, Oxfordshire OX17 2BS
**Tel:** 01295756300
**Web:** www.wg-plc.com
**Reg No:** 3967650 **Estd:** 1998 Public Limited Company
**Line of Business:** Management activities of holding companies
**Issued Capital:** £3,788,924
**Directors:** P D Fowler, Sir W H Ross, Sir M A Parkenham, M G Wood, S P Fowler, R W Worrall, I R Selby
**Co. Secretary:** Ian Selby
**Responsibilities**
**Senior:** Nicholas Mearing Smith *(Senior Finance Administrator)*
**Finance:** Nicholas Mearing Smith *(Senior Finance Administrator)*
**US SIC:** 6711 **UK SIC:** 83962
**Auditors:** Grant Thornton UK LLP
**Bankers:** HSBC Bank plc (40-09-02)

| | 31-12-13 | 31-12-12 | 31-12-11 |
|---|---|---|---|
| TO | 7,629,000 | 9,462,000 | 10,065,000 |
| P/L | (1,991,000) | (1,650,000) | (1,984,000) |
| NW | 1,748,000 | (1,350,000) | (485,000) |
| WC | 765,000 | (292,000) | (348,000) |
| Emp. | 201 | 184 | 64 |

DUNS 21-496-6017
## The Westminster Highview House
Scorguie Avenue, Inverness, Inverness-Shire IV3 8SD
**Tel:** 01463-711331
**Web:** www.barchester.com
**Estd:** 2000 Proprietorship
**Line of Business:** Nursing homes
**Proprietor:** Mrs O Macrea
**Responsibilities**
**Senior:** Ola Macrea *(Manager)*
**US SIC:** 8051 **UK SIC:** 95100
**Employees:** 104

DUNS 51-986-2270
## Westminster Homecare Ltd
Symal House, London NW9 0HU
**Tel:** 01159821331 **Fax:** 020-8205-7095
**Web:** http://westminsterhomecare.co.uk
**Reg No:** 3353584 **Estd:** 1999 Private Limited Company
**Line of Business:** Home care service providers
**Issued Capital:** £250,000
**Directors:** J Patel, S C Radia
**Co. Secretary:** Shreya Patel
**Responsibilities**
**Senior:** Dan Burnett *(Manager)*, Craig Gilbear *(Manager)*
**Admin:** Pamela Parchment *(Coordinator)*
**Branches:** Westminster Homecare Ltd, 20 Queen Street, Ipswich, Suffolk IP1 1SS
**US SIC:** 8091, 8321
**UK SIC:** 95200, 96111
**Auditors:** Leftley Rowe & Co
**Bankers:** HSBC Bank plc (40-08-42)

| | 31-12-13 | 31-12-12 | 31-12-11 |
|---|---|---|---|
| TO | 33,925,991 | 25,427,065 | 21,779,689 |
| P/L | 1,855,183 | 2,401,411 | 1,622,622 |
| NW | 2,406,734 | 4,093,420 | 2,307,050 |
| WC | 3,832,803 | 3,118,281 | 1,997,882 |
| Emp. | 2,571 | 1,831 | 1,633 |

DUNS 50-045-9060
## The Westminster Hotel Ltd
**(Subsidiary of:** Westminster Trading & Property Group Ltd)
312 Mansfield Road, Nottingham, Nottinghamshire NG5 2EF
**Tel:** 01159-555000
**Web:** www.bestwestern.co.uk
**Reg No:** 2311762 **Estd:** 1983 Private Limited Company
**Line of Business:** Hotels and motels without restaurant
**Issued Capital:** £100
**Principals:** A P Morris *(Managing)*, Ms S Morris
**Co. Secretary:** Alan Morris
**Responsibilities**
**Senior:** Robert Carr *(Operations Manager)*, Anil Khanna *(Proprietor)*
**Marketing:** Phil Rea *(General Manager)*
**HR:** Phil Rea *(General Manager)*
**Health & Safety:** Phil Rea *(General Manager)*
**Facilities:** Phil Rea *(General Manager)*
**Branches:** The Westminster Hotel Ltd, Wollaton St, Nottingham, Nottinghamshire NG1 5FW
**US SIC:** 7011, 5812
**UK SIC:** 66500, 66110
**Auditors:** Bentley Jennison

| | 31-12-13 | 31-12-12 | 31-12-11 |
|---|---|---|---|
| TA | 1,011,780 | 1,011,780 | 1,011,780 |
| NW | 100 | 100 | 100 |

DUNS 22-847-1363
## Westminster Kingsway College
211 Grays Inn Road, London WC1X 8RA
**Tel:** 0870 060 9800
**Web:** www.westking.ac.uk
**Estd:** 2000
**Line of Business:** College
**Director:** Ms C Burgess
**Branches:** Westminster Kingsway College, 27 Peter Street, London W1F 0AJ
**US SIC:** 8221 **UK SIC:** 93100
**Bankers:** Barclays Bank Plc (20-90-69)
**Employees:** 450

DUNS 28-985-1222
## Westminster Mind
Radstock House, London SW1W 9LX
**Tel:** 02072598100 **Fax:** 02072598138
**Web:** www.westminstermind.org.uk
**Reg No:** 1796928 **VAT No:** 576951196
**Estd:** 1984 Private Company Limited By Guarantee
**Line of Business:** Other human health activities
**Directors:** J C Thompson, J Mcconnell, Mrs A Clark, R Saturley, Ms G M Reynolds, J S Seidman, P W Moorsom, M C Jones
**Responsibilities**
**Senior:** Janice Horsman *(Manager)*
**Branches:** Westminster Mind, 4 Sutherland Avenue, London W9 2HQ
**US SIC:** 8091, 8321
**UK SIC:** 95200, 96111
**Auditors:** Sayer Vincent
**Bankers:** The Royal Bank Of Scotland Plc (16-00-48)

| | 31-03-14 | 31-03-13 | 31-03-12 |
|---|---|---|---|
| TO | 2,166,549 | 2,063,619 | 2,121,218 |
| P/L | (39,813) | (102,921) | 3,945 |
| NW | 1,079,504 | 1,119,317 | 1,222,238 |
| WC | 238,666 | 834,684 | 1,124,197 |
| Emp. | 76 | 39 | 84 |

DUNS 21-286-1000
## Westminster Motor Insurance Association Ltd
21 Buckingham Palace Road, London SW1W 0QT
**Tel:** 02078343700
**Web:** www.wmia.co.uk
**Line of Business:** Pension companies
**US SIC:** 6371 **UK SIC:** 82002
**Employees:** 100

DUNS 21-783-8971
## Westminster Muslim Welfare Trust
Dryburgh Hall, Abbots Manor, London SW1V 4ET
**Estd:** 2011 Partnership
**Line of Business:** Information services
**Partners:** S Miah, M Miah
**Responsibilities**
**Senior:** Shaista Miah *(Chairman)*
**US SIC:** 7399 **UK SIC:** 83954
**Employees:** 100

DUNS 64-263-1964
## Westminster School
17 Deans Yard, London SW1P 3PB
**Tel:** 020-7963-1000
**Estd:** 1888
**Line of Business:** Schools (independent)
**Responsibilities**
**Finance:** Chris Silcock *(Bursar)*
**IT:** Richard Hindley *(Head of IT)*
**HR:** Chris Silcock *(Bursar)*
**Health & Safety:** Chris Silcock *(Bursar)*
**Facilities:** Douglas Heathcote *(Clerk of Works)*
**Purchasing:** Chris Silcock *(Bursar)*
**Branches:** Westminster School, Headmasters Office, North Street, Maidstone, Kent ME17 3HL
**US SIC:** 8211 **UK SIC:** 93200
**Auditors:** Crowe Clark Whitehill LLP
**Employees:** 360
**Turnover:** £24,103,000

DUNS 50-147-1627
## The Westminster Society for People With Learning Disabilities
16a Croxley Road, London W9 3HL
**Tel:** 020-8968-7376 **Fax:** 02089689165
**Web:** www.wspld.org.uk
**Reg No:** 2325273 **Estd:** 1988 Private Company Limited By Guarantee
**Line of Business:** Other adult and other education not elsewhere classified
**Trading Style:** People With Learning Disabilty, Westminster Society for People With Learning Disabilty
**Directors:** J H Smith, Mrs A M Caro, Ms C M Slater, Ms C S Hallett, Ms H Bach, Mrs A J Blacklaw, Ms J R Rohde, Mrs S J Rodwell
**Co. Secretary:** Gabby Machell
**Responsibilities**
**Senior:** Lynne Brooke *(Trustee)*, David Ive *(Director)*, David Obaze *(Manager)*, Myra Round *(Director)*, Anne Villiers *(Director)*
**Finance:** Andrew Bown *(Head of Finance)*
**IT:** Lawrence Gatens *(IT Coordinator)*
**HR:** Sharon Grant *(Human Resources Manager)*
**Operations:** Mandy Crowford *(Director, Services, Housing Se)*
**Branches:** The Westminster Society For People With Learning Disabilities, 100 Shirland Road, London W9 2EQ
**US SIC:** 7399, 6732
**UK SIC:** 83954, 83100
**Auditors:** Baker Tilly
**Bankers:** National Westminster Bank Plc (60-80-05)

| | 31-03-14 | 31-03-13 | 31-03-12 |
|---|---|---|---|
| TO | 8,522,826 | 8,160,678 | 8,225,743 |
| P/L | (168,267) | (147,418) | 11,536 |
| NW | 9,117,645 | 9,166,032 | 8,614,248 |
| WC | 392,897 | 548,348 | 582,021 |
| Emp. | 282 | 264 | 271 |

DUNS 23-650-6288 Imp
## The Westminster Wire Factory Ltd
9 Westminster Road, Wareham, Dorset BH20 4SN
**Tel:** 01929-550085
**Web:** www.westminsterwire.com
**Reg No:** 3645831 **VAT No:** 723591434
**Estd:** 1998 Private Limited Company
**Line of Business:** Display equipment and fixtures
**Issued Capital:** £3
**Principals:** D A Sowry - House *(Managing)*, M W Sowry - House *(Financial)*, J Malling
**Co. Secretary:** Terry Trace
**Responsibilities**
**Senior:** Mark Sowry *(Financial Director)*
**Finance:** Mark Sowry *(Financial Director)*
**IT:** Mark Sowry *(Financial Director)*
**HR:** Mark Sowry *(Financial Director)*
**Health & Safety:** Mark Sowry *(Financial Director)*
**US SIC:** 2599, 3999
**UK SIC:** 46720, 49590
**Auditors:** Richard Allen & Associates

| | 31-01-14 | 31-01-13 | 31-01-12 |
|---|---|---|---|
| TA | 2,334,257 | 2,381,098 | 2,371,740 |
| NW | 988,595 | 898,723 | 714,831 |
| WC | (33,051) | 40,247 | (4,891) |

DUNS 42-331-9318
## Westmoreland Civil Engineering Ltd
Pitman Road, Denaby Main, Doncaster, South Yorkshire DN12 4LJ
**Tel:** 01709867476
**Web:** www.westmorelandce.co.uk
**Reg No:** 3144957 **Estd:** 2011 Private Limited Company
**Line of Business:** Civil engineers
**Issued Capital:** £3,000
**Directors:** A S Dobb, A Westmoreland
**US SIC:** 8911 **UK SIC:** 83701
**Auditors:** Smith Craven

| | 31-12-13 | 31-12-12 | 31-12-11 |
|---|---|---|---|
| TA | 1,250,615 | 1,483,576 | 1,525,734 |
| NW | 312,816 | 374,929 | 372,530 |
| WC | (116,806) | (119,331) | (182,214) |

DUNS 21-750-9227
## Westmoreland (Yorkshire) Holdings Ltd
Kelham Street Industrial Estate, Doncaster, South Yorkshire DN4 3RE
**Tel:** 01302366437
**Web:** www.westmorelandwaste.co.uk
**Reg No:** 7814731 **Estd:** 1996 Private Limited Company
**Line of Business:** Management of real estate on a fee or contract basis
**Issued Capital:** £10,000
**Director:** A Westmoreland
**Responsibilities**
**Senior:** Paul Dixon *(General Manager)*
**US SIC:** 6531 **UK SIC:** 83400

| | 31-03-14 | 31-03-13 | 31-03-12 |
|---|---|---|---|
| TA | 10,000 | 10,000 | 10,000 |
| NW | 10,000 | 10,000 | 10,000 |

DUNS 34-547-7843
## Westmorland Ltd
Westmorland Place, Orton, Penrith, Cumbria CA10 3SB
**Tel:** 01539624511 **Fax:** 01539 624354
**Web:** www.westmorland.com
**Reg No:** 5357857 **Estd:** 2011 Private Limited Company
**Line of Business:** Representative office
**Trading Style:** Toys@rheged / Toy Shop (Rheged)
**Issued Capital:** £146
**Directors:** L King, Ms J Lane, B M Gray, J C Dunning, Mrs S B Dunning, Ms J Lane
**Responsibilities**
**Senior:** Barbara Dunning *(Manager)*
**Marketing:** C Logan-Stephens *(Senior Marketing Executive)*
**IT:** Julie Pattison *(It Manager)*
**US SIC:** 5411, 7011, 5812
**UK SIC:** 64100, 66500, 66110
**Auditors:** KPMG LLP

**Bankers:** Barclays Bank Plc (20-66-97)

| | 01-07-13 | 01-07-12 | 03-07-11 |
|---|---|---|---|
| TO | 40,624,000 | 39,294,000 | 38,734,000 |
| P/L | 1,485,000 | 857,000 | 1,555,000 |
| NW | 18,414,000 | 15,475,000 | 16,730,000 |
| WC | (4,856,000) | (3,839,000) | (1,422,000) |
| Emp. | 507 | 530 | 549 |

DUNS 22-273-5388

## Westoe Taxis Ltd
48 Dean Road, South Shields, Tyne and Wear NE33 4DZ
**Tel:** 01914564511
**Reg No:** 4291461 **Estd:** 2001 Private Limited Company
**Line of Business:** Taxis and private hire vehicles
**Issued Capital:** £100
**Directors:** M Bradley, P Stobbs, G Davies
**Co. Secretary:** Gary Davies
**Responsibilities**
**Senior:** Nicole Cameron (Manager), Graham Robson (Manager)
**US SIC:** 4121 **UK SIC:** 72200

| | 30-09-13 | 30-09-12 | 30-09-11 |
|---|---|---|---|
| TA | 74,760 | 100,144 | 101,503 |
| NW | 22,969 | 44,544 | 36,026 |
| WC | 22,204 | 40,877 | 30,439 |

DUNS 22-544-8430                                    Exp

## Westok Structural Services Ltd
Horbury Junction, Wakefield, West Yorkshire WF4 5ER
**Tel:** 01924264121 **Fax:** 01924280030
**Web:** www.asdwestok.co.uk
**Reg No:** 1959143 **VAT No:** 461423077
**Estd:** 2002 Private Limited Company
**Line of Business:** Steel fabricators
**Export Markets:** Europe; Far East
**US SIC:** 1622 **UK SIC:** 50200
**Auditors:** RSM Robson Rhodes
**Bankers:** HSBC Bank plc (40-27-15)
**Employees:** 110
**Turnover:** £6,297,000

DUNS 21-735-0206                                    Imp-Exp

## Westomatic Vending Services Ltd
(Subsidiary of: Brintor Group Ltd)
Unit 7-8, Forde Court, Forde Road, Newton Abbot, Devon TQ12 4BT
**Tel:** 01626323100
**Web:** www.westomatic.com
**Reg No:** 0873813 **VAT No:** 141385384
**Estd:** 1966 Private Limited Company
**Line of Business:** Manufacturers of vending machines
**Issued Capital:** £50,000
**Managing Director:** R J Brinsley
**Co. Secretary:** Ashley Rote
**Responsibilities**
**Senior:** Fergus Camier (Manager), Jon Elliott (Product Coordinator)
**Finance:** Kathryn Avery (Financial Director), Anthony Brinsley (Finance Director)
**Sales:** Tony Greensill (Sales Manager)
**Operations:** Phil Kidd (Senior Design Engineer)
**Purchasing:** Barry Craig (Purchasing Manager)
**Engineering:** Phil Kidd (Senior Design Engineer)
**US SIC:** 3549, 5084
**UK SIC:** 32212, 61490
**Auditors:** Francis Clark
**Bankers:** Barclays Bank Plc (20-60-88)

| | 30-09-13 | 30-09-12 | 30-09-11 |
|---|---|---|---|
| TA | 3,403,151 | 4,291,529 | 4,321,046 |
| NW | 1,679,005 | 1,878,730 | 1,861,445 |
| WC | 1,007,229 | 1,299,554 | 558,314 |

DUNS 21-782-6278

## Weston & Somerset Mercury
32 Waterloo Street, Weston-Super-Mare, Avon BS23 1LW
**Web:** www.thewestonmercury.co.uk
**Estd:** 1982 Proprietorship
**Line of Business:** Newspapers publishing
**Proprietor:** B Driscoll
**US SIC:** 2711 **UK SIC:** 47512
**Employees:** 68

DUNS 23-266-0436

## Weston Area Health N H S Trust
Weston General Hospital, Grange Road, Weston-Super-Mare, Avon BS23 4TQ
**Tel:** 01934-636363
**Web:** www.waht.nhs.uk
**Estd:** 2002
**Line of Business:** Nhs clinics
**Issued Capital:** £1
**Principals:** C Creswick (Chairman), R Little (Financial), L Read, Dr G Reah, G Paine, I Turner, Ms J Ferguson, Ms S Calverley

**Responsibilities**
**Senior:** Bronwen Bishop (Manager), Nick Gallego (Medical Director)
**Marketing:** Caroline Welch (Marketing Manager)
**HR:** Alison Kingscott (Human Resources Manager)
**Health & Safety:** Lee Prossor (Health & Safety Officer)
**Facilities:** Clive Duran (Estates Manager)
**Branches:** Weston Area Health N H S Trust, Ebdon Ct, Trenleigh Dr, Weston-Super-Mare, Avon BS22 0LT
**US SIC:** 8062 **UK SIC:** 95100
**Employees:** 1,700

DUNS 73-673-6385                                    Exp

## Weston Beamor Holdings Ltd
3-8 Vyse Street, Hockley, Birmingham, West Midlands B18 6LT
**Tel:** 01212364772 **Fax:** 0121-236-8100
**Web:** www.westonbeamor.co.uk
**Reg No:** 4933065 **Estd:** 2003 Private Limited Company
**Line of Business:** Manufacturers and repair of jewellery
**Export Sales:** £2,513,905
**Trading Style:** Domino Jewellery
**Issued Capital:** £1,500,200
**Directors:** A J Morton, P E Fuller, N C Isaac, R P Pearson, D J Boddy
**Co. Secretary:** Mrs Vivian Fuller
**Responsibilities**
**Senior:** Andrew Sollitt (Sales & Marketing Director)
**Marketing:** Andrew Sollitt (Sales & Marketing Director)
**Sales:** Andrew Sollitt (Sales & Marketing Director)
**HR:** Michelle Stuart (Personnel Manager)
**US SIC:** 3911, 5094
**UK SIC:** 49101, 61900

| | 31-12-13 | 31-12-12 | 31-12-11 |
|---|---|---|---|
| TO | 31,492,913 | 30,547,139 | 23,664,328 |
| P/L | 952,985 | 2,003,025 | 1,698,782 |
| NW | 5,188,067 | 4,690,468 | 6,673,610 |
| WC | 4,164,965 | 3,536,387 | 5,580,245 |
| Emp. | 179 | 175 | 118 |

DUNS 23-234-5983

## Weston College
Bristol Road Lower Weston Lodge, Weston-Super-Mare, Avon BS23 2PJ
**Tel:** 01934411411
**Web:** www.weston.ac.uk
**Estd:** 1998
**Line of Business:** Further education schools and colleges
**Director:** G Williams
**Branches:** Weston College, Somerset Square, Bristol, Avon BS1 6RT
**US SIC:** 8221 **UK SIC:** 93100
**Bankers:** Lloyds TSB Bank plc (30-93-14)
**Employees:** 550

DUNS 21-332-6528

## Weston Favell
Booth Lane South, Northampton, Northamptonshire NN3 3EZ
**Tel:** 01604402121
**Web:** www.westonfavellacademy.org
**Estd:** 2002 Proprietorship
**Line of Business:** Schools (local authority)
**Proprietor:** J Howard
**US SIC:** 8211 **UK SIC:** 93200
**Employees:** 180

DUNS 22-160-7711

## Weston Group Plc
Weston Group Business Centre, Bishops Stortford, Hertfordshire CM22 6PU
**Tel:** 01279873333 **Fax:** 01279873378
**Web:** www.weston-group.co.uk
**Reg No:** 4179330 **Estd:** 2001 Public Limited Company
**Line of Business:** Management activities of holding companies
**Issued Capital:** £870,009
**Directors:** M A Chapman, J G Wood, R J Downing, M W Alden, S P Bickel, S R Thomas, S A Miles-Brown
**Co. Secretary:** Robert Weston
**Responsibilities**
**Senior:** Sue Woodlands (Secretary)
**Sales:** Jane Stocks (Human Resources Manager)
**IT:** Scott Rainger (Technical Director)
**HR:** Jane Stocks (Human Resources Manager)
**US SIC:** 6711 **UK SIC:** 83962
**Bankers:** HSBC Bank plc (40-01-06)

| | 31-07-14 | 31-07-13 | 31-07-12 |
|---|---|---|---|
| TO | 116,427,000 | 115,329,000 | 88,321,000 |
| P/L | 6,525,000 | 7,159,000 | 5,211,000 |
| NW | 27,723,000 | 23,934,000 | 19,827,000 |
| WC | 80,814,000 | 94,409,000 | 100,808,000 |
| Emp. | 210 | 186 | 206 |

DUNS 50-422-2589

## Weston Hospicecare Ltd
Jackson Barstow House, 28 Thornbury Road, Uphill, Weston-Super-Mare, Avon BS23 4YQ
**Tel:** 01934423900
**Web:** www.westonhospicecare.org.uk
**Reg No:** 2414541 **Estd:** 1989 Private Company Limited By Guarantee
**Line of Business:** Hospital activities
**Directors:** Ms M Michael, Mrs I Keeley, Ms D Litten, Mrs G Taylor, Ms J E Driscoll, A C Roche, J M Hutson, Mrs H J Emery
**Co. Secretary:** Mrs Gillian Auden
**Responsibilities**
**Senior:** John Katsouris (Director), Angela Smythe (Director), Michael Wolfman (Director)
**Marketing:** Diana Sorrell (Marketing Manager)
**Branches:** Weston Hospicecare Ltd, 193 Milton Road, Weston-Super-Mare, Avon BS22 8EF
**US SIC:** 7399, 6732
**UK SIC:** 83954, 83100
**Auditors:** Brooking Ruse & Co
**Bankers:** Lloyds TSB Bank plc (30-99-51)

| | 31-03-14 | 31-03-13 | 31-03-12 |
|---|---|---|---|
| TO | 4,918,945 | 4,308,070 | 4,144,022 |
| P/L | 259,913 | 175,111 | 65,238 |
| NW | 7,212,469 | 6,983,590 | 6,616,451 |
| WC | 1,363,284 | 1,162,794 | 747,698 |
| Emp. | 146 | 152 | 150 |

DUNS 21-771-0141

## Weston House
123 Moss Street, Keith, Banffshire AB55 5EZ
**Web:** www.craigardcare.com
**Estd:** 2011 Proprietorship
**Line of Business:** Medical nursing home activities
**Proprietor:** Mrs K Roy
**Responsibilities**
**Admin:** Louise Nicole (Administrator)
**US SIC:** 8051 **UK SIC:** 95100
**Employees:** 60

DUNS 29-873-4401

## Weston Park Foundation
Weston-Under-Lizard, Weston-Under-Lizard, Shifnal, Shropshire TF11 8LE
**Tel:** 01952852100 **Fax:** 01952-850430
**Web:** www.weston-park.com
**Reg No:** 2076097 **Estd:** 1986 Private Company Limited By Guarantee
**Line of Business:** Social work activities without accommodation
**Directors:** Viscount A M Bridgeman, A W Kenyon, W H Montgomery, Hon R E Paterson, M G Bridgeman, T L Forester, R C Sawtell
**Co. Secretary:** John Gregory
**Responsibilities**
**Marketing:** Andrea Webster (Marketing Executive)
**Admin:** Elizabeth Birch (Personal Assistant)
**US SIC:** 8321 **UK SIC:** 96111
**Auditors:** Hall Livesey Brown
**Bankers:** National Westminster Bank Plc (55-50-05)

| | 31-12-13 | 31-12-12 | 31-12-11 |
|---|---|---|---|
| TO | 2,908,846 | 3,345,185 | 3,158,530 |
| P/L | (486,228) | 364,659 | 58,865 |
| NW | 18,256,323 | 18,185,900 | 17,626,417 |
| WC | 1,683,853 | 2,040,631 | 1,853,295 |
| Emp. | 71 | 72 | 74 |

DUNS 23-794-4913

## Weston Park Nursing Care Centre
Moss Lane, Macclesfield, Cheshire SK11 7XE
**Tel:** 01625-613280
**Web:** www.fshc.co.uk
**Estd:** 1987 Proprietorship
**Line of Business:** Nursing homes
**Proprietor:** G Taylor
**Responsibilities**
**Senior:** Gill Dyson (General Manager), Jacinta Lowton (Home Manager), Maggie Smith (General Manager)
**HR:** Jacinta Lowton (Home Manager)
**US SIC:** 8051 **UK SIC:** 95100
**Employees:** 90

DUNS 21-745-9491

## The Weston Road Academy
Blackheath Lane, Stafford, Staffordshire ST18 0YG
**Web:** www.westonroad.staffs.sch.uk
**Reg No:** 7778406 **Estd:** 2011 Private Company Limited By Guarantee
**Line of Business:** General secondary education
**Directors:** P Glover, A W Jackson, D A Moore, Ms S Burgess, M S Wilebur, I G Wise, M Fiddler, Ms A Davidson

**Responsibilities**
**Senior:** Justin Hales (Director), Alec Heath (Director), Mandy Hunter (Director), Ann Kingman (Director), Andrew Locke (Director), Teresa Merchant-Murphy (Director), Aileen Perry (Director), Sarah Rivers (Director)
**US SIC:** 8211 **UK SIC:** 93200
**Bankers:** Lloyds TSB Bank plc (30-00-02)

| | 31-08-14 | 31-08-13 | 31-08-12 |
|---|---|---|---|
| TO | 4,339,000 | 4,380,000 | 13,644,802 |
| P/L | (282,000) | (239,000) | 9,397,711 |
| NW | 8,269,000 | 9,020,000 | 9,250,711 |
| WC | 91,000 | 104,000 | 142,081 |
| Emp. | 90 | 89 | 90 |

DUNS 76-846-1691

## Weston Williamson Ltd
12 Valentine Place, London SE1 8QH
**Tel:** 020-7403-2665
**Web:** www.westonwilliamson.com
**Reg No:** 2605767 **Estd:** 1991 Private Limited Company
**Line of Business:** Architects
**Trading Style:** Weston Williamson Limited
**Issued Capital:** £1,011
**Directors:** A P Weston, R Naybour, S J Humphreys
**Co. Secretary:** Christopher Williamson
**Responsibilities**
**Finance:** Ana Buigas (Accountant)
**US SIC:** 8911 **UK SIC:** 83701
**Auditors:** Lee Associates
**Bankers:** Lloyds TSB Bank plc (30-95-52)

| | 31-03-14 | 31-10-13 | 31-03-12 |
|---|---|---|---|
| TO | 824,414 | 3,748,136 | 3,789,987 |
| P/L | 139,937 | 166,255 | 930,760 |
| NW | 1,566,776 | 1,458,308 | 1,458,002 |
| WC | 462,461 | 515,266 | 1,276,740 |

DUNS 22-514-5192

## Westonbirt Schools Ltd
Westonbirt, Tetbury, Gloucestershire GL8 8QG
**Tel:** 01666881400
**Web:** www.westonbirt.gloucs.sch.uk
**Reg No:** 0230224 **Estd:** 1928 Private Company Limited By Guarantee
**Line of Business:** General secondary education
**Directors:** Mrs S S Pennie, Mrs S Whitfield, T B Gaffney, M C Pyper, Mrs P K Broomhead, C J Wyld, Mrs J D Greenwood, S G Smith
**Co. Secretary:** Michael Porter
**Responsibilities**
**Senior:** Duncan Battishill (Director), Susan Castle (govenour), rob Collinson (govenour), Ian Etchells (Manager), H Falkenburg (Govenour), Philippa Leggate (Director), Dermot Mcmeekin (Director), Henrietta Metters (Director)
**US SIC:** 8211, 6399
**UK SIC:** 93200, 82001
**Auditors:** Saffery Champness
**Bankers:** Barclays Bank Plc (20-71-02)

| | 31-07-13 | 31-07-12 | 31-07-11 |
|---|---|---|---|
| TO | 6,364,750 | 6,643,204 | 6,746,350 |
| P/L | 97,650 | 337,619 | 559,960 |
| NW | 6,188,022 | 6,052,543 | 5,507,105 |
| WC | (329,456) | (334,570) | (678,660) |
| Emp. | 101 | 101 | 100 |

DUNS 21-735-6443

## Westover Holdings Ltd
378-380 Charminster Road, Bournemouth, Dorset BH8 9SA
**Web:** www.westovergroup.co.uk
**Reg No:** 0714373 **VAT No:** 504535176
**Estd:** 1962 Private Limited Company
**Line of Business:** Sale of new motor vehicles
**Trading Style:** Westover Jaguar, Westover Alfa Romeo
**Issued Capital:** £111,812
**Principals:** P C Wood (Managing), K J Martin, Ms J C Wood, Mrs C G Turner
**Co. Secretary:** Ms Marion Stevens
**Responsibilities**
**Senior:** Claire Gist Turner (Director)
**Branches:** Westover Holdings Ltd, 149-153 Wareham Rd, Wimborne, Dorset BH21 3LB
**US SIC:** 5511, 7539
**UK SIC:** 65100, 67100
**Auditors:** Michael Kay & Co

| | 31-12-13 | 31-12-12 | 31-12-11 |
|---|---|---|---|
| TO | 211,870,629 | 180,867,539 | 162,998,745 |
| P/L | 5,872,172 | 5,207,051 | 4,407,690 |
| NW | 29,617,058 | 26,085,237 | 22,821,244 |
| WC | 9,711,666 | 10,603,538 | 7,472,136 |
| Emp. | 551 | 526 | 520 |

DUNS 21-345-4064

## Westow House
79 Westow Hill, Upper Norwood, London SE19 1TX
**Tel:** 020-8670-0654
**Web:** www.westowhouse.com
**Estd:** 2004 Proprietorship
**Line of Business:** Public house
**Proprietor:** A Tomas

**Responsibilities**
**Senior:** Justin Hutton *(Manager)*
**US SIC:** 5813 **UK SIC:** 66200
**Employees:** 70

**DUNS 21-002-1028**
## Westpac Banking Corporation
**(Subsidiary of:** Westpac Banking Corporation)
63 St Mary Axe, London EC3A 8LE
**Tel:** 02076217000 **Fax:** 02076217433
**Web:** www.westpac.com.au
**Reg No:** 0000138FC **Estd:** 1908 Foreign Company
**Line of Business:** Banks
**Trading Style:** Global Transaction Banking
**Directors:** Ms C A Deans, R A Johnston, L P Maxsted, G M Cairns, J B Burd, R W Reid, Ms E B Bryan, L A Davis
**Co. Secretary:** Ms Ilana Atlas
**Responsibilities**
**Senior:** P Baillieu *(Director)*, William Capp *(Director)*, Ewwn Crouch *(Director)*, Llewellyn Edwards *(Director)*, Robert Elstone *(Director)*, Peter Hawkins *(Director)*, Gail Kelly *(Director)*, Michelle Marchhart *(Manager)*, Peter Marriott *(Director)*, Graham Reaney *(Director)*, Julie Thorburn *(Director)*
**Finance:** Lorraine Burton *(Senior Tax Manager)*, Brian Hartzer *(CEO Australian Financial Servi)*, Leonie Mason *(Financial Planning)*
**Branches:** 14 Kingsway, London
**US SIC:** 6012 **UK SIC:** 81402
**Bankers:** Bank Of England (10-00-00)

**DUNS 21-585-0224**
## Westpoint Veterinary Group
Bridgelands Farm, Ingrams Green, Midhurst, West Sussex GU29 0LJ
**Web:** www.westpointfarmvets.co.uk
**Estd:** 2011 Partnership
**Line of Business:** Veterinary activities
**Partners:** R Drysdale, D Ball
**Responsibilities**
**Senior:** Keith Baxter *(Head Vet)*
**US SIC:** 0741 **UK SIC:** 95601
**Employees:** 100

**DUNS 21-733-7952**
## Westram Transport Ltd
Brickyard Lane, Melton, North Ferriby, North Humberside HU14 3HB
**Tel:** 01482635440 **Fax:** 01482635470
**Web:** www.westram.co.uk
**Reg No:** 7685469 **Estd:** 1986 Private Limited Company
**Line of Business:** Freight transport by road not elsewhere classified
**Issued Capital:** £100
**Director:** M J Swan
**Co. Secretary:** Martin Swan
**Responsibilities**
**Senior:** Nigel Reed *(Manager)*
**US SIC:** 4213 **UK SIC:** 72300

| | 31-10-13 | 31-10-12 |
|---|---|---|
| TA | 100 | 100 |
| NW | 100 | 100 |

**DUNS 23-091-5340**
## Westridge Group Ltd
Ruskin House, Bodiam, Robertsbridge, East Sussex TN32 5UP
**Tel:** 01580830600
**Web:** www.westridgeconstruction.co.uk
**Reg No:** 2612379 **Estd:** 1990 Private Limited Company
**Line of Business:** Management activities of construction holding companies
**Trading Style:** Westridge Surveying Services
**Issued Capital:** £43
**Directors:** J V Sinden, S A Smith, W P Marley
**Co. Secretary:** Marc Walker
**US SIC:** 6711, 8911
**UK SIC:** 83962, 83701
**Auditors:** Deeks Evans Audit Services Ltd

| | 28-02-14 | 28-02-13 | 29-02-12 |
|---|---|---|---|
| TO | 36,539,858 | 26,545,823 | 29,085,252 |
| P/L | 250,446 | 222,029 | 694,254 |
| NW | 1,315,714 | 1,126,729 | 2,057,210 |
| WC | 411,240 | 195,604 | 1,215,731 |
| Emp. | 158 | 145 | 185 |

**DUNS 21-892-0346**
## Wests Garage (Cambridge) Ltd
**(Subsidiary of:** West's Garage (H) (Cambridge) Ltd)
217 Newmarket Road, Cambridge, Cambridgeshire CB5 8HD
**Tel:** 01223351616 **Fax:** 01223467684
**Web:** www.westsrenault.co.uk
**Reg No:** 0562554 **VAT No:** 213812495
**Estd:** 1956 Private Limited Company
**Line of Business:** Car dealers (new & used)
**Issued Capital:** £128,557

**Managing Director:** R J West
**Co. Secretary:** Richard West
**Responsibilities**
**Senior:** Terry Starling *(Manager)*
**Marketing:** S Horncastle *(Marketing Director)*
**Branches:** Wests Garage (Cambridge) Ltd, 11 Church Street, Newmarket, Suffolk CB8 7EH
**US SIC:** 5511, 5521, 5531
**UK SIC:** 65100
**Auditors:** Lakin Rose
**Bankers:** Barclays Bank Plc (20-17-35)

| | 30-12-13 | 31-12-12 | 31-12-11 |
|---|---|---|---|
| TO | 27,449,073 | 22,095,163 | 25,497,826 |
| P/L | (4,197,529) | (137,132) | (364,862) |
| NW | (1,507,089) | 3,030,056 | 3,504,497 |
| WC | (1,896,747) | 2,773,911 | 3,685,993 |
| Emp. | 82 | 86 | 95 |

**DUNS 21-579-7797**
## Westvale House Care Home
Old Hall Road, Old Hall, Warrington, Cheshire WA5 9PA
**Tel:** 01925571266
**Web:** www.barchester.com
**Estd:** 1989 Proprietorship
**Line of Business:** Nursing homes
**Proprietor:** Mrs S Slone
**Responsibilities**
**Senior:** Hayley Bebbington *(Manager)*, Sylvia Sloan *(CEO, Managing Director)*
**US SIC:** 8051 **UK SIC:** 95100
**Employees:** 105

**DUNS 77-480-6160**
## Westward Care Ltd
Pennington Cyt Care Home, Leeds, West Yorkshire LS11 6TT
**Tel:** 01132284041 **Fax:** 01132-284045
**Web:** www.westwardcare.co.uk
**Reg No:** 2969357 **Estd:** 1994 Private Limited Company
**Line of Business:** Other human health activities
**Issued Capital:** £3,335,946
**Principals:** P G Hodkinson *(Managing)*, N A Stubbs, Ms B Gregory, D T Spencer
**Co. Secretary:** Mrs Gail Lawton
**US SIC:** 8091 **UK SIC:** 95200
**Auditors:** Freedman Ross
**Bankers:** National Westminster Bank Plc (60-60-05)

| | 31-03-14 | 31-03-13 | 31-03-12 |
|---|---|---|---|
| TO | 4,892,888 | 5,648,763 | 5,520,783 |
| P/L | 524,756 | 503,930 | 200,042 |
| NW | 9,421,799 | 9,083,786 | 8,677,291 |
| WC | (493,998) | 324,084 | (26,965) |
| Emp. | 187 | 196 | 212 |

**DUNS 22-196-6422**
## Westward Energy Services Ltd
**(Subsidiary of:** Asar Holdings Ltd)
Energy House, Alloy Industrial Estate, Pontardawe, Swansea, West Glamorgan SA8 4EN
**Tel:** 01792-862424 **Fax:** 01792830354
**Web:** www.westwardservices.com
**Reg No:** 4214763 **Estd:** 2001 Private Limited Company
**Line of Business:** Boilers servicing and repairs
**Issued Capital:** £1,000
**Director:** A T Slattery
**Co. Secretary:** Andrew Robinson
**Responsibilities**
**Health & Safety:** Kelly King *(Commercial Service Controller)*
**US SIC:** 3567 **UK SIC:** 32452
**Auditors:** Newby Castleman

| | 31-03-14 | 31-03-13 | 31-03-12 |
|---|---|---|---|
| TO | 3,812,885 | 4,562,313 | 5,127,041 |
| P/L | 231,326 | 239,372 | 286,347 |
| NW | 818,809 | 636,965 | 452,863 |
| WC | 678,205 | 513,013 | 332,188 |

**DUNS 23-761-6722**
## Westward Pathfinder
11 The Strand, Barnstaple, Devon EX31 1EU
**Tel:** 01271345851
**Web:** www.path-finder.org.uk
**Reg No:** 3755311 **Estd:** 1999 Private Company Limited By Guarantee
**Line of Business:** Other adult and other education not elsewhere classified
**Directors:** S J Keable, Ms L Grigg, F W Adam, W J Ratcliffe
**Co. Secretary:** Richard Curry
**Branches:** Westward Pathfinder, Fishleigh Court, Fishleigh Road, Roundswell Business Park, Barnstaple, Devon EX31 3UD
**US SIC:** 8299 **UK SIC:** 93300
**Bankers:** National Westminster Bank Plc (53-61-21)

| | 31-12-13 | 31-12-12 | 31-12-11 |
|---|---|---|---|
| TO | 1,698,081 | 1,842,315 | 1,672,900 |
| P/L | 14,097 | 35,448 | (88,570) |
| NW | 239,948 | 213,351 | 165,403 |
| WC | 198,708 | 224,505 | 26,322 |
| Emp. | 55 | 58 | 53 |

**DUNS 21-810-7593**
## The Westway Information Centre
140 Ladbroke Grove, London W10 5ND
**Tel:** 02075984437
**Web:** www.rbkc.gov.uk
**Estd:** 2012
**Line of Business:** Compulsory social security activities
**Responsibilities**
**Senior:** Christopher Luke *(Head of Social Work)*
**US SIC:** 7399 **UK SIC:** 83954
**Employees:** 150

**DUNS 22-037-4768**
## Westway Services Ltd
**(Subsidiary of:** Westway Services Holdings (2010) Ltd.)
Artemis, Ruislip, Middlesex HA4 6QE
**Tel:** 020-8833-7263 **Fax:** 020-8833-7293
**Web:** www.westwayservices.com
**Reg No:** 4039888 **Estd:** 2007 Private Limited Company
**Line of Business:** Servicing af freezers and refrigerators
**Issued Capital:** £1,000
**Directors:** D E Steventon, A Donnell, Ms V J Hale
**Co. Secretary:** Ms Vivien Hale
**Responsibilities**
**Senior:** Carl Brooks *(Manager)*, Karen Stubbings *(HR Manager)*
**HR:** Karen Stubbings *(HR Manager)*
**Operations:** Tim Andrew *(Operations Director)*, Nick Tanti *(Operations Director)*
**Engineering:** Jamie Dale *(Senior Contract Manager)*
**US SIC:** 1799 **UK SIC:** 50000
**Auditors:** BDO LLP
**Bankers:** The Royal Bank Of Scotland Plc (16-00-63)

| | 28-02-14 | 28-02-13 | 29-02-12 |
|---|---|---|---|
| TO | 30,017,884 | 22,273,345 | 23,113,542 |
| P/L | 4,205,415 | 2,768,998 | 1,030,900 |
| NW | 13,844,947 | 10,562,695 | 8,479,114 |
| WC | 13,762,672 | 10,501,302 | 8,393,041 |
| Emp. | 281 | 238 | 227 |

**DUNS 21-210-8794**
## Westwood Court Care Home
Westwood Court Care Home, Well Street, Winsford, Cheshire CW7 1HZ
**Tel:** 01606-594786
**Web:** www.leytonhealthcare.co.uk
**Estd:** 1996
**Line of Business:** Nursing homes
**Proprietor:** Mrs G Capner
**US SIC:** 8051 **UK SIC:** 95100
**Employees:** 61

**DUNS 21-041-3110**
## Westwood Language College for Girls
Spurgeon Road, London SE19 3UG
**Tel:** 02086-531661
**Web:** www.harrisuppernorwood.org.uk
**Estd:** 2003 Partnership
**Line of Business:** Schools (foundation)
**Trading Style:** Harris Academy Upper Norwood
**Partners:** Ms K Benton, Ms M Hedley
**Responsibilities**
**Finance:** Lucie Hicks *(Bursar)*
**Marketing:** Pat Stannard *(Human Resources & Quality Assu)*
**Health & Safety:** Pat Stannard *(Human Resources & Quality Assu)*
**Facilities:** Bruce Agombar *(Premises Manager)*
**US SIC:** 8211, 8249
**UK SIC:** 93200, 93300
**Employees:** 88

**DUNS 23-682-7341**
## Westwood Lodge
Brookview, Helmsman Way, Wigan, Lancashire WN3 5DJ
**Tel:** 01942-829999
**Web:** www.meridiancare.co.uk
**Estd:** 1991 Proprietorship
**Line of Business:** Nursing homes
**Proprietor:** S Lace
**Responsibilities**
**Senior:** Catherine Stott *(Manager)*
**US SIC:** 8051, 8091
**UK SIC:** 95100, 95200
**Employees:** 70

**DUNS 23-228-3056**
## Westwood School
Blithbury, Rugeley, Staffordshire WS15 3JQ
**Tel:** 01889504400
**Web:** www.priorygroup.com
**Line of Business:** Schools (special)

**Responsibilities**
**Senior:** Joan Pierson *(CEO, Managing Director)*
**US SIC:** 8299 **UK SIC:** 93300
**Employees:** 130

**DUNS 57-032-6421**
## Wetheralds Painters & Decorators Ltd
Yorkshire House, Grape Street, Leeds, West Yorkshire LS10 1BX
**Tel:** 01132-449995 **Fax:** 01132-449943
**Web:** www.wetheralds.co.uk
**Reg No:** 2873386 **Estd:** 1993 Private Limited Company
**Line of Business:** Painters and decorators
**Issued Capital:** £12,000
**Director:** M Murphy
**US SIC:** 1721 **UK SIC:** 50400
**Auditors:** Lindley Adams

| | 31-08-14 | 31-08-13 | 31-08-12 |
|---|---|---|---|
| TA | 1,404,280 | 1,074,279 | 565,391 |
| NW | 531,588 | 385,049 | 206,534 |
| WC | 464,332 | 301,391 | 163,592 |

**DUNS 28-979-9108**
## Wetherby Electrical Contractors Ltd
**(Subsidiary of:** Wetherby Electrical Holdings Ltd)
Unit 15, York, North Yorkshire YO26 7RD
**Tel:** 01423-359745 **Fax:** 01423357031
**Web:** www.wetherbyelectrical.co.uk
**Reg No:** 1774042 **Estd:** 1984 Private Limited Company
**Line of Business:** Electrical contractors and electricians
**Issued Capital:** £100
**Principals:** S R Moss *(Managing)*, M Graham
**Co. Secretary:** Lesley Stringfellow
**US SIC:** 1731 **UK SIC:** 50300
**Auditors:** Harris & Co
**Bankers:** Lloyds TSB Bank plc (30-93-91)

| | 30-04-14 | 30-04-13 | 30-04-12 |
|---|---|---|---|
| TO | N/A | N/A | 6,360,145 |
| P/L | N/A | N/A | (25,916) |
| NW | 694,981 | 550,639 | 758,298 |
| WC | 672,149 | 516,316 | 715,429 |
| Emp. | N/A | N/A | 47 |

**DUNS 21-235-3551** **Imp-Exp**
## Wetherby Shade Card Co Ltd
**(Subsidiary of:** Tucker & Oxley Ltd)
Grangefield Industrial Estate, Stanningley, Pudsey, West Yorkshire LS28 6QJ
**Tel:** 01132577381
**Web:** www.wetherby-shade-card.co.uk
**Reg No:** 0632398 **VAT No:** 179991488
**Estd:** 1959 Private Limited Company
**Line of Business:** Other manufacturing not elsewhere classified
**Export Markets:** U S A
**Issued Capital:** £50,000
**Directors:** J M Brazill, B P Mcculla
**Co. Secretary:** Ms Miranda Tunbridge
**Responsibilities**
**Facilities:** Nigel Hogg *(Production Manager)*
**Engineering:** Michael Coggins *(Chief Engineer)*, Nigel Hogg *(Production Manager)*
**US SIC:** 3999 **UK SIC:** 49590
**Auditors:** Brown Butler
**Bankers:** HSBC Bank plc (40-27-15)

| | 30-09-14 | 30-09-13 | 30-09-12 |
|---|---|---|---|
| TA | 3,021,037 | 2,937,977 | 2,912,333 |
| NW | 2,186,152 | 2,184,155 | 2,170,130 |
| WC | 1,515,387 | 1,467,938 | 1,523,141 |

**DUNS 21-194-8880**
## Wetton Cleaning Services Ltd
Wetton House, London SE1 5JX
**Tel:** 08454334101
**Web:** www.wettons.co.uk
**Reg No:** 0473038 **Estd:** 1949 Private Limited Company
**Line of Business:** Traditional cleaning activities
**Trading Style:** Wettons Cleaning
**Issued Capital:** £8,587
**Principals:** Ms N Holmes *(Managing)*, J S Baker *(Financial)*, J Baker
**US SIC:** 7349 **UK SIC:** 92300
**Auditors:** Charterhouse (Accountants) LLP
**Bankers:** Barclays Bank Plc (20-14-33)

| | 31-03-14 | 31-03-13 | 31-03-12 |
|---|---|---|---|
| TO | 27,828,938 | 30,465,465 | 28,701,002 |
| P/L | 285,236 | 1,041,162 | 1,260,708 |
| NW | 910,391 | 1,572,781 | 1,148,813 |
| WC | (343,473) | 276,268 | (155,295) |
| Emp. | 2,018 | 2,202 | 2,145 |

DUNS 21-853-9969

## Weve Ltd

Milton Gate, 60 Chiswell Street, London EC1Y 4AG
**Tel:** 02036672000
**Web:** www.weve.com
**Reg No:** 8178832 **Estd:** 2012 Private Limited Company
**Line of Business:** Telecom consultants
**Issued Capital:** £27,185,103
**Directors:** D J Plumb, J J Rees, N Parbutt, P Modi, G Mcquade
**Co. Secretary:** A G Secretarial Limited
**US SIC:** 4899 **UK SIC:** 79020

| | 31-12-13 |
|---|---|
| TO | 12,762,000 |
| P/L | (24,776,000) |
| NW | 6,308,000 |
| WC | 3,937,000 |
| Emp. | 70 |

DUNS 28-990-7446 Exp

## Wexas Ltd

Dorset House, London SE1 9NT
**Tel:** 02075893315 **Fax:** 02078380837
**Web:** www.wexas.com
**Reg No:** 1820489 **Estd:** 1970 Private Limited Company
**Line of Business:** Activities of travel agencies
**Export Markets:** Worldwide
**Issued Capital:** £1,000,000
**Principals:** Dr I M Wilson *(Chairman)*, G Vaughan Brown, Ms J E Wilson, Miss K H Gershon, M N Wilson
**Co. Secretary:** Dr Ian Wilson
**Responsibilities**
**Senior:** Sarah Strang *(Marketing Director)*
**Marketing:** Sarah Strang *(Marketing Director)*
**Sales:** Fiona Garner *(Sales Manager)*, Gordon Mowatt *(Sales Director)*
**US SIC:** 4722 **UK SIC:** 77001
**Auditors:** BDO Stoy Hayward
**Bankers:** Coutts & Co (18-00-14)

| | 31-12-13 | 31-12-12 | 31-12-11 |
|---|---|---|---|
| TO | 17,001,083 | 17,193,105 | 20,885,040 |
| P/L | 350,828 | 330,706 | 50,995 |
| NW | 6,268,344 | 5,613,398 | 5,221,450 |
| WC | (993,581) | (1,570,044) | (1,897,836) |
| Emp. | 110 | 122 | 133 |

DUNS 22-747-8864 Exp

## The Wey Group International

Premier House Sprint Industrial Estate, West Byfleet, Surrey KT14 7NW
**Tel:** 01932345345
**Web:** www.weygroup.co.uk
**VAT No:** 584358896 **Estd:** 1983 Partnership
**Line of Business:** Couriers
**Export Markets:** Worldwide
**Partners:** P Barnes, C Jacobs
**Branches:** Wimbledon
**US SIC:** 4213, 4511
**UK SIC:** 72300, 75000
**Bankers:** Lloyds TSB Bank plc (30-99-80)
**Employees:** 100

DUNS 21-847-4167

## The Wey Valley School & Sports College

The Wey Valley School Dorchest, Weymouth, Dorset DT3 5AN
**Tel:** 01305817059
**Web:** www.weyvalley.dorset.sch.uk
**Reg No:** 8128803 **Estd:** 2012 Private Company Limited By Guarantee
**Line of Business:** General secondary education
**Directors:** M L Hogben, Mrs J L Mellor, Ms D M Day, P B Quinn, N C Evans, Miss D P Rhodes, P C Thomas, Ms F V Webb
**Co. Secretary:** Robert Cole
**Responsibilities**
**Senior:** Margaret Eaglestone *(Director)*, Dan Emery *(Director)*, Leslie Gardner *(Director)*
**US SIC:** 8211 **UK SIC:** 93200
**Bankers:** Lloyds TSB Bank plc (30-99-56)

| | 31-08-14 | 31-08-13 |
|---|---|---|
| TO | 5,922,006 | 4,775,337 |
| P/L | 231,498 | (1,067,442) |
| NW | (1,361,944) | (1,413,442) |
| WC | 186,450 | 46,481 |
| Emp. | 108 | 114 |

DUNS 21-716-3457

## Weydon School

Weydon Lane, Farnham, Surrey GU9 8UG
**Tel:** 01252725052
**Web:** www.weydonschool.surrey.sch.uk
**Reg No:** 7552535 **Estd:** 1998 Private Company Limited By Guarantee
**Line of Business:** General secondary education
**Directors:** B J Hurn, C Hyland, Mrs C Bradley, Ms S Rees, R K Lee, N D Pow, J K Impey, M J Field
**Co. Secretary:** Mrs Nina Jex
**Responsibilities**
**Senior:** Angela Adam *(Director)*, Louise Barber *(Director)*, Claire Booth *(Director)*, Peter Brinsden *(Director)*, James Cheyne *(Director)*, Julia Crocker *(Director)*, Ralph Johnson *(Director)*, Maria Mason *(Director)*, Rachel Swan *(Director)*
**US SIC:** 8211 **UK SIC:** 93200
**Bankers:** HSBC Bank plc (40-00-00)

| | 31-08-14 | 31-08-13 | 31-08-12 |
|---|---|---|---|
| TO | 11,849,577 | 7,936,545 | 24,317,959 |
| P/L | 4,904,000 | 1,511,666 | 15,394,279 |
| NW | 21,306,945 | 16,799,945 | 15,265,279 |
| WC | 2,837,303 | 2,024,831 | 825,692 |
| Emp. | 107 | 153 | 150 |

DUNS 23-664-6303

## Weymouth & Portland Borough Council

Municipal Offices, North Quay, Weymouth, Dorset DT4 8TA
**Tel:** 01305838000 **Fax:** 01305-760971
**Web:** www.dorsetforyou.com
**VAT No:** 187201957 **Estd:** 1974 Incorporate By Act Of Parliament
**Line of Business:** Central government
**Directors:** I Locke, R Burgess, D Tattersall, D Furley
**Responsibilities**
**Senior:** Tom Grainger *(CEO, Managing Director)*
**Finance:** Jason Vaughan *(Senior Finance Administrator)*
**HR:** Steve Barratt *(Human Resources Manager)*
**Purchasing:** Julia Long *(Procurement Officer)*
**Branches:** Weymouth & Portland Borough Council, 217 Wakeham, Portland, Dorset DT5 1HS
**US SIC:** 9121 **UK SIC:** 91110
**Bankers:** The Co-Operative Bank Plc (08-90-02)
**Employees:** 200

DUNS 42-397-8964

## Weymouth College

Cranford Avenue, Weymouth, Dorset DT4 7LQ
**Tel:** 01305761100
**Web:** www.weymouth.ac.uk
**Estd:** 1993
**Line of Business:** Further education schools and colleges
**Director:** P Done
**Responsibilities**
**Senior:** Alan Birks *(Manager)*, Elizabeth Myles *(Manager)*, Susan Ratcliffe *(Manager)*, Jennifer Stiling *(Manager)*
**IT:** Marie Prentice *(Computer Operations Manager)*, Phil Templeton *(IT Manager)*
**Branches:** Weymouth College, Enterprise Connection The 5 Burr, Dorchester, Dorset DT1 3GR
**US SIC:** 8221 **UK SIC:** 93100
**Employees:** 600

DUNS 23-743-3532

## W.F. Support Services Ltd

Site D Reedlands Road, Clay Flatts Industrial Estate, Workington, Cumbria CA14 3YF
**Tel:** 01900870000
**Web:** www.wfcleaning.co.uk
**Reg No:** 3737557 **Estd:** 1999 Private Limited Company
**Line of Business:** Cleaning contracting commercial
**Issued Capital:** £2
**Director:** Mrs J Walker
**Co. Secretary:** Michael Walker
**US SIC:** 6531, 7349
**UK SIC:** 83400, 92300
**Auditors:** JFW Robinson & Co

| | 31-05-13 | 31-05-12 | 31-05-11 |
|---|---|---|---|
| TA | 932,398 | 779,488 | 704,396 |
| NW | 133,596 | 116,198 | 146,315 |
| WC | 37,292 | 10,960 | 57,438 |

DUNS 77-897-4704

## Wfel Holdings Ltd

**(Subsidiary of:** Krauss-Maffei Wegmann Gmbh & Co. Kg)
Wfel Sir Richard Fairey Road, Heaton Chapel, Stockport, Cheshire SK4 5DY
**Tel:** 01612350304
**Web:** www.wfel.com
**Reg No:** 5801100 **Estd:** 2006 Private Limited Company
**Line of Business:** Manufacture of other special purpose machinery not elsewhere classified
**Export Sales:** £49,234,000
**Issued Capital:** £15,629,771
**Directors:** R Ketzel, M G Houghton, I G Wilson, J Weber, P N Grady, H Rieder
**Co. Secretary:** Patrick Grady
**US SIC:** 3999 **UK SIC:** 49590
**Auditors:** Deloitte LLP
**Bankers:** Barclays Bank Plc (20-33-70)

| | 31-12-13 | 31-12-12 | 31-12-11 |
|---|---|---|---|
| TO | 51,963,000 | 39,658,000 | 36,168,000 |
| P/L | 16,165,000 | 8,735,000 | 2,377,000 |
| NW | 18,355,000 | (945,000) | (24,006,000) |
| WC | 10,903,000 | (4,375,000) | 7,634,000 |
| Emp. | 81 | 83 | 87 |

DUNS 21-631-3445

## Wfl (Uk) Ltd

Causeway End, Brinkworth, Chippenham, Wiltshire SN15 5DN
**Tel:** 01666510345
**Web:** www.watsonfuels.co.uk
**Reg No:** 0594001 **VAT No:** 195046059
**Estd:** 1957 Private Limited Company
**Line of Business:** Wholesale of other fuels and related products
**Trading Style:** Linton Fuel Oils, Watson Fuels
**Issued Capital:** £357,160
**Directors:** W N Declaris, G G Rutherford, C J White, A F Watson, J R Cole, R B Crowell, Ms A B Urban
**Co. Secretary:** Dentons Secretaries Limited
**Responsibilities**
**Health & Safety:** Tony Richards *(Health & Safety Officer)*
**Branches:** Wfl (Uk) Ltd, Churchtown Service Station, Garstang By Pass Road, Preston, Lancashire PR3 0HQ
**US SIC:** 5052 **UK SIC:** 61200
**Auditors:** Grant Thornton UK LLP
**Bankers:** Barclays Bank Plc (20-71-03)

**Following financial data are in thousands**

| | 30-04-14 | 30-04-13 | 30-04-12 |
|---|---|---|---|
| TO | 1,338,745 | 1,246,989 | 1,041,364 |
| P/L | 7,058 | 12,804 | 441 |
| NW | 31,671 | 25,124 | 16,211 |
| WC | 4,394 | 1,811 | (5,780) |
| Emp. | 680 | 676 | 690 |

DUNS 23-078-1312

## Wg Tanker Group Ltd

Leek Road, Waterhouses, Stoke-On-Trent, Staffordshire ST10 3HN
**Tel:** 01538308383 **Fax:** 01538-308133
**Web:** www.wgtanker.com
**Reg No:** 2872193 **Estd:** 1999 Private Limited Company
**Line of Business:** Sale of motor vehicles
**Export Sales:** £200,033
**Trading Style:** Wg Tanker Services Ltd
**Issued Capital:** £10,000
**Director:** I Buxton
**Co. Secretary:** William Smart
**Responsibilities**
**Sales:** Jeff Morris *(Sales Manager)*
**Health & Safety:** Michelle Smart *(Health & Safety Officer)*
**US SIC:** 5511, 7539
**UK SIC:** 65100, 67100
**Auditors:** Howsons
**Bankers:** Barclays Bank Plc (20-48-70)

| | 31-03-14 | 31-03-13 | 31-03-12 |
|---|---|---|---|
| TO | 8,665,248 | 8,155,638 | 8,277,000 |
| P/L | 198,999 | 288,466 | 299,000 |
| NW | 3,807,187 | 3,709,294 | 2,829,000 |
| WC | (284,359) | (291,799) | (541,000) |
| Emp. | 87 | 85 | 87 |

DUNS 73-597-2304

## Wgsn Ltd

**(Subsidiary of:** The Scott Trust Ltd)
Airw1, 2nd Floor, 20 Air Street, London W1B 5AN
**Tel:** 02077156200 **Fax:** 02076927843
**Web:** www.wgsn.com
**Reg No:** 4858491 **Estd:** 2003 Private Limited Company
**Line of Business:** Other publishing
**Export Sales:** £21,416,000
**Issued Capital:** £12,145,015
**Directors:** D A Painter, Ms A J Gradden, J P Neto
**Co. Secretary:** Ms Shanny Looi
**Responsibilities**
**Senior:** Sue Barrett *(Manager)*, Steve Newbold *(Global Managing Director)*
**Marketing:** Amanda Carr *(Specialist)*, Catrin Davies *(Associate Travel and Arts Edit)*, Angela Rumsey *(Global Retail Editor)*, Rachael Taylor *(Marketing Director)*, Lisa Yam *(Regional Business Director, Re)*
**Sales:** Angela Rumsey *(Global Retail Editor)*
**IT:** Steve Weiss *(SVP, Technology)*
**Operations:** Vilislava Petrova *(Head of Content)*
**US SIC:** 2741, 7399
**UK SIC:** 47541, 83954
**Auditors:** KPMG LLP

| | 31-12-13 | 31-12-12 | 31-12-11 |
|---|---|---|---|
| TO | 26,502,000 | 25,690,000 | 24,729,000 |
| P/L | (6,803,000) | 5,846,000 | 8,196,000 |
| NW | 36,116,000 | 41,066,000 | 35,917,000 |
| WC | 29,387,000 | 31,822,000 | 28,160,000 |
| Emp. | 204 | 196 | 221 |

DUNS 22-637-0310

## W.H. Barley (Transport & Storage) Ltd

Old Wolverton Road, Old Wolverton, Milton Keynes, Buckinghamshire MK12 5NL
**Tel:** 01908227222
**Web:** www.whbarley.co.uk
**Reg No:** 1597030 **Estd:** 1981 Private Limited Company
**Line of Business:** Other supporting land transport activities
**Issued Capital:** £1,000
**Principals:** P W Barber *(Managing)*, Ms K L Barber, Miss E V Barber, S P Latchford
**Co. Secretary:** Peter Barber
**Responsibilities**
**Senior:** Clive Keech *(Manager)*
**Marketing:** Tris Anley *(Sales & Marketing Manager)*
**Sales:** Tris Anley *(Sales & Marketing Manager)*
**IT:** Tris Anley *(Sales & Marketing Manager)*
**HR:** Alex Newman *(Human Resources Manager)*
**Health & Safety:** Alex Newman *(Human Resources Manager)*
**Operations:** Tris Anley *(Sales & Marketing Manager)*
**US SIC:** 4789 **UK SIC:** 77002
**Auditors:** John Needham & Co
**Bankers:** Lloyds TSB Bank plc (30-15-53)

| | 30-06-14 | 30-06-13 | 30-06-12 |
|---|---|---|---|
| TO | 6,333,573 | 5,248,550 | 4,932,284 |
| P/L | 213,971 | 127,423 | 122,719 |
| NW | 3,273,297 | 2,521,216 | 2,474,509 |
| WC | (82,674) | (92,690) | (23,791) |
| Emp. | 78 | 68 | 66 |

DUNS 22-522-3023 Imp-Exp

## W.H. Bence (Coachworks) Ltd

Great Western Business Park, Bristol, Avon BS37 5NG
**Web:** www.whbence.co.uk
**Reg No:** 1708157 **VAT No:** 398701217
**Estd:** 1983 Private Limited Company
**Line of Business:** Truck & bus body manufacturers
**Export Markets:** France, Belgium, Sweden, Germany
**Export Sales:** £289,531
**Issued Capital:** £100
**Managing Director:** J H Brown
**Co. Secretary:** Mrs Susan Brown
**Responsibilities**
**Senior:** Huw Owen *(Manager)*
**US SIC:** 3713, 3715
**UK SIC:** 35201, 35220
**Auditors:** Waddingtons
**Bankers:** Barclays Bank Plc (20-13-42)

| | 31-03-14 | 31-03-13 | 31-03-12 |
|---|---|---|---|
| TO | 6,941,434 | 6,884,478 | 5,743,697 |
| P/L | 40,067 | (154,903) | 3,190 |
| NW | 577,590 | 524,629 | 625,451 |
| WC | 24,046 | 156,853 | 272,497 |
| Emp. | 45 | 50 | 60 |

DUNS 22-669-8108 Exp

## W.H. Davis Ltd

**(Subsidiary of:** Portchester Equity Ltd)
Langwith Road, Mansfield, Nottinghamshire NG20 9SA
**Tel:** 01623741600 **Fax:** 01623744474
**Web:** www.whdavis.co.uk
**Reg No:** 1797397 **VAT No:** 401665773
**Estd:** 1984 Private Limited Company
**Line of Business:** Manufacturers of containers
**Export Markets:** Africa, Europe and U S A
**Issued Capital:** £19,500
**Directors:** M Thistlehwayte, T C Sharpe, D C Harbord, D A Horner, D M Hast, I A Whelpton, A Markwell, S C Greenwood
**Co. Secretary:** Mark Jackson
**Responsibilities**
**Senior:** Robin Thistlethw *(Director)*
**HR:** Craig Charlesworth *(Human Resources Manager)*
**Health & Safety:** Craig Charlesworth *(Human Resources Manager)*
**Branches:** W.h. Davis Ltd, Stonebroom Indstl Est, Alfreton, Derbyshire DE55 6LQ
**US SIC:** 3999, 3799
**UK SIC:** 49590, 36502
**Auditors:** Blueprint Audit
**Bankers:** HSBC Bank plc (40-27-29)

| | 30-09-13 | 30-09-12 | 30-09-11 |
|---|---|---|---|
| TO | 22,123,526 | 10,903,456 | 8,435,619 |
| P/L | 2,126,923 | 518,186 | 478,225 |
| NW | 4,793,652 | 3,397,219 | 3,256,478 |
| WC | 3,854,343 | 2,508,014 | 2,506,372 |
| Emp. | 140 | 108 | 93 |

DUNS 23-878-9049

## W.H. Ireland Group Plc

11 St James's Square, Manchester M2 6WH
**Tel:** 01618322174 **Fax:** 01618-198-897
**Web:** www.wh-ireland.co.uk
**Reg No:** 3870190 **VAT No:** 727149034
**Estd:** 1999 Public Limited Company

**Line of Business:** Financial intermediation not elsewhere classified
**Issued Capital:** £1,184,470
**Directors:** D J Cowland, R E Lee, T M Steel, R J Lowe, R W Killingbeck
**Co. Secretary:** Miss Katy Mitchell
**Responsibilities**
**IT:** David Hallstead *(IT Manager)*
**Health & Safety:** Mike Burnes *(Facilities Manager)*
**Facilities:** Mike Burnes *(Facilities Manager)*
**Branches:** W.h. Ireland Group Plc, 11 St. James's Square, Manchester M2 6WH
**US SIC:** 6111, 7399
**UK SIC:** 81501, 83954
**Auditors:** BDO LLP
**Bankers:** Bank Of Scotland (80-02-16)

| | 30-11-13 | 30-11-12 | 30-11-11 |
|---|---|---|---|
| TA | 50,939,000 | 52,353,000 | 41,769,000 |
| P/L | 1,652,000 | (177,000) | (1,441,000) |
| NW | 12,177,000 | 11,105,000 | 11,315,000 |
| WC | 7,830,000 | 6,065,000 | 6,977,000 |
| Emp. | 229 | 217 | 187 |

DUNS 21-725-1792 **Imp**

## W.H. Kemp (Electrics) Ltd

**(Subsidiary of:** Hazelhurst Holdings Ltd)
Cory Way, West Wilts Trading Estate, Westbury, Wiltshire BA13 4QT
**Tel:** 01373-823322 **Fax:** 01373-824411
**Web:** www.whkemp.co.uk
**Reg No:** 0895665 **VAT No:** 138105195
**Estd:** 1967 Private Limited Company
**Line of Business:** Manufacturers cable and wire equipment
**Trading Style:** W.H. Kemp (Electrics) Ltd
**Issued Capital:** £80
**Director:** J P Wyatt
**Co. Secretary:** Mrs Lisa Wyatt
**Responsibilities**
**Senior:** Ann Hazelhurst *(Company Secretayr)*
**Admin:** Lynette Wilmot *(Administration Manager)*
**HR:** Lynette Wilmot *(Administration Manager)*
**Health & Safety:** Lynette Wilmot *(Administration Manager)*
**US SIC:** 3357 **UK SIC:** 22470
**Auditors:** Monahans
**Bankers:** Lloyds TSB Bank plc (30-00-01)

| | 31-01-14 | 31-01-13 | 31-01-12 |
|---|---|---|---|
| TA | 2,332,504 | 2,259,513 | 1,863,221 |
| NW | 1,695,069 | 1,550,516 | 1,399,032 |
| WC | 1,717,119 | 1,663,867 | 1,331,162 |

DUNS 21-259-3859

## W.H. Oddie Ltd

325 Leeds Road, Nelson, Lancashire BB9 8RW
**Tel:** 01282614570
**Web:** www.oddiescakes.co.uk
**Reg No:** 0363671 **VAT No:** 174660941
**Estd:** 1905 Private Limited Company
**Line of Business:** Retail sale of bread, cakes, flour confectionery and sugar confectionery
**Issued Capital:** £4,350
**Principals:** W H Oddie *(Managing)*, Miss L J Oddie, J Oddie
**Co. Secretary:** Ms Jenifer Oddie
**Responsibilities**
**Senior:** Lynne Birchell *(Manageress)*
**Finance:** Deborah Husband *(Financial Controller)*
**Sales:** Carol Clough *(Sales Manager)*
**IT:** Andy Howells *(Bakery Manager)*
**Health & Safety:** Maureen Turner *(Health & Safety Officer)*
**Facilities:** Andy Howells *(Bakery Manager)*
**Operations:** Carol Clough *(Sales Manager)*, Deborah Husband *(Financial Controller)*, Maureen Turner *(Health & Safety Officer)*
**Engineering:** Andy Howells *(Bakery Manager)*
**Branches:** W.h. Oddie Ltd, 10 Market St, Colne, Lancashire BB8 0HR
**US SIC:** 5462 **UK SIC:** 64100
**Auditors:** Cassons
**Bankers:** National Westminster Bank Plc (01-02-20)

| | 25-10-14 | 26-10-13 | 27-10-12 |
|---|---|---|---|
| TA | 2,622,022 | 2,556,221 | 2,593,610 |
| NW | 2,256,912 | 2,262,026 | 2,271,176 |
| WC | 447,447 | 377,649 | 297,183 |

DUNS 53-606-1633

## W.H. Smith & Sons Holdings Ltd

Water Orton Lane, Minworth, Sutton Coldfield, West Midlands B76 9BG
**Web:** www.whs-tools.co.uk
**Reg No:** 3411415 **VAT No:** 670312758
**Estd:** 1933 Private Limited Company
**Line of Business:** Plastic injection moulding
**Export Sales:** £4,741,000
**Issued Capital:** £10,000
**Directors:** C G Smith, F H Smith, B J Smith, J H Smith
**Co. Secretary:** Peter Rushton
**Responsibilities**
**IT:** Matthew Tetley *(IT Manager)*
**US SIC:** 3079 **UK SIC:** 48360
**Auditors:** KPMG

| | 02-05-14 | 26-04-13 | 27-05-12 |
|---|---|---|---|
| TO | 41,771,000 | 34,724,000 | 22,510,000 |
| P/L | 4,802,000 | 2,039,000 | 1,062,000 |
| NW | 17,996,000 | 14,055,000 | 12,481,000 |
| WC | 9,007,000 | 5,194,000 | 4,119,000 |
| Emp. | 667 | 603 | 443 |

DUNS 21-115-8526 **Imp**

## Wh Smith High Street Ltd

**(Subsidiary of:** Wh Smith Plc)
Greenbridge Road, Swindon, Wiltshire SN3 3LD
**Tel:** 0845-604-6543
**Web:** www.whsmith.co.uk
**Reg No:** 6560339 **VAT No:** 238554836
**Estd:** 2008 Private Limited Company
**Line of Business:** Retail sale of books, newspapers and stationery
**Trading Style:** Funky Pigeon
**Issued Capital:** £308,000,001
**Directors:** R J Moorhead, I Houghton, S Clarke
**Co. Secretary:** Ian Houghton
**US SIC:** 5942, 5941
**UK SIC:** 65300, 65400
**Auditors:** Deloitte LLP

| | 31-08-13 | 31-08-12 | 31-08-11 |
|---|---|---|---|
| TO | 702,436,000 | 757,740,000 | 804,891,000 |
| P/L | 44,170,000 | 47,589,000 | 48,530,000 |
| NW | 144,077,000 | 185,324,000 | 147,832,000 |
| WC | 57,154,000 | 93,279,000 | 55,504,000 |

DUNS 73-949-4198

## Wh Smith Plc

Greenbridge Road, Swindon, Wiltshire SN3 3LD
**Web:** www.whsmith.co.uk
**Reg No:** 5202036 **Estd:** 2004 Public Limited Company
**Line of Business:** Management activities of holding companies
**Trading Style:** Wh Smith
**Issued Capital:** £27,364,807
**Directors:** S Clarke, H E Stauton, Ms A V Durbin, J W Hall, R J Moorhead, Ms S C Baxter
**Co. Secretary:** Ian Houghton
**Responsibilities**
**Finance:** Mark Sabin *(Risk Director)*
**Marketing:** Angus Hayman *(E-commerce Director)*, Paul Tavener *(Brand Director)*, Timothy Whitehead *(Strategic Insights Analyst)*
**Health & Safety:** Mark Sabin *(Risk Director)*
**Branches:** Wh Smith Plc, Stratford Railway Station, Station Street, London E15 1AZ
**US SIC:** 6711 **UK SIC:** 83962
**Auditors:** Deloitte LLP

Following financial data are in thousands

| | 31-08-14 | 31-08-13 | 31-08-12 |
|---|---|---|---|
| TO | 1,161,000 | 1,186,000 | 1,243,000 |
| P/L | 112,000 | 108,000 | 102,000 |
| NW | 45,000 | 47,000 | 95,000 |
| WC | (59,000) | (55,000) | (49,000) |
| Emp. | 14,391 | 14,723 | 16,086 |

DUNS 34-547-2182

## Wh Solo Holdings Ltd

105 Jermyn Street, St James, London SW1Y 6EE
**Tel:** 020-7839-4444
**Web:** www.walkerhamill.com
**Reg No:** 5357273 **Estd:** 2005 Private Limited Company
**Line of Business:** Labour recruitment and provision of personnel
**Export Sales:** £21,000
**Issued Capital:** £86,000
**Directors:** T J Smith, C G Townsend, Ms N A Bowring, D L Craig
**Co. Secretary:** Nilesh Katwa
**US SIC:** 7361 **UK SIC:** 83954

| | 28-02-14 | 28-02-13 | 29-02-12 |
|---|---|---|---|
| TO | 12,392,000 | 11,753,000 | 14,692,495 |
| P/L | 398,000 | (479,000) | 514,920 |
| NW | (1,241,000) | (1,821,000) | (1,718,978) |
| WC | (663,000) | (909,000) | (715,036) |
| Emp. | 47 | 48 | 52 |

DUNS 23-679-5670

## Wh Stephens

34 Duncan Close, Moulton Park Industrial Estate, Northampton, Northamptonshire NN3 6WL
**Tel:** 02890663123
**Web:** www.whstephens.com
**VAT No:** 252808753 **Estd:** 1985 Partnership
**Line of Business:** Quantity surveyors
**Partners:** G R Simon, W J Warnock, J Tully, A F Finlay, K Patterson, M Scullion
**Responsibilities**
**Senior:** John Leeding *(Partner)*, Darren Press *(Partner)*, Joe Tully *(Partner)*, Billy Wallace *(Health & Safety Officer)*
**Admin:** Anne Montgomery *(Administration Manager)*
**HR:** Anne Montgomery *(Administration Manager)*
**Health & Safety:** Billy Wallace *(Health & Safety Officer)*
**Facilities:** Joe Tully *(Partner)*
**Branches:** Wh Stephens, 34 Duncan Close, Northampton, Northamptonshire NN3 6WL
**US SIC:** 7397 **UK SIC:** 83702
**Employees:** 65

DUNS 21-834-1790 **Imp-Exp**

## W.H. Tildesley Ltd

Clifford Works, Bow Street, Willenhall, West Midlands WV13 2AN
**Tel:** 01902366440 **Fax:** 01902-366216
**Web:** www.whtildesley.com
**Reg No:** 0188101 **VAT No:** 431476265
**Estd:** 1874 Private Limited Company
**Line of Business:** Metal finishing and polishing services
**Export Markets:** W Europe, Australia, Middle East, Canada, Africa, U S A
**Export Sales:** £228,411
**Issued Capital:** £19,828
**Directors:** T R Tildesley, Ms A L Richardson
**Co. Secretary:** John Tildesley
**Responsibilities**
**Admin:** Denise Clorley *(Administrator)*
**IT:** Bruce Burden *(Technical Manager)*
**Operations:** Steve Reed *(Quality Manager)*
**Engineering:** Bruce Burden *(Technical Manager)*
**US SIC:** 3499 **UK SIC:** 31694
**Auditors:** Lancaster Haskins LLP
**Bankers:** HSBC Bank plc (40-46-35)

| | 30-06-14 | 30-06-13 | 30-06-12 |
|---|---|---|---|
| TO | 3,180,526 | 3,267,331 | N/A |
| P/L | 36,642 | 14,633 | N/A |
| NW | 5,746,366 | 5,684,396 | 5,071,282 |
| WC | 1,411,416 | 1,200,958 | 1,537,926 |
| Emp. | 51 | 51 | N/A |

DUNS 34-593-2685 **Imp**

## Whale & Dolphin Conservation

Brookfield, Rowden Lane, Chippenham, Wiltshire SN15 2AS
**Tel:** 01249-449500
**Web:** www.wdcs.org
**Reg No:** 2737421 **Estd:** 1992 Private Company Limited By Guarantee
**Line of Business:** Conservation organisations
**Directors:** Mrs S J Pope, J N Gerard-Leigh, P Smith, P H Kelland, G M Adams, A J Reed
**Co. Secretary:** Mrs Mary Bryan
**Responsibilities**
**Senior:** Liza Antrim *(Manager)*, Chris Butler-Stroud *(Chief Executive)*
**Marketing:** Danny Groves *(Press Officer)*, Chris Vick *(Marketing Director)*
**Operations:** Nicola Hodgins *(International Projects Manager)*
**US SIC:** 8321 **UK SIC:** 96111
**Auditors:** KPMG
**Bankers:** Barclays Bank Plc (20-37-75)

| | 30-09-13 | 30-09-12 | 30-09-11 |
|---|---|---|---|
| TO | 2,977,818 | 4,357,552 | 3,718,564 |
| P/L | (709,443) | 897,770 | 64,777 |
| NW | 780,831 | 1,490,274 | 592,504 |
| WC | 708,016 | 1,438,563 | 557,300 |
| Emp. | 58 | 54 | 48 |

DUNS 22-233-4422 **Imp-Exp**

## Whale Tankers Ltd

Ravenshaw, Solihull, West Midlands B91 2SU
**Tel:** 0121-704-5700
**Web:** www.whale.co.uk
**Reg No:** 4251423 **VAT No:** 849745079
**Estd:** 2001 Private Limited Company
**Line of Business:** Manufacture of other special purpose machinery not elsewhere classified
**Export Sales:** £613,902
**Issued Capital:** £729,000
**Directors:** K N Van Hagen, R H Turner, C J Anderson, M D Warmington
**Co. Secretary:** Paul Newman
**Responsibilities**
**Senior:** Keith Hagen *(Manager)*
**Engineering:** Andy Ellis *(Engineering Manager)*, Glen Mason *(Production Manager)*
**US SIC:** 3559, 3999
**UK SIC:** 32863, 49590
**Auditors:** Dafferns LLP

| | 31-12-13 | 31-12-12 | 31-12-11 |
|---|---|---|---|
| TO | 26,194,795 | 22,588,913 | 20,192,227 |
| P/L | 1,836,237 | 669,664 | 79,638 |
| NW | 4,971,969 | 3,323,014 | 1,902,435 |
| WC | 2,674,324 | 2,053,765 | 1,881,159 |
| Emp. | 209 | 197 | 179 |

DUNS 21-205-8390 **Imp-Exp**

## Whaleys (Bradford) Ltd

Harris Court, Bradford, West Yorkshire BD7 4EQ
**Tel:** 01274-576-718 **Fax:** 0127521309
**Web:** www.whaleys.co.uk
**Reg No:** 0252859 **VAT No:** 179968969
**Estd:** 1869 Private Limited Company
**Line of Business:** Fabric retailers
**Export Markets:** Worldwide
**Trading Style:** Whaleys (Bradford) Ltd
**Issued Capital:** £20,201
**Principals:** J F Mcilvenny *(Chairman and Managing)*, Mrs A J Rayner, Ms R J Mcllvenny, P J Mcilvenny
**Co. Secretary:** Stephen Baker
**Responsibilities**
**Senior:** Kevin Woodhead *(General Manager)*
**Marketing:** Barry Hardisty *(Sales Manager)*
**Sales:** Barry Hardisty *(Sales Manager)*
**IT:** Kevin Woodhead *(General Manager)*
**US SIC:** 5714, 2394
**UK SIC:** 64700, 45560
**Bankers:** Lloyds TSB Bank plc (30-91-12)

| | 31-10-14 | 31-10-13 | 31-10-12 |
|---|---|---|---|
| TA | 4,656,865 | 4,026,720 | 3,716,144 |
| NW | 3,800,095 | 3,326,337 | 2,967,452 |
| WC | 3,655,827 | 3,152,968 | 2,519,280 |

DUNS 36-811-1423

## Whalley Range Amateur Football Club

Kings Road, Manchester M21 0XX
**Tel:** 01618812618
**Estd:** 1901
**Line of Business:** Racecourses and racetracks
**Principals:** S Cafferty *(Chairman)*, R Lapsey
**Responsibilities**
**Senior:** Keith Filds *(Chief Executive)*
**US SIC:** 7999 **UK SIC:** 97913
**Employees:** 71

DUNS 21-225-9541

## Wharton Clinic

Wharton Primary Health Centre, Crook Lane, Winsford, Cheshire CW7 3GY
**Tel:** 01606542501
**Web:** www.whartonmedicalclinic.com
**Estd:** 1967 Proprietorship
**Line of Business:** Nhs clinics
**Proprietor:** Mrs B Cooper
**Responsibilities**
**Senior:** Andrea Hayden *(Administration Manager)*
**US SIC:** 8062 **UK SIC:** 95100
**Employees:** 70

DUNS 29-581-7878

## Wharton Construction Ltd

Kellaw Road, Darlington, County Durham DL1 4YA
**Web:** www.whartonconstructionltd.co.uk
**Reg No:** 1943490 **VAT No:** 409214964
**Estd:** 1985 Private Limited Company
**Line of Business:** Building construction contractors
**Issued Capital:** £20,000
**Principals:** P Wharton *(Managing)*, J Cutting *(Financial)*, C P Lee, M R Wharton
**Co. Secretary:** Mrs Sandra Wharton
**Responsibilities**
**Health & Safety:** Gary Minns *(Construction Manager)*
**US SIC:** 1522, 1541
**UK SIC:** 50100
**Bankers:** Barclays Bank Plc (20-25-29)

| | 30-09-13 | 30-09-12 | 30-09-11 |
|---|---|---|---|
| TA | 1,692,192 | 2,088,972 | 1,564,419 |
| NW | 1,027,400 | 1,007,347 | 974,785 |
| WC | 888,533 | 877,881 | 828,941 |

DUNS 21-814-1018

## Whartons Nurseries Ltd

**(Subsidiary of:** Whartons Holdings Ltd)
South Green, Harleston Road, Pulham St Mary, Diss, Norfolk IP21 4RP
**Tel:** 01379-606020 **Fax:** 01379608983
**Web:** www.whartons.co.uk
**Reg No:** 0441069 **VAT No:** 106047016
**Estd:** 1947 Private Limited Company
**Line of Business:** Nurserymen
**Trading Style:** Whartons Nurseries Ltd
**Issued Capital:** £5,000
**Principals:** R J Wharton *(Managing)*, P J Wharton
**Co. Secretary:** Ms Mary Wharton
**US SIC:** 0851 **UK SIC:** 02000
**Auditors:** Larking Gowen
**Bankers:** Barclays Bank Plc (20-92-08)

| | 31-08-13 | 31-08-12 | 31-08-11 |
|---|---|---|---|
| TA | 2,326,703 | 2,027,819 | 2,425,951 |
| NW | 1,197,812 | 1,198,633 | 1,182,370 |
| WC | 1,215,737 | 1,216,191 | 1,182,295 |

DUNS 23-875-3235 **Imp**

## What More U K Ltd

**(Subsidiary of:** 0404 Investments Ltd)
Pendle Court, Unit 4, Shuttleworth Mead Business P, Burnley, Lancashire BB12 7NG
**Tel:** 01282-677030 **Fax:** 01282-772778
**Web:** www.manuplastic.com
**Reg No:** 3866672 **VAT No:** 748318117
**Estd:** 1999 Private Limited Company
**Line of Business:** Plastic injection moulding
**Export Sales:** £5,959,006
**Trading Style:** What More U K Ltd

**Issued Capital:** £1,700,010
**Directors:** I Sellick, Ms V Hargreaves, J A Grimshaw, Ms J M Holt, A Riley, A M Holt, R S Tout
**Co. Secretary:** Ms Josephine Dyson
**US SIC:** 3079 **UK SIC:** 48360
**Auditors:** CLB Coopers

| | 31-12-13 | 31-12-12 | 31-12-11 |
|---|---|---|---|
| TO | 38,319,872 | 39,278,373 | 38,345,361 |
| P/L | 4,146,375 | 3,852,891 | 2,644,666 |
| NW | 11,525,589 | 10,154,058 | 7,213,241 |
| WC | 1,763,085 | 2,882,377 | (828,456) |
| Emp. | 153 | 153 | 149 |

DUNS 34-653-0962 Imp

## What Stores Ltd

(**Subsidiary of:** Celebration Investments Ltd)
507 Newport Road, Cardiff, South Glamorgan CF23 9AD
**Tel:** 029-2048-6380
**Reg No:** 5458586 **Estd:** 2007 Private Limited Company
**Line of Business:** Departmental stores
**Issued Capital:** £100
**Directors:** Ms H C Rajani, P Rajani, Miss S Rajani, Ms H C Rajani
**US SIC:** 5399 **UK SIC:** 65600

| | 30-06-13 | 30-06-12 | 30-06-11 |
|---|---|---|---|
| TO | 11,233,064 | 10,044,365 | 11,847,674 |
| P/L | 506,720 | 798,094 | 1,068,646 |
| NW | 1,857,190 | 1,410,335 | 997,437 |
| WC | 1,014,655 | 883,461 | 951,121 |
| Emp. | 121 | 105 | 111 |

DUNS 21-620-9643 Exp

## Whatman International Ltd

(**Subsidiary of:** General Electric Company)
Springfield Mill, James Whatman Way, Sandling Road, Maidstone, Kent ME14 2LE
**Tel:** 01622676670
**Web:** www.gehealthcare.com
**Reg No:** 0106789 **Estd:** 1910 Private Limited Company
**Line of Business:** Paper and pulp mills
**Export Markets:** U S A, Western Europe, S America, Africa, S & S E Asia, Australasia, Canada
**Trading Style:** Ge Healthcare
**Issued Capital:** £62,296,941
**Directors:** Ms M Vavassori, K P Murphy, E R Roman
**Co. Secretary:** Andrew Lester
**Responsibilities**
**Senior:** Vollmer Bomfim *(General Manager)*, Kevin Bussey *(General Manager)*, John Case *(Manager)*, Jan Erneberg *(Manager)*
**Branches:** Whatman International Ltd, Springfield Mill, Sandling Road, Maidstone, Kent ME14 2LE
**US SIC:** 2611, 2631
**UK SIC:** 47101, 47017
**Auditors:** PricewaterhouseCoopers LLP
**Bankers:** National Westminster Bank Plc (60-60-08)

| | 31-12-13 | 31-12-12 | 31-12-11 |
|---|---|---|---|
| TO | 35,913,000 | 33,390,000 | 35,101,000 |
| P/L | 9,640,000 | 7,480,000 | (1,634,000) |
| NW | 213,467,000 | 204,205,000 | 196,331,000 |
| WC | (13,713,000) | (23,954,000) | 199,563,000 |
| Emp. | 109 | 123 | 137 |

DUNS 39-761-5279

## What's on Tickets Ltd

Dane Mill Roadhurst Lane, Congleton, Cheshire CW12 1LA
**Tel:** 01260271145 **Fax:** 01260288666
**Web:** www.circus-starr.co.uk
**Reg No:** 2198551 **VAT No:** 482247341
**Estd:** 1988 Private Limited Company
**Line of Business:** Live theatrical presentation
**Trading Style:** Circus Starr
**Issued Capital:** £3
**Director:** Ms C A Briggs
**Responsibilities**
**Finance:** Michelle Crossley *(Senior Finance Administrator)*
**Marketing:** Terri Lowe *(PR & Marketing Coordinator)*
**US SIC:** 7922 **UK SIC:** 97412
**Bankers:** Barclays Bank Plc (20-53-77)

| | 31-12-13 | 31-12-12 | 31-12-11 |
|---|---|---|---|
| TA | 27,370 | 6,730 | 18,094 |
| NW | 387 | (2,725) | (28,292) |
| WC | 387 | (2,725) | (28,292) |

DUNS 21-445-6980

## W.H.B. Sutherland Ltd

43 Victoria Street, Kirkwall, Orkney KW15 1DN
**Tel:** 01856-873240
**Web:** www.whbsutherland.ik.com
**Reg No:** 0033752SC **VAT No:** 265306073
**Estd:** 1959 Private Limited Company
**Line of Business:** Representative office
**Trading Style:** Sutherland's Chemist
**Issued Capital:** £8,879
**Directors:** E Clyde, H Clyde Jnr
**Co. Secretary:** Ms Iris Clyde
**Responsibilities**
**Senior:** Hugh Clyde *(Director)*, Torquil Clyde *(Manager)*
**Finance:** Torquil Clyde *(Manager)*
**Admin:** Sue Foubister *(Office Manager)*
**HR:** Sue Foubister *(Office Manager)*
**Health & Safety:** Caroline MacGuire *(General Manager)*
**Branches:** W.h.b. Sutherland Ltd, 16 Traill Street, Thurso, Caithness KW14 8EJ
**US SIC:** 5912, 7395
**UK SIC:** 64300, 49300
**Auditors:** Foubister & Bain
**Bankers:** The Royal Bank Of Scotland Plc (83-24-07)

| | 31-03-14 | 31-03-13 | 31-03-12 |
|---|---|---|---|
| TA | 2,100,193 | 2,280,723 | 2,433,136 |
| NW | 991,472 | 1,032,610 | 881,070 |
| WC | 105,731 | 171,857 | 44,701 |

DUNS 21-202-2602 Exp

## W.H.Bowker Ltd

Holme Road, Bamber Bridge, Preston, Lancashire PR5 6BP
**Tel:** 01772-628800
**Web:** www.bowkertransport.co.uk
**Reg No:** 0364757 **VAT No:** 175696415
**Estd:** 1919 Private Limited Company
**Line of Business:** Road haulage and transport services
**Issued Capital:** £162,000
**Principals:** W H Bowker *(Chairman and Managing)*, Ms V Bowker, Ms H Bowker, A P Bowker, W H Bowker, K N Bowker, Ms C J Bowker, K N Bowker
**Co. Secretary:** Darren Thomason
**Responsibilities**
**Senior:** Elizabeth Griffiths *(Director)*, Dennis Turner *(Manager)*, Geoffrey Whittle *(Manager)*
**Finance:** Nigel Bellis *(Financial Director)*
**Marketing:** Dennis Turner *(Manager)*
**IT:** Jason Tiffen *(Computer Operations Manager)*, Geff Whittle *(Data Communications Manager)*
**Health & Safety:** Alan Partington *(Health & Safety Officer)*
**Facilities:** Jim Roach *(Facilities Manager)*
**Purchasing:** Nigel Bellis *(Financial Director)*, Peter Osterbyhansen *(Purchasing Manager)*
**Branches:** W.h.bowker Ltd, Old Jamaica Rd, London SE16 4SU
**US SIC:** 4789, 4226
**UK SIC:** 77002, 77003
**Auditors:** PM&M
**Bankers:** Lloyds TSB Bank plc (30-90-87)

| | 31-12-13 | 31-12-12 | 31-12-11 |
|---|---|---|---|
| TO | 114,155,000 | 105,203,000 | 87,237,000 |
| P/L | 1,899,000 | 2,071,000 | 1,369,000 |
| NW | 10,119,000 | 9,429,000 | 7,936,000 |
| WC | (701,000) | 21,000 | 840,000 |
| Emp. | 356 | 344 | 316 |

DUNS 23-894-1749

## Wheal Jane Ltd

Fairbrook House, Clover Nook Road, Cotes Park Industrial Estate, Somercotes, Alfreton, Derbyshire DE55 4RF
**Tel:** 01872560200 **Fax:** 01773842109
**Web:** www.camon-contracting.co.uk
**Reg No:** 3885040 **Estd:** 1999 Private Limited Company
**Line of Business:** Sanitation, remediation and similar activities
**Issued Capital:** £20,000
**Directors:** G J Stephens, D Evans, M Giddings, D M Giddings, B J Ballard
**Co. Secretary:** Graham Stephens
**US SIC:** 4959, 5039
**UK SIC:** 92110, 61300
**Auditors:** Grant Thornton
**Bankers:** National Westminster Bank Plc (52-21-34)

| | 28-02-14 | 28-02-13 | 29-02-12 |
|---|---|---|---|
| TA | 2,254,072 | 2,060,053 | 1,623,125 |
| NW | 1,518,674 | 1,098,938 | 850,243 |
| WC | 1,253,751 | 842,727 | 564,455 |

DUNS 34-972-0354

## Wheatbridge Development Llp

30 Wheatbridge Road, Chesterfield, Derbyshire S40 2AB
**Tel:** 01246277287
**Web:** www.wheatbridge.co.uk
**Reg No:** 0318876OC **Estd:** 2006
**Line of Business:** Doctors
**US SIC:** 8011 **UK SIC:** 95300

| | 31-03-14 | 31-03-13 | 31-03-12 |
|---|---|---|---|
| TA | 9,730,131 | 9,846,344 | 9,784,332 |
| NW | 2,372,554 | 2,372,554 | 2,208,980 |
| WC | 85,237 | 216,086 | 166,508 |

DUNS 49-131-3409

## Wheatcroft (Worksop) Ltd

(**Subsidiary of:** Wheatcroft Motor Holdings Ltd)
Old Manton Wood Colliery Site, Retford Road, Worksop, Nottinghamshire S80 2RZ
**Tel:** 01909501111 **Fax:** 01909-482648
**Web:** www.walkersmotorgroup.co.uk
**Reg No:** 3105115 **Estd:** 2008 Private Limited Company
**Line of Business:** Car dealers (new & used)
**Trading Style:** Walkers of Worksop
**Issued Capital:** £161,560
**Principals:** J Wheatcroft *(Managing)*, P Wheatcroft, Motors Directors Limited, D R Bowden
**Co. Secretary:** Motors Secretaries Limited
**US SIC:** 5511 **UK SIC:** 65100
**Auditors:** Grant Thornton
**Bankers:** National Westminster Bank Plc (60-70-08)

| | 31-12-13 | 31-12-12 | 31-12-11 |
|---|---|---|---|
| TO | 15,183,229 | 12,871,854 | 10,661,180 |
| P/L | 37,981 | 120,063 | 26,559 |
| NW | 1,194,577 | 1,291,301 | 1,245,411 |
| WC | 274,743 | 386,981 | 358,704 |
| Emp. | 48 | 50 | 51 |

DUNS 21-213-1671

## Wheatlands Nursing Home

Larbert Road, Bonnybridge, Stirlingshire FK4 1ED
**Tel:** 01324814561
**Web:** www.balhousiecare.co.uk
**Estd:** 1989 Partnership
**Line of Business:** Nursing homes
**Partner:** Mrs J Davis
**Responsibilities**
**Senior:** Grace Sloan *(Home Manager)*, Ian Smallwood *(Home Manager)*
**US SIC:** 8051 **UK SIC:** 95100
**Employees:** 53

DUNS 52-004-0692

## Wheatley M & E Services Ltd

Lotherton Court, Lotherton Way, Leeds, West Yorkshire LS25 2JY
**Tel:** 01132877411
**Web:** www.mesonelectrical.com
**Reg No:** 3371035 **Estd:** 2011 Private Limited Company
**Line of Business:** Bridge, tunnel & elevated road builders
**Trading Style:** Wheatley Mechanical and Electrical Building Services, Meson Electrical Services
**Issued Capital:** £20,080
**Director:** N P Wheatley
**Co. Secretary:** Mrs Dawn Downie
**Responsibilities**
**Senior:** James Hennigan *(Manager)*
**US SIC:** 1622, 1731, 1711
**UK SIC:** 50200, 50300
**Auditors:** Clough & Co LLP

| | 31-03-14 | 31-03-13 | 31-03-12 |
|---|---|---|---|
| TA | 1,116,551 | 1,876,098 | 1,579,789 |
| NW | 230,480 | 167,441 | 150,146 |
| WC | 180,671 | 111,633 | 92,783 |

DUNS 23-636-9500

## Wheatley Park School

Holton, Wheatley, Holton, Oxford, Oxfordshire OX33 1QH
**Tel:** 01865-872441
**Web:** www.wheatleyparkschool.co.uk
**Estd:** 1974
**Line of Business:** Schools (local authority)
**Directors:** N Young, Ms I Bull
**Responsibilities**
**IT:** Roger Nixon *(IT Manager)*
**US SIC:** 8211 **UK SIC:** 93200
**Bankers:** Lloyds TSB Bank plc (30-96-35)
**Employees:** 160

DUNS 29-107-0233

## Wheaton Uk Ltd

(**Subsidiary of:** Wheaton Industries Inc.)
Transpennine Trading Estate, Rochdale, Lancashire OL11 2PX
**Tel:** 01706-356444
**Web:** http://wheaton-uk.com
**Reg No:** 1515665 **VAT No:** 306344091
**Estd:** 1980 Private Limited Company
**Line of Business:** Laboratory supplies
**Export Sales:** £1,095,570
**Issued Capital:** £100,000
**Directors:** W Brinster, T E Kohut, G T Topping
**Responsibilities**
**Senior:** Peter Elmore *(Manager)*, Lynda Elmore *(Manager)*, Brian Eves *(Stores Manager)*, Danine Freeman *(Manager)*
**HR:** Jane Camps *(Human Resources Manager)*
**Health & Safety:** Jane Camps *(Human Resources Manager)*
**Purchasing:** Brett Kuczer *(Purchasing Officer)*
**Fleet:** Brian Eves *(Stores Manager)*
**US SIC:** 5199 **UK SIC:** 61900
**Auditors:** HLB Kidsons
**Bankers:** National Westminster Bank Plc (56-00-09)

| | 31-12-13 | 31-12-12 | 31-12-11 |
|---|---|---|---|
| TO | 7,254,933 | 7,204,251 | 8,778,496 |
| P/L | 928,589 | 687,759 | 830,928 |
| NW | 5,761,068 | 5,100,495 | 4,580,104 |
| WC | 5,190,839 | 4,456,279 | 3,996,157 |
| Emp. | 94 | 89 | 88 |

DUNS 45-883-5493

## Wheatsheaf Investments Ltd

The Quarry Hill Road, Eccleston, Chester, Cheshire CH4 9HQ
**Tel:** 01244670970
**Web:** www.wheatsheafinvestments.com
**Reg No:** 3221116 **Estd:** 1996 Private Limited Company
**Line of Business:** Management activities of holding companies
**Issued Capital:** £10,813,821
**Directors:** G P Ramsbottom, F A Scott, J H Newsum, W B Kendall, P L Doyle
**Co. Secretary:** Geoffrey Chadwick
**US SIC:** 6711 **UK SIC:** 83962
**Auditors:** Deloitte & Touche
**Bankers:** HSBC Bank plc (40-17-14)

| | 31-03-14 | 31-03-13 | 31-03-12 |
|---|---|---|---|
| TO | 32,777,000 | 33,980,000 | 37,766,000 |
| P/L | (2,457,000) | (156,000) | (9,111,000) |
| NW | 41,199,000 | 20,765,000 | 20,937,000 |
| WC | 12,941,000 | 5,788,000 | 7,733,000 |
| Emp. | 370 | 330 | 379 |

DUNS 21-783-4994

## Wheatstone Inn

Centre Seven, Gloucester, Gloucestershire GL4 3HR
**Tel:** 01452634360
**Web:** www.chefandbrewer.com
**Estd:** 2001 Proprietorship
**Line of Business:** Public house
**Proprietor:** A Bacon
**Responsibilities**
**Senior:** Alistair Baker *(Branch Manager)*, Kerry Paine *(General Manager)*
**US SIC:** 5813 **UK SIC:** 66200
**Employees:** 76

DUNS 21-882-5966 Imp

## Wheelabrator Group Ltd

(**Subsidiary of:** Wgh Holding Corp)
Unit 5 Sandy Lane Business Park, Sandy Lane, Coventry, West Midlands CV1 4DQ
**Tel:** 02476258811 **Fax:** 01619-290-381
**Web:** www.noricangroup.com
**Reg No:** 0033672 **VAT No:** 561007967
**Estd:** 1908 Private Limited Company
**Line of Business:** Metal finishing and polishing services
**Export Sales:** £15,442,000
**Trading Style:** Norican Group, Spencer Halstead, Tightman Wheelabrator, Bct Spares / Impact Finishers
**Issued Capital:** £1,374,353
**Directors:** A J Matsuyama, I Bird
**Co. Secretary:** Neil Moseley
**Responsibilities**
**Senior:** Christian Tyroll *(Site Manager)*
**Branches:** Wheelabrator Group Ltd, 107-109 Whitby Rd, Slough, Berkshire SL1 3DR
**US SIC:** 3499, 3291
**UK SIC:** 31694, 24600
**Auditors:** BDO LLP
**Bankers:** HSBC Bank plc (40-41-07)

| | 31-12-13 | 31-12-12 | 31-12-11 |
|---|---|---|---|
| TO | 29,747,000 | 34,392,000 | 32,489,000 |
| P/L | 2,921,000 | 870,000 | (684,000) |
| NW | 22,326,000 | 19,342,000 | 18,559,000 |
| WC | 28,705,000 | 25,902,000 | 24,472,000 |
| Emp. | 123 | 126 | 132 |

DUNS 67-208-8507

## Wheelbase Holdings Ltd

Lower Eccleshill Road, Darwen, Lancashire BB3 0RP
**Tel:** 01254-819399
**Web:** www.wheelbase.net
**Reg No:** 6017040 **Estd:** 2006 Private Limited Company
**Line of Business:** Management activities of production holding companies
**Trading Style:** Wheelbase Engineering
**Issued Capital:** £1,600,000
**Director:** S D Pickles
**Co. Secretary:** Christopher Pickles
**US SIC:** 6711 **UK SIC:** 83962

| | 30-09-13 | 30-09-12 | 30-09-11 |
|---|---|---|---|
| TO | 7,093,671 | 6,674,921 | 4,881,673 |
| P/L | 584,484 | 373,249 | 363,080 |
| NW | 2,075,790 | 1,514,736 | 1,362,906 |
| WC | 1,128,555 | 663,875 | 601,466 |
| Emp. | 90 | 89 | 62 |

DUNS 50-458-5852
## Wheeldon Brothers Ltd
Wheeldon House Prime Enterprise Park, Prime Park Way, Derby, Derbyshire DE1 3QB
**Web:** www.wheeldon.co.uk
**Reg No:** 2441153 **Estd:** 1989 Private Limited Company
**Line of Business:** Residential property developers
**Trading Style:** Wheeldon Homes
**Issued Capital:** £1,436,481
**Directors:** E P Parkin, J H Parkin, P W Parkin
**Co. Secretary:** David Brookes
**Branches:** Wheeldon Brothers Ltd, Roman Road, Derby, Derbyshire DE1 3RX
**US SIC:** 6552, 1541, 6531, 6519
**UK SIC:** 85000, 50100, 83400
**Auditors:** Mabe Allen LLP
**Bankers:** National Westminster Bank Plc (60-12-01)

| | 30-06-14 | 30-06-13 | 30-06-12 |
|---|---|---|---|
| TO | 11,009,106 | 12,458,400 | 9,213,808 |
| P/L | 1,382,037 | 1,172,555 | 603,059 |
| NW | 9,011,766 | 8,576,529 | 7,945,192 |
| WC | 12,939,558 | 10,794,799 | 8,539,679 |
| Emp. | 106 | 93 | 76 |

DUNS 23-523-5223
## Wheeldon Brothers Waste Ltd
Unit 8 Yeargate Industrial Estate, Bury, Lancashire BL9 7HT
**Tel:** 0161-764-8888
**Web:** www.wheeldonbrothers.co.uk
**Reg No:** 0843156 **VAT No:** 146288742
**Estd:** 1991 Private Limited Company
**Line of Business:** Skip hire
**Issued Capital:** £9,786
**Principals:** J B Wheeldon *(Managing)*, Mrs G M Wheeldon *(Managing)*, J E Wheeldon, J M Wheeldon
**Co. Secretary:** Mrs Susan Ward
**Branches:** Wheeldon Brothers Waste Ltd, Moss Lane, Oldham, Lancashire OL2 6HR
**US SIC:** 4953 **UK SIC:** 92110
**Auditors:** A E Tupman & Co
**Bankers:** Barclays Bank Plc (20-16-08)

| | 31-07-14 | 31-07-13 | 31-07-12 |
|---|---|---|---|
| TO | 8,430,633 | 6,187,170 | 5,526,044 |
| P/L | 380,612 | 369,557 | 130,685 |
| NW | 3,829,637 | 3,687,497 | 3,417,852 |
| WC | 2,421,802 | 1,840,199 | 1,499,202 |
| Emp. | 91 | 66 | 62 |

DUNS 73-712-6599
## Wheeler Higgins Ltd
13 Silver Road, London W12 7RR
**Tel:** 02087351000
**Web:** www.ctshirts.co.uk
**Reg No:** 2914928 **Estd:** 1994 Private Limited Company
**Line of Business:** Representative office
**Trading Style:** Charles Tyrwhitt
**Issued Capital:** £1,000
**Director:** N C Wheeler
**Co. Secretary:** Peter Higgins
**Branches:** Wheeler Higgins Ltd, 47 Pingle Drive, Bicester, Oxfordshire OX26 6WD
**US SIC:** 5961 **UK SIC:** 65600
**Auditors:** PricewaterhouseCoopers LLP
**Bankers:** National Westminster Bank Plc (60-40-05)

| | 03-08-13 | 28-07-12 | 30-08-11 |
|---|---|---|---|
| TA | 9,423,000 | 9,423,000 | 9,423,000 |
| P/L | 142,000 | 98,000 | 52,000 |
| NW | 1,337,000 | 1,323,000 | 1,239,000 |
| WC | (6,696,000) | (6,710,000) | (5,309,000) |

DUNS 22-558-9928
## Wheeler's (Westbury) Ltd
31 D Link Road, Westbury, Wiltshire BA13 4JB
**Fax:** 01373858045
**Web:** www.wheelers-westbury.co.uk
**Reg No:** 1682288 **VAT No:** 328201781
**Estd:** 1974 Private Limited Company
**Line of Business:** Electrical contractors and electricians
**Issued Capital:** £14,600
**Principals:** R A Norris *(Managing)*, T W Meehan, G Caldicott, K Borgeat
**Co. Secretary:** Mrs Carol Norris
**Responsibilities**
**IT:** Stewart Ackland *(IT Manager)*
**US SIC:** 6711, 7399
**UK SIC:** 83962, 83954
**Auditors:** Berkeley Hall Ltd
**Bankers:** National Westminster Bank Plc (60-21-40)

| | 31-12-13 | 31-12-12 | 31-12-11 |
|---|---|---|---|
| TO | 8,636,660 | 8,464,867 | 8,256,240 |
| P/L | 625,000 | 393,237 | 559,601 |
| NW | 2,649,840 | 2,149,714 | 1,818,150 |
| WC | 2,333,024 | 1,846,378 | 1,551,033 |
| Emp. | 81 | 79 | 81 |

DUNS 21-811-1448
## Wheelhouse Restaurant & Bar
Millennium Wheel Drive, Camelon, Falkirk, Stirlingshire FK1 4AD
**Tel:** 01324673490
**Web:** www.wheelhousefalkirk.com
**Estd:** 2012
**Line of Business:** Restaurants
**Proprietor:** M Binnie
**US SIC:** 5812 **UK SIC:** 66110
**Employees:** 50

DUNS 42-365-9317 **Imp**
## Wheelies
Kingsway Business Centre Kingsway, Swansea, West Glamorgan SA5 4DL
**Tel:** 01792-583000
**Web:** www.wheelies.co.uk
**VAT No:** 484544617 **Estd:** 1988 Partnership
**Line of Business:** Bicycle and accessory retailers
**Partners:** K Jones, M Jones
**Branches:** 34 Uplands Cres, Swansea
**US SIC:** 6311 **UK SIC:** 82002
**Bankers:** HSBC Bank plc (40-43-31)
**Employees:** 60

DUNS 21-602-3185
## Wheelpower
Guttmann Road, Aylesbury, Buckinghamshire HP21 9PA
**Tel:** 01296395995
**Web:** www.wheelpower.org.uk
**Estd:** 2002
**Line of Business:** Operation of other sports arenas and stadiums not elsewhere classified
**Responsibilities**
**Senior:** Martin Mcelhatton *(Chief Executive)*
**US SIC:** 7999 **UK SIC:** 97913
**Employees:** 82

DUNS 21-065-4506
## Wheely Clean Bins
2d Mossgiel Road, Cumbernauld, Glasgow, Lanarkshire G67 2EY
**Estd:** 1991 Proprietorship
**Line of Business:** Blast cleaning
**Proprietor:** K Anderson
**US SIC:** 1799 **UK SIC:** 50000
**Employees:** 350

DUNS 22-503-6573
## Whelan & Grant (Holdings) Ltd
Clare House, Thames Street, Walton-On-Thames, Surrey KT12 2PU
**Web:** www.whelanandgrant.com
**Reg No:** 1165940 **VAT No:** 219268451
**Estd:** 1974 Private Limited Company
**Line of Business:** Building of complete constructions or parts thereof; civil engineering
**Trading Style:** Whelan & Grant Contractors Ltd
**Issued Capital:** £1,000
**Directors:** L N Grant, J J Whelan, S E George, M Ottway
**Co. Secretary:** Ms Catherine Grant
**Responsibilities**
**Senior:** Peter Cusack *(Finance Director)*, Brian Gilbert *(Manager)*, Russell White *(Manager)*
**Finance:** Peter Cusack *(Finance Director)*
**US SIC:** 7399 **UK SIC:** 83954
**Auditors:** Deloitte & Touche
**Bankers:** The Royal Bank Of Scotland Plc (16-01-23)

| | 30-06-14 | 30-06-13 | 30-06-12 |
|---|---|---|---|
| TO | 24,386,379 | 21,965,726 | 20,198,916 |
| P/L | 2,053,940 | 915,940 | 956,176 |
| NW | 9,342,652 | 8,362,506 | 7,989,633 |
| WC | 8,965,751 | 7,927,615 | 7,635,535 |
| Emp. | 101 | 88 | 83 |

DUNS 22-767-9768
## Whelan Environmental Services Ltd
**(Subsidiary of:** Jarron Developments Ltd)
Lindon Road, Brownhills, Walsall, West Midlands WS8 7BB
**Tel:** 0800626274
**Reg No:** 1250398 **Estd:** 1976 Private Limited Company
**Line of Business:** Sanitation, remediation and similar activities
**Trading Style:** Merlin Oils
**Issued Capital:** £55
**Director:** B J Cackett
**Co. Secretary:** Ms Lynda Headley
**US SIC:** 4959 **UK SIC:** 92110
**Bankers:** HSBC Bank plc (40-11-36)

| | 31-12-13 | 31-12-12 | 31-12-11 |
|---|---|---|---|
| TA | 55 | 55 | 55 |
| NW | 55 | 55 | 55 |

DUNS 22-687-7355
## Wherry Hotel
Bridge Road, Oulton Broad, Lowestoft, Suffolk NR32 3LN
**Web:** www.elizabethhotels.co.uk
**Estd:** 1988 Partnership
**Line of Business:** Hotels
**Partners:** D Iredale, A Braithwaite
**Responsibilities**
**Senior:** Ian Cate *(General Manager)*, Tim Kenworthy *(General Manager)*
**US SIC:** 7011 **UK SIC:** 66500
**Bankers:** National Westminster Bank Plc (53-50-03)
**Employees:** 55

DUNS 23-261-1483
## Wherry Housing Association Ltd
6 Central Avenue, Norwich, Norfolk NR7 0HR
**Tel:** 01983521114 **Fax:** 01603700404
**Web:** www.circle.org.uk
**Reg No:** 0026622IP **VAT No:** 532893036
**Estd:** 1990 Friendly Society
**Line of Business:** Housing associations societies trusts & co-operatives
**Principals:** K G Shipman *(Chairman)*, S Beadle, Mrs T Ripley, P Matthew, R Shelton, N Price, J Walters, Mrs C Savory
**Co. Secretary:** P Lewis
**Responsibilities**
**Senior:** C Chaundy-Brain *(Director)*, B Dennison *(Director)*, E Ede *(Director)*, Sue Staders *(Manager)*
**Finance:** Jodie Cunnington-Brock *(Financial Manager)*, James Francis *(Financial Director)*
**Admin:** Kim Bingham *(Personal Assistant)*
**Branches:** Wherry Housing Association Ltd, Maingay House, Abbots Close, Aylsham, Norwich, Norfolk NR11 6HQ
**US SIC:** 8321 **UK SIC:** 96111
**Auditors:** KPMG
**Bankers:** National Westminster Bank Plc (60-15-31)

| | 31-03-12 | 31-03-11 | 31-03-10 |
|---|---|---|---|
| TO | 30,651,000 | 30,920,000 | 32,223,000 |
| P/L | (1,837,000) | 1,261,000 | 173,000 |
| NW | (916,000) | 649,000 | (488,000) |
| WC | (261,701,000) | (252,831,000) | (246,017,000) |
| Emp. | 89 | 86 | 78 |

DUNS 21-102-1060
## Whessoe Engineering Ltd
Whessoe Technology Centre, Morton Palms, Darlington, County Durham DL1 4WB
**Tel:** 01325390000 **Fax:** 01325-390001
**Web:** www.whessoe.co.uk
**Reg No:** 6453867 **Estd:** 2007 Private Limited Company
**Line of Business:** Other engineering activities
**Export Sales:** £3,832,000
**Trading Style:** Whessoe Computing Systems
**Issued Capital:** £100
**Directors:** S U Kim, Y H Hyun
**Responsibilities**
**Senior:** Will Mcnaughton *(General Manager)*, Hyun Yi *(Manager)*
**Branches:** Whessoe Engineering Ltd, Whessoe Technology Centre, Alderman Best Way, Darlington, County Durham DL1 4WB
**US SIC:** 8911 **UK SIC:** 83701
**Auditors:** KPMG LLP

| | 31-12-13 | 31-12-12 | 31-12-11 |
|---|---|---|---|
| TO | 4,619,000 | 2,794,000 | 2,391,000 |
| P/L | 1,368,000 | (1,635,000) | (20,000) |
| NW | 1,793,000 | (2,685,000) | (603,000) |
| WC | 1,353,000 | (2,941,000) | (952,000) |
| Emp. | 58 | 60 | 7 |

DUNS 21-906-1223
## Wheyfeed Ltd
**(Subsidiary of:** Stichting Administratiekantoor Forfarmers)
Melton Road, Stanton-On-The-Wolds, Keyworth, Nottingham, Nottinghamshire NG12 5PJ
**Web:** www.wheyfeed.co.uk
**Reg No:** 0696243 **Estd:** 1961 Private Limited Company
**Line of Business:** Farming of swine
**Export Sales:** £346,899
**Issued Capital:** £5,977
**Directors:** F G Thomson, I Gardner, A E Traas, Y M Knoop
**Co. Secretary:** Andrew Gillard
**Responsibilities**
**Senior:** Stuart Bridge *(Manager)*, Liz Shilton *(Sales Director)*
**Sales:** Liz Shilton *(Sales Director)*
**US SIC:** 0213, 5153
**UK SIC:** 01001, 61100
**Auditors:** Higson & Co

**Bankers:** Lloyds TSB Bank plc (30-18-98)

| | 31-05-13 | 31-05-12 | 31-05-11 |
|---|---|---|---|
| TO | 10,021,405 | 5,870,881 | 9,210,024 |
| P/L | 398,568 | 74,305 | 144,945 |
| NW | 1,274,059 | 1,166,540 | 1,085,857 |
| WC | (208,649) | (45,444) | (119,994) |
| Emp. | 82 | 68 | 80 |

DUNS 21-114-7284
## W.H.Good Group Ltd
W.H.G.H. Limited, Carrs Industrial Estate, Rossendale, Lancashire BB4 5JT
**Web:** www.whgood.co.uk
**Reg No:** 6551875 **Estd:** 2008 Private Limited Company
**Line of Business:** Management activities of holding companies
**Issued Capital:** £2,190,300
**Directors:** P M Sumner, D P Sumner, J Sumner
**Co. Secretary:** Paul Sumner
**Responsibilities**
**Senior:** John Lowson *(Manager)*
**US SIC:** 6711 **UK SIC:** 83962
**Bankers:** National Westminster Bank Plc (01-07-29)

| | 30-04-14 | 30-04-13 | 30-04-12 |
|---|---|---|---|
| TO | 12,024,173 | 13,073,872 | 12,461,799 |
| P/L | 1,175,663 | 1,160,814 | 497,243 |
| NW | 1,849,392 | 1,147,044 | 286,792 |
| WC | 2,865,571 | 2,241,162 | 1,501,305 |
| Emp. | 57 | 57 | 65 |

DUNS 21-705-2062
## Whickham Villa Care Centre
8 Millfield Road, Whickham, Newcastle-Upon-Tyne, Tyne and Wear NE16 4QA
**Web:** www.whickhamvilla.co.uk
**Estd:** 1984 Partnership
**Line of Business:** Nursing home for the elderly with 30 beds
**Partners:** Ms E Gallen, J Gallen
**Responsibilities**
**Marketing:** Kristel Gardner *(General Manager)*
**Sales:** Kristel Gardner *(General Manager)*
**HR:** Kristel Gardner *(General Manager)*
**Health & Safety:** Kristel Gardner *(General Manager)*
**Facilities:** Kristel Gardner *(General Manager)*
**Operations:** Kristel Gardner *(General Manager)*
**US SIC:** 8091, 8051
**UK SIC:** 95200, 95100
**Bankers:** Lloyds TSB Bank plc (30-91-50)
**Employees:** 100

DUNS 77-930-4401
## Whim Hall Nursing Home Ltd
Whim Estate, Lamancha, West Linton, Peeblesshire EH46 7BD
**Tel:** 01968678434
**Reg No:** 0157295SC **Estd:** 1995 Private Limited Company
**Line of Business:** Medical nursing home activities
**Issued Capital:** £100
**Directors:** Ms K A Hartland, G M Hartland
**Co. Secretary:** Dr Andrew Hartland
**US SIC:** 8051 **UK SIC:** 95100
**Auditors:** Adams Moore Audit Ltd
**Bankers:** Clydesdale Bank Plc (82-62-30)

| | 31-03-14 | 31-10-13 | 31-03-12 |
|---|---|---|---|
| NW | (279,906) | (279,906) | (279,706) |

DUNS 29-761-7367 **Imp**
## Whincroft Ltd
**(Subsidiary of:** Smeeth Holdings Ltd)
West House, Shearway Business Park, Pent Road, Folkestone, Kent CT19 4RJ
**Tel:** 01303297888 **Fax:** 01303-297877
**Web:** www.westdesignproducts.co.uk
**Reg No:** 2024811 **VAT No:** 444994213
**Estd:** 1986 Private Limited Company
**Line of Business:** Other retail sale in specialised stores not elsewhere classified
**Export Sales:** £553,194
**Trading Style:** Cross's
**Issued Capital:** £2,667
**Principals:** Mrs M Bray *(Managing)*, Mrs J C Pillai, O J Bray
**Co. Secretary:** Michael Bray
**Branches:** Whincroft Ltd, 119 Sandgate Road, Folkestone, Kent CT20 2BL
**US SIC:** 5199 **UK SIC:** 61900
**Auditors:** Illegible Auditor Name
**Bankers:** Girobank Plc (72-00-00)

| | 31-01-14 | 31-01-13 | 31-01-12 |
|---|---|---|---|
| TO | 15,259,145 | 13,666,630 | 12,294,891 |
| P/L | 1,048,281 | 150,258 | 8,786 |
| NW | 4,244,930 | 3,383,911 | 3,201,986 |
| WC | 2,377,248 | 1,672,332 | 1,210,361 |
| Emp. | 128 | 126 | 131 |

**DUNS 29-631-4156**
### Whinney Hill Stone Sales Ltd
(**Subsidiary of:** Suez Environnement Company)
Church Buildings Warth Road, Bury, Lancashire BL9 9NG
**Reg No:** 1957453 **VAT No:** 441919836
**Estd:** 1986 Private Limited Company
**Line of Business:** Other mining and quarrying not elsewhere classified
**Issued Capital:** £1,000
**Directors:** C A Chapron, D C Palmer-Jones
**Co. Secretary:** Mark Thompson
**Branches:** Whinney Hill Stone Sales Ltd, Whinney Hill Quarry, Whinney Hill Rd, Accrington, Lancashire BB5 5EN
**US SIC:** 1499 **UK SIC:** 23960
**Auditors:** Blueprint Audit Ltd
**Bankers:** National Westminster Bank Plc (01-01-42)

|    | 31-12-13 | 31-12-12 | 31-12-11 |
|----|----------|----------|----------|
| TA | 4,574,000 | 4,574,000 | 4,574,000 |
| NW | 4,574,000 | 4,574,000 | 4,574,000 |

**DUNS 76-983-1330**
### Whipp & Bourne Ltd
(**Subsidiary of:** Melrose Industries Plc)
Hawker Siddeley Switchgear, 2 Broadfield Distribution Centre, Heywood, Lancashire OL10 2TU
**Tel:** 01706632051 **Fax:** 01706-674236
**Web:** www.manchesterhasit.co.uk
**Reg No:** 2641487 **Estd:** 1991 Private Limited Company
**Line of Business:** Holding companies management activities
**Trading Style:** F K I Switchgear
**Issued Capital:** £703
**Directors:** G P Martin, S A Peckham, G E Barnes
**Co. Secretary:** Adam Westley
**US SIC:** 6711, 3643
**UK SIC:** 83962, 34203
**Auditors:** Ernst & Young LLP
Following financial data are in thousands

|    | 31-12-13 | 31-12-12 | 31-12-11 |
|----|----------|----------|----------|
| TA | 1,481,670 | 1,457,756 | 1,549,695 |
| P/L | 23,914 | 308,061 | 11,239 |
| NW | 1,481,670 | 1,457,756 | 1,549,695 |

**DUNS 21-826-5148**
### Whippet Coaches Ltd
(**Subsidiary of:** Tower Transit Group Ltd)
Buckingway Business Park, Rowles Way, Swavesey, Cambridge, Cambridgeshire CB24 4UG
**Tel:** 01954230011
**Web:** www.go-whippet.co.uk
**Reg No:** 0520428 **VAT No:** 213543985
**Estd:** 1953 Private Limited Company
**Line of Business:** Bus operators and stations
**Issued Capital:** £3,000
**Directors:** A D Leishman, N E Smith, P R Cox
**Co. Secretary:** Paul Cox
**US SIC:** 4119 **UK SIC:** 72200
**Auditors:** Kinnaird Hill
**Bankers:** Lloyds TSB Bank plc (30-94-47)

|    | 31-03-14 | 31-03-13 | 31-03-12 |
|----|----------|----------|----------|
| TA | 3,116,291 | 2,967,973 | 3,005,145 |
| NW | 2,315,451 | 2,322,781 | 2,256,434 |
| WC | 154,572 | 70,410 | 448,279 |

**DUNS 23-261-6933**
### Whipps Cross University Hospital Nhs Trust
Whipps Cross Hospital, London E11 1NR
**Tel:** 02085356502
**Web:** www.bartshealth.nhs.uk
**Estd:** 2001
**Line of Business:** Public sector hospital activities, including nhs trusts
**Issued Capital:** £1
**Principals:** G Barnes (Personnel), D Ward, A Morris, Dr L Moore, Dr J Hogan, Dr A Hakim, Ms C Geddes, Ms S Brown
**Responsibilities**
**Senior:** Peter Marrice (Executive Director)
**Marketing:** Mark Graver (Assistant Director, Communicat)
**Admin:** Helen Ferguson (Clerical Officer)
**HR:** Norma French (Human Resources Director), Simon Quantrill (Training Director)
**Branches:** Whipps Cross University Hospital Nhs Trust, Whipps Cross Hospital, Whipps Cross Road, London E11 1NR
**US SIC:** 9121, 8062
**UK SIC:** 91110, 95100
**Employees:** 3,500

**DUNS 29-044-8844**
### Whipsnade Wild Animal Park Ltd
(**Subsidiary of:** Zoological Society of London)
Whipsnade, Dunstable, Bedfordshire LU6 2LF
**Tel:** 01582872171 **Fax:** 01582-872649
**Web:** www.zsl.org
**Reg No:** 0990860 **Estd:** 1931 Private Limited Company
**Line of Business:** A zoo
**Issued Capital:** £196,000
**Directors:** Mrs A L Smith, P Rutteman
**Co. Secretary:** Ms Amanda Smith
**Responsibilities**
**Senior:** Ralph Armond (Manager)
**US SIC:** 8421, 7996
**UK SIC:** 97700, 97913
**Auditors:** Ernst & Young

|    | 31-12-13 | 31-12-12 | 31-12-11 |
|----|----------|----------|----------|
| TO | 3,373,016 | 2,915,310 | 2,840,920 |
| NW | 356,567 | 356,567 | 356,567 |
| WC | 356,567 | 356,567 | 356,567 |

**DUNS 21-775-3054**
### Whipton Hospital
Whipton Hospital, Hospital Lane, Exeter, Devon EX1 3RB
**Tel:** 01392208333
**Estd:** 1989 Proprietorship
**Line of Business:** Health authorities
**Proprietor:** Ms L Cooper
**Responsibilities**
**Senior:** Cathy Weeks (Matron)
**US SIC:** 8062 **UK SIC:** 95100
**Employees:** 100

**DUNS 22-804-0465**					Imp-Exp
### Whirlowdale Trading Co Ltd
Canklow Meadows Industrial Estate, Rotherham, South Yorkshire S60 2XL
**Tel:** 01709-829061
**Web:** www.whirlowdale.com
**Reg No:** 1202861 **VAT No:** 173830067
**Estd:** 1975 Private Limited Company
**Line of Business:** Packing crate and pallet suppliers
**Export Markets:** Netherlands; Belgium; France
**Export Sales:** £381,126
**Issued Capital:** £5,079
**Principals:** A Pearce (Sales), J M Fisher, M Russell, Ms C M Pearce
**Co. Secretary:** Andrew Pearce
**Responsibilities**
**Finance:** Graham Cheesebrough (Finance Director)
**Admin:** Jayne Hatton (Human Resources Manager)
**HR:** Jayne Hatton (Human Resources Manager)
**Purchasing:** Julie Swift (Purchase Ledger)
**Branches:** Whirlowdale Trading Co Ltd, The Willows, New Road, Rainham, Essex RM13 9ED
**US SIC:** 2449, 3079, 5199
**UK SIC:** 46402, 48360, 61900
**Auditors:** Hebblethwaites
**Bankers:** National Westminster Bank Plc (56-00-66)

|    | 31-03-14 | 31-03-13 | 31-03-12 |
|----|----------|----------|----------|
| TO | 15,876,452 | 17,324,935 | 18,267,265 |
| P/L | 917,739 | 113,209 | 1,390,697 |
| NW | 4,842,232 | 4,507,588 | 4,527,684 |
| WC | 2,918,697 | 2,921,218 | 2,973,095 |
| Emp. | 79 | 76 | 71 |

**DUNS 50-005-6247**					Imp
### Whirlpool (Uk) Ltd
(**Subsidiary of:** Whirlpool Corporation)
209 Purley Way, Croydon, Surrey CR9 4RY
**Tel:** 020-8649-5000 **Fax:** 020-8649-5060
**Web:** www.whirlpool.co.uk
**Reg No:** 2295156 **Estd:** 1988 Private Limited Company
**Line of Business:** Domestic appliances (servicing and repairs)
**Export Sales:** £198,000
**Issued Capital:** £12,000,000
**Directors:** D J Harrison, Miss N Matthews
**Co. Secretary:** Miss Nicola Matthews
**Responsibilities**
**Senior:** Irene Lenarduzzi (Director)
**HR:** Samantha Poole (Partner)
**Health & Safety:** Samantha Poole (Partner)
**Branches:** Whirlpool (Uk) Ltd, Transfesa Rd, Tonbridge, Kent TN12 6UY
**US SIC:** 5064, 3629
**UK SIC:** 61500, 34350
**Auditors:** Ernst & Young LLP
**Bankers:** Bank Of America, Na (16-50-50)

|    | 31-12-13 | 31-12-12 | 31-12-11 |
|----|----------|----------|----------|
| TO | 52,657,000 | 58,350,000 | 78,842,000 |
| P/L | 417,000 | 2,573,000 | 924,000 |
| NW | 19,312,000 | 20,960,000 | 20,169,000 |
| WC | 20,141,000 | 20,352,000 | 18,908,000 |
| Emp. | 78 | 94 | 113 |

**DUNS 49-432-1334**					Exp
### Whispering Smith Group Plc
Rajan House, 61 Great Ducie Street, Manchester M3 1RR
**Tel:** 01618313700 **Fax:** 0161-834-3716
**Web:** www.whisperingsmith.com
**Reg No:** 3143117 **Estd:** 1996 Public Limited Company
**Line of Business:** Holding company for subsidiaries engaged as clothing wholesalers and property investments
**Export Markets:** Worldwide
**Export Sales:** £8,844,743
**Issued Capital:** £300,000
**Director:** S Kumar
**Co. Secretary:** Rajan Kumar
**Branches:** Whispering Smith Group Plc, 245 Briscoe Lane, Manchester M40 2ST
**US SIC:** 6711, 5136
**UK SIC:** 83962, 61600
**Auditors:** DTE Business Advisers Ltd
**Bankers:** Barclays Bank Plc (20-16-08)

|    | 31-03-14 | 31-03-13 | 31-03-12 |
|----|----------|----------|----------|
| TO | 43,613,185 | 41,555,838 | 48,360,116 |
| P/L | 2,956,925 | 262,576 | 189,701 |
| NW | 33,308,506 | 31,046,712 | 30,931,551 |
| WC | 26,825,098 | 25,414,803 | 25,172,797 |
| Emp. | 116 | 111 | 131 |

**DUNS 21-326-4482**
### Whispering Willows Beauty Treatment
169 Glasgow Road, Dumbarton, Dunbartonshire G82 1RH
**Tel:** 01389-730700
**Web:** www.whisperingwillows.co.uk
**Estd:** 2008 Proprietorship
**Line of Business:** Beauty salons
**Responsibilities**
**Senior:** Alaine Welsh (Manager)
**US SIC:** 7231 **UK SIC:** 98200
**Employees:** 50

**DUNS 21-592-1049**
### Whistable Medical Practice Estuary View Medical Centre
Boorman Way Estuary View Business Park, Whitstable, Kent CT5 3SE
**Tel:** 01227284300
**Web:** www.whistablemedicalpractice.co.uk
**Estd:** 2010
**Line of Business:** Doctors
**Trading Style:** Vision Care
**Manager:** Ms C Nelson
**US SIC:** 8011 **UK SIC:** 95300
**Employees:** 50

**DUNS 42-429-4655**
### Whistl Uk Ltd
(**Subsidiary of:** Postnl N.V.)
Unit 1 Globeside Business Park, Fieldhouse Lane, Marlow, Buckinghamshire SL7 1HZ
**Tel:** 01628-891-644
**Web:** www.tntpost.co.uk
**Reg No:** 4417047 **Estd:** 2002 Private Limited Company
**Line of Business:** Courier activities other than national post activities
**Trading Style:** Tnt Post
**Issued Capital:** £36,897,152
**Directors:** N M Wells, M K Parmar, N G Polglass
**Co. Secretary:** John Evans
**Responsibilities**
**Senior:** Charles Neilson (Manager), Angus Russell (Manager)
**Branches:** Whistl Uk Ltd, 2-6 Frances Road, Windsor, Berkshire SL4 3AA
**US SIC:** 4311 **UK SIC:** 79010
**Auditors:** PricewaterhouseCoopers LLP
**Bankers:** HSBC Bank plc (40-35-43)

|    | 31-12-13 | 31-12-12 | 31-12-11 |
|----|----------|----------|----------|
| TO | 574,953,000 | 554,584,000 | 455,961,000 |
| P/L | (8,108,000) | 5,747,000 | 1,382,000 |
| NW | 19,891,000 | 26,269,000 | 22,247,000 |
| WC | 5,748,000 | 13,194,000 | 5,697,000 |
| Emp. | 1,725 | 1,228 | 818 |

**DUNS 23-117-5758**
### Whistledawn Ltd
214 Whitegate Drive, Blackpool, Lancashire FY3 9JL
**Tel:** 01253-316160 **Fax:** 01253316511
**Web:** www.northern-care.co.uk
**Reg No:** 3695088 **Estd:** 2011 Private Limited Company
**Line of Business:** Children's homes
**Trading Style:** Northern Care
**Issued Capital:** £200,002
**Directors:** W J Grace, Hx Management Limited
**Co. Secretary:** William Grace
**Responsibilities**
**Senior:** Kurt Denby (Chief Executive), Lisa Lattuca (Manager)
**Branches:** Whistledawn Ltd, 334 St. Annes Road, Blackpool, Lancashire FY4 2QN
**US SIC:** 8321 **UK SIC:** 96111

**Auditors:** Nick Brajkovich Ltd
**Bankers:** Bank Of Scotland (12-08-95)

|    | 31-01-13 | 31-01-12 | 31-01-11 |
|----|----------|----------|----------|
| TO | 25,046,349 | 24,308,310 | 24,119,145 |
| P/L | (984,946) | (2,304,937) | (861,056) |
| NW | 1,914,498 | 1,981,276 | 2,390,154 |
| WC | 5,144,005 | 3,893,953 | 2,530,237 |
| Emp. | 729 | 679 | 625 |

**DUNS 21-136-2814**
### The Whistledown Inn
6-7 Seaview, Warrenpoint, Newry, Co Down BT34 3NH
**Tel:** 028-4175-4174
**Web:** www.thewhistledownhotel.com
**Estd:** 1995 Proprietorship
**Line of Business:** Restaurant - pub food
**Proprietor:** C Mcavoy
**Responsibilities**
**Senior:** Colin McAvoy (Proprietor), Sarah Mcavoy (Partner)
**US SIC:** 7011 **UK SIC:** 66500
**Employees:** 50

**DUNS 22-718-2821**					Imp-Exp
### Whistles Ltd
(**Subsidiary of:** Whistles Holdings Ltd)
183 Eversholt Street, London NW1 1BU
**Fax:** 02073910970
**Web:** www.whistles.co.uk
**Reg No:** 1514754 **VAT No:** 918505615
**Estd:** 2008 Private Limited Company
**Line of Business:** Retail sale of clothing
**Export Markets:** Europe
**Export Sales:** £300,000
**Issued Capital:** £2,146
**Directors:** Ms J E Shepherdson, P G Mickler
**Co. Secretary:** Philip Mickler
**Responsibilities**
**Senior:** Laura Maynard (Manager)
**Branches:** Whistles Ltd, 19 Hill Street, Richmond, Surrey TW9 1SX
**US SIC:** 5699 **UK SIC:** 64500
**Auditors:** KPMG LLP
**Bankers:** HSBC Bank plc (40-05-15)

|    | 25-01-14 | 26-01-13 | 28-01-12 |
|----|----------|----------|----------|
| TO | 55,200,000 | 48,600,000 | 39,100,000 |
| P/L | 2,500,000 | 1,600,000 | (600,000) |
| NW | 6,300,000 | 4,500,000 | 2,200,000 |
| WC | 300,000 | (500,000) | (2,300,000) |
| Emp. | 630 | 571 | 537 |

**DUNS 76-921-1897**
### Whistlestop Foods Ltd
(**Subsidiary of:** S S P Group Plc)
Platform 19-15, Victoria Station, London SW1V 1JU
**Tel:** 020-7976-5533
**Web:** www.compass-group.co.uk
**Reg No:** 2618538 **Estd:** 1991 Private Limited Company
**Line of Business:** Convenience stores
**Issued Capital:** £200,000
**Directors:** M Rainbow, M E Collins, J D Brook, L L Tait, J O Davies
**Co. Secretary:** Mrs Helen Byrne
**Responsibilities**
**Senior:** Tyrone Hylton (Manager)
**Branches:** Whistlestop Foods Ltd, Euston Station Colonnade, Euston Station, London NW1 2DY
**US SIC:** 5411, 5921
**UK SIC:** 64100, 64200
**Auditors:** KPMG LLP
**Bankers:** Barclays Bank Plc (20-78-98)

|    | 25-09-13 | 26-09-12 | 28-09-11 |
|----|----------|----------|----------|
| TO | 2,601,052 | 2,478,214 | 2,466,983 |
| NW | 200,000 | 200,000 | 200,000 |

**DUNS 21-931-3566**					Imp-Exp
### Whiston Industries Ltd
Oak Street, Cradley Heath, West Midlands B64 5JY
**Tel:** 01384-560606 **Fax:** 01384-638182
**Web:** www.whistonindustries.com
**Reg No:** 1061381 **VAT No:** 278059132
**Estd:** 1963 Private Limited Company
**Line of Business:** Precision engineers
**Export Markets:** U S A; European Union (E U)
**Issued Capital:** £210,000
**Technical Director:** B A Whiston
**Co. Secretary:** Robert Whiston
**Responsibilities**
**Finance:** Jayson Allen (Senior Finance Administrator)
**Purchasing:** John Deeley (Purchasing Manager)
**US SIC:** 3542 **UK SIC:** 32212
**Auditors:** Thorpe Thompson
**Bankers:** National Westminster Bank Plc (60-02-35)

|    | 31-12-13 | 31-12-12 | 31-12-11 |
|----|----------|----------|----------|
| TA | 11,912,134 | 11,029,219 | 9,304,363 |
| NW | 4,811,569 | 4,578,125 | 4,355,938 |
| WC | 3,035,032 | 2,805,070 | 2,540,702 |

DUNS 21-109-1297

## Whitaker & Leach Ltd

Florence House, Chase Way, Bradford, West Yorkshire BD5 8HW
**Tel:** 01274-391460 **Fax:** 01274722363
**Web:** www.whitakerandleach.co.uk
**Reg No:** 6508830 **VAT No:** 303392977
**Estd:** 1946 Private Limited Company
**Line of Business:** Building construction contractors
**Trading Style:** Whitaker & Leach Ltd
**Issued Capital:** £1,000
**Director:** J S Wood
**Co. Secretary:** Robert Leach
**Responsibilities**
**Facilities:** Paul Gooch *(Workshop Manager)*
**US SIC:** 1522 **UK SIC:** 50100
**Bankers:** National Westminster Bank Plc (56-00-36)

| | 31-03-14 | 31-03-13 | 31-03-12 |
|---|---|---|---|
| TA | 2,735,580 | 2,811,547 | 2,712,890 |
| NW | 665,068 | 400,929 | 269,992 |
| WC | (445,425) | (684,304) | (802,266) |

DUNS 21-315-8926 **Imp**

## Whitaker Fibres Ltd

**(Subsidiary of:** Curtis Wool Direct Holdings Ltd)
Cashmere Works, Birksland Street, Bradford, West Yorkshire BD3 9SX
**Web:** www.haworthscouring.co.uk
**Reg No:** 1029047 **VAT No:** 180960943
**Estd:** 1971 Private Limited Company
**Line of Business:** Textile design and production
**Trading Style:** Haworth Scouring Co
**Issued Capital:** £2,500
**Directors:** D Isbecque, S W Curtis, K Linnes, Ms K B Lajord, M M Curtis, D N Gisbourne, M Sollerud, T L Holgate
**Co. Secretary:** Daniel Isbecque
**Responsibilities**
**Senior:** Neil Sagar *(Production Director)*, Timothy Whitaker *(Manager)*
**Finance:** Sarah Hodginson *(Management Accountant)*
**Engineering:** Neil Sagar *(Production Director)*
**US SIC:** 2269 **UK SIC:** 43702
**Auditors:** Baker Tilly
**Bankers:** National Westminster Bank Plc (56-00-36)

| | 31-12-13 | 31-12-12 | 31-12-11 |
|---|---|---|---|
| TO | 5,058,401 | 5,031,060 | 6,316,982 |
| P/L | (56,748) | 89,060 | 533,909 |
| NW | 2,148,171 | 2,237,957 | 2,198,411 |
| WC | 27,027 | 16,010 | 53,731 |
| Emp. | 48 | 71 | 62 |

DUNS 21-240-8074 **Imp-Exp**

## Whitakers Chocolates Ltd

85 Keighley Road, Skipton, North Yorkshire BD23 2NA
**Tel:** 01756792531
**Web:** www.whitakerschocolates.com
**Reg No:** 0697955 **Estd:** 1961 Private Limited Company
**Line of Business:** Manufacture of sugar confectionery
**Issued Capital:** £4,100
**Principals:** R J Whitaker *(Chairman)*, W R Whitaker *(Managing)*
**Co. Secretary:** Mrs Sally Thorpe
**Responsibilities**
**Marketing:** Deborah Berisford *(Marketing Manager)*
**US SIC:** 2065 **UK SIC:** 42142
**Auditors:** Robertshaw & Myers
**Bankers:** HSBC Bank plc (40-42-06)

| | 31-12-13 | 31-12-12 | 31-12-11 |
|---|---|---|---|
| TO | 10,914,229 | 10,108,758 | 10,302,000 |
| P/L | 526,030 | 502,362 | 300,865 |
| NW | 2,969,967 | 2,753,617 | 2,513,935 |
| WC | 1,714,988 | 1,497,893 | 1,341,957 |
| Emp. | 145 | 140 | 144 |

DUNS 21-051-0152 **Imp**

## Whitbread Group Plc

**(Subsidiary of:** Whitbread Plc)
College House, Payton Street, Stratford-Upon-Avon, Warwickshire CV37 6UQ
**Tel:** 08715279282 **Fax:** 01582-396-875
**Web:** www.premierinn.com
**Reg No:** 0029423 **VAT No:** 243292864
**Estd:** 1889 Public Limited Company
**Line of Business:** Hotels
**Export Sales:** £82,500,000
**Trading Style:** Costa Coffee, Premier Inn, Beefeater Grill / Brewers Fayre, Taybarns / Table Table
**Issued Capital:** £122,653,638
**Directors:** R Baker, N T Cadbury, A Harrison, Ms L H Smalley
**Co. Secretary:** Simon Barratt
**Responsibilities**
**Senior:** Lisa Henshall *(Operations Manager)*
**Branches:** Whitbread Group Plc, Bath Road, Reading, Berkshire RG7 5RT
**US SIC:** 7011, 5812, 2082
**UK SIC:** 66500, 66110, 42702
**Auditors:** Ernst & Young LLP
**Bankers:** Barclays Bank Plc (20-00-00)
**Following financial data are in thousands**

| | 27-02-14 | 28-02-13 | 01-02-12 |
|---|---|---|---|
| TO | 2,294,300 | 2,030,000 | 1,778,000 |
| P/L | 342,800 | 337,700 | 300,500 |
| NW | 1,462,500 | 1,181,100 | 888,300 |
| WC | (365,800) | (374,900) | (401,100) |
| Emp. | 36,447 | 33,716 | 30,484 |

DUNS 39-977-5857

## Whitbread Hotel (Bournemouth) Ltd

**(Subsidiary of:** Whitbread Plc)
St Michaels Road, Bournemouth, Dorset BH2 5DU
**Tel:** 01202557702
**Web:** www.highcliffgrill.co.uk
**Reg No:** 2273817 **Estd:** 1988 Private Limited Company
**Line of Business:** Hotels
**Issued Capital:** £100,000
**Directors:** S C Barratt, R W Fairhurst
**Co. Secretary:** Whitbread Secretaries Limited
**Branches:** Whitbread Hotel (Bournemouth) Ltd, 105 St. Michaels Road, Bournemouth, Dorset BH2 5DU
**US SIC:** 7011 **UK SIC:** 66500

| | 27-02-14 | 28-02-13 | 01-02-12 |
|---|---|---|---|
| TA | 4,040,000 | 4,040,000 | 4,040,000 |
| NW | 4,040,000 | 4,040,000 | 4,040,000 |

DUNS 21-242-0442

## Whitbread Hotel Company Ltd

**(Subsidiary of:** Whitbread Plc)
Oakley House, Luton, Bedfordshire LU4 9QH
**Tel:** 01582-499499
**Web:** www./www.whitbread.co.uk
**Reg No:** 0224163 **Estd:** 1927 Private Limited Company
**Line of Business:** Hotels
**Trading Style:** Whitbread Hotel Company Ltd
**Issued Capital:** £18,081,262
**Directors:** P J Dempsey, J Forrest
**Co. Secretary:** Russell Fairhurst
**Responsibilities**
**Senior:** Ian Chesire *(Chairman of Committee)*, Paul Flaum *(Managing Director Restaurants)*, Andy Harrison *(Chief Executive)*, Susan Hooper *(Non-Executive Director)*, Paul MacPherson *(President/ Managing Director)*, Susan Taylor-Martin *(Non-Executive Director)*
**Finance:** Alexanda Jones *(Revenue Business Analyst)*
**Admin:** Liz Delany *(PA)*
**HR:** Amanda Brady *(HR Director)*, Helen Hardy *(HR Director)*, Maria Horn *(Talent and Leadership Developm)*, Ruth Jackson *(Head of HR)*, Julie Tindale *(Head of HR Transformation)*
**Branches:** Whitbread Hotel Company Ltd, 28 West Green, Newton Aycliffe, County Durham DL5 6PE
**US SIC:** 7011, 5813
**UK SIC:** 66500, 66200
**Auditors:** Ernst & Young LLP

| | 27-02-14 | 28-02-13 | 01-02-12 |
|---|---|---|---|
| TO | 4,451,504 | 4,241,204 | 4,315,843 |
| P/L | 7,540,571 | 7,455,497 | 10,542,427 |
| NW | 174,760,793 | 168,966,322 | 163,340,876 |
| WC | 142,084,617 | 135,466,055 | 129,113,557 |
| Emp. | 70 | 68 | 72 |

DUNS 21-239-9711 **Imp-Exp**

## Whitby & Chandler Ltd

**(Subsidiary of:** Abco Seals Holdings Ltd)
Witchan Works, Green Road, Sheffield, South Yorkshire S36 6PH
**Tel:** 01226-370380 **Fax:** 01226-767138
**Web:** www.whitby-chandler.co.uk
**Reg No:** 0191878 **VAT No:** 172967721
**Estd:** 1923 Private Limited Company
**Line of Business:** Manufacturers of gaskets
**Export Markets:** Republic of Ireland, Middle East, U S A
**Trading Style:** Wcl
**Issued Capital:** £28,290
**Directors:** I D Cratchley, P Thompson
**Co. Secretary:** Graham Haworth
**Responsibilities**
**Senior:** Alan Streets *(Production Manager)*
**Operations:** Alan Streets *(Production Manager)*
**Purchasing:** Roland Gill *(Purchasing Manager)*
**Engineering:** Alan Streets *(Production Manager)*
**US SIC:** 5531, 3079
**UK SIC:** 65100, 48360
**Auditors:** Barber Harrison & Platt
**Bankers:** The Royal Bank Of Scotland Plc (16-23-17)

| | 30-06-13 | 30-06-12 | 30-06-11 |
|---|---|---|---|
| TA | 2,736,296 | 2,727,991 | 2,692,044 |
| NW | 1,730,346 | 1,679,520 | 1,636,388 |
| WC | 1,261,570 | 1,279,429 | 1,259,073 |

DUNS 23-288-1870

## Whitby Community College

Prospect Hill, Whitby, North Yorkshire YO21 1LA
**Tel:** 01947-602406
**Web:** www.ccwhitby.co.uk
**Estd:** 1949
**Line of Business:** Schools (foundation)
**Principals:** Ms R Totton, M Mercer
**Responsibilities**
**IT:** Tom Hutchinson *(Senior IT Executive)*
**US SIC:** 8211 **UK SIC:** 93200
**Employees:** 107

DUNS 21-776-7830

## Whitby Hospital

Springhill, Whitby, North Yorkshire YO21 1DP
**Tel:** 01947604851
**Estd:** 2011 Proprietorship
**Line of Business:** Hospitals
**Proprietor:** Mrs E Rigden
**Responsibilities**
**Senior:** Sarah King *(Locality Manager)*
**US SIC:** 8062 **UK SIC:** 95100
**Employees:** 323

DUNS 22-819-0211 **Imp-Exp**

## Whitby Seafoods Ltd

Stainsacre Lane Industrial Estate, Fairfield Way, Whitby, North Yorkshire YO22 4PU
**Tel:** 01947-606101 **Fax:** 01947-820589
**Web:** www.whitby-seafoods.com
**Reg No:** 1869220 **VAT No:** 422561868
**Estd:** 1985 Private Limited Company
**Line of Business:** Frozen foods (wholesale)
**Export Markets:** Europe
**Export Sales:** £512,882
**Issued Capital:** £42,000
**Principals:** J G Whittle *(Managing)*, D J Whittle, D A Wormald, Ms L M Whittle, E J Whittle, P W Farnsworth
**Co. Secretary:** Stephen Wormald
**Responsibilities**
**Senior:** John Cowden *(Manager)*, Laura Troughton *(Sales Director)*
**Marketing:** Kimberley McGloin *(Human Resources Manager)*
**Sales:** Laura Troughton *(Sales Director)*
**IT:** Susan Crow *(Technical Manager)*
**HR:** Kimberley McGloin *(Human Resources Manager)*
**Health & Safety:** Susan Crow *(Technical Manager)*
**Facilities:** Andy Bijl *(Engineering Manager)*
**Engineering:** Andy Bijl *(Engineering Manager)*
**US SIC:** 5149 **UK SIC:** 61700
**Auditors:** M Wasley Chapman & Co
**Bankers:** HSBC Bank plc (40-46-24)

| | 31-12-13 | 31-12-12 | 31-12-11 |
|---|---|---|---|
| TO | 32,440,785 | 31,506,324 | 25,468,090 |
| P/L | 858,962 | 772,375 | 848,034 |
| NW | 5,200,063 | 4,457,487 | 3,591,263 |
| WC | 1,343,949 | 959,527 | 1,093,971 |
| Emp. | 281 | 264 | 205 |

DUNS 21-802-1894

## Whitcliffe Mount School

Turnsteads Avenue, Cleckheaton, West Yorkshire BD19 3AQ
**Tel:** 01274851152
**Web:** www.whitcliffemount.co.uk
**Estd:** 2011
**Line of Business:** Schools (local authority)
**Trading Style:** Whitcliffe Mount School
**Responsibilities**
**Senior:** J Templar *(Head Mistress)*
**Finance:** Helen Whiteford *(Senior Finance Administrator)*
**US SIC:** 8211 **UK SIC:** 93200
**Employees:** 200

DUNS 21-041-2480

## White Acres

White Cross, Newquay, Cornwall TR8 4LW
**Tel:** 01726-862100
**Web:** www.parkdeanholidays.com
**Estd:** 2010 Partnership
**Line of Business:** Holidays (self catering)
**Partners:** K Lucock, A Benson
**US SIC:** 7021 **UK SIC:** 66500
**Employees:** 100

DUNS 22-191-3176

## White & Case (Europe) Llp

5 Old Broad Street, London EC2N 1DW
**Fax:** 020-7532-1001
**Web:** www.whitecase.com
**Reg No:** 0300102OC **Estd:** 1971 Limited Partnership
**Line of Business:** Solicitors
**Export Sales:** £20,985,906
**US SIC:** 8111 **UK SIC:** 83500
**Auditors:** Baker Tilly UK Audit LLP

| | 31-12-13 | 31-12-12 | 31-12-11 |
|---|---|---|---|
| TO | 20,994,877 | 20,786,690 | 1,156,608 |
| P/L | (803,893) | N/A | (225,791) |
| WC | 6,601,299 | 7,212,711 | 424,626 |
| Emp. | 193 | 132 | 7 |

DUNS 21-724-5414 **Imp-Exp**

## White & Co Plc

**(Subsidiary of:** Whitport Ltd)
Bottings Industrial Estate, Southampton, Hampshire SO30 2DY
**Tel:** 08000094558
**Web:** www.whiteandcompany.co.uk
**Reg No:** 0052204 **VAT No:** 107360791
**Estd:** 1897 Public Limited Company
**Line of Business:** Freight services
**Export Sales:** £2,216,573
**Issued Capital:** £1,000,000
**Principals:** M Howson-Green *(Chairman)*, R J Nicklinson *(Managing)*, D J Pateman *(Financial)*, S C Fassoms, I M Palmer, I D Nicholson
**Co. Secretary:** David Hoare
**Responsibilities**
**Senior:** Michael Howson-green *(Director & Chairman)*, Lynne Snow *(Fleet Manager)*
**Marketing:** Louis Spies *(Sales & Marketing Manager)*
**Sales:** Louis Spies *(Sales & Marketing Manager)*
**Fleet:** Lynne Snow *(Fleet Manager)*
**Branches:** White & Co Plc, Unit G Bar End Industrial Estate, Winchester, Hampshire SO23 9NP
**US SIC:** 4213 **UK SIC:** 72300
**Auditors:** Westlake Clark
**Bankers:** Lloyds TSB Bank plc (30-96-11)

| | 31-01-14 | 31-01-13 | 31-01-12 |
|---|---|---|---|
| TO | 24,527,518 | 24,074,408 | 23,176,080 |
| P/L | 148,874 | 292,661 | (585,747) |
| NW | 1,789,880 | 1,683,476 | 1,327,185 |
| WC | 855,493 | 402,821 | 675,746 |
| Emp. | 466 | 479 | 472 |

DUNS 21-786-2968

## White Arrow Logistics

4 The Fort, Walthew House Lane Martland Park, Wigan, Lancashire WN5 0LX
**Tel:** 01942213535
**Web:** www.whitearrowlogistics.com
**Estd:** 2011 Proprietorship
**Line of Business:** Warehouses
**Proprietor:** N Hoae
**Responsibilities**
**Senior:** Nick Hoare *(Warehouse Director)*
**US SIC:** 4213 **UK SIC:** 72300
**Employees:** 150

DUNS 21-209-8094

## White Ash Brook Nursing Home

Thwaites Road, Oswaldtwistle, Accrington, Lancashire BB5 4QR
**Tel:** 01254-394163
**Web:** www.harbourhealthcare.co.uk
**Estd:** 1987 Proprietorship
**Line of Business:** Nursing homes
**Proprietor:** Mrs H Marsh
**Responsibilities**
**Senior:** Janet Powers *(Manager)*, Lianne Webb *(Manager)*, Cheryl Wildman *(Interim Manager)*
**US SIC:** 8051 **UK SIC:** 95100
**Employees:** 54

DUNS 39-777-3706

## White Bros. (N'cle-on-Tyne) Ltd

Unit 4-5 Gosforth Industrial Estate, Christon Road, Newcastle-Upon-Tyne, Tyne and Wear NE3 1XD
**Tel:** 01912130455 **Fax:** 01912-841351
**Web:** www.whitebros.co.uk
**Reg No:** 2201035 **VAT No:** 175842731
**Estd:** 1884 Private Limited Company
**Line of Business:** Steel fabricators
**Issued Capital:** £20,000
**Principals:** P J Harding *(Managing)*, S P Roberts, G Wragby
**Responsibilities**
**Senior:** Neville Ferguson *(Manager)*
**Marketing:** Paul Banning *(Sales & Marketing Manager)*
**Sales:** Paul Banning *(Sales & Marketing Manager)*
**US SIC:** 1622 **UK SIC:** 50200
**Auditors:** Tait Walker
**Bankers:** Lloyds TSB Bank plc (30-93-55)

| | 31-12-13 | 31-12-12 | 31-12-11 |
|---|---|---|---|
| TA | 1,640,404 | 1,593,968 | 1,565,138 |
| NW | 821,696 | 730,189 | 679,990 |
| WC | 487,266 | 439,604 | 458,429 |

DUNS 23-676-8805
## White Clarke Automotive Solutions Ltd
(Subsidiary of: White Clarke Technologies Ltd)
White Clarke House, Woodlands Business Park Breckland, Linford Wood, Milton Keynes, Buckinghamshire MK14 6FG
Tel: 08707872211
Web: www.nexusplc.com
Reg No: 3671481 Estd: 1980 Private Limited Company
Line of Business: Management activities of holding companies
Trading Style: White Clarke Group
Issued Capital: £732,375
Directors: E D White, P Scanlon
Co. Secretary: Peter Blease
US SIC: 6711 UK SIC: 83962
Auditors: haysmacintyre
Bankers: Bank Of Scotland (12-09-49)

| | 31-12-13 | 31-12-12 | 31-12-11 |
|---|---|---|---|
| TO | 6,520,905 | 7,861,090 | 7,381,074 |
| P/L | (67,968) | (1,061,670) | (220,389) |
| NW | (554,569) | (549,832) | 511,839 |
| WC | 1,539,917 | 1,428,567 | (74,966) |
| Emp. | 159 | 182 | 163 |

DUNS 21-041-3484
## White Clarke Group
White Clarke House Woodlands Business, Park, 4 Breckland, Linford Wood, Milton Keynes, Buckinghamshire MK14 6FG
Tel: 01908-576600
Web: www.whiteclarkegroup.com
Line of Business: Other computer related activities
Trading Style: White Clarke Group
US SIC: 7379 UK SIC: 83940
Employees: 100

DUNS 53-630-7291     Imp
## White Clarke Group Ltd
White Clarke House, Milton Keynes, Buckinghamshire MK14 6FG
Tel: 01908 576 699
Web: www.whiteclarkegroup.com
Reg No: 3435619 Estd: 1997 Private Limited Company
Line of Business: Other software consultancy and supply
Issued Capital: £3,229
Co. Secretary: Edward White
Responsibilities
Senior: Dara Clarke (CEO)
Marketing: Denise Canvin (PR Manager), Anna Lepp (Marketing Manager)
US SIC: 7399, 5081
UK SIC: 83954, 61490
Auditors: haysmacintyre

| | 31-12-13 | 31-12-12 | 31-12-11 |
|---|---|---|---|
| TO | 25,958,690 | 22,916,162 | 23,702,674 |
| P/L | 2,486,697 | 1,039,827 | 1,143,430 |
| NW | 5,242,977 | 3,922,850 | 3,251,576 |
| WC | 5,304,279 | 3,342,507 | 3,113,595 |
| Emp. | 238 | 225 | 225 |

DUNS 23-222-6741
## The White Co
1 Derry Street, London W8 5HY
Web: www.thewhitecompany.com
Estd: 1993 Proprietorship
Line of Business: Mail order houses
Proprietor: Mrs C Rucker
Responsibilities
Senior: Jane Perks (Director of Human Resources)
HR: Jane Perks (Director of Human Resources)
US SIC: 5961 UK SIC: 65600
Employees: 250

DUNS 21-617-3171
## The White Company
88 George Street, Edinburgh, Midlothian EH2 3BU
Tel: 01313000605
Web: www.thewhitecompany.com
Estd: 2011
Line of Business: Departmental stores
Responsibilities
Senior: Tony Campbell (Manager)
US SIC: 5399 UK SIC: 65600
Employees: 78

DUNS 77-545-4861
## The White Company (U.K.) Ltd
1 Derry Street, London W8 5HY
Tel: 08447364222 Fax: 08456-788151
Web: www.thewhitecompany.com
Reg No: 2998082 VAT No: 830479132
Estd: 1993 Private Limited Company
Line of Business: Drapery, curtain & upholstery retailers
Export Sales: £7,998,000
Issued Capital: £100
Directors: W J Kernan, L A Campbell, Ms B C Rucker, N C Wheeler

Co. Secretary: Philip Clarke
Branches: The White Company (U.k.) Ltd, 15 Northgate Street, Bath, Avon BA1 5AS
US SIC: 5714, 5699, 5961
UK SIC: 64700, 64500, 65600
Auditors: BDO LLP
Bankers: Lloyds TSB Bank plc (30-00-02)

| | 29-03-14 | 30-03-13 | 31-03-12 |
|---|---|---|---|
| TO | 143,780,000 | 125,624,000 | 115,991,000 |
| P/L | 6,538,000 | 4,748,000 | 4,481,000 |
| NW | 13,656,000 | 9,379,000 | 6,401,000 |
| WC | (2,269,000) | (1,296,000) | (6,109,000) |
| Emp. | 1,113 | 997 | 979 |

DUNS 21-415-3632     Imp
## White Cube
48 Hoxton Square, London N1 6PB
Tel: 02079305373
Web: www.whitecube.com
Estd: 1993 Proprietorship
Line of Business: Operation of arts facilities
Proprietor: J Jopling
Branches: Jay Jopling, 25-26 Masons Yard, London SW1Y 6BU
US SIC: 7911 UK SIC: 97913
Employees: 93

DUNS 21-391-6197
## White Digital Media
Grosvenor House, Prince Of Wales Road, Norwich, Norfolk NR1 1NS
Tel: 01603217530
Web: www.wdmgroup.com
Estd: 2007 Proprietorship
Line of Business: Internet publishers
Proprietor: G White
Responsibilities
Senior: Kiron Chavda (Manager)
US SIC: 7379 UK SIC: 83940
Employees: 50

DUNS 21-856-2495
## The White Hills Park Federation Trust
Bramcote College Moor Lane, Bramcote, Nottingham, Nottinghamshire NG9 3GA
Tel: 01159170424
Web: www.whpfederation.org
Reg No: 8195720 Estd: 2012 Private Company Limited By Guarantee
Line of Business: General secondary education
Directors: A E Bird, S Limbachia, C R Peebles, T L Jones, Dr M Wallace, Mrs F R Brittle, P Heery, Reverend W Plimmer
Co. Secretary: Michael Powell
Responsibilities
Senior: Zoe Armitage (Senior Teacher), Julie Francis (Director), Paul Hearey (Executive Head), Cheryl Heath (Director), Stanley Heptinstall (Director), Tina Launchbury (Director), Karen Sandy (Director), Simon Theobald (Manager), Simon Tonks (Director), Caryn Welch (Director)
US SIC: 8211 UK SIC: 93200
Bankers: Lloyds TSB Bank plc (30-12-51)

| | 31-08-14 | 31-08-13 |
|---|---|---|
| TO | 10,020,000 | 46,337,000 |
| P/L | (549,000) | 36,766,000 |
| NW | 35,320,000 | 36,121,000 |
| WC | 222,000 | 649,000 |
| Emp. | 178 | 174 |

DUNS 21-596-3675
## The White Horse
16 Newburgh Street, London W1F 7RY
Tel: 02074949748
Web: www.nicholsonspubs.co.uk
Estd: 2011 Proprietorship
Line of Business: Managed public houses and bars
Proprietor: L Jarvey
Responsibilities
Senior: Julie Hall (Manager)
US SIC: 5813 UK SIC: 66200
Employees: 200

DUNS 28-933-0458
## White Horse Caravan Co Ltd
Paddock Lane, Selsey, Chichester, West Sussex PO20 9EJ
Tel: 01243-604121
Web: www.bennleisure.co.uk
Reg No: 1538949 VAT No: 193019564
Estd: 1959 Private Limited Company
Line of Business: Camping sites, including caravan sites
Trading Style: Bunn Leisure
Issued Capital: £80,000
Principals: J B Bunn (Managing), Ms C M Breen, M A Caven, Ms E S Bunn, E H Bunn, C H Bunn, Ms D H Honeybunn
Co. Secretary: John Bunn
Responsibilities
Senior: Kim Bennett (Manager)
Facilities: Paul Dines (Maintenance Manager)

Branches: White Horse Caravan Co Ltd, West Sands Caravan Park, Mill Lane, Chichester, West Sussex PO20 9BH
US SIC: 7033 UK SIC: 66701
Auditors: Lewis Golden & Co
Bankers: Lloyds TSB Bank plc (30-18-30)

| | 31-01-14 | 31-01-13 | 31-01-12 |
|---|---|---|---|
| TO | 23,027,352 | 21,282,735 | 20,030,661 |
| P/L | 3,110,740 | (3,283,049) | 2,418,877 |
| NW | 14,034,574 | 12,329,069 | 15,764,385 |
| WC | 4,461,008 | 3,270,191 | 10,239,974 |
| Emp. | 222 | 238 | 294 |

DUNS 21-707-3972
## White Horse Contractors Ltd
Blakes Oak Farm, Lodge Hill, Abingdon, Oxfordshire OX14 2JD
Tel: 01865736272
Web: www.whitehorsecontractors.co.uk
Reg No: 0589121 VAT No: 199870686
Estd: 1957 Private Limited Company
Line of Business: Drainage contractors
Issued Capital: £270,000
Principals: Mrs R E Binning (Chairman), J Koster (Managing), J R Binning, J R Binning, G Kneller
Co. Secretary: Mrs Ruth Binning
Responsibilities
Senior: Mick Cross (Workshop Foreman), Sally Merola (Accountant)
Finance: Amanda Turnbull (Accountant)
Marketing: James Coney (Business Development Manager)
HR: Philip Matchwick (Plant Manager)
Health & Safety: Philip Matchwick (Plant Manager)
Facilities: Philip Matchwick (Plant Manager)
Purchasing: Philip Matchwick (Plant Manager)
Fleet: Philip Matchwick (Plant Manager)
US SIC: 4952, 8911
UK SIC: 92120, 83701
Auditors: CV Thames Valley Ltd
Bankers: Barclays Bank Plc (20-01-09)

| | 31-03-14 | 31-03-13 | 30-03-11 |
|---|---|---|---|
| TO | 9,846,682 | 12,624,016 | 17,445,312 |
| P/L | (303,300) | (1,281,144) | 218,472 |
| NW | 3,197,486 | 3,501,717 | 4,211,209 |
| WC | 59,410 | 250,266 | 1,205,913 |
| Emp. | 73 | 83 | 92 |

DUNS 21-840-4133
## The White Horse Federation
The White Horse Federation, Plymouth Street, Swindon, Wiltshire SN1 2LB
Tel: 01793818603
Web: www.thewhitehorsefederation.org.uk
Reg No: 8075785 Estd: 2012 Private Company Limited By Guarantee
Line of Business: Primary education
Directors: Ms J Jarvis, Ms L Saunders, C J Hopton, M H Wolton, N Capstick, S Hagan, Mrs L Connor, M Collins
Co. Secretary: Mrs Lorna Haydon
Responsibilities
Senior: Hayley Brown (Business Director), Bradley Owen (Director)
US SIC: 8211 UK SIC: 93200
Bankers: Lloyds TSB Bank plc (30-18-86)

| | 31-08-14 | 31-08-13 |
|---|---|---|
| TO | 13,697,665 | 23,778,464 |
| P/L | 2,067,108 | 14,158,247 |
| NW | 15,408,355 | 14,057,247 |
| WC | 3,164,828 | 2,241,300 |
| Emp. | 258 | 195 |

DUNS 21-586-3486
## White Horse Leisure & Tennis Ctr
Audlett Drive, Abingdon, Oxfordshire OX14 3PJ
Tel: 01235-540700
Web: www.whltc.co.uk
Estd: 2009 Proprietorship
Line of Business: Physical well-being activities
Proprietor: D Johns
Responsibilities
Finance: Laura New (Financial Manager)
US SIC: 7299 UK SIC: 98902
Employees: 200

DUNS 21-291-8044
## White House
Ashmans Road, Beccles, Suffolk NR34 9NS
Tel: 01502717683
Web: www.healthcarehomes.co.uk
Estd: 1987 Partnership
Line of Business: Residential care establishments
Partners: T R Mason, T Mason
Responsibilities
Senior: Julie Knights (Manager), Terry Mason (Home Manager)
US SIC: 8321 UK SIC: 96111
Employees: 50

DUNS 21-782-4016
## White House Depot
White House Depot, Kingston Road, Ashford, Middlesex TW15 3SE
Tel: 01784446411
Estd: 2011 Proprietorship
Line of Business: Local government
Proprietor: Mrs J Taylor
US SIC: 3549 UK SIC: 32212
Employees: 100

DUNS 21-498-3848
## The White House Hotel
Herm Island, Guernsey, Channel Islands GY1 3HR
Tel: 01481750075
Web: www.herm.com
Line of Business: Hotels
Director: A Hayworth
Responsibilities
Senior: Sion Jones (General Manager), Nigel Waylen (Head Chef)
Marketing: Sion Jones (General Manager)
Sales: Sion Jones (General Manager)
HR: Sion Jones (General Manager)
Purchasing: Sion Jones (General Manager)
US SIC: 7011 UK SIC: 66500
Employees: 50

DUNS 21-748-6323
## White Knight Door 2 Door Ltd
(Subsidiary of: H.Tomlins Ltd)
73 Horsell Moor, Woking, Surrey GU21 4NL
Tel: 08454591276 Fax: 01483-762272
Web: www.white-knight.co.uk
Reg No: 0381306 Estd: 1924 Private Limited Company
Line of Business: Laundries
Issued Capital: £16,000
Directors: P H Tomlins, R W Adams
Responsibilities
Senior: Manoh Gangar (General Manager), Julian Woolcock (Director)
Branches: White Knight Door 2 Door Ltd, 2 Station Approach, West Byfleet, Surrey KT14 6NG
US SIC: 7219 UK SIC: 98110
Auditors: Menzies
Bankers: National Westminster Bank Plc (60-23-40)

| | 31-12-13 | 31-12-12 | 31-12-11 |
|---|---|---|---|
| TO | N/A | 2,480,907 | 2,586,793 |
| P/L | (80,049) | 5,570 | 3,244 |
| NW | 17,458 | 97,507 | 91,937 |

DUNS 23-327-3452
## White Knight Laundry Services
73 Horsell Moor, Woking, Surrey GU21 4NL
Tel: 01483-762567
Web: www.white-knight.co.uk
Estd: 2002 Proprietorship
Line of Business: Washing and dry cleaning of textile and fur products
Proprietor: A Lanceman
Responsibilities
Senior: Colin Dawe (Manager), Manoj Gangarh (Manager), Alan Tomlins (Manager)
Admin: Sharon Connolly (Office Manager)
Engineering: Sally Carey (Production Manager), Sally Novak (Production Manager)
US SIC: 7219 UK SIC: 98110
Employees: 85

DUNS 42-439-6971
## White Label Productions Ltd
(Subsidiary of: Edicis Communications Group Ltd)
45-51 Whitfield Street, London W1T 4HD
Tel: 02030316100 Fax: 02030316101
Web: www.whitelabelproductions.co.uk
Reg No: 4427330 Estd: 2002 Private Limited Company
Line of Business: Advertising, radio, tv and other media
Issued Capital: £1,000
Directors: D R Childs, D H Tubbs, Ms C D Grant
US SIC: 7319, 7399, 7339
UK SIC: 83800, 83954

| | 31-05-13 | 31-05-12 | 31-05-11 |
|---|---|---|---|
| TO | 3,072,000 | 3,991,000 | 3,915,000 |
| P/L | 152,000 | 414,000 | 412,000 |
| NW | 1,387,000 | 1,386,000 | 977,000 |
| WC | 1,290,000 | 1,290,000 | 926,000 |

DUNS 28-870-2855     Imp
## White Light Ltd
(Subsidiary of: Wlh Ltd)
Merton Industrial Estate, 20 Jubilee Way, London SW19 3WL
Tel: 02082544800
Web: www.whitelight.ltd.uk
Reg No: 1031687 VAT No: 234041115
Estd: 1971 Private Limited Company

**Line of Business:** Live theatrical presentation
**Export Sales:** £1,254,283
**Issued Capital:** £531,250
**Principals:** J Simpson *(Managing)*, P Threadgold, S R Needle, C J Nicholls, B A Raven, R M Wilson, D J Isherwood
**Co. Secretary:** Paul Millington
**Branches:** White Light Ltd, Ft, 18 Parsons Green, London SW6 4UH
**US SIC:** 7922 **UK SIC:** 97412
**Auditors:** Alliotts
**Bankers:** Lloyds TSB Bank plc (30-93-23)

| | 31-03-14 | 31-03-13 | 31-03-12 |
|---|---|---|---|
| TO | 18,640,026 | 19,719,003 | 20,140,879 |
| P/L | 147,982 | 309,732 | 413,476 |
| NW | 2,258,995 | 3,267,922 | 3,586,599 |
| WC | (1,459,499) | (659,745) | (512,769) |
| Emp. | 159 | 147 | 141 |

DUNS 21-410-7055
## White Lodge Beefeater
81 Bridgwater Road, Taunton, Somerset TA1 2DU
**Web:** www.beefeater.co.uk
**Estd:** 1989 Proprietorship
**Line of Business:** Restaurant - english
**Proprietor:** N Green
**US SIC:** 5812 **UK SIC:** 66110
**Employees:** 91

DUNS 29-285-4502
## White Lodge Centre
Holloway Hill, Lyne, Chertsey, Surrey KT16 0AE
**Tel:** 01932-567131 **Fax:** 01932-570589
**Web:** www.whitelodgecentre.co.uk
**Reg No:** 1592351 **Estd:** 1981 Private Limited Company
**Line of Business:** Day and care centres
**Trading Style:** White Lodge School
**Directors:** D B Meller, Ms K Taylor, C D Bolton, G J Logan, A E Erickson, Dr V P Bignell, Mrs J Choules, P A Draycott
**Responsibilities**
**Senior:** Sarah Dade *(Manager)*, Janet Deal *(Manager)*, Julia Disney *(Manager)*, Lesley Robbins *(Manager)*
**Branches:** White Lodge Centre, 102 Woodbridge Rd, Guildford, Surrey GU1 4PY
**US SIC:** 8321 **UK SIC:** 96111
**Auditors:** Baker Tilly
**Bankers:** National Westminster Bank Plc (60-23-34)

| | 31-03-14 | 31-03-13 | 31-03-12 |
|---|---|---|---|
| TO | 2,267,000 | 2,235,000 | 2,166,000 |
| P/L | (148,000) | (136,000) | (97,000) |
| NW | 6,762,000 | 6,910,000 | 7,046,000 |
| WC | 559,000 | 581,000 | 599,000 |
| Emp. | 74 | 73 | 71 |

DUNS 21-158-6358
## White Lodge Medical Services Ltd
**(Subsidiary of:** Magnolia Medical Llp)
White Lodge Surgery, 68 Silver Street, Enfield, Middlesex EN1 3EW
**Tel:** 02083634156
**Web:** www.doctorinenfield.co.uk
**Reg No:** 6859832 **Estd:** 2009 Private Limited Company
**Line of Business:** Doctors
**Issued Capital:** £175,000
**Directors:** S Salam, Dr A Patel, H Grewal, N K Amin, Dr B Garland
**US SIC:** 8011 **UK SIC:** 95300

| | 31-10-13 | 31-10-12 | 31-10-11 |
|---|---|---|---|
| TA | 714,760 | 785,869 | 834,459 |
| NW | (2,730) | (5,059) | (139,141) |
| WC | 198,956 | 230,802 | 120,652 |

DUNS 21-809-0282
## White Meadows Primary School
Whitelea Road, Wick, Littlehampton, West Sussex BN17 7JL
**Tel:** 01903731774
**Web:** www.whitemeadows.w-sussex.sch.uk
**Estd:** 2012
**Line of Business:** Schools (foundation)
**Responsibilities**
**Senior:** Yvonne Brailsford *(Head Of School)*
**US SIC:** 8211 **UK SIC:** 93200
**Employees:** 50

DUNS 21-328-3674
## White Moss Horticulture Ltd
North Perimeter Road, Liverpool, Merseyside L33 3AP
**Tel:** 0151-547-2979
**Web:** www.whitemoss.co.uk
**Reg No:** 0490603 **VAT No:** 163737744
**Estd:** 1951 Private Limited Company
**Line of Business:** Turf suppliers and contractors
**Issued Capital:** £1,432
**Managing Director:** S W Washington
**Co. Secretary:** Mrs Helen Silvano
**US SIC:** 5999, 4959
**UK SIC:** 65600, 92110
**Auditors:** J & D Pennington
**Bankers:** National Westminster Bank Plc (60-12-25)

| | 31-08-13 | 31-08-12 | 31-08-11 |
|---|---|---|---|
| TO | 7,442,710 | N/A | N/A |
| P/L | 515,548 | N/A | N/A |
| NW | 7,356,328 | 7,034,903 | 2,570,660 |
| WC | 422,842 | 255,760 | 1,051,025 |
| Emp. | 65 | N/A | N/A |

DUNS 73-709-8884
## White Post Farm Centre Ltd
Mansfield Road, Newark, Nottinghamshire NG22 8HL
**Tel:** 01623-882977 **Fax:** 01623-883499
**Web:** http://whitepostfarmcentre.co.uk
**Reg No:** 4968580 **Estd:** 2003 Private Limited Company
**Line of Business:** Other entertainment activities not elsewhere classified
**Issued Capital:** £40,000
**Directors:** S D Rouse, Ms R L Allott
**Co. Secretary:** Ms Christina Mathoon
**Responsibilities**
**Health & Safety:** Buzz Hope *(Health & Safety Officer)*
**US SIC:** 7999, 8421
**UK SIC:** 97913, 97700

| | 31-12-13 | 31-12-12 | 31-12-11 |
|---|---|---|---|
| TA | 1,062,959 | 1,100,728 | 1,172,746 |
| NW | 285,148 | 193,756 | 199,119 |
| WC | (259,425) | (321,070) | (236,919) |

DUNS 21-771-8685
## White Rock Primary School
Davies Avenue, Paignton, Devon TQ4 7AW
**Tel:** 01803843175
**Web:** www.whiterockprimaryschool.co.uk
**Estd:** 2011 Partnership
**Line of Business:** Schools (local authority)
**Partners:** N Furness, Mrs L Elliott, Mrs L Elliott
**Responsibilities**
**Senior:** David Theobald *(Head Teacher)*, Sarah Tomkinson *(Head Teacher)*
**US SIC:** 8211 **UK SIC:** 93200
**Employees:** 60

DUNS 50-440-4385
## White Rose Environmental Operations Ltd
**(Subsidiary of:** Stericycle Inc.)
Ambulance Station, Woodbridge Road East, Ipswich, Suffolk IP4 5PG
**Tel:** 01473729096
**Reg No:** 2428371 **Estd:** 1989 Private Limited Company
**Line of Business:** Hospitals
**Issued Capital:** £1,000
**Director:** J P Johnston
**Branches:** White Rose Environmental Operations Ltd, Pannell House, 6 Queen Street, Leeds, West Yorkshire LS1 2TW
**US SIC:** 4953, 4952
**UK SIC:** 92110, 92120
**Bankers:** National Westminster Bank Plc (60-60-05)

| | 31-12-13 | 31-12-12 | 31-12-11 |
|---|---|---|---|
| TA | 1,642,000 | 1,642,000 | 1,642,000 |
| NW | 2,000 | 2,000 | 2,000 |

DUNS 21-038-1635
## White Rose Medical Centre
White Rose Way, New Tredegar, Gwent NP24 6DF
**Tel:** 01443837183
**Web:** www.larchwoodcare.co.uk
**Estd:** 1990
**Line of Business:** Children's homes
**Partners:** Dr P Prasad, B Prasad, Mrs A Durdidge
**Responsibilities**
**Senior:** Stephen Prosser *(General Manager)*, Jayne Thomas *(General Manager)*
**US SIC:** 8321 **UK SIC:** 96111
**Employees:** 50

DUNS 21-031-9313
## White Star Line
40 Greek Street, London W1D 4EB
**Tel:** 02077347333
**Web:** www.whitestarline.org.uk
**Line of Business:** Licensed restaurants
**Responsibilities**
**Senior:** Gamal Lahoud *(CEO, Managing Director)*
**Finance:** Suellen Souza *(Accounts Officer)*
**Sales:** C Macnamara *(Senior Sales Executive)*
**HR:** Jimmy Lahoud *(Human Resources Manager)*
**US SIC:** 5812 **UK SIC:** 66110
**Employees:** 50

DUNS 21-664-3799 **Imp**
## White Stuff Group Ltd
Canterbury Court, Kennington Park, 1-3 Brixton Road, London SW9 6DE
**Tel:** 01162389106
**Web:** www.whitestuff.com
**Reg No:** 7186923 **Estd:** 2010 Private Limited Company
**Line of Business:** Ladies fashionwear (retail)
**Export Sales:** £2,879,000
**Issued Capital:** £390
**Directors:** V M Gwilliam, Mrs A D Hewitt, G T Treves, M D Newman, W G Yuill, J P Seigal, S G Thomas, N C Mather
**Co. Secretary:** Mrs Rebecc Kong
**US SIC:** 5621, 5699
**UK SIC:** 64500
**Auditors:** KPMG LLP

| | 03-05-14 | 27-04-13 | 28-05-12 |
|---|---|---|---|
| TO | 115,685,000 | 99,538,000 | 89,324,000 |
| P/L | 9,470,000 | 5,131,000 | (67,066,000) |
| NW | 15,964,000 | 9,009,000 | 3,820,000 |
| WC | 4,117,000 | 611,000 | (2,879,000) |
| Emp. | 1,592 | 1,543 | 1,542 |

DUNS 50-112-6411 **Imp-Exp**
## White Stuff Ltd
**(Subsidiary of:** White Stuff Group Ltd)
Canterbury Court, 1-3 Brixton Road, London SW9 6DE
**Tel:** 02077358133
**Web:** www.whitestuff.com
**Reg No:** 2319237 **VAT No:** 503415783
**Estd:** 1988 Private Limited Company
**Line of Business:** Fashion shops
**Export Markets:** E U
**Export Sales:** £2,879,000
**Issued Capital:** £3,830
**Directors:** G T Treves, M D Newman, Mrs A D Hewitt, V M Gwilliam, N C Mather, S G Thomas, J P Seigal
**Co. Secretary:** Mrs Rebecca Kong
**Responsibilities**
**Marketing:** Becky Barraclough *(Press Officer)*
**Admin:** Phil Game *(Office Manager)*
**Health & Safety:** Phil Game *(Office Manager)*
**Facilities:** Phil Game *(Office Manager)*
**Branches:** White Stuff Ltd, 228 High Street, Guildford, Surrey GU1 3JD
**US SIC:** 5699 **UK SIC:** 64500
**Auditors:** KPMG LLP

| | 03-05-14 | 27-04-13 | 28-05-12 |
|---|---|---|---|
| TO | 115,685,000 | 99,538,000 | 89,324,000 |
| P/L | 12,095,000 | 7,756,000 | 2,824,000 |
| NW | 19,808,000 | 10,688,000 | 4,954,000 |
| WC | 7,961,000 | 2,290,000 | (1,745,000) |
| Emp. | 1,592 | 1,543 | 1,542 |

DUNS 21-738-6346
## White Young Green Consulting Ltd
1 Locksley Business Park, Montgomery Road, Belfast BT6 9UP
**Tel:** 02890706000 **Fax:** 02890706000
**Web:** www.wyg.com
**Reg No:** 0003673NF **Estd:** 2004 Private Limited Company
**Line of Business:** Engineering consultative and design activities
**Directors:** R Hartley, W Brayson, D Ford, M L Taylor, M Whitwell, R G Mccaffrey, P Downie, T Wilson
**Co. Secretary:** Robert Hartley
**Responsibilities**
**Senior:** Kenneth Archibald *(Director)*, David Ellyatt *(Director)*, Terry Everall *(Director)*, Michael Procter *(Director)*, John Purvis *(Director)*, Sidney Winter *(Director)*
**Finance:** Beverley McCallum *(Finance Manager)*
**Marketing:** Susie Nixon *(Office Manager)*
**Sales:** David Alderson *(Planning Director)*
**Admin:** Susie Nixon *(Office Manager)*
**Operations:** Barry Turner *(Associate Director Management)*
**Branches:** White Young Green Consulting Ltd, 39 George Street, Edinburgh, Midlothian EH2 2HN
**US SIC:** 8999, 8911
**UK SIC:** 83954, 83701

DUNS 76-958-6926
## The Whitechapel Centre
Langsdale Street, Liverpool, Merseyside L3 8DT
**Tel:** 0151-207-7617
**Web:** www.whitechapelcentre.co.uk
**Reg No:** 2623071 **Estd:** 1991 Private Company Limited By Guarantee
**Line of Business:** Non-charitable social work activities without accommodation
**Trading Style:** The Whitechapel Centre
**Directors:** D E Antrobus, Ms M M Brown, Ms V Metcalf Mbe, T Walsh, T Crolley, Mrs C Mcguire, B Kearsley Obe, R F Moore
**Co. Secretary:** David Carter
**Responsibilities**
**Senior:** Barbara Burgess *(Manager)*, Daivd Porter *(Chief Executive)*, Kenneth Vance *(Manager)*
**HR:** Judith Bulmer *(Human Resources Manager)*
**US SIC:** 8321 **UK SIC:** 96111
**Auditors:** Bresnan Walsh
**Bankers:** National Westminster Bank Plc (53-70-44)

| | 31-03-14 | 31-03-13 | 31-03-12 |
|---|---|---|---|
| TO | 2,394,577 | 2,269,104 | 1,966,576 |
| P/L | 36,854 | 105,487 | 89,596 |
| NW | 1,593,451 | 1,556,597 | 1,451,110 |
| WC | 593,127 | 556,596 | 451,109 |
| Emp. | 84 | 78 | 66 |

DUNS 21-773-6819
## Whitechapel Community Trust Cic
85 Myrdle Street, London E1 1HL
**Tel:** 02073776909
**Estd:** 2011 Proprietorship
**Line of Business:** Community networks
**Proprietor:** L Rahman
**Responsibilities**
**Senior:** Luther Rahman *(Director)*
**US SIC:** 8699 **UK SIC:** 96902
**Employees:** 50

DUNS 22-092-5494
## Whitechapel Gallery Trustee Ltd
77-82 Whitechapel High Street, London E1 7QX
**Tel:** 02075227888
**Web:** www.whitechapel.org
**Reg No:** 4093862 **Estd:** 1901 Private Limited Company
**Line of Business:** Operation of arts facilities
**Directors:** Ms A Gallagher, F Moussavi, R Islam, R B Taylor, Ms S Conrad, A Ganguli, C M Medvei, Ms M H Eisler
**Co. Secretary:** Miss Clare Hawkins
**Responsibilities**
**Senior:** Duncan Ackery *(Director)*, Stephen Escritt *(Manager)*, Michael Keith *(Manager)*, Dominic Palfreyman *(Director)*, Catherine Petitgas *(Director)*, Alice Rawsthorn *(Director)*, Rohan Silva *(Director)*
**US SIC:** 7911 **UK SIC:** 97913
**Employees:** 70

DUNS 85-610-0532
## Whiteconcierge Ltd
**(Subsidiary of:** Axa Direction Juridique Centrale)
Worldwide House, Thorpe Wood, Peterborough, Cambridgeshire PE3 6SB
**Fax:** 01733-862001
**Web:** www.whiteconcierge.com
**Reg No:** 6203706 **VAT No:** 915766008
**Estd:** 2007 Private Limited Company
**Line of Business:** Call centres
**Export Sales:** £6,537,350
**Issued Capital:** £1,000,000
**Directors:** R A Ewers, M J Oldham, F Regimbeau, J Renson, Mrs G Colella, J P Breeze, Ms S Latil
**Co. Secretary:** Siu Yau
**Responsibilities**
**Marketing:** Maria Gautsch *(Relations Manager)*
**US SIC:** 7399 **UK SIC:** 83954
**Auditors:** RSM Tenon Audit Ltd

| | 31-12-13 | 31-12-12 | 30-12-12 |
|---|---|---|---|
| TO | 8,146,749 | 4,614,699 | 6,922,776 |
| P/L | 725,395 | 1,046,954 | 298,768 |
| NW | 2,646,211 | 2,619,343 | 1,767,436 |
| WC | 2,527,458 | 2,380,196 | 1,485,757 |
| Emp. | 142 | 153 | 149 |

DUNS 29-009-0125
## Whitecross Dental Care Ltd
**(Subsidiary of:** Adp Primary Care Services Ltd)
Europa House Europa Trading Estate, Stoneclough Roa, Manchester M26 1GG
**Tel:** 01983754633
**Web:** www.idhgroup.co.uk
**Reg No:** 0244415 **Estd:** 1929 Private Limited Company
**Line of Business:** Dentists
**Issued Capital:** £3,500,932
**Directors:** C G Davies, B Moroney, Ms D L Lee, T J Scicluna, R C Ablett, M Prasad, Dr S R Williams, W H Robson
**Co. Secretary:** William Robson
**Branches:** Whitecross Dental Care Ltd, Imperial Hall, Unit 4, London EC1V 2NR
**US SIC:** 8021 **UK SIC:** 95400
**Auditors:** PricewaterhouseCoopers LLP
**Bankers:** National Westminster Bank Plc (50-41-01)

| | 31-03-14 | 31-03-13 | 31-03-12 |
|---|---|---|---|
| TO | 138,793,000 | 122,265,000 | 111,933,000 |
| P/L | 10,180,000 | 11,249,000 | 11,310,000 |
| NW | (46,641,000) | (34,359,000) | (23,592,000) |
| WC | 18,375,000 | 32,154,000 | 39,212,000 |
| Emp. | 2,199 | 1,950 | 1,805 |

DUNS 57-840-0038
## Whitecross Healthcare Ltd
(**Subsidiary of:** Adp Primary Care Services Ltd)
Camden Clinic, 51 Kentish Town Road, London NW1 8NX
**Tel:** 02072420088
**Reg No:** 2893060 **Estd:** 1989 Private Limited Company
**Line of Business:** Management activities of holding companies
**Trading Style:** Pan
**Issued Capital:** £763,978
**Directors:** W H Robson, Dr S R Williams, T J Scicluna, Ms D L Lee
**Co. Secretary:** William Robson
**Branches:** Whitecross Healthcare Ltd, 106 Putney High Street, London SW15 1RG
**US SIC:** 6711, 8021
**UK SIC:** 83962, 95400
**Auditors:** KPMG
**Bankers:** The Royal Bank Of Scotland Plc (16-00-02)

| | 31-03-14 | 31-03-13 | 31-03-12 |
|---|---|---|---|
| TA | 16,942,000 | 16,942,000 | 16,942,000 |
| NW | 2,016,000 | 2,016,000 | 2,016,000 |
| WC | (8,485,000) | (8,485,000) | (8,485,000) |

DUNS 21-748-0988
## Whitecross Hereford
Three Elms Road, Hereford, Herefordshire HR4 0RN
**Tel:** 01432376080
**Web:** www.whitecross.hereford.sch.uk
**Reg No:** 7793019 **Estd:** 2011 Private Company Limited By Guarantee
**Line of Business:** General secondary education
**Directors:** B Chave, Mrs J Land, P J Foulkes, Mrs R Morris, L J Rogers, Mrs D S Goodall, K Shannon, Mrs D J Strutt
**Co. Secretary:** Ms Julie Higgs
**Responsibilities**
**Senior:** Melanie Bryans *(Director)*, Wendy Davies *(Director)*, Fiona Morris *(Director)*, Charlotte Thomas *(Director)*
**US SIC:** 8211 **UK SIC:** 93200

| | 31-08-14 | 31-08-13 |
|---|---|---|
| TO | 4,751,962 | 3,175,196 |
| P/L | 66,304 | (539,251) |
| NW | (477,947) | (476,251) |
| WC | 714,625 | 640,474 |
| Emp. | 86 | 93 |

DUNS 77-933-7104
## Whitefield Nursing Home Ltd
25 Service Street, Glasgow, Lanarkshire G66 7JW
**Tel:** 01360-310014 **Fax:** 01360-310042
**Web:** www.fshc.co.uk
**Reg No:** 0157455SC **Estd:** 1995 Private Limited Company
**Line of Business:** Nursing homes
**Issued Capital:** £135,000
**Directors:** B R Taberner, Ms M C Royston, I R Smith
**Co. Secretary:** Mrs Abigail Mattison
**Responsibilities**
**Senior:** Teresa Dogherty *(Manager)*, Dominic Kay *(Manager)*
**US SIC:** 8051 **UK SIC:** 95100
**Auditors:** Sinclair Wood & Co
**Bankers:** Clydesdale Bank Plc (82-69-32)

| | 31-12-13 | 31-12-12 | 31-12-11 |
|---|---|---|---|
| TO | 1,553,000 | 1,668,000 | 1,847,000 |
| P/L | 214,000 | 216,000 | 512,000 |
| NW | 3,522,000 | 3,308,000 | 3,092,000 |
| WC | 2,109,000 | 1,823,000 | 1,610,000 |
| Emp. | 70 | 73 | 78 |

DUNS 21-735-3392
## Whitefield School
Claremont Road, London NW2 1TR
**Tel:** 02084554114
**Web:** www.whitefield.barnet.sch.uk
**Reg No:** 7697281 **Estd:** 2011 Private Company Limited By Guarantee
**Line of Business:** Schools (local authority)
**Directors:** W Forsyth, Mrs N A Manaf, Ms E K Rymer, Ms A Bolton, Ms J Williams, Ms C Chamberlain, Dr M P Page, Ms C Harrison
**Co. Secretary:** Mrs Sandra Scott
**Responsibilities**
**Senior:** Martin Lavelle *(Head Teacher)*, Ann Mullerkins *(Director)*
**US SIC:** 8211 **UK SIC:** 93200
**Bankers:** The Co-Operative Bank Plc (08-02-28)

| | 31-08-14 | 31-08-13 | 31-08-12 |
|---|---|---|---|
| TO | 6,615,235 | 6,710,727 | 27,148,025 |
| P/L | (404,904) | (141,414) | 20,185,204 |
| NW | 19,603,886 | 19,653,790 | 19,890,204 |
| WC | 673,391 | 694,036 | 531,481 |
| Emp. | 121 | 111 | 110 |

DUNS 21-038-4676
## Whitefields Schools and Centre
Macdonald Road, London E17 4AZ
**Tel:** 020-8531-3426
**Web:** www.whitefield.ogr.uk
**Estd:** 1998
**Line of Business:** Schools (foundation)
**Trading Style:** Whitefields Schools and Centre
**Responsibilities**
**Senior:** Elaine Colquhoun *(Principal)*, Laura Tease *(Principal)*
**US SIC:** 8211 **UK SIC:** 93200
**Employees:** 119

DUNS 21-705-2923
## Whitefriars Canterbury Unit Trust
14 Gravel Walk, Canterbury, Kent CT1 2TF
**Tel:** 01227-826760
**Web:** www.whitefriars-canterbury.co.uk
**Estd:** 2009 Proprietorship
**Line of Business:** Other letting of own property
**Proprietor:** P Scutt
**US SIC:** 7399 **UK SIC:** 83954
**Employees:** 100

DUNS 21-727-8568
## Whitefriars Housing Group Ltd
9 Little Park Street, Coventry, West Midlands CV1 2UR
**Tel:** 02476767111
**Web:** www.whitefriarshousing.co.uk
**Reg No:** 0030092IP
**Partnership**
**Line of Business:** Non-charitable social work activities with accommodation
**Partners:** Mrs V Allsopp, D Round
**Responsibilities**
**Senior:** Pat Brandum *(Chief Executive Officer)*
**Finance:** Karen Iceton *(Head of Business and Contracts)*
**Marketing:** Gail Cooper *(Anti-Social Behaviour Team Man)*, John Halton *(Assistant Director, Developmen)*, Karen Iceton *(Head of Business and Contracts)*, Michael Park *(Development Manager)*, Terry Rollings *(Relations Executive)*, Joanna Selby *(Relations Manager)*
**Facilities:** Rachel Hobbs *(Director, Housing Services)*, Kam Sidhu *(?Head of Tenancy Support)*, Hayley Smith *(Resident Support Officer)*, Brian Tidman *(Head of Estate Management)*
**Operations:** Leisa Dixon *(Area Services Manager)*, Tony Marsella *(Service Manager)*, Sylvia Patrick *(Service Development Officer)*
**US SIC:** 8321 **UK SIC:** 96111
**Auditors:** Mazars LLP

| | 31-03-12 | 31-03-11 | 31-03-10 |
|---|---|---|---|
| TO | 72,351,000 | 67,419,000 | 66,041,000 |
| P/L | 8,955,000 | 6,906,000 | 3,518,000 |
| NW | (63,169,000) | (76,186,000) | (95,574,000) |
| WC | 1,678,000 | 3,246,000 | 3,543,000 |
| Emp. | 615 | 603 | 619 |

DUNS 21-579-7856
## Whitefriars Sailing Club
North End Lake 26, Ashton Keynes, Swindon, Wiltshire SN6 6QR
**Tel:** 01285861670
**Web:** www.wfsc.co.uk
**Estd:** 1978 Partnership
**Line of Business:** Sports clubs
**Partners:** C Stout, R Wheelan
**Responsibilities**
**Senior:** Rupert Wheelan *(Chairman)*
**US SIC:** 7999 **UK SIC:** 97913
**Employees:** 60

DUNS 22-661-1002
## Whitegates Estate Agency Ltd
(**Subsidiary of:** Martinco Plc)
4 Bruntcliffe Way, Morley, Morley, Leeds, West Yorkshire LS27 0JG
**Tel:** 01132-539166
**Web:** www.whitegates.co.uk
**Reg No:** 0757788 **Estd:** 1963 Private Limited Company
**Line of Business:** Estate agents
**Trading Style:** Experience Franchising
**Issued Capital:** £6,101,600
**Directors:** R W Martin, D A Raggett, I Wilson
**Co. Secretary:** David Raggett
**Responsibilities**
**Senior:** Michael Stoop *(Manager)*
**Branches:** Whitegates Estate Agency Ltd, Whitegates Estate Agency Ltd, 22 Central Parade, Cleckheaton, West Yorkshire BD19 3RU
**US SIC:** 6531 **UK SIC:** 83400
**Auditors:** PricewaterhouseCoopers LLP
**Bankers:** Barclays Bank Plc (20-11-81)

| | 31-12-13 | 31-12-12 | 31-12-11 |
|---|---|---|---|
| TO | 611,506 | 550,233 | 595,963 |
| P/L | 290,684 | (25,950) | 123,502 |
| NW | 1,369,418 | 1,106,868 | 1,128,807 |
| WC | 1,802,570 | 1,612,863 | 1,773,095 |

DUNS 76-363-8863 Imp
## Whiteghyll Plastics Ltd
3 City Road, Bradford, West Yorkshire BD8 8ER
**Tel:** 01274-307306
**Web:** www.whiteghyll.co.uk
**Reg No:** 2550414 **Estd:** 1990 Private Limited Company
**Line of Business:** Maintenance and repair of motor vehicles
**Issued Capital:** £2,220
**Directors:** R Egan, J Dinnewell, K A Wilson
**Co. Secretary:** Ms Ruth Farmer
**Responsibilities**
**HR:** Colin Storton *(Human Resources Manager)*
**Purchasing:** Colin Storton *(Human Resources Manager)*
**Engineering:** Colin Storton *(Human Resources Manager)*
**US SIC:** 3999 **UK SIC:** 49590
**Auditors:** Naylor Wintersgill
**Bankers:** HSBC Bank plc (40-25-10)

| | 31-12-13 | 31-12-12 | 31-12-11 |
|---|---|---|---|
| TO | 7,477,889 | 7,149,331 | 4,885,222 |
| P/L | 559,109 | 247,747 | (45,139) |
| NW | 1,453,005 | 1,789,898 | 1,654,440 |
| WC | 786,297 | 621,423 | 627,878 |
| Emp. | 84 | 71 | 46 |

DUNS 29-520-6395 Imp
## Whitehall Fabrications Ltd
Whitehall House, Bruntcliffe Lane, Leeds, West Yorkshire LS27 0LZ
**Tel:** 01132223000 **Fax:** 01430861863
**Web:** www.whitehall-uk.com
**Reg No:** 1883845 **VAT No:** 477045236
**Estd:** 1985 Private Limited Company
**Line of Business:** Joinery installation
**Trading Style:** Whitehall Worksurfaces
**Issued Capital:** £4,500
**Principals:** M F Greenwood *(Managing)*, S Daniels
**Co. Secretary:** Michael Greenwood
**Responsibilities**
**Senior:** Martyn Beattie *(Production Director)*, Craig Wall *(Warehouse Manager)*
**Engineering:** Martyn Beattie *(Production Director)*
**Branches:** Whitehall Fabrications Ltd, Unit 15, Hartcliffe Way, Bristol, Avon BS3 5RJ
**US SIC:** 7399 **UK SIC:** 83954
**Auditors:** Gleek Cadman Ross
**Bankers:** Lloyds TSB Bank plc (30-00-05)

| | 31-12-13 | 31-12-12 | 31-12-11 |
|---|---|---|---|
| TA | 1,416,921 | 1,534,845 | 1,530,850 |
| NW | 503,626 | 528,131 | 524,668 |
| WC | 438,124 | 483,663 | 490,552 |

DUNS 21-662-2021 Imp
## Whitehall Garden Centre (Holdings) Ltd
Corsham Road, Lacock, Chippenham, Wiltshire SN15 2LZ
**Tel:** 01249730204
**Web:** www.whitehallgardencentre.co.uk
**Reg No:** 7176171 **Estd:** 2010 Private Limited Company
**Line of Business:** Management activities of holding companies
**Trading Style:** Whithall Garden Center
**Issued Capital:** £28,636
**Directors:** Mrs C J Self, P R Self
**Responsibilities**
**Senior:** Phyllis Self *(Manager)*
**US SIC:** 6711 **UK SIC:** 83962

| | 31-12-13 | 31-12-12 | 31-12-11 |
|---|---|---|---|
| TO | 9,906,886 | 9,633,211 | 10,290,893 |
| P/L | 408,770 | 215,475 | 397,295 |
| NW | 5,425,595 | 5,315,875 | 5,329,424 |
| WC | (812,579) | (2,204,926) | (2,341,481) |
| Emp. | 172 | 169 | 187 |

DUNS 22-770-1778
## Whitehead Building Services Ltd
(**Subsidiary of:** Evol (Wales) Ltd)
Lanyon House, Mission Court, Newport, Gwent NP20 2DW
**Tel:** 01633-242450 **Fax:** 01633-242451
**Web:** www.whiteheadbuildingservices.co.uk
**Reg No:** 1394970 **VAT No:** 337607350
**Estd:** 1978 Private Limited Company
**Line of Business:** Other construction work involving special trades
**Issued Capital:** £1,300
**Directors:** R Morton, I L Cummings, M J Parry, N Williams, W D Reid, Mrs J Cummings
**Co. Secretary:** Rhys Morton
**US SIC:** 1799, 3629
**UK SIC:** 50000, 34350
**Auditors:** UHY Peacheys
**Bankers:** Barclays Bank Plc (20-60-58)

| | 30-11-13 | 30-11-12 | 30-11-11 |
|---|---|---|---|
| TO | 23,341,345 | 17,456,373 | 18,811,908 |
| P/L | 336,238 | 174,971 | 163,616 |
| NW | 1,886,254 | 1,622,459 | 1,501,195 |
| WC | 1,864,971 | 1,570,924 | 1,417,128 |
| Emp. | 114 | 104 | 101 |

DUNS 22-841-1310
## Whitehead Monckton
Monkdown House, Lidsing Road, Maidstone, Kent ME14 3EL
**Web:** www.whitehead-monckton.co.uk
**Estd:** 2001 Partnership
**Line of Business:** Solicitors
**Partners:** J P Jones, T C Monckton, R Coombe, Miss D J Harrison, R P Rogers, A J Robbins, R J Horton, M W Hardcastle
**Responsibilities**
**Senior:** Alexander Bak *(Associate)*, Daniel Bridgland *(Associate)*, Robert Coombe *(Partner and Head of Commercial)*, Jade Darvill *(Personal Injury Executive)*, Janet Goode *(Head of Commercial)*, Andrea Houston *(Partner)*, Christopher Longden *(Manager)*, Tim Monckton *(Partner)*, Adrian Robbins *(Partner)*, Kerin Speedie *(Partner)*, Peter Still *(Partner)*, R Stogdon *(Partner)*, Vicky Stoodley *(Partner)*, Garry Warman *(Associate)*, Matthew Woodhams *(Partner)*
**Finance:** Lynn Miller *(Financial Manager)*, Katie White *(Finance Manager)*
**Sales:** Julie Collier *(Business Development Director)*, Janet Goode *(Head of Commercial)*
**Admin:** Lisa Brown *(Legal Secretary)*, Mandy Coltham *(Personal Assistant)*, Amanada Morrison *(Secretary)*, Claire Smithers *(Legal Secretary)*, Donna morris *(Secretary)*
**HR:** Fiona Beal *(Human Resources)*
**Branches:** Whitehead Monckton, 37 High Street, Tenterden, Kent TN30 6BJ
**US SIC:** 8111, 7392
**UK SIC:** 83500, 83951
**Employees:** 50

DUNS 21-717-2554
## Whitehill Community Academy Multi-Academy Trust
Occupation Lane, Halifax, West Yorkshire HX2 9RL
**Tel:** 01422240874
**Reg No:** 7559439 **Estd:** 2011 Private Company Limited By Guarantee
**Line of Business:** Primary education
**Directors:** P A Smith, J M Craven, Mrs L J Waugh, S D Allen, J R Sayles, S D Taylor, I M Chappell, R Hepplestone
**Co. Secretary:** Mrs Anne Farnell
**Responsibilities**
**Senior:** Ian Hesselden *(Director)*
**US SIC:** 8211 **UK SIC:** 93200
**Bankers:** Yorkshire Bank Plc (05-04-49)

| | 31-08-14 | 31-08-13 | 31-08-12 |
|---|---|---|---|
| TO | 4,864,989 | 2,595,380 | 8,916,970 |
| P/L | 1,493,687 | (67,649) | 5,550,943 |
| NW | 6,738,981 | 5,276,293 | 5,296,943 |
| WC | 566,711 | 167,294 | 68,656 |
| Emp. | 83 | 58 | 73 |

DUNS 50-641-3223
## Whitehills Care Home
Scholars Gate, East Kilbride, Glasgow, Lanarkshire G75 9JL
**Tel:** 01355-579758
**Web:** www.thistlehealthcare.co.uk
**Estd:** 2003 Partnership
**Line of Business:** Residential care establishments
**Partners:** Mrs J Mcewan, Mrs P Chalmers
**Responsibilities**
**Senior:** Janice McEwan *(Manager)*
**US SIC:** 8321 **UK SIC:** 96111
**Employees:** 140

DUNS 21-557-5638
## Whitehills Health and Community Care Centre
Station Road, Forfar, Angus DD8 3DY
**Tel:** 01307475222
**Web:** www.nhstayside.scot.nhs.uk
**Proprietorship**
**Line of Business:** Hospitals
**Proprietor:** Mrs L Kemp
**US SIC:** 8062 **UK SIC:** 95100
**Employees:** 280

DUNS 23-730-6543
## Whitehorse Caterers
69 Beach Street, Deal, Kent CT14 6HY
**VAT No:** 414166378 **Estd:** 2012 Partnership
**Line of Business:** Restaurants
**Principals:** S Bentley, Mrs J Flavell *(Partner)*, W E Flavell *(Partner)*
**Responsibilities**
**Senior:** Mick Walls *(Proprietor)*
**Branches:** Whitehorse Caterers, 1 High St, Deal, Kent CT14 7AA

**US SIC:** 5812  **UK SIC:** 66110
**Bankers:** Barclays Bank Plc (20-02-62)
**Employees:** 50

DUNS 21-928-4163  *Imp*
## Whitehouse Construction Co. Ltd
(Subsidiary of: Brell Ewart Holdings Ltd)
Unit 3, Ewart House, Blenheim Road,
Ashbourne, Derbyshire DE6 1JU
**Fax:** 01335-346546
**Web:** www.whitehouseconstruction.co.uk
**Reg No:** 1331981 **VAT No:** 295396506
**Estd:** 1977 Private Limited Company
**Line of Business:** Civil engineers
**Issued Capital:** £10,000
**Principals:** B P Ewart *(Managing)*,
D B Renshaw, Ms J M Ewart-Sear,
R Jamieson, Ms S A Ewart, S Mckeown
**Co. Secretary:** Robert Ewart-Sear
**Responsibilities**
**Senior:** Katherine Ewart *(Manager)*, Victoria
Ewart *(Manager)*, Robert Sear *(Accountant)*
**Finance:** Robert Sear *(Accountant)*
**IT:** P Stanhope *(IT Manager)*
**Facilities:** Ashley Jackson *(Plant Manager)*
**Purchasing:** Ashley Jackson *(Plant Manager)*
**US SIC:** 1541  **UK SIC:** 50100
**Auditors:** Ashgates Corporate Services Ltd
**Bankers:** The Royal Bank Of Scotland Plc
(16-12-15)

|  | 30-06-14 | 30-06-13 | 30-06-12 |
|---|---|---|---|
| TO | 10,049,535 | 7,992,798 | 7,974,400 |
| P/L | 150,498 | 115,680 | 147,333 |
| NW | 1,319,843 | 1,207,585 | 1,115,835 |
| WC | 1,213,968 | 1,101,465 | 993,768 |
| Emp. | 82 | 74 | 68 |

DUNS 21-092-9654
## The Whitehouse Nursing Home
Gillison Close, Letchworth, Hertfordshire
SG6 1QL
**Tel:** 01462-485852
**Estd:** 1992 Proprietorship
**Line of Business:** Medical nursing home
activities
**Proprietor:** Y Tayob
**Responsibilities**
**Senior:** Alnashir Janmohammed *(Manager)*,
Renaud Sockalingum *(Manager)*
**US SIC:** 8051  **UK SIC:** 95100
**Employees:** 112

DUNS 51-627-1186
## Whitehouse Retail Group
65 Buncrana Road, Londonderry, Co
Londonderry BT48 8LB
**Tel:** 02871362498
**Web:** www.whitehouseretaillimited.com
**Estd:** 1975 Proprietorship
**Line of Business:** Supermarkets
**Proprietor:** D Barber
**Responsibilities**
**Senior:** Lisa Ryans *(General Manager)*
**US SIC:** 5411  **UK SIC:** 64100
**Bankers:** Ulster Bank Ltd (98-09-80)
**Employees:** 50

DUNS 21-764-5404
## Whiteladies Health Centre
Whiteladies Health Centre, Whatley Road,
Bristol, Avon BS8 2PU
**Tel:** 01179731201
**Web:** www.whiteladiesmedical.nhs.uk
**Estd:** 1973 Partnership
**Line of Business:** Doctors
**Partners:** Mrs A Shiner, Ms L Zerouali
**US SIC:** 8011  **UK SIC:** 95300
**Employees:** 50

DUNS 21-037-0196
## Whiteley Community Association
Gull Coppice, Whiteley, Fareham, Hampshire
PO15 7LA
**Tel:** 01489881190
**Web:** www.whiteley-community.co.uk
**Estd:** 1996
**Line of Business:** Community centres
**Proprietor:** Mrs L Pennington
**US SIC:** 6732  **UK SIC:** 83100
**Employees:** 50

DUNS 23-224-1471
## Whiteley Homes Trust
Whiteley Village, Walton On Tham, Walton-On-Thames, Surrey KT12 4BF
**Tel:** 01932857821
**Web:** www.whiteleyvillage.org.uk
**Reg No:** 0244305 **Estd:** 2003 Private
Unlimited Company
**Line of Business:** Non-charitable social
work activities with accommodation

**Responsibilities**
**Senior:** Michael Roycroft *(Wardon)*
**Branches:** Whiteley Homes Trust, Circle Rd,
Walton-On-Thames, Surrey KT12 4DP
**US SIC:** 8321  **UK SIC:** 96111
**Employees:** 120

DUNS 21-756-7704
## Whiteline (Group) Ltd
26-36 Hawthorn Road, Eastbourne, East
Sussex BN23 6QA
**Tel:** 01323723724 **Fax:** 08707749196
**Web:** www.whiteline.co.uk
**Reg No:** 7859392 **Estd:** 2011 Private
Limited Company
**Line of Business:** Other business activities
not elsewhere classified
**Issued Capital:** £600
**Directors:** C H St John, J R Corby,
T R Gourmand
**Responsibilities**
**Senior:** Steven Millen *(Manager)*
**US SIC:** 7399  **UK SIC:** 83954
**Bankers:** Barclays Bank Plc (20-27-91)

|  | 31-12-13 | 31-12-12 | 31-12-11 |
|---|---|---|---|
| TO | 12,961,516 | 10,992,020 | 10,017,841 |
| P/L | 1,018,530 | 629,070 | 389,362 |
| NW | 1,351,326 | 1,087,744 | 1,162,295 |
| WC | 1,334,812 | 801,064 | 780,845 |
| Emp. | 102 | 121 | 95 |

DUNS 34-572-5378  *Imp-Exp*
## Whitelink Seafoods Ltd
Maxwell Place Industrial Estate,
Fraserburgh, Aberdeenshire AB43 9SX
**Tel:** 01346-518-828
**Web:** www.whitelink.com
**Reg No:** 0138829SC **VAT No:** 267596505
**Estd:** 1974 Private Limited Company
**Line of Business:** Fish processing activities.
**Export Markets:** European Union (E U);
Europe
**Issued Capital:** £120,000
**Directors:** J Sutherland, A B Sutherland,
G Sutherland
**Co. Secretary:** Ms Marie Sutherland
**US SIC:** 5146  **UK SIC:** 61700
**Auditors:** Johnston Carmichael LLP
**Bankers:** Bank Of Scotland (80-06-86)

|  | 30-06-13 | 30-06-12 | 30-06-11 |
|---|---|---|---|
| TO | 45,929,710 | 46,738,091 | 50,690,375 |
| P/L | 371,276 | 424,017 | 379,315 |
| NW | 6,474,760 | 6,063,900 | 5,492,041 |
| WC | 3,152,780 | 671,983 | 1,695,627 |
| Emp. | 136 | 138 | 133 |

DUNS 21-016-4383  *Imp*
## Whitemeadow Furniture Ltd
(Subsidiary of: Whitemeadow Group
Holdings Ltd)
Unit 1 Export Drive, Sutton-In-Ashfield,
Nottinghamshire NG17 6AF
**Tel:** 01623555660 **Fax:** 01623-553-366
**Web:** www.whitemeadowfurniture.co.uk
**Reg No:** 6386737 **Estd:** 2007 Private
Limited Company
**Line of Business:** Upholstering
**Export Sales:** £650,945
**Issued Capital:** £28,873
**Directors:** I Oscroft, A Kitchen, P G Garnett,
P Wesson
**Responsibilities**
**Finance:** Michael Clarridge *(Financial Controller)*
**Admin:** Heather Clarkson *(Training Manager)*
**IT:** Robyn Edwards *(Computer Manager)*
**HR:** Heather Clarkson *(Training Manager)*
**US SIC:** 2599  **UK SIC:** 46720
**Auditors:** PKF (UK) LLP

|  | 31-12-13 | 31-12-12 | 31-12-11 |
|---|---|---|---|
| TO | 21,521,533 | 19,842,342 | 22,910,236 |
| P/L | 366,795 | 296,174 | 47,619 |
| NW | 112,707 | (361,583) | (705,032) |
| WC | (178,644) | (452,912) | (616,017) |
| Emp. | 212 | 223 | 222 |

DUNS 23-718-3165
## Whitemountain Quarries Ltd
(Subsidiary of: Lagan Group (Holdings) Ltd)
11b Sheepwalk Road, Lisburn, Co Antrim
BT28 3RD
**Tel:** 028-9250-1000 **Fax:** 028-9250-1100
**Web:** www.whitemountain.co.uk
**Reg No:** 0018140NI **Estd:** 1983 Private
Limited Company
**Line of Business:** Other mining and
quarrying not elsewhere classified
**Issued Capital:** £100
**Directors:** M F Kelly, S G Mccann,
L P Mcdonald, A M Mullan, K J Lagan
**Co. Secretary:** Declan Canavan
**Responsibilities**
**Facilities:** John Donaghy *(Facilities Manager)*
**Engineering:** Francisco Martin *(Production Manager)*
**Branches:** Whitemountain Quarries Ltd, 125
Upper Springfield Road, Belfast, Belfast
BT17 0LU
**US SIC:** 1499  **UK SIC:** 23960

**Auditors:** PricewaterhouseCoopers LLP
**Bankers:** Northern Bank Ltd (95-01-03)

|  | 31-12-13 | 31-12-12 | 31-12-11 |
|---|---|---|---|
| TO | 73,107,871 | 63,137,147 | 52,261,181 |
| P/L | 5,657,663 | 4,666,996 | 3,066,244 |
| NW | 35,896,738 | 30,236,775 | 25,556,408 |
| WC | 30,306,985 | 24,335,447 | 18,992,920 |
| Emp. | 170 | 168 | 185 |

DUNS 21-708-3856  *Imp-Exp*
## White(Packaging) Jacob Ltd
Riverside Industrial Estate, Riverside Way,
Dartford, Kent DA1 5BY
**Tel:** 01322-272531
**Web:** www.jacobwhite.com
**Reg No:** 1003647 **VAT No:** 714232667
**Estd:** 1911 Private Limited Company
**Line of Business:** Manufacture of other
general purpose machinery not elsewhere
classified
**Export Markets:** Worldwide
**Issued Capital:** £10,000
**Principals:** P A Colwell *(Managing)*,
D M Smith *(Financial)*, G J Thornton,
M J Taylor
**Co. Secretary:** Mrs Carla Colwell
**Responsibilities**
**Senior:** James Colwell *(Chairperson)*
**US SIC:** 3549  **UK SIC:** 32212
**Auditors:** Perrys
**Bankers:** Barclays Bank Plc (20-25-42)

|  | 31-12-13 | 31-12-12 | 31-12-11 |
|---|---|---|---|
| TA | 2,701,896 | 3,043,534 | 3,204,268 |
| NW | 774,190 | 739,636 | 891,375 |
| WC | 642,702 | 665,530 | 619,028 |

DUNS 23-682-1666
## Whitepost Healthcare Group
Shrewsbury Road, Redhill, Surrey RH1 6BH
**Tel:** 01737-764664
**Web:** www.whiteposthealthcare.co.uk
**Estd:** 1986 Partnership
**Line of Business:** Medical nursing home
activities
**Partners:** Ms U David, Dr A David,
Dr P J David
**Responsibilities**
**Finance:** Shamim David *(Finance Director)*
**Branches:** Whitepost Healthcare Group,
Cranbrook Rd, Tonbridge, Kent TN12 0ER
**US SIC:** 8051  **UK SIC:** 95100
**Bankers:** Barclays Bank Plc (20-37-16)
**Employees:** 150

DUNS 22-868-0203
## Whiterigg Nurseries
1 Southport Road, Eccleston, Chorley,
Lancashire PR7 6ET
**Estd:** 1973 Proprietorship
**Line of Business:** Garden centres
**Proprietor:** R H Wrigley
**US SIC:** 0161  **UK SIC:** 01001
**Bankers:** HSBC Bank plc (40-42-30)
**Employees:** 70

DUNS 21-018-0275
## White's Bakery Ltd
Charles Street, Barnsley, South Yorkshire
S70 5AF
**Tel:** 01226-203457
**Web:** www.whitesbakery.co.uk
**Reg No:** 6399039 **Estd:** 2007 Private
Limited Company
**Line of Business:** Bakers and confectioners
supplies
**Issued Capital:** £100
**Director:** J D White
**Co. Secretary:** Ms Kirsty Acklam
**US SIC:** 2051, 5462
**UK SIC:** 41960, 64100

|  | 31-03-14 | 31-03-13 | 31-03-12 |
|---|---|---|---|
| TA | 421,180 | 339,521 | 327,094 |
| NW | 115,961 | 27,622 | 2,588 |
| WC | 41,162 | (26,802) | (54,612) |

DUNS 23-300-3768
## White's Club
37-38 St James's Street, London SW1A 1JG
**Estd:** 2013
**Line of Business:** Clubs social and
associations
**Chairman:** J Hambro
**Responsibilities**
**Facilities:** Ray McGuinley *(Facilities Manager)*
**US SIC:** 8699  **UK SIC:** 96902
**Employees:** 46

DUNS 23-676-4473
## Whites Engineering Ltd
Mill Lane, South Witham, Grantham,
Lincolnshire NG33 5QN
**Tel:** 01572-767177
**Web:** www.whitesrecycling.co.uk
**Reg No:** 3671019 **VAT No:** 728408032
**Estd:** 2006 Private Limited Company
**Line of Business:** Collection and treatment
of other waste
**Trading Style:** Whites Recycling

**Issued Capital:** £100
**Principals:** C D Tyler *(Managing)*, A G White
**US SIC:** 3031  **UK SIC:** 48123
**Auditors:** Streets & Co
**Bankers:** Barclays Bank Plc (20-01-96)

|  | 31-03-14 | 31-03-13 | 31-03-12 |
|---|---|---|---|
| TO | 14,957,528 | 12,272,264 | N/A |
| P/L | 2,005,227 | 1,347,822 | N/A |
| NW | 5,267,382 | 2,887,992 | 211,920 |
| WC | 2,414,186 | 1,212,234 | (515,001) |
| Emp. | 131 | 120 | N/A |

DUNS 21-730-7248  *Imp*
## Whites Material Handling Ltd
(Subsidiary of: F & B Profiles (Holdings) Ltd)
6-12 Dixon Road, Bristol, Avon BS4 5QW
**Tel:** 01179720006
**Web:** www.whitesmh.co.uk
**Reg No:** 1248229 **Estd:** 1976 Private
Limited Company
**Line of Business:** Manufacturers and
suppliers of industrial machinery
**Export Sales:** £1,263,510
**Issued Capital:** £1,000
**Principals:** P H White *(Managing)*,
R F Avery
**Co. Secretary:** Ms Lisa Sinclair
**Responsibilities**
**IT:** Ian Groves *(Computer Manager)*
**Health & Safety:** Lee Adams *(Health & Safety Officer)*
**Purchasing:** Steve Lasson *(Buyer)*
**US SIC:** 3559, 3531
**UK SIC:** 32863, 32541
**Auditors:** PKF (UK) LLP
**Bankers:** Bank Of Scotland (12-05-77)

|  | 31-03-14 | 31-03-13 | 31-03-12 |
|---|---|---|---|
| TO | 6,907,842 | 5,633,002 | 5,622,448 |
| P/L | 243,206 | 147,851 | 120,939 |
| NW | 2,235,374 | 2,033,298 | 1,909,202 |
| WC | 1,379,229 | 1,682,548 | 1,598,644 |
| Emp. | 49 | 48 | 44 |

DUNS 21-731-3931  *Exp*
## Whites Transport Ltd
Laundry Road, Minster, Ramsgate, Kent
CT12 4HY
**Tel:** 01843-821377
**Web:** www.whitestransport.co.uk
**Reg No:** 0539226 **Estd:** 1954 Private
Limited Company
**Line of Business:** Road haulage and
transport services
**Export Markets:** France, Germany, Spain
**Issued Capital:** £1,000
**Directors:** C D White, J C White
**Co. Secretary:** Jonathan White
**Branches:** Whites Transport Ltd, Dale La,
Elmsall Way, Pontefract, West Yorkshire
WF9 2XX
**US SIC:** 4789, 4712
**UK SIC:** 77002
**Auditors:** Norman Brisk & Co
**Bankers:** National Westminster Bank Plc
(60-04-27)

|  | 30-09-13 | 30-09-12 | 30-09-11 |
|---|---|---|---|
| TA | 3,250,445 | 2,393,992 | 3,310,271 |
| NW | 2,545,660 | 1,823,742 | 1,569,074 |
| WC | 2,083,438 | 270,940 | (45,385) |

DUNS 21-585-3645
## Whitestone Weavers
Brenda Road, Hartlepool, Cleveland TS25
2BP
**Web:** www.whitestone.co.uk
**Estd:** 2011
**Line of Business:** Manufacture of other
carpets and rugs
**Proprietor:** S Byrne
**US SIC:** 2279  **UK SIC:** 43852
**Employees:** 90

DUNS 21-918-2201  *Imp-Exp*
## Whitford Ltd
(Subsidiary of: Whitford Worldwide
Company)
11 Stuart Road, Runcorn, Cheshire WA7
1TS
**Tel:** 01928571000 **Fax:** 01928-571010
**Web:** www.whitfordww.com
**Reg No:** 0959015 **Estd:** 1969 Private
Limited Company
**Line of Business:** Coating companies
**Export Markets:** E U, Middle East, India, S
Africa; Europe
**Export Sales:** £16,219,000
**Issued Capital:** £14,416
**Principals:** Ms A S Willis *(Managing)*,
D P Willis, M J Garnett
**Co. Secretary:** David Johnson
**Responsibilities**
**Marketing:** Rachel Howarth *(Marketing Manager)*
**US SIC:** 2891  **UK SIC:** 25620
**Auditors:** Grant Thornton UK LLP

**Bankers:** Lloyds TSB Bank plc (30-95-42)

| | 31-12-13 | 31-12-12 | 31-12-11 |
|---|---|---|---|
| TO | 21,996,000 | 19,672,000 | 19,383,000 |
| P/L | 2,206,000 | 510,000 | 2,224,000 |
| NW | 7,463,000 | 5,739,000 | 5,370,000 |
| WC | 3,114,000 | 1,558,000 | 5,051,000 |
| Emp. | 87 | 85 | 76 |

DUNS 21-098-5261 Exp

## Whitford Plastics Ltd

11 Stuart Road, Manor Park, Runcorn, Cheshire WA7 1TH
**Tel:** 01928571896 **Fax:** 01928-571010
**Web:** www.whitfordww.com
**Reg No:** 6426159 **Estd:** 2007 Private Limited Company
**Line of Business:** Manufacture of other plastic products
**Issued Capital:** £1
**Director:** Ms A S Willis
**Co. Secretary:** David Johnson
**Responsibilities**
**Operations:** Geoff Barnett *(Quality Assurance Manager)*
**US SIC:** 3079, 2891
**UK SIC:** 48360, 25620

| | 31-12-13 | 31-12-12 | 31-12-11 |
|---|---|---|---|
| TA | 1 | 1 | 1 |
| NW | 1 | 1 | 1 |

DUNS 22-540-9523

## The Whitgift Foundation

North End, Croydon, Surrey CR9 1SS
**Tel:** 02086808499
**Web:** www.whitgiftfoundation.co.uk
**Estd:** 1905
**Line of Business:** Other business activities not elsewhere classified
**Directors:** R J Smith, E R Nicholson
**Responsibilities**
**Senior:** Martin Corney *(Clerk Of The Foundation)*
**Admin:** Michelle Mcclatchie *(Office Manager)*
**Branches:** The Whitgift Foundation, 76 Brighton Road, South Croydon, Surrey CR2 6AB
**US SIC:** 7399, 8211, 6732
**UK SIC:** 83954, 93200, 83100
**Auditors:** haysmacintyre
**Bankers:** National Westminster Bank Plc (56-00-46)
**Employees:** 523
**Turnover:** £40,738,507

DUNS 73-465-2675

## Whiting & Hammond Ltd

The Little Brown Jug Chiddingstone, Causeway, Tonbridge, Kent TN11 8JJ
**Tel:** 01892-871042
**Web:** www.thecrickertersinn.co.uk
**Reg No:** 4729318 **Estd:** 2003 Private Limited Company
**Line of Business:** Licensed restaurants
**Issued Capital:** £799
**Directors:** B K Whiting, Ms J E Whiting
**Co. Secretary:** Christopher Hammond
**US SIC:** 5812, 5813
**UK SIC:** 66110, 66200
**Auditors:** Gary Sargeant & Co

| | 30-09-13 | 30-09-12 | 30-09-11 |
|---|---|---|---|
| TO | 9,177,697 | 8,204,383 | N/A |
| P/L | 280,087 | 221,570 | N/A |
| NW | 651,026 | 517,696 | 415,005 |
| WC | 198,174 | (25,724) | 23,657 |
| Emp. | 275 | 282 | N/A |

DUNS 76-417-4496

## Whiting Landscape Holdings Ltd

Wildmoor Lane, Wildmoor, Bromsgrove, Worcestershire B61 0RJ
**Web:** www.whitinglandscape.co.uk
**Reg No:** 2559320 **VAT No:** 551518648
**Estd:** 1987 Private Limited Company
**Line of Business:** Other construction work involving special trades
**Issued Capital:** £61,000
**Directors:** M Murphy, D E Griffiths, B W Bridges
**Co. Secretary:** Laurence Upcott
**Responsibilities**
**Senior:** Colin Spear *(Manager)*
**Health & Safety:** Michael Ganner *(General Manager)*
**Purchasing:** Michael Ganner *(General Manager)*
**US SIC:** 1799 **UK SIC:** 50000
**Auditors:** Grant Thornton UK LLP
**Bankers:** Bank Of Scotland (12-05-65)

| | 30-06-14 | 30-06-13 | 30-06-12 |
|---|---|---|---|
| TO | 7,747,084 | 8,461,727 | 8,213,641 |
| P/L | 470,038 | 137,692 | 160,136 |
| NW | 1,253,067 | 1,290,768 | 1,160,112 |
| WC | 387,295 | 427,788 | 310,293 |
| Emp. | 96 | 101 | 99 |

DUNS 21-776-6584

## Whitkirk Primary School

Templegate Walk, Leeds, West Yorkshire LS15 0EU
**Tel:** 01132606203
**Web:** www.whitkirk.leeds.sch.uk
**Estd:** 1997
**Line of Business:** Schools (local authority)
**US SIC:** 8211 **UK SIC:** 93200
**Employees:** 50

DUNS 76-486-3304

## Whitland Engineering Ltd

**(Subsidiary of:** Celtic Process Systems Ltd)
West Street, Whitland, Dyfed SA34 0AE
**Tel:** 01994-240442
**Web:** www.whitlandengineering.co.uk
**Reg No:** 2566083 **VAT No:** 557852990
**Estd:** 1987 Private Limited Company
**Line of Business:** Other engineering activities
**Trading Style:** Whitland Engineering Ltd
**Issued Capital:** £100
**Directors:** J A Donovan, J L Owen, W H Davies
**Co. Secretary:** Eurig Jones
**US SIC:** 8911 **UK SIC:** 83701
**Auditors:** Llewelyn Davies & Co
**Bankers:** National Westminster Bank Plc (56-00-42)

| | 31-10-13 | 31-10-12 | 31-10-11 |
|---|---|---|---|
| TA | 2,629,633 | 1,889,629 | 2,763,498 |
| NW | 574,464 | 606,193 | 720,643 |
| WC | 342,197 | 495,310 | 708,158 |

DUNS 21-782-7335

## Whitleigh Primary School

Lancaster Gardens, Plymouth, Devon PL5 4AA
**Tel:** 01752706383
**Web:** www.whitleigh-pri.plymouth.sch.uk
**Estd:** 1956 Proprietorship
**Line of Business:** Schools (local authority)
**Proprietor:** I Cording
**US SIC:** 8211 **UK SIC:** 93200
**Employees:** 70

DUNS 21-780-5227

## Whitley Bay High School

Deneholm, Whitley Bay, Tyne and Wear NE25 9AS
**Tel:** 01912008800
**Web:** www.whitleybayhighschool.org
**Estd:** 2011 Proprietorship
**Line of Business:** Schools (local authority)
**Proprietor:** A Chedburn
**US SIC:** 8211 **UK SIC:** 93200
**Employees:** 150

DUNS 28-943-9903

## Whitley Hall Hotel Ltd

**(Subsidiary of:** Hlw 229 Ltd)
Elliot Lane, Grenoside, Sheffield, South Yorkshire S35 8NR
**Tel:** 01142-454444
**Web:** www.whitleyhall.com
**Reg No:** 1593427 **Estd:** 1981 Private Limited Company
**Line of Business:** Hotels and motels without restaurant
**Issued Capital:** £336,556
**Directors:** Ms A Stanley, R D Broadbent
**Co. Secretary:** Robert Broadbent
**Responsibilities**
**Senior:** Karen Hirst *(Financial Director)*
**Finance:** Karen Hirst *(Financial Director)*
**US SIC:** 7011, 5812
**UK SIC:** 66500, 66110
**Auditors:** Hollis & Co Ltd
**Bankers:** HSBC Bank plc (40-17-04)

| | 31-12-13 | 31-12-12 | 31-12-11 |
|---|---|---|---|
| TO | 2,262,397 | 2,274,759 | 2,081,925 |
| P/L | 124,490 | 209,826 | 154,266 |
| NW | 4,313,215 | 4,377,827 | 4,365,971 |
| WC | (776,908) | (921,073) | (1,080,000) |
| Emp. | 62 | 63 | 60 |

DUNS 21-014-9174

## Whitley Stimpson Management Llp

Penrose House, 67 Hightown Road, Banbury, Oxfordshire OX16 9BE
**Tel:** 01295270200 **Fax:** 01295-271784
**Web:** www.whitleystimpson.co.uk
**Reg No:** 0331505OC **Estd:** 1990 Private Limited Company
**Line of Business:** Accounting and auditing activities
**Responsibilities**
**Senior:** Alison Anson *(Senior Partner)*, Richard Hancock *(Partner)*, Owen Kyffin *(Designated Limited Liability P)*, Tim Wallbank *(Corporate Finance Partner)*
**Finance:** Alison Anson *(Senior Partner)*, Heather Finnigan *(Accounting Technician)*, Tim Wallbank *(Corporate Finance Partner)*
**Branches:** Whitley Stimpson Management Llp, 7 Hughenden Avenue, Manor Courtyard, High Wycombe, Buckinghamshire HP13 5RE
**US SIC:** 8931 **UK SIC:** 83600

| | 06-04-14 | 31-12-12 | 31-04-11 |
|---|---|---|---|
| TA | 1,780,043 | 1,429,243 | 1,380,014 |
| NW | 870,000 | 810,000 | 1,010,000 |
| WC | 1,251,196 | 1,102,455 | 909,173 |

DUNS 21-686-6277 Imp-Exp

## Whitman Laboratories Ltd

Bedford Road, Petersfield, Petersfield, Hampshire GU32 3DD
**Tel:** 01730266522
**Web:** www.esteelauder.com
**Reg No:** 0005824FC **VAT No:** 193310674
**Estd:** 1966
**Line of Business:** Manufacturers of cosmetics
**Directors:** R J Aquilina, S P Gibson, S P Gibson, B G Leworthy, M J Gladman, D J Hunt, F H Langhammer
**Co. Secretary:** Paul Konney
**Responsibilities**
**Senior:** Mark Osmond *(Warehouse Manager)*, Adrian Parish *(MIS Manager)*
**Marketing:** Adrian Parish *(MIS Manager)*
**IT:** Adrian Parish *(MIS Manager)*
**US SIC:** 2844 **UK SIC:** 25820
**Bankers:** National Westminster Bank Plc (60-16-26)

DUNS 73-596-5514

## Whitminster Inn Ltd

Bristol Road, Whitminster, Gloucester, Gloucestershire GL2 7NY
**Tel:** 01452-740234
**Web:** www.whitminsterinn.co.uk
**Reg No:** 4857785 **Estd:** 1981 Private Limited Company
**Line of Business:** Licensed restaurants
**Issued Capital:** £2
**Directors:** K W Chiu, J Mcgoldrick
**Co. Secretary:** Ms Claire Mcgoldrick
**US SIC:** 5813 **UK SIC:** 66200

| | 31-03-14 | 31-03-13 | 31-03-12 |
|---|---|---|---|
| TA | 127,018 | 123,545 | 121,987 |
| NW | (217,605) | (132,575) | (131,699) |
| WC | (238,683) | (160,708) | (156,901) |

DUNS 23-231-3601

## Whitmore Vale Housing Association Ltd

Whitmore Vale House, Churt Road, Hindhead, Surrey GU26 6NL
**Web:** www.whitmorevale.co.uk
**Reg No:** 0019760IP **Estd:** 1973 Friendly Society
**Line of Business:** Other letting of own property
**Principals:** W Lindop *(Chairman)*, R Kelly, R C Farrant, Ms B Cook, N Peck, Mrs I Lindop
**Co. Secretary:** Ms Jean Wilcock
**Responsibilities**
**Senior:** Ryan Kelley *(Chief Executive)*, hillory hall *(chairman)*
**Branches:** Whitmore Vale Housing Association Ltd, Beaufort House, Chobham Road, Woking, Surrey GU21 2TD
**US SIC:** 7399 **UK SIC:** 83954
**Auditors:** Wise & Co
**Employees:** 50

DUNS 50-334-9698 Imp-Exp

## Whitmore's Timber Co. Ltd

Main Road, Claybrooke Magna, Lutterworth, Leicestershire LE17 5AQ
**Tel:** 01455-209121 **Fax:** 01455-209041
**Web:** www.whitmores.co.uk
**Reg No:** 2359578 **VAT No:** 531956240
**Estd:** 1989 Private Limited Company
**Line of Business:** Saw milling and planing of wood, impregnation of wood
**Export Markets:** Worldwide
**Export Sales:** £22,956
**Issued Capital:** £694,250
**Directors:** C A Smee, P Gaskell, A P Rankine
**Co. Secretary:** Nigel Bazeley
**Responsibilities**
**Senior:** Richard Loveridge *(Manager)*
**US SIC:** 2421 **UK SIC:** 46101
**Auditors:** Harold Sharp
**Bankers:** Bank Of Scotland (80-20-00)

| | 31-07-13 | 31-07-12 | 31-07-11 |
|---|---|---|---|
| TO | 11,432,766 | 12,240,636 | 10,669,267 |
| P/L | 4,164 | 46,930 | 49,459 |
| NW | 1,679,286 | 1,678,089 | 1,638,756 |
| WC | 1,667,880 | 2,005,095 | 1,945,885 |
| Emp. | 64 | 65 | 56 |

DUNS 21-713-3263

## Whitport Ltd

12 Winchester Road The Precinct, Eastleigh, Hampshire SO53 2GA
**Tel:** 02380274555
**Reg No:** 0062172 **Estd:** 1899 Private Limited Company
**Line of Business:** Road haulage and transport services
**Export Sales:** £2,438,991
**Trading Style:** Whitport Ltd
**Issued Capital:** £4,000,000
**Directors:** R W White, R J Nicklinson, Mrs R C Owers, D A Hoare, R H Jeans
**Co. Secretary:** Roy Nicklinson
**Branches:** Whitport Ltd, Bottings Industrial Estate, Southampton, Hampshire SO30 2DY
**US SIC:** 4789, 4226
**UK SIC:** 77002, 77003
**Auditors:** Westlake Clark
**Bankers:** Lloyds TSB Bank plc (30-96-11)

| | 31-01-14 | 31-01-13 | 31-01-12 |
|---|---|---|---|
| TO | 26,340,149 | 25,682,256 | 24,894,082 |
| P/L | 1,067,610 | 349,075 | (144,239) |
| NW | 10,068,926 | 9,355,122 | 9,208,526 |
| WC | 1,050,253 | (224,190) | (550,857) |
| Emp. | 476 | 489 | 478 |

DUNS 21-154-8001

## Whittaker Group Ltd

Upper Hindwells, Stonehaven, Kincardineshire AB39 3UT
**Tel:** 01569-762018
**Web:** www.whittakereng.com
**Reg No:** 0355700SC **VAT No:** 384706331
**Estd:** 1912 Private Limited Company
**Line of Business:** Engineers (general)
**Export Sales:** £1,016,874
**Trading Style:** Whittaker Engineering
**Issued Capital:** £1,000
**Directors:** K Whittaker, Ms J E Whittaker
**Co. Secretary:** Stronachs Secretaries Limited
**US SIC:** 8911 **UK SIC:** 83701

| | 31-12-13 | 31-12-12 | 31-12-11 |
|---|---|---|---|
| TO | 11,298,596 | 20,614,247 | 11,845,999 |
| P/L | (281,487) | 4,484,717 | 1,911,473 |
| NW | 8,474,960 | 8,454,583 | 5,146,421 |
| WC | 1,600,788 | 2,604,424 | 666,455 |
| Emp. | 99 | 102 | 92 |

DUNS 34-848-4010

## Whittan Group Ltd

Link House, Halesfield 6, Telford, Shropshire TF7 4LN
**Tel:** 01952-682251 **Fax:** 01952581810
**Web:** www.polypal.co.uk
**Reg No:** 5647349 **Estd:** 2006 Private Limited Company
**Line of Business:** Management activities of holding companies
**Export Sales:** £38,885,000
**Issued Capital:** £3,551
**Directors:** R W Wood, M H Bailey, J L Heathcote, C Macdonald, A Butler, S Comfort
**Co. Secretary:** Jatinder Nurpuri
**Responsibilities**
**Senior:** Andrew Sumner *(Manager)*
**US SIC:** 6711 **UK SIC:** 83962
**Auditors:** KPMG LLP

| | 31-03-14 | 31-03-13 | 31-03-12 |
|---|---|---|---|
| TO | 109,708,000 | 129,856,000 | 117,419,000 |
| P/L | (2,420,000) | 390,000 | (3,822,000) |
| NW | (40,701,000) | (41,041,000) | (59,561,000) |
| WC | 9,954,000 | 10,504,000 | 11,538,000 |
| Emp. | 627 | 654 | 651 |

DUNS 21-144-6627 Imp

## Whittard Trading Ltd

**(Subsidiary of:** Eso Investments Llp)
Windrush House, Windrush Park Road, Witney, Oxfordshire OX29 7DX
**Tel:** 01993893715
**Web:** www.whittard.co.uk
**Reg No:** 6753147 **Estd:** 2008 Private Limited Company
**Line of Business:** Other retail sale in non-specialised stores
**Export Sales:** £3,088,208
**Trading Style:** Whittard of Chelsea
**Issued Capital:** £1
**Directors:** A M Dunhill, G R Brand, R W Fulford, N J Smith
**Co. Secretary:** Nathan Smith
**Responsibilities**
**Senior:** Sara Halton *(Manager)*
**US SIC:** 5399, 5999
**UK SIC:** 65600
**Auditors:** Hazlewoods LLP
**Bankers:** Lloyds TSB Bank plc (77-27-09)

| | 28-12-13 | 29-12-12 | 24-12-11 |
|---|---|---|---|
| TO | 29,074,308 | 31,776,926 | 31,481,889 |
| P/L | 252,646 | 72,430 | (970,884) |
| NW | (4,524,212) | (4,829,455) | (4,956,562) |
| WC | (5,851,141) | (6,049,265) | (4,524,786) |
| Emp. | 449 | 579 | 608 |

DUNS 73-621-9374

## Whittingham Riddell L L P

Belmont House, Shrewsbury Business Park, Shrewsbury, Shropshire SY2 6LG
**Web:** www.whittinghamriddell.co.uk
**Reg No:** 0305421OC **Estd:** 2003
**Line of Business:** Accounting and auditing activities
**Responsibilities**
**Senior:** Duncan Montgomery *(Designated Limited Liability P)*

**US SIC:** 8931  **UK SIC:** 83600
**Auditors:** Illegible Auditor's Name

| | 31-03-14 | 31-03-13 | 31-03-12 |
|---|---|---|---|
| TO | 8,598,431 | 7,016,889 | 6,901,743 |
| P/L | 1,998,381 | 1,480,032 | 1,592,893 |
| NW | 2,516,887 | 3,044,154 | 2,984,978 |
| WC | 2,751,024 | 2,705,490 | 2,546,379 |

DUNS 54-864-0739

### Whittington Hospital N H S Trust

St Marys Wing, Highgate Hill, London N19 5NF
**Web:** www.whittington.nhs.co.uk
**Line of Business:** Public sector hospital activities, including nhs trusts
**Issued Capital:** £1
**Principals:** R Martin (Financial), Mrs M Boltwood (Personnel), Mrs S Harrington, P Ient, Dr Y Koh, Ms C I Clark, Ms F Smith
**Co. Secretary:** Ms Susan Sorensen
**US SIC:** 8062, 8091
**UK SIC:** 95100, 95200
**Employees:** 2,000

DUNS 28-875-6133

### Whittington Moor Printing Works Ltd

(**Subsidiary of:** Gamble Investments Ltd)
Units 4-5, Stonegravels Lane, Chesterfield, Derbyshire S41 7LF
**Tel:** 01246221892
**Web:** www.wmpw.co.uk
**Reg No:** 1105180  **VAT No:** 127449263
**Estd:** 1973 Private Limited Company
**Line of Business:** Printing not elsewhere classified
**Issued Capital:** £2,236
**Director:** P M Gamble
**Co. Secretary:** Bernard Mackie
**Responsibilities**
**Senior:** Tim Parrott (Manager)
**Finance:** Tim Parrott (Manager)
**IT:** Tim Parrott (Manager)
**Engineering:** Tim Parrott (Manager)
**US SIC:** 2752  **UK SIC:** 47544
**Auditors:** McBoyle & Co
**Bankers:** Lloyds TSB Bank plc (30-91-93)

| | 31-10-14 | 31-10-13 | 31-10-12 |
|---|---|---|---|
| TA | 1,878,346 | 1,754,432 | 1,406,264 |
| NW | 425,071 | 338,525 | 267,137 |
| WC | 170,054 | 158,280 | (1,864) |

DUNS 22-770-4152

### Whittle Coach Bus & Holidays

Foley Business Park, Stourport Road, Kidderminster, Worcestershire DY11 7QL
**Web:** www.whittlecoach.co.uk
**VAT No:** 159289910  **Estd:** 1999 Partnership
**Line of Business:** Coach and bus hire
**Trading Style:** Whittle Coach Bus and Holidays
**Partners:** R A Whittle, Mrs D L Whittle
**Responsibilities**
**Senior:** Andrew McKinnnon (Transport Manager), David Shipp (General Manager)
**Fleet:** Andrew McKinnnon (Transport Manager)
**Branches:** Whittle Coach Bus & Holidays, 11 Whitburn St, Bridgnorth, Shropshire WV16 4QN
**US SIC:** 4119  **UK SIC:** 72200
**Bankers:** Lloyds TSB Bank plc (30-94-70)
**Employees:** 50

DUNS 29-544-6934

### Whittle Jones Group Ltd

Lynton House, Ackhurst Business Park, Foxhole Road, Chorley, Lancashire PR7 1NY
**Web:** www.whittlejones.com
**Reg No:** 1911331  **VAT No:** 604788129
**Estd:** 1989 Private Limited Company
**Line of Business:** Surveyors and valuers
**Trading Style:** Whittle Jones
**Issued Capital:** £1,050
**Directors:** Miss K Revitt, T R Parkinson, G S Brown, D M Lee, M J Grindrod, J C Kay
**Co. Secretary:** Mrs Joanne Patel
**Responsibilities**
**Senior:** John Marrow (Regional Property Manager)
**Branches:** Whittle Jones Group Ltd, Unit 221, 95 Spencer Street, Birmingham, West Midlands B18 6DA
**US SIC:** 8911  **UK SIC:** 83701
**Auditors:** KPMG LLP

| | 31-03-14 | 31-03-13 | 31-03-12 |
|---|---|---|---|
| TO | 2,916,000 | 2,870,000 | 2,372,000 |
| NW | 78,000 | 78,000 | 78,000 |
| WC | (28,000) | (42,000) | (30,000) |
| Emp. | 53 | 56 | 57 |

DUNS 73-993-7535

### Whittle Movers Holdings Ltd

Charnley Fold Lane, Bamber Bridge, Preston, Lancashire PR5 6AA
**Tel:** 01772626573  **Fax:** 01772627770
**Web:** www.whittle.co.uk
**Reg No:** 5244189  **Estd:** 2004 Private Limited Company
**Line of Business:** Management activities of holding companies
**Issued Capital:** £50,000
**Directors:** Mrs P Morris, J J Morris, A D Williams
**US SIC:** 6711, 4226
**UK SIC:** 83962, 77003
**Auditors:** CLB Coopers

| | 31-01-14 | 31-01-13 | 31-01-12 |
|---|---|---|---|
| TA | 359 | 359 | 359 |
| P/L | N/A | N/A | 472,656 |
| NW | 359 | 359 | 359 |
| Emp. | N/A | N/A | 3 |

DUNS 53-644-8574

### Whittle Painting Group Ltd

(**Subsidiary of:** Roy Hankinson (Holdings) Ltd)
Ryan House Ryan Business Park, Radford Road, Nottingham, Nottinghamshire NG7 7DH
**Tel:** 08707892020  **Fax:** 01159-771472
**Web:** www.hankinsongroup.co.uk
**Reg No:** 3450309  **Estd:** 1903 Private Limited Company
**Line of Business:** Painting and glazing
**Issued Capital:** £114,000
**Directors:** I A Thomas, S R Hankinson
**Responsibilities**
**Finance:** Nat Varatheesan (Finance Controller)
**US SIC:** 1721  **UK SIC:** 50400
**Auditors:** Deloitte & Touche
**Bankers:** Bank Of Scotland (12-09-26)

| | 31-10-13 | 31-10-12 | 31-10-11 |
|---|---|---|---|
| TA | 446,627 | 446,627 | 446,627 |
| NW | 218,457 | 218,457 | 218,457 |

DUNS 21-912-6893

### Whittle Painting Nottingham Ltd

(**Subsidiary of:** Roy Hankinson (Holdings) Ltd)
Ryan House Ryan Business Park, Radford Road, Nottingham, Nottinghamshire NG7 7DH
**Tel:** 01159708770  **Fax:** 01159771472
**Web:** www.whittleprogrammed.co.uk
**Reg No:** 1157420  **Estd:** 1974 Private Limited Company
**Line of Business:** Painting contractors
**Trading Style:** P M S
**Issued Capital:** £100,000
**Directors:** I A Thomas, S R Hankinson
**US SIC:** 1721  **UK SIC:** 50400
**Auditors:** Deloitte & Touche
**Bankers:** Bank Of Scotland (12-09-26)

| | 31-10-13 | 31-10-12 | 31-10-11 |
|---|---|---|---|
| TA | 507,101 | 507,101 | 507,101 |
| NW | 507,101 | 507,101 | 507,101 |

DUNS 23-913-5440

### Whittle Pharmacies Ltd

Whittle Brook Pharmacy, Chorley, Lancashire PR6 7HW
**Tel:** 01257-262536
**Reg No:** 3903928  **Estd:** 1998 Private Limited Company
**Line of Business:** Dispensing chemists
**Trading Style:** Whittle Pharmacies Ltd
**Issued Capital:** £440
**Directors:** V Patel, U Patel
**Branches:** Whittle Pharmacies Ltd, 285 Kingsway, Rochdale, Lancashire OL16 4AT
**US SIC:** 5912, 8091
**UK SIC:** 64300, 95200

| | 31-01-14 | 31-01-13 | 31-01-12 |
|---|---|---|---|
| TO | 6,316,928 | 6,461,327 | 6,729,265 |
| P/L | 195,261 | 209,981 | 171,845 |
| NW | 1,525,032 | 1,236,675 | 938,275 |
| WC | 857,661 | 546,787 | 513,966 |
| Emp. | 58 | 59 | 69 |

DUNS 28-868-4467

### Whittle Property Management Ltd

(**Subsidiary of:** G3 Whittle Ltd)
Castle Heights, 72 Maid Marian Way, Nottingham, Nottinghamshire NG1 6BJ
**Tel:** 01159411121
**Web:** www.whittlerealty.com
**Reg No:** 1005855  **Estd:** 1908 Private Limited Company
**Line of Business:** Property Management
**Issued Capital:** £245,950
**Principals:** S C Whittle (Managing), Ms G M Minogue, Ms S M Whittle
**Co. Secretary:** Ms Gillian Minogue
**US SIC:** 6512  **UK SIC:** 85000
**Auditors:** Cooper-Parry

**Bankers:** National Westminster Bank Plc (56-00-61)

| | 31-03-14 | 31-03-13 | 31-03-12 |
|---|---|---|---|
| TA | 237,888 | 237,888 | 237,888 |
| NW | 237,888 | 237,888 | 237,888 |

DUNS 21-761-1340

### Whittlebury Hall & Spa Ltd

(**Subsidiary of:** Whittlebury Hall Ltd)
Whittlebury Hall, West Park, Towcester, Northamptonshire NN12 8QH
**Tel:** 08454000001
**Web:** www.whittleburyhall.co.uk
**Reg No:** 7839199  **Estd:** 2011 Private Limited Company
**Line of Business:** Other tourist assistance activities not elsewhere classified
**Issued Capital:** £1
**Directors:** B Zechner, M Stott
**US SIC:** 7999  **UK SIC:** 97913

| | 31-12-13 | 31-12-12 |
|---|---|---|
| TO | 14,349,052 | 13,894,829 |
| P/L | 1,569,471 | 1,317,769 |
| NW | 2,112,587 | 1,317,766 |
| WC | 1,017,121 | 463,984 |
| Emp. | 313 | 295 |

DUNS 21-774-8804

### Whitwick St John the Baptist C of E Primary School

Parsonwood Hill, Whitwick, Coalville, Leicestershire LE67 5AT
**Tel:** 01530832116
**Web:** www.whitwickce.leics.sch.uk
**Estd:** 2011 Partnership
**Line of Business:** Primary education
**Partners:** Mrs P Baldry, Mrs C Killip, Mrs P Baldry
**US SIC:** 8211  **UK SIC:** 93200
**Employees:** 55

DUNS 23-826-7269

### Whitworth Chemists Ltd

6 Snowdonia Avenue, Scunthorpe, South Humberside DN15 8NL
**Tel:** 01724846648  **Fax:** 01724847284
**Web:** www.whitworthchemists.co.uk
**Reg No:** 3818717  **Estd:** 1999 Private Limited Company
**Line of Business:** Chemists dispensing
**Issued Capital:** £1,375,000
**Directors:** J B Badenhorst, Mrs S Vernon, Mrs D A Bradley, R W Bradley
**Co. Secretary:** Ms Dorothy Bradley
**Responsibilities**
**Health & Safety:** Trevor Eden (Health & Safety Officer)
**Branches:** Whitworth Chemists Ltd, 25 Westcliffe Dr, Blackpool, Lancashire FY3 7BJ
**US SIC:** 5912  **UK SIC:** 64300
**Auditors:** Arthur Wigglesworth & Co
**Bankers:** The Royal Bank Of Scotland Plc (16-00-01)

| | 31-03-14 | 31-03-13 | 31-03-12 |
|---|---|---|---|
| TO | N/A | 23,306,600 | 23,866,899 |
| P/L | N/A | 917,093 | 965,690 |
| NW | (5,737,345) | (6,065,191) | (6,824,043) |
| WC | (1,445,927) | (1,050,167) | (2,246,390) |
| Emp. | N/A | 282 | 277 |

DUNS 21-778-6022

### Whitworth Community High School

Hall Street, Rochdale, Lancashire OL12 8TL
**Tel:** 01706860492
**Web:** www.whitworth.lancs.sch.uk
**Estd:** 2011 Proprietorship
**Line of Business:** Schools (local authority)
**Proprietor:** Ms M Holt
**Responsibilities**
**Senior:** Gill Middlemas (Head Teacher)
**US SIC:** 8211  **UK SIC:** 93200
**Employees:** 100

DUNS 21-034-5147

### Whitworth Hall Country Park Hotel

24 High Street, Spennymoor, County Durham DL16 6DB
**Tel:** 01388811772
**Web:** www.whitworthhall.co.uk
**Estd:** 2012 Partnership
**Line of Business:** Chocolate fountains
**Partners:** A Lax, P Lawson, Mrs J Cartwright Lax
**Responsibilities**
**Senior:** Elizabeth Malpas (General Manager)
**HR:** Jill Lax (Human Resources Manager)
**US SIC:** 7011  **UK SIC:** 66500
**Employees:** 80

DUNS 21-232-9212

### Whitworth Hospital

330 Bakewell Road, Matlock, Derbyshire DE4 2JD
**Tel:** 01629-580211
**Web:** www.derbyshirecountypct.nhs.uk
**Estd:** 2002 Proprietorship
**Line of Business:** Hospitals
**Proprietor:** Mrs W Hulland
**Responsibilities**
**Senior:** Wilma Hulland (Manager), Jonathan Sanderson (General Manager), Karen Sherlock (Matron)
**Health & Safety:** Karen Sherlock (Matron)
**Facilities:** Karen Sherlock (Matron)
**US SIC:** 8062  **UK SIC:** 95100
**Employees:** 117

DUNS 71-887-4592  Imp

### Whitworths Ltd

(**Subsidiary of:** Apricot Topco Ltd)
Orchard House, Irthlingborough, Wellingborough, Northamptonshire NN9 5DB
**Tel:** 01933-653-000
**Web:** www.whitworths.co.uk
**Reg No:** 5269846  **VAT No:** 755698668
**Estd:** 2004 Private Limited Company
**Line of Business:** Food packers
**Export Sales:** £2,450,000
**Issued Capital:** £1
**Directors:** P D Unsworth, P A Utting
**Co. Secretary:** Daniel Jarman
**Responsibilities**
**Senior:** Tina Robinson (HR Manager), Colin Stephens (Manager)
**Sales:** Colin Stephens (Manager)
**HR:** Tina Robinson (HR Manager)
**Purchasing:** Neil Dickens (Procurement Director)
**US SIC:** 7399, 5149
**UK SIC:** 83954, 61700
**Auditors:** Deloitte LLP
**Bankers:** Lloyds TSB Bank plc (30-99-26)

| | 03-05-14 | 27-04-13 | 30-05-12 |
|---|---|---|---|
| TO | 157,205,000 | 144,840,000 | 144,894,000 |
| P/L | 7,053,000 | 11,811,000 | 5,440,000 |
| NW | 43,433,000 | 37,643,000 | 28,580,000 |
| WC | 49,560,000 | 43,966,000 | 34,835,000 |
| Emp. | 366 | 370 | 350 |

DUNS 38-543-5292

### Who Cares? Scotland

Oswald Chambers, 5 Oswald Street, Glasgow, Lanarkshire G1 4QR
**Tel:** 0141-226-4441
**Web:** www.whocaresscotland.org
**Reg No:** 0173232SC  **Estd:** 1997 Private Limited Company
**Line of Business:** Activities of other membership organisations not elsewhere classified
**Directors:** Mrs E Delaney, Ms A G Fowlie, M Friess, F Molyneux, A Lorimer, D J Early, Mrs C L Bell, D R Bowen
**Responsibilities**
**Senior:** Duncan Dunlop (Chief Executive), Sally-Ann Grant (Director), Joseph Rankin (Director)
**Finance:** Linda McCracken (Administration Manager)
**Admin:** Linda McCracken (Administration Manager)
**Facilities:** Linda McCracken (Administration Manager)
**US SIC:** 8699  **UK SIC:** 96902
**Auditors:** The Kelvin Partnership

| | 31-03-14 | 31-03-13 | 31-03-12 |
|---|---|---|---|
| TO | 1,919,206 | 1,689,824 | 1,607,750 |
| P/L | 148,106 | 24,823 | (40,323) |
| NW | 432,025 | 283,919 | 259,096 |
| WC | 409,326 | 259,065 | 231,352 |
| Emp. | 59 | 53 | 44 |

DUNS 21-223-4915

### Wholesale Glass Co

Unit 1, Tramsheds Industrial Estate, Coomber Way, Croydon, Surrey CR0 4TQ
**Tel:** 02086643768
**Web:** www.wholesaleglasscompany.co.uk
**Estd:** 2004 Proprietorship
**Line of Business:** Glass merchants
**Proprietor:** R Jones
**US SIC:** 5039  **UK SIC:** 61300
**Employees:** 50

DUNS 23-184-9659

### Whowhatwherewhenwhy

Queens Quay, Belfast BT3 9QQ
**Tel:** 028-9046-7700  **Fax:** 028-9046-7707
**Web:** www.w5online.co.uk
**Reg No:** 0037861NI  **Estd:** 2000 Private Company Limited By Guarantee
**Line of Business:** Preservation of historical sites and buildings
**Trading Style:** W5
**Directors:** R A Murphy, D E Porter, Mrs W S Gillies, Professor T Harrison, Dr C A O'Mullan
**Co. Secretary:** Antony Payne

**Responsibilities**
**Senior:** Sally Montgomery *(Manager)*
**Operations:** Richard Gapper *(Operations Manager)*
**US SIC:** 8411 **UK SIC:** 97700
**Auditors:** Northern Ireland Audit Office
**Bankers:** The Bank Of Ireland (90-21-27)

| | 31-03-14 | 31-03-13 | 31-03-12 |
|---|---|---|---|
| TO | 2,962,980 | 2,786,595 | 2,666,540 |
| P/L | 145,848 | (434,566) | (341,156) |
| NW | 1,051,292 | 905,444 | 1,340,010 |
| WC | 222,956 | 229,031 | 261,036 |
| Emp. | 49 | 53 | 51 |

DUNS 21-022-3459 Imp-Exp
## W.H.Palmer & Co.(Industries) Ltd
Charringtons House, The Causeway, Bishops Stortford, Hertfordshire CM23 2ER
**Tel:** 01279-658464
**Web:** www.alcohols.co.uk
**Reg No:** 0727228 **Estd:** 1839 Private Limited Company
**Line of Business:** Wholesale of chemical products
**Export Markets:** Worldwide
**Export Sales:** £4,842,930
**Trading Style:** Alcohols
**Issued Capital:** £100,000
**Principals:** A J Wallis *(Managing)*, J Alton, M H Colling
**Co. Secretary:** Robert Ling
**Responsibilities**
**Senior:** Simon Read *(Manager)*
**US SIC:** 5161 **UK SIC:** 61200
**Auditors:** F W Stephens & Co
**Bankers:** National Westminster Bank Plc (60-05-37)

| | 31-12-13 | 31-12-12 | 31-12-11 |
|---|---|---|---|
| TO | 24,470,065 | 22,246,056 | 21,809,619 |
| P/L | 1,711,935 | 1,059,751 | 969,770 |
| NW | 8,575,051 | 7,626,565 | 6,205,939 |
| WC | 6,048,421 | 5,113,729 | 4,545,175 |
| Emp. | 46 | 48 | 46 |

DUNS 21-622-4402
## W.Hurst & Son.(I.W.) Ltd
29-33 Holyrood Street, Newport, Isle of Wight PO30 5AX
**Tel:** 01983-523636
**Web:** www.tryhurstfirst.co.uk
**Reg No:** 0693444 **VAT No:** 107359866
**Estd:** 1961 Private Limited Company
**Line of Business:** Diy shops
**Issued Capital:** £4,075
**Principals:** R D Mclaughlin *(Managing)*, D J Bowley, Mrs J E Williams, Miss A M Reed, Mrs M Bradley, P M Hartnell
**Branches:** W.hurst & Son.(I.w.) Ltd, 17-18 High Street, Cowes, Isle Of Wight PO31 7RZ
**US SIC:** 5251, 5732, 5699, 5999
**UK SIC:** 64800, 64500, 65600
**Auditors:** A.H. Cross & Co
**Bankers:** Lloyds TSB Bank plc (30-95-99)

| | 31-05-13 | 31-05-12 | 31-05-11 |
|---|---|---|---|
| TO | 4,592,758 | 4,624,655 | 4,883,563 |
| P/L | 263,265 | 260,203 | 303,419 |
| NW | 7,067,871 | 6,828,993 | 6,787,103 |
| WC | 2,510,778 | 2,430,399 | 2,362,165 |
| Emp. | 90 | 95 | 92 |

DUNS 21-583-6449
## Whyte & Mackay
South Lumley Street, Grangemouth, Stirlingshire FK3 8NF
**Tel:** 01324667120
**Web:** www.whyteandmackay.com
**Estd:** 2011 Proprietorship
**Line of Business:** Bottlers
**Proprietor:** D Forsyth
**US SIC:** 2086 **UK SIC:** 42831
**Employees:** 150

DUNS 21-401-0548 Imp
## Whyte and Mackay Ltd
**(Subsidiary of:** Emperador Uk Ltd)
Dalmore House, 310 St Vincent Street, Glasgow, Lanarkshire G2 5RG
**Tel:** 01412485771 **Fax:** 0141-221-1993
**Web:** www.whyteandmackay.co.uk
**Reg No:** 0014456SC **VAT No:** 556618711
**Estd:** 1927 Private Limited Company
**Line of Business:** Manufacture of distilled potable alcoholic beverages
**Trading Style:** Whyte & Mackay Brands, Invergordon Distillers
**Issued Capital:** £178,973,000
**Directors:** Dr A C Tan, W S Co, J C Vilardell, B H Donaghey, J D Bohorquez
**Responsibilities**
**Marketing:** Nick Garland *(Global Sales & Marketing Direc)*, Jen McCormick *(Global Brand Manager - Glayva)*
**Sales:** Nick Garland *(Global Sales & Marketing Direc)*, S Lawrie *(Sales Director)*, Stephen Watt *(Sales Director)*
**IT:** Alister Campbell *(It Manager)*, Bernadette Dunsmuir *(IT Manager)*
**HR:** Wendy Ellen *(Human Resources Assistant)*, Liz Patrick *(HR Administrator)*
**Branches:** Whyte and Mackay Ltd, Kyndal International Ltd, Golfview Terrace, Invergordon, Ross-Shire IV18 0HP
**US SIC:** 2085 **UK SIC:** 42402
**Auditors:** PricewaterhouseCoopers LLP
**Bankers:** Barclays Bank Plc (20-33-70)

| | 31-03-14 | 31-03-13 | 31-03-12 |
|---|---|---|---|
| TO | 231,093,000 | 263,395,000 | 227,217,000 |
| P/L | 12,148,000 | 33,555,000 | 26,341,000 |
| NW | 382,907,000 | 366,271,000 | 336,718,000 |
| WC | 346,395,000 | (151,389,000) | (185,524,000) |
| Emp. | 414 | 429 | 439 |

DUNS 22-205-5837
## Whyte Crane Hire Ltd
**(Subsidiary of:** Whyte Cranes Holding Ltd)
Tipperty Industrial Centre, Tipperty, Ellon, Aberdeenshire AB41 8LZ
**Tel:** 01224-729000 **Fax:** 01224729001
**Web:** www.whytecranes.com
**Reg No:** 0219628SC **Estd:** 2002 Private Limited Company
**Line of Business:** Cargo handling
**Issued Capital:** £100
**Director:** L W Whyte
**Co. Secretary:** Stronachs Secretaries Limited
**Responsibilities**
**Senior:** Jennifer Whyte *(Manager)*
**US SIC:** 4712 **UK SIC:** 77002
**Auditors:** Hohnston Carmichael
**Bankers:** The Royal Bank Of Scotland Plc (83-15-08)

| | 30-06-14 | 30-06-13 | 30-06-12 |
|---|---|---|---|
| TO | 10,540,751 | 11,682,821 | 11,366,719 |
| P/L | 558,136 | 601,738 | 284,126 |
| NW | 2,712,582 | 4,272,170 | 3,962,517 |
| WC | (2,115,786) | (3,112,318) | (4,470,655) |
| Emp. | 107 | 98 | 94 |

DUNS 21-158-3950 Imp-Exp
## Whyte Group Ltd
Marlborough House, 298 Regents Park Road, London N3 2UA
**Tel:** 020-8346-5946 **Fax:** 02083494589
**Web:** www.whytechemicals.co.uk
**Reg No:** 1286190 **Estd:** 1976 Private Limited Company
**Line of Business:** Management activities of holding companies
**Export Markets:** E U
**Export Sales:** £64,013,000
**Issued Capital:** £500,000
**Principals:** M M Whyte *(Managing)*, B S Rattan *(Financial)*, G Gupta, Dr A M Rosenberg-Whyte, A Mittra, A Mittra, Ms L Whyte
**Responsibilities**
**Senior:** Paul Bloom *(Finance Director)*
**Finance:** Paul Bloom *(Finance Director)*
**US SIC:** 6711, 5161
**UK SIC:** 83962, 61200
**Auditors:** UHY Hacker Young
**Bankers:** HSBC Bank plc (40-03-28)

| | 30-06-14 | 31-12-12 | 31-06-11 |
|---|---|---|---|
| TO | 133,127,000 | 80,734,000 | 107,276,000 |
| P/L | 332,000 | 59,000 | (65,000) |
| NW | 8,327,000 | 8,159,000 | 8,137,000 |
| WC | 219,000 | 802,000 | 380,000 |
| Emp. | 164 | 177 | 180 |

DUNS 21-779-1173
## Wick High School
West Banks Avenue, Wick, Caithness KW1 5LU
**Tel:** 01955603333
**Estd:** 2011 Proprietorship
**Line of Business:** Schools (local authority)
**Proprietor:** L Gunn
**Responsibilities**
**Senior:** Thomas Mcintyre *(Head Teacher)*
**US SIC:** 8211 **UK SIC:** 93200
**Employees:** 82

DUNS 22-529-3521 Imp
## Wick Hill Group Ltd
River Court, Albert Drive, Woking, Surrey GU21 5RP
**Web:** www.wickhill.co.uk
**Reg No:** 1250558 **VAT No:** 641309952
**Estd:** 1976 Private Limited Company
**Line of Business:** Wholesale of computers, computer peripheral equipment and software
**Issued Capital:** £100,000
**Principals:** I A Kilpatrick *(Managing)*, K Ward, Ms K Kilpatrick, H S Scherff
**Co. Secretary:** Graham Hitchens
**Responsibilities**
**Marketing:** Barry Mattcott *(Marketing Manager)*
**Branches:** Wick Hill Group Ltd, Rivercourt, Albert Drive, Woking, Surrey GU21 5RP
**US SIC:** 5081 **UK SIC:** 61490
**Auditors:** Menzies LLP
**Bankers:** The Royal Bank Of Scotland Plc (15-10-00)

| | 31-03-14 | 31-03-13 | 31-03-12 |
|---|---|---|---|
| TO | 69,935,000 | 49,967,000 | 45,283,000 |
| P/L | 2,895,000 | 423,000 | 805,000 |
| NW | 4,000,000 | 1,937,000 | 1,670,000 |
| WC | 3,553,000 | 1,579,000 | 1,310,000 |
| Emp. | 119 | 110 | 93 |

DUNS 29-484-2109
## Wickes Building Supplies Ltd
**(Subsidiary of:** Travis Perkins Plc)
120-138 Station Road, Harrow, Middlesex HA1 2QB
**Tel:** 02089012000 **Fax:** 020-8901-2036
**Web:** www.wickes.co.uk
**Reg No:** 1840419 **Estd:** 1972 Private Limited Company
**Line of Business:** Diy shops
**Trading Style:** Wickes
**Issued Capital:** £25,317,000
**Directors:** M R Meech, A D Morrison, N Bell, A D Buffin, J P Carter, S King, I Preedy, R D Proctor
**Co. Secretary:** Tpg Management Services Limited
**Responsibilities**
**Senior:** simon king *(manager director)*
**Marketing:** Ketan Mistry *(Email Marketing Manager)*
**Sales:** Gary West *(Trading Manager)*
**Facilities:** Sophia Stephens *(Operations Manager)*
**Operations:** martin robert *(operations director)*
**Purchasing:** David Furness *(Operations Director)*
**Branches:** Wickes Building Supplies Ltd, Walmley Ash Road, Sutton Coldfield, West Midlands B76 1FG
**US SIC:** 5999, 5039
**UK SIC:** 65600, 61300
**Auditors:** Deloitte LLP
**Bankers:** National Westminster Bank Plc (50-00-00)

| | 28-12-13 | 29-12-12 | 31-12-11 |
|---|---|---|---|
| TO | 972,038,000 | 976,136,000 | 980,450,000 |
| P/L | 49,441,000 | 55,550,000 | 40,375,000 |
| NW | 298,859,000 | 273,471,000 | 230,250,000 |
| WC | 190,248,000 | 164,682,000 | 125,150,000 |
| Emp. | 5,479 | 5,729 | 5,783 |

DUNS 29-867-0100
## Wickes Ltd
**(Subsidiary of:** Travis Perkins Plc)
38-40 Croydon Road, West Wickham, Kent BR4 9HT
**Tel:** 02084629209 **Fax:** 02084627079
**Web:** www.wickes.co.uk
**Reg No:** 2070200 **Estd:** 1987 Private Limited Company
**Line of Business:** Diy shops
**Issued Capital:** £27,570,940
**Directors:** J P Carter, M R Meech, A D Buffin
**Co. Secretary:** Tpg Management Services Limited
**Responsibilities**
**Senior:** Philip Gay *(Store Manager)*
**Branches:** Wickes Ltd, Bellfield Rd, High Wycombe, Buckinghamshire HP13 5HN
**US SIC:** 6711, 5251
**UK SIC:** 83962, 64800
**Auditors:** Deloitte & Touche LLP
**Bankers:** Barclays Bank Plc (20-00-00)

| | 28-12-13 | 29-12-12 | 31-12-11 |
|---|---|---|---|
| TA | 338,747,000 | 338,747,000 | 338,747,000 |
| NW | 143,382,000 | 143,382,000 | 143,382,000 |
| WC | 43,824,000 | 43,824,000 | 43,824,000 |

DUNS 21-681-3220 Imp
## Wickham Laboratories Ltd
**(Subsidiary of:** Wickham Laboratories Holdings Ltd)
Hoeford Point, Barwell Lane, Gosport, Hampshire PO13 0AU
**Fax:** 01329 226688
**Web:** www.wickhamlabs.co.uk
**Reg No:** 0752951 **VAT No:** 109060207
**Estd:** 1963 Private Limited Company
**Line of Business:** Research and laboratory based activities
**Issued Capital:** £2,822,500
**Principals:** W B Cartmell *(Managing)*, P J Paice, C A Bishop
**Co. Secretary:** Ms Joan Cartmell
**Responsibilities**
**IT:** A McKay *(Computer Manager)*
**Branches:** Wickham Laboratories Ltd, Hoeford Point, Barwell Lane, Gosport, Hampshire PO13 0AU
**US SIC:** 7391, 7397
**UK SIC:** 94000, 83702
**Auditors:** Nexia Smith & Williamson
**Bankers:** Barclays Bank Plc (20-30-89)

| | 31-03-14 | 31-03-13 | 31-03-12 |
|---|---|---|---|
| TO | 6,099,011 | 4,699,767 | 4,249,505 |
| P/L | 1,035,096 | (338,252) | (355,395) |
| NW | 3,414,956 | 2,486,385 | 821,344 |
| WC | (456,775) | (2,055,138) | (340,401) |
| Emp. | 89 | 93 | 89 |

DUNS 21-730-9962 Exp
## Wickham Laboratories(S.P.F Farms) Ltd
**(Subsidiary of:** Wickham Laboratories Holdings Ltd)
Winchester Road, Wickham, Fareham, Hampshire PO17 5EU
**Fax:** 01329834362
**Web:** www.wickhamlabs.co.uk
**Reg No:** 1027852 **VAT No:** 109060403
**Estd:** 1971 Private Limited Company
**Line of Business:** Research and laboratory based activities
**Export Markets:** Worldwide
**Issued Capital:** £100,550
**Director:** W B Cartmell
**Co. Secretary:** Ms Joan Cartmell
**US SIC:** 7391 **UK SIC:** 94000
**Auditors:** BKL Blueprint
**Employees:** 70

DUNS 53-645-4036
## Wickham Theatre Trust
62 Corkscrew Hill, West Wickham, Kent BR4 9BA
**Tel:** 02087779989
**Web:** www.theatre62.wordpress.com
**Reg No:** 3450828 **Estd:** 1997 Private Limited Company
**Line of Business:** Artistic and literary creation and interpretation
**Directors:** Mrs S G Campbell, J B Heather, Ms R E Aylward, P J Swinge, Ms S J Elgar, I A James, I Munday, S P Scott
**Co. Secretary:** Ms Samantha Elgar
**Responsibilities**
**Senior:** Pauline Hart *(Manager)*, Bernard Hemsley *(Manager)*, Christene Lever *(Director)*, Alice London *(Director)*, Pauline Whalley *(Manager)*
**US SIC:** 7999 **UK SIC:** 97913
**Auditors:** Ron Hoyle

| | 31-12-13 | 31-12-12 | 31-12-11 |
|---|---|---|---|
| TO | 43,340 | 39,298 | 40,366 |
| P/L | (2,930) | (1,237) | 8,652 |
| NW | 116,963 | 118,605 | 117,361 |
| WC | 47,846 | 43,488 | 36,244 |

DUNS 49-387-8367 Imp-Exp
## Wickman Coventry Ltd
**(Subsidiary of:** Ima Srl)
Automatic House, Discovery Way, Leofric Business Park, Binley, Coventry, West Midlands CV3 2TD
**Tel:** 024-7654-7900 **Fax:** 02476547920
**Web:** www.wickman.co.uk
**Reg No:** 3134891 **Estd:** 1995 Private Limited Company
**Line of Business:** Manufacturers of machine tools
**Export Sales:** £2,675,317
**Issued Capital:** £1,173,410
**Directors:** R Dodd, O A Coyne, C P Barrett
**Co. Secretary:** Ian Gill
**Responsibilities**
**Senior:** Dean Powell *(Financial Director)*
**Finance:** Dean Powell *(Financial Director)*
**IT:** Donald Atkins *(IT Manager)*
**HR:** Joe Ferrara *(Human Resources Manager)*
**US SIC:** 3542, 5084
**UK SIC:** 32212, 61490
**Auditors:** Gane Jackson Scott LLP
**Bankers:** HSBC Bank plc (40-46-35)

| | 31-12-13 | 31-12-12 | 31-12-11 |
|---|---|---|---|
| TO | 6,834,718 | 7,290,144 | N/A |
| P/L | 99,908 | 164,901 | N/A |
| NW | 1,401,745 | 1,170,865 | 1,026,087 |
| WC | 2,599,295 | 2,577,818 | 2,088,922 |
| Emp. | 49 | 33 | N/A |

DUNS 21-692-6633
## Wicksteed Charitable Trust
Barton Road, Kettering, Northamptonshire NN15 6NJ
**Tel:** 01536512475 **Fax:** 01536518948
**Web:** www.wicksteedpark.co.uk
**Reg No:** 7394789 **Estd:** 2010 Private Company Limited By Guarantee
**Line of Business:** Amusement park activities
**Trading Style:** Wicksteed Park Limited
**Directors:** C Bowen, R Hunt, Mrs L Groves, Ms D A Tarry, C J Pykett, O C Wicksteed, P J Clarke, G D Keevill
**Responsibilities**
**Senior:** Alistair Macnee *(Manager)*, Alasdair Mcknee *(Manager)*
**Marketing:** Hayley Ryan *(Relations Manager)*
**US SIC:** 7996 **UK SIC:** 97913
**Bankers:** National Westminster Bank Plc (53-61-33)

| | 28-02-14 | 28-02-13 | 28-02-12 |
|---|---|---|---|
| TO | 1,290,866 | 10,678,951 | 2,343,171 |
| P/L | (377,275) | 6,009,463 | 2,347,736 |
| NW | 7,981,399 | 8,405,018 | 2,347,736 |
| WC | 5,963,304 | 6,263,142 | (520,601) |
| Emp. | 192 | 186 | 203 |

DUNS 22-103-4338
## Wicksteedathome Ltd
(**Subsidiary of:** Jardentome Ltd)
Digby Street, Kettering, Northamptonshire NN16 8YJ
**Tel:** 01536-517028
**Web:** www.wicksteed.co.uk
**Reg No:** 4122750 **Estd:** 2000 Private Limited Company
**Line of Business:** Other non-store retail sale
**Trading Style:** Wicksteed Leisure Ltd
**Issued Capital:** £1
**Director:** Lord G P Howard
**Co. Secretary:** Mitchell Barratt
**US SIC:** 5963 **UK SIC:** 65600

| | 31-12-13 | 31-12-12 | 31-12-11 |
|---|---|---|---|
| TA | 1 | 1 | 1 |
| NW | 1 | 1 | 1 |

DUNS 34-512-9725
## Wider Options (3) Ltd
(**Subsidiary of:** Barclays Plc)
Turnpike Gate House, Alcester Heath, Alcester, Warwickshire B49 5JG
**Tel:** 01789-767800
**Web:** www.optionsgroup.co.uk
**Reg No:** 5323908 **Estd:** 2000 Private Limited Company
**Line of Business:** Social work activities with accommodation
**Trading Style:** Options Group
**Issued Capital:** £100
**Directors:** Mrs J R Worsley, G Baker, Mrs R L Northall, R J Cooke, D N Garman
**Responsibilities**
**Senior:** Alison Lord *(Chief Executive)*, Tony Welch *(Manager)*
**Branches:** Wider Options (3) Ltd, The Rhydd, Worcester, Worcestershire WR8 0AD
**US SIC:** 8321 **UK SIC:** 96111
**Auditors:** Heathcote & Coleman LLP

| | 31-03-14 | 31-03-13 | 31-03-12 |
|---|---|---|---|
| TO | 5,185,946 | 4,508,344 | 4,319,348 |
| P/L | 424,467 | 213,307 | 1,824,620 |
| NW | (1,572,161) | (1,748,477) | (1,800,382) |
| WC | 475,549 | 221,778 | 430,813 |
| Emp. | 151 | 125 | 121 |

DUNS 22-210-2118
## Wider Options Ltd
(**Subsidiary of:** Barclays Plc)
Turnpike Gate House, Alcester Heath, Alcester, Warwickshire B49 5JG
**Tel:** 01724-733777
**Web:** www.optionsgroup.co.uk
**Reg No:** 4228353 **Estd:** 2001 Private Limited Company
**Line of Business:** Adult and other education not elsewhere classified
**Trading Style:** Wider Options Ltd
**Issued Capital:** £500,000
**Directors:** D N Garman, G Baker, R J Cooke, Mrs R L Northall, Mrs J R Worsley
**Responsibilities**
**Senior:** Clive Firman *(Manager)*, Suzanne Green *(Manager)*, Alison Lord *(Manager)*, Tommy Macdonald Milner *(Manager)*
**US SIC:** 8249, 8091, 7021
**UK SIC:** 93300, 95200, 66500
**Bankers:** Barclays Bank Plc (20-00-50)

| | 31-03-14 | 31-03-13 | 31-03-12 |
|---|---|---|---|
| TO | 7,858,673 | 7,770,883 | 7,715,477 |
| P/L | 795,028 | 988,479 | 1,287,765 |
| NW | 13,650,376 | 12,656,339 | 11,767,892 |
| WC | 2,161,558 | 1,205,386 | 686,043 |
| Emp. | 270 | 257 | 242 |

DUNS 23-377-6710
## Wider Plan Ltd
11?16 Chestnut Court, Redditch, Worcestershire B96 6EW
**Tel:** 08006127550 **Fax:** 01527 895455
**Web:** www.widerplan.com
**Reg No:** 5207145 **VAT No:** 883846961
**Estd:** 2004 Private Limited Company
**Line of Business:** Childcare services
**Issued Capital:** £300
**Directors:** J W Richardson, Mrs L C Payne, C K Chalmers
**Co. Secretary:** Alison Chalmers
**US SIC:** 8299 **UK SIC:** 93300
**Auditors:** TaxAssist Accountants
**Bankers:** Lloyds TSB Bank plc (30-98-21)

| | 28-02-13 | 29-02-12 | 28-02-11 |
|---|---|---|---|
| TO | 2,050,765 | 1,829,762 | 1,351,900 |
| P/L | 488,366 | 427,541 | 190,534 |
| NW | 847,679 | 497,479 | 228,123 |
| WC | (106,214) | (410,894) | 207,621 |

DUNS 21-630-9634
## Widex Uk Ltd
Winster House, Lakeside, Chester Business Park, Chester, Cheshire CH4 9QT
**Web:** www.widex.co.uk
**Reg No:** 7094822 **Estd:** 2009 Private Limited Company
**Line of Business:** Hearing aid suppliers
**Trading Style:** Widex Uk
**Issued Capital:** £1
**Directors:** J F Andersen, J Jensen, C M Jensen
**Co. Secretary:** Stuart Styles
**Responsibilities**
**Senior:** Jon Billings *(general manager)*
**Finance:** David Gartlon *(Financial controller)*
**US SIC:** 3841 **UK SIC:** 37201

| | 30-04-14 | 30-04-13 | 30-04-12 |
|---|---|---|---|
| TO | 7,355,027 | 8,933,191 | 8,486,015 |
| P/L | 3,360,527 | (733,881) | (10,785) |
| NW | 4,138,559 | (2,596,967) | (1,877,664) |
| WC | 5,629,570 | 610,827 | 991,849 |
| Emp. | 53 | 55 | 50 |

DUNS 21-596-7427
## Widnes Hall Residential Care Home
Widnes Lodge, Coronation Drive, Widnes, Cheshire WA8 8BL
**Tel:** 01514208500
**Web:** www.idealcarehomes.co.uk
**Estd:** 2011 Proprietorship
**Line of Business:** Residential care establishments
**Proprietor:** Mrs S Mccann
**Responsibilities**
**Senior:** Amanda Ashton *(Home Manager)*, Sue McCann *(Proprietor)*
**US SIC:** 8321 **UK SIC:** 96111
**Employees:** 50

DUNS 21-163-7457 **Imp**
## Widney Manufacturing Ltd
(**Subsidiary of:** Widney Manufacturing Holdings Ltd)
Plume Street, Birmingham, West Midlands B6 7SA
**Tel:** 01213275500
**Web:** www.widney.co.uk
**Reg No:** 6899084 **Estd:** 1969 Private Limited Company
**Line of Business:** General mechanical engineering
**Issued Capital:** £1
**Directors:** S L Roberts, J E Brookes, M I Devers
**Co. Secretary:** Matt Devers
**Responsibilities**
**Sales:** Roger Cox *(Sales Manager)*
**IT:** Sue Boucker *(IT Manager)*
**US SIC:** 3999 **UK SIC:** 49590
**Auditors:** HMT Assurance LLP

| | 30-09-13 | 30-09-12 | 30-09-11 |
|---|---|---|---|
| TO | 10,834,053 | 11,557,967 | 10,819,245 |
| P/L | 753,996 | 723,283 | 908,378 |
| NW | 2,642,374 | 2,060,517 | 1,468,505 |
| WC | 2,310,227 | 1,716,888 | 1,454,855 |
| Emp. | 135 | 133 | 121 |

DUNS 64-089-6742 **Imp**
## Wieden & Kennedy U K Ltd
(**Subsidiary of:** Kennedy Wieden Inc)
16 Hanbury Street, London E1 6QR
**Tel:** 02071947000 **Fax:** 020-7194-7100
**Web:** www.wklondon.com
**Reg No:** 3484979 **Estd:** 1998 Private Limited Company
**Line of Business:** Advertising
**Trading Style:** Wieden & Kennedy U K Limited
**Issued Capital:** £2
**Directors:** D G Wieden, N Christie, D W Luhr
**Co. Secretary:** Bronwen Hemming
**Responsibilities**
**Senior:** Clare Delaney *(Manager)*
**US SIC:** 7311 **UK SIC:** 83800
**Auditors:** Ernst & Young LLP
**Bankers:** National Westminster Bank Plc (50-00-00)

| | 31-12-13 | 31-12-12 | 31-12-11 |
|---|---|---|---|
| TO | 26,298,676 | 17,502,167 | 20,648,326 |
| P/L | 3,446,953 | (388,727) | (1,784,560) |
| NW | 4,523,022 | 1,371,654 | 1,764,235 |
| WC | 5,228,152 | 2,179,090 | 1,422,149 |
| Emp. | 161 | 123 | 186 |

DUNS 71-917-9447
## Wienerberger Ltd
(**Subsidiary of:** Wienerberger Ag)
Brooks Drive, Cheadle, Cheshire SK8 3SA
**Tel:** 01614918200 **Fax:** 01902 880432
**Web:** www.wienerberger.co.uk
**Reg No:** 5299520 **VAT No:** 145133788
**Estd:** 1944 Private Limited Company
**Line of Business:** Manufacture of bricks, tiles and construction products, in baked clay
**Trading Style:** Terca
**Issued Capital:** £81,120,552
**Directors:** H A Schwarzmayr, C Domenig, P Stevenson
**Co. Secretary:** Michael Grace
**Responsibilities**
**Senior:** Bert Koekoek *(CEO)*, Heimo Scheuch *(Manager)*
**IT:** Tim Horgan *(IT Helpdesk Manager)*
**Branches:** Wienerberger Ltd, Ewhurst Works, Dorking, Surrey RH5 5QH
**US SIC:** 3251 **UK SIC:** 24100
**Auditors:** KPMG LLP

| | 31-12-13 | 31-12-12 | 31-12-11 |
|---|---|---|---|
| TO | 107,152,000 | 87,707,000 | 92,926,000 |
| P/L | (8,545,000) | (12,865,000) | (8,148,000) |
| NW | 40,137,000 | 47,377,000 | 74,525,000 |
| WC | (25,181,000) | (15,699,000) | (46,246,000) |
| Emp. | 562 | 578 | 614 |

DUNS 23-709-2903
## Wigan and Leigh College
Po Box 53, Parson's Walk, Wigan, Lancashire WN1 1RS
**Tel:** 01942 761600
**Web:** www.wigan-leigh.ac.uk
**Line of Business:** Training centres
**Trading Style:** Travel Shop
**Principals:** N J Crawford *(Financial)*, Mrs M Murdin
**Responsibilities**
**Senior:** Katherine Hurst *(Principal)*
**US SIC:** 8221, 4722
**UK SIC:** 93100, 77001
**Bankers:** The Co-Operative Bank Plc (08-90-58)
**Employees:** 1,100

DUNS 21-784-4086
## Wigan & Leigh Community Drug Team
Coops Business Centre, Dorning Street, Wigan, Lancashire WN1 1HR
**Tel:** 01942027070
**Estd:** 2011 Proprietorship
**Line of Business:** Drug counselling
**Proprietor:** Ms C Marsh
**US SIC:** 8321 **UK SIC:** 96111
**Employees:** 80

DUNS 28-960-3870
## Wigan & Leigh Hospice
5-9 Norfolk Street, Newtown, Wigan, Lancashire WN5 9BJ
**Tel:** 01942821065
**Web:** www.wlh.org.uk
**Reg No:** 1677155 **Estd:** 1995 Private Company Limited By Guarantee
**Line of Business:** Other human health activities
**Directors:** Mrs P Payne, P R Williams, Mrs M S Evans, D P Mayes, Ms M Reid, W Brown, Doctor S E Kenward
**Co. Secretary:** Ms Janet Anderton
**Responsibilities**
**Finance:** Alan Baron *(Financial Director)*
**IT:** Alan Baron *(Financial Director)*
**Purchasing:** Alan Baron *(Financial Director)*
**Branches:** Wigan & Leigh Hospice, Kildare Street, Wigan, Lancashire WN2 3HZ
**US SIC:** 8091 **UK SIC:** 95200
**Auditors:** Taits
**Bankers:** HSBC Bank plc (40-46-32)

| | 31-12-13 | 31-12-12 | 31-12-11 |
|---|---|---|---|
| TO | 4,877,808 | 5,453,385 | 4,955,292 |
| P/L | 650,920 | 1,520,684 | 1,402,155 |
| NW | 10,778,604 | 10,045,702 | 8,459,386 |
| WC | 5,727,807 | 6,313,330 | 4,902,396 |
| Emp. | 89 | 75 | 69 |

DUNS 21-040-2302
## Wigan and Leigh Nhs Trust
The Elms, Wigan Lane, Wigan, Lancashire WN1 2NP
**Tel:** 01942244000
**Web:** www.wiganleigh.nhs.uk
**Estd:** 2003
**Line of Business:** Libraries
**Trading Style:** Wwl Trust
**Responsibilities**
**Senior:** Silas Nicholls *(Director of Strategy and Plann)*, Umesh Prabhu *(Medical Director)*
**Finance:** Rob Forster *(Director of Finance and IT)*
**Marketing:** Silas Nicholls *(Director of Strategy and Plann)*
**HR:** Jon Lenney *(Director of HR and Organisatio)*
**US SIC:** 8231 **UK SIC:** 97700
**Employees:** 4,553

DUNS 21-005-7458
## Wigan Athletic Fc Community Trust
Basinghall Buildings, Upper Basinghall Street, Leeds, West Yorkshire LS1 5HR
**Tel:** 08706090500
**Web:** www.laticscommunity.org
**Reg No:** 6303512 **Estd:** 1977 Private Company Limited By Guarantee
**Line of Business:** Other sporting activities not elsewhere classified
**Directors:** P R Williams, J H Jackson, D A Culshaw, P Ivory, Ms B Spencer
**Responsibilities**
**Senior:** Aaron Lecroy *(Head Of Community)*
**US SIC:** 7999 **UK SIC:** 97913
**Bankers:** Barclays Bank Plc (20-96-37)

| | 31-12-13 | 31-12-12 | 31-12-11 |
|---|---|---|---|
| TO | 680,125 | 560,930 | 307,857 |
| P/L | 79,963 | 106,072 | (36,432) |
| NW | 275,294 | 195,331 | 89,259 |
| WC | 193,956 | 141,312 | 29,826 |
| Emp. | 50 | 28 | 19 |

DUNS 21-677-0444
## Wigan Athletic Holdings Ltd
Jjb Stadium, Lorie Drive, Robin Park, Wigan, Lancashire WN5 0UH
**Tel:** 01942231321
**Reg No:** 7283993 **Estd:** 2010 Private Limited Company
**Line of Business:** Operation of sports arenas and stadiums
**Issued Capital:** £2,173,374,054
**Directors:** D J Sharpe, D Whelan, Mrs P M Whelan
**US SIC:** 7941 **UK SIC:** 97911
**Bankers:** Barclays Bank Plc (20-30-47)

| | 31-05-14 | 31-05-13 | 31-05-12 |
|---|---|---|---|
| TO | 39,321,082 | 58,457,607 | 43,564,769 |
| P/L | (23,752,964) | (2,822,932) | (4,111,916) |
| NW | 18,637,422 | 6,477,693 | 3,601,085 |
| WC | (4,966,536) | (19,631,810) | (22,633,695) |
| Emp. | 307 | 276 | 274 |

DUNS 21-748-4489
## Wigan Council
Town Hall, Library Street, Wigan, Lancashire WN1 1YN
**Tel:** 08456769443
**Web:** www.qualitysolicitors.com
**Estd:** 2007
**Line of Business:** Solicitors
**Trading Style:** Rose Bridge High School, Leigh Building Services, Standish Community High School
**Directors:** N Ash, Mrs K Aldred, M Aldred, K Anderson
**Responsibilities**
**Senior:** Kealey Mulligan *(Strategic Manager)*
**HR:** Alison McKenzie-Folan *(Human Resources Manager)*
**Health & Safety:** Brian Holt *(Health & Safety Officer)*
**Operations:** Martin Kimber *(Environmental Director)*
**Branches:** Wigan Council, Mornington Road, Wigan, Lancashire WN2 4LG
**US SIC:** 8299, 9121, 8211
**UK SIC:** 93300, 91110, 93200
**Employees:** 10,000

DUNS 21-068-0886
## Wigan Firestation
Fire Station, Robin Park Road, Wigan, Lancashire WN5 0UU
**Tel:** 01942650103
**Estd:** 2011 Proprietorship
**Line of Business:** Fire stations
**Proprietor:** J Hardy
**Responsibilities**
**Senior:** Steve Sheridan *(Manager)*
**US SIC:** 9224 **UK SIC:** 91400
**Employees:** 120

DUNS 73-365-7410
## Wigan Leisure & Culture Enterprises Ltd
Haigh Stables Complex, Wigan, Lancashire WN2 1PE
**Tel:** 01942-828508
**Web:** www.wlct.org
**Reg No:** 4639273 **Estd:** 2003 Private Limited Company
**Line of Business:** Eating establishments
**Issued Capital:** £1
**Directors:** P J Burt, G W Cross, S G Murray, D A Lea, K P Gascoigne
**Co. Secretary:** Kevin Gascoigne
**Responsibilities**
**Health & Safety:** Kay Bardgett *(Executive Director Wellbeing D)*
**US SIC:** 5812, 0729, 9121, 7261
**UK SIC:** 66110, 01003, 91110, 98902
**Bankers:** The Co-Operative Bank Plc (08-90-00)

| | 31-03-14 | 31-03-13 | 31-03-12 |
|---|---|---|---|
| TO | 5,108,852 | 4,504,926 | 4,373,917 |
| P/L | 4,086 | 5,442 | 317,714 |
| NW | 34,262 | 32,040 | 61,489 |
| WC | 21,732 | 30,279 | 46,663 |

DUNS 73-350-9561
## Wigan Leisure & Culture Trust
Robin Park Loire Drive, Wigan, Lancashire WN5 0UL
**Tel:** 01942828550
**Web:** www.wlct.org
**Reg No:** 4624607 **Estd:** 2002 Private Company Limited By Guarantee
**Line of Business:** Agricultural service activities; landscape gardening
**Trading Style:** Ossett Steel Services Limited
**Directors:** G W Cross, P G Farrington, T Bradshaw, D A Lea, A Wiggans, E Smethurst, Ms M Kerr, M Watson

**Co. Secretary:** Kevin Gascoigne
**Responsibilities**
**Senior:** Della Bartle *(Director)*, Brendan Bowen *(Director)*, Jean Garlick *(Manager)*, William Hampson *(Manager)*
**HR:** Patricia Grimshaw *(Human Resources Manager)*
**Branches:** Wigan Leisure & Culture Trust, Gathurst La, Wigan, Lancashire WN6 8HA
**US SIC:** 0729, 7911, 8411, 7941
**UK SIC:** 01003, 97913, 97700, 97911
**Auditors:** Grant Thornton UK LLP
**Bankers:** The Co-Operative Bank Plc (08-90-92)

| | 31-03-14 | 31-03-13 | 31-03-12 |
|---|---|---|---|
| TO | 30,707,237 | 32,306,867 | 33,641,230 |
| P/L | (78,055) | (640,252) | 1,833,042 |
| NW | (2,525,941) | (7,203,165) | (1,717,408) |
| WC | (349,687) | (634,975) | (607,225) |
| Emp. | 788 | 832 | 641 |

DUNS 57-841-7628
## Wigan Link
Dorbcrest House, 20 Lowe Mill Lane, Hindley, Wigan, Lancashire WN2 3AF
**Tel:** 01865310199
**Web:** www.wiganlink.co.uk
**Reg No:** 2894707 **Estd:** 1994 Private Limited Company
**Line of Business:** Social work activities without accommodation
**Directors:** Ms M M Welch, R Short
**Co. Secretary:** Nigel Robinson
**Responsibilities**
**Senior:** Philip Gavin *(Manager)*, Norman Welch *(operations director)*
**US SIC:** 8321 **UK SIC:** 96111
**Auditors:** Lathams
**Bankers:** National Westminster Bank Plc (60-24-02)

| | 31-03-14 | 31-03-13 | 31-03-12 |
|---|---|---|---|
| TO | 1,545,541 | 1,627,561 | 1,616,494 |
| P/L | 4,452 | 3,912 | 30,862 |
| NW | 217,407 | 212,955 | 209,043 |
| WC | 216,689 | 211,582 | 207,244 |
| Emp. | 81 | 85 | 104 |

DUNS 22-962-1487
## Wigan Metropolitan Borough Council
Town Hall, Library Street, Wigan, Lancashire WN1 1YN
**Tel:** 01942-244991
**Web:** www.wigan.gov.uk
**Line of Business:** Central Government
**Trading Style:** Wigan Youth Offending Team: New Lodge Centre, Westleigh High School, Orrell Newfold County the Our Ladys Rc School
**Principals:** D Smith *(Financial)*, P Grayling, S Jones, A P Hardy, A P Hardy, I Kell, I Kell, F Costello
**Responsibilities**
**Senior:** Sandra Baines *(Manager)*, Darren Barton *(Manager)*, Keith Benson *(Manager)*, Terry Bolton *(Manager)*, Heather Bush *(Manager)*, Angela Durkin *(Manager)*, Mavis Fitzpatrick *(Manager)*, Carmel Foster-Devine *(Manager)*, Danny Gent *(Manager)*, Richard Helmn *(Manager)*, Karen Holland *(Manager)*, Tony Hollinrake *(Board Member)*, Julie Jeffers *(Manager)*, Dawn Jones *(Manager)*, Mary MacDonald *(Manager)*, Caroline Maffia *(Chairman)*, Refat Mahmood *(Manager)*, Eleanor Mansell *(Manager)*, Helene Mason *(Manager)*, Lee Matthews *(Manager)*, Lisa Middlehurst *(Manager)*, Vicky Perry *(Manager)*, Diana Powell *(Manager)*, John Roughley *(Manager)*, Andrew Smallshaw *(Manager)*, Michell Woodburn *(Manager)*
**Finance:** Andrew Hull *(Finance Manager)*
**Marketing:** Claire Gomersall (Walsh) *(Marketing Officer)*, Nicola Lowe *(Community Engagement)*
**Sales:** Michelle Kemp *(Business Development Manager)*, Julie McGregor *(Business Development Manager)*, Steve McGuckian *(Business Development Manager)*, Allen Sankey *(Sales Manager)*, Ron Sherwood *(Business Development Manager)*
**IT:** Allison Hughes *(IT Manager)*
**HR:** Ellen Belshaw *(Training Director)*, Eric Bradbury *(Training Director)*, John Brewder *(Training Director)*, Nick Burdekin *(Training Director)*, Joanne Edwards *(Training Director)*, Sue Elliott *(Training Director)*, Lynda Jackson *(Human Resources Manager)*, Justine Silcock *(Training Director)*
**Operations:** Steve Corns *(Production and Operations Mana)*, Gilly Hodgkinson *(Production and Operations Mana)*, Sheila Martland *(Production and Operations Mana)*, Steve Sargent *(Production and Operations Mana)*
**Fleet:** John Derbyshire *(Fleet Manager)*
**Engineering:** Paul Fairhurst *(Infrastructure Manager)*, Mike Purcell *(Technical Engineer)*
**Branches:** Wigan Metropolitan Borough Council, Wigan Life Centre, The Wiend, Wigan, Lancashire WN1 1NH
**US SIC:** 9121, 8211
**UK SIC:** 91110, 93200
**Employees:** 10,000

DUNS 28-830-4777
## Wigan Rugby League Club Ltd
Loire Drive, Robin Park, Wigan, Lancashire WN5 0UZ
**Tel:** 01942762889
**Web:** www.dwstadium.com
**Reg No:** 0174692 **VAT No:** 727052056
**Estd:** 1921 Private Limited Company
**Line of Business:** Operation of sports arenas and stadiums
**Issued Capital:** £128,000
**Directors:** K J Radlinski, J J Higham, D J Tully, I F Lenagan
**Co. Secretary:** David Tully
**Responsibilities**
**Marketing:** Sue France *(Sales & Marketing Manager)*, Nick Hollis *(Computer Manager)*
**Sales:** Sue France *(Sales & Marketing Manager)*
**Admin:** Steve Reeves *(Office Manager)*
**IT:** Nick Hollis *(Computer Manager)*
**HR:** Jane Birch *(Human Resources Manager)*, Carol Madden *(Human Resources Manager)*
**Branches:** Wigan Rugby League Club Ltd, Wigan Square, The Galleries, Wigan, Lancashire WN1 1AW
**US SIC:** 7941 **UK SIC:** 97911
**Auditors:** Fairhurst
**Bankers:** Barclays Bank Plc (20-96-37)

| | 30-11-13 | 30-11-12 | 30-11-11 |
|---|---|---|---|
| TO | 6,652,881 | 6,202,183 | 6,189,387 |
| P/L | 108,324 | 27,804 | 126,857 |
| NW | (2,356,338) | (2,397,879) | (2,263,383) |
| WC | (4,099,918) | (4,123,336) | (3,907,634) |
| Emp. | 76 | 76 | 76 |

DUNS 76-934-9937
## Wigan Specsavers Ltd
34-36 Marketgate Shopping Centre, Wigan, Lancashire WN1 1JS
**Tel:** 01942824480
**Web:** www.specsavers.co.uk
**Reg No:** 2487622 **Estd:** 1990 Private Limited Company
**Line of Business:** Other retail sale in specialised stores not elsewhere classified
**Issued Capital:** £100
**Directors:** Mrs M L Perkins, G B Gardner, Mrs S Gardner
**Co. Secretary:** Specsavers Optical Group Limited
**US SIC:** 5999 **UK SIC:** 65600
**Auditors:** Newland Mallett Garner

| | 30-09-13 | 30-09-12 | 30-09-11 |
|---|---|---|---|
| TA | 293,613 | 123,612 | 138,122 |
| NW | 89,048 | (343,688) | (259,969) |
| WC | 9,973 | (396,444) | (321,745) |

DUNS 73-938-0884
## Wiggin Llp
Jessop House, Cheltenham, Gloucestershire GL50 3WG
**Web:** www.wiggin.co.uk
**Reg No:** 0308767OC **Estd:** 2001
**Line of Business:** Solicitors
**Export Sales:** £3,659,501
**Responsibilities**
**Senior:** Simon Baggs *(Non-designated Limited Liabili)*, Susan Crawford *(Non-designated Limited Liabili)*, Neil Gillard *(Non-designated Limited Liabili)*, Ciaran Hickey *(Non-designated Limited Liabili)*, Medwyn Jones *(Non-designated Limited Liabili)*, Miles Ketley *(Non-designated Limited Liabili)*, Neil Parkes *(Non-designated Limited Liabili)*, Marcus Rowland *(Non-designated Limited Liabili)*, Ross Sylvester *(Non-designated Limited Liabili)*, Benjamin Whitelock *(Non-designated Limited Liabili)*
**IT:** Graham Ferrer *(IT Manager)*
**US SIC:** 8111 **UK SIC:** 83500
**Auditors:** BDO Stoy Hayward LLP

| | 31-03-14 | 31-03-13 | 31-03-12 |
|---|---|---|---|
| TO | 15,910,876 | 12,982,371 | 12,423,374 |
| P/L | 53,424 | 75,644 | 45,556 |
| NW | (7,918) | 2,838,977 | (12,818) |
| WC | 4,026,048 | 1,798,730 | 2,145,009 |
| Emp. | 92 | 89 | 79 |

DUNS 73-902-4375
## Wight Salads Group Ltd
(**Subsidiary of:** Siel - S.G.P.S. S.A.)
Unit 1 Bognor Road, Chichester, West Sussex PO20 1NW
**Tel:** 01243819600 **Fax:** 02392415701
**Web:** www.wightsaladsgroup.com
**Reg No:** 5156134 **Estd:** 2004 Private Limited Company
**Line of Business:** Management activities of other non-financial holding companies not elsewhere classified
**Trading Style:** Wight Salads Group Ltd
**Issued Capital:** £24,587
**Directors:** J H Santos, Dr. S D Rothwell, P B Moug, K Fairbrass, T J Brinsmead
**Co. Secretary:** Keith Fairbrass
**Responsibilities**
**Senior:** Jack Cox *(Supply Chain Manager)*, Nicholas Stenning *(Manager)*, Bryan Winch *(Manager)*
**HR:** Tracy Gilgallon *(Human Resources Manager)*
**Health & Safety:** Tracy Gilgallon *(Human Resources Manager)*
**Operations:** Jack Cox *(Supply Chain Manager)*
**Purchasing:** Bob Paine *(Purchasing Manager)*
**US SIC:** 6711 **UK SIC:** 83962
**Auditors:** PricewaterhouseCoopers LLP

| | 31-12-13 | 31-12-12 | 31-12-11 |
|---|---|---|---|
| TO | 44,367,000 | 39,325,000 | 32,950,000 |
| P/L | (3,111,000) | (1,394,000) | (5,194,000) |
| NW | (2,927,000) | 566,000 | 516,000 |
| WC | (13,620,000) | (10,985,000) | (7,668,000) |
| Emp. | 312 | 268 | 325 |

DUNS 29-050-0024
## Wightlink Ltd
(**Subsidiary of:** Macquarie Group Limited)
Gunwharf Road, Portsmouth, Hampshire PO1 2LA
**Tel:** 08713761000
**Web:** www.wightlink.co.uk
**Reg No:** 1059267 **VAT No:** 651201288
**Estd:** 1995 Private Limited Company
**Line of Business:** Boat excursion operators
**Issued Capital:** £17,495,253
**Directors:** G I Parsons, R Kew, R Abel, Ms R Copper
**Co. Secretary:** Jonathan Pascoe
**Responsibilities**
**Facilities:** Elwyn Dop *(Marine Operations Manager)*
**Branches:** Wightlink Ltd, Piergate Kiosk, Esplanade, Ryde, Isle Of Wight PO33 2HE
**US SIC:** 4452 **UK SIC:** 74002
**Auditors:** PricewaterhouseCoopers LLP
**Bankers:** Barclays Bank Plc (20-19-90)

| | 29-03-14 | 30-03-13 | 31-03-12 |
|---|---|---|---|
| TO | 59,668,000 | 59,836,000 | 59,436,000 |
| P/L | 12,943,000 | 9,477,000 | 8,146,000 |
| NW | 125,068,000 | 108,447,000 | 96,186,000 |
| WC | 56,541,000 | 42,024,000 | 33,259,000 |
| Emp. | 256 | 290 | 302 |

DUNS 22-273-0728
## Wightlink Shipping Ltd
(**Subsidiary of:** Macquarie Group Limited)
Gunwharf Terminal, Gunwharf Road, Portsmouth, Hampshire PO1 2LA
**Tel:** 02392855226
**Web:** www.wightlink.co.uk
**Reg No:** 4291021 **Estd:** 2001 Private Limited Company
**Line of Business:** Freight sea and coastal water transport
**Issued Capital:** £2
**Directors:** G I Parsons, R Kew, R Abel, Ms R Copper
**Co. Secretary:** Jonathan Pascoe
**US SIC:** 4411 **UK SIC:** 74001
**Auditors:** Ernst & Young LLP

| | 29-03-14 | 30-03-13 | 31-03-12 |
|---|---|---|---|
| TA | 2 | 2 | 2 |
| NW | 2 | 2 | 2 |

DUNS 21-620-0113
## Wightman & Parrish Ltd
Station Road Industrial Estate, Hailsham, East Sussex BN27 2QA
**Tel:** 01323-440444 **Fax:** 01323440244
**Web:** www.wp.co.uk
**Reg No:** 0139002 **VAT No:** 190157175
**Estd:** 1915 Private Limited Company
**Line of Business:** China and glassware wholesalers
**Trading Style:** Medirite
**Issued Capital:** £49,100
**Principals:** M R Parrish *(Managing)*, N B Parrish
**Co. Secretary:** Mrs Pamela Parrish
**US SIC:** 8091 **UK SIC:** 95200
**Auditors:** Knill James
**Bankers:** Barclays Bank Plc (20-49-76)

| | 31-12-13 | 31-12-12 | 31-12-11 |
|---|---|---|---|
| TO | 14,181,612 | 13,909,748 | 13,083,063 |
| P/L | 32,114 | 300,121 | 56,996 |
| NW | 4,663,813 | 4,719,859 | 4,511,609 |
| WC | 2,035,390 | 2,031,297 | 1,816,953 |
| Emp. | 117 | 126 | 128 |

DUNS 37-891-4188 **Imp**
## Wigmore Medical Ltd
(**Subsidiary of:** Dilazar Ltd)
23 Wigmore Street, London W1U 1PL
**Tel:** 020-7491-0111
**Web:** www.wigmoremedical.com
**Reg No:** 3310740 **Estd:** 2002 Private Limited Company
**Line of Business:** Wholesale of pharmaceutical goods
**Export Sales:** £2,592,848
**Trading Style:** Wigmore Pharmacy
**Issued Capital:** £10,000
**Directors:** R Eghiayan, J D Burr, M Avedissian
**Co. Secretary:** Bedros Eghiayan
**Responsibilities**
**Senior:** Peder Eghiayan *(Co Owner)*, Kaspar Kasparian *(Financial Controller)*
**Finance:** Kaspar Kasparian *(Financial Controller)*
**Operations:** Archie Tashjian *(Operations Manager)*
**US SIC:** 5122, 5999
**UK SIC:** 61800, 65600
**Auditors:** Baker Tilly UK Audit LLP
**Bankers:** Barclays Bank Plc (20-03-53)

| | 31-12-13 | 31-12-12 | 31-12-11 |
|---|---|---|---|
| TO | 23,916,526 | 22,074,972 | 21,546,569 |
| P/L | 1,027,749 | 358,285 | 598,055 |
| NW | 2,353,245 | 1,665,998 | 2,767,668 |
| WC | 2,042,408 | 1,377,788 | 2,360,695 |
| Emp. | 51 | 46 | 36 |

DUNS 23-993-3542
## Wigtown District Council
Council Offices, Sun Street, Stranraer, Wigtownshire DG9 7JJ
**Tel:** 01776702151
**Web:** www.dgcouncil.net.uk
**Estd:** 2011
**Line of Business:** Day and care centres
**Principals:** G Lawson *(Financial)*, S Atkinson, R Chalmers, D Johnstone, A Geddes
**Responsibilities**
**Senior:** Carmel Jones *(Manager)*
**Branches:** Wigtown District Council, Leswalt High Road, Stranraer, Wigtownshire DG9 0AL
**US SIC:** 9121 **UK SIC:** 91110
**Bankers:** The Royal Bank Of Scotland Plc (83-27-14)
**Employees:** 80

DUNS 22-507-7080 **Imp-Exp**
## Wika Instruments Ltd
(**Subsidiary of:** Wika Alexander Wiegand Se & Co. Kg)
4 Wells Place Gatton Park Business, Centre, Redhill, Surrey RH1 3LG
**Tel:** 01737-644008 **Fax:** 01737-644403
**Web:** www.wika.co.uk
**Reg No:** 1032313 **VAT No:** 218272961
**Estd:** 1971 Private Limited Company
**Line of Business:** Manufacture of electronic instruments and appliances for measuring, checking, testing, navigating and other purposes, except industrial process control equipment
**Export Markets:** Middle East
**Export Sales:** £11,212,492
**Issued Capital:** £100,000
**Director:** A K Wiegand
**Co. Secretary:** David Phillips
**Responsibilities**
**HR:** Valerie Holliman *(Human Resources Manager)*
**Health & Safety:** Karen Florence *(Health & Safety Officer)*, Debby Martin *(Health & Safety Officer)*
**US SIC:** 3829 **UK SIC:** 37100
**Auditors:** Rodl & Partner Ltd
**Bankers:** Barclays Bank Plc (20-24-61)

| | 31-12-13 | 31-12-12 | 31-12-11 |
|---|---|---|---|
| TO | 29,552,626 | 23,266,582 | 19,538,844 |
| P/L | 3,047,670 | 2,313,596 | 1,922,001 |
| NW | 10,763,426 | 11,082,037 | 9,713,554 |
| WC | 5,929,619 | 7,125,041 | 5,626,646 |
| Emp. | 97 | 61 | 50 |

DUNS 77-903-8863
## Wil-Lec Grp Ltd
18-24 Kent Street, Grimsby, South Humberside DN32 7DG
**Tel:** 08009158670
**Web:** www.wil-lec.co.uk
**Reg No:** 5808955 **Estd:** 2006 Private Limited Company
**Line of Business:** Installation of electrical wiring and fittings
**Issued Capital:** £100
**Director:** S Wilson
**Co. Secretary:** Ms Shiela Wilson
**US SIC:** 1731 **UK SIC:** 50300

| | 31-05-14 | 31-05-13 | 31-05-12 |
|---|---|---|---|
| TA | 268,031 | 100 | 100 |
| NW | (3,789) | 100 | 100 |
| WC | 18,669 | N/A | N/A |

DUNS 71-902-4270
## Wila Group Ltd
Unit 8-10 The Quadrangle, Downsview Road, Wantage, Oxfordshire OX12 9FA
**Tel:** 01235773500 **Fax:** 01235-773533
**Web:** www.wila.com
**Reg No:** 5284454 **Estd:** 2004 Private Limited Company
**Line of Business:** Management activities of holding companies
**Export Sales:** £12,685,706
**Issued Capital:** £34,484

**Directors:** P Le Manquais, M H Collett, Mrs C L Styles, A Henrlch
**US SIC:** 6711 **UK SIC:** 83962
**Auditors:** Grant Thornton UK LLP
**Bankers:** Barclays Bank Plc (20-03-84)

| | 31-12-13 | 31-12-12 | 31-12-11 |
|---|---|---|---|
| TO | 16,632,310 | 17,399,644 | 16,353,330 |
| P/L | (131,750) | 432,354 | (590,498) |
| NW | 1,669,659 | 1,942,067 | 1,593,420 |
| WC | 995,252 | 1,299,744 | 949,439 |
| Emp. | 124 | 114 | 117 |

DUNS 63-454-5362

## Wilberforce Chambers

8 New Square, London WC2A 3QP
**Tel:** 020-7306-0102
**Web:** www.wilberforce.co.uk
**Estd:** 1940 Proprietorship
**Line of Business:** Barristers
**Proprietors:** E Nugie, E Nugie
**US SIC:** 8111 **UK SIC:** 83500
**Employees:** 70

DUNS 21-706-3371

## Wilberforce College

Saltshouse Road, Hull, North Humberside HU8 9HD
**Tel:** 01482711688
**Web:** www.wilberforce.ac.uk
**Estd:** 1988
**Line of Business:** First-degree level higher education
**Director:** Dr S Jungnitz
**Responsibilities**
**Senior:** Stephan Jungnitz *(Head Teacher)*
**Finance:** Bob Overament *(Senior Finance Administrator)*
**US SIC:** 8221 **UK SIC:** 93100
**Employees:** 200

DUNS 22-210-2852

## The Wilberforce Trust

Wilberforce House, North Moor Road, Huntington, York, North Yorkshire YO32 9QN
**Tel:** 01904760037 **Fax:** 01904768203
**Web:** www.wilberforcetrust.org.uk
**Reg No:** 4228432 **Estd:** 2001 Private Company Limited By Guarantee
**Line of Business:** Disability services
**Directors:** J P Kennedy, R C Cordier, Mrs E S Grierson, K Goodey, Mrs S Hawkesworth, S J Cluderay, L G Twiss, S J Cowell
**Co. Secretary:** Mrs Philippa Crowther
**Responsibilities**
**Senior:** Caroline Hide *(Service Manager)*
**US SIC:** 8321 **UK SIC:** 96111
**Bankers:** Barclays Bank Plc (20-99-56)

| | 31-03-14 | 31-03-13 | 31-03-12 |
|---|---|---|---|
| TO | 2,557,546 | 2,580,603 | 2,692,089 |
| P/L | 51,532 | (41,146) | 105,225 |
| NW | 9,275,049 | 9,045,957 | 8,900,300 |
| WC | 456,259 | 645,060 | 439,148 |
| Emp. | 85 | 87 | 85 |

DUNS 76-697-7268

## Wilby Ltd

(**Subsidiary of:** Wilby Holdings Ltd)
17 Charles Street, Halifax, West Yorkshire HX1 1NA
**Tel:** 01422358525 **Fax:** 01422-357367
**Web:** www.wilbyltd.co.uk
**Reg No:** 2592184 **Estd:** 1991 Private Limited Company
**Line of Business:** Insurance - commercial
**Issued Capital:** £1,334,500
**Principals:** P M Wilby *(Chairman)*, R D Blackburn, M Studholme, M R Shaw
**Co. Secretary:** Kenneth Gardiner
**Responsibilities**
**Senior:** Janet Moody *(Commercial Manager)*
**Marketing:** Anthony Haywood *(Sales & Marketing Manager)*
**Sales:** Anthony Haywood *(Sales & Marketing Manager)*, Janet Moody *(Commercial Manager)*
**HR:** Janet Moody *(Commercial Manager)*
**Health & Safety:** Mark Dalton *(Health & Safety Consultant)*, Andrew Voice *(Health & Safety Consultant)*
**Purchasing:** Janet Moody *(Commercial Manager)*
**US SIC:** 6411, 6399
**UK SIC:** 83200, 82001
**Auditors:** RSM Tenon Audit Ltd
**Bankers:** Barclays Bank Plc (20-35-84)

| | 31-08-13 | 31-08-12 | 31-08-11 |
|---|---|---|---|
| TA | 4,779,347 | 4,724,529 | 4,088,188 |
| NW | 1,037,856 | 584,608 | 1,128,281 |
| WC | 959,571 | 820,293 | 1,066,784 |

DUNS 21-686-1831 **Imp-Exp**

## Wilcomatic Ltd

(**Subsidiary of:** Comprehensive Service Facilities Ltd)
Commerce Park, 19 Commerce Way, Croydon, Surrey CR0 4YL
**Tel:** 020-8649-5760 **Fax:** 02086832070
**Web:** www.wilcomatic.co.uk
**Reg No:** 0910387 **VAT No:** 219807938
**Estd:** 1967 Private Limited Company
**Line of Business:** Other business activities not elsewhere classified
**Export Markets:** worldwide
**Issued Capital:** £506,052
**Director:** K C Pay
**Co. Secretary:** Selwyn Rodrigues
**Responsibilities**
**Health & Safety:** Ruby Diaz *(Quality & Environmental Manage)*
**Purchasing:** Mark Arthur *(Purchasing Manager)*
**Branches:** Wilcomatic Ltd, Commerce Way, Unit 5, Croydon, Surrey CR0 4YL
**US SIC:** 7399, 7699
**UK SIC:** 83954, 67303
**Auditors:** PricewaterhouseCoopers LLP
**Bankers:** Svenska Handelsbanken Ab (publ) (40-51-62)

| | 28-02-14 | 28-02-13 | 29-02-12 |
|---|---|---|---|
| TO | 12,844,502 | 12,697,359 | 13,227,000 |
| P/L | 254,491 | 300,743 | 792,000 |
| NW | 4,972,932 | 4,915,782 | 4,990,000 |
| WC | 4,679,300 | 4,718,385 | 4,528,000 |
| Emp. | 133 | 133 | 122 |

DUNS 21-690-6214 **Imp-Exp**

## Wilcox & Co.(Limousines)Ltd

(**Subsidiary of:** Wilcox & Co (Guernsey) Ltd)
21-25 Lower Road, Gerrards Cross, Buckinghamshire SL9 9AL
**Tel:** 01753480600 **Fax:** 01753-880023
**Web:** www.limousines.co.uk
**Reg No:** 0649545 **Estd:** 1960 Private Limited Company
**Line of Business:** Manufacturers of cars
**Export Markets:** E U, U S A, Canada
**Export Sales:** £42,225
**Issued Capital:** £1,800
**Principals:** P D Wilcox *(Managing)*, L M Wilcox
**Co. Secretary:** Martin Mcclelland
**Responsibilities**
**Senior:** Martin Templett *(Director & General Manager)*, Peter Wilcox *(Manager)*
**Health & Safety:** Phil Oastler *(Service Manager)*
**US SIC:** 3711 **UK SIC:** 35101
**Auditors:** Ernst & Young LLP
**Bankers:** Lloyds TSB Bank plc (30-13-30)

| | 31-03-14 | 31-03-13 | 31-03-12 |
|---|---|---|---|
| TO | 24,027,986 | 21,662,312 | 20,860,175 |
| P/L | 2,470,656 | 1,243,894 | 504,611 |
| NW | 3,809,653 | 3,840,719 | 2,821,654 |
| WC | 2,006,070 | 2,342,645 | 1,634,546 |
| Emp. | 176 | 159 | 161 |

DUNS 64-106-5396 **Exp**

## Wilcox Commercial Vehicles Ltd

Blenheim Way, Northfields Industrial Estate, Market De, Peterborough, Cambridgeshire PE6 8LD
**Tel:** 01778-345151 **Fax:** 01778-347269
**Web:** www.wilcox.uk.com
**Reg No:** 4106720 **VAT No:** 763611629
**Estd:** 2000 Private Limited Company
**Line of Business:** Manufacture of bodies (coachwork) for motor vehicles (except caravans)
**Export Sales:** £356,903
**Issued Capital:** £10,000
**Director:** C J Bartlett
**Co. Secretary:** Vito Ronzano
**Responsibilities**
**Finance:** Martyn Dennis *(Financial Manager)*
**US SIC:** 3715, 3799
**UK SIC:** 35220, 36502
**Auditors:** Rawlinsons
**Bankers:** Barclays Bank Plc (20-18-27)

| | 30-11-13 | 30-11-12 | 30-11-11 |
|---|---|---|---|
| TO | 15,512,483 | 12,254,271 | 11,174,747 |
| P/L | 1,158,620 | 539,904 | 242,464 |
| NW | 2,598,588 | 1,965,885 | 1,798,031 |
| WC | 1,673,443 | 1,028,739 | 761,361 |
| Emp. | 80 | 73 | 69 |

DUNS 21-619-2014

## Wildcats

The Headrow, Leeds, West Yorkshire LS1 5RB
**Tel:** 08703851513
**Web:** www.wildcatsworld.com
**Estd:** 2011
**Line of Business:** Nightclub
**Responsibilities**
**Senior:** Julie Warszylewicz *(Marketing Manager)*
**US SIC:** 5813 **UK SIC:** 66200
**Employees:** 70

DUNS 34-841-1166

## The Wilde Group Ltd.

Harlestone Firs, Harlestone Road, New Duston, Northampton, Northamptonshire NN5 6UJ
**Tel:** 01604586000
**Web:** www.cemfencing.co.uk
**Reg No:** 2804618 **VAT No:** 623688420
**Estd:** 2002 Private Limited Company
**Line of Business:** Steel fabricators
**Trading Style:** C E M Fencing, N R G Fabrication, Wooden Supplies, D J C Joinery
**Issued Capital:** £3,761
**Managing Director:** S I Wilde
**Co. Secretary:** Mrs Sara Wilde
**Branches:** The Wilde Group Ltd., Harlestone Road, Harlestone Road, New Duston, Northampton, Northamptonshire NN5 6UJ
**US SIC:** 2431, 3441, 5039
**UK SIC:** 46300, 32042, 61300
**Auditors:** R.J. McMorran
**Bankers:** The Royal Bank Of Scotland Plc (16-26-27)

| | 30-09-13 | 30-09-12 | 30-09-11 |
|---|---|---|---|
| TO | 7,778,484 | N/A | N/A |
| P/L | 211,819 | N/A | N/A |
| NW | 1,772,111 | 1,750,058 | 1,805,877 |
| WC | 462,128 | 507,955 | 812,888 |
| Emp. | 95 | N/A | N/A |

DUNS 21-716-5599

## Wildern School

Wildern Lane, Hedge End, Southampton, Hampshire SO30 4EJ
**Tel:** 01489783473
**Web:** www.hants.sch.uk
**Reg No:** 7554117 **Estd:** 2011 Private Company Limited By Guarantee
**Line of Business:** General secondary education
**Directors:** Ms H S Manton, W J Hatton, Mrs H Mair, Ms E C Walsh, A P Jardine, C N Bloom, Ms M Litton, J A Riddell
**Responsibilities**
**Senior:** Theodore Emtage *(Director)*, Carolyn Hughan *(Director)*, Ruth Saw *(Director)*, Karen Wigley *(Director)*
**US SIC:** 8211 **UK SIC:** 93200

| | 31-08-14 | 31-08-13 | 31-08-12 |
|---|---|---|---|
| TO | 11,351,162 | 11,070,074 | 10,568,044 |
| P/L | 69,392 | 316,800 | 131,607 |
| NW | 26,269,583 | 26,288,191 | 26,051,491 |
| WC | 2,124,954 | 2,424,411 | 2,660,283 |
| Emp. | 289 | 306 | 331 |

DUNS 57-062-0575 **Imp**

## The Wildfowl & Wetlands Trust

Bowditch, Slimbridge, Gloucester, Gloucestershire GL2 7BT
**Tel:** 01453891900
**Web:** www.wwt.org.uk
**Reg No:** 2882729 **Estd:** 1946 Private Company Limited By Guarantee
**Line of Business:** Other tourist assistance activities not elsewhere classified
**Trading Style:** Wetlands Advisory Service
**Directors:** Ms A Carragher, P M Duncan, P D Day, S J Tonge, L D Jones, Sir G H Fry, Dr A E Brown, A Driver
**Co. Secretary:** Stuart Leed
**Responsibilities**
**Senior:** Barnaby Briggs *(Director)*, George Russell *(Director)*, MArtin Spray *(Manager)*
**Branches:** The Wildfowl & Wetlands Trust, Arundel Wildfowl & Wetland Centre, Offham, Arundel, West Sussex BN18 9PB
**US SIC:** 7999 **UK SIC:** 97913
**Auditors:** PricewaterhouseCoopers
**Bankers:** National Westminster Bank Plc (60-09-02)

| | 31-03-14 | 31-03-13 | 31-03-12 |
|---|---|---|---|
| TO | 24,363,000 | 17,203,000 | 16,931,000 |
| P/L | 5,069,000 | (725,000) | (839,000) |
| NW | 35,517,000 | 29,798,000 | 32,048,000 |
| WC | 7,749,000 | 2,981,000 | 3,522,000 |
| Emp. | 364 | 368 | 363 |

DUNS 76-258-8150

## Wildfowl & Wetlands Trust (Trading) Ltd

Wwt Wetland Centre, Gloucester, Gloucestershire GL2 7BT
**Tel:** 01453891222
**Web:** www.wwtconsulting.co.uk
**Reg No:** 2541350 **Estd:** 1946 Private Limited Company
**Line of Business:** Other retail sale in non-specialised stores
**Trading Style:** The Wildfowl & Wetlands Trust
**Issued Capital:** £350,000
**Directors:** S Sajid, B B Strachan, Ms R Seymour, M C Spray, I M Wilson, Ms E N Spencer
**Co. Secretary:** Stuart Leed
**Responsibilities**
**Senior:** Emma Alesworth *(Associate Director)*, Matthew Simpson *(Associate Director)*, Rebecca Woodward *(Associate Director)*
**Branches:** Wildfowl & Wetlands Trust (Trading) Ltd, Martin Mere, Fish Lane, Ormskirk, Lancashire L40 0TA
**US SIC:** 5399, 5812
**UK SIC:** 65600, 66110
**Auditors:** Pricewaterhousecoopers
**Bankers:** National Westminster Bank Plc (60-09-02)

| | 31-03-14 | 31-03-13 | 31-03-12 |
|---|---|---|---|
| TO | 4,208,951 | 3,937,828 | 4,262,186 |
| P/L | (20,562) | (4,632) | 16,423 |
| NW | 415,093 | 435,655 | 440,287 |
| WC | 169,704 | 144,168 | 188,733 |
| Emp. | 99 | 102 | 107 |

DUNS 21-820-9682

## Wildgoose Construction Ltd

Horsefair House, Alfreton, Derbyshire DE55 7BY
**Tel:** 01773546400 **Fax:** 01773545930
**Web:** www.wildgooseconstruction.co.uk
**Reg No:** 0178605 **VAT No:** 401691283
**Estd:** 1896 Private Limited Company
**Line of Business:** Development and selling of real estate
**Issued Capital:** £19,000
**Principals:** T B Walker *(Managing)*, B Bennett, J N Wildgoose, D L Withers, Mrs L R Harcourt, Mrs M J Wildgoose
**Co. Secretary:** David Withers
**Responsibilities**
**Health & Safety:** Paul Metcalfe-Smith *(Health & Safety Officer)*
**Branches:** Wildgoose Construction Ltd, Fartown Grange, 28 Spaines Road, Huddersfield, West Yorkshire HD2 2QA
**US SIC:** 1522, 2421, 1541
**UK SIC:** 50100, 46101
**Auditors:** PKF (UK) LLP
**Bankers:** Bank Of Scotland (12-18-68)

| | 30-09-13 | 30-09-12 | 30-09-11 |
|---|---|---|---|
| TO | 25,216,459 | 32,405,469 | 35,615,119 |
| P/L | 204,178 | 346,419 | 352,668 |
| NW | 2,776,615 | 2,713,999 | 2,447,524 |
| WC | 2,016,175 | 1,648,270 | 1,047,456 |
| Emp. | 68 | 71 | 76 |

DUNS 21-637-8778 **Imp**

## Wildings Ltd

165 Commercial Street, Newport, Gwent NP20 1UL
**Tel:** 01633-262861
**Web:** www.wildingsonline.co.uk
**Reg No:** 0119916 **VAT No:** 134101722
**Estd:** 1874 Private Limited Company
**Line of Business:** Other retail sale in non-specialised stores
**Trading Style:** Wildings
**Issued Capital:** £20,000
**Principals:** P H Pease *(Chairman)*, P R James *(Managing)*, Ms F A Clark, Ms F Clark
**Co. Secretary:** Arthur James
**Branches:** Wildings Ltd, 14 High Street, Bristol, Avon BS35 2AQ
**US SIC:** 5399 **UK SIC:** 65600
**Auditors:** Arthur Gait & Co
**Bankers:** HSBC Bank plc (40-34-27)

| | 31-01-14 | 31-01-13 | 31-01-12 |
|---|---|---|---|
| TO | 4,464,096 | 4,494,287 | 4,498,274 |
| P/L | 31,714 | 91,235 | (32,508) |
| NW | 3,349,276 | 3,324,922 | 2,726,341 |
| WC | 811,122 | 755,636 | 676,397 |
| Emp. | 112 | 112 | 114 |

DUNS 50-595-1681

## The Wildlife Trust for Bedfordshire Cambridgeshire and Northamptonshire

The Manor House, Broad Street, Great Cambourne, Cambridge, Cambridgeshire CB23 6DH
**Web:** www.wildlifebcnp.org
**Reg No:** 2534145 **Estd:** 1990 Private Company Limited By Guarantee
**Line of Business:** Conservation organisations
**Trading Style:** Wildlife Trust Bcnp
**Directors:** Mrs K F Silcock, Ms L Doughty, P C Solon, Sir J J Robinson, Dr J M Bishop, W L Parker, M Baker, Professor W Stephens
**Co. Secretary:** Ms Fiona Chesterton
**Responsibilities**
**Senior:** Charles Chadwyck Healey *(Chairman)*, Brian Evershan *(CEO)*, David Gowing *(Trustee)*, Tony Juniper *(Director)*, Stewart Lane *(Director)*, Angela Scott *(Accounts & Administration Mana)*, Matthew Walpole *(Director)*
**Branches:** The Wildlife Trust For Bedfordshire, Cambridgeshire and Northamptonshi, The Wildlife Trust, Priory Country Park, Bedford, Bedfordshire MK41 9DJ
**US SIC:** 8699, 9121
**UK SIC:** 96902, 91110
**Auditors:** Saffery Champness

**Bankers:** Barclays Bank Plc (20-17-19)

| | 31-03-14 | 31-03-13 | 31-03-12 |
|---|---|---|---|
| TO | 6,902,889 | 5,102,183 | 4,374,971 |
| P/L | 1,998,939 | 393,360 | (20,959) |
| NW | 20,036,605 | 18,048,497 | 17,659,596 |
| WC | 3,303,137 | 3,107,515 | 3,148,368 |
| Emp. | 89 | 93 | 89 |

DUNS 54-382-9006

## The Wildlife Trusts (Pension Trustee) Ltd

The Kiln Waterside, Mather Road, Newark, Nottinghamshire NG24 1WT
**Tel:** 01636677711 **Fax:** 01636-670001
**Web:** www.wildlifetrusts.org
**Reg No:** 3267860 **Estd:** 1990 Private Limited Company
**Line of Business:** Environmental consultants
**Trading Style:** The Wildlife Trusts
**Issued Capital:** £7
**Directors:** S E Crooks, G W Evans, Ms A J Forsyth, T Hudson, Mrs H L Croft, Mrs V A O'Connor
**Co. Secretary:** Capita Employee Benefits Limited
**Responsibilities**
**Senior:** Stephanie Hilbourne *(Chief Executive)*, Colin Raven *(Director)*
**IT:** Sandra Rhodes *(IT Manager)*
**HR:** Patience Thody *(Human Resources Manager)*
**Health & Safety:** Patience Thody *(Human Resources Manager)*
**Purchasing:** Patience Thody *(Human Resources Manager)*
**US SIC:** 6371 **UK SIC:** 82002

| | 31-03-14 | 31-03-13 | 31-03-12 |
|---|---|---|---|
| TA | 7 | 7 | 7 |
| NW | 7 | 7 | 7 |

DUNS 21-775-7213

## Wildridings County Primary School

Wildridings, Bracknell, Berkshire RG12 7DX
**Tel:** 01344425483
**Web:** www.wildridings.ik.org
**Estd:** 1968 Proprietorship
**Line of Business:** Schools (local authority)
**Proprietor:** Miss J Evans
**US SIC:** 8211 **UK SIC:** 93200
**Employees:** 50

DUNS 21-732-2171

## Wildtree Hotels Ltd

**(Subsidiary of:** Wildtree Hotels (2010) Ltd)
12-22 Pinner Road Roxborough Bridge, Harrow, Middlesex HA1 4HZ
**Tel:** 020-8427-3435 **Fax:** 020-8861-1370
**Web:** www.harrowhotel.co.uk
**Reg No:** 1064700 **VAT No:** 223922185
**Estd:** 1972 Private Limited Company
**Line of Business:** Hotels
**Trading Style:** The Quality Harrow Hotel
**Issued Capital:** £100
**Principals:** S H Flash *(Managing)*, Ms R F Angel
**Co. Secretary:** Ms Rebecca Flash
**Responsibilities**
**Senior:** Robert Algar *(General Manager)*, Wayne Hilton *(Conference Manager)*
**HR:** Robert Algar *(General Manager)*
**Health & Safety:** Robert Algar *(General Manager)*
**Purchasing:** Wayne Hilton *(Conference Manager)*
**Branches:** Wildtree Hotels Ltd, 27-29 Upton Road, Watford, Hertfordshire WD18 0JF
**US SIC:** 7011 **UK SIC:** 66500
**Auditors:** Newman & Partners
**Bankers:** HSBC Bank plc (40-45-27)

| | 31-03-14 | 31-03-13 | 31-03-12 |
|---|---|---|---|
| TA | 2,576,661 | 2,538,978 | 2,660,646 |
| NW | 2,114,598 | 1,676,776 | 1,810,734 |
| WC | 113,613 | (222,709) | (87,552) |

DUNS 21-296-1700 **Imp**

## Wiley Accessories Ltd.

St Pegs Mill, Thornhill Beck Lane, Brighouse, West Yorkshire HD6 4AH
**Fax:** 01484475802
**Web:** www.wileys.co.uk
**Reg No:** 1087243 **VAT No:** 180173088
**Estd:** 1968 Private Limited Company
**Line of Business:** Import and export agents
**Issued Capital:** £5,600
**Principals:** J L Wiley *(Managing)*, Mrs S Wiley, Mrs C R Burbidge, G N Roberts
**Co. Secretary:** Ms Andrea Bacon
**US SIC:** 4712 **UK SIC:** 77002
**Auditors:** Barber Harrison & Platt
**Bankers:** HSBC Bank plc (40-13-15)

| | 30-10-13 | 30-10-12 | 30-10-11 |
|---|---|---|---|
| TO | N/A | 6,598,495 | 9,368,463 |
| P/L | N/A | 33,538 | 348,677 |
| NW | 1,968,767 | 2,250,083 | 2,250,735 |
| WC | 1,324,489 | 1,430,486 | 1,193,972 |
| Emp. | N/A | 46 | 52 |

DUNS 28-861-5859

## Wilf Gilbert(Staffordshire)Ltd

**(Subsidiary of:** Gilbert (Holdings) Ltd)
Po Box 1123, Solihull, West Midlands B90 3BA
**Tel:** 0121-733-3121
**Web:** http://webstarter.easily.co.uk
**Reg No:** 0901341 **Estd:** 1967 Private Limited Company
**Line of Business:** Bookmakers and turf accountants
**Issued Capital:** £4
**Directors:** G G Gilbert, G T Gilbert, G R Gilbert
**Co. Secretary:** Wilf Gilbert (Sports) Limited
**Branches:** Wilf Gilbert(Staffordshire)ltd, Roseville Precinct, Castle St, Bilston, West Midlands WV14 9EP
**US SIC:** 7999 **UK SIC:** 97913
**Auditors:** Henn & Westwood

| | 31-12-13 | 31-12-12 | 31-12-11 |
|---|---|---|---|
| TO | 16,542,564 | 16,132,913 | 18,972,501 |
| P/L | 131,826 | 76,931 | (79,633) |
| NW | 149,510 | 494,998 | 429,092 |
| WC | (639,171) | (397,543) | (584,630) |
| Emp. | 97 | 99 | 107 |

DUNS 21-718-4090

## The Wilf Ward Family Trust

5 Westgate Westgate, Pickering, North Yorkshire YO18 8BA
**Tel:** 01751474740
**Web:** www.wilfward.org.uk
**Reg No:** 7568318 **Estd:** 2011 Private Company Limited By Guarantee
**Line of Business:** Charitable social work activities with accommodation
**Trading Style:** The Wilf Ward Family Trust
**Directors:** Mrs L E Rawnsley, W L Denness, N J Shaw, P Fletcher, M B Smith, Mrs K A Stead
**Co. Secretary:** Mrs Catherine Sell
**Responsibilities**
**Senior:** Rosemary Coles *(Director)*
**US SIC:** 8321 **UK SIC:** 96111
**Bankers:** Barclays Bank Plc (20-67-75)

| | 31-03-14 | 31-03-13 | 31-03-12 |
|---|---|---|---|
| TO | 18,988,381 | 18,210,231 | 18,167,903 |
| P/L | 631,651 | 819,665 | 372,199 |
| NW | 19,082,795 | 18,092,944 | 16,917,151 |
| WC | 5,651,329 | 4,962,626 | 5,111,533 |
| Emp. | 1,166 | 1,104 | 1,126 |

DUNS 21-228-7347

## Wilford Harvester

Wilford House, 1 Clifton Lane, Nottingham, Nottinghamshire NG11 7AT
**Tel:** 0115-9819756
**Web:** www.harvester.co.uk
**Estd:** 2002 Proprietorship
**Line of Business:** Restaurant - english
**Proprietor:** Miss Z Price
**Responsibilities**
**Senior:** Helen Chambers-Kirk *(General Manager)*
**US SIC:** 5812 **UK SIC:** 66110
**Employees:** 93

DUNS 21-209-8222 **Exp**

## Wilfred Scruton Ltd

Providence Foundry, Driffield, North Humberside YO25 3QQ
**Tel:** 01262470221
**Web:** www.wilfredscruton.co.uk
**Reg No:** 0496990 **VAT No:** 167540453
**Estd:** 1951 Private Limited Company
**Line of Business:** Agricultural engineers
**Export Markets:** France; Denmark; Norway
**Issued Capital:** £18,300
**Directors:** Miss J M Scruton, I J Scruton, R G Bower, G W Scruton, R W Gillett, Ms S A Scruton
**Co. Secretary:** Peter Scruton
**Branches:** Wilfred Scruton Ltd, The Garage, Weaverthorpe, Malton, North Yorkshire YO17 8TG
**US SIC:** 8911, 5084
**UK SIC:** 83701, 61490
**Auditors:** Moore Stephens
**Bankers:** Barclays Bank Plc (20-43-47)

| | 31-12-13 | 31-12-12 | 31-12-11 |
|---|---|---|---|
| TO | 21,243,867 | 22,445,130 | 18,680,799 |
| P/L | 278,963 | 369,128 | 355,466 |
| NW | 2,169,826 | 2,123,675 | 1,931,017 |
| WC | 1,862,943 | 1,539,192 | 1,329,786 |
| Emp. | 48 | 46 | 45 |

DUNS 22-513-1598 **Exp**

## Wilfred T Fry Ltd

**(Subsidiary of:** Fry Wealth Ltd)
Crescent House, Crescent Road, Worthing, West Sussex BN11 1RN
**Tel:** 01903231545
**Web:** www.thefrygroup.co.uk
**Reg No:** 0212927 **VAT No:** 238916532
**Estd:** 1926 Private Limited Company
**Line of Business:** Activities auxiliary to insurance and pension funding
**Export Markets:** Worldwide
**Export Sales:** £5,574,000
**Issued Capital:** £500,000
**Directors:** S J Tucker, R H Rennison, J J Woodley, J D Walford, A P Bailey
**Co. Secretary:** Richard Butler
**Responsibilities**
**Admin:** Angela Parrish *(Office Manager)*
**HR:** Angela Parrish *(Office Manager)*
**Purchasing:** Angela Parrish *(Office Manager)*
**Branches:** Wilfred T Fry Ltd, Broadwalk House, Southernhay West, Exeter, Devon EX1 1WF
**US SIC:** 6411 **UK SIC:** 83200
**Auditors:** Carpenter Box
**Bankers:** Lloyds TSB Bank plc (30-99-93)

| | 31-03-14 | 31-03-13 | 31-03-12 |
|---|---|---|---|
| TO | 13,505,599 | 13,007,880 | 10,991,277 |
| P/L | (415,101) | (227,570) | 594,245 |
| NW | (8,018,125) | (8,193,910) | (7,037,934) |
| WC | 1,406,333 | 1,206,187 | 1,292,307 |
| Emp. | 154 | 155 | 132 |

DUNS 21-825-8853 **Exp**

## Wilfreda Luxury Coaches Ltd

Apex House, Church Lane, Adwick-Le-Street, Doncaster, South Yorkshire DN6 7AY
**Tel:** 01302330330 **Fax:** 01302-330204
**Web:** www.wilfreda.co.uk
**Reg No:** 0474455 **VAT No:** 126406980
**Estd:** 1949 Private Limited Company
**Line of Business:** Other passenger land transport
**Export Markets:** Europe
**Trading Style:** Wilfreda Beehive, Access Travel
**Issued Capital:** £100,000
**Directors:** P G Haxby, P A Scholey, N G Haxby
**Co. Secretary:** Ms Susan Scholey
**US SIC:** 4141 **UK SIC:** 72102
**Auditors:** Hope Agar Ltd
**Bankers:** Yorkshire Bank Plc (05-04-14)

| | 30-09-13 | 30-09-12 | 30-09-11 |
|---|---|---|---|
| TA | 5,227,604 | 5,170,745 | 4,548,863 |
| NW | 1,123,764 | 957,247 | 598,296 |
| WC | (639,061) | (651,686) | (460,753) |

DUNS 21-118-3793 **Imp**

## Wilfrid Whittington Ltd

Victoria Park Way, Netherfield, Nottingham, Nottinghamshire NG4 2PA
**Tel:** 01159-875500
**Reg No:** 0612790 **VAT No:** 117500994
**Estd:** 1955 Private Limited Company
**Line of Business:** Florists wholesale
**Trading Style:** Whittingtons Florist Sundries
**Issued Capital:** £4,650
**Directors:** B Perkins, B W Perkins, B J Perkins
**Co. Secretary:** Christopher Samples
**Branches:** Wilfrid Whittington Ltd, B12 Wholesale Fruit & Flower Market, Clarke Road, Nottingham, Nottingham, Nottinghamshire NG2 3JJ
**US SIC:** 5199 **UK SIC:** 61900
**Auditors:** Hacker Young
**Bankers:** National Westminster Bank Plc (54-21-07)

| | 31-03-14 | 31-03-13 | 31-03-12 |
|---|---|---|---|
| TO | 7,378,122 | 7,745,577 | 7,271,246 |
| P/L | 624,198 | 646,182 | 250,517 |
| NW | 3,130,576 | 2,691,308 | 2,276,645 |
| WC | 1,225,472 | 1,204,483 | 849,355 |
| Emp. | 90 | 86 | 88 |

DUNS 21-726-1709

## The Wilkes Partnership Llp

41 Church Street, Birmingham, West Midlands B3 2RT
**Web:** www.wilkes.co.uk
**Reg No:** 0364479OC **Estd:** 1998
**Line of Business:** Solicitors
**Responsibilities**
**Senior:** Timothy Coplestone *(Non-designated Limited Liabili)*, Carl Csukas *(Non-designated Limited Liabili)*, Kathryn Hackett *(Non-designated Limited Liabili)*, Andrew Hasnip *(Non-designated Limited Liabili)*, Julia Morgan *(Non-designated Limited Liabili)*, Duncan Smyth *(Non-designated Limited Liabili)*, Susan Vogel *(Non-designated Limited Liabili)*
**Marketing:** J Royal *(Marketing Manager)*
**US SIC:** 8111 **UK SIC:** 83500

| | 30-04-14 | 30-04-13 | 30-04-12 |
|---|---|---|---|
| TO | 9,435,210 | 6,752,923 | N/A |
| P/L | 2,842,304 | 2,009,514 | N/A |
| NW | 1,183,226 | 878,443 | 615,357 |
| WC | 3,443,718 | 2,938,921 | 2,525,791 |
| Emp. | 120 | 74 | N/A |

DUNS 21-705-5429

## Wilkies

Treefield Industrial Estate, Gelderd Road, Morley, Leeds, West Yorkshire LS27 7JU
**Tel:** 01133079955
**Web:** www.wilkies-sales.co.uk
**Estd:** 2009
**Line of Business:** Distribution service providers
**Partners:** P Waterhouse, P Waterhouse
**US SIC:** 5713 **UK SIC:** 64700
**Employees:** 80

DUNS 21-632-0135 **Imp-Exp**

## Wilkin & Sons Ltd

112 Colchester Road, White Colne, Colchester, Essex CO6 2PP
**Web:** www.tiptree.com
**Reg No:** 0026233 **VAT No:** 802673247
**Estd:** 2012 Private Limited Company
**Line of Business:** Manufacture of other food products not elsewhere classified
**Export Markets:** UK, Europe, North America, Middle and Far East, Others
**Export Sales:** £6,766,000
**Trading Style:** Tiptree Jam
**Issued Capital:** £1,000,000
**Principals:** P J Wilkin *(Chairman and Managing)*, I K Thurgood *(Sales)*, S A James, C W Newenham, W W Scott, S P Goodfellow
**Co. Secretary:** Mrs Roseanne Offord
**Responsibilities**
**Senior:** Tony Moore *(Logistics Manager)*
**Facilities:** Tsveta Lihareva *(Facilities Manager)*
**Operations:** Kevin Townsend *(Environment Officer)*
**Branches:** Wilkin & Sons Ltd, Basin Road, Maldon, Essex CM9 4RS
**US SIC:** 2099, 2052
**UK SIC:** 42399, 41970
**Auditors:** Baker Tilly UK Audit LLP
**Bankers:** Barclays Bank Plc (20-97-40)

| | 31-12-13 | 31-12-12 | 31-12-11 |
|---|---|---|---|
| TO | 35,613,000 | 34,917,000 | 30,892,000 |
| P/L | 557,000 | 2,256,000 | 1,043,000 |
| NW | 15,193,000 | 14,783,000 | 12,571,000 |
| WC | 9,039,000 | 8,891,000 | 7,684,000 |
| Emp. | 461 | 439 | 415 |

DUNS 34-821-3500

## Wilkin Chapman Group Ltd

**(Subsidiary of:** Wilkin Chapman Llp)
New Oxford House, Town Hall Square, Grimsby, South Humberside DN31 1HE
**Fax:** 01472360198
**Web:** www.wilkinchapman.co.uk
**Reg No:** 5620938 **Estd:** 1953 Private Limited Company
**Line of Business:** Solicitors
**Issued Capital:** £1
**Directors:** Ms J Whittaker, J M Carlton
**Co. Secretary:** Ms Janet Ward
**US SIC:** 8111 **UK SIC:** 83500
**Auditors:** Baker Tilly UK Audit LLP

| | 31-03-14 | 31-03-13 | 31-03-12 |
|---|---|---|---|
| TA | 1,262,097 | 1,161,277 | 768,863 |
| NW | (2,106,999) | (1,937,999) | (1,868,999) |
| WC | 1 | 1 | (309,999) |

DUNS 21-152-9609

## Wilkin Chapman Llp

25 Osborne Street, Grimsby, South Humberside DN31 1EY
**Tel:** 01472347112
**Web:** www.wilkinchapman.co.uk
**Reg No:** 0343261OC **Estd:** 1910 Private Limited Company
**Line of Business:** Solicitors
**Responsibilities**
**Senior:** Lesley Archer *(Non-designated Limited Liabili)*, Lisa Boileau *(Non-designated Limited Liabili)*, Nigel Burn *(Non-designated Limited Liabili)*, Tean Butcher *(Non-designated Limited Liabili)*, Russell Eke *(Non-designated Limited Liabili)*, Christopher Grocock *(Non-designated Limited Liabili)*, Lisa Howes *(Non-designated Limited Liabili)*, Claire Parker *(Non-designated Limited Liabili)*, Ian Sherburn *(Non-designated Limited Liabili)*
**US SIC:** 8111 **UK SIC:** 83500

| | 31-03-14 | 31-03-13 | 31-03-12 |
|---|---|---|---|
| TO | 18,120,922 | 16,488,952 | 16,542,069 |
| NW | (312,500) | N/A | N/A |
| WC | 7,907,969 | 7,143,990 | 6,805,954 |
| Emp. | 301 | 295 | 296 |

DUNS 21-757-0780

## Wilkins Kennedy Llp

Bridge House, 4 Borough High Street, Lambeth, London SE1 9QR
**Tel:** 02074-031-877
**Web:** www.wilkinskennedy.com
**Reg No:** 0370220OC **Estd:** 1882
**Line of Business:** Accounting and auditing activities
**Responsibilities**
**Senior:** Anthony Cork *(Non-designated Limited Liabili)*, Daniel Garside *(Non-designated Limited Liabili)*, Julian Golding *(Non-designated Limited Liabili)*, Daniel Graves *(Non-designated Limited Liabili)*, Sarah Hannaford *(Non-designated Limited Liabili)*, Sandra Harrison *(Non-designated Limited Liabili)*, Martin Macdonald *(Non-designated Limited Liabili)*, Alison Nayler *(Non-designated Limited Liabili)*, Nicholas Parrett *(Non-designated Limited Liabili)*

**Branches:** Wilkins Kennedy Llp, 92 London Street, Reading, Berkshire RG1 4SJ
**US SIC:** 8931   **UK SIC:** 83600
**Auditors:** Harmer Slater Ltd
**Bankers:** Allied Irish Bank (gb) (23-84-82)

| | 30-04-14 | 30-04-13 |
|---|---|---|
| TO | 33,657,874 | 30,403,611 |
| P/L | 89,223 | 89,419 |
| NW | (5,717,657) | (3,273,964) |
| WC | 9,618,020 | 9,863,791 |
| Emp. | 484 | 405 |

DUNS 64-108-2420
## Wilkins Kennedy Trustees Ltd
Gladstone House, Egham, Surrey TW20 9HY
**Tel:** 01784435561 **Fax:** 01784430584
**Web:** www.wilkinskennedy.com
**Reg No:** 4511662  **Estd:** 2002 Private Limited Company
**Line of Business:** Management activities of holding companies
**Issued Capital:** £2
**Directors:** K J Walmsley, M R Hall
**Responsibilities**
**Senior:** Andy Coghlan (Partner, Director of WK Corpor), Amanda Magagnin (Partner), Linda Penny (Partner), Tommy White (Partner)
**Finance:** Charles Baynes (Senior Finance Administrator)
**IT:** Vishal Biniwale (Network, Security Manager)
**US SIC:** 6711  **UK SIC:** 83962

| | 31-08-14 | 31-08-13 | 31-08-12 |
|---|---|---|---|
| TA | 2 | 2 | 2 |
| NW | 2 | 2 | 2 |

DUNS 29-094-9544  Imp
## The Wilkinson Corporation Ltd
Shield Drive, Wardley Industrial Estate, Manchester M28 2WD
**Tel:** 01617938127
**Web:** www.wilkinsonstar.com
**Reg No:** 1451522  **Estd:** 1979 Private Limited Company
**Line of Business:** Television goods wholesalers
**Export Sales:** £516,987
**Issued Capital:** £40,008
**Managing Director:** J A Wilkinson
**Co. Secretary:** Ms Elaine Wilkinson
**Responsibilities**
**Marketing:** Alistair Baker (Senior Marketing Executive)
**Sales:** Paul Dempster (Export Manager)
**IT:** Cathy Ashcroft (IT Manager)
**US SIC:** 5064  **UK SIC:** 61500
**Auditors:** Barlow Andrews
**Bankers:** National Westminster Bank Plc (60-22-46)

| | 30-11-13 | 30-11-12 | 30-11-11 |
|---|---|---|---|
| TO | 7,379,551 | 7,817,451 | 9,079,325 |
| P/L | 567 | (166,685) | (176,005) |
| NW | 348,988 | 345,945 | 518,924 |
| WC | 842,076 | 615,184 | 527,881 |
| Emp. | 56 | 67 | 101 |

DUNS 21-003-6741
## Wilkinson Eyre Group Ltd
33 Bowling Green Lane, London EC1R 0BJ
**Tel:** 020-7608-7900
**Web:** www.wilkinsoneyre.com
**Reg No:** 6287618  **Estd:** 2007 Private Limited Company
**Line of Business:** Architects
**Export Sales:** £4,250,196
**Trading Style:** Wilkinson Eyre Architects
**Issued Capital:** £144
**Directors:** C J Wilkinson, O J Tyler, P Baker, D K Bettison, G S Critchlow
**Co. Secretary:** James Eyre
**US SIC:** 8911  **UK SIC:** 83701
**Auditors:** BDO LLP
**Bankers:** HSBC Bank plc (40-33-33)

| | 31-03-14 | 31-03-13 | 31-03-12 |
|---|---|---|---|
| TO | 14,794,617 | 9,367,686 | 10,323,437 |
| P/L | 2,691,909 | 627,389 | 922,637 |
| NW | (1,393,241) | (3,417,277) | (3,885,245) |
| WC | 807,266 | 388,765 | 1,245,388 |
| Emp. | 141 | 117 | 124 |

DUNS 21-585-0997
## Wilkinson Facilities Services
Baker Road, Nelson Park West, Cramlington, Northumberland NE23 1WL
**Tel:** 01670700150
**Web:** www.wilkinson.co.uk
**Estd:** 2011 Proprietorship
**Line of Business:** Property maintenance services
**Proprietor:** S Leadbitter
**US SIC:** 1799  **UK SIC:** 50000
**Employees:** 90

DUNS 21-087-8661
## Wilkinson Woodward
11 Fountain Street, Halifax, West Yorkshire HX1 1LU
**Web:** www.wilkinsonwoodward.co.uk
**Estd:** 2012 Partnership
**Line of Business:** Solicitors
**Partners:** A M Crabtree, D Horsman, R Scott, R Woodward, Mrs M Cawthorn
**Responsibilities**
**Senior:** P Manock (Partner)
**Finance:** Angela Dent-Smith (Chief Cashier)
**Admin:** Jane Spears (Administrator)
**HR:** Jane Spears (Administrator)
**Health & Safety:** Jane Spears (Administrator)
**Facilities:** Jane Spears (Administrator)
**US SIC:** 8111  **UK SIC:** 83500
**Employees:** 60

DUNS 54-846-3967
## Wilkinson's
2 Market Place, Ashton-Under-Lyne, Lancashire OL6 7JU
**Tel:** 0161-339-9408
**Web:** www.wilko.com
**Estd:** 2002 Proprietorship
**Line of Business:** Other retail sale in non-specialised stores
**Proprietor:** N Whitehouse
**US SIC:** 5399  **UK SIC:** 65600
**Employees:** 90

DUNS 21-582-3207
## Wilkinsons
41 St George's Street, Canterbury, Kent CT1 2LE
**Tel:** 01227379850
**Web:** www.wilko.com
**Estd:** 2011 Proprietorship
**Line of Business:** Departmental stores
**Proprietor:** D Bowden
**US SIC:** 5399  **UK SIC:** 65600
**Employees:** 80

DUNS 21-818-5106  Imp
## Wilko Retail Ltd
J K House, Po Box 20, Roebuck Way, Manton Wood, Worksop, Nottinghamshire S80 3YY
**Tel:** 08000329329
**Web:** http://corporate.wilkinsonplus.com
**Reg No:** 0365335  **VAT No:** 125596651
**Estd:** 1930 Private Limited Company
**Line of Business:** Supermarkets
**Trading Style:** Wilko, Wilkinson
**Issued Capital:** £33,098
**Directors:** S P Toal, S H Sinclair, Ms L J Wilkinson, I A Ellis
**Co. Secretary:** Alison Edgerton
**Responsibilities**
**Marketing:** Fiona Gunn (Sales & Marketing Manager)
**Sales:** Fiona Gunn (Sales & Marketing Manager)
**IT:** Ritin Patel (Computer Manager), peter truman (Computer Manager)
**Facilities:** Leigh Oldfield (Maintenance Manager)
**Branches:** Wilko Retail Ltd, 196 Bradfield Road, Sheffield, South Yorkshire S6 2BY
**US SIC:** 5411, 5999
**UK SIC:** 64100, 65600
**Auditors:** Cooper Parry Group Ltd
Following financial data are in thousands

| | 01-02-14 | 02-02-13 | 27-02-12 |
|---|---|---|---|
| TO | 1,462,843 | 1,529,668 | 1,565,400 |
| P/L | 27,612 | 27,512 | 22,736 |
| NW | 248,295 | 230,431 | 230,479 |
| WC | 57,212 | 20,043 | (7,882) |
| Emp. | 21,648 | 22,897 | 23,229 |

DUNS 23-779-5955
## W.I.L.L. Wirral Independent Living & Learning
12 Tower Quays Tower Road, Birkenhead, Merseyside CH41 1BP
**Web:** www.willwirral.org.uk
**Reg No:** 3772855  **Estd:** 2002 Private Company Limited By Guarantee
**Line of Business:** Social work activities without accommodation
**Directors:** K Houghton, Mrs J Price, Mrs C Hood, J Engwall, Mrs J Murphy, Mrs H Solomon, Mrs V Rea, Mrs C Thomson
**Responsibilities**
**Senior:** Dave Large (Manager)
**US SIC:** 8321, 6732
**UK SIC:** 96111, 83100

| | 31-05-13 | 31-05-12 | 31-05-11 |
|---|---|---|---|
| TO | 1,096,527 | 725,458 | 711,138 |
| P/L | 65,555 | 47,784 | 100,858 |
| NW | 366,427 | 307,993 | 260,209 |
| WC | 354,134 | 295,511 | 247,227 |
| Emp. | 70 | 47 | 30 |

DUNS 28-848-5097
## Willan Homes Ltd
(**Subsidiary of:** Willan Group Ltd)
2 Brooklands Road, Sale, Cheshire M33 3SS
**Tel:** 01619731234
**Web:** www.willan.co.uk
**Reg No:** 0678791  **Estd:** 1960 Private Limited Company
**Line of Business:** Single-Family Housing Constructors
**Trading Style:** Bpd
**Issued Capital:** £500
**Director:** A P Stewart
**Co. Secretary:** Mrs Alison Booth
**Responsibilities**
**IT:** Hamish Mcmurray (Senior IT Executive)
**Facilities:** George Annable (Senior Management Surveyor), Toby Holmes (Commercial Lettings Surveyor)
**US SIC:** 1521  **UK SIC:** 50100
**Auditors:** PricewaterhouseCoopers

| | 31-03-14 | 31-03-13 | 31-03-12 |
|---|---|---|---|
| TA | 255,822 | 255,822 | 255,822 |
| NW | 500 | 500 | 500 |
| WC | 500 | 500 | 500 |

DUNS 38-782-1655
## Willard Electrical Services Ltd
Leigh Road, Chichester, West Sussex PO19 8TS
**Tel:** 01243784711
**Web:** www.painemanwaring.com
**Estd:** 2007 Partnership
**Line of Business:** Art restoration
**Partners:** J Willard, P Willard
**Responsibilities**
**Senior:** Malcolm Wain (Manager)
**Finance:** Malcolm Wain (Manager)
**HR:** Malcolm Wain (Manager)
**Health & Safety:** Malcolm Wain (Manager)
**US SIC:** 7699  **UK SIC:** 67303
**Employees:** 50

DUNS 21-584-8642
## Willenhall Fire Station
Fire Station, Clarkes Lane, Willenhall, West Midlands WV13 1HT
**Tel:** 01213807553
**Web:** www.wmfs.net
**Estd:** 2011 Proprietorship
**Line of Business:** Fire service activities
**Proprietor:** S Ward
**Responsibilities**
**Senior:** Mark Flannigan (Manager)
**US SIC:** 9224  **UK SIC:** 91400
**Employees:** 50

DUNS 21-222-9064
## Willenhall Practice
Remembrance Road, Coventry, West Midlands CV3 3DG
**Tel:** 02476304299
**Web:** www.nhs.net
**Estd:** 2010 Proprietorship
**Line of Business:** Doctors
**Proprietor:** Mrs S Williams
**Responsibilities**
**Senior:** Amanda Lanigan (Practice Manager)
**US SIC:** 8021  **UK SIC:** 95400
**Employees:** 50

DUNS 21-764-7609
## Willenhall Primary Care Centre
Remembrance Road, Coventry, West Midlands CV3 3DG
**Tel:** 02476304888
**Estd:** 2004
**Line of Business:** Nhs clinics
**US SIC:** 7011  **UK SIC:** 66500
**Employees:** 50

DUNS 21-215-3365  Exp
## Willerby Holiday Homes Ltd.
(**Subsidiary of:** Scaid Investments Ltd)
Imperial House, 1251 Hedon Road, Hull, North Humberside HU9 5NA
**Fax:** 01482-711482
**Web:** www.willerby.com
**Reg No:** 0387583  **Estd:** 1944 Private Limited Company
**Line of Business:** Manufacture of caravans
**Export Sales:** £5,249,428
**Issued Capital:** £5,100,000
**Directors:** C D Jeffrey, P J White
**Co. Secretary:** Bernard Murphy
**Responsibilities**
**Senior:** I Burville (Chief Executive)
**Health & Safety:** Gary Youngson (Health & Safety Officer)
**Facilities:** Graham Kemp (Facilities Manager)
**Operations:** Will Dennett (Purchasing Manager), Graham Kemp (Facilities Manager)

**Purchasing:** Will Dennett (Purchasing Manager)
**Engineering:** Dennis Hope (Engineering Manager)
**US SIC:** 3792  **UK SIC:** 35230
**Auditors:** Deloitte & Touche LLP
**Bankers:** National Westminster Bank Plc (56-00-06)

| | 28-09-13 | 29-09-12 | 01-09-11 |
|---|---|---|---|
| TO | 99,974,306 | 93,274,731 | 120,944,998 |
| P/L | 2,015,560 | (2,266,207) | 11,105,268 |
| NW | 69,776,121 | 69,884,481 | 73,875,107 |
| WC | 68,457,652 | 68,398,504 | 72,262,052 |
| Emp. | 639 | 685 | 820 |

DUNS 39-905-0590
## Willerby Landscapes (Holdings) Ltd
Bridge Nurseries, Green Lane, Four Elms, Edenbridge, Kent TN8 6RN
**Web:** www.willerby-landscapes.co.uk
**Reg No:** 2230149  **VAT No:** 367658012
**Estd:** 1988 Private Limited Company
**Line of Business:** Management activities of construction holding companies
**Trading Style:** Willerby Landscapes (Holdings) Ltd
**Issued Capital:** £102,000
**Principals:** J A Melmoe (Managing), R N Davies, M G Ainscow
**Co. Secretary:** Peter Smith
**Responsibilities**
**Health & Safety:** Colin Caplehorne (Health & Safety Manager)
**US SIC:** 6711, 0729
**UK SIC:** 83962, 01003
**Auditors:** Ledger Sparks
**Bankers:** National Westminster Bank Plc (55-70-13)

| | 30-06-14 | 30-06-13 | 30-06-12 |
|---|---|---|---|
| TO | 13,771,488 | 9,213,868 | 12,751,213 |
| P/L | 645,775 | 636,039 | 1,001,956 |
| NW | 3,088,397 | 2,799,416 | 2,694,886 |
| WC | 1,772,859 | 1,470,647 | 1,376,295 |
| Emp. | 93 | 81 | 90 |

DUNS 21-776-5326
## Willesborough Infant School
Church Road, Willesborough, Willesborough, Ashford, Kent TN24 0JZ
**Tel:** 01233624165
**Web:** www.willesborough-infants.kent.sch.uk
**Estd:** 1994 Partnership
**Line of Business:** Schools (local authority)
**Partners:** Mrs J Parsons, Mrs J Tarsons
**Responsibilities**
**Senior:** Fran Rusbridee (Head Teacher)
**US SIC:** 8211  **UK SIC:** 93200
**Employees:** 50

DUNS 21-165-6249
## Willesborough Junior School
Highfield Road, Willesborough, Ashford, Kent TN24 0JU
**Tel:** 01233-620405
**Web:** www.willesborough-js.kent.sch.uk
**Estd:** 1998
**Line of Business:** Schools (local authority)
**Director:** Mrs E Pettersen
**Responsibilities**
**Senior:** Jennie King (Head Teacher)
**US SIC:** 8211  **UK SIC:** 93200
**Employees:** 69

DUNS 85-598-5739
## Willesden Hospital
Robson Avenue, London NW10 3RY
**Tel:** 02084387000
**Web:** www.brentpct.nhs.uk
**Estd:** 2010 Proprietorship
**Line of Business:** Nhs clinics
**Proprietor:** Easton
**Responsibilities**
**Senior:** Mark Easten (CEO, Managing Director), Noel O'Farrell (Hospital Manager), Polly Poglase (Communications Manager)
**US SIC:** 8062  **UK SIC:** 95100
**Employees:** 300

DUNS 22-626-7318  Exp
## Willett International Ltd
4 & 5 Ermine Centre, Lancaster Way, Huntingdon, Cambridgeshire PE29 6XX
**Tel:** 08702-405542
**Reg No:** 1689892  **VAT No:** 576641510
**Estd:** 1983 Private Limited Company
**Line of Business:** Holding companies management activities
**Export Markets:** Worldwide
**Issued Capital:** £1
**Directors:** K G Ward, F T Mcfaden
**Co. Secretary:** Pavan Khanna
**Branches:** Willett International Ltd, 2 Newmans Row, Willett House, High Wycombe, Buckinghamshire HP12 3RE
**US SIC:** 6711, 3559
**UK SIC:** 83962, 32863
**Auditors:** Ernst & Young LLP

**Bankers:** HSBC Bank plc (40-42-08)

| | 31-12-13 | 31-12-12 | 31-12-11 |
|---|---|---|---|
| TA | 3,064,000 | 3,064,000 | 3,057,000 |
| P/L | N/A | 7,000 | 6,000 |
| NW | 3,064,000 | 3,064,000 | 3,057,000 |

DUNS 73-956-4560
### Willi Betz Uk Ltd
Office 16, Epsilon House, 1-5 West Road
Epsilon Terrace, Ipswich, Suffolk IP3 9FJ
**Tel:** 01473276184 **Fax:** 01394270010
**Web:** www.willibetz.com
**Reg No:** 5208158 **Estd:** 2011 Private Limited Company
**Line of Business:** Road haulage and transport services
**Issued Capital:** £75,000
**Directors:** Y Koppejan, N Van Den Boogaard
**Responsibilities**
**Senior:** Shan Wassermeyer *(Manager)*
**US SIC:** 4789 **UK SIC:** 77002
**Auditors:** Ensors

| | 31-12-13 | 31-12-12 | 31-12-11 |
|---|---|---|---|
| TO | N/A | N/A | 8,267,891 |
| P/L | N/A | N/A | (468,653) |
| NW | (3,788,875) | (3,924,084) | (4,100,395) |
| WC | (3,804,620) | (3,945,161) | (4,102,106) |
| Emp. | N/A | N/A | 49 |

DUNS 23-067-7254
### William A. Lewis Engineering Ltd
(**Subsidiary of:** Lewis & Sons Holdings Ltd)
Harlescott Lane, Shrewsbury, Shropshire SY1 3AD
**Tel:** 01743-450005
**Web:** www.walewis.co.uk
**Reg No:** 2790973 **Estd:** 1993 Private Limited Company
**Line of Business:** Engineers (general)
**Issued Capital:** £1,000
**Principals:** S W Lewis *(Managing)*, G S Lewis, D J Howells, P J Lewis
**Co. Secretary:** Geoffrey Lewis
**US SIC:** 8911, 3499
**UK SIC:** 83701, 31694
**Auditors:** Whittingham Riddell
**Bankers:** National Westminster Bank Plc (55-50-05)

| | 31-12-13 | 31-12-12 | 31-12-11 |
|---|---|---|---|
| TA | 1,405,659 | 1,115,167 | 1,833,005 |
| NW | 396,792 | 542,332 | 851,972 |
| WC | 396,792 | 542,292 | 851,932 |

DUNS 21-244-7080
### William Anelay Ltd
Murton Way, Osbaldwick, York, North Yorkshire YO19 5UW
**Tel:** 01904-412624
**Web:** www.williamanelay.co.uk
**Reg No:** 0218686 **VAT No:** 168892895
**Estd:** 1927 Private Limited Company
**Line of Business:** Stonemasons
**Trading Style:** William Anelay Ltd
**Issued Capital:** £110,000
**Principals:** C T Anelay *(Managing)*, T J Donlon, A C Townend, A Bowers
**Co. Secretary:** Charles Anelay
**US SIC:** 1799 **UK SIC:** 50000
**Auditors:** Grabutt & Elliott
**Bankers:** National Westminster Bank Plc (56-00-70)

| | 30-06-13 | 30-06-12 | 30-06-11 |
|---|---|---|---|
| TO | 25,442,185 | 23,134,447 | 13,697,359 |
| P/L | 307,968 | 454,004 | 397,666 |
| NW | 1,744,424 | 1,501,016 | 1,165,042 |
| WC | 1,737,995 | 1,118,484 | 516,747 |
| Emp. | 99 | 99 | 101 |

DUNS 21-172-6077
### William Armes Holdings Ltd
Church Field Road, Sudbury, Suffolk CO10 2YA
**Tel:** 01787372988
**Web:** www.william-armes.co.uk
**Reg No:** 6967132 **Estd:** 2009 Private Limited Company
**Line of Business:** Other letting of own property
**Issued Capital:** £182,800
**Directors:** Mrs J K Bosman, Birketts Directors Limited, M E Gipson
**Co. Secretary:** Philip Holroyd
**US SIC:** 6519 **UK SIC:** 85000

| | 31-12-13 | 31-12-12 | 31-12-11 |
|---|---|---|---|
| TA | 2,807,077 | 2,862,588 | 2,888,762 |
| NW | 1,604,493 | 1,608,699 | 1,583,896 |
| WC | (26,783) | (10,822) | (25,683) |

DUNS 21-310-8475 **Imp-Exp**
### William Beckett Plastics Ltd
Unit 5a, Shepcote Way, Sheffield, South Yorkshire S9 1TH
**Tel:** 01142-434399
**Web:** www.beckettplastics.com
**Reg No:** 1304215 **VAT No:** 646445031
**Estd:** 1973 Private Limited Company
**Line of Business:** Plastic injection moulding
**Issued Capital:** £60,000
**Principals:** W A Beckett *(Managing)*, Ms K Goodison *(Financial)*, P D Stocks
**Co. Secretary:** Mrs Linda Beckett
**Responsibilities**
**Sales:** claudia collins *(Exports Manager)*
**US SIC:** 3079 **UK SIC:** 48360
**Auditors:** HLB Kidsons
**Bankers:** The Royal Bank Of Scotland Plc (16-00-08)

| | 31-12-13 | 31-12-12 | 31-12-11 |
|---|---|---|---|
| TA | 1,633,289 | 1,813,932 | 1,881,853 |
| NW | 732,890 | 730,901 | 751,043 |
| WC | 197,851 | 219,612 | 263,142 |

DUNS 21-244-7379
### William Birch & Sons Ltd
Link Road Court, Osbaldwick, York, North Yorkshire YO10 3JQ
**Tel:** 01904411411 **Fax:** 01904-428428
**Web:** www.williambirch.co.uk
**Reg No:** 0129834 **VAT No:** 168874506
**Estd:** 1874 Private Limited Company
**Line of Business:** Plant hire and leasing
**Issued Capital:** £50,000
**Directors:** P Goyea, C W Birch
**Co. Secretary:** Alistair Birch
**Branches:** William Birch & Sons Ltd, Osbaldwick Link Road, York, North Yorkshire YO19 5JA
**US SIC:** 1799, 1541
**UK SIC:** 50000, 50100
**Auditors:** Forster, Stott & Co
**Bankers:** Barclays Bank Plc (20-99-56)

| | 31-12-13 | 31-12-12 | 31-12-11 |
|---|---|---|---|
| TO | 20,535,782 | 16,209,202 | 19,342,765 |
| P/L | (151,027) | (264,337) | 60,520 |
| NW | 12,405,609 | 12,534,579 | 12,319,501 |
| WC | 2,797,609 | 2,543,145 | 3,181,719 |
| Emp. | 81 | 84 | 92 |

DUNS 23-621-8728
### William Blair International Ltd
(**Subsidiary of:** Wbc Holdings L.P.)
The Broadgate Tower, 20 Primrose Street, London EC2A 2EW
**Tel:** 0779110000 **Fax:** 020-7868-4420
**Web:** www.williamblair.com
**Reg No:** 3619027 **Estd:** 1998 Private Limited Company
**Line of Business:** Financial intermediation not elsewhere classified
**Issued Capital:** £3,100,000
**Directors:** J Moore, M Gooch, R A Mastrangelo, J Zindel, J R Ettelson, R W Smirl, A J Simon, Ms M R Seitz
**Co. Secretary:** Arthur Simon
**US SIC:** 6111 **UK SIC:** 81501
**Auditors:** Ernst & Young LLP
**Bankers:** The Royal Bank Of Scotland Plc (83-00-81)

| | 31-12-13 | 31-12-12 | 31-12-11 |
|---|---|---|---|
| TA | 25,344,564 | 17,744,752 | 13,716,421 |
| P/L | 8,404,602 | 6,616,035 | 2,817,521 |
| NW | 19,327,936 | 12,970,210 | 8,055,878 |
| WC | 16,994,577 | 10,469,150 | 6,050,405 |
| Emp. | 55 | 43 | 35 |

DUNS 85-598-5253
### William Booth Infant School
Notintone Street, Nottingham, Nottinghamshire NG2 4QF
**Tel:** 01159-155821
**Web:** www.wix.com
**Estd:** 2005 Proprietorship
**Line of Business:** Schools (local authority)
**Proprietor:** A Mattison
**Responsibilities**
**Senior:** Gary Fullwood *(Head Teacher)*, Andrew Mattison *(Head Teacher)*
**US SIC:** 8211 **UK SIC:** 93200
**Employees:** 80

DUNS 21-069-2997
### William Budd Health Centre
Downton Road, Bristol, Avon BS4 1WH
**Tel:** 01179449700
**Estd:** 2003 Partnership
**Line of Business:** Doctors
**Partners:** Dr C Mason, Dr T Dean, Dr C Sailsbury, Dr A R Peters, Dr S Peterson
**Responsibilities**
**Senior:** Marie King *(Practice Manager)*
**US SIC:** 8011 **UK SIC:** 95300
**Employees:** 50

DUNS 21-455-9247
### William Coates Ltd.
37 Mallusk Road, Newtownabbey, Co Antrim BT36 4PP
**Tel:** 028-9034-2560
**Web:** www.williamcoates.com
**Reg No:** 0005996NI **VAT No:** 252775739
**Estd:** 1964 Private Limited Company
**Line of Business:** Electrical contractors and electricians
**Issued Capital:** £40,500
**Directors:** W P Dickson, Mrs M Weir, M W Weir, D Gould, P R Weir
**Co. Secretary:** Desmond Gould
**Responsibilities**
**Senior:** Edwin Backler *(Manager)*, Michael Dowds *(Director)*, Paul Wear *(Proprietor)*
**US SIC:** 1731, 1711
**UK SIC:** 50300
**Auditors:** Jones Peters
**Bankers:** Ulster Bank Ltd (98-01-10)

| | 31-05-14 | 31-05-13 | 31-05-12 |
|---|---|---|---|
| TO | 10,650,081 | 8,495,080 | 7,500,618 |
| P/L | 31,705 | 308,901 | 116,337 |
| NW | 1,669,482 | 1,685,165 | 1,428,220 |
| WC | 788,740 | 850,270 | 886,345 |
| Emp. | 63 | 56 | 55 |

DUNS 36-480-0409
### William Cook Holdings Ltd
Parkway Avenue, Parkway Industrial Estate, Sheffield, South Yorkshire S9 4UL
**Tel:** 01388528248
**Web:** www.william-cook.co.uk
**Reg No:** 3283010 **Estd:** 1902 Private Limited Company
**Line of Business:** Management activities of production holding companies
**Export Sales:** £29,032,000
**Issued Capital:** £377,247
**Directors:** K J Grayley, A J Cook
**Co. Secretary:** Michael Hodgson
**US SIC:** 6711 **UK SIC:** 83962
**Auditors:** KPMG LLP
**Bankers:** The Royal Bank Of Scotland Plc (16-23-37)

| | 29-03-14 | 30-03-13 | 31-03-12 |
|---|---|---|---|
| TO | 61,071,000 | 83,662,000 | 72,855,000 |
| P/L | 2,493,000 | 14,225,000 | 8,995,000 |
| NW | 49,542,000 | 46,792,000 | 36,290,000 |
| WC | 21,111,000 | 23,954,000 | 14,849,000 |
| Emp. | 736 | 816 | 701 |

DUNS 21-217-0849 **Imp-Exp**
### William Cook Leeds Ltd
(**Subsidiary of:** William Cook Holdings Ltd)
Pontefract Lane, Cross Green, Leeds, West Yorkshire LS9 0DQ
**Tel:** 01132-496363 **Fax:** 01132-491376
**Web:** www.william-cook.co.uk
**Reg No:** 0053475 **VAT No:** 168873117
**Estd:** 1900 Private Limited Company
**Line of Business:** Die casting equipment and services
**Export Sales:** £12,418,993
**Issued Capital:** £550,000
**Principals:** K J Grayley *(Managing)*, A J Cook
**Co. Secretary:** Michael Houghton
**Responsibilities**
**Sales:** Roland Dixon *(Senior Sales Executive)*, David Walshaw *(Sales Manager)*
**IT:** David Semmence *(Senior IT Executive)*
**Purchasing:** Stewart Wright *(Purchasing Manager)*
**US SIC:** 3559 **UK SIC:** 32863
**Auditors:** KPMG LLP
**Bankers:** Barclays Bank Plc (20-76-89)

| | 29-03-14 | 30-03-13 | 31-03-12 |
|---|---|---|---|
| TO | 20,646,719 | 29,666,489 | 28,292,466 |
| P/L | 1,336,355 | 4,318,584 | 3,030,421 |
| NW | 5,712,951 | 7,125,974 | 5,374,736 |
| WC | 1,130,702 | 2,293,018 | 574,211 |
| Emp. | 199 | 236 | 215 |

DUNS 21-819-2888
### William Davis Ltd
(**Subsidiary of:** Broadthorpe Ltd)
Forest Field, Forest Road, Loughborough, Leicestershire LE11 3NS
**Tel:** 01509-231181
**Web:** www.williamdavis.co.uk
**Reg No:** 0468397 **VAT No:** 114635196
**Estd:** 1935 Private Limited Company
**Line of Business:** Building construction contractors
**Issued Capital:** £9,000,000
**Principals:** E Davis *(Chairman)*, G S Higgins *(Managing)*, T Higgins
**Co. Secretary:** Geoffrey Pearson
**Responsibilities**
**Senior:** Matt Colloby *(Business Development Manager)*, Eddie Davis *(Chairman)*, Julian Shaw *(Maintenance Manager)*
**Finance:** Richard Cornes *(Partnerships Director)*
**Marketing:** Matt Colloby *(Business Development Manager)*, Georgina Newcombe *(Sales and Marketing Director)*
**Sales:** Matt Colloby *(Business Development Manager)*, Georgina Newcombe *(Sales and Marketing Director)*
**HR:** Rebecca Hinchley *(HR & Training Officer)*
**Facilities:** Julian Shaw *(Maintenance Manager)*
**Operations:** Nigel Radcliffe *(Production Manager)*, Martyn Tharratt *(Project Manager)*
**Purchasing:** Terry Hopper *(Purchasing Manager)*
**Engineering:** Nigel Radcliffe *(Production Manager)*
**Branches:** William Davis Ltd, 3 Gold Ave, Rugby, Warwickshire CV22 7FB
**US SIC:** 1522 **UK SIC:** 50100
**Auditors:** PricewaterhouseCoopers LLP
**Bankers:** Barclays Bank Plc (20-52-69)

| | 31-05-14 | 31-05-13 | 31-05-12 |
|---|---|---|---|
| TO | 67,502,000 | 57,401,000 | 73,834,000 |
| P/L | 9,289,000 | 2,471,000 | 5,910,000 |
| NW | 98,271,000 | 91,124,000 | 90,888,000 |
| WC | 97,916,000 | 91,727,000 | 91,598,000 |
| Emp. | 314 | 302 | 358 |

DUNS 21-758-6082
### William De Ferrers School
Trinity Square South, Chelmsford, Essex CM3 5JU
**Web:** www.williamdeferrers.essex.sch.uk
**Reg No:** 7552735 **Estd:** 2011 Private Limited Company
**Line of Business:** General secondary education
**Directors:** G A Garner, Mrs F Engelbrecht, Ms B Stannard, T Chamberlin, Mrs L L Smith, Mrs D A Warman, P Acton, Mrs K Raymont
**Co. Secretary:** Ms Susan Newby
**Responsibilities**
**Senior:** Janice Gilroy *(Director)*, Susan Hillman *(Director)*, Malcolm Lyall *(Director)*, Neal Mcgowan *(Director)*, Una O'Neill *(Director)*, Adrian Phelps-Knights *(Director)*
**IT:** Farook Patel *(IT Support)*
**US SIC:** 8211 **UK SIC:** 93200

| | 31-08-14 | 31-08-13 | 31-08-12 |
|---|---|---|---|
| TO | 11,736,443 | 11,268,366 | 25,125,623 |
| P/L | (31,411) | (342,069) | 9,155,604 |
| NW | 8,370,124 | 8,019,535 | 8,494,604 |
| WC | 998,097 | 503,970 | 595,711 |
| Emp. | 283 | 227 | 215 |

DUNS 36-834-5039
### William Duncan & Co
30 Miller Road, Ayr, Ayrshire KA7 2AY
**Tel:** 01292-265071
**Web:** www.williamduncan.co.uk
**Estd:** 1974 Partnership
**Line of Business:** Accounting and auditing activities
**Trading Style:** William Duncan & Co
**Partners:** R Ferguson, J Wallis, J Laurie, A Pickles
**Responsibilities**
**Senior:** Stephen Bargh *(Partner)*, Hazel Murphy *(Partner)*
**Branches:** William Duncan & Co, Dalblair House, 46 Dalblair Road, Ayr, Ayrshire KA7 1UQ
**US SIC:** 8931 **UK SIC:** 83600
**Employees:** 46

DUNS 21-162-3413
### William Edward School & Sports College
Stifford Clays Road, Grays, Essex RM16 3NJ
**Tel:** 01375-486000
**Web:** www.williameduards.thurrock.sch.uk
**Estd:** 2002 Proprietorship
**Line of Business:** Schools (local authority)
**Proprietor:** Ms B Watson
**Responsibilities**
**Senior:** Stephen Munday *(Head Teacher)*
**US SIC:** 8211 **UK SIC:** 93200
**Employees:** 184

DUNS 21-817-5560
### William Freer Ltd
360 Melton Road, Leicester, Leicestershire LE4 7SL
**Tel:** 01162-689660 **Fax:** 01162-689650
**Web:** www.williamfreer.co.uk
**Reg No:** 0229334 **Estd:** 1928 Private Limited Company
**Line of Business:** Plumbing
**Issued Capital:** £69,560
**Principals:** R W Freer *(Chairman)*, M J Whitehead *(Managing)*
**Co. Secretary:** Richard Freer
**Responsibilities**
**Senior:** Stuart Whitehead *(Operations Manager)*
**Marketing:** Stuart Whitehead *(Operations Manager)*
**Admin:** Jade Russell *(Office Manager)*
**Facilities:** Stuart Whitehead *(Operations Manager)*
**Branches:** William Freer Ltd, Mowbeck House, Alexandra Road, Grantham, Lincolnshire NG31 7AS
**US SIC:** 1711, 7699
**UK SIC:** 50300, 67303
**Auditors:** JWPCreers
**Bankers:** Barclays Bank Plc (20-49-11)

| | 31-12-13 | 31-12-12 | 31-12-11 |
|---|---|---|---|
| TO | 8,664,318 | 11,071,670 | 10,207,626 |
| P/L | (424,729) | (78,717) | 239,857 |
| NW | 5,209,566 | 5,582,009 | 4,926,917 |
| WC | 1,267,977 | 1,692,740 | 2,377,931 |
| Emp. | 114 | 117 | 112 |

## DUNS 21-003-6048
### William Gibbons Group Ltd
Po Box 103, 26 Planetary Road, Willenhall, West Midlands WV13 3XT
**Tel:** 01902730011 **Fax:** 01902865835
**Web:** www.williamgibbons.co.uk
**Reg No:** 6287023 **Estd:** 2007 Private Limited Company
**Line of Business:** Management activities of holding companies
**Issued Capital:** £4,150
**Director:** D A Gibbons
**Co. Secretary:** Donald Gibbons
**US SIC:** 6711 **UK SIC:** 83962
**Bankers:** Lloyds TSB Bank plc (30-13-66)

|  | 31-03-14 | 31-03-13 | 31-03-12 |
|---|---|---|---|
| TO | 38,032,693 | 39,688,823 | 41,674,445 |
| P/L | 1,128,438 | 2,194,594 | 2,942,122 |
| NW | (5,088,759) | (6,638,718) | (9,102,616) |
| WC | (284,241) | (22,668) | (423,734) |
| Emp. | 373 | 340 | 312 |

## DUNS 21-589-1417    Imp-Exp
### William Grant & Company Ltd
16 Coney Road, Londonderry, Co Londonderry BT48 8JP
**Tel:** 02871352232 **Fax:** 02871 352461
**Reg No:** 0000477NI **VAT No:** 253459646
**Estd:** 1911 Private Limited Company
**Line of Business:** Production of meat products
**Export Markets:** Republic Of Ireland
**Issued Capital:** £1,760
**Directors:** E V Grant, V Grant
**Co. Secretary:** Vincent Grant
**Responsibilities**
**Marketing:** Harold Bond (Marketing Manager)
**Facilities:** Gerry Magee (Engineering Manager)
**Engineering:** Gerry Magee (Engineering Manager)
**US SIC:** 2013 **UK SIC:** 41223
**Auditors:** Hill Vellacott
**Bankers:** The Bank Of Ireland (90-49-74)

|  | 06-06-13 | 06-06-12 | 06-06-11 |
|---|---|---|---|
| TO | 13,502,025 | 13,910,151 | 12,876,884 |
| P/L | (104,203) | (169,300) | 8,354 |
| NW | 4,131,232 | 4,085,271 | 4,254,571 |
| WC | 3,410,102 | 3,529,306 | 3,641,707 |
| Emp. | 56 | 56 | 57 |

## DUNS 23-784-0215    Exp
### William Grant & Sons Enterprises Ltd
(**Subsidiary of:** William Grant & Sons Holdings Ltd)
Independence Road, 84 Lower Mortlake Road, Richmond, Surrey TW9 2HS
**Tel:** 020-8332-1188 **Fax:** 02083321695
**Web:** www.glenfiddich.com
**Reg No:** 0196614SC **Estd:** 1887 Private Limited Company
**Line of Business:** Distilleries
**Trading Style:** William Grant & Sons Ltd
**Issued Capital:** £10,000
**Directors:** G J Bargeton, E J Henderson
**Responsibilities**
**Marketing:** Kate Athanasi (Marketing Director), Shayne Hoyne (Marketing Director)
**Sales:** Maurice Doyle (Business Development Director)
**Admin:** Sue Read (Office Manager)
**IT:** Kevan Osnowski (IT Administrator)
**HR:** Jane Golding (Human Resources Business Partn), Sue Read (Office Manager)
**Health & Safety:** Sue Read (Office Manager)
**Facilities:** Sue Read (Office Manager)
**Purchasing:** Sue Read (Office Manager)
**US SIC:** 2085 **UK SIC:** 42402
**Auditors:** Ernst & Young LLP

|  | 31-12-13 | 31-12-12 | 31-12-11 |
|---|---|---|---|
| TA | 132,913,000 | 108,925,000 | 108,890,000 |
| P/L | 23,900,000 | 23,854,000 | 11,059,000 |
| NW | 114,480,000 | 90,593,000 | 66,703,000 |
| WC | 6,480,000 | (17,407,000) | (41,297,000) |

## DUNS 76-854-0973    Exp
### William Grant & Sons Ltd
(**Subsidiary of:** William Grant & Sons Holdings Ltd)
Phoenix Crescent, Strathclyde Bu, Bellshill, Lanarkshire ML4 3AN
**Tel:** 01698843843 **Fax:** 01698 844788
**Web:** www.williamgrant.com
**Reg No:** 0131772SC **VAT No:** 554690029
**Estd:** 1986 Private Limited Company
**Line of Business:** Distilleries
**Export Markets:** Worldwide
**Issued Capital:** £343,670
**Directors:** Mrs S J David, S J Hunt, Ms R A Mcginness, B T Thomson, M Lamont, P G Gordon, A P Hopkins
**Responsibilities**
**Senior:** Maurice Doyle (Manager), Gerry McEntee (Warehouse Manager), Nicholas Swan (Manager), George Tait (Manager)
**Sales:** Allan Lowndes (Sales Director)

**Health & Safety:** Barrie Dexter (Health & Safety Officer)
**Facilities:** William French (Maintenance Manager)
**Operations:** Barrie Dexter (Health & Safety Officer)
**Purchasing:** Ken McKinley (Purchasing Director)
**Branches:** William Grant & Sons Ltd, Girvan Distillery, Grangestone Industrial Estate, Girvan, Ayrshire KA26 9PT
**US SIC:** 2085, 2083
**UK SIC:** 42402, 42702
**Auditors:** Ernst & Young LLP
**Bankers:** The Royal Bank Of Scotland Plc (83-07-06)

|  | 31-12-13 | 31-12-12 | 31-12-11 |
|---|---|---|---|
| TA | 249,040,000 | 283,552,000 | 285,440,000 |
| P/L | (766,000) | (2,095,000) | (2,217,000) |
| NW | (9,658,000) | (10,384,000) | (9,748,000) |
| WC | (121,405,000) | (112,049,000) | (108,466,000) |
| Emp. | 114 | 103 | 85 |

## DUNS 23-589-2973    Imp
### William Grant & Sons Uk Ltd
(**Subsidiary of:** William Grant & Sons Holdings Ltd)
Form One, 17 Bartley Woods Business Park, Bartley Way, Hook, Hampshire RG27 9XA
**Tel:** 01256748100 **Fax:** 02380-311-111
**Web:** www.williamgrant.com
**Reg No:** 2288241 **VAT No:** 643394331
**Estd:** 1942 Private Limited Company
**Line of Business:** Wholesale of wine, beer, spirits and other alcoholic beverages
**Trading Style:** William Grants & Sons
**Issued Capital:** £200,000
**Directors:** P H Rochford, P G Hancock, C W Mason, S J Hunt
**Co. Secretary:** William Payne
**Responsibilities**
**Senior:** Gemma Hayes (Facilities Manager)
**Marketing:** Andrea Mills (Customer Marketing Manager)
**Sales:** Karen Brookbank (Sales Director)
**HR:** Lorna Hunt (Human Resources Manager)
**Facilities:** Gemma Hayes (Facilities Manager), Geoff Whittaker (Facilities Manager)
**US SIC:** 5182, 4213, 7319
**UK SIC:** 61700, 72300, 83800
**Auditors:** Ernst & Young LLP
**Bankers:** National Westminster Bank Plc (56-00-68)

|  | 31-12-13 | 31-12-12 | 31-12-11 |
|---|---|---|---|
| TO | 113,546,000 | 118,106,000 | 126,024,000 |
| P/L | 500,000 | 500,000 | 479,000 |
| NW | 774,000 | 572,000 | 487,000 |
| WC | (115,000) | (560,000) | (939,000) |
| Emp. | 142 | 140 | 127 |

## DUNS 22-283-0320
### William Gray Construction Ltd
36 Longman Drive, Inverness, Inverness-Shire IV1 1SU
**Tel:** 01463-712072
**Web:** www.williamgray.co.uk
**Reg No:** 0224032SC **Estd:** 2001 Private Limited Company
**Line of Business:** Building construction contractors
**Issued Capital:** £5,000
**Principals:** W H Gray (Managing), D H Murray, Miss P Fox
**Co. Secretary:** Ms Barbara Gray
**Branches:** William Gray Construction Ltd, Lochside, Dingwall, Ross-Shire IV7 8LA
**US SIC:** 6552, 1541, 1522, 1751
**UK SIC:** 85000, 50100, 50400
**Auditors:** Saffery Champness

|  | 31-12-13 | 31-12-12 | 31-12-11 |
|---|---|---|---|
| TO | N/A | N/A | 5,719,224 |
| P/L | N/A | N/A | 5,176 |
| NW | 222,821 | 146,471 | 1,085,432 |
| WC | 157,638 | 69,047 | 980,512 |
| Emp. | N/A | N/A | 43 |

## DUNS 21-262-6741
### William Grimshaw & Sons Ltd
(**Subsidiary of:** Pentagon Motor Holdings Ltd)
Bury New Road, Manchester M25 3BD
**Tel:** 01617987000 **Fax:** 01617730800
**Web:** www.grimshaws.co.uk
**Reg No:** 0338830 **VAT No:** 389705989
**Estd:** 1938 Private Limited Company
**Line of Business:** Sale of new motor vehicles
**Issued Capital:** £18,100
**Directors:** Motors Directors Limited, G P Hall, T Reeve
**Co. Secretary:** Motors Secretaries Limited
**Responsibilities**
**Senior:** Alan Grimshaw (Manager), William Myles (Financial Director)
**Finance:** William Myles (Financial Director)
**Sales:** Janine Templeman (Fleet Manager)
**IT:** Andy Cryer (IT Manager), Alan Grimshaw (Manager)
**Health & Safety:** Alan Grimshaw (Manager)

**Operations:** Neil Saville (Fleet Operations Manager)
**US SIC:** 5511 **UK SIC:** 65100
**Auditors:** John Goulding & Co
**Bankers:** Barclays Bank Plc (20-54-58)

|  | 31-12-13 | 31-12-12 | 31-12-11 |
|---|---|---|---|
| TO | 49,653,708 | 42,739,911 | 48,581,863 |
| P/L | (196,339) | (141,892) | (318,792) |
| NW | 245,947 | 442,286 | 584,178 |
| WC | (668,212) | (434,683) | (305,385) |
| Emp. | 65 | 71 | 69 |

## DUNS 21-824-9191    Imp-Exp
### William Hackett Chains Ltd
(**Subsidiary of:** William Hackett Chains Holdings Ltd)
Maypole Fields, Cradley, Halesowen, West Midlands B63 2QE
**Tel:** 01384569431
**Web:** www.williamhackett.co.uk
**Reg No:** 0343086 **VAT No:** 462370653
**Estd:** 1980 Private Limited Company
**Line of Business:** Manufacturers of chains
**Issued Capital:** £1,958
**Directors:** B Burgess, A Lloyd, R T Bell, T J Burgess, R Corston, I Kelly, Mrs E A Burgess
**Co. Secretary:** Adrian Lloyd
**Responsibilities**
**Marketing:** Stuart Mullins (Director - Harrow Products)
**Sales:** Andrea Bayliss (Sales Administrator), Victoria Mukhina (Sales Administrator)
**Admin:** Andrea Bayliss (Sales Administrator), Victoria Mukhina (Sales Administrator)
**Fleet:** Mark Homer (Assistant Works Manager)
**Engineering:** Chris Wiggins (Utilities Marine and Bespoke C)
**Branches:** William Hackett Chains Ltd, Oak Drive, Alnwick, Northumberland NE66 2EU
**US SIC:** 3568, 3469
**UK SIC:** 32613, 31200
**Auditors:** Cox Jerome
**Bankers:** National Westminster Bank Plc (60-09-39)

|  | 31-08-13 | 31-08-12 | 31-08-11 |
|---|---|---|---|
| TO | 12,574,333 | 11,106,740 | 11,135,264 |
| P/L | 518,688 | 1,329,111 | 1,346,443 |
| NW | 3,344,396 | 3,232,985 | 3,114,500 |
| WC | 4,405,539 | 2,162,560 | 1,749,865 |
| Emp. | 46 | 43 | 37 |

## DUNS 76-896-5360
### William Hare Group Ltd
Brandlesholme House, Brandlesholme Road, Bury, Lancashire BL8 1JJ
**Fax:** 01616090409
**Web:** www.hare.com
**Reg No:** 2616280 **Estd:** 1991 Private Limited Company
**Line of Business:** Management activities of holding companies
**Issued Capital:** £35,000
**Directors:** Ms S K Hodgkiss, T G Haughey, Ms J Hodgkiss, D M Hodgkiss, P M Norris, C D Evans
**Co. Secretary:** Philip Norris
**Responsibilities**
**Senior:** Bartle Hodgkiss (Manager)
**Finance:** Phil Coventry (Accountant)
**US SIC:** 6711 **UK SIC:** 83962
**Auditors:** Horsfield & Smith
**Bankers:** Lloyds TSB Bank plc (30-16-82)

|  | 31-12-13 | 31-12-12 | 31-12-11 |
|---|---|---|---|
| TO | 157,520,000 | 179,458,000 | 177,158,000 |
| P/L | 1,883,000 | (1,811,000) | (6,823,000) |
| NW | 40,056,000 | 39,036,000 | 41,500,000 |
| WC | 24,390,000 | 22,589,000 | 23,104,000 |
| Emp. | 1,741 | 1,768 | 1,659 |

## DUNS 21-584-1528
### The William Henry
1 Frederick Place, Weymouth, Dorset DT4 8HQ
**Tel:** 01305763730
**Web:** www.jdwetherspoon.co.uk
**Estd:** 2011
**Line of Business:** Public house
**Responsibilities**
**Senior:** Steve Newstead (Manager)
**US SIC:** 5813 **UK SIC:** 66200
**Employees:** 55

## DUNS 23-259-6775
### William Henry Smith School
Boothroyd Lane, Brighouse, West Yorkshire HD6 3JW
**Web:** www.whsschool.org.uk
**Estd:** 1962
**Line of Business:** Other adult and other education not elsewhere classified
**Director:** B J Heneghan
**Responsibilities**
**Senior:** Caroline Booth (School Business Manager), Andy Christie (Deputy Principal), Brendan Heneghan (Principal), Lynne Reeve (Head of Support Services)

**Finance:** Samantha Child (Purchasing Manager), Vicki Quinn (Finance Assistant), Lynne Reeve (Head of Support Services)
**IT:** Jonathan Kerry (ICT Manager), Jordan Willars (ICT Support)
**HR:** Brendan Loughnane (Vice Principal), Judy Moorhouse (HR Assistant)
**Health & Safety:** Lynne Reeve (Head of Support Services)
**Facilities:** Michael Fairbank (Premises Manager)
**Purchasing:** Samantha Child (Purchasing Manager)
**US SIC:** 8299 **UK SIC:** 93300
**Employees:** 80

## DUNS 28-874-2034
### William Hepworth (Huddersfield) Ltd
(**Subsidiary of:** Brighton Holdings Ltd)
650-652 Leeds Road, Huddersfield, West Yorkshire HD2 1UB
**Tel:** 01484-514541
**Web:** www.hepworthhonda.co.uk
**Reg No:** 1085226 **VAT No:** 182312289
**Estd:** 2005 Private Limited Company
**Line of Business:** Sale of new motor vehicles
**Trading Style:** Hepworth Honda
**Issued Capital:** £56,842
**Chairman:** F Brighton
**Co. Secretary:** Stephen Brighton
**Branches:** William Hepworth (Huddersfield) Ltd, Keighley Rd, Bradford, West Yorkshire BD9 4JR
**US SIC:** 5511 **UK SIC:** 65100
**Auditors:** Bentley Jennson
**Bankers:** Barclays Bank Plc (20-48-46)

|  | 31-12-13 | 31-12-12 | 31-12-11 |
|---|---|---|---|
| TO | 17,714,511 | 16,997,052 | 17,842,786 |
| P/L | 172,947 | 221,434 | 96,653 |
| NW | 1,550,296 | 1,511,784 | 1,327,639 |
| WC | 1,461,148 | 1,419,295 | 1,222,326 |
| Emp. | 50 | 53 | 56 |

## DUNS 22-194-3983
### William Hill Plc
Greenside House, 50 Station Road, London N22 7TP
**Tel:** 020-8918-3600 **Fax:** 020-8918-3726
**Web:** www.williamhill.co.uk
**Reg No:** 4212563 **Estd:** 2003 Public Limited Company
**Line of Business:** Gambling and betting activities
**Export Sales:** £223,100,000
**Trading Style:** William Hill
**Issued Capital:** £86,580
**Directors:** Mrs G Harvey, Ms I Walsh, D S Lowden, G Davis, J Henderson, A G Highfield, S R Gardner, N Cooper
**Co. Secretary:** Luke Thomas
**Branches:** William Hill Plc, William Hill Bookmakers, 48 Union Street, Aberdeen, Aberdeenshire AB10 1BB
**US SIC:** 7999 **UK SIC:** 97913
**Auditors:** Deloitte LLP
**Following financial data are in thousands**

|  | 31-12-13 | 01-01-13 | 27-12-11 |
|---|---|---|---|
| TO | 1,486,500 | 1,276,900 | 1,136,700 |
| P/L | 257,000 | 277,700 | 187,400 |
| NW | (831,500) | (411,000) | (510,600) |
| WC | (55,900) | (83,300) | (93,200) |
| Emp. | 17,089 | 16,883 | 15,937 |

## DUNS 21-735-5144
### William Howard School (An Academy) Ltd
Longtown Road, Brampton, Cumbria CA8 1AR
**Tel:** 01697745700
**Web:** www.williamhoward.cumbria.sch.uk
**Reg No:** 7698631 **Estd:** 2011 Private Company Limited By Guarantee
**Line of Business:** Schools (local authority)
**Directors:** Ms R Hayton, Mrs K Mcallister, Ms S F Goodliffe, Ms R Wagstaff, Mrs A Fullerton, N Polmear, Ms M Payne, Mrs C Cartwright
**Co. Secretary:** Mrs Deborah Edwards
**Responsibilities**
**Senior:** Euan Cartwright (Director), Lorrayne Hughes (Director), Karen McAllister (Director)
**US SIC:** 8211 **UK SIC:** 93200
**Bankers:** Barclays Bank Plc (20-18-47)

|  | 31-08-14 | 31-08-13 | 31-08-12 |
|---|---|---|---|
| TO | 8,816,000 | 9,378,000 | 14,107,116 |
| P/L | (350,000) | 548,000 | 3,896,121 |
| NW | 3,848,000 | 4,417,000 | 3,771,121 |
| WC | 235,000 | 326,000 | 262,681 |
| Emp. | 185 | 187 | 188 |

## DUNS 21-687-0725
### William Hughes (Civil Engineering) Ltd
Talwrn, Llangefni, Gwynedd LL77 7TG
**Tel:** 01248-750193 **Fax:** 01248-723709
**Web:** www.williamhughes.com
**Reg No:** 1112626 **VAT No:** 159301765

**Estd:** 1973 Private Limited Company
**Line of Business:** Collection and treatment of sewage
**Issued Capital:** £6,000
**Director:** I Hughes
**Co. Secretary:** Thomas Hughes
**US SIC:** 4952, 1541, 1629
**UK SIC:** 92120, 50100, 50000
**Auditors:** J Emyr Thomas & Co
**Bankers:** National Westminster Bank Plc (53-81-02)

| | 31-03-14 | 31-03-13 | 31-03-12 |
|---|---|---|---|
| TO | 5,949,998 | 4,637,146 | 6,367,030 |
| P/L | 102,069 | 426,014 | 644,895 |
| NW | 3,890,812 | 3,890,693 | 3,621,899 |
| WC | 3,156,727 | 3,174,342 | 2,839,695 |
| Emp. | 51 | 48 | 61 |

DUNS 21-014-2246    **Imp**

## William Hughes Ltd

(Subsidiary of: High Tension Wires Ltd)
Station Road Business Park, Station Road, Sturminster Newton, Dorset DT10 2RZ
**Tel:** 01963-363377
**Web:** www.wmhughes.co.uk
**Reg No:** 0243035 **VAT No:** 233078773
**Estd:** 1790 Private Limited Company
**Line of Business:** Manufacture of fasteners, screw machine products, chains and springs
**Export Sales:** £1,530,220
**Issued Capital:** £6,700
**Principals:** M I Hughes (Managing), Mrs E P Burgon
**Co. Secretary:** Ms Clara Hughes
**Branches:** William Hughes Ltd, Llyn Alaw Water Treatment Works, Holyhead, Gwynedd LL65 4TW
**US SIC:** 3452, 3496
**UK SIC:** 31371, 31694
**Auditors:** H Graham King & Co
**Bankers:** National Westminster Bank Plc (60-04-24)

| | 31-12-13 | 31-12-12 | 31-12-11 |
|---|---|---|---|
| TO | 8,017,416 | N/A | 6,167,456 |
| P/L | 221,954 | N/A | (132,180) |
| NW | 765,118 | 590,177 | 684,449 |
| WC | 228,954 | (26,025) | 656,919 |
| Emp. | 91 | N/A | N/A |

DUNS 23-048-6490

## William J Furber

Unit 1 Prees Industrial Estate, Shrewsbury Road, Whitchurch, Shropshire SY13 2DJ
**Web:** www.wjfurber.co.uk
**Estd:** 1966 Proprietorship
**Line of Business:** Car accessories and parts
**Proprietor:** W J Furber
**Branches:** William J Furber, Telesales, Roving Bridge, Whitchurch, Shropshire SY13 2RT
**US SIC:** 5531, 5199
**UK SIC:** 65100, 61900
**Employees:** 60

DUNS 21-214-7300    **Exp**

## William Jackson & Son Ltd

The Riverside Building, Hessle, North Humberside HU13 0DZ
**Tel:** 01482224939 **Fax:** 01482223217
**Web:** www.wjfg.co.uk
**Reg No:** 0506672 **Estd:** 1952 Private Limited Company
**Line of Business:** Manufacture of other food products not elsewhere classified
**Trading Style:** Tryton Foods W J S, Jacksons Family Food Stores, Cryston Motor Group, Jackson Bakers Jackson Stores
**Issued Capital:** £1,601,753
**Directors:** P Mountifield, N G Soutar, G M Urmston, N A Oughtred, Ms S Wyse, T J Cooper-Jones, A Wheelwright
**Co. Secretary:** Gary Urmston
**Responsibilities**
**HR:** Sue Argent (Group Recruitment & Community)
**Branches:** William Jackson & Son Ltd, Melrose House, Yarm Road, Stockton-On-Tees, Cleveland TS18 3RP
**US SIC:** 2099, 5462
**UK SIC:** 42399, 64100
**Auditors:** PricewaterhouseCoopers LLP
**Bankers:** Lloyds TSB Bank plc (30-97-51)

| | 26-04-14 | 27-04-13 | 28-04-12 |
|---|---|---|---|
| TO | 268,467,000 | 228,547,000 | 179,477,000 |
| P/L | 15,465,000 | 12,603,000 | 11,117,000 |
| NW | 72,361,000 | 54,500,000 | 81,967,000 |
| WC | 17,659,000 | 18,290,000 | 16,502,000 |
| Emp. | 1,960 | 1,729 | 1,376 |

DUNS 29-346-0440

## William Jackson Bakery (Export) Ltd

(Subsidiary of: William Jackson & Son Ltd)
40 Derringham Street, Hull, North Humberside HU3 1EW
**Tel:** 01482882665 **Fax:** 01482-588237
**Web:** www.jacksonsbakery.co.uk
**Reg No:** 0367860 **Estd:** 1998 Private Limited Company

**Line of Business:** Manufacture of bread; manufacture of fresh pastry goods and cakes
**Issued Capital:** £250,000
**Directors:** S Ball, Wjs Executives Limited, T J Maplethorpe
**Co. Secretary:** Gary Urmston
**US SIC:** 2051 **UK SIC:** 41960
**Auditors:** PricewaterhouseCoopers

| | 26-04-14 | 27-04-13 | 28-04-12 |
|---|---|---|---|
| TO | 3,887,000 | 4,102,000 | 3,926,000 |
| P/L | 273,000 | 287,000 | 275,000 |
| NW | 1,936,000 | 1,728,000 | 1,510,000 |
| WC | 1,936,000 | N/A | 1,510,000 |

DUNS 22-775-0338

## William Jones Schools Foundation

The Haberdashers Company, Haberdashers Hall, 18 West Smithfield, London EC1A 9HQ
**Web:** www.haberdashers.co.uk
**Estd:** 1891
**Line of Business:** Other tourist or short-stay accommodation
**Trading Style:** Haberdashers Monmouth Schools
**Directors:** Mrs P Phillips, D A Loffhagen, Haberdashers Co
**Responsibilities**
**Senior:** Helen Davy (Headmistress)
**Marketing:** Sarah Lee (Marketing Director)
**IT:** Tom Arrand (Deputy Head)
**HR:** Tom Arrand (Deputy Head)
**Health & Safety:** Tessa Norgrove (Bursar)
**Operations:** Sarah Lee (Marketing Director)
**Branches:** William Jones Schools Foundation, Haberdashers Monmouth Schools , 37-39 St Marys Street , NP25 3DD Monmouth
**US SIC:** 7021 **UK SIC:** 66500
**Auditors:** Saffery Champness
**Bankers:** Lloyds TSB Bank plc (30-95-11)

| | 31-08-12 | 31-08-11 | 31-08-10 |
|---|---|---|---|
| TO | 19,667,000 | 19,882,000 | 19,093,000 |
| P/L | (876,000) | 98,000 | 493,000 |
| NW | 83,436,000 | 82,586,000 | 77,978,000 |
| WC | 3,477,000 | 1,955,000 | 1,974,000 |
| Emp. | 403 | 406 | 390 |

DUNS 22-954-5520

## William Kendrick & Sons Ltd

Tasker Street, Walsall, West Midlands WS1 3QP
**Tel:** 01922-622263
**Web:** www.kendrick.co.uk
**Reg No:** 1142445 **Estd:** 1873 Private Limited Company
**Line of Business:** Building services
**Trading Style:** Kendrick Construction
**Issued Capital:** £36,542
**Principals:** A W Kendrick (Chairman and Managing), W D Kendrick
**Co. Secretary:** Paul Sharp
**Responsibilities**
**Senior:** Peter Farmer (Manager)
**Purchasing:** John Sproston (Purchasing Manager)
**US SIC:** 6552, 6531, 7399
**UK SIC:** 85000, 83400, 83954
**Auditors:** RSM Bentley Jennison
**Bankers:** HSBC Bank plc (40-45-19)

| | 30-06-13 | 31-03-12 | 31-06-11 |
|---|---|---|---|
| TO | 40,042,102 | 27,078,615 | 32,042,506 |
| P/L | (210,155) | 384,981 | 682,071 |
| NW | 20,721,797 | 20,972,307 | 20,993,603 |
| WC | 15,542,351 | 15,076,489 | 13,552,200 |
| Emp. | 96 | 100 | 107 |

DUNS 21-812-1341    **Imp-Exp**

## William Kenyon & Sons Ltd

P O Box 33, Chapel Field Works, Railway Street, Hyde, Cheshire SK14 4RP
**Tel:** 0161-308-6030 **Fax:** 01613086046
**Web:** www.williamkenyon.co.uk
**Reg No:** 0094366 **VAT No:** 146352277
**Estd:** 1958 Private Limited Company
**Line of Business:** Ropes and cables
**Export Markets:** Worldwide
**Export Sales:** £11,589,580
**Issued Capital:** £338,981
**Principals:** C G Kenyon (Chairman and Managing), Mrs H M Kenyon, W Kenyon, Mrs M Kenyon, Ms S A Kenyon
**Co. Secretary:** Piers Kenyon
**Responsibilities**
**Finance:** Rowena Mellor (Finance Director)
**Branches:** William Kenyon & Sons Ltd, 16 Cross Street, Leamington Spa, Warwickshire CV32 4PX
**US SIC:** 6711 **UK SIC:** 83962
**Auditors:** Nasmith Coutts & Co
**Bankers:** National Westminster Bank Plc (01-00-39)

| | 31-03-14 | 31-03-13 | 31-03-12 |
|---|---|---|---|
| TO | 12,045,360 | 11,117,140 | 11,311,040 |
| P/L | 881,144 | 436,550 | 610,405 |
| NW | 12,190,777 | 13,211,591 | 12,817,396 |
| WC | 8,501,249 | 10,077,864 | 9,637,162 |
| Emp. | 102 | 100 | 95 |

DUNS 21-833-5719    **Imp-Exp**

## William King Ltd

Atlas Centre, Union Road, West Bromwich, West Midlands B70 9DR
**Tel:** 01215004100
**Web:** www.williamking.co.uk
**Reg No:** 0498601 **VAT No:** 277724718
**Estd:** 1820 Private Limited Company
**Line of Business:** Wholesale of metals and ores
**Export Sales:** £4,258,000
**Issued Capital:** £100,000
**Principals:** E M Worley (Managing), K R Hirst, A J Worley, Mrs R M Graville, J Moore
**Co. Secretary:** Dipak Patel
**Responsibilities**
**Senior:** Carl Cook (Operations Manager), Peter Ullathorne (Manager)
**IT:** Cliff Gwilliam (Non-PC Systems Manager)
**Health & Safety:** Robert Byatt (health & Safety Officer)
**Facilities:** Carl Cook (Operations Manager)
**Operations:** Carl Cook (Operations Manager)
**Engineering:** Carl Cook (Operations Manager)
**US SIC:** 5051 **UK SIC:** 61200
**Auditors:** PricewaterhouseCoopers LLP
**Bankers:** Barclays Bank Plc (20-07-71)

| | 30-06-14 | 30-06-13 | 30-06-12 |
|---|---|---|---|
| TO | 97,638,000 | 97,878,000 | 98,646,000 |
| P/L | 2,093,000 | 813,000 | 526,000 |
| NW | 28,673,000 | 28,553,000 | 26,365,000 |
| WC | 23,681,000 | 21,945,000 | 20,826,000 |
| Emp. | 197 | 187 | 187 |

DUNS 21-618-1537

## William Lacey Sustainable Homes Ltd

(Subsidiary of: William Lacey Group Ltd)
William Lacey Group, Woking, Surrey GU22 9AF
**Tel:** 01483-880770
**Reg No:** 0858372 **Estd:** 1905 Private Limited Company
**Line of Business:** Holding companies management activities
**Issued Capital:** £1,000
**Director:** C T Lacey
**US SIC:** 1522 **UK SIC:** 50100
**Auditors:** Charles Stuart
**Bankers:** National Westminster Bank Plc (60-11-13)

| | 30-09-13 | 30-09-12 | 30-09-11 |
|---|---|---|---|
| TA | 1,000 | 1,000 | 1,000 |
| NW | 1,000 | 1,000 | 1,000 |

DUNS 50-565-4988    **Imp-Exp**

## William Lamb Footwear Ltd

Bottom Boat Road, Stanley, Wakefield, West Yorkshire WF3 4AY
**Tel:** 01924820282 **Fax:** 01924-836936
**Web:** www.wlamb.co.uk
**Reg No:** 2513251 **VAT No:** 412165981
**Estd:** 1887 Private Limited Company
**Line of Business:** Manufacture of footwear
**Export Markets:** Republic of Ireland & Europe
**Export Sales:** £727,806
**Issued Capital:** £2
**Principals:** S H Lamb (Chairman), C Hargreaves, Ms J Watson, A N Cook, P R Ablett, Miss C J Lamb
**Co. Secretary:** David Ratcliffe
**Responsibilities**
**Senior:** Thomas Freeman (Manager)
**Branches:** William Lamb Footwear Ltd, Skopos Mills, Bradford Rd, Batley, West Yorkshire WF17 5LZ
**US SIC:** 7399 **UK SIC:** 83954
**Auditors:** KPMG LLP

| | 31-12-13 | 31-12-12 | 31-12-11 |
|---|---|---|---|
| TO | 54,320,992 | 44,023,301 | 39,020,502 |
| P/L | 2,875,690 | 1,831,781 | 1,676,949 |
| NW | 5,296,465 | 4,342,483 | 4,172,122 |
| WC | 4,662,673 | 3,682,655 | 3,560,027 |
| Emp. | 102 | 90 | 93 |

DUNS 21-309-7074    **Exp**

## William Lee Ltd

Callywhite Lane, Dronfield, Dronfield, South Yorkshire S18 2XU
**Tel:** 01246-416155
**Reg No:** 0711234 **Estd:** 1889 Private Limited Company
**Line of Business:** Manufacture of basic iron and steel and of ferro-alloys
**Export Markets:** Sweden
**Directors:** J R Tickell, W J Maclean
**Branches:** Station Rd Oakengates Telford Shropshire
**US SIC:** 3325 **UK SIC:** 31110
**Bankers:** Barclays Bank Plc (20-97-78)
**Employees:** 400

DUNS 21-444-1222    **Imp-Exp**

## William Lockie & Company Ltd

27-28 Drumlanrig Square, Hawick, Roxburghshire TD9 0AW
**Tel:** 01450-372645
**Web:** www.williamlockie.com
**Reg No:** 0023788SC **VAT No:** 269633129
**Estd:** 1946 Private Limited Company
**Line of Business:** Manufacturers and wholesalers of knitwear
**Export Markets:** U S A, W Europe, Middle East, Japan, Australia
**Export Sales:** £4,885,795
**Issued Capital:** £9,000
**Principals:** D Nuttall (Managing), R J Nuttall, Ms J J Thorburn, M R Thorburn
**Co. Secretary:** Ms Hazel Graham
**Responsibilities**
**Finance:** Irene McRobert (Office Manager)
**Admin:** Irene McRobert (Office Manager)
**HR:** Irene McRobert (Office Manager)
**Engineering:** Roger Nuttall (Technical, Production Manager)
**US SIC:** 2253 **UK SIC:** 43632
**Auditors:** Ernst & Young LLP
**Bankers:** The Royal Bank Of Scotland Plc (83-23-01)

| | 01-02-14 | 01-02-13 | 01-02-12 |
|---|---|---|---|
| TO | 6,038,377 | 6,200,703 | 6,004,358 |
| P/L | 530,451 | 801,468 | 819,534 |
| NW | 2,672,848 | 2,923,080 | 2,590,028 |
| WC | 4,348,208 | 4,299,213 | 4,087,588 |
| Emp. | 137 | 138 | 130 |

DUNS 54-377-8195

## William Morgan Group Ltd

Bedford Road Northampton, Northampton, Northamptonshire NN1 5SZ
**Tel:** 01604-232000
**Web:** www.wollaston.co.uk
**Reg No:** 3265603 **Estd:** 1997 Private Limited Company
**Line of Business:** Sale of new motor vehicles
**Issued Capital:** £100,000
**Directors:** C W Le Fevre, T G Bramall, M H Allard
**Co. Secretary:** Paul Newsome
**Responsibilities**
**Senior:** Max Cruttwell (Business Manager)
**US SIC:** 5511, 5521, 7539, 5571
**UK SIC:** 65100, 67100
**Auditors:** Macintyre Hudson
**Bankers:** National Westminster Bank Plc (55-70-37)

| | 31-12-13 | 31-12-12 | 31-12-11 |
|---|---|---|---|
| TO | 123,736,464 | 87,566,473 | 53,830,747 |
| P/L | 644,212 | 252,337 | (53,940) |
| NW | (2,116,212) | (2,830,872) | 196,065 |
| WC | 2,152,650 | 2,712,919 | 2,051,798 |
| Emp. | 253 | 184 | 115 |

DUNS 28-916-2349

## William Morris (Camphill) Community Ltd

Chipmans Platt, Stonehouse, Gloucestershire GL10 3SH
**Tel:** 01453824025
**Web:** www.wmcc.ac.uk
**Reg No:** 1448003 **Estd:** 1979 Private Limited Company
**Line of Business:** Other adult and other education not elsewhere classified
**Directors:** N Ferguson, Ms L Crociani-Windland, G Barton, S A Parker, D Geula, Ms J M Pullen
**Co. Secretary:** Stephen Parker
**Responsibilities**
**Senior:** Eva Cerolini (Manager)
**US SIC:** 8299, 8091, 8321
**UK SIC:** 93300, 95200, 96111
**Auditors:** Wenn Townsend
**Bankers:** National Westminster Bank Plc (55-61-08)

| | 31-03-13 | 31-03-12 | 31-03-11 |
|---|---|---|---|
| TO | 2,739,078 | 2,585,254 | 2,344,138 |
| P/L | (2,100) | 79,035 | (28,027) |
| NW | 1,919,690 | 2,676,222 | 2,594,485 |
| WC | 506,926 | 699,296 | 576,907 |
| Emp. | 92 | 85 | 78 |

DUNS 22-720-6349    **Imp**

## William Morris Endeavor Entertainment (U.K.) Ltd

Centre Point, 103 New Oxford Street, London WC1A 1DD
**Tel:** 020-7534-6800 **Fax:** 020-7534-6900
**Web:** www.wmeentertainment.com
**Reg No:** 0841344 **Estd:** 1965 Private Limited Company
**Line of Business:** Entertainment agencies
**Issued Capital:** £1,000
**Directors:** Ms A Z Emanuel, J H Lublin, P Grosslight, P W Whitesell
**Co. Secretary:** Mitre Secretaries Limited
**Responsibilities**
**Senior:** Robert Silverton (Head of Operations), James Wiatt (Manager)
**US SIC:** 7999 **UK SIC:** 97913
**Auditors:** PricewaterhouseCoopers LLP

**Bankers:** National Westminster Bank Plc (51-50-14)

| | 31-12-13 | 31-12-12 | 31-12-11 |
|---|---|---|---|
| TO | 8,126,987 | 9,448,968 | 7,067,879 |
| P/L | (831,214) | 996,406 | 323,790 |
| NW | (5,810,280) | (4,978,040) | (5,972,298) |
| WC | (6,273,521) | (5,220,167) | (6,250,668) |
| Emp. | 64 | 54 | 51 |

DUNS 21-587-7028     **Imp**

## William Morton Ltd
137 Shawbridge Street, Glasgow, Lanarkshire G43 1QQ
**Fax:** 0141-649-7074
**Reg No:** 0056257SC **VAT No:** 309011502
**Estd:** 1983 Private Limited Company
**Line of Business:** Wholesale of wine, beer, spirits and other alcoholic beverages
**Trading Style:** Cheviot U K Wine Agencies, Inverarity
**Issued Capital:** £6,248
**Principals:** S G Russell (Managing), H J Jagielko, D M Campbell, A Bulloch, J D Turnbull, Ms G I Smith, Mrs C A Jagielko
**Co. Secretary:** Brian Robertson
**Responsibilities**
**Senior:** W Armstrong (Partner)
**Marketing:** J Gillitan (Sales & Marketing Director)
**Sales:** J Gillitan (Sales & Marketing Director)
**IT:** Morag Hodge (Computer Operations Manager)
**US SIC:** 5182 **UK SIC:** 61700
**Auditors:** Campbell Dallas LLP
**Bankers:** Clydesdale Bank Plc (82-53-03)

| | 30-09-13 | 30-09-12 | 30-09-11 |
|---|---|---|---|
| TO | 51,152,364 | 47,256,873 | 44,814,859 |
| P/L | 303,252 | 198,270 | 121,516 |
| NW | 1,033,288 | 742,050 | 1,779,614 |
| WC | 2,295,943 | 2,046,339 | 2,028,291 |
| Emp. | 152 | 140 | 116 |

DUNS 21-582-6348

## William Munro Construction (Highland) Ltd
River Drive, Teaninich Industrial Estate, Alness, Ross-Shire IV17 0PG
**Tel:** 01349-882373
**Web:** www.munrohighland.co.uk
**Reg No:** 0061834SC **VAT No:** 296563021
**Estd:** 1977 Private Limited Company
**Line of Business:** Building construction contractors
**Issued Capital:** £20,000
**Directors:** R D Munro, J Munro
**US SIC:** 1541, 1795
**UK SIC:** 50100, 50000
**Auditors:** Ernst & Young
**Bankers:** Bank Of Scotland (80-05-30)

| | 30-09-13 | 30-09-12 | 30-09-11 |
|---|---|---|---|
| TO | 10,618,658 | 11,185,015 | 10,824,904 |
| P/L | 573,758 | 660,748 | 433,300 |
| NW | 2,899,197 | 2,405,976 | 2,236,025 |
| WC | 240,885 | (351,003) | (728,085) |
| Emp. | 52 | 49 | 41 |

DUNS 21-445-1452

## William Murchland & Company Ltd
(**Subsidiary of:** Arete Developments Ltd)
10-16 Grange Street, Kilmarnock, Ayrshire KA1 2AR
**Tel:** 01563-525051
**Web:** www.murchland.co.uk
**Reg No:** 0030230SC **VAT No:** 262998019
**Estd:** 1954 Private Limited Company
**Line of Business:** Plumbing
**Issued Capital:** £8,000
**Directors:** A N Mctaggart, A G Mctaggart
**Co. Secretary:** Andrew Mctaggart
**US SIC:** 1711 **UK SIC:** 50300
**Auditors:** Smith & Wallace & Co
**Bankers:** Bank Of Scotland (80-08-53)

| | 31-07-13 | 31-07-12 | 31-07-11 |
|---|---|---|---|
| TA | 1,118,994 | 1,120,074 | 836,201 |
| NW | 64,449 | 169,060 | 362,837 |
| WC | (177,860) | (55,432) | 114,439 |

DUNS 29-528-3121

## William Nicol (Aberdeen) Ltd
Unit 27 29 Barclayhill Place, Aberdeen, Aberdeenshire AB12 4PF
**Tel:** 01224782100
**Web:** www.williamnicol.co.uk
**Reg No:** 0092415SC **VAT No:** 430040910
**Estd:** 1985 Private Limited Company
**Line of Business:** Road haulage and transport services
**Trading Style:** William Nicol (Aberdeen) Ltd
**Issued Capital:** £20,000
**Managing Director:** B Nicol
**Co. Secretary:** Laurie & Co
**Branches:** William Nicol (Aberdeen) Ltd, Badentoy Crescent, Badentoy Industrial Estate, Aberdeen, Aberdeenshire AB12 4YD
**US SIC:** 4789, 8999
**UK SIC:** 77002, 83954
**Auditors:** Bain Henry Reid

**Bankers:** Bank Of Scotland (80-05-11)

| | 30-09-13 | 30-09-12 | 30-09-11 |
|---|---|---|---|
| TO | 9,194,376 | 8,513,183 | N/A |
| P/L | 1,718,092 | 1,470,408 | N/A |
| NW | 7,883,015 | 6,934,722 | 6,047,478 |
| WC | 420,278 | 632,267 | 368,740 |
| Emp. | 46 | 45 | N/A |

DUNS 21-041-2267

## William Patten Primary School
Stoke Newington Road, London N16 7UY
**Tel:** 02079237803
**Web:** www.williampatten.hackney.sch.uk
**Estd:** 1991 Proprietorship
**Line of Business:** Nursery schools
**Proprietor:** Mrs K Kale
**US SIC:** 8211 **UK SIC:** 93200
**Employees:** 60

DUNS 22-714-2494     **Imp**

## The William Pears Group of Companies Ltd
(**Subsidiary of:** William Pears Group Ltd)
2 Old Brewery Mews, London NW3 1PZ
**Tel:** 02074333333
**Web:** www.williampears.co.uk
**Reg No:** 0556533 **Estd:** 2010 Private Limited Company
**Line of Business:** Management activities of holding companies
**Issued Capital:** £21,510
**Principals:** M A Pears (Managing), T S Pears, Wpg Registrars Limited
**Co. Secretary:** David Pears
**US SIC:** 6711, 7399
**UK SIC:** 83962, 83954
**Auditors:** Arram Berlyn Gardner
**Bankers:** Barclays Bank Plc (20-03-53)

| | 30-04-14 | 30-04-13 | 30-04-12 |
|---|---|---|---|
| TO | 20,703,402 | 15,103,762 | 9,831,343 |
| P/L | 35,754,935 | 12,730,377 | 218,735,861 |
| NW | 28,318,208 | 73,719,400 | 365,677,583 |
| WC | (295,808,187) | (244,881,671) | 136,156,618 |
| Emp. | 43 | 92 | 89 |

DUNS 28-824-0468

## William Purves (Funeral Directors) Ltd
Oakvale Funeral Home, 106 Whitehouse Loan, Edinburgh, Midlothian EH9 1BD
**Web:** www.williampurves.co.uk
**Reg No:** 0060678SC **Estd:** 1976 Private Limited Company
**Line of Business:** Funeral and related activities
**Issued Capital:** £1,000
**Directors:** J T Purves, J B Morris, A Purves, C J Brown
**Co. Secretary:** Roger Pagan
**Responsibilities**
**Marketing:** Tim Purves (Manager)
**Sales:** Tim Purves (Manager)
**Branches:** William Purves (Funeral Directors) Ltd, 6 Braid Road, Edinburgh, Midlothian EH10 6AD
**US SIC:** 7261 **UK SIC:** 98902
**Auditors:** Dalgliesh & Tullo
**Bankers:** The Royal Bank Of Scotland Plc (83-06-08)

| | 30-09-14 | 30-09-13 | 30-09-12 |
|---|---|---|---|
| TO | 9,967,062 | 9,675,102 | 8,788,976 |
| P/L | 1,456,868 | 1,287,409 | 591,991 |
| NW | 4,367,668 | 4,089,076 | 3,593,099 |
| WC | (214,909) | (18,519) | 322,816 |
| Emp. | 83 | 80 | 81 |

DUNS 21-024-4646     **Imp**

## William Reed Holdings Ltd
Broadfield Park, Brighton Road, Pease Pottage, Crawley, West Sussex RH11 9RT
**Tel:** 01293613400 **Fax:** 01293-403180
**Web:** www.william-reed.co.uk
**Reg No:** 0224823 **Estd:** 1861 Private Limited Company
**Line of Business:** Management activities of holding companies
**Export Sales:** £9,909,000
**Issued Capital:** £990,000
**Principals:** C C Reed (Managing), T S Barratt, A L Reed, R A Oscroft, N H Lawes, G N Perren
**Co. Secretary:** Nicholas Reed
**Responsibilities**
**Senior:** Robert Robert (Manager)
**US SIC:** 6711 **UK SIC:** 83962
**Auditors:** PricewaterhouseCoopers LLP
**Bankers:** The Royal Bank Of Scotland Plc (15-10-00)

| | 31-03-14 | 31-03-13 | 31-03-12 |
|---|---|---|---|
| TO | 46,938,000 | 36,886,000 | 39,162,000 |
| P/L | 4,774,000 | 70,000 | 2,052,000 |
| NW | 13,104,000 | 8,270,000 | 5,753,000 |
| WC | 7,817,000 | 5,503,000 | 2,977,000 |
| Emp. | 340 | 342 | 363 |

DUNS 77-111-0897

## William Russell Ltd
William Russell House, Lightwater, Surrey GU18 5SS
**Tel:** 01276-486455 **Fax:** 01276486466
**Web:** www.william-russell.com
**Reg No:** 2687939 **Estd:** 1992 Private Limited Company
**Line of Business:** Insurance services
**Export Sales:** £7,718,988
**Issued Capital:** £10,000
**Principals:** Ms I A Cooper (Managing), J W Cooper, W M Cooper
**Responsibilities**
**Senior:** Nicola Haward (claims manager)
**Finance:** Keith Olding (Financial Director)
**Admin:** Jessica Cooper (Consultant)
**Engineering:** Tim Coyne (International Technical Manage)
**US SIC:** 6311, 6399
**UK SIC:** 82002, 82001
**Auditors:** Smith Pearman
**Bankers:** National Westminster Bank Plc (60-24-20)

| | 31-12-13 | 31-12-12 | 31-12-11 |
|---|---|---|---|
| TO | 7,857,198 | 7,877,825 | 7,931,921 |
| P/L | 2,285,963 | 2,097,284 | 2,605,385 |
| NW | 6,892,672 | 6,144,618 | 4,573,041 |
| WC | 5,187,848 | 4,410,038 | 2,790,036 |
| Emp. | 55 | N/A | N/A |

DUNS 51-650-5641

## William Simpson & Son
40 Hanover Street, Stranraer, Wigtownshire DG9 7RP
**Tel:** 01776-703193
**Estd:** 1972 Partnership
**Line of Business:** Retail sale of bread, cakes, flour confectionery and sugar confectionery
**Proprietor:** W Simpson
**Responsibilities**
**Senior:** Terry Simpson (IT Manager)
**IT:** Terry Simpson (IT Manager)
**Branches:** William Simpson & Son, 104 Dalrymple Street, Girvan, Ayrshire KA26 9BT
**US SIC:** 5462 **UK SIC:** 64100
**Employees:** 60

DUNS 21-922-3724     **Imp-Exp**

## William Sinclair Holdings Plc
Firth Road, Lincoln, Lincolnshire LN6 7AH
**Tel:** 01522-537561 **Fax:** 01522513609
**Web:** www.william-sinclair.co.uk
**Reg No:** 1392876 **Estd:** 1978 Public Limited Company
**Line of Business:** Management activities of holding companies
**Export Markets:** Europe, Middle East & Far East & Other
**Export Sales:** £595,000
**Trading Style:** William Sinclair Horticulture
**Issued Capital:** £4,256,012
**Directors:** P J Rush, K S Piggott, T R King
**Co. Secretary:** Peter Williams
**Responsibilities**
**Senior:** Bernard Burns (Manager), Hugh Etheridge (Manager)
**IT:** Brian Denton (Computer Manager)
**HR:** Kelly Trown (Human Resources Manager)
**Health & Safety:** Greg Sutherland (Production Director)
**Purchasing:** Alicia Pollard (Purchasing Director)
**Engineering:** Greg Sutherland (Production Director)
**Branches:** William Sinclair Holdings Plc, Malvern Road, Knottingley, West Yorkshire WF11 8EG
**US SIC:** 6711 **UK SIC:** 83962
**Auditors:** PricewaterhouseCoopers LLP
**Bankers:** Lloyds TSB Bank plc (30-00-00)

| | 30-09-13 | 30-09-12 | 30-09-11 |
|---|---|---|---|
| TO | 46,479,000 | 48,240,000 | 54,263,000 |
| P/L | (1,182,000) | (404,000) | 3,182,000 |
| NW | 12,410,000 | 12,827,000 | 15,853,000 |
| WC | 2,274,000 | 11,328,000 | 16,205,000 |
| Emp. | 335 | 318 | 346 |

DUNS 21-312-3755

## William Smith (Wakefield) Ltd
Red House Farm, Staintondale, Scarborough, North Yorkshire YO13 0HA
**Tel:** 01723-870728
**Reg No:** 0288166 **VAT No:** 169534531
**Estd:** 1890 Private Limited Company
**Line of Business:** Growing of cereals and other crops not elsewhere classified
**Issued Capital:** £500
**Managing Director:** W D Smith
**Co. Secretary:** Ms Christine Smith
**US SIC:** 0119, 5199
**UK SIC:** 01001, 61900
**Auditors:** Walter Dawson & Son

**Bankers:** National Westminster Bank Plc (54-30-46)

| | 31-03-14 | 31-03-13 | 31-03-12 |
|---|---|---|---|
| TO | 15,124,162 | 13,699,236 | 13,035,870 |
| P/L | 823,685 | 834,604 | 841,062 |
| NW | 4,824,611 | 4,107,899 | 3,482,508 |
| WC | (181,761) | (103,387) | 338,621 |
| Emp. | 146 | 136 | 126 |

DUNS 21-451-0562     **Exp**

## William Stephen (Bakers) Ltd
Unit 21 Dunfermline Business Park, Primrose Lane, Rosyth, Dunfermline, Fife KY11 2RN
**Web:** www.stephensbakery.com
**Reg No:** 0032964SC **VAT No:** 269503930
**Estd:** 1873 Private Limited Company
**Line of Business:** Bakers shops
**Export Markets:** Republic Of Ireland
**Trading Style:** Bakers & Confectioners
**Issued Capital:** £7,600
**Directors:** A Sarafilovic, E D Chisholm, Ms R Sarafilovic
**Co. Secretary:** Alexander Sarafilovic
**Responsibilities**
**IT:** Robert McPherson (Technical Manager)
**Health & Safety:** Robert McPherson (Technical Manager)
**Operations:** Robert McPherson (Technical Manager)
**Branches:** William Stephen (Bakers) Ltd, 124 Fraser Avenue, Inverkeithing, Fife KY11 1EH
**US SIC:** 5462 **UK SIC:** 64100
**Auditors:** PKF (UK) LLP
**Bankers:** The Royal Bank Of Scotland Plc (83-33-00)

| | 30-06-13 | 30-06-12 | 30-06-11 |
|---|---|---|---|
| TO | 7,778,508 | N/A | N/A |
| P/L | 1,101,024 | N/A | N/A |
| NW | 75,040 | 43,054 | 33,725 |
| WC | (7,790) | (172,796) | (329,964) |
| Emp. | 145 | N/A | N/A |

DUNS 21-241-5558

## William Strike Ltd
(**Subsidiary of:** Klondyke Group Ltd)
Beancross, Falkirk, Stirlingshire FK2 0XS
**Tel:** 01642710419
**Web:** www.klondyke.co.uk
**Reg No:** 0096366 **Estd:** 1908 Private Limited Company
**Line of Business:** Other retail sale in specialised stores not elsewhere classified
**Trading Style:** William Strike of Klondyte
**Issued Capital:** £29,961
**Principals:** E D Mcghee (Managing), W D Yardley (Managing), Mrs S Allan, D A Robb, R J Hewitt, W J Stewart, D J Hustwayte, D Abbott
**Co. Secretary:** Mrs Dorothy Gault
**Branches:** William Strike Ltd, Parwoods Nursery, Darlington Road, Northallerton, North Yorkshire DL6 2PW
**US SIC:** 5999 **UK SIC:** 65600
**Auditors:** Baker Tilly
**Bankers:** National Westminster Bank Plc (55-61-00)

| | 29-09-13 | 30-09-12 | 02-09-11 |
|---|---|---|---|
| TO | 46,374,056 | 43,601,198 | 46,933,515 |
| P/L | 3,163,751 | 1,925,094 | 2,983,107 |
| NW | 19,391,726 | 16,888,873 | 15,327,473 |
| WC | 14,753,481 | 12,090,880 | 10,858,584 |
| Emp. | 852 | 836 | 846 |

DUNS 21-400-8989

## William Sword Ltd
Groveside Bakeries, 8 Limekilns Road, Glasgow, Lanarkshire G67 2TX
**Tel:** 01236-725094
**Web:** www.williamsword.co.uk
**Reg No:** 0028343SC **Estd:** 1951 Private Limited Company
**Line of Business:** Bakers shops
**Issued Capital:** £56,000
**Managing Directors:** G D Sword, J D Sword
**Co. Secretary:** George Sword
**Responsibilities**
**Admin:** Janice Greer (Office Manager)
**HR:** Janice Greer (Office Manager)
**Purchasing:** Janice Greer (Office Manager)
**Branches:** William Sword Ltd, Abbey Health Centre, East Abbey Street, Arbroath, Angus DD11 1EN
**US SIC:** 5462 **UK SIC:** 64100
**Auditors:** Campbell Dallas
**Bankers:** Bank Of Scotland (80-13-13)

| | 31-03-14 | 31-03-13 | 31-03-12 |
|---|---|---|---|
| TA | 2,609,343 | 2,358,941 | 2,142,798 |
| NW | 1,400,566 | 1,141,270 | 1,051,321 |
| WC | 149,902 | 27,950 | (48,863) |

DUNS 67-215-5780

## William Thompson Group Holdings Ltd
William Thompson Group Holdings, Main Street, Malton, North Yorkshire YO17 6TA
**Tel:** 01904-488388
**Web:** www.thompsons-feeds.co.uk
**Reg No:** 6045349 **Estd:** 2007 Private Limited Company

**Line of Business:** Management activities of production holding companies
**Issued Capital:** £185,725
**Directors:** A M Richardson, R C Rook, A C Brader, J M Drury
**US SIC:** 6711 **UK SIC:** 83962

| | 30-09-14 | 30-04-13 | 30-09-12 |
|---|---|---|---|
| TO | N/A | 32,491,813 | 28,070,346 |
| P/L | N/A | 2,370,895 | 934,084 |
| NW | 185,725 | 2,151,242 | 1,268,144 |
| WC | N/A | 761,189 | 725,821 |
| Emp. | N/A | 49 | 48 |

DUNS 21-562-1681

## William Tracey Ltd

**(Subsidiary of:** Dcc Plc)
Unit 49, Burnbrae Road, Paisley, Renfrewshire PA3 3BD
**Tel:** 01505-321000 **Fax:** 01505-335555
**Web:** www.wmtracey.co.uk
**Reg No:** 0057052SC **VAT No:** 836430139
**Estd:** 1948 Private Limited Company
**Line of Business:** Refuse systems
**Issued Capital:** £14,184
**Directors:** S H Cairns, C C Macdonald, T Davy, R B Stevenson, G J Mcdonald, B J Power, M T Tracey
**Co. Secretary:** Mrs Jane Stewart
**Branches:** William Tracey Ltd, Pinwhinnie Recovery Site, Raebog Rd, Glenmavis, Airdrie, Lanarkshire ML6 0NW
**US SIC:** 4953, 5093, 3341
**UK SIC:** 92110, 62200, 22470
**Auditors:** PricewaterhouseCoopers
**Bankers:** Bank Of Scotland (80-05-54)

| | 31-03-14 | 31-03-13 | 31-03-12 |
|---|---|---|---|
| TO | 57,790,206 | 55,504,793 | 56,413,211 |
| P/L | 4,862,586 | 4,626,776 | 4,558,178 |
| NW | 28,750,114 | 26,408,654 | 27,768,105 |
| WC | 5,245,148 | 1,749,456 | 2,602,148 |
| Emp. | 412 | 399 | 423 |

DUNS 21-931-2907 Imp

## William Turner & Son (Stockport) Ltd

Conway Centre, Stockport, Cheshire SK5 7PS
**Tel:** 01614753570
**Web:** www.william-turner.co.uk
**Reg No:** 1819061 **Estd:** 1969 Private Limited Company
**Line of Business:** Manufacture of workwear
**Issued Capital:** £300
**Directors:** D G Turner, A M Smith, J J Turner
**Co. Secretary:** Daniel Turner
**Responsibilities**
**Sales:** Tracy Holt *(Sales Executive)*, Cath O' Neill *(Sales Executive)*, Jenny Sivori *(Sales Executive)*
**US SIC:** 2328 **UK SIC:** 45340
**Auditors:** Robert Whowell & Partners
**Bankers:** National Westminster Bank Plc (01-03-93)

| | 30-09-14 | 30-09-13 | 30-09-12 |
|---|---|---|---|
| TO | 9,397,190 | 8,538,491 | 8,155,687 |
| P/L | 1,121,229 | 633,042 | 653,577 |
| NW | 5,127,381 | 4,414,211 | 4,073,484 |
| WC | 4,532,540 | 3,847,249 | 3,549,974 |
| Emp. | 111 | 111 | 111 |

DUNS 21-882-2195

## William Twigg (Matlock) Ltd

26 Bakewell Road, Matlock, Derbyshire DE4 3AU
**Tel:** 01629-566-51
**Web:** www.twiggs.co.uk
**Reg No:** 0420697 **VAT No:** 125424494
**Estd:** 1905 Private Limited Company
**Line of Business:** Steel stockholders
**Trading Style:** Twiggs
**Issued Capital:** £52,212
**Principals:** D W Allen *(Managing)*, Mrs S E Allen *(Financial)*, R Tarbatt
**Co. Secretary:** Mrs Sheila Allen
**Responsibilities**
**Senior:** Alan Boden *(Steel Yard Manager)*, richard tarbatt *(Director)*
**IT:** richard tarbatt *(Director)*
**Health & Safety:** Alan Boden *(Steel Yard Manager)*
**Facilities:** Alan Boden *(Steel Yard Manager)*
**Operations:** Alan Boden *(Steel Yard Manager)*
**US SIC:** 5051, 5074, 3441
**UK SIC:** 61200, 61300, 32042
**Auditors:** Grant Thornton UK LLP
**Bankers:** The Royal Bank Of Scotland Plc (16-25-21)

| | 31-03-14 | 31-03-13 | 31-03-12 |
|---|---|---|---|
| TO | 5,868,115 | 6,309,924 | 6,992,860 |
| P/L | 5,534 | 21,688 | 157,969 |
| NW | 2,816,767 | 2,572,262 | 2,557,871 |
| WC | 2,134,949 | 1,811,577 | 1,755,755 |
| Emp. | 60 | 58 | 62 |

DUNS 22-956-8498 Imp-Exp

## William Vere (Holdings) Ltd

Chapel Lane, Sands, High Wycombe, Buckinghamshire HP12 4BG
**Tel:** 01494448000
**Web:** www.irtpholdings.com
**Reg No:** 1607387 **Estd:** 1982 Private Limited Company
**Line of Business:** Management activities of holding companies
**Export Markets:** European Union (E U)
**Export Sales:** £349,028
**Trading Style:** Verco
**Issued Capital:** £4,720,000
**Director:** D W Vere
**Co. Secretary:** Jeff Roberts
**US SIC:** 6711, 2599
**UK SIC:** 83962, 46720
**Auditors:** Lancasters (Accountants) Ltd
**Bankers:** Barclays Bank Plc (20-40-71)

| | 31-12-13 | 31-12-12 | 31-12-11 |
|---|---|---|---|
| TO | 11,311,554 | 10,660,888 | 10,677,156 |
| P/L | 47,630 | (278,519) | (186,906) |
| NW | 12,814,003 | 12,779,763 | 13,066,681 |
| WC | 4,717,813 | 4,502,635 | 4,525,719 |
| Emp. | 101 | 104 | 109 |

DUNS 36-529-8710

## William West & Sons (Ilkeston) Ltd

Furnace Road, Ilkeston, Derbyshire DE7 5BX
**Tel:** 01159-325783
**Web:** www.west-transport.co.uk
**Reg No:** 3289941 **Estd:** 1900 Private Limited Company
**Line of Business:** Road haulage and transport services
**Issued Capital:** £400
**Managing Director:** M S Major
**Co. Secretary:** Ms Diane Ormsby
**Responsibilities**
**Finance:** Jon Richmond *(Accountant)*
**IT:** Jon Richmond *(Accountant)*
**Operations:** Jon Richmond *(Accountant)*
**Branches:** William West & Sons (Ilkeston) Ltd, Back Brierley Street, Heywood, Lancashire OL10 1PE
**US SIC:** 4789, 4226
**UK SIC:** 77002, 77003
**Auditors:** Grant Thornton UK LLP
**Bankers:** National Westminster Bank Plc (60-11-37)

| | 31-07-14 | 31-07-13 | 31-07-12 |
|---|---|---|---|
| TO | 13,044,995 | 14,494,079 | 12,454,458 |
| P/L | (377,488) | (145,058) | (8,428) |
| NW | 2,191,878 | 2,957,488 | 3,082,697 |
| WC | 788,690 | 457,936 | 793,761 |
| Emp. | 171 | 160 | 148 |

DUNS 21-712-1042

## William Willett Learning Trust

Hawkwood Lane, Chislehurst, Kent BR7 5PS
**Tel:** 02084673263
**Web:** www.cooperstc.com
**Reg No:** 7520128 **Estd:** 1987 Private Company Limited By Guarantee
**Line of Business:** Schools (local authority)
**Directors:** R H Brown, J E Norris, K G Cromwell, Ms L A Stuart, Mrs A Rush, D B Viles, Ms C A Singleton, J C Cliff
**Co. Secretary:** Robert Carling
**Responsibilities**
**Senior:** Raymond Humby *(Director)*, Sarah Macneil *(Director)*, Jill Nettleingham Davys *(Director)*, Shelly Puxty *(Head Teacher)*, Shirley Puxty *(Director)*
**US SIC:** 8211 **UK SIC:** 93200

| | 31-08-13 | 31-08-12 | 31-08-11 |
|---|---|---|---|
| TO | 10,684,000 | 9,548,000 | 34,045,000 |
| P/L | 2,163,000 | 1,635,000 | 29,706,000 |
| NW | 33,508,000 | 31,105,000 | 29,790,000 |
| WC | 911,000 | 1,678,000 | 867,000 |
| Emp. | 149 | 159 | 161 |

DUNS 51-710-6118

## William Wilson & Son

1 School Wynd, Kilbirnie, Ayrshire KA25 7AY
**Estd:** 1986 Proprietorship
**Line of Business:** Plumbers
**Proprietor:** A Wilson
**Responsibilities**
**Senior:** Harry Willson *(Proprietor)*
**US SIC:** 1711 **UK SIC:** 50300
**Bankers:** Clydesdale Bank Plc (82-65-28)
**Employees:** 59

DUNS 21-400-7247

## William Wilson Ltd.

**(Subsidiary of:** Wolseley Plc)
Hareness Road, Altens Industrial Estate, Aberdeen, Aberdeenshire AB12 3QA
**Web:** www.electric-center.co.uk
**Reg No:** 0014691SC **VAT No:** 362023393
**Estd:** 1900 Private Limited Company
**Line of Business:** Agents involved in the sale of timber and building materials
**Trading Style:** Electric Centre
**Issued Capital:** £3,829,784
**Directors:** Wolseley Uk Directors Limited, M A Ronchetti
**Co. Secretary:** Ms Vanessa French
**Branches:** William Wilson Ltd., Unit A Kirkgate Business Centre Stennard Island, Wakefield, West Yorkshire WF1 5DL
**US SIC:** 5072, 5064, 5074, 5199
**UK SIC:** 61500, 61300, 61900
**Auditors:** PricewaterhouseCoopers LLP
**Bankers:** Bank Of Scotland (12-21-37)

| | 31-07-13 | 31-07-12 | 31-07-11 |
|---|---|---|---|
| TO | 68,370,000 | 70,468,000 | 208,650,000 |
| P/L | 10,218,000 | 10,997,000 | 9,634,000 |
| NW | 39,271,000 | 30,682,000 | 22,677,000 |
| WC | 26,157,000 | 20,386,000 | 13,900,000 |
| Emp. | 269 | 246 | 845 |

DUNS 21-609-6123

## Williams & Griffin Ltd

**(Subsidiary of:** Fenwick Limited)
152 High Street, Colchester, Essex CO1 1PN
**Tel:** 01206-571212
**Web:** www.williegee.com
**Reg No:** 0740079 **VAT No:** 102798079
**Estd:** 1962 Private Limited Company
**Line of Business:** Departmental stores
**Issued Capital:** £185,850
**Directors:** N A Fenwick, M A Fenwick
**Co. Secretary:** Miss Jill Anders
**Responsibilities**
**Senior:** Carl Milton *(Manager)*
**IT:** Paul Kearse *(?Inventory Control & IT Suppor)*
**Branches:** Hawkins Rd, Colchester
**US SIC:** 5411 **UK SIC:** 64100
**Auditors:** PricewaterhouseCoopers LLP
**Bankers:** HSBC Bank plc (40-18-04)

| | 31-01-14 | 25-01-13 | 27-01-12 |
|---|---|---|---|
| TA | 4,323,187 | 4,323,187 | 4,323,187 |
| NW | 3,598,713 | 3,598,713 | 3,598,713 |
| WC | 3,598,713 | 3,598,713 | 3,598,713 |

DUNS 21-621-6333 Imp-Exp

## Williams & Oakey Engineering Co Ltd

Radstock Road, Midsomer Norton, Bath, Avon BA3 2AA
**Tel:** 01761413010
**Web:** www.williams-oakey.co.uk
**Reg No:** 1305201 **VAT No:** 318702956
**Estd:** 1977 Private Limited Company
**Line of Business:** Precision engineers
**Export Markets:** Germany
**Issued Capital:** £100,000
**Directors:** R W Oakey, S Oakey, R G Williams
**Co. Secretary:** Ms Fiona Taylor
**Responsibilities**
**Senior:** Mike Moon *(Tool Room Manager)*, Muriel Williams *(Manager)*, Ewart Williams *(Manager)*
**HR:** Terry Edgell *(Works Manager)*
**Facilities:** Terry Edgell *(Works Manager)*
**Purchasing:** Michael Lampert *(Purchasing Manager)*
**Engineering:** Terry Edgell *(Works Manager)*
**US SIC:** 8911 **UK SIC:** 83701
**Auditors:** Robson Taylor
**Bankers:** Lloyds TSB Bank plc (30-95-57)

| | 31-03-14 | 31-03-13 | 31-03-12 |
|---|---|---|---|
| TO | 4,541,803 | 7,166,495 | 6,934,656 |
| P/L | (216,647) | 488,495 | 810,704 |
| NW | 2,354,733 | 2,685,874 | 2,500,709 |
| WC | 989,821 | 1,209,324 | 844,841 |
| Emp. | 87 | 97 | 95 |

DUNS 21-606-2133

## Williams Automobiles Ltd

Totteroak Courtyard, Horton, Bristol, Avon BS37 6QG
**Tel:** 01454315112
**Web:** www.williamsautomobiles.com
**Reg No:** 0408695 **VAT No:** 137765245
**Estd:** 1946 Private Limited Company
**Line of Business:** Car dealers (new & used)
**Issued Capital:** £2,600
**Chairman:** R F Williams
**Co. Secretary:** John Williams
**Responsibilities**
**Senior:** Kevin Harrington *(Parts Manager)*
**Branches:** Williams Automobiles Ltd, 16-20 Fishponds Road, Bristol, Avon BS5 6SA
**US SIC:** 5511, 5531
**UK SIC:** 65100
**Auditors:** Robert Brown & Co
**Bankers:** Lloyds TSB Bank plc (30-00-01)

| | 31-12-13 | 31-12-12 | 31-12-11 |
|---|---|---|---|
| TO | N/A | N/A | 4,719,465 |
| P/L | N/A | N/A | (266,470) |
| NW | 3,770,119 | 3,616,430 | 3,271,048 |
| WC | 591,871 | 495,561 | 458,589 |
| Emp. | N/A | N/A | 10 |

DUNS 22-897-2345

## Williams (Bolton) Ltd

**(Subsidiary of:** Williams Motor Co.(Holdings)ltd)
Vincent Way, Bolton, Lancashire BL3 2NB
**Tel:** 01204900900
**Web:** www.williamsboltonbmw.co.uk
**Reg No:** 1811598 **Estd:** 1985 Private Limited Company
**Line of Business:** Car dealers (new & used)
**Issued Capital:** £100
**Director:** N J Cook
**Responsibilities**
**Senior:** Jean Roberts *(Manager)*
**US SIC:** 5511, 5531
**UK SIC:** 65100
**Auditors:** Baker Tilly
**Bankers:** HSBC Bank plc (40-31-23)

| | 31-12-13 | 31-12-12 | 31-12-11 |
|---|---|---|---|
| TA | 6,021,000 | 6,021,000 | 6,021,000 |
| NW | 6,021,000 | 6,021,000 | 6,021,000 |

DUNS 50-527-2518

## Williams De Broe Ltd

**(Subsidiary of:** Investec Plc)
100 Wood Street, London EC2V 7AN
**Tel:** 02075971234 **Fax:** 02070727501
**Web:** www.wdebroe.com
**Reg No:** 2485266 **Estd:** 1990 Private Limited Company
**Line of Business:** Investment consultants
**Trading Style:** Investec
**Issued Capital:** £10,000
**Directors:** M Rigby, I W Hooley, Mrs J E Price, J P Wragg
**Co. Secretary:** David Miller
**Responsibilities**
**Senior:** Tony Lee *(Manager)*, Adrian Quin *(Head Of Office)*
**Finance:** Andrew Butler-Cassar *(Corporate Development Director)*
**IT:** Reg Pressney *(IT Manager)*
**Branches:** Williams De Broe Ltd, 2 Fouberts Place, London W1F 7AD
**US SIC:** 6111 **UK SIC:** 81501
**Auditors:** PricewaterhouseCoopers LLP
**Bankers:** National Westminster Bank Plc (54-21-21)

| | 31-03-14 | 31-03-13 | 31-03-12 |
|---|---|---|---|
| TA | 5,400,000 | 9,816,000 | 54,882,000 |
| P/L | (425,000) | (8,118,000) | 4,927,000 |
| NW | 4,092,000 | 9,331,000 | 13,527,000 |
| WC | 735,000 | 3,560,000 | 5,972,000 |
| Emp. | N/A | 326 | 309 |

DUNS 56-962-6542

## Williams (Fasteners) Ltd

Unit 4a, Shepcote Way, Tinsley Industrial Estate, Hillsborough, Sheffield, South Yorkshire S9 1TH
**Tel:** 01142565200 **Fax:** 01142565210
**Web:** www.williamsfasteners.com
**Reg No:** 2851687 **Estd:** 1870 Private Limited Company
**Line of Business:** Manufacturers of bolts and fixings
**Trading Style:** Williams Bros of Sheffield
**Issued Capital:** £100,000
**Director:** A G Searles
**Co. Secretary:** Ms Susan Battersby
**Responsibilities**
**Senior:** Tina Searles *(Manager)*, Barry Ward *(Manager)*
**US SIC:** 3452 **UK SIC:** 31371
**Auditors:** Locke Williams Associates LLP

| | 31-03-14 | 31-03-13 | 31-03-12 |
|---|---|---|---|
| TO | 7,323,730 | 6,912,098 | 7,227,878 |
| P/L | 30,735 | (45,444) | 131,946 |
| NW | 1,067,342 | 1,040,743 | 1,116,187 |
| WC | 941,234 | 964,241 | 983,806 |
| Emp. | 74 | 70 | 72 |

DUNS 21-703-1729

## Williams Grand Prix Holdings Plc

Grove, Wantage, Oxfordshire OX12 0DQ
**Tel:** 01235777700
**Web:** www.williamsf1.com
**Reg No:** 7475805 **Estd:** 2010 Public Limited Company
**Line of Business:** Management activities of holding companies
**Trading Style:** Williams Grand Prix Holdings
**Issued Capital:** £500,000
**Directors:** Miss C V Williams, N C Rose, M P O'Driscoll, R W Charlton, J J Cowdry, A R Kinch, M Biddle
**Co. Secretary:** Mark Biddle
**Responsibilities**
**Senior:** Torger Wolff *(Manager)*
**US SIC:** 6711 **UK SIC:** 83962
**Auditors:** KPMG LLP
**Bankers:** Barclays Bank Plc (20-61-51)

| | 31-12-13 | 31-12-12 | 31-12-11 |
|---|---|---|---|
| TO | 130,426,649 | 126,969,081 | 104,535,384 |
| P/L | 11,741,785 | (4,983,617) | 7,402,057 |
| NW | 49,710,000 | 37,684,477 | 42,128,800 |
| WC | 6,057,617 | 22,617 | 9,538,603 |
| Emp. | 635 | 616 | 515 |

DUNS 23-232-4921 Imp-Exp

## Williams Industrial Services Ltd

Unit 5-7 Hydepark Commercial Centre, Newtownabbey, Co Antrim BT36 4PY
**Tel:** 02890 838999
**Web:** www.wis-ni.com
**Reg No:** 0028974NI **Estd:** 1981 Private Limited Company

**Line of Business:** Instrumentation consultants and engineers
**Export Markets:** Republic of Ireland and U S A
**Issued Capital:** £144,919
**Directors:** G W Caves, T D Picking, J P Toner, R J Bell
**Co. Secretary:** Thomas Picking
**US SIC:** 3999, 3643
**UK SIC:** 49590, 34203
**Auditors:** Muir & Addy
**Bankers:** First Trust Bank (aib Group (uk) Plc) (93-84-91)

| | 31-05-14 | 31-05-13 | 31-05-12 |
|---|---|---|---|
| TO | 20,526,685 | 20,527,357 | 20,176,113 |
| P/L | 1,043,420 | 537,702 | 1,012,624 |
| NW | 2,599,478 | 2,404,268 | 3,085,557 |
| WC | 3,275,380 | 2,065,479 | 2,456,467 |
| Emp. | 141 | 134 | 158 |

DUNS 39-345-6413 Imp
## Williams Lea Ltd
(**Subsidiary of:** Deutsche Post Ag)
29 St John's Lane, Farringdon, London EC1M 4NA
**Tel:** 02077724400
**Web:** www.williamslea.com
**Reg No:** 2119266 **Estd:** 1901 Private Limited Company
**Line of Business:** Other business activities not elsewhere classified
**Export Sales:** £16,619,000
**Issued Capital:** £500,000
**Directors:** D R Ellerton, Ms A Lattimore, S J Faulkner, S D Trood, M A Pierleoni
**Co. Secretary:** Exel Secretarial Services Limite
**Responsibilities**
**Health & Safety:** Keith McIlroy *(Health & Safety Officer)*
**Branches:** Williams Lea Ltd, Weavers Court, Unit 19A, Belfast, Belfast BT12 5GH
**US SIC:** 7399 **UK SIC:** 83954
**Auditors:** PricewaterhouseCoopers LLP
**Bankers:** National Westminster Bank Plc (60-08-23)

| | 31-12-13 | 31-12-12 | 31-12-11 |
|---|---|---|---|
| TO | 344,885,000 | 310,862,000 | 346,626,000 |
| P/L | 9,485,000 | 8,592,000 | 7,920,000 |
| NW | 55,748,000 | 48,685,000 | 40,047,000 |
| WC | 33,317,000 | 24,408,000 | 17,520,000 |
| Emp. | 2,728 | 2,855 | 3,039 |

DUNS 22-814-6858 Imp-Exp
## Williams Lea Uk Ltd.
(**Subsidiary of:** Deutsche Post Ag)
Foxbridge Way, Normanton Industrial Estate, Normanton, West Yorkshire WF6 1TN
**Tel:** 01924-890000 **Fax:** 01924-245444
**Web:** www.williamslea.com
**Reg No:** 1650602 **VAT No:** 363880234
**Estd:** 1982 Private Limited Company
**Line of Business:** Printers general
**Export Markets:** Hong Kong
**Issued Capital:** £67,000
**Directors:** Ms A Lattimore, S D Trood
**Co. Secretary:** Exel Secretarial Services Limite
**Responsibilities**
**Senior:** Justin Barton *(Manager)*, Kevin Bibbs *(Warehouse Manager)*, Conor Davey *(Manager)*
**Branches:** Williams Lea Uk Ltd., Unit B, Mildred Sylvester Way, Normanton, West Yorkshire WF6 1TA
**US SIC:** 2752, 5999
**UK SIC:** 47544, 65600
**Auditors:** Ernst & Young LLP
**Bankers:** Barclays Bank Plc (20-11-81)

| | 31-12-13 | 31-12-12 | 31-12-11 |
|---|---|---|---|
| TA | 306,592 | 305,062 | 321,000 |
| P/L | (882) | 2,291 | 19,000 |
| NW | 304,385 | 305,062 | 302,000 |
| WC | 304,385 | N/A | 302,000 |

DUNS 21-936-6056 Imp
## Williams Medical Holdings Ltd
(**Subsidiary of:** Dcc Plc)
The Whitbread Centre, The Terrace, Tredegar, Gwent NP22 5XD
**Tel:** 01685-844724
**Web:** www.wms.co.uk
**Reg No:** 6228280 **Estd:** 2007 Private Limited Company
**Line of Business:** Management activities of holding companies
**Export Sales:** £952,204
**Trading Style:** Williams Medicals Supplies Limited
**Issued Capital:** £1,115,000
**Directors:** L Deacon, C F Costigan, H L Hamer, R Mcevoy
**Co. Secretary:** Anthony O'Connor
**Responsibilities**
**Senior:** Mark Advani *(Manager)*
**Finance:** William Armstrong *(Finance Manager)*
**US SIC:** 6711 **UK SIC:** 83962

**Auditors:** KPMG LLP

| | 31-07-13 | 31-07-12 | 31-07-11 |
|---|---|---|---|
| TO | 57,433,844 | 56,385,697 | 53,255,256 |
| P/L | (444,268) | (740,374) | (926,489) |
| NW | (27,691,587) | (28,266,737) | (28,485,493) |
| WC | 6,803,917 | 5,038,712 | 4,562,015 |
| Emp. | 154 | 153 | 162 |

DUNS 21-230-3267
## Williams Motor Co.(Holdings)Ltd
326 Chester Road, Manchester M16 9EZ
**Tel:** 01619070340 **Fax:** 0161-907-0326
**Web:** www.williamsgroup.co.uk
**Reg No:** 0597708 **VAT No:** 146880638
**Estd:** 1914 Private Limited Company
**Line of Business:** Sale of new motor vehicles
**Issued Capital:** £261,395
**Principals:** Ms M M Orton Williams *(Chairman)*, N J Cook *(Managing)*, N J Dunning, Ms A M Cook
**Responsibilities**
**Finance:** Jean Roberts *(Manager)*
**Branches:** Williams Motor Co.(Holdings)ltd, 6 Hadfield Street, Manchester M16 9FG
**US SIC:** 5511, 5521, 7539, 5531
**UK SIC:** 65100, 67100
**Auditors:** Baker Tilly UK Audit LLP
**Bankers:** Barclays Bank Plc (27-99-00)

| | 31-12-13 | 31-12-12 | 31-12-11 |
|---|---|---|---|
| TO | 320,773,000 | 308,176,000 | 273,730,000 |
| P/L | 5,001,000 | 4,612,000 | 1,606,000 |
| NW | 29,666,000 | 26,382,000 | 23,380,000 |
| WC | 8,440,000 | 5,309,000 | 2,746,000 |
| Emp. | 614 | 578 | 580 |

DUNS 23-581-3610
## Williams of Swansea Ltd
Prydwen Road Fforestfach Trading Estate, Swansea, West Glamorgan SA5 4HW
**Tel:** 01792-582546
**Web:** www.williamsofswansea.co.uk
**Reg No:** 3579111 **Estd:** 1998 Private Limited Company
**Line of Business:** Wholesale of other household goods not elsewhere classified
**Export Sales:** £254,679
**Issued Capital:** £200,000
**Principals:** R J Coode *(Managing)*, R F Strawford, D G Leach
**Co. Secretary:** Anthony Mark
**US SIC:** 5199 **UK SIC:** 61900
**Auditors:** Griffith & Miles

| | 31-12-13 | 31-12-12 | 31-12-11 |
|---|---|---|---|
| TO | 6,300,300 | 6,841,593 | 7,583,879 |
| P/L | 115,786 | 227,395 | 228,087 |
| NW | 1,235,235 | 1,473,982 | 1,622,772 |
| WC | 1,090,951 | 1,323,049 | 1,461,984 |
| Emp. | 53 | 58 | 61 |

DUNS 28-843-8682
## Williams Rochdale Ltd
(**Subsidiary of:** Williams Motor Co.(Holdings)ltd)
Trans Pennine Trading Estate, Gorrells Way At The End Of The, Rochdale, Lancashire OL11 2PX
**Tel:** 01706-717700
**Web:** www.williamsminirochdale.co.uk
**Reg No:** 0594908 **Estd:** 1973 Private Limited Company
**Line of Business:** Car dealers (new & used)
**Trading Style:** Williams Bmw
**Issued Capital:** £1,000
**Directors:** N J Cook, Ms M M Orton Williams, N J Dunning
**Responsibilities**
**Senior:** Tony Corolla *(Dealer Principal)*
**Finance:** Irene Howarth *(Finance Director)*, Cameron poli *(Finance Manager)*
**Sales:** Steve Aslam *(Sales Manager)*, Paul DiClemente *(Sales Manager)*, Lee Potter *(Sales Manager)*
**Branches:** Williams Rochdale Ltd, Trans Pennine Trading Estate Gor, Rochdale, Lancashire OL11 2PX
**US SIC:** 5511 **UK SIC:** 65100
**Auditors:** Baker Tilly

| | 31-12-13 | 31-12-12 | 31-12-11 |
|---|---|---|---|
| TA | 1,702,000 | 1,702,000 | 1,702,000 |
| NW | 1,702,000 | 1,702,000 | 1,702,000 |

DUNS 21-629-8307
## Williams Shipping Holdings Ltd
Manor House Avenue, Southampton, Hampshire SO15 0LF
**Tel:** 02380237330 **Fax:** 02380772422
**Web:** www.williams-shipping.co.uk
**Reg No:** 0376891 **VAT No:** 370067174
**Estd:** 2012 Private Limited Company
**Line of Business:** Equine transportation and horse boxes
**Export Sales:** £502,848
**Trading Style:** Williams Shipping Transport, Williams Shipping Marines, Williams Shipping Cabins and Container, Williams Shipping Lubrican
**Issued Capital:** £103,021
**Principals:** J E Williams *(Managing)*, J R Williams, Mrs B D Williams, P J Williams
**Co. Secretary:** Colin Williams
**Branches:** Williams Shipping Holdings Ltd, Captain Superintendents Building, The Dockyard, Pembroke Dock, Dyfed SA72 6TD
**US SIC:** 4789, 4226
**UK SIC:** 77002, 77003
**Auditors:** Fiander Tovell & Co
**Bankers:** National Westminster Bank Plc (56-00-68)

| | 30-09-14 | 30-09-13 | 30-09-12 |
|---|---|---|---|
| TO | 12,253,072 | 12,142,890 | 11,921,745 |
| P/L | 1,171,834 | 747,260 | 896,670 |
| NW | 7,760,667 | 7,468,129 | 7,407,407 |
| WC | (2,038,682) | (1,449,170) | (1,143,245) |
| Emp. | 78 | 81 | 84 |

DUNS 39-956-9771
## Williams Southern Ltd
(**Subsidiary of:** Williamsbuild Management Ltd)
Southern House, Eagle Road, Plympton, Plymouth, Devon PL7 5HZ
**Tel:** 01752201300 **Fax:** 01752-201299
**Web:** www.williamsbuild.com
**Reg No:** 2262602 **VAT No:** 491603838
**Estd:** 1988 Private Limited Company
**Line of Business:** Construction of domestic buildings
**Trading Style:** Williams Southern Ltd
**Issued Capital:** £2,880
**Directors:** R R Williams, J D Whittaker
**Co. Secretary:** Ms Linda Williams
**US SIC:** 1522, 8911
**UK SIC:** 50100, 83701
**Auditors:** Bishop Fleming
**Bankers:** Barclays Bank Plc (20-68-10)

| | 31-07-13 | 31-07-12 | 31-07-11 |
|---|---|---|---|
| TO | 37,355,361 | 29,859,914 | 27,152,197 |
| P/L | 608,410 | 657,908 | 665,938 |
| NW | 2,832,793 | 2,387,651 | 2,914,332 |
| WC | 2,269,866 | 1,671,392 | 2,284,894 |
| Emp. | 106 | 102 | 91 |

DUNS 49-386-4698 Imp
## Williams Tanker Services Ltd
Howley Park Road East, Morley, Leeds, West Yorkshire LS27 0SW
**Tel:** 01132897990 **Fax:** 01132-897778
**Web:** www.williamsts.com
**Reg No:** 3133504 **Estd:** 1995 Private Limited Company
**Line of Business:** Repairing cleaning and maintenance of tanks
**Export Sales:** £90,040
**Issued Capital:** £1,000
**Directors:** Mrs K E Thompson, B E Williams
**Co. Secretary:** Bruce Williams
**Branches:** Williams Tanker Services Ltd, Howley Park Road East, Morley, Leeds, West Yorkshire LS27 0BN
**US SIC:** 7349, 7539
**UK SIC:** 92300, 67100
**Auditors:** Jolliffe Cork LLP
**Bankers:** National Westminster Bank Plc (60-14-34)

| | 31-12-13 | 31-12-12 | 31-12-11 |
|---|---|---|---|
| TO | 8,412,742 | N/A | N/A |
| P/L | 705,821 | N/A | N/A |
| NW | 3,124,538 | 2,617,705 | 2,089,149 |
| WC | 850,624 | 155,099 | 23,807 |
| Emp. | 52 | N/A | N/A |

DUNS 21-722-1795 Imp-Exp
## Williams Trade Supplies Ltd
13-19 Standard Way, Fareham, Hampshire PO16 8XB
**Tel:** 01329226500
**Web:** www.williams.uk.com
**Reg No:** 1864711 **VAT No:** 107767064
**Estd:** 1972 Private Limited Company
**Line of Business:** Wholesale of hardware, plumbing and heating equipment and supplies
**Export Markets:** Germany
**Trading Style:** Williams & Co
**Issued Capital:** £5,025
**Principals:** M T Williams *(Chairman and Managing)*, Mrs A Williams, R Stafford
**Co. Secretary:** Ms Rachel Moore
**Responsibilities**
**Senior:** Ray Stafford *(Manager)*
**Branches:** Williams Trade Supplies Ltd, Unit 3-4 Amey Industrial Estate, Frenchmans Road, Petersfield, Hampshire GU32 3AN
**US SIC:** 7399, 5065
**UK SIC:** 83954, 61500
**Auditors:** taylorcocks
**Bankers:** National Westminster Bank Plc (56-00-64)

| | 30-11-13 | 30-11-12 | 30-11-11 |
|---|---|---|---|
| TO | 36,930,655 | 27,111,784 | 21,404,715 |
| P/L | 2,538,388 | 1,335,547 | 1,401,430 |
| NW | 7,221,840 | 5,357,873 | 4,440,285 |
| WC | 6,686,597 | 4,882,765 | 4,030,039 |
| Emp. | 154 | 134 | 108 |

DUNS 64-263-2111
## Williamson & Soden
Stanton House, 54 Stratford Road, Solihull, West Midlands B90 3LS
**Tel:** 01217338000
**Web:** www.williamsonandsoden.co.uk
**Estd:** 1996 Partnership
**Line of Business:** Solicitors
**Partners:** I Williamson, J Soden
**Responsibilities**
**Senior:** Paul Gilkes *(Manager)*, John Soden *(Founding Partner)*
**Branches:** Williamson & Soden, 100 Windsor Street South, Birmingham, West Midlands B7 4HZ
**US SIC:** 8111 **UK SIC:** 83500
**Employees:** 60

DUNS 22-108-9928
## Williamson-Dickie Europe Holdings Ltd
(**Subsidiary of:** Williamson-Dickie Holding Company L.L.C.)
Second Avenue, Midsomer Norton, Midsomer Norton, Bath, Avon BA3 4BH
**Tel:** 01761410732 **Fax:** 01761414825
**Web:** www.dickies-uk.co.uk
**Reg No:** 4128248 **Estd:** 2000 Private Limited Company
**Line of Business:** Holding companies management activities
**Issued Capital:** £5
**Directors:** P C Williamson, D K Searle, K M Ehrlich
**Co. Secretary:** Ms Sarah Deverill
**Responsibilities**
**Senior:** Christine Dark *(Manager)*, Barrie Tidball *(Manager)*
**Branches:** Williamson-Dickie Europe Holdings Ltd, Metropole House, 5 Metropole Lane, Glasgow, Lanarkshire G1 4NH
**US SIC:** 7394 **UK SIC:** 84000
**Auditors:** PricewaterhouseCoopers LLP
**Bankers:** HSBC Bank plc (40-14-12)

| | 31-12-13 | 31-12-12 | 31-12-11 |
|---|---|---|---|
| TO | 92,908,000 | 90,744,000 | 90,451,000 |
| P/L | 4,665,000 | 3,152,000 | 4,139,000 |
| NW | 39,121,000 | 36,940,000 | 30,733,000 |
| WC | 32,330,000 | 29,897,000 | 23,314,000 |
| Emp. | 473 | 443 | 457 |

DUNS 22-608-0158 Imp-Exp
## Williamson-Dickie Europe Ltd
(**Subsidiary of:** Williamson-Dickie Holding Company L.L.C.)
Second Avenue Westfield Trading, Bath, Avon BA3 4BH
**Tel:** 01761410041 **Fax:** 01761-414825
**Web:** www.dickies.com
**Reg No:** 1757853 **VAT No:** 543372451
**Estd:** 1983 Private Limited Company
**Line of Business:** Holding companies management activities
**Export Markets:** Europe
**Issued Capital:** £88,250
**Directors:** M A Strange, K M Ehrlich, Ms J A Clay, P C Williamson, Mrs S Cooper, M Morton, D K Searle
**Co. Secretary:** Ms Sarah Deverill
**US SIC:** 2389, 5661
**UK SIC:** 45393, 64600
**Auditors:** Grant Thornton UK LLP
**Bankers:** HSBC Bank plc (40-14-13)

| | 31-12-13 | 31-12-12 | 31-12-11 |
|---|---|---|---|
| TO | 56,229,000 | 54,024,000 | 53,991,000 |
| P/L | 3,279,000 | 1,962,000 | 2,387,000 |
| NW | 24,344,000 | 21,110,000 | 19,325,000 |
| WC | 17,043,000 | 15,207,000 | 13,396,000 |
| Emp. | 266 | 250 | 247 |

DUNS 21-444-5975
## The Williamson Group Ltd
5, Inverness, Inverness-Shire IV1 1TD
**Tel:** 01463236600 **Fax:** 01463222764
**Web:** www.williamsongroup.com
**Reg No:** 0032547SC **VAT No:** 266687605
**Estd:** 1957 Private Limited Company
**Line of Business:** Wholesalers of fruit and vegetable
**Export Sales:** £446,615
**Issued Capital:** £2,000
**Directors:** J W Williamson, G V Williamson, M A Williamson
**Co. Secretary:** Mrs Crystelle Williamson
**Branches:** The Williamson Group Ltd, 1 High Street, Beauly, Inverness-Shire IV4 7BY
**US SIC:** 5148, 5147
**UK SIC:** 61700
**Auditors:** Scott Oswald
**Bankers:** Bank Of Scotland (80-91-26)

| | 31-12-13 | 31-12-12 | 31-12-11 |
|---|---|---|---|
| TO | 8,921,827 | 7,983,243 | 8,111,520 |
| P/L | 171,370 | (8,826) | 57,418 |
| NW | 1,091,023 | 991,086 | 997,055 |
| WC | (239,585) | (418,702) | (307,661) |
| Emp. | 74 | 77 | 76 |

**DUNS 21-677-9651**
## Williamson Morton Thornton Llp
Torrington House, 47 Holywell Hill, St Albans, Hertfordshire AL1 1HD
**Tel:** 01727838255
**Web:** www.wmtllp.com
**Reg No:** 0355827OC **Estd:** 2010
**Line of Business:** Accounting activities
**US SIC:** 8931 **UK SIC:** 83600

|     | 31-03-14  | 31-03-13  | 31-03-12  |
|-----|-----------|-----------|-----------|
| TA  | 1,600,860 | 1,915,630 | 1,748,263 |
| NW  | 375,565   | 411,091   | 309,005   |
| WC  | 1,159,088 | 1,487,180 | 1,408,571 |

**DUNS 21-718-6009**
## The Williamson Trust
Maidstone Road, Rochester, Kent ME1 3EL
**Tel:** 01634818303
**Web:** www.thewilliamsontrust.co.uk
**Reg No:** 7569727 **Estd:** 2011 Private Company Limited By Guarantee
**Line of Business:** Educational training
**Directors:** C Dimmick, Dr G P Holden, M E Costello, L J Mc Veigh, F Cook, S J Marsden, D G Kesby, R J Carter
**Co. Secretary:** Ms Julie Freeman
**Responsibilities**
**Senior:** Peter Clough (Director), Graham Cottle (Director)
**US SIC:** 8299 **UK SIC:** 93300

|     | 31-08-13   | 31-08-12   |
|-----|------------|------------|
| TO  | 23,274,243 | 58,685,464 |
| P/L | 4,358,726  | 39,824,553 |
| NW  | 36,494,469 | 33,970,010 |
| WC  | 2,245,910  | 1,535,527  |
| Emp.| 372        | 299        |

**DUNS 21-606-3415**
## Williamsons Solicitors
23 Exchange Street, Driffield, North Humberside YO25 6LF
**Tel:** 01377252022
**Web:** www.ivesonandatkin.inspace.com
**Estd:** 1994
**Line of Business:** Solicitors
**Proprietor:** B Cook
**Responsibilities**
**Senior:** Bill Waddington (Manager)
**US SIC:** 8111 **UK SIC:** 83500
**Employees:** 120

**DUNS 23-319-9210**
## Willington Garden Centre
Sandy Road, Willington, Bedford, Bedfordshire MK44 3QP
**Tel:** 01234838777
**Web:** www.frostsgardencentres.co.uk
**Estd:** 1973 Partnership
**Line of Business:** Garden centres
**Trading Style:** Frosts At Willington
**Partners:** A E Frost, Mrs C M Godber, J C Frost, R T Godber
**Responsibilities**
**Senior:** Angela Wilson (Centre Manager)
**Branches:** Frost Garden Centre, Brampton Garden Centre. Buckden Road, Brampton, Cambs. PE28 4NF Huntingdon
**US SIC:** 5999, 0161
**UK SIC:** 65600, 01001
**Employees:** 100

**DUNS 23-653-9941**
## Willington Ltd
1st Floor, London W1W 8QX
**Tel:** 01515491082
**Reg No:** 3649149 **Estd:** 1998 Private Limited Company
**Line of Business:** Business services
**Export Sales:** £44,342,000
**Issued Capital:** £3,900,000
**Directors:** M S Baskerville, R M Robinow, J J Robinow
**Co. Secretary:** R.E.A. Services Limited
**US SIC:** 7399 **UK SIC:** 83954
**Auditors:** PKF (UK) LLP

|     | 31-12-13   | 31-12-12   | 31-12-11   |
|-----|------------|------------|------------|
| TO  | 63,464,000 | 42,341,000 | 19,048,000 |
| P/L | 1,725,000  | 911,000    | 669,000    |
| NW  | 12,197,000 | 10,694,000 | 4,857,000  |
| WC  | 5,535,000  | 4,948,000  | 535,000    |
| Emp.| 85         | 77         | 58         |

**DUNS 21-726-3102** **Imp-Exp**
## Willis Brecknell & Co Ltd
(**Subsidiary of:** Wabtec Uk Holdings Ltd)
Po Box 10, Chard, Somerset TA20 2DE
**Tel:** 01460260700 **Fax:** 01460-66122
**Web:** www.brecknell-willis.co.uk
**Reg No:** 0306444 **VAT No:** 323432394
**Estd:** 1894 Private Limited Company
**Line of Business:** Manufacture of other transport equipment not elsewhere classified
**Export Sales:** £20,221,491
**Issued Capital:** £6,000,000
**Directors:** C J Weatherall, A R Whitefield, D J Bailey, P D Dugan, D M Seitz

**Responsibilities**
**Senior:** Michael Bostelmann (Manager), Martin Perfect (Financial Director)
**Finance:** Martin Perfect (Financial Director)
**HR:** Claire White (Human Resources Manager)
**Purchasing:** Nigel Heselton (Purchasing Manager)
**Engineering:** Steve Fielder (Engineering Manager)
**US SIC:** 3799 **UK SIC:** 36502
**Auditors:** Saffery Champness
**Bankers:** Barclays Bank Plc (20-85-26)

|     | 31-12-13   | 31-12-12   | 31-12-11   |
|-----|------------|------------|------------|
| TO  | 34,300,019 | 37,325,901 | 38,011,545 |
| P/L | 2,287,864  | 2,348,405  | 4,249,978  |
| NW  | 17,166,102 | 16,754,425 | 15,952,261 |
| WC  | 11,657,387 | 12,149,683 | 10,472,879 |
| Emp.| 220        | 216        | 218        |

**DUNS 22-943-5037**
## Willis Brothers
Fields Farm, Houndings Lane, Sandbach, Cheshire CW11 4HJ
**VAT No:** 279677583 **Estd:** 1965 Partnership
**Line of Business:** Drainage contractors
**Partners:** S A Willis, F A Willis, D T Willis
**US SIC:** 4952 **UK SIC:** 92120
**Bankers:** The Royal Bank Of Scotland Plc (16-31-13)
**Employees:** 50

**DUNS 77-960-4636**
## Willis Construction Ltd
Unit 6, Mellyn Mair Business Centre, Wentloog Avenue Lamby Industrial Park, Cardiff, South Glamorgan CF3 2EX
**Tel:** 02920797073
**Web:** www.willisconstruction.co.uk
**Reg No:** 3063831 **VAT No:** 667192505
**Estd:** 1995 Private Limited Company
**Line of Business:** Building construction contractors
**Issued Capital:** £10,000
**Directors:** P M Jenkins, R S Jeremy, G N Williams
**Co. Secretary:** Ms Christine Williams
**Responsibilities**
**Senior:** Bob Humphreys (Manager), June Way (Office Manager)
**Sales:** June Way (Office Manager)
**Admin:** June Way (Office Manager)
**HR:** Paul Cachia (Health & Safety and Training C)
**Health & Safety:** Paul Cachia (Health & Safety and Training C)
**Operations:** Glynn Grey (Operations Manager)
**US SIC:** 1522 **UK SIC:** 50100
**Auditors:** Hughes & Co
**Bankers:** HSBC Bank plc (40-16-17)

|     | 30-09-13  | 30-09-12  | 30-09-11  |
|-----|-----------|-----------|-----------|
| TO  | 6,792,101 | 7,500,897 | N/A       |
| P/L | 348,075   | 400,529   | N/A       |
| NW  | 1,889,319 | 1,735,602 | 1,565,374 |
| WC  | 1,565,888 | 1,355,825 | 1,600,940 |
| Emp.| 67        | 81        | N/A       |

**DUNS 21-032-0073** **Exp**
## Willis Ltd
(**Subsidiary of:** Willis Group Holdings Public Limited Company)
51 Lime Street, London EC3M 7DQ
**Tel:** 020-3124-6000 **Fax:** 020 3124 8223
**Web:** www.willis.com
**Reg No:** 0181116 **Estd:** 1922 Private Limited Company
**Line of Business:** Insurance brokers
**Export Markets:** U S A, E U, Asia & The Pacific & The Middle East & Africa
**Trading Style:** Willis Group Holdings, Fine Art Jewellery & Specie
**Directors:** Ms S J Turvill, S W Gaffney, N P Perry, A J Rivers, D J Martin, A P Dickinson, D V Paige, Ms C Powell
**Co. Secretary:** Alistair Peel
**Responsibilities**
**Senior:** Donald Bailey (Chairman and Chief Executive), Justin Blackmore (Manager), Chris Dear (News Director), Jeremy Hanley (Director), James Vickers (Director)
**Finance:** Matthew Spratt (Director of IT and Project Aud)
**Marketing:** Chris Dear (News Director), Thierry Saada (Sales & Marketing Manager), Laura Wheaton (Head of Marketing)
**Sales:** Bob Choppen (Executive Director of UK Retai), Thierry Saada (Sales & Marketing Manager)
**IT:** Matt Davy (IT Director), Nick Friar (IT Manager), Tony Millings (Technology Procurement Manager), Matthew Spratt (Director of IT and Project Aud)
**HR:** Celia Brown (EVP & HR Director), Craig Morgans (Head of Resourcing)
**Health & Safety:** Trudi Gilbert (Health & Safety Officer)
**Engineering:** Martin Walsh (Technical Specialist)
**Branches:** Willis Ltd, 55-57 St. Benedicts Street, Norwich, Norfolk NR2 4PQ
**US SIC:** 6411, 6399

**UK SIC:** 83200, 82001
**Auditors:** Deloitte LLP
**Bankers:** Lloyds TSB Bank plc (30-00-02)
**Employees:** 3,693
**Turnover:** £993,000,000

**DUNS 21-617-6404**
## Willmott Dixon Holdings Ltd
(**Subsidiary of:** Hardwicke Investments Ltd)
Spirella 2, Letchworth, Hertfordshire SG6 4GY
**Web:** www.willmottdixongroup.co.uk
**Reg No:** 0198032 **VAT No:** 197737796
**Estd:** 1924 Private Limited Company
**Line of Business:** Development and selling of real estate
**Issued Capital:** £100,000,000
**Directors:** C Enticknap, A J Telfer, C J Sheridan, R J Willmott, C S Durkin, P R Smith, J E Porritt
**Co. Secretary:** Ms Wendy Mcwilliams
**Responsibilities**
**Admin:** Bridgette Sawford (Executive Secretary)
**Branches:** Willmott Dixon Holdings Ltd, Hitchin Road, Shefford, Bedfordshire SG17 5JS
**US SIC:** 1522, 1541, 6711
**UK SIC:** 50100, 83962
**Auditors:** PKF (UK) LLP
**Bankers:** HSBC Bank plc (40-05-18)
Following financial data are in thousands

|     | 31-12-13  | 31-12-12  | 31-12-11  |
|-----|-----------|-----------|-----------|
| TO  | 1,023,610 | 1,033,997 | 1,052,137 |
| P/L | 12,974    | 15,678    | 21,148    |
| NW  | 99,807    | 96,270    | 89,258    |
| WC  | 82,314    | 84,238    | 86,537    |
| Emp.| 3,078     | 3,145     | 2,852     |

**DUNS 29-052-5633**
## Willmott Dixon Premises Ltd
(**Subsidiary of:** Hardwicke Investments Ltd)
Hitchin Road, Shefford, Bedfordshire SG17 5JA
**Tel:** 01462-814455
**Web:** www.willmottdixon.co.uk
**Reg No:** 1093332 **Estd:** 1973 Private Limited Company
**Line of Business:** Management of real estate on a fee or contract basis
**Issued Capital:** £20,000
**Directors:** R J Willmott, C Enticknap, Ms W J Mcwilliams, D I Canney
**Co. Secretary:** Laurence Holdcroft
**Responsibilities**
**Senior:** Robert Eyre (Manager)
**US SIC:** 6531 **UK SIC:** 83400
**Bankers:** HSBC Bank plc (40-05-18)

|     | 31-12-13 | 31-12-12 | 31-12-11 |
|-----|----------|----------|----------|
| TA  | 13,511   | 13,511   | 13,511   |
| NW  | 13,511   | 13,511   | 13,511   |

**DUNS 21-681-2883**
## Willmott's Transport Ltd
(**Subsidiary of:** Admp Group Ltd)
Waterlip, Shepton Mallet, Somerset BA4 4RN
**Fax:** 01749-880337
**Web:** www.willmottsdjb.com
**Reg No:** 0701449 **VAT No:** 130311046
**Estd:** 1961 Private Limited Company
**Line of Business:** Storage and warehousing
**Issued Capital:** £5,000
**Directors:** D C Willmott, A M Stott, D J Buxton
**US SIC:** 4226, 4213
**UK SIC:** 77003, 72300
**Auditors:** Raymond Wright & Co
**Bankers:** National Westminster Bank Plc (60-02-05)

|     | 31-12-13  | 31-12-12  | 31-12-11  |
|-----|-----------|-----------|-----------|
| TO  | 5,691,069 | 5,161,605 | N/A       |
| P/L | 161,047   | 206,360   | 94,906    |
| NW  | 1,272,858 | 1,291,870 | 648,596   |
| WC  | (745,288) | (536,600) | (256,341) |
| Emp.| 59        | 52        | 57        |

**DUNS 21-782-8405**
## Willoughby Grange Nursing Home
Willoughby Road, Boston, Lincolnshire PE21 9EG
**Tel:** 01205357836
**Web:** www.fshc.co.uk
**Estd:** 1991 Proprietorship
**Line of Business:** Residential care establishments
**Proprietor:** Mrs B Roach
**US SIC:** 8321 **UK SIC:** 96111
**Employees:** 51

**DUNS 28-879-2195**
## Willover Property Ltd
155 Duffield Road, Derby, Derbyshire DE22 1AH
**Web:** www.stanleyhousenursinghome.co.uk
**Reg No:** 1154443 **Estd:** 1974 Private Limited Company

**Line of Business:** Other human health activities
**Trading Style:** Stanley House Nursing Home, Abbydale Nursing Home
**Issued Capital:** £22,500
**Director:** R J Shepperson
**Co. Secretary:** Michael Shepperson
**Responsibilities**
**Senior:** Karen Jenkinson (Home Manager)
**HR:** Karen Jenkinson (Home Manager)
**Health & Safety:** Karen Jenkinson (Home Manager)
**Facilities:** Karen Jenkinson (Home Manager)
**US SIC:** 8091 **UK SIC:** 95200
**Auditors:** Thornton Springer
**Bankers:** HSBC Bank plc (40-28-04)

|     | 31-03-14  | 31-03-13  | 31-03-12  |
|-----|-----------|-----------|-----------|
| TA  | 4,607,204 | 2,917,762 | 2,822,168 |
| NW  | 4,421,638 | 2,669,324 | 2,609,568 |
| WC  | 709,964   | 675,599   | 651,500   |

**DUNS 21-585-9259**
## The Willow Brook Shopping Centre Management
Savages Wood, Bradley Stoke, Bristol, Avon BS32 8BS
**Tel:** 01454205040
**Web:** www.willowbrookcentre.co.uk
**Estd:** 2011 Proprietorship
**Line of Business:** Shopping centres
**Proprietor:** S Lahive
**Responsibilities**
**Senior:** Scott Lahive (Manager), Andy Wynn (Centre Manager)
**US SIC:** 5399 **UK SIC:** 65600
**Employees:** 100

**DUNS 21-227-8080**
## Willow Court Residential Home
Aldwickbury Crescent, Harpenden, Hertfordshire AL5 5SD
**Tel:** 01582-466244
**Web:** www.quantumcare.co.uk
**Estd:** 2001
**Line of Business:** Residential care establishments
**Partners:** Ms K Coles, Miss C Flattley
**US SIC:** 8321 **UK SIC:** 96111
**Employees:** 50

**DUNS 21-878-8705**
## Willow Dene School
Willow Dene School, Swingate Lane, London SE18 2JD
**Tel:** 02088549841
**Web:** www.willowdeneschool.co.uk
**Estd:** 2012
**Line of Business:** Schools (special)
**Responsibilities**
**Senior:** Rachel Harrison (Head of School)
**US SIC:** 8299 **UK SIC:** 93300
**Employees:** 120

**DUNS 55-060-1025**
## Willow Grange Rest Home
119 St Bernards Road, Solihull, West Midlands B92 7DH
**Tel:** 0121-708-0804
**Web:** www.alphacarehomes.co.uk
**Estd:** 2003 Proprietorship
**Line of Business:** Rest and retirement homes
**Proprietor:** Mrs N Pudney
**US SIC:** 8321 **UK SIC:** 96111
**Employees:** 50

**DUNS 21-039-9005**
## Willow Park Housing Trust
8 Poundswick Lane, Manchester M22 9TA
**Tel:** 0800-633-5500
**Web:** www.willowparkenterprise.com
**Estd:** 1999 Partnership
**Line of Business:** Housing associations societies trusts & co-operatives
**Partners:** J Doherty, A Percival
**Responsibilities**
**Finance:** Shahida Latif-Haider (Head of Finance)
**HR:** Vivian Proctor (Human Resources Manager)
**US SIC:** 6531 **UK SIC:** 83400
**Employees:** 55

**DUNS 23-715-7107**
## Willow Park Housing Trust Ltd
Willow Park Housing Trust, Manchester M22 9TA
**Tel:** 01619460055 **Fax:** 01619469507
**Web:** www.willow-park.co.uk
**Reg No:** 3710937 **Estd:** 1999 Private Limited Company
**Line of Business:** Other letting of own property
**Issued Capital:** £2

**Directors:** R P Wakefield, Mrs S E Loose, Ms S A Morris, D Chorlton, M F Williams, Ms F L Shone, B O'Neil, T Judge
**Co. Secretary:** Richard Coughlan
**Responsibilities**
**Senior:** Dennis Finnegan *(Manager)*, Joe Leigh *(Manager)*
**Finance:** Mike Gerrard *(Financial Director)*
**US SIC:** 6519 **UK SIC:** 85000
**Auditors:** RSM Robson Rhodes LLP

| | 31-03-14 | 31-03-13 | 31-03-12 |
|---|---|---|---|
| TO | 36,283,000 | 34,591,398 | 32,626,715 |
| P/L | 1,905,000 | (1,994,529) | 673,452 |
| NW | 122,838,000 | 120,455,601 | 117,533,552 |
| WC | 7,283,000 | 2,662,649 | 4,181,435 |
| Emp. | 377 | 384 | 363 |

DUNS 21-291-0496
## Willow Tree Day Nursery
Chingford Avenue, Clacton-On-Sea, Essex CO15 4US
**Web:** www.willowtreechildrenscentre.co.uk
**Estd:** 1987 Proprietorship
**Line of Business:** Nursery schools
**Proprietor:** Mrs B Dearsley
**Responsibilities**
**Senior:** Christina Hart *(Manager)*
**US SIC:** 8211 **UK SIC:** 93200
**Employees:** 52

DUNS 64-252-6073
## Willowbank Nursing Home
5-7 Barwick Road, Leeds, West Yorkshire LS15 8SE
**Tel:** 01132234603
**Web:** www.mmcg.co.uk
**Estd:** 2002 Partnership
**Line of Business:** Nursing homes
**Partners:** Mrs A Prentice, D Prentice
**Responsibilities**
**Senior:** Linda Oram *(Nurse Care Manager)*, Herbert Prentice *(Manager)*, Anne Prentice *(Director)*
**US SIC:** 8051 **UK SIC:** 95100
**Employees:** 46

DUNS 34-977-5697
## Willowbeck Health Care Ltd
**(Subsidiary of:** Exemplar Health Care Partnerships Ltd)
95 Holywell Road, Sheffield, South Yorkshire S4 8AR
**Tel:** 01142617771 **Fax:** 01142619779
**Web:** www.exemplarhc.com
**Reg No:** 5772982 **Estd:** 2006 Private Limited Company
**Line of Business:** Nursing homes
**Issued Capital:** £1
**Directors:** Mrs L Thomas, E D Craig, Ms T Duke, Mrs T J Clarkson, D Rowe-Bewick, D Collinge
**Co. Secretary:** Mrs Tracy Clarkson
**US SIC:** 8051, 8321
**UK SIC:** 95100, 96111

| | 31-03-14 | 31-03-13 | 25-03-12 |
|---|---|---|---|
| TO | 4,508,277 | 4,272,719 | 4,194,187 |
| P/L | 319,275 | 497,278 | 695,093 |
| NW | (2,973,134) | 389,227 | 517,283 |
| WC | 835,230 | 149,220 | 380,761 |
| Emp. | 156 | 155 | 155 |

DUNS 21-583-2748
## Willowbrook Foods
38 Jubilee Road, Newtownards, Co Down BT23 4YH
**Tel:** 07816784397
**Web:** www.sliceofheavenni.co.uk
**Estd:** 2011 Proprietorship
**Line of Business:** Misc Food Preparation Manufacturers
**Proprietor:** Miss A Nelson
**US SIC:** 2099 **UK SIC:** 42399
**Employees:** 50

DUNS 23-184-6333
## Willowbrook Foods Ltd
50a Whiterock Road, Killinchy, Killinchy, Newtownards, Co Down BT23 6PT
**Tel:** 02897541603 **Fax:** 02897542208
**Web:** www.willowbrookfoods.co.uk
**Reg No:** 0037757NI **Estd:** 2000 Private Unlimited Company
**Line of Business:** Processing and preserving of fruit and vegetables not elsewhere classified
**Issued Capital:** £10,000
**Director:** W Mccann
**Co. Secretary:** Mrs Janine Mccann
**Responsibilities**
**Senior:** Maurice Johnson *(Manager)*
**HR:** Andrea Nelson *(Human Resources Manager)*
**US SIC:** 2099, 7399
**UK SIC:** 42399, 83954
**Auditors:** ASM (M) Ltd
**Bankers:** Ulster Bank Ltd (98-04-45)

| | 31-01-14 | 31-01-13 | 31-01-12 |
|---|---|---|---|
| TO | 19,453,638 | 19,171,062 | 19,866,028 |
| P/L | 232,103 | (289,538) | (279,440) |
| NW | 5,002,127 | 4,898,095 | 5,119,779 |
| WC | (1,495,378) | (1,607,293) | (1,044,876) |
| Emp. | 103 | 109 | 122 |

DUNS 34-845-3804
## Willowbrook Hospice
Portico Lane, Eccleston Park, Prescot, Merseyside L34 2QT
**Tel:** 01514308736
**Web:** www.willowbrook.org.uk
**Reg No:** 2808633 **Estd:** 1998 Private Company Limited By Guarantee
**Line of Business:** Hospices
**Directors:** D Corf, J G Spencer, R Macmillan, A J Chick, Lady K Pilkington, K Stringer, Dr K Beeby, Dr M G Van Dessel
**Co. Secretary:** Geoffrey Slater
**Responsibilities**
**Senior:** Elaine Inglesby *(Director)*, Philip Nee *(Director)*
**Finance:** Val Southcote *(Financial Administrator)*
**HR:** Dympna Gelling *(Human Resources Manager)*
**Facilities:** Jane Finnerty *(Outreach Services Manager)*, Val Haller *(Facilities Manager)*
**Operations:** Chris Haywood *(Head of Hospice Services)*, Nicky Saunders *(Fundraising Manager)*
**Purchasing:** Carol Varey *(Trading Company Manager)*
**US SIC:** 8062 **UK SIC:** 95100
**Auditors:** Livesey Spottiswood
**Bankers:** National Westminster Bank Plc (60-70-08)

| | 31-03-14 | 31-03-13 | 31-03-12 |
|---|---|---|---|
| TO | 3,861,142 | 3,588,638 | 3,102,934 |
| P/L | 262,386 | 148,722 | 31,525 |
| NW | 4,798,831 | 4,533,920 | 4,343,178 |
| WC | 582,532 | 508,372 | 359,230 |
| Emp. | 77 | 70 | 66 |

DUNS 21-782-1962
## Willowbrook School
Summer Lane, Exeter, Devon EX4 8NN
**Tel:** 01392466208
**Web:** www.willowbrook.devon.sch.uk
**Estd:** 2011 Proprietorship
**Line of Business:** Schools (local authority)
**Proprietor:** Mrs M Marlow
**US SIC:** 8211 **UK SIC:** 93200
**Employees:** 50

DUNS 21-685-9046
## Willowburn Sports & Leisure Centre
Willowburn Avenue, Alnwick, Northumberland NE66 2JH
**Tel:** 01665-605030
**Web:** www.activenorthumberland.org.uk
**Estd:** 2002 Proprietorship
**Line of Business:** Other sporting activities not elsewhere classified
**Proprietor:** P Halliwell
**Responsibilities**
**Senior:** Peter Halliwell *(Manager)*
**US SIC:** 7999 **UK SIC:** 97913
**Bankers:** Barclays Bank Plc (20-58-17)
**Employees:** 50

DUNS 21-781-3918
## Willowmead Residential Care Homes
Wickham Bishops Road, Hatfield Peverel, Chelmsford, Essex CM3 2JL
**Tel:** 01245381787
**Web:** www.goldcarehomes.com
**Estd:** 2001 Partnership
**Line of Business:** Residential care establishments
**Partners:** R Gidar, S Gidar, J Gidar, Ms K Hirst
**Responsibilities**
**Senior:** Tracey Wash *(Manager)*
**US SIC:** 8321 **UK SIC:** 96111
**Employees:** 50

DUNS 21-580-6743
## The Willows Care Centre
14-16 The Lant, Shepshed, Loughborough, Leicestershire LE12 9PD
**Web:** www.fshc.co.uk
**Estd:** 2006 Proprietorship
**Line of Business:** Nursing homes
**Proprietor:** Miss L Knowles
**US SIC:** 8051 **UK SIC:** 95100
**Employees:** 50

DUNS 21-223-6106
## The Willows Care Home
7 Norbriggs Road, Woodthorpe, Mastin Moor, Chesterfield, Derbyshire S43 3BW
**Tel:** 01246280539
**Web:** www.priorygroup.com
**Estd:** 1991
**Line of Business:** Residential care establishments
**Proprietor:** Miss T Godley
**Responsibilities**
**Senior:** William Duncan-Carr *(Food & Beverage Manager)*
**US SIC:** 8321 **UK SIC:** 96111
**Employees:** 50

DUNS 21-879-9358
## The Willows Care Uk
Woodside Resource Centre, Cavendish Road, Middlesbrough, Cleveland TS4 3EB
**Tel:** 01642828146
**Web:** www.careuk.com
**Estd:** 2012
**Line of Business:** Children's homes
**Responsibilities**
**Senior:** Helen Nutton *(Manager)*
**US SIC:** 8321 **UK SIC:** 96111
**Employees:** 70

DUNS 21-585-1548
## Willows Counselling Service
11 Prospect Place, Swindon, Wiltshire SN1 3LQ
**Tel:** 01793426650
**Web:** www.willowscounselling.org.uk
**Estd:** 2011 Proprietorship
**Line of Business:** Counselling & advice services
**Proprietor:** Mrs G Price
**Responsibilities**
**Senior:** Ron Headon *(Centre Manager)*
**US SIC:** 8321 **UK SIC:** 96111
**Employees:** 100

DUNS 21-207-0804
## The Willows Nursing & Residential Home
105-107 Coventry Road, Market Harborough, Leicestershire LE16 9BX
**Tel:** 01858463177
**Web:** www.willowsnursinghome.co.uk
**Estd:** 1981 Partnership
**Line of Business:** Clinics private
**Partners:** J Cooper, Mrs J Riddett, J Cooper, Mrs M V Cooper
**US SIC:** 8051, 6732
**UK SIC:** 95100, 83100
**Employees:** 50

DUNS 21-168-9422
## The Willows Nursing Home
Nevin Road, Blacon, Chester, Cheshire CH1 5RP
**Tel:** 01244-374023
**Web:** www.willows-carehome.co.uk
**Estd:** 1994 Partnership
**Line of Business:** Nursing homes
**Partners:** V Hussain, Mrs A Hussain, N Hussain, M Hussain
**Responsibilities**
**Senior:** Alison Plstlef *(Home Manager)*, Maria Sabo *(Home Manager)*
**US SIC:** 8051 **UK SIC:** 95100
**Employees:** 60

DUNS 22-955-0058
## Willstan Ltd
**(Subsidiary of:** William Hill Plc)
369 Newtownards Road, Belfast BT4 1AJ
**Tel:** 02890450925 **Fax:** 028-9046-0805
**Web:** www.williamhill.co.uk
**Reg No:** 0004101NI **Estd:** 1958 Private Limited Company
**Line of Business:** Gambling and betting activities
**Trading Style:** William Hall
**Issued Capital:** £176,130
**Director:** Ms J Whiteley
**Co. Secretary:** Dennis Read
**Branches:** Willstan Ltd, Charlotte St, Ballymoney, Co Antrim BT53 6AY
**US SIC:** 7999 **UK SIC:** 97913
**Auditors:** PricewaterhouseCoopers LLP

| | 31-12-13 | 01-01-13 | 27-12-11 |
|---|---|---|---|
| TO | 121,820,000 | 122,638,000 | 125,041,000 |
| P/L | 4,005,000 | 2,656,000 | 2,218,000 |
| NW | 40,105,000 | 36,064,000 | 33,417,000 |
| WC | 34,712,000 | 30,797,000 | 28,030,000 |

DUNS 73-268-2674
## Wilman Universal Group Ltd
Universal Buildings, Green Lane, Hounslow, Middlesex TW4 6DF
**Tel:** 02085704455
**Reg No:** 4542000 **Estd:** 2002 Private Limited Company
**Line of Business:** Other manufacturing not elsewhere classified
**Issued Capital:** £1,000
**Director:** R M Cook
**Co. Secretary:** Robert Cook
**US SIC:** 3999 **UK SIC:** 49590

| | 31-10-13 | 31-10-12 | 31-10-11 |
|---|---|---|---|
| TO | 20,666,539 | 19,733,238 | 23,378,077 |
| P/L | 390,320 | 334,893 | 152,211 |
| NW | 2,193,054 | 2,032,741 | 2,063,962 |
| WC | 2,268,366 | 1,363,100 | 1,639,160 |
| Emp. | 145 | 134 | 136 |

DUNS 21-323-2206
## Wilmington Grammar Sch for Boys
Wilmington Hall, Common Lane, Dartford, Kent DA2 7DA
**Tel:** 01322-223090
**Web:** www.wgsb.org.uk
**Estd:** 2002 Proprietorship
**Line of Business:** Schools (foundation)
**Proprietor:** A Williamson
**US SIC:** 8211 **UK SIC:** 93200
**Employees:** 80

DUNS 21-733-3734
## Wilmington Grammar School for Girls
Wilmington Grange Parsons Lane, Wilmington, Dartford, Kent DA2 7BB
**Tel:** 01322226351
**Web:** www.wgsg.co.uk
**Reg No:** 7682332 **Estd:** 2011 Private Company Limited By Guarantee
**Line of Business:** General secondary education
**Directors:** R S Sandu, A J Smith, P J Hammond, Ms B J Clark, Ms M Dooley, J E Price, G Rogers, A Ojo
**Co. Secretary:** Ronald Dale
**Responsibilities**
**Senior:** George Benson *(Director)*, Diane Connell *(Director)*, Sara Kemsley *(Director)*, Donna Lodge *(Head Teacher)*, Peter Mcrae *(Director)*
**US SIC:** 8211 **UK SIC:** 93200
**Bankers:** Lloyds TSB Bank plc (30-00-00)

| | 31-08-14 | 31-08-13 | 31-08-12 |
|---|---|---|---|
| TO | 4,378,000 | 4,933,000 | 14,192,000 |
| P/L | 28,000 | 664,000 | 9,173,000 |
| NW | 9,807,000 | 9,720,000 | 9,078,000 |
| WC | 798,000 | 753,000 | 753,000 |
| Emp. | 74 | 72 | 68 |

DUNS 77-751-3367 **Exp**
## Wilmington Group Plc
6-14 Underwood Street, London EC2A 2BS
**Web:** www.wilmington.co.uk
**Reg No:** 3015847 **Estd:** 1995 Public Limited Company
**Line of Business:** Management activities of holding companies
**Export Markets:** Overseas
**Export Sales:** £32,889,000
**Trading Style:** International Company Profile (Icp)
**Issued Capital:** £4,305,157
**Directors:** M Asplin, D R Carter, P Ros, Ms N E Schwarz, C J Brady, T B Garthwaite, A M Foye
**Co. Secretary:** Ms Linda Wake
**Responsibilities**
**Senior:** Richard Cockton *(Manager)*, Kasia Rafalat *(Manager)*
**Finance:** Richard Cockton *(Manager)*
**Marketing:** Tanya Noronha *(Senior Marketing Executive)*
**Sales:** Paula Pusey *(Senior Sales Executive)*
**IT:** Mike Kent *(Head of IT)*, Jason Philpott *(Senior IT Executive)*
**Branches:** Wilmington Group Plc, Po Box 100, CT10 1UJ Broadstairs
**US SIC:** 6711, 2721
**UK SIC:** 83962, 47522
**Auditors:** PricewaterhouseCoopers LLP
**Bankers:** Barclays Bank Plc (20-20-62)

| | 30-06-14 | 30-06-13 | 30-06-12 |
|---|---|---|---|
| TO | 90,024,000 | 85,048,000 | 85,326,000 |
| P/L | 8,592,000 | 5,116,000 | 6,328,000 |
| NW | (53,192,000) | (53,206,000) | (54,519,000) |
| WC | (15,585,000) | (12,125,000) | (15,816,000) |
| Emp. | 850 | 804 | 819 |

DUNS 50-587-5328
## Wilmington Healthcare Ltd
**(Subsidiary of:** Wilmington Group Plc)
Beechwood House, Basildon, Essex SS15 6EF
**Tel:** 01268-495600
**Web:** www.binleys.com
**Reg No:** 2530185 **Estd:** 1991 Private Limited Company
**Line of Business:** Database development services
**Trading Style:** Binleys
**Issued Capital:** £100
**Principals:** Mrs A Brinzer *(Managing)*, Ms L A Wake, A M Foye, P Ros
**Co. Secretary:** Daniel Barton

**Responsibilities**
**Senior:** Steve Bint *(Warehouse Manager)*, Amy Brinzer *(Manager)*, Walter Brinzer *(Manager)*, Richard Cockton *(Manager)*, Rory Conwell *(Manager)*, Sarah Drury *(Senior Sales Executive)*, Ajay Taneja *(Manager)*
**Marketing:** Sarah Eglington *(Marketing Manager)*
**Sales:** Sarah Drury *(Senior Sales Executive)*
**Admin:** Yvonne Arnold *(Office Manager)*, Jane Grace *(Office Manager)*
**IT:** James Hollington *(Systems Support Technician)*
**HR:** Yvonne Arnold *(Office Manager)*, Jane Grace *(Office Manager)*
**US SIC:** 7374, 8999
**UK SIC:** 83940, 83954
**Auditors:** PKF
**Bankers:** Lloyds TSB Bank plc (30-96-09)

| | 30-06-13 | 30-06-12 | 30-06-11 |
|---|---|---|---|
| TO | 7,499,221 | 8,017,719 | 7,435,664 |
| P/L | 1,032,218 | 1,128,116 | 532,085 |
| NW | 1,049,078 | 1,399,423 | 2,970,792 |
| WC | 525,539 | 790,287 | 2,319,181 |
| Emp. | 116 | 117 | 117 |

DUNS 42-343-3762
## Wilmington Manor Nursing Home
Common Lane, Dartford, Kent DA2 7BA
**Tel:** 01322288746
**Web:** www.bupa.co.uk
**Estd:** 1992 Proprietorship
**Line of Business:** Nursing homes
**Proprietor:** Miss M Bazeley
**US SIC:** 8051 **UK SIC:** 95100
**Employees:** 70

DUNS 52-001-3699 **Imp**
## Wilmington Publishing & Information Ltd
**(Subsidiary of:** Wilmington Group Plc)
6-14 Underwood Street, London N1 7JQ
**Tel:** 02074900049 **Fax:** 01207-566 8318
**Web:** www.icpcredit.com
**Reg No:** 3368442 **VAT No:** 899372551
**Estd:** 1997 Private Limited Company
**Line of Business:** Publishing of books
**Export Sales:** £2,676,138
**Trading Style:** International Company Profile
**Issued Capital:** £50,000
**Directors:** A M Foye, P Ros, Ms L A Wake
**Co. Secretary:** Daniel Barton
**Responsibilities**
**Senior:** Richard Cockton *(Manager)*
**US SIC:** 2731, 2721
**UK SIC:** 47532, 47522
**Auditors:** PricewaterhouseCoopers LLP
**Bankers:** Barclays Bank Plc (20-20-62)

| | 30-06-13 | 30-06-12 | 30-06-11 |
|---|---|---|---|
| TO | 14,426,005 | 18,079,123 | 19,194,341 |
| P/L | 2,992,924 | 1,550,740 | 4,309,008 |
| NW | (13,647,953) | (16,819,732) | (18,148,943) |
| WC | (41,248,872) | (44,603,056) | (45,395,587) |
| Emp. | 174 | 240 | 247 |

DUNS 73-287-2440
## Wilmoths Holdings Ltd
91-93 Eastbourne Road, Willingdon, Eastbourne, East Sussex BN20 9NR
**Tel:** 01323-488000
**Web:** www.wilmoths.co.uk
**Reg No:** 4561051 **Estd:** 2002 Private Limited Company
**Line of Business:** Sale of new motor vehicles
**Export Sales:** £50,887
**Issued Capital:** £100
**Directors:** D Froude, J J Wilmoth
**Co. Secretary:** Ms Zoe Wilmoth
**US SIC:** 5511 **UK SIC:** 65100

| | 31-12-13 | 31-12-12 | 31-12-11 |
|---|---|---|---|
| TO | 39,573,866 | 32,427,115 | 30,984,378 |
| P/L | 546,663 | 303,294 | 252,618 |
| NW | 3,499,261 | 3,097,119 | 2,886,538 |
| WC | (1,931,912) | (2,175,028) | (1,330,433) |
| Emp. | 90 | 80 | 83 |

DUNS 29-582-4361 **Imp**
## Wilo (U.K.) Ltd
**(Subsidiary of:** Caspar Ludwig Opländer Stiftung)
Second Avenue, Burton-On-Trent, Staffordshire DE14 2WJ
**Tel:** 01283523000 **Fax:** 01283-523099
**Web:** www.wilo.co.uk
**Reg No:** 1944189 **VAT No:** 428445049
**Estd:** 1985 Private Limited Company
**Line of Business:** Pumps sales and servicing
**Issued Capital:** £500,000
**Directors:** A J O'Brien, G A Mannus, M Stiebing
**Co. Secretary:** Andrew O'Brien
**US SIC:** 5084 **UK SIC:** 61490
**Auditors:** BDO Stoy Hayward
**Bankers:** Barclays Bank Plc (20-25-85)

| | 31-12-13 | 31-12-12 | 31-12-11 |
|---|---|---|---|
| TO | 20,371,095 | 18,385,834 | 16,401,998 |
| P/L | 1,214,916 | 802,990 | 357,945 |
| NW | 2,110,004 | 1,716,268 | 932,775 |
| WC | 1,509,264 | 962,312 | (64,480) |
| Emp. | 88 | 88 | 88 |

DUNS 23-503-6188
## Wilson & Co. (Motor Sales) Ltd
Hewitts Avenue, Humberston, Grimsby, South Humberside DN36 4SE
**Tel:** 01472-290290 **Fax:** 01472-699991
**Web:** www.wilsonandco.com
**Reg No:** 3503183 **Estd:** 1992 Private Limited Company
**Line of Business:** Sale of new motor vehicles
**Trading Style:** Wilson & Co
**Issued Capital:** £1,047,477
**Directors:** R Wilson, Motors Directors Limited
**Co. Secretary:** Motors Secretaries Limited
**Responsibilities**
**Senior:** Darren Bradford *(Manager)*, Keith West *(Manager)*
**IT:** Simon Keyworth *(Computer Manager)*
**Branches:** Wilson & Co. (Motor Sales) Ltd, Standish Street, Chorley, Lancashire PR7 3AH
**US SIC:** 5511 **UK SIC:** 65100
**Auditors:** Grant Thornton
**Bankers:** National Westminster Bank Plc (60-70-08)

| | 31-12-13 | 31-12-12 | 31-12-11 |
|---|---|---|---|
| TO | 66,890,970 | 69,084,585 | 66,688,511 |
| P/L | 884,924 | 955,681 | 627,932 |
| NW | 3,574,083 | 3,153,324 | 2,612,443 |
| WC | 839,775 | 536,588 | 110,689 |
| Emp. | 233 | 199 | 207 |

DUNS 21-161-7849
## Wilson Browne Llp
41 Meadow Road, Kettering, Northamptonshire NN16 8TL
**Tel:** 01536-410041
**Web:** www.wilsonbrowne.co.uk
**Reg No:** 0345105OC **Estd:** 2009 Private Limited Company
**Line of Business:** Solicitors
**Responsibilities**
**Senior:** Laura Carter *(Non-designated Limited Liabili)*, Jane Forsyth *(Non-designated Limited Liabili)*, Rachel Hawkins *(Non-designated Limited Liabili)*, Neelam Maher *(Non-designated Limited Liabili)*, Deena Tate *(Non-designated Limited Liabili)*, Louise Tyler *(Non-designated Limited Liabili)*, Helen York *(Non-designated Limited Liabili)*
**US SIC:** 8111 **UK SIC:** 83500
**Bankers:** Barclays Bank Plc (20-45-77)

| | 31-03-14 | 31-03-13 | 31-03-12 |
|---|---|---|---|
| TO | 6,515,820 | 5,772,889 | 6,280,689 |
| P/L | 8,547 | 1,611 | 151 |
| NW | N/A | N/A | (2,500) |
| WC | 2,495,920 | 2,097,130 | 1,882,902 |
| Emp. | 136 | 139 | 161 |

DUNS 50-439-4222
## Wilson Construction Ltd
Salcoats House, 37-43 Cutlers Road, Chelmsford, Essex CM3 5WA
**Tel:** 01245-428282
**Web:** www.wilsonconstruction.com
**Reg No:** 2427375 **VAT No:** 466010766
**Estd:** 1989 Private Limited Company
**Line of Business:** Groundwork contractors
**Issued Capital:** £1,000
**Managing Director:** C B Wilson
**Co. Secretary:** Mrs Sharon Wilson
**US SIC:** 1622 **UK SIC:** 50200
**Auditors:** Carlton Baker Clarke Ltd
**Bankers:** Barclays Bank Plc (20-79-73)

| | 31-03-14 | 31-03-13 | 31-03-12 |
|---|---|---|---|
| TA | 786,993 | 526,079 | 549,729 |
| NW | 359,007 | 305,246 | 313,642 |
| WC | 336,331 | 280,801 | 287,199 |

DUNS 22-502-0163
## Wilson Electrical Distributors Ltd
2 Balfour Road Balfour Business Centre, Southall, Middlesex UB2 5BD
**Tel:** 02085744218 **Fax:** 01483454722
**Web:** www.wilsonelectrical.com
**Reg No:** 1479269 **VAT No:** 225512687
**Estd:** 1982 Private Limited Company
**Line of Business:** Wholesale of radio and television goods; wholesale of electrical household appliances not elsewhere classified
**Issued Capital:** £54,600
**Directors:** P Davies, D R Williams
**Co. Secretary:** Alexander Powell
**Responsibilities**
**Senior:** Brian Woodley *(General Manager)*
**Branches:** Wilson Electrical Distributors Ltd, 7 North Lane, Aldershot, Hampshire GU12 4QF
**US SIC:** 5064, 5074
**UK SIC:** 61500, 61300
**Auditors:** Morgan Brown & Spofforth
**Bankers:** HSBC Bank plc (40-42-13)

| | 31-03-14 | 31-03-13 | 31-03-12 |
|---|---|---|---|
| TO | 15,024,557 | 14,107,613 | 14,243,771 |
| P/L | 874,832 | 798,791 | 692,237 |
| NW | 3,911,944 | 3,232,072 | 2,623,281 |
| WC | 2,772,517 | 2,305,430 | 2,055,518 |
| Emp. | 65 | 62 | 58 |

DUNS 21-858-4269
## Wilson Field Group Ltd
The Manor House, 260 Ecclesall Road South, Sheffield, South Yorkshire S11 9PS
**Tel:** 08724365592
**Reg No:** 8212364 **Estd:** 2012 Private Limited Company
**Line of Business:** Management activities of holding companies
**Issued Capital:** £1,000
**Directors:** Ms L Hogg, N J Wilson, Ms J Fantom
**US SIC:** 6711 **UK SIC:** 83962
**Bankers:** Chelsea Building Society (08-02-55)

| | 31-08-13 |
|---|---|
| TO | 6,324,389 |
| P/L | 152,158 |
| NW | 902,317 |
| WC | 655,198 |
| Emp. | 95 |

DUNS 34-604-3979
## Wilson Gibb Management Services Ltd
**(Subsidiary of:** F & D Holdings Ltd)
31-33 Albert Street, Motherwell, Lanarkshire ML1 1PR
**Tel:** 01698275444
**Web:** www.driverhire.co.uk
**Reg No:** 0140165SC **Estd:** 1992 Private Limited Company
**Line of Business:** Labour recruitment and provision of personnel
**Trading Style:** D H Workforce, Driver Hire
**Issued Capital:** £36,000
**Director:** D A Gibb
**Co. Secretary:** Ms Fiona Thompson
**Responsibilities**
**Operations:** Stevie Thompson *(Operations Manager)*
**US SIC:** 7361 **UK SIC:** 83954
**Bankers:** Bank Of Scotland (80-12-39)

| | 31-03-14 | 31-03-13 | 31-03-12 |
|---|---|---|---|
| TO | 7,244,975 | 5,970,880 | 5,708,689 |
| P/L | 271,721 | (224,224) | 40,614 |
| NW | 3,192,571 | 2,984,485 | 3,156,146 |
| WC | 3,302,583 | 3,094,953 | 3,269,478 |
| Emp. | 287 | 288 | 401 |

DUNS 23-453-3185
## Wilson Gunn
5th Floor, Manchester M3 2JA
**Tel:** 01618279400
**Web:** www.wilsongunn.com
**Estd:** 1999 Proprietorship
**Line of Business:** Activities of patent and copyright agents
**Proprietor:** A Bubb
**Responsibilities**
**Senior:** David Slattery *(Partner)*
**Admin:** Clare Nicholson *(Head of Human Resources)*
**HR:** Clare Nicholson *(Head of Human Resources)*
**Health & Safety:** Mary Rowlinson *(Head of Facilities)*
**Facilities:** Mary Rowlinson *(Head of Facilities)*
**US SIC:** 7399 **UK SIC:** 83954
**Employees:** 48

DUNS 21-227-1643
## Wilson Hospital
Cranmer Road, Mitcham, Surrey CR4 4TP
**Tel:** 020-86483021
**Web:** www.nhs.uk
**Estd:** 2000
**Line of Business:** Hospitals
**Trading Style:** Wilson Hospital
**Proprietor:** J Welch
**Responsibilities**
**Facilities:** Steve Curran *(Head of Facilities)*
**US SIC:** 8062 **UK SIC:** 95100
**Employees:** 125

DUNS 77-500-8469
## Wilson Imports Ltd
**(Subsidiary of:** Iain Wilson Holdings Ltd)
1 Queen Elizabeth Avenue, Hillington Industrial Estate, Hillington Park, Glasgow, Lanarkshire G52 4NQ
**Web:** www.wilsonimports.net
**Reg No:** 0153737SC **VAT No:** 652947996
**Estd:** 1994 Private Limited Company
**Line of Business:** Import and export agents
**Issued Capital:** £2
**Managing Director:** I Wilson
**Co. Secretary:** Mrs Maureen Wilson
**Responsibilities**
**Senior:** Lynn Mcneilage *(Proprietor)*
**Branches:** Wilson Imports Ltd, Cotswold Enterprise Centre, Unit 4, Luton, Bedfordshire LU1 4AJ
**US SIC:** 5136, 5139, 7399
**UK SIC:** 61600, 83954
**Auditors:** Grant Thornton UK LLP
**Bankers:** HSBC Bank plc (40-22-47)

| | 31-12-13 | 31-12-12 | 31-12-11 |
|---|---|---|---|
| TO | 49,934,866 | 41,096,416 | 32,563,424 |
| P/L | 1,359,216 | 795,789 | 116,352 |
| NW | 2,261,893 | 910,976 | 2,308,587 |
| WC | 2,801,117 | 751,538 | 2,392,775 |
| Emp. | 88 | 72 | 62 |

DUNS 28-859-3916
## Wilson Insurance Broking Group Ltd
Wilson House, 1-3 Waverley Street, Nottingham, Nottinghamshire NG7 4HG
**Fax:** 01159-420459
**Web:** www.wilorg.com
**Reg No:** 0862690 **Estd:** 1965 Private Limited Company
**Line of Business:** Insurance brokers
**Issued Capital:** £1,100
**Directors:** Sir C D Naish, Miss C J Perkins, G A Cormack, Ms A K Prow, J J Prow
**Co. Secretary:** Ms Olga Prow
**Responsibilities**
**Senior:** Ian Baguley *(Manager)*, Roy Costa *(Manager)*, Charlotte Prow *(Manager)*
**Finance:** Richard Dilley *(Finance Manager)*
**Marketing:** Ped Briggs *(Markting manager)*
**Sales:** Mike Reed *(Account Director)*
**US SIC:** 6411 **UK SIC:** 83200
**Auditors:** Clayton & Brewill
**Bankers:** National Westminster Bank Plc (60-80-09)

| | 31-03-14 | 31-03-13 | 31-03-12 |
|---|---|---|---|
| TO | 3,165,908 | 3,274,869 | 3,432,387 |
| P/L | 7,764 | 39,563 | 13,941 |
| NW | (2,109,588) | (1,893,242) | (1,777,836) |
| WC | (151,539) | (157,392) | (93,701) |
| Emp. | 48 | 54 | 64 |

DUNS 39-970-3495
## Wilson James Ltd
**(Subsidiary of:** Wilson James Group Ltd)
648-656 London Road, Westcliff-On-Sea, Essex SS0 9HR
**Tel:** 01702-346222
**Web:** www.wilsonjames.co.uk
**Reg No:** 2269560 **VAT No:** 546153938
**Estd:** 1988 Private Limited Company
**Line of Business:** Other construction work involving special trades
**Issued Capital:** £25,000
**Principals:** M R Dobson *(Managing)*, G Sullivan, S D Lowden
**Co. Secretary:** Mark Abraham
**Responsibilities**
**Admin:** Hayley Lord *(Business Systems Administrator)*
**IT:** James Carruthers *(Computer Administrator)*, Hayley Lord *(Business Systems Administrator)*
**HR:** Gemma Quirke *(Human Resources Director)*
**Health & Safety:** Sean McKeeman *(Health & Safety Officer)*
**Fleet:** Ron Dickin *(Operations Director-Security S)*
**Branches:** Wilson James Ltd, Edward House, Cores End Road, Bourne End, Buckinghamshire SL8 5AL
**US SIC:** 1799, 7393
**UK SIC:** 50000, 83954
**Auditors:** KPMG LLP
**Bankers:** Lloyds TSB Bank plc (30-91-85)

| | 31-07-14 | 31-07-13 | 31-07-12 |
|---|---|---|---|
| TO | 104,566,000 | 112,490,000 | 100,150,000 |
| P/L | 2,365,000 | 3,463,000 | 3,874,000 |
| NW | 16,547,000 | 14,556,000 | 11,629,000 |
| WC | 15,196,000 | 13,835,000 | 12,367,000 |
| Emp. | 2,652 | 3,053 | 2,630 |

DUNS 23-985-1165
## Wilson Nesbitt
Albert Street, Belfast BT12 4HQ
**Tel:** 028-9032-3864
**Web:** www.wilsonnesbitt.com
**Estd:** 1982 Partnership
**Line of Business:** Solicitors
**Partners:** G Nesbitt, P Hunt, J Young, C Worthington
**Branches:** Wilson Nesbitt, 33 Hamilton Road, Bangor, Co Down BT20 4LF
**US SIC:** 8111, 7392
**UK SIC:** 83500, 83951
**Bankers:** First Trust Bank (aib Group (uk) Plc) (93-82-03)
**Employees:** 90

DUNS 51-601-6701 **Imp**

## Wilson Tool International Europe Ltd

(**Subsidiary of:** Wilson Tool International Inc.)
Unit B2 Stirling Court, Stirling Road, South Marston Industrial Estate, Swindon, Wiltshire SN3 4TQ
**Tel:** 01793829060 **Fax:** 01793831945
**Web:** www.wilsontool.com
**Reg No:** 5882186 **Estd:** 2006 Private Limited Company
**Line of Business:** Builders merchants
**Export Sales:** £16,338,990
**Issued Capital:** £42
**Directors:** B Robinson, C Blackwell
**Co. Secretary:** Richard Renner
**Responsibilities**
**Senior:** James Bin *(Manager)*, Ian Mccartney *(Business Manager)*
**Sales:** Ian Mccartney *(Business Manager)*
**US SIC:** 5072 **UK SIC:** 61500

| | 31-12-13 | 31-12-12 | 31-12-11 |
|---|---|---|---|
| TO | 19,347,491 | 18,349,227 | 19,114,666 |
| P/L | 424,207 | 1,195,971 | 1,964,037 |
| NW | 15,070,805 | 14,867,582 | 14,292,774 |
| WC | 8,614,058 | 8,442,413 | 8,324,774 |
| Emp. | 183 | 182 | 157 |

DUNS 22-288-0481

## Wilson Vale Catering Management Ltd

Unit 1, Ivanhoe Office Park, Ivanhoe Park Way, Ashby-De-La-Zouch, Leicestershire LE65 2AB
**Tel:** 01530-563100 **Fax:** 01530-563023
**Web:** www.wilsonvale.co.uk
**Reg No:** 4306005 **Estd:** 2002 Private Limited Company
**Line of Business:** Catering
**Issued Capital:** £52,631
**Directors:** A S Wilson, Ms C J Vale
**Co. Secretary:** Ms Esther Brookes
**Responsibilities**
**Senior:** Marion Speed *(Development Manager)*
**Marketing:** Marion Speed *(Development Manager)*
**US SIC:** 5812 **UK SIC:** 66110
**Auditors:** BSN Associates Ltd

| | 31-12-13 | 31-12-12 | 31-12-11 |
|---|---|---|---|
| TO | 18,030,166 | 17,150,458 | 15,129,604 |
| P/L | 1,275,533 | 1,090,468 | 837,053 |
| NW | 932,924 | 537,070 | 331,448 |
| WC | 427,618 | 200,661 | 165,301 |
| Emp. | 505 | 486 | 466 |

DUNS 21-482-3168

## Wilsons Auction

6 Kilwinning Road, Dalry, Ayrshire KA24 4LG
**Tel:** 01294-833444
**Web:** www.wilsonsauctions.com
**Estd:** 1997 Proprietorship
**Line of Business:** Other business activities not elsewhere classified
**Proprietor:** G Wilson
**Responsibilities**
**Senior:** Stephanie Benton *(General Manager)*
**Marketing:** David Keenan *(IT Operations)*
**Sales:** Gillian Frew *(Auction Support)*, Matt Peden *(Property Department Executive)*, Leanne Sherrie *(Auction Support)*, Marion Watson *(Auction Support Manager)*, Claire Wilson *(Auction Support)*
**US SIC:** 7399 **UK SIC:** 83954
**Employees:** 50

DUNS 22-928-8675

## Wilson's Auctions Ltd

22 Mallusk Road, Newtownabbey, Co Antrim BT36 4PP
**Tel:** 02890342626 **Fax:** 02890342528
**Web:** www.wilsonsauctions.com
**Reg No:** 0011967NI **Estd:** 2012 Private Limited Company
**Line of Business:** Auctioneers and valuers
**Export Sales:** £2,116,065
**Issued Capital:** £20
**Directors:** F Wilson, Ms R Wilson, P A Johnston, G Wilson, A M Wilson, C Wilson
**Co. Secretary:** Ian Wilson
**Responsibilities**
**Senior:** John Ardill *(Fleet Manager)*
**Sales:** John Ardill *(Fleet Manager)*, Grace Fenton *(Auction Support)*, Maeve Heaney *(Auction Support)*, Richard McFetridge *(Plant, Machinery & Commercial)*, Craig Walker *(Auction Support Manager)*
**Branches:** Wilson's Auctions Ltd, Lynn Holms, Kilwinning Road, Dalry, Ayrshire KA24 4LB
**US SIC:** 7399 **UK SIC:** 83954
**Auditors:** Hanna Thompson

**Bankers:** Northern Bank Ltd (95-01-01)

| | 31-03-14 | 31-03-13 | 31-03-12 |
|---|---|---|---|
| TO | 10,853,753 | 10,441,183 | 9,140,716 |
| P/L | 292,827 | 1,537,270 | 724,544 |
| NW | 5,542,433 | 6,842,287 | 8,214,076 |
| WC | (5,073,001) | (3,478,249) | (3,515,476) |
| Emp. | 145 | 143 | 141 |

DUNS 21-032-0826

## Wilsons Automobiles & Coachworks Ltd

Nonsuch Industrial Estate, Kiln Lane, Epsom, Surrey KT17 1DH
**Tel:** 01372736000
**Web:** www.wilsons.co.uk
**Reg No:** 0272743 **Estd:** 1904 Private Limited Company
**Line of Business:** Car dealers (new & used)
**Issued Capital:** £164,100
**Principals:** I A Wilson *(Chairman)*, P Turner, T Wilson, J P Butler, W Gumienny, Ms M Fenwick, D M Wheatcroft, Mrs G Storr
**Co. Secretary:** Mrs Teresa Wilson
**Branches:** Wilsons Automobiles & Coachworks Ltd, Unit 1, 137 Holywood Road, Belfast, Belfast BT4 3BE
**US SIC:** 5511, 5521
**UK SIC:** 65100
**Auditors:** Simpson Wreford & Partners
**Bankers:** Barclays Bank Plc (20-82-94)

| | 31-12-13 | 31-12-12 | 31-12-11 |
|---|---|---|---|
| TO | 74,867,585 | 61,319,518 | 60,677,517 |
| P/L | 2,277,877 | 686,684 | 439,069 |
| NW | 19,221,192 | 17,492,762 | 16,997,507 |
| WC | 7,107,041 | 6,203,597 | 5,469,330 |
| Emp. | 193 | 199 | 209 |

DUNS 42-471-6868

## Wilsons Country Ltd

(**Subsidiary of:** Joyus Investments Ltd)
25 Carn Road, Portadown, Craigavon, Co Armagh BT63 5WG
**Tel:** 028-3839-1029 **Fax:** 028-3839-1042
**Web:** www.wilsonscountry.com
**Reg No:** 0025583NI **Estd:** 1991 Private Limited Company
**Line of Business:** Other retail sale of food, beverages and tobacco in specialised stores
**Issued Capital:** £25,706
**Directors:** L H Cunningham, A Wilson, Ms J Wilson
**Co. Secretary:** Ian Gibson
**Responsibilities**
**Senior:** Norman Forbes *(Manager)*, William Lochart *(Manager)*
**Marketing:** Joanne Weir *(Senior Marketing Executive)*
**Sales:** Ruth Pollock *(Senior Sales Executive)*
**IT:** Ryan Cosgrove *(IT Manager)*
**Operations:** Gillian Garvin *(Technical, Production Manager)*
**Purchasing:** Brian Lockhart *(Purchasing Manager)*
**US SIC:** 5499 **UK SIC:** 64100
**Auditors:** Flynn Moore

| | 27-07-13 | 31-07-12 | 31-07-11 |
|---|---|---|---|
| TO | 17,596,890 | 13,387,780 | 16,010,582 |
| P/L | (165,005) | 271,277 | 519,535 |
| NW | 5,326,118 | 5,654,228 | 5,508,166 |
| WC | (835,234) | (850,335) | (641,520) |
| Emp. | 81 | 92 | 116 |

DUNS 29-845-1501 **Imp-Exp**

## Wilsons Ltd

(**Subsidiary of:** Henley Management Company)
Old North Road, Huntingdon, Cambridgeshire PE28 5XN
**Tel:** 01487833600 **Fax:** 01480-456425
**Web:** www.wilsonsmetals.com
**Reg No:** 2048485 **Estd:** 1986 Private Limited Company
**Line of Business:** Wholesale of metals and ores
**Export Markets:** Italy; U S A; Middle East
**Export Sales:** £1,811,866
**Trading Style:** Amari Metals
**Issued Capital:** £50,002
**Directors:** R W Colburn, J E Digby, B A King
**Co. Secretary:** Mrs Morag Hale
**Responsibilities**
**Senior:** Colin Fairman *(Manager)*, Morag Thorpe *(Manager)*
**Sales:** Cathy Garrett *(Sales Executive)*, Angela Marsden *(Sales Executive)*
**Purchasing:** Ashley Brand *(Buyer)*
**Branches:** Wilsons Ltd, Unit 5 & 6 Webb Ind Est, 49-53 Sutherland Rd, Waithamstow, London E17 6BJ
**US SIC:** 5051, 5199
**UK SIC:** 61200, 61900
**Auditors:** Grant Thornton UK LLP
**Bankers:** HSBC Bank plc (40-45-27)

| | 31-12-13 | 31-12-12 | 31-12-11 |
|---|---|---|---|
| TO | 15,785,117 | 15,553,258 | 13,892,280 |
| P/L | (645,574) | 598,182 | 934,568 |
| NW | 10,440,814 | 10,988,256 | 15,041,719 |
| WC | 9,964,938 | 10,561,772 | 14,671,475 |
| Emp. | N/A | 74 | 72 |

DUNS 21-458-7313 **Imp**

## Wilsons of Rathkenny Ltd

381 Cushendall Road, Ballymena, Co Antrim BT43 6QB
**Tel:** 028-2175-8261
**Web:** www.wilsonsofrathkenny.co.uk
**Reg No:** 0006176NI **Estd:** 1964 Private Limited Company
**Line of Business:** New & used motor vehicle dealers
**Trading Style:** Wilsons of Rathkenny Ltd
**Issued Capital:** £20,345
**Directors:** D Wilson, J Wilson
**Co. Secretary:** Ms Mary Wilson
**Branches:** Wilsons Of Rathkenny Ltd, 381 Cushendall Rd, Ballymena, Co Antrim BT43 6QB
**US SIC:** 5511, 5521, 7539
**UK SIC:** 65100, 67100
**Auditors:** Wilsons
**Bankers:** First Trust Bank (aib Group (uk) Plc) (93-80-17)

| | 31-12-13 | 31-12-12 | 31-12-11 |
|---|---|---|---|
| TO | 29,770,970 | 24,234,470 | 21,893,101 |
| P/L | 757,961 | 253,927 | 248,262 |
| NW | 7,836,871 | 7,297,923 | 7,152,781 |
| WC | 1,410,576 | 910,364 | 868,557 |
| Emp. | 74 | 74 | 75 |

DUNS 21-714-3054

## Wilson's School

Mollison Drive, Wallington, Surrey SM6 9JW
**Tel:** 02087732931
**Web:** www.wilsonsschool.sutton.sch.uk
**Reg No:** 7536970 **Estd:** 2011 Private Company Limited By Guarantee
**Line of Business:** Schools (local authority)
**Directors:** R S Allen, N J Gardner, D Eynon, M G Creamore, C R Peckover, Ms E A Nash, T Kimber, I M Bawa
**Co. Secretary:** Caitlin Lowe
**Responsibilities**
**Senior:** Beverley Barry *(Director)*, Susan Billin *(Director)*, D Charnock *(Head Teacher)*, Ian Downes *(Director)*, Bozena Mcmillan *(Director)*, Julian Pearcey *(Director)*, Marek Polniaszek *(Director)*, Lynne Smithard *(Director)*, Stephen Wisson *(Director)*
**US SIC:** 8211, 8221
**UK SIC:** 93200, 93100
**Bankers:** HSBC Bank plc (40-18-41)

| | 31-08-14 | 31-08-13 | 31-08-12 |
|---|---|---|---|
| TO | 6,959,693 | 6,448,101 | 6,310,474 |
| P/L | 738,239 | 76,359 | (7,026) |
| NW | (253,655) | (566,894) | (643,253) |
| WC | 355,766 | 372,024 | 316,278 |
| Emp. | 96 | 97 | 97 |

DUNS 21-000-9948

## Wilsons Solicitors Llp

Steynings House, Summerlock Approach, Salisbury, Wiltshire SP2 7RJ
**Tel:** 01722-412412
**Web:** www.wilsonslaw.com
**Reg No:** 0328787OC **Estd:** 2007 Private Limited Company
**Line of Business:** Solicitors
**Responsibilities**
**Senior:** Timothy Clayden *(Partner)*, Adam Herbert *(Non-designated Limited Liabili)*, Jane Lonergan *(Non-designated Limited Liabili)*, Andrew O'Keefe *(Non-designated Limited Liabili)*, Dominic Ogden *(Non-designated Limited Liabili)*, Moira Protani *(Non-designated Limited Liabili)*, James Ritchie *(Non-designated Limited Liabili)*, Peter Steer *(Partner)*, Belinda Watson *(Non-designated Limited Liabili)*, Charlotte Watts *(Non-designated Limited Liabili)*, Torsten White *(Non-designated Limited Liabili)*
**US SIC:** 8111 **UK SIC:** 83500
**Bankers:** Barclays Bank Plc (20-33-83)

| | 30-04-14 | 30-04-13 | 30-04-12 |
|---|---|---|---|
| TO | 12,552,132 | 11,831,183 | 12,694,987 |
| P/L | 4,272,988 | 2,276,641 | 3,152,413 |
| NW | 3,832,383 | 2,330,036 | 3,616,848 |
| WC | 6,620,372 | 2,925,961 | 5,303,370 |
| Emp. | 125 | 140 | 144 |

DUNS 22-803-3601

## Wiltel Ltd

Royal Square, Bowness On Windermere, Windermere, Cumbria LA23 3EB
**Tel:** 01539-443060
**Web:** www.hyltens.co.uk
**Reg No:** 0883435 **Estd:** 1966 Private Limited Company
**Line of Business:** Restaurants
**Trading Style:** Gibbys Restaurant
**Issued Capital:** £3,200
**Principals:** I P Wilson *(Managing)*, M K Wilson, S T Wilson
**Co. Secretary:** Kevin Wilson
**Responsibilities**
**Senior:** Sarah Taylforth *(General Manager)*
**Branches:** Wiltel Ltd, Ash St, Bowness On Windermere, Windermere, Cumbria LA23 3EB
**US SIC:** 5812 **UK SIC:** 66110
**Auditors:** Armstrong Watson

**Bankers:** Barclays Bank Plc (20-10-03)

| | 28-02-14 | 28-02-13 | 29-02-12 |
|---|---|---|---|
| TA | 3,329,480 | 3,072,245 | 2,896,561 |
| NW | 2,843,985 | 2,663,769 | 2,526,458 |
| WC | 1,489,118 | 1,435,603 | 1,261,397 |

DUNS 57-032-5498 **Imp-Exp**

## Wilton Bradley Ltd

Unit 8, Newton Abbot, Devon TQ12 6TL
**Tel:** 01626835400
**Web:** www.wiltonbradley.com
**Reg No:** 2873284 **VAT No:** 631120694
**Estd:** 1989 Private Limited Company
**Line of Business:** Mens & boys clothing wholesalers
**Export Sales:** £1,075,677
**Issued Capital:** £260,000
**Principals:** A W Bradley *(Managing)*, P K Arrowsmith
**Co. Secretary:** Mrs Leigh Cheetham
**US SIC:** 5136, 5199, 5399, 5961
**UK SIC:** 61600, 61900, 65600
**Auditors:** Francis Clark LLP
**Bankers:** Barclays Bank Plc (20-60-88)

| | 31-12-13 | 31-12-12 | 31-12-11 |
|---|---|---|---|
| TO | 17,714,701 | 16,247,524 | 17,909,601 |
| P/L | (134,604) | (46,138) | 576,003 |
| NW | 5,411,474 | 5,543,227 | 5,584,690 |
| WC | 1,954,137 | 2,111,907 | 2,285,308 |
| Emp. | 192 | 191 | 189 |

DUNS 73-705-9217

## The Wilton Carpet Factory Ltd

(**Subsidiary of:** Avon Valley Holdings Ltd)
The Wilton Shopping Village, Salisbury, Wiltshire SP2 0AY
**Tel:** 01722-746000
**Web:** www.wiltoncarpets.com
**Reg No:** 4964598 **VAT No:** 927298387
**Estd:** 2003 Private Limited Company
**Line of Business:** Manufacture of carpets and rugs
**Export Sales:** £949,066
**Trading Style:** Wilton Carpets Commercial
**Issued Capital:** £1
**Directors:** S M King, D Clemo, R H Load, A B Whittle, C S Brammall
**Co. Secretary:** Peter Le Count
**Responsibilities**
**Senior:** Terrence Rossitter *(Manager)*
**Sales:** Christopher Brammer *(Senior Sales Executive)*
**IT:** Andy Corkhill *(IT Manager)*
**US SIC:** 2279 **UK SIC:** 43852
**Auditors:** CW Fellowes Ltd

| | 31-08-13 | 01-09-12 | 03-08-11 |
|---|---|---|---|
| TO | 7,344,352 | 6,812,877 | N/A |
| P/L | 111,119 | 106,190 | N/A |
| NW | 565,352 | 475,081 | 392,069 |
| WC | 727,043 | 657,442 | 569,669 |
| Emp. | 104 | 109 | N/A |

DUNS 73-942-5403 **Imp**

## Wilton Engineering Services Ltd

(**Subsidiary of:** Pimco 2852 Ltd)
Port Clarence Road, Port Clarence, Middlesbrough, Cleveland TS2 1RZ
**Web:** www.wilton-group.com
**Reg No:** 2945270 **VAT No:** 633358048
**Estd:** 1994 Private Limited Company
**Line of Business:** Engineers (general)
**Export Sales:** £991,766
**Issued Capital:** £919
**Directors:** Ms C Stobbs, S B Pearson, P J Johnson, W Scott, S Glenn
**Co. Secretary:** Ms Christine Stobbs
**Responsibilities**
**Senior:** James Keegan *(Manager)*
**Health & Safety:** Steven Atter *(Health & Safety Manager)*, Lee Gordon *(Health & Safety Officer)*
**US SIC:** 8911, 3499
**UK SIC:** 83701, 31694
**Auditors:** UNW LLP
**Bankers:** Yorkshire Bank Plc (05-09-34)

| | 30-06-13 | 30-06-12 | 30-06-11 |
|---|---|---|---|
| TO | 42,379,850 | 68,085,498 | 46,917,167 |
| P/L | 4,476,074 | 4,013,238 | 3,057,719 |
| NW | 13,339,408 | 11,033,564 | 7,405,434 |
| WC | 10,885,423 | 8,945,110 | 6,447,397 |
| Emp. | 341 | 383 | 229 |

DUNS 29-671-5238

## Wilton House Ltd

73 - 77 London Road, Shenley, Radlett, Hertfordshire WD7 9BW
**Tel:** 01923858272 **Fax:** 01923856760
**Web:** www.wiltonhousecarehomes.com
**Reg No:** 1997746 **Estd:** 1986 Private Limited Company
**Line of Business:** Other human health activities
**Issued Capital:** £200
**Director:** V S Ramoutar
**Responsibilities**
**Senior:** Alan Reekhaye *(Proprietor)*
**Finance:** Alan Reekhaye *(Proprietor)*
**Health & Safety:** Siji Sebastian *(Home Manager)*

**Facilities:** Alan Reekhaye *(Proprietor)*
**Operations:** Siji Sebastian *(Home Manager)*
**Branches:** Wilton House Ltd, 49 Stratford Rd, Watford, Hertfordshire WD17 4NY
**US SIC:** 8091 **UK SIC:** 95200
**Auditors:** Benjamin Kay & Brummer
**Bankers:** Bank Of Scotland (80-02-10)

| | 31-03-13 | 31-03-12 | 31-03-11 |
|---|---|---|---|
| TO | 5,281,680 | 4,999,230 | 4,876,453 |
| P/L | 2,040,323 | 1,958,492 | 1,573,008 |
| NW | 12,039,020 | 10,611,202 | 9,249,884 |
| WC | 15,031,492 | 11,794,051 | 10,872,517 |
| Emp. | 109 | 113 | 111 |

DUNS 23-115-2067
## Wilton Manor Nursing Centre
Wilton Avenue, Southampton, Hampshire SO15 2HA
**Tel:** 023-8023-0555
**Estd:** 1994
**Line of Business:** Nursing homes
**Proprietor:** Mrs S Welham
**Responsibilities**
**Senior:** Kerry Brown *(Manager)*
**US SIC:** 8051 **UK SIC:** 95100
**Employees:** 78

DUNS 21-036-9933
## Wiltshire Air Ambulance Appeal
Unit E4, Avon Way, Langley Park, Chippenham, Wiltshire SN15 1GG
**Tel:** 08451221423
**Web:** www.wiltshireairambulance.co.uk
**Line of Business:** Associations
**Trading Style:** Wiltshire Air Ambulance Appeal Charitable Trust
**US SIC:** 8699 **UK SIC:** 96902
**Employees:** 70

DUNS 34-806-0711
## Wiltshire & Somerset Colleges Partnership Ltd
Wellington Road, Taunton, Somerset TA1 5AX
**Tel:** 01823-366341
**Web:** www.thecollegespartnership.co.uk
**Reg No:** 5606069 **Estd:** 2005 Private Company Limited By Guarantee
**Line of Business:** Adult and other education not elsewhere classified
**Trading Style:** Wiltshire & Somerset Colleges Partnership Ltd
**Directors:** A Ford, Mrs A Burnside, J P Olosunde, Ms R S Davies, J Wills
**Co. Secretary:** Ms Elizabeth Hurst
**Responsibilities**
**Senior:** Michael Crabbe *(Director)*, Diane Dale *(Manager)*, Nick Moore *(Director)*
**Admin:** Diane Dale *(Manager)*, Nick Moore *(Director)*
**US SIC:** 8249 **UK SIC:** 93300
**Bankers:** Barclays Bank Plc (20-85-26)

| | 31-07-13 | 31-07-12 | 31-07-11 |
|---|---|---|---|
| TO | 6,314,867 | 4,882,769 | 4,776,053 |
| P/L | 25,979 | 49,627 | 50,000 |
| NW | 726,274 | 687,228 | 657,177 |
| WC | 650,626 | 717,985 | 677,608 |
| Emp. | 119 | 101 | 100 |

DUNS 21-618-7996
## Wiltshire & Swindon History Centre
Cocklebury Road, Chippenham, Wiltshire SN15 3QN
**Tel:** 01249705500
**Web:** www.wshc.eu
**Estd:** 2011
**Line of Business:** Other tourist assistance activities not elsewhere classified
**Responsibilities**
**Senior:** Peter Tyas *(Manager Arts & Archive)*
**US SIC:** 7999 **UK SIC:** 97913
**Employees:** 50

DUNS 23-998-4792
## Wiltshire College
College Road, Trowbridge, Wiltshire BA14 0ES
**Tel:** 01225350035
**Web:** www.wiltshire.ac.uk
**Estd:** 1955
**Line of Business:** Further education schools and colleges
**Trading Style:** Wiltshire College Trowbridge
**Director:** G Bright
**Responsibilities**
**Senior:** Diane Dale *(Principal)*
**Marketing:** Paul Duff *(IT Director)*
**IT:** Paul Duff *(IT Director)*
**Branches:** Wiltshire College, The Avenue, Warminster, Wiltshire BA12 9AA
**US SIC:** 8221, 8249
**UK SIC:** 93100, 93300
**Bankers:** Lloyds TSB Bank plc (30-98-75)
**Employees:** 650

DUNS 23-265-2339
## Wiltshire Constabulary Air Support Unit
New Park Street, Devizes, Wiltshire SN10 1DZ
**Tel:** 08454087000 **Fax:** 01380-734-176
**Web:** www.wiltshire-pa.gov.uk
**Estd:** 1839 Incorporate By Act Of Parliament
**Line of Business:** Police hq & call centre
**Trading Style:** Wiltshire Police
**Principals:** R C Denning *(Financial)*, Miss E Neville, W R Girven
**Responsibilities**
**Senior:** Kieran Kilgallen *(Chief Executive)*
**Branches:** Wiltshire Constabulary Air Support Unit, Trowbridge Police Station, Polebarn Road, Trowbridge, Wiltshire BA14 7EP
**US SIC:** 9221 **UK SIC:** 91300
**Employees:** 500

DUNS 21-879-2461
## Wiltshire Council Children & Families
Monkton Park Offices, Monkton Park, Chippenham, Wiltshire SN15 1ER
**Tel:** 01249707900
**Estd:** 2012
**Line of Business:** The dss
**US SIC:** 8321 **UK SIC:** 96111
**Employees:** 80

DUNS 21-041-5934
## Wiltshire Fire & Rescue Service
Fire Station, Ashley Road, Salisbury, Wiltshire SP2 7TN
**Tel:** 01722439300
**Web:** www.wiltsfire.gov.uk
**Proprietorship**
**Line of Business:** Fire stations
**Proprietors:** I Rennie, I Rennie
**Responsibilities**
**Senior:** Michael Bagnall *(Station Manager)*
**US SIC:** 9224 **UK SIC:** 91400
**Employees:** 100

DUNS 42-439-3432
## Wiltshire Heavy Building Materials Ltd
(**Subsidiary of:** Wiltshire Heavy Building Materials (Group) Ltd)
65 St Mary St Chippenham, Chippenham, Wiltshire SN15 3JF
**Tel:** 01225773600
**Web:** www.wiltshirehbm.com
**Reg No:** 4427023 **Estd:** 2002 Private Limited Company
**Line of Business:** Transportation consultants
**Issued Capital:** £210
**Directors:** J D Brown, P Brown, M K Mcquaid
**Co. Secretary:** Ms Tracey Mcquaid
**US SIC:** 4712 **UK SIC:** 77002
**Auditors:** Dutton Mander Duffill
**Bankers:** Lloyds TSB Bank plc (77-50-14)

| | 31-05-13 | 31-05-12 | 31-05-11 |
|---|---|---|---|
| TO | 7,270,244 | N/A | N/A |
| P/L | 615,108 | N/A | N/A |
| NW | 965,350 | 757,950 | 642,486 |
| WC | 458,415 | 269,395 | 99,752 |
| Emp. | 52 | N/A | N/A |

DUNS 21-754-3235
## Wiltshire Nhs Primary Care Trust
Southgate House, Pans Lane, Devizes, Wiltshire SN10 5EQ
**Tel:** 01380728899
**Web:** www.wiltshire.nhs.uk
**Estd:** 2003 Partnership
**Line of Business:** Primary care trusts
**Partners:** Miss B Smith, Reverend J James
**Responsibilities**
**HR:** Suzanne Tewkesbury *(director of human resources)*
**US SIC:** 8062 **UK SIC:** 95100
**Employees:** 200

DUNS 28-856-7811
## The Wilverley Association
The Rise, Brockenhurst, Hampshire SO42 7SJ
**Tel:** 01590623418
**Web:** www.newforestcarehomes.org.uk
**Reg No:** 0817104 **Estd:** 1964 Private Company Limited By Guarantee
**Line of Business:** Other human health activities
**Trading Style:** Forest Oaks, Little Haven
**Directors:** A B Bates, Mrs A M White, Ms A C Hawksworth, Ms P H Hilborn, A G Jennings, Dr J R Lang
**Co. Secretary:** Mrs Gail Pussard

**Responsibilities**
**Senior:** Norman Blacker *(Acting Business Manager)*, Gemma Domingo *(Manager)*
**US SIC:** 8091, 8321
**UK SIC:** 95200, 96111
**Auditors:** Westlake Clark
**Bankers:** Bank Of Scotland (12-09-61)

| | 31-03-14 | 31-03-13 | 31-03-12 |
|---|---|---|---|
| TO | 3,288,223 | 2,838,124 | 3,016,530 |
| P/L | 251,082 | (40,411) | 135,728 |
| NW | 4,721,084 | 4,395,839 | 4,249,663 |
| WC | (176,134) | (377,563) | (266,825) |
| Emp. | 115 | 125 | 123 |

DUNS 34-864-2971 Imp
## Wimberly Allison Tong & Goo (Uk) Ltd
6 Little Portland Street, London W1W 7JE
**Fax:** 02079066660
**Web:** www.watg.com
**Reg No:** 5663701 **Estd:** 2005 Private Limited Company
**Line of Business:** Architectural activities
**Issued Capital:** £1,000
**Directors:** M Seyle, J T Heyes, P Priebe
**Co. Secretary:** Peter Priebe
**Responsibilities**
**Senior:** Doug Morris *(Manager)*
**US SIC:** 8911 **UK SIC:** 83701
**Auditors:** Saffery Champness
**Bankers:** Barclays Bank Plc (20-03-53)

| | 31-12-13 | 31-12-12 | 31-12-11 |
|---|---|---|---|
| TO | 10,075,095 | 9,414,865 | 10,467,851 |
| P/L | (878,053) | (2,198,821) | (857,678) |
| NW | (34,863) | 717,688 | 2,403,800 |
| WC | (319,796) | 373,801 | 2,021,031 |
| Emp. | 52 | 51 | 51 |

DUNS 23-708-8240
## Wimbledon College Art
Merton Hall Road, London SW19 3QA
**Web:** www.arts.ac.uk
**Estd:** 2002
**Line of Business:** Schools and colleges (art)
**Director:** Prof R Bugg
**Responsibilities**
**Senior:** Dominic Kane *(Manager)*, Margaret Kane *(Manager)*
**Finance:** Maggie Sedwell *(Finance Manager)*
**Marketing:** Elsie King *(Press and Communications Offic)*
**Admin:** Maggie Sedwell *(Finance Manager)*
**IT:** Sabrina Samsoodin *(IT Manager)*
**HR:** Ken Burrell *(Payroll Manager)*, Nick Rogers *(Human Resources Director)*
**Health & Safety:** Eleanor Pirie *(Head of Health & Safety)*
**Branches:** Wimbledon College Art, First Floor-Purchase Ledger Department, 5 Richbell Pl, London WC1N 3LA
**US SIC:** 8249 **UK SIC:** 93300
**Employees:** 70
**Turnover:** £7,258,000

DUNS 34-749-9741
## Wimbledon College Ltd
Edge Hill, London SW19 4NS
**Tel:** 02089462533
**Web:** www.wimbledoncollege.org.uk
**Reg No:** 2783713 **Estd:** 1993 Private Limited Company
**Line of Business:** Other letting of own property
**Issued Capital:** £1,000
**Director:** A J Laing
**Co. Secretary:** Philip Murphy
**Responsibilities**
**Admin:** Annette Lawlor *(Secretary)*
**US SIC:** 6519 **UK SIC:** 85000
**Auditors:** Michael Jellicoe

| | 31-03-14 | 31-03-13 | 31-03-12 |
|---|---|---|---|
| TA | 113,547 | 84,929 | 41,750 |
| NW | 415 | 2,765 | 2,765 |
| WC | 415 | 2,765 | 2,765 |

DUNS 23-082-7540
## Wimbledon College Prep School
Donhead Lodge, 33 Edge Hill, London SW19 4NP
**Tel:** 020-8946-7000
**Web:** www.donhead.org.uk
**Estd:** 1997
**Line of Business:** Schools (independent)
**Trading Style:** Donhead
**Director:** C Mcgrath
**Responsibilities**
**Senior:** G Macgrath *(Head Teacher)*
**US SIC:** 8211 **UK SIC:** 93200
**Employees:** 70

DUNS 21-030-5028
## The Wimbledon Guild of Social Welfare
Guild House, 30-32 Worple Road, London SW19 4EF
**Tel:** 020-8946-0735
**Web:** www.wimbledonguild.co.uk
**Line of Business:** Charities and charitable organisations
**Responsibilities**
**Senior:** Wendy Perdmore *(Ceo)*
**US SIC:** 8699 **UK SIC:** 96902
**Employees:** 56

DUNS 28-833-2380
## The Wimbledon Squash & Badminton Courts Ltd
(**Subsidiary of:** Wimbledon Racquets & Fitness Club Ltd)
Cranbrook Road, London SW19 4HD
**Tel:** 02089475806
**Web:** www.wsbc.co.uk
**Reg No:** 0314509 **Estd:** 1936 Private Limited Company
**Line of Business:** Other sporting activities not elsewhere classified
**Trading Style:** Wmbledon Squash & Badminton Club
**Issued Capital:** £3,600
**Directors:** Miss J Lacey, P J Stevens, A D Cain, W Wildo, B Chant, R Pratt, R P Hunter
**Responsibilities**
**Senior:** Jason Beever *(General Manager)*
**US SIC:** 7999 **UK SIC:** 97913
**Auditors:** Hepburn & Co

| | 30-09-13 | 30-09-12 | 30-09-11 |
|---|---|---|---|
| TA | 18,003 | 18,003 | 18,003 |
| NW | 10,111 | 10,111 | 10,111 |

DUNS 64-754-0277
## Wimbledon Studio Theatre
Wimbledon Theatre, 93 The Broadway, London SW19 1QG
**Tel:** 02085457900
**Web:** www.atgtickets.com
**Proprietorship**
**Line of Business:** Management of real estate on a fee or contract basis
**Proprietor:** Ms M Sarrington
**Responsibilities**
**Senior:** Samantha Bain *(General Manager)*, Gavin Shuman *(Manager)*
**US SIC:** 6531 **UK SIC:** 83400
**Employees:** 155

DUNS 77-611-3573
## Wimborne First School Play Clubs
School Lane, Wimborne, Dorset BH21 1HQ
**Tel:** 01202-882532 **Fax:** 01202883135
**Web:** www.wimbornefirst.dorset.sch.uk
**Reg No:** 3001881 **Estd:** 1994 Private Limited Company
**Line of Business:** Schools (local authority)
**Directors:** Ms S Allman, L L Griffiths
**Co. Secretary:** Alistair Gemmell
**Responsibilities**
**Senior:** Sarah Lynch *(Head Teacher)*, Michael Weatherley *(Manager)*
**US SIC:** 8211 **UK SIC:** 93200

| | 31-12-13 | 31-12-12 | 31-12-11 |
|---|---|---|---|
| TO | 55,154 | 61,100 | 50,608 |
| P/L | (5,647) | 5,368 | 4,942 |
| NW | 11,312 | 16,958 | 12,662 |
| WC | 11,312 | 16,958 | 12,662 |

DUNS 23-735-5172
## Wims Ltd
Jewry House, Jewry Street, Winchester, Hampshire SO23 8RZ
**Web:** www.iprotectinsurance.co.uk
**Reg No:** 3729853 **Estd:** 1999 Private Limited Company
**Line of Business:** Insurance services
**Issued Capital:** £50,000
**Directors:** J D Monkcom, N P Preston
**Co. Secretary:** Gareth Sampson
**US SIC:** 6411 **UK SIC:** 83200
**Bankers:** National Westminster Bank Plc (55-81-26)

| | 30-06-14 | 30-06-13 | 30-06-12 |
|---|---|---|---|
| TO | 3,107,625 | 2,395,430 | 2,279,745 |
| P/L | 829,296 | 398,289 | 467,272 |
| NW | 1,909,977 | 1,466,269 | 1,220,897 |
| WC | 911,424 | 540,691 | 408,225 |
| Emp. | 54 | 43 | 37 |

DUNS 34-976-0905 Imp
## Win Technologies (Uk) Ltd
(**Subsidiary of:** City Views Limited)
2nd Floor North The Forum, London NW1 0EG
**Tel:** 02071213180 **Fax:** 087 0441 9489
**Web:** www.wintechnologies.net
**Reg No:** 5771461 **VAT No:** 893648566
**Estd:** 2006 Private Limited Company

**Line of Business:** Marketing consultants
**Issued Capital:** £1,000
**Directors:** G Menashe, T G Whyles, B J Susskind
**Co. Secretary:** Neal Menashe
**Responsibilities**
**Senior:** Christelle Evraurd *(Personal Assistant)*
**US SIC:** 7392 **UK SIC:** 83951
**Bankers:** Allied Irish Bank (gb) (23-83-97)

| | 31-12-13 | 31-12-12 | 31-12-11 |
|---|---|---|---|
| TO | 24,554,357 | 20,716,373 | 16,197,053 |
| P/L | 1,383,647 | 1,134,069 | 824,049 |
| NW | 3,670,456 | 2,661,127 | 1,849,035 |
| WC | 2,106,686 | 1,576,145 | 1,008,630 |
| Emp. | 253 | 217 | 210 |

DUNS 49-395-4762
## Winander Group Holdings Ltd
Winander House, Glebe Road, Windermere, Cumbria LA23 3HE
**Tel:** 01539443360 **Fax:** 01539-440341
**Web:** www.windermere-lakecruises.co.uk
**Reg No:** 3139467 **Estd:** 1940 Private Limited Company
**Line of Business:** Management activities of holding companies
**Issued Capital:** £5,451,177
**Directors:** T R Cowherd, E G Fallowfield, A J Rothwell, J R Thompson, Ms A R Howson, Ms S Sproat, L Micklethwaite, N Wilkinson
**Co. Secretary:** Andrew Simon
**Responsibilities**
**Senior:** Allan Brockbank *(Director)*, Martin Dennison *(Director)*, Maureen Fleming *(Director)*, Katrina Hardman *(Director)*, Evelyn Twaddle *(Director)*
**Branches:** Winander Group Holdings Ltd, Rectory Rd Glebe Coach Pk, Windermere, Cumbria LA23 3HB
**US SIC:** 6711, 7392
**UK SIC:** 83962, 83951
**Auditors:** Garbutt & Elliott Ltd
**Bankers:** Barclays Bank Plc (20-45-28)

| | 31-01-14 | 31-01-13 | 31-01-12 |
|---|---|---|---|
| TO | 8,656,571 | 7,827,330 | 8,138,159 |
| P/L | 2,167,063 | 1,634,637 | 1,966,576 |
| NW | 6,333,444 | 5,531,295 | 4,758,304 |
| WC | 3,360,394 | 2,649,878 | 1,948,885 |
| Emp. | 156 | 157 | 138 |

DUNS 51-636-0570
## Winash Ltd
9 Albert Road, Clevedon, Avon BS21 7RP
**Tel:** 01275-873129
**Web:** www.winash.co.uk
**Reg No:** 5953260 **Estd:** 2006 Private Limited Company
**Line of Business:** Social work activities with accommodation
**Issued Capital:** £100
**Director:** Ms H J House
**Co. Secretary:** Bryan Wood
**US SIC:** 8321 **UK SIC:** 96111

| | 31-03-14 | 31-03-13 | 31-03-12 |
|---|---|---|---|
| TA | 229,478 | 287,888 | 219,116 |
| NW | (100,667) | (85,606) | (131,434) |
| WC | 44,592 | 61,341 | 11,698 |

DUNS 77-165-5768 **Exp**
## Winbro Group Technologies Ltd
**(Subsidiary of:** Flow Grinding Corp.)
Unit 7 Stenson Road Whitwick Business, Park, Coalville, Leicestershire LE67 4JP
**Tel:** 01530516000 **Fax:** 01530-516-001
**Web:** www.winbrogroup.com
**Reg No:** 2707834 **VAT No:** 558784677
**Estd:** 1992 Private Limited Company
**Line of Business:** Sales of machine tools
**Export Markets:** Countries Worldwide
**Export Sales:** £13,118,138
**Trading Style:** Winbro Advanced Machining
**Issued Capital:** £83,526
**Directors:** L P Bromham, T J Barnett, R J Folwell, R Wagstaff, R M Arbon, Dr. W Perry, M G Whitmore, A M Lawson
**Responsibilities**
**Senior:** John Stackouse *(Manager)*
**IT:** Phil Antill *(IT Manager)*
**US SIC:** 5251, 3621
**UK SIC:** 64800, 34201
**Auditors:** Grant Thornton UK LLP
**Bankers:** National Westminster Bank Plc (60-60-06)

| | 31-12-13 | 31-12-12 | 31-12-11 |
|---|---|---|---|
| TO | 18,771,518 | 18,888,195 | 18,545,725 |
| P/L | 1,100,144 | 3,078,131 | 2,593,379 |
| NW | 8,088,754 | 7,052,344 | 4,747,713 |
| WC | 7,296,598 | 7,334,299 | 5,079,189 |
| Emp. | 157 | 147 | 131 |

DUNS 22-002-1128
## Winbur Building
The Old Substation, Queens Driv, Nottingham, Nottinghamshire NG2 1AP
**Tel:** 08456047081
**Estd:** 2010 Proprietorship
**Line of Business:** Multi-disciplined building and construction company
**Proprietor:** R Irwin
**Responsibilities**
**Senior:** RICHARD IRWIN *(Proprietor)*
**US SIC:** 1531 **UK SIC:** 50100
**Bankers:** Lloyds TSB Bank plc (77-22-08)
**Employees:** 48

DUNS 23-646-1815
## Wincanton Community Sports Centre
West Hill, Wincanton, Somerset BA9 9SP
**Tel:** 01963-824400
**Web:** www.wincantonsports.co.uk
**Reg No:** 3641430 **Estd:** 1998 Private Unlimited Company
**Line of Business:** Operation of other sports arenas and stadiums not elsewhere classified
**Directors:** H T Ellard, G C Gibbs, N S Engert, Miss S Forshaw, N C Colbert, D B Osborne, S J Miller, C P Fenton
**Co. Secretary:** Howard Ellard
**Responsibilities**
**Senior:** Rex Calvert *(Board Member)*, Alfred Chinnock *(Board Member)*
**US SIC:** 7999 **UK SIC:** 97913
**Bankers:** National Westminster Bank Plc (60-24-09)

| | 31-03-14 | 31-03-13 | 31-03-12 |
|---|---|---|---|
| TO | 336,221 | 614,978 | 654,147 |
| P/L | (3,342) | (41,551) | (6,712) |
| NW | 1,544 | 4,886 | 46,437 |
| WC | (610) | 122 | 34,584 |
| Emp. | 49 | 50 | 50 |

DUNS 21-635-5719 **Imp-Exp**
## Wincanton Engineering Ltd
**(Subsidiary of:** Tetra Laval Holdings B.V.)
Bradley Junction Industrial Estate, Leeds Road, Huddersfield, West Yorkshire HD2 1UR
**Tel:** 01935-818800 **Fax:** 01935-818818
**Web:** www.tetrapak.com
**Reg No:** 0209985 **VAT No:** 469768472
**Estd:** 1925 Private Limited Company
**Line of Business:** Manufacture of machinery for food, beverage and tobacco processing
**Export Markets:** U S A; Canada
**Issued Capital:** £55,000
**Directors:** M Boxall, M Stendahl
**US SIC:** 3551 **UK SIC:** 32441
**Bankers:** National Westminster Bank Plc (56-00-34)

| | 31-12-13 | 31-12-12 | 31-12-11 |
|---|---|---|---|
| TA | 55,000 | 145,000 | 55,000 |
| NW | 55,000 | 145,000 | 55,000 |

DUNS 22-160-1938
## Wincanton Plc
Methuen Park, Chippenham, Wiltshire SN14 0WT
**Tel:** 01249-710-000 **Fax:** 01249-710-001
**Web:** www.wincanton.co.uk
**Reg No:** 4178808 **VAT No:** 768958448
**Estd:** 1925 Public Limited Company
**Line of Business:** Miscellaneous transportation services
**Issued Capital:** £12,174,729
**Directors:** A M Colman, P Venables, E M Born, M T Sawkins, D J Radcliffe, G Mcfaull, P D Dean, S Oades
**Co. Secretary:** Mrs Alison Dowling
**Responsibilities**
**Senior:** Jonson Cox *(Manager)*, Charles Phillips *(Manager)*, Nigel Sullivan *(Manager)*
**Marketing:** Holly Porter *(Marketing Director)*
**IT:** Simon Deane *(IT Director)*
**HR:** Wendy Vaughan *(Human Resources Director)*
**Facilities:** Sally Robinson *(Facilities Manager)*
**Branches:** Wincanton Plc, Pontyfelin Roa, Pontypool, Gwent NP4 0NY
**US SIC:** 4789, 4226, 4712, 7392
**UK SIC:** 77002, 77003, 83951
**Auditors:** KPMG Audit PLC
**Following financial data are in thousands**

| | 31-03-14 | 31-03-13 | 31-03-12 |
|---|---|---|---|
| TO | 1,098,300 | 1,086,800 | 1,202,800 |
| P/L | 34,900 | 24,800 | (47,400) |
| NW | (355,500) | (400,900) | (391,600) |
| WC | (95,200) | (101,900) | (103,300) |
| Emp. | 15,440 | 15,700 | 18,400 |

DUNS 57-828-7591 **Imp**
## Wincanton Print Co Ltd
Wessex Way, Wincanton Business Park, Wincanton, Somerset BA9 9RR
**Tel:** 0196333643
**Web:** www.wincanton-print.com
**Reg No:** 2886990 **VAT No:** 639449987
**Estd:** 1994 Private Limited Company
**Line of Business:** Printers general
**Trading Style:** Wincanton Print Co.Ltd
**Issued Capital:** £100
**Director:** S W Taylor
**Co. Secretary:** Ms Tania Graham
**Responsibilities**
**Senior:** Ian Gatfield *(Production Director)*, Peter Vallis *(Marketing Manager)*
**Marketing:** Peter Vallis *(Marketing Manager)*
**Sales:** Peter Vallis *(Marketing Manager)*
**HR:** Ian Gatfield *(Production Director)*
**Health & Safety:** Ian Gatfield *(Production Director)*
**Operations:** Ian Gatfield *(Production Director)*
**Engineering:** Ian Gatfield *(Production Director)*
**US SIC:** 2752, 2721
**UK SIC:** 47544, 47522
**Auditors:** Burton Sweet
**Bankers:** National Westminster Bank Plc (60-24-09)

| | 31-05-13 | 31-05-12 | 31-05-11 |
|---|---|---|---|
| TA | 3,102,231 | 3,371,288 | 3,704,411 |
| NW | 224,192 | 217,133 | 221,605 |
| WC | (133,536) | (164,844) | (162,033) |

DUNS 21-830-9243
## Winch & Blatch Ltd
29 Market Hill, Sudbury, Suffolk CO10 2EN
**Tel:** 01787-373737
**Web:** www.winchblatch.co.uk
**Reg No:** 0401911 **VAT No:** 102354814
**Estd:** 1945 Private Limited Company
**Line of Business:** Departmental stores
**Issued Capital:** £9,000
**Managing Director:** R J Blatch
**Co. Secretary:** Mrs Judith Blatch
**Branches:** Winch & Blatch Ltd, King Street, Sudbury, Suffolk CO10 2EH
**US SIC:** 5399 **UK SIC:** 00000
**Auditors:** Griffin Chapman
**Bankers:** Lloyds TSB Bank plc (30-98-31)

| | 01-02-14 | 26-01-13 | 28-02-12 |
|---|---|---|---|
| TA | 1,541,075 | 1,677,145 | 1,740,535 |
| NW | 1,247,166 | 1,329,569 | 1,357,503 |
| WC | 295,062 | 375,055 | 365,481 |

DUNS 21-723-3945
## Winchcombe School
Greet Road, Winchcombe, Cheltenham, Gloucestershire GL54 5LB
**Fax:** 01242604211
**Web:** www.winchcombe.gloucs.sch.uk
**Reg No:** 7606409 **Estd:** 2011 Private Company Limited By Guarantee
**Line of Business:** Schools (local authority)
**Directors:** A R Wilcock, Mrs S J Proctor, P N Grimshaw, Mrs A J Peck, C M Holliday, A W Grainger
**Co. Secretary:** Ms Pauline Shaw
**US SIC:** 8211 **UK SIC:** 93200
**Auditors:** Randall & Payne LLP

| | 31-08-14 | 31-08-13 | 31-08-12 |
|---|---|---|---|
| TO | 2,982,000 | 2,893,000 | 10,165,000 |
| P/L | 73,000 | 64,000 | 6,203,000 |
| NW | 6,058,000 | 6,220,000 | 6,129,000 |
| WC | 428,000 | 273,000 | 134,000 |
| Emp. | 55 | 54 | 76 |

DUNS 23-082-9959
## Wincheap Primary School
Hollowmede, Canterbury, Kent CT1 3SD
**Tel:** 01227-464134
**Web:** www.wincheap.kent.sch.uk
**Estd:** 1930
**Line of Business:** Schools (local authority)
**Director:** Mrs R Jenner
**Responsibilities**
**Senior:** Clive Close *(Head Teacher)*
**US SIC:** 8211 **UK SIC:** 93200
**Employees:** 60

DUNS 22-883-8280
## Winchester City Council
City Offices, Colebrook Street, Winchester, Hampshire SO23 9LJ
**Tel:** 01962840222 **Fax:** 01962-841365
**Web:** www.winchester.gov.uk
**VAT No:** 189408424 **Estd:** 1974 Incorporate By Act Of Parliament
**Line of Business:** Museums & art galleries
**Principals:** Ms S Bowden *(Financial)*, F Lyon *(Financial)*, D H Cowan
**Responsibilities**
**Senior:** Simon Eden *(Chief Executive)*, Ross Turle *(Executive)*, Stephen Whetnall *(Chief Operating Officer)*
**Finance:** Eloise Appleby *(Assistant Director of Economy)*, Alexis Garlick *(Financial Director)*
**Marketing:** Rachel Gander *(Tourism Marketing and Developm)*, Steve Lincoln *(Community Planning Manager)*, Simon Maggs *(Housing Strategy and Developme)*, Kathleen Mcculloch *(e-Communications & Development)*, Steven Tillbury *(Data Communications Manager)*
**Sales:** Alison Woods *(Business Development Officer)*
**IT:** Tony Fawcett *(Head of IT)*, Jane Maughan *(Business Support)*
**Health & Safety:** Bob Cole *(Health & Safety Officer)*
**Facilities:** Andrew Kingston *(Head of Property Services)*, Simon Maggs *(Housing Strategy and Developme)*
**Operations:** Stuart Dunbar-Dempsey *(Open Space Project Officer)*, Richard Hein *(Parking, Concessionary Travel)*, James Jenkison *(Principal Planning Officer)*, Bob Merrett *(Environmental Health Director)*, Stephen Whetnall *(Chief Operating Officer)*
**Purchasing:** Debbie Chick *(Purchasing Officer)*
**Engineering:** Corinne Phillips *(Traffic Engineer)*
**Branches:** Winchester City Council, Victoria House, Victoria Road, Winchester, Hampshire SO23 7BP
**US SIC:** 9121 **UK SIC:** 91110
**Bankers:** National Westminster Bank Plc (55-81-26)
**Employees:** 600

DUNS 23-082-7904
## Winchester College
College Street, Winchester, Hampshire SO23 9NA
**Tel:** 01962-621100
**Web:** www.winchestercollege.org
**Estd:** 1990
**Line of Business:** Schools (independent)
**Principals:** Dr R Townsend, D Clementi, Dr J Shaw, Prof A Ryan, R Fox, R Woods, M Loveday, Prof D Hanna
**Responsibilities**
**Senior:** Andrew Longmore *(Partner)*
**Admin:** Kate Ross *(PA to the Directors and Office)*
**US SIC:** 8211 **UK SIC:** 93200
**Auditors:** Crowe Clark Whitehill LLP

| | 31-08-12 | 31-08-11 | 31-08-10 |
|---|---|---|---|
| TO | 26,428,000 | 24,348,000 | 22,858,000 |
| P/L | 2,736,000 | 1,574,000 | 947,000 |
| NW | 138,304,000 | 132,230,000 | 117,767,000 |
| WC | 6,766,000 | 3,823,000 | 2,718,000 |
| Emp. | 356 | 354 | 359 |

DUNS 77-707-1085 **Imp-Exp**
## Winchester Growers Ltd
**(Subsidiary of:** Fieldlink Nv)
Herdgate Lane, Pinchbeck, Spalding, Lincolnshire PE11 3UP
**Tel:** 01775680261 **Fax:** 01775-680814
**Web:** www.winchestergrowers.co.uk
**Reg No:** 3007729 **VAT No:** 656504920
**Estd:** 1995 Private Limited Company
**Line of Business:** Farming (arable)
**Export Markets:** Worldwide
**Export Sales:** £1,871,346
**Issued Capital:** £10,408,000
**Principals:** Dr G J Flint *(Managing)*, R M Baker, A A Forrester, M D Harpham
**Co. Secretary:** Richard Baker
**Responsibilities**
**IT:** Anne Howard *(Senior IT Executive)*
**Branches:** Winchester Growers Ltd, Varfell Farm, Long Rock, Penzance, Cornwall TR20 8AQ
**US SIC:** 5199, 0119
**UK SIC:** 61900, 01001
**Auditors:** Ernst & Young LLP
**Bankers:** National Westminster Bank Plc (55-81-26)

| | 31-12-13 | 31-12-12 | 31-12-11 |
|---|---|---|---|
| TO | 49,813,642 | 50,960,865 | 51,465,577 |
| P/L | (963,975) | 582,347 | 487,642 |
| NW | 2,889,659 | 4,134,619 | 3,523,223 |
| WC | (2,004,850) | 63,408 | 220,630 |
| Emp. | 332 | 314 | 253 |

DUNS 21-617-3078
## The Winchester Hotel
Worthy Lane, Winchester, Hampshire SO23 7AB
**Tel:** 01962709988
**Web:** www.thewinchesterhotel.co.uk
**Estd:** 1991
**Line of Business:** Hotels
**Proprietor:** J Gettings
**Responsibilities**
**Senior:** Paul Eaves *(General Manager)*
**US SIC:** 7011 **UK SIC:** 66500
**Employees:** 50

DUNS 21-614-5314
## Winchester House Medical Centre
Independents Road, London SE3 9LF
**Tel:** 02082974500
**Web:** www.bmihealthcare.co.uk
**Estd:** 2012
**Line of Business:** Hospitals
**Responsibilities**
**Senior:** Carole Sibley *(House Manager)*
**US SIC:** 8091 **UK SIC:** 95200
**Employees:** 50

DUNS 28-843-8963

## Winchester House School Trust Ltd

44 High Street, Brackley, Northamptonshire NN13 7AZ
**Tel:** 01280-702483
**Web:** www.winchester-house.org
**Reg No:** 0595630 **Estd:** 1957 Private Company Limited By Guarantee
**Line of Business:** General secondary education
**Directors:** A R Heygate, M H Wetherill, Mrs J C Harris, T E Purton, J S Moule, R P Fordham, R S Greaves, G E Seligman
**Co. Secretary:** Mrs Sarah Budd
**Responsibilities**
**Senior:** Emma Goldsmith *(Head Teacher)*, Josephine Hearnden *(Director)*, Mark Seymor *(Head Teacher)*, Hugh Smith *(Director)*
**US SIC:** 8211 **UK SIC:** 93200
**Auditors:** Upstone Blencowe
**Bankers:** Lloyds TSB Bank plc (30-11-08)

| | 31-08-13 | 31-08-12 | 31-08-11 |
|---|---|---|---|
| TO | 4,465,016 | 4,272,970 | 4,277,062 |
| P/L | 47,654 | 89,851 | (51,676) |
| NW | 3,436,912 | 3,389,258 | 3,299,407 |
| WC | 374,576 | 394,818 | 284,042 |
| Emp. | 135 | 133 | 136 |

DUNS 21-724-8905

## Winchester Motor Co Ltd

43 St Cross Road, Winchester, Hampshire SO23 9PU
**Tel:** 01962866331
**Web:** www.volkswagen.co.uk
**Reg No:** 1033289 **VAT No:** 188207051
**Estd:** 1971 Private Limited Company
**Line of Business:** Car dealers (new & used)
**Issued Capital:** £50,000
**Principals:** R K Mills-Goodlet *(Chairman)*, M A Mills Goodlet *(Managing)*
**Co. Secretary:** Ms Lynda Mills Goodlet
**US SIC:** 5511 **UK SIC:** 65100
**Auditors:** Rossell Hicks
**Bankers:** Barclays Bank Plc (20-97-01)

| | 30-04-14 | 30-04-13 | 30-04-12 |
|---|---|---|---|
| TO | 21,874,294 | 14,845,232 | 13,665,104 |
| P/L | 222,099 | (46,812) | 53,568 |
| NW | 2,499,471 | 2,299,257 | 2,349,665 |
| WC | 1,002,363 | 776,144 | 900,155 |
| Emp. | 57 | 53 | 46 |

DUNS 21-776-8610

## Winchester Retreat & Conference Centre

Old Alresford, Alresford, Hampshire SO24 9DH
**Web:** www.oldalresfordplace.co.uk
**Estd:** 1961 Partnership
**Line of Business:** Places of worship
**Trading Style:** The Old Alresford Place Conference & Training Centre
**Partners:** Mrs A Southern, P Lippiett, C Harbidge, Mrs A Wakeham, J Turpin
**US SIC:** 8661 **UK SIC:** 96600
**Employees:** 50

DUNS 21-105-9146

## Winckworth Sherwood Llp

Minerva House, 5 Montague Close, London SE1 9BB
**Tel:** 020-7593-5000
**Web:** www.wslaw.co.uk
**Reg No:** 0334359OC **Estd:** 2002
**Line of Business:** Solicitors
**Responsibilities**
**Senior:** Robert Botkai *(Non-designated Limited Liabili)*, Owen Carew-Jones *(Non-designated Limited Liabili)*, Emma Chadwick *(Non-designated Limited Liabili)*, Francesco Ferrari *(Non-designated Limited Liabili)*, Alison Gorlov *(Non-designated Limited Liabili)*, Aiden Hargreaves-Smith *(Non-designated Limited Liabili)*, Paul Irving *(Non-designated Limited Liabili)*, Jo-Anne Keddie *(Non-designated Limited Liabili)*, Eleanor Kilminster *(Non-designated Limited Liabili)*, Roderick Macdougald *(Non-designated Limited Liabili)*, Johnathan Mitchell *(Office Manager)*, Louis Robert *(Non-designated Limited Liabili)*, Andrea Squires *(Non-designated Limited Liabili)*, David Von Hagen *(Non-designated Limited Liabili)*
**Admin:** Johnathan Mitchell *(Office Manager)*
**Purchasing:** Johnathan Mitchell *(Office Manager)*
**US SIC:** 8111 **UK SIC:** 83500
**Bankers:** The Royal Bank Of Scotland Plc (16-08-83)

| | 31-03-14 | 31-03-13 | 31-03-12 |
|---|---|---|---|
| TO | 30,484,282 | 25,867,247 | 23,885,628 |
| P/L | (346,886) | N/A | 56,618 |
| NW | 12,536,949 | 3,577,944 | 3,572,124 |
| WC | 13,979,993 | 12,116,882 | 11,377,093 |
| Emp. | 243 | 268 | 233 |

DUNS 52-571-0083

## Wind Prospect Group Ltd

Lewins Place, Lewins Mead, Bristol, Avon BS1 2NR
**Tel:** 01173017151
**Web:** www.windprospect.com
**Reg No:** 3254615 **VAT No:** 691678288
**Estd:** 1992 Private Limited Company
**Line of Business:** Production of electricity
**Export Sales:** £7,968,444
**Issued Capital:** £967
**Directors:** B Allan, R Barker, E P Cameron
**Co. Secretary:** Alexander Hannah
**Responsibilities**
**Senior:** Colin Palmer *(Manager)*
**Branches:** Wind Prospect Group Ltd, Bede House, Belmont Business Park, Durham, County Durham DH1 1TW
**US SIC:** 4911 **UK SIC:** 16101
**Auditors:** Elliott Bunker Ltd
**Bankers:** HSBC Bank plc (40-47-20)

| | 31-12-13 | 31-12-12 | 31-12-11 |
|---|---|---|---|
| TO | 16,954,137 | 18,069,187 | 22,193,342 |
| P/L | (3,060,127) | (3,762,004) | (964,946) |
| NW | (6,656,455) | (3,927,641) | 130,612 |
| WC | (2,794,238) | 586,891 | 1,063,762 |
| Emp. | 194 | 190 | 195 |

DUNS 21-714-4078

## Wind Towers (Scotland) Ltd

(**Subsidiary of:** Sse Plc)
Inveralmond House, 200 Dunkeld Road, Perth, Perthshire PH1 3AQ
**Tel:** 01586 555 000
**Web:** www.windtowersscotland.com
**Reg No:** 0394018SC **Estd:** 2011 Private Limited Company
**Line of Business:** Manufacture of metal structures and parts of structures
**Export Sales:** £4,632,814
**Trading Style:** Wind Towers Scotland
**Issued Capital:** £319,808
**Directors:** A J Breugelmans, A D Biggar, M A Mcghie, C D Farrell, B C Davidson
**Co. Secretary:** Ms Samantha Coyne
**US SIC:** 3441 **UK SIC:** 32042
**Auditors:** KPMG Audit PLC

| | 31-03-14 | 31-03-13 | 31-03-11 |
|---|---|---|---|
| TO | 8,359,243 | 7,204,540 | 2,595,106 |
| P/L | (2,529,310) | (4,622,076) | (1,648,411) |
| NW | 2,195,133 | 4,378,826 | 8,562,324 |
| WC | 3,809,044 | 1,346,031 | 6,190,523 |
| Emp. | 123 | 113 | 93 |

DUNS 21-914-0852 **Imp**

## Windboats Marine Ltd

Norwich Road, Norwich, Norfolk NR12 8RX
**Tel:** 01603-782236
**Web:** www.windboats.co.uk
**Reg No:** 1188752 **VAT No:** 282020788
**Estd:** 1974 Private Limited Company
**Line of Business:** Building and repairing of pleasure and sporting boats
**Issued Capital:** £2,000
**Director:** O D James
**Co. Secretary:** Mrs Yvonne James
**Responsibilities**
**Senior:** Frank Berry *(Manager)*
**HR:** Clive Howard *(General Manager)*
**US SIC:** 3732 **UK SIC:** 36102
**Auditors:** Johnson Holmes & Co
**Bankers:** HSBC Bank plc (40-35-09)

| | 31-03-14 | 31-03-13 | 31-03-12 |
|---|---|---|---|
| TO | N/A | 3,017,765 | N/A |
| P/L | N/A | 355,091 | N/A |
| NW | 2,842,214 | 3,161,643 | 2,890,797 |
| WC | 1,681,360 | 1,992,425 | 1,705,737 |
| Emp. | N/A | 61 | N/A |

DUNS 34-640-7104 **Imp-Exp**

## Winder Power Ltd

(**Subsidiary of:** Winder Power Holdings Ltd)
Grangefield House Richardshaw Road, Pudsey, West Yorkshire LS28 6QS
**Tel:** 01132-555666
**Web:** www.winderpower.com
**Reg No:** 5446559 **VAT No:** 860040268
**Estd:** 1961 Private Limited Company
**Line of Business:** Manufacture of electric motors, generators and transformers
**Export Sales:** £472,864
**Issued Capital:** £75,758
**Directors:** W J Evans, P D Matthews, L R Mackenzie, A P Pinkney
**Co. Secretary:** William Evans
**Responsibilities**
**Purchasing:** Nigel Keene *(Purchasing Manager)*
**US SIC:** 3621, 3643
**UK SIC:** 34201, 34203
**Bankers:** Barclays Bank Plc (20-11-81)

| | 31-03-14 | 31-03-13 | 31-03-12 |
|---|---|---|---|
| TO | 14,600,752 | 14,381,774 | 10,819,577 |
| P/L | 730,268 | 1,200,937 | 482,506 |
| NW | 3,852,819 | 3,417,797 | 2,723,857 |
| WC | 2,934,967 | 2,616,618 | 1,811,800 |
| Emp. | 93 | 87 | 75 |

DUNS 21-581-7749

## Windermere Grange Care Home

Windermere Road, Middlesbrough, Cleveland TS5 5DH
**Tel:** 01642815594
**Estd:** 2011 Proprietorship
**Line of Business:** Residential care establishments
**Proprietor:** Mrs P Edgerton
**Responsibilities**
**Senior:** Michelle Clark *(Manager)*
**US SIC:** 8321 **UK SIC:** 96111
**Employees:** 60

DUNS 29-525-2472

## Windermere Iron Steamboat Company Ltd

(**Subsidiary of:** Winander Group Holdings Ltd)
Lakeside Pier, Ulverston, Cumbria LA12 8AS
**Tel:** 01539-531188 **Fax:** 01539-531947
**Web:** www.windermere-lakecruises.co.uk
**Reg No:** 1892921 **Estd:** 1985 Private Limited Company
**Line of Business:** Passenger inland water transport
**Issued Capital:** £100
**Principals:** L Micklethwaite *(Managing)*, J R Thompson, A J Simon, J Woodburn, N Wilkinson, E G Fallowfield, W J Bewley, T R Cowherd
**Responsibilities**
**Senior:** Allan Brockbank *(Director)*
**Marketing:** Jacqui O' Connor *(Press Officer)*
**US SIC:** 4459 **UK SIC:** 72603
**Bankers:** Barclays Bank Plc (20-45-28)

| | 31-01-14 | 31-01-13 | 31-01-12 |
|---|---|---|---|
| TA | 100 | 100 | 100 |
| NW | 100 | 100 | 100 |

DUNS 22-813-9804

## Windermere Marina Village Ltd

(**Subsidiary of:** New Era Holdings Ltd)
The Marina, Bowness-On-Windermere Marina, Bowness-On-Windermere, Windermere, Cumbria LA23 3JQ
**Web:** www.wmv.co.uk
**Reg No:** 0422332 **Estd:** 1988 Private Limited Company
**Line of Business:** Holiday centres and holiday villages
**Trading Style:** Windermere Marina
**Issued Capital:** £1,357,027
**Managing Directors:** J M Dearden, Mrs E R Ainscough
**Co. Secretary:** Mrs Shona Taylor
**Responsibilities**
**Facilities:** Hannah Sewell *(Accommodation Manager)*
**US SIC:** 7032, 7011
**UK SIC:** 66702, 66500
**Auditors:** KPMG
**Bankers:** HSBC Bank plc (40-46-32)

| | 31-03-14 | 31-03-13 | 31-03-12 |
|---|---|---|---|
| TA | 14,281,209 | 14,700,556 | 12,703,166 |
| NW | 11,357,665 | 11,296,013 | 11,243,366 |
| WC | (297,803) | 563,574 | 1,021,790 |

DUNS 39-793-5958

## Windfall Films Ltd

(**Subsidiary of:** Argonon Ltd)
One Underwood Row, London N1 7LZ
**Tel:** 020-7251-7676
**Web:** www.windfallfilms.com
**Reg No:** 2205891 **Estd:** 1987 Private Limited Company
**Line of Business:** Television activities
**Issued Capital:** £1,500
**Principals:** D P Dugan *(Managing)*, I Duncan, M K Obradovic, Mrs L E Bessell-Martin, C J Massarella, C J Burstall
**Co. Secretary:** Neptune Secretaries Limited
**Responsibilities**
**Senior:** Oliver Morse *(Company Director)*
**Marketing:** Kate Barker *(Producer/Director)*, Paul Shepard *(Editor)*
**Admin:** Martha Pitwood *(Office Manager)*
**HR:** Julie Duncan *(Human Resources Manager)*
**Operations:** Cherry Brewer *(Line Producer)*, Jason Hendriksen *(Production Manager)*, Birte Pedersen *(Head of Production)*
**US SIC:** 4833 **UK SIC:** 97411
**Auditors:** West & Co

| | 28-02-14 | 28-08-13 | 28-02-12 |
|---|---|---|---|
| TO | 6,747,733 | 16,449,045 | N/A |
| P/L | 206,003 | 1,218,444 | N/A |
| NW | 3,139,471 | 2,933,468 | 1,155,845 |
| WC | 3,025,013 | 2,832,627 | 1,067,586 |
| Emp. | 63 | 54 | N/A |

DUNS 23-386-6909

## Windhoist Ltd

(**Subsidiary of:** Windhoist Holdings Limited)
1 Dunlop Place, Meadowhead Industrial Estate, Irvine, Irvine, Ayrshire KA11 5BJ
**Tel:** 01294204860 **Fax:** 01294278422
**Web:** www.windhoist.co.uk
**Reg No:** 0278511SC **Estd:** 2005 Private Limited Company
**Line of Business:** Other construction work involving special trades
**Export Sales:** £5,391,805
**Issued Capital:** £2,000
**Co. Secretary:** Hugh Mcnally
**Responsibilities**
**Senior:** Jack Neill *(Workshop Manager)*
**US SIC:** 1799, 7399
**UK SIC:** 50000, 83954
**Auditors:** John A. Webb & Co
**Bankers:** The Bank Of Ireland (83-91-12)

| | 31-12-13 | 31-12-12 | 31-12-11 |
|---|---|---|---|
| TO | 21,418,867 | 26,546,556 | N/A |
| P/L | 2,468,050 | 4,213,888 | N/A |
| NW | 7,673,878 | 6,206,740 | 3,444,473 |
| WC | 11,961,634 | 6,839,098 | (3,806,362) |
| Emp. | 165 | 126 | N/A |

DUNS 29-823-0657

## The Windhorse Trust

17 Newmarket Road, Cambridge, Cambridgeshire CB5 8EG
**Tel:** 01223868600
**Web:** www.windhorse.biz
**Reg No:** 1990430 **Estd:** 1986 Private Company Limited By Guarantee
**Line of Business:** Activities of religious organisations
**Directors:** R P Staunton, R E Jones, T Pilchick, B L Murphy, A C Ernst Kennedy, D Thakkar
**Co. Secretary:** Robert Jones
**US SIC:** 8661 **UK SIC:** 96600
**Auditors:** Chater Allan
**Bankers:** HSBC Bank plc (40-17-32)

| | 31-03-14 | 31-03-13 | 31-03-12 |
|---|---|---|---|
| TO | 9,724,035 | 10,691,340 | 10,153,860 |
| P/L | (1,292,189) | (74,544) | (13,743) |
| NW | 7,295,752 | 8,587,942 | 8,662,486 |
| WC | 2,925,654 | 3,171,833 | 3,228,876 |
| Emp. | 197 | 176 | 174 |

DUNS 21-233-0717

## Windjammer Cafe & Bistro

11 Priory Street, Milford Haven, Dyfed SA73 2AD
**Tel:** 01646693999
**Estd:** 2002 Proprietorship
**Line of Business:** Restaurants
**Proprietor:** S Barton
**US SIC:** 5812 **UK SIC:** 66110
**Employees:** 99

DUNS 49-118-8264

## Windjen Power Ltd

(**Subsidiary of:** Work Panel Ltd)
Bod Hyfryd, Tan Y Graig Road, Llysfaen, Colwyn Bay, Clwyd LL29 8TH
**Tel:** 01492-517534
**Reg No:** 3099443 **Estd:** 1995 Private Limited Company
**Line of Business:** Electricity generating equipment
**Issued Capital:** £100
**Director:** D G Jones
**Co. Secretary:** Ms Elaine Jones
**Responsibilities**
**Senior:** Alun Evans *(Financial Controller)*
**Finance:** Alun Evans *(Financial Controller)*
**US SIC:** 6711 **UK SIC:** 83962

| | 31-03-14 | 31-03-13 | 31-03-12 |
|---|---|---|---|
| TA | 1,045,343 | 1,049,953 | 1,061,571 |
| NW | 895,343 | 899,109 | 909,086 |
| WC | 895,341 | 899,107 | 909,084 |

DUNS 21-636-2965 **Imp**

## Windles Group Manufacturing Ltd

5-8 Drakes Drive Meadow View, Aylesbury, Buckinghamshire HP18 9EQ
**Tel:** 01844201683 **Fax:** 01844201695
**Web:** www.windlesgroup.co.uk
**Reg No:** 7277210 **Estd:** 1984 Private Limited Company
**Line of Business:** Printing not elsewhere classified
**Trading Style:** Windles Group Manufacturing Ltd
**Issued Capital:** £200
**Directors:** W T Marr, Ms C L Podmore, Ms A C Norcott, B A Podmore
**Co. Secretary:** William Marr
**Responsibilities**
**Senior:** Dennis Podmore *(Manager)*
**Marketing:** Paul Stirland *(sales & marketing director)*
**Sales:** Paul Stirland *(sales & marketing director)*
**Health & Safety:** Philip Shipley *(operations director)*

**Facilities:** Philip Shipley *(operations director)*
**US SIC:** 2752 **UK SIC:** 47544

| | 31-05-13 | 31-05-12 | 31-05-11 |
|---|---|---|---|
| TO | 8,141,280 | 8,113,240 | N/A |
| P/L | (68,330) | 142,304 | N/A |
| NW | 3,630,562 | 3,837,930 | 3,762,767 |
| WC | 2,424,542 | 2,243,894 | 1,813,516 |
| Emp. | 70 | 68 | N/A |

DUNS 21-674-9551
## Windlesham House School
London Road, Washington, Pulborough, West Sussex RH20 4AY
**Tel:** 01903874700
**Web:** www.windlesham.com
**Estd:** 2002
**Line of Business:** General secondary education
**Directors:** S Holiday, N Ryan
**US SIC:** 8211 **UK SIC:** 93200
**Employees:** 156

DUNS 28-880-6060
## Windlesham School Trust Ltd
190 Dyke Road, Brighton, East Sussex BN1 5AA
**Web:** www.windleshamschool.co.uk
**Reg No:** 1172432 **Estd:** 1948 Private Limited Company
**Line of Business:** Schools (independent)
**Directors:** N D Baxter, G Rowlands-Hempel, Doctor E J Eadie, Mrs O A Mannion Watson
**Co. Secretary:** Graham Rowlands-Hempel
**Responsibilities**
**Senior:** Graham Rowlands-hempel *(Director)*
**US SIC:** 8211 **UK SIC:** 93200
**Auditors:** BDO Stoy Hayward
**Bankers:** Barclays Bank Plc (20-12-75)

| | 31-08-13 | 31-08-12 | 31-08-11 |
|---|---|---|---|
| TO | 1,748,041 | 1,674,234 | 1,552,989 |
| P/L | 138,178 | 105,573 | 108,260 |
| NW | 2,030,580 | 1,892,492 | 1,786,780 |
| WC | 414,217 | 240,348 | 112,238 |
| Emp. | 56 | 54 | 51 |

DUNS 23-667-9309
## Windmill Care Ltd
Windmill House, Alveston Road, Bristol, Avon BS32 4PH
**Tel:** 01454-413818 **Fax:** 01454423752
**Web:** www.windmillcare.com
**Reg No:** 3662801 **Estd:** 1998 Private Limited Company
**Line of Business:** Non-charitable social work activities with accommodation
**Issued Capital:** £1,000
**Directors:** Ms K R Collacott, R A Dawes
**Co. Secretary:** Leonard Collacott
**Responsibilities**
**Senior:** Richard Devison *(Manager)*
**US SIC:** 8321 **UK SIC:** 96111
**Auditors:** William Price & Co

| | 31-12-13 | 31-12-12 | 31-12-11 |
|---|---|---|---|
| TO | 3,475,479 | 3,308,692 | N/A |
| P/L | 768,060 | 330,729 | N/A |
| NW | 1,624,878 | 1,010,901 | 720,815 |
| WC | 427,073 | 700,252 | (147,531) |
| Emp. | 129 | 107 | N/A |

DUNS 23-682-5923
## Windmill Court Nursing & Residential Home
St Minver, Wadebridge, Cornwall PL27 6RD
**Estd:** 1989 Partnership
**Line of Business:** Non-charitable social work activities with accommodation
**US SIC:** 8321 **UK SIC:** 96111
**Employees:** 50

DUNS 22-667-9231 Exp
## Windmill (Dormco) Ltd
(**Subsidiary of:** Domes of Silence Holdings Ltd)
Whitley Way, Airfield Industrial Estate, Ashbourne, Derbyshire DE6 1LG
**Tel:** 01335348987 **Fax:** 01335-346350
**Reg No:** 1740033 **VAT No:** 646665111
**Estd:** 1983 Private Limited Company
**Line of Business:** Plastic extrusion manufacturers, subject acts an agents for Cirqual PLC.
**Export Markets:** Poland; Germany; Singapore
**Trading Style:** Unilux
**Issued Capital:** £860,000
**Director:** M S Meyer
**US SIC:** 3079, 2891
**UK SIC:** 48360, 25620
**Auditors:** PricewaterhouseCoopers
**Bankers:** Barclays Bank Plc (20-53-30)

| | 30-06-11 |
|---|---|
| NW | (360) |

DUNS 23-931-7998 Exp
## Windmill Extrusions Ltd
(**Subsidiary of:** Domes of Silence Holdings Ltd)
Whitley Way, Ashbourne, Derbyshire DE6 1LG
**Tel:** 01335-344554 **Fax:** 01335-346350
**Web:** www.windmill-unilux.com
**Reg No:** 3921669 **Estd:** 2000 Private Limited Company
**Line of Business:** Manufacturers of plastic products
**Export Sales:** £350,399
**Issued Capital:** £7,389,243
**Directors:** M S Meyer, P K Jones
**Responsibilities**
**Senior:** Bryn Morgan *(General Manager)*
**US SIC:** 2821 **UK SIC:** 25140

| | 30-06-14 | 30-06-13 | 30-06-12 |
|---|---|---|---|
| TO | 5,489,544 | 5,561,577 | 6,193,476 |
| P/L | 118,552 | (33,838) | 17,805 |
| NW | 5,046,292 | 4,897,733 | 4,896,207 |
| WC | 4,625,090 | 4,404,309 | 4,175,639 |
| Emp. | 68 | 65 | 69 |

DUNS 52-527-9808
## Windmill Group (Uk) Ltd.
Windmill Lane, Denton, Manchester M34 2JF
**Tel:** 01613209119 **Fax:** 0161-320-4747
**Web:** www.windmillgroup.uk.com
**Reg No:** 3233847 **Estd:** 1996 Private Limited Company
**Line of Business:** Demolition contractors
**Trading Style:** Windmill Group (Uk) Ltd
**Issued Capital:** £2
**Director:** A J Kelly
**Responsibilities**
**Marketing:** Maureen Whittaker *(Marketing Coordinator)*
**Admin:** Mike Knight *(Office Manager)*
**IT:** Mike Knight *(Office Manager)*
**HR:** Mike Knight *(Office Manager)*
**Health & Safety:** Mike Knight *(Office Manager)*
**Facilities:** Mike Knight *(Office Manager)*
**Purchasing:** Mike Knight *(Office Manager)*
**US SIC:** 1795 **UK SIC:** 50000
**Auditors:** Downham Morris Mayer & Co

| | 31-12-13 | 31-12-12 | 31-12-11 |
|---|---|---|---|
| TA | 1,106,406 | 1,046,407 | 811,625 |
| NW | 327,855 | 307,519 | 245,784 |
| WC | (9,616) | (5,433) | 23,694 |

DUNS 45-806-1751
## Windmill Hills Care Home Ltd
Newbiggin Lane, Newcastle-Upon-Tyne, Tyne and Wear NE5 1NA
**Tel:** 08000858904 **Fax:** 0191-490-1986
**Web:** www.execcaregroup.co.uk
**Reg No:** 3164158 **Estd:** 1996 Private Limited Company
**Line of Business:** Other human health activities
**Issued Capital:** £2
**Directors:** M C Glowasky, D M Harrison
**Co. Secretary:** Geoffrey Brown
**US SIC:** 8091 **UK SIC:** 95200
**Auditors:** The Charlton Williamson Partnership LLP
**Bankers:** Yorkshire Bank Plc (05-02-57)

| | 31-03-13 | 31-10-11 | 31-03-10 |
|---|---|---|---|
| TO | 3,657,022 | 1,454,358 | 1,423,730 |
| P/L | 70,376 | 34,847 | 21,149 |
| NW | (2,190,105) | 156,669 | 135,451 |
| WC | (4,692,246) | 864,096 | 976,891 |
| Emp. | 129 | 70 | 71 |

DUNS 21-228-2018
## Windmill House Nursing Home
77 Toll Road, Cellardyke, Anstruther, Fife KY10 3HZ
**Tel:** 01333-314300
**Web:** www.windmillhousecarehome.co.uk
**Estd:** 2002 Partnership
**Line of Business:** Medical nursing home activities
**Partners:** Mrs A Rusack, Mrs L Rusack
**Responsibilities**
**Senior:** Ailson Rusack *(Home Manager)*
**Admin:** Karen Steel *(Office Manager)*
**IT:** Karen Steel *(Office Manager)*
**HR:** Ailson Rusack *(Home Manager)*
**Facilities:** Ailson Rusack *(Home Manager)*
**US SIC:** 8051 **UK SIC:** 95100
**Employees:** 54

DUNS 23-555-9072 Imp
## Windmill Organics Ltd
34a Clifton Road, Kingston-Upon-Thames, Surrey KT2 6PH
**Tel:** 02085 472775 **Fax:** 02085 469942
**Web:** www.windmillorganics.com
**Reg No:** 3554199 **Estd:** 1998 Private Limited Company
**Line of Business:** Organic food production and supply
**Issued Capital:** £1,000
**Director:** N Mcdonald
**Co. Secretary:** Donata Berger
**US SIC:** 5499, 2834
**UK SIC:** 64100, 25700
**Auditors:** Arthur G. Mead Ltd

| | 31-12-13 | 31-12-12 | 30-12-12 |
|---|---|---|---|
| TO | 23,442,542 | 11,763,054 | 12,315,750 |
| P/L | 4,308,318 | 1,927,514 | 2,057,867 |
| NW | 12,619,513 | 9,526,419 | 8,307,007 |
| WC | 10,980,416 | 7,771,541 | 7,943,765 |
| Emp. | 47 | 43 | 41 |

DUNS 21-164-0979
## Windmill Primary School
Windmill Lane, Raunds, Wellingborough, Northamptonshire NN9 6LA
**Tel:** 01933-623121
**Web:** www.windmillprimary.co.uk
**Estd:** 1971
**Line of Business:** Schools (foundation)
**Chairman:** D Moreton
**Responsibilities**
**Senior:** Michelle Ginn *(Head Teacher)*
**US SIC:** 8211 **UK SIC:** 93200
**Employees:** 50

DUNS 23-859-4790
## Window Build
55-56 Lewis Road, Cardiff, South Glamorgan CF24 5EB
**Tel:** 029-2030-7200
**Web:** www.windowbuild.co.uk
**Estd:** 1989 Proprietorship
**Line of Business:** Manufacturers of window frames
**Proprietors:** D Hanson, D Hanson
**Responsibilities**
**Finance:** Natasha Moore *(Management Accountant)*
**IT:** Ryan Churches *(Computer Manager)*
**Operations:** Martin Bosomworth *(Production Manager)*
**Engineering:** Martin Bosomworth *(Production Manager)*
**US SIC:** 3442 **UK SIC:** 31420
**Employees:** 160

DUNS 34-862-4776
## The Window Bureau Ltd
Unit 5 8, Station Lane, Birtley, Chester-Le-Street, County Durham DH3 1DQ
**Tel:** 0191-410-9333 **Fax:** 01914105593
**Web:** www.wbgroup.co.uk
**Reg No:** 2814410 **VAT No:** 569547681
**Estd:** 1981 Private Limited Company
**Line of Business:** Manufacture of other plastic products
**Trading Style:** W B Group
**Issued Capital:** £86
**Directors:** D Pitcher, Miss C J Craggs, A T Craggs, M Tindle, Mrs A L Griffin, K Craggs
**Co. Secretary:** Ms Andrea Griffin
**US SIC:** 3079 **UK SIC:** 48360
**Auditors:** Clive Owen & Co LLP
**Bankers:** National Westminster Bank Plc (52-30-44)

| | 31-12-13 | 31-12-12 | 31-12-11 |
|---|---|---|---|
| TA | 1,848,682 | 1,322,339 | 1,162,846 |
| NW | 800,422 | 458,695 | 351,467 |
| WC | 564,145 | 220,015 | 74,617 |

DUNS 22-519-9017
## Window Fitters Mate Ltd
(**Subsidiary of:** Sig Plc)
4 The Pentex Centre, Bolton Close, Uckfield, East Sussex TN22 1PH
**Tel:** 01825760505
**Web:** www.wfm.co.uk
**Reg No:** 1712782 **Estd:** 1987 Private Limited Company
**Line of Business:** Double glazing suppliers
**Issued Capital:** £84
**Director:** I Jackson
**Co. Secretary:** Richard Monro
**Responsibilities**
**Senior:** Christopher Bow *(Manager)*, Michael Chivers *(Manager)*, Bob French *(Branch Manager)*
**Branches:** Window Fitters Mate Ltd, 71 Windmill Road, Luton, Bedfordshire LU1 3XL
**US SIC:** 1721, 3231
**UK SIC:** 50400, 24791
**Bankers:** National Westminster Bank Plc (52-41-00)

| | 31-12-13 | 31-12-12 | 31-12-11 |
|---|---|---|---|
| TA | 84 | 84 | 84 |
| NW | 84 | 84 | 84 |

DUNS 23-445-4150
## The Window Store
Tor Park Road, Paignton, Devon TQ4 7PL
**Tel:** 01803-554355
**Web:** www.windowstoreplastics.co.uk
**Estd:** 1984 Proprietorship
**Line of Business:** Manufacturers of plastic products
**Proprietor:** S Rose
**US SIC:** 2821 **UK SIC:** 25140
**Employees:** 50

DUNS 21-613-7927 Imp
## Windowflowers Ltd
(**Subsidiary of:** Window Boxes Ltd)
Grove Road, Burnham, Slough, Berkshire SL1 8DT
**Fax:** 01628-604047
**Web:** www.windowflowers.com
**Reg No:** 0427413 **VAT No:** 537879289
**Estd:** 1947 Private Limited Company
**Line of Business:** Floral and plant displays
**Issued Capital:** £3,920
**Principals:** A C Gradden *(Managing)*, M E Watson-Smyth
**Co. Secretary:** Mrs Miranda Arkell
**Responsibilities**
**Senior:** Miles Smyth *(Manager)*
**US SIC:** 5999 **UK SIC:** 65600
**Auditors:** MacIntyre Hudson LLP
**Bankers:** Lloyds TSB Bank plc (30-94-28)

| | 31-12-13 | 31-12-12 | 31-12-11 |
|---|---|---|---|
| TA | 1,444,646 | 1,570,687 | 1,216,233 |
| NW | 403,149 | 472,704 | 445,381 |
| WC | (118,828) | (61,152) | (43,068) |

DUNS 21-588-6386
## Windowmate
Unit 2 68 Balloo Road, Bangor, Co Down BT19 7PG
**Tel:** 02895622500
**Web:** www.windowmateupvc.com
**Estd:** 2007
**Line of Business:** Double glazing installers
**Responsibilities**
**Senior:** Thomas Mcallister *(Branch Manager)*
**US SIC:** 1721 **UK SIC:** 50400
**Employees:** 60

DUNS 28-827-3402
## Windows Catering Company (Four) Ltd
21 Royal Exchange Square, Glasgow, Lanarkshire G1 3AJ
**Tel:** 01412482111 **Fax:** 01412487160
**Web:** www.dimaggios.co.uk
**Reg No:** 0083732SC **Estd:** 2002 Private Limited Company
**Line of Business:** Restaurant - italian
**Trading Style:** Di Maggios
**Issued Capital:** £20,000
**Principals:** M L Gizzi *(Managing)*, G A Conetta
**Co. Secretary:** Mario Gizzi
**Responsibilities**
**Senior:** Giuseppe Conetta *(Director)*, Ching Mellan *(Reservations Manager)*, Akif Polat *(General Manager)*
**Branches:** Windows Catering Company (Four) Ltd, The Boardwalk, Stroud Rd, Glasgow, Lanarkshire G75 0YA
**US SIC:** 5812 **UK SIC:** 66110
**Auditors:** Baker Tilly Audit Ltd

| | 03-05-14 | 27-04-13 | 30-05-11 |
|---|---|---|---|
| TO | N/A | N/A | 18,449,338 |
| P/L | N/A | N/A | (1,823,599) |
| NW | 48,888 | 20,001 | (117,381) |
| WC | 48,888 | 20,001 | (392,242) |
| Emp. | N/A | N/A | 419 |

DUNS 28-951-7286
## Windrush Garage Ltd
57 Farnham Road, Slough, Berkshire SL1 3TN
**Tel:** 01753-670200
**Web:** www.windrush.co.uk
**Reg No:** 1631994 **VAT No:** 370174272
**Estd:** 1982 Private Limited Company
**Line of Business:** Car dealers (new & used)
**Issued Capital:** £334,000
**Principals:** A P Rosner *(Managing)*, T S Attwood, Mrs S Rosner
**Co. Secretary:** Leigh Chappell
**Responsibilities**
**Senior:** Keith Mountaney *(Parts Manager)*
**Finance:** Lee Chappell *(Financial Director)*
**IT:** Brian Furness *(IT Systems Manager)*
**Health & Safety:** Brian Furness *(IT Systems Manager)*
**US SIC:** 5511, 5521
**UK SIC:** 65100
**Auditors:** Nyman Libson Paul
**Bankers:** Lloyds TSB Bank plc (77-91-66)

| | 31-12-13 | 31-12-12 | 31-12-11 |
|---|---|---|---|
| TO | 33,353,904 | 28,578,870 | 27,865,697 |
| P/L | 184,818 | 93,346 | (77,209) |
| NW | 636,337 | 536,075 | 418,430 |
| WC | (77,200) | (8,217) | (201,534) |
| Emp. | 85 | 89 | 93 |

DUNS 21-197-9604
## Windsmoor Ltd
(**Subsidiary of:** Sun Capital Partners Inc.)
Windsmoor, Seaham, County Durham SR7 0PZ
**Tel:** 08447705838
**Web:** www.windsmoor.co.uk
**Reg No:** 0869809 **VAT No:** 589932568
**Estd:** 1933 Private Limited Company

**Line of Business:** Offices of holding companies
**Trading Style:** Jacques Vert
**Issued Capital:** £1,113,415
**Directors:** Ms T Tideman, Ms J C Bennett
**Co. Secretary:** Mrs Amanda Fogg
**Branches:** Windsmoor Ltd, Unit 1 Bowburn North Indstl Est, Durham, County Durham DH6 5PF
**US SIC:** 6711 **UK SIC:** 83962
**Bankers:** HSBC Bank plc (40-05-30)

| | 25-01-14 | 26-01-13 | 28-01-12 |
|---|---|---|---|
| TA | 8,707,780 | 8,707,780 | 8,707,780 |
| NW | 5,935,868 | 5,935,868 | 5,935,868 |
| WC | 3,163,747 | 3,163,747 | 3,163,747 |

DUNS 23-230-6530
## Windsor & District Housing Association Ltd
Parkside House, Windsor, Berkshire SL4 1BY
**Tel:** 01753-777400 **Fax:** 01753-777499
**Web:** www.radian.co.uk
**Reg No:** 0027877IP **Estd:** 1993 Friendly Society
**Line of Business:** Industrial and providence housing association
**Trading Style:** Windsor Housing
**Chairman:** Ms D Lawson
**Co. Secretary:** Colin Sherriff
**Responsibilities**
**Senior:** Gemma Stephenson (Community Development Officer)
**Branches:** Windsor & District Housing Association Ltd, Brockenhurst Rd, Ascot, Berkshire SL5 9DF
**US SIC:** 6531 **UK SIC:** 83400
**Bankers:** Barclays Bank Plc (20-97-09)

| | 31-03-12 | 31-03-11 | 31-03-10 |
|---|---|---|---|
| TO | 24,610,000 | 23,307,000 | 22,901,000 |
| P/L | (1,235,000) | 3,693,000 | (588,000) |
| NW | 190,379,000 | 172,606,000 | 146,529,000 |
| WC | 7,882,000 | (2,130,000) | (2,092,000) |
| Emp. | 58 | 61 | 52 |

DUNS 21-579-7983
## Windsor & Maidenhead Community Mental Health Team
Nicholsons Walk, Maidenhead, Berkshire SL6 1LB
**Tel:** 01628640200
**Estd:** 1988 Proprietorship
**Line of Business:** Hospitals
**Proprietor:** Mrs B Fairbairn
**US SIC:** 8091 **UK SIC:** 95200
**Employees:** 50

DUNS 21-579-8014
## Windsor Court
Bartholomew Avenue, Goole, North Humberside DN14 6YN
**Web:** www.hc-one.co.uk
**Estd:** 1997 Proprietorship
**Line of Business:** Medical nursing home activities
**Proprietor:** Mrs K Green Smith
**US SIC:** 8051 **UK SIC:** 95100
**Employees:** 68

DUNS 64-263-2210
## Windsor Court Nursing Home
The Avenue, Wallsend, Tyne and Wear NE28 6SD
**Web:** www.ladhargroupcarehomes.co.uk
**Estd:** 1996 Proprietorship
**Line of Business:** Medical nursing home activities
**Proprietor:** B Ladhar
**US SIC:** 8051 **UK SIC:** 95100
**Employees:** 50

DUNS 50-349-1623    Imp
## Windsor Engineering (Hull) Ltd
Citadel Trading Park, Citadel Way, Hull, North Humberside HU9 1TQ
**Tel:** 01482-329996 **Fax:** 01482-229942
**Web:** www.windsor-mh.co.uk
**Reg No:** 2371193 **VAT No:** 501047700
**Estd:** 1989 Private Limited Company
**Line of Business:** Plant hire and leasing
**Trading Style:** Windsor Engineering (Hull) Limited
**Issued Capital:** £1,000
**Principals:** G Burton (Managing), A Lane, S P Burton, J G Burton
**Co. Secretary:** Mark Harrison
**Branches:** Windsor Engineering (Hull) Limited, Fairfield House, Sleaford, Lincolnshire NG34 8SX
**US SIC:** 7394, 3534
**UK SIC:** 84000, 32553
**Auditors:** Dutton Moore

**Bankers:** HSBC Bank plc (40-25-18)

| | 31-07-13 | 31-07-12 | 31-07-11 |
|---|---|---|---|
| TO | 13,615,395 | 11,150,287 | 10,228,488 |
| P/L | 740,738 | 449,625 | (43,965) |
| NW | 3,344,218 | 2,740,373 | 2,346,727 |
| WC | (1,092,638) | (1,561,633) | (1,615,653) |
| Emp. | 108 | 100 | 97 |

DUNS 21-585-1788
## Windsor Farm Shop
Datchet Road, Old Windsor, Windsor, Berkshire SL4 2RQ
**Tel:** 01753-623800
**Web:** www.windsorfarmshop.co.uk
**Estd:** 2001 Proprietorship
**Line of Business:** Farm shops
**Proprietor:** C Murray
**Responsibilities**
**Senior:** Martin Gorsuch (General Manager)
**Admin:** Lianne Bradford (Office Administrator)
**US SIC:** 0729 **UK SIC:** 01003
**Employees:** 99

DUNS 21-585-3756
## Windsor Group
Unit 7 9, Romsey Industrial Estate, Greatbridge Road, Romsey, Hampshire SO51 0AD
**Tel:** 01794527420
**Web:** www.windsorproducts.com
**Estd:** 2010
**Line of Business:** Health & safety products
**US SIC:** 5999 **UK SIC:** 65600
**Employees:** 250

DUNS 23-082-8365
## Windsor High School
Richmond Street, Halesowen, West Midlands B63 4BB
**Tel:** 0121-550-1452
**Web:** www.windsor.dudley.sch.uk
**Estd:** 1991
**Line of Business:** Schools (local authority)
**Principals:** K Bissell (Chairman), K W Sorrell
**US SIC:** 8211 **UK SIC:** 93200
**Bankers:** Lloyds TSB Bank plc (30-93-75)
**Employees:** 80

DUNS 21-395-9793
## Windsor House
1 Woolwich Manor Way, London E6 5NT
**Tel:** 02075113840
**Web:** www.brewersfayre.co.uk
**Estd:** 2007 Proprietorship
**Line of Business:** Restaurant - english
**Proprietor:** L Stone
**Responsibilities**
**Senior:** Jarrod Green (Manager)
**US SIC:** 5812 **UK SIC:** 66110
**Employees:** 70

DUNS 21-314-6272
## Windsor Leisure Centre
Stovell Road, Windsor, Berkshire SL4 5JB
**Tel:** 01753842191
**Web:** www.rbwm.gov.uk
**Estd:** 2011 Proprietorship
**Line of Business:** Alternative medical treatments and therapies
**Proprietor:** J Spencer
**Responsibilities**
**Senior:** Jes Spencer (Centre Manager)
**Finance:** Richard May (Business Development Manager)
**HR:** Linda Ambrose (Human Resources Manager)
**Facilities:** Jes Spencer (Centre Manager)
**Operations:** Jes Spencer (Centre Manager)
**Purchasing:** Jes Spencer (Centre Manager)
**US SIC:** 7299 **UK SIC:** 98902
**Employees:** 300

DUNS 21-322-4343
## Windsor Nursing Home
232 Victoria Road East, Hebburn, Tyne and Wear NE31 1YQ
**Estd:** 1993 Proprietorship
**Line of Business:** Residential care establishments
**Proprietor:** Dr V Vinayak
**US SIC:** 8321 **UK SIC:** 96111
**Employees:** 52

DUNS 23-233-0709
## Windsor Voice Services
Fairacre House, Tinkers Lane Dedworth Road, Windsor, Berkshire SL4 4LE
**Web:** www.dot2taxi.co.uk
**Estd:** 1994 Partnership
**Line of Business:** Taxis and private hire vehicles
**Partners:** K Dyer, M Smith
**US SIC:** 4121 **UK SIC:** 72200
**Employees:** 47

DUNS 21-832-0075
## Windsors (Wallasey) Ltd
Harrison Drive, Wallasey, Merseyside CH45 3HP
**Tel:** 01516396181
**Web:** www.windsors.uk.com
**Reg No:** 0301435 **VAT No:** 163544171
**Estd:** 1922 Private Limited Company
**Line of Business:** New & used motor vehicle dealers
**Issued Capital:** £15,564
**Principals:** D M Tuomey (Managing), Mrs K Tuomey, J M Stockdale
**Co. Secretary:** Philip Mccormick
**Responsibilities**
**HR:** Paula Brown (Human Resources Manager)
**Health & Safety:** Paula Brown (Human Resources Manager)
**Operations:** Steve Burdett (Service Manager)
**Purchasing:** Steve Burdett (Service Manager)
**Branches:** Windsors (Wallasey) Ltd, Milner Road, Wirral, Merseyside CH60 5RZ
**US SIC:** 5511, 5521, 7539, 5531
**UK SIC:** 65100, 67100
**Auditors:** McEwan Wallace
**Bankers:** HSBC Bank plc (40-10-22)

| | 31-05-14 | 31-05-13 | 31-05-12 |
|---|---|---|---|
| TO | 27,301,702 | 25,301,067 | 23,038,382 |
| P/L | 382,817 | 654,513 | 233,352 |
| NW | 5,238,324 | 5,347,076 | 5,215,240 |
| WC | 944,363 | 902,828 | 677,424 |
| Emp. | 72 | 72 | 74 |

DUNS 22-519-6393    Imp
## Windward Marine Ltd
Bath Road, Lymington, Hampshire SO41 3RU
**Tel:** 01590673698 **Fax:** 08451300720
**Web:** www.force4.co.uk
**Reg No:** 1013726 **Estd:** 1971 Private Limited Company
**Line of Business:** Catalogue shops
**Export Sales:** £353,467
**Trading Style:** Force 4 Chandlery
**Issued Capital:** £65,445
**Directors:** P R Mcluskie, N D Paramor, L A Parr, R W Young, Ms S E Radford
**US SIC:** 4469, 5699, 5999, 5961
**UK SIC:** 76300, 64500, 65600
**Auditors:** Hextall Meakin
**Bankers:** Lloyds TSB Bank plc (30-92-06)

| | 31-10-13 | 31-10-12 | 31-10-11 |
|---|---|---|---|
| TO | 11,566,225 | 10,344,582 | 9,997,271 |
| P/L | 631,366 | 467,392 | 450,112 |
| NW | 2,236,470 | 1,871,816 | 1,596,790 |
| WC | 2,120,440 | 1,733,191 | 1,448,120 |
| Emp. | 88 | 68 | 61 |

DUNS 50-648-4799
## Windwhistle Post Office
7 Loxton Road, Weston-Super-Mare, Avon BS23 4QX
**Tel:** 01934-625145
**Web:** www.postoffice.co.uk
**Estd:** 1989 Partnership
**Line of Business:** Post offices
**Partners:** Mrs J S Page, A J Page
**US SIC:** 4311, 5999
**UK SIC:** 79010, 65600
**Bankers:** HSBC Bank plc (40-01-01)
**Employees:** 70

DUNS 21-485-4817
## Windyhall Nursing Home
3 Southpark Road, Ayr, Ayrshire KA7 2TL
**Web:** www.carehome.co.uk
**Estd:** 1984 Partnership
**Line of Business:** Nursing homes
**Partners:** J Murdoch, Mrs M Murdoch
**Responsibilities**
**Senior:** Isabel Wyatt (Home Manager)
**Finance:** Beth McIntyre (Financial Administrator)
**IT:** Isabel Wyatt (Home Manager)
**HR:** Isabel Wyatt (Home Manager)
**Health & Safety:** Isabel Wyatt (Home Manager)
**Facilities:** Isabel Wyatt (Home Manager)
**Operations:** Isabel Wyatt (Home Manager)
**Purchasing:** Beth McIntyre (Financial Administrator)
**US SIC:** 8051 **UK SIC:** 95100
**Employees:** 58

DUNS 22-913-5777    Imp
## Windymains Sawmills Ltd
(Subsidiary of: Figaro Ltd)
Windymains, Humbie, East Lothian EH36 5PA
**Tel:** 01875321950 **Fax:** 01875-833326
**Web:** www.windymainstimber.co.uk
**Reg No:** 0011581M **VAT No:** 328606648
**Estd:** 1978 Private Limited Company
**Line of Business:** Saw milling and planing of wood, impregnation of wood
**Trading Style:** Windymains Timber Ltd

**Issued Capital:** £2,283,434
**Principals:** J J Harrison (Managing), J Bruce, Ms M S Harrison, J Bruce
**Co. Secretary:** James Cowan
**US SIC:** 2421 **UK SIC:** 46101
**Bankers:** HSBC Bank plc (40-20-44)
**Employees:** 50

DUNS 28-865-5897    Imp
## Wine & Spirit Education Trust
International House, 39-45 Bermondsey Street, London SE1 3XF
**Tel:** 020-7089-3800
**Web:** www.wsetglobal.com
**Reg No:** 0964179 **Estd:** 2005 Private Company Limited By Guarantee
**Line of Business:** Adult and other education not elsewhere classified
**Export Sales:** £4,046,068
**Directors:** J P Driver, J C Simpson, N A Hyde, Ms M F Randall, S W Thorpe, M J Turner, A J Hawes, T Christensen
**Co. Secretary:** Ms Angela Fordham
**Responsibilities**
**Senior:** Janet Bangs (Office Manager)
**Marketing:** Antony Moss (Director of Strategic Planning), Kate Powell (Online Communications Manager), David Wrigley (Global Communications Director)
**Sales:** Catherine Boot (Business Development Manager), Jude Mullins (International Business Develop), Simon Robertson-Macleod (Business Development Manager), Rosemary Rogers (Business Development Manager)
**Admin:** Janet Bangs (Office Manager), Owen Barritt (Librarian), Isabelle Dufton (Examinations Administrator)
**Operations:** John Townley (Quality Assurance Manager)
**Purchasing:** Joseph Beddoe (Wine Buyer)
**Branches:** Wine & Spirit Education Trust, Post Office La, Nottingham, Nottinghamshire NG13 0JL
**US SIC:** 8249 **UK SIC:** 93300
**Auditors:** Coulthards MacKenzie
**Bankers:** National Westminster Bank Plc (56-00-18)

| | 31-07-14 | 31-07-13 | 31-07-12 |
|---|---|---|---|
| TO | 7,634,091 | 6,750,788 | 5,784,388 |
| P/L | 1,156,595 | 1,287,226 | 764,044 |
| NW | 8,305,307 | 7,148,712 | 5,861,486 |
| WC | 1,861,105 | 2,613,398 | 3,488,535 |
| Emp. | 79 | 69 | 63 |

DUNS 23-716-4199    Imp
## Wineflair (Belfast) Ltd
(Subsidiary of: Liquorland Ltd)
8 West Bank Road, Belfast Harbour Estated, Belfast BT3 9JL
**Tel:** 028-9077-3990 **Fax:** 02890370566
**Web:** www.wineflair.net
**Reg No:** 0019803NI **Estd:** 1986 Private Limited Company
**Line of Business:** Representative office
**Trading Style:** Wineflair, Chateau
**Issued Capital:** £502
**Directors:** C D Mckay, H F Cushnahan, N J Mackinlay, R Hall, Mrs A Carson, R Hughes, A Mcguinness
**Branches:** Wineflair (Belfast) Ltd, 85-87 Glen Road, Andersonstown, Belfast, Belfast BT11 8BD
**US SIC:** 7399, 5993
**UK SIC:** 83954, 64200
**Auditors:** McClure Watters
**Bankers:** First Trust Bank (aib Group (uk) Plc) (93-80-92)

| | 30-09-13 | 30-09-12 | 30-09-11 |
|---|---|---|---|
| TO | 24,934,291 | 20,862,511 | 35,346,095 |
| P/L | 683,256 | 165,551 | 520,861 |
| NW | 10,328,655 | 11,108,945 | 11,009,513 |
| WC | 10,241,195 | 10,212,546 | 10,558,133 |
| Emp. | 253 | 253 | 263 |

DUNS 21-591-1310
## Winelodge
58 Bridge Road, Lowestoft, Suffolk NR32 3LR
**Tel:** 01502587642
**Web:** www.winelodge.co.uk
**Estd:** 2011 Proprietorship
**Line of Business:** Bars
**Proprietor:** D Pickess
**US SIC:** 5813 **UK SIC:** 66200
**Employees:** 50

DUNS 22-928-9400
## Winemark the Winemerchants Ltd
(Subsidiary of: Golf Holdings Limited)
3 Duncrue Place, Belfast BT3 9BU
**Tel:** 02890746274
**Web:** www.winemark.com
**Reg No:** 0012743NI **Estd:** 1978 Private Limited Company
**Line of Business:** Retail sale of alcoholic and other beverages
**Trading Style:** Winemark
**Issued Capital:** £100

**Directors:** P M Hunt, J O Hunt, R J Davis, P Hunt, R Davis, J P Hunt, J P Hunt, J O Hunt
**Co. Secretary:** William Wilson
**Branches:** Winemark The Winemerchants Ltd, 190 Saintfield Road, Belfast, Belfast BT8 6NN
**US SIC:** 5921, 5993
**UK SIC:** 64200
**Auditors:** James P. Convery & Co
**Bankers:** Northern Bank Ltd (95-00-05)

| | 31-12-13 | 31-12-12 | 31-12-11 |
|---|---|---|---|
| TO | 19,080,255 | 19,633,065 | 20,779,908 |
| P/L | 468,493 | 1,751,330 | 966,132 |
| NW | 16,062,881 | 15,852,803 | 15,544,038 |
| WC | 6,947,775 | 6,626,978 | 5,088,622 |
| Emp. | 244 | 258 | 281 |

DUNS 77-009-4811

## Winep 52 Ltd

(**Subsidiary of:** Epwin Group Plc)
Stafford Park 6, Telford, Shropshire TF3 3AT
**Tel:** 01952280550
**Web:** www.e-strategy.net
**Reg No:** 2659759 **VAT No:** 864450710
**Estd:** 1991 Private Limited Company
**Line of Business:** Home improvement
**Trading Style:** Swish Window & Door Systems, Telford Extrusions, Wrekin Windows
**Issued Capital:** £4,000,000
**Director:** J A Bednall
**Co. Secretary:** Epwin Secretaries Limited
**US SIC:** 5719 **UK SIC:** 64700

| | 31-12-13 | 31-12-12 | 31-12-11 |
|---|---|---|---|
| TA | 4,034,662 | 4,034,662 | 4,034,662 |
| NW | 4,034,662 | 4,034,662 | 4,004,002 |

DUNS 29-876-6437

## Winep 55 Ltd

(**Subsidiary of:** Epwin Group Plc)
Alders Way Yalberton Industrial Estate, Paignton, Devon TQ4 7QE
**Tel:** 01803-697197
**Web:** www.epwin.co.uk
**Reg No:** 2079769 **VAT No:** 668461107
**Estd:** 1986 Private Limited Company
**Line of Business:** Conservatories
**Trading Style:** The Apwin Group
**Issued Capital:** £10,000
**Director:** J A Bednall
**Co. Secretary:** Epwin Secretaries Limited
**Responsibilities**
**Senior:** Paul Hazel *(Manager)*, Richard Rawson *(Manager)*, Jim Rawson *(Manager)*, Sean Rice *(Manager)*
**Finance:** Michelle Day *(Credit Control)*
**HR:** Martin Manning *(Hr Director)*
**Health & Safety:** Bill Feasey *(Health & Safety Manager)*
**Engineering:** Gordon Cowell *(Maintenance Manager)*
**Branches:** Stafford Park 6, Telford, Shropshire TF3 3AT
**US SIC:** 3441, 3079
**UK SIC:** 32042, 48360

| | 31-12-13 | 31-12-12 | 31-12-11 |
|---|---|---|---|
| TA | 109,909 | 109,909 | 109,909 |
| NW | 109,909 | 109,909 | 109,909 |

DUNS 21-910-5400

## Winfield Engineering Ltd

Alma Park Road, Grantham, Lincolnshire NG31 9SE
**Tel:** 01476567105
**Web:** www.winfieldengineering.com
**Reg No:** 1188208 **Estd:** 1974 Private Limited Company
**Line of Business:** Sheet metal fabricators
**Issued Capital:** £1,000
**Principals:** S P Winfield *(Managing)*, Mrs S Winfield
**Co. Secretary:** Simon Winfield
**Responsibilities**
**Senior:** Alan Hardisty *(Manager)*
**US SIC:** 3469 **UK SIC:** 31200
**Auditors:** Duncan & Toplis
**Bankers:** National Westminster Bank Plc (60-09-09)

| | 30-04-14 | 30-04-13 | 30-04-12 |
|---|---|---|---|
| TA | 2,461,454 | 1,989,575 | 1,802,440 |
| NW | 1,177,569 | 1,052,695 | 1,019,858 |
| WC | 422,888 | 286,690 | 630,875 |

DUNS 21-012-9762

## Winfield Shoe Co Ltd

(**Subsidiary of:** Winfield Holdings Ltd)
Mill Street, Rossendale, Lancashire BB4 5JW
**Tel:** 01706831952 **Fax:** 01706218207
**Web:** www.winfieldsoutdoors.co.uk
**Reg No:** 6359798 **Estd:** 2007 Private Limited Company
**Line of Business:** Health & fitness club
**Trading Style:** Winfields Megastore
**Issued Capital:** £1
**Directors:** D Winfield, Mrs J Winfield
**Co. Secretary:** Ms Janine Winfield
**Responsibilities**
**HR:** June Siminiuk *(Human Resources Manager)*
**Facilities:** Jamie Woods *(Maintenance Manager)*
**Branches:** Winfield Shoe Co Ltd, Winfield Shoe Co Ltd, Hazel Mill, Rossendale, Lancashire BB4 5DD
**US SIC:** 7399 **UK SIC:** 83954

| | 31-01-14 | 31-01-13 | 31-01-12 |
|---|---|---|---|
| TA | 1 | 1 | 1 |
| NW | 1 | 1 | 1 |

DUNS 73-560-4147 **Imp**

## Wing Hong & Co Ltd

(**Subsidiary of:** New Leaf Investments Ltd)
55 George Street, Newcastle-Upon-Tyne, Tyne and Wear NE4 7JN
**Tel:** 01912723888 **Fax:** 01912-723999
**Web:** www.winghong.co.uk
**Reg No:** 4822242 **Estd:** 2003 Private Limited Company
**Line of Business:** Supermarkets
**Issued Capital:** £1
**Director:** D Cheng
**Co. Secretary:** Ken Cheng
**Branches:** Wing Hong & Co Ltd, 45-51 Stowell Street, Newcastle-Upon-Tyne, Newcastle Upon Tyne, Tyne and Wear NE1 4YB
**US SIC:** 5149, 5147, 5499
**UK SIC:** 61700, 64100
**Bankers:** Lloyds TSB Bank plc (30-93-55)

| | 31-07-13 | 31-07-12 | 31-07-11 |
|---|---|---|---|
| TO | 7,357,066 | 8,133,910 | 7,784,438 |
| P/L | (222,365) | 16,637 | 208,145 |
| NW | (56,992) | 147,648 | 131,162 |
| WC | 42,011 | 95,498 | 68,746 |
| Emp. | 55 | 51 | 52 |

DUNS 42-402-0449

## Wing Security Ltd

Wing House Herne Manor Farm, Park Road, Toddington, Dunstable, Bedfordshire LU5 6HH
**Fax:** 01525878088
**Web:** www.wingsecurity.co.uk
**Reg No:** 4389731 **Estd:** 1988 Private Limited Company
**Line of Business:** Security and related activities
**Issued Capital:** £1,000
**Director:** R P Dickens
**Co. Secretary:** Mark Austin
**Responsibilities**
**Senior:** Carole Collins *(Manager)*
**US SIC:** 8999 **UK SIC:** 83954
**Auditors:** AVN BeyondProfit

| | 30-04-14 | 30-04-13 | 30-04-12 |
|---|---|---|---|
| TA | 45,584 | 9,211 | 108,665 |
| NW | 15,871 | 3,471 | 36,871 |
| WC | 15,871 | 3,471 | 19,709 |

DUNS 73-915-0592

## Wingate Ltd

Wingate House, Rutherford Road, Basingstoke, Hampshire RG24 8QD
**Tel:** 01256-330000
**Reg No:** 5168477 **Estd:** 2004 Private Limited Company
**Line of Business:** Holding companies management activities
**Issued Capital:** £58,333
**Director:** P Frewin
**Co. Secretary:** Mark Frewin
**US SIC:** 6711 **UK SIC:** 83962
**Auditors:** RSM Tenon Ltd
**Bankers:** National Westminster Bank Plc (60-02-49)

| | 30-09-13 | 30-09-12 | 30-09-11 |
|---|---|---|---|
| TO | 30,955,018 | 32,173,120 | 30,814,443 |
| P/L | 1,599,072 | 1,602,931 | 1,484,765 |
| NW | 7,440,487 | 6,720,713 | 6,008,232 |
| WC | 6,412,742 | 5,616,101 | 5,000,447 |
| Emp. | 193 | 224 | 228 |

DUNS 21-209-8243

## Wingfield Nursing Home

Oakridge Court, Bingley, West Yorkshire BD16 4TA
**Estd:** 2012 Proprietorship
**Line of Business:** Clinics private
**Proprietor:** Dr A Ghoneim
**Responsibilities**
**Senior:** Emma Rushen *(Home Manager)*
**Finance:** Lucy Hudson *(Administrator)*
**Health & Safety:** Tareck Ghoneim *(Health & Safety Officer)*
**Facilities:** Elliott Moseley *(Facilities Manager)*
**US SIC:** 8051 **UK SIC:** 95100
**Employees:** 46

DUNS 21-312-2559

## Wingrove Motor Company Ltd

Silverlink Retail Park, Silverlink, Wallsend, Tyne and Wear NE28 9ND
**Tel:** 01912953000
**Web:** www.wingrovemotors.citroen.co.uk
**Reg No:** 0207803 **VAT No:** 176117953
**Estd:** 1925 Private Limited Company
**Line of Business:** Sale of new motor vehicles
**Issued Capital:** £155,000
**Principals:** P Dalkin *(Managing)*, Mrs L Parker
**Co. Secretary:** Peter Dalkin
**Responsibilities**
**Senior:** Louise Dalkin *(Proprietor)*
**Branches:** Wingrove Motor Company Ltd, Stephenson Building, 173 Elswick Road, Newcastle Upon Tyne, Tyne and Wear NE4 6SQ
**US SIC:** 5511, 5521, 7539, 5531
**UK SIC:** 65100, 67100
**Auditors:** R Tait Walker & Co
**Bankers:** Barclays Bank Plc (20-59-97)

| | 31-12-13 | 31-12-12 | 31-12-12 |
|---|---|---|---|
| TO | 22,654,488 | 15,535,542 | 22,689,309 |
| P/L | 58,285 | 132,921 | (546,380) |
| NW | 2,120,221 | 2,075,443 | 1,955,733 |
| WC | 49,903 | 66,198 | (88,288) |
| Emp. | 74 | 73 | 74 |

DUNS 21-774-1947

## Wingrove Primary School

Hadrian Road, Newcastle-upon-Tyne, Tyne and Wear NE4 9HN
**Tel:** 01912735842
**Web:** www.wingrove.newcastle.sch.uk
**Estd:** 1993 Proprietorship
**Line of Business:** Primary education
**Proprietor:** Mrs D Harland
**Responsibilities**
**Senior:** Jane Mullarkey *(Head Teacher)*
**US SIC:** 8211 **UK SIC:** 93200
**Employees:** 50

DUNS 73-353-4262

## Wings Education Ltd

(**Subsidiary of:** Kedleston Education Ltd)
Whassett, Milnthorpe, Cumbria LA7 7DN
**Tel:** 01539-562006
**Web:** www.wingsschool.co.uk
**Reg No:** 4627039 **Estd:** 2003 Private Limited Company
**Line of Business:** Schools (independent)
**Trading Style:** Wings School
**Issued Capital:** £83,334
**Directors:** D Brosnan, A R Hurran, P Brosnan, A R Hurran
**Responsibilities**
**Senior:** Jon Hather *(Manager)*, Donagh Mckillop *(Principal)*, Pam Redican *(CEO, Managing Director)*
**Finance:** Heidi Boardman *(Financial Accountant)*, Heidi Cooke *(Senior Finance Administrator)*
**IT:** Stuart Billarroel *(IT Manager)*
**US SIC:** 8211 **UK SIC:** 93200

| | 31-12-12 | 31-12-11 | 31-12-10 |
|---|---|---|---|
| TO | 14,905,804 | 11,518,204 | 8,730,914 |
| P/L | 8,374,629 | 6,002,451 | 4,099,236 |
| NW | 20,185,261 | 13,872,199 | 9,468,917 |
| WC | 8,984,101 | 2,687,066 | 90,206 |
| Emp. | 186 | 161 | 130 |

DUNS 71-882-6402 **Imp**

## Winkontent Ltd

(**Subsidiary of:** Winkorp Ag)
Midori House, London W1U 4EG
**Tel:** 02077254343
**Web:** www.winkreative.com
**Reg No:** 5265119 **Estd:** 2006 Private Limited Company
**Line of Business:** Publishing of journals and periodicals
**Export Sales:** £12,509,263
**Trading Style:** Winkreative
**Issued Capital:** £800,000
**Directors:** Ms S Vandenbroucke, Winkontent Ag, J T Brule, R G Atkinson
**Co. Secretary:** Milford Secretaries Limited
**Responsibilities**
**Senior:** Ariel Childs *(Manager)*
**US SIC:** 2721, 4833
**UK SIC:** 47522, 97411
**Auditors:** UHY Hacker Young LLP

| | 31-12-13 | 31-12-12 | 31-12-11 |
|---|---|---|---|
| TO | 14,772,145 | 13,087,278 | N/A |
| P/L | 578,994 | 512,451 | N/A |
| NW | (1,355,053) | (1,868,853) | (2,423,580) |
| WC | 1,259,330 | 801,526 | 249,093 |
| Emp. | 74 | 79 | N/A |

DUNS 21-016-6362

## Winks London Ltd

Palladium House, 1-4 Argyll Street, London W1F 7LD
**Tel:** 02071187118
**Web:** www.winkslondon.com
**Reg No:** 6388272 **Estd:** 2007 Private Limited Company
**Line of Business:** Physical well-being activities
**Issued Capital:** £1
**Director:** H Kobayashi
**Co. Secretary:** Arnaud Lambillon
**Responsibilities**
**Senior:** Willow Woodworth *(Client Services Manager)*
**US SIC:** 8999 **UK SIC:** 83954

| | 31-12-13 | 31-12-12 | 31-12-11 |
|---|---|---|---|
| TA | 104,492 | 84,262 | 140,635 |
| NW | (146,005) | (125,396) | (37,655) |
| WC | 97,079 | (125,396) | (37,655) |

DUNS 39-791-8954 **Imp-Exp**

## Winlock Security Ltd

(**Subsidiary of:** Easyfit Hardware Ltd)
Unit B, Hortonwood 31, Telford, Shropshire TF1 7GS
**Tel:** 01952602250 **Fax:** 01952602255
**Web:** www.winlock.co.uk
**Reg No:** 2204121 **VAT No:** 489056210
**Estd:** 1987 Private Limited Company
**Line of Business:** Distribution service providers
**Issued Capital:** £200,000
**Directors:** M L Davidsen, A T Parker
**Co. Secretary:** Mrs Marisa Parker
**Responsibilities**
**Senior:** Paul Dupre-Smith *(Manager)*
**Sales:** Nathan Hutchon *(Area Sales Manager)*
**Operations:** Glenn Tonks *(Technical, Production Manager)*
**Purchasing:** Davinia Britnell *(Customer Service and Supply Ch)*
**Engineering:** Martin Murdoch *(Technical Manager)*
**US SIC:** 3499, 3442
**UK SIC:** 31694, 31420
**Auditors:** Deloitte & Touche
**Bankers:** Lloyds TSB Bank plc (30-99-63)

| | 31-12-13 | 31-12-12 | 31-12-11 |
|---|---|---|---|
| TO | N/A | 5,716,361 | 7,056,136 |
| P/L | N/A | 5,403 | (234,637) |
| NW | 122,888 | 416,665 | 347,859 |
| WC | 334,321 | 354,415 | 266,714 |
| Emp. | N/A | 43 | 48 |

DUNS 21-882-8580 **Exp**

## Winmau Dartboard Co Ltd

(**Subsidiary of:** Winmau Holdings Ltd)
South Road, Bridgend Industrial Estate, Bridgend, Mid Glamorgan CF31 3PT
**Tel:** 01656-767042
**Web:** www.winmau.com
**Reg No:** 0624584 **VAT No:** 102255130
**Estd:** 1959 Private Limited Company
**Line of Business:** Operation of other sports arenas and stadiums not elsewhere classified
**Export Markets:** Worldwide
**Issued Capital:** £485,000
**Principals:** A Milton *(Financial)*, A G Bluck, V C Bluck
**US SIC:** 7999, 4712
**UK SIC:** 97913, 77002
**Auditors:** Broomfield & Alexander Ltd
**Bankers:** Barclays Bank Plc (20-74-05)

| | 31-12-13 | 31-12-12 | 31-12-11 |
|---|---|---|---|
| TA | 2,922,481 | 2,742,715 | 2,368,753 |
| NW | 1,233,666 | 1,025,465 | 857,025 |
| WC | 1,233,666 | 1,025,465 | 857,025 |

DUNS 21-098-0892 **Imp-Exp**

## Winn & Coales International Ltd

Denso House, 33-35 Chapel Road, London SE27 0TR
**Tel:** 020-8670-7511
**Web:** www.thedensogroup.com
**Reg No:** 1012752 **Estd:** 1883 Private Limited Company
**Line of Business:** Management activities of holding companies
**Export Markets:** Far East, Australasia, U S A, Middle East, Africa
**Trading Style:** Denso
**Issued Capital:** £900,000
**Principals:** D Winn *(Chairman)*, J R Burton *(Managing)*, Dr K F Erskine, C P Winn, B R Dunsterville
**Responsibilities**
**Finance:** Sean Ahearne *(Financial Director)*
**Marketing:** Martin Lowe *(Marketing Manager)*
**Health & Safety:** Alec Bryan *(Health & Safety Officer)*
**Facilities:** Robert Tilley *(Maintenance Manager)*
**US SIC:** 6711, 2899
**UK SIC:** 83962, 25670
**Auditors:** Kingston Smith LLP
**Bankers:** Barclays Bank Plc (20-00-00)

| | 30-06-14 | 30-06-13 | 30-06-12 |
|---|---|---|---|
| TO | 51,120,000 | 54,229,000 | 49,063,000 |
| P/L | 8,838,000 | 10,998,000 | 8,743,000 |
| NW | 38,033,000 | 34,111,000 | 28,629,000 |
| WC | 26,414,000 | 25,515,000 | 21,731,000 |
| Emp. | 203 | 208 | 258 |

DUNS 73-828-7270
### Winn Solicitors Ltd
**(Subsidiary of:** Continental Shelf 556 Ltd)
Brinkburn Street, Byker, Newcastle-Upon-Tyne, Tyne and Wear NE6 1PL
**Tel:** 01912761000
**Web:** www.winnsolicitors.com
**Reg No:** 5084463 **Estd:** 2004 Private Limited Company
**Line of Business:** Solicitors
**Issued Capital:** £1,000
**Directors:** C Birkett, Miss D Winn, G Bashey, I S Richardson
**Co. Secretary:** Jeffery Winn
**Responsibilities**
**Senior:** Fiona Livingstone *(House Manager)*, Geoffrey Winn *(Proprietor)*
**Admin:** Emma Errington *(Administrator)*
**US SIC:** 8111 **UK SIC:** 83500
**Auditors:** Tait Walker
**Bankers:** Barclays Bank Plc (20-59-42)

| | 31-03-14 | 31-03-13 | 31-03-12 |
|---|---|---|---|
| TO | 16,897,588 | 17,150,779 | 14,572,928 |
| P/L | 3,655,011 | 5,845,585 | 5,781,154 |
| NW | 7,354,394 | 13,529,423 | 9,348,771 |
| WC | 5,192,704 | 11,423,053 | 6,381,044 |
| Emp. | 252 | 241 | 196 |

DUNS 21-771-0059
### Winnicott Centre
The Winnicott Centre, 195-197 Hathersage Road, Manchester M13 0JE
**Tel:** 01612489494
**Estd:** 1993 Proprietorship
**Line of Business:** Nhs clinics
**Proprietor:** Mrs T Gregory
**US SIC:** 8062 **UK SIC:** 95100
**Employees:** 60

DUNS 22-189-7908 **Imp**
### Winning Moves International Ltd
7 Praed Street, London W2 1NJ
**Tel:** 020-7262-9696
**Web:** www.winningmoves.co.uk
**Reg No:** 4207931 **VAT No:** 815282829
**Estd:** 2001 Private Limited Company
**Line of Business:** Management activities of holding companies
**Export Sales:** £9,929,944
**Trading Style:** Winning Moves Uk Limited
**Issued Capital:** £6,352
**Directors:** R P Knights, P Griffin, M Mierau, A A Tahir, M A Hauser, L I Frenkel, R Herbert, D J Ripley
**Responsibilities**
**Senior:** Denis Ferry *(Manager)*, Thomas Kremer *(Manager)*, Michael Meyers *(Director)*, Philip Orbanes *(Director)*, Alexandre Swain *(Director)*
**Marketing:** Carl Cliss *(Marketing Director)*
**US SIC:** 6711, 5042
**UK SIC:** 83962, 61900

| | 31-03-14 | 31-12-12 | 31-03-11 |
|---|---|---|---|
| TO | 19,730,271 | 16,006,766 | 15,655,704 |
| P/L | 261,670 | 309,373 | (671,309) |
| NW | 3,667,744 | 3,383,253 | 5,562,421 |
| WC | 3,565,660 | 5,076,281 | 4,396,683 |
| Emp. | 62 | 56 | 45 |

DUNS 21-003-6040
### Winning Pitch Ltd
Innovation Centre, 131 Mount Pleasant, Liverpool, Merseyside L3 5TF
**Tel:** 01513315007 **Fax:** 0151 331 5007
**Web:** www.winning-pitch.co.uk
**Reg No:** 6287017 **Estd:** 2011 Private Limited Company
**Line of Business:** Life coaching
**Issued Capital:** £52,194
**Directors:** J Leach, R A Newey, R M Briddock, P C Smart, J Keane
**Co. Secretary:** Mrs Heather Lomas
**Responsibilities**
**Senior:** Nick Roach *(Manager)*
**Marketing:** Nick Roach *(Manager)*
**US SIC:** 8299 **UK SIC:** 93300
**Auditors:** CLB Coopers

| | 31-03-14 | 31-03-13 | 30-03-12 |
|---|---|---|---|
| TO | 7,889,965 | 3,023,396 | 2,908,955 |
| P/L | 1,113,767 | 435,645 | 119,926 |
| NW | 1,066,155 | 732,545 | 405,581 |
| WC | 5,874,550 | 1,916,395 | 1,526,184 |
| Emp. | 71 | 53 | 35 |

DUNS 21-734-7546
### The Winnock Hotel (Drymen) Ltd
The Square, Drymen, Glasgow, Lanarkshire G63 0BL
**Tel:** 01360-660245
**Web:** www.winnockhotel.com
**Reg No:** 0296009SC **Estd:** 1968 Private Limited Company
**Line of Business:** Hotels
**Trading Style:** The Winnock Hotel (Drymen) Ltd
**Issued Capital:** £1
**Director:** E J Warnes
**Co. Secretary:** David Warnes
**Responsibilities**
**Admin:** Gillian McCann *(Office Manager)*
**Facilities:** George Peterson *(Maintenance Manager)*
**Purchasing:** Gillian McCann *(Office Manager)*
**US SIC:** 7011 **UK SIC:** 66500

| | 31-01-14 | 31-01-13 | 31-01-12 |
|---|---|---|---|
| TA | 1,431,461 | 1,256,915 | 1,187,034 |
| NW | 408,769 | 210,614 | 79,699 |
| WC | 104,320 | (130,688) | (285,494) |

DUNS 23-636-9344
### The Winns Primary School
Fleeming Road, London E17 5ET
**Tel:** 020-8527-1872
**Web:** www.thewinnsprimaryschool.co.uk
**Estd:** 1995
**Line of Business:** Primary education
**Directors:** A D Forrest, Ms J Jopp
**US SIC:** 8211 **UK SIC:** 93200
**Employees:** 100

DUNS 50-361-2459
### Winn's Security Services Ltd
700 London Road, Westcliff-On-Sea, Essex SS0 9HQ
**Tel:** 01702-719100 **Fax:** 01202-719020
**Web:** www.winnssecurity.co.uk
**Reg No:** 2378158 **Estd:** 1980 Private Limited Company
**Line of Business:** Security and related activities
**Issued Capital:** £44,850
**Director:** A L Davies
**Co. Secretary:** Robert Stillwell
**US SIC:** 7393 **UK SIC:** 83954
**Auditors:** E J Clouder & Co
**Bankers:** National Westminster Bank Plc (54-30-60)

| | 30-09-13 | 30-09-12 | 30-09-11 |
|---|---|---|---|
| TA | 557,336 | 485,793 | 633,672 |
| NW | 142,755 | 41,159 | 55,953 |
| WC | 136,421 | 31,154 | 50,156 |

DUNS 21-585-8862
### Winray Care Housing
Office 6, Upper Ground South, 5 Blackhorse Lane, London E17 6DS
**Tel:** 02085278861
**Web:** www.winraycarehousing.com
**Estd:** 2010 Proprietorship
**Line of Business:** Home care service providers
**Proprietor:** Miss R Williams
**US SIC:** 8091 **UK SIC:** 95200
**Employees:** 50

DUNS 21-210-8984
### Winscombe Hall
Winscombe Court, Winscombe, Avon BS25 1DE
**Tel:** 01934-843553
**Web:** www.cedarscaregroup.co.uk
**Estd:** 1989 Proprietorship
**Line of Business:** Nursing homes
**Proprietor:** R Lekhani
**Responsibilities**
**Senior:** Kate Sweeting *(Home Manager)*, Rachael Williams *(Manager)*, Ty Yilmaz *(Proprietor)*
**US SIC:** 8051 **UK SIC:** 95100
**Employees:** 55

DUNS 21-771-2287
### Winsor
54 The Avenue, Minehead, Somerset TA24 5AW
**Tel:** 01643707870
**Web:** www.sanctuary-care.co.uk
**Estd:** 1995
**Line of Business:** Nursing homes
**Responsibilities**
**Senior:** Patricia Blackett *(Manager)*, Mandy Ricketts *(Manager)*
**US SIC:** 8051 **UK SIC:** 95100
**Employees:** 50

DUNS 73-675-4701
### Winsor Bishop Ltd
41-43 London Street, Norwich, Norfolk NR2 1HU
**Tel:** 01603-620638
**Web:** www.winsorbishop.co.uk
**Reg No:** 4934858 **Estd:** 2003 Private Limited Company
**Line of Business:** Jewellery retailers
**Issued Capital:** £40,001
**Directors:** E Sykes, Mrs T Von Moll, Mrs S J Fulford
**Co. Secretary:** Anthony Woodward
**Responsibilities**
**Senior:** Sophie Croyden *(Manager)*, Robert Croydon *(Manager)*
**US SIC:** 3911 **UK SIC:** 49101

| | 31-03-14 | 31-03-13 | 31-03-12 |
|---|---|---|---|
| TO | 8,989,189 | 8,525,647 | N/A |
| P/L | 969,049 | 664,855 | N/A |
| NW | 2,562,358 | 1,970,734 | 1,218,629 |
| WC | 2,536,018 | 1,812,457 | 1,196,813 |
| Emp. | 52 | 48 | N/A |

DUNS 73-570-2651
### Winstanley & Co Ltd
**(Subsidiary of:** Winstanley Holdings Ltd)
Racecourse Road, Pershore, Worcestershire WR10 2DG
**Tel:** 01386-552278
**Web:** www.winstanleyco.co.uk
**Reg No:** 4831995 **VAT No:** 864415319
**Estd:** 2003 Private Limited Company
**Line of Business:** Steel fabricators
**Export Sales:** £213,661
**Issued Capital:** £170,189
**Principals:** R A Smith *(Managing)*, N C Annis
**Co. Secretary:** Warwick Kendrick
**US SIC:** 1622 **UK SIC:** 50200
**Auditors:** Crowther Beard LLP

| | 31-08-14 | 31-08-13 | 31-08-12 |
|---|---|---|---|
| TO | 6,303,770 | 5,179,944 | 3,977,566 |
| P/L | 385,102 | 216,709 | 207,168 |
| NW | 2,393,851 | 2,102,908 | 1,833,986 |
| WC | 86,582 | (155,498) | (330,723) |
| Emp. | 84 | 79 | 79 |

DUNS 22-557-2825
### Winter Gardens Pavilion
Town Hall, Weston-Super-Mare, Avon BS23 1AQ
**Tel:** 01934417117
**Web:** www.thewintergardens.com
**Line of Business:** Letting of conference and exhibition centres
**Principals:** J W Councillor *(Chairman)*, C A Stephens, J C Wiltshire, T E Simpkins, M J Turnbull
**Branches:** Winter Gardens Pavilion, Hutton Moor Road, Weston-Super-Mare, Avon BS22 8LY
**US SIC:** 7399 **UK SIC:** 83954
**Employees:** 50

DUNS 21-158-7403
### Winter Rule Llp
Lowin House Tregolls Road, Truro, Cornwall TR1 2NA
**Tel:** 01872-276477
**Web:** www.francisclark.co.uk
**Reg No:** 0344405OC **Estd:** 2009 Private Limited Company
**Line of Business:** Accounting activities
**Responsibilities**
**Senior:** Thomas Roach *(Designated Limited Liability P)*
**US SIC:** 8931 **UK SIC:** 83600
**Auditors:** Price Bailey LLP
**Bankers:** Barclays Bank Plc (20-87-94)

| | 30-11-11 |
|---|---|
| TO | 2,830,226 |
| Emp. | 91 |

DUNS 21-879-8142
### Winterbourne Care Centre
London Road, Salisbury, Wiltshire SP1 3HP
**Tel:** 01722428210
**Web:** www.caringhomes.org
**Estd:** 2012
**Line of Business:** Residential care establishments
**Responsibilities**
**Senior:** Helen Pessell *(Manager)*
**US SIC:** 8321 **UK SIC:** 96111
**Employees:** 100

DUNS 39-928-0387
### Winterflood Securities Ltd
**(Subsidiary of:** Close Brothers Group Plc)
The Atrium Building, London EC4R 2GA
**Tel:** 020-3100-0000 **Fax:** 020-7623-9482
**Web:** www.winterflood.com
**Reg No:** 2242204 **Estd:** 1988 Private Limited Company
**Line of Business:** Financial intermediation not elsewhere classified
**Trading Style:** Market Maker
**Issued Capital:** £120,292
**Principals:** B M Winterflood *(Managing)*, P J Yarrow, I A Throssell, J C Moseley, J A Howell, P P Prebensen, R J Meaney, S M Rafferty
**Co. Secretary:** James Stapleton
**Responsibilities**
**Senior:** Spencer Crooks *(Director)*, Jeremy Hansford *(Finance Director)*, Leslie Hartt *(Executive)*, Gareth Henderson *(Executive)*, Julian Palfreyman *(Chief Executive)*
**Finance:** Jeremy Hansford *(Finance Director)*
**Marketing:** Spencer Crooks *(Director)*
**Sales:** Julian Dixon *(Sales Executive)*, Ben Fitzjohn *(Retail Sales Trader)*
**Admin:** Carly Cheeseman *(Executive Assistant)*
**US SIC:** 6111 **UK SIC:** 81501
**Auditors:** Deloitte LLP
**Bankers:** The Royal Bank Of Scotland Plc (16-04-00)

| | 31-07-14 | 31-07-13 | 31-07-12 |
|---|---|---|---|
| TA | 638,805,564 | 601,463,238 | 603,089,192 |
| P/L | 26,677,696 | 15,400,070 | 16,794,296 |
| NW | 78,147,225 | 75,452,551 | 73,850,427 |
| WC | 69,760,417 | 67,182,830 | 68,966,687 |
| Emp. | 223 | 201 | 205 |

DUNS 21-739-2919 **Imp**
### Winterhalter Ltd
**(Subsidiary of:** Winterhalter Holding Gmbh)
Winterhalter House, Roebuck Way, Knowlhill, Milton Keynes, Buckinghamshire MK5 8WH
**Tel:** 01908-359000 **Fax:** 01908-359060
**Web:** www.winterhalter.co.uk
**Reg No:** 0992463 **VAT No:** 230049017
**Estd:** 1970 Private Limited Company
**Line of Business:** Manufacture of electric domestic appliances
**Export Sales:** £530,374
**Issued Capital:** £6,350,100
**Principals:** D Smithson *(Managing)*, V Faller, J Mackay, P Huber, J Winterhalter, R Winterhalter, A K Blake, A M Salter
**Co. Secretary:** David Parsons
**Responsibilities**
**Senior:** Peter Alsworth *(Director)*, Claire Burke *(Manager)*, Stephen Kinkead *(Managing Director)*, Jason MacKay *(Facilities Manager)*, Barry Spicer *(Parts Manager)*
**Marketing:** Paul Crowley *(Marketing Manager)*
**IT:** Neil Tolchard *(IT Manager)*
**Health & Safety:** Jason MacKay *(Facilities Manager)*
**Facilities:** Jason MacKay *(Facilities Manager)*
**Operations:** Jason MacKay *(Facilities Manager)*
**US SIC:** 3639, 5084
**UK SIC:** 34600, 61490
**Auditors:** Grant Thornton UK LLP
**Bankers:** HSBC Bank plc (40-19-30)

| | 31-12-13 | 31-12-12 | 31-12-11 |
|---|---|---|---|
| TO | 22,307,451 | 20,962,803 | 21,387,476 |
| P/L | 170,262 | 785,404 | 77,150 |
| NW | 6,987,895 | 6,817,442 | 4,341,817 |
| WC | 334,070 | 188,339 | (2,359,702) |
| Emp. | 100 | 90 | 91 |

DUNS 21-628-6460
### Winterhill Largo Ltd
6 Anchor Court, Commercial Road, Blackburn, Darwen, Lancashire BB3 0DB
**Tel:** 01254763183 **Fax:** 01254873957
**Web:** www.winterhilllargo.com
**Reg No:** 7077517 **Estd:** 2009 Private Limited Company
**Line of Business:** Management activities of holding companies
**Issued Capital:** £1,060,000
**Directors:** Mrs A J Duckworth, N G Duckworth
**US SIC:** 6711 **UK SIC:** 83962
**Auditors:** Crowe Clark Whitehill LLP

| | 31-01-13 | 31-01-12 | 31-01-11 |
|---|---|---|---|
| TO | 3,420,388 | 3,005,094 | 2,727,707 |
| P/L | 325,699 | (83,634) | 106,866 |
| NW | (466,798) | (649,210) | (20,280) |
| WC | (318,459) | (437,246) | (158,649) |
| Emp. | 49 | 41 | 37 |

DUNS 77-059-6302
### Winters Electrical Services Ltd
Henson House, Henson Road, Crawley, West Sussex RH10 1EP
**Tel:** 01293-843800 **Fax:** 01293529502
**Web:** www.winterselectrical.co.uk
**Reg No:** 2671206 **VAT No:** 602948735
**Estd:** 2006 Private Limited Company
**Line of Business:** Installation of electrical wiring and fittings
**Issued Capital:** £1,000
**Principals:** M J Winters *(Managing)*, M J Flynn, C J Rothery, C A Henderson
**Co. Secretary:** Ms Gillian Thredder
**Responsibilities**
**Senior:** Rob Costidell *(Manager)*
**Branches:** Winters Electrical Services Ltd, Ingate Place, Battersea, London, London SW8 3NS
**US SIC:** 1731 **UK SIC:** 50300
**Auditors:** James Todd & Co

| | 31-10-13 | 31-10-12 | 31-10-11 |
|---|---|---|---|
| TO | 14,819,722 | 17,920,745 | 16,467,506 |
| P/L | 804,168 | 619,459 | 514,725 |
| NW | 4,010,010 | 3,410,534 | 2,966,609 |
| WC | 3,831,539 | 3,173,862 | 2,682,615 |
| Emp. | 50 | 64 | 61 |

DUNS 29-210-6283
## Winterthur Financial Services U K Ltd
(**Subsidiary of:** Axa Direction Juridique Centrale)
Winterthur Way, Basingstoke, Hampshire RG21 6SZ
**Tel:** 01256-470707 **Fax:** 01256-798348
**Web:** www.winterthur.com
**Reg No:** 0823355 **Estd:** 1995 Private Limited Company
**Line of Business:** Management activities of holding companies
**Trading Style:** Axa Uk
**Issued Capital:** £62,757,151
**Directors:** M J Kellard, A J Purvis, D R Cheeseman
**Co. Secretary:** Jeremy Small
**Responsibilities**
**Senior:** Jean Drouffe *(Group Finance Director)*
**Branches:** Winterthur Financial Services U K Ltd, 86 Plungington Rd, Preston, Lancashire PR1 7RA
**US SIC:** 6711 **UK SIC:** 83962
**Auditors:** KPMG Audit PLC
**Bankers:** Barclays Bank Plc (20-00-00)

| | 31-12-13 | 31-12-12 | 31-12-11 |
|---|---|---|---|
| TO | 218,497,000 | 282,709,000 | 295,192,000 |
| P/L | (28,767,000) | (29,048,000) | (33,042,000) |
| NW | (20,121,000) | 12,106,000 | 1,459,000 |
| WC | (14,576,000) | 1,456,000 | 2,729,000 |
| Emp. | 1,476 | 2,092 | 2,194 |

DUNS 23-997-6009 Imp
## Winterwood Farms Ltd
Chartway Street, East Sutton, Maidstone, Kent ME17 3DN
**Tel:** 01622-844286
**Web:** www.winterwood.co.uk
**Reg No:** 3985775 **VAT No:** 303768265
**Estd:** 2000 Private Limited Company
**Line of Business:** Growing of cereals and other crops not elsewhere classified
**Issued Capital:** £100
**Principals:** S M Taylor *(Managing)*, T Gilham
**Co. Secretary:** Mrs Jacqueline Taylor
**US SIC:** 7399 **UK SIC:** 83954
**Auditors:** Day, Smith & Hunter
**Bankers:** National Westminster Bank Plc (60-60-08)

| | 31-03-13 | 31-03-12 | 31-03-11 |
|---|---|---|---|
| TO | 31,175,205 | 28,363,807 | 24,264,854 |
| P/L | 837,572 | 373,204 | 1,192,767 |
| NW | 4,309,343 | 3,652,845 | 3,372,424 |
| WC | 2,384,058 | 1,815,368 | 1,822,799 |
| Emp. | 181 | 179 | 187 |

DUNS 73-497-4434
## Wintle Heating & Plumbing Holdings Ltd
19a Mansion Close, Moulton Park Industrial Estate, Northampton, Northamptonshire NN3 6RU
**Tel:** 01604-790800 **Fax:** 01604790808
**Web:** www.wintle.co.uk
**Reg No:** 4760745 **Estd:** 1966 Private Limited Company
**Line of Business:** Plumbers
**Issued Capital:** £14,827
**Director:** P P Wintle
**Co. Secretary:** Mrs Carole Osborne
**Responsibilities**
**Senior:** Richard Jenson *(Manager)*
**Finance:** Liam Wood *(Accounts Clerk)*
**HR:** Stuart Jeffs *(Human Resources Manager)*
**US SIC:** 1711 **UK SIC:** 50300

| | 30-09-13 | 30-09-12 | 30-09-11 |
|---|---|---|---|
| TO | 8,423,061 | 9,669,647 | 9,137,058 |
| P/L | 209,044 | 46,986 | 27,734 |
| NW | 283,398 | 359,634 | 735,850 |
| WC | 1,213,760 | 1,215,686 | 1,258,900 |
| Emp. | 75 | 84 | 84 |

DUNS 37-892-4641 Imp
## Winton Capital Management Ltd
Grove House, 27 Hammersmith Grove, London W6 0NE
**Web:** www.wintoncapital.com
**Reg No:** 3311531 **Estd:** 2003 Private Limited Company
**Line of Business:** Security broking and related activities
**Issued Capital:** £2,386,354
**Directors:** Ms A B Rentoul, R Patel, D W Harding, M D Beddall
**Co. Secretary:** Temple Secretarial Limited
**Responsibilities**
**Finance:** Nagin Dhayatker *(Finance Director)*
**US SIC:** 6211, 7392
**UK SIC:** 83100, 83951
**Auditors:** KPMG LLP
**Bankers:** Lloyds TSB Bank plc (30-94-65)

| | 31-12-13 | 31-12-12 | 31-12-11 |
|---|---|---|---|
| TA | 305,246,000 | 199,013,000 | 199,753,000 |
| P/L | 199,186,000 | 78,813,000 | 221,393,000 |
| NW | 221,116,000 | 158,928,000 | 147,644,000 |
| WC | 215,591,000 | 154,632,000 | 142,615,000 |
| Emp. | 281 | 262 | 218 |

DUNS 21-322-8583
## Winton Nursing Home
Wallop House, Stockbridge, Hampshire SO20 8HE
**Tel:** 01264-781366
**Web:** www.amesburyabbey.com
**Estd:** 1972 Proprietorship
**Line of Business:** Nursing homes
**Proprietor:** Mrs M Cornelius-Reid
**US SIC:** 8051 **UK SIC:** 95100
**Employees:** 70

DUNS 22-232-3441 Exp
## Wintwire Ltd
Oxspring Wire Mills, Sheffield Road, Oxspring, Sheffield, South Yorkshire S36 8YW
**Tel:** 01226-763081
**Web:** www.wintwire.co.uk
**Reg No:** 4250311 **VAT No:** 809237131
**Estd:** 2003 Private Limited Company
**Line of Business:** Wire drawing
**Issued Capital:** £100
**Directors:** R M Turner, B A Turner
**Co. Secretary:** Ms Sally Wilson
**Responsibilities**
**IT:** Craig Charlesworth *(It Manager)*
**Operations:** Christopher Mosley *(Operations Manager)*
**US SIC:** 3315 **UK SIC:** 22340

| | 31-05-14 | 31-05-13 | 31-05-12 |
|---|---|---|---|
| TA | 989,653 | 871,666 | 1,084,187 |
| NW | 116,601 | 122,316 | 117,367 |
| WC | (10,107) | 2,110 | (26,467) |

DUNS 51-601-4201
## Winvic Group Ltd
19 Tenter Road, Moulton Park Industrial Estate, Northampton, Northamptonshire NN3 6PZ
**Web:** www.winvic.co.uk
**Reg No:** 5881912 **Estd:** 2006 Private Limited Company
**Line of Business:** Construction of commercial buildings
**Issued Capital:** £850
**Directors:** D J Ward, S W Hunt
**Co. Secretary:** Simon Girardier
**US SIC:** 1541 **UK SIC:** 50100
**Bankers:** National Westminster Bank Plc (56-00-60)

| | 31-01-14 | 31-01-13 | 31-01-12 |
|---|---|---|---|
| TO | 146,410,092 | 111,504,531 | 154,104,077 |
| P/L | 4,487,765 | 3,075,739 | 4,209,416 |
| NW | 8,279,923 | 8,165,032 | 6,138,020 |
| WC | 8,198,927 | 8,113,599 | 6,021,487 |
| Emp. | 92 | 75 | 72 |

DUNS 21-748-4203 Imp-Exp
## Wipak U K Ltd
(**Subsidiary of:** Wihuri International Oy)
Unit 3 Buttington Cross Enterprise Park, Welshpool, Powys SY21 8SL
**Tel:** 01938-555255 **Fax:** 01938-555277
**Web:** www.wipak.com
**Reg No:** 1251293 **VAT No:** 289705606
**Estd:** 1976 Private Limited Company
**Line of Business:** Manufacturers of packaging materials
**Export Markets:** Finaland and E U
**Issued Capital:** £3,500,000
**Principals:** A Aarnio Wihuri *(Chairman)*, M H Aarnio-Wihuri, M J Rovamaa, J M Hellgren
**Co. Secretary:** Philip Wolstenholme
**Responsibilities**
**Senior:** Jaako Knuutila *(Manager)*, Marja Wihuri *(Manager)*
**Finance:** Lesley Draper *(Financial Controller)*, Lesley Tittensor *(Financial Controller)*
**Admin:** Jonathan Andrews *(ITAdministrator)*
**IT:** Jonathan Andrews *(ITAdministrator)*, Andrew Newbold *(Technical Manager)*
**Operations:** Andrew Newbold *(Technical Manager)*
**Branches:** Wipak U K Ltd, 17 Tormarton Road, Badminton, Avon GL9 1HP
**US SIC:** 2654, 5199
**UK SIC:** 47280, 61900
**Auditors:** KPMG LLP
**Bankers:** HSBC Bank plc (40-33-33)

| | 31-12-13 | 31-12-12 | 31-12-11 |
|---|---|---|---|
| TO | 20,102,000 | 17,046,000 | 15,944,000 |
| P/L | 1,256,000 | 1,187,000 | 942,000 |
| NW | 4,414,000 | 4,375,000 | 4,190,000 |
| WC | 2,100,000 | (1,441,000) | (1,790,000) |
| Emp. | 89 | 79 | 76 |

DUNS 23-021-6959 Imp
## Wipro Ltd
(**Subsidiary of:** Wipro Limited)
3 Sheldon Square, London W2 6HY
**Tel:** 020 7432 8500 **Fax:** 02072865703
**Web:** www.wipro.com
**Reg No:** 0019088FC **Estd:** 2012 Foreign Company
**Line of Business:** Other software consultancy and supply
**Directors:** S C Senapaty, M K Sharma, T Kurlen, V Joshi, W A Owens
**Co. Secretary:** Venkatesan Ramachandran
**Responsibilities**
**Senior:** Amandeep Bhandal *(Office Manager)*
**Marketing:** Sacha Meckler *(Regulatory and Business Develo)*
**Admin:** Amandeep Bhandal *(Office Manager)*
**US SIC:** 7379 **UK SIC:** 83940

DUNS 22-652-9170
## Wipro Uk Ltd
(**Subsidiary of:** Wipro Limited)
2nd Floor, 120 New Cavendish Street, London W1W 6XX
**Web:** www.saic.com
**Reg No:** 1396396 **VAT No:** 599547464
**Estd:** 1990 Private Limited Company
**Line of Business:** Public relations activities
**Export Sales:** £12,780,000
**Issued Capital:** £706,725
**Directors:** S Lakshmanan, N Khandelwal
**Co. Secretary:** Navneet Khandelwal
**Branches:** Wipro Uk Ltd, Berkshire House, Queen Street, Maidenhead, Berkshire SL6 1NF
**US SIC:** 7399, 7379
**UK SIC:** 83954, 83940
**Auditors:** Deloitte LLP
**Bankers:** National Westminster Bank Plc (60-13-35)

| | 31-03-14 | 31-03-13 | 31-03-12 |
|---|---|---|---|
| TO | 50,519,000 | 49,972,000 | 54,320,000 |
| P/L | 4,033,000 | 1,512,000 | 16,740,000 |
| NW | 12,483,000 | 9,717,000 | 8,555,000 |
| WC | 10,522,000 | 7,585,000 | 6,237,000 |
| Emp. | 370 | 383 | 446 |

DUNS 21-321-6997
## Wira Technology Group Ltd
Ring Road, West Park, Leeds, West Yorkshire LS16 6EB
**Tel:** 07866778836 **Fax:** 0113-230-4195
**Web:** www.wirabusinesspark.com
**Reg No:** 0151519 **Estd:** 2011 Private Company Limited By Guarantee
**Line of Business:** Business and commerce centres
**Trading Style:** Wira Instrumentation
**Director:** S Donnelly
**Co. Secretary:** Mark Greenwood
**Responsibilities**
**Senior:** Russell Thomas *(Building Manager)*
**US SIC:** 7392 **UK SIC:** 83951
**Auditors:** Peat Marwick McLintock
**Bankers:** HSBC Bank plc (40-27-15)
**Employees:** 400

DUNS 21-108-8695 Imp-Exp
## Wire Belt Co Ltd
(**Subsidiary of:** Wire Belt Company of America)
Unit B Castle Road, Sittingbourne, Kent ME10 3RF
**Tel:** 01795-421771
**Web:** www.wirebelt.co.uk
**Reg No:** 0716510 **VAT No:** 202937774
**Estd:** 1962 Private Limited Company
**Line of Business:** Conveyor belts and systems
**Export Markets:** Australia, New Zealand, Thailand, Singapore, Malaysia, European Union (E U); U S A; Africa; Middle East
**Export Sales:** £5,809,305
**Issued Capital:** £54,875
**Principals:** P C Winter *(Managing)*, R A Tomsett, D L Greer
**Responsibilities**
**Senior:** Allan Munday *(Accountant)*
**Finance:** Allan Munday *(Accountant)*
**IT:** Allan Munday *(Accountant)*
**US SIC:** 3534 **UK SIC:** 32553
**Auditors:** KPMG
**Bankers:** HSBC Bank plc (40-15-05)

| | 31-12-13 | 31-12-12 | 31-12-11 |
|---|---|---|---|
| TO | 10,377,173 | 7,468,854 | 7,341,374 |
| P/L | 1,255,204 | 949,545 | 1,009,326 |
| NW | 12,044,245 | 11,478,226 | 10,896,670 |
| WC | 7,035,725 | 7,793,940 | 7,196,238 |
| Emp. | 144 | 103 | 98 |

DUNS 21-589-3229
## Wired Red
Shepley Street, Audenshaw, Manchester M34 5JD
**Tel:** 03337774444
**Web:** www.brother.co.uk
**Estd:** 1889
**Line of Business:** Computer consumables suppliers
**Responsibilities**
**Senior:** Shirley Turner *(Communications Manager)*
**Facilities:** Maggie Robinson *(Facilities Manager)*
**US SIC:** 5081 **UK SIC:** 61490
**Employees:** 250

DUNS 23-857-0738 Imp
## Wireless Energy Management Systems International Ltd
(**Subsidiary of:** Wheb Ventures 2 (Scotgp) Lp)
The Mission, Wellington Street, Stockport, Cheshire SK1 3AH
**Tel:** 0161-475-1777
**Web:** www.wems.co.uk
**Reg No:** 3848754 **Estd:** 1999 Private Limited Company
**Line of Business:** Management activities of holding companies
**Export Sales:** £55,249
**Trading Style:** Wems
**Issued Capital:** £1,363
**Directors:** C P Bithell, C M Irwin, P T Summers, J J Blower, G C Barber
**Responsibilities**
**Senior:** Ivan Mckeever *(Manager)*
**US SIC:** 6711, 8911
**UK SIC:** 83962, 83701
**Auditors:** Grant Thornton UK LLP
**Bankers:** The Royal Bank Of Scotland Plc (16-00-01)

| | 31-12-13 | 31-07-13 | 31-12-12 |
|---|---|---|---|
| TO | 3,353,649 | 10,268,855 | 12,204,138 |
| P/L | (481,867) | 862,915 | 775,857 |
| NW | 904,023 | 1,150,957 | 1,163,827 |
| WC | 971,378 | 1,216,562 | 2,194,886 |
| Emp. | 95 | 91 | 78 |

DUNS 23-506-5914 Imp
## Wireline Engineering Ltd
Technology House, Blackburn Business Par, Aberdeen, Aberdeenshire AB21 0PS
**Tel:** 01224-798000 **Fax:** 01224791410
**Web:** www.wireline-engineering.com
**Reg No:** 0182768SC **VAT No:** 699669241
**Estd:** 1998 Private Limited Company
**Line of Business:** Service activities incidental to oil and gas extraction excluding surveying
**Issued Capital:** £360,000
**Directors:** A S Inglis, W S Petrie, B Semple, R N Hall, D Mitchell, A Gordon
**Co. Secretary:**
Pinsent Masons Secretarial Limit
**Responsibilities**
**Senior:** Magnus Wardel *(Engineering Manager)*
**US SIC:** 1389, 7394
**UK SIC:** 13000, 84000

| | 28-02-14 | 28-02-13 | 29-02-12 |
|---|---|---|---|
| TA | 6,855,086 | 6,532,654 | 6,784,824 |
| NW | 4,750,356 | 4,593,814 | 4,580,430 |
| WC | 3,288,398 | 2,940,831 | 2,779,443 |

DUNS 39-670-9008 Exp
## Wirquin Ltd
(**Subsidiary of:** Force 5)
Warmsworth Halt Industrial Estate, Doncaster, South Yorkshire DN4 9LS
**Tel:** 01709770001 **Fax:** 01302792191
**Web:** www.cmesansys.com
**Reg No:** 2136997 **VAT No:** 918530030
**Estd:** 1987 Private Limited Company
**Line of Business:** Manufacturers of sanitary ware
**Export Markets:** Saudi Arabia, Rest of Middle East, Eire, E U Countries & Worldwide
**Export Sales:** £7,012,000
**Issued Capital:** £5,000,100
**Directors:** D Le Coent, G Le Coent
**Responsibilities**
**Senior:** Robert Balcam *(Finance.Director)*
**Finance:** Robert Balcam *(Finance.Director)*
**Marketing:** Manjit Lall *(Marketing Manager)*
**HR:** Tracy Cunningham *(Human Resources Manager)*
**Health & Safety:** Eric Merchant *(Maintenance Manager)*
**Facilities:** Eric Merchant *(Maintenance Manager)*
**Engineering:** Eric Merchant *(Maintenance Manager)*
**Branches:** Wirquin Ltd, Unit 2, Fifth Avenue, Dukinfield, Cheshire SK16 4PP
**US SIC:** 3079, 2599
**UK SIC:** 48360, 46720
**Auditors:** RSM Tenon Audit Ltd

**Bankers:** Investec Bank (uk) Ltd (30-00-72)

| | 31-12-13 | 31-12-12 | 31-12-11 |
|---|---|---|---|
| TO | 22,368,000 | 22,237,000 | 22,166,000 |
| P/L | (610,000) | (1,286,000) | (4,150,000) |
| NW | 1,944,000 | 2,554,000 | 3,840,000 |
| WC | 8,734,000 | 8,044,000 | 4,873,000 |
| Emp. | 227 | 234 | 261 |

DUNS 77-007-9838

## The Wirral Autistic Society

Unit C Oak House, Bromborough, Wirral, Merseyside CH62 3PA
**Tel:** 0151-334-7510 **Fax:** 01513341762
**Web:** www.wirral.autistic.org
**Reg No:** 2658268 **Estd:** 1991 Private Company Limited By Guarantee
**Line of Business:** Charities and charitable organisations
**Directors:** A D Davies, E Behan, Mrs K N Beddow, M J Battersby, Professor H Dobson, P R Mcgrory, Ms A Reddy, J T Kennedy
**Co. Secretary:** Philip Wells
**Responsibilities**
**Senior:** Gerald Adamson *(Director)*, Dianne Asher *(Chief Executive)*, Barrie Bradburn *(Manager)*, Michael Fortune *(Director)*, Ruth Morley *(Director)*
**Branches:** The Wirral Autistic Society, 134 Allport Rd, Wirral, Merseyside CH62 6BB
**US SIC:** 8091 **UK SIC:** 95200
**Auditors:** Morris & Co
**Bankers:** HSBC Bank plc (40-15-04)

| | 31-03-14 | 31-03-13 | 31-03-12 |
|---|---|---|---|
| TO | 15,775,520 | 13,479,944 | 12,132,445 |
| P/L | 133,720 | 266,722 | 311,217 |
| NW | 4,840,264 | 1,745,544 | 2,643,822 |
| WC | 1,038,566 | 968,807 | 716,033 |
| Emp. | 750 | 613 | 520 |

DUNS 21-584-0631

## Wirral Borough Council

250 Cleveland Street, Birkenhead, Merseyside CH41 3QL
**Tel:** 01516478335
**Web:** www.wirral.gov.uk
**Estd:** 2011
**Line of Business:** Department of transport
**Proprietor:** B Jones
**Responsibilities**
**Senior:** Geoff Turnock *(Head Of Transport)*
**Purchasing:** Geoff Turnock *(Head Of Transport)*
**Branches:** Wirral Borough Council, Westminster House, Hamilton Street, CH41 5FN Birkenhead
**US SIC:** 9121 **UK SIC:** 91110
**Employees:** 200

DUNS 29-885-4720

## Wirral Christian Centre Trust Ltd

1 Woodchurch Road, Birkenhead, Merseyside CH41 2UE
**Tel:** 01516538307
**Web:** www.wccuk.org
**Reg No:** 2088322 **Estd:** 1987 Private Company Limited By Guarantee
**Line of Business:** Places of worship
**Trading Style:** Wirral Christian Centre
**Principals:** Rev P A Epton *(Chairman)*, Dr A K Adegoke, G J Epton, R Dixon, R N Fisher, Dr O S Kehinde
**Co. Secretary:** Mrs Karen Fisher
**Responsibilities**
**Senior:** Nick Weyman *(Manager)*
**Branches:** Leasowe, Birkenhead.
**US SIC:** 8321 **UK SIC:** 96111
**Auditors:** Hailwood & Co
**Bankers:** Lloyds TSB Bank plc (77-48-23)

| | 31-03-14 | 31-03-13 | 31-03-12 |
|---|---|---|---|
| TO | 1,716,930 | 1,342,135 | 1,243,974 |
| P/L | 191,325 | 13,102 | 141,938 |
| NW | 3,680,174 | 3,488,849 | 3,465,247 |
| WC | (151,045) | (326,667) | (258,054) |
| Emp. | 53 | 49 | 41 |

DUNS 21-740-1411

## Wirral Grammar School for Boys

Cross Lane, Bebington, Wirral, Merseyside CH63 3AQ
**Tel:** 01516440908
**Web:** www.wirralgrammarboys.com
**Reg No:** 7734231 **Estd:** 1931 Private Company Limited By Guarantee
**Line of Business:** Schools (local authority)
**Directors:** Dr G D Patel, A G Lawrence, Mrs A F Whitehead, Mrs R L Miller, P G Ronayne, Mrs C P Mclachlan, E P Thomas, D G Elliott
**Responsibilities**
**Senior:** Sheila Clarke Mbe *(Director)*, Brian Edmondson *(Director)*, David Hazeldine *(Director)*, Stephen Schofield *(Director)*
**Finance:** Eddie Reilly *(Senior Finance Administrator)*
**Admin:** Debbie Richards *(Administrator)*
**IT:** Lee Wakelam *(PC Manager)*, Jeremy Woodham *(Head of IT)*
**US SIC:** 8211 **UK SIC:** 93200

**Bankers:** Lloyds TSB Bank plc (77-17-13)

| | 31-08-13 | 31-08-12 |
|---|---|---|
| TO | 6,019,024 | 16,063,826 |
| P/L | 54,521 | 10,391,516 |
| NW | 10,356,037 | 10,230,516 |
| WC | 444,537 | 236,457 |
| Emp. | 90 | 94 |

DUNS 28-929-2070

## Wirral Hospice St John's

Mount Road, Higher Bebington, Wirral, Merseyside CH63 6JE
**Tel:** 0151-334-2778
**Web:** www.wirralhospice.org
**Reg No:** 1518364 **Estd:** 1980 Private Company Limited By Guarantee
**Line of Business:** Hospices
**Directors:** Dr P J Cuthbertson, C M Pope, Ms H R Staveley Taylor, P S Shepherd, A J Denye, Dr S Brennan, Dr B C Oates, G M Ridgway
**Co. Secretary:** John Pentland
**Responsibilities**
**Senior:** Martin Greaney *(Manager)*
**Marketing:** Lesley Woodhead *(Fundraising Manager)*
**HR:** Paul Lashbrook *(Human Resources Manager)*
**Health & Safety:** Paul Lashbrook *(Human Resources Manager)*
**Branches:** Wirral Hospice St John's, Charity Shop, 118 Victoria Road, Wallasey, Merseyside CH45 2JF
**US SIC:** 8091, 8321
**UK SIC:** 95200, 96111
**Auditors:** Grant Thornton
**Bankers:** HSBC Bank plc (40-10-22)

| | 31-03-14 | 31-03-13 | 31-03-12 |
|---|---|---|---|
| TO | 5,519,207 | 4,598,053 | 4,421,313 |
| P/L | 1,082,122 | 300,638 | 531,020 |
| NW | 10,973,877 | 9,488,206 | 8,660,236 |
| WC | 1,730,205 | 1,421,895 | 1,691,453 |
| Emp. | 140 | 140 | 121 |

DUNS 23-951-3158

## Wirral Hospice St Johns Enterprises Ltd

254 Telegraph Road, Wirral, Merseyside CH60 7SG
**Tel:** 01513426030
**Web:** www.stjohnshospice.org
**Reg No:** 3940685 **Estd:** 1983 Private Limited Company
**Line of Business:** Hospices
**Issued Capital:** £2
**Directors:** Ms J Gorry, S Burrows, C M Pope, G M Ridgway, P S Shepherd, A J Denye, Ms P A Hunter, Ms H R Staveley Taylor
**Co. Secretary:** John Pentland
**US SIC:** 8321 **UK SIC:** 96111
**Auditors:** Baker Tilly
**Bankers:** HSBC Bank plc (40-10-22)

| | 31-03-14 | 31-03-13 | 31-03-12 |
|---|---|---|---|
| TO | 85,908 | 88,961 | 98,755 |
| NW | 2 | 2 | 2 |
| WC | 2 | 2 | 2 |

DUNS 23-193-0652

## Wirral Information Resource for Equality & Diversity Ltd

Unit 7 Wirral Business Park, Arrowe Brook Road, Wirral, Merseyside CH49 1SX
**Tel:** 08448801500
**Web:** www.wired.me.uk
**Reg No:** 2997803 **Estd:** 2003 Private Limited Company
**Line of Business:** Other service activities not elsewhere classified
**Trading Style:** Wired
**Directors:** C Russell, A J Welch, K G Murphy, L G Brown, Dr P A Dufton, W E Woods
**US SIC:** 8999, 6732
**UK SIC:** 83954, 83100
**Auditors:** Bailey Page & Roper
**Bankers:** National Westminster Bank Plc (01-07-02)

| | 31-03-14 | 31-03-13 | 31-03-12 |
|---|---|---|---|
| TO | 2,067,683 | 2,088,199 | 2,176,559 |
| P/L | (283,940) | (190,192) | 777,484 |
| NW | 449,430 | 719,489 | 909,682 |
| WC | 399,234 | 657,185 | 830,633 |

DUNS 22-944-4146

## Wirral Metropolitan Borough Council

Town Hall, Brighton Street, Wallasey, Merseyside CH44 8ED
**Web:** www.wirral.gov.uk
**VAT No:** 165565540 **Estd:** 2011
**Line of Business:** Tourist information offices
**Principals:** A Worthington, A White, D Richard, Ms C Baker *(Manager)*, J Agass
**Co. Secretary:** Philip Manson
**Responsibilities**
**Senior:** Juggy Landay *(Destination Marketing Manager)*
**Marketing:** Gill Rutter *(Press Officer)*
**IT:** Marge Evans *(Senior IT Executive)*
**HR:** Chris Hyams *(Head of Personnel)*, Huw Wilkie *(Staff Development Manager)*
**Health & Safety:** Mark Camborne *(Health & Safety Officer)*
**Operations:** Gill Rutter *(Press Officer)*
**Purchasing:** Ray Williams *(Head of Procurement)*
**Branches:** Wirral Metropolitan Borough Council, Warden, Black Horse Clo, Wirral, Merseyside CH48 6HD
**US SIC:** 9121 **UK SIC:** 91110
**Bankers:** National Westminster Bank Plc (60-05-07)
**Employees:** 9,531

DUNS 42-429-9360

## Wirral Metropolitan College

Conway Park Campus, Europa Boulevard, Conway Park, Birkenhead, Merseyside CH41 4NT
**Tel:** 01515517777
**Web:** www.wmc.ac.uk
**Estd:** 1995 Proprietorship
**Line of Business:** Schools (foundation)
**Director:** R Dowd
**Branches:** Wirral Metropolitan College, Summerhill Ho, Beechwood Dr, Prenton, Merseyside CH43 7ZU
**US SIC:** 8211 **UK SIC:** 93200
**Employees:** 600

DUNS 73-652-7057

## Wirral Partnership Homes Ltd

Hamilton Street, Birkenhead, Merseyside CH41 4AA
**Tel:** 01516063000 **Fax:** 01516063001
**Web:** www.magentaliving.org.uk
**Reg No:** 4912562 **Estd:** 2003 Private Company Limited By Guarantee
**Line of Business:** Housing associations societies trusts & co-operatives
**Trading Style:** Magenta Living
**Directors:** Mrs E M Roberts, S Foulkes, Ms D E Roberts, D G Clark, J E Green, J E Fedden, Ms A Green, S Whittingham
**Co. Secretary:** Patrick Mccarthy
**Responsibilities**
**Senior:** Lynne Bunting *(Manager)*, Thomas Harney *(Manager)*, Jean Mcintosh *(Director)*, Michael Parkin *(Director)*, Muriel Wilkinson *(Director)*
**HR:** Joanne Francom *(Human Resources Manager)*
**Branches:** Wirral Partnership Homes Ltd, Whitfield Ct, Birkenhead, Merseyside CH42 0LR
**US SIC:** 6519 **UK SIC:** 85000
**Auditors:** Grant Thornton UK LLP
**Bankers:** The Royal Bank Of Scotland Plc (15-00-00)

| | 31-03-14 | 31-03-13 | 31-03-12 |
|---|---|---|---|
| TO | 56,814,000 | 53,984,000 | 59,616,000 |
| P/L | 4,388,000 | (3,529,000) | 7,855,000 |
| NW | 51,793,000 | 43,470,000 | 51,973,000 |
| WC | 7,547,000 | 12,505,000 | 12,927,000 |
| Emp. | 534 | 527 | 507 |

DUNS 23-271-8184

## Wirral Primary Care Trust

Old Market House, Birkenhead, Wirral, Merseyside CH41 5AL
**Tel:** 01516 510 011
**Line of Business:** Primary Care Trust. Accountability: Each Trust Board is directly accountable to the Secertary of State via the N H S Executive.
**Trading Style:** Nhs Wirral
**Issued Capital:** £1
**Director:** Ms A Cook
**Responsibilities**
**Senior:** Phil Jennings *(Chairperson)*
**Branches:** Wirral Primary Care Trust, 3 Port Causeway, Wirral, Merseyside CH62 4NH
**US SIC:** 8062 **UK SIC:** 95100
**Employees:** 350

DUNS 54-864-0432

## Wirral University Teaching Hospital Nhs Foundation Trust

Arrowe Park Hospital, Arrowe Park Road, Wirral, Merseyside CH49 5PE
**Tel:** 0151 678 5111
**Web:** www.wirral.nhs.uk
**Estd:** 2001 Incorporate By Act Of Parliament
**Line of Business:** Hospitals
**Director:** F G Burns
**Responsibilities**
**Senior:** Pamela Leonard *(Manager)*
**Branches:** Wirral University Teaching Hospital Nhs Foundation Trust, Fender Way, Prenton, Merseyside CH43 9QS
**US SIC:** 8062 **UK SIC:** 95100
**Auditors:** St James' Square

| | 31-03-14 | 31-03-13 | 31-03-12 |
|---|---|---|---|
| TO | 300,889,000 | 296,992,000 | 253,796,000 |
| P/L | 1,506,000 | 6,270,000 | 6,599,000 |
| NW | 140,483,000 | 143,042,000 | 140,929,000 |
| WC | (3,784,000) | 1,700,000 | 3,107,000 |
| Emp. | 4,928 | 4,823 | 4,763 |

DUNS 77-785-6865 Imp

## Wirtgen Ltd

**(Subsidiary of:** Wirtgen Group Gmbh)
Reinhard House, Whisby Road, Lincoln, Lincolnshire LN6 3QW
**Tel:** 01522-889200 **Fax:** 01522-889222
**Web:** www.wirtgen.co.uk
**Reg No:** 3026300 **VAT No:** 646670024
**Estd:** 1987 Private Limited Company
**Line of Business:** Manufacturers of plant machinery
**Export Sales:** £3,133,131
**Issued Capital:** £500,000
**Directors:** P J Higginson, P F Holmes
**Co. Secretary:** John Bainbridge
**Responsibilities**
**Senior:** Andy Kent *(Manager)*, Stefan Wirtgen *(President)*
**Marketing:** Melanie Leggett *(Sales & Marketing Manager)*
**Sales:** Richard Allsopp *(Sales Manager - Road Technolog)*, Melanie Leggett *(Sales & Marketing Manager)*, Terry Watson *(Sales Manager)*
**IT:** Hayley Carpenter *(Computer Manager)*, Chris Rockey *(IT Manager)*
**Health & Safety:** Mervyn Fox *(Health & Safety Officer)*
**Operations:** Phil Bean *(Product Specialist)*, Russell Wilkinson *(Product Leader (Crushing & Scr)*, Neil Woodward *(Product Specialist)*
**US SIC:** 3531, 1799
**UK SIC:** 32541, 50000
**Auditors:** Streets Audit LLP
**Bankers:** National Westminster Bank Plc (60-13-15)

| | 31-12-13 | 31-12-12 | 31-12-11 |
|---|---|---|---|
| TO | 54,232,212 | 36,648,095 | 37,578,594 |
| P/L | 1,403,311 | 1,040,826 | 1,371,079 |
| NW | 9,108,246 | 8,454,554 | 7,675,634 |
| WC | 6,896,451 | 6,255,763 | 5,454,300 |
| Emp. | N/A | 54 | 53 |

DUNS 49-001-6466

## Wirth Research Ltd

Unit D4 Telford Road, Bicester, Oxfordshire OX26 4LD
**Tel:** 01869355260
**Web:** www.wirthresearch.com
**Reg No:** 3069609 **Estd:** 1996 Private Limited Company
**Line of Business:** Research and experimental development on natural sciences and engineering
**Export Sales:** £2,419,478
**Issued Capital:** £20
**Directors:** D J Davies, N J Wirth, M Y Fieldsend, S P Crompton
**Co. Secretary:** Mrs Louise Wirth
**Branches:** Wirth Research Ltd, Unit A11-A12, Telford Road, Bicester, Oxfordshire OX26 4LD
**US SIC:** 7391 **UK SIC:** 94000
**Auditors:** Webb House Ltd
**Bankers:** National Westminster Bank Plc (60-01-35)

| | 31-03-14 | 31-03-13 | 31-03-12 |
|---|---|---|---|
| TO | 9,973,890 | 11,486,411 | 11,545,617 |
| P/L | 264,249 | 483,162 | (1,566,176) |
| NW | 2,919,155 | 2,572,011 | 1,960,113 |
| WC | 2,035,950 | 1,628,479 | 1,251,017 |
| Emp. | 76 | 59 | 58 |

DUNS 22-215-9522

## Wisbech Grammar School

North Brink, Wisbech, Cambridgeshire PE13 1JX
**Tel:** 01945-583631
**Web:** www.wgs.cambs.sch.uk
**Reg No:** 4234021 **Estd:** 2001 Private Limited Company
**Line of Business:** Schools (independent)
**Directors:** H K Mccurdy, P P Hobday, Ms E C Morris, Professor J R Raven, P S King, C M Goad, Dr D Barter, Mrs C R Mair
**Co. Secretary:** Group Captain Jonathan Wheeler
**Responsibilities**
**Senior:** Rupert Calleja *(Director)*, Frederick Grounds *(Manager)*, Stephen Halls *(Bursar)*, Jeffrey Hazel *(Manager)*, Colin Kolbert *(Manager)*, Ian Maclachlan *(Director)*, Sara Meekins *(Director)*, Fiona Sconce *(Director)*, Frederick Treasure *(Director)*
**Marketing:** James MacDonald *(Marketing Manager)*
**HR:** Stephen Halls *(Bursar)*, Christine Noxon *(HR Manager)*
**US SIC:** 8211 **UK SIC:** 93200
**Bankers:** Barclays Bank Plc (20-97-34)

| | 31-07-13 | 31-07-12 | 31-07-11 |
|---|---|---|---|
| TO | 5,710,240 | 5,803,001 | 5,734,518 |
| P/L | (55,716) | 157,759 | 138,925 |
| NW | 12,194,341 | 12,080,979 | 11,946,113 |
| WC | 5,808,695 | 5,827,069 | 6,624,197 |
| Emp. | 117 | 115 | 112 |

DUNS 21-585-0196
## Wisdon Court Day Centre
Wisden Road, Stevenage, Hertfordshire SG1 5JD
**Tel:** 01438727220
**Estd:** 2011 Proprietorship
**Line of Business:** Day and care centres
**Proprietor:** Mrs T Fletcher
**US SIC:** 8321 **UK SIC:** 96111
**Employees:** 60

DUNS 21-144-1125
## Wise Ability Ltd
Cathedral Court, 46 Church Street, Sheffield, South Yorkshire S1 2GN
**Tel:** 01142725365
**Web:** www.wiseability.co.uk
**Reg No:** 6749024 **Estd:** 2008 Private Company Limited By Guarantee
**Line of Business:** Local government
**Directors:** Ms P F Toop, Z M Duff, J L Bateup, Professor J Graffam, A B Urquhart, Ms E Rozario, Ms A Leyden
**Co. Secretary:** Ms Patricia Toop
**Branches:** Wise Ability Ltd, Newebury House, South Grove, Rotherham, South Yorkshire S60 2AF
**US SIC:** 9121 **UK SIC:** 91110

| | 30-06-14 | 30-06-13 | 30-06-12 |
|---|---|---|---|
| TO | 3,598,947 | 2,791,158 | 2,744,585 |
| P/L | 48,792 | (306,162) | 295,770 |
| NW | (878,695) | (927,487) | (621,325) |
| WC | 737,259 | 575,324 | 591,830 |
| Emp. | 100 | 82 | 56 |

DUNS 21-712-3416
## Wise Academies
Wise Academies Head Office, Borodin Avenue, Sunderland, Tyne and Wear SR5 4NX
**Tel:** 01915536916
**Web:** www.wiseacademies.co.uk
**Reg No:** 7521946 **Estd:** 2011 Private Company Limited By Guarantee
**Line of Business:** Primary education
**Directors:** P J Smith, Ms N Fountain, Ms N S Vokes, R Symonds, Ms Z Carr, J G Wood, Ms M E Stephenson, R Symonds
**Responsibilities**
**Senior:** Jeanette Clennell *(Director)*, Evonne Hodgson *(Director)*, Ashley Humble *(Director)*, Donna Weiss *(Director)*
**US SIC:** 8211 **UK SIC:** 93200
**Bankers:** Lloyds TSB Bank plc (77-20-01)

| | 31-08-14 | 31-08-13 | 31-08-12 |
|---|---|---|---|
| TO | 7,226,000 | 10,634,126 | 5,423,182 |
| P/L | (649,000) | 4,584,972 | 2,974,320 |
| NW | 6,917,000 | 7,346,192 | 3,001,220 |
| WC | 1,347,000 | 1,291,687 | 412,438 |
| Emp. | 139 | 226 | 96 |

DUNS 76-433-4876
## Wise Catering Ltd
Unit T, Hazel Road Willments Industrial Estate, Southampton, Hampshire SO19 7HS
**Tel:** 02380439280
**Web:** www.wisecatering.co.uk
**Reg No:** 2562441 **Estd:** 1990 Private Limited Company
**Line of Business:** Catering
**Trading Style:** Wise Catering
**Issued Capital:** £900
**Director:** J H Wharton Davies
**Co. Secretary:** Christopher Treacher
**US SIC:** 5812 **UK SIC:** 66110
**Auditors:** Fiander Tovell & Co

| | 29-09-14 | 29-09-13 | 29-09-12 |
|---|---|---|---|
| TA | 466,236 | 408,626 | 528,138 |
| NW | 89,614 | 95,049 | 92,573 |
| WC | (21,265) | (7,440) | (34,703) |

DUNS 76-998-8288
## Wise Employment (Swindon) Ltd
103-104 Commercial Road, Swindon, Wiltshire SN1 5PL
**Tel:** 01793416650 **Fax:** 01793430086
**Web:** www.wiseemployment.co.uk
**Reg No:** 2653264 **Estd:** 1991 Private Limited Company
**Line of Business:** Labour recruitment and provision of personnel
**Issued Capital:** £16,500
**Director:** Mrs J D Robinson
**Co. Secretary:** Keith Robinson
**Branches:** Wise Employment (Swindon) Ltd, First Floor, 176 Fore Street, Exeter, Devon EX4 3AX
**US SIC:** 7361 **UK SIC:** 83954
**Auditors:** Morris Owen
**Bankers:** HSBC Bank plc (40-43-41)

| | 31-12-13 | 31-12-12 | 31-12-11 |
|---|---|---|---|
| TO | 11,678,414 | 13,240,905 | 16,438,231 |
| P/L | 25,850 | (132,772) | 119,197 |
| NW | 647,316 | 813,137 | 1,046,506 |
| WC | 412,964 | 546,326 | 767,134 |
| Emp. | 65 | 66 | 69 |

DUNS 50-532-7700
## Wise Financial Services Ltd
Wey Court West, Union Road, Farnham, Surrey GU9 7PT
**Tel:** 01252-711244
**Web:** www.wiseandco.co.uk
**Reg No:** 2490704 **Estd:** 1992 Private Limited Company
**Line of Business:** Accounting activities
**Trading Style:** Wise & Co
**Issued Capital:** £2,000
**Director:** F E Blackmore
**Co. Secretary:**
Southern Secretarial Services Li
**Responsibilities**
**Senior:** Deborah Chamberlain *(Practice Manager)*, Bob Lock *(Partner)*, Stephen South *(Partner)*
**Branches:** Wise Financial Services Ltd, Sovereign House 155 To 157 High Street, Aldershot, Hampshire GU11 1TT
**US SIC:** 8931 **UK SIC:** 83600

| | 30-09-13 | 30-09-12 | 30-09-11 |
|---|---|---|---|
| TA | 15,869 | 17,888 | 108,472 |
| NW | 2,103 | 2,118 | 2,000 |
| WC | 2,103 | 2,118 | 2,000 |

DUNS 22-911-1729
## The Wise Group
72 Charlotte Street, Glasgow, Lanarkshire G1 5DW
**Tel:** 01413033131
**Web:** www.thewisegroup.co.uk
**Reg No:** 0091095SC **Estd:** 1984 Private Company Limited By Guarantee
**Line of Business:** Career information services
**Directors:** Ms G E Callaghan, G O'Sullivan, Ms M Morrison, Ms S P Young, D Campbell, S L Patrick, K S Anderson, D Mcnulty
**Co. Secretary:** Ms Margaret Maclean
**Responsibilities**
**Senior:** Peter Cheney *(Manager)*, Archibald Kirkwood Of Kirkhope *(Director)*, Desmond McNulty *(Director)*, Gavin Nicol *(Director)*, Laurie Russell *(Chief Executive)*, George Ryan *(Manager)*, James Stretton *(Chairman)*
**Finance:** Carron Garmory *(Finance Director)*
**Marketing:** Bernadette Milligan *(Communication Director)*
**Branches:** The Wise Group, Unit 15 Atlas Rd Indstl Est, Glasgow, Lanarkshire G21 4TP
**US SIC:** 7361, 8249
**UK SIC:** 83954, 93300
**Auditors:** Scott-Moncrieff
**Bankers:** Bank Of Scotland (80-83-33)

| | 31-12-13 | 31-12-12 | 31-12-11 |
|---|---|---|---|
| TO | 8,224,199 | 8,462,609 | 1,646,720 |
| P/L | (437,451) | (3,487,221) | 657,423 |
| NW | 4,030,510 | 4,467,962 | 9,086,687 |
| WC | 2,110,043 | 2,419,318 | 5,553,315 |
| Emp. | 201 | 365 | 549 |

DUNS 21-837-4505
## Wise Owl Trust
Briscoe Lane Academy, Briscoe Lane, Manchester M40 2TB
**Tel:** 01616811783
**Web:** www.wiseowltrust.com
**Reg No:** 8053288 **Estd:** 2012 Private Company Limited By Guarantee
**Line of Business:** Primary education
**Directors:** G Larder, D Savage, I Chadwick, Ms L Marks
**Responsibilities**
**Senior:** Christopher Oshawghnessy *(Executive Principle)*
**US SIC:** 8211 **UK SIC:** 93200
**Bankers:** The Co-Operative Bank Plc (08-00-50)

| | 31-08-14 | 31-08-13 |
|---|---|---|
| TO | 4,435,526 | 9,458,255 |
| P/L | (9,739) | 6,280,795 |
| NW | 5,698,055 | 5,991,795 |
| WC | 673,950 | 541,727 |
| Emp. | 108 | 125 |

DUNS 23-716-9581
## Wisecall Claims Assistance Ltd
**(Subsidiary of:** Kindertons 2013 Ltd)
St Andrews House, Riverside Road, Sunderland, Tyne and Wear SR5 3JG
**Tel:** 08458735500 **Fax:** 08707871129
**Web:** www.wisecall.co.uk
**Reg No:** 3711784 **Estd:** 1999 Private Limited Company
**Line of Business:** Non-life insurance
**Issued Capital:** £200
**Directors:** S Faun, C J Latham
**Responsibilities**
**Senior:** Julie Mcgeever *(Manager)*, Donald Rodger *(Manager)*
**US SIC:** 6399 **UK SIC:** 82001
**Bankers:** The Royal Bank Of Scotland Plc (16-19-22)

| | 28-02-14 | 28-02-13 | 30-02-12 |
|---|---|---|---|
| TO | 3,993,929 | N/A | N/A |
| P/L | (84,548) | N/A | N/A |
| NW | (418,988) | (334,694) | (553,434) |
| WC | 802,978 | 929,496 | 503,090 |

DUNS 42-328-5352
## Wiseman Lee Solicitors
9-11 Cambridge Park, London E11 2PU
**Tel:** 02082151174
**Web:** www.wiseman.co.uk
**VAT No:** 248756127 **Estd:** 1953 Partnership
**Line of Business:** Solicitors
**Partners:** Mrs P Daly, J Smith, P Kaufman, P Wershof, D Wershof, P Le Rasle, D Inkpin, J Diamond
**Branches:** Wiseman Lee Solicitors, 229 Hoe Street, London E17 9PP
**US SIC:** 8111 **UK SIC:** 83500
**Bankers:** National Westminster Bank Plc (60-07-18)
**Employees:** 90

DUNS 21-783-8794
## Wishaw Housing Area Office
236 Main Street, Wishaw, Lanarkshire ML2 7ND
**Tel:** 01698302920
**Estd:** 2011 Proprietorship
**Line of Business:** Housing associations societies trusts & co-operatives
**Proprietor:** Mrs G Whitehead
**US SIC:** 8321 **UK SIC:** 96111
**Employees:** 50

DUNS 21-225-4707
## Wishaw Social Work
Kings House, 14-16 King Street, Wishaw, Lanarkshire ML2 8BS
**Tel:** 01698-348200
**Web:** www.northlan.gov.uk
**Estd:** 2002 Proprietorship
**Line of Business:** The dss
**Proprietor:** T Cowan
**US SIC:** 8321 **UK SIC:** 96111
**Employees:** 180

DUNS 39-720-7523
## The Wisley Golf Club Plc
Ripley Road, Woking, Surrey GU23 7LT
**Tel:** 01483-211022 **Fax:** 01483-211662
**Web:** www.thewisley.com
**Reg No:** 2169672 **VAT No:** 503518573
**Estd:** 1987 Public Limited Company
**Line of Business:** Other sporting activities not elsewhere classified
**Issued Capital:** £18,750,000
**Directors:** C J Day, J Langston, G C Atterbury, R F Lane, V Chandler, Ms S Lee, J Carter-Meggs
**Co. Secretary:** Robert Nesbitt
**Responsibilities**
**Senior:** Anthony Jansen *(Manager)*, Wayne Sheffield *(Chief Executive)*, Brian Stopp *(Manager)*
**US SIC:** 7999 **UK SIC:** 97913
**Auditors:** Deloitte & Touche
**Bankers:** Bank Of Scotland (12-09-61)

| | 31-12-13 | 31-12-12 | 31-12-11 |
|---|---|---|---|
| TO | 5,078,523 | 4,831,503 | 4,831,627 |
| P/L | (89,697) | (103,744) | (117,213) |
| NW | 19,800,150 | 19,891,970 | 19,996,125 |
| WC | (501,512) | (607,206) | (244,367) |
| Emp. | 98 | 97 | 94 |

DUNS 21-038-9170
## Wistaston Westfield Infant School
Church Lane, Crewe, Cheshire CW2 8EZ
**Tel:** 01270663619
**Web:** www.wistaston.cheshire.sch.uk
**Estd:** 1996
**Line of Business:** Schools (local authority)
**Trading Style:** Wistaston Church Lane Primary School
**Partner:** G Prince
**US SIC:** 8211 **UK SIC:** 93200
**Employees:** 50

DUNS 21-745-1729
## Witchford Village College
Manor Road, Ely, Cambridgeshire CB6 2JA
**Tel:** 01353662053
**Web:** www.witchfordvc.co.uk
**Reg No:** 7772516 **Estd:** 2011 Private Company Limited By Guarantee
**Line of Business:** General secondary education
**Directors:** J Peryer, G Dewey, A F Boobyer, R P Birch, Ms S Mckenzie, Mrs F J Dyer, Ms J E Lucas, P Blackwell
**Responsibilities**
**Senior:** Tracy Anderson *(Director)*, Karin Tahir *(Director)*
**IT:** Gareth Sandy *(PC Manager)*, Jeremy Simmonds *(Director of ICT)*
**Facilities:** Gavin Peasey *(Site Manager)*
**US SIC:** 8211 **UK SIC:** 93200

**Auditors:** Baker Tilly UK Audit LLP

| | 31-08-14 | 31-08-13 | 31-08-12 |
|---|---|---|---|
| TO | 4,744,704 | 4,480,698 | 10,671,059 |
| P/L | (246,129) | (59,670) | 6,267,277 |
| NW | 5,615,478 | 6,157,607 | 6,162,277 |
| WC | 610,354 | 573,163 | 544,253 |
| Emp. | 107 | 102 | 94 |

DUNS 36-519-0821
## Witham Hall Preparatory School
Witham On The Hill, Bourne, Lincolnshire PE10 0JJ
**Tel:** 01778-590222
**Web:** www.withamhall.co.uk
**Estd:** 1997
**Line of Business:** General secondary education
**Directors:** D Telfer, Mrs S Telfer
**US SIC:** 8211 **UK SIC:** 93200
**Employees:** 50

DUNS 21-781-6406
## Withensea Holiday Park
Waxholme Road, Withernsea, North Humberside HU19 2BS
**Tel:** 01964612189
**Web:** www.parkresorts.co.uk
**Estd:** 2011 Proprietorship
**Line of Business:** Other tourist or short-stay accommodation
**Proprietor:** S Morris
**Responsibilities**
**Senior:** Richard Gissing *(Manager)*
**US SIC:** 7021 **UK SIC:** 66500
**Employees:** 100

DUNS 53-621-4653
## Witherbys Ltd
P W S Ltd, London EC1R 0ET
**Tel:** 02070178600 **Fax:** 02073367493
**Web:** www.witherbysonline.com
**Reg No:** 3426548 **Estd:** 1997 Private Limited Company
**Line of Business:** Printing not elsewhere classified
**Issued Capital:** £1,333
**Director:** J Greene
**Co. Secretary:** William Kelly
**US SIC:** 2752 **UK SIC:** 47544

| | 30-09-14 | 30-09-13 | 30-09-12 |
|---|---|---|---|
| TA | 2,559,226 | 2,450,258 | 2,632,479 |
| NW | 892,216 | 819,228 | 805,954 |
| WC | 400,931 | 339,241 | 358,911 |

DUNS 64-748-3676
## Withers & Rogers
Nicholas Wilson House, 6 Dormer Place, Leamington Spa, Warwickshire CV32 5AE
**Web:** www.withersrogers.com
**Partnership**
**Line of Business:** Activities of patent and copyright agents
**Partner:** D Bannerman
**Responsibilities**
**HR:** Tracey Wykes *(Human Resources Manager)*
**Health & Safety:** Tracey Wykes *(Human Resources Manager)*
**Branches:** Withers & Rogers, 4 Dyers Buildings Holborn, Chichester, West Sussex PO20 7HJ
**US SIC:** 7399 **UK SIC:** 83954
**Employees:** 50

DUNS 34-521-7686
## Withers & Rogers Group Llp
Golding House, Claybrook Road, London W6 8NA
**Tel:** 02076633500
**Web:** www.withersrogers.co.uk
**Reg No:** 0310991OC **VAT No:** 849768160
**Estd:** 2005
**Line of Business:** Law firm, trademark attorney
**Export Sales:** £18,392,223
**Responsibilities**
**Senior:** Simon Beck *(Non-designated Limited Liabili)*, Michael Blatchford *(Manager)*, Richard Bunn *(Manager)*, David Croston *(Non-designated Limited Liabili)*, Nick Dougan *(Manager)*, Matthew Howell *(Non-designated Limited Liabili)*, James Ribeiro *(Non-designated Limited Liabili)*, John-Paul Rooney *(Non-designated Limited Liabili)*, Adrian Tombling *(Non-designated Limited Liabili)*, Nicholas Wallin *(Non-designated Limited Liabili)*, Callum Wardle *(Non-designated Limited Liabili)*, Joanna Westwood *(Non-designated Limited Liabili)*
**Finance:** Michael Blatchford *(Manager)*
**Branches:** Withers & Rogers Group Llp, Nicholas Wilson Ho, Dormer Place, Leamington Spa, Warwickshire CV32 5AE
**US SIC:** 8111 **UK SIC:** 83500
**Auditors:** Horwath Clark Whitehill LLP

**Bankers:** Barclays Bank Plc (20-37-75)

| | 31-03-14 | 31-03-13 | 31-03-12 |
|---|---|---|---|
| TO | 32,824,673 | 30,241,869 | 27,653,045 |
| WC | 5,659,888 | 5,364,586 | 4,803,517 |
| Emp. | 125 | 108 | 96 |

DUNS 34-521-7702

## Withers & Rogers Renewals Llp

4 More, London Riverside, London SE1 2AU
**Tel:** 02079403600
**Web:** www.withersrogers.co.uk
**Reg No:** 0310993OC **Estd:** 2005
**Line of Business:** Legal activities
**US SIC:** 8111 **UK SIC:** 83500
**Auditors:** Horwath Clark Whitehill LLP

| | 31-03-14 | 31-03-13 | 31-03-12 |
|---|---|---|---|
| TA | 1,143,666 | 1,026,338 | 879,175 |
| NW | 385,722 | N/A | N/A |
| WC | 585,722 | 404,942 | 413,445 |

DUNS 42-351-5712

## Withers Llp

16 Old Bailey, London EC4M 7EG
**Web:** www.withersworldwide.com
**Reg No:** 0301149OC **Estd:** 2001
**Line of Business:** Solicitors
**Principals:** T Burns, S Davis, Mrs A J Paines, D Moise, H Haeri, A C Terry, J S Riches, Ms S V Cormack
**Responsibilities**
**Senior:** Elaine Aarons *(Partner)*, Julia Abrey *(Partner)*, Christine Blackman *(Manager)*, Jeffry Blomberg *(Designated Limited Liability P)*, Paul Brecknell *(Designated Limited Liability P)*, James Brockway *(Designated Limited Liability P)*, James Carolan *(Designated Limited Liability P)*, Richard Cassell *(Partner)*, Dora Clarke *(Partner)*, Christopher Coffin *(Designated Limited Liability P)*, Emma Copestake *(Partner)*, James Copson *(Designated Limited Liability P)*, Rupert Cowper-Coles *(Partner, Media & Reputation)*, Philip Digennaro *(Designated Limited Liability P)*, Sophie Dworetzsky *(Designated Limited Liability P)*, Dawn Goodman *(Designated Limited Liability P)*, Michael Gouriet *(Designated Limited Liability P)*, David Guin *(Designated Limited Liability P)*, Edward Hoskyns Abrahall *(Designated Limited Liability P)*, Bertie Hoskyns-Abrahall *(Partner)*, Anthony Indaimo *(Designated Limited Liability P)*, Daniel Isaac *(Designated Limited Liability P)*, Mitchell Kops *(Designated Limited Liability P)*, Jay Krause *(Designated Limited Liability P)*, Julian Lipson *(Designated Limited Liability P)*, Roberto Moruzzi *(Partner)*, Robin Paul *(Partner)*, Denis Petkovic *(Partner)*, Kurt Rademacher *(Partner)*, Margret Robinson *(Manager)*, Francis Rojas *(Partner, New Office)*, Susan Satchell *(Partner)*, Meriel Schindler *(Partner)*, Henry Stuart *(Partner)*, Jeremy Wakeham *(Partner)*
**Finance:** Ann Cogdell *(Trust Manager)*, Simon Eldridge *(International Finance Director)*, Mike Timms *(Global Finance Director)*
**Admin:** Noelle Brown *(Secretary)*, Paulin Drewett *(Secretary)*
**IT:** Angela Conner *(IT Manager)*, Ian Goodley *(Deputy Head of IT)*
**HR:** Simon Luckett *(Human Resources Director)*, Cara Willis *(Human Resources Assistant)*
**Health & Safety:** Stephen Laver *(Health & Safety Officer)*
**Operations:** Peter Gibbons *(Operations Director)*
**US SIC:** 8111 **UK SIC:** 83500
**Auditors:** Deloitte & Touche LLP

| | 01-07-13 | 01-07-12 | 01-07-11 |
|---|---|---|---|
| TO | 80,453,456 | 80,524,587 | 75,710,527 |
| P/L | 15,702,874 | 20,951,575 | 19,264,262 |
| NW | 5,097,310 | 8,056,073 | 9,945,243 |
| WC | 13,942,019 | 17,802,201 | 17,813,165 |
| Emp. | 539 | 519 | 482 |

DUNS 73-613-8848

## Witherslack Care Ltd

**(Subsidiary of:** Witherslack Group (Holdings) Ltd)
Black Moss Lane, Ormskirk, Lancashire L39 4TW
**Tel:** 01695578734
**Reg No:** 4874778 **Estd:** 2003 Private Limited Company
**Line of Business:** Committee managed organisations
**Issued Capital:** £100
**Directors:** H C Tennant, M Davey, P D Jones
**Co. Secretary:** Craig Baxter
**US SIC:** 8699 **UK SIC:** 96902
**Auditors:** BDO LLP

| | 31-08-13 | 31-08-12 | 31-08-11 |
|---|---|---|---|
| TO | N/A | 6,786,212 | 5,676,158 |
| P/L | N/A | 1,376,391 | 1,058,282 |
| NW | 100 | 100 | 10,509 |
| WC | N/A | N/A | (269,486) |
| Emp. | N/A | N/A | 100 |

DUNS 21-699-8122

## Witherslack Group (Holdings) Ltd

Lupton Tower Lupton, Carnforth, Lancashire LA6 2PR
**Tel:** 01695578558
**Web:** www.witherslackgroup.co.uk
**Reg No:** 7449888 **Estd:** 2010 Private Limited Company
**Line of Business:** Management activities of other non-financial holding companies not elsewhere classified
**Issued Capital:** £205,440
**Directors:** P D Jones, J Titmuss, M Davey, A S Holloway, H C Tennant, J F Bowers, Mrs J Jones, M A Barrow
**US SIC:** 6711 **UK SIC:** 83962

| | 31-08-14 | 31-08-13 | 31-08-12 |
|---|---|---|---|
| TO | 34,726,775 | 29,793,988 | 25,476,955 |
| P/L | (273,564) | (744,693) | (1,356,750) |
| NW | (26,307,605) | (26,308,108) | (26,089,343) |
| WC | (12,068,565) | (8,375,851) | (7,781,050) |
| Emp. | 641 | 592 | 496 |

DUNS 23-082-9587

## Withington Girl's School

100 Wellington Road, Manchester M14 6BL
**Tel:** 0161-224-1077
**Web:** www.withington.manchester.sch.uk
**Estd:** 1910
**Line of Business:** Schools (independent)
**Director:** Mrs M Kenyon
**Responsibilities**
**Finance:** Sharon Senn *(Bursar)*
**IT:** Andrew Lockett *(Network Manager)*
**US SIC:** 8211 **UK SIC:** 93200
**Employees:** 110

DUNS 21-802-2460

## Withington Hospital Stroke Club

Nell Lane, Manchester M20 2LR
**Tel:** 01614345555
**Web:** www.manchester.nhs.uk
**Estd:** 1977
**Line of Business:** Public sector hospital activities, including nhs trusts
**Principals:** D Whyster, Mrs I Whyster
**Responsibilities**
**Senior:** Tom Pickup *(Hospital Manager)*
**IT:** David Phoenix-Stone *(IT Manager)*
**US SIC:** 8062, 8699
**UK SIC:** 95100, 96902
**Employees:** 4,400

DUNS 21-230-3580

## The Withy Grove Stores Ltd

35-39 Withy Grove, Manchester M4 2BJ
**Tel:** 01618348768
**Web:** www.safesatwithygrove.co.uk
**Reg No:** 0118224 **Estd:** 1850 Private Limited Company
**Line of Business:** Suppliers and installers of safes
**Issued Capital:** £4,300
**Managing Directors:** B K Solomon, A D Solomon
**Co. Secretary:** Brian Solomon
**US SIC:** 3499 **UK SIC:** 31694
**Auditors:** Ernst & Young
**Bankers:** National Westminster Bank Plc (01-10-01)

| | 30-04-14 | 30-04-13 | 30-04-12 |
|---|---|---|---|
| TA | 128,345 | 204,093 | 233,164 |
| NW | 85,127 | 162,481 | 198,442 |
| WC | 68,991 | 140,226 | 167,150 |

DUNS 23-633-0205

## Withy King

North Bailey House, New Inn Hall Street, Oxford, Oxfordshire OX1 2EA
**Web:** www.withyking.co.uk
**VAT No:** 194619332 **Estd:** 2011 Partnership
**Line of Business:** Solicitors
**Principals:** Ms T N Evans, J M Stonham, R A Peet *(Partner)*, S R Woods *(Partner)*, Ms M Wakeman *(Partner)*, M L King *(Partner)*, V W Gatter *(Partner)*, D Atkinson *(Partner)*
**Responsibilities**
**Senior:** James Barnatt *(Partner)*, Simon Bassett *(Partner)*, A Battson *(Partner)*
**Branches:** Withy King, 121 Cowley Road, Oxford, Oxfordshire OX4 3TH
**US SIC:** 8111 **UK SIC:** 83500
**Bankers:** Lloyds TSB Bank plc (30-96-35)
**Employees:** 100

DUNS 21-710-7752

## Withy King Llp

5-6 Northumberland Buildings, Bath, Avon BA1 2JE
**Web:** www.withyking.co.uk
**Reg No:** 0361361OC **Estd:** 2011
**Line of Business:** Solicitors
**Responsibilities**
**Senior:** Philip Banks-Welsh *(Partner)*, Anne Battson *(Partner)*, Jessica Bent *(Partner)*, Stuart Brazington *(Partner)*, Ian Carrier *(Non-designated Limited Liabili)*, David Cavaliero *(Non-designated Limited Liabili)*, Simon Clegg *(Partner)*, Peter Foskett *(Non-designated Limited Liabili)*, Louise Garcia *(Partner)*, Louise Hart *(Non-designated Limited Liabili)*, Sharon Macdonald *(Non-designated Limited Liabili)*, Katharine Mortimer *(Partner, Corporate Services)*, Amanda Noyce *(Partner)*, Shaun O'Halloran *(Partner for Finance & Operatio)*, Caroline Preist *(Partner)*, Kerstin Scheel *(Partner)*, Sarah Sibley *(Partner)*, Tony Spiers *(Partner)*, Angus Williams *(Partner)*
**Finance:** Dayton Little *(Tax and Trust Manager)*, Nick Martin *(Tax and Trust Manager)*, Shaun O'Halloran *(Partner for Finance & Operatio)*
**US SIC:** 8111 **UK SIC:** 83500
**Bankers:** HSBC Bank plc (40-09-19)

| | 30-04-14 | 30-04-13 | 30-04-12 |
|---|---|---|---|
| TO | 18,488,992 | 17,212,420 | 16,399,041 |
| P/L | 1,647,394 | 1,900,841 | 2,380,298 |
| NW | 4,952,527 | 4,659,166 | 5,354,189 |
| WC | 7,855,868 | 7,061,447 | 6,946,913 |
| Emp. | 236 | 213 | N/A |

DUNS 21-766-6324

## Witness Service Magistrates Court

St Aldates, Oxford, Oxfordshire OX1 1TL
**Tel:** 01865727753
**Web:** www.justice.gov.uk
**Estd:** 2011
**Line of Business:** Justice and judicial activities
**Responsibilities**
**Senior:** Rosemary Dilsaver *(Service Delivery Manager)*
**US SIC:** 8999 **UK SIC:** 83954
**Employees:** 50

DUNS 21-780-8115

## Witney Community Hospital

Welch Way, Witney, Oxfordshire OX28 6JJ
**Tel:** 01993209400
**Web:** www.nhs.uk
**Estd:** 2011 Proprietorship
**Line of Business:** Hospitals
**Proprietor:** Miss J Pointer
**US SIC:** 8062 **UK SIC:** 95100
**Employees:** 149

DUNS 39-776-7567

## Witney Four Pillars Hotel Ltd

**(Subsidiary of:** Spire Bidco Hotels Ltd)
Ducklington Lane, Witney, Oxfordshire OX8 4TJ
**Tel:** 01993-779777
**Web:** www.four-pillars.co.uk
**Reg No:** 2200412 **Estd:** 1989 Private Limited Company
**Line of Business:** Hotels
**Trading Style:** The Witney Four Pillars Hotel
**Issued Capital:** £50,000
**Directors:** J C Bradshaw, J A Burrell, A G Troy, T M Tolley, Ms S Broughton
**Responsibilities**
**Senior:** Anna Bambrock *(General Manager)*, Rex Clayton *(Manager)*
**HR:** Simone Cook *(Human Resources Manager)*, Jo Wherle *(HR Manager)*
**US SIC:** 7011, 5812
**UK SIC:** 66500, 66110
**Auditors:** Cannon Williamson Ltd

| | 31-12-13 | 31-12-12 | 31-12-11 |
|---|---|---|---|
| TO | 2,918,389 | 2,860,850 | 2,900,168 |
| P/L | 208,874 | 115,506 | 157,777 |
| NW | 919,789 | 804,482 | 717,070 |
| WC | 2,260,506 | 2,076,729 | 2,695,068 |
| Emp. | 73 | 77 | 78 |

DUNS 51-605-1278

## Witt & Son Properties Ltd

**(Subsidiary of:** Witt & Son Uk Holdings Ltd)
Witt House, Brookwoods Industrial Estate, Burrwood Way, Holywell Green, Halifax, West Yorkshire HX4 9BH
**Tel:** 01422378131
**Web:** www.wittandson.co.uk
**Reg No:** 5885579 **Estd:** 2006 Private Limited Company
**Line of Business:** Development and selling of real estate
**Trading Style:** Witt & Son Properties Ltd
**Issued Capital:** £1
**Director:** Dr H T Witt
**Co. Secretary:** Karsten Witt
**US SIC:** 6552, 8911
**UK SIC:** 85000, 83701
**Bankers:** Lloyds TSB Bank plc (30-93-76)

| | 31-12-13 | 31-12-12 | 31-12-11 |
|---|---|---|---|
| TA | 167,088 | 150,185 | 150,185 |
| NW | 1 | 1 | 1 |
| WC | 1 | 1 | 1 |

DUNS 22-708-8622 **Exp**

## Wittington Investments Ltd

10 Grosvenor Street, London W1K 4QY
**Web:** www.abf.co.uk
**Reg No:** 0366054 **Estd:** 1941 Private Limited Company
**Line of Business:** Manufacture of other food products not elsewhere classified
**Export Markets:** Australia; New Zealand; North America; Republic Of Ireland
**Export Sales:** £7,312,000
**Issued Capital:** £431,011
**Directors:** G G Weston, Sir H A Djanogly, C D Mason, G G Weston, Mrs E S Adamo, S C Hancock, W G Weston, G H Weston
**Co. Secretary:** Ms Amanda Geday
**Responsibilities**
**Senior:** Anna Hobhouse *(Director)*
**Branches:** Wittington Investments Ltd, Lancaster Way Business Park, Ely, Cambridgeshire CB6 3NW
**US SIC:** 6711, 2099
**UK SIC:** 83962, 42399
**Auditors:** KPMG Audit PLC
**Bankers:** Bank Of Scotland (12-11-03)
**Following financial data are in thousands**

| | 13-09-14 | 14-09-13 | 15-09-12 |
|---|---|---|---|
| TO | 13,063,000 | 13,417,000 | 12,350,000 |
| P/L | 1,044,000 | 887,000 | 782,000 |
| NW | 3,169,000 | 2,784,000 | 2,351,000 |
| WC | 1,813,000 | 1,763,000 | 1,471,000 |
| Emp. | 119,371 | 113,447 | 107,046 |

DUNS 85-606-3883

## Wixted & Co Ltd

57 Putney Bridge Road, London SW18 1NP
**Tel:** 020-8877-8700 **Fax:** 020-8877-8701
**Web:** www.insurancebwi.co.uk
**Reg No:** 6243291 **Estd:** 2007 Private Limited Company
**Line of Business:** Solicitors
**Trading Style:** Wixted & Co Limited
**Issued Capital:** £200
**Director:** T P Wixted
**Co. Secretary:** Ms Jane Green
**US SIC:** 8111 **UK SIC:** 83500
**Bankers:** Barclays Bank Plc (20-00-00)

| | 31-10-13 | 31-10-12 | 31-10-11 |
|---|---|---|---|
| TO | 11,212,520 | 13,036,101 | 10,859,297 |
| P/L | 2,919,615 | 5,276,933 | 4,091,764 |
| NW | 13,831,955 | 12,533,121 | 8,828,405 |
| WC | 13,737,258 | 12,478,865 | 8,787,267 |
| Emp. | 103 | 89 | 83 |

DUNS 76-680-8141

## W.J. Findon & Son Ltd

Bordon Hill Nurseries, Stratford-Upon-Avon, Warwickshire CV37 9RY
**Tel:** 01789292792
**Web:** www.bordonhill.com
**Reg No:** 2588990 **Estd:** 1991 Private Limited Company
**Line of Business:** Growing of vegetables, horticultural specialities and nursery products
**Issued Capital:** £2
**Co. Secretary:** David Findon
**US SIC:** 0161 **UK SIC:** 01001

| | 30-04-14 | 30-04-13 | 30-04-12 |
|---|---|---|---|
| TA | 2 | 2 | 2 |
| NW | 2 | 2 | 2 |

DUNS 49-249-8431 **Imp-Exp**

## W.J. Furse & Co Ltd

**(Subsidiary of:** Abb Ltd)
Wilford Road, Nottingham, Nottinghamshire NG2 1EB
**Tel:** 01159-643700 **Fax:** 01159-860538
**Web:** www.furse.com
**Reg No:** 3118288 **VAT No:** 657807987
**Estd:** 1893 Private Limited Company
**Line of Business:** Other non-ferrous metal production
**Export Markets:** Middle East; Far East; E U
**Trading Style:** W.J. Furse & Co Ltd / Thomas & Betts
**Issued Capital:** £1,691,726
**Directors:** F J Van Belle, D L Alyea
**Co. Secretary:** William Smith Jr
**US SIC:** 3339, 3496, 3661
**UK SIC:** 22470, 31694, 34410
**Auditors:** KPMG LLP
**Bankers:** Bank Of America, Na (16-50-50)

| | 31-12-13 | 31-12-12 | 31-12-11 |
|---|---|---|---|
| TO | 8,389,000 | 8,146,000 | 8,140,000 |
| P/L | 1,409,000 | 2,683,000 | 2,109,000 |
| NW | 6,773,000 | 5,124,000 | 2,182,000 |
| WC | 5,280,000 | 3,785,000 | 909,000 |
| Emp. | 148 | 139 | 139 |

DUNS 28-942-7254 **Imp**

## Wj Groundwater Ltd

**(Subsidiary of:** Wj Management Ltd)
Bournehall House, Bushey, Hertfordshire WD23 3EE
**Web:** www.wjgl.com
**Reg No:** 1586827 **VAT No:** 367004564
**Estd:** 2010 Private Limited Company
**Line of Business:** Speciality design activities
**Export Sales:** £8,540,439
**Issued Capital:** £3,463

**Principals:** Dr T O Roberts (Managing), Dr G J Holmes, R M Fielden, P F Turner
**Co. Secretary:** Stevyn Harris
**Branches:** Wj Groundwater Ltd, Fir Tree Farm, 30 Bumpers Lane, Chester, Cheshire CH1 6QE
**US SIC:** 4941, 8911
**UK SIC:** 17000, 83701
**Auditors:** Lees
**Bankers:** National Westminster Bank Plc (60-04-17)

|  | 30-04-14 | 30-04-13 | 30-04-12 |
|---|---|---|---|
| TO | 16,423,921 | 10,848,835 | 7,869,013 |
| P/L | 2,680,507 | 1,744,868 | 834,498 |
| NW | 7,226,229 | 5,703,283 | 4,385,096 |
| WC | 5,383,437 | 4,331,295 | 3,151,543 |
| Emp. | 138 | 120 | 114 |

DUNS 50-523-4765
## W.J. Holdings Ltd
Unit 4 Phoenix Park Bayton Road, Coventry, West Midlands CV7 9QN
**Tel:** 02476360211 **Fax:** 02476-368219
**Web:** www.mcscontrolsystems.co.uk
**Reg No:** 2481568 **Estd:** 1990 Private Limited Company
**Line of Business:** Manufacture of other electrical equipment not elsewhere classified
**Issued Capital:** £54,188
**Principals:** S C Poole (Managing), K J Parsons (Financial), P Isaacs, S S Foster, R Armstrong
**Co. Secretary:** David Tucker
**US SIC:** 3629, 8999
**UK SIC:** 34350, 83954
**Auditors:** Moffat Gilbert

|  | 31-08-13 | 30-11-12 | 30-08-11 |
|---|---|---|---|
| TO | 8,402,749 | 11,075,232 | 10,527,601 |
| P/L | 150,950 | (1,034,791) | 252,638 |
| NW | 437,107 | 282,349 | 1,309,347 |
| WC | (18,798) | (156,039) | 962,518 |
| Emp. | 140 | 142 | 134 |

DUNS 57-615-9222    Imp
## Wj North Ltd
(Subsidiary of: Wj Linkline Group Ltd)
7 Brock Way, Newcastle, Staffordshire ST5 6AZ
**Tel:** 01782381780
**Web:** www.wjroadmarkings.com
**Reg No:** 2884681 **Estd:** 1994 Private Limited Company
**Line of Business:** Other construction work involving special trades
**Issued Capital:** £95
**Directors:** M Webb, W D Johnston
**Co. Secretary:** Nigel Bayley
**Responsibilities**
**Admin:** Nick Gee (Office Manager), Sue Palk (Commercial Administrator Manag)
**HR:** Jimmy Smallwood (Training Manager / Special Pro)
**Operations:** Andy Walker (Commercial Manager)
**Purchasing:** Kevin Gannon (Contract Manager), Nick Holt (Contracts Manager), Gethin Horsley (Contract Manager)
**Branches:** W J Roadmarkings Ltd, Unit 2 Ainley Industrial Estate, Elland, West Yorkshire HX5 9JP
**US SIC:** 1799 **UK SIC:** 50000
**Auditors:** Bentley Jennison

|  | 31-01-14 | 31-01-13 | 31-01-12 |
|---|---|---|---|
| TO | 18,297,687 | 19,520,985 | 16,187,765 |
| P/L | 1,461,243 | 1,437,657 | 1,280,975 |
| NW | 4,390,264 | 4,675,925 | 3,683,559 |
| WC | 4,160,192 | 7,533,237 | 2,246,813 |
| Emp. | 121 | 124 | 113 |

DUNS 22-544-9768
## W.J. Watkins & Son Ltd
Highfield, Holsworthy Beacon, Holsworthy, Devon EX22 7NF
**Tel:** 01409-261242
**Web:** www.freshlay.co.uk
**Reg No:** 1285475 **Estd:** 1962 Private Limited Company
**Line of Business:** Dairy farmers
**Issued Capital:** £842,900
**Principals:** D J Watkins (Chairman), Ms C E Watkins, Ms H C Cobbledick
**Co. Secretary:** David Watkins
**Responsibilities**
**Senior:** Donald Watkins (Manager)
**HR:** Debbie Maunder (Poultry Farm Manager)
**Branches:** W.j. Watkins & Son Ltd, Worden Farm, Holsworthy, Devon EX22 7NT
**US SIC:** 0241, 0214, 0259
**UK SIC:** 01001
**Auditors:** Simpkins Edwards
**Bankers:** Lloyds TSB Bank plc (30-94-91)

|  | 25-04-14 | 26-04-13 | 27-04-12 |
|---|---|---|---|
| TO | 12,686,114 | 10,238,347 | 12,841,214 |
| P/L | 449,055 | 1,657,558 | 150,384 |
| NW | 5,750,448 | 5,089,691 | 3,132,389 |
| WC | 3,587,557 | 2,218,725 | 1,227,432 |
| Emp. | 52 | 55 | 88 |

DUNS 21-812-6944    Imp
## W.J.Aldiss Ltd
Oxborough Lane, Fakenham, Norfolk NR21 8AF
**Tel:** 01328862381 **Fax:** 01328-855327
**Web:** www.wjaldiss.co.uk
**Reg No:** 0421363 **VAT No:** 104657875
**Estd:** 1892 Private Limited Company
**Line of Business:** Retail sale of furniture, lighting equipment and household articles not elsewhere classified
**Trading Style:** Aldiss of Fakenham & Norwich
**Issued Capital:** £26,450
**Principals:** T C Aldiss (Managing), Ms A C Kump, P Clifford, Ms C Aldiss, Mrs P S Aldiss, E Kump
**Co. Secretary:** Timothy Summers
**Responsibilities**
**Senior:** Gavin Secker (Store Manager)
**IT:** Dax Jupp (Computer Manager)
**Health & Safety:** Tony Woodham (Health & Safety Officer)
**Branches:** W.j.aldiss Ltd, White Lodge Business Park, Unit 2, Norwich, Norfolk NR4 6DG
**US SIC:** 5719, 5699
**UK SIC:** 64700, 64500
**Auditors:** Grant Thornton UK LLP
**Bankers:** Barclays Bank Plc (20-30-81)

|  | 28-09-13 | 29-09-12 | 01-09-11 |
|---|---|---|---|
| TO | 16,462,164 | 15,576,522 | 16,165,637 |
| P/L | 271,035 | 90,508 | 80,819 |
| NW | 2,552,646 | 2,517,374 | 2,440,998 |
| WC | (254,113) | (160,680) | (203,006) |
| Emp. | 178 | 181 | 180 |

DUNS 21-007-8002
## W.J.Daniel & Company Ltd
120-124 Peascod Street, Windsor, Berkshire SL4 1DP
**Tel:** 01753801000
**Web:** www.danielstores.co.uk
**Reg No:** 0259919 **VAT No:** 226704963
**Estd:** 1904 Private Limited Company
**Line of Business:** Other retail sale in non-specialised stores
**Trading Style:** Daniels Department Store, Daniels of Windsor
**Issued Capital:** £97,000
**Principals:** P W Daniel (Chairman and Managing), W J Daniel (Managing), Mrs T N Durkin (Managing), S M Daniel, Ms H J Marion, A J Durkin, A A Daniel
**Co. Secretary:** William Daniel
**Responsibilities**
**HR:** Sarah Daniel (Personnel Officer)
**Branches:** W.j.daniel & Company Ltd, 121/125 Peascod Street, Windsor, Berkshire SL4 1DP
**US SIC:** 5399 **UK SIC:** 65600
**Auditors:** Shipleys LLP
**Bankers:** HSBC Bank plc (40-02-26)

|  | 02-02-14 | 27-01-13 | 29-02-12 |
|---|---|---|---|
| TO | 11,491,404 | 10,697,105 | 11,448,249 |
| P/L | (3,814,249) | (30,719) | 303,944 |
| NW | 21,997,624 | 19,141,866 | 17,343,618 |
| WC | (4,195,956) | (4,035,872) | (4,390,230) |
| Emp. | 125 | 137 | 163 |

DUNS 49-485-9853
## Wjec Cbac Ltd
245 Western Avenue, Cardiff, South Glamorgan CF5 2YX
**Tel:** 02920265136
**Web:** www.wjec.co.uk
**Reg No:** 3150875 **Estd:** 1948 Private Limited Company
**Line of Business:** Primary education
**Directors:** E W Williams, Mrs E M Williams, H J David, M T Evans, D Huse, P S Haley, J R Magill, Mrs P A Passaro
**Co. Secretary:** Mrs Rachel Elias-Lee
**Responsibilities**
**Senior:** Edward Dickenson (Director), Denise Preece (Director)
**US SIC:** 8211, 8249
**UK SIC:** 93200, 93300
**Auditors:** Pricewaterhouse Coopers
**Bankers:** Barclays Bank Plc (20-18-15)

|  | 30-09-13 | 30-09-12 | 30-09-11 |
|---|---|---|---|
| TO | 39,896,000 | 40,670,000 | 39,746,000 |
| P/L | 4,550,000 | 5,385,000 | 5,881,000 |
| NW | 22,529,000 | 19,472,000 | 15,496,000 |
| WC | 21,841,000 | 17,836,000 | 12,240,000 |
| Emp. | 360 | 345 | 329 |

DUNS 21-602-6617
## W.J.King(Garages) Ltd
70-88 Park View Road, Welling, Kent DA16 1SF
**Tel:** 020-8303-1234 **Fax:** 020-8298-6433
**Web:** www.wjking.com
**Reg No:** 0647053 **VAT No:** 434999401
**Estd:** 1960 Private Limited Company
**Line of Business:** Sale of new motor vehicles
**Issued Capital:** £100
**Principals:** Mrs J M King (Managing), W J King, Mrs O King
**Co. Secretary:** Ms Olivia King

**Responsibilities**
**IT:** Nick Stocker (Computer Manager)
**HR:** Allan Nash (Human Resources Manager)
**Health & Safety:** Allan Nash (Human Resources Manager)
**Branches:** W.j.king(Garages) Ltd, 91-101 Bromley Common, Bromley, Kent BR2 9RW
**US SIC:** 5511, 5541
**UK SIC:** 65100, 65200
**Auditors:** Stephen M Fryer
**Bankers:** HSBC Bank plc (40-19-04)

|  | 30-04-14 | 30-04-13 | 30-04-12 |
|---|---|---|---|
| TO | 107,763,515 | 101,252,706 | 100,158,508 |
| P/L | 2,268,835 | 2,248,763 | 935,463 |
| NW | 34,979,316 | 33,233,567 | 31,522,036 |
| WC | 17,319,487 | 15,529,589 | 13,773,035 |
| Emp. | 330 | 337 | 359 |

DUNS 21-220-9183    Imp-Exp
## W.J.Leech & Sons Ltd
275 Derby Road, Bootle, Merseyside L20 8PL
**Tel:** 0151-933-9334
**Web:** www.wjleech.com
**Reg No:** 0485220 **VAT No:** 387389193
**Estd:** 1950 Private Limited Company
**Line of Business:** Trailers and semi-trailers
**Export Markets:** Europe and worldwide
**Trading Style:** Leech Group
**Issued Capital:** £41,500
**Principals:** A T Leech (Chairman), Mrs W E Maitland, D A Leech
**Co. Secretary:** Mrs Annette Leech
**Responsibilities**
**Senior:** Lorna Greggory (Office Manager)
**Admin:** Lorna Greggory (Office Manager)
**IT:** Wendy Leech (IT Director)
**Purchasing:** Sue Donnelly (Purchasing Officer)
**Branches:** W.j.leech & Sons Ltd, 61 Osborn Rd, Bedford, Bedfordshire MK45 4NY
**US SIC:** 3715 **UK SIC:** 35220
**Auditors:** Chadwick LLP
**Bankers:** National Westminster Bank Plc (60-13-20)

|  | 31-03-14 | 30-06-13 | 30-03-12 |
|---|---|---|---|
| TA | 1,552,793 | 1,454,581 | 1,457,806 |
| NW | 798,155 | 685,368 | 551,914 |
| WC | 510,180 | 375,218 | 219,074 |

DUNS 23-302-6850
## Wjm Building Services Ltd
574-576 Ballysillan Road, Belfast BT14 6RN
**Tel:** 028-9071-0000 **Fax:** 028-9039-1062
**Web:** www.whttp:
**Reg No:** 0043406NI **Estd:** 1983 Private Limited Company
**Line of Business:** Building construction contractors
**Issued Capital:** £1,000
**Directors:** A Pascoe, M Mcdowell, M Magee, G Meikle
**Co. Secretary:** Mrs Joan Meikle
**Responsibilities**
**Senior:** Billy Meikle (Manager)
**HR:** Yvonne Crosby (Human Resources Manager)
**US SIC:** 1522 **UK SIC:** 50100

|  | 30-09-13 | 30-09-12 | 30-09-11 |
|---|---|---|---|
| TO | 16,735,461 | 13,368,798 | 9,035,938 |
| P/L | 232,331 | 338,581 | 228,320 |
| NW | 1,434,350 | 1,342,942 | 1,150,114 |
| WC | 1,050,244 | 967,403 | 787,410 |
| Emp. | 98 | 78 | N/A |

DUNS 21-139-5504
## Wk Finn Kelcey
Stourside Place, 35-41 Station Road, Ashford, Kent TN23 1PP
**Web:** www.wilkinskennedy.com
**Estd:** 1924 Partnership
**Line of Business:** Accounting activities
**Trading Style:** Wilkens Kennedy Fkc
**Principals:** J R Finn-Kelcey, B N White (Partner), R S Pickard (Partner), M D Bushell (Partner), H J Summerfield (Partner), H Ellison (Partner), M R Bates (Partner), E Manning (Partner)
**Responsibilities**
**Marketing:** Pauline Piddock (Office Administrator)
**Admin:** Pauline Piddock (Office Administrator)
**HR:** Pauline Piddock (Office Administrator)
**Health & Safety:** Pauline Piddock (Office Administrator)
**Purchasing:** Pauline Piddock (Office Administrator)
**Branches:** Wk Finn Kelcey, 22 Cheriton Gdns, Folkestone, Kent CT20 2AS
**US SIC:** 8931, 7392
**UK SIC:** 83600, 83951
**Bankers:** National Westminster Bank Plc (60-01-21)
**Employees:** 70

DUNS 21-835-1827
## Wkb Waterlooville Ltd
Elettra Avenue, Waterlooville, Hampshire PO7 7XW
**Tel:** 02392233888
**Reg No:** 8036131 **Estd:** 2012 Private Limited Company
**Line of Business:** Management activities of holding companies
**Issued Capital:** £2,250,000
**Directors:** Mrs J C Wood, S T Wood, G G Harmar, D N Kilby, M W Fenlon
**Co. Secretary:** Mrs Tracey Gibbs
**US SIC:** 6711 **UK SIC:** 83962

|  | 31-12-13 | 31-12-12 |
|---|---|---|
| TO | 29,212,106 | 12,940,966 |
| P/L | 372,421 | 37,449 |
| NW | 2,581,319 | 2,259,702 |
| WC | 720,686 | (2,067,951) |
| Emp. | 70 | 79 |

DUNS 28-940-6217    Imp
## W.K.W. Precision Engineering Company Ltd
Shaw Royd Works, Shaw Lane, Halifax, West Yorkshire HX3 9HD
**Web:** www.wkw-eng.co.uk
**Reg No:** 1576936 **VAT No:** 333625764
**Estd:** 1981 Private Limited Company
**Line of Business:** Manufacture of other general purpose machinery not elsewhere classified
**Issued Capital:** £47,304
**Principals:** R A Wyatt (Managing), Ms S J Calder, A R Wyatt
**Co. Secretary:** Richard Wyatt
**Responsibilities**
**Health & Safety:** Chris Steele (Quality Inspector)
**US SIC:** 3549 **UK SIC:** 32212
**Auditors:** Spenser Wilson & Co
**Bankers:** Lloyds TSB Bank plc (30-93-76)

|  | 31-07-14 | 31-07-13 | 31-07-12 |
|---|---|---|---|
| TA | 3,770,281 | 3,686,050 | 3,136,174 |
| NW | 2,545,825 | 2,249,982 | 2,028,691 |
| WC | 1,237,400 | 828,928 | 853,537 |

DUNS 21-030-8219
## W.L. Agencies Ltd
Rjj House, Haven Exchange South, Felixstowe, Suffolk IP11 2QE
**Tel:** 01394695550
**Reg No:** 0898648 **Estd:** 2013 Private Limited Company
**Line of Business:** Freight forwarders
**Issued Capital:** £1,000
**Directors:** Ms A C Bagert, S I Bagert
**Branches:** Seftob Ho, Exchange Bldg, Liverpool Merseyside
**US SIC:** 4712 **UK SIC:** 77002
**Bankers:** HSBC Bank plc (40-18-51)

|  | 31-12-13 | 31-12-12 | 31-12-11 |
|---|---|---|---|
| TA | 226,951 | 99,564 | 100,743 |
| NW | 99,761 | 97,564 | 98,427 |
| WC | 98,714 | 96,168 | 96,682 |

DUNS 21-572-3537    Imp
## W.L. Gore & Associates (U.K.) Ltd
(Subsidiary of: W. L. Gore & Associates Inc.)
Kirkton South Road, Livingston, West Lothian EH54 7BT
**Fax:** 01506-462270
**Web:** www.gorefabrics.com
**Reg No:** 0856254 **VAT No:** 268637809
**Estd:** 1965 Private Limited Company
**Line of Business:** Manufacture of other textiles not elsewhere classified
**Export Sales:** £110,878,000
**Trading Style:** Gore-Tex
**Issued Capital:** £10,003,000
**Directors:** R A Pheely, R Doak, F M Mccollam
**Co. Secretary:** John Kings
**Responsibilities**
**Marketing:** John Jefferson (Senior Marketing Executive), John Overdijking (Associate)
**HR:** Lynn Pearson (Human Resources Manager)
**Branches:** W.l. Gore & Associates (U.k.) Ltd, Kirkton South, Livingston, West Lothian EH54 7BT
**US SIC:** 2299, 3079
**UK SIC:** 43992, 48360
**Bankers:** Bank Of Scotland (80-06-55)

|  | 31-03-14 | 31-03-13 | 31-03-12 |
|---|---|---|---|
| TO | 136,977,000 | 112,249,000 | 136,285,000 |
| P/L | 22,444,000 | 11,123,000 | 30,365,000 |
| NW | 83,428,000 | 84,973,000 | 86,792,000 |
| WC | 74,205,000 | 76,882,000 | 72,207,000 |
| Emp. | 402 | 424 | 413 |

DUNS 22-954-3590    Exp
## W.L. Shareholding Company Ltd
Eagle Works, Walton Well Road, Oxford, Oxfordshire OX2 6EE
**Tel:** 01865-311411 **Fax:** 01865510535
**Reg No:** 0608514 **VAT No:** 194447434

**Estd:** 1958 Private Limited Company
**Line of Business:** Management activities of holding companies
**Export Markets:** Western Europe, South and South East Asia, Africa, Middle East and Australasia
**Issued Capital:** £134,808
**Principals:** C R Dick *(Chairman)*, C R Levick, R I Dick, P R Turner, J C Dick
**Co. Secretary:** Ms Felicity Dick
**Responsibilities**
**Senior:** Anthony Winckworth *(Manager)*
**US SIC:** 6711, 3643
**UK SIC:** 83962, 34203
**Auditors:** Wenn Townsend
**Bankers:** Barclays Bank Plc (20-65-18)

| | 31-12-13 | 31-12-12 | 31-12-11 |
|---|---|---|---|
| TO | 152,057,000 | 125,238,000 | 94,466,000 |
| P/L | 14,834,000 | 6,830,000 | 640,000 |
| NW | 70,112,000 | 62,946,000 | 58,407,000 |
| WC | 35,842,000 | 30,198,000 | 24,103,000 |
| Emp. | 1,090 | 872 | 706 |

DUNS 28-847-1394
## W.L.Dairies(Leominster)Ltd
Green Street, Hereford, Herefordshire HR1 2QW
**Tel:** 01568-612676
**Web:** www.bart-dairies.co.uk
**Reg No:** 0654528 **Estd:** 1997 Private Limited Company
**Line of Business:** Other non-store retail sale
**Issued Capital:** £3,700
**Director:** P A Matthews
**Co. Secretary:** John Matthews
**US SIC:** 5963, 6519
**UK SIC:** 65600, 85000
**Auditors:** Hawkins Priday

| | 31-03-14 | 31-03-13 | 31-03-12 |
|---|---|---|---|
| TA | 1,832,015 | 1,878,941 | 1,826,144 |
| NW | 1,807,471 | 1,823,071 | 1,737,924 |
| WC | 19,436 | (2,296) | (31,383) |

DUNS 21-675-1461
## W.L.Vallance Ltd
**(Subsidiary of:** W.L.Vallance (Holdings) Ltd)
5 Roundhead Road, Heathfield Industrial Estate, Newton Abbot, Devon TQ12 6SQ
**Tel:** 01626204204
**Web:** www.vallancetransport.co.uk
**Reg No:** 0689776 **Estd:** 1947 Private Limited Company
**Line of Business:** Road haulage and transport services
**Issued Capital:** £5,000
**Principals:** N Vallance *(Managing)*, M J Vallance
**Co. Secretary:** Nicholas Vallance
**Branches:** Harefield, Plymouth
**US SIC:** 4789 **UK SIC:** 77002
**Auditors:** KPMG
**Bankers:** Barclays Bank Plc (20-60-88)

| | 30-09-13 | 30-09-12 | 30-09-11 |
|---|---|---|---|
| TA | 2,752,255 | 2,656,163 | 2,695,739 |
| NW | 1,380,273 | 1,177,151 | 1,014,861 |
| WC | 286,240 | 211,901 | 92,147 |

DUNS 21-682-0530 **Imp**
## W.L.West & Sons Ltd
Selham, Petworth, West Sussex GU28 0PJ
**Tel:** 01798-861611
**Web:** www.wlwest.co.uk
**Reg No:** 0577291 **VAT No:** 193177639
**Estd:** 1957 Private Limited Company
**Line of Business:** Timber merchants
**Issued Capital:** £7,336
**Principals:** S Smith *(Sales)*, R G West, Miss H Rickards, M J West
**Co. Secretary:** David West
**US SIC:** 2421, 2431, 5039
**UK SIC:** 46101, 46300, 61300
**Auditors:** Watling & Hirst
**Bankers:** Barclays Bank Plc (20-20-62)

| | 31-03-14 | 31-03-13 | 31-03-12 |
|---|---|---|---|
| TA | 2,328,264 | 2,334,198 | 2,425,738 |
| NW | 824,651 | 798,300 | 937,340 |
| WC | (381,217) | (374,907) | (173,002) |

DUNS 21-317-4980
## Wm. Armstrong (Longtown) Ltd
Townfoot, Longtown, Carlisle, Cumbria CA6 5LY
**Tel:** 01228-791242 **Fax:** 01228792242
**Web:** www.warmstrong.co.uk
**Reg No:** 0706029 **VAT No:** 256276835
**Estd:** 1961 Private Limited Company
**Line of Business:** Road haulage and transport services
**Issued Capital:** £16,008
**Directors:** D G Armstrong, G W Armstrong, Mrs J M Whyberd
**Co. Secretary:** Ms Debbie Winter
**Responsibilities**
**Senior:** Cyril Armstrong *(Manager)*
**US SIC:** 4789 **UK SIC:** 77002
**Auditors:** Armstrong Watson

**Bankers:** HSBC Bank plc (40-30-22)

| | 31-03-14 | 31-03-13 | 31-03-12 |
|---|---|---|---|
| TO | 22,258,131 | 20,908,017 | 19,854,285 |
| P/L | 351,115 | 327,400 | 309,261 |
| NW | 997,286 | 871,561 | 724,135 |
| WC | (3,079,950) | (2,655,956) | (1,982,457) |
| Emp. | 210 | 199 | 199 |

DUNS 22-020-1763
## Wm Barrowcliffe & Sons Ltd
Thornfield Estate Hooton Street, Off Carlton Road, Nottingham, Nottinghamshire NG3 2NJ
**Tel:** 01159505402
**Web:** www.barrowcliffes.com
**Reg No:** 4022995 **Estd:** 2000 Private Limited Company
**Line of Business:** Processing and preserving of fruit and vegetables not elsewhere classified
**Issued Capital:** £225,100
**Directors:** E T Sutherland, L Miller, A A Archer
**Co. Secretary:** Roy Irish
**Responsibilities**
**Marketing:** Nick Sutherland *(Sales & Marketing Director)*
**Sales:** Nick Sutherland *(Sales & Marketing Director)*
**IT:** Jeremy Dawson *(Computer Manager)*
**HR:** Stefan Cufeniuk *(Human Resources Manager)*
**Health & Safety:** Stefan Cufeniuk *(Human Resources Manager)*
**Facilities:** Tony Parish *(Engineering Manager)*
**Engineering:** Tony Parish *(Engineering Manager)*
**US SIC:** 2033 **UK SIC:** 41473
**Auditors:** UHY Hacker Young
**Bankers:** The Royal Bank Of Scotland Plc (16-26-32)

| | 31-08-14 | 31-08-13 | 31-08-12 |
|---|---|---|---|
| TA | 225,100 | 225,100 | 225,100 |
| NW | 225,100 | 225,100 | 225,100 |

DUNS 28-923-4023
## W.M. Brown (Kingshurst) Ltd
351 Warwick Road, Solihull, West Midlands B91 1BQ
**Tel:** 01217645505 **Fax:** 0121-776-4269
**Web:** www.lccweb.co.uk
**Reg No:** 1487430 **VAT No:** 346122185
**Estd:** 1980 Private Limited Company
**Line of Business:** Dispensing chemists
**Issued Capital:** £10,937
**Principals:** W M Brown *(Managing)*, Mrs J L Elliott, M A O'Donnell, Ms S Richardson, J M Brown
**Co. Secretary:** Mrs Maureen Brown
**Responsibilities**
**Senior:** Mike Odonal *(Manager)*
**Branches:** W.m. Brown (Kingshurst) Ltd, Southfield Road, Hinckley, Leicestershire LE10 1UA
**US SIC:** 5912 **UK SIC:** 64300
**Auditors:** Burgis & Bullock
**Bankers:** Yorkshire Bank Plc (05-06-76)

| | 31-07-13 | 31-07-12 | 31-07-11 |
|---|---|---|---|
| TO | 6,049,787 | 6,241,096 | 6,699,510 |
| P/L | 425,844 | 575,329 | 67,825 |
| NW | 2,230,395 | 1,861,548 | 1,368,338 |
| WC | 1,306,928 | 1,011,961 | 388,451 |
| Emp. | 71 | 68 | 67 |

DUNS 34-887-3717
## Wm Hamilton & Sons Ltd
Whitehill Farm, Larkhall, Lanarkshire ML9 3PR
**Tel:** 01698793292
**Web:** www.allisonsflowers.co.uk
**Reg No:** 0295966SC **VAT No:** 260377954
**Estd:** 2011 Private Limited Company
**Line of Business:** Freight transport by road not elsewhere classified
**Issued Capital:** £1,316
**Directors:** G R Hamilton, D B Hamilton, R T Hamilton
**Co. Secretary:** Duncan Graham
**Responsibilities**
**Senior:** Grace Hamilton *(Manager)*, Allison Walker *(Proprietor)*
**US SIC:** 4213 **UK SIC:** 72300
**Auditors:** Graham & Co (Accountants) Ltd

| | 31-03-14 | 31-03-13 | 31-03-12 |
|---|---|---|---|
| TO | 12,794,062 | 11,956,862 | 10,729,933 |
| P/L | 2,885,789 | 3,019,114 | 2,537,323 |
| NW | 13,224,772 | 8,732,038 | 6,659,937 |
| WC | 3,824,268 | 2,298,583 | 1,597,270 |
| Emp. | 75 | 71 | 67 |

DUNS 76-945-5981
## W.M. Ironwork Ltd
Barttridge Bridge, Newton Tracey, Barnstaple, Devon EX31 3PN
**Tel:** 01271858444
**Web:** www.wmironwork.co.uk
**Reg No:** 1840433 **VAT No:** 142925176
**Estd:** 1977 Private Limited Company
**Line of Business:** Manufacture of other fabricated metal products not elsewhere classified

**Issued Capital:** £100,000
**Directors:** C H West, Mrs P C West
**Co. Secretary:** Stuart West
**US SIC:** 3499, 1796
**UK SIC:** 31694, 50400
**Auditors:** David M. Jenkins & Co Accountants

| | 30-06-14 | 30-06-13 | 30-06-12 |
|---|---|---|---|
| TA | 1,437,864 | 1,225,386 | 1,143,814 |
| NW | 765,332 | 659,290 | 594,395 |
| WC | 633,349 | 549,150 | 470,194 |

DUNS 77-908-6573
## Wm. Lillico & Son (Holdings) Ltd
The Forstal Beddow Way, Aylesford, Kent ME20 7BT
**Tel:** 01622718062
**Web:** www.lillico.co.uk
**Reg No:** 5811948 **Estd:** 2006 Private Limited Company
**Line of Business:** Management activities of holding companies
**Export Sales:** £2,522,111
**Issued Capital:** £80,000
**Directors:** Mrs J Newman Rogers, Mrs V C Harrison, Mrs J E Parker, P C Walker, Mrs H M Steele, R E Steele
**Co. Secretary:** David Chapman
**Responsibilities**
**Senior:** Mike Booth *(Manager)*
**US SIC:** 6711 **UK SIC:** 83962

| | 31-03-14 | 31-03-13 | 31-03-12 |
|---|---|---|---|
| TO | 27,485,686 | 30,901,606 | 28,363,481 |
| P/L | 94,305 | 98,149 | 1,085,014 |
| NW | 8,075,033 | 8,919,513 | 8,947,502 |
| WC | 6,997,471 | 7,156,179 | 6,992,566 |
| Emp. | 77 | 80 | 84 |

DUNS 21-441-8105
## Wm. Martin & Co. (Marine) Ltd
Cirrus Building, Paisley, Renfrewshire PA3 2SJ
**Tel:** 01418436300 **Fax:** 01418436390
**Web:** www.morganashurst.com
**Reg No:** 0025769SC **VAT No:** 260496160
**Estd:** 2009 Private Limited Company
**Line of Business:** Airfreight forwarding services
**Trading Style:** Kuehne & Nagel
**Issued Capital:** £3,928
**Director:** C B Smith
**Co. Secretary:** Peterkins Robertson Paul
**Responsibilities**
**Senior:** Harry Thorburn *(CEO, Managing Director)*
**Admin:** Lindsey Verlague *(Administration Manager)*
**Branches:** Wm. Martin & Co. (Marine) Ltd, Cargo Ho, 10 Watt Rd, Glasgow, Lanarkshire G52 4RY
**US SIC:** 4511, 4722
**UK SIC:** 75000, 77001
**Auditors:** JRD Partnership
**Bankers:** The Royal Bank Of Scotland Plc (83-07-06)

| | 31-12-13 | 31-12-12 | 31-12-11 |
|---|---|---|---|
| TA | 332,407 | 334,644 | 336,024 |
| NW | 194,336 | 196,344 | 198,113 |
| WC | 194,336 | 196,344 | 198,113 |

DUNS 21-205-1973 **Imp-Exp**
## Wm Morrison Supermarkets P L C
New Park Street, Hamilton, Lanarkshire ML3 0BN
**Tel:** 01698-457-722 **Fax:** 08456-116-737
**Web:** www.morrisons.co.uk
**Reg No:** 0358949 **VAT No:** 343475355
**Estd:** 1940 Public Limited Company
**Line of Business:** Retail sale in non-specialised stores (excluding ctns) not holding an alcohol licence with food, beverages or tobacco predominating
**Issued Capital:** £232,622,987
**Directors:** A T Higginson, T Strain, P G Cox, Mrs J E Waterous, R Gillingwater, Ms P L Hughes
**Co. Secretary:** Mark Amsden
**Responsibilities**
**Senior:** Timothy Philips *(Chief Executive)*
**Marketing:** Michael Bates *(Marketing Director)*
**Sales:** Mark Gunter *(Stores Operations Director)*
**HR:** Norman Pickavance *(Group Personnel Director)*
**Facilities:** Terry Hartwell *(Property Director)*
**Purchasing:** Martin Weekes *(Purchasing Director)*
**Branches:** Wm Morrison Supermarkets P L C, Wm Morrison Supermarkets Plc, Titwood Road, Glasgow, Lanarkshire G41 4DA
**US SIC:** 5411, 5921
**UK SIC:** 64100, 64200
**Auditors:** KPMG Audit PLC

**Bankers:** HSBC Bank plc (40-13-15)
**Following financial data are in thousands**

| | 02-02-14 | 03-02-13 | 29-02-12 |
|---|---|---|---|
| TO | 17,680,000 | 18,116,000 | 17,663,000 |
| P/L | (176,000) | 879,000 | 947,000 |
| NW | 4,234,000 | 4,815,000 | 5,094,000 |
| WC | (1,443,000) | (992,000) | (981,000) |
| Emp. | 127,403 | 128,705 | 131,207 |

DUNS 21-930-7212 **Imp**
## Wm. Nelstrop & Co. Ltd
Albion Flour Mills, Stockport, Cheshire SK4 1TZ
**Tel:** 0161-480-3071 **Fax:** 0161-480-0325
**Web:** www.nelstrop.co.uk
**Reg No:** 0260082 **VAT No:** 157617838
**Estd:** 2002 Private Limited Company
**Line of Business:** Manufacture of breakfast cereals and cereals-based foods
**Export Sales:** £8,568,978
**Trading Style:** Nelstrops the Family Miller
**Issued Capital:** £28,674
**Principals:** C J Nelstrop *(Chairman)*, C H Syers, M B Nelstrop, A P Nelstrop, Dr G A Nelstrop, P A Roberts, S J Roberts
**Responsibilities**
**Senior:** Damon Escott *(Operations Manager)*
**Sales:** Damon Escott *(Operations Manager)*
**Admin:** Sarah Merret *(Sales & Administration Executi)*
**IT:** Damon Escott *(Operations Manager)*
**HR:** Michael Barclay *(Personnel Manager)*, Damon Escott *(Operations Manager)*
**Health & Safety:** Michael Barclay *(Personnel Manager)*
**Operations:** Michael Barclay *(Personnel Manager)*, Damon Escott *(Operations Manager)*
**Purchasing:** Damon Escott *(Operations Manager)*
**US SIC:** 2041 **UK SIC:** 41600
**Auditors:** BDO LLP
**Bankers:** National Westminster Bank Plc (01-08-38)

| | 31-03-14 | 31-03-13 | 31-03-12 |
|---|---|---|---|
| TO | 55,130,342 | 50,575,664 | 51,188,276 |
| P/L | (113,132) | (1,638,225) | (39,417) |
| NW | 18,307,935 | 18,478,415 | 19,948,704 |
| WC | 13,801,480 | 13,902,645 | 15,472,244 |
| Emp. | 53 | 54 | 54 |

DUNS 21-640-7841
## Wm. Nicholls & Company (Crickhowell) Ltd
19 High Street, Crickhowell, Powys NP8 1BD
**Tel:** 01873-811616
**Web:** www.nichollsfeeds.co.uk
**Reg No:** 1499976 **VAT No:** 337767321
**Estd:** 1925 Private Limited Company
**Line of Business:** Wholesale of grain, seeds and animal feeds
**Trading Style:** Nicholls, Nicholls Department Store
**Issued Capital:** £2,000
**Directors:** R Tomlinson, T J Davies
**Co. Secretary:** Ms Katie Sinclair
**Responsibilities**
**Senior:** Tracey Nicholls *(Manager)*
**Branches:** Wm. Nicholls & Company (Crickhowell) Ltd, 19-20 High Street, Brecon, Powys LD3 7AL
**US SIC:** 5153, 5699, 5963
**UK SIC:** 61100, 64500, 65600
**Auditors:** W.J. James & Co
**Bankers:** National Westminster Bank Plc (51-61-02)

| | 28-01-14 | 28-01-13 | 31-01-12 |
|---|---|---|---|
| TO | 8,488,184 | 7,962,656 | 7,065,756 |
| P/L | 393,152 | 185,698 | 141,309 |
| NW | 2,375,319 | 2,066,674 | 1,930,245 |
| WC | 1,773,563 | 1,408,291 | 1,600,927 |
| Emp. | 91 | 90 | 84 |

DUNS 28-840-6960
## Wm.Allison & Sons Ltd
7 South Church Road, Bishop Auckland, County Durham DL14 7LB
**Tel:** 01388-603245
**Web:** www.william-allison.co.uk
**Reg No:** 0533478 **VAT No:** 258663228
**Estd:** 1954 Private Limited Company
**Line of Business:** Monumental masons
**Issued Capital:** £18,300
**Managing Director:** M N Allison
**Co. Secretary:** Paul Allison
**US SIC:** 0291, 1429, 4213, 7261
**UK SIC:** 01001, 23102, 72300, 98902
**Auditors:** HLB Kidsons
**Bankers:** Lloyds TSB Bank plc (30-92-52)

| | 30-06-13 | 30-06-12 | 30-06-11 |
|---|---|---|---|
| TO | 3,997,440 | 4,198,283 | 3,788,191 |
| P/L | 113,542 | 394,503 | 177,593 |
| NW | 3,273,775 | 3,280,530 | 3,031,736 |
| WC | 618,041 | 883,708 | 725,389 |
| Emp. | 56 | 55 | 55 |

DUNS 28-846-1296
## Wmc Retail Partners Plc
21 Market Street, Wellington, Telford, Shropshire TF1 1DT
**Tel:** 01952-242019
**Web:** www.wellingtonmarkets.co.uk
**Reg No:** 0636475 **Estd:** 1959 Public Limited Company
**Line of Business:** Art and craft material sales and supply
**Issued Capital:** £3,365,012
**Directors:** M P Ball, M Chadwick, Ms S J Hewett, A B Sparrow, J Lord Lee Of Trafford
**Co. Secretary:** Paul Fice
**Responsibilities**
**Senior:** Lisa Kirby *(Manager)*
**Branches:** Wmc Retail Partners Plc, Regent House, 5 Queen Street, Leeds, West Yorkshire LS1 2TW
**US SIC:** 6519 **UK SIC:** 85000
**Auditors:** KPMG
**Bankers:** Lloyds TSB Bank plc (30-18-55)

| | 31-12-13 | 31-12-12 | 31-12-11 |
|---|---|---|---|
| TO | 6,200,000 | 6,932,000 | 6,861,000 |
| P/L | 276,000 | (11,000) | (443,000) |
| NW | 3,335,000 | 3,141,000 | 3,417,000 |
| WC | (821,000) | (1,734,000) | (5,716,000) |
| Emp. | 58 | 76 | 81 |

DUNS 21-216-1822 **Imp**
## W.McClure Ltd
The Garage, Windermere, Cumbria LA23 1BX
**Tel:** 01539-442636 **Fax:** 01539-488560
**Web:** www.wmcclure.co.uk
**Reg No:** 0685360 **VAT No:** 533438353
**Estd:** 2013 Private Limited Company
**Line of Business:** Catering food and drink suppliers
**Issued Capital:** £64,333
**Directors:** Mrs J C Foster, M Hutchinson, M P Mcclure, B K Mcclure, W K Mcclure
**Co. Secretary:** Matthew Mcclure
**Responsibilities**
**Senior:** Sharyn Farrar *(H&S)*, Alan Hart *(Manager)*, Duncan Rose *(Accountant)*
**Finance:** Duncan Rose *(Accountant)*
**Marketing:** Duncan Rose *(Accountant)*
**Admin:** Mike Edmonds *(Administration Manager)*
**IT:** Mike Edmonds *(Administration Manager)*
**HR:** Mike Edmonds *(Administration Manager)*
**Health & Safety:** Sharyn Farrar *(H&S)*
**US SIC:** 5149, 5411
**UK SIC:** 61700, 64100
**Auditors:** Stables, Thompson & Briscoe
**Bankers:** HSBC Bank plc (40-47-01)

| | 28-02-14 | 28-02-13 | 29-02-12 |
|---|---|---|---|
| TO | 15,553,209 | 13,106,049 | 11,023,245 |
| P/L | 401,798 | 342,639 | 315,292 |
| NW | 1,646,360 | 1,330,945 | 1,073,321 |
| WC | 328,924 | 254,730 | 355,718 |
| Emp. | 107 | 89 | 85 |

DUNS 23-695-5790
## Wmf United Kingdom Ltd
(**Subsidiary of:** Kkr & Co. L.P.)
31 Riverside Way, Cowley, Uxbridge, Middlesex UB8 2YF
**Tel:** 01895816100 **Fax:** 01895816105
**Web:** www.wmf.uk.com
**Reg No:** 3690400 **Estd:** 2006 Private Limited Company
**Line of Business:** Wholesale of other household goods not elsewhere classified
**Export Sales:** £729,425
**Issued Capital:** £150,000
**Directors:** M Gansloser, Ms J A Green
**Responsibilities**
**Senior:** Florian Lehmann *(Manager)*
**Branches:** Wmf United Kingdom Ltd, 31 Riverside Way, Uxbridge, Middlesex UB8 2YF
**US SIC:** 5199, 3639
**UK SIC:** 61900, 34600
**Auditors:** Blick Rothenberg
**Bankers:** HSBC Bank plc (40-17-07)

| | 31-12-13 | 31-12-12 | 31-12-11 |
|---|---|---|---|
| TO | 10,907,366 | 11,012,922 | 12,187,173 |
| P/L | 1,270,063 | 942,456 | 1,556,952 |
| NW | 8,338,647 | 7,361,653 | 6,658,682 |
| WC | 8,358,815 | 7,444,165 | 6,801,550 |
| Emp. | 54 | 54 | 52 |

DUNS 23-586-6261 **Imp**
## Wmg Management Europe Ltd
(**Subsidiary of:** Wasserman Media Group Llc)
33-34 Soho Square, London W1D 3QU
**Tel:** 020-7009-6000 **Fax:** 02033301053
**Web:** www.wmgllc.com
**Reg No:** 3584251 **Estd:** 1998 Private Limited Company
**Line of Business:** Sports management services
**Issued Capital:** £1,910,252
**Directors:** Miss T E Schroeder, M Watts, F K Ecvet, C Wasserman, Ms J C Quillan
**Co. Secretary:** Miss Trista Schroeder
**Responsibilities**
**Senior:** David Kogan *(CO-Managing director)*, Sara Munds *(Co-Managing Director)*
**Operations:** Tim Chadwick *(Chief Operating Officer, Europ)*
**Branches:** Wmg Management Europe Ltd, Unit 7 Hockley Court, 2401 Stratford Road, Hockley Heath, Solihull, West Midlands B94 6NW
**US SIC:** 7999 **UK SIC:** 97913
**Auditors:** Deloitte LLP
**Bankers:** Coutts & Co (18-00-02)

| | 31-12-13 | 31-12-12 | 31-12-11 |
|---|---|---|---|
| TO | 23,702,000 | 13,435,000 | 13,326,000 |
| P/L | (3,930,000) | (3,926,000) | (527,000) |
| NW | (14,419,000) | (5,749,000) | (3,562,000) |
| WC | (14,796,000) | (5,240,000) | (1,563,000) |
| Emp. | 69 | 55 | 39 |

DUNS 21-240-0287
## Wmi Ltd
(**Subsidiary of:** Wincro Holdings Ltd)
Wincobank Steel Works 3 Fife Street, Sheffield, South Yorkshire S9 1NJ
**Tel:** 01142422171 **Fax:** 01142434306
**Reg No:** 0386397 **Estd:** 1944 Private Limited Company
**Line of Business:** Manufacture of basic iron and steel and of ferro-alloys
**Trading Style:** Wincro Metal Industries
**Issued Capital:** £26,666
**Director:** P Butler
**Co. Secretary:** Martin Swann
**US SIC:** 3325, 3442
**UK SIC:** 31110, 31420
**Bankers:** Barclays Bank Plc (20-76-89)

| | 31-03-14 | 31-03-13 | 31-03-12 |
|---|---|---|---|
| TA | 1,064,993 | 1,064,993 | 1,064,993 |
| NW | 1,064,993 | 1,064,993 | 1,064,993 |

DUNS 21-917-3051
## Wm.Print Ltd
45-47 Frederick Street, Walsall, West Midlands WS2 9NE
**Tel:** 01922-643008
**Web:** www.wmprint.co.uk
**Reg No:** 1019091 **VAT No:** 100547419
**Estd:** 1971 Private Limited Company
**Line of Business:** Representative office
**Issued Capital:** £20,002
**Principals:** G A Cooper *(Managing)*, R A Green
**Co. Secretary:** Gary Cooper
**Responsibilities**
**Senior:** John Burrows *(Works Manager)*
**Branches:** Wm.print Ltd, Bellmans Yard, High Street, Newport, Shropshire TF10 7AJ
**US SIC:** 5081, 2711
**UK SIC:** 61490, 47512
**Auditors:** KPMG

| | 30-09-13 | 30-09-12 | 30-09-11 |
|---|---|---|---|
| TA | 1,492,918 | 1,706,452 | 1,647,024 |
| NW | 386,452 | 449,087 | 426,919 |
| WC | (217,640) | (61,722) | (55,159) |

DUNS 21-200-9500 **Imp-Exp**
## Wm.Smith & Sons (Barnard Castle) Ltd
Grove Works, Queen Street, Barnard Castle, County Durham DL12 8JQ
**Tel:** 01833-690305
**Web:** www.williamsmith.co.uk
**Reg No:** 0844451 **Estd:** 1952 Private Limited Company
**Line of Business:** Sign and nameplate equipment
**Export Sales:** £96,283
**Trading Style:** William Smith
**Issued Capital:** £10,000
**Principals:** M A Smith *(Managing)*, Mrs N L Smith, Mrs L A Hennedy, R J Smith
**Co. Secretary:** Lesley Smith
**Responsibilities**
**Senior:** Gerry McDonald *(General Manager)*
**IT:** Gerry McDonald *(General Manager)*
**HR:** Sue Brook *(Human Resources Manager)*
**Health & Safety:** Gerry McDonald *(General Manager)*
**Operations:** Gerry McDonald *(General Manager)*
**Purchasing:** Gerry McDonald *(General Manager)*
**Engineering:** Gerry McDonald *(General Manager)*
**US SIC:** 5199, 3079
**UK SIC:** 61900, 48360
**Auditors:** Rainbow Straughan & Elliott
**Bankers:** Barclays Bank Plc (20-25-29)

| | 31-03-14 | 31-03-13 | 31-03-12 |
|---|---|---|---|
| TO | 15,508,197 | 14,076,277 | 14,509,312 |
| P/L | (16,906) | 389,941 | 637,526 |
| NW | 3,695,377 | 3,713,703 | 3,409,517 |
| WC | 3,313,897 | 3,292,028 | 2,920,484 |
| Emp. | 82 | 84 | 80 |

DUNS 39-962-9765
## Wmsnt (Holdings) Ltd
80 Park Road, Aston, Birmingham, West Midlands B6 5PL
**Web:** www.ringandride.org
**Reg No:** 2263123 **VAT No:** 486686871
**Estd:** 2009 Private Company Limited By Guarantee
**Line of Business:** Bus operators and stations
**Trading Style:** Ring and Ride
**Directors:** F A Green, R J Brooks, I Pearson, A C Aston, Mrs J C Lucas, Ms J Robinson, Mrs J A Robson, M G Kemp
**Co. Secretary:** Mrs Alex Mcquinn
**Responsibilities**
**Senior:** Tom Ansell *(Manager)*, Paul Beecham *(Manager)*, David Frater *(Manager)*, Peter Maggs *(Chief Executive)*, Des Rogers *(Operations Manager)*, Renee Spector *(Manager)*
**Marketing:** Des Rogers *(Operations Manager)*
**Sales:** Des Rogers *(Operations Manager)*
**Branches:** Wmsnt (Holdings) Ltd, Pool Street, Wolverhampton, West Midlands WV2 4HN
**US SIC:** 4119 **UK SIC:** 72200
**Auditors:** Deloitte & Touche
**Bankers:** Unity Trust Bank Plc (08-60-01)

| | 31-03-14 | 31-03-13 | 31-03-12 |
|---|---|---|---|
| TO | 19,534,664 | 18,330,604 | 16,765,129 |
| P/L | (246,639) | (175,771) | (720,712) |
| NW | 6,437,359 | 6,578,092 | 6,623,872 |
| WC | 767,083 | 1,000,070 | 1,004,427 |
| Emp. | 767 | 755 | 699 |

DUNS 21-405-7184
## W.N. Lindsay Ltd
Gladsmuir Granary, Tranent, East Lothian EH33 1EJ
**Tel:** 01875852151
**Web:** www.wnlindsay.com
**Reg No:** 0015288SC **VAT No:** 270412295
**Estd:** 1864 Private Limited Company
**Line of Business:** Grain wholesalers
**Trading Style:** W N Lindsay
**Issued Capital:** £150,000
**Directors:** G A Lindsay, G R Baird, A W Stephen, A D Lindsay, D Hardie, H J Thomson, J N Lindsay
**Co. Secretary:** Douglas Henderson
**Responsibilities**
**Senior:** Anthony Nixon *(Chairman)*
**Finance:** Keith Henderson *(Financial Director)*
**Branches:** W.n. Lindsay Ltd, Gordons Granaries, Banff, Banffshire AB45 1GF
**US SIC:** 5153, 0729
**UK SIC:** 61100, 01003
**Auditors:** PricewaterhouseCoopers LLP
**Bankers:** Bank Of Scotland (80-08-23)

| | 31-05-14 | 31-05-13 | 31-05-12 |
|---|---|---|---|
| TO | 114,119,716 | 114,782,739 | 105,398,842 |
| P/L | 2,405,737 | 2,663,130 | 2,481,864 |
| NW | 11,892,600 | 10,718,360 | 9,156,501 |
| WC | 4,705,975 | 4,671,482 | 4,687,967 |
| Emp. | 47 | 47 | 46 |

DUNS 50-001-6605
## Wns Global Services (Uk) Ltd
(**Subsidiary of:** Wns (Holdings) Ltd)
Assistance Court, Ipswich, Suffolk IP1 1HT
**Tel:** 08448540660 **Fax:** 0844 854 0611
**Web:** www.wns.com
**Reg No:** 2292251 **Estd:** 1988 Private Limited Company
**Line of Business:** Activities auxiliary to insurance and pension funding
**Trading Style:** W N S Assistance
**Issued Capital:** £50,505
**Directors:** S K Das, R D Gillette
**Co. Secretary:** Ms Danielle Head
**Branches:** Wns Global Services (Uk) Ltd, Unit 3, Polo Grounds, Pontypool, Gwent NP4 0TW
**US SIC:** 7399 **UK SIC:** 83954
**Auditors:** Grant Thornton UK LLP
**Bankers:** Barclays Bank Plc (20-98-07)

| | 31-03-14 | 31-03-13 | 31-03-12 |
|---|---|---|---|
| TO | 51,207,000 | 39,882,000 | 77,249,000 |
| P/L | 5,553,000 | 3,593,000 | 5,709,000 |
| NW | 19,500,000 | 31,121,000 | 28,604,000 |
| WC | 9,055,000 | 35,876,000 | 43,028,000 |
| Emp. | 309 | 260 | 256 |

DUNS 23-778-9966 **Imp**
## Wnt (Uk) Ltd
(**Subsidiary of:** Ceratizit Sa)
Sheffield Airport Business Park, Sheffield, South Yorkshire S9 1XU
**Tel:** 01142496249
**Web:** www.wnt.de
**Reg No:** 3772242 **Estd:** 1999 Private Limited Company
**Line of Business:** Sales of machine tools
**Export Sales:** £2,076,518
**Issued Capital:** £1,000,000
**Directors:** G Knienieder, J P O'Hara, C Sun
**Co. Secretary:** Tony Pennington
**US SIC:** 5251 **UK SIC:** 64800
**Auditors:** Grant Thornton
**Bankers:** Barclays Bank Plc (20-91-48)

| | 28-02-14 | 28-02-13 | 29-02-12 |
|---|---|---|---|
| TO | 21,283,631 | 20,203,813 | 18,007,886 |
| P/L | 3,131,854 | 3,019,624 | 1,834,060 |
| NW | 3,446,113 | 3,646,500 | 1,370,753 |
| WC | 3,065,771 | 3,265,286 | 1,713,418 |
| Emp. | 47 | 49 | 48 |

DUNS 22-600-6435
## Woburn Enterprises Ltd
Woburn Abbey, Woburn, Milton Keynes, Buckinghamshire MK17 9WA
**Tel:** 01525290666
**Web:** www.woburn.co.uk
**Reg No:** 0966094 **Estd:** 1999 Private Limited Company
**Line of Business:** Hotels and motels without restaurant
**Trading Style:** Inn At Woburn, Woburn Abbey
**Issued Capital:** £89,495
**Directors:** The Hon C W Cayzer, P V Lindon, L R Russell, A I Russell Fifteenth Duke Of Bedfor, T F How
**Co. Secretary:** Kevin Shurrock
**Responsibilities**
**Senior:** David Bouchet *(Restaurant Manager)*, Ricahrd Carr *(General Manager)*, Sue Crowley *(General Manager)*
**Finance:** Carol Bury *(Head of Accounts)*
**Marketing:** Dawn Jones *(Senior Marketing Executive)*
**Facilities:** Ricahrd Carr *(General Manager)*
**US SIC:** 8421, 5813
**UK SIC:** 97700, 66200
**Auditors:** Saffery Champness
**Bankers:** National Westminster Bank Plc (60-23-19)

| | 31-12-13 | 31-12-12 | 31-12-11 |
|---|---|---|---|
| TO | 66,716 | N/A | N/A |
| P/L | 64,829 | (28,747) | 365,469 |
| NW | 7,484,209 | 7,494,790 | 7,527,469 |
| WC | (225,424) | (155,307) | (44,883) |

DUNS 77-826-3079
## Woburn House Conference Centre Ltd
(**Subsidiary of:** Universities Uk)
Woburn House, 20-24 Tavistock Square, London WC1H 9HQ
**Tel:** 02074194111
**Web:** www.woburnhouse.co.uk
**Reg No:** 3031467 **Estd:** 2001 Private Limited Company
**Line of Business:** Letting of conference and exhibition centres
**Issued Capital:** £2
**Directors:** Ms N Dandridge, J Holmes
**US SIC:** 6519 **UK SIC:** 85000
**Auditors:** Horwath Clark Whitehill
**Bankers:** National Westminster Bank Plc (60-80-07)

| | 31-07-14 | 31-07-13 | 31-07-12 |
|---|---|---|---|
| TO | 677,330 | 806,778 | 709,099 |
| P/L | (16,831) | (8,602) | 1,092 |
| NW | 10,757 | 27,588 | 36,191 |
| WC | (58,869) | (12,442) | (19,503) |

DUNS 51-562-7420
## Woburn Safari Park
Woburn Park, Milton Keynes, Buckinghamshire MK17 9QN
**Tel:** 01525290407
**Web:** www.woburnsafari.co.uk
**Estd:** 1970 Partnership
**Line of Business:** Botanical and zoological gardens and nature reserve activities
**Trading Style:** Junglies Gift Shop
**Partners:** W Woburn Safari Park Ltd, Bedford Estates
**Responsibilities**
**Senior:** Celia Deeley *(Chief Executive)*
**Finance:** P Critcher *(Senior Finance Administrator)*
**Marketing:** Abigail Crowley *(Marketing Manager)*
**HR:** Denise Roscorn *(Human Resources Manager)*
**Branches:** Woburn Safari Park, Woburn Park, Milton Keynes, Buckinghamshire MK17 9QN
**US SIC:** 8421 **UK SIC:** 97700
**Bankers:** National Westminster Bank Plc (60-24-19)
**Employees:** 50

DUNS 34-887-9693 **Imp-Exp**
## Wockhardt Uk Holdings Ltd
(**Subsidiary of:** Wockhardt Limited)
Ash Road North, Wrexham, Clwyd LL13 9UF
**Tel:** 01978-661261
**Web:** www.wockhardt.co.uk
**Reg No:** 2825053 **VAT No:** 625129846
**Estd:** 1993 Private Limited Company
**Line of Business:** Management activities of holding companies
**Export Markets:** Worldwide
**Export Sales:** £30,633,000

**Trading Style:** Wockhardt Uk
**Issued Capital:** £275,048
**Directors:** N Wynne, S Singh
**Co. Secretary:** James Higgins
**Responsibilities**
**Senior:** Habil Khorakiwala *(Manager)*
**Facilities:** Cilla Lacey *(Facilities Manager)*
**US SIC:** 6711, 2834, 5122
**UK SIC:** 83962, 25700, 61800
**Auditors:** Menzies LLP
**Bankers:** Lloyds TSB Bank plc (30-95-42)

| | 31-03-14 | 31-03-13 | 31-03-12 |
|---|---|---|---|
| TO | 30,750,000 | 29,581,000 | 27,727,000 |
| P/L | 1,626,000 | 1,445,000 | 1,051,000 |
| NW | 16,068,000 | 15,301,000 | 12,884,000 |
| WC | 6,603,000 | 7,148,000 | 6,928,000 |
| Emp. | 291 | 282 | 274 |

DUNS 21-579-8053
## Woden Community Resource Centre
Vicarage Road, Wednesfield, Wolverhampton, West Midlands WV11 1SF
**Tel:** 01902553494
**Web:** www.wolverhampton.gov.uk
**Estd:** 2001 Proprietorship
**Line of Business:** The dss
**Proprietor:** P Watlin
**Responsibilities**
**Senior:** Paul Watling *(CEO, Managing Director)*
**US SIC:** 8321 **UK SIC:** 96111
**Employees:** 60

DUNS 21-605-5168
## Wodensfield Primary School
Woden Avenue, Wolverhampton, West Midlands WV11 1PW
**Tel:** 01902556350
**Estd:** 1990
**Line of Business:** Primary education
**Proprietor:** Mrs J Herriman
**US SIC:** 8211 **UK SIC:** 93200
**Employees:** 50

DUNS 21-213-1846
## Woffington House Nursing Home
Rear Earl Street, Tredegar, Gwent NP22 3QW
**Tel:** 01495-717667
**Web:** www.craegmoor.co.uk
**Estd:** 1987 Proprietorship
**Line of Business:** Residential care establishments
**Proprietor:** Mrs J Jane
**Responsibilities**
**Senior:** Julya Jayne *(Home Manager)*, Heather Llewellyn *(Manager)*
**HR:** Julya Jayne *(Home Manager)*
**Health & Safety:** Julya Jayne *(Home Manager)*
**Facilities:** Julya Jayne *(Home Manager)*
**US SIC:** 8321, 6732
**UK SIC:** 96111, 83100
**Employees:** 49

DUNS 21-116-3449 **Imp**
## Woking Borough Council
Civic Offices, Gloucester Square, Woking, Surrey GU21 6YL
**Tel:** 01483-755855 **Fax:** 01483275318
**Web:** www.woking.gov.uk
**Estd:** 1974 Incorporate By Act Of Parliament
**Line of Business:** Local government
**Principals:** M Ray *(Financial)*, P Russell
**Responsibilities**
**Senior:** Geoff McManus *(Head of Environmental Services)*, Michela Mercer *(Planning & Regulation)*, Ray Morgan *(Chief Executive)*, Daniel Ogle *(Facilities Manager)*
**Finance:** Ray Morgan *(Chief Executive)*
**Marketing:** Andrew Gresham *(Web Master)*
**IT:** Vince Barnard *(Service Desk Manager)*, Dave Fayers *(Computer Operations Manager)*
**Fleet:** Daniel Ogle *(Facilities Manager)*
**Branches:** Woking Borough Council, Ashridge Road, Wokingham, Berkshire RG40 1PG
**US SIC:** 9121 **UK SIC:** 91110
**Auditors:** KPMG LLP
**Bankers:** Lloyds TSB Bank plc (30-99-80)

| | 31-03-13 |
|---|---|
| TO | 72,122,000 |
| P/L | (1,190,000) |
| NW | 156,931,000 |
| WC | (26,501,000) |
| Emp. | 600 |

DUNS 23-251-9426
## Woking College
Rydens Way, Woking, Surrey GU22 9DL
**Tel:** 01483-761036
**Web:** www.woking.ac.uk
**Estd:** 1977
**Line of Business:** Colleges (higher education)
**Directors:** M Clinton, M Ingram
**Responsibilities**
**Finance:** Kathryn Mercer *(Head of College Finance)*
**Marketing:** Jill Herst *(Senior Marketing Executive)*
**Admin:** Celia Bottomley *(Registrar)*, Kirsty Crook *(PA to the Principal)*
**IT:** Nathan Paul *(ICT Infrastructure Manager)*
**US SIC:** 8221 **UK SIC:** 93100
**Employees:** 56

DUNS 21-777-8215
## Woking High School
Morton Road, Woking, Surrey GU21 4TJ
**Web:** www.wokinghigh.surrey.sch.uk
**Estd:** 2002 Proprietorship
**Line of Business:** Schools (local authority)
**Proprietor:** Mrs J Abbott
**US SIC:** 8211 **UK SIC:** 93200
**Employees:** 140

DUNS 23-966-6121
## Woking Hospice
Hill View Road, Woking, Surrey GU22 7HW
**Tel:** 01483-881750
**Web:** www.wokinghospice.co.uk
**Reg No:** 3955487 **Estd:** 2000 Private Limited Company
**Line of Business:** Medical practice activities
**Directors:** Ms M Jenner, Rev B D Prothero, R H Lofting, Ms H P Dudley, M L Riggs, Dr C J Dunstan, Dr A M Green, D A Perry
**Co. Secretary:** Nigel Harding
**Responsibilities**
**Senior:** Michael Addison *(Manager)*, Malcolm Fellowes Freeman *(Manager)*, Simon Oxley *(Director)*, Dorothy Stickney *(Director)*
**US SIC:** 8011 **UK SIC:** 95300

| | 31-03-14 | 31-03-13 | 31-03-12 |
|---|---|---|---|
| TO | 8,689,378 | 6,976,266 | 6,160,308 |
| P/L | 1,358,167 | 74,286 | 521,096 |
| NW | 5,496,760 | 4,138,593 | 4,064,307 |
| WC | 3,583,760 | 2,716,808 | 2,577,091 |
| Emp. | 161 | 167 | 133 |

DUNS 21-030-4844
## Wokingham Borough Council
Shute End, Wokingham, Berkshire RG40 1BN
**Tel:** 01189-746000
**Web:** www.wokingham.gov.uk
**Partnership**
**Line of Business:** General (overall) public service activities
**Partners:** Mrs S Law, P Brecknock, M Moon, Ms W Woodock, P Watson, D Patterson
**Responsibilities**
**Senior:** Andrew Couldrick *(Chief Exucutive)*
**Finance:** Graham Ebers *(Head of Finance)*
**HR:** Tracey Coppard *(Learning & Development Coordin)*
**Health & Safety:** Veronica Glenister *(Health & Safety Manager)*
**US SIC:** 9121 **UK SIC:** 91110
**Employees:** 1,000

DUNS 21-129-2849
## Woldingham School
Marden Park, Woldingham, Caterham, Surrey CR3 7YA
**Tel:** 01883-349431 **Fax:** 01883-348653
**Web:** www.woldinghamschool.co.uk
**Reg No:** 6636665 **Estd:** 2008 Private Company Limited By Guarantee
**Line of Business:** General secondary education
**Directors:** W Crothers, I P Tyler, T Woffenden, A J Stoker, N P Crapp, Miss M Bouchard, R H Parkinson, M L Redman
**Co. Secretary:** Niall Campbell
**Responsibilities**
**Senior:** Neill Campbell *(Busaur)*, Vivienne Durham *(Manager)*, Alexandra Maule *(Director)*, M Ribbins *(Principal)*, Jayne Triffitt *(Headmistress)*
**Finance:** Neill Campbell *(Busaur)*, Gerry Hunt *(Bursar)*
**Marketing:** Gerry Hunt *(Bursar)*
**Admin:** Sue Hooper *(Office Manager)*
**IT:** Paul Island *(Senior IT Executive)*, Doug Tillin *(Computer Manager)*
**HR:** Gerry Hunt *(Bursar)*, Doug Tillin *(Computer Manager)*
**Health & Safety:** Gerry Hunt *(Bursar)*
**Facilities:** Gerry Hunt *(Bursar)*
**Purchasing:** Laureen McGuire *(Purchasing Clerk)*
**US SIC:** 8211 **UK SIC:** 93200
**Bankers:** Barclays Bank Plc (20-24-61)

| | 31-07-14 | 31-07-13 | 31-07-12 |
|---|---|---|---|
| TO | 14,396,317 | 13,908,998 | 14,266,769 |
| P/L | 773,366 | 444,244 | 1,829,461 |
| NW | 16,426,927 | 15,655,804 | 15,215,442 |
| WC | (2,187,904) | (1,329,400) | (1,611,871) |
| Emp. | 172 | 170 | 176 |

DUNS 23-932-1099 **Imp**
## Wolf Corporation Ltd
**(Subsidiary of:** Dp Partnership Ltd)
Waterside Industrial Estate, Doulton Road, Rowley Regis, West Midlands B65 8JG
**Tel:** 01384632915
**Web:** www.mcm.uk
**Reg No:** 3921934 **Estd:** 2000 Private Limited Company
**Line of Business:** Management activities of holding companies
**Export Sales:** £31,621
**Issued Capital:** £20,000
**Principals:** P Sloan *(Managing)*, Mrs D Clarke Brereton
**US SIC:** 6711, 2821
**UK SIC:** 83962, 25140
**Auditors:** Mazars

| | 30-09-13 | 30-09-12 | 30-09-11 |
|---|---|---|---|
| TO | 2,895,865 | 3,194,211 | 4,053,696 |
| P/L | 151,391 | 147,428 | 237,282 |
| NW | 1,652,496 | 1,531,414 | 1,429,261 |
| WC | 656,901 | 671,489 | 670,498 |
| Emp. | 61 | 64 | 80 |

DUNS 21-958-9708
## Wolferstans Llp
60-66 North Hill, Plymouth, Devon PL4 8EP
**Tel:** 01752663295
**Web:** www.wolferstans.com
**Reg No:** 0387390OC **Estd:** 2013
**Line of Business:** Solicitors
**US SIC:** 8999 **UK SIC:** 83954
**Employees:** 1,400

DUNS 21-390-4549
## Wolfes Burger Connoisseurs
111 Old Dundonald Road, Dundonald, Belfast BT16 1XT
**Tel:** 028-90480377
**Web:** www.wolfesburgers.co.uk
**Estd:** 2009 Proprietorship
**Line of Business:** Licensed restaurants
**Proprietor:** Miss O Hall
**US SIC:** 5812 **UK SIC:** 66110
**Employees:** 50

DUNS 29-583-3248 **Exp**
## Wolff Olins Ltd
10 Regents Wharf, All Saints Street, London N1 9RL
**Tel:** 02077137733 **Fax:** 02077130217
**Web:** www.wolffolins.com
**Reg No:** 1945130 **Estd:** 1965 Private Limited Company
**Line of Business:** Limited company registration services
**Export Markets:** Worldwide
**Export Sales:** £8,618,474
**Issued Capital:** £2
**Directors:** Ms K S Ashman, B Boylan, P D Trueman
**Co. Secretary:** Mrs Sally Bray
**Responsibilities**
**Senior:** Sairah Ashman *(Manager)*
**Marketing:** Rose Bentley *(Sales & Marketing Director)*, Gilles Guilbert *(Marketing Director)*, Victoria Matthews *(Communications Manager)*
**Sales:** Rose Bentley *(Sales & Marketing Director)*, Paige Reilly *(Operations Director)*
**HR:** Simone Flecther *(HR Coordinator)*, S. Fletcher *(Human Resources Director)*, Ellen O'Connor *(Head of Human Resources)*
**Operations:** Rose Bentley *(Sales & Marketing Director)*, Paige Reilly *(Operations Director)*
**US SIC:** 8111 **UK SIC:** 83500
**Auditors:** KPMG Audit PLC
**Bankers:** Bank Of Scotland (12-01-03)

| | 31-12-13 | 31-12-12 | 31-12-11 |
|---|---|---|---|
| TO | 12,701,726 | 11,401,000 | 10,411,000 |
| P/L | 2,700,073 | 1,986,000 | 1,295,000 |
| NW | 5,649,734 | 5,025,000 | 4,792,000 |
| WC | 5,651,152 | 5,018,000 | 4,571,000 |
| Emp. | 93 | 87 | 83 |

DUNS 21-778-8946
## Wolfmet
Hibernia Way, Stretford, Manchester M32 0ZD
**Tel:** 01618645454
**Web:** www.wolfmet.com
**Estd:** 2011 Proprietorship
**Line of Business:** Manufacture of basic chemicals
**Proprietor:** G Williams
**US SIC:** 2869 **UK SIC:** 25120
**Employees:** 150

DUNS 28-860-4168
## Wolseley (Group Services) Ltd
**(Subsidiary of:** Wolseley Plc)
Park View 1220, Arlington Business Park, Theald, Reading, Berkshire RG7 4GA
**Tel:** 01189-298700 **Fax:** 01189-298701
**Web:** www.wolseley.com
**Reg No:** 0880371 **Estd:** 2007 Private Limited Company
**Line of Business:** Representative office
**Issued Capital:** £153,413,191
**Directors:** S N Oakland, J W Martin, R I Shoylekov
**Co. Secretary:** Graham Middlemiss
**Responsibilities**
**Senior:** Tom Brophy *(Manager)*
**Finance:** Matthew Webb *(Financial controller)*
**Marketing:** Mark Fearon *(Director of Group Communicatio)*
**US SIC:** 7399 **UK SIC:** 83954
**Auditors:** PricewaterhouseCoopers LLP
**Bankers:** Lloyds TSB Bank plc (30-00-03)

| | 31-07-13 | 31-07-12 | 31-07-11 |
|---|---|---|---|
| TA | 119,879,000 | 170,829,000 | 101,308,000 |
| P/L | 2,112,000 | 21,071,000 | 6,943,000 |
| NW | 64,802,000 | 55,792,000 | (94,590,000) |
| WC | 56,708,000 | 109,098,000 | 27,798,000 |
| Emp. | 101 | 104 | 102 |

DUNS 21-706-2862
## Wolseley Plc
The Wolseley Center, Leamington Spa, Warwickshire CV31 3HH
**Tel:** 01926-705-000 **Fax:** 01189-298-701
**Web:** www.wolseley.co.uk
**Reg No:** 0106605J **Estd:** 1889 Private Limited Company
**Line of Business:** Builders
**Export Sales:** £1.138E + 10
**Principals:** G Davis *(Chairman)*, J W Martin *(Financial)*, F W Roach, I K Meakins, M Clarke, J I Murray, N M Stein, Ms T Bamford
**Co. Secretary:** Richard Shoylekov
**Responsibilities**
**Senior:** Tom Brophy *(Manager)*, Keith Dorling *(Managing Director, Burdens)*, Karen Finn *(Human Resources Director)*, Rob Gladwin *(Managing Director-Plumb and Pa)*, Jeremy Maxwell *(Multichannel Director)*, Lee Newman *(Managing Director-Pipe and Cli)*, Michael Wareing CMG *(Non-Executive Director)*
**Marketing:** Gary Hitchens *(Head of Strategy)*, Suki Lehal *(New Strategy Development Manag)*, Denis Turcotte *(Relations Manager)*, Gail Van Dijk *(Marketing Manager)*, Phil Viner *(Senior Product Manager)*
**Sales:** Andy McEwen *(Business Development Manager)*, Alice Wadsworth *(Business Development Superviso)*
**IT:** Julian Simmons *(Business Systems Manager)*
**HR:** Karen Finn *(Human Resources Director)*, Andrew Shorter *(HR Business Partner)*
**Operations:** Mehlran Aborzpour *(Project Manager)*, Stuart Evers *(Project Manager Infrastructure)*, Scott Holleyhead *(Project Manager)*, Paul Raynor *(Operations Director)*, Joanne Woodworth *(Project Manager)*
**US SIC:** 6711, 5074
**UK SIC:** 83962, 61300
**Auditors:** PricewaterhouseCoopers LLP
**Following financial data are in thousands**

| | 31-07-13 |
|---|---|
| TO | 13,154,000 |
| P/L | 473,000 |
| NW | 1,807,000 |
| WC | 1,445,000 |
| Emp. | 39,995 |

DUNS 21-590-9885
## Wolseley Uk
Wainwright Road, Worcester, Worcestershire WR4 9FA
**Tel:** 01905752499
**Web:** www.wolseley.co.uk
**Estd:** 2011 Proprietorship
**Line of Business:** Distribution service providers
**Proprietor:** S Sorrinson
**US SIC:** 4712 **UK SIC:** 77002
**Employees:** 113

DUNS 52-560-2439 **Imp-Exp**
## Wolsey Ltd
**(Subsidiary of:** Wolsey Acquisitions Uk Ltd)
2 New Star Road, Leicester, Leicestershire LE4 9JD
**Web:** www.wolsey.com
**Reg No:** 3246062 **Estd:** 1996 Private Limited Company
**Line of Business:** Wholesale of clothing and footwear
**Issued Capital:** £339,716
**Directors:** D A Brown, J Hargreaves
**Co. Secretary:** Danny Brown

**Responsibilities**
**Senior:** Alan Mapletoft *(Warehouse Manager)*
**Marketing:** Sophie Hickerton *(Group Marketing Manager)*, Louis Wolcott *(Group Brand Director)*
**IT:** Steve Brighty *(I T Support)*
**Health & Safety:** Alan Mapletoft *(Warehouse Manager)*
**Facilities:** Alan Mapletoft *(Warehouse Manager)*
**US SIC:** 5136, 2251
**UK SIC:** 61600, 43631
**Auditors:** PricewaterhouseCoopers LLP
**Bankers:** Barclays Bank Plc (20-35-81)

| | 28-02-14 | 28-02-13 | 29-02-12 |
|---|---|---|---|
| TO | 6,424,000 | 8,191,000 | 8,029,000 |
| P/L | (6,184,000) | (4,477,000) | (2,777,000) |
| NW | (9,460,000) | (3,272,000) | 1,214,000 |
| WC | (1,730,000) | 1,019,000 | 590,000 |
| Emp. | 97 | 99 | 92 |

DUNS 57-056-2850
## Wolsey Securities Ltd
**(Subsidiary of:** Wolsey Group Ltd)
Munro House, Portsmouth Road, Cobham, Surrey KT11 1PA
**Fax:** 01932586801
**Web:** www.wolsey.net
**Reg No:** 2881264 **Estd:** 1993 Private Limited Company
**Line of Business:** Financial products (direct)
**Issued Capital:** £95
**Directors:** S M Ratcliffe, S W O'Brien, M A Ratcliffe
**Co. Secretary:** Paul Robinson
**Responsibilities**
**Senior:** Tanya Draper *(Personal Assistant)*
**Branches:** Wolsey Securities Ltd, 174 Woodplumpton Rd, Preston, Lancashire PR4 0TA
**US SIC:** 6552, 7392
**UK SIC:** 85000, 83951
**Auditors:** BDO Stoy Hayward LLP
**Bankers:** Bank Of Scotland (80-20-00)

| | 31-12-13 | 31-12-12 | 31-12-11 |
|---|---|---|---|
| TO | 635,969 | 431,949 | 381,084 |
| P/L | 60,271 | 161,642 | 258,590 |
| NW | 992,321 | 932,050 | 770,408 |
| WC | 992,321 | 931,094 | 766,848 |

DUNS 50-593-1550 **Imp-Exp**
## Wolstenholme Machine Knives Ltd
**(Subsidiary of:** Tgw (Holdings) Ltd)
Clough Bank Works, Sheffield, South Yorkshire S4 8BT
**Tel:** 01142445600 **Fax:** 01143446556
**Web:** www.wolstenholme.co.uk
**Reg No:** 2532135 **VAT No:** 534101102
**Estd:** 1908 Private Limited Company
**Line of Business:** Manufacturers of machine tools
**Export Sales:** £6,197,646
**Trading Style:** T G Wolstenholme & Sons
**Issued Capital:** £10,000
**Principals:** R J Wolstenholme *(Managing)*, D Clowes, N J Harrison, I K Brazewell, S J Corbett
**Co. Secretary:** Mrs Lisa Street
**Responsibilities**
**Senior:** Donald Stain *(Manager)*, Davyd Wilkinson *(Manager)*
**US SIC:** 3542 **UK SIC:** 32212
**Auditors:** Hawsons

| | 31-03-14 | 31-03-13 | 31-03-12 |
|---|---|---|---|
| TO | 8,140,954 | 7,586,771 | 7,437,396 |
| P/L | 762,879 | 1,150,192 | 1,170,629 |
| NW | 6,605,152 | 5,935,482 | 4,982,974 |
| WC | 5,877,034 | 6,762,899 | 5,626,730 |
| Emp. | 87 | 82 | 88 |

DUNS 21-712-2480 **Exp**
## Wolters Kluwer (Uk) Ltd
**(Subsidiary of:** Wolters Kluwer N.V.)
145 London Road, Kingston-Upon-Thames, Surrey KT2 6SR
**Tel:** 02082471100
**Web:** www.wolterskluwer.co.uk
**Reg No:** 0450650 **VAT No:** 318328852
**Estd:** 2012 Private Limited Company
**Line of Business:** Publishing of books
**Trading Style:** Wolters Kluwer U K, Croner, Cch
**Issued Capital:** £10,000
**Directors:** S P Crompton, S Fernandez-Lopez, Ms D Williams, J Goudie
**Co. Secretary:** John Goudie
**Responsibilities**
**Senior:** Cathy Wolfe *(Chief Executive)*
**Marketing:** Ros Marks *(Marketing Manager)*, Clare Moore *(Communications Manager)*
**HR:** Andrew Ayers *(Personnel Director)*
**Health & Safety:** John Mahon *(Facilities Manager)*
**Facilities:** John Mahon *(Facilities Manager)*
**Branches:** Wolters Kluwer (Uk) Ltd, Reward House, Diamond Way, Stone, Staffordshire ST15 0SD
**US SIC:** 2731 **UK SIC:** 47532
**Auditors:** KPMG LLP
**Bankers:** HSBC Bank plc (40-42-18)

| | 31-12-13 | 31-12-12 | 31-12-11 |
|---|---|---|---|
| TO | 78,671,000 | 82,590,000 | 91,013,000 |
| P/L | 2,489,000 | 4,389,000 | 2,511,000 |
| NW | (10,383,000) | (14,988,000) | (16,842,000) |
| WC | 10,967,000 | 6,494,000 | 6,378,000 |
| Emp. | 725 | 785 | 796 |

DUNS 29-584-8642
## Wolverhampton Citizens Advice Bureaux
Snow Hill, Wolverhampton, West Midlands WV2 4AD
**Tel:** 01902572200
**Web:** www.citizensadvice.org.uk
**Reg No:** 1946618 **Estd:** 1985 Private Company Limited By Guarantee
**Line of Business:** Non-charitable social work activities without accommodation
**Directors:** P Paul, K Purchase, Ms N K Reehal, Ms G Patel, J M Smith, N W Cheesewright, Ms L M Jones, A Llazari
**Co. Secretary:** Jeremy Vanes
**Responsibilities**
**Senior:** Brian Chindendere *(Trustee)*, Jonathan Crockett *(Director)*, Harry Dodd *(Director)*, Antony Lee *(Trustee)*, Francis Reeves *(Director)*, Ranjit Sahota *(Manager)*
**US SIC:** 8321 **UK SIC:** 96111
**Auditors:** Neal & Co
**Bankers:** Barclays Bank Plc (20-97-78)

| | 31-03-14 | 31-03-13 | 31-03-12 |
|---|---|---|---|
| TO | 1,450,608 | 1,299,141 | 1,419,406 |
| P/L | (49,686) | 104 | (17,468) |
| NW | 1,045,952 | 1,095,638 | 1,095,534 |
| WC | 318,790 | 354,115 | 339,493 |
| Emp. | 53 | 47 | 50 |

DUNS 22-989-5453 **Imp**
## Wolverhampton City Council
Civic Centre, St Peters Square, Wolverhampton, West Midlands WV1 1DA
**Tel:** 08453303313
**Web:** www.wolverhampton.gov.uk
**Estd:** 1999
**Line of Business:** Local government
**Trading Style:** Wmbc, Registration of Births Deaths & Marriages, The Maltings Daycentre
**Principals:** B Bailey *(Financial)*, R Roberts, D B Anderson
**Responsibilities**
**Senior:** John Allez *(Manager)*, Linda Banbury *(Manager)*, Heather Clark *(Superintendent Registrar)*, Michelle Earp-Gaskell *(Team Manager)*, Fiona Gough *(Manager)*, Sarah Norman *(Strategic Director)*, Earl Piggott-Smith *(Manager)*, Simon Warren *(Chief Executive)*, Kerry Webb *(Proprietor)*
**Marketing:** Sue Handy *(Marketing Manager)*
**Sales:** Mel Potter *(Business Development Manager)*, Joanne Woodcock *(Senior Sales Executive)*
**IT:** Mike Cattell *(Solution Architect)*
**HR:** Caroline Lane *(Workforce Development and Lear)*, Kathy Roper *(Training Director)*
**Operations:** Amy Baker *(Production and Operations Mana)*
**Purchasing:** Mike Brooker *(Purchasing Manager)*, Lynn Brunsdon *(Purchasing Director)*, Alex Marsden *(Purchasing Manager)*, Valerie Powers *(Purchasing Manager)*
**Branches:** Wolverhampton City Council, Unit 5, Kennedy Road, Wolverhampton, West Midlands WV10 0LL
**US SIC:** 9121 **UK SIC:** 91110
**Employees:** 12,500

DUNS 22-767-3340 **Imp-Exp**
## Wolverhampton Electroplating Ltd
Wood Lane, Wolverhampton, West Midlands WV10 8HN
**Tel:** 01902-397333
**Web:** www.anochrome-group.co.uk
**Reg No:** 1583889 **VAT No:** 361874924
**Estd:** 1981 Private Limited Company
**Line of Business:** Treatment and coating of metals
**Export Markets:** Republic of Ireland; Netherlands
**Trading Style:** W E P
**Issued Capital:** £100
**Directors:** S M Rolls, R T Gray, J S Oliver, P A James
**Co. Secretary:** Malcolm Oliver
**US SIC:** 3999 **UK SIC:** 49590
**Auditors:** T.J. Saxon
**Bankers:** HSBC Bank plc (40-45-19)

| | 31-03-14 | 31-03-13 | 31-03-12 |
|---|---|---|---|
| TA | 5,300,268 | 4,369,382 | 4,799,015 |
| NW | 4,072,693 | 3,353,944 | 2,708,958 |
| WC | 2,567,086 | 1,665,257 | 1,518,193 |

DUNS 21-165-6660
## Wolverhampton Girl's High School
Tettenhall Road, Wolverhampton, West Midlands WV6 0BY
**Tel:** 01902551515
**Web:** www.wghs.org.uk
**Estd:** 1911
**Line of Business:** Schools (foundation)
**Director:** Mrs D James
**Responsibilities**
**Senior:** Julie Lawton *(Head Teacher)*, Trudi Young *(Head Teacher)*
**Finance:** Jane Oliver *(Business Manager)*
**Marketing:** Jane Oliver *(Business Manager)*
**Admin:** Jane Oliver *(Business Manager)*
**Health & Safety:** Jane Oliver *(Business Manager)*
**Facilities:** Mark Dugmore *(Site Manager)*
**US SIC:** 8211 **UK SIC:** 93200
**Employees:** 60

DUNS 21-125-8414
## Wolverhampton Grammar School Ltd
Compton Road, Wolverhampton, West Midlands WV3 9RB
**Tel:** 01902421326
**Web:** www.wgs.org.uk
**Reg No:** 6610261 **Estd:** 1989 Private Company Limited By Guarantee
**Line of Business:** Schools (independent)
**Directors:** J Patel, Mrs S H Cawdell, J E Sage, C Tatton, M E Brooker, Mrs A Brennan, R G Purshouse, P A Hawthorne
**Co. Secretary:** Mrs Penelope Rudge
**Responsibilities**
**Senior:** Anne-marie Brennan *(Director)*, Kathy Crewe-Read *(Head Teacher)*, Tazmina Crisp *(Director)*, Vincent Darby *(Principal)*, Keith Madelin *(Director)*, Jacqueline Orledge *(governor)*, Philip Sims *(Director)*
**IT:** Paul Hancox *(IT Manager)*
**Facilities:** Keith Flavell *(Site Manager)*
**US SIC:** 8211 **UK SIC:** 93200
**Bankers:** Allied Irish Bank (gb) (23-85-85)

| | 31-08-13 | 31-08-12 | 31-08-11 |
|---|---|---|---|
| TO | 7,587,796 | 7,406,892 | 6,620,769 |
| P/L | 656,709 | 589,034 | 375,048 |
| NW | 10,338,554 | 9,445,563 | 8,801,921 |
| WC | (622,076) | (797,200) | (1,433,905) |
| Emp. | 127 | 126 | 118 |

DUNS 54-896-4410
## Wolverhampton Health Care N H S Trust
West Park Rehabilitation Hospital, Park Road West, Wolverhampton, West Midlands WV1 4PW
**Tel:** 01902444000
**Web:** www.wolverhamptonhealth.nhs.uk
**Line of Business:** Hospital. "Accountability: Each Trust Board is directly accountable to the Secretary of State via The N H S Executive."
**Principals:** G Urwin *(Financial)*, M Pyrah
**Responsibilities**
**Senior:** John Crockett *(CEO Managing Director)*
**Branches:** Wolverhampton Health Care N H S Trust, 19 Raynor Road, Wolverhampton, West Midlands WV10 9QY
**US SIC:** 8062 **UK SIC:** 95100
**Employees:** 1,600

DUNS 22-766-3184 **Exp**
## Wolverhampton Pressings Co Ltd
**(Subsidiary of:** Firstmain Investments Ltd)
Fordhouse Road, Bushbury, Wolverhampton, West Midlands WV10 9DZ
**Tel:** 01902307799 **Fax:** 01902-721026
**Web:** www.wolvespressings.com
**Reg No:** 1145374 **VAT No:** 346318945
**Estd:** 1973 Private Limited Company
**Line of Business:** Other engineering activities
**Issued Capital:** £120,000
**Directors:** Mrs L A Smith, A J Smith
**Responsibilities**
**Senior:** Steve Croot *(Maintenance Manager)*, Peter McInnes *(Manager)*
**Sales:** Nigel Betteridge *(Sales Director)*
**Facilities:** Steve Croot *(Maintenance Manager)*
**Purchasing:** Grace Jurance *(Purchasing Manager)*
**US SIC:** 8911 **UK SIC:** 83701
**Auditors:** Baker Tilly UK Audit LLP
**Bankers:** Barclays Bank Plc (20-07-71)

| | 30-01-14 | 31-01-13 | 31-01-12 |
|---|---|---|---|
| TA | 1,539,219 | 1,468,134 | 1,357,212 |
| NW | 342,781 | 563,682 | 655,251 |
| WC | 77,063 | 406,998 | 314,076 |

DUNS 39-706-9741
## Wolverhampton Racecourse Ltd
**(Subsidiary of:** Arena Racing Corporation Ltd)
Dunstall Park, Wolverhampton, West Midlands WV6 0PE
**Tel:** 01902421421 **Fax:** 08702200107
**Web:** www.wolverhampton-racecourse.co.uk
**Reg No:** 2159607 **Estd:** 1999 Private Limited Company
**Line of Business:** Operation of sports arenas and stadiums
**Trading Style:** Wolverhampton Racecourse, Holiday Inn Woverhampton Garden Court
**Issued Capital:** £100
**Principals:** W A Parker *(Financial)*, S A Nahum, R I Renton, P C Odriscoll, D A Roberts, K S Robertson, A B Kelly
**Co. Secretary:** Ms Megan Langridge
**Responsibilities**
**Marketing:** Charlotte Buckland *(Hospitality and Sponsorship Sa)*, Lesley Gross *(Hospitality and Sponsorship Sa)*
**Sales:** Charlotte Buckland *(Hospitality and Sponsorship Sa)*, Lesley Gross *(Hospitality and Sponsorship Sa)*
**Admin:** Fergus Cameron *(Clerk)*
**IT:** Adam Gray *(Support Services Manager)*
**HR:** Stella Postins *(Human Resources Manager)*
**Health & Safety:** Stella Postins *(Human Resources Manager)*
**Operations:** Karen Billingsley *(Project Executive)*, Adam Gray *(Support Services Manager)*
**US SIC:** 7941 **UK SIC:** 97911
**Auditors:** BDO Stoy Hayward
**Bankers:** Bank Of Scotland (80-20-00)

| | 31-12-13 | 31-12-12 | 31-12-11 |
|---|---|---|---|
| TO | 15,690,366 | 13,976,021 | 10,919,998 |
| P/L | 3,626,906 | 1,303,104 | 367,752 |
| NW | 11,537,080 | 7,962,938 | 6,712,592 |
| WC | (841,748) | (4,393,772) | (7,009,586) |
| Emp. | 54 | 52 | 52 |

DUNS 29-849-8346
## Wolverhampton Wanderers Football Club (1986) Ltd
**(Subsidiary of:** Bridgemere Properties Ltd)
Molineux Stadium, Waterloo Road, Wolverhampton, West Midlands WV1 4QR
**Tel:** 08712222220 **Fax:** 01902-687006
**Web:** www.wolves.co.uk
**Reg No:** 1989823 **VAT No:** 431485656
**Estd:** 1866 Private Limited Company
**Line of Business:** Other sporting activities not elsewhere classified
**Issued Capital:** £3,000,000
**Directors:** S P Morgan, J F Bowater, J D Moxey, J Gough
**Co. Secretary:** Richard Skirrow
**Branches:** Wolverhampton Wanderers Football Club (1986) Ltd, Victoria House, Mander Centre, Wolverhampton, West Midlands WV1 3PS
**US SIC:** 7999 **UK SIC:** 97913
**Auditors:** Deloitte LLP
**Bankers:** HSBC Bank plc (40-47-11)

| | 31-05-13 | 31-05-12 | 31-05-11 |
|---|---|---|---|
| TO | 32,122,000 | 60,646,000 | 64,401,000 |
| P/L | (30,439,000) | 5,760,000 | 9,163,000 |
| NW | (11,176,000) | 978,000 | (3,908,000) |
| WC | 38,786,000 | 36,757,000 | 32,286,000 |
| Emp. | 265 | 261 | 251 |

DUNS 22-265-2153 **Imp-Exp**
## Wolverine Europe Ltd
**(Subsidiary of:** Wolverine World Wide Inc.)
Kings Place, 90 York Way, London N1 9AG
**Tel:** 02078600100
**Web:** www.wolverineworldwide.com
**Reg No:** 4283166 **Estd:** 1901 Private Limited Company
**Line of Business:** Manufacturers of footwear
**Export Sales:** £12,145,753
**Trading Style:** Merrell, Hush Puppies, Hytest, Bates
**Issued Capital:** £10,000
**Directors:** B W Krueger, D T Grimes, J M Macleod
**Co. Secretary:** Ms Jennifer Miller
**Responsibilities**
**Senior:** Kenneth Grady *(Manager)*, Dan Le-Vesconte *(Manager)*, David Rist *(Manager)*
**Finance:** Bruce Condon *(Financial Director)*
**IT:** Liz Smith *(European IT Manager)*
**Branches:** Wolverine Europe Ltd, Park La Ho, Broad St, Glasgow, Lanarkshire G40 2QW
**US SIC:** 3149 **UK SIC:** 45100
**Auditors:** Ernst & Young LLP
**Bankers:** The Chase Manhattan Bank (60-91-41)

| | 28-12-13 | 29-12-12 | 31-12-11 |
|---|---|---|---|
| TO | 66,211,178 | 70,638,787 | 91,503,321 |
| P/L | (4,826,474) | 947,427 | (2,543,714) |
| NW | 22,377,506 | 25,454,401 | 23,604,986 |
| WC | 26,676,350 | 31,000,261 | 28,664,160 |
| Emp. | 208 | 191 | 191 |

DUNS 38-765-0708
## Wolverley Court Residential Home
Wolverley Court Wolverley Road, Kidderminster, Worcestershire DY10 3RP
**Tel:** 01562850201
**Estd:** 1990 Proprietorship
**Line of Business:** Residential care establishments
**Principals:** B Moore, A Sadik *(Proprietor)*
**US SIC:** 8321 **UK SIC:** 96111
**Bankers:** Lloyds TSB Bank plc (30-94-70)
**Employees:** 60

DUNS 73-965-8297
## Wolviston Group Ltd
Wolviston House 5 Falcon Court, Preston Farm, Stockton-On-Tees, Cleveland TS18 3TS
**Tel:** 01642615792
**Web:** www.wolviston.com
**Reg No:** 5216781 **Estd:** 2004 Private Limited Company
**Line of Business:** Management activities of holding companies
**Export Sales:** £407,687
**Issued Capital:** £60
**Director:** Ms S Micklewright
**Co. Secretary:** Graham Bell
**US SIC:** 6711, 7361
**UK SIC:** 83962, 83954

| | 31-08-13 | 31-08-12 | 31-08-11 |
|---|---|---|---|
| TO | 29,296,827 | 30,395,036 | 31,174,941 |
| P/L | 977,974 | 995,142 | 913,857 |
| NW | 2,736,880 | 2,079,990 | 1,373,679 |
| WC | 2,705,161 | 2,050,216 | 1,354,424 |
| Emp. | 382 | 374 | 455 |

DUNS 36-806-6510
## Wombourne Leisure Centre
Ounsdale High School, Ounsdale Road, Wolverhampton, West Midlands WV5 8BJ
**Tel:** 01902-898202
**Web:** www.sstaffs.gov.uk
**Estd:** 2002 Proprietorship
**Line of Business:** Leisure centres
**Proprietor:** P Wheaton
**Responsibilities**
**Senior:** Sarah Bagnall *(Manager)*
**US SIC:** 7999 **UK SIC:** 97913
**Employees:** 100

DUNS 21-242-7871
## Women & Girls Network
P O Box 13095, London W14 0FE
**Tel:** 02076104678
**Web:** www.wgn.org.uk
**Proprietorship**
**Line of Business:** Counselling & advice services
**Proprietor:** Mrs R Sharif
**Responsibilities**
**Senior:** Akima Thomas *(Manager)*, Gurpreet Virdee *(Manager)*
**US SIC:** 8699 **UK SIC:** 96902
**Employees:** 50

DUNS 51-617-0060
## Wonga Group Ltd
88 Crawford Street, London W1H 2EJ
**Tel:** 08712885704
**Web:** www.instantcashsolutions.co.uk
**Reg No:** 5897177 **Estd:** 2007 Private Limited Company
**Line of Business:** Management activities of other non-financial holding companies not elsewhere classified
**Issued Capital:** £2,045
**Directors:** Mrs S De Rycker, I A Ahmed, A Dillon, Ms L C Bowden, A K Haste, R M Klein, B Liautaud
**Co. Secretary:** Justin Hubble
**US SIC:** 6711 **UK SIC:** 83962
**Auditors:** PricewaterhouseCoopers LLP
**Bankers:** HSBC Bank plc (40-04-03)

| | 31-12-13 | 31-12-12 | 31-12-11 |
|---|---|---|---|
| TO | 314,711,000 | 309,290,000 | 184,674,000 |
| P/L | 39,694,000 | 84,476,000 | 62,427,000 |
| NW | 176,180,000 | 179,224,000 | 118,370,000 |
| WC | 166,222,000 | 175,732,000 | 116,294,000 |
| Emp. | 550 | 325 | 131 |

DUNS 21-602-0164
## Wood & Co
Bumpers Way, Chippenham, Wiltshire SN14 6NG
**Tel:** 01249444777
**Estd:** 1802 Partnership
**Line of Business:** Book retailers
**Partners:** D Locke, C G Awine, E G Allen, Ms M Allen
**Branches:** 12 Old Bond St, Bath Avon BA1 1BR. (Tel: 0225-445347)
**US SIC:** 5942, 2752
**UK SIC:** 65300, 47544
**Bankers:** Barclays Bank Plc (20-05-06)
**Employees:** 50

DUNS 56-951-5638 **Imp-Exp**
## Wood & Douglas Ltd
**(Subsidiary of:** Ultra Electronics Holdings Plc)
Baughurst Road, Tadley, Hampshire RG26 5LP
**Tel:** 01189-811444
**Web:** www.woodanddouglas.co.uk
**Reg No:** 2844692 **VAT No:** 614786422
**Estd:** 1978 Private Limited Company
**Line of Business:** Radio equipment
**Export Markets:** Worldwide
**Export Sales:** £3,485,499
**Trading Style:** Wood & Douglas Limited
**Issued Capital:** £70,000
**Directors:** Ms M E Waldner, M Anderson, M Clayton, R Sharma
**Co. Secretary:** Ms Sharon Harris
**Responsibilities**
**Senior:** Patricia Lovelock *(Head of Administration)*, Minaxi Patel *(Manager)*, Sally Wallace *(Purchaser)*
**Admin:** Patricia Lovelock *(Head of Administration)*
**HR:** Patricia Lovelock *(Head of Administration)*, Sally Wallace *(Purchaser)*
**Health & Safety:** Patricia Lovelock *(Head of Administration)*
**Purchasing:** Sally Wallace *(Purchaser)*
**US SIC:** 3662, 3661
**UK SIC:** 34430, 34410
**Auditors:** Sargent & Co
**Bankers:** HSBC Bank plc (40-09-18)

| | 31-08-13 | 31-08-12 | 31-08-11 |
|---|---|---|---|
| TO | 8,012,642 | N/A | N/A |
| P/L | 1,104,079 | N/A | N/A |
| NW | 2,873,329 | 2,144,706 | 2,058,906 |
| WC | 2,344,908 | 1,647,324 | 1,867,756 |

DUNS 54-837-6771
## Wood & Sons
Unit 7 Baulker Lane, Clipstone Village, Mansfield, Nottinghamshire NG21 9BG
**Web:** www.wilsonsworktops.co.uk
**Estd:** 2011 Partnership
**Line of Business:** Marble and granite suppliers
**Partner:** J H Wood
**Responsibilities**
**Senior:** Bertie Wilson *(Proprietor)*
**US SIC:** 5039 **UK SIC:** 61300
**Employees:** 50

DUNS 21-681-7668 **Imp-Exp**
## Wood & Wood International Signs Ltd
**(Subsidiary of:** Fitzwilton Ltd)
Heron Road, Sowton Industrial Estate, Exeter, Devon EX2 7LX
**Fax:** 01392-252358
**Web:** www.woodandwood.co.uk
**Reg No:** 0926425 **VAT No:** 344752155
**Estd:** 1968 Private Limited Company
**Line of Business:** Sign and nameplate equipment
**Export Sales:** £263,182
**Issued Capital:** £125,000
**Directors:** R C Robinson, K C Mcgoran, D W Roxburgh
**Co. Secretary:** Nicholas Jeal
**Responsibilities**
**Health & Safety:** Martyn Batho *(Operations Manager)*
**Operations:** Martyn Batho *(Operations Manager)*
**Branches:** Wood & Wood International Signs Ltd, St. Johnsall Saints School, Exton St, London SE1 8UE
**US SIC:** 2599, 7399
**UK SIC:** 46720, 83954
**Auditors:** pricewaterhouseCoopers
**Bankers:** National Westminster Bank Plc (56-00-63)

| | 31-12-13 | 31-12-12 | 31-12-11 |
|---|---|---|---|
| TO | 5,226,340 | 4,318,502 | 5,084,931 |
| P/L | 223,421 | (95,727) | 173,378 |
| NW | 2,741,242 | 2,570,911 | 2,653,591 |
| WC | 2,661,193 | 2,490,136 | 2,566,482 |
| Emp. | 54 | 51 | 50 |

DUNS 21-214-0917 **Imp-Exp**
## Wood Auto Supplies Ltd
**(Subsidiary of:** Rga Newco (2012) Ltd)
Colne Road, Huddersfield, West Yorkshire HD1 3ES
**Web:** www.woodauto.co.uk
**Reg No:** 0851509 **Estd:** 1926 Private Limited Company
**Line of Business:** Sale of motor vehicle parts and accessories
**Export Markets:** Countries worldwide
**Issued Capital:** £100
**Principals:** R E Heywood *(Managing)*, G J Heywood
**Co. Secretary:** Alan Stead
**Responsibilities**
**Senior:** Daniel Crines *(Stores Manager)*
**Facilities:** Daniel Crines *(Stores Manager)*
**Branches:** Wood Auto Supplies Ltd, 4B Locksley Dr, Belfast, Belfast BT10 0BH
**US SIC:** 5531, 3629
**UK SIC:** 65100, 34350
**Auditors:** Connelly & Co
**Bankers:** Barclays Bank Plc (20-43-04)

| | 31-03-14 | 31-03-13 | 31-03-12 |
|---|---|---|---|
| TO | 8,519,188 | 7,782,040 | 7,924,393 |
| P/L | 176,202 | 234,425 | 66,785 |
| NW | 3,231,190 | 3,111,265 | 2,908,790 |
| WC | 3,604,404 | 3,498,043 | 3,231,974 |
| Emp. | 67 | 56 | 60 |

DUNS 21-722-7670
## Wood End Academy
Vernon Rise, Greenford, Middlesex UB6 0EQ
**Web:** www.woodend-jun.ealing.sch.uk
**Reg No:** 7601680 **Estd:** 2011 Private Company Limited By Guarantee
**Line of Business:** Primary education
**Directors:** D I Goss, U C Mannan, Ms J E Phillpot, Ms L Smith, L W Stainbank, M Arshad, Ms J A Evans, Ms A Cobden
**Co. Secretary:** Ms Sarah Lindsey
**Responsibilities**
**Senior:** Anne Hayes *(Director)*, Maureen Hider *(Director)*, Christine Lambi *(Director)*, Paul Morrison *(Director)*
**US SIC:** 8211 **UK SIC:** 93200
**Bankers:** Barclays Bank Plc (20-49-08)

| | 31-08-14 | 31-08-13 | 31-08-12 |
|---|---|---|---|
| TO | 5,154,199 | 2,226,365 | 1,868,867 |
| P/L | 2,822,348 | 157,214 | 73,025 |
| NW | 11,892,743 | 9,003,395 | 8,827,181 |
| WC | 962,000 | 810,562 | 677,764 |
| Emp. | 61 | 60 | 54 |

DUNS 21-802-3674
## Wood End School Parent Teacher Association
Yeomans Avenue, Harpenden, Hertfordshire AL5 3EF
**Tel:** 01582-761636
**Web:** www.woodend.herts.sch.uk
**Estd:** 1996 Proprietorship
**Line of Business:** General secondary education
**Proprietor:** Mrs R Cornish
**Responsibilities**
**Senior:** Diane John *(Head Teacher)*
**US SIC:** 8211 **UK SIC:** 93200
**Employees:** 50

DUNS 22-251-7042
## Wood Energy Ltd
**(Subsidiary of:** Strong Energy Solutions Ltd)
Energy House, Wotton-Under-Edge, Gloucestershire GL12 8QH
**Tel:** 0845-070-7338 **Fax:** 08450707339
**Web:** www.woodenergy.com
**Reg No:** 4269709 **Estd:** 2001 Private Limited Company
**Line of Business:** Manufacture of electricity distribution and control apparatus
**Issued Capital:** £109,824
**Directors:** J Tomlinson, T Mcleman, F Murtagh
**Co. Secretary:** Fergal Murtagh
**Responsibilities**
**Senior:** Robin Cotton *(Manager)*, Jeremy Margetson *(Sales Director)*, Paul Neilson *(Manager)*, Laurel Remington *(Manager)*, Gail Watkins *(Manager)*
**Finance:** Paul Neilson *(Manager)*
**Sales:** Jeremy Margetson *(Sales Director)*
**Admin:** Heidi Plant *(Office Manager)*
**Engineering:** Keith Mckendrick *(Technical Manager)*
**US SIC:** 3643, 1711
**UK SIC:** 34203, 50300
**Auditors:** PricewaterhouseCoopers LLP

| | 31-10-13 | 31-10-12 | 31-10-11 |
|---|---|---|---|
| TA | 1,667,928 | 2,098,909 | 3,170,692 |
| NW | 223,304 | 219,947 | 1,108,484 |
| WC | 680,025 | 216,138 | 1,096,177 |

DUNS 21-714-4983
## Wood Green Academy
Wood Green Road, Wednesbury, West Midlands WS10 9QU
**Tel:** 01215564131
**Web:** www.woodgreenhigh.sandwell.sch.uk
**Reg No:** 7538389 **Estd:** 2011 Private Company Limited By Guarantee
**Line of Business:** General secondary education
**Directors:** Ms T A Simpson, Ms D Bannister Mbe, M J Langley, Mrs J Hawkins, M A Patel, J Topham, Ms N J Brant, K J Byrne
**Co. Secretary:** Peter Hesslegrave
**Responsibilities**
**Senior:** Gurnam Berdesha *(Director)*, Amanda Birch *(Director)*, John Blackband *(Director)*, Darren Fellows *(Director)*, Gerald Gould *(Director)*, Dilip Patidar *(Director)*, Christine Preece *(Director)*
**US SIC:** 8211 **UK SIC:** 93200

**Bankers:** The Co-Operative Bank Plc (08-90-01)

| | 31-03-14 | 31-03-13 | 31-03-12 |
|---|---|---|---|
| TO | 9,543,172 | 10,381,560 | 31,694,933 |
| P/L | 245,135 | 500,715 | 22,431,863 |
| NW | 22,133,581 | 22,155,578 | 21,751,863 |
| WC | 1,928,716 | 1,976,424 | 1,198,235 |
| Emp. | 169 | 166 | 162 |

DUNS 29-870-7050
## Wood Green Animal Shelters
King's Bush Farm, Huntingdon, Cambridgeshire PE29 2NH
**Tel:** 08442488181 **Fax:** 01480832389
**Web:** www.woodgreen.org.uk
**Reg No:** 2073930 **VAT No:** 538263532
**Estd:** 1924 Private Company Limited By Guarantee
**Line of Business:** Activities of other membership organisations not elsewhere classified
**Trading Style:** Kings Bush Trading
**Directors:** J M Cousins, Ms J M South, Dr C E Manser, C K Byles, C P Alder, R Auld, Ms A Y Au, Mrs P L Gee
**Co. Secretary:** Sean Fear
**Responsibilities**
**Senior:** Jan Alabaster *(Director)*, Dennis Baker *(CEO, Managing Director)*, Celia Waldron *(Director)*
**Finance:** Paul Edmond *(Finance Director)*
**Branches:** Wood Green Animal Shelters, 601 Lordship Lane, London N22 5LG
**US SIC:** 8699, 0752
**UK SIC:** 96902, 01003
**Auditors:** Price Bailey
**Bankers:** Singer & Friedlander Ltd (60-01-56)

| | 31-03-14 | 31-03-13 | 31-03-12 |
|---|---|---|---|
| TO | 8,981,370 | 8,093,675 | 8,495,317 |
| P/L | 383,016 | (526,113) | (532,069) |
| NW | 23,137,400 | 22,459,252 | 22,249,987 |
| WC | 4,367,063 | 4,201,719 | 4,465,716 |
| Emp. | 218 | 200 | 219 |

DUNS 21-590-2629
## Wood Green Crown Court
Lordship Lane, London N22 5LF
**Tel:** 02088264100
**Web:** www.gov.uk
**Estd:** 2011 Proprietorship
**Line of Business:** Courts
**Proprietor:** Mrs A Rogers
**Responsibilities**
**Senior:** Janine Ince *(Court Manager)*
**US SIC:** 9211 **UK SIC:** 91200
**Employees:** 50

DUNS 73-470-3643
## Wood Group Engineering International Ltd
**(Subsidiary of:** John Wood Group P.L.C.)
John Wood House, Greenwell Road, East Tullos Industrial Estate, Aberdeen, Aberdeenshire AB12 3AX
**Tel:** 01224851200 **Fax:** 01224-851166
**Web:** www.woodgroup.com
**Reg No:** 0247871SC **Estd:** 2003 Private Limited Company
**Line of Business:** Other engineering activities
**Issued Capital:** £1
**Directors:** W G Setter, R M Brown
**Co. Secretary:** Robert Brown
**Responsibilities**
**Senior:** Leslie Hinder *(Manager)*
**Sales:** Dave Buchan *(Commercial Director)*
**HR:** Ross McCrae *(Human Resources Manager)*
**Health & Safety:** Phil Ley *(Health & Safety Officer)*
**US SIC:** 8911 **UK SIC:** 83701

| | 31-12-13 | 31-12-12 | 31-12-11 |
|---|---|---|---|
| TA | 1 | 1 | 1 |
| NW | 1 | 1 | 1 |

DUNS 73-906-0510
## Wood Group Industrial Services Ltd
**(Subsidiary of:** John Wood Group P.L.C.)
Kirkstone House, St Omers Road, Gateshead, Tyne and Wear NE11 9EZ
**Tel:** 0191-493-2600
**Web:** www.pyeroy.co.uk
**Reg No:** 5159696 **Estd:** 2004 Private Limited Company
**Line of Business:** Other construction work involving special trades
**Export Sales:** £4,348,000
**Issued Capital:** £126,941
**Directors:** Mrs S Ventress, H M Pelham, D A Stewart, S J Nicol
**Co. Secretary:** Robert Brown
**Responsibilities**
**Senior:** Douglas Spence *(fin)*
**Finance:** Douglas Spence *(fin)*
**US SIC:** 1799 **UK SIC:** 50000
**Auditors:** Baker Tilly UK Audit LLP

**Bankers:** Yorkshire Bank Plc (05-06-23)

| | 31-12-13 | 31-12-12 | 31-12-11 |
|---|---|---|---|
| TO | 106,482,000 | 88,910,227 | 73,849,754 |
| P/L | 5,976,000 | 4,414,039 | 2,884,196 |
| NW | 22,426,000 | 18,112,454 | 16,296,393 |
| WC | 16,848,000 | 11,130,408 | 11,074,280 |
| Emp. | 1,595 | 1,363 | 1,118 |

DUNS 22-622-2347 **Exp**

## Wood Group Kenny Ltd

(**Subsidiary of:** John Wood Group P.L.C.)
Compass Point, 79-87 Kingston Road, Staines, Middlesex TW18 1DT
**Tel:** 01784-417200 **Fax:** 01784-417283
**Web:** www.woodgroupkenny.com
**Reg No:** 1398385 **VAT No:** 296428713
**Estd:** 1978 Private Limited Company
**Line of Business:** Engineering related scientific and technical consulting activities
**Export Markets:** E U, Middle East, Africa
**Export Sales:** £22,950,000
**Issued Capital:** £300,000
**Directors:** D W Baker, G J Williams, B Middleton, C B Mckinnon, S J Wayman
**Co. Secretary:** Robert Brown
**Responsibilities**
**Senior:** Steven Peett *(Manager)*
**Branches:** Wood Group Kenny Ltd, Caledonian House, 234 Union Street, Aberdeen, Aberdeenshire AB10 1TN
**US SIC:** 8911 **UK SIC:** 83701
**Auditors:** PricewaterhouseCoopers LLP
**Bankers:** Clydesdale Bank Plc (82-60-10)

| | 31-12-13 | 31-12-12 | 31-12-11 |
|---|---|---|---|
| TO | 93,226,000 | 69,842,000 | 55,673,000 |
| P/L | 5,390,000 | 8,793,000 | 7,690,000 |
| NW | 5,985,000 | 1,603,000 | 4,441,000 |
| WC | 6,136,000 | 1,470,000 | 5,172,000 |
| Emp. | 317 | 235 | 189 |

DUNS 34-902-6984

## Wood Group Psn Ltd

(**Subsidiary of:** John Wood Group P.L.C.)
Wellheads Place, Wellheads Industrial Estate, Aberdeen, Aberdeenshire AB21 7GB
**Tel:** 01224777777
**Web:** www.woodgroup-psn.com
**Reg No:** 0296737SC **VAT No:** 877960557
**Estd:** 2006 Private Limited Company
**Line of Business:** Service activities incidental to oil and gas extraction excluding surveying
**Trading Style:** P S N World
**Issued Capital:** £1,000,000
**Directors:** D A Stewart, S J Nicol, W G Setter, A C Webster, R M Brown
**Co. Secretary:** Robert Brown
**US SIC:** 1389 **UK SIC:** 13000
**Auditors:** PricewaterhouseCoopers LLP
**Bankers:** Bank Of Scotland (80-05-17)

| | 31-12-13 | 31-12-12 | 31-12-11 |
|---|---|---|---|
| TO | 413,037,000 | 401,760,000 | 306,584,000 |
| P/L | 3,391,000 | 16,404,000 | 15,248,000 |
| NW | (7,774,000) | (11,806,000) | (24,107,000) |
| WC | (9,061,000) | (11,008,000) | (26,612,000) |
| Emp. | 1,664 | 1,595 | 1,596 |

DUNS 21-599-8622

## Wood Hall Hotel Spa

Trip Lane, Linton, Wetherby, West Yorkshire LS22 4JA
**Tel:** 01937587271
**Web:** www.handpicked.co.uk
**Estd:** 2011
**Line of Business:** Hotels
**Responsibilities**
**Senior:** Gordon Burniston *(Manager)*, Terniston Gordon *(Manager)*, Andrew Wainwright *(Manager)*
**US SIC:** 7011 **UK SIC:** 66500
**Employees:** 100

DUNS 21-212-0179

## Wood Lodge

Wood Lodge, 50 Mill Hill, Castlewellan, Co Down BT31 9NB
**Tel:** 028-4377-8511
**Web:** www.lodgecare.com
**Estd:** 1982
**Line of Business:** Nursing homes
**Proprietor:** L Lavery
**Responsibilities**
**Senior:** Berni McArdle *(Home Manager)*
**US SIC:** 8051 **UK SIC:** 95100
**Employees:** 70

DUNS 22-254-0978

## Wood Mackenzie Ltd

(**Subsidiary of:** Lloyds Banking Group Plc)
2 Exchange Place, 5 Semple Street, Edinburgh, Midlothian EH3 8BL
**Tel:** 01312-434400
**Web:** www.woodmacresearch.com
**Reg No:** 0222302SC **VAT No:** 865211825
**Estd:** 2002 Private Limited Company
**Line of Business:** Management and business consultants
**Export Sales:** £186,260,000
**Issued Capital:** £409,542
**Directors:** S Halliday, P A Marshall, P D Gregory
**Co. Secretary:** Brian Aird
**Responsibilities**
**Senior:** Kristen Oosterhof *(Manager)*
**Marketing:** Joelle Coldicott *(Head of Marketing)*, Francesca Levoir *(Marketing Manager)*, Kirsty Mitchell *(Senior Marketing Manager)*, Doug Montgomery *(Global Head of Sales and Marke)*, Andy Todd *(Head of EMEARC Sales & Marketi)*, Gael Williamson *(Marketing Manager)*
**Sales:** Doug Montgomery *(Global Head of Sales and Marke)*, Andy Todd *(Head of EMEARC Sales & Marketi)*
**Admin:** Sonia Mallan *(Assistant)*
**IT:** Philip Boyle *(IT Strategy & Enterprise Archi)*, Jamie Scotland *(Business Systems Manager)*
**HR:** Sharon Edwards-Grant *(Human Resources Manager)*
**Engineering:** John Meagher *(Global Gas Product Manager)*
**US SIC:** 1389 **UK SIC:** 13000
**Auditors:** Deloitte LLP
**Bankers:** Bank Of Scotland (80-20-00)

| | 31-12-13 | 31-12-12 | 31-12-11 |
|---|---|---|---|
| TO | 212,804,000 | 190,820,000 | 158,305,000 |
| P/L | 86,935,000 | 79,642,000 | 66,105,000 |
| NW | 224,988,000 | 143,225,000 | 68,302,000 |
| WC | 272,326,000 | 206,898,000 | 118,813,000 |
| Emp. | 923 | 829 | 703 |

DUNS 21-263-2657

## Wood-Mitchell Building Group Plc

Sunnyfield Works Lowtown, Pudsey, West Yorkshire LS28 9AD
**Tel:** 01132-571727
**Web:** www.woodmitchell.co.uk
**Reg No:** 1126943 **VAT No:** 180842362
**Estd:** 1971 Public Limited Company
**Line of Business:** Other building completion
**Trading Style:** Wood-Mitchell Joinery, Wood-Mitchell Construction, Wood-Mitchell Shopfitting Naylor Plumbing & Heating, Laister Decorators Pestige Flooring
**Issued Capital:** £50,000
**Directors:** P R Snook, Mrs V M Snook
**Co. Secretary:** Paul Snook
**Responsibilities**
**Senior:** Jeffrey Swithenbank *(Manager)*
**Facilities:** Paul Crashley *(Maintenance Manager)*
**US SIC:** 1799, 2599, 1721
**UK SIC:** 50000, 46720, 50400
**Auditors:** BDO Stoy Hayward LLP
**Bankers:** National Westminster Bank Plc (60-60-05)

| | 30-09-13 | 30-09-12 | 30-09-11 |
|---|---|---|---|
| TO | 12,226,380 | 12,318,523 | 12,127,222 |
| P/L | (411,924) | (393,644) | 44,571 |
| NW | 1,635,583 | 2,097,441 | 2,509,463 |
| WC | 920,533 | 1,328,862 | 1,740,439 |
| Emp. | 119 | 119 | 123 |

DUNS 21-830-2966 **Imp**

## Wood Mitchell Printers Ltd

(**Subsidiary of:** Wood Mitchell & Co Ltd)
Festival Way, Stoke-On-Trent, Staffordshire ST1 5BB
**Tel:** 01782-202440
**Web:** www.wood-mitchell.co.uk
**Reg No:** 0083016 **VAT No:** 278963590
**Estd:** 1901 Private Limited Company
**Line of Business:** Printing not elsewhere classified
**Issued Capital:** £18,090
**Principals:** W E Hancock *(Managing)*, S R Mitchell *(Financial)*, C H Mitchell, R S Mitchell
**Responsibilities**
**Sales:** Andrew Cadman *(Sales Manager)*
**Operations:** Andrew Snape *(Production Manager)*
**Engineering:** Andrew Snape *(Production Manager)*
**US SIC:** 2752 **UK SIC:** 47544
**Auditors:** K P M G
**Bankers:** Lloyds TSB Bank plc (30-93-83)

| | 31-03-14 | 31-03-13 | 31-03-12 |
|---|---|---|---|
| TO | N/A | N/A | 4,393,552 |
| P/L | N/A | N/A | 28,484 |
| NW | 488,439 | 701,454 | 487,629 |
| WC | 527,071 | 361,617 | 376,116 |
| Emp. | N/A | N/A | 39 |

DUNS 21-022-9795 **Imp-Exp**

## Wood Petty & Co Ltd

(**Subsidiary of:** Brands of Distinction Ltd)
Livingstone Road, Andover, Hampshire SP10 5NS
**Tel:** 01264-345500 **Fax:** 01264-332025
**Web:** www.pettywood.co.uk
**Reg No:** 0082419 **VAT No:** 235683350
**Estd:** 1904 Private Limited Company
**Line of Business:** Non-specialised wholesale of food, beverages and tobacco
**Export Markets:** E U
**Export Sales:** £2,969,438
**Issued Capital:** £1,543,823
**Directors:** J Potter, M J Cole, S Cuthbertson
**Co. Secretary:** Sean Linehan
**Responsibilities**
**Finance:** Sean Lynham *(Head of Finance)*
**US SIC:** 5149 **UK SIC:** 61700
**Auditors:** BDO LLP
**Bankers:** Bank Of Scotland (12-08-81)

| | 28-03-14 | 29-03-13 | 30-03-12 |
|---|---|---|---|
| TO | 48,925,352 | 50,348,398 | 50,092,935 |
| P/L | 854,856 | 715,434 | 1,237,277 |
| NW | 6,149,774 | 5,311,778 | 5,399,020 |
| WC | 6,063,296 | 5,803,175 | 5,662,289 |
| Emp. | 103 | 104 | 103 |

DUNS 23-223-9327

## The Wood Veterinary Group

125 Bristol Road, Gloucester, Gloucestershire GL2 4NB
**Web:** www.woodvet.co.uk
**Estd:** 1950 Partnership
**Line of Business:** Veterinary activities
**Partners:** P Woods, R Blowey, C Watson, G Stevens
**Responsibilities**
**Senior:** Emma Mcewan *(Practice Administrator)*
**Branches:** The Wood Veterinary Group, The Cattle Market, St Oswalds Road, Gloucester, Gloucester, Gloucestershire GL1 2SJ
**US SIC:** 0741 **UK SIC:** 95601
**Employees:** 52

DUNS 73-483-4067 **Imp-Exp**

## Woodall Nicholson Ltd

(**Subsidiary of:** Woodall Nicholson Holdings Ltd)
Wigan Road, Westhoughton, Bolton, Lancashire BL5 2EE
**Tel:** 01942-815600 **Fax:** 01942815115
**Web:** www.woodall-nicholson.co.uk
**Reg No:** 4747125 **Estd:** 1992 Private Limited Company
**Line of Business:** Manufacturers of vans and trucks
**Trading Style:** Mellor Coachcraft, Mellor Coachcraft, Mellor Vancraft
**Issued Capital:** £105,000
**Directors:** D T Jackson, B J Davidson, M Barlow, G K Hudson
**Co. Secretary:** Daniel Jackson
**Responsibilities**
**IT:** Charles Sorry *(Senior IT Executive)*
**US SIC:** 3711, 3713
**UK SIC:** 35101, 35201
**Auditors:** Tenon Audit Ltd
**Bankers:** HSBC Bank plc (40-31-24)

| | 31-12-13 | 31-12-12 | 31-12-11 |
|---|---|---|---|
| TO | 25,694,603 | 22,100,226 | 15,021,040 |
| P/L | 2,135,081 | 1,620,915 | 93,884 |
| NW | 6,369,123 | 4,740,225 | 3,436,179 |
| WC | 5,223,253 | 3,747,427 | 2,517,285 |
| Emp. | 192 | 171 | 158 |

DUNS 73-386-1772

## The Woodard Corporation

High Street, Abbots Bromley, Abbots Bromley, Rugeley, Staffordshire WS15 3BW
**Tel:** 01283840120
**Reg No:** 4659710 **Estd:** 2003 Private Company Limited By Guarantee
**Line of Business:** Primary education
**Trading Style:** St Augustine Academy
**Directors:** Mrs J C Richardson, S G Alder, M E Hartley, L M Barley, R Mansell, Ms M F Holman, Ms L Ayres, Dr I Bishop
**Co. Secretary:** Michael Corcoran
**Responsibilities**
**Senior:** Thomas Fremantle *(Director)*, Peter Southern *(Director)*
**Branches:** The Woodard Corporation, Saltash, Oakwood Road, Maidstone, Kent ME16 8AL
**US SIC:** 8211, 7392
**UK SIC:** 93200, 83951
**Auditors:** Grant Thornton UK LLP
**Bankers:** Lloyds TSB Bank plc (30-97-62)

| | 31-08-13 | 31-08-12 | 31-08-11 |
|---|---|---|---|
| TO | 169,160,000 | 224,395,000 | 146,270,000 |
| P/L | 9,782,000 | 73,198,000 | 7,159,000 |
| NW | 170,584,000 | 159,401,000 | 89,130,000 |
| WC | (1,184,000) | (9,303,000) | (7,582,000) |
| Emp. | 3,332 | 3,372 | 3,159 |

DUNS 22-555-3627

## Woodard Schools (Western Division) Ltd

1 The Sanctuary, London SW1P 3JT
**Tel:** 01823285920 **Fax:** 020-7222-7502
**Web:** www.facultyoffice.org.uk
**Reg No:** 1182633 **Estd:** 1974 Private Limited Company
**Line of Business:** Adult and other education not elsewhere classified
**Trading Style:** Central Office
**Issued Capital:** £100
**Directors:** R H Knight, B D Clover, D R Bilton
**Co. Secretary:** David Cudworth
**Branches:** Woodard Schools (Western Division) Ltd, Kingston Road, Taunton, Somerset TA2 8AA
**US SIC:** 8249, 8221
**UK SIC:** 93300, 93100
**Auditors:** A C Mole & Sons
**Bankers:** National Westminster Bank Plc (60-80-06)

| | 31-08-13 | 31-08-12 | 31-08-11 |
|---|---|---|---|
| TA | 100 | 100 | 100 |
| NW | 100 | 100 | 100 |

DUNS 73-348-5655

## Woodbay Ltd

98 Eglinton Road, Ardrossan, Ayrshire KA22 8NN
**Tel:** 01294-602915
**Reg No:** 0241458SC **Estd:** 2002 Private Limited Company
**Line of Business:** Residential care establishments
**Issued Capital:** £80
**Directors:** B A Collins, Mrs L Wanless
**Co. Secretary:** Nigel Wanless
**US SIC:** 8051 **UK SIC:** 95100

| | 31-03-14 | 31-03-13 | 31-03-12 |
|---|---|---|---|
| TA | 2,598,247 | 2,543,554 | 2,413,098 |
| NW | 1,363,459 | 1,209,498 | 1,068,169 |
| WC | 123,838 | 327,695 | 144,137 |

DUNS 23-993-3419

## Woodbridge School

Burkitt Road, Woodbridge, Suffolk IP12 4JH
**Tel:** 01394615000
**Web:** www.woodbridge.suffolk.sch.uk
**Estd:** 1990
**Line of Business:** Schools (independent)
**Responsibilities**
**Senior:** Neil Tetley *(Headmaster)*
**IT:** James Hillman *(IT Coordinator)*
**Branches:** Woodbridge School, The Abbey School, Cumberland Street, Woodbridge, Suffolk IP12 1DS
**US SIC:** 8211, 8299
**UK SIC:** 93200, 93300
**Bankers:** Barclays Bank Plc (20-98-07)
**Employees:** 180

DUNS 21-015-7573

## Woodbury Park Hotel & Golf Club Ltd

Woodbury Castle, Exeter, Devon EX5 1JJ
**Tel:** 01395233382
**Web:** www.woodburypark.co.uk
**Reg No:** 6381443 **Estd:** 2007 Private Limited Company
**Line of Business:** Hotels
**Issued Capital:** £1,000
**Director:** R B Hawkins
**Co. Secretary:** Ms Susan Paine
**Responsibilities**
**Senior:** Joe Hammond *(General Manager)*
**US SIC:** 7011 **UK SIC:** 66500
**Bankers:** Lloyds TSB Bank plc (30-93-15)

| | 31-03-14 | 31-03-13 | 31-03-12 |
|---|---|---|---|
| TO | 4,283,408 | 4,115,188 | 4,006,635 |
| P/L | 927,162 | 15,224 | 50,083 |
| NW | (351,353) | (1,165,170) | (1,263,922) |
| WC | (531,100) | (1,120,659) | (1,723,353) |
| Emp. | 115 | 114 | 117 |

DUNS 21-745-5918

## Woodchurch High School

Carr Bridge Road, Wirral, Merseyside CH49 7NG
**Tel:** 01516775257
**Reg No:** 7775671 **Estd:** 2011 Private Company Limited By Guarantee
**Line of Business:** Schools (local authority)
**Directors:** Mrs A C Whorton, Mrs G E Astle, Mrs S L Broderick, Dr M R Gilbertson, Ms R Phillips, M R Brown, Ms J M Merry, D J Cumberland
**Co. Secretary:** Ms Susan Rogers
**Responsibilities**
**Senior:** Alan Brimage *(Governor)*, Simon Burke *(Director)*, Maureen Cain *(Director)*, Margaret Cronin *(Director)*, Elizabeth Renshaw *(Director)*
**US SIC:** 8211 **UK SIC:** 93200
**Bankers:** Barclays Bank Plc (20-50-36)

| | 31-08-14 | 31-08-13 |
|---|---|---|
| TO | 8,716,288 | 34,601,129 |
| P/L | (354,870) | 26,881,061 |
| NW | 26,330,190 | 26,820,061 |
| WC | 2,627,199 | 2,305,399 |
| Emp. | 243 | 235 |

DUNS 28-945-6923

## Woodclay Ltd

Broadgate, Broadway Bsns Park, Chadderton, Oldham, Lancashire OL9 9XE
**Tel:** 01616881200
**Web:** www.widdop.co.uk
**Reg No:** 1601417 **Estd:** 1981 Private Limited Company
**Line of Business:** Wholesale of other household goods not elsewhere classified
**Export Sales:** £3,004,589
**Trading Style:** Widdop Bingham & Co
**Issued Capital:** £1,866
**Principals:** R Illingworth *(Chairman)*, R S Illingworth *(Managing)*, M A Illingworth
**Co. Secretary:** Christopher Illingworth

**US SIC:** 5199 **UK SIC:** 61900
**Auditors:** Wheawill & Sudworth
**Bankers:** Lloyds TSB Bank plc (30-96-26)

| | 30-09-13 | 30-09-12 | 30-09-11 |
|---|---|---|---|
| TO | 26,669,629 | 23,902,783 | 22,706,166 |
| P/L | 3,823,517 | 3,479,010 | 2,955,255 |
| NW | 9,786,013 | 13,227,117 | 10,637,498 |
| WC | 7,562,831 | 10,920,270 | 8,269,964 |
| Emp. | 134 | 130 | 124 |

DUNS 21-587-4743
## Woodcot Lodge Care Home
12 Rowner Road, Lee-On-The-Solent, Hampshire PO13 0EW
**Tel:** 02392520085
**Web:** www.fshc.co.uk
**Estd:** 2011 Proprietorship
**Line of Business:** Residential care establishments
**Proprietor:** Mrs C Bezer
**Responsibilities**
**Senior:** Judiph Houghart *(Manager)*
**US SIC:** 8321 **UK SIC:** 96111
**Employees:** 50

DUNS 64-072-9315 **Imp**
## Woodcote Green Nurseries Ltd
4a Woodmansterne Lane, Wallington, Surrey SM6 0SU
**Tel:** 02086476838
**Web:** www.woodcotegreen.com
**Reg No:** 3468372 **Estd:** 1997 Private Limited Company
**Line of Business:** Garden centres
**Issued Capital:** £100
**Managing Director:** C M Milan
**Co. Secretary:** Andrew Rollinson
**Responsibilities**
**Senior:** Lawrence Newton *(Manager)*
**Marketing:** Philip Barnden *(General Manager)*
**IT:** Hannah Manning *(IT Senior Section Leader)*
**Facilities:** Jon Hoare *(Facilities Manager)*
**US SIC:** 5999 **UK SIC:** 65600
**Auditors:** BDO Stoy Hayward
**Bankers:** HSBC Bank plc (40-45-17)

| | 31-08-13 | 31-08-12 | 31-08-11 |
|---|---|---|---|
| TO | 12,625,672 | 10,751,762 | 11,085,634 |
| P/L | 855,081 | 534,111 | 654,377 |
| NW | 2,140,530 | 1,638,800 | 1,420,760 |
| WC | 201,768 | (361,941) | (107,146) |
| Emp. | 119 | 106 | 102 |

DUNS 55-072-1328
## Woodcroft Nursery School
Whitakers Way, Loughton, Essex IG10 1SQ
**Tel:** 020-8508-1369
**Web:** www.woodcroftschool.net
**Estd:** 1963
**Line of Business:** Nursery schools
**Proprietor:** Mrs M Newton
**US SIC:** 8299 **UK SIC:** 93300
**Employees:** 60

DUNS 21-178-6490
## Woodcroft Veterinary Group Ltd
Cheadle Hulme Veterinary Hospital 2-4, Queens Road, Cheadle Hulme, Cheadle, Cheshire SK8 5LU
**Tel:** 01614858444
**Web:** www.woodcroftvets.com
**Reg No:** 7013686 **Estd:** 2009 Private Limited Company
**Line of Business:** Veterinary activities
**Issued Capital:** £240
**Directors:** D Wiggins, L Atkinson, P H Locke, Ms P Connolly, A P Oldfield, M Allington, D Parker
**US SIC:** 0741 **UK SIC:** 95601

| | 31-05-13 | 31-05-12 | 31-05-11 |
|---|---|---|---|
| TO | 4,636,245 | N/A | N/A |
| P/L | 388,846 | N/A | N/A |
| NW | (1,235,680) | (1,602,837) | (191,252) |
| WC | (313,065) | (359,658) | (89,444) |
| Emp. | 114 | N/A | N/A |

DUNS 34-833-2375
## Woodfines Llp
Exchange Building, 16 St Cuthberts Street, Bedford, Bedfordshire MK40 3JG
**Tel:** 01234-270600
**Web:** www.woodfines.co.uk
**Reg No:** 0316334OC **Estd:** 2005
**Line of Business:** Solicitors
**Responsibilities**
**Senior:** Nigel Ashton *(Non-designated Limited Liabili)*, Alun Butler *(Non-designated Limited Liabili)*, Denise Davies *(Non-designated Limited Liabili)*, John Leadbeater *(Non-designated Limited Liabili)*, Iain Macaskill *(Non-designated Limited Liabili)*, Stephen Ridyard *(Non-designated Limited Liabili)*
**US SIC:** 8111 **UK SIC:** 83500

**Auditors:** MacIntyre Hudson LLP

| | 31-03-14 | 31-03-13 | 31-03-12 |
|---|---|---|---|
| TO | 7,197,792 | 6,011,263 | 6,081,705 |
| NW | 2,714,339 | N/A | N/A |
| WC | 2,272,829 | 1,913,002 | 1,931,251 |
| Emp. | 95 | 91 | 97 |

DUNS 21-322-1877
## Woodford County High School for Girls
High Road, Woodford Green, Essex IG8 9LA
**Tel:** 020-8504-0611
**Web:** www.woodford.redbridge.sch.uk
**Estd:** 1922 Proprietorship
**Line of Business:** Schools (foundation)
**Proprietor:** Miss H Cleland
**Responsibilities**
**Senior:** Jo Pomeroy *(Head Teacher)*
**US SIC:** 8211 **UK SIC:** 93200
**Employees:** 85

DUNS 28-845-2782
## Woodford Green Preparatory School Ltd
Glengall Road, Woodford Green, Essex IG8 0BZ
**Tel:** 020-8504-5045
**Web:** www.woodfordgreenprep.co.uk
**Reg No:** 0621311 **Estd:** 1959 Private Company Limited By Guarantee
**Line of Business:** Primary education
**Directors:** Mrs P Y Fisher, Mrs E A Hare, Mrs J A Deeks, Ms E J Sparks, A Halford, M Townsend, G T Dunn, Ms A E Quaife Odonnell
**Co. Secretary:** Glen Jones
**Responsibilities**
**Senior:** A Blackhurst *(Head Teacher)*, Tracey Campbell *(Manager)*, Jacqueline Hart *(Headmistress)*, Keith Percy *(Governor)*, Afshan Shamas *(Governor)*, Jo Youldon *(Head of Administration)*
**Admin:** Dawn Layton *(SChool Secretary)*, Jo Youldon *(Head of Administration)*
**IT:** Teresa Barnes *(Computer Manager)*
**HR:** Jacqueline Hart *(Headmistress)*
**Purchasing:** Jo Youldon *(Head of Administration)*
**Branches:** Woodford Green Preparatory School Ltd, Litchaton Way, Plymouth, Devon PL7 4RB
**US SIC:** 8211, 6732
**UK SIC:** 93200, 83100
**Auditors:** Cooper Paul
**Bankers:** HSBC Bank plc (40-47-14)

| | 31-08-14 | 31-08-13 | 31-08-12 |
|---|---|---|---|
| TO | 3,099,969 | 2,980,225 | 2,908,261 |
| P/L | 78,519 | 87,591 | 69,612 |
| NW | 3,260,375 | 3,181,857 | 3,094,266 |
| WC | 444,674 | 369,855 | 427,085 |
| Emp. | 48 | 49 | 49 |

DUNS 57-021-5558
## Woodford Heating & Energy Ltd
**(Subsidiary of:** Woodford Heating Holdings Ltd)
Unit 17, Forest Trading Estate, Priestley Way, Walthamstow, London E17 6AL
**Tel:** 02085310004
**Web:** www.woodfordheating.com
**Reg No:** 2868418 **VAT No:** 466603535
**Estd:** 1994 Private Limited Company
**Line of Business:** Plumbers
**Issued Capital:** £100
**Principals:** R S Alderslade *(Managing)*, S T Abbott
**US SIC:** 1711 **UK SIC:** 50300
**Auditors:** Learer Roberts
**Bankers:** Barclays Bank Plc (20-52-74)

| | 31-01-14 | 31-01-13 | 31-01-12 |
|---|---|---|---|
| TO | 12,184,434 | N/A | N/A |
| P/L | 309,462 | N/A | N/A |
| NW | 1,886,335 | 1,711,228 | 1,425,329 |
| WC | 1,784,430 | 1,605,757 | 1,348,241 |
| Emp. | 64 | N/A | N/A |

DUNS 21-551-1242
## Woodford House Nursing Home
The Green, Trysull, Wolverhampton, West Midlands WV5 7HW
**Tel:** 01902-324264
**Web:** www.woodford-house.co.uk
**Estd:** 2000 Partnership
**Line of Business:** Nursing homes
**Partners:** Mrs J Mcdonath, C Goodall, K Bedwood
**Responsibilities**
**Senior:** Julie Mcdonough *(Partner)*
**US SIC:** 8051 **UK SIC:** 95100
**Employees:** 64

DUNS 23-434-0750
## Woodford Park Garden Centre
Chester Road, Woodford, Stockport, Cheshire SK7 1QS
**Tel:** 01614390745
**Web:** www.notcutts.co.uk
**Estd:** 2002 Proprietorship
**Line of Business:** Garden centres
**Proprietor:** A Jenkins
**US SIC:** 5999 **UK SIC:** 65600
**Employees:** 160

DUNS 29-887-7366
## Woodgate & Clark Ltd
The Red House, King Street, West Malling, Kent ME19 6QT
**Tel:** 01732-848077
**Web:** www.woodgate-clark.co.uk
**Reg No:** 2090698 **Estd:** 1987 Private Limited Company
**Line of Business:** Activities auxiliary to insurance and pension funding
**Issued Capital:** £10,000
**Director:** R G Clark
**Co. Secretary:** Michael Woodgate
**Responsibilities**
**HR:** Nic Fordyce *(Human Resources Manager)*
**Health & Safety:** Barbara Weatherill *(Health & Safety Officer)*
**Branches:** Woodgate & Clark Ltd, Astra House, Christy Way, Southfields, Basildon, Essex SS15 6TQ
**US SIC:** 7399, 6411
**UK SIC:** 83954, 83200
**Auditors:** Rushton Osborne & Co Ltd

| | 30-04-14 | 30-04-13 | 30-04-12 |
|---|---|---|---|
| TO | 9,974,168 | 9,378,451 | 8,713,749 |
| P/L | 2,500,108 | 1,532,180 | 1,450,314 |
| NW | 4,807,653 | 4,240,545 | 4,093,718 |
| WC | 4,431,507 | 3,866,466 | 3,722,267 |
| Emp. | 124 | 131 | 128 |

DUNS 29-859-0571
## Woodgrange Laundry Ltd
407 Green Street, London E13 9AU
**Tel:** 020-8552-1231 **Fax:** 020-8503-4112
**Web:** www.blossomandbrowne.com
**Reg No:** 2062328 **Estd:** 1986 Private Limited Company
**Line of Business:** Washing and dry cleaning of textile and fur products
**Issued Capital:** £51,000
**Directors:** Mrs F S Browne, J B Browne
**Co. Secretary:** Daniel Browne
**Branches:** Woodgrange Laundry Ltd, 160 Regents Park Road, London NW1 8XN
**US SIC:** 7219 **UK SIC:** 98110
**Auditors:** Bristow Burrell

| | 30-09-14 | 30-09-13 | 30-09-12 |
|---|---|---|---|
| TA | 1,405,929 | 1,285,175 | 1,322,495 |
| NW | 119,833 | 45,504 | (21,075) |
| WC | (209,630) | (266,753) | (310,626) |

DUNS 21-467-9172
## Woodgreen Nursing Home
27 Wood Green Road, Wednesbury, West Midlands WS10 9AX
**Tel:** 0121-556-0381
**Estd:** 2003 Proprietorship
**Line of Business:** Medical nursing home activities
**Proprietor:** W H Morrall
**Responsibilities**
**Senior:** Rosemarie Eagleton *(home manager)*
**Finance:** Gregory Morrall *(Finance Director)*
**US SIC:** 8051 **UK SIC:** 95100
**Employees:** 60

DUNS 21-462-5597
## Woodhall Park Nursing Home
Derby Road, Risley, Derby, Derbyshire DE72 3SS
**Tel:** 01159-490444
**Web:** www.woodhallparknursinghome.co.uk
**Estd:** 1989
**Line of Business:** Medical nursing home activities
**Partners:** Mrs A Dunkley, Mrs A Dunkly
**Responsibilities**
**Senior:** Patricia Betts *(matron)*, Sue Featherstone *(Manager)*
**US SIC:** 8051 **UK SIC:** 95100
**Employees:** 48

DUNS 77-950-3143
## Woodhall Spa Estate Management Co Ltd
**(Subsidiary of:** Woodhall Spa Land Holdings Ltd)
The National Golf Centre, The Broadway, Woodhall Spa, Lincolnshire LN10 6PU
**Tel:** 01526-351803 **Fax:** 01526-351817
**Web:** www.woodhallspagolf.com
**Reg No:** 3056116 **Estd:** 1995 Private Limited Company

**Line of Business:** Other letting of own property
**Issued Capital:** £6,500,001
**Directors:** P J Holt, S J Keighley, J A Grayson, M D Hepworth, J M Pitts
**US SIC:** 6519 **UK SIC:** 85000
**Auditors:** PKF
**Bankers:** Lloyds TSB Bank plc (30-94-39)

| | 31-10-13 | 31-10-12 | 31-10-11 |
|---|---|---|---|
| TO | 113,879 | 100,229 | 103,959 |
| P/L | 100,187 | 24,261 | 13,864 |
| NW | 6,035,645 | 5,944,605 | 5,930,544 |
| WC | 19,062 | (23,978) | (17,039) |

DUNS 21-233-1323 **Exp**
## Woodhead Bros
Markethill Industrial Estate, Markethill Road, Turriff, Aberdeenshire AB53 4PA
**Tel:** 01888-563751
**Web:** www.morrisons.co.uk
**Estd:** 2013 Proprietorship
**Line of Business:** Animal by-product processing
**Proprietor:** A Thomson
**Responsibilities**
**Senior:** Michael Tough *(General Manager)*
**Facilities:** Malcolm Baillie *(Engineering Manager)*
**Engineering:** Malcolm Baillie *(Engineering Manager)*
**US SIC:** 2013 **UK SIC:** 41223
**Employees:** 300

DUNS 21-163-0760
## Woodhorn Charitable Trust
Queen Elizabeth Ii Country Park, Ashington, Northumberland NE63 9YF
**Tel:** 01670-528080
**Web:** www.experiencewoodhorn.com
**Reg No:** 6893854 **Estd:** 2009 Private Company Limited By Guarantee
**Line of Business:** Library and archive activities
**Directors:** J M Carr-Ellison, D B Ronn, P J Robinson, P A Browell, I Lavery, R B Charlton, Ms P J Wilkinson, J Browne-Swinburne
**Responsibilities**
**Senior:** Lesley Rickerby *(Manager)*
**US SIC:** 8231, 8411
**UK SIC:** 97700
**Bankers:** Cafcash Ltd (40-52-40)

| | 31-03-14 | 31-03-13 | 31-03-12 |
|---|---|---|---|
| TO | 3,023,580 | 2,353,262 | 1,830,380 |
| P/L | 564,912 | 218,839 | (271,618) |
| NW | 1,569,412 | 1,004,500 | 785,661 |
| WC | 1,568,046 | 873,016 | 524,059 |
| Emp. | 49 | 44 | 48 |

DUNS 54-862-0236
## Woodhouse College
Woodhouse Road, London N12 9EY
**Tel:** 020-8445-1210
**Web:** www.woodhouse.ac.uk
**Estd:** 2004
**Line of Business:** Colleges (higher education)
**Responsibilities**
**Finance:** Clive Winters *(Senior Finance Administrator)*
**IT:** Colin Everitt *(Senior IT Executive)*
**US SIC:** 8221 **UK SIC:** 93100
**Employees:** 83

DUNS 21-017-7004
## Woodhouse Healthcare Services Ltd
5-7 Skelton Lane, Woodhouse, Sheffield, South Yorkshire S13 7LY
**Tel:** 01142880004
**Web:** www.woodhousehealthcentre.co.uk
**Reg No:** 6396490 **Estd:** 2007 Private Limited Company
**Line of Business:** Chemists dispensing
**Issued Capital:** £100
**Directors:** Dr N W Smith, Dr C A Mitchell, Mrs A J Smith, Dr A D Mcginty, Dr M J Spinks, Dr P Mcginty, Dr N P Anumba
**Co. Secretary:** Gordon Osborne
**Responsibilities**
**Senior:** Stewart Kelly *(Manager)*, Zachary Mcmurray *(Manager)*
**US SIC:** 5912 **UK SIC:** 64300

| | 31-10-13 | 31-10-12 | 31-10-11 |
|---|---|---|---|
| TA | 688,951 | 690,282 | 554,339 |
| NW | 202,701 | 257,873 | 229,108 |
| WC | 222,219 | 282,107 | N/A |

DUNS 21-507-0629
## Woodhurst Nursing Home
Old Bridgend, Carluke, Lanarkshire ML8 4HN
**Tel:** 01555772164
**Web:** www.canterbury-care.com
**Estd:** 1985 Proprietorship
**Line of Business:** Nursing homes
**Proprietor:** Dr E Kerr

**Responsibilities**
Senior: Dawn Mccormick (Manager)
US SIC: 8051 UK SIC: 95100
Employees: 88

---

DUNS 21-579-8118
## Woodingdean Primary School
Warren Road, Brighton, East Sussex BN2 6BB
Tel: 01273680811
Web: www.woodingdeanprimaryschool.co.uk
Estd: 1997 Proprietorship
Line of Business: Schools (local authority)
Proprietor: Mrs G Hutchins
**Responsibilities**
Senior: Jonathan Whitfield (Head Teacher)
US SIC: 8211 UK SIC: 93200
Employees: 65

---

DUNS 21-738-3026
## Woodkirk Academy Trust
Rein Road, Tingley, Wakefield, West Yorkshire WF3 1JQ
Tel: 01133368140 Fax: 01132526456
Web: www.woodkirkacademy.co.uk
Reg No: 7720181 Estd: 2011 Private Company Limited By Guarantee
Line of Business: Schools (foundation)
Directors: J Westwood, I West, A R Aiston, G F Beacon, L Zwalf, S Alleston, N Bilton, Mrs K Grey
Co Secretary: Steven Outcliffe
**Responsibilities**
Senior: Sharon Anderson (Director), William Bartholomew (Director), Judith Elliott (Director), Dennis Fisher (Director), Anthony Grayson (Director), Ashley Rawlins (Director), Janet Standage (Director)
US SIC: 8211 UK SIC: 93200

| | 31-08-13 | 31-08-12 |
|---|---|---|
| TO | 9,831,000 | 21,579,000 |
| P/L | (116,000) | 12,162,000 |
| NW | 11,740,000 | 11,688,000 |
| WC | 1,470,000 | 1,411,000 |
| Emp. | 198 | 180 |

---

DUNS 57-020-9833
## Woodland Commercial Ltd
292 Worton Road, Isleworth, Middlesex TW7 6EL
Tel: 020-8560-0010
Web: www.woodlandcommercial.co.uk
Reg No: 2867824 Estd: 1993 Private Limited Company
Line of Business: Builders
Issued Capital: £100
Director: S P Archer
Co. Secretary: Kevin Furey
US SIC: 1799, 1522
UK SIC: 50000, 50100
Auditors: Crick Heitman
Bankers: Barclays Bank Plc (20-42-73)

| | 31-10-13 | 31-10-12 | 31-10-11 |
|---|---|---|---|
| TA | 2,210,964 | 1,670,682 | 1,705,199 |
| NW | 214,290 | 263,176 | 309,879 |
| WC | 206,864 | 258,445 | 302,689 |

---

DUNS 23-176-8883
## Woodland Grange Training Centre
Development & Conference Centre, Old Milverton Lane, Leamington Spa, Warwickshire CV32 6RN
Tel: 01926-336621
Web: www.eef.co.uk
Estd: 1970
Line of Business: Activities of private training providers
Director: A Taylor
**Responsibilities**
Senior: David Vaughton (Manager)
Finance: Louise Shore (Finance Director)
US SIC: 8299 UK SIC: 93300
Employees: 60

---

DUNS 34-649-4599   Imp
## Woodland Group Ltd
Woodland House, Montrose Road, Chelmsford, Essex CM2 6TE
Tel: 01245 619900 Fax: 01245 619688
Web: www.woodland-group.com
Reg No: 5455052 Estd: 2005 Private Limited Company
Line of Business: Freight services
Export Sales: £77,073,000
Issued Capital: £16,605,001
Director: K G Stevens
Co. Secretary: John Stubbings
**Responsibilities**
Senior: Sean Kerby (Manager)
US SIC: 6711, 4712
UK SIC: 83962, 77002
Auditors: Grant Thornton UK LLP

---

Bankers: The Royal Bank Of Scotland Plc (83-04-25)

| | 31-12-13 | 31-12-12 | 31-12-11 |
|---|---|---|---|
| TO | 107,958,000 | 104,802,000 | 88,017,000 |
| P/L | 1,483,000 | 832,000 | 683,000 |
| NW | 7,553,000 | 5,993,000 | 5,061,000 |
| WC | 5,551,000 | 3,763,000 | 2,433,000 |
| Emp. | 484 | 501 | 410 |

---

DUNS 21-534-5401
## Woodland Health Care
Middle Warberry Road, Torquay, Devon TQ1 1RN
Tel: 01803-296809
Estd: 1988
Line of Business: Nursing homes
Trading Style: Woodland House
Proprietor: Mrs K Gwiliam
US SIC: 8051 UK SIC: 95100
Employees: 47

---

DUNS 21-778-4454
## Woodland Hospital
Rothwell Road, Kettering, Northamptonshire NN16 8XF
Tel: 01536414515
Web: www.woodlandhospital.co.uk
Estd: 2011
Line of Business: Hospitals
**Responsibilities**
Senior: Tania Terblanche (Manager)
US SIC: 8062 UK SIC: 95100
Employees: 100

---

DUNS 21-718-1656
## Woodland Middle School Academy
Malham Close, Flitwick, Bedford, Bedfordshire MK45 1NP
Tel: 01525750400
Web: www.woodlandacademy.co.uk
Reg No: 7566455 Estd: 1998 Private Company Limited By Guarantee
Line of Business: Schools (local authority)
Directors: J Conquest, Ms C Davis, C James-Reynolds, A Bowerbank, A Lees, Ms M Wilsmore
Co. Secretary: Ms Anne Knudsen
US SIC: 8211 UK SIC: 93200

| | 31-08-14 | 31-08-13 | 31-08-12 |
|---|---|---|---|
| TO | 2,704,482 | 2,724,181 | 7,856,878 |
| P/L | (138,521) | (130,460) | 4,053,474 |
| NW | 3,612,493 | 3,887,014 | 3,990,474 |
| WC | 437,757 | 404,978 | 346,204 |
| Emp. | 51 | 55 | 57 |

---

DUNS 29-656-6086
## The Woodland Trust
Kempton Way, Grantham, Lincolnshire NG31 6LL
Tel: 01476-581-135
Web: www.woodlandtrust.org.uk
Reg No: 1982873 VAT No: 520611104
Estd: 1972 Private Company Limited By Guarantee
Line of Business: Forestry and logging
Directors: H W Battcock, R J Sykes, Dr J N Nicholls, T J Rollinson, J S Marshall, Ms G M Lambert, E M Mannis, P J Macdonald
Co. Secretary: Mrs Helga Edwards
**Responsibilities**
Senior: Sue Holden (Chief Executive), Anne Lightowler (Human Resources Manager)
Marketing: Philip Shipway (Sales & Marketing Manager)
Sales: Philip Shipway (Sales & Marketing Manager)
IT: Lionel Wilson (Computer Manager)
HR: Anne Lightowler (Human Resources Manager), L Stanley (Human Resources Manager)
Health & Safety: Marcus Bond (Facilities Manager)
Facilities: Marcus Bond (Facilities Manager)
Branches: The Woodland Trust, Jayrise, Bristol, Avon BS40 7UT
US SIC: 0851, 8421, 8699
UK SIC: 02000, 97700, 96902
Auditors: haysmacintyre
Bankers: Lloyds TSB Bank plc (30-93-58)

| | 31-12-13 | 31-12-12 | 31-12-11 |
|---|---|---|---|
| TO | 33,397,000 | 31,878,000 | 26,997,000 |
| P/L | 6,748,000 | 6,682,000 | 1,399,000 |
| NW | 123,548,000 | 114,985,000 | 107,601,000 |
| WC | 12,753,000 | 9,176,000 | 9,730,000 |
| Emp. | 291 | 291 | 291 |

---

DUNS 21-013-0932
## Woodland Trust Farming Ltd
Kempton Way, Grantham, Lincolnshire NG31 6LL
Tel: 01476-581111
Web: www.woodlandtrust.org.uk
Reg No: 6360791 Estd: 2007 Private Limited Company
Line of Business: Representative office
Issued Capital: £100
Directors: E M Mannis, Professor J I Drori, Dr J N Nicholls

---

Co. Secretary: Mrs Helga Edwards
**Responsibilities**
Senior: Sian Atkinson (Senior Manager), Kaye Brennan (Executive), Merle Dekanski (Executive), Amanda Holmes (General Manager), Jerry Langford (Wales Director), Michelle Mccaughtry (Executive), Becky Speight (Chief Executive Officer), Loma Templeton (General Manager)
Finance: Alison Chmiel (Trustee, Finance Committee)
Marketing: Kaye Coates (Communications Officer), Rob Croxall (Head Of Membership), Katie Downing-Howitt (Digital Marketing Manager), Sue East (Corporate Fundraiser), Andrew Fairbum (Development Manager), Rory Francis (Public Relations and Press Off), Phil Shipway (Sales & Marketing Manager)
Sales: Phil Shipway (Sales & Marketing Manager)
IT: Richard Otter (Head of IT)
HR: L Stanley (Human Resources Manager)
Health & Safety: Marcus Bond (Facilities Manager)
Facilities: Roy Barlow (Site Manager), Marcus Bond (Facilities Manager), Gary Haley (Site Manager)
Operations: Gregor Fulton (Project Manager), Gordon Pfetscher (Operations Manager), Jennie Ryan (Project Officer)
Engineering: Tim Kirwin (Officer)
US SIC: 0119, 0241, 0214, 0851
UK SIC: 01001, 02000

| | 31-12-13 | 31-12-12 | 31-12-11 |
|---|---|---|---|
| TO | 1,183,000 | 975,000 | 651,000 |

---

DUNS 21-039-2426
## Woodlands
Minstead Avenue, Southampton, Hampshire SO18 5FW
Web: www.paintpotsnursery.co.uk
Estd: 2012 Proprietorship
Line of Business: Pre school education
**Responsibilities**
Senior: Emma Nicholson (Manager)
US SIC: 8211 UK SIC: 93200
Employees: 200

---

DUNS 23-954-7354
## Woodlands & Hill Brow Ltd
(Subsidiary of: Hill Brow Group Ltd)
Beacon Hill Road, Ewshot, Farnham, Surrey GU10 5DB
Tel: 01252-850236 Fax: 01252-851436
Web: www.woodland-hillbrow.co.uk
Reg No: 3944030 Estd: 2000 Private Limited Company
Line of Business: Non-charitable social work activities with accommodation
Issued Capital: £999
Directors: Ms G A Lee, G Martinez, A J Lee
Co. Secretary: Gareth Lee
US SIC: 8321 UK SIC: 96111

| | 31-03-14 | 31-03-13 | 31-03-12 |
|---|---|---|---|
| TO | 6,180,575 | N/A | N/A |
| P/L | 1,607,452 | N/A | N/A |
| NW | 3,015,043 | 2,014,004 | 1,167,165 |
| WC | 2,754,319 | 1,702,684 | 800,125 |
| Emp. | 155 | N/A | N/A |

---

DUNS 54-905-0193
## Woodlands Community School
Blenheim Drive, Allestree, Derby, Derbyshire DE22 2LW
Tel: 01332551921
Web: www.woodlands.derby.sch.uk
Estd: 2012
Line of Business: Schools (foundation)
Chairman: Dr J Spincer
US SIC: 8211 UK SIC: 93200
Employees: 140

---

DUNS 21-782-1765
## Woodlands County Infant School
Higham School Road, Tonbridge, Kent TN10 4BB
Tel: 01732353655
Web: www.woodland-infant.kent.sch.uk
Estd: 1999 Proprietorship
Line of Business: Schools (local authority)
Proprietor: Ms S Morgan
US SIC: 8211 UK SIC: 93200
Employees: 50

---

DUNS 21-770-6809
## Woodlands Court Residential Home
Boston Road, Kirton, Boston, Lincolnshire PE20 1DS
Tel: 01205723355
Web: www.woodlandscourt.org
Estd: 2011 Proprietorship
Line of Business: Residential care establishments
Proprietor: Mrs S Woodings

---

**Responsibilities**
Senior: Amanda Perrins (Manager)
US SIC: 8321 UK SIC: 96111
Employees: 50

---

DUNS 77-929-7733
## Woodlands (Gb) Ltd
(Subsidiary of: Woodlands Homecare (Group) Ltd)
Woodlands House, Station Road, Leeds, West Yorkshire LS18 5NL
Web: www.woodlands-sheds.com
Reg No: 5832492 Estd: 1979 Private Limited Company
Line of Business: Timber merchants
Issued Capital: £100
Co. Secretary: David Moran
US SIC: 5072 UK SIC: 61500

| | 30-11-14 | 30-11-13 | 30-11-12 |
|---|---|---|---|
| TA | 100 | 100 | 100 |
| NW | 100 | 100 | 100 |

---

DUNS 21-213-3177   Imp
## Woodlands Homecare Ltd
(Subsidiary of: Woodlands Homecare (Group) Ltd)
Calverley Bridge, Calverley Lane, Leeds, West Yorkshire LS13 1NP
Web: www.woodlands-sheds.com
Reg No: 0132673 Estd: 1913 Private Limited Company
Line of Business: Manufacture of other products of wood
Trading Style: Woodlands Garden Sheds
Issued Capital: £1,675
Principals: D J Moran (Financial), Mrs J M Moran, Ms J Moran
Co. Secretary: Ross Moran
**Responsibilities**
Senior: Eric Moran (Managing Director, Director)
Purchasing: Gary Claughton (Purchasing Manager)
US SIC: 2499, 5072, 5251
UK SIC: 46500, 61500, 64800
Auditors: Wild & Co
Bankers: National Westminster Bank Plc (60-60-05)

| | 30-11-13 | 30-11-12 | 30-11-11 |
|---|---|---|---|
| TA | 6,539,935 | 5,611,246 | 5,696,251 |
| P/L | 843,267 | 1,112,116 | 943,824 |
| NW | 3,514,424 | 2,871,069 | 1,971,584 |
| WC | 2,921,260 | 2,361,608 | 1,373,139 |
| Emp. | 88 | 75 | 75 |

---

DUNS 21-615-1157
## Woodlands Hospital
Morton Park Way, Town Centre, Darlington, County Durham DL1 4PL
Web: www.woodlandshealthcare.com
Estd: 2011 Proprietorship
Line of Business: Hospitals
Proprietor: Mrs D Dobbs
US SIC: 7011 UK SIC: 66500
Employees: 122

---

DUNS 21-207-0903
## Woodlands Manor Nursing Home
Ruffet Road, Kendleshire, Winterbourne, Bristol, Avon BS36 1AN
Tel: 01454-250593
Web: www.woodlandsmanorcarehome.co.uk
Estd: 1994 Partnership
Line of Business: Nursing homes
Partners: D J Jenkins, Mrs L M Jenkins
**Responsibilities**
Senior: Lynne Jenkins (Manager), Pauline Rodman (Home Manager)
Health & Safety: Cheryl Lawrence (Home Manager)
Facilities: Cheryl Lawrence (Home Manager)
US SIC: 8051 UK SIC: 95100
Employees: 55

---

DUNS 23-187-3654
## Woodlands Nursing Home
Sands Lane, Mirfield, West Yorkshire WF14 8HJ
Tel: 01924-491570
Web: www.craegmoor.co.uk
Estd: 2002 Proprietorship
Line of Business: Nursing homes
Proprietor: Ms J Westwood
**Responsibilities**
Senior: Lyn Hawkins (Manager)
US SIC: 8051 UK SIC: 95100
Employees: 70

---

DUNS 23-113-8004
## Woodlands Primary School
The Crescent, Doncaster, South Yorkshire DN6 7RG
Tel: 01302-722367
Estd: 1988 Proprietorship
Line of Business: Schools (local authority)

**Proprietor:** J Mcenaney
**US SIC:** 8211 **UK SIC:** 93200
**Employees:** 65

DUNS 21-782-2553
## Woodlands School
Regent Walk, Aberdeen, Aberdeenshire AB24 1SX
**Tel:** 01224524393
**Estd:** 2005 Partnership
**Line of Business:** Schools (special)
**Partner:** Mrs C Stirton
**US SIC:** 8299 **UK SIC:** 93300
**Employees:** 60

DUNS 28-906-8819
## Woodlands Schools Ltd
Hutton Manor, 428 Rayleigh Road, Hutton, Brentwood, Essex CM13 1SD
**Tel:** 01277245580 **Fax:** 01314493034
**Web:** www.woodlandsschools.co.uk
**Reg No:** 1389757 **Estd:** 1978 Private Limited Company
**Line of Business:** Primary education
**Issued Capital:** £75,000
**Directors:** Mrs C A Beeston, J K Lewis, B K Lewis, Mrs J Y Lewis, Mrs L Lewis
**Responsibilities**
**Senior:** Debbie Cook *(Admissions Officer)*
**US SIC:** 8211 **UK SIC:** 93200
**Auditors:** Grant Thornton
**Bankers:** The Royal Bank Of Scotland Plc (15-10-00)

| | 31-08-13 | 31-08-12 | 31-08-11 |
|---|---|---|---|
| TA | 2,840,257 | 3,078,251 | 3,163,020 |
| NW | 452,027 | 295,850 | 272,557 |
| WC | (802,930) | (881,569) | (734,820) |

DUNS 42-316-2551
## Woodleigh Beeches
Lakin Road, Warwick, Warwickshire CV34 5BW
**Tel:** 01926410281
**Proprietorship**
**Line of Business:** Hospitals
**Director:** P Farenden
**US SIC:** 8062 **UK SIC:** 95100
**Employees:** 2,000

DUNS 28-960-3714
## Woodley Hotels Ltd
15-25 Hogarth Road, London SW5 0QJ
**Tel:** 020-7373-4502 **Fax:** 020-7373-5115
**Web:** www.woodleygroup.co.uk
**Reg No:** 1677114 **VAT No:** 394625520
**Estd:** 1985 Private Limited Company
**Line of Business:** Hotels
**Trading Style:** The Enterprise
**Issued Capital:** £425,002
**Principals:** V D Dhrona *(Managing)*, B D Dhrona
**Co. Secretary:** Girishkumar Dhrona
**Responsibilities**
**Senior:** Ramesh Maden *(Health & Safety Director)*
**Health & Safety:** Ramesh Maden *(Health & Safety Director)*
**Branches:** Woodley Hotels Ltd, 119 Ainsworth Road, Manchester M26 4FD
**US SIC:** 7011, 6111
**UK SIC:** 66500, 81501
**Auditors:** Clayton Stark & Co
**Bankers:** Syndicate Bank (60-92-67)

| | 31-03-14 | 31-03-13 | 31-03-12 |
|---|---|---|---|
| TA | 23,933,820 | 45,135,691 | 40,680,272 |
| P/L | 313,919 | 353,615 | 108,687 |
| NW | 19,468,708 | 34,880,258 | 29,863,515 |
| WC | 3,532,013 | (2,072,987) | (1,873,983) |
| Emp. | 159 | 156 | 159 |

DUNS 64-081-3580
## Woodlodge Products Ltd
Babdown Airfield, Tetbury, Gloucestershire GL8 8YL
**Tel:** 01666501000
**Web:** www.woodlodge.co.uk
**Reg No:** 3476579 **VAT No:** 710938540
**Estd:** 1997 Private Limited Company
**Line of Business:** Wholesale of chemical products
**Issued Capital:** £100
**Director:** M K Wooldridge
**Co. Secretary:** Geoffrey Wooldridge
**US SIC:** 5199, 3263
**UK SIC:** 61900, 24893
**Auditors:** Wilson Sandford (Brighton) Ltd
**Bankers:** Lloyds TSB Bank plc (77-66-01)

| | 30-06-14 | 30-06-13 | 30-06-12 |
|---|---|---|---|
| TO | 14,487,191 | 11,875,512 | 11,523,137 |
| P/L | 961,534 | 97,517 | 494,853 |
| NW | 6,939,290 | 6,245,833 | 6,173,875 |
| WC | 6,235,982 | 5,454,957 | 5,306,842 |
| Emp. | 92 | 92 | 90 |

DUNS 29-663-0080
## Woodmace Ltd
21-23 Willis Way, Poole, Dorset BH15 3AP
**Tel:** 01202667785
**Web:** www.woodmace.co.uk
**Reg No:** 1989748 **VAT No:** 423522287
**Estd:** 1986 Private Limited Company
**Line of Business:** Building of complete constructions or parts thereof; civil engineering
**Issued Capital:** £100
**Principals:** J Oak *(Managing)*, N G Cooper
**Co. Secretary:** Mrs Tracey Fisher
**Responsibilities**
**Senior:** Jackie Thorpe *(Office Manager)*
**Finance:** Tracey Orchard *(Accountant)*
**Purchasing:** Dean McCarthy *(Buyer)*
**US SIC:** 1541, 1799
**UK SIC:** 50100, 50000
**Auditors:** Carter & Coley
**Bankers:** National Westminster Bank Plc (56-00-35)

| | 31-03-14 | 31-03-13 | 31-03-12 |
|---|---|---|---|
| TO | 13,244,647 | 12,507,337 | 12,324,981 |
| P/L | 122,897 | (124,704) | 107,510 |
| NW | 1,257,834 | 1,161,686 | 1,262,872 |
| WC | 237,582 | 417,216 | 789,444 |
| Emp. | 110 | 115 | 116 |

DUNS 28-931-0310
## Woodman Wine Bars Ltd
44 Tiddington Road, Stratford-Upon-Avon, Warwickshire CV37 7BA
**Tel:** 02086616542
**Reg No:** 1527958 **Estd:** 1979 Private Limited Company
**Line of Business:** Bars
**Trading Style:** Legends Nightclub
**Issued Capital:** £104
**Director:** A P Dumpress
**Co. Secretary:** Stuart Myers
**US SIC:** 5813 **UK SIC:** 66200
**Bankers:** Barclays Bank Plc (20-29-90)

| | 30-04-14 | 30-04-13 | 30-04-12 |
|---|---|---|---|
| TA | 635,092 | 607,982 | 540,933 |
| NW | 619,515 | 567,557 | 514,485 |
| WC | 78,942 | 26,984 | (26,088) |

DUNS 21-634-2105
## Woodmansterne Ltd
1 Boulevard, Blackmoor Lane, Watford, Hertfordshire WD18 8UW
**Tel:** 01923-200600 **Fax:** 01932200600
**Web:** www.woodmansterne.co.uk
**Reg No:** 0549875 **Estd:** 1955 Private Limited Company
**Line of Business:** Publishing of books
**Trading Style:** Woodmansterne Publications
**Issued Capital:** £2,500
**Managing Director:** P A Woodmansterne
**Co. Secretary:** Mrs Julia Britton
**Responsibilities**
**Senior:** Helen Mclaughlin *(Accounts Manager)*
**Finance:** Helen Mclaughlin *(Accounts Manager)*
**US SIC:** 2731 **UK SIC:** 47532
**Auditors:** Reeves & Neylan

| | 31-03-14 | 31-03-13 | 31-03-12 |
|---|---|---|---|
| TA | 5,000 | 5,000 | 5,000 |
| NW | 5,000 | 5,000 | 5,000 |

DUNS 21-781-7968
## Woodmill High School
Shields Road, Dunfermline, Fife KY11 4ER
**Tel:** 01383602406
**Web:** www.fife-education.org.uk
**Estd:** 2002 Proprietorship
**Line of Business:** Schools (local authority)
**Proprietor:** M Gilmour
**Responsibilities**
**Senior:** Michael Gilmour *(Head Teacher)*, Sandy Mcintosh *(Head Teacher)*
**Sales:** Margaret West *(Business Manager)*
**US SIC:** 8211 **UK SIC:** 93200
**Employees:** 120

DUNS 23-970-8584
## Woodnet
Woodland Enterprise Centre, Hastings Road, Flimwell, Wadhurst, East Sussex TN5 7PR
**Tel:** 01580879547
**Web:** www.woodnet.org.uk
**Reg No:** 3959651 **Estd:** 2000 Private Limited Company
**Line of Business:** Research and laboratory based activities
**Directors:** A W Penrose, C Yarrow, D P Lambert
**Co. Secretary:** David Saunders
**US SIC:** 0851, 7391, 8299
**UK SIC:** 02000, 94000, 93300
**Auditors:** C. Roughton

| | 31-03-14 | 31-03-13 | 31-03-12 |
|---|---|---|---|
| TO | N/A | 434 | 688 |
| P/L | N/A | 7,826 | (265) |
| NW | (5,295) | (11,665) | (19,491) |
| WC | (5,296) | (11,666) | (19,492) |

DUNS 21-781-0271
## Woodnewton Learning Community
Rowlett Road, Corby, Northamptonshire NN17 2NU
**Tel:** 01536265173
**Web:** www.woodnewton.northants.sch.uk
**Estd:** 1990 Proprietorship
**Line of Business:** Schools (foundation)
**Proprietor:** Mrs E Wallace
**Responsibilities**
**Senior:** Ellen Wallace *(Head Teacher)*
**US SIC:** 8211 **UK SIC:** 93200
**Employees:** 120

DUNS 34-712-3924
## Woodpecker Timber Ltd
Hunt House Sawmills, Clowstop, Kidderminster, Worcestershire DY14 9HY
**Tel:** 01299832611
**Web:** www.mmtimber.co.uk
**Reg No:** 5516334 **Estd:** 2005 Private Limited Company
**Line of Business:** Manufacturers and suppliers of coat hangers
**Issued Capital:** £4
**Co. Secretary:** Nigel Poyner
**US SIC:** 2499 **UK SIC:** 46500

| | 31-07-13 | 31-07-12 | 31-07-11 |
|---|---|---|---|
| TA | 4 | 4 | 4 |
| NW | 4 | 4 | 4 |

DUNS 29-768-4953
## Woods Bagot Europe Ltd
**(Subsidiary of:** Woods Bagot Holdings Pty. Ltd.)
46-48 Foley Street, London W1W 7TY
**Web:** www.woodsbagot.com
**Reg No:** 2031503 **Estd:** 1986 Private Limited Company
**Line of Business:** Architects
**Export Sales:** £3,306,262
**Issued Capital:** £10,000
**Directors:** J French, J J Clarke, N Karalis
**Co. Secretary:**
Barlow Robbins Secretariat Limit
**Responsibilities**
**Senior:** Earle Arney *(Manager)*, S Reimke *(Manager)*, Rob Steul *(Manager)*
**Finance:** Girish Shah *(Finance Director)*
**IT:** Jonathan McGrath *(IT Manager)*
**HR:** Mimie Sama *(HR Manager)*
**US SIC:** 8911 **UK SIC:** 83701
**Auditors:** Moulton Johnson
**Bankers:** HSBC Bank plc (40-08-43)

| | 30-06-14 | 30-06-13 | 30-06-12 |
|---|---|---|---|
| TO | 5,595,809 | 6,861,929 | 8,449,530 |
| P/L | (552,347) | 665,188 | (521,790) |
| NW | (810,117) | (361,069) | (843,462) |
| WC | 174,392 | 2,175,872 | 1,810,577 |
| Emp. | 52 | 50 | 71 |

DUNS 77-442-1101
## Woods Building Services Ltd
Woods House, Harlow, Essex CM20 2DP
**Tel:** 08445760278 **Fax:** 01279-444-632
**Web:** www.aawoods.co.uk
**Reg No:** 2951763 **Estd:** 2012 Private Limited Company
**Line of Business:** Asbestos products & removal
**Trading Style:** Aa Woods Asbestos Abatement
**Issued Capital:** £1,000
**Directors:** D Petri, D J Pienaar
**Co. Secretary:** Mrs Tara Petri
**Responsibilities**
**Senior:** Ralph Waghorn *(Contracts Manager)*
**Branches:** Woods Building Services Ltd, Kings Road Industrial Estate, Kings Road, Tyseley, Birmingham, West Midlands B11 2AX
**US SIC:** 1799, 4959
**UK SIC:** 50000, 92110
**Auditors:** Maynard Heady LLP

| | 31-12-13 | 31-03-13 | 31-12-11 |
|---|---|---|---|
| TO | 7,391,967 | 13,790,686 | 7,130,904 |
| P/L | 380,671 | (402,795) | 3,266 |
| NW | 660,423 | 329,804 | 732,501 |
| WC | 265,478 | (74,795) | 386,859 |
| Emp. | 120 | N/A | N/A |

DUNS 21-927-4560
## Woods Coaches Ltd
223 Gloucester Crescent, Wigston, Leicestershire LE18 4YR
**Tel:** 01162-786374 **Fax:** 01162-477819
**Web:** www.woodscoaches.com
**Reg No:** 0968555 **VAT No:** 114591777
**Estd:** 1969 Private Limited Company
**Line of Business:** Other tourist assistance activities not elsewhere classified
**Issued Capital:** £10,000
**Directors:** R Stevens, A W Cotton
**Co. Secretary:** Ms Jacqueline Bates
**Responsibilities**
**Senior:** Ian Trigg *(Engineering Director)*
**Marketing:** Alison Wayman *(Marketing Manager)*
**Facilities:** Ian Trigg *(Engineering Director)*
**Engineering:** Ian Trigg *(Engineering Director)*
**US SIC:** 7999, 4142
**UK SIC:** 97913, 72102
**Auditors:** McGregors Corporate
**Bankers:** HSBC Bank plc (40-46-33)

| | 31-03-14 | 31-12-12 | 31-03-11 |
|---|---|---|---|
| TA | 1,638,853 | 1,345,081 | 1,240,618 |
| NW | 43,833 | 387,837 | 367,193 |
| WC | (501,792) | (101,123) | 62,518 |

DUNS 23-671-0765
## The Woods Group Ltd
**(Subsidiary of:** Woods Consolidated Ltd)
Bumpers Way, Bumpers Farm, Chippenham, Wiltshire SN14 6NG
**Tel:** 01249-653444
**Web:** www.woodsresponse.co.uk
**Reg No:** 3665861 **Estd:** 1993 Private Limited Company
**Line of Business:** National post activities
**Trading Style:** Woods the Printers
**Issued Capital:** £41,927
**Directors:** A Taylor, I P Scarr, N P Baker, J W Lowndes, B J Dix
**Co. Secretary:** Barry Dix
**Responsibilities**
**Senior:** Raymond Dias *(Manager)*, Rachael Shutter *(Manager)*, Roger Shutter *(Manager)*, Patricia Shutter *(Manager)*, Andrew Shutter *(Manager)*, Andy Wiltshire *(Manager)*
**Finance:** Laura Illsley *(Senior Accounts Manager)*
**Sales:** Kathryn Russell *(Account Manager)*
**IT:** Dave Sully *(IT Manager)*
**Operations:** Mike Beel *(Operations Manager)*
**Purchasing:** Gemma Ward *(Purchasing Manager)*
**US SIC:** 7399 **UK SIC:** 83954
**Auditors:** Baker Tilly UK Audit LLP

| | 31-03-14 | 31-03-13 | 31-03-12 |
|---|---|---|---|
| TO | 9,318,152 | 8,080,040 | 5,993,079 |
| P/L | 1,007,463 | 699,361 | 632,481 |
| NW | 4,438,594 | 3,476,877 | 2,939,055 |
| WC | 3,697,049 | 2,684,400 | 1,741,363 |
| Emp. | 69 | 65 | 66 |

DUNS 39-667-0283
## Woods Hardwick Ltd
**(Subsidiary of:** Woods Hardwick Group Ltd)
1517 Goldinfton Road, 20 Grove Place, Bedford, Bedfordshire MK40 3NH
**Tel:** 01234-268862 **Fax:** 01234-353034
**Web:** www.woodshardwick.com
**Reg No:** 2133642 **VAT No:** 479305421
**Estd:** 1987 Private Limited Company
**Line of Business:** Other engineering activities
**Export Sales:** £21,391
**Issued Capital:** £27,654
**Directors:** J G Freeman, T J Francis, M R Appleyard, C H Wilson, J A Leonard
**Co. Secretary:** Alan Brown
**Responsibilities**
**Senior:** Karl Myhill *(Manager)*, Gary Surkitt *(Manager)*
**US SIC:** 8911, 7392
**UK SIC:** 83701, 83951
**Auditors:** Macintyre Hudson
**Bankers:** National Westminster Bank Plc (60-02-13)

| | 30-09-13 | 30-09-12 | 30-09-11 |
|---|---|---|---|
| TO | 2,376,743 | 2,648,401 | 2,271,978 |
| P/L | 543,559 | 293,490 | 259,746 |
| NW | 4,429,959 | 3,995,885 | 4,062,990 |
| WC | 4,441,666 | 4,005,883 | 4,088,251 |

DUNS 28-932-4790
## Woods Reisen Ltd
211 Gloucester Crescent, Wigston, Leicestershire LE18 4YH
**Tel:** 01162786377 **Fax:** 01162477819
**Web:** www.woodscoaches.com
**Reg No:** 1535604 **Estd:** 1980 Private Limited Company
**Line of Business:** Other scheduled passenger land transport not elsewhere classified
**Trading Style:** Woods Coaches
**Issued Capital:** £1,000
**Directors:** A W Cotton, R Stevens
**Responsibilities**
**Senior:** Ian Trigg *(Manager)*
**US SIC:** 4119 **UK SIC:** 72200
**Auditors:** McGregors Corporate

| | 31-03-14 | 31-12-12 | 31-03-11 |
|---|---|---|---|
| TA | 419,623 | 251,538 | 315,390 |
| NW | 52,536 | 41,015 | 43,449 |
| WC | 52,536 | 41,015 | 43,449 |

DUNS 23-248-4647
## Woods Supermarkets Ltd
16-22 Main Street, Richhill, Armagh, Co Armagh BT61 9PW
**Tel:** 02838871210 **Fax:** 02838871030
**Web:** www.shop.supervalu.ie
**Reg No:** 0041119NI **Estd:** 2002 Private Limited Company
**Line of Business:** Retail sale in non-specialised stores (excluding ctns) not holding an alcohol licence with food, beverages or tobacco predominating
**Issued Capital:** £3
**Directors:** J R Woods, P J Woods, Ms M M Woods
**Co. Secretary:** Joseph Woods
**US SIC:** 5199 **UK SIC:** 61900

| | 31-07-13 | 31-07-12 | 31-07-11 |
|---|---|---|---|
| TA | 3,552,974 | 3,570,764 | 3,752,541 |
| P/L | N/A | N/A | 131,076 |
| NW | 664,938 | 536,566 | 464,687 |
| WC | (288,221) | (358,971) | (380,726) |
| Emp. | N/A | N/A | 3 |

DUNS 21-783-4781
## Woodside Care Home
Woodside Street, Coatbridge, Lanarkshire ML5 1EL
**Tel:** 01236442000
**Estd:** 2011 Proprietorship
**Line of Business:** Medical nursing home activities
**Proprietor:** Mrs M Mcmcrum
**Responsibilities**
**Senior:** Marie McMcrum *(Proprietor)*
**US SIC:** 8051 **UK SIC:** 95100
**Employees:** 80

DUNS 23-285-3473
## Woodside Farms Ltd
Woodside Farm Flats Lane Hocquarde, Lane Rue Coutanche, Trinity, Jersey, Channel Islands JE3 5DU
**Tel:** 01534-865969
**Reg No:** 0012820J **Estd:** 1977 Private Limited Company
**Line of Business:** Farming (mixed)
**Issued Capital:** £9
**Directors:** Ms E S Hathaway, C P Gallichan
**US SIC:** 0291 **UK SIC:** 01001
**Employees:** 100

DUNS 21-209-8375
## Woodside Hall
Polegate Road, Hailsham, East Sussex BN27 3PQ
**Tel:** 01323-841670
**Web:** www.woodsidehall-nh.co.uk
**Estd:** 1988 Proprietorship
**Line of Business:** Nursing homes
**Proprietor:** C Canganatra
**US SIC:** 8051 **UK SIC:** 95100
**Employees:** 59

DUNS 21-443-5331
## Woodside Haulage (G B) Ltd
**(Subsidiary of:** Woodside Haulage (Holdings) Ltd)
Unit 280 Carnfield Place, Walton Summit Industrial Estate, Bamber Bridge, Preston, Lancashire PR5 8AN
**Tel:** 01772-323381 **Fax:** 01772-627020
**Web:** www.woodsides.com
**Reg No:** 0042664SC **Estd:** 1922 Private Limited Company
**Line of Business:** Road haulage and transport services
**Issued Capital:** £31,000
**Director:** R G Woodside
**Co. Secretary:** Robert Woodside
**Responsibilities**
**Senior:** Chris McMahon *(General Manager)*
**HR:** Keith Ashcroft *(Training Officer)*
**Health & Safety:** Keith Ashcroft *(Training Officer)*
**Purchasing:** Chris McMahon *(General Manager)*
**Branches:** Woodside Haulage (G B) Ltd, Lauriston Rd, Grangemouth, Stirlingshire FK3 8EX
**US SIC:** 4789 **UK SIC:** 77002
**Auditors:** Crawford Sedgwick & Co
**Bankers:** The Royal Bank Of Scotland Plc (83-27-14)

| | 31-03-14 | 31-03-13 | 31-03-12 |
|---|---|---|---|
| TA | 697,125 | 697,125 | 697,125 |
| NW | 697,125 | 697,125 | 697,125 |

DUNS 22-929-5324 **Exp**
## Woodside Haulage (Holdings) Ltd
61 Carrickfergus Road, Ballynure, Ballyclare, Co Antrim BT39 9QJ
**Tel:** 028-9335-2255
**Web:** www.woodsides.com
**Reg No:** 0013212NI **Estd:** 1978 Private Limited Company
**Line of Business:** Freight transport by road not elsewhere classified
**Export Markets:** other EC countries
**Export Sales:** £1,910,260
**Issued Capital:** £299,998
**Directors:** R J Woodside, Ms M Woodside
**Co. Secretary:** Robert Woodside
**Responsibilities**
**Senior:** John Woodside *(Manager)*
**US SIC:** 4213 **UK SIC:** 72300
**Auditors:** Crawford Sedgwick & Co
**Bankers:** Ulster Bank Ltd (98-02-80)

| | 31-03-14 | 31-03-13 | 31-03-12 |
|---|---|---|---|
| TO | 51,361,634 | 46,869,919 | 43,116,895 |
| P/L | 999,565 | 958,949 | 882,795 |
| NW | 16,908,262 | 16,346,082 | 15,716,340 |
| WC | 1,811,284 | 2,236,139 | 2,157,160 |
| Emp. | 405 | 364 | 360 |

DUNS 21-753-0804
## Woodside High School
White Hart Lane, London N22 5QJ
**Tel:** 02088896761
**Web:** www.woodsidehighschool.co.uk
**Reg No:** 7831292 **Estd:** 2011 Private Company Limited By Guarantee
**Line of Business:** Schools (local authority)
**Directors:** Dr P J Graham, Ms S M Davidson, Mrs C A Humm, D E Palmer, J S Adekunle, R H Stripe, G A Kelly, J D Blake
**Responsibilities**
**Senior:** Samuel Freedman *(Director)*, Noreen Graham *(Director)*, Margaret Mccartan *(Director)*, Miranda Smith *(Director)*
**IT:** Colin Keywood *(IT Manager)*
**US SIC:** 8211 **UK SIC:** 93200
**Bankers:** National Westminster Bank Plc (60-07-38)

| | 31-08-14 | 31-08-13 | 31-08-12 |
|---|---|---|---|
| TO | 7,671,329 | 7,805,285 | 27,891,722 |
| P/L | 7,262 | 145,983 | 21,581,857 |
| NW | 21,208,102 | 21,701,840 | 21,469,857 |
| WC | 1,386,030 | 929,008 | 387,910 |
| Emp. | 147 | 146 | 144 |

DUNS 64-256-0882
## Woodside Priamary School
Clifton Road, Aberdeen, Aberdeenshire AB24 4EA
**Tel:** 01224-484778
**Web:** www.aberdeen-education.org.uk
**Estd:** 1904
**Line of Business:** Schools (local authority)
**Director:** Mrs C Johnstone
**US SIC:** 8211 **UK SIC:** 93200
**Employees:** 57

DUNS 73-722-4811
## Woodside Saltash Ltd
**(Subsidiary of:** Manuplas Offshore Ltd)
18 Estover Road, Plymouth, Devon PL6 7PY
**Tel:** 01752-771740 **Fax:** 01752-769696
**Web:** www.manuplas.co.uk
**Reg No:** 4980832 **Estd:** 2003 Private Limited Company
**Line of Business:** Manufacture of other plastic products
**Issued Capital:** £1,000
**Director:** A P Wickham
**Co. Secretary:** Ms Claire Mollet
**Responsibilities**
**Senior:** David Hamnett *(Manager)*, Charles Willday *(Manager)*
**US SIC:** 3079, 1611
**UK SIC:** 48360, 50200
**Auditors:** Paul Webster & Associates
**Bankers:** HSBC Bank plc (40-40-15)

| | 31-03-14 | 31-12-12 | 31-03-11 |
|---|---|---|---|
| TA | 1,000,000 | 3,210,338 | 2,076,874 |
| NW | 1,000,000 | 1,399,193 | 1,149,360 |
| WC | N/A | 681,783 | 750,747 |

DUNS 21-099-6197
## Woodspeen Training Group Plc
44 Southampton Buildings, London WC2A 1AP
**Tel:** 01274721391
**Web:** www.woodspeentraining.co.uk
**Reg No:** 6434555 **Estd:** 2007 Public Limited Company
**Line of Business:** Management activities of holding companies
**Issued Capital:** £3,578,620
**Directors:** C C Prior, C G Hellyer
**Co. Secretary:** Ms Lynn Chandler
**US SIC:** 6711 **UK SIC:** 83962
**Auditors:** BDO LLP

| | 31-07-13 | 31-07-12 | 31-07-11 |
|---|---|---|---|
| TO | 4,013,333 | 6,547,870 | 5,711,583 |
| P/L | (428,023) | (1,415,570) | (1,263,889) |
| NW | 2,693,243 | 2,990,631 | 3,543,411 |
| WC | 2,473,737 | 2,845,262 | 3,463,434 |
| Emp. | 127 | 177 | 153 |

DUNS 57-001-4324 **Imp-Exp**
## Woodstock Leabank Office Furniture Ltd
**(Subsidiary of:** Marplace (Number 633) Ltd)
Corrie Way, Bredbury Park Industrial Estate, Bredbury, Stockport, Cheshire SK6 2ST
**Tel:** 01614945868
**Web:** www.woodstockleabank.co.uk
**Reg No:** 2861506 **VAT No:** 616402175
**Estd:** 1995 Private Limited Company
**Line of Business:** Wholesale of furniture
**Issued Capital:** £300
**Principals:** J Omalley *(Managing)*, P D Atherton, T Ingham
**Co. Secretary:** Ms Louise Ryalls
**Responsibilities**
**Senior:** Joseph O'Malley *(Managing Director)*
**Branches:** Woodstock Leabank Office Furniture Ltd, Greenway Centre Doncaster Road, Bristol, Avon BS10 5PY
**US SIC:** 5021 **UK SIC:** 61500
**Auditors:** CLB Coopers
**Bankers:** The Co-Operative Bank Plc (08-90-00)

| | 30-06-14 | 30-06-13 | 30-06-12 |
|---|---|---|---|
| TO | 8,316,424 | 8,310,932 | 6,780,147 |
| P/L | 58,009 | 17,684 | 122,263 |
| NW | 1,171,640 | 548,150 | 1,030,972 |
| WC | 170,450 | (474,476) | (239,692) |
| Emp. | 60 | 64 | 55 |

DUNS 21-213-1879
## Woodstock Nursing Home
35 North Upton Lane, Barnwood, Barnwood, Gloucester, Gloucestershire GL4 3TD
**Web:** www.woodstocknursinghome.co.uk
**Estd:** 1985 Partnership
**Line of Business:** Nursing homes
**Partners:** J W Barnes, Mrs M R Barnes
**Responsibilities**
**Senior:** Millie Barns *(Proprietor)*
**US SIC:** 8051 **UK SIC:** 95100
**Employees:** 47

DUNS 73-269-0479
## Woodstock Products Ltd
Woodstock Buildings, 9c Windermere Road, London N19 5SG
**Tel:** 02072814866
**Web:** www.woodstockproductsinc.com
**Reg No:** 4542812 **Estd:** 2002 Private Limited Company
**Line of Business:** Manufacture of builders carpentry and joinery
**Issued Capital:** £100
**Director:** J Mcwalter
**Co. Secretary:** James Mcwalter
**US SIC:** 2431 **UK SIC:** 46300

| | 30-09-14 | 30-09-13 | 30-09-12 |
|---|---|---|---|
| TA | 56,368 | 32,045 | 39,554 |
| NW | 51,519 | 30,897 | 31,877 |
| WC | 47,230 | 25,485 | 23,002 |

DUNS 42-362-1924 **Imp**
## Woodthorpe Hall Garden Centres Ltd
Woodthorpe, Alford, Lincolnshire LN13 0DD
**Tel:** 01507450509
**Web:** www.britishgardencentres.com
**Reg No:** 4349805 **VAT No:** 809086124
**Estd:** 1986 Private Limited Company
**Line of Business:** Other retail sale in specialised stores not elsewhere classified
**Trading Style:** Brigg Garden Centre
**Issued Capital:** £1,000
**Directors:** C E Stubbs, R J Stubbs
**Co. Secretary:** Mrs Phillippa Stubbs
**Responsibilities**
**Senior:** Diane Rudkin *(Manager)*, Tasha Virgo *(Manager)*
**Branches:** Woodthorpe Hall Garden Centres Ltd, Woodthorpe Hall, Alford, Lincolnshire LN13 0DD
**US SIC:** 5999 **UK SIC:** 65600
**Auditors:** H.W. Skegness
**Bankers:** HSBC Bank plc (40-30-26)

| | 31-12-13 | 31-12-12 | 31-12-11 |
|---|---|---|---|
| TO | 20,706,684 | 17,622,189 | 17,056,473 |
| P/L | 1,310,442 | 1,170,743 | 1,163,087 |
| NW | 7,177,657 | 6,267,096 | 5,340,799 |
| WC | 2,487,059 | 1,869,723 | 1,141,094 |
| Emp. | 432 | 381 | 343 |

DUNS 23-310-8534
## Woodvale Construction Company
59 Crevenagh Road, Omagh, Co Tyrone BT79 0EX
**Tel:** 028-8224-2867
**Estd:** 1980 Partnership
**Line of Business:** Builders
**Trading Style:** Woodvale Construction Company
**Partners:** W D Scott, Mrs I Ewing
**US SIC:** 1522, 1541, 1622
**UK SIC:** 50100, 50200
**Employees:** 50

DUNS 42-417-8635
## Woodward & Falconer Pubs Co. Ltd
The Goshawk, Station Road, Mouldsworth, Chester, Cheshire CH3 8AJ
**Tel:** 01928-740977
**Web:** www.woodwardandfalconer.com
**Reg No:** 4405591 **Estd:** 2002 Private Limited Company
**Line of Business:** Representative office
**Issued Capital:** £100
**Directors:** J A Woodward, D C Falconer
**Co. Secretary:** Adrian Evans
**Branches:** Woodward & Falconer Pubs Co. Ltd, The Goshawk, Station Road, Chester, Cheshire CH3 8AJ
**US SIC:** 7399, 5813
**UK SIC:** 83954, 66200
**Bankers:** Girobank Plc (72-00-00)

| | 31-03-14 | 31-03-13 | 31-03-12 |
|---|---|---|---|
| TO | 6,058,325 | 5,876,602 | 5,854,765 |
| P/L | (126,567) | 118,803 | 134,491 |
| NW | 328,838 | 424,078 | 304,329 |
| WC | (731,670) | (475,173) | (504,894) |
| Emp. | 154 | 162 | 163 |

DUNS 23-196-2072 **Imp**
## Woodward International Inc
**(Subsidiary of:** Woodward Inc.)
5 Shawfarm Road, Prestwick, Ayrshire KA9 2TR
**Tel:** 01292677600 **Fax:** 01292-474231
**Web:** www.woodward.com
**Reg No:** 0000753SF **Estd:** 1997 Foreign Company
**Line of Business:** Manufacture of aircraft and spacecraft
**Trading Style:** Woodward Aircraft Controls Prestwick Inc
**Director:** S A Patel
**Responsibilities**
**Finance:** Frank Edwards *(Financial Controller)*
**IT:** Neale Lawson *(Computer Manager)*
**Health & Safety:** Sandy Simpson *(Quality Manager)*
**Purchasing:** Gordon Home *(Purchasing Manager)*
**US SIC:** 3721 **UK SIC:** 36400

DUNS 23-719-0053
## Woodwin (Catering) Ltd
**(Subsidiary of:** Treetops Holding Company)
18 Diviny Drive, Craigavon, Co Armagh BT63 5WE
**Tel:** 028-3835-1530
**Web:** www.hungryhousefoods.com
**Reg No:** 0016978NI **Estd:** 1981 Private Limited Company
**Line of Business:** Secretarial and translation activities
**Trading Style:** Hungry House Sandwiches
**Issued Capital:** £150,000
**Director:** Ms D G Irwin
**Co. Secretary:** Harold Irwin
**US SIC:** 7399 **UK SIC:** 83954
**Auditors:** Barry Thompson & Co

| | 30-09-13 | 30-09-12 | 30-09-11 |
|---|---|---|---|
| TA | 1,111,577 | 1,394,927 | 1,515,277 |
| NW | 230,000 | 334,300 | 312,248 |
| WC | (415,115) | (285,502) | (369,443) |

DUNS 73-529-0764
## Wookey Hole Ltd
One New Street, Wells, Somerset BA5 2LA
**Tel:** 01749672243
**Web:** www.wookey.co.uk
**Reg No:** 4791696 **Estd:** 2003 Private Limited Company
**Line of Business:** Combat game operators
**Issued Capital:** £2,250,000
**Director:** D J Medley
**US SIC:** 7999 **UK SIC:** 97913
**Bankers:** Barclays Bank Plc (20-90-56)

| | 28-02-14 | 28-02-13 | 29-02-12 |
|---|---|---|---|
| TO | 3,581,523 | 3,691,079 | 3,532,305 |
| P/L | 263,442 | 252,314 | 299,324 |
| NW | 2,195,766 | 2,075,750 | 1,969,187 |
| WC | (1,283,847) | (1,242,872) | (1,069,852) |
| Emp. | 85 | 90 | 86 |

DUNS 21-636-2905
## Wool & Bovington Motors Ltd
Station Garage, Wareham Road, Wool, Wareham, Dorset BH20 6HQ
**Tel:** 01929462263
**Web:** www.wool-bovington.co.uk
**Reg No:** 0675228 **Estd:** 1920 Private Limited Company
**Line of Business:** Car and commercial vehicle repairs
**Trading Style:** Rapid Fit
**Issued Capital:** £2,000
**Directors:** T C Pyne, S F Pyne
**Co. Secretary:** Nicholas Pyne
**Responsibilities**
**Senior:** Richard Custard *(Parts Manager)*, Bob Flint *(General Manager)*, John Marchant *(Manager)*

**Finance:** Jeremy Pretty (*Financial Controller*)
**US SIC:** 7539, 5531, 5521
**UK SIC:** 67100, 65100
**Auditors:** Trevor Jones & Co
**Bankers:** National Westminster Bank Plc (56-00-35)

| | 31-05-13 | 31-05-12 | 31-05-11 |
|---|---|---|---|
| TO | 11,637,988 | 10,816,820 | 10,866,486 |
| P/L | (33,342) | (139,258) | 61,026 |
| NW | 1,475,340 | 1,505,296 | 1,629,037 |
| WC | (246,637) | (210,342) | (111,389) |
| Emp. | 63 | 58 | 61 |

DUNS 33-984-2668
## Woolacombe Bay Holiday Park
Sandy Lane, Ilfracombe, Devon EX34 7AH
**Tel:** 01271-870343
**Web:** www.woolacombe.co.uk
**Estd:** 1960 Partnership
**Line of Business:** Holiday parks and camps
**Partners:** R Lancaster, R Lancaster
**Responsibilities**
**Senior:** Aidan Glover (*General Manager*)
**Finance:** Helen Larcomb (*Administration Manager*)
**Admin:** Helen Larcomb (*Administration Manager*)
**HR:** Helen Larcomb (*Administration Manager*)
**Facilities:** Aidan Glover (*General Manager*)
**Purchasing:** Aidan Glover (*General Manager*)
**US SIC:** 7021 **UK SIC:** 66500
**Employees:** 100

DUNS 21-623-2876
## Wooldot Ltd
Coatham Avenue, Aycliffe Industrial Estate, Newton Aycliffe, County Durham DL5 6DB
**Tel:** 01325-300777
**Reg No:** 0746083 **Estd:** 1963 Private Limited Company
**Line of Business:** Car Components Manufacturing
**Issued Capital:** £67,056
**Principals:** M D Rimington, C Jewett, G M Marshall
**Co. Secretary:** Mark Blanshard
**US SIC:** 3714 **UK SIC:** 35300
**Bankers:** Barclays Bank Plc (20-25-29)
**Employees:** 100

DUNS 64-745-9932
## The Woolgate Shopping Centre
Market Square, Witney, Oxfordshire OX28 6AP
**Tel:** 01993-778370
**Web:** www.woolgateshoppingcentre.co.uk
**Estd:** 2010 Proprietorship
**Line of Business:** Shopping centres
**Proprietor:** R Hartnell
**US SIC:** 5399 **UK SIC:** 65600
**Employees:** 300

DUNS 21-587-9768    Imp-Exp
## Woollard & Henry Ltd
(**Subsidiary of:** Woollard & Henry Holdings Ltd)
Stoneywood Park, Stoneywood Road, Dyce, Aberdeen, Aberdeenshire AB21 7DZ
**Web:** www.woollardandhenry.com
**Reg No:** 0036131SC **VAT No:** 266547430
**Estd:** 1873 Private Limited Company
**Line of Business:** Engineers (general)
**Export Markets:** Worldwide
**Trading Style:** Woollard & Henry Ltd
**Issued Capital:** £8,400
**Directors:** P Mcdougall, S P Daniels, E A Gillespie
**Co. Secretary:** Frederick Bowden
**Responsibilities**
**Senior:** Craig Watson (*Employee Director*)
**US SIC:** 8911 **UK SIC:** 83701
**Auditors:** Isaac McCutcheon
**Bankers:** Clydesdale Bank Plc (82-69-23)

| | 31-03-14 | 31-03-13 | 31-03-12 |
|---|---|---|---|
| TA | 5,448,559 | 5,912,715 | 5,217,949 |
| NW | 3,900,573 | 3,835,560 | 3,312,376 |
| WC | 3,241,953 | 3,173,149 | 2,733,656 |

DUNS 33-983-9110    Exp
## Woollen Spinners
Wellington Mills, 70 Plover Road, Huddersfield, West Yorkshire HD3 3HR
**Web:** www.woollenspinners.com
**Estd:** 2010 Proprietorship
**Line of Business:** Wholesale suppliers of yarn
**Proprietor:** R Wood
**US SIC:** 2299 **UK SIC:** 43992
**Employees:** 50

DUNS 21-324-9816    Exp
## Woolley Bros. (Wholesale Meats) Ltd
Rother Valley Way, Holbrook, Sheffield, South Yorkshire S20 3RW
**Tel:** 01142470814
**Web:** www.woolleybrothers.co.uk
**Reg No:** 1416010 **VAT No:** 308243283
**Estd:** 1979 Private Limited Company
**Line of Business:** Abattoirs
**Export Markets:** E U
**Export Sales:** £9,551,535
**Issued Capital:** £6,000
**Director:** P J Woolley
**Co. Secretary:** Steven Woolley
**US SIC:** 2013, 5147
**UK SIC:** 41223, 61700
**Auditors:** Philip Barnes & Co Ltd
**Bankers:** Barclays Bank Plc (20-55-62)

| | 31-12-13 | 31-12-12 | 31-12-11 |
|---|---|---|---|
| TO | 45,275,079 | 45,805,715 | 46,993,821 |
| P/L | 1,230,851 | 250,708 | 1,386,663 |
| NW | 6,249,918 | 5,775,187 | 5,709,970 |
| WC | 3,666,076 | 3,079,753 | 3,025,738 |
| Emp. | 88 | 80 | 71 |

DUNS 22-767-3183    Exp
## Woolley Gmc Engineering Co Ltd
(**Subsidiary of:** R A Shield Holdings Ltd)
Torrington Avenue, Coventry, West Midlands CV4 9AP
**Tel:** 02476-362371
**Web:** www.woolley-gmc.co.uk
**Reg No:** 1352834 **VAT No:** 307147282
**Estd:** 1978 Private Limited Company
**Line of Business:** Engineers (general)
**Export Markets:** France; U S A
**Issued Capital:** £125
**Directors:** B J O'Connor, C R Shield, J Cooper
**Co. Secretary:** Christopher Shield
**Responsibilities**
**Senior:** Malcolm Morley (*Manager*)
**Sales:** Clifford Holmes (*Sales Director*)
**Branches:** Woolley Gmc Engineering Co Ltd, South Site, Torrington Avenue, Coventry, West Midlands CV4 9AQ
**US SIC:** 8911 **UK SIC:** 83701
**Auditors:** Thomas May & Co
**Bankers:** Lloyds TSB Bank plc (30-92-33)

| | 31-10-13 | 31-10-12 | 31-10-11 |
|---|---|---|---|
| TO | 21,270,861 | 21,336,645 | 17,832,635 |
| P/L | 474,136 | 482,344 | 1,066,473 |
| NW | 4,256,115 | 3,831,169 | 3,460,039 |
| WC | 295,030 | 273,151 | 1,111,110 |
| Emp. | 106 | 119 | 97 |

DUNS 53-640-1490
## Woolovers Ltd
Wool Overs House, Victoria Gardens, Burgess Hill, West Sussex RH15 9NB
**Tel:** 01444 870970
**Web:** www.woolovers.co.uk
**Reg No:** 3445676 **Estd:** 1997 Private Limited Company
**Line of Business:** Retail sale via mail order house
**Issued Capital:** £2
**Managing Director:** M Shenton
**Co. Secretary:** Mrs Clare Shenton
**US SIC:** 5961 **UK SIC:** 65600
**Auditors:** Antrams
**Bankers:** Lloyds TSB Bank plc (30-91-44)

| | 31-03-14 | 31-03-13 | 31-03-12 |
|---|---|---|---|
| TO | 20,116,388 | 15,217,953 | 10,809,821 |
| P/L | 3,493,205 | 1,839,204 | 1,121,670 |
| NW | 7,494,616 | 5,060,770 | 3,766,665 |
| WC | 6,074,730 | 3,377,920 | 1,780,287 |
| Emp. | 86 | 58 | 45 |

DUNS 21-777-2101
## Woolpack Beefeater
Maidstone Road A20, Hothfield, Ashford, Kent TN26 1AP
**Tel:** 01233713000
**Estd:** 1982 Proprietorship
**Line of Business:** Managed public houses and bars
**Proprietor:** J Holden
**US SIC:** 5813 **UK SIC:** 66200
**Employees:** 100

DUNS 21-764-9192
## Woolpit Health Centre
Heath Road, Woolpit, Bury St Edmunds, Suffolk IP30 9QU
**Tel:** 01359240298
**Web:** www.numarkpharmacists.com
**Estd:** 2011
**Line of Business:** Doctors
**Responsibilities**
**Senior:** Sallie Crouch (*Practice Manager*)
**US SIC:** 8011 **UK SIC:** 95300
**Employees:** 70

DUNS 22-638-4972
## Woolsey Morris & Kennedy
100 Station Road, Sidcup, Kent DA15 7DT
**Web:** www.wmk-law.com
**Partnership**
**Line of Business:** Solicitors
**Partner:** I Hollinsworth
**Responsibilities**
**Senior:** Isabel Elliott (*Partner*), Charlotte Parry-Jones (*Partner*)
**Admin:** Lynn Clements (*Personal Assistant*), Stephanie Partridge (*Personal Assistant*)
**IT:** Ian Motton (*IT Manager*)
**HR:** Ian Motton (*IT Manager*)
**US SIC:** 8111 **UK SIC:** 83500
**Employees:** 50

DUNS 22-045-3752    Imp
## Wooltex U.K. Ltd
Woodland Mill, Dale Street, Longwood, Huddersfield, West Yorkshire HD3 4TG
**Web:** www.wooltexuk.com
**Reg No:** 4047701 **VAT No:** 755730516
**Estd:** 1997 Private Limited Company
**Line of Business:** Manufacture of other textiles not elsewhere classified
**Issued Capital:** £5,000
**Principals:** P Timmins (*Managing*), Kvadrat A/S
**Co. Secretary:** Ms Paula Timmins
**US SIC:** 2299 **UK SIC:** 43992
**Auditors:** Wheawill & Sadworth
**Bankers:** HSBC Bank plc (40-22-28)

| | 31-12-13 | 31-12-12 | 31-12-11 |
|---|---|---|---|
| TO | 16,467,873 | 13,765,823 | 7,800,171 |
| P/L | 2,265,871 | 1,673,786 | 493,913 |
| NW | 2,252,768 | 2,014,196 | 742,590 |
| WC | 1,327,738 | 1,429,947 | 339,560 |
| Emp. | 61 | 58 | 53 |

DUNS 21-210-9057
## Woolton Manor Nursing Home
High Street, Woolton, Liverpool, Merseyside L25 7TB
**Tel:** 0151-421-0801
**Estd:** 1996 Proprietorship
**Line of Business:** Residential care establishments
**Proprietor:** M Chowdry
**Responsibilities**
**Senior:** Yousef Chacodry (*Proprietor*), Ian Smallwood (*Manager*)
**US SIC:** 8321 **UK SIC:** 96111
**Employees:** 80

DUNS 21-411-8615
## Woolworths Group Pension Scheme
3rd Floor City Exchange, 11 Albion Street, Leeds, West Yorkshire LS1 5ES
**Tel:** 01132617101
**Web:** www.capita.co.uk
**Estd:** 2001 Proprietorship
**Line of Business:** Pension companies
**Proprietor:** Miss A Cox
**US SIC:** 6371 **UK SIC:** 82002
**Employees:** 100

DUNS 21-740-9872
## Wootton Academy Trust
Hall End, Wootton, Bedford, Bedfordshire MK43 9HT
**Tel:** 01234767123
**Web:** www.homepage.wootton.beds.sch.uk
**Reg No:** 7740758 **Estd:** 2011 Private Company Limited By Guarantee
**Line of Business:** General secondary education
**Directors:** M G Gleeson, A S Metcalf, Professor T Stephenson, R E Shribbs, Mrs A Mathers, Dr S K Peace, D Clare, Ms H Donnellan
**Co. Secretary:** Mrs Ann Mathers
**Responsibilities**
**Senior:** Jonathan Billington (*Director*), Caroline Godfrey (*Director*), Simon O'Toole (*Director*)
**US SIC:** 8211 **UK SIC:** 93200
**Bankers:** Lloyds TSB Bank plc (30-00-00)

| | 31-08-14 | 31-08-13 | 31-08-12 |
|---|---|---|---|
| TO | 24,030,000 | 7,424,000 | 25,325,000 |
| P/L | 16,037,000 | 316,000 | 19,095,000 |
| NW | 35,040,000 | 19,208,000 | 18,877,000 |
| WC | 2,074,000 | 1,166,000 | 686,000 |
| Emp. | 138 | 144 | 210 |

DUNS 23-998-1772
## Worcester & District Health Authority
Shrub Hill Road, Worcester, Worcestershire WR4 9GX
**Web:** www.worcsmhp.nhs.uk
**Line of Business:** Healthcare companies
**Trading Style:** Evesham Community Healthcare, Devenal House Surgery, Thornloe Lodge Surgery

**Principals:** A J Prescott (*Chairman*), J C Waits (*Managing*), K J Gittans (*Financial*), J C Walls, Dr B Mccloskey
**Responsibilities**
**Senior:** Ros Keeton (*Chief Executive*), B McCloskey (*Principal*)
**HR:** Alison Wilmott-Miller (*Human Resources Director*)
**Facilities:** Irving Steeper (*Facilities Manager*)
**Branches:** Worcester & District Health Authority, 172 Worcester Rd, Malvern, Worcestershire WR14 1AA
**US SIC:** 8091, 9121
**UK SIC:** 95200, 91110
**Employees:** 100

DUNS 21-835-6988
## Worcester Carsales Ltd
(**Subsidiary of:** Worcester Carsales (Holdings) Ltd)
C/O T Wall Garages, High Street, Pensnett, Brierley Hill, West Midlands DY6 8XB
**Tel:** 01384672910
**Web:** www.crysler.co.uk
**Reg No:** 0595935 **VAT No:** 274736726
**Estd:** 1954 Private Limited Company
**Line of Business:** Car dealers (new & used)
**Trading Style:** City & County
**Issued Capital:** £1,314,980
**Director:** Mrs F E Grieveson
**Co. Secretary:** Stuart Grieveson
**Branches:** Worcester Carsales Ltd, Trindle Road, Dudley, West Midlands DY2 7AZ
**US SIC:** 5511, 5521, 5531
**UK SIC:** 65100
**Auditors:** Ballard Dale Syree Watson LLP
**Bankers:** Lloyds TSB Bank plc (30-99-90)

| | 31-12-13 | 31-12-12 | 31-12-11 |
|---|---|---|---|
| TO | 71,764,166 | 62,399,089 | 59,105,836 |
| P/L | 1,718,115 | 1,146,149 | 625,806 |
| NW | 5,780,041 | 4,862,420 | 4,376,222 |
| WC | 6,856,639 | 6,225,710 | 5,962,072 |
| Emp. | 243 | 235 | 236 |

DUNS 28-893-2478
## Worcester Cathedral Enterprises Ltd
Chapter Office, 8 College Yard, Worcester, Worcestershire WR1 2LA
**Tel:** 01905732900
**Web:** www.worcestercathedral.co.uk
**Reg No:** 1298811 **Estd:** 1977 Private Limited Company
**Line of Business:** Places of worship
**Issued Capital:** £4
**Directors:** P J Seward, S D White, Mrs C A Blackwell, G A Harris, The Very Reverend P G Atkinson
**Co. Secretary:** Leslie West
**US SIC:** 8661, 5812
**UK SIC:** 96600, 66110
**Auditors:** Rabjohns

| | 31-03-14 | 31-03-13 | 31-03-12 |
|---|---|---|---|
| TA | 64,815 | 69,875 | 80,633 |
| NW | 27,800 | 11,609 | 11,609 |
| WC | 27,800 | 11,609 | 11,609 |

DUNS 21-154-3978
## Worcester Citizens Advice Bureau & Whabac
The Hopmarket, Worcester, Worcestershire WR1 1DL
**Tel:** 0844111303
**Web:** www.cabwhabac.org.uk
**Reg No:** 6827297 **Estd:** 2009 Private Company Limited By Guarantee
**Line of Business:** Social work activities without accommodation
**Directors:** Ms H J Fenton, G V Hughes, M E Jenkins, P Y Griffith, B Griffiths, Ms A Mobberley, Dr J D Williams, D A Tibbutt
**Co. Secretary:** Martyn Saunders
**Responsibilities**
**Senior:** Simon Lister (*Director*), Iain Pugh (*Director*)
**US SIC:** 8321 **UK SIC:** 96111
**Auditors:** Richards Sandy Partnership
**Bankers:** Unity Trust Bank Plc (08-60-01)

| | 31-03-14 | 31-03-13 | 31-03-12 |
|---|---|---|---|
| TO | 1,367,923 | 1,486,002 | 1,332,759 |
| P/L | 47,564 | 98,500 | 37,893 |
| NW | 1,193,886 | 1,146,322 | 1,047,822 |
| WC | 788,083 | 743,900 | 642,722 |
| Emp. | 45 | 50 | 53 |

DUNS 23-673-6760
## Worcester College Enterprises Ltd
Walton Street, Oxford, Oxfordshire OX1 2HB
**Web:** www.worc.ox.ac.uk
**Reg No:** 3668358 **Estd:** 1998 Private Limited Company
**Line of Business:** Other business activities not elsewhere classified
**Issued Capital:** £2
**Directors:** J A Forrest, Professor A J Bate, Doctor J M Crawley Quinn
**Co. Secretary:** Mrs Caroline Fabes

**US SIC:** 7399 **UK SIC:** 83954

| | 31-07-14 | 31-07-13 | 30-07-12 |
|---|---|---|---|
| TO | 262,148 | N/A | N/A |
| NW | 2 | 2 | 2 |
| WC | 2 | N/A | N/A |

DUNS 22-983-5582

## Worcester College of Technology

Deansway, Worcester, Worcestershire WR1 2JF
**Tel:** 01905725555
**Web:** www.worcester.ac.uk
**Estd:** 2012
**Line of Business:** Nursery schools
**Trading Style:** Worcester College of Technology
**Principals:** H Spence *(Financial)*, J Henderson, A Hardwicke
**Responsibilities**
**Senior:** Emma Lockwood *(Manager)*, Stewart Loverick *(Principal)*
**Marketing:** Rachel Gowers *(Marketing Manager)*
**HR:** Berni Long *(Head of Learning & Development)*
**Health & Safety:** Angie Moss *(Health & Safety Officer)*
**Facilities:** Alex Taylor *(Facilities Manager)*
**Purchasing:** Adam Connolly *(Purchasing Manager)*
**Branches:** Worcester College Of Technology, School Of Art & Design, Barbourne Road, Worcester, Worcestershire WR1 1RT
**US SIC:** 8221 **UK SIC:** 93100
**Employees:** 16

DUNS 64-118-2519

## Worcester Community Housing Ltd

Progress House, Central Park, Worcester, Worcestershire WR5 1DU
**Tel:** 01905670100 **Fax:** 01905670101
**Web:** www.wchnet.co.uk
**Reg No:** 4521505 **Estd:** 2002 Private Limited Company
**Line of Business:** Other letting of own property
**Directors:** G P Williams, M G Davies, S Williams, M G Moyles, D A Thompson, A J Milner, C B Almgill, F J Bentley
**Co. Secretary:** Andy Howarth
**Responsibilities**
**Senior:** Cathy Jackson *(Director)*, Stewart Mountfield *(Chief Executive)*
**Branches:** Worcester Community Housing Ltd, 35 Wells Road, Worcester, Worcestershire WR5 1NN
**US SIC:** 6519 **UK SIC:** 85000
**Bankers:** Barclays Bank Plc (20-98-61)

| | 31-03-14 | 31-03-13 | 31-03-12 |
|---|---|---|---|
| TO | 24,418,000 | 23,056,000 | 19,841,000 |
| P/L | 6,196,000 | 4,876,000 | 3,216,000 |
| NW | 138,663,000 | 28,522,000 | 24,888,000 |
| WC | 11,000 | 735,000 | 439,000 |
| Emp. | 178 | 195 | 190 |

DUNS 28-832-2589

## The Worcester Diocesan Board of Finance Ltd

The Old Palace, Deansway, Worcester, Worcestershire WR1 2JE
**Tel:** 0190520537 **Fax:** 01905-612302
**Web:** www.cofe-worcester.org.uk
**Reg No:** 0271752 **Estd:** 1932 Private Limited Company
**Line of Business:** Religious organisations and places of worship
**Trading Style:** Worcester Diocesan Board of Finance
**Directors:** Ms R B Stephens, Reverend P G Harrison, J G Inge, N J Groarke, A Pettersen, D S Hargreaves, P J Seward, D Southall
**Co. Secretary:** Robert Higham
**Responsibilities**
**Senior:** Anthony Attwood *(Manager)*, Richard Court *(Director)*, Stuart Currie *(Director)*, David Hoskin *(Director)*, John Layton *(Director)*, Robin Lunn *(Director)*, Garth Nathaniel *(Director)*, Andrew Quinn *(Director)*, Susan Renshaw *(Director)*, Graham Usher *(Director)*
**IT:** John Layton *(Director)*
**US SIC:** 8661 **UK SIC:** 96600
**Auditors:** John Yelland & Co
**Bankers:** Lloyds TSB Bank plc (30-99-90)

| | 31-12-13 | 31-12-12 | 31-12-11 |
|---|---|---|---|
| TO | 8,083,000 | 7,872,000 | 8,100,000 |
| P/L | 63,000 | 247,000 | 7,000 |
| NW | 60,052,000 | 54,694,000 | 52,324,000 |
| WC | 3,826,000 | 2,981,000 | 1,917,000 |
| Emp. | 47 | 46 | 38 |

DUNS 23-600-4008

## Worcester Electrical Distributors Ltd

Unit F7-F8, Worcester, Worcestershire WR3 8SG
**Tel:** 01905-755110
**Web:** www.worcesterelectrical.co.uk
**Reg No:** 2203536 **VAT No:** 487802018
**Estd:** 1988 Private Limited Company
**Line of Business:** Wholesale of hardware, plumbing and heating equipment and supplies
**Trading Style:** Electrical Control Supplies
**Issued Capital:** £100
**Principals:** R A Rushton *(Chairman)*, N W Butler *(Managing)*
**Branches:** Worcester Electrical Distributors Ltd, Unit 1, Long Acre, Birmingham, West Midlands B7 5JD
**US SIC:** 5074 **UK SIC:** 61300
**Auditors:** Derek Young & Co

| | 31-03-14 | 31-03-13 | 31-03-12 |
|---|---|---|---|
| TO | 12,651,768 | 12,673,846 | 12,777,608 |
| P/L | 335,854 | 408,853 | 583,276 |
| NW | 972,123 | 864,142 | 616,012 |
| WC | 759,727 | 706,915 | 436,027 |
| Emp. | 75 | 75 | 68 |

DUNS 21-341-7924

## Worcester Journal

Berrows House Hylton Road, Worcester, Worcestershire WR2 5JX
**Tel:** 01905748300
**Web:** www.worcesternews.co.uk
**Estd:** 1995 Partnership
**Line of Business:** Newspapers publishing
**Partners:** N Carpenter, P Hunter, P Davidson, P Radburn
**Responsibilities**
**Senior:** Sue Griffiths *(Classifieds Manager)*
**US SIC:** 2711 **UK SIC:** 47512
**Employees:** 120

DUNS 55-067-5078

## Worcester Lodge

30-32 Castle Road, Clevedon, Avon BS21 7DE
**Estd:** 1983 Proprietorship
**Line of Business:** Non-charitable social work activities with accommodation
**Proprietor:** S Millhouse
**Responsibilities**
**Senior:** Shelley Hollbrow *(Manager)*
**US SIC:** 8321 **UK SIC:** 96111
**Employees:** 48

DUNS 73-800-4923

## Worcester Y M C A

Henwick Road, Worcester, Worcestershire WR2 5NS
**Tel:** 01905741008 **Fax:** 01905-422969
**Web:** www.ymcaworcester.org.uk
**Reg No:** 5056873 **Estd:** 2004 Private Company Limited By Guarantee
**Line of Business:** Other tourist or short-stay accommodation
**Directors:** P J Simpson, Dr S L Brush
**Co. Secretary:** Howard Berry
**US SIC:** 7021, 8249
**UK SIC:** 66500, 93300
**Auditors:** BDWM
**Bankers:** Barclays Bank Plc (20-84-17)

| | 31-03-14 | 31-03-13 | 31-03-12 |
|---|---|---|---|
| TO | 1,655,644 | 1,401,084 | N/A |
| P/L | 53,698 | (76,442) | N/A |
| NW | 506,085 | 452,386 | 528,828 |
| WC | 101,222 | 34,250 | 89,984 |
| Emp. | 58 | 50 | N/A |

DUNS 23-223-8605

## Worcestershire Acute Hospital N H S Trust

Worcestershire Royal Infirmary, Charles Hastings Way, Worcester, Worcestershire WR5 1DD
**Tel:** 01905-763333
**Web:** www.worcsacute.nhs.uk
**Estd:** 2000
**Line of Business:** Hospital Accountability: Each trust board is directly accountable to the Secretary of State via the NHS Executive
**Trading Style:** Worcestershire Royal Infirmary, Alexandra Hospital League of Friends
**Issued Capital:** £1
**Principals:** Ms N Trigg *(Chairman)*, M O'Riordan *(Chairman)*, M Stevens *(Financial)*, J Crawshaw *(Personnel)*, P Milligan, J Rostill, Ms J Rhead, H Turner
**Responsibilities**
**Senior:** Rosemary Adams *(Non Executive Member)*, John Burbeck *(Non-Executive Director)*, Brian Mc Ginty *(Non-Executive Director)*, Lynn Todd *(Non-Executive Director)*
**HR:** Helen Blanchard *(Director of HR)*
**Facilities:** Peter Male *(Facilities Manager)*
**Branches:** Worcestershire Acute Hospital N H S Trust, Bewdley Road, Kidderminster, Worcestershire DY11 6RJ
**US SIC:** 9121, 8062
**UK SIC:** 91110, 95100
**Employees:** 5,693

DUNS 23-035-9643

## Worcestershire County Council

County Hall, Spetchley Road, Worcester, Worcestershire WR5 2NP
**Tel:** 01905-763-763
**Web:** www.worcestershire.gov.uk
**Estd:** 1899
**Line of Business:** Local government
**Principals:** E Moore *(Chairman)*, P Birch, J Hobbs, R Harling, Ms D Tilley, Ms G Quinton, E Clarke, Ms T Haines
**Responsibilities**
**Senior:** Clare Marchants *(Chief Executive Officer)*
**IT:** Brian Brumhead *(IT Manager)*, Malcolm Follis *(Software Manager)*, Alan Woolliscroft *(Computer Manager)*
**Health & Safety:** Christine Birch *(Health & Safety Officer)*, Clive Werrett *(Health & Safety Officer)*
**Fleet:** Andy Baker *(Sustainable Transport Manager)*, Madeleine Sumner *(Community Transport Officer)*
**Branches:** Worcestershire County Council, Old Coach Road, Droitwich, Worcestershire WR9 8BD
**US SIC:** 9121 **UK SIC:** 91110
**Employees:** 1,500

DUNS 21-761-9821

## Worcestershire Health and Care Nhs Trust

Unit 19, Isaac Maddox House, Shrub Hill Industrial Estate, Worcester, Worcestershire WR4 9RW
**Tel:** 01905733658
**Web:** www.hacw.nhs.uk
**Estd:** 2012
**Line of Business:** Health authorities
**Principals:** R Mackie *(Financial)*, Ms J Ditheridge, B Creaney, S Trickett, Ms S Brennan, Ms S Dugan, D Priestnall, P Lachecki
**Responsibilities**
**Senior:** Gill Gramann *(Non-Executive Director)*
**US SIC:** 9121 **UK SIC:** 91110
**Employees:** 3,600

DUNS 36-518-0756

## Worcestershire Pct

County Hall, Spetchley Road, Worcester, Worcestershire WR5 2NP
**Tel:** 01905760010
**Web:** www.worcestershirehealth.nhs.uk
**VAT No:** 654419428 **Estd:** 2012
**Line of Business:** Representative office
**Trading Style:** Worcestershire Primary Care Trust
**Director:** P Bates
**Responsibilities**
**Senior:** Stella Baldwin *(Board Member)*, Simon Hairsnape *(Director, Delivery)*, Sue Home *(Executive)*, Frances Howie *(Assistant Director of Public H)*, Jonathan Leach *(Board Member)*, Vicky Preece *(Manager)*, Sonia Spurr *(Manager)*
**Finance:** Brian Hanford *(Financial Accountant)*
**HR:** Mandy Childs *(Executive)*
**Branches:** Worcestershire Pct, Crossgate House, Crossgate Road, Redditch, Worcestershire B98 7SN
**US SIC:** 9121, 8062
**UK SIC:** 91110, 95100
**Bankers:** Bank Of England (10-14-99)
**Employees:** 200

DUNS 42-480-9403

## Word Marketing Ltd

6a Forresters Road, Burbage, Hinckley, Leicestershire LE10 2RX
**Tel:** 01455-614333
**Web:** www.wordassociation.co.uk
**Reg No:** 4468518 **Estd:** 1998 Private Limited Company
**Line of Business:** Marketing consultants
**Trading Style:** Word Association
**Issued Capital:** £100
**Director:** M Thomas
**US SIC:** 7392, 7311
**UK SIC:** 83951, 83800
**Auditors:** McCranor Kirby Smale Ltd
**Bankers:** National Westminster Bank Plc (56-00-45)

| | 30-06-13 | 30-06-12 | 30-06-11 |
|---|---|---|---|
| TA | 216,675 | 211,163 | 241,879 |
| NW | 118,855 | 115,814 | 160,606 |
| WC | 102,176 | 109,245 | 153,441 |

DUNS 50-019-1796 **Exp**

## Wordbank Ltd

55 Greek Street, London W1D 3DT
**Tel:** 02074327300
**Web:** www.wordbank.com
**Reg No:** 2299752 **Estd:** 1988 Private Limited Company
**Line of Business:** Other publishing
**Export Markets:** Worldwide
**Issued Capital:** £10,500
**Principals:** K D Grant-Dalton *(Managing)*, Princess E M Galitzine, G M Husbands
**Responsibilities**
**Sales:** Marie-Helene Mahy *(New Business Manager)*
**US SIC:** 2741 **UK SIC:** 47541
**Auditors:** Hextall Meakin
**Bankers:** Lloyds TSB Bank plc (30-91-31)

| | 31-03-14 | 31-03-13 | 31-03-12 |
|---|---|---|---|
| TO | 1,958,159 | N/A | 5,440,881 |
| P/L | (47,374) | N/A | (96,986) |
| NW | 100 | 681,852 | 1,059,074 |
| WC | N/A | 477,558 | 824,210 |

DUNS 21-226-5123

## Wordsley Hall

Mill Street, Wordsley, Stourbridge, West Midlands DY8 5SX
**Tel:** 01384-571606
**Web:** www.minstercaregroup.co.uk
**Estd:** 1987 Partnership
**Line of Business:** Residential care establishments
**Partners:** N Nauth, Mrs S Nauth
**Responsibilities**
**Senior:** Km Costello *(General Manager)*
**US SIC:** 8321 **UK SIC:** 96111
**Employees:** 50

DUNS 54-891-8093

## The Wordsworth Trust

Dove Cottage, Grasmere, Ambleside, Cumbria LA22 9SH
**Tel:** 01539435544
**Web:** www.wordsworth.org.uk
**Reg No:** 3442086 **Estd:** 1997 Private Company Limited By Guarantee
**Line of Business:** Museums & art galleries
**Directors:** Ms J H Cooke, J S Collier, C A Sebag-Montefiore, Mrs E R Ainscough, Ms J S Uglow, Professor F R Sampson, D M Heal, Mrs D R Matthews
**Co. Secretary:** Adrian Cowl
**Responsibilities**
**Senior:** Geoffrey Bindman *(Manager)*, Mary Chuck *(Director)*, Michael Mcgregor *(Manager)*, Lucy Peltz *(Director)*, Seamus Perry *(Director)*, Nicholas Roe *(Director)*, Lynn Shepherd *(Director)*, Charles Sturgis *(Manager)*
**HR:** Carrie Taylor *(Visitor Services Manager)*
**Health & Safety:** Carrie Taylor *(Visitor Services Manager)*
**Facilities:** Carrie Taylor *(Visitor Services Manager)*
**US SIC:** 7911, 8231
**UK SIC:** 97913, 97700
**Auditors:** KPMG LLP
**Bankers:** Barclays Bank Plc (20-45-28)

| | 31-12-13 | 31-12-12 | 31-12-11 |
|---|---|---|---|
| TO | 1,576,000 | 1,499,000 | 1,491,000 |
| P/L | 106,000 | (6,000) | 77,000 |
| NW | 13,852,000 | 13,514,000 | 13,512,000 |
| WC | 684,000 | 757,000 | 818,000 |
| Emp. | 47 | 39 | 39 |

DUNS 77-001-4819

## Wordwave International Ltd

(**Subsidiary of:** Smith Bernal Group Ltd)
190 Fleet Street, London EC4A 2AG
**Tel:** 02074041400 **Fax:** 020-7404-1424
**Web:** www.merrioocoorporation.com
**Reg No:** 2656370 **Estd:** 1991 Private Limited Company
**Line of Business:** Publishing of software
**Export Sales:** £1,328,496
**Trading Style:** Merrill Legal Solutions
**Issued Capital:** £100
**Directors:** R H Nazarian, R R Atterbury
**Responsibilities**
**Senior:** Anne Kiss *(Director Of Resourcing)*, Jayne Perry *(Uk Director)*
**Marketing:** Lorraine Medcraft *(Marketing Manager)*
**Sales:** Lorraine Medcraft *(Marketing Manager)*
**Admin:** Martin Brookes *(Office Manager)*
**IT:** Jacques Dewet *(Senior IT Executive)*
**US SIC:** 7372, 9211
**UK SIC:** 83940, 91200
**Auditors:** PricewaterhouseCoopers LLP
**Bankers:** National Westminster Bank Plc (51-50-03)

| | 31-01-14 | 31-01-13 | 31-01-12 |
|---|---|---|---|
| TO | 11,408,206 | 14,095,599 | 15,045,008 |
| P/L | (25,641) | 123,881 | 290,788 |
| NW | 2,160,851 | 3,135,474 | 5,634,861 |
| WC | 1,872,390 | 2,700,258 | 6,710,025 |
| Emp. | 78 | 104 | 114 |

DUNS 29-537-0282 **Imp**

## Worgas Burners Ltd

**(Subsidiary of:** Worgas Bruciatori Srl)
Unit 3 Wincobank Way, Alfreton, Derbyshire DE55 2FX
**Tel:** 01773 864870 **Fax:** 01773864871
**Web:** www.worgas.com
**Reg No:** 1904016 **VAT No:** 421806868
**Estd:** 1985 Private Limited Company
**Line of Business:** Gas equipment wholesalers
**Issued Capital:** £330,000
**Directors:** G G Berthold, F Pisano
**Responsibilities**
**Senior:** James Maxfield *(Manager)*, Renzo Vecchi *(Manager)*
**US SIC:** 5074 **UK SIC:** 61300
**Auditors:** Somers Baker Prince Kurz LLP
**Bankers:** Barclays Bank Plc (20-55-62)

| | 31-12-13 | 31-03-13 | 31-12-12 |
|---|---|---|---|
| TA | 3,957,895 | 3,906,388 | 3,495,965 |
| NW | 814,795 | 947,718 | 797,458 |
| WC | 313,661 | 498,245 | 585,927 |

DUNS 21-741-7805

## The Work Foundation Alliance Ltd

21 Palmer Street, London SW1H 0AD
**Tel:** 020 7076 3512
**Web:** www.theworkfoundation.com
**Reg No:** 7746776 **Estd:** 2011 Private Company Limited By Guarantee
**Line of Business:** Business and management consultancy activities not elsewhere classified
**Directors:** Mrs S J Randall-Paley, T Levitt, Dame C M Black, Prof S J Cox, G Johnes, G Parker, D J Barron
**Co. Secretary:** Geoffrey Fielding
**Responsibilities**
**Senior:** Ian Brinkley *(Manager)*
**US SIC:** 7392 **UK SIC:** 83951
**Bankers:** National Westminster Bank Plc (01-54-90)

| | 31-07-13 | 31-07-12 |
|---|---|---|
| TO | 3,186,703 | N/A |
| P/L | (320,915) | N/A |
| NW | (320,915) | N/A |
| WC | 65,189 | N/A |
| Emp. | 48 | N/A |

DUNS 23-750-7095

## Work Group P L C

11th Floor Marble Arch Tower, 55 Bryanston Street, London W1H 7AA
**Fax:** 020-7492-0001
**Web:** www.workgroup.plc.uk
**Reg No:** 3744673 **Estd:** 1999 Public Limited Company
**Line of Business:** Labour recruitment and provision of personnel
**Issued Capital:** £572,449
**Directors:** K G Cameron, S J Howard, Ms R R Colledge
**Co. Secretary:** David Hooper
**Responsibilities**
**Senior:** Julian Maslen *(Financial Director)*
**Finance:** Julian Maslen *(Financial Director)*
**US SIC:** 7361 **UK SIC:** 83954
**Auditors:** PricewaterhouseCoopers LLP
**Bankers:** Barclays Bank Plc (20-00-00)

| | 31-12-13 | 31-12-12 | 31-12-11 |
|---|---|---|---|
| TO | 10,435,000 | 18,386,000 | 21,698,000 |
| P/L | (1,345,000) | (8,167,000) | 59,000 |
| NW | 1,563,000 | 994,000 | 1,384,000 |
| WC | 1,154,000 | 323,000 | 1,023,000 |
| Emp. | 106 | 167 | 180 |

DUNS 21-779-7341

## Work Solutions

6-10 Hanover Street, Manchester M4 4BB
**Tel:** 01618283230
**Web:** www.economic-solutions.co.uk
**Estd:** 2011
**Line of Business:** Employment and recruitment companies and consultants
**Responsibilities**
**Senior:** Julie Mcmenamin *(Service Manager)*
**US SIC:** 7361 **UK SIC:** 83954
**Employees:** 60

DUNS 21-319-1831

## Workers' Educational Association

4 Luke Street, London EC2A 4XW
**Web:** www.wea.org.uk
**Reg No:** 2806910 **Estd:** 1903 Private Company Limited By Guarantee
**Line of Business:** Adult and other education not elsewhere classified
**Trading Style:** W E A
**Directors:** L Smith, F Islam, R K Taylor, J E Taylor, Ms A E King, F Islam, M Crilly, Mrs R S Mayes
**Co. Secretary:** Ipcep Ltd
**Responsibilities**
**Senior:** Colin Barnes *(Director)*, Richard Bolsin *(General Secretary)*, Charles Lynch *(Director)*, Ruth Tanner *(Director)*, Gordon Vowles *(Director)*
**Branches:** Workers Educational Association, North West Region Regional Office, Suite 405, Cotton Exchange, Old Hall Street,, Liverpool, Merseyside L3 9JR
**US SIC:** 8249 **UK SIC:** 93300
**Auditors:** Crowe Clark Whitehill LLP
**Bankers:** The Royal Bank Of Scotland Plc (15-00-00)

| | 31-07-13 | 31-07-12 | 31-07-11 |
|---|---|---|---|
| TO | 28,047,000 | 28,654,000 | 30,087,000 |
| P/L | (503,000) | 348,000 | 67,000 |
| NW | 4,842,000 | 4,004,000 | 3,404,000 |
| WC | 4,497,000 | 5,477,000 | 4,995,000 |
| Emp. | 707 | 685 | 744 |

DUNS 42-414-1190

## Workforce Training Services Ltd

90-120 Peter Pan Industrial Estate, Springfield Road, Belfast BT12 7AJ
**Tel:** 028-9024-7016 **Fax:** 02890238436
**Web:** www.workforceonline.org
**Reg No:** 0031308NI **Estd:** 1990 Private Limited Company
**Line of Business:** Training services
**Directors:** D Lynn, H Mccarry, J Mcauley, Mrs J M Maguire, Mrs H A Ferguson, J F Deery, F Cullen, Ms C M Mccorry
**Co. Secretary:** Gerard Mcgrath
**Responsibilities**
**Senior:** Philip Toner *(Director)*
**US SIC:** 8299 **UK SIC:** 93300
**Auditors:** M P Fitzmaurice & Co
**Bankers:** Northern Bank Ltd (95-01-26)

| | 31-03-14 | 31-03-13 | 31-03-12 |
|---|---|---|---|
| TO | 3,016,734 | 3,048,487 | 3,100,358 |
| P/L | 133,607 | 269,743 | 446,809 |
| NW | 4,067,894 | 1,860,653 | 3,797,545 |
| WC | 1,317,875 | 1,448,740 | 1,208,359 |
| Emp. | 50 | 50 | 49 |

DUNS 23-856-3972

## The Working Health Co Ltd

13 St Marys Street, Stamford, Lincolnshire PE9 2DE
**Tel:** 01780-754954 **Fax:** 01780-754560
**Web:** www.workinghealth.co.uk
**Reg No:** 3848209 **Estd:** 1999 Private Limited Company
**Line of Business:** Health clubs
**Issued Capital:** £200
**Directors:** A J Bennett, R N Holmes
**Co. Secretary:** Ms Valerie Marsden Holmes
**US SIC:** 7299, 7999
**UK SIC:** 98902, 97913

| | 31-12-13 | 31-12-12 | 31-12-11 |
|---|---|---|---|
| TA | 69,724 | 129,915 | 77,102 |
| NW | (71,483) | (78,364) | (99,254) |
| WC | (75,312) | (90,533) | (117,002) |

DUNS 50-641-8354

## Working Links

4th Floor Cobourg House, 32 Mayflower Street, Plymouth, Devon PL1 1QX
**Tel:** 01752672007
**Web:** www.workinglinks.co.uk
**Estd:** 2000
**Line of Business:** Employment and recruitment companies and consultants
**Proprietor:** Ms H Thomas
**Responsibilities**
**Senior:** Heidi Ondrak *(Performance Manager)*
**US SIC:** 7361 **UK SIC:** 83954
**Employees:** 70

DUNS 23-954-3882

## Working Links (Employment) Ltd

Pennant House, St Catherine St And Apos;s Corner, Pontypridd, Mid Glamorgan CF37 2TB
**Tel:** 08009179262 **Fax:** 02070-107-832
**Web:** www.workinglinks.co.uk
**Reg No:** 3943678 **Estd:** 2000 Private Limited Company
**Line of Business:** Labour recruitment and provision of personnel
**Trading Style:** Working Links
**Issued Capital:** £400
**Directors:** W Cook, E G Crouch, P A Scales, D P Whitham, P R Andrew, J J Halliwell, Ms U Banerjee, M G Watkins
**Co. Secretary:** Anthony Hunter
**Responsibilities**
**Senior:** Brege Burkes *(Chief Executive Officer)*, Catherine Yeomans *(Director)*
**Finance:** Clive Pitts *(Implementation and Finance Dir)*
**HR:** Claire Davey *(Human Resources Manager)*
**Health & Safety:** Maggie Taylor *(Health & Safety Manager)*
**Branches:** Working Links (Employment) Ltd, Provident Wks, Newdigate St, Nottingham, Nottinghamshire NG7 4FD
**US SIC:** 7361 **UK SIC:** 83954
**Auditors:** Grant Thornton UK LLP
**Bankers:** The Royal Bank Of Scotland Plc (83-22-04)

| | 30-09-14 | 30-09-13 | 30-09-12 |
|---|---|---|---|
| TO | 86,283,000 | 81,368,000 | 73,997,000 |
| P/L | 2,526,000 | (6,816,000) | 15,493,000 |
| NW | 12,827,000 | 10,912,000 | 16,781,000 |
| WC | 12,505,000 | 10,583,000 | 17,836,000 |
| Emp. | 771 | 931 | 905 |

DUNS 22-731-5975

## Working Mens Club & Institute Union Ltd

Club Union House, 253-256 Upper Street, London N1 1RY
**Tel:** 02072260221 **Fax:** 020-7354-1847
**Web:** www.wmciu.org
**Reg No:** 0002766IP **VAT No:** 233122709
**Estd:** 1862 Friendly Society
**Line of Business:** Clubs social and associations
**Trading Style:** Services to Clubs
**Principals:** D J Dormer *(President)*, D J Macmahon, C J Wright, C P Hughes, R Mills, K Brown, J Lindsay, T Little
**Responsibilities**
**Senior:** K Barrowcliffe *(Principal)*, H Drysdale *(Principal)*, A Garnett *(Principal)*, Stephen Goulding *(General Manager)*, B Guess *(Principal)*, W Laverick *(Director)*, R Linstead *(Principal)*, Mick McGlasham *(General Secretary)*
**Branches:** Working Mens Club & Institute Union Ltd, 534 Hyde Road, Manchester M18 7AA
**US SIC:** 8699, 8999
**UK SIC:** 96902, 83954
**Bankers:** The Co-Operative Bank Plc (08-90-36)
**Employees:** 150

DUNS 76-912-2227

## Working Mens College

44 Crowndale Road, London NW1 1TR
**Tel:** 02072554700
**Web:** www.wmcollege.ac.uk
**Reg No:** 0008894 **Estd:** 1874 Private Company Limited By Guarantee
**Line of Business:** Sub-degree level higher education
**Trading Style:** Working Men's College
**Directors:** P J Badman, Ms A Hall, A Quadir, Ms J Esnard, Ms B A Byrne, Mrs P Whittle, Professor A F Marmot, Ms K O Bell
**Co. Secretary:** Alan Conway
**Responsibilities**
**Senior:** Severine Campos *(Director)*, Lucy De Groot *(Director)*, Satnam Gill *(Principal)*, Helen Hammond *(Director)*, Tony Jennings *(Manager)*, Shingo Nakatani *(Manager)*, David Offenbach *(Director)*, Peter Ptashko *(Director)*, Bennett Rodomsky *(Central Services Manager)*, Michal Sasadeusz *(Director)*, Tom Schuller *(Director)*, Tulip Siddiq *(Director)*
**Health & Safety:** Satnam Gill *(Principal)*
**Facilities:** Bennett Rodomsky *(Central Services Manager)*
**Purchasing:** Bennett Rodomsky *(Central Services Manager)*
**US SIC:** 8221 **UK SIC:** 93100
**Auditors:** Buzzacott LLP
**Bankers:** National Westminster Bank Plc (60-04-24)

| | 31-07-14 | 31-07-13 | 31-07-12 |
|---|---|---|---|
| TO | 5,809,000 | 5,172,490 | 4,638,879 |
| P/L | 586,000 | 136,064 | 328,315 |
| NW | 10,015,000 | 9,408,863 | 8,542,602 |
| WC | 1,107,000 | 607,947 | 626,938 |
| Emp. | 107 | 97 | 85 |

DUNS 21-551-1176

## The Workington Playgoers

Theatre Royal, Washington Street, Workington, Cumbria CA14 3AW
**Estd:** 1935 Proprietorship
**Line of Business:** Theatre services run by members of the commitee
**Principals:** J Hool *(Chairman)*, Mrs G Walker
**US SIC:** 7922, 8699
**UK SIC:** 97412, 96902
**Employees:** 120

DUNS 23-259-7088

## Workman & Partners

Alliance Health, 12 Caxton Street, London SW1H 0QS
**Tel:** 020-7227-6200
**Web:** www.workman.co.uk
**Estd:** 1985 Partnership
**Line of Business:** Estate management services
**Partners:** J Laundon, J Laundon, Ms C Sim, P Hiberd, S Newton, P Hibberd, S Newton, J Bates
**Responsibilities**
**Senior:** Richard Kingston *(Partner)*, Robert Yeo *(Partner)*
**Branches:** Workman & Partners, Hanover House 30 32, Charlotte Street, Manchester M1 4FD
**US SIC:** 6531 **UK SIC:** 83400
**Employees:** 100

DUNS 84-694-0351

## Workman Llp

The Heights, 59-65 Lowlands Road, Harrow, Middlesex HA1 3AW
**Tel:** 02084 265155 **Fax:** 02072 276204
**Web:** www.workman.co.uk
**Reg No:** 0327825OC **Estd:** 1991 Private Limited Company
**Line of Business:** Estate management services
**Export Sales:** £839,877
**Responsibilities**
**Senior:** Colette Berwitz *(Non-designated Limited Liabili)*, Gordon Birdwood *(Non-designated Limited Liabili)*, Jeremy Forester *(Non-designated Limited Liabili)*, Wendy Ibbetson *(Non-designated Limited Liabili)*, Matthew Pateman *(Non-designated Limited Liabili)*, Keith Stock *(Security)*
**US SIC:** 7397 **UK SIC:** 83702
**Auditors:** RPG Crouch Chapman LLP

| | 30-04-14 | 30-04-13 | 30-04-12 |
|---|---|---|---|
| TO | 43,692,091 | 33,693,238 | 29,990,113 |
| P/L | 7,580,243 | 2,911,318 | 6,089,809 |
| NW | 8,823,525 | 4,995,622 | 4,041,989 |
| WC | 6,658,719 | 3,143,187 | 2,904,066 |
| Emp. | 738 | 557 | 533 |

DUNS 39-677-8284

## Workmates & Daniel Owen Ltd

Hadwyn House, Field Road, Reading, Berkshire RG1 6AP
**Tel:** 01214567620 **Fax:** 0121-456-7621
**Web:** www.workmates.co.uk
**Reg No:** 2142070 **VAT No:** 438285526
**Estd:** 1987 Private Limited Company
**Line of Business:** Employment and recruitment companies and consultants
**Issued Capital:** £193
**Principals:** R O Andrews *(Managing)*, A P Tigg
**Co. Secretary:** Philip Andrews
**Responsibilities**
**Senior:** Sean Bridgeman *(Manager)*
**Branches:** Workmates & Daniel Owen Ltd, 28 Baldwin Street, Bristol, Avon BS1 1NG
**US SIC:** 7361 **UK SIC:** 83954
**Auditors:** James & Cowper
**Bankers:** National Westminster Bank Plc (60-17-21)

| | 30-06-13 | 30-06-12 | 30-06-11 |
|---|---|---|---|
| TO | 29,259,612 | 16,708,034 | 35,266,543 |
| P/L | 655,142 | 385,319 | 435,997 |
| NW | 991,627 | 887,516 | 775,956 |
| WC | 880,885 | 777,920 | 654,571 |
| Emp. | 67 | 64 | 53 |

DUNS 21-034-4618

## Workplace by Design

South Court, Sharston Road, Manchester M22 4SN
**Tel:** 01619987571
**Web:** www.wpbd.co.uk
**Proprietorship**
**Line of Business:** Architectural and engineering activities and related technical consultancy
**Proprietor:** S Fasulo
**US SIC:** 7399 **UK SIC:** 83954
**Employees:** 50

DUNS 23-777-5809

## Workplace Management (Westminster) Ltd

**(Subsidiary of:** Bell Rock Bidco Ltd)
Sunningdale Centre, Sunningdale Road, Leicester, Leicestershire LE3 1UR
**Tel:** 01162016800 **Fax:** 01344-457208
**Web:** www.sgp.co.uk
**Reg No:** 3770853 **Estd:** 1999 Private Limited Company
**Line of Business:** Other business activities not elsewhere classified
**Issued Capital:** £1
**Directors:** D C Wilton, M J Holt
**Co. Secretary:** David Wilton
**US SIC:** 7399 **UK SIC:** 83954
**Auditors:** Unknown Auditor

| | 31-12-13 | 31-12-12 | 31-12-11 |
|---|---|---|---|
| TA | 2 | 1 | 1 |
| NW | 2 | 1 | 1 |

DUNS 23-977-7894 **Imp**

## Workplace Systems International Ltd

(**Subsidiary of:** Wasp Management Software Ltd)
Precedent Drive, Rooksley, Milton Keynes, Buckinghamshire MK13 8PP
**Tel:** 01908-242042 **Fax:** 01908251321
**Web:** www.workplacesystems.com
**Reg No:** 3966381 **Estd:** 2000 Private Limited Company
**Line of Business:** Other computer related activities
**Trading Style:** Workplace Systems
**Issued Capital:** £8,174,423
**Directors:** D G Farquhar, R O'Dulaing, R Odulaing, A T Lloyd, P J Reading
**Responsibilities**
**Senior:** Barney Quinn *(Non Executive)*, Bernard Quinn *(Non-Executive Director)*
**Engineering:** Alex Davis *(Chief Technology Officer)*
**US SIC:** 7379, 6711
**UK SIC:** 83940, 83962
**Auditors:** Mazars LLP

| | 31-12-13 | 31-12-12 | 31-12-11 |
|---|---|---|---|
| TO | 9,673,000 | 10,565,000 | 8,176,000 |
| P/L | (1,699,000) | 81,000 | 344,000 |
| NW | (152,000) | 1,467,000 | 2,658,000 |
| WC | (1,166,000) | 1,039,000 | 2,467,000 |
| Emp. | 136 | 135 | 128 |

DUNS 34-893-0236

## Works Infrastructure (Holdings) Ltd

(**Subsidiary of:** Downer Edi Limited)
4100 Park Approach, Leeds, West Yorkshire LS15 8GB
**Tel:** 01133970890 **Fax:** 01133-970469
**Web:** www.works.co.uk
**Reg No:** 5690610 **VAT No:** 551840253
**Estd:** 2006 Private Limited Company
**Line of Business:** Management activities of holding companies
**Issued Capital:** £11,500,000
**Directors:** A Titter, C Bruyn, P J Tompkins
**Co. Secretary:** Ian Warburton
**Branches:** Works Infrastructure (Holdings) Ltd, Sillcon House, Graythorp Industrial Estate, Hartlepool, Cleveland TS25 2DF
**US SIC:** 6711, 1541
**UK SIC:** 83962, 50100
**Auditors:** Deloitte LLP
**Bankers:** HSBC Bank plc (40-41-07)

| | 31-12-13 | 31-12-12 | 30-12-11 |
|---|---|---|---|
| TA | 450,100 | 16,634,894 | 7,454,883 |
| P/L | (19,303,014) | (578,875) | (16,690,043) |
| NW | 450,100 | (21,804,615) | (21,225,738) |
| WC | N/A | (21,804,615) | (21,725,738) |

DUNS 21-115-4486 **Imp**

## The Works Stores Ltd

5 Kingsbury Road Midpoint Park, Sutton Coldfield, West Midlands B76 1RN
**Tel:** 01213136000
**Web:** www.theworks.co.uk
**Reg No:** 6557400 **VAT No:** 931381535
**Estd:** 2008 Private Limited Company
**Line of Business:** Other retail sale in non-specialised stores
**Trading Style:** The Works
**Issued Capital:** £250,267
**Directors:** S Joseph, Ms A S Bennett, A Solomon, N J Wood, P K Hughes, T Scott, K G Keaney
**Co. Secretary:** Ms Victoria Norrish
**Responsibilities**
**Senior:** Lloyd Hughes *(Manager)*, David Luper *(Manager)*
**US SIC:** 5399 **UK SIC:** 65600
**Auditors:** KPMG LLP
**Bankers:** HSBC Bank plc (40-12-24)

| | 27-04-14 | 28-04-13 | 29-04-12 |
|---|---|---|---|
| TO | 127,960,000 | 122,781,000 | 121,491,000 |
| P/L | 5,838,000 | 2,669,000 | 4,261,000 |
| NW | 10,022,000 | 5,729,000 | 4,425,000 |
| WC | 3,895,000 | (792,000) | 2,917,000 |
| Emp. | 1,253 | 2,370 | 2,357 |

DUNS 77-548-0155

## The Works (U.K.) Ltd

18-22 Canal Wharf, Holbeck, Leeds, West Yorkshire LS11 5PS
**Tel:** 01133201130
**Web:** www.theworksrec.co.uk
**Reg No:** 2998539 **Estd:** 1994 Private Limited Company
**Line of Business:** Labour recruitment and provision of personnel
**Issued Capital:** £1,070
**Principals:** C Suttle-Burton *(Managing)*, Ms R L Hannan, Miss G M Johnson, A M Izzard
**Co. Secretary:** Brian Gee
**Branches:** The Works (U.k.) Ltd, 6 Eldon Arcade, Barnsley, South Yorkshire S70 2JP
**US SIC:** 7361 **UK SIC:** 83954
**Auditors:** Watson Buckle LLP
**Bankers:** HSBC Bank plc (40-13-15)

| | 30-09-13 | 30-09-12 | 30-09-11 |
|---|---|---|---|
| TO | 7,151,092 | N/A | N/A |
| P/L | 57,503 | N/A | N/A |
| NW | 223,976 | 183,491 | 184,623 |
| WC | 200,560 | 146,402 | 136,028 |
| Emp. | 101 | N/A | N/A |

DUNS 23-561-6906 **Imp**

## Workshare Ltd

(**Subsidiary of:** Skydox Ltd)
10-20 Fashion Street, Whitechapel, London E1 6PX
**Tel:** 020-7426-0000
**Web:** www.workshare.com
**Reg No:** 3559880 **Estd:** 1998 Private Limited Company
**Line of Business:** Computer software (development)
**Trading Style:** Workshare Technology
**Principals:** B A Hadfield *(Managing)*, R J Rowson, B A Foy
**Co. Secretary:** Peter Shiner
**Responsibilities**
**Senior:** Jim Caccavo *(Manager)*, Alan Fraser *(Manager)*, John Laing *(Manager)*
**Finance:** Valentine Bala *(Vice President of Finance)*
**Engineering:** John Safa *(Vice President of Engineering)*
**US SIC:** 7379 **UK SIC:** 83940
**Auditors:** Deloitte & Touche LLP
**Bankers:** National Westminster Bank Plc (51-50-03)

| | 31-12-13 | 31-12-12 | -12- |
|---|---|---|---|
| TO | 7,384,000 | 5,488,000 | N/A |
| P/L | (2,632,000) | (472,000) | N/A |
| NW | 3,286,000 | 6,095,000 | N/A |
| WC | (2,462,000) | 4,252,000 | N/A |
| Emp. | 84 | 52 | 98 |

DUNS 23-789-5268

## The Workshop Uk Ltd

Sclattie Quarry Industrial Estate, Bankhead Avenue, Bucksburn, Aberdeen, Aberdeenshire AB21 9EG
**Tel:** 01224-710391 **Fax:** 01224-715383
**Web:** www.theworkshop.uk.com
**Reg No:** 0196886SC **VAT No:** 735292819
**Estd:** 1999 Private Limited Company
**Line of Business:** Caterers
**Issued Capital:** £100
**Principals:** A W Henderson *(Managing)*, Ms J M Murray, Mrs N A Fong
**Co. Secretary:** Raeburn Christie Clark & Wallace
**US SIC:** 5812 **UK SIC:** 66110
**Auditors:** Simpson Forsyth

| | 31-12-13 | 31-12-12 | 31-12-11 |
|---|---|---|---|
| TA | 1,317,682 | 1,099,324 | 892,110 |
| NW | 581,141 | 503,055 | 403,473 |
| WC | 456,751 | 316,411 | 242,881 |

DUNS 28-921-1229

## Worksop Industrial Tippers Ltd

Unit 2a, Coach Crescent, Worksop, Nottinghamshire S81 8AD
**Tel:** 01909-475500
**Web:** www.witrans.co.uk
**Reg No:** 1474782 **Estd:** 1980 Private Limited Company
**Line of Business:** Other supporting land transport activities
**Issued Capital:** £1,000
**Principals:** P S Brown *(Managing)*, Mrs J A Brown
**Co. Secretary:** Philip Brown
**US SIC:** 4789 **UK SIC:** 77002
**Auditors:** Arnold J R Slaney & Co
**Bankers:** National Westminster Bank Plc (60-24-30)

| | 30-04-14 | 30-04-13 | 30-04-12 |
|---|---|---|---|
| TO | 4,147,820 | 4,222,575 | N/A |
| P/L | 361,860 | 355,446 | N/A |
| NW | 2,744,894 | 2,533,810 | 2,326,519 |
| WC | 1,723,459 | 1,492,802 | 1,242,070 |
| Emp. | 50 | 52 | N/A |

DUNS 36-802-5086

## Worksop Leisure Centre

Valley Road, Worksop, Nottinghamshire S81 7EN
**Tel:** 01909-473937
**Web:** www.bpl.org.uk
**Estd:** 1972 Proprietorship
**Line of Business:** Other sporting activities not elsewhere classified
**Proprietor:** D Rose
**Responsibilities**
**Senior:** Phill Richardson *(Manager)*
**US SIC:** 7999 **UK SIC:** 97913
**Employees:** 60

DUNS 77-932-1277

## Workspace 14 Ltd

(**Subsidiary of:** Workspace Group Plc)
Chester House Kennington Park, 1-3 Brixton Road, London SW9 6DE
**Tel:** 02072477614
**Reg No:** 5834831 **Estd:** 2006 Private Limited Company
**Line of Business:** Other letting of own property
**Issued Capital:** £363,620,321
**Directors:** G C Clemett, Dr C J Pieroni, A R Boag, J P Hopkins
**Co. Secretary:** Miss Carmelina Carfora
**US SIC:** 6519 **UK SIC:** 85000

| | 31-03-14 | 31-03-13 | 31-03-12 |
|---|---|---|---|
| TO | 38,961,493 | 36,770,534 | 35,595,794 |
| P/L | 9,048,973 | 11,702,709 | 11,786,626 |
| NW | 425,089,678 | 324,067,755 | 292,337,396 |
| WC | (125,180,514) | 95,652,791 | 92,889,822 |

DUNS 23-213-6713

## Workspace (Draperstown) Ltd

Business Centre, Tobermore Road, Draperstown, Magherafelt, Co Londonderry BT45 7AG
**Web:** www.workspace.org.uk
**Reg No:** 0018240NI **Estd:** 1985 Private Company Limited By Guarantee
**Line of Business:** Management and business consultants
**Trading Style:** Energy Initiatives, Rural College, Plantation Centre of Ulster
**Directors:** Ms C Mccoy, L G O'Kane, W H Mckeown, P Mcshane, D J Heron, Dr M Mc Allister, G Mawhinney, B Mcguigan
**Co. Secretary:** Robin Gawne
**Responsibilities**
**Senior:** Sammantha Mccloskey *(Director)*
**Branches:** Workspace (Draperstown) Ltd, 50 High St, Magherafelt, Co Londonderry BT45 7AD
**US SIC:** 7392, 7941
**UK SIC:** 83951, 97911
**Auditors:** E & M Associates
**Bankers:** First Trust Bank (aib Group (uk) Plc) (93-87-93)

| | 31-03-14 | 31-03-13 | 31-03-12 |
|---|---|---|---|
| TO | 12,547,068 | 10,511,937 | 9,431,966 |
| P/L | (38,226) | 338,559 | 191,124 |
| NW | 5,301,525 | 5,282,616 | 5,047,797 |
| WC | 471,063 | 337,430 | 180,556 |
| Emp. | 254 | 222 | 4 |

DUNS 29-823-5839

## Workspace Group Plc

Canterbury Court, 1-3 Brixton Road, London SW9 6DE
**Tel:** 02071383300
**Web:** www.workspace.co.uk
**Reg No:** 2041612 **VAT No:** 524739140
**Estd:** 1986 Public Limited Company
**Line of Business:** Other letting of own property
**Trading Style:** The Leather Market
**Issued Capital:** £145,319,600
**Directors:** J P Hopkins, D J Russell, S A Hubbard, C F Girling, G C Clemett, D J Kitchen, Dr M V Moloney
**Co. Secretary:** Miss Carmelina Carfora
**Responsibilities**
**Marketing:** James Friedenthal *(Commercial Manager)*
**IT:** Maddy Carragher *(Computer Operations Manager)*
**HR:** Synthia Charlery *(Human Resources Manager)*
**Branches:** Workspace Group Plc, 10 Barley Mow Passage, London W4 4PH
**US SIC:** 6519, 6531
**UK SIC:** 85000, 83400
**Auditors:** PricewaterhouseCoopers LLP
**Bankers:** Barclays Bank Plc (20-30-47)

| | 31-03-14 | 31-03-13 | 31-03-12 |
|---|---|---|---|
| TO | 73,600,000 | 69,500,000 | 67,300,000 |
| P/L | 252,500,000 | 76,400,000 | 48,500,000 |
| NW | 725,700,000 | 499,900,000 | 435,100,000 |
| WC | (24,900,000) | (16,800,000) | (4,000,000) |
| Emp. | 182 | 170 | 164 |

DUNS 21-809-3125

## Workstation Specialists

Stephenson's Way, Wyvern Business Park, Chaddesden, Derby, Derbyshire DE21 6LY
**Web:** www.workstationspecialists.com
**Estd:** 1993
**Line of Business:** Computer systems and software (sales)
**US SIC:** 7379 **UK SIC:** 83940
**Employees:** 60

DUNS 76-496-9135

## Workstream Construction Services Ltd

(**Subsidiary of:** Recruitment Assets Ltd)
Newton Morrell Farm, Bicester, Oxfordshire OX27 8AG
**Tel:** 01280-848888 **Fax:** 01280849031
**Web:** www.workstream.co.uk
**Reg No:** 2566955 **Estd:** 1989 Private Limited Company
**Line of Business:** Employment and recruitment companies and consultants
**Issued Capital:** £50,000
**Directors:** M F Hancock, K A Alderton
**Responsibilities**
**Senior:** Ben Alderton *(Regional Manager)*, William Manoe *(Manager)*
**US SIC:** 7361 **UK SIC:** 83954
**Auditors:** Richard Anthony & Co

| | 31-01-14 | 31-01-13 | 31-01-12 |
|---|---|---|---|
| TO | 14,858,339 | 16,677,194 | 15,403,592 |
| P/L | 395,804 | 411,682 | 242,829 |
| NW | 815,946 | 643,497 | 524,293 |
| WC | 604,885 | 405,779 | 290,795 |
| Emp. | 60 | 67 | 65 |

DUNS 21-585-5354 **Imp-Exp**

## Workstrings International Ltd

(**Subsidiary of:** Superior Energy Services (Uk) Ltd)
Pitmedden Road Industrial Estate, Kirkton Avenue, Dyce, Aberdeen, Aberdeenshire AB21 0BF
**Tel:** 01224-724900
**Web:** www.workstrings.com
**Reg No:** 1083092 **VAT No:** 553022185
**Estd:** 1972 Private Limited Company
**Line of Business:** Plant and tool hire
**Export Markets:** Worldwide
**Trading Style:** Workstrings International
**Issued Capital:** £100
**Directors:** R Taylor, D D Dunlap, W B Masters
**Co. Secretary:** Md Secretaries Limited
**Responsibilities**
**Senior:** Mike Collie *(Manager)*, Russell Crofts *(Manager)*, Mike Delahoussaye *(Manager)*, Barry Moir *(Manager)*
**Finance:** Nicola Inkster *(Financial Controller)*
**Marketing:** Amanda Jenkins *(Commercial Executive)*
**Sales:** Amanda Jenkins *(Commercial Executive)*
**Admin:** Vicki Morrison *(Administrator)*
**HR:** Linda Ross *(Human Resources Manager)*
**Health & Safety:** Alex Selbie *(Facilities Manager)*
**Facilities:** Alex Selbie *(Facilities Manager)*
**Branches:** Workstrings International Ltd, Units 1 & 2 Enterprise Court Gapton Hall Industri, Great Yarmouth, Norfolk NR31 0ND
**US SIC:** 1389 **UK SIC:** 13000
**Auditors:** PricewaterhouseCoopers
**Bankers:** Bank Of Scotland (80-06-60)

| | 31-12-13 | 31-12-12 | 31-12-11 |
|---|---|---|---|
| TO | 47,403,000 | 32,680,000 | 26,278,000 |
| P/L | 16,628,000 | 4,748,000 | (2,072,000) |
| NW | 79,275,000 | 63,685,000 | 60,279,000 |
| WC | 47,164,000 | 31,573,000 | 25,961,000 |
| Emp. | 87 | 67 | 69 |

DUNS 52-031-7397

## Worktop Fabrications Ltd

Wingate Close, Nottingham, Nottinghamshire NG8 4LP
**Tel:** 01159-425549
**Web:** www.worktopfabrications.co.uk
**Reg No:** 3398221 **Estd:** 1997 Private Limited Company
**Line of Business:** Joinery installation
**Issued Capital:** £100,000
**Directors:** N Pitcher, A Green, Mrs A Pitcher, G Thompson, I Danby, A Pitcher
**Co. Secretary:** John Bryant
**Responsibilities**
**Senior:** David Pitcher *(Manager)*
**Sales:** Isley Jakeman *(UK sales manager)*
**US SIC:** 7399 **UK SIC:** 83954
**Auditors:** John Bryant
**Bankers:** National Westminster Bank Plc (60-01-10)

| | 31-03-14 | 31-03-13 | 31-03-12 |
|---|---|---|---|
| TO | 12,364,444 | 10,461,282 | 9,406,471 |
| P/L | 542,249 | 335,841 | 83,449 |
| NW | 2,262,496 | 1,857,212 | 1,591,044 |
| WC | 2,048,946 | 1,496,926 | 1,263,224 |
| Emp. | 66 | 65 | 66 |

DUNS 22-136-0360

## Workwithus.Org Ltd

Mansfield Traquair Centre, 15 Mansfield Place, Edinburgh, Midlothian EH3 6BB
**Tel:** 01314748030
**Web:** www.workwithus.org
**Reg No:** 0215516SC **Estd:** 2001 Private Limited Company
**Line of Business:** Other computer related activities

**Issued Capital:** £100
**Directors:** M P Sime, Ms F Campbell, Ms E Scouller
**Co. Secretary:** Alastair Dutton
**US SIC:** 7379 **UK SIC:** 83940

| | 31-03-14 | 31-03-13 | 31-03-12 |
|---|---|---|---|
| TO | 138,580 | 130,734 | 148,920 |
| P/L | (1,861) | (3,180) | 20 |
| NW | 698 | 2,559 | 5,738 |
| WC | 698 | 2,559 | 5,738 |

DUNS 23-974-6592

## World Advertising Research Center Ltd

(**Subsidiary of:** Warc Ltd)
Farm Road, Henley-On-Thames, Oxfordshire RG9 1EJ
**Tel:** 02074678100 **Fax:** 02074678101
**Web:** www.warc.com
**Reg No:** 3963340 **Estd:** 2000 Private Limited Company
**Line of Business:** Book publishers
**Issued Capital:** £2
**Director:** M J Waterson
**Co. Secretary:** Darren Blundy
**US SIC:** 2731 **UK SIC:** 47532

| | 31-03-14 | 31-03-13 | 31-03-12 |
|---|---|---|---|
| TA | 2 | 2 | 2 |
| NW | 2 | 2 | 2 |

DUNS 22-026-9257

## World Animal Protection

5th Floor 222 Gray's Inn Road, London WC1X 8HB
**Web:** www.wspa.org.uk
**Reg No:** 4029540 **Estd:** 2000 Private Company Limited By Guarantee
**Line of Business:** Veterinary activities
**Directors:** H Maij-Weggen, Ms N Hatendi, C Luke, Ms C Vega Leon, Ms M Meredith, J Nhan-O'Reilly, M R Watts, Dr C Krishna
**Co. Secretary:** Stephen Corri
**Responsibilities**
**Senior:** Mike Baker *(Director General)*, Dominique Bierhaalder *(Director)*
**HR:** Christina Ware *(Human Resources Officer)*
**US SIC:** 7399 **UK SIC:** 83954
**Auditors:** Grant Thornton UK LLP
**Bankers:** The Co-Operative Bank Plc (08-90-61)

| | 31-12-13 | 31-12-12 | 31-12-11 |
|---|---|---|---|
| TO | 27,892,000 | 24,991,000 | 29,022,000 |
| P/L | (1,089,000) | (3,318,000) | 5,335,000 |
| NW | 11,079,000 | 11,790,000 | 14,921,000 |
| WC | 7,143,000 | 7,984,000 | 11,130,000 |
| Emp. | 224 | 204 | 154 |

DUNS 50-598-7446

## World Cancer Research Fund

22 Bedford Square, London WC1B 3HH
**Tel:** 02073434200
**Web:** www.wcrf.org
**Reg No:** 2536180 **Estd:** 1998 Private Company Limited By Guarantee
**Line of Business:** Charities and charitable organisations
**Trading Style:** W C R F
**Directors:** A R Cooper, Ms S A Pepper, L I Isaacson, P Mccarty, J H Bunn
**Co. Secretary:**
Reed Smith Corporate Services Li
**Responsibilities**
**Senior:** Marilyn Gentry *(Chief Executive)*, Peter McCarty *(Director)*
**Marketing:** Teresa Nightingale *(Sales & Marketing Manager)*, Andy Wilks *(Press and PR Programme Manager)*
**Sales:** Teresa Nightingale *(Sales & Marketing Manager)*
**Admin:** Rachel Marlew *(Secretary)*
**HR:** Penny McCarthy *(Human Resources Manager)*
**US SIC:** 8699 **UK SIC:** 96902
**Auditors:** KPMG
**Bankers:** Barclays Bank Plc (20-20-15)

| | 30-09-13 | 30-09-12 | 30-09-11 |
|---|---|---|---|
| TO | 8,622,905 | 8,962,031 | 8,627,936 |
| P/L | 280,152 | 149,448 | 448,249 |
| NW | 6,342,636 | 4,831,938 | 5,931,362 |
| WC | 5,944,696 | 5,326,808 | 4,762,488 |
| Emp. | 46 | 44 | 48 |

DUNS 23-821-4816

## World Careers Network Plc

5 Seventh Avenue, London E12 5JL
**Tel:** 02089-469876 **Fax:** 02089469855
**Web:** www.wcn.co.uk
**Reg No:** 3813540 **Estd:** 1999 Public Limited Company
**Line of Business:** Career information services
**Export Sales:** £785,852
**Trading Style:** Wcn
**Issued Capital:** £7,656
**Directors:** D J Earland, D K Moore, C E Hipps
**Co. Secretary:** Paul Hipps
**Responsibilities**
**Senior:** Tariq Mustafa *(General Manager)*
**Facilities:** Tariq Mustafa *(General Manager)*

**Purchasing:** Brendon Potter *(Purchasing Manager)*
**US SIC:** 7361 **UK SIC:** 83954
**Auditors:** BDO LLP

| | 31-07-14 | 31-07-13 | 31-07-12 |
|---|---|---|---|
| TO | 8,583,571 | 7,246,342 | 7,156,306 |
| P/L | 2,474,784 | 1,843,549 | 1,981,355 |
| NW | 8,133,218 | 6,587,527 | 5,436,539 |
| WC | 8,025,076 | 6,487,251 | 5,307,690 |
| Emp. | 89 | 83 | 79 |

DUNS 23-541-9897

## World Cleaners Ltd

Shackles Dock, Silverdale Road, Hayes, Middlesex UB3 3BN
**Tel:** 020-8848-7755 **Fax:** 020-8848-7733
**Web:** www.worldcleanersltd.co.uk
**Reg No:** 3540598 **Estd:** 1998 Private Limited Company
**Line of Business:** Commercial premises cleaning
**Issued Capital:** £1
**Director:** B Balasuresh
**US SIC:** 7349 **UK SIC:** 92300
**Auditors:** Tamsons

| | 31-05-14 | 31-05-13 | 31-05-12 |
|---|---|---|---|
| TA | 505,631 | 671,209 | 633,431 |
| NW | 139,918 | 103,999 | 21,581 |
| WC | 83,106 | 41,326 | (300,163) |

DUNS 21-154-3491 **Imp**

## World Courier (U.K.) Ltd

(**Subsidiary of:** World Courier Group Sarl)
Spitfire House Cargo Terminal, Turnhouse Road, Edinburgh Airport, Edinburgh, Midlothian EH12 0AL
**Fax:** 020-7928-7105
**Web:** www.worldcourier.co.uk
**Reg No:** 1194193 **VAT No:** 245029085
**Estd:** 1974 Private Limited Company
**Line of Business:** Couriers
**Issued Capital:** £10,603,872
**Principals:** J C Butler *(Managing)*, S L Clifford, G Anspach
**Co. Secretary:** Faisal Rahmatullah
**Responsibilities**
**Senior:** Philip O'brien *(Manager)*
**Health & Safety:** Damion Jones *(Health & Safety Officer)*
**Branches:** World Courier (U.k.) Ltd, Suite 1 Millbrook Business Centre, Floats Road, Roundthorn Industrial Estate, Manchester M23 9YJ
**US SIC:** 4213, 4511
**UK SIC:** 72300, 75000
**Auditors:** Deloitte & Touche
**Bankers:** The Royal Bank Of Scotland Plc (16-00-42)

| | 30-09-13 | 31-12-12 | 31-09-11 |
|---|---|---|---|
| TO | 26,569,646 | 35,401,623 | 32,733,647 |
| P/L | 160,706 | (1,600,031) | 5,220,699 |
| NW | 14,259,872 | 14,111,241 | 15,655,917 |
| WC | 634,271 | 635,521 | 4,619,144 |
| Emp. | 165 | 153 | 163 |

DUNS 73-765-1252

## World First Uk Ltd

Millbank Tower, 21-24 Millbank, London SW1P 4QP
**Web:** www.worldfirst.com
**Reg No:** 5022388 **Estd:** 2004 Private Limited Company
**Line of Business:** Financial intermediation not elsewhere classified
**Export Sales:** £1,629,747,000
**Issued Capital:** £1,000,000
**Directors:** Sir D C Clementi, Miss E J Dobson, M Batsvik-Miller, K A Griswold, B E Bernstein, A L Sullivan, N J Robinson, J R Quin
**Co. Secretary:** Mrs Rosheen Fischer
**Responsibilities**
**Marketing:** Summer Wilson *(Marketing Executive)*
**US SIC:** 6111 **UK SIC:** 81501
**Auditors:** haysmacintyre

| | 31-01-14 | 31-01-13 | 31-01-12 |
|---|---|---|---|
| TA | 54,358,000 | 44,264,000 | 37,518,000 |
| P/L | 7,864,000 | 5,395,000 | 4,494,000 |
| NW | 11,473,000 | 9,627,000 | 6,521,000 |
| WC | 11,314,000 | 9,454,000 | 6,434,000 |
| Emp. | 188 | 133 | 110 |

DUNS 21-667-2620

## World Fuel Services Aviation Ltd

(**Subsidiary of:** Wfs Uk Holding Partnership Li Lp)
62 Buckingham Gate, London SW1E 6AJ
**Tel:** 01293 400333
**Web:** https://www.wfscorp.com
**Reg No:** 7209006 **Estd:** 2010 Private Limited Company
**Line of Business:** Wholesale of other fuels and related products
**Directors:** Ms A B Urban, C J White, W N Declaris
**Co. Secretary:**
Reed Smith Corporate Services Li
**Responsibilities**
**IT:** Tom Bernard *(IT Manager)*

**US SIC:** 5052 **UK SIC:** 61200
**Employees:** 200
**Turnover:** £314,138,947

DUNS 73-585-4031 **Imp**

## World Fuel Services Europe Ltd

(**Subsidiary of:** Wfs Uk Holding Partnership Li Lp)
8th Floor, 62 Buckingham Gate, London SW1E 6AJ
**Tel:** 020 7808 5000 **Fax:** 020 7808 5088
**Web:** www.wfscorp.com
**Reg No:** 4846814 **VAT No:** 835972195
**Estd:** 2006 Private Limited Company
**Line of Business:** Wholesale of petroleum and petroleum products
**Directors:** Ms A B Urban, R D Mcmichael, J R Cole, C J White, C M Velazquez, W N Declaris, A Saleem
**Co. Secretary:** Dentons Secretaries Limited
**Branches:** World Fuel Services Europe Ltd, Portland House, Bressenden Place, London SW1E 5BH
**US SIC:** 5171, 5052
**UK SIC:** 61200
**Auditors:** PricewaterhouseCoopers LLP
**Bankers:** HSBC Bank plc (40-05-15)
**Employees:** 69
**Turnover:** £3,800,284,097

DUNS 64-254-0199

## World Horse Welfare

Anne Colvin House, Snetterton, Norwich, Norfolk NR16 2LR
**Tel:** 01953-498-682
**Web:** www.worldhorsewelfare.org
**Estd:** 1927
**Line of Business:** Animal welfare and care organisations
**Principals:** G Maitland-Carew *(Chairman)*, Lord M Allenby
**Responsibilities**
**IT:** Dale Gedge *(Computer Manager)*
**Branches:** World Horse Welfare, Anne Colvin House, Norwich, Norfolk NR16 2LR
**US SIC:** 8321, 0214
**UK SIC:** 96111, 01001
**Employees:** 50

DUNS 21-100-0085

## World of Books Ltd

(**Subsidiary of:** A World of Buzz Ltd)
Mulberry House, Woods Way, Goring-By-Sea, Worthing, West Sussex BN12 4QY
**Tel:** 01903507544
**Web:** www.worldofbooks.com
**Reg No:** 6437594 **Estd:** 2007 Private Limited Company
**Line of Business:** Retail sale of books, newspapers and stationery
**Export Sales:** £4,850,264
**Issued Capital:** £1,000
**Directors:** K C Blair, S Boobyer, A Maxfield, S B Downes, B Maxfield
**Co. Secretary:** Stephen Boobyer
**US SIC:** 5942 **UK SIC:** 65300

| | 31-10-13 | 31-10-12 | 31-10-11 |
|---|---|---|---|
| TO | 22,754,004 | 18,659,090 | 15,320,074 |
| P/L | 681,115 | 1,373,682 | 715,773 |
| NW | 1,730,018 | 1,308,903 | 537,171 |
| WC | 1,238,806 | 856,597 | 495,073 |
| Emp. | 322 | 290 | 214 |

DUNS 50-496-1616

## World of Golf (U K) Ltd

(**Subsidiary of:** Leisure Property Group Ltd)
Wyvern Estate, Beverley Way, New Malden, Surrey KT3 4PH
**Tel:** 020-8949-9200
**Web:** www.worldofgolf.co.uk
**Reg No:** 2464315 **Estd:** 1990 Private Limited Company
**Line of Business:** Theatrical agencies
**Issued Capital:** £86,000
**Director:** D Whittaker
**Co. Secretary:** Edward Haddon
**Branches:** Beverley Pk Golf Range, Beverley Way, New Malden
**US SIC:** 7999 **UK SIC:** 97913
**Bankers:** Bank Of Scotland (12-01-03)

| | 31-07-13 | 31-07-12 | 31-07-11 |
|---|---|---|---|
| TA | 86,000 | 86,000 | 86,000 |
| NW | 86,000 | 86,000 | 86,000 |

DUNS 23-291-2626

## World Society for the Protection of Animals

Camelford House 87-90, Albert Embankment, London SE1 7TP
**Tel:** 02075875000
**Web:** www.wspa.org.uk
**Estd:** 1900
**Line of Business:** Animal welfare and care organisations
**Trading Style:** W S P A

**Director:** A Dickson
**US SIC:** 8321 **UK SIC:** 96111
**Employees:** 100

DUNS 85-599-5226

## World Trade Group (Holdings) Ltd

(**Subsidiary of:** Atlas 90 Holdings Ltd)
90 Union Street, London SE1 0NW
**Tel:** 02079221228
**Reg No:** 6217575 **Estd:** 2007 Private Limited Company
**Line of Business:** Activities of conference organisers
**Export Sales:** £17,568,974
**Issued Capital:** £72,327
**Directors:** M Berard, R L Stanton
**US SIC:** 7999 **UK SIC:** 97913
**Auditors:** Grant Thornton UK LLP

| | 30-06-13 | 30-06-12 | 31-06-11 |
|---|---|---|---|
| TO | 22,475,211 | 27,488,463 | 15,674,656 |
| P/L | 1,382,234 | 1,354,428 | 2,181,674 |
| NW | 1,033,578 | 1,619,697 | 1,039,233 |
| WC | 620,716 | 984,799 | 687,588 |
| Emp. | 265 | 287 | 218 |

DUNS 37-970-8118 **Imp**

## World Trade Group Ltd

(**Subsidiary of:** Kester Capital Llp)
90 Union Street, London SE1 0NW
**Tel:** 020-7202-7500
**Web:** www.wtgevents.com
**Reg No:** 3278627 **Estd:** 1996 Private Limited Company
**Line of Business:** Conference related services
**Export Sales:** £8,792,063
**Issued Capital:** £84,250
**Directors:** M Berard, R L Stanton
**Responsibilities**
**Senior:** Dan Drori *(Group Sales Director)*
**Marketing:** Lawrence Allen *(Marketing Manager)*
**Sales:** Lawrence Allen *(Marketing Manager)*, Dan Drori *(Group Sales Director)*
**IT:** B Peat *(Computer Manager)*
**HR:** Ceri Barratt *(Human Resources Manager)*
**Health & Safety:** Ceri Barratt *(Human Resources Manager)*
**Operations:** Ben Ruffell *(Consultant)*
**Engineering:** Caroline Mather *(Group Events Director, Product)*
**US SIC:** 7399, 7999
**UK SIC:** 83954, 97913
**Auditors:** Grant Thornton UK LLP
**Bankers:** National Westminster Bank Plc (60-40-05)

| | 30-06-13 | 30-06-12 | 31-06-11 |
|---|---|---|---|
| TO | 13,698,300 | 18,036,266 | 10,404,562 |
| P/L | 162,898 | 91,100 | 1,280,488 |
| NW | 301,913 | (70,096) | 356,058 |
| WC | (29,183) | (526,832) | 92,359 |
| Emp. | 174 | 172 | 143 |

DUNS 21-032-4182 **Imp**

## World Transport Agency Ltd

(**Subsidiary of:** Sommer Holdings Ltd)
Thameside House, Kingsway Business Park, Oldfield Road, Hampton, Middlesex TW12 2HD
**Fax:** 02087832114
**Web:** www.wtagroup.com
**Reg No:** 0129014 **VAT No:** 235976624
**Estd:** 1913 Private Limited Company
**Line of Business:** Freight forwarders
**Export Sales:** £9,446,329
**Trading Style:** W T A
**Issued Capital:** £23,800
**Principals:** C E Sommer *(Chairman)*, G W Lawler *(Managing)*, A Hilton, A R Butler, J D Sommer, T Kuehn, Miss E C Evans
**Co. Secretary:** Charles Wegener
**Responsibilities**
**Senior:** Kelvin Edmundson *(Manager)*
**Sales:** David Berkshire *(Sales Director)*
**HR:** Carol Goodyear *(Human Resources Manager)*
**Health & Safety:** Michelle Beasley-Hill *(IT)*, Dave Brown *(Health & Safety)*
**Branches:** World Transport Agency Ltd, Furness House, Furness Quay, Salford, Lancashire M50 3XZ
**US SIC:** 4712 **UK SIC:** 77002
**Auditors:** Menzies LLP
**Bankers:** HSBC Bank plc (40-08-32)

| | 30-06-13 | 30-06-12 | 30-06-11 |
|---|---|---|---|
| TO | 56,106,010 | 61,911,942 | 58,463,680 |
| P/L | 782,846 | 1,436,757 | 1,531,164 |
| NW | 2,321,955 | 2,075,099 | 3,102,744 |
| WC | 2,165,547 | 1,912,962 | 2,956,724 |
| Emp. | 92 | 85 | 85 |

DUNS 22-731-9878 **Imp-Exp**

## World Vision U K

World Vision House, Opal Drive, Milton Keynes, Buckinghamshire MK15 0ZR
**Tel:** 01908841000
**Web:** www.worldvision.org.uk
**Reg No:** 1675552 **Estd:** 1982 Private Company Limited By Guarantee
**Line of Business:** Development and selling of real estate
**Trading Style:** World Vision
**Directors:** M R Sheard, M R Parsons, S W Phelps, R P Izard, Ms A E Laszlo, J C Thomas, Ms V M Dias, K R Malcouronne
**Co. Secretary:** Jonathan Bailey
**Responsibilities**
**Senior:** Justin Byworth *(Chief Executive)*, Marie-Eve Coulomb *(Director)*, Dorothea Hodge *(Manager)*
**Marketing:** Sally Bownes *(Head of Media and Communicatio)*, Bev Jarvis-Pearson *(Marketing Manager)*
**IT:** David Allsopp *(Head of ICTand Operations)*
**Health & Safety:** Ian Turvey *(Facilities Manager)*
**Facilities:** Ian Turvey *(Facilities Manager)*
**US SIC:** 6552 **UK SIC:** 85000
**Auditors:** Deloitte & Touche LLP
**Bankers:** The Co-Operative Bank Plc (08-90-13)

| | 30-09-13 | 30-09-12 | 30-09-11 |
|---|---|---|---|
| TO | 66,742,000 | 68,789,000 | 67,925,000 |
| P/L | (3,680,000) | 125,000 | 583,000 |
| NW | 14,544,000 | 19,131,000 | 17,000,000 |
| WC | 11,598,000 | 15,165,000 | 14,680,000 |
| Emp. | 206 | 221 | 193 |

DUNS 23-864-6181 **Imp**

## Worldmark Uk Ltd

(**Subsidiary of:** Worldmark International Holdings Ltd)
4 Redwood Crescent, East Kilbride, Glasgow, Lanarkshire G74 5PA
**Tel:** 01355-249191 **Fax:** 01355-230875
**Web:** www.worldmark.com
**Reg No:** 0200673SC **Estd:** 1999 Private Limited Company
**Line of Business:** Printing not elsewhere classified
**Export Sales:** £30,166,000
**Issued Capital:** £4,000,000
**Director:** W Graham
**Co. Secretary:** Francis Duffin
**US SIC:** 2752 **UK SIC:** 47544
**Auditors:** Deloitte LLP
**Bankers:** The Royal Bank Of Scotland Plc (16-13-18)

| | 31-12-13 | 31-12-12 | 31-12-11 |
|---|---|---|---|
| TO | 33,368,000 | 33,229,000 | 36,069,000 |
| P/L | 1,224,000 | 3,865,000 | 6,738,000 |
| NW | 33,665,000 | 32,075,000 | 27,864,000 |
| WC | 44,971,000 | 43,005,000 | 35,523,000 |
| Emp. | 257 | 287 | 306 |

DUNS 23-995-3362 **Imp**

## Worldone Research Ltd

Unity Wharf, London SE1 2BH
**Tel:** 020-7252-1118
**Web:** www.worldone.com
**Reg No:** 3983598 **VAT No:** 761384325
**Estd:** 2000 Private Limited Company
**Line of Business:** Market research organisations
**Issued Capital:** £533,408
**Directors:** J M Wright, P Kirk
**Responsibilities**
**Senior:** Morten Kirk *(Manager)*, Gerard Smith *(Manager)*
**Operations:** Oran Hallale *(SVP Global Operations)*
**US SIC:** 7392 **UK SIC:** 83951
**Auditors:** BDO LLP

| | 31-12-13 | 31-12-12 | 31-12-11 |
|---|---|---|---|
| TO | 24,548,885 | 31,375,534 | 34,766,628 |
| P/L | (8,287,882) | (5,313,556) | (3,646,600) |
| NW | (12,802,667) | (4,521,418) | 813,757 |
| WC | (13,379,166) | (5,191,949) | 489,894 |
| Emp. | 68 | 165 | 183 |

DUNS 34-792-9916

## Worldpay Ap Ltd.

(**Subsidiary of:** Ship Investor & Cy Sca)
60 Charlotte Street, London W1T 2DD
**Tel:** 020 7436 7851 **Fax:** 02071175307
**Web:** www.envoyservices.com
**Reg No:** 5593466 **VAT No:** 873050141
**Estd:** 2006 Private Limited Company
**Line of Business:** Financial intermediation not elsewhere classified
**Export Sales:** £26,727,000
**Issued Capital:** £259
**Directors:** R Kalifa, M E O'Brien, F P De Kort, P J Mcgriskin, P E Jansen
**Co. Secretary:** Mark O'Brien
**US SIC:** 6111, 7399
**UK SIC:** 81501, 83954
**Auditors:** Riches & Co
**Bankers:** Barclays Bank Plc (20-36-47)

| | 31-12-13 | 31-12-12 | 31-12-11 |
|---|---|---|---|
| TA | 176,687,000 | 104,376,753 | 65,782,193 |
| P/L | 4,323,000 | 1,936,598 | (367,667) |
| NW | 11,277,000 | 8,104,411 | 5,153,748 |
| WC | 8,298,000 | 3,908,212 | 4,296,545 |
| Emp. | 76 | 69 | 71 |

DUNS 53-619-6140

## Worldpay Ltd

(**Subsidiary of:** Ship Investor & Cy Sca)
270-289 The Science Park, Cambridge, Cambridgeshire CB4 0WG
**Tel:** 08453016251 **Fax:** 08703661275
**Web:** www.worldpay.com
**Reg No:** 3424752 **Estd:** 1997 Private Limited Company
**Line of Business:** Other business activities not elsewhere classified
**Trading Style:** Worldpay Limited
**Issued Capital:** £165,000
**Directors:** F P De Kort, P E Jansen, R M Kalifa, A J Connolly
**Responsibilities**
**Senior:** Dave Hobday *(Manager)*, Raghav Prasad *(Manager)*, Elizabeth Shurdom *(Manager)*
**Admin:** Jackie Harrow *(Office Manager)*
**HR:** Andy Doyle *(Chief Human Resources Officer)*
**Health & Safety:** Jackie Harrow *(Office Manager)*
**Facilities:** Jackie Harrow *(Office Manager)*
**US SIC:** 7399 **UK SIC:** 83954
**Auditors:** Deloitte LLP
**Bankers:** National Westminster Bank Plc (60-12-03)

| | 31-12-13 | 31-12-12 | 31-12-11 |
|---|---|---|---|
| TO | 152,537,000 | 121,167,000 | 107,237,000 |
| P/L | 12,439,000 | 12,850,000 | 20,547,000 |
| NW | 22,631,000 | 35,711,000 | 29,469,000 |
| WC | 20,517,000 | 33,829,000 | 26,402,000 |
| Emp. | 46 | 61 | 257 |

DUNS 21-681-0815 **Imp**

## Worldpay (Uk) Ltd

(**Subsidiary of:** Ship Investor & Cy Sca)
The Walbrook Building, London EC4N 8AF
**Web:** www.worldpay.com
**Reg No:** 7316500 **Estd:** 2010 Private Limited Company
**Line of Business:** Other business activities not elsewhere classified
**Export Sales:** £39,000,000
**Trading Style:** Streamline
**Issued Capital:** £1,033,504,702
**Directors:** A J Connolly, P E Jansen, R Kalifa, D A Hobday
**Responsibilities**
**Senior:** Floris de Kort *(Managing Director - E-commerce)*
**Finance:** Rob Hornby *(Chief Separation Officer)*
**Marketing:** Damon Anderson *(Vice President, Product Manage)*, Kevin Dallas *(Chief Marketing Officer)*, Jenna Dore *(Marketing Campaign Manager)*, Floris de Kort *(Managing Director - E-commerce)*
**Sales:** Russell Curzon *(Sales Director)*, Shane Happach *(Chief Commercial Officer - E-C)*, Clare Haskins *(Head of Sales)*, Paul McManus *(Business Development Manager)*
**IT:** Shane Happach *(Chief Commercial Officer - E-C)*
**US SIC:** 7399 **UK SIC:** 83954
**Auditors:** KPMG LLP
**Bankers:** The Royal Bank Of Scotland Plc (15-00-00)

**Following financial data are in thousands**

| | 31-12-13 | 31-12-12 | 31-12-11 |
|---|---|---|---|
| TO | 1,516,000 | 1,406,000 | 1,512,000 |
| P/L | 28,000 | 55,000 | 118,000 |
| NW | 427,000 | 373,000 | 301,000 |
| WC | 259,000 | 271,000 | 241,000 |
| Emp. | 2,180 | 2,427 | 1,144 |

DUNS 28-946-6831 **Imp-Exp**

## Worlds Apart Ltd

(**Subsidiary of:** Worlds Apart Holdings Ltd)
Unit 3 St Columb Major Business Park, Hurling Way, St Columb, Cornwall TR9 6SX
**Tel:** 08456022119
**Web:** http://worldsapart.com
**Reg No:** 1606138 **VAT No:** 237857524
**Estd:** 1982 Private Limited Company
**Line of Business:** Manufacturers of games, toys and sporting products
**Export Markets:** E U
**Issued Capital:** £105,555
**Principals:** J G Stewart *(Managing)*, S M Birchenough *(Managing)*, N T Shinner, A C Cooper, B C Lawton
**Co. Secretary:** Brian Lawton
**Responsibilities**
**Finance:** Craig Norton *(Financial Controller)*
**IT:** Andy Butterworth *(IT Manager)*
**HR:** Bethan Roberts *(Human Resources Manager)*, Jackie Walsh *(Human Resources Manager)*
**Health & Safety:** Bethan Roberts *(Human Resources Manager)*, Jackie Walsh *(Human Resources Manager)*
**Facilities:** Bethan Roberts *(Human Resources Manager)*, Jackie Walsh *(Human Resources Manager)*
**US SIC:** 3949 **UK SIC:** 49420
**Auditors:** KPMG LLP
**Bankers:** Lloyds TSB Bank plc (30-97-86)

| | 31-12-13 | 31-12-12 | 31-12-11 |
|---|---|---|---|
| TA | 11,023,983 | 12,731,198 | 10,663,671 |
| P/L | 1,081,128 | 968,812 | 57,822 |
| NW | 3,113,604 | 2,648,099 | 2,307,451 |
| WC | 2,525,577 | 1,756,468 | 1,615,012 |
| Emp. | 81 | 84 | 85 |

DUNS 73-315-2339

## Worldview Ltd

Telephone House, 3rd & 4th Floor, Lancaster, Lancashire LA3 1BS
**Tel:** 08455-211-680 **Fax:** 08455-211-681
**Web:** www.worldviewlimited.com
**Reg No:** 4588973 **Estd:** 2001 Private Limited Company
**Line of Business:** Other tourist or short-stay accommodation
**Issued Capital:** £198
**Directors:** Mrs D M Parker, V Parker, D Parker
**Co. Secretary:** Stuart Parker
**US SIC:** 7021 **UK SIC:** 66500
**Auditors:** RSM Tenon Ltd

| | 30-11-13 | 30-11-12 | 30-11-11 |
|---|---|---|---|
| TA | 891,766 | 895,564 | 736,120 |
| NW | 353,759 | 495,108 | 291,009 |
| WC | 313,882 | 468,853 | 254,829 |

DUNS 39-930-1563 **Imp**

## Worldwide Clinical Trials Uk Ltd

(**Subsidiary of:** Wct Holdings Ltd)
Isaac Newton Centre, Nottingham Science & Technology Park, Nottingham, Nottinghamshire NG7 2RH
**Tel:** 01159-567711
**Web:** www.wwctrials.com
**Reg No:** 2244384 **Estd:** 2009 Private Limited Company
**Line of Business:** Research and laboratory based activities
**Issued Capital:** £105
**Directors:** M R Denvir, F Dorigotti, P Suffredini, D M Butler, A Carta
**Co. Secretary:** Dentons Secretaries Limited
**Responsibilities**
**Senior:** Anthony Merriman *(Facilities Manager)*
**US SIC:** 7391, 7397
**UK SIC:** 94000, 83702
**Auditors:** PKF
**Bankers:** National Westminster Bank Plc (60-15-49)

| | 31-12-13 | 31-12-12 | 31-12-11 |
|---|---|---|---|
| TO | N/A | N/A | 4,059,643 |
| P/L | N/A | N/A | 679,641 |
| NW | 3,230,440 | 3,230,440 | 3,230,440 |
| WC | N/A | N/A | 3,230,440 |
| Emp. | N/A | N/A | 145 |

DUNS 21-807-0453

## Worldwide Flight Services

Building F Cargo Terminal 1, Gatwick Airport West, London Gatwick Airport, Horley, Surrey RH6 0SQ
**Tel:** 01293555490
**Web:** www.worldwideflightservices.co.uk
**Estd:** 2012
**Line of Business:** Animal transportation services
**Responsibilities**
**Senior:** Andrew Willett *(General Manager)*
**US SIC:** 4712 **UK SIC:** 77002
**Employees:** 50

DUNS 23-896-7488

## Worldwide Flight Services Ltd

(**Subsidiary of:** Lbo France Gestion)
Building 552, Shoreham Road East, London Heathrow Airport, Hounslow, Middlesex TW6 3UA
**Tel:** 02085645550 **Fax:** 01132391110
**Reg No:** 3887506 **Estd:** 1999 Private Limited Company
**Line of Business:** Other supporting air transport activities
**Export Sales:** £1,199,656
**Issued Capital:** £3,582,552
**Directors:** P I Roberts, O P Bijaoui
**Co. Secretary:** Steven Greenhalgh
**US SIC:** 4582 **UK SIC:** 76400
**Auditors:** Inghams
**Bankers:** National Westminster Bank Plc (55-50-39)

| | 31-12-13 | 31-12-12 | 31-12-11 |
|---|---|---|---|
| TO | 66,517,367 | 62,365,347 | 55,951,164 |
| P/L | 3,217,909 | 4,219,145 | 1,185,327 |
| NW | 2,427,984 | 429,867 | (1,930,164) |
| WC | 2,147,520 | 146,775 | (1,037,716) |
| Emp. | 630 | 522 | 476 |

DUNS 23-815-4897 **Imp**

## Worldwide Foods (Birmingham) Ltd

360 Coventry Road, Small Heath, Birmingham, West Midlands B10 0XE
**Tel:** 01217534391 **Fax:** 0121-771-1439
**Web:** www.nisatodaysfoodstores.com
**Reg No:** 3807718 **Estd:** 2002 Private Limited Company
**Line of Business:** Supermarkets
**Issued Capital:** £1,000
**Director:** M A Alam
**Responsibilities**
**Senior:** Wasif Amjad *(Manager)*, Kashif Javed *(Manager)*
**US SIC:** 5411 **UK SIC:** 64100
**Auditors:** Tenon Ltd
**Bankers:** National Westminster Bank Plc (01-07-44)

| | 30-05-13 | 30-05-12 | 30-05-11 |
|---|---|---|---|
| TO | 12,170,983 | 12,004,108 | N/A |
| P/L | 171,843 | 199,396 | N/A |
| NW | 207,922 | 238,798 | 260,308 |
| WC | (1,555,821) | (1,467,911) | (1,143,680) |
| Emp. | 49 | 56 | N/A |

DUNS 23-839-4741

## Worldwide Fruit Ltd

Apple Way, Wardentree Lane, Pinchbeck, Spalding, Lincolnshire PE11 3BB
**Tel:** 01775-717000
**Web:** www.worldwidefruit.co.uk
**Reg No:** 3831143 **VAT No:** 740920155
**Estd:** 2000 Private Limited Company
**Line of Business:** Wholesalers of fruit and vegetable
**Export Sales:** £1,916,000
**Issued Capital:** £500,000
**Principals:** G Clark *(Financial)*, A T Fissette, A M Hulbert, L P Morrish, H R Hamster, P Mansfield, R A Hinge
**Responsibilities**
**Senior:** Robert Balicki *(Chief Executive)*, David Candy *(Operations Manager)*, Gordan Clark *(Financial Director)*
**Finance:** Gordan Clark *(Financial Director)*
**Marketing:** Steve Maxwell *(Commercial Director)*
**Sales:** Steve Maxwell *(Commercial Director)*
**Admin:** Gordan Clark *(Financial Director)*
**Facilities:** David Candy *(Operations Manager)*
**Operations:** David Candy *(Operations Manager)*, Steve Maxwell *(Commercial Director)*
**Purchasing:** Steve Maxwell *(Commercial Director)*
**Fleet:** David Candy *(Operations Manager)*
**Branches:** Worldwide Fruit Ltd, Unit 68-69, Harvey Drive, Whitstable, Kent CT5 3QT
**US SIC:** 5148, 4712
**UK SIC:** 61700, 77002
**Auditors:** Burgess Hodgson
**Bankers:** National Westminster Bank Plc (55-50-36)

| | 28-06-14 | 29-06-13 | 30-06-12 |
|---|---|---|---|
| TO | 116,101,000 | 113,248,000 | 104,432,000 |
| P/L | 2,009,000 | 1,538,000 | 1,765,000 |
| NW | 3,160,000 | 2,592,000 | 1,655,000 |
| WC | (523,000) | (414,000) | (1,694,000) |
| Emp. | 257 | 257 | 235 |

DUNS 23-575-0242

## Worldwide Leisure Group Ltd

(**Subsidiary of:** G. I. H. Ltd)
Woodland Point, Wootton Mount, Bournemouth, Dorset BH1 1PJ
**Tel:** 08717816800
**Web:** www.wwlg.co.uk
**Reg No:** 3572985 **Estd:** 1998 Private Limited Company
**Line of Business:** Timeshare operations
**Trading Style:** The Paradise Group
**Issued Capital:** £60
**Director:** G J Siden
**Co. Secretary:** Mrs Diane Norman
**Responsibilities**
**Senior:** Louise Speight *(Office Manager)*
**Branches:** Worldwide Leisure Group Ltd, 1st Floor, 55-56 Worcester St, Kidderminster, Worcestershire DY10 1EL
**US SIC:** 7021 **UK SIC:** 66500
**Auditors:** KPMG

| | 31-12-13 | 31-12-12 | 31-12-11 |
|---|---|---|---|
| TO | 2,032,362 | 2,092,178 | 3,028,589 |
| P/L | (142,167) | (10,483) | (175,397) |
| NW | 386,536 | 688,515 | (191,441) |
| WC | (549,964) | (200,745) | 293,866 |
| Emp. | 80 | 81 | 99 |

DUNS 76-797-9487 **Imp**

## Worldwide Oilfield Machine (U K) Ltd

(**Subsidiary of:** Worldwide Oilfield Machine Inc.)
7 St Machar Road, Aberdeen, Aberdeenshire AB24 2UU
**Tel:** 01224484400
**Web:** www.womusa.com
**Reg No:** 0131097SC **VAT No:** 658321723

**Estd:** 2010 Private Limited Company
**Line of Business:** Drilling and boring equipment
**Export Sales:** £4,441,228
**Issued Capital:** £200,000
**Directors:** S S Puranik, D J Ayrton, W G Kinnear
**Co. Secretary:** Neil Gordon
**US SIC:** 3531 **UK SIC:** 32541
**Auditors:** Deloitte & Touche
**Bankers:** Clydesdale Bank Plc (82-62-22)

| | 31-12-13 | 31-12-12 | 30-12-12 |
|---|---|---|---|
| TO | 17,483,872 | 9,755,482 | 10,834,739 |
| P/L | 1,794,167 | 1,389,380 | 987,651 |
| NW | 4,625,381 | 3,253,015 | 1,856,506 |
| WC | 3,003,636 | 1,758,442 | 1,448,366 |
| Emp. | 61 | 51 | 45 |

DUNS 22-247-2230
## Worldwide Recruitment Solutions Ltd
First Floor Bowdon House, 4 Scott Drive, Altrincham, Cheshire WA15 8AB
**Tel:** 01619262525 **Fax:** 0161-926-4647
**Web:** www.worldwide-rs.com
**Reg No:** 4265209 **Estd:** 2001 Private Limited Company
**Line of Business:** Employment and recruitment companies and consultants
**Export Sales:** £19,084,394
**Issued Capital:** £128
**Directors:** F J Dunleavy, M R Brown, M D Wells
**Co. Secretary:** Luana Brown
**US SIC:** 7361 **UK SIC:** 83954

| | 31-12-13 | 31-12-12 | 31-12-11 |
|---|---|---|---|
| TO | 22,450,294 | N/A | N/A |
| P/L | 1,673,878 | N/A | N/A |
| NW | 2,489,425 | 1,576,787 | 615,826 |
| WC | 2,462,364 | 1,569,232 | 620,343 |
| Emp. | 49 | N/A | N/A |

DUNS 23-079-7714 Exp
## Worldwing Investments Ltd
(**Subsidiary of:** Wittington Investments Ltd)
Pataks Foods Ltd, Kiribati Way, Leigh, Lancashire WN7 5RS
**Fax:** 01942272500
**Reg No:** 2778854 **VAT No:** 707723730
**Estd:** 1993 Private Limited Company
**Line of Business:** Management activities of holding companies
**Export Markets:** Australia, U S A, Canada, Netherlands, France, Ireland
**Issued Capital:** £3,344,153
**Directors:** S P White, A J Mayhew
**Co. Secretary:** Mrs Rosalyn Schofield
**US SIC:** 6711 **UK SIC:** 83962
**Auditors:** Baker Tilly UK Audit LLP
**Bankers:** HSBC Bank plc (40-12-41)

| | 14-09-13 | 15-09-12 | 17-09-11 |
|---|---|---|---|
| TA | 3,850,545 | 3,847,324 | 4,341,646 |
| P/L | 10,005,221 | 10,008,679 | 2,316,259 |
| NW | 3,848,685 | 3,844,691 | 3,838,190 |
| WC | 517,533 | 513,539 | 507,038 |

DUNS 42-346-7658
## Worleyparsons Europe Ltd
(**Subsidiary of:** Worleyparsons Limited)
Parkview, Great West Road, Brentford, Middlesex TW8 9AZ
**Tel:** 020 8326 5000 **Fax:** 020 8710 0220
**Web:** www.worleyparsons.com
**Reg No:** 4334425 **VAT No:** 945648483
**Estd:** 2001 Private Limited Company
**Line of Business:** Architectural activities
**Issued Capital:** £1,000,000
**Directors:** Mrs B Connell, A Wood, M J Stirling, S Holt, A Gordon, C Ashton, M O Daly
**Co. Secretary:** Victor Jibuike
**Responsibilities**
**Senior:** Stuart Bradie *(Manager)*, John Grill *(Manager)*, Mark Southey *(Managing Director Minerals and)*
**Sales:** Phil Penfold *(Business Development Director)*
**IT:** Seamus Flannagan *(IT Manager)*
**HR:** Helen Sheehy *(HR Manager)*
**Operations:** Liege Robson *(Project Director)*
**Engineering:** James Assem *(Principal Hydrogeologist)*, Morgan Sales *(Lead Environmental Engineer)*
**Branches:** Worleyparsons Europe Ltd, Signal Point, Bredbury Park Way, Stockport, Cheshire SK6 2SN
**US SIC:** 8911 **UK SIC:** 83701
**Auditors:** Ernst & Young LLP
**Bankers:** HSBC Bank plc (40-02-50)

| | 30-06-14 | 30-06-13 | 30-06-12 |
|---|---|---|---|
| TO | 287,720,000 | 265,762,000 | 284,862,000 |
| P/L | (5,222,000) | 18,768,000 | 8,505,000 |
| NW | 274,599,000 | 282,642,000 | 270,986,000 |
| WC | 35,692,000 | 12,367,000 | 2,830,000 |
| Emp. | 685 | 711 | 624 |

DUNS 28-993-9274 Exp
## Wormald Industrial Property Ltd
Grimshaw Lane, Manchester M40 2AX
**Tel:** 01612052321
**Reg No:** 1834858 **Estd:** 2013 Private Limited Company
**Line of Business:** Business services
**Issued Capital:** £2
**Directors:** A Bowie, P Schieser
**Co. Secretary:** Anton Alphonsus
**US SIC:** 7399 **UK SIC:** 83954

| | 30-09-13 | 30-09-12 | 30-09-11 |
|---|---|---|---|
| TA | 1 | 1 | 1 |
| NW | (508,756) | (508,756) | (508,756) |
| WC | (508,756) | N/A | N/A |

DUNS 28-829-8755
## Worplesdon Golf Club Estates Ltd
Heath House Road, Woking, Surrey GU22 0RA
**Tel:** 01483-472277
**Web:** www.worplesdongc.co.uk
**Reg No:** 0136913 **Estd:** 1914 Private Limited Company
**Line of Business:** Golf clubs
**Trading Style:** Worplesdon Golf Club
**Issued Capital:** £9
**Directors:** A N Mcarthur, J E Phillips, J Hargreaves, A J Rickard, B O Lloyd, D I Hough, D Swanston, J J Caplan
**Co. Secretary:** Christopher Lomas
**Responsibilities**
**Senior:** Rodney Bond *(Manager)*, James Christine *(Manager)*, Stephen Gebbie *(Director)*, Michael Stearn *(Manager)*, Andrew Swanston *(Manager)*
**US SIC:** 6531, 7999
**UK SIC:** 83400, 97913
**Bankers:** The Royal Bank Of Scotland Plc (16-19-26)

| | 31-12-13 | 31-12-12 | 31-12-11 |
|---|---|---|---|
| TA | 331,922 | 343,827 | 405,310 |
| NW | 149,055 | 148,960 | 148,864 |
| WC | N/A | N/A | 51,258 |

DUNS 23-667-5229
## The Worshipful Co of Mercers
Worshipful Company Of Mercers, London EC2V 8HE
**Tel:** 020-7726-4991
**Web:** www.mercers.co.uk
**Estd:** 1985
**Line of Business:** Committee managed organisations
**Trading Style:** The Mercers Company
**Directors:** Selbourne, F F Fenwick, J A Watney, Mrs M Mcgregor, R Pope
**Responsibilities**
**Senior:** Richard Westmacott *(Manager)*
**Branches:** The Worshipful Co Of Mercers, Mercers Hall, Ironmonger Lane, London EC2V 8HE
**US SIC:** 8699 **UK SIC:** 96902
**Auditors:** PricewaterhouseCoopers LLP
**Bankers:** Bank Of England (10-00-00)
**Employees:** 46
**Turnover:** £16,180,000

DUNS 21-664-4646
## Worsley Park Golf Club
Walkden Road, Worsley, Manchester M28 2QT
**Tel:** 01619752043
**Web:** www.marriott.co.uk
**Estd:** 1998
**Line of Business:** Hotels and motels without restaurant
**US SIC:** 7011 **UK SIC:** 66500
**Employees:** 250

DUNS 23-685-3870 Imp
## Worsley Plant Ltd
Road Beta, Brooks Lane, Middlewich, Cheshire CW10 0QF
**Tel:** 01606-835544 **Fax:** 01606-835522
**Web:** www.worsleyplant.co.uk
**Reg No:** 3680407 **Estd:** 1995 Private Limited Company
**Line of Business:** Building of complete constructions or parts thereof; civil engineering
**Issued Capital:** £1
**Director:** S E Heron
**Co. Secretary:** Ms Elizabeth Oldfield
**US SIC:** 1541, 1799
**UK SIC:** 50100, 50000

| | 31-12-13 | 31-12-12 | 31-12-11 |
|---|---|---|---|
| TA | 3,084,357 | 2,582,026 | 2,152,955 |
| NW | 1,569,036 | 1,119,206 | 1,007,496 |
| WC | 556,731 | 326,965 | 354,656 |

DUNS 36-532-0808
## Worth Abbey
Paddockhurst Road, Turners Hill, Crawley, West Sussex RH10 4SB
**Reg No:** 4475556 **Estd:** 2002 Private Limited Company
**Line of Business:** Activities of religious organisations
**Directors:** R L Jolly, M E Mcgee, P V Fludder, J M Barrett, P M Williams, C A Murray, A Da Costa Fernandes
**Co. Secretary:** Mark Sweeting
**Responsibilities**
**Senior:** James Cutts *(Manager)*
**US SIC:** 8661 **UK SIC:** 96600
**Bankers:** Bank Of Scotland (12-12-68)

| | 31-08-13 | 31-08-12 | 31-08-11 |
|---|---|---|---|
| TO | 13,336,478 | 12,951,149 | 12,439,254 |
| P/L | 613,649 | 1,342,992 | 1,134,241 |
| NW | 19,597,773 | 18,648,493 | 17,079,477 |
| WC | (2,492,148) | (3,359,714) | (2,622,078) |
| Emp. | 179 | 173 | 162 |

DUNS 23-343-6653
## Worth School
Paddockhurst Road, Turners Hill, Crawley, West Sussex RH10 4SD
**Web:** www.worthschool.co.uk
**Reg No:** 4476558 **Estd:** 2002 Private Limited Company
**Line of Business:** General secondary education
**Directors:** B J Elwes, Ms A Andreotti, J B Guyatt, J F Scherer, P L Cutts, R L Jolly, N Deeming, D R Buxton
**Co. Secretary:** Mark Sweeting
**Responsibilities**
**Senior:** Gino Carminati *(Headmaster)*, Christina Fitzsimons *(Director)*, Gordon Moore *(Director)*, Fiona Newton *(Director)*
**Marketing:** Olivia Henley *(Marketing Manager)*
**Admin:** Jenny Griggs *(Administrator)*, Yvonne Lorraine *(Registrar)*
**IT:** Stuart Blackhurst *(Computer Manager)*
**HR:** Joan Riddell *(Human Resources Manager)*, James Whitehead *(Deputy Head)*
**Fleet:** Andrew McMahon *(Transport Manager)*
**US SIC:** 8211, 8661
**UK SIC:** 93200, 96600
**Auditors:** Crowe Clark Whitehill LLP
**Bankers:** Bank Of Scotland (12-12-68)

| | 31-08-13 | 31-08-12 | 31-08-11 |
|---|---|---|---|
| TO | 12,468,772 | 11,961,955 | 11,127,774 |
| P/L | N/A | N/A | (8,108) |
| WC | 1,705,774 | 1,829,258 | 1,580,892 |
| Emp. | 158 | 153 | 142 |

DUNS 50-648-1576
## Worthing & Southlands
Hospitals Nhs Trust, Lyndhurst Road, Worthing, West Sussex BN11 2DH
**Web:** www.worthinghospital.nhs.uk
**Estd:** 1995
**Line of Business:** General medical and surgical hospitals
**Responsibilities**
**IT:** Simon Steeles *(Head of Procurement & IT)*
**US SIC:** 8062 **UK SIC:** 95100
**Employees:** 3,000

DUNS 23-642-9734
## Worthing Borough Council
Town Hall, Chapel Road, Worthing, West Sussex BN11 1HA
**Tel:** 01903-239999
**Web:** www.worthing.gov.uk
**Estd:** 1890
**Line of Business:** Local government
**Director:** M Ball
**Responsibilities**
**Senior:** Russ Akehurst *(Executive)*, Alex Bailey *(Chief Executive Officer)*, Ann Barlow *(Chairman)*, Rhian Francis *(Partner)*, Tony Lucas *(Executive)*, Diana Peek *(General Manager)*, Christine Ryder *(Head of Adur homes)*
**Marketing:** Janice Fraser *(Tourism Development & Marketin)*
**Admin:** Elaine Lefebour *(Administrator)*
**IT:** Mark Gawley *(ICT Services Manager)*, Vicky Lamburn *(IT Officer)*
**Health & Safety:** Jacqui Cooke *(Community Safety Manager)*
**Facilities:** Bryan Curtis *(Principal Engineer)*, Andy Edwards *(Parks and Shore Manager)*, Amanda Lowes *(Housing Services Manager)*
**Operations:** James Appleton *(Executive Head of Planning, Re)*
**Purchasing:** Martin Hosier *(Business Services Administrato)*
**Engineering:** Cliff Harrison *(Executive Head of Technical Se)*
**Branches:** Worthing Borough Council, 87 Pelham Rd, Worthing, West Sussex BN13 1JA
**US SIC:** 9121 **UK SIC:** 91110
**Bankers:** Lloyds TSB Bank plc (30-99-93)
**Employees:** 700

DUNS 77-167-8141
## Worthing Churches Homeless Projects
13 Grafton Road, Worthing, West Sussex BN11 1QP
**Tel:** 01903235208
**Web:** www.wchp.org.uk
**Reg No:** 2708334 **Estd:** 1992 Private Limited Company
**Line of Business:** Other tourist or short-stay accommodation
**Directors:** Reverend J K Eldridge, J M Saunders, R Skipp, Dr L J Rockall, Ms S Roff, T V Wolstenholme, M J Hodson, Ms P A Maggs
**Co. Secretary:** Miss Carol Fletcher
**Responsibilities**
**Senior:** Paul Burtenshaw *(Director)*
**US SIC:** 7021 **UK SIC:** 66500
**Bankers:** National Westminster Bank Plc (60-24-31)

| | 31-03-14 | 31-03-13 | 31-03-12 |
|---|---|---|---|
| TO | 1,495,937 | 1,739,510 | 1,361,773 |
| P/L | (92,633) | 236,622 | (60,320) |
| NW | 2,834,883 | 2,927,516 | 2,690,894 |
| WC | 529,214 | 597,012 | 333,494 |
| Emp. | 46 | 39 | 39 |

DUNS 21-329-2811
## Worthing College
1 Sanditon Way, Worthing, West Sussex BN14 9FD
**Tel:** 01903275755
**Web:** www.worthing.ac.uk
**Estd:** 1999
**Line of Business:** Further education schools and colleges
**Responsibilities**
**Senior:** Peter Corrigan *(Principal)*
**Branches:** Worthing College, 53 Queens Road, Brighton, East Sussex BN1 3XB
**US SIC:** 8221 **UK SIC:** 93100
**Employees:** 250

DUNS 23-518-1901
## Worthing Homes Ltd
Davison House, North Street, Worthing, West Sussex BN11 1ER
**Fax:** 01903-703111
**Web:** www.worthing-homes.org.uk
**Reg No:** 3517244 **Estd:** 1999 Private Limited Company
**Line of Business:** Housing associations societies trusts & co-operatives
**Trading Style:** Worthing Homes
**Issued Capital:** £70
**Directors:** C D Polden, I J Flitcroft, M G Richardson, P J Howard, Ms H J Cook, Dr H M Mercer, D I Jagger, M J Mcjennett
**Co. Secretary:** Julian Pitcher
**Responsibilities**
**Senior:** Noel Atkins *(Manager)*, Virginia Hewlett *(Manager)*, Trevor Lewin *(Director)*, Mark Swindall *(Manager)*
**Marketing:** Suzanne Newman *(Marketing & Communications Coo)*
**Health & Safety:** Vic Horswell *(Health & Safety Officer)*
**US SIC:** 6519 **UK SIC:** 85000
**Auditors:** Deloitte & Touche LLP
**Bankers:** Lloyds TSB Bank plc (30-99-93)

| | 31-03-14 | 31-03-13 | 31-03-12 |
|---|---|---|---|
| TO | 18,682,000 | 16,725,000 | 14,940,000 |
| P/L | 4,457,000 | 3,175,000 | 2,218,000 |
| NW | 13,820,000 | 8,647,000 | 5,467,000 |
| WC | 3,788,000 | 1,043,000 | 8,871,000 |
| Emp. | 96 | 100 | 87 |

DUNS 34-919-9851 Imp
## Worthvision Ltd
(**Subsidiary of:** Blue Elephant International Ltd)
32 Bryanston Street, London W1H 7EG
**Tel:** 020-7224-0055 **Fax:** 020-7224-1144
**Web:** www.laportedesindes.com
**Reg No:** 2834678 **VAT No:** 653692119
**Estd:** 1996 Private Limited Company
**Line of Business:** Restaurants
**Issued Capital:** £300,000
**Directors:** S Alexander Mody, K A Steppe
**Co. Secretary:** Thaviseuth Phouthavong
**Responsibilities**
**Senior:** Patrick Henrotin *(Manager)*, Mehernosh Mody *(Health & Safety Officer)*, Nooror Somany *(Manager)*, Michel Steppe *(Manager)*
**Finance:** Patrick Henrotin *(Manager)*
**Health & Safety:** Mehernosh Mody *(Health & Safety Officer)*
**US SIC:** 5812 **UK SIC:** 66110
**Auditors:** HLB AV Audit Plc
**Bankers:** Barclays Bank Plc (20-35-90)

| | 31-12-13 | 31-12-12 | 31-12-11 |
|---|---|---|---|
| TO | 3,411,902 | 3,405,052 | 3,328,642 |
| P/L | 180,159 | 168,844 | 132,877 |
| NW | 2,061,464 | 1,825,304 | 1,704,643 |
| WC | 1,996,245 | 1,736,470 | 1,588,041 |
| Emp. | 74 | 74 | 76 |

**DUNS 21-309-6035**

## Wortlea Estates (Leeds) Ltd

Whitehall Road, Leeds, West Yorkshire LS12 5NL
**Tel:** 01132-634222 **Fax:** 01132792564
**Web:** www.ringways.co.uk
**Reg No:** 0758842 **Estd:** 1963 Private Limited Company
**Line of Business:** Holding companies management activities
**Trading Style:** Ringways Motor Group
**Issued Capital:** £147,283
**Directors:** D H Innes, G B Roberts, Mrs E M Innes, Ms J L Terry, R N Roberts, R H Innes
**Co. Secretary:** Guy Roberts
**US SIC:** 6711, 5511
**UK SIC:** 83962, 65100
**Auditors:** PricewaterhouseCoopers LLP
**Bankers:** Yorkshire Bank Plc (05-01-36)

|      | 31-12-13   | 31-12-12   | 31-12-11   |
|------|------------|------------|------------|
| TO   | 63,888,380 | 59,830,279 | 95,300,186 |
| P/L  | (126,846)  | 577,398    | (458,804)  |
| NW   | 3,599,697  | 3,726,543  | 3,748,044  |
| WC   | (1,180,078)| (1,032,601)| (1,004,615)|
| Emp. | 131        | 126        | 207        |

**DUNS 34-747-5688**

## Wortley Byers Llp

1 Cathedral Place, Brentwood, Essex CM14 4ES
**Tel:** 01277268368
**Web:** www.wortleybyers.co.uk
**Reg No:** 0311066OC
**Partnership**
**Line of Business:** Solicitors
**Responsibilities**
**Senior:** Michael Callaghan (Non-designated Limited Liabili), Robert Hawkings (Designated Limited Liability P)
**US SIC:** 8111 **UK SIC:** 83500

|     | 31-12-13  | 31-12-12  | 31-12-11  |
|-----|-----------|-----------|-----------|
| TA  | 1,153,957 | 1,177,236 | 1,296,816 |
| NW  | 731,874   | 563,797   | N/A       |
| WC  | 824,492   | 695,297   | 963,388   |

**DUNS 21-549-9554**

## Wotton House

Guildford Road, Wotton, Dorking, Surrey RH5 6HS
**Tel:** 01306730000
**Web:** www.principal-hayley.com
**Estd:** 2012
**Line of Business:** Other tourist assistance activities not elsewhere classified
**Trading Style:** Hayley Conference Centre
**Proprietor:** M Wilson
**Responsibilities**
**Senior:** Thomas Armes (General Manager)
**US SIC:** 7999 **UK SIC:** 97913
**Employees:** 200

**DUNS 21-613-6623**

## Wow

4 Churchill Way, Cardiff, South Glamorgan CF10 2DW
**Tel:** 02920666247
**Web:** www.wowbarcardiff.co.uk
**Estd:** 2011
**Line of Business:** Managed public houses and bars
**Responsibilities**
**Senior:** Gareth Crossman (Manager), Victoria Roffi (Manager)
**US SIC:** 5813 **UK SIC:** 66200
**Employees:** 49

**DUNS 77-888-6101**

## Wozair Ltd

5-6 Saracen Close, Gillingham Business Park, Gillingham, Kent ME8 0QN
**Web:** www.wozair.com
**Reg No:** 3039016 **Estd:** 1995 Private Limited Company
**Line of Business:** Air conditioning equipment
**Export Sales:** £22,753,304
**Issued Capital:** £17,000
**Directors:** A R Brooks, K H Pleace, P M Azzopardi
**Co. Secretary:** Simon Collins
**Responsibilities**
**Senior:** Francis Sayle (Operations Manager)
**Finance:** Sue Chevis (Accounts Manager)
**IT:** Anoj Perera (Computer Manager)
**Facilities:** Francis Sayle (Operations Manager)
**Operations:** Francis Sayle (Operations Manager)
**Engineering:** Francis Sayle (Operations Manager)
**US SIC:** 3585 **UK SIC:** 32841
**Auditors:** McCabe Ford Williams
**Bankers:** Barclays Bank Plc (20-23-97)

|      | 31-12-13   | 31-12-12   | 31-12-11   |
|------|------------|------------|------------|
| TO   | 32,190,397 | 26,942,975 | 30,898,517 |
| P/L  | 2,713,903  | 2,601,915  | 3,177,807  |
| NW   | 7,979,382  | 7,126,682  | 5,063,869  |
| WC   | 7,319,748  | 6,491,938  | 4,478,688  |
| Emp. | 134        | 100        | 90         |

**DUNS 73-880-0916**

## Wp Sk Holdings Ltd

**(Subsidiary of:** Wp Midco3 Ltd)
Safety Kleen House, Isleworth, Middlesex TW7 5XB
**Web:** www.safetykleeneurope.com
**Reg No:** 5134411 **Estd:** 2004 Private Limited Company
**Line of Business:** Management activities of holding companies
**Issued Capital:** £100,001
**Directors:** P R Mauguy, G M Baldock, K Buchborn-Klos
**Co. Secretary:** Geoffrey Baldock
**US SIC:** 6711 **UK SIC:** 83962
**Auditors:** PricewaterhouseCoopers LLP

|    | 28-12-13   | 29-12-12   | 31-12-11   |
|----|------------|------------|------------|
| TA | 46,000,000 | 46,000,000 | 46,000,000 |
| NW | 46,000,000 | 46,000,000 | 46,000,000 |

**DUNS 28-884-2412**

## Wpf Therapy Ltd

23 Magdalen Street, London SE1 2EN
**Tel:** 020 7378 2000 **Fax:** 020 7378 2010
**Web:** www.wpf.org.uk
**Reg No:** 1214251 **Estd:** 1969 Private Company Limited By Guarantee
**Line of Business:** Other human health activities
**Trading Style:** W P S Therapy Ltd
**Directors:** P C Lee, S Holland, J A Gare, Mrs J J Peart
**Responsibilities**
**Senior:** Elizabeth Marin-Curtoud (Chauir of Trustees), Justyna Sugalska (Manager)
**Branches:** Wpf Therapy Ltd, Porthkerry Rd Methodist Church, Annex Rommily Rd, Barry, South Glamorgan CF62 7ER
**US SIC:** 8091, 8299
**UK SIC:** 95200, 93300
**Auditors:** Goldwins Ltd
**Bankers:** HSBC Bank plc (40-02-06)

|      | 30-09-13  | 30-09-12  | 30-09-11  |
|------|-----------|-----------|-----------|
| TO   | 1,842,778 | 1,764,956 | 1,691,827 |
| P/L  | 28,854    | 57,988    | 86,319    |
| NW   | 1,762,077 | 1,698,137 | 1,615,216 |
| WC   | (556,262) | (593,822) | (687,547) |
| Emp. | 98        | 102       | 105       |

**DUNS 76-894-4217**

## Wpg Ltd

**(Subsidiary of:** Wpg Holdings Ltd)
Printing House, Severn Farm Industrial Estate, Welshpool, Powys SY21 7DF
**Tel:** 01938552260
**Web:** www.wpg-group.com
**Reg No:** 2613569 **VAT No:** 161112614
**Estd:** 1991 Private Limited Company
**Line of Business:** Lithographic printers
**Trading Style:** Welshpool Printing Group
**Issued Capital:** £73,825
**Principals:** P E Jones (Managing), D C Greatorex, B E Jones, J A Bebb, I D Jones, G J Williams
**Co. Secretary:** Paul Jones
**Responsibilities**
**Senior:** Graham Pierce (Manager)
**US SIC:** 2752 **UK SIC:** 47544
**Bankers:** National Westminster Bank Plc (55-70-40)

|    | 31-03-14  | 31-03-13  | 31-03-12  |
|----|-----------|-----------|-----------|
| TA | 1,992,958 | 2,101,537 | 2,001,915 |
| NW | 1,180,935 | 1,075,976 | 1,075,867 |
| WC | 72,918    | (21,749)  | 73,293    |

**DUNS 21-117-1692**

## Wpi Group Ltd

Wpi House King St Trading Estate, Middlewich, Cheshire CW10 9LF
**Tel:** 01606737380
**Web:** www.wpigroup.co.uk
**Reg No:** 6570652 **Estd:** 2008 Private Limited Company
**Line of Business:** Building of complete constructions or parts thereof; civil engineering
**Issued Capital:** £300
**Directors:** A W Hoose, S M Igoe, M J Igoe, Miss K M Igoe, W Igoe, Mrs C M Stubbs
**US SIC:** 1541 **UK SIC:** 50100
**Bankers:** HSBC Bank plc (40-39-01)

|      | 31-10-13   | 31-10-12   | 31-10-11   |
|------|------------|------------|------------|
| TO   | 22,371,231 | 17,719,221 | 15,027,928 |
| P/L  | 5,299,801  | 179,608    | 401,327    |
| NW   | 7,181,421  | 3,153,009  | 2,990,546  |
| WC   | 4,147,019  | 415,570    | 540,870    |
| Emp. | 115        | 106        | 96         |

**DUNS 76-638-3921** **Exp**

## Wpl Ltd

**(Subsidiary of:** N-Ov8 Group Ltd)
1-2 Aston Road, Waterlooville, Hampshire PO7 7UX
**Tel:** 023-9224-2600
**Web:** www.wpl.co.uk
**Reg No:** 2583411 **Estd:** 1991 Private Limited Company
**Line of Business:** Water treatment services
**Export Markets:** Europe
**Export Sales:** £262,944

**Trading Style:** Wpl Limited
**Issued Capital:** £66,522
**Directors:** R J Gundry, A Baird, D Parkinson, S J Kimber, Ms J C Gregory, M G Mansfield, M J Palin, Ms I Knights
**Co. Secretary:** Gareth Jones
**US SIC:** 4941 **UK SIC:** 17000
**Auditors:** BDO LLP
**Bankers:** National Westminster Bank Plc (56-00-68)

|     | 31-12-13  | 31-12-12  | 31-12-11  |
|-----|-----------|-----------|-----------|
| TO  | 7,968,892 | 7,732,236 | 9,721,341 |
| P/L | 182,868   | 27,187    | 786,257   |
| NW  | 794,261   | 780,072   | 923,045   |
| WC  | 133,764   | 117,202   | 351,025   |
| Emp.| 61        | 65        | 66        |

**DUNS 34-851-4688**

## Wpp Holdings Ltd

51 Staines Road West, Sunbury-On-Thames, Middlesex TW16 7AH
**Tel:** 01932-781641 **Fax:** 01932765590
**Web:** www.wppgroup.co.uk
**Reg No:** 2812340 **Estd:** 1993 Private Limited Company
**Line of Business:** Planning supervisors
**Issued Capital:** £100
**Directors:** K F Twining, G J Street
**Co. Secretary:** Keith Crosby
**Responsibilities**
**Senior:** Inga James (Personal Assistant)
**Branches:** Wpp Holdings Ltd, 7-8 Conduit Street, London W1S 2XF
**US SIC:** 6711 **UK SIC:** 00002

|    | 30-04-14 | 30-04-13 | 30-04-12 |
|----|----------|----------|----------|
| TA | 100      | 100      | 100      |
| NW | 100      | 100      | 100      |

**DUNS 21-878-4436**

## Wpp Plc

27 Farm Street, London W1J 5RJ
**Tel:** 020-7408-2204 **Fax:** 020-7493-6819
**Web:** www.wpp.com
**Reg No:** 0111714J **Estd:** 2012 Public Limited Company
**Line of Business:** Advertising agency services
**Export Sales:** £9,605,400,000
**Trading Style:** Wpp
**US SIC:** 7319, 7333
**UK SIC:** 83800, 83953
**Auditors:** Deloitte LLP
**Following financial data are in thousands**

|      | 31-12-13    | 31-12-12    |
|------|-------------|-------------|
| TO   | 11,019,400  | 10,373,100  |
| P/L  | 1,295,800   | 1,091,900   |
| NW   | (3,553,800) | (4,473,600) |
| WC   | (22,000)    | (671,900)   |
| Emp. | 117,115     | 114,490     |

**DUNS 76-979-9248** **Imp-Exp**

## Wrafton Laboratories Ltd

**(Subsidiary of:** Perrigo Uk Finco Limited Partnership)
Wrafton, Braunton, Devon EX33 2DL
**Tel:** 01271-815815
**Web:** www.perrigouk.com
**Reg No:** 2638733 **VAT No:** 585684189
**Estd:** 1992 Private Limited Company
**Line of Business:** Manufacture of basic pharmaceutical products
**Export Markets:** Middle East, Russia
**Export Sales:** £3,102,000
**Trading Style:** Perrigo
**Issued Capital:** £660,796
**Directors:** M A Tucker, P M O'Sullivan, P Thompson, R P Howard
**Co. Secretary:** Niall Kavanagh
**Responsibilities**
**Sales:** Stephen Duke (Head of Sales - Store Brand), Cass Khan (Head of European Business Deve)
**IT:** Phyllis Amos (Itms Technician)
**Engineering:** Phyllis Amos (Itms Technician)
**US SIC:** 2834 **UK SIC:** 25700
**Auditors:** BDO Stoy Hayward LLP
**Bankers:** HSBC Bank plc (40-09-13)

|      | 29-06-13   | 30-06-12   | 25-06-11   |
|------|------------|------------|------------|
| TO   | 44,331,000 | 40,284,000 | 38,380,000 |
| P/L  | 2,488,000  | 1,378,000  | 76,000     |
| NW   | 11,417,000 | 9,502,000  | 8,506,000  |
| WC   | 1,675,000  | 200,000    | (787,000)  |
| Emp. | 467        | 448        | 419        |

**DUNS 39-947-1440**

## Wragge & Co Ltd

**(Subsidiary of:** Wragge Lawrence Graham & Co Llp)
55 Colmore Row, Birmingham, West Midlands B3 2AS
**Tel:** 01212331000 **Fax:** 0870-904-1099
**Web:** www.wragge.com
**Reg No:** 2253188 **Estd:** 1988 Private Limited Company
**Line of Business:** Solicitors
**Issued Capital:** £2
**Directors:** Mrs S Ayres, Ingleby Holdings Limited
**Co. Secretary:** Ingleby Nominees Limited

**US SIC:** 8111 **UK SIC:** 83500

|    | 30-04-14 | 30-04-13 | 30-04-12 |
|----|----------|----------|----------|
| TA | 2        | 2        | 2        |
| NW | 2        | 2        | 2        |

**DUNS 73-459-9181**

## Wragge Lawrence Graham & Co Llp

55 Colmore Row, Birmingham, West Midlands B3 2AS
**Web:** www.wragge-law.com
**Reg No:** 0304378OC **Estd:** 1834
**Line of Business:** Solicitors
**Responsibilities**
**Senior:** Bernadine Adkins (Partner), Patrick Arben (Partner), Gareth Baker (Manager), Simon Baylis (Partner), Richard Black (Non-designated Limited Liabili), Christopher Brennan (Manager), Christopher Brierley (Non-designated Limited Liabili), Alexandra Brodie (Non-designated Limited Liabili), Robert Caddick (Partner), Charles Chamberlain (Non-designated Limited Liabili), Mark Chester (Non-designated Limited Liabili), Martin Chitty (Non-designated Limited Liabili), Baljit Chohan (Partner), Giles Clifford (Partner), Philip Clissitt (Non-designated Limited Liabili), Jason Coates (Non-designated Limited Liabili), Ed Colreavy (Manager), Helen Davenport (Manager), Susan Dearden (Non-designated Limited Liabili), Patrick Duxbury (Non-designated Limited Liabili), Jane Fielding (Partner), Anna Fletcher (Manager), Andrew Galla (Partner), Elizabeth Gane (Manager), Derek Goodban (Partner), Richard Goold (Partner), Davinia Gransbury (Partner), Mark Greenburgh (Partner), David Hamlett (Partner), Jenny Hardy (Manager), Mark Hick (Partner), Samantha Holland (Manager), Colin Hurt (Partner), Jack Jacovou (Partner), Cerryg Jones (Partner), Luke Kempton (Partner), Jacqueline Knox (Partner), Michael Luckman (Partner), Andrew Manning-Cox (Partner), Gayle McFarlane (Manager), Julia McNaught (Manager), Sally Mewies (Partner), Jeremy Millington (Partner), Ashley Mitchell (Partner), Joe Morris (Manager), Duncan Murphy (Partner), Andrew Nugent Smith (Manager), Lee Nuttall (Partner), Claire O'Brien (Manager), David Pettingale (Manager), Emma Pioli (Partner and Head of Asset Mana), Quentin Poole (Senior Partner), Ravi Randhawa (Manager), Dominic Richardson (Manager), Clark Sargent (Partner), Peter Shave (Partner), Derek Southall (Partner), Graham Spalding (Manager), Greg Standing (Partner), Chris Towle (Manager), Ian Weatherall (Partner), Kirsten Whitfield (Manager), Daniel Wood (Partner), Gus Wood (Partner), Graham Wrigglesworth (Manager)
**Finance:** Penny Sanders (Director - Financial Services)
**Marketing:** Gayle Biddle (Corporate Communications Execu), Nicola Lynch (Business Development Executive)
**Sales:** Nicola Lynch (Business Development Executive)
**Admin:** Clare Barrett (Personal Assistant), Julie Dipple (Personal Assistant), Louise Hewins (Personal Assistant), Claire Logan (Personal Secretary), Kelly Mahoney (Legal Secretary), Carol Warnock (Secretary)
**IT:** Andrew Lawton Smith (Head of Enterprise), Andy Rudall (BIS Operations & Programme Man)
**HR:** Julie Caudle (Head of Resourcing and Reward), Hayley Mee (Recruitment Assistant)
**Branches:** Wragge Lawrence Graham & Co Llp, 3 Waterhouse Square, 142 Holborn, London EC1N 2SW
**US SIC:** 8111 **UK SIC:** 83500
**Auditors:** Deloitte LLP
**Bankers:** Lloyds TSB Bank plc (30-13-66)

|      | 30-04-14    | 30-04-13    | 30-04-12    |
|------|-------------|-------------|-------------|
| TO   | 121,171,000 | 120,543,000 | 118,229,000 |
| P/L  | 724,000     | 703,000     | 762,000     |
| WC   | 27,073,000  | 50,483,000  | 44,728,000  |
| Emp. | 854         | 960         | 988         |

**DUNS 57-014-4964**

## Wragge Lawrence Graham & Co Services Ltd

**(Subsidiary of:** Wragge Lawrence Graham & Co Llp)
4 More London Riverside, London SE1 2AU
**Tel:** 020-7379-0000
**Web:** www.lg-legal.com
**Reg No:** 2865108 **Estd:** 2004 Private Limited Company
**Line of Business:** Solicitors
**Issued Capital:** £2
**Directors:** H P Maule, A Witts
**Responsibilities**
**Senior:** Andrew Wittes (senior partner)
**US SIC:** 8111 **UK SIC:** 83500

**Auditors:** Nexia Smith & Williamson

| | 30-04-14 | 30-04-13 | 30-04-12 |
|---|---|---|---|
| TO | 16,578,151 | 16,160,542 | 17,364,659 |
| P/L | 569,300 | 212,566 | 246,820 |
| NW | 59,441 | 44,335 | 44,335 |
| WC | 59,441 | 44,335 | 44,335 |
| Emp. | 201 | 223 | 257 |

DUNS 21-739-0004 **Imp-Exp**

## Wrap Film Systems Ltd

(**Subsidiary of:** Wrap Film Holdings Ltd)
Hortonwood 45, Telford, Shropshire TF1 7FA
**Tel:** 01952-678-800 **Fax:** 01952-678-801
**Web:** www.wrapfilm.com
**Reg No:** 1243964 **VAT No:** 927113244
**Estd:** 1996 Private Limited Company
**Line of Business:** Catering equipment
**Export Markets:** E U
**Export Sales:** £9,413,023
**Issued Capital:** £25,000
**Directors:** J L Crook, A R Brown, B Canfield, Ms C A Campbell
**Co. Secretary:** Michael Florey
**Responsibilities**
**Senior:** Gordon Rooney *(Manager)*, Mo Tyrer *(Production Planner)*
**IT:** James Coburn *(IT Administrator)*, Robey Tucker *(Materials Manager)*
**Facilities:** Robey Tucker *(Materials Manager)*
**Purchasing:** Robey Tucker *(Materials Manager)*
**Engineering:** Robey Tucker *(Materials Manager)*
**US SIC:** 3334, 3079, 2654
**UK SIC:** 22451, 48360, 47280
**Auditors:** Mazars LLP
**Bankers:** Barclays Bank Plc (20-33-70)

| | 31-12-13 | 31-12-12 | 31-12-11 |
|---|---|---|---|
| TO | 54,369,561 | 51,823,144 | 51,046,980 |
| P/L | 3,674,246 | 3,622,441 | 2,544,994 |
| NW | 18,678,342 | 15,526,980 | 12,550,213 |
| WC | 16,827,688 | 13,477,425 | 10,235,320 |
| Emp. | 315 | 303 | 267 |

DUNS 34-835-4312

## Wrapid Group Ltd

250 Thornton Road, Bradford, West Yorkshire BD1 2LB
**Web:** www.wrapid.co.uk
**Reg No:** 5634670 **Estd:** 2005 Private Limited Company
**Line of Business:** Management activities of holding companies
**Export Sales:** £2,285,402
**Issued Capital:** £76
**Directors:** J R Clark, Ms N Dillon
**Co. Secretary:** Stephen York
**Responsibilities**
**Senior:** William Birkinhead *(Manager)*
**US SIC:** 6711 **UK SIC:** 83962
**Auditors:** Dafferns LLP

| | 31-12-13 | 31-12-12 | 31-12-11 |
|---|---|---|---|
| TO | 15,927,910 | 16,248,356 | 16,775,918 |
| P/L | 363,603 | 207,610 | 317,968 |
| NW | (2,523,249) | (3,036,710) | (3,433,120) |
| WC | (673,297) | (627,761) | (544,907) |
| Emp. | 117 | 110 | 109 |

DUNS 21-782-0528

## Wray Common Primary School

Kendal Close, Reigate, Surrey RH2 0LR
**Tel:** 01737761254
**Web:** www.wray-common.surrey.sch.uk
**Estd:** 1998 Proprietorship
**Line of Business:** Schools (local authority)
**Proprietor:** Mrs D Robins
**Responsibilities**
**Senior:** Lloyd Murphy *(Head Teacher)*
**US SIC:** 8211 **UK SIC:** 93200
**Employees:** 60

DUNS 21-230-2837

## Wray Common Private Nursing Home

Wray Common Road, Reigate, Surrey RH2 0ND
**Web:** www.wraycommon.co.uk
**Estd:** 1978
**Line of Business:** Nursing homes
**Proprietor:** S Segal
**US SIC:** 8051 **UK SIC:** 95100
**Employees:** 60

DUNS 39-956-4830 **Imp-Exp**

## Wrc P.L.C.

Frankland Road, Swindon, Wiltshire SN5 8YF
**Web:** www.wrcplc.co.uk
**Reg No:** 2262098 **VAT No:** 527180453
**Estd:** 1988 Public Limited Company
**Line of Business:** Research institutions and organisations
**Export Markets:** Europe, U S A, Canada, S & S E Asia
**Export Sales:** £1,377,000
**Issued Capital:** £580,000
**Directors:** R Zocchi, M W Smith, R E Chapman, A K Griffiths
**Co. Secretary:** Anthony Griffiths
**Responsibilities**
**Senior:** Denise Bennett *(Manager)*, Sarah France *(Environmental Assessment Manag)*, Andy Godley *(Senior Consultant)*, Karen McLintock *(Manager)*, Paul Rumsby *(Chairman)*
**Marketing:** Ian Dawes *(Business Analyst)*, Faye Deacon *(Website Developer)*, Jayne Matwiejczyk *(Sales & Marketing Manager)*
**Sales:** Margarita Cabrera *(Business Development Manager,)*, Elizabeth Gimmler *(Key Account Director)*, Jayne Matwiejczyk *(Sales & Marketing Manager)*
**Admin:** Martine Gibbons *(Secretary)*, Jayne Matwiejczyk *(Sales & Marketing Manager)*, Shirley Peters *(Receptionist)*
**HR:** Joann Malham *(Human Resources Advisor)*
**Health & Safety:** Roderick Palfrey *(Quality Manager)*
**Operations:** Sarah France *(Environmental Assessment Manag)*, Mike Hing *(Design Manager)*, Jayne Matwiejczyk *(Sales & Marketing Manager)*, Julia Trew *(Senior Project Manager)*, Carmen Waylen *(Senior Project Manager)*
**Purchasing:** Mike Hing *(Design Manager)*
**Engineering:** Victoria Benson *(Engineer)*, Glenn Dillon *(Senior Engineer)*, Jeremy Dudley *(Engineer)*, Joanne Hulance *(Senior Engineer)*, Kathy Lewin *(Technical Specialist)*, Steve Nixon *(Senior Technical Manager)*
**US SIC:** 7391, 7399
**UK SIC:** 94000, 83954
**Auditors:** KPMG LLP
**Bankers:** HSBC Bank plc (40-24-10)

| | 31-03-14 | 31-03-13 | 31-03-12 |
|---|---|---|---|
| TO | 7,955,000 | 8,848,000 | 8,192,000 |
| P/L | (990,000) | (675,000) | (444,000) |
| NW | (25,511,000) | (24,906,000) | (20,561,000) |
| WC | 1,664,000 | 1,784,000 | 1,221,000 |
| Emp. | 111 | 117 | 121 |

DUNS 21-639-2563

## W.R.Davies(Motors) Ltd

Pool Road, Newtown, Powys SY16 3AH
**Tel:** 01686623440 **Fax:** 01686-629009
**Web:** www.morrisons.co.uk
**Reg No:** 0347316 **VAT No:** 158907233
**Estd:** 1938 Private Limited Company
**Line of Business:** Sale of new motor vehicles
**Issued Capital:** £1,828
**Principals:** J R Davies *(Managing)*, D J Conway, N D Sullivan
**Co. Secretary:** Bernard Pritchard
**Responsibilities**
**Senior:** William Pritchard *(Manager)*
**Branches:** W.r.davies(Motors) Ltd, Salop Road, Welshpool, Powys SY21 7ES
**US SIC:** 5511, 5521, 7539, 5531
**UK SIC:** 65100, 67100
**Auditors:** D R E & Co
**Bankers:** HSBC Bank plc (40-46-07)

| | 31-12-13 | 31-12-12 | 31-12-11 |
|---|---|---|---|
| TO | 80,550,712 | 73,942,665 | 72,600,596 |
| P/L | 840,212 | 171,614 | 367,377 |
| NW | 3,693,372 | 2,901,555 | 3,464,241 |
| WC | (952,252) | (1,300,619) | (1,029,448) |
| Emp. | 254 | 250 | 243 |

DUNS 73-775-7513

## The Wrekin Housing Group Ltd

Colliers Way, Old Park, Telford, Shropshire TF3 4AW
**Tel:** 01952217100
**Web:** www.wrekinhousingtrust.org.uk
**Reg No:** 5032634 **Estd:** 1998 Private Company Limited By Guarantee
**Line of Business:** Construction of domestic buildings
**Directors:** S J Price, J Wood, M R Lawton, C N Cullen, Mrs S Lane, Mrs A Ward
**Co. Secretary:** Christopher Horton
**US SIC:** 1522, 6531, 6519
**UK SIC:** 50100, 83400, 85000
**Bankers:** Barclays Bank Plc (20-07-71)

| | 31-03-14 | 31-03-13 | 31-03-12 |
|---|---|---|---|
| TO | 68,596,000 | 65,076,000 | 59,400,000 |
| P/L | 17,615,000 | 17,111,000 | 18,289,000 |
| NW | 62,640,000 | 34,816,000 | 26,781,000 |
| WC | 5,241,000 | 7,284,000 | 6,055,000 |
| Emp. | 823 | 749 | 731 |

DUNS 28-830-4462

## The Wrekin Old Hall Trust Ltd

Sutherland Road, Telford, Shropshire TF1 3BH
**Tel:** 01952-265600 **Fax:** 01952415068
**Web:** www.wrekincollege.com
**Reg No:** 0172472 **VAT No:** 162112804
**Estd:** 1921 Private Limited Company
**Line of Business:** General secondary education
**Trading Style:** Wrekin College
**Issued Capital:** £1,537
**Directors:** Mrs A J Dixon, Mrs P A Hunt, T Shaw, N A Wilkie, Mrs V L Hughes-Hines, M D Halewood, H W Campion, R D Bubbers
**Co. Secretary:** Michael Porter
**Responsibilities**
**Senior:** Andrew Huxley *(Director)*, Robert Mottram *(Director)*
**Facilities:** Bernard Crone *(Facilities Manager)*
**US SIC:** 8211 **UK SIC:** 93200
**Auditors:** Binder Harnlyn
**Bankers:** Barclays Bank Plc (20-03-84)

| | 31-07-13 | 31-07-12 | 31-07-11 |
|---|---|---|---|
| TO | 8,497,312 | 8,631,928 | 8,983,686 |
| P/L | (70,618) | 319,159 | 897,953 |
| NW | 18,784,624 | 18,855,242 | 18,536,083 |
| WC | 1,448,050 | 1,651,729 | 1,077,919 |
| Emp. | 177 | 176 | 174 |

DUNS 21-098-0120

## Wren Academy

Hilton Avenue, London N12 9HB
**Tel:** 020-8492-6000 **Fax:** 02084926010
**Web:** www.wrenacademy.org
**Reg No:** 6422162 **Estd:** 2007 Private Company Limited By Guarantee
**Line of Business:** General secondary education
**Directors:** The Reverend J P Caperon, Ms C Ogunsanya, Mrs S J Tidey, C E Kiernan, Mrs D J Dieppe, M Whitworth, Ms K Archer, Dr C J Bisdorff
**Co. Secretary:** Marc Lewis
**Responsibilities**
**Senior:** Sylvia Duthie *(Director)*, Mark Mcaulay *(Director)*, Marc Rawcliffe *(Director)*, Vincent Sagua *(Director)*
**Health & Safety:** Debra Griffiths *(Facilities Manager)*
**Facilities:** Debra Griffiths *(Facilities Manager)*
**US SIC:** 8211 **UK SIC:** 93200

| | 31-08-14 | 31-08-13 | 31-08-12 |
|---|---|---|---|
| TO | 6,994,469 | 6,097,746 | 5,468,666 |
| P/L | (580,471) | (504,802) | (425,153) |
| NW | 22,947,216 | 24,619,687 | 25,222,489 |
| WC | 108,503 | 358,782 | 527,185 |
| Emp. | 111 | 106 | 91 |

DUNS 23-932-5553

## Wren Hall Nursing Home Ltd

234 Nottingham Road, Selston, Nottingham, Nottinghamshire NG16 6AB
**Tel:** 01773-581203
**Web:** www.wrenhall.com
**Reg No:** 3922399 **Estd:** 1989 Private Limited Company
**Line of Business:** Nursing homes
**Issued Capital:** £100
**Directors:** R P Kesari, Mrs J Leach, Ms A Astle
**Co. Secretary:** Dr Veenarayan Kesari
**Responsibilities**
**HR:** Marion North *(Training & Quality Coordinator)*
**Health & Safety:** Jason Elliott *(Facilities Manager)*
**Facilities:** Jason Elliott *(Facilities Manager)*
**US SIC:** 8051 **UK SIC:** 95100
**Bankers:** Yorkshire Bank Plc (05-03-68)

| | 31-03-14 | 31-03-13 | 31-03-12 |
|---|---|---|---|
| TA | 3,187,650 | 3,168,109 | 3,314,413 |
| NW | 737,375 | 698,238 | 731,395 |
| WC | (83,495) | (16,313) | (13,085) |

DUNS 21-150-6703

## Wren Living Ltd

Ferry Road, Goole, North Humberside DN14 7UL
**Tel:** 08454041000 **Fax:** 08715 285001
**Web:** www.wrenliving.com
**Reg No:** 6799478 **Estd:** 2009 Private Limited Company
**Line of Business:** Retail sale of furniture, lighting equipment and household articles not elsewhere classified
**Trading Style:** Wren Kitchens and Bedrooms
**Issued Capital:** £100
**Directors:** A L Sanchez, M J Pullan
**Co. Secretary:** Miss Jane Oldfield
**Responsibilities**
**Senior:** Malcolm Healey *(Manager)*
**Operations:** David Fenner *(Operations Manager)*
**US SIC:** 5719, 2599, 1751
**UK SIC:** 64700, 46720, 50400
**Auditors:** PricewaterhouseCoopers LLP
**Bankers:** The Royal Bank Of Scotland Plc (16-23-17)

| | 31-12-13 | 31-12-12 | 31-12-11 |
|---|---|---|---|
| TO | 135,960,671 | 81,412,650 | 43,441,925 |
| P/L | (3,964,464) | (9,834,202) | (18,133,789) |
| NW | (10,588,241) | (33,067,777) | (23,560,257) |
| WC | (1,998,001) | (29,805,335) | (24,949,437) |
| Emp. | 1,217 | 702 | 514 |

DUNS 42-459-6455

## Wrenco Contractors (Holdings) Ltd

25 Stratford Road, Liverpool, Merseyside L19 3RE
**Tel:** 0151-520-2323
**Web:** www.wrenco.co.uk
**Reg No:** 4447308 **Estd:** 2002 Private Limited Company
**Line of Business:** Building construction contractors
**Trading Style:** Wrenco Contractors (Holdings) Ltd
**Issued Capital:** £3,753
**Director:** T Carney
**Co. Secretary:** Brendan Bolland
**Branches:** Wrenco Contractors (Holdings) Ltd, Sidcup Road, Manchester M23 9PH
**US SIC:** 1522 **UK SIC:** 50100
**Bankers:** Barclays Bank Plc (20-51-01)

| | 31-05-13 | 31-05-12 | 31-05-11 |
|---|---|---|---|
| TO | 5,632,436 | 4,260,677 | 7,547,715 |
| P/L | 11,818 | 42,600 | 45,817 |
| NW | 813,921 | 837,041 | 890,966 |
| WC | 571,650 | 511,289 | 461,632 |
| Emp. | 54 | 60 | 69 |

DUNS 21-317-3917 **Exp**

## Wrengate Ltd

(**Subsidiary of:** Wrengate Holdings Ltd)
Wrengate House, 221 Palatine Road, Didsbury, Manchester M20 2EE
**Tel:** 0161-438-1000
**Web:** www.wrengate.co.uk
**Reg No:** 1172978 **Estd:** 1974 Private Limited Company
**Line of Business:** Management activities of other non-financial holding companies not elsewhere classified
**Export Markets:** Rest of World
**Issued Capital:** £1,000,000
**Principals:** Dr N G Musry *(Chairman and Managing)*, R Musry, A P Musry
**Responsibilities**
**Senior:** Nicky Gates *(Operations Manager)*
**Operations:** Nicky Gates *(Operations Manager)*
**US SIC:** 6711, 5133
**UK SIC:** 83962, 61600
**Auditors:** PKF

| | 30-04-14 | 30-04-13 | 30-04-12 |
|---|---|---|---|
| TA | 21,717,699 | 18,080,593 | 15,678,433 |
| NW | 14,793,943 | 13,070,377 | 13,040,201 |
| WC | 8,680,805 | 8,513,032 | 8,460,358 |

DUNS 21-325-1049

## Wrenn School

Doddington Road, Wellingborough, Northamptonshire NN8 2JJ
**Tel:** 01933-222793
**Web:** www.wrenn.northants.sch.uk
**Estd:** 1996
**Line of Business:** Schools (local authority)
**Director:** Mrs S Shepherd
**Responsibilities**
**Senior:** Christine Hunt *(Deputy Head)*
**Finance:** Jevon Corbett *(Bursar)*
**IT:** Frank Morris *(Senior IT Executive)*
**US SIC:** 8211 **UK SIC:** 93200
**Employees:** 100

DUNS 21-234-0037

## Wrens Shop

Church Road, East Knoyle, Salisbury, Wiltshire SP3 6AE
**Estd:** 2006 Proprietorship
**Line of Business:** Convenience stores
**Proprietor:** P Eggington
**US SIC:** 5411 **UK SIC:** 64100
**Employees:** 70

DUNS 28-847-6633

## W.R.Evans(Chemist) Ltd

Manor House, Merlin Way, Quarry Hill Industrial Estate, Ilkeston, Derbyshire DE7 4RA
**Tel:** 01159-440222
**Web:** www.wrevans.co.uk
**Reg No:** 0664125 **VAT No:** 616702944
**Estd:** 1966 Private Limited Company
**Line of Business:** Chemists dispensing
**Trading Style:** Manor Pharmacy
**Issued Capital:** £14,600
**Directors:** S M Allan, A T Evans, Ms A Evans, R E Mcdonald, P E Isaac, I C Mckenzie, D R Evans, Ms E J Evans
**Co. Secretary:** Peter Isaac
**Branches:** W.r.evans(Chemist) Ltd, 35 Plains Road, Nottingham, Nottinghamshire NG3 5JU
**US SIC:** 5912 **UK SIC:** 64300
**Auditors:** Royston Parkin Ltd
**Bankers:** HSBC Bank plc (40-25-29)

| | 31-07-13 | 31-07-12 | 31-07-11 |
|---|---|---|---|
| TO | 73,262,432 | 74,167,524 | 75,692,335 |
| P/L | 4,410,215 | 3,677,467 | 2,949,300 |
| NW | 3,085,636 | 587,695 | (1,293,943) |
| WC | 3,173,214 | 1,315,714 | 1,175,482 |
| Emp. | 653 | 640 | 635 |

DUNS 21-558-5754

## Wrexham and Prestige Taxis

Yale House, Brook Street, Wrexham, Clwyd LL13 7LL
**Tel:** 01978291899
**Web:** www.wrexhamandprestigetaxis.co.uk
**VAT No:** 482433445 **Estd:** 1982 Proprietorship
**Line of Business:** Taxis
**Proprietor:** M Coates
**US SIC:** 4121, 7512
**UK SIC:** 72200, 84801
**Employees:** 90

DUNS 21-704-4676

## Wrexham County Borough Council

The Guildhall, Wrexham, Clwyd LL11 1AY
**Tel:** 01978-292012
**Web:** www.wrexham.gov.uk
**Estd:** 1996 Incorporate By Act Of Parliament
**Line of Business:** Administration of the state and the economic and social policy of the community
**Trading Style:** Human Resources Department
**Principals:** M Scholes *(Financial)*, D A Griffin, B Goodall, P Walton, T Garner, M C Simkins, M Russell
**Branches:** Wrexham County Borough Council, Llanelian, Colwyn Bay, Clwyd LL29 8YY
**US SIC:** 9121 **UK SIC:** 91110
**Bankers:** National Westminster Bank Plc (55-81-42)
**Employees:** 6,000

DUNS 77-896-7666

## Wrexham Football Club (2006) Ltd

(**Subsidiary of:** Wrexham Village Ltd)
Racecourse Ground, Wrexham, Clwyd LL11 2AH
**Tel:** 01978313001 **Fax:** 01978357821
**Web:** www.wrexhamfootballclub.com
**Reg No:** 5800501 **Estd:** 2006 Private Limited Company
**Line of Business:** Other tourist assistance activities not elsewhere classified
**Issued Capital:** £100,000
**Co. Secretary:** Geoffrey Moss
**US SIC:** 7999 **UK SIC:** 97913
**Auditors:** Baker Tilly UK Audit LLP

| | 30-06-13 | 30-06-12 | 30-06-11 |
|---|---|---|---|
| TA | 401,590 | 401,590 | 1,393,337 |
| NW | (1,431,039) | (1,431,039) | (417,185) |
| WC | N/A | N/A | (503,715) |

DUNS 58-159-3654

## Wrexham Hospice & Cancer Support Centre Foundation

Nightingale House, Chester Road, Wrexham, Clwyd LL11 2SJ
**Tel:** 01978-316800
**Web:** www.nightingalehouse.co.uk
**Reg No:** 2906838 **Estd:** 1995 Private Company Limited By Guarantee
**Line of Business:** Hospices
**Trading Style:** Nightingale House
**Directors:** Dr N W Braid, G G Greasley, Dr J Duguid, Mrs E Griffiths, Ms J Lowe, Mrs P R Valentine, A P Morse, Dr H Paterson
**Co. Secretary:** Ms Pamela Valentine
**Responsibilities**
**HR:** Robert Bound *(Human Resources Manager)*, Pat Walmsley *(Human Resources Manager)*
**Health & Safety:** Tracy Livingstone *(Matron)*
**Operations:** Tracy Livingstone *(Matron)*
**Branches:** Wrexham Hospice & Cancer Support Centre Foundation, Nightingale House, Chester Road, Wrexham, Clwyd LL11 2SJ
**US SIC:** 8091, 8062
**UK SIC:** 95200, 95100
**Auditors:** Conways
**Bankers:** HSBC Bank plc (40-47-26)

| | 31-12-13 | 31-12-12 | 31-12-11 |
|---|---|---|---|
| TO | 3,856,436 | 3,553,966 | 3,299,972 |
| P/L | 490,635 | 91,758 | (1,910) |
| NW | 5,954,777 | 5,294,778 | 5,116,433 |
| WC | 1,502,660 | 1,037,239 | 958,497 |
| Emp. | 76 | 82 | 76 |

DUNS 21-232-5234

## Wrexham Volkswagen

Rhosrobin Industrial Estate, Llay New Road, Wrexham, Clwyd LL11 4BG
**Tel:** 01978340600
**Web:** www.wrexham.volkswagon.co.uk
**Estd:** 1989 Proprietorship
**Line of Business:** Car dealers (used)
**Proprietor:** M Donnelly
**US SIC:** 5521 **UK SIC:** 65100
**Employees:** 47

DUNS 21-034-4384

## Wrexham Waterworld

Holt Street, Wrexham, Clwyd LL13 8DH
**Tel:** 01978-297300
**Web:** www.wrexham.gov.uk
**Estd:** 1998 Proprietorship
**Line of Business:** Operation of sports arenas and stadiums
**Proprietor:** M Drew
**Responsibilities**
**Senior:** Mark Drew *(General Manager)*
**Health & Safety:** Greg Ryan *(Maintenance Manager)*
**Facilities:** Greg Ryan *(Maintenance Manager)*
**US SIC:** 7941 **UK SIC:** 97911
**Employees:** 60

DUNS 42-344-4801

## Wrfc Trading Ltd

Sixways Stadium, Worcester, Worcestershire WR3 8ZE
**Tel:** 08451296751
**Web:** www.davidlloyd.co.uk
**Reg No:** 3160145 **Estd:** 1996 Private Limited Company
**Line of Business:** Health clubs
**Trading Style:** Worcester Warriors
**Issued Capital:** £16,070,834
**Directors:** R D Murray, G R Allen, C C Glossop, R G Colley, J J O'Toole, J R Crabtree, G W Bolsover, C Duckworth
**Co. Secretary:** Richard Colley
**Responsibilities**
**Senior:** Wayne Isaac *(General Manager)*
**Marketing:** Tom Rider *(marketing manager)*
**Health & Safety:** Helen Grayer *(facilities manager)*
**US SIC:** 7299 **UK SIC:** 98902
**Auditors:** Bishop Fleming Rabjohns
**Bankers:** National Westminster Bank Plc (60-24-28)

| | 30-06-13 | 30-06-12 | 30-06-11 |
|---|---|---|---|
| TO | 8,930,199 | 8,643,409 | 7,605,132 |
| P/L | (3,226,827) | (1,685,876) | (3,465,670) |
| NW | (4,477,106) | (5,652,876) | (1,157,203) |
| WC | (1,453,920) | (1,550,270) | (3,305,507) |
| Emp. | 273 | 342 | 316 |

DUNS 23-553-8324

## Wrg Group Ltd

(**Subsidiary of:** Wrg Worldwide Ltd)
The Tower Building, Trinity Way, Manchester M3 7BF
**Tel:** 01619 209500
**Web:** www.wrg.uk.com
**Reg No:** 3552198 **Estd:** 1976 Private Limited Company
**Line of Business:** Management activities of holding companies
**Export Sales:** £26,464,000
**Issued Capital:** £900
**Directors:** N A Bale, C Halliday, C Gosling, D M Sharrock
**Co. Secretary:** Steven Kinsey
**US SIC:** 6711 **UK SIC:** 83962
**Auditors:** KPMG LLP

| | 31-10-13 | 31-10-12 | 31-10-11 |
|---|---|---|---|
| TO | 48,115,000 | 66,765,491 | 44,686,103 |
| P/L | (85,000) | 2,426,522 | 2,724,443 |
| NW | 739,000 | 2,270,833 | 285,922 |
| WC | 2,177,000 | 3,089,609 | 1,419,770 |
| Emp. | 177 | 136 | 111 |

DUNS 50-136-4772 **Imp**

## Wright & Offland Holdings Ltd

Floats Glass House, Floats Road, Manchester M23 9NJ
**Tel:** 01619468000 **Fax:** 0161-946-8090
**Web:** www.floatglass.co.uk
**Reg No:** 2322362 **VAT No:** 603541476
**Estd:** 1988 Private Limited Company
**Line of Business:** Management activities of production holding companies
**Trading Style:** Float Glass Industries
**Issued Capital:** £85,700
**Principals:** R E Offland *(Chairman)*, K B Offland *(Managing)*, M E Offland, C E Offland, Ms D E Golding, Ms J A Stepney, D M Offland
**Co. Secretary:** Christopher Edwards
**US SIC:** 6711 **UK SIC:** 83962
**Auditors:** Booth Ainsworth
**Bankers:** HSBC Bank plc (40-31-24)

| | 30-04-14 | 30-04-13 | 30-04-12 |
|---|---|---|---|
| TO | 22,088,904 | 20,329,281 | 20,278,353 |
| P/L | 486,161 | 575,085 | 43,368 |
| NW | 5,134,084 | 5,010,569 | 4,885,921 |
| WC | 492,663 | (43,679) | (558,434) |
| Emp. | 166 | 150 | 160 |

DUNS 21-332-4007

## Wright Build Ltd.

(**Subsidiary of:** John Turner Holdings Ltd)
Crab Tree Lane, Atherton, Manchester M46 0AG
**Tel:** 01942883312
**Web:** www.wrightbuild.org.uk
**Reg No:** 1401191 **VAT No:** 294964206
**Estd:** 2008 Private Limited Company
**Line of Business:** Building services
**Issued Capital:** £100
**Directors:** J D Haigh, J J Clarke, L J Lillywhite, L D Mckenzie
**Co. Secretary:** Stephen Crookes
**Responsibilities**
**Finance:** Kaye Lillywhite *(Commercial Manager)*
**Marketing:** Kaye Lillywhite *(Commercial Manager)*
**Purchasing:** Lee Rawson *(Purchasing Manager)*
**US SIC:** 1622, 1731, 1796
**UK SIC:** 50200, 50300, 50400
**Auditors:** CLB Coopers
**Bankers:** National Westminster Bank Plc (60-01-28)

| | 31-03-14 | 31-03-13 | 31-03-12 |
|---|---|---|---|
| TO | 4,190,431 | 3,149,321 | 2,762,894 |
| P/L | 141,606 | 168,604 | 122,295 |
| NW | 1,260,020 | 1,136,912 | 1,002,331 |
| WC | 1,110,983 | 987,786 | 863,401 |

DUNS 21-109-3072

## Wright Farm Produce Ltd

Rutland, Taylors Meanygate, Tarleton, Preston, Lancashire PR4 6XB
**Tel:** 01772-812704
**Web:** www.wrightfarmproduce.co.uk
**Reg No:** 6510209 **VAT No:** 930019854
**Estd:** 2008 Private Limited Company
**Line of Business:** Growing of vegetables, horticultural specialities and nursery products
**Issued Capital:** £200
**Director:** C P Wright
**Co. Secretary:** Ms Kathryn Wright
**US SIC:** 0161 **UK SIC:** 01001
**Bankers:** HSBC Bank plc (40-24-14)

| | 31-03-14 | 31-03-13 | 31-03-12 |
|---|---|---|---|
| TA | 1,483,504 | 1,114,672 | 1,177,174 |
| NW | 1,052,133 | (159,570) | (163,745) |
| WC | 503,028 | 321,349 | 293,306 |

DUNS 21-830-7756

## Wright Fenn & Manson Ltd

43-45 Kings Terrace, London W1S 3AS
**Tel:** 02078748700
**Web:** www.nicolefarhi.com
**Reg No:** 8002796 **Estd:** 2012 Private Limited Company
**Line of Business:** Wholesale of clothing and footwear
**Trading Style:** Nicole Farhi Fashion Limited
**Issued Capital:** £1
**Directors:** Ms M Adams, Mrs A J Seabourne, M J Doctors, Mrs D A Dooley
**Responsibilities**
**Senior:** Jane Eskriett *(Manager)*, Monica Kan *(Manager)*
**IT:** Tom Brooke *(IT Manager)*
**US SIC:** 5136, 5699
**UK SIC:** 61600, 64500
**Auditors:** Baker Tilly UK Audit LLP

| | 25-01-14 | 30-03-13 |
|---|---|---|
| TO | 5,185,924 | 11,608,172 |
| P/L | (2,859,708) | (4,764,642) |
| NW | (7,114,350) | (4,254,642) |
| WC | (7,329,601) | (4,286,345) |
| Emp. | 50 | 100 |

DUNS 28-827-4129

## Wright Hardware Ltd

95 Main Street, Prestwick, Ayrshire KA9 1JS
**Tel:** 01292-477324
**Web:** www.opendi.co.uk
**Reg No:** 0084114SC **Estd:** 1983 Private Limited Company
**Line of Business:** Retail sale of hardware, paints and glass
**Trading Style:** Wright"s Hardware Ltd, Home Hardware
**Issued Capital:** £100,000
**Principals:** J H Ferguson *(Managing)*, B L Ferguson
**Co. Secretary:** Mrs Celia Ferguson
**Branches:** Wright Hardware Ltd, Wright Hardware Ltd, 42 Dalrymple Street, Girvan, Ayrshire KA26 9BU
**US SIC:** 5251 **UK SIC:** 64800
**Auditors:** J.B. Colvan & Partners
**Bankers:** The Royal Bank Of Scotland Plc (83-26-43)

| | 31-12-13 | 31-12-12 | 31-12-11 |
|---|---|---|---|
| TO | 10,265,970 | 9,465,486 | 9,283,920 |
| P/L | 57,354 | 314,455 | 275,886 |
| NW | 2,794,570 | 2,750,500 | 2,460,440 |
| WC | 3,433,840 | 3,219,003 | 3,056,235 |
| Emp. | 122 | 102 | 101 |

DUNS 34-804-3345

## Wright Hassall Llp

Olympus Avenue, Tachbrook Park, Warwick, Warwickshire CV34 6BF
**Tel:** 01926 886688
**Web:** www.wrighthassall.co.uk
**Reg No:** 0315843OC **Estd:** 2005
**Line of Business:** Solicitors
**Responsibilities**
**Senior:** Peter Abell *(Partner)*, Peter Beddoes *(Senior Partner)*, Gemma Carson *(Partner)*, Justin Creed *(Partner)*, Marian Dixon *(Partner -Business Immigration)*, John Dormer *(Partner)*, Humphrey Halford *(Partner)*, James Hillard *(Designated Limited Liability P)*, Anthony Jarman *(Designated Limited Liability P)*, Carol Matthews *(Designated Limited Liability P)*, Claire McGinnity *(Partner)*, John Rouse *(Partner)*
**Finance:** Peter Beddoes *(Senior Partner)*, Alan Darby *(Director of Tax)*
**Marketing:** Jane Senior *(Marketing Manager)*
**Admin:** Eileen Osborne *(Legal Secretary)*
**HR:** Gemma Faulkner *(HR Legal Consultant)*, Paula Mcgill *(Human Resources Manager)*
**Facilities:** Rachael Sales *(Facilities Officer)*
**Operations:** James Hillard *(Designated Limited Liability P)*
**US SIC:** 8111 **UK SIC:** 83500
**Auditors:** Hazlewoods LLP
**Bankers:** Lloyds TSB Bank plc (30-16-93)

| | 31-12-13 | 31-12-12 | 31-12-11 |
|---|---|---|---|
| TO | 13,910,132 | 13,458,125 | 13,544,148 |
| P/L | 108,435 | 104,587 | N/A |
| NW | 423,316 | 732,535 | 439,697 |
| WC | 4,585,394 | 4,923,108 | 4,849,840 |
| Emp. | 220 | 220 | 214 |

DUNS 21-404-5304 **Imp-Exp**

## Wright Health Group Ltd

Kingsway West, Dundee, Angus DD2 3QD
**Tel:** 01382833866 **Fax:** 0800374511
**Web:** www.wright-cottrell.co.uk
**Reg No:** 0007906SC **VAT No:** 268991395
**Estd:** 1898 Private Limited Company
**Line of Business:** Manufacture of medical and surgical equipment and orthopaedic appliances
**Export Markets:** Africa, USA, All Other Countries
**Export Sales:** £21,208,000
**Trading Style:** Wright-Cottrell
**Issued Capital:** £332,000
**Principals:** I L Matheson *(Managing)*, D J Millner, N J Graham, Sir A M Grossart
**Co. Secretary:** Ms Karen Souter
**Responsibilities**
**Senior:** Serena Dell *(Regional Manager)*
**Sales:** Neil Worrall *(Equipment Sales Manager)*
**IT:** Irene Kennedy *(Group IT Manager)*
**HR:** Marie Davies *(HR Manager)*
**Fleet:** Barbara Cavanagh *(Export Manager)*
**Branches:** Wright Health Group Ltd, Oakwell Court, Unit 6, Batley, West Yorkshire WF17 9LU
**US SIC:** 3841, 8021
**UK SIC:** 37201, 95400
**Auditors:** KPMG LLP
**Bankers:** Clydesdale Bank Plc (82-44-04)

| | 31-12-13 | 31-12-12 | 31-12-11 |
|---|---|---|---|
| TO | 49,169,000 | 52,138,000 | 56,150,000 |
| P/L | 915,000 | 1,569,000 | 3,026,000 |
| NW | 14,957,000 | 16,042,000 | 16,464,000 |
| WC | 13,561,000 | 15,137,000 | 15,584,000 |
| Emp. | 372 | 393 | 419 |

DUNS 23-681-9293

## Wright Leisure (Purchasing) Co. Ltd.

Hillview Place, Alexandria, Dunbartonshire G83 0QD
**Tel:** 01389754543 **Fax:** 01389-720232
**Web:** www.wrightleisure.com
**Reg No:** 0191630SC **Estd:** 2000 Private Limited Company
**Line of Business:** Wholesale of wine, beer, spirits and other alcoholic beverages
**Issued Capital:** £100
**Director:** A Wright
**Co. Secretary:** Ms Linda Wright
**Branches:** Wright Leisure (Purchasing) Co. Ltd., 41-43 Main St, Alexandria, Dunbartonshire G83 0DY
**US SIC:** 5182 **UK SIC:** 61700

| | 31-12-13 | 31-12-12 | 31-12-11 |
|---|---|---|---|
| TA | 55,659 | 109,575 | 29,503 |
| NW | (16,898) | (20,593) | (17,570) |
| WC | (16,898) | (24,393) | (19,270) |

DUNS 28-970-9479 **Imp**

## Wright Manufacturing Services Ltd

Avenue Farm Industrial Estate, Stratford-Upon-Avon, Warwickshire CV37 0HR
**Tel:** 01789299859
**Web:** www.wrightmfg.co.uk
**Reg No:** 1731086 **Estd:** 1983 Private Limited Company
**Line of Business:** Sales of machine tools
**Issued Capital:** £100
**Principals:** W J Wright *(Managing)*, W R Wright, Mrs J Wright, K S Joyce
**US SIC:** 5251, 5084
**UK SIC:** 64800, 61490
**Auditors:** Guard D Oyly

**Bankers:** Barclays Bank Plc (20-98-61)

| | 31-08-13 | 31-08-12 | 31-08-11 |
|---|---|---|---|
| TA | 1,730,271 | 1,525,897 | 1,392,388 |
| NW | 1,163,359 | 1,090,473 | 988,571 |
| WC | 869,567 | 841,514 | 724,350 |

DUNS 21-033-2298

## Wright Robinson Sports College

Abbey Hey Lane, Abbey Hey, Manchester M18 8RL
**Tel:** 0161-370-5121
**Web:** www.wrightrobinson.co.uk
**Estd:** 2002 Proprietorship
**Line of Business:** Schools (local authority)
**Proprietor:** N Beischer
**Responsibilities**
**Finance:** Lindsey Elkes *(Financial Director)*
**Health & Safety:** Ken Halliwell *(Health & Safety Officer)*
**Facilities:** Lindsey Elkes *(Financial Director)*
**US SIC:** 8221 **UK SIC:** 93100
**Employees:** 150

DUNS 23-611-1642

## Wright Steel Construction Ltd

Foxhill Farm Stables, Foxhill Road, Northampton, Northamptonshire NN6 7BG
**Tel:** 01788-510529 **Fax:** 01788510728
**Web:** www.h2o-irrigation.co.uk
**Reg No:** 3608399 **Estd:** 1998 Private Limited Company
**Line of Business:** Irrigation systems design and development
**Issued Capital:** £100
**Director:** N R Palmer
**US SIC:** 0729 **UK SIC:** 01003
**Auditors:** KPMG

| | 31-01-14 | 31-01-13 | 31-01-12 |
|---|---|---|---|
| TA | 100 | 100 | 100 |
| NW | 100 | 100 | 100 |

DUNS 21-123-6691

## Wright-Way Cleaning & Maintenance Services Ltd

Middle Fen Farm, Earith Road, Cambridge, Cambridgeshire CB24 5LT
**Tel:** 01954212405
**Web:** www.wright-way.co.uk
**Reg No:** 6695089 **Estd:** 2003 Private Limited Company
**Line of Business:** Cleaning contracting domestic
**Issued Capital:** £99
**Director:** P M Wright
**Co. Secretary:** Ms Jill Cleaver-Wright
**US SIC:** 7349 **UK SIC:** 92300

| | 30-09-13 | 30-09-12 | 30-09-11 |
|---|---|---|---|
| TA | 168,144 | 158,970 | 145,959 |
| NW | 80,917 | 55,246 | 2,115 |
| WC | 63,679 | 38,894 | 17,709 |

DUNS 23-265-3878

## Wrights Accident Repair Centres Ltd

533 Saintfield Road, Carryduff, Belfast BT8 8ES
**Tel:** 02890817181
**Web:** www.warcni.co.uk
**Reg No:** 0041722NI **Estd:** 2001 Private Limited Company
**Line of Business:** Maintenance and repair of motor vehicles
**Issued Capital:** £100
**Directors:** R M Wright, W D Wright, R D Wright
**Co. Secretary:** Ms Mary Wright
**US SIC:** 7539 **UK SIC:** 67100

| | 31-10-13 | 31-10-12 | 31-10-11 |
|---|---|---|---|
| TO | 11,939,547 | 11,480,725 | 12,003,199 |
| P/L | 1,593,744 | 1,321,383 | 1,122,114 |
| NW | 6,115,633 | 5,672,727 | 4,807,050 |
| WC | 4,073,964 | 3,568,355 | 2,767,662 |
| Emp. | 161 | 166 | 175 |

DUNS 23-119-5087 **Imp-Exp**

## Wrights Group Ltd

**(Subsidiary of:** The Cornerstone Group Ltd)
Fenaghy Road Galgorm Industrial Estate, Ballymena, Co Antrim BT42 1PY
**Tel:** 02825 641212 **Fax:** 02825 649703
**Web:** www.wright-bus.com
**Reg No:** 0036890NI **VAT No:** 778584265
**Estd:** 1946 Private Limited Company
**Line of Business:** Other business activities not elsewhere classified
**Issued Capital:** £1,450,200
**Directors:** W T Wright, M Johnston, Mrs L R Rock, Mrs A A Knowles, J P Mcgarry, R A Barr, J B Mclaughlin, J M Nodder
**Co. Secretary:** Mrs Sara-Ann Macdonald
**Responsibilities**
**Senior:** Steven Francey *(Director)*
**US SIC:** 7399 **UK SIC:** 83954
**Auditors:** Stevenson & Wilson

**Bankers:** The Bank Of Ireland (90-20-55)

| | 30-09-13 | 30-09-12 | 30-09-11 |
|---|---|---|---|
| TO | 178,906,758 | N/A | N/A |
| P/L | 4,014,345 | N/A | N/A |
| NW | 21,153,006 | 4,865,200 | 3,450,200 |
| WC | 18,698,467 | 3,165,000 | 1,750,000 |
| Emp. | 1,369 | N/A | N/A |

DUNS 21-914-6610 **Exp**

## Wrights Pies (Shelton) Ltd

8 Campbell Place, Stoke-On-Trent, Staffordshire ST4 1LX
**Tel:** 01782848169 **Fax:** 01270-504350
**Web:** www.wrightspies.co.uk
**Reg No:** 0526954 **VAT No:** 278906508
**Estd:** 1953 Private Limited Company
**Line of Business:** Bakers shops
**Export Markets:** Worldwide
**Issued Capital:** £10,115
**Principals:** D J Wright *(Managing)*, P D Wright *(Managing)*, Ms L Smith, N Carruthers, Mrs A J Harding, D R Yendole, P J Wright
**Co. Secretary:** Peter Wright
**Responsibilities**
**Senior:** Yvonne Collis *(Manager)*, Angela Storey *(General Manager)*
**Branches:** Wrights Pies (Shelton) Ltd, Wrights Pies, 49 High Street, Newcastle, Staffordshire ST5 1PN
**US SIC:** 5462, 2099
**UK SIC:** 64100, 42399
**Auditors:** Hardwickes
**Bankers:** Lloyds TSB Bank plc (30-93-83)

| | 04-01-14 | 04-01-13 | 04-01-12 |
|---|---|---|---|
| TO | 38,013,444 | 38,157,865 | 34,745,143 |
| P/L | 2,896,217 | 2,948,845 | 553,419 |
| NW | 17,977,371 | 16,104,691 | 14,213,991 |
| WC | 3,708,785 | 3,112,626 | 1,470,805 |
| Emp. | 430 | 441 | 451 |

DUNS 39-029-0880 **Imp**

## Wrights Plastics Ltd

Brandon Way, West Bromwich, West Midlands B70 8JH
**Tel:** 0121-580-3080
**Web:** www.wrightsplastics.co.uk
**Reg No:** 2108847 **VAT No:** 100676405
**Estd:** 1969 Private Limited Company
**Line of Business:** Manufacture of other plastic products
**Trading Style:** Wrights Plastics Ltd
**Issued Capital:** £8,500
**Co. Secretary:** Michael Wright
**Responsibilities**
**Senior:** Gary Oakley *(Works Manager)*
**Admin:** Craig Skeldon *(Administrator)*
**US SIC:** 3079, 2599
**UK SIC:** 48360, 46720
**Auditors:** Moore Stephens
**Bankers:** HSBC Bank plc (40-26-23)

| | 30-04-14 | 30-04-13 | 30-04-12 |
|---|---|---|---|
| TO | 6,480,272 | 4,552,572 | 4,848,078 |
| P/L | 920,601 | 178,306 | 345,096 |
| NW | 3,905,795 | 3,175,359 | 3,639,392 |
| WC | 2,812,852 | 2,286,918 | 2,883,510 |
| Emp. | 76 | 71 | 70 |

DUNS 21-634-7237 **Imp**

## The Wrigley Company Ltd

**(Subsidiary of:** Mars Incorporated)
Estover, Plymouth, Devon PL6 7PR
**Tel:** 01752-701107
**Web:** www.wrigley.com
**Reg No:** 0210533 **VAT No:** 143000925
**Estd:** 1925 Private Limited Company
**Line of Business:** Manufacturers of confectionery
**Export Sales:** £33,845,000
**Issued Capital:** £11,250,000
**Directors:** P A Owings, C J Moss, M Andrews, A R Gedeller, O R Morton
**Co. Secretary:** Colin Moss
**Responsibilities**
**Senior:** George Bojewski *(Manager)*, Ian Burton *(Manager)*, Ellen Kollar *(Manager)*, Duncan McCulloch *(Manager)*, Hamish Thompson *(Manager)*
**Marketing:** Toby Baker *(Marketing Director)*
**US SIC:** 2065 **UK SIC:** 42142
**Auditors:** PricewaterhouseCoopers LLP
**Bankers:** National Westminster Bank Plc (56-00-63)

| | 28-12-13 | 29-12-12 | 31-12-11 |
|---|---|---|---|
| TO | 245,188,000 | 229,702,000 | 194,415,000 |
| P/L | 63,919,000 | 56,223,000 | 40,257,000 |
| NW | 11,867,000 | 20,604,000 | 29,816,000 |
| WC | 25,143,000 | 32,604,000 | 33,130,000 |
| Emp. | 508 | 494 | 474 |

DUNS 34-932-1807

## Wrigleys Solicitors Llp

19 Cookridge Street, Leeds, West Yorkshire LS2 3AG
**Tel:** 01132-446100
**Web:** www.wrigleys.co.uk
**Reg No:** 0318186OC **Estd:** 1990 Partnership
**Line of Business:** Solicitors
**Trading Style:** Wrigleys

**Responsibilities**
**Senior:** Christopher Billingtin *(Non-designated Limited Liabili)*, Lynne Bradey *(Non-designated Limited Liabili)*, Edward Bromet *(Non-designated Limited Liabili)*, Andrew Chart *(Partner)*, Peter Greswold *(Non-designated Limited Liabili)*, Marie-Louise Hamilton *(Non-designated Limited Liabili)*, Sylvie Nunn *(Partner)*, Andrew Wriglesworth *(Non-designated Limited Liabili)*, William Wrigley *(Non-designated Limited Liabili)*
**Admin:** Diane Robershaw *(Office Manager)*
**US SIC:** 8111 **UK SIC:** 83500

| | 30-04-14 | 30-04-13 | 30-04-12 |
|---|---|---|---|
| TO | 10,779,552 | 10,338,458 | 9,764,748 |
| WC | 6,083,183 | 6,279,297 | 5,780,349 |
| Emp. | 147 | 139 | 137 |

DUNS 23-909-2849

## Wring Group Ltd

Vale Lane, Bristol, Avon BS3 5RU
**Tel:** 01179-231-320
**Web:** www.wringgroup.co.uk
**Reg No:** 3899806 **Estd:** 1999 Private Limited Company
**Line of Business:** Demolition contractors
**Issued Capital:** £1,000
**Director:** D S Wring
**Co. Secretary:** John Wring
**Responsibilities**
**Senior:** Alec Wallace *(Manager)*
**Finance:** Sam laing *(Financial Manager)*
**Purchasing:** Lee Edwards *(Purchasing Manager)*
**Branches:** Wring Group Limited, Unit 5, Heron Works, Exeter, Devon EX2 7LL
**US SIC:** 1795, 1799
**UK SIC:** 50000
**Auditors:** Houghton Stone
**Bankers:** Barclays Bank Plc (20-33-83)

| | 31-08-13 | 31-08-12 | 31-08-11 |
|---|---|---|---|
| TO | 10,418,020 | 7,726,378 | 7,862,847 |
| P/L | 688,362 | 532,061 | 219,996 |
| NW | 4,406,518 | 3,987,479 | 3,422,130 |
| WC | 655,062 | 655,925 | 1,037,282 |
| Emp. | 85 | 86 | 77 |

DUNS 23-323-6871

## Wrings Transport

Unit 3-5 Severn View Industrial Park, Central Avenue, Hallen, Bristol, Avon BS10 7SD
**Tel:** 01179-384646
**Web:** www.wrings.co.uk
**Estd:** 2001 Partnership
**Line of Business:** Road haulage and transport services
**Partners:** R Wring, S Wring, Mrs L Wring, M Wring
**US SIC:** 4789 **UK SIC:** 77002
**Employees:** 60

DUNS 22-636-8108 **Imp**

## Writtle College

Lordship Road, Chelmsford, Essex CM1 3RR
**Tel:** 01245424200
**Web:** www.writtle.ac.uk
**VAT No:** 282797312 **Estd:** 1896
**Line of Business:** Colleges (technical and agricultural)
**Principals:** R Knight *(Financial)*, Prof M Alder
**Responsibilities**
**Senior:** Nigel Kirby *(Senior Manager)*, Alan Roscoe *(Executive)*, Marcus Walker *(General Manager)*
**Finance:** Robert Edes *(Financial Director)*
**Marketing:** Caroline Benyon *(Marketing Manager)*, Rebecca Hughes *(Press Officer)*
**IT:** Mike Coe *(IT Manager)*
**Facilities:** Patricia Everitt *(Property Manager)*
**US SIC:** 8221, 8249
**UK SIC:** 93100, 93300
**Bankers:** Barclays Bank Plc (20-19-95)
**Employees:** 347
**Turnover:** £22,482,000

DUNS 73-975-6273

## Writtle Holdings Ltd

30 Park Street, London SE1 9EQ
**Tel:** 02078426950
**Web:** www.writtleholdings.co.uk
**Reg No:** 5226380 **Estd:** 2004 Private Limited Company
**Line of Business:** Management activities of other non-financial holding companies not elsewhere classified
**Export Sales:** £14,986,000
**Issued Capital:** £6,583,457
**Directors:** A Sutcliffe, R W Seymour, R G Saysell, D H Powell, R C Williams, N D Stern, A J Wright, A W Lucas
**Co. Secretary:** Matthew Gilmore
**Responsibilities**
**Senior:** Kevin Mackenzie *(Director)*

**US SIC:** 7399 **UK SIC:** 83954

| | 31-12-13 | 31-12-12 | 31-12-11 |
|---|---|---|---|
| TO | 88,559,000 | 88,865,000 | 62,892,367 |
| P/L | 5,927,000 | 3,599,000 | 2,999,547 |
| NW | 5,190,000 | 2,856,000 | 962,224 |
| WC | 3,711,000 | 1,574,000 | (1,052,766) |
| Emp. | 942 | 837 | 617 |

DUNS 53-635-5696

## Wrixon Security Services Ltd

Broxbournebury Mansion, White Stubbs Lane, Broxbourne, Hertfordshire EN10 7PY
**Tel:** 01992-442244 **Fax:** 01992442270
**Web:** www.wrixoncare.co.uk
**Reg No:** 3440357 **Estd:** 1995 Private Limited Company
**Line of Business:** Social work activities without accommodation
**Issued Capital:** £100
**Co. Secretary:** Mrs Janice Wrixon
**Responsibilities**
**Senior:** Carla Wrixon *(Manager)*, Patrick Wrixon *(Manager)*
**US SIC:** 8321 **UK SIC:** 96111

| | 31-03-14 | 31-03-13 | 31-03-12 |
|---|---|---|---|
| TA | 886,199 | 938,890 | 649,180 |
| NW | 414,649 | 502,131 | 398,328 |
| WC | 370,418 | 443,277 | 355,546 |

DUNS 77-241-8505

## Wrn Broadcast Ltd

Wyvil Road, London SW8 2TJ
**Web:** www.wrnbroadcast.com
**Reg No:** 2712443 **VAT No:** 610084389
**Estd:** 1992 Private Limited Company
**Line of Business:** Television and radio station operators
**Export Sales:** £6,078,946
**Issued Capital:** £90,000
**Principals:** K H Miosga *(Managing)*, D G Travis, J B Cohen, D A Treadway, N P Thompson, S P Blake, T Ashburner
**Responsibilities**
**Facilities:** Darren Howells *(Facilities & Infrastructure Ma)*
**US SIC:** 4833 **UK SIC:** 97411
**Auditors:** Kingston Smith LLP
**Bankers:** Barclays Bank Plc (20-65-18)

| | 31-12-13 | 31-12-12 | 31-12-11 |
|---|---|---|---|
| TO | 11,032,687 | 9,992,555 | 9,507,785 |
| P/L | 536,337 | 348,507 | 352,770 |
| NW | 1,503,133 | 1,192,801 | 1,014,370 |
| WC | (1,320,154) | (583,679) | (558,556) |
| Emp. | 49 | 46 | 47 |

DUNS 21-730-8060

## Wrotham School

Borough Green Road, Wrotham, Sevenoaks, Kent TN15 7RD
**Tel:** 01732884207 **Fax:** 01732882178
**Web:** www.wrotham.kent.sch.uk
**Reg No:** 7662701 **Estd:** 2011 Private Company Limited By Guarantee
**Line of Business:** General secondary education
**Directors:** D J Lewis, P Cole, Dr D Price, E K Moe, Mrs S Smith, Ms J S Finney, K B Williams, K E Skinner
**Responsibilities**
**Senior:** Philip Broszek *(Director)*, Sean Toher *(Director)*
**Finance:** Donna Emirali *(Senior Finance Administrator)*
**IT:** Ian Game *(IT Manager)*
**US SIC:** 8211 **UK SIC:** 93200
**Bankers:** National Westminster Bank Plc (60-19-02)

| | 31-08-13 |
|---|---|
| TO | 11,748,852 |
| P/L | 10,030,074 |
| NW | 9,223,074 |
| WC | 72,789 |
| Emp. | 79 |

DUNS 22-114-2271

## Wroxall Abbey Estate Ltd

Birmingham Road, Wroxall, Warwick, Warwickshire CV35 7NB
**Tel:** 01926-484470 **Fax:** 01926485206
**Web:** www.wroxall.com
**Reg No:** 4133415 **Estd:** 2000 Private Limited Company
**Line of Business:** Hotels
**Issued Capital:** £5,464,680
**Directors:** G Howlett, J M Kent, J E Clarkson, A C Fox
**Co. Secretary:** Keith Churchman
**Responsibilities**
**Senior:** Anthony George *(General Manager)*
**Finance:** Jonathan Outram *(Financial Controller)*
**HR:** Linda Carrington *(Human Resources Manager)*, Penny Turner *(Human Resources Manager)*
**Health & Safety:** Linda Carrington *(Human Resources Manager)*, Penny Turner *(Human Resources Manager)*
**US SIC:** 7011 **UK SIC:** 66500

**Bankers:** The Royal Bank Of Scotland Plc (16-18-30)

| | 30-04-13 | 30-04-12 | 30-04-11 |
|---|---|---|---|
| TO | 1,864,864 | 1,563,335 | 1,996,197 |
| P/L | (537,717) | 2,936,181 | (365,541) |
| NW | 7,838,749 | 8,376,466 | (218,147) |
| WC | (728,777) | (751,821) | (1,177,417) |
| Emp. | 67 | 63 | 67 |

DUNS 28-958-8857

## Wroxham Barns Ltd

**(Subsidiary of:** Menutex Ltd)
Tunstead Road, Hoveton, Norwich, Norfolk NR12 8QU
**Tel:** 01603783762 **Fax:** 01603-781401
**Web:** www.wroxhambarns.co.uk
**Reg No:** 1669296 **VAT No:** 373124078
**Estd:** 1983 Private Limited Company
**Line of Business:** Other retail sale in specialised stores not elsewhere classified
**Issued Capital:** £100
**Director:** I A Russell
**Co. Secretary:** Ms Susan Petrie
**US SIC:** 5999 **UK SIC:** 65600
**Bankers:** Lloyds TSB Bank plc (30-96-17)

| | 29-12-13 | 30-12-12 | 01-12-12 |
|---|---|---|---|
| TA | 1,014,565 | 955,262 | 942,502 |
| NW | (119,965) | (7,670) | 25,624 |
| WC | (323,508) | (185,657) | (317,507) |

DUNS 21-834-8109

## The Wroxham Foundation

The Wroxham School, Wroxham Gardens, Potters Bar, Hertfordshire EN6 3DJ
**Tel:** 01707660905
**Reg No:** 8033193 **Estd:** 2012 Private Company Limited By Guarantee
**Line of Business:** Primary education
**Directors:** A J Borden, Mrs A Hill-Stratemeier, Mrs B De Rivaz, C T Presho, A Bull, Mrs A M Peacock, M Vandewalle, B K Smith
**Co. Secretary:** Miss Helen Bugg
**Responsibilities**
**Senior:** Stephen Davy *(Director)*, Simon Hersom *(Director)*
**US SIC:** 8211 **UK SIC:** 93200
**Bankers:** Barclays Bank Plc (20-95-61)

| | 31-08-14 | 31-08-13 |
|---|---|---|
| TO | 1,573,319 | 4,150,786 |
| P/L | 31,419 | 2,461,660 |
| NW | 2,396,079 | 2,479,660 |
| WC | 186,149 | 102,702 |
| Emp. | 46 | 49 |

DUNS 22-678-8842 **Imp**

## W.R.R.Pedley & Co. Ltd

**(Subsidiary of:** C&F Group Holdings Ltd)
Ann Street, Willenhall, West Midlands WV13 1EW
**Tel:** 01902-366060
**Web:** www.wrr-pedley.com
**Reg No:** 0362615 **VAT No:** 100154934
**Estd:** 1940 Private Limited Company
**Line of Business:** Manufacture of other fabricated metal products not elsewhere classified
**Issued Capital:** £140,000
**Principals:** C M Carver *(Managing)*, Ms C M Stokes, W G Devlson, Ms D S Carver, M D Jackson, B A Rollason
**Co. Secretary:** David Foster
**US SIC:** 3499 **UK SIC:** 31694
**Auditors:** BDO LLP
**Bankers:** HSBC Bank plc (40-46-35)

| | 31-03-14 | 31-03-13 | 31-03-12 |
|---|---|---|---|
| TO | 4,269,969 | 4,231,365 | 4,435,725 |
| P/L | 59,222 | 229,507 | 112,746 |
| NW | 2,954,738 | 2,940,845 | 2,813,488 |
| WC | 2,459,428 | 2,612,033 | 2,478,146 |
| Emp. | 82 | 70 | 78 |

DUNS 21-239-7467 **Exp**

## W.R.Swann & Co. Ltd

Owlerton Green, Sheffield, South Yorkshire S6 2BJ
**Tel:** 01142-344231 **Fax:** 01142-314966
**Web:** www.swann-morton.com
**Reg No:** 0457231 **Estd:** 1948 Private Limited Company
**Line of Business:** Manufacturers of instruments for medical purposes
**Export Markets:** Africa; Asia; Australasia; U S A
**Export Sales:** £17,204,971
**Trading Style:** Swann Morton
**Issued Capital:** £198,000
**Directors:** R J Whiteley, C L Taylor, M J Mcginley
**Co. Secretary:** Michael Hirst
**US SIC:** 3841 **UK SIC:** 37201
**Auditors:** Landin Wilcock & Co
**Bankers:** Barclays Bank Plc (20-76-89)

| | 31-10-13 | 31-10-12 | 31-10-11 |
|---|---|---|---|
| TO | 25,710,891 | 24,815,098 | 23,577,501 |
| P/L | 1,739,464 | 1,751,029 | 1,517,001 |
| NW | 18,401,361 | 18,717,625 | 16,600,572 |
| WC | 10,966,366 | 10,462,013 | 9,688,599 |
| Emp. | 388 | 372 | 381 |

DUNS 29-522-4364

## Ws Atkins Plc

Epsom Gateway, 2 Ashley Avenue, Epsom, Surrey KT18 5AL
**Tel:** 02890788600 **Fax:** 01372 740055
**Web:** www.atkinsglobal.com
**Reg No:** 1885586 **Estd:** 2011 Public Limited Company
**Line of Business:** Other engineering activities
**Export Sales:** £800,700,000
**Trading Style:** Atkins Group
**Issued Capital:** £522,259
**Directors:** Ms F J Clutterbuck, T C Leppert, Doctor K Rajagopal, U Krueger, A G Langlands, A E Cook, A J Cullens, H S Drewett
**Co. Secretary:** Mrs Helen Baker
**Responsibilities**
**Senior:** Chris Birdsong *(CEO Atkins - Asia Pacific and)*, Tim Budd *(Associate Director)*, Sandra Burch *(HR Business Partner)*, James Busby *(Operations Director)*, Valerie Evans *(Associate Director, Design)*, David Haboubi *(Head of International Nuclear)*, Jim Hale *(Client Delivery Director)*, Gregg Holland *(Chairman)*, John Inglis *(Commercial Director)*, Christina Leafe *(Director - Land Development)*, Guy Ledger *(Operations Director)*, John McSheen *(Business Development Director)*, Simon Moon *(Managing Director of Design)*, Tom O' Malley *(Managing Director - Ireland)*, Jennifer Sang *(Marketing Director - China)*, Samson Sin *(Managing Director - China)*, Alan Skates *(Manager)*, Andy Southern *(Head of Transport Planning)*, David Tonkin *(Chief Executive Officer - UK)*, David Whitmore *(Engineering and technical dire)*, Mike Woolgar *(MD of Environmental and water)*
**Marketing:** John Drever *(?Innovation Director)*, Matt Grayson *(Group PR Director)*, Emilie Moore *(Marketing Coordinator)*, Dyon Peoples *(Marketing Communications Manag)*, Louisa Perry *(Communications Manager)*, Matt Sanderson *(Marketing Manager)*, Jennifer Sang *(Marketing Director - China)*, Richard Seston *(Communications Manager)*, Jane Sheils *(Group PR manager)*
**Sales:** Philip Bullen *(Business Development Manager)*, Simon Demetriou *(Business Development Manager)*, John Inglis *(Commercial Director)*, Jake Master *(Business Development Manager)*, Callum McLaurin *(Commercial and Continuous Impr)*, John McSheen *(Business Development Director)*
**Admin:** Jane Bird *(Personal Assistant)*, Victoria Thompson *(?PA to Group Communications Di)*
**IT:** Tim Featherstone-Griffin *(Product Director: Business Tra)*
**HR:** Sandra Burch *(HR Business Partner)*
**Health & Safety:** Rita Bailie *(Health & Safety Officer)*
**Facilities:** Phil Malem *(Facilities Director)*
**Operations:** James Busby *(Operations Director)*, David Haboubi *(Head of International Nuclear)*, Andy Hughes *(Director - Dams and Resources,)*, Guy Ledger *(Operations Director)*, Mike Pearson *(Airports Director)*
**Fleet:** Farshid Kamali *(Director Highways and Transpor)*, Barry Schulz *(Transportation Group Company P)*, Andy Southern *(Head of Transport Planning)*
**Engineering:** Eric Chui *(Divisional Director and Head o)*, Richard Engledow *(Chief Engineer)*, Pankaj Garg *(Senior Engineer)*, Ian Gee *(Ground Engineering Director)*, Derek Harper *(Head of Generation)*, Rachel House *(Engineering Consultant)*, John Jennow *(Chief Engineer)*, Anna Lachut *(Assistant Engineer)*, Don Lamont *(Principle Engineer)*, Paul Littler *(Technical Director)*, Richard Neuling *(Chartered Civil Engineer)*, Glenda Pereira Romero *(Process Engineer)*, Reka Sanders *(Principal Engineer)*, Andrew Stenning *(?Technical Director)*, Simon Tinley *(Engineering Manager)*, David Whitmore *(Engineering and technical dire)*
**Branches:** Ws Atkins Plc, Cornerstone House, Stafford Park 13, Telford, Shropshire TF3 3AZ
**US SIC:** 8911, 7392
**UK SIC:** 83701, 83951
**Auditors:** PricewaterhouseCoopers LLP
**Following financial data are in thousands**

| | 31-03-14 | 31-03-13 | 31-03-12 |
|---|---|---|---|
| TO | 1,750,100 | 1,705,200 | 1,711,100 |
| P/L | 114,200 | 103,300 | 135,500 |
| NW | (109,400) | (107,000) | (132,000) |
| WC | 143,800 | 92,200 | 3,400 |
| Emp. | 16,530 | 16,600 | 16,453 |

DUNS 76-722-4397

## Ws East Anglia Ltd

**(Subsidiary of:** George Thurlow & Sons (Holdings) Ltd)
Station Road, Great Yarmouth, Norfolk NR31 0HB
**Tel:** 01493603677 **Fax:** 01493-440562
**Web:** www.warwickshubrook.co.uk
**Reg No:** 2596913 **VAT No:** 595072321
**Estd:** 1991 Private Limited Company
**Line of Business:** Management activities of holding companies
**Issued Capital:** £175,001
**Directors:** G B Osborn, S Bottomley, S N Grylls, J R Thurlow
**Co. Secretary:** Philip Addinall
**Branches:** Ws East Anglia Ltd, Station Road, Beccles, Suffolk NR34 9QQ
**US SIC:** 6711, 7539
**UK SIC:** 83962, 67100
**Auditors:** PKF
**Bankers:** National Westminster Bank Plc (55-81-45)

| | 31-12-13 | 31-12-12 | 31-12-11 |
|---|---|---|---|
| TA | 3,998,000 | 3,998,000 | 3,998,000 |
| NW | 3,998,000 | 3,998,000 | 3,998,000 |

DUNS 21-608-5258

## W.S. Hunt's Transport Ltd

**(Subsidiary of:** W.S. Hunt's Holdings Ltd)
Brox Road, Chertsey, Surrey KT16 0LZ
**Tel:** 01279414111
**Web:** www.w-s-hunt.co.uk
**Reg No:** 0466642 **Estd:** 1927 Private Limited Company
**Line of Business:** Other supporting land transport activities
**Issued Capital:** £44,150
**Principals:** G W Truett *(Managing)*, P J Truett
**Co. Secretary:** Malcolm Hunt
**Branches:** W.s. Hunt's Transport Ltd, 111 High St, Swadlincote, Derbyshire DE12 7JB
**US SIC:** 4789, 4213
**UK SIC:** 77002, 72300
**Auditors:** G & G B Young
**Bankers:** Barclays Bank Plc (20-90-56)

| | 31-03-14 | 31-03-13 | 31-03-12 |
|---|---|---|---|
| TA | 1,209,786 | 1,100,024 | 1,108,421 |
| NW | 331,707 | 351,286 | 392,205 |
| WC | (37,591) | (79,841) | 23,367 |

DUNS 73-542-4009

## Wsbl Ltd

**(Subsidiary of:** Wsbl Holdings Ltd)
Durbar Mill, Hereford Road, Blackburn, Lancashire BB1 3JU
**Tel:** 01254-583825
**Web:** www.wsbl.co.uk
**Reg No:** 4804705 **Estd:** 2003 Private Limited Company
**Line of Business:** Manufacture of other rubber products
**Issued Capital:** £1
**Directors:** W Price, R W Long
**Co. Secretary:** Ms Norah Long
**Responsibilities**
**Senior:** Barry Pugh *(General Manager)*
**Operations:** Barry Pugh *(General Manager)*
**US SIC:** 3069, 3079
**UK SIC:** 48123, 48360

| | 31-12-13 | 31-12-12 | 31-12-11 |
|---|---|---|---|
| TA | 3,182,557 | 3,224,728 | 3,055,801 |
| NW | 1,765,461 | 1,431,030 | 1,367,413 |
| WC | 536,645 | 442,014 | 341,666 |

DUNS 23-876-3952

## W.S.L. Ltd

Canal Court 152 154, High Street, Brentford, Middlesex TW8 8JA
**Tel:** 02083800333
**Web:** www.wsl-ltd.co.uk
**Reg No:** 3867748 **Estd:** 1992 Private Limited Company
**Line of Business:** Legal activities
**Trading Style:** Will Writing Services London
**Issued Capital:** £1,021
**Director:** J Donohoe
**Co. Secretary:** Geralyn Donohoe
**Branches:** W.s.l. Ltd, Canal Ct, 152-154 High St, Brentford, Middlesex TW8 8JA
**US SIC:** 8111 **UK SIC:** 83500
**Auditors:** Macnair Mason
**Bankers:** National Westminster Bank Plc (60-50-06)

| | 31-03-14 | 31-03-13 | 31-03-12 |
|---|---|---|---|
| TA | 1,350,836 | 1,201,312 | 1,160,385 |
| NW | 544,390 | 402,473 | 351,441 |
| WC | 504,716 | 367,117 | 305,286 |

DUNS 23-813-2786

## Wsm Communications Ltd

**(Subsidiary of:** Corbis Corporation)
111 Salusbury Road, London NW6 6RG
**Tel:** 020-7183-4610
**Web:** www.wsmcommunications.com
**Reg No:** 3805586 **Estd:** 1999 Private Limited Company
**Line of Business:** Management and business consultants
**Issued Capital:** £1,472,500
**Directors:** Ms A E Skurczynska, Ms C L Keeley, J Schick
**Co. Secretary:** Ms Anna Skurczynska
**Responsibilities**
**Senior:** Nicholas Addecott *(Office Manager)*, Adrian De La Touche *(Manager)*, Chris O'donoghue *(Manager)*, Harry Owen *(Events Director)*, Matt Shepstone *(Financial Controller)*
**US SIC:** 7392 **UK SIC:** 83951

| | 31-03-13 | 31-03-12 | 31-03-11 |
|---|---|---|---|
| TA | 4,291,716 | 2,822,718 | 2,992,839 |
| NW | 1,397,777 | 1,378,745 | 1,205,335 |
| WC | 1,338,186 | 1,301,877 | 1,158,735 |

DUNS 23-886-5682 **Exp**

## Wsp Cel Ltd

**(Subsidiary of:** Wsp Holding Uk Ltd)
Cel House, Westwood Way, Westwood Business Park, Coventry, West Midlands CV4 8HS
**Tel:** 024-7686-2000
**Web:** www.wspcel.com
**Reg No:** 3877626 **VAT No:** 747809784
**Estd:** 1999 Private Limited Company
**Line of Business:** Specialised building trade contractors
**Export Markets:** China
**Export Sales:** £3,106,000
**Issued Capital:** £111,334
**Directors:** A C Noble, K Doherty, N C Barnes, S N Maguire, J Ratliff
**Responsibilities**
**Senior:** Ian Barter *(Commercial Director)*, Roger Burley *(Engineering Director)*
**Finance:** David Hollinghead *(Financial Manager)*
**Sales:** Iain Turner *(Commercial Manager)*
**HR:** Ian Barter *(Commercial Director)*, Roger Burley *(Engineering Director)*
**Facilities:** Iain Turner *(Commercial Manager)*
**Engineering:** Roger Burley *(Engineering Director)*
**Branches:** Wsp Cel Ltd, Ideas Project Engineering Ltd, Unit 304, Penarth, South Glamorgan CF64 5SY
**US SIC:** 1799 **UK SIC:** 50000
**Auditors:** PricewaterhouseCoopers LLP
**Bankers:** HSBC Bank plc (40-11-04)

| | 31-12-13 | 31-12-12 | 31-12-11 |
|---|---|---|---|
| TO | 10,929,000 | 11,905,000 | 10,301,000 |
| P/L | 450,000 | 1,442,000 | 1,680,000 |
| NW | 4,767,000 | 4,659,000 | 3,578,000 |
| WC | 3,492,000 | 2,931,000 | 1,886,000 |
| Emp. | 108 | 117 | 104 |

DUNS 22-705-3915

## Wsp Environmental Ltd

**(Subsidiary of:** Groupe Wsp Global Inc)
The Victoria, Salford, Lancashire M50 3SP
**Tel:** 01618862400
**Web:** www.wspgroup.com
**Reg No:** 1152332 **VAT No:** 629527024
**Estd:** 1995 Private Limited Company
**Line of Business:** Engineers (consulting)
**Trading Style:** W S P
**Issued Capital:** £20,000
**Directors:** Dr P K Dollin, M W Naysmith
**Responsibilities**
**Senior:** Anders Karlsson *(Manager)*, Adrian Nickols *(Manager)*
**Branches:** Wsp Environmental Ltd, Elton Lodge, Newton Rd, Leeds, West Yorkshire LS7 4HE
**US SIC:** 8911, 7397
**UK SIC:** 83701, 83702
**Auditors:** PricewaterhouseCoopers LLP
**Bankers:** Barclays Bank Plc (20-03-53)

| | 31-12-13 | 31-12-12 | 31-12-11 |
|---|---|---|---|
| TO | 30,151,000 | 31,157,000 | 28,549,000 |
| P/L | 1,345,000 | (1,380,000) | 753,000 |
| NW | 874,000 | (1,016,000) | 233,000 |
| WC | 241,000 | (877,000) | 279,000 |
| Emp. | 333 | 351 | 304 |

DUNS 21-743-5372

## Wsp Textiles Ltd

**(Subsidiary of:** Ludus Capital Ltd)
Lodgemore Mills, Stroud, Gloucestershire GL5 3EJ
**Tel:** 01453764456
**Web:** www.wsptextiles.com
**Reg No:** 7759993 **Estd:** 2011 Private Limited Company
**Line of Business:** Manufacture of other textiles not elsewhere classified
**Issued Capital:** £70,000
**Directors:** T E Chaloner, N D Hammond, M W Henderson, M Fallows, D Smith, D Kettell
**Co. Secretary:** Ewen Hamilton
**US SIC:** 2299 **UK SIC:** 43992

| | 01-12-13 | 02-12-12 |
|---|---|---|
| TO | 16,747,000 | 17,946,000 |
| P/L | 1,823,000 | 873,000 |
| NW | (2,303,000) | (3,883,000) |
| WC | 5,083,000 | 3,587,000 |
| Emp. | 153 | 152 |

DUNS 28-906-0493 **Exp**

## Wsp Uk Ltd

**(Subsidiary of:** Groupe Wsp Global Inc)
Wsp House 70 Chancery Lane, London WC2A 1AF
**Tel:** 020-7314-5000
**Web:** www.wspgroup.com
**Reg No:** 1383511 **Estd:** 1978 Private Limited Company
**Line of Business:** Engineering related scientific and technical consulting activities
**Export Markets:** E U; Middle East; South Africa; Mauritius
**Issued Capital:** £1,000
**Directors:** M P Rogerson, A C Noble, Dr P K Dollin, M W Naysmith, P Tremble, J R Harvey, J Ratliff
**Branches:** Wsp Uk Limited, 66-68 Hills Road, Cambridge, Cambridgeshire CB2 1LA
**US SIC:** 8911, 7399
**UK SIC:** 83701, 83954
**Auditors:** PricewaterhouseCoopers LLP
**Bankers:** Barclays Bank Plc (20-05-75)

| | 31-12-13 | 31-12-12 | 31-12-11 |
|---|---|---|---|
| TO | 191,872,000 | 167,490,000 | 175,471,000 |
| P/L | 5,971,000 | 3,027,000 | (789,000) |
| NW | 9,766,000 | 5,187,000 | 2,284,000 |
| WC | 9,876,000 | 5,267,000 | 2,032,000 |
| Emp. | 1,513 | 1,467 | 1,625 |

DUNS 22-771-2262 **Imp**

## W.S.Scott & Co. Ltd

8 Fish & Poultry Market, Pershore St Wholesale Markets Precinct, Birmingham, West Midlands B5 6UE
**Tel:** 0121-622-3848 **Fax:** 01216223847
**Web:** www.wsscott.co.uk
**Reg No:** 0612042 **Estd:** 1958 Private Limited Company
**Line of Business:** Fish merchants (wholesale)
**Issued Capital:** £3,000
**Managing Director:** J R Davis
**Co. Secretary:** Ms Rachel Davis
**Responsibilities**
**Senior:** Michael Monnington *(Manager)*
**US SIC:** 5146 **UK SIC:** 61700
**Auditors:** Wenham Major
**Bankers:** HSBC Bank plc (40-41-27)

| | 31-03-14 | 31-03-13 | 31-03-12 |
|---|---|---|---|
| TA | 1,153,623 | 992,555 | 1,021,625 |
| NW | 113,592 | 130,914 | 126,975 |
| WC | 60,205 | 80,548 | 74,549 |

DUNS 34-582-0885 **Imp**

## Wt Emea Acquisition Ltd

**(Subsidiary of:** Francisco Partners Management Llc)
Mallard Court, Market Square, Staines, Middlesex TW18 4RH
**Tel:** 01784-415-700 **Fax:** 01784415777
**Web:** www.webtrends.com
**Reg No:** 5389904 **Estd:** 2005 Private Limited Company
**Line of Business:** Other computer related activities
**Export Sales:** £10,158,000
**Trading Style:** Webtrends
**Issued Capital:** £1
**Directors:** N P Sharp, J Davis
**Co. Secretary:** Ari Lee
**Responsibilities**
**Senior:** Suk Kim *(Manager)*, Kristen Magnuson Decozio *(Manager)*, Alex Yoder *(CEO)*
**Admin:** Alex Yoder *(CEO)*
**US SIC:** 7379 **UK SIC:** 83940

| | 30-06-13 | 30-06-12 | 30-06-11 |
|---|---|---|---|
| TO | 18,090,000 | 16,102,000 | 14,076,000 |
| P/L | 111,000 | 247,000 | 152,000 |
| NW | 1,032,000 | 872,000 | 614,000 |
| WC | 1,584,000 | 2,782,000 | 905,000 |
| Emp. | 71 | 72 | 62 |

DUNS 29-650-1539 **Exp**

## W.T. Hills Ltd

**(Subsidiary of:** W T Hills Holdings (2005) Ltd)
Pole House, Old Ide Lane, Exeter, Devon EX2 9RY
**Tel:** 01392-218010
**Web:** www.wthills.com
**Reg No:** 1976259 **Estd:** 2002 Private Limited Company
**Line of Business:** Architects
**Export Markets:** West Europe, Middle East, Canada and U.S.A.
**Trading Style:** Hills
**Issued Capital:** £867,896
**Directors:** P H Rumbelow, P R Sowden, A R Hill
**Co. Secretary:** Peter Churchill
**Responsibilities**
**Senior:** Lloyd Husband *(Associate Director)*
**Branches:** W.t. Hills Ltd, Pole House, Old Ide Lane, Exeter, Devon EX2 9RY
**US SIC:** 7397 **UK SIC:** 83702
**Auditors:** Francis Clark
**Bankers:** Lloyds TSB Bank plc (30-93-14)

| | 31-07-13 | 31-07-12 | 31-07-11 |
|---|---|---|---|
| TA | 1,779,099 | 1,773,645 | 1,724,039 |
| NW | 1,210,844 | 1,122,546 | 1,214,633 |
| WC | 1,282,198 | 1,220,278 | 1,314,247 |

DUNS 21-807-8038 **Imp**

## W.T. Parker Group Ltd.

**(Subsidiary of:** W T Parker Holdings Ltd)
24-28 Moor Street, Burton-On-Trent, Staffordshire DE14 3SX
**Tel:** 08000853828
**Web:** www.wtparker.co.uk
**Reg No:** 0480127 **VAT No:** 289178403
**Estd:** 1922 Private Limited Company
**Line of Business:** Management activities of holding companies
**Export Sales:** £87,269
**Issued Capital:** £190,000
**Directors:** J M Parker, Ms R E Pizzey, T W Parker, K A Booth, A W Owen, S T Smyth, A J Benton
**Co. Secretary:** Mrs Susan Blackmore
**Responsibilities**
**IT:** Peter Dicken *(IT Manager)*
**Operations:** Nigel Bonner *(Technical, Production Manager)*
**US SIC:** 6711 **UK SIC:** 83962
**Auditors:** PKF Cooper Parry Group Ltd
**Bankers:** HSBC Bank plc (40-15-20)

| | 28-02-14 | 28-02-13 | 29-02-12 |
|---|---|---|---|
| TO | 64,476,540 | 50,652,980 | 54,413,686 |
| P/L | 2,546,261 | 2,366,308 | 2,535,783 |
| NW | 8,258,776 | 8,384,021 | 9,937,453 |
| WC | 9,452,249 | 9,085,985 | 8,608,497 |
| Emp. | 455 | 453 | 437 |

DUNS 67-205-6699

## Wtg Technologies Ltd

**(Subsidiary of:** Wtg Technologies Group Ltd)
Fifth Floor, 76 Hammersmith Road, 76 Hammersmith Road, London W14 8UD
**Tel:** 02073398600
**Web:** www.webtechnologygroup.co.uk
**Reg No:** 6035710 **Estd:** 2006 Private Limited Company
**Line of Business:** Other software consultancy and supply
**Trading Style:** Redtech Technology Group
**Issued Capital:** £96
**Directors:** J H Steventon, R Bacchus
**Co. Secretary:** Reza Bacchus
**US SIC:** 7379 **UK SIC:** 83940
**Auditors:** BDO LLP

| | 31-03-14 | 31-03-13 | 31-03-12 |
|---|---|---|---|
| TO | 4,462,168 | 4,185,442 | 5,069,640 |
| P/L | 8,809 | (616,782) | (1,170,833) |
| NW | 189,898 | 156,119 | 707,954 |
| WC | 222,563 | 355,685 | 605,531 |

DUNS 21-213-7962 **Imp**

## W.T.Johnson & Sons(Huddersfield) Ltd

Bankfield Mills, Wakefield Road, Moldgreen, Huddersfield, West Yorkshire HD5 9BB
**Tel:** 01484-549965
**Web:** www.wtjohnson.co.uk
**Reg No:** 0531016 **VAT No:** 184513166
**Estd:** 1954 Private Limited Company
**Line of Business:** Dyers
**Issued Capital:** £9,770
**Principals:** P T Johnson *(Chairman)*, P T Johnson *(Managing)*, D P Johnson
**Co. Secretary:** Paul Johnson
**Responsibilities**
**Finance:** Alison Hargreaves *(Accountant)*
**Purchasing:** Jeremy McKinnell *(Buyer)*
**US SIC:** 2269 **UK SIC:** 43702
**Auditors:** Royce Peeling Green Ltd
**Bankers:** Barclays Bank Plc (20-43-04)

| | 30-04-14 | 30-04-13 | 30-04-12 |
|---|---|---|---|
| TO | 5,930,618 | 5,499,152 | 4,834,265 |
| P/L | (57,468) | (357,189) | 228,282 |
| NW | 4,692,778 | 4,658,260 | 4,993,419 |
| WC | 308,682 | 1,021,120 | 1,106,320 |
| Emp. | 105 | 92 | 86 |

DUNS 22-678-4296 **Imp-Exp**

## Wulfrun Specialised Fasteners Ltd

**(Subsidiary of:** Trimas Corporation)
Unit 3, Wolverhampton, West Midlands WV10 6PZ
**Tel:** 08448732226 **Fax:** 01902-875969
**Web:** www.wulfrunfasteners.co.uk
**Reg No:** 2009570 **VAT No:** 559309513
**Estd:** 1986 Private Limited Company
**Line of Business:** Manufacturers of bolts and fixings
**Export Markets:** Netherlands; Norway; Republic of Ireland
**Export Sales:** £633,755
**Issued Capital:** £100
**Directors:** D M Wathen, K P Allen, A M Zeffiro, J A Sherbin
**Responsibilities**
**Finance:** Julie Lamsdale *(Senior Finance Director)*
**US SIC:** 3452 **UK SIC:** 31371
**Auditors:** BKR Haines Watts
**Bankers:** National Westminster Bank Plc (01-00-90)

| | 31-12-13 | 30-06-13 | 31-12-12 |
|---|---|---|---|
| TO | 2,956,385 | 5,768,199 | N/A |
| P/L | (73,477) | 270,562 | N/A |
| NW | 1,927,173 | 1,987,550 | 1,758,674 |
| WC | 527,537 | 1,294,752 | 1,326,864 |
| Emp. | 96 | 88 | N/A |

DUNS 23-321-1569

## Wulvern Housing Ltd

2nd Floor Finance Department, Electra Way, Crewe, Cheshire CW1 6GW
**Fax:** 01270506258
**Web:** www.wulvernhousing.org.uk
**Reg No:** 0029307IP **Estd:** 2003 Friendly Society
**Line of Business:** Housing associations societies trusts & co-operatives
**Principals:** D Williams *(Chairman)*, R Huntley, J Taylor, Ms L Snow, T Beard, Ms B Shaw, S Hargreaves, W Gethings
**Responsibilities**
**Senior:** Sasha Deepwell *(Deputy Chief Executive)*, Brian Dykes *(Director)*, Graham Eades *(Chairman)*, Sue Lock *(Chief Executive Officer)*, Ray Westwood *(Director)*
**Finance:** Diane Jones *(Executive Director (Finance &)*
**Marketing:** Sue Crum *(Regeneration Manager)*
**Facilities:** Nicole Kershaw *(Executive Director (Customers)*
**Operations:** Julie-ann Ankers *(Director Operations)*
**US SIC:** 8321 **UK SIC:** 96111
**Auditors:** KPMG LLP
**Bankers:** National Westminster Bank Plc (60-06-23)

| | 31-03-12 | 31-03-11 | 31-03-10 |
|---|---|---|---|
| TO | 21,529,000 | 19,995,000 | 19,694,000 |
| P/L | (1,305,000) | 1,373,000 | (2,650,000) |
| NW | (4,161,000) | (27,163,000) | (35,356,000) |
| WC | 1,321,000 | 555,000 | (1,299,000) |
| Emp. | 209 | 201 | 213 |

DUNS 21-153-7360 **Imp**

## Wurth U K Ltd

**(Subsidiary of:** Adolf Würth Gmbh & Co Kg)
1 Centurion Way, Erith, Kent DA18 4AE
**Tel:** 0870-598-7841 **Fax:** 01483412805
**Web:** www.wurth.co.uk
**Reg No:** 1124802 **VAT No:** 204272209
**Estd:** 1973 Private Limited Company
**Line of Business:** Fasteners and fixings
**Issued Capital:** £95,000
**Directors:** A R Dagnall, S Oftedal
**Co. Secretary:** Andrew Dagnall
**Responsibilities**
**Senior:** Ivor Jones *(Logistics Manager)*, Wayne Moss *(Manager)*, Reinhold Wurth *(Manager)*
**Marketing:** Martin Chaillis *(Purchasing Manager)*, Angela Smith *(Marketing Manager)*
**Sales:** Wayne Moss *(Manager)*
**Facilities:** Ivor Jones *(Logistics Manager)*
**Purchasing:** Martin Chaillis *(Purchasing Manager)*
**Fleet:** Ivor Jones *(Logistics Manager)*
**Branches:** Wurth U K Ltd, Ameiva Point, Portsmouth, Hampshire PO3 5QP
**US SIC:** 3452, 5039, 5074
**UK SIC:** 31371, 61300
**Auditors:** Ernst & Young LLP
**Bankers:** HSBC Bank plc (40-02-50)

| | 31-12-13 | 31-12-12 | 31-12-11 |
|---|---|---|---|
| TO | 53,224,000 | 54,296,000 | 56,011,000 |
| P/L | 10,001,000 | (2,321,000) | (4,077,000) |
| NW | 7,907,000 | (3,641,000) | (1,300,000) |
| WC | (613,000) | (18,573,000) | (16,654,000) |
| Emp. | 614 | 655 | 713 |

DUNS 21-625-2650

## Ww Martin Ltd

Dane Park Road, Ramsgate, Kent CT11 7LT
**Tel:** 01843-591-584 **Fax:** 01843-596-333
**Web:** www.wwmartin.co.uk
**Reg No:** 0504927 **VAT No:** 201440725
**Estd:** 1952 Private Limited Company
**Line of Business:** Construction of commercial buildings
**Issued Capital:** £16,008
**Directors:** N R Peck, M R Darling, D A Barker, J E Higgens, I D Posnett, Ms J C Robinson
**Co. Secretary:** Neil Peck
**Responsibilities**
**Senior:** Gary Simmons *(Manager)*
**US SIC:** 1541, 1522
**UK SIC:** 50100
**Auditors:** Reeves & Co LLP
**Bankers:** Lloyds TSB Bank plc (30-96-93)

| | 28-02-14 | 28-02-13 | 29-02-12 |
|---|---|---|---|
| TO | 28,028,197 | 20,392,643 | 22,844,082 |
| P/L | 95,205 | 91,934 | 86,196 |
| NW | 974,367 | 890,439 | 750,063 |
| WC | 292,866 | 199,921 | 95,514 |
| Emp. | 91 | 89 | 98 |

DUNS 21-114-3262

## Ww Truck & Bus Ltd

Unit 201, Bristol, Avon BS11 8AP
**Tel:** 01179-823741 **Fax:** 01179235087
**Web:** www.volvotrucks.com
**Reg No:** 6548649 **VAT No:** 936434413
**Estd:** 2000 Private Limited Company
**Line of Business:** Van and truck dealers
**Trading Style:** Wales and West Truck and Buses
**Issued Capital:** £250,000
**Directors:** R J Millar, W Nairn
**Co. Secretary:** Jeffrey Clarke
**Responsibilities**
**Senior:** B Nairne *(Manager)*
**Branches:** Ww Truck & Bus Ltd, Clarke Ave, Portmarsh Indstl Est, Calne, Wiltshire SN11 9BS
**US SIC:** 5511, 7539
**UK SIC:** 65100, 67100
**Auditors:** Grant Thornton UK LLP
**Bankers:** Lloyds TSB Bank plc (30-00-03)

| | 31-12-13 | 31-12-12 | 31-12-11 |
|---|---|---|---|
| TO | 50,296,463 | 42,188,011 | 39,974,828 |
| P/L | 889,342 | 443,662 | 218,136 |
| NW | 1,488,113 | 836,293 | 518,587 |
| WC | 605,825 | 32,502 | (249,179) |
| Emp. | 184 | 183 | 176 |

DUNS 57-001-3623 **Imp**

## Ww (Uk) Ltd

1300 Aztec West, Almondsbury, Bristol, Avon BS32 4RX
**Tel:** 01454207360
**Web:** www.tcoffice.co.uk
**Reg No:** 2861426 **Estd:** 1993 Private Limited Company
**Line of Business:** Office furniture and equipment suppliers
**Export Sales:** £870,567
**Trading Style:** Tc Group
**Issued Capital:** £1,000
**Directors:** Ms P L Webb, G S Wooler, M James, C Facey, A T Hickman, A Warren, D A Wooler
**Responsibilities**
**Senior:** Judith Reyner *(Home Manager)*
**Admin:** Janice Muncaster *(Administrator)*
**Health & Safety:** Judith Reyner *(Home Manager)*
**Facilities:** Mark Harriman *(Maintenance Manager)*
**Operations:** Judith Reyner *(Home Manager)*
**US SIC:** 2599 **UK SIC:** 46720
**Auditors:** Riley

| | 30-04-14 | 30-04-13 | 30-04-12 |
|---|---|---|---|
| TO | 19,644,469 | 17,817,658 | 19,107,086 |
| P/L | (57,840) | (312,068) | 643,376 |
| NW | 2,194,178 | 2,532,418 | 2,899,565 |
| WC | (475,344) | (207,583) | 423,905 |
| Emp. | 75 | 77 | 67 |

DUNS 22-013-6944 **Imp**

## Wwf-Uk

Panda House, Weyside Park, Catteshall Lane, Godalming, Surrey GU7 1XR
**Tel:** 01483-426-444 **Fax:** 01483-426-409
**Web:** www.wwf.org.uk
**Reg No:** 4016725 **VAT No:** 733761821
**Estd:** 2000 Private Company Limited By Guarantee
**Line of Business:** Other publishing
**Trading Style:** World Wildlife Fund
**Directors:** M R Chambers, Miss N S Gross, Ms G M Mace, Sir M Dixon, D M Phillips, A W Reicher, R J Sambrook, Sir A T Cahn
**Co. Secretary:** Simon Major
**Responsibilities**
**Senior:** Keith Allott *(Head of Climate Change)*, Abdelilah Kasem *(Director)*
**Finance:** Dermot Heffernan *(Director of Resources)*
**Marketing:** Adrian Cockle *(Digital Innovation Manager)*, Joe Dix *(Website Manager)*, Amy Langridge *(Communications Manager)*, Claire Lowe *(Head of Online Marketing)*, Kate Randerson *(Head of Brand Communication)*
**IT:** Peter Best *(Head of Facilities)*
**HR:** Ajay Barai *(Training & Development Manager)*, Karen Gravestock *(Head of Human Resources)*
**Health & Safety:** Peter Best *(Head of Facilities)*
**Facilities:** Peter Best *(Head of Facilities)*
**Purchasing:** Peter Best *(Head of Facilities)*
**US SIC:** 2741, 8911, 8699
**UK SIC:** 47541, 83701, 96902
**Auditors:** Crowe Clark Whitehill LLP
**Bankers:** The Co-Operative Bank Plc (08-02-28)

| | 30-06-14 | 30-06-13 | 30-06-12 |
|---|---|---|---|
| TO | 62,952,000 | 59,980,000 | 66,177,000 |
| P/L | 727,000 | 1,358,000 | 7,041,000 |
| NW | 47,883,000 | 46,516,000 | 43,911,000 |
| WC | 14,214,000 | 17,160,000 | 27,405,000 |
| Emp. | 295 | 299 | 312 |

DUNS 21-786-3477
## Wwrd United Kingdom
Mustang Drive, Stafford, Staffordshire ST16 1GW
**Tel:** 01785272030
**Estd:** 2011 Proprietorship
**Line of Business:** Distribution service providers
**Proprietor:** Beech
**Responsibilities**
**Senior:** Shaun Davies *(Manager)*
**US SIC:** 4712 **UK SIC:** 77002
**Employees:** 150

DUNS 21-151-4169 Imp
## Wwrd United Kingdom Ltd
**(Subsidiary of:** Wwrd Group Midco Limited)
Wedgwood Drive, Barlaston, Stoke-On-Trent, Staffordshire ST12 9ER
**Tel:** 01782204141 **Fax:** 01782204402
**Web:** www.wwrd.com
**Reg No:** 6805116 **VAT No:** 946915581
**Estd:** 2009 Private Limited Company
**Line of Business:** Wholesale of china and glassware, wallpaper and cleaning materials
**Trading Style:** Waterford Wedgwood Uk
**Issued Capital:** £100,001
**Directors:** P H De Villemejane, A G Jones
**Co. Secretary:** Ms Mary Murray
**US SIC:** 5199 **UK SIC:** 61900
**Auditors:** KPMG LLP
**Bankers:** Bank Of America, Na (30-16-35)

| | 05-04-14 | 30-03-13 | 31-04-12 |
|---|---|---|---|
| TO | 103,571,000 | 111,142,000 | 105,460,000 |
| P/L | (3,763,000) | 3,590,000 | (3,424,000) |
| NW | (32,839,000) | (25,242,000) | (26,281,000) |
| WC | 14,336,000 | 25,634,000 | 29,901,000 |
| Emp. | 647 | 671 | 712 |

DUNS 50-415-1622
## W.Wright Electrical Ltd
87 Princess Street, Sheffield, South Yorkshire S4 7UU
**Tel:** 01142-766576 **Fax:** 01142-766527
**Web:** www.wrightelec.co.uk
**Reg No:** 2412032 **VAT No:** 308070388
**Estd:** 1978 Private Limited Company
**Line of Business:** Electrical contractors and electricians
**Issued Capital:** £100
**Principals:** W Wright *(Managing)*, J I Willmott
**Co. Secretary:** Ms Sandra Wright
**US SIC:** 1731, 1711
**UK SIC:** 50300
**Auditors:** Robinson Linell
**Bankers:** HSBC Bank plc (40-41-08)

| | 30-11-14 | 30-11-13 | 30-11-12 |
|---|---|---|---|
| TA | 2,117,231 | 2,602,948 | 1,991,011 |
| NW | 1,515,542 | 1,368,993 | 1,024,881 |
| WC | 1,208,827 | 1,088,757 | 789,671 |

DUNS 21-363-5933
## Www DOOR2DOOR Deliveries Co Uk
7 Vectis Road, Gosport, Hampshire PO12 2QD
**Web:** www.door2door-deliveries.co.uk
**Proprietorship**
**Line of Business:** Circular distribution activities
**Proprietor:** B Seeney
**Responsibilities**
**Senior:** Brian Seeney *(Proprietor)*
**US SIC:** 4311, 7319, 7311
**UK SIC:** 79010, 83800
**Employees:** 500

DUNS 29-328-2489 Imp
## Www.Cruise.Co.Uk Ltd
**(Subsidiary of:** Risk Capital Partners Llp)
Grosvenor House, Prospect Hill, Redditch, Worcestershire B97 4DL
**Tel:** 08004086200 **Fax:** 0121-445-6177
**Web:** www.cruise.co.uk
**Reg No:** 1827977 **VAT No:** 389432022
**Estd:** 2012 Private Limited Company
**Line of Business:** Activities of travel agencies
**Trading Style:** Cruise Collection
**Issued Capital:** £548,523
**Principals:** A J Gardner *(Managing)*, J M Conlon
**Branches:** Www.cruise.co.uk Ltd, 111 Peartree Ave, Southampton, Hampshire SO19 7JJ
**US SIC:** 4722 **UK SIC:** 77001
**Auditors:** KPMG LLP
**Bankers:** National Westminster Bank Plc (60-04-05)

| | 30-11-13 | 30-11-12 | 30-11-11 |
|---|---|---|---|
| TO | 16,437,557 | 10,107,866 | 7,272,287 |
| P/L | 1,434,875 | 1,353,415 | 358,192 |
| NW | 2,131,753 | 1,065,544 | 1,365,832 |
| WC | 2,943,565 | 1,573,465 | 1,845,872 |
| Emp. | 108 | 87 | 61 |

DUNS 21-133-8932
## Www.Nakedwines.Com Ltd
**(Subsidiary of:** Wiv Wein International Ag)
Holland Court, Norwich, Norfolk NR1 4DY
**Tel:** 01603-281-800 **Fax:** 01603-615-503
**Web:** https://www.nakedwines.com
**Reg No:** 6672317 **Estd:** 2008 Private Limited Company
**Line of Business:** Wine manufacturers & wholesalers
**Trading Style:** Naked Wines
**Issued Capital:** £5,472
**Directors:** R Gormley, E W Fitzgerald
**Responsibilities**
**Senior:** Amy Fulcher *(Manager)*, Rowlan Gormley *(Managing Director)*, Andreas Pieroth *(Manager)*
**Operations:** Diane Pearce *(Operations Director)*
**US SIC:** 2084, 5182
**UK SIC:** 42611, 61700
**Auditors:** Ernst & Young LLP

| | 31-12-13 | 31-12-12 | 31-12-11 |
|---|---|---|---|
| TO | 38,669,825 | 34,867,429 | 22,168,763 |
| P/L | 1,483,572 | 962,698 | (1,814,584) |
| NW | (2,602,553) | (3,687,590) | (5,316,523) |
| WC | 1,363,212 | (3,772,884) | (5,357,733) |
| Emp. | 80 | 67 | N/A |

DUNS 23-038-7813 Exp
## Wxyz Ltd
Po Box 155, Bradford, West Yorkshire BD4 6ST
**Tel:** 01274 654700 **Fax:** 01274654769
**Web:** www.astracast.co.uk
**Reg No:** 2744335 **Estd:** 1992 Private Limited Company
**Line of Business:** Other manufacturing not elsewhere classified
**Trading Style:** Fordham Pland, Astracast by Jacuzzi
**Issued Capital:** £500,000
**Responsibilities**
**IT:** Yvonne Taylor *(Group IT Manager)*
**Purchasing:** Kevin Bailey *(Purchasing Manager)*
**US SIC:** 3999, 3499
**UK SIC:** 49590, 31694
**Bankers:** The Royal Bank Of Scotland Plc (16-23-37)

| | 30-03-13 | 01-10-11 | 03-03-10 |
|---|---|---|---|
| TA | 500,000 | 500,000 | 500,000 |
| NW | 500,000 | 500,000 | 500,000 |

DUNS 21-312-9638 Imp
## Wybone Ltd
Mason Way, Hoyland, Barnsley, South Yorkshire S74 9TF
**Tel:** 01226-744010
**Web:** www.wybone.co.uk
**Reg No:** 0952455 **VAT No:** 182088650
**Estd:** 1969 Private Limited Company
**Line of Business:** Manufacture of glass fibres
**Issued Capital:** £200
**Managing Directors:** S R Cooper, C E Wyatt
**Co. Secretary:** Mrs Mary Gascoigne
**Responsibilities**
**Senior:** Olivia Burton *(Administrator)*
**Finance:** Joanne Sagar *(Accounts Manager)*
**Admin:** Olivia Burton *(Administrator)*
**HR:** Dawn Tucker *(Human Resources Officer)*
**Health & Safety:** Dawn Tucker *(Human Resources Officer)*
**Purchasing:** Michael Scholey *(Purchasing Manager)*
**Branches:** Wybone Ltd, 16 Blackberry La, Four Marks, Alton, Hampshire GU34 5BN
**US SIC:** 3229, 3841
**UK SIC:** 24791, 37201
**Auditors:** Angus Nordon & Co
**Bankers:** Yorkshire Bank Plc (05-02-27)

| | 30-04-14 | 30-04-13 | 30-04-12 |
|---|---|---|---|
| TA | 3,814,661 | 3,971,397 | 3,837,577 |
| NW | 2,054,817 | 1,844,546 | 1,748,307 |
| WC | 733,862 | 425,376 | 745,641 |

DUNS 53-632-9154
## Wyborn Hotels Ltd
High Street, Lyndhurst, Hampshire SO43 7NF
**Tel:** 02380282922
**Web:** www.crownhotel-lyndhurst.co.uk
**Reg No:** 3437795 **Estd:** 1997 Private Limited Company
**Line of Business:** Hotels
**Issued Capital:** £54,002
**Directors:** I D Dunn, L R Dunn
**Co. Secretary:** Ms Margaret Dunn
**Responsibilities**
**Senior:** Andrew Moody *(Manager)*
**Branches:** Wyborn Hotels Ltd, 1 The Arcade, Newbury, Berkshire RG14 5AD
**US SIC:** 7011 **UK SIC:** 66500
**Auditors:** David Gamblin

**Bankers:** Barclays Bank Plc (20-71-03)

| | 29-09-13 | 30-09-12 | 02-09-11 |
|---|---|---|---|
| TO | 2,339,237 | 2,811,316 | 3,615,689 |
| P/L | (473,363) | 71,518 | 233,499 |
| NW | 3,359,868 | 5,834,175 | 6,291,098 |
| WC | 89,625 | (419,244) | (329,470) |
| Emp. | 78 | 142 | 144 |

DUNS 21-751-7697
## Wyboston Lakes Ltd
Wyboston Lakes, Great North Road, Bedford, Bedfordshire MK44 3AL
**Tel:** 08452300666 **Fax:** 01480-223000
**Web:** www.wybostonlakes.co.uk
**Reg No:** 1122944 **Estd:** 1973 Private Limited Company
**Line of Business:** Development and selling of real estate
**Issued Capital:** £50,000
**Principals:** K N Hollis *(Managing)*, Ms J Chapman, S R Hutchinson, C R Hutchinson, M C Jones, C A Warner, D H Barford
**Co. Secretary:** Ms Julie Ireland
**Responsibilities**
**Senior:** Gill Holloway *(Senior Marketing Executive)*, Olivier Six *(Manager)*
**Marketing:** Johnathan Hollis *(Marketing Executive)*, Gill Holloway *(Senior Marketing Executive)*, Tony Knox *(Business Development Manager)*
**Sales:** Clive Bache *(Sales Director)*, Carol Brice *(Corporate Sales Manager)*, Laura Footner *(National Sales Manager)*, Liz Incledon-Webber *(Business Development Executive)*, Julia Moses *(Business Development Manager)*, Rachael Waldron *(National Sales Manager)*
**Branches:** Wyboston Lakes Ltd, Wyboston Lakes, The Bungalow, Bedford, Bedfordshire MK44 3AL
**US SIC:** 7999, 7399
**UK SIC:** 97913, 83954
**Auditors:** Norton Lewis & Co
**Bankers:** HSBC Bank plc (40-43-36)

| | 31-12-13 | 31-12-12 | 31-12-11 |
|---|---|---|---|
| TO | 13,511,764 | 12,428,686 | 12,016,434 |
| P/L | 160,122 | (170,105) | 268,344 |
| NW | 28,474,294 | 28,302,811 | 28,528,637 |
| WC | 1,772,588 | 1,739,026 | 5,594,061 |
| Emp. | 293 | 272 | 248 |

DUNS 22-029-7282
## Wycar Leys Ltd
**(Subsidiary of:** Taylor Hogan Healthcare Ltd)
Kirklington Road, Bilsthorpe, Newark, Nottinghamshire NG22 8TT
**Tel:** 01623871752
**Web:** www.wycarleys.co.uk
**Reg No:** 4032322 **Estd:** 1988 Private Limited Company
**Line of Business:** Other human health activities
**Issued Capital:** £8,000
**Directors:** J R Talbot, I J Taylor
**US SIC:** 8091 **UK SIC:** 95200
**Auditors:** PKF (UK) LLP
**Bankers:** The Royal Bank Of Scotland Plc (16-18-18)

| | 30-09-13 | 30-09-12 | 30-09-11 |
|---|---|---|---|
| TO | 3,264,370 | 3,337,146 | 3,287,639 |
| P/L | 70,149 | 93,103 | (57,124) |
| NW | 6,947,408 | 6,957,736 | 6,909,615 |
| WC | 72,692 | (2,693) | (101,854) |
| Emp. | 105 | 106 | 104 |

DUNS 23-225-7139
## Wychavon District Council
Civic Centre, Queen Elizabeth Drive, Pershore, Worcestershire WR10 1PT
**Tel:** 01386-565000
**Web:** www.wychavon.gov.uk
**Estd:** 2010
**Line of Business:** Local government
**Principals:** S Pritchard *(Managing)*, S Pritchard, W S Nott
**Responsibilities**
**Senior:** Vic Alison *(Deputy Managing Director)*, Sally Griffiths *(Executive)*, Jack Haggerty *(Line Manager)*, Lynn Stevens *(Parks Officer)*, Martin Tout *(Land Terrier Officer)*
**Finance:** Andy Poppleton *(Welfare Benefits & Money Advis)*
**Marketing:** Maureen Cook *(Communications Manager)*
**Sales:** Tim Deakin *(Development Manager)*, Denise Ditchburn *(Promotions & Monitoring Assist)*, Cheryl Peters *(Business Improvement Manager)*
**Admin:** Sally Jacques *(Administrator)*
**IT:** Nigel Winters *(IT Manager)*
**Facilities:** Mark Haslam *(Property Services Manager)*
**Branches:** Wychavon District Council, Main Street, Pershore, Worcestershire WR10 3NB
**US SIC:** 9121 **UK SIC:** 91110
**Employees:** 300

DUNS 23-316-3497
## Wychavon Leisure Community Association Ltd
King Georges Way, Pershore, Worcestershire WR10 1QU
**Tel:** 01386562931 **Fax:** 01386562940
**Web:** www.wychavonleisure.co.uk
**Reg No:** 0028894IP **Estd:** 1999 Friendly Society
**Line of Business:** Leisure centres
**Trading Style:** Wychavon Leisure Centre
**Responsibilities**
**Senior:** Kay Mcbride *(centre manager)*
**Marketing:** Sharon Keen *(Marketing Manager)*
**Facilities:** Kay Mcbride *(centre manager)*
**Operations:** Mark O"Shea *(Head of Operations)*
**US SIC:** 7999 **UK SIC:** 97913
**Employees:** 300

DUNS 21-551-8155
## Wychbury Care Services
350-352 Hagley Road, Stourbridge, West Midlands DY9 0QY
**Tel:** 01562883358
**Estd:** 1983 Partnership
**Line of Business:** Residential care for the elderly
**Partners:** D G Johnson, Mrs A K Johnson
**US SIC:** 8361 **UK SIC:** 96112
**Employees:** 61

DUNS 28-835-0226
## Wychwood School Ltd
72-74 Banbury Road, Oxford, Oxfordshire OX2 6JR
**Web:** www.wychwoodschool.org
**Reg No:** 0380424 **Estd:** 1943 Private Limited Company
**Line of Business:** Schools (local authority)
**Trading Style:** Wychwood School
**Issued Capital:** £500
**Directors:** A F Stewart, Mrs R J Hayes, Mrs N J King, Ms D J Pluck, Ms M C Crawford, W R Briant, Mrs K Rogers, Mrs A S Hunter
**Co. Secretary:** Ian Williams
**Responsibilities**
**Senior:** David Clews *(Director)*, Paul Hall *(Director)*, Daisy Hay *(Director)*, Nigel Rice *(Manager)*, Susan Winfield Digby *(Headmistress)*
**Finance:** Amanda Drake-Brockman *(Bursar)*
**Admin:** Susan Grainger *(Head Secretary)*
**HR:** Susan Winfield Digby *(Headmistress)*
**US SIC:** 8211 **UK SIC:** 93200
**Auditors:** Critchleys
**Bankers:** Barclays Bank Plc (20-65-18)

| | 31-08-13 | 31-08-12 | 31-08-11 |
|---|---|---|---|
| TO | 1,584,673 | 1,683,325 | 1,947,566 |
| P/L | (367,679) | (185,947) | 95,765 |
| NW | 1,885,011 | 2,252,690 | 2,438,637 |
| WC | 156,371 | 523,133 | 657,718 |
| Emp. | 51 | 57 | 60 |

DUNS 21-908-1411 Imp
## Wyckham Blackwell Ltd
**(Subsidiary of:** Wyckham Blackwell Group Ltd)
Old Station Road, Hampton-In-Arden, Solihull, West Midlands B92 0HB
**Tel:** 01675-442233
**Web:** www.wyckham-blackwell.co.uk
**Reg No:** 1073927 **VAT No:** 110705228
**Estd:** 1972 Private Limited Company
**Line of Business:** Manufacture of builders carpentry and joinery
**Trading Style:** Wyckham Blackwell Ltd
**Issued Capital:** £10,000
**Director:** C H Golby
**Co. Secretary:** Henry Taylor
**Responsibilities**
**Senior:** David Himmons *(Director)*
**US SIC:** 2431, 1761
**UK SIC:** 46300, 50400
**Auditors:** Weatherer Bailey Bragg
**Bankers:** National Westminster Bank Plc (51-61-26)

| | 31-03-14 | 31-03-13 | 31-03-12 |
|---|---|---|---|
| TA | 1,734,804 | 1,531,733 | 1,673,159 |
| NW | 798,470 | 1,094,586 | 1,173,029 |
| WC | 633,021 | 902,465 | 960,208 |

DUNS 73-493-2655
## Wyclean Group Ltd
4 The Valley Centre, Gordon Road, High Wycombe, Buckinghamshire HP13 6EQ
**Tel:** 01494473338 **Fax:** 01494473350
**Web:** www.wycleangroup.co.uk
**Reg No:** 4756722 **Estd:** 1984 Private Limited Company
**Line of Business:** Management of real estate on a fee or contract basis
**Issued Capital:** £100
**Directors:** M T Hughes, Mrs K P Goncalves
**Responsibilities**
**Operations:** Bernard Gallyot *(Director of Operations)*

**US SIC:** 6531 **UK SIC:** 83400
**Auditors:** Seymour Taylor Audit Ltd

| | 31-12-13 | 31-12-12 | 31-12-11 |
|---|---|---|---|
| TA | 2,013,300 | 1,994,210 | 1,892,070 |
| NW | 214,707 | 5,256 | (85,882) |
| WC | 185,413 | (44,084) | (155,692) |

DUNS 34-864-3664

## Wycliffe Bible Translators Ltd.

Wycombe Road, Saunderton, High Wycombe, Buckinghamshire HP14 4BF
**Web:** www.wycliffe.org.uk
**Reg No:** 5663771 **Estd:** 1964
**Line of Business:** Religious organisations and places of worship
**Directors:** M J Clark, Wycliffe Uk Ltd
**Responsibilities**
**Senior:** Eddie Arthur *(Manager)*, Katherine Caroe *(Manager)*, Peter Grainger *(Manager)*
**Finance:** Barrie Prebble *(Finance Director)*
**US SIC:** 8661 **UK SIC:** 96600
**Employees:** 160

DUNS 23-551-0328

## Wycliffe College (Incorporated)

Bath Road, Stonehouse, Gloucestershire GL10 2JQ
**Tel:** 01453822432
**Web:** www.wycliffe.co.uk
**Reg No:** 0255632 **Estd:** 1931 Private Company Limited By Guarantee
**Line of Business:** Schools (independent)
**Trading Style:** Wycliffe College (Incorporated)
**Directors:** Mrs K R Fife, I H Paling, Group Captain G E Reid, Mrs S J Lacey, J Slater, J C Pritchard, T G Hale, Brigadier R J Bacon
**Co. Secretary:** Andrew Golding
**Responsibilities**
**Senior:** Gillian Camm *(Manager)*, Caroline Duckworth *(Director)*, Bernet Ward *(Head Teacher)*, Jeremy Williams *(Director)*
**Marketing:** Melanie Gray *(Marketing Manager)*
**Facilities:** Amanda Bromley *(Facilities Coordinator)*
**Branches:** Wycliffe College (Incorporated), Ryeford Hall, Ebley Road, Stonehouse, Gloucestershire GL10 2LD
**US SIC:** 8211 **UK SIC:** 93200
**Auditors:** Griffiths Marshall
**Bankers:** Lloyds TSB Bank plc (30-98-29)

| | 31-08-14 | 31-08-13 | 31-08-12 |
|---|---|---|---|
| TO | 13,152,123 | 12,917,016 | 13,278,710 |
| P/L | 962,853 | 1,027,184 | 1,330,027 |
| NW | 21,508,646 | 20,545,793 | 19,518,609 |
| WC | (2,156,473) | (711,849) | (1,529,660) |
| Emp. | 345 | 340 | 334 |

DUNS 23-635-6929

## Wycombe High School for Girls

Marlow Road, High Wycombe, Buckinghamshire HP11 1TB
**Tel:** 01494-523961
**Web:** www.whs.bucks.sch.uk
**Estd:** 1901
**Line of Business:** General secondary education
**Directors:** Ms M N Pilkington, Mrs E J Duffy, Ms P Nower
**Responsibilities**
**Senior:** Sharon Cromie *(Head Teacher)*
**US SIC:** 8211 **UK SIC:** 93200
**Bankers:** National Westminster Bank Plc (60-01-31)
**Employees:** 130

DUNS 73-878-1215

## Wycombe Wanderers Football Club Ltd

Adams Park, Hillbottom Road, Sands Industrial Estate, High Wycombe, Buckinghamshire HP12 4HJ
**Tel:** 01494-472100
**Web:** www.wycombewanderers.co.uk
**Reg No:** 5132509 **Estd:** 1986 Private Limited Company
**Line of Business:** Operation of other sports arenas and stadiums not elsewhere classified
**Issued Capital:** £1,360,900
**Directors:** D J Roberton, D F Cook, A J Howard
**Co. Secretary:** Miss Kelly Francis
**Responsibilities**
**Senior:** Ivor Beeks *(Manager)*, Stephen Hayes *(Manager)*, Brian Kane *(Manager)*, David McGee *(Manager)*, David McGregor *(General Manager)*
**Sales:** Corina Francis *(Head of Commercial Sales -)*, Becci Redmond *(Commercial Executive)*
**US SIC:** 7999, 8999
**UK SIC:** 97913, 83954
**Auditors:** H W

**Bankers:** Lloyds TSB Bank plc (30-94-28)

| | 30-06-13 | 30-06-12 | 30-06-11 |
|---|---|---|---|
| TO | 3,493,391 | 4,643,651 | 4,503,980 |
| P/L | (1,029,897) | 3,682,693 | (1,252,623) |
| NW | (1,394,865) | (367,468) | (3,074,390) |
| WC | (1,703,320) | (758,481) | (2,108,655) |
| Emp. | N/A | 104 | 110 |

DUNS 23-265-1807

## Wye Valley Demolition Ltd

Lloyd George House Fordshill Road, Hereford, Herefordshire HR2 6NS
**Tel:** 01432361691 **Fax:** 01432-361689
**Web:** www.wye-valley-demolition.co.uk
**Reg No:** 4293062 **Estd:** 2011 Private Limited Company
**Line of Business:** Demolition and wrecking of buildings; earth moving
**Issued Capital:** £2
**Director:** A R Howell
**Co. Secretary:** Ms Susan Howell
**Responsibilities**
**Senior:** Gavin Pettigrew *(Advertising Manager)*
**Sales:** Gavin Pettigrew *(Advertising Manager)*
**US SIC:** 1795 **UK SIC:** 50000
**Auditors:** Cole Bishop & Co

| | 31-08-14 | 31-08-13 | 31-08-12 |
|---|---|---|---|
| TA | 1,645,770 | 2,070,089 | 2,001,042 |
| NW | 595,187 | 1,888,766 | 1,743,597 |
| WC | 1,034,423 | 1,888,766 | 1,743,607 |

DUNS 21-123-5715

## Wye Valley Green Energy Ltd

Lloyd George House, Fordshill Road, Hereford, Herefordshire HR2 6NS
**Tel:** 01432361695
**Web:** www.wyevalley.co.uk
**Reg No:** 6678572 **Estd:** 2008 Private Limited Company
**Line of Business:** Agricultural shows
**Issued Capital:** £2
**Directors:** A R Howell, T B David
**US SIC:** 7399 **UK SIC:** 83954

| | 31-08-13 | 31-08-12 | 31-08-11 |
|---|---|---|---|
| TA | 2 | 2 | 2 |
| NW | 2 | 2 | 2 |

DUNS 64-070-1025 **Imp**

## Wyevale Garden Centres G&L Ltd

**(Subsidiary of:** London 58 Limited)
Smallway, Congresbury, Bristol, Avon BS49 5AA
**Tel:** 01934875700
**Web:** www.g-l.co.uk
**Reg No:** 3465908 **Estd:** 1997 Private Limited Company
**Line of Business:** Other retail sale in specialised stores not elsewhere classified
**Trading Style:** The Garden & Leisure Group Limited
**Issued Capital:** £28,938,317
**Directors:** N O Steinmeyer, D C Murray, K M Bradshaw
**Co. Secretary:** Nils Steinmeyer
**Responsibilities**
**Senior:** Bruno Lanthier *(Manager)*, Daniel Metivet *(Manager)*
**Branches:** Wyevale Garden Centres G&l Ltd, 454 Bridgnorth Rd, Shipley, Wolverhampton, West Midlands WV6 7AJ
**US SIC:** 5999 **UK SIC:** 65600
**Auditors:** PricewaterhouseCoopers LLP
**Bankers:** Barclays Bank Plc (20-33-83)

| | 29-12-13 | 31-12-12 | 31-12-11 |
|---|---|---|---|
| TO | 38,142,000 | 37,625,000 | 40,306,000 |
| P/L | (2,040,000) | (769,000) | (923,000) |
| NW | 23,291,000 | 25,337,000 | 32,580,000 |
| WC | 2,732,000 | 2,764,000 | 3,102,000 |
| Emp. | 526 | 530 | 546 |

DUNS 29-646-2773

## Wyevale Garden Centres Holdings Ltd

**(Subsidiary of:** London 58 Limited)
258 Bath Road, Slough, Berkshire SL1 4DX
**Tel:** 01332514268 **Fax:** 01753696541
**Web:** www.wyevale.co.uk
**Reg No:** 1972554 **Estd:** 1985 Private Limited Company
**Line of Business:** Garden centres
**Issued Capital:** £48,150,692
**Directors:** N O Steinmeyer, K M Bradshaw, S T Murphy
**Co. Secretary:** Nils Steinmeyer
**Branches:** Wyevale Garden Centres Holdings Ltd, Bulbourne Road, Tring, Hertfordshire HP23 5HF
**US SIC:** 6711 **UK SIC:** 83962
**Auditors:** Deloitte LLP
**Bankers:** Barclays Bank Plc (20-39-64)

| | 29-12-13 | 30-12-12 | 25-12-11 |
|---|---|---|---|
| TO | 70,370,000 | 67,247,000 | 73,144,000 |
| P/L | (5,233,000) | 1,959,000 | 4,625,000 |
| NW | 257,411,000 | 298,778,000 | 300,830,000 |
| WC | (163,173,000) | (164,180,000) | (163,962,000) |
| Emp. | N/A | 3,305 | 3,019 |

DUNS 21-613-3090 **Imp**

## Wyevale Garden Centres Ltd

**(Subsidiary of:** London 58 Limited)
Syon Park, London Road, Brentford, Middlesex TW8 8JF
**Tel:** 02083261200
**Web:** www.thegardencentregroup.co.uk
**Reg No:** 0662286 **Estd:** 1960 Private Limited Company
**Line of Business:** Other retail sale in specialised stores not elsewhere classified
**Issued Capital:** £6,450
**Directors:** N O Steinmeyer, K M Bradshaw, S T Murphy
**Co. Secretary:** Nils Steinmeyer
**Responsibilities**
**Senior:** Stephen Pitcher *(Purchasing Director)*, Lorraine Robertson *(Marketing Director)*
**Marketing:** Lorraine Robertson *(Marketing Director)*
**Purchasing:** Stephen Pitcher *(Purchasing Director)*
**Branches:** Wyevale Garden Centres Ltd, Rougham Road, Bury St Edmunds, Bury St. Edmunds, Suffolk IP33 2RN
**US SIC:** 5999 **UK SIC:** 65600
**Auditors:** Deloitte LLP
**Bankers:** Barclays Bank Plc (20-39-64)

| | 29-12-13 | 30-12-12 | 25-12-11 |
|---|---|---|---|
| TO | 261,811,000 | 259,234,000 | 263,657,000 |
| P/L | (4,732,000) | (20,145,000) | 586,000 |
| NW | 27,369,000 | 32,938,000 | 50,833,000 |
| WC | (50,226,000) | (7,729,000) | 3,610,000 |

DUNS 29-633-6647

## Wyg Engineering Ltd

**(Subsidiary of:** Wyg Plc)
Arndale Court, Otley Road Arndale Centre, Leeds, West Yorkshire LS6 2UJ
**Tel:** 01132787111 **Fax:** 01132-783487
**Web:** www.wyg.com
**Reg No:** 1959704 **VAT No:** 431032608
**Estd:** 1964 Private Limited Company
**Line of Business:** Other engineering activities
**Trading Style:** White Young
**Issued Capital:** £85,300
**Directors:** T A Holden, A J Gillespie
**Co. Secretary:** Gareth Arber
**Responsibilities**
**Senior:** Glen Thorn *(Manager)*
**Branches:** Wyg Engineering Ltd, 2 St James Gate, Newcastle-Upon-Tyne, Newcastle Upon Tyne, Tyne and Wear NE1 4AD
**US SIC:** 8911 **UK SIC:** 83701
**Auditors:** PricewaterhouseCoopers LLP
**Bankers:** Lloyds TSB Bank plc (30-00-05)

| | 31-03-14 | 31-03-13 | 31-03-12 |
|---|---|---|---|
| TO | 21,292,000 | 20,411,000 | 17,084,000 |
| P/L | 2,553,000 | 853,000 | (243,000) |
| NW | 10,834,000 | 8,456,000 | 7,906,000 |
| WC | 18,644,000 | 18,048,000 | 15,440,000 |
| Emp. | 227 | 202 | 256 |

DUNS 77-938-2225

## Wyg Environment Planning Transport Ltd

**(Subsidiary of:** Wyg Plc)
Arndale Court, Arndale Centre, Otley Road, Leeds, West Yorkshire LS6 2UJ
**Tel:** 02920829200
**Web:** www.wyg.com
**Reg No:** 3050297 **Estd:** 2008 Private Limited Company
**Line of Business:** Urban planning and landscape architectural activities
**Issued Capital:** £2
**Directors:** T A Holden, M K Davies, A J Gillespie
**Co. Secretary:** Benjamin Whitworth
**Responsibilities**
**Senior:** Neil Denison *(Manager)*
**US SIC:** 8911 **UK SIC:** 83701
**Auditors:** PricewaterhouseCoopers LLP

| | 31-03-14 | 31-03-13 | 31-03-12 |
|---|---|---|---|
| TO | 31,749,000 | 32,222,000 | 36,030,000 |
| P/L | 2,405,000 | 1,000,000 | (9,990,000) |
| NW | 32,301,000 | 29,916,000 | 28,916,000 |
| WC | 12,040,000 | 9,611,000 | 8,948,000 |
| Emp. | 330 | 364 | 386 |

DUNS 73-545-5813

## Wyg Management Services Ltd

**(Subsidiary of:** Wyg Plc)
Arndale Court, Arndale Centre, Otley Road, Leeds, West Yorkshire LS6 2UJ
**Web:** www.tweeds.co.uk
**Reg No:** 4807864 **Estd:** 1952 Private Limited Company
**Line of Business:** Business and management consultancy activities not elsewhere classified
**Trading Style:** Tweeds
**Issued Capital:** £7,037,498
**Directors:** C D Anderson, T A Holden, A J Gillespie
**Co. Secretary:** Benjamin Whitworth
**US SIC:** 7392, 8911

**UK SIC:** 83951, 83701
**Auditors:** PricewaterhouseCoopers LLP

| | 31-03-14 | 31-03-13 | 31-03-12 |
|---|---|---|---|
| TO | 14,313,000 | 14,477,000 | 12,501,000 |
| P/L | 1,814,000 | 1,072,000 | (712,000) |
| NW | 8,655,000 | 6,841,000 | 5,769,000 |
| WC | 10,073,000 | 10,870,000 | 8,390,000 |
| Emp. | 113 | 131 | 130 |

DUNS 29-506-3192 **Exp**

## Wyg Plc

Arndale Court, Arndale Centre, Otley Road, Leeds, West Yorkshire LS6 2UJ
**Tel:** 02072507500 **Fax:** 01132-783487
**Web:** www.wyg.com
**Reg No:** 1869543 **Estd:** 1984 Public Limited Company
**Line of Business:** Management activities of holding companies
**Export Sales:** £54,003,000
**Trading Style:** White Young Green Consulting, White Young Green (Ireland)
**Issued Capital:** £69,247
**Directors:** G D Olver, P C Hamer, S V Cummins, R M Mctighe, R G Barr, D J Jeffcoat
**Co. Secretary:** Benjamin Whitworth
**Branches:** Wyg Plc, 2 St James Gate, Newcastle-Upon-Tyne, Newcastle Upon Tyne, Tyne and Wear NE1 4AD
**US SIC:** 6711, 7392, 8911
**UK SIC:** 83962, 83951, 83701
**Auditors:** Deloitte LLP
**Bankers:** National Westminster Bank Plc (60-00-01)

| | 31-03-14 | 31-03-13 | 31-03-12 |
|---|---|---|---|
| TO | 126,914,000 | 125,744,000 | 139,864,000 |
| P/L | 1,777,000 | (3,307,000) | 11,878,000 |
| NW | 2,231,000 | 183,000 | 609,000 |
| WC | 17,098,000 | 21,088,000 | 27,997,000 |
| Emp. | 1,230 | 1,306 | 1,470 |

DUNS 23-635-7786

## Wyggeston & Queen Elizabeth I College

University Road, Leicester, Leicestershire LE1 7RJ
**Web:** www.wqeic.ac.uk
**Estd:** 1877
**Line of Business:** General secondary education
**Principals:** B Smith *(Financial)*, Dr R Wilkinson
**Responsibilities**
**HR:** Lewis Clifford *(Training Manager)*, Rachel Cooper *(Human Resources Manager)*
**US SIC:** 8211 **UK SIC:** 93200
**Employees:** 248

DUNS 23-356-4801

## Wyke College

Bricknell Avenue, Hull, North Humberside HU5 4NT
**Tel:** 01482-346347
**Web:** www.wyke.ac.uk
**Estd:** 1997
**Line of Business:** Sixth form colleges
**Principals:** Mrs P Cook, A Woodcock, J Darmody, Dr R Smith, M Rogerson, Dr I Taylor
**Responsibilities**
**Senior:** Jay Trivedy *(Principal)*, Elizabeth Younger *(Manager)*
**IT:** Bill Jackson *(IT Coordinator)*
**US SIC:** 8211 **UK SIC:** 93200
**Bankers:** Lloyds TSB Bank plc (30-94-44)
**Employees:** 160

DUNS 21-683-1081 **Imp-Exp**

## Wyke Farms Ltd

White House Farm, Bruton, Somerset BA10 0PQ
**Fax:** 01749-813495
**Web:** www.wykefarms.com
**Reg No:** 0751654 **VAT No:** 130163618
**Estd:** 1937 Private Limited Company
**Line of Business:** Cheese makers
**Export Markets:** Spain; Belgium; France; Germany
**Export Sales:** £4,168,000
**Trading Style:** Wyke Farm
**Issued Capital:** £1,075,770
**Principals:** R J Clothier *(Managing)*, D J Clothier, Mrs G L Clothier, R T Clothier, R W Clothier, T J Clothier, A W Wilson
**Co. Secretary:** Paul Hardwick
**Responsibilities**
**IT:** Jason Fewell *(Engineering Manager)*
**HR:** Tim Hake *(Human Resources Manager)*
**Health & Safety:** Tim Hake *(Human Resources Manager)*
**Branches:** Wyke Farms Ltd, Unit 2-4, Bennetts Field Trading Estate, Wincanton, Somerset BA9 9DT
**US SIC:** 2021 **UK SIC:** 41302
**Auditors:** PricewaterhouseCoopers LLP

## Wyre Housing Association Ltd

**Bankers:** Barclays Bank Plc (20-99-40)

| | 31-03-13 | 31-03-12 | 31-03-11 |
|---|---|---|---|
| TO | 59,820,000 | 59,260,000 | 59,075,000 |
| P/L | 2,429,000 | 2,181,000 | 1,243,000 |
| NW | 13,940,000 | 12,432,000 | 11,046,000 |
| WC | 15,103,000 | 2,089,000 | 8,652,000 |
| Emp. | 218 | 207 | 233 |

DUNS 21-774-4953

## Wyke Regis C of E Junior School

High Street, Wyke Regis, Weymouth, Dorset DT4 9NU
**Tel:** 01305786041
**Web:** www.wykeregisjun.co.uk
**Estd:** 1997 Proprietorship
**Line of Business:** General secondary education
**Proprietor:** C Saunders
**US SIC:** 8211 **UK SIC:** 93200
**Employees:** 50

DUNS 21-124-8350

## Wylie & Bisset Llp

168 Bath Street, Glasgow, Lanarkshire G2 4TP
**Tel:** 0141 566 7000
**Web:** www.trust-deeds-scotland.co.uk
**Reg No:** 0301911SO **Estd:** 2008
**Line of Business:** Accounting activities
**Responsibilities**
**Senior:** Ross Mclauchlan (Non-designated Limited Liabili)
**US SIC:** 8621, 7399
**UK SIC:** 96311, 83954

| | 31-03-14 | 31-03-13 | 31-03-12 |
|---|---|---|---|
| TA | 3,039,715 | 2,963,560 | 2,787,360 |
| NW | N/A | N/A | (35,000) |
| WC | 975,150 | 1,448,690 | 1,464,817 |

DUNS 22-616-7641     Exp

## Wyman Dillon Ltd

Silverhill, Rudgeway, Bristol, Avon BS35 3NS
**Tel:** 01454200000
**Web:** www.wymandillon.co.uk
**Reg No:** 1266200 **VAT No:** 286191532
**Estd:** 1976 Private Limited Company
**Line of Business:** Market research and public opinion polling
**Export Markets:** Germany, Belgium & Portugal
**Issued Capital:** £38,000
**Managing Director:** A A Douglas
**Co. Secretary:** Peter Deacon
**Responsibilities**
**Senior:** Linda Dare (General Manager)
**Marketing:** Linda Dare (General Manager)
**HR:** Linda Dare (General Manager)
**Health & Safety:** Linda Dare (General Manager)
**Operations:** Linda Dare (General Manager)
**Purchasing:** Linda Dare (General Manager)
**US SIC:** 7392 **UK SIC:** 83951
**Auditors:** Unknown Auditor
**Bankers:** Lloyds TSB Bank plc (30-94-83)

| | 31-05-14 | 31-05-13 | 31-05-12 |
|---|---|---|---|
| TA | 313,189 | 321,579 | 348,910 |
| NW | 183,685 | 194,835 | 194,264 |
| WC | 131,819 | 146,228 | 129,792 |

DUNS 57-831-9147     Imp

## Wyman-Gordon Ltd

(**Subsidiary of:** Precision Castparts Corp.)
Wyman Gordon Complex, 1a Houstoun Road, Livingston, West Lothian EH54 5BZ
**Tel:** 01506-446200
**Web:** www.wyman-gordon.com
**Reg No:** 2889486 **VAT No:** 634860919
**Estd:** 1883 Private Limited Company
**Line of Business:** Metal finishing and polishing services
**Issued Capital:** £12,903,225
**Directors:** R P Becker, S C Blackmore, Mrs S R Hagel, K Buck, A R Milner, R S Pattee, Ms R A Beyer
**Co. Secretary:** Scott Sinclair
**Responsibilities**
**Senior:** Nigel Tutton (Manager)
**Branches:** Wyman-Gordon Ltd, Houstoun Road, Livingston, West Lothian EH54 5BZ
**US SIC:** 3499, 3469
**UK SIC:** 31694, 31200
**Auditors:** Deloitte LLP
**Bankers:** Clydesdale Bank Plc (82-45-05)

| | 30-03-14 | 31-03-13 | 01-03-12 |
|---|---|---|---|
| TO | 133,936,000 | 142,145,000 | 128,104,000 |
| P/L | 25,447,000 | 33,131,000 | 23,715,000 |
| NW | 71,114,000 | 48,059,000 | 31,316,000 |
| WC | 72,357,000 | 48,797,000 | 23,234,000 |
| Emp. | 354 | 371 | 370 |

DUNS 21-661-2941

## Wymondham College Enterprises Ltd

(**Subsidiary of:** Wymondham College)
Golf Links Road, Wymondham, Norfolk NR18 9SZ
**Tel:** 01953609000 **Fax:** 01953603313
**Web:** www.wymondhamcollege.org
**Reg No:** 7169209 **Estd:** 2010 Private Limited Company
**Line of Business:** General secondary education
**Issued Capital:** £2
**Directors:** J S Taylor, P J Rout
**Responsibilities**
**Senior:** Melvyn Roffe (Principal)
**IT:** Dave Tonnison (Senior IT Executive)
**US SIC:** 8211 **UK SIC:** 93200

| | 28-02-14 | 28-02-13 | 28-02-12 |
|---|---|---|---|
| TO | N/A | 15,971 | 23,984 |
| P/L | N/A | (357) | (26,526) |
| NW | 654 | 1,580 | 1,937 |
| WC | 654 | 1,580 | 1,937 |

DUNS 36-802-5334

## Wymondham Leisure Centre

Wymondham Leisure Centre, Norwich Road, Wymondham, Norfolk NR18 0NT
**Tel:** 01953607171
**Web:** www.south-norfolk.gov.uk
**Proprietorship**
**Line of Business:** Leisure centres
**Responsibilities**
**Senior:** Kate Martin (Manager)
**US SIC:** 7999 **UK SIC:** 97913
**Employees:** 80

DUNS 23-138-4348

## Wyn Construction Ltd

Hill Top, Durham, County Durham DH7 9RL
**Tel:** 01913733374
**Web:** www.wyn-construction-ltd.co.uk
**Reg No:** 2732520 **Estd:** 1992 Private Limited Company
**Line of Business:** Civil engineers
**Trading Style:** Wyn Construction Ltd
**Issued Capital:** £1,700
**Directors:** D Cowie, D Ginsberg, M Horner, A Cowie
**Co. Secretary:** Roy Bainbridge
**Responsibilities**
**Health & Safety:** Ed Page (health & safety manager)
**US SIC:** 1522 **UK SIC:** 50100
**Auditors:** John Alderdice & Son

| | 31-08-13 | 31-08-12 | 31-08-11 |
|---|---|---|---|
| TO | 10,076,041 | 13,211,878 | 10,710,882 |
| P/L | 110,146 | 172,339 | 122,493 |
| NW | 1,938,903 | 1,851,229 | 1,717,640 |
| WC | 1,344,399 | 1,297,279 | 1,255,560 |
| Emp. | 99 | 114 | 98 |

DUNS 21-209-8482

## Wyncourt

162 Park Road, Timperley, Altrincham, Cheshire WA15 6QH
**Web:** www.wyncourtnursinghome.com
**Estd:** 1982 Partnership
**Line of Business:** Accommodation advice
**Partners:** Mrs S Mattinson, H Mattinson
**Responsibilities**
**Facilities:** Ged Martin (Maintenance Manager)
**US SIC:** 8091 **UK SIC:** 95200
**Bankers:** The Royal Bank Of Scotland Plc (16-12-11)
**Employees:** 50

DUNS 21-714-4872

## Wyndeham Grange Ltd

Butts Road, Brighton, East Sussex BN42 4EJ
**Tel:** 01273-592244
**Web:** www.wyndeham.co.uk
**Reg No:** 0553857 **VAT No:** 191249750
**Estd:** 1905 Private Limited Company
**Line of Business:** Manufacturers of albums
**Issued Capital:** £740,586
**Directors:** P Utting, R Day, Mrs Z Repman, R C Fookes, Mrs D Read, R E Kingston
**Co. Secretary:** Mrs Zoe Repman
**Responsibilities**
**Senior:** Bryan Bedson (Manager), Kenneth Bridle (Manager), Paul Hollebone (Manager), Ian Tarry (Manager)
**Branches:** Wyndeham Grange Ltd, Vigilant Ho, 120 Wilton Rd, London SW1V 1JZ
**US SIC:** 2752 **UK SIC:** 47544
**Auditors:** Baker Tilly
**Bankers:** Barclays Bank Plc (20-12-75)

| | 31-12-13 | 31-12-12 | 31-12-11 |
|---|---|---|---|
| TO | 9,537,020 | 9,616,583 | 8,871,051 |
| P/L | 497,163 | 798,177 | 515,423 |
| NW | 3,819,866 | 3,409,180 | 2,718,455 |
| WC | 2,842,683 | 2,274,192 | 1,396,834 |
| Emp. | 75 | 75 | 69 |

DUNS 76-670-9596

## Wyndeham Heron Ltd

(**Subsidiary of:** Walstead Investments Ltd)
14c Colchester Road Bentalls Complex, Maldon, Essex CM9 4NW
**Tel:** 01621-877777
**Web:** www.wyndeham.co.uk
**Reg No:** 2586277 **VAT No:** 594549390
**Estd:** 1991 Private Limited Company
**Line of Business:** Printing not elsewhere classified
**Export Sales:** £1,016,000
**Issued Capital:** £161,650
**Directors:** Mrs Z Repman, P Utting, R E Kingston, Mrs D Read, R C Fookes
**Co. Secretary:** Mrs Zoe Repman
**US SIC:** 2752 **UK SIC:** 47544
**Auditors:** Baker Tilly UK Audit LLP
**Bankers:** Bank Of Scotland (80-31-20)

| | 31-12-13 | 31-12-12 | 31-12-11 |
|---|---|---|---|
| TO | 24,616,000 | 26,757,000 | 29,665,000 |
| P/L | (1,964,000) | 983,000 | (11,004,000) |
| NW | (6,004,000) | (4,040,000) | (5,023,000) |
| WC | (13,083,000) | (12,243,000) | (14,777,000) |
| Emp. | 193 | 231 | 294 |

DUNS 21-227-3517

## Wyndham Grand

Chelsea Harbour, London SW10 0XG
**Tel:** 02073008443
**Web:** www.wyndham.com
**Estd:** 2010 Proprietorship
**Line of Business:** Hairdressing and other beauty treatment
**Proprietor:** P Constandinos
**Responsibilities**
**Senior:** Gianluca Beltrame (Restaurant Manager), Xavier Montembault (Operations director), Jay Witzel (CEO, Managing Director)
**HR:** Sharon Panesar (HR Manager)
**Operations:** Xavier Montembault (Operations director)
**US SIC:** 7231 **UK SIC:** 98200
**Employees:** 160

DUNS 22-115-1777     Imp

## Wyndham Hotel Group Europe Ltd

(**Subsidiary of:** Wyndham Worldwide Corporation)
The Triangle, 5-17 Hammersmith Grove, London W6 0LG
**Tel:** 02087626600 **Fax:** 020-8762-6678
**Web:** www.wyndham.com
**Reg No:** 4134294 **Estd:** 2001 Private Limited Company
**Line of Business:** Other business activities not elsewhere classified
**Issued Capital:** £1
**Director:** R M Barros
**Co. Secretary:** Jeremy Barker
**Responsibilities**
**Senior:** Michael Poynter (Manager)
**Marketing:** Sandra Van den Bossche (Development Administration Man)
**US SIC:** 7399 **UK SIC:** 83954
**Auditors:** Deloitte & Touche LLP
**Bankers:** The Royal Bank Of Scotland Plc (16-01-70)

| | 31-12-13 | 31-12-12 | 31-12-11 |
|---|---|---|---|
| TO | 7,424,000 | 2,611,000 | 4,827,000 |
| P/L | 69,000 | (303,000) | 2,711,000 |
| NW | 318,000 | (15,209,000) | (16,710,000) |
| WC | 223,000 | (15,392,000) | (16,973,000) |
| Emp. | 46 | 46 | 36 |

DUNS 77-141-3481

## Wynnstay Group P.L.C.

Eagle House, Llansantffraid, Powys SY22 6AQ
**Web:** www.wynnstay.co.uk
**Reg No:** 2704051 **VAT No:** 159186630
**Estd:** 1974 Public Limited Company
**Line of Business:** Agricultural merchants
**Issued Capital:** £4,185,509
**Directors:** H J Richards, D A Evans, K R Greetham, P M Kirkham, Lord Carlile Of Berriew Qc, J J Mccarthy
**Co. Secretary:** Bryan Roberts
**Responsibilities**
**Senior:** Wyn Hughes (President)
**Fleet:** Zack Edwards (Logistics Manager)
**Branches:** Wynnstay Group P.L.c., 1 Maesyllan, Llanidloes, Powys SY18 6DF
**US SIC:** 5159 **UK SIC:** 61100
**Auditors:** Whittingham Riddell LLP
**Bankers:** HSBC Bank plc (40-35-32)

| | 31-10-14 | 31-10-13 | 31-10-12 |
|---|---|---|---|
| TO | 413,558,000 | 413,481,000 | 375,776,000 |
| P/L | 8,493,000 | 8,021,000 | 7,760,000 |
| NW | 59,962,000 | 54,474,000 | 41,260,000 |
| WC | 40,967,000 | 38,449,000 | 24,231,000 |
| Emp. | 981 | 901 | 833 |

DUNS 39-818-5785

## Wynnstay Oswestry Ltd

43 Church Street, Oswestry, Shropshire SY11 2SZ
**Tel:** 01691-655261
**Web:** www.wynnstayhotel.com
**Reg No:** 2217629 **Estd:** 1988 Public Limited Company
**Line of Business:** Hotels
**Trading Style:** The Wynnstay Hotel
**Issued Capital:** £1,300,003
**Principals:** B Woodward (Chairman and Managing), N A Woodward, G W Woodward
**Co. Secretary:** Timothy Woodward
**Responsibilities**
**Senior:** Max Senatore (Restaurant Manager), Sebastiano Siddi (Manager)
**Finance:** Sian Jeffells (Credit Controller)
**Marketing:** Sebastiano Siddi (Manager)
**Sales:** Sebastiano Siddi (Manager)
**HR:** Sebastiano Siddi (Manager)
**Health & Safety:** Sebastiano Siddi (Manager)
**Facilities:** Bernie Watson (Maintenance Manager)
**Purchasing:** Sebastiano Siddi (Manager)
**US SIC:** 7011 **UK SIC:** 66500
**Auditors:** Turner Peachey
**Bankers:** National Westminster Bank Plc (60-16-04)

| | 01-05-14 | 02-05-13 | 03-05-12 |
|---|---|---|---|
| TO | 1,900,824 | 1,836,925 | 1,761,777 |
| P/L | 55,495 | 20,652 | (53,497) |
| NW | £1,182,334 | £1,149,270 | £1,127,602 |
| WC | (202,910) | (182,540) | (170,407) |
| Emp. | 65 | 62 | 65 |

DUNS 23-329-6289     Imp-Exp

## Wynyard Import Consultants

11 Wellington Drive, Wynyard Park, Billingham, Cleveland TS22 5QJ
**Estd:** 2001 Proprietorship
**Line of Business:** Wholesalers of closed circuit television equipment and also importer of security systems from Chinese Company Hik Vision Security Systems
**Proprietor:** J Cooper
**US SIC:** 5065 **UK SIC:** 61500
**Bankers:** HSBC Bank plc (40-12-01)
**Employees:** 60

DUNS 23-664-6493

## Wyre Borough Council

Wyre Civic Centre, Breck Road, Poulton-Le-Fylde, Lancashire FY6 7PU
**Web:** www.wyre.gov.uk
**Estd:** 1974
**Line of Business:** Local government
**Directors:** B Parsonage, K A Hunter
**Responsibilities**
**HR:** Philippa Davies (Corporate Director of Resource)
**Fleet:** Marianne Hesketh (Head of Transformation)
**Branches:** Wyre Borough Council, Brighton Avenue, Thornton-Cleveleys, Lancashire FY5 2AA
**US SIC:** 9121 **UK SIC:** 91110
**Bankers:** National Westminster Bank Plc (60-08-26)
**Employees:** 500

DUNS 23-810-7999

## Wyre Forest District Council

Town Hall, Vicar Street, Kidderminster, Worcestershire DY10 1DB
**Tel:** 01562 732928
**Web:** www.wyreforestdc.gov.uk
**Estd:** 1974
**Line of Business:** General (overall) public service activities
**Principals:** J Gordon (Chairman), A S Dick, W Delin, G Craddock, N Broome
**Branches:** Wyre Forest District Council, Load Street, Bewdley, Worcestershire DY12 2AE
**US SIC:** 9121 **UK SIC:** 91110
**Bankers:** Barclays Bank Plc (20-46-06)
**Employees:** 120

DUNS 42-469-5609

## Wyre Housing Association Ltd

Regenda House, Northgate Close, Bolton, Lancashire BL6 6PQ
**Tel:** 01204814000 **Fax:** 01204-814555
**Web:** www.regenda.org.uk
**Reg No:** 0028191IP **Estd:** 2011 Friendly Society
**Line of Business:** Cycle shops
**Trading Style:** Regenda Group
**Directors:** I Henderson, J Squires
**Responsibilities**
**Senior:** Graham Mcmurray (Proprietor), Heather Mcmurray (Partner)
**Branches:** Wyre Housing Association Ltd, Chatsworth Avenue, Fleetwood, Lancashire FY7 8RN
**US SIC:** 6732 **UK SIC:** 83100

**Bankers:** Barclays Bank Plc (20-10-03)
**Employees:** 63
**Turnover:** £12,645,000

DUNS 34-866-6525

## Wyse Group Ltd

14 Sheridan Terrace, Hove, East Sussex BN3 5AE
**Tel:** 01273773409 **Fax:** 01797-229100
**Web:** www.wysegroup.co.uk
**Reg No:** 5665971 **Estd:** 2006 Private Limited Company
**Line of Business:** Employment and recruitment companies and consultants
**Issued Capital:** £100
**Director:** J W Johnson-Watts
**Co. Secretary:** James Stevenson-Hamilton
**Responsibilities**
**Senior:** Mick O'donnell *(Regional Director)*
**US SIC:** 7361 **UK SIC:** 83954

| | 31-03-14 | 31-03-13 | 31-03-12 |
|---|---|---|---|
| TO | 10,991,413 | 11,675,323 | 13,306,306 |
| P/L | 293,943 | 130,159 | 4,065 |
| NW | 1,831,292 | 1,610,418 | 1,518,323 |
| WC | 1,252,282 | 932,847 | 696,746 |
| Emp. | 114 | 123 | 154 |

DUNS 21-899-3801

## Wyselabour Ltd

(**Subsidiary of:** Wyse (Holdings) Ltd)
Lancaster Road, Cressex Business Park, High Wycombe, Buckinghamshire HP12 3QP
**Tel:** 08081681675
**Web:** www.wysegroup.co.uk
**Reg No:** 6084909 **Estd:** 2007 Private Limited Company
**Line of Business:** Other construction work involving special trades
**Issued Capital:** £100
**Directors:** J R Stevenson-Hamilton, J W Johnson-Watts
**Co. Secretary:** James Stevenson Hamilton
**US SIC:** 1799, 7361
**UK SIC:** 50000, 83954

| | 31-03-14 | 31-03-13 | 31-03-12 |
|---|---|---|---|
| TO | 8,143,644 | N/A | 9,877,552 |
| P/L | 23,650 | N/A | (96,002) |
| NW | 30,861 | 15,945 | 116,201 |
| WC | 21,177 | 154 | 101,508 |
| Emp. | 8 | N/A | N/A |

DUNS 73-274-8624

## Wythenshawe Forum Trust Ltd

Forum Square, Manchester M22 5RX
**Tel:** 0161-935-4000
**Web:** www.wythenshaweforum.co.uk
**Reg No:** 4548636 **Estd:** 2002 Private Company Limited By Guarantee
**Line of Business:** Operation of other sports arenas and stadiums not elsewhere classified
**Trading Style:** The Forum
**Directors:** Mrs M K Karwat, G Evans, C Hemingway, N Fairlamb, D Halsall, E P O'Rourke, A Rogers, Reverend S M Edwards
**Co. Secretary:**
Manchester Professional Services
**Responsibilities**
**Senior:** Ashraf Bakhat *(Director)*, Tom Barber *(Building Manager)*, Brenda Grixti *(Manager)*
**US SIC:** 8211 **UK SIC:** 93200
**Bankers:** The Co-Operative Bank Plc (08-90-00)

| | 31-03-14 | 31-03-13 | 31-03-12 |
|---|---|---|---|
| TO | N/A | 2,550,843 | 2,539,011 |
| P/L | N/A | 5,738 | 26,138 |
| NW | (39,000) | (240,000) | (79,000) |
| WC | (455,176) | (462,146) | (469,218) |
| Emp. | N/A | 52 | 48 |

DUNS 23-659-8863

## Wyvern Cargo Distribution Ltd

(**Subsidiary of:** Wyvern Holdings Ltd)
Broom Road, Poole, Dorset BH12 4NR
**Tel:** 01202307500 **Fax:** 01933-317894
**Web:** www.wyverneasyfast.com
**Reg No:** 3654831 **Estd:** 1998 Private Limited Company
**Line of Business:** Freight transport by road not elsewhere classified
**Issued Capital:** £10,000
**Principals:** E Sparrowhawk *(Managing)*, C R Hawkins, J S Probert
**Co. Secretary:** Stephen Bennett
**Responsibilities**
**Senior:** Matthew Whiley *(Manager)*
**US SIC:** 4213 **UK SIC:** 72300

| | 31-03-14 | 31-03-13 | 31-03-12 |
|---|---|---|---|
| NW | (623) | (623) | (623) |

DUNS 22-557-9481

## Wyvern Cargo Ltd

Broom Road, Poole, Dorset BH12 4NR
**Tel:** 01202307550
**Web:** www.wyverncargo.com
**Reg No:** 1690595 **VAT No:** 355925723
**Estd:** 1983 Private Limited Company
**Line of Business:** Other supporting land transport activities
**Issued Capital:** £10,000
**Principals:** J S Probert *(Managing)*, C R Hawkins, E Sparrowhawk, Mrs L Probert
**Co. Secretary:** Stephen Bennett
**Responsibilities**
**Senior:** Matthew Whiley *(Manager)*
**Branches:** Wyvern Cargo Ltd, Broom Road, Poole, Dorset BH12 4NR
**US SIC:** 4789, 4226
**UK SIC:** 77002, 77003
**Auditors:** Mazars LLP
**Bankers:** Barclays Bank Plc (20-68-79)

| | 31-03-14 | 31-03-13 | 31-03-12 |
|---|---|---|---|
| TO | 12,485,022 | 12,362,058 | 12,083,438 |
| P/L | 498,776 | 360,349 | 376,597 |
| NW | 3,006,676 | 2,626,871 | 2,360,870 |
| WC | 439,095 | 532,614 | 349,051 |
| Emp. | 109 | 106 | 98 |

# X

DUNS 22-809-3308 **Imp**

## X-Cel Superturn (Gb) Ltd

Millstone Works, 32 Atlas Way, Sheffield, South Yorkshire S4 7QQ
**Tel:** 01142-432898
**Web:** www.x-cel.com
**Reg No:** 1710788 **VAT No:** 308953440
**Estd:** 1975 Private Limited Company
**Line of Business:** Manufacture of other fabricated metal products not elsewhere classified
**Issued Capital:** £2,830
**Principals:** A N Taylor *(Managing)*, J Kirk, D Barton-Phillips, Ms L T Furniss-Plant, J M Marsh, A J Hall
**Co. Secretary:** Ms Leanne Furniss-Plant
**Responsibilities**
**Senior:** Mark Burrell *(Sales Director)*, Joanne Crampin *(Deputy Managing Director)*
**HR:** Sharon Crofts *(Human Resources Manager)*
**Branches:** X-Cel Superturn (Gb) Ltd, 70 Hoyland Rd, Sheffield, South Yorkshire S3 8AB
**US SIC:** 3499 **UK SIC:** 31694
**Auditors:** Warneford Gibbs
**Bankers:** National Westminster Bank Plc (60-01-33)

| | 31-03-14 | 31-03-13 | 31-03-12 |
|---|---|---|---|
| TO | 23,483,920 | 19,073,035 | 14,099,435 |
| P/L | 3,698,322 | 1,865,756 | 1,768,992 |
| NW | 8,511,083 | 6,412,523 | 4,684,472 |
| WC | 3,739,455 | 2,322,143 | 1,494,518 |
| Emp. | 138 | 114 | 80 |

DUNS 21-807-1500

## X D P

Unit 1 Biggar Road Industrial Es, Biggar Road, Cleland, Motherwell, Lanarkshire ML1 5PB
**Web:** www.xdp.co.uk
**Estd:** 2011
**Line of Business:** Post offices
**US SIC:** 4311 **UK SIC:** 79010
**Employees:** 60

DUNS 49-395-6502

## X D P Ltd

Curdworth House Fair View Industrial, Estate, Kingsbury Road, Curdworth, Sutton Coldfield, West Midlands B76 9EE
**Fax:** 01675-475853
**Web:** www.xdp.co.uk
**Reg No:** 3139661 **VAT No:** 669669752
**Estd:** 1995 Private Limited Company
**Line of Business:** Road haulage and transport services
**Trading Style:** Express Despatch
**Issued Capital:** £100,000
**Directors:** C A Walters, L S John, Ms I Wayte
**Co. Secretary:** Mrs Valda Townsend
**Branches:** X D P Ltd, Emmanuel St, Preston, Lancashire PR1 7LN
**US SIC:** 4789 **UK SIC:** 77002
**Auditors:** B K R Haines Watts

| | 31-07-13 | 31-07-12 | 31-07-11 |
|---|---|---|---|
| TO | 26,132,213 | 22,871,321 | 20,512,295 |
| P/L | 36,009 | 414,737 | 333,927 |
| NW | 1,624,838 | 1,656,884 | 1,343,194 |
| WC | 994,624 | 1,314,985 | 1,054,892 |
| Emp. | 136 | 129 | 123 |

DUNS 77-079-7165

## X F M Ltd

(**Subsidiary of:** Global Radio Group Limited)
Xfm London 104.9, London WC2H 7LA
**Tel:** 08701211049 **Fax:** 02077666601
**Web:** www.xfm.co.uk
**Reg No:** 2672315 **Estd:** 1991 Private Limited Company
**Line of Business:** Radio activities
**Trading Style:** Global
**Issued Capital:** £300,000
**Directors:** S G Miron, M D Connole, R F Park
**Co. Secretary:** Clive Potterell
**US SIC:** 4832 **UK SIC:** 97411
**Auditors:** KPMG Audit Plc
**Bankers:** Bank Of Scotland (12-01-03)

| | 31-03-14 | 31-03-13 | 31-03-12 |
|---|---|---|---|
| TO | 3,865,000 | 2,873,000 | 2,813,000 |
| P/L | (1,381,000) | (1,816,000) | (1,753,000) |
| NW | (24,338,000) | (22,942,000) | (22,016,000) |
| WC | N/A | (22,942,000) | (22,016,000) |
| Emp. | 3 | N/A | N/A |

DUNS 21-580-6335

## X L Contractors

West End Road, Southampton, Hampshire SO18 6TE
**Tel:** 02380444420
**Web:** www.excelcontractors.co.uk
**Estd:** 2006 Proprietorship
**Line of Business:** Blast cleaning
**Proprietor:** D Tanna
**US SIC:** 1799 **UK SIC:** 50000
**Employees:** 80

DUNS 23-914-9599 **Imp-Exp**

## X L Video Ltd

Unit 2 Eastman Way, Hemel Hempstead, Hertfordshire HP2 7DU
**Tel:** 01442849400
**Web:** www.xlvideo.com
**Reg No:** 3905302 **Estd:** 2000 Private Limited Company
**Line of Business:** Hire and rental of television goods
**Export Sales:** £8,328,000
**Issued Capital:** £1,387
**Directors:** J M Hooker, I H Gibson, P D Mercer, R Burford, M S Mellows, L Spencer, M Whittall
**Co. Secretary:** Ian Gibson
**Responsibilities**
**Senior:** Lucas Covers *(Group CEO)*
**US SIC:** 7394 **UK SIC:** 84000
**Auditors:** KPMG LLP

| | 31-10-13 | 31-10-12 | 31-10-11 |
|---|---|---|---|
| TO | 24,335,000 | 21,593,000 | 25,991,000 |
| P/L | 412,000 | 944,000 | 1,551,000 |
| NW | 4,487,000 | 4,351,000 | 3,894,000 |
| WC | (936,000) | 477,000 | 1,231,000 |
| Emp. | 99 | 101 | 101 |

DUNS 50-013-1792 **Imp**

## X P Plc

(**Subsidiary of:** Xp Power Limited)
14-16 Horseshoe Park, Reading, Berkshire RG8 7JW
**Tel:** 01189-845515
**Web:** www.xppower.com
**Reg No:** 2297983 **VAT No:** 491713143
**Estd:** 1988 Public Limited Company
**Line of Business:** Manufacturers of electronic equipment and components
**Export Sales:** £4,666,000
**Trading Style:** X P Power
**Issued Capital:** £156,200
**Directors:** M T Brabham, D J Penny, S M Elliot, S W Head, R Bartlett, G R Bocock, S J Willis, P M Garner
**Co. Secretary:** Jonathan Rhodes
**Responsibilities**
**Senior:** Anne Honeyman *(Director)*, James Peters *(Manager)*
**Branches:** X P Plc, Unit 19, Deacon Way, Reading, Berkshire RG30 6QG
**US SIC:** 3679 **UK SIC:** 34542
**Auditors:** PricewaterhouseCoopers LLP
**Bankers:** Coutts & Co (18-00-02)

| | 31-12-13 | 31-12-12 | 31-12-11 |
|---|---|---|---|
| TO | 15,412,000 | 13,976,000 | 15,727,000 |
| P/L | 1,374,000 | 1,904,000 | 1,166,000 |
| NW | 3,530,000 | 2,266,000 | 2,842,000 |
| WC | (7,416,000) | (8,965,000) | (8,224,000) |
| Emp. | 76 | 73 | 74 |

DUNS 21-808-4532

## X-Pharmarcy

4 Progress Business Centre, Whittle Parkway, Slough, Berkshire SL1 6DQ
**Tel:** 01628668811
**Estd:** 2012
**Line of Business:** Drug stores outlets
**Trading Style:** Touchwood Pharmacy
**Responsibilities**
**Senior:** Sarook Ahmed *(Manager)*
**US SIC:** 5912 **UK SIC:** 64300
**Employees:** 150

DUNS 29-655-2094 **Imp-Exp**

## X-Tek Systems Ltd

(**Subsidiary of:** Nikon Corporation)
Unit 5 Icknield Way Industrial E, Tring, Hertfordshire HP23 4JX
**Web:** www.xtekxray.com
**Reg No:** 1981536 **Estd:** 1986 Private Limited Company
**Line of Business:** Manufacture of electronic industrial process control equipment
**Export Sales:** £16,575,000
**Issued Capital:** £500,100
**Director:** H Kosawa
**Co. Secretary:** Hideyuki Sonobe
**Responsibilities**
**Senior:** Bart Coppenolle *(Manager)*
**US SIC:** 3823, 3832, 3559
**UK SIC:** 37100, 37320, 32863
**Auditors:** Deloitte LLP
**Bankers:** National Westminster Bank Plc (60-10-33)

| | 31-03-14 | 31-03-13 | 31-03-12 |
|---|---|---|---|
| TO | 19,468,000 | 13,593,000 | 16,041,000 |
| P/L | (979,000) | 564,000 | 50,000 |
| NW | (4,290,000) | (3,263,000) | (3,827,000) |
| WC | (5,288,000) | (4,324,000) | (4,759,000) |
| Emp. | 84 | 78 | 66 |

DUNS 89-669-6226 **Exp**

## Xaar Plc

316 Milton Road Science Park, Cambridge, Cambridgeshire CB4 0XR
**Tel:** 01223-423663 **Fax:** 01223-423590
**Web:** www.xaar.com
**Reg No:** 3320972 **VAT No:** 700266478
**Estd:** 1997 Public Limited Company
**Line of Business:** Computer consumables suppliers
**Trading Style:** Xaar
**Issued Capital:** £7,473,832
**Directors:** R G Williams, A P Bevis, E D Creutzmann, E C Wiggans, D Cheesman, I N Dinwoodie, P J Lawler, R M Barham
**Co. Secretary:** Alexander Bevis
**Responsibilities**
**Senior:** Vince Badcock *(Head of IT)*, Philip Eaves *(Sales & Marketing Director)*, Graham Tweedale *(Production Manager)*
**Marketing:** Sarah Dodd *(Marketing Specialist)*, Philip Eaves *(Sales & Marketing Director)*
**Sales:** Philip Eaves *(Sales & Marketing Director)*, Steve Knight *(Sales Manager)*
**Admin:** Debbie Smith *(Facilities Manager)*
**IT:** Vince Badcock *(Head of IT)*, Keith Brookes *(Software Manager)*, Christopher Culshaw *(IT Manager)*, Kevin Mcintyre *(IT Technical Services Manager)*, Werner Zapka *(Head of Advanced ApplicationT)*
**HR:** Josh Solanki *(Human Resources Manager)*
**Health & Safety:** Debbie Smith *(Facilities Manager)*
**Facilities:** Debbie Smith *(Facilities Manager)*
**Operations:** Greg Lockett *(Manufacturing Director)*, Marguerite Quinn *(Product Manager)*, Debbie Smith *(Facilities Manager)*, Graham Tweedale *(Production Manager)*, Ted Wiggans *(Operations Director)*
**Purchasing:** Peter Lavender *(Engineering Manager)*
**Engineering:** Peter Lavender *(Engineering Manager)*, Graham Tweedale *(Production Manager)*
**US SIC:** 3679, 7391, 3953
**UK SIC:** 34542, 94000, 49541
**Auditors:** Deloitte LLP
**Bankers:** Barclays Bank Plc (20-17-19)

| | 31-12-13 | 31-12-12 | 31-12-11 |
|---|---|---|---|
| TO | 137,128,000 | 86,304,000 | 68,706,000 |
| P/L | 40,087,000 | 15,701,000 | 9,126,000 |
| NW | 105,935,000 | 69,384,000 | 56,241,000 |
| WC | 62,795,000 | 42,249,000 | 27,954,000 |
| Emp. | 692 | 502 | 461 |

DUNS 21-028-3819

## Xact Industrial

60 Vauxhall Road, Liverpool, Merseyside L3 6DL
**Tel:** 0151-479-3020
**Web:** www.xactpack.co.uk
**Estd:** 1935 Proprietorship
**Line of Business:** Manufacture of machinery for food, beverage and tobacco processing
**Proprietor:** D Hughes
**Responsibilities**
**Senior:** Barry Baldock *(Sales Director)*
**Sales:** Barry Baldock *(Sales Director)*
**US SIC:** 3551 **UK SIC:** 32441
**Employees:** 50

DUNS 50-485-6790

## Xafinity Consulting Ltd

(**Subsidiary of:** Xafinity Group Holdings (Reading) Ltd)
Phoenix House, Reading, Berkshire RG1 1NB
**Tel:** 01189-583-683 **Fax:** 01199-185-095
**Web:** www.xafinity.com
**Reg No:** 2459442 **VAT No:** 544173550
**Estd:** 1990 Private Limited Company
**Line of Business:** Business and management consultancy activities not elsewhere classified
**Trading Style:** Xafinity Consulting, Xafinity
**Issued Capital:** £342,500

**Directors:** B O Bramhall, R J Birmingham, I R Moore, R W Thompson, Ms C A Noble, J P Hunt
**Responsibilities**
**Senior:** Andrew Amor *(Facilities Manager)*
**Finance:** Andy Bowsher *(Director of Self Invested Pens)*, Paul Darlow *(Head of Proposition Developmen)*, Alisdair Marnoch *(Financial Director)*
**Marketing:** Patrick Wynne *(Marketing Director)*
**Admin:** Neil Macbeth *(Director, Reading)*
**HR:** Fiona Lawrance *(Senior Consultant - HR Trustee)*
**Health & Safety:** Andrew Amor *(Facilities Manager)*
**Facilities:** Andrew Amor *(Facilities Manager)*
**Branches:** Xafinity Consulting Limited, Wilson House, Waterberry Drive, Waterlooville, Hampshire PO7 7XX
**US SIC:** 7392 **UK SIC:** 83951
**Auditors:** PricewaterhouseCoopers LLP
**Bankers:** HSBC Bank plc (40-38-04)

| | 31-03-14 | 31-12-12 | 31-03-11 |
|---|---|---|---|
| TO | 53,102,000 | 39,771,000 | 37,319,000 |
| P/L | 13,418,000 | 13,002,000 | 11,153,000 |
| NW | 20,140,000 | 8,600,000 | 14,869,000 |
| WC | 20,995,000 | 10,959,000 | 31,074,000 |
| Emp. | 347 | 330 | 317 |

**DUNS 21-867-2539**

## Xafinity (Reading) Ltd
**(Subsidiary of:** Xafinity Group Holdings (Reading) Ltd)
Phoenix House 1 Station Hill, Reading, Berkshire RG1 1NB
**Tel:** 01189185118
**Web:** www.natpen.co.uk
**Reg No:** 8279362 **Estd:** 2012 Private Limited Company
**Line of Business:** Management activities of other non-financial holding companies not elsewhere classified
**Directors:** J P Hunt, R W Thompson, R J Birmingham, I R Moore, Ms C A Noble
**US SIC:** 6711 **UK SIC:** 83962

| | 31-03-14 |
|---|---|
| TO | 51,637,000 |
| P/L | 2,090,000 |
| NW | (67,241,000) |
| WC | (21,240,000) |
| Emp. | 394 |

**DUNS 22-287-5069**

## Xafinity Trustees Ltd
**(Subsidiary of:** Xafinity Group Holdings (Reading) Ltd)
27 Kings Road, Reading, Berkshire RG1 3AR
**Tel:** 01189-513700 **Fax:** 0870-762-7281
**Web:** www.xafinity.com
**Reg No:** 4305500 **Estd:** 2001 Private Limited Company
**Line of Business:** Other business activities not elsewhere classified
**Issued Capital:** £2
**Directors:** R J Birmingham, J P Hunt
**Responsibilities**
**Senior:** Sharon Atherton *(Manager)*, Wayne Story *(Manager)*
**IT:** Andrew Docherty *(IT Manager)*
**US SIC:** 7399 **UK SIC:** 83954

| | 31-03-14 | 31-12-12 | 31-03-11 |
|---|---|---|---|
| TA | 1,212 | 1,212 | 1,212 |
| NW | 1,212 | 1,212 | 1,212 |

**DUNS 22-233-6799**

## Xanadu Tec Ltd
91 Delamere Road, London W5 3JP
**Tel:** 08451082840 **Fax:** 0870-831-3467
**Web:** www.xanadutec.com
**Reg No:** 4251641 **Estd:** 2001 Private Limited Company
**Line of Business:** Data processing
**Issued Capital:** £1,000
**Managing Director:** R Dhawan
**Co. Secretary:** Aradhika Dhawan
**US SIC:** 7374 **UK SIC:** 83940

| | 31-07-13 | 31-07-12 | 31-07-11 |
|---|---|---|---|
| TA | 1,089,295 | 841,869 | 724,099 |
| NW | 742,789 | 601,583 | 489,839 |
| WC | 739,125 | 596,761 | 486,105 |

**DUNS 21-510-3339**

## Xaverian College
Lower Park Road, Manchester M14 5RB
**Tel:** 0161-224-1781
**Web:** www.xaverian.ac.uk
**Estd:** 2002 Partnership
**Line of Business:** Sixth form colleges
**Responsibilities**
**Senior:** Karen Crow *(Manager)*
**Finance:** Mike Davey *(Finance Manager)*
**IT:** Lynn Bainbridge *(CIS Manager)*
**US SIC:** 8221 **UK SIC:** 93100
**Employees:** 137

**DUNS 21-110-6244** Imp

## Xbite Ltd
X H Q, Ravenshorn Way, Renishaw, Sheffield, South Yorkshire S21 3WY
**Tel:** 08444145296
**Web:** www.xbite.co.uk
**Reg No:** 6520821 **Estd:** 2008 Private Limited Company
**Line of Business:** Other non-store retail sale
**Export Sales:** £13,653,557
**Issued Capital:** £2
**Directors:** P M Ravilious, N A Whitehead, S Brereton
**Co. Secretary:** Mrs Keely Whitehead
**Responsibilities**
**Senior:** Jill Kay *(Human Resources Manager)*
**US SIC:** 5963 **UK SIC:** 65600

| | 30-06-13 | 30-06-12 | 30-06-11 |
|---|---|---|---|
| TO | 21,490,813 | 23,306,337 | N/A |
| P/L | 621,584 | 515,960 | N/A |
| NW | 457,464 | 3,641 | (898,193) |
| WC | 560,096 | 390,950 | (191,971) |
| Emp. | 62 | 42 | N/A |

**DUNS 23-979-1945**

## Xbridge Ltd
**(Subsidiary of:** Xbridge Holdings Ltd)
Milbank House Finsbury Square, London EC2A 2DX
**Fax:** 020-7378-7378
**Web:** www.simplybusiness.co.uk
**Reg No:** 3967717 **Estd:** 2000 Private Limited Company
**Line of Business:** Computer software (development)
**Trading Style:** Simply Business
**Issued Capital:** £866
**Directors:** B J Hollowood, C Slater, P B Cartwright, Dr D T Kelly, J Stockwood
**Responsibilities**
**Senior:** Arvinder Mangat *(Manager)*
**US SIC:** 6411 **UK SIC:** 83200
**Auditors:** PricewaterhouseCoopers

| | 31-12-13 | 31-12-12 | 31-12-11 |
|---|---|---|---|
| TO | 25,081,000 | 22,876,000 | 19,549,000 |
| P/L | 2,675,000 | 2,174,000 | 454,000 |
| NW | 7,214,000 | 124,000 | (2,136,000) |
| WC | 10,074,000 | 806,000 | 4,388,000 |
| Emp. | 226 | 189 | 167 |

**DUNS 42-414-3688**

## Xc Trains Ltd
**(Subsidiary of:** Bundesrepublik Deutschland)
5th Floor, Cannon House, 18 Priory Queensway, Birmingham, West Midlands B4 6BS
**Web:** www.crosscountrytrains.co.uk
**Reg No:** 4402048 **Estd:** 1844 Private Limited Company
**Line of Business:** Transport via railways
**Issued Capital:** £2
**Directors:** J L Roberts, Ms M F Earl, J R Higgins, Ms A Furlong, A J Cooper, W Rogers, D A Watkin
**Co. Secretary:** Mrs Lorna Edwards
**Responsibilities**
**Senior:** Rachel Baldwin *(Director)*, Elizabeth Thorpe *(Manager)*
**HR:** Maria Zywica *(Human Resources Director)*
**Operations:** Helen Waters *(Production Director)*
**US SIC:** 4011 **UK SIC:** 71000
**Auditors:** PricewaterhouseCoopers LLP

| | 31-12-13 | 31-12-12 | 31-12-11 |
|---|---|---|---|
| TO | 552,536,000 | 501,577,000 | 387,163,000 |
| P/L | 15,190,000 | 17,154,000 | (27,234,000) |
| NW | 33,074,000 | 5,539,000 | (6,622,000) |
| WC | 18,178,000 | 4,304,000 | (11,719,000) |
| Emp. | 1,695 | 1,639 | 1,629 |

**DUNS 21-111-3197**

## Xceed Group Ltd
1 Alie Street, London E1 8DE
**Tel:** 02074800030
**Web:** www.xceedgroup.com
**Reg No:** 6526750 **Estd:** 2008 Private Limited Company
**Line of Business:** Management activities of other non-financial holding companies not elsewhere classified
**Export Sales:** £1,283,599
**Issued Capital:** £300
**Directors:** J P Casserly, J R Turner, G F Stewart
**US SIC:** 6711, 7392
**UK SIC:** 83962, 83951

| | 30-11-13 | 30-11-12 | 30-11-11 |
|---|---|---|---|
| TO | 15,185,280 | 16,343,387 | 13,740,435 |
| P/L | 1,975,898 | 21,913 | 2,090,617 |
| NW | 1,273,918 | 246,565 | 626,891 |
| WC | 1,235,779 | 192,963 | 581,506 |
| Emp. | 69 | 58 | 45 |

**DUNS 34-985-1753**

## Xceed Training Ltd
16 Windermere Close, Mansfield Woodhouse, Mansfield, Nottinghamshire NG19 9FD
**Tel:** 01623627264 **Fax:** 01623427978
**Web:** www.xceedtraining.co.uk
**Reg No:** 5780352 **Estd:** 2006 Private Limited Company
**Line of Business:** Activities of private training providers
**Issued Capital:** £100
**Director:** G R Townsend
**Co. Secretary:** Ms Bronwyn Tyler
**US SIC:** 8299 **UK SIC:** 93300

| | 31-10-14 | 31-10-13 | 31-10-12 |
|---|---|---|---|
| TA | 35,059 | 32,891 | 37,325 |
| NW | 8,008 | 894 | 2,845 |
| WC | 5,791 | (1,613) | (498) |

**DUNS 29-352-9285** Imp-Exp

## Xcel Power Systems Ltd.
**(Subsidiary of:** Emrise Electronics Ltd)
Cobbswood Industrial Estate, Brunswick Road, Ashford, Kent TN23 1EL
**Tel:** 01233642211
**Web:** www.dcdautos.com
**Reg No:** 0575679 **VAT No:** 571928708
**Estd:** 1956 Private Limited Company
**Line of Business:** Wind generation equipment and windmills
**Export Markets:** U S A; European Union (E U)
**Export Sales:** £317,719
**Issued Capital:** £10,000
**Directors:** C T Oliva, R L Weller
**Co. Secretary:** Graham Jefferies
**Responsibilities**
**Senior:** Derry May *(Proprietor)*
**Branches:** Xcel Power Systems Ltd., 197 Church Rd, Reading, Berkshire RG6 1HW
**US SIC:** 5521 **UK SIC:** 65100
**Auditors:** BDO Stoy Hayward
**Bankers:** Lloyds TSB Bank plc (30-98-08)

| | 31-12-13 | 31-12-12 | 31-12-11 |
|---|---|---|---|
| TO | 4,416,496 | 4,512,112 | 3,515,589 |
| P/L | 203,036 | 477,380 | 37,099 |
| NW | 4,784,518 | 4,824,234 | 4,463,207 |
| WC | 4,488,961 | 4,754,034 | 4,433,997 |
| Emp. | 49 | 49 | 47 |

**DUNS 22-288-1612**

## Xchanging Claims Services Ltd
34 Leadenhall Street, London EC3A 1AX
**Tel:** 020-7780-6999 **Fax:** 020-7780-6998
**Web:** www.xchanging.com
**Reg No:** 4306133 **Estd:** 2001 Private Limited Company
**Line of Business:** Activities auxiliary to financial intermediation not elsewhere classified
**Issued Capital:** £4,001
**Directors:** D G Turner, A M Pell, K J Rainer, T A Bolt, J E Gregory
**Co. Secretary:** Ms Anna Myburgh
**Responsibilities**
**Senior:** Ian Beaton *(Manager)*, Paul Bermingham *(Director)*, Paul Swain *(Manager)*
**US SIC:** 6111 **UK SIC:** 81501
**Auditors:** PricewaterhouseCoopers LLP
**Bankers:** National Westminster Bank Plc (60-00-01)

| | 31-12-13 | 31-12-12 | 31-12-11 |
|---|---|---|---|
| TA | 19,200,000 | 19,313,000 | 17,386,000 |
| P/L | 6,909,000 | 8,523,000 | 7,490,000 |
| NW | 5,576,000 | 6,773,000 | 5,632,000 |
| WC | 4,845,000 | 6,548,000 | 5,560,000 |
| Emp. | 308 | 341 | 349 |

**DUNS 21-579-8210**

## Xchanging Ins Sure Services
Ins-Sure House, Folkestone, Kent CT20 2RJ
**Tel:** 01303850111
**Web:** www.xchanging.com
**Estd:** 2004 Partnership
**Line of Business:** Actuaries
**Partners:** D Fisher, D Andrews, M Pell, M Taylor, P George
**Responsibilities**
**IT:** Mike Maple *(?End User Computer Manager)*, Alison Wilcox *(IT Manager)*
**US SIC:** 6411 **UK SIC:** 83200
**Employees:** 150

**DUNS 77-915-8224**

## Xchanging Plc
34 Leadenhall Street, London EC3A 1AX
**Tel:** 0203604699 **Fax:** 02077806998
**Web:** www.xchanging.com
**Reg No:** 5819018 **Estd:** 2006 Public Limited Company
**Line of Business:** Business and management consultancy activities not elsewhere classified
**Issued Capital:** £12,015,546

**Directors:** S D Wilson, I D Cormack, K Lever, E G Unwin, M J Paulin, D G Bauernfeind, W G Thomas, S Srivastava
**Co. Secretary:** Christopher Fussell
**Branches:** Xchanging Plc, 34 Leadenhall Street, London EC3A 1AX
**US SIC:** 7392, 7399
**UK SIC:** 83951, 83954
**Auditors:** PricewaterhouseCoopers LLP
**Bankers:** Lloyds TSB Bank plc (30-00-02)

| | 31-12-13 | 31-12-12 | 31-12-11 |
|---|---|---|---|
| TO | 526,400,000 | 668,300,000 | 651,200,000 |
| P/L | 78,300,000 | 41,500,000 | (2,500,000) |
| NW | (7,100,000) | (51,000,000) | (53,000,000) |
| WC | 26,000,000 | 23,500,000 | 17,100,000 |
| Emp. | 7,929 | 8,122 | 7,930 |

**DUNS 22-201-8322**

## Xchanging Procurement Services Ltd
**(Subsidiary of:** Xchanging Plc)
34 Leadenhall Street, London EC3A 1AX
**Tel:** 02036046999 **Fax:** 01772-677001
**Web:** www.xchanging.com
**Reg No:** 4220043 **Estd:** 2001 Private Limited Company
**Line of Business:** Management activities of holding companies
**Export Sales:** £118,000
**Trading Style:** Xchanging
**Issued Capital:** £1
**Directors:** N Ford, Ms P A Dreghorn, D J Royer
**Responsibilities**
**Senior:** John Andre *(Manager)*, Margaret Spink *(Manager)*, Stephen Trainor *(Manager)*
**US SIC:** 6711 **UK SIC:** 83962
**Auditors:** PricewaterhouseCoopers LLP
**Bankers:** Lloyds TSB Bank plc (30-00-02)

| | 31-12-13 | 31-12-12 | 31-12-11 |
|---|---|---|---|
| TO | 176,141,000 | 161,612,000 | 142,672,000 |
| P/L | 145,000 | 4,056,000 | (01,000) |
| NW | 4,091,000 | 3,790,000 | 464,000 |
| WC | 2,867,000 | 3,782,000 | 1,677,000 |
| Emp. | 176 | 196 | 193 |

**DUNS 67-153-2302**

## Xconnect Services Ltd
**(Subsidiary of:** Xconnect Global Networks Ltd)
Cooper House, Regents Park Road, London N3 2JX
**Tel:** 020-8371-4800
**Web:** www.xconnect.net
**Reg No:** 6011610 **VAT No:** 912558818
**Estd:** 2006 Private Limited Company
**Line of Business:** Telecommunication networks
**Issued Capital:** £100
**Directors:** O Finkelstein, A Katz
**Co. Secretary:** Neil Cohen
**Responsibilities**
**Senior:** E Eli *(Chief Executive Officer)*, Eli Katz *(Chief Executive Officer)*
**US SIC:** 7379 **UK SIC:** 83940

| | 31-12-13 | 31-12-12 | 31-12-11 |
|---|---|---|---|
| TA | 9,000 | 9,000 | 9,000 |
| NW | 9,000 | 9,000 | 9,000 |

**DUNS 22-705-1752**

## Xenith Document Systems Ltd
**(Subsidiary of:** Xenith Managed Services Ltd)
11-13 Wakley Street, London EC1V 7LT
**Tel:** 02074172000 **Fax:** 020-7417-2093
**Web:** www.xenith.co.uk
**Reg No:** 1406243 **Estd:** 1978 Private Limited Company
**Line of Business:** Other service activities not elsewhere classified
**Export Sales:** £301,940
**Trading Style:** Xenith Document System
**Issued Capital:** £3,493
**Principals:** N A Carlile *(Managing)*, J G Milligan, S T Allaway, Ms S Page
**Co. Secretary:** Ms Sarah Page
**Responsibilities**
**Marketing:** Feroze Engineer *(Marketing Manager)*
**IT:** Muhammad Khan *(Computer Manager)*
**US SIC:** 8999 **UK SIC:** 83954
**Auditors:** Oppenheim Scroxton
**Bankers:** National Westminster Bank Plc (56-00-18)

| | 31-03-14 | 31-03-13 | 31-03-12 |
|---|---|---|---|
| TO | 14,980,216 | 15,955,982 | 14,170,020 |
| P/L | 2,150,429 | 1,921,769 | 1,766,609 |
| NW | 7,816,111 | 5,889,591 | 4,281,760 |
| WC | 7,724,712 | 5,763,698 | 4,150,067 |
| Emp. | 56 | 54 | 49 |

DUNS 42-465-1342 **Imp**

## Xention Ltd

**(Subsidiary of:** Xention Pharma Ltd)
Unit 3 Iconix Park, London Road, Pampisford, Cambridge, Cambridgeshire CB22 3EG
**Tel:** 01223-493900
**Web:** www.xention.com
**Reg No:** 4452808 **Estd:** 2002 Private Limited Company
**Line of Business:** Research institutions and organisations
**Issued Capital:** £369,202
**Directors:**
Newmedia Spark Directors Limited, H A Slootweg, Dr K T Cunningham, Prof W Hartwig, A O'Connell, Dr K G Mccullagh, B X Montanari
**Co. Secretary:** Ms Rebecca Hemsley
**Responsibilities**
**Senior:** Graham Fagg *(Manager)*, June Powter *(Administrator)*
**Admin:** June Powter *(Administrator)*
**US SIC:** 7391 **UK SIC:** 94000
**Auditors:** Deloitte & Touche LLP

| | 31-10-13 | 31-10-12 | 31-10-11 |
|---|---|---|---|
| TA | 5,475,000 | 3,657,000 | 3,348,226 |
| NW | 2,821,000 | (919,000) | 1,065,589 |
| WC | 2,663,000 | (1,343,000) | 556,960 |

DUNS 21-812-5683

## Xentrall Shared Services

Town Hall, Feethams, Darlington, County Durham DL1 5QT
**Tel:** 01642527890
**Web:** www.xentrall.org.uk
**Estd:** 2009
**Line of Business:** Employment and recruitment companies and consultants
**Responsibilities**
**IT:** David Reese *(ICT Infrastructure Team Leader)*, Steven Vaughan *(Senior IT Support Technician)*
**Branches:** Xentrall Shared Services, Po Box 877, Stockton-On-Tees, Cleveland TS19 1JA
**US SIC:** 8321, 9121
**UK SIC:** 96111, 91110
**Employees:** 100

DUNS 29-015-3311

## Xeon Smiles Uk Ltd

**(Subsidiary of:** Zermatt Investments Limited)
6c Cae Meillion, Caerphilly, Mid Glamorgan CF83 1SN
**Tel:** 02920887838 **Fax:** 029-2088-1898
**Web:** www.jameshull.co.uk
**Reg No:** 0479564 **Estd:** 1950 Private Limited Company
**Line of Business:** Dentists
**Issued Capital:** £15,000,100
**Directors:** Dr G C Pullen, J J Ash, Dr P Slevin, Dr J F Perry
**Co. Secretary:** Oasis Healthcare Limited
**Responsibilities**
**Senior:** Kaylee Crocker *(Practice Manager)*
**Branches:** Xeon Smiles Uk Ltd, Superdrug Stores Plc, Unit 21, Tredegar, Gwent NP22 3EJ
**US SIC:** 8021 **UK SIC:** 95400
**Auditors:** Deloitte LLP
**Bankers:** Bank Of Scotland (80-07-14)

| | 31-12-13 | 31-12-12 | 30-12-12 |
|---|---|---|---|
| TO | 40,713,491 | 32,159,675 | 54,404,169 |
| P/L | 896,811 | (1,919,909) | (5,641,679) |
| NW | (8,330,427) | (44,465,179) | (42,545,270) |
| WC | (13,715,630) | (47,526,301) | (45,834,894) |
| Emp. | 512 | 580 | 460 |

DUNS 73-694-5168

## Xeretec Group Holdings Ltd

Oaklands Business Centre, Ashridge House, Wokingham, Berkshire RG41 2FD
**Tel:** 01189-770123
**Web:** http://xeretec.co.uk
**Reg No:** 4953382 **Estd:** 2003 Private Limited Company
**Line of Business:** Management activities of holding companies
**Export Sales:** £3,190,954
**Issued Capital:** £1,500
**Directors:** W J Beard, S J Hawkins, A G Jenkins
**Co. Secretary:** Ms Karina Smith
**US SIC:** 6711, 7399
**UK SIC:** 83962, 83954

| | 31-08-13 | 31-08-12 | 31-08-11 |
|---|---|---|---|
| TO | 35,422,656 | 21,107,498 | 20,204,231 |
| P/L | 2,945,581 | 1,360,175 | 1,082,464 |
| NW | (282,271) | (999,155) | (321,373) |
| WC | (157,029) | (131,338) | (690,804) |
| Emp. | 148 | 84 | 67 |

DUNS 29-654-1998 **Imp**

## Xerox It Services Ltd

**(Subsidiary of:** Xerox Corporation)
Hortonwood 37, Telford, Shropshire TF1 7GT
**Tel:** 01952607000
**Web:** www.xeroxitservices.co.uk
**Reg No:** 1980455 **VAT No:** 438125751
**Estd:** 1986 Private Limited Company
**Line of Business:** Hardware consultancy
**Export Sales:** £4,147,310
**Issued Capital:** £100,000
**Directors:** S Graham, K L Taylor
**Co. Secretary:** James Peffer
**US SIC:** 7399 **UK SIC:** 83954
**Auditors:** BDO LLP
**Bankers:** National Westminster Bank Plc (60-11-01)

| | 31-12-13 | 31-12-12 | 31-12-11 |
|---|---|---|---|
| TO | 32,647,434 | 38,311,816 | 40,718,441 |
| P/L | 3,749,695 | 867,856 | (598,328) |
| NW | 4,387,773 | (425,467) | (1,552,025) |
| WC | (2,739,798) | (1,347,252) | (1,327,731) |
| Emp. | 167 | 197 | 223 |

DUNS 21-024-2194 **Imp**

## Xerox Ltd

**(Subsidiary of:** Xerox Corporation)
Bridge House, Oxford Road, Uxbridge, Middlesex UB8 1HS
**Tel:** 08709 005 608
**Web:** www.xerox.co.uk
**Reg No:** 0575914 **VAT No:** 232364682
**Estd:** 1960 Private Limited Company
**Line of Business:** Computer stationery
**Export Sales:** £1,905,680,000
**Issued Capital:** £30,050,407
**Directors:** Mrs P L Fisher, J H Guers, X Heiss
**Co. Secretary:** Michael Barrett
**Responsibilities**
**Senior:** David Bachelor *(Senior Manager)*, Marcus Childs *(General Manager)*, Shaun Pantling *(Director)*
**Branches:** Xerox Ltd, 10-14 Bath Road, Slough, Berkshire SL1 3SA
**US SIC:** 5942, 5399
**UK SIC:** 65300, 65600
**Auditors:** PricewaterhouseCoopers LLP
**Bankers:** National Westminster Bank Plc (60-50-03)

**Following financial data are in thousands**

| | 31-12-13 | 31-12-12 | 31-12-11 |
|---|---|---|---|
| TO | 2,324,000 | 2,323,000 | 2,512,000 |
| P/L | (13,000) | 583,000 | 145,000 |
| NW | 1,836,000 | 1,928,000 | 1,502,000 |
| WC | 444,000 | 504,000 | 343,000 |
| Emp. | 1,400 | 1,600 | 1,500 |

DUNS 21-713-8536 **Imp**

## Xerox (Uk) Ltd

**(Subsidiary of:** Xerox Corporation)
Bridge House, Oxford Road, Uxbridge, Middlesex UB8 1HS
**Tel:** 01895251133 **Fax:** 01895-254095
**Web:** www.xerox.co.uk
**Reg No:** 0330754 **Estd:** 1937 Private Limited Company
**Line of Business:** Wholesale of other office machinery and equipment
**Trading Style:** Xerox
**Issued Capital:** £1,500,100
**Directors:** Mrs M C Odriscoll, D S Cassidy, Ms M E Richards, F J Mooney, O J Dehon
**Co. Secretary:** Michael Barett
**Responsibilities**
**Senior:** David Bachelor *(Senior Manager)*, Ursula Burns *(Chief Executive Officer)*, Alan Charnley *(Manager)*, Marcus Childs *(General Manager)*, Tom Maddison *(Corporate Senior Vice Presiden)*, Shaun Pantling *(Corporate Vice President Direc)*, Russell Peacock *(CEO, Managing Director)*
**Finance:** Ian Branch *(CFO for UK)*
**Marketing:** Bernie Gooch *(General Manager)*, Chris Hawkesworth *(Global Marketing Program Mngr)*, Darrell Minards *(Head of Marketing)*, Nav Moulavi *(UK Events and Direct Marketing)*, Nick Stainton *(Marketing)*, Alexandra Voss *(Marketing Executive)*
**Sales:** Paul Batten *(?Global Sales Enablement Manag)*
**IT:** Beth Waddington *(IT Manager)*
**HR:** Maurice Marciano *(HR Director for Europe)*
**Health & Safety:** Keith Filler *(Health & Safety Officer)*
**Branches:** Xerox (Uk) Ltd, Stokes House, 17-25 College Square East, Belfast, Belfast BT1 6DH
**US SIC:** 5081, 7379
**UK SIC:** 61490, 83940
**Auditors:** PricewaterhouseCoopers LLP
**Bankers:** National Westminster Bank Plc (60-50-03)

| | 31-12-13 | 31-12-12 | 31-12-11 |
|---|---|---|---|
| TO | 258,700,000 | 296,000,000 | 428,300,000 |
| P/L | 8,000,000 | 24,100,000 | 29,600,000 |
| NW | 233,100,000 | 223,100,000 | 240,000,000 |
| WC | 232,600,000 | 221,400,000 | 215,400,000 |
| Emp. | 2,237 | 2,458 | 2,531 |

DUNS 21-035-7737

## Xervon Palmers Ltd

**(Subsidiary of:** Rethmann Se & Co. Kg)
331 Charles Street, Glasgow, Lanarkshire G21 2QA
**Tel:** 0141-553-4030 **Fax:** 01256-385971
**Web:** www.xervonpalmers.com
**Reg No:** 0159161 **Estd:** 1880 Private Limited Company
**Line of Business:** Other construction work involving special trades
**Issued Capital:** £320,000
**Principals:** I Mcfarlane *(Marketing)*, D Morrison
**Co. Secretary:** Miss Catherine Meighan
**Responsibilities**
**Senior:** Ian Macfarlane *(Business Development Director)*, Andrew O'Connor *(Ops Man)*
**Marketing:** Ian Macfarlane *(Business Development Director)*
**Branches:** Xervon Palmers Ltd, Kiln La, Western Indstl Area, Bracknell, Berkshire RG12 1NA
**US SIC:** 1799, 7394
**UK SIC:** 50000, 84000
**Auditors:** KPMG LLP
**Bankers:** National Westminster Bank Plc (56-00-68)

| | 31-12-13 | 31-12-12 | 30-12-11 |
|---|---|---|---|
| TO | 27,551,000 | 53,732,000 | 37,182,000 |
| P/L | 677,000 | (5,821,000) | (10,256,000) |
| NW | 736,000 | 59,000 | (3,120,000) |
| WC | 2,189,000 | (3,800,000) | (9,448,000) |
| Emp. | 322 | 575 | 770 |

DUNS 22-820-9805 **Imp**

## Xiros Ltd

Springfield House, White House Lane, Yeadon, Leeds, West Yorkshire LS19 7UE
**Web:** www.xiros.eu.com
**Reg No:** 1664824 **VAT No:** 405680756
**Estd:** 1982 Private Limited Company
**Line of Business:** Manufacturers of instruments for medical purposes
**Issued Capital:** £50,000
**Principals:** Doctor B B Seedhom *(Chairman and Managing)*, P Duckworth, Doctor A E Ostell, Dr R Henney, Dr D D Haut Junior
**Co. Secretary:** Dr Roland Henney
**Responsibilities**
**Senior:** Donald Haut *(Director)*, Adrian Howe *(Manager)*
**Finance:** Adrian Howe *(Manager)*
**Marketing:** Dawn McGuire *(Sales & Marketing Coordinator)*
**Sales:** Dawn McGuire *(Sales & Marketing Coordinator)*
**Facilities:** Dave Wardle *(Service Coordinator)*
**Branches:** Unit 8 Robinson Indstl Est, Shaftesbury Sq, Derby Derbyshire DE3 2NL.
**US SIC:** 3841 **UK SIC:** 37201
**Auditors:** Mazars LLP
**Bankers:** Bank Of Scotland (12-08-83)

| | 31-03-14 | 31-03-13 | 31-03-12 |
|---|---|---|---|
| TO | 5,575,269 | 4,819,442 | 4,148,426 |
| P/L | 693,538 | 555,326 | 281,194 |
| NW | 5,252,612 | 4,351,662 | 3,784,723 |
| WC | 2,803,803 | 2,593,279 | 2,370,674 |
| Emp. | 86 | 85 | 80 |

DUNS 21-675-1274

## Xix Management Ltd

Unit 33 Ransomes Dock Business C, 35-37 Parkgate Road, London SW11 4NP
**Tel:** 02078011976 **Fax:** 02078011920
**Web:** www.xixentertainment.com
**Reg No:** 7269120 **Estd:** 2002 Private Limited Company
**Line of Business:** Other artistic and literary creation and interpretation
**Issued Capital:** £100
**Director:** R C Dodds
**Co. Secretary:** Abogado Nominees Limited
**Responsibilities**
**Senior:** Thomas Benson *(Vice President)*, Mark Blackford *(Manager)*, Simon Fuller *(Manager)*, Howard Tytel *(Manager)*
**US SIC:** 8999 **UK SIC:** 83954
**Bankers:** Coutts & Co (18-00-02)

| | 31-12-13 | 31-12-12 | 31-12-11 |
|---|---|---|---|
| TO | 7,366,703 | 8,156,499 | N/A |
| P/L | (2,372,908) | (1,270,295) | N/A |
| NW | (8,028,734) | (5,376,002) | (3,769,126) |
| WC | (11,513,902) | (3,086,886) | (1,890,180) |
| Emp. | 99 | 89 | N/A |

DUNS 23-841-4002 **Imp**

## Xl Joinery Ltd

**(Subsidiary of:** Right Balance Sdn Bhd)
Bradford Road, Batley, West Yorkshire WF17 8NE
**Tel:** 01924350500 **Fax:** 01924-350525
**Web:** www.xljoinery.co.uk
**Reg No:** 3833043 **VAT No:** 740714843
**Estd:** 1999 Private Limited Company
**Line of Business:** Wholesale of wood, construction materials and sanitary equipment
**Issued Capital:** £1,250,000
**Directors:** A F Mohamad, J N Kamaruddin, K Md Nor
**Co. Secretary:** Robert Reah
**Responsibilities**
**Senior:** Dan Furness *(Warehouse Manager)*, Roy Parker *(Operations Director)*
**IT:** Roy Parker *(Operations Director)*
**HR:** Sara Tweddle *(Customer Services Controller)*
**Health & Safety:** Roy Parker *(Operations Director)*
**Facilities:** Roy Parker *(Operations Director)*
**Operations:** Sara Tweddle *(Customer Services Controller)*
**US SIC:** 5039, 5074
**UK SIC:** 61300
**Auditors:** Clough & Co LLP
**Bankers:** HSBC Bank plc (40-47-06)

| | 31-12-13 | 31-12-12 | 31-12-11 |
|---|---|---|---|
| TO | 26,741,560 | 23,036,069 | 22,314,016 |
| P/L | 1,303,109 | 1,202,239 | 1,197,157 |
| NW | 5,764,939 | 4,767,300 | 3,865,911 |
| WC | 5,715,944 | 4,697,098 | 3,809,873 |
| Emp. | 60 | 63 | 60 |

DUNS 34-864-4402 **Imp**

## Xl Services Uk Ltd

**(Subsidiary of:** Xl Group Plc.)
Office 208, Birmingham, West Midlands B1 2JB
**Tel:** 01216988631 **Fax:** 020-7469-1000
**Web:** www.xlgroup.com
**Reg No:** 2816304 **Estd:** 1993 Private Limited Company
**Line of Business:** Other business activities not elsewhere classified
**Export Sales:** £59,819,169
**Trading Style:** Xl Services Uk Limited
**Issued Capital:** £40,072,005
**Directors:** S C Barrett, N D Russell, A P Pitchford, Miss T A Coletta
**Co. Secretary:** Sean Wastie
**Responsibilities**
**Senior:** Tony Giacco *(Senior Vice President)*, Michael Mcgavick *(Chief Executive Officer)*, Jacob Rosengarten *(Executive Vice President and C)*
**Finance:** Jean-Luc Allard *(Chief Actuary - Financial Repo)*, Alex Blanco *(Chief Underwriting Officer)*, Gavin Bruce-Smythe *(Chief Underwriting Officer)*, Thomas Burke *(Head of Alternatives)*, Peter Porrino *(CFO)*
**Operations:** Myron Hendry *(Executive Vice President and C)*, Jamie Veghte *(Reinsurance Operations)*
**Engineering:** Robin Arendt *(Enterprise Technology and Stra)*
**US SIC:** 7399 **UK SIC:** 83954
**Auditors:** PricewaterhouseCoopers LLP
**Bankers:** Barclays Bank Plc (20-00-00)

| | 31-12-13 | 31-12-12 | 31-12-11 |
|---|---|---|---|
| TO | 177,534,291 | 157,880,811 | 138,909,603 |
| P/L | 963,518 | (1,616,310) | 2,944,942 |
| NW | 11,016,987 | 12,082,732 | 16,328,010 |
| WC | 31,081,558 | 29,072,109 | 32,708,609 |
| Emp. | 835 | 783 | 776 |

DUNS 23-912-1176

## Xln Telecom Ltd.

**(Subsidiary of:** Hamsard 3209 Ltd)
69 Bondway, London SW8 1SQ
**Tel:** 02077935533
**Web:** www.xlntelecom.co.uk
**Reg No:** 3902543 **Estd:** 2000 Private Limited Company
**Line of Business:** Telecommunications
**Issued Capital:** £205
**Directors:** N F Conaghan, C Nellemann
**Co. Secretary:** Panayiotis Koullas
**Branches:** Xln Telecom Ltd., 282 Streatham High Road, London SW16 6HE
**US SIC:** 4899 **UK SIC:** 79020
**Auditors:** Deloitte LLP

| | 31-03-14 | 31-03-13 | 31-03-12 |
|---|---|---|---|
| TO | 49,316,653 | 48,861,717 | 49,193,969 |
| P/L | 11,358,962 | 9,009,253 | 8,234,542 |
| NW | 37,363,939 | 28,563,347 | 21,651,412 |
| WC | 37,148,991 | 28,239,570 | 21,208,969 |
| Emp. | 236 | 253 | 276 |

DUNS 67-215-4221

## The Xmod Ltd

Traquair Road, Innerleithen, Peeblesshire EH44 6PD
**Tel:** 01450818191
**Web:** www.thexmod.com
**Reg No:** 0314265SC **Estd:** 2008 Private Limited Company
**Line of Business:** Other retail sale in specialised stores not elsewhere classified
**Issued Capital:** £200
**Director:** A Bain
**Co. Secretary:** Gordon Bain
**US SIC:** 5961 **UK SIC:** 65600

| | 31-01-14 | 31-01-13 | 31-01-12 |
|---|---|---|---|
| TA | 356,370 | 365,946 | 149,951 |
| NW | 96,228 | 102,382 | 55,695 |
| WC | (68,667) | (195,636) | 30,345 |

DUNS 21-919-2267

## Xnp Ltd

(**Subsidiary of:** Northpoint Group Ltd.)
Globe Lane, Dukinfield, Cheshire SK16 4UY
**Tel:** 01613-304551 **Fax:** 0161-339-7169
**Web:** www.northpoint.ltd.uk
**Reg No:** 1325752 **VAT No:** 560845041
**Estd:** 1977 Private Limited Company
**Line of Business:** Treatment and coating of metals
**Trading Style:** Northpiont Ltd
**Issued Capital:** £1,044,728
**Principals:** H Tomes (*Marketing*),
P Dawson, G P Marshall
**Co. Secretary:** Simon Quiligotti
**Responsibilities**
**Sales:** Dominika Dziedzic (*Fence Coating Account Manager*), Tracey Rawlinson (*Pipe & Fence Coating Account M*), Amanda Whittingham (*Senior Fence Coating Account M*)
**US SIC:** 3398 **UK SIC:** 31380
**Auditors:** Grant Thornton UK LLP
**Bankers:** The Co-Operative Bank Plc (08-90-00)
**Employees:** 81

DUNS 21-669-9878

## Xodus Group (Holdings) Ltd

(**Subsidiary of:** Chiyoda Corporation)
Xodus House, 50 Huntly Street, Aberdeen, Aberdeenshire AD10 1RO
**Tel:** 01224628300
**Web:** www.xodus.com
**Reg No:** 0377287SC **Estd:** 2010 Private Limited Company
**Line of Business:** Engineers (consulting)
**Issued Capital:** £13,990,200
**Directors:** S K Swindell, W Van Der Zande, C A Manson, M Kumagai, Mrs E J Merchant, T Kariya, K Nakagaki
**Co. Secretary:** Shinji Kusunoki
**Branches:** Xodus Group (Holdings) Ltd, Cheapside House / 138, Cheapside, London EC2V 6BJ
**US SIC:** 8911 **UK SIC:** 83701
**Auditors:** Deloitte LLP

| | 31-12-13 | 31-12-12 | 31-12-11 |
|---|---|---|---|
| TO | 75,934,000 | 61,102,000 | 33,129,000 |
| P/L | (10,084,000) | (448,000) | (312,000) |
| NW | (17,330,000) | (1,565,000) | (3,846,000) |
| WC | 8,252,000 | 12,426,000 | 2,379,000 |
| Emp. | 475 | 348 | 243 |

DUNS 21-719-4950

## Xograph Healthcare Ltd

Xograph House, Ebley Road, Stonehouse, Gloucestershire GL10 2LU
**Tel:** 01453820320 **Fax:** 01453 820 321
**Web:** www.xograph.com
**Reg No:** 0918971 **VAT No:** 103177801
**Estd:** 1967 Private Limited Company
**Line of Business:** X-ray facilities and services
**Export Sales:** £972,707
**Issued Capital:** £5,600
**Principals:** P C Staff (*Managing*), N H Staff
**Co. Secretary:** Peter Staff
**US SIC:** 3841, 8011
**UK SIC:** 37201, 95300
**Auditors:** RSM Tenon Audit Ltd

| | 31-05-13 | 31-05-12 | 31-05-11 |
|---|---|---|---|
| TO | 10,238,402 | 10,984,208 | 9,359,850 |
| P/L | 211,848 | 542,121 | 692,747 |
| NW | 1,757,670 | 1,567,116 | 1,667,187 |
| WC | 1,761,412 | 1,869,224 | 2,014,916 |
| Emp. | 57 | 54 | 59 |

DUNS 23-959-2343

## Xoomworks Ltd

Dunstan House 14a, St Cross Street, London EC1N 8XA
**Tel:** 020-7400-6120 **Fax:** 020-7831-2171
**Web:** www.xoomworks.com
**Reg No:** 3948354 **Estd:** 2000 Private Limited Company
**Line of Business:** Management and business consultants
**Export Sales:** £2,118,576
**Issued Capital:** £693,191
**Directors:** S C Jackson, A A Kazmi, A S Baring
**Co. Secretary:** Malcolm Clark
**Responsibilities**
**Senior:** Nicolas Hutchins (*Manager*)
**Marketing:** Andy Law (*Chief Marketing Officer*)
**Sales:** Nicolas Henry (*Head of Business Intelligence*)
**Admin:** Charlene Huskinson (*Office Manager*)
**IT:** Martin Denham (*?Head of Technology*)
**Operations:** Jamie Holmes (*Operations Director*)
**Purchasing:** Ian Dagg (*Head of Procurement Consulting*)
**US SIC:** 7392 **UK SIC:** 83951

**Auditors:** Hillier Hopkins LLP

| | 30-06-13 | 30-06-12 | 30-06-11 |
|---|---|---|---|
| TO | 6,419,927 | 5,502,613 | 4,332,729 |
| P/L | (313,074) | (1,000,954) | (809,520) |
| NW | 1,080,076 | 1,871,140 | 2,933,804 |
| WC | 1,012,104 | 1,821,338 | 2,000,534 |
| Emp. | 90 | 73 | 65 |

DUNS 21-855-3448

## Xpressions 4 U Ltd

(**Subsidiary of:** Raptor Capital Ltd)
3rd Floor Paternoster House, 65 St Paul's Churchyard, London EC4M 8AB
**Tel:** 02087 567 793 **Fax:** 02087 567 799
**Web:** www.xpressionsgifts.co.uk
**Reg No:** 8188964 **Estd:** 2012 Private Limited Company
**Line of Business:** Other retail sale in non-specialised stores
**Export Sales:** £613,559
**Trading Style:** The Expressions Gift Company
**Issued Capital:** £100
**Directors:** C S Shah, N Valamootoo, K D Shah
**US SIC:** 5399 **UK SIC:** 65600
**Bankers:** National Westminster Bank Plc (60-10-10)

| | 30-04-14 | 30-04-13 |
|---|---|---|
| TO | 13,634,652 | 6,039,168 |
| P/L | 695,600 | 557,032 |
| NW | 953,888 | 418,568 |
| WC | 921,026 | 375,456 |
| Emp. | 49 | 50 |

DUNS 49-131-4738   *Imp*

## Xstrahl Ltd

The Coliseum, Watchmoor Park, Camberley, Surrey GU15 3YL
**Tel:** 01276462696 **Fax:** 01276684205
**Web:** www.xstrahl.com
**Reg No:** 3105256 **Estd:** 1995 Private Limited Company
**Line of Business:** Manufacturers of medical equipment
**Export Sales:** £9,160,072
**Trading Style:** Gulmay LImited
**Issued Capital:** £17,181
**Directors:** A Mullen, A Treverton, Ms A Tulk, J S Hall, S W Duncan, M C Robinson
**Co. Secretary:** Mrs Amanda Tulk
**Branches:** Xstrahl Ltd, Unit 2 Maybrook Industrial Estate, Maybrook Road, Walsall, West Midlands WS8 7DG
**US SIC:** 3841 **UK SIC:** 37201
**Bankers:** National Westminster Bank Plc (60-22-03)

| | 30-09-13 | 30-09-12 | 30-09-11 |
|---|---|---|---|
| TO | 10,819,282 | N/A | N/A |
| P/L | 1,682,939 | N/A | N/A |
| NW | 3,352,543 | 2,516,083 | 1,694,064 |
| WC | 3,149,927 | 2,564,454 | 1,534,484 |
| Emp. | 52 | N/A | N/A |

DUNS 23-993-1525

## Xtrac Transmissions Ltd

Gables Way, Thatcham, Berkshire RG19 4ZA
**Tel:** 01635-293800
**Web:** www.xtrac.com
**Reg No:** 3981388 **Estd:** 2000 Private Limited Company
**Line of Business:** Motor sport preparation
**Export Sales:** £24,460,000
**Issued Capital:** £1,219,889
**Directors:** P Digby, C A Hawkins, S J Lane, A P Moore
**Co. Secretary:** Stephen Lane
**Responsibilities**
**Finance:** Peter Ayling (*Financial Controller*)
**Marketing:** Adam Bach (*Business Manager*), Ben Green (*Business Manager*), Varun Lakshman (*Business Manager*), James Setter (*Senior Business Manager*), Natalie Stevenson (*Business Manager*)
**IT:** Mike Gooding (*Head of IT*)
**HR:** Kelly Packman (*HR Officer*)
**Engineering:** Martin Halley (*Chief Engineer*)
**US SIC:** 3714 **UK SIC:** 35300
**Bankers:** Barclays Bank Plc (20-11-74)

| | 30-09-13 | 30-09-12 | 30-09-11 |
|---|---|---|---|
| TO | 35,582,000 | 40,164,000 | 36,064,000 |
| P/L | (97,000) | 3,642,000 | 618,000 |
| NW | 20,555,000 | 23,244,000 | 15,231,000 |
| WC | 11,557,000 | 13,371,000 | 6,266,000 |
| Emp. | 270 | 266 | 243 |

DUNS 29-551-1158   *Exp*

## Xtrakter Ltd

(**Subsidiary of:** Marketaxess Holdings Inc.)
5 Aldermanbury Square, London EC2V 7HR
**Tel:** 02036553500 **Fax:** 02078490934
**Web:** www.xtrakter.com
**Reg No:** 1917944 **VAT No:** 446931626
**Estd:** 2008 Private Limited Company
**Line of Business:** Other business activities not elsewhere classified
**Export Markets:** Worldwide
**Trading Style:** I C M A
**Issued Capital:** £115,485
**Directors:** J N Rucker, J L Waight, R M Mcvey, P S Brine

**Co. Secretary:** Mrs Miranda Morad
**Responsibilities**
**Senior:** Bernard Frenay (*Manager*), Sue Fuller (*Manager*), Yannic Weber (*Manager*)
**US SIC:** 7399 **UK SIC:** 83954
**Auditors:** PricewaterhouseCoopers LLP
**Bankers:** Barclays Bank Plc (20-26-46)

| | 31-12-13 | 31-12-12 | 31-12-11 |
|---|---|---|---|
| TO | 14,265,000 | 15,181,000 | 15,041,000 |
| P/L | 587,000 | 2,055,000 | 2,377,000 |
| NW | 5,666,000 | 6,312,000 | 4,672,000 |
| WC | 4,939,000 | 5,252,000 | 2,922,000 |
| Emp. | 63 | 73 | 72 |

DUNS 21-736-0754   *Imp*

## Xtralis Holdings Uk Ltd

Focus 31, Mark Road, Hemel Hempstead Industrial Estate, Hemel Hempstead, Hertfordshire HP2 7BW
**Tel:** 01442242330
**Web:** www.xtralis.com
**Reg No:** 5704221 **Estd:** 2006 Private Limited Company
**Line of Business:** Management activities of other non-financial holding companies not elsewhere classified
**Export Sales:** £24,525,932
**Issued Capital:** £8,430,443
**Directors:** S Samhouri, D J Mcgraw
**Co. Secretary:** David Mcgraw
**Responsibilities**
**Senior:** Nick Cartas (*Manager*)
**US SIC:** 3999 **UK SIC:** 49590

| | 30-06-13 | 30-06-12 | 30-06-11 |
|---|---|---|---|
| TO | 35,780,956 | 36,665,352 | 27,394,682 |
| P/L | (15,687,886) | (3,595,627) | (2,293,401) |
| NW | (34,080,987) | (27,960,505) | (22,599,379) |
| WC | (34,344,540) | (11,812,326) | (7,137,504) |
| Emp. | 113 | 107 | 63 |

DUNS 42-329-8129

## Xtralite Ltd

Unit 7-9, Spencer Road, Blyth, Northumberland NE24 5TG
**Tel:** 01670-354157
**Web:** www.xtralite.co.uk
**Reg No:** 4317568 **Estd:** 2001 Private Limited Company
**Line of Business:** Other manufacturing not elsewhere classified
**Issued Capital:** £1
**Director:** R W Tweedy
**Co. Secretary:** Ms Deborah Smith
**US SIC:** 3999 **UK SIC:** 49590

| | 31-12-13 | 31-12-12 | 31-12-11 |
|---|---|---|---|
| TA | 1 | 1 | 1 |
| NW | 1 | 1 | 1 |

DUNS 42-416-4999   *Imp*

## Xtratherm U K Ltd

(**Subsidiary of:** Leanort Ltd)
Park Road, Holmewood Industrial Park, Holmewood, Chesterfield, Derbyshire S42 5UY
**Tel:** 01246858100 **Fax:** 01246857447
**Web:** www.xtratherm.com
**Reg No:** 4404208 **Estd:** 2004 Private Limited Company
**Line of Business:** Cladding and insulation materials
**Trading Style:** Xtratherm Uk
**Issued Capital:** £2
**Principals:** E J Hynes (*Managing*), S K Steenson, E Hynes, B Rafferty, Ms T Hynes
**Co. Secretary:** Gerald Beggy
**US SIC:** 3079, 2822
**UK SIC:** 48360, 25150
**Auditors:** Deloitte & Touche
**Bankers:** The Bank Of Ireland (30-14-58)

| | 31-12-13 | 31-12-12 | 31-12-11 |
|---|---|---|---|
| TO | 96,664,597 | 93,941,436 | 55,525,007 |
| P/L | 1,278,913 | 2,674,377 | 1,982,576 |
| NW | 8,451,036 | 7,442,789 | 4,928,540 |
| WC | 3,885,448 | 2,653,677 | 261,660 |
| Emp. | 122 | 114 | 108 |

DUNS 52-572-0645   *Exp*

## Xtreme Information Ltd

(**Subsidiary of:** Ebiquity Plc)
45 Fouberts Place, London W1F 7QH
**Tel:** 02075751800
**Web:** www.xtremeinformation.com
**Reg No:** 3255646 **VAT No:** 725937800
**Estd:** 1997 Private Limited Company
**Line of Business:** Advertising agency services
**Trading Style:** Ebiquity Private Limited Company
**Issued Capital:** £3,820,637
**Directors:** N V Manning, M E Greenlees, A W Beach
**Co. Secretary:** Andrew Beach
**Responsibilities**
**Senior:** Jeffrey Stevenson (*Manager*)
**US SIC:** 7319 **UK SIC:** 83800
**Auditors:** BDO LLP

| | 30-04-14 | 30-04-12 |
|---|---|---|
| TO | N/A | 2,001,000 |
| P/L | N/A | 665,000 |
| NW | 65,000 | N/A |
| Emp. | N/A | 31 |

DUNS 21-613-3066   *Exp*

## Xylem Dewatering Solutions Uk Ltd

(**Subsidiary of:** Xylem Inc.)
Coneygar Road, Cirencester, Gloucestershire GL7 5BX
**Fax:** 01285-750352
**Web:** www.xyleminc.com
**Reg No:** 0254887 **VAT No:** 274374148
**Estd:** 1877 Private Limited Company
**Line of Business:** Manufacture of pumps
**Export Markets:** Worldwide
**Export Sales:** £19,090,000
**Issued Capital:** £500,000
**Directors:** B C May, J E Mowbray
**Co. Secretary:** Mrs Catharine Smith
**Responsibilities**
**Senior:** David Braithwaite (*Manager*)
**Marketing:** Jane Skinner (*Sales & Marketing Manager*)
**Sales:** Jane Skinner (*Sales & Marketing Manager*)
**IT:** Jon Le-Bon (*IT Manager*)
**Purchasing:** Julie Roche (*Buyer*)
**US SIC:** 3561 **UK SIC:** 32870
**Auditors:** Tenon Ltd
**Bankers:** The Royal Bank Of Scotland Plc (16-04-00)

| | 31-12-13 | 31-12-12 | 31-12-11 |
|---|---|---|---|
| TO | 22,219,000 | 28,849,000 | 34,795,000 |
| P/L | 894,000 | 6,555,000 | 7,571,000 |
| NW | 19,221,000 | 18,771,000 | 13,404,000 |
| WC | 20,731,000 | 19,040,000 | 14,917,000 |
| Emp. | 90 | 129 | 129 |

DUNS 21-809-5644

## Xylem Water Solutions Uk Ltd

(**Subsidiary of:** Xylem Inc.)
Private Road 1, Colwick Industrial Estate, Nottingham, Nottinghamshire NG4 2AN
**Tel:** 01159 400111 **Fax:** 01159 400444
**Web:** www.xylemwatersolutions.com
**Reg No:** 0479504 **Estd:** 2010 Private Limited Company
**Line of Business:** Collection, purification and distribution of water
**Export Sales:** £10,942,000
**Trading Style:** Itt Www Projects, Godwin Pumps
**Issued Capital:** £5,100,250
**Directors:** R Grund, D J Lewis, Mrs K L Pay
**Co. Secretary:** Mrs Melanie Sowter
**Responsibilities**
**Senior:** Peter Lewington (*Manager*)
**Marketing:** Louise McIntyre (*General Manager*)
**Sales:** Peter Lewington (*Manager*)
**IT:** Mike Pursey (*IT Manager*)
**HR:** Brian Blackmore (*Human Resources Manager*)
**Facilities:** Alan Mawby (*Purchasing Manager*), Paul Whiteside (*Facilities Manager*)
**Purchasing:** Alan Mawby (*Purchasing Manager*)
**Branches:** Xylem Water Solutions Uk Ltd, Busby Stoop Trad Est, Ripon Rd, North Yorkshire Thirsk
**US SIC:** 4941 **UK SIC:** 17000
**Auditors:** Deloitte LLP
**Bankers:** National Westminster Bank Plc (56-00-09)

| | 31-12-13 | 31-12-12 | 31-12-11 |
|---|---|---|---|
| TO | 113,354,000 | 78,979,000 | 68,039,000 |
| P/L | 1,691,000 | 4,532,000 | 2,665,000 |
| NW | 18,185,000 | 7,560,000 | 4,289,000 |
| WC | 8,874,000 | 2,595,000 | 354,000 |
| Emp. | 516 | 314 | 286 |

DUNS 28-978-1262   *Imp-Exp*

## Xyz Machine Tools Ltd

(**Subsidiary of:** Southwestern Industries Inc.)
Woodlands Business Park, Tiverton, Devon EX16 7LL
**Tel:** 01823674200
**Web:** www.xyzmachinetools.com
**Reg No:** 1765883 **Estd:** 1984 Private Limited Company
**Line of Business:** Sales of machine tools
**Export Markets:** worldwide markets
**Issued Capital:** £100
**Principals:** N Atherton (*Managing*), R W Leonhard
**Co. Secretary:** Keith Wilson
**US SIC:** 5251, 5199
**UK SIC:** 64800, 61900
**Auditors:** Francis Clark
**Bankers:** Lloyds TSB Bank plc (30-96-06)

| | 30-04-14 | 30-04-13 | 30-04-12 |
|---|---|---|---|
| TO | 25,358,604 | 24,829,466 | 22,883,626 |
| P/L | 4,866,788 | 5,032,077 | 4,521,228 |
| NW | 22,724,911 | 18,474,949 | 17,661,262 |
| WC | 17,559,427 | 15,542,144 | 14,735,757 |
| Emp. | 68 | 67 | 58 |

# Y

DUNS 39-993-2417
## Yacht Havens Group Ltd
Kings Saltern Road, Lymington, Hampshire SO41 3QD
**Tel:** 01590679971
**Web:** www.havenrestaurant.co.uk
**Reg No:** 2281758 **Estd:** 2001 Private Limited Company
**Line of Business:** Restaurant - seafood
**Issued Capital:** £36,061
**Principals:** D H Kalis *(Managing)*, N H Case, D I Kalis, Miss C R Elder, Mrs H J Grew, T H Case
**Co. Secretary:** Dirk Kalis
**US SIC:** 6711, 4469
**UK SIC:** 83962, 76300
**Auditors:** Andrews & Palmer
**Bankers:** Lloyds TSB Bank plc (30-95-32)

| | 31-03-14 | 31-03-13 | 31-03-12 |
|---|---|---|---|
| TO | 13,744,416 | 12,101,758 | 12,273,063 |
| P/L | 3,819,511 | 4,690,600 | 4,815,617 |
| NW | 25,734,724 | 26,768,088 | 23,930,519 |
| WC | (3,114,864) | 864,297 | (4,694,504) |
| Emp. | 117 | 102 | 107 |

DUNS 34-914-9877
## Yachting Investors Group Ltd
8th Floor Berkeley Square House, Berkeley Square, London W1J 6DB
**Tel:** 02076474030
**Web:** www.yiguk.com
**Reg No:** 5711989 **Estd:** 2006 Private Limited Company
**Line of Business:** Management activities of other non-financial holding companies not elsewhere classified
**Issued Capital:** £4
**Directors:** J M Mcdonald, M Mogilevsky
**US SIC:** 6711, 7392
**UK SIC:** 83962, 83951

| | 31-12-13 | 31-12-12 | 31-12-11 |
|---|---|---|---|
| TO | 55,165,000 | 35,326,000 | 25,946,000 |
| P/L | (3,778,000) | (1,474,000) | (6,800,000) |
| NW | (3,046,000) | 55,000 | 1,541,000 |
| WC | (31,480,000) | (28,777,000) | (25,960,000) |
| Emp. | 116 | 127 | 139 |

DUNS 21-157-1302
## The Yachting Monthly Ltd
(**Subsidiary of:** Time Warner Inc.)
Kip Marina, Main Street, Inverkip, Greenock, Renfrewshire PA16 0AS
**Tel:** 01475528825
**Web:** www.equiom.je
**Reg No:** 1403675 **Estd:** 1909 Private Limited Company
**Line of Business:** Newspapers publishing
**Issued Capital:** £2
**Directors:** Dr C L Meredith, M A Rich, S J May, J J Bairstow
**Co. Secretary:** Ms Lauren Klein
**Responsibilities**
**Senior:** Scott Cornu *(Operations Officer)*
**US SIC:** 2711 **UK SIC:** 47512
**Bankers:** National Westminster Bank Plc (56-00-03)

| | 31-12-13 | 31-12-12 | 31-12-11 |
|---|---|---|---|
| TA | 2 | 155,080 | 77,541 |
| NW | 2 | 2 | 2 |
| WC | N/A | 2 | 2 |

DUNS 28-986-9257
## Yachtlease Ltd
Unit 2 Therm Road, Hull, North Humberside HU8 7BF
**Tel:** 01482620988
**Reg No:** 1805157 **Estd:** 1984 Private Limited Company
**Line of Business:** Other recreational activities not elsewhere classified
**Issued Capital:** £100
**Principals:** W E Clark *(Managing)*, E C Clark, Ms K O'Callaghan
**Co. Secretary:** Miss Vanessa Birch
**US SIC:** 7999 **UK SIC:** 97913
**Auditors:** Arthur Andersen
**Bankers:** Bank Of Scotland (12-16-30)
**Employees:** 154

DUNS 23-736-2582
## Yahooı Uk Services Ltd
(**Subsidiary of:** Yahoo Inc.)
125 Shaftesbury Avenue, London WC2H 8AD
**Tel:** 02071311000 **Fax:** 020-7131-1001
**Web:** www.yahoo.co.uk
**Reg No:** 3730602 **Estd:** 1999 Private Limited Company
**Line of Business:** Other computer related activities
**Issued Capital:** £2
**Directors:** J Talley, A Kothari
**Co. Secretary:** Ms Katherine Pawson
**Responsibilities**
**Senior:** Abigail Harris-Deans *(Legal Director)*, Edward Holden *(Manager)*
**Marketing:** Andrew Cocker *(Marketing Director)*
**IT:** James Bird *(IT Manager)*
**US SIC:** 7399, 7374
**UK SIC:** 83954, 83940
**Auditors:** PricewaterhouseCoopers
**Bankers:** HSBC Bank plc (40-41-27)

| | 31-12-13 | 31-12-12 | 31-12-11 |
|---|---|---|---|
| TO | 38,552,000 | 36,951,000 | 41,178,000 |
| P/L | 1,599,000 | 3,133,000 | 3,995,000 |
| NW | 9,827,000 | 5,261,000 | 28,574,000 |
| WC | 12,137,000 | 5,982,000 | 26,029,000 |
| Emp. | 200 | 230 | 289 |

DUNS 21-102-4035
## Yakira Group Ltd
83 Sefton Lane, Liverpool, Merseyside L31 8BU
**Tel:** 01515262626
**Web:** www.yakiragroup.com
**Reg No:** 6456147 **Estd:** 2007 Private Limited Company
**Line of Business:** Management activities of other non-financial holding companies not elsewhere classified
**Export Sales:** £9,180,259
**Issued Capital:** £3,875,061
**Directors:** Ms J A Anderson, M J Carberry, L Johnston, D M Thorn, J G Conway
**Co. Secretary:** Simon Granger
**US SIC:** 6711 **UK SIC:** 83962
**Bankers:** HSBC Bank plc (40-16-33)

| | 30-06-13 | 30-06-12 | 30-06-11 |
|---|---|---|---|
| TO | 16,082,854 | 15,191,829 | 13,007,389 |
| P/L | 1,517,525 | 1,876,106 | 839,690 |
| NW | 2,571,518 | 2,632,352 | 2,682,645 |
| WC | 2,671,486 | 2,647,315 | 2,699,932 |
| Emp. | 72 | 75 | 68 |

DUNS 21-585-3707
## Yale College
Bersham Road, Wrexham, Clwyd LL13 7UH
**Tel:** 01978311222
**Web:** www.cambria.ac.uk
**Estd:** 2010 Proprietorship
**Line of Business:** Further education schools and colleges
**Proprietor:** W Roberts
**Responsibilities**
**Senior:** Nick Tyson *(Executive Director)*
**US SIC:** 8221 **UK SIC:** 93100
**Employees:** 60

DUNS 21-319-5134
## Yale Materials Handling Uk Ltd
(**Subsidiary of:** Hyster-Yale Materials Handling Inc.)
Unit C, Orbital Way, Cannock, Staffordshire WS11 8XW
**Tel:** 03301239814 **Fax:** 01922-742469
**Web:** www.yale-uk.com
**Reg No:** 1228726 **VAT No:** 166209659
**Estd:** 1975 Private Limited Company
**Line of Business:** Wholesale of other machinery for use in industry, trade and navigation
**Trading Style:** Yale Uk
**Issued Capital:** £142
**Directors:** C A Bittenbender, C Wilson, R Mock, K C Schilling
**Branches:** Yale Materials Handling Uk Ltd, 143 Rimrose Road, Bootle, Merseyside L20 4XQ
**US SIC:** 5084 **UK SIC:** 61490
**Auditors:** Duncan Sheard Glass
**Bankers:** HSBC Bank plc (40-12-26)
**Employees:** 131

DUNS 28-991-8740 **Imp-Exp**
## Yale University Press London
47 Bedford Square, London WC1B 3DP
**Tel:** 02074314422
**Web:** www.yalebooks.co.uk
**Reg No:** 1825760 **VAT No:** 233525875
**Estd:** 1961 Private Company Limited By Guarantee
**Line of Business:** Publishing of books
**Export Markets:** Worldwide
**Directors:** Ms D K Robinson, T W Faber, A W Mcphail, Ms K Brown, J Donatich, Ms M C Highsmith, R K Fisher, F Bennett
**Co. Secretary:** Miss Emma Duncalf
**Responsibilities**
**Senior:** Robert Baldock *(Manager)*, Donal Burke *(Manager)*, Fionnuala Duggan *(Director)*, John Rollins *(Director)*, Peter Salovey *(Director)*
**US SIC:** 2731 **UK SIC:** 47532
**Auditors:** Baker Tilly
**Bankers:** National Westminster Bank Plc (60-40-04)

| | 30-06-13 | 30-06-12 | 30-06-11 |
|---|---|---|---|
| TO | 7,246,793 | 8,179,000 | 7,370,499 |
| P/L | (78,058) | 602,585 | 310,505 |
| NW | 2,955,367 | 3,033,425 | 2,430,840 |
| WC | 2,913,782 | 3,011,267 | 2,409,994 |
| Emp. | 59 | 55 | 55 |

DUNS 21-733-0117 **Imp**
## Yamaha Motor (U K) Ltd
(**Subsidiary of:** Yamaha Motor Co. Ltd.)
Sopwith Drive, Weybridge, Surrey KT13 0UZ
**Tel:** 01932-358000
**Web:** www.yamaha-motor.co.uk
**Reg No:** 1006420 **VAT No:** 235837250
**Estd:** 1971 Private Limited Company
**Line of Business:** Sale of motor vehicles
**Issued Capital:** £2,400,000
**Directors:** K Kuwata, A Sunnotel, L J Neesham
**Co. Secretary:** Lee Neesham
**Responsibilities**
**Senior:** Takahiro Fujimura *(Manager)*, Shigeo Hayakawa *(Manager)*, Kazunori Masuda *(Manager)*
**Finance:** Takahiro Fujimura *(Manager)*
**Marketing:** Jeff Turner *(Marketing Manager)*
**Sales:** Martin Carey *(Divisional Manager)*
**IT:** Mark Knight *(Computer Operations Controller)*
**US SIC:** 5511 **UK SIC:** 65100
**Auditors:** Deloitte LLP

| | 31-12-13 | 31-12-12 | 31-12-11 |
|---|---|---|---|
| TO | 57,032,000 | 52,436,000 | 60,451,000 |
| P/L | (396,000) | (3,167,000) | (703,000) |
| NW | (13,680,000) | (7,633,000) | (4,456,000) |
| WC | (12,227,000) | (11,371,000) | (7,927,000) |
| Emp. | 51 | 61 | 67 |

DUNS 21-635-8188 **Imp**
## Yamaha Music Europe Gmbh (Uk)
(**Subsidiary of:** Yamaha Corporation)
Sherbourne Drive, Tilbrook, Milton Keynes, Buckinghamshire MK7 8BL
**Tel:** 01908366700
**Web:** www.yamahamusiceducation.co.uk
**Reg No:** 0029516FC **Estd:** 2010 Foreign Company
**Line of Business:** Other service activities not elsewhere classified
**Directors:** K Masayuki, M Takahashi, H Sasagi, H Sasaki
**US SIC:** 8999 **UK SIC:** 83954

DUNS 36-483-3942 **Exp**
## Yamato Transport Europe B V
(**Subsidiary of:** Yamato Holdings Co. Ltd.)
Unit 1g The Ridgeway, Iver, Buckinghamshire SL0 9JQ
**Tel:** 01753657657 **Fax:** 01753-657658
**Web:** www.yamatoeurope.com
**Reg No:** 0025319FC **Estd:** 2004 Foreign Company
**Line of Business:** Freight forwarders
**Directors:** S Shirai, R G Bakker, K Maeda, K Koshijima
**Responsibilities**
**Health & Safety:** Marcus Marsh *(Deputy Branch Manager)*
**Facilities:** Marcus Marsh *(Deputy Branch Manager)*
**US SIC:** 4712, 4213
**UK SIC:** 77002, 72300

DUNS 42-438-8759
## Yang Ming (Uk) Ltd
2nd Floor 210 South Street, Romford, Essex RM1 1TG
**Tel:** 01708 776 900 **Fax:** 01708 776 929
**Web:** www.yangming.co.uk
**Reg No:** 3311986 **Estd:** 1997 Private Limited Company
**Line of Business:** Freight sea and coastal water transport
**Export Sales:** £397,356,009
**Issued Capital:** £1,500,000
**Directors:** S Hsu, C H Yeh, T Chia
**Co. Secretary:** Simon Williams
**Responsibilities**
**Senior:** Tom Campbell *(General Manager)*, Silas Hsu *(Manager)*
**Finance:** RoseMarie Dodd *(Credit Control)*, Graham Lewis *(Principal Accounts)*, Frank Lu *(Chief Accountant)*, Hinal Makhani *(Credit Controller)*, Kashif Nadeem *(Finance Manager)*
**Marketing:** Dawn Bale *(Booking Coordinator)*, Denise Tarrant *(Booking Coordinator)*
**Sales:** Malcolm Ashton *(Sales Ledger Assistant)*, Tracy Jacobson *(Sales Coordinator)*, Jasmine Skelton *(Sales Coordinator)*, Rory Wang *(Deputy Manager of Business Dev)*
**IT:** Joe Chan *(IT Manager)*, Paul Pun *(Computer Manager)*
**Operations:** Alyson Challis *(Import Operation Manager)*
**Purchasing:** Rima Lukminaite *(Purchase Ledger)*
**Fleet:** Terry Miles *(Transport Manager)*
**Branches:** Yang Ming (Uk) Ltd, Valentines House 51 69 Ilford Hill, Ilford, Essex IG1 2DG
**US SIC:** 4411 **UK SIC:** 74001
**Auditors:** Deloitte LLP
**Bankers:** HSBC Bank plc (40-25-27)

| | 31-12-13 | 31-12-12 | 31-12-11 |
|---|---|---|---|
| TO | 404,398,954 | 419,347,505 | 464,077,480 |
| P/L | (5,133,634) | 7,519,935 | (31,156,925) |
| NW | (50,089,196) | (46,231,728) | (56,725,650) |
| WC | (43,918,076) | (42,327,522) | (55,819,587) |
| Emp. | 59 | 61 | 63 |

DUNS 23-706-4857 **Imp**
## Yang Sing Ltd
34 Princess Street, Manchester M1 4JY
**Tel:** 0161-236-2200
**Web:** www.yang-sing.com
**Reg No:** 3701666 **Estd:** 1999 Private Limited Company
**Line of Business:** Restaurant - chinese
**Issued Capital:** £2
**Director:** H S Yeung
**US SIC:** 5812 **UK SIC:** 66110
**Auditors:** Baker Tilly

| | 30-04-14 | 30-04-13 | 30-04-12 |
|---|---|---|---|
| TA | 596,762 | 697,394 | 524,099 |
| NW | (234,378) | (295,338) | (349,017) |
| WC | (264,493) | (304,012) | (353,003) |

DUNS 23-531-4361 **Imp-Exp**
## Yankee Candle Co (Europe) Ltd
Poplar Way East, Cabbot Park, Bristol, Avon BS11 0YH
**Tel:** 01173161200 **Fax:** 01454-454510
**Web:** www.yankeecandle.co.uk
**Reg No:** 3530345 **Estd:** 1998 Private Limited Company
**Line of Business:** Wholesale of other household goods not elsewhere classified
**Export Sales:** £30,429,174
**Issued Capital:** £100
**Directors:** J E Capps, R T Sansone
**Co. Secretary:** Benjamin Preston
**Responsibilities**
**Senior:** Jonathan Fontana *(President)*, Hannah Jenkins *(Sales & Marketing Manager)*, Harlan Kent *(Ceo)*, James Perley *(Manager)*
**Marketing:** Michaela Lee *(Sales & Marketing Manager)*
**Sales:** Michaela Lee *(Sales & Marketing Manager)*
**US SIC:** 5199 **UK SIC:** 61900
**Bankers:** HSBC Bank plc (40-13-32)

| | 31-12-13 | 31-12-12 | 31-12-11 |
|---|---|---|---|
| TO | 82,851,549 | 67,500,532 | 59,674,312 |
| P/L | 3,221,806 | 2,053,093 | 1,117,539 |
| NW | 9,481,550 | 7,035,222 | 5,436,620 |
| WC | 4,909,088 | 30,782,602 | 22,794,029 |
| Emp. | 214 | 164 | 113 |

DUNS 21-321-9454 **Imp-Exp**
## Yara Phosyn Ltd
(**Subsidiary of:** Yara International Asa)
Manor Place, Pocklington Industrial Estate, Pocklington, York, North Yorkshire YO42 1DN
**Web:** www.yara.com
**Reg No:** 1035807 **VAT No:** 368372619
**Estd:** 1971 Private Limited Company
**Line of Business:** Nutritionists
**Export Markets:** Worldwide
**Issued Capital:** £93,724
**Directors:** L Lycett, Doctor G Paulson
**Co. Secretary:** Ms Lynne Gorbutt
**Responsibilities**
**Senior:** Tove Andersen *(Manager)*, Clyde Dealtry *(Non-PC Systems Manager)*, Nina Kleiv *(Manager)*
**Sales:** Roger Brogden *(Business Manager - Liquids)*
**Admin:** Pat Auton *(HR Service Specialist & Office)*
**IT:** Clyde Dealtry *(Non-PC Systems Manager)*
**HR:** Pat Auton *(HR Service Specialist & Office)*
**US SIC:** 2873 **UK SIC:** 25130
**Auditors:** Deloitte LLP
**Bankers:** Bank Of Scotland (12-08-83)

| | 31-12-13 | 31-12-12 | 31-12-11 |
|---|---|---|---|
| TA | 544,000 | 544,000 | 544,000 |
| NW | 544,000 | 544,000 | 544,000 |

DUNS 21-807-7306
## Yara Restaurant
29 London Road, Wilmslow, Cheshire SK9 7JT
**Tel:** 01625584040
**Web:** www.yara2eat.co.uk
**Estd:** 2012
**Line of Business:** Managed public houses and bars
**Proprietor:** F Sabbah
**US SIC:** 5813 **UK SIC:** 66200
**Employees:** 100

DUNS 23-826-1700
## Yara Uk Ltd
(**Subsidiary of:** Yara International Asa)
Stapleford Cottage, Tarporley, Cheshire CW6 0ET
**Tel:** 01829741512
**Web:** www.yara.co.uk
**Reg No:** 3818176 **Estd:** 1843 Private Limited Company
**Line of Business:** Conference centres and facilities
**Export Sales:** £206,513,000
**Issued Capital:** £49,441,000
**Directors:** L Lycett, J E Prew, T Knutsen, R C Cattermole, B K Axelsen, B F Lamaison, C S Grey
**Co. Secretary:** Ms Lynne Gorbutt
**Responsibilities**
**Senior:** Tove Anderson *(Manager)*, Ben Maison *(Manager)*
**Marketing:** Rosie Carne *(Senior Marketing Executive)*
**Branches:** Yara Uk Ltd, Manor Place, Pocklington Industrial Estate, Pocklington, York, North Yorkshire YO42 1NP
**US SIC:** 2873, 7399
**UK SIC:** 25130, 83954
**Auditors:** Deloitte LLP

| | 31-12-13 | 31-12-12 | 31-12-11 |
|---|---|---|---|
| TO | 698,593,000 | 668,501,000 | 632,837,000 |
| P/L | 62,889,000 | 98,169,000 | 123,944,000 |
| NW | 219,428,000 | 231,055,000 | 148,607,000 |
| WC | 157,391,000 | 178,589,000 | 101,068,000 |
| Emp. | 271 | 266 | 269 |

DUNS 21-263-1337
## Yarborough Ltd
(**Subsidiary of:** Shepherd Distribution Services Ltd)
Unit 9, Sheffield, South Yorkshire S12 2AX
**Tel:** 01142-531355
**Web:** www.shepherd-distribution.co.uk
**Reg No:** 0660908 **VAT No:** 172954440
**Estd:** 1946 Private Limited Company
**Line of Business:** Freight transport by road not elsewhere classified
**Issued Capital:** £8,000
**Directors:** L D Abel, I A Davis
**US SIC:** 4213 **UK SIC:** 72300
**Auditors:** H W
**Bankers:** Lloyds TSB Bank plc (77-74-15)

| | 31-07-14 | 31-07-13 | 31-07-12 |
|---|---|---|---|
| TO | 8,388,979 | 7,272,281 | 7,179,620 |
| P/L | 468,806 | 405,717 | 519,132 |
| NW | 7,052,497 | 6,773,524 | 6,517,337 |
| WC | 6,846,264 | 6,250,238 | 5,983,583 |
| Emp. | 108 | 101 | 99 |

DUNS 21-772-2935
## Yarborough Primary School
Yarrow Road, Grimsby, South Humberside DN34 4JU
**Tel:** 01472237772
**Web:** www.yarborough.eschools.co.uk
**Estd:** 1959 Proprietorship
**Line of Business:** Schools (local authority)
**Proprietor:** S Carr
**Responsibilities**
**Senior:** Jackie Bishop *(Business Manager)*, Chris Jessup *(Head Teacher)*
**US SIC:** 8211 **UK SIC:** 93200
**Employees:** 60

DUNS 21-122-2178
## Yarbourgh Leisure Centre
Riseholme Road, Lincoln, Lincolnshire LN1 3SP
**Tel:** 01522-873600
**Web:** www.yarboroughleisure.co.uk
**Proprietorship**
**Line of Business:** Leisure centres
**Proprietor:** S Blackbourn
**US SIC:** 7999, 7996
**UK SIC:** 97913
**Employees:** 50

DUNS 21-597-2626
## Yardley Grange Care Services
465 Church Road, Yardley, Birmingham, West Midlands B33 8NY
**Tel:** 0121-789-7188
**Estd:** 1988
**Line of Business:** Nursing homes
**Partners:** A Martin, Mrs J King
**US SIC:** 8051 **UK SIC:** 95100
**Employees:** 56

DUNS 23-989-7317
## Yardley Great Trust
31 Old Brookside, Birmingham, West Midlands B33 8QL
**Tel:** 0121-784-7889
**Web:** www.ygt.org.uk
**Estd:** 1987
**Line of Business:** Charities and charitable organisations
**Chairman:** Mrs I Aylin
**Branches:** Yardley Great Trust, 2 Foliot Fields, Birmingham, West Midlands B25 8RF
**US SIC:** 8321 **UK SIC:** 96111
**Auditors:** Clement Keys
**Employees:** 52
**Turnover:** £1,893,581

DUNS 21-697-6004
## Yardley Primary School
Hawkwood Crescent, London E4 7PH
**Tel:** 02085293671 **Fax:** 02085293229
**Web:** www.yardleyprimary.co.uk
**Reg No:** 7432995 **Estd:** 2010 Private Company Limited By Guarantee
**Line of Business:** Schools (local authority)
**Directors:** Ms J Stenton, P M Wilford, Mrs D L Burke, N J Clear, M Callaghan, Miss J L Hemsted, M J Keane, Mrs S Fisher
**Co. Secretary:** Ms Joan Easton
**Responsibilities**
**Senior:** Leigh Clothier *(Director)*, Susan Emerson *(Director)*, Ann Finnis *(Director)*
**US SIC:** 8211 **UK SIC:** 93200
**Bankers:** The Royal Bank Of Scotland Plc (16-00-08)

| | 31-08-14 | 31-08-13 | 31-08-12 |
|---|---|---|---|
| TO | 2,345,000 | 2,398,000 | 1,790,000 |
| P/L | (46,000) | 172,000 | 4,000 |
| NW | 3,198,000 | 3,011,000 | 2,825,000 |
| WC | 945,000 | 875,000 | 647,000 |
| Emp. | 42 | 59 | 42 |

DUNS 21-040-6262
## Yardleys School
Reddings Lane, Tyseley, Birmingham, West Midlands B11 3EY
**Tel:** 01214-646821
**Web:** www.yardleys-vle.org
**Estd:** 2002 Partnership
**Line of Business:** Schools (local authority)
**Partners:** Mrs R Hughes, Mrs H Jones
**Responsibilities**
**Senior:** Rose-Mary Hughes *(Head Teacher)*
**IT:** Danjit Rana *(Senior IT Executive)*
**US SIC:** 8211 **UK SIC:** 93200
**Employees:** 105

DUNS 21-880-2624
## Yarls Wood Immigration Centre
The Pines, Thurleigh Road, Milton Ernest, Bedford, Bedfordshire MK44 1RF
**Tel:** 01234821000
**Estd:** 2012
**Line of Business:** Social work activities without accommodation
**US SIC:** 8321 **UK SIC:** 96111
**Employees:** 500

DUNS 21-780-9889
## Yarm School
The Friarage, Yarm, Cleveland TS15 9EJ
**Tel:** 01642786023
**Web:** www.yarmschool.org
**Estd:** 2011 Proprietorship
**Line of Business:** Schools (independent)
**Proprietor:** D Dunn
**US SIC:** 8211 **UK SIC:** 93200
**Employees:** 1,000

DUNS 21-775-4173
## Yarnfield Park Training & Conference Centre
Yarnfield Park, Yarnfield, Stone, Staffordshire ST15 0NL
**Tel:** 01785762906
**Web:** www.bt.com
**Estd:** 2011
**Line of Business:** Conference centres and facilities
**US SIC:** 8299 **UK SIC:** 93300
**Employees:** 100

DUNS 21-779-7283
## Yarnspinners Primary Health Care Centre Nelson
Carr Road, Nelson, Lancashire BB9 7SR
**Tel:** 01282657600
**Web:** www.elht.nhs.uk
**Estd:** 2011 Proprietorship
**Line of Business:** Health centres
**Proprietor:** Mrs J Walmsley
**US SIC:** 8091 **UK SIC:** 95200
**Employees:** 50

DUNS 22-663-6876
## Yarnton Nurseries
Yarnton Nurseries, Sandy Lane, Yarnton, Kidlington, Oxfordshire OX5 1PA
**Tel:** 01865842141
**Web:** www.yarnton-nurseries-garden-ctre.co.uk
**Estd:** 1968 Partnership
**Line of Business:** Other retail sale in specialised stores not elsewhere classified
**Partners:** R G Wallbridge, N H Wallbridge
**US SIC:** 5199, 5999
**UK SIC:** 61900, 65600
**Bankers:** Lloyds TSB Bank plc (30-96-35)
**Employees:** 50

DUNS 28-845-4598
## Yarrells Preparatory School Ltd.
Yarrells Drive, Poole, Dorset BH16 5EU
**Tel:** 01202-622229
**Web:** www.yarrells.co.uk
**Reg No:** 0624143 **Estd:** 1959 Private Limited Company
**Line of Business:** Schools (independent)
**Issued Capital:** £100
**Directors:** R N Covell, C J Covell
**Co. Secretary:** Mrs Natalie Covell
**Responsibilities**
**Senior:** Charlotte Oosthuizen *(Headmistress)*
**US SIC:** 8211 **UK SIC:** 93200
**Auditors:** Mazars Neville Russell

| | 31-08-13 | 31-08-12 | 31-08-11 |
|---|---|---|---|
| TA | 1,873,401 | 1,659,553 | 1,645,976 |
| NW | 990,577 | 861,456 | 873,472 |
| WC | 114,214 | 296,399 | 298,243 |

DUNS 23-206-9260
## Yarrow Housing Ltd
216 Goldhawk Road, London W12 9NX
**Tel:** 020-8735-4600 **Fax:** 02087354601
**Web:** www.yarrowhousing.org.uk
**Reg No:** 0026315IP **Estd:** 1988 Friendly Society
**Line of Business:** Home care and help services
**Principals:** Ms J Hamelton *(Chairman)*, T Hughes, Ms R Farrar
**Responsibilities**
**Senior:** Christine Aloyo *(Manager)*, Jean Chapple *(Vice Chairman)*, Raj Mungur *(Associato Director of Care and)*
**Finance:** Fatahi Onibudo *(Financial Director)*
**IT:** Ray Mayston *(IT Manager)*
**HR:** Margaret Spiers *(Human Resources Manager)*
**Operations:** Diana Cadogan *(Director of Organisational Dev)*, Lindy Shufflebotham *(Director of Operations)*
**Branches:** Yarrow Housing Ltd, 2 Elmfield Way, London W9 3TU
**US SIC:** 8811 **UK SIC:** 99000
**Auditors:** Valentine Marke Stevens
**Bankers:** Barclays Bank Plc (20-35-90)
**Employees:** 209
**Turnover:** £8,393,605

DUNS 51-726-7050
## Yas Restaurant
7 Hammersmith Road, West Kensington, London W14 8XJ
**Tel:** 02076039148
**Web:** www.yasrestaurant.com
**Estd:** 2007 Proprietorship
**Line of Business:** Licensed restaurants
**Proprietor:** S Eshraghi
**US SIC:** 5812, 5813
**UK SIC:** 66110, 66200
**Employees:** 80

DUNS 76-398-7229 **Imp-Exp**
## Yaskawa Electric Uk Ltd
(**Subsidiary of:** Yaskawa Electric Corporation)
1 Hunt Hill, Cumbernauld, Glasgow, Lanarkshire G68 9LF
**Tel:** 01236735000
**Web:** www.yaskawa.co.uk
**Reg No:** 0128373SC **Estd:** 1990 Private Limited Company
**Line of Business:** Manufacture of other electrical equipment not elsewhere classified
**Export Markets:** Worldwide
**Export Sales:** £31,390,485
**Issued Capital:** £3,000,000
**Directors:** A Kumage, M Zenke, K Takamiya, H Ushijima
**Co. Secretary:** Toshio Kawasaki
**Responsibilities**
**Senior:** Fumio Ando *(Manager)*, Yoshikatsu Minami *(Manager)*, Junichi Nakano *(Manager)*, Hiroshi Ogasawara *(Manager)*
**US SIC:** 3629, 3661
**UK SIC:** 34350, 34410
**Auditors:** Ernst & Young LLP
**Bankers:** The Royal Bank Of Scotland Plc (83-17-31)

| | 28-02-14 | 28-02-13 | 29-02-12 |
|---|---|---|---|
| TO | 31,390,485 | 27,521,662 | 30,295,051 |
| P/L | 1,590,623 | 168,702 | (688,352) |
| NW | 10,550,368 | 9,377,406 | 9,292,295 |
| WC | 7,825,195 | 6,081,230 | 5,340,271 |
| Emp. | 124 | 122 | 145 |

DUNS 22-527-6732
## Yateley Industries for the Disabled Ltd
Mill Lane, Yateley, Hampshire GU46 7TF
**Web:** www.yateleyindustries.co.uk
**Reg No:** 0448920 **VAT No:** 199312436
**Estd:** 1948 Private Company Limited By Guarantee
**Line of Business:** Regulation of the activities of agencies that provide health care, education, cultural services and other social services excluding social security
**Directors:** I Head, Mrs S A Brettell, E E Fillingham, R Grimwood, G R Barwick, Mrs H J Gover, J Haynes
**Co. Secretary:** Patrick Mclarry
**Responsibilities**
**Finance:** Janet Higginbottom *(Financial Manager)*
**IT:** Janet Higginbottom *(Financial Manager)*
**Health & Safety:** Karen Palmer *(Production Manager)*
**Facilities:** Karen Palmer *(Production Manager)*
**Engineering:** Karen Palmer *(Production Manager)*
**US SIC:** 8999, 6732
**UK SIC:** 83954, 83100
**Auditors:** Menzies
**Bankers:** Barclays Bank Plc (20-16-99)

| | 31-03-14 | 31-03-13 | 31-03-12 |
|---|---|---|---|
| TO | 1,125,081 | 1,074,911 | 1,029,860 |
| P/L | 31,302 | (133,654) | 20,503 |
| NW | 617,900 | 586,598 | 720,252 |
| WC | (15,905) | (29,694) | 93,771 |
| Emp. | 111 | 102 | 77 |

DUNS 23-579-8931
## Yateley Manor School Ltd
Council Offices, Reading Road, Yateley, Hampshire GU46 7RP
**Tel:** 01252872198
**Web:** www.yateley-tc.gov.uk
**Reg No:** 0966437 **Estd:** 1947 Private Limited Company
**Line of Business:** General secondary education
**Directors:** Dr C J Clark, G Pearson, S V Sharp, J Lonsdale, H J Garland, Ms J E Roberts, S A Gorys, M Riley
**Co. Secretary:** Brandon Ashton
**Responsibilities**
**Senior:** Joe French *(Board of Governors - Member)*, Eila Huxford *(Board of Governors - Member)*, Fergus Livingstone *(Board of Governors - Member)*, Royston Truman *(Board of Governors - Member)*
**Finance:** Karen Farr *(Assistant Bursar)*
**Marketing:** Penny Charles *(Marketing Assistant)*
**Facilities:** Richard Nickless *(Head of Maintenance)*
**US SIC:** 8211 **UK SIC:** 93200
**Auditors:** Smith & Williamson
**Bankers:** Allied Irish Bank (gb) (23-84-85)

| | 31-08-14 | 31-08-13 | 31-08-12 |
|---|---|---|---|
| TO | 4,491,023 | 4,346,146 | 4,252,911 |
| P/L | 268,209 | 155,457 | 169,289 |
| NW | 5,562,346 | 5,294,137 | 5,138,680 |
| WC | 1,262,194 | 1,089,792 | 408,999 |
| Emp. | 120 | 117 | 103 |

DUNS 21-773-2038
## Yates's
411 Promenade, Blackpool, Lancashire FY1 6BQ
**Tel:** 01253406070
**Web:** www.weareyates.com
**Estd:** 2002 Proprietorship
**Line of Business:** Public house
**Proprietor:** P Myers
**US SIC:** 5813 **UK SIC:** 66200
**Employees:** 60

DUNS 21-747-4808
## Yattendon Group Plc
Barn Close, Burnt Hill, Thatcham, Berkshire RG18 0UX
**Tel:** 01635-203929 **Fax:** 01635-203921
**Web:** www.yit.co.uk
**Reg No:** 0288238 **VAT No:** 112447796
**Estd:** 1934 Public Limited Company
**Line of Business:** Newspapers publishing
**Export Sales:** £12,527,000
**Issued Capital:** £5,308,284
**Principals:** Lord R P Iliffe *(Chairman)*, D S Fordham, M G Spencer, S P Sadler, F A Austin, The Honourable E R Iliffe
**Co. Secretary:** Catherine Fleming
**Responsibilities**
**Senior:** Michael Lawrence *(Non-Executive Director)*
**Branches:** Yattendon Group Plc, 12 North Street, Bishops Stortford, Bishop's Stortford, Hertfordshire CM23 2LQ
**US SIC:** 6711, 4469
**UK SIC:** 83962, 76300
**Auditors:** Ernst & Young LLP

**Bankers:** Lloyds TSB Bank plc (77-18-00)

| | 31-03-14 | 07-01-13 | 31-03-11 |
|---|---|---|---|
| TO | 74,450,000 | 89,716,000 | 102,918,000 |
| P/L | 5,754,000 | (2,966,000) | (2,120,000) |
| NW | 220,752,000 | 207,073,000 | 226,786,000 |
| WC | 1,503,000 | (14,011,000) | (16,414,000) |
| Emp. | 388 | 955 | 1,021 |

DUNS 23-082-7433
## Yattendon School
Oakwood Road, Horley, Surrey RH6 7BZ
**Tel:** 01293734100
**Web:** www.yattendon.org
**Estd:** 1989
**Line of Business:** Schools (local authority)
**Director:** T Clarke
**US SIC:** 8211 **UK SIC:** 93200
**Employees:** 50

DUNS 21-418-8777
## Yauatcha
15 Broadwick Street, London W1F 0DL
**Tel:** 020-74948888
**Web:** www.yauatcha.com
**Estd:** 2004 Proprietorship
**Line of Business:** Restaurant - chinese
**Proprietor:** A Yau
**Responsibilities**
**Senior:** Helenka Pallester (General Manager)
**US SIC:** 5812 **UK SIC:** 66110
**Employees:** 77

DUNS 21-728-2874
## Yavneh College
Hillside Avenue, Borehamwood, Hertfordshire WD6 1HL
**Tel:** 02087365580
**Web:** www.yavnehcollege.org
**Reg No:** 7643712 **Estd:** 2011 Private Company Limited By Guarantee
**Line of Business:** Schools (independent)
**Directors:** S H Rosenberg, M E Frazer, Mrs S A Nyman, D Ardeman, R M Gilbert, A Maurice, J S Reback, Mrs D Morris
**Co. Secretary:** Mrs Hayley Fraser
**Responsibilities**
**Senior:** Daniel Album (Director), Tanya Charlton (Director), Dena Coleman (Head Teacher), Rolanda Hyams (Director), Heidi Krianes (Director), Spencer Lewis (Director), Adam Newbey (Director), Bradley Raphael (Director)
**US SIC:** 8211 **UK SIC:** 93200

| | 31-08-13 | 31-08-12 |
|---|---|---|
| TO | 5,201,241 | 5,517,196 |
| P/L | (156,955) | (241,693) |
| NW | (488,148) | (342,193) |
| WC | (161,275) | (39,127) |
| Emp. | 99 | 94 |

DUNS 22-704-1704    **Imp-Exp**
## Yazaki Europe Ltd
(Subsidiary of: Yazaki Co. Ltd.)
Unit 1-3, Zodiac, Hemel Hempstead, Hertfordshire HP2 7SJ
**Tel:** 01442-292400 **Fax:** 01442-292444
**Web:** www.yazaki-europe.com
**Reg No:** 1490660 **VAT No:** 345614654
**Estd:** 1980 Private Limited Company
**Line of Business:** Manufacture of electricity distribution and control apparatus
**Export Markets:** Worldwide
**Export Sales:** £1,302,628,000
**Issued Capital:** £45,000,000
**Directors:** K Nishimoto, Y Tsuji, H Ichikawa, K Matsunaga, Dr H Rudolph, Dr M R Rummel
**Co. Secretary:** Dr Michael Rummel
**Responsibilities**
**Senior:** Kim Dixon (Operations Manager), Volker Heuzeroth (Chairman), Pareshkumar Mehta (Manager), Rudiger Wachendorff (President)
**HR:** Mandy Roden (Hr Manager)
**Branches:** Yazaki Europe Ltd, Fifth Avenue Business Park, Gateshead, Tyne and Wear NE11 0BL
**US SIC:** 3643, 5199
**UK SIC:** 34203, 61900
**Auditors:** PricewaterhouseCoopers LLP
**Following financial data are in thousands**

| | 31-03-14 | 31-03-13 | 31-03-12 |
|---|---|---|---|
| TO | 1,437,551 | 1,002,206 | 904,216 |
| P/L | 4,841 | 1,379 | (3,479) |
| NW | (820) | (18,466) | 23,695 |
| WC | 8,720 | 859 | 21,404 |
| Emp. | 1,517 | 1,047 | 979 |

DUNS 22-155-5894
## Ybc Cleaning Services Ltd
161 North Lane, Aldershot, Hampshire GU12 4TA
**Tel:** 01252-338873
**Web:** www.ybccleaning.co.uk
**Reg No:** 4174249 **Estd:** 1996 Private Limited Company
**Line of Business:** Cleaning contracting commercial
**Issued Capital:** £100

**Principals:** Y B Chhetri (Managing), M Kc, Ms M A Blackman
**Responsibilities**
**Senior:** Ewa Skorek (Office Administrator)
**US SIC:** 7349 **UK SIC:** 92300

| | 31-03-14 | 31-03-13 | 31-03-12 |
|---|---|---|---|
| TA | 2,023,692 | 2,191,599 | 2,073,410 |
| NW | 1,589,756 | 1,693,076 | 1,412,892 |
| WC | 1,055,428 | 1,254,616 | 1,033,774 |

DUNS 34-970-4218
## Ybs Holdings Ltd
Access Works, Martin Street, Birstall, Batley, West Yorkshire WF17 9PJ
**Tel:** 01924-471955
**Reg No:** 5765802 **Estd:** 2006 Private Limited Company
**Line of Business:** Plumbing
**Issued Capital:** £1,000
**Directors:** A D Sutcliffe, G Mitchell
**Co. Secretary:** Amos Harrison
**US SIC:** 1711 **UK SIC:** 50300
**Auditors:** Ford Campbell Freedman LLP
**Bankers:** Yorkshire Bank Plc (05-00-20)

| | 30-06-14 | 30-06-13 | 30-06-12 |
|---|---|---|---|
| TO | 22,043,459 | 18,315,123 | 18,454,453 |
| P/L | 1,200,669 | 680,688 | 1,014,415 |
| NW | 352,196 | (268,806) | (849,777) |
| WC | 17,879 | (563,226) | (838,623) |
| Emp. | 56 | 58 | 60 |

DUNS 73-753-6677
## Y.Co Group Ltd
18 Coulson Street, London SW3 3NB
**Tel:** 02075841801 **Fax:** 02075891802
**Web:** www.ycogroup.com
**Reg No:** 5011189 **Estd:** 2004 Public Limited Company
**Line of Business:** Management activities of holding companies
**Issued Capital:** £169,708
**Directors:** S Hoffman, C N Birkett, P H Jay, G Wright, C H Evans-Pollard
**Co. Secretary:** Ralph Crane
**Responsibilities**
**Senior:** Scott Lidbetter (Non-Executive Chairman), Rishi Malliwal (Non-Executive Director)
**IT:** Nigel Blackbourn (Project Manager)
**US SIC:** 6711 **UK SIC:** 83962
**Auditors:** Jeffreys Henry LLP
**Bankers:** Coutts & Co (18-00-02)

| | 31-12-13 | 31-12-12 | 31-12-11 |
|---|---|---|---|
| TO | 19,041,015 | 27,292,258 | 16,570,652 |
| P/L | (461,245) | (7,403,698) | (4,113,074) |
| NW | 1,464,998 | 1,633,993 | 1,465,477 |
| WC | 977,106 | 833,089 | 704,942 |
| Emp. | 74 | 72 | 70 |

DUNS 21-615-0903
## Yeadon Way
Yeadon Way, Blackpool, Lancashire FY1 6BF
**Tel:** 01253340618
**Web:** www.brewersfayre.co.uk
**Estd:** 2011
**Line of Business:** Bars
**Responsibilities**
**Senior:** Alan Murdock (General Manager)
**US SIC:** 5813 **UK SIC:** 66200
**Employees:** 50

DUNS 21-585-6475
## Yearsley
Belle Eau Park, Bilsthorpe, Newark, Nottinghamshire NG22 8TX
**Tel:** 01623873719
**Web:** www.yearsley.co.uk
**Estd:** 2011
**Line of Business:** Frozen food processors and distributors
**Responsibilities**
**Senior:** Nigel Welsh (Site Manager)
**US SIC:** 5149 **UK SIC:** 61700
**Employees:** 200

DUNS 21-582-5230
## Yearsley Group
Garonor Way, Royal Portbury Dock, Portbury, Bristol, Avon BS20 7XE
**Tel:** 01275378750
**Web:** www.yearsley.co.uk
**Estd:** 2011 Proprietorship
**Line of Business:** Catering food and drink suppliers
**Proprietor:** P Chapman
**US SIC:** 5149 **UK SIC:** 61700
**Employees:** 55

DUNS 21-227-1101
## Yearsley Is Group
Tupton Way, Holmewood Industrial Park, Holmewood, Chesterfield, Derbyshire S42 5BX
**Tel:** 01706694672
**Web:** www.yearsley.co.uk
**Estd:** 2011
**Line of Business:** Road haulage and transport services

**Responsibilities**
**Senior:** Steve Walsh (General Manager)
**US SIC:** 4789 **UK SIC:** 77002
**Employees:** 84

DUNS 21-009-5016
## Yellow Advertiser Ltd
(Subsidiary of: Tindle Press Holdings Ltd)
Acorn House, Great Oaks, Basildon, Essex SS14 1AH
**Tel:** 01268503428
**Web:** www.yellowadvertiser.co.uk
**Reg No:** 6332840 **Estd:** 2007 Private Limited Company
**Line of Business:** Publishing of newspapers
**Issued Capital:** £1
**Directors:** Mrs W D Craig, S Wood, Mrs K L Fyfield, Sir R S Tindle
**Co. Secretary:** Mrs Kathryn Fyfield
**Responsibilities**
**Finance:** Jane Butt (Finance Manager)
**US SIC:** 2711 **UK SIC:** 47512
**Bankers:** Lloyds TSB Bank plc (30-93-74)

| | 31-03-14 | 31-03-13 | 31-03-12 |
|---|---|---|---|
| TO | 3,444,676 | 4,172,637 | 4,874,813 |
| P/L | (146,433) | (490,955) | (283,077) |
| NW | (749,127) | (636,292) | (260,054) |
| WC | (764,520) | (646,459) | (287,728) |
| Emp. | 47 | 58 | 67 |

DUNS 64-714-1811
## Yellow Cab Co
Parade House, 36 Bedminster Parade, Bristol, Avon BS3 4HS
**Tel:** 01179-231515
**Web:** www.yellowcabsbristol.co.uk
**Estd:** 2004 Proprietorship
**Line of Business:** Taxi operation
**Proprietor:** S Poulton
**Responsibilities**
**Finance:** Emily Lenthall (Accounts Manager)
**US SIC:** 4121 **UK SIC:** 72200
**Employees:** 100

DUNS 23-962-4435
## Yeo Group Ltd
123 Undercliff Road West, Felixstowe, Suffolk IP11 2AF
**Tel:** 01394-282958
**Web:** www.alexcafebar.co.uk
**Reg No:** 3951437 **Estd:** 2000 Private Limited Company
**Line of Business:** Restaurant - english
**Trading Style:** The Alex
**Issued Capital:** £1,000
**Principals:** T Yeo (Managing), Mrs J D Yeo
**Co. Secretary:** Ms Marilyn Goodwin
**US SIC:** 5812 **UK SIC:** 66110

| | 31-03-14 | 31-03-13 | 31-03-12 |
|---|---|---|---|
| TA | 1,003,455 | 1,198,129 | 1,155,988 |
| NW | 641,371 | 869,798 | 808,110 |
| WC | (15,316) | (35,753) | (26,104) |

DUNS 21-683-1040    **Imp**
## Yeo Paull Ltd
Coat Road, Martock, Somerset TA12 6EX
**Tel:** 01935822204
**Web:** www.paulls.co.uk
**Reg No:** 0048482 **VAT No:** 357899675
**Estd:** 1896 Private Limited Company
**Line of Business:** Builders merchants
**Issued Capital:** £80,000
**Principals:** P C Paull (Managing), D C Paull, M B Russell, J H Paull
**Co. Secretary:** Philip Paull
**Branches:** Yeo Paull Ltd, 2A Town St, Shepton Mallet, Somerset BA4 5BG
**US SIC:** 6519 **UK SIC:** 85000
**Auditors:** Beer Aplin
**Bankers:** Lloyds TSB Bank plc (30-00-01)

| | 31-12-13 | 31-12-12 | 31-12-11 |
|---|---|---|---|
| TA | 1,797,804 | 1,522,101 | 1,483,779 |
| NW | 1,708,130 | 1,444,276 | 1,422,742 |
| WC | (32,468) | 111,421 | 94,828 |

DUNS 22-506-4443    **Imp-Exp**
## Yeo Valley Farms (Production) Ltd
The Mendip Centre, Rhodyate, Bristol, Avon BS40 7YE
**Web:** www.yeovalley.co.uk
**Reg No:** 1283809 **Estd:** 1976 Private Limited Company
**Line of Business:** Representative office
**Export Markets:** E U
**Export Sales:** £1,834,772
**Issued Capital:** £37,233
**Principals:** T W Mead (Managing), S P Page, A J Fenton, A J Carne, G T Hayes
**Co. Secretary:** Karl Tucker
**Responsibilities**
**Marketing:** Ben Cull (Head of Marketing), Tom Depass (Head Of Communications)
**Sales:** Adrian Khan (Commercial Director)
**HR:** Terry Kelly (Human Resources Manager)
**Health & Safety:** Terry Kelly (Human Resources Manager)
**US SIC:** 2026, 2023, 2024

**UK SIC:** 41301, 41303, 42130
**Auditors:** Nexia Smith & Williamson
**Bankers:** Barclays Bank Plc (20-13-42)

| | 02-06-13 | 27-05-12 | 29-06-11 |
|---|---|---|---|
| TO | 261,016,302 | 228,689,907 | 201,701,660 |
| P/L | 4,711,320 | 3,505,298 | 1,524,539 |
| NW | 12,721,854 | 10,140,429 | 7,519,439 |
| WC | 10,449,759 | 10,092,756 | 7,499,182 |
| Emp. | 1,657 | 1,492 | 1,404 |

DUNS 22-909-1640
## Yeoman (Morvern) Ltd
(Subsidiary of: Holcim U K Holdings Ltd)
Rhugh Garbh Depot, Barcaldine, Oban, Argyll PA37 1SE
**Tel:** 01631730441
**Web:** www.fosteryeoman.com
**Reg No:** 0074406SC **Estd:** 1981 Private Limited Company
**Line of Business:** Manufacturers of stone articles
**Trading Style:** Aggriagate Industries
**Issued Capital:** £10,000
**Directors:** N Lander, J F Bowater
**Responsibilities**
**Senior:** Guy Edwards (Manager), Darren Loftas (Quarry Manager)
**Branches:** Yeoman (Morvern) Ltd, Glensander Quarry Operations, Rhughgareh Depot,, Oban, Argyll PA37 1SE
**US SIC:** 1429 **UK SIC:** 23102
**Auditors:** KPMG
**Bankers:** National Westminster Bank Plc (60-30-21)

| | 31-12-13 | 31-12-12 | 31-12-11 |
|---|---|---|---|
| TA | 10,000 | 10,000 | 10,000 |
| NW | 10,000 | 10,000 | 10,000 |

DUNS 77-540-0351
## Yeomans Canyon Tours Ltd
Old School Lane, Hereford, Herefordshire HR1 1EX
**Tel:** 01432356206 **Fax:** 01432-356206
**Web:** www.yeomanscoachholidays.com
**Reg No:** 2995289 **Estd:** 1988 Private Limited Company
**Line of Business:** Coach and bus hire
**Trading Style:** Yeomans Canyon Travel
**Issued Capital:** £100
**Director:** N D Yeomans
**Co. Secretary:** Mrs Susan Yeomans
**US SIC:** 4722 **UK SIC:** 77001

| | 31-03-14 | 31-03-13 | 31-03-12 |
|---|---|---|---|
| TA | 150,622 | 165,841 | 191,967 |
| NW | 5,298 | 3,961 | 3,941 |
| WC | 5,298 | 3,961 | 3,941 |

DUNS 39-884-9091
## Yeomans Canyon Travel Ltd
The Travel Centre, Old School Lane, Hereford, Herefordshire HR1 1EX
**Tel:** 01432356201 **Fax:** 01432352290
**Web:** www.yeomanscoachholidays.com
**Reg No:** 2225073 **Estd:** 1988 Private Limited Company
**Line of Business:** Other scheduled passenger land transport not elsewhere classified
**Issued Capital:** £20,000
**Managing Director:** N D Yeomans
**Co. Secretary:** Mrs Susan Yeomans
**Responsibilities**
**Senior:** Sue Perkins (Accounts Manager)
**Finance:** Sue Perkins (Accounts Manager)
**US SIC:** 4722, 7999
**UK SIC:** 77001, 97913
**Auditors:** Cockett & Co Ltd

| | 31-03-14 | 31-03-13 | 31-03-12 |
|---|---|---|---|
| TO | 4,407,196 | 4,488,861 | 4,657,048 |
| P/L | 134,067 | 72,924 | 179,393 |
| NW | 2,292,781 | 2,189,133 | 2,105,397 |
| WC | (380,035) | (582,269) | (616,614) |
| Emp. | 113 | 113 | 113 |

DUNS 29-575-8932
## Yeomans Ltd
Yeomans Road, Worthing, West Sussex BN13 3NS
**Tel:** 01903694499 **Fax:** 01903694093
**Web:** www.yeomans.co.uk
**Reg No:** 1937745 **VAT No:** 430669550
**Estd:** 1993 Private Limited Company
**Line of Business:** Car dealers (new & used)
**Trading Style:** Yeoman's
**Issued Capital:** £1,000,000
**Directors:** T S Lander, J R Smith, K L Newitt, Miss K S Smith, Miss H F Smith
**Co. Secretary:** Anthony Brooks
**Branches:** Yeomans Ltd, 52-54 Horsham Road, Littlehampton, West Sussex BN17 6DN
**US SIC:** 5511, 5531
**UK SIC:** 65100
**Auditors:** George Hay & Co
**Bankers:** Lloyds TSB Bank plc (30-12-05)

| | 31-12-13 | 31-12-12 | 31-12-11 |
|---|---|---|---|
| TO | 151,795,082 | 137,959,598 | 131,697,870 |
| P/L | 2,678,418 | 3,745,401 | 2,389,837 |
| NW | 17,531,601 | 15,574,967 | 12,918,770 |
| WC | 7,806,933 | 7,251,858 | 5,553,685 |
| Emp. | 355 | 336 | 331 |

DUNS 21-838-1617
## Yeomans Outdoors Ltd
Unit A, Ireland Industrial Estate, Griffen Close, Staveley, Chesterfield, Derbyshire S43 3LJ
**Tel:** 01246477513
**Web:** www.yeomansoutdoors.co.uk
**Reg No:** 8058714 **Estd:** 2012 Private Limited Company
**Line of Business:** Representative office
**Issued Capital:** £100
**Directors:** D M Forsey, J Kinnaird, B J Leach, P K Drake
**Co. Secretary:** Cameron Olsen
**US SIC:** 5941, 5699
**UK SIC:** 65400, 64500

| | 31-05-13 |
|---|---|
| TO | 13,466,698 |
| P/L | (381,444) |
| NW | (381,344) |
| WC | (454,029) |
| Emp. | 362 |

DUNS 23-680-7012
## Yeovil College
Mudford Road, Yeovil, Somerset BA21 4DR
**Tel:** 01935-423921
**Web:** www.yeovil.ac.uk
**Estd:** 1959
**Line of Business:** Further education schools and colleges
**Principals:** C Ball *(Financial)*, Mrs M Mckenna, N Kershaw, Ms J Knott, R Atkins
**Responsibilities**
**Senior:** James Hampton *(Principal)*
**Finance:** Janice Tipper *(Head of Finance)*
**IT:** Craig Cullen *(Head of IT Services)*
**Branches:** Yeovil College, 72-74 Middle Street, Yeovil, Somerset BA20 1LU
**US SIC:** 8221 **UK SIC:** 93100
**Employees:** 500

DUNS 54-864-5266
## Yeovil District Hospital Nhs Foundation Trust
Yeovil District Hospital, Higher Kingston, Yeovil, Somerset BA21 4AT
**Tel:** 01935-475-122
**Web:** www.yeovilhospital.nhs.uk
**Estd:** 2006
**Line of Business:** Nhs clinics
**Issued Capital:** £1
**Principals:** P Wyman Cbe *(Chairman)*, P Mears, Mrs A Ellingworth, Mrs G Waldron, M Aichroth, A Russell, J Buckley, Ms S Jones
**Responsibilities**
**Senior:** David Brock *(Divisional General Manager)*, Maddie Groves *(Associate Director - Nursing a)*, Jonathan Higman *(Director of Operations)*, Pippa Moger *(Finance Director)*, Dean Stevens *(Assistant Finance Director)*, Peter Wyman CBE *(Chairperson)*
**Finance:** James Kirton *(Head of Fundraising)*, Pippa Moger *(Finance Director)*, Dean Stevens *(Assistant Finance Director)*, Libby Walters *(Deputy Financial Director)*
**Marketing:** Amy Mercer *(Communications Officer)*
**Sales:** Andy Hind *(Commercial Manager)*
**Admin:** Nicola Webber *(Membership Officer)*
**Operations:** Jonathan Higman *(Director of Operations)*
**Branches:** Yeovil District Hospital Nhs Foundation Trust, Yeovil District Hospital, Higher Kingston, Yeovil, Somerset BA21 4AT
**US SIC:** 9121, 8062
**UK SIC:** 91110, 95100
**Auditors:** KPMG LLP

| | 31-03-14 | 31-03-13 | 31-03-12 |
|---|---|---|---|
| TO | 117,922,000 | 116,369,000 | 98,025,000 |
| P/L | (435,000) | 372,000 | 797,000 |
| NW | 56,936,000 | 54,593,000 | 55,549,000 |
| WC | 4,461,000 | 4,456,000 | 3,656,000 |
| Emp. | 1,728 | 1,728 | 1,712 |

DUNS 28-830-7036
## The Yeovil Football & Athletic Club Ltd
**(Subsidiary of:** Yeovil Town Holdings Ltd)
Huish Park, Lufton Way, Lufton, Yeovil, Somerset BA22 8YF
**Tel:** 01935-423662 **Fax:** 01935-473956
**Web:** www.ytfc.net
**Reg No:** 0189754 **Estd:** 1895 Private Limited Company
**Line of Business:** Sports clubs
**Trading Style:** The Yeovil Town Football Club
**Issued Capital:** £1,707,214
**Principals:** J R Fry *(Chairman)*, A V Chamberlain, S P Allinson, W D Lee, A M Rossiter, B E Willis, R E Budden, N Hayward
**Co. Secretary:** William Lee
**Responsibilities**
**Senior:** Jean Cotton *(Manager)*, James Hillier *(Stadium Manager)*, Adrian Hopper *(Manager)*, Dot Smith *(Executive)*
**Finance:** Sue Linney *(Accounts Assistant)*, Pete O' Riordan *(Accountant)*
**Marketing:** Martin Mcconachie *(Website Administrator, Commerc)*
**Sales:** Sue Linney *(Accounts Assistant)*
**IT:** James Hillier *(Stadium Manager)*
**HR:** James Hillier *(Stadium Manager)*
**Health & Safety:** James Hillier *(Stadium Manager)*
**Facilities:** James Hillier *(Stadium Manager)*
**Purchasing:** James Hillier *(Stadium Manager)*
**US SIC:** 7999 **UK SIC:** 97913
**Auditors:** Illegible
**Bankers:** National Westminster Bank Plc (60-19-12)

| | 30-06-13 | 30-06-12 | 30-06-11 |
|---|---|---|---|
| TA | 1,908,599 | 1,841,830 | 1,873,848 |
| NW | 518,172 | 977,986 | 926,235 |
| WC | (551,217) | (82,051) | (154,442) |

DUNS 85-610-2512 **Exp**
## Yeovil Precision Castings Ltd
**(Subsidiary of:** Coker (Holdings) Ltd)
11 Buckland Road, Yeovil, Somerset BA21 5EF
**Tel:** 01935426271
**Web:** www.yeovilperciision.co.uk
**Reg No:** 6203909 **Estd:** 2007 Private Limited Company
**Line of Business:** Base metal industries
**Issued Capital:** £580,000
**Director:** S Murray
**Co. Secretary:** Steven Docherty
**Responsibilities**
**Engineering:** Michelle Tuck *(Production Assistant)*, Des Wilson *(Production Manager)*
**US SIC:** 3325, 7397
**UK SIC:** 31110, 83702

| | 31-03-14 | 31-03-13 | 31-03-12 |
|---|---|---|---|
| TA | 2,752,430 | 3,666,079 | 3,182,768 |
| NW | 834,706 | 1,456,384 | 1,189,584 |
| WC | 668,410 | 410,267 | 418,954 |

DUNS 77-010-6581
## Yes/No Productions Ltd
The Old Market, Upper Market Street, Hove, East Sussex BN3 1AS
**Tel:** 01273-711151 **Fax:** 01273-737538
**Web:** www.yesnoproductions.co.uk
**Reg No:** 2660520 **Estd:** 2011 Private Limited Company
**Line of Business:** Film production services and studios
**Export Sales:** £3,537,359
**Issued Capital:** £2
**Directors:** W L Cresswell, Ms L Mcnicholas
**Co. Secretary:** Stephen Mc Nicholas
**Responsibilities**
**Senior:** Loretta Sacco *(joint managing director)*
**Marketing:** Loretta Sacco *(joint managing director)*
**US SIC:** 7819, 7922
**UK SIC:** 97111, 97412
**Auditors:** Victor Boorman & Co
**Bankers:** Allied Irish Bank (gb) (23-83-95)

| | 31-12-13 | 31-12-12 | 31-12-11 |
|---|---|---|---|
| TO | 7,443,858 | 7,153,051 | 7,059,458 |
| P/L | 276,902 | 615,446 | 672,568 |
| NW | 4,897,520 | 5,267,328 | 4,760,890 |
| WC | 3,653,006 | 3,657,779 | 3,105,061 |
| Emp. | 54 | 25 | 9 |

DUNS 21-752-8188
## YeS2 Ltd
**(Subsidiary of:** Vasanta Group Holdings Ltd)
K House Sheffield Business Park, Europa Link, Sheffield, South Yorkshire S9 1XU
**Tel:** 0845 108 1888 **Fax:** 0845 108 1889
**Web:** www.yes2solutions.com
**Reg No:** 7829258 **Estd:** 2011 Private Limited Company
**Line of Business:** Business services
**Trading Style:** Gb Office Group
**Issued Capital:** £1
**Directors:** A P Gale, S Haworth, A Butler, R R Baldrey
**Branches:** YES2 Ltd, The Genesis Centre, North Staffs Business Centre, Innovation Way, Stoke-On-Trent, Staffordshire ST6 4BF
**US SIC:** 7399 **UK SIC:** 83954

| | 31-12-13 | 31-01-13 |
|---|---|---|
| TO | 7,531,000 | 10,535,891 |
| P/L | (629,000) | (2,685,574) |
| NW | (2,298,000) | (3,927,174) |
| WC | 314,000 | (2,940,203) |
| Emp. | 59 | 65 |

DUNS 21-960-1858
## Yew Holdings Ltd
**(Subsidiary of:** Dignity Plc)
Grovehill Road, Beverley, North Humberside HU17 0JJ
**Tel:** 01482882537
**Reg No:** 6141773 **Estd:** 2007 Private Limited Company
**Line of Business:** Funeral services
**Issued Capital:** £118
**Directors:** A R Davies, R H Portman, S L Whittern, M K Mccollum
**Co. Secretary:** Richard Portman
**US SIC:** 7261 **UK SIC:** 98902
**Auditors:** PricewaterhouseCoopers LLP

| | 27-12-13 | 25-01-13 | 31-12-12 |
|---|---|---|---|
| TO | 2,360,989 | 15,146,798 | 30,243,401 |
| P/L | 26,392,608 | 1,230,234 | 1,833,745 |
| NW | 33,723,356 | (2,548,630) | (11,093,951) |
| WC | 33,723,356 | (24,487,487) | (31,919,484) |
| Emp. | 114 | 202 | 199 |

DUNS 21-787-7946
## Yew Tree Care Centre
Yew Tree Avenue, Redcar, Cleveland TS10 4QG
**Tel:** 01642489480
**Web:** www.yewtree-care.co.uk
**Estd:** 2011 Proprietorship
**Line of Business:** Other human health activities
**Proprietor:** Ms N Melling
**Responsibilities**
**Senior:** Maureen Mclean *(Care Manager)*
**US SIC:** 8091 **UK SIC:** 95200
**Employees:** 80

DUNS 22-265-0447
## Yew Tree Care Ltd
North End Road, Arundel, West Sussex BN18 0DU
**Tel:** 02085592995 **Fax:** 02085449682
**Web:** www.churchfieldscare.co.uk
**Reg No:** 4283031 **Estd:** 1901 Private Limited Company
**Line of Business:** Other human health activities
**Issued Capital:** £10,000
**Director:** R K Patel
**Co. Secretary:** Mrs Laxmi Patel
**US SIC:** 8091 **UK SIC:** 95200
**Auditors:** Sterling
**Bankers:** Barclays Bank Plc (20-24-61)

| | 31-03-14 | 31-03-13 | 31-03-12 |
|---|---|---|---|
| TA | 1,590,322 | 1,837,730 | 1,795,910 |
| NW | (179,099) | (200,792) | (386,771) |
| WC | (164,179) | (78,988) | (198,368) |

DUNS 21-781-7187
## Yew Tree Community School
Alcester Street, Chadderton, Oldham, Lancashire OL9 8LD
**Tel:** 01612845464
**Estd:** 1965 Proprietorship
**Line of Business:** Schools (local authority)
**Proprietor:** Mrs M Buckley
**US SIC:** 8211 **UK SIC:** 93200
**Employees:** 104

DUNS 29-511-3930
## Yh Training Services Ltd
37-39 Falsgrave Road, Scarborough, North Yorkshire YO12 5EA
**Tel:** 08005422848
**Web:** www.yh-group.co.uk
**Reg No:** 1874612 **VAT No:** 390399225
**Estd:** 1984 Private Limited Company
**Line of Business:** Training providers
**Issued Capital:** £1,705
**Principals:** F H Mcmahon *(Managing)*, S L Mcmahon, Ms C P Mcmahon
**Co. Secretary:** Ms Samantha Crosier
**Responsibilities**
**Senior:** Jean Schneider *(Branch Manager)*
**HR:** Joanne Sellers *(Employee Development Manager)*
**Branches:** Yh Training Services Ltd, Dunslow Ct, Scarborough, North Yorkshire YO11 3XT
**US SIC:** 8299, 8999
**UK SIC:** 93300, 83954
**Auditors:** Ingham & Co
**Bankers:** Barclays Bank Plc (20-75-92)

| | 31-07-13 | 31-07-12 | 31-07-11 |
|---|---|---|---|
| TA | 1,166,508 | 1,047,574 | 979,238 |
| NW | 440,968 | 326,526 | 275,120 |
| WC | 69,594 | 1,333 | (39,402) |

DUNS 28-832-4775
## Yha (England & Wales)
Trevelyan House, Matlock, Derbyshire DE4 3YH
**Web:** www.yha.org.uk
**Reg No:** 0282555 **VAT No:** 598385666
**Estd:** 1930 Private Company Limited By Guarantee
**Line of Business:** Hostels
**Directors:** J F Templeton, H W Alcock, Ms N J Scrivings, V Talwar, R Pugh, P Shearman, Ms H J Maurice-Jones, Dr N Cornelius
**Co. Secretary:** Ms Caroline White
**Responsibilities**
**Senior:** Lindsey Fairbrother *(Director)*, Anthony Gaines *(Director)*, Nicholas Hardwick *(Director)*, Harry Horton *(Director)*, Ian Maginnis *(Director)*, Patricia Mckenna *(Director)*, Margo Muris *(Director)*, Josephine Murray *(Director)*, Paula Yates *(Director)*
**Marketing:** Joe Lynch *(Director of Sales, Marketing a)*
**Sales:** Jamie Hutchinson *(Sales Manager)*, Joe Lynch *(Director of Sales, Marketing a)*
**IT:** Glynn Steers *(Technical Services Director)*
**HR:** Karen Shotbolt *(People Director)*
**Facilities:** Jake Chalmers *(Director of Property)*
**Branches:** Yha (England & Wales), Holland House Holland Park, London W8 6LU
**US SIC:** 7021, 7011
**UK SIC:** 66500
**Auditors:** Grant Thornton U K LLP
**Bankers:** Barclays Bank Plc (20-39-07)

| | 28-02-14 | 28-02-13 | 29-02-12 |
|---|---|---|---|
| TO | 45,233,000 | 44,094,000 | 45,436,000 |
| P/L | 1,369,000 | 1,181,000 | 1,028,000 |
| NW | 45,055,000 | 44,252,000 | 42,993,000 |
| WC | (9,218,000) | (6,626,000) | (8,960,000) |
| Emp. | 1,228 | 1,148 | 1,184 |

DUNS 34-716-2310 **Imp**
## Yianis Fscr Ltd
**(Subsidiary of:** Yianis Holdings Ltd)
46 Westferry Circus, London E14 8RS
**Tel:** 02075101999 **Fax:** 020 7510-1998
**Web:** www.fourseasons.com
**Reg No:** 5519934 **Estd:** 2003 Private Limited Company
**Line of Business:** Hotels
**Trading Style:** Four Seasons Hotel Canary Wharf
**Issued Capital:** £2
**Directors:** L Hadjiioannou, Y T Christodoulou
**Co. Secretary:** Richard Short
**Responsibilities**
**Senior:** Lynn Broutman *(General Manager)*, Michael Patel *(General Manager)*
**Finance:** John Kentish-Barnes *(Financial Director)*
**Marketing:** Andrew Pert *(Marketing Director)*
**IT:** Kalayan Ramam *(IT Manager)*
**HR:** Barbara Kentish Barnes *(Training Manager)*
**Health & Safety:** Eric Ramlot *(Security Manager)*
**Operations:** Eric Ramlot *(Security Manager)*
**US SIC:** 7011 **UK SIC:** 66500
**Auditors:** Langley Group LLP

| | 30-04-14 | 30-04-13 | 30-04-12 |
|---|---|---|---|
| TO | 12,655,490 | 12,592,198 | 12,292,197 |
| P/L | (1,540,843) | (1,598,743) | (1,569,298) |
| NW | (10,773,772) | (9,232,929) | (7,634,186) |
| WC | (9,713,875) | (10,349,214) | (8,740,173) |
| Emp. | 157 | 146 | 146 |

DUNS 21-094-3929
## Yiewsley Health Centre
28 High Street, West Drayton, Middlesex UB7 7DP
**Web:** www.rosedalelighting.com
**Estd:** 1994 Partnership
**Line of Business:** Chemists dispensing
**Trading Style:** Yiewsley Family Practice
**Partners:** Dr G F Chana, Dr I Raj
**Responsibilities**
**Senior:** Devinder Virdee *(Proprietor)*
**US SIC:** 8091 **UK SIC:** 95200
**Employees:** 87

DUNS 21-614-1465
## Yjl Infrastructure Ltd
**(Subsidiary of:** Renew Holdings Plc.)
39 Cornhill, London EC3V 3ND
**Tel:** 02075223220
**Web:** www.amco-construction.co.uk
**Reg No:** 0649330 **Estd:** 1960 Private Limited Company
**Line of Business:** Construction of commercial buildings
**Trading Style:** Amco Construction
**Issued Capital:** £600,000
**Directors:**
Renew Corporate Director Limited, B W May
**Co. Secretary:** Lovell Nominees Limited
**US SIC:** 1541, 1799
**UK SIC:** 50100, 50000
**Auditors:** KPMG Audit Plc
**Bankers:** Barclays Bank Plc (20-00-30)

| | 30-09-14 | 30-09-13 | 30-09-12 |
|---|---|---|---|
| TO | N/A | 213,000 | 7,459,000 |
| P/L | 29,000 | (14,000) | 1,407,000 |
| NW | 654,000 | 625,000 | 746,000 |
| WC | 654,000 | 625,000 | 750,000 |

DUNS 21-091-1087 **Imp-Exp**

## Ykk (U.K.) Ltd

**(Subsidiary of:** Ykk Corporation)
Whitehouse Industrial Estate, Runcorn, Cheshire WA7 3BW
**Tel:** 01928593800
**Web:** www.ykkfastening.com
**Reg No:** 0893599 **VAT No:** 577541117
**Estd:** 1966 Private Limited Company
**Line of Business:** Manufacturers of slide fasteners
**Export Markets:** Worldwide
**Issued Capital:** £1,000,000
**Directors:** P T Byrne, N Igarashi
**Responsibilities**
**Senior:** Tony Reillt *(Manager)*
**IT:** Graham Lewtas *(IT Manager)*
**Operations:** Robbie Wright *(Maintenance Manager)*
**Engineering:** Robbie Wright *(Maintenance Manager)*
**Branches:** Ykk (U.k.) Ltd, 340 Aston Lane South, Runcorn, Cheshire WA7 3BW
**US SIC:** 3452 **UK SIC:** 31371
**Auditors:** Ernst & Young LLP
**Bankers:** Barclays Bank Plc (20-77-67)

| | 31-03-14 | 31-03-13 | 31-03-12 |
|---|---|---|---|
| TO | 21,058,242 | 18,112,602 | 17,130,285 |
| P/L | 1,541,400 | 1,312,690 | 950,380 |
| NW | 4,047,981 | 4,662,382 | 3,923,789 |
| WC | 7,022,851 | 5,423,944 | 4,976,937 |
| Emp. | 97 | 81 | 81 |

DUNS 64-116-3415

## Ymca Black Country Group

38 Carters Green, West Bromwich, West Midlands B70 9LG
**Tel:** 0121 524 1950
**Web:** www.wbymca.org.uk
**Reg No:** 4116412 **Estd:** 2000 Private Unlimited Company
**Line of Business:** Other tourist or short-stay accommodation
**Directors:** Ms C Taylor, G M Stonyer, Mrs H M Bloxham, J S Oakley, T Palfreyman, M A Fussell, E S Moore, Ms B M Moore
**Co. Secretary:** Stephen Clay
**Responsibilities**
**Senior:** Manjit Poonia *(Director)*
**Marketing:** Stephen Bavington *(Marketing Manager)*
**HR:** Natalie Gilliland *(Human Resources Manager)*
**Health & Safety:** Michael Rossington *(Health & Safety Officer)*
**US SIC:** 7021, 7379, 8249
**UK SIC:** 66500, 83940, 93300
**Auditors:** Mazars LLP
**Bankers:** National Westminster Bank Plc (01-09-31)

| | 31-03-14 | 31-03-13 | 31-03-12 |
|---|---|---|---|
| TO | 5,537,828 | 5,349,353 | 5,534,057 |
| P/L | 178,559 | 253,527 | 93,705 |
| NW | 6,928,772 | 5,769,514 | 5,402,537 |
| WC | 2,743,467 | 2,333,086 | 2,010,003 |
| Emp. | 219 | 230 | 231 |

DUNS 23-563-3992

## Ymca Cambridgeshire & Peterborough

Queen Anne House, Gonville Place, Cambridge, Cambridgeshire CB1 1ND
**Tel:** 01223-356998
**Web:** www.theymca.org.uk
**Reg No:** 3561613 **Estd:** 1998 Private Unlimited Company
**Line of Business:** Activities of religious organisations
**Directors:** A Chandler, I M Dow, Ms M Sanders, Mrs J S Inman, Mrs A Pauling, Ms A K Maclean, E N Cappitt
**Co. Secretary:** Neil Portor
**Responsibilities**
**Senior:** Martin Forbes *(Manager)*, Robert Higginbottom *(Manager)*, Elizabeth Mather *(Manager)*
**US SIC:** 8661, 7999
**UK SIC:** 96600, 97913
**Auditors:** Deloitte & Touche
**Bankers:** Lloyds TSB Bank plc (30-13-55)

| | 31-03-14 | 31-03-13 | 31-03-12 |
|---|---|---|---|
| TO | 3,025,981 | 2,865,222 | 2,987,325 |
| P/L | 247,398 | 403,901 | 199,359 |
| NW | 3,457,405 | 3,210,007 | 2,806,106 |
| WC | 2,091,628 | 1,950,846 | 1,888,242 |
| Emp. | 71 | 66 | 75 |

DUNS 77-958-4127

## Ymca Derbyshire.

London Road, Alvaston, Derby, Derbyshire DE24 8UT
**Tel:** 01332579550
**Web:** www.ymcaderbyshire.org.uk
**Reg No:** 3061837 **Estd:** 1995 Private Limited Company
**Line of Business:** Hostels
**Trading Style:** Y M C A Derbyshire
**Directors:** D J Greatorex, Mrs M A Gordon, R J Swainson, Mrs H C Disney, Mrs E J Fothergill, D J Ayling, A P Trenier, Mrs H M Wigglesworth
**Co. Secretary:** Mrs Gillian Sewell
**Responsibilities**
**Senior:** Graham Ashurst *(Manager)*, Oliver Charles *(Manager)*, Andrew Flack *(Director)*, Peter Posner *(Director)*, David smith *(finance director)*
**Finance:** David smith *(finance director)*
**US SIC:** 7021, 5812, 8249, 8321
**UK SIC:** 66500, 66110, 93300, 96111
**Auditors:** Weeks Rhodes & Co
**Bankers:** National Westminster Bank Plc (60-12-01)

| | 31-03-14 | 31-03-13 | 31-03-12 |
|---|---|---|---|
| TO | 2,330,000 | 3,260,000 | 2,917,000 |
| P/L | (30,000) | 135,000 | 100,000 |
| NW | 1,794,000 | 1,812,000 | 1,677,000 |
| WC | 658,000 | 825,000 | 643,000 |
| Emp. | 96 | 106 | 105 |

DUNS 23-862-1747

## Ymca Downslink Group

17 Marmion Road, Hove, East Sussex BN3 5FS
**Tel:** 01273731724
**Web:** www.sussexcentralymca.org.uk
**Reg No:** 3853734 **Estd:** 1919 Private Company Limited By Guarantee
**Line of Business:** Social work activities
**Directors:** A Wilson, J A Slater, Mrs D A Pepper, Mrs I Beatty, S J Stokes, J R Lister, R D Nerurkar, P C Jeffrey
**Co. Secretary:** Peter Brayne
**Responsibilities**
**Senior:** Peter Mcmahon *(Director)*, Richard Smillie *(Director)*
**Branches:** Ymca Downslink Group, 10-12 Goldstone Villas, Hove, East Sussex BN3 3RF
**US SIC:** 7399, 8699
**UK SIC:** 83954, 96902
**Auditors:** Clark Brownscombe
**Bankers:** The Royal Bank Of Scotland Plc (16-14-24)

| | 31-03-14 | 31-03-13 | 31-03-12 |
|---|---|---|---|
| TO | 8,872,914 | 7,532,571 | 6,608,535 |
| P/L | (104,252) | 1,407,834 | 120,189 |
| NW | 3,176,054 | 3,280,963 | 1,169,398 |
| WC | (561,125) | (335,392) | (291,212) |
| Emp. | 303 | 285 | 327 |

DUNS 42-349-0577

## Ymca Fairthorne Group

Fairthorne Manor, Curdridge, Southampton, Hampshire SO30 2GH
**Tel:** 01489785228
**Web:** www.ymca-fg.org
**Reg No:** 4336719 **Estd:** 2001 Private Company Limited By Guarantee
**Line of Business:** Outdoor leisure pursuit organisers and equipment
**Trading Style:** Ymca Fairthorne Manor
**Directors:** Mrs C J Hillier, M B Morrall, M H Cranston, Professor W A Couchman, Ms A Smith, C R Carnegy, Ms S J Littlemore, Dr C Laws
**Co. Secretary:** Christopher Hand
**Responsibilities**
**Senior:** Sheila Clark *(Director)*, Ian Creek *(Director)*, Malcolm Hogg *(Manager)*, Craig Philbrick *(Manager)*, Michael Tilbury *(Manager)*
**US SIC:** 8699 **UK SIC:** 96902
**Auditors:** BDO Stoy Hayward LLP
**Bankers:** Barclays Bank Plc (20-69-34)

| | 31-12-13 | 31-12-12 | 31-12-11 |
|---|---|---|---|
| TO | 6,664,960 | 6,281,258 | 6,182,309 |
| P/L | (70,770) | 8,668 | 55,586 |
| NW | 7,504,226 | 7,824,996 | 7,816,327 |
| WC | 154,608 | 694,188 | 724,644 |
| Emp. | 297 | 290 | 280 |

DUNS 77-485-3964

## Ymca London South West

St James House, Surbiton, Surrey KT6 4QH
**Tel:** 020-8399-5427
**Web:** www.ymca.org.uk
**Reg No:** 2971930 **Estd:** 1994 Private Company Limited By Guarantee
**Line of Business:** Hostels
**Directors:** Ms T E Ray, A D Worthington, A J May, Mrs V A Hancock, Dr I D Beith, S C Tanner, M J Parker, Ms H E Jones
**Co. Secretary:** Stuart Leamy
**Responsibilities**
**Senior:** Debbie Camp *(Manager)*, Caroline Chalke *(Manager)*, Jean Fogg *(Manager)*, William Holland *(Manager)*
**Branches:** Ymca London South West, Lower Ham Road, Kingston Upon Thames, Surrey KT2 5BH
**US SIC:** 7021, 7999, 8661
**UK SIC:** 66500, 97913, 96600
**Auditors:** PKF (UK) LLP
**Bankers:** The Co-Operative Bank Plc (83-91-26)

| | 31-03-14 | 31-03-13 | 31-03-12 |
|---|---|---|---|
| TO | 9,307,015 | 8,745,143 | 8,394,122 |
| P/L | 319,741 | 349,906 | 54,088 |
| NW | 9,028,877 | 8,784,145 | 8,326,444 |
| WC | 2,216,615 | 672,549 | 1,302,378 |
| Emp. | 208 | 371 | 358 |

DUNS 29-864-3529

## Ymca Norfolk

35-37 Exchange Street, Norwich, Norfolk NR2 1LP
**Web:** www.ymca-norfolk.org.uk
**Reg No:** 2067523 **Estd:** 1986 Private Limited Company
**Line of Business:** Other tourist or short-stay accommodation
**Directors:** Ms A B Aves, R W Pennington, Ms C M Hutchinson, P G Macdonald, F P Harmer, J E Shelton, M J Aust, Ms R J Gascoyne-Richards
**Co. Secretary:** Tim Sweeting
**Responsibilities**
**Senior:** Doreen Betts *(Manager)*, Rosemary English *(Manager)*, Kay Fisher *(Director)*, Donna Kitchen *(Operations Manager)*, Julie Oaks *(Manager)*, John Rockliff *(Board Member)*
**Finance:** Susie Knights *(Fundraising Manager)*, Diane Page *(Head of Finance)*
**Sales:** Jason Beattie *(Business Development Director)*
**IT:** Peter Atthill *(ICT Manager)*
**Facilities:** Abigail Canham *(Head of Housing)*, Dean Hazell *(Facilities Manager)*
**US SIC:** 7021 **UK SIC:** 66500
**Auditors:** Larking Gowen
**Bankers:** Barclays Bank Plc (20-62-53)

| | 30-03-14 | 31-03-13 | 01-03-12 |
|---|---|---|---|
| TO | 3,373,019 | 3,185,498 | 3,381,110 |
| P/L | 450,644 | (119,885) | 97,077 |
| NW | 2,779,994 | 1,977,725 | 2,097,610 |
| WC | 671,021 | 501,601 | 720,196 |
| Emp. | 83 | 92 | 93 |

DUNS 77-139-9185

## Ymca North Tyneside

3rd Floor Ymca Building, Church Way, North Shields, Tyne and Wear NE29 0AB
**Tel:** 01916432298
**Web:** www.northtynesidecarers.org.uk
**Reg No:** 2703063 **Estd:** 1995 Private Company Limited By Guarantee
**Line of Business:** Charities and charitable organisations
**Directors:** J Smith, J W Hawksworth, S J Clark, I Pearson, D Hodgson, S J Mckinlay, R Ariss, Mrs L Stewart
**Co. Secretary:** Dean Titterton
**Responsibilities**
**Senior:** Douglas Bailey *(Director)*, Claire Easton *(Centre Manager)*, Pamela Groom *(Manager)*, Zena Lethbridge *(Manager)*, Johanne Mears *(Manager)*, Deborah Shearer *(Director)*
**US SIC:** 4899 **UK SIC:** 79020
**Auditors:** Rowlands
**Bankers:** Lloyds TSB Bank plc (30-96-15)

| | 31-03-14 | 31-03-13 | 31-03-12 |
|---|---|---|---|
| TO | 959,061 | 1,071,739 | 1,046,466 |
| P/L | (112,404) | (134,625) | (65,659) |
| NW | 4,786,320 | 4,901,941 | 5,039,794 |
| WC | (183,612) | 148,345 | 293,020 |
| Emp. | 52 | 57 | 56 |

DUNS 23-865-0639

## Ymca Thames Gateway (South) Ltd

Round House, Overy Street, Dartford, Kent DA1 1UP
**Tel:** 01322282030 **Fax:** 01322-294798
**Web:** www.ymcathamesgateway.org.uk
**Reg No:** 3856563 **Estd:** 1883 Private Limited Company
**Line of Business:** Technical and vocational secondary education
**Trading Style:** Dartford Y.M.C.A Nursery
**Directors:** N Fenton, K F Moore, A G Hilton, Mrs A S Ojo, A R Bassam, P Larmond, D J Thomas, Mrs K L Dudley
**Co. Secretary:** Kenneth Moore
**Responsibilities**
**Senior:** Denise Hattons *(Manager)*, Geoff Rofe *(Director)*
**HR:** Alison Costello *(Human Resources Officer)*
**US SIC:** 8249, 8321, 8999
**UK SIC:** 93300, 96111, 83954
**Auditors:** Hedley Dunk

| | 31-03-14 | 31-03-13 | 31-03-12 |
|---|---|---|---|
| TO | 1,514,189 | 1,537,934 | 2,106,547 |
| P/L | (58,685) | (371,914) | (640,227) |
| NW | 2,841,024 | 2,899,709 | 3,271,623 |
| WC | (156,432) | (422,021) | (194,755) |
| Emp. | 95 | 84 | 87 |

DUNS 42-391-4451

## Ymca Training

55 High Street, Banbury, Oxfordshire OX16 5JJ
**Web:** www.ymcatraining.org.uk
**Reg No:** 4379109 **Estd:** 2002 Private Company Limited By Guarantee
**Line of Business:** Technical and vocational secondary education
**Directors:** Ms P Campbell, D H Bennison, A P Smith, R A Hayward, P G Rogerson, Ms S R Morton
**Co. Secretary:** Andrew Chesters
**Responsibilities**
**Senior:** Clive Bodley *(board memeber)*, Jane Burns *(board member)*, Jean Fogg *(board member)*, Susan Hammond *(Manager)*, Andrew Haxell *(Manager)*, Ann Lindsey *(Chief Executive)*
**Branches:** Ymca Training, Brookfield House, 193-195 Wallington Road South, Stockport, Cheshire SK2 6NG
**US SIC:** 8249, 8661
**UK SIC:** 93300, 96600
**Auditors:** Baker Tilly UK Audit LLP
**Bankers:** Barclays Bank Plc (20-00-00)

| | 31-03-14 | 31-03-13 | 31-03-12 |
|---|---|---|---|
| TO | 11,456,000 | 13,608,000 | 14,545,000 |
| P/L | (3,899,000) | 188,000 | (2,647,000) |
| NW | (3,184,000) | 715,000 | 527,000 |
| WC | (3,250,000) | 1,332,000 | 998,000 |
| Emp. | 367 | 371 | 466 |

DUNS 77-744-1676

## Ymca Wolverhampton

29-31 Temple Street, Wolverhampton, West Midlands WV2 4AN
**Tel:** 01902371550
**Web:** www.ymca-wolverhampton.co.uk
**Reg No:** 3012233 **Estd:** 1995 Private Limited Company
**Line of Business:** Non-charitable social work activities with accommodation
**Directors:** G M Stonyer, Mrs D R Walton, T Palfreyman, J S Oakley, P W Walker, J R Rowe, E S Moore, Mrs H M Bloxham
**Co. Secretary:** Stephen Clay
**Responsibilities**
**Senior:** Manjit Poonia *(Director)*, Pauline Tomlinson *(Acting Chief Executive)*
**Finance:** Jill Law *(Head of Finance)*
**Branches:** Ymca Wolverhampton, Aelfgar House, Church Street, Rugeley, Staffordshire WS15 2WH
**US SIC:** 8321, 8249
**UK SIC:** 96111, 93300
**Auditors:** Muras Baker Jones & Co
**Bankers:** Barclays Bank Plc (20-97-78)

| | 31-03-14 | 31-03-13 | 31-03-12 |
|---|---|---|---|
| TO | 2,053,749 | 2,221,497 | 2,625,645 |
| P/L | (3,238) | (45,763) | (61,112) |
| NW | 1,680,576 | 1,683,814 | 1,729,577 |
| WC | 1,298,214 | 1,237,804 | 1,117,584 |
| Emp. | 96 | 110 | 98 |

DUNS 85-612-0050

## Ymddiriedolaeth Gofalwyr Gogledd Cymru - Gwasanaethau Gofal Croe

Heritage Gate, Abergele Road, Colwyn Bay, Clwyd LL29 8BW
**Tel:** 01492546143
**Web:** www.nwcrossroads.org.uk
**Reg No:** 6205600 **Estd:** 2007 Private Company Limited By Guarantee
**Line of Business:** Social work activities without accommodation
**Directors:** D Brydon, E L Gibson, Mrs H P Stevens, J A Rees, Ms R Jones
**Co. Secretary:** Mrs Alison Jones
**US SIC:** 8321 **UK SIC:** 96111
**Bankers:** National Westminster Bank Plc (60-17-30)

| | 31-03-14 | 31-03-13 | 31-03-12 |
|---|---|---|---|
| TO | 521,689 | 528,362 | 563,820 |
| P/L | (24,113) | (8,032) | (129,241) |
| NW | 217,815 | 241,928 | 249,960 |
| WC | 217,815 | 240,466 | 247,036 |
| Emp. | 49 | 53 | 65 |

DUNS 21-592-7277

## Yo Sushi

Coventry Street, London W1D 7DH
**Tel:** 02074342724
**Web:** www.yosushi.co.uk
**Estd:** 2000
**Line of Business:** Restaurant - japanese
**Proprietor:** C Czyz
**Responsibilities**
**Senior:** Warren Bailey *(Manager)*
**US SIC:** 5812 **UK SIC:** 66110
**Employees:** 49

DUNS 77-537-9613

## Yo Sushi Uk Ltd

**(Subsidiary of:** Quilvest Sa)
95 Farringdon Road, London EC1R 3BT
**Tel:** 02078410700
**Web:** www.yosushi.com
**Reg No:** 2994470 **Estd:** 1994 Private Limited Company
**Line of Business:** Licensed restaurants
**Export Sales:** £893,553
**Trading Style:** Yo Below
**Issued Capital:** £1,000
**Directors:** A M Campbell, V Hall, Ms A Vickers, R Rowland
**Co. Secretary:** Andrew Campbell
**Responsibilities**
**IT:** Billy Waters *(IT Manager)*
**Branches:** Yo Sushi Uk Ltd, 1 Fulham Broadway, London SW6 1AA
**US SIC:** 5812 **UK SIC:** 66110

**Auditors:** Rees Pollock
**Bankers:** National Westminster Bank Plc (60-12-13)

| | 01-12-13 | 25-11-12 | 27-12-11 |
|---|---|---|---|
| TO | 71,046,785 | 62,628,343 | 57,672,805 |
| P/L | 4,693,872 | 2,193,366 | 3,882,420 |
| NW | 20,714,700 | 15,858,708 | 13,242,176 |
| WC | 14,217,878 | 8,452,680 | 5,661,144 |
| Emp. | 1,614 | 1,531 | 1,549 |

DUNS 55-072-1815
## Yoakley House
Yoakley House, St Peters Road, Margate, Kent CT9 4AN
**Web:** www.michaelyoakley.co.uk
**Estd:** 1981
**Line of Business:** Residential care establishments
**Principals:** Mrs P Heigham *(Chairman)*, Mrs S Piper *(Manager)*
**Responsibilities**
**Senior:** Julie Wickenden *(Manager)*
**US SIC:** 8699, 8321
**UK SIC:** 96902, 96111
**Employees:** 52

DUNS 73-947-4786
## Yodel Delivery Network Ltd
(**Subsidiary of:** Yodel Distribution Holdings Ltd)
(It Department Only), Atlantic Pavilion, Albert Dock, Liverpool, Merseyside L3 4AE
**Tel:** 01513008644 **Fax:** 01925812273
**Web:** www.myyodel.co.uk
**Reg No:** 5200072 **Estd:** 2010 Private Limited Company
**Line of Business:** Freight transport by road not elsewhere classified
**Trading Style:** Hdnl, Yodel
**Issued Capital:** £484,000,000
**Directors:** N A Lloyd, R Stead, M Seal, P L Peters, H M Barclay, R J Neal, A S Barclay, K Basnett
**Co. Secretary:** March Secretarial Services Limit
**Responsibilities**
**Senior:** Bryan Gaunt *(Manager)*, Tony McVeigh *(Manager)*
**HR:** Simon Kettle *(Training Manager)*
**Health & Safety:** Campbell Fitch *(Health & Safety Director)*
**Branches:** Yodel Delivery Network Ltd, 3 Barnes Wallis Road, Fareham, Hampshire PO15 5ST
**US SIC:** 7399, 4789
**UK SIC:** 83954, 77002
**Auditors:** Deloitte LLP

| | 30-06-13 | 30-06-12 | 30-06-11 |
|---|---|---|---|
| TO | 379,024,000 | 535,142,000 | 723,563,000 |
| P/L | (98,297,000) | (66,937,000) | (131,836,000) |
| NW | 33,798,000 | 77,379,000 | (163,000) |
| WC | (7,041,000) | 22,584,000 | (5,047,000) |
| Emp. | 4,545 | 7,090 | 10,907 |

DUNS 52-533-1765
## Yodel Ltd
Unit 20 Ffordd Maelgwyn, Tremarl Industrial Estate, Llandudno Junction, Gwynedd LL31 9PN
**Tel:** 01604766423
**Reg No:** 3237701 **Estd:** 1996 Private Limited Company
**Line of Business:** Freight transport by road not elsewhere classified
**Issued Capital:** £1,000
**Branches:** Yodel Ltd, 2 Bertha Park View, Perth, Perthshire PH1 3JE
**US SIC:** 7399 **UK SIC:** 83954

| | 31-12-12 | 31-12-11 | 31-12-10 |
|---|---|---|---|
| TA | 73,307 | 38,729 | 33,687 |
| NW | 16,447 | 15,626 | 9,604 |
| WC | 16,447 | 15,626 | 9,604 |

DUNS 73-595-8634
## Yodel Network Ltd
(**Subsidiary of:** Yodel Distribution Holdings Ltd)
First Floor, Skyways House, Speke Road, Liverpool, Merseyside L70 1AB
**Tel:** 08000830411 **Fax:** 0161-636-7475
**Reg No:** 4857082 **Estd:** 2003 Private Limited Company
**Line of Business:** Direct mail advertising services
**Issued Capital:** £1
**Directors:** March Company Director Limited, P L Peters
**Co. Secretary:** March Secretarial Services Limit
**Branches:** Yodel Network Ltd, 12th Floor Arndale Ho, Market St, Manchester M60 6EQ
**US SIC:** 7331 **UK SIC:** 83800

| | 30-06-13 | 30-06-12 | 30-06-11 |
|---|---|---|---|
| TA | 1 | 1 | 1 |
| NW | 1 | 1 | 1 |

DUNS 21-775-6300
## Yoden Care Complex
Hesleden Road, Blackhall Colliery, Hartlepool, Cleveland TS27 4LH
**Tel:** 01915860294
**Web:** www.countrywidecarehomes.co.uk
**Estd:** 2011 Proprietorship
**Line of Business:** Residential care establishments
**Proprietor:** Mrs M Garrett
**Responsibilities**
**Senior:** Maxine Lee *(Home Manager)*
**US SIC:** 8321 **UK SIC:** 96111
**Employees:** 70

DUNS 34-888-2866
## Yogo Group Ltd
Woodgate Studios 2 8, Games Road, Barnet, Hertfordshire EN4 9HN
**Tel:** 02089206626
**Web:** www.yogogroup.com
**Reg No:** 5686098 **Estd:** 2006 Private Limited Company
**Line of Business:** Management activities of construction holding companies
**Issued Capital:** £100
**Director:** G Philippou
**US SIC:** 6711 **UK SIC:** 83962

| | 31-03-13 | 31-03-12 | 31-03-11 |
|---|---|---|---|
| TA | 302 | 302 | 302 |
| NW | (7,905) | (7,005) | (5,145) |
| WC | (8,107) | (7,207) | (5,347) |

DUNS 29-824-8907 **Imp-Exp**
## Yokogawa United Kingdom Ltd
(**Subsidiary of:** Yokogawa Electric Corporation)
17 Stuart Road, Runcorn, Cheshire WA7 1TR
**Web:** www.yokogawa.co.uk
**Reg No:** 2042994 **VAT No:** 452965227
**Estd:** 1986 Private Limited Company
**Line of Business:** Control system equipment
**Export Markets:** Worldwide
**Export Sales:** £2,233,199
**Issued Capital:** £6,500,001
**Directors:** S M Rogers, H J Van Den Berg
**Co. Secretary:** Carl Ramsden
**Responsibilities**
**Senior:** William Groot *(Manager)*, Desmond Irvine *(Manager)*
**US SIC:** 3643, 5084
**UK SIC:** 34203, 61490
**Auditors:** Deloitte & Touche
**Bankers:** National Westminster Bank Plc (01-10-01)

| | 31-03-14 | 31-03-13 | 31-03-12 |
|---|---|---|---|
| TO | 25,045,867 | 22,624,886 | 17,484,443 |
| P/L | 694,075 | (354,055) | 461,478 |
| NW | 3,140,347 | 2,165,347 | (980,598) |
| WC | 1,602,159 | 597,951 | (2,435,449) |
| Emp. | 81 | 76 | 83 |

DUNS 64-102-2954 **Imp**
## Yoo Holdings Ltd
2 Bentinck Street, London W1U 2FA
**Tel:** 02070090100 **Fax:** 02070090200
**Web:** www.yoo.com
**Reg No:** 4505775 **Estd:** 2002 Private Limited Company
**Line of Business:** Management of real estate on a fee or contract basis
**Issued Capital:** £1,667
**Directors:** J S Johal, J Hitchcock, P Starck
**Co. Secretary:** Anthony Patel
**Responsibilities**
**Finance:** Ayodeji Oladehin *(Accountant)*, Kien Phu *(Project Accountant)*, Zoran Stepanovic *(Finance Controller)*
**Marketing:** Yvette Costi *(Marketing Manager)*, Jay Durnan *(Marketing Manager)*, Hannah Godwin *(Marketing Executive)*, Phillip Haller *(Chief Marketing Officer)*, Emma Hamilton *(Digital Marketing Manager)*
**Sales:** Rebecca Jaques *(Business Development Manager)*
**IT:** Wassim El Bizri *(IT Manager)*, Emma Hamilton *(Digital Marketing Manager)*
**US SIC:** 6531 **UK SIC:** 83400

| | 31-12-13 | 31-12-12 | 31-12-11 |
|---|---|---|---|
| TO | 10,739,807 | 13,947,653 | 9,136,995 |
| P/L | 911,237 | 1,864,074 | 572,856 |
| NW | 15,547,321 | 14,789,772 | 13,079,690 |
| WC | 17,472,115 | 15,716,105 | 11,964,475 |
| Emp. | 48 | 42 | 35 |

DUNS 76-722-6426
## Yoplait Uk Ltd
(**Subsidiary of:** Sodim Sas)
St Andrew's House, Esher, Surrey KT10 9TA
**Tel:** 01372-476000 **Fax:** 01372476111
**Web:** www.yoplait.co.uk
**Reg No:** 2597128 **VAT No:** 600354002
**Estd:** 1991 Private Limited Company
**Line of Business:** Non-specialised wholesale of food, beverages and tobacco
**Issued Capital:** £1
**Directors:** R Bouchier, O Faujour
**Responsibilities**
**Senior:** Stephane Dalyac *(Manager)*, Lucien Fa *(Chairman)*, StUphane Leconte *(Director)*, Emeline Mettania *(IT Manager)*
**IT:** Emeline Mettania *(IT Manager)*
**Purchasing:** Liz Edwards *(Supply Chain Manager)*
**Branches:** Yoplait Uk Ltd, 1 Copse Rd, Yeovil, Somerset BA22 8RN
**US SIC:** 5199, 5143
**UK SIC:** 61900, 61700
**Auditors:** Ernst & Young LLP
**Bankers:** National Westminster Bank Plc (60-10-33)

| | 30-04-14 | 30-04-13 | 30-04-12 |
|---|---|---|---|
| TO | 147,988,000 | 145,407,000 | 117,214,000 |
| P/L | 18,886,000 | 24,112,000 | 19,328,000 |
| NW | 16,475,000 | 13,720,000 | 12,323,000 |
| WC | 8,808,000 | 13,471,000 | 11,796,000 |
| Emp. | 54 | 47 | 46 |

DUNS 21-583-3160
## York & Albany
127-129 Parkway, London NW1 7PS
**Tel:** 02073875700
**Web:** www.gordonramsay.com
**Estd:** 2011 Proprietorship
**Line of Business:** Hotels
**Proprietor:** G Ramsay
**Responsibilities**
**Senior:** Ahmed Ameziane *(Manager)*, Jeremy Gibbs *(Manager)*, Lucy Sliwka *(Hotel Manager)*
**US SIC:** 7011 **UK SIC:** 66500
**Employees:** 80

DUNS 21-041-2049
## York Archaeological Trust
47 Aldwark, York, North Yorkshire YO1 7BX
**Tel:** 01904-663000
**Web:** www.iadb.co.uk
**Estd:** 1974 Proprietorship
**Line of Business:** Software consultancy and supply
**Proprietor:** P Nicholson
**Responsibilities**
**Senior:** Kevin Cockayne *(Manager)*, Ailsa Mainman *(Manager)*
**Finance:** Karen Bettsworth *(Human Resources Manager)*
**IT:** Jon Brownridge *(IT Manager)*
**HR:** Karen Bettsworth *(Human Resources Manager)*
**Operations:** David Aspden *(Operations & Contracts Manager)*
**Engineering:** Ian Milsted *(Field Officer)*
**US SIC:** 7379 **UK SIC:** 83940
**Employees:** 117

DUNS 28-913-1393
## York Archaeological Trust for Excavation & Research Ltd
Jorvik Viking Centre, York, North Yorkshire YO1 9WT
**Tel:** 01904615505
**Web:** www.jorvik-viking-centre.co.uk
**Reg No:** 1430801 **VAT No:** 433524666
**Estd:** 1984 Private Company Limited By Guarantee
**Line of Business:** Misc special bldg trade contractors
**Trading Style:** Jorvik Viking Centre
**Directors:** Professor S T Driscoll, M R Watson, T Suthers, A C Hall, Professor R K Morris, Ms E M Heaps, Ms H M Dobson, Dr D R Neave
**Co. Secretary:** Peter Nicholson
**Responsibilities**
**Senior:** Jean Hunter-Didrichsen *(Director)*, Graham Wilford *(Director)*
**Admin:** Rachel Acey *(Office Manager)*
**Branches:** York Archaeological Trust For Excavation & Research Ltd, St. Saviourgate, York, North Yorkshire YO1 8NN
**US SIC:** 1799, 7399, 8411
**UK SIC:** 50000, 83954, 97700
**Auditors:** Barron & Barron
**Bankers:** Barclays Bank Plc (20-99-56)

| | 31-03-14 | 31-03-13 | 31-03-12 |
|---|---|---|---|
| TO | 6,407,004 | 5,992,055 | 6,023,141 |
| P/L | (212,997) | (521,146) | (381,381) |
| NW | 2,093,374 | 1,978,946 | 2,572,178 |
| WC | 330,762 | 490,006 | 842,308 |
| Emp. | 158 | 163 | 146 |

DUNS 49-249-3838
## The York Brewery Co. Ltd.
(**Subsidiary of:** Mitchell's Brewery Ltd)
12 Toft Green, York, North Yorkshire YO1 6JT
**Tel:** 01904-621162 **Fax:** 01904-621216
**Web:** www.york-brewery.co.uk
**Reg No:** 3117802 **VAT No:** 647465703
**Estd:** 1995 Private Limited Company
**Line of Business:** Brewers
**Issued Capital:** £50,100
**Directors:** A M Barker, D Lowe, J R Barker, Ms J Hodge
**Co. Secretary:** David Lowe
**Branches:** The York Brewery Co. Ltd., 27 Colliergate, York, North Yorkshire YO1 8BN
**US SIC:** 2082 **UK SIC:** 42702
**Auditors:** Clive Owen & Co
**Bankers:** National Westminster Bank Plc (56-00-70)

| | 26-02-14 | 26-02-13 | 26-02-12 |
|---|---|---|---|
| TO | 4,100,000 | 3,443,000 | 3,252,000 |
| P/L | 169,000 | (46,000) | 229,000 |
| NW | 1,089,000 | 932,000 | 956,000 |
| WC | 464,000 | 277,000 | 282,000 |
| Emp. | 57 | 59 | 57 |

DUNS 45-871-8285
## York C E E Holdings Ltd
(**Subsidiary of:** Johnson Controls Inc.)
Waterberry Drive, Waterlooville, Hampshire PO7 7YH
**Tel:** 01268246000
**Reg No:** 3214234 **Estd:** 1996 Private Limited Company
**Line of Business:** Holding companies management activities
**Trading Style:** Johnson Controls Ltd
**Issued Capital:** £636,096
**Directors:** B Cadwallader, M Ayre
**US SIC:** 6711 **UK SIC:** 83962
**Auditors:** KPMG

| | 30-09-13 | 30-09-12 | 30-09-11 |
|---|---|---|---|
| TA | 35,951,000 | 35,641,000 | 2,476,000 |
| P/L | 1,032,000 | 33,161,000 | (2,000) |
| NW | 35,948,000 | 34,935,000 | 1,774,000 |
| WC | 35,933,000 | 34,920,000 | 403,000 |

DUNS 20 000 0004
## York Centre for Voluntary Service
15-17 Priory Street, York, North Yorkshire YO1 6ET
**Tel:** 01904639968
**Web:** www.ilsyork.org.uk
**Reg No:** 0493550 **Estd:** 1996 Private Limited Company
**Line of Business:** Pre school education
**Trading Style:** Priory Street Nursery
**Directors:** G L Collett, L P Lennox, G T Wood, Mrs S E Mason, Mrs A T Jessop, C J Welch, M Hick, Mrs A B Collins
**Co. Secretary:** Luke Barnett
**Responsibilities**
**Senior:** Kerry Fletcher *(Acting Manager)*, Charlotte Hall *(Manager)*, Roderick Peet *(Director)*
**Branches:** York Centre For Voluntary Service, 1 Brownlow St, York, North Yorkshire YO31 8LW
**US SIC:** 8211 **UK SIC:** 93200
**Auditors:** Creers
**Bankers:** National Westminster Bank Plc (56-00-70)

| | 31-03-14 | 31-03-13 | 31-03-12 |
|---|---|---|---|
| TO | 1,166,171 | 1,097,673 | 1,224,983 |
| P/L | (150,767) | (191,590) | 167,020 |
| NW | 1,571,678 | 1,691,306 | 1,831,782 |
| WC | 96,729 | 370,495 | 578,184 |
| Emp. | 45 | 73 | 39 |

DUNS 50-508-5506
## York Childcare Ltd
The Pavilion, York, North Yorkshire YO23 6NP
**Tel:** 01904409763
**Web:** www.yorkchildcare.co.uk
**Reg No:** 2476480 **Estd:** 1990 Private Company Limited By Guarantee
**Line of Business:** Creches
**Directors:** Mrs K Dean, Ms J L Armistead, Mrs C Harvey, Mrs S C Lawson, C H Jenkins, Ms J C Spittle
**Co. Secretary:** Christopher Jenkins
**Responsibilities**
**Senior:** Karen Mawson *(General Manager)*
**Branches:** York Childcare Ltd, Rawcliffe Lane, York, North Yorkshire YO30 6NP
**US SIC:** 8211, 6732
**UK SIC:** 93200, 83100
**Auditors:** Creers
**Bankers:** HSBC Bank plc (40-47-31)

| | 31-03-14 | 31-03-13 | 31-03-12 |
|---|---|---|---|
| TO | 1,005,552 | 976,330 | 928,674 |
| P/L | (36,462) | 14,237 | 3,661 |
| NW | 190,786 | 227,248 | 213,011 |
| WC | 74,074 | 112,475 | 102,578 |
| Emp. | 64 | 57 | 58 |

DUNS 56-938-5321
## York Conferences Ltd
Heslington Hall Heslington, York, North Yorkshire YO10 5DD
**Web:** www.yorkconferences.com
**Reg No:** 2838054 **Estd:** 1993 Private Limited Company
**Line of Business:** Retail sale in non-specialised stores with food, beverages or tobacco predominating
**Issued Capital:** £50,000
**Directors:** J M Greenwood, J C Lindley, Dr D J Duncan
**Co. Secretary:** Michael Slade
**US SIC:** 5411, 7011
**UK SIC:** 64100, 66500

**Bankers:** HSBC Bank plc (40-47-31)

| | 31-07-14 | 31-07-13 | 31-07-12 |
|---|---|---|---|
| TO | 9,283,106 | 8,420,971 | 4,587,017 |
| P/L | 1,109,347 | N/A | N/A |
| NW | 50,000 | 50,000 | 50,000 |
| WC | 50,000 | 50,000 | 50,000 |
| Emp. | 206 | 184 | 33 |

DUNS 21-582-5892

### York High School

Cornlands Road, York, North Yorkshire YO24 3WZ
**Tel:** 01904555500
**Web:** www.yorkhighschool.co.uk
**Estd:** 2011 Proprietorship
**Line of Business:** Education services
**Proprietor:** I Parnaby
**US SIC:** 8299 **UK SIC:** 93300
**Employees:** 130

DUNS 21-732-0951

### York House (Meat Products) Ltd

(**Subsidiary of:** York House Foods Ltd)
Shannon Place, Potton, Sandy, Bedfordshire SG19 2YH
**Tel:** 01767260114 **Fax:** 01767-262165
**Web:** www.yorkhousefoods.com
**Reg No:** 0992229 **VAT No:** 196261736
**Estd:** 1995 Private Limited Company
**Line of Business:** Meat wholesalers
**Export Sales:** £32,919
**Issued Capital:** £2,378
**Directors:** M N Pallister, I J Affleck
**Co. Secretary:** Trevor Michelson
**Responsibilities**
**Senior:** Clive Pattle *(Distribution Manager)*
**Marketing:** Paul Popham *(Business Development Manager)*
**Sales:** Chris Filus *(Sales Manager)*
**Health & Safety:** Clive Pattle *(Distribution Manager)*
**Engineering:** Dave Vince *(Chief Engineer)*
**Branches:** Manningtree
**US SIC:** 5147 **UK SIC:** 61700
**Auditors:** Baker Tilly UK Audit LLP
**Bankers:** Barclays Bank Plc (20-07-71)

| | 31-12-13 | 31-12-12 | 31-12-11 |
|---|---|---|---|
| TO | 23,355,191 | 23,887,150 | 21,225,983 |
| P/L | 1,109,565 | 1,006,063 | 1,570,720 |
| NW | 6,040,955 | 5,190,162 | 4,414,833 |
| WC | 4,799,374 | 4,033,079 | 3,385,266 |
| Emp. | 71 | 75 | 79 |

DUNS 21-309-9096 Exp

### York Linings International Ltd

(**Subsidiary of:** Cape Plc)
Millfield Industrial Estate, Wheldrake, York, North Yorkshire YO19 6NA
**Tel:** 01904449777 **Fax:** 01904-449888
**Web:** www.yorklinings.com
**Reg No:** 1159919 **Estd:** 1974 Private Limited Company
**Line of Business:** Engineers (general)
**Export Markets:** South Africa, Malta, Rumania & Norway
**Export Sales:** £1,477,000
**Issued Capital:** £100,000
**Directors:** Mrs V A George, M Hooper, S P Roberts
**Co. Secretary:** Richard Allan
**US SIC:** 6711, 1711
**UK SIC:** 83962, 50300
**Auditors:** Kay Johnson Gee
**Bankers:** Bank Of Scotland (12-16-30)

| | 31-12-13 | 31-12-12 | 31-12-11 |
|---|---|---|---|
| TO | 9,233,000 | 13,367,000 | 16,239,000 |
| P/L | (178,000) | 893,000 | 781,000 |
| NW | 1,745,000 | 2,397,000 | 3,008,000 |
| WC | 1,360,000 | 1,924,000 | 2,511,000 |
| Emp. | 83 | 122 | 111 |

DUNS 23-584-5935

### York Mailing Ltd

(**Subsidiary of:** York Mailing Group Ltd)
Airfield Industrial Estate, York Road, Elvington, York, North Yorkshire YO41 4AU
**Tel:** 01904-608050 **Fax:** 01904-608040
**Web:** www.yorkmailing.co.uk
**Reg No:** 3582268 **VAT No:** 974824772
**Estd:** 1998 Private Limited Company
**Line of Business:** Printers general
**Export Sales:** £11,388,793
**Issued Capital:** £230,000
**Directors:** C W Ingram, S T Goodman
**Co. Secretary:** Michael Newbould
**Responsibilities**
**Finance:** Jacqui Newbould *(Accounts Manager)*
**Admin:** Jacqui Newbould *(Accounts Manager)*
**IT:** Derek Burrows *(Commercial Manager)*
**HR:** Jacqui Newbould *(Accounts Manager)*
**US SIC:** 2752 **UK SIC:** 47544
**Auditors:** Deloitte LLP

**Bankers:** National Westminster Bank Plc (60-08-46)

| | 31-05-13 | 31-05-12 | 31-05-11 |
|---|---|---|---|
| TO | 40,099,822 | 36,793,759 | 32,474,875 |
| P/L | 1,173,024 | 1,012,208 | 1,115,608 |
| NW | 12,736,679 | 12,375,469 | 11,482,147 |
| WC | 7,038,444 | 6,790,446 | 7,527,054 |
| Emp. | 100 | 137 | 128 |

DUNS 42-394-0290 Imp

### York Museums & Gallery Trust

St Mary And Apos;s Lodge, Marygate, York, North Yorkshire YO1 7DR
**Web:** www.yorkmuseumstrust.org.uk
**Reg No:** 4381647 **Estd:** 2005 Private Company Limited By Guarantee
**Line of Business:** Museum activities
**Trading Style:** York Museums & Gallery Trust
**Directors:** Ms N Carmody, S E Lusty, Ms J C Atchison, Miss L E Harrison, Mrs J M Bell, N Barnes, Miss S J Drummond, E F Waterson
**Co. Secretary:** Alan Wadsworth
**Responsibilities**
**Senior:** Fiona Burton *(Volunteers Manager)*, John Lawton *(Director)*, Patrick Scott *(Director)*
**Marketing:** Charlotte Dootson *(Marketing Manager)*
**Sales:** Michael Woodward *(Commercial Director)*
**US SIC:** 7399 **UK SIC:** 83954
**Bankers:** HSBC Bank plc (40-47-31)

| | 31-03-14 | 31-03-13 | 31-03-12 |
|---|---|---|---|
| TO | 7,685,635 | 6,805,530 | 6,043,062 |
| P/L | 1,694,211 | 638,278 | (109,540) |
| NW | 4,181,716 | 3,188,978 | 2,550,700 |
| WC | 2,682,324 | 2,457,969 | 1,673,815 |
| Emp. | 94 | 93 | 91 |

DUNS 22-817-9362

### The York Race Committee

The Racecourse, Knavesmire Road, York, North Yorkshire YO23 1EX
**Tel:** 01904638971
**Web:** www.yorkracecourse.co.uk
**Estd:** 1842
**Line of Business:** Racecourses and racetracks
**Responsibilities**
**Senior:** Marquis of Artington *(Designated Limited Liability P)*
**Branches:** The York Race Committee, Tadcaster Road, York, North Yorkshire YO24 1QG
**US SIC:** 7999 **UK SIC:** 97913
**Auditors:** Garbutt & Elliott LLP
**Bankers:** Barclays Bank Plc (20-99-56)

| | 31-10-12 | 31-10-11 | 31-10-10 |
|---|---|---|---|
| TA | 12,031,000 | 12,470,000 | 11,053,000 |
| P/L | 278,000 | 1,564,000 | 794,000 |
| NW | 12,008,000 | 12,003,000 | 10,843,000 |
| WC | 11,908,000 | 11,903,000 | 10,743,000 |
| Emp. | 48 | 48 | 48 |

DUNS 21-605-5417

### York Road Junior School

York Road, Dartford, Kent DA1 1SQ
**Tel:** 01322224453
**Web:** www.yorkroadacademy.org.uk
**Estd:** 1981
**Line of Business:** Schools (local authority)
**Proprietor:** N Hodgess
**Responsibilities**
**Senior:** Karen Major *(Head Teacher)*, Caroline Sadler *(Head Of School)*
**IT:** Karen Brooker *(Senior IT Executive)*
**US SIC:** 8211 **UK SIC:** 93200
**Employees:** 50

DUNS 64-095-2185

### York St John University

Lord Mayors Walk, York, North Yorkshire YO31 7EX
**Tel:** 01904876654
**Web:** www.yorksj.ac.uk
**Reg No:** 4498683 **Estd:** 2002 Private Company Limited By Guarantee
**Line of Business:** First-degree level higher education
**Directors:** Mrs C A Clelland, Mrs M Pavlou, S Milner, R E France, Ms H J Hanstock, Mrs A M Green, Ms A Lees, T F Butler
**Co. Secretary:** Ms Alison Kennell
**Responsibilities**
**Senior:** Haleh Afshar *(Director)*, Jonothan Booth *(Director)*, Russell Davidson *(Director)*, John Hadjioannou *(Director)*, Laura Jackson *(Director)*
**US SIC:** 8221 **UK SIC:** 93100
**Bankers:** Barclays Bank Plc (20-99-56)

| | 31-07-14 | 31-07-13 | 31-07-12 |
|---|---|---|---|
| TO | 54,864,000 | 49,178,000 | 44,512,000 |
| P/L | 4,930,000 | 2,387,000 | 1,063,000 |
| NW | 97,639,000 | 67,928,000 | 62,090,000 |
| WC | 9,678,000 | 10,855,000 | 9,491,000 |
| Emp. | 617 | 587 | 557 |

DUNS 23-503-7905

### York Station Taxis Ltd

York Railway Station, Station Road, York, North Yorkshire YO24 1AY
**Tel:** 01904-623332 **Fax:** 01904-658396
**Web:** www.yorkstationtaxis.co.uk
**Reg No:** 3503049 **Estd:** 2000 Private Limited Company
**Line of Business:** Taxi operation
**Issued Capital:** £37
**Directors:** K Hatfield, B J Trotter, K G Pitts
**Co. Secretary:** Brendan Trotter
**Responsibilities**
**Senior:** Paul Brolly *(Proprietor)*, Martin Coombs *(Manager)*
**US SIC:** 4121 **UK SIC:** 72200

| | 31-03-14 | 31-03-13 | 31-03-12 |
|---|---|---|---|
| TA | 127,547 | 122,104 | 78,142 |
| NW | 64,916 | 60,611 | 47,585 |
| WC | 45,199 | 40,203 | 33,122 |

DUNS 23-222-9943

### York Teaching Hospital Nhs Foundation Trust

Scarborough Hospital, Woodlands Drive, Scarborough, North Yorkshire YO12 6QL
**Tel:** 01723368111
**Web:** www.yorkhospitals.nhs.uk
**Estd:** 2002
**Line of Business:** Hospitals
**Trading Style:** Scarborough Hospital, Bridlington Hospital
**Issued Capital:** £1
**Principals:** A Rose *(Chairman)*, A Bertram *(Financial)*, P Crowley, Ms P Hayward, Dr A Turnbull
**Responsibilities**
**Senior:** Michael Carlisle *(Chairman)*, James Hayward *(Manager)*, Deborah McInerny *(Non Executive Member)*, Denise Potter *(Manager)*, Alan Raymond *(Non Executive Member)*
**Finance:** Richard Mellor *(Financial Director)*
**IT:** Gary Hughs *(PC Manager)*
**Branches:** York Teaching Hospital Nhs Foundation Trust, 703 Leeds & Bradford Road, Pudsey, West Yorkshire LS28 6PE
**US SIC:** 8062 **UK SIC:** 95100
**Employees:** 2,500

DUNS 54-864-1364 Imp

### York Teaching Hospital Nhs Foundation Trust

Wigginton Road, York, North Yorkshire YO31 8HE
**Tel:** 01904-631313
**Web:** www.yorkhealthservices.org
**Estd:** 1970
**Line of Business:** Hospitals
**Issued Capital:** £1
**Principals:** A Bertram *(Financial)*, Ms P Hayward *(Personnel)*, P Crowley, P Hutton, P Ashton, Ms L Palazzo, Ms L Raper, A Rose
**Responsibilities**
**Senior:** Elizabeth McManus *(Chief Nurse)*, Michael Sweet *(Non Executive Member)*
**Admin:** Tina Ivel *(Administrator)*
**IT:** Stuart Cassidy *(IT Service Manager)*
**Operations:** Amanda Clark *(Project Executive)*
**Branches:** York Teaching Hospital Nhs Foundation Trust, 59 Huntington Road, York, North Yorkshire YO31 8RL
**US SIC:** 8062, 8091, 6732
**UK SIC:** 95100, 95200, 83100
**Auditors:** Grant Thornton UK LLP

| | 31-03-14 | 31-03-13 | 31-03-12 |
|---|---|---|---|
| TO | 431,850,000 | 387,180,000 | 257,553,000 |
| P/L | 49,000 | 1,386,000 | 647,000 |
| NW | 226,210,000 | 174,439,000 | 101,286,000 |
| WC | 25,945,000 | 7,394,000 | 4,614,000 |
| Emp. | 7,318 | 6,747 | 5,017 |

DUNS 77-973-7779

### York Telecom Ltd

(**Subsidiary of:** York Telecom Corporation)
3 Hazelwood, Lime Tree Way, Chineham Business Park, Chineham, Basingstoke, Hampshire RG24 8WZ
**Tel:** 01256-372-700 **Fax:** 01256-372-716
**Reg No:** 5942331 **Estd:** 2006 Private Limited Company
**Line of Business:** Telecom consultants
**Export Sales:** £34
**Issued Capital:** £485
**Directors:** K R Gyford, R Gaboury, Y Wang, A V Lowe
**Co. Secretary:** Ms Judith Pulig
**US SIC:** 4899 **UK SIC:** 79020
**Auditors:** Baker Tilly UK Audit LLP

| | 31-12-13 | 31-12-12 | 31-12-11 |
|---|---|---|---|
| TO | 8,325,028 | 8,176,733 | N/A |
| P/L | (931,350) | (240,403) | N/A |
| NW | (4,052,945) | (3,470,657) | 10,202 |
| WC | (2,452,980) | 123,207 | 68,469 |
| Emp. | 53 | 35 | N/A |

DUNS 73-396-3375

### York Theatre Royal Enterprises Ltd

St Leonards Place, York, North Yorkshire YO1 7HD
**Tel:** 01904-658162 **Fax:** 01904611534
**Web:** www.yorktheatreroyal.co.uk
**Reg No:** 2909939 **Estd:** 1994 Private Limited Company
**Line of Business:** Licensed restaurants
**Issued Capital:** £2
**Directors:** G Kennedy, T Cantrell, J J Rebbeck
**Co. Secretary:** Mrs Janis Smyth
**Responsibilities**
**Senior:** Vicky Biles *(General Manager)*
**US SIC:** 5812 **UK SIC:** 66110

| | 31-03-14 | 31-03-13 | 31-03-12 |
|---|---|---|---|
| TA | 223,708 | 112,631 | 220,005 |
| NW | 7,876 | 7,876 | 21,651 |
| WC | 7,876 | 7,876 | 21,651 |

DUNS 73-492-4108

### Yorkare Homes Ltd

Brantingham Thorpe Hall, Brantingham, Brough, North Humberside HU15 1QG
**Tel:** 01482665063
**Web:** www.yorkarehomes.co.uk
**Reg No:** 4755842 **Estd:** 2003 Private Limited Company
**Line of Business:** Home care service providers
**Issued Capital:** £4,250,000
**Directors:** J J Garton, Miss E C Garton, J R Garton, L J Garton
**Co. Secretary:** Mrs Evonne Garton
**US SIC:** 8091 **UK SIC:** 95200

| | 31-05-14 | 31-05-13 | 31-05-12 |
|---|---|---|---|
| TO | 2,126,772 | 1,415,305 | N/A |
| P/L | (130,531) | (21,153) | N/A |
| NW | 3,939,327 | 4,070,346 | 4,088,249 |
| WC | (3,149,144) | 41,543 | 445,173 |
| Emp. | 102 | 79 | N/A |

DUNS 28-960-7764

### Yorkcloud Ltd

(**Subsidiary of:** Lakeside Hotel Windermere Ltd)
Newby Bridge, Ulverston, Cumbria LA12 8AT
**Tel:** 01539530001 **Fax:** 01539-531699
**Web:** www.lakesidehotel.co.uk
**Reg No:** 1679025 **Estd:** 2002 Private Limited Company
**Line of Business:** Hotels
**Trading Style:** Lakeside Hotel
**Issued Capital:** £92,400
**Principals:** N R Talbot *(Managing)*, C Wilson, D M Snowdon, C J Malpas
**Co. Secretary:** Arthur Bailes
**Branches:** Lakeside Hotel, Newby Bridge, Cumbria LA12 8AT (Tel : 05395-31207)
**US SIC:** 7011 **UK SIC:** 66500
**Auditors:** E J Williams & Co
**Bankers:** National Westminster Bank Plc (01-08-93)

| | 31-01-14 | 31-01-13 | 31-01-12 |
|---|---|---|---|
| TO | 4,657,397 | 4,327,831 | 4,686,672 |
| P/L | 159,196 | 36,099 | 245,217 |
| NW | 2,621,975 | 2,547,234 | 2,567,659 |
| WC | (1,196,302) | (1,571,688) | (1,503,523) |
| Emp. | 114 | 112 | 113 |

DUNS 21-778-9123

### Yorkhill Childrens Hospital

Dalnair Street, Glasgow, Lanarkshire G3 8SJ
**Tel:** 01412016917
**Web:** www.yorkhill.org
**Estd:** 1999 Proprietorship
**Line of Business:** Fund raising services charitable and non charitable
**Proprietor:** J Best
**Responsibilities**
**Senior:** Shona Cardle *(Chief Executive)*, John Hughan *(Manager)*, Alison Rennie *(Manager)*, Robert Scully *(Manager)*, Brian Simmers *(Manager)*
**US SIC:** 8062 **UK SIC:** 95100
**Employees:** 1,000

DUNS 23-480-4581

### Yorkshire Agricultural Society

Great Yorkshire Showground, Railway Road, Harrogate, North Yorkshire HG2 8NZ
**Web:** www.pavilionsofharrogate.co.uk
**Reg No:** 1666751 **Estd:** 1982 Private Company Limited By Guarantee
**Line of Business:** Conference centres and facilities
**Trading Style:** Yorkshire Event Centre
**Directors:** W V Cowling, G C Lane-Fox, R Copley, Mrs C I Bromet, J S Crabtree, C D Forbes Adam, S F Theakston, C E Mills
**Co. Secretary:** Nigel Pulling
**US SIC:** 8699, 6531
**UK SIC:** 96902, 83400
**Auditors:** PricewaterhouseCoopers

**Bankers:** National Westminster Bank Plc (56-00-70)

| | 31-12-13 | 31-12-12 | 31-12-11 |
|---|---|---|---|
| TO | 8,810,315 | 6,029,378 | 7,871,917 |
| P/L | 438,714 | (1,669,431) | 312,790 |
| NW | 25,383,298 | 23,062,341 | 24,062,455 |
| WC | (1,390,085) | (1,627,069) | (478,847) |
| Emp. | 89 | 92 | 93 |

DUNS 21-878-1687
### Yorkshire & Humber Postgraduate Deanery
Willow Approach, Leeds, West Yorkshire LS4 2HE
**Tel:** 0113 3431557
**Web:** www.yorksandhumberdeanery.nhs.uk
**Estd:** 2012
**Line of Business:** Training centres
**Director:** D Wilkinson
**Responsibilities**
**Senior:** Julie Hunsberger *(Business Manager)*
**Branches:** Yorkshire and The Humber Postgraduate Deanery, Don Valley House, Sheffield S4 7UQ Savile Street East
**US SIC:** 8299 **UK SIC:** 93300
**Employees:** 170

DUNS 29-491-5897
### Yorkshire Bank Home Loans Ltd
**(Subsidiary of:** National Australia Bank Limited)
20 Merrion Way, Leeds, West Yorkshire LS2 8NZ
**Tel:** 08453550845
**Reg No:** 1855020 **Estd:** 1984 Private Limited Company
**Line of Business:** Activities of mortgage finance companies
**Issued Capital:** £100
**Directors:** N P Somerset, J Shovelin, I D Smith, M J Hart
**Co. Secretary:** Miss Lorna Mcmillan
**US SIC:** 6111, 8999
**UK SIC:** 81501, 83954
**Auditors:** Ernst & Young LLP
**Bankers:** Yorkshire Bank Plc (05-00-01)
**Following financial data are in thousands**

| | 30-09-14 | 30-09-13 | 30-09-12 |
|---|---|---|---|
| TA | 1,451,181 | 4,498,648 | 4,567,726 |
| P/L | 29,760 | 32,219 | 150,050 |
| NW | 25,398 | 27,172 | 102,566 |
| WC | (1,383,584) | (4,404,660) | (4,394,330) |

DUNS 21-218-9252
### Yorkshire Bank Plc
**(Subsidiary of:** National Australia Bank Limited)
20 Merrion Way, Leeds, West Yorkshire LS2 8NZ
**Tel:** 01138072000 **Fax:** 01132 472620
**Web:** www.ybonline.co.uk
**Reg No:** 0117413 **Estd:** 1859 Public Limited Company
**Line of Business:** Financial intermediation not elsewhere classified
**Issued Capital:** £251,125,000
**Directors:** T Slater, I D Smith, K J Malkin
**Co. Secretary:** Miss Lorna Mcmillan
**Responsibilities**
**Marketing:** Stephen Glass *(Marketing Manager)*
**IT:** John Crane *(Head of IT)*
**HR:** Arthur Willett *(Human Resources Manager)*
**Branches:** Yorkshire Bank Plc, Business Banking Centre, Heavens Walk, Doncaster, South Yorkshire DN4 5HZ
**US SIC:** 6111 **UK SIC:** 81501
**Employees:** 3,640

DUNS 23-546-9611
### Yorkshire Building Society Charitable Foundation
Yorkshire House, Yorkshire Drive, Bradford, West Yorkshire BD5 8LJ
**Tel:** 01274740740
**Web:** www.yorkshirebuildingsociety.co.uk
**Reg No:** 3545437 **Estd:** 1998 Private Limited Company
**Line of Business:** Building societies
**Directors:** A M Caton, C L Parrish, Mrs L A Oakes, C J Faulkner
**Co. Secretary:** Mrs Ann Fitzpatrick
**US SIC:** 6012, 7399
**UK SIC:** 81402, 83954
**Auditors:** Deloitte LLP
**Bankers:** National Westminster Bank Plc (56-00-36)

| | 31-12-13 | 31-12-12 | 31-12-11 |
|---|---|---|---|
| TA | 141,992 | 245,041 | 432,129 |
| P/L | (9,164) | (120,430) | (127,348) |
| NW | 138,542 | 147,706 | 268,136 |
| WC | 138,542 | 147,706 | 268,136 |

DUNS 50-532-2289
### Yorkshire Cable Communications Ltd
**(Subsidiary of:** The Depository Trust & Clearing Corporation)
Mayfair Business Park, Broad Lane, Bradford, West Yorkshire BD4 8PW
**Tel:** 01274732244 **Fax:** 01274-828400
**Web:** www.telewest.co.uk
**Reg No:** 2490136 **VAT No:** 607130283
**Estd:** 1990 Private Limited Company
**Line of Business:** Television licence suppliers
**Trading Style:** Yorkshire Cable
**Issued Capital:** £5,180,877
**Directors:** R D Dunn, M O Hifzi
**Co. Secretary:** Ms Gillian James
**US SIC:** 4833, 4899, 7379
**UK SIC:** 97411, 79020, 83940
**Auditors:** KPMG Audit Plc
**Bankers:** Barclays Bank Plc (20-11-81)

| | 31-12-13 | 31-12-12 | 31-12-11 |
|---|---|---|---|
| TO | 32,544,000 | 34,631,000 | 31,098,000 |
| P/L | 132,541,000 | (4,902,000) | 20,969,000 |
| NW | (219,461,000) | (352,002,000) | (347,100,000) |
| WC | (266,141,000) | (404,033,000) | (406,033,000) |

DUNS 21-201-6281
### Yorkshire Caravans of Bawtry Ltd
Doncaster Road, Doncaster, South Yorkshire DN11 8NA
**Tel:** 01302-710366
**Web:** www.yorkshirecaravans.com
**Reg No:** 0688060 **VAT No:** 419772522
**Estd:** 1931 Private Limited Company
**Line of Business:** Other retail sale in specialised stores not elsewhere classified
**Trading Style:** Yorkshire Caravans, Y C Leisure
**Issued Capital:** £20,000
**Directors:** J R Goulden, Mrs J B Goulden Smith
**Co. Secretary:** John Siddall
**Responsibilities**
**Facilities:** Stuart McCaig *(Operations Manager)*
**Branches:** Yorkshire Caravans Of Bawtry Ltd, Great North Road, Doncaster, South Yorkshire DN10 6DG
**US SIC:** 5999, 5931
**UK SIC:** 65600, 65400
**Bankers:** HSBC Bank plc (40-19-20)

| | 31-03-14 | 31-03-13 | 30-03-11 |
|---|---|---|---|
| TA | 2,711,735 | 2,746,865 | 3,034,844 |
| NW | 227,313 | 215,585 | 469,082 |
| WC | (153,557) | (170,313) | 18,311 |

DUNS 38-782-5284
### The Yorkshire Clinic
Bradford Road, Bingley, West Yorkshire BD16 1TW
**Tel:** 01274550600
**Web:** www.theyorkshireclinic.co.uk
**Estd:** 2011 Proprietorship
**Line of Business:** Hospitals
**General Manager:** K Hague
**US SIC:** 8062 **UK SIC:** 95100
**Employees:** 400

DUNS 21-204-2535
### Yorkshire Co-Operatives Ltd
Sunwin House, 65 Sunbridge Road, Bradford, West Yorkshire BD1 2NB
**Tel:** 01535-653426 **Fax:** 01535-657970
**Reg No:** 0015568IP **Estd:** 1960 Friendly Society
**Line of Business:** Grocery Stores
**Trading Style:** Food Fairs, Maurice Leach & Son, Late Shop, Food Market
**Principals:** T Wood *(Chairman)*, Ms J Mitchell, J M Prestale, T Finn, N Cox Jp, A E Drake, J Leeson, P Barraclough
**Co. Secretary:** P Marks
**Responsibilities**
**Senior:** N Cox JP *(Director)*, Alec Gardiner *(Director)*
**Branches:** Yorkshire Co-Operatives Ltd, 4 Gladstone Court, Bolton, Lancashire BL4 7EU
**US SIC:** 5411 **UK SIC:** 64100
**Auditors:** Burton & Co
**Bankers:** The Co-Operative Bank Plc (08-90-72)
**Employees:** 5,795

DUNS 23-275-0443
### Yorkshire Coast College of Further & Higher Education
Lady Ediths Drive, Scarborough, North Yorkshire YO12 5RN
**Tel:** 01723-372105
**Web:** www.yorkshirecoastcollege.ac.uk
**Estd:** 1993 Proprietorship
**Line of Business:** Further education schools and colleges
**Proprietor:** Mrs B Hodge
**Responsibilities**
**Senior:** Debbie Erwin *(Warehouse Manager)*, Tim Obrien *(Principal)*, Clare Wareing *(Principal)*
**Finance:** Beverley Dye *(Financial Director)*
**IT:** Mick Mullane *(IT Coordinator)*
**HR:** Louise Hanks *(Human Resources Manager)*, John Parnham *(Human Resources Manager)*
**Purchasing:** Beverley Dye *(Financial Director)*
**Branches:** Yorkshire Coast College Of Further & Higher Education, Westwood Campus, Valley Bridge Parade, Scarborough, North Yorkshire YO11 2PL
**US SIC:** 8221, 8249, 8211
**UK SIC:** 93100, 93300, 93200
**Employees:** 225

DUNS 42-450-6215
### Yorkshire Coast Homes Ltd
Brook House, Scarborough, North Yorkshire YO12 7BH
**Tel:** 03450655656 **Fax:** 01723-343055
**Web:** www.ych.org.uk
**Reg No:** 4438271 **Estd:** 2002 Private Company Limited By Guarantee
**Line of Business:** Housing associations societies trusts & co-operatives
**Directors:** G Priestley, M Donohue-Moncrieff, I Kitson, A G Evans, Mrs S Balding, S J Perry, Mrs R E Fox, Mrs J Jones
**Co. Secretary:** Shaun Tymon
**Responsibilities**
**Senior:** Steve Aldrige *(Chief Executive)*, Sheila Buckle *(Director)*, Anita Ferguson *(Director)*, Jane Mortimer *(Director)*, Raymond Tedds *(Director)*
**Marketing:** Sarah Bird *(Marketing Manager)*, Debbie Gordon *(Office Manager)*
**Admin:** Debbie Gordon *(Office Manager)*
**IT:** Linda Woodward *(Computer Manager)*
**HR:** Debbie Gordon *(Office Manager)*
**Health & Safety:** Debbie Gordon *(Office Manager)*
**Facilities:** Sarah Bird *(Marketing Manager)*, Debbie Gordon *(Office Manager)*
**Operations:** Sarah Bird *(Marketing Manager)*, Bill Miller *(Director of Operations)*
**Branches:** Yorkshire Coast Homes Ltd, Gatesgarth Close, Scarborough, North Yorkshire YO12 5PA
**US SIC:** 8321 **UK SIC:** 96111
**Bankers:** National Westminster Bank Plc (54-41-24)

| | 31-03-14 | 31-03-13 | 31-03-12 |
|---|---|---|---|
| TO | 19,320,000 | 19,303,000 | 17,481,000 |
| P/L | 2,478,000 | 1,663,000 | 85,000 |
| NW | 25,256,000 | 18,202,000 | 17,158,000 |
| WC | 6,870,000 | (9,084,000) | 1,088,000 |
| Emp. | 207 | 124 | 111 |

DUNS 21-827-0841 **Exp**
### Yorkshire Copper Tube
**(Subsidiary of:** Intek Group Spa)
East Lancashire Road, Liverpool, Merseyside L33 7TU
**Tel:** 01515462700
**Web:** www.yorkshirecoppertube.com
**Reg No:** 0375576 **VAT No:** 565871305
**Estd:** 1942 Private Limited Company
**Line of Business:** Manufacturers of brass and copper
**Issued Capital:** £3,261,093
**Director:** F Thiele
**Co. Secretary:** John Dodd
**Responsibilities**
**Senior:** Christoph Geyer *(Manager)*, Ronald McLean *(Manager)*, Roelf Reins *(Manager)*, Italo Romano *(Manager)*
**IT:** Malcolm Mackenzie *(Senior IT Executive)*, Richard Marland *(IT Operations Manager)*
**US SIC:** 3331 **UK SIC:** 22461
**Auditors:** Deloitte & Touche LLP
**Bankers:** Lloyds TSB Bank plc (30-95-11)

| | 31-12-13 | 30-12-12 | 31-12-11 |
|---|---|---|---|
| TA | 294,000 | 294,000 | 294,000 |
| NW | 276,000 | 276,000 | 276,000 |
| WC | 258,000 | 258,000 | 258,000 |

DUNS 22-815-3391
### Yorkshire County Cricket Club
Headingley Carnegie Stadium, Kirkstall Lane, Leeds, West Yorkshire LS6 3DP
**Tel:** 08435043099
**Web:** www.yorkshireccc.com
**Reg No:** 0028929IP **VAT No:** 169706723
**Estd:** 1863 Friendly Society
**Line of Business:** Sports clubs
**Directors:** C A Hassell, P W Townend
**Responsibilities**
**Senior:** Mark Arthur *(Chief Executive)*
**US SIC:** 5813 **UK SIC:** 66200
**Auditors:** Grant Thornton
**Bankers:** National Westminster Bank Plc (60-60-05)
**Employees:** 50

DUNS 64-739-1606
### Yorkshire Dales National Park
Colvend, Skipton, North Yorkshire BD23 5LB
**Tel:** 01756751600
**Web:** www.yorkshiredales.org.uk
**Estd:** 2010
**Line of Business:** Parks & gardens
**Director:** Ms H Hancock
**Responsibilities**
**Senior:** David Butterworth *(CEO, Managing Director)*
**Branches:** Yorkshire Dales National Park, 13-15 Burnley Road, Todmorden, Lancashire OL14 7BU
**US SIC:** 8411 **UK SIC:** 97700
**Employees:** 50

DUNS 21-880-0245
### Yorkshire Electricity Board
New York Road, Shiremoor, Newcastle-Upon-Tyne, Tyne and Wear NE27 0LP
**Tel:** 01912294401
**Estd:** 2012
**Line of Business:** Wholesale of other electronic parts and equipment
**Responsibilities**
**Senior:** Phil Moat *(Administrator)*
**US SIC:** 5065 **UK SIC:** 61500
**Employees:** 200

DUNS 21-701-8269
### Yorkshire Electricity Distribution Ltd
**(Subsidiary of:** Northern Powergrid Holdings Co)
Cargo Fleet Lane, Middlesbrough, Middlesbrough, Cleveland TS3 8DG
**Tel:** 08450702703 **Fax:** 01912294603
**Web:** www.ce-electricuk.com
**Reg No:** 7465398 **Estd:** 2000 Private Limited Company
**Line of Business:** Business services
**Issued Capital:** £1
**Director:** J Elliott
**US SIC:** 7399 **UK SIC:** 83954

| | 31-12-13 | 31-12-12 | 31-12-11 |
|---|---|---|---|
| TA | 1 | 1 | 1 |
| NW | 1 | 1 | 1 |

DUNS 23-617-6822
### Yorkshire Electricity Group Plc
**(Subsidiary of:** Northern Powergrid Holdings Co)
Wetherby Road, Leeds, West Yorkshire LS14 3HS
**Tel:** 0800-668-877
**Reg No:** 2366995 **Estd:** 1989 Public Limited Company
**Line of Business:** Management activities of other non-financial holding companies not elsewhere classified
**Issued Capital:** £108,593,832
**Directors:** Dr P A Jones, P J Goodman, T E Fielden, Dr J M France
**Co. Secretary:** John Elliott
**Branches:** Yorkshire Electricity Group Plc, Linewood App, Leeds, West Yorkshire LS1 1QZ
**US SIC:** 6711, 4932
**UK SIC:** 83962, 16200
**Auditors:** Deloitte LLP
**Bankers:** National Westminster Bank Plc (60-60-05)

| | 31-12-13 | 31-12-12 | 31-12-11 |
|---|---|---|---|
| TO | 514,000 | 469,000 | 435,000 |
| P/L | 51,997,000 | 53,309,000 | 53,876,000 |
| NW | 537,161,000 | 487,957,000 | 437,907,000 |
| WC | 146,961,000 | 97,557,000 | (19,231,000) |

DUNS 21-584-1382
### Yorkshire Envelope Co
Unit 42 Castlefields Industrial Estate, Bingley, West Yorkshire BD16 2AG
**Tel:** 01274518890
**Web:** www.yorkshireenvelopes.com
**Estd:** 2011 Proprietorship
**Line of Business:** Envelopes
**Proprietor:** Miss S Jackson
**US SIC:** 2648 **UK SIC:** 47231
**Employees:** 58

DUNS 21-135-1709 **Imp**
### Yorkshire Fittings Ltd
**(Subsidiary of:** Aalberts Industries N.V.)
Haigh Park Road, Leeds, West Yorkshire LS10 1TT
**Tel:** 01132701104 **Fax:** 01132719803
**Reg No:** 6681938 **VAT No:** 418013192
**Estd:** 2008 Private Limited Company
**Line of Business:** Forging, pressing, stamping and roll forming of metal; powder metallurgy
**Trading Style:** Pegler Yorkshire Group
**Issued Capital:** £1
**Directors:** I M Howarth, B Liddle
**Co. Secretary:** Kevin Parker

**Responsibilities**
**Senior:** M Beardall *(Proprietor)*, Mike Saunders *(Manager)*
**Sales:** Graham Brian *(Sales Manager)*, Chris Hird *(Area Sales Manager)*, Steve Molson *(Divisional Sales Manager)*, Billy Ritchie *(Regional Manager (Commercial))*
**Facilities:** Mick Hinchcliff *(Facilities Manager)*
**Purchasing:** Roger Ablett *(Supply Chain Director)*
**US SIC:** 3469, 3317
**UK SIC:** 31200, 22200

| | 31-12-13 | 31-12-12 | 31-12-10 |
|---|---|---|---|
| TA | 1 | 1 | 1 |
| NW | 1 | 1 | 1 |

DUNS 21-776-6966
## Yorkshire Flowerpots
Clough Green, Barnsley, South Yorkshire S75 4AD
**Tel:** 01226794059
**Web:** www.yorkshireflowerpots.co.uk
**Estd:** 2011 Proprietorship
**Line of Business:** Manufacturers of pottery
**Proprietor:** Mrs L Huston
**US SIC:** 3269 **UK SIC:** 24894
**Employees:** 225

DUNS 23-554-5741 **Imp**
## Yorkshire Fur Fabrics Ltd
Fairfield Mills, Queen Street South, Huddersfield, West Yorkshire HD1 3DU
**Web:** www.yorkshirefurfabrics.co.uk
**Reg No:** 3552926 **VAT No:** 721209179
**Estd:** 1998 Private Limited Company
**Line of Business:** Manufacturers of clothing and fabrics
**Export Sales:** £2,673,252
**Issued Capital:** £312,622
**Directors:** M D Oldroyd, K S Rai, B S Hayer
**Co. Secretary:** Richard Tordoff
**Branches:** Yorkshire Fur Fabrics Ltd, Elm Street, Huddersfield, West Yorkshire HD8 9DZ
**US SIC:** 2389, 5133
**UK SIC:** 45393, 61600
**Auditors:** Mazars LLP
**Bankers:** Bank Of Scotland (12-08-83)

| | 30-06-14 | 30-06-13 | 30-06-12 |
|---|---|---|---|
| TO | 7,986,759 | 6,981,418 | 8,261,636 |
| P/L | 285,129 | 31,729 | 118,611 |
| NW | 1,584,185 | 1,517,147 | 1,614,251 |
| WC | 1,422,824 | 1,318,373 | 1,376,359 |
| Emp. | 54 | 54 | 53 |

DUNS 23-285-2897
## Yorkshire Metropolitan Housing Association Ltd
Dysons Chambers, Leeds, West Yorkshire LS1 6ER
**Tel:** 01138256000
**Web:** www.yorkshirehousing.co.uk
**Reg No:** 0017752IP **VAT No:** 477025538
**Estd:** 1974 Friendly Society
**Line of Business:** Housing associations societies trusts & co-operatives
**Trading Style:** Y M H A
**Principals:** M J Simpson *(Chairman)*, P Knowles *(Financial)*, Ms C Moran, W Payne, M Stammers, R Council, Mrs D Ardron, K Smith
**Responsibilities**
**Senior:** Eryl Edwards *(Principal)*, Nadhia Hussain *(Head of Housing)*, Michael Meadowcroft *(Principal)*
**Finance:** Tansy Hepton *(Director of Resources)*
**Sales:** Ged Walsh *(Business & Development Directo)*
**HR:** Tracy Marsden *(Human Resources Manager)*
**Facilities:** Nadhia Khan *(Head of Housing)*
**Purchasing:** Tansy Hepton *(Director of Resources)*
**Branches:** Yorkshire Metropolitan Housing Association Ltd, 49 Church St, Barnsley, South Yorkshire S70 2AH
**US SIC:** 8321 **UK SIC:** 96111
**Bankers:** National Westminster Bank Plc (56-00-54)
**Employees:** 126

DUNS 21-262-2385
## Yorkshire Post Newspapers Ltd
(**Subsidiary of:** Johnston Press Plc)
P O Box 168, Leeds, West Yorkshire LS1 1RF
**Tel:** 01132-432701 **Fax:** 01132443430
**Web:** www.yorkshireposttoday.co.uk
**Reg No:** 0002899 **Estd:** 1866 Private Limited Company
**Line of Business:** The Notes to the accounts for the period ending 28.12.2013 state that the subject acts as an agent for Johnston Publishing Ltd.
**Issued Capital:** £690,000
**Directors:** A G Highfield, D J King
**Co. Secretary:** Peter Mccall
**Responsibilities**
**Senior:** Andy Allen *(Commercial Director)*, Grant Murray *(Finance Director)*
**Finance:** Grant Murray *(Finance Director)*
**Sales:** Mike Pennington *(Commercial Director)*
**HR:** Carrie Playford *(Training Manager)*
**Branches:** Yorkshire Post Newspapers Ltd, Hennymoor House, 9-11 Manor Row, Bradford, West Yorkshire BD1 4PB
**US SIC:** 2711 **UK SIC:** 47512
**Auditors:** Deloitte LLP
**Bankers:** Lloyds TSB Bank plc (30-91-79)

| | 28-12-13 | 29-12-12 | 31-12-11 |
|---|---|---|---|
| TO | 10,169,000 | 10,483,000 | 12,617,000 |
| NW | 88,532,000 | 88,532,000 | 88,532,000 |
| WC | 88,532,000 | 88,532,000 | N/A |
| Emp. | 311 | 291 | 437 |

DUNS 53-609-5433
## Yorkshire Poultry Products Ltd
(**Subsidiary of:** Gs Group (Uk) Ltd)
182 Hammerton Street, Bradford, West Yorkshire BD3 9RD
**Tel:** 01274-745505 **Fax:** 01274-736993
**Web:** www.yorkshirepoultry.com
**Reg No:** 3414780 **Estd:** 1997 Private Limited Company
**Line of Business:** Abattoirs
**Issued Capital:** £1,000
**Directors:** G J Sarwar, G Mujitba, M I Sarwar
**Co. Secretary:** Mohammed Mustafa
**Responsibilities**
**Senior:** John Farwar *(Manager)*, Ghulam Mustafa *(Manager)*, Jallani Sarwar *(Manager)*, Hassan Sarwar *(Manager)*
**Finance:** Afnez Malek *(Finance Director)*
**Marketing:** George Jallani *(Marketing Manager)*, Jallani Sarwar *(Manager)*
**Sales:** Jallani Sarwar *(Manager)*
**HR:** Liequat Hussain *(Head of Human Resources)*
**Facilities:** Ray White *(General Manager)*
**US SIC:** 2013 **UK SIC:** 41223

| | 31-07-13 | 31-01-12 | 31-07-11 |
|---|---|---|---|
| TO | 51,146,193 | 37,417,371 | 31,801,464 |
| P/L | (960,078) | 280,464 | (484,926) |
| NW | 112,968 | 937,941 | 739,837 |
| WC | (1,717,284) | (1,089,773) | (1,348,181) |
| Emp. | 118 | 117 | 114 |

DUNS 22-803-3981 **Imp**
## Yorkshire Purchasing Organisation
41 Industrial Street, Wakefield, West Yorkshire WF4 5EG
**Tel:** 01924834834 **Fax:** 01924834926
**Web:** www.ypo.co.uk
**VAT No:** 642720651 **Estd:** 1944 Incorporate By Act Of Parliament
**Line of Business:** Central government
**Trading Style:** Y P O
**Director:** D J Phillipson
**Responsibilities**
**IT:** Simon Gaukroger *(Computer Operations Manager)*
**HR:** Julie Wray *(Head of HR and People Support)*
**Branches:** Yorkshire Purchasing Organisation, Hanover St, Bolton, Lancashire BL1 4TG
**US SIC:** 9121 **UK SIC:** 91110
**Bankers:** The Co-Operative Bank Plc (08-90-20)
**Employees:** 400

DUNS 29-526-4949
## Yorkshire Repak Ltd
Summer Lane, Barnsley, South Yorkshire S70 2NP
**Tel:** 01226-204747
**Web:** www.yorkshirerepak.com
**Reg No:** 1894028 **Estd:** 1985 Private Limited Company
**Line of Business:** Packagers
**Export Sales:** £2,478,622
**Issued Capital:** £251,000
**Principals:** N Askham *(Managing)*, Mrs D Askham, T M Foy
**Co. Secretary:** Neil Askham
**US SIC:** 7399, 8999
**UK SIC:** 83954
**Auditors:** Garbutt & Elliott Ltd
**Bankers:** Barclays Bank Plc (20-77-62)

| | 31-05-14 | 31-05-13 | 31-05-12 |
|---|---|---|---|
| TO | 11,669,709 | 9,270,738 | 11,956,372 |
| P/L | 1,853,471 | 1,466,138 | 2,789,147 |
| NW | 3,502,614 | 2,775,101 | 3,693,224 |
| WC | 3,625,437 | 2,890,800 | 3,685,335 |
| Emp. | 425 | 354 | 433 |

DUNS 64-103-9318
## Yorkshire Sculpture Park
Bretton Lane, Wakefield, West Yorkshire WF4 4LB
**Tel:** 01924832631 **Fax:** 01924-832600
**Web:** www.ysp.co.uk
**Reg No:** 3498700 **Estd:** 1998 Private Unlimited Company
**Line of Business:** Operation of arts facilities
**Directors:** Dr I M Roscoe, J E Foster, G T Worthington, Professor P A Clegg, Ms S J Wilkinson, Rt Hon A Milburn, P Box, R G Nabarro
**Co. Secretary:** Paul Rogers
**Responsibilities**
**Senior:** Alan Bowness *(Director)*, Francis Carnwath *(Trustee)*, Judith Collins *(Director)*, Maria De Peverelli *(Director)*, Phillip King *(Director)*, Rodney Walker *(Director)*
**Marketing:** Anna Neville *(Marketing Officer)*
**Admin:** Jane Appleyard *(Administrator)*
**US SIC:** 7911 **UK SIC:** 97913
**Auditors:** Baker Tilly UK Audit LLP
**Bankers:** Lloyds TSB Bank plc (30-99-01)

| | 31-03-14 | 31-03-13 | 31-03-12 |
|---|---|---|---|
| TO | 5,698,235 | 5,651,298 | 7,296,096 |
| P/L | 94,490 | 79,932 | 2,020,870 |
| NW | 15,005,751 | 14,911,261 | 14,831,329 |
| WC | 1,001,121 | 1,706,827 | 1,570,351 |
| Emp. | 178 | 158 | 148 |

DUNS 21-290-6630 **Exp**
## Yorkshire Television Ltd
(**Subsidiary of:** Itv Plc)
Television House, 104 Kirkstall Road, Leeds, West Yorkshire LS3 1JS
**Tel:** 01132227000
**Web:** www.yorkshire-television.tv
**Reg No:** 0899713 **Estd:** 1967 Private Limited Company
**Line of Business:** Television activities
**Export Markets:** Worldwide
**Issued Capital:** £3
**Directors:** Ms E K Irving, Ms H J Tautz
**Branches:** Yorkshire Television Ltd, 23 Prospect St, Prospect Centre, Hull, North Humberside HU2 8PN
**US SIC:** 4833 **UK SIC:** 97411
**Auditors:** KPMG Audit PLC
**Bankers:** National Westminster Bank Plc (60-60-05)

| | 31-12-13 | 31-12-12 | 31-12-11 |
|---|---|---|---|
| TA | 3 | 3 | 3 |
| NW | 3 | 3 | 3 |

DUNS 22-147-2470
## Yorkshire Tiger Ltd
(**Subsidiary of:** Bundesrepublik Deutschland)
1 Admiral Way, Doxford International Business P, Sunderland, Tyne and Wear SR3 3XP
**Tel:** 01484538603 **Fax:** 01484453628
**Web:** www.tracky.co.uk
**Reg No:** 4166041 **Estd:** 2001 Private Limited Company
**Line of Business:** Rail transport services
**Issued Capital:** £1
**Directors:** R A Bowler, N P Featham, D Cocker
**Co. Secretary:** Mrs Lorna Edwards
**Responsibilities**
**Senior:** Mark Knot *(Operations Manager)*
**Finance:** Mark Knot *(Operations Manager)*
**IT:** Mark Knot *(Operations Manager)*
**HR:** Mark Knot *(Operations Manager)*
**Health & Safety:** Mark Knot *(Operations Manager)*
**Facilities:** Mark Knot *(Operations Manager)*
**US SIC:** 4011 **UK SIC:** 71000
**Auditors:** N.R. Barton & Co

| | 31-12-13 | 30-04-13 | 30-12-12 |
|---|---|---|---|
| TO | 4,745,000 | N/A | N/A |
| P/L | 214,000 | N/A | N/A |
| NW | 56,000 | (176,047) | (591,971) |
| WC | (2,258,000) | 1,070,720 | 430,962 |
| Emp. | 118 | N/A | N/A |

DUNS 21-239-2666 **Imp**
## The Yorkshire Tile Co Ltd
Hill Street, Sheffield, South Yorkshire S2 4SP
**Tel:** 01142731133
**Web:** www.ytctiles.com
**Reg No:** 1181030 **VAT No:** 646776784
**Estd:** 1974 Private Limited Company
**Line of Business:** Wholesale of wood, construction materials and sanitary equipment
**Trading Style:** Nortile
**Issued Capital:** £255
**Principals:** S Firth *(Managing)*, Ms H G Morrison, C Morrison, S A Firth
**Co. Secretary:** Matthew Webster
**Responsibilities**
**Senior:** Steffan Firth *(Managing Director)*
**Finance:** Steffan Firth *(Managing Director)*
**Marketing:** Steffan Firth *(Managing Director)*
**IT:** Jordan Mawbey *(IT Manager)*, Jan Mawbey *(IT Manager)*
**HR:** Chris Hiley *(General Manager)*
**Health & Safety:** Chris Hiley *(General Manager)*
**Facilities:** Chris Hiley *(General Manager)*
**Purchasing:** Chris Hiley *(General Manager)*
**Branches:** The Yorkshire Tile Co Ltd, York Road Trading Estate, Doncaster, South Yorkshire DN5 8PT
**US SIC:** 5039, 5999
**UK SIC:** 61300, 65600
**Auditors:** Marriott Gibbs Rees Wallis
**Bankers:** National Westminster Bank Plc (56-00-09)

| | 31-12-13 | 31-12-12 | 31-12-11 |
|---|---|---|---|
| TA | 1,321,077 | 1,510,611 | 1,649,845 |
| NW | 436,667 | 447,731 | 447,155 |
| WC | 323,697 | 316,758 | 325,964 |

DUNS 89-622-0340
## Yorkshire Trade Windows Ltd
(**Subsidiary of:** Mkc (Yorkshire) Ltd)
Carr Wood Road, Castleford, West Yorkshire WF10 4PT
**Tel:** 01977668877 **Fax:** 01977-668855
**Web:** www.yorkshiretradewindows.co.uk
**Reg No:** 3315698 **Estd:** 1997 Private Limited Company
**Line of Business:** Manufacture of builders carpentry and joinery of metal
**Issued Capital:** £1,000
**Directors:** R D Williams, S L Drewell, Mrs E Drewell, G Amos
**US SIC:** 3442, 1721
**UK SIC:** 31420, 50400
**Auditors:** The HSA Partnership
**Bankers:** Barclays Bank Plc (20-89-68)

| | 31-03-14 | 31-03-13 | 31-03-12 |
|---|---|---|---|
| TA | 2,645,948 | 2,477,934 | 2,707,920 |
| NW | 710,888 | 629,274 | 647,552 |
| WC | 346,731 | 99,520 | 283,597 |

DUNS 21-694-9076
## Yorkshire Vets Ltd
515 Bradford Road, Thornbury, Bradford, West Yorkshire BD3 7BA
**Tel:** 01274663301
**Web:** www.yorkshirevets.co.uk
**Reg No:** 7412259 **Estd:** 2010 Private Limited Company
**Line of Business:** Veterinary activities
**Issued Capital:** £55,000
**Directors:** Ms R M Marchewka, J T Kinvig, S K Robertson, R J Wilkinson, R S Duggal, E R Morton, A R Watt, D J Roberts
**Responsibilities**
**Senior:** Jeanette Broxup *(Manager)*, Sharon Sanderson *(Practice Manager)*
**US SIC:** 0741 **UK SIC:** 95601

| | 31-12-13 | 31-12-12 | 31-12-11 |
|---|---|---|---|
| TO | 3,979,006 | 3,888,809 | 3,687,628 |
| P/L | 826,784 | 853,707 | 755,796 |
| NW | (1,137,100) | (1,742,491) | (2,443,750) |
| WC | (470,567) | (865,165) | (719,287) |
| Emp. | 69 | 68 | 68 |

DUNS 23-785-4901
## Yorkshire Water Ltd
(**Subsidiary of:** Kelda Holdings Limited)
Po Box 52, Bradford, West Yorkshire BD3 7YD
**Tel:** 01274-691111 **Fax:** 01274372800
**Web:** www.yorkshirewater.co.uk
**Reg No:** 3778498 **Estd:** 1999 Private Limited Company
**Line of Business:** Water companies
**Issued Capital:** £100
**Director:** Mrs C B Forrest
**Co. Secretary:** Robert Hill
**Responsibilities**
**Senior:** Stuart Mcfarlane *(Manager)*
**IT:** James Lockwood *(IT Director)*
**Operations:** Paul Straw *(Water Regulation Inspector)*, Nathan Sunderland *(Asset Strategy Project Manager)*
**US SIC:** 4941 **UK SIC:** 17000

| | 31-03-14 | 31-03-13 | 31-03-12 |
|---|---|---|---|
| TA | 100 | 100 | 100 |
| NW | 100 | 100 | 100 |

DUNS 77-818-4655
## Yorkshire Water Projects Ltd
(**Subsidiary of:** Kelda Holdings Limited)
Western House, Western Way, Buttershaw, Bradford, West Yorkshire BD6 2SZ
**Tel:** 01274600222
**Reg No:** 3028361 **Estd:** 1995 Private Limited Company
**Line of Business:** Other business activities not elsewhere classified
**Issued Capital:** £2
**Director:** Mrs C B Forrest
**Co. Secretary:** Robert Hill
**US SIC:** 7399, 7339
**UK SIC:** 83954
**Auditors:** Price Waterhouse

| | 31-03-14 | 31-03-13 | 31-03-12 |
|---|---|---|---|
| NW | (2,532,340) | (2,532,340) | (2,532,340) |

DUNS 23-662-3377
## Yorkshire Water Services Ltd
(**Subsidiary of:** Kelda Holdings Limited)
Po Box 52, Bradford, West Yorkshire BD3 7YD
**Fax:** 01274372800
**Web:** www.yorkshirewater.com
**Reg No:** 2366682 **Estd:** 1989 Private Limited Company
**Line of Business:** Water authorities
**Issued Capital:** £10,000,000

**Directors:** R O'Toole, Mrs P J Rogerson, R Parry Jones, A L Rabin, C S Haysom, K I Whiteman, R D Flint, Mrs K M Pinnock
**Co. Secretary:** Mrs Chantal Forrest
**Responsibilities**
**Senior:** Nevil Muncaster *(Director)*
**Branches:** Yorkshire Water Services Ltd, Knostrop Treatment Works, Knowsthorpe Lane, Leeds, West Yorkshire LS9 0PJ
**US SIC:** 4941, 4952
**UK SIC:** 17000, 92120
**Auditors:** PricewaterhouseCoopers LLP
**Bankers:** National Westminster Bank Plc (60-60-05)
**Following financial data are in thousands**

| | 31-03-14 | 31-03-13 | 31-03-12 |
|---|---|---|---|
| TO | 984,200 | 936,200 | 893,600 |
| P/L | 142,200 | 186,200 | 68,500 |
| NW | 2,607,600 | 2,554,000 | 2,576,600 |
| WC | 1,139,700 | 1,121,200 | 1,110,600 |
| Emp. | 2,415 | 2,509 | 2,489 |

DUNS 23-566-7094
## Yorkshire Wildlife Trust
1 St Georges Place, York, North Yorkshire YO24 1GN
**Web:** www.northseawildlife.org.uk
**Reg No:** 0409650 **Estd:** 1946 Private Company Limited By Guarantee
**Line of Business:** Conservation organisations
**Directors:** Ms L Farnell, Mrs C Packer, H Williamson, Ms V Scholfield, C Macintosh, Mrs J Royle, R E Missin, R J Donner
**Co. Secretary:** Alison Wright
**Responsibilities**
**Senior:** David Counsel *(Director)*, John Macarthur *(Director)*, Charles Mclaren *(Director)*, Warren Meads *(Manager)*, Andrew Mendus *(Director)*, Mark Pratt *(Manager)*, David Sharrod *(Manager)*, Robert Stoneman *(Chief Executive)*
**Marketing:** Jonathan Leadley *(Head of Fundraising & Communic)*
**Sales:** Jonathan Leadley *(Head of Fundraising & Communic)*
**Admin:** Mike Hewitt *(Administration Coordinator)*
**Facilities:** Mike Hewitt *(Administration Coordinator)*
**Branches:** Yorkshire Wildlife Trust, Kirkstall Valley Nature Reserve, Hollybush Lane, Leeds, West Yorkshire LS5 3BP
**US SIC:** 8321, 8699
**UK SIC:** 96111, 96902
**Auditors:** Creers
**Bankers:** Barclays Bank Plc (20-99-56)

| | 31-03-14 | 31-03-13 | 31-03-12 |
|---|---|---|---|
| TO | 5,724,598 | 5,032,960 | 4,438,391 |
| P/L | 231,812 | 379,830 | 301,273 |
| NW | 7,160,067 | 6,899,325 | 6,444,568 |
| WC | 1,308,814 | 1,216,821 | 843,345 |
| Emp. | 93 | 96 | 94 |

DUNS 22-681-5397
## Yorkwold Pigpro Ltd
Field House Farm, Scarborough Road, Driffield, North Humberside YO25 5UY
**Web:** www.farmline.com
**Reg No:** 1046828 **Estd:** 1972 Private Limited Company
**Line of Business:** Representative office
**Issued Capital:** £8,590
**Directors:** R Beckett, J W Dewhirst, T C Dewhirst, R J Dewhirst
**Co. Secretary:** Joseph Dewhirst
**Responsibilities**
**Senior:** Martin Colebrook *(Manager)*
**IT:** Janet Yeadon *(Computer Manager)*
**Branches:** Yorkwold Pigpro Ltd, Cowder Farm, Cowden, Hull, North Humberside HU11 4UH
**US SIC:** 0213, 0119
**UK SIC:** 01001
**Auditors:** PricewaterhouseCoopers
**Bankers:** National Westminster Bank Plc (60-07-05)

| | 28-02-14 | 28-02-13 | 26-02-12 |
|---|---|---|---|
| TO | 20,563,258 | 17,013,615 | 16,019,007 |
| P/L | 2,387,391 | 1,515,179 | 1,248,519 |
| NW | 11,890,704 | 10,119,199 | 8,990,976 |
| WC | 6,227,845 | 4,470,689 | 5,213,418 |
| Emp. | 76 | 74 | 68 |

DUNS 77-038-3610
## Yorwaste Ltd
Mount View, Northallerton, North Yorkshire DL6 2YD
**Tel:** 01609774400 **Fax:** 01609-772327
**Web:** www.yorwaste.co.uk
**Reg No:** 2666908 **VAT No:** 602101519
**Estd:** 1991 Private Limited Company
**Line of Business:** Collection and treatment of other waste
**Trading Style:** Yorwaste
**Issued Capital:** £4,526,000
**Principals:** S A Grieve *(Managing)*, T R Harrison-Topham, J Phillips, D R Bowe, M H Buckley
**Co. Secretary:** Paul Harrison
**Responsibilities**
**Senior:** Arthur Barker *(Manager)*, Steve Worsley *(Site Manager)*
**Sales:** Eric Flint *(Business Development Manager)*, Mark Moorhouse *(Business Sales Consultant)*
**Branches:** Yorwaste Ltd, Harewood Whinn, Tinker Lane, York, North Yorkshire YO23 3RR
**US SIC:** 4953, 3341
**UK SIC:** 92110, 22470
**Auditors:** PricewaterhouseCoopers LLP
**Bankers:** Yorkshire Bank Plc (05-06-31)

| | 31-03-14 | 31-03-13 | 31-03-12 |
|---|---|---|---|
| TO | 43,926,872 | 42,266,175 | 45,624,833 |
| P/L | 366,090 | (348,978) | 2,809,279 |
| NW | 11,521,991 | 10,831,525 | 10,470,532 |
| WC | 7,375,519 | 7,391,395 | 7,527,765 |
| Emp. | 227 | 236 | 239 |

DUNS 22-836-8726
## The You Trust
Fareham House, 69 High Street, Fareham, Hampshire PO16 7BB
**Tel:** 01329825930
**Web:** www.lifeyouwant.org.uk
**Reg No:** 1898188 **Estd:** 1985 Private Company Limited By Guarantee
**Line of Business:** Representative office
**Directors:** Ms T A Short, Ms P H Smith, B Sparks, S J Pitt, Dr. J A Grunstein, Ms S J Linham, Ms A Ridley, Ms A J Devoil
**Responsibilities**
**Senior:** James Fullarton *(Director)*, Colin How *(Director)*, Sandra Lewis *(Director)*, Graeme Quar *(Director)*, Penelope Rowlinson *(Director)*, Norman Rowlinson *(Director)*, Nicola Youern *(Chief Executive)*
**Finance:** Jonathan Crutchfield *(Finance Director)*
**HR:** J Cracknell *(Human Resources Manager)*, V Steenton *(Training Manager)*
**Health & Safety:** Tracie Bascombe *(Health & Safety Officer)*
**Facilities:** Tracie Bascombe *(Health & Safety Officer)*
**Branches:** The You Trust, 55 Greywell Rd, Havant, Hampshire PO9 5AH
**US SIC:** 8091, 8321, 8999
**UK SIC:** 95200, 96111, 83954
**Auditors:** Morris Crocker
**Bankers:** Lloyds TSB Bank plc (30-13-95)

| | 31-03-14 | 31-03-13 | 31-03-12 |
|---|---|---|---|
| TO | 8,311,000 | 11,129,000 | 11,605,000 |
| P/L | (8,000) | (198,000) | (8,000) |
| NW | 3,389,000 | 3,397,000 | 3,595,000 |
| WC | 1,390,000 | 1,310,000 | 1,466,000 |
| Emp. | 239 | 319 | 316 |

DUNS 38-549-4125
## Youdevise Ltd
3 Copthall Avenue, London EC2R 7BH
**Web:** www.timgroup.com
**Reg No:** 3331176 **VAT No:** 769612785
**Estd:** 1997 Private Limited Company
**Line of Business:** Other software consultancy and supply
**Trading Style:** Youdevise Ltd
**Issued Capital:** £166,314
**Directors:** J Jeffery, R Beaulieu, J Hurst, R Koppel, A P Battersby
**Co. Secretary:** Colin Berthoud
**Responsibilities**
**IT:** Gareth Houston *(IT Manager)*
**US SIC:** 7379, 7372
**UK SIC:** 83940
**Auditors:** The Gallagher Partnership LLP

| | 31-12-13 | 31-12-12 | 31-12-11 |
|---|---|---|---|
| TO | 10,444,186 | 9,207,655 | 9,065,061 |
| P/L | (1,382,051) | (1,736,581) | (1,165,982) |
| NW | (4,401,011) | (3,170,725) | (1,104,163) |
| WC | (3,336,798) | (2,007,899) | (1,781,925) |
| Emp. | 92 | 92 | 91 |

DUNS 23-610-0389
## Yougov Plc
50 Featherstone Street, London EC1Y 8RT
**Web:** www.yougov.com
**Reg No:** 3607311 **Estd:** 1998 Private Limited Company
**Line of Business:** Market research organisations
**Issued Capital:** £194,406
**Directors:** Ms R B Leith, J N Jones, S Shakespeare, R G Parry, R D Rivers, B W Elliot, P L Bazalgette
**Co. Secretary:** Alan Newman
**Responsibilities**
**Marketing:** Nathalie Hinrichsen *(Head of Marketing)*
**Sales:** Kyle Skeates *(Senior Business Development Ex)*
**US SIC:** 7392 **UK SIC:** 83951
**Auditors:** PricewaterhouseCoopers LLP
**Bankers:** National Westminster Bank Plc (56-00-64)

| | 31-07-14 | 31-07-13 | 31-07-12 |
|---|---|---|---|
| TO | 67,375,000 | 62,551,000 | 58,145,000 |
| P/L | 733,000 | 1,486,000 | 440,000 |
| NW | 11,279,000 | 13,073,000 | 11,166,000 |
| WC | 8,393,000 | 11,040,000 | 10,272,000 |
| Emp. | 578 | 502 | 482 |

DUNS 21-032-6286
## Young & Co's Brewery Plc
Riverside House, London SW18 1NH
**Tel:** 020-8875-7000
**Web:** www.youngs.co.uk
**Reg No:** 0032762 **Estd:** 1890 Public Limited Company
**Line of Business:** Hotels
**Issued Capital:** £6,036,191
**Principals:** P W Whitehead *(Financial)*, N M Bryan, T C Sligo-Young, E J Turner, R J Clevely, Ms P A Corzine, R M Lambert, D M Page
**Co. Secretary:** Anthony Schroeder
**Responsibilities**
**Senior:** Patrick Dardis *(Director)*, Stephen Goodyear *(Chief Executive)*
**Sales:** Patrick Dardis *(Director)*
**IT:** Shakeel Khan *(Network Manager)*, Andrew Maynard *(IT Director)*, Daniel Venturini *(IT Manager)*
**Health & Safety:** Neville Brent *(Health & Safety Officer)*
**Branches:** Young & Co's Brewery Plc, 183 London Road, Isleworth, Middlesex TW7 5BQ
**US SIC:** 7011, 5813
**UK SIC:** 66500, 66200
**Auditors:** Ernst & Young LLP
**Bankers:** The Royal Bank Of Scotland Plc (16-04-00)

| | 31-03-14 | 01-04-13 | 02-03-12 |
|---|---|---|---|
| TO | 210,768,000 | 193,677,000 | 178,964,000 |
| P/L | 26,560,000 | 22,319,000 | (7,494,000) |
| NW | 359,236,000 | 314,119,000 | 297,259,000 |
| WC | (21,549,000) | (19,119,000) | (12,409,000) |
| Emp. | 3,357 | 3,242 | 2,985 |

DUNS 23-728-9488
## Young & Rubicam Development (Holdings) Ltd
**(Subsidiary of:** Wpp Plc)
Greater London House, Hampstead Road, London NW1 7QP
**Tel:** 02076116569 **Fax:** 020-7611-6011
**Web:** www.rkcryr.com
**Reg No:** 3723506 **Estd:** 1999 Private Limited Company
**Line of Business:** Planning, creation and placement of advertising activities
**Issued Capital:** £121,409,002
**Directors:** I G Paul, M M Pienaar, I C Pinilla, Doctor B J Kelly
**Co. Secretary:** Helina Mazur
**US SIC:** 7311 **UK SIC:** 83800
**Auditors:** Deloitte LLP
**Bankers:** National Westminster Bank Plc (60-80-07)

| | 31-12-13 | 31-12-12 | 31-12-11 |
|---|---|---|---|
| TA | 156,328,000 | 153,670,000 | 155,626,000 |
| P/L | 2,658,000 | (1,956,000) | (2,044,000) |
| NW | 156,192,000 | 153,534,000 | 155,490,000 |
| WC | 7,075,000 | 4,417,000 | 4,417,000 |

DUNS 21-032-6450
## Young & Rubicam Group Ltd
**(Subsidiary of:** Wpp Plc)
Greater London House, Hampstead Road, London NW1 7QP
**Tel:** 02073879366 **Fax:** 02076-116668
**Web:** www.yr.com
**Reg No:** 0390845 **VAT No:** 232168974
**Estd:** 1944 Private Limited Company
**Line of Business:** Advertising agency services
**Export Sales:** £47,263,000
**Trading Style:** Young & Rubicam Advertising, Wundermann Automotive
**Issued Capital:** £25,100
**Directors:** I C Pinilla, M M Pienaar, Doctor B J Kelly, I G Paul
**Co. Secretary:** Helina Mazur
**Responsibilities**
**Senior:** Pegi Lehane *(Director Information)*, Ali Power *(Art Buyer)*
**Sales:** Alexandra Gluck *(New Business Assistant)*
**Branches:** Young & Rubicam Group Ltd, The Burrows Building, 5 Rayleigh Road, Hutton, Brentwood, Essex CM13 1AB
**US SIC:** 6711, 7311
**UK SIC:** 83962, 83800
**Auditors:** Deloitte & Touche LLP
**Bankers:** National Westminster Bank Plc (60-80-07)

| | 31-12-13 | 31-12-12 | 31-12-11 |
|---|---|---|---|
| TO | 169,987,000 | 208,099,000 | 210,369,000 |
| P/L | 14,025,000 | 2,820,000 | 8,915,000 |
| NW | 14,651,000 | 91,343,000 | 88,941,000 |
| WC | 11,699,000 | 86,764,000 | 82,706,000 |
| Emp. | 828 | 955 | 1,025 |

DUNS 52-537-0862
## Young Devon
10 Erme Road, Ivybridge, Devon PL21 0AB
**Tel:** 01752691511 **Fax:** 01752-895411
**Web:** www.youngdevon.org
**Reg No:** 3240655 **Estd:** 1948 Private Limited Company
**Line of Business:** Activities of other membership organisations not elsewhere classified
**Trading Style:** D Y A
**Directors:** R C Stevens, R M Kirk, Mrs S Robbie, Mrs D A Conduit, M J Huddleson
**Responsibilities**
**Senior:** Dudley Booth *(Manager)*, Thomas Corben *(Manager)*, Kerstin Neason *(Manager)*, Linda Pow *(Manager)*, David Strudwick *(Manager)*
**Branches:** Young Devon, 2-6 Wilder Road, Ilfracombe, Devon EX34 8BN
**US SIC:** 8699 **UK SIC:** 96902
**Auditors:** Shaun Walbridge & Co
**Bankers:** Lloyds TSB Bank plc (30-94-58)

| | 31-03-14 | 31-03-13 | 31-03-12 |
|---|---|---|---|
| TO | 2,878,855 | 4,472,455 | 3,614,962 |
| P/L | 13,884 | 7,521 | (23,281) |
| NW | 152,904 | 139,020 | 131,499 |
| WC | (252,739) | (257,514) | (246,045) |
| Emp. | 97 | 108 | 67 |

DUNS 28-850-4699
## Young Enterprise
Peterley House, Peterley Road, Cowley, Oxford, Oxfordshire OX4 2TZ
**Tel:** 01865-776845 **Fax:** 01865-775671
**Web:** www.y-e.org.uk
**Reg No:** 0712260 **Estd:** 1963 Private Company Limited By Guarantee
**Line of Business:** Misc schools & educational services
**Directors:** Mrs M White, J B Fox, J W Froomberg, G Denham, Ms S T Lewis, Mrs V Pell, O Thoresen, D W Walter
**Co. Secretary:** Derek Walmsley
**Responsibilities**
**Senior:** Sheena Amin *(Trustee)*, Celia Carlsen *(Manager)*, Kevin Dundas *(Manager)*, Suzanne Fairbairn *(Manager)*, Judith Felton *(Director)*, Andrew Firr *(General Manager)*, Tony Hewitt *(Manager)*, Catherine Marchant *(Acting Chief Executive)*, Gene McLeod *(Manager)*, Michael Merchieca *(Chief Executive)*, Pam Oddy *(Area Manager North East & Cumb)*, Julie Pond *(Area Manager)*, Jazz Rayet *(Trustee)*, Jaswinder Rayet *(Director)*, William Salomon *(Honorary President)*
**Marketing:** Marie Harper *(Business Relationships Manager)*
**Sales:** Sally Hopkins *(Account Manager)*, Eileen Jackson *(Sales Manager)*
**HR:** Katie Kavanagh *(Personnel Officer)*
**Operations:** Sharon Davies *(Chief Operating Officer)*, Eira Guest *(Operations Manager)*
**Branches:** Young Enterprise, University Of Ulster, Jordanstown Shore Road, Newtownabbey, Co Antrim BT37 0QB
**US SIC:** 8299, 8211, 8249, 8221
**UK SIC:** 93300, 93200, 93100
**Auditors:** Critchleys Chartered Accountants
**Bankers:** HSBC Bank plc (40-35-35)

| | 31-07-14 | 31-07-13 | 31-07-12 |
|---|---|---|---|
| TO | 6,304,000 | 6,404,000 | 5,011,000 |
| P/L | 130,000 | 117,000 | (1,043,000) |
| NW | 1,661,000 | 1,558,000 | 1,659,000 |
| WC | 1,556,000 | 1,533,000 | 1,652,000 |
| Emp. | 130 | 124 | 143 |

DUNS 42-439-5721
## Young Enterprise Northern Ireland
145-149 Donegall Pass, Belfast BT7 1DT
**Tel:** 028-9032-7003
**Web:** www.yeni.co.uk
**Reg No:** 0032769NI **Estd:** 1997 Private Company Limited By Guarantee
**Line of Business:** Training services
**Directors:** Ms A M Mcgowan, P Cassidy, C H Russell, D Murphy, T P Griffiths, C J Conway, Dr A C Lennon, Ms U M Barker
**Responsibilities**
**Senior:** Carol Sitzsimmons *(Chief Executive)*
**US SIC:** 8299, 8699
**UK SIC:** 93300, 96902
**Auditors:** PricewaterhouseCoopers LLP
**Bankers:** Northern Bank Ltd (95-03-25)

| | 31-07-14 | 31-07-13 | 31-07-12 |
|---|---|---|---|
| TO | 1,098,000 | 2,518,000 | 2,504,000 |
| P/L | 63,000 | (31,000) | 30,000 |
| NW | 799,000 | 736,000 | 767,000 |
| WC | 796,000 | 731,000 | 827,000 |
| Emp. | 28 | 46 | 48 |

DUNS 73-772-8399
## Young Foundations Ltd
2 Acrefield Road, Birkenhead, Merseyside CH42 8LD
**Tel:** 01325-366365
**Web:** www.youngfoundations.com
**Reg No:** 5029887 **Estd:** 2004 Private Limited Company
**Line of Business:** Other human health activities
**Issued Capital:** £1
**Directors:** Mrs J Adey, N S Kelly
**Co. Secretary:** Roberto Pino
**Responsibilities**
**Senior:** Brian Dunham *(Md)*

**Branches:** Young Foundations Ltd, Meadholme, Dene Gr, Darlington, County Durham DL3 9LU
**US SIC:** 8091 **UK SIC:** 95200
**Bankers:** The Royal Bank Of Scotland Plc (16-17-31)

| | 30-06-14 | 30-06-13 | 30-06-12 |
|---|---|---|---|
| TO | 5,279,469 | 5,765,858 | 9,424,000 |
| P/L | (100,741) | 500,388 | (4,142,000) |
| NW | 3,703,793 | 3,850,132 | 504,000 |
| WC | (340,548) | (270,922) | (4,552,000) |
| Emp. | 116 | 123 | 128 |

DUNS 71-917-7763 Imp
## Young Living (Europe) Ltd.
(**Subsidiary of:** Yl Holdings Inc)
12 Harvard Way, Huntingdon, Cambridgeshire PE28 0NN
**Tel:** 01480-862840 **Fax:** 01480455088
**Web:** www.youngliving.com
**Reg No:** 5299340 **Estd:** 2004 Private Limited Company
**Line of Business:** Health food retailers
**Export Sales:** £17,034,900
**Issued Capital:** £2
**Directors:** R G Phillips, J F Doughty
**Responsibilities**
**Senior:** Simon Payton *(Manager)*
**Operations:** Simon Payton *(Manager)*
**US SIC:** 5499 **UK SIC:** 64100

| | 31-12-13 | 31-12-12 | 31-12-11 |
|---|---|---|---|
| TO | 17,533,651 | 13,085,078 | 11,411,058 |
| P/L | 731,977 | 1,305,788 | 1,784,627 |
| NW | 3,860,930 | 4,286,090 | 3,936,487 |
| WC | 2,675,490 | 3,125,232 | 2,843,658 |
| Emp. | 54 | 44 | 38 |

DUNS 23-872-1559
## Young Offenders Institute
Bedfont Road, Feltham, Middlesex TW13 4ND
**Tel:** 02088445000 **Fax:** 020-8893-7496
**Incorporate By Act Of Parliament**
**Line of Business:** Hm prisons
**Director:** I Ward
**Responsibilities**
**Senior:** N Pascoe *(Manager)*
**US SIC:** 8321 **UK SIC:** 96111
**Employees:** 550

DUNS 21-584-8632
## Young Peoples Services
Moss Street, Blackburn, Lancashire BB1 5JT
**Tel:** 01254298622
**Web:** www.blackburn.gov.uk
**Estd:** 2011 Proprietorship
**Line of Business:** Community projects
**Proprietor:** J Ratcliffe
**Responsibilities**
**Senior:** Imran Akuji *(Head Of Services)*
**US SIC:** 8699 **UK SIC:** 96902
**Employees:** 100

DUNS 50-396-3480
## Young Samuel Chambers (Y S C) Ltd
(**Subsidiary of:** Ysc Holdings Ltd)
Y S C Building, 49-51 Floral Street, London WC2E 9DA
**Tel:** 02075205555 **Fax:** 02075205556
**Web:** www.ysc.com
**Reg No:** 2402857 **Estd:** 1990 Private Limited Company
**Line of Business:** Business and management consultancy activities not elsewhere classified
**Export Sales:** £10,219,000
**Trading Style:** Y S C
**Issued Capital:** £34,497
**Principals:** Dr G Bains *(Managing)*, S Jawa, Doctor K Rowe, R Sharrock, Dr D D Anciano
**Responsibilities**
**Finance:** Benn Latham *(Finance Director)*
**Marketing:** Adele Preater *(Client Business Manager)*
**Admin:** Claire Baldock *(Personal Assistant)*, Lucy Ball *(Personal Assistant)*
**HR:** Amy Strong *(Human Resources Manager)*
**US SIC:** 7392, 7399
**UK SIC:** 83951, 83954
**Auditors:** BDO Stoy Hayward LLP
**Bankers:** National Westminster Bank Plc (60-00-01)

| | 30-04-14 | 30-04-13 | 30-04-12 |
|---|---|---|---|
| TO | 24,222,000 | 25,577,000 | 22,645,000 |
| P/L | 4,307,000 | 4,171,000 | 1,968,000 |
| NW | 13,149,000 | 3,290,000 | 6,355,000 |
| WC | 7,299,000 | 3,982,000 | 2,330,000 |
| Emp. | 135 | 149 | 149 |

DUNS 21-213-8882
## Young Street Chambers
76 Quay Street, Manchester M3 4PR
**Web:** www.youngstreetchambers.com
**Estd:** 2003 Proprietorship
**Line of Business:** Barristers
**Proprietor:** J Mcgoldrick
**US SIC:** 8111 **UK SIC:** 83500
**Employees:** 55

DUNS 28-881-9295
## The Young Vic Co
66 The Cut, Southwark, London SE1 8LZ
**Tel:** 02079222922 **Fax:** 02079228401
**Web:** www.youngvic.org
**Reg No:** 1188209 **Estd:** 1989 Private Company Limited By Guarantee
**Line of Business:** Art centres
**Trading Style:** Young Vic Theatre
**Directors:** Ms S E Hall, Ms K H Mchugh, Ms C A Lake, Mrs R J Skinner, Ms J Storie, P A Mckenna, B Winters, I Lewis
**Co. Secretary:** Sean Egan
**Responsibilities**
**Senior:** Murray Cooper-Melchiors *(Box Office Manager)*, Patrick Handley *(Director)*, Rory Kinnear *(Director)*, David Lan *(Artistic Director)*, Anna Lane *(Director)*, Steven Tompkins *(Director)*
**Marketing:** Libby Ridley *(Marketing Manager)*
**HR:** Frederica Notley *(General Manager)*
**Health & Safety:** Frederica Notley *(General Manager)*
**Facilities:** Frederica Notley *(General Manager)*
**US SIC:** 7911 **UK SIC:** 97913
**Auditors:** W H Payne & Co
**Bankers:** Allied Irish Bank (gb) (23-84-82)

| | 31-03-14 | 31-03-13 | 31-03-12 |
|---|---|---|---|
| TO | 7,544,585 | 6,108,706 | 6,164,734 |
| P/L | (7,345) | (543,901) | (307,582) |
| NW | 10,743,542 | 10,750,887 | 11,294,788 |
| WC | 520,861 | 290,813 | 564,189 |
| Emp. | 65 | 61 | 61 |

DUNS 34-635-9743 Imp
## Youngman Group Ltd
(**Subsidiary of:** Werner Access Products Uk Holdings Ltd)
The Causeway, Maldon, Essex CM9 4LJ
**Tel:** 01621-745900 **Fax:** 01621-745701
**Web:** www.youngmangroup.com
**Reg No:** 5442058 **Estd:** 2005 Private Limited Company
**Line of Business:** Manufacture of other fabricated metal products not elsewhere classified
**Export Sales:** £6,755,000
**Trading Style:** Youngman Group
**Issued Capital:** £627,813
**Directors:** P A Bentley, J Bungay, W T Allen, J J Stapleton, P Sullivan, C Owen
**Co. Secretary:** Geoffrey Hartenstein
**Responsibilities**
**Marketing:** Stuart Proudfoot *(Marketing Manager)*
**IT:** Rod Ibinson *(Computer Manager)*
**US SIC:** 3499, 5199
**UK SIC:** 31694, 61900
**Auditors:** Grant Thornton UK LLP

| | 30-06-13 | 30-06-12 | 30-06-11 |
|---|---|---|---|
| TO | 33,072,990 | 33,606,408 | 34,543,613 |
| P/L | 22,897 | (628,849) | 98,630 |
| NW | 3,187,446 | 3,201,607 | 3,699,462 |
| WC | 5,480,166 | 5,145,575 | 5,539,405 |
| Emp. | 206 | 200 | 185 |

DUNS 21-125-6822
## Youngs Container Transport Ltd
(**Subsidiary of:** Y C T Holdings Ltd)
Beacon Hill Industrial Estate, Botany Way, Purfleet, Essex RM19 1SR
**Tel:** 01708868081 **Fax:** 01708862769
**Web:** www.ytgroup.com
**Reg No:** 6608709 **Estd:** 2008 Private Limited Company
**Line of Business:** Freight transport by road not elsewhere classified
**Trading Style:** Youngs Container Tpt
**Issued Capital:** £4
**Director:** B E Walker
**US SIC:** 4213 **UK SIC:** 72300

| | 31-03-14 | 31-08-13 | 31-03-12 |
|---|---|---|---|
| TA | 2,089,206 | 2,254,211 | 1,079,396 |
| NW | (1,153,572) | (809,892) | (1,684,575) |
| WC | (453,572) | (409,892) | (92,567) |

DUNS 23-373-1863
## Your Bottom Line Ltd
Unit 22 Batley Enterprise Centre, Batley, West Yorkshire WF17 8LL
**Tel:** 01924-478669 **Fax:** 01133-087549
**Web:** www.ybloffice.co.uk
**Reg No:** 5182393 **VAT No:** 898276746
**Estd:** 2004 Private Limited Company
**Line of Business:** Other retail sale in non-specialised stores
**Issued Capital:** £100
**Director:** J Howarth
**Co. Secretary:** Ms Suzanne Howarth
**US SIC:** 5399 **UK SIC:** 65600

| | 31-12-13 | 31-12-12 | 31-12-11 |
|---|---|---|---|
| TA | 43,153 | 39,220 | 58,455 |
| NW | 6,397 | 5,225 | 4,389 |
| WC | 5,176 | 2,725 | 2,224 |

DUNS 21-813-7620
## Your Choice (Barnet) Ltd
Barnet House 1255 High Road, Whetstone, London N20 0EJ
**Tel:** 08003895225
**Web:** www.yourchoicebarnet.com
**Reg No:** 7873969 **Estd:** 2011 Private Limited Company
**Line of Business:** Social work activities without accommodation
**Issued Capital:** £1
**Directors:** Ms T D Lees, Mrs R N Touloui, T P Rogers, N C Turner
**Co. Secretary:** Troy Henshall
**US SIC:** 8321 **UK SIC:** 96111
**Bankers:** The Co-Operative Bank Plc (08-90-78)

| | 31-03-14 | 31-03-13 |
|---|---|---|
| TO | 5,331,000 | 7,099,000 |
| P/L | (1,019,000) | (241,000) |
| NW | (4,710,000) | (3,600,000) |
| WC | (606,000) | 785,000 |
| Emp. | 137 | 155 |

DUNS 21-228-3387
## Your Communications
Unit 2005 The Crescent, Solihull Parkway, Birmingham Business Park, Birmingham, West Midlands B37 7YE
**Tel:** 08001957000
**Web:** www.yourcommunications.com
**Line of Business:** Telecom services
**US SIC:** 4899 **UK SIC:** 79020
**Employees:** 897

DUNS 21-730-0364
## Your Electrical Supplies Service & Solutions (A) Ltd
Unit B Foxbridge Way, Normanton Industrial Estate, Normanton, West Yorkshire WF6 1TN
**Tel:** 08448-464-555 **Fax:** 08448-803-651
**Web:** www.yessselectrical.co.uk
**Reg No:** 7656807 **Estd:** 2011 Private Limited Company
**Line of Business:** Wholesale of other machinery for use in industry, trade and navigation
**Trading Style:** Yesss Electrical
**Issued Capital:** £2,000,001
**Directors:** A P Singleton, M Q Nolan, G K Lockwood, M A Abbey
**Co. Secretary:** Sisec Limited
**US SIC:** 7399, 5064
**UK SIC:** 83954, 61500
**Auditors:** KPMG LLP

| | 30-04-14 | 30-04-13 | 31-04-12 |
|---|---|---|---|
| TO | 56,889,000 | 4,627,847 | N/A |
| P/L | (15,599,000) | (16,951,699) | (102,047) |
| NW | (15,153,000) | (13,553,745) | 3,397,954 |
| WC | 1,492,000 | 271,074 | 3,394,363 |
| Emp. | 377 | 152 | 194 |

DUNS 71-866-2567
## Your Golf Travel Ltd
Clerks Court, 18-20 Farringdon Lane, London EC1R 3AU
**Tel:** 08001936630 **Fax:** 01292286424
**Web:** www.yourgolftravel.com
**Reg No:** 5250279 **Estd:** 2004 Private Limited Company
**Line of Business:** Travel agency activities
**Issued Capital:** £80,000
**Directors:** R A Marshall, A J Harding
**Co. Secretary:** John Williams
**Responsibilities**
**Senior:** Oliver Gunning *(Associate Director)*, Tom MacFarlane *(Associate Director)*
**Marketing:** Euan Gillan *(Head of Product Marketing & St)*, Andrew Manduca *(Email Marketing Manager)*, Craig Stephenson *(UK Product & Contracts Manager)*
**US SIC:** 7999, 4722
**UK SIC:** 97913, 77001

| | 31-03-14 | 31-03-13 | 31-03-11 |
|---|---|---|---|
| TO | 47,803,445 | 53,573,764 | 35,123,584 |
| P/L | 1,283,360 | 738,348 | 785,320 |
| NW | 4,715,545 | 1,810,363 | 1,292,644 |
| WC | 395,839 | (376,071) | (721,817) |
| Emp. | 95 | 79 | 66 |

DUNS 49-082-0123
## Your Health Ltd
(**Subsidiary of:** Farrowdale Properties Limited)
Holford House Holford Court, Hearthcote Road, Swadlincote, Derbyshire DE11 9BX
**Tel:** 01283226581
**Web:** www.yourhealthgroup.co.uk
**Reg No:** 3087838 **Estd:** 2013 Private Limited Company
**Line of Business:** Medical nursing home activities
**Issued Capital:** £2
**Directors:** Ms B J Davison Shaw, D Shaw
**Responsibilities**
**Senior:** Vicky Weller *(General Manager)*
**Branches:** Your Health Ltd, Cedar Court Nursing Home, Bretby, Burton-On-Trent, Staffordshire DE15 0QX
**US SIC:** 7399 **UK SIC:** 83954
**Auditors:** Buckler Spencer Ltd

| | 30-11-13 | 30-11-12 | 30-11-11 |
|---|---|---|---|
| TO | 5,896,520 | N/A | N/A |
| P/L | 433,944 | N/A | N/A |
| NW | 408,841 | (56,174) | (356,836) |
| WC | (2,161,264) | (417,019) | (364,761) |
| Emp. | 276 | N/A | N/A |

DUNS 21-600-4946
## Your Homes Newcastle
Unit 5 Greenfinch Way, Newcastle-Upon-Tyne, Tyne and Wear NE15 8NX
**Web:** www.yhn.org.uk
**Estd:** 2011 Proprietorship
**Line of Business:** Housing associations societies trusts & co-operatives
**Proprietor:** J Wylie
**US SIC:** 8321 **UK SIC:** 96111
**Employees:** 70

DUNS 73-820-3046
## Your Homes Newcastle Ltd
Y H N House, Benton Park Road, Newcastle-Upon-Tyne, Tyne and Wear NE7 7LX
**Fax:** 01912788789
**Web:** www.yhn.org.uk
**Reg No:** 5076256 **VAT No:** 837546595
**Estd:** 2004 Private Company Limited By Guarantee
**Line of Business:** Other letting of own property
**Directors:** Ms A V Dunn, A J Moore, Ms L Middlemiss, Ms D Huddart, J D Stokel-Walker, N Shukla, Ms L Stephenson, J Mccarty
**Co. Secretary:** Mrs Jill Davison
**Responsibilities**
**Senior:** George Allison *(Director)*, Judith Common *(Director)*, Philip Dibbs *(Director)*, Lisa Doherty *(Director)*, David Down *(Director)*, Robert Higgins *(Manager)*, Ammar Mirza *(Director)*, Julie Purvis *(Director)*, Elaine Snaith *(Director)*, Marion Talbot *(Director)*
**Branches:** Your Homes Newcastle Ltd, Park Rd, Newcastle-Upon-Tyne, Newcastle Upon Tyne, Tyne and Wear NE4 7EP
**US SIC:** 6519 **UK SIC:** 85000
**Auditors:** Ernst & Young LLP

| | 31-03-14 | 31-03-13 | 31-03-12 |
|---|---|---|---|
| TO | 31,094,000 | 33,002,000 | 32,923,000 |
| P/L | 12,000 | N/A | 156,000 |
| NW | 33,000 | 22,000 | 160,000 |
| WC | 33,000 | 22,000 | 2,065,000 |
| Emp. | 875 | 853 | 830 |

DUNS 21-558-5198
## Your Housing Group Ltd
Apex House, 266 Moseley Road, Levenshulme, Manchester M19 2LH
**Tel:** 01612482300
**Web:** www.harvesthousing.org.uk
**Reg No:** 0030666IP **Estd:** 2009 Friendly Society
**Line of Business:** Social work activities
**Responsibilities**
**Senior:** Brian Cronan *(CEO)*, Adrian Davids *(Manager)*, Robert Huntbach *(Manager)*, Dennis Small *(Manager)*
**US SIC:** 6732 **UK SIC:** 83100
**Auditors:** BDO LLP

| | 31-03-12 | 31-03-11 | 31-03-10 |
|---|---|---|---|
| TO | 83,581,000 | 82,314,000 | 77,433,000 |
| P/L | 6,778,000 | 8,241,000 | 3,474,000 |
| NW | 69,586,000 | 85,058,000 | 73,254,000 |
| WC | 26,464,000 | 16,812,000 | 765,000 |
| Emp. | 592 | 622 | 557 |

DUNS 22-555-9640
## Your-Move.Co.U K Ltd
(**Subsidiary of:** Lsl Property Services Plc)
Newcastle House, Albany Court, Newcastle Business Park, Newcastle-Upon-Tyne, Tyne and Wear NE4 7YB
**Tel:** 01912334000 **Fax:** 01912334700
**Web:** www.your-move.co.uk
**Reg No:** 1864469 **Estd:** 1984 Private Limited Company
**Line of Business:** Real estate agencies
**Issued Capital:** £7,476,000
**Directors:** P Hardy, Mrs L Charles-Jones, S Cox, J C Mcauley, J A Cooke, A S Gill
**Co. Secretary:** Mrs Sapna Fitzgerald
**Responsibilities**
**Senior:** gordon Fowlis *(Manager)*, William Fowlis *(Director)*
**Marketing:** Jackie Fell *(Marketing Manager)*
**Health & Safety:** Karen Morgan *(Facilities Manager)*
**Facilities:** Karen Morgan *(Facilities Manager)*
**Purchasing:** Karen Morgan *(Facilities Manager)*
**Branches:** Your-Move.co.u K Ltd, 714 London Road, Aylesford, Kent ME20 6BL
**US SIC:** 6531, 8911

**UK SIC:** 83400, 83701
**Auditors:** Ernst & Young LLP
**Bankers:** Barclays Bank Plc (20-59-61)

| | 31-12-13 | 31-12-12 | 31-12-11 |
|---|---|---|---|
| TO | 77,599,000 | 70,257,000 | 64,568,000 |
| P/L | 5,434,000 | 2,725,000 | 256,000 |
| NW | 16,357,000 | 11,985,000 | 9,820,000 |
| WC | 11,722,000 | 9,133,000 | 6,695,000 |
| Emp. | 1,943 | 1,765 | 1,695 |

DUNS 34-655-2693
## Your World Recruitment Ltd
(**Subsidiary of:** Your World Recruitment Group Ltd)
4th Floor, 5 Devonshire Square L, London Uk, London EC2M 4YD
**Tel:** 020 7220 0811 **Fax:** 020 7220 0810
**Web:** www.yourworldmedical.com
**Reg No:** 5460751 **VAT No:** 976050409
**Estd:** 2005 Private Limited Company
**Line of Business:** Employment and recruitment companies and consultants
**Issued Capital:** £20,000
**Directors:** R J Phillips, A Moss
**Co. Secretary:** Ms Sally Moss
**Responsibilities**
**Senior:** Gemma Calder *(Office Manager)*
**US SIC:** 7361 **UK SIC:** 83954
**Auditors:** Pentins Business Advisers Ltd
**Bankers:** HSBC Bank plc (40-20-23)

| | 31-12-13 | 31-12-12 | 31-12-11 |
|---|---|---|---|
| TO | 26,629,856 | 17,032,611 | 16,582,886 |
| P/L | 846,601 | 301,098 | (171,392) |
| NW | 622,062 | 117,731 | 30,795 |
| WC | 626,618 | 371,493 | 110,361 |
| Emp. | 61 | 43 | N/A |

DUNS 23-913-6539 **Imp**
## Yourcash Ltd
(**Subsidiary of:** Yourcash Solutions Ltd)
Willow House, Breckland, Linford Wood, Milton Keynes, Buckinghamshire MK14 6EU
**Tel:** 01908574100
**Web:** www.yourcash.com
**Reg No:** 3904039 **Estd:** 2000 Private Limited Company
**Line of Business:** Cash machines
**Trading Style:** Yourcash Limited
**Issued Capital:** £100,000
**Directors:** Ms J B Campbell, W F Raynal, P Aratoon, E Ogilvie
**Co. Secretary:** Peter Aratoon
**Responsibilities**
**Senior:** Deborah Esslemont *(Manager)*, Devendra Kumar *(Manager)*, Ian Masterson *(Warehouse Manager)*, Mark Pauley *(Sales Manager)*
**Marketing:** Anthony Chan *(Marketing Manager)*
**Sales:** Stuart Oniell *(Sales Manager)*, Mark Pauley *(Sales Manager)*
**IT:** Lee Middleton *(Computer Manager)*
**Facilities:** Shelly Flood *(Facilities Manager)*
**US SIC:** 3579 **UK SIC:** 33010
**Auditors:** Deloitte & Touche LLP
**Bankers:** National Westminster Bank Plc (60-14-55)

| | 31-12-13 | 31-12-12 | 31-12-11 |
|---|---|---|---|
| TO | 19,651,000 | 22,781,000 | 24,847,000 |
| P/L | (553,000) | 695,000 | 1,303,000 |
| NW | 3,178,000 | 17,846,000 | 17,175,000 |
| WC | (2,098,000) | 12,393,000 | 11,025,000 |
| Emp. | 86 | 86 | 78 |

DUNS 57-807-2316
## Yours Clothing Ltd
(**Subsidiary of:** Ak Retail Holdings Ltd)
1184 Lincoln Road, Peterborough, Cambridgeshire PE4 6LA
**Tel:** 01733383890 **Fax:** 01933-419819
**Web:** www.yoursclothing.co.uk
**Reg No:** 2886196 **Estd:** 1994 Private Limited Company
**Line of Business:** Armed service outfitters
**Issued Capital:** £200
**Directors:** Ms D A Torr, R S Dorka, A R Killingsworth, R J Thurlow, S Hatteea
**Co. Secretary:** David Preece
**Branches:** Yours Clothing Ltd, 14A King St, Thetford, Norfolk IP24 2AP
**US SIC:** 5621 **UK SIC:** 64500
**Auditors:** Ensors
**Bankers:** Barclays Bank Plc (20-67-37)

| | 02-02-14 | 03-02-13 | 29-02-12 |
|---|---|---|---|
| TO | 32,098,001 | 26,620,026 | 23,458,585 |
| P/L | 2,267,773 | 1,433,928 | 25,194 |
| NW | 3,515,248 | 1,395,411 | 338,964 |
| WC | 1,764,778 | 59,455 | (755,877) |
| Emp. | 445 | 426 | 338 |

DUNS 23-123-8218
## Youth Action Northern Ireland Ltd
14 College Square North, Belfast BT1 6AS
**Tel:** 028-9024-0551 **Fax:** 028-9024-0556
**Web:** www.youthaction.org
**Reg No:** 0035317NI **Estd:** 1998 Private Company Limited By Guarantee
**Line of Business:** Youth centres and associations
**Directors:** C Maneely, Ms S P Ballantine, Dr A M Gray, C Maneely, Miss A M Barnett, J NIcholson, B W Hannaway, R D Gould
**Responsibilities**
**Senior:** Martin McMullan *(Assistant Director / Area Base)*, Susan Mccullough *(Director)*, June Trimble MBE *(Manager)*
**Finance:** Colleen McGivern *(Financial Officer)*
**Marketing:** Anne McTaggart *(Fundraising Manager)*
**Admin:** Shirley Moore *(Coordinator of Services and Ad)*, Elspeth Webb *(Administration Officer)*
**Operations:** Elaine Lavery *(Quality Assurance Coordinator)*, Martin McMullan *(Assistant Director / Area Base)*
**US SIC:** 8699 **UK SIC:** 96902
**Bankers:** Northern Bank Ltd (95-01-28)

| | 31-12-13 | 31-12-12 | 31-12-11 |
|---|---|---|---|
| TO | 1,935,734 | 1,862,319 | 2,037,877 |
| P/L | 46,931 | 81,450 | 47,200 |
| NW | 3,850,151 | 3,803,220 | 3,721,770 |
| WC | 906,343 | 807,024 | 663,075 |
| Emp. | 58 | 53 | 61 |

DUNS 21-602-0991
## Youth Connexions
County Hall High Street, Newport, Isle of Wight PO30 1UD
**Web:** www.iwight.com
**Estd:** 1994
**Line of Business:** Information services
**Proprietor:** S Dear
**US SIC:** 7399 **UK SIC:** 83954
**Employees:** 50

DUNS 22-639-9277
## Youth Hostels Association (England & Wales)
Trevelyan House, Matlock, Derbyshire DE4 3YH
**Web:** www.yha.org.uk
**Reg No:** 0301657IP **VAT No:** 198022453
**Estd:** 1930 Friendly Society
**Line of Business:** Charities and charitable organisations
**Trading Style:** Youth Hostels Association (England & Wales)
**Principals:** D Hanson *(Chairman)*, C Logan *(Managing)*, T Pagan *(Financial)*, Ms L Lloyd *(Marketing)*
**Branches:** Youth Hostels Association (England & Wales), Elmscott, Hartland, Bideford, Devon EX39 6ES
**US SIC:** 8699 **UK SIC:** 96902
**Auditors:** Grant Thornton
**Bankers:** Barclays Bank Plc (20-74-09)
**Employees:** 150

DUNS 21-748-3275
## The Youth Justice Agency of Northern Ireland
41 -43 Waring Street, Belfast BT1 2DY
**Tel:** 02890316400
**Web:** www.youthjusticeagencyni.gov.uk
**Estd:** 2012
**Line of Business:** Central government
**Trading Style:** Youth Justice Agency
**Responsibilities**
**Senior:** Tony O'neill *(Manager)*
**US SIC:** 9121 **UK SIC:** 91110
**Employees:** 100

DUNS 23-304-2121
## The Youth Justice Board
102 Petty France, London SW1H 9AJ
**Tel:** 02033345300 **Fax:** 02033342250
**Web:** www.yjb.gov.uk
**Estd:** 1998 Incorporate By Act Of Parliament
**Line of Business:** General (overall) public service activities
**Principals:** Lord N Warner *(Chairman)*, C Wilson, Dr H Williamson Cbe, R Allen B A A D, Dr T Nutale, Mrs A Scott Jp, L Whyte, J Mosley
**Responsibilities**
**Senior:** Lin Hinnigan *(Chief Executive Officer)*, Graig Watkins *(Corporate Services Manager)*
**Operations:** Daniel Craig *(Media Manager)*
**Branches:** The Youth Justice Board, Lindisfarne Court, Unit 38E, Jarrow, Tyne and Wear NE32 3HG
**US SIC:** 9121 **UK SIC:** 91110
**Employees:** 250

DUNS 21-879-1089
## Youth Offending Service
4640 Kingsgate, Cascade Way, Oxford Business Park South, Oxford, Oxfordshire OX4 2SU
**Tel:** 01865816500
**Web:** www.oxfordshire.gov.uk
**Estd:** 2012
**Line of Business:** Probation services
**Responsibilities**
**Senior:** Amrik Panaser *(Youth Offending Service Manage)*
**US SIC:** 9121 **UK SIC:** 91110
**Employees:** 60

DUNS 21-588-0524
## The Youth Offending Team
Ivybank, 45 St Davids Hill, Exeter, Devon EX4 4DN
**Tel:** 01392-384978
**Web:** www.devon.gov.uk
**Estd:** 2011 Proprietorship
**Line of Business:** Probation services
**Proprietor:** S Walker
**Responsibilities**
**Senior:** Jim Wood *(Area Manager)*
**US SIC:** 9211 **UK SIC:** 91200
**Employees:** 50

DUNS 21-233-3196
## Youth Offending Team
Tolladine Road, Worcester, Worcestershire WR4 9NB
**Tel:** 01905-732200
**Estd:** 2007 Proprietorship
**Line of Business:** The dss
**Proprietor:** K Barham
**US SIC:** 8321 **UK SIC:** 96111
**Employees:** 60

DUNS 21-232-3137
## Youth Service
Council Offices, Wellington Road, Ashton-Under-Lyne, Lancashire OL6 6DL
**Tel:** 01613428355
**Web:** www.tameside.gov.uk
**Estd:** 2002
**Line of Business:** Local government
**Responsibilities**
**Senior:** Steven Pleasent *(Chief Executive)*
**US SIC:** 9121 **UK SIC:** 91110
**Employees:** 3,000

DUNS 22-161-6043 **Imp**
## Youth Sport Trust
Loughborough Park, 2 Oakwood Drive, Loughborough, Leicestershire LE11 3QF
**Fax:** 01509-210-851
**Web:** www.youthsporttrust.org
**Reg No:** 4180163 **Estd:** 2001 Private Company Limited By Guarantee
**Line of Business:** Schools (leisure based activities)
**Trading Style:** Yst
**Directors:** Mrs L B Gadd, Ms S E Munday, B I Stimson, M Woods, J D Edwards, T P Hollingsworth, Viscount C Mackintosh Of Halifax, Baroness S C Campbell
**Co. Secretary:** Ms Joanne Simpson
**Responsibilities**
**Senior:** Sophie Goldschmidt *(Director)*, Steve Grainger *(Chief Executive)*, Christopher Grant *(Director)*, Melanie Honnor *(Director)*, Thelma Probert *(Manager)*, Hellen shuttleworth *(Human Resources Manager)*, john steele *(CEo)*
**Marketing:** Sarah Collinson *(Marketing Manager)*
**HR:** Lorraine Baldock *(Human Resources Manager)*, Hellen shuttleworth *(Human Resources Manager)*
**Health & Safety:** Lorraine Baldock *(Human Resources Manager)*
**Branches:** Youth Sport Trust, Walkden House, 10 Melton Street, London NW1 2EB
**US SIC:** 8299 **UK SIC:** 93300
**Auditors:** Baker Tilly UK Audit LLP
**Bankers:** Bank Of Scotland (12-11-01)

| | 31-03-14 | 31-03-13 | 31-03-12 |
|---|---|---|---|
| TO | 17,948,997 | 15,175,729 | 24,275,071 |
| P/L | 901,024 | (1,718,011) | (586,360) |
| NW | 8,088,191 | 7,187,167 | 8,905,178 |
| WC | 7,753,391 | 6,901,151 | 8,567,550 |
| Emp. | 95 | 91 | 89 |

DUNS 28-871-5758
## Youth With A Mission Ltd
6 Highfield Oval Ambrose Lane, Harpenden, Hertfordshire AL5 4BX
**Tel:** 01582463300
**Web:** www.ywamharpenden.org
**Reg No:** 1049516 **VAT No:** 490408741
**Estd:** 1972 Private Company Limited By Guarantee
**Line of Business:** Activities of religious organisations
**Principals:** L Green *(Chairman)*, C Tinnion, K L Shreeves, S C Mayers, M A Venning, Ms J A Wright, H B Clarke, D F Lambert
**Responsibilities**
**Senior:** Peter Irwin Clark *(Director)*, John Peachey *(Manager)*, John Pugh-Smith *(Director)*
**Branches:** Youth With A Mission Ltd, Youth With A Mission, Kings Lodge, Nuneaton, Warwickshire CV10 0TZ
**US SIC:** 7399 **UK SIC:** 83954
**Auditors:** Mazars Neville Russell
**Bankers:** National Westminster Bank Plc (60-06-20)

| | 31-08-13 | 31-08-12 | 31-08-11 |
|---|---|---|---|
| TO | 2,991,616 | 3,170,745 | 3,120,501 |
| P/L | 60,936 | 44,564 | 565,509 |
| NW | 6,326,163 | 6,265,228 | 6,220,664 |
| WC | 586,804 | 539,708 | 544,281 |

DUNS 21-680-2865
## Youview Tv Ltd
10 Lower Thames Street, Third Floor, London EC3R 6YT
**Tel:** 02033557955
**Web:** www.youview.com
**Reg No:** 7308805 **Estd:** 2010 Private Limited Company
**Line of Business:** Radio activities
**Issued Capital:** £43
**Directors:** A W Green, P A Thornton-Jones, K O Clifton, S P Duffy, P Dunthorne, G Whitehead, T Harrison, S J Pitts
**Co. Secretary:** Mrs Christina Pettit
**US SIC:** 4832, 4833
**UK SIC:** 97411
**Auditors:** KPMG LLP

| | 31-03-14 | 31-03-13 | 31-03-12 |
|---|---|---|---|
| TO | 43,076,000 | 44,444,000 | 32,664,000 |
| P/L | 921,000 | 1,027,000 | 797,000 |
| NW | 1,406,000 | 2,201,000 | 578,000 |
| WC | 1,303,000 | 2,058,000 | 447,000 |
| Emp. | 99 | 55 | 29 |

DUNS 76-388-7965 **Exp**
## Ypm 2012 Ltd
(**Subsidiary of:** A N M Group Ltd)
Aston Street, Sheffield, South Yorkshire S2 5BD
**Tel:** 01977658000
**Web:** www.anmgroup.co.uk
**Reg No:** 2555685 **VAT No:** 600041324
**Estd:** 1990 Private Limited Company
**Line of Business:** Wholesale of meat and meat products
**Export Markets:** W Europe
**Issued Capital:** £2,000,000
**Directors:** D Brown, J B Mcintosh, J I Farquharson, M T Macaulay, J S Cruickshank, J F Gregor, J W Gordon, P J Chapman
**Co. Secretary:** Lc Secretaries Limited
**Responsibilities**
**Senior:** John Fowlie *(Manager)*, Patrick Machray *(Director)*, Grant Rogerson *(Director)*, Andrew Tucker *(Manager)*
**Finance:** Andrew Tucker *(Manager)*
**Admin:** Margaret Scholey *(Administration Manager)*
**HR:** Margaret Scholey *(Administration Manager)*
**Engineering:** Darren Dennison *(Production Manager)*
**US SIC:** 5147, 5423
**UK SIC:** 61700, 64100
**Auditors:** Williamson & Dunn

| | 31-12-13 | 31-12-12 | 31-12-11 |
|---|---|---|---|
| TO | 117 | 39,569,999 | 53,279,717 |
| P/L | 3,121,150 | (6,374,259) | (1,426,851) |
| NW | N/A | (3,121,150) | 2,793,608 |
| WC | N/A | (4,146,150) | (535,653) |
| Emp. | N/A | 98 | 130 |

DUNS 23-222-4746
## Ysgol Bryn Elian High School
Windsor Drive, Colwyn Bay, Clwyd LL29 8HU
**Tel:** 01492-518215
**Web:** www.brynelian.conwy.sch.uk
**Estd:** 1975
**Line of Business:** General secondary education
**Director:** S K Matthews
**Responsibilities**
**Senior:** Eichne Hughes *(Manager)*
**Finance:** Brian Crossland *(Finance Director)*
**US SIC:** 8211 **UK SIC:** 93200
**Employees:** 85

DUNS 21-706-3525
## Ysgol Clywedog
Ruthin Road, Wrexham, Clwyd LL13 7UB
**Tel:** 01978 346800
**Web:** www.clywedog.org
**Estd:** 2010
**Line of Business:** Schools (local authority)
**Responsibilities**
**Senior:** Martin Hulland *(Head Teacher)*
**US SIC:** 8211 **UK SIC:** 93200
**Employees:** 100

DUNS 21-579-8276
## Ysgol Crug Glas
Croft Street, Swansea, West Glamorgan SA1 1QA
**Tel:** 01792652388
**Web:** https://swansea-edunet.gov.uk
**Estd:** 1954 Proprietorship
**Line of Business:** Schools (special)
**Proprietor:** P Martin

**Responsibilities**
**IT:** Joanne Watkins *(Network, Security Manager)*
**US SIC:** 8299 **UK SIC:** 93300
**Employees:** 60

DUNS 21-772-7422
## Ysgol David Hughes
Pentraeth Road, Menai Bridge, Gwynedd LL59 5SS
**Tel:** 01248712287
**Web:** http://ysgoldavidhughes.org
**Estd:** 2002 Partnership
**Line of Business:** General secondary education
**Partners:** Dr B Jones, Mrs H Evans, M Harris
**Responsibilities**
**Senior:** Huw Aemyr-Williams *(Head Teacher)*, Darren Harris *(Partner)*
**IT:** Glenda Jone *(Senior IT Executive)*
**US SIC:** 8211 **UK SIC:** 93200
**Employees:** 100

DUNS 21-772-5461
## Ysgol Gyfun Cwm Rhymni
Gellihaf Road, Blackwood, Gwent NP12 3UY
**Tel:** 01443875227
**Web:** www.cwmrhymni.com
**Estd:** 1988 Partnership
**Line of Business:** Schools (local authority)
**Partners:** S Phillips, H Mathias, O At Dafydd
**Responsibilities**
**IT:** Marion John *(Senior IT Executive)*
**US SIC:** 8211 **UK SIC:** 93200
**Employees:** 100

DUNS 21-773-8622
## Ysgol Gyfun Garth Olwg
Main Road, Pontypridd, Mid Glamorgan CF38 1DX
**Tel:** 01443219580
**Estd:** 1990 Proprietorship
**Line of Business:** Schools (local authority)
**Proprietor:** P Griffiths
**US SIC:** 8211 **UK SIC:** 93200
**Employees:** 70

DUNS 21-033-9327
## Ysgol Gysun Penweddig
Llanbadarn Road, Llanon, Dyfed SY23 3QN
**Tel:** 01970-639499
**Web:** www.penweddig.ceredigion.sch.uk
**Estd:** 2001 Proprietorship
**Line of Business:** Schools (foundation)
**Proprietor:** G Isan
**Responsibilities**
**Senior:** Gwenallt Isan *(Head Teacher)*
**US SIC:** 8211 **UK SIC:** 93200
**Employees:** 75

DUNS 21-880-4488
## Ysgol Pen Coch
Prince Of Wales Avenue, Flint, Clwyd CH6 5NF
**Tel:** 01352792730
**Web:** www.flintshire.gov.uk
**Estd:** 2012
**Line of Business:** Adult education locations
**Responsibilities**
**Senior:** Ange Anderson *(Head Teacher)*
**US SIC:** 8299 **UK SIC:** 93300
**Employees:** 60

DUNS 21-499-9760
## Ysgol Pen-y-Bryn
Wentworth Avenue, Colwyn Bay, Clwyd LL29 6DD
**Tel:** 01492531260
**Web:** www.ysgolpenybryn.com
**Estd:** 1987 Proprietorship
**Line of Business:** Schools (foundation)
**Principals:** J Roberts, J Maclennan *(Proprietor)*
**US SIC:** 8211 **UK SIC:** 93200
**Employees:** 60

DUNS 21-582-3450
## Ysgolbrobanw Junior School
Walter Road, Ammanford, Dyfed SA18 2NF
**Tel:** 01269592481
**Web:** www.brobanw.amdro.org.uk
**Estd:** 2011 Proprietorship
**Line of Business:** Schools (local authority)
**Partners:** Mrs M Davies, Ms M Davies
**US SIC:** 8211 **UK SIC:** 93200
**Employees:** 91

DUNS 64-256-1153
## Ysgolion - Schools
Bethel Road, Caernarfon, Gwynedd LL55 1HW
**Tel:** 01286673076
**Web:** www.syrhughowen.gwynedd.sch.uk
**Estd:** 2012 Proprietorship
**Line of Business:** Schools (local authority)
**Proprietor:** D Williams
**Responsibilities**
**Senior:** Paul Matthews-Jones *(Head Teacher)*
**US SIC:** 8211 **UK SIC:** 93200
**Employees:** 60

DUNS 54-904-3719
## Ysguborwen Nursing Home
Ysguborwen, Aberdare, Mid Glamorgan CF44 0AX
**Tel:** 01685-872606
**Web:** www.ysguborwen.com
**Estd:** 1990 Partnership
**Line of Business:** Nursing homes
**Trading Style:** Ysguborwen House
**Partners:** M Slater, Mrs S Slater
**Responsibilities**
**Senior:** Jackie Owens *(Manager)*, Debbie Strong *(General Manager)*
**IT:** Cerys Sansom *(Admin)*
**HR:** Jackie Owens *(Manager)*
**Facilities:** Jackie Owens *(Manager)*
**US SIC:** 8051, 6732
**UK SIC:** 95100, 83100
**Bankers:** Lloyds TSB Bank plc (30-90-54)
**Employees:** 100

DUNS 22-021-7066
## Yss Ltd
Training & Enterprise Centre, 13 - 17 Carden Street, Worcester, Worcestershire WR1 2AT
**Tel:** 01299-252300
**Web:** www.yss.org.uk
**Reg No:** 4024428 **Estd:** 2000 Private Limited Company
**Line of Business:** Social work activities without accommodation
**Directors:** I W Richards, Ms S J Mcfarlane, Ms G Furse, H M Barker, Mrs P Bradbury, Ms C A Driscoll, Ms S D Kelley, R Peel
**Co. Secretary:** Ian Richards
**US SIC:** 8321 **UK SIC:** 96111
**Bankers:** Lloyds TSB Bank plc (30-99-90)

| | 31-03-14 | 31-03-13 | 31-03-12 |
|---|---|---|---|
| TO | 1,792,008 | 1,728,648 | 2,001,229 |
| P/L | 41,237 | (192,365) | (6,656) |
| NW | 404,217 | 362,980 | 555,345 |
| WC | 392,316 | 318,507 | 503,116 |
| Emp. | 55 | 55 | 69 |

DUNS 21-168-0371
## Ystrad Mynach College
Ystrad Mynach Campus, Twyn Road, Hengoed, Mid Glamorgan CF82 7XR
**Web:** www.ystrad-mynach.ac.uk
**Estd:** 1969
**Line of Business:** Further education schools and colleges
**Director:** B Davies
**Branches:** Ystrad Mynach College, Training & Technology Centre, 19 High St, Bargoed, Mid Glamorgan CF81 8RA
**US SIC:** 8221 **UK SIC:** 93100
**Employees:** 500

DUNS 23-775-3343 **Imp**
## Ytc Ltd
Maclaren House Skerne Road, Driffield, North Humberside YO25 6PN
**Tel:** 01377272278
**Web:** www.yugiohtradingcard.co.uk
**Reg No:** 3768619 **VAT No:** 282256258
**Estd:** 2008 Private Limited Company
**Line of Business:** Manufacture of other wearing apparel and accessories not elsewhere classified
**Trading Style:** Yorkshire Trading Co, Yorkshire Clothing Co
**Issued Capital:** £1,000
**Directors:** R D Nichols, A T Nichols, P J Nichols
**Co. Secretary:** Ms Deborah Bath
**Responsibilities**
**HR:** Samantha O'Neale *(Personnel Manager)*
**Health & Safety:** Samantha O'Neale *(Personnel Manager)*
**Branches:** Ytc Ltd, Bedford Street, North Shields, Tyne and Wear NE29 6QH
**US SIC:** 2389, 5963, 5961
**UK SIC:** 45393, 65600
**Auditors:** White & Hoggard
**Bankers:** HSBC Bank plc (40-40-22)

| | 31-10-13 | 31-10-12 | 31-10-11 |
|---|---|---|---|
| TO | 23,893,781 | 21,541,124 | 20,700,541 |
| P/L | 2,201,794 | 1,483,751 | 469,280 |
| NW | 9,124,271 | 7,896,413 | 6,634,937 |
| WC | 836,631 | 1,154,779 | 2,103,060 |
| Emp. | 351 | 324 | 319 |

DUNS 73-716-1930
## Ytm Furniture Ltd
Grove Road, Pontefract, West Yorkshire WF8 1EE
**Tel:** 01977705020
**Web:** www.ytmfurniture.com
**Reg No:** 4974761 **VAT No:** 660376337
**Estd:** 1981 Private Limited Company
**Line of Business:** Manufacture of other office and shop furniture
**Issued Capital:** £2
**Director:** A C Davies
**Co. Secretary:** Damien Duffy
**US SIC:** 2599, 2517
**UK SIC:** 46720, 46714
**Auditors:** D'Arcy-Howard Castleford Ltd
**Bankers:** Lloyds TSB Bank plc (30-99-01)

| | 31-12-13 | 31-12-12 | 31-12-11 |
|---|---|---|---|
| TA | 2 | 2 | 2 |
| NW | 2 | 2 | 2 |

DUNS 28-946-5098 **Imp**
## Ytm Group Ltd
Innovation House, Castleford, West Yorkshire WF10 5NP
**Tel:** 01977665050 **Fax:** 01977511155
**Web:** www.ytmfurniture.com
**Reg No:** 1605310 **Estd:** 1981 Private Limited Company
**Line of Business:** Manufacturers of upholstered chairs and seats
**Issued Capital:** £250
**Principals:** P Duffy *(Managing)*, D P Duffy, A C Davies
**Co. Secretary:** Dominic Duffy
**Responsibilities**
**HR:** Joanne Stones *(Human Resources Manager)*
**Health & Safety:** Joanne Stones *(Human Resources Manager)*
**US SIC:** 2599, 2517
**UK SIC:** 46720, 46714
**Auditors:** D"Arcy-Howard Castleford Ltd
**Bankers:** Lloyds TSB Bank plc (30-99-01)

| | 31-12-13 | 31-12-12 | 31-12-11 |
|---|---|---|---|
| TO | 6,789,445 | 8,617,579 | 8,357,719 |
| P/L | (493,531) | 523,820 | 273,434 |
| NW | 485,862 | 981,402 | 926,283 |
| WC | (507,491) | (50,852) | (102,754) |
| Emp. | 129 | 129 | 105 |

DUNS 42-440-6564 **Imp**
## Yuanda (Uk) Co. Ltd
(**Subsidiary of:** Tricor Subscribers Limited)
12th Floor 125 Old Broad Street, London EC2N 1AR
**Tel:** 02075627766 **Fax:** 02087-9390759
**Web:** www.yuanda-europe.com
**Reg No:** 4428369 **VAT No:** 799188449
**Estd:** 2003 Private Limited Company
**Line of Business:** Building services
**Issued Capital:** £500,000
**Directors:** F W Lee, R Tong, D Baumeler, A J Lazenby
**Co. Secretary:** Dominik Baumeler
**US SIC:** 1799, 3442, 1751
**UK SIC:** 50000, 31420, 50400
**Auditors:** Carter Backer Winter LLP
**Bankers:** Bank Of China (40-50-37)

| | 31-12-13 | 31-12-12 | 31-12-11 |
|---|---|---|---|
| TO | 46,285,583 | 43,910,776 | 7,701,976 |
| P/L | (1,522,277) | (3,631,414) | (3,555,235) |
| NW | (8,339,208) | (6,816,931) | (3,185,517) |
| WC | (8,479,484) | (7,038,307) | (3,463,353) |
| Emp. | 52 | 51 | 41 |

DUNS 42-399-4610 **Imp**
## Yuasa Battery Europe Ltd
(**Subsidiary of:** Gs Yuasa Corporation)
Unit 13 Hants Rise, South Marston Industrial Estate, Swindon, Wiltshire SN3 4TG
**Tel:** 01793833555 **Fax:** 0121-325-5602
**Web:** www.yuasaeurope.com
**Reg No:** 4387136 **Estd:** 1995 Private Limited Company
**Line of Business:** Manufacture of accumulators, primary cells and primary batteries
**Export Sales:** £111,605,000
**Issued Capital:** £27,500,000
**Directors:** A Furukawa, M Furumi, M Yamamura, S Sugitani, P Marciano
**Co. Secretary:** Gareth Beale
**Responsibilities**
**Senior:** John Houmoller *(Manager)*
**US SIC:** 3692, 6711
**UK SIC:** 34321, 83962
**Auditors:** Deloitte LLP
**Bankers:** The Sumitomo Bank, Ltd (40-51-25)

| | 31-12-13 | 31-12-12 | 31-12-11 |
|---|---|---|---|
| TO | 183,759,000 | 169,832,000 | 168,526,000 |
| P/L | 2,321,000 | (2,976,000) | 3,714,000 |
| NW | 16,954,000 | 15,361,000 | 19,319,000 |
| WC | 19,900,000 | 18,280,000 | 23,653,000 |
| Emp. | 561 | 490 | 485 |

DUNS 22-759-8505 **Imp-Exp**
## Yuasa Battery (U K) Ltd
(**Subsidiary of:** Gs Yuasa Corporation)
Unit 22 Rassau Industrial Estate, Rassau, Ebbw Vale, Gwent NP23 5SD
**Tel:** 01495350121 **Fax:** 08708500265
**Web:** www.yuasa-battery.co.uk
**Reg No:** 1561536 **VAT No:** 356518536
**Estd:** 1981 Private Limited Company
**Line of Business:** Manufacturers of batteries
**Export Markets:** Europe; Asia
**Export Sales:** £75,195,949
**Issued Capital:** £10,000,000
**Directors:** S Sugitani, M Yamamura
**Co. Secretary:** Gareth Beale
**Responsibilities**
**Senior:** Wayne Turner *(Logistics Manager)*
**Health & Safety:** Selwyn Thomas *(Environmental Manager)*
**Facilities:** Shaun Gardner *(Plant Manager)*
**Operations:** Selwyn Thomas *(Environmental Manager)*
**Purchasing:** Tyron Williams *(Chief Buyer)*
**Fleet:** Wayne Turner *(Logistics Manager)*
**Engineering:** Shaun Gardner *(Plant Manager)*, Robert West *(Engineer)*
**US SIC:** 3692 **UK SIC:** 34321
**Auditors:** Deloitte LLP
**Bankers:** Lloyds TSB Bank plc (30-92-97)

| | 31-12-13 | 31-12-12 | 31-12-11 |
|---|---|---|---|
| TO | 148,656,650 | 131,610,803 | 116,638,173 |
| P/L | (2,379,737) | (6,418,982) | 137,717 |
| NW | (4,591,367) | (2,875,202) | 3,427,500 |
| WC | 3,019,007 | 4,412,552 | 11,289,737 |
| Emp. | 401 | 342 | 343 |

DUNS 21-246-7784
## Yue Yee House
303 Greenbrow Road, Manchester M23 2UH
**Tel:** 01614988884
**Estd:** 2002
**Line of Business:** Take-away food shops
**US SIC:** 5812 **UK SIC:** 66110
**Employees:** 84

DUNS 22-900-7976
## Yuill & Dodds Ltd
Unit 6, Hamilton, Lanarkshire ML3 0ED
**Tel:** 01698720700 **Fax:** 01698720709
**Web:** www.yuill-and-dodds.co.uk
**Reg No:** 0088529SC **VAT No:** 260716863
**Estd:** 1952 Private Limited Company
**Line of Business:** Other supporting land transport activities
**Issued Capital:** £970,823
**Directors:** Ms K L Kerr, B A Yuill, J B Waddell
**Co. Secretary:** Ms Letitia Yuill
**US SIC:** 4789 **UK SIC:** 77002
**Auditors:** French Duncan LLP
**Bankers:** Clydesdale Bank Plc (82-70-03)

| | 30-11-13 | 31-07-12 | 31-11-11 |
|---|---|---|---|
| TO | 16,347,120 | 10,500,347 | 11,153,892 |
| P/L | 70,429 | 37,442 | (454,414) |
| NW | 248,843 | 178,414 | 140,972 |
| WC | (1,358,357) | (1,696,607) | (1,844,618) |
| Emp. | 90 | 87 | 98 |

DUNS 76-347-9508 **Imp**
## Yusen Logistics (Uk) Ltd
(**Subsidiary of:** Nippon Yusen Kabushiki Kaisha)
Grange Park 1 Cheaney Drive Grange Park, Northampton, Northamptonshire NN4 5FB
**Tel:** 01604-748500 **Fax:** 01604 748515
**Web:** www.uk.yusen-logistics.com
**Reg No:** 2548297 **VAT No:** 593411144
**Estd:** 1991 Private Limited Company
**Line of Business:** Other scheduled air transport
**Export Sales:** £111,113,000
**Issued Capital:** £44,130,000
**Principals:** I G Veitch *(Managing)*, T Moriya, S Ando, Ms D A Hardy, K A Appleton
**Co. Secretary:** Mark Bent
**Responsibilities**
**Senior:** Hiroyuki Okamoto *(Chief Representative)*, Kazuyuki Suzuki *(Manager)*
**Branches:** Yusen Logistics (Uk) Ltd, Bradbourne Drive, Tilbrook, Milton Keynes, Buckinghamshire MK7 8BN
**US SIC:** 4511, 4411, 4226
**UK SIC:** 75000, 74001, 77003
**Auditors:** Deloitte LLP
**Bankers:** Barclays Bank Plc (20-00-00)

| | 29-03-14 | 30-03-13 | 31-03-12 |
|---|---|---|---|
| TO | 234,613,000 | 218,826,000 | 213,513,000 |
| P/L | 3,037,000 | 2,477,000 | 2,355,000 |
| NW | 15,974,000 | 14,932,000 | 15,169,000 |
| WC | (1,334,000) | 3,796,000 | 4,514,000 |
| Emp. | 1,407 | 1,441 | 1,469 |

DUNS 50-395-8571
## Yvonne Arnaud Theatre (Vanbrugh Club) Ltd
(**Subsidiary of:** Yvonne Arnaud Theatre Management Ltd)
Millbrook, Guildford, Surrey GU1 3UX
**Tel:** 07912991141
**Web:** www.yvonne-arnaud.co.uk
**Reg No:** 2402362 **Estd:** 2005 Private Limited Company
**Line of Business:** Theatres & concert halls
**Trading Style:** The Vanbrugh Club, Yvonne Arnaud Management, Yvonne Arnaud Theatre Catering, Yvonne Arnaud Theatre Stage Scenery
**Issued Capital:** £250,000
**Directors:** N Acomb, Mrs P M Grayburn

**Co. Secretary:** Ms Carmela Amaddio
**Responsibilities**
**Finance:** Sarah Gatwood (Financial Director)
**IT:** Neil Scudder (Head of IT)
**US SIC:** 7922, 6531
**UK SIC:** 97412, 83400
**Auditors:** Smith & Williamson

|  | 05-04-14 | 05-04-13 | 05-04-12 |
|---|---|---|---|
| TA | 239,178 | 239,178 | 239,178 |
| NW | 239,178 | 239,178 | 239,178 |

---

**DUNS 29-577-4459**

## Ywc Group Ltd

Hellaby Industrial Estate, Rotherham, South Yorkshire S66 8HN
**Tel:** 01709702227 **Fax:** 01709-700648
**Web:** www.yorkshirewindows.com
**Reg No:** 1939258 **Estd:** 1980 Private Limited Company
**Line of Business:** Double glazing installers
**Issued Capital:** £60,800
**Principals:** M S Yarlett (Managing), K Taylor, S R Cousins, R A Carter, I R Chester, S R Cousins
**Responsibilities**
**Senior:** Robert Keenan (Manager), Eddie Rigby (General Manager)
**Finance:** Eddie Rigby (General Manager)
**Marketing:** Alan Willert (Commercial Manager)
**Sales:** Alan Willert (Commercial Manager)
**Health & Safety:** Eddie Rigby (General Manager)
**Engineering:** Eddie Rigby (General Manager)
**Branches:** Ywc Group Ltd, 304 Meadowhead, Sheffield, South Yorkshire S8 7UJ
**US SIC:** 1721, 1796
**UK SIC:** 50400
**Auditors:** Michael A. Jarvis & Co
**Bankers:** The Royal Bank Of Scotland Plc (16-34-22)

|  | 31-03-14 | 31-03-13 | 31-03-12 |
|---|---|---|---|
| TO | 11,116,748 | 13,967,351 | 12,674,441 |
| P/L | (752,839) | (79,008) | (510,051) |
| NW | 1,192,247 | 1,939,242 | 2,003,996 |
| WC | (137,374) | 248,578 | 226,156 |
| Emp. | 140 | 155 | 155 |

---

**DUNS 21-781-1883**

## Ywca Doncaster Women's Centre

21 Cleveland Street, Doncaster, South Yorkshire DN1 3EH
**Tel:** 01302309800
**Web:** www.platform51.org
**Estd:** 1982 Proprietorship
**Line of Business:** Charities and charitable organisations
**Proprietor:** Miss D Derbyshire
**US SIC:** 6732 **UK SIC:** 83100
**Employees:** 46

---

**DUNS 28-829-8805**

## Ywca England & Wales

Clarendon House, Oxford, Oxfordshire OX1 3EJ
**Tel:** 01865304200
**Web:** www.ywca.org.uk
**Reg No:** 0137113 **VAT No:** 233648951
**Estd:** 1855 Private Company Limited By Guarantee
**Line of Business:** Social work activities without accommodation
**Trading Style:** Y W C A
**Directors:** Ms K Devlin, Ms R Clapson, Ms D S Mattinson, M D Le Comte, M G Pilgrim, Baroness S J Nye, Ms T C Leathers, Ms A C Birtles
**Co. Secretary:** Dr Carole Easton
**Responsibilities**
**Senior:** Donna Dickenson (Director), Michelle Mitchell (Director), Penny Newman (Chief Executive Officer), Neeta Patel (Director)
**Marketing:** Francois Gallais (Head of Fundraising)
**Branches:** Ywca England & Wales, 328 Wells Road, Bristol, Avon BS4 2QL
**US SIC:** 8321, 6732
**UK SIC:** 96111, 83100
**Auditors:** Buzzacott LLP
**Bankers:** National Westminster Bank Plc (56-00-14)

|  | 31-03-14 | 31-03-13 | 31-03-12 |
|---|---|---|---|
| TO | 2,092,000 | 3,384,000 | 4,780,000 |
| P/L | (2,705,000) | (2,970,000) | (2,442,000) |
| NW | 22,455,000 | 23,935,000 | 24,097,000 |
| WC | 444,000 | 385,000 | 211,000 |
| Emp. | 58 | 85 | 183 |

---

# Z

---

**DUNS 21-472-8367**

## Z Denning

116 Church Lane East, Aldershot, Hampshire GU11 3HN
**Tel:** 01252-319738
**Web:** www.manorplacecarehome.com
**Estd:** 2000 Proprietorship
**Line of Business:** Nursing homes
**Proprietors:** Dr Z Denning, Dr Z Denning
**US SIC:** 8051 **UK SIC:** 95100
**Employees:** 150

---

**DUNS 51-986-1470** **Imp**

## Z-Tech Control Systems Ltd

Unit 4 Meridian, Buckingway Business Park, Anderson Road, Swavesey, Cambridge, Cambridgeshire CB24 4AE
**Tel:** 01223-653-500 **Fax:** 01223-653-501
**Web:** www.z-tech.co.uk
**Reg No:** 3353499 **Estd:** 1997 Private Limited Company
**Line of Business:** Control system equipment
**Issued Capital:** £8,320
**Directors:** M A Tempset, W J Oliver, J D Bull
**Co. Secretary:** Michael Swinhoe
**Branches:** Z-Tech Control Systems Ltd, Unit B13-B14, 10 Prestons Road, London E14 9RL
**US SIC:** 7399 **UK SIC:** 83954
**Auditors:** Streets Audit LLP
**Bankers:** Svenska Handelsbanken Ab (publ) (40-51-62)

|  | 30-04-14 | 30-04-13 | 30-04-12 |
|---|---|---|---|
| TO | 11,080,105 | 10,362,628 | 7,557,044 |
| P/L | 1,134,016 | 582,521 | 704,945 |
| NW | 2,389,841 | 1,733,991 | 1,505,842 |
| WC | 964,507 | 530,354 | 477,134 |
| Emp. | 143 | 131 | 89 |

---

**DUNS 21-224-2229**

## Zachary Merton Hospital

Zachary Merton Community Hospital, Glenville Road, Littlehampton, West Sussex BN16 2EB
**Tel:** 01903858100
**Web:** www.nhs.uk
**Estd:** 1906 Proprietorship
**Line of Business:** Hospitals
**Proprietor:** Mrs L Squires Early
**Responsibilities**
**Senior:** Simon Neill (Community Matron)
**US SIC:** 8062 **UK SIC:** 95100
**Employees:** 49

---

**DUNS 34-829-2942**

## Zaha Hadid Holdings Ltd

10 Bowling Green Lane, London EC1R 0BQ
**Tel:** 02072535147
**Reg No:** 5628725 **Estd:** 2005 Private Limited Company
**Line of Business:** Architectural activities
**Export Sales:** £46,586,949
**Issued Capital:** £100
**Directors:** N P Calvert, Dame Z M Hadid
**Co. Secretary:** Nigel Calvert
**US SIC:** 8911 **UK SIC:** 83701
**Bankers:** National Westminster Bank Plc (60-19-26)

|  | 30-04-14 | 30-04-13 | 30-04-12 |
|---|---|---|---|
| TO | 47,570,305 | 36,929,421 | 34,491,861 |
| P/L | 5,743,677 | 4,142,342 | 1,940,089 |
| NW | 16,041,618 | 11,785,937 | 8,724,559 |
| WC | 8,914,396 | 8,165,292 | 4,769,755 |
| Emp. | 418 | 354 | 304 |

---

**DUNS 71-904-5705** **Imp**

## Zamir Telecom Ltd

City Reach, 7th Floor, 5 Greenwich View Place, Millharbour, London E14 9NN
**Web:** www.zamirtelecom.com
**Reg No:** 5286517 **VAT No:** 907449605
**Estd:** 2004 Private Limited Company
**Line of Business:** Telecom consultants
**Issued Capital:** £100
**Director:** M N Zamir
**Co. Secretary:** Mohammed Bhuiyan
**Responsibilities**
**Senior:** Naufal Zamir (Manager)
**US SIC:** 4899 **UK SIC:** 79020
**Auditors:** Zaidi & Co
**Bankers:** HSBC Bank plc (40-02-44)

|  | 30-11-13 | 30-11-12 | 30-11-11 |
|---|---|---|---|
| TO | 20,308,562 | 24,160,476 | 22,607,211 |
| P/L | 85,575 | 192,246 | 174,501 |
| NW | (1,117,333) | (1,084,802) | 289,460 |
| WC | (2,824,728) | 2,565,404 | 1,946,000 |
| Emp. | 49 | 52 | 45 |

---

**DUNS 21-621-0464**

## Zara

M S U, 2 Churchill Square, Brighton, East Sussex BN1 2TD
**Tel:** 01273740180
**Web:** www.zara.com
**Estd:** 2011 Proprietorship
**Line of Business:** Retail sale of other men's clothing
**Proprietor:** Mrs K Aicken
**Responsibilities**
**Senior:** Henning Muller (Store Manager)
**US SIC:** 5611 **UK SIC:** 64500
**Employees:** 50

---

**DUNS 21-772-6098**

## Zara

Prince Charles Drive Brent Cross, Shopping Centre, London NW4 3FP
**Tel:** 02084576550
**Web:** www.zara.com
**Estd:** 1988 Partnership
**Line of Business:** Fashion shops
**Partners:** J Romay, J Rios, M Shearwood, A Ferrandez, J Castellano Rios
**Responsibilities**
**Senior:** Joanna Jucha (Manager)
**US SIC:** 5699 **UK SIC:** 64500
**Employees:** 1,116

---

**DUNS 73-645-9723**

## Zara Home Uk Ltd

(Subsidiary of: Pontegadea Inversiones Sl)
129 Regent Street, London W1B 4HT
**Tel:** 02074320040
**Web:** www.zarahome.com
**Reg No:** 4906026 **Estd:** 2003 Private Limited Company
**Line of Business:** Retail sale of furniture, lighting equipment and household articles not elsewhere classified
**Issued Capital:** £4,900,000
**Directors:** J M Romay De La Colina, Ms E M Cardenas Botas, V C Gonzalez Criado
**Co. Secretary:** Athenaeum Secretaries Limited
**Branches:** Zara Home Uk Ltd, Princes Street, Edinburgh, Midlothian EH2 3AA
**US SIC:** 5719 **UK SIC:** 64700
**Auditors:** KPMG LLP

|  | 31-01-14 | 31-01-13 | 31-01-12 |
|---|---|---|---|
| TO | 12,987,000 | 11,161,000 | 8,797,000 |
| P/L | 1,357,000 | 975,000 | (191,000) |
| NW | 4,843,000 | 3,832,000 | 3,143,000 |
| WC | 1,958,000 | 1,989,000 | 455,000 |
| Emp. | 83 | 77 | 79 |

---

**DUNS 39-932-1595** **Exp**

## Zara U.K. Ltd

(Subsidiary of: Pontegadea Inversiones Sl)
120 Regent Street, London W1B 5FE
**Tel:** 020-7851-4300 **Fax:** 020-7851-4301
**Web:** www.zara.com
**Reg No:** 2245999 **Estd:** 1988 Private Limited Company
**Line of Business:** Representative office
**Export Markets:** Spain
**Issued Capital:** £76,000,000
**Directors:** R Renon Tunez, A Canete Diaz, J M Romay De La Colina
**Co. Secretary:** Athenaeum Secretaries Limited
**Responsibilities**
**Senior:** Lorenzo Marcheselli (Manager)
**Finance:** Stephanie Lebreton (Financial Director)
**IT:** Lander Siasi (IT Manager)
**HR:** Vanessa Corley (Human Resources Director)
**Health & Safety:** Adam Mason (Facilities Manager)
**Facilities:** Adam Mason (Facilities Manager)
**Branches:** Zara U.k. Ltd, 129-132 Briggate, Leeds, West Yorkshire LS1 6BR
**US SIC:** 5621 **UK SIC:** 64500
**Auditors:** Deloitte LLP

|  | 31-01-14 | 31-01-13 | 31-01-12 |
|---|---|---|---|
| TO | 457,817,000 | 442,740,000 | 368,847,000 |
| P/L | 33,945,000 | 51,790,000 | 19,349,000 |
| NW | 100,781,000 | 80,241,000 | 112,679,000 |
| WC | 30,802,000 | 15,554,000 | 49,673,000 |
| Emp. | 2,810 | 2,893 | 2,571 |

---

**DUNS 54-429-1198** **Imp**

## Zaun Ltd

Steel Drive, Wolverhampton, West Midlands WV10 9ED
**Tel:** 01902796699
**Web:** www.zaun.co.uk
**Reg No:** 3275214 **VAT No:** 687521110
**Estd:** 1996 Private Limited Company
**Line of Business:** Security activities
**Export Sales:** £572,193
**Issued Capital:** £22,940
**Directors:** A R Henman, S M Foden
**Co. Secretary:** Mrs Mandy Smith
**Branches:** Zaun Ltd, Steel Drive, Wolverhampton, West Midlands WV10 9ED

---

**US SIC:** 7393, 3499, 3442
**UK SIC:** 83954, 31694, 31420
**Bankers:** Barclays Bank Plc (20-07-71)

|  | 31-12-13 | 31-12-12 | 31-12-11 |
|---|---|---|---|
| TO | 7,110,187 | 10,125,711 | 11,122,329 |
| P/L | 667,563 | 1,400,169 | 1,021,942 |
| NW | 6,234,993 | 5,773,596 | 4,762,969 |
| WC | 3,234,328 | 2,801,146 | 1,847,725 |
| Emp. | 61 | 78 | 76 |

---

**DUNS 21-760-1994**

## Zavarco Plc

Gainsborough House, 33 Throgmorton Street, London EC2N 2BR
**Tel:** 02071-565274 **Fax:** 020715-65001
**Web:** www.vasseti.co.uk
**Reg No:** 7687158 **Estd:** 2011 Private Limited Company
**Line of Business:** Telecom consultants
**Directors:** Ms T M Abd Aziz, T Hock Peng, V Varanyananda
**Co. Secretary:** Uk Company Secretaries Ltd
**Responsibilities**
**Senior:** Gustav Brunner (Manager), Pushpan Murugiah (Manager), Syed Nasir (Manager), Hirofumi Ouchi (Manager)
**US SIC:** 4899, 6733
**UK SIC:** 79020, 83100
**Auditors:** UHY Hacker Young LLP
**Employees:** 115
**Turnover:** £67,711,000

---

**DUNS 23-732-1836**

## Zayo Group Uk Ltd

(Subsidiary of: Communications Infrastructure Investments Llc)
Brandon House, 180 Borough High Street, London SE1 1LW
**Fax:** 02072209001
**Web:** www.abovenet.co.uk
**Reg No:** 3726666 **VAT No:** 740474736
**Estd:** 1999 Private Limited Company
**Line of Business:** Other computer related activities
**Trading Style:** Zayo
**Issued Capital:** £60,618,567
**Directors:** K Desgarennes, D P Caruso, S E Beer
**Co. Secretary:** Abogado Nominees Limited
**Responsibilities**
**Senior:** Adam Buckby (Manager)
**Marketing:** Fiona Burke (Marketing Manager), Michael Katz (EU Carrier Relations Manager)
**Sales:** Samuel Thorpe (Account Manager)
**IT:** Kevin Fenn (Project Manager)
**US SIC:** 4899 **UK SIC:** 79020
**Auditors:** BDO Stoy Hayward LLP
**Bankers:** Barclays Bank Plc (20-00-00)

|  | 30-06-13 | 31-12-11 | 31-06-10 |
|---|---|---|---|
| TO | 53,212,031 | 28,937,181 | 25,203,922 |
| P/L | 15,497,517 | 7,232,146 | 4,481,535 |
| NW | 41,608,415 | 27,687,556 | 16,599,404 |
| WC | 16,540,903 | 12,118,678 | 8,351,069 |
| Emp. | 56 | 89 | 85 |

---

**DUNS 21-616-8752**

## Zebedees

5 Stone Cross Business Centre, Lewes Road, Laughton, Lewes, East Sussex BN8 6BN
**Estd:** 1998 Partnership
**Line of Business:** Caterers mobile
**Partners:** P Oates, S Parsons
**US SIC:** 5812 **UK SIC:** 66110
**Employees:** 80

---

**DUNS 51-625-9640**

## Zebra Projects (Holdings) Ltd

(Subsidiary of: Zebra Projects Holdings (2008) Ltd)
1 Newhams Row, London SE1 3UZ
**Tel:** 02079409040 **Fax:** 020-7940-9098
**Web:** www.zebweb.co.uk
**Reg No:** 5905850 **Estd:** 1998 Private Limited Company
**Line of Business:** Management activities of holding companies
**Issued Capital:** £800
**Director:** M J Mason
**Co. Secretary:** Ms Jessica Howard
**US SIC:** 6711 **UK SIC:** 83962

|  | 31-12-13 | 31-12-12 | 31-12-11 |
|---|---|---|---|
| TA | 980,018 | 789,993 | 791,536 |
| NW | 815,009 | 760,024 | 762,041 |
| WC | 28,582 | (26,403) | (24,386) |

---

**DUNS 57-056-0771** **Imp**

## Zebra Technologies Europe Ltd

(Subsidiary of: Zebra Technologies Corporation)
3 Millboard Road Dukes Meadow, Bourne End, Buckinghamshire SL8 5XF
**Tel:** 01628556000 **Fax:** 01628556001
**Web:** www.zebra.com
**Reg No:** 2881068 **VAT No:** 636005662
**Estd:** 1969 Private Limited Company

**Line of Business:** Printing production equipment and machinery
**Directors:** T R Naughton, J L Kaput, S M Piercey, R F Rodericks, A A Ford
**Co. Secretary:** Pitsec Limited
**Responsibilities**
**Senior:** Anders Gustafsson *(CEO)*
**Finance:** Mike Wyllie *(Account Consultant)*
**Sales:** Gary Malcolm *(Pre-sales Technical Specialist)*
**Operations:** Mike Forrester *(Operations Manager)*
**US SIC:** 7379, 3559
**UK SIC:** 83940, 32863
**Auditors:** Ernst & Young LLP
**Employees:** 301
**Turnover:** £328,942,000

DUNS 34-622-7770
## Zebra Technologies Preston Ltd
(**Subsidiary of:** Azzurri Communications Ltd)
Pittman Way, Fulwood, Preston, Lancashire PR2 9ZD
**Tel:** 01772-797555 **Fax:** 01772-693000
**Web:** www.zebra.com
**Reg No:** 2756652 **Estd:** 1992 Private Limited Company
**Line of Business:** Bar-code equipment software etc
**Issued Capital:** £549,990
**Directors:** R F Rodericks, S M Piercey
**Co. Secretary:** Pitsec Limited
**Responsibilities**
**Operations:** Muir Hutton *(Technical, Production Manager)*
**Engineering:** Muir Hutton *(Technical, Production Manager)*
**US SIC:** 7399, 2752
**UK SIC:** 83954, 47544

| | 31-12-13 | 31-12-12 | 31-12-11 |
|---|---|---|---|
| TA | 1,924,000 | 1,924,000 | 1,924,000 |
| NW | 1,924,000 | 1,924,000 | 1,924,000 |

DUNS 76-838-1105
## Zee & Co. Ltd
Unit 1-2, New Court Business Park, Perry Road, Harlow, Essex CM18 7NS
**Tel:** 01279432078 **Fax:** 01279-424080
**Web:** www.zeeandco.co.uk
**Reg No:** 2604329 **Estd:** 1991 Private Limited Company
**Line of Business:** Retail sale of clothing
**Issued Capital:** £500
**Directors:** Mrs J Reynolds, Mrs J R Johnstone
**Co. Secretary:** Stephen Reynolds
**Responsibilities**
**Health & Safety:** Helena Pisula *(Facilities Manager)*
**Facilities:** Helena Pisula *(Facilities Manager)*
**Branches:** Zee & Co. Ltd, Zee & Co Ltd, 4-6 Cranbrook Road, Ilford, Essex IG1 4DJ
**US SIC:** 5699 **UK SIC:** 64500
**Auditors:** Mead Turner & Co Ltd
**Bankers:** Barclays Bank Plc (20-44-22)

| | 30-04-14 | 30-04-13 | 30-04-12 |
|---|---|---|---|
| TO | 6,656,573 | 7,375,739 | 7,738,508 |
| P/L | 348,000 | (41,924) | 99,064 |
| NW | 1,299,080 | 1,090,667 | 1,148,948 |
| WC | 1,162,686 | 1,038,290 | 1,323,182 |
| Emp. | 88 | 91 | 97 |

DUNS 21-229-4306
## Zeera Indian Cuisine
853 Manchester Road, Rochdale, Lancashire OL11 2UY
**Tel:** 01706-655334
**Web:** www.zeeraonline.co.uk
**Estd:** 2005 Proprietorship
**Line of Business:** Licensed restaurants
**Proprietor:** R Ullah
**Responsibilities**
**Senior:** Abdul Kadir *(Manager)*
**US SIC:** 5812 **UK SIC:** 66110
**Employees:** 60

DUNS 50-007-0982 **Imp-Exp**
## Zehnder Group Uk Ltd
(**Subsidiary of:** Zehnder Group Uk Holdings Ltd)
Unit 4, Camberley, Surrey GU15 3AD
**Tel:** 01276605855 **Fax:** 0127624058
**Web:** www.zehnder.co.uk
**Reg No:** 2296696 **VAT No:** 717624039
**Estd:** 1969 Private Limited Company
**Line of Business:** Plumbers merchants
**Export Markets:** E U, Australia
**Export Sales:** £2,121,435
**Issued Capital:** £3,500,002
**Directors:** Ms D M Gosden, Dr H Zehnder, C Peysson, M A Twohig
**Co. Secretary:** Ms Doreen Gosden
**Responsibilities**
**Senior:** B Herbett *(Manager)*, Tony Twohig *(Manager)*
**US SIC:** 5074 **UK SIC:** 61300
**Bankers:** National Westminster Bank Plc (52-41-37)

| | 31-12-13 | 31-12-12 | 31-12-11 |
|---|---|---|---|
| TO | 30,149,644 | 27,526,811 | 26,135,830 |
| P/L | 1,444,756 | 395,085 | 111,658 |
| NW | 4,549,023 | 3,770,798 | 3,260,029 |
| WC | 3,813,497 | 3,051,916 | 2,916,817 |
| Emp. | 94 | 92 | 95 |

DUNS 21-260-0639 **Imp-Exp**
## Zell-Em Group Ltd
210 Watson Road, Blackpool, Lancashire FY4 3EF
**Web:** www.bestplate.com
**Reg No:** 0720285 **Estd:** 1942 Private Limited Company
**Line of Business:** Sign and nameplate suppliers
**Export Markets:** Central America, Africa, Europe
**Export Sales:** £12,284
**Issued Capital:** £26,250
**Principals:** G Zell *(Chairman)*, T Mcnamee *(Managing)*
**Co. Secretary:** Mrs Barbara Zell
**Responsibilities**
**Senior:** Rick Kenny *(Technical Development Manager)*
**Finance:** Roger Neild *(Financial Director)*
**IT:** Rick Kenny *(Technical Development Manager)*
**Engineering:** Rick Kenny *(Technical Development Manager)*
**US SIC:** 2599, 6711
**UK SIC:** 46720, 83962
**Auditors:** Blick Rothenberg
**Bankers:** National Westminster Bank Plc (60-03-04)

| | 30-06-13 | 30-06-12 | 30-06-11 |
|---|---|---|---|
| TO | 10,376,706 | 9,865,702 | 8,968,668 |
| P/L | 811,604 | 422,352 | 63,946 |
| NW | 4,163,586 | 3,755,969 | 3,530,549 |
| WC | 3,177,677 | 2,567,978 | 2,335,630 |
| Emp. | 75 | 87 | 100 |

DUNS 49-122-6353
## Zen Internet Ltd
Sandbrook Park, Sandbrook Way, Rochdale, Lancashire OL11 1RY
**Tel:** 08450589000 **Fax:** 08450589005
**Web:** www.zen.co.uk
**Reg No:** 3101568 **VAT No:** 646889668
**Estd:** 1995 Private Limited Company
**Line of Business:** Other computer related activities
**Trading Style:** Zen Internet
**Issued Capital:** £10,000
**Directors:** S Warburton, Mrs C Taylor, R Tang
**Co. Secretary:** Russell Hill
**Responsibilities**
**Marketing:** Andrew Sanderson *(Marketing Manager)*
**IT:** John Pickersgill *(System Operations Manager)*
**Facilities:** Michael Marland *(Facilities Manager)*
**Branches:** Zen Internet Ltd, Globe Park, Moss Bridge Road, Rochdale, Lancashire OL16 5EB
**US SIC:** 7379 **UK SIC:** 83940
**Auditors:** RSM Tenon Audit Ltd
**Bankers:** HSBC Bank plc (40-39-01)

| | 30-09-13 | 30-09-12 | 30-09-11 |
|---|---|---|---|
| TO | 47,363,295 | 45,604,950 | 43,097,768 |
| P/L | 267,462 | 1,109,345 | 1,008,707 |
| NW | 8,153,231 | 8,576,233 | 8,160,166 |
| WC | (569,139) | 2,266,956 | 2,209,403 |
| Emp. | 428 | 414 | 399 |

DUNS 42-374-0369
## Zenda Ltd
St Helens Parade, Southsea, Hampshire PO4 0RN
**Tel:** 02392-731281
**Web:** www.royalbeachhotel.co.uk
**Reg No:** 4361665 **Estd:** 2002 Private Limited Company
**Line of Business:** Hotels
**Trading Style:** Zenda Ltd
**Issued Capital:** £25
**Directors:** G Murphy, F Yeganeh
**Co. Secretary:** Jay Laundon
**Responsibilities**
**Senior:** Christopher Gilmore *(general manager)*
**Finance:** Tracy Curt *(deputy manager)*
**Health & Safety:** Tracy Curt *(deputy manager)*
**Branches:** Zenda Ltd, Royal Beach Hotel, St. Helens Parade, Southsea, Hampshire PO4 0RN
**US SIC:** 7011 **UK SIC:** 66500
**Bankers:** The Royal Bank Of Scotland Plc (15-10-00)

| | 31-08-14 | 31-08-13 | 31-08-12 |
|---|---|---|---|
| TO | 3,032,798 | 2,939,411 | 2,733,282 |
| P/L | 261,242 | 223,826 | 17,635 |
| NW | 957,628 | (482,346) | (646,028) |
| WC | (501,582) | (323,339) | (447,548) |
| Emp. | 102 | 97 | 90 |

DUNS 23-867-6766
## Zendor/Gsi Commerce Ltd
Unit 26, Broadgate, Oldham Broadway Business Park, Chadderto, Oldham, Lancashire OL9 9XA
**Tel:** 0161-332-7900 **Fax:** 0161-332-7901
**Web:** www.gsicommerce.eu
**Reg No:** 3859136 **Estd:** 1999 Private Limited Company
**Line of Business:** Business information services
**Issued Capital:** £101
**Directors:** P Depaul, P D Cataldo, M Kliger
**Co. Secretary:** Taylor Wessing Secretaries Limit
**Responsibilities**
**Senior:** Scott Rosenberg *(Manager)*
**US SIC:** 7399 **UK SIC:** 83954
**Auditors:** Deloitte LLP
**Bankers:** HSBC Bank plc (40-31-23)

| | 31-12-13 | 31-12-12 | 31-12-11 |
|---|---|---|---|
| TO | 19,671,736 | 13,834,449 | 12,927,505 |
| P/L | (1,376,057) | (4,952,819) | (2,918,508) |
| NW | (14,203,016) | (15,027,047) | (10,074,228) |
| WC | (14,671,163) | (15,449,138) | (10,826,710) |
| Emp. | 100 | 102 | 131 |

DUNS 34-916-7788
## Zenith Bank (Uk) Ltd
(**Subsidiary of:** Zenith Bank Plc)
39 Cornhill, London EC3V 3ND
**Tel:** 020-7105-3950
**Web:** www.zenith-bank.co.uk
**Reg No:** 5713749 **Estd:** 2006 Private Limited Company
**Line of Business:** Banks and financial institutions
**Issued Capital:** £65,001,000
**Directors:** L C Llewellyn, J Ovia, D Somers, Q R Aylward, A U Uzoebo, P Amangbo, J R Weguelin
**Co. Secretary:** Mrs Susan Mcbride
**Responsibilities**
**Senior:** Godwin Emefiele *(Group Chief Executive Director)*, Renier Lemmens *(Non Executive Director)*
**Finance:** John Shea *(Head of Finance & Operations)*, Paul Whippy *(Treasurer)*
**US SIC:** 6012 **UK SIC:** 81402
**Auditors:** KPMG Audit PLC
**Bankers:** Barclays Bank Plc (20-03-80)

| | 31-12-13 | 31-12-12 | 31-12-11 |
|---|---|---|---|
| TA | 849,996,476 | 611,063,730 | 497,041,885 |
| P/L | 10,059,745 | 6,928,088 | 5,104,963 |
| NW | 74,039,581 | 66,315,634 | 43,624,795 |
| WC | 73,531,401 | 65,376,237 | (119,623,572) |
| Emp. | 52 | 46 | 38 |

DUNS 42-405-2327
## Zenith Contractors Ltd
Unit 4 205 Torrington Avenue, Coventry, West Midlands CV4 9UT
**Tel:** 02476 687167
**Web:** www.zenithcontractors.co.uk
**Reg No:** 4392942 **Estd:** 2002 Private Limited Company
**Line of Business:** Cleaning activities not elsewhere classified
**Trading Style:** Zenith Contractors Limited
**Issued Capital:** £4,082
**Principals:** M Hancox *(Managing)*, A Irwin, C Richards
**Co. Secretary:** Ms Dorothy Hancox
**Responsibilities**
**Senior:** Jill Reay *(Director)*
**US SIC:** 7349, 7341
**UK SIC:** 92300
**Auditors:** Prime

| | 31-03-14 | 31-03-13 | 31-03-12 |
|---|---|---|---|
| TA | 705,876 | 603,683 | 856,420 |
| NW | 240,037 | 237,509 | 218,712 |
| WC | 222,898 | 214,890 | 191,179 |

DUNS 21-672-0309
## Zenith Ef Ltd
(**Subsidiary of:** Accelerate Acquisitions Ltd)
Anglia House, 1-3 Woodhall Road Holly Park Mills, Pudsey, West Yorkshire LS28 5QS
**Tel:** 01132565565
**Web:** www.zenith.co.uk
**Reg No:** 7245395 **Estd:** 2006 Private Limited Company
**Line of Business:** Car, van and truck leasing and contract hire
**Trading Style:** Zenith
**Issued Capital:** £1
**Directors:** T P Buchan, R A Butler, M T Phillips
**Co. Secretary:** Ms Sally Jones
**US SIC:** 7512 **UK SIC:** 84801

| | 31-03-14 | 31-03-13 | 31-03-12 |
|---|---|---|---|
| TO | 836,000 | 586,000 | 1,237,000 |
| P/L | 86,000 | 107,000 | 185,000 |
| NW | 527,000 | 431,000 | 341,000 |
| WC | (3,403,000) | (1,952,000) | (2,770,000) |

DUNS 21-138-2423
## Zenith Hygiene Group Plc
Zenith House, Hatfield, Hertfordshire AL9 7JE
**Tel:** 01707-270-260
**Web:** http://zhgplc.com
**Reg No:** 6707511 **VAT No:** 859964253
**Estd:** 1996 Public Limited Company
**Line of Business:** Cleaning materials and equipment
**Export Sales:** £1,644,000
**Issued Capital:** £5,101,987
**Directors:** S Fink, M A Cronk, R D Francis, Mrs A J Pettitt, S P Bower
**Co. Secretary:** Alison Pettitt
**Responsibilities**
**Senior:** Tony Clough *(Technical Director)*, Tony Cousins *(Sales Director)*, Rupert Felsing *(Board Member)*, Bakhtiar Hanan *(Group Purchasing Director)*, Derek Lafbery *(Director of Special Projects)*, Alan O' Neill *(Depot Manager)*, Raxs Patel *(IT Director)*
**Sales:** Tony Cousins *(Sales Director)*
**IT:** Raxs Patel *(IT Director)*
**Operations:** Derek Lafbery *(Director of Special Projects)*, David McIlroy *(Operations Director, Ireland)*
**Purchasing:** Bakhtiar Hanan *(Group Purchasing Director)*
**Engineering:** Tony Clough *(Technical Director)*
**US SIC:** 2841, 5199
**UK SIC:** 25810, 61900
**Auditors:** Baker Tilly UK Audit LLP
**Bankers:** The Royal Bank Of Scotland Plc (15-00-00)

| | 28-02-14 | 28-02-13 | 29-02-12 |
|---|---|---|---|
| TO | 42,533,000 | 37,484,000 | 35,055,000 |
| P/L | (392,000) | (612,000) | (1,514,000) |
| NW | (6,541,000) | (6,732,000) | (6,973,000) |
| WC | (4,394,000) | (3,380,000) | (4,128,000) |
| Emp. | 325 | 303 | 313 |

DUNS 76-722-1146 **Imp-Exp**
## Zenith International Ltd
7 Kingsmead Square, Bath, Avon BA1 2AB
**Fax:** 01225-327901
**Web:** www.zenithinternational.com
**Reg No:** 2596583 **VAT No:** 543548827
**Estd:** 1991 Private Limited Company
**Line of Business:** Management and business consultants
**Export Markets:** E U
**Issued Capital:** £32,220
**Principals:** R C Hall *(Chairman)*, M Wilton, D M Finlayson, Mrs K E Amey, Mrs E C Renfrew, G S Roethenbaugh
**Co. Secretary:** Mrs Kathryn Amey
**Responsibilities**
**Senior:** Owen Phillips *(Manager)*
**Marketing:** Linda Leonard *(Events Manager)*
**Operations:** Gordon Robinson *(Production and Operations Mana)*
**Branches:** Zenith International Ltd, The Old Rectory, Warminster, Wiltshire BA12 0AH
**US SIC:** 7399 **UK SIC:** 83954
**Auditors:** O'Donovan & Co
**Bankers:** National Westminster Bank Plc (60-02-05)

| | 31-12-13 | 31-12-12 | 31-12-11 |
|---|---|---|---|
| TA | 639,142 | 610,993 | 780,000 |
| NW | 331,962 | 322,553 | 379,639 |
| WC | 279,979 | 211,276 | 203,638 |

DUNS 22-767-1930
## Zenith Nursery
Station Road, Offenham, Evesham, Worcestershire WR11 8LW
**Tel:** 01386-831959
**Estd:** 1978 Partnership
**Line of Business:** Nurserymen
**Partners:** G Barone, Mrs N Barone
**Responsibilities**
**Senior:** Frank Barone *(Manager)*
**US SIC:** 0851 **UK SIC:** 02000
**Bankers:** Barclays Bank Plc (20-98-61)
**Employees:** 50

DUNS 73-723-0115 **Imp**
## Zenith Oilfield Technology Ltd
(**Subsidiary of:** General Electric Company)
Unit 8 Thainstone Business Park, Inverurie, Aberdeenshire AB51 5TB
**Tel:** 01467628866 **Fax:** 01467629857
**Web:** www.zenithoilfield.com
**Reg No:** 0260113SC **VAT No:** 829287880
**Estd:** 2004 Private Limited Company
**Line of Business:** Oil and gas exploration services
**Export Sales:** £35,677,000
**Issued Capital:** £106,123
**Directors:** E Gray, R K Holsey, Jr, G J Davie
**Co. Secretary:** Jordan Company Secretaries Limit
**Responsibilities**
**Senior:** Ronal Holsey *(Director)*
**Finance:** Richard Hamilton *(Financial Director)*
**Marketing:** Karen Grant *(Marketing Manager)*

**Sales:** Keith Kettlewell *(Sales Director)*, Ismail Mohamed *(International Sales and Operat)*, Eddie Moore *(International Sales and Operat)*, Wessam Nasser *(International Sales & Operatio)*
**Operations:** Eddie Moore *(International Sales and Operat)*, Wessam Nasser *(International Sales & Operatio)*
**US SIC:** 1389, 3829
**UK SIC:** 13000, 37100
**Auditors:** Deloitte LLP
**Bankers:** HSBC Bank plc (40-01-25)

| | 31-12-13 | 31-12-12 | 31-12-12 |
|---|---|---|---|
| TO | 35,685,000 | 18,935,055 | 26,675,137 |
| P/L | 9,335,000 | 4,887,614 | 7,012,447 |
| NW | 27,576,000 | 18,663,128 | 14,312,661 |
| WC | 27,040,000 | 18,148,634 | 13,746,240 |
| Emp. | 109 | 97 | 90 |

DUNS 73-929-3335
## Zenith Packaging Ltd
**(Subsidiary of:** Wymoon Capital Ltd)
Unit 1 Cambrian Industrial Park, Tonypandy, Mid Glamorgan CF40 2XX
**Tel:** 01443441100
**Web:** www.zenith-media.co.uk
**Reg No:** 5182330 **Estd:** 2004 Private Limited Company
**Line of Business:** Printing not elsewhere classified
**Trading Style:** Zenith Media
**Issued Capital:** £1,305,004
**Directors:** Mrs H Mooney, J Mooney
**Co. Secretary:** John Mooney
**Responsibilities**
**Senior:** Keith John *(Manager)*, Maxwell Moody *(Manager)*, Mark Partridge *(Operations Director)*, Geoffrey Walters *(Manager)*
**US SIC:** 2752 **UK SIC:** 47544
**Auditors:** Houghton Stone
**Bankers:** National Westminster Bank Plc (56-00-64)

| | 31-03-14 | 31-03-13 | 31-03-12 |
|---|---|---|---|
| TO | 5,805,593 | N/A | N/A |
| P/L | 14,293 | N/A | N/A |
| NW | 1,797,817 | 468,295 | 158,806 |
| WC | (62,439) | (139,843) | (382,840) |
| Emp. | 75 | N/A | N/A |

DUNS 21-614-4360
## Zenith Plumbpoint Ltd
**(Subsidiary of:** Travis Perkins Plc)
Frog Island, Northridge Place, Leicester, Leicestershire LE3 5AG
**Tel:** 01162515888 **Fax:** 01162-514335
**Web:** www.ptsplumbing.co.uk
**Reg No:** 0640740 **Estd:** 1929 Private Limited Company
**Line of Business:** Wholesale of hardware, plumbing and heating equipment and supplies
**Trading Style:** P T S
**Issued Capital:** £50,036
**Directors:** A D Buffin, J P Carter, Tp Directors Ltd
**Branches:** Zenith Plumbpoint, Colchester Avenue, Cardiff, South Glamorgan CF3 7UG
**US SIC:** 5074, 5084
**UK SIC:** 61300, 61490

| | 31-12-13 | 31-12-12 | 31-12-11 |
|---|---|---|---|
| TA | 2,955,455 | 2,955,455 | 2,955,455 |
| NW | 2,955,455 | 2,875,455 | 2,955,455 |

DUNS 21-110-1532
## Zenith Staybrite Ltd
**(Subsidiary of:** Entu (Uk) Plc)
7 Road One, Industrial Estate, Winsford, Cheshire CW7 3PZ
**Tel:** 01932 266800
**Web:** www.zenithhome.co.uk
**Reg No:** 6516827 **Estd:** 2008 Private Limited Company
**Line of Business:** Painting contractors
**Issued Capital:** £100
**Directors:** Miss N J Cook, S R Drew, G A Burton
**Branches:** Zenith Staybrite Ltd, Abbey Farm Commercial Park, Norwich, Norfolk NR10 3JU
**US SIC:** 1721 **UK SIC:** 50400
**Auditors:** Beever & Struthers
**Bankers:** Barclays Bank Plc (20-54-58)

| | 31-10-13 | 31-10-12 | 31-10-11 |
|---|---|---|---|
| TO | 33,373,749 | 36,272,507 | 30,171,000 |
| P/L | 2,568,448 | 1,036,454 | 585,000 |
| NW | 3,910,184 | 1,510,494 | 1,425,000 |
| WC | 5,023,233 | 3,443,534 | 3,513,000 |
| Emp. | 71 | 108 | 66 |

DUNS 29-760-9182 Imp
## Zenith Survey Equipment Ltd
Paragon House, 33 Church Street, Ossett, West Yorkshire WF5 9DN
**Tel:** 01924-263346
**Web:** www.zenithsurvey.co.uk
**Reg No:** 2024095 **VAT No:** 722036768
**Estd:** 1986 Private Limited Company
**Line of Business:** Surveying instruments
**Issued Capital:** £6
**Principals:** T F Long *(Managing)*, S Rhodes
**Co. Secretary:** Paul Finney
**Branches:** Zenith Survey Equipment Ltd, 2 River Court, Brighouse Road, Middlesbrough, Cleveland TS2 1RT
**US SIC:** 3832 **UK SIC:** 37320
**Auditors:** Mazars Neville Russell
**Bankers:** Lloyds TSB Bank plc (30-00-05)

| | 28-02-14 | 28-02-13 | 29-02-12 |
|---|---|---|---|
| TO | 7,297,608 | 6,497,643 | 6,712,111 |
| P/L | 482,778 | 337,246 | 188,099 |
| NW | 2,435,675 | 2,103,508 | 2,043,068 |
| WC | 651,632 | 496,364 | 263,731 |
| Emp. | 84 | 82 | 78 |

DUNS 39-968-1170
## Zenith Vehicle Contracts Ltd
**(Subsidiary of:** Accelerate Acquisitions Ltd)
Anglia House, Pudsey, West Yorkshire LS28 5QS
**Tel:** 0844 848 8091 **Fax:** 01132-564877
**Web:** www.zenith.co.uk
**Reg No:** 2267701 **VAT No:** 606926039
**Estd:** 1989 Private Limited Company
**Line of Business:** Renting of automobiles
**Trading Style:** Zenith
**Issued Capital:** £142,189
**Principals:** M T Phillips *(Financial)*, M Connor, Ms C G Rose, A Kirby, R A Butler, T P Buchan, I M Hughes
**Co. Secretary:** Mrs Sally Jones
**Responsibilities**
**Finance:** Tommy Snowden *(Accountant)*
**Marketing:** Philip Jerome *(Sales & Marketing Director)*
**Sales:** Philip Jerome *(Sales & Marketing Director)*
**Purchasing:** Chris Woodcock *(Head of Purchasing)*
**US SIC:** 7512 **UK SIC:** 84801
**Auditors:** Deloitte LLP
**Bankers:** National Westminster Bank Plc (56-00-36)

| | 31-03-14 | 31-03-13 | 31-03-12 |
|---|---|---|---|
| TO | 166,522,000 | 156,113,000 | 140,343,000 |
| P/L | 9,307,000 | 11,399,000 | 6,660,000 |
| NW | 1,493,000 | 4,823,000 | 2,782,000 |
| WC | 81,839,000 | 74,673,000 | 60,414,000 |
| Emp. | 203 | 184 | 172 |

DUNS 21-394-5247
## Zenith Windows
41 Osborne Road, Southsea, Hampshire PO5 3LS
**Web:** www.zenithwindows.co.uk
**Estd:** 1994 Proprietorship
**Line of Business:** Double glazing installers
**Proprietor:** A Daley
**US SIC:** 1721 **UK SIC:** 50400
**Employees:** 60

DUNS 29-557-0543
## Zenithoptimedia Ltd
**(Subsidiary of:** Publicis Groupe S.A.)
24 Percy Street, London W1T 2BS
**Tel:** 02079611000 **Fax:** 02079611001
**Web:** www.zenithoptimedia.com
**Reg No:** 1921320 **Estd:** 1985 Private Limited Company
**Line of Business:** Advertising, radio, tv and other media
**Export Sales:** £366,000
**Issued Capital:** £200,264
**Directors:** Ms B L Rowe, A C Sayliss
**Co. Secretary:** Raj Basran
**Responsibilities**
**Finance:** Jonathan Barnard *(Head of Forecasting)*
**Marketing:** Laura Cullum *(Marketing Director)*, Olivier Harwood-Matthews *(Marketing & New Business Direc)*
**HR:** Rudi Symons *(Training Manager)*
**Health & Safety:** Egle Gabalyte *(Facilities Manager)*
**Facilities:** Egle Gabalyte *(Facilities Manager)*
**US SIC:** 7319 **UK SIC:** 83800
**Auditors:** Ernst & Young LLP

| | 31-12-13 | 31-12-12 | 31-12-11 |
|---|---|---|---|
| TO | 34,418,000 | 629,321,000 | 636,339,000 |
| P/L | 6,804,000 | 8,742,000 | 7,794,000 |
| NW | 4,663,000 | 6,276,000 | 4,614,000 |
| WC | 3,803,000 | 5,029,000 | 2,683,000 |
| Emp. | 370 | 370 | 330 |

DUNS 22-853-5910
## Zenoffice Ltd
**(Subsidiary of:** Stat Co Ltd)
Unit 13 Gateway Crescent, Broadway Business Park, Chadderton, Oldham, Lancashire OL9 9XB
**Tel:** 08451232980 **Fax:** 08451232981
**Web:** www.zenoffice.com
**Reg No:** 1189115 **Estd:** 1974 Private Limited Company
**Line of Business:** Commercial stationery supplies
**Trading Style:** Platen Bethune
**Issued Capital:** £100
**Directors:** M S Waterhouse, Mrs S Hitchman, L J Kerr, G B Davie
**Co. Secretary:** Ms Monique Schles
**Responsibilities**
**Senior:** Zen Office *(Office Suppliers)*
**US SIC:** 5942, 5199
**UK SIC:** 65300, 61900
**Auditors:** Bennett Brooks & Co Ltd
**Bankers:** Barclays Bank Plc (20-51-01)

| | 31-12-13 | 31-12-12 | 31-12-11 |
|---|---|---|---|
| TO | 9,424,165 | N/A | N/A |
| P/L | 84,457 | N/A | N/A |
| NW | 3,565 | (48,996) | (97,483) |
| WC | (575,423) | (636,832) | (608,394) |
| Emp. | 59 | N/A | N/A |

DUNS 73-303-9858
## Zensar Technologies (Uk) Ltd
**(Subsidiary of:** Zensar Technologies Limited)
Thames Central, 8th Floor, North Suite, Hatfield Road, Slough, Berkshire SL1 1QE
**Tel:** 01753-692700
**Web:** www.zensar.com
**Reg No:** 4577853 **Estd:** 2002 Private Limited Company
**Line of Business:** Hardware consultancy
**Export Sales:** £3,166,054
**Trading Style:** Zensar Technologies U K Limited
**Issued Capital:** £50,000
**Directors:** G Natarajan, P K Mohapatra
**Responsibilities**
**Health & Safety:** Wendy Huggins *(operations manager)*
**US SIC:** 7379 **UK SIC:** 83940

| | 31-03-14 | 31-03-13 | 31-03-12 |
|---|---|---|---|
| TO | 23,147,733 | 21,552,052 | 22,805,982 |
| P/L | 2,657,191 | 1,624,169 | 1,369,471 |
| NW | 5,280,986 | 4,245,659 | 3,012,080 |
| WC | 5,229,864 | 4,180,348 | 2,960,105 |
| Emp. | 173 | 112 | 47 |

DUNS 50-318-7197 Imp-Exp
## Zeon Chemicals Europe Ltd
**(Subsidiary of:** Zeon Corporation)
Sully Moors Road, Penarth, South Glamorgan CF64 5ZE
**Web:** www.zeon.co.uk
**Reg No:** 2343599 **VAT No:** 531719159
**Estd:** 1989 Private Limited Company
**Line of Business:** Manufacture of other rubber products
**Export Markets:** Worldwide
**Export Sales:** £28,657,000
**Issued Capital:** £23,300,000
**Director:** H Takahashi
**Co. Secretary:**
Secretarial Appointments Limited
**US SIC:** 3069, 5199
**UK SIC:** 48123, 61900
**Auditors:** Ernst & Young LLP
**Bankers:** The Dai-Ichi Kangyo Bank, Ltd. (40-50-69)

| | 31-12-13 | 31-12-12 | 31-12-11 |
|---|---|---|---|
| TO | 41,795,000 | 41,308,000 | 49,347,000 |
| P/L | 541,000 | 895,000 | 2,435,000 |
| NW | 18,519,000 | 18,535,000 | 18,087,000 |
| WC | 12,875,000 | 14,092,000 | 13,581,000 |
| Emp. | 88 | 87 | 88 |

DUNS 21-163-8978 Imp-Exp
## Zeon Ltd
**(Subsidiary of:** Herald Group Limited)
39-41 Waterloo Road, London NW2 7TT
**Tel:** 02082081833 **Fax:** 020-8208-0350
**Web:** www.zeonltd.co.uk
**Reg No:** 1459158 **Estd:** 1979 Private Limited Company
**Line of Business:** Wholesale of jewellery
**Export Markets:** the Far East; Europe; Canada; U S A; E Europe
**Issued Capital:** £2,949,167
**Directors:** Ms Y F Li, Ms M Bloch, G Tang, T K Cheung, S Gilham, Y S Thong, R D Dorfman, T G Lawrance
**Co. Secretary:** Jitendra Dabasia
**Responsibilities**
**Senior:** Richard Tibber *(Manager)*
**Health & Safety:** Ralph Will *(Health & Safety Officer)*
**Facilities:** Richard Tibber *(Manager)*
**Branches:** Zeon Ltd, 1 Swinstead Close, Nottingham, Nottinghamshire NG8 3JG
**US SIC:** 5094 **UK SIC:** 61900
**Auditors:** KPMG
**Bankers:** The Hongkong And Shanghai Banking Corporation Ltd (40-48-69)

| | 31-03-14 | 31-03-13 | 31-03-12 |
|---|---|---|---|
| TO | 8,222,000 | 8,870,000 | 8,838,000 |
| P/L | (1,511,000) | (742,000) | (685,000) |
| NW | (92,000) | 938,000 | 1,668,000 |
| WC | (2,513,000) | (4,215,000) | (4,397,000) |
| Emp. | 71 | 81 | 95 |

DUNS 22-757-5024 Exp
## Zep Uk Ltd
**(Subsidiary of:** Hale Group (Widnes) Ltd)
Tanhouse Lane, Widnes, Cheshire WA8 0RD
**Tel:** 0151-422-1000
**Web:** www.zep.co.uk
**Reg No:** 1428569 **VAT No:** 344063379
**Estd:** 1967 Private Limited Company
**Line of Business:** Chemicals and allied products
**Trading Style:** Zep Uk
**Issued Capital:** £838,200
**Directors:** R P Collins, M R Bachmann, A Brighenti
**Responsibilities**
**Senior:** Philip Hale *(Manager)*
**IT:** Keith Dooley *(IT Manager)*
**US SIC:** 2899 **UK SIC:** 25670
**Auditors:** BDO LLP
**Bankers:** Barclays Bank Plc (20-55-34)

| | 31-08-13 | 31-08-12 | 31-08-11 |
|---|---|---|---|
| TO | 6,184,044 | 3,135,669 | 4,727,732 |
| P/L | (562,052) | 117,784 | 244,355 |
| NW | 3,025,187 | 4,382,932 | 4,282,102 |
| WC | (1,388,519) | (987,382) | 1,538,204 |
| Emp. | 52 | 46 | 48 |

DUNS 21-909-2665 Imp-Exp
## Zephyr Racing Pennants Ltd
Midland Road, Thrapston, Kettering, Northamptonshire NN14 4LX
**Tel:** 01832-734484 **Fax:** 01832733064
**Web:** www.zephyr-flags.co.uk
**Reg No:** 0951407 **VAT No:** 120138426
**Estd:** 1955 Private Limited Company
**Line of Business:** Manufacture of household textiles
**Export Markets:** Worldwide
**Trading Style:** Zephyr Flags & Banners
**Issued Capital:** £14,180
**Principals:** C E Skey *(Chairman and Managing)*, S C Skey
**Responsibilities**
**Senior:** Paula Glass *(Warehouse Manager)*, Bryan Skey *(Manager)*
**Finance:** Richard Deer *(Accounts Manager)*
**Engineering:** David Althorpe *(Engineering Manager)*
**Branches:** Zephyr Racing Pennants Ltd, 16-17 High St, Tring, Hertfordshire HP23 5AH
**US SIC:** 2392 **UK SIC:** 45550
**Auditors:** K S Goring & Co
**Bankers:** National Westminster Bank Plc (53-61-33)

| | 31-12-13 | 31-12-12 | 31-12-11 |
|---|---|---|---|
| TA | 2,168,303 | 2,047,246 | 1,940,294 |
| NW | 1,248,137 | 1,048,139 | 1,027,108 |
| WC | 727,167 | 574,833 | 484,556 |

DUNS 63-450-9939
## Zermansky & Partners
10 Butts Court, Leeds, West Yorkshire LS1 5JS
**Web:** www.zermansky-solicitors.com
**Estd:** 1957 Partnership
**Line of Business:** Solicitors
**Trading Style:** Zermansky & Partners
**Partner:** N Taylor
**Responsibilities**
**Senior:** Judith Glynn *(Senior Partner)*, carl gallagher *(partner)*
**US SIC:** 8111 **UK SIC:** 83500
**Employees:** 20

DUNS 21-685-9598
## Zero Carbon Energy Ltd
499 Bideford Green, Leighton Buzzard, Bedfordshire LU7 2UA
**Tel:** 07749941594
**Web:** www.zero-carbon-energy.co.uk
**Reg No:** 7353348 **Estd:** 2010 Private Limited Company
**Line of Business:** Other service activities not elsewhere classified
**Issued Capital:** £2
**Directors:** D T Ridgeway, S Giles
**US SIC:** 1711 **UK SIC:** 50300

| | 31-08-13 | 31-08-12 | 31-08-11 |
|---|---|---|---|
| TA | 1,738 | 2,690 | 2,690 |
| NW | 1,325 | (1,002) | (1,002) |
| WC | 1,325 | (1,002) | (1,002) |

DUNS 23-481-6791 Imp
## Zerographic Systems Ltd
Dunston Hall, Dunston, Stafford, Staffordshire ST18 9AB
**Tel:** 01785711800 **Fax:** 08707876788
**Web:** www.zerographic.com
**Reg No:** 2602222 **Estd:** 1991 Private Limited Company
**Line of Business:** Manufacture of machinery for paper and paperboard production
**Trading Style:** Zerographic Systems Ltd
**Issued Capital:** £15,000
**Director:** Ms M A Corbett
**Co. Secretary:** Kevin Corbett
**Responsibilities**
**Sales:** Gavin Burborough *(Senior Sales Executive)*
**IT:** Shaun Talbot *(Senior IT Executive)*
**US SIC:** 3579 **UK SIC:** 33010
**Auditors:** Bsn Associates Ltd

| | 30-04-14 | 30-04-13 | 30-04-12 |
|---|---|---|---|
| TO | 9,936,375 | 8,389,619 | 10,562,679 |
| P/L | 268,839 | 17,719 | (515,035) |
| NW | 1,661,435 | 1,394,185 | 1,281,558 |
| WC | 152,586 | 25,504 | 133,280 |
| Emp. | 57 | 66 | 82 |

DUNS 28-974-9855 **Imp**

## Zerpetz Ltd

(**Subsidiary of:** Grinsty Holdings Ltd)
Arrow Business Park, Redditch, Worcestershire B98 8YN
**Tel:** 01527-514151
**Web:** www.arrowvale.co.uk
**Reg No:** 1751418 **VAT No:** 389224030
**Estd:** 1988 Private Limited Company
**Line of Business:** Electronic equipment (assembly)
**Trading Style:** Arrowvale Electronics
**Issued Capital:** £25,000
**Principals:** M P Thompson *(Managing)*, D J Gonnella, R J Amos
**Co. Secretary:** Gordon Sutherland
**Responsibilities**
**Senior:** Roger Beavon *(Manager)*
**Purchasing:** Emma Beard *(Senior Buyer)*
**US SIC:** 3643 **UK SIC:** 34203
**Auditors:** Clement Keys
**Bankers:** Barclays Bank Plc (20-27-17)

| | 30-06-13 | 30-06-12 | 30-06-11 |
|---|---|---|---|
| TA | 2,501,172 | 2,309,963 | 2,351,357 |
| NW | 1,672,398 | 1,592,477 | 1,510,198 |
| WC | 1,662,447 | 1,579,212 | 1,492,511 |

DUNS 21-135-5178

## Zest Investment Group Ltd

16 High Street, Yarm, Cleveland TS15 9AE
**Tel:** 01325288803
**Reg No:** 6684578 **Estd:** 2008 Private Limited Company
**Line of Business:** Management activities of holding companies
**Issued Capital:** £300
**Directors:** P H Scott, G K Sizer
**Responsibilities**
**Senior:** Edmund Coyle *(Director)*
**US SIC:** 6711 **UK SIC:** 83962
**Bankers:** Ulster Bank Ltd (98-00-10)

| | 30-09-13 | 30-09-12 | 30-09-11 |
|---|---|---|---|
| TO | 8,876,291 | N/A | 70,000 |
| P/L | (180,229) | (137,257) | (46,940) |
| NW | 6,793,724 | (268,862) | (131,605) |
| WC | (24,318,477) | 5,112,538 | 5,347,752 |
| Emp. | 400 | 2 | 2 |

DUNS 51-983-5920

## Zeta Compliance Services Ltd

(**Subsidiary of:** Zeta Compliance Group Plc)
Zeta House Avboury, House Lane, Upper Heyford, Bicester, Oxfordshire OX26 2UA
**Tel:** 08449994109 **Fax:** 01869-238071
**Web:** www.fineapply.com
**Reg No:** 3351062 **VAT No:** 927452020
**Estd:** 1997 Private Limited Company
**Line of Business:** Management of real estate on a fee or contract basis
**Issued Capital:** £830
**Directors:** R G Nicoll, S D Cooke, G D Brown, D B Downer
**Co. Secretary:** Graham Brown
**US SIC:** 6531 **UK SIC:** 83400
**Auditors:** James Cowper LLP

| | 31-01-14 | 31-01-13 | 31-01-12 |
|---|---|---|---|
| TO | 3,068,435 | 2,166,625 | 2,300,442 |
| P/L | 147,835 | (90,777) | 135,055 |
| NW | 1,015,476 | 868,129 | 956,289 |
| WC | 995,920 | 840,818 | 938,914 |
| Emp. | 47 | 34 | 37 |

DUNS 71-927-1277

## Zetar Ltd

(**Subsidiary of:** Zuckerraffinerie Tangermünde Fr. Meyers Sohn Holdi)
Unit 1000, Highgate Studios, 53-79 Highgate Road, London NW5 1TL
**Tel:** 02072849500
**Web:** www.zetarplc.com
**Reg No:** 5308258 **Estd:** 2004 Private Limited Company
**Line of Business:** Manufacture of cocoa and chocolate confectionery
**Export Sales:** £10,625,000
**Issued Capital:** £1,437,095
**Directors:** I M Blackburn, C H Beecham
**Responsibilities**
**Senior:** Susan Fadil *(Manager)*
**Finance:** Mark Stott *(Finance Director)*
**Sales:** Dave Clack *(Commercial Director)*
**US SIC:** 2066, 6711
**UK SIC:** 42141, 83962
**Auditors:** Grant Thornton UK LLP

| | 31-12-13 | 30-04-13 | 30-12-12 |
|---|---|---|---|
| TO | 91,026,000 | 136,498,000 | 128,258,000 |
| P/L | 2,048,000 | 231,000 | 2,854,000 |
| NW | 20,965,000 | 19,439,000 | 16,634,000 |
| WC | 4,124,000 | 4,899,000 | 4,444,000 |
| Emp. | 1,412 | 1,479 | 1,408 |

DUNS 39-927-1188 **Imp**

## Zetes Ltd

(**Subsidiary of:** Zetes Industries Sa)
Horizon, Honey Lane, Hurley, Maidenhead, Berkshire SL6 6RJ
**Tel:** 08452303500 **Fax:** 01628501896
**Web:** www.zetes.co.uk
**Reg No:** 2241256 **VAT No:** 543190851
**Estd:** 1988 Private Limited Company
**Line of Business:** Other software consultancy and supply
**Issued Capital:** £13,970,000
**Directors:** A Wirtz, J F Jacques, A Driesen
**Co. Secretary:** Eoin Oshea
**Responsibilities**
**Senior:** Alec Harrow *(Manager)*, Marco Malaihollo *(Manager)*
**Sales:** Francesca Smart *(Business Development Manager)*
**HR:** Naomi Jones *(Human Resources Manager)*
**Fleet:** Sam Gaines *(Head of Transport and Logistic)*
**Branches:** Zetes Ltd, Unit B, Buckhurst Road, Ascot, Berkshire SL5 7PW
**US SIC:** 7399, 7379
**UK SIC:** 83954, 83940
**Auditors:** Collards
**Bankers:** Barclays Bank Plc (20-05-06)

| | 31-12-13 | 31-12-12 | 31-12-11 |
|---|---|---|---|
| TO | 14,415,717 | 18,356,582 | 21,217,278 |
| P/L | (1,448,980) | (909,363) | (839,582) |
| NW | 2,227,093 | 3,676,073 | 4,585,436 |
| WC | 1,601,453 | 2,890,007 | 3,555,306 |
| Emp. | 76 | 79 | 92 |

DUNS 21-597-2672

## The Zetter Hotel

86-88 Clerkenwell Road, London EC1M 5RJ
**Tel:** 02073244444
**Web:** www.thezetter.com
**Estd:** 2011 Proprietorship
**Line of Business:** Hotels and motels without restaurant
**Proprietor:** J Catifeoglou
**Responsibilities**
**Senior:** Ashley Ely *(General Manager)*, Brian Tapson *(General Manager)*
**US SIC:** 7011 **UK SIC:** 66500
**Employees:** 100

DUNS 22-126-1311 **Imp**

## Zeus Packaging (Uk) Ltd

(**Subsidiary of:** Zeus Packaging Group Limited)
Gunnels Wood Road Aspect One, Stevenage, Hertfordshire SG1 2DG
**Tel:** 01438-777000 **Fax:** 01438-777002
**Web:** www.zeuspackaging.com
**Reg No:** 4145121 **Estd:** 1987 Private Limited Company
**Line of Business:** Agents specialising in the sale of particular products or ranges of products not elsewhere classified
**Export Sales:** £497,650
**Trading Style:** Zeus Packaging Group
**Issued Capital:** £4,186
**Director:** B O'Sullivan
**Co. Secretary:** Tlt Secretaries Limited
**Responsibilities**
**IT:** Chris Pilbeam *(Senior IT Executive)*
**Purchasing:** Nicki Hutton *(Purchasing Manager)*
**Branches:** Zeus Packaging (Uk) Ltd, Unit 9, Jackson Street, Coalville, Leicestershire LE67 3NR
**US SIC:** 5199 **UK SIC:** 61900
**Auditors:** Deloitte & Touche
**Bankers:** Lloyds TSB Bank plc (30-16-64)

| | 31-12-13 | 31-12-12 | 31-12-11 |
|---|---|---|---|
| TO | 31,866,627 | 30,890,095 | 30,062,720 |
| P/L | 1,509,906 | 1,644,274 | 1,443,700 |
| NW | 4,968,887 | 3,905,108 | 2,512,795 |
| WC | 4,724,094 | 4,821,272 | 3,346,279 |
| Emp. | 94 | 91 | 91 |

DUNS 49-075-6988 **Imp**

## Zeus Technology Ltd

(**Subsidiary of:** Riverbed Technology Inc.)
The Jeffreys Building, Cambridge, Cambridgeshire CB4 0DS
**Tel:** 01223388500 **Fax:** 01223388501
**Web:** www.riverbed.com
**Reg No:** 3085230 **Estd:** 1995 Private Limited Company
**Line of Business:** Computer software (development)
**Trading Style:** Riverbed Technology
**Issued Capital:** £6,657,698
**Directors:** J M Kennelly, M J Palu
**Co. Secretary:** Brett Nissenberg
**Responsibilities**
**Senior:** Nicholas Brisbourne *(Manager)*, David Day *(Manager)*, Charles Hobley *(Manager)*, Travis Reed *(Manager)*
**Marketing:** Vanessa Cross *(Director, Marketing Communicat)*
**US SIC:** 7379 **UK SIC:** 83940
**Auditors:** PKF Littlejohn LLP
**Bankers:** Barclays Bank Plc (20-17-19)

| | 31-12-12 | 31-12-11 |
|---|---|---|
| TO | N/A | 2,406,465 |
| P/L | (750,215) | 44,153,880 |
| NW | N/A | 45,589,737 |
| WC | N/A | 45,589,737 |
| Emp. | N/A | 60 |

DUNS 50-348-3265 **Imp-Exp**

## Zf Lemforder Uk Ltd

(**Subsidiary of:** Zeppelin-Stiftung)
Heath Road, Wednesbury, West Midlands WS10 8BH
**Tel:** 012152 64441 **Fax:** 01215 263579
**Web:** www.zf.com
**Reg No:** 2370396 **VAT No:** 547666502
**Estd:** 1989 Private Limited Company
**Line of Business:** Manufacturers of vehicle components
**Export Markets:** E U, U S A, Mexico
**Export Sales:** £3,405,000
**Trading Style:** Division C Plant Darlaston
**Issued Capital:** £7,000,000
**Directors:** C Haedge, P Buckermann, T Somerfield, B R Wrenbeck
**Co. Secretary:** Philip Mauldridge
**Responsibilities**
**Marketing:** Bruce Jones *(Commercial Director)*
**Sales:** R Homer *(Sales Manager)*, Bruce Jones *(Commercial Director)*
**HR:** Fulger Sam *(Chief Buyer)*
**Facilities:** Mike Lester *(Engineering Manager)*
**Engineering:** Mike Lester *(Engineering Manager)*
**Branches:** Zf Lemforder Uk Ltd, Starley Way, Birmingham, West Midlands B37 7GN
**US SIC:** 8911 **UK SIC:** 83701
**Auditors:** PricewaterhouseCoopers LLP
**Bankers:** Lloyds TSB Bank plc (30-99-06)

| | 31-12-13 | 31-12-12 | 31-12-11 |
|---|---|---|---|
| TO | 223,986,000 | 161,224,000 | 148,273,000 |
| P/L | 6,154,000 | 2,056,000 | 2,379,000 |
| NW | 16,116,000 | 13,397,000 | 10,530,000 |
| WC | 9,000 | (2,457,000) | 358,000 |
| Emp. | 337 | 330 | 318 |

DUNS 21-913-3956 **Imp-Exp**

## Zf Services Uk Ltd

(**Subsidiary of:** Zeppelin-Stiftung)
Abbeyfield Road, Nottingham, Nottinghamshire NG7 2SX
**Tel:** 03332401123 **Fax:** 01159-869261
**Web:** www.zf.com
**Reg No:** 1137722 **VAT No:** 118224200
**Estd:** 1973 Private Limited Company
**Line of Business:** Motor factors
**Export Markets:** Worldwide
**Export Sales:** £3,681,000
**Trading Style:** Zf Services
**Issued Capital:** £4,000,000
**Directors:** T Henne, P Dellai, J Kotak, G J Truckel
**Co. Secretary:** Jiten Kotak
**Responsibilities**
**Senior:** Alois Ludwig *(Chairman of the Board)*, Simon Scarth *(Logistics Manager)*
**Marketing:** Nina Sargeant *(Marketing Coordinator)*
**HR:** Paula Saunders *(Human Resources Manager)*
**Health & Safety:** Peter Fedorow *(Quality Manager)*, Jamie Reilly *(Heath & Safety Manager)*
**Facilities:** Darren Hutchinson *(Facilities Controller)*
**Operations:** John Millward *(Rail & Wind Turbine Production)*
**Purchasing:** Christopher Adcock *(Operations Director)*
**Fleet:** Simon Scarth *(Logistics Manager)*
**Engineering:** Christopher Adcock *(Operations Director)*
**US SIC:** 5531 **UK SIC:** 65100
**Auditors:** Ernst & Young LLP
**Bankers:** Barclays Bank Plc (20-63-25)

| | 31-12-13 | 31-12-12 | 31-12-11 |
|---|---|---|---|
| TO | 62,335,000 | 54,568,000 | 41,820,000 |
| P/L | 3,799,000 | 1,206,000 | 2,240,000 |
| NW | 10,323,000 | 1,321,000 | 2,401,000 |
| WC | 17,682,000 | 9,110,000 | 8,358,000 |
| Emp. | 195 | 196 | 162 |

DUNS 21-213-7426 **Imp-Exp**

## Z.Hinchliffe & Sons Ltd

(**Subsidiary of:** Harold Hinchliffe Ltd)
Hartcliffe Mills, Wakefield Road, Denby Dale, Huddersfield, West Yorkshire HD8 8QL
**Tel:** 01484-862207
**Web:** www.zhinchliffe.co.uk
**Reg No:** 0078708 **VAT No:** 183473545
**Estd:** 1850 Private Limited Company
**Line of Business:** Wholesale suppliers of yarn
**Export Markets:** Worldwide
**Export Sales:** £6,917,734
**Issued Capital:** £254,968
**Directors:** G A Wilby, J H Hinchliffe, J R Hinchliffe
**Co. Secretary:** John Glennon
**Responsibilities**
**Senior:** Richard Knutte *(Maintenance Manager)*, Richard Suarez *(Dyehouse Manager)*, George Wilby *(Manager)*
**Finance:** George Wilby *(Manager)*
**Health & Safety:** George Wilby *(Manager)*
**Facilities:** Richard Knutte *(Maintenance Manager)*, Richard Suarez *(Dyehouse Manager)*
**Operations:** Kevin Kaye *(Dyehouse Manager)*, Richard Suarez *(Dyehouse Manager)*
**Purchasing:** George Wilby *(Manager)*
**Branches:** Z.hinchliffe & Sons Ltd, 11A Drakemyre, Dalry, Ayrshire KA24 5JD
**US SIC:** 2299 **UK SIC:** 43992
**Auditors:** Wheawill & Sudworth Ltd
**Bankers:** HSBC Bank plc (40-25-10)

| | 30-06-13 | 30-06-12 | 30-06-11 |
|---|---|---|---|
| TO | 14,673,690 | 14,642,577 | 17,585,844 |
| P/L | (1,105,689) | (236,511) | 976,570 |
| NW | 19,673,523 | 20,815,175 | 21,562,658 |
| WC | 17,409,817 | 18,728,560 | 19,038,936 |
| Emp. | 229 | 235 | 245 |

DUNS 39-761-9164

## Zibrant Ltd

(**Subsidiary of:** Sodexo)
2 Millennium Way Prospect Place, Derby, Derbyshire DE24 8HG
**Tel:** 01332-292-979 **Fax:** 08434794101
**Web:** www.zibrant.com
**Reg No:** 2198966 **VAT No:** 496328310
**Estd:** 1987 Private Limited Company
**Line of Business:** Corporate entertainment and hospitality
**Trading Style:** Zibrant Live!
**Issued Capital:** £100,000
**Directors:** N P Cooper, D C Boden, Ms F A Sharpe, Ms H Mccabe
**Co. Secretary:** Darren Boden
**Responsibilities**
**Senior:** Helen McCabe *(Managing Director of Operation)*
**Marketing:** Penny McGrigor *(Head of Brand & Marketing)*
**Admin:** Pam Sharple *(Administration Officer)*
**Facilities:** Pam Sharple *(Administration Officer)*
**Branches:** Zibrant Ltd, Sandford House, Catteshall Lane, Godalming, Surrey GU7 1LG
**US SIC:** 7999 **UK SIC:** 97913
**Auditors:** Grant Thornton UK LLP
**Bankers:** National Westminster Bank Plc (60-12-01)

| | 31-12-13 | 31-12-12 | 31-12-11 |
|---|---|---|---|
| TO | 11,034,754 | 13,965,176 | 18,098,368 |
| P/L | 34,056 | 75,589 | 891,943 |
| NW | 2,040,226 | 2,140,999 | 1,394,198 |
| WC | (362,669) | (317,265) | (1,656,146) |
| Emp. | 178 | 185 | 216 |

DUNS 23-558-6729

## Zim Uk Ltd

Room 249, India Building, Water Street, Liverpool, Merseyside L2 0QD
**Tel:** 0151-258-1118 **Fax:** 01512581117
**Web:** www.zim.com
**Reg No:** 3556934 **VAT No:** 707942029
**Estd:** 1998 Private Limited Company
**Line of Business:** Shipping companies
**Issued Capital:** £200
**Directors:** S Dotan, Ms S Dahan Nagar, S E Sutherland
**Responsibilities**
**Senior:** Rafael Ari *(Manager)*, Isaac Brauner *(Manager)*
**Finance:** Karen Musker *(Finance Supervisor)*, Thomas Warburton *(Credit Control Supervisor)*
**Operations:** Peter Leonard *(Marine Operations Manager)*
**Fleet:** Paul Blundell *(Logistics Manager)*, Miroslawa Kadys *(Transport Supervisor)*
**Branches:** Zim Uk Ltd, Marlin House, Kings Road, Immingham, Lincolnshire DN40 1AW
**US SIC:** 4712 **UK SIC:** 77002
**Auditors:** Carter Backer Winter
**Bankers:** HSBC Bank plc (40-29-08)

| | 31-12-13 | 31-12-12 | 31-12-11 |
|---|---|---|---|
| TO | 2,218,800 | 2,239,213 | 2,231,870 |
| P/L | 43,506 | 43,906 | 43,762 |
| NW | 562,436 | 530,802 | 512,409 |
| WC | 514,735 | 465,367 | 431,689 |
| Emp. | 54 | 58 | 61 |

DUNS 22-554-8841 **Imp-Exp**

## Zimmer Ltd

(**Subsidiary of:** Zimmer Holdings Inc.)
The Courtyard, Lancaster Place, Swindon, Wiltshire SN3 4FP
**Tel:** 01793-584500
**Web:** www.zimmer.co.uk
**Reg No:** 0740767 **VAT No:** 332744662
**Estd:** 1979 Private Limited Company
**Line of Business:** Wholesale of pharmaceutical goods
**Export Sales:** £680,000
**Issued Capital:** £31,628,250
**Directors:** M D Humphris, J Cresser Brown, B Melzi, A Massarella
**Co. Secretary:** Christopher Jefferis
**Responsibilities**
**Senior:** Clive Ridgwell *(Manager)*
**US SIC:** 5122 **UK SIC:** 61800
**Auditors:** PricewaterhouseCoopers LLP

**Bankers:** National Westminster Bank Plc
(60-21-40)

|  | 31-12-13 | 31-12-12 | 31-12-11 |
|---|---|---|---|
| TO | 76,338,000 | 75,005,000 | 67,980,000 |
| P/L | 3,885,000 | 4,094,000 | 3,739,000 |
| NW | 60,292,000 | 56,649,000 | 54,920,000 |
| WC | 53,387,000 | 50,339,000 | 48,660,000 |
| Emp. | 113 | 116 | 115 |

---

DUNS 21-726-3530

## Zinc Ahead Holdings Ltd

(Subsidiary of: Mineral Newco Ltd)
4240 Nash Court, John Smith Drive Oxford
Business, Oxford, Oxfordshire OX4 2RU
**Tel:** 01865398170
**Reg No:** 7628900  **Estd:** 2011 Private
Limited Company
**Line of Business:** Other software
consultancy and supply
**Export Sales:** £9,604,558
**Issued Capital:** £1,190
**Directors:** J A Brown, Ms Z Cottrell, D Ely,
D Eaton
**US SIC:** 7379  **UK SIC:** 83940
**Bankers:** HSBC Bank plc (40-35-43)

|  | 31-03-14 | 31-03-13 | 31-03-12 |
|---|---|---|---|
| TO | 12,558,764 | 9,287,952 | 7,411,070 |
| P/L | 1,294,110 | 1,166,351 | 2,345,285 |
| NW | 1,120,191 | 3,506,421 | 2,942,368 |
| WC | 790,429 | 4,498,747 | 2,710,062 |
| Emp. | 94 | 65 | 50 |

---

DUNS 49-110-5128

## Zinc Bar & Grill Ltd

(Subsidiary of: W2d2 Ltd)
Unit 5a, The Corn Exchange, 37 Hanging
Ditch, Manchester M4 3TR
**Tel:** 01618274200  **Fax:** 020-7403-4580
**Web:** www.zincbar.co.uk
**Reg No:** 3096889  **Estd:** 1999 Private
Limited Company
**Line of Business:** Restaurants
**Issued Capital:** £100
**Directors:** S J Walker, V Lord
**Co. Secretary:** John Hammond
**Branches:** Zinc Bar & Grill Ltd, 14 John
Dalton Street, Manchester M2 6JR
**US SIC:** 5812  **UK SIC:** 66110
**Auditors:** Ernst & Young LLP

|  | 31-03-12 |
|---|---|
| P/L | 2,335,000 |

---

DUNS 77-120-0607

## Zincast Foundry Ltd

(Subsidiary of: Zincast (Holdings) Ltd)
Strawberry Lane, Willenhall, West Midlands
WV13 3NG
**Tel:** 01902606226  **Fax:** 01902-634607
**Web:** www.zincast.co.uk
**Reg No:** 2692531  **VAT No:** 559683385
**Estd:** 1926 Private Limited Company
**Line of Business:** Foundries
**Issued Capital:** £10,000
**Principals:** F E Heath (Managing),
Ms B J Heath, P A Heath
**Co. Secretary:** Ms Susan Heath
**US SIC:** 3325  **UK SIC:** 31110
**Auditors:** Horwath Clark Whitehill
**Bankers:** Barclays Bank Plc (20-97-78)

|  | 31-08-13 | 31-08-12 | 31-08-11 |
|---|---|---|---|
| TA | 1,117,003 | 1,155,786 | 1,289,484 |
| NW | 216,681 | 214,753 | 213,191 |
| WC | 54,146 | 42,776 | 52,386 |

---

DUNS 23-807-8021

## Zincox Resources Plc

Knightway House, Park Street, Bagshot,
Surrey GU19 5AQ
**Tel:** 01276-450100  **Fax:** 01276-850281
**Web:** www.zincox.com
**Reg No:** 3800208  **Estd:** 2000 Public Limited
Company
**Line of Business:** Mining of metals
**Trading Style:** Zincox Resources
**Directors:** A C Woollett, Dr R G Beddows,
S C Hall, G S Dalal, J Z Dewalens,
G D Lafferty
**Co. Secretary:** Ian Halliwell
**Responsibilities**
**Senior:** Jeremy Saville (Non-Executive
Director.)
**US SIC:** 1099, 3332, 3339, 3341
**UK SIC:** 21000, 22470
**Auditors:** Grant Thornton UK LLP
**Bankers:** HSBC Bank plc (40-16-33)
**Employees:** 8
**Turnover:** £27,522,000

---

DUNS 21-595-5456

## Zion Community Health & Resource Centre

339 Stretford Road, Manchester M15 4ZY
**Tel:** 0161-226-5412
**Web:** www.zioncentre.co.uk
**Estd:** 2002
**Line of Business:** Activities of other
membership organisations not elsewhere
classified
**Proprietor:** Ms F Selvan
**Responsibilities**
**Senior:** Paul Mathis (Operations Manager)
**Operations:** Jennifer Horton (Operations
Manager)
**US SIC:** 8699  **UK SIC:** 96902
**Employees:** 200

---

DUNS 76-995-3191                          Imp

## Zip Heaters (Uk) Ltd

(Subsidiary of: Zip Holdco 1 Pty Limited)
Bertie Ward Way, Dereham, Norfolk NR19
1TE
**Tel:** 08706088888
**Web:** www.zipheaters.co.uk
**Reg No:** 2649782  **VAT No:** 688630685
**Estd:** 1991 Private Limited Company
**Line of Business:** Heating equipment sales
and service
**Issued Capital:** £20,000
**Directors:** B Chertkow, J A Doumani,
C J Binnie, S P Delahanty
**Co. Secretary:** Christopher Hannant
**Responsibilities**
**Senior:** Kevin Samuel (Manager)
**IT:** John Steedman (Commercial Manager)
**HR:** Maria Fosbrook (Human Resources
Manager)
**Health & Safety:** John Steedman
(Commercial Manager)
**Facilities:** Philippa Syder (Support
Operations Manager)
**Purchasing:** Claire Hayden (Purchasing
Manager)
**Branches:** Zip Heaters (Uk) Ltd, R4 Unit
Tenterfields Business Park, Burnley Road,
Luddendenfoot, Halifax, West Yorkshire HX2
6EQ
**US SIC:** 3999  **UK SIC:** 49590
**Auditors:** PricewaterhouseCoopers LLP
**Bankers:** HSBC Bank plc (40-08-53)

|  | 30-06-13 | 30-06-12 | 30-06-11 |
|---|---|---|---|
| TA | 14,953,798 | 13,016,703 | 9,359,134 |
| P/L | 3,198,986 | 2,434,856 | 2,370,839 |
| NW | 6,388,473 | 5,402,296 | 4,656,666 |
| WC | 5,821,286 | 5,030,938 | 4,500,281 |
| Emp. | 158 | 134 | 121 |

---

DUNS 73-251-3820

## Zipcar (Uk) Ltd

(Subsidiary of: Avis Budget Group Inc.)
Melbury House, London SW19 7QW
**Tel:** 03332409000
**Web:** www.zipcar.co.uk
**Reg No:** 4525217  **VAT No:** 832428339
**Estd:** 2004 Private Limited Company
**Line of Business:** Vehicle rental (car)
**Issued Capital:** £622,177
**Directors:** M W Walker, W S Deaver,
D B Wyshner, M K Tucker
**Co. Secretary:** Mark Walker
**Responsibilities**
**Senior:** Brett Akker (Manager)
**Finance:** Andrew Valentine (Finance
Director)
**Marketing:** Dave McKean (CRM Manager)
**US SIC:** 7512  **UK SIC:** 84801
**Auditors:** Baker Tilly UK Audit LLP

|  | 31-12-13 | 31-12-12 | 31-12-11 |
|---|---|---|---|
| TO | 28,278,000 | 27,596,000 | 24,800,000 |
| P/L | (1,222,000) | (3,657,000) | (4,573,000) |
| NW | (13,181,000) | (13,624,000) | (9,967,000) |
| WC | (20,769,000) | (22,901,000) | (19,706,000) |
| Emp. | 205 | 201 | 198 |

---

DUNS 21-590-5351

## Zippos Circus

Longcopse Farm, Newbury, Berkshire RG20
0LD
**Tel:** 07836641277
**Web:** www.zipposcircus.co.uk
**Estd:** 2011
**Line of Business:** Entertainers
**Proprietor:** M Burton
**US SIC:** 7922  **UK SIC:** 97412
**Employees:** 70

---

DUNS 34-731-7336                          Imp

## Zirax Ltd

68 Lombard Street, London EC3V 9LJ
**Tel:** 02078681694  **Fax:** 02078681800
**Web:** www.zirax.com
**Reg No:** 5533825  **Estd:** 2005 Private
Limited Company

---

**Line of Business:** Business and
management consultancy activities not
elsewhere classified
**Directors:** N Louis, S V Belichenko
**Co. Secretary:** Clyde Secretaries Limited
**Responsibilities**
**Senior:** Valery Andosov (Head of Corporate
project Spec), Mikhail Baranov (Owner),
Matthias Durst (Manager)
**Sales:** Sergey Mizitov (Business
Development Manager), Anna Shevchenko
(Overseas Business Development)
**US SIC:** 7392, 7399
**UK SIC:** 83951, 83954
**Auditors:** Goodman Jones LLP
**Employees:** 252
**Turnover:** £64,422,000

---

DUNS 55-062-2591

## Zoar Residential Home

Merion Street, Clydach Vale, Tonypandy, Mid
Glamorgan CF40 1QU
**Tel:** 01443432262
**Estd:** 1990 Proprietorship
**Line of Business:** Individual & Family Social
Services
**Proprietor:** M Saunders
**US SIC:** 8321  **UK SIC:** 96111
**Employees:** 48

---

DUNS 21-117-7316                          Exp

## Zodiac Interconnect Uk Ltd

(Subsidiary of: Zodiac Aerospace Cs20001)
220 Bedford Avenue, Slough, Berkshire SL1
4RY
**Tel:** 01753-896600  **Fax:** 01753-896601
**Web:** www.icore.co.uk
**Reg No:** 0874618  **Estd:** 1929 Private
Limited Company
**Line of Business:** Manufacture of other
plastic products
**Export Sales:** £16,641,000
**Trading Style:** Zodiac
**Issued Capital:** £100
**Directors:** C M Stuttard, J J Jegou,
O G Zarrouati
**Co. Secretary:**
Athenaeum Secretaries Limited
**Responsibilities**
**Senior:** Gregory Burland (Technical
Director), David Gostelow (Warehouse
Manager)
**Marketing:** Gregory Burland (Technical
Director)
**Sales:** Gregory Burland (Technical Director)
**IT:** Gregory Burland (Technical Director),
Kieron Marshall (IT Manager)
**HR:** Peter Shorrocks (Human Resources
Director)
**Health & Safety:** Peter Shorrocks (Human
Resources Director)
**Operations:** David Bayliss (Quality Control
Manager)
**US SIC:** 3079, 3661
**UK SIC:** 48360, 34410
**Auditors:** Ernst & Young LLP
**Bankers:** National Westminster Bank Plc
(50-00-00)

|  | 31-08-13 | 31-08-12 | 31-08-11 |
|---|---|---|---|
| TO | 21,215,000 | 23,549,000 | 20,634,000 |
| P/L | 2,394,000 | 2,652,000 | 2,051,000 |
| NW | 8,739,000 | 6,468,000 | 4,049,000 |
| WC | 7,818,000 | 5,434,000 | 3,490,000 |
| Emp. | 117 | 122 | 118 |

---

DUNS 21-160-4533

## Zodiac Maritime Ltd

6th Floor, 1 Hanover Street, London W1S
1YZ
**Tel:** 02073332222
**Web:** www.zodiac-maritime.com
**Reg No:** 1240802  **Estd:** 1976 Private
Limited Company
**Line of Business:** Ships agents
**Trading Style:** Zodiac Maritime Agencies
Limited
**Issued Capital:** £90,000
**Directors:** S A Gontha, D M Ofer, D G Ofer
**Co. Secretary:** Chaim Klein
**Responsibilities**
**Senior:** Eyal Ofer (Chairman), Rami Zingher
(Manager)
**Finance:** Darren Abbabial (Financial
Director)
**Admin:** Glen Easlea (Administration
Manager)
**Health & Safety:** Mark Rawson (Health &
Safety Officer)
**Facilities:** Glen Easlea (Administration
Manager)
**Purchasing:** Ivelin Krastev (Purchasing
Manager)
**US SIC:** 4712  **UK SIC:** 77002
**Auditors:** KPMG LLP

---

**Bankers:** The Chase Manhattan Bank
(60-92-42)

|  | 31-12-13 | 31-12-12 | 31-12-11 |
|---|---|---|---|
| TO | 33,287,607 | 46,384,575 | 44,577,645 |
| P/L | 5,236,281 | 10,683,900 | 7,883,644 |
| NW | 8,031,917 | 7,092,420 | 8,880,269 |
| WC | 5,135,695 | 3,499,302 | 4,911,226 |
| Emp. | 170 | 168 | 176 |

---

DUNS 21-025-5030                          Imp

## Zodiac Seats Uk Ltd

(Subsidiary of: Zodiac Aerospace Cs20001)
Kestrel House, Lakeside, Cwmbran, Gwent
NP44 3HQ
**Tel:** 01633793500
**Web:** www.contouraerospace.co.uk
**Reg No:** 0278391  **VAT No:** 346413367
**Estd:** 2005 Private Limited Company
**Line of Business:** Manufacture of parts and
accessories for motor vehicles and their
engines
**Export Sales:** £168,126,000
**Trading Style:** Contour Aerospace Seating
+ Contour, Britax Aircraft Seating, Heath
Techna
**Issued Capital:** £25,864,297
**Directors:** P A Strothers, C L Novella,
Zodiac Aerospace Sa, M A Knafo
**Co. Secretary:**
Pinsent Masons Secretarial Limit
**Branches:** Zodiac Seats Uk Limited,
Watchmoor Point, Camberley, Surrey GU15
3AH
**US SIC:** 3999  **UK SIC:** 49590
**Auditors:** KPMG LLP
**Bankers:** Barclays Bank Plc (20-07-71)

|  | 31-08-13 | 31-08-12 | 31-08-11 |
|---|---|---|---|
| TO | 175,326,000 | 86,872,000 | 160,944,000 |
| P/L | 15,044,000 | 1,946,000 | 19,148,000 |
| NW | 47,814,000 | 40,093,000 | 26,838,000 |
| WC | 49,262,000 | 37,390,000 | 22,494,000 |
| Emp. | 1,080 | 1,094 | 1,065 |

---

DUNS 42-458-6969

## Zoe's Place Trust

1 Mill Street, Leamington Spa, W,
Leamington Spa, Warwickshire CV31 1ES
**Tel:** 01926889633
**Web:** www.zoes-place.org.uk
**Reg No:** 4446416  **Estd:** 2002 Private
Company Limited By Guarantee
**Line of Business:** Charities and charitable
organisations
**Directors:** Reverend P D Mcguire,
Professor S Sinha, J J Scarisbrick
**Co. Secretary:** Ms Joan Stainsby
**Responsibilities**
**Senior:** Lisa Retford (Group Finance
Manager)
**US SIC:** 8062  **UK SIC:** 95100
**Auditors:** Tom Carroll Associates Ltd
**Bankers:** National Westminster Bank Plc
(60-12-35)

|  | 30-06-14 | 30-06-13 | 30-06-12 |
|---|---|---|---|
| TO | 3,375,624 | 2,719,259 | 2,464,577 |
| P/L | 453,858 | (77,635) | (408,525) |
| NW | 3,337,521 | 2,883,663 | 2,961,298 |
| WC | 1,517,301 | 1,139,739 | 1,062,374 |
| Emp. | 92 | 115 | 110 |

---

DUNS 21-845-8095

## Zoetis Uk Ltd

(Subsidiary of: Zoetis Animal Health Ltd)
5th Floor 6 St Andrew Street, London EC4A
3AE
**Tel:** 08453008034
**Web:** www.vetsupportplus.com
**Reg No:** 8116609  **Estd:** 2012 Private
Limited Company
**Line of Business:** Wholesale of
pharmaceutical goods
**Issued Capital:** £67,788,255
**Directors:** N W Robinson, J M Hanley
**US SIC:** 5122  **UK SIC:** 61800

|  | 30-11-13 |
|---|---|
| TO | 113,927,000 |
| P/L | 3,625,000 |
| NW | 6,501,000 |
| WC | 6,486,000 |
| Emp. | 160 |

---

DUNS 45-846-3338

## Zok International Group Ltd

(Subsidiary of: Airworthy Ltd)
Airworthy House, Elsted, Midhurst, West
Sussex GU29 0JT
**Fax:** 03337002728
**Web:** www.zok.com
**Reg No:** 3193013  **Estd:** 1982 Private
Limited Company
**Line of Business:** Manufacturers of
chemicals
**Issued Capital:** £1,000
**Directors:** K G Cartwright, Ms R Horton,
R C Johnson
**Responsibilities**
**Senior:** Ruth Schofield (Manager)
**US SIC:** 2899  **UK SIC:** 25670

**Auditors:** Grant Thornton
**Bankers:** HSBC Bank plc (40-00-96)

|     | 31-12-13 | 31-12-12 | 31-12-11 |
|-----|----------|----------|----------|
| TA  | 892,273  | 931,856  | 649,330  |
| NW  | 477,140  | 440,265  | 343,917  |
| WC  | 396,167  | 340,144  | 243,531  |

DUNS 21-583-0624

## Zolfo Cooper
107 West Regent Street, Glasgow,
Lanarkshire G2 2BA
**Tel:** 01413538600
**Web:** www.zolfocooper.com
**Estd:** 2011 Proprietorship
**Line of Business:** Insolvency practitioners
**Proprietor:** M Mcpherson
**Responsibilities**
**Senior:** Elizabeth Mackay (Senior Partner)
**US SIC:** 6111  **UK SIC:** 81501
**Employees:** 50

DUNS 21-138-1867

## Zolfo Cooper Llp
10 Fleet Place, London EC4M 7RB
**Tel:** 02073325000 **Fax:** 02073325001
**Web:** www.europe.zolfocooper.com
**Reg No:** 0340361OC  **Estd:** 2008 Private
Limited Company
**Line of Business:** Financial management
**Export Sales:** £7,107,723
**Responsibilities**
**Senior:** Alastair Beveridge (Non-designated
Limited Liabili), Tony Brierley (Partner),
Ryan Grant (Non-designated Limited Liabili),
Fraser Gray (Non-designated Limited
Liabili), Charles Holder (Non-designated
Limited Liabili), Anne Laing (Non-designated
Limited Liabili), Elizabeth Mackay (Non-
designated Limited Liabili), Anne Okeefe
(Non-designated Limited Liabili), Gordon
Stevenson (Non-designated Limited Liabili)
**Marketing:** Nina Grayson (Marketing
Executive)
**Fleet:** Lana Anderson (Head of International
Events &)
**US SIC:** 8999  **UK SIC:** 83954

|     | 31-03-14   | 31-03-13   | 31-03-12   |
|-----|------------|------------|------------|
| TO  | 37,991,119 | 50,741,769 | 48,873,043 |
| P/L | 21,713,871 | 20,658,086 | 19,415,266 |
| NW  | 6,225,724  | 3,907,570  | 1,367,852  |
| WC  | 22,789,251 | 10,372,850 | 14,893,163 |

DUNS 22-956-3978

## Zoltan Engineering Co Ltd
Cromwell Road, Bredbruy, Stockport,
Cheshire SK6 2RH
**Tel:** 0161-430-3173 **Fax:** 0161-430-8643
**Web:** www.ctl-eng.com
**Reg No:** 0955189  **Estd:** 1969 Private
Limited Company
**Line of Business:** General mechanical
engineering
**Export Sales:** £5,089,264
**Trading Style:** Ctl Engineering
**Issued Capital:** £17,600
**Directors:** D A Davidson, S D Kirk,
I H Booth, C W Booth, K M Ness,
J M Ferguson
**Co. Secretary:** Mark Kynaston
**US SIC:** 8911  **UK SIC:** 83701
**Auditors:** Hurst & Co
**Bankers:** HSBC Bank plc (40-43-10)

|     | 31-12-13  | 31-12-12  | 31-12-11  |
|-----|-----------|-----------|-----------|
| TO  | 9,509,047 | 8,231,160 | 7,764,097 |
| P/L | 508,092   | 187,475   | 230,330   |
| NW  | 1,718,291 | 1,260,745 | 1,358,009 |
| WC  | 271,572   | 87,803    | (436,605) |
| Emp.| 82        | 81        | 80        |

DUNS 21-589-6929                          **Imp-Exp**

## Zonal Retail Data Systems Ltd
1 Tanfield, Edinburgh, Midlothian EH3 5DA
**Tel:** 01314778200
**Web:** www.zonal.co.uk
**Reg No:** 0069596SC  **Estd:** 1979 Private
Limited Company
**Line of Business:** Wholesale of other office
machinery and equipment
**Export Markets:** Eire
**Export Sales:** £590,770
**Issued Capital:** £1,045
**Principals:** S J Mclean (Managing),
R A Mclean (Financial), H S Mclean,
P M Edwards, Ms B J Mclean, C D Plucknett,
R Hammond, J A Mclean
**Co. Secretary:** Carl Plucknett
**Responsibilities**
**Senior:** Gordon Black (Warehouse
Manager), Clive Consterdine (Director)
**IT:** Scott Baillie (IT Manager)
**HR:** Catriona Dick (Human Resources
Manager)
**Facilities:** Brian Cairncross (Maintenance
Manager)
**Branches:** Zonal Retail Data Systems Ltd,
Forth House 70 High Street, Aylesbury,
Buckinghamshire HP18 0LB

---

**US SIC:** 5081  **UK SIC:** 61490
**Auditors:** Blueprint Audit Ltd
**Bankers:** Clydesdale Bank Plc (82-45-05)

|     | 30-06-13   | 30-06-12   | 30-06-11   |
|-----|------------|------------|------------|
| TO  | 41,313,171 | 36,165,915 | 29,900,207 |
| P/L | 158,667    | 989,388    | 2,725,511  |
| NW  | 9,080,373  | 9,897,579  | 9,269,772  |
| WC  | 3,746,605  | 4,747,596  | 4,373,145  |
| Emp.| 260        | 230        | 192        |

DUNS 21-596-3814

## The Zone
St Andrews Road, Huddersfield, West
Yorkshire HD1 6PT
**Tel:** 01484484134
**Web:** www.thezone.uk.com
**Estd:** 2011 Proprietorship
**Line of Business:** Children's activity
playcentres
**Proprietor:** P France
**US SIC:** 8699  **UK SIC:** 96902
**Employees:** 50

DUNS 64-074-7536

## Zone Contractors Ltd
116 Summer Road, Erdington, Birmingham,
West Midlands B23 6DY
**Tel:** 0121-693-6226
**Web:** www.zonecontractors.co.uk
**Reg No:** 4478131  **Estd:** 2002 Private
Limited Company
**Line of Business:** Construction of domestic
buildings
**Issued Capital:** £100
**Director:** J Munnelly
**Co. Secretary:** Cornelius Allen
**US SIC:** 1541, 1522
**UK SIC:** 50100

|     | 31-03-14  | 31-03-13  | 31-03-12  |
|-----|-----------|-----------|-----------|
| TA  | 2,091,420 | 1,548,688 | 1,900,528 |
| NW  | 189,199   | 75,260    | 576,953   |
| WC  | (141,271) | (248,827) | 451,558   |

DUNS 52-036-5727                              **Imp**

## Zone Ltd
Unit 10 South Baileygate Baileygate,
Industrial Estate, Pontefract, West Yorkshire
WF8 2LN
**Tel:** 020-7267-4774 **Fax:** 020-7267-1119
**Web:** www.thisiszone.com
**Reg No:** 3402993  **Estd:** 1997 Private
Limited Company
**Line of Business:** Multimedia publishers and
producers
**Issued Capital:** £162,169
**Principals:** J S Freedman (Managing),
M D Parnell, J Kelly, M I Nunny, D Mills,
Ms A Mckenna, J Davie, J E Simmons
**Co. Secretary:** Ms Anna Kissin
**Responsibilities**
**Senior:** Thomas Chandos (Manager)
**US SIC:** 7372  **UK SIC:** 83940
**Auditors:** Harris & Trotter

|     | 31-12-13   | 31-12-12 | 31-12-11 |
|-----|------------|----------|----------|
| TO  | 10,383,922 | N/A      | N/A      |
| P/L | 408,715    | N/A      | N/A      |
| NW  | 652,595    | 734,618  | 777,166  |
| WC  | (424,211)  | 557,407  | 595,259  |
| Emp.| 123        | N/A      | N/A      |

DUNS 21-922-2379

## Zonegate Ltd
6 Hewell Road, Barnt Green, Birmingham,
West Midlands B45 8NE
**Tel:** 01214452632 **Fax:** 01332331237
**Web:** www.tonyshandyman.co.uk
**Reg No:** 1076448  **VAT No:** 109384759
**Estd:** 1999 Private Limited Company
**Line of Business:** Retail sale of hardware,
paints and glass
**Trading Style:** Tonys Handiman
**Issued Capital:** £2
**Managing Director:** A J Balls
**Co. Secretary:** Mrs Judith Balls
**Responsibilities**
**Senior:** April Jones (Sales Assistant)
**Branches:** Zonegate Ltd, 6 Hewell Road,
Birmingham, West Midlands B45 8NE
**US SIC:** 5251  **UK SIC:** 64800
**Auditors:** Rigby Harrison
**Bankers:** Barclays Bank Plc (20-71-45)

|     | 31-08-13 | 31-08-12 | 31-08-11 |
|-----|----------|----------|----------|
| TA  | 297,441  | 384,526  | 440,262  |
| NW  | 242,399  | 323,122  | 366,767  |
| WC  | 242,399  | 323,122  | 366,767  |

DUNS 36-534-3466

## Zonemedia Management Ltd
(**Subsidiary of:** Amc Uk Topco Ltd)
4 Queen Studios, 117-121 Salusbury Road,
London NW6 6RG
**Tel:** 020-7328-8808 **Fax:** 02073288858
**Web:** www.zonevision.com
**Reg No:** 3290575  **Estd:** 1996 Private
Limited Company

---

**Line of Business:** Television activities
**Issued Capital:** £10,000
**Directors:** D Verwer, M P Moriarty,
J G Gallagher, R Andree Wiltens
**Co. Secretary:** Andrew Fischer
**US SIC:** 4833  **UK SIC:** 97411
**Auditors:** KPMG LLP

|     | 31-12-13   | 31-12-12   | 31-12-11   |
|-----|------------|------------|------------|
| TO  | 20,657,579 | 19,164,854 | 18,504,489 |
| P/L | 3,195,000  | 3,254,119  | 953,766    |
| NW  | 12,996,391 | 9,001,585  | 5,221,989  |
| WC  | 11,859,864 | 7,516,519  | 3,633,346  |
| Emp.| 192        | 178        | 165        |

DUNS 23-492-7846                              **Imp**

## Zones (Uk) Ltd
(**Subsidiary of:** Zones (Emea) Ltd)
12-16 Westland Place, London N1 7LP
**Tel:** 020-7608-7676
**Web:** www.ukzones.com
**Reg No:** 2823778  **VAT No:** 606036080
**Estd:** 1993 Private Limited Company
**Line of Business:** Other computer related
activities
**Export Sales:** £6,860,328
**Issued Capital:** £650,000
**Principals:** A D Kaye (Managing),
R Mcfadden, F H Lalji
**Co. Secretary:** Trevor Boyd
**Branches:** Zones (Uk) Ltd, Edge Business
Centre Humber Road, London NW2 6EW
**US SIC:** 7379  **UK SIC:** 83940
**Auditors:** Jeffreys Henry LLP
**Bankers:** Barclays Bank Plc (20-65-82)

|     | 31-12-13   | 31-12-12   | 31-12-11  |
|-----|------------|------------|-----------|
| TO  | 23,656,303 | 20,922,069 | N/A       |
| P/L | (115,381)  | 39,613     | N/A       |
| NW  | 997,565    | 1,121,134  | 1,102,556 |
| WC  | 734,754    | 877,369    | 1,064,416 |
| Emp.| 62         | 49         | N/A       |

DUNS 23-867-4258

## Zoo Digital Group Plc
The Tower, Sheffield, South Yorkshire S1
4QL
**Web:** www.zoodigitalgroup.com
**Reg No:** 3858881  **Estd:** 2001 Public Limited
Company
**Line of Business:** Computer software
(development)
**Directors:** R D Jeynes, S A Green, G Doran
**Co. Secretary:** Mrs Helen Gilder
**Responsibilities**
**Marketing:** Adam Prichard (Commercial
Director)
**Operations:** Duncan Wain (Chief Operating
Officer)
**Engineering:** Phil Corio (Chief Technical
Officer)
**US SIC:** 7379  **UK SIC:** 83940
**Auditors:** PKF (UK) LLP
**Bankers:** The Royal Bank Of Scotland Plc
(16-00-08)
**Employees:** 35
**Turnover:** £9,562,000

DUNS 22-701-2275                              **Imp**

## Zoological Society of London
Outer Circle, London NW1 4RY
**Tel:** 020-7722-3333
**Web:** www.zsl.org
**Reg No:** 0000749RC  **Estd:** 1988
Incorporate By Act Of Parliament
**Line of Business:** A zoo
**Trading Style:** Zsl, Institute of Zoology,
London Zoo, Whipsnade Wild Animal Park
**Directors:** P J Wrangle, Prof R A Mcneil,
Sir M J Field Chapple, P H Denton
**Responsibilities**
**Senior:** Matthew Gollock (Assistant
Manager), Noelle Kumpel (Manager), R
McNeil (Principal), Mike Russell (Financial
Director), Armi Torrechilla (Manager), Adrian
Walls (Team Leader, Birds)
**Finance:** Idrish Dudhwala (Administrator,
Finance), Mike Russell (Financial Director)
**Marketing:** Rhiannon Bates (VIP Liaison and
Press Officer), Rebecca Blanchard (Press
Officer), Rowena Fisher (Media), Lynsey
Ford (Press Officer), Amy Harris (Publishing
& Media Manager), Nicola Kelly
(Publications Officer), Clare Murray
(Development Executive), Daniel Sprawson
(Digital Communications Manager)
**Sales:** Teague Flannery (Development
Executive)
**Admin:** Lucy Cannock (Development
Administrator), Idrish Dudhwala
(Administrator, Finance)
**IT:** Amrit Dehal (Administrator), Amy Harris
(Publishing & Media Manager)
**HR:** Karen Turnbull (Human Resources
Manager)

---

**Operations:** Jonathan Baillie (Director of
Conservation Progr), George Busby (Project
Manager), Sanjay Gubbi (Production and
Operations Mana), Heather Koldewey (Head
of Global Conservation Pr), Natasha Pauli
(Program Manager), Paul Pearce-Kelly
(Senior Curator Invertebrates a), Jurgenne
Primavera (Manager)
**Engineering:** Chris Ransom (Program
Manager)
**Branches:** Zoological Society Of London, 49
Regents Park, Exeter, Devon EX1 2NZ
**US SIC:** 8699, 8421
**UK SIC:** 96902, 97700
**Auditors:** Ernst & Young LLP
**Bankers:** The Royal Bank Of Scotland Plc
(16-00-38)
**Employees:** 600
**Turnover:** £26,499,000

DUNS 23-417-0277

## Zoom Fulfilment Services Ltd
Unit 6 Leconfield Estate, Cleator Moor,
Cumbria CA25 5QB
**Tel:** 01946818140 **Fax:** 01946818131
**Web:** www.zoomfs.com
**Reg No:** 5585269  **VAT No:** 878493849
**Estd:** 2006 Private Limited Company
**Line of Business:** Mail order houses
**Issued Capital:** £88,670
**Director:** J Beale
**Co. Secretary:** Francis Mckee
**Responsibilities**
**Senior:** Rashpal Gill (Manager), Eleanor
Powell (Client service manager)
**IT:** John Spargo (IT Manager)
**Operations:** Eleanor Powell (Client service
manager)
**US SIC:** 5961, 7339
**UK SIC:** 65600, 83954
**Bankers:** Bank Of Scotland (12-18-05)

|     | 31-01-14  | 31-01-13  | 31-01-12  |
|-----|-----------|-----------|-----------|
| TA  | 1,934,215 | 1,747,548 | 1,416,905 |
| NW  | 1,084,353 | 886,306   | 731,793   |
| WC  | 792,226   | 739,669   | 593,590   |

DUNS 45-859-2144                              **Imp**

## Zorba Delicacies Ltd
(**Subsidiary of:** Entrepreneurial Food Group
Llc)
Plateau, Ebbw Vale, Gwent NP23 5SD
**Tel:** 01495-301-999
**Web:** www.zorbafoods.co.uk
**Reg No:** 3205254  **Estd:** 1996 Private
Limited Company
**Line of Business:** Manufacture of other food
products not elsewhere classified
**Trading Style:** Lava Foods
**Issued Capital:** £100
**Directors:** C Nash, D R Roberts,
N A Horsman
**Co. Secretary:** Richard Shippee
**Responsibilities**
**Senior:** Tim Henderson-Ross (Manager)
**Branches:** Zorba Delicacies Ltd, Unit 12-13,
Rassau Industrial Estate, Ebbw Vale, Gwent
NP23 5SD
**US SIC:** 2099  **UK SIC:** 42399
**Auditors:** Wingrave Yeats Partnership LLP
**Bankers:** HSBC Bank plc (40-16-18)

|     | 30-09-13   | 30-09-12   | 30-09-11   |
|-----|------------|------------|------------|
| TO  | 47,672,000 | 43,907,000 | 38,342,000 |
| P/L | 2,233,000  | 2,125,000  | 1,941,000  |
| NW  | 17,138,000 | 14,481,000 | 13,071,000 |
| WC  | 11,126,000 | 8,141,000  | 6,219,000  |
| Emp.| 293        | 277        | 265        |

DUNS 21-583-7766                              **Imp**

## Zot Engineering Ltd
Inveresk Mills Industrial Park, Musselburgh,
Midlothian EH21 7UQ
**Tel:** 0131-653-6834 **Fax:** 0131-653-6025
**Web:** www.zot.co.uk
**Reg No:** 0057167SC  **VAT No:** 271600877
**Estd:** 1975 Private Limited Company
**Line of Business:** Sheet metal fabricators
**Export Sales:** £1,671,249
**Issued Capital:** £136,000
**Principals:** C Antonelli (Financial),
J R Cross, A J Millar, C Antonelli
**Responsibilities**
**Senior:** Robin Laing (Maintenance Director),
Durk Molly (Manager)
**IT:** Gary Kerr (Technical Manager), Mike
Sullivan (Support Systems Manager)
**Facilities:** Robin Laing (Maintenance
Director)
**Engineering:** Alan Stevenson (Technical
Engineer)
**Branches:** Zot Engineering Ltd, St.
Columbas College, Newtown St Boswells,
Melrose, Roxburghshire TD6 0SG
**US SIC:** 3679, 3629
**UK SIC:** 34542, 34350
**Auditors:** Dalgliesh & Tullo

**Bankers:** Bank Of Scotland (80-17-68)

| | 28-02-14 | 28-02-13 | 29-02-12 |
|---|---|---|---|
| TO | 13,738,427 | 13,252,521 | 14,513,435 |
| P/L | 626,493 | 766,198 | 771,456 |
| NW | 6,336,112 | 5,761,279 | 5,134,270 |
| WC | 2,523,410 | 2,145,011 | 2,513,605 |
| Emp. | 217 | 217 | 220 |

DUNS 77-270-1298 **Exp**

## Zotefoams Plc

675 Mitcham Road, E Croydon, Croydon, Surrey CR9 3AL
**Tel:** 020-8664-1600
**Web:** www.zotefoams.com
**Reg No:** 2714645 **VAT No:** 843861703
**Estd:** 1992 Public Limited Company
**Line of Business:** Manufacture of other builders ware of plastic
**Export Markets:** Worldwide
**Export Sales:** £35,155,000
**Issued Capital:** £1,991,566
**Principals:** N G Howard *(Chairman)*, D B Stirling *(Managing)*, C G Hurst *(Financial)*, S P Good, Ms A C Bromfield, R J Clowes, Ms M Clayton
**Co. Secretary:** James Kindell
**Responsibilities**
**Sales:** Chris Endres *(Business Development Manager)*, Stewart Hendry *(Global Business Unit Manager)*
**Engineering:** Gary Morton *(Engineering Manager)*
**US SIC:** 3079, 6711
**UK SIC:** 48360, 83962
**Auditors:** PricewaterhouseCoopers LLP
**Bankers:** Barclays Bank Plc (20-00-00)

| | 31-12-13 | 31-12-12 | 31-12-11 |
|---|---|---|---|
| TO | 44,634,000 | 47,188,000 | 44,208,000 |
| P/L | 3,856,000 | 5,926,000 | 5,465,000 |
| NW | 34,098,000 | 30,442,000 | 29,523,000 |
| WC | 14,039,000 | 14,868,000 | 10,529,000 |
| Emp. | 298 | 295 | 273 |

DUNS 21-890-3891

## Zpg Ltd

(**Subsidiary of:** Rothermere Continuation Limited)
2nd Floor, London SE1 0LH
**Tel:** 08445021000 **Fax:** 03338001001
**Web:** www.zoopla.co.uk
**Reg No:** 6074771 **Estd:** 2007 Private Limited Company
**Line of Business:** Marketing consultants
**Issued Capital:** £4,085
**Directors:** S Morana, A E Chesterman
**Co. Secretary:** Edward Staple
**Responsibilities**
**Marketing:** Dave Thompson *(Media Manager)*
**US SIC:** 7319, 7374
**UK SIC:** 83800, 83940
**Auditors:** Deloitte LLP

| | 30-09-13 | 30-09-12 | 31-09-11 |
|---|---|---|---|
| TO | 64,498,000 | 26,844,277 | 13,816,236 |
| P/L | 28,287,000 | 3,561,133 | (890,030) |
| NW | 30,750,000 | 15,185,259 | 2,811,549 |
| WC | 21,674,000 | 14,506,623 | 2,651,876 |
| Emp. | 172 | 145 | 81 |

DUNS 50-554-7059 **Imp**

## Zs Associates International Inc

(**Subsidiary of:** Zs Associates Inc.)
Level 8, 338 Euston Road, London NW1 3BG
**Tel:** 020-7915-4200
**Web:** www.zsassociates.com
**Reg No:** 0015486FC **Estd:** 1998 Foreign Company
**Line of Business:** Management and business consultants
**Director:** A A Zoltners
**Co. Secretary:** Prabhakant Sinha
**Responsibilities**
**Senior:** Stuart Alderton *(Principal)*, Ianin Fratter *(Office Managing Principal)*
**IT:** Jyotiranjan Singh *(IT Consultant)*
**US SIC:** 7392 **UK SIC:** 83951

DUNS 22-251-3975 **Imp**

## Zte (Uk) Ltd

(**Subsidiary of:** Zte Corporation)
5th Floor Profile West, Brentford, Middlesex TW8 9ES
**Tel:** 02034282000 **Fax:** 02082317140
**Web:** www.zteuk.co.uk
**Reg No:** 4269408 **Estd:** 2001 Private Limited Company
**Line of Business:** Other business activities not elsewhere classified
**Issued Capital:** £841,478
**Directors:** X J Shi, Mrs C Jia, Miss Y Ying
**Co. Secretary:** Miss Yan Ying
**US SIC:** 7399 **UK SIC:** 83954

**Auditors:** Silver Levene

| | 31-12-13 | 31-12-12 | 31-12-11 |
|---|---|---|---|
| TO | 9,049,956 | 23,219,803 | 39,266,325 |
| P/L | (1,665,807) | (3,665,125) | (2,000,604) |
| NW | (14,163,335) | (12,497,528) | (8,832,403) |
| WC | 1,088,767 | 2,479,229 | 6,796,067 |
| Emp. | 55 | 73 | 73 |

DUNS 49-096-5258

## Zubrance Ltd

Healey Old Mills, Healey Road, Ossett, West Yorkshire WF5 8NE
**Tel:** 07803183388
**Web:** www.zubrance.co.uk
**Reg No:** 3092937 **VAT No:** 647545118
**Estd:** 1952 Private Limited Company
**Line of Business:** Manufacture of other food products not elsewhere classified
**Trading Style:** New Ivory Sauces
**Issued Capital:** £9,144
**Principals:** R N Whitehead *(Managing)*, A P Jones
**Co. Secretary:** Adam Jones
**US SIC:** 2099, 2079
**UK SIC:** 42399, 41150
**Auditors:** Baker Tilly UK Audit LLP
**Bankers:** Barclays Bank Plc (20-48-46)

| | 28-06-14 | 29-06-13 | 23-06-12 |
|---|---|---|---|
| TO | 25,756,000 | 31,379,000 | 29,871,000 |
| P/L | 704,000 | (363,000) | 1,042,000 |
| NW | 5,465,000 | 5,277,000 | 4,598,000 |
| WC | 2,524,000 | 2,803,000 | 1,810,000 |
| Emp. | 303 | 303 | 100 |

DUNS 21-694-6558 **Imp-Exp**

## Zuken Ltd

(**Subsidiary of:** Zuken Inc.)
1500 Aztec West, Almondsbury, Almondsbury, Bristol, Avon BS32 4RF
**Tel:** 01454-207800 **Fax:** 01454-207803
**Web:** www.zuken.com
**Reg No:** 0956340 **Estd:** 1965 Private Limited Company
**Line of Business:** Computer software (development)
**Export Markets:** India; S Africa; Europe
**Export Sales:** £6,154,000
**Trading Style:** Zuken-Redac
**Issued Capital:** £8,550,042
**Directors:** K Kariya, J Katsube, S Yukawa
**Co. Secretary:** Mark Sandham
**Responsibilities**
**Senior:** Gerhard Lipski *(Manager)*, Vivienne Long *(Shipping Officer)*
**Marketing:** Mark Knight *(Marketing Systems Manager)*
**Sales:** Gerhard Lipski *(Manager)*
**HR:** Bronwen Llewellyn-Evans *(Human Resources Manager)*, Leeca Rose *(Human Resources and Operations)*
**Health & Safety:** Bronwen Llewellyn-Evans *(Human Resources Manager)*
**Purchasing:** Vivienne Long *(Shipping Officer)*
**Engineering:** Chris Hambleton *(Deputy Engineering General Man)*
**US SIC:** 7379 **UK SIC:** 83940
**Auditors:** Arthur Andersen
**Bankers:** Barclays Bank Plc (20-00-00)

| | 31-03-14 | 31-03-13 | 31-03-12 |
|---|---|---|---|
| TO | 6,978,000 | 7,671,000 | 7,680,000 |
| P/L | (278,000) | (205,000) | (43,000) |
| NW | (1,932,000) | (1,614,000) | (1,409,000) |
| WC | (2,353,000) | (2,009,000) | (1,818,000) |
| Emp. | 54 | 56 | 57 |

DUNS 56-962-5536 **Imp**

## Zumtobel Lighting Ltd

(**Subsidiary of:** Zumtobel Group Ag)
Chiltern Park, Chiltern Hill, Chalfont St Peter, Gerrards Cross, Buckinghamshire SL9 9FG
**Tel:** 01753482650
**Web:** www.zumtobelcomp.com
**Reg No:** 2851586 **Estd:** 1993 Private Limited Company
**Line of Business:** Installation of electrical wiring and fittings
**Issued Capital:** £3,190,000
**Director:** M Boucher
**Co. Secretary:**
St John'S Square Secretaries Ltd
**Responsibilities**
**Senior:** Harry Barnett *(Sales Director)*
**Sales:** Harry Barnett *(Sales Director)*
**HR:** Harry Barnett *(Sales Director)*
**US SIC:** 1731 **UK SIC:** 50300
**Auditors:** Arthur Andersen
**Bankers:** Bank Austria Ag (40-52-11)

| | 30-04-13 | 30-04-12 | 30-04-11 |
|---|---|---|---|
| TO | 36,059,000 | 41,274,000 | 37,098,000 |
| P/L | 677,000 | 1,829,000 | (4,620,000) |
| NW | 1,202,000 | 795,000 | (3,234,000) |
| WC | 563,000 | 642,000 | (3,263,000) |
| Emp. | 90 | 91 | 70 |

DUNS 21-579-8340

## Zurich

6th Floor Whitefriars, Lewins Mead, Bristol, Avon BS1 2NT
**Tel:** 01179291031
**Web:** www.zurich.co.uk
**Estd:** 1977 Partnership
**Line of Business:** Activities auxiliary to insurance and pension funding
**Partner:** M Bresnan
**Responsibilities**
**Senior:** Geoffrey Bacon *(Business Manager)*, Nick Jeffery *(Branch Manager)*
**US SIC:** 6411 **UK SIC:** 83200
**Employees:** 99

DUNS 50-482-8674

## Zurich Assurance Ltd

(**Subsidiary of:** Zurich Insurance Group Ag)
Uk Life Centre, Station Road, Swindon, Wiltshire SN1 1EL
**Tel:** 01793-514514 **Fax:** 01242221554
**Web:** www.zurich.co.uk
**Reg No:** 2456671 **Estd:** 1990 Private Limited Company
**Line of Business:** Life insurance
**Issued Capital:** £236,131,734
**Directors:** I C Stuart, G P Shaughnessy, J T Butler, N A Burnet, C S Fairclough, J R Sykes
**Co. Secretary:**
Zurich Corporate Secretary (Uk)
**Responsibilities**
**HR:** Amanda Chester *(Human Resources Manager)*
**Health & Safety:** Nick Mansfield *(Health & Safety Officer)*
**Branches:** Zurich Assurance Ltd, Unit 9, The Postings, Kirkcaldy, Fife KY1 1HN
**US SIC:** 6311 **UK SIC:** 82002
**Auditors:** PricewaterhouseCoopers LLP
**Following financial data are in thousands**

| | 31-12-13 | 31-12-12 | 31-12-11 |
|---|---|---|---|
| TO | 652,000 | 2,962,000 | 2,963,000 |
| P/L | 30,000 | (18,000) | (60,000) |
| NW | 1,171,000 | 539,000 | 582,000 |
| WC | (30,000) | (313,000) | (261,000) |

DUNS 89-621-5225

## Zurich Financial Services (Ukisa) Nominees Ltd

(**Subsidiary of:** Zurich Insurance Group Ag)
3 Minster Court Mincing Lane, London EC3R 7DD
**Tel:** 02076483200
**Web:** www.zurich.com
**Reg No:** 3315204 **Estd:** 1997 Private Limited Company
**Line of Business:** Financial services
**Issued Capital:** £2
**Directors:** J Vaughan-Williams, Mrs E Skuse, Mrs A Gibson
**Co. Secretary:**
Zurich Corporate Secretary (Uk)
**US SIC:** 6111, 6211
**UK SIC:** 81501, 83100

| | 31-12-13 | 31-12-12 | 31-12-11 |
|---|---|---|---|
| TA | 3 | 3 | 3 |
| NW | 2 | 2 | 2 |
| WC | N/A | 1 | N/A |

DUNS 29-885-7558

## Zurich Independent Wealth Management Ltd

(**Subsidiary of:** Allied Dunbar Assurance Plc)
47 Brunswick Place, London N1 6EB
**Tel:** 01793506000
**Web:** www.zurich.co.uk
**Reg No:** 2088643 **Estd:** 1987 Private Limited Company
**Line of Business:** Financial services
**Trading Style:** Openwork Market Solutions
**Issued Capital:** £16,190,000
**Directors:** D P Sims, A P Kenmir, G P Shaughnessy, N J Evans
**Co. Secretary:**
Zurich Corporate Secretary (Uk)
**Responsibilities**
**Senior:** Darren Dodwel *(Manager)*, Amanda Knott *(Manager)*, Marcus Nagel *(Manager)*, Corina Ross *(Manager)*
**Branches:** Zurich Independent Wealth Management Ltd, Springburn Shopping Centre, Unit 1, Glasgow, Lanarkshire G21 1TS
**US SIC:** 6111 **UK SIC:** 81501
**Auditors:** PricewaterhouseCoopers

| | 31-12-13 | 31-12-12 | 31-12-11 |
|---|---|---|---|
| TA | 428,008 | 484,082 | 600,330 |
| P/L | 89,634 | (34,767) | (314,852) |
| NW | 394,555 | 325,918 | 352,326 |
| WC | 394,555 | 325,918 | 498,112 |

DUNS 22-609-2856

## Zurich Insurance Company (U.K.) Ltd

(**Subsidiary of:** Zurich Insurance Group Ag)
The Zurich Centre, 3000b Parkway, Fareham, Hampshire PO15 7JZ
**Tel:** 01793514514
**Web:** www.zurich.co.uk
**Reg No:** 0376989 **Estd:** 2012 Private Limited Company
**Line of Business:** Insurance companies and agents
**Trading Style:** Zurich Group
**Issued Capital:** £250,000
**Directors:** Mrs R J Hine, N A Freshwater
**Co. Secretary:** Philip Lampshire
**Responsibilities**
**Senior:** Steven Richardson *(Director)*, Martin Senn *(Partner)*
**Marketing:** Kristian Westcott *(Digital Marketing Executive)*
**Purchasing:** Pete Tart *(Chief Procurement Officer, Eur)*
**Branches:** Zurich Insurance Company (U.k.) Ltd, Zurich Insurance Co, Po Box 568, Leeds, West Yorkshire LS1 2AA
**US SIC:** 6411, 7399
**UK SIC:** 83200, 83954
**Auditors:** PricewaterhouseCoopers LLP
**Bankers:** National Westminster Bank Plc (56-00-64)

| | 31-12-13 | 31-12-12 | 31-12-11 |
|---|---|---|---|
| TA | 2,302,986 | 2,297,123 | 2,292,014 |
| P/L | 8,005 | 8,743 | 9,252 |
| NW | 2,301,119 | 2,294,975 | 2,288,371 |
| WC | 2,301,117 | 2,294,973 | 2,288,369 |

DUNS 22-865-5775 **Exp**

## Zurich International Life Ltd

(**Subsidiary of:** Zurich Insurance Group Ag)
43-51 Athol Street, Douglas, Isle of Man IM99 1EF
**Tel:** 01624671666 **Fax:** 01624-662038
**Web:** www.zurichbankinternational.com
**Reg No:** 0020126M **Estd:** 1982 Private Limited Company
**Line of Business:** Banks and financial institutions
**Export Markets:** Middle East, Far East, Scandinavia, S America
**Trading Style:** Zurich International
**Issued Capital:** £20,600,000
**Principals:** L Tyrer *(Managing)*, J D Pattie, T M Naskret
**Co. Secretary:** Lee Tyrer
**Responsibilities**
**Senior:** Mark Waterhouse *(Manager)*
**US SIC:** 6411 **UK SIC:** 83200
**Bankers:** HSBC Bank plc (40-19-38)
**Employees:** 400

DUNS 21-418-4956

## Zurich Municipal

Zurich House, 2 Gladiator Way, Farnborough, Hampshire GU14 6GB
**Tel:** 01252-387780
**Line of Business:** Life assurance services
**US SIC:** 6411 **UK SIC:** 83200
**Employees:** 500

DUNS 21-913-8492 **Imp**

## Zwanenberg Food Uk Ltd

(**Subsidiary of:** Vleesexport Centrale Eindhoven B.V.)
Minsterley, Shrewsbury, Shropshire SY5 0BD
**Tel:** 01743791232
**Web:** www.zwanenberg.nl
**Reg No:** 1032611 **VAT No:** 159054261
**Estd:** 1971 Private Limited Company
**Line of Business:** Production, processing and preserving of meat and meat products
**Export Sales:** £23,482
**Trading Style:** Rea Valley (Canned Meat) Ltd, Puredrive Fine Foods, Rea Valley
**Issued Capital:** £2,500,000
**Directors:** J D Ashmore, M A Burdekin, A T Van Der Laan, Ms J E Higginson, A M Higginson, Ms J C Stevers-Van Der Laan, R E Lotgerink, A M Van Der Laan
**Co. Secretary:** Peter Mcdonald
**Responsibilities**
**Senior:** Mitch Higginson *(Manager)*
**Facilities:** Andy Morgan *(Maintenance Manager)*
**US SIC:** 2011, 5147
**UK SIC:** 41210, 61700
**Auditors:** Whittingham Riddell LLP

**Bankers:** The Royal Bank Of Scotland Plc
(16-31-23)

|     | 31-12-13 | 31-12-12 | 31-12-11 |
|-----|----------|----------|----------|
| TO  | 46,409,490 | 42,173,552 | 46,019,050 |
| P/L | (910,856) | (1,734,428) | 354,169 |
| NW  | 16,347,282 | 17,375,534 | 18,968,452 |
| WC  | 5,586,905 | 7,188,886 | 8,286,792 |
| Emp. | 536 | 310 | 311 |

DUNS 21-920-9221
## Zycko Group Ltd
Inda House, South Cerney, Cirencester,
Gloucestershire GL7 5TQ
**Tel:** 01285868517
**Web:** www.zycko.com
**Reg No:** 8367867 **Estd:** 2013 Private
Limited Company
**Line of Business:** Management activities of
other non-financial holding companies not
elsewhere classified
**Export Sales:** £50,261,000
**Directors:** D R Galton-Fenzi, R J Sweet,
N J Moglia, K I Wood
**Co. Secretary:** Matthew Smith
**US SIC:** 6711 **UK SIC:** 83962

|     | 31-03-14 | 31-03-13 |
|-----|----------|----------|
| TO  | 89,939,000 | N/A |
| P/L | (189,000) | N/A |
| NW  | 4,765,000 | (785,000) |
| WC  | 4,376,000 | (1,376,000) |
| Emp. | 163 | N/A |

DUNS 23-886-9759                                    Imp
## Zycko Ltd
(**Subsidiary of:** Zycko Group Ltd)
India House, The Mallards, Cirencester,
Gloucestershire GL7 5TQ
**Tel:** 01285-868500 **Fax:** 01285-868501
**Web:** www.zycko.com
**Reg No:** 3878046 **VAT No:** 742329048
**Estd:** 1999 Private Limited Company
**Line of Business:** Wholesale of computers,
computer peripheral equipment and software
**Export Sales:** £38,883,000
**Issued Capital:** £2

---

**Directors:** K I Wood, D R Galton Fenzi,
N J Moglia, R J Sweet
**Co. Secretary:** Matthew Smith
**Responsibilities**
**Marketing:** Gemma Matthews (Marketing
Campaign Manager)
**IT:** Paul Wignall (Computer Manager)
**Operations:** David Hopper (COO)
**US SIC:** 5081, 5065
**UK SIC:** 61490, 61500
**Auditors:** Deloitte LLP
**Bankers:** Lloyds TSB Bank plc (77-88-88)

|     | 31-03-14 | 31-03-13 | 31-03-12 |
|-----|----------|----------|----------|
| TO  | 77,212,000 | 83,625,000 | 79,409,000 |
| P/L | 203,000 | 1,431,000 | 1,854,000 |
| NW  | 6,739,000 | 6,588,000 | 8,113,000 |
| WC  | 6,528,000 | 6,287,000 | 7,912,000 |
| Emp. | 65 | 69 | 69 |

DUNS 77-956-7890
## Zyro Ltd
Thirsk Industrial Park, York Road, Thirsk,
North Yorkshire YO7 3BX
**Tel:** 01845-521700
**Web:** www.zyro.co.uk
**Reg No:** 3060232 **Estd:** 1995 Public Limited
Company
**Line of Business:** Cycle accessories
**Issued Capital:** £80,000
**Principals:** S J Ellison (Managing),
M H Barker, A Budd
**Co. Secretary:** Ms Julie Ellison
**US SIC:** 3751 **UK SIC:** 36330
**Auditors:** MGI Watson Buckle LLP
**Bankers:** Lloyds TSB Bank plc (30-93-91)

|     | 31-12-13 | 31-12-12 | 31-12-11 |
|-----|----------|----------|----------|
| TO  | 28,265,484 | 36,162,784 | 28,513,320 |
| P/L | 3,262,758 | 5,049,903 | 4,618,334 |
| NW  | 10,203,261 | 12,230,250 | 8,457,767 |
| WC  | 6,931,052 | 10,394,793 | 6,727,486 |
| Emp. | 115 | 102 | 97 |

---

DUNS 49-338-3335
## Zytek Automotive Ltd
(**Subsidiary of:** Continental Ag)
Lancaster Road, Fradley Park, Lichfield,
Staffordshire WS13 8RY
**Tel:** 01543412400
**Web:** www.zytek.co.uk
**Reg No:** 3125253 **Estd:** 1996 Private
Limited Company
**Line of Business:** Research and
experimental development on natural
sciences and engineering
**Export Sales:** £4,786,187
**Issued Capital:** £2
**Directors:** N R Heslington,
Miss K A Diamond
**Co. Secretary:** Miss Kerry Diamond
**Responsibilities**
**Senior:** Stephen Tremble (Sales and
Marketing Director)
**Marketing:** Stephen Tremble (Sales and
Marketing Director)
**Sales:** Stephen Tremble (Sales and
Marketing Director)
**US SIC:** 7391 **UK SIC:** 94000
**Auditors:** Chantrey Vellacott DFK LLP
**Bankers:** National Westminster Bank Plc
(60-12-51)

|     | 31-12-13 | 31-12-12 | 31-12-11 |
|-----|----------|----------|----------|
| TO  | 7,136,799 | 14,764,921 | 28,086,158 |
| P/L | (2,791,475) | (28,817) | 1,183,860 |
| NW  | (498,440) | 3,367,035 | 2,878,253 |
| WC  | (2,048,939) | 1,388,995 | 2,373,011 |
| Emp. | 146 | 143 | 151 |

DUNS 49-338-3293                                    Imp
## Zytek Group Ltd
(**Subsidiary of:** Continental Ag)
Lancaster Road, Lichfield, Staffordshire
WS13 8RY
**Web:** www.zytekautomotive.co.uk
**Reg No:** 3125249 **Estd:** 1995 Private
Limited Company
**Line of Business:** Other manufacturing not
elsewhere classified
**Issued Capital:** £97,347

---

**Directors:** N R Heslington,
Miss K A Diamond
**Co. Secretary:** Miss Kerry Diamond
**Responsibilities**
**Marketing:** Steve Tremble (Sales And
Marketing Director)
**Sales:** Steve Tremble (Sales And Marketing
Director)
**IT:** Neil Cheeseman (Program Manager)
**Engineering:** Michal Orczynski (Application
Engineer - Pure El)
**US SIC:** 3999, 8911
**UK SIC:** 49590, 83701
**Auditors:** Bentley Jennison

|     | 31-12-13 | 31-12-12 | 31-12-11 |
|-----|----------|----------|----------|
| TA  | 3,308,490 | 3,308,490 | 3,309,113 |
| P/L | N/A | (668) | N/A |
| NW  | 1,808,490 | 1,808,490 | 1,809,158 |
| WC  | 1,808,490 | 1,808,490 | 1,809,158 |

DUNS 23-890-2451                                    Imp-Exp
## Zytronic P L C
Whiteley Road, Blaydon-On-Tyne, Tyne and
Wear NE21 5NJ
**Tel:** 0191-414-5511 **Fax:** 0191-414-0545
**Web:** www.zytronic.co.uk
**Reg No:** 3881244 **Estd:** 1999 Public Limited
Company
**Line of Business:** Management activities of
holding companies
**Export Sales:** £17,646,000
**Issued Capital:** £149,052
**Directors:** Sir D R Chapman, D J Buffham,
M Cambridge, T G Davies, Mrs C L Smith
**Co. Secretary:** Mrs Claire Smith
**Responsibilities**
**Senior:** Kenneth Oakley (Manager)
**US SIC:** 6711 **UK SIC:** 83962
**Auditors:** Ernst & Young LLP
**Bankers:** Lloyds TSB Bank plc (30-16-91)

|     | 30-09-14 | 30-09-13 | 30-09-12 |
|-----|----------|----------|----------|
| TO  | 18,886,000 | 17,282,000 | 20,424,000 |
| P/L | 3,261,000 | 1,939,000 | 4,195,000 |
| NW  | 16,640,000 | 14,648,000 | 14,064,000 |
| WC  | 11,273,000 | 8,923,000 | 7,757,000 |
| Emp. | 169 | 182 | 207 |